132ND YEAR

WISDEN

CRICKETERS' ALMANACK

1995

EDITED BY MATTHEW ENGEL

PUBLISHED BY JOHN WISDEN & CO LTD

Cased edition ISBN 0 947766 24 3 £23.50
Soft cover edition ISBN 0 947766 25 1 £23.50
Leather bound edition ISBN 0 947766 27 8 £200
(Limited edition of 100)

JOHN WISDEN & CO LTD
25 Down Road, Merrow, Guildford, Surrey GU1 2PY
Tel: 01483 570358 Fax: 01483 33153

WISDEN CRICKETERS' ALMANACK

Editor: Matthew Engel, The Oaks, Newton St Margarets, Herefordshire HR2 0QN.
Assistant editor: Harriet Monkhouse. Production editor: Christine Forrest.
Advertisement manager: Colin Ackehurst.

Computer typeset by Spottiswoode Ballantyne Ltd, Colchester

Printed and bound in Great Britain by Clays Ltd, St Ives plc
Distributed by The Penguin Group

PREFACE

There are pains and pleasures in editing *Wisden*. Chief among the pleasures is being responsible for the selection of the Five Cricketers of the Year, an award which, since 1889, has developed into the game's Hall of Fame. It is gratifying and a little frightening to discover the importance attached to this throughout the cricketing world.

People often ask, so this seems a good opportunity to restate the three rules relating to this award, each of which might reasonably be challenged. The first is that no one may be chosen twice. The selection would often be stronger if this rule were abolished and it might be fun to pick Graham Gooch for the tenth time, or whatever. But the concept of an award emerged from the biographical articles rather than the other way around, and the tradition on this point is very powerful.

The second is that the choice is based primarily on the previous English season, which sometimes means that September's cert looks a bit shaky come springtime. It might be better to consider all the cricket in a calendar year, but as the quantity of international cricket grows uncontrollably, it is hard to know how anyone could come up with a coherent selection. And nearly all the world's best cricketers do play in England some time in their careers.

The third rule is that the choice is the editor's alone. No doubt one could construct a committee of the game's great and good to take on the burden. However, that would probably put an end to the occasional offbeat, even eccentric, selections which are part of the Five Cricketers' charm. The dictatorial method of choosing Cricketers of the Year has not been appreciably less successful than, say, the selection of England teams.

And frankly, the editor of *Wisden* deserves a perk. "The question of space becomes more and more pressing," Sydney Pardon wrote in his preface exactly a hundred years ago. But he did not have to contend with nine major countries playing vast quantities of Tests and one-day internationals. The return of South Africa and the arrival of Zimbabwe mean we are approaching the point where the survival of *Wisden* as a single volume is becoming a matter of concern.

In my judgment, *Wisden* has to provide a full record of all international cricket and of UK domestic cricket – but it cannot be a mere statistical record, it has to debate the issues and convey the flavour of the game as it is now played.

To preserve these core functions, I have taken two hard decisions; both may be regarded as experimental. In 1988, when my predecessor discontinued full scorecards of domestic matches round the world, he spared the Sheffield Shield because "no annual publication provides this information". Well, Australia is a grown-up country now and two excellent books cover this ground: the *ABC Australian Cricket Almanac* and *Allan's Australian Cricket Annual*.

I have also omitted the Index to Cricketers, which was in any case primarily an index to players in the Cricket Records rather than the entire volume. Before the complaints start, I would draw readers' attention to the Contents on page five, and the Index to Records on page 106, which should provide a very clear route map through *Wisden*.

The responsibility for these decisions is mine. If, as I hope, in all other respects, the 1995 *Wisden* is better than ever, the credit for that should be shared among all our contributors but especially the board and management committee of John Wisden & Co; Harriet Monkhouse, the assistant editor; Christine Forrest, the production editor; Peter Bather and Mike Smith of our typesetters Spottiswoode Ballantyne; plus Gordon Burling, Bill Frindall, John Kitchin, Andrew Radd and Roy Smart. My special thanks to my colleagues on *The Guardian* and, above all, to Hilary and Laurie, my wife and son.

MATTHEW ENGEL

Newton St Margarets, Herefordshire,
February 1995

LIST OF CONTRIBUTORS

Paul Allott
Jack Arlidge
Chris Aspin
Jack Bailey
Philip Bailey
Jack Bannister
Frank Baron
Colin Bateman
Greg Baum
Trevor Bayley
Brian Bearshaw
Mike Berry
Scyld Berry
Edward Bevan
Bidhan Kumar
John Bishop
J. Watson Blair
Christopher Booker
Robert Brooke
Colin Bryden
John Callaghan
Charlie Chelliah
Ted Corbett
Mike Coward
Tony Cozier
Jon Culley
John Curtis
Gareth A. Davies
Geoffrey Dean
Tim de Lisle
Norman de Mesquita
Patrick Eagar
John Etheridge
Brian Fell
Paton Fenton
T. J. Finlayson
David Foot
Bill Frindall
David Frith
Nigel Fuller
Simone Gambino
Andrew Gidley
Russell Grant
David Hallett
Maurice F. Hankey
David Hardy
Peter Hargreaves
Norman Harris
Andy Heading
Murray Hedgcock
Simon Hewitt
Frank Heydenrych
Eric Hill
Philip Hoare
Derek Hodgson
Grenville Holland
David Hopps
Gerald Howat
Doug Insole
Jai Kumar Shah
John Jameson
John A. Kaminsky
Abid Ali Kazi
John Kitchin
Peter Knight
Alan Lee
Mark Lees
David Llewellyn
Nick Lucy
Steven Lynch
John MacKinnon
Christopher Martin-Jenkins
R. Mohan
Chris Moore
Glenn Moore
Graham Morris
Gerald Mortimer
David Munden
Pat Murphy
Mike Neasom
Mark Nicholas
Graham Otway
Stanley Perlman
Terry Power
Derek Pringle
Qamar Ahmed
Andrew Radd
Amanda Ripley
Dicky Rutnagur
Carol Salmon
Derek Scott
Brian Scovell
Mike Selvey
Ross Setford
Fraser M. Simm
Andrew Simpson-Parker
Jasmer Singh
Bill Smith
Peter Snape
Richard Stilgoe
Tanjeeb Ahsan Saad
John Thicknesse
Derek Thursby
David Townsend
Sudhir Vaidya
Gerry Vaidyasekera
John Ward
Paul Weaver
J. R. Webber
Tim Wellock
John Woodcock
Roger Wootton
Terry Yates-Round

Thanks are also accorded to the following for checking the scorecards of first-class matches: Michael Ayers, Geoff Blackburn, Caroline Byatt, Len Chandler, Bill Davies, Alex Davis, Byron Denning, Jack Foley, Peter Gordon, Brian Hunt, Vic Isaacs, Bert Jenkins, Malcolm Jones, David Kendix, Tony Kingston, Reg May, David Oldam, Gordon Stringfellow, Stan Tacey, Muriel Tinsley, Tony Weld and Roy Wilkinson.

The editor also acknowledges with gratitude assistance from the following: Gowton Achaibar, David Armstrong, Mike Averis, Kim Baloch, Peter Baxter, June Bayliss, Dick Brittenden, James Colabavala, Andrew Collomosse, Geoffrey Copinger, Nick Crockford, Brian Croudy, Steven Dobrow, Dudley Doust, Tom Engel, Ric Finlay, Ghulam Mustafa Khan, Lee Glanville, Robin Gordon-Walker, Maria Grant, David Green, Bob Harragan, Leo Harrison, Les Hatton, Col. Malcolm Havergal, S. Hicks, Lt-Col. K. Hitchcock, W. F. Hughes, Colin Ingleby-Mackenzie, Ken Ingman, David Jeater, Kate Jenkins, Louise Kent, Rajesh Kumar, David Lacey, Keith Lodge, Malcolm Lorimer, M. P. Mapagunaratne, Robin Marlar, Nick Mason, Colin Maynard, Mohandas Menon, Allan Miller, Arthur Milton, Andrew Nickolds, Qasim E. Noorani, Christopher Paul, Francis Payne, S. S. Perera, S. Pervez Qaiser, Roger Phillips, David Rayvern Allen, Rex Roberts, Dan Ruparel, Ahmad Saidullah, Anthony Sampson, Andrew Samson, Geoffrey Saulez, Jonathan Smith, Karen Spink, Neil Stacey, Richard Streeton, Bob Thomas, David Walsh, Jim Watts, Wendy Wimbush and Peter Wynne-Thomas.

The production of *Wisden* would not be possible without the support and co-operation of many other cricket officials, writers and lovers of the game. To them all, many thanks.

CONTENTS

Part One: Comment

Part Two: Records

Part Three: English Cricket in 1994

Part Four: Overseas Cricket in 1993-94

Part Five: Administration and Laws

Part Six: Miscellaneous

Addresses of first-class and minor counties can now be found on pages 1287-1288.

A more detailed index to Cricket Records appears on pages 106-110. The index to the Laws may be found on pages 1291-1292 and an index of Test matches played in 1994-95 on pages 1400-1401.

Index of Fillers

PART ONE: COMMENT

NOTES BY THE EDITOR

On a July morning in 1994, Warwickshire lost the toss against Derbyshire and were forced to bat on a green pitch at Queen's Park, Chesterfield. Of the 22 participants, 21 found batting anywhere between difficult and impossible and, but for the one exception, the Test and County Cricket Board's pitchfinder-general, Harry Brind, might well have been racing up the motorway, siren wailing, to consider the question of a 25-point deduction.

Brian Lara scored a century before lunch, a performance of effortless, almost superhuman, dominance. It was not his most famous innings of 1994, perhaps not – who can say? – his best. But, by happy chance, I was there. So were a couple of thousand others. For every one of us, the memory of his batting on a summer's day on one of the world's most beautiful cricket grounds will remain in our personal treasure-house as long as the mind's eye still functions.

A year ago these Notes mourned the retirement of Ian Botham, David Gower and Viv Richards and wondered whether a new generation could bring forth similar giants to replace them. Then along came Lara. Thus the game renews itself, by a process as mysterious and magical as the springtime.

No cricketer in history has had a sequence like Lara had in 1994, when he broke the world's two most important batting records within seven weeks. It requires a certain cast of mind to want to score 375 and 501; Gower would not have been interested, no more would Jack Hobbs. But though he is a calculator, Lara is also an instinctive entertainer; in him, the three often irreconcilable aims of a professional cricketer – personal success, collective success and pleasure for the onlooker – come together in glorious conjunction.

On distant fields – they did not collide in 1994 – Shane Warne did the same, continuing the revival of leg-spin, and concluding the calendar year by taking a Test match hat-trick at Melbourne and effectively retaining the Ashes for Australia. Warne's statistics were not as spectacular, but he provided an extra, psychological, dimension. There were moments in the early part of the Ashes series when, if he had said he had devised a way of making the ball explode in mid-air, the England batsmen would have worried about their technique for avoiding the fragments.

The cricketing battle changes subtly all the time. As I write, in an English midwinter, both men have fallen a little from the topmost pinnacle. Both will have times when playing cricket will seem infinitely harder than it did for much of 1994. None the less, everyone who has seen them play has been brushed by greatness. Before we go on to nag at the game's problems, we should pause, rejoice and give thanks.

Time for a World Championship

The most immediate problem facing the game is little discussed: England remains the home of cricketing self-analysis, and the greatest triumph of English cricket (amidst its manifest failures) has been to maintain and enhance the status of Test cricket as the game's apogee. Full-length, i.e. five-match, Test series are extinct where neither England nor Australia are involved. And even West Indies v Australia this year is down to four matches.

One-day internationals, in a bewildering variety of competitions with no legitimacy beyond the profit motive, continue to attract vast crowds from Ahmedabad to Wellington. In Test cricket the picture is very patchy indeed: suddenly encouraging in South Africa after a slow start on their return; in India, often better in the smaller and less blasé cities; variable in the West Indies, except when boosted by English mass tourism; excellent in Australia at the moment but, one suspects, heavily dependent on the team's success; dismal in Pakistan, New Zealand, Sri Lanka and Zimbabwe.

It is hard to explain why a Test match between two mighty sides, Pakistan and Australia, should attract crowds barely touching four figures in Lahore, not a city famous for its range of competing leisure attractions. Tickets are often too expensive; it is cheaper and easier to watch one day rather than five; live TV coverage may be a hindrance.

But Test cricket, crucially, depends on context. It needs a five-Test series (six is too long) for the personalities to emerge and the battle to capture the public imagination. These half-hearted one-off Tests rarely work.

There is a possible solution which would cost next to nothing, could bring in major sponsorship, and would give shape to the present mish-mash of world cricket, raise the game's profile and give it something it badly needs: a true world champion team to go alongside the one-day world champions, who are after all the winners of just one tournament.

All the Test countries need do is undertake to play at least one Test home and away against all the others in a four-year cycle, which they are edging towards anyway. (In this context, it is worth saying that England's decision to play six Tests against West Indies in 1995 instead of inviting Zimbabwe is a rather churlish and unworthy exception.)

In an Ashes series, the World Championship would merely be a subplot and the whole series could count in the final table: two points, say, for the winner; one each if it were drawn. For countries which just played a single Test against each other, then the one game would count for everything. It would thus add particular pith to the matches that now seem least important. There is no reason why this Championship could not be instituted almost at once. It can do no harm and could be very good for the game.

The Ashes really should go to Australia

It is easy to see why England might fear such a Championship: someone might eventually propose that the bottom country be relegated. The full analysis of the 1994-95 Ashes series, in keeping with ancient custom, will appear in the 1996 *Wisden*, though as an interim service the scorecards of this most resonant of cricketing contests appear on pages 1405-1409.

The consequences of this remarkable series cannot be ignored, as they provide yet more threads in the seamless story of cricket, and the ongoing saga of the adventures of England's raggle-taggle army. Despite their defeat in Adelaide, Australia's victories in Brisbane, Melbourne and Perth ensure that they retain the Ashes, which they have held since 1989, at least until 1997. On some reckonings this sequence is already the most one-sided ever.

Australia retain the Ashes theoretically, anyway. As every schoolboy used and ought to know, the urn and its contents rest permanently in the museum at Lord's. This is, of course, legally as it should be: they were given to MCC in 1927. But the Ashes is no longer a contest between a mother-country and its colonial offshoot, far from it; it is a battle between two independent nations. Works of art are transported round the world. It would be in keeping with MCC's historic mission if it were to agree that the trophy should be displayed in the country that holds them.

Such a move would generate enormous public interest in both nations and give a huge emotional charge to the moment the Ashes changed hands. This would not just be an act of generosity. It would be terrific for English cricket's long-term well-being: children could then be taken to Lord's, forced to stare at the empty plinth and swear that they would help bring about the urn's return. There is no single reason why England lose so often at cricket, but it is easy to underestimate the power of symbolism and patriotism and passion.

It cannot be irrelevant to England's long-term failures that so many of their recent Test players were either born overseas and/or spent their formative years as citizens of other countries. In the heat of Test cricket, there is a difference between a cohesive team with a common goal, and a coalition of individuals whose major ambitions are for themselves.

Successive England captains have all been aware of this. It is not a question of race. And of course there have been many fine and committed performances from players with all kinds of disparate backgrounds. But several of these players only came to England to play as professionals. There is a vast difference between wanting to play Test cricket and wanting to play for England. The overall effect has been to create a climate in which, as *The Independent* put it, "some of our lot play for their country because they get paid for it."

Why? Oh why?

As England were losing to a team from the Australian Cricket Academy at North Sydney Oval late in 1994, one of the most telling but not necessarily the worst of the many humiliations English cricket has suffered these past few years, a plane appeared (not thought on this occasion to be carrying David Gower) and sky-wrote the word WHY? in the clear blue sky.

The question apparently related to Sydney Airport's new runway, not cricket. But, invisibly, it hung there all tour, even after the victory in Adelaide. England are never boring: each time they plummet to a previously uncharted depth, they stage an improbable leap upwards; they were bowled out under 100 three times in 1994, but invariably came back to score a startling victory a Test or two later. None the less, each depth does seem to be lower than the last. I have never seen a team as dismal and demoralised as the England side that slouched around the field on the fourth day of the Melbourne Test. Each time this happens the Why-ing gets more frenzied and less enlightening.

Much of it emanates from the press box, which is not an environment designed for original thought. But, though no one seems to be able to answer the question, everyone seems to know what to do about it. From 1913, when the bigger counties backed off from a threat to break away from the rest, until the 1990s, the idea of two divisions in the County Championship was one of those ideas that rarely got an airing outside the letters columns of the cricket magazines. In the past 12 months, it has been paraded by many writers as the solution to England's problems with the certainty usually reserved for revealed truth. Just as hurriedly and thoughtlessly, the counties tossed it out at their meeting in December 1994.

Such a scheme could have infinitely more far-reaching effects than its enthusiasts have contemplated. Yes, it would make some Championship matches more pressurised. But it bears no relation to the present evenly spread division of power (consider the recent gyrations in the county table of Glamorgan, Warwickshire and Worcestershire); it would lead to a full-blown transfer system, probably within hours; and it could destroy what the counties actually do well – spotting the talent that is around, and keeping professional cricket alive and within easy reach of the vast majority of the population.

In practice, it could even damage the national team's prospects, because the pressure on teams to stay in the higher division might create club-country battles for the leading players' attention that would be irreconcilable in a short English summer. It seems to me that those who seek to reform English cricket are sometimes a bit too rapid in demanding the chucking out of not only the baby with the bathwater, but the bath itself.

But the counties have got to start doing some hard thinking, especially about the amount of one-day cricket they play. In 1995, having returned to a zonal system in the Benson and Hedges Cup, every county will play between 22 and 30 competitive one-day matches; 241 are scheduled in all, an unprecedented figure. In the face of all the evidence of the damage this form of the game is doing to English players' technique, this is grotesque and disgraceful.

Since the counties are most unlikely to get rid of the wretched Sunday League, I propose a small but, I think, elegant interim reform. In future, the Benson and Hedges Cup should be restricted to the top eight Championship teams of the previous season. This would cut out 50 of the least-watched one-day games, avoid the unjust April knockouts of 1993 and 1994, and add more vigour to some of the late-summer mid-table four-day games.

A year of Illingworth

Overall, it is possible to get far too hung up on the tortured logic which suggests that, because Australia beat England, the way to reverse this must be to copy everything Australia does. Australia has only six state teams: quick! get rid of a dozen counties. Australia has a Cricket Academy: gotta-getta-Cricket-Academy. Actually, there has been an Academy of sorts in England for ages, the Lord's groundstaff. But the MCC Young Cricketers now generally provide a second chance for players who have not been signed by a county. A new structure would be useful only if it were very carefully designed to fit in with what the counties do well (scooping up talent) and what they do badly (making the most of it). To be truthful, the most important asset Australia has over England is its climate, which could be matched only by towing Great Britain a thousand miles nearer the Equator, a proceeding likely to be ruled out on grounds of practicality and cost.

Amidst all this, it is very easy to ignore what is in front of our noses. In 1994-95 Australia had a better cricket team than England. But the gap between the players' inherent abilities was nowhere near as great as some of the performances suggested. Whereas Australia appeared to approach Test cricket open to the best and most up-to-date methods in everything from technical analysis and fitness training to media relations, much of England's thinking proceeded on the basis that what was good enough for our forefathers was good enough now. England, even more than the counties, continue to fail hopelessly to make the most of their human resources.

In March 1994, the counties, as constituents of the TCCB, did try and do something about this. Faced with two contending former England captains as candidates to succeed Ted Dexter as chairman of selectors, they made the surprisingly imaginative decision of choosing Ray Illingworth instead of the safer figure of M. J. K. Smith. Illingworth at once announced that, though he would be heading a committee of five, he would be taking full control of England's affairs, diminishing the role of both the team manager, Keith Fletcher, and the captain, Mike Atherton.

An extraordinary 12 months followed. Illingworth's approach was very different from the po-faced taciturnity that has long been the norm in English cricket. He spoke from the start as though he possessed the answers. Indeed, he spoke non-stop, making individual judgments and criticisms even while players were in the midst of preparing for or playing Test matches in both the West Indies and Australia. Modern warfare is usually accompanied by the sound of armchair generals chuntering over the airwaves about the correct way to invade Kuwait City or Port Stanley; it is not a role normally played by the serving commander-in-chief.

Illingworth abandoned Dexter's elaborate system of observers, making it clear that he would be relying on his observations and intuition. When he did not get his way in the re-styled committee (containing Brian Bolus and Fred Titmus as well as Fletcher and Atherton) he made that clear too. But there was no evidence that his judgments were any less fallible than anyone else's. His assessments of cricketing character were often awry, hence his preference for Martin McCague ahead of Angus Fraser in the initial selection for the Australian tour; he appeared not even to understand the extent to which Australian wickets have slowed up over the past 20 years. Everyone respects Illingworth's feel for the game; but he sometimes seemed to forget that one of the beauties of this most complex pastime is that no one ever has a monopoly of cricketing wisdom. One began to feel that the right adjective was the one that never attached to him in his playing days: amateurish.

Illingworth then went out to Australia for two Tests on the traditional TCCB-funded trip, which past chairmen of selectors used rather like state visits. He arrived with England already 1-0 down and was greeted by some sections of the travelling press as a saviour, which from their point of view he was, since his comments could fill columns of newsprint. In contrast, the tour manager – the same M. J. K. Smith whose approach had been implicitly rejected by the counties in their vote – who was nominally in control, refused to play a part in the explanations of England's performances. The Duke of Norfolk, as manager in 1962-63, was infinitely less remote.

There were edges to this farce that were very serious indeed: England were beaten so badly in Melbourne that one sensed the Australians starting to regard the whole country, not just its cricketers, as a laughing-stock. No one knew who was in charge. The tensions were obvious, overwhelming and, as I write, unresolved, with the captain and one selector, Titmus, firing messages to each other in print about a policy of concentrating on young players, which

Atherton wanted and Titmus did not. The situation increased Fletcher's tendency to fatalistic pessimism at a time when England needed an optimist. The tour was organised in a shambolic way, and it must never happen again.

If power is to lie with the chairman of selectors rather than the team manager, then he has to give the job the dedication and commitment he is entitled to expect from his players. He should be the tour manager, taking full responsibility, backed up by keen young coaches and an administrator to cope with the logistics and day-to-day public relations. It is not necessary to be a former England captain to get baggage off carousels.

Who benefits?

One of the nastier shocks of growing up is discovering that not every professional sportsman cares quite as deeply about winning every match as a young supporter might. It is not a problem unique to county cricket, but the set-up actively encourages lack of ambition. In that sense, the proponents of two divisions have identified a genuine problem.

Benefits date back to days when professionals were low-caste journeymen who needed a helping hand to prevent them ending up in the workhouse. They continue because cricket enthusiasts regard them as a worthy form of charity, and because the taxman looks on kindly. A good benefit can double a player's career income. On the one hand, waiting for this opportunity promotes loyalty to a club, though of a rather selfish and calculating kind. On the other, it creates a culture of time-serving and mediocrity.

Followers of county cricket, perhaps because they prefer the humbler virtues, like to reward the players they have come to know, never mind that they might have done only just enough each year to cling on to their contract. Excellence often makes the British uncomfortable.

County captains, mindful of the way things work, are reluctant to dump old sweats in favour of someone unproven but threatening. It will take a long time to end the benefit system: to harness spectators' generosity more productively, to pay players more but to shift the emphasis towards success rather than muddling through. Following the new TV deal, which will bring in £60 million over the next four years, English cricket has money enough to begin the process. It is time to do so.

A whole new Board game

In the next year or so the various administrative bodies that have ruled English cricket for the past 27 years are to be merged into something that will probably be called the English Cricket Board. For most people, the main effect may be that they will learn to stop saying, "Look what those fools at the TCCB have done now," and say instead, "Look what those fools at the ECB have done now." The danger with these reorganisations is always that more people are hired to push the same amount of paper round and everyone involved gets a handsome pay rise and a better car.

However, since the new Board will control cricket at all levels, it will be in a position to try to bring about the urgent changes that are needed below first-class level. There is a huge amount to be done; in this volume the tattered state of things is revealed even in a section as gentle as League Cricket in England and Wales, which tells of the way overseas players, especially itinerant Australians, manage to dominate the game in the innermost recesses of the country.

Nominally, cricket already has not one but two Second Divisions – but the Minor Counties Championship, now that Durham have departed, is contested by clubs with minimal ambition for themselves (imagine a football club that did not want to be promoted) and is increasingly dominated by ex-first-class players on the way down; there are hardly any potential first-class players on the way up. It might profitably be merged with the Second Eleven Championship, with the first-class teams using nearby counties as "farm clubs", as happens in American baseball.

There is a need for more elite leagues, as Micky Stewart has been saying, especially round the major population centres, getting away from limited-overs games and the 2.30-start-if-everyone-turns-up-on-time mentality. There is a need to recognise that there are not two universities in England but 80, containing a very large percentage of the country's 18 to 22-year-olds, and in many of these institutions cricket is close to collapse because of the contraction of the summer term and a shortage of funds.

The disaster that has overtaken cricket in the state schools has long been recognised, but hardly addressed. Many thousand boys attend sixth-form colleges; but in these schools, funding exists only for "specific vocational qualifications", which makes cricket a very low priority indeed, unless pupils are doing Physical Education A-Level. The concerned rhetoric of the Prime Minister is very different from his government's policy.

It would also help if the new organisation were less instinctively secretive than the old one. The Board will have a massive constituency of county members and players, which could make it even harder to control democratically than the TCCB. But is there any reason why it should not publish its accounts? Above all, it is going to need strong leadership. In 1990 the counties replaced Raman Subba Row with Frank Chamberlain as chairman, a clear decision not to have an activist in charge. It is time to change again. The game does not need dictatorship; it does need direction.

Unfamiliar action, familiar reaction

Possibly the most bizarre cricketing moment in 1994 was the conversation that took place between Ossie Wheatley, then the chairman of the TCCB cricket committee, and a former Test bowler whose anonymity we will preserve. Wheatley was giving details of his conversations with an Indian rocket scientist working for NASA who had explained to him the aerodynamic principles behind reverse swing. "Horsefeathers" (or something like that), said the Test player. "There's no such thing as reverse swing. It's a complete con."

This was just a postscript to the affair that for a week convulsed English cricket: when Mike Atherton appeared to perform what was officially called, with splendid coyness, "unfamilar action" on the ball as Darren Gough was trying to induce reverse swing. The details of the Saturday of the Lord's Test against South Africa are reported elsewhere in *Wisden*. Several months on, the TV pictures remain puzzling, Atherton's evasiveness remains discreditable. What is hard to re-create is the febrile atmosphere of the time in which every saloon bar in the land was unanimous that Atherton was cheating, while those best-placed to know how to fiddle with a cricket ball were least convinced – or did not even believe reverse swing existed.

We shall never know the truth unless and until Atherton publishes his memoirs with a chapter headed "Bang to Rights: Of course I did it". But perhaps even Atherton did not know quite what he was doing and why: the human mind is complex and captaining England is a very stressful job.

But, according to old team-mates, Atherton bowled with dust in his pockets in his leg-spinning days when he was definitely not trying to reverse swing it. Traditional British justice and common sense suggest that we should not destroy the career of any sportsman unless the evidence of his malfeasance is absolutely clear-cut – and, before anyone says anything, this is not out of line with what *Wisden* said about the Pakistani bowlers in similar circumstances two years ago.

However, the modern British way is to damn people first and ask questions later; it is an attitude of mind promoted by our newspapers and it is having an insidious effect on national life. The American Ring Lardner wrote a short story called *The Champ*, about a boxer who got away with every kind of evil because he was the champ; had Lardner been British he would have written the story the other way round. Atherton was the right choice to captain England. Nothing has happened to change that. He has made mistakes but has a sense of what needs to be done, and deserves the chance to bring that to fruition. That should not be tossed away lightly, by him or the rest of us.

In Fantasyland

Maybe, in the end, 1994 will be remembered as the year when Fantasy Cricket took a grip of the land. Four of Britain's national newspapers ran competitions in which readers were invited to compile their own elevens made up of any of the players in the County Championship; the runs and wickets they got in the Championship then counted in the competition.

The best-organised of these was in the *Daily Telegraph*, which attracted 132,537 entrants, who all had to pay 75p each. The sole prize was a trip to Australia, costing, say, a thousand pounds or two. It is not necessary to be Einstein to work out that this constitutes a rather less favourable form of gambling than a bent fruit machine or the three-card trick.

But it was an awfully good game, infinitely better than the footballing equivalent, because cricket's individual and statistical nature is perfect for the purpose. It began to take over cricket conversation: "Poor old Bloggins of Loamshire has just fallen downstairs and broken every bone in his body." "Damn, he's in my fantasy team." The editor of *Wisden* came 36,952nd. As I was saying, no one has a monopoly of cricketing wisdom.

Ah, Nostalgia!

After the rained-out one-day international between England and New Zealand in May, a woman from Chelmsford wrote to the *Daily Express* to congratulate the BBC for showing an old match from 1979 instead. "It was a joy to watch cricket of yesteryear when the crowds were happy and there was no abuse or rowdiness."

Ah, yes: 1979, the Golden Age of the game – the Packer schism, sledging, Lillee's aluminium bat, bouncer wars. . . . No abuse or rowdiness, indeed! We live in the age of Lara and Warne. A love of cricket goes together with an appreciation of the past. But, for heaven's sake, don't overdo it.

LOOKING AT LARA

SIX VIEWS OF HIS TWO RECORD-BREAKING INNINGS

THE COACH

Bob Woolmer, the Warwickshire coach in 1994, is believed to be the only man to have seen both Hanif Mohammad's old record 499 and Lara's 501.

It was a freak that I saw the Hanif innings. I was at prep school at Tonbridge and my father was working in Karachi. I was flown out on a BOAC Comet 4. That was a story in itself: we were actually forced down by fighters in Baghdad, where there was political trouble. I was 11 and I was very scared. Dad dropped me at the ground at Karachi where Hanif was closing in on the record and then he went to work. I don't remember much about it. There was a big crowd, a matting wicket, a very rough outfield and a bloke getting run out. My father asked me what happened and I said: "Well, someone got 499, Dad." Lara's innings is a bit clearer in my mind. At lunch, Brian said to me, "What score's the first-class record?" I said, "499. You're not going for that?" He said, "Well, are you thinking of declaring?" And Dermot Reeve said, "Well, sort of. We'll see how it goes." So it was agreed he could at least go for the Warwickshire record, 305, and I said to Dermot, "Let him go the whole way." He was just so single-minded, it was always inevitable, almost mystical. I don't think I remember any one shot in the innings so much as a Sunday League stroke at Taunton a couple of weeks earlier, against Payne of Somerset, when he flat-batted him into the old stand. I just remember him getting the 501 and his face. He signed a picture for me of his pull with the front foot off the ground. He put: "Try to teach this one, coach." I shall frame that.

Note: Mushtaq Mohammad, who played in the Karachi match, raced to Edgbaston from his office in Birmingham, having been tipped off by a phone call when Lara was past 450, but arrived too late.

THE SCORER

Alex Davis, a retired quantity surveyor and Warwickshire scorer since 1990, was also the scorer on the England tour of the West Indies. He is thus believed to be the only man to have watched every ball of both Lara's record-breaking innings.

For me, the two innings are very different, because the first I was doing manually in a scorebook, whereas the second I was doing on the computer and a manual scoresheet, so I was working twice as hard. And the second one was scored at such a rate, we kept having to answer the phone to the press to give the details of each of the fifties. At one time the pressman said: "Shall I stay on for the next 50?" The advantage of the computer is that it does do the adding-up for you, so you don't have to do so much cross-checking. When there's 800 runs on the board that makes a difference. There wasn't a problem of space, because I was doing it on a linear system, down the page. But then I copied it on to the standard scoresheet. Fortunately, with the 375, Simmons and Williams were out for eight and three, so there was loads of space to spread Lara. With the other one it wasn't so easy because of the runs the other players made, so I had to dodge round the spaces. So far as I know, I'm the only person who saw both all the way through. A lot of people didn't bother coming to Edgbaston on the Monday because the game looked completely dead and we had a semi-final at The Oval on the Tuesday. Mike Smith, who was the England manager in Antigua, missed it. My wife Christine normally comes and she never misses a ball: she used to score for Warwickshire Colts and she saw all the 375. But the general feeling was it wouldn't be much of a day. I got a terrible telling off for not ringing up. But she'd have had to come in on public transport from Solihull. And you can't do that with cricket. It used to happen when our son played: she used to ring up and tell me he was doing well and by the time I got there he'd be out.

THE BOWLER

Anderson Cummins, the Barbadian fast bowler, was 12th man for West Indies during the 375, but was playing for Durham and on the opposing side for the 501.

I had a good idea he was capable of record-breaking innings after seeing his 277 against Australia at Sydney. He's the type of individual who wants to be the best at what he does and that means going for records. He was running into form when he made his 375 against England. It was a very flat wicket and he set his stall out to produce something big. I don't think there was much else England could have done. With that sort of ability and determination, it was going to be very difficult to dislodge him. He started slowly but confidently. He didn't miss much. He has the natural art of picking the gaps and he played better and better. I never thought of the record until he was past 200, but we were all behind him to go for it. We had won the series and we knew it was something he wanted. When he made his 501 against Durham we bowled very well at him early on. We tried to exploit him stepping across his stumps early in his innings and we had our chances. He could have been out first ball. Knowing the type of player he is, I knew he would go for it if I banged one in. It lobbed off the end of his bat just out of my reach. He was on ten when I bowled him with a no-ball. It was a deliberate leg-stump yorker and he stepped inside it. But he started to play really well after about 90 minutes at the crease. I had batted on the pitch and I knew it was as flat as hell, and the way the game went it was set up for Lara to do something like that. Things usually go better for people who really believe in themselves. He was helped by the short boundary, which meant he could clip the ball off his stumps and it would go for six, but I was very impressed by his stamina. I knew he had the ability, but to concentrate for that long and keep going was amazing. I don't think anybody thought we had given it to him. Nobody flagged and we stuck at it right to the end. People forget that the match ended in a draw. We could have set something up to give them a target, but we were a bowler short because David Graveney was injured and at that stage of the Championship we didn't want to give anybody points.

THE BATSMAN

Keith Piper, the Warwickshire wicket-keeper, batted with Lara through the last 165 of his 501.

I'm not one for records, but he told me that 424 was his first target. Then, when he went past that score, he said that 500 was next. He didn't say much, just told me to keep concentrating. All through the season he kept on saying that if he batted for an hour, then he shouldn't get out and he expected a hundred. Yet he was so relaxed about everything that I felt none of the pressure I expected batting with someone who finally scored 390 that day. When he got hit on the helmet by John Morris towards 5.30 p.m., I went down the pitch to see if he knew what I knew. I'd checked with both umpires, and they told me that we could not claim the extra half-hour and so I told Brian that he had two balls left to go from 497 to 500. He just nodded and smashed the next ball through the covers for four. Brian's the best I've ever seen. The first thing I noticed about him was his backlift, which is the biggest and highest I've seen. Normally, that leads to looseness and mistakes but, once he is in perfect position at the top, he lets the arms go with such timing that he does something I have never seen before. He will bring the bat down straight, looking as though he must play the ball somewhere between mid-off and mid-on. Then, in the last part of the stroke, he will open or close the face of the bat and the ball scorches away square of the wicket. A lot of people talk about his power, and he does hit the ball hard, but it is the timing that beats the field and gives the impression he is always finding the gaps. He is like a squash player: the timing comes from playing the ball late under eye and head level. That's why he seldom hits the fielders.

THE JOURNALIST

John Thicknesse of the Evening Standard *was one of a handful of reporters to cover the 375 and to rush down to catch the end of the 501.*

There were 45 fours in Lara's 375 and I can recall only one that did not go where he intended – an edge off Caddick at 286 that would have been a chest-high catch to first slip if Thorpe had not been moved out in the hope of saving runs. If any given stroke brought Lara more boundaries than any other it was probably the extra-cover drive. But the shot I shall remember longest was the pull off Lewis with which he went from 365 to 369 – less because it gave him sole possession of the record than because it hit the advertising hoardings almost exactly where Richards smashed Botham with what has always been my favourite stroke in his 56-ball hundred in 1985-86. As a right hander, Richards was batting at the opposite end from Lara, and, rather than pulling a short ball, he was scything one at full stretch that, left to itself, would have been a leg-side wide. It was a fast good-length ball from Botham bowled from wide of the crease, pitching a few inches outside Richards's leg stump – arguably the hardest type of ball to hit in cricket. Somehow it was entirely fitting that eight years later Lara's record-breaking stroke went to almost the same spot. It was a marvellous

[*Graham Morris*

BRITANNIC ASSURANCE CHAMPIONSHIP

MATCH BETWEEN WARWICKSHIRE AND DURHAM
PLAYED AT EDGBASTON
ON 2nd 3rd 4th and 6th JUNE 1994
UMPIRES T.E. JESTY / P.B. WIGHT
SIDE WINNING TOSS DURHAM who elected to bat
SCORERS ALEX E. DAVIS : B. HUNT
INNINGS FIRST OF WARWICKSHIRE

ORDER	BATSMEN	RUNS AS SCORED	4/6	Balls Recd.	HOW OUT	BOWLER	Totals
1	OSTLER D.P.	[illegible]	2	8	c SCOTT (wkt)	CUMMINS	8
2	TWOSE R.G.	[illegible]	9	35	c COX	BROWN	51
3	LARA B.C.	[illegible]	62 10	427	NOT OUT		501
4	PENNEY T.L.	[illegible]	3 1	186	c HUTTON	BAINBRIDGE	44
5	SMITH P.A.	[illegible]	2	31	LBW	CUMMINS	12
6	PIPER K.J. (wk)	[illegible]	19 1	161	NOT OUT		116
7	REEVE D.A. (cpt)	DID NOT BAT					
8	SMITH N.M.K.						
9	DAVIS R.P.						
10	SMALL G.C.						
11	MUNTON T.A.						732

REMARKS: 3/6 Tea 66-1, Close 210-2; 4/6 Rain No Play in the day; 6/6 Lunch 483-2, Tea 686-4

Extras: Byes 4, Leg byes 4 ... 22; Wides 2 ... 2; No balls ... 26 — 78

	1	2	3	4	5	6	7	8	9	10
Overs	2.2	26.1	81.2	90.4						
FALL OF WICKETS	8	123	437	486						
BATSMAN OUT	OSTLER 8	TWOSE 51	PENNEY 44	SMITH P. 12						
NOT OUT	TWOSE	LARA	297	326						

TOTAL 810 for 4 wkts declared. 135.5 overs. 483 mins

Lara and 350 ... 400 ... 450 ... 500

Alex E. Davis

[*Roger Wootton*

Top: Sir Garfield Sobers goes on to the field to congratulate Lara as he passes Sobers's own Test record. *Above:* Warwickshire scorer Alex Davis's scorebook of the 501.

piece of luck that, when Lara scored his 501 not out seven Mondays later, England were wrapping up an innings win over New Zealand at Trent Bridge, which, with Jack Bannister at the wheel, proved to be no more than an hour's fast drive away. We arrived at Edgbaston in time for the last 130, witnessing another aspect of Lara's cricket: his fitness. Tiring, was he, after six hours at the crease? Pigs might fly. At 396 he hit an extra-cover drive 18 inches short of the distant Rae Bank boundary . . . and sprinted to 400 with an all-run four.

THE MAN HIMSELF

In 1994, Brian Lara was, beyond dispute, the greatest batsman in the world.

The 375 in the Antigua Test match was on a marble top of a pitch, ideal for batting. I knew if we won the toss we would make a big score and it did cross my mind it would give me a chance of scoring another double-hundred in Tests. But it was only after the first day's play, when I was on 164, that I thought it might be a big innings, maybe a world record. The next morning I started carefully, playing out two maiden overs from Angus Fraser. I knew it was up to me. If I kept my concentration and didn't do anything rash, I knew I had a chance of making history. I was not too tense. The tension only got to me in the early hours of the next morning when I woke much earlier than usual, and my mind was churning over what it would mean to me if I managed to score 46 more runs. My whole life flashed through my mind. I thought of all the people who had faith in me. I knew I couldn't let them down. The year before in Australia I was given a chance of breaking the record when I passed 200 in the Sydney Test but was run out on 277. That was the best innings of my career and still is. Most players never have a second opportunity. I knew I had to do it this time. The Antiguan innings was chanceless. I played a little sketchily on the third morning but I didn't give a chance. The one that went wide of Jack Russell's glove was a foot or so away from him. The 501 at Edgbaston was different in so many respects. The pitch was not quite so good but the outfield was faster. And obviously Durham's attack wasn't anywhere near as good as England's. On the Friday night I batted so poorly that I was bowled off a no-ball and dropped behind by Chris Scott at 18. "Jeez, I hope he doesn't go on and get a hundred," he said. At tea I went to the nets to try and correct the faults in my batting. It was unbelievable that both records should be broken in such a short space of time. The 375 was more important because it was in a Test match, but I will cherish both records. Test cricket is the highest form of cricket and to have broken the record of Sir Garfield Sobers in a Test in the West Indies meant more to me than anything I had achieved before. If only my father who did so much for me had been there to share the moment with me.

Interviews by Matthew Engel, Tim Wellock, Jack Bannister and Brian Scovell of the Daily Mail. *Lara's full account of the two innings can be found in his book,* Beating the Field (*Partridge Press*).

THE ROAD TO 375

PROGRESSIVE TEST INDIVIDUAL RECORD SCORES

				Minutes	6s	4s	Total	%
165*	C. Bannerman	A v E, Melbourne	March 15, 16, 1877	290	–	18	245	67.34
211	W. L. Murdoch	A v E, The Oval	August 11, 12, 1884	480	–	24	551	38.29
287	R. E. Foster	E v A, Sydney	December 12, 14, 1903	419	–	37	577	49.74
325	A. Sandham	E v WI, Kingston	April 3, 4, 5, 1930	600	–	27†	849	38.28
334	D. G. Bradman	A v E, Leeds	July 11, 12, 1930	383	–	46	566	59.01
336*	W. R. Hammond	E v NZ, Auckland	March 31, April 1, 1933	318	10	34	548-7d	61.31
364	L. Hutton	E v A, The Oval	August 20, 22, 23, 1938	797	–	35	903-7d	40.31
365*	G. S. Sobers	WI v P, Kingston	February 27, 28, March 1, 1958	614	–	38	790-3d	46.20
375	B. C. Lara	WI v E, St John's	April 16, 17, 18, 1994	766	–	45	593-5d	63.23

† Sandham's score of 325 also included one 7 and one 5.

OTHER SCORES OVER 300

				Minutes	6s	4s	Total	%
337	Hanif Mohammad	P v WI, Bridgetown	January 20, 21, 22, 23, 1958	970	–	24	657-8d	51.29
333	G. A. Gooch	E v I, Lord's	July 26, 27, 1990	627	3	43	653-4d	50.99
311	R. B. Simpson	A v E, Manchester	July 23, 24, 25, 1964	762	1	23	656-8d	47.40
310*	J. H. Edrich	E v NZ, Leeds	July 8, 9, 1965	532	5	52	546-4d	56.77
307	R. M. Cowper	A v E, Melbourne	February 12, 14, 16, 1966	727	–	20	543-8d	56.53
304	D. G. Bradman	A v E, Leeds	July 21, 23, 1934	430	2	43	584	52.05
302	L. G. Rowe	WI v E, Bridgetown	March 7, 9, 10, 1974	612	6	36	596-8d	50.67

Note: An accurate record of balls received is not possible for most of these innings. Lara faced 538 balls, Gooch 485 and Rowe 430.

THE ROAD TO 501

PROGRESSIVE FIRST-CLASS INDIVIDUAL RECORD SCORES

				Minutes	*6s*	*4s*	*Total*	*%*
344	W. G. Grace	MCC v Kent, Canterbury	August 11, 12, 1876	380	–	51	557-9	61.75
424	A. C. MacLaren	Lancashire v Somerset, Taunton	July 15, 16, 1895	470	1	62	801	52.93
429	W. H. Ponsford	Victoria v Tasmania, Melbourne	February 3, 5, 1923	477	–	42	1,059	40.50
437	W. H. Ponsford	Victoria v Queensland, Melbourne	December 16, 17, 1927	621	–	42	793	55.10
452*	D. G. Bradman	NSW v Queensland, Sydney	January 4, 6, 1930	415	–	49	761-8d	59.39
499	Hanif Mohammad	Karachi v Bahawalpur, Karachi	January 8, 9, 11, 1959	635	–	64	772-7d	64.63
501*	B. C. Lara	Warwickshire v Durham, Birmingham	June 3, 4, 6, 1994	474	10	62	810-4d	61.85

OTHER SCORES OVER 400

				Minutes	*6s*	*4s*	*Total*	*%*
443*	B. B. Nimbalkar	Maharashtra v Kathiawar, Poona	December 16, 17, 18, 1948	494	1	50	826-4	53.63
428	Aftab Baloch	Sind v Baluchistan, Karachi	February 18, 19, 20, 1974	584	–	25?	951-7d	45.00
405*	G. A. Hick	Worcestershire v Somerset, Taunton	May 5, 6, 1988	555	11	35	628-7d	64.49

Note: An accurate record of balls received is possible only for Hick's innings (469) and Lara's (427).

Statistics by Philip Bailey

[*Hulton-Deutsch Collection*

One of Peter May's most characteristic shots. The match was Surrey v Derbyshire at The Oval in 1952 and the wicket-keeper was George Dawkes.

PETER MAY 1929-1994

AN APPRECIATION

By DOUG INSOLE

Six years after the Second World War, Peter May came into the England team against South Africa at Headingley and scored 138 with enormous style. It was the most exciting thing to have happened in English cricket since Len Hutton's 364 at The Oval 13 years earlier. England's batting heroes in the years before that were, inevitably, players like Hutton, Washbrook, Compton and Edrich who had begun to make their reputations in pre-war days. But May's first Test innings against South Africa heralded the arrival of a new generation and ushered in for England the most successful decade in their cricketing history.

Now, 44 years on, I think he remains the best batsman England has produced since the war. His batting did not have Compton's flair and charm, but at the peak of his form he could be dazzling – there was one occasion when I was skippering Essex against Surrey and I felt distinct twinges of regret when we got him out. His basic technique was very sound, and he was an outstanding front-foot player, especially on the on side, where I have not seen his equal.

He seemed to thrive in difficult situations. It would be wrong to say he liked them, but he faced up to them with that determination that was so much a part of his temperament. His confidence depended on habit. He avoided going into the nets on a morning when he was likely to be batting, and he very seldom watched the play before going to the wicket. Indeed, if the opening batsmen were playing and missing a lot, he would retire to the back of the dressing-room, out of sight and sound. His concentration on the task ahead was absolute, and it was not easy to get much sense out of him during this pregnant period.

Sometimes this could boil over into superstition. On the South African tour of 1956-57, Peter began with four consecutive hundreds. At a reception in Salisbury (now Harare), the city's Mayor presented him with a live duck and expressed the patriotic hope that it might have a debilitating effect on his future performances. From that point on, he struggled to reach double figures. After getting out to yet another magnificent catch late in the Test series he came back to the dressing-room, threw his bat on his bag, and said, "That ---- duck." He did not often swear.

When Peter took over the captaincy of England from Len Hutton in 1955, he had very little experience of leading a side. But he was liked and respected by those who played under him and he got the best out of them. He was never a soft touch: he was loyal to his players and they were aware of it, but he could be distinctly uncharitable if that loyalty was not returned and he was quick to punish lack of effort, or stupidity, as distinct from naïveté.

His tactical approach was straightforward. He was not adventurous, but it might be said that he had no need to be. The attacks at his command, for Surrey and England, were very strong, and he depended on his established bowlers to do their job. He would set out with a plan and he was not easily deflected from it. During his magnificent unbeaten 285 against West Indies at Edgbaston in 1957, a few of us tried to persuade him to declare earlier than he did, but he had set his heart on saving the match and wanted to make absolutely certain of that before considering the prospect of winning it. Since he and Colin Cowdrey had got England out of a really dire situation, it was not difficult to sympathise.

Peter May was likeable, modest, and also extremely sensitive. When England were being beaten in Australia in 1958-59 while the "throwing" controversy was at its height, he was criticised by some newspapers for spending his spare time on the tour with his fiancée Virginia when he might, in their opinion, have been better employed in the nets. He resented bitterly that his wife-to-be should have been dragged into what he regarded as a totally unjustified personal attack, and he never subsequently had quite the same appetite for the game.

He became ill and returned home during the West Indies tour the following winter, and medical opinion was that stress was a major cause. Much later, in the 1980s, when he was chairman of selectors, he was hurt by the virulence of some of the criticism directed at him when England were performing badly. Previous experience had shown him what to expect, but the intervening years had barely diminished his vulnerability.

Those he permitted to get close to him were well aware that Peter had a lively sense of humour, and was very good company indeed. Together with Peter Richardson, he and I made a recording of a version of Cole Porter's "Let's Do It" that we had written and performed for the team's Saturday Night Club in South Africa, and Peter did his vocal stuff with great gusto and considerable enjoyment.

When we were co-selectors, I watched hundreds of hours of Test cricket with him. He was a very sound judge of a player and, while he was an exacting critic, he was in no way dismissive of the skills and abilities of modern cricketers. He was a traditionalist as an administrator, and worked hard to sustain high standards of behaviour on the field. He was not stuffy about it and was prepared to concede that in changing times it was unreasonable not to accept modern manifestations of delight. What he could not condone was dissent and the general pressurising of umpires. His influence on such matters was exerted quietly and positively, but he often said that he did not find it easy to communicate his views to the younger generation of cricketers.

Until cricket tours changed his winters, Peter was a useful footballer, at inside forward for Cambridge and occasionally for Pegasus, the Oxford and Cambridge side that had a highly successful run in amateur football in the 1950s. He did the basic things well – his ball control was good and his passing accurate – but he was a bit short on pace and panache.

Peter's family was the most important thing in his life. His father-in-law was Harold Gilligan, so there was a cricketing pedigree, but Virginia, while recognising the importance of cricket, was and is greatly interested in horses. So, in their turn, were the four daughters of whom Peter was immensely proud. He was perhaps an unlikely stable lad, but it had seemed possible over the past few years that he might turn up at Lord's with the odd wisp of straw in his hair. The family's togetherness was eloquently demonstrated during the last few months of his life. I doubt whether Peter had an enemy. His friends will miss him greatly. Cricket has lost a great player and one of its finest ambassadors.

Doug Insole played nine Tests for England and was Peter May's vice-captain in South Africa in 1956-57. He was subsequently chairman of both the Test selectors and the TCCB. An obituary of Peter May appears on page 1389.

CHEATING: THE SECRET HISTORY

By DEREK PRINGLE

Cheating, in any sport, is an emotive subject. In cricket the stigma attached to "illegal practices" is even greater, for the game has been a byword for fair play wherever English is spoken since its beginnings on the downland of southern England. Yet as the line between what constitutes fair and unfair play becomes ever more blurred, the notion of ungentlemanly conduct, once seen as underpinning cricket's charm, has become its burden.

In professional cricket what may be rigidly set down in the black and white of the law could have been slowly bent by the players for generations, ending up as an accepted practice. Perhaps these customs have been endured rather than lauded, but they can be condemned without reservation only by people who have never used the office phone to find out the Test score or taken a paper clip from the stationery cupboard. As I was working on this piece, a former colleague accused the Essex and Lancashire teams of agreeing a tit-for-tat exchange of matches in 1991, which was news to me. But it was a reminder that anyone who has played cricket may be living in a glass house, and throwing stones can be very dangerous indeed.

Any team sport has to be designed to provide a close contest; this is what gives sport its appeal, to both players and spectators. In cricket the internal dynamic has always been between bat and ball. But it is a battle that is constantly in flux as conditions change and new methods and techniques evolve. When imbalances have occurred, the laws of the game have often been amended to prevent anyone gaining too much of an advantage.

In recent years, however, the balance has swung only one way and almost every law change has been made to hinder the bowler. First there was the limitation placed on leg-side fielders, with only two allowed behind square. This came about as a direct result of the Bodyline series. As Bruce Harris, author of *Jardine Justified*, observed at the time: "So used are batsmen to being on top that, when a form of attack is evolved to put bowlers on terms again, up rises a wail of protest." This holds true today, except that most of the protests come not from the players, but from the commentators and press.

In 1963, the back-foot no-ball law was altered to prevent bowlers dragging until they were bowling from 18 yards. Then came the covering of pitches, by far the most emasculating of all the changes that favour bat over ball. But there have been further limitations, to the size of the seam, to the number of bouncers per over and so on. In contrast, the only significant change of any benefit to the bowler was the alteration of the lbw law to discourage a batsman padding the ball away without playing a stroke, which was done more to appease bored spectators than disgruntled bowlers.

When you add in all the technological advances favouring batsmen, such as heavy but well-balanced bats and better protective gear like helmets, thigh pads and chest guards, a pattern builds up. Since an increasing amount of time is spent playing one-day cricket, a form of the game specifically designed for batting, it is hardly surprising that bowlers begin to suspect that the people who run the game have lost interest, for commercial reasons, in maintaining the ancient balance.

Cricketers have always crossed over into unfairness in seeking to gain the advantage. In the late 18th century, when cricket was very largely a gambling game, whole teams were bribed to throw matches. In 1817, William Lambert, the greatest batsman of his era, was forced out of cricket for corruption. Around the same time, there was a farcical match between England and Nottinghamshire in which both sides had sold the match, so batsmen were trying to get out to bowlers who were doing their best to avoid taking wickets.

W. G. Grace, the first cricketing superstar, was regularly guilty of "irksome subterfuges within the law". He was also a notorious sledger. In 1921, J. W. H. T. Douglas, the England captain in Australia, supposedly threatened to report Arthur Mailey for illegally using resin to grip the ball – until Mailey pointed out that Douglas's own thumbnail had been worn to the flesh picking the seam for his own bowlers.

Until recently most infractions were either ignored by the umpires, or sorted out with a quiet word in the ear of either the culprit or the captain. One umpire just stared at the ball, as treated by an England fast bowler, and said: "You better take six wickets with that or there'll be trouble." The media and television, in particular, have changed all that. As Graham Gooch put it: "What for years were accepted but mildly frowned-upon practices, like picking the seam, have now been labelled cheating. That's a big word. What people would once have had a bit of a laugh about in the bar is now being flatly denied. Nobody wants to be labelled a cheat. It's all the media's fault for going overboard to get their story." The *Sunday Mirror* recently quoted Geoff Boycott admitting that Yorkshire players in his day sometimes played around with the ball. Three of the first 55 words were "bombshell", "incredible" and "sensationally".

So administrators have clamped down on practices like seam-lifting, using lipsalve to maintain the shine and, horror of horrors, batsmen getting their spikes into the pitch to break it up once their team is in the ascendancy. All these actions are premeditated. In a court of law, a premeditated crime is considered far worse than one committed on the spur of the moment. But in cricket these have traditionally been regarded far more lightly than the behaviour of the chancer who on the spur of the moment refuses to walk or claims a catch on the bounce.

Picking the seam has been endemic to the professional game for years. Usually, that is the action of the individual bowler not only to try and get an advantage over the batsmen but to get one over on his fellow-bowlers by taking more wickets than them and keeping his place in the team. A professional playing a team game has more than one objective in his mind.

In contrast, keeping the ball shiny by using lipsalve requires a team effort. Very often, at county level, this has been sanctioned not only by the captain but also by the ex-players who are umpires. There was an incident that reputedly took place in the law-abiding surroundings of Tunbridge Wells, of all places, where the visiting slip fielders returned the ball to the fast bowler before they had time to rub in whatever substance was being used that day. The bowler bellowed out: "What's this greasy stuff someone's put all over the ball?"

"In my day, everyone cleaned the seam," recalled the former Northamptonshire and England bowler Frank Tyson. "You had to, playing on uncovered wickets. Inevitably, the seam would get lifted as well. Some sides were notorious for it. Brylcreem and hair oil would also find their way on to the ball. Both were widely used as part of the fashion of the day. Of course, it was no bloody use to me. I had no hair to put it on even then."

This was in clear contravention of the Laws and yet, until recently, this sort of thing was far more acceptable than a batsman not walking, though this was not in breach of any written rule. It may have something to do with the fact that, when the distinction still existed, batsmen were a mixture of amateurs and professionals, whereas bowlers were far more likely to be professional. As Bob Appleyard, the former Yorkshire and England bowler, confirmed, when asked if everyone in his day walked: "Ay, mostly. But those who didn't were more likely to be professional." It was, perhaps, easier for amateurs to live up to gentlemanly notions of fair play than for professionals who had a living to scrape together.

However, gentlemanliness always had its limits. In the 1960s and 1970s some well-known batsmen were believed to have built up unblemished reputations for walking when an edged catch was obvious, but standing their ground when less obvious chances were offered in more critical situations, relying on their good name to be given not out. This was a very English phenomenon. Ray Lindwall says none of his contemporaries ever walked – except Neil Harvey, once, for lbw in a Test match.

"To walk or not to walk?" was still a debate on the England tour of Australia in 1982-83. The rest of the world had stopped walking at Test level at least a decade earlier, but England held a team meeting in which Ian Botham vehemently insisted that, if anyone walked, it would be over his dead body. His argument was that England would be getting no favours from Australian umpires and probably bad decisions too. Several players felt uncomfortable with this line and in the end Bob Willis, as captain, left it up to the individual.

Not walking might break the spirit of the game, but it is harder for batsmen to break the Laws. When "Shock" White walked out in the 18th century with a bat wider than the stumps it was not then illegal; and Dennis Lillee was not breaking any existing law when he used an aluminium bat against England in 1979-80. However, it is not unknown for lead weights to be put in the back of bats to make them bottom-heavy, and bowlers these days get annoyed by batsmen using fibreglass tape, which has an abrasive effect on the ball, rather than Elastoplast to bind their bats. No one screams that anyone should be drummed out of the game for this.

Thus fair play is largely a notion that affects bowlers. And far from being a blessing, it is becoming an encumbrance for players as the game finds itself a vehicle for moral and behavioural issues far beyond its compass. The word "cheat" has been much bandied round in the past three seasons when first the Pakistani fast bowlers and then England captain Mike Atherton were accused of illegally helping the ball reverse swing.

The discovery of reverse swing is a perfect example of man's triumph over an unhelpful environment in order to survive. Playing on grassless pitches of low bounce with hard, bare outfields, where cricket balls rapidly deteriorate, Pakistan's bowlers developed a method of swinging an old ball. It requires a creation of opposites on the ball's surface, a kind of Yin and Yang effect where one side is kept smooth and damp while the other is allowed to roughen but is kept scrupulously dry. It has to be a team effort, for any dampness on the rough side will negate the swing.

This has not always been achieved legally, and Imran Khan has admitted once using a bottle-top to scratch one side of the ball to speed up its deterioration. But not long ago, roughing up a ball by rubbing it in the dirt was accepted practice. One county captain was seen to do the job against the concrete on the pavilion steps. Granted, it was done in those days to improve the grip for the spinners, but where's the difference?

So was Atherton cheating? To my eyes, there was no evidence that he was taking any action to alter the state of the ball and there is no regulation to stop a player having a pocketful of soil. There is a danger now that the authorities will be panicked into rewriting the Laws yet again. The contest between bat and ball will work best with a minimum of fuss and a maximum of self-regulation.

Derek Pringle played 30 Tests for England between 1982 and 1992. He is now cricket correspondent of the Independent on Sunday.

YEAR OF GRACE, 1895

This year marks the centenary of one of the most remarkable cricket seasons ever, when the Golden Age of the game was close to its zenith and the greatest of all cricketers reached previously uncharted peaks. Dr W. G. Grace had been in poor form, by his standards, for some years before 1895, which was not surprising since he was about to celebrate his 47th birthday that July.

He did not play a first-class match until May 9, for MCC against Sussex, when he made 103, his 99th century. After failing twice for MCC against Yorkshire, he returned home to Bristol for Gloucestershire v Somerset. In weather so cold that tradition says he batted with snowflakes in his beard, Grace not merely became the first man to score a hundred hundreds but went on to make 288. He followed this a week later with 257 against Kent and, on May 30, hit 169 against Middlesex at Lord's to become the first man to score 1,000 runs in May, a feat emulated only twice since.

"The years had rolled away," wrote Bernard Darwin later, "and for this one year W. G. once more stood supreme as in the 'seventies . . . the unbeatable, the unbowlable." Three national testimonials were launched, raising more than £9,000 between them; and *The Times* suggested, unavailingly, that he ought to be in the Birthday Honours.

A fine spring meant that batting records were broken all over England. As Grace was scoring his 288, Nottinghamshire were making 726 against Sussex, the highest total in county cricket. This, however, was surpassed in July when Lancashire made 801 at Taunton and A. C. MacLaren scored 424, which remained the highest first-class score in the world for almost three decades. It was also the summer when K. S. Ranjitsinhji first batted, brilliantly, for Sussex. It was still possible to bowl: Tom Richardson of Surrey took 290 wickets. In September, *Punch* marked the season in verse:

Yet ne'er before three heroes have I seen
More apt and splendid on the well-rolled green;
Men of one skill, though varying in race –
MacLaren, Ranjitsinhji, Grand old Grace.

Centenary dates in 1995: May 17 – Grace's 100th 100; May 30 – Grace's 1,000 in May; July 16 – MacLaren's 424.

THE RECORD-BREAKERS RETIRE

1. ALLAN BORDER – 11,174 TEST RUNS

By MIKE COWARD

Allan Border, who retired in May 1994 as Test cricket's highest run-scorer, committed the greater part of a long and distinguished career to re-establishing the credibility and image of Australian cricket. A self-effacing man of simple tastes and pleasures, Border served at the most tempestuous time in cricket history, and came to represent the indomitable spirit of the Australian game. As it grappled with two schisms, the first over World Series Cricket, the second over the provocative actions of the mercenaries in South Africa, it was debilitated and destabilised as never before and cried out for a figure of Bradmanesque dimensions to return it to its rightful and influential position on the world stage.

Into the breach strode earnest Allan Robert Border, a working-class boy, born at Cremorne on the north shore of Sydney Harbour, who grew up over the road from the Mosman Oval that now bears his name. At one time he was a beach bum, who was cajoled from his indolence and indifference by the noted coach and former England Test player, Barry Knight. But Border, standing just 5ft 9in, bestrode the Test match arena like a colossus for more than 15 years.

When he retired 11 weeks before his 39th birthday, after fulfilling his ambition to lead Australia in South Africa, Border was entitled to be ranked alongside Sir Donald Bradman as the greatest of Australian cricketers. Certainly no one since Sir Donald has done more to advance Australian cricket throughout the world – particularly in developing countries.

Border's batting cannot really stand comparison with Bradman but many of his achievements go far beyond the Bradmanesque – 156 Test matches, 153 of them consecutive, on 36 grounds in eight different Test-playing countries (Sir Donald played 52 Tests on ten grounds, all in Australia and England); 11,174 runs at 50.56 with 27 centuries and 63 fifties; 93 consecutive Test matches as captain; 156 catches; 273 limited-overs appearances, 178 as captain, including Australia's victory in the 1987 World Cup final. All of these accomplishments are in a league of their own and some may remain so; Sunil Gavaskar, the only other scorer of more than 10,000 Test runs, doubts that Border's run record will ever be broken.

Yet only in the twilight of his career did Border become even faintly interested in his statistical achievements. Essentially he was an unromantic, uncomplicated but uncompromising workman-cricketer. It is problematical whether Border, unlike Bradman, has ever understood his place in history. He reinvigorated Australian cricket and provided it with stability, direction and enthusiasm; this was the most significant of his many contributions and the one which gave him the greatest satisfaction. There is a remarkable set of figures to underscore the extent of the stability Border provided. From the time he succeeded his fragile friend Kim Hughes on December 7, 1984 until his captaincy ended on March 29, 1994, opposing countries commissioned 38 captains – 21 of them against Australia. From his first Test, at Melbourne, on December 29, 1978, he played with and against 361 different players.

To gain a true appreciation of Border, it is necessary to examine his formative years in the leadership when his team was scorned and he was disturbingly close to a breakdown. In 1985 when Australian cricket reached its nadir and a collection of leading players defected to South Africa, Border, the least political of men, was dragged into a black hole of depression. He was barely four months into his term of office – while he forgave them, he never forgot the hurt caused by those team-mates who pursued the dollar rather than the dream, and opted to play in South Africa. For a man who placed such store in team loyalty, it was a cruel lesson. When he retired, Border reflected: "I felt very let down. We were playing in Sharjah and everyone was having a beer and saying that the team was starting to get it together. There was that sort of talk. You feel such a fool when you then read in the paper that blokes you have trusted, who have told you how great the future looks, are going to South Africa."

Many of his attitudes were formed and much of his philosophy as a captain formulated at this time when Australia were not expected to win and, in the main, did not. The dire circumstances of the day compelled him to think defensively, and it was not until 1989 when he engineered a memorable 4-0 eclipse of a dispirited England that there was a measure of optimism and aggression about his leadership. But while his entitlement to the job was hardly ever questioned, the negativism of his captaincy was the area that most occupied the attention of his critics. In mitigation, he insisted that the circumstances of his time had made it impossible for him to develop a totally positive philosophy. He evolved into an enterprising captain when he was finally in charge of able and ambitious men, as was evidenced by his thoughtful and often bold use of the leg-spinner Shane Warne. In this period, some English critics felt that Australia's approach was getting too hard; that might say more about them than about Border.

With customary candour, he often pleaded guilty to periods of moodiness and regretted that, at least in the dressing-room, his instinct was to internalise his deepest thoughts and feelings. Paradoxically, he was an expansive and articulate spokesman, and was much admired by the media for being accessible, courteous and forthright. So he had good reason to resent the "Captain Grumpy" tag foisted upon him by the tabloids.

With few, if any, exceptions, his team-mates and employers indulged his contrariness; it was infrequent and irritating rather than damaging. Indeed, the fact that his actions and reactions were always so commonplace, so human, made him an endearing as well as an enduring champion. Essentially, he was an ordinary soul who accomplished extraordinary deeds. For a suburban family man, with an unselfconscious hankering for a beer around a backyard barbecue, Border became an exceptionally worldly cricketer. That he was able to expunge many of the prejudices and preconceptions amongst his team-mates about playing cricket in the Third World was another of the outstanding legacies of his captaincy.

The fact that his technique and temperament allowed him to play productively in the most extreme conditions and situations was perhaps the true gauge of his greatness. Indeed, the tougher the predicament the more resolute and more resourceful was his batting. He averaged 56.57 in 70 overseas Tests. In Australia, he averaged 45.94 in 86 Tests. And he averaged fractionally more as captain (50.94) than as non-captain (50.01) – further confirmation of his red-blooded response to challenge.

[*Patrick Eagar*

Above: Kapil Dev bowling against South Africa at Durban, November 1992. *Below:* Allan Border, on the way to a double-century against England at Headingley, July 1993.

[*Patrick Eagar*

While he was never numbered among the poetic left-handers, it is erroneous to categorise him as just an accumulator of runs. In his pomp, he hooked and pulled as well as he square cut and drove in front of point. For many years he was bracketed with Javed Miandad, another eminent and indefatigable scrapper, as the foremost player of slow bowling in the world. Furthermore, Border was blessed with all-round skills. He was a sure catch anywhere, but especially at slip, and in the limited-overs game earned an impressive reputation for his ability to throw down the stumps from any angle within the circle. And while he was self-deprecating about his left-arm orthodox spin bowling, he once took 11 wickets in a Sydney Test against West Indies. But that was no balm for his disappointment at being unable to defeat West Indies in a Test series and so legitimately claim for Australia the unofficial title of world champion. At Adelaide in 1992-93 he went within two runs of attaining the goal.

His retirement from the captaincy and Test cricket was messy, an unfortunate situation caused, more than anything, by a misunderstanding between Border and the Australian Cricket Board. It should have been done with style. But he handed to Mark Taylor the most precious gift of all – a stable, committed, educated, enterprising and hard-edged elite cricket team. Australian cricket will forever be in the debt of AB, the cricketer's cricketer, the people's cricketer and a bloody good bloke with it.

Mike Coward is cricket columnist for The Australian.

2. KAPIL DEV – 434 TEST WICKETS

By MIKE SELVEY

Perhaps the hardest thing to appreciate about Kapil Dev finally exchanging his cricket box for the TV commentary box is the fact that he was only 35 years old when he did so. Well, give or take a bit maybe: he might be a touch more geriatric than that; it is often suggested that at the time he was born, whenever that was, it was not necessarily the custom in northern India to register the year of birth. But that misses the point: however old he was, he seemed to have been around for a lot longer, prancing in to shore up the Indian attack and joyfully retrieving an innings with uninhibited squeaky-clean hitting. An Indian team without him will never seem quite the same.

With his departure comes the end of an era that has been blessed with a quartet of all-rounders unmatched in the history of the game, beginning in the early 1970s with Richard – later Sir Richard – Hadlee and Imran Khan, progressing to the laddo Botham, and finally, with his Test debut in October 1978, to the man who became known to his countrymen as the Haryana Hurricane.

What deeds from these four! Between them, they took 1,610 Test wickets and scored 17,379 runs. With the possible exception of Hadlee, each was equipped technically to play international cricket as a specialist in either role. But what a contrast: Hadlee the Inquisitor, with a surgeon's touch and an accountant's brain; Imran, the haughty, proud Pathan; Botham, the bull elephant who lived cricket and life on the edge and Kapil, flamboyant and cavalier, charming but deadly. Today, Wasim Akram alone is left to carry a torch for the standards set by these four.

Kapil has perhaps been regarded as the most lightweight of the group. But with 434 wickets and 5,248 runs, he is the one who proved, in the end, to be the most prolific with both ball and bat. That has much to do with the fact that he played 131 Tests compared with Hadlee's 86, Imran's 88 and Botham's 102. And, as the last to survive, he was in a position to make sure that he finished top of the heap. But he laid out his credentials as soon as he entered Test cricket. His teeth may have flashed a disarming smile but this was a formidable competitor worthy of his fierce Punjabi ancestors.

Kapil has always regarded bowling as his primary role. And on February 8, 1994 he took the wicket of the Sri Lankan, Hashan Tillekeratne, to go past Hadlee's world record haul of 431 wickets. For the latter part of his career, it had been a hard slog, chipping away bit by bit at the target, like someone climbing a rock face and gradually running out of handholds with the top of the pitch in sight. Towards the end the years caught up and he was reduced to little more than medium-pace, with away-swing going invitingly early.

But it hadn't always been so. In his prime, he was much like the young, lithe Botham, with pace enough – goaded by the irrational Indian belief that their bowlers were born only to beguile – to render footwork leaden. This was accompanied by snaking late out-swing, helped by a contortionist's action so far round that it presented his left shoulder-blade to the batsman, and a wicked break-back that struck with the speed of a cobra. Superficially, his bowling may have lacked Hadlee's relentlessly searching examination, or Imran's leaping, muscular pace, or Botham's bludgeon and will-power, but it was deceptively effective for all that.

Yet in the fullness of time, he may be remembered more for his carefree, hawk-eyed batting. He was helped by the fact that he was an all-rounder and so had the freedom to play as he did: one discipline fuelled the other. The rate at which he was capable of scoring was phenomenal. At Lord's in 1982, he brought the England bowling to its knees, hitting 13 fours and three sixes, an innings of 89 that came from just 55 balls, well on course then for what would have been the fastest Test century in history. And in his last Lord's Test, in 1990 – Gooch's match – he scored the 24 India required to save the follow-on by hitting Eddie Hemmings for four successive straight sixes while the last man, Hirwani, blinked myopically at the other end and got out next ball.

And yet perhaps his finest moment came not in a Test but in a limited-overs international against Zimbabwe, not even a Test-playing nation then, at, improbably enough, Tunbridge Wells. In 1983, it was Kapil's lot to lead India in the World Cup, and he found himself at the crease on a damp pitch, with the scoreboard reading 17 for five. He was to play what he has described as "the innings of a lifetime", scoring an unbeaten 175 as India reached 266 for eight and went on to win the game.

Eventually, they progressed to the final at Lord's where, against all the odds, they beat West Indies, then arguably the most potent cricket force ever to set foot on the ground. Kapil and India showed they could be taken, and an illusion was shattered: West Indies have not won the World Cup since.

Mike Selvey, who played three Tests for England, is cricket correspondent of The Guardian.

TALKING A GOOD GAME

50 YEARS OF CRICKET SOCIETIES

By MURRAY HEDGCOCK

It is odd that it took the English so many years after they invented cricket to devise an organisation in which people could talk about the game, or just listen to others talking about it for them. But now it is anniversary time. The Cricket Society, based in London and the most senior of the 40 or so societies now flourishing worldwide, celebrates its half-century this year; the umbrella organisation, the Council of Cricket Societies, turned 25 in 1994.

There was a forerunner. The Cricketana Society was launched in London on October 21, 1929 "for collectors of cricket literature, prints, records, trophies etc. and to assist members in their hobby". It was too esoteric for its own good, and withered away in the 1930s.

But during the war many servicemen abroad thought wistfully of the summer game and in *The Cricketer* Spring Annual in 1945, Antony Weigall, an accountant and Kent supporter, suggested that statisticians should link up. A meeting that November at 15 Great Scotland Yard drew just eight enthusiasts. They went ahead, again on the elitist track, forming the Society of Cricket Statisticians, with membership "limited to cricket statisticians and collectors of cricketana". Weigall was elected chairman, with the writer S. C. Caple as secretary and the BBC scorer Roy Webber as his assistant.

A prime object of the new society was a bibliography of cricket: a start was made in 1947 – the project ebbed and flowed, until Tim Padwick of Guildhall Library masterminded the invaluable reference book that was finally published by the Library Association in 1977.

The group was soon renamed the Cricket Society, to underline its widening interests, but it still found problems in gaining recognition. Then, in September 1950, Sir Pelham Warner, the MCC President, spoke at a dinner: this seal of approval set the society on its way. Just as the North-South divide exists in English culture, politics and cricket, it has been a feature of the cricket society movement: for years there was a frosty relationship between London and Yorkshire. The Cricket Society, as a London-based organisation with a worldwide membership and a metropolitan flavour, saw itself as the keystone. But in Leeds, the society's northern branch had made a unilateral declaration of independence as the Northern Cricket Society in January 1948, months before their southern cousins adopted a similar name. They therefore claimed to be the senior society, and strong characters on each side argued the respective cases.

This led to The Curious Incident Of The *Wisden* Report, when the 1979 Almanack ran an article on the society movement, written by Ron Yeomans, a Yorkshireman with a Truemanesque belief that the White Rose county came first in all things. A year later, *Wisden* recorded with some embarrassment that Yeomans had devoted his entire article, with the exception of a single paragraph, to societies north of the Trent: the new edition paid belated tribute to London.

Relations are warm today, but the movement in England, like brass bands, flourishes particularly north of Watford, as the list of societies on page 1289 will confirm. Yorkshire remains the heartland, with at least eight different societies. But it is the Cricket Society which sums up the reasoning behind the entire movement with its stated aim: "To support the game of cricket at all levels wherever it is played, regardless of race, colour or creed." With a worldwide membership of 2,000-plus, it draws hundreds to spring and autumn dinners addressed by anyone from MPs to showbiz stars; the society runs its own team, has built an extensive library, and produces a journal twice yearly contributing substantially to research and discourse on the game.

Since 1970 the society, whose president is the former Test batsman and MCC Treasurer Hubert Doggart, has provided Lord's Easter coaching places for promising youngsters, and it awards trophies to outstanding young players. The society team has developed from amateurish beginnings to lively elevens fielded regularly: the first tour was Paris in 1954, and others have gone as far as Hong Kong, Australia, Barbados and Philadelphia. Strange team members have surfaced now and then: cricket secretary Jeremy Burford recalls Garfield Hambly playing at 82, and "the anonymous Belgian boy of 16 who was 'given' to our team in Brussels and made top score". The most newsworthy activity of the Northern Cricket Society has been its annual Boxing Day match, begun in 1949, and played mostly at Alwoodley. Most games have beaten the weather, even snow.

The venues of the different societies range from the echoes-of-empire splendour of the National Liberal Club and the Royal Overseas League (The Cricket Society), and the tradition-rich atmosphere of the Trent Bridge Long Room (Nottingham Cricket Lovers' Society), to the spartan canteen of Ross Sports Club at Grimsby (Lincolnshire CLS). Speakers run the gamut of the game. Current Test players (when they can be persuaded) are most highly prized; former players, often happy to recall days in the limelight, are regulars. Umpires and groundsmen, scorers and statisticians, broadcasters and journalists, administrators and collectors of cricketana all cheer the faithful. Attendances can top three hundred at the Essex Society and the Lancashire and Cheshire, in the Chelmsford and Old Trafford pavilions, down to a dozen or so at the smaller outposts.

In the 1960s, the National Cricket Association suggested a linking body, to be represented on the NCA: the Council of Cricket Societies was set up in 1969 with Ron Yeomans as founder chairman. The council seat on the NCA has allowed it to put the case for members' concerns: grassroots cricket, the highest standards of sportsmanship – and maximum BBC broadcast coverage.

The council is eager to encourage new societies, especially those involving the young, such as the groups at Oxford and Cambridge plus several public schools. These are the butterflies of the movement: for a time there can be enthusiasm sparked by an individual or a small band of devotees, but it is sometimes hard to guarantee speakers an audience, especially in institutions where a lecture is hardly a novelty. One cricket writer was disappointed to get just 15 for his talk at Oxford only to be reassured: "We got nine for Colin Cowdrey."

Australia is the overseas hub of the movement, today's societies having had a short-lived forerunner in the Victorian city of Geelong. In 1950 local cricketers Roy Brown and David Shaw (his brother John later played for

Victoria) formed the Geelong Cricketers' Club. The first speaker was Lindsay Hassett – a Geelong man, also a cousin of the Shaws, and at that time leading Australia against Freddie Brown's England tourists. Six hundred people packed Geelong West Town Hall to hear Hassett – with Ian Johnson – speak and answer questions, including the topic of the day: Was Sid Barnes being deliberately excluded from the Australian team? The next meeting, addressed by Bodyline series umpire George Hele, drew an audience of ten – a reminder that cricket history as distinct from current cricket is the interest of a minority.

The club lapsed, but in 1967 Melbourne solicitor Andrew Joseph contacted local subscribers to the late Rowland Bowen's *Cricket Quarterly* in the hope they might get together, and the Australian Cricket Society was the result. This has sparked active societies in the other major Australian cities. Melbourne remains the busiest, with a hyperactive president, Colin Barnes, who is able to charm/cajole/bribe/intimidate a flow of Test and Sheffield Shield players into addressing meetings. Societies have been increasingly active in South Africa, Zimbabwe, New Zealand and India, all guaranteeing hospitality to overseas visitors.

But for a society that epitomises the character of the movement, it is impossible to go beyond Wombwell, founded in 1950 by one of the personalities of the cricket society world. This is the extraordinary Jack Sokell, who has given a small Yorkshire mining village on the outskirts of Barnsley its own unique fame. Sokell, who was made an MBE in 1994, is tireless in organisation. Most societies meet once a month in the winter; Wombwell meets and has a speaker once a week.

Sokell is Wombwell born and bred: his society is a major influence in the community, running everything from fashion shows and beauty contests to jazz nights and dances, as well as cricket coaching sessions. He still voices mock resentment that his committee in the 1960s talked him out of hiring a rock group. Members felt the £50 fee was far too much for a group no one knew, nor ever would. Silly name, too – the Beatles.

Johnny Wardle was Wombwell's first speaker, followed by Yardley, Hutton, Bowes, Trueman, Duckworth, Hendren, George Pope, Leyland, Close and the Bedsers. Any society speakers' secretary in the 1990s would gasp at such a galaxy, wondering at the cost (in fact no more than bare expenses at most), because it is a rare star today who agrees to shine except at a price. Many society members are retired, with limited funds, and subscriptions are kept to a few pounds a year, which does not allow for heavy fees to guest speakers. This has become one of the most pragmatic functions of the Council of Cricket Societies – to provide a forum where officers exchange information on which names talk well and come cheap. The game lost its innocence for many organisers when they discovered that even youngsters not yet awarded a county cap would insist their agents negotiate a fee for their services. The council has more than once reminded the Cricketers' Association that society members are often the most hardworking of county supporters and help to organise benefits – so players might in return look kindly on requests to speak.

Great names have commended the movement. Sir Donald Bradman, when accepting life membership of the Australian Society, declared: "The great thing about this society is that it is working in the interests of the game of cricket." And John Arlott said that the Cricket Society "has never sought to do more than to serve and enjoy the game, which is the reason for its existence".

But true to the tradition of cricket that behind a serene, ordered exterior often lie dark depths and unexplained mysteries, the veteran collector and statistician Geoffrey Copinger just once lifted the protective veil. Recording that he did not take part in the Cricket Society team's first overseas tour, to Paris, Copinger commented: "Perhaps this is just as well, for I understand that one member never really recovered." What on earth, one asks, could have happened on that legendary excursion in this simple, innocent, sporting, dedicated world of the cricket society movement?

Murray Hedgcock has been a London columnist of The Australian *since 1971. He has been a member of both the Cricket Society and the Australian Cricket Society for even longer.*

THE VAGRANT GYPSY LIFE

150 YEARS OF I ZINGARI

By JOHN WOODCOCK

The widespread increase in competitive club and village cricket in the late 1960s and through the 1970s presented many long-established and well-run private clubs with an awkward problem. I am thinking, for example, of the constituent county clubs with euphonious names, such as the Devon Dumplings and the Hampshire Hogs, as well as the more nomadic Free Foresters and Incogniti and Cryptics and Buccaneers and Arabs, and the oldest and perhaps most illustrious of them all, I Zingari. Even MCC, with their 300 out-matches a year, began to find it more difficult to put a strong side into the field.

In 1960 there was very little league cricket south of the Midlands. Now, the great majority of town and village clubs throughout the country are in a league of some kind or other, and need to find, in so far as it is possible, a settled side. There is also the national club knockout, the national village championship, and countless other relatively new competitions. The wandering clubs suddenly found it more difficult to fulfil their commitments to the extent to which they were accustomed, or to recruit suitably competent and socially suitable members. The sort of players they had always relied upon became less regularly available. Fixture lists had to be cut back; in some cases, dissolution threatened. None has ridden the crisis – for that, to many, is what it was – more surely than IZ, founded 150 years ago and still with a language and a status of its own.

On July 4, 1845, its founders, J. L. Baldwin, Frederic and Spencer Ponsonby (to become the Earl of Bessborough and Sir Spencer Ponsonby-Fane respectively) and R. P. Long, dined together at the Blenheim Hotel in Bond Street, following a match that day against Harrow School. There and then they formed a club, for the purpose of fostering amateur cricket, christened it and framed the rules. Next day they informed William Boland, a barrister with an extensive practice and a formidable presence, that he was Perpetual President and 20 of their friends that they were now members of I Zingari (the gypsies).

The rules were half-serious and half-comic ("The Entrance fee be nothing and the Annual Subscription do not exceed the Entrance.") and many of them survive today, including the ordinance to "keep your promise, keep your temper and keep your wicket up". The affirmation of amateurism was important, mainly because most sides in those days employed professionals, or "given men", to bolster them, whereas the Zingaros preferred to do without one. Colours of black, red and gold ("out of darkness, through fire, into light") were chosen, and attracted such attention that in the late 1860s MCC appropriated them, except that they kept to the red and gold and left out the black. (For the next 100 years or so the MCC "egg and bacon" tie and cravat were rarely worn – it was considered bourgeois to be seen in them. Today, however, on the first morning of a Test match at Lord's, the pavilion is a blaze of red and gold.)

Excellence was of the essence to IZ. Patronised by royalty, acknowledged in high society and careful whom they chose to play for them, they were very soon able to turn out a side strong enough to hold its own against any professional eleven, besides reading like a table of precedence. By 1877, IZ were beating Yorkshire at the Scarborough Festival, and in 1882 and 1884 they had a fixture against the touring Australians. Their last first-class match was against a Gentlemen of England XI at Lord's in 1904. At the time, a fully representative Gentlemen's side would have consisted mostly of IZ. But the days of quite such high glory were numbered. With their activities being suspended during the two wars, when many of the country house grounds on which they played came under the plough, the club had to rely upon its renown – one could justifiably say its mystique – and the devotion of its senior members to hold its place.

Since 1867, *Wisden* has made a point of publishing the results of all I Zingari matches, a service provided for no other private club. In 1884, in its heyday, IZ played 52 days' cricket (one three-day, 19 two-day and 11 one-day matches). In 1994 they played 24 one-day matches and one of two days. The results are on page 857.

Because Boland was made Perpetual President in 1845, the club's senior living officer is called not the President but the Governor, who is currently the former Middlesex and England captain, George Mann. To Sir William Becher, though, IZ owes its greatest modern debt. In 1839, six years before the dinner in Bond Street, one of Becher's forbears gave his name to the brook at which so many hopes have been dashed in the Grand National at Aintree. "Billy" Becher himself, secretary from 1953 to 1993, has given much of his own life to keeping the Zingaric spirit alive, and ensuring that in 1995, its 150th year, IZ remains the most urbane of clubs.

John Woodcock was cricket correspondent of The Times *from 1954 to 1987 and editor of* Wisden *from 1981 to 1986.*

FIVE CRICKETERS OF THE YEAR

DEVON MALCOLM

Devon Malcolm is an unlikely hero. He can be erratic, he is hopelessly short-sighted, and at times he is wildly inaccurate. But he possesses an athleticism and physical strength which he combines with an ungainly, almost unco-ordinated delivery to produce bowling which at best is lightning fast and straight, and at worst searches in vain for the cut strip.

Ask any South African cricketer and they will have just one memory of the man. Fearsomely fast, searingly straight and awesomely aggressive, devastating Devon was the hero of The Oval in 1994. His nine for 57 in the second innings demolished and demoralised South Africa in a way that only outstanding fast bowling can. The analysis was the sixth-best in the history of Test cricket and it elevated Malcolm into English cricketing folklore.

Since twin tours were introduced in England in 1965, no team had ever come back to win or draw a three-match series after falling one behind. England in their selection threw caution to the wind, abandoning hope of fielding a balanced attack in favour of all-out speed. Malcolm was delivered from Chesterfield and Eastbourne and thrust into his favourite arena.

The Oval's pitch with its generous pace and bounce provided him with an ideal surface on which to perform and rejuvenate his flagging career. Malcolm felt he had been publicly humiliated when sent away from the Lord's Test match against New Zealand 24 hours before the game. Sensibly, he retained a faith in his own ability and also a respect for the England captain, Mike Atherton, who as an accomplished opening batsman realises more than most the unsettling effect of raw pace.

DEVON EUGENE MALCOLM was born on February 22, 1963 in Kingston, Jamaica. His father, Albert, supported the family by working in England, and his mother, Brendalee, died when Devon was five, leaving him to be brought up by his grandmother in the Jamaican town of St Elizabeth. At school he enjoyed all sports, particularly sprinting, cricket and football. But it was not until he went to join his father in Sheffield in 1979, and began studying at Richmond College, that his cricketing talent was recognised. The college had a cricket team, but it was made up of old boys and staff and Devon became the first student member.

He kept taking five wickets and on his own admission kept scaring people, so much so that his prowess was highlighted in the *Sheffield Star*. In 1981 he played in the same Yorkshire schools side as Ashley Metcalfe and progressed via Sheffield Caribbean and Sheffield United to selection for the Yorkshire League XI which played the county side in April 1984. His two prized scalps that afternoon were Geoffrey Boycott and Martyn Moxon, both clean bowled.

That performance must have left Yorkshire wondering if the Kingston on Malcolm's birth certificate might be the Hull variety rather than the Jamaican. But at that stage the strict Yorkshire-born policy applied. He signed for Derbyshire later that season. He told Phil Russell, the Derbyshire coach, that he didn't want any money for playing, he would play for the love of it. His love of the game has been sorely tested since that day, his career being a constant roller-coaster of selections and non-selections for both Derbyshire and England. Derbyshire, with a large stock of seam bowlers, have had a policy of rest and rotation, believing this is in the best interests of the player, though Malcolm himself thrives on hard work.

Nevertheless, Malcolm was and always will be a "raw" quick bowler, who will remain indebted to Russell for encouraging him to bowl as fast as possible, and to his fellow Jamaican and team-mate at Derby, Michael Holding, who emphasised the levels of concentration that were needed to bowl fast and highlighted the one single factor that transforms Malcolm, more than any other bowler, from also-ran to danger-man: "Follow through straight."

Since qualifying to play for England, by residence, in 1987, and his triumph at The Oval he played 28 Test matches and took 98 wickets at an average of 35. These are hardly startling figures and reflect the erratic nature of his career. But by the winter of 1989-90 his strike bowling capabilities were well recognised, and his waywardness countered and complemented by a partnership with the admirably straight Angus Fraser. The duo bowled England to an improbable victory in Jamaica, where Malcolm blew away the West Indians' key batsmen in the second innings, and to the verge of victory in Port-of-Spain where a match analysis of ten for 137 gave him his best and most aggressive performance to date.

His dislike of the generally slower and flatter pitches in England and his apparent inability to adapt to these conditions limited his appearances to the extent that by 1993 he was chosen only for the Oval Test, where he took six wickets against the hitherto rampant Australians. With a West Indies tour coming up after that, he was a natural choice to lead the attack in the winter, but the first serious injury of his career, picked up in the Jamaica Test, scuppered his chances of glory. And when he was dropped again after one Test against New Zealand in 1994, many thought that, at 31, he was finished as a Test cricketer. No one, not even Malcolm at his most resolute, could have dreamed what was to follow when he came back to face South Africa at The Oval.

After a first-day argument, that he describes as "healthy", with his captain over the bowling of bouncers at de Villiers and Donald (Atherton wanted them delivered, Malcolm didn't), events conspired to produce his definitive fast bowling performance. Inspired by the batting efforts of DeFreitas and Gough on Friday evening, goaded into retaliation by a blow between the eyes from a de Villiers bouncer, and kept calm by the reggae on his Walkman in the dressing-room, Devon bowled England to victory and himself into the history books.

P.S. Tradition dictates that we have to mention his batting. He was once officially described, by Conrad Hunte in his capacity as Test match referee, as "one of the worst No. 11s in the game". It is entertaining, though. – Paul Allott.

TIM MUNTON

Sometimes events on the cricket field unfold with just the right amount of symmetry. The gods that determine such things handled matters efficiently at the end of Warwickshire's historic summer. On a grey evening at Bristol on Sunday, September 18, the catch which sealed Warwickshire's third trophy of the summer was taken by Tim Munton. The tall, heavy-boned seam bowler dived low to take a classy catch at mid-wicket that must have threatened his cold hamstrings. Munton's team-mates simply accepted that splendid effort as further proof that the big fellow's influence on a remarkable summer was as massive as the brilliant Brian Lara's. None of them quibbled when Munton announced that the ball which had secured Warwickshire the Sunday League title that day would not be prised from his personal trophy cabinet.

Press the rewind button a further 16 days to a sunlit afternoon at Edgbaston as Warwickshire's players saluted their home crowd from the balcony after the County Championship was clinched with an innings win over Hampshire. The players were individually cheered, with the genius of Lara admiringly acclaimed. Yet the biggest cheer, one laced with affection and respect, went to Tim Munton. That was not just for an outstanding personal season, nor for his golden run as stand-in captain for the injured Dermot Reeve, but also for Munton's high standards of professionalism, his durability and his approachability. The supporters had not forgotten Munton's selfless performances in many undistinguished seasons for the club, his tireless commitment to his job, his willingness to meet every autograph request and to exchange cheery banter at any time of his working day. Reeve judged the situation perfectly that day on the Edgbaston balcony, as he insisted that the Championship pennant should be handed over to his vice-captain. A record of eight Championship wins out of nine games under Munton's leadership in 1994 speaks for itself.

Munton's success with the ball last season was almost overshadowed by the side's remarkable record under his captaincy. He blossomed under the responsibilities of leadership, using his genial personality to steer a middle course through a dressing-room that contained its fair share of voluble characters. Working as a sales representative for a local brewery in recent winters has given him a wider perspective on life and an insight into the different ways that individuals deal with stressful situations. Munton came to be known as "Captain Sensible" for his ability to defuse tensions and capitalise on the genuine friendship the Warwickshire players felt for each other. Reeve and the director of cricket, Bob Woolmer, were equally subtle in their differing approaches to personal interactions in a long, draining season, and the corporate *bonhomie* they engendered was crucial as Warwickshire made history in 1994.

Munton knew before the season began that, in the absence of Allan Donald, there would be far more pressure on him to fire out top batsmen. "I worked hard on the weights during the winter, building up my stamina and strength, because I was prepared for a strike bowler's role, rather than my usual supporting role as the miserly stock bowler. I was prepared to concede a few more runs, attack the stumps more and bowl more bouncers. I also went around the wicket on occasions – something I'd always been loath to do – and it got me a few wickets at vital times. I was definitely a yard quicker and could still bowl as many overs." The result was his biggest haul of first-class wickets in a season, 81, and widespread sympathy when he was not included in England's touring parties for the winter. Typically, Munton simply got on with his job, kept his own counsel when he was overlooked, and rejoiced in his team's success.

TIMOTHY ALAN MUNTON was born in Melton Mowbray, Leicestershire, on July 30, 1965 and for as long as he can remember he wanted to play cricket. Encouraged by his parents, Alan and Brenda, he played for the county second team while still at King Edward VII Upper School. For three seasons, Munton improved gradually in Leicestershire's Second Eleven, but as the county had a strong array of experienced seam bowlers, he could not break into the first team and was never offered a contract. "Not making the grade at first-class level was a huge blow for me, because I desperately wanted to play for my home county. But it proved a blessing in disguise." Warwickshire signed him at the end of the 1984 season and, with Bob Willis just retired and the club short of seam bowling, Munton soon prospered. "I got on a steep learning curve quickly and picked up valuable experience that was denied other seamers of my age who couldn't get a look-in elsewhere." David Brown, then Warwickshire's manager, and his successor Bob Cottam were invaluable mentors to Munton, and he willingly drank in the practical knowledge of the two former England fast bowlers. It was Cottam who made the major breakthrough with Munton in the winter of 1989-90, teaching him the subtleties of swing bowling. Within two years he was playing for England.

In his two Tests against Pakistan, Munton was not quite at his best, but he was considered good enough to be in the squad for every Test that summer – yet he was not selected for England's winter tour of India and Sri Lanka. Nor did any member of the England hierarchy bother contacting him with an encouraging word. That offended Munton's sense of good manners, but he buckled further to the task of improving his bowling and tactical appreciation. "That's why I wasn't too upset at missing out on England selection in 1994. If I wasn't going to be picked for a tour in '92, I couldn't allow myself to be optimistic, even though I was now a better bowler."

Yet he has enough pride in his performance to hope for further England selection, although his main hope is that Warwickshire's *annus mirabilis* does not prove to be illusory. Married to Helen, with two small children, Tim Munton is a cricketer at peace with himself, quietly aware of his own worth, but the quintessential team man. It is typical that he has been Warwickshire's representative for the Cricketers' Association, the body that represents the players' interests: with his high personal integrity and playing reputation, he is a handy fellow to have on your side around the negotiating table.

Above all, Munton is the very antithesis of the unflattering image that some modern Test cricketers have carved out. Not for him the crass agent, the obsession with the mobile phone and the skulking in the dressing-room, waiting for the supporters to melt away. His infinite capacity for taking pains has brought him deserved status and popularity. "I can't believe how lucky I have been when the summit of my ambitions was just to play county cricket. I've got England caps, a full trophy cabinet and a stack of friendships that will last." And universal respect from all sections of the cricket industry. Not that Tim Munton would ever say that. – Pat Murphy.

STEVE RHODES

Rarely has a modern English player made such a smooth transition into Test cricket as Steve Rhodes. What made his instant acclimatisation even more striking was that he had been on the fringe of the side for the best part of a decade, and was close to his 30th birthday, before he won the recognition he deserved.

Rhodes finished his first England summer with 26 catches, two stumpings and a batting average in his six Tests of 55.50. He also emerged with a heartfelt tribute from his captain, Mike Atherton, who named the Worcestershire wicket-keeper as his player of the year. Rhodes had been installed almost immediately as a respected senior pro, and well before the season had run its course had become one of Atherton's most trusted advisers. His approach is one of total involvement; he knows no other way to play.

English county standards have often been maligned in recent years, but here was a player who promoted the advantages of a lengthy county upbringing. Rhodes's spirit had been unquenchable through the long years without Test recognition and the knowledge he gleaned had become widely admired. When his chance came, he pursued it with the energy and enthusiasm of a yapping terrier tearing at a slipper.

Throughout the summer, whatever situation England might have found themselves in, Rhodes exuded energy, chivvying and chattering, bombarding his team-mates with a stream of leg-pulls, worldly-wise comments and tactical insights. Critics who had once wondered about the minutiae of his style were instead massively impressed by his substance. One had to think long and hard in September to recall a chance he might have missed. Arguably, no wicket-keeper in the world at the present time gives his captain, or his bowlers, more.

With his jutting chin, defiant expression and professional outlook, Rhodes was an integral part of what appeared in the summer to be a tougher, more positive England – the most visible proof of the change of emphasis introduced by the new chairman of selectors, Ray Illingworth. He had been raised in the West Riding only a few miles from Illingworth's home in Pudsey. Their spiritual home, in both cases, was the Bradford League. Rhodes was exactly the type of player which the Bradford League presents as its essence, an indefatigable competitor who gives or asks no quarter.

His debut Test innings – 49 against New Zealand at Trent Bridge – identified him as a worthy Test No. 7, but it was the manner in which he staved off defeat at Lord's, batting for more than two hours for 24 not out, that caused Illingworth to sing his praises. "There was a brave little Yorkie out there," Illingworth trumpeted. There was an uncompromising one, too. To salvage a draw, Rhodes had not been averse to a little obvious time-wasting. Such professionalism was greeted with sporadic distaste, but it brought no criticism from New Zealand's captain, Ken Rutherford, who judged it gamesmanship within acceptable limits. Though his form was to wobble in the winter, by the time the South Africans had departed, Rhodes possessed an air of permanence.

STEVEN JOHN RHODES was born in Bradford, Yorkshire, on June 17, 1964 and was a pupil of Carlton-Bolling School in Bradford. His father, Billy, kept wicket for Nottinghamshire in the early 1960s, but it was quite by chance that his son's own interest was fired. Rooting around a cupboard one day when he was ten, he discovered a pair of Billy's old stumping gloves and so loved the feel of them that it was not long before tennis balls were thumping against the wall of the family's paper shop.

Rhodes quickly made an impression in Yorkshire's age-group sides, joined Saltaire in the Bradford League and, at 15, he was offered his first Worcestershire contract. His immediate ambitions rested with his native Yorkshire but, although he made his first-class debut for them against the Sri Lankans at Abbeydale Park in 1981, his progress was blocked by David Bairstow, a red-blooded and popular 'keeper who was in no mood to retire graciously. Rhodes's predictable departure from Yorkshire in the autumn of 1984 caused much dismay throughout the county, not least for the coach, Doug Padgett. The manner of his leaving was quite exceptional: Yorkshire's general committee, then at its most divided, voted narrowly to ask Bairstow if he would retain the captaincy, but relinquish the gloves to Rhodes. Bairstow immediately and volcanically refused, leaving the committee to retreat from the lava flow.

Worcestershire has proved a more than satisfying home. Rhodes has played a full and enthusiastic part in their two Championships and four one-day trophies since 1987, and graduated to the vice-captaincy in 1993. The advent of four-day cricket has been the making of his batting, allowing him the opportunity to develop from being a regular maker of spritely thirties and forties to a batsman with seven first-class centuries to his name. His maiden England representative hundred, for the A team against Border in East London in 1993-94, was a landmark which afforded him special pleasure and one he had yearned for the evening before the game.

Rhodes was lavishly praised during his first England tour, for the B squad in Sri Lanka in 1985-86. He was selected for the 1988-89 tour of India, which was then abandoned for political reasons, and, although he made his one-day debut against Australia the following year, he was discarded for Jack Russell when the Tests began. Four more A tours followed, to Zimbabwe, Sri Lanka, the West Indies and South Africa, all of them approached with enthusiastic professionalism. England's call was a long time coming. Let him enjoy the acclaim. – David Hopps.

KEPLER WESSELS

He led them in from the cold, a modest man with a private face and a lion's heart. It is not how many times you fall down, he assured them, but how many times you stand up. His moral is that you must never give up.

And so, on such simple and strong virtues, Kepler Wessels has shepherded South Africa from a quarter of a century of numbing isolation to a position of honour and respect in world cricket. If, a decade ago, someone had told you that this Afrikaner, who was opening the batting for Australia at the time, would lead South Africa to victory over England at Lord's, you would have worried about their marbles. But there he stood, in the shimmering heat of an unlikely British July, his arms aloft in exultation. Not only had South Africa crushed England by 356 runs on their return to the home of cricket but their captain had made yet another careful, crucial century when his team had needed it most.

KEPLER CHRISTOFFEL WESSELS was born in Bloemfontein on September 14, 1957 and as a member of the Dutch Reformed Church, he learned the discipline and self-justification that were his people's hallmark. He was educated at Grey College and, though gifted at both boxing and tennis, he insisted on learning about cricket, a game not previously linked with the traditions of Afrikanerdom. His insistence intensified as a generation of South African heroes emerged in the late 1960s to embarrass Australia and threaten the world.

As a schoolboy prodigy – mentioned in the same breath as Graeme Pollock for his free and uncomplicated style – he sometimes found himself excluded from South African Schools teams in which he should have played. Then, with South Africa firmly exiled from Test cricket, he set his own course. He arrived at Sussex when he was only 18, and was there for five fruitful, if at times uncomfortable, seasons. But when he was barely past 21, he emigrated to Australia. The initial lure was Kerry Packer's World Series Cricket; the ultimate goal a place in the Australian Test team. It is important not to underestimate the extraordinary gamble that Wessels was taking. He had come from the most introverted part of an introverted country, where national pride burst from the chest of the revered rugby players. And this shy, slightly scared but extraordinarily ambitious 21-year-old cricketer just upped and left, with his cricket bat and his dream.

After a heady baptism under Ian Chappell in the cauldron of World Series Cricket, he settled in Brisbane and during his four years of qualification for Australia became, with Allan Border, the toughest nut in Queensland. When chosen to play in his first Test match in November 1982 at his adopted home ground, the Gabba, he responded to the jibes about his nationality by making 162 and driving Botham and Willis, heroes of Headingley 16 months earlier, to distraction. And there Wessels stayed, happy at heart amongst the bluntest Australians and a virtual ever-present in the Test team. And then three years later, as abruptly as he had arrived, he went, forced out of Australian cricket amid false accusations of recruiting for the rebel tour of South Africa. He flew back to South Africa, shaken but sad. He signed, against his better judgment, to play for the Australian rebels *against* the country of his birth, while at the same time taking on the captaincy of Eastern Province, leading a desolate team off the floor and in just three years taking them to the Currie Cup.

He was selected *for* South Africa against Mike Gatting's rebels, but was so badly received by the senior Springbok players who had stayed put through the years of isolation that he withdrew from the team, amidst accusations of being a quitter who wanted to have his cake and eat it. Just 21 months later he was shaking the hand of Mother Teresa and batting for South Africa in an official international match, in the improbable setting of Eden Gardens, Calcutta. He was his country's most valuable, most travelled cricketer and was rewarded as such when he was selected ahead of Clive Rice to lead the 1992 World Cup campaign.

From that day, to the announcement of his retirement from the captaincy last November, the boy from Bloemfontein has seen South African cricket through the most extraordinary years of their history. He has not been everyone's cup of tea; he can be aloof, unsmiling and, at times, unsympathetic, but his inspiration has been remarkable. In the Sydney Test in January last year, his team marvelled at his indifference to a hand so badly smashed that he sat in hospital with an anti-infection drip. His response was to push the shattered finger into a heavy splint, promote himself two places in the order and bat virtually one-handed to convince the boys that victory was possible. And, quite famously, it was – by five runs.

He is not a pretty batsman – the limpets to the crease rarely are – but he is an indispensable one. In defence, he sits on the ball, consuming it and extracting its venom with a dead bat or an obstinate pad. In attack, he nudges past point and square leg, only occasionally allowing a flourish through extra cover or, at his most rampant, a punch over mid-wicket. He is efficient but ugly; uninteresting but packed full of substance. When he came to the crease at Lord's, South Africa were a fidgety 35 for two; when he left it, minutes before the close, to a tired, uncharacteristic stroke, his team had responded to his spirit and his determination and were on course for their remarkable victory.

Confronted by innumerable obstacles, Kepler Wessels has hunted down his ambitions with a grim determination that has misled his detractors. That he does not see cricket as wildly funny is neither relevant nor realistic; he has given it his best shot, applying a conviction and resolution that most men could scarcely imagine. Throughout, he has endured as much criticism as praise but has always gutsed it out when others might have quit. "All through my career I have tried to beat the odds," he says. "I want to be remembered as someone who got stronger as the going got tougher." – Mark Nicholas.

BRIAN LARA

The unparalleled glut of batting records that fell to Brian Lara between April and June 1994 amazed the cricket world and gained global attention beyond the game's narrow confines. It also prompted an outpouring of national pride in his native Trinidad & Tobago where he was showered with honours and gifts. Yet, while there was understandable joy, there was no real surprise among many of his countrymen at the left-hander's achievement, simply the feeling that his inevitable date with destiny had arrived rather more suddenly than expected.

Trinidadians craved the arrival of a batting superstar they, alone of all the territories that comprise West Indies cricket, had lacked, and Lara had long since provided unmistakable signs that he would fill the void. Even the most cock-eyed optimist could not have foreseen his virtually simultaneous eclipse of both Sir Garfield Sobers's Test and Hanif Mohammad's first-class records, but those who had followed his development from the time he first played organised cricket were never in any doubt that it was within the potential of his talent and ambition. There was even talk, not entirely prompted by the euphoria of the moment, that Lara himself would surpass his own standards by the time he was through.

Such confident assessments were based on solid evidence. As a stripling of a lad at Fatima College, in Port-of-Spain, Lara had reeled off seven centuries in a single season of the national inter-school competition at the age of 15. In the annual West Indies' under-19 championships, he created new standards, averaging over 50 in his four years. In only his second first-class match, when he was not yet 19, he held firm for more than five hours to score 92 against Trinidad & Tobago's sporting arch-rivals, Barbados, whose attack was led by Joel Garner and Malcolm Marshall.

Nor was the Trinidadian public alone in its early appraisal. Lara was made captain of the West Indies team to the Youth World Cup in Australia in 1988 and the West Indies B team to Zimbabwe the following year, ahead of older and more seasoned contenders. On his return, aged 20, he was appointed Trinidad & Tobago's youngest ever captain. If his advance to a

EXCELSIOR!

[*Graham Morris*

Brian Lara reaches his world record 501 not out.

IN TRIUMPH, HUMILITY

[*Graham Morris*

Brian Lara kisses the ground at St John's Antigua, after breaking the world Test record on his way to scoring 375.

UNFAMILIAR ACTION

[*Patrick Eagar/BBC TV*

Mike Atherton, the England captain, during the Lord's Test. Some experts and, according to a poll, 100 per cent of *Daily Mirror* readers thought he was cheating. Atherton vigorously denied it.

TROUBLE IN PARADISE

[*Ross Setford, Popperfoto*

Crowd trouble reached even New Zealand in 1993. Ata-ur-Rehman is led from the field at Eden Park, Auckland, after being hit by a bottle at a one-day international.

V

ENGLAND'S GLORY

[*Graham Morris*

Angus Fraser leads the celebrations as he has Keith Arthurton caught behind on his way to eight for 75 and a stunning England victory in the Test at Bridgetown, where West Indies had not lost in 59 years.

ENGLAND'S SHAME

[*Graham Morris*

The moment of truth for England as Chris Lewis is caught at Port-of-Spain and they are all out for 46, their lowest score of the century.

PUT OUT MORE FLAGS

[*Graham Morris*

South Africa's dressing-room balcony as they head for a 356-run win over England and a smaller victory over MCC regulations prohibiting the display of flags.

FIVE CRICKETERS OF THE YEAR

[*Patrick Eagar*

KEPLER WESSELS

FIVE CRICKETERS OF THE YEAR

[*David Munden*

STEVE RHODES

FIVE CRICKETERS OF THE YEAR

[*Patrick Eagar*

TIM MUNTON

FIVE CRICKETERS OF THE YEAR

[*David Munden*

DEVON MALCOLM

FIVE CRICKETERS OF THE YEAR

[*Graham Morris*

BRIAN LARA

permanent place in the West Indies Test team was inordinately delayed – he made his debut in Viv Richards' absence in Pakistan in December 1990 and did not reappear until April 1992, against South Africa, after Richards had retired – it was through no lack of claim on his part. Even after he set a new, if temporary, record for the highest aggregate in the Red Stripe Cup, with 627 runs in the five matches, he was kept on hold.

The simultaneous exits of Richards, Gordon Greenidge and Jeffrey Dujon after the 1991 tour of England finally made a place vacant and Lara immediately became the hub around which the reconstituted batting revolved. When West Indies faltered in the 1992 World Cup, he alone sparkled. Used as opener, he announced his arrival on the world stage with 333 runs in the eight matches at an average of 47.57. More than half were accumulated in boundaries as he rattled on at a striking-rate of 81.61 per 100 balls.

In common with almost all other players, Lara was not satisfied to be judged on the artificiality of the shortened game and it was his 277 in Sydney in January 1993, in his fifth Test, that confirmed what Trinidadians had long since taken for granted, that here was the newest in the long line of great West Indian batsmen. One of his predecessors, now team cricket manager, Rohan Kanhai, called it "one of the greatest innings I have ever seen". Its immediate value was that it inspired a revival of West Indian spirits that led to the conversion of a 1-0 series deficit at the time to an eventual 2-1 triumph; its long-term significance was that it established Lara as batting leader of a team still searching for a central figure in the absence of Richards.

It also reinforced Lara's self-confidence, never in short supply but always essential in the make-up of a champion sportsman. While receiving his award as Trinidad & Tobago's 1993 Sportsman of the Year, he was asked what might be his goals for 1994. "To get a few centuries, maybe a double, even a triple," he replied. He proceeded to exceed even his own expectations.

Leading Trinidad & Tobago in the Red Stripe Cup, he reclaimed his old aggregate record with 715 runs in the five matches. His 180 against Jamaica was an astonishing innings, scored out of 219 while he was at the wicket; his partners contributed 21. It was merely a preview of what was to follow. Within five months, the memory even of that extraordinary performance had been eclipsed by his 375 in the Antigua Test against England and his unique sequence of seven centuries in eight innings, the next six for Warwickshire in the English County Championship, culminating with his unbeaten 501 against Durham.

It was final confirmation for Trinidadians of what they had recognised for some time. According to Winston, one of his elder brothers, the Lara family "knew he was something special even before he was ten". The second-youngest of seven sons and four daughters of Bunty and Pearl Lara, BRIAN CHARLES LARA was born on May 2, 1969 in Cantaro, a village in the verdant Santa Cruz Valley, half an hour's drive from Port-of-Spain. His father was superintendent at a government agricultural station. The boy's fascination for, and mastery of, ball games was evident almost from the time he could walk. According to Winston, he would use a broom stick and a lime or a marble as a ball and knock up against the garage door. As he got older, he would defy his brothers to get him out with a tennis ball. It was typical West Indian rural life – except that Lara was fortunate in having a family that recognised his rare talent and did everything to encourage and develop it.

When he was three, his father gave him a cut-down bat. When he was six, his father and his sister, Agnes, enrolled him at the Harvard Club coaching clinic in Port-of-Spain and would take him there and back every Sunday. Although he was good enough at soccer to gain selection to the national youth training squad – where he struck up a lasting friendship with Dwight Yorke, now with Aston Villa – his father insisted his future lay with cricket and influenced him to stick to it. He was taken to major matches at the Queen's Park Oval where he saw the leading players of the day in action. Roy Fredericks, the West Indies opener, was an early favourite for he was, after all, small, left-handed and a dasher. When his father died in 1988, Lara's grief was deep and understandable. His guidance had extended beyond cricket. Dedicating his 375 to his memory, Lara said: "I had some bad influences in my time and, if my parents weren't there to straighten me out, things might have gone haywire."

Another mentor was Joey Carew, the former West Indies opening batsman. As soon as Carew saw Lara play, in Fatima College junior teams captained by his sons, he took a keen interest, gaining him membership of Queen's Park, the island's strongest club team, and carefully, but not overbearingly, monitoring his development. On leaving Fatima, Lara was academically qualified enough to consider a career in accountancy but it was only a fleeting thought. Cricket, it was obvious, would be his profession. But Lara is from the island renowned for its carnival, and he knows how to enjoy himself beyond the boundary. Like Sobers and so many other cricketers, he has become addicted to golf, which he plays right-handed and increasingly well, and is an avid fan of horse-racing. His boyish good looks and easy-going manner, not to mention his fame and fortune, render him a vulnerable bachelor.

There is another more threatening consequence of his sudden success and stardom. It places on him an awesome responsibility that not all celebrated young sportsmen can properly handle. With satellite television now spanning the globe, Lara has become cricket's first truly international megastar. Public expectations will be excessive, and the non-cricketing demands on him persistent.

There are pressures that the great players of the past – even Bradman, Sobers and Viv Richards – did not have to contend with to the same extent. Temperament, as much as talent, is now likely to dictate Brian Lara's future. – Tony Cozier.

AN ALTERNATIVE FIVE

By DAVID HOPPS

Every year *Wisden* chooses Five Cricketers of the Year and often the selection includes one of the game's lesser stars, who has worked away in county cricket for many years without the glamour of international recognition. They usually get called "stalwarts" and "salt of the earth".

But, as well as all the cricketers, there is a far bigger band of stalwarts who keep the professional circuit alive without getting any recognition, sometimes without getting any money. There are the umpires, scorers and groundsmen, of course. But there are hundreds of others, as well, in all kinds of jobs.

This year, as well as the Five Cricketers, we have chosen five other people. Without them, in different ways, first-class cricket would be impossible. But they are only a sample, chosen almost at random. They stand for dozens of others. There are people like Vince Miller, who has been printing the scorecards under the Grand Stand at Lord's since 1958, Lilian Byrne, who has answered the MCC telephones since 1972, Peter Lees, long-time presiding genius of the Lord's press bar, Graham Jones, the steward, and Eddie Rickard, the dressing-room attendant, both at Swansea from just after the war into the 1990s. There are many more. We could only pick five.

The first of them is undoubtedly the best-known. Amongst professional cricketers she is a legendary figure. Last year, NANCY DOYLE was made an honorary MBE and received her honour inside the Long Room at Lord's, which was a far more appropriate setting than Buckingham Palace. Her domain, however, is upstairs, where she is manageress of both the players' and committee dining rooms. Nancy Doyle has never read a cookery book, claiming she could never follow a written recipe. She never uses scales, much preferring guesswork, and has changed little from the basic method taught to her by the nuns at her convent school in Mullingar. That means a typical menu, as on one day of the Lord's Test against New Zealand last summer, might read: roast chicken with chips and two veg, followed by jam roly-poly with a choice of custard, cream or ice cream. The players love it.

Nancy first worked at Lord's as a casual waitress in 1961, transferring to the players' dining room the following year. In all those years, she says, she has never had a complaint, not even the time when she dropped hot apple pie and custard over Wilf Slack's lap during a Middlesex Championship match. Wilf quietly assured her it was no problem, accepted another helping and, after changing his trousers, went back out to complete a double-century.

During Tests, Nancy prepares about a hundred meals for players, committee and office staff and about 60 at every county match. She unfalteringly protects the Lord's dress code: no jeans, tracksuits or shorts in the players' dining room, no jackets to be removed in the committee dining room. During Tests against India, Pakistan or Sri Lanka, her daughter Jeanette, a nurse, takes leave to help her; Nancy cannot cook curries.

She professes scant knowledge of cricket, although Sir Colin Cowdrey first taught her that "it wasn't rounders", which has left her with a soft spot for Kent ever since. Her loyalty to her players is unshakeable. She claims never to have been asked for a hangover cure. Nancy plans to serve out the 1995 season, then "see what happens". Everyone hopes retirement is a good while away yet, but when it comes woe betide anyone who makes a fuss of her by baking her a cake.

BERT BARDEN was also contemplating retirement as the season drew to a close last September. At 83, he was one of the county game's most senior servants and beginning to suspect that age was catching up with him.

In the hectic build-up to a big limited-overs occasion, there are few more taxing jobs than that of manning the Chelmsford members' car park. Bert, as Essex's chief car parking steward, has been responsible for keeping order when tempers are becoming frayed. There have been times when merely not being run over in the rush for parking places has been some kind of achievement. If 33 years as a bus driver for Eastern National left him with a poor opinion of driving standards, he is equally unimpressed at the parking skills of the great cricketing public.

"They all know they have to park properly," he said, "but some of them have to reverse three or four times to get into a space, even if it's at the end of a row. When I was on the buses, I used to complain about women drivers, just like everybody else, but I've come to learn that the women park much more neatly than the men do. Perhaps it's because they know I'm keeping a keen eye on them."

Since the death of his wife, Kathleen, more than ten years ago, the camaraderie of the county circuit has been a blessing. He admits openly to long, lonely winters, which he is able to escape each spring with the first smell of freshly-mown grass. "I get very depressed in the winter," he said, "but Essex have been good to me. There are one or two nasty pieces of work about, and we have to watch out for the West Ham mob on Sundays down at Ilford, but 99 per cent of people are well behaved and friendly. It's good company; in fact, it's been good company since I watched my first Essex match more than 70 years ago."

His active involvement with Essex began in the early 1980s. Bert was in the garden shed, doing some carpentry and listening to the football on the radio; Kathleen was in the greenhouse, tuned instead to the local BBC station, where an appeal for stewards went out. "I went down for an interview," he said. "They didn't ask me much. It seemed that if you could walk and breathe, you were up to the job." In his quieter moments, Bert Barden has had the fortune to see some excellent cricket in the past 13 seasons. He has also had the chance to utter, more than once, that immortal line: "You can't come in here without a pass."

Consider the history of Trent Bridge, and the Dalling family should, by rights, immediately spring to mind. The name figures prominently in the county's history, with four men boasting more than a century's service to Nottinghamshire. HARRY DALLING served as ground superintendent at Trent Bridge ("responsible for everything outside the boundary rope") for 42 years until 1991. No one ever believed that retirement would end his

Nancy Doyle [*Patrick Eagar*

Harry Dalling [*Andy Heading, Empics*

Steve Howes [*Patrick Eagar*

Bert Barden [*Mark Lees,* Essex Chronicle

Keith Partridge [*Frank Baron,* The Guardian

connection with the club and last season, aged 73, he was still performing a variety of supporting roles, most recognisably as one of the voices on the Trent Bridge public address.

Harry Dalling was born in Nottingham and has never had any inclination to leave it. Today, he still lives only six minutes' walk from the ground. His father, Frank Dalling, was ground superintendent for 22 years; Harry's younger brother, also Frank, was head groundsman for 26 years until the mid-1970s; and now Frank's son, know as Frank junior, is assistant to the present groundsman, Ron Allsopp.

Harry has never married. "I've often been asked why," he said, "but I don't know a woman who would have tolerated the hours that I've spent at the ground. My first love has always been cricket and I don't feel that I've missed anything. I've had so many happy memories."

Those memories include the Championship win in 1929 when, as a child, he glimpsed Harold Larwood and Bill Voce, and the day he dismissed Jim Laker for 49 in a benefit match. "I thought I fired one in just short of a length. He called it a long hop, but I was proud of it all the same," he said.

"The family have been privileged to serve Nottinghamshire over the years," he said. "Trent Bridge is an exquisite sight and has a very special atmosphere, even when it's empty. When it's full, the place sends a shiver down your spine. And what's pleasing is that it has retained its character throughout all the changes."

More than a decade has passed since computerised scoreboards began to change the face of English county grounds. For detailed information, the advantages of the best of them are undeniable, but if they remain for a century and more, they will never achieve the same solid and restful qualities of their manual predecessors. Wooden scoreboards, in all their alternative forms, help to form the character of the ground they grace.

STEVE HOWES therefore gains prominence, not just for himself, but for the building he represents. For the past 13 years, he has been particularly responsible for the smooth running of the scoreboard at The Oval, the most efficient in the country. Only in cricket, and perhaps only in England, could a scoreboard encourage such affection. But cricket is a statistical game, its conclusion revealed over a considerable period of time. When major records are broken – Lancashire's 863 against Surrey in 1990, the highest Championship total this century; or Devon Malcolm's nine wickets for 57 runs against South Africa last year – The Oval scoreboard unfailingly poses for another round of photographs.

For most of the 1980s, Steve worked the box alongside his brother, Andrew, and they drew pride from their reputation for speed and accuracy. The advent of a second, electronic scoreboard on the ground a few years ago provided another incentive to maintain the highest standards. Recognition can easily depart and Steve admits that he used to feel a flutter of nerves before the start of a Test. "One year a number on the hundreds fell horizontal and no one could see it," he said. "I watched the Test highlights that evening and nearly had a heart attack."

The Oval box is now more than 40 years old and is struggling to disguise its age. Figures have been known to drop from the windows without warning – thankfully, there have been no recorded incidents of spectators being injured by Last Man's score – and are temporarily repaired with a hastily applied nail or screw. The box is spartan: a couple of chairs, a stool (Steve's preference), and a portable radio, tuned whenever possible to Test Match Special. There is not even a kettle in the box; they tried it once, but remembering to bring along a pint of fresh milk proved too challenging.

Steve took time out in 1990 to gain a degree in leisure management at Thames Valley University. But he returned in 1994, and the retirement in the autumn of Harry Brind caused him to move up a rung to "No. 4" on the groundstaff. The only drawback with his promotion is that it might end his scoreboard duties, traditionally the novice's role.

Approaching his mid-thirties, Steve wonders about "a proper job". But The Oval exerts a powerful pull: the renewal of old acquaintances, the charting of a player's career from its infancy, the discovery of the "same old boys in the same old seats" year upon year. "And you have to be mad on cricket to watch as much as I do," he said.

In his two passionate loves, cricket and classical music, KEITH PARTRIDGE has something in common with Sir Neville Cardus. When he is not at Hove or Horsham watching his beloved Sussex, Keith listens to Mozart and Brahms. There, the similarities must end. Cardus never tramped around a county ground all day selling lottery tickets. But he would have recognised that it is the untiring and unheralded contribution of cricket lovers like Keith that guards the future of the game.

Keith is handicapped and partially sighted, but he has consistently risen above such misfortune to be one of Sussex's staunchest and most committed supporters. He is a familiar sight during Sussex home matches, and sells lottery tickets throughout the county, from Chichester to Crawley to Rye. The only payment he receives is his train fare and the cost of his lunch. He was a young man when he moved, with his parents, to Brighton from London in the early 1960s, just before Sussex won their first trophy, the inaugural Gillette Cup, in 1963.

"It was a great time to be a Sussex member," he recalled. "Ted Dexter and Jim Parks were batting, John Snow played for England for the first time in 1965 and then we had Tony Greig." But Keith was not satisfied with taking an inactive pleasure in the county's success. In 1968, he began to attend the Sussex Cricket Society's monthly winter meetings and then started to raise money for the club. He has barely stopped for breath since. He now raises about £5,000 a year for Sussex: Christmas draw tickets, the Derby draw and the year-round lottery tickets. It may be small beer compared to the modern might of the TCCB handout, but it is community involvement at its finest.

David Hopps is a cricket writer on The Guardian.

PART TWO: RECORDS

TEST CRICKETERS

FULL LIST FROM 1877 TO AUGUST 28, 1994

These lists have been compiled on a home and abroad basis, appearances abroad being printed in *italics*.

Abbreviations. E: England. A: Australia. SA: South Africa. WI: West Indies. NZ: New Zealand. In: India. P: Pakistan. SL: Sri Lanka. Z: Zimbabwe.

All appearances are placed in this order of seniority. Hence, any England cricketer playing against Australia in England has that achievement recorded first and the remainder of his appearances at home (if any) set down before passing to matches abroad. The figures immediately following each name represent the total number of appearances in *all* Tests.

The two Tests played between Sri Lanka and Pakistan in 1994-95 have been included.

Where the season embraces two different years, the first year is given; i.e. 1876 indicates 1876-77.

ENGLAND

Number of Test cricketers: 570

Abel, R. 13: v A 1888 (3) 1896 (3) 1902 (2); *v A 1891 (3); v SA 1888 (2)*
Absolom, C. A. 1: *v A 1878*
Agnew, J. P. 3: v A 1985 (1); v WI 1984 (1); v SL 1984 (1)
Allen, D. A. 39: v A 1961 (4) 1964 (1); v SA 1960 (2); v WI 1963 (2) 1966 (1); v P 1962 (4); *v A 1962 (1) 1965 (4); v SA 1964 (4); v WI 1959 (5); v NZ 1965 (3); v In 1961 (5); v P 1961 (3)*
Allen, G. O. B. 25: v A 1930 (1) 1934 (2); v WI 1933 (1); v NZ 1931 (3); v In 1936 (3); *v A 1932 (5) 1936 (5); v WI 1947 (3); v NZ 1932 (2)*
Allom, M. J. C. 5: *v SA 1930 (1); v NZ 1929 (4)*
Allott, P. J. W. 13: v A 1981 (1) 1985 (4); v WI 1984 (3); v In 1982 (2); v SL 1984 (1); *v In 1981 (1); v SL 1981 (1)*
Ames, L. E. G. 47: v A 1934 (5) 1938 (2); v SA 1929 (1) 1935 (4); v WI 1933 (3); v NZ 1931 (3) 1937 (3); v In 1932 (1); *v A 1932 (5) 1936 (5); v SA 1938 (5); v WI 1929 (4) 1934 (4); v NZ 1932 (2)*
Amiss, D. L. 50: v A 1968 (1) 1975 (2) 1977 (2); v WI 1966 (1) 1973 (3) 1976 (1); v NZ 1973 (3); v In 1967 (2) 1971 (1) 1974 (3); v P 1967 (1) 1971 (3) 1974 (3); *v A 1974 (5) 1976 (1); v WI 1973 (5) v NZ 1974 (2); v In 1972 (3) 1976 (5); v P 1972 (3)*
Andrew, K. V. 2: v WI 1963 (1); *v A 1954 (1)*
Appleyard, R. 9: v A 1956 (1); v SA 1955 (1); v P 1954 (1); *v A 1954 (4); v NZ 1954 (2)*
Archer, A. G. 1: *v SA 1898*
Armitage, T. 2: *v A 1876 (2)*
Arnold, E. G. 10: v A 1905 (4); v SA 1907 (2); *v A 1903 (4)*
Arnold, G. G. 34: v A 1972 (3) 1975 (1); v WI 1973 (3); v NZ 1969 (1) 1973 (3); v In 1974 (2); v P 1967 (2) 1974 (3); *v A 1974 (4); v WI 1973 (3); v NZ 1974 (2); v In 1972 (4); v P 1972 (3)*
Arnold, J. 1: v NZ 1931
Astill, W. E. 9: *v SA 1927 (5); v WI 1929 (4)*
Atherton, M. A. 40: v A 1989 (2) 1993 (6); v SA 1994 (3); v WI 1991 (5); v NZ 1990 (3) 1994 (3); v In 1990 (3); v P 1992 (3); *v A 1990 (5); v WI 1993 (5); v In 1992 (1); v SL 1992 (1)*
Athey, C. W. J. 23: v A 1980 (1); v WI 1988 (1); v NZ 1986 (3); v In 1986 (2); v P 1987 (4); *v A 1986 (5) 1987 (1); v WI 1980 (2); v NZ 1987 (1); v P 1987 (3)*
Attewell, W. 10: v A 1890 (1); *v A 1884 (5) 1887 (1) 1891 (3)*

Bailey, R. J. 4: v WI 1988 (1); *v WI 1989 (3)*
Bailey, T. E. 61: v A 1953 (5) 1956 (4); v SA 1951 (2) 1955 (5); v WI 1950 (2) 1957 (4); v NZ 1949 (4) 1958 (4); v P 1954 (3); *v A 1950 (4) 1954 (5) 1958 (5); v SA 1956 (5); v WI 1953 (5); v NZ 1950 (2) 1954 (2)*

Bairstow, D. L. 4: v A 1980 (1); v WI 1980 (1); v In 1979 (1); *v WI 1980 (1)*
Bakewell, A. H. 6: v SA 1935 (2); v WI 1933 (1); v NZ 1931 (2); *v In 1933 (1)*
Balderstone, J. C. 2: v WI 1976 (2)
Barber, R. W. 28: v A 1964 (1) 1968 (1); v SA 1960 (1) 1965 (3); v WI 1966 (2); v NZ 1965 (3); *v A 1965 (5); v SA 1964 (4); v In 1961 (5); v P 1961 (3)*
Barber, W. 2: v SA 1935 (2)
Barlow, G. D. 3: v A 1977 (1); *v In 1976 (2)*
Barlow, R. G. 17: v A 1882 (1) 1884 (3) 1886 (3); *v A 1881 (4) 1882 (4) 1886 (2)*
Barnes, S. F. 27: v A 1902 (1) 1909 (3) 1912 (3); v SA 1912 (3); *v A 1901 (3) 1907 (5) 1911 (5); v SA 1913 (4)*
Barnes, W. 21: v A 1880 (1) 1882 (1) 1884 (2) 1886 (2) 1888 (3) 1890 (2); *v A 1882 (4) 1884 (5) 1886 (1)*
Barnett, C. J. 20: v A 1938 (3) 1948 (1); v SA 1947 (3); v WI 1933 (1); v NZ 1937 (3); v In 1936 (1); *v A 1936 (5); v In 1933 (3)*
Barnett, K. J. 4: v A 1989 (3); v SL 1988 (1)
Barratt, F. 5: v SA 1929 (1); *v NZ 1929 (4)*
Barrington, K. F. 82: v A 1961 (5) 1964 (5) 1968 (3); v SA 1955 (2) 1960 (4) 1965 (3); v WI 1963 (5) 1966 (2); v NZ 1965 (2); v In 1959 (5) 1967 (3); v P 1962 (4) 1967 (3); *v A 1962 (5) 1965 (5); v SA 1964 (5); v WI 1959 (5) 1967 (5); v NZ 1962 (3); v In 1961 (5) 1963 (1); v P 1961 (2)*
Barton, V. A. 1: *v SA 1891*
Bates, W. 15: *v A 1881 (4) 1882 (4) 1884 (5) 1886 (2)*
Bean, G. 3: *v A 1891 (3)*
Bedser, A. V. 51: v A 1948 (5) 1953 (5); v SA 1947 (2) 1951 (5) 1955 (1); v WI 1950 (3); v NZ 1949 (2); v In 1946 (3) 1952 (4); v P 1954 (2); *v A 1946 (5) 1950 (5) 1954 (1); v SA 1948 (5); v NZ 1946 (1) 1950 (2)*
Benjamin, J. E. 1: v SA 1994
Benson, M. R. 1: v In 1986
Berry, R. 2: v WI 1950 (2)
Bicknell, M. P. 2: v A 1993 (2)
Binks, J. G. 2: *v In 1963 (2)*
Bird, M. C. 10: *v SA 1909 (5) 1913 (5)*
Birkenshaw, J. 5: *v WI 1973 (2); v In 1972 (2); v P 1972 (1)*
Blakey, R. J. 2: *v In 1992 (2)*
Bligh, Hon. I. F. W. 4: *v A 1882 (4)*
Blythe, C. 19: v A 1905 (1) 1909 (2); v SA 1907 (3); *v A 1901 (5) 1907 (1); v SA 1905 (5) 1909 (2)*
Board, J. H. 6: *v SA 1898 (2) 1905 (4)*
Bolus, J. B. 7: v WI 1963 (2); *v In 1963 (5)*
Booth, M. W. 2: *v SA 1913 (2)*
Bosanquet, B. J. T. 7: v A 1905 (3); *v A 1903 (4)*
Botham, I. T. 102: v A 1977 (2) 1980 (1) 1981 (6) 1985 (6) 1989 (3); v WI 1980 (5) 1984 (5) 1991 (1); v NZ 1978 (3) 1983 (4) 1986 (1); v In 1979 (4) 1982 (3); v P 1978 (3) 1982 (3) 1987 (5) 1992 (2); v SL 1984 (1) 1991 (1); *v A 1978 (6) 1979 (3) 1982 (5) 1986 (4); v WI 1980 (4) 1985 (5); v NZ 1977 (3) 1983 (3) 1991 (1); v In 1979 (1) 1981 (6); v P 1983 (1); v SL 1981 (1)*
Bowden, M. P. 2: *v SA 1888 (2)*
Bowes, W. E. 15: v A 1934 (3) 1938 (2); v SA 1935 (4); v WI 1939 (2); v In 1932 (1) 1946 (1); *v A 1932 (1); v NZ 1932 (1)*
Bowley, E. H. 5: v SA 1929 (2); *v NZ 1929 (3)*
Boycott, G. 108: v A 1964 (4) 1968 (3) 1972 (2) 1977 (3) 1980 (1) 1981 (6); v SA 1965 (2); v WI 1966 (4) 1969 (3) 1973 (3) 1980 (5); v NZ 1965 (2) 1969 (3) 1973 (3) 1978 (2); v In 1967 (2) 1971 (1) 1974 (1) 1979 (4); v P 1967 (1) 1971 (2); *v A 1965 (5) 1970 (5) 1978 (6) 1979 (3); v SA 1964 (5); v WI 1967 (5) 1973 (5) 1980 (4); v NZ 1965 (2) 1977 (3); v In 1979 (1) 1981 (4); v P 1977 (3)*
Bradley, W. M. 2: v A 1899 (2)
Braund, L. C. 23: v A 1902 (5); v SA 1907 (3); *v A 1901 (5) 1903 (5) 1907 (5)*
Brearley, J. M. 39: v A 1977 (5) 1981 (4); v WI 1976 (2); v NZ 1978 (3); v In 1979 (4); v P 1978 (3); *v A 1976 (1) 1978 (6) 1979 (3); v In 1976 (5) 1979 (1); v P 1977 (2)*
Brearley, W. 4: v A 1905 (2) 1909 (1); v SA 1912 (1)
Brennan, D. V. 2: v SA 1951 (2)
Briggs, John 33: v A 1886 (3) 1888 (3) 1893 (2) 1896 (1) 1899 (1); *v A 1884 (5) 1886 (2) 1887 (1) 1891 (3) 1894 (5) 1897 (5); v SA 1888 (2)*
Broad, B. C. 25: v A 1989 (2); v WI 1984 (4) 1988 (2); v P 1987 (4); v SL 1984 (1); *v A 1986 (5) 1987 (1); v NZ 1987 (3); v P 1987 (3)*
Brockwell, W. 7: v A 1893 (1) 1899 (1); *v A 1894 (5)*

Bromley-Davenport, H. R. 4: *v SA 1895 (3) 1898 (1)*
Brookes, D. 1: *v WI 1947*
Brown, A. 2: *v In 1961 (1); v P 1961 (1)*
Brown, D. J. 26: v A 1968 (4); v SA 1965 (2); v WI 1966 (1) 1969 (3); v NZ 1969 (1); v In 1967 (2): *v A 1965 (4); v WI 1967 (4); v NZ 1965 (2); v P 1968 (3)*
Brown, F. R. 22: v A 1953 (1); v SA 1951 (5); v WI 1950 (1); v NZ 1931 (2) 1937 (1) 1949 (2); v In 1932 (1); *v A 1950 (5); v NZ 1932 (2) 1950 (2)*
Brown, G. 7: v A 1921 (3); *v SA 1922 (4)*
Brown, J. T. 8: v A 1896 (2) 1899 (1); *v A 1894 (5)*
Buckenham, C. P. 4: *v SA 1909 (4)*
Butcher, A. R. 1: v In 1979
Butcher, R. O. 3: *v WI 1980 (3)*
Butler, H. J. 2: v SA 1947 (1); *v WI 1947 (1)*
Butt, H. R. 3: *v SA 1895 (3)*

Caddick, A. R. 8: v A 1993 (4); *v WI 1993 (4)*
Calthorpe, Hon. F. S. G. 4: *v WI 1929 (4)*
Capel, D. J. 15: v A 1989 (1); v WI 1988 (2); v P 1987 (1); *v A 1987 (1); v WI 1989 (4); v NZ 1987 (3); v P 1987 (3)*
Carr, A. W. 11: v A 1926 (4); v SA 1929 (2); *v SA 1922 (5)*
Carr, D. B. 2: *v In 1951 (2)*
Carr, D. W. 1: v A 1909
Cartwright, T. W. 5: v A 1964 (2); v SA 1965 (1); v NZ 1965 (1); *v SA 1964 (1)*
Chapman, A. P. F. 26: v A 1926 (4) 1930 (4); v SA 1924 (2); v WI 1928 (3); *v A 1924 (4) 1928 (4); v SA 1930 (5)*
Charlwood, H. R. J. 2: *v A 1876 (2)*
Chatterton, W. 1: *v SA 1891*
Childs, J. H. 2: v WI 1988 (2)
Christopherson, S. 1: v A 1884
Clark, E. W. 8: v A 1934 (2); v SA 1929 (1); v WI 1933 (2); *v In 1933 (3)*
Clay, J. C. 1: v SA 1935
Close, D. B. 22: v A 1961 (1); v SA 1955 (1); v WI 1957 (2) 1963 (5) 1966 (1) 1976 (3); v NZ 1949 (1); v In 1959 (1) 1967 (3); v P 1967 (3); *v A 1950 (1)*
Coldwell, L. J. 7: v A 1964 (2); v P 1962 (2); *v A 1962 (2); v NZ 1962 (1)*
Compton, D. C. S. 78: v A 1938 (4) 1948 (5) 1953 (5) 1956 (1); v SA 1947 (5) 1951 (4) 1955 (5); v WI 1939 (3) 1950 (1); v NZ 1937 (1) 1949 (4); v In 1946 (3) 1952 (2); v P 1954 (4); *v A 1946 (5) 1950 (4) 1954 (4); v SA 1948 (5) 1956 (5); v WI 1953 (5); v NZ 1946 (1) 1950 (2)*
Cook, C. 1: v SA 1947
Cook, G. 7: v In 1982 (3); *v A 1982 (3); v SL 1981 (1)*
Cook, N. G. B. 15: v A 1989 (3); v WI 1984 (3); v NZ 1983 (2); *v NZ 1983 (1); v P 1983 (3) 1987 (3)*
Cope, G. A. 3: *v P 1977 (3)*
Copson, W. H. 3: v SA 1947 (1); v WI 1939 (2)
Cornford, W. L. 4: *v NZ 1929 (4)*
Cottam, R. M. H. 4: *v In 1972 (2); v P 1968 (2)*
Coventry, Hon. C. J. 2: *v SA 1888 (2)*
Cowans, N. G. 19: v A 1985 (1); v WI 1984 (1); v NZ 1983 (4); *v A 1982 (4); v NZ 1983 (2); v In 1984 (5); v P 1983 (2)*
Cowdrey, C. S. 6: v WI 1988 (1); *v In 1984 (5)*
Cowdrey, M. C. 114: v A 1956 (5) 1961 (4) 1964 (3) 1968 (4); v SA 1955 (1) 1960 (5) 1965 (3); v WI 1957 (5) 1963 (2) 1966 (4); v NZ 1958 (4) 1965 (3); v In 1959 (5); v P 1962 (4) 1967 (2) 1971 (1); *v A 1954 (5) 1958 (5) 1962 (5) 1965 (4) 1970 (3) 1974 (5); v SA 1956 (5); v WI 1959 (5) 1967 (5); v NZ 1954 (2) 1958 (2) 1962 (3) 1965 (3) 1970 (1); v In 1963 (3); v P 1968 (3)*
Coxon, A. 1: v A 1948
Cranston, J. 1: v A 1890
Cranston, K. 8: v A 1948 (1); v SA 1947 (3); *v WI 1947 (4)*
Crapp, J. F. 7: v A 1948 (3); *v SA 1948 (4)*
Crawford, J. N. 12: v SA 1907 (2); *v A 1907 (5); v SA 1905 (5)*
Crawley, J. P. 3: v SA 1994 (3)
Curtis, T. S. 5: v A 1989 (3); v WI 1988 (2)
Cuttell, W. R. 2: *v SA 1898 (2)*

Dawson, E. W. 5: *v SA 1927 (1); v NZ 1929 (4)*
Dean, H. 3: v A 1912 (2); v SA 1912 (1)
DeFreitas, P. A. J. 39: v A 1989 (1) 1993 (1); v SA 1994 (3); v WI 1988 (3) 1991 (5); v NZ 1990 (2) 1994 (3); v P 1987 (1) 1992 (2); v SL 1991 (1); *v A 1986 (4) 1990 (3); v WI 1989 (2); v NZ 1987 (2) 1991 (3); v In 1992 (1); v P 1987 (2)*
Denness, M. H. 28: v A 1975 (1); v NZ 1969 (1); v In 1974 (3); v P 1974 (3); *v A 1974 (5); v WI 1973 (5); v NZ 1974 (2); v In 1972 (5); v P 1972 (3)*
Denton, D. 11: v A 1905 (1); *v SA 1905 (5) 1909 (5)*
Dewes, J. G. 5: v A 1948 (1); v WI 1950 (2); *v A 1950 (2)*
Dexter, E. R. 62: v A 1961 (5) 1964 (5) 1968 (2); v SA 1960 (5); v WI 1963 (5); v NZ 1958 (1) 1965 (2); v In 1959 (2); v P 1962 (5); *v A 1958 (2) 1962 (5); v SA 1964 (5); v WI 1959 (5); v NZ 1958 (2) 1962 (3); v In 1961 (5); v P 1961 (3)*
Dilley, G. R. 41: v A 1981 (3) 1989 (2); v WI 1980 (3) 1988 (4); v NZ 1983 (1) 1986 (2); v In 1986 (2); v P 1987 (4); *v A 1979 (2) 1986 (4) 1987 (1); v WI 1980 (4); v NZ 1987 (3); v In 1981 (4); v P 1983 (1) 1987 (1)*
Dipper, A. E. 1: v A 1921
Doggart, G. H. G. 2: v WI 1950 (2)
D'Oliveira, B. L. 44: v A 1968 (2) 1972 (5); v WI 1966 (4) 1969 (3); v NZ 1969 (3); v In 1967 (2) 1971 (3); v P 1967 (3) 1971 (3); *v A 1970 (6); v WI 1967 (5); v NZ 1970 (2); v P 1968 (3)*
Dollery, H. E. 4: v A 1948 (2); v SA 1947 (1); v WI 1950 (1)
Dolphin, A. 1: *v A 1920*
Douglas, J. W. H. T. 23: v A 1912 (1) 1921 (5); v SA 1924 (1); *v A 1911 (5) 1920 (5) 1924 (1); v SA 1913 (5)*
Downton, P. R. 30: v A 1981 (1) 1985 (6); v WI 1984 (5) 1988 (3); v In 1986 (1); v SL 1984 (1); *v WI 1980 (3) 1985 (5); v In 1984 (5)*
Druce, N. F. 5: *v A 1897 (5)*
Ducat, A. 1: v A 1921
Duckworth, G. 24: v A 1930 (5); v SA 1924 (1) 1929 (4) 1935 (1); v WI 1928 (1); v In 1936 (3); *v A 1928 (5); v SA 1930 (3); v NZ 1932 (1)*
Duleepsinhji, K. S. 12: v A 1930 (4); v SA 1929 (1); v NZ 1931 (3); *v NZ 1929 (4)*
Durston, F. J. 1: v A 1921

Edmonds, P. H. 51: v A 1975 (2) 1985 (5); v NZ 1978 (3) 1983 (2) 1986 (3); v In 1979 (4) 1982 (3) 1986 (2); v P 1978 (3) 1987 (5); *v A 1978 (1) 1986 (5); v WI 1985 (3); v NZ 1977 (3); v In 1984 (5); v P 1977 (2)*
Edrich, J. H. 77: v A 1964 (3) 1968 (5) 1972 (5) 1975 (4); v SA 1965 (1); v WI 1963 (3) 1966 (1) 1969 (3) 1976 (2); v NZ 1965 (1) 1969 (3); v In 1967 (2) 1971 (3) 1974 (3); v P 1971 (3) 1974 (3); *v A 1965 (5) 1970 (6) 1974 (4); v WI 1967 (5); v NZ 1965 (3) 1970 (2) 1974 (2); v In 1963 (2); v P 1968 (3)*
Edrich, W. J. 39: v A 1938 (4) 1948 (5) 1953 (3); v SA 1947 (4); v WI 1950 (2); v NZ 1949 (4); v In 1946 (1); v P 1954 (1); *v A 1946 (5) 1954 (4); v SA 1938 (5); v NZ 1946 (1)*
Elliott, H. 4: v WI 1928 (1); *v SA 1927 (1); v In 1933 (2)*
Ellison, R. M. 11: v A 1985 (2); v WI 1984 (1); v In 1986 (1); v SL 1984 (1); *v WI 1985 (3); v In 1984 (3)*
Emburey, J. E. 63: v A 1980 (1) 1981 (4) 1985 (6) 1989 (3) 1993 (1); v WI 1980 (3) 1988 (3); v NZ 1978 (1) 1986 (2); v In 1986 (3); v P 1987 (4); v SL 1988 (1); *v A 1978 (4) 1986 (5) 1987 (1); v WI 1980 (4) 1985 (4); v NZ 1987 (3); v In 1979 (1) 1981 (3) 1992 (1); v P 1987 (3); v SL 1981 (1) 1992 (1)*
Emmett, G. M. 1: v A 1948
Emmett, T. 7: *v A 1876 (2) 1878 (1) 1881 (4)*
Evans, A. J. 1: v A 1921
Evans, T. G. 91: v A 1948 (5) 1953 (5) 1956 (5); v SA 1947 (5) 1951 (3) 1955 (3); v WI 1950 (3) 1957 (5); v NZ 1949 (4) 1958 (5); v In 1946 (1) 1952 (4) 1959 (2); v P 1954 (4); *v A 1946 (4) 1950 (5) 1954 (4) 1958 (3); v SA 1948 (3) 1956 (5); v WI 1947 (4) 1953 (4); v NZ 1946 (1) 1950 (2) 1954 (2)*

Fagg, A. E. 5: v WI 1939 (1); v In 1936 (2); *v A 1936 (2)*
Fairbrother, N. H. 10: v NZ 1990 (3); v P 1987 (1); *v NZ 1987 (2); v In 1992 (2); v P 1987 (1); v SL 1992 (1)*
Fane, F. L. 14: *v A 1907 (4); v SA 1905 (5) 1909 (5)*
Farnes, K. 15: v A 1934 (2) 1938 (4); *v A 1936 (2); v SA 1938 (5); v WI 1934 (2)*
Farrimond, W. 4: v SA 1935 (1); *v SA 1930 (2); v WI 1934 (1)*

Fender, P. G. H. 13: v A 1921 (2); v SA 1924 (2) 1929 (1); *v A 1920 (3); v SA 1922 (5)*
Ferris, J. J. 1: *v SA 1891*
Fielder, A. 6: *v A 1903 (2) 1907 (4)*
Fishlock, L. B. 4: v In 1936 (2) 1946 (1); *v A 1946 (1)*
Flavell, J. A. 4: v A 1961 (2) 1964 (2)
Fletcher, K. W. R. 59: v A 1968 (1) 1972 (1) 1975 (2); v WI 1973 (3); v NZ 1969 (2) 1973 (3); v In 1971 (2) 1974 (3); v P 1974 (3); *v A 1970 (5) 1974 (5) 1976 (1); v WI 1973 (4); v NZ 1970 (1) 1974 (2); v In 1972 (5) 1976 (3) 1981 (6); v P 1968 (3) 1972 (3); v SL 1981 (1)*
Flowers, W. 8: v A 1893 (1); *v A 1884 (5) 1886 (2)*
Ford, F. G. J. 5: *v A 1894 (5)*
Foster, F. R. 11: v A 1912 (3); v SA 1912 (3); *v A 1911 (5)*
Foster, N. A. 29: v A 1985 (1) 1989 (3) 1993 (1); v WI 1984 (1) 1988 (2); v NZ 1983 (1) 1986 (1); v In 1986 (1); v P 1987 (5); v SL 1988 (1); *v A 1987 (1); v WI 1985 (3); v NZ 1983 (2); v In 1984 (2); v P 1983 (2) 1987 (2)*
Foster, R. E. 8: v SA 1907 (3); *v A 1903 (5)*
Fothergill, A. J. 2: *v SA 1888 (2)*
Fowler, G. 21: v WI 1984 (5); v NZ 1983 (2); v P 1982 (1); v SL 1984 (1); *v A 1982 (3); v NZ 1983 (2); v In 1984 (5); v P 1983 (2)*
Fraser, A. R. C. 21: v A 1989 (3) 1993 (1); v SA 1994 (2); v NZ 1994 (3); v In 1990 (3); *v A 1990 (3); v WI 1989 (2) 1993 (4)*
Freeman, A. P. 12: v SA 1929 (3); v WI 1928 (3); *v A 1924 (2); v SA 1927 (4)*
French, B. N. 16: v NZ 1986 (3); v In 1986 (2); v P 1987 (4); *v A 1987 (1); v NZ 1987 (3); v P 1987 (3)*
Fry, C. B. 26: v A 1899 (5) 1902 (3) 1905 (4) 1909 (3) 1912 (3); v SA 1907 (3) 1912 (3); *v SA 1895 (2)*

Gatting, M. W. 74: v A 1980 (1) 1981 (6) 1985 (6) 1989 (1) 1993 (2); v WI 1980 (4) 1984 (1) 1988 (2); v NZ 1983 (2) 1986 (3); v In 1986 (3); v P 1982 (3) 1987 (5); *v A 1986 (5) 1987 (1); v WI 1980 (1) 1985 (1); v NZ 1977 (1) 1983 (2) 1987 (3); v In 1981 (5) 1984 (5) 1992 (3); v P 1977 (1) 1983 (3) 1987 (3); v SL 1992 (1)*
Gay, L. H. 1: *v A 1894*
Geary, G. 14: v A 1926 (2) 1930 (1) 1934 (2); v SA 1924 (1) 1929 (2); *v A 1928 (4); v SA 1927 (2)*
Gibb, P. A. 8: v In 1946 (2); *v A 1946 (1); v SA 1938 (5)*
Gifford, N. 15: v A 1964 (2) 1972 (3); v NZ 1973 (2); v In 1971 (2); v P 1971 (2); *v In 1972 (2); v P 1972 (2)*
Gilligan, A. E. R. 11: v SA 1924 (4); *v A 1924 (5); v SA 1922 (2)*
Gilligan, A. H. H. 4: *v NZ 1929 (4)*
Gimblett, H. 3: v WI 1939 (1); v In 1936 (2)
Gladwin, C. 8: v SA 1947 (2); v NZ 1949 (1); *v SA 1948 (5)*
Goddard, T. W. 8: v A 1930 (1); v WI 1939 (2); v NZ 1937 (2); *v SA 1938 (3)*
Gooch, G. A. 113: v A 1975 (2) 1980 (1) 1981 (5) 1985 (6) 1989 (5) 1993 (6); v SA 1994 (3); v WI 1980 (5) 1988 (5) 1991 (5); v NZ 1978 (3) 1986 (3) 1990 (3) 1994 (3); v In 1979 (4) 1986 (3) 1990 (3); v P 1978 (2) 1992 (5); v SL 1988 (1) 1991 (1); *v A 1978 (6) 1979 (2) 1990 (4); v WI 1980 (4) 1985 (5) 1989 (2); v NZ 1991 (3); v In 1979 (1) 1981 (6) 1992 (2); v P 1987 (3); v SL 1981 (1)*
Gough, D. 4: v SA 1994 (3); v NZ 1994 (1)
Gover, A. R. 4: v NZ 1937 (2); v In 1936 (1) 1946 (1)
Gower, D. I. 117: v A 1980 (1) 1981 (5) 1985 (6) 1989 (6); v WI 1980 (1) 1984 (5) 1988 (4); v NZ 1978 (3) 1983 (4) 1986 (3); v In 1979 (4) 1982 (3) 1986 (2) 1990 (3); v P 1978 (3) 1982 (3) 1987 (5) 1992 (3); v SL 1984 (1); *v A 1978 (6) 1979 (3) 1982 (5) 1986 (5) 1990 (5); v WI 1980 (4) 1985 (5); v NZ 1983 (3); v In 1979 (1) 1981 (6) 1984 (5); v P 1983 (3); v SL 1981 (1)*
Grace, E. M. 1: v A 1880
Grace, G. F. 1: v A 1880
Grace, W. G. 22: v A 1880 (1) 1882 (1) 1884 (3) 1886 (3) 1888 (3) 1890 (2) 1893 (2) 1896 (3) 1899 (1); *v A 1891 (3)*
Graveney, T. W. 79: v A 1953 (5) 1956 (2) 1968 (5); v SA 1951 (1) 1955 (5); v WI 1957 (4) 1966 (4) 1969 (1); v NZ 1958 (4); v In 1952 (4) 1967 (3); v P 1954 (3) 1962 (4) 1967 (3); *v A 1954 (2) 1958 (5) 1962 (3); v WI 1953 (5) 1967 (5); v NZ 1954 (2) 1958 (2); v In 1951 (4); v P 1968 (3)*
Greenhough, T. 4: v SA 1960 (1); v In 1959 (3)
Greenwood, A. 2: *v A 1876 (2)*
Greig, A. W. 58: v A 1972 (5) 1975 (4) 1977 (5); v WI 1973 (3) 1976 (5); v NZ 1973 (3); v In 1974 (3); v P 1974 (3); *v A 1974 (6) 1976 (1); v WI 1973 (5); v NZ 1974 (2); v In 1972 (5) 1976 (5); v P 1972 (3)*

Greig, I. A. 2: v P 1982 (2)
Grieve, B. A. F. 2: *v SA 1888 (2)*
Griffith, S. C. 3: *v SA 1948 (2); v WI 1947 (1)*
Gunn, G. 15: v A 1909 (1); *v A 1907 (5) 1911 (5); v WI 1929 (4)*
Gunn, J. 6: v A 1905 (1); *v A 1901 (5)*
Gunn, W. 11: v A 1888 (2) 1890 (2) 1893 (3) 1896 (1) 1899 (1); *v A 1886 (2)*

Haig, N. E. 5: v A 1921 (1); *v WI 1929 (4)*
Haigh, S. 11: v A 1905 (2) 1909 (1) 1912 (1); *v SA 1898 (2) 1905 (5)*
Hallows, C. 2: v A 1921 (1); v WI 1928 (1)
Hammond, W. R. 85: v A 1930 (5) 1934 (5) 1938 (4); v SA 1929 (4) 1935 (5); v WI 1928 (3) 1933 (3) 1939 (3); v NZ 1931 (3) 1937 (3); v In 1932 (1) 1936 (2) 1946 (3); *v A 1928 (5) 1932 (5) 1936 (5) 1946 (4); v SA 1927 (5) 1930 (5) 1938 (5); v WI 1934 (4); v NZ 1932 (2) 1946 (1)*
Hampshire, J. H. 8: v A 1972 (1) 1975 (1); v WI 1969 (2); *v A 1970 (2); v NZ 1970 (2)*
Hardinge, H. T. W. 1: v A 1921
Hardstaff, J. 5: *v A 1907 (5)*
Hardstaff, J. jun. 23: v A 1938 (2) 1948 (1); v SA 1935 (1); v WI 1939 (3); v NZ 1937 (3); v In 1936 (2) 1946 (2); *v A 1936 (5) 1946 (1); v WI 1947 (3)*
Harris, Lord 4: v A 1880 (1) 1884 (2); *v A 1878 (1)*
Hartley, J. C. 2: *v SA 1905 (2)*
Hawke, Lord 5: *v SA 1895 (3) 1898 (2)*
Hayes, E. G. 5: v A 1909 (1); v SA 1912 (1); *v SA 1905 (3)*
Hayes, F. C. 9: v WI 1973 (3) 1976 (2); *v WI 1973 (4)*
Hayward, T. W. 35: v A 1896 (2) 1899 (5) 1902 (1) 1905 (5) 1909 (1); v SA 1907 (3); *v A 1897 (5) 1901 (5) 1903 (5); v SA 1895 (3)*
Hearne, A. 1: *v SA 1891*
Hearne, F. 2: *v SA 1888 (2)*
Hearne, G. G. 1: *v SA 1891*
Hearne, J. T. 12: v A 1896 (3) 1899 (3); *v A 1897 (5); v SA 1891 (1)*
Hearne, J. W. 24: v A 1912 (3) 1921 (1) 1926 (1); v SA 1912 (2) 1924 (3); *v A 1911 (5) 1920 (2) 1924 (4); v SA 1913 (3)*
Hemmings, E. E. 16: v A 1989 (1); v NZ 1990 (3); v In 1990 (3); v P 1982 (2); *v A 1982 (3) 1987 (1) 1990 (1); v NZ 1987 (1); v P 1987 (1)*
Hendren, E. H. 51: v A 1921 (2) 1926 (5) 1930 (2) 1934 (4); v SA 1924 (5) 1929 (4); v WI 1928 (1); *v A 1920 (5) 1924 (5) 1928 (5); v SA 1930 (5); v WI 1929 (4) 1934 (4)*
Hendrick, M. 30: v A 1977 (3) 1980 (1) 1981 (2); v WI 1976 (2) 1980 (2); v NZ 1978 (2); v In 1974 (3) 1979 (4); v P 1974 (2); *v A 1974 (2) 1978 (5); v NZ 1974 (1) 1977 (1)*
Heseltine, C. 2: *v SA 1895 (2)*
Hick, G. A. 29: v A 1993 (3); v SA 1994 (3); v WI 1991 (4); v NZ 1994 (3); v P 1992 (4); *v WI 1993 (5); v NZ 1991 (3); v In 1992 (3); v SL 1992 (1)*
Higgs, K. 15: v A 1968 (1); v WI 1966 (5); v SA 1965 (1); v In 1967 (1); v P 1967 (3); *v A 1965 (1); v NZ 1965 (3)*
Hill, A. 2: *v A 1876 (2)*
Hill, A. J. L. 3: *v SA 1895 (3)*
Hilton, M. J. 4: v SA 1951 (1); v WI 1950 (1); *v In 1951 (2)*
Hirst, G. H. 24: v A 1899 (1) 1902 (4) 1905 (3) 1909 (4); v SA 1907 (3); *v A 1897 (4) 1903 (5)*
Hitch, J. W. 7: v A 1912 (1) 1921 (1); v SA 1912 (1); *v A 1911 (3) 1920 (1)*
Hobbs, J. B. 61: v A 1909 (3) 1912 (3) 1921 (1) 1926 (5) 1930 (5); v SA 1912 (3) 1924 (4) 1929 (1); v WI 1928 (2); *v A 1907 (4) 1911 (5) 1920 (5) 1924 (5) 1928 (5); v SA 1909 (5) 1913 (5)*
Hobbs, R. N. S. 7: v In 1967 (3); v P 1967 (1) 1971 (1); *v WI 1967 (1); v P 1968 (1)*
Hollies, W. E. 13: v A 1948 (1); v SA 1947 (3); v WI 1950 (2); v NZ 1949 (4); *v WI 1934 (3)*
Holmes, E. R. T. 5: v SA 1935 (1); *v WI 1934 (4)*
Holmes, P. 7: v A 1921 (1); v In 1932 (1); *v SA 1927 (5)*
Hone, L. 1: *v A 1878*
Hopwood, J. L. 2: v A 1934 (2)
Hornby, A. N. 3: v A 1882 (1) 1884 (1); *v A 1878 (1)*
Horton, M. J. 2: v In 1959 (2)
Howard, N. D. 4: *v In 1951 (4)*
Howell, H. 5: v A 1921 (1); v SA 1924 (1); *v A 1920 (3)*
Howorth, R. 5: v SA 1947 (1); *v WI 1947 (4)*
Humphries, J. 3: *v A 1907 (3)*
Hunter, J. 5: *v A 1884 (5)*

Hussain, N. 7: v A 1993 (4); *v WI 1989 (3)*
Hutchings, K. L. 7: v A 1909 (2); *v A 1907 (5)*
Hutton, L. 79: v A 1938 (3) 1948 (4) 1953 (5); v SA 1947 (5) 1951 (5); v WI 1939 (3) 1950 (3); v NZ 1937 (3) 1949 (4); v In 1946 (3) 1952 (4); v P 1954 (2); *v A 1946 (5) 1950 (5) 1954 (5); v SA 1938 (4) 1948 (5); v WI 1947 (2) 1953 (5); v NZ 1950 (2) 1954 (2)*
Hutton, R. A. 5: v In 1971 (3); v P 1971 (2)

Iddon, J. 5: v SA 1935 (1); *v WI 1934 (4)*
Igglesden, A. P. 3: v A 1989 (1); *v WI 1993 (2)*
Ikin, J. T. 18: v SA 1951 (3) 1955 (1); v In 1946 (2) 1952 (2); *v A 1946 (5); v NZ 1946 (1); v WI 1947 (4)*
Illingworth, R. 61: v A 1961 (2) 1968 (3) 1972 (5); v SA 1960 (4); v WI·1966 (2) 1969 (3) 1973 (3); v NZ 1958 (1) 1965 (1) 1969 (3) 1973 (3); v In 1959 (2) 1967 (3) 1971 (3); v P 1962 (1) 1967 (1) 1971 (3); *v A 1962 (2) 1970 (6); v WI 1959 (5); v NZ 1962 (3) 1970 (2)*
Illingworth, R. K. 2: v WI 1991 (2)
Ilott, M. C. 3: v A 1993 (3)
Insole, D. J. 9: v A 1956 (1); v SA 1955 (1); v WI 1950 (1) 1957 (1); *v SA 1956 (5)*

Jackman, R. D. 4: v P 1982 (2); *v WI 1980 (2)*
Jackson, F. S. 20: v A 1893 (2) 1896 (3) 1899 (5) 1902 (5) 1905 (5)
Jackson, H. L. 2: v A 1961 (1); v NZ 1949 (1)
Jameson, J. A. 4: v In 1971 (2); *v WI 1973 (2)*
Jardine, D. R. 22: v WI 1928 (2) 1933 (2); v NZ 1931 (3); v In 1932 (1); *v A 1928 (5) 1932 (5); v NZ 1932 (1); v In 1933 (3)*
Jarvis, P. W. 9: v A 1989 (2); v WI 1988 (2); *v NZ 1987 (2); v In 1992 (2), v SL 1992 (1)*
Jenkins, R. O. 9: v WI 1950 (2); v In 1952 (2); *v SA 1948 (5)*
Jessop, G. L. 18: v A 1899 (1) 1902 (4) 1905 (1) 1909 (2); v SA 1907 (3) 1912 (2); *v A 1901 (5)*
Jones, A. O. 12: v A 1899 (1) 1905 (2) 1909 (2); *v A 1901 (5) 1907 (2)*
Jones, I. J. 15: v WI 1966 (2); *v A 1965 (4); v WI 1967 (5); v NZ 1965 (3); v In 1963 (1)*
Jupp, H. 2: *v A 1876 (2)*
Jupp, V. W. C. 8: v A 1921 (2); v WI 1928 (2); *v SA 1922 (4)*

Keeton, W. W. 2: v A 1934 (1); v WI 1939 (1)
Kennedy, A. S. 5: *v SA 1922 (5)*
Kenyon, D. 8: v A 1953 (2); v SA 1955 (3); *v In 1951 (3)*
Killick, E. T. 2: v SA 1929 (2)
Kilner, R. 9: v A 1926 (4); v SA 1924 (2); *v A 1924 (3)*
King, J. H. 1: v A 1909
Kinneir, S. P. 1: *v A 1911*
Knight, A. E. 3: *v A 1903 (3)*
Knight, B. R. 29: v A 1968 (2); v WI 1966 (1) 1969 (3); v NZ 1969 (2); v P 1962 (2); *v A 1962 (1) 1965 (2); v NZ 1962 (3) 1965 (2); v In 1961 (4) 1963 (5); v P 1961 (2)*
Knight, D. J. 2: v A 1921 (2)
Knott, A. P. E. 95: v A 1968 (5) 1972 (5) 1975 (4) 1977 (5) 1981 (2); v WI 1969 (3) 1973 (3) 1976 (5) 1980 (4); v NZ 1969 (3) 1973 (3); v In 1971 (3) 1974 (3); v P 1967 (2) 1971 (3) 1974 (3); *v A 1970 (6) 1974 (6) 1976 (1); v WI 1967 (2) 1973 (5); v NZ 1970 (1) 1974 (2); v In 1972 (5) 1976 (5); v P 1968 (3) 1972 (3)*
Knox, N. A. 2: v SA 1907 (2)

Laker, J. C. 46: v A 1948 (3) 1953 (3) 1956 (5); v SA 1951 (2) 1955 (1); v WI 1950 (1) 1957 (4); v NZ 1949 (1) 1958 (4); v In 1952 (4); v P 1954 (1); *v A 1958 (4); v SA 1956 (5); v WI 1947 (4) 1953 (4)*
Lamb, A. J. 79: v A 1985 (6) 1989 (1); v WI 1984 (5) 1988 (4) 1991 (4); v NZ 1983 (4) 1986 (1) 1990 (3); v In 1982 (3) 1986 (2) 1990 (3); v P 1982 (3) 1992 (2); v SL 1984 (1) 1988 (1); *v A 1982 (5) 1986 (5) 1990 (3); v WI 1985 (5) 1989 (4); v NZ 1983 (3) 1991 (3); v In 1984 (5); v P 1983 (3)*
Langridge, James 8: v SA 1935 (1); v WI 1933 (2); v In 1936 (1) 1946 (1); *v In 1933 (3)*
Larkins, W. 13: v A 1981 (1); v WI 1980 (3); *v A 1979 (1) 1990 (3); v WI 1989 (4); v In 1979 (1)*
Larter, J. D. F. 10: v SA 1965 (2); v NZ 1965 (1); v P 1962 (1); *v NZ 1962 (3); v In 1963 (3)*
Larwood, H. 21: v A 1926 (2) 1930 (3); v SA 1929 (3); v WI 1928 (2); v NZ 1931 (1); *v A 1928 (5) 1932 (5)*
Lathwell, M. N. 2: v A 1993 (2)
Lawrence, D. V. 5: v WI 1991 (2); v SL 1988 (1) 1991 (1); *v NZ 1991 (1)*

Leadbeater, E. 2: *v In 1951 (2)*
Lee, H. W. 1: *v SA 1930*
Lees, W. S. 5: *v SA 1905 (5)*
Legge, G. B. 5: *v SA 1927 (1); v NZ 1929 (4)*
Leslie, C. F. H. 4: *v A 1882 (4)*
Lever, J. K. 21: v A 1977 (3); v WI 1980 (1); v In 1979 (1) 1986 (1); *v A 1976 (1) 1978 (1) 1979 (1); v NZ 1977 (1); v In 1976 (5) 1979 (1) 1981 (2); v P 1977 (3)*
Lever, P. 17: v A 1972 (1) 1975 (1); v In 1971 (1); v P 1971 (3); *v A 1970 (5) 1974 (2); v NZ 1970 (2) 1974 (2)*
Leveson Gower, H. D. G. 3: *v SA 1909 (3)*
Levett, W. H. V. 1: *v In 1933*
Lewis, A. R. 9: v NZ 1973 (1); *v In 1972 (5); v P 1972 (3)*
Lewis, C. C. 25: v A 1993 (2); v WI 1991 (2); v NZ 1990 (1); v In 1990 (2); v P 1992 (5); v SL 1991 (1); *v A 1990 (1); v WI 1993 (5); v NZ 1991 (2); v In 1992 (3); v SL 1992 (1)*
Leyland, M. 41: v A 1930 (3) 1934 (5) 1938 (1); v SA 1929 (5) 1935 (4); v WI 1928 (1) 1933 (1); v In 1936 (2); *v A 1928 (1) 1932 (5) 1936 (5); v SA 1930 (5); v WI 1934 (3)*
Lilley, A. A. 35: v A 1896 (3) 1899 (4) 1902 (5) 1905 (5) 1909 (5); v SA 1907 (3); *v A 1901 (5) 1903 (5)*
Lillywhite, James jun. 2: *v A 1876 (2)*
Lloyd, D. 9: v In 1974 (2); v P 1974 (3); *v A 1974 (4)*
Lloyd, T. A. 1: v WI 1984
Loader, P. J. 13: v SA 1955 (1); v WI 1957 (2); v NZ 1958 (3); v P 1954 (1); *v A 1958 (2); v SA 1956 (4)*
Lock, G. A. R. 49: v A 1953 (2) 1956 (4) 1961 (3); v SA 1955 (3); v WI 1957 (3) 1963 (3); v NZ 1958 (5); v In 1952 (2); v P 1962 (3); *v A 1958 (4); v SA 1956 (1); v WI 1953 (5) 1967 (2); v NZ 1958 (2); v In 1961 (5); v P 1961 (2)*
Lockwood, W. H. 12: v A 1893 (2) 1899 (1) 1902 (4); *v A 1894 (5)*
Lohmann, G. A. 18: v A 1886 (3) 1888 (3) 1890 (2) 1896 (1); *v A 1886 (2) 1887 (1) 1891 (3); v SA 1895 (3)*
Lowson, F. A. 7: v SA 1951 (2) 1955 (1); *v In 1951 (4)*
Lucas, A. P. 5: v A 1880 (1) 1882 (1) 1884 (2); *v A 1878 (1)*
Luckhurst, B. W. 21: v A 1972 (4); v WI 1973 (2); v In 1971 (3); v P 1971 (3); *v A 1970 (5) 1974 (2); v NZ 1970 (2)*
Lyttelton, Hon. A. 4: v A 1880 (1) 1882 (1) 1884 (2)

Macaulay, G. G. 8: v A 1926 (1); v SA 1924 (1); v WI 1933 (2); *v SA 1922 (4)*
MacBryan, J. C. W. 1: v SA 1924
McCague, M. J. 2: v A 1993 (2)
McConnon, J. E. 2: v P 1954 (2)
McGahey, C. P. 2: *v A 1901 (2)*
MacGregor, G. 8: v A 1890 (2) 1893 (3); *v A 1891 (3)*
McIntyre, A. J. W. 3: v SA 1955 (1); v WI 1950 (1); *v A 1950 (1)*
MacKinnon, F. A. 1: *v A 1878*
MacLaren, A. C. 35: v A 1896 (2) 1899 (4) 1902 (5) 1905 (4) 1909 (5); *v A 1894 (5) 1897 (5) 1901 (5)*
McMaster, J. E. P. 1: *v SA 1888*
Makepeace, J. W. H. 4: *v A 1920 (4)*
Malcolm, D. E. 28: v A 1989 (1) 1993 (1); v SA 1994 (1); v WI 1991 (2); v NZ 1990 (3) 1994 (1); v In 1990 (3); v P 1992 (3); *v A 1990 (5); v WI 1989 (4) 1993 (1); v In 1992 (2); v SL 1992 (1)*
Mallender, N. A. 2: v P 1992 (2)
Mann, F. G. 7: v NZ 1949 (2); *v SA 1948 (5)*
Mann, F. T. 5: *v SA 1922 (5)*
Marks, V. J. 6: v NZ 1983 (1); v P 1982 (1); *v NZ 1983 (1); v P 1983 (3)*
Marriott, C. S. 1: v WI 1933
Martin, F. 2: v A 1890 (1); *v SA 1891 (1)*
Martin, J. W. 1: v SA 1947
Mason, J. R. 5: *v A 1897 (5)*
Matthews, A. D. G. 1: v NZ 1937
May, P. B. H. 66: v A 1953 (2) 1956 (5) 1961 (4); v SA 1951 (2) 1955 (5); v WI 1957 (5); v NZ 1958 (5); v In 1952 (4) 1959 (3); v P 1954 (4); *v A 1954 (5) 1958 (5); v SA 1956 (5); v WI 1953 (5) 1959 (3); v NZ 1954 (2) 1958 (2)*
Maynard, M. P. 4: v A 1993 (2); v WI 1988 (1); *v WI 1993 (1)*

Mead, C. P. 17: v A 1921 (2); *v A 1911 (4) 1928 (1); v SA 1913 (5) 1922 (5)*
Mead, W. 1: v A 1899
Midwinter, W. E. 4: *v A 1881 (4)*
Milburn, C. 9: v A 1968 (2); v WI 1966 (4); v In 1967 (1); v P 1967 (1); *v P 1968 (1)*
Miller, A. M. 1: *v SA 1895*
Miller, G. 34: v A 1977 (2); v WI 1976 (1) 1984 (2); v NZ 1978 (2); v In 1979 (3) 1982 (1); v P 1978 (3) 1982 (1); *v A 1978 (6) 1979 (1) 1982 (5); v WI 1980 (1); v NZ 1977 (3); v P 1977 (3)*
Milligan, F. W. 2: *v SA 1898 (2)*
Millman, G. 6: v P 1962 (2); *v In 1961 (2); v P 1961 (2)*
Milton, C. A. 6: v NZ 1958 (2); v In 1959 (2); *v A 1958 (2)*
Mitchell, A. 6: v SA 1935 (2); v In 1936 (1); *v In 1933 (3)*
Mitchell, F. 2: *v SA 1898 (2)*
Mitchell, T. B. 5: v A 1934 (2); v SA 1935 (1); *v A 1932 (1); v NZ 1932 (1)*
Mitchell-Innes, N. S. 1: v SA 1935
Mold, A. W. 3: v A 1893 (3)
Moon, L. J. 4: *v SA 1905 (4)*
Morley, F. 4: v A 1880 (1); *v A 1882 (3)*
Morris, H. 3: v WI 1991 (2); v SL 1991 (1)
Morris, J. E. 3: v In 1990 (3)
Mortimore, J. B. 9: v A 1964 (1); v In 1959 (2); *v A 1958 (1); v NZ 1958 (2); v In 1963 (3)*
Moss, A. E. 9: v A 1956 (1); v SA 1960 (2); v In 1959 (3); *v WI 1953 (1) 1959 (2)*
Moxon, M. D. 10: v A 1989 (1); v WI 1988 (2); v NZ 1986 (2); v P 1987 (1); *v A 1987 (1); v NZ 1987 (3)*
Munton, T. A. 2: v P 1992 (2)
Murdoch, W. L. 1: *v SA 1891*
Murray, J. T. 21: v A 1961 (5); v WI 1966 (1); v In 1967 (3); v P 1962 (3) 1967 (1); *v A 1962 (1); v SA 1964 (1); v NZ 1962 (1) 1965 (1); v In 1961 (3); v P 1961 (1)*

Newham, W. 1: *v A 1887*
Newport, P. J. 3: v A 1989 (1); v SL 1988 (1); *v A 1990 (1)*
Nichols, M. S. 14: v A 1930 (1); v SA 1935 (4); v WI 1933 (1) 1939 (1); *v NZ 1929 (4); v In 1933 (3)*

Oakman, A. S. M. 2: v A 1956 (2)
O'Brien, Sir T. C. 5: v A 1884 (1) 1888 (1); *v SA 1895 (3)*
O'Connor, J. 4: v SA 1929 (1); *v WI 1929 (3)*
Old, C. M. 46: v A 1975 (3) 1977 (2) 1980 (1) 1981 (2); v WI 1973 (1) 1976 (2) 1980 (1); v NZ 1973 (2) 1978 (1); v In 1974 (3); v P 1974 (3) 1978 (3); *v A 1974 (2) 1976 (1) 1978 (1); v WI 1973 (4) 1980 (1); v NZ 1974 (1) 1977 (2); v In 1972 (4) 1976 (4); v P 1972 (1) 1977 (1)*
Oldfield, N. 1: v WI 1939

Padgett, D. E. V. 2: v SA 1960 (2)
Paine, G. A. E. 4: *v WI 1934 (4)*
Palairet, L. C. H. 2: v A 1902 (2)
Palmer, C. H. 1: *v WI 1953*
Palmer, K. E. 1: *v SA 1964*
Parfitt, P. H. 37: v A 1964 (4) 1972 (3); v SA 1965 (2); v WI 1969 (1); v NZ 1965 (2); v P 1962 (5); *v A 1962 (2); v SA 1964 (5); v NZ 1962 (3) 1965 (3); v In 1961 (2) 1963 (3); v P 1961 (2)*
Parker, C. W. L. 1: v A 1921
Parker, P. W. G. 1: v A 1981
Parkhouse, W. G. A. 7: v WI 1950 (2); v In 1959 (2); *v A 1950 (2); v NZ 1950 (1)*
Parkin, C. H. 10: v A 1921 (4); v SA 1924 (1); *v A 1920 (5)*
Parks, J. H. 1: v NZ 1937
Parks, J. M. 46: v A 1964 (5); v SA 1960 (5) 1965 (3); v WI 1963 (4) 1966 (4); v NZ 1965 (3); v P 1954 (1); *v A 1965 (5); v SA 1964 (5); v WI 1959 (1) 1967 (3); v NZ 1965 (2); v In 1963 (5)*
Pataudi sen., Nawab of, 3: v A 1934 (1); *v A 1932 (2)*
Paynter, E. 20: v A 1938 (4); v WI 1939 (2); v NZ 1931 (1) 1937 (2); v In 1932 (1); *v A 1932 (3); v SA 1938 (5); v NZ 1932 (2)*
Peate, E. 9: v A 1882 (1) 1884 (3) 1886 (1); *v A 1881 (4)*
Peebles, I. A. R. 13: v A 1930 (2); v NZ 1931 (3); *v SA 1927 (4) 1930 (4)*
Peel, R. 20: v A 1888 (3) 1890 (1) 1893 (1) 1896 (1); *v A 1884 (5) 1887 (1) 1891 (3) 1894 (5)*
Penn, F. 1: v A 1880

Perks, R. T. D. 2: v WI 1939 (1); *v SA 1938 (1)*
Philipson, H. 5: *v A 1891 (1) 1894 (4)*
Pigott, A. C. S. 1: *v NZ 1983*
Pilling, R. 8: v A 1884 (1) 1886 (1) 1888 (1); *v A 1881 (4) 1887 (1)*
Place, W. 3: *v WI 1947 (3)*
Pocock, P. I. 25: v A 1968 (1); v WI 1976 (2) 1984 (2); v SL 1984 (1); *v WI 1967 (2) 1973 (4); v In 1972 (4) 1984 (5); v P 1968 (1) 1972 (3)*
Pollard, R. 4: v A 1948 (2); v In 1946 (1); *v NZ 1946 (1)*
Poole, C. J. 3: *v In 1951 (3)*
Pope, G. H. 1: v SA 1947
Pougher, A. D. 1: *v SA 1891*
Price, J. S. E. 15: v A 1964 (2) 1972 (1); v In 1971 (3); v P 1971 (1); *v SA 1964 (4); v In 1963 (4)*
Price, W. F. F. 1: v A 1938
Prideaux, R. M. 3: v A 1968 (1); *v P 1968 (2)*
Pringle, D. R. 30: v A 1989 (2); v WI 1984 (3) 1988 (4) 1991 (4); v NZ 1986 (1); v In 1982 (3) 1986 (3); v P 1982 (1) 1992 (3); v SL 1988 (1); *v A 1982 (3); v NZ 1991 (2)*
Pullar, G. 28: v A 1961 (5); v SA 1960 (3); v In 1959 (3); v P 1962 (2); *v A 1962 (4); v WI 1959 (5); v In 1961 (3); v P 1961 (3)*

Quaife, W. G. 7: v A 1899 (2); *v A 1901 (5)*

Radford, N. V. 3: v NZ 1986 (1); v In 1986 (1); *v NZ 1987 (1)*
Radley, C. T. 8: v NZ 1978 (3); v P 1978 (3); *v NZ 1977 (2)*
Ramprakash, M. R. 14: v A 1993 (1); v WI 1991 (5); v P 1992 (3); v SL 1991 (1); *v WI 1993 (4)*
Randall, D. W. 47: v A 1977 (5); v WI 1984 (1); v NZ 1983 (3); v In 1979 (3) 1982 (3); v P 1982 (3); *v A 1976 (1) 1978 (6) 1979 (2) 1982 (4); v NZ 1977 (3) 1983 (3); v In 1976 (4); v P 1977 (3) 1983 (3)*
Ranjitsinhji, K. S. 15: v A 1896 (2) 1899 (5) 1902 (3); *v A 1897 (5)*
Read, H. D. 1: v SA 1935
Read, J. M. 17: v A 1882 (1) 1890 (2) 1893 (1); *v A 1884 (5) 1886 (2) 1887 (1) 1891 (3); v SA 1888 (2)*
Read, W. W. 18: v A 1884 (2) 1886 (3) 1888 (3) 1890 (2) 1893 (2); *v A 1882 (4) 1887 (1); v SA 1891 (1)*
Reeve, D. A. 3: *v NZ 1991 (3)*
Relf, A. E. 13: v A 1909 (1); *v A 1903 (2); v SA 1905 (5) 1913 (5)*
Rhodes, H. J. 2: v In 1959 (2)
Rhodes, S. J. 6: v SA 1994 (3); v NZ 1994 (3)
Rhodes, W. 58: v A 1899 (3) 1902 (5) 1905 (4) 1909 (4) 1912 (3) 1921 (1) 1926 (1); v SA 1912 (3); *v A 1903 (5) 1907 (5) 1911 (5) 1920 (5); v SA 1909 (5) 1913 (5); v WI 1929 (4)*
Richards, C. J. 8: v WI 1988 (2); v P 1987 (1); *v A 1986 (5)*
Richardson, D. W. 1: v WI 1957
Richardson, P. E. 34: v A 1956 (5); v WI 1957 (5) 1963 (1); v NZ 1958 (4); *v A 1958 (4); v SA 1956 (5); v NZ 1958 (2); v In 1961 (5); v P 1961 (3)*
Richardson, T. 14: v A 1893 (1) 1896 (3); *v A 1894 (5) 1897 (5)*
Richmond, T. L. 1: v A 1921
Ridgway, F. 5: *v In 1951 (5)*
Robertson, J. D. 11: v SA 1947 (1); v NZ 1949 (1); *v WI 1947 (4); v In 1951 (5)*
Robins, R. W. V. 19: v A 1930 (2); v SA 1929 (1) 1935 (3); v WI 1933 (2); v NZ 1931 (1) 1937 (3); v In 1932 (1) 1936 (2); *v A 1936 (4)*
Robinson, R. T. 29: v A 1985 (6) 1989 (1); v In 1986 (1); v P 1987 (5); v SL 1988 (1); *v A 1987 (1); v WI 1985 (4); v NZ 1987 (3); v In 1984 (5); v P 1987 (2)*
Roope, G. R. J. 21: v A 1975 (1) 1977 (2); v WI 1973 (1); v NZ 1973 (3) 1978 (1); v P 1978 (3); *v NZ 1977 (3); v In 1972 (2); v P 1972 (2) 1977 (3)*
Root, C. F. 3: v A 1926 (3)
Rose, B. C. 9: v WI 1980 (3); *v WI 1980 (1); v NZ 1977 (2); v P 1977 (3)*
Royle, V. P. F. A. 1: *v A 1878*
Rumsey, F. E. 5: v A 1964 (1); v SA 1965 (1); v NZ 1965 (3)
Russell, A. C. 10: v A 1921 (2); *v A 1920 (4); v SA 1922 (4)*
Russell, R. C. 36: v A 1989 (6); v WI 1991 (4); v NZ 1990 (3); v In 1990 (3); v P 1992 (3); v SL 1988 (1) 1991 (1); *v A 1990 (3); v WI 1989 (4) 1993 (5); v NZ 1991 (3)*
Russell, W. E. 10: v SA 1965 (1); v WI 1966 (2); v P 1967 (1); *v A 1965 (1); v NZ 1965 (3); v In 1961 (1); v P 1961 (1)*

Salisbury, I. D. K. 7: v SA 1994 (1); v P 1992 (2); *v WI 1993 (2); v In 1992 (2)*
Sandham, A. 14: v A 1921 (1); v SA 1924 (2); *v A 1924 (2); v SA 1922 (5); v WI 1929 (4)*
Schultz, S. S. 1: *v A 1878*
Scotton, W. H. 15: v A 1884 (1) 1886 (3); *v A 1881 (4) 1884 (5) 1886 (2)*
Selby, J. 6: *v A 1876 (2) 1881 (4)*
Selvey, M. W. W. 3: v WI 1976 (2); *v In 1976 (1)*
Shackleton, D. 7: v SA 1951 (1); v WI 1950 (1) 1963 (4); *v In 1951 (1)*
Sharp, J. 3: v A 1909 (3)
Sharpe, J. W. 3: v A 1890 (1); *v A 1891 (2)*
Sharpe, P. J. 12: v A 1964 (2); v WI 1963 (3) 1969 (3); v NZ 1969 (3); *v In 1963 (1)*
Shaw, A. 7: v A 1880 (1); *v A 1876 (2) 1881 (4)*
Sheppard, Rev. D. S. 22: v A 1956 (2); v WI 1950 (1) 1957 (2); v In 1952 (2); v P 1954 (2) 1962 (2); *v A 1950 (2) 1962 (5); v NZ 1950 (1) 1963 (3)*
Sherwin, M. 3: v A 1888 (1); *v A 1886 (2)*
Shrewsbury, A. 23: v A 1884 (3) 1886 (3) 1890 (2) 1893 (3); *v A 1881 (4) 1884 (5) 1886 (2) 1887 (1)*
Shuter, J. 1: v A 1888
Shuttleworth, K. 5: v P 1971 (1); *v A 1970 (2); v NZ 1970 (2)*
Sidebottom, A. 1: v A 1985
Simpson, R. T. 27: v A 1953 (3); v SA 1951 (3); v WI 1950 (3); v NZ 1949 (2); v In 1952 (2); v P 1954 (3); *v A 1950 (5) 1954 (1); v SA 1948 (1); v NZ 1950 (2) 1954 (2)*
Simpson-Hayward, G. H. 5: *v SA 1909 (5)*
Sims, J. M. 4: v SA 1935 (1); v In 1936 (1); *v A 1936 (2)*
Sinfield, R. A. 1: v A 1938
Slack, W. N. 3: v In 1986 (1); *v WI 1985 (2)*
Smailes, T. F. 1: v In 1946
Small, G. C. 17: v A 1989 (1); v WI 1988 (1); v NZ 1986 (2) 1990 (3); *v A 1986 (2) 1990 (4); v WI 1989 (4)*
Smith, A. C. 6: *v A 1962 (4); v NZ 1962 (2)*
Smith, C. A. 1: *v SA 1888*
Smith, C. I. J. 5: v NZ 1937 (1); *v WI 1934 (4)*
Smith, C. L. 8: v NZ 1983 (2); v In 1986 (1); *v NZ 1983 (2); v P 1983 (3)*
Smith, D. 2: v SA 1935 (2)
Smith, D. M. 2: *v WI 1985 (2)*
Smith, D. R. 5: *v In 1961 (5)*
Smith, D. V. 3: v WI 1957 (3)
Smith, E. J. 11: v A 1912 (3); v SA 1912 (3); *v A 1911 (4); v SA 1913 (1)*
Smith, H. 1: v WI 1928
Smith, M. J. K. 50: v A 1961 (1) 1972 (3); v SA 1960 (4) 1965 (3); v WI 1966 (1); v NZ 1958 (3) 1965 (3); v In 1959 (2); *v A 1965 (5); v SA 1964 (5); v WI 1959 (5); v NZ 1965 (3); v In 1961 (4) 1963 (5); v P 1961 (3)*
Smith, R. A. 53: v A 1989 (5) 1993 (5); v WI 1988 (2) 1991 (4); v NZ 1990 (3) 1994 (3); v In 1990 (3); v P 1992 (5); v SL 1988 (1) 1991 (1); *v A 1990 (5); v WI 1989 (4) 1993 (5); v NZ 1991 (3); v In 1992 (3); v SL 1992 (1)*
Smith, T. P. B. 4: v In 1946 (1); *v A 1946 (2); v NZ 1946 (1)*
Smithson, G. A. 2: *v WI 1947 (2)*
Snow, J. A. 49: v A 1968 (5) 1972 (5) 1975 (4); v SA 1965 (1); v WI 1966 (3) 1969 (3) 1973 (1) 1976 (3); v NZ 1965 (1) 1969 (2) 1973 (3); v In 1967 (3) 1971 (2); v P 1967 (1); *v A 1970 (6); v WI 1967 (4); v P 1968 (2)*
Southerton, J. 2: *v A 1876 (2)*
Spooner, R. H. 10: v A 1905 (2) 1909 (2) 1912 (3); v SA 1912 (3)
Spooner, R. T. 7: v SA 1955 (1); *v In 1951 (5); v WI 1953 (1)*
Stanyforth, R. T. 4: *v SA 1927 (4)*
Staples, S. J. 3: *v SA 1927 (3)*
Statham, J. B. 70: v A 1953 (1) 1956 (3) 1961 (4); v SA 1951 (2) 1955 (4) 1960 (5) 1965 (1); v WI 1957 (3) 1963 (2); v NZ 1958 (2); v In 1959 (3); v P 1954 (4) 1962 (3); *v A 1954 (5) 1958 (4) 1962 (5); v SA 1956 (4); v WI 1953 (4) 1959 (3); v NZ 1950 (1) 1954 (2); v In 1951 (5)*
Steel, A. G. 13: v A 1880 (1) 1882 (1) 1884 (3) 1886 (3) 1888 (1); *v A 1882 (4)*
Steele, D. S. 8: v A 1975 (3); v WI 1976 (5)
Stephenson, J. P. 1: v A 1989
Stevens, G. T. S. 10: v A 1926 (2); *v SA 1922 (1) 1927 (5); v WI 1929 (2)*
Stevenson, G. B. 2: *v WI 1980 (1); v In 1979 (1)*

Stewart, A. J. 43: v A 1993 (6); v SA 1994 (3); v WI 1991 (1); v NZ 1990 (3) 1994 (3); v P 1992 (5); v SL 1991 (1); *v A 1990 (5); v WI 1989 (4) 1993 (5); v NZ 1991 (3); v In 1992 (3); v SL 1992 (1)*
Stewart, M. J. 8: v WI 1963 (4); v P 1962 (2); *v In 1963 (2)*
Stoddart, A. E. 16: v A 1893 (3) 1896 (2); *v A 1887 (1) 1891 (3) 1894 (5) 1897 (2)*
Storer, W. 6: v A 1899 (1); *v A 1897 (5)*
Street, G. B. 1: *v SA 1922*
Strudwick, H. 28: v A 1921 (2) 1926 (5); v SA 1924 (1); *v A 1911 (1) 1920 (4) 1924 (5); v SA 1909 (5) 1913 (5)*
Studd, C. T. 5: v A 1882 (1); *v A 1882 (4)*
Studd, G. B. 4: *v A 1882 (4)*
Subba Row, R. 13: v A 1961 (5); v SA 1960 (4); v NZ 1958 (1); v In 1959 (1); *v WI 1959 (2)*
Such, P. M. 8: v A 1993 (5); v NZ 1994 (3)
Sugg, F. H. 2: v A 1888 (2)
Sutcliffe, H. 54: v A 1926 (5) 1930 (4) 1934 (4); v SA 1924 (5) 1929 (5) 1935 (2); v WI 1928 (3) 1933 (2); v NZ 1931 (2); v In 1932 (1); *v A 1924 (5) 1928 (4) 1932 (5); v SA 1927 (5); v NZ 1932 (2)*
Swetman, R. 11: v In 1959 (3); *v A 1958 (2); v WI 1959 (4); v NZ 1958 (2)*

Tate, F. W. 1: v A 1902
Tate, M. W. 39: v A 1926 (5) 1930 (5); v SA 1924 (5) 1929 (3) 1935 (1); v WI 1928 (3); v NZ 1931 (1); *v A 1924 (5) 1928 (5); v SA 1930 (5); v NZ 1932 (1)*
Tattersall, R. 16: v A 1953 (1); v SA 1951 (5); v P 1954 (1); *v A 1950 (2); v NZ 1950 (2); v In 1951 (5)*
Tavaré, C. J. 31: v A 1981 (2) 1989 (1); v WI 1980 (2) 1984 (1); v NZ 1983 (4); v In 1982 (3); v P 1982 (3); v SL 1984 (1); *v A 1982 (5); v NZ 1983 (2); v In 1981 (6); v SL 1981 (1)*
Taylor, J. P. 2: v NZ 1994 (1); *v In 1992 (1)*
Taylor, K. 3: v A 1964 (1); v In 1959 (2)
Taylor, L. B. 2: v A 1985 (2)
Taylor, R. W. 57: v A 1981 (3); v NZ 1978 (3) 1983 (4); v In 1979 (3) 1982 (3); v P 1978 (3) 1982 (3); *v A 1978 (6) 1979 (3) 1982 (5); v NZ 1970 (1) 1977 (3) 1983 (3); v In 1979 (1) 1981 (6); v P 1977 (3) 1983 (3); v SL 1981 (1)*
Tennyson, Hon. L. H. 9: v A 1921 (4); *v SA 1913 (5)*
Terry, V. P. 2: v WI 1984 (2)
Thomas, J. G. 5: v NZ 1986 (1); *v WI 1985 (4)*
Thompson, G. J. 6: v A 1909 (1); *v SA 1909 (5)*
Thomson, N. I. 5: *v SA 1964 (5)*
Thorpe, G. P. 10: v A 1993 (3); v SA 1994 (2); *v WI 1993 (5)*
Titmus, F. J. 53: v A 1964 (5); v SA 1955 (2) 1965 (3); v WI 1963 (4) 1966 (3); v NZ 1965 (3); v P 1962 (2) 1967 (2); *v A 1962 (5) 1965 (5) 1974 (4); v SA 1964 (5); v WI 1967 (2); v NZ 1962 (3); v In 1963 (5)*
Tolchard, R. W. 4: *v In 1976 (4)*
Townsend, C. L. 2: v A 1899 (2)
Townsend, D. C. H. 3: *v WI 1934 (3)*
Townsend, L. F. 4: *v WI 1929 (1); v In 1933 (3)*
Tremlett, M. F. 3: *v WI 1947 (3)*
Trott, A. E. 2: *v SA 1898 (2)*
Trueman, F. S. 67: v A 1953 (1) 1956 (2) 1961 (4) 1964 (4); v SA 1955 (1) 1960 (5); v WI 1957 (5) 1963 (5); v NZ 1958 (5) 1965 (2); v In 1952 (4) 1959 (5); v P 1962 (4); *v A 1958 (3) 1962 (5); v WI 1953 (3) 1959 (5); v NZ 1958 (2) 1962 (2)*
Tufnell, N. C. 1: *v SA 1909*
Tufnell, P. C. R. 18: v A 1993 (2); v SA 1994 (1); v WI 1991 (1); v P 1992 (1); v SL 1991 (1); *v A 1990 (4); v WI 1993 (2); v NZ 1991 (3); v In 1992 (2); v SL 1992 (1)*
Turnbull, M. J. 9: v WI 1933 (2); v In 1936 (1); *v SA 1930 (5); v NZ 1929 (1)*
Tyldesley, E. 14: v A 1921 (3) 1926 (1); v SA 1924 (1); v WI 1928 (3); *v A 1928 (1); v SA 1927 (5)*
Tyldesley, J. T. 31: v A 1899 (2) 1902 (5) 1905 (5) 1909 (4); v SA 1907 (3); *v A 1901 (5) 1903 (5); v SA 1898 (2)*
Tyldesley, R. K. 7: v A 1930 (2); v SA 1924 (4); *v A 1924 (1)*
Tylecote, E. F. S. 6: v A 1886 (2); *v A 1882 (4)*
Tyler, E. J. 1: *v SA 1895*
Tyson, F. H. 17: v A 1956 (1); v SA 1955 (2); v P 1954 (1); *v A 1954 (5) 1958 (2); v SA 1956 (2); v NZ 1954 (2) 1958 (2)*

Ulyett, G. 25: v A 1882 (1) 1884 (3) 1886 (3) 1888 (2) 1890 (1); *v A 1876 (2) 1878 (1) 1881 (4) 1884 (5) 1887 (1); v SA 1888 (2)*
Underwood, D. L. 86: v A 1968 (4) 1972 (2) 1975 (4) 1977 (5); v WI 1966 (2) 1969 (2) 1973 (3) 1976 (5) 1980 (1); v NZ 1969 (3) 1973 (1); v In 1971 (1) 1974 (3); v P 1967 (2) 1971 (1) 1974 (3); *v A 1970 (5) 1974 (5) 1976 (1) 1979 (3); v WI 1973 (4); v NZ 1970 (2) 1974 (2); v In 1972 (4) 1976 (5) 1979 (1) 1981 (6); v P 1968 (3) 1972 (2); v SL 1981 (1)*

Valentine, B. H. 7: *v SA 1938 (5); v In 1933 (2)*
Verity, H. 40: v A 1934 (5) 1938 (4); v SA 1935 (4); v WI 1933 (2) 1939 (1); v NZ 1931 (2) 1937 (1); v In 1936 (3); *v A 1932 (4) 1936 (5); v SA 1938 (5); v NZ 1932 (1); v In 1933 (3)*
Vernon, G. F. 1: *v A 1882*
Vine, J. 2: *v A 1911 (2)*
Voce, W. 27: v NZ 1931 (1) 1937 (1); v In 1932 (1) 1936 (1) 1946 (1); *v A 1932 (4) 1936 (5) 1946 (2); v SA 1930 (5); v WI 1929 (4); v NZ 1932 (2)*

Waddington, A. 2: *v A 1920 (2)*
Wainwright, E. 5: v A 1893 (1); *v A 1897 (4)*
Walker, P. M. 3: v SA 1960 (3)
Walters, C. F. 11: v A 1934 (5); v WI 1933 (3); *v In 1933 (3)*
Ward, A. 5: v WI 1976 (1); v NZ 1969 (3); v P 1971 (1)
Ward, A. 7: v A 1893 (2); *v A 1894 (5)*
Wardle, J. H. 28: v A 1953 (3) 1956 (1); v SA 1951 (2) 1955 (3); v WI 1950 (1) 1957 (1); v P 1954 (4); *v A 1954 (4); v SA 1956 (4); v WI 1947 (1) 1953 (2); v NZ 1954 (2)*
Warner, P. F. 15: v A 1909 (1) 1912 (1); v SA 1912 (1); *v A 1903 (5); v SA 1898 (2) 1905 (5)*
Warr, J. J. 2: *v A 1950 (2)*
Warren, A. R. 1: v A 1905
Washbrook, C. 37: v A 1948 (4) 1956 (3); v SA 1947 (5); v WI 1950 (2); v NZ 1937 (1) 1949 (2); v In 1946 (3); *v A 1946 (5) 1950 (5); v SA 1948 (5); v NZ 1946 (1) 1950 (1)*
Watkin, S. L. 3: v A 1993 (1); v WI 1991 (2)
Watkins, A. J. 15: v A 1948 (1); v NZ 1949 (1); v In 1952 (3); *v SA 1948 (5); v In 1951 (5)*
Watson, W. 23: v A 1953 (3) 1956 (2); v SA 1951 (5) 1955 (1); v NZ 1958 (2); v In 1952 (1); *v A 1958 (2); v WI 1953 (5); v NZ 1958 (2)*
Webbe, A. J. 1: *v A 1878*
Wellard, A. W. 2: v A 1938 (1); v NZ 1937 (1)
Wharton, A. 1: v NZ 1949
Whitaker, J. J. 1: *v A 1986*
White, C. 4: v SA 1994 (1); v NZ 1994 (3)
White, D. W. 2: v *P 1961 (2)*
White, J. C. 15: v A 1921 (1) 1930 (1); v SA 1929 (3); v WI 1928 (1); *v A 1928 (5); v SA 1930 (4)*
Whysall, W. W. 4: v A 1930 (1); *v A 1924 (3)*
Wilkinson, L. L. 3: *v SA 1938 (3)*
Willey, P. 26: v A 1980 (1) 1981 (4) 1985 (1); v WI 1976 (2) 1980 (5); v NZ 1986 (1); v In 1979 (1); *v A 1979 (3); v WI 1980 (4) 1985 (4)*
Williams, N. F. 1: v In 1990
Willis, R. G. D. 90: v A 1977 (5) 1981 (6); v WI 1973 (1) 1976 (2) 1980 (4) 1984 (3); v NZ 1978 (3) 1983 (4); v In 1974 (1) 1979 (3) 1982 (3); v P 1974 (1) 1978 (3) 1982 (2); *v A 1970 (4) 1974 (5) 1976 (1) 1978 (6) 1979 (3) 1982 (5); v WI 1973 (3); v NZ 1970 (1) 1977 (3) 1983 (3); v In 1976 (5) 1981 (5); v P 1977 (3) 1983 (1); v SL 1981 (1)*
Wilson, C. E. M. 2: *v SA 1898 (2)*
Wilson, D. 6: *v NZ 1970 (1); v In 1963 (5)*
Wilson, E. R. 1: *v A 1920*
Wood, A. 4: v A 1938 (1); v WI 1939 (3)
Wood, B. 12: v A 1972 (1) 1975 (3); v WI 1976 (1); v P 1978 (1); *v NZ 1974 (2); v In 1972 (3); v P 1972 (1)*
Wood, G. E. C. 3: v SA 1924 (3)
Wood, H. 4: v A 1888 (1); *v SA 1888 (2) 1891 (1)*
Wood, R. 1: *v A 1886*
Woods S. M. J. 3: *v SA 1895 (3)*
Woolley, F. E. 64: v A 1909 (1) 1912 (3) 1921 (5) 1926 (5) 1930 (2) 1934 (1); v SA 1912 (3) 1924 (5) 1929 (3); v NZ 1931 (1); v In 1932 (1); *v A 1911 (5) 1920 (5) 1924 (5); v SA 1909 (5) 1913 (5) 1922 (5); v NZ 1929 (4)*

Woolmer, R. A. 19: v A 1975 (2) 1977 (5) 1981 (2); v WI 1976 (5) 1980 (2); *v A 1976 (1); v In 1976 (2)*
Worthington, T. S. 9: v In 1936 (2); *v A 1936 (3); v NZ 1929 (4)*
Wright, C. W. 3: *v SA 1895 (3)*
Wright, D. V. P. 34: v A 1938 (3) 1948 (1); v SA 1947 (4); v WI 1939 (3) 1950 (1); v NZ 1949 (1); v In 1946 (2); *v A 1946 (5) 1950 (5); v SA 1938 (3) 1948 (3); v NZ 1946 (1) 1950 (2)*
Wyatt, R. E. S. 40: v A 1930 (1) 1934 (4); v SA 1929 (2) 1935 (5); v WI 1933 (2); v In 1936 (1); *v A 1932 (5) 1936 (2); v SA 1927 (5) 1930 (5); v WI 1929 (2) 1934 (4); v NZ 1932 (2)*
Wynyard, E. G. 3: v A 1896 (1); *v SA 1905 (2)*

Yardley, N. W. D. 20: v A 1948 (5); v SA 1947 (5); v WI 1950 (3); *v A 1946 (5); v SA 1938 (1); v NZ 1946 (1)*
Young, H. I. 2: v A 1899 (2)
Young, J. A. 8: v A 1948 (3); v SA 1947 (1); v NZ 1949 (2); *v SA 1948 (2)*
Young, R. A. 2: *v A 1907 (2)*

AUSTRALIA

Number of Test cricketers: 359

a'Beckett, E. L. 4: v E 1928 (2); v SA 1931 (1); *v E 1930 (1)*
Alderman, T. M. 41: v E 1982 (1) 1990 (4); v WI 1981 (2) 1984 (3) 1988 (2); v NZ 1989 (1); v P 1981 (3) 1989 (2); v SL 1989 (2); *v E 1981 (6) 1989 (6); v WI 1983 (3) 1990 (1); v NZ 1981 (3) 1989 (1); v P 1982 (1)*
Alexander, G. 2: v E 1884 (1); *v E 1880 (1)*
Alexander, H. H. 1: v E 1932
Allan, F. E. 1: v E 1878
Allan, P. J. 1: v E 1965
Allen, R. C. 1: v E 1886
Andrews, T. J. E. 16: v E 1924 (3); *v E 1921 (5) 1926 (5); v SA 1921 (3)*
Angel, J. 1: v WI 1992
Archer, K. A. 5: v E 1950 (3); v WI 1951 (2)
Archer, R. G. 19: v E 1954 (4); v SA 1952 (1); *v E 1953 (3) 1956 (5); v WI 1954 (5); v P 1956 (1)*
Armstrong, W. W. 50: v E 1901 (4) 1903 (3) 1907 (5) 1911 (5) 1920 (5); v SA 1910 (5); *v E 1902 (5) 1905 (5) 1909 (5) 1921 (5); v SA 1902 (3)*

Badcock, C. L. 7: v E 1936 (3); *v E 1938 (4)*
Bannerman, A. C. 28: v E 1878 (1) 1881 (3) 1882 (4) 1884 (4) 1886 (1) 1887 (1) 1891 (3); *v E 1880 (1) 1882 (1) 1884 (3) 1888 (3) 1893 (3)*
Bannerman, C. 3: v E 1876 (2) 1878 (1)
Bardsley, W. 41: v E 1911 (4) 1920 (5) 1924 (3); v SA 1910 (5); *v E 1909 (5) 1912 (3) 1921 (5) 1926 (5); v SA 1912 (3) 1921 (3)*
Barnes, S. G. 13: v E 1946 (4); v In 1947 (3); *v E 1938 (1) 1948 (4); v NZ 1945 (1)*
Barnett, B. A. 4: *v E 1938 (4)*
Barrett, J. E. 2: *v E 1890 (2)*
Beard, G. R. 3: *v P 1979 (3)*
Benaud, J. 3: v P 1972 (2); *v WI 1972 (1)*
Benaud, R. 63: v E 1954 (5) 1958 (5) 1962 (5); v SA 1952 (4) 1963 (4); v WI 1951 (1) 1960 (5); *v E 1953 (3) 1956 (5) 1961 (4); v SA 1957 (5); v WI 1954 (5); v In 1956 (3) 1959 (5); v P 1956 (1) 1959 (3)*
Bennett, M. J. 3: v WI 1984 (2); *v E 1985 (1)*
Blackham, J. McC. 35: v E 1876 (2) 1878 (1) 1881 (4) 1882 (4) 1884 (2) 1886 (1) 1887 (1) 1891 (3) 1894 (1); *v E 1880 (1) 1882 (1) 1884 (3) 1886 (3) 1888 (3) 1890 (2) 1893 (3)*
Blackie, D. D. 3: v E 1928 (3)
Bonnor, G. J. 17: v E 1882 (4) 1884 (3); *v E 1880 (1) 1882 (1) 1884 (3) 1886 (2) 1888 (3)*
Boon, D. C. 89: v E 1986 (4) 1987 (1) 1990 (5); v SA 1993 (3); v WI 1984 (3) 1988 (5) 1992 (5); v NZ 1985 (3) 1987 (3) 1989 (1) 1993 (3); v In 1985 (3) 1991 (5); v P 1989 (2); v SL 1987 (1) 1989 (2); *v E 1985 (4) 1989 (6) 1993 (6); v SA 1993 (3); v WI 1990 (5); v NZ 1985 (3) 1989 (1) 1992 (3); v In 1986 (3); v P 1988 (3); v SL 1992 (3)*

Booth, B. C. 29: v E 1962 (5) 1965 (3); v SA 1963 (4); v P 1964 (1); *v E 1961 (2) 1964 (5); v WI 1964 (5); v In 1964 (3); v P 1964 (1)*

Border, A. R. 156: v E 1978 (3) 1979 (3) 1982 (5) 1986 (5) 1987 (1) 1990 (5); v SA 1993 (3); v WI 1979 (3) 1981 (3) 1984 (5) 1988 (5) 1992 (5); v NZ 1980 (3) 1985 (3) 1987 (3) 1989 (1) 1993 (3); v In 1980 (3) 1985 (3) 1991 (5); v P 1978 (2) 1981 (3) 1983 (5) 1989 (3); v SL 1987 (1) 1989 (2); *v E 1980 (1) 1981 (6) 1985 (6) 1989 (6) 1993 (6); v SA 1993 (3); v WI 1983 (5) 1990 (5); v NZ 1981 (3) 1985 (3) 1989 (1) 1992 (3); v In 1979 (6) 1986 (3); v P 1979 (3) 1982 (3) 1988 (3); v SL 1982 (1) 1992 (3)*

Boyle, H. F. 12: v E 1878 (1) 1881 (4) 1882 (1) 1884 (1); *v E 1880 (1) 1882 (1) 1884 (3)*

Bradman, D. G. 52: v E 1928 (4) 1932 (4) 1936 (5) 1946 (5); v SA 1931 (5); v WI 1930 (5); v In 1947 (5); *v E 1930 (5) 1934 (5) 1938 (4) 1948 (5)*

Bright, R. J. 25: v E 1979 (1); v WI 1979 (1); v NZ 1985 (1); v In 1985 (3); *v E 1977 (3) 1980 (1) 1981 (5); v NZ 1985 (2); v In 1986 (3); v P 1979 (3) 1982 (2)*

Bromley, E. H. 2: v E 1932 (1); *v E 1934 (1)*

Brown, W. A. 22: v E 1936 (2); v In 1947 (3); *v E 1934 (5) 1938 (4) 1948 (2); v SA 1935 (5); v NZ 1945 (1)*

Bruce, W. 14: v E 1884 (2) 1891 (3) 1894 (4); *v E 1886 (2) 1893 (3)*

Burge, P. J. P. 42: v E 1954 (1) 1958 (1) 1962 (3) 1965 (4); v SA 1963 (5); v WI 1960 (2); *v E 1956 (3) 1961 (5) 1964 (5); v SA 1957 (1); v WI 1954 (1); v In 1956 (3) 1959 (2) 1964 (3); v P 1959 (2) 1964 (1)*

Burke, J. W. 24: v E 1950 (2) 1954 (2) 1958 (5); v WI 1951 (1); *v E 1956 (5); v SA 1957 (5); v In 1956 (3); v P 1956 (1)*

Burn, K. E. 2: *v E 1890 (2)*

Burton, F. J. 2: v E 1886 (1) 1887 (1)

Callaway, S. T. 3: v E 1891 (2) 1894 (1)

Callen, I. W. 1: v In 1977

Campbell, G. D. 4: v P 1989 (1); v SL 1989 (1); *v E 1989 (1); v NZ 1989 (1)*

Carkeek, W. 6: *v E 1912 (3); v SA 1912 (3)*

Carlson, P. H. 2: v E 1978 (2)

Carter, H. 28: v E 1907 (5) 1911 (5) 1920 (2); v SA 1910 (5); *v E 1909 (5) 1921 (4); v SA 1921 (2)*

Chappell, G. S. 87: v E 1970 (5) 1974 (6) 1976 (1) 1979 (3) 1982 (5); v WI 1975 (6) 1979 (3) 1981 (3); v NZ 1973 (3) 1980 (3); v In 1980 (3); v P 1972 (3) 1976 (3) 1981 (3) 1983 (5); *v E 1972 (5) 1975 (4) 1977 (5) 1980 (1); v WI 1972 (5); v NZ 1973 (3) 1976 (2) 1981 (3); v P 1979 (3); v SL 1982 (1)*

Chappell, I. M. 75: v E 1965 (2) 1970 (6) 1974 (6) 1979 (2); v WI 1968 (5) 1975 (6) 1979 (1); v NZ 1973 (3); v In 1967 (4); v P 1964 (1) 1972 (3); *v E 1968 (5) 1972 (5) 1975 (4); v SA 1966 (5) 1969 (4); v WI 1972 (5); v NZ 1973 (3); v In 1969 (5)*

Chappell, T. M. 3: *v E 1981 (3)*

Charlton, P. C. 2: *v E 1890 (2)*

Chipperfield, A. G. 14: v E 1936 (3); *v E 1934 (5) 1938 (1); v SA 1935 (5)*

Clark, W. M. 10: v In 1977 (5); v P 1978 (1); *v WI 1977 (4)*

Colley, D. J. 3: *v E 1972 (3)*

Collins, H. L. 19: v E 1920 (5) 1924 (5); *v E 1921 (3) 1926 (3); v SA 1921 (3)*

Coningham, A. 1: v E 1894

Connolly, A. N. 29: v E 1965 (1) 1970 (1); v SA 1963 (3); v WI 1968 (5); v In 1967 (3); *v E 1968 (5); v SA 1969 (4); v In 1964 (2) 1969 (5)*

Cooper, B. B. 1: v E 1876

Cooper, W. H. 2: v E 1881 (1) 1884 (1)

Corling, G. E. 5: *v E 1964 (5)*

Cosier, G. J. 18: v E 1976 (1) 1978 (2); v WI 1975 (3); v In 1977 (4); v P 1976 (3); *v WI 1977 (3); v NZ 1976 (2)*

Cottam, W. J. 1: v E 1886

Cotter, A. 21: v E 1903 (2) 1907 (2) 1911 (4); v SA 1910 (5); *v E 1905 (3) 1909 (5)*

Coulthard, G. 1: v E 1881

Cowper, R. M. 27: v E 1965 (4); v In 1967 (4); v P 1964 (1); *v E 1964 (1) 1968 (4); v SA 1966 (5); v WI 1964 (5); v In 1964 (2); v P 1964 (1)*

Craig, I. D. 11: v SA 1952 (1); *v E 1956 (2); v SA 1957 (5); v In 1956 (2); v P 1956 (1)*

Crawford, W. P. A. 4: *v E 1956 (1); v In 1956 (3)*

Darling, J. 34: v E 1894 (5) 1897 (5) 1901 (3); *v E 1896 (3) 1899 (5) 1902 (5) 1905 (5); v SA 1902 (3)*

Darling, L. S. 12: v E 1932 (2) 1936 (1); *v E 1934 (4); v SA 1935 (5)*

Darling, W. M. 14: v E 1978 (4); v In 1977 (1); v P 1978 (1); *v WI 1977 (3); v In 1979 (5)*
Davidson, A. K. 44: v E 1954 (3) 1958 (5) 1962 (5); v WI 1960 (4); *v E 1953 (5) 1956 (2) 1961 (5); v SA 1957 (5); v In 1956 (1) 1959 (5); v P 1956 (1) 1959 (3)*
Davis, I. C. 15: v E 1976 (1); v NZ 1973 (3); v P 1976 (3); *v E 1977 (3); v NZ 1973 (3) 1976 (2)*
Davis, S. P. 1: *v NZ 1985*
De Courcy, J. H. 3: *v E 1953 (3)*
Dell, A. R. 2: v E 1970 (1); v NZ 1973 (1)
Dodemaide, A. I. C. 10: v E 1987 (1); v WI 1988 (2); v NZ 1987 (1); v SL 1987 (1); *v P 1988 (3); v SL 1992 (2)*
Donnan, H. 5: v E 1891 (2); *v E 1896 (3)*
Dooland, B. 3: v E 1946 (2); v In 1947 (1)
Duff, R. A. 22: v E 1901 (4) 1903 (5); *v E 1902 (5) 1905 (5); v SA 1902 (3)*
Duncan, J. R. F. 1: v E 1970
Dyer, G. C. 6: v E 1986 (1) 1987 (1); v NZ 1987 (3); v SL 1987 (1)
Dymock, G. 21: v E 1974 (1) 1978 (3) 1979 (3); v WI 1979 (2); v NZ 1973 (1); v P 1978 (1); *v NZ 1973 (2); v In 1979 (5); v P 1979 (3)*
Dyson, J. 30: v E 1982 (5); v WI 1981 (2) 1984 (3); v NZ 1980 (3); v In 1977 (3) 1980 (3); *v E 1981 (5); v NZ 1981 (3); v P 1982 (3)*

Eady, C. J. 2: v E 1901 (1); *v E 1896 (1)*
Eastwood, K. H. 1: v E 1970
Ebeling, H. I. 1: *v E 1934*
Edwards, J. D. 3: *v E 1888 (3)*
Edwards, R. 20: v E 1974 (5); v P 1972 (2); *v E 1972 (4) 1975 (4); v WI 1972 (5)*
Edwards, W. J. 3: v E 1974 (3)
Emery, S. H. 4: *v E 1912 (2); v SA 1912 (2)*
Evans, E. 6: v E 1881 (2) 1882 (1) 1884 (1); *v E 1886 (2)*

Fairfax, A. G. 10: v E 1928 (1); v WI 1930 (5); *v E 1930 (4)*
Favell, L. E. 19: v E 1954 (4) 1958 (2); v WI 1960 (4); *v WI 1954 (2); v In 1959 (4); v P 1959 (3)*
Ferris, J. J. 8: v E 1886 (2) 1887 (1); *v E 1888 (3) 1890 (2)*
Fingleton, J. H. 18: v E 1932 (3) 1936 (5); v SA 1931 (1); *v E 1938 (4); v SA 1935 (5)*
Fleetwood-Smith, L. O'B. 10: v E 1936 (3); *v E 1938 (4); v SA 1935 (3)*
Francis, B. C. 3: *v E 1972 (3)*
Freeman, E. W. 11: v WI 1968 (4); v In 1967 (2); *v E 1968 (2); v SA 1969 (2); v In 1969 (1)*
Freer, F. W. 1: v E 1946

Gannon, J. B. 3: v In 1977 (3)
Garrett, T. W. 19: v E 1876 (2) 1878 (1) 1881 (3) 1882 (3) 1884 (3) 1886 (2) 1887 (1); *v E 1882 (1) 1886 (3)*
Gaunt, R. A. 3: v SA 1963 (1); *v E 1961 (1); v SA 1957 (1)*
Gehrs, D. R. A. 6: v E 1903 (1); v SA 1910 (4); *v E 1905 (1)*
Giffen, G. 31: v E 1881 (3) 1882 (4) 1884 (3) 1891 (3) 1894 (5); *v E 1882 (1) 1884 (3) 1886 (3) 1893 (3) 1896 (3)*
Giffen, W. F. 3: v E 1886 (1) 1891 (2)
Gilbert, D. R. 9: v NZ 1985 (3); v In 1985 (2); *v E 1985 (1); v NZ 1985 (1); v In 1986 (2)*
Gilmour, G. J. 15: v E 1976 (1); v WI 1975 (5); v NZ 1973 (2); v P 1976 (3); *v E 1975 (1); v NZ 1973 (1) 1976 (2)*
Gleeson, J. W. 29: v E 1970 (5); v WI 1968 (5); v In 1967 (4); *v E 1968 (5) 1972 (3); v SA 1969 (4); v In 1969 (3)*
Graham, H. 6: v E 1894 (2); *v E 1893 (3) 1896 (1)*
Gregory, D. W. 3: v E 1876 (2) 1878 (1)
Gregory, E. J. 1: v E 1876
Gregory, J. M. 24: v E 1920 (5) 1924 (5) 1928 (1); *v E 1921 (5) 1926 (5); v SA 1921 (3)*
Gregory, R. G. 2: v E 1936 (2)
Gregory, S. E. 58: v E 1891 (1) 1894 (5) 1897 (5) 1901 (5) 1903 (4) 1907 (2) 1911 (1); *v E 1890 (2) 1893 (3) 1896 (3) 1899 (5) 1902 (5) 1905 (3) 1909 (5) 1912 (3); v SA 1902 (3) 1912 (3)*
Grimmett, C. V. 37: v E 1924 (1) 1928 (5) 1932 (3); v SA 1931 (5); v WI 1930 (5); *v E 1926 (3) 1930 (5) 1934 (5); v SA 1935 (5)*
Groube, T. U. 1: *v E 1880*
Grout, A. T. W. 51: v E 1958 (5) 1962 (2) 1965 (5); v SA 1963 (5); v WI 1960 (5); *v E 1961 (5) 1964 (5); v SA 1957 (5); v WI 1964 (5); v In 1959 (4) 1964 (1); v P 1959 (3) 1964 (1)*
Guest, C. E. J. 1: v E 1962

Hamence, R. A. 3: v E 1946 (1); v In 1947 (2)
Hammond, J. R. 5: *v WI 1972 (5)*
Harry, J. 1: v E 1894
Hartigan, R. J. 2: v E 1907 (2)
Hartkopf, A. E. V. 1: v E 1924
Harvey, M. R. 1: v E 1946
Harvey, R. N. 79: v E 1950 (5) 1954 (5) 1958 (5) 1962 (5); v SA 1952 (5); v WI 1951 (5) 1960 (4); v In 1947 (2); *v E 1948 (2) 1953 (5) 1956 (5) 1961 (5); v SA 1949 (5) 1957 (4); v WI 1954 (5); v In 1956 (3) 1959 (5); v P 1956 (1) 1959 (3)*
Hassett, A. L. 43: v E 1946 (5) 1950 (5); v SA 1952 (5); v WI 1951 (4); v In 1947 (4); *v E 1938 (4) 1948 (5) 1953 (5); v SA 1949 (5); v NZ 1945 (1)*
Hawke, N. J. N. 27: v E 1962 (1) 1965 (4); v SA 1963 (4); v In 1967 (1); v P 1964 (1); *v E 1964 (5) 1968 (2); v SA 1966 (2); v WI 1964 (5); v In 1964 (1); v P 1964 (1)*
Hayden, M. L. 1: *v SA 1993*
Hazlitt, G. R. 9: v E 1907 (2) 1911 (1); *v E 1912 (3); v SA 1912 (3)*
Healy, I. A. 62: v E 1990 (5); v SA 1993 (3); v WI 1988 (5) 1992 (5); v NZ 1989 (1) 1993 (3); v In 1991 (5); v P 1989 (3); v SL 1989 (2); *v E 1989 (6) 1993 (6); v SA 1993 (3); v WI 1990 (5); v NZ 1989 (1) 1992 (3); v P 1988 (3); v SL 1992 (3)*
Hendry, H. S. T. L. 11: v E 1924 (1) 1928 (4); *v E 1921 (4); v SA 1921 (2)*
Hibbert, P. A. 1: v In 1977
Higgs, J. D. 22: v E 1978 (5) 1979 (1); v WI 1979 (1); v NZ 1980 (3); v In 1980 (2); *v WI 1977 (4); v In 1979 (6)*
Hilditch, A. M. J. 18: v E 1978 (1); v WI 1984 (2); v NZ 1985 (1); v P 1978 (2); *v E 1985 (6); v In 1979 (6)*
Hill, C. 49: v E 1897 (5) 1901 (5) 1903 (5) 1907 (5) 1911 (5); v SA 1910 (5); *v E 1896 (3) 1899 (3) 1902 (5) 1905 (5); v SA 1902 (3)*
Hill, J. C. 3: *v E 1953 (2); v WI 1954 (1)*
Hoare, D. E. 1: v WI 1960
Hodges, J. R. 2: v E 1876 (2)
Hogan, T. G. 7: v P 1983 (1); *v WI 1983 (5); v SL 1982 (1)*
Hogg, R. M. 38: v E 1978 (6) 1982 (3); v WI 1979 (2) 1984 (4); v NZ 1980 (2); v In 1980 (2); v P 1978 (2) 1983 (4); *v E 1981 (2); v WI 1983 (4); v In 1979 (6); v SL 1982 (1)*
Hohns, T. V. 7: v WI 1988 (2); *v E 1989 (5)*
Hole, G. B. 18: v E 1950 (1) 1954 (3); v SA 1952 (4); v WI 1951 (5); *v E 1953 (5)*
Holland, R. G. 11: v WI 1984 (3); v NZ 1985 (3); v In 1985 (1); *v E 1985 (4)*
Hookes, D. W. 23: v E 1976 (1) 1982 (5); v WI 1979 (1); v NZ 1985 (2); v In 1985 (2); *v E 1977 (5); v WI 1983 (5); v P 1979 (1); v SL 1982 (1)*
Hopkins, A. J. Y. 20: v E 1901 (2) 1903 (5); *v E 1902 (5) 1905 (3) 1909 (2); v SA 1902 (3)*
Horan, T. P. 15: v E 1876 (1) 1878 (1) 1881 (4) 1882 (4) 1884 (4); *v E 1882 (1)*
Hordern, H. V. 7: v E 1911 (5); v SA 1910 (2)
Hornibrook, P. M. 6: v E 1928 (1); *v E 1930 (5)*
Howell, W. P. 18: v E 1897 (3) 1901 (4) 1903 (3); *v E 1899 (5) 1902 (1); v SA 1902 (2)*
Hughes, K. J. 70: v E 1978 (6) 1979 (3) 1982 (5); v WI 1979 (3) 1981 (3) 1984 (4); v NZ 1980 (3); v In 1977 (2) 1980 (3); v P 1978 (2) 1981 (3) 1983 (5); *v E 1977 (1) 1980 (1) 1981 (6); v WI 1983 (5); v NZ 1981 (3); v In 1979 (6); v P 1979 (3) 1982 (3)*
Hughes, M. G. 53: v E 1986 (4) 1990 (4); v WI 1988 (4) 1992 (5); v NZ 1987 (1) 1989 (1); v In 1985 (1) 1991 (5); v P 1989 (3); v SL 1987 (1) 1989 (2); *v E 1989 (6) 1993 (6); v SA 1993 (2); v WI 1990 (5); v NZ 1992 (3)*
Hunt, W. A. 1: v SA 1931
Hurst, A. G. 12: v E 1978 (6); v NZ 1973 (1); v In 1977 (1); v P 1978 (2); *v In 1979 (2)*
Hurwood, A. 2: v WI 1930 (2)

Inverarity, R. J. 6: v WI 1968 (1); *v E 1968 (2) 1972 (3)*
Iredale, F. A. 14: v E 1894 (5) 1897 (4); *v E 1896 (2) 1899 (3)*
Ironmonger, H. 14: v E 1928 (2) 1932 (4); v SA 1931 (4); v WI 1930 (4)
Iverson, J. B. 5: v E 1950 (5)

Jackson, A. A. 8: v E 1928 (2); v WI 1930 (4); *v E 1930 (2)*
Jarman, B. N. 19: v E 1962 (3); v WI 1968 (4); v In 1967 (4); v P 1964 (1); *v E 1968 (4); v In 1959 (1) 1964 (2)*
Jarvis, A. H. 11: v E 1884 (3) 1894 (4); *v E 1886 (2) 1888 (2)*
Jenner, T. J. 9: v E 1970 (2) 1974 (2); v WI 1975 (1); *v WI 1972 (4)*

Jennings, C. B. 6: *v E 1912 (3); v SA 1912 (3)*
Johnson I. W. 45: v E 1946 (4) 1950 (5) 1954 (4); v SA 1952 (1); v WI 1951 (4); v In 1947 (4); *v E 1948 (4) 1956 (5); v SA 1949 (5); v WI 1954 (5); v NZ 1945 (1); v In 1956 (2); v P 1956 (1)*
Johnson, L. J. 1: v In 1947
Johnston W. A. 40: v E 1950 (5) 1954 (4); v SA 1952 (5); v WI 1951 (5); v In 1947 (4); *v E 1948 (5) 1953 (3); v SA 1949 (5); v WI 1954 (4)*
Jones, D. M. 52: v E 1986 (5) 1987 (1) 1990 (5); v WI 1988 (3); v NZ 1987 (3) 1989 (1); v In 1991 (5); v P 1989 (3); v SL 1987 (1) 1989 (2); *v E 1989 (6); v WI 1983 (2) 1990 (5); v NZ 1989 (1); v In 1986 (3); v P 1988 (3); v SL 1992 (3)*
Jones, E. 19: v E 1894 (1) 1897 (5) 1901 (2); *v E 1896 (3) 1899 (5) 1902 (2); v SA 1902 (1)*
Jones, S. P. 12: v E 1881 (2) 1884 (4) 1886 (1) 1887 (1); *v E 1882 (1) 1886 (3)*
Joslin, L. R. 1: v In 1967
Julian, B. P. 2: *v E 1993 (2)*

Kelleway, C. 26: v E 1911 (4) 1920 (5) 1924 (5) 1928 (1); v SA 1910 (5); *v E 1912 (3); v SA 1912 (3)*
Kelly, J. J. 36: v E 1897 (5) 1901 (5) 1903 (5); *v E 1896 (3) 1899 (5) 1902 (5) 1905 (5); v SA 1902 (3)*
Kelly, T. J. D. 2: v E 1876 (1) 1878 (1)
Kendall, T. 2: v E 1876 (2)
Kent, M. F. 3: *v E 1981 (3)*
Kerr, R. B. 2: v NZ 1985 (2)
Kippax, A. F. 22: v E 1924 (1) 1928 (5) 1932 (1); v SA 1931 (4); v WI 1930 (5); *v E 1930 (5) 1934 (1)*
Kline L. F. 13: v E 1958 (2); v WI 1960 (2); *v SA 1957 (5); v In 1959 (3); v P 1959 (1)*

Laird, B. M. 21: v E 1979 (2); v WI 1979 (3) 1981 (3); v P 1981 (3); *v E 1980 (1); v NZ 1981 (3); v P 1979 (3) 1982 (3)*
Langer, J. L. 5: v WI 1992 (2); *v NZ 1992 (3)*
Langley, G. R. A. 26: v E 1954 (2); v SA 1952 (5); v WI 1951 (5); *v E 1953 (4) 1956 (3); v WI 1954 (4); v In 1956 (2); v P 1956 (1)*
Laughlin, T. J. 3: v E 1978 (1); *v WI 1977 (2)*
Laver, F. 15: v E 1901 (1) 1903 (1); *v E 1899 (4) 1905 (5) 1909 (4)*
Lawry, W. M. 67: v E 1962 (5) 1965 (5) 1970 (5); v SA 1963 (5); v WI 1968 (5); v In 1967 (4); v P 1964 (1); *v E 1961 (5) 1964 (5) 1968 (4); v SA 1966 (5) 1969 (4); v WI 1964 (5); v In 1964 (3) 1969 (5); v P 1964 (1)*
Lawson, G. F. 46: v E 1982 (5) 1986 (1); v WI 1981 (1) 1984 (5) 1988 (1); v NZ 1980 (1) 1985 (2) 1989 (1); v P 1983 (5); v SL 1989 (1); *v E 1981 (3) 1985 (6) 1989 (6); v WI 1983 (5); v P 1982 (3)*
Lee, P. K. 2: v E 1932 (1); v SA 1931 (1)
Lillee, D. K. 70: v E 1970 (2) 1974 (6) 1976 (1) 1979 (3) 1982 (1); v WI 1975 (5) 1979 (3) 1981 (3); v NZ 1980 (3); v In 1980 (3); v P 1972 (3) 1976 (3) 1981 (3) 1983 (5); *v E 1972 (5) 1975 (4) 1980 (1) 1981 (6); v WI 1972 (1); v NZ 1976 (2) 1981 (3); v P 1979 (3); v SL 1982 (1)*
Lindwall, R. R. 61: v E 1946 (4) 1950 (5) 1954 (4) 1958 (2); v SA 1952 (4); v WI 1951 (5); v In 1947 (5); *v E 1948 (5) 1953 (5) 1956 (4); v SA 1949 (4); v WI 1954 (5); v NZ 1945 (1); v In 1956 (3) 1959 (2); v P 1956 (1) 1959 (2)*
Love, H. S. B. 1: v E 1932
Loxton, S. J. E. 12: v E 1950 (3); v In 1947 (1); *v E 1948 (3); v SA 1949 (5)*
Lyons, J. J. 14: v E 1886 (1) 1891 (3) 1894 (3) 1897 (1); *v E 1888 (1) 1890 (2) 1893 (3)*

McAlister, P. A. 8: v E 1903 (2) 1907 (4); *v E 1909 (2)*
Macartney, C. G. 35: v E 1907 (5) 1911 (1) 1920 (2); v SA 1910 (4); *v E 1909 (5) 1912 (3) 1921 (5) 1926 (5); v SA 1912 (3) 1921 (2)*
McCabe, S. J. 39: v E 1932 (5) 1936 (5); v SA 1931 (5); v WI 1930 (5); *v E 1930 (5) 1934 (5) 1938 (4); v SA 1935 (5)*
McCool, C. L. 14: v E 1946 (5); v In 1947 (3); *v SA 1949 (5) v NZ 1945 (1)*
McCormick, E. L. 12: v E 1936 (4); *v E 1938 (3); v SA 1935 (5)*
McCosker, R. B. 25: v E 1974 (3) 1976 (1) 1979 (2); v WI 1975 (4) 1979 (1); v P 1976 (3); *v E 1975 (4) 1977 (5); v NZ 1976 (2)*
McDermott, C. J. 58: v E 1986 (1) 1987 (1) 1990 (2); v SA 1993 (3); v WI 1984 (2) 1988 (2) 1992 (5); v NZ 1985 (2) 1987 (3) 1993 (3); v In 1985 (2) 1991 (5); v SL 1987 (1); *v E 1985 (6) 1993 (2); v SA 1993 (3); v WI 1990 (5); v NZ 1985 (2) 1992 (3); v In 1986 (2); v SL 1992 (3)*
McDonald, C. C. 47: v E 1954 (2) 1958 (5); v SA 1952 (5); v WI 1951 (1) 1960 (5); *v E 1956 (5) 1961 (3); v SA 1957 (5); v WI 1954 (5); v In 1956 (2) 1959 (5); v P 1956 (1) 1959 (3)*
McDonald, E. A. 11: v E 1920 (3); *v E 1921 (5); v SA 1921 (3)*

McDonnell, P. S. 19: v E 1881 (4) 1882 (3) 1884 (2) 1886 (2) 1887 (1); *v E 1880 (1) 1884 (3) 1888 (3)*
McGrath, G. D. 5: v SA 1993 (1); v NZ 1993 (2); *v SA 1993 (2)*
McIlwraith, J. 1: *v E 1886*
Mackay K. D. 37: v E 1958 (5) 1962 (3); v WI 1960 (5); *v E 1956 (3) 1961 (5); v SA 1957 (5); v In 1956 (3) 1959 (5); v P 1959 (3)*
McKenzie, G. D. 60: v E 1962 (5) 1965 (4) 1970 (3); v SA 1963 (5); v WI 1968 (5); v In 1967 (2); v P 1964 (1); *v E 1961 (3) 1964 (5) 1968 (5); v SA 1966 (5) 1969 (3); v WI 1964 (5); v In 1964 (3) 1969 (5); v P 1964 (1)*
McKibbin, T. R. 5: v E 1894 (1) 1897 (2); *v E 1896 (2)*
McLaren, J. W. 1: v E 1911
Maclean, J. A. 4: v E 1978 (4)
McLeod, C. E. 17: v E 1894 (1) 1897 (5) 1901 (2) 1903 (3); *v E 1899 (1) 1905 (5)*
McLeod, R. W. 6: v E 1891 (3); *v E 1893 (3)*
McShane, P. G. 3: v E 1884 (1) 1886 (1) 1887 (1)
Maddocks, L. V. 7: v E 1954 (3); *v E 1956 (2); v WI 1954 (1); v In 1956 (1)*
Maguire, J. N. 3: v P 1983 (1); *v WI 1983 (2)*
Mailey, A. A. 21: v E 1920 (5) 1924 (5); *v E 1921 (3) 1926 (5); v SA 1921 (3)*
Mallett, A. A. 38: v E 1970 (2) 1974 (5) 1979 (1); v WI 1968 (1) 1975 (6) 1979 (1); v NZ 1973 (3); v P 1972 (2); *v E 1968 (1) 1972 (2) 1975 (4) 1980 (1); v SA 1969 (1); v NZ 1973 (3); v In 1969 (5)*
Malone, M. F. 1: *v E 1977*
Mann, A. L. 4: v In 1977 (4)
Marr, A. P. 1: v E 1884
Marsh, G. R. 50: v E 1986 (5) 1987 (1) 1990 (5); v WI 1988 (5); v NZ 1987 (3); v In 1985 (3) 1991 (4); v P 1989 (2); v SL 1987 (1); *v E 1989 (6); v WI 1990 (5); v NZ 1985 (3) 1989 (1); v In 1986 (3); v P 1988 (3)*
Marsh, R. W. 96: v E 1970 (6) 1974 (6) 1976 (1) 1979 (3) 1982 (5); v WI 1975 (6) 1979 (3) 1981 (3); v NZ 1973 (3) 1980 (3); v In 1980 (3); v P 1972 (3) 1976 (3) 1981 (3) 1983 (5); *v E 1972 (5) 1975 (4) 1977 (5) 1980 (1) 1981 (6); v WI 1972 (5); v NZ 1973 (3) 1976 (2) 1981 (3); v P 1979 (3) 1982 (3)*
Martin, J. W. 8: v SA 1963 (1); v WI 1960 (3); *v SA 1966 (1); v In 1964 (2); v P 1964 (1)*
Martyn, D. R. 7: v SA 1993 (2); v WI 1992 (4); *v NZ 1992 (1)*
Massie, H. H. 9: v E 1881 (4) 1882 (3) 1884 (1); *v E 1882 (1)*
Massie, R. A. L. 6: v P 1972 (2); *v E 1972 (4)*
Matthews, C. D. 3: v E 1986 (2); v WI 1988 (1)
Matthews, G. R. J. 33: v E 1986 (4) 1990 (5); v WI 1984 (1) 1992 (2); v NZ 1985 (3); v In 1985 (3); v P 1983 (2); *v E 1985 (1); v WI 1983 (1) 1990 (2); v NZ 1985 (3); v In 1986 (3); v SL 1992 (3)*
Matthews, T. J. 8: v E 1911 (2); *v E 1912 (3); v SA 1912 (3)*
May, T. B. A. 19: v SA 1993 (3); v WI 1988 (3) 1992 (1); v NZ 1987 (1) 1993 (2); *v E 1993 (5); v SA 1993 (1); v P 1988 (3)*
Mayne, E. R. 4: *v E 1912 (1); v SA 1912 (1) 1921 (2)*
Mayne, L. C. 6: *v SA 1969 (2); v WI 1964 (3); v In 1969 (1)*
Meckiff, I. 18: v E 1958 (4); v SA 1963 (1); v WI 1960 (2); *v SA 1957 (4); v In 1959 (5); v P 1959 (2)*
Meuleman, K. D. 1: *v NZ 1945*
Midwinter, W. E. 8: v E 1876 (2) 1882 (1) 1886 (2); *v E 1884 (3)*
Miller, K. R. 55: v E 1946 (5) 1950 (5) 1954 (4); v SA 1952 (4); v WI 1951 (5); v In 1947 (5); *v E 1948 (5) 1953 (5) 1956 (5); v SA 1949 (5); v WI 1954 (5); v NZ 1945 (1); v P 1956 (1)*
Minnett, R. B. 9: v E 1911 (5); *v E 1912 (1); v SA 1912 (3)*
Misson, F. M. 5: v WI 1960 (3); *v E 1961 (2)*
Moody, T. M. 8: v NZ 1989 (1); v In 1991 (1); v P 1989 (1); v SL 1989 (2); *v SL 1992 (3)*
Moroney, J. R. 7: v E 1950 (1); v WI 1951 (1); *v SA 1949 (5)*
Morris, A. R. 46: v E 1946 (5) 1950 (5) 1954 (4); v SA 1952 (5); v WI 1951 (4); v In 1947 (4); *v E 1948 (5) 1953 (5); v SA 1949 (5); v WI 1954 (4)*
Morris, S. 1: v E 1884
Moses, H. 6: v E 1886 (2) 1887 (1) 1891 (2) 1894 (1)
Moss, J. K. 1: v P 1978
Moule, W. H. 1: *v E 1880*
Murdoch, W. L. 18: v E 1876 (1) 1878 (1) 1881 (4) 1882 (4) 1884 (1); *v E 1880 (1) 1882 (1) 1884 (3) 1890 (2)*
Musgrove, H. 1: v E 1884

Nagel, L. E. 1: v E 1932
Nash, L. J. 2: v E 1936 (1); v SA 1931 (1)
Nitschke, H. C. 2: v SA 1931 (2)
Noble, M. A. 42: v E 1897 (4) 1901 (5) 1903 (5) 1907 (5); *v E 1899 (5) 1902 (5) 1905 (5) 1909 (5); v SA 1902 (3)*
Noblet, G. 3: v SA 1952 (1); v WI 1951 (1); *v SA 1949 (1)*
Nothling, O. E. 1: v E 1928

O'Brien, L. P. J. 5: v E 1932 (2) 1936 (1); *v SA 1935 (2)*
O'Connor, J. D. A. 4: v E 1907 (3); *v E 1909 (1)*
O'Donnell, S. P. 6: v NZ 1985 (1); *v E 1985 (5)*
Ogilvie, A. D. 5: v In 1977 (3); *v WI 1977 (2)*
O'Keeffe, K. J. 24: v E 1970 (2) 1976 (1); v NZ 1973 (3); v P 1972 (2) 1976 (3); *v E 1977 (3); v WI 1972 (5); v NZ 1973 (3) 1976 (2)*
Oldfield, W. A. 54: v E 1920 (3) 1924 (5) 1928 (5) 1932 (4) 1936 (5); v SA 1931 (5); v WI 1930 (5); *v E 1921 (1) 1926 (5) 1930 (5) 1934 (5); v SA 1921 (1) 1935 (5)*
O'Neill, N. C. 42: v E 1958 (5) 1962 (5); v SA 1963 (4); v WI 1960 (5); *v E 1961 (5) 1964 (4); v WI 1964 (4); v In 1959 (5) 1964 (2); v P 1959 (3)*
O'Reilly, W. J. 27: v E 1932 (5) 1936 (5); v SA 1931 (2); *v E 1934 (5) 1938 (4); v SA 1935 (5); v NZ 1945 (1)*
Oxenham, R. K. 7: v E 1928 (3); v SA 1931 (1); v WI 1930 (3)

Palmer, G. E. 17: v E 1881 (4) 1882 (4) 1884 (2); *v E 1880 (1) 1884 (3) 1886 (3)*
Park, R. L. 1: v E 1920
Pascoe, L. S. 14: v E 1979 (2); v WI 1979 (1) 1981 (1); v NZ 1980 (3); v In 1980 (3); *v E 1977 (3) 1980 (1)*
Pellew, C. E. 10: v E 1920 (4); *v E 1921 (5); v SA 1921 (1)*
Phillips, W. B. 27: v WI 1984 (2); v NZ 1985 (3); v In 1985 (3); v P 1983 (5); *v E 1985 (6); v WI 1983 (5); v NZ 1985 (3)*
Phillips, W. N. 1: v In 1991
Philpott, P. I. 8: v E 1965 (3); *v WI 1964 (5)*
Ponsford, W. H. 29: v E 1924 (5) 1928 (2) 1932 (3); v SA 1931 (4); v WI 1930 (5); *v E 1926 (2) 1930 (4) 1934 (4)*
Pope, R. J. 1: v E 1884

Rackemann, C. G. 12: v E 1982 (1) 1990 (1); v WI 1984 (1); v NZ 1989 (1); v P 1983 (2) 1989 (3); v SL 1989 (1); *v WI 1983 (1); v NZ 1989 (1)*
Ransford, V. S. 20: v E 1907 (5) 1911 (5); v SA 1910 (5); *v E 1909 (5)*
Redpath, I. R. 66: v E 1965 (1) 1970 (6) 1974 (6); v SA 1963 (1); v WI 1968 (5) 1975 (6); v In 1967 (3); v P 1972 (3); *v E 1964 (5) 1968 (5); v SA 1966 (5) 1969 (4); v WI 1972 (5); v NZ 1973 (3); v In 1964 (2) 1969 (5); v P 1964 (1)*
Reedman, J. C. 1: v E 1894
Reid, B. A. 27: v E 1986 (5) 1990 (4); v WI 1992 (1); v NZ 1987 (2); v In 1985 (3) 1991 (2); *v WI 1990 (2); v NZ 1985 (3); v In 1986 (2); v P 1988 (3)*
Reiffel, P. R. 12: v SA 1993 (2); v NZ 1993 (2); v In 1991 (1); *v E 1993 (3); v SA 1993 (1); v NZ 1992 (3)*
Renneberg, D. A. 8: v In 1967 (3); *v SA 1966 (5)*
Richardson, A. J. 9: v E 1924 (4); *v E 1926 (5)*
Richardson, V. Y. 19: v E 1924 (3) 1928 (2) 1932 (5); *v E 1930 (4); v SA 1935 (5)*
Rigg, K. E. 8: v E 1936 (3); v SA 1931 (4); v WI 1930 (1)
Ring, D. T. 13: v SA 1952 (5); v WI 1951 (5); v In 1947 (1); *v E 1948 (1) 1953 (1)*
Ritchie, G. M. 30: v E 1986 (4); v WI 1984 (1); v NZ 1985 (3); v In 1985 (2); *v E 1985 (6); v WI 1983 (5); v NZ 1985 (3); v In 1986 (3); v P 1982 (3)*
Rixon, S. J. 13: v WI 1984 (3); v In 1977 (5); *v WI 1977 (5)*
Robertson, W. R. 1: v E 1884
Robinson, R. D. 3: *v E 1977 (3)*
Robinson, R. H. 1: v E 1936
Rorke, G. F. 4: v E 1958 (2); *v In 1959 (2)*
Rutherford, J. W. 1: *v In 1956*
Ryder, J. 20: v E 1920 (5) 1924 (3) 1928 (5); *v E 1926 (4); v SA 1921 (3)*

Saggers, R. A. 6: *v E 1948 (1); v SA 1949 (5)*
Saunders, J. V. 14: v E 1901 (1) 1903 (2) 1907 (5); *v E 1902 (4); v SA 1902 (2)*
Scott, H. J. H. 8: v E 1884 (2); *v E 1884 (3) 1886 (3)*
Sellers, R. H. D. 1: *v In 1964*
Serjeant, C. S. 12: v In 1977 (4); *v E 1977 (3); v WI 1977 (5)*
Sheahan, A. P. 31: v E 1970 (2); v WI 1968 (5); v NZ 1973 (2); v In 1967 (4); v P 1972 (2); *v E 1968 (5) 1972 (2); v SA 1969 (4); v In 1969 (5)*
Shepherd, B. K. 9: v E 1962 (2); v SA 1963 (4); v P 1964 (1); *v WI 1964 (2)*
Sievers, M. W. 3: v E 1936 (3)
Simpson, R. B. 62: v E 1958 (1) 1962 (5) 1965 (3); v SA 1963 (5); v WI 1960 (5); v In 1967 (3) 1977 (5); v P 1964 (1); *v E 1961 (5) 1964 (5); v SA 1957 (5) 1966 (5); v WI 1964 (5) 1977 (5); v In 1964 (3); v P 1964 (1)*
Sincock, D. J. 3: v E 1965 (1); v P 1964 (1); *v WI 1964 (1)*
Slater, K. N. 1: v E 1958
Slater, M. J. 15: v SA 1993 (3); v NZ 1993 (3); *v E 1993 (6); v SA 1993 (3)*
Sleep, P. R. 14: v E 1986 (3) 1987 (1); v NZ 1987 (3); v P 1978 (1) 1989 (1); v SL 1989 (1); *v In 1979 (2); v P 1982 (1) 1988 (1)*
Slight, J. 1: *v E 1880*
Smith, D. B. M. 2: *v E 1912 (2)*
Smith, S. B. 3: *v WI 1983 (3)*
Spofforth, F. R. 18: v E 1876 (1) 1878 (1) 1881 (1) 1882 (4) 1884 (3) 1886 (1); *v E 1882 (1) 1884 (3) 1886 (3)*
Stackpole, K. R. 43: v E 1965 (2) 1970 (6); v WI 1968 (5); v NZ 1973 (3); v P 1972 (1); *v E 1972 (5); v SA 1966 (5) 1969 (4); v WI 1972 (4); v NZ 1973 (3); v In 1969 (5)*
Stevens, G. B. 4: *v In 1959 (2); v P 1959 (2)*

Taber, H. B. 16: v WI 1968 (1); *v E 1968 (1); v SA 1966 (5) 1969 (4); v In 1969 (5)*
Tallon, D. 21: v E 1946 (5) 1950 (5); v In 1947 (5); *v E 1948 (4) 1953 (1); v NZ 1945 (1)*
Taylor, J. M. 20: v E 1920 (5) 1924 (5); *v E 1921 (5) 1926 (3); v SA 1921 (2)*
Taylor, M. A. 54: v E 1990 (5); v SA 1993 (3); v WI 1988 (2) 1992 (4); v NZ 1989 (1) 1993 (3); v In 1991 (5); v P 1989 (3); v SL 1989 (2); *v E 1989 (6) 1993 (6); v SA 1993 (2); v WI 1990 (5); v NZ 1989 (1) 1992 (3); v SL 1992 (3)*
Taylor, P. L. 13: v E 1986 (1) 1987 (1); v WI 1988 (2); v In 1991 (2); v P 1989 (2); v SL 1987 (1); *v WI 1990 (1); v NZ 1989 (1); v P 1988 (2)*
Thomas, G. 8: v E 1965 (3); *v WI 1964 (5)*
Thoms, G. R. 1: v WI 1951
Thomson, A. L. 4: v E 1970 (4)
Thomson, J. R. 51: v E 1974 (5) 1979 (1) 1982 (4); v WI 1975 (6) 1979 (1) 1981 (2); v In 1977 (5); v P 1972 (1) 1976 (1) 1981 (3); *v E 1975 (4) 1977 (5) 1985 (2); v WI 1977 (5); v NZ 1981 (3); v P 1982 (3)*
Thomson, N. F. D. 2: v E 1876 (2)
Thurlow, H. M. 1: v SA 1931
Toohey, P. M. 15: v E 1978 (5) 1979 (1); v WI 1979 (1); v In 1977 (5); *v WI 1977 (3)*
Toshack, E. R. H. 12: v E 1946 (5); v In 1947 (2); *v E 1948 (4); v NZ 1945 (1)*
Travers, J. P. F. 1: v E 1901
Tribe, G. E. 3: v E 1946 (3)
Trott, A. E. 3: v E 1894 (3)
Trott, G. H. S. 24: v E 1891 (3) 1894 (5) 1897 (5); *v E 1888 (3) 1890 (2) 1893 (3) 1896 (3)*
Trumble, H. 32: v E 1894 (1) 1897 (5) 1901 (5) 1903 (4); *v E 1890 (2) 1893 (3) 1896 (3) 1899 (5) 1902 (3); v SA 1902 (1)*
Trumble, J. W. 7: v E 1884 (4); *v E 1886 (3)*
Trumper, V. T. 48: v E 1901 (5) 1903 (5) 1907 (5) 1911 (5); v SA 1910 (5); *v E 1899 (5) 1902 (5) 1905 (5) 1909 (5); v SA 1902 (3)*
Turner, A. 14: v WI 1975 (6); v P 1976 (3); *v E 1975 (3); v NZ 1976 (2)*
Turner, C. T. B. 17: v E 1886 (2) 1887 (1) 1891 (3) 1894 (3); *v E 1888 (3) 1890 (2) 1893 (3)*

Veivers, T. R. 21: v E 1965 (4); v SA 1963 (3); v P 1964 (1); *v E 1964 (5); v SA 1966 (4); v In 1964 (3); v P 1964 (1)*
Veletta, M. R. J. 8: v E 1987 (1); v WI 1988 (2); v NZ 1987 (3); v P 1989 (1); v SL 1987 (1)

Waite, M. G. 2: *v E 1938 (2)*
Walker, M. H. N. 34: v E 1974 (6) 1976 (1); v WI 1975 (3); v NZ 1973 (1); v P 1972 (2) 1976 (2); *v E 1975 (4) 1977 (5); v WI 1972 (5); v NZ 1973 (3) 1976 (2)*
Wall, T. W. 18: v E 1928 (1) 1932 (4); v SA 1931 (3); v WI 1930 (1); *v E 1930 (5) 1934 (4)*
Walters, F. H. 1: v E 1884
Walters, K. D. 74: v E 1965 (5) 1970 (6) 1974 (6) 1976 (1); v WI 1968 (4); v NZ 1973 (3) 1980 (3); v In 1967 (2) 1980 (3); v P 1972 (1) 1976 (3); *v E 1968 (5) 1972 (4) 1975 (4) 1977 (5); v SA 1969 (4); v WI 1972 (5); v NZ 1973 (3) 1976 (2); v In 1969 (5)*
Ward, F. A. 4: v E 1936 (3); *v E 1938 (1)*
Warne, S. K. 26: v SA 1993 (3); v WI 1992 (4); v NZ 1993 (3); v In 1991 (2); *v E 1993 (6); v SA 1993 (3); v NZ 1992 (3); v SL 1992 (2)*
Watkins, J. R. 1: v P 1972
Watson, G. D. 5: *v E 1972 (2); v SA 1966 (3)*
Watson, W. J. 4: v E 1954 (1); *v WI 1954 (3)*
Waugh, M. E. 36: v E 1990 (2); v SA 1993 (3); v WI 1992 (5); v NZ 1993 (3); v In 1991 (4); *v E 1993 (6); v SA 1993 (3); v WI 1990 (5); v NZ 1992 (2); v SL 1992 (3)*
Waugh, S. R. 65: v E 1986 (5) 1987 (1) 1990 (3); v SA 1993 (1); v WI 1988 (5) 1992 (5); v NZ 1987 (3) 1989 (1) 1993 (3); v In 1985 (2); v P 1989 (3); v SL 1987 (1) 1989 (2); *v E 1989 (6) 1993 (6); v SA 1993 (3); v WI 1990 (2); v NZ 1985 (3) 1989 (1) 1992 (3); v In 1986 (3); v P 1988 (3)*
Wellham, D. M. 6: v E 1986 (1); v WI 1981 (1); v P 1981 (2); *v E 1981 (1) 1985 (1)*
Wessels, K. C. 24: v E 1982 (4); v WI 1984 (5); v NZ 1985 (1); v P 1983 (5); *v E 1985 (6); v WI 1983 (2); v SL 1982 (1)*
Whatmore, D. F. 7: v P 1978 (2); *v In 1979 (5)*
Whitney, M. R. 12: v WI 1988 (1) 1992 (1); v NZ 1987 (1); v In 1991 (3); *v E 1981 (2); v WI 1990 (2); v SL 1992 (2)*
Whitty, W. J. 14: v E 1911 (2); v SA 1910 (5); *v E 1909 (1) 1912 (3); v SA 1912 (3)*
Wiener, J. M. 6: v E 1979 (2); v WI 1979 (2); *v P 1979 (2)*
Wilson, J. W. 1: *v In 1956*
Wood, G. M. 59: v E 1978 (6) 1982 (1); v WI 1981 (3) 1984 (5) 1988 (3); v NZ 1980 (3); v In 1977 (1) 1980 (3); v P 1978 (1) 1981 (3); *v E 1980 (1) 1981 (6) 1985 (5); v WI 1977 (5) 1983 (1); v NZ 1981 (3); v In 1979 (2); v P 1982 (3) 1988 (3); v SL 1982 (1)*
Woodcock, A. J. 1: v NZ 1973
Woodfull, W. M. 35: v E 1928 (5) 1932 (5); v SA 1931 (5); v WI 1930 (5); *v E 1926 (5) 1930 (5) 1934 (5)*
Woods, S. M. J. 3: *v E 1888 (3)*
Woolley, R. D. 2: *v WI 1983 (1); v SL 1982 (1)*
Worrall, J. 11: v E 1884 (1) 1887 (1) 1894 (1) 1897 (1); *v E 1888 (3) 1899 (4)*
Wright, K. J. 10: v E 1978 (2); v P 1978 (2); *v In 1979 (6)*

Yallop, G. N. 39: v E 1978 (6); v WI 1975 (3) 1984 (1); v In 1977 (1); v P 1978 (1) 1981 (1) 1983 (5); *v E 1980 (1) 1981 (6); v WI 1977 (4); v In 1979 (6); v P 1979 (3); v SL 1982 (1)*
Yardley, B. 33: v E 1978 (4) 1982 (5); v WI 1981 (3); v In 1977 (1) 1980 (2); v P 1978 (1) 1981 (3); *v WI 1977 (5); v NZ 1981 (3); v In 1979 (3); v P 1982 (2); v SL 1982 (1)*

Zoehrer, T. J. 10: v E 1986 (4); *v NZ 1985 (3); v In 1986 (3)*

SOUTH AFRICA

Number of Test cricketers: 257

Adcock, N. A. T. 26: v E 1956 (5); v A 1957 (5); v NZ 1953 (5) 1961 (2); *v E 1955 (4) 1960 (5)*
Anderson, J. H. 1: v A 1902
Ashley, W. H. 1: v E 1888

Bacher, A. 12: v A 1966 (5) 1969 (4); *v E 1965 (3)*
Balaskas, X. C. 9: v E 1930 (2) 1938 (1); v A 1935 (3); *v E 1935 (1); v NZ 1931 (2)*
Barlow, E. J. 30: v E 1964 (5); v A 1966 (5) 1969 (4); v NZ 1961 (5); *v E 1965 (3); v A 1963 (5); v NZ 1963 (3)*
Baumgartner, H. V. 1: v E 1913

Beaumont, R. 5: v E 1913 (2); *v E 1912 (1); v A 1912 (2)*
Begbie, D. W. 5: v E 1948 (3); v A 1949 (2)
Bell, A. J. 16: v E 1930 (3); *v E 1929 (3) 1935 (3); v A 1931 (5); v NZ 1931 (2)*
Bisset, M. 3: v E 1898 (2) 1909 (1)
Bissett, G. F. 4: v E 1927 (4)
Blanckenberg, J. M. 18: v E 1913 (5) 1922 (5); v A 1921 (3); *v E 1924 (5)*
Bland, K. C. 21: v E 1964 (5); v A 1966 (1); v NZ 1961 (5); *v E 1965 (3); v A 1963 (4); v NZ 1963 (3)*
Bock, E. G. 1: v A 1935
Bond, G. E. 1: v E 1938
Bosch, T. 1: *v WI 1991*
Botten, J. T. 3: *v E 1965 (3)*
Brann, W. H. 3: v E 1922 (3)
Briscoe, A. W. 2: v E 1938 (1); v A 1935 (1)
Bromfield, H. D. 9: v E 1964 (3); v NZ 1961 (5); *v E 1965 (1)*
Brown, L. S. 2: *v A 1931 (1); v NZ 1931 (1)*
Burger, C. G. de V. 2: v A 1957 (2)
Burke, S. F. 2: v E 1964 (1); v NZ 1961 (1)
Buys, I. D. 1: v E 1922

Cameron, H. B. 26: v E 1927 (5) 1930 (5); *v E 1929 (4) 1935 (5); v A 1931 (5); v NZ 1931 (2)*
Campbell, T. 5: v E 1909 (4); *v E 1912 (1)*
Carlstein, P. R. 8: v A 1957 (1); *v E 1960 (5); v A 1963 (2)*
Carter, C. P. 10: v E 1913 (2); v A 1921 (3); *v E 1912 (2) 1924 (3)*
Catterall, R. H. 24: v E 1922 (5) 1927 (5) 1930 (4); *v E 1924 (5) 1929 (5)*
Chapman, H. W. 2: v E 1913 (1); v A 1921 (1)
Cheetham, J. E. 24: v E 1948 (1); v A 1949 (3); v NZ 1953 (5); *v E 1951 (5) 1955 (3); v A 1952 (5); v NZ 1952 (2)*
Chevalier, G. A. 1: v A 1969
Christy, J. A. J. 10: v E 1930 (1); *v E 1929 (2); v A 1931 (5); v NZ 1931 (2)*
Chubb, G. W. A. 5: *v E 1951 (5)*
Cochran, J. A. K. 1: v E 1930
Coen, S. K. 2: v E 1927 (2)
Commaille, J. M. M. 12: v E 1909 (5) 1927 (2); *v E 1924 (5)*
Conyngham, D. P. 1: v E 1922
Cook, F. J. 1: v E 1895
Cook, S. J. 3: v In 1992 (2); *v SL 1993 (1)*
Cooper, A. H. C. 1: v E 1913
Cox, J. L. 3: v E 1913 (3)
Cripps, G. 1: v E 1891
Crisp, R. J. 9: v A 1935 (4); *v E 1935 (5)*
Cronje, W. J. 16: v A 1993 (3); v In 1992 (3); *v E 1994 (3); v A 1993 (3); v WI 1991 (1); v SL 1993 (3)*
Cullinan, D. J. 8: v In 1992 (1); *v E 1994 (1); v A 1993 (3); v SL 1993 (3)*
Curnow, S. H. 7: v E 1930 (3); *v A 1931 (4)*

Dalton, E. L. 15: v E 1930 (1) 1938 (4); v A 1935 (1); *v E 1929 (1) 1935 (4); v A 1931 (2); v NZ 1931 (2)*
Davies, E. Q. 5: v E 1938 (3); v A 1935 (2)
Dawson, O. C. 9: v E 1948 (4); *v E 1947 (5)*
Deane, H. G. 17: v E 1927 (5) 1930 (2); *v E 1924 (5) 1929 (5)*
de Villiers, P. S. 9: v A 1993 (3); *v E 1994 (3); v A 1993 (3)*
Dixon, C. D. 1: v E 1913
Donald, A. A. 17: v A 1993 (3); v In 1992 (4); *v E 1994 (3); v A 1993 (3); v WI 1991 (1); v SL 1993 (3)*
Dower, R. R. 1: v E 1898
Draper, R. G. 2: v A 1949 (2)
Duckworth, C. A. R. 2: v E 1956 (2)
Dumbrill, R. 5: v A 1966 (2); *v E 1965 (3)*
Duminy, J. P. 3: v E 1927 (2); *v E 1929 (1)*
Dunell, O. R. 2: v E 1888 (2)
Du Preez, J. H. 2: v A 1966 (2)

Du Toit, J. F. 1: v E 1891
Dyer, D. V. 3: *v E 1947 (3)*

Eksteen, C. E. 1: *v SL 1993*
Elgie, M. K. 3: v NZ 1961 (3)
Endean, W. R. 28: v E 1956 (5); v A 1957 (5); v NZ 1953 (5); *v E 1951 (1) 1955 (5); v A 1952 (5); v NZ 1952 (2)*

Farrer, W. S. 6: v NZ 1961 (3); *v NZ 1963 (3)*
Faulkner, G. A. 25: v E 1905 (5) 1909 (5); *v E 1907 (3) 1912 (3) 1924 (1); v A 1910 (5) 1912 (3)*
Fellows-Smith, J. P. 4: *v E 1960 (4)*
Fichardt, C. G. 2: v E 1891 (1) 1895 (1)
Finlason, C. E. 1: v E 1888
Floquet, C. E. 1: v E 1909
Francis, H. H. 2: v E 1898 (2)
Francois, C. M. 5: v E 1922 (5)
Frank, C. N. 3: v A 1921 (3)
Frank, W. H. B. 1: v E 1895
Fuller, E. R. H. 7: v A 1957 (1); *v E 1955 (2); v A 1952 (2); v NZ 1952 (2)*
Fullerton, G. M. 7: v A 1949 (2); *v E 1947 (2) 1951 (3)*
Funston, K. J. 18: v E 1956 (3); v A 1957 (5); v NZ 1953 (3); *v A 1952 (5); v NZ 1952 (2)*

Gamsy, D. 2: v A 1969 (2)
Gleeson, R. A. 1: v E 1895
Glover, G. K. 1: v E 1895
Goddard, T. L. 41: v E 1956 (5) 1964 (5); v A 1957 (5) 1966 (5) 1969 (3); *v E 1955 (5) 1960 (5); v A 1963 (5); v NZ 1963 (3)*
Gordon, N. 5: v E 1938 (5)
Graham, R. 2: v E 1898 (2)
Grieveson, R. E. 2: v E 1938 (2)
Griffin, G. M. 2: *v E 1960 (2)*

Hall, A. E. 7: v E 1922 (4) 1927 (2) 1930 (1)
Hall, G. G. 1: v E 1964
Halliwell, E. A. 8: v E 1891 (1) 1895 (3) 1898 (1); v A 1902 (3)
Halse, C. G. 3: *v A 1963 (3)*
Hands, P. A. M. 7: v E 1913 (5); v A 1921 (1); *v E 1924 (1)*
Hands, R. H. M. 1: v E 1913
Hanley, M. A. 1: v E 1948
Harris, T. A. 3: v E 1948 (1); *v E 1947 (2)*
Hartigan, G. P. D. 5: v E 1913 (3); *v E 1912 (1); v A 1912 (1)*
Harvey, R. L. 2: v A 1935 (2)
Hathorn, C. M. H. 12: v E 1905 (5); v A 1902 (3); *v E 1907 (3); v A 1910 (1)*
Hearne, F. 4: v E 1891 (1) 1895 (3)
Hearne, G. A. L. 3: v E 1922 (2); *v E 1924 (1)*
Heine, P. S. 14: v E 1956 (5); v A 1957 (4); v NZ 1961 (1); *v E 1955 (4)*
Henry, O. 3: v In 1992 (3)
Hime, C. F. W. 1: v E 1895
Hudson, A. C. 16: v A 1993 (3); v In 1992 (4); *v E 1994 (2); v A 1993 (3); v WI 1991 (1); v SL 1993 (3)*
Hutchinson, P. 2: v E 1888 (2)

Ironside, D. E. J. 3: v NZ 1953 (3)
Irvine, B. L. 4: v A 1969 (4)

Johnson, C. L. 1: v E 1895

Keith, H. J. 8: v E 1956 (3); *v E 1955 (4); v A 1952 (1)*
Kempis, G. A. 1: v E 1888
Kirsten, G. 9: v A 1993 (3); *v E 1994 (3); v A 1993 (3)*
Kirsten, P. N. 12: v A 1993 (3); v In 1992 (4); *v E 1994 (3); v A 1993 (1); v WI 1991 (1)*
Kotze, J. J. 3: v A 1902 (2); *v E 1907 (1)*

Kuiper, A. P. 1: *v WI 1991*
Kuys, F. 1: v E 1898

Lance, H. R. 13: v A 1966 (5) 1969 (3); v NZ 1961 (2); *v E 1965 (3)*
Langton, A. B. C. 15: v E 1938 (5); v A 1935 (5); *v E 1935 (5)*
Lawrence, G. B. 5: v NZ 1961 (5)
Le Roux, F. le S. 1: v E 1913
Lewis, P. T. 1: v E 1913
Lindsay, D. T. 19: v E 1964 (3); v A 1966 (5) 1969 (2); *v E 1965 (3); v A 1963 (3); v NZ 1963 (3)*
Lindsay, J. D. 3: *v E 1947 (3)*
Lindsay, N. V. 1: v A 1921
Ling, W. V. S. 6: v E 1922 (3); v A 1921 (3)
Llewellyn, C. B. 15: v E 1895 (1) 1898 (1); v A 1902 (3); *v E 1912 (3); v A 1910 (5) 1912 (2)*
Lundie, E. B. 1: v E 1913

Macaulay, M. J. 1: v E 1964
McCarthy, C. N. 15: v E 1948 (5); v A 1949 (5); *v E 1951 (5)*
McGlew, D. J. 34: v E 1956 (1); v A 1957 (5); v NZ 1953 (5) 1961 (5); *v E 1951 (2) 1955 (5) 1960 (5); v A 1952 (4); v NZ 1952 (2)*
McKinnon, A. H. 8: v E 1964 (2); v A 1966 (2); v NZ 1961 (1); *v E 1960 (1) 1965 (2)*
McLean, R. A. 40: v E 1956 (5) 1964 (2); v A 1957 (4); v NZ 1953 (4) 1961 (5); *v E 1951 (3) 1955 (5) 1960 (5); v A 1952 (5); v NZ 1952 (2)*
McMillan, B. M. 13: v A 1993 (3); v In 1992 (4); *v E 1994 (3); v A 1993 (1); v SL 1993 (2)*
McMillan, Q. 13: v E 1930 (5); *v E 1929 (2); v A 1931 (4); v NZ 1931 (2)*
Mann, N. B. F. 19: v E 1948 (5); v A 1949 (5); *v E 1947 (5) 1951 (4)*
Mansell, P. N. F. 13: *v E 1951 (2) 1955 (4); v A 1952 (5); v NZ 1952 (2)*
Markham, L. A. 1: v E 1948
Marx, W. F. E. 3: v A 1921 (3)
Matthews, C. R. 11: v A 1993 (3); v In 1992 (3); *v E 1994 (3); v A 1993 (2)*
Meintjes, D. J. 2: v E 1922 (2)
Melle, M. G. 7: v A 1949 (2); *v E 1951 (1); v A 1952 (4)*
Melville, A. 11: v E 1938 (5) 1948 (1); *v E 1947 (5)*
Middleton, J. 6: v E 1895 (2) 1898 (2); v A 1902 (2)
Mills, C. 1: v E 1891
Milton, W. H. 3: v E 1888 (2) 1891 (1)
Mitchell, B. 42: v E 1930 (5) 1938 (5) 1948 (5); v A 1935 (5); *v E 1929 (5) 1935 (5) 1947 (5); v A 1931 (5); v NZ 1931 (2)*
Mitchell, F. 3: *v E 1912 (1); v A 1912 (2)*
Morkel, D. P. B. 16: v E 1927 (5); *v E 1929 (5); v A 1931 (5); v NZ 1931 (1)*
Murray, A. R. A. 10: v NZ 1953 (4); *v A 1952 (4); v NZ 1952 (2)*

Nel, J. D. 6: v A 1949 (5) 1957 (1)
Newberry, C. 4: v E 1913 (4)
Newson, E. S. 3: v E 1930 (1) 1938 (2)
Nicholson, F. 4: v A 1935 (4)
Nicolson, J. F. W. 3: v E 1927 (3)
Norton, N. O. 1: v E 1909
Nourse, A. D. 34: v E 1938 (5) 1948 (5); v A 1935 (5) 1949 (5); *v E 1935 (4) 1947 (5) 1951 (5)*
Nourse, A. W. 45: v E 1905 (5) 1909 (5) 1913 (5) 1922 (5); v A 1902 (3) 1921 (3); *v E 1907 (3) 1912 (3) 1924 (5); v A 1910 (5) 1912 (3)*
Nupen, E. P. 17: v E 1922 (4) 1927 (5) 1930 (3); v A 1921 (2) 1935 (1); *v E 1924 (2)*

Ochse, A. E. 2: v E 1888 (2)
Ochse, A. L. 3: v E 1927 (1); *v E 1929 (2)*
O'Linn, S. 7: v NZ 1961 (2); *v E 1960 (5)*
Owen-Smith, H. G. 5: *v E 1929 (5)*

Palm, A. W. 1: v E 1927
Parker, G. M. 2: *v E 1924 (2)*
Parkin, D. C. 1: v E 1891
Partridge, J. T. 11: v E 1964 (3); *v A 1963 (5); v NZ 1963 (3)*
Pearse, O. C. 3: *v A 1910 (3)*

Pegler, S. J. 16: v E 1909 (1); *v E 1912 (3) 1924 (5); v A 1910 (4) 1912 (3)*
Pithey, A. J. 17: v E 1956 (3) 1964 (5); *v E 1960 (2); v A 1963 (4); v NZ 1963 (3)*
Pithey, D. B. 8: v A 1966 (2); *v A 1963 (3); v NZ 1963 (3)*
Plimsoll, J. B. 1: *v E 1947*
Pollock, P. M. 28: v E 1964 (5); v A 1966 (5) 1969 (4); v NZ 1961 (3); *v E 1965 (3); v A 1963 (5); v NZ 1963 (3)*
Pollock, R. G. 23: v E 1964 (5); v A 1966 (5) 1969 (4); *v E 1965 (3); v A 1963 (5); v NZ 1963 (1)*
Poore, R. M. 3: v E 1895 (3)
Pothecary, J. E. 3: *v E 1960 (3)*
Powell, A. W. 1: v E 1898
Prince, C. F. H. 1: v E 1898
Pringle, M. W. 3: v In 1992 (2); *v WI 1991 (1)*
Procter, M. J. 7: v A 1966 (3) 1969 (4)
Promnitz, H. L. E. 2: v E 1927 (2)

Quinn, N. A. 12: v E 1930 (1); *v E 1929 (4); v A 1931 (5); v NZ 1931 (2)*

Reid, N. 1: v A 1921
Rhodes, J. N. 16: v A 1993 (3); v In 1992 (4); *v E 1994 (3); v A 1993 (3); v SL 1993 (3)*
Richards, A. R. 1: v E 1895
Richards, B. A. 4: v A 1969 (4)
Richards, W. H. 1: v E 1888
Richardson, D. J. 17: v A 1993 (3); v In 1992 (4); *v E 1994 (3); v A 1993 (3); v WI 1991 (1); v SL 1993 (3)*
Robertson, J. B. 3: v A 1935 (3)
Rose-Innes, A. 2: v E 1888 (2)
Routledge, T. W. 4: v E 1891 (1) 1895 (3)
Rowan, A. M. B. 15: v E 1948 (5); *v E 1947 (5) 1951 (5)*
Rowan, E. A. B. 26: v E 1938 (4) 1948 (4); v A 1935 (3) 1949 (5); *v E 1935 (5) 1951 (5)*
Rowe, G. A. 5: v E 1895 (2) 1898 (2); v A 1902 (1)
Rushmere, M. W. 1: *v WI 1991*

Samuelson, S. V. 1: v E 1909
Schultz, B. N. 5: v In 1992 (2); *v SL 1993 (3)*
Schwarz, R. O. 20: v E 1905 (5) 1909 (4); *v E 1907 (3) 1912 (1); v A 1910 (5) 1912 (2)*
Seccull, A. W. 1: v E 1895
Seymour, M. A. 7: v E 1964 (2); v A 1969 (1); *v A 1963 (4)*
Shalders, W. A. 12: v E 1898 (1) 1905 (5); v A 1902 (3); *v E 1907 (3)*
Shepstone, G. H. 2: v E 1895 (1) 1898 (1)
Sherwell, P. W. 13: v E 1905 (5); *v E 1907 (3); v A 1910 (5)*
Siedle, I. J. 18: v E 1927 (1) 1930 (5); v A 1935 (5); *v E 1929 (3) 1935 (4)*
Sinclair, J. H. 25: v E 1895 (3) 1898 (2) 1905 (5) 1909 (4); v A 1902 (3); *v E 1907 (3); v A 1910 (5)*
Smith, C. J. E. 3: v A 1902 (3)
Smith, F. W. 3: v E 1888 (2) 1895 (1)
Smith, V. I. 9: v A 1949 (3) 1957 (1); *v E 1947 (4) 1955 (1)*
Snell, R. P. 4: *v A 1993 (1); v WI 1991 (1); v SL 1993 (2)*
Snooke, S. D. 1: *v E 1907*
Snooke, S. J. 26: v E 1905 (5) 1909 (5) 1922 (3); *v E 1907 (3) 1912 (3); v A 1910 (5) 1912 (2)*
Solomon, W. R. 1: v E 1898
Stewart, R. B. 1: v E 1888
Stricker, L. A. 13: v E 1909 (4); *v E 1912 (2); v A 1910 (5) 1912 (2)*
Susskind, M. J. 5: *v E 1924 (5)*
Symcox, P. L. 5: *v A 1993 (2); v SL 1993 (3)*

Taberer, H. M. 1: v A 1902
Tancred, A. B. 2: v E 1888 (2)
Tancred, L. J. 14: v E 1905 (5) 1913 (1); v A 1902 (3); *v E 1907 (1) 1912 (2); v A 1912 (2)*
Tancred, V. M. 1: v E 1898
Tapscott, G. L. 1: v E 1913
Tapscott, L. E. 2: v E 1922 (2)
Tayfield, H. J. 37: v E 1956 (5); v A 1949 (5) 1957 (5); v NZ 1953 (5); *v E 1955 (5) 1960 (5); v A 1952 (5); v NZ 1952 (2)*

Taylor, A. I. 1: v E 1956
Taylor, D. 2: v E 1913 (2)
Taylor, H. W. 42: v E 1913 (5) 1922 (5) 1927 (5) 1930 (4); v A 1921 (3); *v E 1912 (3) 1924 (5) 1929 (3); v A 1912 (3) 1931 (5); v NZ 1931 (1)*
Theunissen, N. H. G. de J. 1: v E 1888
Thornton, P. G. 1: v A 1902
Tomlinson, D. S. 1: *v E 1935*
Traicos, A. J. 3: v A 1969 (3)
Trimborn, P. H. J. 4: v A 1966 (3) 1969 (1)
Tuckett, L. 9: v E 1948 (4); *v E 1947 (5)*
Tuckett, L. R. 1: v E 1913
Twentyman-Jones, P. S. 1: v A 1902

van der Bijl, P. G. V. 5: v E 1938 (5)
Van der Merwe, E. A. 2: v A 1935 (1); *v E 1929 (1)*
Van der Merwe, P. L. 15: v E 1964 (2); v A 1966 (5); *v E 1965 (3); v A 1963 (3); v NZ 1963 (2)*
Van Ryneveld, C. B. 19: v E 1956 (5); v A 1957 (4); v NZ 1953 (5); *v E 1951 (5)*
Varnals, G. D. 3: v E 1964 (3)
Viljoen, K. G. 27: v E 1930 (3) 1938 (4) 1948 (2); v A 1935 (4); *v E 1935 (4) 1947 (5); v A 1931 (4); v NZ 1931 (1)*
Vincent, C. L. 25: v E 1927 (5) 1930 (5); *v E 1929 (4) 1935 (4); v A 1931 (5); v NZ 1931 (2)*
Vintcent, C. H. 3: v E 1888 (2) 1891 (1)
Vogler, A. E. E. 15: v E 1905 (5) 1909 (5); *v E 1907 (3); v A 1910 (2)*

Wade, H. F. 10: v A 1935 (5); *v E 1935 (5)*
Wade, W. W. 11: v E 1938 (3) 1948 (5); v A 1949 (3)
Waite, J. H. B. 50: v E 1956 (5) 1964 (2); v A 1957 (5); v NZ 1953 (5) 1961 (5); *v E 1951 (4) 1955 (5) 1960 (5); v A 1952 (5) 1963 (4); v NZ 1952 (2) 1963 (3)*
Walter, K. A. 2: v NZ 1961 (2)
Ward, T. A. 23: v E 1913 (5) 1922 (5); v A 1921 (3); *v E 1912 (2) 1924 (5); v A 1912 (3)*
Watkins, J. C. 15: v E 1956 (2); v A 1949 (3); v NZ 1953 (3); *v A 1952 (5); v NZ 1952 (2)*
Wesley, C. 3: *v E 1960 (3)*
Wessels, K. C. 16: v A 1993 (3); v In 1992 (4); *v E 1994 (3); v A 1993 (2); v WI 1991 (1); SL 1993 (3)*
Westcott, R. J. 5: v A 1957 (2); v NZ 1953 (3)
White, G. C. 17: v E 1905 (5) 1909 (4); *v E 1907 (3) 1912 (2); v A 1912 (3)*
Willoughby, J. T. I. 2: v E 1895 (2)
Wimble, C. S. 1: v E 1891
Winslow, P. L. 5: v A 1949 (2); *v E 1955 (3)*
Wynne, O. E. 6: v E 1948 (3); v A 1949 (3)

Zulch, J. W. 16: v E 1909 (5) 1913 (3); v A 1921 (3); *v A 1910 (5)*

WEST INDIES

Number of Test cricketers: 205

Achong, E. 6: v E 1929 (1) 1934 (2); *v E 1933 (3)*
Adams, J. C. 9: v E 1993 (5); v SA 1991 (1); *v A 1992 (3)*
Alexander, F. C. M. 25: v E 1959 (5); v P 1957 (5); *v E 1957 (2); v A 1960 (5); v In 1958 (5); v P 1958 (3)*
Ali, Imtiaz 1: v In 1975
Ali, Inshan 12: v E 1973 (2); v A 1972 (3); v In 1970 (1); v P 1976 (1); v NZ 1971 (3); *v E 1973 (1); v A 1975 (1)*
Allan, D. W. 5: v A 1964 (1); v In 1961 (2); *v E 1966 (2)*
Allen, I. B. A. 2: *v E 1991 (2)*
Ambrose, C. E. L. 48: v E 1989 (3) 1993 (5); v A 1990 (5); v SA 1991 (1); v In 1988 (4); v P 1987 (3) 1992 (3); *v E 1988 (5) 1991 (5); v A 1988 (5) 1992 (5); v P 1990 (3); v SL 1993 (1)*
Arthurton, K. L. T. 20: v E 1993 (5); v SA 1991 (1); v In 1988 (4); v P 1992 (3); *v E 1988 (1); v A 1992 (5); v SL 1993 (1)*

Asgarali, N. 2: *v E 1957 (2)*
Atkinson, D. St E. 22: v E 1953 (4); v A 1954 (4); v P 1957 (1); *v E 1957 (2); v A 1951 (2); v NZ 1951 (1) 1955 (4); v In 1948 (4)*
Atkinson, E. St E. 8: v P 1957 (3); *v In 1958 (3); v P 1958 (2)*
Austin, R. A. 2: v A 1977 (2)

Bacchus, S. F. A. F. 19: v A 1977 (2); *v E 1980 (5); v A 1981 (2); v In 1978 (6); v P 1980 (4)*
Baichan, L. 3: *v A 1975 (1); v P 1974 (2)*
Baptiste, E. A. E. 10: v E 1989 (1); v A 1983 (3); *v E 1984 (5); v In 1983 (1)*
Barrett, A. G. 6: v E 1973 (2); v In 1970 (2); *v In 1974 (2)*
Barrow, I. 11: v E 1929 (1) 1934 (1); *v E 1933 (3) 1939 (1); v A 1930 (5)*
Bartlett, E. L. 5: *v E 1928 (1); v A 1930 (4)*
Benjamin, K. C. G. 7: v E 1993 (5); v SA 1991 (1); *v A 1992 (1)*
Benjamin, W. K. M. 16: v E 1993 (5); v In 1988 (1); v P 1987 (3) 1992 (2); *v E 1988 (3); v In 1987 (1); v SL 1993 (1)*
Best, C. A. 8: v E 1985 (3) 1989 (3); *v P 1990 (2)*
Betancourt, N. 1: v E 1929
Binns, A. P. 5: v A 1954 (1); v In 1952 (1); *v NZ 1955 (3)*
Birkett, L. S. 4: *v A 1930 (4)*
Bishop, I. R. 18: v E 1989 (4); v In 1988 (4); v P 1992 (2); *v A 1992 (5); v P 1990 (3)*
Boyce, K. D. 21: v E 1973 (4); v A 1972 (4); v In 1970 (1); *v E 1973 (3); v A 1975 (4); v In 1974 (3); v P 1974 (2)*
Browne, C. R. 4: v E 1929 (2); *v E 1928 (2)*
Butcher, B. F. 44: v E 1959 (2) 1967 (5); v A 1964 (5); *v E 1963 (5) 1966 (5) 1969 (3); v A 1968 (5); v NZ 1968 (3); v In 1958 (5) 1966 (3); v P 1958 (3)*
Butler, L. 1: v A 1954
Butts, C. G. 7: v NZ 1984 (1); *v NZ 1986 (1); v In 1987 (3); v P 1986 (2)*
Bynoe, M. R. 4: *v In 1966 (3); v P 1958 (1)*

Camacho, G. S. 11: v E 1967 (5); v In 1970 (2); *v E 1969 (2); v A 1968 (2)*
Cameron, F. J. 5: *v In 1948 (5)*
Cameron, J. H. 2: *v E 1939 (2)*
Carew, G. M. 4: v E 1934 (1) 1947 (2); *v In 1948 (1)*
Carew, M. C. 19: v E 1967 (1); v NZ 1971 (3); v In 1970 (3); *v E 1963 (2) 1966 (1) 1969 (1); v A 1968 (5); v NZ 1968 (3)*
Challenor, G. 3: *v E 1928 (3)*
Chanderpaul, S. 4: v E 1993 (4)
Chang, H. S. 1: *v In 1978*
Christiani, C. M. 4: v E 1934 (4)
Christiani, R. J. 22: v E 1947 (4) 1953 (1); v In 1952 (2); *v E 1950 (4); v A 1951 (5); v NZ 1951 (1); v In 1948 (5)*
Clarke, C. B. 3: *v E 1939 (3)*
Clarke, S. T. 11: v A 1977 (1); *v A 1981 (1); v In 1978 (5); v P 1980 (4)*
Constantine, L. N. 18: v E 1929 (3) 1934 (3); *v E 1928 (3) 1933 (1) 1939 (3); v A 1930 (5)*
Croft, C. E. H. 27: v E 1980 (4); v A 1977 (2); v P 1976 (5); *v E 1980 (3); v A 1979 (3) 1981 (3); v NZ 1979 (3); v P 1980 (4)*
Cummins, A. C. 3: v P 1992 (2); *v A 1992 (1)*

Da Costa, O. C. 5: v E 1929 (1) 1934 (1); *v E 1933 (3)*
Daniel, W. W. 10: v A 1983 (2); v In 1975 (1); *v E 1976 (4); v In 1983 (3)*
Davis, B. A. 4: v A 1964 (4)
Davis, C. A. 15: v A 1972 (2); v NZ 1971 (5); v In 1970 (4); *v E 1969 (3); v A 1968 (1)*
Davis, W. W. 15: v A 1983 (1); v NZ 1984 (2); v In 1982 (1); *v E 1984 (1); v In 1983 (6) 1987 (4)*
De Caires, F. I. 3: v E 1929 (3)
Depeiza, C. C. 5: v A 1954 (3); *v NZ 1955 (2)*
Dewdney, T. 9: v A 1954 (2); v P 1957 (3); *v E 1957 (1); v NZ 1955 (3)*
Dowe, U. G. 4: v A 1972 (1); v NZ 1971 (1); v In 1970 (2)
Dujon, P. J. L. 81: v E 1985 (4) 1989 (4); v A 1983 (5) 1990 (5); v NZ 1984 (4); v In 1982 (5) 1988 (4); v P 1987 (3); *v E 1984 (5) 1988 (5) 1991 (5); v A 1981 (3) 1984 (5) 1988 (5); v NZ 1986 (3); v In 1983 (6) 1987 (4); v P 1986 (3) 1990 (3)*

Edwards, R. M. 5: *v A 1968 (2); v NZ 1968 (3)*

Ferguson, W. 8: v E 1947 (4) 1953 (1); *v In 1948 (3)*
Fernandes, M. P. 2: v E 1929 (1); *v E 1928 (1)*
Findlay, T. M. 10: v A 1972 (1); v NZ 1971 (5); v In 1970 (2); *v E 1969 (2)*
Foster, M. L. C. 14: v E 1973 (1); v A 1972 (4) 1977 (1); v NZ 1971 (3); v In 1970 (2); v P 1976 (1); *v E 1969 (1) 1973 (1)*
Francis, G. N. 10: v E 1929 (1); *v E 1928 (3) 1933 (1); v A 1930 (5)*
Frederick, M. C. 1: v E 1953
Fredericks, R. C. 59: v E 1973 (5); v A 1972 (5); v NZ 1971 (5); v In 1970 (4) 1975 (4); v P 1976 (5); *v E 1969 (3) 1973 (3) 1976 (5); v A 1968 (4) 1975 (6); v NZ 1968 (3); v In 1974 (5); v P 1974 (2)*
Fuller, R. L. 1: v E 1934
Furlonge, H. A. 3: v A 1954 (1); *v NZ 1955 (2)*

Ganteaume, A. G. 1: v E 1947
Garner, J. 58: v E 1980 (4) 1985 (5); v A 1977 (2) 1983 (5); v NZ 1984 (4); v In 1982 (4); v P 1976 (5); *v E 1980 (5) 1984 (5); v A 1979 (3) 1981 (3) 1984 (5); v NZ 1979 (3) 1986 (2); v P 1980 (3)*
Gaskin, B. B. M. 2: v E 1947 (2)
Gibbs, G. L. R. 1: v A 1954
Gibbs, L. R. 79: v E 1967 (5) 1973 (5); v A 1964 (5) 1972 (5); v NZ 1971 (2); v In 1961 (5) 1970 (1); v P 1957 (4); *v E 1963 (5) 1966 (5) 1969 (3) 1973 (3); v A 1960 (3) 1968 (5) 1975 (6); v NZ 1968 (3); v In 1958 (1) 1966 (3) 1974 (5); v P 1958 (3) 1974 (2)*
Gilchrist, R. 13: v P 1957 (5); *v E 1957 (4); v In 1958 (4)*
Gladstone, G. 1: v E 1929
Goddard, J. D. C. 27: v E 1947 (4); *v E 1950 (4) 1957 (5); v A 1951 (4); v NZ 1951 (2) 1955 (3); v In 1948 (5)*
Gomes, H. A. 60: v E 1980 (4) 1985 (5); v A 1977 (3) 1983 (2); v NZ 1984 (4); v In 1982 (5); *v E 1976 (2) 1984 (5); v A 1981 (3) 1984 (5); v NZ 1986 (3); v In 1978 (6) 1983 (6); v P 1980 (4) 1986 (3)*
Gomez, G. E. 29: v E 1947 (4) 1953 (4); v In 1952 (4); *v E 1939 (2) 1950 (4); v A 1951 (5); v NZ 1951 (1); v In 1948 (5)*
Grant, G. C. 12: v E 1934 (4); *v E 1933 (3); v A 1930 (5)*
Grant, R. S. 7: v E 1934 (4); *v E 1939 (3)*
Gray, A. H. 5: *v NZ 1986 (2); v P 1986 (3)*
Greenidge, A. E. 6: v A 1977 (2); *v In 1978 (4)*
Greenidge, C. G. 108: v E 1980 (4) 1985 (5) 1989 (4); v A 1977 (2) 1983 (5) 1990 (5); v NZ 1984 (4); v In 1982 (5) 1988 (4); v P 1976 (5) 1987 (3); *v E 1976 (5) 1980 (5) 1984 (5) 1988 (4); v A 1975 (2) 1979 (3) 1981 (2) 1984 (5) 1988 (5); v NZ 1979 (3) 1986 (3); v In 1974 (5) 1983 (6) 1987 (3); v P 1986 (3) 1990 (3)*
Greenidge, G. A. 5: v A 1972 (3); v NZ 1971 (2)
Grell, M. G. 1: v E 1929
Griffith, C. C. 28: v E 1959 (1) 1967 (4); v A 1964 (5); *v E 1963 (5) 1966 (5); v A 1968 (3); v NZ 1968 (2); v In 1966 (3)*
Griffith, H. C. 13: v E 1929 (3); *v E 1928 (3) 1933 (2); v A 1930 (5)*
Guillen, S. C. 5: *v A 1951 (3); v NZ 1951 (2)*

Hall, W. W. 48: v E 1959 (5) 1967 (4); v A 1964 (5); v In 1961 (5); *v E 1963 (5) 1966 (5); v A 1960 (5) 1968 (2); v NZ 1968 (1); v In 1958 (5) 1966 (3); v P 1958 (3)*
Harper, R. A. 25: v E 1985 (2); v A 1983 (4); v NZ 1984 (1); *v E 1984 (5) 1988 (3); v A 1984 (2) 1988 (1); v In 1983 (2) 1987 (1); v P 1986 (3); v SL 1993 (1)*
Haynes, D. L. 116: v E 1980 (4) 1985 (5) 1989 (4) 1993 (4); v A 1977 (2) 1983 (5) 1990 (5); v SA 1991 (1); v NZ 1984 (4); v In 1982 (5) 1988 (4); v P 1987 (3) 1992 (3); *v E 1980 (5) 1984 (5) 1988 (4) 1991 (5); v A 1979 (3) 1981 (3) 1984 (5) 1988 (5) 1992 (5); v NZ 1979 (3) 1986 (3); v In 1983 (6) 1987 (4); v P 1980 (4) 1986 (3) 1990 (3); v SL 1993 (1)*
Headley, G. A. 22: v E 1929 (4) 1934 (4) 1947 (1) 1953 (1); *v E 1933 (3) 1939 (3); v A 1930 (5); v In 1948 (1)*
Headley, R. G. A. 2: *v E 1973 (2)*
Hendriks, J. L. 20: v A 1964 (4); v In 1961 (1); *v E 1966 (3) 1969 (1); v A 1968 (5); v NZ 1968 (3); v In 1966 (3)*
Hoad, E. L. G. 4: v E 1929 (1); *v E 1928 (1) 1933 (2)*
Holder, V. A. 40: v E 1973 (1); v A 1972 (3) 1977 (3); v NZ 1971 (4); v In 1970 (3) 1975 (1); v P 1976 (1); *v E 1969 (3) 1973 (2) 1976 (4); v A 1975 (3); v In 1974 (4) 1978 (6); v P 1974 (2)*

Holding, M. A. 60: v E 1980 (4) 1985 (4); v A 1983 (3); v NZ 1984 (3); v In 1975 (4) 1982 (5); *v E 1976 (4) 1980 (5) 1984 (4); v A 1975 (5) 1979 (3) 1981 (3) 1984 (3); v NZ 1979 (3) 1986 (1); v In 1983 (6)*
Holford, D. A. J. 24: v E 1967 (4); v NZ 1971 (5); v In 1970 (1) 1975 (2); v P 1976 (1); *v E 1966 (5); v A 1968 (2); v NZ 1968 (3); v In 1966 (1)*
Holt, J. K. 17: v E 1953 (5); v A 1954 (5); *v In 1958 (5); v P 1958 (2)*
Hooper, C. L. 40: v E 1989 (3); v A 1990 (5); v P 1987 (3) 1992 (3); *v E 1988 (5) 1991 (5); v A 1988 (5) 1992 (4); v In 1987 (3); v P 1990 (3); v SL 1993 (1)*
Howard, A. B. 1: v NZ 1971
Hunte, C. C. 44: v E 1959 (5); v A 1964 (5); v In 1961 (5); v P 1957 (5); *v E 1963 (5) 1966 (5); v A 1960 (5); v In 1958 (5) 1966 (3); v P 1958 (1)*
Hunte, E. A. C. 3: v E 1929 (3)
Hylton, L. G. 6: v E 1934 (4); *v E 1939 (2)*

Johnson, H. H. H. 3: v E 1947 (1); *v E 1950 (2)*
Johnson, T. F. 1: *v E 1939*
Jones, C. M. 4: v E 1929 (1) 1934 (3)
Jones, P. E. 9: v E 1947 (1); *v E 1950 (2); v A 1951 (1); v In 1948 (5)*
Julien, B. D. 24: v E 1973 (5); v In 1975 (4); v P 1976 (1); *v E 1973 (3) 1976 (2); v A 1975 (3); v In 1974 (4); v P 1974 (2)*
Jumadeen, R. R. 12: v A 1972 (1) 1977 (2); v NZ 1971 (1); v In 1975 (4); v P 1976 (1); *v E 1976 (1); v In 1978 (2)*

Kallicharran, A. I. 66: v E 1973 (5); v A 1972 (5) 1977 (5); v NZ 1971 (2); v In 1975 (4); v P 1976 (5); *v E 1973 (3) 1976 (3) 1980 (5); v A 1975 (6) 1979 (3); v NZ 1979 (3); v In 1974 (5) 1978 (6); v P 1974 (2) 1980 (4)*
Kanhai, R. B. 79: v E 1959 (5) 1967 (5) 1973 (5); v A 1964 (5) 1972 (5); v In 1961 (5) 1970 (5); v P 1957 (5); *v E 1957 (5) 1963 (5) 1966 (5) 1973 (3); v A 1960 (5) 1968 (5); v In 1958 (5) 1966 (3); v P 1958 (3)*
Kentish, E. S. M. 2: v E 1947 (1) 1953 (1)
King, C. L. 9: v P 1976 (1); *v E 1976 (3) 1980 (1); v A 1979 (1); v NZ 1979 (3)*
King, F. M. 14: v E 1953 (3); v A 1954 (4); v In 1952 (5); *v NZ 1955 (2)*
King, L. A. 2: v E 1967 (1); v In 1961 (1)

Lambert, C. B. 1: *v E 1991*
Lara, B. C. 16: v E 1993 (5); v SA 1991 (1); v P 1992 (3); *v A 1992 (5); v P 1990 (1); v SL 1993 (1)*
Lashley, P. D. 4: *v E 1966 (2); v A 1960 (2)*
Legall, R. 4: v In 1952 (4)
Lewis, D. M. 3: v In 1970 (3)
Lloyd, C. H. 110: v E 1967 (5) 1973 (5) 1980 (4); v A 1972 (3) 1977 (2) 1983 (4); v NZ 1971 (2); v In 1970 (5) 1975 (4) 1982 (5); v P 1976 (5); *v E 1969 (3) 1973 (3) 1976 (5) 1980 (4) 1984 (5); v A 1968 (4) 1975 (6) 1979 (2) 1981 (3) 1984 (5); v NZ 1968 (3) 1979 (3); v In 1966 (3) 1974 (5) 1983 (6); v P 1974 (2) 1980 (4)*
Logie, A. L. 52: v E 1989 (3); v A 1983 (1) 1990 (5); v NZ 1984 (4); v In 1982 (5) 1988 (4); v P 1987 (3); *v E 1988 (5) 1991 (4); v A 1988 (5); v NZ 1986 (3); v In 1983 (3) 1987 (4); v P 1990 (3)*

McMorris, E. D. A. St J. 13: v E 1959 (4); v In 1961 (4); v P 1957 (1); *v E 1963 (2) 1966 (2)*
McWatt, C. A. 6: v E 1953 (5); v A 1954 (1)
Madray, I. S. 2: v P 1957 (2)
Marshall, M. D. 81: v E 1980 (1) 1985 (5) 1989 (2); v A 1983 (4) 1990 (5); v NZ 1984 (4); v In 1982 (5) 1988 (3); v P 1987 (2); *v E 1980 (4) 1984 (4) 1988 (5) 1991 (5); v A 1984 (5) 1988 (5); v NZ 1986 (3); v In 1978 (3) 1983 (6); v P 1980 (4) 1986 (3) 1990 (3)*
Marshall, N. E. 1: v A 1954
Marshall, R. E. 4: *v A 1951 (2); v NZ 1951 (2)*
Martin, F. R. 9: v E 1929 (1); *v E 1928 (3); v A 1930 (5)*
Martindale, E. A. 10: v E 1934 (4); *v E 1933 (3) 1939 (3)*
Mattis, E. H. 4: v E 1980 (4)
Mendonca, I. L. 2: v In 1961 (2)
Merry, C. A. 2: *v E 1933 (2)*
Miller, R. 1: v In 1952
Moodie, G. H. 1: v E 1934
Moseley, E. A. 2: v E 1989 (2)

Murray, D. A. 19: v E 1980 (4); v A 1977 (3); *v A 1981 (2); v In 1978 (6); v P 1980 (4)*
Murray, D. L. 62: v E 1967 (5) 1973 (5); v A 1972 (4) 1977 (2); v In 1975 (4); v P 1976 (5); *v E 1963 (5) 1973 (3) 1976 (5) 1980 (5); v A 1975 (6) 1979 (3); v NZ 1979 (3); v In 1974 (5); v P 1974 (2)*
Murray, J. R. 12: v E 1993 (5); v P 1992 (3); *v A 1992 (3); v SL 1993 (1)*

Nanan, R. 1: *v P 1980*
Neblett, J. M. 1: v E 1934
Noreiga, J. M. 4: v In 1970 (4)
Nunes, R. K. 4: v E 1929 (1); *v E 1928 (3)*
Nurse, S. M. 29: v E 1959 (1) 1967 (5); v A 1964 (4); v In 1961 (1); *v E 1966 (5); v A 1960 (3) 1968 (5); v NZ 1968 (3); v In 1966 (2)*

Padmore, A. L. 2: v In 1975 (1); *v E 1976 (1)*
Pairaudeau, B. H. 13: v E 1953 (2); v In 1952 (5): *v E 1957 (2); v NZ 1955 (4)*
Parry, D. R. 12: v A 1977 (5); *v NZ 1979 (1); v In 1978 (6)*
Passailaigue, C. C. 1: v E 1929
Patterson, B. P. 28: v E 1985 (5) 1989 (1); v A 1990 (5); v SA 1991 (1); v P 1987 (1); *v E 1988 (2) 1991 (3); v A 1988 (4) 1992 (1); v In 1987 (4); v P 1986 (1)*
Payne, T. R. O. 1: v E 1985
Phillip, N. 9: v A 1977 (3); *v In 1978 (6)*
Pierre, L. R. 1: v E 1947

Rae, A. F. 15: v In 1952 (2); *v E 1950 (4); v A 1951 (3); v NZ 1951 (1); v In 1948 (5)*
Ramadhin, S. 43: v E 1953 (5) 1959 (4); v A 1954 (4); v In 1952 (4); *v E 1950 (4) 1957 (5); v A 1951 (5) 1960 (2); v NZ 1951 (2) 1955 (4); v In 1958 (2); v P 1958 (2)*
Richards, I. V. A. 121: v E 1980 (4) 1985 (5) 1989 (3); v A 1977 (2) 1983 (5) 1990 (5); v NZ 1984 (4); v In 1975 (4) 1982 (5) 1988 (4); v P 1976 (5) 1987 (2); *v E 1976 (4) 1980 (5) 1984 (5) 1988 (5) 1991 (5); v A 1975 (6) 1979 (3) 1981 (3) 1984 (5) 1988 (5); v NZ 1986 (3); v In 1974 (5) 1983 (6) 1987 (4); v P 1974 (2) 1980 (4) 1986 (3)*
Richardson, R. B. 76: v E 1985 (5) 1989 (4) 1993 (4); v A 1983 (5) 1990 (5); v SA 1991 (1); v NZ 1984 (4); v In 1988 (4); v P 1987 (3) 1992 (3); *v E 1988 (3) 1991 (5); v A 1984 (5) 1988 (5) 1992 (5); v NZ 1986 (3); v In 1983 (1) 1987 (4); v P 1986 (3) 1990 (3); v SL 1993 (1)*
Rickards, K. R. 2: v E 1947 (1); *v A 1951 (1)*
Roach, C. A. 16: v E 1929 (4) 1934 (1); *v E 1928 (3) 1933 (3); v A 1930 (5)*
Roberts, A. M. E. 47: v E 1973 (1) 1980 (3); v A 1977 (2); v In 1975 (2) 1982 (5); v P 1976 (5); *v E 1976 (5) 1980 (3); v A 1975 (5) 1979 (3) 1981 (2); v NZ 1979 (2); v In 1974 (5) 1983 (2); v P 1974 (2)*
Roberts, A. T. 1: *v NZ 1955*
Rodriguez, W. V. 5: v E 1967 (1); v A 1964 (1); v In 1961 (2); *v E 1963 (1)*
Rowe, L. G. 30: v E 1973 (5); v A 1972 (3); v NZ 1971 (4); v In 1975 (4); *v E 1976 (2); v A 1975 (6) 1979 (3); v NZ 1979 (3)*

St Hill, E. L. 2: v E 1929 (2)
St Hill, W. H. 3: v E 1929 (1); *v E 1928 (2)*
Scarlett, R. O. 3: v E 1959 (3)
Scott, A. P. H. 1: v In 1952
Scott, O. C. 8: v E 1929 (1); *v E 1928 (2); v A 1930 (5)*
Sealey, B. J. 1: *v E 1933*
Sealy, J. E. D. 11: v E 1929 (2) 1934 (4); *v E 1939 (3); v A 1930 (2)*
Shepherd, J. N. 5: v In 1970 (2); *v E 1969 (3)*
Shillingford, G. C. 7: v NZ 1971 (2); v In 1970 (3); *v E 1969 (2)*
Shillingford, I. T. 4: v A 1977 (1); v P 1976 (3)
Shivnarine, S. 8: v A 1977 (3); *v In 1978 (5)*
Simmons, P. V. 19: v E 1993 (2); v SA 1991 (1); v P 1987 (1) 1992 (3); *v E 1991 (5); v A 1992 (5); v In 1987 (1); v SL 1993 (1)*
Singh, C. K. 2: v E 1959 (2)
Small, J. A. 3: v E 1929 (1); *v E 1928 (2)*
Small, M. A. 2: v A 1983 (1); *v E 1984 (1)*
Smith, C. W. 5: v In 1961 (1); *v A 1960 (4)*
Smith, O. G. 26: v A 1954 (4); v P 1957 (5); *v E 1957 (5); v NZ 1955 (4); v In 1958 (5); v P 1958 (3)*

Sobers, G. S. 93: v E 1953 (1) 1959 (5) 1967 (5) 1973 (4); v A 1954 (4) 1964 (5); v NZ 1971 (5); v In 1961 (5); 1970 (5); v P 1957 (5); *v E 1957 (5) 1963 (5) 1966 (5) 1969 (3) 1973 (3); v A 1960 (5) 1968 (5); v NZ 1955 (4) 1968 (3); v In 1958 (5) 1966 (3); v P 1958 (3)*

Solomon, J. S. 27: v E 1959 (2); v A 1964 (4); v In 1961 (4); *v E 1963 (5); v A 1960 (5); v In 1958 (4); v P 1958 (3)*

Stayers, S. C. 4: v In 1961 (4)

Stollmeyer, J. B. 32: v E 1947 (2) 1953 (5); v A 1954 (2); v In 1952 (5); *v E 1939 (3) 1950 (4); v A 1951 (5); v NZ 1951 (2); v In 1948 (4)*

Stollmeyer, V. H. 1: *v E 1939*

Taylor, J. 3: v P 1957 (1); *v In 1958 (1); v P 1958 (1)*

Trim, J. 4: v E 1947 (1); *v A 1951 (1); v In 1948 (2)*

Valentine, A. L. 36: v E 1953 (3); v A 1954 (3); v In 1952 (5) 1961 (2); v P 1957 (1); *v E 1950 (4) 1957 (2); v A 1951 (5) 1960 (5); v NZ 1951 (2) 1955 (4)*

Valentine, V. A. 2: *v E 1933 (2)*

Walcott, C. L. 44: v E 1947 (4) 1953 (5) 1959 (2); v A 1954 (5); v In 1952 (5); v P 1957 (4); *v E 1950 (4) 1957 (5); v A 1951 (3); v NZ 1951 (2); v In 1948 (5)*

Walcott, L. A. 1: v E 1929

Walsh, C. A. 65: v E 1985 (1) 1989 (3) 1993 (5); v A 1990 (5); v SA 1991 (1); v NZ 1984 (1); v In 1988 (4); v P 1987 (3) 1992 (3); *v E 1988 (5) 1991 (5); v A 1984 (5) 1988 (5) 1992 (5); v NZ 1986 (3); v In 1987 (4); v P 1986 (3) 1990 (3); v SL 1993 (1)*

Watson, C. 7: v E 1959 (5); v In 1961 (1); *v A 1960 (1)*

Weekes, E. D. 48: v E 1947 (4) 1953 (4); v A 1954 (5) v In 1952 (5); v P 1957 (5); *v E 1950 (4) 1957 (5); v A 1951 (5); v NZ 1951 (2) 1955 (4); v In 1948 (5)*

Weekes, K. H. 2: *v E 1939 (2)*

White, W. A. 2: v A 1964 (2)

Wight, C. V. 2: v E 1929 (1); *v E 1928 (1)*

Wight, G. L. 1: v In 1952

Wiles, C. A. 1: *v E 1933*

Willett, E. T. 5: v A 1972 (3); *v In 1974 (2)*

Williams, A. B. 7: v A 1977 (3); *v In 1978 (4)*

Williams, D. 3: v SA 1991 (1); *v A 1992 (2)*

Williams, E. A. V. 4: v E 1947 (3); *v E 1939 (1)*

Williams, S. C. 1: v E 1993

Wishart, K. L. 1: v E 1934

Worrell, F. M. M. 51: v E 1947 (3) 1953 (4) 1959 (4); v A 1954 (4); v In 1952 (5) 1961 (5); *v E 1950 (4) 1957 (5) 1963 (5); v A 1951 (5) 1960 (5); v NZ 1951 (2)*

NEW ZEALAND

Number of Test cricketers: 190

Alabaster, J. C. 21: v E 1962 (2); v WI 1955 (1); v In 1967 (4); *v E 1958 (2); v SA 1961 (5); v WI 1971 (2); v In 1955 (4); v P 1955 (1)*

Allcott, C. F. W. 6: v E 1929 (2); v SA 1931 (1); *v E 1931 (3)*

Anderson, R. W. 9: v E 1977 (3); *v E 1978 (3); v P 1976 (3)*

Anderson, W. M. 1: v A 1945

Andrews, B. 2: *v A 1973 (2)*

Badcock, F. T. 7: v E 1929 (3) 1932 (2); v SA 1931 (2)

Barber, R. T. 1: v WI 1955

Bartlett, G. A. 10: v E 1965 (2); v In 1967 (2); v P 1964 (1); *v SA 1961 (5)*

Barton, P. T. 7: v E 1962 (3); *v SA 1961 (4)*

Beard, D. D. 4: v WI 1951 (2) 1955 (2)

Beck, J. E. F. 8: v WI 1955 (4); *v SA 1953 (4)*

Bell, W. 2: *v SA 1953 (2)*

Bilby, G. P. 2: v E 1965 (2)

Blain, T. E. 11: v A 1992 (2); v P 1993 (3); *v E 1986 (1); v A 1993 (3); v In 1988 (2)*

Blair, R. W. 19: v E 1954 (1) 1958 (2) 1962 (2); v SA 1952 (2) 1963 (3); v WI 1955 (2); *v E 1958 (3); v SA 1953 (4)*

Blunt, R. C. 9: v E 1929 (4); v SA 1931 (2); *v E 1931 (3)*

Bolton, B. A. 2: v E 1958 (2)

Boock, S. L. 30: v E 1977 (3) 1983 (2) 1987 (1); v WI 1979 (3) 1986 (2); v P 1978 (3) 1984 (2) 1988 (1); *v E 1978 (3); v A 1985 (1); v WI 1984 (3); v P 1984 (3); v SL 1983 (3)*

Bracewell, B. P. 6: v P 1978 (1) 1984 (1); *v E 1978 (3); v A 1980 (1)*

Bracewell, J. G. 41: v E 1987 (3); v A 1985 (2) 1989 (1); v WI 1986 (3); v In 1980 (1) 1989 (2); v P 1988 (2); *v E 1983 (4) 1986 (3) 1990 (3); v A 1980 (3) 1985 (2) 1987 (3); v WI 1984 (1); v In 1988 (3); v P 1984 (2); v SL 1983 (2) 1986 (1)*

Bradburn, G. E. 5: v SL 1990 (1); *v P 1990 (3); v SL 1992 (1)*

Bradburn, W. P. 2: v SA 1963 (2)

Brown, V. R. 2: *v A 1985 (2)*

Burgess, M. G. 50: v E 1970 (1) 1977 (3); v A 1973 (1) 1976 (2); v WI 1968 (2); v In 1967 (4) 1975 (3); v P 1972 (3) 1978 (3); *v E 1969 (2) 1973 (3) 1978 (3); v A 1980 (3); v WI 1971 (5); v In 1969 (3) 1976 (3); v P 1969 (3) 1976 (3)*

Burke, C. 1: v A 1945

Burtt, T. B. 10: v E 1946 (1) 1950 (2); v SA 1952 (1); v WI 1951 (2); *v E 1949 (4)*

Butterfield, L. A. 1: v A 1945

Cairns, B. L. 43: v E 1974 (1) 1977 (1) 1983 (3); v A 1976 (1) 1981 (3); v WI 1979 (3); v In 1975 (1) 1980 (3); v P 1978 (3) 1984 (3); v SL 1982 (2); *v E 1978 (2) 1983 (4); v A 1973 (1) 1980 (3) 1985 (1); v WI 1984 (2); v In 1976 (2); v P 1976 (2); v SL 1983 (2)*

Cairns, C. L. 10: v E 1991 (3); v A 1992 (2); v P 1993 (1); v SL 1990 (1); *v A 1989 (1) 1993 (2)*

Cameron, F. J. 19: v E 1962 (3); v SA 1963 (3); v P 1964 (3); *v E 1965 (2); v SA 1961 (5); v In 1964 (1); v P 1964 (2)*

Cave, H. B. 19: v E 1954 (2); v WI 1955 (3); *v E 1949 (4) 1958 (2); v In 1955 (5); v P 1955 (3)*

Chapple, M. E. 14: v E 1954 (1) 1965 (1); v SA 1952 (1) 1963 (3); v WI 1955 (1); *v SA 1953 (5) 1961 (2)*

Chatfield, E. J. 43: v E 1974 (1) 1977 (1) 1983 (3) 1987 (3); v A 1976 (2) 1981 (1) 1985 (3); v WI 1986 (3); v P 1984 (3) 1988 (2); v SL 1982 (2); *v E 1983 (3) 1986 (1); v A 1985 (2) 1987 (2); v WI 1984 (4); v In 1988 (3); v P 1984 (1); v SL 1983 (2) 1986 (1)*

Cleverley, D. C. 2: v SA 1931 (1); v A 1945 (1)

Collinge, R. O. 35: v E 1970 (2) 1974 (2) 1977 (3); v A 1973 (3); v In 1967 (2) 1975 (3); v P 1964 (3) 1972 (2); *v E 1965 (3) 1969 (1) 1973 (3) 1978 (1); v In 1964 (2) 1976 (1); v P 1964 (2) 1976 (2)*

Colquhoun, I. A. 2: v E 1954 (2)

Coney, J. V. 52: v E 1983 (3); v A 1973 (2) 1981 (3) 1985 (3); v WI 1979 (3) 1986 (3); v In 1980 (3); v P 1978 (3) 1984 (3); v SL 1982 (2); *v E 1983 (4) 1986 (3); v A 1973 (2) 1980 (2) 1985 (3); v WI 1984 (4); v P 1984 (3); v SL 1983 (3)*

Congdon, B. E. 61: v E 1965 (3) 1970 (2) 1974 (2) 1977 (3); v A 1973 (3) 1976 (2); v WI 1968 (3); v In 1967 (4) 1975 (3); v P 1964 (3) 1972 (3); *v E 1965 (3) 1969 (3) 1973 (3) 1978 (3); v A 1973 (3); v WI 1971 (5); v In 1964 (3) 1969 (3); v P 1964 (1) 1969 (3)*

Cowie, J. 9: v E 1946 (1); v A 1945 (1); *v E 1937 (3) 1949 (4)*

Cresswell G. F. 3: v E 1950 (2); *v E 1949 (1)*

Cromb, I. B. 5: v SA 1931 (2); *v E 1931 (3)*

Crowe, J. J. 39: v E 1983 (3) 1987 (2); v A 1989 (1); v WI 1986 (3); v P 1984 (3) 1988 (2); v SL 1982 (2); *v.E 1983 (2) 1986 (3); v A 1985 (3) 1987 (3) 1989 (1); v WI 1984 (4); v P 1984 (3); v SL 1983 (3) 1986 (1)*

Crowe, M. D. 70: v E 1983 (3) 1987 (3) 1991 (3); v A 1981 (3) 1985 (3) 1992 (3); v WI 1986 (3); v In 1989 (3); v P 1984 (3) 1988 (2); v SL 1990 (2); *v E 1983 (4) 1986 (3) 1990 (3) 1994 (3); v A 1985 (3) 1987 (3) 1989 (1) 1993 (1); v WI 1984 (4); v P 1984 (3) 1990 (3); v SL 1983 (3) 1986 (1) 1992 (2); v Z 1992 (2)*

Cunis, R. S. 20: v E 1965 (3) 1970 (2); v SA 1963 (1); v WI 1968 (3); *v E 1969 (1); v WI 1971 (5); v In 1969 (3); v P 1969 (2)*

D'Arcy, J. W. 5: *v E 1958 (5)*

Davis, H. T. 1: *v E 1994*

de Groen, R. P. 4: v P 1993 (2); *v A 1993 (2)*

Dempster, C. S. 10: v E 1929 (4) 1932 (2); v SA 1931 (2); *v E 1931 (2)*

Dempster, E. W. 5: v SA 1952 (1); *v SA 1953 (4)*

Dick, A. E. 17: v E 1962 (3); v SA 1963 (2); v P 1964 (2); *v E 1965 (2); v SA 1961 (5); v P 1964 (3)*

Dickinson, G. R. 3: v E 1929 (2); v SA 1931 (1)
Donnelly, M. P. 7: *v E 1937 (3) 1949 (4)*
Doull, S. B. 6: v P 1993 (3); *v A 1993 (2); v Z 1992 (1)*
Dowling, G. T. 39: v E 1962 (3) 1970 (2); v SA 1963 (1); v WI 1968 (3); v In 1967 (4); v P 1964 (2); *v E 1965 (3) 1969 (3); v SA 1961 (4); v WI 1971 (2); v In 1964 (4) 1969 (3); v P 1964 (2) 1969 (3)*
Dunning, J. A. 4: v E 1932 (1); *v E 1937 (3)*

Edgar, B. A. 39: v E 1983 (3); v A 1981 (3) 1985 (3); v WI 1979 (3); v In 1980 (3); v P 1978 (3); v SL 1982 (2); *v E 1978 (3) 1983 (4) 1986 (3); v A 1980 (3) 1985 (3); v P 1984 (3)*
Edwards, G. N. 8: v E 1977 (1); v A 1976 (2); v In 1980 (3); *v E 1978 (2)*
Emery, R. W. G. 2: v WI 1951 (2)

Fisher, F. E. 1: v SA 1952
Fleming, S. P. 4: v In 1993 (1); *v E 1994 (3)*
Foley, H. 1: v E 1929
Franklin, T. J. 21: v E 1987 (3); v A 1985 (1) 1989 (1); v In 1989 (3); v SL 1990 (3); *v E 1983 (1) 1990 (3); v In 1988 (3); v P 1990 (3)*
Freeman, D. L. 2: v E 1932 (2)

Gallichan, N. 1: *v E 1937*
Gedye, S. G. 4: v SA 1963 (3); v P 1964 (1)
Gillespie, S. R. 1: v A 1985
Gray, E. J. 10: *v E 1983 (2) 1986 (3); v A 1987 (1); v In 1988 (1); v P 1984 (2); v SL 1986 (1)*
Greatbatch, M. J. 34: v E 1987 (2) 1991 (1); v A 1989 (1) 1992 (3); v In 1989 (3) 1993 (1); v P 1988 (1) 1992 (1) 1993 (3); v SL 1990 (2); *v E 1990 (3) 1994 (1); v A 1989 (1) 1993 (3); v In 1988 (3); v P 1990 (3); v Z 1992 (2)*
Guillen, S. C. 3: v WI 1955 (3)
Guy, J. W. 12: v E 1958 (2); v WI 1955 (2); *v SA 1961 (2); v In 1955 (5); v P 1955 (1)*

Hadlee, D. R. 26: v E 1974 (2) 1977 (1); v A 1973 (3) 1976 (1); v In 1975 (3); v P 1972 (2); *v E 1969 (2) 1973 (3); v A 1973 (3); v In 1969 (3); v P 1969 (3)*
Hadlee, R. J. 86: v E 1977 (3) 1983 (3) 1987 (1); v A 1973 (2) 1976 (2) 1981 (3) 1985 (3) 1989 (1); v WI 1979 (3) 1986 (3); v In 1975 (2) 1980 (3) 1989 (3); v P 1972 (1) 1978 (3) 1984 (3) 1988 (2); v SL 1982 (2); *v E 1973 (1) 1978 (3) 1983 (4) 1986 (3) 1990 (3); v A 1973 (3) 1980 (3) 1985 (3) 1987 (3); v WI 1984 (4); v In 1976 (3) 1988 (3); v P 1976 (3); v SL 1983 (3) 1986 (1)*
Hadlee, W. A. 11: v E 1946 (1) 1950 (2); v A 1945 (1); *v E 1937 (3) 1949 (4)*
Harford, N. S. 8: *v E 1958 (4); v In 1955 (2); v P 1955 (2)*
Harford, R. I. 3: v In 1967 (3)
Harris, C. Z. 5: v A 1992 (1); v P 1992 (1); *v A 1993 (1); v SL 1992 (2)*
Harris, P. G. Z. 9: v P 1964 (1); *v SA 1961 (5); v In 1955 (1); v P 1955 (2)*
Harris, R. M. 2: v E 1958 (2)
Hart, M. N. 6: v In 1993 (1); v P 1993 (2); *v E 1994 (3)*
Hartland, B. R. 9: v E 1991 (3); v In 1993 (1); v P 1992 (1) 1993 (1); *v E 1994 (1); v SL 1992 (2)*
Haslam, M. J. 2: *v Z 1992 (2)*
Hastings, B. F. 31: v E 1974 (2); v A 1973 (3); v WI 1968 (3); v In 1975 (1); v P 1972 (3); *v E 1969 (3) 1973 (3); v A 1973 (3); v WI 1971 (5); v In 1969 (2); v P 1969 (3)*
Hayes, J. A. 15: v E 1950 (2) 1954 (1); v WI 1951 (2); *v E 1958 (4); v In 1955 (5); v P 1955 (1)*
Henderson, M. 1: v E 1929
Horne, P. A. 4: v WI 1986 (1); *v A 1987 (1); v P 1990 (1); v SL 1986 (1)*
Hough, K. W. 2: v E 1958 (2)
Howarth, G. P. 47: v E 1974 (2) 1977 (3) 1983 (3); v A 1976 (2) 1981 (3); v WI 1979 (3); v In 1980 (3); v P 1978 (3) 1984 (3); v SL 1982 (2); *v E 1978 (3) 1983 (4); v A 1980 (2); v WI 1984 (4); v In 1976 (2); v P 1976 (2); v SL 1983 (3)*
Howarth, H. J. 30: v E 1970 (2) 1974 (2); v A 1973 (3) 1976 (2); v In 1975 (2); v P 1972 (3); *v E 1969 (3) 1973 (2); v WI 1971 (5); v In 1969 (3); v P 1969 (3)*

James, K. C. 11: v E 1929 (4) 1932 (2); v SA 1931 (2); *v E 1931 (3)*
Jarvis, T. W. 13: v E 1965 (1); v P 1972 (3); *v WI 1971 (4); v In 1964 (2); v P 1964 (3)*
Jones, A. H. 37: v E 1987 (1) 1991 (3); v A 1989 (1) 1992 (3); v In 1989 (3); v P 1988 (2) 1992 (1) 1993 (3); v SL 1990 (3); *v E 1990 (3); v A 1987 (3) 1993 (3); v In 1988 (3); v SL 1986 (1) 1992 (2); v Z 1992 (2)*

Kerr, J. L. 7: v E 1932 (2); v SA 1931 (1); *v E 1931 (2) 1937 (2)*
Kuggeleijn, C. M. 2: *v In 1988 (2)*

Larsen, G. R. 1: *v E 1994*
Latham, R. T. 4: v E 1991 (1); v P 1992 (1); *v Z 1992 (2)*
Lees, W. K. 21: v E 1977 (2); v A 1976 (1); v WI 1979 (3); v P 1978 (3); v SL 1982 (2); *v E 1983 (2); v A 1980 (2); v In 1976 (3); v P 1976 (3)*
Leggat, I. B. 1: *v SA 1953*
Leggat, J. G. 9: v E 1954 (1); v SA 1952 (1); v WI 1951 (1) 1955 (1); *v In 1955 (3); v P 1955 (2)*
Lissette, A. F. 2: v WI 1955 (2)
Lowry, T. C. 7: v E 1929 (4); *v E 1931 (3)*

MacGibbon, A. R. 26: v E 1950 (2) 1954 (2); v SA 1952 (1); v WI 1955 (3); *v E 1958 (5); v SA 1953 (5); v In 1955 (5); v P 1955 (3)*
McEwan, P. E. 4: v WI 1979 (1); *v A 1980 (2); v P 1984 (1)*
McGirr, H. M. 2: v E 1929 (2)
McGregor, S. N. 25: v E 1954 (2) 1958 (2); v SA 1963 (3); v WI 1955 (4); v P 1964 (2); *v SA 1961 (5); v In 1955 (4); v P 1955 (3)*
McLeod E. G. 1: v E 1929
McMahon T. G. 5: v WI 1955 (1); *v In 1955 (3); v P 1955 (1)*
McRae, D. A. N. 1: v A 1945
Matheson, A. M. 2: v E 1929 (1); *v E 1931 (1)*
Meale, T. 2: *v E 1958 (2)*
Merritt, W. E. 6: v E 1929 (4); *v E 1931 (2)*
Meuli, E. M. 1: v SA 1952
Milburn, B. D. 3: v WI 1968 (3)
Miller, L. S. M. 13: v SA 1952 (2); v WI 1955 (3); *v E 1958 (4); v SA 1953 (4)*
Mills, J. E. 7: v E 1929 (3) 1932 (1); *v E 1931 (3)*
Moir, A. M. 17: v E 1950 (2) 1954 (2) 1958 (2); v SA 1952 (1); v WI 1951 (2) 1955 (1); *v E 1958 (2); v In 1955 (2); v P 1955 (3)*
Moloney D. A. R. 3: *v E 1937 (3)*
Mooney, F. L. H. 14: v E 1950 (2); v SA 1952 (2); v WI 1951 (2); *v E 1949 (3); v SA 1953 (5)*
Morgan, R. W. 20: v E 1965 (2) 1970 (2); v WI 1968 (1); v P 1964 (2); *v E 1965 (3); v WI 1971 (3); v In 1964 (4); v P 1964 (3)*
Morrison, B. D. 1: v E 1962
Morrison, D. K. 35: v E 1987 (3) 1991 (3); v A 1989 (1) 1992 (3); v In 1989 (3) 1993 (1); v P 1988 (1) 1992 (1) 1993 (2); v SL 1990 (3); *v E 1990 (3); v A 1987 (3) 1989 (1) 1993 (3); v In 1988 (1); v P 1990 (3)*
Morrison, J. F. M. 17: v E 1974 (2); v A 1973 (3) 1981 (3); v In 1975 (3); *v A 1973 (3); v In 1976 (1); v P 1976 (2)*
Motz, R. C. 32: v E 1962 (2) 1965 (3); v SA 1963 (2); v WI 1968 (3); v In 1967 (4); v P 1964 (3); *v E 1965 (3) 1969 (3); v SA 1961 (5); v In 1964 (3); v P 1964 (1)*
Murray, B. A. G. 13: v E 1970 (1); v In 1967 (4); *v E 1969 (2); v In 1969 (3); v P 1969 (3)*

Nash, D. J. 6: v In 1993 (1); *v E 1994 (3); v SL 1992 (1); v Z 1992 (1)*
Newman J. 3: v E 1932 (2); v SA 1931 (1)

O'Sullivan, D. R. 11: v In 1975 (1); v P 1972 (1); *v A 1973 (3); v In 1976 (3); v P 1976 (3)*
Overton, G. W. F. 3: *v SA 1953 (3)*
Owens, M. B. 8: v A 1992 (2); v P 1992 (1) 1993 (1); *v E 1994 (2); v SL 1992 (2)*

Page, M. L. 14: v E 1929 (4) 1932 (2); v SA 1931 (2); *v E 1931 (3) 1937 (3)*
Parker, J. M. 36: v E 1974 (2) 1977 (3); v A 1973 (3) 1976 (2); v WI 1979 (3); v In 1975 (3); v P 1972 (1) 1978 (2); *v E 1973 (3) 1978 (2); v A 1973 (3) 1980 (3); v In 1976 (3); v P 1976 (3)*
Parker, N. M. 3: *v In 1976 (2); v P 1976 (1)*
Parore, A. C. 12: v E 1991 (1); v A 1992 (1); v In 1993 (1); v P 1992 (1); *v E 1990 (1) 1994 (3); v SL 1992 (2); v Z 1992 (2)*
Patel, D. N. 25: v E 1991 (3); v A 1992 (3); v WI 1986 (3); v P 1988 (1) 1992 (1); v SL 1990 (2); *v A 1987 (3) 1989 (1) 1993 (3); v P 1990 (3); v Z 1992 (2)*
Petherick, P. J. 6: v A 1976 (1); *v In 1976 (3); v P 1976 (2)*
Petrie, E. C. 14: v E 1958 (2) 1965 (3); *v E 1958 (5); v In 1955 (2); v P 1955 (2)*
Playle, W. R. 8: v E 1962 (3); *v E 1958 (5)*

Pocock, B. A. 6: v P 1993 (2); *v E 1994 (1); v A 1993 (3)*
Pollard, V. 32: v E 1965 (3) 1970 (1); v WI 1968 (3); v In 1967 (4); v P 1972 (1); *v E 1965 (3) 1969 (3) 1973 (3); v In 1964 (4) 1969 (1); v P 1964 (3) 1969 (3)*
Poore, M. B. 14: v E 1954 (1); v SA 1952 (1); *v SA 1953 (5); v In 1955 (4); v P 1955 (3)*
Priest, M. W. 1: *v E 1990*
Pringle, C. 11: v E 1991 (1); v In 1993 (1); v P 1993 (1); v SL 1990 (2); *v E 1994 (2); v P 1990 (3); v SL 1992 (1)*
Puna, N. 3: v E 1965 (3)

Rabone, G. O. 12: v E 1954 (2); v SA 1952 (1); v WI 1951 (2); *v E 1949 (4); v SA 1953 (3)*
Redmond, R. E. 1: v P 1972
Reid, J. F. 19: v A 1985 (3); v In 1980 (3); v P 1978 (1) 1984 (3); *v A 1985 (3); v P 1984 (3); v SL 1983 (3)*
Reid, J. R. 58: v E 1950 (2) 1954 (2) 1958 (2) 1962 (3); v SA 1952 (2) 1963 (3); v WI 1951 (2) 1955 (4); v P 1964 (3); *v E 1949 (2) 1958 (5) 1965 (3); v SA 1953 (5) 1961 (5); v In 1955 (5) 1964 (4); v P 1955 (3) 1964 (3)*
Roberts, A. D. G. 7: v In 1975 (2); *v In 1976 (3); v P 1976 (2)*
Roberts, A. W. 5: v E 1929 (1); v SA 1931 (2); *v E 1937 (2)*
Robertson, G. K. 1: v A 1985
Rowe, C. G. 1: v A 1945
Rutherford, K. R. 48: v E 1987 (2) 1991 (2); v A 1985 (3) 1989 (1) 1992 (3); v WI 1986 (2); v In 1989 (3) 1993 (1); v P 1992 (1) 1993 (3); v SL 1990 (3); *v E 1986 (1) 1990 (2) 1994 (3); v A 1987 (1) 1993 (3); v WI 1984 (4); v In 1988 (2); v P 1990 (3); v SL 1986 (1) 1992 (2); v Z 1992 (2)*

Scott, R. H. 1: v E 1946
Scott, V. J. 10: v E 1946 (1) 1950 (2); v A 1945 (1); v WI 1951 (2); *v E 1949 (4)*
Shrimpton, M. J. F. 10: v E 1962 (2) 1965 (3) 1970 (2); v SA 1963 (1); *v A 1973 (2)*
Sinclair, B. W. 21: v E 1962 (3) 1965 (3); v SA 1963 (3); v In 1967 (2); v P 1964 (2); *v E 1965 (3); v In 1964 (2); v P 1964 (3)*
Sinclair, I. M. 2: v WI 1955 (2)
Smith, F. B. 4: v E 1946 (1); v WI 1951 (1); *v E 1949 (2)*
Smith, H. D. 1: v E 1932
Smith, I. D. S. 63: v E 1983 (3) 1987 (3) 1991 (2); v A 1981 (3) 1985 (3) 1989 (1); v WI 1986 (3); v In 1980 (3) 1989 (3); v P 1984 (3) 1988 (2); v SL 1990 (3); *v E 1983 (2) 1986 (2) 1990 (2); v A 1980 (1) 1985 (3) 1987 (3) 1989 (1); v WI 1984 (4); v In 1988 (3); v P 1984 (3) 1990 (3); v SL 1983 (3) 1986 (1)*
Snedden, C. A. 1: v E 1946
Snedden, M. C. 25: v E 1983 (1) 1987 (2); v A 1981 (3) 1989 (1); v WI 1986 (1); v In 1980 (3) 1989 (3); v SL 1982 (2); *v E 1983 (1) 1990 (3); v A 1985 (1) 1987 (1) 1989 (1); v In 1988 (1); v SL 1986 (1)*
Sparling, J. T. 11: v E 1958 (2) 1962 (1); v SA 1963 (2); *v E 1958 (3); v SA 1961 (3)*
Stirling, D. A. 6: *v E 1986 (2); v WI 1984 (1); v P 1984 (3)*
Su'a, M. L. 11: v E 1991 (2); v A 1992 (2); v P 1992 (1); *v A 1993 (2); v SL 1992 (2); v Z 1992 (2)*
Sutcliffe, B. 42: v E 1946 (1) 1950 (2) 1954 (2) 1958 (2); v SA 1952 (2); v WI 1951 (2) 1955 (2); *v E 1949 (4) 1958 (4) 1965 (1); v SA 1953 (5); v In 1955 (5) 1964 (4); v P 1955 (3) 1964 (3)*

Taylor, B. R. 30: v E 1965 (1); v WI 1968 (3); v In 1967 (3); v P 1972 (3); *v E 1965 (2) 1969 (2) 1973 (3); v WI 1971 (4); v In 1964 (3) 1969 (2); v P 1964 (3) 1969 (1)*
Taylor, D. D. 3: v E 1946 (1); v WI 1955 (2)
Thomson, K. 2: v In 1967 (2)
Thomson, S. A. 11: v E 1991 (1); v In 1989 (1) 1993 (1); v P 1993 (3); v SL 1990 (2); *v E 1994 (3)*
Tindill, E. W. T. 5: v E 1946 (1); v A 1945 (1); *v E 1937 (3)*
Troup, G. B. 15: v A 1981 (2) 1985 (2); v WI 1979 (3); v In 1980 (2); v P 1978 (2); *v A 1980 (2); v WI 1984 (1); v In 1976 (1)*
Truscott, P. B. 1: v P 1964
Turner, G. M. 41: v E 1970 (2) 1974 (2); v A 1973 (3) 1976 (2); v WI 1968 (3); v In 1975 (3); v P 1972 (3); v SL 1982 (2); *v E 1969 (2) 1973 (3); v A 1973 (2); v WI 1971 (5); v In 1969 (3) 1976 (3); v P 1969 (1) 1976 (2)*

Vance, R. H. 4: v E 1987 (1); v P 1988 (2); *v A 1989 (1)*
Vaughan, J. T. C. 1: *v SL 1992*
Vivian, G. E. 5: *v WI 1971 (4); v In 1964 (1)*
Vivian, H. G. 7: v E 1932 (1); v SA 1931 (1); *v E 1931 (2) 1937 (3)*

Wadsworth, K. J. 33: v E 1970 (2) 1974 (2); v A 1973 (3); v In 1975 (3); v P 1972 (3); *v E 1969 (3) 1973 (3); v A 1973 (3); v WI 1971 (5); v In 1969 (3); v P 1969 (3)*
Wallace, W. M. 13: v E 1946 (1) 1950 (2); v A 1945 (1); v SA 1952 (2); *v E 1937 (3) 1949 (4)*
Ward, J. T. 8: v SA 1963 (1); v In 1967 (1); v P 1964 (1); *v E 1965 (1); v In 1964 (4)*
Watson, W. 15: v E 1991 (1); v A 1992 (2); v SL 1990 (3); *v E 1986 (2); v A 1989 (1) 1993 (1); v P 1990 (3); v Z 1992 (2)*
Watt, L. 1: v E 1954
Webb, M. G. 3: v E 1970 (1); v A 1973 (1); *v WI 1971 (1)*
Webb, P. N. 2: v WI 1979 (2)
Weir, G. L. 11: v E 1929 (3) 1932 (2); v SA 1931 (2); *v E 1931 (3) 1937 (1)*
White, D. J. 2: *v P 1990 (2)*
Whitelaw, P. E. 2: v E 1932 (2)
Wright, J. G. 82: v E 1977 (3) 1983 (3) 1987 (3) 1991 (3); v A 1981 (3) 1985 (2) 1989 (1) 1992 (3); v WI 1979 (3) 1986 (3); v In 1980 (3) 1989 (3); v P 1978 (3) 1984 (3) 1988 (2); v SL 1982 (2) 1990 (3); *v E 1978 (2) 1983 (3) 1986 (3) 1990 (3); v A 1980 (3) 1985 (3) 1987 (3) 1989 (1); v WI 1984 (4); v In 1988 (3); v P 1984 (3); v SL 1983 (3) 1992 (2)*

Young, B. A. 8: v In 1993 (1); v P 1993 (3); *v E 1994 (3); v A 1993 (1)*
Yuile, B. W. 17: v E 1962 (2); v WI 1968 (3); v In 1967 (1); v P 1964 (3); *v E 1965 (1); v In 1964 (3) 1969 (1); v P 1964 (1) 1969 (2)*

INDIA

Number of Test cricketers: 200

Abid Ali, S. 29: v E 1972 (4); v A 1969 (1); v WI 1974 (2); v NZ 1969 (3); *v E 1971 (3) 1974 (3); v A 1967 (4); v WI 1970 (5); v NZ 1967 (4)*
Adhikari, H. R. 21: v E 1951 (3); v A 1956 (2); v WI 1948 (5) 1958 (1); v P 1952 (2); *v E 1952 (3); v A 1947 (5)*
Amarnath, L. 24: v E 1933 (3) 1951 (3); v WI 1948 (5); v P 1952 (5); *v E 1946 (3); v A 1947 (5)*
Amarnath, M. 69: v E 1976 (2) 1984 (5); v A 1969 (1) 1979 (1) 1986 (3); v WI 1978 (2) 1983 (3) 1987 (3); v NZ 1976 (3); v P 1983 (2) 1986 (5); v SL 1986 (2); *v E 1979 (2) 1986 (2); v A 1977 (5) 1985 (3); v WI 1975 (4) 1982 (5); v NZ 1975 (3); v P 1978 (3) 1982 (6) 1984 (2); v SL 1985 (2)*
Amarnath, S. 10: v E 1976 (2): *v WI 1975 (2); v NZ 1975 (3); v P 1978 (3)*
Amar Singh 7: v E 1933 (3); *v E 1932 (1) 1936 (3)*
Amir Elahi 1: *v A 1947*
Amre, P. K. 11: v E 1992 (3); v Z 1992 (1); *v SA 1992 (4); v SL 1993 (3)*
Ankola, S. A. 1: *v P 1989*
Apte, A. L. 1: *v E 1959*
Apte, M. L. 7: v P 1952 (2); *v WI 1952 (5)*
Arshad Ayub 13: v WI 1987 (4); v NZ 1988 (3); *v WI 1988 (4); v P 1989 (2)*
Arun, B. 2: v SL 1986 (2)
Arun Lal 16: v WI 1987 (4); v NZ 1988 (3); v P 1986 (1); v SL 1982 (1); *v WI 1988 (4); v P 1982 (3)*
Azad, K. 7: v E 1981 (3); v WI 1983 (2); v P 1983 (1); *v NZ 1980 (1)*
Azharuddin, M. 62: v E 1984 (3) 1992 (3); v A 1986 (3); v WI 1987 (3); v NZ 1988 (3); v P 1986 (5); v SL 1986 (1) 1990 (1) 1993 (3); v Z 1992 (1); *v E 1986 (3) 1990 (3); v A 1985 (3) 1991 (5); v SA 1992 (4); v WI 1988 (3); v NZ 1989 (3) 1993 (1); v P 1989 (4); v SL 1985 (3) 1993 (3); v Z 1992 (1)*

Baig, A. A. 10: v A 1959 (3); v WI 1966 (2); v P 1960 (3); *v E 1959 (2)*
Banerjee, S. A. 1: v WI 1948
Banerjee, S. N. 1: v WI 1948
Banerjee, S. T. 1: *v A 1991*
Baqa Jilani, M. 1: *v E 1936*
Bedi, B. S. 67: v E 1972 (5) 1976 (5); v A 1969 (5); v WI 1966 (2) 1974 (4) 1978 (3); v NZ 1969 (3) 1976 (3); *v E 1967 (3) 1971 (3) 1974 (3) 1979 (3); v A 1967 (2) 1977 (5); v WI 1970 (5) 1975 (4); v NZ 1967 (4) 1975 (2); v P 1978 (3)*
Bhandari, P. 3: v A 1956 (1); v NZ 1955 (1); *v P 1954 (1)*
Bhat, A. R. 2: v WI 1983 (1); v P 1983 (1)

Binny, R. M. H. 27: v E 1979 (1); v WI 1983 (6); v P 1979 (6) 1983 (2) 1986 (3); *v E 1986 (3); v A 1980 (1) 1985 (2); v NZ 1980 (1); v P 1984 (1); v SL 1985 (1)*
Borde, C. G. 55: v E 1961 (5) 1963 (5); v A 1959 (5) 1964 (3) 1969 (1); v WI 1958 (4) 1966 (3); v NZ 1964 (4); v P 1960 (5); *v E 1959 (4) 1967 (3); v A 1967 (4); v WI 1961 (5); v NZ 1967 (4)*

Chandrasekhar, B. S. 58: v E 1963 (4) 1972 (5) 1976 (5); v A 1964 (2); v WI 1966 (3) 1974 (4) 1978 (4); v NZ 1964 (2) 1976 (3); *v E 1967 (3) 1971 (3) 1974 (2) 1979 (1); v A 1967 (2) 1977 (5); v WI 1975 (4); v NZ 1975 (3); v P 1978 (3)*
Chauhan, C. P. S. 40: v E 1972 (2); v A 1969 (1) 1979 (6); v WI 1978 (6); v NZ 1969 (2); v P 1979 (6); *v E 1979 (4); v A 1977 (4) 1980 (3); v NZ 1980 (3); v P 1978 (3)*
Chauhan, R. K. 11: v E 1992 (3); v SL 1993 (3); v Z 1992 (1); *v NZ 1993 (1); v SL 1993 (3)*
Chowdhury, N. R. 2: v E 1951 (1); v WI 1948 (1)
Colah, S. H. M. 2: v E 1933 (1); *v E 1932 (1)*
Contractor, N. J. 31: v E 1961 (5); v A 1956 (1) 1959 (5); v WI 1958 (5); v NZ 1955 (4); v P 1960 (5); *v E 1959 (4); v WI 1961 (2)*

Dani, H. T. 1: v P 1952
Desai, R. B. 28: v E 1961 (4) 1963 (2); v A 1959 (3); v WI 1958 (1); v NZ 1964 (3); v P 1960 (5); *v E 1959 (5); v A 1967 (1); v WI 1961 (3); v NZ 1967 (1)*
Dilawar Hussain 3: v E 1933 (2); *v E 1936 (1)*
Divecha, R. V. 5: v E 1951 (2); v P 1952 (1); *v E 1952 (2)*
Doshi, D. R. 33: v E 1979 (1) 1981 (6); v A 1979 (6); v P 1979 (6) 1983 (1); v SL 1982 (1); *v E 1982 (3); v A 1980 (3); v NZ 1980 (2); v P 1982 (4)*
Durani, S. A. 29: v E 1961 (5) 1963 (5) 1972 (3); v A 1959 (1) 1964 (3); v WI 1966 (1); v NZ 1964 (3); *v WI 1961 (5) 1970 (3)*

Engineer, F. M. 46: v E 1961 (4) 1972 (5); v A 1969 (5); v WI 1966 (1) 1974 (5); v NZ 1964 (4) 1969 (2); *v E 1967 (3) 1971 (3) 1974 (3); v A 1967 (4); v WI 1961 (3); v NZ 1967 (4)*

Gadkari, C. V. 6: *v WI 1952 (3); v P 1954 (3)*
Gaekwad, A. D. 40: v E 1976 (4) 1984 (3); v WI 1974 (3) 1978 (5) 1983 (6); v NZ 1976 (3); v P 1983 (3); *v E 1979 (2); v A 1977 (1); v WI 1975 (3) 1982 (5); v P 1984 (2)*
Gaekwad, D. K. 11: v WI 1958 (1); v P 1952 (2) 1960 (1); *v E 1952 (1) 1959 (4); v WI 1952 (2)*
Gaekwad, H. G. 1: v P 1952
Gandotra, A. 2: v A 1969 (1); v NZ 1969 (1)
Gavaskar, S. M. 125: v E 1972 (5) 1976 (5) 1979 (1) 1981 (6) 1984 (5); v A 1979 (6) 1986 (3); v WI 1974 (2) 1978 (6) 1983 (6); v NZ 1976 (3); v P 1979 (6) 1983 (3) 1986 (4); v SL 1982 (1) 1986 (3); *v E 1971 (3) 1974 (3) 1979 (4) 1982 (3) 1986 (3); v A 1977 (5) 1980 (3) 1985 (3); v WI 1970 (4) 1975 (4) 1982 (5); v NZ 1975 (3) 1980 (3); v P 1978 (3) 1982 (6) 1984 (2); v SL 1985 (3)*
Ghavri, K. D. 39: v E 1976 (3) 1979 (1); v A 1979 (6); v WI 1974 (3) 1978 (6); v NZ 1976 (2); v P 1979 (6); *v E 1979 (4); v A 1977 (3) 1980 (3); v NZ 1980 (1); v P 1978 (1)*
Ghorpade, J. M. 8: v A 1956 (1); v WI 1958 (1); v NZ 1955 (1); *v E 1959 (3); v WI 1952 (2)*
Ghulam Ahmed 22: v E 1951 (2); v A 1956 (2); v WI 1948 (3) 1958 (2); v NZ 1955 (1); v P 1952 (4); *v E 1952 (4); v P 1954 (4)*
Gopalan, M. J. 1: v E 1933
Gopinath, C. D. 8: v E 1951 (3); v A 1959 (1); v P 1952 (1); *v E 1952 (1); v P 1954 (2)*
Guard, G. M. 2: v A 1959 (1); v WI 1958 (1)
Guha, S. 4: v A 1969 (3); *v E 1967 (1)*
Gul Mahomed 8: v P 1952 (2); *v E 1946 (1); v A 1947 (5)*
Gupte, B. P. 3: v E 1963 (1); v NZ 1964 (1); v P 1960 (1)
Gupte, S. P. 36: v E 1951 (1) 1961 (2); v A 1956 (3); v WI 1958 (5); v NZ 1955 (5); v P 1952 (2) 1960 (3); *v E 1959 (5); v WI 1952 (5); v P 1954 (5)*
Gursharan Singh 1: *v NZ 1989*

Hafeez, A. 3: *v E 1946 (3)*
Hanumant Singh 14: v E 1963 (2); v A 1964 (3); v WI 1966 (2); v NZ 1964 (4) 1969 (1); *v E 1967 (2)*
Hardikar, M. S. 2: v WI 1958 (2)
Hazare, V. S. 30: v E 1951 (5); v WI 1948 (5); v P 1952 (3); *v E 1946 (3) 1952 (4); v A 1947 (5); v WI 1952 (5)*

Hindlekar, D. D. 4: *v E 1936 (1) 1946 (3)*
Hirwani, N. D. 14: v WI 1987 (1); v NZ 1988 (3); v SL 1990 (1); *v E 1990 (3); v WI 1988 (3); v NZ 1989 (3)*

Ibrahim, K. C. 4: v WI 1948 (4)
Indrajitsinhji, K. S. 4: v A 1964 (3); v NZ 1969 (1)
Irani, J. K. 2: *v A 1947 (2)*

Jadeja, A. D. 3: *v SA 1992 (3)*
Jahangir Khan, M. 4: *v E 1932 (1) 1936 (3)*
Jai, L. P. 1: v E 1933
Jaisimha, M. L. 39: v E 1961 (5) 1963 (5); v A 1959 (1) 1964 (3); v WI 1966 (2); v NZ 1964 (4) 1969 (1); v P 1960 (4); *v E 1959 (1); v A 1967 (2); v WI 1961 (4) 1970 (3); v NZ 1967 (4)*
Jamshedji, R. J. 1: v E 1933
Jayantilal, K. 1: *v WI 1970*
Joshi, P. G. 12: v E 1951 (2); v A 1959 (1); v WI 1958 (1); v P 1952 (1) 1960 (1); *v E 1959 (3); v WI 1952 (3)*

Kambli, V. G. 11: v E 1992 (3); v SL 1993 (3); v Z 1992 (1); *v NZ 1993 (1); v SL 1993 (3)*
Kanitkar, H. S. 2: v WI 1974 (2)
Kapil Dev 131: v E 1979 (1) 1981 (6) 1984 (4) 1992 (3); v A 1979 (6) 1986 (3); v WI 1978 (6) 1983 (6) 1987 (4); v NZ 1988 (3); v P 1979 (6) 1983 (3) 1986 (5); v SL 1982 (1) 1986 (3) 1990 (1) 1993 (3); v Z 1992 (1); *v E 1979 (4) 1982 (3) 1986 (3) 1990 (3); v A 1980 (3) 1985 (3) 1991 (5); v SA 1992 (4); v WI 1982 (5) 1988 (4); v NZ 1980 (3) 1989 (3) 1993 (1); v P 1978 (3) 1982 (6) 1984 (2) 1989 (4); v SL 1985 (3) 1993 (3); v Z 1992 (1)*
Kardar, A. H. (*see* Hafeez)
Kenny, R. B. 5: v A 1959 (4); v WI 1958 (1)
Kirmani, S. M. H. 88: v E 1976 (5) 1979 (1) 1981 (6) 1984 (5); v A 1979 (6); v WI 1978 (6) 1983 (6); v NZ 1976 (3); v P 1979 (6) 1983 (3); v SL 1982 (1); *v E 1982 (3); v A 1977 (5) 1980 (3) 1985 (3); v WI 1975 (4) 1982 (5); v NZ 1975 (3) 1980 (3); v P 1978 (3) 1982 (6) 1984 (2)*
Kischenchand, G. 5: v P 1952 (1); *v A 1947 (4)*
Kripal Singh, A. G. 14: v E 1961 (3) 1963 (2); v A 1956 (2) 1964 (1); v WI 1958 (1); v NZ 1955 (4); *v E 1959 (1)*
Krishnamurthy, P. 5: *v WI 1970 (5)*
Kulkarni, R. R. 3: v A 1986 (1); v P 1986 (2)
Kulkarni, U. N. 4: *v A 1967 (3); v NZ 1967 (1)*
Kumar, V. V. 2: v E 1961 (1); v P 1960 (1)
Kumble, A. 17: v E 1992 (3); v SL 1993 (3); v Z 1992 (1); *v E 1990 (1); v SA 1992 (4); v NZ 1993 (1); v SL 1993 (3); v Z 1992 (1)*
Kunderan, B. K. 18: v E 1961 (1) 1963 (5); v A 1959 (3); v WI 1966 (2); v NZ 1964 (1); v P 1960 (2); *v E 1967 (2); v WI 1961 (2)*

Lall Singh 1: *v E 1932*
Lamba, R. 4: v WI 1987 (1); v SL 1986 (3)

Madan Lal 39: v E 1976 (2) 1981 (6); v WI 1974 (2) 1983 (3); v NZ 1976 (1); v P 1983 (3); v SL 1982 (1); *v E 1974 (2) 1982 (3) 1986 (1); v A 1977 (2); v WI 1975 (4) 1982 (2); v NZ 1975 (3); v P 1982 (3) 1984 (1)*
Maka, E. S. 2: v P 1952 (1); *v WI 1952 (1)*
Malhotra, A. 7: v E 1981 (2) 1984 (1); v WI 1983 (3); *v E 1982 (1)*
Maninder Singh 35: v A 1986 (3); v WI 1983 (4) 1987 (3); v P 1986 (4); v SL 1986 (3); v Z 1992 (1); *v E 1986 (3); v WI 1982 (3); v P 1982 (5) 1984 (1) 1989 (3); v SL 1985 (2)*
Manjrekar, S. V. 30: v WI 1987 (1); v SL 1990 (1) 1993 (3); *v E 1990 (3); v A 1991 (5); v SA 1992 (4); v WI 1988 (4); v NZ 1989 (3) 1993 (1); v P 1989 (4); v Z 1992 (1)*
Manjrekar, V. L. 55: v E 1951 (2) 1961 (5) 1963 (4); v A 1956 (3) 1964 (3); v WI 1958 (4); v NZ 1955 (5) 1964 (1); v P 1952 (3) 1960 (5); *v E 1952 (4) 1959 (2); v WI 1952 (4) 1961 (5); v P 1954 (5)*
Mankad, A. V. 22: v E 1976 (1); v A 1969 (5); v WI 1974 (1); v NZ 1969 (2) 1976 (3); *v E 1971 (3) 1974 (1); v A 1977 (3); v WI 1970 (3)*
Mankad, V. 44: v E 1951 (5); v A 1956 (3); v WI 1948 (5) 1958 (2); v NZ 1955 (4); v P 1952 (4); *v E 1946 (3) 1952 (3); v A 1947 (5); v WI 1952 (5); v P 1954 (5)*
Mansur Ali Khan (*see* Pataudi)

Mantri, M. K. 4: v E 1951 (1); *v E 1952 (2); v P 1954 (1)*
Meherhomji, K. R. 1: *v E 1936*
Mehra, V. L. 8: v E 1961 (1) 1963 (2); v NZ 1955 (2); *v WI 1961 (3)*
Merchant, V. M. 10: v E 1933 (3) 1951 (1); *v E 1936 (3) 1946 (3)*
Milkha Singh, A. G. 4: v E 1961 (1); v A 1959 (1); v P 1960 (2)
Modi, R. S. 10: v E 1951 (1); v WI 1948 (5); v P 1952 (1); *v E 1946 (3)*
Mongia, N. R. 4: v SL 1993 (3); *v NZ 1993 (1)*
More, K. S. 49: v E 1992 (3); v A 1986 (2); v WI 1987 (4); v NZ 1988 (3); v P 1986 (5); v SL 1986 (3) 1990 (1); *v E 1986 (3) 1990 (3); v A 1991 (3); v SA 1992 (4); v WI 1988 (4); v NZ 1989 (3); v P 1989 (4); v SL 1993 (3); v Z 1992 (1)*
Muddiah, V. M. 2: v A 1959 (1); v P 1960 (1)
Mushtaq Ali, S. 11: v E 1933 (2) 1951 (1); v WI 1948 (3); *v E 1936 (3) 1946 (2)*

Nadkarni, R. G. 41: v E 1961 (1) 1963 (5); v A 1959 (5) 1964 (3); v WI 1958 (1) 1966 (1); v NZ 1955 (1) 1964 (4); v P 1960 (4); *v E 1959 (4); v A 1967 (3); v WI 1961 (5); v NZ 1967 (4)*
Naik, S. S. 3: v WI 1974 (2); *v E 1974 (1)*
Naoomal Jeoomal 3: v E 1933 (2); *v E 1932 (1)*
Narasimha Rao, M. V. 4: v A 1979 (2); v WI 1978 (2)
Navle, J. G. 2: v E 1933 (1); *v E 1932 (1)*
Nayak, S. V. 2: *v E 1982 (2)*
Nayudu, C. K. 7: v E 1933 (3); *v E 1932 (1) 1936 (3)*
Nayudu, C. S. 11: v E 1933 (2) 1951 (1); *v E 1936 (2) 1946 (2); v A 1947 (4)*
Nazir Ali, S. 2: v E 1933 (1); *v E 1932 (1)*
Nissar, Mahomed 6: v E 1933 (2); *v E 1932 (1) 1936 (3)*
Nyalchand, S. 1: v P 1952

Pai, A. M. 1: v NZ 1969
Palia, P. E. 2: *v E 1932 (1) 1936 (1)*
Pandit, C. S. 5: v A 1986 (2); *v E 1986 (1); v A 1991 (2)*
Parkar, G. A. 1: *v E 1982*
Parkar, R. D. 2: v E 1972 (2)
Parsana, D. D. 2: v WI 1978 (2)
Patankar, C. T. 1: v NZ 1955
Pataudi sen., Nawab of, 3: *v E 1946 (3)*
Pataudi jun., Nawab of (now Mansur Ali Khan) 46: v E 1961 (3) 1963 (5) 1972 (3); v A 1964 (3) 1969 (5); v WI 1966 (3) 1974 (4); v NZ 1964 (4) 1969 (3); *v E 1967 (3); v A 1967 (3); v WI 1961 (3); v NZ 1967 (4)*
Patel, B. P. 21: v E 1976 (5); v WI 1974 (3); v NZ 1976 (3); *v E 1974 (2); v A 1977 (2); v WI 1975 (3); v NZ 1975 (3)*
Patel, J. M. 7: v A 1956 (2) 1959 (3); v NZ 1955 (1); *v P 1954 (1)*
Patel, R. 1: v NZ 1988
Patiala, Yuvraj of, 1: v E 1933
Patil, S. M. 29: v E 1979 (1) 1981 (4) 1984 (2); v WI 1983 (2); v P 1979 (2) 1983 (3); v SL 1982 (1); *v E 1982 (2); v A 1980 (3); v NZ 1980 (3); v P 1982 (4) 1984 (2)*
Patil, S. R. 1: v NZ 1955
Phadkar, D. G. 31: v E 1951 (4); v A 1956 (1); v WI 1948 (4) 1958 (1); v NZ 1955 (4); v P 1952 (2); *v E 1952 (4); v A 1947 (4); v WI 1952 (4); v P 1954 (3)*
Prabhakar, M. 33: v E 1984 (2) 1992 (3); v SL 1990 (1) 1993 (3); v Z 1992 (1); *v E 1990 (3); v A 1991 (5); v SA 1992 (4); v NZ 1989 (3); v P 1989 (4); v SL 1993 (3); v Z 1992 (1)*
Prasanna, E. A. S. 49: v E 1961 (1) 1972 (3) 1976 (4); v A 1969 (5); v WI 1966 (1) 1974 (5); v NZ 1969 (3); *v E 1967 (3) 1974 (2); v A 1967 (4) 1977 (4); v WI 1961 (1) 1970 (3) 1975 (1); v NZ 1967 (4) 1975 (3); v P 1978 (2)*
Punjabi, P. H. 5: *v P 1954 (5)*

Rai Singh, K. 1: *v A 1947*
Rajinder Pal 1: v E 1963
Rajindernath, V. 1: v P 1952
Rajput, L. S. 2: *v SL 1985 (2)*
Raju, S. L. V. 18: v E 1992 (3); v SL 1990 (1) 1993 (3); *v A 1991 (4); v SA 1992 (2); v NZ 1989 (2) 1993 (1); v SL 1993 (1); v Z 1992 (1)*
Raman, W. V. 8: v WI 1987 (1); v NZ 1988 (1); *v SA 1992 (1); v WI 1988 (1); v NZ 1989 (3); v Z 1992 (1)*

Ramaswami, C. 2: *v E 1936 (2)*
Ramchand, G. S. 33: v A 1956 (3) 1959 (5); v WI 1958 (3); v NZ 1955 (5); v P 1952 (3); *v E 1952 (4); v WI 1952 (5); v P 1954 (5)*
Ramji, L. 1: v E 1933
Rangachary, C. R. 4: v WI 1948 (2); *v A 1947 (2)*
Rangnekar, K. M. 3: *v A 1947 (3)*
Ranjane, V. B. 7: v E 1961 (3) 1963 (1); v A 1964 (1); v WI 1958 (1); *v WI 1961 (1)*
Razdan, V. 2: *v P 1989 (2)*
Reddy, B. 4: *v E 1979 (4)*
Rege, M. R. 1: v WI 1948
Roy, A. 4: v A 1969 (2); v NZ 1969 (2)
Roy, Pankaj 43: v E 1951 (5); v A 1956 (3) 1959 (5); v WI 1958 (5); v NZ 1955 (3); v P 1952 (3) 1960 (1); *v E 1952 (4) 1959 (5); v WI 1952 (4); v P 1954 (5)*
Roy, Pranab 2: v E 1981 (2)

Sandhu, B. S. 8: v WI 1983 (1); *v WI 1982 (4); v P 1982 (3)*
Sardesai, D. N. 30: v E 1961 (1) 1963 (5) 1972 (1); v A 1964 (3) 1969 (1); v WI 1966 (2); v NZ 1964 (3); *v E 1967 (1) 1971 (3); v A 1967 (2); v WI 1961 (3) 1970 (5)*
Sarwate, C. T. 9: v E 1951 (1); v WI 1948 (2); *v E 1946 (1); v A 1947 (5)*
Saxena, R. C. 1: *v E 1967*
Sekar, T. A. P. 2: *v P 1982 (2)*
Sen, P. 14: v E 1951 (2); v WI 1948 (5); v P 1952 (2); *v E 1952 (2); v A 1947 (3)*
Sengupta, A. K. 1: v WI 1958
Sharma, Ajay 1: v WI 1987
Sharma, Chetan 23: v E 1984 (3); v A 1986 (2); v WI 1987 (3); v SL 1986 (2); *v E 1986 (2); v A 1985 (2); v WI 1988 (4); v P 1984 (2); v SL 1985 (3)*
Sharma, Gopal 5: v E 1984 (1); v P 1986 (2); v SL 1990 (1); *v SL 1985 (1)*
Sharma, P. 5: v E 1976 (2); v WI 1974 (2); *v WI 1975 (1)*
Sharma, Sanjeev 2: v NZ 1988 (1); *v E 1990 (1)*
Shastri, R. J. 80: v E 1981 (6) 1984 (5); v A 1986 (3); v WI 1983 (6) 1987 (4); v NZ 1988 (3); v P 1983 (2) 1986 (5); v SL 1986 (3) 1990 (1); *v E 1982 (3) 1986 (3) 1990 (3); v A 1985 (3) 1991 (3); v SA 1992 (3); v WI 1982 (5) 1988 (4); v NZ 1980 (3); v P 1982 (2) 1984 (2) 1989 (4); v SL 1985 (3); v Z 1992 (1)*
Shinde, S. G. 7: v E 1951 (3); v WI 1948 (1); *v E 1946 (1) 1952 (2)*
Shodhan, R. H. 3: v P 1952 (1); *v WI 1952 (2)*
Shukla, R. C. 1: v SL 1982
Sidhu, N. S. 31: v E 1992 (3); v WI 1983 (2); v NZ 1988 (3); v SL 1993 (3); v Z 1992 (1); *v E 1990 (3); v A 1991 (3); v WI 1988 (4); v NZ 1989 (1) 1993 (1); v P 1989 (4); v SL 1993 (3)*
Sivaramakrishnan, L. 9: v E 1984 (5); *v A 1985 (2); v WI 1982 (1); v SL 1985 (1)*
Sohoni, S. W. 4: v E 1951 (1); *v E 1946 (2); v A 1947 (1)*
Solkar, E. D. 27: v E 1972 (5) 1976 (1); v A 1969 (4); v WI 1974 (4); v NZ 1969 (1); *v E 1971 (3) 1974 (3); v WI 1970 (5) 1975 (1)*
Sood, M. M. 1: v A 1959
Srikkanth, K. 43: v E 1981 (4) 1984 (2); v A 1986 (3); v WI 1987 (4); v NZ 1988 (3); v P 1986 (5); v SL 1986 (3); *v E 1986 (3); v A 1985 (3) 1991 (4); v P 1982 (2) 1989 (4); v SL 1985 (3)*
Srinath, J. 12: *v A 1991 (5); v SA 1992 (3); v NZ 1993 (1); v SL 1993 (2); v Z 1992 (1)*
Srinivasan, T. E. 1: *v NZ 1980*
Subramanya, V. 9: v WI 1966 (2); v NZ 1964 (1); *v E 1967 (2); v A 1967 (2); v NZ 1967 (2)*
Sunderram, G. 2: v NZ 1955 (2)
Surendranath, R. 11: v A 1959 (2); v WI 1958 (2); v P 1960 (2); *v E 1959 (5)*
Surti, R. F. 26: v E 1963 (1); v A 1964 (2) 1969 (1); v WI 1966 (2); v NZ 1964 (1) 1969 (2); v P 1960 (2); *v E 1967 (2); v A 1967 (4); v WI 1961 (5); v NZ 1967 (4)*
Swamy, V. N. 1: v NZ 1955

Tamhane, N. S. 21: v A 1956 (3) 1959 (1); v WI 1958 (4); v NZ 1955 (4); v P 1960 (2); *v E 1959 (2); v P 1954 (5)*
Tarapore, K. K. 1: v WI 1948
Tendulkar, S. R. 32: v E 1992 (3); v SL 1990 (1) 1993 (3); v Z 1992 (1); *v E 1990 (3); v A 1991 (5); v SA 1992 (4); v NZ 1989 (3) 1993 (1); v P 1989 (4); v SL 1993 (3); v Z 1992 (1)*

Umrigar, P. R. 59: v E 1951 (5) 1961 (4); v A 1956 (3) 1959 (3); v WI 1948 (1) 1958 (5); v NZ 1955 (5); v P 1952 (5) 1960 (5); *v E 1952 (4) 1959 (4); v WI 1952 (5) 1961 (5); v P 1954 (5)*

Vengsarkar, D. B. 116: v E 1976 (1) 1979 (1) 1981 (6) 1984 (5); v A 1979 (6) 1986 (2); v WI 1978 (6) 1983 (5) 1987 (3); v NZ 1988 (3); v P 1979 (5) 1983 (1) 1986 (5); v SL 1982 (1) 1986 (3) 1990 (1); *v E 1979 (4) 1982 (3) 1986 (3) 1990 (3); v A 1977 (5) 1980 (3) 1985 (3) 1991 (5); v WI 1975 (2) 1982 (5) 1988 (4); v NZ 1975 (3) 1980 (3) 1989 (2); v P 1978 (3) 1982 (6) 1984 (2); v SL 1985 (3)*

Venkataraghavan, S. 57: v E 1972 (2) 1976 (1); v A 1969 (5) 1979 (3); v WI 1966 (2) 1974 (2) 1978 (6); v NZ 1964 (4) 1969 (2) 1976 (3); v P 1983 (2); *v E 1967 (1) 1971 (3) 1974 (2) 1979 (4); v A 1977 (1); v WI 1970 (5) 1975 (3) 1982 (5); v NZ 1975 (1)*

Venkataramana, M. 1: *v WI 1988*

Viswanath, G. R. 91: v E 1972 (5) 1976 (5) 1979 (1) 1981 (6); v A 1969 (4) 1979 (6); v WI 1974 (5) 1978 (6); v NZ 1976 (3); v P 1979 (6); v SL 1982 (1); *v E 1971 (3) 1974 (3) 1979 (4) 1982 (3); v A 1977 (5) 1980 (3); v WI 1970 (3) 1975 (4); v NZ 1975 (3) 1980 (3); v P 1978 (3) 1982 (6)*

Viswanath, S. 3: *v SL 1985 (3)*

Vizianagram, Maharaj Kumar of, Sir Vijay A. 3: *v E 1936 (3)*

Wadekar, A. L. 37: v E 1972 (5); v A 1969 (5); v WI 1966 (2); v NZ 1969 (3); *v E 1967 (3) 1971 (3) 1974 (3); v A 1967 (4); v WI 1970 (5); v NZ 1967 (4)*

Wassan, A. S. 4: *v E 1990 (1); v NZ 1989 (3)*

Wazir Ali, S. 7: v E 1933 (3); *v E 1932 (1) 1936 (3)*

Yadav, N. S. 35: v E 1979 (1) 1981 (1) 1984 (4); v A 1979 (5) 1986 (3); v WI 1983 (3); v P 1979 (5) 1986 (4); v SL 1986 (2); *v A 1980 (2) 1985 (3); v NZ 1980 (1); v P 1984 (1)*

Yadav, V. S. 1: v Z 1992

Yajurvindra Singh 4: v E 1976 (2); v A 1979 (1); *v E 1979 (1)*

Yashpal Sharma 37: v E 1979 (1) 1981 (2); v A 1979 (6); v WI 1983 (1); v P 1979 (6) 1983 (3); v SL 1982 (1); *v E 1979 (3) 1982 (3); v A 1980 (3); v WI 1982 (5); v NZ 1980 (1); v P 1982 (2)*

Yograj Singh 1: *v NZ 1980*

Note: Hafeez, on going later to Oxford University, took his correct name, Kardar.

PAKISTAN

Number of Test cricketers: 132

Aamer Malik 13: v E 1987 (2); v A 1988 (1); v WI 1990 (1); v In 1989 (4); *v A 1989 (2); v WI 1987 (1); v NZ 1988 (2)*

Aamir Nazir 2: *v WI 1992 (1); v NZ 1993 (1)*

Aamir Sohail 16: v Z 1993 (3); *v E 1992 (5); v WI 1992 (2); v NZ 1992 (1) 1993 (3); v SL 1994 (2)*

Abdul Kadir 4: v A 1964 (1); *v A 1964 (1); v NZ 1964 (2)*

Abdul Qadir 67: v E 1977 (3) 1983 (3) 1987 (3); v A 1982 (3) 1988 (3); v WI 1980 (2) 1986 (3) 1990 (2); v NZ 1984 (3) 1990 (2); v In 1982 (5) 1984 (1) 1989 (4); v SL 1985 (3); *v E 1982 (3) 1987 (4); v A 1983 (5); v WI 1987 (3); v NZ 1984 (2) 1988 (2); v In 1979 (3) 1986 (3); v SL 1985 (2)*

Afaq Hussain 2: v E 1961 (1); *v A 1964 (1)*

Aftab Baloch 2: v WI 1974 (1); v NZ 1969 (1)

Aftab Gul 6: v E 1968 (2); v NZ 1969 (1); *v E 1971 (3)*

Agha Saadat Ali 1: v NZ 1955

Agha Zahid 1: v WI 1974

Akram Raza 6: v WI 1990 (1); v In 1989 (1); v SL 1991 (1); *v NZ 1993 (2); v SL 1994 (1)*

Alim-ud-Din 25: v E 1961 (2); v A 1956 (1) 1959 (1); v WI 1958 (1); v NZ 1955 (3); v In 1954 (5); *v E 1954 (3) 1962 (3); v WI 1957 (5); v In 1960 (1)*

Amir Elahi 5: *v In 1952 (5)*

Anil Dalpat 9: v E 1983 (3); v NZ 1984 (3); *v NZ 1984 (3)*

Anwar Hussain 4: *v In 1952 (4)*

Anwar Khan 1: *v NZ 1978*

Aqib Javed 14: v NZ 1990 (3); v SL 1991 (3); *v E 1992 (5); v A 1989 (1); v NZ 1988 (1) 1992 (1)*

Arif Butt 3: *v A 1964 (1); v NZ 1964 (2)*

Ashfaq Ahmed 1: v Z 1993

Ashraf Ali 8: v E 1987 (3); v In 1984 (2); v SL 1981 (2) 1985 (1)

Asif Iqbal 58: v E 1968 (3) 1972 (3); v A 1964 (1); v WI 1974 (2); v NZ 1964 (3) 1969 (3) 1976 (3); v In 1978 (3); *v E 1967 (3) 1971 (3) 1974 (3); v A 1964 (1) 1972 (3) 1976 (3) 1978 (2); v WI 1976 (5); v NZ 1964 (3) 1972 (3) 1978 (2); v In 1979 (6)*

Asif Masood 16: v E 1968 (2) 1972 (1); v WI 1974 (2); v NZ 1969 (1); *v E 1971 (3) 1974 (3); v A 1972 (3) 1976 (1)*
Asif Mujtaba 19: v E 1987 (1); v WI 1986 (2); v Z 1993 (3); *v E 1992 (5); v WI 1992 (3); v NZ 1992 (1) 1993 (2); v SL 1994 (2)*
Ata-ur-Rehman 9: v Z 1993 (3); *v E 1992 (1); v WI 1992 (3); v NZ 1993 (2)*
Atif Rauf 1: *v NZ 1993*
Azeem Hafeez 18: v E 1983 (2); v NZ 1984 (3); v In 1984 (2); *v A 1983 (5); v NZ 1984 (3); v In 1983 (3)*
Azhar Khan 1: v A 1979
Azmat Rana 1: v A 1979

Basit Ali 11: v Z 1993 (3); *v WI 1992 (3); v NZ 1993 (3); v SL 1994 (2)*
Burki, J. 25: v E 1961 (3); v A 1964 (1); v NZ 1964 (3) 1969 (1); *v E 1962 (5) 1967 (3); v A 1964 (1); v NZ 1964 (3); v In 1960 (5)*

D'Souza, A. 6: v E 1961 (2); v WI 1958 (1); *v E 1962 (3)*

Ehtesham-ud-Din 5: v A 1979 (1); *v E 1982 (1); v In 1979 (3)*

Farooq Hamid 1: *v A 1964*
Farrukh Zaman 1: v NZ 1976
Fazal Mahmood 34: v E 1961 (1); v A 1956 (1) 1959 (2); v WI 1958 (3); v NZ 1955 (2); v In 1954 (4); *v E 1954 (4) 1962 (2); v WI 1957 (5); v In 1952 (5) 1960 (5)*

Ghazali, M. E. Z. 2: *v E 1954 (2)*
Ghulam Abbas 1: *v E 1967*
Gul Mahomed 1: v A 1956

Hanif Mohammad 55: v E 1961 (3) 1968 (3); v A 1956 (1) 1959 (3) 1964 (1); v WI 1958 (1); v NZ 1955 (3) 1964 (3) 1969 (1); v In 1954 (5); *v E 1954 (4) 1962 (5) 1967 (3); v A 1964 (1); v WI 1957 (5); v NZ 1964 (3); v In 1952 (5) 1960 (5)*
Haroon Rashid 23: v E 1977 (3); v A 1979 (2) 1982 (3); v In 1982 (1); v SL 1981 (2); *v E 1978 (3) 1982 (1); v A 1976 (1) 1978 (1); v WI 1976 (5); v NZ 1978 (1)*
Haseeb Ahsan 12: v E 1961 (2); v A 1959 (1); v WI 1958 (1); *v WI 1957 (3); v In 1960 (5)*

Ibadulla, K. 4: v A 1964 (1); *v E 1967 (2); v NZ 1964 (1)*
Ijaz Ahmed 19: v E 1987 (3); v A 1988 (3); v WI 1990 (3); *v E 1987 (4); v A 1989 (3); v WI 1987 (2); v In 1986 (1)*
Ijaz Butt 8: v A 1959 (2); v WI 1958 (3); *v E 1962 (3)*
Ijaz Faqih 5: v WI 1980 (1); *v A 1981 (1); v WI 1987 (2); v In 1986 (1)*
Imran Khan 88: v A 1979 (2) 1982 (3); v WI 1980 (4) 1986 (3) 1990 (3); v NZ 1976 (3); v In 1978 (3) 1982 (6) 1989 (4); v SL 1981 (1) 1985 (3) 1991 (3); *v E 1971 (1) 1974 (3) 1982 (3) 1987 (5); v A 1976 (3) 1978 (2) 1981 (3) 1983 (2) 1989 (3); v WI 1976 (5) 1987 (3); v NZ 1978 (2) 1988 (2); v In 1979 (5) 1986 (5); v SL 1985 (3)*
Imtiaz Ahmed 41: v E 1961 (3); v A 1956 (1) 1959 (3); v WI 1958 (3); v NZ 1955 (3); v In 1954 (5); *v E 1954 (4) 1962 (4); v WI 1957 (5); v In 1952 (5) 1960 (5)*
Intikhab Alam 47: v E 1961 (2) 1968 (3) 1972 (3); v A 1959 (1) 1964 (1); v WI 1974 (2); v NZ 1964 (3) 1969 (3) 1976 (3); *v E 1962 (3) 1967 (3) 1971 (3) 1974 (3); v A 1964 (1) 1972 (3); v WI 1976 (1); v NZ 1964 (3) 1972 (3); v In 1960 (3)*
Inzamam-ul-Haq 16: v Z 1993 (3); *v E 1992 (4); v WI 1992 (3); v NZ 1992 (1) 1993 (3); v SL 1994 (2)*
Iqbal Qasim 50: v E 1977 (3) 1987 (3); v A 1979 (3) 1982 (2) 1988 (3); v WI 1980 (4); v NZ 1984 (3); v In 1978 (3) 1982 (2); v SL 1981 (3); *v E 1978 (3); v A 1976 (3) 1981 (2); v WI 1976 (2); v NZ 1984 (1); v In 1979 (6) 1983 (1) 1986 (3)*
Israr Ali 4: v A 1959 (2); *v In 1952 (2)*

Jalal-ud-Din 6: v A 1982 (1); v In 1982 (2) 1984 (2); v SL 1985 (1)
Javed Akhtar 1: *v E 1962*
Javed Miandad 124: v E 1977 (3) 1987 (3); v A 1979 (3) 1982 (3) 1988 (3); v WI 1980 (4) 1986 (3) 1990 (2); v NZ 1976 (3) 1984 (3) 1990 (3); v In 1978 (3) 1982 (6) 1984 (2) 1989 (4); v SL 1981 (3) 1985 (3) 1991 (3); v Z 1993 (3); *v E 1978 (3) 1982 (3) 1987 (5) 1992 (5); v A 1976 (3) 1978 (2) 1981 (3) 1983 (5) 1989 (3); v WI 1976 (1) 1987 (3) 1992 (3); v NZ 1978 (3) 1984 (3) 1988 (2) 1992 (1); v In 1979 (6) 1983 (3) 1986 (4); v SL 1985 (3)*

Kabir Khan 1: *v SL 1994*
Kardar, A. H. 23: v A 1956 (1); v NZ 1955 (3); v In 1954 (5); *v E 1954 (4); v WI 1957 (5); v In 1952 (5)*
Khalid Hassan 1: *v E 1954*
Khalid Wazir 2: *v E 1954 (2)*
Khan Mohammad 13: v A 1956 (1); v NZ 1955 (3); v In 1954 (4); *v E 1954 (2); v WI 1957 (2); v In 1952 (1)*

Liaqat Ali 5: v E 1977 (2); v WI 1974 (1); *v E 1978 (2)*

Mahmood Hussain 27: v E 1961 (1); v WI 1958 (3); v NZ 1955 (1); v In 1954 (5); *v E 1954 (2) 1962 (3); v WI 1957 (3); v In 1952 (4) 1960 (5)*
Majid Khan 63: v E 1968 (3) 1972 (3); v A 1964 (1) 1979 (3); v WI 1974 (2) 1980 (4); v NZ 1964 (3) 1976 (3); v In 1978 (3) 1982 (1); v SL 1981 (1); *v E 1967 (3) 1971 (2) 1974 (3) 1982 (1); v A 1972 (3) 1976 (3) 1978 (2) 1981 (3); v WI 1976 (5); v NZ 1972 (3) 1978 (2); v In 1979 (6)*
Mansoor Akhtar 19: v A 1982 (3); v WI 1980 (2); v In 1982 (3); v SL 1981 (1); *v E 1982 (3) 1987 (5); v A 1981 (1) 1989 (1)*
Manzoor Elahi 4: v NZ 1984 (1); v In 1984 (1); *v In 1986 (2)*
Maqsood Ahmed 16: v NZ 1955 (2); v In 1954 (5); *v E 1954 (4); v In 1952 (5)*
Masood Anwar 1: v WI 1990
Mathias, Wallis 21: v E 1961 (1); v A 1956 (1) 1959 (2); v WI 1958 (3); v NZ 1955 (1); *v E 1962 (3); v WI 1957 (5); v In 1960 (5)*
Miran Bux 2: v In 1954 (2)
Mohammad Aslam 1: *v E 1954*
Mohammad Farooq 7: v NZ 1964 (3); *v E 1962 (2); v In 1960 (2)*
Mohammad Ilyas 10: v E 1968 (2); v NZ 1964 (3); *v E 1967 (1); v A 1964 (1); v NZ 1964 (3)*
Mohammad Munaf 4: v E 1961 (2); v A 1959 (2)
Mohammad Nazir 14: v E 1972 (1); v WI 1980 (4); v NZ 1969 (3); *v A 1983 (3); v In 1983 (3)*
Mohsin Kamal 7: v E 1983 (1); v SL 1985 (1); *v E 1987 (4); v SL 1985 (1)*
Mohsin Khan 48: v E 1977 (1) 1983 (3); v A 1982 (3); v WI 1986 (3); v NZ 1984 (2); v In 1982 (6) 1984 (2); v SL 1981 (2) 1985 (2); *v E 1978 (3) 1982 (3); v A 1978 (1) 1981 (2) 1983 (5); v NZ 1978 (1) 1984 (3); v In 1983 (3); v SL 1985 (3)*
Moin Khan 11: v WI 1990 (2); v SL 1991 (3); *v E 1992 (4); v WI 1992 (2)*
Mudassar Nazar 76: v E 1977 (3) 1983 (1) 1987 (3); v A 1979 (3) 1982 (3) 1988 (3); v WI 1986 (2); v NZ 1984 (3); v In 1978 (2) 1982 (6) 1984 (2); v SL 1981 (1) 1985 (3) ; *v E 1978 (3) 1982 (3) 1987 (5); v A 1976 (1) 1978 (1) 1981 (3) 1983 (5); v WI 1987 (3); v NZ 1978 (1) 1984 (3) 1988 (2); v In 1979 (5) 1983 (3); v SL 1985 (3)*
Mufasir-ul-Haq 1: *v NZ 1964*
Munir Malik 3: v A 1959 (1); *v E 1962 (2)*
Mushtaq Ahmed 15: v WI 1990 (2); v Z 1993 (2); *v E 1992 (5); v A 1989 (1); v WI 1992 (1); v NZ 1992 (1) 1993 (1); v SL 1994 (2)*
Mushtaq Mohammad 57: v E 1961 (3) 1968 (3) 1972 (3); v WI 1958 (1) 1974 (2); v NZ 1969 (2) 1976 (3); v In 1978 (3); *v E 1962 (5) 1967 (3) 1971 (3) 1974 (3); v A 1972 (3) 1976 (3) 1978 (2); v WI 1976 (5); v NZ 1972 (2) 1978 (3); v In 1960 (5)*

Nadeem Abbasi 3: v In 1989 (3)
Nadeem Ghauri 1: *v A 1989*
Nadeem Khan 1: *v WI 1992*
Nasim-ul-Ghani 29: v E 1961 (2); v A 1959 (2) 1964 (1); v WI 1958 (3); *v E 1962 (5) 1967 (2); v A 1964 (1) 1972 (1); v WI 1957 (5); v NZ 1964 (3); v In 1960 (4)*
Naushad Ali 6: v NZ 1964 (3); *v NZ 1964 (3)*
Naved Anjum 2: v NZ 1990 (1); v In 1989 (1)
Nazar Mohammad 5: *v In 1952 (5)*
Nazir Junior (*see* Mohammad Nazir)
Niaz Ahmed 2: v E 1968 (1); *v E 1967 (1)*

Pervez Sajjad 19: v E 1968 (1) 1972 (2); v A 1964 (1); v NZ 1964 (3) 1969 (3); *v E 1971 (3); v NZ 1964 (3) 1972 (3)*

Qasim Omar 26: v E 1983 (3); v WI 1986 (3); v NZ 1984 (3); v In 1984 (2); v SL 1985 (3); *v A 1983 (5); v NZ 1984 (3); v In 1983 (1); v SL 1985 (3)*

Ramiz Raja 48: v E 1983 (2) 1987 (3); v A 1988 (3); v WI 1986 (3) 1990 (2); v NZ 1990 (3); v In 1989 (4); v SL 1985 (1) 1991 (3); *v E 1987 (2) 1992 (5); v A 1989 (2); v WI 1987 (3) 1992 (3); v NZ 1992 (1); v In 1986 (5); v SL 1985 (3)*
Rashid Khan 4: v SL 1981 (2); *v A 1983 (1); v NZ 1984 (1)*
Rashid Latif 11: v Z 1993 (3); *v E 1992 (1); v WI 1992 (1); v NZ 1992 (1) 1993 (3); v SL 1994 (2)*
Rehman, S. F. 1: *v WI 1957*
Rizwan-uz-Zaman 11: v WI 1986 (1); v SL 1981 (2); *v A 1981 (1); v NZ 1988 (2); v In 1986 (5)*

Sadiq Mohammad 41: v E 1972 (3) 1977 (2); v WI 1974 (1) 1980 (3); v NZ 1969 (3) 1976 (3); v In 1978 (1); *v E 1971 (3) 1974 (3) 1978 (3); v A 1972 (3) 1976 (2); v WI 1976 (5); v NZ 1972 (3); v In 1979 (3)*
Saeed Ahmed 41: v E 1961 (3) 1968 (3); v A 1959 (3) 1964 (1); v WI 1958 (3); v NZ 1964 (3); *v E 1962 (5) 1967 (3) 1971 (1); v A 1964 (1) 1972 (2); v WI 1957 (5); v NZ 1964 (3); v In 1960 (5)*
Saeed Anwar 6: v WI 1990 (1); *v NZ 1993 (3); v SL 1994 (2)*
Salah-ud-Din 5: v E 1968 (1); v NZ 1964 (3) 1969 (1)
Saleem Jaffer 14: v E 1987 (1); v A 1988 (2); v WI 1986 (1); v NZ 1990 (2); v In 1989 (1); v SL 1991 (2); *v WI 1987 (1); v NZ 1988 (2); v In 1986 (2)*
Salim Altaf 21: v E 1972 (3); v NZ 1969 (2); v In 1978 (1); *v E 1967 (2) 1971 (2); v A 1972 (3) 1976 (2); v WI 1976 (3); v NZ 1972 (3)*
Salim Malik 77: v E 1983 (3) 1987 (3); v A 1988 (3); v WI 1986 (1) 1990 (3); v NZ 1984 (3) 1990 (3); v In 1982 (6) 1984 (2) 1989 (4); v SL 1981 (2) 1985 (3) 1991 (3); *v E 1987 (5) 1992 (5); v A 1983 (3) 1989 (1); v WI 1987 (3); v NZ 1984 (3) 1988 (2) 1992 (1) 1993 (3); v In 1983 (2) 1986 (5); v SL 1985 (3) 1994 (2)*
Salim Yousuf 32: v A 1988 (3); v WI 1986 (3) 1990 (1); v NZ 1990 (3); v In 1989 (1); v SL 1981 (1) 1985 (2); *v E 1987 (5); v A 1989 (3); v WI 1987 (3); v NZ 1988 (2); v In 1986 (5)*
Sarfraz Nawaz 55: v E 1968 (1) 1972 (2) 1977 (2) 1983 (3); v A 1979 (3); v WI 1974 (2) 1980 (2); v NZ 1976 (3); v In 1978 (3) 1982 (6); *v E 1974 (3) 1978 (2) 1982 (1); v A 1972 (2) 1976 (2) 1978 (2) 1981 (3) 1983 (3); v WI 1976 (4); v NZ 1972 (3) 1978 (3)*
Shafiq Ahmed 6: v E 1977 (3); v WI 1980 (2); *v E 1974 (1)*
Shafqat Rana 5: v E 1968 (2); v A 1964 (1); v NZ 1969 (2)
Shahid Israr 1: v NZ 1976
Shahid Mahboob 1: v In 1989
Shahid Mahmood 1: *v E 1962*
Shahid Saeed 1: v In 1989
Shakeel Ahmed 1: *v WI 1992*
Sharpe, D. 3: v A 1959 (3)
Shoaib Mohammad 42: v E 1983 (1) 1987 (1); v A 1988 (3); v WI 1990 (3); v NZ 1984 (1) 1990 (3); v In 1989 (4); v SL 1985 (1) 1991 (3); v Z 1993 (3); *v E 1987 (4) 1992 (1); v A 1989 (3); v WI 1987 (3); v NZ 1984 (1) 1988 (2); v In 1983 (2) 1986 (3)*
Shuja-ud-Din 19: v E 1961 (2); v A 1959 (3); v WI 1958 (3); v NZ 1955 (3); v In 1954 (5); *v E 1954 (3)*
Sikander Bakht 26: v E 1977 (2); v WI 1980 (1); v NZ 1976 (1); v In 1978 (2) 1982 (1); *v E 1978 (3) 1982 (2); v A 1978 (2) 1981 (3); v WI 1976 (1); v NZ 1978 (3); v In 1979 (5)*

Tahir Naqqash 15: v A 1982 (3); v In 1982 (2); v SL 1981 (3); *v E 1982 (2); v A 1983 (1); v NZ 1984 (1); v In 1983 (3)*
Talat Ali 10: v E 1972 (3); *v E 1978 (2); v A 1972 (1); v NZ 1972 (1) 1978 (3)*
Taslim Arif 6: v A 1979 (3); v WI 1980 (2); *v In 1979 (1)*
Tauseef Ahmed 34: v E 1983 (2) 1987 (2); v A 1979 (3) 1988 (3); v WI 1986 (3); v NZ 1984 (1) 1990 (2); v In 1984 (1); v SL 1981 (3) 1985 (1); v Z 1993 (1); *v E 1987 (2); v A 1989 (3); v NZ 1988 (1); v In 1986 (4); v SL 1985 (2)*

Waqar Hassan 21: v A 1956 (1) 1959 (1); v WI 1958 (1); v NZ 1955 (3); v In 1954 (5); *v E 1954 (4); v WI 1957 (1); v In 1952 (5)*
Waqar Younis 31: v WI 1990 (3); v NZ 1990 (3); v In 1989 (2); v SL 1991 (3); v Z 1993 (3); *v E 1992 (5); v A 1989 (3); v WI 1992 (3); v NZ 1992 (1) 1993 (3); v SL 1994 (2)*
Wasim Akram 55: v E 1987 (2); v WI 1986 (2) 1990 (3); v NZ 1990 (2); v In 1989 (4); v SL 1985 (3) 1991 (3); v Z 1993 (2); *v E 1987 (5) 1992 (4); v A 1989 (3); v WI 1987 (3) 1992 (3); v NZ 1984 (2) 1992 (1) 1993 (3); v In 1986 (5); v SL 1985 (3) 1994 (2)*
Wasim Bari 81: v E 1968 (3) 1972 (3) 1977 (3); v A 1982 (3); v WI 1974 (2) 1980 (2); v NZ 1969 (3) 1976 (2); v In 1978 (3) 1982 (6); *v E 1967 (3) 1971 (3) 1974 (3) 1978 (3) 1982 (3); v A 1972 (3) 1976 (3) 1978 (2) 1981 (3) 1983 (5); v WI 1976 (5); v NZ 1972 (3) 1978 (3); v In 1979 (6) 1983 (3)*

Wasim Raja 57: v E 1972 (1) 1977 (3) 1983 (3); v A 1979 (3); v WI 1974 (2) 1980 (4); v NZ 1976 (1) 1984 (1); v In 1982 (1) 1984 (1); v SL 1981 (3); *v E 1974 (2) 1978 (3) 1982 (1); v A 1978 (1) 1981 (3) 1983 (2); v WI 1976 (5); v NZ 1972 (3) 1978 (3) 1984 (2); v In 1979 (6) 1983 (3)*
Wazir Mohammad 20: v A 1956 (1) 1959 (1); v WI 1958 (3); v NZ 1955 (2); v In 1954 (5); *v E 1954 (2); v WI 1957 (5); v In 1952 (1)*

Younis Ahmed 4: v NZ 1969 (2); *v In 1986 (2)*

Zaheer Abbas 78: v E 1972 (2) 1983 (3); v A 1979 (2) 1982 (3); v WI 1974 (2) 1980 (3); v NZ 1969 (1) 1976 (3) 1984 (3); v In 1978 (3) 1982 (6) 1984 (2); v SL 1981 (1) 1985 (2); *v E 1971 (3) 1974 (3) 1982 (3); v A 1972 (3) 1976 (3) 1978 (2) 1981 (2) 1983 (5); v WI 1976 (3); v NZ 1972 (3) 1978 (2) 1984 (2); v In 1979 (5) 1983 (3)*
Zahid Fazal 6: v WI 1990 (3); v SL 1991 (3)
Zakir Khan 2: v In 1989 (1); *v SL 1985 (1)*
Zulfiqar Ahmed 9: v A 1956 (1); v NZ 1955 (3); *v E 1954 (2); v In 1952 (3)*
Zulqarnain 3: *v SL 1985 (3)*

SRI LANKA

Number of Test cricketers: 63

Ahangama, F. S. 3: v In 1985 (3)
Amalean, K. N. 2: v P 1985 (1); *v A 1987 (1)*
Amerasinghe, A. M. J. G. 2: v NZ 1983 (2)
Anurasiri, S. D. 17: v A 1992 (3); v WI 1993 (1); v NZ 1986 (1) 1992 (2); v P 1985 (2); *v E 1991 (1); v In 1986 (1) 1993 (3); v P 1991 (3)*
Atapattu, M. S. 3: v A 1992 (1); *v In 1990 (1) 1993 (1)*

Dassanayake, P. B. 9: v SA 1993 (3); v WI 1993 (1); v P 1994 (2); *v In 1993 (3)*
de Alwis, R. G. 11: v A 1982 (1); v NZ 1983 (3); v P 1985 (2); *v A 1987 (1); v NZ 1982 (1); v In 1986 (3)*
de Mel, A. L. F. 17: v E 1981 (1); v A 1982 (1); v In 1985 (3); v P 1985 (3); *v E 1984 (1); v In 1982 (1) 1986 (1); v P 1981 (3) 1985 (3)*
de Silva, A. M. 3: v E 1992 (1); v In 1993 (2)
de Silva, D. S. 12: v E 1981 (1); v A 1982 (1); v NZ 1983 (3); *v E 1984 (1); v NZ 1982 (2); v In 1982 (1); v P 1981 (3)*
de Silva, E. A. R. 10: v In 1985 (1); v P 1985 (1); *v A 1989 (2); v NZ 1990 (3); v In 1986 (3)*
de Silva, G. R. A. 4: v E 1981 (1); *v In 1982 (1); v P 1981 (2)*
de Silva, P. A. 43: v E 1992 (1); v A 1992 (3); v SA 1993 (3); v WI 1993 (1); v NZ 1992 (2); v In 1985 (3) 1993 (3); v P 1985 (3) 1994 (2); *v E 1984 (1) 1988 (1) 1991 (1); v A 1987 (1) 1989 (2); v NZ 1990 (3); v In 1986 (3) 1990 (1) 1993 (3); v P 1985 (3) 1991 (3)*
Dharmasena, H. D. P. K. 4: v SA 1993 (2); v P 1994 (2)
Dias, R. L. 20: v E 1981 (1); v A 1982 (1); v NZ 1983 (2) 1986 (1); v In 1985 (3); v P 1985 (1); *v E 1984 (1); v In 1982 (1) 1986 (3); v P 1981 (3) 1985 (3)*

Fernando, E. R. N. S. 5: v A 1982 (1); v NZ 1983 (2); *v NZ 1982 (2)*

Goonatillake, H. M. 5: v E 1981 (1); *v In 1982 (1); v P 1981 (3)*
Gunasekera, Y. 2: *v NZ 1982 (2)*
Guneratne, R. P. W. 1: v A 1982
Gurusinha, A. P. 28: v E 1992 (1); v A 1992 (3); v SA 1993 (1); v NZ 1986 (1) 1992 (2); v In 1993 (3); v P 1985 (2) 1994 (1); *v E 1991 (1); v A 1989 (2); v NZ 1990 (3); v In 1986 (3) 1990 (1); v P 1985 (1) 1991 (3)*

Hathurusinghe, U. C. 18: v E 1992 (1); v A 1992 (3); v SA 1993 (3); v NZ 1992 (2); v In 1993 (3); *v E 1991 (1); v NZ 1990 (2); v P 1991 (3)*

Jayasekera, R. S. A. 1: *v P 1981*
Jayasuriya S. T. 15: v E 1992 (1); v A 1992 (2); v SA 1993 (2); v WI 1993 (1); v In 1993 (1); v P 1994 (1); *v E 1991 (1); v NZ 1990 (2); v In 1993 (1); v P 1991 (3)*

Jeganathan, S. 2: *v NZ 1982 (2)*
John, V. B. 6: v NZ 1983 (3); *v E 1984 (1); v NZ 1982 (2)*
Jurangpathy, B. R. 2: v In 1985 (1); *v In 1986 (1)*

Kalpage, R. S. 7: v SA 1993 (1); v WI 1993 (1); v In 1993 (1); v P 1994 (1); *v In 1993 (3)*
Kaluperuma, L. W. 2: v E 1981 (1); *v P 1981 (1)*
Kaluperuma, S. M. S. 4: v NZ 1983 (3); *v A 1987 (1)*
Kaluwitharana, R. S. 3: v A 1992 (2); v In 1993 (1)
Kuruppu, D. S. B. P. 4: v NZ 1986 (1); *v E 1988 (1) 1991 (1); v A 1987 (1)*
Kuruppuarachchi, A. K. 2: v NZ 1986 (1); v P 1985 (1)

Labrooy, G. F. 9: *v E 1988 (1); v A 1987 (1) 1989 (2); v NZ 1990 (3); v In 1986 (1) 1990 (1)*
Liyanage, D. K. 8: v A 1992 (2); v SA 1993 (1); v NZ 1992 (2); v In 1993 (2); *v In 1993 (1)*

Madugalle, R. S. 21: v E 1981 (1); v A 1982 (1); v NZ 1983 (3) 1986 (1); v In 1985 (3); *v E 1984 (1) 1988 (1); v A 1987 (1); v NZ 1982 (2); v In 1982 (1); v P 1981 (3) 1985 (3)*
Madurasinghe, A. W. R. 3: v A 1992 (1); *v E 1988 (1); v In 1990 (1)*
Mahanama, R. S. 29: v E 1992 (1); v A 1992 (3); v SA 1993 (3); v WI 1993 (1); v NZ 1986 (1) 1992 (2); v In 1993 (3); v P 1985 (2) 1994 (2); *v E 1991 (1); v A 1987 (1) 1989 (2); v NZ 1990 (1); v In 1990 (1) 1993 (3); v P 1991 (2)*
Mendis, L. R. D. 24: v E 1981 (1); v A 1982 (1); v NZ 1983 (3) 1986 (1); v In 1985 (3); v P 1985 (3); *v E 1984 (1) 1988 (1); v In 1982 (1) 1986 (3); v P 1981 (3) 1985 (3)*
Muralitharan, M. 14: v E 1992 (1); v A 1992 (2); v SA 1993 (3); v WI 1993 (1); v NZ 1992 (1); v In 1993 (2); v P 1994 (1); *v In 1993 (3)*

Pushpakumara, K. R. 1: v P 1994

Ramanayake, C. P. H. 18: v E 1992 (1); v A 1992 (3); v SA 1993 (2); v NZ 1992 (1); v In 1993 (1); *v E 1988 (1) 1991 (1); v A 1987 (1) 1989 (2); v NZ 1990 (3); v P 1991 (2)*
Ranasinghe, A. N. 2: *v In 1982 (1); v P 1981 (1)*
Ranatunga, A. 51: v E 1981 (1) 1992 (1); v A 1982 (1) 1992 (3); v SA 1993 (3); v WI 1993 (1); v NZ 1983 (3) 1986 (1) 1992 (2); v In 1985 (3) 1993 (3); v P 1985 (3) 1994 (2); *v E 1984 (1) 1988 (1); v A 1987 (1) 1989 (2); v NZ 1990 (3); v In 1982 (1) 1986 (3) 1990 (1) 1993 (3); v P 1981 (2) 1985 (3) 1991 (3)*
Ranatunga, D. 2: *v A 1989 (2)*
Ranatunga, S. 1: v P 1994
Ratnayake, R. J. 23: v A 1982 (1); v NZ 1983 (1) 1986 (1); v In 1985 (3); v P 1985 (1); *v E 1991 (1); v A 1989 (1); v NZ 1982 (2) 1990 (3); v In 1986 (2) 1990 (1); v P 1985 (3) 1991 (3)*
Ratnayeke, J. R. 22: v NZ 1983 (2) 1986 (1); v P 1985 (3); *v E 1984 (1) 1988 (1); v A 1987 (1) 1989 (2); v NZ 1982 (2); v In 1982 (1) 1986 (3); v P 1981 (2) 1985 (3)*

Samarasekera, M. A. R. 4: *v E 1988 (1); v A 1989 (1); v In 1990 (1); v P 1991 (1)*
Samaraweera, D. P. 5: v WI 1993 (1); v P 1994 (1); *v In 1993 (3)*
Senanayake, C. P. 3: *v NZ 1990 (3)*
Silva, S. A. R. 9: v In 1985 (3); v P 1985 (1); *v E 1984 (1) 1988 (1); v NZ 1982 (1); v P 1985 (2)*

Tillekeratne, H. P. 25: v E 1992 (1); v A 1992 (1); v SA 1993 (3); v WI 1993 (1); v NZ 1992 (2); v In 1993 (3); v P 1994 (2); *v E 1991 (1); v A 1989 (1); v NZ 1990 (3); v In 1990 (1) 1993 (3); v P 1991 (3)*

Vaas, W. P. U. J. C. 1: v P 1994

Warnapura, B. 4: v E 1981 (1); *v In 1982 (1); v P 1981 (2)*
Warnaweera, K. P. J. 10: v E 1992 (1); v NZ 1992 (2); v In 1993 (3); v P 1985 (1) 1994 (1); *v NZ 1990 (1); v In 1990 (1)*
Weerasinghe, C. D. U. S. 1: v In 1985
Wettimuny, M. D. 2: *v NZ 1982 (2)*
Wettimuny, S. 23: v E 1981 (1); v A 1982 (1); v NZ 1983 (3); v In 1985 (3); v P 1985 (3); *v E 1984 (1); v NZ 1982 (2); v In 1986 (3); v P 1981 (3) 1985 (3)*
Wickremasinghe, A. G. D. 3: v NZ 1992 (2); *v A 1989 (1)*
Wickremasinghe, G. P. 13: v A 1992 (1); v SA 1993 (2); v WI 1993 (1); v In 1993 (2); v P 1994 (1); *v In 1993 (3); v P 1991 (3)*
Wijegunawardene, K. I. W. 2: *v E 1991 (1); v P 1991 (1)*
Wijesuriya, R. G. C. E. 4: *v P 1981 (1) 1985 (3)*
Wijetunge, P. K. 1: v SA 1993

ZIMBABWE

Number of Test cricketers: 22

Arnott, K. J. 4: v NZ 1992 (2); v In 1992 (1); *v In 1992 (1)*
Brain, D. H. 4: v NZ 1992 (1); *v In 1992 (1); v P 1993 (2)*
Brandes, E. A. 6: v NZ 1992 (1); v In 1992 (1); *v In 1992 (1); v P 1993 (3)*
Briant, G. A. 1: *v In 1992*
Bruk-Jackson, G. K. 2: *v P 1993 (2)*
Burmester, M. G. 3: v NZ 1992 (2); v In 1992 (1)
Campbell, A. D. R. 7: v NZ 1992 (2); v In 1992 (1); *v In 1992 (1); v P 1993 (3)*
Crocker, G. J. 3: v NZ 1992 (2); v In 1992 (1)
Dekker, M. H. 3: *v P 1993 (3)*
Flower, A. 7: v NZ 1992 (2); v In 1992 (1); *v In 1992 (1); v P 1993 (3)*
Flower, G. W. 7: v NZ 1992 (2); v In 1992 (1); *v In 1992 (1); v P 1993 (3)*
Houghton, D. L. 7: v NZ 1992 (2); v In 1992 (1); *v In 1992 (1); v P 1993 (3)*
James, W. R. 1: *v P 1993*
Jarvis, M. P. 2: v NZ 1992 (1); v In 1992 (1)
Peall, S. G. 2: *v P 1993 (2)*
Pycroft, A. J. 3: v NZ 1992 (2); v In 1992 (1)
Ranchod, U. 1: *v In 1992*
Rennie, J. A. 2: *v P 1993 (2)*
Shah, A. H. 2: v NZ 1992 (1); *v In 1992 (1)*
Streak, H. H. 3: *v P 1993 (3)*
Traicos, A. J. 4: v NZ 1992 (2); v In 1992 (1); *v In 1992 (1)*
Whittall, G. J. 3: *v P 1993 (3)*

TWO COUNTRIES

Fourteen cricketers have appeared for two countries in Test matches, namely:

Amir Elahi, *India and Pakistan.*
J. J. Ferris, *Australia and England.*
S. C. Guillen, *West Indies and NZ.*
Gul Mahomed, *India and Pakistan.*
F. Hearne, *England and South Africa.*
A. H. Kardar, *India and Pakistan.*
W. E. Midwinter, *England and Australia.*
F. Mitchell, *England and South Africa.*
W. L. Murdoch, *Australia and England.*
Nawab of Pataudi, sen., *England and India.*
A. J. Traicos, *South Africa and Zimbabwe.*
A. E. Trott, *Australia and England.*
K. C. Wessels, *Australia and South Africa.*
S. M. J. Woods, *Australia and England.*

ENGLAND v REST OF THE WORLD

In 1970, owing to the cancellation of the South African tour to England, a series of matches was arranged, with the trappings of a full Test series, between England and the Rest of the World. It was played for the Guinness Trophy.

The following were awarded England caps for playing against the Rest of the World in that series, although the five matches played are now generally considered not to have rated as full Tests: D. L. Amiss (1), G. Boycott (2), D. J. Brown (2), M. C. Cowdrey (4), M. H. Denness (1), B. L. D'Oliveira (4), J. H. Edrich (2), K. W. R. Fletcher (4), A. W. Greig (3), R. Illingworth (5), A. Jones (1), A. P. E. Knott (5), P. Lever (1), B. W. Luckhurst (5), C. M. Old (2), P. J. Sharpe (1), K. Shuttleworth (1), J. A. Snow (5), D. L. Underwood (3), A. Ward (1), D. Wilson (2).

The following players represented the Rest of the World: E. J. Barlow (5), F. M. Engineer (2), L. R. Gibbs (4), Intikhab Alam (5), R. B. Kanhai (5), C. H. Lloyd (5), G. D. McKenzie (3), D. L. Murray (3), Mushtaq Mohammad (2), P. M. Pollock (1), R. G. Pollock (5), M. J. Procter (5), B. A. Richards (5), G. S. Sobers (5).

LIMITED-OVERS INTERNATIONAL CRICKETERS

The following players have appeared in limited-overs internationals but had not represented their countries in Test matches by August 28, 1994:

England D. G. Cork, I. J. Gould, G. W. Humpage, T. E. Jesty, J. D. Love, M. A. Lynch, M. J. Smith, S. D. Udal, C. M. Wells.

Australia M. G. Bevan, G. A. Bishop, D. W. Fleming, S. F. Graf, R. J. McCurdy, K. H. MacLeay, G. D. Porter, J. D. Siddons, G. S. Trimble, A. K. Zesers.

South Africa D. J. Callaghan, C. E. B. Rice, D. B. Rundle, T. G. Shaw, E. O. Simons, E. L. R. Stewart, C. J. P. G. van Zyl, M. Yachad.

West Indies R. S. Gabriel, R. C. Haynes, R. I. C. Holder, M. R. Pydanna, P. A. Wallace.

New Zealand B. R. Blair, P. G. Coman, M. W. Douglas, B. G. Hadlee, R. T. Hart, B. J. McKechnie, E. B. McSweeney, J. P. Millmow, R. G. Petrie, R. B. Reid, S. J. Roberts, L. W. Stott, R. J. Webb, J. W. Wilson.

G. R. Larsen appeared for New Zealand in 55 limited-overs internationals before making his Test debut.

India A. C. Bedade, Bhupinder Singh, sen., G. Bose, V. B. Chandrasekhar, S. C. Ganguly, R. S. Ghai, S. C. Khanna, S. P. Mukherjee, A. K. Patel, B. K. V. Prasad, Randhir Singh, R. P. Singh, R. R. Singh, Sudhakar Rao.

Pakistan Aamer Hameed, Aamer Hanif, Arshad Khan, Arshad Pervez, Ghulam Ali, Haafiz Shahid, Hasan Jamil, Iqbal Sikandar, Irfan Bhatti, Mansoor Rana, Maqsood Rana, Masood Iqbal, Moin-ul-Atiq, Naeem Ahmed, Naseer Malik, Parvez Mir, Saadat Ali, Sajid Ali, Sajjad Akbar, Salim Pervez, Shakil Khan, Sohail Fazal, Tanvir Mehdi, Wasim Haider, Zahid Ahmed.

Sri Lanka U. U. Chandana, D. L. S. de Silva, G. N. de Silva, E. R. Fernando, T. L. Fernando, U. N. K. Fernando, F. R. M. Goonatillake, A. A. W. Gunawardene, P. D. Heyn, S. A. Jayasinghe, S. H. U. Karnain, M. Munasinghe, A. R. M. Opatha, S. P. Pasqual, K. G. Perera, H. S. M. Pieris, S. K. Ranasinghe, N. Ranatunga, N. L. K. Ratnayake, A. P. B. Tennekoon, M. H. Tissera, D. M. Vonhagt, A. P. Weerakkody, S. R. de S. Wettimuny, R. P. A. H. Wickremaratne.

Zimbabwe R. D. Brown, I. P. Butchart, K. M. Curran, K. G. Duers, E. A. Essop-Adam, C. N. Evans, D. A. G. Fletcher, J. G. Heron, V. R. Hogg, M. A. Meman, G. A. Paterson, G. E. Peckover, P. W. E. Rawson, A. C. Waller.

CRICKET RECORDS

Amended by BILL FRINDALL to end of the 1994 season in England
(Including Pakistan's matches in Sri Lanka in July and August 1994.)

Unless stated to be of a minor character, all records apply only to first-class cricket. This is traditionally considered to have started in 1815, after the Napoleonic War.

* Denotes not out or an unbroken partnership.

(A), (SA), (WI), (NZ), (I), (P), (SL) or (Z) indicates either the nationality of the player, or the country in which the record was made.

FIRST-CLASS RECORDS

BATTING RECORDS

BOWLING RECORDS

ALL-ROUND RECORDS

WICKET-KEEPING RECORDS

FIELDING RECORDS

TEAM RECORDS

TEST MATCH RECORDS

BATTING RECORDS

BOWLING RECORDS

ALL-ROUND RECORDS

WICKET-KEEPING RECORDS

FIELDING RECORDS

TEAM RECORDS

CAPTAINCY

UMPIRING

TEST SERIES

LIMITED-OVERS INTERNATIONAL RECORDS

MISCELLANEOUS

FIRST-CLASS RECORDS

BATTING RECORDS

HIGHEST INDIVIDUAL SCORES

501*	B. C. Lara	Warwickshire v Durham at Birmingham	1994
499	Hanif Mohammad	Karachi v Bahawalpur at Karachi	1958-59
452*	D. G. Bradman	NSW v Queensland at Sydney	1929-30
443*	B. B. Nimbalkar	Maharashtra v Kathiawar at Poona	1948-49

437	W. H. Ponsford	Victoria v Queensland at Melbourne	1927-28
429	W. H. Ponsford	Victoria v Tasmania at Melbourne	1922-23
428	Aftab Baloch	Sind v Baluchistan at Karachi	1973-74
424	A. C. MacLaren	Lancashire v Somerset at Taunton	1895
405*	G. A. Hick	Worcestershire v Somerset at Taunton	1988
385	B. Sutcliffe	Otago v Canterbury at Christchurch	1952-53
383	C. W. Gregory	NSW v Queensland at Brisbane	1906-07
377	S. V. Manjrekar	Bombay v Hyderabad at Bombay	1990-91
375	B. C. Lara	West Indies v England at St John's	1993-94
369	D. G. Bradman	South Australia v Tasmania at Adelaide	1935-36
366	N. H. Fairbrother	Lancashire v Surrey at The Oval	1990
366	M. V. Sridhar	Hyderabad v Andhra at Secunderabad	1993-94
365*	C. Hill	South Australia v NSW at Adelaide	1900-01
365*	G. S. Sobers	West Indies v Pakistan at Kingston	1957-58
364	L. Hutton	England v Australia at The Oval	1938
359*	V. M. Merchant	Bombay v Maharashtra at Bombay	1943-44
359	R. B. Simpson	NSW v Queensland at Brisbane	1963-64
357*	R. Abel	Surrey v Somerset at The Oval	1899
357	D. G. Bradman	South Australia v Victoria at Melbourne	1935-36
356	B. A. Richards	South Australia v Western Australia at Perth	1970-71
355*	G. R. Marsh	Western Australia v South Australia at Perth	1989-90
355	B. Sutcliffe	Otago v Auckland at Dunedin	1949-50
352	W. H. Ponsford	Victoria v NSW at Melbourne	1926-27
350	Rashid Israr	Habib Bank v National Bank at Lahore	1976-77
345	C. G. Macartney	Australians v Nottinghamshire at Nottingham	1921
344*	G. A. Headley	Jamaica v Lord Tennyson's XI at Kingston	1931-32
344	W. G. Grace	MCC v Kent at Canterbury	1876
343*	P. A. Perrin	Essex v Derbyshire at Chesterfield	1904
341	G. H. Hirst	Yorkshire v Leicestershire at Leicester	1905
340*	D. G. Bradman	NSW v Victoria at Sydney	1928-29
340	S. M. Gavaskar	Bombay v Bengal at Bombay	1981-82
338*	R. C. Blunt	Otago v Canterbury at Christchurch	1931-32
338	W. W. Read	Surrey v Oxford University at The Oval	1888
337*	Pervez Akhtar	Railways v Dera Ismail Khan at Lahore	1964-65
337*	D. J. Cullinan	Transvaal v Northern Transvaal at Johannesburg	1993-94
337†	Hanif Mohammad	Pakistan v West Indies at Bridgetown	1957-58
336*	W. R. Hammond	England v New Zealand at Auckland	1932-33
336	W. H. Ponsford	Victoria v South Australia at Melbourne	1927-28
334	D. G. Bradman	Australia v England at Leeds	1930
333	K. S. Duleepsinhji	Sussex v Northamptonshire at Hove	1930
333	G. A. Gooch	England v India at Lord's	1990
332	W. H. Ashdown	Kent v Essex at Brentwood	1934
331*	J. D. Robertson	Middlesex v Worcestershire at Worcester	1949
325*	H. L. Hendry	Victoria v New Zealanders at Melbourne	1925-26
325	A. Sandham	England v West Indies at Kingston	1929-30
325	C. L. Badcock	South Australia v Victoria at Adelaide	1935-36
324	J. B. Stollmeyer	Trinidad v British Guiana at Port-of-Spain	1946-47
324	Waheed Mirza	Karachi Whites v Quetta at Karachi	1976-77
323	A. L. Wadekar	Bombay v Mysore at Bombay	1966-67
322	E. Paynter	Lancashire v Sussex at Hove	1937
322	I. V. A. Richards	Somerset v Warwickshire at Taunton	1985
321	W. L. Murdoch	NSW v Victoria at Sydney	1881-82
320	R. Lamba	North Zone v West Zone at Bhilai	1987-88
319	Gul Mahomed	Baroda v Holkar at Baroda	1946-47
318*	W. G. Grace	Gloucestershire v Yorkshire at Cheltenham	1876
317	W. R. Hammond	Gloucestershire v Nottinghamshire at Gloucester	1936
317	K. R. Rutherford	New Zealanders v D. B. Close's XI at Scarborough	1986
316*	J. B. Hobbs	Surrey v Middlesex at Lord's	1926
316*	V. S. Hazare	Maharashtra v Baroda at Poona	1939-40
316	R. H. Moore	Hampshire v Warwickshire at Bournemouth	1937
315*	T. W. Hayward	Surrey v Lancashire at The Oval	1898
315*	P. Holmes	Yorkshire v Middlesex at Lord's	1925

315*	A. F. Kippax	NSW v Queensland at Sydney	1927-28
314*	C. L. Walcott	Barbados v Trinidad at Port-of-Spain	1945-46
313*	S. J. Cook	Somerset v Glamorgan at Cardiff	1990
313	H. Sutcliffe	Yorkshire v Essex at Leyton	1932
313	W. V. Raman	Tamil Nadu v Goa at Panjim	1988-89
312*	W. W. Keeton	Nottinghamshire v Middlesex at The Oval‡	1939
312*	J. M. Brearley	MCC Under-25 v North Zone at Peshawar	1966-67
311*	G. M. Turner	Worcestershire v Warwickshire at Worcester	1982
311	J. T. Brown	Yorkshire v Sussex at Sheffield	1897
311	R. B. Simpson	Australia v England at Manchester	1964
311	Javed Miandad	Karachi Whites v National Bank at Karachi	1974-75
310*	J. H. Edrich	England v New Zealand at Leeds	1965
310	H. Gimblett	Somerset v Sussex at Eastbourne	1948
309	V. S. Hazare	The Rest v Hindus at Bombay	1943-44
308*	F. M. M. Worrell	Barbados v Trinidad at Bridgetown	1943-44
307*	T. N. Lazard	Boland v W. Province at Worcester, Cape Province	1993-94
307	M. C. Cowdrey	MCC v South Australia at Adelaide	1962-63
307	R. M. Cowper	Australia v England at Melbourne	1965-66
306*	A. Ducat	Surrey v Oxford University at The Oval	1919
306*	E. A. B. Rowan	Transvaal v Natal at Johannesburg	1939-40
306*	D. W. Hookes	South Australia v Tasmania at Adelaide	1986-87
305*	F. E. Woolley	MCC v Tasmania at Hobart	1911-12
305*	F. R. Foster	Warwickshire v Worcestershire at Dudley	1914
305*	W. H. Ashdown	Kent v Derbyshire at Dover	1935
304*	A. W. Nourse	Natal v Transvaal at Johannesburg	1919-20
304*	P. H. Tarilton	Barbados v Trinidad at Bridgetown	1919-20
304*	E. D. Weekes	West Indians v Cambridge University at Cambridge	1950
304	R. M. Poore	Hampshire v Somerset at Taunton	1899
304	D. G. Bradman	Australia v England at Leeds	1934
303*	W. W. Armstrong	Australians v Somerset at Bath	1905
303*	Mushtaq Mohammad	Karachi Blues v Karachi University at Karachi	1967-68
303*	Abdul Azeem	Hyderabad v Tamil Nadu at Hyderabad	1986-87
302*	P. Holmes	Yorkshire v Hampshire at Portsmouth	1920
302*	W. R. Hammond	Gloucestershire v Glamorgan at Bristol	1934
302*	Arjan Kripal Singh	Tamil Nadu v Goa at Panjim	1988-89
302	W. R. Hammond	Gloucestershire v Glamorgan at Newport	1939
302	L. G. Rowe	West Indies v England at Bridgetown	1973-74
301*	E. H. Hendren	Middlesex v Worcestershire at Dudley	1933
301	W. G. Grace	Gloucestershire v Sussex at Bristol	1896
300*	V. T. Trumper	Australians v Sussex at Hove	1899
300*	F. B. Watson	Lancashire v Surrey at Manchester	1928
300*	Imtiaz Ahmed	PM's XI v Commonwealth XI at Bombay	1950-51
300	J. T. Brown	Yorkshire v Derbyshire at Chesterfield	1898
300	D. C. S. Compton	MCC v N. E. Transvaal at Benoni	1948-49
300	R. Subba Row	Northamptonshire v Surrey at The Oval	1958

† *Hanif Mohammad batted for 16 hours 10 minutes – the longest innings in first-class cricket.*
‡ *Played at The Oval because Lord's was required for Eton v Harrow.*
Note: W. V. Raman (313) and Arjan Kripal Singh (302*) provide the only instance of two triple-hundreds in the same innings.

HIGHEST SCORE FOR EACH FIRST-CLASS COUNTY

Derbyshire	274	G. Davidson v Lancashire at Manchester	1896
Durham	204	J. E. Morris v Warwickshire at Birmingham	1994
Essex	343*	P. A. Perrin v Derbyshire at Chesterfield	1904
Glamorgan	287*	D. E. Davies v Gloucestershire at Newport	1939
Gloucestershire	318*	W. G. Grace v Yorkshire at Cheltenham	1876

Hampshire	316	R. H. Moore v Warwickshire at Bournemouth	1937
Kent	332	W. H. Ashdown v Essex at Brentwood	1934
Lancashire	424	A. C. MacLaren v Somerset at Taunton	1895
Leicestershire	261	P. V. Simmons v Northamptonshire at Leicester	1994
Middlesex	331*	J. D. Robertson v Worcestershire at Worcester	1949
Northamptonshire	300	R. Subba Row v Surrey at The Oval	1958
Nottinghamshire	312*	W. W. Keeton v Middlesex at The Oval†	1939
Somerset	322	I. V. A. Richards v Warwickshire at Taunton	1985
Surrey	357*	R. Abel v Somerset at The Oval	1899
Sussex	333	K. S. Duleepsinhji v Northamptonshire at Hove	1930
Warwickshire	501*	B. C. Lara v Durham at Birmingham	1994
Worcestershire	405*	G. A. Hick v Somerset at Taunton	1988
Yorkshire	341	G. H. Hirst v Leicestershire at Leicester	1905

† *Played at The Oval because Lord's was required for Eton v Harrow.*

HIGHEST SCORE AGAINST EACH FIRST-CLASS COUNTY

Derbyshire	343*	P. A. Perrin (Essex) at Chesterfield	1904
Durham	501*	B. C. Lara (Warwickshire) at Birmingham	1994
Essex	332	W. H. Ashdown (Kent) at Brentwood	1934
Glamorgan	313*	S. J. Cook (Somerset) at Cardiff	1990
Gloucestershire	296	A. O. Jones (Nottinghamshire) at Nottingham	1903
Hampshire	302*	P. Holmes (Yorkshire) at Portsmouth	1920
Kent	344	W. G. Grace (MCC) at Canterbury	1876
Lancashire	315*	T. W. Hayward (Surrey) at The Oval	1898
Leicestershire	341	G. H. Hirst (Yorkshire) at Leicester	1905
Middlesex	316*	J. B. Hobbs (Surrey) at Lord's	1926
Northamptonshire	333	K. S. Duleepsinhji (Sussex) at Hove	1930
Nottinghamshire	345	C. G. Macartney (Australians) at Nottingham	1921
Somerset	424	A. C. MacLaren (Lancashire) at Taunton	1895
Surrey	366	N. H. Fairbrother (Lancashire) at The Oval	1990
Sussex	322	E. Paynter (Lancashire) at Hove	1937
Warwickshire	322	I. V. A. Richards (Somerset) at Taunton	1985
Worcestershire	331*	J. D. Robertson (Middlesex) at Worcester	1949
Yorkshire	318*	W. G. Grace (Gloucestershire) at Cheltenham	1876

DOUBLE-HUNDRED ON DEBUT

227	T. Marsden	Sheffield & Leicester v Nottingham at Sheffield	1826
207	N. F. Callaway†	New South Wales v Queensland at Sydney	1914-15
240	W. F. E. Marx	Transvaal v Griqualand West at Johannesburg	1920-21
200*	A. Maynard	Trinidad v MCC at Port-of-Spain	1934-35
232*	S. J. E. Loxton	Victoria v Queensland at Melbourne	1946-47
215*	G. H. G. Doggart	Cambridge University v Lancashire at Cambridge	1948
202	J. Hallebone	Victoria v Tasmania at Melbourne	1951-52
230	G. R. Viswanath	Mysore v Andhra at Vijayawada	1967-68
260	A. A. Muzumdar	Bombay v Haryana at Faridabad	1993-94

† *In his only first-class innings. He was killed in action in France in 1917.*

TWO SEPARATE HUNDREDS ON DEBUT

148 and 111	A. R. Morris	New South Wales v Queensland at Sydney	1940-41
152 and 102*	N. J. Contractor	Gujarat v Baroda at Baroda	1952-53
132* and 110	Aamer Malik	Lahore "A" v Railways at Lahore	1979-80

Notes: J. S. Solomon, British Guiana, scored a hundred in each of his first three innings in first-class cricket: 114* v Jamaica; 108 v Barbados in 1956-57; 121 v Pakistanis in 1957-58.

R. Watson-Smith, Border, scored 310 runs before he was dismissed in first-class cricket, including not-out centuries in his first two innings: 183* v Orange Free State and 125* v Griqualand West in 1969-70.

G. R. Viswanath and D. M. Wellham alone have scored a hundred on their debut in both first-class cricket and Test cricket. Viswanath scored 230 for Mysore v Andhra in 1967-68 and 137 for India v Australia in 1969-70. Wellham scored 100 for New South Wales v Victoria in 1980-81 and 103 for Australia v England in 1981.

HUNDRED ON DEBUT IN BRITAIN

(The following list does not include instances of players who have previously appeared in first-class cricket outside the British Isles or who performed the feat before 1965. Full lists of earlier instances are in *Wisdens* prior to 1984.)

108	D. R. Shepherd	Gloucestershire v Oxford University at Oxford	1965
110*	A. J. Harvey-Walker	Derbyshire v Oxford University at Burton upon Trent	†1971
173	J. Whitehouse	Warwickshire v Oxford University at Oxford	1971
106	J. B. Turner	Minor Counties v Pakistanis at Jesmond	1974
112	J. A. Claughton	Oxford University v Gloucestershire at Oxford	†1976
100*	A. W. Lilley	Essex v Nottinghamshire at Nottingham	†1978
146*	J. S. Johnson	Minor Counties v Indians at Wellington	1979
110	N. R. Taylor	Kent v Sri Lankans at Canterbury	1979
146*	D. G. Aslett	Kent v Hampshire at Bournemouth	1981
116	M. D. Moxon	Yorkshire v Essex at Leeds	†1981
100	D. A. Banks	Worcestershire v Oxford University at Oxford	1983
122	A. A. Metcalfe	Yorkshire v Nottinghamshire at Bradford	1983
117*	K. T. Medlycott	Surrey v Cambridge University at Banstead	‡1984
101*	N. J. Falkner	Surrey v Cambridge University at Banstead	‡1984
106	A. C. Storie	Northamptonshire v Hampshire at Northampton	†1985
102	M. P. Maynard	Glamorgan v Yorkshire at Swansea	1985
117*	R. J. Bartlett	Somerset v Oxford University at Oxford	1986
100*	P. D. Bowler	Leicestershire v Hampshire at Leicester	1986
145	I. L. Philip	Scotland v Ireland at Glasgow	1986
114*	P. D. Atkins	Surrey v Cambridge University at The Oval	1988
100	B. M. W. Patterson	Scotland v Ireland at Dumfries	1988
116*	J. J. B. Lewis	Essex v Surrey at The Oval	1990
117	J. D. Glendenen	Durham v Oxford University at Oxford	1992
109	J. R. Wileman	Nottinghamshire v Cambridge U. at Nottingham	1992
123	A. J. Hollioake	Surrey v Derbyshire at Ilkeston	†1993

† *In his second innings.*
‡ *The only instance in England of two players performing the feat in the same match.*

TWO DOUBLE-HUNDREDS IN A MATCH

A. E. Fagg	244	202*	Kent v Essex at Colchester	1938

TRIPLE-HUNDRED AND HUNDRED IN A MATCH

G. A. Gooch	333	123	England v India at Lord's	1990

DOUBLE-HUNDRED AND HUNDRED IN A MATCH

C. B. Fry	125	229	Sussex v Surrey at Hove	1900
W. W. Armstrong	157*	245	Victoria v South Australia at Melbourne.	1920-21
H. T. W. Hardinge	207	102*	Kent v Surrey at Blackheath	1921
C. P. Mead	113	224	Hampshire v Sussex at Horsham	1921
K. S. Duleepsinhji	115	246	Sussex v Kent at Hastings	1929
D. G. Bradman	124	225	Woodfull's XI v Ryder's XI at Sydney	1929-30
B. Sutcliffe	243	100*	New Zealanders v Essex at Southend	1949
M. R. Hallam	210*	157	Leicestershire v Glamorgan at Leicester	1959
M. R. Hallam	203*	143*	Leicestershire v Sussex at Worthing	1961
Hanumant Singh	109	213*	Rajasthan v Bombay at Bombay	1966-67
Salah-ud-Din	256	102*	Karachi v East Pakistan at Karachi	1968-69
K. D. Walters	242	103	Australia v West Indies at Sydney	1968-69
S. M. Gavaskar	124	220	India v West Indies at Port-of-Spain	1970-71
L. G. Rowe	214	100*	West Indies v New Zealand at Kingston	1971-72
G. S. Chappell	247*	133	Australia v New Zealand at Wellington	1973-74
L. Baichan	216*	102	Berbice v Demerara at Georgetown	1973-74
Zaheer Abbas	216*	156*	Gloucestershire v Surrey at The Oval	1976
Zaheer Abbas	230*	104*	Gloucestershire v Kent at Canterbury	1976
Zaheer Abbas	205*	108*	Gloucestershire v Sussex at Cheltenham	1977
Saadat Ali	141	222	Income Tax v Multan at Multan	1977-78
Talat Ali	214*	104	PIA v Punjab at Lahore	1978-79
Shafiq Ahmad	129	217*	National Bank v MCB at Karachi	1978-79
D. W. Randall	209	146	Notts. v Middlesex at Nottingham	1979
Zaheer Abbas	215*	150*	Gloucestershire v Somerset at Bath	1981
Qasim Omar	210*	110	MCB v Lahore at Lahore	1982-83
A. I. Kallicharran	200*	117*	Warwicks. v Northants at Birmingham	1984
Rizwan-uz-Zaman	139	217*	PIA v PACO at Lahore	1989-90
G. A. Hick	252*	100*	Worcs. v Glamorgan at Abergavenny	1990
N. R. Taylor	204	142	Kent v Surrey at Canterbury	1990
N. R. Taylor	111	203*	Kent v Sussex at Hove	1991
W. V. Raman	226	120	Tamil Nadu v Haryana at Faridabad	1991-92
A. J. Lamb	209	107	Northants v Warwicks. at Northampton.	1992
G. A. Gooch	101	205	Essex v Worcestershire at Worcester	1994

TWO SEPARATE HUNDREDS IN A MATCH

Eight times: Zaheer Abbas.

Seven times: W. R. Hammond.

Six times: J. B. Hobbs, G. M. Turner.

Five times: C. B. Fry, G. A. Gooch.

Four times: D. G. Bradman, G. S. Chappell, J. H. Edrich, L. B. Fishlock, T. W. Graveney, C. G. Greenidge, H. T. W. Hardinge, E. H. Hendren, Javed Miandad, G. L. Jessop, P. A. Perrin, B. Sutcliffe, H. Sutcliffe.

Three times: Agha Zahid, L. E. G. Ames, G. Boycott, I. M. Chappell, D. C. S. Compton, S. J. Cook, M. C. Cowdrey, D. Denton, K. S. Duleepsinhji, R. E. Foster, R. C. Fredericks, S. M. Gavaskar, W. G. Grace, G. Gunn, M. R. Hallam, Hanif Mohammad, M. J. Harris, T. W. Hayward, V. S. Hazare, D. W. Hookes, L. Hutton, A. Jones, D. M. Jones, P. N. Kirsten, R. B. McCosker, P. B. H. May, C. P. Mead, H. Morris, Rizwan-uz-Zaman, R. T. Robinson, A. C. Russell, Sadiq Mohammad, J. T. Tyldesley, K. C. Wessels.

Twice: Ali Zia, D. L. Amiss, C. W. J. Athey, L. Baichan, Basit Ali, D. C. Boon, A. R. Border, B. J. T. Bosanquet, R. J. Boyd-Moss, A. R. Butcher, M. D. Crowe, C. C. Dacre, G. M. Emmett, A. E. Fagg, L. E. Favell, H. Gimblett, C. Hallows, R. A. Hamence, A. L. Hassett, M. L. Hayden, D. L. Haynes, G. A. Headley, G. A. Hick, D. M. Jones, A. I. Kallicharran, J. H. King, A. F. Kippax, A. J. Lamb, J. G. Langridge, H. W. Lee, E. Lester, C. B. Llewellyn, C. G. Macartney, M. P. Maynard, C. A. Milton, A. R. Morris, P. H. Parfitt, Nawab of Pataudi jun., E. Paynter, C. Pinch, R. G. Pollock, R. M. Prideaux, Qasim Omar, W. Rhodes, B. A. Richards, I. V. A. Richards, Pankaj Roy, Salim Malik, James Seymour, Shafiq Ahmad, R. B. Simpson, C. L. Smith, G. S. Sobers, M. A. Taylor, N. R. Taylor, E. Tyldesley, C. L. Walcott, T. R. Ward, W. W. Whysall, G. N. Yallop.

Notes: W. Lambert scored 107 and 157 for Sussex v Epsom at Lord's in 1817 and it was not until W. G. Grace made 130 and 102* for South of the Thames v North of the Thames at Canterbury in 1868 that the feat was repeated.

Zaheer Abbas scored a double-hundred and a hundred in the same match for Gloucestershire four times, on each occasion without being dismissed.

C. J. B. Wood, 107* and 117* for Leicestershire v Yorkshire at Bradford in 1911, and S. J. Cook, 120* and 131* for Somerset v Nottinghamshire at Nottingham in 1989, are alone in carrying their bats and scoring hundreds in each innings.

FOUR HUNDREDS OR MORE IN SUCCESSION

Six in succession: D. G. Bradman 1938-39; C. B. Fry 1901; M. J. Procter 1970-71.

Five in succession: B. C. Lara 1993-94/1994; E. D. Weekes 1955-56.

Four in succession: C. W. J. Athey 1987; M. Azharuddin 1984-85; M. G. Bevan 1990-91; A. R. Border 1985; D. G. Bradman 1931-32, 1948/1948-49; D. C. S. Compton 1946-47; N. J. Contractor 1957-58; S. J. Cook 1989; K. S. Duleepsinhji 1931; C. B. Fry 1911; C. G. Greenidge 1986; W. R. Hammond 1936-37, 1945/1946; H. T. W. Hardinge 1913; T. W. Hayward 1906; J. B. Hobbs 1920, 1925; D. W. Hookes 1976-77; P. N. Kirsten 1976-77; J. G. Langridge 1949; C. G. Macartney 1921; K. S. McEwan 1977; P. B. H. May 1956-57; V. M. Merchant 1941-42; A. Mitchell 1933; Nawab of Pataudi sen. 1931; Rizwan-uz-Zaman 1989-90; L. G. Rowe 1971-72; Pankaj Roy 1962-63; Sadiq Mohammad 1976; Saeed Ahmed 1961-62; M. V. Sridhar 1990-91/1991-92; H. Sutcliffe 1931, 1939; E. Tyldesley 1926; W. W. Whysall 1930; F. E. Woolley 1929; Zaheer Abbas 1970-71, 1982-83.

Notes: T. W. Hayward (Surrey v Nottinghamshire and Leicestershire) and D. W. Hookes (South Australia v Queensland and New South Wales) are the only players listed above to score two hundreds in two successive matches. Hayward scored his in six days, June 4-9, 1906.

The most fifties in consecutive innings is ten – by E. Tyldesley in 1926 and by D. G. Bradman in the 1947-48 and 1948 seasons.

MOST HUNDREDS IN A SEASON

Eighteen: D. C. S. Compton 1947.
Sixteen: J. B. Hobbs 1925.
Fifteen: W. R. Hammond 1938.
Fourteen: H. Sutcliffe 1932.
Thirteen: G. Boycott 1971, D. G. Bradman 1938, C. B. Fry 1901, W. R. Hammond 1933 and 1937, T. W. Hayward 1906, E. H. Hendren 1923, 1927 and 1928, C. P. Mead 1928, H. Sutcliffe 1928 and 1931.

Since 1969 (excluding G. Boycott – above)

Twelve: G. A. Gooch 1990.
Eleven: S. J. Cook 1991, Zaheer Abbas 1976.
Ten: G. A. Hick 1988, H. Morris 1990, G. M. Turner 1970, Zaheer Abbas 1981.

MOST DOUBLE-HUNDREDS IN A SEASON

Six: D. G. Bradman 1930.
Five: K. S. Ranjitsinhji 1900; E. D. Weekes 1950.
Four: Arun Lal 1986-87; C. B. Fry 1901; W. R. Hammond 1933, 1934; E. H. Hendren 1929-30; V. M. Merchant 1944-45; G. M. Turner 1971-72.
Three: L. E. G. Ames 1933; Arshad Pervez 1977-78; D. G. Bradman 1930-31, 1931-32, 1934, 1935-36, 1936-37, 1938, 1939-40; W. J. Edrich 1947; C. B. Fry 1903, 1904; M. W. Gatting 1994; G. A. Gooch 1994; W. R. Hammond 1928, 1928-29, 1932-33, 1938; J. Hardstaff jun. 1937, 1947; V. S. Hazare 1943-44; E. H. Hendren 1925; J. B. Hobbs 1914, 1926; L. Hutton 1949; D. M. Jones 1991-92; A. I. Kallicharran 1982; V. G. Kambli 1992-93; P. N. Kirsten 1980; R. S. Modi 1944-45; Nawab of Pataudi sen. 1933; W. H. Ponsford 1927-28, 1934; W. V. Raman 1988-89; K. S. Ranjitsinhji 1901; I. V. A. Richards 1977; R. B. Simpson 1963-64; P. R. Umrigar 1952, 1959; F. B. Watson 1928.

MOST HUNDREDS IN A CAREER

(35 or more)

			Total	*100th 100*				
		100s	*Inns*	*Season*	*Inns*	*400+*	*300+*	*200+*
1	J. B. Hobbs	197	1,315	1923	821	0	1	16
2	E. H. Hendren	170	1,300	1928-29	740	0	1	22
3	W. R. Hammond	167	1,005	1935	679	0	4	36
4	C. P. Mead	153	1,340	1927	892	0	0	13
5	G. Boycott	151	1,014	1977	645	0	0	10
6	H. Sutcliffe	149	1,088	1932	700	0	1	17
7	F. E. Woolley	145	1,532	1929	1,031	0	1	9
8	L. Hutton	129	814	1951	619	0	1	11
9	W. G. Grace	126	1,493	1895	1,113	0	3	13
10	D. C. S. Compton	123	839	1952	552	0	1	9
11	T. W. Graveney	122	1,223	1964	940	0	0	7
12	D. G. Bradman	117	338	1947-48	295	1	6	37
13	I. V. A. Richards	114	796	1988-89	658	0	1	10
14	**G. A. Gooch**	**112**	**888**	**1992-93**	**820**	**0**	**1**	**12**
15	Zaheer Abbas	108	768	1982-83	658	0	0	10
16	A. Sandham	107	1,000	1935	871	0	1	11
	M. C. Cowdrey	107	1,130	1973	1,035	0	1	3
18	T. W. Hayward	104	1,138	1913	1,076	0	1	8
19	J. H. Edrich	103	979	1977	945	0	1	4
	G. M. Turner	103	792	1982	779	0	1	10
21	E. Tyldesley	102	961	1934	919	0	0	7
	L. E. G. Ames	102	951	1950	915	0	0	9
	D. L. Amiss	102	1,139	1986	1,081	0	0	3

E. H. Hendren, D. G. Bradman and I. V. A. Richards scored their 100th hundreds in Australia, G. A. Gooch scored his in India. His record includes his century in South Africa in 1981-82, which is no longer accepted by ICC. Zaheer Abbas scored his in Pakistan. Zaheer Abbas and G. Boycott did so in Test matches.

Most double-hundreds scored by batsmen not included in the above list:

Sixteen: C. B. Fry.

Fourteen: C. G. Greenidge, K. S. Ranjitsinhji.

Thirteen: W. H. Ponsford (including two 400s and two 300s), J. T. Tyldesley.

Twelve: P. Holmes, Javed Miandad, R. B. Simpson.

Eleven: J. W. Hearne, V. M. Merchant.

Ten: S. M. Gavaskar, J. Hardstaff, jun., V. S. Hazare, A. Shrewsbury, R. T. Simpson.

J. W. Hearne	96
C. B. Fry	94
C. G. Greenidge	92
A. I. Kallicharran	87
W. J. Edrich	86
A. J. Lamb	**86**
G. S. Sobers	86
J. T. Tyldesley	86
P. B. H. May	85
R. E. S. Wyatt	85
J. Hardstaff, jun.	83
R. B. Kanhai	83
M. W. Gatting	**82**
S. M. Gavaskar	81
Javed Miandad	**80**
M. Leyland	80
B. A. Richards	80
C. H. Lloyd	79
G. A. Hick	**77**
K. F. Barrington	76
J. G. Langridge	76
C. Washbrook	76
H. T. W. Hardinge	75
R. Abel	74
G. S. Chappell	74
D. Kenyon	74
K. S. McEwan	74
Majid Khan	73
Mushtaq Mohammad	72
J. O'Connor	72
W. G. Quaife	72
K. S. Ranjitsinhji	72
D. Brookes	71
A. C. Russell	71
D. Denton	69
M. J. K. Smith	69

A. R. Border **68**
R. E. Marshall 68
M. D. Crowe **67**
R. N. Harvey 67
P. Holmes 67
J. D. Robertson 67
P. A. Perrin.......... 66
R. G. Pollock 64
R. T. Simpson........ 64
S. J. Cook **63**
K. W. R. Fletcher 63
G. Gunn 62
V. S. Hazare 60
G. H. Hirst 60
R. B. Simpson........ 60
P. F. Warner......... 60
I. M. Chappell 59
A. L. Hassett......... 59
D. L. Haynes......... **59**
A. Shrewsbury........ 59
J. G. Wright 59
A. E. Fagg........... 58
P. H. Parfitt 58
W. Rhodes........... 58
W. Larkins **57**
L. B. Fishlock 56
A. Jones............. 56
C. A. Milton 56
C. Hallows........... 55
Hanif Mohammad 55
D. B. Vengsarkar 55
W. Watson 55
K. C. Wessels **55**
D. J. Insole 54
W. W. Keeton........ 54
W. Bardsley.......... 53
B. F. Davison 53
A. E. Dipper......... 53
D. I. Gower.......... 53
G. L. Jessop 53
P. N. Kirsten......... **53**
James Seymour 53
Shafiq Ahmad........ 53
D. C. Boon........... **52**
E. H. Bowley......... 52
D. B. Close 52
A. Ducat 52
D. W. Randall 52
E. R. Dexter 51
J. M. Parks 51
R. T. Robinson **51**
W. W. Whysall 51
B. C. Broad **50**
G. Cox, jun. 50
H. E. Dollery 50
K. S. Duleepsinhji 50
H. Gimblett.......... 50
W. M. Lawry 50
Sadiq Mohammad..... 50
F. B. Watson......... 50

C. W. J. Athey **49**
C. G. Macartney...... 49
M. J. Stewart 49
K. G. Suttle.......... 49
P. R. Umrigar........ 49
W. M. Woodfull 49
C. J. Barnett 48
W. Gunn 48
E. G. Hayes 48
B. W. Luckhurst...... 48
M. J. Procter......... 48
C. E. B. Rice **48**
C. J. Tavaré 48
M. E. Waugh......... **48**
A. C. MacLaren 47
P. W. G. Parker 47
W. H. Ponsford....... 47
C. L. Smith 47
M. R. Benson **46**
A. R. Butcher 46
J. Iddon 46
A. R. Morris 46
C. T. Radley 46
Younis Ahmed 46
W. W. Armstrong..... 45
Asif Iqbal 45
L. G. Berry 45
J. M. Brearley 45
A. W. Carr 45
C. Hill 45
N. C. O'Neill 45
E. Paynter 45
Rev. D. S. Sheppard... 45
R. A. Smith **45**
K. D. Walters 45
K. J. Barnett **44**
H. H. I. Gibbons 44
V. M. Merchant 44
A. Mitchell 44
P. E. Richardson 44
B. Sutcliffe........... 44
G. R. Viswanath...... 44
P. Willey 44
E. J. Barlow 43
B. L. D'Oliveira 43
J. H. Hampshire...... 43
A. F. Kippax 43
J. W. H. Makepeace .. 43
James Langridge...... 42
Mudassar Nazar 42
H. W. Parks 42
T. F. Shepherd 42
V. T. Trumper 42
M. J. Harris 41
G. D. Mendis 41
K. R. Miller 41
A. D. Nourse 41
J. H. Parks 41
R. M. Prideaux....... 41
G. Pullar 41

W. E. Russell 41
N. R. Taylor **41**
M. Azharuddin......... **40**
R. C. Fredericks...... 40
J. Gunn 40
M. J. Smith.......... 40
C. L. Walcott 40
D. M. Young......... 40
Arshad Pervez........ 39
W. H. Ashdown 39
J. B. Bolus........... 39
W. A. Brown......... 39
R. J. Gregory 39
D. M. Jones.......... **39**
J. E. Morris.......... **39**
W. R. D. Payton...... 39
J. R. Reid 39
F. M. M. Worrell 39
I. T. Botham 38
F. L. Bowley 38
P. J. P. Burge 38
J. F. Crapp 38
D. Lloyd 38
V. L. Manjrekar 38
M. D. Moxon **38**
A. W. Nourse 38
N. Oldfield 38
Rev. J. H. Parsons 38
W. W. Read 38
J. Sharp............. 38
L. J. Todd 38
J. Arnold 37
G. Brown............ 37
G. Cook............. 37
G. M. Emmett 37
H. W. Lee 37
T. M. Moody......... **37**
H. Morris **37**
M. A. Noble 37
B. P. Patel........... 37
H. S. Squires 37
R. T. Virgin 37
C. J. B. Wood........ 37
N. F. Armstrong...... 36
G. Fowler........... **36**
E. Oldroyd........... 36
W. Place 36
V. P. Terry **36**
A. L. Wadekar 36
E. D. Weekes 36
T. S. Curtis **35**
C. S. Dempster 35
D. R. Jardine 35
T. E. Jesty........... 35
Rizwan-uz-Zaman **35**
Salim Malik.......... **35**
B. H. Valentine....... 35
G. M. Wood 35

Bold type denotes those who played in 1993-94 and 1994 seasons.

3,000 RUNS IN A SEASON

	Season	*I*	*NO*	*R*	*HS*	*100s*	*Avge*
D. C. S. Compton	1947	50	8	3,816	246	18	90.85
W. J. Edrich	1947	52	8	3,539	267*	12	80.43
T. W. Hayward	1906	61	8	3,518	219	13	66.37
L. Hutton	1949	56	6	3,429	269*	12	68.58
F. E. Woolley........	1928	59	4	3,352	198	12	60.94
H. Sutcliffe	1932	52	7	3,336	313	14	74.13
W. R. Hammond.....	1933	54	5	3,323	264	13	67.81
E. H. Hendren	1928	54	7	3,311	209*	13	70.44
R. Abel.............	1901	68	8	3,309	247	7	55.15
W. R. Hammond.....	1937	55	5	3,252	217	13	65.04
M. J. K. Smith	1959	67	11	3,245	200*	8	57.94
E. H. Hendren	1933	65	9	3,186	301*	11	56.89
C. P. Mead	1921	52	6	3,179	280*	10	69.10
T. W. Hayward	1904	63	5	3,170	203	11	54.65
K. S. Ranjitsinhji.....	1899	58	8	3,159	197	8	63.18
C. B. Fry	1901	43	3	3,147	244	13	78.67
K. S. Ranjitsinhji.....	1900	40	5	3,065	275	11	87.57
L. E. G. Ames	1933	57	5	3,058	295	9	58.80
J. T. Tyldesley	1901	60	5	3,041	221	9	55.29
C. P. Mead	1928	50	10	3,027	180	13	75.67
J. B. Hobbs	1925	48	5	3,024	266*	16	70.32
E. Tyldesley	1928	48	10	3,024	242	10	79.57
W. E. Alley	1961	64	11	3,019	221*	11	56.96
W. R. Hammond.....	1938	42	2	3,011	271	15	75.27
E. H. Hendren	1923	51	12	3,010	200*	13	77.17
H. Sutcliffe	1931	42	11	3,006	230	13	96.96
J. H. Parks..........	1937	63	4	3,003	168	11	50.89
H. Sutcliffe	1928	44	5	3,002	228	13	76.97

Notes: W. G. Grace scored 2,739 runs in 1871 – the first batsman to reach 2,000 runs in a season. He made ten hundreds and twice exceeded 200, with an average of 78.25 in all first-class matches.

The highest aggregate in a season since the reduction of County Championship matches in 1969 is 2,755 by S. J. Cook (42 innings) in 1991.

2,000 RUNS IN A SEASON

Since Reduction of Championship Matches in 1969

Five times: G. A. Gooch 2,746 (1990), 2,559 (1984), 2,324 (1988), 2,208 (1985), 2,023 (1993).

Three times: D. L. Amiss 2,239 (1984), 2,110 (1976), 2,030 (1978); S. J. Cook 2,755 (1991), 2,608 (1990), 2,241 (1989); M. W. Gatting 2,257 (1984), 2,057 (1991), 2,000 (1992); G. A. Hick 2,713 (1988), 2,347 (1990), 2,004 (1986); G. M. Turner 2,416 (1973), 2,379 (1970), 2,101 (1981).

Twice: G. Boycott 2,503 (1971), 2,051 (1970); J. H. Edrich 2,238 (1969), 2,031 (1971); A. I. Kallicharran 2,301 (1984), 2,120 (1982); Zaheer Abbas 2,554 (1976), 2,306 (1981).

Once: M. Azharuddin 2,016 (1991); J. B. Bolus 2,143 (1970); P. D. Bowler 2,044 (1992); B. C. Broad 2,226 (1990); A. R. Butcher 2,116 (1990); C. G. Greenidge 2,035 (1986); M. J. Harris 2,238 (1971); D. L. Haynes 2,346 (1990); Javed Miandad 2,083 (1981); A. J. Lamb 2,049 (1981); B. C. Lara 2,066 (1994); K. S. McEwan 2,176 (1983); Majid Khan 2,074 (1972); A. A. Metcalfe 2,047 (1990); H. Morris 2,276 (1990); D. W. Randall 2,151 (1985); I. V. A. Richards 2,161 (1977); R. T. Robinson 2,032 (1984); M. A. Roseberry 2,044 (1992); C. L. Smith 2,000 (1985); R. T. Virgin 2,223 (1970); D. M. Ward 2,072 (1990); M. E. Waugh 2,072 (1990).

1,000 RUNS IN A SEASON MOST TIMES

(Includes Overseas Tours and Seasons)

28 times: W. G. Grace 2,000 (6); F. E. Woolley 3,000 (1), 2,000 (12).
27 times: M. C. Cowdrey 2,000 (2); C. P. Mead 3,000 (2), 2,000 (9).
26 times: G. Boycott 2,000 (3); J. B. Hobbs 3,000 (1), 2,000 (16).
25 times: E. H. Hendren 3,000 (3), 2,000 (12).
24 times: D. L. Amiss 2,000 (3); W. G. Quaife 2,000 (1); H. Sutcliffe 3,000 (3), 2,000 (12).
23 times: A. Jones.
22 times: T. W. Graveney 2,000 (7); W. R. Hammond 3,000 (3), 2,000 (9).
21 times: D. Denton 2,000 (5); J. H. Edrich 2,000 (6); W. Rhodes 2,000 (2).
20 times: D. B. Close; K. W. R. Fletcher; G. Gunn; T. W. Hayward 3,000 (2), 2,000 (8); James Langridge 2,000 (1); J. M. Parks 2,000 (3); A. Sandham 2,000 (8); M. J. K. Smith 3,000 (1), 2,000 (5); C. Washbrook 2,000 (2).
19 times: G. A. Gooch 2,000 (5); J. W. Hearne 2,000 (4); G. H. Hirst 2,000 (3); D. Kenyon 2,000 (7); E. Tyldesley 3,000 (1), 2,000 (5); J. T. Tyldesley 3,000 (1), 2,000 (4).
18 times: L. G. Berry 2,000 (1); H. T. W. Hardinge 2,000 (5); R. E. Marshall 2,000 (6); P. A. Perrin; G. M. Turner 2,000 (3); R. E. S. Wyatt 2,000 (5).
17 times: L. E. G. Ames 3,000 (1), 2,000 (5); T. E. Bailey 2,000 (1); D. Brookes 2,000 (6); D. C. S. Compton 3,000 (1), 2,000 (5); M. W. Gatting 2,000 (3); C. G. Greenidge 2,000 (1); L. Hutton 3,000 (1), 2,000 (8); J. G. Langridge 2,000 (11); M. Leyland 2,000 (3); I. V. A. Richards 2,000 (1); K. G. Suttle 2,000 (1); Zaheer Abbas 2,000 (2).
16 times: D. G. Bradman 2,000 (4); D. E. Davies 2,000 (1); E. G. Hayes 2,000 (2); C. A. Milton 2,000 (1); J. O'Connor 2,000 (4); C. T. Radley; James Seymour 2,000 (1); C. J. Tavaré.
15 times: G. Barker; K. F. Barrington 2,000 (3); E. H. Bowley 2,000 (4); M. H. Denness; A. E. Dipper 2,000 (5); H. E. Dollery 2,000 (2); W. J. Edrich 3,000 (1), 2,000 (8); J. H. Hampshire; P. Holmes 2,000 (7); Mushtaq Mohammad; R. B. Nicholls 2,000 (1); P. H. Parfitt 2,000 (3); W. G. A. Parkhouse 2,000 (1); B. A. Richards 2,000 (1); J. D. Robertson 2,000 (9); G. S. Sobers; M. J. Stewart 2,000 (1).

Notes: F. E. Woolley reached 1,000 runs in 28 consecutive seasons (1907-1938), C. P. Mead in 27 (1906-1936).

Outside England, 1,000 runs in a season has been reached most times by D. G. Bradman (in 12 seasons in Australia).

Three batsmen have scored 1,000 runs in a season in each of four different countries: G. S. Sobers in West Indies, England, India and Australia; M. C. Cowdrey and G. Boycott in England, South Africa, West Indies and Australia.

HIGHEST AGGREGATES OUTSIDE ENGLAND

	Season	I	NO	R	HS	100s	Avge
In Australia							
D. G. Bradman	1928-29	24	6	1,690	340*	7	93.88
In South Africa							
J. R. Reid...........	1961-62	30	2	1,915	203	7	68.39
In West Indies							
E. H. Hendren.......	1929-30	18	5	1,765	254*	6	135.76
In New Zealand							
M. D. Crowe	1986-87	21	3	1,676	175*	8	93.11
In India							
C. G. Borde	1964-65	28	3	1,604	168	6	64.16
In Pakistan							
Saadat Ali	1983-84	27	1	1,649	208	4	63.42
In Sri Lanka							
P. A. de Silva	1992-93	22	1	1,308	231	3	62.28

In Zimbabwe

D. L. Houghton......	1989-90	9	1	701	202	3	87.62

Note: In more than one country, the following aggregates of over 2,000 runs have been recorded:

	Season	*I*	*NO*	*R*	*HS*	*100s*	*Avge*
M. Amarnath (P/I/WI)	1982-83	34	6	2,234	207	9	79.78
J. R. Reid (SA/A/NZ).	1961-62	40	2	2,188	203	7	57.57
S. M. Gavaskar (I/P) .	1978-79	30	6	2,121	205	10	88.37
R. B. Simpson (I/P/A/WI)........	1964-65	34	4	2,063	201	8	68.76

LEADING BATSMEN IN AN ENGLISH SEASON

(Qualification: 8 innings)

Season	*Leading scorer*	*Runs*	*Avge*	*Top of averages*	*Runs*	*Avge*
1946	D. C. S. Compton ...	2,403	61.61	W. R. Hammond ...	1,783	84.90
1947	D. C. S. Compton ...	3,816	90.85	D. C. S. Compton ..	3,816	90.85
1948	L. Hutton	2,654	64.73	D. G. Bradman.....	2,428	89.92
1949	L. Hutton	3,429	68.58	J. Hardstaff........	2,251	72.61
1950	R. T. Simpson.......	2,576	62.82	E. Weekes.........	2,310	79.65
1951	J. D. Robertson	2,917	56.09	P. B. H. May	2,339	68.79
1952	L. Hutton	2,567	61.11	D. S. Sheppard	2,262	64.62
1953	W. J. Edrich........	2,557	47.35	W. A. Johnston.....	102	102.00†
1954	D. Kenyon	2,636	51.68	D. C. S. Compton ..	1,524	58.61
1955	D. J. Insole.........	2,427	42.57	D. J. McGlew......	1,871	58.46
1956	T. W. Graveney	2,397	49.93	K. Mackay	1,103	52.52
1957	T. W. Graveney	2,361	49.18	P. B. H. May	2,347	61.76
1958	P. B. H. May	2,231	63.74	P. B. H. May	2,231	63.74
1959	M. J. K. Smith......	3,245	57.94	V. L. Manjrekar	755	68.63
1960	M. J. K. Smith......	2,551	45.55	R. Subba Row	1,503	55.66
1961	W. E. Alley.........	3,019	56.96	W. M. Lawry	2,019	61.18
1962	J. H. Edrich	2,482	51.70	R. T. Simpson......	867	54.18
1963	J. B. Bolus..........	2,190	41.32	G. S. Sobers	1,333	47.60
1964	T. W. Graveney	2,385	54.20	K. F. Barrington....	1,872	62.40
1965	J. H. Edrich	2,319	62.67	M. C. Cowdrey.....	2,093	63.42
1966	A. R. Lewis.........	2,198	41.47	G. S. Sobers	1,349	61.31
1967	C. A. Milton........	2,089	46.42	K. F. Barrington....	2,059	68.63
1968	B. A. Richards	2,395	47.90	G. Boycott.........	1,487	64.65
1969	J. H. Edrich	2,238	69.93	J. H. Edrich	2,238	69.93
1970	G. M. Turner	2,379	61.00	G. S. Sobers	1,742	75.73
1971	G. Boycott..........	2,503	100.12	G. Boycott.........	2,503	100.12
1972	Majid Khan	2,074	61.00	G. Boycott.........	1,230	72.35
1973	G. M. Turner	2,416	67.11	G. M. Turner	2,416	67.11
1974	R. T. Virgin	1,936	56.94	C. H. Lloyd........	1,458	63.39
1975	G. Boycott..........	1,915	73.65	R. B. Kanhai	1,073	82.53
1976	Zaheer Abbas	2,554	75.11	Zaheer Abbas	2,554	75.11
1977	I. V. A. Richards	2,161	65.48	R. P. Baker........	215	71.66‡
1978	D. L. Amiss	2,030	53.42	C. E. B. Rice	1,871	66.82
1979	K. C. Wessels.......	1,800	52.94	G. Boycott.........	1,538	102.53
1980	P. N. Kirsten	1,895	63.16	A. J. Lamb	1,797	66.55
1981	Zaheer Abbas	2,306	88.69	Zaheer Abbas	2,306	88.69
1982	A. I. Kallicharran....	2,120	66.25	G. M. Turner	1,171	90.07
1983	K. S. McEwan	2,176	64.00	I. V. A. Richards ...	1,204	75.25
1984	G. A. Gooch........	2,559	67.34	C. G. Greenidge....	1,069	82.23
1985	G. A. Gooch........	2,208	71.22	I. V. A. Richards ...	1,836	76.50
1986	C. G. Greenidge.....	2,035	67.83	J. G. Bracewell.....	386	77.20§

Season	Leading scorer	Runs	Avge	Top of averages	Runs	Avge
1987	G. A. Hick	1,879	52.19	M. D. Crowe	1,627	67.79
1988	G. A. Hick	2,713	77.51	R. A. Harper	622	77.75
1989	S. J. Cook	2,241	60.56	D. M. Jones	1,510	88.82
1990	G. A. Gooch	2,746	101.70	G. A. Gooch	2,746	101.70
1991	S. J. Cook	2,755	81.02	C. L. Hooper	1,501	93.81
1992	P. D. Bowler	2,044	65.93	Salim Malik	1,184	78.93
	M. A. Roseberry	2,044	56.77			
1993	G. A. Gooch	2,023	63.21	G. Yates	367	91.75‖
1994	B. C. Lara	2,066	89.82	J. D. Carr	1,543	90.76

† *Johnston had 17 innings with 16 not outs, highest score 28*.*
‡ *Baker had 12 innings with 9 not outs, highest score 77*.*
§ *Bracewell had 11 innings with 6 not outs, highest score 110.*
‖ *Yates had 10 innings with 6 not outs, highest score 134*.*

Note: The highest average recorded in an English season was 115.66 (2,429 runs, 26 innings) by D. G. Bradman in 1938.

25,000 RUNS IN A CAREER

Dates in italics denote the first half of an overseas season; i.e. *1945* denotes the 1945-46 season.

		Career	R	I	NO	HS	100s	Avge
1	J. B. Hobbs	1905-34	61,237	1,315	106	316*	197	50.65
2	F. E. Woolley	1906-38	58,969	1,532	85	305*	145	40.75
3	E. H. Hendren	1907-38	57,611	1,300	166	301*	170	50.80
4	C. P. Mead	1905-36	55,061	1,340	185	280*	153	47.67
5	W. G. Grace	1865-1908	54,896	1,493	105	344	126	39.55
6	W. R. Hammond	1920-51	50,551	1,005	104	336*	167	56.10
7	H. Sutcliffe	1919-45	50,138	1,088	123	313	149	51.95
8	G. Boycott	1962-86	48,426	1,014	162	261*	151	56.83
9	T. W. Graveney	1948-*71*	47,793	1,223	159	258	122	44.91
10	T. W. Hayward	1893-1914	43,551	1,138	96	315*	104	41.79
11	D. L. Amiss	1960-87	43,423	1,139	126	262*	102	42.86
12	M. C. Cowdrey	1950-76	42,719	1,130	134	307	107	42.89
13	A. Sandham	1911-*37*	41,284	1,000	79	325	107	44.82
14	**G. A. Gooch**	**1973-94**	**40,174**	**888**	**72**	**333**	**112**	**49.23**
15	L. Hutton	1934-60	40,140	814	91	364	129	55.51
16	M. J. K. Smith	1951-75	39,832	1,091	139	204	69	41.84
17	W. Rhodes	1898-1930	39,802	1,528	237	267*	58	30.83
18	J. H. Edrich	1956-78	39,790	979	104	310*	103	45.47
19	R. E. S. Wyatt	1923-57	39,405	1,141	157	232	85	40.04
20	D. C. S. Compton	1936-64	38,942	839	88	300	123	51.85
21	E. Tyldesley	1909-36	38,874	961	106	256*	102	45.46
22	J. T. Tyldesley	1895-1923	37,897	994	62	295*	86	40.66
23	K. W. R. Fletcher	1962-88	37,665	1,167	170	228*	63	37.77
24	C. G. Greenidge	1970-92	37,354	889	75	273*	92	45.88
25	J. W. Hearne	1909-36	37,252	1,025	116	285*	96	40.98
26	L. E. G. Ames	1926-51	37,248	951	95	295	102	43.51
27	D. Kenyon	1946-67	37,002	1,159	59	259	74	33.63
28	W. J. Edrich	1934-58	36,965	964	92	267*	86	42.39
29	J. M. Parks	1949-76	36,673	1,227	172	205*	51	34.76
30	D. Denton	1894-1920	36,479	1,163	70	221	69	33.37
31	G. H. Hirst	1891-1929	36,323	1,215	151	341	60	34.13
32	I. V. A. Richards	*1971*-93	36,212	796	62	322	114	49.33
33	A. Jones	1957-83	36,049	1,168	72	204*	56	32.89
34	W. G. Quaife	1894-1928	36,012	1,203	185	255*	72	35.37
35	R. E. Marshall	*1945*-72	35,725	1,053	59	228*	68	35.94
36	G. Gunn	1902-32	35,208	1,061	82	220	62	35.96

		Career	*R*	*I*	*NO*	*HS*	*100s*	*Avge*
37	D. B. Close	1949-86	34,994	1,225	173	198	52	33.26
38	Zaheer Abbas	*1965-86*	34,843	768	92	274	108	51.54
39	J. G. Langridge	1928-55	34,380	984	66	250*	76	37.45
40	G. M. Turner	*1964-82*	34,346	792	101	311*	103	49.70
41	C. Washbrook	1933-64	34,101	906	107	251*	76	42.67
42	M. Leyland	1920-48	33,660	932	101	263	80	40.50
43	H. T. W. Hardinge	1902-33	33,519	1,021	103	263*	75	36.51
44	R. Abel	1881-1904	33,124	1,007	73	357*	74	35.46
45	A. I. Kallicharran	*1966*-90	32,650	834	86	243*	87	43.64
46	C. A. Milton	1948-74	32,150	1,078	125	170	56	33.73
47	J. D. Robertson	1937-59	31,914	897	46	331*	67	37.50
48	J. Hardstaff, jun.	1930-55	31,847	812	94	266	83	44.35
49	**M. W. Gatting**	**1975-94**	**31,785**	**740**	**116**	**258**	**82**	**50.93**
50	James Langridge	1924-53	31,716	1,058	157	167	42	35.20
51	K. F. Barrington	1953-68	31,714	831	136	256	76	45.63
52	C. H. Lloyd	*1963*-86	31,232	730	96	242*	79	49.26
53	**A. J. Lamb**	***1972-94***	**31,131**	**744**	**104**	**294**	**86**	**48.64**
54	Mushtaq Mohammad	*1956*-85	31,091	843	104	303*	72	42.07
55	C. B. Fry	1892-*1921*	30,886	658	43	258*	94	50.22
56	D. Brookes	1934-59	30,874	925	70	257	71	36.10
57	P. Holmes	1913-35	30,573	810	84	315*	67	42.11
58	R. T. Simpson	*1944*-63	30,546	852	55	259	64	38.32
59	L. G. Berry	1924-51	30,225	1,056	57	232	45	30.25
	K. G. Suttle	1949-71	30,225	1,064	92	204*	49	31.09
61	P. A. Perrin	1896-1928	29,709	918	91	343*	66	35.92
62	P. F. Warner	1894-1929	29,028	875	75	244	60	36.28
63	R. B. Kanhai	*1954-81*	28,774	669	82	256	83	49.01
64	J. O'Connor	1921-39	28,764	903	79	248	72	34.90
65	**Javed Miandad**	***1973-93***	**28,647**	**631**	**95**	**311**	**80**	**53.44**
66	T. E. Bailey	1945-67	28,641	1,072	215	205	28	33.42
67	D. W. Randall	1972-93	28,456	827	81	237	52	38.14
68	E. H. Bowley	1912-34	28,378	859	47	283	52	34.94
69	B. A. Richards	*1964-82*	28,358	576	58	356	80	54.74
70	G. S. Sobers	*1952*-74	28,315	609	93	365*	86	54.87
71	A. E. Dipper	1908-32	28,075	865	69	252*	53	35.27
72	D. G. Bradman	*1927-48*	28,067	338	43	452*	117	95.14
73	J. H. Hampshire	1961-84	28,059	924	112	183*	43	34.55
74	P. B. H. May	1948-63	27,592	618	77	285*	85	51.00
75	B. F. Davison	*1967-87*	27,453	766	79	189	53	39.96
76	Majid Khan	*1961-84*	27,444	700	62	241	73	43.01
77	A. C. Russell	1908-30	27,358	717	59	273	71	41.57
78	E. G. Hayes	1896-1926	27,318	896	48	276	48	32.21
79	A. E. Fagg	1932-57	27,291	803	46	269*	58	36.05
80	James Seymour	1900-26	27,237	911	62	218*	53	32.08
81	P. H. Parfitt	1956-*73*	26,924	845	104	200*	58	36.33
82	G. L. Jessop	1894-1914	26,698	855	37	286	53	32.63
83	K. S. McEwan	*1972-91*	26,628	705	67	218	74	41.73
84	D. E. Davies	1924-54	26,564	1,032	80	287*	32	27.90
85	A. Shrewsbury	1875-1902	26,505	813	90	267	59	36.65
86	M. J. Stewart	1954-72	26,492	898	93	227*	49	32.90
87	C. T. Radley	1964-87	26,441	880	134	200	46	35.44
88	**W. Larkins**	**1972-94**	**26,405**	**819**	**54**	**252**	**57**	**34.51**
89	D. I. Gower	1975-93	26,339	727	70	228	53	40.08
90	**C. E. B. Rice**	***1969-93***	**26,331**	**766**	**123**	**246**	**48**	**40.95**
91	Younis Ahmed	*1961-86*	26,073	762	118	221*	46	40.48
92	P. E. Richardson	1949-65	26,055	794	41	185	44	34.60
93	M. H. Denness	1959-80	25,886	838	65	195	33	33.48
94	S. M. Gavaskar	*1966*-87	25,834	563	61	340	81	51.46
95	J. W. H. Makepeace	1906-30	25,799	778	66	203	43	36.23

		Career	R	I	NO	HS	100s	Avge
96	W. Gunn	1880-1904	25,691	850	72	273	48	33.02
97	W. Watson	1939-64	25,670	753	109	257	55	39.86
98	G. Brown	1908-33	25,649	1,012	52	232*	37	26.71
99	G. M. Emmett	1936-59	25,602	865	50	188	37	31.41
100	J. B. Bolus	1956-75	25,598	833	81	202*	39	34.03
101	**A. R. Border**	***1976-93***	**25,551**	**589**	**91**	**205**	**68**	**51.30**
102	W. E. Russell	1956-72	25,525	796	64	193	41	34.87
103	C. J. Barnett	1927-*53*	25,389	821	45	259	48	32.71
104	L. B. Fishlock	1931-52	25,376	699	54	253	56	39.34
105	D. J. Insole	1947-63	25,241	743	72	219*	54	37.61
106	J. M. Brearley	1961-83	25,185	768	102	312*	45	37.81
107	J. Vine	1896-1922	25,171	920	79	202	34	29.92
108	R. M. Prideaux	1958-*74*	25,136	808	75	202*	41	34.29
109	J. H. King	1895-1925	25,122	988	69	227*	34	27.33
110	J. G. Wright	*1975-92*	25,073	636	44	192	59	42.35

Bold type denotes those who played in 1993-94 and 1994 seasons.

Note: Some works of reference provide career figures which differ from those in this list, owing to the exclusion or inclusion of matches recognised or not recognised as first-class by *Wisden*.

Current Players with 20,000 Runs

	Career	R	I	NO	HS	100s	Avge
D. L. Haynes	*1976*-94	24,219	596	69	255*	59	45.95
G. A. Hick	*1983*-94	23,124	450	46	405*	77	57.23
C. W. J. Athey	1976-94	22,751	703	68	184	49	35.82
R. T. Robinson	1978-94	22,637	605	76	220*	51	42.79
B. C. Broad	1979-94	21,892	613	38	227*	50	38.07
K. C. Wessels	*1973*-94	21,318	469	41	254	55	49.80
P. N. Kirsten	*1973*-94	20,920	521	57	271	53	45.08
S. J. Cook	*1972-93*	20,676	463	55	313*	63	50.67
K. J. Barnett	1979-94	20,565	581	54	239*	44	39.02

CAREER AVERAGE OVER 50

(Qualification: 10,000 runs)

Avge		Career	I	NO	R	HS	100s
95.14	D. G. Bradman	*1927-48*	338	43	28,067	452*	117
71.22	V. M. Merchant	*1929-51*	229	43	13,248	359*	44
65.18	W. H. Ponsford	*1920-34*	235	23	13,819	437	47
64.99	W. M. Woodfull	*1921-34*	245	39	13,388	284	49
58.24	A. L. Hassett	*1932-53*	322	32	16,890	232	59
58.19	V. S. Hazare	*1934-66*	365	45	18,621	316*	60
57.23	**G. A. Hick**	***1983-94***	**450**	**46**	**23,124**	**405***	**77**
57.22	A. F. Kippax	*1918-35*	256	33	12,762	315*	43
56.83	G. Boycott	1962-86	1,014	162	48,426	261*	151
56.70	**M. E. Waugh**	***1985-93***	**296**	**43**	**14,346**	**229***	**48**
56.55	C. L. Walcott	*1941-63*	238	29	11,820	314*	40
56.37	K. S. Ranjitsinhji	1893-1920	500	62	24,692	285*	72
56.22	R. B. Simpson	*1952-77*	436	62	21,029	359	60
56.10	W. R. Hammond	1920-51	1,005	104	50,551	336*	167
55.85	**M. D. Crowe**	***1979-94***	**393**	**58**	**18,710**	**299**	**67**
55.51	L. Hutton	1934-60	814	91	40,140	364	129
55.34	E. D. Weekes	*1944*-64	241	24	12,010	304*	36
54.87	G. S. Sobers	*1952*-74	609	93	28,315	365*	86

Avge		*Career*	*I*	*NO*	*R*	*HS*	*100s*
54.74	B. A. Richards	*1964-82*	576	58	28,358	356	80
54.67	R. G. Pollock	*1960-86*	437	54	20,940	274	64
54.24	F. M. M. Worrell	*1941-64*	326	49	15,025	308*	39
53.78	R. M. Cowper	*1959-69*	228	31	10,595	307	26
53.67	A. R. Morris	*1940-63*	250	15	12,614	290	46
53.44	**Javed Miandad**	***1973-93***	**631**	**95**	**28,647**	**311**	**80**
52.86	D. B. Vengsarkar	*1975-91*	390	52	17,868	284	55
52.80	**M. Azharuddin**	***1981-94***	**247**	**27**	**11,617**	**226**	**40**
52.32	Hanif Mohammad	*1951-75*	371	45	17,059	499	55
52.27	P. R. Umrigar	*1944-67*	350	41	16,154	252*	49
52.20	G. S. Chappell	*1966-83*	542	72	24,535	247*	74
51.95	H. Sutcliffe	1919-45	1,088	123	50,138	313	149
51.85	D. C. S. Compton	1936-64	839	88	38,942	300	123
51.65	**D. M. Jones**	***1981-93***	**295**	**32**	**13,586**	**248**	**39**
51.54	Zaheer Abbas	*1965-86*	768	92	34,843	274	108
51.53	A. D. Nourse	*1931-52*	269	27	12,472	260*	41
51.46	S. M. Gavaskar	*1966-87*	563	61	25,834	340	81
51.44	W. A. Brown	*1932-49*	284	15	13,838	265*	39
51.30	**A. R. Border**	***1976-93***	**589**	**91**	**25,551**	**205**	**68**
51.00	P. B. H. May	1948-63	618	77	27,592	285*	85
50.95	N. C. O'Neill	*1955-67*	306	34	13,859	284	45
50.93	**M. W. Gatting**	**1975-94**	**740**	**116**	**31,785**	**258**	**82**
50.93	R. N. Harvey	*1946-62*	461	35	21,699	231*	67
50.90	W. M. Lawry	*1955-71*	417	49	18,734	266	50
50.90	A. V. Mankad	*1963-82*	326	71	12,980	265	31
50.80	E. H. Hendren	1907-38	1,300	166	57,611	301*	170
50.67	**S. J. Cook**	***1972-93***	**463**	**55**	**20,676**	**313***	**63**
50.65	J. B. Hobbs	1905-34	1,315	106	61,237	316*	197
50.22	C. B. Fry	1892-*1921*	658	43	30,886	258*	94
50.01	Shafiq Ahmad	*1967-90*	449	58	19,555	217*	53

Bold type denotes those who played first-class cricket in 1993-94 and 1994 seasons or on the Pakistan tour of Sri Lanka in 1994-95.

FASTEST FIFTIES

Minutes			
11	C. I. J. Smith (66)	Middlesex v Gloucestershire at Bristol	1938
14	S. J. Pegler (50)	South Africans v Tasmania at Launceston	1910-11
14	F. T. Mann (53)	Middlesex v Nottinghamshire at Lord's	1921
14	H. B. Cameron (56)	Transvaal v Orange Free State at Johannesburg	1934-35
14	C. I. J. Smith (52)	Middlesex v Kent at Maidstone	1935

Note: The following fast fifties were scored in contrived circumstances when runs were given from full tosses and long hops to expedite a declaration: C. C. Inman (8 minutes), Leicestershire v Nottinghamshire at Nottingham, 1965; G. Chapple (10 minutes), Lancashire v Glamorgan at Manchester, 1993; T. M. Moody (11 minutes), Warwickshire v Glamorgan at Swansea, 1990; A. J. Stewart (14 minutes), Surrey v Kent at Dartford, 1986; M. P. Maynard (14 minutes), Glamorgan v Yorkshire at Cardiff, 1987.

FASTEST HUNDREDS

Minutes			
35	P. G. H. Fender (113*)	Surrey v Northamptonshire at Northampton	1920
40	G. L. Jessop (101)	Gloucestershire v Yorkshire at Harrogate	1897
40	Ahsan-ul-Haq (100*)	Muslims v Sikhs at Lahore	1923-24
42	G. L. Jessop (191)	Gentlemen of South v Players of South at Hastings	1907
43	A. H. Hornby (106)	Lancashire v Somerset at Manchester	1905
43	D. W. Hookes (107)	South Australia v Victoria at Adelaide	1982-83
44	R. N. S. Hobbs (100)	Essex v Australians at Chelmsford	1975

Notes: The fastest recorded authentic hundred in terms of balls received was scored off 34 balls by D. W. Hookes (above).

Research of the scorebook has shown that P. G. H. Fender scored his hundred from between 40 and 46 balls. He contributed 113 to an unfinished sixth-wicket partnership of 171 in 42 minutes with H. A. Peach.

E. B. Alletson (Nottinghamshire) scored 189 out of 227 runs in 90 minutes against Sussex at Hove in 1911. It has been estimated that his last 139 runs took 37 minutes.

The following fast hundreds were scored in contrived circumstances when runs were given from full tosses and long hops to expedite a declaration: G. Chapple (21 minutes), Lancashire v Glamorgan at Manchester, 1993; T. M. Moody (26 minutes), Warwickshire v Glamorgan at Swansea, 1990; S. J. O'Shaughnessy (35 minutes), Lancashire v Leicestershire at Manchester, 1983; C. M. Old (37 minutes), Yorkshire v Warwickshire at Birmingham, 1977; N. F. M. Popplewell (41 minutes), Somerset v Gloucestershire at Bath, 1983.

FASTEST DOUBLE-HUNDREDS

Minutes			
113	R. J. Shastri (200*)	Bombay v Baroda at Bombay	1984-85
120	G. L. Jessop (286)	Gloucestershire v Sussex at Hove	1903
120	C. H. Lloyd (201*)	West Indians v Glamorgan at Swansea	1976
130	G. L. Jessop (234)	Gloucestershire v Somerset at Bristol	1905
131	V. T. Trumper (293)	Australians v Canterbury at Christchurch	1913-14

FASTEST TRIPLE-HUNDREDS

Minutes			
181	D. C. S. Compton (300)	MCC v N. E. Transvaal at Benoni	1948-49
205	F. E. Woolley (305*)	MCC v Tasmania at Hobart	1911-12
205	C. G. Macartney (345)	Australians v Nottinghamshire at Nottingham	1921
213	D. G. Bradman (369)	South Australia v Tasmania at Adelaide	1935-36

300 RUNS IN ONE DAY

390*	B. C. Lara	Warwickshire v Durham at Birmingham	1994
345	C. G. Macartney	Australians v Nottinghamshire at Nottingham	1921
334	W. H. Ponsford	Victoria v New South Wales at Melbourne	1926-27
333	K. S. Duleepsinhji	Sussex v Northamptonshire at Hove	1930
331*	J. D. Robertson	Middlesex v Worcestershire at Worcester	1949
325*	B. A. Richards	S. Australia v W. Australia at Perth	1970-71
322†	E. Paynter	Lancashire v Sussex at Hove	1937
322	I. V. A. Richards	Somerset v Warwickshire at Taunton	1985
318	C. W. Gregory	New South Wales v Queensland at Brisbane	1906-07
317	K. R. Rutherford	New Zealanders v D. B. Close's XI at Scarborough	1986
316†	R. H. Moore	Hampshire v Warwickshire at Bournemouth	1937
315*	R. C. Blunt	Otago v Canterbury at Christchurch	1931-32
312*	J. M. Brearley	MCC Under-25 v North Zone at Peshawar	1966-67
311*	G. M. Turner	Worcestershire v Warwickshire at Worcester	1982
311*	N. H. Fairbrother	Lancashire v Surrey at The Oval	1990
309*	D. G. Bradman	Australia v England at Leeds	1930
307*	W. H. Ashdown	Kent v Essex at Brentwood	1934
306*	A. Ducat	Surrey v Oxford University at The Oval	1919
305*	F. R. Foster	Warwickshire v Worcestershire at Dudley	1914

† *E. Paynter's 322 and R. H. Moore's 316 were scored on the same day: July 28, 1937.*

These scores do not necessarily represent the complete innings. *See page 106.*

1,000 RUNS IN MAY

	Runs	Avge
W. G. Grace, May 9 to May 30, 1895 (22 days):		
13, 103, 18, 25, 288, 52, 257, 73*, 18, 169	1,016	112.88
Grace was within two months of completing his 47th year.		
W. R. Hammond, May 7 to May 31, 1927 (25 days):		
27, 135, 108, 128, 17, 11, 99, 187, 4, 30, 83, 7, 192, 14	1,042	74.42
Hammond scored his 1,000th run on May 28, thus equalling Grace's record of 22 days.		
C. Hallows, May 5 to May 31, 1928 (27 days):		
100, 101, 51*, 123, 101*, 22, 74, 104, 58, 34*, 232	1,000	125.00

1,000 RUNS IN APRIL AND MAY

T. W. Hayward, April 16 to May 31, 1900:		
120*, 55, 108, 131*, 55, 193, 120, 5, 6, 3, 40, 146, 92	1,074	97.63
D. G. Bradman, April 30 to May 31, 1930:		
236, 185*, 78, 9, 48*, 66, 4, 44, 252*, 32, 47*	1,001	143.00
On April 30 Bradman was 75 not out.		
D. G. Bradman, April 30 to May 31, 1938:		
258, 58, 137, 278, 2, 143, 145*, 5, 30*	1,056	150.85
Bradman scored 258 on April 30, and his 1,000th run on May 27.		
W. J. Edrich, April 30 to May 31, 1938:		
104, 37, 115, 63, 20*, 182, 71, 31, 53*, 45, 15, 245, 0, 9, 20*	1,010	84.16
Edrich was 21 not out on April 30. All his runs were scored at Lord's.		
G. M. Turner, April 24 to May 31, 1973:		
41, 151*, 143, 85, 7, 8, 17*, 81, 13, 53, 44, 153*, 3, 2, 66*, 30, 10*, 111	1,018	78.30
G. A. Hick, April 17 to May 29, 1988:		
61, 37, 212, 86, 14, 405*, 8, 11, 6, 7, 172	1,019	101.90
Hick scored a record 410 runs in April, and his 1,000th run on May 28.		

1,000 RUNS IN TWO SEPARATE MONTHS

Only four batsmen, C. B. Fry, K. S. Ranjitsinhji, H. Sutcliffe and L. Hutton, have scored over 1,000 runs in each of two months in the same season. L. Hutton, by scoring 1,294 in June 1949, made more runs in a single month than anyone else. He also made 1,050 in August 1949.

MOST RUNS SCORED OFF ONE OVER

(All instances refer to six-ball overs)

36	G. S. Sobers	off M. A. Nash, Nottinghamshire v Glamorgan at Swansea (six sixes)	1968
36	R. J. Shastri	off Tilak Raj, Bombay v Baroda at Bombay (six sixes)	1984-85
34	E. B. Alletson	off E. H. Killick, Nottinghamshire v Sussex at Hove (46604446; including two no-balls)	1911
34	F. C. Hayes	off M. A. Nash, Lancashire v Glamorgan at Swansea (646666)	1977
32	I. T. Botham	off I. R. Snook, England XI v Central Districts at Palmerston North (466466)	1983-84
32	P. W. G. Parker	off A. I. Kallicharran, Sussex v Warwickshire at Birmingham (466664)	1982
32	I. R. Redpath	off N. Rosendorff, Australians v Orange Free State at Bloemfontein (666644)	1969-70
32	C. C. Smart	off G. Hill, Glamorgan v Hampshire at Cardiff (664664)	1935

Notes: The following instances have been excluded from the above table because of the bowlers' compliance: 34 – M. P. Maynard off S. A. Marsh, Glamorgan v Kent at Swansea, 1992; 34 – G. Chapple off P. A. Cottey, Lancashire v Glamorgan at Manchester, 1993; 32 – C. C. Inman off N. W. Hill, Leicestershire v Nottinghamshire at Nottingham, 1965; 32 – T. E. Jesty off R. J. Boyd-Moss, Hampshire v Northamptonshire at Southampton, 1984; 32 – G. Chapple off P. A. Cottey, Lancashire v Glamorgan at Manchester, 1993. Chapple's 34 and 32 came off successive overs from Cottey.

The greatest number of runs scored off an eight-ball over is 34 (40446664) by R. M. Edwards off M. C. Carew, Governor-General's XI v West Indians at Auckland, 1968-69.

In a Shell Trophy match against Canterbury at Christchurch in 1989-90, R. H. Vance (Wellington), acting on the instructions of his captain, deliberately conceded 77 runs in an over of full tosses which contained 17 no-balls and, owing to the umpire's understandable miscalculation, only five legitimate deliveries.

MOST SIXES IN AN INNINGS

15	J. R. Reid (296)	Wellington v N. Districts at Wellington	1962-63
14	Shakti Singh (128)	Himachal Pradesh v Haryana at Dharmsala	1990-91
13	Majid Khan (147*)	Pakistanis v Glamorgan at Swansea	1967
13	C. G. Greenidge (273*)	D. H. Robins' XI v Pakistanis at Eastbourne	1974
13	C. G. Greenidge (259)	Hampshire v Sussex at Southampton	1975
13	G. W. Humpage (254)	Warwickshire v Lancashire at Southport	1982
13	R. J. Shastri (200*)	Bombay v Baroda at Bombay	1984-85
12	Gulfraz Khan (207)	Railways v Universities at Lahore	1976-77
12	I. T. Botham (138*)	Somerset v Warwickshire at Birmingham	1985
12	R. A. Harper (234)	Northamptonshire v Gloucestershire at Northampton	1986
12	D. M. Jones (248)	Australians v Warwickshire at Birmingham	1989
12	D. N. Patel (204)	Auckland v Northern Districts at Auckland	1991-92
12	W. V. Raman (206)	Tamil Nadu v Kerala at Madras	1991-92
11	C. K. Nayudu (153)	Hindus v MCC at Bombay	1926-27
11	C. J. Barnett (194)	Gloucestershire v Somerset at Bath	1934
11	R. Benaud (135)	Australians v T. N. Pearce's XI at Scarborough	1953
11	R. Bora (126)	Assam v Tripura at Gauhati	1987-88
11	G. A. Hick (405*)	Worcestershire v Somerset at Taunton	1988

Note: W. J. Stewart (Warwickshire) hit 17 sixes in the match v Lancashire, at Blackpool, 1959: ten in his first innings of 155 and seven in his second innings of 125.

MOST SIXES IN A SEASON

80	I. T. Botham	1985
66	A. W. Wellard	1935
57	A. W. Wellard	1936
57	A. W. Wellard	1938
51	A. W. Wellard	1933

MOST BOUNDARIES IN AN INNINGS

	4s/6s			
72	62/10	B. C. Lara (501*)	Warwickshire v Durham at Birmingham	1994
68	68/–	P. A. Perrin (343*)	Essex v Derbyshire at Chesterfield	1904
64	64/–	Hanif Mohammad (499)	Karachi v Bahawalpur at Karachi	1958-59
63	62/1	A. C. MacLaren (424)	Lancashire v Somerset at Taunton	1895
57	52/5	J. H. Edrich (310*)	England v New Zealand at Leeds	1965
55	55/–	C. W. Gregory (383)	NSW v Queensland at Brisbane	1906-07
55	53/2	G. R. Marsh (355*)	W. Australia v S. Australia at Perth	1989-90
54	53/1	G. H. Hirst (341)	Yorkshire v Leicestershire at Leicester	1905
54	51/2†	S. V. Manjrekar (377)	Bombay v Hyderabad at Bombay	1990-91

	4s/6s			
53	53/–	A. W. Nourse (304*)	Natal v Transvaal at Johannesburg ...	1919-20
53	45/8	K. R. Rutherford (317)	New Zealanders v D. B. Close's XI at Scarborough	1986
52	47/5	N. H. Fairbrother (366)	Lancashire v Surrey at The Oval	1990
51	47/4	C. G. Macartney (345)	Australians v Notts. at Nottingham ...	1921
51	50/1	B. B. Nimbalkar (443*)	Maharashtra v Kathiawar at Poona ...	1948-49
50	46/4	D. G. Bradman (369)	S. Australia v Tasmania at Adelaide ..	1935-36
50	47/–‡	A. Ducat (306*)	Surrey v Oxford U. at The Oval......	1919
50	35/15	J. R. Reid (296)	Wellington v N. Districts at Wellington	1962-63
50	42/8	I. V. A. Richards (322)	Somerset v Warwickshire at Taunton .	1985

† Plus one five.
‡ Plus three fives.

HIGHEST PARTNERSHIPS

577	V. S. Hazare (288) and Gul Mahomed (319), fourth wicket, Baroda v Holkar at Baroda	1946-47
574*	F. M. M. Worrell (255*) and C. L. Walcott (314*), fourth wicket, Barbados v Trinidad at Port-of-Spain	1945-46
561	Waheed Mirza (324) and Mansoor Akhtar (224*), first wicket, Karachi Whites v Quetta at Karachi	1976-77
555	P. Holmes (224*) and H. Sutcliffe (313), first wicket, Yorkshire v Essex at Leyton	1932
554	J. T. Brown (300) and J. Tunnicliffe (243), first wicket, Yorkshire v Derbyshire at Chesterfield	1898
502*	F. M. M. Worrell (308*) and J. D. C. Goddard (218*), fourth wicket, Barbados v Trinidad at Bridgetown	1943-44
490	E. H. Bowley (283) and J. G. Langridge (195), first wicket, Sussex v Middlesex at Hove	1933
487*	G. A. Headley (344*) and C. C. Passailaigue (261*), sixth wicket, Jamaica v Lord Tennyson's XI at Kingston	1931-32
475	Zahir Alam (257) and L. S. Rajput (239), second wicket, Assam v Tripura at Gauhati	1991-92
470	A. I. Kallicharran (230*) and G. W. Humpage (254), fourth wicket, Warwickshire v Lancashire at Southport	1982

HIGHEST PARTNERSHIPS FOR EACH WICKET

The following lists include all stands above 400; otherwise the top ten for each wicket.

First Wicket

561	Waheed Mirza and Mansoor Akhtar, Karachi Whites v Quetta at Karachi	1976-77
555	P. Holmes and H. Sutcliffe, Yorkshire v Essex at Leyton................	1932
554	J. T. Brown and J. Tunnicliffe, Yorkshire v Derbyshire at Chesterfield	1898
490	E. H. Bowley and J. G. Langridge, Sussex v Middlesex at Hove	1933
456	E. R. Mayne and W. H. Ponsford, Victoria v Queensland at Melbourne ...	1923-24
451*	S. Desai and R. M. H. Binny, Karnataka v Kerala at Chikmagalur.......	1977-78
431	M. R. J. Veletta and G. R. Marsh, Western Australia v South Australia at Perth	1989-90
428	J. B. Hobbs and A. Sandham, Surrey v Oxford University at The Oval....	1926
424	I. J. Siedle and J. F. W. Nicolson, Natal v Orange Free State at Bloemfontein	1926-27
421	S. M. Gavaskar and G. A. Parkar, Bombay v Bengal at Bombay........	1981-82
418	Kamal Najamuddin and Khalid Alvi, Karachi v Railways at Karachi.....	1980-81
413	V. Mankad and Pankaj Roy, India v New Zealand at Madras	1955-56
405	C. P. S. Chauhan and M. S. Gupte, Maharashtra v Vidarbha at Poona ...	1972-73

Second Wicket

475 Zahir Alam and L. S. Rajput, Assam v Tripura at Gauhati 1991-92
465* J. A. Jameson and R. B. Kanhai, Warwicks. v Gloucestershire at Birmingham 1974
455 K. V. Bhandarkar and B. B. Nimbalkar, Maharashtra v Kathiawar at Poona 1948-49
451 W. H. Ponsford and D. G. Bradman, Australia v England at The Oval ... 1934
446 C. C. Hunte and G. S. Sobers, West Indies v Pakistan at Kingston 1957-58
429* J. G. Dewes and G. H. G. Doggart, Cambridge U. v Essex at Cambridge . 1949
426 Arshad Pervez and Mohsin Khan, Habib Bank v Income Tax at Lahore .. 1977-78
415 A. D. Jadeja and S. V. Manjrekar, Indians v Bowl XI at Springs......... 1992-93
403 G. A. Gooch and P. J. Prichard, Essex v Leicestershire at Chelmsford 1990
398 A. Shrewsbury and W. Gunn, Nottinghamshire v Sussex at Nottingham ... 1890

Third Wicket

467 A. H. Jones and M. D. Crowe, New Zealand v Sri Lanka at Wellington .. 1990-91
456 Khalid Irtiza and Aslam Ali, United Bank v Multan at Karachi 1975-76
451 Mudassar Nazar and Javed Miandad, Pakistan v India at Hyderabad 1982-83
445 P. E. Whitelaw and W. N. Carson, Auckland v Otago at Dunedin 1936-37
434 J. B. Stollmeyer and G. E. Gomez, Trinidad v British Guiana at Port-of-Spain 1946-47
424* W. J. Edrich and D. C. S. Compton, Middlesex v Somerset at Lord's 1948
413 D. J. Bicknell and D. M. Ward, Surrey v Kent at Canterbury 1990
410 R. S. Modi and L. Amarnath, India in England v The Rest at Calcutta ... 1946-47
405 A. D. Jadeja and A. S. Kaypee, Haryana v Services at Faridabad 1991-92
399 R. T. Simpson and D. C. S. Compton, MCC v N. E. Transvaal at Benoni . 1948-49

Fourth Wicket

577 V. S. Hazare and Gul Mahomed, Baroda v Holkar at Baroda............ 1946-47
574* C. L. Walcott and F. M. M. Worrell, Barbados v Trinidad at Port-of-Spain 1945-46
502* F. M. M. Worrell and J. D. C. Goddard, Barbados v Trinidad at Bridgetown 1943-44
470 A. I. Kallicharran and G. W. Humpage, Warwicks. v Lancs. at Southport . 1982
462* D. W. Hookes and W. B. Phillips, South Australia v Tasmania at Adelaide 1986-87
448 R. Abel and T. W. Hayward, Surrey v Yorkshire at The Oval 1899
425* A. Dale and I. V. A. Richards, Glamorgan v Middlesex at Cardiff 1993
424 I. S. Lee and S. O. Quin, Victoria v Tasmania at Melbourne 1933-34
411 P. B. H. May and M. C. Cowdrey, England v West Indies at Birmingham. 1957
410 G. Abraham and P. Balan Pandit, Kerala v Andhra at Palghat 1959-60
402 W. Watson and T. W. Graveney, MCC v British Guiana at Georgetown .. 1953-54
402 R. B. Kanhai and K. Ibadulla, Warwicks. v Notts. at Nottingham 1968

Note: The partnership between A. Dale and I. V. A. Richards includes 13 runs for no-balls under TCCB playing conditions. Under the Laws of Cricket, only five runs would have resulted from six no-balls bowled in this partnership.

Fifth Wicket

464* M. E. Waugh and S. R. Waugh, New South Wales v Western Australia at Perth 1990-91
405 S. G. Barnes and D. G. Bradman, Australia v England at Sydney 1946-47
397 W. Bardsley and C. Kelleway, New South Wales v South Australia at Sydney 1920-21
393 E. G. Arnold and W. B. Burns, Worcestershire v Warwickshire at Birmingham 1909
360 U. M. Merchant and M. N. Raiji, Bombay v Hyderabad at Bombay...... 1947-48
355 Altaf Shah and Tariq Bashir, HBFC v Multan at Multan 1976-77
355 A. J. Lamb and J. J. Strydom, OFS v Eastern Province at Bloemfontein .. 1987-88
347 D. Brookes and D. W. Barrick, Northamptonshire v Essex at Northampton 1952
344 M. C. Cowdrey and T. W. Graveney, MCC v South Australia at Adelaide. 1962-63
343 R. I. Maddocks and J. Hallebone, Victoria v Tasmania at Melbourne 1951-52

Note: The Waugh twins achieved the first instance of brothers each scoring a double-hundred in the same first-class innings. Their partnership includes 20 runs for no-balls under ACB playing conditions. Under the Laws of Cricket, only seven runs would have resulted from ten no-balls bowled in this partnership.

Sixth Wicket

487*	G. A. Headley and C. C. Passailaigue, Jamaica v Lord Tennyson's XI at Kingston	1931-32
428	W. W. Armstrong and M. A. Noble, Australians v Sussex at Hove	1902
411	R. M. Poore and E. G. Wynyard, Hampshire v Somerset at Taunton	1899
376	R. Subba Row and A. Lightfoot, Northamptonshire v Surrey at The Oval	1958
371	V. M. Merchant and R. S. Modi, Bombay v Maharashtra at Bombay	1943-44
356	W. V. Raman and A. Kripal Singh, Tamil Nadu v Goa at Panjim	1988-89
353	Salah-ud-Din and Zaheer Abbas, Karachi v East Pakistan at Karachi	1968-69
346	J. H. W. Fingleton and D. G. Bradman, Australia v England at Melbourne	1936-37
332	N. G. Marks and G. Thomas, New South Wales v South Australia at Sydney	1958-59
323	E. H. Hendren and J. W. H. T. Douglas, MCC v Victoria at Melbourne	1920-21

Seventh Wicket

347	D. St E. Atkinson and C. C. Depeiza, West Indies v Australia at Bridgetown	1954-55
344	K. S. Ranjitsinhji and W. Newham, Sussex v Essex at Leyton	1902
340	K. J. Key and H. Philipson, Oxford University v Middlesex at Chiswick Park	1887
336	F. C. W. Newman and C. R. N. Maxwell, Sir J. Cahn's XI v Leicestershire at Nottingham	1935
335	C. W. Andrews and E. C. Bensted, Queensland v New South Wales at Sydney	1934-35
325	G. Brown and C. H. Abercrombie, Hampshire v Essex at Leyton	1913
323	E. H. Hendren and L. F. Townsend, MCC v Barbados at Bridgetown	1929-30
308	Waqar Hassan and Imtiaz Ahmed, Pakistan v New Zealand at Lahore	1955-56
301	C. C. Lewis and B. N. French, Nottinghamshire v Durham at Chester-le-Street	1993
299	B. Mitchell and A. Melville, Transvaal v Griqualand West at Kimberley	1946-47

Eighth Wicket

433	V. T. Trumper and A. Sims, A. Sims' Aust. XI v Canterbury at Christchurch	1913-14
292	R. Peel and Lord Hawke, Yorkshire v Warwickshire at Birmingham	1896
270	V. T. Trumper and E. P. Barbour, New South Wales v Victoria at Sydney	1912-13
263	D. R. Wilcox and R. M. Taylor, Essex v Warwickshire at Southend	1946
255	E. A. V. Williams and E. A. Martindale, Barbados v Trinidad at Bridgetown	1935-36
249*	Shaukat Mirza and Akram Raza, Habib Bank v PNSC at Lahore	1993-94
246	L. E. G. Ames and G. O. B. Allen, England v New Zealand at Lord's	1931
243	R. J. Hartigan and C. Hill, Australia v England at Adelaide	1907-08
242*	T. J. Zoehrer and K. H. MacLeay, W. Australia v New South Wales at Perth	1990-91
240	Gulfraz Khan and Raja Sarfraz, Railways v Universities at Lahore	1976-77

Ninth Wicket

283	J. Chapman and A. Warren, Derbyshire v Warwickshire at Blackwell	1910
251	J. W. H. T. Douglas and S. N. Hare, Essex v Derbyshire at Leyton	1921
245	V. S. Hazare and N. D. Nagarwalla, Maharashtra v Baroda at Poona	1939-40
244*	Arshad Ayub and M. V. Ramanamurthy, Hyderabad v Bihar at Hyderabad	1986-87
239	H. B. Cave and I. B. Leggat, Central Districts v Otago at Dunedin	1952-53
232	C. Hill and E. Walkley, South Australia v New South Wales at Adelaide	1900-01
231	P. Sen and J. Mitter, Bengal v Bihar at Jamshedpur	1950-51
230	D. A. Livingstone and A. T. Castell, Hampshire v Surrey at Southampton	1962
226	C. Kelleway and W. A. Oldfield, New South Wales v Victoria at Melbourne	1925-26
225	W. W. Armstrong and E. A. Windsor, Australian XI v The Rest at Sydney	1907-08

Tenth Wicket

307	A. F. Kippax and J. E. H. Hooker, New South Wales v Victoria at Melbourne	1928-29
249	C. T. Sarwate and S. N. Banerjee, Indians v Surrey at The Oval	1946
235	F. E. Woolley and A. Fielder, Kent v Worcestershire at Stourbridge	1909
233	Ajay Sharma and Maninder Singh, Delhi v Bombay at Bombay	1991-92
230	R. W. Nicholls and W. Roche, Middlesex v Kent at Lord's	1899
228	R. Illingworth and K. Higgs, Leicestershire v Northamptonshire at Leicester	1977
218	F. H. Vigar and T. P. B. Smith, Essex v Derbyshire at Chesterfield	1947
211	M. Ellis and T. J. Hastings, Victoria v South Australia at Melbourne	1902-03
196*	Nadim Yousuf and Maqsood Kundi, MCB v National Bank at Lahore	1981-82
192	H. A. W. Bowell and W. H. Livsey, Hampshire v Worcs. at Bournemouth	1921

UNUSUAL DISMISSALS

Handled the Ball

J. Grundy	MCC v Kent at Lord's	1857
G. Bennett	Kent v Sussex at Hove	1872
W. H. Scotton	Smokers v Non-Smokers at East Melbourne	1886-87
C. W. Wright	Nottinghamshire v Gloucestershire at Bristol	1893
E. Jones	South Australia v Victoria at Melbourne	1894-95
A. W. Nourse	South Africans v Sussex at Hove	1907
E. T. Benson	MCC v Auckland at Auckland	1929-30
A. W. Gilbertson	Otago v Auckland at Auckland	1952-53
W. R. Endean	South Africa v England at Cape Town	1956-57
P. J. P. Burge	Queensland v New South Wales at Sydney	1958-59
Dildar Awan	Services v Lahore at Lahore	1959-60
M. Mehra	Railways v Delhi at Delhi	1959-60
Mahmood-ul-Hasan	Karachi University v Railways-Quetta at Karachi	1960-61
Ali Raza	Karachi Greens v Hyderabad at Karachi	1961-62
Mohammad Yusuf	Rawalpindi v Peshawar at Peshawar	1962-63
A. Rees	Glamorgan v Middlesex at Lord's	1965
Pervez Akhtar	Multan v Karachi Greens at Sahiwal	1971-72
Javed Mirza	Railways v Punjab at Lahore	1972-73
R. G. Pollock	Eastern Province v Western Province at Cape Town	1973-74
C. I. Dey	Northern Transvaal v Orange Free State at Bloemfontein	1973-74
Nasir Valika	Karachi Whites v National Bank at Karachi	1974-75
Haji Yousuf	National Bank v Railways at Lahore	1974-75
Masood-ul-Hasan	PIA v National Bank B at Lyallpur	1975-76
D. K. Pearse	Natal v Western Province at Cape Town	1978-79
A. M. J. Hilditch	Australia v Pakistan at Perth	1978-79
Musleh-ud-Din	Railways v Lahore at Lahore	1979-80
Jalal-ud-Din	IDBP v Habib Bank at Bahawalpur	1981-82
Mohsin Khan	Pakistan v Australia at Karachi	1982-83
D. L. Haynes	West Indies v India at Bombay	1983-84
K. Azad	Delhi v Punjab at Amritsar	1983-84
Athar A. Khan	Allied Bank v HBFC at Sialkot	1983-84
A. N. Pandya	Saurashtra v Baroda at Baroda	1984-85
G. L. Linton	Barbados v Windward Islands at Bridgetown	1985-86
R. B. Gartrell	Tasmania v Victoria at Melbourne	1986-87
R. Nayyar	Himachal Pradesh v Punjab at Una	1988-89
R. Weerawardene	Moratuwa v Nomads SC at Colombo	1988-89
A. M. Kane	Vidarbha v Railways at Nagpur	1989-90
P. Bali	Jammu and Kashmir v Services at Delhi	1991-92
M. J. Davis	Northern Transvaal B v OFS B at Bloemfontein	1991-92
J. T. C. Vaughan	Emerging Players v England XI at Hamilton	1991-92
G. A. Gooch	England v Australia at Manchester	1993

Obstructing the Field

C. A. Absolom	Cambridge University v Surrey at The Oval	1868
T. Straw	Worcestershire v Warwickshire at Worcester	1899
T. Straw	Worcestershire v Warwickshire at Birmingham	1901
J. P. Whiteside	Leicestershire v Lancashire at Leicester	1901
L. Hutton	England v South Africa at The Oval	1951
J. A. Hayes	Canterbury v Central Districts at Christchurch	1954-55
D. D. Deshpande	Madhya Pradesh v Uttar Pradesh at Benares	1956-57
K. Ibadulla	Warwickshire v Hampshire at Coventry	1963
Qaiser Khan	Dera Ismail Khan v Railways at Lahore	1964-65
Ijaz Ahmed	Lahore Greens v Lahore Blues at Lahore	1973-74
Qasim Feroze	Bahawalpur v Universities at Lahore	1974-75
T. Quirk	Northern Transvaal v Border at East London	1978-79
Mahmood Rashid	United Bank v Muslim Commercial Bank at Bahawalpur	1981-82
Arshad Ali	Sukkur v Quetta at Quetta	1983-84
H. R. Wasu	Vidarbha v Rajasthan at Akola	1984-85
Khalid Javed	Railways v Lahore at Lahore	1985-86
C. Binduhewa	Singha SC v Sinhalese SC at Colombo	1990-91

Hit the Ball Twice

H. E. Bull	MCC v Oxford University at Lord's	1864
H. R. J. Charlwood	Sussex v Surrey at Hove	1872
R. G. Barlow	North v South at Lord's	1878
P. S. Wimble	Transvaal v Griqualand West at Kimberley	1892-93
G. B. Nicholls	Somerset v Gloucestershire at Bristol	1896
A. A. Lilley	Warwickshire v Yorkshire at Birmingham	1897
J. H. King	Leicestershire v Surrey at The Oval	1906
A. P. Binns	Jamaica v British Guiana at Georgetown	1956-57
K. Bhavanna	Andhra v Mysore at Guntur	1963-64
Zaheer Abbas	PIA A v Karachi Blues at Karachi	1969-70
Anwar Miandad	IDBP v United Bank at Lahore	1979-80
Anwar Iqbal	Hyderabad v Sukkur at Hyderabad	1983-84
Iqtidar Ali	Allied Bank v Muslim Commercial Bank at Lahore	1983-84
Aziz Malik	Lahore Division v Faisalabad at Sialkot	1984-85
Javed Mohammad	Multan v Karachi Whites at Sahiwal	1986-87
Shahid Pervez	Jammu and Kashmir v Punjab at Srinigar	1986-87

BOWLING RECORDS

TEN WICKETS IN AN INNINGS

	O	*M*	*R*		
E. Hinkly (Kent)				v England at Lord's	1848
*J. Wisden (North)				v South at Lord's	1850
V. E. Walker (England)	43	17	74	v Surrey at The Oval	1859
V. E. Walker (Middlesex)	44.2	5	104	v Lancashire at Manchester	1865
G. Wootton (All England)	31.3	9	54	v Yorkshire at Sheffield	1865
W. Hickton (Lancashire)	36.2	19	46	v Hampshire at Manchester	1870
S. E. Butler (Oxford)	24.1	11	38	v Cambridge at Lord's	1871
James Lillywhite (South)	60.2	22	129	v North at Canterbury	1872
A. Shaw (MCC)	36.2	8	73	v North at Lord's	1874
E. Barratt (Players)	29	11	43	v Australians at The Oval	1878
G. Giffen (Australian XI)	26	10	66	v The Rest at Sydney	1883-84
W. G. Grace (MCC)	36.2	17	49	v Oxford University at Oxford	1886
G. Burton (Middlesex)	52.3	25	59	v Surrey at The Oval	1888
†A. E. Moss (Canterbury)	21.3	10	28	v Wellington at Christchurch	1889-90
S. M. J. Woods (Cambridge U.)	31	6	69	v Thornton's XI at Cambridge	1890
T. Richardson (Surrey)	15.3	3	45	v Essex at The Oval	1894
H. Pickett (Essex)	27	11	32	v Leicestershire at Leyton	1895
E. J. Tyler (Somerset)	34.3	15	49	v Surrey at Taunton	1895
W. P. Howell (Australians)	23.2	14	28	v Surrey at The Oval	1899
C. H. G. Bland (Sussex)	25.2	10	48	v Kent at Tonbridge	1899
J. Briggs (Lancashire)	28.5	7	55	v Worcestershire at Manchester	1900
A. E. Trott (Middlesex)	14.2	5	42	v Somerset at Taunton	1900
F. Hinds (A. B. St Hill's XI)	19.1	6	36	v Trinidad at Port-of-Spain	1900-01
A. Fielder (Players)	24.5	1	90	v Gentlemen at Lord's	1906
E. G. Dennett (Gloucestershire)	19.4	7	40	v Essex at Bristol	1906
A. E. E. Vogler (E. Province)	12	2	26	v Griqualand W. at Johannesburg	1906-07
C. Blythe (Kent)	16	7	30	v Northants at Northampton	1907
A. Drake (Yorkshire)	8.5	0	35	v Somerset at Weston-s-Mare	1914
W. Bestwick (Derbyshire)	19	2	40	v Glamorgan at Cardiff	1921
A. A. Mailey (Australians)	28.4	5	66	v Gloucestershire at Cheltenham	1921
C. W. L. Parker (Glos.)	40.3	13	79	v Somerset at Bristol	1921
T. Rushby (Surrey)	17.5	4	43	v Somerset at Taunton	1921
J. C. White (Somerset)	42.2	11	76	v Worcestershire at Worcester	1921
G. C. Collins (Kent)	19.3	4	65	v Nottinghamshire at Dover	1922
H. Howell (Warwickshire)	25.1	5	51	v Yorkshire at Birmingham	1923

	O	M	R		
A. S. Kennedy (Players)	22.4	10	37	v Gentlemen at The Oval	1927
G. O. B. Allen (Middlesex)	25.3	10	40	v Lancashire at Lord's	1929
A. P. Freeman (Kent)	42	9	131	v Lancashire at Maidstone	1929
G. Geary (Leicestershire)	16.2	8	18	v Glamorgan at Pontypridd	1929
C. V. Grimmett (Australians)	22.3	8	37	v Yorkshire at Sheffield	1930
A. P. Freeman (Kent)	30.4	8	53	v Essex at Southend	1930
H. Verity (Yorkshire)	18.4	6	36	v Warwickshire at Leeds	1931
A. P. Freeman (Kent)	36.1	9	79	v Lancashire at Manchester	1931
V. W. C. Jupp (Northants)	39	6	127	v Kent at Tunbridge Wells	1932
H. Verity (Yorkshire)	19.4	16	10	v Nottinghamshire at Leeds	1932
T. W. Wall (South Australia)	12.4	2	36	v New South Wales at Sydney	1932-33
T. B. Mitchell (Derbyshire)	19.1	4	64	v Leicestershire at Leicester	1935
J. Mercer (Glamorgan)	26	10	51	v Worcestershire at Worcester	1936
T. W. J. Goddard (Glos.)	28.4	4	113	v Worcestershire at Cheltenham	1937
T. F. Smailes (Yorkshire)	17.1	5	47	v Derbyshire at Sheffield	1939
E. A. Watts (Surrey)	24.1	8	67	v Warwickshire at Birmingham	1939
*W. E. Hollies (Warwickshire)	20.4	4	49	v Notts. at Birmingham	1946
J. M. Sims (East)	18.4	2	90	v West at Kingston	1948
T. E. Bailey (Essex)	39.4	9	90	v Lancashire at Clacton	1949
J. K. Graveney (Glos.)	18.4	2	66	v Derbyshire at Chesterfield	1949
R. Berry (Lancashire)	36.2	9	102	v Worcestershire at Blackpool	1953
S. P. Gupte (President's XI)	24.2	7	78	v Combined XI at Bombay	1954-55
J. C. Laker (Surrey)	46	18	88	v Australians at The Oval	1956
J. C. Laker (England)	51.2	23	53	v Australia at Manchester	1956
G. A. R. Lock (Surrey)	29.1	18	54	v Kent at Blackheath	1956
K. Smales (Nottinghamshire)	41.3	20	66	v Gloucestershire at Stroud	1956
P. M. Chatterjee (Bengal)	19	11	20	v Assam at Jorhat	1956-57
J. D. Bannister (Warwickshire)	23.3	11	41	v Comb. Services at Birmingham‡	1959
A. J. G. Pearson (Cambridge U.)	30.3	8	78	v Leics. at Loughborough	1961
N. I. Thomson (Sussex)	34.2	19	49	v Warwickshire at Worthing	1964
P. J. Allan (Queensland)	15.6	3	61	v Victoria at Melbourne	1965-66
I. J. Brayshaw (W. Australia)	17.6	4	44	v Victoria at Perth	1967-68
Shahid Mahmood (Karachi Whites)	25	5	58	v Khairpur at Karachi	1969-70
E. E. Hemmings (International XI)	49.3	14	175	v West Indies XI at Kingston	1982-83
P. Sunderam (Rajasthan)	22	5	78	v Vidarbha at Jodhpur	1985-86
S. T. Jefferies (W. Province)	22.5	7	59	v Orange Free State at Cape Town	1987-88
Imran Adil (Bahawalpur)	22.5	3	92	v Faisalabad at Faisalabad	1989-90
G. P. Wickremasinghe (Sinhalese SC)	19.2	5	41	v Kalutara at Colombo (SSC)	1991-92
R. L. Johnson (Middlesex)	18.5	6	45	v Derbyshire at Derby	1994

** J. Wisden and W. E. Hollies achieved the feat without the direct assistance of a fielder. Wisden's ten were all bowled; Hollies bowled seven and had three lbw.*

† On debut in first-class cricket. ‡ Mitchells & Butlers Ground.

Note: The following instances were achieved in 12-a-side matches:

E. M. Grace (MCC)	32.2	7	69	v Gents of Kent at Canterbury	1862
W. G. Grace (MCC)	46.1	15	92	v Kent at Canterbury	1873

OUTSTANDING ANALYSES

	O	M	R	W		
H. Verity (Yorkshire)	19.4	16	10	10	v Nottinghamshire at Leeds	1932
G. Elliott (Victoria)	19	17	2	9	v Tasmania at Launceston	1857-58
Ahad Khan (Railways)	6.3	4	7	9	v Dera Ismail Khan at Lahore	1964-65
J. C. Laker (England)	14	12	2	8	v The Rest at Bradford	1950
D. Shackleton (Hampshire)	11.1	7	4	8	v Somerset at Weston-s-Mare	1955
E. Peate (Yorkshire)	16	11	5	8	v Surrey at Holbeck	1883

	O	M	R	W		
F. R. Spofforth (Australians)	8.3	6	3	7	v England XI at Birmingham	1884
W. A. Henderson (N.E. Transvaal)	9.3	7	4	7	v Orange Free State at Bloemfontein	1937-38
Rajinder Goel (Haryana)	7	4	4	7	v Jammu and Kashmir at Chandigarh	1977-78
V. I. Smith (South Africans)	4.5	3	1	6	v Derbyshire at Derby	1947
S. Cosstick (Victoria)	21.1	20	1	6	v Tasmania at Melbourne	1868-69
Israr Ali (Bahawalpur)	11	10	1	6	v Dacca U. at Bahawalpur	1957-58
A. D. Pougher (MCC)	3	3	0	5	v Australians at Lord's	1896
G. R. Cox (Sussex)	6	6	0	5	v Somerset at Weston-s-Mare	1921
R. K. Tyldesley (Lancashire)	5	5	0	5	v Leicestershire at Manchester	1924
P. T. Mills (Gloucestershire)	6.4	6	0	5	v Somerset at Bristol	1928

MOST WICKETS IN A MATCH

19-90	J. C. Laker	England v Australia at Manchester	1956
17-48	C. Blythe	Kent v Northamptonshire at Northampton	1907
17-50	C. T. B. Turner	Australians v England XI at Hastings	1888
17-54	W. P. Howell	Australians v Western Province at Cape Town	1902-03
17-56	C. W. L. Parker	Gloucestershire v Essex at Gloucester	1925
17-67	A. P. Freeman	Kent v Sussex at Hove	1922
17-89	W. G. Grace	Gloucestershire v Nottinghamshire at Cheltenham	1877
17-89	F. C. L. Matthews	Nottinghamshire v Northants at Nottingham	1923
17-91	H. Dean	Lancashire v Yorkshire at Liverpool	1913
17-91	H. Verity	Yorkshire v Essex at Leyton	1933
17-92	A. P. Freeman	Kent v Warwickshire at Folkestone	1932
17-103	W. Mycroft	Derbyshire v Hampshire at Southampton	1876
17-106	G. R. Cox	Sussex v Warwickshire at Horsham	1926
17-106	T. W. J. Goddard	Gloucestershire v Kent at Bristol	1939
17-119	W. Mead	Essex v Hampshire at Southampton	1895
17-137	W. Brearley	Lancashire v Somerset at Manchester	1905
17-159	S. F. Barnes	England v South Africa at Johannesburg	1913-14
17-201	G. Giffen	South Australia v Victoria at Adelaide	1885-86
17-212	J. C. Clay	Glamorgan v Worcestershire at Swansea	1937

SIXTEEN OR MORE WICKETS IN A DAY

17-48	C. Blythe	Kent v Northamptonshire at Northampton	1907
17-91	H. Verity	Yorkshire v Essex at Leyton	1933
17-106	T. W. J. Goddard	Gloucestershire v Kent at Bristol	1939
16-38	T. Emmett	Yorkshire v Cambridgeshire at Hunslet	1869
16-52	J. Southerton	South v North at Lord's	1875
16-69	T. G. Wass	Nottinghamshire v Lancashire at Liverpool	1906
16-38	A. E. E. Vogler	E. Province v Griqualand West at Johannesburg	1906-07
16-103	T. G. Wass	Nottinghamshire v Essex at Nottingham	1908
16-83	J. C. White	Somerset v Worcestershire at Bath	1919

FOUR WICKETS WITH CONSECUTIVE BALLS

J. Wells	Kent v Sussex at Brighton	1862
G. Ulyett	Lord Harris's XI v New South Wales at Sydney	1878-79
G. Nash	Lancashire v Somerset at Manchester	1882
J. B. Hide	Sussex v MCC and Ground at Lord's	1890
F. J. Shacklock	Nottinghamshire v Somerset at Nottingham	1893
A. D. Downes	Otago v Auckland at Dunedin	1893-94
F. Martin	MCC and Ground v Derbyshire at Lord's	1895

A. W. Mold	Lancashire v Nottinghamshire at Nottingham	1895
W. Brearley†	Lancashire v Somerset at Manchester	1905
S. Haigh	MCC v Army XI at Pretoria	1905-06
A. E. Trott‡	Middlesex v Somerset at Lord's	1907
F. A. Tarrant	Middlesex v Gloucestershire at Bristol	1907
A. Drake	Yorkshire v Derbyshire at Chesterfield	1914
S. G. Smith	Northamptonshire v Warwickshire at Birmingham	1914
H. A. Peach	Surrey v Sussex at The Oval	1924
A. F. Borland	Natal v Griqualand West at Kimberley	1926-27
J. E. H. Hooker†	New South Wales v Victoria at Sydney	1928-29
R. K. Tyldesley†	Lancashire v Derbyshire at Derby	1929
R. J. Crisp	Western Province v Griqualand West at Johannesburg	1931-32
R. J. Crisp	Western Province v Natal at Durban	1933-34
A. R. Gover	Surrey v Worcestershire at Worcester	1935
W. H. Copson	Derbyshire v Warwickshire at Derby	1937
W. A. Henderson	N.E. Transvaal v Orange Free State at Bloemfontein	1937-38
F. Ridgway	Kent v Derbyshire at Folkestone	1951
A. K. Walker§	Nottinghamshire v Leicestershire at Leicester	1956
S. N. Mohol	President's XI v Combined XI at Poona	1965-66
P. I. Pocock	Surrey v Sussex at Eastbourne	1972
S. S. Saini†	Delhi v Himachal Pradesh at Delhi	1988-89
D. Dias	W. Province (Suburbs) v Central Province at Colombo	1990-91

† *Not all in the same innings.*

‡ *Trott achieved another hat-trick in the same innings of this, his benefit match.*

§ *Walker dismissed Firth with the last ball of the first innings and Lester, Tompkin and Smithson with the first three balls of the second innings, a feat without parallel.*

Notes: In their match with England at The Oval in 1863, Surrey lost four wickets in the course of a four-ball over from G. Bennett.

Sussex lost five wickets in the course of the final (six-ball) over of their match with Surrey at Eastbourne in 1972. P. I. Pocock, who had taken three wickets in his previous over, captured four more, taking in all seven wickets with 11 balls, a feat unique in first-class matches. (The eighth wicket fell to a run-out.)

HAT-TRICKS

Double Hat-Trick

Besides Trott's performance, which is given in the preceding section, the following instances are recorded of players having performed the hat-trick twice in the same match, Rao doing so in the same innings.

A. Shaw	Nottinghamshire v Gloucestershire at Nottingham	1884
T. J. Matthews	Australia v South Africa at Manchester	1912
C. W. L. Parker	Gloucestershire v Middlesex at Bristol	1924
R. O. Jenkins	Worcestershire v Surrey at Worcester	1949
J. S. Rao	Services v Northern Punjab at Amritsar	1963-64
Amin Lakhani	Combined XI v Indians at Multan	1978-79

Five Wickets in Six Balls

W. H. Copson	Derbyshire v Warwickshire at Derby	1937
W. A. Henderson	N.E. Transvaal v Orange Free State at Bloemfontein	1937-38
P. I. Pocock	Surrey v Sussex at Eastbourne	1972

Most Hat-Tricks

Seven times: D. V. P. Wright.

Six times: T. W. J. Goddard, C. W. L. Parker.

Five times: S. Haigh, V. W. C. Jupp, A. E. G. Rhodes, F. A. Tarrant.

Four times: R. G. Barlow, J. T. Hearne, J. C. Laker, G. A. R. Lock, G. G. Macaulay, T. J. Matthews, M. J. Procter, T. Richardson, F. R. Spofforth, F. S. Trueman.

Three times: W. M. Bradley, H. J. Butler, S. T. Clarke, W. H. Copson, R. J. Crisp, J. W. H. T. Douglas, J. A. Flavell, A. P. Freeman, G. Giffen, K. Higgs, A. Hill, W. A. Humphreys, R. D. Jackman, R. O. Jenkins, A. S. Kennedy, W. H. Lockwood, E. A. McDonald, T. L. Pritchard, J. S. Rao, A. Shaw, J. B. Statham, M. W. Tate, H. Trumble, D. Wilson, G. A. Wilson.

Twice (current players only): E. E. Hemmings, M. D. Marshall, Shahid Ali Khan, P. A. Smith, C. J. van Heerden.

HAT-TRICK ON DEBUT

H. Hay	South Australia v Lord Hawke's XI at Unley, Adelaide	1902-03
H. A. Sedgwick	Yorkshire v Worcestershire at Hull	1906
V. B. Ranjane	Maharashtra v Saurashtra at Poona	1956-57
J. S. Rao	Services v Jammu & Kashmir at Delhi	1963-64
R. O. Estwick	Barbados v Guyana at Bridgetown	1982-83
S. A. Ankola	Maharashtra v Gujarat at Poona	1988-89
J. Srinath	Karnataka v Hyderabad at Secunderabad	1989-90
S. P. Mukherjee	Bengal v Hyderabad at Secunderabad	1989-90

Notes: R. R. Phillips (Border) took a hat-trick in his first over in first-class cricket (v Eastern Province at Port Elizabeth, 1939-40) having previously played in four matches without bowling.

J. S. Rao took two more hat-tricks in his next match.

250 WICKETS IN A SEASON

	Season	*O*	*M*	*R*	*W*	*Avge*
A. P. Freeman	1928	1,976.1	423	5,489	304	18.05
A. P. Freeman	1933	2,039	651	4,549	298	15.26
T. Richardson	1895‡	1,690.1	463	4,170	290	14.37
C. T. B. Turner**	1888†	2,427.2	1,127	3,307	283	11.68
A. P. Freeman	1931	1,618	360	4,307	276	15.60
A. P. Freeman	1930	1,914.3	472	4,632	275	16.84
T. Richardson	1897‡	1,603.4	495	3,945	273	14.45
A. P. Freeman	1929	1,670.5	381	4,879	267	18.27
W. Rhodes	1900	1,553	455	3,606	261	13.81
J. T. Hearne	1896	2,003.1	818	3,670	257	14.28
A. P. Freeman	1932	1,565.5	404	4,149	253	16.39
W. Rhodes	1901	1,565	505	3,797	251	15.12

† *Indicates 4-ball overs;* ‡ *5-ball overs.*
** *Exclusive of matches not reckoned as first-class.*

Notes: In four consecutive seasons (1928-31), A. P. Freeman took 1,122 wickets, and in eight consecutive seasons (1928-35), 2,090 wickets. In each of these eight seasons he took over 200 wickets.

T. Richardson took 1,005 wickets in four consecutive seasons (1894-97).

In 1896, J. T. Hearne took his 100th wicket as early as June 12. In 1931, C. W. L. Parker did the same and A. P. Freeman obtained his 100th wicket a day later.

LEADING BOWLERS IN AN ENGLISH SEASON

(Qualification: 10 wickets in 10 innings)

Season	Leading wicket-taker	Wkts	Avge	Top of averages	Wkts	Avge
1946	W. E. Hollies	184	15.60	A. Booth	111	11.61
1947	T. W. J. Goddard	238	17.30	J. C. Clay	65	16.44
1948	J. E. Walsh	174	19.56	J. C. Clay	41	14.17
1949	R. O. Jenkins	183	21.19	T. W. J. Goddard	160	19.18
1950	R. Tattersall	193	13.59	R. Tattersall	193	13.59
1951	R. Appleyard	200	14.14	R. Appleyard	200	14.14
1952	J. H. Wardle	177	19.54	F. S. Trueman	61	13.78
1953	B. Dooland	172	16.58	C. J. Knott	38	13.71
1954	B. Dooland	196	15.48	J. B. Statham	92	14.13
1955	G. A. R. Lock	216	14.49	R. Appleyard	85	13.01
1956	D. J. Shepherd	177	15.36	G. A. R. Lock	155	12.46
1957	G. A. R. Lock	212	12.02	G. A. R. Lock	212	12.02
1958	G. A. R. Lock	170	12.08	H. L. Jackson	143	10.99
1959	D. Shackleton	148	21.55	J. B. Statham	139	15.01
1960	F. S. Trueman	175	13.98	J. B. Statham	135	12.31
1961	J. A. Flavell	171	17.79	J. A. Flavell	171	17.79
1962	D. Shackleton	172	20.15	C. Cook	58	17.13
1963	D. Shackleton	146	16.75	C. C. Griffith	119	12.83
1964	D. Shackleton	142	20.40	J. A. Standen	64	13.00
1965	D. Shackleton	144	16.08	H. J. Rhodes	119	11.04
1966	D. L. Underwood	157	13.80	D. L. Underwood	157	13.80
1967	T. W. Cartwright	147	15.52	D. L. Underwood	136	12.39
1968	R. Illingworth	131	14.36	O. S. Wheatley	82	12.95
1969	R. M. H. Cottam	109	21.04	A. Ward	69	14.82
1970	D. J. Shepherd	106	19.16	Majid Khan	11	18.81
1971	L. R. Gibbs	131	18.89	G. G. Arnold	83	17.12
1972	T. W. Cartwright B. Stead	98 98	18.64 20.38	I. M. Chappell	10	10.60
1973	B. S. Bedi	105	17.94	T. W. Cartwright	89	15.84
1974	A. M. E. Roberts	119	13.62	A. M. E. Roberts	119	13.62
1975	P. G. Lee	112	18.45	A. M. E. Roberts	57	15.80
1976	G. A. Cope	93	24.13	M. A. Holding	55	14.38
1977	M. J. Procter	109	18.04	R. A. Woolmer	19	15.21
1978	D. L. Underwood	110	14.49	D. L. Underwood	110	14.49
1979	D. L. Underwood J. K. Lever	106 106	14.85 17.30	J. Garner	55	13.83
1980	R. D. Jackman	121	15.40	J. Garner	49	13.93
1981	R. J. Hadlee	105	14.89	R. J. Hadlee	105	14.89
1982	M. D. Marshall	134	15.73	R. J. Hadlee	61	14.57
1983	J. K. Lever D. L. Underwood	106 106	16.28 19.28	Imran Khan	12	7.16
1984	R. J. Hadlee	117	14.05	R. J. Hadlee	117	14.05
1985	N. V. Radford	101	24.68	R. M. Ellison	65	17.20
1986	C. A. Walsh	118	18.17	M. D. Marshall	100	15.08
1987	N. V. Radford	109	20.81	R. J. Hadlee	97	12.64
1988	F. D. Stephenson	125	18.31	M. D. Marshall	42	13.16
1989	D. R. Pringle S. L. Watkin	94 94	18.64 25.09	T. M. Alderman	70	15.64
1990	N. A. Foster	94	26.61	I. R. Bishop	59	19.05
1991	Waqar Younis	113	14.65	Waqar Younis	113	14.65
1992	C. A. Walsh	92	15.96	C. A. Walsh	92	15.96
1993	S. L. Watkin	92	22.80	Wasim Akram	59	19.27
1994	M. M. Patel	90	22.86	C. E. L. Ambrose	77	14.45

100 WICKETS IN A SEASON

Since Reduction of Championship Matches in 1969

Five times: D. L. Underwood 110 (1978), 106 (1979), 106 (1983), 102 (1971), 101 (1969).

Four times: J. K. Lever 116 (1984), 106 (1978), 106 (1979), 106 (1983).

Twice: B. S. Bedi 112 (1974), 105 (1973); T. W. Cartwright 108 (1969), 104 (1971); N. A. Foster 105 (1986), 102 (1991); N. Gifford 105 (1970), 104 (1983); R. J. Hadlee 117 (1984), 105 (1981); P. G. Lee 112 (1975), 101 (1973); M. D. Marshall 134 (1982), 100 (1986); M. J. Procter 109 (1977), 108 (1969); N. V. Radford 109 (1987), 101 (1985); F. J. Titmus 105 (1970), 104 (1971).

Once: J. P. Agnew 101 (1987); I. T. Botham 100 (1978); K. E. Cooper 101 (1988); R. M. H. Cottam 109 (1969); D. R. Doshi 101 (1980); J. E. Emburey 103 (1983); L. R. Gibbs 131 (1971); R. N. S. Hobbs 102 (1970); Intikhab Alam 104 (1971); R. D. Jackman 121 (1980); A. M. E. Roberts 119 (1974); P. J. Sainsbury 107 (1971); Sarfraz Nawaz 101 (1975); M. W. W. Selvey 101 (1978); D. J. Shepherd 106 (1970); F. D. Stephenson 125 (1988); C. A. Walsh 118 (1986); Waqar Younis 113 (1991); D. Wilson 102 (1969).

100 WICKETS IN A SEASON MOST TIMES

(Includes Overseas Tours and Seasons)

23 times: W. Rhodes 200 wkts (3).

20 times: D. Shackleton (In successive seasons – 1949 to 1968 inclusive).

17 times: A. P. Freeman 300 wkts (1), 200 wkts (7).

16 times: T. W. J. Goddard 200 wkts (4), C. W. L. Parker 200 wkts (5), R. T. D. Perks, F. J. Titmus.

15 times: J. T. Hearne 200 wkts (3), G. H. Hirst 200 wkts (1), A. S. Kennedy 200 wkts (1).

14 times: C. Blythe 200 wkts (1), W. E. Hollies, G. A. R. Lock 200 wkts (2), M. W. Tate 200 wkts (3), J. C. White.

13 times: J. B. Statham.

12 times: J. Briggs, E. G. Dennett 200 wkts (1), C. Gladwin, D. J. Shepherd, N. I. Thomson, F. S. Trueman.

11 times: A. V. Bedser, G. Geary, S. Haigh, J. C. Laker, M. S. Nichols, A. E. Relf.

10 times: W. Attewell, W. G. Grace, R. Illingworth, H. L. Jackson, V. W. C. Jupp, G. G. Macaulay 200 wkts (1), W. Mead, T. B. Mitchell, T. Richardson 200 wkts (3), J. Southerton 200 wkts (1), R. K. Tyldesley, D. L. Underwood, J. H. Wardle, T. G. Wass, D. V. P. Wright.

9 times: W. E. Astill, T. E. Bailey, W. E. Bowes, C. Cook, R. Howorth, J. Mercer, A. W. Mold 200 wkts (2), J. A. Newman, C. F. Root 200 wkts (1), A. Shaw 200 wkts (1), H. Verity 200 wkts (3).

8 times: T. W. Cartwright, H. Dean, J. A. Flavell, A. R. Gover 200 wkts (2), H. Larwood, G. A. Lohmann 200 wkts (3), R. Peel, J. M. Sims, F. A. Tarrant, R. Tattersall, G. J. Thompson, G. E. Tribe, A. W. Wellard, F. E. Woolley, J. A. Young.

100 WICKETS IN A SEASON OUTSIDE ENGLAND

W		*Season*	*Country*	*R*	*Avge*
116	M. W. Tate	1926-27	India/Ceylon	1,599	13.78
107	Ijaz Faqih	1985-86	Pakistan	1,719	16.06
106	C. T. B. Turner....	1887-88	Australia	1,441	13.59
106	R. Benaud	1957-58	South Africa	2,056	19.39
104	S. F. Barnes.......	1913-14	South Africa	1,117	10.74
104	Sajjad Akbar	1989-90	Pakistan	2,328	22.38
103	Abdul Qadir	1982-83	Pakistan	2,367	22.98

1,500 WICKETS IN A CAREER

Dates in italics denote the first half of an overseas season; i.e. *1970* denotes the 1970-71 season.

		Career	*W*	*R*	*Avge*
1	W. Rhodes	1898-1930	4,187	69,993	16.71
2	A. P. Freeman	1914-36	3,776	69,577	18.42
3	C. W. L. Parker	1903-35	3,278	63,817	19.46
4	J. T. Hearne	1888-1923	3,061	54,352	17.75
5	T. W. J. Goddard	1922-52	2,979	59,116	19.84
6	W. G. Grace	1865-1908	2,876	51,545	17.92
7	A. S. Kennedy	1907-36	2,874	61,034	21.23
8	D. Shackleton	1948-69	2,857	53,303	18.65
9	G. A. R. Lock	1946-*70*	2,844	54,709	19.23
10	F. J. Titmus	1949-82	2,830	63,313	22.37
11	M. W. Tate	1912-37	2,784	50,571	18.16
12	G. H. Hirst	1891-1929	2,739	51,282	18.72
13	C. Blythe	1899-1914	2,506	42,136	16.81
14	D. L. Underwood	1963-87	2,465	49,993	20.28
15	W. E. Astill	1906-39	2,431	57,783	23.76
16	J. C. White	1909-37	2,356	43,759	18.57
17	W. E. Hollies	1932-57	2,323	48,656	20.94
18	F. S. Trueman	1949-69	2,304	42,154	18.29
19	J. B. Statham	1950-68	2,260	36,999	16.37
20	R. T. D. Perks	1930-55	2,233	53,770	24.07
21	J. Briggs	1879-1900	2,221	35,431	15.95
22	D. J. Shepherd	1950-72	2,218	47,302	21.32
23	E. G. Dennett	1903-26	2,147	42,571	19.82
24	T. Richardson	1892-1905	2,104	38,794	18.43
25	T. E. Bailey	1945-67	2,082	48,170	23.13
26	R. Illingworth	1951-83	2,072	42,023	20.28
27	N. Gifford	1960-88	2,068	48,731	23.56
	F. E. Woolley	1906-38	2,068	41,066	19.85
29	G. Geary	1912-38	2,063	41,339	20.03
30	D. V. P. Wright	1932-57	2,056	49,307	23.98
31	J. A. Newman	1906-30	2,032	51,111	25.15
32	†A. Shaw	1864-97	2,027	24,580	12.12
33	S. Haigh	1895-1913	2,012	32,091	15.94
34	H. Verity	1930-39	1,956	29,146	14.90
35	W. Attewell	1881-1900	1,951	29,896	15.32
36	J. C. Laker	1946-*64*	1,944	35,791	18.41
37	A. V. Bedser	1939-60	1,924	39,279	20.41
38	W. Mead	1892-1913	1,916	36,388	18.99
39	A. E. Relf	1900-21	1,897	39,724	20.94
40	P. G. H. Fender	1910-36	1,894	47,458	25.05
41	J. W. H. T. Douglas	1901-30	1,893	44,159	23.32
42	J. H. Wardle	1946-*67*	1,846	35,027	18.97
43	G. R. Cox	1895-1928	1,843	42,136	22.86
44	G. A. Lohmann	1884-97	1,841	25,295	13.73
45	J. W. Hearne	1909-36	1,839	44,926	24.42
46	G. G. Macaulay	1920-35	1,837	32,440	17.65
47	M. S. Nichols	1924-39	1,833	39,666	21.63
48	J. B. Mortimore	1950-75	1,807	41,904	23.18
49	C. Cook	1946-64	1,782	36,578	20.52
50	R. Peel	1882-99	1,752	28,442	16.23
51	H. L. Jackson	1947-63	1,733	30,101	17.36
52	J. K. Lever	1967-89	1,722	41,772	24.25
53	T. P. B. Smith	1929-52	1,697	45,059	26.55
54	J. Southerton	1854-79	1,681	24,290	14.44
55	A. E. Trott	*1892*-1911	1,674	35,317	21.09
56	A. W. Mold	1889-1901	1,673	26,010	15.54

		Career	W	R	Avge
57	T. G. Wass	1896-1920	1,666	34,092	20.46
58	V. W. C. Jupp	1909-38	1,658	38,166	23.01
59	C. Gladwin	1939-58	1,653	30,265	18.30
60	W. E. Bowes	1928-47	1,639	27,470	16.76
61	A. W. Wellard	1927-50	1,614	39,302	24.35
62	P. I. Pocock	1964-86	1,607	42,648	26.53
63	**M. D. Marshall**	***1977-94***	**1,602**	**30,579**	**19.08**
64	N. I. Thomson	1952-72	1,597	32,867	20.58
65	J. Mercer	1919-47	1,591	37,210	23.38
	G. J. Thompson	1897-1922	1,591	30,058	18.89
67	J. M. Sims	1929-53	1,581	39,401	24.92
68	T. Emmett	1866-88	1,571	21,314	13.56
	Intikhab Alam	*1957*-82	1,571	43,474	27.67
70	B. S. Bedi	*1961-81*	1,560	33,843	21.69
71	W. Voce	1927-52	1,558	35,961	23.08
72	A. R. Gover	1928-48	1,555	36,753	23.63
73	T. W. Cartwright	1952-77	1,536	29,357	19.11
	K. Higgs	1958-86	1,536	36,267	23.61
75	James Langridge	1924-53	1,530	34,524	22.56
76	J. A. Flavell	1949-67	1,529	32,847	21.48
77	C. F. Root	1910-33	1,512	31,933	21.11
	F. A. Tarrant	*1898-1936*	1,512	26,450	17.49
79	R. K. Tyldesley	1919-35	1,509	25,980	17.21
80	**J. E. Emburey**	**1973-94**	**1,503**	**38,956**	**25.91**
81	**E. E. Hemmings**	**1966-94**	**1,500**	**43,961**	**29.30**

Bold type denotes those who played in 1993-94 and 1994 seasons.

† *The figures for A. Shaw exclude one wicket for which no analysis is available.*

Note: Some works of reference provide career figures which differ from those in this list, owing to the exclusion or inclusion of matches recognised or not recognised as first-class by *Wisden.*

Current Player with 1,000 Wickets

	Career	W	R	Avge
C. A. Walsh	*1981*-94	1,213	27,152	22.38

ALL-ROUND RECORDS

HUNDRED AND TEN WICKETS IN AN INNINGS

V. E. Walker, England v Surrey at The Oval; 20*, 108, ten for 74, and four for 17. 1859
W. G. Grace, MCC v Oxford University at Oxford; 104, two for 60, and ten for 49. 1886

Note: E. M. Grace, for MCC v Gentlemen of Kent in a 12-a-side match at Canterbury in 1862, scored 192* and took five for 77 and ten for 69.

TWO HUNDRED RUNS AND SIXTEEN WICKETS

G. Giffen, South Australia v Victoria at Adelaide; 271, nine for 96, and seven for 70. 1891-92

HUNDRED IN EACH INNINGS AND FIVE WICKETS TWICE

G. H. Hirst, Yorkshire v Somerset at Bath; 111, 117*, six for 70, and five for 45. 1906

HUNDRED IN EACH INNINGS AND TEN WICKETS

B. J. T. Bosanquet, Middlesex v Sussex at Lord's; 103, 100*, three for 75, and eight for 53 1905
F. D. Stephenson, Nottinghamshire v Yorkshire at Nottingham; 111, 117, four for 105, and seven for 117 1988

HUNDRED AND HAT-TRICK

G. Giffen, Australians v Lancashire at Manchester; 13, 113, and six for 55 including hat-trick 1884
W. E. Roller, Surrey v Sussex at The Oval; 204, four for 28 including hat-trick, and two for 16. (Unique instance of 200 and hat-trick.) 1885
W. B. Burns, Worcestershire v Gloucestershire at Worcester; 102*, three for 56 including hat-trick, and two for 21 1913
V. W. C. Jupp, Sussex v Essex at Colchester; 102, six for 61 including hat-trick, and six for 78 1921
R. E. S. Wyatt, MCC v Ceylon at Colombo; 124 and five for 39 including hat-trick. 1926-27
L. N. Constantine, West Indians v Northamptonshire at Northampton; seven for 45 including hat-trick, 107, and six for 67 1928
D. E. Davies, Glamorgan v Leicestershire at Leicester; 139, four for 27, and three for 31 including hat-trick 1937
V. M. Merchant, Dr C. R. Pereira's XI v Sir Homi Mehta's XI at Bombay; 1, 142, three for 31 including hat-trick, and no wicket for 17 1946-47
M. J. Procter, Gloucestershire v Essex at Westcliff-on-Sea; 51, 102, three for 43, and five for 30 including hat-trick (all lbw) 1972
M. J. Procter, Gloucestershire v Leicestershire at Bristol; 122, no wkt for 32, and seven for 26 including hat-trick 1979

Note: W. G. Grace, for MCC v Kent in a 12-a-side match at Canterbury in 1874, scored 123 and took five for 82 and six for 47 including a hat-trick.

SEASON DOUBLES

2,000 Runs and 200 Wickets

1906	G. H. Hirst	2,385 runs and 208 wickets

3,000 Runs and 100 Wickets

1937	J. H. Parks	3,003 runs and 101 wickets

2,000 Runs and 100 Wickets

	Season	*R*	*W*
W. G. Grace	1873	2,139	106
W. G. Grace	1876	2,622	129
C. L. Townsend	1899	2,440	101
G. L. Jessop	1900	2,210	104
G. H. Hirst	1904	2,501	132
G. H. Hirst	1905	2,266	110
W. Rhodes	1909	2,094	141
W. Rhodes	1911	2,261	117
F. A. Tarrant	1911	2,030	111
J. W. Hearne	1913	2,036	124
J. W. Hearne	1914	2,116	123
F. E. Woolley	1914	2,272	125
J. W. Hearne	1920	2,148	142
V. W. C. Jupp	1921	2,169	121
F. E. Woolley	1921	2,101	167
F. E. Woolley	1922	2,022	163
F. E. Woolley	1923	2,091	101
L. F. Townsend	1933	2,268	100
D. E. Davies	1937	2,012	103
James Langridge	1937	2,082	101
T E Bailey	1959	2,011	100

1,000 Runs and 200 Wickets

	Season	R	W		Season	R	W
A. E. Trott	1899	1,175	239	M. W. Tate	1923	1,168	219
A. E. Trott	1900	1,337	211	M. W. Tate	1924	1,419	205
A. S. Kennedy	1922	1,129	205	M. W. Tate	1925	1,290	228

1,000 Runs and 100 Wickets

Sixteen times: W. Rhodes.
Fourteen times: G. H. Hirst.
Ten times: V. W. C. Jupp.
Nine times: W. E. Astill.
Eight times: T. E. Bailey, W. G. Grace, M. S. Nichols, A. E. Relf, F. A. Tarrant, M. W. Tate†, F. J. Titmus, F. E. Woolley.
Seven times: G. E. Tribe.
Six times: P. G. H. Fender, R. Illingworth, James Langridge.
Five times: J. W. H. T. Douglas, J. W. Hearne, A. S. Kennedy, J. A. Newman.
Four times: E. G. Arnold, J. Gunn, R. Kilner, B. R. Knight.
Three times: W. W. Armstrong (Australians), L. C. Braund, G. Giffen (Australians), N. E. Haig, R. Howorth, C. B. Llewellyn, J. B. Mortimore, Ray Smith, S. G. Smith, L. F. Townsend, A. W. Wellard.

† *M. W. Tate also scored 1,193 runs and took 116 wickets for MCC in first-class matches on the 1926-27 MCC tour of India and Ceylon.*

Note: R. J. Hadlee (1984) and F. D. Stephenson (1988) are the only players to perform the feat since the reduction of County Championship matches. A complete list of those performing the feat before then will be found on p. 202 of the 1982 *Wisden.*

Wicket-Keeper's Double

	Season	R	D
L. E. G. Ames	1928	1,919	122
L. E. G. Ames	1929	1,795	128
L. E. G. Ames	1932	2,482	104
J. T. Murray	1957	1,025	104

20,000 RUNS AND 2,000 WICKETS IN A CAREER

	Career	R	Avge	W	Avge	Doubles
W. E. Astill........	1906-39	22,731	22.55	2,431	23.76	9
T. E. Bailey........	1945-67	28,641	33.42	2,082	23.13	8
W. G. Grace.......	1865-1908	54,896	39.55	2,876	17.92	8
G. H. Hirst........	1891-1929	36,323	34.13	2,739	18.72	14
R. Illingworth......	1951-83	24,134	28.06	2,072	20.28	6
W. Rhodes	1898-1930	39,802	30.83	4,187	16.71	16
M. W. Tate........	1912-37	21,717	25.01	2,784	18.16	8
F. J. Titmus	1949-82	21,588	23.11	2,830	22.37	8
F. E. Woolley	1906-38	58,969	40.75	2,068	19.85	8

WICKET-KEEPING RECORDS

MOST DISMISSALS IN AN INNINGS

9 (8ct, 1st)	Tahir Rashid	Habib Bank v PACO at Gujranwala	1992-93
8 (all ct)	A. T. W. Grout	Queensland v Western Australia at Brisbane	1959-60
8 (all ct)†	D. E. East	Essex v Somerset at Taunton	1985
8 (all ct)	S. A. Marsh‡	Kent v Middlesex at Lord's	1991
8 (6ct, 2st)	T. J. Zoehrer	Australians v Surrey at The Oval	1993
7 (4ct, 3st)	E. J. Smith	Warwickshire v Derbyshire at Birmingham	1926
7 (6ct, 1st)	W. Farrimond	Lancashire v Kent at Manchester	1930
7 (all ct)	W. F. F. Price	Middlesex v Yorkshire at Lord's	1937
7 (3ct, 4st)	D. Tallon	Queensland v Victoria at Brisbane	1938-39
7 (all ct)	R. A. Saggers	New South Wales v Combined XI at Brisbane	1940-41
7 (1ct, 6st)	H. Yarnold	Worcestershire v Scotland at Dundee	1951
7 (4ct, 3st)	J. Brown	Scotland v Ireland at Dublin	1957
7 (6ct, 1st)	N. Kirsten	Border v Rhodesia at East London	1959-60
7 (all ct)	M. S. Smith	Natal v Border at East London	1959-60
7 (all ct)	K. V. Andrew	Northamptonshire v Lancashire at Manchester	1962
7 (all ct)	A. Long	Surrey v Sussex at Hove	1964
7 (all ct)	R. M. Schofield	Central Districts v Wellington at Wellington	1964-65
7 (all ct)	R. W. Taylor	Derbyshire v Glamorgan at Derby	1966
7 (6ct, 1st)	H. B. Taber	New South Wales v South Australia at Adelaide	1968-69
7 (6ct, 1st)	E. W. Jones	Glamorgan v Cambridge University at Cambridge.	1970
7 (6ct, 1st)	S. Benjamin	Central Zone v North Zone at Bombay	1973-74
7 (all ct)	R. W. Taylor	Derbyshire v Yorkshire at Chesterfield	1975
7 (6ct, 1st)	Shahid Israr	Karachi Whites v Quetta at Karachi	1976-77
7 (4ct, 3st)	Wasim Bari	PIA v Sind at Lahore	1977-78
7 (all ct)	J. A. Maclean	Queensland v Victoria at Melbourne	1977-78
7 (5ct, 2st)	Taslim Arif	National Bank v Punjab at Lahore	1978-79
7 (all ct)	Wasim Bari	Pakistan v New Zealand at Auckland	1978-79
7 (all ct)	R. W. Taylor	England v India at Bombay	1979-80
7 (all ct)	D. L. Bairstow	Yorkshire v Derbyshire at Scarborough	1982
7 (6ct, 1st)	R. B. Phillips	Queensland v New Zealanders at Bundaberg	1982-83
7 (3ct, 4st)	Masood Iqbal	Habib Bank v Lahore at Lahore	1982-83
7 (3ct, 4st)	Arif-ud-Din	United Bank v PACO at Sahiwal	1983-84
7 (6ct, 1st)	R. J. East	OFS v Western Province B at Cape Town	1984-85
7 (all ct)	B. A. Young	Northern Districts v Canterbury at Christchurch	1986-87
7 (all ct)	D. J. Richardson	Eastern Province v OFS at Bloemfontein	1988-89
7 (6ct, 1st)	Dildar Malik	Multan v Faisalabad at Sahiwal	1988-89
7 (all ct)	W. K. Hegg	Lancashire v Derbyshire at Chesterfield	1989
7 (all ct)	Imran Zia	Bahawalpur v Faisalabad at Faisalabad	1989-90
7 (all ct)	I. D. S. Smith	New Zealand v Sri Lanka at Hamilton	1990-91
7 (all ct)	J. F. Holyman	Tasmania v Western Australia at Hobart	1990-91
7 (all ct)	P. J. L. Radley	OFS v Western Province at Cape Town	1990-91
7 (all ct)	C. P. Metson	Glamorgan v Derbyshire at Chesterfield	1991
7 (all ct)	H. M. de Vos	W. Transvaal v E. Transvaal at Potchefstroom	1993-94
7 (all ct)	P. Kirsten	Griqualand West v W. Transvaal at Potchefstroom	1993-94
7 (6ct, 1st)	S. A. Marsh	Kent v Durham at Canterbury	1994
7 (all ct)	K. J. Piper	Warwickshire v Essex at Birmingham	1994
7 (6ct, 1st)	K. J. Piper	Warwickshire v Derbyshire at Chesterfield	1994

† *The first eight wickets to fall.* ‡ *S. A. Marsh also scored 108*.*

WICKET-KEEPERS' HAT-TRICKS

W. H. Brain, Gloucestershire v Somerset at Cheltenham, 1893 – three stumpings off successive balls from C. L. Townsend.

G. O. Dawkes, Derbyshire v Worcestershire at Kidderminster, 1958 – three catches off successive balls from H. L. Jackson.

R. C. Russell, Gloucestershire v Surrey at The Oval, 1986 – three catches off successive balls from C. A. Walsh and D. V. Lawrence (2).

MOST DISMISSALS IN A MATCH

12 (8ct, 4st)	E. Pooley	Surrey v Sussex at The Oval	1868
12 (9ct, 3st)	D. Tallon	Queensland v New South Wales at Sydney	1938-39
12 (9ct, 3st)	H. B. Taber	New South Wales v South Australia at Adelaide.	1968-69
11 (all ct)	A. Long	Surrey v Sussex at Hove	1964
11 (all ct)	R. W. Marsh	Western Australia v Victoria at Perth	1975-76
11 (all ct)	D. L. Bairstow	Yorkshire v Derbyshire at Scarborough	1982
11 (all ct)	W. K. Hegg	Lancashire v Derbyshire at Chesterfield	1989
11 (all ct)	A. J. Stewart	Surrey v Leicestershire at Leicester	1989
11 (all ct)	T. J. Nielsen	South Australia v Western Australia at Perth	1990-91
11 (10ct, 1st)	I. A. Healy	Australians v N. Transvaal at Verwoerdburg	1993-94
11 (10ct, 1st)	K. J. Piper	Warwickshire v Derbyshire at Chesterfield	1994
10 (5ct, 5st)	H. Phillips	Sussex v Surrey at The Oval	1872
10 (2ct, 8st)	E. Pooley	Surrey v Kent at The Oval	1878
10 (9ct, 1st)	T. W. Oates	Nottinghamshire v Middlesex at Nottingham	1906
10 (1ct, 9st)	F. H. Huish	Kent v Surrey at The Oval	1911
10 (9ct, 1st)	J. C. Hubble	Kent v Gloucestershire at Cheltenham	1923
10 (8ct, 2st)	H. Elliott	Derbyshire v Lancashire at Manchester	1935
10 (7ct, 3st)	P. Corrall	Leicestershire v Sussex at Hove	1936
10 (9ct, 1st)	R. A. Saggers	New South Wales v Combined XI at Brisbane	1940-41
10 (all ct)	A. E. Wilson	Gloucestershire v Hampshire at Portsmouth	1953
10 (7ct, 3st)	B. N. Jarman	South Australia v New South Wales at Adelaide.	1961-62
10 (all ct)	L. A. Johnson	Northamptonshire v Sussex at Worthing	1963
10 (all ct)	R. W. Taylor	Derbyshire v Hampshire at Chesterfield	1963
10 (8ct, 2st)	L. A. Johnson	Northamptonshire v Warwickshire at Birmingham	1965
10 (9ct, 1st)	R. C. Jordon	Victoria v South Australia at Melbourne	1970-71
10 (all ct)	R. W. Marsh†	Western Australia v South Australia at Perth	1976-77
10 (6ct, 4st)	Taslim Arif	National Bank v Punjab at Lahore	1978-79
10 (9ct, 1st)	Arif-ud-Din	United Bank v Karachi B at Karachi	1978-79
10 (all ct)	R. W. Taylor	England v India at Bombay	1979-80
10 (all ct)	R. J. Parks	Hampshire v Derbyshire at Portsmouth	1981
10 (9ct, 1st)	A. Ghosh	Bihar v Assam at Bhagalpur	1981-82
10 (8ct, 2st)	Z. Parkar	Bombay v Maharashtra at Bombay	1981-82
10 (all ct)	R. V. Jennings	Transvaal v Arosa Sri Lankans at Johannesburg	1982-83
10 (9ct, 1st)	Kamal Najamuddin	Karachi v Lahore at Multan	1982-83
10 (all ct)	D. A. Murray	West Indies XI v South Africa at Port Elizabeth.	1983-84
10 (7ct, 3st)	Azhar Abbas	Bahawalpur v Lahore City Greens at Bahawalpur	1983-84
10 (7ct, 3st)	B. N. French	Nottinghamshire v Oxford University at Oxford.	1984
10 (8ct, 2st)	R. J. Ryall	Western Province v Transvaal at Cape Town	1984-85
10 (all ct)	S. J. Rixon	Australian XI v South Africa at Johannesburg	1985-86
10 (8ct, 2st)	Anil Dalpat	Karachi v United Bank at Lahore	1985-86
10 (all ct)	R. V. Jennings	Transvaal v Northern Transvaal at Verwoerdburg	1986-87
10 (all ct)	S. J. Rixon	Australian XI v South Africa at Johannesburg	1986-87
10 (all ct)	R. V. Jennings	Transvaal v Orange Free State at Johannesburg	1986-87
10 (9ct, 1st)	C. J. Richards	Surrey v Sussex at Guildford	1987
10 (all ct)	C. W. Scott	Nottinghamshire v Derbyshire at Derby	1988
10 (all ct)	D. J. Richardson	Eastern Province v OFS at Bloemfontein	1988-89
10 (all ct)	A. N. Aymes	Hampshire v Oxford University at Oxford	1989
10 (all ct)	L. R. Fernando	Moratuwa v Panadura at Moratuwa	1989-90
10 (all ct)	Imran Zia	Bahawalpur v Faisalabad at Faisalabad	1989-90
10 (9ct, 1st)	D. J. Richardson	Eastern Province v N. Transvaal at Verwoerdburg	1989-90
10 (all ct)	H. M. de Vos	Western Transvaal v Eastern Transvaal at Potchefstroom	1993-94
10 (all ct)	N. R. Mongia	Rest of India v Punjab at Ludhiana	1993-94
10 (all ct)	W. K. Hegg	Lancashire v Yorkshire at Leeds	1994

† *R. W. Marsh also scored 104.*

MOST DISMISSALS IN A SEASON

128 (79ct, 49st)	L. E. G. Ames	Kent	1929
122 (70ct, 52st)	L. E. G. Ames	Kent	1928
110 (63ct, 47st)	H. Yarnold	Worcestershire	1949
107 (77ct, 30st)	G. Duckworth	Lancashire	1928
107 (96ct, 11st)	J. G. Binks	Yorkshire	1960
104 (40ct, 64st)	L. E. G. Ames	Kent	1932
104 (82ct, 22st)	J. T. Murray	Middlesex	1957
102 (69ct, 33st)	F. H. Huish	Kent	1913
102 (95ct, 7st)	J. T. Murray	Middlesex	1960
101 (62ct, 39st)	F. H. Huish	Kent	1911
101 (85ct, 16st)	R. Booth	Worcestershire	1960
100 (91ct, 9st)	R. Booth	Worcestershire	1964

MOST DISMISSALS IN A CAREER

Dates in italics denote the first half of an overseas season; i.e. *1914* denotes the 1914-15 season.

		Career	*M*	*Ct*	*St*	*Total*
1	R. W. Taylor	1960-88	639	1,473	176	1,649
2	J. T. Murray	1952-75	635	1,270	257	1,527
3	H. Strudwick	1902-27	675	1,242	255	1,497
4	A. P. E. Knott	1964-85	511	1,211	133	1,344
5	F. H. Huish	1895-1914	497	933	377	1,310
6	B. Taylor	1949-73	572	1,083	211	1,294
7	D. Hunter	1889-1909	548	906	347	1,253
8	H. R. Butt	1890-1912	550	953	275	1,228
9	J. H. Board	1891-*1914*	525	852	355	1,207
10	H. Elliott	1920-47	532	904	302	1,206
11	J. M. Parks	1949-76	739	1,088	93	1,181
12	R. Booth	1951-70	468	948	178	1,126
13	L. E. G. Ames	1926-51	593	703	418	1,121
14	D. L. Bairstow	1970-90	459	961	138	1,099
15	G. Duckworth	1923-47	504	753	343	1,096
16	H. W. Stephenson	1948-64	462	748	334	1,082
17	J. G. Binks	1955-75	502	895	176	1,071
18	T. G. Evans	1939-69	465	816	250	1,066
19	A. Long	1960-80	452	922	124	1,046
20	G. O. Dawkes	1937-61	482	895	148	1,043
21	R. W. Tolchard	1965-83	483	912	125	1,037
22	W. L. Cornford	1921-47	496	675	342	1,017

Current Players with 500 Dismissals

	Career	*M*	*Ct*	*St*	*Total*
B. N. French	1976-94	358	814	100	914
R. C. Russell	1981-94	301	701	94	795
S. J. Rhodes	1981-94	259	642	83	725
S. A. Marsh	1982-94	211	497	40	537
C. P. Metson	1981-94	204	491	41	532
D. Ripley	1984-94	212	464	65	529

FIELDING RECORDS

(Excluding wicket-keepers)

MOST CATCHES IN AN INNINGS

7	M. J. Stewart	Surrey v Northamptonshire at Northampton	1957
7	A. S. Brown	Gloucestershire v Nottinghamshire at Nottingham	1966

MOST CATCHES IN A MATCH

10	W. R. Hammond†	Gloucestershire v Surrey at Cheltenham	1928
8	W. B. Burns	Worcestershire v Yorkshire at Bradford	1907
8	F. G. Travers	Europeans v Parsees at Bombay	1923-24
8	A. H. Bakewell	Northamptonshire v Essex at Leyton	1928
8	W. R. Hammond	Gloucestershire v Worcestershire at Cheltenham	1932
8	K. J. Grieves	Lancashire v Sussex at Manchester	1951
8	C. A. Milton	Gloucestershire v Sussex at Hove	1952
8	G. A. R. Lock	Surrey v Warwickshire at The Oval	1957
8	J. M. Prodger	Kent v Gloucestershire at Cheltenham	1961
8	P. M. Walker	Glamorgan v Derbyshire at Swansea	1970
8	Masood Anwar	Rawalpindi v Lahore Division at Rawalpindi	1983-84
8	M. C. J. Ball	Gloucestershire v Yorkshire at Cheltenham	1994

† *Hammond also scored a hundred in each innings.*

MOST CATCHES IN A SEASON

78	W. R. Hammond	1928
77	M. J. Stewart	1957
73	P. M. Walker	1961
71	P. J. Sharpe	1962
70	J. Tunnicliffe	1901
69	J. G. Langridge	1955
69	P. M. Walker	1960
66	J. Tunnicliffe	1895
65	W. R. Hammond	1925
65	P. M. Walker	1959
65	D. W. Richardson	1961
64	K. F. Barrington	1957
64	G. A. R. Lock	1957
63	J. Tunnicliffe	1896
63	J. Tunnicliffe	1904
63	K. J. Grieves	1950
63	C. A. Milton	1956
61	J. V. Wilson	1955
61	M. J. Stewart	1958

Note: The most catches by a fielder since the reduction of County Championship matches in 1969 is 49 by C. J. Tavaré in 1978.

MOST CATCHES IN A CAREER

Dates in italics denote the first half of an overseas season; i.e. *1970* denotes the 1970-71 season.

1,018	F. E. Woolley (1906-38)
887	W. G. Grace (1865-1908)
830	G. A. R. Lock (1946-*70*)
819	W. R. Hammond (1920-51)
813	D. B. Close (1949-86)
784	J. G. Langridge (1928-55)
764	W. Rhodes (1898-1930)
758	C. A. Milton (1948-74)
754	E. H. Hendren (1907-38)

Most Catches by Current Players

510	G. A. Gooch (1973-94)
434	J. E. Emburey (1973-94)
423	M. W. Gatting (1975-94)
401	C. E. B. Rice (*1969-93*)
399	C. W. J. Athey (1976-94)

TEAM RECORDS

HIGHEST TOTALS

1,107	Victoria v New South Wales at Melbourne	1926-27
1,059	Victoria v Tasmania at Melbourne	1922-23
951-7 dec.	Sind v Baluchistan at Karachi	1973-74
944-6 dec.	Hyderabad v Andhra at Secunderabad	1993-94
918	New South Wales v South Australia at Sydney	1900-01
912-8 dec.	Holkar v Mysore at Indore	1945-46
912-6 dec.†	Tamil Nadu v Goa at Panjim	1988-89
910-6 dec.	Railways v Dera Ismail Khan at Lahore	1964-65
903-7 dec.	England v Australia at The Oval	1938
887	Yorkshire v Warwickshire at Birmingham	1896
868†	North Zone v West Zone at Bhilai	1987-88
863	Lancashire v Surrey at The Oval	1990
855-6 dec.†	Bombay v Hyderabad at Bombay	1990-91

† *Tamil Nadu's total of 912-6 dec. included 52 penalty runs from their opponents' failure to meet the required bowling rate. North Zone's total of 868 included 68 and Bombay's total of 855-6 dec. included 48.*

HIGHEST FOR EACH FIRST-CLASS COUNTY

Derbyshire	645	v Hampshire at Derby	1898
Durham	625-6 dec.	v Derbyshire at Chesterfield	1994
Essex	761-6 dec.	v Leicestershire at Chelmsford	1990
Glamorgan	587-8 dec.	v Derbyshire at Cardiff	1951
Gloucestershire	653-6 dec.	v Glamorgan at Bristol	1928
Hampshire	672-7 dec.	v Somerset at Taunton	1899
Kent	803-4 dec.	v Essex at Brentwood	1934
Lancashire	863	v Surrey at The Oval	1990
Leicestershire	701-4 dec.	v Worcestershire at Worcester	1906
Middlesex	642-3 dec.	v Hampshire at Southampton	1923
Northamptonshire	636-6 dec.	v Essex at Chelmsford	1990
Nottinghamshire	739-7 dec.	v Leicestershire at Nottingham	1903
Somerset	675-9 dec.	v Hampshire at Bath	1924
Surrey	811	v Somerset at The Oval	1899
Sussex	705-8 dec.	v Surrey at Hastings	1902
Warwickshire	810-4 dec.	v Durham at Birmingham	1994
Worcestershire	633	v Warwickshire at Worcester	1906
Yorkshire	887	v Warwickshire at Birmingham	1896

HIGHEST AGAINST EACH FIRST-CLASS COUNTY

Derbyshire	662	by Yorkshire at Chesterfield	1898
Durham	810-4 dec.	by Warwickshire at Birmingham	1994
Essex	803-4 dec.	by Kent at Brentwood	1934
Glamorgan	657-7 dec.	by Warwickshire at Birmingham	1994
Gloucestershire	774-7 dec.	by Australians at Bristol	1948
Hampshire	742	by Surrey at The Oval	1909
Kent	676	by Australians at Canterbury	1921
Lancashire	707-9 dec.	by Surrey at The Oval	1990
Leicestershire	761-6 dec.	by Essex at Chelmsford	1990
Middlesex	665	by West Indians at Lord's	1939

Northamptonshire	670-9 dec.	by Sussex at Hove	1921
Nottinghamshire	706-4 dec.	by Surrey at Nottingham	1947
Somerset	811	by Surrey at The Oval	1899
Surrey	863	by Lancashire at The Oval	1990
Sussex	726	by Nottinghamshire at Nottingham	1895
Warwickshire	887	by Yorkshire at Birmingham	1896
Worcestershire	701-4 dec.	by Leicestershire at Worcester	1906
Yorkshire	630	by Somerset at Leeds	1901

LOWEST TOTALS

12	Oxford University v MCC and Ground at Oxford	†1877
12	Northamptonshire v Gloucestershire at Gloucester	1907
13	Auckland v Canterbury at Auckland	1877-78
13	Nottinghamshire v Yorkshire at Nottingham	1901
14	Surrey v Essex at Chelmsford	1983
15	MCC v Surrey at Lord's	1839
15	Victoria v MCC at Melbourne	†1903-04
15	Northamptonshire v Yorkshire at Northampton	†1908
15	Hampshire v Warwickshire at Birmingham (Following on, Hampshire scored 521 and won by 155 runs.)	1922
16	MCC and Ground v Surrey at Lord's	1872
16	Derbyshire v Nottinghamshire at Nottingham	1879
16	Surrey v Nottinghamshire at The Oval	1880
16	Warwickshire v Kent at Tonbridge	1913
16	Trinidad v Barbados at Bridgetown	1942-43
16	Border v Natal at East London (first innings)	1959-60
17	Gentlemen of Kent v Gentlemen of England at Lord's	1850
17	Gloucestershire v Australians at Cheltenham	1896
18	The Bs v England at Lord's	1831
18	Kent v Sussex at Gravesend	†1867
18	Tasmania v Victoria at Melbourne	1868-69
18	Australians v MCC and Ground at Lord's	†1896
18	Border v Natal at East London (second innings)	1959-60
19	Sussex v Surrey at Godalming	1830
19	Sussex v Nottinghamshire at Hove	†1873
19	MCC and Ground v Australians at Lord's	1878
19	Wellington v Nelson at Nelson	1885-86

† *Signifies that one man was absent.*

Note: At Lord's in 1810, The Bs, with one man absent, were dismissed by England for 6.

LOWEST TOTAL IN A MATCH

34	(16 and 18) Border v Natal at East London	1959-60
42	(27 and 15) Northamptonshire v Yorkshire at Northampton	1908

Note: Northamptonshire batted one man short in each innings.

LOWEST FOR EACH FIRST-CLASS COUNTY

Derbyshire	16	v Nottinghamshire at Nottingham	1879
Durham	83	v Lancashire at Manchester	1993
Essex	30	v Yorkshire at Leyton	1901
Glamorgan	22	v Lancashire at Liverpool	1924
Gloucestershire	17	v Australians at Cheltenham	1896
Hampshire	15	v Warwickshire at Birmingham	1922
Kent	18	v Sussex at Gravesend	1867
Lancashire	25	v Derbyshire at Manchester	1871
Leicestershire	25	v Kent at Leicester	1912
Middlesex	20	v MCC at Lord's	1864
Northamptonshire	12	v Gloucestershire at Gloucester	1907
Nottinghamshire	13	v Yorkshire at Nottingham	1901
Somerset	25	v Gloucestershire at Bristol	1947
Surrey	14	v Essex at Chelmsford	1983
Sussex	19	v Nottinghamshire at Hove	1873
Warwickshire	16	v Kent at Tonbridge	1913
Worcestershire	24	v Yorkshire at Huddersfield	1903
Yorkshire	23	v Hampshire at Middlesbrough	1965

LOWEST AGAINST EACH FIRST-CLASS COUNTY

Derbyshire	23	by Hampshire at Burton upon Trent	1958
Durham	73	by Oxford University at Oxford	1994
Essex	14	by Surrey at Chelmsford	1983
Glamorgan	33	by Leicestershire at Ebbw Vale	1965
Gloucestershire	12	by Northamptonshire at Gloucester	1907
Hampshire	23	by Yorkshire at Middlesbrough	1965
Kent	16	by Warwickshire at Tonbridge	1913
Lancashire	22	by Glamorgan at Liverpool	1924
Leicestershire	24	by Oxford University at Oxford	1985
Middlesex	31	by Gloucestershire at Bristol	1924
Northamptonshire	33	by Lancashire at Northampton	1977
Nottinghamshire	16	by Derbyshire at Nottingham	1879
	16	by Surrey at The Oval	1880
Somerset	22	by Gloucestershire at Bristol	1920
Surrey	16	by MCC at Lord's	1872
Sussex	18	by Kent at Gravesend	1867
Warwickshire	15	by Hampshire at Birmingham	1922
Worcestershire	30	by Hampshire at Worcester	1903
Yorkshire	13	by Nottinghamshire at Nottingham	1901

HIGHEST MATCH AGGREGATES

2,376 for 37 wickets	Maharashtra v Bombay at Poona	1948-49
2,078 for 40 wickets	Bombay v Holkar at Bombay	1944-45
1,981 for 35 wickets	England v South Africa at Durban	1938-39
1,929 for 39 wickets	New South Wales v South Australia at Sydney	1925-26
1,911 for 34 wickets	New South Wales v Victoria at Sydney	1908-09
1,905 for 40 wickets	Otago v Wellington at Dunedin	1923-24

In Britain

1,808 for 20 wickets	Sussex v Essex at Hove	1993
1,723 for 31 wickets	England v Australia at Leeds	1948
1,650 for 19 wickets	Surrey v Lancashire at The Oval	1990
1,641 for 16 wickets	Glamorgan v Worcestershire at Abergavenny	1990
1,614 for 30 wickets	England v India at Manchester	1990
1,603 for 28 wickets	England v India at Lord's	1990
1,601 for 29 wickets	England v Australia at Lord's	1930
1,578 for 37 wickets	Sussex v Kent at Hove	1991
1,570 for 29 wickets	Essex v Kent at Chelmsford	1988
1,570 for 29 wickets	Derbyshire v Durham at Chesterfield	1994
1,536 for 27 wickets	Northamptonshire v Middlesex at Northampton	1994
1,531 for 31 wickets	Kent v Essex at Maidstone	1993
1,530 for 19 wickets	Essex v Leicestershire at Chelmsford	1990
1,527 for 23 wickets	Middlesex v Essex at Uxbridge	1994
1,509 for 36 wickets	Somerset v Worcestershire at Taunton	1990
1,507 for 28 wickets	England v West Indies at The Oval	1976
1,502 for 28 wickets	MCC v New Zealanders at Lord's	1927

LOWEST AGGREGATE IN A COMPLETED MATCH

105 for 31 wickets MCC v Australians at Lord's 1878

Note: The lowest aggregate since 1900 is 158 for 22 wickets, Surrey v Worcestershire at The Oval, 1954.

HIGHEST FOURTH-INNINGS TOTALS

(Unless otherwise stated, the side making the runs won the match.)

654-5	England v South Africa at Durban (After being set 696 to win. The match was left drawn on the tenth day.)	1938-39
604	Maharashtra v Bombay at Poona (After being set 959 to win.)	1948-49
576-8	Trinidad v Barbados at Port-of-Spain (After being set 672 to win. Match drawn on fifth day.)	1945-46
572	New South Wales v South Australia at Sydney (After being set 593 to win.)	1907-08
529-9	Combined XI v South Africans at Perth (After being set 579 to win. Match drawn on fourth day.)	1963-64
518	Victoria v Queensland at Brisbane (After being set 753 to win.)	1926-27
507-7	Cambridge University v MCC and Ground at Lord's	1896
506-6	South Australia v Queensland at Adelaide	1991-92
502-6	Middlesex v Nottinghamshire at Nottingham (Game won by an unfinished stand of 271; a county record.)	1925
502-8	Players v Gentlemen at Lord's	1900
500-7	South African Universities v Western Province at Stellenbosch	1978-79

LARGEST VICTORIES

Largest Innings Victories

Inns and 851 runs:	Railways (910-6 dec.) v Dera Ismail Khan (Lahore)	1964-65
Inns and 666 runs:	Victoria (1,059) v Tasmania (Melbourne)	1922-23
Inns and 656 runs:	Victoria (1,107) v New South Wales (Melbourne)	1926-27
Inns and 605 runs:	New South Wales (918) v South Australia (Sydney)	1900-01
Inns and 579 runs:	England (903-7 dec.) v Australia (The Oval)	1938
Inns and 575 runs:	Sind (951-7 dec.) v Baluchistan (Karachi)	1973-74
Inns and 527 runs:	New South Wales (713) v South Australia (Adelaide)	1908-09
Inns and 517 runs:	Australians (675) v Nottinghamshire (Nottingham)	1921

Largest Victories by Runs Margin

685 runs:	New South Wales (235 and 761-8 dec.) v Queensland (Sydney)	1929-30
675 runs:	England (521 and 342-8 dec.) v Australia (Brisbane)	1928-29
638 runs:	New South Wales (304 and 770) v South Australia (Adelaide)	1920-21
625 runs:	Sargodha (376 and 416) v Lahore Municipal Corporation (Faisalabad)	1978-79
609 runs:	Muslim Commercial Bank (575 and 282-0 dec.) v WAPDA (Lahore).	1977-78
573 runs:	Sinhalese SC (395-7 dec. and 350-2 dec.) v Sebastianites C and AC (63 and 109) at Colombo	1990-91
571 runs:	Victoria (304 and 649) v South Australia (Adelaide)	1926-27
562 runs:	Australia (701 and 327) v England (The Oval)	1934

Victory Without Losing a Wicket

Lancashire (166-0 dec. and 66-0) beat Leicestershire by ten wickets (Manchester)	1956
Karachi A (277-0 dec.) beat Sind A by an innings and 77 runs (Karachi)	1957-58
Railways (236-0 dec. and 16-0) beat Jammu and Kashmir by ten wickets (Srinagar)	1960-61
Karnataka (451-0 dec.) beat Kerala by an innings and 186 runs (Chikmagalur)	1977-78

TIED MATCHES IN FIRST-CLASS CRICKET

Since 1948 a tie has been recognised only when the scores are level with all the wickets down in the fourth innings.

The following are the instances since then:

D. G. Bradman's XI v A. L. Hassett's XI at Melbourne	1948-49
Hampshire v Kent at Southampton	1950
Sussex v Warwickshire at Hove	1952
Essex v Lancashire at Brentwood	1952
Northamptonshire v Middlesex at Peterborough	1953
Yorkshire v Leicestershire at Huddersfield	1954
Sussex v Hampshire at Eastbourne	1955
Victoria v New South Wales at Melbourne	1956-57
T. N. Pearce's XI v New Zealanders at Scarborough	1958
Essex v Gloucestershire at Leyton	1959
Australia v West Indies (First Test) at Brisbane	1960-61
Bahawalpur v Lahore B at Bahawalpur	1961-62
Hampshire v Middlesex at Portsmouth	1967
England XI v England Under-25 XI at Scarborough	1968
Yorkshire v Middlesex at Bradford	1973
Sussex v Essex at Hove	1974
South Australia v Queensland at Adelaide	1976-77
Central Districts v England XI at New Plymouth	1977-78
Victoria v New Zealanders at Melbourne	1982-83
Muslim Commercial Bank v Railways at Sialkot	1983-84
Sussex v Kent at Hastings	1984

Northamptonshire v Kent at Northampton 1984
Eastern Province B v Boland at Albany SC, Port Elizabeth 1985-86
Natal B v Eastern Province B at Pietermaritzburg 1985-86
India v Australia (First Test) at Madras 1986-87
Gloucestershire v Derbyshire at Bristol 1987
Bahawalpur v Peshawar at Bahawalpur 1988-89
Wellington v Canterbury at Wellington 1988-89
Sussex v Kent at Hove . . . . . †1991
Nottinghamshire v Worcestershire at Nottingham 1993

† *Sussex (436) scored the highest total to tie a first-class match.*

MATCHES BEGUN AND FINISHED ON FIRST DAY

Since 1900. A fuller list may be found in the Wisden *of 1981 and preceding editions.*

Yorkshire v Worcestershire at Bradford, May 7 1900
MCC and Ground v London County at Lord's, May 20 1903
Transvaal v Orange Free State at Johannesburg, December 30 1906
Middlesex v Gentlemen of Philadelphia at Lord's, July 20 1908
Gloucestershire v Middlesex at Bristol, August 26 1909
Eastern Province v Orange Free State at Port Elizabeth, December 26 1912
Kent v Sussex at Tonbridge, June 21 1919
Lancashire v Somerset at Manchester, May 21 1925
Madras v Mysore at Madras, November 4 1934
Ireland v New Zealanders at Dublin, September 11 1937
Derbyshire v Somerset at Chesterfield, June 11 1947
Lancashire v Sussex at Manchester, July 12 1950
Surrey v Warwickshire at The Oval, May 16 1953
Somerset v Lancashire at Bath, June 6 (H. F. T. Buse's benefit) 1953
Kent v Worcestershire at Tunbridge Wells, June 15 1960

TEST MATCH RECORDS

Note: This section covers all Tests up to August 28, 1994.

BATTING RECORDS

HIGHEST INDIVIDUAL INNINGS

375	B. C. Lara	West Indies v England at St John's	1993-94
365*	G. S. Sobers	West Indies v Pakistan at Kingston	1957-58
364	L. Hutton	England v Australia at The Oval	1938
337	Hanif Mohammad	Pakistan v West Indies at Bridgetown	1957-58
336*	W. R. Hammond	England v New Zealand at Auckland	1932-33
334	D. G. Bradman	Australia v England at Leeds	1930
333	G. A. Gooch	England v India at Lord's	1990
325	A. Sandham	England v West Indies at Kingston	1929-30
311	R. B. Simpson	Australia v England at Manchester	1964
310*	J. H. Edrich	England v New Zealand at Leeds	1965
307	R. M. Cowper	Australia v England at Melbourne	1965-66
304	D. G. Bradman	Australia v England at Leeds	1934
302	L. G. Rowe	West Indies v England at Bridgetown	1973-74
299*	D. G. Bradman	Australia v South Africa at Adelaide	1931-32
299	M. D. Crowe	New Zealand v Sri Lanka at Wellington	1990-91
291	I. V. A. Richards	West Indies v England at The Oval	1976
287	R. E. Foster	England v Australia at Sydney	1903-04
285*	P. B. H. May	England v West Indies at Birmingham	1957
280*	Javed Miandad	Pakistan v India at Hyderabad	1982-83
278	D. C. S. Compton	England v Pakistan at Nottingham	1954
277	B. C. Lara	West Indies v Australia at Sydney	1992-93
274	R. G. Pollock	South Africa v Australia at Durban	1969-70
274	Zaheer Abbas	Pakistan v England at Birmingham	1971
271	Javed Miandad	Pakistan v New Zealand at Auckland	1988-89
270*	G. A. Headley	West Indies v England at Kingston	1934-35
270	D. G. Bradman	Australia v England at Melbourne	1936-37
268	G. N. Yallop	Australia v Pakistan at Melbourne	1983-84
267	P. A. de Silva	Sri Lanka v New Zealand at Wellington	1990-91
266	W. H. Ponsford	Australia v England at The Oval	1934
262*	D. L. Amiss	England v West Indies at Kingston	1973-74
261	F. M. M. Worrell	West Indies v England at Nottingham	1950
260	C. C. Hunte	West Indies v Pakistan at Kingston	1957-58
260	Javed Miandad	Pakistan v England at The Oval	1987
259	G. M. Turner	New Zealand v West Indies at Georgetown	1971-72
258	T. W. Graveney	England v West Indies at Nottingham	1957
258	S. M. Nurse	West Indies v New Zealand at Christchurch	1968-69
256	R. B. Kanhai	West Indies v India at Calcutta	1958-59
256	K. F. Barrington	England v Australia at Manchester	1964
255*	D. J. McGlew	South Africa v New Zealand at Wellington	1952-53
254	D. G. Bradman	Australia v England at Lord's	1930
251	W. R. Hammond	England v Australia at Sydney	1928-29
250	K. D. Walters	Australia v New Zealand at Christchurch	1976-77
250	S. F. A. F. Bacchus	West Indies v India at Kanpur	1978-79

The highest individual innings for India and Zimbabwe are:

236*	S. M. Gavaskar	India v West Indies at Madras	1983-84
121	D. L. Houghton	Zimbabwe v India at Harare	1992-93

HUNDRED ON TEST DEBUT

C. Bannerman (165*)	Australia v England at Melbourne	1876-77
W. G. Grace (152)	England v Australia at The Oval	1880
H. Graham (107)	Australia v England at Lord's	1893

†K. S. Ranjitsinhji (154*)	England v Australia at Manchester	1896
†P. F. Warner (132*)	England v South Africa at Johannesburg	1898-99
†R. A. Duff (104)	Australia v England at Melbourne	1901-02
R. E. Foster (287)	England v Australia at Sydney	1903-04
G. Gunn (119)	England v Australia at Sydney	1907-08
†R. J. Hartigan (116)	Australia v England at Adelaide	1907-08
†H. L. Collins (104)	Australia v England at Sydney	1920-21
W. H. Ponsford (110)	Australia v England at Sydney	1924-25
A. A. Jackson (164)	Australia v England at Adelaide	1928-29
†G. A. Headley (176)	West Indies v England at Bridgetown	1929-30
J. E. Mills (117)	New Zealand v England at Wellington	1929-30
Nawab of Pataudi sen. (102)	England v Australia at Sydney	1932-33
B. H. Valentine (136)	England v India at Bombay	1933-34
†L. Amarnath (118)	India v England at Bombay	1933-34
†P. A. Gibb (106)	England v South Africa at Johannesburg	1938-39
S. C. Griffith (140)	England v West Indies at Port-of-Spain	1947-48
A. G. Ganteaume (112)	West Indies v England at Port-of-Spain	1947-48
†J. W. Burke (101*)	Australia v England at Adelaide	1950-51
P. B. H. May (138)	England v South Africa at Leeds	1951
R. H. Shodhan (110)	India v Pakistan at Calcutta	1952-53
B. H. Pairaudeau (115)	West Indies v India at Port-of-Spain	1952-53
†O. G. Smith (104)	West Indies v Australia at Kingston	1954-55
A. G. Kripal Singh (100*)	India v New Zealand at Hyderabad	1955-56
C. C. Hunte (142)	West Indies v Pakistan at Bridgetown	1957-58
C. A. Milton (104*)	England v New Zealand at Leeds	1958
†A. A. Baig (112)	India v England at Manchester	1959
Hanumant Singh (105)	India v England at Delhi	1963-64
Khalid Ibadulla (166)	Pakistan v Australia at Karachi	1964-65
B. R. Taylor (105)	New Zealand v India at Calcutta	1964-65
K. D. Walters (155)	Australia v England at Brisbane	1965-66
J. H. Hampshire (107)	England v West Indies at Lord's	1969
†G. R. Viswanath (137)	India v Australia at Kanpur	1969-70
G. S. Chappell (108)	Australia v England at Perth	1970-71
‡L. G. Rowe (214, 100*)	West Indies v New Zealand at Kingston	1971-72
A. I. Kallicharran (100*)	West Indies v New Zealand at Georgetown	1971-72
R. E. Redmond (107)	New Zealand v Pakistan at Auckland	1972-73
†F. C. Hayes (106*)	England v West Indies at The Oval	1973
†C. G. Greenidge (107)	West Indies v India at Bangalore	1974-75
†L. Baichan (105*)	West Indies v Pakistan at Lahore	1974-75
G. J. Cosier (109)	Australia v West Indies at Melbourne	1975-76
S. Amarnath (124)	India v New Zealand at Auckland	1975-76
Javed Miandad (163)	Pakistan v New Zealand at Lahore	1976-77
†A. B. Williams (100)	West Indies v Australia at Georgetown	1977-78
†D. M. Wellham (103)	Australia v England at The Oval	1981
†Salim Malik (100*)	Pakistan v Sri Lanka at Karachi	1981-82
K. C. Wessels (162)	Australia v England at Brisbane	1982-83
W. B. Phillips (159)	Australia v Pakistan at Perth	1983-84
§M. Azharuddin (110)	India v England at Calcutta	1984-85
D. S. B. P. Kuruppu (201*)	Sri Lanka v New Zealand at Colombo (CCC)	1986-87
†M. J. Greatbatch (107*)	New Zealand v England at Auckland	1987-88
M. E. Waugh (138)	Australia v England at Adelaide	1990-91
A. C. Hudson (163)	South Africa v West Indies at Bridgetown	1991-92
R. S. Kaluwitharana (132*)	Sri Lanka v Australia at Colombo (SSC)	1992-93
D. L. Houghton (121)	Zimbabwe v India at Harare	1992-93
P. K. Amre (103)	India v South Africa at Durban	1992-93
†G. P. Thorpe (114*)	England v Australia at Nottingham	1993

† *In his second innings of the match.*

‡ *L. G. Rowe is the only batsman to score a hundred in each innings on debut.*

§ *M. Azharuddin is the only batsman to score hundreds in each of his first three Tests.*

Note: L. Amarnath and S. Amarnath provide the only instance of a father and son scoring a hundred on debut.

300 RUNS IN FIRST TEST

314	L. G. Rowe (214, 100*)	West Indies v New Zealand at Kingston	1971-72
306	R. E. Foster (287, 19)	England v Australia at Sydney	1903-04

TWO SEPARATE HUNDREDS IN A TEST

Three times: S. M. Gavaskar v West Indies (1970-71), v Pakistan (1978-79), v West Indies (1978-79).

Twice in one series: C. L. Walcott v Australia (1954-55).

Twice: H. Sutcliffe v Australia (1924-25), v South Africa (1929); G. A. Headley v England (1929-30 and 1939); G. S. Chappell v New Zealand (1973-74), v West Indies (1975-76); ‡A. R. Border v Pakistan (1979-80), v New Zealand (1985-86).

Once: W. Bardsley v England (1909); A. C. Russell v South Africa (1922-23); W. R. Hammond v Australia (1928-29); E. Paynter v South Africa (1938-39); D. C. S. Compton v Australia (1946-47); A. R. Morris v England (1946-47); A. Melville v England (1947); B. Mitchell v England (1947); D. G. Bradman v India (1947-48); V. S. Hazare v Australia (1947-48); E. D. Weekes v India (1948-49); J. Moroney v South Africa (1949-50); G. S. Sobers v Pakistan (1957-58); R. B. Kanhai v Australia (1960-61); Hanif Mohammad v England (1961-62); R. B. Simpson v Pakistan (1964-65); K. D. Walters v West Indies (1968-69); †L. G. Rowe v New Zealand (1971-72); I. M. Chappell v New Zealand (1973-74); G. M. Turner v Australia (1973-74); C. G. Greenidge v England (1976); G. P. Howarth v England (1977-78); L. R. D. Mendis v India (1982-83); Javed Miandad v New Zealand (1984-85); D. M. Jones v Pakistan (1989-90); G. A. Gooch v India (1990); A. H. Jones v Sri Lanka (1990-91); A. P. Gurusinha v New Zealand (1990-91); A. J. Stewart v West Indies (1993-94).

† *L. G. Rowe's two hundreds were on his Test debut.*

‡ *A. R. Border scored 150* and 153 against Pakistan to become the first batsman to score 150 in each innings of a Test match.*

TRIPLE-HUNDRED AND HUNDRED IN SAME TEST

G. A. Gooch (England)	333 and 123 v India at Lord's	1990

The only instance in first-class cricket.

DOUBLE-HUNDRED AND HUNDRED IN SAME TEST

K. D. Walters (Australia)	242 and 103 v West Indies at Sydney	1968-69
S. M. Gavaskar (India)	124 and 220 v West Indies at Port-of-Spain	1970-71
†L. G. Rowe (West Indies)	214 and 100* v New Zealand at Kingston	1971-72
G. S. Chappell (Australia)	247* and 133 v New Zealand at Wellington	1973-74

† *On Test debut.*

MOST RUNS IN A SERIES

	T	*I*	*NO*	*R*	*HS*	*100s*	*Avge*		
D. G. Bradman	5	7	0	974	334	4	139.14	A v E	1930
W. R. Hammond	5	9	1	905	251	4	113.12	E v A	1928-29
M. A. Taylor	6	11	1	839	219	2	83.90	A v E	1989
R. N. Harvey	5	9	0	834	205	4	92.66	A v SA	1952-53
I. V. A. Richards	4	7	0	829	291	3	118.42	WI v E	1976
C. L. Walcott	5	10	0	827	155	5	82.70	WI v A	1954-55

	T	I	NO	R	HS	100s	Avge		
G. S. Sobers......	5	8	2	824	365*	3	137.33	WI v P	1957-58
D. G. Bradman...	5	9	0	810	270	3	90.00	A v E	1936-37
D. G. Bradman...	5	5	1	806	299*	4	201.50	A v SA	1931-32
B. C. Lara.......	5	8	0	798	375	2	99.75	WI v E	1993-94
E. D. Weekes....	5	7	0	779	194	4	111.28	WI v I	1948-49
†S. M. Gavaskar..	4	8	3	774	220	4	154.80	I v WI	1970-71
Mudassar Nazar..	6	8	2	761	231	4	126.83	P v I	1982-83
D. G. Bradman...	5	8	0	758	304	2	94.75	A v E	1934
D. C. S. Compton.	5	8	0	753	208	4	94.12	E v SA	1947
‡G. A. Gooch....	3	6	0	752	333	3	125.33	E v I	1990

† *Gavaskar's aggregate was achieved in his first Test series.*
‡ *G. A. Gooch is alone in scoring 1,000 runs in Test cricket during an English season with 1,058 runs in 11 innings against New Zealand and India in 1990.*

1,000 TEST RUNS IN A CALENDAR YEAR

	T	I	NO	R	HS	100s	Avge	Year
I. V. A. Richards (WI)........	11	19	0	1,710	291	7	90.00	1976
S. M. Gavaskar (I)...........	18	27	1	1,555	221	5	59.80	1979
G. R. Viswanath (I)..........	17	26	3	1,388	179	5	60.34	1979
R. B. Simpson (A)...........	14	26	3	1,381	311	3	60.04	1964
D. L. Amiss (E).............	13	22	2	1,379	262*	5	68.95	1974
S. M. Gavaskar (I)...........	18	32	4	1,310	236*	5	46.78	1983
G. A. Gooch (E).............	9	17	1	1,264	333	4	79.00	1990
D. C. Boon (A)..............	16	25	5	1,241	164*	4	62.05	1993
M. A. Taylor (A).............	11	20	1	1,219	219	4	64.15	1989†
G. S. Sobers (WI)............	7	12	3	1,193	365*	5	132.55	1958
D. B. Vengsarkar (I)..........	18	27	4	1,174	146*	5	51.04	1979
K. J. Hughes (A).............	15	28	4	1,163	130*	2	48.45	1979
D. C. S. Compton (E).........	9	15	1	1,159	208	6	82.78	1947
C. G. Greenidge (WI)........	14	22	4	1,149	223	4	63.83	1984
M. A. Taylor (A).............	15	23	2	1,106	170	4	52.66	1993
A. R. Border (A).............	11	20	3	1,099	196	4	64.64	1985
D. M. Jones (A).............	11	18	3	1,099	216	4	73.26	1989
I. T. Botham (E).............	14	22	0	1,095	208	3	49.77	1982
K. W. R. Fletcher (E)........	13	22	4	1,090	178	2	60.55	1973
M. Amarnath (I).............	14	24	1	1,077	120	4	46.82	1983
A. R. Border (A).............	14	27	3	1,073	162	3	44.70	1979
C. Hill (A)..................	12	21	2	1,061	142	2	55.84	1902
D. I. Gower (E).............	14	25	2	1,061	114	1	46.13	1982
D. I. Gower (E).............	14	25	1	1,059	136	2	44.12	1986
W. M. Lawry (A)............	14	27	2	1,056	157	2	42.24	1964
S. M. Gavaskar (I)...........	9	15	2	1,044	205	4	80.30	1978
G. A. Gooch (E).............	9	17	1	1,040	174	3	65.00	1991
K. F. Barrington (E)..........	12	22	2	1,039	132*	3	51.95	1963
E. R. Dexter (E).............	11	15	1	1,038	205	2	74.14	1962
K. F. Barrington (E)..........	10	17	4	1,032	172	4	79.38	1961
Mohsin Khan (P)............	10	17	3	1,029	200	4	73.50	1982
D. G. Bradman (A)..........	8	13	4	1,025	201	5	113.88	1948
S. M. Gavaskar (I)...........	11	20	1	1,024	156	4	53.89	1976
A. R. Border (A).............	11	19	3	1,000	140	5	62.50	1986

† *The year of his debut.*

Notes: The earliest date for completing 1,000 runs is May 3 by M. Amarnath in 1983.

D. G. Bradman scored 1,005 runs in five consecutive Tests, all against England, in 1936-37 and 1938: 13, 270, 26, 212, 169, 51, 144*, 18, 102*.

MOST RUNS IN A CAREER

(Qualification: 2,000 runs)

ENGLAND

		T	I	NO	R	HS	100s	Avge
1	**G. A. Gooch**	**113**	**205**	**6**	**8,655**	**333**	**20**	**43.49**
2	D. I. Gower	117	204	18	8,231	215	18	44.25
3	G. Boycott	108	193	23	8,114	246*	22	47.72
4	M. C. Cowdrey	114	188	15	7,624	182	22	44.06
5	W. R. Hammond	85	140	16	7,249	336*	22	58.45
6	L. Hutton	79	138	15	6,971	364	19	56.67
7	K. F. Barrington	82	131	15	6,806	256	20	58.67
8	D. C. S. Compton	78	131	15	5,807	278	17	50.06
9	J. B. Hobbs	61	102	7	5,410	211	15	56.94
10	I. T. Botham	102	161	6	5,200	208	14	33.54
11	J. H. Edrich	77	127	9	5,138	310*	12	43.54
12	T. W. Graveney	79	123	13	4,882	258	11	44.38
13	A. J. Lamb	79	139	10	4,656	142	14	36.09
14	H. Sutcliffe	54	84	9	4,555	194	16	60.73
15	P. B. H. May	66	106	9	4,537	285*	13	46.77
16	E. R. Dexter	62	102	8	4,502	205	9	47.89
17	A. P. E. Knott	95	149	15	4,389	135	5	32.75
18	M. W. Gatting	74	129	14	4,227	207	9	36.75
19	**R. A. Smith**	**53**	**97**	**14**	**3,677**	**175**	**9**	**44.30**
20	D. L. Amiss	50	88	10	3,612	262*	11	46.30
21	A. W. Greig	58	93	4	3,599	148	8	40.43
22	E. H. Hendren	51	83	9	3,525	205*	7	47.63
23	F. E. Woolley	64	98	7	3,283	154	5	36.07
24	K. W. R. Fletcher	59	96	14	3,272	216	7	39.90
25	**A. J. Stewart**	**43**	**78**	**5**	**2,982**	**190**	**7**	**40.84**
26	**M. A. Atherton**	**40**	**74**	**1**	**2,917**	**151**	**7**	**39.95**
27	M. Leyland	41	65	5	2,764	187	9	46.06
28	C. Washbrook	37	66	6	2,569	195	6	42.81
29	B. L. D'Oliveira	44	70	8	2,484	158	5	40.06
30	D. W. Randall	47	79	5	2,470	174	7	33.37
31	W. J. Edrich	39	63	2	2,440	219	6	40.00
32	T. G. Evans	91	133	14	2,439	104	2	20.49
33	L. E. G. Ames	47	72	12	2,434	149	8	40.56
34	W. Rhodes	58	98	21	2,325	179	2	30.19
35	T. E. Bailey	61	91	14	2,290	134*	1	29.74
36	M. J. K. Smith	50	78	6	2,278	121	3	31.63
37	P. E. Richardson	34	56	1	2,061	126	5	37.47

AUSTRALIA

		T	I	NO	R	HS	100s	Avge
1	**A. R. Border**	**156**	**265**	**44**	**11,174**	**205**	**27**	**50.56**
2	G. S. Chappell	87	151	19	7,110	247*	24	53.86
3	D. G. Bradman	52	80	10	6,996	334	29	99.94
4	**D. C. Boon**	**89**	**160**	**18**	**6,564**	**200**	**18**	**46.22**
5	R. N. Harvey	79	137	10	6,149	205	21	48.41
6	K. D. Walters	74	125	14	5,357	250	15	48.26
7	I. M. Chappell	75	136	10	5,345	196	14	42.42
8	W. M. Lawry	67	123	12	5,234	210	13	47.15
9	R. B. Simpson	62	111	7	4,869	311	10	46.81
10	I. R. Redpath	66	120	11	4,737	171	8	43.45
11	K. J. Hughes	70	124	6	4,415	213	9	37.41
12	**M. A. Taylor**	**54**	**97**	**6**	**4,275**	**219**	**12**	**46.97**
13	R. W. Marsh	96	150	13	3,633	132	3	26.51
14	D. M. Jones	52	89	11	3,631	216	11	46.55

		T	*I*	*NO*	*R*	*HS*	*100s*	*Avge*
15	A. R. Morris	46	79	3	3,533	206	12	46.48
16	**S. R. Waugh**	**65**	**98**	**18**	**3,495**	**177***	**7**	**43.68**
17	C. Hill	49	89	2	3,412	191	7	39.21
18	G. M. Wood	59	112	6	3,374	172	9	31.83
19	V. T. Trumper	48	89	8	3,163	214*	8	39.04
20	C. C. McDonald	47	83	4	3,107	170	5	39.32
21	A. L. Hassett	43	69	3	3,073	198*	10	46.56
22	K. R. Miller	55	87	7	2,958	147	7	36.97
23	W. W. Armstrong	50	84	10	2,863	159*	6	38.68
24	G. R. Marsh	50	93	7	2,854	138	4	33.18
25	K. R. Stackpole	43	80	5	2,807	·207	7	37.42
26	N. C. O'Neill	42	69	8	2,779	181	6	45.55
27	G. N. Yallop	39	70	3	2,756	268	8	41.13
28	S. J. McCabe	39	62	5	2,748	232	6	48.21
29	W. Bardsley	41	66	5	2,469	193*	6	40.47
30	W. M. Woodfull	35	54	4	2,300	161	7	46.00
31	P. J. P. Burge	42	68	8	2,290	181	4	38.16
32	S. E. Gregory	58	100	7	2,282	201	4	24.53
33	R. Benaud	63	97	7	2,201	122	3	24.45
34	**M. E. Waugh**	**36**	**57**	**4**	**2,177**	**139***	**6**	**41.07**
35	C. G. Macartney	35	55	4	2,131	170	7	41.78
36	W. H. Ponsford	29	48	4	2,122	266	7	48.22
37	R. M. Cowper	27	46	2	2,061	307	5	46.84
38	**I. A. Healy**	**62**	**90**	**10**	**2,057**	**113***	**2**	**25.71**

SOUTH AFRICA

		T	*I*	*NO*	*R*	*HS*	*100s*	*Avge*
1	B. Mitchell	42	80	9	3,471	189*	8	48.88
2	A. D. Nourse	34	62	7	2,960	231	9	53.81
3	H. W. Taylor	42	76	4	2,936	176	7	40.77
4	E. J. Barlow	30	57	2	2,516	201	6	45.74
4	T. L. Goddard	41	78	5	2,516	112	1	34.46
6	D. J. McGlew	34	64	6	2,440	255*	7	42.06
7	J. H. B. Waite	50	86	7	2,405	134	4	30.44
8	R. G. Pollock	23	41	4	2,256	274	7	60.97
9	A. W. Nourse	45	83	8	2,234	111	1	29.78
10	R. A. McLean	40	73	3	2,120	142	5	30.28

K. C. Wessels has scored 2,788 runs in 40 Tests: 1,761 (average 42.95) in 24 Tests for Australia, and 1,027 (average 38.03) in 16 Tests for South Africa.

WEST INDIES

		T	*I*	*NO*	*R*	*HS*	*100s*	*Avge*
1	I. V. A. Richards	121	182	12	8,540	291	24	50.23
2	G. S. Sobers	93	160	21	8,032	365*	26	57.78
3	C. G. Greenidge	108	185	16	7,558	226	19	44.72
4	C. H. Lloyd	110	175	14	7,515	242*	19	46.67
5	**D. L. Haynes**	**116**	**202**	**25**	**7,487**	**184**	**18**	**42.29**
6	R. B. Kanhai	79	137	6	6,227	256	15	47.53
7	**R. B. Richardson**	**76**	**130**	**11**	**5,445**	**194**	**15**	**45.75**
8	E. D. Weekes	48	81	5	4,455	207	15	58.61
9	A. I. Kallicharran	66	109	10	4,399	187	12	44.43
10	R. C. Fredericks	59	109	7	4,334	169	8	42.49
11	F. M. M. Worrell	51	87	9	3,860	261	9	49.48
12	C. L. Walcott	44	74	7	3,798	220	15	56.68
13	P. J. L. Dujon	81	115	11	3,322	139	5	31.94
14	C. C. Hunte	44	78	6	3,245	260	8	45.06
15	H. A. Gomes	60	91	11	3,171	143	9	39.63

		T	I	NO	R	HS	100s	Avge
16	B. F. Butcher	44	78	6	3,104	209*	7	43.11
17	S. M. Nurse	29	54	1	2,523	258	6	47.60
18	A. L. Logie	52	78	9	2,470	130	2	35.79
19	G. A. Headley	22	40	4	2,190	270*	10	60.83
20	J. B. Stollmeyer	32	56	5	2,159	160	4	42.33
21	L. G. Rowe	30	49	2	2,047	302	7	43.55

NEW ZEALAND

		T	I	NO	R	HS	100s	Avge
1	J. G. Wright	82	148	7	5,334	185	12	37.82
2	**M. D. Crowe**	**70**	**120**	**11**	**5,230**	**299**	**17**	**47.98**
3	B. E. Congdon	61	114	7	3,448	176	7	32.22
4	J. R. Reid	58	108	5	3,428	142	6	33.28
5	R. J. Hadlee	86	134	19	3,124	151*	2	27.16
6	G. M. Turner	41	73	6	2,991	259	7	44.64
7	**A. H. Jones**	**37**	**70**	**7**	**2,898**	**186**	**7**	**46.00**
8	B. Sutcliffe	42	76	8	2,727	230*	5	40.10
9	M. G. Burgess	50	92	6	2,684	119*	5	31.20
10	J. V. Coney	52	85	14	2,668	174*	3	37.57
11	G. P. Howarth	47	83	5	2,531	147	6	32.44
12	G. T. Dowling	39	77	3	2,306	239	3	31.16
13	**K. R. Rutherford**	**48**	**85**	**7**	**2,119**	**107***	**3**	**27.16**

INDIA

		T	I	NO	R	HS	100s	Avge
1	S. M. Gavaskar	125	214	16	10,122	236*	34	51.12
2	D. B. Vengsarkar	116	185	22	6,868	166	17	42.13
3	G. R. Viswanath	91	155	10	6,080	222	14	41.93
4	**Kapil Dev**	**131**	**184**	**15**	**5,248**	**163**	**8**	**31.05**
5	M. Amarnath	69	113	10	4,378	138	11	42.50
6	**M. Azharuddin**	**62**	**88**	**3**	**4,020**	**199**	**14**	**47.29**
7	R. J. Shastri	80	121	14	3,830	206	11	35.79
8	P. R. Umrigar	59	94	8	3,631	223	12	42.22
9	V. L. Manjrekar	55	92	10	3,208	189*	7	39.12
10	C. G. Borde	55	97	11	3,061	177*	5	35.59
11	Nawab of Pataudi jun.	46	83	3	2,793	203*	6	34.91
12	S. M. H. Kirmani	88	124	22	2,759	102	2	27.04
13	F. M. Engineer	46	87	3	2,611	121	2	31.08
14	Pankaj Roy	43	79	4	2,442	173	5	32.56
15	V. S. Hazare	30	52	6	2,192	164*	7	47.65
16	A. L. Wadekar	37	71	3	2,113	143	1	31.07
17	V. Mankad	44	72	5	2,109	231	5	31.47
18	C. P. S. Chauhan	40	68	2	2,084	97	0	31.57
19	K. Srikkanth	43	72	3	2,062	123	2	29.88
20	M. L. Jaisimha	39	71	4	2,056	129	3	30.68
21	**S. R. Tendulkar**	**32**	**45**	**5**	**2,023**	**165**	**7**	**50.57**
22	D. N. Sardesai	30	55	4	2,001	212	5	39.23

PAKISTAN

		T	I	NO	R	HS	100s	Avge
1	**Javed Miandad**	**124**	**189**	**21**	**8,832**	**280***	**23**	**52.57**
2	Zaheer Abbas	78	124	11	5,062	274	12	44.79
3	Mudassar Nazar	76	116	8	4,114	231	10	38.09
4	**Salim Malik**	**77**	**111**	**19**	**4,040**	**165**	**11**	**43.91**
5	Majid Khan	63	106	5	3,931	167	8	38.92
6	Hanif Mohammad	55	97	8	3,915	337	12	43.98

		T	I	NO	R	HS	100s	Avge
7	Imran Khan	88	126	25	3,807	136	6	37.69
8	Mushtaq Mohammad	57	100	7	3,643	201	10	39.17
9	Asif Iqbal	58	99	7	3,575	175	11	38.85
10	Saeed Ahmed	41	78	4	2,991	172	5	40.41
11	Wasim Raja	57	92	14	2,821	125	4	36.16
12	Mohsin Khan	48	79	6	2,709	200	7	37.10
13	**Shoaib Mohammad**	**42**	**63**	**7**	**2,622**	**203***	**7**	**46.82**
14	Sadiq Mohammad	41	74	2	2,579	166	5	35.81
15	Ramiz Raja	48	78	5	2,243	122	2	30.72
16	Imtiaz Ahmed	41	72	1	2,079	209	3	29.28

SRI LANKA

		T	I	NO	R	HS	100s	Avge
1	**A. Ranatunga**	**51**	**86**	**4**	**2,804**	**135***	**4**	**34.19**
2	**P. A. de Silva**	**43**	**74**	**3**	**2,760**	**267**	**7**	**38.87**

ZIMBABWE: The highest aggregate is 499, average 55.44, by **A. Flower** in 7 Tests.

Bold type denotes those who played Test cricket in 1993-94 and 1994 seasons or Sri Lanka v Pakistan in 1994-95.

HIGHEST CAREER AVERAGES

(Qualification: 20 innings)

Avge		T	I	NO	R	HS	100s
99.94	D. G. Bradman (A)	52	80	10	6,996	334	29
62.61	**B. C. Lara (WI)**	**16**	**26**	**0**	**1,628**	**375**	**3**
60.97	R. G. Pollock (SA)	23	41	4	2,256	274	7
60.83	G. A. Headley (WI)	22	40	4	2,190	270*	10
60.73	H. Sutcliffe (E)	54	84	9	4,555	194	16
59.23	E. Paynter (E)	20	31	5	1,540	243	4
58.67	K. F. Barrington (E)	82	131	15	6,806	256	20
58.61	E. D. Weekes (WI)	48	81	5	4,455	207	15
58.45	W. R. Hammond (E)	85	140	16	7,249	336*	22
57.78	G. S. Sobers (WI)	93	160	21	8,032	365*	26
56.94	J. B. Hobbs (E)	61	102	7	5,410	211	15
56.68	C. L. Walcott (WI)	44	74	7	3,798	220	15
56.67	L. Hutton (E)	79	138	15	6,971	364	19
55.00	E. Tyldesley (E)	14	20	2	990	122	3
54.20	C. A. Davis (WI)	15	29	5	1,301	183	4
53.86	G. S. Chappell (A)	87	151	19	7,110	247*	24
53.81	A. D. Nourse (SA)	34	62	7	2,960	231	9
52.57	**Javed Miandad (P)**	**124**	**189**	**21**	**8,832**	**280***	**23**
51.62	J. Ryder (A)	20	32	5	1,394	201*	3
51.12	S. M. Gavaskar (I)	125	214	16	10,122	236*	34
50.57	**S. R. Tendulkar (I)**	**32**	**45**	**5**	**2,023**	**165**	**7**
50.56	**A. R. Border (A)**	**156**	**265**	**44**	**11,174**	**205**	**27**
50.23	I. V. A. Richards (WI)	121	182	12	8,540	291	24
50.06	D. C. S. Compton (E)	78	131	15	5,807	278	17

Bold type denotes those who played Test cricket in 1993-94 and 1994 seasons.

MOST HUNDREDS

	Total	200+	Inns	*Opponents* E	A	SA	WI	NZ	I	P	SL	Z
S. M. Gavaskar (I)	34	4	214	4	8	–	13	2	–	5	2	–
D. G. Bradman (A)	29	12	80	19	–	4	2	–	4	–	–	–
A. R. Border (A)	**27**	**2**	**265**	**8**	**–**	**–**	**3**	**5**	**4**	**6**	**1**	**–**
G. S. Sobers (WI)	26	2	160	10	4	–	–	1	8	3	–	–
G. S. Chappell (A)	24	4	151	9	–	–	5	3	1	6	0	–
I. V. A. Richards (WI)	24	3	182	8	5	–	–	1	8	2	–	–
Javed Miandad (P)	**23**	**6**	**189**	**2**	**6**	**–**	**2**	**7**	**5**	**–**	**1**	**–**
G. Boycott (E)	22	1	193	–	7	1	5	2	4	3	–	–
M. C. Cowdrey (E)	22	0	188	–	5	3	6	2	3	3	–	–
W. R. Hammond (E)	22	7	140	–	9	6	1	4	2	–	–	–
R. N. Harvey (A)	21	2	137	6	–	8	3	–	4	0	–	–
K. F. Barrington (E)	20	1	131	–	5	2	3	3	3	4	–	–
G. A. Gooch (E)	**20**	**2**	**205**	**–**	**4**	**–**	**5**	**4**	**5**	**1**	**1**	**–**
C. G. Greenidge (WI)	19	4	185	7	4	–	–	2	5	1	–	–
L. Hutton (E)	19	4	138	–	5	4	5	3	2	0	–	–
C. H. Lloyd (WI)	19	1	175	5	6	–	–	0	7	1	–	–
D. C. Boon (A)	**18**	**1**	**160**	**6**	**–**	**–**	**3**	**3**	**6**	**0**	**0**	**–**
D. I. Gower (E)	18	2	204	–	9	–	1	4	2	2	0	–
D. L. Haynes (WI)	**18**	**0**	**202**	**5**	**5**	**0**	**–**	**3**	**2**	**3**	**–**	**–**
D. C. S. Compton (E)	17	2	131	–	5	7	2	2	0	1	–	–
M. D. Crowe (NZ)	**17**	**1**	**120**	**5**	**3**	**–**	**3**	**–**	**1**	**2**	**2**	**1**
D. B. Vengsarkar (I)	17	0	185	5	2	–	6	0	–	2	2	–
H. Sutcliffe (E)	16	0	84	–	8	6	0	2	0	–	–	–
J. B. Hobbs (E)	15	1	102	–	12	2	1	–	–	–	–	–
R. B. Kanhai (WI)	15	2	137	5	5	–	–	–	4	1	–	–
R. B. Richardson (WI)	**15**	**0**	**130**	**4**	**8**	**0**	**–**	**1**	**2**	**0**	**–**	**–**
C. L. Walcott (WI)	15	1	74	4	5	–	–	1	4	1	–	–
K. D. Walters (A)	15	2	125	4	–	0	6	3	1	1	–	–
E. D. Weekes (WI)	15	2	81	3	1	–	–	3	7	1	–	–

The most double-hundreds by batsmen not qualifying for the above list is four by Zaheer Abbas (12 hundreds for Pakistan) and three by R. B. Simpson (10 hundreds for Australia).

Bold type denotes those who played Test cricket in 1993-94 and 1994 seasons. Dashes indicate that a player did not play against the country concerned.

CARRYING BAT THROUGH TEST INNINGS

(Figures in brackets show side's total)

A. B. Tancred	26*	(47)	South Africa v England at Cape Town	1888-89
J. E. Barrett	67*	(176)	Australia v England at Lord's	1890
R. Abel	132*	(307)	England v Australia at Sydney	1891-92
P. F. Warner	132*	(237)	England v South Africa at Johannesburg	1898-99
W. W. Armstrong	159*	(309)	Australia v South Africa at Johannesburg	1902-03
J. W. Zulch	43*	(103)	South Africa v England at Cape Town	1909-10
W. Bardsley	193*	(383)	Australia v England at Lord's	1926
W. M. Woodfull	30*	(66)‡	Australia v England at Brisbane	1928-29
W. M. Woodfull	73*	(193)†	Australia v England at Adelaide	1932-33
W. A. Brown	206*	(422)	Australia v England at Lord's	1938
L. Hutton	202*	(344)	England v West Indies at The Oval	1950
L. Hutton	156*	(272)	England v Australia at Adelaide	1950-51
Nazar Mohammad	124*	(331)	Pakistan v India at Lucknow	1952-53
F. M. M. Worrell	191*	(372)	West Indies v England at Nottingham	1957
T. L. Goddard	56*	(99)	South Africa v Australia at Cape Town	1957-58

D. J. McGlew	127* (292)	South Africa v New Zealand at Durban	1961-62
C. C. Hunte	60* (131)	West Indies v Australia at Port-of-Spain	1964-65
G. M. Turner	43* (131)	New Zealand v England at Lord's	1969
W. M. Lawry	49* (107)	Australia v India at Delhi	1969-70
W. M. Lawry	60* (116)†	Australia v England at Sydney	1970-71
G. M. Turner	223* (386)	New Zealand v West Indies at Kingston	1971-72
I. R. Redpath	159* (346)	Australia v New Zealand at Auckland	1973-74
G. Boycott	99* (215)	England v Australia at Perth	1979-80
S. M. Gavaskar	127* (286)	India v Pakistan at Faisalabad	1982-83
Mudassar Nazar	152* (323)	Pakistan v India at Lahore	1982-83
S. Wettimuny	63* (144)	Sri Lanka v New Zealand at Christchurch	1982-83
D. C. Boon	58* (103)	Australia v New Zealand at Auckland	1985-86
D. L. Haynes	88* (211)	West Indies v Pakistan at Karachi	1986-87
G. A. Gooch	154* (252)	England v West Indies at Leeds	1991
D. L. Haynes	75* (176)	West Indies v England at The Oval	1991
A. J. Stewart	69* (175)	England v Pakistan at Lord's	1992
D. L. Haynes	143* (382)	West Indies v Pakistan at Port-of-Spain	1992-93
M. H. Dekker	68* (187)	Zimbabwe v Pakistan at Rawalpindi	1993-94

† *One man absent.* ‡ *Two men absent.*

Notes: G. M. Turner (223*) holds the record for the highest score by a player carrying his bat through a Test innings. He is also the youngest player to do so, being 22 years 63 days old when he first achieved the feat (1969).

G. A. Gooch (61.11%) holds the record for the highest percentage of a side's total by anyone carrying his bat throughout a Test innings.

Nazar Mohammad and Mudassar Nazar provide the only instance of a father and son carrying their bat through a Test innings.

D. L. Haynes, who is alone in achieving this feat on three occasions, also opened the batting and was last man out in each innings for West Indies v New Zealand at Dunedin, 1979-80.

FASTEST FIFTIES

Minutes			
28	J. T. Brown	England v Australia at Melbourne	1894-95
29	S. A. Durani	India v England at Kanpur	1963-64
30	E. A. V. Williams	West Indies v England at Bridgetown	1947-48
30	B. R. Taylor	New Zealand v West Indies at Auckland	1968-69
33	C. A. Roach	West Indies v England at The Oval	1933
34	C. R. Browne	West Indies v England at Georgetown	1929-30

The fastest fifties in terms of balls received (where recorded) are:

Balls			
30	Kapil Dev	India v Pakistan at Karachi (2nd Test)	1982-83
32	I. V. A. Richards	West Indies v India at Kingston	1982-83
32	I. T. Botham	England v New Zealand at The Oval	1986
33	R. C. Fredericks	West Indies v Australia at Perth	1975-76
33	Kapil Dev	India v Pakistan at Karachi	1978-79
33	Kapil Dev	India v England at Manchester	1982
33	A. J. Lamb	England v New Zealand at Auckland	1991-92

FASTEST HUNDREDS

Minutes			
70	J. M. Gregory	Australia v South Africa at Johannesburg	1921-22
75	G. L. Jessop	England v Australia at The Oval	1902
78	R. Benaud	Australia v West Indies at Kingston	1954-55
80	J. H. Sinclair	South Africa v Australia at Cape Town	1902-03
81	I. V. A. Richards	West Indies v England at St John's	1985-86
86	B. R. Taylor	New Zealand v West Indies at Auckland	1968-69

The fastest hundreds in terms of balls received (where recorded) are:

Balls			
56	I. V. A. Richards	West Indies v England at St John's	1985-86
67	J. M. Gregory	Australia v South Africa at Johannesburg	1921-22
71	R. C. Fredericks	West Indies v Australia at Perth	1975-76
74	Kapil Dev	India v Sri Lanka at Kanpur	1986-87
76	G. L. Jessop	England v Australia at The Oval	1902
77	Majid Khan	Pakistan v New Zealand at Karachi	1976-77

FASTEST DOUBLE-HUNDREDS

Minutes			
214	D. G. Bradman	Australia v England at Leeds	1930
223	S. J. McCabe	Australia v England at Nottingham	1938
226	V. T. Trumper	Australia v South Africa at Adelaide	1910-11
234	D. G. Bradman	Australia v England at Lord's	1930
240	W. R. Hammond	England v New Zealand at Auckland	1932-33
241	S. E. Gregory	Australia v England at Sydney	1894-95
245	D. C. S. Compton	England v Pakistan at Nottingham	1954

The fastest double-hundreds in terms of balls received (where recorded) are:

Balls			
220	I. T. Botham	England v India at The Oval	1982
232	C. G. Greenidge	West Indies v England at Lord's	1984
240	C. H. Lloyd	West Indies v India at Bombay	1974-75
241	Zaheer Abbas	Pakistan v India at Lahore	1982-83
242	D. G. Bradman	Australia v England at The Oval	1934
242	I. V. A. Richards	West Indies v Australia at Melbourne	1984-85

FASTEST TRIPLE-HUNDREDS

Minutes			
288	W. R. Hammond	England v New Zealand at Auckland	1932-33
336	D. G. Bradman	Australia v England at Leeds	1930

MOST RUNS IN A DAY BY A BATSMAN

309	D. G. Bradman	Australia v England at Leeds	1930
295	W. R. Hammond	England v New Zealand at Auckland	1932-33
273	D. C. S. Compton	England v Pakistan at Nottingham	1954
271	D. G. Bradman	Australia v England at Leeds	1934

SLOWEST INDIVIDUAL BATTING

2* in 81 minutes	P. C. R. Tufnell, England v India at Bombay	1992-93
3* in 100 minutes	J. T. Murray, England v Australia at Sydney	1962-63
5 in 102 minutes	Nawab of Pataudi jun., India v England at Bombay	1972-73
7 in 123 minutes	G. Miller, England v Australia at Melbourne	1978-79
9 in 132 minutes	R. K. Chauhan, India v Sri Lanka at Ahmedabad	1993-94
10* in 133 minutes	T. G. Evans, England v Australia at Adelaide	1946-47
16* in 147 minutes	D. B. Vengsarkar, India v Pakistan at Kanpur	1979-80
17* in 166 minutes	G. M. Ritchie, Australia v India at Sydney	1985-86
18 in 194 minutes	W. R. Playle, New Zealand v England at Leeds	1958
19 in 217 minutes	M. D. Crowe, New Zealand v Sri Lanka at Moratuwa	1983-84
25 in 242 minutes	D. K. Morrison, New Zealand v Pakistan at Faisalabad	1990-91

28* in 250 minutes	J. W. Burke, Australia v England at Brisbane	1958-59
31 in 264 minutes	K. D. Mackay, Australia v England at Lord's	1956
34* in 271 minutes	Younis Ahmed, Pakistan v India at Ahmedabad	1986-87
35 in 332 minutes	C. J. Tavaré, England v India at Madras	1981-82
55 in 336 minutes	B. A. Edgar, New Zealand v Australia at Wellington	1981-82
57 in 346 minutes	G. S. Camacho, West Indies v England at Bridgetown	1967-68
58 in 367 minutes	Ijaz Butt, Pakistan v Australia at Karachi	1959-60
60 in 390 minutes	D. N. Sardesai, India v West Indies at Bridgetown	1961-62
62 in 408 minutes	Ramiz Raja, Pakistan v West Indies at Karachi	1986-87
68 in 458 minutes	T. E. Bailey, England v Australia at Brisbane	1958-59
99 in 505 minutes	M. L. Jaisimha, India v Pakistan at Kanpur	1960-61
105 in 575 minutes	D. J. McGlew, South Africa v Australia at Durban	1957-58
114 in 591 minutes	Mudassar Nazar, Pakistan v England at Lahore	1977-78
120* in 609 minutes	J. J. Crowe, New Zealand v Sri Lanka, Colombo (CCC)	1986-87
146* in 655 minutes	M. J. Greatbatch, New Zealand v Australia at Perth	1989-90
163 in 720 minutes	Shoaib Mohammad, Pakistan v New Zealand at Wellington	1988-89
201* in 777 minutes	D. S. B. P. Kuruppu, Sri Lanka v New Zealand at Colombo (CCC)	1986-87
337 in 970 minutes	Hanif Mohammad, Pakistan v West Indies at Bridgetown.	1957-58

Note: The longest any batsman in all first-class innings has taken to score his first run is 97 minutes by T. G. Evans for England against Australia at Adelaide, 1946-47.

SLOWEST HUNDREDS

557 minutes	Mudassar Nazar, Pakistan v England at Lahore	1977-78
545 minutes	D. J. McGlew, South Africa v Australia at Durban	1957-58
516 minutes	J. J. Crowe, New Zealand v Sri Lanka, Colombo (CCC)	1986-87
500 minutes	S. V. Manjrekar, India v Zimbabwe at Harare	1992-93
488 minutes	P. E. Richardson, England v South Africa at Johannesburg	1956-57

Notes: The slowest hundred for any Test in England is 458 minutes (329 balls) by K. W. R. Fletcher, England v Pakistan, The Oval, 1974.

The slowest double-hundred in a Test was scored in 777 minutes (548 balls) by D. S. B. P. Kuruppu for Sri Lanka v New Zealand at Colombo (CCC), 1986-87, on his debut. It is also the slowest-ever first-class double-hundred.

HIGHEST PARTNERSHIPS FOR EACH WICKET

413 for 1st	V. Mankad (231)/Pankaj Roy (173)	I v NZ	Madras	1955-56
451 for 2nd	W. H. Ponsford (266)/D. G. Bradman (244).	A v E	The Oval	1934
467 for 3rd	A. H. Jones (186)/M. D. Crowe (299)	NZ v SL	Wellington	1990-91
411 for 4th	P. B. H. May (285*)/M. C. Cowdrey (154)	E v WI	Birmingham	1957
405 for 5th	S. G. Barnes (234)/D. G. Bradman (234)	A v E	Sydney	1946-47
346 for 6th	J. H. W. Fingleton (136)/D. G. Bradman (270)	A v E	Melbourne	1936-37
347 for 7th	D. St E. Atkinson (219)/C. C. Depeiza (122)	WI v A	Bridgetown	1954-55
246 for 8th	L. E. G. Ames (137)/G. O. B. Allen (122)	E v NZ	Lord's	1931
190 for 9th	Asif Iqbal (146)/Intikhab Alam (51)	P v E	The Oval	1967
151 for 10th	B. F. Hastings (110)/R. O. Collinge (68*)	NZ v P	Auckland	1972-73

PARTNERSHIPS OF 300 AND OVER

467	for 3rd	A. H. Jones (186)/M. D. Crowe (299)	NZ v SL	Wellington	1990-91
451	for 2nd	W. H. Ponsford (266)/D. G. Bradman (244)	A v E	The Oval	1934
451	for 3rd	Mudassar Nazar (231)/Javed Miandad (280*)	P v I	Hyderabad	1982-83
446	for 2nd	C. C. Hunte (260)/G. S. Sobers (365*)	WI v P	Kingston	1957-58
413	for 1st	V. Mankad (231)/Pankaj Roy (173)	I v NZ	Madras	1955-56
411	for 4th	P. B. H. May (285*)/M. C. Cowdrey (154)	E v WI	Birmingham	1957
405	for 5th	S. G. Barnes (234)/D. G. Bradman (234)	A v E	Sydney	1946-47
399	for 4th	G. S. Sobers (226)/F. M. M. Worrell (197*)	WI v E	Bridgetown	1959-60

397	for 3rd	Qasim Omar (206)/Javed Miandad (203*)	P v SL	Faisalabad	1985-86
388	for 4th	W. H. Ponsford (181)/D. G. Bradman (304)	A v E	Leeds	1934
387	for 1st	G. M. Turner (259)/T. W. Jarvis (182)	NZ v WI	Georgetown	1971-72
382	for 2nd	L. Hutton (364)/M. Leyland (187)	E v A	The Oval	1938
382	for 1st	W. M. Lawry (210)/R. B. Simpson (201)	A v WI	Bridgetown	1964-65
370	for 3rd	W. J. Edrich (189)/D. C. S. Compton (208)	E v SA	Lord's	1947
369	for 2nd	J. H. Edrich (310*)/K. F. Barrington (163)	E v NZ	Leeds	1965
359	for 1st	L. Hutton (158)/C. Washbrook (195)	E v SA	Johannesburg	1948-49
351	for 2nd	G. A. Gooch (196)/D. I. Gower (157)	E v A	The Oval	1985
350	for 4th	Mushtaq Mohammad (201)/Asif Iqbal (175)	P v NZ	Dunedin	1972-73
347	for 7th	D. St E. Atkinson (219)/C. C. Depeiza (122)	WI v A	Bridgetown	1954-55
346	for 6th	J. H. Fingleton (136)/D. G. Bradman (270)	A v E	Melbourne	1936-37
344*	for 2nd	S. M. Gavaskar (182*)/D. B. Vengsarkar (157*)	I v WI	Calcutta	1978-79
341	for 3rd	E. J. Barlow (201)/R. G. Pollock (175)	SA v A	Adelaide	1963-64
338	for 3rd	E. D. Weekes (206)/F. M. M. Worrell (167)	WI v E	Port-of-Spain	1953-54
336	for 4th	W. M. Lawry (151)/K. D. Walters (242)	A v WI	Sydney	1968-69
332*	for 5th	A. R. Border (200*)/S. R. Waugh (157*)	A v E	Leeds	1993
331	for 2nd	R. T. Robinson (148)/D. I. Gower (215)	E v A	Birmingham	1985
329	for 1st	G. R. Marsh (138)/M. A. Taylor (219)	A v E	Nottingham	1989
323	for 1st	J. B. Hobbs (178)/W. Rhodes (179)	E v A	Melbourne	1911-12
322	for 4th	Javed Miandad (153*)/Salim Malik (165)	P v E	Birmingham	1992
319	for 3rd	A. Melville (189)/A. D. Nourse (149)	SA v E	Nottingham	1947
316†	for 3rd	G. R. Viswanath (222)/Yashpal Sharma (140)	I v E	Madras	1981-82
308	for 7th	Waqar Hassan (189)/Imtiaz Ahmed (209)	P v NZ	Lahore	1955-56
308	for 3rd	R. B. Richardson (154)/I. V. A. Richards (178)	WI v A	St John's	1983-84
308	for 3rd	G. A. Gooch (333)/A. J. Lamb (139)	E v I	Lord's	1990
303	for 3rd	I. V. A. Richards (232)/A. I. Kallicharran (97)	WI v E	Nottingham	1976
303	for 3rd	M. A. Atherton (135)/R. A. Smith (175)	E v WI	St John's	1993-94
301	for 2nd	A. R. Morris (182)/D. G. Bradman (173*)	A v E	Leeds	1948

† 415 runs were scored for this wicket in two separate partnerships: D. B. Vengsarkar retired hurt when he and Viswanath had added 99 runs.

BOWLING RECORDS

MOST WICKETS IN AN INNINGS

10-53	J. C. Laker	England v Australia at Manchester	1956
9-28	G. A. Lohmann	England v South Africa at Johannesburg	1895-96
9-37	J. C. Laker	England v Australia at Manchester	1956
9-52	R. J. Hadlee	New Zealand v Australia at Brisbane	1985-86
9-56	Abdul Qadir	Pakistan v England at Lahore	1987-88
9-57	D. E. Malcolm	England v South Africa at The Oval	1994
9-69	J. M. Patel	India v Australia at Kanpur	1959-60
9-83	Kapil Dev	India v West Indies at Ahmedabad	1983-84
9-86	Sarfraz Nawaz	Pakistan v Australia at Melbourne	1978-79
9-95	J. M. Noreiga	West Indies v India at Port-of-Spain	1970-71
9-102	S. P. Gupte	India v West Indies at Kanpur	1958-59
9-103	S. F. Barnes	England v South Africa at Johannesburg	1913-14
9-113	H. J. Tayfield	South Africa v England at Johannesburg	1956-57
9-121	A. A. Mailey	Australia v England at Melbourne	1920-21
8-7	G. A. Lohmann	England v South Africa at Port Elizabeth	1895-96
8-11	J. Briggs	England v South Africa at Cape Town	1888-89
8-29	S. F. Barnes	England v South Africa at The Oval	1912
8-29	C. E. H. Croft	West Indies v Pakistan at Port-of-Spain	1976-77
8-31	F. Laver	Australia v England at Manchester	1909
8-31	F. S. Trueman	England v India at Manchester	1952
8-34	I. T. Botham	England v Pakistan at Lord's	1978
8-35	G. A. Lohmann	England v Australia at Sydney	1886-87
8-38	L. R. Gibbs	West Indies v India at Bridgetown	1961-62
8-43†	A. E. Trott	Australia v England at Adelaide	1894-95

8-43	H. Verity	England v Australia at Lord's	1934
8-43	R. G. D. Willis	England v Australia at Leeds	1981
8-45	C. E. L. Ambrose	West Indies v England at Bridgetown	1989-90
8-51	D. L. Underwood	England v Pakistan at Lord's	1974
8-52	V. Mankad	India v Pakistan at Delhi	1952-53
8-53	G. B. Lawrence	South Africa v New Zealand at Johannesburg	1961-62
8-53†	R. A. L. Massie	Australia v England at Lord's	1972
8-55	V. Mankad	India v England at Madras	1951-52
8-56	S. F. Barnes	England v South Africa at Johannesburg	1913-14
8-58	G. A. Lohmann	England v Australia at Sydney	1891-92
8-58	Imran Khan	Pakistan v Sri Lanka at Lahore	1981-82
8-59	C. Blythe	England v South Africa at Leeds	1907
8-59	A. A. Mallett	Australia v Pakistan at Adelaide	1972-73
8-60	Imran Khan	Pakistan v India at Karachi	1982-83
8-61†	N. D. Hirwani	India v West Indies at Madras	1987-88
8-65	H. Trumble	Australia v England at The Oval	1902
8-68	W. Rhodes	England v Australia at Melbourne	1903-04
8-69	H. J. Tayfield	South Africa v England at Durban	1956-57
8-69	Sikander Bakht	Pakistan v India at Delhi	1979-80
8-70	S. J. Snooke	South Africa v England at Johannesburg	1905-06
8-71	G. D. McKenzie	Australia v West Indies at Melbourne	1968-69
8-72	S. Venkataraghavan	India v New Zealand at Delhi	1964-65
8-75†	N. D. Hirwani	India v West Indies at Madras	1987-88
8-75	A. R. C. Fraser	England v West Indies at Bridgetown	1993-94
8-76	E. A. S. Prasanna	India v New Zealand at Auckland	1975-76
8-79	B. S. Chandrasekhar	India v England at Delhi	1972-73
8-81	L. C. Braund	England v Australia at Melbourne	1903-04
8-83	J. R. Ratnayeke	Sri Lanka v Pakistan at Sialkot	1985-86
8-84†	R. A. L. Massie	Australia v England at Lord's	1972
8-85	Kapil Dev	India v Pakistan at Lahore	1982-83
8-86	A. W. Greig	England v West Indies at Port-of-Spain	1973-74
8-87	M. G. Hughes	Australia v West Indies at Perth	1988-89
8-92	M. A. Holding	West Indies v England at The Oval	1976
8-94	T. Richardson	England v Australia at Sydney	1897-98
8-97	C. J. McDermott	Australia v England at Perth	1990-91
8-103	I. T. Botham	England v West Indies at Lord's	1984
8-104†	A. L. Valentine	West Indies v England at Manchester	1950
8-106	Kapil Dev	India v Australia at Adelaide	1985-86
8-107	B. J. T. Bosanquet	England v Australia at Nottingham	1905
8-107	N. A. Foster	England v Pakistan at Leeds	1987
8-112	G. F. Lawson	Australia v West Indies at Adelaide	1984-85
8-126	J. C. White	England v Australia at Adelaide	1928-29
8-141	C. J. McDermott	Australia v England at Manchester	1985
8-143	M. H. N. Walker	Australia v England at Melbourne	1974-75

† *On Test debut.*

Note: The best for Zimbabwe is 5-42 by D. H. Brain against Pakistan at Lahore, 1993-94.

OUTSTANDING ANALYSES

	O	*M*	*R*	*W*		
J. C. Laker (E)	51.2	23	53	10	v Australia at Manchester	1956
G. A. Lohmann (E)	14.2	6	28	9	v South Africa at Johannesburg	1895-96
J. C. Laker (E)	16.4	4	37	9	v Australia at Manchester	1956
G. A. Lohmann (E)	9.4	5	7	8	v South Africa at Port Elizabeth	1895-96
J. Briggs (E)	14.2	5	11	8	v South Africa at Cape Town	1888-89
J. Briggs (E)	19.1	11	17	7	v South Africa at Cape Town	1888-89
M. A. Noble (A)	7.4	2	17	7	v England at Melbourne	1901-02
W. Rhodes (E)	11	3	17	7	v Australia at Birmingham	1902
A. E. R. Gilligan (E)	6.3	4	7	6	v South Africa at Birmingham	1924
S. Haigh (E)	11.4	6	11	6	v South Africa at Cape Town	1898-99
D. L. Underwood (E)	11.6	7	12	6	v New Zealand at Christchurch	1970-71

	O	*M*	*R*	*W*		
S. L. V. Raju (I)	17.5	13	12	6	v Sri Lanka at Chandigarh	1990-91
H. J. Tayfield (SA)	14	7	13	6	v New Zealand at Johannesburg.	1953-54
C. T. B. Turner (A)	18	11	15	6	v England at Sydney	1886-87
M. H. N. Walker (A)	16	8	15	6	v Pakistan at Sydney	1972-73
E. R. H. Toshack (A)	2.3	1	2	5	v India at Brisbane	1947-48
H. Ironmonger (A)	7.2	5	6	5	v South Africa at Melbourne	1931-32
Pervez Sajjad (P)	12	8	5	4	v New Zealand at Rawalpindi	1964-65
K. Higgs (E)	9	7	5	4	v New Zealand at Christchurch.	1965-66
P. H. Edmonds (E)	8	6	6	4	v Pakistan at Lord's	1978
J. C. White (E)	6.3	2	7	4	v Australia at Brisbane	1928-29
J. H. Wardle (E)	5	2	7	4	v Australia at Manchester	1953
R. Appleyard (E)	6	3	7	4	v New Zealand at Auckland	1954-55
R. Benaud (A)	3.4	3	0	3	v India at Delhi	1959-60

MOST WICKETS IN A MATCH

19-90	J. C. Laker	England v Australia at Manchester	1956
17-159	S. F. Barnes	England v South Africa at Johannesburg	1913-14
16-136†	N. D. Hirwani	India v West Indies at Madras	1987-88
16-137†	R. A. L. Massie	Australia v England at Lord's	1972
15-28	J. Briggs	England v South Africa at Cape Town	1888-89
15-45	G. A. Lohmann	England v South Africa at Port Elizabeth	1895-96
15-99	C. Blythe	England v South Africa at Leeds	1907
15-104	H. Verity	England v Australia at Lord's	1934
15-123	R. J. Hadlee	New Zealand v Australia at Brisbane	1985-86
15-124	W. Rhodes	England v Australia at Melbourne	1903-04
14-90	F. R. Spofforth	Australia v England at The Oval	1882
14-99	A. V. Bedser	England v Australia at Nottingham	1953
14-102	W. Bates	England v Australia at Melbourne	1882-83
14-116	Imran Khan	Pakistan v Sri Lanka at Lahore	1981-82
14-124	J. M. Patel	India v Australia at Kanpur	1959-60
14-144	S. F. Barnes	England v South Africa at Durban	1913-14
14-149	M. A. Holding	West Indies v England at The Oval	1976
14-199	C. V. Grimmett	Australia v South Africa at Adelaide	1931-32

† *On Test debut.*

Notes: The best for South Africa is 13-165 by H. J. Tayfield against Australia at Melbourne, 1952-53. The best for Sri Lanka is 9-125 by R. J. Ratnayake against India at Colombo (PSS), 1985-86. The best for Zimbabwe is 8-114 by H. H. Streak against Pakistan at Rawalpindi, 1993-94.

MOST WICKETS IN A SERIES

	T	*R*	*W*	*Avge*		
S. F. Barnes	4	536	49	10.93	England v South Africa.	1913-14
J. C. Laker	5	442	46	9.60	England v Australia	1956
C. V. Grimmett	5	642	44	14.59	Australia v South Africa	1935-36
T. M. Alderman	6	893	42	21.26	Australia v England	1981
R. M. Hogg	6	527	41	12.85	Australia v England	1978-79
T. M. Alderman	6	712	41	17.36	Australia v England	1989
Imran Khan	6	558	40	13.95	Pakistan v India	1982-83
A. V. Bedser	5	682	39	17.48	England v Australia	1953
D. K. Lillee	6	870	39	22.30	Australia v England	1981
M. W. Tate	5	881	38	23.18	England v Australia	1924-25
W. J. Whitty	5	632	37	17.08	Australia v South Africa	1910-11
H. J. Tayfield	5	636	37	17.18	South Africa v England.	1956-57
A. E. E. Vogler	5	783	36	21.75	South Africa v England.	1909-10
A. A. Mailey	5	946	36	26.27	Australia v England	1920-21
G. A. Lohmann	3	203	35	5.80	England v South Africa.	1895-96
B. S. Chandrasekhar	5	662	35	18.91	India v England	1972-73
M. D. Marshall	5	443	35	12.65	West Indies v England	1988

MOST WICKETS IN A CAREER

(Qualification: 100 wickets)

ENGLAND

		T	*Balls*	*R*	*W*	*Avge*	*5W/i*	*10W/m*
1	I. T. Botham	102	21,815	10,878	383	28.40	27	4
2	R. G. D. Willis	90	17,357	8,190	325	25.20	16	—
3	F. S. Trueman	67	15,178	6,625	307	21.57	17	3
4	D. L. Underwood	86	21,862	7,674	297	25.83	17	6
5	J. B. Statham	70	16,056	6,261	252	24.84	9	1
6	A. V. Bedser	51	15,918	5,876	236	24.89	15	5
7	J. A. Snow	49	12,021	5,387	202	26.66	8	1
8	J. C. Laker	46	12,027	4,101	193	21.24	9	3
9	S. F. Barnes	27	7,873	3,106	189	16.43	24	7
10	G. A. R. Lock	49	13,147	4,451	174	25.58	9	3
11	M. W. Tate	39	12,523	4,055	155	26.16	7	1
12	F. J. Titmus	53	15,118	4,931	153	32.22	7	—
13	J. E. Emburey	63	15,211	5,564	147	37.85	6	—
14	H. Verity	40	11,173	3,510	144	24.37	5	2
15	C. M. Old	46	8,858	4,020	143	28.11	4	—
16	A. W. Greig	58	9,802	4,541	141	32.20	6	2
17	G. R. Dilley	41	8,192	4,107	138	29.76	6	—
18	T. E. Bailey	61	9,712	3,856	132	29.21	5	1
19	W. Rhodes	58	8,231	3,425	127	26.96	6	1
20	**P. A. J. DeFreitas**	**39**	**8,572**	**4,027**	**125**	**32.21**	**4**	**—**
	P. H. Edmonds	51	12,028	4,273	125	34.18	2	—
22	D. A. Allen	39	11,297	3,779	122	30.97	4	—
	R. Illingworth	61	11,934	3,807	122	31.20	3	—
24	J. Briggs	33	5,332	2,095	118	17.75	9	4
25	G. G. Arnold	34	7,650	3,254	115	28.29	6	—
26	G. A. Lohmann	18	3,821	1,205	112	10.75	9	5
27	D. V. P. Wright	34	8,135	4,224	108	39.11	6	1
28	J. H. Wardle	28	6,597	2,080	102	20.39	5	1
29	R. Peel	20	5,216	1,715	101	16.98	5	1
30	C. Blythe	19	4,546	1,863	100	18.63	9	4

AUSTRALIA

		T	*Balls*	*R*	*W*	*Avge*	*5W/i*	*10W/m*
1	D. K. Lillee	70	18,467	8,493	355	23.92	23	7
2	R. Benaud	63	19,108	6,704	248	27.03	16	1
3	G. D. McKenzie	60	17,681	7,328	246	29.78	16	3
4	**C. J. McDermott**	**58**	**13,400**	**6,694**	**231**	**28.97**	**9**	**2**
5	R. R. Lindwall	61	13,650	5,251	228	23.03	12	—
6	C. V. Grimmett	37	14,513	5,231	216	24.21	21	7
7	**M. G. Hughes**	**53**	**12,285**	**6,017**	**212**	**28.38**	**7**	**1**
8	J. R. Thomson	51	10,535	5,601	200	28.00	8	—
9	A. K. Davidson	44	11,587	3,819	186	20.53	14	2
10	G. F. Lawson	46	11,118	5,501	180	30.56	11	2
11	K. R. Miller	55	10,461	3,906	170	22.97	7	1
	T. M. Alderman	41	10,181	4,616	170	27.15	14	1
13	W. A. Johnston	40	11,048	3,826	160	23.91	7	—
14	W. J. O'Reilly	27	10,024	3,254	144	22.59	11	3
15	H. Trumble	32	8,099	3,072	141	21.78	9	3

		T	Balls	R	W	Avge	5W/i	10W/m
16	M. H. N. Walker	34	10,094	3,792	138	27.47	6	—
17	A. A. Mallett	38	9,990	3,940	132	29.84	6	1
18	B. Yardley	33	8,909	3,986	126	31.63	6	1
19	R. M. Hogg	38	7,633	3,503	123	28.47	6	2
20	M. A. Noble	42	7,159	3,025	121	25.00	9	2
21	**S. K. Warne**	**26**	**7,985**	**2,780**	**116**	**23.96**	**5**	**1**
22	B. A. Reid	27	6,244	2,784	113	24.63	5	2
23	I. W. Johnson	45	8,780	3,182	109	29.19	3	—
24	G. Giffen	31	6,457	2,791	103	27.09	7	1
25	A. N. Connolly	29	7,818	2,981	102	29.22	4	—
26	C. T. B. Turner	17	5,179	1,670	101	16.53	11	2

SOUTH AFRICA

		T	Balls	R	W	Avge	5W/i	10W/m
1	H. J. Tayfield	37	13,568	4,405	170	25.91	14	2
2	T. L. Goddard	41	11,736	3,226	123	26.22	5	—
3	P. M. Pollock	28	6,522	2,806	116	24.18	9	1
4	N. A. T. Adcock	26	6,391	2,195	104	21.10	5	—

WEST INDIES

		T	Balls	R	W	Avge	5W/i	10W/m
1	M. D. Marshall	81	17,584	7,876	376	20.94	22	4
2	L. R. Gibbs	79	27,115	8,989	309	29.09	18	2
3	J. Garner	58	13,169	5,433	259	20.97	7	—
4	M. A. Holding	60	12,680	5,898	249	23.68	13	2
5	G. S. Sobers	93	21,599	7,999	235	34.03	6	—
6	**C. A. Walsh**	**65**	**13,197**	**5,824**	**222**	**26.23**	**6**	**1**
7	**C. E. L. Ambrose**	**48**	**11,809**	**4,616**	**219**	**21.07**	**11**	**3**
8	A. M. E. Roberts	47	11,136	5,174	202	25.61	11	2
9	W. W. Hall	48	10,421	5,066	192	26.38	9	1
10	S. Ramadhin	43	13,939	4,579	158	28.98	10	1
11	A. L. Valentine	36	12,953	4,215	139	30.32	8	2
12	C. E. H. Croft	27	6,165	2,913	125	23.30	3	—
13	V. A. Holder	40	9,095	3,627	109	33.27	3	—

NEW ZEALAND

		T	Balls	R	W	Avge	5W/i	10W/m
1	R. J. Hadlee	86	21,918	9,611	431	22.29	36	9
2	B. L. Cairns	43	10,628	4,280	130	32.92	6	1
3	E. J. Chatfield	43	10,360	3,958	123	32.17	3	1
4	**D. K. Morrison**	**35**	**7,532**	**4,181**	**120**	**34.84**	**8**	**—**
5	R. O. Collinge	35	7,689	3,392	116	29.24	3	—
6	B. R. Taylor	30	6,334	2,953	111	26.60	4	—
7	J. G. Bracewell	41	8,403	3,653	102	35.81	4	1
8	R. C. Motz	32	7,034	3,148	100	31.48	5	—

INDIA

		T	Balls	R	W	Avge	5W/i	10W/m
1	**Kapil Dev**	**131**	**27,740**	**12,867**	**434**	**29.64**	**23**	**2**
2	B. S. Bedi	67	21,364	7,637	266	28.71	14	1
3	B. S. Chandrasekhar	58	15,963	7,199	242	29.74	16	2
4	E. A. S. Prasanna	49	14,353	5,742	189	30.38	10	2
5	V. Mankad	44	14,686	5,236	162	32.32	8	2
6	S. Venkataraghavan	57	14,877	5,634	156	36.11	3	1
7	R. J. Shastri	80	15,751	6,185	151	40.96	2	—
8	S. P. Gupte	36	11,284	4,403	149	29.55	12	1
9	D. R. Doshi	33	9,322	3,502	114	30.71	6	—
10	K. D. Ghavri	39	7,042	3,656	109	33.54	4	—
11	N. S. Yadav	35	8,349	3,580	102	35.09	3	—

PAKISTAN

		T	Balls	R	W	Avge	5W/i	10W/m
1	Imran Khan	88	19,458	8,258	362	22.81	23	6
2	Abdul Qadir	67	17,126	7,742	236	32.80	15	5
3	**Wasim Akram**	**55**	**12,484**	**5,378**	**235**	**22.88**	**16**	**3**
4	**Waqar Younis**	**31**	**6,411**	**3,382**	**180**	**18.78**	**19**	**4**
5	Sarfraz Nawaz	55	13,927	5,798	177	32.75	4	1
6	Iqbal Qasim	50	13,019	4,807	171	28.11	8	2
7	Fazal Mahmood	34	9,834	3,434	139	24.70	13	4
8	Intikhab Alam	47	10,474	4,494	125	35.95	5	2

SRI LANKA: The highest aggregate is 73 wickets, average 35.10, by R. J. Ratnayake in 23 Tests.

ZIMBABWE: The highest aggregate is 18 wickets, average 23.94, by **D. H. Brain** in 4 Tests.

Bold type denotes those who played Test cricket in 1993-94 and 1994 seasons or Sri Lanka v Pakistan in 1994-95.

WICKET WITH FIRST BALL IN TEST CRICKET

	Batsman dismissed			
A. Coningham	A. C. MacLaren	A v E	Melbourne	1894-95
W. M. Bradley	F. Laver	E v A	Manchester	1899
E. G. Arnold	V. T. Trumper	E v A	Sydney	1903-04
G. G. Macaulay	G. A. L. Hearne	E v SA	Cape Town	1922-23
M. W. Tate	M. J. Susskind	E v SA	Birmingham	1924
M. Henderson	E. W. Dawson	NZ v E	Christchurch	1929-30
H. D. Smith	E. Paynter	NZ v E	Christchurch	1932-33
T. F. Johnson	W. W. Keeton	WI v E	The Oval	1939
R. Howorth	D. V. Dyer	E v SA	The Oval	1947
Intikhab Alam	C. C. McDonald	P v A	Karachi	1959-60
R. K. Illingworth	P. V. Simmons	E v WI	Nottingham	1991

HAT-TRICKS

F. R. Spofforth	Australia v England at Melbourne	1878-79
W. Bates	England v Australia at Melbourne	1882-83
J. Briggs	England v Australia at Sydney	1891-92
G. A. Lohmann	England v South Africa at Port Elizabeth	1895-96
J. T. Hearne	England v Australia at Leeds	1899
H. Trumble	Australia v England at Melbourne	1901-02
H. Trumble	Australia v England at Melbourne	1903-04
T. J. Matthews† / T. J. Matthews	Australia v South Africa at Manchester	1912
M. J. C. Allom‡	England v New Zealand at Christchurch	1929-30
T. W. J. Goddard	England v South Africa at Johannesburg	1938-39
P. J. Loader	England v West Indies at Leeds	1957
L. F. Kline	Australia v South Africa at Cape Town	1957-58
W. W. Hall	West Indies v Pakistan at Lahore	1958-59
G. M. Griffin	South Africa v England at Lord's	1960
L. R. Gibbs	West Indies v Australia at Adelaide	1960-61
P. J. Petherick‡	New Zealand v Pakistan at Lahore	1976-77
C. A. Walsh§	West Indies v Australia at Brisbane	1988-89
M. G. Hughes§	Australia v West Indies at Perth	1988-89

† *T. J. Matthews did the hat-trick in each innings of the same match.*
‡ *On Test debut.*
§ *Not all in the same innings.*

FOUR WICKETS IN FIVE BALLS

M. J. C. Allom	England v New Zealand at Christchurch *On debut, in his eighth over: W-WWW*	1929-30
C. M. Old	England v Pakistan at Birmingham *Sequence interrupted by a no-ball: WW-WW*	1978
Wasim Akram	Pakistan v West Indies at Lahore (*WW-WW*)	1990-91

MOST BALLS BOWLED IN A TEST

S. Ramadhin (West Indies) sent down 774 balls in 129 overs against England at Birmingham, 1957. It was the most delivered by any bowler in a Test, beating H. Verity's 766 for England against South Africa at Durban, 1938-39. In this match Ramadhin also bowled the most balls (588) in any single first-class innings, including Tests.

ALL-ROUND RECORDS

100 RUNS AND FIVE WICKETS IN AN INNINGS

England					
A. W. Greig	148	6-164	v West Indies	Bridgetown	1973-74
I. T. Botham	103	5-73	v New Zealand	Christchurch	1977-78
I. T. Botham	108	8-34	v Pakistan	Lord's	1978
I. T. Botham	114	6-58 7-48	v India	Bombay	1979-80
I. T. Botham	149*	6-95	v Australia	Leeds	1981
I. T. Botham	138	5-59	v New Zealand	Wellington	1983-84
Australia					
C. Kelleway	114	5-33	v South Africa	Manchester	1912
J. M. Gregory	100	7-69	v England	Melbourne	1920-21
K. R. Miller	109	6-107	v West Indies	Kingston	1954-55
R. Benaud	100	5-84	v South Africa	Johannesburg	1957-58

South Africa					
J. H. Sinclair	106	6-26	v England	Cape Town	1898-99
G. A. Faulkner	123	5-120	v England	Johannesburg	1909-10
West Indies					
D. St E. Atkinson	219	5-56	v Australia	Bridgetown	1954-55
O. G. Smith	100	5-90	v India	Delhi	1958-59
G. S. Sobers	104	5-63	v India	Kingston	1961-62
G. S. Sobers	174	5-41	v England	Leeds	1966
New Zealand					
B. R. Taylor†	105	5-86	v India	Calcutta	1964-65
India					
V. Mankad	184	5-196	v England	Lord's	1952
P. R. Umrigar	172*	5-107	v West Indies	Port-of-Spain	1961-62
Pakistan					
Mushtaq Mohammad	201	5-49	v New Zealand	Dunedin	1972-73
Mushtaq Mohammad	121	5-28	v West Indies	Port-of-Spain	1976-77
Imran Khan	117	6-98 5-82	v India	Faisalabad	1982-83
Wasim Akram	123	5-100	v Australia	Adelaide	1989-90

† *On debut.*

100 RUNS AND FIVE DISMISSALS IN AN INNINGS

D. T. Lindsay	182	6ct	SA v A	Johannesburg	1966-67
I. D. S. Smith	113*	4ct, 1st	NZ v E	Auckland	1983-84
S. A. R. Silva	111	5ct	SL v I	Colombo (PSS)	1985-86

100 RUNS AND TEN WICKETS IN A TEST

A. K. Davidson	44 80	5-135 6-87	A v WI	Brisbane	1960-61
I. T. Botham	114	6-58 7-48	E v I	Bombay	1979-80
Imran Khan	117	6-98 5-82	P v I	Faisalabad	1982-83

1,000 RUNS AND 100 WICKETS IN A CAREER

	Tests	*Runs*	*Wkts*	*Tests for Double*
England				
T. E. Bailey	61	2,290	132	47
†I. T. Botham	102	5,200	383	21
J. E. Emburey	63	1,705	147	46
A. W. Greig	58	3,599	141	37
R. Illingworth	61	1,836	122	47
W. Rhodes	58	2,325	127	44
M. W. Tate	39	1,198	155	33
F. J. Titmus	53	1,449	153	40
Australia				
R. Benaud	63	2,201	248	32
A. K. Davidson	44	1,328	186	34
G. Giffen	31	1,238	103	30
M. G. Hughes	**53**	**1,032**	**212**	**52**
I. W. Johnson	45	1,000	109	45
R. R. Lindwall	61	1,502	228	38
K. R. Miller	55	2,958	170	33
M. A. Noble	42	1,997	121	27

	Tests	Runs	Wkts	Tests for Double
South Africa				
T. L. Goddard	41	2,516	123	36
West Indies				
M. D. Marshall	81	1,810	376	49
†G. S. Sobers	93	8,032	235	48
New Zealand				
J. G. Bracewell	41	1,001	102	41
R. J. Hadlee	86	3,124	431	28
India				
Kapil Dev	**131**	**5,248**	**434**	**25**
V. Mankad	44	2,109	162	23
R. J. Shastri	80	3,830	151	44
Pakistan				
Abdul Qadir	67	1,029	236	62
Imran Khan	88	3,807	362	30
Intikhab Alam	47	1,493	125	41
Sarfraz Nawaz	55	1,045	177	55
Wasim Akram	**55**	**1,205**	**235**	**45**

Bold type denotes those who played Test cricket in 1993-94 and 1994 seasons or Sri Lanka v Pakistan in 1994-95.

† I. T. Botham (120 catches) and G. S. Sobers (109) are the only players to have achieved the treble of 1,000 runs, 100 wickets and 100 catches.

WICKET-KEEPING RECORDS

Most Dismissals in an Innings

7 (all ct)	Wasim Bari	Pakistan v New Zealand at Auckland	1978-79
7 (all ct)	R. W. Taylor	England v India at Bombay	1979-80
7 (all ct)	I. D. S. Smith	New Zealand v Sri Lanka at Hamilton	1990-91
6 (all ct)	A. T. W. Grout	Australia v South Africa at Johannesburg	1957-58
6 (all ct)	D. T. Lindsay	South Africa v Australia at Johannesburg	1966-67
6 (all ct)	J. T. Murray	England v India at Lord's	1967
6 (5ct, 1st)	S. M. H. Kirmani	India v New Zealand at Christchurch	1975-76
6 (all ct)	R. W. Marsh	Australia v England at Brisbane	1982-83
6 (all ct)	S. A. R. Silva	Sri Lanka v India at Colombo (SSC)	1985-86
6 (all ct)	R. C. Russell	England v Australia at Melbourne	1990-91

Note: The most stumpings in an innings is 5 by K. S. More for India v West Indies at Madras in 1987-88.

Most Dismissals in a Test

10 (all ct)	R. W. Taylor	England v India at Bombay	1979-80
9 (8ct, 1st)	G. R. A. Langley	Australia v England at Lord's	1956
9 (all ct)	D. A. Murray	West Indies v Australia at Melbourne	1981-82
9 (all ct)	R. W. Marsh	Australia v England at Brisbane	1982-83
9 (all ct)	S. A. R. Silva	Sri Lanka v India at Colombo (SSC)	1985-86
9 (8ct, 1st)	S. A. R. Silva	Sri Lanka v India at Colombo (PSS)	1985-86
9 (all ct)	D. J. Richardson	South Africa v India at Port Elizabeth	1992-93
9 (all ct)	Rashid Latif	Pakistan v New Zealand at Auckland	1993-94
8 (all ct)	J. J. Kelly	Australia v England at Sydney	1901-02

8 (6ct, 2st)	L. E. G. Ames	England v West Indies at The Oval	1933
8 (all ct)	G. R. A. Langley	Australia v West Indies at Kingston	1954-55
8 (6ct, 2st)	A. T. W. Grout	Australia v Pakistan at Lahore	1959-60
8 (all ct)	A. T. W. Grout	Australia v England at Lord's	1961
8 (all ct)	J. M. Parks	England v New Zealand at Christchurch	1965-66
8 (all ct)	D. T. Lindsay	South Africa v Australia at Johannesburg	1966-67
8 (7ct, 1st)	H. B. Taber	Australia v South Africa at Johannesburg	1966-67
8 (all ct)	Wasim Bari	Pakistan v England at Leeds	1971
8 (all ct)	R. W. Marsh	Australia v West Indies at Melbourne	1975-76
8 (all ct)	R. W. Marsh	Australia v New Zealand at Christchurch	1976-77
8 (7ct, 1st)	R. W. Marsh	Australia v India at Sydney	1980-81
8 (all ct)	W. K. Lees	New Zealand v Sri Lanka at Wellington	1982-83
8 (all ct)	R. W. Marsh	Australia v England at Adelaide	1982-83
8 (all ct)	I. D. S. Smith	New Zealand v Sri Lanka at Hamilton	1990-91
8 (6ct, 2st)	I. A. Healy	Australia v West Indies at Adelaide	1992-93
8 (all ct)	J. R. Murray	West Indies v Australia at Perth	1992-93
8 (all ct)	D. J. Richardson	South Africa v Sri Lanka at Colombo (SSC)	1993-94

Notes: S. A. R. Silva made 18 dismissals in two successive Tests.

The most stumpings in a match is 6 by K. S. More for India v West Indies at Madras in 1987-88.

Most Dismissals in a Series

(*Played in 5 Tests unless otherwise stated*)

28 (all ct)	R. W. Marsh	Australia v England	1982-83
26 (23ct, 3st)	J. H. B. Waite	South Africa v New Zealand	1961-62
26 (all ct)	R. W. Marsh	Australia v West Indies (6 Tests)	1975-76
26 (21ct, 5st)	I. A. Healy	Australia v England (6 Tests)	1993
24 (22ct, 2st)	D. L. Murray	West Indies v England	1963
24 (all ct)	D. T. Lindsay	South Africa v Australia	1966-67
24 (21ct, 3st)	A. P. E. Knott	England v Australia (6 Tests)	1970-71
24 (all ct)	I. A. Healy	Australia v England	1990-91
23 (16ct, 7st)	J. H. B. Waite	South Africa v New Zealand	1953-54
23 (22ct, 1st)	F. C. M. Alexander	West Indies v England	1959-60
23 (20ct, 3st)	A. T. W. Grout	Australia v West Indies	1960-61
23 (21ct, 2st)	A. E. Dick	New Zealand v South Africa	1961-62
23 (21ct, 2st)	R. W. Marsh	Australia v England	1972
23 (22ct, 1st)	A. P. E. Knott	England v Australia (6 Tests)	1974-75
23 (all ct)	R. W. Marsh	Australia v England (6 Tests)	1981
23 (all ct)	P. J. L. Dujon	West Indies v Australia	1990-91
23 (19ct, 4st)	I. A. Healy	Australia v West Indies	1992-93
22 (all ct)	S. J. Rixon	Australia v India	1977-78
22 (21ct, 1st)	S. A. R. Silva	Sri Lanka v India (3 Tests)	1985-86
21 (15ct, 6st)	H. Strudwick	England v South Africa	1913-14
21 (13ct, 8st)	R. A. Saggers	Australia v South Africa	1949-50
21 (16ct, 5st)	G. R. A. Langley	Australia v West Indies	1951-52
21 (20ct, 1st)	A. T. W. Grout	Australia v England	1961
21 (all ct)	R. W. Marsh	Australia v Pakistan	1983-84
20 (16ct, 4st)	D. Tallon	Australia v England	1946-47
20 (16ct, 4st)	G. R. A. Langley	Australia v West Indies (4 Tests)	1954-55
20 (18ct, 2st)	T. G. Evans	England v South Africa	1956-57
20 (17ct, 3st)	A. T. W. Grout	Australia v England	1958-59
20 (19ct, 1st)	H. B. Taber	Australia v South Africa	1966-67
20 (18ct, 2st)	R. W. Taylor	England v Australia (6 Tests)	1978-79
20 (19ct, 1st)	P. J. L. Dujon	West Indies v Australia	1983-84
20 (19ct, 1st)	P. R. Downton	England v Australia (6 Tests)	1985
20 (all ct)	P. J. L. Dujon	West Indies v England	1988

Most Dismissals in a Career

		T	*Ct*	*St*	*Total*
1	R. W. Marsh (Australia)	96	343	12	355
2	P. J. L. Dujon (West Indies)	81	267	5	272
3	A. P. E. Knott (England)	95	250	19	269
4	Wasim Bari (Pakistan)	81	201	27	228
5	T. G. Evans (England)	91	173	46	219
6	**I. A. Healy (Australia)**	**62**	**191**	**14**	**205**
7	S. M. H. Kirmani (India)	88	160	38	198
8	D. L. Murray (West Indies)	62	181	8	189
9	A. T. W. Grout (Australia)	51	163	24	187
10	I. D. S. Smith (New Zealand)	63	168	8	176
11	R. W. Taylor (England)	57	167	7	174
12	J. H. B. Waite (South Africa)	50	124	17	141
13	**K. S. More (India)**	**49**	**110**	**20**	**130**
13	W. A. S. Oldfield (Australia)	54	78	52	130
15	J. M. Parks (England)	46	103	11	114
16	Salim Yousuf (Pakistan)	32	91	13	104

Notes: The records for P. J. L. Dujon and J. M. Parks each include two catches taken when not keeping wicket in two and three Tests respectively.

The most dismissals for other countries are Sri Lanka 34 (S. A. R. Silva 33ct, 1st in 9 Tests) and Zimbabwe 16 (**A. Flower** 14ct, 2st in 6 Tests as wicket-keeper).

Bold type denotes those who played Test cricket in 1993-94.

FIELDING RECORDS

(Excluding wicket-keepers)

Most Catches in an Innings

5	V. Y. Richardson	Australia v South Africa at Durban	1935-36
5	Yajurvindra Singh	India v England at Bangalore	1976-77
5	M. Azharuddin	India v Pakistan at Karachi	1989-90
5	K. Srikkanth	India v Australia at Perth	1991-92

Most Catches in a Test

7	G. S. Chappell	Australia v England at Perth	1974-75
7	Yajurvindra Singh	India v England at Bangalore	1976-77
7	H. P. Tillekeratne	Sri Lanka v New Zealand at Colombo (SSC)	1992-93
6	A. Shrewsbury	England v Australia at Sydney	1887-88
6	A. E. E. Vogler	South Africa v England at Durban	1909-10
6	F. E. Woolley	England v Australia at Sydney	1911-12
6	J. M. Gregory	Australia v England at Sydney	1920-21
6	B. Mitchell	South Africa v Australia at Melbourne	1931-32
6	V. Y. Richardson	Australia v South Africa at Durban	1935-36
6	R. N. Harvey	Australia v England at Sydney	1962-63
6	M. C. Cowdrey	England v West Indies at Lord's	1963
6	E. D. Solkar	India v West Indies at Port-of-Spain	1970-71
6	G. S. Sobers	West Indies v England at Lord's	1973
6	I. M. Chappell	Australia v New Zealand at Adelaide	1973-74
6	A. W. Greig	England v Pakistan at Leeds	1974
6	D. F. Whatmore	Australia v India at Kanpur	1979-80
6	A. J. Lamb	England v New Zealand at Lord's	1983
6	R. B. Richardson	West Indies v South Africa at Bridgetown	1991-92
6	G. A. Hick	England v Pakistan at Leeds	1992
6	B. A. Young	New Zealand v Pakistan at Auckland	1993-94
6	J. C. Adams	West Indies v England at Kingston	1993-94

Most Catches in a Series

15	J. M. Gregory	Australia v England	1920-21
14	G. S. Chappell	Australia v England (6 Tests)	1974-75
13	R. B. Simpson	Australia v South Africa	1957-58
13	R. B. Simpson	Australia v West Indies	1960-61

Most Catches in a Career

A. R. Border (Australia)	**156 in 156 matches**
G. S. Chappell (Australia)	122 in 87 matches
I. V. A. Richards (West Indies)	122 in 121 matches
I. T. Botham (England)	120 in 102 matches
M. C. Cowdrey (England)	120 in 114 matches
R. B. Simpson (Australia)	110 in 62 matches
W. R. Hammond (England)	110 in 85 matches
G. S. Sobers (West Indies)	109 in 93 matches
S. M. Gavaskar (India)	108 in 125 matches
I. M. Chappell (Australia)	105 in 75 matches
G. A. Gooch (England)	**103 in 113 matches**

Bold type denotes players who played Test cricket in 1993-94 and 1994 seasons.

TEAM RECORDS

HIGHEST INNINGS TOTALS

903-7 dec.	England v Australia at The Oval	1938
849	England v West Indies at Kingston	1929-30
790-3 dec.	West Indies v Pakistan at Kingston	1957-58
758-8 dec.	Australia v West Indies at Kingston	1954-55
729-6 dec.	Australia v England at Lord's	1930
708	Pakistan v England at The Oval	1987
701	Australia v England at The Oval	1934
699-5	Pakistan v India at Lahore	1989-90
695	Australia v England at The Oval	1930
687-8 dec.	West Indies v England at The Oval	1976
681-8 dec.	West Indies v England at Port-of-Spain	1953-54
676-7	India v Sri Lanka at Kanpur	1986-87
674-6	Pakistan v India at Faisalabad	1984-85
674	Australia v India at Adelaide	1947-48
671-4	New Zealand v Sri Lanka at Wellington	1990-91
668	Australia v West Indies at Bridgetown	1954-55
659-8 dec.	Australia v England at Sydney	1946-47
658-8 dec.	England v Australia at Nottingham	1938
657-8 dec.	Pakistan v West Indies at Bridgetown	1957-58
656-8 dec.	Australia v England at Manchester	1964
654-5	England v South Africa at Durban	1938-39
653-4 dec.	England v India at Lord's	1990
653-4 dec.	Australia v England at Leeds	1993
652-7 dec.	England v India at Madras	1984-85
652-8 dec.	West Indies v England at Lord's	1973
652	Pakistan v India at Faisalabad	1982-83
650-6 dec.	Australia v West Indies at Bridgetown	1964-65

The highest innings for the countries not mentioned above are:

622-9 dec.	South Africa v Australia at Durban	1969-70
547-8 dec.	Sri Lanka v Australia at Colombo (SSC)	1992-93
456	Zimbabwe v India at Harare	1992-93

HIGHEST FOURTH-INNINGS TOTALS

To win

406-4	India (needing 403) v West Indies at Port-of-Spain	1975-76
404-3	Australia (needing 404) v England at Leeds	1948
362-7	Australia (needing 359) v West Indies at Georgetown	1977-78
348-5	West Indies (needing 345) v New Zealand at Auckland	1968-69
344-1	West Indies (needing 342) v England at Lord's	1984

To tie

347	India v Australia at Madras	1986-87

To draw

654-5	England (needing 696 to win) v South Africa at Durban	1938-39
429-8	India (needing 438 to win) v England at The Oval	1979
423-7	South Africa (needing 451 to win) v England at The Oval	1947
408-5	West Indies (needing 836 to win) v England at Kingston	1929-30

To lose

445	India (lost by 47 runs) v Australia at Adelaide	1977-78
440	New Zealand (lost by 38 runs) v England at Nottingham	1973
417	England (lost by 45 runs) v Australia at Melbourne	1976-77
411	England (lost by 193 runs) v Australia at Sydney	1924-25

MOST RUNS IN A DAY (BOTH SIDES)

588	England (398-6), India (190-0) at Manchester (2nd day)	1936
522	England (503-2), South Africa (19-0) at Lord's (2nd day)	1924
508	England (221-2), South Africa (287-6) at The Oval (3rd day)	1935

MOST RUNS IN A DAY (ONE SIDE)

503	England (503-2) v South Africa at Lord's (2nd day)	1924
494	Australia (494-6) v South Africa at Sydney (1st day)	1910-11
475	Australia (475-2) v England at The Oval (1st day)	1934
471	England (471-8) v India at The Oval (1st day)	1936
458	Australia (458-3) v England at Leeds (1st day)	1930
455	Australia (455-1) v England at Leeds (2nd day)	1934

MOST WICKETS IN A DAY

27	England (18-3 to 53 out and 62) v Australia (60) at Lord's (2nd day)	1888
25	Australia (112 and 48-5) v England (61) at Melbourne (1st day)	1901-02

HIGHEST MATCH AGGREGATES

Runs	*Wkts*			*Days played*
1,981	35	South Africa v England at Durban	1938-39	10†
1,815	34	West Indies v England at Kingston	1929-30	9‡
1,764	39	Australia v West Indies at Adelaide	1968-69	5
1,753	40	Australia v England at Adelaide	1920-21	6

Runs	*Wkts*			*Days played*
1,723	31	England v Australia at Leeds	1948	5
1,661	36	West Indies v Australia at Bridgetown	1954-55	6

† *No play on one day.* ‡ *No play on two days.*

LOWEST INNINGS TOTALS

26	New Zealand v England at Auckland	1954-55
30	South Africa v England at Port Elizabeth	1895-96
30	South Africa v England at Birmingham	1924
35	South Africa v England at Cape Town	1898-99
36	Australia v England at Birmingham	1902
36	South Africa v Australia at Melbourne	1931-32
42	Australia v England at Sydney	1887-88
42	New Zealand v Australia at Wellington	1945-46
42†	India v England at Lord's	1974
43	South Africa v England at Cape Town	1888-89
44	Australia v England at The Oval	1896
45	England v Australia at Sydney	1886-87
45	South Africa v Australia at Melbourne	1931-32
46	England v West Indies at Port-of-Spain	1993-94
47	South Africa v England at Cape Town	1888-89
47	New Zealand v England at Lord's	1958

The lowest innings for the countries not mentioned above are:

53	West Indies v Pakistan at Faisalabad	1986-87
62	Pakistan v Australia at Perth	1981-82
71	Sri Lanka v Pakistan at Kandy	1994-95
134	Zimbabwe v Pakistan at Karachi (DS)	1993-94

† *Batted one man short.*

FEWEST RUNS IN A FULL DAY'S PLAY

95 At Karachi, October 11, 1956. Australia 80 all out; Pakistan 15 for two (first day, 5½ hours).

104 At Karachi, December 8, 1959. Pakistan 0 for no wicket to 104 for five v Australia (fourth day, 5½ hours).

106 At Brisbane, December 9, 1958. England 92 for two to 198 all out v Australia (fourth day, 5 hours). *England were dismissed five minutes before the close of play, leaving no time for Australia to start their second innings.*

112 At Karachi, October 15, 1956. Australia 138 for six to 187 all out; Pakistan 63 for one (fourth day, 5½ hours).

115 At Karachi, September 19, 1988. Australia 116 for seven to 165 all out and 66 for five following on v Pakistan (fourth day, 5½ hours).

117 At Madras, October 19, 1956. India 117 for five v Australia (first day, 5½ hours).

117 At Colombo (SSC), March 21, 1984. New Zealand 6 for no wicket to 123 for four (fifth day, 5 hours 47 minutes).

In England

151 At Lord's, August 26, 1978. England 175 for two to 289 all out; New Zealand 37 for seven (third day, 6 hours).

159 At Leeds, July 10, 1971. Pakistan 208 for four to 350 all out; England 17 for one (third day, 6 hours).

LOWEST MATCH AGGREGATES

(For a completed match)

Runs	*Wkts*			*Days played*
234	29	Australia v South Africa at Melbourne	1931-32	3†
291	40	England v Australia at Lord's	1888	2

Runs	*Wkts*			*Days played*
295	28	New Zealand v Australia at Wellington	1945-46	2
309	29	West Indies v England at Bridgetown	1934-35	3
323	30	England v Australia at Manchester	1888	2

† *No play on one day.*

YOUNGEST TEST PLAYERS

Years	*Days*			
15	124	Mushtaq Mohammad	Pakistan v West Indies at Lahore	1958-59
16	189	Aqib Javed	Pakistan v New Zealand at Wellington	1988-89
16	205	S. R. Tendulkar	India v Pakistan at Karachi	1989-90
16	221	Aftab Baloch	Pakistan v New Zealand at Dacca	1969-70
16	248	Nasim-ul-Ghani	Pakistan v West Indies at Bridgetown	1957-58
16	352	Khalid Hassan	Pakistan v England at Nottingham	1954
17	5	Zahid Fazal	Pakistan v West Indies at Karachi	1990-91
17	69	Ata-ur-Rehman	Pakistan v England at Birmingham	1992
17	118	L. Sivaramakrishnan	India v West Indies at St John's	1982-83
17	122	J. E. D. Sealy	West Indies v England at Bridgetown	1929-30
17	189	C. D. U. S. Weerasinghe	Sri Lanka v India at Colombo (PSS)	1985-86
17	193	Maninder Singh	India v Pakistan at Karachi	1982-83
17	239	I. D. Craig	Australia v South Africa at Melbourne	1952-53
17	245	G. S. Sobers	West Indies v England at Kingston	1953-54
17	265	V. L. Mehra	India v New Zealand at Bombay	1955-56
17	300	Hanif Mohammad	Pakistan v India at Delhi	1952-53
17	341	Intikhab Alam	Pakistan v Australia at Karachi	1959-60
17	364	Waqar Younis	Pakistan v India at Karachi	1989-90

Note: The youngest Test players for countries not mentioned above are: England – D. B. Close, 18 years 149 days, v New Zealand at Manchester, 1949; New Zealand – D. L. Freeman, 18 years 197 days, v England at Christchurch, 1932-33; South Africa – A. E. Ochse, 19 years 1 day, v England at Port Elizabeth, 1888-89; Zimbabwe – H. H. Streak, 19 years 260 days, v Pakistan at Karachi (DS), 1993-94.

OLDEST PLAYERS ON TEST DEBUT

Years	*Days*			
49	119	J. Southerton	England v Australia at Melbourne	1876-77
47	284	Miran Bux	Pakistan v India at Lahore	1954-55
46	253	D. D. Blackie	Australia v England at Sydney	1928-29
46	237	H. Ironmonger	Australia v England at Brisbane	1928-29
42	242	N. Betancourt	West Indies v England at Port-of-Spain	1929-30
41	337	E. R. Wilson	England v Australia at Sydney	1920-21
41	27	R. J. D. Jamshedji	India v England at Bombay	1933-34
40	345	C. A. Wiles	West Indies v England at Manchester	1933
40	295	O. Henry	South Africa v India at Durban	1992-93
40	216	S. P. Kinneir	England v Australia at Sydney	1911-12
40	110	H. W. Lee	England v South Africa at Johannesburg	1930-31
40	56	G. W. A. Chubb	South Africa v England at Nottingham	1951
40	37	C. Ramaswami	India v England at Manchester	1936

Note: The oldest Test player on debut for New Zealand was H. M. McGirr, 38 years 101 days, v England at Auckland, 1929-30; for Sri Lanka, D. S. de Silva, 39 years 251 days, v England at Colombo (PSS), 1981-82; for Zimbabwe, M. P. Jarvis, 36 years 317 days, v India at Harare, 1992-93. A. J. Traicos was 45 years 154 days old when he made his debut for Zimbabwe (v India at Harare, 1992-93) having played 3 Tests for South Africa in 1969-70.

OLDEST TEST PLAYERS

(Age on final day of their last Test match)

Years	*Days*			
52	165	W. Rhodes	England v West Indies at Kingston	1929-30
50	327	H. Ironmonger	Australia v England at Sydney	1932-33
50	320	W. G. Grace	England v Australia at Nottingham	1899
50	303	G. Gunn	England v West Indies at Kingston	1929-30
49	139	J. Southerton	England v Australia at Melbourne	1876-77
47	302	Miran Bux	Pakistan v India at Peshawar	1954-55
47	249	J. B. Hobbs	England v Australia at The Oval	1930
47	87	F. E. Woolley	England v Australia at The Oval	1934
46	309	D. D. Blackie	Australia v England at Adelaide	1928-29
46	206	A. W. Nourse	South Africa v England at The Oval	1924
46	202	H. Strudwick	England v Australia at The Oval	1926
46	41	E. H. Hendren	England v West Indies at Kingston	1934-35
45	304	A. J. Traicos	Zimbabwe v India at Delhi	1992-93
45	245	G. O. B. Allen	England v West Indies at Kingston	1947-48
45	215	P. Holmes	England v India at Lord's	1932
45	140	D. B. Close	England v West Indies at Manchester	1976

MOST TEST APPEARANCES

156 A. R. Border (Australia)
131 Kapil Dev (India)
125 S. M. Gavaskar (India)
124 Javed Miandad (Pakistan)
121 I. V. A. Richards (West Indies)
117 D. I. Gower (England)
116 D. L. Haynes (West Indies)
116 D. B. Vengsarkar (India)
114 M. C. Cowdrey (England)
113 G. A. Gooch (England)
110 C. H. Lloyd (West Indies)
108 G. Boycott (England)
108 C. G. Greenidge (West Indies)
102 I. T. Botham (England)

The most appearances for New Zealand is 86 by R. J. Hadlee, for South Africa 50 by J. H. B. Waite, for Sri Lanka 51 by **A. Ranatunga** and for Zimbabwe 7 by **A. D. R. Campbell**, **A. Flower**, **G. W. Flower** and **D. L. Houghton**.

Bold type denotes those who played Test cricket in 1993-94 or 1994 seasons or Sri Lanka v Pakistan in 1994-95.

MOST CONSECUTIVE TEST APPEARANCES

153	A. R. Border (Australia)	March 1979 to March 1994
106	S. M. Gavaskar (India)	January 1975 to February 1987
87	G. R. Viswanath (India)	March 1971 to February 1983
85	G. S. Sobers (West Indies)	April 1955 to April 1972
72	D. L. Haynes (West Indies)	December 1979 to June 1988
71	I. M. Chappell (Australia)	January 1966 to February 1976
66	Kapil Dev (India)	October 1978 to December 1984
65	I. T. Botham (England)	February 1978 to March 1984
65	Kapil Dev (India)	January 1985 to March 1994
65	A. P. E. Knott (England)	March 1971 to August 1977

The most consecutive Test appearances for the countries not mentioned above are:

58†	J. R. Reid (New Zealand)	July 1949 to July 1965
53	Javed Miandad (Pakistan)	December 1977 to January 1984
45†	A. W. Nourse (South Africa)....	October 1902 to August 1924
30*	P. A. de Silva (Sri Lanka)	February 1988 to August 1994

The most for Zimbabwe is 7 (as above).

* *Sequence still in progress.*
† *Indicates complete Test career.*

CAPTAINCY

MOST TESTS AS CAPTAIN

	P	*W*	*L*	*D*		*P*	*W*	*L*	*D*
A. R. Border (A)	**93**	**32**	**22**	**38***	G. A. Gooch (E)	34	10	12	12
C. H. Lloyd (WI)	74	36	12	26	Javed Miandad (P)	34	14	6	14
I. V. A. Richards (WI)	50	27	8	15	Kapil Dev (I)	34	4	7	22*
G. S. Chappell (A)	48	21	13	14	J. R. Reid (NZ)	34	3	18	13
Imran Khan (P)	48	14	8	26	D. I. Gower (E)	32	5	18	9
S. M. Gavaskar (I)	47	9	8	30	J. M. Brearley (E)	31	18	4	9
P. B. H. May (E)	41	20	10	11	R. Illingworth (E)	31	12	5	14
Nawab of Pataudi jun. (I)	40	9	19	12	I. M. Chappell (A)	30	15	5	10
R. B. Simpson (A)	39	12	12	15	E. R. Dexter (E)	30	9	7	14
G. S. Sobers (WI)	39	9	10	20	G. P. Howarth (NZ)	30	11	7	12

* *One match tied.*

Most Tests as captain of countries not mentioned above:

	P	*W*	*L*	*D*
A. Ranatunga (SL)	**24**	**2**	**10**	**12**
H. W. Taylor (SA)	18	1	10	7
D. L. Houghton (Z)	4	0	2	2

Notes: A. R. Border captained Australia in 93 consecutive Tests.

W. W. Armstrong (Australia) captained his country in the most Tests without being defeated: ten matches with eight wins and two draws.

I. T. Botham (England) captained his country in the most Tests without ever winning: 12 matches with eight draws and four defeats.

Bold type denotes those who were captains in the 1993-94 season or Sri Lanka v Pakistan in 1994-95.

UMPIRING

MOST TEST MATCHES

		First Test	*Last Test*
59	**H. D. Bird (England)**	**1973**	**1994**
48	F. Chester (England)	1924	1955
42	C. S. Elliott (England)	1957	1974
36	D. J. Constant (England)	1971	1988
33	J. S. Buller (England)	1956	1969
33	A. R. Crafter (Australia)	1978-79	1991-92
32	R. W. Crockett (Australia)	1901-02	1924-25
31	D. Sang Hue (West Indies)	1961-62	1980-81

Note: H. D. Bird's total includes three Tests in Zimbabwe and three Tests in West Indies in 1992-93, and two Tests in New Zealand in 1993-94. C. S. Elliott's total includes one Test in New Zealand in 1970-71.

Bold type indicates an umpire who stood in 1993-94 or 1994 seasons.

SUMMARY OF ALL TEST MATCHES

To August 28, 1994

	Opponents	Tests	Won by E	A	SA	WI	NZ	I	P	SL	Z	Tied	Drawn
England	v Australia	280	89	108	–	–	–	–	–	–	–	–	83
	v South Africa	105	47	–	19	–	–	–	–	–	–	–	39
	v West Indies	109	25	–	–	46	–	–	–	–	–	–	38
	v New Zealand	75	34	–	–	–	4	–	–	–	–	–	37
	v India	81	31	–	–	–	–	14	–	–	–	–	36
	v Pakistan	52	14	–	–	–	–	–	7	–	–	–	31
	v Sri Lanka	5	3	–	–	–	–	–	–	1	–	–	1
Australia	v South Africa	59	–	31	13	–	–	–	–	–	–	–	15
	v West Indies	77	–	30	–	26	–	–	–	–	–	1	20
	v New Zealand	32	–	13	–	–	7	–	–	–	–	–	12
	v India	50	–	24	–	–	–	8	–	–	–	1	17
	v Pakistan	34	–	12	–	–	–	–	9	–	–	–	13
	v Sri Lanka	7	–	4	–	–	–	–	–	0	–	–	3
South Africa	v West Indies	1	–	–	0	1	–	–	–	–	–	–	–
	v New Zealand	17	–	–	9	–	2	–	–	–	–	–	6
	v India	4	–	–	1	–	–	0	–	–	–	–	3
	v Sri Lanka	3	–	–	1	–	–	–	–	0	–	–	2
West Indies	v New Zealand	24	–	–	–	8	4	–	–	–	–	–	12
	v India	62	–	–	–	26	–	6	–	–	–	–	30
	v Pakistan	31	–	–	–	12	–	–	7	–	–	–	12
	v Sri Lanka	1	–	–	–	0	–	–	–	0	–	–	1
New Zealand	v India	32	–	–	–	–	6	12	–	–	–	–	14
	v Pakistan	36	–	–	–	–	4	–	16	–	–	–	16
	v Sri Lanka	11	–	–	–	–	4	–	–	1	–	–	6
	v Zimbabwe	2	–	–	–	–	1	–	–	–	0	–	1
India	v Pakistan	44	–	–	–	–	–	4	7	–	–	–	33
	v Sri Lanka	14	–	–	–	–	–	7	–	1	–	–	6
	v Zimbabwe	2	–	–	–	–	–	1	–	–	0	–	1
Pakistan	v Sri Lanka	14	–	–	–	–	–	–	8	1	–	–	5
	v Zimbabwe	3	–	–	–	–	–	–	2	–	0	–	1
		1,267	243	222	43	119	32	52	56	4	0	2	494

	Tests	*Won*	*Lost*	*Drawn*	*Tied*	*Toss Won*
England	707	243	199	265	–	348
Australia	539	222	152	163	2	271
South Africa	189	43	81	65	–	91
West Indies	305	119	72	113	1	158
New Zealand	229	32	93	104	–	116
India	289	52	96	140	1	144
Pakistan	214	56	47	111	–	108
Sri Lanka	55	4	27	24	–	28
Zimbabwe	7	0	4	3	–	3

ENGLAND v AUSTRALIA

Captains

Season	*England*	*Australia*	*T*	*E*	*A*	*D*
1876-77	James Lillywhite	D. W. Gregory	2	1	1	0
1878-79	Lord Harris	D. W. Gregory	1	0	1	0
1880	Lord Harris	W. L. Murdoch	1	1	0	0
1881-82	A. Shaw	W. L. Murdoch	4	0	2	2
1882	A. N. Hornby	W. L. Murdoch	1	0	1	0

THE ASHES

Captains

Season	*England*	*Australia*	*T*	*E*	*A*	*D*	*Held by*
1882-83	Hon. Ivo Bligh	W. L. Murdoch	4*	2	2	0	E
1884	Lord Harris[1]	W. L. Murdoch	3	1	0	2	E
1884-85	A. Shrewsbury	T. P. Horan[2]	5	3	2	0	E
1886	A. G. Steel	H. J. H. Scott	3	3	0	0	E

	Captains						
Season	*England*	*Australia*	*T*	*E*	*A*	*D*	*Held by*
1886-87	A. Shrewsbury	P. S. McDonnell	2	2	0	0	E
1887-88	W. W. Read	P. S. McDonnell	1	1	0	0	E
1888	W. G. Grace[3]	P. S. McDonnell	3	2	1	0	E
1890†	W. G. Grace	W. L. Murdoch	2	2	0	0	E
1891-92	W. G. Grace	J. McC. Blackham	3	1	2	0	A
1893	W. G. Grace[4]	J. McC. Blackham	3	1	0	2	E
1894-95	A. E. Stoddart	G. Giffen[5]	5	3	2	0	E
1896	W. G. Grace	G. H. S. Trott	3	2	1	0	E
1897-98	A. E. Stoddart[6]	G. H. S. Trott	5	1	4	0	A
1899	A. C. MacLaren[7]	J. Darling	5	0	1	4	A
1901-02	A. C. MacLaren	J. Darling[8]	5	1	4	0	A
1902	A. C. MacLaren	J. Darling	5	1	2	2	A
1903-04	P. F. Warner	M. A. Noble	5	3	2	0	E
1905	Hon. F. S. Jackson	J. Darling	5	2	0	3	E
1907-08	A. O. Jones[9]	M. A. Noble	5	1	4	0	A
1909	A. C. MacLaren	M. A. Noble	5	1	2	2	A
1911-12	J. W. H. T. Douglas	C. Hill	5	4	1	0	E
1912	C. B. Fry	S. E. Gregory	3	1	0	2	E
1920-21	J. W. H. T. Douglas	W. W. Armstrong	5	0	5	0	A
1921	Hon. L. H. Tennyson[10]	W. W. Armstrong	5	0	3	2	A
1924-25	A. E. R. Gilligan	H. L. Collins	5	1	4	0	A
1926	A. W. Carr[11]	H. L. Collins[12]	5	1	0	4	E
1928-29	A. P. F. Chapman[13]	J. Ryder	5	4	1	0	E
1930	A. P. F. Chapman[14]	W. M. Woodfull	5	1	2	2	A
1932-33	D. R. Jardine	W. M. Woodfull	5	4	1	0	E
1934	R. E. S. Wyatt[15]	W. M. Woodfull	5	1	2	2	A
1936-37	G. O. B. Allen	D. G. Bradman	5	2	3	0	A
1938†	W. R. Hammond	D. G. Bradman	4	1	1	2	A
1946-47	W. R. Hammond[16]	D. G. Bradman	5	0	3	2	A
1948	N. W. D. Yardley	D. G. Bradman	5	0	4	1	A
1950-51	F. R. Brown	A. L. Hassett	5	1	4	0	A
1953	L. Hutton	A. L. Hassett	5	1	0	4	E
1954-55	L. Hutton	I. W. Johnson[17]	5	3	1	1	E
1956	P. B. H. May	I. W. Johnson	5	2	1	2	E
1958-59	P. B. H. May	R. Benaud	5	0	4	1	A
1961	P. B. H. May[18]	R. Benaud[19]	5	1	2	2	A
1962-63	E. R. Dexter	R. Benaud	5	1	1	3	A
1964	E. R. Dexter	R. B. Simpson	5	0	1	4	A
1965-66	M. J. K. Smith	R. B. Simpson[20]	5	1	1	3	A
1968	M. C. Cowdrey[21]	W. M. Lawry[22]	5	1	1	3	A
1970-71†	R. Illingworth	W. M. Lawry[23]	6	2	0	4	E
1972	R. Illingworth	I. M. Chappell	5	2	2	1	E
1974-75	M. H. Denness[24]	I. M. Chappell	6	1	4	1	A
1975	A. W. Greig[25]	I. M. Chappell	4	0	1	3	A
1976-77‡	A. W. Greig	G. S. Chappell	1	0	1	0	—
1977	J. M. Brearley	G. S. Chappell	5	3	0	2	E
1978-79	J. M. Brearley	G. N. Yallop	6	5	1	0	E
1979-80‡	J. M. Brearley	G. S. Chappell	3	0	3	0	—
1980‡	I. T. Botham	G. S. Chappell	1	0	0	1	—
1981	J. M. Brearley[26]	K. J. Hughes	6	3	1	2	E
1982-83	R. G. D. Willis	G. S. Chappell	5	1	2	2	A
1985	D. I. Gower	A. R. Border	6	3	1	2	E
1986-87	M. W. Gatting	A. R. Border	5	2	1	2	E
1987-88‡	M. W. Gatting	A. R. Border	1	0	0	1	—
1989	D. I. Gower	A. R. Border	6	0	4	2	A
1990-91	G. A. Gooch[27]	A. R. Border	5	0	3	2	A
1993	G. A. Gooch[28]	A. R. Border	6	1	4	1	A
	In Australia		145	51	70	24	
	In England		135	38	38	59	
	Totals		280	89	108	83	

* *The Ashes were awarded in 1882-83 after a series of three matches which England won 2-1. A fourth unofficial match was played, each innings being played on a different pitch, and this was won by Australia.*

† *The matches at Manchester in 1890 and 1938 and at Melbourne (Third Test) in 1970-71 were abandoned without a ball being bowled and are excluded.*

‡ *The Ashes were not at stake in these series.*

Notes: The following deputised for the official touring captain or were appointed by the home authority for only a minor proportion of the series:
[1]A. N. Hornby (First). [2]W. L. Murdoch (First), H. H. Massie (Third), J. McC. Blackham (Fourth). [3]A. G. Steel (First). [4]A. E. Stoddart (First). [5]J. McC. Blackham (First). [6]A. C. MacLaren (First, Second and Fifth). [7]W. G. Grace (First). [8]H. Trumble (Fourth and Fifth). [9]F. L. Fane (First, Second and Third). [10]J. W. H. T. Douglas (First and Second). [11]A. P. F. Chapman (Fifth). [12]W. Bardsley (Third and Fourth). [13]J. C. White (Fifth). [14]R. E. S. Wyatt (Fifth). [15]C. F. Walters (First). [16]N. W. D. Yardley (Fifth). [17]A. R. Morris (Second). [18]M. C. Cowdrey (First and Second). [19]R. N. Harvey (Second). [20]B. C. Booth (First and Third). [21]T. W. Graveney (Fourth). [22]B. N. Jarman (Fourth). [23]I. M. Chappell (Seventh). [24]J. H. Edrich (Fourth). [25]M. H. Denness (First). [26]I. T. Botham (First and Second). [27]A. J. Lamb (First). [28]M. A. Atherton (Fifth and Sixth).

HIGHEST INNINGS TOTALS

For England	in England: 903-7 dec. at The Oval	1938
	in Australia: 636 at Sydney	1928-29
For Australia	in England: 729-6 dec. at Lord's	1930
	in Australia: 659-8 dec. at Sydney	1946-47

LOWEST INNINGS TOTALS

For England	in England: 52 at The Oval	1948
	in Australia: 45 at Sydney	1886-87
For Australia	in England: 36 at Birmingham	1902
	in Australia: 42 at Sydney	1887-88

INDIVIDUAL HUNDREDS

For England (199)

R. Abel (1)		
132*‡	Sydney	1891-92
L. E. G. Ames (1)		
120	Lord's	1934
M. A. Atherton (1)		
105	Sydney	1990-91
R. W. Barber (1)		
185	Sydney	1965-66
W. Barnes (1)		
134	Adelaide	1884-85
C. J. Barnett (2)		
129	Adelaide	1936-37
126	Nottingham	1938
K. F. Barrington (5)		
132*	Adelaide	1962-63
101	Sydney	1962-63
256	Manchester	1964
102	Adelaide	1965-66
115	Melbourne	1965-66
I. T. Botham (4)		
119*	Melbourne	1979-80
149*	Leeds	1981
118	Manchester	1981
138	Brisbane	1986-87
G. Boycott (7)		
113	The Oval	1964
142*	Sydney	1970-71
119*	Adelaide	1970-71
107	Nottingham	1977
191	Leeds	1977
128*	Lord's	1980
137	The Oval	1981
L. C. Braund (2)		
103*	Adelaide	1901-02
102	Sydney	1903-04
J. Briggs (1)		
121	Melbourne	1884-85
B. C. Broad (4)		
162	Perth	1986-87
116	Adelaide	1986-87
112	Melbourne	1986-87
139	Sydney	1987-88
J. T. Brown (1)		
140	Melbourne	1894-95
A. P. F. Chapman (1)		
121	Lord's	1930
D. C. S. Compton (5)		
102†	Nottingham	1938
147 / 103*	Adelaide	1946-47
184	Nottingham	1948
145*	Manchester	1948

M. C. Cowdrey (5)
102 Melbourne .. 1954-55
100* Sydney 1958-59
113 Melbourne .. 1962-63
104 Melbourne .. 1965-66
104 Birmingham . 1968
M. H. Denness (1)
188 Melbourne .. 1974-75
E. R. Dexter (2)
180 Birmingham . 1961
174 Manchester .. 1964
B. L. D'Oliveira (2)
158 The Oval 1968
117 Melbourne .. 1970-71
K. S. Duleepsinhji (1)
173† Lord's 1930
J. H. Edrich (7)
120† Lord's 1964
109 Melbourne .. 1965-66
103 Sydney 1965-66
164 The Oval 1968
115* Perth 1970-71
130 Adelaide 1970-71
175 Lord's 1975
W. J. Edrich (2)
119 Sydney 1946-47
111 Leeds 1948
K. W. R. Fletcher (1)
146 Melbourne .. 1974-75
R. E. Foster (1)
287† Sydney 1903-04
C. B. Fry (1)
144 The Oval 1905
M. W. Gatting (3)
160 Manchester .. 1985
100* Birmingham . 1985
100 Adelaide 1986-87
G. A. Gooch (4)
196 The Oval 1985
117 Adelaide 1990-91
133 Manchester .. 1993
120 Nottingham . 1993
D. I. Gower (9)
102 Perth 1978-79
114 Adelaide 1982-83
166 Nottingham . 1985
215 Birmingham . 1985
157 The Oval 1985
136 Perth 1986-87
106 Lord's 1989
100 Melbourne .. 1990-91
123 Sydney 1990-91
W. G. Grace (2)
152† The Oval 1880
170 The Oval 1886
T. W. Graveney (1)
111 Sydney 1954-55
A. W. Greig (1)
110 Brisbane 1974-75
G. Gunn (2)
119† Sydney 1907-08
122* Sydney 1907-08
W. Gunn (1)
102* Manchester .. 1893

W. R. Hammond (9)
251 Sydney 1928-29
200 Melbourne .. 1928-29
119* } Adelaide 1928-29
177 }
113 Leeds 1930
112 Sydney 1932-33
101 Sydney 1932-33
231* Sydney 1936-37
240 Lord's 1938
J. Hardstaff jun. (1)
169* The Oval 1938
T. W. Hayward (2)
130 Manchester .. 1899
137 The Oval 1899
J. W. Hearne (1)
114 Melbourne .. 1911-12
E. H. Hendren (3)
127* Lord's 1926
169 Brisbane 1928-29
132 Manchester .. 1934
J. B. Hobbs (12)
126* Melbourne .. 1911-12
187 Adelaide 1911-12
178 Melbourne .. 1911-12
107 Lord's 1912
122 Melbourne .. 1920-21
123 Adelaide 1920-21
115 Sydney 1924-25
154 Melbourne .. 1924-25
119 Adelaide 1924-25
119 Lord's 1926
100 The Oval 1926
142 Melbourne .. 1928-29
K. L. Hutchings (1)
126 Melbourne .. 1907-08
L. Hutton (5)
100† Nottingham . 1938
364 The Oval 1938
122* Sydney 1946-47
156*‡ Adelaide 1950-51
145 Lord's 1953
Hon. F. S. Jackson (5)
103 The Oval 1893
118 The Oval 1899
128 Manchester .. 1902
144* Leeds 1905
113 Manchester .. 1905
G. L. Jessop (1)
104 The Oval 1902
A. P. E. Knott (2)
106* Adelaide 1974-75
135 Nottingham . 1977
A. J. Lamb (1)
125 Leeds 1989
M. Leyland (7)
137† Melbourne .. 1928-29
109 Lord's 1934
153 Manchester .. 1934
110 The Oval 1934
126 Brisbane 1936-37
111* Melbourne .. 1936-37
187 The Oval 1938

B. W. Luckhurst (2)
131 Perth 1970-71
109 Melbourne .. 1970-71
A. C. MacLaren (5)
120 Melbourne .. 1894-95
109 Sydney 1897-98
124 Adelaide 1897-98
116 Sydney 1901-02
140 Nottingham . 1905
J. W. H. Makepeace (1)
117 Melbourne .. 1920-21
P. B. H. May (3)
104 Sydney 1954-55
101 Leeds 1956
113 Melbourne .. 1958-59
C. P. Mead (1)
182* The Oval 1921
Nawab of Pataudi sen. (1)
102† Sydney 1932-33
E. Paynter (1)
216* Nottingham . 1938
D. W. Randall (3)
174† Melbourne .. 1976-77
150 Sydney 1978-79
115 Perth 1982-83
K. S. Ranjitsinhji (2)
154*† Manchester .. 1896
175 Sydney 1897-98
W. W. Read (1)
117 The Oval 1884
W. Rhodes (1)
179 Melbourne .. 1911-12
C. J. Richards (1)
133 Perth 1986-87
P. E. Richardson (1)
104 Manchester .. 1956
R. T. Robinson (2)
175† Leeds 1985
148 Birmingham . 1985
A. C. Russell (3)
135* Adelaide 1920-21
101 Manchester .. 1921
102* The Oval 1921
R. C. Russell (1)
128* Manchester .. 1989
J. Sharp (1)
105 The Oval 1909
Rev. D. S. Sheppard (2)
113 Manchester .. 1956
113 Melbourne .. 1962-63
A. Shrewsbury (3)
105* Melbourne .. 1884-85
164 Lord's 1886
106 Lord's 1893
R. T. Simpson (1)
156* Melbourne .. 1950-51
R. A. Smith (2)
143 Manchester .. 1989
101 Nottingham . 1989
A. G. Steel (2)
135* Sydney 1882-83
148 Lord's 1884

A. E. Stoddart (2)
134 Adelaide 1891-92
173 Melbourne .. 1894-95
R. Subba Row (2)
112† Birmingham . 1961
137 The Oval.... 1961
H. Sutcliffe (8)
115† Sydney 1924-25
176 } Melbourne .. 1924-25
127 }
143 Melbourne .. 1924-25
161 The Oval.... 1926
135 Melbourne .. 1928-29
161 The Oval.... 1930
194 Sydney 1932-33
G. P. Thorpe (1)
114*† Nottingham . 1993
J. T. Tyldesley (3)
138 Birmingham . 1902
100 Leeds 1905
112* The Oval.... 1905
G. Ulyett (1)
149 Melbourne .. 1881-82
A. Ward (1)
117 Sydney 1894-95
C. Washbrook (2)
112 Melbourne .. 1946-47
143 Leeds 1948
W. Watson (1)
109† Lord's 1953
F. E. Woolley (2)
133* Sydney 1911-12
123 Sydney 1924-25
R. A. Woolmer (3)
149 The Oval.... 1975
120 Lord's 1977
137 Manchester.. 1977

† *Signifies hundred on first appearance in England–Australia Tests.*
‡ *Carried his bat.*
Note: In consecutive innings in 1928-29, W. R. Hammond scored 251 at Sydney, 200 and 32 at Melbourne, and 119* and 177 at Adelaide.

For Australia (224)

W. W. Armstrong (4)
133* Melbourne .. 1907-08
158 Sydney 1920-21
121 Adelaide 1920-21
123* Melbourne .. 1920-21
C. L. Badcock (1)
118 Melbourne .. 1936-37
C. Bannerman (1)
165*† Melbourne .. 1876-77
W. Bardsley (3)
136 } The Oval.... 1909
130 }
193*‡ Lord's 1926
S. G. Barnes (2)
234 Sydney 1946-47
141 Lord's 1948
G. J. Bonnor (1)
128 Sydney 1884-85
D. C. Boon (6)
103 Adelaide 1986-87
184* Sydney 1987-88
121 Adelaide 1990-91
164* Lord's 1993
101 Nottingham . 1993
107 Leeds 1993
B. C. Booth (2)
112 Brisbane 1962-63
103 Melbourne .. 1962-63
A. R. Border (8)
115 Perth 1979-80
123* Manchester.. 1981
106* The Oval.... 1981
196 Lord's 1985
146* Manchester.. 1985
125 Perth 1986-87
100* Adelaide 1986-87
200* Leeds 1993
D. G. Bradman (19)
112 Melbourne .. 1928-29
123 Melbourne .. 1928-29
131 Nottingham . 1930
254 Lord's 1930
334 Leeds 1930
232 The Oval.... 1930
103* Melbourne .. 1932-33
304 Leeds 1934
244 The Oval.... 1934
270 Melbourne .. 1936-37
212 Adelaide 1936-37
169 Melbourne .. 1936-37
144* Nottingham . 1938
102* Lord's 1938
103 Leeds 1938
187 Brisbane 1946-47
234 Sydney 1946-47
138 Nottingham . 1948
173* Leeds 1948
W. A. Brown (3)
105 Lord's 1934
133 Nottingham . 1938
206*‡ Lord's 1938
P. J. P. Burge (4)
181 The Oval.... 1961
103 Sydney 1962-63
160 Leeds 1964
120 Melbourne .. 1965-66
J. W. Burke (1)
101*† Adelaide 1950-51
G. S. Chappell (9)
108† Perth 1970-71
131 Lord's 1972
113 The Oval ... 1972
144 Sydney 1974-75
102 Melbourne .. 1974-75
112 Manchester.. 1977
114 Melbourne .. 1979-80
117 Perth 1982-83
115 Adelaide 1982-83
I. M. Chappell (4)
111 Melbourne .. 1970-71
104 Adelaide 1970-71
118 The Oval.... 1972
192 The Oval.... 1975
H. L. Collins (3)
104† Sydney 1920-21
162 Adelaide 1920-21
114 Sydney 1924-25
R. M. Cowper (1)
307 Melbourne .. 1965-66
J. Darling (3)
101 Sydney 1897-98
178 Adelaide 1897-98
160 Sydney 1897-98
R. A. Duff (2)
104† Melbourne .. 1901-02
146 The Oval.... 1905
J. Dyson (1)
102 Leeds 1981
R. Edwards (2)
170* Nottingham . 1972
115 Perth 1974-75
J. H. Fingleton (2)
100 Brisbane 1936-37
136 Melbourne .. 1936-37
G. Giffen (1)
161 Sydney 1894-95
H. Graham (2)
107† Lord's 1893
105 Sydney 1894-95
J. M. Gregory (1)
100 Melbourne .. 1920-21
S. E. Gregory (4)
201 Sydney 1894-95
103 Lord's 1896
117 The Oval.... 1899
112 Adelaide 1903-04
R. J. Hartigan (1)
116† Adelaide 1907-08

R. N. Harvey (6)
112† Leeds 1948
122 Manchester 1953
162 Brisbane 1954-55
167 Melbourne 1958-59
114 Birmingham 1961
154 Adelaide 1962-63
A. L. Hassett (4)
128 Brisbane 1946-47
137 Nottingham 1948
115 Nottingham 1953
104 Lord's 1953
I. A. Healy (1)
102* Manchester 1993
H. S. T. L. Hendry (1)
112 Sydney 1928-29
A. M. J. Hilditch (1)
119 Leeds 1985
C. Hill (4)
188 Melbourne 1897-98
135 Lord's 1899
119 Sheffield 1902
160 Adelaide 1907-08
T. P. Horan (1)
124 Melbourne 1881-82
K. J. Hughes (3)
129 Brisbane 1978-79
117 Lord's 1980
137 Sydney 1982-83
F. A. Iredale (2)
140 Adelaide 1894-95
108 Manchester 1896
A. A. Jackson (1)
164† Adelaide 1928-29
D. M. Jones (3)
184* Sydney 1986-87
157 Birmingham 1989
122 The Oval 1989
C. Kelleway (1)
147 Adelaide 1920-21
A. F. Kippax (1)
100 Melbourne 1928-29
W. M. Lawry (7)
130 Lord's 1961
102 Manchester 1961
106 Manchester 1964
166 Brisbane 1965-66
119 Adelaide 1965-66
108 Melbourne 1965-66
135 The Oval 1968
R. R. Lindwall (1)
100 Melbourne 1946-47
J. J. Lyons (1)
134 Sydney 1891-92
C. G. Macartney (5)
170 Sydney 1920-21
115 Leeds 1921
133* Lord's 1926
151 Leeds 1926
109 Manchester 1926

S. J. McCabe (4)
187* Sydney 1932-33
137 Manchester 1934
112 Melbourne 1936-37
232 Nottingham 1938
C. L. McCool (1)
104* Melbourne 1946-47
R. B. McCosker (2)
127 The Oval 1975
107 Nottingham 1977
C. C. McDonald (2)
170 Adelaide 1958-59
133 Melbourne 1958-59
P. S. McDonnell (3)
147 Sydney 1881-82
103 The Oval 1884
124 Adelaide 1884-85
C. E. McLeod (1)
112 Melbourne 1897-98
G. R. Marsh (2)
110† Brisbane 1986-87
138 Nottingham 1989
R. W. Marsh (1)
110* Melbourne 1976-77
G. R. J. Matthews (1)
128 Sydney 1990-91
K. R. Miller (3)
141* Adelaide 1946-47
145* Sydney 1950-51
109 Lord's 1953
A. R. Morris (8)
155 Melbourne 1946-47
122 }
124* } Adelaide 1946-47
105 Lord's 1948
182 Leeds 1948
196 The Oval 1948
206 Adelaide 1950-51
153 Brisbane 1954-55
W. L. Murdoch (2)
153* The Oval 1880
211 The Oval 1884
M. A. Noble (1)
133 Sydney 1903-04
N. C. O'Neill (2)
117 The Oval 1961
100 Adelaide 1962-63
C. E. Pellew (2)
116 Melbourne 1920-21
104 Adelaide 1920-21
W. H. Ponsford (5)
110† Sydney 1924-25
128 Melbourne 1924-25
110 The Oval 1930
181 Leeds 1934
266 The Oval 1934
V. S. Ransford (1)
143* Lord's 1909

I. R. Redpath (2)
171 Perth 1970-71
105 Sydney 1974-75
A. J. Richardson (1)
100 Leeds 1926
V. Y. Richardson (1)
138 Melbourne 1924-25
G. M. Ritchie (1)
146 Nottingham 1985
J. Ryder (2)
201* Adelaide 1924-25
112 Melbourne 1928-29
H. J. H. Scott (1)
102 The Oval 1884
R. B. Simpson (2)
311 Manchester 1964
225 Adelaide 1965-66
M. J. Slater (1)
152 Lord's 1993
K. R. Stackpole (3)
207 Brisbane 1970-71
136 Adelaide 1970-71
114 Nottingham 1972
J. M. Taylor (1)
108 Sydney 1924-25
M. A. Taylor (4)
136† Leeds 1989
219 Nottingham 1989
124 Manchester 1993
111 Lord's 1993
G. H. S. Trott (1)
143 Lord's 1896
V. T. Trumper (6)
135* Lord's 1899
104 Manchester 1902
185* Sydney 1903-04
113 Adelaide 1903-04
166 Sydney 1907-08
113 Sydney 1911-12
K. D. Walters (4)
155† Brisbane 1965-66
115 Melbourne 1965-66
112 Brisbane 1970-71
103 Perth 1974-75
M. E. Waugh (2)
138† Adelaide 1990-91
137 Birmingham 1993
S. R. Waugh (3)
177* Leeds 1989
152* Lord's 1989
157* Leeds 1993
D. M. Wellham (1)
103† The Oval 1981
K. C. Wessels (1)
162† Brisbane 1982-83
G. M. Wood (3)
100 Melbourne 1978-79
112 Lord's 1980
172 Nottingham 1985

W. M. Woodfull (6)						**G. N. Yallop** (3)		
141	Leeds	1926	107	Melbourne	1928-29	102†	Brisbane	1978-79
117	Manchester	1926	102	Melbourne	1928-29	121	Sydney	1978-79
111	Sydney	1928-29	155	Lord's	1930	114	Manchester	1981

† *Signifies hundred on first appearance in England–Australia Tests.*
‡ *Carried his bat.*

Notes: D. G. Bradman's scores in 1930 were 8 and 131 at Nottingham, 254 and 1 at Lord's, 334 at Leeds, 14 at Manchester, and 232 at The Oval.

D. G. Bradman scored a hundred in eight successive Tests against England in which he batted – three in 1936-37, three in 1938 and two in 1946-47. He was injured and unable to bat at The Oval in 1938.

W. H. Ponsford and K. D. Walters each hit hundreds in their first two Tests.

C. Bannerman and H. Graham each scored their maiden hundred in first-class cricket in their first Test.

No right-handed batsman has obtained two hundreds for Australia in a Test match against England, and no left-handed batsman for England against Australia.

H. Sutcliffe, in his first two games for England, scored 59 and 115 at Sydney and 176 and 127 at Melbourne in 1924-25. In the latter match, which lasted into the seventh day, he was on the field throughout except for 86 minutes, namely 27 hours and 52 minutes.

C. Hill made 98 and 97 at Adelaide in 1901-02, and F. E. Woolley 95 and 93 at Lord's in 1921.

H. Sutcliffe in 1924-25, C. G. Macartney in 1926 and A. R. Morris in 1946-47 made three hundreds in consecutive innings.

J. B. Hobbs and H. Sutcliffe shared 11 first-wicket three-figure partnerships.

L. Hutton and C. Washbrook twice made three-figure stands in each innings, at Adelaide in 1946-47 and at Leeds in 1948.

H. Sutcliffe, during his highest score of 194, v Australia in 1932-33, took part in three stands each exceeding 100, viz. 112 with R. E. S. Wyatt for the first wicket, 188 with W. R. Hammond for the second wicket, and 123 with the Nawab of Pataudi sen. for the third wicket. In 1903-04 R. E. Foster, in his historic innings of 287, added 192 for the fifth wicket with L. C. Braund, 115 for the ninth with A. E. Relf, and 130 for the tenth with W. Rhodes.

When L. Hutton scored 364 at The Oval in 1938 he added 382 for the second wicket with M. Leyland, 135 for the third wicket with W. R. Hammond and 215 for the sixth wicket with J. Hardstaff jun.

D. C. S. Compton and A. R. Morris at Adelaide in 1946-47 provided the first instance of a player on each side hitting two separate hundreds in a Test match.

G. S. and I. M. Chappell at The Oval in 1972 provide the first instance in Test matches of brothers each scoring hundreds in the same innings.

RECORD PARTNERSHIPS FOR EACH WICKET

For England

323 for 1st	J. B. Hobbs and W. Rhodes at Melbourne	1911-12
382 for 2nd†	L. Hutton and M. Leyland at The Oval	1938
262 for 3rd	W. R. Hammond and D. R. Jardine at Adelaide	1928-29
222 for 4th	W. R. Hammond and E. Paynter at Lord's	1938
206 for 5th	E. Paynter and D. C. S. Compton at Nottingham	1938
215 for 6th	L. Hutton and J. Hardstaff jun. at The Oval	1938
	G. Boycott and A. P. E. Knott at Nottingham	1977
143 for 7th	F. E. Woolley and J. Vine at Sydney	1911-12
124 for 8th	E. H. Hendren and H. Larwood at Brisbane	1928-29
151 for 9th	W. H. Scotton and W. W. Read at The Oval	1884
130 for 10th†	R. E. Foster and W. Rhodes at Sydney	1903-04

For Australia

329 for 1st	G. R. Marsh and M. A. Taylor at Nottingham	1989
451 for 2nd†	W. H. Ponsford and D. G. Bradman at The Oval	1934
276 for 3rd	D. G. Bradman and A. L. Hassett at Brisbane	1946-47
388 for 4th†	W. H. Ponsford and D. G. Bradman at Leeds	1934
405 for 5th†‡	S. G. Barnes and D. G. Bradman at Sydney	1946-47
346 for 6th†	J. H. Fingleton and D. G. Bradman at Melbourne	1936-37

165 for 7th	C. Hill and H. Trumble at Melbourne	1897-98
243 for 8th†	R. J. Hartigan and C. Hill at Adelaide	1907-08
154 for 9th†	S. E. Gregory and J. McC. Blackham at Sydney	1894-95
127 for 10th†	J. M. Taylor and A. A. Mailey at Sydney	1924-25

† *Denotes record partnership against all countries.*
‡ *Record fifth-wicket partnership in first-class cricket.*

MOST RUNS IN A SERIES

England in England	732 (average 81.33)	D. I. Gower	1985
England in Australia	905 (average 113.12)	W. R. Hammond	1928-29
Australia in England	974 (average 139.14)	D. G. Bradman	1930
Australia in Australia	810 (average 90.00)	D. G. Bradman	1936-37

TEN WICKETS OR MORE IN A MATCH

For England (36)

13-163 (6-42, 7-121)	S. F. Barnes, Melbourne	1901-02
14-102 (7-28, 7-74)	W. Bates, Melbourne	1882-83
10-105 (5-46, 5-59)	A. V. Bedser, Melbourne	1950-51
14-99 (7-55, 7-44)	A. V. Bedser, Nottingham	1953
11-102 (6-44, 5-58)	C. Blythe, Birmingham	1909
11-176 (6-78, 5-98)	I. T. Botham, Perth	1979-80
10-253 (6-125, 4-128)	I. T. Botham, The Oval	1981
11-74 (5-29, 6-45)	J. Briggs, Lord's	1886
12-136 (6-49, 6-87)	J. Briggs, Adelaide	1891-92
10-148 (5-34, 5-114)	J. Briggs, The Oval	1893
10-104 (6-77, 4-27)†	R. M. Ellison, Birmingham	1985
10-179 (5-102, 5-77)†	K. Farnes, Nottingham	1934
10-60 (6-41, 4-19)	J. T. Hearne, The Oval	1896
11-113 (5-58, 6-55)	J. C. Laker, Leeds	1956
19-90 (9-37, 10-53)	J. C. Laker, Manchester	1956
10-124 (5-96, 5-28)	H. Larwood, Sydney	1932-33
11-76 (6-48, 5-28)	W. H. Lockwood, Manchester	1902
12-104 (7-36, 5-68)	G. A. Lohmann, The Oval	1886
10-87 (8-35, 2-52)	G. A. Lohmann, Sydney	1886-87
10-142 (8-58, 2-84)	G. A. Lohmann, Sydney	1891-92
12-102 (6-50, 6-52)†	F. Martin, The Oval	1890
11-68 (7-31, 4-37)	R. Peel, Manchester	1888
15-124 (7-56, 8-68)	W. Rhodes, Melbourne	1903-04
10-156 (5-49, 5-107)†	T. Richardson, Manchester	1893
11-173 (6-39, 5-134)	T. Richardson, Lord's	1896
13-244 (7-168, 6-76)	T. Richardson, Manchester	1896
10-204 (8-94, 2-110)	T. Richardson, Sydney	1897-98
11-228 (6-130, 5-98)†	M. W. Tate, Sydney	1924-25
11-88 (5-58, 6-30)	F. S. Trueman, Leeds	1961
10-130 (4-45, 6-85)	F. H. Tyson, Sydney	1954-55
10-82 (4-37, 6-45)	D. L. Underwood, Leeds	1972
11-215 (7-113, 4-102)	D. L. Underwood, Adelaide	1974-75
15-104 (7-61, 8-43)	H. Verity, Lord's	1934
10-57 (6-41, 4-16)	W. Voce, Brisbane	1936-37
13-256 (5-130, 8-126)	J. C. White, Adelaide	1928-29
10-49 (5-29, 5-20)	F. E. Woolley, The Oval	1912

For Australia (38)

10-151 (5-107, 5-44)	T. M. Alderman, Leeds	1989
10-239 (4-129, 6-110)	L. O'B. Fleetwood-Smith, Adelaide	1936-37
10-160 (4-88, 6-72)	G. Giffen, Sydney	1891-92
11-82 (5-45, 6-37)†	C. V. Grimmett, Sydney	1924-25
10-201 (5-107, 5-94)	C. V. Grimmett, Nottingham	1930
10-122 (5-65, 5-57)	R. M. Hogg, Perth	1978-79
10-66 (5-30, 5-36)	R. M. Hogg, Melbourne	1978-79
12-175 (5-85, 7-90)†	H. V. Hordern, Sydney	1911-12
10-161 (5-95, 5-66)	H. V. Hordern, Sydney	1911-12
10-164 (7-88, 3-76)	E. Jones, Lord's	1899
11-134 (6-47, 5-87)	G. F. Lawson, Brisbane	1982-83
10-181 (5-58, 5-123)	D. K. Lillee, The Oval	1972
11-165 (6-26, 5-139)	D. K. Lillee, Melbourne	1976-77
11-138 (6-60, 5-78)	D. K. Lillee, Melbourne	1979-80
11-159 (7-89, 4-70)	D. K. Lillee, The Oval	1981
11-85 (7-58, 4-27)	C. G. Macartney, Leeds	1909
11-157 (8-97, 3-60)	C. J. McDermott, Perth	1990-91
10-302 (5-160, 5-142)	A. A. Mailey, Adelaide	1920-21
13-236 (4-115, 9-121)	A. A. Mailey, Melbourne	1920-21
16-137 (8-84, 8-53)†	R. A. L. Massie, Lord's	1972
10-152 (5-72, 5-80)	K. R. Miller, Lord's	1956
13-77 (7-17, 6-60)	M. A. Noble, Melbourne	1901-02
11-103 (5-51, 6-52)	M. A. Noble, Sheffield	1902
10-129 (5-63, 5-66)	W. J. O'Reilly, Melbourne	1932-33
11-129 (4-75, 7-54)	W. J. O'Reilly, Nottingham	1934
10-122 (5-66, 5-56)	W. J. O'Reilly, Leeds	1938
11-165 (7-68, 4-97)	G. E. Palmer, Sydney	1881-82
10-126 (7-65, 3-61)	G. E. Palmer, Melbourne	1882-83
13-148 (6-97, 7-51)	B. A. Reid, Melbourne	1990-91
13-110 (6-48, 7-62)	F. R. Spofforth, Melbourne	1878-79
14-90 (7-46, 7-44)	F. R. Spofforth, The Oval	1882
11-117 (4-73, 7-44)	F. R. Spofforth, Sydney	1882-83
10-144 (4-54, 6-90)	F. R. Spofforth, Sydney	1884-85
12-89 (6-59, 6-30)	H. Trumble, The Oval	1896
10-128 (4-75, 6-53)	H. Trumble, Manchester	1902
12-173 (8-65, 4-108)	H. Trumble, The Oval	1902
12-87 (5-44, 7-43)	C. T. B. Turner, Sydney	1887-88
10-63 (5-27, 5-36)	C. T. B. Turner, Lord's	1888

† *Signifies ten wickets or more on first appearance in England–Australia Tests.*

Note: J. Briggs, J. C. Laker, T. Richardson in 1896, R. M. Hogg, A. A. Mailey, H. Trumble and C. T. B. Turner took ten wickets or more in successive Tests. J. Briggs was omitted, however, from the England team for the first Test match in 1893.

MOST WICKETS IN A SERIES

England in England	46 (average 9.60)	J. C. Laker	1956
England in Australia	38 (average 23.18)	M. W. Tate	1924-25
Australia in England	42 (average 21.26)	T. M. Alderman (6 Tests)	1981
Australia in Australia	41 (average 12.85)	R. M. Hogg (6 Tests)	1978-79

WICKET-KEEPING – MOST DISMISSALS

	M	*Ct*	*St*	*Total*
†R. W. Marsh (Australia)	42	141	7	148
A. P. E. Knott (England)	34	97	8	105
†W. A. Oldfield (Australia)	38	59	31	90
A. A. Lilley (England)	32	65	19	84
A. T. W. Grout (Australia)	22	69	7	76
T. G. Evans (England)	31	63	12	75

† *The number of catches by R. W. Marsh (141) and stumpings by W. A. Oldfield (31) are respective records in England–Australia Tests.*

SCORERS OF OVER 2,000 RUNS

	T	I	NO	R	HS	Avge
D. G. Bradman	37	63	7	5,028	334	89.78
J. B. Hobbs	41	71	4	3,636	187	54.26
A. R. Border	47	82	19	3,548	200*	56.31
D. I. Gower	42	77	4	3,269	215	44.78
G. Boycott	38	71	9	2,945	191	47.50
W. R. Hammond	33	58	3	2,852	251	51.85
H. Sutcliffe	27	46	5	2,741	194	66.85
C. Hill	41	76	1	2,660	188	35.46
J. H. Edrich	32	57	3	2,644	175	48.96
G. S. Chappell	35	65	8	2,619	144	45.94
M. C. Cowdrey	43	75	4	2,433	113	34.26
L. Hutton	27	49	6	2,428	364	56.46
R. N. Harvey	37	68	5	2,416	167	38.34
G. A. Gooch	37	69	0	2,387	196	34.59
V. T. Trumper	40	74	5	2,263	185*	32.79
W. M. Lawry	29	51	5	2,233	166	48.54
S. E. Gregory	52	92	7	2,193	201	25.80
W. W. Armstrong	42	71	9	2,172	158	35.03
I. M. Chappell	30	56	4	2,138	192	41.11
K. F. Barrington	23	39	6	2,111	256	63.96
A. R. Morris	24	43	2	2,080	206	50.73

BOWLERS WITH 100 WICKETS

	T	Balls	R	W	5W/i	Avge
D. K. Lillee	29	8,516	3,507	167	11	21.00
I. T. Botham	36	8,479	4,093	148	9	27.65
H. Trumble	31	7,895	2,945	141	9	20.88
R. G. D. Willis	35	7,294	3,346	128	7	26.14
M. A. Noble	39	6,845	2,860	115	9	24.86
R. R. Lindwall	29	6,728	2,559	114	6	22.44
W. Rhodes	41	5,791	2,616	109	6	24.00
S. F. Barnes	20	5,749	2,288	106	12	21.58
C. V. Grimmett	22	9,224	3,439	106	11	32.44
D. L. Underwood	29	8,000	2,770	105	4	26.38
A. V. Bedser	21	7,065	2,859	104	7	27.49
G. Giffen	31	6,457	2,791	103	7	27.09
W. J. O'Reilly	19	7,864	2,587	102	8	25.36
R. Peel	20	5,216	1,715	101	5	16.98
C. T. B. Turner	17	5,195	1,670	101	11	16.53
T. M. Alderman	17	4,717	2,117	100	11	21.17
J. R. Thomson	21	4,951	2,418	100	5	24.18

RESULTS ON EACH GROUND

In England

THE OVAL (31)

England (14) 1880, 1886, 1888, 1890, 1893, 1896, 1902, 1912, 1926, 1938, 1953, 1968, 1985, 1993.

Australia (5) 1882, 1930, 1934, 1948, 1972.

Drawn (12) 1884, 1899, 1905, 1909, 1921, 1956, 1961, 1964, 1975, 1977, 1981, 1989.

MANCHESTER (26)

England (7) 1886, 1888, 1905, 1956, 1972, 1977, 1981.

Australia (6) 1896, 1902, 1961, 1968, 1989, 1993.

Drawn (13) 1884, 1893, 1899, 1909, 1912, 1921, 1926, 1930, 1934, 1948, 1953, 1964, 1985.

The scheduled matches in 1890 and 1938 were abandoned without a ball bowled and are excluded.

LORD'S (30)
England (5) 1884, 1886, 1890, 1896, 1934.
Australia (12) 1888, 1899, 1909, 1921, 1930, 1948, 1956, 1961, 1972, 1985, 1989, 1993.
Drawn (13) 1893, 1902, 1905, 1912, 1926, 1938, 1953, 1964, 1968, 1975, 1977, 1980, 1981.

NOTTINGHAM (17)
England (3) 1905, 1930, 1977.
Australia (5) 1921, 1934, 1948, 1981, 1989.
Drawn (9) 1899, 1926, 1938, 1953, 1956, 1964, 1972, 1985, 1993.

LEEDS (21)
England (6) 1956, 1961, 1972, 1977, 1981, 1985.
Australia (7) 1909, 1921, 1938, 1948, 1964, 1989, 1993.
Drawn (8) 1899, 1905, 1926, 1930, 1934, 1953, 1968, 1975.

BIRMINGHAM (9)
England (3) 1909, 1981, 1985.
Australia (2) 1975, 1993.
Drawn (4) 1902, 1961, 1968, 1989.

SHEFFIELD (1)
Australia (1) 1902.

In Australia

MELBOURNE (49)
England (18) *1876, 1882, 1884*(2), *1894*(2), *1903, 1907, 1911*(2), *1924, 1928, 1950, 1954, 1962, 1974, 1982, 1986.*
Australia (24) *1876, 1878, 1882, 1891, 1897*(2), *1901*(2), *1903, 1907, 1920*(2), *1924, 1928, 1932, 1936*(2), *1950, 1958*(2), *1976, 1978, 1979, 1990.*
Drawn (7) *1881*(2), *1946, 1965*(2), *1970, 1974.*

One scheduled match in 1970-71 was abandoned without a ball bowled and is excluded.

SYDNEY (49)
England (20) *1882, 1886*(2), *1887, 1894, 1897, 1901, 1903*(2), *1911, 1928, 1932*(2), *1936, 1954, 1965, 1970*(2), *1978*(2).
Australia (23) *1881*(2), *1882, 1884*(2), *1891, 1894, 1897, 1901, 1907*(2), *1911, 1920*(2), *1924*(2), *1946*(2), *1950, 1962, 1974, 1979, 1986.*
Drawn (6) *1954, 1958, 1962, 1982, 1987, 1990.*

ADELAIDE (25)
England (7) *1884, 1891, 1911, 1928, 1932, 1954, 1978.*
Australia (13) *1894, 1897, 1901, 1903, 1907, 1920, 1924, 1936, 1950, 1958, 1965, 1974, 1982.*
Drawn (5) *1946, 1962, 1970, 1986, 1990.*

BRISBANE Exhibition Ground (1)
England (1) *1928.*

BRISBANE Woolloongabba (14)
England (4) *1932, 1936, 1978, 1986.*
Australia (7) *1946, 1950, 1954, 1958, 1974, 1982, 1990.*
Drawn (3) *1962, 1965, 1970.*

PERTH (7)

England (1) *1978.*

Australia (3) *1974, 1979, 1990.*

Drawn (3) *1970, 1982, 1986.*

For Tests in Australia the first year of the season is given in italics; i.e. *1876* denotes the 1876-77 season.

ENGLAND v SOUTH AFRICA

	Captains					
Season	*England*	*South Africa*	*T*	*E*	*SA*	*D*
1888-89	C. A. Smith[1]	O. R. Dunell[2]	2	2	0	0
1891-92	W. W. Read	W. H. Milton	1	1	0	0
1895-96	Lord Hawke[3]	E. A. Halliwell[4]	3	3	0	0
1898-99	Lord Hawke	M. Bisset	2	2	0	0
1905-06	P. F. Warner	P. W. Sherwell	5	1	4	0
1907	R. E. Foster	P. W. Sherwell	3	1	0	2
1909-10	H. D. G. Leveson Gower[5]	S. J. Snooke	5	2	3	0
1912	C. B. Fry	F. Mitchell[6]	3	3	0	0
1913-14	J. W. H. T. Douglas	H. W. Taylor	5	4	0	1
1922-23	F. T. Mann	H. W. Taylor	5	2	1	2
1924	A. E. R. Gilligan[7]	H. W. Taylor	5	3	0	2
1927-28	R. T. Stanyforth[8]	H. G. Deane	5	2	2	1
1929	J. C. White[9]	H. G. Deane	5	2	0	3
1930-31	A. P. F. Chapman	H. G. Deane[10]	5	0	1	4
1935	R. E. S. Wyatt	H. F. Wade	5	0	1	4
1938-39	W. R. Hammond	A. Melville	5	1	0	4
1947	N. W. D. Yardley	A. Melville	5	3	0	2
1948-49	F. G. Mann	A. D. Nourse	5	2	0	3
1951	F. R. Brown	A. D. Nourse	5	3	1	1
1955	P. B. H. May	J. E. Cheetham[11]	5	3	2	0
1956-57	P. B. H. May	C. B. van Ryneveld[12]	5	2	2	1
1960	M. C. Cowdrey	D. J. McGlew	5	3	0	2
1964-65	M. J. K. Smith	T. L. Goddard	5	1	0	4
1965	M. J. K. Smith	P. L. van der Merwe	3	0	1	2
1994	M. A. Atherton	K. C. Wessels	3	1	1	1
	In South Africa		58	25	13	20
	In England		47	22	6	19
	Totals		105	47	19	39

Notes: The following deputised for the official touring captain or were appointed by the home authority for only a minor proportion of the series:

[1]M. P. Bowden (Second). [2]W. H. Milton (Second). [3]Sir T. C. O'Brien (First). [4]A. R. Richards (Third). [5]F. L. Fane (Fourth and Fifth). [6]L. J. Tancred (Second and Third). [7]J. W. H. T. Douglas (Fourth). [8]G. T. S. Stevens (Fifth). [9]A. W. Carr (Fourth and Fifth). [10]E. P. Nupen (First), H. B. Cameron (Fourth and Fifth). [11]D. J. McGlew (Third and Fourth). [12]D. J. McGlew (Second).

HIGHEST INNINGS TOTALS

For England in England: 554-8 dec. at Lord's 1947
in South Africa: 654-5 at Durban 1938-39

For South Africa in England: 538 at Leeds 1951
in South Africa: 530 at Durban 1938-39

LOWEST INNINGS TOTALS

For England	in England: 76 at Leeds	1907
	in South Africa: 92 at Cape Town	1898-99
For South Africa	in England: 30 at Birmingham	1924
	in South Africa: 30 at Port Elizabeth	1895-96

INDIVIDUAL HUNDREDS

For England (88)

R. Abel (1)		
120	Cape Town	1888-89
L. E. G. Ames (2)		
148*	The Oval	1935
115	Cape Town	1938-39
K. F. Barrington (2)		
148*	Durban	1964-65
121	Johannesburg	1964-65
G. Boycott (1)		
117	Pt Elizabeth	1964-65
L. C. Braund (1)		
104†	Lord's	1907
D. C. S. Compton (7)		
163†	Nottingham	1947
208	Lord's	1947
115	Manchester	1947
113	The Oval	1947
114	Johannesburg	1948-49
112	Nottingham	1951
158	Manchester	1955
M. C. Cowdrey (3)		
101	Cape Town	1956-57
155	The Oval	1960
105	Nottingham	1965
D. Denton (1)		
104	Johannesburg	1909-10
E. R. Dexter (1)		
172	Johannesburg	1964-65
J. W. H. T. Douglas (1)		
119†	Durban	1913-14
W. J. Edrich (3)		
219	Durban	1938-39
189	Lord's	1947
191	Manchester	1947
F. L. Fane (1)		
143	Johannesburg	1905-06
C. B. Fry (1)		
129	The Oval	1907
P. A. Gibb (2)		
106†	Johannesburg	1938-39
120	Durban	1938-39
W. R. Hammond (6)		
138*	Birmingham	1929
101*	The Oval	1929
136*	Durban	1930-31
181	Cape Town	1938-39
120	Durban	1938-39
140	Durban	1938-39
T. W. Hayward (1)		
122	Johannesburg	1895-96
E. H. Hendren (2)		
132	Leeds	1924
142	The Oval	1924
G. A. Hick (1)		
110	Leeds	1994
A. J. L. Hill (1)		
124	Cape Town	1895-96
J. B. Hobbs (2)		
187	Cape Town	1909-10
211	Lord's	1924
L. Hutton (4)		
100	Leeds	1947
158	Johannesburg	1948-49
123	Johannesburg	1948-49
100	Leeds	1951
D. J. Insole (1)		
110*	Durban	1956-57
M. Leyland (2)		
102	Lord's	1929
161	The Oval	1935
F. G. Mann (1)		
136*	Pt Elizabeth	1948-49
P. B. H. May (3)		
138†	Leeds	1951
112	Lord's	1955
117	Manchester	1955
C. P. Mead (3)		
102	Johannesburg	1913-14
117	Pt Elizabeth	1913-14
181	Durban	1922-23
P. H. Parfitt (1)		
122*	Johannesburg	1964-65
J. M. Parks (1)		
108*	Durban	1964-65
E. Paynter (3)		
117 100	†Johannesburg	1938-39
243	Durban	1938-39
G. Pullar (1)		
175	The Oval	1960
W. Rhodes (1)		
152	Johannesburg	1913-14
P. E. Richardson (1)		
117†	Johannesburg	1956-57
R. W. V. Robins (1)		
108	Manchester	1935
A. C. Russell (2)		
140 111	Durban	1922-23
R. T. Simpson (1)		
137	Nottingham	1951
M. J. K. Smith (1)		
121	Cape Town	1964-65
R. H. Spooner (1)		
119†	Lord's	1912
H. Sutcliffe (6)		
122	Lord's	1924
102	Johannesburg	1927-28
114	Birmingham	1929
100	Lord's	1929
104 109*	The Oval	1929
M. W. Tate (1)		
100*	Lord's	1929
E. Tyldesley (2)		
122	Johannesburg	1927-28
100	Durban	1927-28
J. T. Tyldesley (1)		
112	Cape Town	1898-99
B. H. Valentine (1)		
112	Cape Town	1938-39
P. F. Warner (1)		
132*†‡	Johannesburg	1898-99
C. Washbrook (1)		
195	Johannesburg	1948-49
A. J. Watkins (1)		
111	Johannesburg	1948-49
H. Wood (1)		
134*	Cape Town	1891-92
F. E. Woolley (3)		
115*	Johannesburg	1922-23
134*	Lord's	1924
154	Manchester	1929
R. E. S. Wyatt (2)		
113	Manchester	1929
149	Nottingham	1935

For South Africa (60)

E. J. Barlow (1)
138 Cape Town . . 1964-65
K. C. Bland (2)
144* Johannesburg 1964-65
127 The Oval 1965
R. H. Catterall (3)
120 Birmingham . 1924
120 Lord's 1924
119 Durban 1927-28
E. L. Dalton (2)
117 The Oval 1935
102 Johannesburg 1938-39
W. R. Endean (1)
116* Leeds 1955
G. A. Faulkner (1)
123 Johannesburg 1909-10
T. L. Goddard (1)
112 Johannesburg 1964-65
C. M. H. Hathorn (1)
102 Johannesburg 1905-06
P. N. Kirsten (1)
104 Leeds 1994
D. J. McGlew (2)
104* Manchester . . 1955
133 Leeds 1955
R. A. McLean (3)
142 Lord's 1955
100 Durban 1956-57
109 Manchester . . 1960
A. Melville (4)
103 Durban 1938-39
189 }
104* } Nottingham . 1947
117 Lord's 1947
B. Mitchell (7)
123 Cape Town . . 1930-31
164* Lord's 1935
128 The Oval 1935
109 Durban 1938-39
120 }
189* } The Oval 1947
120 Cape Town . . 1948-49
A. D. Nourse (7)
120 Cape Town . . 1938-39
103 Durban 1938-39
149 Nottingham . 1947
115 Manchester . . 1947
112 Cape Town . . 1948-49
129* Johannesburg 1948-49
208 Nottingham . 1951
H. G. Owen-Smith (1)
129 Leeds 1929
A. J. Pithey (1)
154 Cape Town . . 1964-65
R. G. Pollock (2)
137 Pt Elizabeth . 1964-65
125 Nottingham . 1965
E. A. B. Rowan (2)
156* Johannesburg 1948-49
236 Leeds 1951
P. W. Sherwell (1)
115 Lord's 1907
I. J. Siedle (1)
141 Cape Town . . 1930-31
J. H. Sinclair (1)
106 Cape Town . . 1898-99
H. W. Taylor (7)
109 Durban 1913-14
176 Johannesburg 1922-23
101 Johannesburg 1922-23
102 Durban 1922-23
101 Johannesburg 1927-28
121 The Oval 1929
117 Cape Town . . 1930-31
P. G. V. van der Bijl (1)
125 Durban 1938-39
K. G. Viljoen (1)
124 Manchester . . 1935
W. W. Wade (1)
125 Pt Elizabeth . 1948-49
J. H. B. Waite (1)
113 Manchester . . 1955
K. C. Wessels (1)
105† Lord's 1994
G. C. White (2)
147 Johannesburg 1905-06
118 Durban 1909-10
P. L. Winslow (1)
108 Manchester . . 1955

† *Signifies hundred on first appearance in England–South Africa Tests. K. C. Wessels had earlier scored 162 on his Test debut for Australia against England at Brisbane in 1982-83.*
‡ *P. F. Warner carried his bat through the second innings.*
A. Melville's four hundreds were made in successive Test innings.
H. Wood scored the only hundred of his career in a Test match.

RECORD PARTNERSHIP FOR EACH WICKET

For England

359	for 1st†	L. Hutton and C. Washbrook at Johannesburg	1948-49
280	for 2nd	P. A. Gibb and W. J. Edrich at Durban	1938-39
370	for 3rd†	W. J. Edrich and D. C. S. Compton at Lord's	1947
197	for 4th	W. R. Hammond and L. E. G. Ames at Cape Town	1938-39
237	for 5th	D. C. S. Compton and N. W. D. Yardley at Nottingham	1947
206*	for 6th	K. F. Barrington and J. M. Parks at Durban	1964-65
115	for 7th	M. C. Bird and J. W. H. T. Douglas at Durban	1913-14
154	for 8th	C. W. Wright and H. R. Bromley-Davenport at Johannesburg	1895-96
71	for 9th	H. Wood and J. T. Hearne at Cape Town	1891-92
92	for 10th	A. C. Russell and A. E. R. Gilligan at Durban	1922-23

For South Africa

260	for 1st†	I. J. Siedle and B. Mitchell at Cape Town	1930-31
198	for 2nd†	E. A. B. Rowan and C. B. van Ryneveld at Leeds	1951
319	for 3rd	A. Melville and A. D. Nourse at Nottingham	1947
214	for 4th†	H. W. Taylor and H. G. Deane at The Oval	1929
157	for 5th†	A. J. Pithey and J. H. B. Waite at Johannesburg	1964-65
171	for 6th	J. H. B. Waite and P. L. Winslow at Manchester	1955
123	for 7th	H. G. Deane and E. P. Nupen at Durban	1927-28

109* for 8th	B. Mitchell and L. Tuckett at The Oval	1947
137 for 9th†	E. L. Dalton and A. B. C. Langton at The Oval	1935
103 for 10th†	H. G. Owen-Smith and A. J. Bell at Leeds	1929

† *Denotes record partnership against all countries.*

MOST RUNS IN A SERIES

England in England	753 (average 94.12)	D. C. S. Compton	1947
England in South Africa	653 (average 81.62)	E. Paynter	1938-39
South Africa in England	621 (average 69.00)	A. D. Nourse	1947
South Africa in South Africa	582 (average 64.66)	H. W. Taylor	1922-23

TEN WICKETS OR MORE IN A MATCH

For England (24)

11-110 (5-25, 6-85)†	S. F. Barnes, Lord's	1912
10-115 (6-52, 4-63)	S. F. Barnes, Leeds	1912
13-57 (5-28, 8-29)	S. F. Barnes, The Oval	1912
10-105 (5-57, 5-48)	S. F. Barnes, Durban	1913-14
17-159 (8-56, 9-103)	S. F. Barnes, Johannesburg	1913-14
14-144 (7-56, 7-88)	S. F. Barnes, Durban	1913-14
12-112 (7-58, 5-54)	A. V. Bedser, Manchester	1951
11-118 (6-68, 5-50)	C. Blythe, Cape Town	1905-06
15-99 (8-59, 7-40)	C. Blythe, Leeds	1907
10-104 (7-46, 3-58)	C. Blythe, Cape Town	1909-10
15-28 (7-17, 8-11)	J. Briggs, Cape Town	1888-89
13-91 (6-54, 7-37)†	J. J. Ferris, Cape Town	1891-92
10-207 (7-115, 3-92)	A. P. Freeman, Leeds	1929
12-171 (7-71, 5-100)	A. P. Freeman, Manchester	1929
12-130 (7-70, 5-60)	G. Geary, Johannesburg	1927-28
11-90 (6-7, 5-83)	A. E. R. Gilligan, Birmingham	1924
10-119 (4-64, 6-55)	J. C. Laker, The Oval	1951
15-45 (7-38, 8-7)†	G. A. Lohmann, Port Elizabeth	1895-96
12-71 (9-28, 3-43)	G. A. Lohmann, Johannesburg	1895-96
10-138 (1-81, 9-57)	D. E. Malcolm, The Oval	1994
11-97 (6-63, 5-34)	J. B. Statham, Lord's	1960
12-101 (7-52, 5-49)	R. Tattersall, Lord's	1951
12-89 (5-53, 7-36)	J. H. Wardle, Cape Town	1956-57
10-175 (5-95, 5-80)	D. V. P. Wright, Lord's	1947

For South Africa (6)

11-112 (4-49, 7-63)†	A. E. Hall, Cape Town	1922-23
11-150 (5-63, 6-87)	E. P. Nupen, Johannesburg	1930-31
10-87 (5-53, 5-34)	P. M. Pollock, Nottingham	1965
12-127 (4-57, 8-70)	S. J. Snooke, Johannesburg	1905-06
13-192 (4-79, 9-113)	H. J. Tayfield, Johannesburg	1956-57
12-181 (5-87, 7-94)	A. E. E. Vogler, Johannesburg	1909-10

† *Signifies ten wickets or more on first appearance in England–South Africa Tests.*

Note: S. F. Barnes took ten wickets or more in his first five Tests v South Africa and in six of his seven Tests v South Africa. A. P. Freeman and G. A. Lohmann took ten wickets or more in successive matches.

MOST WICKETS IN A SERIES

England in England	34 (average 8.29)	S. F. Barnes	1912
England in South Africa	49 (average 10.93)	S. F. Barnes	1913-14
South Africa in England	26 (average 21.84)	H. J. Tayfield	1955
South Africa in England	26 (average 22.57)	N. A. T. Adcock	1960
South Africa in South Africa	37 (average 17.18)	H. J. Tayfield	1956-57

ENGLAND v WEST INDIES

	Captains					
Season	England	West Indies	T	E	WI	D
1928	A. P. F. Chapman	R. K. Nunes	3	3	0	0
1929-30	Hon. F. S. G. Calthorpe	E. L. G. Hoad[1]	4	1	1	2
1933	D. R. Jardine[2]	G. C. Grant	3	2	0	1
1934-35	R. E. S. Wyatt	G. C. Grant	4	1	2	1
1939	W. R. Hammond	R. S. Grant	3	1	0	2
1947-48	G. O. B. Allen[3]	J. D. C. Goddard[4]	4	0	2	2
1950	N. W. D. Yardley[5]	J. D. C. Goddard	4	1	3	0
1953-54	L. Hutton	J. B. Stollmeyer	5	2	2	1
1957	P. B. H. May	J. D. C. Goddard	5	3	0	2
1959-60	P. B. H. May[6]	F. C. M. Alexander	5	1	0	4

THE WISDEN TROPHY

	Captains						
Season	England	West Indies	T	E	WI	D	Held by
1963	E. R. Dexter	F. M. M. Worrell	5	1	3	1	WI
1966	M. C. Cowdrey[7]	G. S. Sobers	5	1	3	1	WI
1967-68	M. C. Cowdrey	G. S. Sobers	5	1	0	4	E
1969	R. Illingworth	G. S. Sobers	3	2	0	1	E
1973	R. Illingworth	R. B. Kanhai	3	0	2	1	WI
1973-74	M. H. Denness	R. B. Kanhai	5	1	1	3	WI
1976	A. W. Greig	C. H. Lloyd	5	0	3	2	WI
1980	I. T. Botham	C. H. Lloyd[8]	5	0	1	4	WI
1980-81†	I. T. Botham	C. H. Lloyd	4	0	2	2	WI
1984	D. I. Gower	C. H. Lloyd	5	0	5	0	WI
1985-86	D. I. Gower	I. V. A. Richards	5	0	5	0	WI
1988	J. E. Emburey[9]	I. V. A. Richards	5	0	4	1	WI
1989-90‡	G. A. Gooch[10]	I. V. A. Richards[11]	4	1	2	1	WI
1991	G. A. Gooch	I. V. A. Richards	5	2	2	1	WI
1993-94	M. A. Atherton	R. B. Richardson[12]	5	1	3	1	WI
	In England		59	16	26	17	
	In West Indies		50	9	20	21	
	Totals		109	25	46	38	

† The Second Test, at Georgetown, was cancelled owing to political pressure and is excluded.
‡ The Second Test, at Georgetown, was abandoned without a ball being bowled and is excluded.

Notes: The following deputised for the official touring captain or were appointed by the home authority for only a minor proportion of the series:

[1]N. Betancourt (Second), M. P. Fernandes (Third), R. K. Nunes (Fourth). [2]R. E. S. Wyatt (Third). [3]K. Cranston (First). [4]G. A. Headley (First), G. E. Gomez (Second). [5]F. R. Brown (Fourth). [6]M. C. Cowdrey (Fourth and Fifth). [7]M. J. K. Smith (First), D. B. Close (Fifth). [8]I. V. A. Richards (Fifth). [9]M. W. Gatting (First), C. S. Cowdrey (Fourth), G. A. Gooch (Fifth). [10]A. J. Lamb (Fourth and Fifth). [11]D. L. Haynes (Third). [12]C. A. Walsh (Fifth).

HIGHEST INNINGS TOTALS

For England in England: 619-6 dec. at Nottingham 1957
in West Indies: 849 at Kingston 1929-30

For West Indies in England: 687-8 dec. at The Oval 1976
in West Indies: 681-8 dec. at Port-of-Spain 1953-54

LOWEST INNINGS TOTALS

For England in England: 71 at Manchester 1976
in West Indies: 46 at Port-of-Spain 1993-94

For West Indies in England: 86 at The Oval 1957
in West Indies: 102 at Bridgetown 1934-35

INDIVIDUAL HUNDREDS

For England (93)

L. E. G. Ames (3)
105 Port-of-Spain 1929-30
149 Kingston.... 1929-30
126 Kingston.... 1934-35
D. L. Amiss (4)
174 Port-of-Spain 1973-74
262* Kingston.... 1973-74
118 Georgetown . 1973-74
203 The Oval.... 1976
M. A. Atherton (2)
144 Georgetown . 1993-94
135 St John's.... 1993-94
A. H. Bakewell (1)
107† The Oval.... 1933
K. F. Barrington (3)
128† Bridgetown.. 1959-60
121 Port-of-Spain 1959-60
143 Port-of-Spain 1967-68
G. Boycott (5)
116 Georgetown . 1967-68
128 Manchester.. 1969
106 Lord's...... 1969
112 Port-of-Spain 1973-74
104* St John's.... 1980-81
D. C. S. Compton (2)
120† Lord's...... 1939
133 Port-of-Spain 1953-54
M. C. Cowdrey (6)
154† Birmingham . 1957
152 Lord's...... 1957
114 Kingston.... 1959-60
119 Port-of-Spain 1959-60
101 Kingston.... 1967-68
148 Port-of-Spain 1967-68
E. R. Dexter (2)
136*† Bridgetown.. 1959-60
110 Georgetown . 1959-60
J. H. Edrich (1)
146 Bridgetown.. 1967-68
T. G. Evans (1)
104 Manchester.. 1950
K. W. R. Fletcher (1)
129* Bridgetown.. 1973-74
G. Fowler (1)
106 Lord's...... 1984

G. A. Gooch (5)
123 Lord's...... 1980
116 Bridgetown.. 1980-81
153 Kingston.... 1980-81
146 Nottingham . 1988
154*‡ Leeds 1991
D. I. Gower (1)
154* Kingston.... 1980-81
T. W. Graveney (5)
258 Nottingham . 1957
164 The Oval.... 1957
109 Nottingham . 1966
165 The Oval.... 1966
118 Port-of-Spain 1967-68
A. W. Greig (3)
148 Bridgetown.. 1973-74
121 Georgetown . 1973-74
116 Leeds 1976
S. C. Griffith (1)
140† Port-of-Spain 1947-48
W. R. Hammond (1)
138 The Oval.... 1939
J. H. Hampshire (1)
107† Lord's...... 1969
F. C. Hayes (1)
106*† The Oval.... 1973
E. H. Hendren (2)
205* Port-of-Spain 1929-30
123 Georgetown . 1929-30
J. B. Hobbs (1)
159 The Oval.... 1928
L. Hutton (5)
196† Lord's...... 1939
165* The Oval.... 1939
202*‡ The Oval.... 1950
169 Georgetown . 1953-54
205 Kingston.... 1953-54
R. Illingworth (1)
113 Lord's...... 1969
D. R. Jardine (1)
127 Manchester.. 1933
A. P. E. Knott (1)
116 Leeds 1976
A. J. Lamb (6)
110 Lord's...... 1984
100 Leeds 1984
100* Manchester.. 1984
113 Lord's...... 1988
132 Kingston.... 1989-90
119 Bridgetown.. 1989-90

P. B. H. May (3)
135 Port-of-Spain 1953-54
285* Birmingham . 1957
104 Nottingham . 1957
C. Milburn (1)
126* Lord's...... 1966
J. T. Murray (1)
112† The Oval.... 1966
J. M. Parks (1)
101*† Port-of-Spain 1959-60
W. Place (1)
107 Kingston.... 1947-48
P. E. Richardson (2)
126 Nottingham . 1957
107 The Oval.... 1957
J. D. Robertson (1)
133 Port-of-Spain 1947-48
A. Sandham (2)
152† Bridgetown.. 1929-30
325 Kingston.... 1929-30
M. J. K. Smith (1)
108 Port-of-Spain 1959-60
R. A. Smith (3)
148* Lord's...... 1991
109 The Oval ... 1991
175 St John's.... 1993-94
D. S. Steele (1)
106† Nottingham . 1976
A. J. Stewart (2)
118 }
143 } Bridgetown.. 1993-94
R. Subba Row (1)
100† Georgetown . 1959-60
E. Tyldesley (1)
122† Lord's...... 1928
C. Washbrook (2)
114† Lord's...... 1950
102 Nottingham . 1950
W. Watson (1)
116† Kingston.... 1953-54
P. Willey (2)
100* The Oval.... 1980
102* St John's.... 1980-81

For West Indies (103)

J. C. Adams (1)		
137	Georgetown	1993-94
K. L. T. Arthurton (1)		
126	Kingston	1993-94
I. Barrow (1)		
105	Manchester	1933
C. A. Best (1)		
164	Bridgetown	1989-90
B. F. Butcher (2)		
133	Lord's	1963
209*	Nottingham	1966
G. M. Carew (1)		
107	Port-of-Spain	1947-48
C. A. Davis (1)		
103	Lord's	1969
P. J. L. Dujon (1)		
101	Manchester	1984
R. C. Fredericks (3)		
150	Birmingham	1973
138	Lord's	1976
109	Leeds	1976
A. G. Ganteaume (1)		
112†	Port-of-Spain	1947-48
H. A. Gomes (2)		
143	Birmingham	1984
104*	Leeds	1984
C. G. Greenidge (7)		
134 } 101 }	Manchester	1976
115	Leeds	1976
214*	Lord's	1984
223	Manchester	1984
103	Lord's	1988
149	St John's	1989-90
D. L. Haynes (5)		
184	Lord's	1980
125	The Oval	1984
131	St John's	1985-86
109	Bridgetown	1989-90
167	St John's	1989-90
G. A. Headley (8)		
176†	Bridgetown	1929-30
114 } 112 }	Georgetown	1929-30
223	Kingston	1929-30
169*	Manchester	1933
270*	Kingston	1934-35
106 } 107 }	Lord's	1939
D. A. J. Holford (1)		
105*	Lord's	1966
J. K. Holt (1)		
166	Bridgetown	1953-54
C. L. Hooper (1)		
111	Lord's	1991
C. C. Hunte (3)		
182	Manchester	1963
108*	The Oval	1963
135	Manchester	1966
B. D. Julien (1)		
121	Lord's	1973
A. I. Kallicharran (2)		
158	Port-of-Spain	1973-74
119	Bridgetown	1973-74
R. B. Kanhai (5)		
110	Port-of-Spain	1959-60
104	The Oval	1966
153	Port-of-Spain	1967-68
150	Georgetown	1967-68
157	Lord's	1973
B. C. Lara (2)		
167	Georgetown	1993-94
375	St John's	1993-94
C. H. Lloyd (5)		
118†	Port-of-Spain	1967-68
113*	Bridgetown	1967-68
132	The Oval	1973
101	Manchester	1980
100	Bridgetown	1980-81
S. M. Nurse (2)		
137	Leeds	1966
136	Port-of-Spain	1967-68
A. F. Rae (2)		
106	Lord's	1950
109	The Oval	1950
I. V. A. Richards (8)		
232†	Nottingham	1976
135	Manchester	1976
291	The Oval	1976
145	Lord's	1980
182*	Bridgetown	1980-81
114	St John's	1980-81
117	Birmingham	1984
110*	St John's	1985-86
R. B. Richardson (4)		
102	Port-of-Spain	1985-86
160	Bridgetown	1985-86
104	Birmingham	1991
121	The Oval	1991
C. A. Roach (2)		
122	Bridgetown	1929-30
209	Georgetown	1929-30
L. G. Rowe (3)		
120	Kingston	1973-74
302	Bridgetown	1973-74
123	Port-of-Spain	1973-74
O. G. Smith (2)		
161†	Birmingham	1957
168	Nottingham	1957
G. S. Sobers (10)		
226	Bridgetown	1959-60
147	Kingston	1959-60
145	Georgetown	1959-60
102	Leeds	1963
161	Manchester	1966
163*	Lord's	1966
174	Leeds	1966
113*	Kingston	1967-68
152	Georgetown	1967-68
150*	Lord's	1973
C. L. Walcott (4)		
168*	Lord's	1950
220	Bridgetown	1953-54
124	Port-of-Spain	1953-54
116	Kingston	1953-54
E. D. Weekes (3)		
141	Kingston	1947-48
129	Nottingham	1950
206	Port-of-Spain	1953-54
K. H. Weekes (1)		
137	The Oval	1939
F. M. M. Worrell (6)		
131*	Georgetown	1947-48
261	Nottingham	1950
138	The Oval	1950
167	Port-of-Spain	1953-54
191*‡	Nottingham	1957
197*	Bridgetown	1959-60

† *Signifies hundred on first appearance in England–West Indies Tests. S. C. Griffith provides the only instance for England of a player hitting his maiden century in first-class cricket in his first Test.*
‡ *Carried his bat.*

RECORD PARTNERSHIPS FOR EACH WICKET

For England

212	for 1st	C. Washbrook and R. T. Simpson at Nottingham	1950
266	for 2nd	P. E. Richardson and T. W. Graveney at Nottingham	1957
303	for 3rd	M. A. Atherton and R. A. Smith at St John's	1993-94
411	for 4th†	P. B. H. May and M. C. Cowdrey at Birmingham	1957

150	for 5th	A. J. Stewart and G. P. Thorpe at Bridgetown	1993-94
163	for 6th	A. W. Greig and A. P. E. Knott at Bridgetown	1973-74
197	for 7th†	M. J. K. Smith and J. M. Parks at Port-of-Spain	1959-60
217	for 8th	T. W. Graveney and J. T. Murray at The Oval	1966
109	for 9th	G. A. R. Lock and P. I. Pocock at Georgetown	1967-68
128	for 10th	K. Higgs and J. A. Snow at The Oval	1966

For West Indies

298	for 1st†	C. G. Greenidge and D. L. Haynes at St John's	1989-90
287*	for 2nd	C. G. Greenidge and H. A. Gomes at Lord's	1984
338	for 3rd†	E. D. Weekes and F. M. M. Worrell at Port-of-Spain	1953-54
399	for 4th†	G. S. Sobers and F. M. M. Worrell at Bridgetown	1959-60
265	for 5th†	S. M. Nurse and G. S. Sobers at Leeds	1966
274*	for 6th†	G. S. Sobers and D. A. J. Holford at Lord's	1966
155*	for 7th‡	G. S. Sobers and B. D. Julien at Lord's	1973
99	for 8th	C. A. McWatt and J. K. Holt at Georgetown	1953-54
150	for 9th	E. A. E. Baptiste and M. A. Holding at Birmingham	1984
67*	for 10th	M. A. Holding and C. E. H. Croft at St John's	1980-81

† *Denotes record partnership against all countries.*
‡ *231 runs were added for this wicket in two separate partnerships: G. S. Sobers retired ill and was replaced by K. D. Boyce when 155 had been added.*

TEN WICKETS OR MORE IN A MATCH

For England (11)

11-98 (7-44, 4-54)	T. E. Bailey, Lord's	1957
10-93 (5-54, 5-39)	A. P. Freeman, Manchester	1928
13-156 (8-86, 5-70)	A. W. Greig, Port-of-Spain	1973-74
11-48 (5-28, 6-20)	G. A. R. Lock, The Oval	1957
10-137 (4-60, 6-77)	D. E. Malcolm, Port-of-Spain	1989-90
11-96 (5-37, 6-59)†	C. S. Marriott, The Oval	1933
10-142 (4-82, 6-60)	J. A. Snow, Georgetown	1967-68
10-195 (5-105, 5-90)†	G. T. S. Stevens, Bridgetown	1929-30
11-152 (6-100, 5-52)	F. S. Trueman, Lord's	1963
12-119 (5-75, 7-44)	F. S. Trueman, Birmingham	1963
11-149 (4-79, 7-70)	W. Voce, Port-of-Spain	1929-30

For West Indies (13)

10-127 (2-82, 8-45)	C. E. L. Ambrose, Bridgetown	1989-90
11-84 (5-60, 6-24)	C. E. L. Ambrose, Port-of-Spain	1993-94
11-147 (5-70, 6-77)†	K. D. Boyce, The Oval	1973
11-229 (5-137, 6-92)	W. Ferguson, Port-of-Spain	1947-48
11-157 (5-59, 6-98)†	L. R. Gibbs, Manchester	1963
10-106 (5-37, 5-69)	L. R. Gibbs, Manchester	1966
14-149 (8-92, 6-57)	M. A. Holding, The Oval	1976
10-96 (5-41, 5-55)†	H. H. H. Johnson, Kingston	1947-48
10-92 (6-32, 4-60)	M. D. Marshall, Lord's	1988
11-152 (5-66, 6-86)	S. Ramadhin, Lord's	1950
10-123 (5-60, 5-63)	A. M. E. Roberts, Lord's	1976
11-204 (8-104, 3-100)†	A. L. Valentine, Manchester	1950
10-160 (4-121, 6-39)	A. L. Valentine, The Oval	1950

† *Signifies ten wickets or more on first appearance in England–West Indies Tests.*

Note: F. S. Trueman took ten wickets or more in successive matches.

ENGLAND v NEW ZEALAND

	Captains					
Season	*England*	*New Zealand*	*T*	*E*	*NZ*	*D*
1929-30	A. H. H. Gilligan	T. C. Lowry	4	1	0	3
1931	D. R. Jardine	T. C. Lowry	3	1	0	2
1932-33	D. R. Jardine[1]	M. L. Page	2	0	0	2
1937	R. W. V. Robins	M. L. Page	3	1	0	2
1946-47	W. R. Hammond	W. A. Hadlee	1	0	0	1
1949	F. G. Mann[2]	W. A. Hadlee	4	0	0	4
1950-51	F. R. Brown	W. A. Hadlee	2	1	0	1
1954-55	L. Hutton	G. O. Rabone	2	2	0	0
1958	P. B. H. May	J. R. Reid	5	4	0	1
1958-59	P. B. H. May	J. R. Reid	2	1	0	1
1962-63	E. R. Dexter	J. R. Reid	3	3	0	0
1965	M. J. K. Smith	J. R. Reid	3	3	0	0
1965-66	M. J. K. Smith	B. W. Sinclair[3]	3	0	0	3
1969	R. Illingworth	G. T. Dowling	3	2	0	1
1970-71	R. Illingworth	G. T. Dowling	2	1	0	1
1973	R. Illingworth	B. E. Congdon	3	2	0	1
1974-75	M. H. Denness	B. E. Congdon	2	1	0	1
1977-78	G. Boycott	M. G. Burgess	3	1	1	1
1978	J. M. Brearley	M. G. Burgess	3	3	0	0
1983	R. G. D. Willis	G. P. Howarth	4	3	1	0
1983-84	R. G. D. Willis	G. P. Howarth	3	0	1	2
1986	M. W. Gatting	J. V. Coney	3	0	1	2
1987-88	M. W. Gatting	J. J. Crowe[4]	3	0	0	3
1990	G. A. Gooch	J. G. Wright	3	1	0	2
1991-92	G. A. Gooch	M. D. Crowe	3	2	0	1
1994	M. A. Atherton	K. R. Rutherford	3	1	0	2
	In New Zealand		35	13	2	20
	In England		40	21	2	17
	Totals		75	34	4	37

Notes: The following deputised for the official touring captain or were appointed by the home authority for only a minor proportion of the series:

[1]R. E. S. Wyatt (Second). [2]F. R. Brown (Third and Fourth). [3]M. E. Chapple (First). [4]J. G. Wright (Third).

HIGHEST INNINGS TOTALS

For England in England: 567-8 dec. at Nottingham 1994
in New Zealand: 593-6 dec. at Auckland 1974-75

For New Zealand in England: 551-9 dec. at Lord's 1973
in New Zealand: 537 at Wellington 1983-84

LOWEST INNINGS TOTALS

For England in England: 158 at Birmingham 1990
in New Zealand: 64 at Wellington 1977-78

For New Zealand in England: 47 at Lord's 1958
in New Zealand: 26 at Auckland 1954-55

INDIVIDUAL HUNDREDS

For England (79)

Score	Venue	Season
G. O. B. Allen (1)		
122†	Lord's	1931
L. E. G. Ames (2)		
137†	Lord's	1931
103	Christchurch	1932-33
D. L. Amiss (2)		
138*†	Nottingham	1973
164*	Christchurch	1974-75
M. A. Atherton (3)		
151†	Nottingham	1990
101	Nottingham	1994
111	Manchester	1994
T. E. Bailey (1)		
134*	Christchurch	1950-51
K. F. Barrington (3)		
126†	Auckland	1962-63
137	Birmingham	1965
163	Leeds	1965
I. T. Botham (3)		
103	Christchurch	1977-78
103	Nottingham	1983
138	Wellington	1983-84
E. H. Bowley (1)		
109	Auckland	1929-30
G. Boycott (2)		
115	Leeds	1973
131	Nottingham	1978
B. C. Broad (1)		
114†	Christchurch	1987-88
D. C. S. Compton (2)		
114	Leeds	1949
116	Lord's	1949
M. C. Cowdrey (2)		
128*	Wellington	1962-63
119	Lord's	1965
M. H. Denness (1)		
181	Auckland	1974-75
E. R. Dexter (1)		
141	Christchurch	1958-59
B. L. D'Oliveira (1)		
100	Christchurch	1970-71
K. S. Duleepsinhji (2)		
117	Auckland	1929-30
109	The Oval	1931
J. H. Edrich (3)		
310*†	Leeds	1965
115	Lord's	1969
155	Nottingham	1969
W. J. Edrich (1)		
100	The Oval	1949
K. W. R. Fletcher (2)		
178	Lord's	1973
216	Auckland	1974-75
G. Fowler (1)		
105†	The Oval	1983
M. W. Gatting (1)		
121	The Oval	1986
G. A. Gooch (4)		
183	Lord's	1986
154	Birmingham	1990
114	Auckland	1991-92
210	Nottingham	1994
D. I. Gower (4)		
111†	The Oval	1978
112*	Leeds	1983
108	Lord's	1983
131	The Oval	1986
A. W. Greig (1)		
139†	Nottingham	1973
W. R. Hammond (4)		
100*	The Oval	1931
227	Christchurch	1932-33
336*	Auckland	1932-33
140	Lord's	1937
J. Hardstaff jun. (2)		
114†	Lord's	1937
103	The Oval	1937
L. Hutton (3)		
100	Manchester	1937
101	Leeds	1949
206	The Oval	1949
B. R. Knight (1)		
125†	Auckland	1962-63
A. P. E. Knott (1)		
101	Auckland	1970-71
A. J. Lamb (3)		
102*†	The Oval	1983
137*	Nottingham	1983
142	Wellington	1991-92
G. B. Legge (1)		
196	Auckland	1929-30
P. B. H. May (3)		
113*	Leeds	1958
101	Manchester	1958
124*	Auckland	1958-59
C. A. Milton (1)		
104*†	Leeds	1958
P. H. Parfitt (1)		
131*†	Auckland	1962-63
C. T. Radley (1)		
158	Auckland	1977-78
D. W. Randall (2)		
164	Wellington	1983-84
104	Auckland	1983-84
P. E. Richardson (1)		
100†	Birmingham	1958
J. D. Robertson (1)		
121†	Lord's	1949
P. J. Sharpe (1)		
111	Nottingham	1969
R. T. Simpson (1)		
103†	Manchester	1949
A. J. Stewart (3)		
148	Christchurch	1991-92
107	Wellington	1991-92
119	Lord's	1994
H. Sutcliffe (2)		
117†	The Oval	1931
109*	Manchester	1931
C. J. Tavaré (1)		
109†	The Oval	1983
C. Washbrook (1)		
103*	Leeds	1949

For New Zealand (38)

Score	Venue	Season
J. G. Bracewell (1)		
110	Nottingham	1986
M. G. Burgess (2)		
104	Auckland	1970-71
105	Lord's	1973
J. V. Coney (1)		
174*	Wellington	1983-84
B. E. Congdon (3)		
104	Christchurch	1965-66
176	Nottingham	1973
175	Lord's	1973
J. J. Crowe (1)		
128	Auckland	1983-84
M. D. Crowe (5)		
100	Wellington	1983-84
106	Lord's	1986
143	Wellington	1987-88
142	Lord's	1994
115	Manchester	1994
C. S. Dempster (2)		
136	Wellington	1929-30
120	Lord's	1931
M. P. Donnelly (1)		
206	Lord's	1949
T. J. Franklin (1)		
101	Lord's	1990
M. J. Greatbatch (1)		
107*†	Auckland	1987-88
W. A. Hadlee (1)		
116	Christchurch	1946-47
G. P. Howarth (3)		
122 102	Auckland	1977-78
123	Lord's	1978
A. H. Jones (1)		
143	Wellington	1991-92

J. E. Mills (1)
117† Wellington . . 1929-30
M. L. Page (1)
104 Lord's 1931
J. M. Parker (1)
121 Auckland . . . 1974-75
V. Pollard (2)
116 Nottingham . 1973
105* Lord's 1973

J. R. Reid (1)
100 Christchurch. 1962-63
K. R. Rutherford (1)
107* Wellington . . 1987-88
B. W. Sinclair (1)
114 Auckland . . . 1965-66
I. D. S. Smith (1)
113* Auckland . . . 1983-84

B. Sutcliffe (2)
101 Manchester . . 1949
116 Christchurch. 1950-51
J. G. Wright (4)
130 Auckland . . . 1983-84
119 The Oval 1986
103 Auckland . . . 1987-88
116 Wellington . . 1991-92

† *Signifies hundred on first appearance in England–New Zealand Tests.*

RECORD PARTNERSHIPS FOR EACH WICKET

For England

223	for 1st	G. Fowler and C. J. Tavaré at The Oval	1983
369	for 2nd	J. H. Edrich and K. F. Barrington at Leeds	1965
245	for 3rd	W. R. Hammond and J. Hardstaff jun. at Lord's	1937
266	for 4th	M. H. Denness and K. W. R. Fletcher at Auckland	1974-75
242	for 5th	W. R. Hammond and L. E. G. Ames at Christchurch	1932-33
240	for 6th†	P. H. Parfitt and B. R. Knight at Auckland	1962-63
149	for 7th	A. P. E. Knott and P. Lever at Auckland	1970-71
246	for 8th†	L. E. G. Ames and G. O. B. Allen at Lord's	1931
163*	for 9th†	M. C. Cowdrey and A. C. Smith at Wellington	1962-63
59	for 10th	A. P. E. Knott and N. Gifford at Nottingham	1973

For New Zealand

276	for 1st	C. S. Dempster and J. E. Mills at Wellington	1929-30
241	for 2nd†	J. G. Wright and A. H. Jones at Wellington	1991-92
210	for 3rd	B. A. Edgar and M. D. Crowe at Lord's	1986
155	for 4th	M. D. Crowe and M. J. Greatbatch at Wellington	1987-88
180	for 5th	M. D. Crowe and S. A. Thomson at Lord's	1994
141	for 6th	M. D. Crowe and A. C. Parore at Manchester	1994
117	for 7th	D. N. Patel and C. L. Cairns at Christchurch	1991-92
104	for 8th	D. A. R. Moloney and A. W. Roberts at Lord's	1937
118	for 9th	J. V. Coney and B. L. Cairns at Wellington	1983-84
57	for 10th	F. L. H. Mooney and J. Cowie at Leeds	1949

† *Denotes record partnership against all countries.*

TEN WICKETS OR MORE IN A MATCH

For England (8)

11-140 (6-101, 5-39)	I. T. Botham, Lord's	1978
10-149 (5-98, 5-51)	A. W. Greig, Auckland	1974-75
11-65 (4-14, 7-51)	G. A. R. Lock, Leeds	1958
11-84 (5-31, 6-53)	G. A. R. Lock, Christchurch	1958-59
11-147 (4-100, 7-47)†	P. C. R. Tufnell, Christchurch	1991-92
11-70 (4-38, 7-32)†	D. L. Underwood, Lord's	1969
12-101 (6-41, 6-60)	D. L. Underwood, The Oval	1969
12-97 (6-12, 6-85)	D. L. Underwood, Christchurch	1970-71

For New Zealand (5)

10-144 (7-74, 3-70)	B. L. Cairns, Leeds	1983
10-140 (4-73, 6-67)	J. Cowie, Manchester	1937
10-100 (4-74, 6-26)	R. J. Hadlee, Wellington	1977-78
10-140 (6-80, 4-60)	R. J. Hadlee, Nottingham	1986
11-169 (6-76, 5-93)	D. J. Nash, Lord's	1994

† *Signifies ten wickets or more on first appearance in England–New Zealand Tests.*

Note: D. L. Underwood took 12 wickets in successive matches against New Zealand in 1969 and 1970-71.

HAT-TRICK AND FOUR WICKETS IN FIVE BALLS

M. J. C. Allom, in his first Test match, v New Zealand at Christchurch in 1929-30, dismissed C. S. Dempster, T. C. Lowry, K. C. James, and F. T. Badcock to take four wickets in five balls (w-www).

ENGLAND v INDIA

	Captains					
Season	*England*	*India*	*T*	*E*	*I*	*D*
1932	D. R. Jardine	C. K. Nayudu	1	1	0	0
1933-34	D. R. Jardine	C. K. Nayudu	3	2	0	1
1936	G. O. B. Allen	Maharaj of Vizianagram	3	2	0	1
1946	W. R. Hammond	Nawab of Pataudi sen.	3	1	0	2
1951-52	N. D. Howard[1]	V. S. Hazare	5	1	1	3
1952	L. Hutton	V. S. Hazare	4	3	0	1
1959	P. B. H. May[2]	D. K. Gaekwad[3]	5	5	0	0
1961-62	E. R. Dexter	N. J. Contractor	5	0	2	3
1963-64	M. J. K. Smith	Nawab of Pataudi jun.	5	0	0	5
1967	D. B. Close	Nawab of Pataudi jun.	3	3	0	0
1971	R. Illingworth	A. L. Wadekar	3	0	1	2
1972-73	A. R. Lewis	A. L. Wadekar	5	1	2	2
1974	M. H. Denness	A. L. Wadekar	3	3	0	0
1976-77	A. W. Greig	B. S. Bedi	5	3	1	1
1979	J. M. Brearley	S. Venkataraghavan	4	1	0	3
1979-80	J. M. Brearley	G. R. Viswanath	1	1	0	0
1981-82	K. W. R. Fletcher	S. M. Gavaskar	6	0	1	5
1982	R. G. D. Willis	S. M. Gavaskar	3	1	0	2
1984-85	D. I. Gower	S. M. Gavaskar	5	2	1	2
1986	M. W. Gatting[4]	Kapil Dev	3	0	2	1
1990	G. A. Gooch	M. Azharuddin	3	1	0	2
1992-93	G. A. Gooch[5]	M. Azharuddin	3	0	3	0
	In England		38	21	3	14
	In India		43	10	11	22
	Totals		81	31	14	36

Notes: The 1932 Indian touring team was captained by the Maharaj of Porbandar but he did not play in the Test match.

The following deputised for the official touring captain or were appointed by the home authority for only a minor proportion of the series:

[1]D. B. Carr (Fifth). [2]M. C. Cowdrey (Fourth and Fifth). [3]Pankaj Roy (Second). [4]D. I. Gower (First). [5]A. J. Stewart (Second).

HIGHEST INNINGS TOTALS

For England in England: 653-4 dec. at Lord's 1990
in India: 652-7 dec. at Madras.......... 1984-85

For India in England: 606-9 dec. at The Oval 1990
in India: 591 at Bombay 1992-93

LOWEST INNINGS TOTALS

For England in England: 101 at The Oval 1971
in India: 102 at Bombay.......... 1981-82

For India in England: 42 at Lord's 1974
in India: 83 at Madras 1976-77

INDIVIDUAL HUNDREDS

For England (72)

D. L. Amiss (2)
188 Lord's 1974
179 Delhi 1976-77
M. A. Atherton (1)
131 Manchester 1990
K. F. Barrington (3)
151* Bombay 1961-62
172 Kanpur 1961-62
113* Delhi 1961-62
I. T. Botham (5)
137 Leeds 1979
114 Bombay 1979-80
142 Kanpur 1981-82
128 Manchester 1982
208 The Oval 1982
G. Boycott (4)
246*† Leeds 1967
155 Birmingham 1979
125 The Oval 1979
105 Delhi 1981-82
M. C. Cowdrey (3)
160 Leeds 1959
107 Calcutta 1963-64
151 Delhi 1963-64
M. H. Denness (2)
118 Lord's 1974
100 Birmingham 1974
E. R. Dexter (1)
126* Kanpur 1961-62
B. L. D'Oliveira (1)
109† Leeds 1967
J. H. Edrich (1)
100* Manchester 1974
T. G. Evans (1)
104 Lord's 1952
K. W. R. Fletcher (2)
113 Bombay 1972-73
123* Manchester 1974
G. Fowler (1)
201 Madras 1984-85
M. W. Gatting (3)
136 Bombay 1984-85
207 Madras 1984-85
183* Birmingham 1986
G. A. Gooch (5)
127 Madras 1981-82
114 Lord's 1986
333 }
123 } Lord's 1990
116 Manchester 1990
D. I. Gower (2)
200*† Birmingham 1979
157* The Oval 1990
T. W. Graveney (2)
175† Bombay 1951-52
151 Lord's 1967
A. W. Greig (3)
148 Bombay 1972-73
106 Lord's 1974
103 Calcutta 1976-77
W. R. Hammond (2)
167 Manchester 1936
217 The Oval 1936
J. Hardstaff jun. (1)
205* Lord's 1946
G. A. Hick (1)
178 Bombay 1992-93
L. Hutton (2)
150 Lord's 1952
104 Manchester 1952
R. Illingworth (1)
107 Manchester 1971
B. R. Knight (1)
127 Kanpur 1963-64
A. J. Lamb (3)
107 The Oval 1982
139 Lord's 1990
109 Manchester 1990
A. R. Lewis (1)
125 Kanpur 1972-73
C. C. Lewis (1)
117 Madras 1992-93
D. Lloyd (1)
214* Birmingham 1974
B. W. Luckhurst (1)
101 Manchester 1971
P. B. H. May (1)
106 Nottingham 1959
P. H. Parfitt (1)
121 Kanpur 1963-64
G. Pullar (2)
131 Manchester 1959
119 Kanpur 1961-62
D. W. Randall (1)
126 Lord's 1982
R. T. Robinson (1)
160 Delhi 1984-85
D. S. Sheppard (1)
119 The Oval 1952
M. J. K. Smith (1)
100† Manchester 1959
R. A. Smith (2)
100*† Lord's 1990
121* Manchester 1990
C. J. Tavaré (1)
149 Delhi 1981-82
B. H. Valentine (1)
136† Bombay 1933-34
C. F. Walters (1)
102 Madras 1933-34
A. J. Watkins (1)
137*† Delhi 1951-52
T. S. Worthington (1)
128 The Oval 1936

For India (60)

L. Amarnath (1)
118† Bombay 1933-34
M. Azharuddin (6)
110† Calcutta 1984-85
105 Madras 1984-85
122 Kanpur 1984-85
121 Lord's 1990
179 Manchester 1990
182 Calcutta 1992-93
A. A. Baig (1)
112† Manchester 1959
F. M. Engineer (1)
121 Bombay 1972-73
S. M. Gavaskar (4)
101 Manchester 1974
108 Bombay 1976-77
221 The Oval 1979
172 Bangalore 1981-82
Hanumant Singh (1)
105† Delhi 1963-64
V. S. Hazare (2)
164* Delhi 1951-52
155 Bombay 1951-52
M. L. Jaisimha (2)
127 Delhi 1961-62
129 Calcutta 1963-64
V. G. Kambli (1)
224 Bombay 1992-93
Kapil Dev (2)
116 Kanpur 1981-82
110 The Oval 1990
S. M. H. Kirmani (1)
102 Bombay 1984-85
B. K. Kunderan (2)
192 Madras 1963-64
100 Delhi 1963-64
V. L. Manjrekar (3)
133 Leeds 1952
189* Delhi 1961-62
108 Madras 1963-64
V. Mankad (1)
184 Lord's 1952
V. M. Merchant (3)
114 Manchester 1936
128 The Oval 1946
154 Delhi 1951-52

Mushtaq Ali (1)
112 Manchester.. 1936

R. G. Nadkarni (1)
122* Kanpur..... 1963-64

Nawab of Pataudi jun. (3)
103 Madras..... 1961-62
203* Delhi....... 1963-64
148 Leeds...... 1967

S. M. Patil (1)
129* Manchester.. 1982

D. G. Phadkar (1)
115 Calcutta.... 1951-52

Pankaj Roy (2)
140 Bombay.... 1951-52
111 Madras..... 1951-52

R. J. Shastri (4)
142 Bombay.... 1984-85
111 Calcutta.... 1984-85
100 Lord's...... 1990
187 The Oval... 1990

N. S. Sidhu (1)
106 Madras..... 1992-93

S. R. Tendulkar (2)
119* Manchester.. 1990
165 Madras..... 1992-93

P. R. Umrigar (3)
130* Madras..... 1951-52
118 Manchester.. 1959
147* Kanpur..... 1961-62

D. B. Vengsarkar (5)
103 Lord's...... 1979
157 Lord's...... 1982
137 Kanpur..... 1984-85
126* Lord's...... 1986
102* Leeds...... 1986

G. R. Viswanath (4)
113 Bombay.... 1972-73
113 Lord's...... 1979
107 Delhi....... 1981-82
222 Madras..... 1981-82

Yashpal Sharma (1)
140 Madras..... 1981-82

† *Signifies hundred on first appearance in England–India Tests.*

Notes: G. A. Gooch's match aggregate of 456 (333 and 123) for England at Lord's in 1990 is the record in Test matches and provides the only instance of a batsman scoring a triple-hundred and a hundred in the same first-class match. His 333 is the highest innings in any match at Lord's.

M. Azharuddin scored hundreds in each of his first three Tests.

RECORD PARTNERSHIPS FOR EACH WICKET

For England

225 for 1st	G. A. Gooch and M. A. Atherton at Manchester	1990
241 for 2nd	G. Fowler and M. W. Gatting at Madras	1984-85
308 for 3rd	G. A. Gooch and A. J. Lamb at Lord's	1990
266 for 4th	W. R. Hammond and T. S. Worthington at The Oval	1936
254 for 5th†	K. W. R. Fletcher and A. W. Greig at Bombay	1972-73
171 for 6th	I. T. Botham and R. W. Taylor at Bombay	1979-80
125 for 7th	D. W. Randall and P. H. Edmonds at Lord's	1982
168 for 8th	R. Illingworth and P. Lever at Manchester	1971
83 for 9th	K. W. R. Fletcher and N. Gifford at Madras	1972-73
70 for 10th	P. J. W. Allott and R. G. D. Willis at Lord's	1982

For India

213 for 1st	S. M. Gavaskar and C. P. S. Chauhan at The Oval	1979
192 for 2nd	F. M. Engineer and A. L. Wadekar at Bombay	1972-73
316 for 3rd†‡	G. R. Viswanath and Yashpal Sharma at Madras	1981-82
222 for 4th†	V. S. Hazare and V. L. Manjrekar at Leeds	1952
214 for 5th†	M. Azharuddin and R. J. Shastri at Calcutta	1984-85
130 for 6th	S. M. H. Kirmani and Kapil Dev at The Oval	1982
235 for 7th†	R. J. Shastri and S. M. H. Kirmani at Bombay	1984-85
128 for 8th	R. J. Shastri and S. M. H. Kirmani at Delhi	1981-82
104 for 9th	R. J. Shastri and Madan Lal at Delhi	1981-82
51 for 10th	R. G. Nadkarni and B. S. Chandrasekhar at Calcutta	1963-64
	S. M. H. Kirmani and Chetan Sharma at Madras	1984-85

† *Denotes record partnership against all countries.*

‡ *415 runs were added between the fall of the 2nd and 3rd wickets: D. B. Vengsarkar retired hurt when he and Viswanath had added 99 runs.*

TEN WICKETS OR MORE IN A MATCH

For England (7)

10-78 (5-35, 5-43)†	G. O. B. Allen, Lord's	1936
11-145 (7-49, 4-96)†	A. V. Bedser, Lord's	1946
11-93 (4-41, 7-52)	A. V. Bedser, Manchester	1946
13-106 (6-58, 7-48)	I. T. Botham, Bombay	1979-80
11-163 (6-104, 5-59)†	N. A. Foster, Madras	1984-85
10-70 (7-46, 3-24)†	J. K. Lever, Delhi	1976-77
11-153 (7-49, 4-104)	H. Verity, Madras	1933-34

For India (4)

10-177 (6-105, 4-72)	S. A. Durani, Madras	1961-62
12-108 (8-55, 4-53)	V. Mankad, Madras	1951-52
10-188 (4-130, 6-58)	Chetan Sharma, Birmingham	1986
12-181 (6-64, 6-117)†	L. Sivaramakrishnan, Bombay	1984-85

† *Signifies ten wickets or more on first appearance in England–India Tests.*

Note: A. V. Bedser took 11 wickets in a match in each of the first two Tests of his career.

ENGLAND v PAKISTAN

	Captains					
Season	*England*	*Pakistan*	*T*	*E*	*P*	*D*
1954	L. Hutton[1]	A. H. Kardar	4	1	1	2
1961-62	E. R. Dexter	Imtiaz Ahmed	3	1	0	2
1962	E. R. Dexter[2]	Javed Burki	5	4	0	1
1967	D. B. Close	Hanif Mohammad	3	2	0	1
1968-69	M. C. Cowdrey	Saeed Ahmed	3	0	0	3
1971	R. Illingworth	Intikhab Alam	3	1	0	2
1972-73	A. R. Lewis	Majid Khan	3	0	0	3
1974	M. H. Denness	Intikhab Alam	3	0	0	3
1977-78	J. M. Brearley[3]	Wasim Bari	3	0	0	3
1978	J. M. Brearley	Wasim Bari	3	2	0	1
1982	R. G. D. Willis[4]	Imran Khan	3	2	1	0
1983-84	R. G. D. Willis[5]	Zaheer Abbas	3	0	1	2
1987	M. W. Gatting	Imran Khan	5	0	1	4
1987-88	M. W. Gatting	Javed Miandad	3	0	1	2
1992	G. A. Gooch	Javed Miandad	5	1	2	2
	In England		34	13	5	16
	In Pakistan		18	1	2	15
	Totals		52	14	7	31

Notes: The following deputised for the official touring captain or were appointed by the home authority for only a minor proportion of the series:

[1]D. S. Sheppard (Second and Third). [2]M. C. Cowdrey (Third). [3]G. Boycott (Third). [4]D. I. Gower (Second). [5]D. I. Gower (Second and Third).

HIGHEST INNINGS TOTALS

For England in England:	558-6 dec. at Nottingham	1954
in Pakistan:	546-8 dec. at Faisalabad	1983-84
For Pakistan in England:	708 at The Oval	1987
in Pakistan:	569-9 dec. at Hyderabad	1972-73

LOWEST INNINGS TOTALS

For England	in England: 130 at The Oval	1954
	in Pakistan: 130 at Lahore	1987-88
For Pakistan	in England: 87 at Lord's	1954
	in Pakistan: 191 at Faisalabad	1987-88

INDIVIDUAL HUNDREDS

For England (44)

D. L. Amiss (3)
112 Lahore 1972-73
158 Hyderabad 1972-73
183 The Oval 1974

C. W. J. Athey (1)
123 Lord's 1987

K. F. Barrington (4)
139† Lahore 1961-62
148 Lord's 1967
109* Nottingham 1967
142 The Oval 1967

I. T. Botham (2)
100† Birmingham 1978
108 Lord's 1978

G. Boycott (3)
121* Lord's 1971
112 Leeds 1971
100* Hyderabad 1977-78

B. C. Broad (1)
116 Faisalabad 1987-88

D. C. S. Compton (1)
278 Nottingham 1954

M. C. Cowdrey (3)
159† Birmingham 1962
182 The Oval 1962
100 Lahore 1968-69

E. R. Dexter (2)
205 Karachi 1961-62
172 The Oval 1962

B. L. D'Oliveira (1)
114* Dacca 1968-69

K. W. R. Fletcher (1)
122 The Oval 1974

M. W. Gatting (2)
124 Birmingham 1987
150* The Oval 1987

G. A. Gooch (1)
135 Leeds 1992

D. I. Gower (2)
152 Faisalabad 1983-84
173* Lahore 1983-84

T. W. Graveney (3)
153 Lord's 1962
114 Nottingham 1962
105 Karachi 1968-69

A. P. E. Knott (1)
116 Birmingham 1971

B. W. Luckhurst (1)
108*† Birmingham 1971

C. Milburn (1)
139 Karachi 1968-69

P. H. Parfitt (4)
111 Karachi 1961-62
101* Birmingham 1962
119 Leeds 1962
101* Nottingham 1962

G. Pullar (1)
165 Dacca 1961-62

C. T. Radley (1)
106† Birmingham 1978

D. W. Randall (1)
105 Birmingham 1982

R. T. Robinson (1)
166† Manchester 1987

R. T. Simpson (1)
101 Nottingham 1954

R. A. Smith (1)
127† Birmingham 1992

A. J. Stewart (1)
190† Birmingham 1992

For Pakistan (33)

Aamir Sohail (1)
205 Manchester 1992

Alim-ud-Din (1)
109 Karachi 1961-62

Asif Iqbal (3)
146 The Oval 1967
104* Birmingham 1971
102 Lahore 1972-73

Hanif Mohammad (3)
111 } Dacca 1961-62
104 }
187* Lord's 1967

Haroon Rashid (2)
122† Lahore 1977-78
108 Hyderabad 1977-78

Imran Khan (1)
118 The Oval 1987

Intikhab Alam (1)
138 Hyderabad 1972-73

Javed Burki (3)
138† Lahore 1961-62
140 Dacca 1961-62
101 Lord's 1962

Javed Miandad (2)
260 The Oval 1987
153* Birmingham 1992

Mohsin Khan (2)
200 Lord's 1982
104 Lahore 1983-84

Mudassar Nazar (3)
114† Lahore 1977-78
124 Birmingham 1987
120 Lahore 1987-88

Mushtaq Mohammad (3)
100* Nottingham 1962
100 Birmingham 1971
157 Hyderabad 1972-73

Nasim-ul Ghani (1)
101 Lord's 1962

Sadiq Mohammad (1)
119 Lahore 1972-73

Salim Malik (3)
116 Faisalabad 1983-84
102 The Oval 1987
165 Birmingham 1992

Wasim Raja (1)
112 Faisalabad 1983-84

Zaheer Abbas (2)
274† Birmingham 1971
240 The Oval 1974

† *Signifies hundred on first appearance in England–Pakistan Tests.*

Note: Three batsmen – Majid Khan, Mushtaq Mohammad and D. L. Amiss – were dismissed for 99 at Karachi, 1972-73: the only instance in Test matches.

RECORD PARTNERSHIPS FOR EACH WICKET

For England

198	for 1st	G. Pullar and R. W. Barber at Dacca	1961-62
248	for 2nd	M. C. Cowdrey and E. R. Dexter at The Oval	1962
227	for 3rd	A. J. Stewart and R. A. Smith at Birmingham	1992
188	for 4th	E. R. Dexter and P. H. Parfitt at Karachi	1961-62
192	for 5th	D. C. S. Compton and T. E. Bailey at Nottingham	1954
153*	for 6th	P. H. Parfitt and D. A. Allen at Birmingham	1962
167	for 7th	D. I. Gower and V. J. Marks at Faisalabad	1983-84
99	for 8th	P. H. Parfitt and D. A. Allen at Leeds	1962
76	for 9th	T. W. Graveney and F. S. Trueman at Lord's	1962
79	for 10th	R. W. Taylor and R. G. D. Willis at Birmingham	1982

For Pakistan

173	for 1st	Mohsin Khan and Shoaib Mohammad at Lahore	1983-84
291	for 2nd†	Zaheer Abbas and Mushtaq Mohammad at Birmingham	1971
180	for 3rd	Mudassar Nazar and Haroon Rashid at Lahore	1977-78
322	for 4th	Javed Miandad and Salim Malik at Birmingham	1992
197	for 5th	Javed Burki and Nasim-ul-Ghani at Lord's	1962
145	for 6th	Mushtaq Mohammad and Intikhab Alam at Hyderabad	1972-73
89	for 7th	Ijaz Ahmed and Salim Yousuf at The Oval	1987
130	for 8th†	Hanif Mohammad and Asif Iqbal at Lord's	1967
190	for 9th†	Asif Iqbal and Intikhab Alam at The Oval	1967
62	for 10th	Sarfraz Nawaz and Asif Masood at Leeds	1974

† *Denotes record partnership against all countries.*

TEN WICKETS OR MORE IN A MATCH

For England (2)

11-83 (6-65, 5-18)†	N. G. B. Cook, Karachi	1983-84
13-71 (5-20, 8-51)	D. L. Underwood, Lord's	1974

For Pakistan (6)

10-194 (5-84, 5-110)	Abdul Qadir, Lahore	1983-84
13-101 (9-56, 4-45)	Abdul Qadir, Lahore	1987-88
10-186 (5-88, 5-98)	Abdul Qadir, Karachi	1987-88
10-211 (7-96, 3-115)	Abdul Qadir, The Oval	1987
12-99 (6-53, 6-46)	Fazal Mahmood, The Oval	1954
10-77 (3-37, 7-40)	Imran Khan, Leeds	1987

† *Signifies ten wickets or more on first appearance in England–Pakistan Tests.*

FOUR WICKETS IN FIVE BALLS

C. M. Old, v Pakistan at Birmingham in 1978, dismissed Wasim Raja, Wasim Bari, Iqbal Qasim and Sikander Bakht to take four wickets in five balls (ww-ww).

ENGLAND v SRI LANKA

	Captains					
Season	*England*	*Sri Lanka*	*T*	*E*	*SL*	*D*
1981-82	K. W. R. Fletcher	B. Warnapura	1	1	0	0
1984	D. I. Gower	L. R. D. Mendis	1	0	0	1
1988	G. A. Gooch	R. S. Madugalle	1	1	0	0
1991	G. A. Gooch	P. A. de Silva	1	1	0	0
1992-93	A. J. Stewart	A. Ranatunga	1	0	1	0
	In England		3	2	0	1
	In Sri Lanka		2	1	1	0
	Totals		5	3	1	1

HIGHEST INNINGS TOTALS

For England in England: 429 at Lord's 1988
in Sri Lanka: 380 at Colombo (SSC) 1992-93

For Sri Lanka in England: 491-7 dec. at Lord's 1984
in Sri Lanka: 469 at Colombo (SSC) 1992-93

LOWEST INNINGS TOTALS

For England in England: 282 at Lord's 1991
in Sri Lanka: 223 at Colombo (PSS) 1981-82

For Sri Lanka in England: 194 at Lord's 1988
in Sri Lanka: 175 at Colombo (PSS) 1981-82

INDIVIDUAL HUNDREDS

For England (4)

G. A. Gooch (1)
174 Lord's 1991

A. J. Lamb (1)
107† Lord's 1984

R. A. Smith (1)
128 Colombo (SSC) 1992-93

A. J. Stewart (1)
113*† Lord's 1991

For Sri Lanka (3)

L. R. D. Mendis (1)
111 Lord's 1984

S. A. R. Silva (1)
102*† Lord's 1984

S. Wettimuny (1)
190 Lord's 1984

† *Signifies hundred on first appearance in England–Sri Lanka Tests.*

BEST BOWLING

Best bowling in an innings for England: 7-70 by P. A. J. DeFreitas at Lord's ... 1991
for Sri Lanka: 5-69 by R. J. Ratnayake at Lord's 1991

RECORD PARTNERSHIPS FOR EACH WICKET

For England

78 for 1st	G. A. Gooch and H. Morris at Lord's	1991
139 for 2nd	G. A. Gooch and A. J. Stewart at Lord's	1991
112 for 3rd	R. A. Smith and G. A. Hick at Colombo (SSC)	1992-93
122 for 4th	R. A. Smith and A. J. Stewart at Colombo (SSC)	1992-93

40 for 5th	A. J. Stewart and I. T. Botham at Lord's	1991
87 for 6th	A. J. Lamb and R. M. Ellison at Lord's	1984
63 for 7th	A. J. Stewart and R. C. Russell at Lord's	1991
20 for 8th	J. E. Emburey and P. W. Jarvis at Colombo (SSC)	1992-93
37 for 9th	P. J. Newport and N. A. Foster at Lord's	1988
40 for 10th	J. E. Emburey and D. E. Malcolm at Colombo (SSC)	1992-93

For Sri Lanka

99 for 1st	R. S. Mahanama and U. C. Hathurusinghe at Colombo (SSC)	1992-93
83 for 2nd	B. Warnapura and R. L. Dias at Colombo (PSS)	1981-82
101 for 3rd	S. Wettimuny and R. L. Dias at Lord's	1984
148 for 4th	S. Wettimuny and A. Ranatunga at Lord's	1984
150 for 5th†	S. Wettimuny and L. R. D. Mendis at Lord's	1984
138 for 6th†	S. A. R. Silva and L. R. D. Mendis at Lord's	1984
74 for 7th	U. C. Hathurusinghe and R. J. Ratnayake at Lord's	1991
29 for 8th	R. J. Ratnayake and C. P. H. Ramanayake at Lord's	1991
83 for 9th†	H. P. Tillekeratne and M. Muralitharan at Colombo (SSC)	1992-93
64 for 10th†	J. R. Ratnayeke and G. F. Labrooy at Lord's	1988

† *Denotes record partnership against all countries.*

AUSTRALIA v SOUTH AFRICA

	Captains					
Season	*Australia*	*South Africa*	*T*	*A*	*SA*	*D*
1902-03*S*	J. Darling	H. M. Taberer[1]	3	2	0	1
1910-11*A*	C. Hill	P. W. Sherwell	5	4	1	0
1912*E*	S. E. Gregory	F. Mitchell[2]	3	2	0	1
1921-22*S*	H. L. Collins	H. W. Taylor	3	1	0	2
1931-32*A*	W. M. Woodfull	H. B. Cameron	5	5	0	0
1935-36*S*	V. Y. Richardson	H. F. Wade	5	4	0	1
1949-50*S*	A. L. Hassett	A. D. Nourse	5	4	0	1
1952-53*A*	A. L. Hassett	J. E. Cheetham	5	2	2	1
1957-58*S*	I. D. Craig	C. B. van Ryneveld[3]	5	3	0	2
1963-64*A*	R. B. Simpson[4]	T. L. Goddard	5	1	1	3
1966-67*S*	R. B. Simpson	P. L. van der Merwe	5	1	3	1
1969-70*S*	W. M. Lawry	A. Bacher	4	0	4	0
1993-94*A*	A. R. Border	K. C. Wessels[5]	3	1	1	1
1993-94*S*	A. R. Border	K. C. Wessels	3	1	1	1
	In South Africa		33	16	8	9
	In Australia		23	13	5	5
	In England		3	2	0	1
	Totals		59	31	13	15

S Played in South Africa. A Played in Australia. E Played in England.

Notes: The following deputised for the official touring captain or were appointed by the home authority for only a minor proportion of the series:

[1]J. H. Anderson (Second), E. A. Halliwell (Third). [2]L. J. Tancred (Third). [3]D. J. McGlew (First). [4]R. Benaud (First). [5]W. J. Cronje (Third).

HIGHEST INNINGS TOTALS

For Australia in Australia:	578 at Melbourne	1910-11
in South Africa:	549-7 dec. at Port Elizabeth	1949-50
For South Africa in Australia:	595 at Adelaide	1963-64
in South Africa:	622-9 dec. at Durban	1969-70

LOWEST INNINGS TOTALS

For Australia in Australia: 111 at Sydney 1993-94
in South Africa: 75 at Durban 1949-50

For South Africa in Australia: 36† at Melbourne 1931-32
in South Africa: 85 at Johannesburg 1902-03

† *Scored 45 in the second innings giving the smallest aggregate of 81 (12 extras) in Test cricket.*

INDIVIDUAL HUNDREDS

For Australia (58)

W. W. Armstrong (2)
159*‡ Johannesburg 1902-03
132 Melbourne .. 1910-11
W. Bardsley (3)
132† Sydney 1910-11
121 Manchester.. 1912
164 Lord's 1912
R. Benaud (2)
122 Johannesburg 1957-58
100 Johannesburg 1957-58
B. C. Booth (2)
169† Brisbane 1963-64
102* Sydney 1963-64
D. G. Bradman (4)
226† Brisbane 1931-32
112 Sydney 1931-32
167 Melbourne .. 1931-32
299* Adelaide 1931-32
W. A. Brown (1)
121 Cape Town .. 1935-36
J. W. Burke (1)
189 Cape Town .. 1957-58
A. G. Chipperfield (1)
109† Durban 1935-36
H. L. Collins (1)
203 Johannesburg 1921-22
J. H. Fingleton (3)
112 Cape Town .. 1935-36
108 Johannesburg 1935-36
118 Durban 1935-36
J. M. Gregory (1)
119 Johannesburg 1921-22
R. N. Harvey (8)
178 Cape Town .. 1949-50
151* Durban 1949-50
100 Johannesburg 1949-50
116 Pt Elizabeth . 1949-50
109 Brisbane 1952-53
190 Sydney 1952-53
116 Adelaide 1952-53
205 Melbourne .. 1952-53
A. L. Hassett (3)
112† Johannesburg 1949-50
167 Pt Elizabeth . 1949-50
163 Adelaide 1952-53
C. Hill (3)
142† Johannesburg 1902-03
191 Sydney 1910-11
100 Melbourne .. 1910-11
C. Kelleway (2)
114 Manchester.. 1912
102 Lord's 1912
W. M. Lawry (1)
157 Melbourne .. 1963-64
S. J. E. Loxton (1)
101† Johannesburg 1949-50
C. G. Macartney (2)
137 Sydney 1910-11
116 Durban 1921-22
S. J. McCabe (2)
149 Durban 1935-36
189* Johannesburg 1935-36
C. C. McDonald (1)
154 Adelaide 1952-53
J. Moroney (2)
118 }
101* } Johannesburg 1949-50
A. R. Morris (2)
111 Johannesburg 1949-50
157 Pt Elizabeth . 1949-50
K. E. Rigg (1)
127† Sydney 1931-32
J. Ryder (1)
142 Cape Town .. 1921-22
R. B. Simpson (1)
153 Cape Town .. 1966-67
K. R. Stackpole (1)
134 Cape Town .. 1966-67
M. A. Taylor (1)
170† Melbourne .. 1993-94
V. T. Trumper (2)
159 Melbourne .. 1910-11
214* Adelaide 1910-11
M. E. Waugh (1)
113* Durban 1993-94
S. R. Waugh (1)
164† Adelaide 1993-94
W. M. Woodfull (1)
161 Melbourne .. 1931-32

For South Africa (38)

E. J. Barlow (5)
114† Brisbane 1963-64
109 Melbourne .. 1963-64
201 Adelaide 1963-64
127 Cape Town .. 1969-70
110 Johannesburg 1969-70
K. C. Bland (1)
126 Sydney 1963-64
W. J. Cronje (1)
122 Johannesburg 1993-94
W. R. Endean (1)
162* Melbourne .. 1952-53
G. A. Faulkner (3)
204 Melbourne .. 1910-11
115 Adelaide 1910-11
122* Manchester.. 1912
C. N. Frank (1)
152 Johannesburg 1921-22
A. C. Hudson (1)
102 Cape Town .. 1993-94
B. L. Irvine (1)
102 Pt Elizabeth . 1969-70
D. T. Lindsay (3)
182 Johannesburg 1966-67
137 Durban 1966-67
131 Johannesburg 1966-67
D. J. McGlew (2)
108 Johannesburg 1957-58
105 Durban 1957-58
A. D. Nourse (2)
231 Johannesburg 1935-36
114 Cape Town .. 1949-50
A. W. Nourse (1)
111 Johannesburg 1921-22
R. G. Pollock (5)
122 Sydney 1963-64
175 Adelaide 1963-64
209 Cape Town .. 1966-67
105 Pt Elizabeth . 1966-67
274 Durban 1969-70
B. A. Richards (2)
140 Durban 1969-70
126 Pt Elizabeth . 1969-70
E. A. B. Rowan (1)
143 Durban 1949-50
J. H. Sinclair (2)
101 Johannesburg 1902-03
104 Cape Town .. 1902-03

S. J. Snooke (1)
103 Adelaide 1910-11

K. G. Viljoen (1)
111 Melbourne .. 1931-32

J. H. B. Waite (2)
115 Johannesburg 1957-58
134 Durban 1957-58

J. W. Zulch (2)
105 Adelaide 1910-11
150 Sydney 1910-11

† *Signifies hundred on first appearance in Australia–South Africa Tests.*
‡ *Carried his bat.*

RECORD PARTNERSHIPS FOR EACH WICKET

For Australia

233 for 1st	J. H. Fingleton and W. A. Brown at Cape Town	1935-36
275 for 2nd	C. C. McDonald and A. L. Hassett at Adelaide	1952-53
242 for 3rd	C. Kelleway and W. Bardsley at Lord's	1912
169 for 4th	M. A. Taylor and M. E. Waugh at Melbourne	1993-94
208 for 5th	A. R. Border and S. R. Waugh at Adelaide	1993-94
108 for 6th	S. R. Waugh and I. A. Healy at Cape Town	1993-94
160 for 7th	R. Benaud and G. D. McKenzie at Sydney	1963-64
83 for 8th	A. G. Chipperfield and C. V. Grimmett at Durban	1935-36
78 for 9th	D. G. Bradman and W. J. O'Reilly at Adelaide	1931-32
	K. D. Mackay and I. Meckiff at Johannesburg	1957-58
82 for 10th	V. S. Ransford and W. J. Whitty at Melbourne	1910-11

For South Africa

176 for 1st	D. J. McGlew and T. L. Goddard at Johannesburg	1957-58
173 for 2nd	L. J. Tancred and C. B. Llewellyn at Johannesburg	1902-03
341 for 3rd†	E. J. Barlow and R. G. Pollock at Adelaide	1963-64
206 for 4th	C. N. Frank and A. W. Nourse at Johannesburg	1921-22
129 for 5th	J. H. B. Waite and W. R. Endean at Johannesburg	1957-58
200 for 6th†	R. G. Pollock and H. R. Lance at Durban	1969-70
221 for 7th	D. T. Lindsay and P. L. van der Merwe at Johannesburg	1966-67
124 for 8th†	A. W. Nourse and E. A. Halliwell at Johannesburg	1902-03
85 for 9th	R. G. Pollock and P. M. Pollock at Cape Town	1966-67
53 for 10th	L. A. Stricker and S. J. Pegler at Adelaide	1910-11

† *Denotes record partnership against all countries.*

TEN WICKETS OR MORE IN A MATCH

For Australia (6)

14-199 (7-116, 7-83)	C. V. Grimmett, Adelaide	1931-32
10-88 (5-32, 5-56)	C. V. Grimmett, Cape Town	1935-36
10-110 (3-70, 7-40)	C. V. Grimmett, Johannesburg	1935-36
13-173 (7-100, 6-73)	C. V. Grimmett, Durban	1935-36
11-24 (5-6, 6-18)	H. Ironmonger, Melbourne	1931-32
12-128 (7-56, 5-72)	S. K. Warne, Sydney	1993-94

For South Africa (3)

10-123 (4-80, 6-43)	P. S. de Villiers, Sydney	1993-94
10-116 (5-43, 5-73)	C. B. Llewellyn, Johannesburg	1902-03
13-165 (6-84, 7-81)	H. J. Tayfield, Melbourne	1952-53

Note: C. V. Grimmett took ten wickets or more in three consecutive matches in 1935-36.

AUSTRALIA v WEST INDIES

Captains

Season	*Australia*	*West Indies*	*T*	*A*	*WI*	*T*	*D*
1930-31*A*	W. M. Woodfull	G. C. Grant	5	4	1	0	0
1951-52*A*	A. L. Hassett[1]	J. D. C. Goddard[2]	5	4	1	0	0
1954-55*W*	I. W. Johnson	D. St E. Atkinson[3]	5	3	0	0	2
1960-61*A*	R. Benaud	F. M. M. Worrell	5	2	1	1	1

THE FRANK WORRELL TROPHY

Season	Captains: Australia	West Indies	T	A	WI	T	D	Held by
1964-65*W*	R. B. Simpson	G. S. Sobers	5	1	2	0	2	WI
1968-69*A*	W. M. Lawry	G. S. Sobers	5	3	1	0	1	A
1972-73*W*	I. M. Chappell	R. B. Kanhai	5	2	0	0	3	A
1975-76*A*	G. S. Chappell	C. H. Lloyd	6	5	1	0	0	A
1977-78*W*	R. B. Simpson	A. I. Kallicharran[4]	5	1	3	0	1	WI
1979-80*A*	G. S. Chappell	C. H. Lloyd[5]	3	0	2	0	1	WI
1981-82*A*	G. S. Chappell	C. H. Lloyd	3	1	1	0	1	WI
1983-84*W*	K. J. Hughes	C. H. Lloyd[6]	5	0	3	0	2	WI
1984-85*A*	A. R. Border[7]	C. H. Lloyd	5	1	3	0	1	WI
1988-89*A*	A. R. Border	I. V. A. Richards	5	1	3	0	1	WI
1990-91*W*	A. R. Border	I. V. A. Richards	5	1	2	0	2	WI
1992-93*A*	A. R. Border	R. B. Richardson	5	1	2	0	2	WI
	In Australia		47	22	16	1	8	
	In West Indies		30	8	10	0	12	
	Totals		77	30	26	1	20	

A Played in Australia. W Played in West Indies.

Notes: The following deputised for the official touring captain or were appointed by the home authority for only a minor proportion of the series:

[1]A. R. Morris (Third). [2]J. B. Stollmeyer (Fifth). [3]J. B. Stollmeyer (Second and Third). [4]C. H. Lloyd (First and Second). [5]D. L. Murray (First). [6]I. V. A. Richards (Second). [7]K. J. Hughes (First and Second).

HIGHEST INNINGS TOTALS

For Australia in Australia: 619 at Sydney 1968-69
in West Indies: 758-8 dec. at Kingston 1954-55

For West Indies in Australia: 616 at Adelaide 1968-69
in West Indies: 573 at Bridgetown 1964-65

LOWEST INNINGS TOTALS

For Australia in Australia: 76 at Perth 1984-85
in West Indies: 90 at Port-of-Spain 1977-78

For West Indies in Australia: 78 at Sydney 1951-52
in West Indies: 109 at Georgetown 1972-73

INDIVIDUAL HUNDREDS

For Australia (74)

R. G. Archer (1)
128 Kingston 1954-55
R. Benaud (1)
121 Kingston 1954-55
D. C. Boon (3)
149 Sydney 1988-89
109* Kingston 1990-91
111 Brisbane 1992-93
B. C. Booth (1)
117 Port-of-Spain 1964-65
A. R. Border (3)
126 Adelaide 1981-82
100* Port-of-Spain 1983-84
110 Melbourne .. 1992-93
D. G. Bradman (2)
223 Brisbane 1930-31
152 Melbourne .. 1930-31
G. S. Chappell (5)
106 Bridgetown .. 1972-73
123 }
109* } ‡Brisbane ... 1975-76
182* Sydney 1975-76
124 Brisbane 1979-80
I. M. Chappell (5)
117† Brisbane 1968-69
165 Melbourne .. 1968-69
106* Bridgetown .. 1972-73
109 Georgetown . 1972-73
156 Perth 1975-76
G. J. Cosier (1)
109† Melbourne .. 1975-76
R. M. Cowper (2)
143 Port-of-Spain 1964-65
102 Bridgetown .. 1964-65
J. Dyson (1)
127*† Sydney 1981-82
R. N. Harvey (3)
133 Kingston 1954-55
133 Port-of-Spain 1954-55
204 Kingston 1954-55

A. L. Hassett (2)
132 Sydney 1951-52
102 Melbourne .. 1951-52
A. M. J. Hilditch (1)
113† Melbourne .. 1984-85
K. J. Hughes (2)
130*† Brisbane 1979-80
100* Melbourne .. 1981-82
D. M. Jones (1)
216 Adelaide 1988-89
A. F. Kippax (1)
146† Adelaide 1930-31
W. M. Lawry (4)
210 Bridgetown .. 1964-65
105 Brisbane 1968-69
205 Melbourne .. 1968-69
151 Sydney 1968-69
R. R. Lindwall (1)
118 Bridgetown .. 1954-55
R. B. McCosker (1)
109* Melbourne .. 1975-76
C. C. McDonald (2)
110 Port-of-Spain 1954-55
127 Kingston 1954-55

K. R. Miller (4)
129 Sydney 1951-52
147 Kingston 1954-55
137 Bridgetown .. 1954-55
109 Kingston 1954-55
A. R. Morris (1)
111 Port-of-Spain 1954-55
N. C. O'Neill (1)
181† Brisbane 1960-61
W. B. Phillips (1)
120 Bridgetown .. 1983-84
W. H. Ponsford (2)
183 Sydney 1930-31
109 Brisbane 1930-31
I. R. Redpath (4)
132 Sydney 1968-69
102 Melbourne .. 1975-76
103 Adelaide 1975-76
101 Melbourne .. 1975-76
C. S. Serjeant (1)
124 Georgetown . 1977-78
R. B. Simpson (1)
201 Bridgetown .. 1964-65

K. R. Stackpole (1)
142 Kingston 1972-73
M. A. Taylor (1)
144 St John's 1990-91
P. M. Toohey (1)
122 Kingston 1977-78
A. Turner (1)
136 Adelaide 1975-76
K. D. Walters (6)
118 Sydney 1968-69
110 Adelaide 1968-69
242 } Sydney 1968-69
103 }
102* Bridgetown .. 1972-73
112 Port-of-Spain 1972-73
M. E. Waugh (2)
139* St John's 1990-91
112 Melbourne .. 1992-93
S. R. Waugh (1)
100 Sydney 1992-93
K. C. Wessels (1)
173 Sydney 1984-85
G. M. Wood (2)
126 Georgetown . 1977-78
111 Perth 1988-89

For West Indies (77)

F. C. M. Alexander (1)
108 Sydney 1960-61
K. L. T. Arthurton (1)
157* Brisbane 1992-93
D. St E. Atkinson (1)
219 Bridgetown .. 1954-55
B. F. Butcher (3)
117 Port-of-Spain 1964-65
101 Sydney 1968-69
118 Adelaide 1968-69
C. C. Depeiza (1)
122 Bridgetown .. 1954-55
P. J. L. Dujon (2)
130 Port-of-Spain 1983-84
139 Perth 1984-85
M. L. C. Foster (1)
125† Kingston 1972-73
R. C. Fredericks (1)
169 Perth 1975-76
H. A. Gomes (6)
101† Georgetown . 1977-78
115 Kingston 1977-78
126 Sydney 1981-82
124* Adelaide 1981-82
127 Perth 1984-85
120* Adelaide 1984-85
C. G. Greenidge (4)
120* Georgetown . 1983-84
127 Kingston 1983-84
104 Adelaide 1988-89
226 Bridgetown .. 1990-91

D. L. Haynes (5)
103* Georgetown . 1983-84
145 Bridgetown .. 1983-84
100 Perth 1988-89
143 Sydney 1988-89
111 Georgetown . 1990-91
G. A. Headley (2)
102* Brisbane 1930-31
105 Sydney 1930-31
C. C. Hunte (1)
110 Melbourne .. 1960-61
A. I. Kallicharran (4)
101 Brisbane 1975-76
127 Port-of-Spain 1977-78
126 Kingston 1977-78
106 Adelaide 1979-80
R. B. Kanhai (5)
117 } Adelaide 1960-61
115 }
129 Bridgetown .. 1964-65
121 Port-of-Spain 1964-65
105 Bridgetown .. 1972-73
B. C. Lara (1)
277 Sydney 1992-93
C. H. Lloyd (6)
129† Brisbane 1968-69
178 Georgetown . 1972-73
149 Perth 1975-76
102 Melbourne .. 1975-76
121 Adelaide 1979-80
114 Brisbane 1984-85

F. R. Martin (1)
123* Sydney 1930-31
S. M. Nurse (2)
201 Bridgetown .. 1964-65
137 Sydney 1968-69
I. V. A. Richards (5)
101 Adelaide 1975-76
140 Brisbane 1979-80
178 St John's 1983-84
208 Melbourne .. 1984-85
146 Perth 1988-89
R. B. Richardson (8)
131* Bridgetown .. 1983-84
154 St John's 1983-84
138 Brisbane 1984-85
122 Melbourne .. 1988-89
106 Adelaide 1988-89
104* Kingston 1990-91
182 Georgetown . 1990-91
109 Sydney 1992-93
L. G. Rowe (1)
107 Brisbane 1975-76
P. V. Simmons (1)
110 Melbourne .. 1992-93
O. G. Smith (1)
104† Kingston 1954-55
G. S. Sobers (4)
132 Brisbane 1960-61
168 Sydney 1960-61
110 Adelaide 1968-69
113 Sydney 1968-69

J. B. Stollmeyer (1)
104 Sydney 1951-52

C. L. Walcott (5)
108 Kingston.... 1954-55
126 } Port-of-Spain 1954-55
110 }
155 } Kingston.... 1954-55
110 }

E. D. Weekes (1)
139 Port-of-Spain 1954-55

A. B. Williams (1)
100† Georgetown . 1977-78

F. M. M. Worrell (1)
108 Melbourne .. 1951-52

† *Signifies hundred on first appearance in Australia–West Indies Tests.*
‡ *G. S. Chappell is the only player to score hundreds in both innings of his first Test as captain.*

Note: F. C. M. Alexander and C. C. Depeiza scored the only hundreds of their careers in a Test match.

RECORD PARTNERSHIPS FOR EACH WICKET

For Australia

382 for 1st†	W. M. Lawry and R. B. Simpson at Bridgetown	1964-65
298 for 2nd	W. M. Lawry and I. M. Chappell at Melbourne	1968-69
295 for 3rd†	C. C. McDonald and R. N. Harvey at Kingston	1954-55
336 for 4th	W. M. Lawry and K. D. Walters at Sydney	1968-69
220 for 5th	K. R. Miller and R. G. Archer at Kingston	1954-55
206 for 6th	K. R. Miller and R. G. Archer at Bridgetown	1954-55
134 for 7th	A. K. Davidson and R. Benaud at Brisbane	1960-61
137 for 8th	R. Benaud and I. W. Johnson at Kingston	1954-55
114 for 9th	D. M. Jones and M. G. Hughes at Adelaide	1988-89
97 for 10th	T. G. Hogan and R. M. Hogg at Georgetown	1983-84

For West Indies

250* for 1st	C. G. Greenidge and D. L. Haynes at Georgetown	1983-84
297 for 2nd	D. L. Haynes and R. B. Richardson at Georgetown	1990-91
308 for 3rd	R. B. Richardson and I. V. A. Richards at St John's	1983-84
198 for 4th	L. G. Rowe and A. I. Kallicharran at Brisbane	1975-76
210 for 5th	R. B. Kanhai and M. L. C. Foster at Kingston	1972-73
165 for 6th	R. B. Kanhai and D. L. Murray at Bridgetown	1972-73
347 for 7th†‡	D. St E. Atkinson and C. C. Depeiza at Bridgetown	1954-55
87 for 8th	P. J. L. Dujon and C. E. L. Ambrose at Port-of-Spain	1990-91
122 for 9th	D. A. J. Holford and J. L. Hendriks at Adelaide	1968-69
56 for 10th	J. Garner and C. E. H. Croft at Brisbane	1979-80

† *Denotes record partnership against all countries.*
‡ *Record seventh-wicket partnership in first-class cricket.*

TEN WICKETS OR MORE IN A MATCH

For Australia (11)

11-96 (7-46, 4-50)	A. R. Border, Sydney	1988-89
11-222 (5-135, 6-87)†	A. K. Davidson, Brisbane	1960-61
11-183 (7-87, 4-96)†	C. V. Grimmett, Adelaide	1930-31
10-115 (6-72, 4-43)	N. J. N. Hawke, Georgetown	1964-65
10-144 (6-54, 4-90)	R. G. Holland, Sydney	1984-85
13-217 (5-130, 8-87)	M. G. Hughes, Perth	1988-89
11-79 (7-23, 4-56)	H. Ironmonger, Melbourne	1930-31
11-181 (8-112, 3-69)	G. F. Lawson, Adelaide	1984-85
10-127 (7-83, 3-44)	D. K. Lillee, Melbourne	1981-82
10-159 (8-71, 2-88)	G. D. McKenzie, Melbourne	1968-69
10-185 (3-87, 7-98)	B. Yardley, Sydney	1981-82

For West Indies (4)

10-120 (6-74, 4-46)	C. E. L. Ambrose, Adelaide	1992-93
10-113 (7-55, 3-58)	G. E. Gomez, Sydney	1951-52
11-107 (5-45, 6-62)	M. A. Holding, Melbourne	1981-82
10-107 (5-69, 5-38)	M. D. Marshall, Adelaide	1984-85

† *Signifies ten wickets or more on first appearance in Australia–West Indies Tests.*

AUSTRALIA v NEW ZEALAND

	Captains					
Season	*Australia*	*New Zealand*	*T*	*A*	*NZ*	*D*
1945-46*N*	W. A. Brown	W. A. Hadlee	1	1	0	0
1973-74*A*	I. M. Chappell	B. E. Congdon	3	2	0	1
1973-74*N*	I. M. Chappell	B. E. Congdon	3	1	1	1
1976-77*N*	G. S. Chappell	G. M. Turner	2	1	0	1
1980-81*A*	G. S. Chappell	G. P. Howarth[1]	3	2	0	1
1981-82*N*	G. S. Chappell	G. P. Howarth	3	1	1	1

TRANS-TASMAN TROPHY

	Captains						
Season	*Australia*	*New Zealand*	*T*	*A*	*NZ*	*D*	*Held by*
1985-86*A*	A. R. Border	J. V. Coney	3	1	2	0	NZ
1985-86*N*	A. R. Border	J. V. Coney	3	0	1	2	NZ
1987-88*A*	A. R. Border	J. J. Crowe	3	1	0	2	A
1989-90*A*	A. R. Border	J. G. Wright	1	0	0	1	A
1989-90*N*	A. R. Border	J. G. Wright	1	0	1	0	NZ
1992-93*N*	A. R. Border	M. D. Crowe	3	1	1	1	NZ
1993-94*A*	A. R. Border	M. D. Crowe[2]	3	2	0	1	A
	In Australia		16	8	2	6	
	In New Zealand		16	5	5	6	
	Totals		32	13	7	12	

A Played in Australia. N Played in New Zealand.

Note: The following deputised for the official touring captain: [1]M. G. Burgess (Second). [2]K. R. Rutherford (Second and Third).

HIGHEST INNINGS TOTALS

For Australia in Australia: 607-6 dec. at Brisbane 1993-94
in New Zealand: 552 at Christchurch 1976-77

For New Zealand in Australia: 553-7 dec. at Brisbane 1985-86
in New Zealand: 484 at Wellington 1973-74

LOWEST INNINGS TOTALS

For Australia in Australia: 162 at Sydney 1973-74
in New Zealand: 103 at Auckland 1985-86

For New Zealand in Australia: 121 at Perth 1980-81
in New Zealand: 42 at Wellington 1945-46

INDIVIDUAL HUNDREDS

For Australia (30)

D. C. Boon (3)
143 Brisbane 1987-88
200 Perth 1989-90
106 Hobart 1993-94

A. R. Border (5)
152* Brisbane 1985-86
140 } Christchurch. 1985-86
114* }
205 Adelaide 1987-88
105 Brisbane 1993-94

G. S. Chappell (3)
247* } Wellington .. 1973-74
133 }
176 Christchurch. 1981-82

I. M. Chappell (2)
145 } Wellington .. 1973-74
121 }

G. J. Gilmour (1)
101 Christchurch. 1976-77

I. A. Healy (1)
113* Perth 1993-94

G. R. Marsh (1)
118 Auckland ... 1985-86

R. W. Marsh (1)
132 Adelaide 1973-74

G. R. J. Matthews (2)
115† Brisbane 1985-86
130 Wellington .. 1985-86

I. R. Redpath (1)
159*‡ Auckland ... 1973-74

M. J. Slater (1)
168 Hobart 1993-94

K. R. Stackpole (1)
122† Melbourne .. 1973-74

M. A. Taylor (1)
142* Perth 1993-94

K. D. Walters (3)
104* Auckland ... 1973-74
250 Christchurch. 1976-77
107 Melbourne .. 1980-81

M. E. Waugh (1)
111 Hobart 1993-94

S. R. Waugh (1)
147* Brisbane 1993-94

G. M. Wood (2)
111† Brisbane 1980-81
100 Auckland ... 1981-82

For New Zealand (19)

J. V. Coney (1)
101* Wellington .. 1985-86

B. E. Congdon (2)
132 Wellington .. 1973-74
107* Christchurch. 1976-77

M. D. Crowe (3)
188 Brisbane 1985-86
137 Christchurch. 1985-86
137 Adelaide 1987-88

B. A. Edgar (1)
161 Auckland ... 1981-82

M. J. Greatbatch (1)
146*† Perth 1989-90

B. F. Hastings (1)
101 Wellington .. 1973-74

A. H. Jones (2)
150 Adelaide 1987-88
143 Perth 1993-94

J. F. M. Morrison (1)
117 Sydney 1973-74

J. M. Parker (1)
108 Sydney 1973-74

J. F. Reid (1)
108† Brisbane 1985-86

K. R. Rutherford (1)
102 Christchurch. 1992-93

G. M. Turner (2)
101 } Christchurch. 1973-74
110* }

J. G. Wright (2)
141 Christchurch. 1981-82
117* Wellington .. 1989-90

† *Signifies hundred on first appearance in Australia–New Zealand Tests.*
‡ *Carried his bat.*

Notes: G. S. and I. M. Chappell at Wellington in 1973-74 provide the only instance in Test matches of brothers both scoring a hundred in each innings and in the same Test.

RECORD PARTNERSHIPS FOR EACH WICKET

For Australia

198 for 1st	M. J. Slater and M. A. Taylor at Perth	1993-94
235 for 2nd	M. J. Slater and D. C. Boon at Hobart	1993-94
264 for 3rd	I. M. Chappell and G. S. Chappell at Wellington	1973-74
150 for 4th	M. E. Waugh and A. R. Border at Hobart	1993-94
213 for 5th	G. M. Ritchie and G. R. J. Matthews at Wellington	1985-86
197 for 6th	A. R. Border and G. R. J. Matthews at Brisbane	1985-86
217 for 7th†	K. D. Walters and G. J. Gilmour at Christchurch	1976-77
93 for 8th	G. J. Gilmour and K. J. O'Keeffe at Auckland	1976-77
69 for 9th	I. A. Healy and C. J. McDermott at Perth	1993-94
60 for 10th	K. D. Walters and J. D. Higgs at Melbourne	1980-81

For New Zealand

111	for 1st	M. J. Greatbatch and J. G. Wright at Wellington	1992-93
128*	for 2nd	J. G. Wright and A. H. Jones at Wellington	1989-90
224	for 3rd	J. F. Reid and M. D. Crowe at Brisbane	1985-86
229	for 4th†	B. E. Congdon and B. F. Hastings at Wellington	1973-74
88	for 5th	J. V. Coney and M. G. Burgess at Perth	1980-81
109	for 6th	K. R. Rutherford and J. V. Coney at Wellington	1985-86
132*	for 7th	J. V. Coney and R. J. Hadlee at Wellington	1985-86
88*	for 8th	M. J. Greatbatch and M. C. Snedden at Perth	1989-90
73	for 9th	H. J. Howarth and D. R. Hadlee at Christchurch	1976-77
124	for 10th	J. G. Bracewell and S. L. Boock at Sydney	1985-86

† *Denotes record partnership against all countries.*

TEN WICKETS OR MORE IN A MATCH

For Australia (2)

10-174 (6-106, 4-68)	R. G. Holland, Sydney	1985-86
11-123 (5-51, 6-72)	D. K. Lillee, Auckland	1976-77

For New Zealand (4)

10-106 (4-74, 6-32)	J. G. Bracewell, Auckland	1985-86
15-123 (9-52, 6-71)	R. J. Hadlee, Brisbane	1985-86
11-155 (5-65, 6-90)	R. J. Hadlee, Perth	1985-86
10-176 (5-109, 5-67)	R. J. Hadlee, Melbourne	1987-88

AUSTRALIA v INDIA

	Captains						
Season	*Australia*	*India*	*T*	*A*	*I*	*T*	*D*
1947-48*A*	D. G. Bradman	L. Amarnath	5	4	0	0	1
1956-57*I*	I. W. Johnson[1]	P. R. Umrigar	3	2	0	0	1
1959-60*I*	R. Benaud	G. S. Ramchand	5	2	1	0	2
1964-65*I*	R. B. Simpson	Nawab of Pataudi jun.	3	1	1	0	1
1967-68*A*	R. B. Simpson[2]	Nawab of Pataudi jun.[3]	4	4	0	0	0
1969-70*I*	W. M. Lawry	Nawab of Pataudi jun.	5	3	1	0	1
1977-78*A*	R. B. Simpson	B. S. Bedi	5	3	2	0	0
1979-80*I*	K. J. Hughes	S. M. Gavaskar	6	0	2	0	4
1980-81*A*	G. S. Chappell	S. M. Gavaskar	3	1	1	0	1
1985-86*A*	A. R. Border	Kapil Dev	3	0	0	0	3
1986-87*I*	A. R. Border	Kapil Dev	3	0	0	1	2
1991-92*A*	A. R. Border	M. Azharuddin	5	4	0	0	1
	In Australia		25	16	3	0	6
	In India		25	8	5	1	11
	Totals		50	24	8	1	17

A Played in Australia. I Played in India.

Notes: The following deputised for the official touring captain or were appointed by the home authority for only a minor proportion of the series:

[1]R. R. Lindwall (Second). [2]W. M. Lawry (Third and Fourth). [3]C. G. Borde (First).

HIGHEST INNINGS TOTALS

For Australia in Australia: 674 at Adelaide 1947-48
in India: 574-7 dec. at Madras 1986-87

For India in Australia: 600-4 dec. at Sydney 1985-86
in India: 517-5 dec. at Bombay 1986-87

LOWEST INNINGS TOTALS

For Australia in Australia: 83 at Melbourne 1980-81
in India: 105 at Kanpur 1959-60

For India in Australia: 58 at Brisbane 1947-48
in India: 135 at Delhi 1959-60

INDIVIDUAL HUNDREDS

For Australia (51)

S. G. Barnes (1)
112 Adelaide 1947-48
D. C. Boon (6)
123† Adelaide 1985-86
131 Sydney 1985-86
122 Madras 1986-87
129* Sydney 1991-92
135 Adelaide 1991-92
107 Perth 1991-92
A. R. Border (4)
162† Madras 1979-80
124 Melbourne .. 1980-81
163 Melbourne .. 1985-86
106 Madras 1986-87
D. G. Bradman (4)
185† Brisbane 1947-48
132 }
127* } Melbourne .. 1947-48
201 Adelaide 1947-48
J. W. Burke (1)
161 Bombay 1956-57
G. S. Chappell (1)
204† Sydney 1980-81
I. M. Chappell (2)
151 Melbourne .. 1967-68
138 Delhi 1969-70

R. M. Cowper (2)
108 Adelaide 1967-68
165 Sydney 1967-68
L. E. Favell (1)
101 Madras 1959-60
R. N. Harvey (4)
153 Melbourne .. 1947-48
140 Bombay 1956-57
114 Delhi 1959-60
102 Bombay 1959-60
A. L. Hassett (1)
198* Adelaide 1947-48
K. J. Hughes (2)
100 Madras 1979-80
213 Adelaide 1980-81
D. M. Jones (2)
210† Madras 1986-87
150* Perth 1991-92
W. M. Lawry (1)
100 Melbourne .. 1967-68
A. L. Mann (1)
105 Perth 1977-78
G. R. Marsh (1)
101 Bombay 1986-87
G. R. J. Matthews (1)
100* Melbourne .. 1985-86
T. M. Moody (1)
101† Perth 1991-92

A. R. Morris (1)
100* Melbourne .. 1947-48
N. C. O'Neill (2)
163 Bombay 1959-60
113 Calcutta 1959-60
G. M. Ritchie (1)
128† Adelaide 1985-86
A. P. Sheahan (1)
114 Kanpur 1969-70
R. B. Simpson (4)
103 Adelaide 1967-68
109 Melbourne .. 1967-68
176 Perth 1977-78
100 Adelaide 1977-78
K. R. Stackpole (1)
103† Bombay 1969-70
M. A. Taylor (1)
100 Adelaide 1991-92
K. D. Walters (1)
102 Madras 1969-70
G. M. Wood (1)
125 Adelaide 1980-81
G. N. Yallop (2)
121† Adelaide 1977-78
167 Calcutta 1979-80

For India (35)

M. Amarnath (2)
100 Perth 1977-78
138 Sydney 1985-86
M. Azharuddin (1)
106 Adelaide 1991-92
N. J. Contractor (1)
108 Bombay 1959-60
S. M. Gavaskar (8)
113† Brisbane 1977-78
127 Perth 1977-78
118 Melbourne .. 1977-78
115 Delhi 1979-80
123 Bombay 1979-80
166* Adelaide 1985-86
172 Sydney 1985-86
103 Bombay 1986-87
V. S. Hazare (2)
116, 145 Adelaide 1947-48

M. L. Jaisimha (1)
101 Brisbane 1967-68
Kapil Dev (1)
119 Madras 1986-87
S. M. H. Kirmani (1)
101* Bombay 1979-80
V. Mankad (2)
116 Melbourne .. 1947-48
111 Melbourne .. 1947-48
Nawab of Pataudi jun. (1)
128*† Madras 1964-65
S. M. Patil (1)
174 Adelaide 1980-81
D. G. Phadkar (1)
123 Adelaide 1947-48
G. S. Ramchand (1)
109 Bombay 1956-57

R. J. Shastri (2)
121* Bombay 1986-87
206 Sydney 1991-92
K. Srikkanth (1)
116 Sydney 1985-86
S. R. Tendulkar (2)
148* Sydney 1991-92
114 Perth 1991-92
D. B. Vengsarkar (2)
112 Bangalore ... 1979-80
164* Bombay 1986-87
G. R. Viswanath (4)
137† Kanpur 1969-70
161* Bangalore ... 1979-80
131 Delhi 1979-80
114 Melbourne .. 1980-81
Yashpal Sharma (1)
100* Delhi 1979-80

† *Signifies hundred on first appearance in Australia–India Tests.*

RECORD PARTNERSHIPS FOR EACH WICKET

For Australia

217	for 1st	D. C. Boon and G. R. Marsh at Sydney	1985-86
236	for 2nd	S. G. Barnes and D. G. Bradman at Adelaide	1947-48
222	for 3rd	A. R. Border and K. J. Hughes at Madras	1979-80
178	for 4th	D. M. Jones and A. R. Border at Madras	1986-87
223*	for 5th	A. R. Morris and D. G. Bradman at Melbourne	1947-48
151	for 6th	T. R. Veivers and B. N. Jarman at Bombay	1964-65
66	for 7th	G. R. J. Matthews and R. J. Bright at Melbourne	1985-86
73	for 8th	T. R. Veivers and G. D. McKenzie at Madras	1964-65
87	for 9th	I. W. Johnson and W. P. A. Crawford at Madras	1956-57
77	for 10th	A. R. Border and D. R. Gilbert at Melbourne	1985-86

For India

192	for 1st	S. M. Gavaskar and C. P. S. Chauhan at Bombay	1979-80
224	for 2nd	S. M. Gavaskar and M. Amarnath at Sydney	1985-86
159	for 3rd	S. M. Gavaskar and G. R. Viswanath at Delhi	1979-80
159	for 4th	D. B. Vengsarkar and G. R. Viswanath at Bangalore	1979-80
196	for 5th	R. J. Shastri and S. R. Tendulkar at Sydney	1991-92
298*	for 6th†	D. B. Vengsarkar and R. J. Shastri at Bombay	1986-87
132	for 7th	V. S. Hazare and H. R. Adhikari at Adelaide	1947-48
127	for 8th	S. M. H. Kirmani and K. D. Ghavri at Bombay	1979-80
81	for 9th	S. R. Tendulkar and K. S. More at Perth	1991-92
94	for 10th	S. M. Gavaskar and N. S. Yadav at Adelaide	1985-86

† *Denotes record partnership against all countries.*

TEN WICKETS OR MORE IN A MATCH

For Australia (11)

11-105 (6-52, 5-53)	R. Benaud, Calcutta	1956-57
12-124 (5-31, 7-93)	A. K. Davidson, Kanpur	1959-60

12-166 (5-99, 7-67)	G. Dymock, Kanpur	1979-80
10-168 (5-76, 5-92)	C. J. McDermott, Adelaide	1991-92
10-91 (6-58, 4-33)†	G. D. McKenzie, Madras	1964-65
10-151 (7-66, 3-85)	G. D. McKenzie, Melbourne	1967-68
10-144 (5-91, 5-53)	A. A. Mallett, Madras	1969-70
10-249 (5-103, 5-146)	G. R. J. Matthews, Madras	1986-87
12-126 (6-66, 6-60)	B. A. Reid, Melbourne	1991-92
11-31 (5-2, 6-29)†	E. R. H. Toshack, Brisbane	1947-48
11-95 (4-68, 7-27)	M. R. Whitney, Perth	1991-92

For India (6)

10-194 (5-89, 5-105)	B. S. Bedi, Perth	1977-78
12-104 (6-52, 6-52)	B. S. Chandrasekhar, Melbourne	1977-78
10-130 (7-49, 3-81)	Ghulam Ahmed, Calcutta	1956-57
11-122 (5-31, 6-91)	R. G. Nadkarni, Madras	1964-65
14-124 (9-69, 5-55)	J. M. Patel, Kanpur	1959-60
10-174 (4-100, 6-74)	E. A. S. Prasanna, Madras	1969-70

† *Signifies ten wickets or more on first appearance in Australia–India Tests.*

AUSTRALIA v PAKISTAN

Season	*Captains* *Australia*	*Pakistan*	*T*	*A*	*P*	*D*
1956-57*P*	I. W. Johnson	A. H. Kardar	1	0	1	0
1959-60*P*	R. Benaud	Fazal Mahmood[1]	3	2	0	1
1964-65*P*	R. B. Simpson	Hanif Mohammad	1	0	0	1
1964-65*A*	R. B. Simpson	Hanif Mohammad	1	0	0	1
1972-73*A*	I. M. Chappell	Intikhab Alam	3	3	0	0
1976-77*A*	G. S. Chappell	Mushtaq Mohammad	3	1	1	1
1978-79*A*	G. N. Yallop[2]	Mushtaq Mohammad	2	1	1	0
1979-80*P*	G. S. Chappell	Javed Miandad	3	0	1	2
1981-82*A*	G. S. Chappell	Javed Miandad	3	2	1	0
1982-83*P*	K. J. Hughes	Imran Khan	3	0	3	0
1983-84*A*	K. J. Hughes	Imran Khan[3]	5	2	0	3
1988-89*P*	A. R. Border	Javed Miandad	3	0	1	2
1989-90*A*	A. R. Border	Imran Khan	3	1	0	2
	In Pakistan		14	2	6	6
	In Australia		20	10	3	7
	Totals		34	12	9	13

A Played in Australia. P Played in Pakistan.

Notes: The following deputised for the official touring captain or were appointed by the home authority for only a minor proportion of the series:

[1]Imtiaz Ahmed (Second). [2]K. J. Hughes (Second). [3]Zaheer Abbas (First, Second and Third).

HIGHEST INNINGS TOTALS

For Australia in Australia:	585 at Adelaide	1972-73
in Pakistan:	617 at Faisalabad	1979-80
For Pakistan in Australia:	624 at Adelaide	1983-84
in Pakistan:	501-6 dec. at Faisalabad	1982-83

LOWEST INNINGS TOTALS

For Australia	in Australia: 125 at Melbourne	1981-82
	in Pakistan: 80 at Karachi	1956-57
For Pakistan	in Australia: 62 at Perth	1981-82
	in Pakistan: 134 at Dacca	1959-60

INDIVIDUAL HUNDREDS

For Australia (37)

J. Benaud (1)
142 Melbourne .. 1972-73
A. R. Border (6)
105† Melbourne .. 1978-79
150* } Lahore 1979-80
153 }
118 Brisbane 1983-84
117* Adelaide 1983-84
113* Faisalabad .. 1988-89
G. S. Chappell (6)
116* Melbourne .. 1972-73
121 Melbourne .. 1976-77
235 Faisalabad .. 1979-80
201 Brisbane 1981-82
150* Brisbane 1983-84
182 Sydney 1983-84
I. M. Chappell (1)
196 Adelaide 1972-73
G. J. Cosier (1)
168 Melbourne .. 1976-77
I. C. Davis (1)
105† Adelaide 1976-77
K. J. Hughes (2)
106 Perth....... 1981-82
106 Adelaide 1983-84
D. M. Jones (2)
116 } Adelaide 1989-90
121* }
R. B. McCosker (1)
105 Melbourne... 1976-77
R. W. Marsh (1)
118† Adelaide 1972-73
N. C. O'Neill (1)
134 Lahore...... 1959-60
W. B. Phillips (1)
159† Perth....... 1983-84
I. R. Redpath (1)
135 Melbourne... 1972-73
G. M. Ritchie (1)
106* Faisalabad .. 1982-83
A. P. Sheahan (1)
127 Melbourne .. 1972-73
R. B. Simpson (2)
153 } †Karachi 1964-65
115 }
M. A. Taylor (2)
101† Melbourne .. 1989-90
101* Sydney 1989-90
K. D. Walters (1)
107 Adelaide 1976-77
K. C. Wessels (1)
179 Adelaide 1983-84
G. M. Wood (1)
100 Melbourne .. 1981-82
G. N. Yallop (3)
172 Faisalabad .. 1979-80
141 Perth 1983-84
268 Melbourne .. 1983-84

For Pakistan (31)

Asif Iqbal (3)
152* Adelaide 1976-77
120 Sydney 1976-77
134* Perth....... 1978-79
Hanif Mohammad (2)
101* Karachi 1959-60
104 Melbourne .. 1964-65
Ijaz Ahmed (2)
122 Faisalabad .. 1988-89
121 Melbourne .. 1989-90
Imran Khan (1)
136 Adelaide ... 1989-90
Javed Miandad (6)
129* Perth....... 1978-79
106* Faisalabad .. 1979-80
138 Lahore 1982-83
131 Adelaide 1983-84
211 Karachi 1988-89
107 Faisalabad .. 1988-89
Khalid Ibadulla (1)
166† Karachi 1964-65
Majid Khan (3)
158 Melbourne .. 1972-73
108 Melbourne .. 1978-79
110* Lahore 1979-80
Mansoor Akhtar (1)
111 Faisalabad .. 1982-83
Mohsin Khan (3)
135 Lahore 1982-83
149 Adelaide 1983-84
152 Melbourne .. 1983-84
Mushtaq Mohammad (1)
121 Sydney 1972-73
Qasim Omar (1)
113 Adelaide 1983-84
Sadiq Mohammad (2)
137 Melbourne .. 1972-73
105 Melbourne .. 1976-77
Saeed Ahmed (1)
166 Lahore 1959-60
Taslim Arif (1)
210* Faisalabad .. 1979-80
Wasim Akram (1)
123 Adelaide 1989-90
Zaheer Abbas (2)
101 Adelaide 1976-77
126 Faisalabad .. 1982-83

† *Signifies hundred on first appearance in Australia–Pakistan Tests.*

RECORD PARTNERSHIPS FOR EACH WICKET

For Australia

134 for 1st	I. C. Davis and A. Turner at Melbourne	1976-77
259 for 2nd	W. B. Phillips and G. N. Yallop at Perth	1983-84
203 for 3rd	G. N. Yallop and K. J. Hughes at Melbourne	1983-84
217 for 4th	G. S. Chappell and G. N. Yallop at Faisalabad	1979-80
171 for 5th	G. S. Chappell and G. J. Cosier at Melbourne	1976-77
	A. R. Border and G. S. Chappell at Brisbane	1983-84
139 for 6th	R. M. Cowper and T. R. Veivers at Melbourne	1964-65
185 for 7th	G. N. Yallop and G. R. J. Matthews at Melbourne	1983-84
117 for 8th	G. J. Cosier and K. J. O'Keeffe at Melbourne	1976-77
83 for 9th	J. R. Watkins and R. A. L. Massie at Sydney	1972-73
52 for 10th	D. K. Lillee and M. H. N. Walker at Sydney	1976-77
	G. F. Lawson and T. M. Alderman at Lahore	1982-83

For Pakistan

249 for 1st†	Khalid Ibadulla and Abdul Kadir at Karachi	1964-65
233 for 2nd	Mohsin Khan and Qasim Omar at Adelaide	1983-84
223* for 3rd	Taslim Arif and Javed Miandad at Faisalabad	1979-80
155 for 4th	Mansoor Akhtar and Zaheer Abbas at Faisalabad	1982-83
186 for 5th	Javed Miandad and Salim Malik at Adelaide	1983-84
191 for 6th	Imran Khan and Wasim Akram at Adelaide	1989-90
104 for 7th	Intikhab Alam and Wasim Bari at Adelaide	1972-73
111 for 8th	Majid Khan and Imran Khan at Lahore	1979-80
56 for 9th	Intikhab Alam and Afaq Hussain at Melbourne	1964-65
87 for 10th	Asif Iqbal and Iqbal Qasim at Adelaide	1976-77

† *Denotes record partnership against all countries.*

TEN WICKETS OR MORE IN A MATCH

For Australia (3)

10-111 (7-87, 3-24)†	R. J. Bright, Karachi	1979-80
10-135 (6-82, 4-53)	D. K. Lillee, Melbourne	1976-77
11-118 (5-32, 6-86)†	C. G. Rackemann, Perth	1983-84

For Pakistan (6)

11-218 (4-76, 7-142)	Abdul Qadir, Faisalabad	1982-83
13-114 (6-34, 7-80)†	Fazal Mahmood, Karachi	1956-57
12-165 (6-102, 6-63)	Imran Khan, Sydney	1976-77
11-118 (4-69, 7-49)	Iqbal Qasim, Karachi	1979-80
11-125 (2-39, 9-86)	Sarfraz Nawaz, Melbourne	1978-79
11-160 (6-62, 5-98)†	Wasim Akram, Melbourne	1989-90

† *Signifies ten wickets or more on first appearance in Australia–Pakistan Tests.*

AUSTRALIA v SRI LANKA

	Captains					
Season	*Australia*	*Sri Lanka*	*T*	*A*	*SL*	*D*
1982-83*S*	G. S. Chappell	L. R. D. Mendis	1	1	0	0
1987-88*A*	A. R. Border	R. S. Madugalle	1	1	0	0
1989-90*A*	A. R. Border	A. Ranatunga	2	1	0	1
1992-93*S*	A. R. Border	A. Ranatunga	3	1	0	2
	In Australia		3	2	0	1
	In Sri Lanka		4	2	0	2
	Totals		7	4	0	3

A Played in Australia. S Played in Sri Lanka.

INNINGS TOTALS

Highest innings total for Australia: 514-4 dec. at Kandy 1982-83
for Sri Lanka: 547-8 dec. at Colombo (SSC) 1992-93

Lowest innings total for Australia: 224 at Hobart 1989-90
for Sri Lanka: 153 at Perth 1987-88

INDIVIDUAL HUNDREDS

For Australia (10)

A. R. Border (1)
106 Moratuwa ... 1992-93
118* Hobart 1989-90
100* Colombo (KS) 1992-93

D. W. Hookes (1)
143*† Kandy 1982-83

D. M. Jones (3)
102† Perth 1987-88

T. M. Moody (1)
106† Brisbane 1989-90

M. A. Taylor (2)
164† Brisbane 1989-90
108 Hobart 1989-90

S. R. Waugh (1)
134* Hobart 1989-90

K. C. Wessels (1)
141† Kandy 1982-83

For Sri Lanka (4)

P. A. de Silva (1)
167 Brisbane 1989-90

A. P. Gurusinha (1)
137 Colombo (SSC) 1992-93

A. Ranatunga (1)
127 Colombo (SSC) 1992-93

R. S. Kaluwitharana (1)
132*† Colombo (SSC) 1992-93

† *Signifies hundred on first appearance in Australia–Sri Lanka Tests.*

BEST BOWLING

Best bowling in an innings for Australia: 5-66 by T. G. Hogan at Kandy 1982-83
for Sri Lanka: 6-66 by R. J. Ratnayake at Hobart ... 1989-90

RECORD PARTNERSHIPS FOR EACH WICKET

For Australia

120	for 1st	G. R. Marsh and D. C. Boon at Perth	1987-88
170	for 2nd	K. C. Wessels and G. N. Yallop at Kandy	1982-83
158	for 3rd	T. M. Moody and A. R. Border at Brisbane	1989-90
163	for 4th	M. A. Taylor and A. R. Border at Hobart	1989-90
155*	for 5th	D. W. Hookes and A. R. Border at Kandy	1982-83
260*	for 6th	D. M. Jones and S. R. Waugh at Hobart	1989-90
129	for 7th	G. R. J. Matthews and I. A. Healy at Moratuwa	1992-93
56	for 8th	G. R. J. Matthews and C. J. McDermott at Colombo (SSC)	1992-93
45	for 9th	I. A. Healy and S. K. Warne at Colombo (SSC)	1992-93
49	for 10th	I. A. Healy and M. R. Whitney at Colombo (SSC)	1992-93

For Sri Lanka

110	for 1st	R. S. Mahanama and U. C. Hathurusinghe at Colombo (KS)	1992-93
92	for 2nd	R. S. Mahanama and A. P. Gurusinha at Colombo (SSC)	1992-93
107	for 3rd	U. C. Hathurusinghe and P. A. de Silva at Colombo (KS)	1992-93
		R. S. Mahanama and P. A. de Silva at Moratuwa	1992-93
230	for 4th	A. P. Gurusinha and A. Ranatunga at Colombo (SSC)	1992-93
116	for 5th	H. P. Tillekeratne and A. Ranatunga at Moratuwa	1992-93
96	for 6th	A. Ranatunga and R. S. Kaluwitharana at Colombo (SSC)	1992-93
144	for 7th†	P. A. de Silva and J. R. Ratnayeke at Brisbane	1989-90
33	for 8th	A. Ranatunga and C. P. H. Ramanayake at Perth	1987-88
44*	for 9th	R. S. Kaluwitharana and A. W. R. Madurasinghe at Colombo (SSC)	1992-93
27	for 10th	P. A. de Silva and C. P. H. Ramanayake at Brisbane	1989-90

† *Denotes record partnership against all countries.*

SOUTH AFRICA v WEST INDIES

	Captains					
Season	*South Africa*	*West Indies*	*T*	*SA*	*WI*	*D*
1991-92*W*	K. C. Wessels	R. B. Richardson	1	0	1	0

W Played in West Indies.

HIGHEST INNINGS TOTALS

For South Africa: 345 at Bridgetown 1991-92

For West Indies: 283 at Bridgetown 1991-92

INDIVIDUAL HUNDREDS

For South Africa (1)

A. C. Hudson (1)
163† Bridgetown.. 1991-92

Highest score for West Indies: 79* by J. C. Adams.

† *Signifies hundred on first appearance in South Africa–West Indies Tests.*

HIGHEST PARTNERSHIPS

For South Africa

125 for 2nd A. C. Hudson and K. C. Wessels at Bridgetown............. 1991-92

For West Indies

99 for 1st D. L. Haynes and P. V. Simmons at Bridgetown 1991-92

BEST MATCH BOWLING ANALYSES

For South Africa

8-158 (4-84, 4-74) R. P. Snell, Bridgetown 1991-92

For West Indies

8-81 (2-47, 6-34) C. E. L. Ambrose, Bridgetown 1991-92

SOUTH AFRICA v NEW ZEALAND

	Captains					
Season	*South Africa*	*New Zealand*	*T*	*SA*	*NZ*	*D*
1931-32*N*	H. B. Cameron	M. L. Page	2	2	0	0
1952-53*N*	J. E. Cheetham	W. M. Wallace	2	1	0	1
1953-54*S*	J. E. Cheetham	G. O. Rabone[1]	5	4	0	1
1961-62*S*	D. J. McGlew	J. R. Reid	5	2	2	1
1963-64*N*	T. L. Goddard	J. R. Reid	3	0	0	3
	In New Zealand		7	3	0	4
	In South Africa		10	6	2	2
	Totals		17	9	2	6

N Played in New Zealand. S Played in South Africa.

Note: The following deputised for the official touring captain:
[1]B. Sutcliffe (Fourth and Fifth).

HIGHEST INNINGS TOTALS

For South Africa in South Africa: 464 at Johannesburg 1961-62
in New Zealand: 524-8 at Wellington 1952-53

For New Zealand in South Africa: 505 at Cape Town 1953-54
in New Zealand: 364 at Wellington 1931-32

LOWEST INNINGS TOTALS

For South Africa in South Africa: 148 at Johannesburg 1953-54
in New Zealand: 223 at Dunedin 1963-64

For New Zealand in South Africa: 79 at Johannesburg 1953-54
in New Zealand: 138 at Dunedin 1963-64

INDIVIDUAL HUNDREDS

For South Africa (11)

X. C. Balaskas (1)
122* Wellington .. 1931-32
J. A. J. Christy (1)
103† Christchurch. 1931-32
W. R. Endean (1)
116 Auckland ... 1952-53
D. J. McGlew (3)
255*† Wellington .. 1952-53
127*‡ Durban 1961-62
120 Johannesburg 1961-62
R. A. McLean (2)
101 Durban 1953-54
113 Cape Town . 1961-62
B. Mitchell (1)
113† Christchurch. 1931-32
A. R. A. Murray (1)
109† Wellington .. 1952-53
J. H. B. Waite (1)
101 Johannesburg 1961-62

For New Zealand (7)

P. T. Barton (1)
109 Pt Elizabeth . 1961-62
P. G. Z. Harris (1)
101 Cape Town . 1961-62
G. O. Rabone (1)
107 Durban 1953-54
J. R. Reid (2)
135 Cape Town . 1953-54
142 Johannesburg 1961-62
B. W. Sinclair (1)
138 Auckland ... 1963-64
H. G. Vivian (1)
100† Wellington .. 1931-32

† *Signifies hundred on first appearance in South Africa–New Zealand Tests.*
‡ *Carried his bat.*

RECORD PARTNERSHIPS FOR EACH WICKET

For South Africa

196 for 1st	J. A. J. Christy and B. Mitchell at Christchurch	1931-32
76 for 2nd	J. A. J. Christy and H. B. Cameron at Wellington	1931-32
112 for 3rd	D. J. McGlew and R. A. McLean at Johannesburg	1961-62
135 for 4th	K. J. Funston and R. A. McLean at Durban	1953-54
130 for 5th	W. R. Endean and J. E. Cheetham at Auckland	1952-53
83 for 6th	K. C. Bland and D. T. Lindsay at Auckland	1963-64
246 for 7th†	D. J. McGlew and A. R. A. Murray at Wellington	1952-53
95 for 8th	J. E. Cheetham and H. J. Tayfield at Cape Town	1953-54
60 for 9th	P. M. Pollock and N. A. T. Adcock at Port Elizabeth	1961-62
47 for 10th	D. J. McGlew and H. D. Bromfield at Port Elizabeth	1961-62

For New Zealand

126	for 1st	G. O. Rabone and M. E. Chapple at Cape Town	1953-54
51	for 2nd	W. P. Bradburn and B. W. Sinclair at Dunedin	1963-64
94	for 3rd	M. B. Poore and B. Sutcliffe at Cape Town	1953-54
171	for 4th	B. W. Sinclair and S. N. McGregor at Auckland	1963-64
174	for 5th	J. R. Reid and J. E. F. Beck at Cape Town	1953-54
100	for 6th	H. G. Vivian and F. T. Badcock at Wellington	1931-32
84	for 7th	J. R. Reid and G. A. Bartlett at Johannesburg	1961-62
73	for 8th	P. G. Z. Harris and G. A. Bartlett at Durban	1961-62
69	for 9th	C. F. W. Allcott and I. B. Cromb at Wellington	1931-32
49*	for 10th	A. E. Dick and F. J. Cameron at Cape Town	1961-62

† *Denotes record partnership against all countries.*

TEN WICKETS OR MORE IN A MATCH

For South Africa (1)

11-196 (6-128, 5-68)† S. F. Burke, Cape Town 1961-62

† *Signifies ten wickets or more on first appearance in South Africa–New Zealand Tests.*

Note: The best match figures by a New Zealand bowler are 8-180 (4-61, 4-119), J. C. Alabaster at Cape Town, 1961-62.

SOUTH AFRICA v INDIA

	Captains					
Season	*South Africa*	*India*	*T*	*SA*	*I*	*D*
1992-93*S*	K. C. Wessels	M. Azharuddin	4	1	0	3

S Played in South Africa.

HIGHEST INNINGS TOTALS

For South Africa: 360-9 dec. at Cape Town 1992-93

For India: 277 at Durban 1992-93

INDIVIDUAL HUNDREDS

For South Africa (2)

W. J. Cronje (1)
135 Pt Elizabeth . 1992-93

K. C. Wessels (1)
118† Durban 1992-93

For India (3)

P. K. Amre (1)
103† Durban 1992-93

Kapil Dev (1)
129 Pt Elizabeth . 1992-93

S. R. Tendulkar (1)
111 Johannesburg 1992-93

† *Signifies hundred on first appearance in South Africa–India Tests.*

HUNDRED PARTNERSHIPS

For South Africa

117 for 2nd A. C. Hudson and W. J. Cronje at Port Elizabeth 1992-93

For India

101 for 8th P. K. Amre and K. S. More at Durban 1992-93

TEN WICKETS OR MORE IN A MATCH

For South Africa (1)

12-139 (5-55, 7-84) A. A. Donald at Port Elizabeth 1992-93

Note: The best match figures by an Indian bowler are 8-113 (2-60, 6-53), A. Kumble at Johannesburg, 1992-93.

SOUTH AFRICA v SRI LANKA

	Captains					
Season	*South Africa*	*Sri Lanka*	*T*	*SA*	*SL*	*D*
1993-94*SL*	K. C. Wessels	A. Ranatunga	3	1	0	2

SL Played in Sri Lanka.

HIGHEST INNINGS TOTALS

For South Africa: 495 at Colombo (SSC) 1993-94

For Sri Lanka: 331 at Moratuwa 1993-94

INDIVIDUAL HUNDREDS

For South Africa (3)

W. J. Cronje (1)
122 Colombo (SSC) 1993-94

D. J. Cullinan (1)
102 Colombo (PSS) 1993-94

J. N. Rhodes (1)
101*† Moratuwa... 1993-94

For Sri Lanka (1)

A. Ranatunga (1)
131† Moratuwa... 1993-94

† *Signifies hundred on first appearance in South Africa–Sri Lanka Tests.*

HUNDRED PARTNERSHIPS

For South Africa

137 for 1st	K. C. Wessels and A. C. Hudson at Colombo (SSC)	1993-94
122 for 6th	D. J. Cullinan and D. J. Richardson at Colombo (PSS)	1993-94
105 for 3rd	W. J. Cronje and D. J. Cullinan at Colombo (SSC)	1993-94
104 for 1st	K. C. Wessels and A. C. Hudson at Moratuwa	1993-94

For Sri Lanka

121 for 5th	P. A. de Silva and A. Ranatunga at Moratuwa	1993-94
103 for 6th	A. Ranatunga and H. P. Tillekeratne at Moratuwa	1993-94
101 for 4th	P. A. de Silva and A. Ranatunga at Colombo (PSS)	1993-94

BEST MATCH BOWLING ANALYSES

For South Africa

9-106 (5-48, 4-58) B. N. Schultz, Colombo (SSC) 1993-94

For Sri Lanka

6-152 (5-104, 1-48) M. Muralitharan, Moratuwa 1993-94

WEST INDIES v NEW ZEALAND

	Captains					
Season	*West Indies*	*New Zealand*	*T*	*WI*	*NZ*	*D*
1951-52*N*	J. D. C. Goddard	B. Sutcliffe	2	1	0	1
1955-56*N*	D. St E. Atkinson	J. R. Reid[1]	4	3	1	0
1968-69*N*	G. S. Sobers	G. T. Dowling	3	1	1	1
1971-72*W*	G. S. Sobers	G. T. Dowling[2]	5	0	0	5
1979-80*N*	C. H. Lloyd	G. P. Howarth	3	0	1	2
1984-85*W*	I. V. A. Richards	G. P. Howarth	4	2	0	2
1986-87*N*	I. V. A. Richards	J. V. Coney	3	1	1	1
	In New Zealand		15	6	4	5
	In West Indies		9	2	0	7
	Totals		24	8	4	12

N Played in New Zealand. W Played in West Indies.

Notes: The following deputised for the official touring captain or were appointed by the home authority for only a minor proportion of the series:
[1]H. B. Cave (First). [2]B. E. Congdon (Third, Fourth and Fifth).

HIGHEST INNINGS TOTALS

For West Indies in West Indies: 564-8 at Bridgetown 1971-72
in New Zealand: 546-6 dec. at Auckland 1951-52

For New Zealand in West Indies: 543-3 dec. at Georgetown 1971-72
in New Zealand: 460 at Christchurch 1979-80

LOWEST INNINGS TOTALS

For West Indies in West Indies: 133 at Bridgetown 1971-72
in New Zealand: 77 at Auckland 1955-56

For New Zealand in West Indies: 94 at Bridgetown 1984-85
in New Zealand: 74 at Dunedin 1955-56

INDIVIDUAL HUNDREDS

By West Indies (25)

M. C. Carew (1)
109† Auckland ... 1968-69
C. A. Davis (1)
183 Bridgetown .. 1971-72
R. C. Fredericks (1)
163 Kingston 1971-72
C. G. Greenidge (2)
100 Port-of-Spain 1984-85
213 Auckland ... 1986-87
D. L. Haynes (3)
105† Dunedin 1979-80
122 Christchurch. 1979-80
121 Wellington .. 1986-87
A. I. Kallicharran (2)
100*† Georgetown . 1971-72
101 Port-of-Spain 1971-72
C. L. King (1)
100* Christchurch. 1979-80
S. M. Nurse (2)
168† Auckland ... 1968-69
258 Christchurch. 1968-69
I. V. A. Richards (1)
105 Bridgetown .. 1984-85
R. B. Richardson (1)
185 Georgetown . 1984-85
L. G. Rowe (3)
214 }
100* } †Kingston ... 1971-72
100 Christchurch. 1979-80
G. S. Sobers (1)
142 Bridgetown .. 1971-72
J. B. Stollmeyer (1)
152 Auckland ... 1951-52
C. L. Walcott (1)
115 Auckland ... 1951-52
E. D. Weekes (3)
123 Dunedin 1955-56
103 Christchurch. 1955-56
156 Wellington .. 1955-56
F. M. M. Worrell (1)
100 Auckland ... 1951-52

By New Zealand (17)

M. G. Burgess (1)
101 Kingston 1971-72
B. E. Congdon (2)
166* Port-of-Spain 1971-72
126 Bridgetown .. 1971-72
J. J. Crowe (1)
112 Kingston 1984-85
M. D. Crowe (3)
188 Georgetown . 1984-85
119 Wellington .. 1986-87
104 Auckland ... 1986-87
B. A. Edgar (1)
127 Auckland ... 1979-80
R. J. Hadlee (1)
103 Christchurch. 1979-80
B. F. Hastings (2)
117* Christchurch. 1968-69
105 Bridgetown .. 1971-72
G. P. Howarth (1)
147 Christchurch. 1979-80
T. W. Jarvis (1)
182 Georgetown . 1971-72
B. R. Taylor (1)
124† Auckland ... 1968-69
G. M. Turner (2)
223*‡ Kingston 1971-72
259 Georgetown . 1971-72
J. G. Wright (1)
138 Wellington .. 1986-87

† *Signifies hundred on first appearance in West Indies–New Zealand Tests.*
‡ *Carried his bat.*

Notes: E. D. Weekes in 1955-56 made three hundreds in consecutive innings.

L. G. Rowe and A. I. Kallicharran each scored hundreds in their first two innings in Test cricket, Rowe being the only batsman to do so in his first match.

RECORD PARTNERSHIPS FOR EACH WICKET

For West Indies

225 for 1st	C. G. Greenidge and D. L. Haynes at Christchurch	1979-80
269 for 2nd	R. C. Fredericks and L. G. Rowe at Kingston	1971-72
185 for 3rd	C. G. Greenidge and R. B. Richardson at Port-of-Spain	1984-85
162 for 4th	E. D. Weekes and O. G. Smith at Dunedin	1955-56
	C. G. Greenidge and A. I. Kallicharran at Christchurch	1979-80
189 for 5th	F. M. M. Worrell and C. L. Walcott at Auckland	1951-52
254 for 6th	C. A. Davis and G. S. Sobers at Bridgetown	1971-72
143 for 7th	D. St E. Atkinson and J. D. C. Goddard at Christchurch	1955-56
83 for 8th	I. V. A. Richards and M. D. Marshall at Bridgetown	1984-85
70 for 9th	M. D. Marshall and J. Garner at Bridgetown	1984-85
31 for 10th	T. M. Findlay and G. C. Shillingford at Bridgetown	1971-72

For New Zealand

387	for 1st†	G. M. Turner and T. W. Jarvis at Georgetown	1971-72
210	for 2nd	G. P. Howarth and J. J. Crowe at Kingston	1984-85
241	for 3rd	J. G. Wright and M. D. Crowe at Wellington	1986-87
175	for 4th	B. E. Congdon and B. F. Hastings at Bridgetown	1971-72
142	for 5th	M. D. Crowe and J. V. Coney at Georgetown	1984-85
220	for 6th	G. M. Turner and K. J. Wadsworth at Kingston	1971-72
143	for 7th	M. D. Crowe and I. D. S. Smith at Georgetown	1984-85
136	for 8th†	B. E. Congdon and R. S. Cunis at Port-of-Spain	1971-72
62*	for 9th	V. Pollard and R. S. Cunis at Auckland	1968-69
41	for 10th	B. E. Congdon and J. C. Alabaster at Port-of-Spain	1971-72

† *Denotes record partnership against all countries.*

TEN WICKETS OR MORE IN A MATCH

For West Indies (1)

11-120 (4-40, 7-80)	M. D. Marshall, Bridgetown	1984-85

For New Zealand (3)

10-124 (4-51, 6-73)†	E. J. Chatfield, Port-of-Spain	1984-85
11-102 (5-34, 6-68)†	R. J. Hadlee, Dunedin	1979-80
10-166 (4-71, 6-95)	G. B. Troup, Auckland	1979-80

† *Signifies ten wickets or more on first appearance in West Indies–New Zealand Tests.*

WEST INDIES v INDIA

	Captains					
Season	*West Indies*	*India*	*T*	*WI*	*I*	*D*
1948-49*I*	J. D. C. Goddard	L. Amarnath	5	1	0	4
1952-53*W*	J. B. Stollmeyer	V. S. Hazare	5	1	0	4
1958-59*I*	F. C. M. Alexander	Ghulam Ahmed[1]	5	3	0	2
1961-62*W*	F. M. M. Worrell	N. J. Contractor[2]	5	5	0	0
1966-67*I*	G. S. Sobers	Nawab of Pataudi jun.	3	2	0	1
1970-71*W*	G. S. Sobers	A. L. Wadekar	5	0	1	4
1974-75*I*	C. H. Lloyd	Nawab of Pataudi jun.[3]	5	3	2	0
1975-76*W*	C. H. Lloyd	B. S. Bedi	4	2	1	1
1978-79*I*	A. I. Kallicharran	S. M. Gavaskar	6	0	1	5
1982-83*W*	C. H. Lloyd	Kapil Dev	5	2	0	3
1983-84*I*	C. H. Lloyd	Kapil Dev	6	3	0	3
1987-88*I*	I. V. A. Richards	D. B. Vengsarkar[4]	4	1	1	2
1988-89*W*	I. V. A. Richards	D. B. Vengsarkar	4	3	0	1
	In India		34	13	4	17
	In West Indies		28	13	2	13
	Totals		62	26	6	30

I Played in India. W Played in West Indies.

Notes: The following deputised for the official touring captain or were appointed by the home authority for only a minor proportion of the series:

[1]P. R. Umrigar (First), V. Mankad (Fourth), H. R. Adhikari (Fifth). [2]Nawab of Pataudi jun. (Third, Fourth and Fifth). [3]S. Venkataraghavan (Second). [4]R. J. Shastri (Fourth).

HIGHEST INNINGS TOTALS

For West Indies in West Indies: 631-8 dec. at Kingston 1961-62
in India: 644-8 dec. at Delhi 1958-59

For India in West Indies: 469-7 at Port-of-Spain 1982-83
in India: 644-7 dec. at Kanpur 1978-79

LOWEST INNINGS TOTALS

For West Indies in West Indies: 214 at Port-of-Spain 1970-71
in India: 127 at Delhi 1987-88

For India in West Indies: 97† at Kingston 1975-76
in India: 75 at Delhi 1987-88

† *Five men absent hurt. The lowest with 11 men batting is 98 at Port-of-Spain, 1961-62.*

INDIVIDUAL HUNDREDS

For West Indies (76)

S. F. A. F. Bacchus (1)
250 Kanpur 1978-79
B. F. Butcher (2)
103 Calcutta 1958-59
142 Madras 1958-59
R. J. Christiani (1)
107† Delhi 1948-49
C. A. Davis (2)
125* Georgetown . 1970-71
105 Port-of-Spain 1970-71
P. J. L. Dujon (1)
110 St John's 1982-83
R. C. Fredericks (2)
100 Calcutta 1974-75
104 Bombay 1974-75
H. A. Gomes (1)
123 Port-of-Spain 1982-83
G. E. Gomez (1)
101† Delhi 1948-49
C. G. Greenidge (5)
107† Bangalore ... 1974-75
154* St John's 1982-83
194 Kanpur 1983-84
141 Calcutta 1987-88
117 Bridgetown . 1988-89
D. L. Haynes (2)
136 St John's 1982-83
112* Bridgetown . 1988-89
J. K. Holt (1)
123 Delhi 1958-59
C. L. Hooper (1)
100* Calcutta 1987-88
C. C. Hunte (1)
101 Bombay 1966-67

A. I. Kallicharran (3)
124† Bangalore ... 1974-75
103* Port-of-Spain 1975-76
187 Bombay 1978-79
R. B. Kanhai (4)
256 Calcutta 1958-59
138 Kingston ... 1961-62
139 Port-of-Spain 1961-62
158* Kingston ... 1970-71
C. H. Lloyd (7)
163 Bangalore ... 1974-75
242* Bombay 1974-75
102 Bridgetown . 1975-76
143 Port-of-Spain 1982-83
106 St John's 1982-83
103 Delhi 1983-84
161* Calcutta 1983-84
A. L. Logie (2)
130 Bridgetown . 1982-83
101 Calcutta 1987-88
E. D. A. McMorris (1)
125† Kingston ... 1961-62
B. H. Pairaudeau (1)
115† Port-of-Spain 1952-53
A. F. Rae (2)
104 Bombay 1948-49
109 Madras 1948-49
I. V. A. Richards (8)
192* Delhi 1974-75
142 Bridgetown . 1975-76
130 Port-of-Spain 1975-76
177 Port-of-Spain 1975-76
109 Georgetown . 1982-83
120 Bombay 1983-84
109* Delhi 1987-88
110 Kingston ... 1988-89

R. B. Richardson (2)
194 Georgetown . 1988-89
156 Kingston ... 1988-89
O. G. Smith (1)
100 Delhi 1958-59
G. S. Sobers (8)
142*† Bombay 1958-59
198 Kanpur 1958-59
106* Calcutta 1958-59
153 Kingston ... 1961-62
104 Kingston ... 1961-62
108* Georgetown . 1970-71
178* Bridgetown . 1970-71
132 Port-of-Spain 1970-71
J. S. Solomon (1)
100* Delhi 1958-59
J. B. Stollmeyer (2)
160 Madras 1948-49
104* Port-of-Spain 1952-53
C. L. Walcott (4)
152† Delhi 1948-49
108 Calcutta 1948-49
125 Georgetown . 1952-53
118 Kingston ... 1952-53
E. D. Weekes (7)
128† Delhi 1948-49
194 Bombay 1948-49
162, 101 } Calcutta 1948-49
207 Port-of-Spain 1952-53
161 Port-of-Spain 1952-53
109 Kingston ... 1952-53
A. B. Williams (1)
111 Calcutta 1978-79
F. M. M. Worrell (1)
237 Kingston ... 1952-53

For India (55)

H. R. Adhikari (1)
114*† Delhi 1948-49
M. Amarnath (3)
101* Kanpur 1978-79
117 Port-of-Spain 1982-83
116 St John's 1982-83
M. L. Apte (1)
163* Port-of-Spain 1952-53
C. G. Borde (3)
109 Delhi 1958-59
121 Bombay 1966-67
125 Madras 1966-67
S. A. Durani (1)
104 Port-of-Spain 1961-62
F. M. Engineer (1)
109 Madras 1966-67
A. D. Gaekwad (1)
102 Kanpur 1978-79
S. M. Gavaskar (13)
116 Georgetown . 1970-71
117* Bridgetown . 1970-71
124 } Port-of-Spain 1970-71
220 }
156 Port-of-Spain 1975-76
102 Port-of-Spain 1975-76
205 Bombay 1978-79
107 } Calcutta 1978-79
182* }
120 Delhi 1978-79
147* Georgetown . 1982-83
121 Delhi 1983-84
236* Madras 1983-84
V. S. Hazare (2)
134* Bombay 1948-49
122 Bombay 1948-49
Kapil Dev (3)
126* Delhi 1978-79
100* Port-of-Spain 1982-83
109 Madras 1987-88
S. V. Manjrekar (1)
108 Bridgetown . 1988-89
V. L. Manjrekar (1)
118 Kingston ... 1952-53
R. S. Modi (1)
112 Bombay 1948-49
Mushtaq Ali (1)
106† Calcutta 1948-49
B. P. Patel (1)
115* Port-of-Spain 1975-76
Pankaj Roy (1)
150 Kingston ... 1952-53
D. N. Sardesai (3)
212 Kingston ... 1970-71
112 Port-of-Spain 1970-71
150 Bridgetown . 1970-71
R. J. Shastri (2)
102 St John's 1982-83
107 Bridgetown . 1988-89
N. S. Sidhu (1)
116 Kingston ... 1988-89
E. D. Solkar (1)
102 Bombay 1974-75
P. R. Umrigar (3)
130 Port-of-Spain 1952-53
117 Kingston ... 1952-53
172* Port-of-Spain 1961-62
D. B. Vengsarkar (6)
157* Calcutta 1978-79
109 Delhi 1978-79
159 Delhi 1983-84
100 Bombay 1983-84
102 Delhi 1987-88
102* Calcutta 1987-88
G. R. Viswanath (4)
139 Calcutta 1974-75
112 Port-of-Spain 1975-76
124 Madras 1978-79
179 Kanpur 1978-79

† *Signifies hundred on first appearance in West Indies–India Tests.*

RECORD PARTNERSHIPS FOR EACH WICKET

For West Indies

296	for 1st	C. G. Greenidge and D. L. Haynes at St John's	1982-83
255	for 2nd	E. D. A. McMorris and R. B. Kanhai at Kingston	1961-62
220	for 3rd	I. V. A. Richards and A. I. Kallicharran at Bridgetown	1975-76
267	for 4th	C. L. Walcott and G. E. Gomez at Delhi	1948-49
219	for 5th	E. D. Weekes and B. H. Pairaudeau at Port-of-Spain	1952-53
250	for 6th	C. H. Lloyd and D. L. Murray at Bombay	1974-75
130	for 7th	C. G. Greenidge and M. D. Marshall at Kanpur	1983-84
124	for 8th†	I. V. A. Richards and K. D. Boyce at Delhi	1974-75
161	for 9th†	C. H. Lloyd and A. M. E. Roberts at Calcutta	1983-84
98*	for 10th	F. M. M. Worrell and W. W. Hall at Port-of-Spain	1961-62

For India

153	for 1st	S. M. Gavaskar and C. P. S. Chauhan at Bombay	1978-79
344*	for 2nd†	S. M. Gavaskar and D. B. Vengsarkar at Calcutta	1978-79
159	for 3rd	M. Amarnath and G. R. Viswanath at Port-of-Spain	1975-76
172	for 4th	G. R. Viswanath and A. D. Gaekwad at Kanpur	1978-79
204	for 5th	S. M. Gavaskar and B. P. Patel at Port-of-Spain	1975-76
170	for 6th	S. M. Gavaskar and R. J. Shastri at Madras	1983-84
186	for 7th	D. N. Sardesai and E. D. Solkar at Bridgetown	1970-71
107	for 8th	Yashpal Sharma and B. S. Sandhu at Kingston	1982-83
143*	for 9th	S. M. Gavaskar and S. M. H. Kirmani at Madras	1983-84
62	for 10th	D. N. Sardesai and B. S. Bedi at Bridgetown	1970-71

† *Denotes record partnership against all countries.*

TEN WICKETS OR MORE IN A MATCH

For West Indies (4)

11-126 (6-50, 5-76)	W. W. Hall, Kanpur	1958-59
11-89 (5-34, 6-55)	M. D. Marshall, Port-of-Spain	1988-89
12-121 (7-64, 5-57)	A. M. E. Roberts, Madras	1974-75
10-101 (6-62, 4-39)	C. A. Walsh, Kingston	1988-89

For India (4)

11-235 (7-157, 4-78)†	B. S. Chandrasekhar, Bombay	1966-67
10-223 (9-102, 1-121)	S. P. Gupte, Kanpur	1958-59
16-136 (8-61, 8-75)†	N. D. Hirwani, Madras	1987-88
10-135 (1-52, 9-83)	Kapil Dev, Ahmedabad	1983-84

† *Signifies ten wickets or more on first appearance in West Indies–India Tests.*

WEST INDIES v PAKISTAN

Season	*Captains* *West Indies*	*Pakistan*	*T*	*WI*	*P*	*D*
1957-58*W*	F. C. M. Alexander	A. H. Kardar	5	3	1	1
1958-59*P*	F. C. M. Alexander	Fazal Mahmood	3	1	2	0
1974-75*P*	C. H. Lloyd	Intikhab Alam	2	0	0	2
1976-77*W*	C. H. Lloyd	Mushtaq Mohammad	5	2	1	2
1980-81*P*	C. H. Lloyd	Javed Miandad	4	1	0	3
1986-87*P*	I. V. A. Richards	Imran Khan	3	1	1	1
1987-88*W*	I. V. A. Richards[1]	Imran Khan	3	1	1	1
1990-91*P*	D. L. Haynes	Imran Khan	3	1	1	1
1992-93*W*	R. B. Richardson	Wasim Akram	3	2	0	1
	In West Indies		16	8	3	5
	In Pakistan		15	4	4	7
	Totals		31	12	7	12

P Played in Pakistan. W Played in West Indies.

Note: The following was appointed by the home authority for only a minor proportion of the series:

[1]C. G. Greenidge (First).

HIGHEST INNINGS TOTALS

For West Indies in West Indies: 790-3 dec. at Kingston 1957-58
in Pakistan: 493 at Karachi 1974-75

For Pakistan in West Indies: 657-8 dec. at Bridgetown 1957-58
in Pakistan: 406-8 dec. at Karachi 1974-75

LOWEST INNINGS TOTALS

For West Indies in West Indies: 127 at Port-of-Spain 1992-93
in Pakistan: 53 at Faisalabad 1986-87

For Pakistan in West Indies: 106 at Bridgetown 1957-58
in Pakistan: 77 at Lahore 1986-87

INDIVIDUAL HUNDREDS

For West Indies (24)

L. Baichan (1)
105*† Lahore 1974-75
P. J. L. Dujon (1)
106* Port-of-Spain 1987-88
R. C. Fredericks (1)
120 Port-of-Spain 1976-77
C. G. Greenidge (1)
100 Kingston.... 1976-77
D. L. Haynes (3)
117 Karachi 1990-91
143*‡ Port-of-Spain 1992-93
125 Bridgetown.. 1992-93

C. L. Hooper (2)
134 Lahore 1990-91
178* St John's.... 1992-93
C. C. Hunte (3)
142† Bridgetown.. 1957-58
260 Kingston.... 1957-58
114 Georgetown . 1957-58
B. D. Julien (1)
101 Karachi 1974-75
A. I. Kallicharran (1)
115 Karachi 1974-75
R. B. Kanhai (1)
217 Lahore 1958-59
C. H. Lloyd (1)
157 Bridgetown.. 1976-77

I. V. A. Richards (2)
120* Multan 1980-81
123 Port-of-Spain 1987-88
I. T. Shillingford (1)
120 Georgetown . 1976-77
G. S. Sobers (3)
365* Kingston.... 1957-58
125 }
109* } Georgetown . 1957-58
C. L. Walcott (1)
145 Georgetown . 1957-58
E. D. Weekes (1)
197† Bridgetown.. 1957-58

For Pakistan (18)

Asif Iqbal (1)
135 Kingston.... 1976-77
Hanif Mohammad (2)
337† Bridgetown.. 1957-58
103 Karachi 1958-59
Imtiaz Ahmed (1)
122 Kingston.... 1957-58
Imran Khan (1)
123 Lahore 1980-81
Inzamam-ul-Haq (1)
123 St John's.... 1992-93

Javed Miandad (2)
114 Georgetown . 1987-88
102 Port-of-Spain 1987-88
Majid Khan (2)
100 Karachi 1974-75
167 Georgetown . 1976-77
Mushtaq Mohammad (2)
123 Lahore 1974-75
121 Port-of-Spain 1976-77

Saeed Ahmed (1)
150 Georgetown . 1957-58
Salim Malik (1)
102 Karachi 1990-91
Wasim Raja (2)
107* Karachi 1974-75
117* Bridgetown.. 1976-77
Wazir Mohammad (2)
106 Kingston.... 1957-58
189 Port-of-Spain 1957-58

† *Signifies hundred on first appearance in West Indies–Pakistan Tests.*
‡ *Carried his bat.*

RECORD PARTNERSHIPS FOR EACH WICKET

For West Indies

182	for 1st	R. C. Fredericks and C. G. Greenidge at Kingston	1976-77
446	for 2nd†	C. C. Hunte and G. S. Sobers at Kingston	1957-58
169	for 3rd	D. L. Haynes and B. C. Lara at Port-of-Spain	1992-93
188*	for 4th	G. S. Sobers and C. L. Walcott at Kingston	1957-58
185	for 5th	E. D. Weekes and O. G. Smith at Bridgetown	1957-58
151	for 6th	C. H. Lloyd and D. L. Murray at Bridgetown	1976-77
70	for 7th	C. H. Lloyd and J. Garner at Bridgetown	1976-77
60	for 8th	C. L. Hooper and A. C. Cummins at St John's	1992-93
61*	for 9th	P. J. L. Dujon and W. K. M. Benjamin at Bridgetown	1987-88
106	for 10th†	C. L. Hooper and C. A. Walsh at St John's	1992-93

For Pakistan

159	for 1st[1]	Majid Khan and Zaheer Abbas at Georgetown	1976-77
178	for 2nd	Hanif Mohammad and Saeed Ahmed at Karachi	1958-59
169	for 3rd	Saeed Ahmed and Wazir Mohammad at Port-of-Spain	1957-58
174	for 4th	Shoaib Mohammad and Salim Malik at Karachi	1990-91
88	for 5th	Basit Ali and Inzamam-ul-Haq at St John's	1992-93
166	for 6th	Wazir Mohammad and A. H. Kardar at Kingston	1957-58
128	for 7th[2]	Wasim Raja and Wasim Bari at Karachi	1974-75

94 for 8th	Salim Malik and Salim Yousuf at Port-of-Spain	1987-88
96 for 9th	Inzamam-ul-Haq and Nadeem Khan at St John's	1992-93
133 for 10th†	Wasim Raja and Wasim Bari at Bridgetown	1976-77

† Denotes record partnership against all countries.

[1] *219 runs were added for this wicket in two separate partnerships: Sadiq Mohammad retired hurt and was replaced by Zaheer Abbas when 60 had been added. The highest partnership by two opening batsmen is 152 by Hanif Mohammad and Imtiaz Ahmed at Bridgetown, 1957-58.*

[2] *Although the seventh wicket added 168 runs against West Indies at Lahore in 1980-81, this comprised two partnerships with Imran Khan adding 72* with Abdul Qadir (retired hurt) and a further 96 with Sarfraz Nawaz.*

TEN WICKETS OR MORE IN A MATCH

For Pakistan (2)

12-100 (6-34, 6-66)	Fazal Mahmood, Dacca	1958-59
11-121 (7-80, 4-41)	Imran Khan, Georgetown	1987-88

Note: The best match figures by a West Indian bowler are 9-95 (8-29, 1-66) by C. E. H. Croft at Port-of-Spain, 1976-77.

WEST INDIES v SRI LANKA

	Captains					
Season	*West Indies*	*Sri Lanka*	*T*	*WI*	*SL*	*D*
1993-94*S*	R. B. Richardson	A. Ranatunga	1	0	0	1

S Played in Sri Lanka.

HIGHEST INNINGS TOTALS

For West Indies:	204 at Moratuwa	1993-94
For Sri Lanka:	190 at Moratuwa	1993-94

Highest score for West Indies: 62 by C. L. Hooper at Moratuwa.
Highest score for Sri Lanka: 53 by P. A. de Silva at Moratuwa.

HIGHEST PARTNERSHIPS

For West Indies

84 for 5th	R. B. Richardson and C. L. Hooper at Moratuwa	1993-94

For Sri Lanka

51 for 7th	R. S. Kalpage and P. B. Dassanayake at Moratuwa	1993-94

BEST MATCH BOWLING ANALYSES

For West Indies

5-51 (4-46, 1-5)	W. K. M. Benjamin, Moratuwa	1993-94

For Sri Lanka

4-47 (4-47)	M. Muralitharan, Moratuwa	1993-94

NEW ZEALAND v INDIA

Season	Captains: New Zealand	India	T	NZ	I	D
1955-56*I*	H. B. Cave	P. R. Umrigar[1]	5	0	2	3
1964-65*I*	J. R. Reid	Nawab of Pataudi jun.	4	0	1	3
1967-68*N*	G. T. Dowling[2]	Nawab of Pataudi jun.	4	1	3	0
1969-70*I*	G. T. Dowling	Nawab of Pataudi jun.	3	1	1	1
1975-76*N*	G. M. Turner	B. S. Bedi[3]	3	1	1	1
1976-77*I*	G. M. Turner	B. S. Bedi	3	0	2	1
1980-81*N*	G. P. Howarth	S. M. Gavaskar	3	1	0	2
1988-89*I*	J. G. Wright	D. B. Vengsarkar	3	1	2	0
1989-90*N*	J. G. Wright	M. Azharuddin	3	1	0	2
1993-94*N*	K. R. Rutherford	M. Azharuddin	1	0	0	1
	In India		18	2	8	8
	In New Zealand		14	4	4	6
	Totals		32	6	12	14

I Played in India. N Played in New Zealand.

Notes: The following deputised for the official touring captain or were appointed by the home authority for a minor proportion of the series:
[1]Ghulam Ahmed (First). [2]B. W. Sinclair (First). [3]S. M. Gavaskar (First).

HIGHEST INNINGS TOTALS

For New Zealand in New Zealand: 502 at Christchurch 1967-68
in India: 462-9 dec. at Calcutta 1964-65

For India in New Zealand: 482 at Auckland 1989-90
in India: 537-3 dec. at Madras 1955-56

LOWEST INNINGS TOTALS

For New Zealand in New Zealand: 100 at Wellington 1980-81
in India: 124 at Hyderabad 1988-89

For India in New Zealand: 81 at Wellington 1975-76
in India: 88 at Bombay 1964-65

INDIVIDUAL HUNDREDS

For New Zealand (21)

M. D. Crowe (1)
113 Auckland ... 1989-90
G. T. Dowling (3)
120 Bombay 1964-65
143 Dunedin 1967-68
239 Christchurch. 1967-68
J. W. Guy (1)
102† Hyderabad .. 1955-56
G. P. Howarth (1)
137* Wellington .. 1980-81
A. H. Jones (1)
170* Auckland ... 1989-90
J. M. Parker (1)
104 Bombay 1976-77
J. F. Reid (1)
123* Christchurch. 1980-81
J. R. Reid (2)
119* Delhi....... 1955-56
120 Calcutta 1955-56
I. D. S. Smith (1)
173 Auckland ... 1989-90
B. Sutcliffe (3)
137*† Hyderabad .. 1955-56
230* Delhi....... 1955-56
151* Calcutta 1964-65
B. R. Taylor (1)
105† Calcutta 1964-65
G. M. Turner (2)
117 Christchurch. 1975-76
113 Kanpur..... 1976-77
J. G. Wright (3)
110 Auckland ... 1980-81
185 Christchurch. 1989-90
113* Napier 1989-90

For India (22)

S. Amarnath (1)
124† Auckland ... 1975-76
M. Azharuddin (1)
192 Auckland ... 1989-90
C. G. Borde (1)
109 Bombay 1964-65
S. M. Gavaskar (2)
116† Auckland ... 1975-76
119 Bombay 1976-77
A. G. Kripal Singh (1)
100*† Hyderabad .. 1955-56
V. L. Manjrekar (3)
118† Hyderabad .. 1955-56
177 Delhi....... 1955-56
102* Madras 1964-65
V. Mankad (2)
223 Bombay 1955-56
231 Madras 1955-56
Nawab of Pataudi jun. (2)
153 Calcutta 1964-65
113 Delhi....... 1964-65
G. S. Ramchand (1)
106* Calcutta 1955-56
Pankaj Roy (2)
100 Calcutta 1955-56
173 Madras 1955-56
D. N. Sardesai (2)
200* Bombay 1964-65
106 Delhi....... 1964-65
N. S. Sidhu (1)
116† Bangalore ... 1988-89
P. R. Umrigar (1)
223† Hyderabad .. 1955-56
G. R. Viswanath (1)
103* Kanpur..... 1976-77
A. L. Wadekar (1)
143 Wellington .. 1967-68

† *Signifies hundred on first appearance in New Zealand–India Tests. B. R. Taylor provides the only instance for New Zealand of a player scoring his maiden hundred in first-class cricket in his first Test.*

RECORD PARTNERSHIPS FOR EACH WICKET

For New Zealand

149	for 1st	T. J. Franklin and J. G. Wright at Napier	1989-90
155	for 2nd	G. T. Dowling and B. E. Congdon at Dunedin	1967-68
222*	for 3rd	B. Sutcliffe and J. R. Reid at Delhi	1955-56
125	for 4th	J. G. Wright and M. J. Greatbatch at Christchurch	1989-90
119	for 5th	G. T. Dowling and K. Thomson at Christchurch	1967-68
87	for 6th	J. W. Guy and A. R. MacGibbon at Hyderabad	1955-56
163	for 7th	B. Sutcliffe and B. R. Taylor at Calcutta	1964-65
103	for 8th	R. J. Hadlee and I. D. S. Smith at Auckland	1989-90
136	for 9th†	I. D. S. Smith and M. C. Snedden at Auckland	1989-90
61	for 10th	J. T. Ward and R. O. Collinge at Madras	1964-65

For India

413	for 1st†	V. Mankad and Pankaj Roy at Madras	1955-56
204	for 2nd	S. M. Gavaskar and S. Amarnath at Auckland	1975-76
238	for 3rd	P. R. Umrigar and V. L. Manjrekar at Hyderabad	1955-56
171	for 4th	P. R. Umrigar and A. G. Kripal Singh at Hyderabad	1955-56
127	for 5th	V. L. Manjrekar and G. S. Ramchand at Delhi	1955-56
193*	for 6th	D. N. Sardesai and Hanumant Singh at Bombay	1964-65
128	for 7th	S. R. Tendulkar and K. S. More at Napier	1989-90
143	for 8th†	R. G. Nadkarni and F. M. Engineer at Madras	1964-65
105	for 9th	S. M. H. Kirmani and B. S. Bedi at Bombay	1976-77
		S. M. H. Kirmani and N. S. Yadav at Auckland	1980-81
57	for 10th	R. B. Desai and B. S. Bedi at Dunedin	1967-68

† *Denotes record partnership against all countries.*

TEN WICKETS OR MORE IN A MATCH

For New Zealand (2)

11-58 (4-35, 7-23)	R. J. Hadlee, Wellington	1975-76
10-88 (6-49, 4-39)	R. J. Hadlee, Bombay	1988-89

For India (2)

11-140 (3-64, 8-76)	E. A. S. Prasanna, Auckland	1975-76
12-152 (8-72, 4-80)	S. Venkataraghavan, Delhi	1964-65

NEW ZEALAND v PAKISTAN

Season	Captains: New Zealand	Captains: Pakistan	T	NZ	P	D
1955-56P	H. B. Cave	A. H. Kardar	3	0	2	1
1964-65N	J. R. Reid	Hanif Mohammad	3	0	0	3
1964-65P	J. R. Reid	Hanif Mohammad	3	0	2	1
1969-70P	G. T. Dowling	Intikhab Alam	3	1	0	2
1972-73N	B. E. Congdon	Intikhab Alam	3	0	1	2
1976-77P	G. M. Turner[1]	Mushtaq Mohammad	3	0	2	1
1978-79N	M. G. Burgess	Mushtaq Mohammad	3	0	1	2
1984-85P	J. V. Coney	Zaheer Abbas	3	0	2	1
1984-85N	G. P. Howarth	Javed Miandad	3	2	0	1
1988-89N†	J. G. Wright	Imran Khan	2	0	0	2
1990-91P	M. D. Crowe	Javed Miandad	3	0	3	0
1992-93N	K. R. Rutherford	Javed Miandad	1	0	1	0
1993-94N	K. R. Rutherford	Salim Malik	3	1	2	0
	In Pakistan		18	1	11	6
	In New Zealand		18	3	5	10
	Totals		36	4	16	16

N Played in New Zealand. P Played in Pakistan.
† *The First Test at Dunedin was abandoned without a ball being bowled and is excluded.*

Note: The following deputised for the official touring captain:
[1]J. M. Parker (Third).

HIGHEST INNINGS TOTALS

For New Zealand in New Zealand 492 at Wellington 1984-85
in Pakistan: 482-6 dec. at Lahore 1964-65

For Pakistan in New Zealand: 616-5 dec. at Auckland 1988-89
in Pakistan: 565-9 dec. at Karachi 1976-77

LOWEST INNINGS TOTALS

For New Zealand in New Zealand: 93 at Hamilton 1992-93
in Pakistan: 70 at Dacca 1955-56

For Pakistan in New Zealand: 169 at Auckland 1984-85
in Pakistan: 102 at Faisalabad 1990-91

INDIVIDUAL HUNDREDS

For New Zealand (21)

M. G. Burgess (2)
119* Dacca 1969-70
111 Lahore 1976-77
J. V. Coney (1)
111* Dunedin 1984-85
M. D. Crowe (2)
174 Wellington .. 1988-89
108* Lahore 1990-91
B. A. Edgar (1)
129† Christchurch. 1978-79
M. J. Greatbatch (1)
133 Hamilton ... 1992-93
B. F. Hastings (1)
110 Auckland ... 1972-73
G. P. Howarth (1)
114 Napier 1978-79
W. K. Lees (1)
152 Karachi 1976-77
S. N. McGregor (1)
111 Lahore 1955-56
R. E. Redmond (1)
107† Auckland ... 1972-73
J. F. Reid (3)
106 Hyderabad .. 1984-85
148 Wellington .. 1984-85
158* Auckland ... 1984-85
J. R. Reid (1)
128 Karachi 1964-65
B. W. Sinclair (1)
130 Lahore 1964-65
S. A. Thomson (1)
120* Christchurch 1993-94
G. M. Turner (1)
110† Dacca 1969-70
J. G. Wright (1)
107 Karachi 1984-85
B. A. Young (1)
120 Christchurch 1993-94

For Pakistan (37)

Asif Iqbal (3)
175 Dunedin 1972-73
166 Lahore 1976-77
104 Napier 1978-79
Basit Ali (1)
103 Christchurch 1993-94
Hanif Mohammad (3)
103 Dacca 1955-56
100* Christchurch. 1964-65
203* Lahore 1964-65
Imtiaz Ahmed (1)
209 Lahore 1955-56
Inzamam-ul-Haq (1)
135* Wellington .. 1993-94
Javed Miandad (7)
163† Lahore 1976-77
206 Karachi 1976-77
160* Christchurch. 1978-79
104 } Hyderabad .. 1984-85
103* }
118 Wellington .. 1988-89
271 Auckland ... 1988-89
Majid Khan (3)
110 Auckland ... 1972-73
112 Karachi 1976-77
119* Napier 1978-79
Mohammad Ilyas (1)
126 Karachi 1964-65
Mudassar Nazar (1)
106 Hyderabad .. 1984-85
Mushtaq Mohammad (3)
201 Dunedin 1972-73
101 Hyderabad .. 1976-77
107 Karachi 1976-77
Sadiq Mohammad (2)
166 Wellington .. 1972-73
103* Hyderabad .. 1976-77
Saeed Ahmed (1)
172 Karachi 1964-65
Saeed Anwar (1)
169 Wellington .. 1993-94
Salim Malik (2)
119* Karachi 1984-85
140 Wellington .. 1993-94
Shoaib Mohammad (5)
163 Wellington .. 1988-89
112 Auckland ... 1988-89
203* Karachi 1990-91
105 Lahore 1990-91
142 Faisalabad .. 1990-91
Waqar Hassan (1)
189 Lahore 1955-56
Zaheer Abbas (1)
135 Auckland ... 1978-79

† *Signifies hundred on first appearance in New Zealand–Pakistan Tests.*

Notes: Mushtaq and Sadiq Mohammad, at Hyderabad in 1976-77, provide the fourth instance in Test matches, after the Chappells (thrice), of brothers each scoring hundreds in the same innings.

Shoaib Mohammad scored his first four hundreds in this series in successive innings.

RECORD PARTNERSHIPS FOR EACH WICKET

For New Zealand

159 for 1st	R. E. Redmond and G. M. Turner at Auckland	1972-73
195 for 2nd	J. G. Wright and G. P. Howarth at Napier	1978-79
178 for 3rd	B. W. Sinclair and J. R. Reid at Lahore	1964-65
128 for 4th	B. F. Hastings and M. G. Burgess at Wellington	1972-73
183 for 5th†	M. G. Burgess and R. W. Anderson at Lahore	1976-77
145 for 6th	J. F. Reid and R. J. Hadlee at Wellington	1984-85
186 for 7th†	W. K. Lees and R. J. Hadlee at Karachi	1976-77
100 for 8th	B. W. Yuile and D. R. Hadlee at Karachi	1969-70
96 for 9th	M. G. Burgess and R. S. Cunis at Dacca	1969-70
151 for 10th†	B. F. Hastings and R. O. Collinge at Auckland	1972-73

For Pakistan

172 for 1st	Ramiz Raja and Shoaib Mohammad at Karachi	1990-91
114 for 2nd	Mohammad Ilyas and Saeed Ahmed at Rawalpindi	1964-65
248 for 3rd	Shoaib Mohammad and Javed Miandad at Auckland	1988-89
350 for 4th†	Mushtaq Mohammad and Asif Iqbal at Dunedin	1972-73
281 for 5th†	Javed Miandad and Asif Iqbal at Lahore	1976-77
217 for 6th†	Hanif Mohammad and Majid Khan at Lahore	1964-65
308 for 7th†	Waqar Hassan and Imtiaz Ahmed at Lahore	1955-56
89 for 8th	Anil Dalpat and Iqbal Qasim at Karachi	1984-85
52 for 9th	Intikhab Alam and Arif Butt at Auckland	1964-65
65 for 10th	Salah-ud-Din and Mohammad Farooq at Rawalpindi	1964-65

† *Denotes record partnership against all countries.*

TEN WICKETS OR MORE IN A MATCH

For New Zealand (1)

11-152 (7-52, 4-100)	C. Pringle, Faisalabad	1990-91

For Pakistan (7)

10-182 (5-91, 5-91)	Intikhab Alam, Dacca	1969-70
11-130 (7-52, 4-78)	Intikhab Alam, Dunedin	1972-73
10-106 (3-20, 7-86)	Waqar Younis, Lahore	1990-91
12-130 (7-76, 5-54)	Waqar Younis, Faisalabad	1990-91
10-128 (5-56, 5-72)	Wasim Akram, Dunedin	1984-85
11-179 (4-60, 7-119)	Wasim Akram, Wellington	1993-94
11-79 (5-37, 6-42)†	Zulfiqar Ahmed, Karachi	1955-56

† *Signifies ten wickets or more on first appearance in New Zealand–Pakistan Tests.*

Note: Waqar Younis's performances were in successive matches.

NEW ZEALAND v SRI LANKA

Season	*Captains* *New Zealand*	*Sri Lanka*	*T*	*NZ*	*SL*	*D*
1982-83*N*	G. P. Howarth	D. S. de Silva	2	2	0	0
1983-84*S*	G. P. Howarth	L. R. D. Mendis	3	2	0	1
1986-87*S*†	J. J. Crowe	L. R. D. Mendis	1	0	0	1
1990-91*N*	M. D. Crowe[1]	A. Ranatunga	3	0	0	3
1992-93*S*	M. D. Crowe	A. Ranatunga	2	0	1	1
	In New Zealand		5	2	0	3
	In Sri Lanka		6	2	1	3
	Totals		11	4	1	6

N Played in New Zealand. S Played in Sri Lanka.

† *The Second and Third Tests were cancelled owing to civil disturbances.*

Note: The following was appointed by the home authority for only a minor proportion of the series:

[1]I. D. S. Smith (Third).

HIGHEST INNINGS TOTALS

For New Zealand in New Zealand: 671-4 at Wellington	1990-91
in Sri Lanka: 459 at Colombo (CCC)	1983-84
For Sri Lanka in New Zealand: 497 at Wellington	1990-91
in Sri Lanka: 397-9 dec. at Colombo (CCC)	1986-87

LOWEST INNINGS TOTALS

For New Zealand in New Zealand: 174 at Wellington	1990-91
in Sri Lanka: 102 at Colombo (SSC)	1992-93
For Sri Lanka in New Zealand: 93 at Wellington	1982-83
in Sri Lanka: 97 at Kandy	1983-84

INDIVIDUAL HUNDREDS

For New Zealand (10)

J. J. Crowe (1)
120* Colombo (CCC) 1986-87

M. D. Crowe (2)
299 Wellington .. 1990-91
107 Colombo (SSC) 1992-93

R. J. Hadlee (1)
151* Colombo (CCC) 1986-87

A. H. Jones (3)
186 Wellington .. 1990-91
122 }
100* } Hamilton ... 1990-91

J. F. Reid (1)
180 Colombo (CCC) 1983-84

K. R. Rutherford (1)
105 Moratuwa ... 1992-93

J. G. Wright (1)
101 Hamilton ... 1990-91

For Sri Lanka (8)

P. A. de Silva (2)
267† Wellington .. 1990-91
123 Auckland ... 1990-91

R. L. Dias (1)
108† Colombo (SSC) 1983-84

A. P. Gurusinha (2)
119 }
102 } Hamilton ... 1990-91

D. S. B. P. Kuruppu (1)
201*† Colombo (CCC) 1986-87

R. S. Mahanama (2)
153 Moratuwa ... 1992-93
109 Colombo (SSC) 1992-93

† *Signifies hundred on first appearance in New Zealand–Sri Lanka Tests.*

Note: A. P. Gurusinha and A. H. Jones at Hamilton in 1990-91 provided the second instance of a player on each side hitting two separate hundreds in a Test match.

RECORD PARTNERSHIPS FOR EACH WICKET

For New Zealand

161	for 1st	T. J. Franklin and J. G. Wright at Hamilton	1990-91
76	for 2nd	J. G. Wright and A. H. Jones at Auckland	1990-91
467	for 3rd†‡	A. H. Jones and M. D. Crowe at Wellington	1990-91
82	for 4th	J. F. Reid and S. L. Boock at Colombo (CCC)	1983-84
151	for 5th	K. R. Rutherford and C. Z. Harris at Moratuwa	1992-93
246*	for 6th†	J. J. Crowe and R. J. Hadlee at Colombo (CCC)	1986-87
30	for 7th	R. J. Hadlee and I. D. S. Smith at Kandy	1983-84
		R. J. Hadlee and J. J. Crowe at Kandy	1983-84
79	for 8th	J. V. Coney and W. K. Lees at Christchurch	1982-83
42	for 9th	W. K. Lees and M. C. Snedden at Christchurch	1982-83
52	for 10th	W. K. Lees and E. J. Chatfield at Christchurch	1982-83

For Sri Lanka

102	for 1st	R. S. Mahanama and U. C. Hathurusinghe at Colombo (SSC)	1992-93
138	for 2nd	R. S. Mahanama and A. P. Gurusinha at Moratuwa	1992-93
159*	for 3rd†[1]	S. Wettimuny and R. L. Dias at Colombo (SSC)	1983-84
178	for 4th	P. A. de Silva and A. Ranatunga at Wellington	1990-91
130	for 5th	R. S. Madugalle and D. S. de Silva at Wellington	1982-83
109*	for 6th[2]	R. S. Madugalle and A. Ranatunga at Colombo (CCC)	1983-84
55	for 7th	A. P. Gurusinha and A. Ranatunga at Hamilton	1990-91
69	for 8th	H. P. Tillekeratne and S. D. Anurasiri at Colombo (SSC)	1992-93
31	for 9th	G. F. Labrooy and R. J. Ratnayake at Auckland	1990-91
		S. T. Jayasuriya and R. J. Ratnayake at Auckland	1990-91
60	for 10th	V. B. John and M. J. G. Amerasinghe at Kandy	1983-84

† *Denotes record partnership against all countries.*
‡ *Record third-wicket partnership in first-class cricket.*
[1] *163 runs were added for this wicket in two separate partnerships: S. Wettimuny retired hurt and was replaced by L. R. D. Mendis when 159 had been added.*
[2] *119 runs were added for this wicket in two separate partnerships: R. S. Madugalle retired hurt and was replaced by D. S. de Silva when 109 had been added.*

TEN WICKETS OR MORE IN A MATCH

For New Zealand (1)

10-102 (5-73, 5-29) R. J. Hadlee, Colombo (CCC) 1983-84

Note: The best match figures by a Sri Lankan bowler are 8-159 (5-86, 3-73), V. B. John at Kandy, 1983-84.

NEW ZEALAND v ZIMBABWE

	Captains					
Season	*New Zealand*	*Zimbabwe*	*T*	*NZ*	*Z*	*D*
1992-93Z	M. D. Crowe	D. L. Houghton	2	1	0	1

Z Played in Zimbabwe.

HIGHEST INNINGS TOTALS

For New Zealand: 335 at Harare 1992-93

For Zimbabwe: 283-9 dec. at Harare 1992-93

INDIVIDUAL HUNDREDS

For New Zealand (2)

M. D. Crowe (1)
140 Harare 1992-93

R. T. Latham (1)
119† Bulawayo ... 1992-93

For Zimbabwe (1)

K. J. Arnott (1)
101*† Bulawayo ... 1992-93

† *Signifies hundred on first appearance in New Zealand–Zimbabwe Tests.*

HUNDRED PARTNERSHIPS

For New Zealand

168 for 4th	M. D. Crowe and K. R. Rutherford at Harare	1992-93
130 for 5th	K. R. Rutherford and D. N. Patel at Harare	1992-93
127 for 2nd	R. T. Latham and A. H. Jones at Bulawayo	1992-93
116 for 1st	M. J. Greatbatch and R. T. Latham at Bulawayo	1992-93
102 for 1st	M. J. Greatbatch and R. T. Latham at Bulawayo	1992-93

For Zimbabwe

107 for 2nd	K. J. Arnott and A. D. R. Campbell at Harare	1992-93
105* for 2nd	K. J. Arnott and A. D. R. Campbell at Bulawayo	1992-93

BEST MATCH BOWLING ANALYSES

For New Zealand

8-131 (2-81, 6-50) D. N. Patel, Harare 1992-93

For Zimbabwe

4-101 (3-49, 1-52) D. H. Brain, Harare 1992-93

INDIA v PAKISTAN

Season	*India* (Captains)	*Pakistan*	*T*	*I*	*P*	*D*
1952-53*I*	L. Amarnath	A. H. Kardar	5	2	1	2
1954-55*P*	V. Mankad	A. H. Kardar	5	0	0	5
1960-61*I*	N. J. Contractor	Fazal Mahmood	5	0	0	5
1978-79*P*	B. S. Bedi	Mushtaq Mohammad	3	0	2	1
1979-80*I*	S. M. Gavaskar[1]	Asif Iqbal	6	2	0	4
1982-83*P*	S. M. Gavaskar	Imran Khan	6	0	3	3
1983-84*I*	Kapil Dev	Zaheer Abbas	3	0	0	3
1984-85*P*	S. M. Gavaskar	Zaheer Abbas	2	0	0	2
1986-87*I*	Kapil Dev	Imran Khan	5	0	1	4
1989-90*P*	K. Srikkanth	Imran Khan	4	0	0	4
	In India		24	4	2	18
	In Pakistan		20	0	5	15
	Totals		44	4	7	33

I Played in India. P Played in Pakistan.

Note: The following was appointed by the home authority for only a minor proportion of the series:
[1]G. R. Viswanath (Sixth).

HIGHEST INNINGS TOTALS

For India in India: 539-9 dec. at Madras 1960-61
in Pakistan: 509 at Lahore 1989-90

For Pakistan in India: 487-9 dec. at Madras 1986-87
in Pakistan: 699-5 at Lahore 1989-90

LOWEST INNINGS TOTALS

For India in India: 106 at Lucknow 1952-53
in Pakistan: 145 at Karachi 1954-55

For Pakistan in India: 116 at Bangalore 1986-87
in Pakistan: 158 at Dacca 1954-55

INDIVIDUAL HUNDREDS

For India (31)

M. Amarnath (4)
109* Lahore 1982-83
120 Lahore 1982-83
103* Karachi 1982-83
101* Lahore 1984-85
M. Azharuddin (3)
141 Calcutta 1986-87
110 Jaipur 1986-87
109 Faisalabad .. 1989-90
C. G. Borde (1)
177* Madras 1960-61
A. D. Gaekwad (1)
201 Jullundur ... 1983-84
S. M. Gavaskar (5)
111 } 137 } Karachi 1978-79
166 Madras 1979-80
127*‡ Faisalabad .. 1982-83
103* Bangalore ... 1983-84
V. S. Hazare (1)
146* Bombay 1952-53
S. V. Manjrekar (2)
113*† Karachi 1989-90
218 Lahore 1989-90
S. M. Patil (1)
127 Faisalabad .. 1984-85
R. J. Shastri (3)
128 Karachi 1982-83
139 Faisalabad .. 1984-85
125 Jaipur 1986-87
R. H. Shodhan (1)
110† Calcutta 1952-53
K. Srikkanth (1)
123 Madras 1986-87
P. R. Umrigar (5)
102 Bombay 1952-53
108 Peshawar ... 1954-55
115 Kanpur 1960-61
117 Madras 1960-61
112 Delhi 1960-61
D. B. Vengsarkar (2)
146* Delhi 1979-80
109 Ahmedabad . 1986-87
G. R. Viswanath (1)
145† Faisalabad .. 1978-79

For Pakistan (41)

Aamer Malik (2)
117 Faisalabad .. 1989-90
113 Lahore 1989-90
Alim-ud-Din (1)
103* Karachi 1954-55
Asif Iqbal (1)
104† Faisalabad .. 1978-79
Hanif Mohammad (2)
142 Bahawalpur . 1954-55
160 Bombay 1960-61
Ijaz Faqih (1)
105† Ahmedabad . 1986-87
Imtiaz Ahmed (1)
135 Madras 1960-61
Imran Khan (3)
117 Faisalabad .. 1982-83
135* Madras 1986-87
109* Karachi 1989-90
Javed Miandad (5)
154*† Faisalabad .. 1978-79
100 Karachi 1978-79
126 Faisalabad .. 1982-83
280* Hyderabad .. 1982-83
145 Lahore 1989-90
Mohsin Khan (1)
101*† Lahore 1982-83
Mudassar Nazar (6)
126 Bangalore ... 1979-80
119 Karachi 1982-83
231 Hyderabad .. 1982-83
152*‡ Lahore 1982-83
152 Karachi 1982-83
199 Faisalabad .. 1984-85
Mushtaq Mohammad (1)
101 Delhi 1960-61
Nazar Mohammad (1)
124*‡ Lucknow ... 1952-53
Qasim Omar (1)
210 Faisalabad .. 1984-85
Ramiz Raja (1)
114 Jaipur 1986-87
Saeed Ahmed (2)
121† Bombay 1960-61
103 Madras 1960-61
Salim Malik (3)
107 Faisalabad .. 1982-83
102* Faisalabad .. 1984-85
102* Karachi 1989-90
Shoaib Mohammad (2)
101 Madras 1986-87
203* Lahore 1989-90
Wasim Raja (1)
125 Jullundur ... 1983-84
Zaheer Abbas (6)
176† Faisalabad .. 1978-79
235* Lahore 1978-79
215 Lahore 1982-83
186 Karachi 1982-83
168 Faisalabad .. 1982-83
168* Lahore 1984-85

† *Signifies hundred on first appearance in India–Pakistan Tests.*
‡ *Carried his bat.*

RECORD PARTNERSHIPS FOR EACH WICKET

For India

200 for 1st	S. M. Gavaskar and K. Srikkanth at Madras	1986-87
135 for 2nd	N. S. Sidhu and S. V. Manjrekar at Karachi	1989-90
190 for 3rd	M. Amarnath and Yashpal Sharma at Lahore	1982-83
186 for 4th	S. V. Manjrekar and R. J. Shastri at Lahore	1989-90
200 for 5th	S. M. Patil and R. J. Shastri at Faisalabad	1984-85
143 for 6th	M. Azharuddin and Kapil Dev at Calcutta	1986-87
155 for 7th	R. M. H. Binny and Madan Lal at Bangalore	1983-84
122 for 8th	S. M. H. Kirmani and Madan Lal at Faisalabad	1982-83
149 for 9th†	P. G. Joshi and R. B. Desai at Bombay	1960-61
109 for 10th†	H. R. Adhikari and Ghulam Ahmed at Delhi	1952-53

For Pakistan

162 for 1st	Hanif Mohammad and Imtiaz Ahmed at Madras	1960-61
250 for 2nd	Mudassar Nazar and Qasim Omar at Faisalabad	1984-85
451 for 3rd†	Mudassar Nazar and Javed Miandad at Hyderabad	1982-83
287 for 4th	Javed Miandad and Zaheer Abbas at Faisalabad	1982-83
213 for 5th	Zaheer Abbas and Mudassar Nazar at Karachi	1982-83
207 for 6th	Salim Malik and Imran Khan at Faisalabad	1982-83
154 for 7th	Imran Khan and Ijaz Faqih at Ahmedabad	1986-87
112 for 8th	Imran Khan and Wasim Akram at Madras	1986-87
60 for 9th	Wasim Bari and Iqbal Qasim at Bangalore	1979-80
104 for 10th	Zulfiqar Ahmed and Amir Elahi at Madras	1952-53

† Denotes record partnership against all countries.

TEN WICKETS OR MORE IN A MATCH

For India (3)

11-146 (4-90, 7-56)	Kapil Dev, Madras	1979-80
10-126 (7-27, 3-99)	Maninder Singh, Bangalore	1986-87
13-131 (8-52, 5-79)†	V. Mankad, Delhi	1952-53

For Pakistan (5)

12-94 (5-52, 7-42)	Fazal Mahmood, Lucknow	1952-53
11-79 (3-19, 8-60)	Imran Khan, Karachi	1982-83
11-180 (6-98, 5-82)	Imran Khan, Faisalabad	1982-83
10-175 (4-135, 6-40)	Iqbal Qasim, Bombay	1979-80
11-190 (8-69, 3-121)	Sikander Bakht, Delhi	1979-80

† Signifies ten wickets or more on first appearance in India–Pakistan Tests.

INDIA v SRI LANKA

	Captains					
Season	*India*	*Sri Lanka*	*T*	*I*	*SL*	*D*
1982-83*I*	S. M. Gavaskar	B. Warnapura	1	0	0	1
1985-86*S*	Kapil Dev	L. R. D. Mendis	3	0	1	2
1986-87*I*	Kapil Dev	L. R. D. Mendis	3	2	0	1
1990-91*I*	M. Azharuddin	A. Ranatunga	1	1	0	0
1993-94*S*	M. Azharuddin	A. Ranatunga	3	1	0	2
1993-94*I*	M. Azharuddin	A. Ranatunga	3	3	0	0
	In India		8	6	0	2
	In Sri Lanka		6	1	1	4
	Totals		14	7	1	6

I Played in India. S Played in Sri Lanka.

HIGHEST INNINGS TOTALS

For India in India: 676-7 at Kanpur	1986-87
in Sri Lanka: 446 at Colombo (PSS)	1993-94
For Sri Lanka in India: 420 at Kanpur	1986-87
in Sri Lanka: 385 at Colombo (PSS)	1985-86

LOWEST INNINGS TOTALS

For India in India: 288 at Chandigarh	1990-91
in Sri Lanka: 198 at Colombo (PSS)	1985-86
For Sri Lanka in India: 82 at Chandigarh	1990-91
in Sri Lanka: 198 at Kandy	1985-86

INDIVIDUAL HUNDREDS

For India (17)

M. Amarnath (2)
116* Kandy...... 1985-86
131 Nagpur..... 1986-87
M. Azharuddin (3)
199 Kanpur..... 1986-87
108 Bangalore... 1993-94
152 Ahmedabad . 1993-94
S. M. Gavaskar (2)
155† Madras..... 1982-83
176 Kanpur..... 1986-87
V. G. Kambli (2)
125 Colombo (SSC) 1993-94
120 Colombo (PSS) 1993-94
Kapil Dev (1)
163 Kanpur..... 1986-87
S. M. Patil (1)
114*† Madras..... 1982-83
N. S. Sidhu (2)
104 Colombo (SSC) 1993-94
124 Lucknow.... 1993-94
S. R. Tendulkar (2)
104* Colombo (SSC) 1993-94
142 Lucknow.... 1993-94
D. B. Vengsarkar (2)
153 Nagpur..... 1986-87
166 Cuttack..... 1986-87

For Sri Lanka (9)

P. A. de Silva (1)
148 Colombo (PSS) 1993-94
R. L. Dias (1)
106 Kandy...... 1985-86
R. S. Madugalle (1)
103 Colombo (SSC) 1985-86
R. S. Mahanama (1)
151 Colombo (PSS) 1993-94
L. R. D. Mendis (3)
105 }
105 } †Madras..... 1982-83
124 Kandy...... 1985-86
A. Ranatunga (1)
111 Colombo (SSC) 1985-86
S. A. R. Silva (1)
111 Colombo (PSS)....... 1985-86

† Signifies hundred on first appearance in India–Sri Lanka Tests.

RECORD PARTNERSHIPS FOR EACH WICKET

For India

171	for 1st	M. Prabhakar and N. S. Sidhu at Colombo (SSC)	1993-94
173	for 2nd	S. M. Gavaskar and D. B. Vengsarkar at Madras	1982-83
173	for 3rd	M. Amarnath and D. B. Vengsarkar at Nagpur	1986-87
163	for 4th	S. M. Gavaskar and M. Azharuddin at Kanpur	1986-87
87	for 5th	M. Azharuddin and S. V. Manjrekar at Bangalore	1993-94
272	for 6th	M. Azharuddin and Kapil Dev at Kanpur	1986-87
78*	for 7th	S. M. Patil and Madan Lal at Madras	1982-83
70	for 8th	Kapil Dev and L. Sivaramakrishnan at Colombo (PSS)	1985-86
67	for 9th	M. Azharuddin and R. K. Chauhan at Ahmedabad	1993-94
29	for 10th	Kapil Dev and Chetan Sharma at Colombo (PSS)	1985-86

For Sri Lanka

159	for 1st†	S. Wettimuny and J. R. Ratnayeke at Kanpur	1986-87
95	for 2nd	S. A. R. Silva and R. S. Madugalle at Colombo (PSS)	1985-86
153	for 3rd	R. L. Dias and L. R. D. Mendis at Madras	1982-83
216	for 4th	R. L. Dias and L. R. D. Mendis at Kandy	1985-86
144	for 5th	R. S. Madugalle and A. Ranatunga at Colombo (SSC)	1985-86
89	for 6th	L. R. D. Mendis and A. N. Ranasinghe at Madras	1982-83
77	for 7th	R. S. Madugalle and D. S. de Silva at Madras	1982-83
40*	for 8th	P. A. de Silva and A. L. F. de Mel at Kandy	1985-86
60	for 9th	H. P. Tillekeratne and A. W. R. Madurasinghe at Chandigarh	1990-91
44	for 10th	R. J. Ratnayake and E. A. R. de Silva at Nagpur	1986-87

† Denotes record partnership against all countries.

TEN WICKETS OR MORE IN A MATCH

For India (3)

11-128 (4-69, 7-59)	A. Kumble, Lucknow	1993-94
10-107 (3-56, 7-51)	Maninder Singh, Nagpur	1986-87
11-125 (5-38, 6-87)	S. L. V. Raju, Ahmedabad	1993-94

Note: The best match figures by a Sri Lankan bowler are 9-125 (4-76, 5-49) by R. J. Ratnayake against India at Colombo (PSS), 1985-86.

INDIA v ZIMBABWE

Season	India (Captains)	Zimbabwe (Captains)	T	I	Z	D
1992-93*Z*	M. Azharuddin	D. L. Houghton	1	0	0	1
1992-93*I*	M. Azharuddin	D. L. Houghton	1	1	0	0
	In India		1	1	0	0
	In Zimbabwe		1	0	0	1
	Totals		2	1	0	1

I Played in India. Z Played in Zimbabwe.

HIGHEST INNINGS TOTALS

For India: 536-7 dec. at Delhi 1992-93

For Zimbabwe: 456 at Harare 1992-93

INDIVIDUAL HUNDREDS

For India (2)

V. G. Kambli (1)
227† Delhi....... 1992-93

S. V. Manjrekar (1)
104† Harare 1992-93

For Zimbabwe (2)

A. Flower (1)
115 Delhi....... 1992-93

D. L. Houghton (1)
121† Harare 1992-93

† *Signifies hundred on first appearance in India–Zimbabwe Tests.*

HUNDRED PARTNERSHIPS

For India

137 for 3rd	V. G. Kambli and S. R. Tendulkar at Delhi	1992-93
107 for 2nd	N. S. Sidhu and V. G. Kambli at Delhi	1992-93
107 for 4th	V. G. Kambli and M. Azharuddin at Delhi	1992-93

For Zimbabwe

192 for 4th†	G. W. Flower and A. Flower at Delhi	1992-93
165 for 6th†	D. L. Houghton and A. Flower at Harare	1992-93
100 for 1st†	K. J. Arnott and G. W. Flower at Harare	1992-93

† *Denotes record partnership against all countries.*

BEST MATCH BOWLING ANALYSES

For India

8-160 (3-90, 5-70) A. Kumble, Delhi 1992-93

For Zimbabwe

5-86 (5-86) A. J. Traicos, Harare 1992-93

PAKISTAN v SRI LANKA

	Captains					
Season	*Pakistan*	*Sri Lanka*	*T*	*P*	*SL*	*D*
1981-82*P*	Javed Miandad	B. Warnapura[1]	3	2	0	1
1985-86*P*	Javed Miandad	L. R. D. Mendis	3	2	0	1
1985-86*S*	Imran Khan	L. R. D. Mendis	3	1	1	1
1991-92*P*	Imran Khan	P. A. de Silva	3	1	0	2
1994-95*S*†	Salim Malik	A. Ranatunga	2	2	0	0
	In Pakistan		9	5	0	4
	In Sri Lanka		5	3	1	1
	Totals		14	8	1	5

P Played in Pakistan. S Played in Sri Lanka.

† *One Test was cancelled owing to the threat of civil disturbances following a general election.*
Note: The following deputised for the official touring captain:
[1]L. R. D. Mendis (Second).

HIGHEST INNINGS TOTALS

For Pakistan in Pakistan: 555-3 at Faisalabad 1985-86
in Sri Lanka: 390 at Colombo (PSS) 1994-95

For Sri Lanka in Pakistan: 479 at Faisalabad 1985-86
in Sri Lanka: 323-3 at Colombo (PSS) 1985-86

LOWEST INNINGS TOTALS

For Pakistan in Pakistan: 221 at Faisalabad 1991-92
in Sri Lanka: 132 at Colombo (CCC) 1985-86

For Sri Lanka in Pakistan: 149 at Karachi 1981-82
in Sri Lanka: 71 at Kandy 1994-95

INDIVIDUAL HUNDREDS

For Pakistan (10)

Haroon Rashid (1)
153† Karachi 1981-82
Inzamam-ul-Haq (1)
100* Kandy...... 1994-95
Javed Miandad (1)
203* Faisalabad .. 1985-86
Mohsin Khan (1)
129 Lahore 1981-82

Qasim Omar (1)
206† Faisalabad .. 1985-86
Ramiz Raja (1)
122 Colombo (PSS)....... 1985-86
Saeed Anwar (1)
136 Colombo (PSS)....... 1994-95

Salim Malik (2)
100*† Karachi 1981-82
101 Sialkot 1991-92
Zaheer Abbas (1)
134† Lahore 1981-82

For Sri Lanka (7)

P. A. de Silva (3)
122† Faisalabad .. 1985-86
105 Karachi 1985-86
127 Colombo (PSS)....... 1994-95

R. L. Dias (1)
109 Lahore 1981-82
A. P. Gurusinha (1)
116* Colombo (PSS)....... 1985-86

A. Ranatunga (1)
135* Colombo (PSS)....... 1985-86
S. Wettimuny (1)
157 Faisalabad .. 1981-82

† *Signifies hundred on first appearance in Pakistan–Sri Lanka Tests.*

RECORD PARTNERSHIPS FOR EACH WICKET

For Pakistan

128 for 1st	Ramiz Raja and Shoaib Mohammad at Sialkot	1991-92
	Saeed Anwar and Aamir Sohail at Colombo (PSS)	1994-95
151 for 2nd	Mohsin Khan and Majid Khan at Lahore	1981-82
397 for 3rd	Qasim Omar and Javed Miandad at Faisalabad	1985-86
162 for 4th	Salim Malik and Javed Miandad at Karachi	1981-82
132 for 5th	Salim Malik and Imran Khan at Sialkot	1991-92
100 for 6th	Zaheer Abbas and Imran Khan at Lahore	1981-82
104 for 7th	Haroon Rashid and Tahir Naqqash at Karachi	1981-82
33 for 8th	Inzamam-ul-Haq and Wasim Akram at Kandy	1994-95
127 for 9th	Haroon Rashid and Rashid Khan at Karachi	1981-82
48 for 10th	Rashid Khan and Tauseef Ahmed at Faisalabad	1981-82

For Sri Lanka

81 for 1st	R. S. Mahanama and U. C. Hathurusinghe at Faisalabad	1991-92
217 for 2nd†	S. Wettimuny and R. L. Dias at Faisalabad	1981-82
85 for 3rd	S. Wettimuny and R. L. Dias at Faisalabad	1985-86
240* for 4th†	A. P. Gurusinha and A. Ranatunga at Colombo (PSS)	1985-86
119 for 5th	P. A. de Silva and H. P. Tillekeratne at Colombo (PSS)	1994-95
121 for 6th	A. Ranatunga and P. A. de Silva at Faisalabad	1985-86
131 for 7th	H. P. Tillekeratne and R. S. Kalpage at Kandy	1994-95
61 for 8th†	R. S. Madugalle and D. S. de Silva at Faisalabad	1981-82
52 for 9th	P. A. de Silva and R. J. Ratnayake at Faisalabad	1985-86
36 for 10th	R. J. Ratnayake and R. G. C. E. Wijesuriya at Faisalabad	1985-86

† *Denotes record partnership against all countries.*

TEN WICKETS OR MORE IN A MATCH

For Pakistan (2)

14-116 (8-58, 6-58)	Imran Khan, Lahore	1981-82
11-119 (6-34, 5-85)	Waqar Younis, Kandy	1994-95

Note: The best match figures by a Sri Lankan bowler are 9-162 (4-103, 5-59), D. S. de Silva at Faisalabad, 1981-82.

PAKISTAN v ZIMBABWE

	Captains					
Season	*Pakistan*	*Zimbabwe*	*T*	*P*	*Z*	*D*
1993-94*P*	Wasim Akram	A. Flower	3	2	0	1

P Played in Pakistan.

Note: The following was appointed by the home authority for only a minor proportion of the series:
Waqar Younis (First).

HIGHEST INNINGS TOTALS

For Pakistan: 423-8 dec. at Karachi (DS) 1993-94
For Zimbabwe: 289 at Karachi (DS) 1993-94

LOWEST INNINGS TOTALS

For Pakistan: 147 at Lahore 1993-94
For Zimbabwe: 134 at Karachi (DS) 1993-94

Highest score for Pakistan: 81 by Shoaib Mohammad at Karachi (DS).
Highest score for Zimbabwe: 75 by A. D. R. Campbell at Rawalpindi.

HUNDRED PARTNERSHIPS

For Pakistan

118* for 2nd Shoaib Mohammad and Asif Mujtaba at Lahore 1993-94

For Zimbabwe

135† for 2nd M. H. Dekker and A. D. R. Campbell at Rawalpindi 1993-94
102 for 2nd M. H. Dekker and A. D. R. Campbell at Rawalpindi 1993-94

† *Denotes record partnership against all countries.*

TEN WICKETS OR MORE IN A MATCH

For Pakistan (1)

13-135 (7-91, 6-44) Waqar Younis, Karachi (DS) 1993-94

Note: The best match figures for Zimbabwe are 8-114 (3-58, 5-56) by H. H. Streak at Rawalpindi, 1993-94.

TEST MATCH GROUNDS

In Chronological Sequence

City and Ground	*First Test Match*		*Tests*
1. Melbourne, Melbourne Cricket Ground	March 15, 1877	A v E	86
2. London, Kennington Oval	September 6, 1880	E v A	77
3. Sydney, Sydney Cricket Ground (No. 1)	February 17, 1882	A v E	80
4. Manchester, Old Trafford	July 11, 1884	E v A	61
5. London, Lord's	July 21, 1884	E v A	92

	City and Ground	*First Test Match*		*Tests*
6.	Adelaide, Adelaide Oval	December 12, 1884	A v E	52
7.	Port Elizabeth, St George's Park	March 12, 1889	SA v E	13
8.	Cape Town, Newlands	March 25, 1889	SA v E	26
9.	Johannesburg, Old Wanderers	March 2, 1896	SA v E	22
	Now the site of Johannesburg Railway Station.			
10.	Nottingham, Trent Bridge	June 1, 1899	E v A	42
11.	Leeds, Headingley	June 29, 1899	E v A	56
12.	Birmingham, Edgbaston	May 29, 1902	E v A	30
13.	Sheffield, Bramall Lane	July 3, 1902	E v A	1
	Sheffield United Football Club have built a stand over the cricket pitch.			
14.	Durban, Lord's	January 21, 1910	SA v E	4
	Ground destroyed and built on.			
15.	Durban, Kingsmead	January 18, 1923	SA v E	21
16.	Brisbane, Exhibition Ground	November 30, 1928	A v E	2
	No longer used for cricket.			
17.	Christchurch, Lancaster Park	January 10, 1930	NZ v E	32
18.	Bridgetown, Kensington Oval	January 11, 1930	WI v E	30
19.	Wellington, Basin Reserve	January 24, 1930	NZ v E	29
20.	Port-of-Spain, Queen's Park Oval	February 1, 1930	WI v E	43
21.	Auckland, Eden Park	February 17, 1930	NZ v E	36
22.	Georgetown, Bourda	February 21, 1930	WI v E	23
23.	Kingston, Sabina Park	April 3, 1930	WI v E	30
24.	Brisbane, Woolloongabba	November 27, 1931	A v SA	36
25.	Bombay, Gymkhana Ground	December 15, 1933	I v E	1
	No longer used for first-class cricket.			
26.	Calcutta, Eden Gardens	January 5, 1934	I v E	27
27.	Madras, Chepauk (Chidambaram Stadium)	February 10, 1934	I v E	21
28.	Delhi, Feroz Shah Kotla	November 10, 1948	I v WI	23
29.	Bombay, Brabourne Stadium	December 9, 1948	I v WI	17
	Rarely used for first-class cricket.			
30.	Johannesburg, Ellis Park	December 27, 1948	SA v E	6
	Mainly a rugby stadium, no longer used for cricket.			
31.	Kanpur, Green Park (Modi Stadium)	January 12, 1952	I v E	16
32.	Lucknow, University Ground	October 25, 1952	I v P	1
	Ground destroyed, now partly under a river bed.			
33.	Dacca, Dacca Stadium	January 1, 1955	P v I	7
	Ceased staging Tests after East Pakistan seceded and became Bangladesh.			
34.	Bahawalpur, Dring (now Bahawal) Stadium	January 15, 1955	P v I	1
	Still used for first-class cricket.			
35.	Lahore, Lawrence Gardens (Bagh-i-Jinnah)	January 29, 1955	P v I	3
	Still used for club and occasional first-class matches.			
36.	Peshawar, Services Ground	February 13, 1955	P v I	1
	Superseded by new stadium.			
37.	Karachi, National Stadium	February 26, 1955	P v I	30
38.	Dunedin, Carisbrook	March 11, 1955	NZ v E	8
39.	Hyderabad, Fateh Maidan (Lal Bahadur Stadium)	November 19, 1955	I v NZ	3
40.	Madras, Corporation Stadium	January 6, 1956	I v NZ	9
	Superseded by rebuilt Chepauk Stadium.			
41.	Johannesburg, Wanderers	December 24, 1956	SA v E	13
42.	Lahore, Gaddafi Stadium	November 21, 1959	P v A	26
43.	Rawalpindi, Pindi Club Ground	March 27, 1965	P v NZ	1
	Superseded by new stadium.			
44.	Nagpur, Vidarbha C.A. Ground	October 3, 1969	I v NZ	3
45.	Perth, Western Australian C.A. Ground	December 11, 1970	A v E	21
46.	Hyderabad, Niaz Stadium	March 16, 1973	P v E	5
47.	Bangalore, Karnataka State C.A. Ground (Chinnaswamy Stadium)	November 22, 1974	I v WI	10
48.	Bombay, Wankhede Stadium	January 23, 1975	I v WI	14
49.	Faisalabad, Iqbal Stadium	October 16, 1978	P v I	16

	City and Ground	First Test Match		Tests
50.	Napier, McLean Park	February 16, 1979	NZ v P	2
51.	Multan, Ibn-e-Qasim Bagh Stadium	December 30, 1980	P v WI	1
52.	St John's (Antigua), Recreation Ground	March 27, 1981	WI v E	8
53.	Colombo, P. Saravanamuttu Stadium	February 17, 1982	SL v E	6
54.	Kandy, Asgiriya Stadium	April 22, 1983	SL v A	6
55.	Jullundur, Burlton Park	September 24, 1983	I v P	1
56.	Ahmedabad, Gujarat Stadium	November 12, 1983	I v WI	3
57.	Colombo, Sinhalese Sports Club Ground	March 16, 1984	SL v NZ	7
58.	Colombo, Colombo Cricket Club Ground	March 24, 1984	SL v NZ	3
59.	Sialkot, Jinnah Stadium	October 27, 1985	P v SL	3
60.	Cuttack, Barabati Stadium	January 4, 1987	I v SL	1
61.	Jaipur, Sawai Mansingh Stadium	February 21, 1987	I v P	1
62.	Hobart, Bellerive Oval	December 16, 1989	A v SL	2
63.	Chandigarh, Sector 16 Stadium	November 23, 1990	I v SL	1
64.	Hamilton, Trust Bank (Seddon) Park	February 22, 1991	NZ v SL	3
65.	Gujranwala, Municipal Stadium	December 20, 1991	P v SL	1
66.	Colombo, Khettarama Stadium	August 28, 1992	SL v A	1
67.	Moratuwa, Tyronne Fernando Stadium	September 8, 1992	SL v A	4
68.	Harare, Harare Sports Club	October 18, 1992	Z v I	2
69.	Bulawayo, Bulawayo Athletic Club	November 1, 1992	Z v NZ	1
70.	Karachi, Defence Stadium	December 1, 1993	P v Z	1
71.	Rawalpindi, Rawalpindi Cricket Stadium	December 9, 1993	P v Z	1
72.	Lucknow, K. D. Singh "Babu" Stadium	January 18, 1994	I v SL	1

FAMILIES IN TEST CRICKET

FATHERS AND SONS

England

M. C. Cowdrey (114 Tests, 1954-55–1974-75) and C. S. Cowdrey (6 Tests, 1984-85–1988).
J. Hardstaff (5 Tests, 1907-08) and J. Hardstaff jun. (23 Tests, 1935–1948).
L. Hutton (79 Tests, 1937–1954-55) and R. A. Hutton (5 Tests, 1971).
F. T. Mann (5 Tests, 1922-23) and F. G. Mann (7 Tests, 1948-49–1949).
J. H. Parks (1 Test, 1937) and J. M. Parks (46 Tests, 1954–1967-68).
M. J. Stewart (8 Tests, 1962–1963-64) and A. J. Stewart (43 Tests, 1989-90–1994).
F. W. Tate (1 Test, 1902) and M. W. Tate (39 Tests, 1924–1935).
C. L. Townsend (2 Tests, 1899) and D. C. H. Townsend (3 Tests, 1934-35).

Australia

E. J. Gregory (1 Test, 1876-77) and S. E. Gregory (58 Tests, 1890–1912).

South Africa

F. Hearne (4 Tests, 1891-92–1895-96) and G. A. L. Hearne (3 Tests, 1922-23–1924).
F. Hearne also played 2 Tests for England in 1888-89.
J. D. Lindsay (3 Tests, 1947) and D. T. Lindsay (19 Tests, 1963-64–1969-70).
A. W. Nourse (45 Tests, 1902-03–1924) and A. D. Nourse (34 Tests, 1935–1951).
L. R. Tuckett (1 Test, 1913-14) and L. Tuckett (9 Tests, 1947–1948-49).

West Indies

G. A. Headley (22 Tests, 1929-30–1953-54) and R. G. A. Headley (2 Tests, 1973).
O. C. Scott (8 Tests, 1928–1930-31) and A. P. H. Scott (1 Test, 1952-53).

New Zealand

W. M. Anderson (1 Test, 1945-46) and R. W. Anderson (9 Tests, 1976-77–1978).
W. P. Bradburn (2 Tests, 1963-64) and G. E. Bradburn (4 Tests, 1990-91).
B. L. Cairns (43 Tests, 1973-74–1985-86) and C. L. Cairns (10 Tests, 1989-90–1993-94).
W. A. Hadlee (11 Tests, 1937–1950-51) and D. R. Hadlee (26 Tests, 1969–1977-78); Sir R. J. Hadlee (86 Tests, 1972-73–1990).
P. G. Z. Harris (9 Tests, 1955-56–1964-65) and C. Z. Harris (5 Tests, 1993-94).
H. G. Vivian (7 Tests, 1931–1937) and G. E. Vivian (5 Tests, 1964-65–1971-72).

India

L. Amarnath (24 Tests, 1933-34–1952-53) and M. Amarnath (69 Tests, 1969-70–1987-88); S. Amarnath (10 Tests, 1975-76–1978-79).

D. K. Gaekwad (11 Tests, 1952–1960-61) and A. D. Gaekwad (40 Tests, 1974-75–1984-85).

Nawab of Pataudi (Iftikhar Ali Khan) (3 Tests, 1946) and Nawab of Pataudi (Mansur Ali Khan) (46 Tests, 1961-62–1974-75).

Nawab of Pataudi sen. also played 3 Tests for England, 1932-33–1934.

V. L. Manjrekar (55 Tests, 1951-52–1964-65) and S. V. Manjrekar (30 Tests, 1987-88–1993-94).

V. Mankad (44 Tests, 1946–1958-59) and A. V. Mankad (22 Tests, 1969-70–1977-78).

Pankaj Roy (43 Tests, 1951-52–1960-61) and Pranab Roy (2 Tests, 1981-82).

India and Pakistan

M. Jahangir Khan (4 Tests, 1932–1936) and Majid Khan (63 Tests, 1964-65–1982-83).

S. Wazir Ali (7 Tests, 1932–1936) and Khalid Wazir (2 Tests, 1954).

Pakistan

Hanif Mohammad (55 Tests, 1954–1969-70) and Shoaib Mohammad (42 Tests, 1983-84–1993-94).

Nazar Mohammad (5 Tests, 1952-53) and Mudassar Nazar (76 Tests, 1976-77–1988-89).

GRANDFATHERS AND GRANDSONS

Australia

V. Y. Richardson (19 Tests, 1924-25–1935-36) and G. S. Chappell (87 Tests, 1970-71–1983-84); I. M. Chappell (75 Tests, 1964-65–1979-80); T. M. Chappell (3 Tests, 1981).

GREAT-GRANDFATHER AND GREAT-GRANDSON

Australia

W. H. Cooper (2 Tests, 1881-82 and 1884-85) and A. P. Sheahan (31 Tests, 1967-68–1973-74).

BROTHERS IN SAME TEST TEAM

England

E. M., G. F. and W. G. Grace: 1 Test, 1880.

C. T. and G. B. Studd: 4 Tests, 1882-83.

A. and G. G. Hearne: 1 Test, 1891-92.

F. Hearne, their brother, played in this match for South Africa.

D. W. and P. E. Richardson: 1 Test, 1957.

Australia

E. J. and D. W. Gregory: 1 Test, 1876-77.

C. and A. C. Bannerman: 1 Test, 1878-79.

G. and W. F. Giffen: 2 Tests, 1891-92.

G. H. S. and A. E. Trott: 3 Tests, 1894-95.

I. M. and G. S. Chappell: 43 Tests, 1970-71–1979-80.

S. R. and M. E. Waugh: 22 Tests, 1990-91–1993-94 – the first instance of twins appearing together.

South Africa

S. J. and S. D. Snooke: 1 Test, 1907.

D. and H. W. Taylor: 2 Tests, 1913-14.

R. H. M. and P. A. M. Hands: 1 Test, 1913-14.

P. N. and G. Kirsten: 7 Tests, 1993-94–1994.

E. A. B. and A. M. B. Rowan: 9 Tests, 1948-49–1951.

P. M. and R. G. Pollock: 23 Tests, 1963-64–1969-70.

A. J. and D. B. Pithey: 5 Tests, 1963-64.

West Indies

G. C. and R. S. Grant: 4 Tests, 1934-35.

J. B. and V. H. Stollmeyer: 1 Test, 1939.

D. St E. and E. St E. Atkinson: 1 Test, 1957-58.

New Zealand

J. J. and M. D. Crowe: 34 Tests, 1983–1989-90.
D. R. and R. J. Hadlee: 10 Tests, 1973–1977-78.
H. J. and G. P. Howarth: 4 Tests, 1974-75–1976-77.
J. M. and N. M. Parker: 3 Tests, 1976-77.
B. P. and J. G. Bracewell: 1 Test, 1980-81.

India

S. Wazir Ali and S. Nazir Ali: 2 Tests, 1932–1933-34.
L. Ramji and Amar Singh: 1 Test, 1933-34.
C. K. and C. S. Nayudu: 4 Tests, 1933-34–1936.
A. G. Kripal Singh and A. G. Milkha Singh: 1 Test, 1961-62.
S. and M. Amarnath: 8 Tests, 1975-76–1978-79.

Pakistan

Wazir and Hanif Mohammad: 18 Tests, 1952-53–1959-60.
Wazir and Mushtaq Mohammad: 1 Test, 1958-59.
Hanif and Mushtaq Mohammad: 19 Tests, 1960-61–1969-70.
Hanif, Mushtaq and Sadiq Mohammad: 1 Test, 1969-70.
Mushtaq and Sadiq Mohammad: 26 Tests, 1969-70–1978–79.
Wasim and Ramiz Raja: 2 Tests, 1983-84.

Sri Lanka

A. and D. Ranatunga: 2 Tests, 1989-90.
A. and S. Ranatunga: 1 Test, 1994-95.
M. D. and S. Wettimuny: 2 Tests, 1982-83.

Zimbabwe

A. and G. W. Flower: 7 Tests, 1992-93–1993-94.

THE ASHES

"In affectionate remembrance of English cricket which died at The Oval, 29th August, 1882. Deeply lamented by a large circle of sorrowing friends and acquaintances, R.I.P. N.B. The body will be cremated and the Ashes taken to Australia."

Australia's first victory on English soil over the full strength of England, on August 29, 1882, inspired a young London journalist, Reginald Shirley Brooks, to write this mock "obituary". It appeared in the *Sporting Times*.

Before England's defeat at The Oval, by seven runs, arrangements had already been made for the Hon. Ivo Bligh, afterwards Lord Darnley, to lead a team to Australia. Three weeks later they set out, now with the popular objective of recovering the Ashes. In the event, Australia won the First Test by nine wickets, but with England winning the next two it became generally accepted that they brought back the Ashes.

It was long accepted that the real Ashes – a small urn believed to contain the ashes of a bail used in the third match – were presented to Bligh by a group of Melbourne women. At the time of the 1982 centenary of The Oval Test match, however, evidence was produced which suggested that these ashes were the remains of a ball and that they were given to the England captain by Sir William Clarke, the presentation taking place before the Test matches in Australia in 1883. The certain origin of the Ashes, therefore, is the subject of some dispute.

After Lord Darnley's death in 1927, the urn was given to MCC by Lord Darnley's Australian-born widow, Florence. It can be seen in the cricket museum at Lord's, together with a red and gold velvet bag, made specially for it, and the scorecard of the 1882 match.

LIMITED-OVERS INTERNATIONAL RECORDS

Note: Limited-overs international matches do not have first-class status.

SUMMARY OF ALL LIMITED-OVERS INTERNATIONALS

To August 24, 1994

	Opponents	*Matches*						*Won by*								*Tied*	*NR*
			E	*A*	*SA*	*WI*	*NZ*	*I*	*P*	*SL*	*Z*	*B*	*C*	*EA*	*UAE*		
England	Australia	55	25	28	–	–	–	–	–	–	–	–	–	–	–	1	1
	South Africa	4	4	–	0	–	–	–	–	–	–	–	–	–	–	–	–
	West Indies	48	20	–	–	26	–	–	–	–	–	–	–	–	–	–	2
	New Zealand	41	21	–	–	–	17	–	–	–	–	–	–	–	–	–	3
	India	29	16	–	–	–	–	13	–	–	–	–	–	–	–	–	–
	Pakistan	36	23	–	–	–	–	–	12	–	–	–	–	–	–	–	1
	Sri Lanka	11	8	–	–	–	–	–	–	3	–	–	–	–	–	–	–
	Zimbabwe	1	0	–	–	–	–	–	–	–	1	–	–	–	–	–	–
	Canada	1	1	–	–	–	–	–	–	–	–	–	0	–	–	–	–
	East Africa	1	1	–	–	–	–	–	–	–	–	–	–	0	–	–	–
Australia	South Africa	16	–	8	8	–	–	–	–	–	–	–	–	–	–	–	–
	West Indies	69	–	26	–	41	–	–	–	–	–	–	–	–	–	1	1
	New Zealand	60	–	41	–	–	17	–	–	–	–	–	–	–	–	–	2
	India	41	–	24	–	–	–	14	–	–	–	–	–	–	–	–	3
	Pakistan	38	–	18	–	–	–	–	17	–	–	–	–	–	–	1	2
	Sri Lanka	25	–	18	–	–	–	–	–	5	–	–	–	–	–	–	2
	Zimbabwe	5	–	4	–	–	–	–	–	–	1	–	–	–	–	–	–
	Bangladesh	1	–	1	–	–	–	–	–	–	–	0	–	–	–	–	–
	Canada	1	–	1	–	–	–	–	–	–	–	–	0	–	–	–	–
South Africa	West Indies	8	–	–	4	4	–	–	–	–	–	–	–	–	–	–	–
	New Zealand	4	–	–	1	–	3	–	–	–	–	–	–	–	–	–	–
	India	13	–	–	7	–	–	6	–	–	–	–	–	–	–	–	–
	Pakistan	4	–	–	1	–	–	–	3	–	–	–	–	–	–	–	–
	Sri Lanka	5	–	–	2	–	–	–	–	2	–	–	–	–	–	–	1
	Zimbabwe	2	–	–	1	–	–	–	–	–	0	–	–	–	–	–	1
West Indies	New Zealand	14	–	–	–	11	2	–	–	–	–	–	–	–	–	–	1
	India	42	–	–	–	30	–	11	–	–	–	–	–	–	–	1	–
	Pakistan	73	–	–	–	50	–	–	21	–	–	–	–	–	–	2	–
	Sri Lanka	19	–	–	–	16	–	–	–	2	–	–	–	–	–	–	1
	Zimbabwe	4	–	–	–	4	–	–	–	–	0	–	–	–	–	–	–
New Zealand	India	33	–	–	–	–	15	18	–	–	–	–	–	–	–	–	–
	Pakistan	34	–	–	–	–	14	–	18	–	–	–	–	–	–	1	1
	Sri Lanka	27	–	–	–	–	20	–	–	6	–	–	–	–	–	–	1
	Zimbabwe	5	–	–	–	–	5	–	–	–	0	–	–	–	–	–	–
	Bangladesh	1	–	–	–	–	1	–	–	–	–	0	–	–	–	–	–
	East Africa	1	–	–	–	–	1	–	–	–	–	–	–	0	–	–	–
India	Pakistan	40	–	–	–	–	–	12	26	–	–	–	–	–	–	–	2
	Sri Lanka	33	–	–	–	–	–	21	–	10	–	–	–	–	–	–	2
	Zimbabwe	10	–	–	–	–	–	9	–	–	0	–	–	–	–	1	–
	Bangladesh	2	–	–	–	–	–	2	–	–	–	0	–	–	–	–	–
	East Africa	1	–	–	–	–	–	1	–	–	–	–	–	0	–	–	–
	U A Emirates	1	–	–	–	–	–	1	–	–	–	–	–	–	0	–	–
Pakistan	Sri Lanka	45	–	–	–	–	–	–	36	8	–	–	–	–	–	–	1
	Zimbabwe	6	–	–	–	–	–	–	6	–	0	–	–	–	–	–	–
	Bangladesh	2	–	–	–	–	–	–	2	–	–	0	–	–	–	–	–
	Canada	1	–	–	–	–	–	–	1	–	–	–	0	–	–	–	–
	U A Emirates	1	–	–	–	–	–	–	1	–	–	–	–	–	0	–	–
Sri Lanka	Zimbabwe	3	–	–	–	–	–	–	–	3	0	–	–	–	–	–	–
	Bangladesh	3	–	–	–	–	–	–	–	3	–	0	–	–	–	–	–
		920	119	169	24	182	95	108	143	42	2	0	0	0	0	8	28

	Matches	*Won*	*Lost*	*Tied*	*No Result*	*% Won (excl. NR)*
West Indies	277	182	86	4	5	66.91
Australia	311	169	128	3	11	56.33
England	227	119	100	1	7	54.09
Pakistan	280	143	126	4	7	52.38
India	245	108	128	2	7	45.37
New Zealand	220	95	116	1	8	44.81
South Africa	56	24	30	0	2	44.44
Sri Lanka	171	42	121	0	8	25.76
Zimbabwe	36	2	32	1	1	5.71
Bangladesh	9	0	9	0	0	–
Canada	3	0	3	0	0	–
East Africa	3	0	3	0	0	–
United Arab Emirates	2	0	2	0	0	–

MOST RUNS

	M	*I*	*NO*	*R*	*HS*	*100s*	*Avge*
D. L. Haynes (West Indies)	238	237	28	8,648	152*	17	41.37
Javed Miandad (Pakistan)	228	215	40	7,327	119*	8	41.86
I. V. A. Richards (West Indies)	187	167	24	6,721	189*	11	47.00
A. R. Border (Australia)	273	252	39	6,524	127*	3	30.62
D. M. Jones (Australia)	164	161	25	6,068	145	7	44.61
R. B. Richardson (West Indies)	202	195	27	5,641	122	5	33.57
C. G. Greenidge (West Indies)	128	127	13	5,134	133*	11	45.03
D. C. Boon (Australia)	162	158	11	5,243	122	5	35.66
Ramiz Raja (Pakistan)	159	158	11	4,915	119*	8	33.43
Salim Malik (Pakistan)	191	172	23	4,755	102	5	31.91
M. Azharuddin (India)	174	161	31	4,661	108*	3	35.85
M. D. Crowe (New Zealand)	134	133	18	4,412	105*	3	38.36
G. R. Marsh (Australia)	117	115	6	4,357	126*	9	39.97
G. A. Gooch (England)	121	118	6	4,229	142	8	37.75
K. Srikkanth (India)	146	145	4	4,092	123	4	29.02
A. J. Lamb (England)	122	118	16	4,010	118	4	39.31

Leading aggregates for other countries are:

	M	*I*	*NO*	*R*	*HS*	*100s*	*Avge*
A. Ranatunga (Sri Lanka)	144	137	25	3,805	98	0	33.97
K. C. Wessels (South Africa)	49	48	4	1,484	90	0	33.72
D. L. Houghton (Zimbabwe)	36	34	0	1,010	142	1	29.70

Note: K. C. Wessels also scored 1,740 runs for Australia.

HIGHEST INDIVIDUAL SCORE FOR EACH COUNTRY

189*	I. V. A. Richards	West Indies v England at Manchester	1984
175*	Kapil Dev	India v Zimbabwe at Tunbridge Wells	1983
171*	G. M. Turner	New Zealand v East Africa at Birmingham	1975
167*	R. A. Smith	England v Australia at Birmingham	1993
145	D. M. Jones	Australia v England at Brisbane	1990-91
142	D. L. Houghton	Zimbabwe v New Zealand at Hyderabad (India)	1987-88
137*	Inzamam-ul-Haq	Pakistan v New Zealand at Sharjah	1993-94
121	R. L. Dias	Sri Lanka v India at Bangalore	1982-83
112*	G. Kirsten	South Africa v Australia at Melbourne	1993-94

MOST HUNDREDS

Total		E	A	SA	WI	NZ	I	P	SL	Z
17	D. L. Haynes (West Indies)	2	6	0	–	2	2	4	1	0
11	C. G. Greenidge (West Indies)	0	1	–	–	3	3	2	1	1
11	I. V. A. Richards (West Indies)	3	3	–	–	1	3	0	1	0
9	G. R. Marsh (Australia)	1	–	0	2	2	3	1	0	0
8	G. A. Gooch (England)	–	4	0	1	1	1	1	0	0
8	Javed Miandad (Pakistan)	1	0	1	1	0	3	–	2	0
8	Ramiz Raja (Pakistan)	1	0	0	1	3	0	–	3	0
7	D. I. Gower (England)	–	2	–	0	3	0	1	1	–
7	D. M. Jones (Australia)	3	–	0	0	2	0	1	1	0
7	Zaheer Abbas (Pakistan)	0	2	–	0	1	3	–	1	–

HIGHEST PARTNERSHIP FOR EACH WICKET

212	for 1st	G. R. Marsh and D. C. Boon	A v I	Jaipur	1986-87
263	for 2nd	Aamir Sohail and Inzamam-ul-Haq	P v NZ	Sharjah	1993-94
224*	for 3rd	D. M. Jones and A. R. Border	A v SL	Adelaide	1984-85
173	for 4th	D. M. Jones and S. R. Waugh	A v P	Perth	1986-87
152	for 5th	I. V. A. Richards and C. H. Lloyd	WI v SL	Brisbane	1984-85
154	for 6th	R. B. Richardson and P. J. L. Dujon	WI v P	Sharjah	1991-92
115	for 7th	P. J. L. Dujon and M. D. Marshall	WI v P	Gujranwala	1986-87
119	for 8th	P. R. Reiffel and S. K. Warne	A v SA	Port Elizabeth	1993-94
126*	for 9th	Kapil Dev and S. M. H. Kirmani	I v Z	Tunbridge Wells	1983
106*	for 10th	I. V. A. Richards and M. A. Holding	WI v E	Manchester	1984

MOST WICKETS

	M	Balls	R	W	BB	4W/i	Avge
Wasim Akram (Pakistan)	174	8,937	5,628	254	5-15	15	22.15
Kapil Dev (India)	220	11,082	6,833	251	5-43	4	27.22
Imran Khan (Pakistan)	175	7,461	4,845	182	6-14	4	26.62
C. J. McDermott (Australia)	116	6,301	4,258	170	5-44	5	25.04
R. J. Hadlee (New Zealand)	115	6,182	3,407	158	5-25	6	21.56
M. D. Marshall (West Indies)	136	7,175	4,233	157	4-18	6	26.96
S. R. Waugh (Australia)	167	6,831	5,067	152	4-33	2	33.33
C. E. L. Ambrose (West Indies)	104	5,579	3,248	151	5-17	8	21.50
Waqar Younis (Pakistan)	88	4,327	3,081	149	6-26	12	20.67
J. Garner (West Indies)	98	5,330	2,752	146	5-31	5	18.84
I. T. Botham (England)	116	6,271	4,139	145	4-31	3	28.54
M. A. Holding (West Indies)	102	5,473	3,034	142	5-26	6	21.36
E. J. Chatfield (New Zealand)	114	6,065	3,618	140	5-34	4	25.84
C. A. Walsh (West Indies)	124	6,622	4,239	134	5-1	6	31.63
Abdul Qadir (Pakistan)	104	5,100	3,453	132	5-44	6	26.15
M. Prabhakar (India)	102	5,056	3,457	129	5-35	5	26.79
R. J. Shastri (India)	150	6,613	4,650	129	5-15	3	36.04
I. V. A. Richards (West Indies)	187	5,644	4,228	118	6-41	3	35.83
M. C. Snedden (New Zealand)	93	4,525	3,237	114	4-34	1	28.39
Mudassar Nazar (Pakistan)	122	4,855	3,431	111	5-28	2	30.90
C. L. Hooper (West Indies)	115	4,642	3,300	110	4-34	1	30.00
S. P. O'Donnell (Australia)	87	4,350	3,102	108	5-13	6	28.72
D. K. Lillee (Australia)	63	3,593	2,145	103	5-34	6	20.82
P. A. J. DeFreitas (England)	87	4,861	3,154	100	4-35	1	31.54

Leading aggregates for other countries are:

	M	Balls	R	W	BB	4W/i	Avge
J. R. Ratnayeke (Sri Lanka)	78	3,573	2,866	85	4-23	1	33.71
A. A. Donald (South Africa)	46	2,456	1,614	62	5-29	2	26.03
E. A. Brandes (Zimbabwe)	23	1,175	987	28	4-21	1	35.25

BEST BOWLING FOR EACH COUNTRY

7-37	Aqib Javed	Pakistan v India at Sharjah	1991-92
7-51	W. W. Davis	West Indies v Australia at Leeds	1983
6-12	A. Kumble	India v West Indies at Calcutta	1993-94
6-14	G. J. Gilmour	Australia v England at Leeds	1975
6-29	S. T. Jayasuriya	Sri Lanka v England at Moratuwa	1992-93
5-20	V. J. Marks	England v New Zealand at Wellington	1983-84
5-23	R. O. Collinge	New Zealand v India at Christchurch	1975-76
5-29	A. A. Donald	South Africa v India at Calcutta	1991-92
4-21	E. A. Brandes	Zimbabwe v England at Albury	1991-92

HAT-TRICKS

Jalal-ud-Din	Pakistan v Australia at Hyderabad	1982-83
B. A. Reid	Australia v New Zealand at Sydney	1985-86
Chetan Sharma	India v New Zealand at Nagpur	1987-88
Wasim Akram	Pakistan v West Indies at Sharjah	1989-90
Wasim Akram	Pakistan v Australia at Sharjah	1989-90
Kapil Dev	India v Sri Lanka at Calcutta	1990-91
Aqib Javed	Pakistan v India at Sharjah	1991-92
D. K. Morrison	New Zealand v India at Napier	1993-94

MOST DISMISSALS IN AN INNINGS

5 (all ct)	R. W. Marsh	Australia v England at Leeds	1981
5 (all ct)	R. G. de Alwis	Sri Lanka v Australia at Colombo (PSS)	1982-83
5 (all ct)	S. M. H. Kirmani	India v Zimbabwe at Leicester	1983
5 (3ct, 2st)	S. Viswanath	India v England at Sydney	1984-85
5 (3ct, 2st)	K. S. More	India v New Zealand at Sharjah	1987-88
5 (all ct)	H. P. Tillekeratne	Sri Lanka v Pakistan at Sharjah	1990-91
5 (3ct, 2st)	N. R. Mongia	India v New Zealand at Auckland	1993-94

MOST DISMISSALS IN A CAREER

	M	*Ct*	*St*	*Total*
P. J. L. Dujon (West Indies)	169	183	21	204
I. A. Healy (Australia)	109	127	19	146
R. W. Marsh (Australia)	92	120	4	124
Salim Yousuf (Pakistan)	86	81	22	103
K. S. More (India)	94	63	27	90
I. D. S. Smith (New Zealand)	98	81	5	86
D. J. Richardson (South Africa)	52	65	8	73
Rashid Latif (Pakistan)	50	53	14	67
Wasim Bari (Pakistan)	51	52	10	62

MOST CATCHES IN AN INNINGS

(Excluding wicket-keepers)

5	J. N. Rhodes	South Africa v West Indies at Bombay	1993-94
4	Salim Malik	Pakistan v New Zealand at Sialkot	1984-85
4	S. M. Gavaskar	India v Pakistan at Sharjah	1984-85
4	R. B. Richardson	West Indies v England at Birmingham	1991
4	K. C. Wessels	South Africa v West Indies at Kingston	1991-92
4	M. A. Taylor	Australia v West Indies at Sydney	1992-93
4	C. L. Hooper	West Indies v Pakistan at Durban	1992-93

Note: While fielding as substitute, J. G. Bracewell held 4 catches for New Zealand v Australia at Adelaide, 1980-81.

MOST CATCHES IN A CAREER

	M	*Ct*		*M*	*Ct*
A. R. Border (A)	273	127	Javed Miandad (P)	228	68
I. V. A. Richards (WI)	187	101	M. Azharuddin (I)	174	68
Kapil Dev (I)	220	71	M. D. Crowe (NZ)	134	64
R. B. Richardson (WI)	202	70	A. L. Logie (WI)	158	61

ALL-ROUND

1,000 Runs and 100 Wickets

	M	*R*	*W*
I. T. Botham (England)	116	2,113	145
R. J. Hadlee (New Zealand)	115	1,751	158
C. L. Hooper (West Indies)	115	2,177	110
Imran Khan (Pakistan)	175	3,709	182
Kapil Dev (India)	220	3,766	251
Mudassar Nazar (Pakistan)	122	2,653	111
S. P. O'Donnell (Australia)	87	1,242	108
M. Prabhakar (India)	102	1,253	129
I. V. A. Richards (West Indies)	187	6,721	118
R. J. Shastri (India)	150	3,108	129
Wasim Akram (Pakistan)	174	1,490	254
S. R. Waugh (Australia)	167	3,401	152

1,000 Runs and 100 Dismissals

	M	*R*	*D*
P. J. L. Dujon (West Indies)	169	1,945	204
R. W. Marsh (Australia)	92	1,225	124

TEAM RECORDS

HIGHEST INNINGS TOTALS

363-7	(55 overs)	England v Pakistan at Nottingham	1992
360-4	(50 overs)	West Indies v Sri Lanka at Karachi	1987-88
338-4	(50 overs)	New Zealand v Bangladesh at Sharjah	1989-90
338-5	(60 overs)	Pakistan v Sri Lanka at Swansea	1983
334-4	(60 overs)	England v India at Lord's	1975
333-8	(45 overs)	West Indies v India at Jamshedpur	1983-84
333-9	(60 overs)	England v Sri Lanka at Taunton	1983
332-3	(50 overs)	Australia v Sri Lanka at Sharjah	1989-90
330-6	(60 overs)	Pakistan v Sri Lanka at Nottingham	1975

Highest totals by other countries are:

313-7	(49.2 overs)	Sri Lanka v Zimbabwe at New Plymouth	1991-92
312-4	(50 overs)	Zimbabwe v Sri Lanka at New Plymouth	1991-92
299-4	(40 overs)	India v Sri Lanka at Bombay	1986-87
288-2	(46.4 overs)	South Africa v India at Delhi	1991-92

HIGHEST TOTALS BATTING SECOND

Winning

313-7	(49.2 overs)	Sri Lanka v Zimbabwe at New Plymouth	1991-92
298-6	(54.5 overs)	New Zealand v England at Leeds	1990
297-6	(48.5 overs)	New Zealand v England at Adelaide	1982-83

Losing

289-7	(40 overs)	Sri Lanka v India at Bombay	1986-87
288-9	(60 overs)	Sri Lanka v Pakistan at Swansea	1983
288-8	(50 overs)	Sri Lanka v Pakistan at Adelaide	1989-90

HIGHEST MATCH AGGREGATES

626-14	(120 overs)	Pakistan v Sri Lanka at Swansea	1983
625-11	(99.2 overs)	Sri Lanka v Zimbabwe at New Plymouth	1991-92
619-19	(118 overs)	England v Sri Lanka at Taunton	1983
604-9	(120 overs)	Australia v Sri Lanka at The Oval	1975
603-11	(100 overs)	Pakistan v Sri Lanka at Adelaide	1989-90

LOWEST INNINGS TOTALS

43	(19.5 overs)	Pakistan v West Indies at Cape Town	1992-93
45	(40.3 overs)	Canada v England at Manchester	1979
55	(28.3 overs)	Sri Lanka v West Indies at Sharjah	1986-87
63	(25.5 overs)	India v Australia at Sydney	1980-81
64	(35.5 overs)	New Zealand v Pakistan at Sharjah	1985-86
69	(28 overs)	South Africa v Australia at Sydney	1993-94
70	(25.2 overs)	Australia v England at Birmingham	1977
70	(26.3 overs)	Australia v New Zealand at Adelaide	1985-86

Note: This section does not take into account those matches in which the number of overs was reduced.

Lowest totals by other countries are:

87	(29.3 overs)	West Indies v Australia at Sydney	1992-93
93	(36.2 overs)	England v Australia at Leeds	1975
99	(36.3 overs)	Zimbabwe v West Indies at Hyderabad, India	1993-94

LARGEST VICTORIES

232 runs	Australia (323-2 in 50 overs) v Sri Lanka (91 in 35.5 overs) at Adelaide	1984-85
206 runs	New Zealand (276-7 in 50 overs) v Australia (70 in 26.3 overs) at Adelaide	1985-86
202 runs	England (334-4 in 60 overs) v India (132-3 in 60 overs) at Lord's	1975

By ten wickets: There have been nine instances of victory by ten wickets.

TIED MATCHES

West Indies 222-5 (50 overs) v Australia 222-9 (50 overs) at Melbourne	1983-84
England 226-5 (55 overs) v Australia 226-8 (55 overs) at Nottingham	1989
West Indies 186-5 (39 overs) v Pakistan 186-9 (39 overs) at Lahore	1991-92
India 126 (47.4 overs) v West Indies 126 (41 overs) at Perth	1991-92
Australia 228-7 (50 overs) v Pakistan 228-9 (50 overs) at Hobart	1992-93
Pakistan 244-6 (50 overs) v West Indies 244-5 (50 overs) at Georgetown	1992-93
India 248-5 (50 overs) v Zimbabwe 248 (50 overs) at Indore	1993-94
Pakistan 161-9 (50 overs) v New Zealand 161 (49.4 overs) at Auckland	1993-94

MOST APPEARANCES

(200 or more)

	Total	*E*	*A*	*SA*	*WI*	*NZ*	*I*	*P*	*SL*	*Z*	*C*	*B*
A. R. Border (A)	273	43	–	15	61	52	38	34	23	5	1	1
D. L. Haynes (WI)	238	35	64	8	–	13	36	65	14	3	–	–
Javed Miandad (P)	228	26	35	3	64	23	34	–	35	6	1	1
Kapil Dev (I)	220	23	40	13	41	29	–	32	31	9	–	2
R. B. Richardson (WI)	202	32	45	8	–	11	31	59	14	2	–	–

Most appearances for other countries:

	Total	*E*	*A*	*SA*	*WI*	*NZ*	*I*	*P*	*SL*	*Z*	*C*	*B*
J. G. Wright (NZ)	149	30	42	–	11	–	21	18	24	2	–	1
A. Ranatunga (SL)	144	9	20	5	15	22	29	39	–	3	–	2
A. J. Lamb (E)	122	–	23	1	26	28	15	22	6	1	–	–
D. J. Richardson (SA)	52	4	16	–	6	3	13	3	5	2	–	–
D. L. Houghton (Z)	36	1	5	2	4	5	10	6	3	–	–	–

WORLD CUP RECORDS 1975-1992

RESULTS SUMMARY

	Played	*Won*	*Lost*	*No Result*
England	34	23	10	1
West Indies	32	22	9	1
Australia	30	17	13	0
Pakistan	31	17	13	1
New Zealand	29	16	13	0
India	29	14	14	1
South Africa	9	5	4	0
Sri Lanka	26	4	20	2
Zimbabwe	20	2	18	0
Canada	3	0	3	0
East Africa	3	0	3	0

WORLD CUP FINALS

1975	WEST INDIES (291-8) beat Australia (274) by 17 runs	Lord's
1979	WEST INDIES (286-9) beat England (194) by 92 runs	Lord's
1983	INDIA (183) beat West Indies (140) by 43 runs	Lord's
1987-88	AUSTRALIA (253-5) beat England (246-8) by seven runs	Calcutta
1991-92	PAKISTAN (249-6) beat England (227) by 22 runs	Melbourne

BATTING RECORDS

Most Runs

	M	*I*	*NO*	*R*	*HS*	*100s*	*Avge*
Javed Miandad (P)	28	27	4	1,029	103	1	44.73
I. V. A. Richards (WI)	23	21	4	1,013	181	3	59.58
G. A. Gooch (E)	21	21	1	897	115	1	44.85
M. D. Crowe (NZ)	21	21	5	880	100*	1	55.00
D. L. Haynes (WI)	25	25	2	854	105	1	37.13
D. C. Boon (A)	16	16	1	815	100	2	54.33

Highest Score

181 I. V. A. Richards WI v SL Karachi 1987-88

Hundred Before Lunch

101 A. Turner A v SL The Oval 1975

Most Hundreds

3 I. V. A. Richards (WI), Ramiz Raja (P)

Highest Partnership for Each Wicket

182	for 1st	R. B. McCosker and A. Turner	A v SL	The Oval	1975
176	for 2nd	D. L. Amiss and K. W. R. Fletcher	E v I	Lord's	1975
195*	for 3rd	C. G. Greenidge and H. A. Gomes	WI v Z	Worcester	1983
149	for 4th	R. B. Kanhai and C. H. Lloyd	WI v A	Lord's	1975
145*	for 5th	A. Flower and A. C. Waller	Z v SL	New Plymouth	1991-92
144	for 6th	Imran Khan and Shahid Mahboob	P v SL	Leeds	1983
75*	for 7th	D. A. G. Fletcher and I. P. Butchart	Z v A	Nottingham	1983
117	for 8th	D. L. Houghton and I. P. Butchart	Z v NZ	Hyderabad (India)	1987-88
126*	for 9th	Kapil Dev and S. M. H. Kirmani	I v Z	Tunbridge Wells	1983
71	for 10th	A. M. E. Roberts and J. Garner	WI v I	Manchester	1983

BOWLING RECORDS

Most Wickets

	Balls	*R*	*W*	*BB*	*4W/i*	*Avge*
Imran Khan (P)	1,017	655	34	4-37	2	19.26
I. T. Botham (E)	1,332	862	30	4-31	1	28.73
Kapil Dev (I)	1,422	892	28	5-43	1	31.85
A. M. E. Roberts (WI)	1,021	552	26	3-32	0	21.23
C. J. McDermott (A)	876	587	26	5-44	2	22.57
Wasim Akram (P)	918	633	25	4-32	1	25.32

Best Bowling

7-51 W. W. Davis WI v A Leeds 1983

Hat-Trick

Chetan Sharma	I v NZ	Nagpur	1987-88

Most Economical Bowling

12-8-6-1	B. S. Bedi	I v EA	Leeds	1975

Most Expensive Bowling

12-1-105-2	M. C. Snedden	NZ v E	The Oval	1983

WICKET-KEEPING RECORDS

Most Dismissals

Wasim Bari (P)	22	(18 ct, 4 st)
P. J. L. Dujon (WI)	20	(19 ct, 1 st)
R. W. Marsh (A)	18	(17 ct, 1 st)
K. S. More (I)	18	(12 ct, 6 st)
D. L. Murray (WI)	16	(16 ct)
D. J. Richardson (SA)	15	(14 ct, 1 st)

Most Dismissals in an Innings

5 (5 ct)	S. M. H. Kirmani	I v Z	Leicester	1983

FIELDING RECORDS

Most Catches

12 C. H. Lloyd (WI), Kapil Kev (I), D. L. Haynes (WI)
10 I. T. Botham (E), A. R. Border (A)

Most Catches in an Innings

3	C. H. Lloyd	WI v SL	Manchester	1975
3	D. A. Reeve	E v P	Adelaide	1991-92
3	Ijaz Ahmed	P v A	Perth	1991-92
3	A. R. Border	A v Z	Hobart	1991-92

MOST APPEARANCES

28 Imran Khan (P), Javed Miandad (P)
26 Kapil Dev (I)
25 A. R. Border (A), D. L. Haynes (WI)

TEAM RECORDS

Highest Total	360-4	West Indies v Sri Lanka	Karachi	1987-88
– Batting Second	313-7	Sri Lanka v Zimbabwe	New Plymouth	1991-92
Lowest Total	45	Canada v England	Manchester	1979
Highest Aggregate	626	Pakistan v Sri Lanka	Swansea	1983

Largest Victories	10 wkts	India beat East Africa	Leeds	1975
	10 wkts	West Indies beat Zimbabwe	Birmingham	1983
	10 wkts	West Indies beat Pakistan	Melbourne	1991-92
	202 runs	England beat India	Lord's	1975
Narrowest Victories	1 wkt	West Indies beat Pakistan	Birmingham	1975
	1 wkt	Pakistan beat West Indies	Lahore	1987-88
	1 run	Australia beat India	Madras	1987-88
	1 run	Australia beat India	Brisbane	1991-92

CAPTAINCY

LIMITED-OVERS INTERNATIONAL CAPTAINS

England (227 matches; 19 captains)

G. A. Gooch 50; M. W. Gatting 37; R. G. D. Willis 29; J. M. Brearley 25; D. I. Gower 24; M. H. Denness 12; I. T. Botham 9; M. A. Atherton 8; A. J. Stewart 6; K. W. R. Fletcher 5; J. E. Emburey 4; A. J. Lamb 4; D. B. Close 3; R. Illingworth 3; G. Boycott 2; N. Gifford 2; A. W. Greig 2; J. H. Edrich 1; A. P. E. Knott 1.

Australia (311 matches; 11 captains)

A. R. Border 178; G. S. Chappell 49; K. J. Hughes 49; I. M. Chappell 11; M. A. Taylor 11; G. R. Marsh 4; G. N. Yallop 4; R. B. Simpson 2; R. J. Bright 1; D. W. Hookes 1; W. M. Lawry 1.

South Africa (56 matches; 3 captains)

K. C. Wessels 46; W. J. Cronje 7; C. E. B. Rice 3.

West Indies (277 matches; 10 captains)

I. V. A. Richards 108; C. H. Lloyd 81; R. B. Richardson 65; C. G. Greenidge 8; D. L. Haynes 7; M. A. Holding 2; R. B. Kanhai 2; D. L. Murray 2; P. J. L. Dujon 1; A. I. Kallicharran 1.

New Zealand (220 matches; 11 captains)

G. P. Howarth 60; M. D. Crowe 44; J. G. Wright 31; J. V. Coney 25; K. R. Rutherford 17; J. J. Crowe 16; M. G. Burgess 8; B. E. Congdon 7; G. M. Turner 7; G. R. Larsen 3; A. H. Jones 2.

India (245 matches; 12 captains)

M. Azharuddin 76; Kapil Dev 74; S. M. Gavaskar 37; D. B. Vengsarkar 18; K. Srikkanth 13; R. J. Shastri 11; S. Venkataraghavan 7; B. S. Bedi 4; A. L. Wadekar 2; M. Amarnath 1; S. M. H. Kirmani 1; G. R. Viswanath 1.

Pakistan (280 matches; 15 captains)

Imran Khan 139; Javed Miandad 62; Wasim Akram 23; Salim Malik 14, Zaheer Abbas 13; Asif Iqbal 6; Abdul Qadir 5; Wasim Bari 5; Mushtaq Mohammad 4; Intikhab Alam 3; Majid Khan 2; Ramiz Raja 1; Salim Malik 1; Sarfraz Nawaz 1; Waqar Younis 1.

Sri Lanka (171 matches; 9 captains)

A. Ranatunga 68; L. R. D. Mendis 61; P. A. de Silva 13; R. S. Madugalle 13; B. Warnapura 8; A. P. B. Tennekoon 4; R. S. Mahanama 2; D. S. de Silva 1; J. R. Ratnayeke 1.

Zimbabwe (36 matches; 4 captains)

D. L. Houghton 17; A. Flower 7; D. A. G. Fletcher 6; A. J. Traicos 6.

Others (17 matches; 5 captains)

Gazi Ashraf (Bangladesh) 7; B. M. Mauricette (Canada) 3; Harilal R. Shah (East Africa) 3; Minhaz-ul-Abedin (Bangladesh) 2; Sultan M. Zarawani (United Arab Emirates) 2.

MISCELLANEOUS

LARGE ATTENDANCES

Test Series

943,000	Australia v England (5 Tests)	1936-37
In England		
549,650	England v Australia (5 Tests)	1953

Test Matches

†350,534	Australia v England, Melbourne (Third Test)	1936-37
325,000+	India v England, Calcutta (Second Test)	1972-73
In England		
158,000+	England v Australia, Leeds (Fourth Test)	1948
137,915	England v Australia, Lord's (Second Test)	1953

Test Match Day

90,800	Australia v West Indies, Melbourne (Fifth Test, 2nd day)	1960-61

Other First-Class Matches in England

80,000+	Surrey v Yorkshire, The Oval (3 days)	1906
78,792	Yorkshire v Lancashire, Leeds (3 days)	1904
76,617	Lancashire v Yorkshire, Manchester (3 days)	1926

Limited-Overs Internationals

‡90,000	India v Pakistan, Calcutta	1986-87
‡90,000	India v South Africa, Calcutta	1991-92
‡90,000	India v South Africa, Calcutta	1993-94
‡90,000	India v West Indies, Calcutta	1993-94
87,182	England v Pakistan, Melbourne (World Cup final)	1991-92
86,133	Australia v West Indies, Melbourne	1983-84

† *Although no official figures are available, the attendance at the Fourth Test between India and England at Calcutta, 1981-82, was thought to have exceeded this figure.*

‡ *No official attendance figures were issued for these games, but 90,000 seats were believed to be occupied. Press reports which gave much higher figures included security guards, food vendors etc., as well as paying spectators.*

LORD'S CRICKET GROUND

Lord's and the MCC were founded in 1787. The Club has enjoyed an uninterrupted career since that date, but there have been three grounds known as Lord's. The first (1787-1810) was situated where Dorset Square now is; the second (1809-13), at North Bank, had to be abandoned owing to the cutting of the Regent's Canal; and the third, opened in 1814, is the present one at St John's Wood. It was not until 1866 that the freehold of Lord's was secured by the MCC. The present pavilion was erected in 1890 at a cost of £21,000.

HIGHEST INDIVIDUAL SCORES MADE AT LORD'S

333	G. A. Gooch	England v India	1990
316*	J. B. Hobbs	Surrey v Middlesex	1926
315*	P. Holmes	Yorkshire v Middlesex	1925

Note: The longest innings in a first-class match at Lord's was played by S. Wettimuny (636 minutes, 190 runs) for Sri Lanka v England, 1984.

HIGHEST TOTALS AT LORD'S

First-Class Matches

729-6 dec.	Australia v England	1930
665	West Indians v Middlesex	1939
653-4 dec.	England v India	1990
652-8 dec.	West Indies v England	1973

Minor Match

735-9 dec.	MCC and Ground v Wiltshire	1888

BIGGEST HIT AT LORD'S

The only known instance of a batsman hitting a ball over the present pavilion at Lord's occurred when A. E. Trott, appearing for MCC against Australians on July 31, August 1, 2, 1899, drove M. A. Noble so far and high that the ball struck a chimney pot and fell behind the building.

MINOR CRICKET

HIGHEST INDIVIDUAL SCORES

628*	A. E. J. Collins, Clark's House v North Town at Clifton College. (A Junior House match. His innings of 6 hours 50 minutes was spread over four afternoons.)	1899
566	C. J. Eady, Break-o'-Day v Wellington at Hobart	1901-02
515	D. R. Havewalla, B.B. and C.I. Rly v St Xavier's at Bombay	1933-34
506*	J. C. Sharp, Melbourne GS v Geelong College at Melbourne	1914-15
502*	Chaman Lal, Mehandra Coll., Patiala v Government Coll., Rupar at Patiala	1956-57
485	A. E. Stoddart, Hampstead v Stoics at Hampstead	1886
475*	Mohammad Iqbal, Muslim Model HS v Islamia HS, Sialkot at Lahore	1958-59
466*	G. T. S. Stevens, Beta v Lambda (University College School House match) at Neasden	1919
459	J. A. Prout, Wesley College v Geelong College at Geelong	1908-09

Note: The highest score in a Minor County match is 323* by F. E. Lacey for Hampshire v Norfolk at Southampton in 1887; the highest in the Minor Counties Championship is 282 by E. Garnett for Berkshire v Wiltshire at Reading in 1908.

HIGHEST PARTNERSHIP

664* for 3rd V. G. Kambli and S. R. Tendulkar, Sharadashram Vidyamandir School v St Xavier's High School at Bombay 1987-88

RECORD HIT

The Rev. W. Fellows, while at practice on the Christ Church ground at Oxford in 1856, drove a ball bowled by Charles Rogers 175 yards from hit to pitch.

THROWING THE CRICKET BALL

140 yards 2 feet, Robert Percival, on the Durham Sands racecourse, Co. Durham c1882
140 yards 9 inches, Ross Mackenzie, at Toronto 1872
140 yards, "King Billy" the Aborigine at Clermont, Queensland 1872

Note: Extensive research has shown that these traditional records are probably authentic, if not necessarily wholly accurate. Modern competitions have failed to produce similar distances although Ian Pont, the Essex all-rounder who also played baseball, was reported to have thrown 138 yards in Cape Town in 1981. There have been speculative reports attributing throws of 150 yards or more to figures as diverse at the South African Test player Colin Bland, the Latvian javelin thrower Janis Lusis, who won a gold medal for the Soviet Union in the 1968 Olympics, and the British sprinter Charley Ransome. The definitive record is still awaited.

DATES OF FORMATION OF COUNTY CLUBS NOW FIRST-CLASS

		Present Club	
County	*First known county organisation*	*Original date*	*Reorganisation, if substantial*
Derbyshire	November 4, 1870	November 4, 1870	—
Durham	January 24, 1874	May 10, 1882	March, 1991
Essex	By May, 1790	January 14, 1876	—
Glamorgan	August 5, 1861	July 6, 1888	—
Gloucestershire	November 3, 1863	1871	—
Hampshire	April 3, 1849	August 12, 1863	July, 1879
Kent	August 6, 1842	March 1, 1859	December 6, 1870
Lancashire	January 12, 1864	January 12, 1864	—
Leicestershire	By August, 1820	March 25, 1879	—
Middlesex	December 15, 1863	February 2, 1864	—
Northamptonshire	1820†	July 31, 1878	—
Nottinghamshire	March/April, 1841	March/April, 1841	December 11, 1866
Somerset	October 15, 1864	August 18, 1875	—
Surrey	August 22, 1845	August 22, 1845	—
Sussex	June 16, 1836	March 1, 1839	August, 1857
Warwickshire	May, 1826	1882	—
Worcestershire	1844	March 5, 1865	—
Yorkshire	March 7, 1861	January 8, 1863	December 10, 1891

† *Town club.*

DATES OF FORMATION OF CLUBS IN THE CURRENT MINOR COUNTIES CHAMPIONSHIP

County	*First known county organisation*	*Present Club*
Bedfordshire	May, 1847	November 3, 1899
Berkshire	By May, 1841	March 17, 1895
Buckinghamshire	November, 1864	January 15, 1891
Cambridgeshire	March 13, 1844	June 6, 1891
Cheshire	1819	September 29, 1908
Cornwall	1813	November 12, 1894
Cumberland	January 2, 1884	April 10, 1948
Devon	1824	November 26, 1899
Dorset	1862 *or* 1871	February 5, 1896
Herefordshire	July 13, 1836	January 9, 1991
Hertfordshire	1838	March 8, 1876
Lincolnshire	1853	September 28, 1906
Norfolk	January 11, 1827	October 14, 1876
Northumberland	1834	December, 1895
Oxfordshire	1787	December 14, 1921
Shropshire	1819 or 1829	June 28, 1956
Staffordshire	November 24, 1871	November 24, 1871
Suffolk	July 27, 1864	August, 1932
Wiltshire	February 24, 1881	January, 1893

CONSTITUTION OF COUNTY CHAMPIONSHIP

There are references in the sporting press to a champion county as early as 1825, but the list is not continuous and in some years only two counties contested the title. The earliest reference in any cricket publication is from 1864, and at this time there were eight leading counties who have come to be regarded as first-class from that date – Cambridgeshire, Hampshire, Kent, Middlesex, Nottinghamshire, Surrey, Sussex and Yorkshire. The newly formed Lancashire club began playing inter-county matches in 1865, Gloucestershire in 1870 and Derbyshire in 1871, and they are therefore regarded as first-class from these respective dates. Cambridgeshire dropped out after 1871, Hampshire, who had not played inter-county matches in certain seasons, after 1885, and Derbyshire after 1887. Somerset, who had played matches against the first-class counties since 1879, were regarded as first-class from 1882 to 1885, and were admitted formally to the Championship in 1891. In 1894, Derbyshire, Essex, Leicestershire and Warwickshire were granted first-class status, but did not compete in the Championship until 1895 when Hampshire returned. Worcestershire, Northamptonshire and Glamorgan were admitted to the Championship in 1899, 1905 and 1921 respectively and are regarded as first-class from these dates. An invitation in 1921 to Buckinghamshire to enter the Championship was declined, owing to the lack of necessary playing facilities, and an application by Devon in 1948 was unsuccessful. Durham were admitted to the Championship in 1992 and were granted first-class status prior to their pre-season tour of Zimbabwe.

MOST COUNTY CHAMPIONSHIP APPEARANCES

762	W. Rhodes	Yorkshire	1898-1930
707	F. E. Woolley	Kent	1906-38
668	C. P. Mead	Hampshire	1906-36
617	N. Gifford	Worcestershire (484), Warwickshire (133)	1960-88
611	W. G. Quaife	Warwickshire	1895-1928
601	G. H. Hirst	Yorkshire	1891-1921

The most appearances for counties not mentioned singly above are:

594	F. J. Titmus	Middlesex	1949-82
591	W. E. Astill	Leicestershire	1906-39
589	D. J. Shepherd	Glamorgan	1950-72
571	C. W. L. Parker	Gloucestershire	1905-35
561	J. Langridge	Sussex	1924-53
544	G. Gunn	Nottinghamshire	1902-32
538	D. Kenyon	Worcestershire	1946-67
536	J. B. Hobbs	Surrey	1905-34
529	K. W. R. Fletcher	Essex	1962-88
526	G. E. Tyldesley	Lancashire	1909-36
506	D. C. Morgan	Derbyshire	1950-69
479	B. A. Langford	Somerset	1953-74
464	D. Brookes	Northamptonshire	1934-59

Notes: The most for Durham (1992-94) is 49 by P. Bainbridge, S. J. E. Brown, D. A. Graveney and W. Larkins. F. J. Titmus also played one match for Surrey (1978). The most appearances by a captain is 407 by Lord Hawke for Yorkshire (1883-1909), by a wicket-keeper 506 by H. Strudwick for Surrey (1902-27) and by an amateur 496 by P. A. Perrin for Essex (1896-1928).

MOST CONSECUTIVE COUNTY CHAMPIONSHIP APPEARANCES

423	K. G. Suttle	Sussex	1954-69
412	J. G. Binks	Yorkshire	1955-69
399	J. Vine	Sussex	1899-1914
344	E. H. Killick	Sussex	1898-1912
326	C. N. Woolley	Northamptonshire	1913-31
305	A. H. Dyson	Glamorgan	1930-47
301	B. Taylor	Essex	1961-72

Notes: J. Vine made 417 consecutive appearances for Sussex in all first-class matches between July 1900 and September 1914.

J. G. Binks did not miss a Championship match for Yorkshire between making his debut in June 1955 and retiring at the end of the 1969 season.

UMPIRES

MOST COUNTY CHAMPIONSHIP APPEARANCES

569	T. W. Spencer	1950-1980
533	F. Chester	1922-1955
516	H. G. Baldwin	1932-1962
470	**P. B. Wight**	**1966-1994**
457	A. Skelding	1931-1958

Bold type denotes an umpire who stood in the 1994 season.

MOST SEASONS ON FIRST-CLASS LIST

31	T. W. Spencer	1950-1980
29	**P. B. Wight**	**1966-1994**
28	F. Chester	1922-1955
27	J. Moss	1899-1929
26	**D. J. Constant**	**1969-1994**
26	W. A. J. West	1896-1925
25	H. G. Baldwin	1932-1962
25	A. Jepson	1960-1984
25	J. G. Langridge	1956-1980
25	**A. G. T. Whitehead**	**1970-1994**

Bold type denotes umpires who stood in the 1994 season.

WISDEN'S CRICKETERS OF THE YEAR, 1889-1995

1889 *Six Great Bowlers of the Year:* J. Briggs, J. J. Ferris, G. A. Lohmann, R. Peel, C. T. B. Turner, S. M. J. Woods.
1890 *Nine Great Batsmen of the Year:* R. Abel, W. Barnes, W. Gunn, L. Hall, R. Henderson, J. M. Read, A. Shrewsbury, F. H. Sugg, A. Ward.
1891 *Five Great Wicket-Keepers:* J. McC. Blackham, G. MacGregor, R. Pilling, M. Sherwin, H. Wood.
1892 *Five Great Bowlers:* W. Attewell, J. T. Hearne, F. Martin, A. W. Mold, J. W. Sharpe.
1893 *Five Batsmen of the Year:* H. T. Hewett, L. C. H. Palairet, W. W. Read, S. W. Scott, A. E. Stoddart.
1894 *Five All-Round Cricketers:* G. Giffen, A. Hearne, F. S. Jackson, G. H. S. Trott, E. Wainwright.
1895 *Five Young Batsmen of the Season:* W. Brockwell, J. T. Brown, C. B. Fry, T. W. Hayward, A. C. MacLaren.
1896 W. G. Grace.
1897 *Five Cricketers of the Season:* S. E. Gregory, A. A. Lilley, K. S. Ranjitsinhji, T. Richardson, H. Trumble.
1898 *Five Cricketers of the Year:* F. G. Bull, W. R. Cuttell, N. F. Druce, G. L. Jessop, J. R. Mason.
1899 *Five Great Players of the Season:* W. H. Lockwood, W. Rhodes, W. Storer, C. L. Townsend, A. E. Trott.
1900 *Five Cricketers of the Season:* J. Darling, C. Hill, A. O. Jones, M. A. Noble, Major R. M. Poore.
1901 *Mr R. E. Foster and Four Yorkshiremen:* R. E. Foster, S. Haigh, G. H. Hirst, T. L. Taylor, J. Tunnicliffe.
1902 L. C. Braund, C. P. McGahey, F. Mitchell, W. G. Quaife, J. T. Tyldesley.
1903 W. W. Armstrong, C. J. Burnup, J. Iremonger, J. J. Kelly, V. T. Trumper.
1904 C. Blythe, J. Gunn, A. E. Knight, W. Mead, P. F. Warner.
1905 B. J. T. Bosanquet, E. A. Halliwell, J. Hallows, P. A. Perrin, R. H. Spooner.
1906 D. Denton, W. S. Lees, G. J. Thompson, J. Vine, L. G. Wright.
1907 J. N. Crawford, A. Fielder, E. G. Hayes, K. L. Hutchings, N. A. Knox.
1908 A. W. Hallam, R. O. Schwarz, F. A. Tarrant, A. E. E. Vogler, T. G. Wass.
1909 *Lord Hawke and Four Cricketers of the Year:* W. Brearley, Lord Hawke, J. B. Hobbs, A. Marshal, J. T. Newstead.
1910 W. Bardsley, S. F. Barnes, D. W. Carr, A. P. Day, V. S. Ransford.
1911 H. K. Foster, A. Hartley, C. B. Llewellyn, W. C. Smith, F. E. Woolley.
1912 *Five Members of the MCC's Team in Australia:* F. R. Foster, J. W. Hearne, S. P. Kinneir, C. P. Mead, H. Strudwick.
1913 John Wisden: Personal Recollections.
1914 M. W. Booth, G. Gunn, J. W. Hitch, A. E. Relf, Hon. L. H. Tennyson.
1915 J. W. H. T. Douglas, P. G. H. Fender, H. T. W. Hardinge, D. J. Knight, S. G. Smith.
1916-17 No portraits appeared.
1918 *School Bowlers of the Year:* H. L. Calder, J. E. D'E. Firth, C. H. Gibson, G. A. Rotherham, G. T. S. Stevens.
1919 *Five Public School Cricketers of the Year:* P. W. Adams, A. P. F. Chapman, A. C. Gore, L. P. Hedges, N. E. Partridge.
1920 *Five Batsmen of the Year:* A. Ducat, E. H. Hendren, P. Holmes, H. Sutcliffe, E. Tyldesley.
1921 P. F. Warner.
1922 H. Ashton, J. L. Bryan, J. M. Gregory, C. G. Macartney, E. A. McDonald.
1923 A. W. Carr, A. P. Freeman, C. W. L. Parker, A. C. Russell, A. Sandham.
1924 *Five Bowlers of the Year:* A. E. R. Gilligan, R. Kilner, G. G. Macaulay, C. H. Parkin, M. W. Tate.
1925 R. H. Catterall, J. C. W. MacBryan, H. W. Taylor, R. K. Tyldesley, W. W. Whysall.

1926 J. B. Hobbs.
1927 G. Geary, H. Larwood, J. Mercer, W. A. Oldfield, W. M. Woodfull.
1928 R. C. Blunt, C. Hallows, W. R. Hammond, D. R. Jardine, V. W. C. Jupp.
1929 L. E. G. Ames, G. Duckworth, M. Leyland, S. J. Staples, J. C. White.
1930 E. H. Bowley, K. S. Duleepsinhji, H. G. Owen-Smith, R. W. V. Robins, R. E. S. Wyatt.
1931 D. G. Bradman, C. V. Grimmett, B. H. Lyon, I. A. R. Peebles, M. J. Turnbull.
1932 W. E. Bowes, C. S. Dempster, James Langridge, Nawab of Pataudi sen., H. Verity.
1933 W. E. Astill, F. R. Brown, A. S. Kennedy, C. K. Nayudu, W. Voce.
1934 A. H. Bakewell, G. A. Headley, M. S. Nichols, L. F. Townsend, C. F. Walters.
1935 S. J. McCabe, W. J. O'Reilly, G. A. E. Paine, W. H. Ponsford, C. I. J. Smith.
1936 H. B. Cameron, E. R. T. Holmes, B. Mitchell, D. Smith, A. W. Wellard.
1937 C. J. Barnett, W. H. Copson, A. R. Gover, V. M. Merchant, T. S. Worthington.
1938 T. W. J. Goddard, J. Hardstaff jun., L. Hutton, J. H. Parks, E. Paynter.
1939 H. T. Bartlett, W. A. Brown, D. C. S. Compton, K. Farnes, A. Wood.
1940 L. N. Constantine, W. J. Edrich, W. W. Keeton, A. B. Sellers, D. V. P. Wright.
1941-46 No portraits appeared.
1947 A. V. Bedser, L. B. Fishlock, V. (M. H.) Mankad, T. P. B. Smith, C. Washbrook.
1948 M. P. Donnelly, A. Melville, A. D. Nourse, J. D. Robertson, N. W. D. Yardley.
1949 A. L. Hassett, W. A. Johnston, R. R. Lindwall, A. R. Morris, D. Tallon.
1950 T. E. Bailey, R. O. Jenkins, J. G. Langridge, R. T. Simpson, B. Sutcliffe.
1951 T. G. Evans, S. Ramadhin, A. L. Valentine, E. D. Weekes, F. M. M. Worrell.
1952 R. Appleyard, H. E. Dollery, J. C. Laker, P. B. H. May, E. A. B. Rowan.
1953 H. Gimblett, T. W. Graveney, D. S. Sheppard, W. S. Surridge, F. S. Trueman.
1954 R. N. Harvey, G. A. R. Lock, K. R. Miller, J. H. Wardle, W. Watson.
1955 B. Dooland, Fazal Mahmood, W. E. Hollies, J. B. Statham, G. E. Tribe.
1956 M. C. Cowdrey, D. J. Insole, D. J. McGlew, H. J. Tayfield, F. H. Tyson.
1957 D. Brookes, J. W. Burke, M. J. Hilton, G. R. A. Langley, P. E. Richardson.
1958 P. J. Loader, A. J. W. McIntyre, O. G. Smith, M. J. Stewart, C. L. Walcott.
1959 H. L. Jackson, R. E. Marshall, C. A. Milton, J. R. Reid, D. Shackleton.
1960 K. F. Barrington, D. B. Carr, R. Illingworth, G. Pullar, M. J. K. Smith.
1961 N. A. T. Adcock, E. R. Dexter, R. A. McLean, R. Subba Row, J. V. Wilson.
1962 W. E. Alley, R. Benaud, A. K. Davidson, W. M. Lawry, N. C. O'Neill.
1963 D. Kenyon, Mushtaq Mohammad, P. H. Parfitt, P. J. Sharpe, F. J. Titmus.
1964 D. B. Close, C. C. Griffith, C. C. Hunte, R. B. Kanhai, G. S. Sobers.
1965 G. Boycott, P. J. P. Burge, J. A. Flavell, G. D. McKenzie, R. B. Simpson.
1966 K. C. Bland, J. H. Edrich, R. C. Motz, P. M. Pollock, R. G. Pollock.
1967 R. W. Barber, B. L. D'Oliveira, C. Milburn, J. T. Murray, S. M. Nurse.
1968 Asif Iqbal, Hanif Mohammad, K. Higgs, J. M. Parks, Nawab of Pataudi jun.
1969 J. G. Binks, D. M. Green, B. A. Richards, D. L. Underwood, O. S. Wheatley.
1970 B. F. Butcher, A. P. E. Knott, Majid Khan, M. J. Procter, D. J. Shepherd.
1971 J. D. Bond, C. H. Lloyd, B. W. Luckhurst, G. M. Turner, R. T. Virgin.
1972 G. G. Arnold, B. S. Chandrasekhar, L. R. Gibbs, B. Taylor, Zaheer Abbas.
1973 G. S. Chappell, D. K. Lillee, R. A. L. Massie, J. A. Snow, K. R. Stackpole.
1974 K. D. Boyce, B. E. Congdon, K. W. R. Fletcher, R. C. Fredericks, P. J. Sainsbury.
1975 D. L. Amiss, M. H. Denness, N. Gifford, A. W. Greig, A. M. E. Roberts.
1976 I. M. Chappell, P. G. Lee, R. B. McCosker, D. S. Steele, R. A. Woolmer.
1977 J. M. Brearley, C. G. Greenidge, M. A. Holding, I. V. A. Richards, R. W. Taylor.
1978 I. T. Botham, M. Hendrick, A. Jones, K. S. McEwan, R. G. D. Willis.
1979 D. I. Gower, J. K. Lever, C. M. Old, C. T. Radley, J. N. Shepherd.
1980 J. Garner, S. M. Gavaskar, G. A. Gooch, D. W. Randall, B. C. Rose.
1981 K. J. Hughes, R. D. Jackman, A. J. Lamb, C. E. B. Rice, V. A. P. van der Bijl.
1982 T. M. Alderman, A. R. Border, R. J. Hadlee, Javed Miandad, R. W. Marsh.
1983 Imran Khan, T. E. Jesty, A. I. Kallicharran, Kapil Dev, M. D. Marshall.
1984 M. Amarnath, J. V. Coney, J. E. Emburey, M. W. Gatting, C. L. Smith.
1985 M. D. Crowe, H. A. Gomes, G. W. Humpage, J. Simmons, S. Wettimuny.
1986 P. Bainbridge, R. M. Ellison, C. J. McDermott, N. V. Radford, R. T. Robinson.
1987 J. H. Childs, G. A. Hick, D. B. Vengsarkar, C. A. Walsh, J. J. Whitaker.

1988 J. P. Agnew, N. A. Foster, D. P. Hughes, P. M. Roebuck, Salim Malik.
1989 K. J. Barnett, P. J. L. Dujon, P. A. Neale, F. D. Stephenson, S. R. Waugh.
1990 S. J. Cook, D. M. Jones, R. C. Russell, R. A. Smith, M. A. Taylor.
1991 M. A. Atherton, M. Azharuddin, A. R. Butcher, D. L. Haynes, M. E. Waugh.
1992 C. E. L. Ambrose, P. A. J. DeFreitas, A. A. Donald, R. B. Richardson, Waqar Younis.
1993 N. E. Briers, M. D. Moxon, I. D. K. Salisbury, A. J. Stewart, Wasim Akram.
1994 D. C. Boon, I. A. Healy, M. G. Hughes, S. K. Warne, S. L. Watkin.
1995 B. C. Lara, D. E. Malcolm, T. A. Munton, S. J. Rhodes, K. C. Wessels.

THE LOST CRICKETER OF THE YEAR

[*Cape Times*

Harry Calder: as pictured in *Wisden* in 1918 . . . and in 1994.

In 1918, in the absence of any first-class cricket, *Wisden* named five public school bowlers as its Cricketers of the Year. Among them was H. L. Calder, for his feats the previous summer as a 16-year-old spin bowler at Cranleigh School.

The years passed. In 1994, we tried to track down the oldest surviving Cricketers of the Year to invite them to the annual *Wisden* dinner – indeed R. E. S. Wyatt, then almost 93 and thought to be the oldest survivor, was present. But there was a small mystery. There was no record of Harry Calder's death. Indeed, there was no record of his life. Cranleigh had no knowledge of what became of him; nor did cricket's best-known old Cranleighan, E. W. Swanton.

However, Robert Brooke, perhaps cricket's most assiduous researcher, had a hint that he had been heard of in Port Elizabeth, South Africa in the 1930s. On the off-chance, Brooke wrote to a newspaper there; a friend read the article and Calder wrote to us from a rest home in Cape Town, not as well as he had been before a stroke in 1992 but, at 93, three months older than Wyatt, very much alive.

Calder's father, Henry, had played for Hampshire in the 1880s and later captained Western Province. The family went back to South Africa in 1921. Henry Calder wanted his son to join the Wanderers Club, but all Harry saw was "a sea of gravel", so he decided to play tennis and golf instead, while he made his living in banking and industry. He never played serious cricket again and, until Brooke got in touch with him, never even knew he was a member of the game's elite. But he was "delighted" to hear the news, 76 years late.

BIRTHS AND DEATHS OF CRICKETERS

The qualifications for inclusion are as follows:

1. All players who have appeared in a Test match or a one-day international for a Test-match playing country.

2. English county players who have appeared in 50 or more first-class matches during their careers and, if dead, were still living ten years ago.

3. Players who appeared in 15 or more first-class matches in the 1994 English season.

4. English county captains, county caps and captains of Oxford and Cambridge Universities who, if dead, were still living ten years ago.

5. All players chosen as *Wisden* Cricketers of the Year, including the Public Schoolboys chosen for the 1918 and 1919 Almanacks. Cricketers of the Year are identified by the italic notation *CY* and year of appearance. A list of the Cricketers of the Year from 1889 to 1995 appears on pages 273-275.

6. Players or personalities not otherwise qualified who are thought to be of sufficient interest to merit inclusion.

Key to abbreviations and symbols

CUCC – Cambridge University, OUCC – Oxford University.

Australian states: NSW – New South Wales, Qld – Queensland, S. Aust. – South Australia, Tas. – Tasmania, Vic. – Victoria, W. Aust. – Western Australia.

Indian teams: Guj. – Gujarat, H'bad – Hyderabad, Ind. Rlwys – Indian Railways, Ind. Serv. – Indian Services, J/K – Jammu and Kashmir, Karn. – Karnataka (Mysore to 1972-73), M. Pradesh – Madhya Pradesh (Central India [C. Ind.] to 1939-40, Holkar to 1954-55, Madhya Bharat to 1956-57), M'tra – Maharashtra, Naw. – Nawanagar, Raja. – Rajasthan, S'tra – Saurashtra (West India [W. Ind.] to 1945-46, Kathiawar to 1949-50), S. Punjab – Southern Punjab (Patiala to 1958-59, Punjab since 1968-69), TC – Travanacore-Cochin (Kerala since 1956-57), TN – Tamil Nadu (Madras to 1959-60), U. Pradesh – Uttar Pradesh (United Provinces [U. Prov.] to 1948-49), Vidarbha (CP & Berar to 1949-50, Madhya Pradesh to 1956-57).

New Zealand provinces: Auck. – Auckland, Cant. – Canterbury, C. Dist. – Central Districts, N. Dist. – Northern Districts, Wgtn – Wellington.

Pakistani teams: ADBP – Agricultural Development Bank of Pakistan, B'pur – Bahawalpur, F'bad – Faisalabad, HBFC – House Building Finance Corporation, HBL – Habib Bank Ltd, I'bad – Islamabad, IDBP – Industrial Development Bank of Pakistan, Kar. – Karachi, MCB – Muslim Commercial Bank, NBP – National Bank of Pakistan, NWFP – North-West Frontier Province, PACO – Pakistan Automobile Corporation, Pak. Rlwys – Pakistan Railways, Pak. Us – Pakistan Universities, PIA – Pakistan International Airlines, PNSC – Pakistan National Shipping Corporation, PWD – Public Works Department, R'pindi – Rawalpindi, UBL – United Bank Ltd, WAPDA – Water and Power Development Authority.

South African provinces: E. Prov. – Eastern Province, E. Tvl – Eastern Transvaal, Griq. W. – Griqualand West, N. Tvl – Northern Transvaal, NE Tvl – North-Eastern Transvaal, OFS – Orange Free State, Rhod. – Rhodesia, Tvl – Transvaal, W. Prov. – Western Province, W. Tvl – Western Transvaal.

Sri Lankan teams: Ant. – Antonians, BRC – Burgher Recreation Club, CCC – Colombo Cricket Club, Mor. – Moratuwa Sports Club, NCC – Nondescripts Cricket Club, Pan. – Panadura Sports Club, Seb. – Sebastianites, SLAF – Air Force, SSC – Sinhalese Sports Club, TU – Tamil Union Cricket and Athletic Club, Under-23 – Board Under-23 XI.

West Indies islands: B'dos – Barbados, BG – British Guiana (Guyana since 1966), Comb. Is. – Combined Islands, Jam. – Jamaica, T/T – Trinidad & Tobago.

Zimbabwean teams: Mash. – Mashonaland, Mat. – Matabeleland, MCD – Mashonaland Country Districts, Under-24 – Mashonaland Under-24.

* *Denotes Test player.* ** *Denotes appeared for two countries. There is a list of Test players country by country from page 57.*
† *Denotes also played for team under its previous name.*

Aamer Hameed (Pak. Us, Lahore, Punjab & OUCC) b Oct. 18, 1954
Aamer Hanif (Kar. & PACO) b Oct. 4, 1971
*Aamer Malik (ADBP, PIA, Multan & Lahore) b Jan. 3, 1963
*Aamir Nazir (I'bad) b Jan. 2, 1971
*Aamir Sohail (HBL, Sargodha & Lahore) b Sept. 14, 1966
Abberley, R. N. (Warwicks.) b April 22, 1944
*a'Beckett, E. L. (Vic.) b Aug. 11, 1907, d June 2, 1989
*Abdul Kadir (Kar. & NBP) b May 10, 1944
*Abdul Qadir (HBL, Lahore & Punjab) b Sept. 15, 1955
*Abel, R. (Surrey; *CY 1890*) b Nov. 30, 1857, d Dec. 10, 1936
Abell, Sir G. E. B. (OUCC, Worcs. & N. Ind.) b June 22, 1904, d Jan. 11, 1989
Aberdare, 3rd Lord (*see* Bruce, Hon. C. N.)
*Abid Ali, S. (H'bad) b Sept. 9, 1941
Abrahams, J. (Lancs.) b July 21, 1952
*Absolom, C. A. (CUCC & Kent) b June 7, 1846, d July 30, 1889
Acfield D. L. (CUCC & Essex) b July 24, 1947
*Achong, E. (T/T) b Feb. 16, 1904, d Aug. 29, 1986
Ackerman, H. M. (Border, NE Tvl, Northants, Natal & W. Prov.) b April 28, 1947
A'Court, D. G. (Glos.) b July 27, 1937
Adam, Sir Ronald, 2nd Bt (Pres. MCC 1946-47) b Oct. 30, 1885, d Dec. 26, 1982
Adams, C. J. (Derbys.) b May 6, 1970
*Adams, J. C. (Jam. & Notts.) b Jan. 9, 1968
Adams, P. W. (Cheltenham & Sussex; *CY 1919*) b Sept. 5, 1900, d Sept. 28, 1962
*Adcock, N. A. T. (Tvl & Natal; *CY 1961*) b March 8, 1931
*Adhikari, H. R. (Guj., Baroda & Ind. Serv.) b July 31, 1919
*Afaq Hussain (Kar., Pak. Us, PIA & PWD) b Dec. 31, 1939
Afford, J. A. (Notts.) b May 12, 1964
*Aftab Baloch (PWD, Kar., Sind, NBP & PIA) b April 1, 1953
*Aftab Gul (Punjab U., Pak. Us & Lahore) b March 31, 1946
*Agha Saadat Ali (Pak. Us, Punjab, B'pur & Lahore) b June 21, 1929
*Agha Zahid (Pak. Us, Punjab, Lahore & HBL) b Jan. 7, 1953
*Agnew, J. P. (Leics; *CY 1988*) b April 4, 1960
*Ahangama, F. S. (SSC) b Sept. 14, 1959
Aird, R. (CUCC & Hants; Sec. MCC 1953-62, Pres. MCC 1968-69) b May 4, 1902, d Aug. 16, 1986
Aislabie, B. (Surrey, Hants, Kent & Sussex; Sec. MCC 1822-42) b Jan. 14, 1774, d June 2, 1842
Aitchison, Rev. J. K. (Scotland) b May 26, 1920, d Feb. 13, 1994
*Akram Raza (Lahore, Sargodha, WAPDA & HBL) b Nov. 22, 1964
*Alabaster, J. C. (Otago) b July 11, 1930
Alcock, C. W. (Sec. Surrey CCC 1872-1907, Editor *Cricket* 1882-1907) b Dec. 2, 1842, d Feb. 26, 1907
Alderman, A. E. (Derbys.) b Oct. 30, 1907, d June 4, 1990
*Alderman, T. M. (W. Aust., Kent & Glos.; *CY 1982*) b June 12, 1956
Aldridge, K. J. (Worcs & Tas.) b March 13, 1935
Alexander of Tunis, 1st Lord (Pres. MCC 1955-56) b Dec. 10, 1891, d June 16, 1969
*Alexander, F. C. M. (CUCC & Jam.) b Nov. 2, 1928
*Alexander, G. (Vic.) b April 22, 1851, d Nov. 6, 1930
*Alexander, H. H. (Vic.) b June 9, 1905, d April 15, 1993
Alikhan, R. I. (Sussex, PIA & Surrey) b Dec. 28, 1962
*Alim-ud-Din (Rajputana, Guj., Sind, B'pur, Kar. & PWD) b Dec. 15, 1930
*Allan, D. W. (B'dos) b Nov. 5, 1937
*Allan, F. E. (Vic.) b Dec. 2, 1849, d Feb. 9, 1917
Allan, J. M. (OUCC, Kent, Warwicks. & Scotland) b April 2, 1932
*Allan, P. J. (Qld) b Dec. 31, 1935
*Allcott, C. F. W. (Auck.) b Oct. 7, 1896, d Nov. 19, 1973
Allen, A. W. (CUCC & Northants) b Dec. 22, 1912
*Allen, D. A. (Glos.) b Oct. 29, 1935
*Allen, Sir G. O. B. (CUCC & Middx; Pres. MCC 1963-64; *special portrait 1987*) b July 31, 1902, d Nov. 29, 1989
*Allen, I. B. A. (Windwards) b Oct. 6, 1965
Allen, M. H. J. (Northants & Derbys.) b Jan. 7, 1933

*Allen, R. C. (NSW) b July 2, 1858, d May 2, 1952
Alletson, E. B. (Notts.) b March 6, 1884, d July 5, 1963
Alley, W. E. (NSW & Som.; *CY 1962*) b Feb. 3, 1919
Alleyne, H. L. (B'dos, Worcs., Natal & Kent) b Feb. 28, 1957
Alleyne, M. W. (Glos.) b May 23, 1968
*Allom, M. J. C. (CUCC & Surrey; Pres. MCC 1969-70) b March 23, 1906
*Allott, P. J. W. (Lancs. & Wgtn) b Sept. 14, 1956
Altham, H. S. (OUCC, Surrey & Hants; Pres. MCC 1959-60) b Nov. 30, 1888, d March 11, 1965
*Amalean, K. N. (SL) b April 7, 1965
*Amarnath, Lala (N. Ind., S. Punjab, Guj., Patiala, U. Pradesh & Ind. Rlwys) b Sept. 11, 1911
*Amarnath, M. (Punjab & Delhi; *CY 1984*) b Sept. 24, 1950
*Amarnath, S. (Punjab & Delhi) b Dec. 30, 1948
*Amar Singh, L. (Patiala, W. Ind. & Naw.) b Dec. 4, 1910, d May 20, 1940
*Ambrose, C. E. L. (Leewards & Northants; *CY 1992*) b Sept. 21, 1963
*Amerasinghe, A. M. J. G. (Nomads & Ant.) b Feb. 2, 1954
*Ames, L. E. G. (Kent; *CY 1929*) b Dec. 3, 1905, d Feb. 26, 1990
**Amir Elahi (Baroda, N. Ind., S. Punjab & B'pur) b Sept. 1, 1908, d Dec. 28, 1980
*Amiss, D. L. (Warwicks.; *CY 1975*) b April 7, 1943
*Amre, P. K. (Ind. Rlwys & Raja.) b Aug. 14, 1968
Anderson, I. S. (Derbys. & Boland) b April 24, 1960
*Anderson, J. H. (W. Prov.) b April 26, 1874, d March 11, 1926
*Anderson, R. W. (Cant., N. Dist., Otago & C. Dist.) b Oct. 2, 1948
*Anderson, W. McD. (Otago, C. Dist. & Cant.) b Oct. 8, 1919, d Dec. 21, 1979
Andrew, C. R. (CUCC) b Feb. 18, 1963
*Andrew, K. V. (Northants) b Dec. 15, 1929
Andrew, S. J. W. (Hants & Essex) b Jan. 27, 1966
*Andrews, B. (Cant., C. Dist. & Otago) b April 4, 1945
*Andrews, T. J. E. (NSW) b Aug. 26, 1890, d Jan. 28, 1970
Andrews, W. H. R. (Som.) b April 14, 1908, d Jan. 9, 1989
*Angel, J. (W. Aust.) b April 22, 1968
Angell, F. L. (Som.) b June 29, 1922
*Anil Dalpat (Kar. & PIA) b Sept. 20, 1963
*Ankola, S. A. (M'tra & Bombay) b March 1, 1968
*Anurasiri, S. D. (Pan.) b Feb. 25, 1966
*Anwar Hussain (N. Ind., Bombay, Sind & Kar.) b July 16, 1920
*Anwar Khan (Kar., Sind & NBP) b Dec. 24, 1955
*Appleyard, R. (Yorks.; *CY 1952*) b June 27, 1924
*Apte, A. L. (Ind. Us, Bombay & Raja.) b Oct. 24, 1934
*Apte, M. L. (Bombay & Bengal) b Oct. 5, 1932
*Aqib Javed (Lahore, PACO, Hants & I'bad) b Aug. 5, 1972
*Archer, A. G. (Worcs.) b Dec. 6, 1871, d July 15, 1935
Archer, G. F. (Notts.) b Sept. 26, 1970
*Archer, K. A. (Qld) b Jan. 17, 1928
*Archer, R. G. (Qld) b Oct. 25, 1933
*Arif Butt (Lahore & Pak. Rlwys) b May 17, 1944
Arlott, John (Writer & Broadcaster) b Feb. 25, 1914, d Dec. 14, 1991
*Armitage, T. (Yorks.) b April 25, 1848, d Sept. 21, 1922
Armstrong, N. F. (Leics.) b Dec. 22, 1892, d Jan. 19, 1990
Armstrong, T. R. (Derbys.) b Oct. 13, 1909
*Armstrong, W. W. (Vic.; *CY 1903*) b May 22, 1879, d July 13, 1947
Arnold, A. P. (Cant. & Northants) b Oct. 16, 1926
*Arnold, E. G. (Worcs.) b Nov. 7, 1876, d Oct. 25, 1942
*Arnold, G. G. (Surrey & Sussex; *CY 1972*) b Sept. 3, 1944
*Arnold, J. (Hants) b Nov. 30, 1907, d April 4, 1984
*Arnott, K. J. (MCD) b March 8, 1961
*Arshad Ayub (H'bad) b Aug. 2, 1958
Arshad Khan (Peshawar, I'bad & Pak. Rlways) b March 22, 1971
Arshad Pervez (Sargodha, Lahore, Pak. Us, Servis Ind., HBL & Punjab) b Oct. 1, 1952
*Arthurton, K. L. T. (Leewards) b Feb. 21, 1965
*Arun, B. (TN) b Dec. 14, 1962
*Arun Lal (Delhi & Bengal) b Aug. 1, 1955
*Asgarali, N. (T/T) b Dec. 28, 1920
Ashdown, W. H. (Kent) b Dec. 27, 1898, d Sept. 15, 1979
*Ashfaq Ahmed (PACO & PIA) b June 6, 1973
*Ashley, W. H. (W. Prov.) b Feb. 10, 1862, d July 14, 1930
*Ashraf Ali (Lahore, Income Tax, Pak Us, Pak Rlwys & UBL) b April 22, 1958
Ashton, C. T. (CUCC & Essex) b Feb. 19, 1901, d Oct. 31, 1942
Ashton, G. (CUCC & Worcs.) b Sept. 27, 1896, d Feb. 6, 1981

Ashton, Sir H. (CUCC & Essex; *CY 1922*; Pres. MCC 1960-61) b Feb. 13, 1898, d June 17,1979
Asif Din, M. (Warwicks.) b Sept. 21, 1960
*Asif Iqbal (H'bad, Kar., Kent, PIA & NBP; *CY 1968*) b June 6, 1943
*Asif Masood (Lahore, Punjab U. & PIA) b Jan. 23, 1946
*Asif Mujtaba (Kar. & PIA) b Nov. 4, 1967
Aslett, D. G. (Kent) b Feb. 12, 1958
Aspinall, R. (Yorks.) b Nov. 26, 1918
*Astill, W. E. (Leics.; *CY 1933*) b March 1, 1888, d Feb. 10, 1948
*Atapattu, M. S. (SSC) b Nov. 22, 1972
*Ata-ur-Rehman (Lahore & PACO) b March 28, 1975
*Atherton, M. A. (CUCC & Lancs.; *CY 1991*) b March 23, 1968
*Athey, C. W. J. (Yorks., Glos. & Sussex) b Sept. 27, 1957
*Atif Rauf (I'bad & ADBP) b March 3, 1964
Atkinson, C. R. M. (Som.) b July 23, 1931, d June 25, 1991
*Atkinson, D. St E. (B'dos & T/T) b Aug. 9, 1926
*Atkinson, E. St E. (B'dos) b Nov. 6, 1927
Atkinson, G. (Som. & Lancs.) b March 29, 1938
Atkinson, J. C. M. (Som. & CUCC) b July 10, 1968
Atkinson, T. (Notts.) b Sept. 27, 1930, d Sept. 2, 1990
*Attewell, W. (Notts.; *CY 1892*) b June 12, 1861, d June 11, 1927
Austin, Sir H. B. G. (B'dos) b July 15, 1877, d July 27, 1943
Austin, I. D. (Lancs.) b May 30, 1966
*Austin, R. A. (Jam.) b Sept. 5, 1954
Avery, A. V. (Essex) b Dec. 19, 1914
Aworth, C. J. (CUCC & Surrey) b Feb. 19, 1953
Ayling, J. R. (Hants) b June 13, 1967
Aylward, J. (Hants & All-England) b 1741, d Dec. 27, 1827
Aymes, A. N. (Hants) b June 4, 1964
*Azad, K. (Delhi) b Jan. 2, 1959
*Azeem Hafeez (Kar., Allied Bank & PIA) b July 29, 1963
*Azhar Khan (Lahore, Punjab, Pak. Us., PIA & HBL) b Sept. 7, 1955
*Azharuddin, M. (H'bad & Derbys.; *CY 1991*) b Feb. 8, 1963
*Azmat Rana (B'pur, PIA, Punjab, Lahore & MCB) b Nov. 3, 1951

Babington, A. M. (Sussex & Glos.) b July 22, 1963
*Bacchus, S. F. A. F. (Guyana, W. Prov. & Border) b Jan. 31, 1954
*Bacher, Dr A. (Tvl) b May 24, 1942
*Badcock, C. L. (Tas. & S. Aust.) b April 10, 1914, d Dec. 13, 1982
*Badcock, F. T. (Wgtn & Otago) b Aug. 9, 1895, d Sept. 19, 1982
*Baichan, L. (Guyana) b May 12, 1946
*Baig, A. A. (H'bad, OUCC & Som.) b March 19, 1939
Bailey, Sir D. T. L. (Glos.) b Aug. 5, 1918
Bailey, J. (Hants) b April 6, 1908, d Feb. 9, 1988
Bailey, J. A. (Essex & OUCC; Sec. MCC 1974-87) b June 22, 1930
*Bailey, R. J. (Northants) b Oct. 28, 1963
*Bailey, T. E. (Essex & CUCC; *CY 1950*) b Dec. 3, 1923
Baillie, A. W. (Sec. MCC 1858-63) b June 22, 1830, d May 10, 1867
Bainbridge, P. (Glos. & Durham; *CY 1986*) b April 16, 1958
*Bairstow, D. L. (Yorks. & Griq. W.) b Sept. 1, 1951
Baker, R. P. (Surrey) b April 9, 1954
*Bakewell, A. H. (Northants; *CY 1934*) b Nov. 2, 1908, d Jan. 23, 1983
Bakker, P. J. (Hants) b Aug. 19, 1957
*Balaskas, X. C. (Griq. W., Border, W. Prov., Tvl & NE Tvl) b Oct. 15, 1910, d May 12, 1994
*Balderstone, J. C. (Yorks. & Leics.) b Nov. 16, 1940
Baldry, D. O. (Middx & Hants) b Dec. 26, 1931
Ball, M. C. J. (Glos.) b April 26, 1970
*Banerjee, S. A. (Bengal & Bihar) b Nov. 1, 1919, d. Sept. 14, 1992
*Banerjee, S. N. (Bengal, Naw., Bihar & M. Pradesh) b Oct. 3, 1911, d Oct. 14, 1980
*Banerjee, S. T. (Bihar) b Feb. 13, 1969
*Bannerman, A. C. (NSW) b March 22, 1854, d Sept. 19, 1924
*Bannerman, Charles (NSW) b July 23, 1851, d Aug. 20, 1930
Bannister, J. D. (Warwicks.; Writer & Broadcaster) b Aug. 23, 1930
*Baptiste, E. A. E. (Kent, Leewards, Northants & E. Prov.) b March 12, 1960
*Baqa Jilani, M. (N. Ind.) b July 20, 1911, d July 2, 1941
Barber, A. T. (OUCC & Yorks.) b June 17, 1905, d March 10, 1985
*Barber, R. T. (Wgtn & C. Dist.) b June 23, 1925
*Barber, R. W. (Lancs., CUCC & Warwicks.; *CY 1967*) b Sept. 26, 1935
*Barber, W. (Yorks.) b April 18, 1901, d Sept. 10, 1968
Barclay, J. R. T. (Sussex & OFS) b Jan. 22, 1954
*Bardsley, W. (NSW; *CY 1910*) b Dec. 6, 1882, d Jan. 20, 1954
Baring, A. E. G. (Hants) b Jan. 21, 1910, d Aug. 29, 1986
Barker, G. (Essex) b July 6, 1931

Barling, H. T. (Surrey) b Sept. 1, 1906, d Jan. 2, 1993
*Barlow, E. J. (Tvl, E. Prov., W. Prov., Derbys. & Boland) b Aug. 12, 1940
*Barlow, G. D. (Middx) b March 26, 1950
*Barlow, R. G. (Lancs.) b May 28, 1851, d July 31, 1919
Barnard, H. M. (Hants) b July 18, 1933
Barnes, A. R. (Sec. Aust. Cricket Board 1960-81) b Sept. 12, 1916, d March 14, 1989
*Barnes, S. F. (Warwicks. & Lancs.; *CY 1910*) b April 19, 1873, d Dec. 26, 1967
*Barnes, S. G. (NSW) b June 5, 1916, d Dec. 16, 1973
*Barnes, W. (Notts.; *CY 1890*) b May 27, 1852, d March 24, 1899
Barnett, A. A. (Middx & Lancs.) b Sept. 11, 1970
*Barnett, B. A. (Vic.) b March 23, 1908, d June 29, 1979
*Barnett, C. J. (Glos.; *CY 1937*) b July 3, 1910, d May 28, 1993
*Barnett, K. J. (Derbys. & Boland; *CY 1989*) b July 17, 1960
Barnwell, C. J. P. (Som.) b June 23, 1914
Baroda, Maharaja of (Manager, Ind. in Eng., 1959) b April 2, 1930, d Sept. 1, 1988
*Barratt, F. (Notts.) b April 12, 1894, d Jan. 29, 1947
Barratt, R. J. (Leics.) b May 3, 1942
*Barrett, A. G. (Jam.) b April 5, 1942
Barrett, B. J. (Auck., C. Dist., Worcs. & N. Dist.) b Nov. 16, 1966
*Barrett, J. E. (Vic.) b Oct. 15, 1866, d Feb. 6, 1916
Barrick, D. W. (Northants) b April 28, 1926
*Barrington, K. F. (Surrey; *CY 1960*) b Nov. 24, 1930, d March 14, 1981
Barron, W. (Lancs. & Northants) b Oct. 26, 1917
*Barrow, I. (Jam.) b Jan. 6, 1911, d April 2, 1979
*Bartlett, E. L. (B'dos) b March 18, 1906, d Dec. 21, 1976
*Bartlett, G. A. (C. Dist. & Cant.) b Feb. 3, 1941
Bartlett, H. T. (CUCC, Surrey & Sussex; *CY 1939*) b Oct. 7, 1914, d June 26, 1988
Bartlett, R. J. (Som.) b Oct. 8, 1966
Bartley, T. J. (Umpire) b March 19, 1908, d April 2, 1964
Barton, M. R. (OUCC & Surrey) b Oct. 14, 1914
*Barton, P. T. (Wgtn) b Oct. 9, 1935
*Barton, V. A. (Kent & Hants) b Oct. 6, 1867, d March 23, 1906
Barwick, S. R. (Glam.) b Sept. 6, 1960
Base, S. J. (W. Prov., Glam., Derbys., Boland & Border) b Jan. 2, 1960
*Basit Ali (Kar. & UBL) b Dec. 13, 1970
Bates, D. L. (Sussex) b May 10, 1933
*Bates, W. (Yorks.) b Nov. 19, 1855, d Jan. 8, 1900
Batty, J. D. (Yorks.) b May 15, 1971
*Baumgartner, H. V. (OFS & Tvl) b Nov. 17, 1883, d April 8, 1938
Baxter, A. D. (Devon, Lancs., Middx & Scotland) b Jan. 20, 1910, d Jan. 28, 1986
*Bean, G. (Notts & Sussex) b March 7, 1864, d March 16, 1923
Bear, M. J. (Essex & Cant.) b Feb. 23, 1934
*Beard, D. D. (C. Dist. & N. Dist.) b Jan. 14, 1920, d July 15, 1982
*Beard, G. R. (NSW) b Aug. 19, 1950
Beauclerk, Lord Frederick (Middx, Surrey & MCC) b May 8, 1773, d April 22, 1850
Beaufort, 10th Duke of (Pres. MCC 1952-53) b April 4, 1900, d Feb. 5, 1984
*Beaumont, R. (Tvl) b Feb. 4, 1884, d May 25, 1958
*Beck, J. E. F. (Wgtn) b Aug. 1, 1934
Bedade, A. C. (Baroda) b Sept. 24, 1966
*Bedi, B. S. (N. Punjab, Delhi & Northants) b Sept. 25, 1946
*Bedser, A. V. (Surrey; *CY 1947*) b July 4, 1918
Bedser, E. A. (Surrey) b July 4, 1918
Beet, G. (Derbys.; Umpire) b April 24, 1886, d Dec. 13, 1946
*Begbie, D. W. (Tvl) b Dec. 12, 1914
Beldham, W. (Hambledon & Surrey) b Feb. 5, 1766, d Feb. 20, 1862
*Bell, A. J. (W. Prov. & Rhod.) b April 15, 1906, d Aug. 2, 1985
Bell, R. V. (Middx & Sussex) b Jan. 7, 1931, d Oct. 26, 1989
*Bell, W. (Cant.) b Sept. 5, 1931
Bellamy, B. W. (Northants) b April 22, 1891, d Dec. 20, 1985
*Benaud, J. (NSW) b May 11, 1944
*Benaud, R. (NSW; *CY 1962*) b Oct. 6, 1930
*Benjamin, J. E. (Warwicks. & Surrey) b Feb. 2, 1961
*Benjamin, K. C. G. (Leewards & Worcs.) b April 8, 1967
*Benjamin, W. K. M. (Leewards, Leics. & Hants) b Dec. 31, 1964
Bennett, D. (Middx) b Dec. 18, 1933
*Bennett, M. J. (NSW) b Oct. 16, 1956
Bennett, N. H. (Surrey) b Sept. 23, 1912
Bennett, R. (Lancs.) b June 16, 1940
Benson, J. D. R. (Leics.) b March 1, 1967
*Benson, M. R. (Kent) b July 6, 1958
Bernard, J. R. (CUCC & Glos.) b Dec. 7, 1938
Berry, L. G. (Leics.) b April 28, 1906, d Feb. 5, 1985
*Berry, R. (Lancs., Worcs. & Derbys.) b Jan. 29, 1926
*Best, C. A. (B'dos & W. Prov.) b May 14, 1959

*Betancourt, N. (T/T) b June 4, 1887, d Oct. 12, 1947
Bevan, M. G. (NSW) b May 8, 1970
Bhalekar, R. B. (M'tra) b Feb. 17, 1952
*Bhandari, P. (Delhi & Bengal) b Nov. 27, 1935
*Bhat, A. R. (Karn.) b April 16, 1958
Bhupinder Singh (Punjab) b April 1, 1965
Bick, D. A. (Middx) b Feb. 22, 1936, d Jan. 13, 1992
Bicknell, D. J. (Surrey) b June 24, 1967
*Bicknell, M. P. (Surrey) b Jan. 14, 1969
Biddulph, K. D. (Som.) b May 29, 1932
*Bilby, G. P. (Wgtn) b May 7, 1941
*Binks, J. G. (Yorks.; *CY 1969*) b Oct. 5, 1935
*Binns, A. P. (Jam.) b July 24, 1929
*Binny, R. M. H. (Karn.) b July 19, 1955
Birch, J. D. (Notts.) b June 18, 1955
Bird, H. D. (Yorks. & Leics.; Umpire) b April 19, 1933
*Bird, M. C. (Lancs. & Surrey) b March 25, 1888, d Dec. 9, 1933
Bird, R. E. (Worcs.) b April 4, 1915, d Feb. 20, 1985
*Birkenshaw, J. (Yorks., Leics. & Worcs.) b Nov. 13, 1940
*Birkett, L. S. (B'dos, BG & T/T) b April 14, 1904
Birrell, H. B. (E. Prov., Rhod. & OUCC) b Dec. 1, 1927
Bishop, G. A. (S. Aust.) b Feb. 25, 1960
*Bishop, I. R. (T/T & Derbys.) b Oct. 24, 1967
*Bisset, Sir Murray (W. Prov.) b April 14, 1876, d Oct. 24, 1931
*Bissett, G. F. (Griq. W., W. Prov. & Tvl) b Nov. 5, 1905, d Nov. 14, 1965
Bissex, M. (Glos.) b Sept. 28, 1944
*Blackham, J. McC. (Vic.; *CY 1891*) b May 11, 1854, d Dec. 28, 1932
*Blackie, D. D. (Vic.) b April 5, 1882, d April 18, 1955
Blackledge, J. F. (Lancs.) b April 15, 1928
*Blain, T. E. (C. Dist.) b Feb. 17, 1962
Blair, B. R. (Otago) b Dec. 27, 1957
*Blair, R. W. (Wgtn & C. Dist.) b June 23, 1932
Blake, D. E. (Hants) b April 27, 1925
Blake, Rev. P. D. S. (OUCC & Sussex) b May 23, 1927
*Blakey, R. J. (Yorks.) b Jan. 15, 1967
*Blanckenberg, J. M. (W. Prov. & Natal) b Dec. 31, 1893, dead
*Bland, K. C. (Rhod., E. Prov. & OFS; *CY 1966*) b April 5, 1938
Blenkiron, W. (Warwicks.) b July 21, 1942
Bligh, Hon. Ivo (*see* 8th Earl of Darnley)
Blundell, Sir E. D. (CUCC & NZ) b May 29, 1907, d Sept. 24, 1984
*Blunt, R. C. (Cant. & Otago; *CY 1928*) b Nov. 3, 1900, d June 22, 1966
*Blythe, C. (Kent; *CY 1904*) b May 30, 1879, d Nov. 8, 1917
*Board, J. H. (Glos.) b Feb. 23, 1867, d April 16, 1924
*Bock, E. G. (Griq. W., Tvl & W. Prov.) b Sept. 17, 1908, d Sept. 5, 1961
Bodkin, P. E. (CUCC) b Sept. 15, 1924, d Sept. 18, 1994
*Bolton, B. A. (Cant. & Wgtn) b May 31, 1935
*Bolus, J. B. (Yorks., Notts. & Derbys.) b Jan. 31, 1934
*Bond, G. E. (W. Prov.) b April 5, 1909, d Aug. 27, 1965
Bond, J. D. (Lancs. & Notts.; *CY 1971*) b May 6, 1932
*Bonnor, G. J. (Vic. & NSW) b Feb. 25, 1855, d June 27, 1912
*Boock, S. L. (Otago & Cant.) b Sept. 20, 1951
*Boon, D. C. (Tas.; *CY 1994*) b Dec. 29, 1960
Boon, T. J. (Leics.) b Nov. 1, 1961
*Booth, B. C. (NSW) b Oct. 19, 1933
Booth, B. J. (Lancs. & Leics.) b Dec. 3, 1935
*Booth, M. W. (Yorks.; *CY 1914*) b Dec. 10, 1886, d July 1, 1916
Booth, P. (Leics.) b Nov. 2, 1952
Booth, P. A. (Yorks. & Warwicks.) b Sept. 5, 1965
Booth, R. (Yorks. & Worcs.) b Oct. 1, 1926
*Borde, C. G. (Baroda & M'tra) b July 21, 1934
*Border, A. R. (NSW, Glos, Qld & Essex; *CY 1982*) b July 27, 1955
Bore, M. K. (Yorks. & Notts.) b June 2, 1947
Borrington, A. J. (Derbys.) b Dec. 8, 1948
*Bosanquet, B. J. T. (OUCC & Middx; *CY 1905*) b Oct. 13, 1877, d Oct. 12, 1936
*Bosch T. (N. Tvl) b March 14, 1966
Bose, G. (Bengal) b May 20, 1947
Boshier, B. S. (Leics.) b March 6, 1932
*Botham, I. T. (Som., Worcs., Durham & Qld; *CY 1978*) b Nov. 24, 1955
*Botten, J. T. (NE Tvl & N. Tvl) b June 21, 1938
Boucher, J. C. (Ireland) b Dec. 22, 1910
Bourne, W. A. (B'dos & Warwicks.) b Nov. 15, 1952
*Bowden, M. P. (Surrey & Tvl) b Nov. 1, 1865, d Feb. 19, 1892
*Bowes, W. E. (Yorks.; *CY 1932*) b July 25, 1908, d Sept. 5, 1987
Bowler, P. D. (Leics., Tas. & Derbys.) b July 30, 1963
*Bowley, E. H. (Sussex & Auck.; *CY 1930*) b June 6, 1890, d July 9, 1974
Bowley, F. L. (Worcs.) b Nov. 9, 1873, d May 31, 1943
Box, T. (Sussex) b Feb. 7, 1808, d July 12, 1876

*Boyce, K. D. (B'dos & Essex; *CY 1974*) b Oct. 11, 1943
*Boycott, G. (Yorks. & N. Tvl; *CY 1965*) b Oct. 21, 1940
Boyd-Moss, R. J. (CUCC & Northants) b Dec. 16, 1959
Boyes, G. S. (Hants) b March 31, 1899, d Feb. 11, 1973
*Boyle, H. F. (Vic.) b Dec. 10, 1847, d Nov. 21, 1907
*Bracewell, B. P. (C. Dist., Otago & N. Dist.) b Sept. 14, 1959
*Bracewell, J. G. (Otago & Auck.) b April 15, 1958
*Bradburn, G. E. (N. Dist.) b May 26, 1966
*Bradburn, W. P. (N. Dist.) b Nov. 24, 1938
*Bradley, W. M. (Kent) b Jan. 2, 1875, d June 19, 1944
*Bradman, Sir D. G. (NSW & S. Aust.; *CY 1931*) b Aug. 27, 1908
Brain, B. M. (Worcs. & Glos.) b Sept. 13, 1940
*Brain, D. H. (Mash.) b Oct. 4, 1964
Bramall, Field-Marshal The Lord (Pres. MCC 1988-89) b Dec. 18, 1923
*Brandes, E. A. (Zimb.) b March 5, 1963
*Brann, W. H. (E. Prov.) b April 4, 1899, d Sept. 22, 1953
Brassington, A. J. (Glos.) b Aug. 9, 1954
*Braund, L. C. (Surrey & Som.; *CY 1902*) b Oct. 18, 1875, d Dec. 23, 1955
Bray, C. (Essex) b April 6, 1898, d Sept. 12, 1993
Brayshaw, I. J. (W. Aust.) b Jan. 14, 1942
Brazier, A. F. (Surrey & Kent) b Dec. 7, 1924
Breakwell, D. (Northants & Som.) b July 2, 1948
*Brearley, J. M. (CUCC & Middx; *CY 1977*) b April 28, 1942
*Brearley, W. (Lancs.; *CY 1909*) b March 11, 1876, d Jan. 13, 1937
*Brennan, D. V. (Yorks.) b Feb. 10, 1920, d Jan. 9, 1985
*Briant, G. A. (Zimb.) b April 11, 1969
Bridge, W. B. (Warwicks.) b May 29, 1938
Bridger, Rev. J. R. (Hants) b April 8, 1920, d July 14, 1986
Brierley, T. L. (Glam., Lancs. & Canada) b June 15, 1910, d Jan. 7, 1989
Briers, N. E. (Leics.; *CY 1993*) b Jan. 15, 1955
*Briggs, John (Lancs.; *CY 1889*) b Oct. 3, 1862, d Jan. 11, 1902
*Bright, R. J. (Vic.) b July 13, 1954
*Briscoe, A. W. (Tvl) b Feb. 6, 1911, d April 22, 1941
*Broad, B. C. (Glos. & Notts.) b Sept. 29, 1957
Broadbent, R. G. (Worcs.) b June 21, 1924, d April 26, 1993
Brocklehurst, B. G. (Som.) b Feb. 18, 1922
*Brockwell, W. (Kimberley & Surrey; *CY 1895*) b Jan. 21, 1865, d June 30, 1935
Broderick, V. (Northants) b Aug. 17, 1920
Brodhurst, A. H. (CUCC & Glos.) b July 21, 1916
*Bromfield, H. D. (W. Prov.) b June 26, 1932
*Bromley, E. H. (W. Aust. & Vic.) b Sept. 2, 1912, d Feb. 1, 1967
*Bromley-Davenport, H. R. (CUCC, Bombay Eur. & Middx) b Aug. 18, 1870, d May 23, 1954
*Brookes, D. (Northants; *CY 1957*) b Oct. 29, 1915
Brookes, W. H. (Editor of *Wisden* 1936-39) b Dec. 5, 1894, d May 28, 1955
Brooks, R. A. (OUCC & Som.) b June 14, 1943
*Brown, A. (Kent) b Oct. 17, 1935
Brown, A. D. (Surrey) b Feb. 11, 1970
Brown, A. S. (Glos.) b June 24, 1936
*Brown, D. J. (Warwicks.) b Jan. 30, 1942
Brown, D. W. J. (Glos.) b Feb. 26, 1942
*Brown, F. R. (CUCC, Surrey & Northants; *CY 1933*; Pres. MCC 1971-72) b Dec. 16, 1910, d July 24, 1991
*Brown, G. (Hants) b Oct. 6, 1887, d Dec. 3, 1964
Brown, J. (Scotland) b Sept. 24, 1931
*Brown, J. T. (Yorks.; *CY 1895*) b Aug. 20, 1869, d Nov. 4, 1904
Brown, K. R. (Middx) b March 18, 1963
*Brown, L. S. (Tvl, NE Tvl & Rhod.) b Nov. 24, 1910, d Sept. 1, 1983
Brown, R. D. (Zimb.) b March 11, 1951
Brown, S. J. E. (Northants & Durham) b June 29, 1969
Brown, S. M. (Middx) b Dec. 8, 1917, d Dec. 28, 1987
*Brown, V. R. (Cant. & Auck.) b Nov. 3, 1959
*Brown, W. A. (NSW & Qld; *CY 1939*) b July 31, 1912
Brown, W. C. (Northants) b Nov. 13, 1900, d Jan. 20, 1986
*Browne, C. R. (B'dos & BG) b Oct. 8, 1890, d Jan. 12, 1964
Bruce, Hon. C. N. (3rd Lord Aberdare) (OUCC & Middx) b Aug. 2, 1885, d Oct. 4, 1957
*Bruce, W. (Vic.) b May 22, 1864, d Aug. 3, 1925
*Bruk-Jackson, G. K. (MCD) b April 25, 1969
Bryan, G. J. (Kent) b Dec. 29, 1902, d April 4, 1991
Bryan, J. L. (CUCC & Kent; *CY 1922*) b May 26, 1896, d April 23, 1985
Bryan, R. T. (Kent) b July 30, 1898, d July 27, 1970
*Buckenham, C. P. (Essex) b Jan. 16, 1876, d Feb. 23, 1937

Buckingham, J. (Warwicks.) b Jan. 21, 1903, d Jan. 25, 1987
Budd, E. H. (Middx & All-England) b Feb. 23, 1785, d March 29, 1875
Budd, W. L. (Hants) b Oct. 25, 1913, d Aug. 23, 1986
Bull, F. G. (Essex; *CY 1898*) b April 2, 1875, d Sept. 16, 1910
Buller, J. S. (Yorks. & Worcs.; Umpire) b Aug. 23, 1909, d Aug. 7, 1970
Burden, M. D. (Hants) b Oct. 4, 1930, d Nov. 9, 1987
*Burge, P. J. P. (Qld; *CY 1965*) b May 17, 1932
*Burger, C. G. de V. (Natal) b July 12, 1935
Burgess, G. I. (Som.) b May 5, 1943
*Burgess, M. G. (Auck.) b July 17, 1944
*Burke, C. (Auck.) b March 22, 1914
*Burke, J. W. (NSW; *CY 1957*) b June 12, 1930, d Feb. 2, 1979
*Burke, S. F. (NE Tvl & OFS) b March 11, 1934
*Burki, Javed (Pak. Us, OUCC, Punjab, Lahore, Kar., R'pindi & NWFP) b May 8, 1938
*Burmester, M. G. (Mash.) b Jan. 24, 1968
*Burn, E. J. K. (K. E.) (Tas.) b Sept. 17, 1862, d July 20, 1956
Burnet, J. R. (Yorks.) b Oct. 11, 1918
Burns, N. D. (Essex, W. Prov. & Som.) b Sept. 19, 1965
Burnup, C. J. (CUCC & Kent; *CY 1903*) b Nov. 21, 1875, d April 5, 1960
Burrough, H. D. (Som.) b Feb. 6, 1909, d April 9, 1994
*Burton, F. J. (Vic. & NSW) b Nov. 2, 1865, d Aug. 25, 1929
*Burtt, T. B. (Cant.) b Jan. 22, 1915, d May 24, 1988
Buse, H. F. T. (Som.) b Aug. 5, 1910, d Feb. 23, 1992
Bushby, M. H. (CUCC) b July 29, 1931
Buss, A. (Sussex) b Sept. 1, 1939
Buss, M. A. (Sussex & OFS) b Jan. 24, 1944
Buswell, J. E. (Northants) b July 3, 1909
Butchart, I. P. (Zimb.) b May 9, 1967
*Butcher, A. R. (Surrey & Glam.; *CY 1991*) b Jan. 7, 1954
*Butcher, B. F. (Guyana; *CY 1970*) b Sept. 3, 1933
Butcher, I. P. (Leics. & Glos.) b July 1, 1962
*Butcher, R. O. (Middx, B'dos & Tas.) b Oct. 14, 1953
*Butler, H. J. (Notts.) b March 12, 1913, d July 17, 1991
*Butler, L. S. (T/T) b Feb. 9, 1929
*Butt, H. R. (Sussex) b Dec. 27, 1865, d Dec. 21, 1928
*Butterfield, L. A. (Cant.) b Aug. 29, 1913
*Butts, C. G. (Guyana) b July 8, 1957
Buxton, I. R. (Derbys.) b April 17, 1938
*Buys, I. D. (W. Prov.) b Feb. 3, 1895, dead
Byas, D. (Yorks.) b Aug. 26, 1963
*Bynoe, M. R. (B'dos) b Feb. 23, 1941

Caccia, Lord (Pres. MCC 1973-74) b Dec. 21, 1905, d Oct. 31, 1990
*Caddick, A. R. (Som.) b Nov. 21, 1968
Caesar, Julius (Surrey & All-England) b March 25, 1830, d March 6, 1878
Caffyn, W. (Surrey & NSW) b Feb. 2, 1828, d Aug. 28, 1919
Caine, C. Stewart (Editor of *Wisden* 1926-33) b Oct. 28, 1861, d April 15, 1933
*Cairns, B. L. (C. Dist., Otago & N. Dist.) b Oct. 10, 1949
*Cairns, C. L. (N. Dist., Notts. & Cant.) b June 13, 1970
Calder, H. L. (Cranleigh; *CY 1918; oldest surviving CY*) b Jan. 24, 1901
Callaghan, D. J. (E. Prov.) b Feb. 1, 1965
*Callaway, S. T. (NSW & Cant.) b Feb. 6, 1868, d Nov. 25, 1923
*Callen, I. W. (Vic. & Boland) b May 2, 1955
*Calthorpe, Hon. F. S. Gough- (CUCC, Sussex & Warwicks.) b May 27, 1892, d Nov. 19, 1935
*Camacho, G. S. (Guyana) b Oct. 15, 1945
*Cameron, F. J. (Jam.) b June 22, 1923
*Cameron, F. J. (Otago) b June 1, 1932
*Cameron, H. B. (Tvl, E. Prov. & W. Prov.; *CY 1936*) b July 5, 1905, d Nov. 2, 1935
*Cameron, J. H. (CUCC, Jam. & Som.) b April 8, 1914
*Campbell, A. D. R. (MCD) b Sept. 23, 1972
*Campbell, G. D. (Tas.) b March 10, 1964
*Campbell, T. (Tvl) b Feb. 9, 1882, d Oct. 5, 1924
Cannings, V. H. D. (Warwicks. & Hants) b April 3, 1919
*Capel, D. J. (Northants & E. Prov.) b Feb. 6, 1963
Caple, R. G. (Middx & Hants) b Dec. 8, 1939
Cardus, Sir Neville (Cricket Writer) b April 3, 1888, d Feb. 27, 1975
*Carew, G. McD. (B'dos) b June 4, 1910, d Dec. 9, 1974
*Carew, M. C. (T/T) b Sept. 15, 1937
*Carkeek, W. (Vic.) b Oct. 17, 1878, d Feb. 20, 1937
*Carlson, P. H. (Qld) b Aug. 8, 1951
*Carlstein, P. R. (OFS, Tvl, Natal & Rhod.) b Oct. 28, 1938
Carpenter, D. (Glos.) b Sept. 12, 1935
Carpenter, R. (Cambs. & Utd England XI) b Nov. 18, 1830, d July 13, 1901
*Carr, A. W. (Notts.; *CY 1923*) b May 21, 1893, d Feb. 7, 1963
*Carr, D. B. (OUCC & Derbys.; *CY 1960*; Sec. TCCB 1974-86) b Dec. 28, 1926

*Carr, D. W. (Kent; *CY 1910*) b March 17, 1872, d March 23, 1950
Carr, J. D. (OUCC & Middx) b June 15, 1963
Carrick, P. (Yorks. & E. Prov.) b July 16, 1952
Carrington, E. (Derbys.) b March 25, 1914
Carse, J. A. (Rhod., W. Prov., E. Prov. & Northants) b Dec. 13, 1958
*Carter, C. P. (Natal & Tvl) b April 23, 1881, d Nov. 8, 1952
*Carter, H. (NSW) b Halifax, Yorks. March 15, 1878, d June 8, 1948
Carter, R. G. (Warwicks.) b April 14, 1933
Carter, R. G. M. (Worcs.) b July 11, 1937
Carter, R. M. (Northants & Cant.) b May 25, 1960
Cartwright, H. (Derbys.) b May 12, 1951
*Cartwright, T. W. (Warwicks., Som. & Glam.) b July 22, 1935
Cass, G. R. (Essex, Worcs. & Tas.) b April 23, 1940
Castell, A. T. (Hants) b Aug. 6, 1943
Castle, F. (Som.) b April 9, 1909
Catt, A. W. (Kent & W. Prov.) b Oct. 2, 1933
*Catterall, R. H. (Tvl, Rhod., Natal & OFS; *CY 1925*) b July 10, 1900, d Jan. 2, 1961
*Cave, H. B. (Wgtn & C. Dist.) b Oct. 10, 1922, d Sept. 15, 1989
Chalk, F. G. H. (OUCC & Kent) b Sept. 7, 1910, d Feb. 17, 1943
*Challenor, G. (B'dos) b June 28, 1888, d July 30, 1947
Chamberlain, W. R. F. (Northants; Chairman TCCB 1990-94) b April 13, 1925
Chandana, U. U. (TU) b May 7, 1972
*Chanderpaul, S. (Guyana) b Aug. 18, 1974
*Chandrasekhar, B. S. (†Karn.; *CY 1972*) b May 17, 1945
Chandrasekhar, V. B. (TN) b Aug. 21, 1961
*Chang, H. S. (Jam.) b July 22, 1952
*Chapman, A. P. F. (Uppingham, OUCC & Kent; *CY 1919*) b Sept. 3, 1900, d Sept. 16, 1961
*Chapman, H. W. (Natal) b June 30, 1890, d Dec. 1, 1941
*Chappell, G. S. (S. Aust., Som. & Qld; *CY 1973*) b Aug. 7, 1948
*Chappell, I. M. (S. Aust. & Lancs.; *CY 1976*) b Sept. 26, 1943
*Chappell, T. M. (S. Aust., W. Aust. & NSW) b Oct. 21, 1952
Chapple, G. (Lancs.) b Jan. 23, 1974
*Chapple, M. E. (Cant. & C. Dist.) b July 25, 1930, d July 31, 1985
*Charlton, P. C. (NSW) b April 9, 1867, d Sept. 30, 1954
*Charlwood, H. R. J. (Sussex) b Dec. 19, 1846, d June 6, 1888
*Chatfield, E. J. (Wgtn) b July 3, 1950
*Chatterton, W. (Derbys.) b Dec. 27, 1861, d March 19, 1913
*Chauhan, C. P. S. (M'tra & Delhi) b July 21, 1947
*Chauhan, R. K. (M. Pradesh) b Dec. 19, 1966
Cheatle, R. G. L. (Sussex & Surrey) b July 31, 1953
*Cheetham, J. E. (W. Prov.) b May 26, 1920, d Aug. 21, 1980
Chester, F. (Worcs.; Umpire) b Jan. 20, 1895, d April 8, 1957
Chesterton, G. H. (OUCC & Worcs.) b July 15, 1922
*Chevalier, G. A. (W. Prov.) b March 9, 1937
*Childs, J. H. (Glos. & Essex; *CY 1987*) b Aug. 15, 1951
*Chipperfield, A. G. (NSW) b Nov. 17, 1905, d July 29, 1987
Chisholm, R. H. E. (Scotland) b May 22, 1927
*Chowdhury, N. R. (Bihar & Bengal) b May 23, 1923, d Dec. 14, 1979
*Christiani, C. M. (BG) b Oct. 28, 1913, d April 4, 1938
*Christiani, R. J. (BG) b July 19, 1920
*Christopherson, S. (Kent; Pres. MCC 1939-45) b Nov. 11, 1861, d April 6, 1949
*Christy, J. A. J. (Tvl & Qld) b Dec. 12, 1904, d Feb. 1, 1971
*Chubb, G. W. A. (Border & Tvl) b April 12, 1911, d Aug. 28, 1982
Clark, D. G. (Kent; Pres. MCC 1977-78) b Jan. 27, 1919
Clark, E. A. (Middx) b April 15, 1937
*Clark, E. W. (Northants) b Aug. 9, 1902, d April 28, 1982
Clark, L. S. (Essex) b March 6, 1914
*Clark, W. M. (W. Aust.) b Sept. 19, 1953
*Clarke, Dr C. B. (B'dos, Northants & Essex) b April 7, 1918, d Oct. 14, 1993
*Clarke, S. T. (B'dos, Surrey, Tvl, OFS & N. Tvl) b Dec. 11, 1954
Clarke, William (Notts.; founded All-England XI & Trent Bridge ground) b Dec. 24, 1798, d Aug. 25, 1856
Clarkson, A. (Yorks. & Som.) b Sept. 5, 1939
Claughton, J. A. (OUCC & Warwicks.) b Sept. 17, 1956
*Clay, J. C. (Glam.) b March 18, 1898, d Aug. 12, 1973
Clay, J. D. (Notts.) b Oct. 15, 1924
Clayton, G. (Lancs. & Som.) b Feb. 3, 1938
Clements, S. M. (OUCC) b April 19, 1956
*Cleverley, D. C. (Auck.) b Dec. 23, 1909
Clift, Patrick B. (Rhod., Leics. & Natal) b July 14, 1953
Clift, Philip B. (Glam.) b Sept. 3, 1918
Clinton, G. S. (Kent, Surrey & Zimb.-Rhod.) b May 5, 1953

*Close, D. B. (Yorks. & Som.; *CY 1964*) b Feb. 24, 1931
Cobb, R. A. (Leics. & Natal) b May 18, 1961
Cobham, 10th Visct (Hon. C. J. Lyttelton) (Worcs.; Pres. MCC 1954) b Aug. 8, 1909, d March 20, 1977
*Cochrane, J. A. K. (Tvl & Griq. W.) b July 15, 1909, d June 15, 1987
Cock, D. F. (Essex) b Oct. 22, 1914, d Sept. 26, 1992
*Coen, S. K. (OFS, W. Prov., Tvl & Border) b Oct. 14, 1902, d Jan. 28, 1967
*Colah, S. M. H. (Bombay, W. Ind. & Naw.) b Sept. 22, 1902, d Sept. 11, 1950
Colchin, Robert ("Long Robin") (Kent & All-England) b Nov. 1713, d April 1750
*Coldwell, L. J. (Worcs.) b Jan. 10, 1933
*Colley, D. J. (NSW) b March 15, 1947
Collin, T. (Warwicks.) b April 7, 1911
*Collinge, R. O. (C. Dist., Wgtn & N. Dist.) b April 2, 1946
Collins, A. E. J. (Clifton Coll. & Royal Engineers) b 1885, d Nov. 11, 1914
*Collins, H. L. (NSW) b Jan. 21, 1888, d May 28, 1959
Collins, R. (Lancs.) b March 10, 1934
*Colquhoun, I. A. (C. Dist.) b June 8, 1924
Coman, P. G. (Cant.) b April 13, 1943
*Commaille, J. M. M. (W. Prov., Natal, OFS & Griq. W.) b Feb. 21, 1883, d July 27, 1956
*Compton, D. C. S. (Middx & Holkar; *CY 1939*) b May 23, 1918
*Coney, J. V. (Wgtn; *CY 1984*) b June 21, 1952
*Congdon, B. E. (C. Dist., Wgtn, Otago & Cant.; *CY 1974*) b Feb. 11, 1938
*Coningham, A. (NSW & Qld) b July 14, 1863, d June 13, 1939
*Connolly, A. N. (Vic. & Middx) b June 29, 1939
Connor, C. A. (Hants) b March 24, 1961
Constable, B. (Surrey) b Feb. 19, 1921
Constant, D. J. (Kent & Leics.; Umpire) b Nov. 9, 1941
*Constantine, Lord L. N. (T/T & B'dos; *CY 1940*) b Sept. 21, 1902, d July 1, 1971
Constantine, L. S. (T/T) b May 25, 1874, d Jan. 5, 1942
*Contractor, N. J. (Guj. & Ind. Rlwys) b March 7, 1934
*Conyngham, D. P. (Natal, Tvl & W. Prov.) b May 10, 1897, d July 7, 1979
*Cook, C. (Glos.) b Aug. 23, 1921
*Cook, F. J. (E. Prov.) b 1870, dead
*Cook, G. (Northants & E. Prov.) b Oct. 9, 1951
*Cook, N. G. B. (Leics. & Northants) b June 17, 1956
*Cook, S. J. (Tvl & Som.; *CY 1990*) b July 31, 1953
Cook, T. E. R. (Sussex) b Jan. 5, 1901, d Jan. 15, 1950
*Cooper, A. H. C. (Tvl) b Sept 2, 1893, d July 18, 1963
*Cooper, B. B. (Middx, Kent & Vic.) b March 15, 1844, d Aug. 7, 1914
Cooper, F. S. Ashley- (Cricket Historian) b March 17, 1877, d Jan. 31, 1932
Cooper, G. C. (Sussex) b Sept. 2, 1936
Cooper, H. P. (Yorks. & N. Tvl) b April 17, 1949
Cooper, K. E. (Notts. & Glos.) b Dec. 27, 1957
*Cooper, W. H. (Vic.) b Sept. 11, 1849, d April 5, 1939
*Cope, G. A. (Yorks.) b Feb. 23, 1947
*Copson, W. H. (Derbys.; *CY 1937*) b April 27, 1908, d Sept. 14, 1971
Cordle, A. E. (Glam.) b Sept. 21, 1940
Cork, D. G. (Derbys.) b Aug. 7, 1971
*Corling, G. E. (NSW) b July 13, 1941
Cornford, J. H. (Sussex) b Dec. 9, 1911, d June 17, 1985
*Cornford, W. L. (Sussex) b Dec. 25, 1900, d Feb. 6, 1964
Corrall, P. (Leics.) b July 16, 1906, d Feb. 1994
Corran, A. J. (OUCC & Notts.) b Nov. 25, 1936
*Cosier, G. J. (Vic., S. Aust. & Qld) b April 25,1953
*Cottam, J. T. (NSW) b Sept. 5, 1867, d Jan. 30, 1897
*Cottam, R. M. H. (Hants & Northants) b Oct. 16, 1944
*Cotter, A. (NSW) b Dec. 3, 1884, d Oct. 31, 1917
Cottey, P. A. (Glam. & E. Tvl) b June 2, 1966
Cotton, J. (Notts. & Leics.) b Nov. 7, 1940
Cottrell, G. A. (CUCC) b March 23, 1945
*Coulthard, G. (Vic.) b Aug. 1, 1856, d Oct. 22, 1883
*Coventry, Hon. C. J. (Worcs.) b Feb. 26, 1867, d June 2, 1929
Coverdale, S. P. (CUCC, Yorks., & Northants) b Nov. 20, 1954
Cowan, M. J. (Yorks.) b June 10, 1933
*Cowans, N. G. (Middx & Hants) b April 17, 1961
*Cowdrey, C. S. (Kent & Glam.) b Oct. 20, 1957
Cowdrey, G. R. (Kent) b June 27, 1964
*Cowdrey, Sir M. C. (OUCC & Kent; *CY 1956*; Pres. MCC 1986-87) b Dec. 24, 1932
*Cowie, J. (Auck.) b March 30, 1912, d June 3, 1994
Cowley, N. G. (Hants & Glam.) b March 1, 1953

*Cowper, R. M. (Vic. & W. Aust.) b Oct. 5, 1940
Cox, A. L. (Northants) b July 22, 1907, d Nov. 1986
Cox, G., jun. (Sussex) b Aug. 23, 1911, d March 30, 1985
Cox, G. R. (Sussex) b Nov. 29, 1873, d March 24, 1949
*Cox, J. L. (Natal) b June 28, 1886, d July 4, 1971
*Coxon, A. (Yorks.) b Jan. 18, 1916
Craig, E. J. (CUCC & Lancs.) b March 26, 1942
*Craig, I. D. (NSW) b June 12, 1935
Cranfield, L. M. (Glos.) b Aug. 29, 1909, d Nov. 18, 1993
Cranmer, P. (Warwicks.) b Sept. 10, 1914, d May 29, 1994
*Cranston, J. (Glos.) b Jan. 9, 1859, d Dec. 10, 1904
*Cranston, K. (Lancs.) b Oct. 20, 1917
*Crapp, J. F. (Glos.) b Oct. 14, 1912, d Feb. 15, 1981
*Crawford, J. N. (Surrey, S. Aust., Wgtn & Otago; *CY 1907*) b Dec. 1, 1886, d May 2, 1963
*Crawford, P. (NSW) b Aug. 3, 1933
Crawley, A. M. (OUCC & Kent; Pres. MCC 1972-73) b April 10, 1908, d Nov. 3, 1993
*Crawley, J. P. (Lancs. & CUCC) b Sept. 21, 1971
Crawley, M. A. (OUCC, Lancs. & Notts.) b Dec. 16, 1967
Cray, S. J. (Essex) b May 29, 1921
*Cresswell, G. F. (Wgtn & C. Dist.) b March 22, 1915, d Jan. 10, 1966
*Cripps, G. (W. Prov.) b Oct. 19, 1865, d July 27, 1943
*Crisp, R. J. (Rhod., W. Prov. & Worcs.) b May 28, 1911, d March 3, 1994
*Crocker, G. J. (MCD) b May 16, 1962
*Croft, C. E. H. (Guyana & Lancs.) b March 15, 1953
Croft, R. D. B. (Glam.) b May 25, 1970
*Cromb, I. B. (Cant.) b June 25, 1905, d March 6, 1984
*Cronje, W. J. (OFS) b Sept. 25, 1969
Crookes, N. S. (Natal) b Nov. 15, 1935
Cross, G. F. (Leics.) b Nov. 15, 1943
*Crowe, J. J. (S. Aust. & Auck.) b Sept. 14, 1958
*Crowe, M. D. (Auck., C. Dist., Som. & Wgtn; *CY 1985*) b Sept. 22, 1962
Crump, B. S. (Northants) b April 25, 1938
Crush, E. (Kent) b April 25, 1917
*Cullinan, D. J. (Border, W. Prov. & Tvl) b March 4, 1967
Cumbes, J. (Lancs., Surrey, Worcs. & Warwicks.) b May 4, 1944
*Cummins, A. C. (B'dos & Durham) b May 7, 1966
*Cunis, R. S. (Auck. & N. Dist.) b Jan. 5, 1941
*Curnow, S. H. (Tvl) b Dec. 16, 1907, d July 28, 1986
Curran, K. M. (Glos., Zimb, Natal & Northants) b Sept. 7, 1959
*Curtis, T. S. (Worcs. & CUCC) b Jan. 15, 1960
Cuthbertson, G. B. (Middx, Sussex & Northants) b March 23, 1901, d August 9, 1993
Cutmore, J. A. (Essex) b Dec. 28, 1898, d Nov. 30, 1985
*Cuttell, W. R. (Lancs.; *CY 1898*) b Sept. 13, 1864, d Dec. 9, 1929

*Da Costa, O. C. (Jam.) b Sept. 11, 1907, d Oct. 1, 1936
Dacre, C. C. (Auck. & Glos.) b May 15, 1899, d Nov. 2, 1975
Daft, Richard (Notts. & All-England) b Nov. 2, 1835, d July 18, 1900
Dakin, G. F. (E. Prov.) b Aug. 13, 1935
Dale, A. (Glam.) b Oct. 24, 1968
*Dalton, E. L. (Natal) b Dec. 2, 1906, d June 3, 1981
*Dani, H. T. (M'tra & Ind. Serv.) b May 24, 1933
*Daniel, W. W. (B'dos, Middx & W. Aust.) b Jan. 16, 1956
*D'Arcy, J. W. (Cant., Wgtn & Otago) b April 23, 1936
Dare, R. (Hants) b Nov. 26, 1921
*Darling, J. (S. Aust.; *CY 1900*) b Nov. 21, 1870, d Jan. 2, 1946
*Darling, L. S. (Vic.) b Aug. 14, 1909, d June 24, 1992
*Darling, W. M. (S. Aust.) b May 1, 1957
*Darnley, 8th Earl of (Hon. Ivo Bligh) (CUCC & Kent; Pres. MCC 1900) b March 13, 1859, d April 10, 1927
*Dassanayake, P. B. (Colts & Under-23) b July 11, 1970
Davey, J. (Glos.) b Sept. 4, 1944
*Davidson, A. K. (NSW; *CY 1962*) b June 14, 1929
Davies, Dai (Glam.; Umpire) b Aug. 26, 1896, d July 16, 1976
Davies, Emrys (Glam.; Umpire) b June 27, 1904, d Nov. 10, 1975
*Davies, E. Q. (E. Prov., Tvl & NE Tvl) b Aug. 26, 1909, d Nov. 11, 1976
Davies, H. D. (Glam.) b July 23, 1932
Davies, H. G. (Glam.) b April 23, 1912, d Sept. 4, 1993
Davies, J. G. W. (CUCC & Kent; Pres. MCC 1985-86) b Sept. 10, 1911, d Nov. 5, 1992
Davies, M. (Glam. & Glos.) b April 18, 1969
Davies, T. (Glam.) b Oct. 25, 1960
*Davis, B. A. (T/T & Glam.) b May 2, 1940

*Davis, C. A. (T/T) b Jan. 1, 1944
Davis, E. (Northants) b March 8, 1922
*Davis, H. T. (Wgtn) b Nov. 30, 1971
*Davis, I. C. (NSW & Qld) b June 25, 1953
Davis, M. R. (Som.) b Feb. 26, 1962
Davis, P. C. (Northants) b May 24, 1915
Davis, R. C. (Glam.) b Jan. 1, 1946
Davis, R. P. (Kent & Warwicks.) b March 18, 1966
*Davis, S. P. (Vic.) b Nov. 8, 1959
*Davis, W. W. (Windwards, Glam., Tas., Northants & Wgtn) b Sept. 18, 1958
Davison, B. F. (Rhod., Leics, Tas. & Glos.) b Dec. 21, 1946
Davison, I. J. (Notts.) b Oct. 4, 1937
Dawkes, G. O. (Leics. & Derbys.) b July 19, 1920
*Dawson, E. W. (CUCC & Leics.) b Feb. 13, 1904, d June 4, 1979
*Dawson, O. C. (Natal & Border) b Sept. 1, 1919
Dawson, R. I. (Glos.) b March 29, 1970
Day, A. P. (Kent; *CY 1910*) b April 10, 1885, d Jan. 22, 1969
*de Alwis, R. G. (SSC) b Feb. 15, 1959
*Dean, H. (Lancs.) b Aug. 13, 1884, d March 12, 1957
*Deane, H. G. (Natal & Tvl) b July 21, 1895, d Oct. 21, 1939
*De Caires, F. I. (BG) b May 12, 1909, d Feb. 2, 1959
*De Courcy, J. H. (NSW) b April 18, 1927
*DeFreitas, P. A. J. (Leics., Lancs., Boland & Derbys.; *CY 1992*) b Feb. 18, 1966
*de Groen, R. P. (Auck. & N. Dist.) b Aug. 5, 1962
*Dekker, M. H. (Mat.) b Dec. 5, 1969
Delisle, G. P. S. (OUCC & Middx) b Dec. 25, 1934
*Dell, A. R. (Qld) b Aug. 6, 1947
*de Mel, A. L. F. (SL) b May 9, 1959
*Dempster, C. S. (Wgtn, Leics., Scotland & Warwicks.; *CY 1932*) b Nov. 15, 1903, d Feb. 14, 1974
*Dempster, E. W. (Wgtn) b Jan. 25, 1925
*Denness, M. H. (Scotland, Kent & Essex; *CY 1975*) b Dec. 1, 1940
Dennett, E. G. (Glos.) b April 27, 1880, d Sept. 14, 1937
Denning, P. W. (Som.) b Dec. 16, 1949
Dennis, F. (Yorks.) b June 11, 1907
Dennis, S. J. (Yorks., OFS & Glam.) b Oct. 18, 1960
*Denton, D. (Yorks.; *CY 1906*) b July 4, 1874, d Feb. 16, 1950
Deodhar, D. B. (M'tra) b Jan. 14, 1892, d Aug. 24, 1993
*Depeiza, C. C. (B'dos) b Oct. 10, 1927
Derrick, J. (Glam.) b Jan. 15, 1963
*Desai, R. B. (Bombay) b June 20, 1939
*de Silva, A. M. (CCC) b Dec. 3, 1963
de Silva, D. L. S. (SL) b Nov. 17, 1956, d April 12, 1980
*de Silva, D. S. (SL) b June 11, 1942
*de Silva, E. A. R. (NCC) b March 28, 1956
de Silva, G. N. (SL) b March 12, 1955
*de Silva, G. R. A. (SL) b Dec. 12, 1952
*de Silva, P. A. (NCC) b Oct. 17, 1965
de Smidt, R. W. (W. Prov., longest-lived known first-class cricketer) b Nov. 24, 1883, d Aug. 3, 1986
Devereux, L. N. (Middx, Worcs. & Glam.) b Oct. 20, 1931
*de Villiers, P. S. (N. Tvl & Kent) b Oct. 12, 1964
*Dewdney, C. T. (Jam.) b Oct. 23, 1933
*Dewes, J. G. (CUCC & Middx) b Oct. 11, 1926
Dews, G. (Worcs.) b June 5, 1921
*Dexter, E. R. (CUCC & Sussex; *CY 1961*) b May 15, 1935
*Dharmasena, H. D. P. K. (TU & Ant.) b April 24, 1971
*Dias, R. L. (CCC) b Oct. 18, 1952
Dibbs, A. H. A. (Pres. MCC 1983-84) b Dec. 9, 1918, d Nov. 28, 1985
*Dick, A. E. (Otago & Wgtn) b Oct. 10, 1936
*Dickinson, G. R. (Otago) b March 11, 1903, d March 17, 1978
*Dilley, G. R. (Kent, Natal & Worcs.) b May 18, 1959
Diment, R. A. (Glos. & Leics.) b Feb. 9, 1927
*Dipper, A. E. (Glos.) b Nov. 9, 1885, d Nov. 7, 1945
*Divecha, R. V. (Bombay, OUCC, Northants, Vidarbha & S'tra) b Oct. 18, 1927
Diver, A. J. D. (Cambs., Middx, Notts. & All-England) b June 6, 1824, d March 25, 1876
Dixon, A. L. (Kent) b Nov. 27, 1933
*Dixon, C. D. (Tvl) b Feb. 12, 1891, d Sept. 9, 1969
Dodds, T. C. (Essex) b May 29, 1919
*Dodemaide, A. I. C. (Vic. & Sussex) b Oct. 5, 1963
*Doggart, G. H. G. (CUCC & Sussex; Pres. MCC 1981-82) b July 18, 1925
*D'Oliveira, B. L. (Worcs.; *CY 1967*) b Oct. 4, 1931
D'Oliveira, D. B. (Worcs.) b Oct. 19, 1960
*Dollery, H. E. (Warwicks. & Wgtn; *CY 1952*) b Oct. 14, 1914, d Jan. 20, 1987
Dollery, K. R. (Qld, Auck., Tas. & Warwicks.) b Dec. 9, 1924
*Dolphin, A. (Yorks.) b Dec. 24, 1885, d Oct. 23, 1942
*Donald, A. A. (OFS & Warwicks.; *CY 1992*) b Oct. 20, 1966
Donelan, B. T. P. (Sussex & Som.) b Jan. 3, 1968

*Donnan, H. (NSW) b Nov. 12, 1864, d Aug. 13, 1956
*Donnelly, M. P. (Wgtn, Cant., Middx, Warwicks. & OUCC; *CY 1948*) b Oct. 17, 1917
*Dooland, B. (S. Aust. & Notts.; *CY 1955*) b Nov. 1, 1923, d Sept. 8, 1980
Dorrinton, W. (Kent & All-England) b April 29, 1809, d Nov. 8, 1848
Dorset, 3rd Duke of (Kent) b March 24, 1745, d July 19, 1799
*Doshi, D. R. (Bengal, Notts., Warwicks. & S'tra) b Dec. 22, 1947
*Douglas, J. W. H. T. (Essex; *CY 1915*) b Sept. 3, 1882, d Dec. 19, 1930
Douglas, M. W. (C. Dist. & Wgtn) b Oct. 20, 1968
*Doull, S. B. (N. Dist.) b Aug. 6, 1969
Dowding, A. L. (OUCC) b April 4, 1929
*Dowe, U. G. (Jam.) b March 29, 1949
*Dower, R. R. (E. Prov.) b June 4, 1876, d Sept. 15, 1964
*Dowling, G. T. (Cant.) b March 4, 1937
*Downton, P. R. (Kent & Middx) b April 4, 1957
*Draper, R. G. (E. Prov. & Griq. W.) b Dec. 24, 1926
Dredge, C. H. (Som.) b Aug. 4, 1954
*Druce, N. F. (CUCC & Surrey; *CY 1898*) b Jan. 1, 1875, d Oct. 27, 1954
Drybrough, C. D. (OUCC & Middx) b Aug. 31, 1938
*D'Souza, A. (Kar., Peshawar & PIA) b Jan. 17, 1939
*Ducat, A. (Surrey; *CY 1920*) b Feb. 16, 1886, d July 23, 1942
*Duckworth, C. A. R. (Natal & Rhod.) b March 22, 1933
*Duckworth, G. (Lancs.; *CY 1929*) b May 9, 1901, d Jan. 5, 1966
Dudleston, B. (Leics., Glos. & Rhod.) b July 16, 1945
Duers, K. G. (Mash.) b June 30, 1960
*Duff, R. A. (NSW) b Aug. 17, 1878, d Dec. 13, 1911
*Dujon, P. J. L. (Jam.; *CY 1989*) b May 28, 1956
*Duleepsinhji, K. S. (CUCC & Sussex; *CY 1930*) b June 13, 1905, d Dec. 5, 1959
*Dumbrill, R. (Natal & Tvl) b Nov. 19, 1938
*Duminy, J. P. (OUCC, W. Prov. & Tvl) b Dec. 16, 1897, d Jan. 31, 1980
*Duncan, J. R. F. (Qld & Vic.) b March 25, 1944
*Dunell, O. R. (E. Prov.) b July 15, 1856, d Oct. 21, 1929
*Dunning, J. A. (Otago & OUCC) b Feb. 6, 1903, d June 24, 1971
*Du Preez, J. H. (Rhod. & Zimb.) b Nov. 14, 1942
*Durani, S. A. (S'tra, Guj. & Raja.) b Dec. 11, 1934
Durose, A. J. (Northants) b Oct. 10, 1944
*Durston, F. J. (Middx) b July 11, 1893, d April 8, 1965
*Du Toit, J. F. (SA) b April 5, 1868, d July 10, 1909
Dye, J. C. J. (Kent, Northants & E. Prov.) b July 24, 1942
Dyer, D. D. (Natal & Tvl) b Dec. 3, 1946
*Dyer, D. V. (Natal) b May 2, 1914, d June 18, 1990
*Dyer, G. C. (NSW) b March 16, 1959
Dyer, R. I. H. B. (Warwicks.) b Dec. 22, 1958
*Dymock, G. (Qld) b July 21, 1945
Dyson, A. H. (Glam.) b July 10, 1905, d June 7, 1978
Dyson, J. (Lancs.) b July 8, 1934
*Dyson, John (NSW) b June 11, 1954

*Eady, C. J. (Tas.) b Oct. 29, 1870, d Dec. 20, 1945
Eagar, E. D. R. (OUCC, Glos. & Hants) b Dec. 8, 1917, d Sept. 13, 1977
Eagar, M. A. (OUCC & Glos.) b March 20, 1934
Eaglestone, J. T. (Middx & Glam.) b July 24, 1923
Ealham, A. G. E. (Kent) b Aug. 30, 1944
Ealham, M. A. (Kent) b Aug. 27, 1969
East, D. E. (Essex) b July 27, 1959
East, R. E. (Essex) b June 20, 1947
Eastman, G. F. (Essex) b April 7, 1903, d March 15, 1991
Eastman, L. C. (Essex & Otago) b June 3, 1897, d April 17, 1941
*Eastwood, K. H. (Vic.) b Nov. 23, 1935
*Ebeling, H. I. (Vic.) b Jan. 1, 1905, d Jan. 12, 1980
Eckersley, P. T. (Lancs.) b July 2, 1904, d Aug. 13, 1940
*Edgar, B. A. (Wgtn) b Nov. 23, 1956
Edinburgh, HRH Duke of (Pres. MCC 1948-49, 1974-75) b June 10, 1921
Edmeades, B. E. A. (Essex) b Sept. 17, 1941
*Edmonds, P. H. (CUCC, Middx & E. Prov.) b March 8, 1951
Edmonds, R. B. (Warwicks.) b March 2, 1941
Edrich, B. R. (Kent & Glam.) b Aug. 18, 1922
Edrich, E. H. (Lancs.) b March 27, 1914, d July 9, 1993
Edrich, G. A. (Lancs.) b July 13, 1918
*Edrich, J. H. (Surrey; *CY 1966*) b June 21, 1937
*Edrich, W. J. (Middx; *CY 1940*) b March 26, 1916, d April 24, 1986
*Edwards, G. N. (C. Dist.) b May 27, 1955
*Edwards, J. D. (Vic.) b June 12, 1862, d July 31, 1911
Edwards, M. J. (CUCC & Surrey) b March 1, 1940

*Edwards, R. (W. Aust. & NSW) b Dec. 1, 1942
*Edwards, R. M. (B'dos) b June 3, 1940
*Edwards, W. J. (W. Aust.) b Dec. 23, 1949
Eele, P. J. (Som.) b Jan. 27, 1935
*Ehtesham-ud-Din (Lahore, Punjab, PIA, NBP & UBL) b Sept. 4, 1950
*Eksteen, C. E. (Tvl) b Dec. 2, 1966
*Elgie, M. K. (Natal) b March 6, 1933
Elliott, C. S. (Derbys.) b April 24, 1912
*Elliott, H. (Derbys.) b Nov. 2, 1891, d Feb. 2, 1976
Ellis, G. P. (Glam.) b May 24, 1950
Ellis, R. G. P. (OUCC & Middx) b Oct. 20 1960
*Ellison, R. M. (Kent & Tas.; *CY 1986*) b Sept. 21, 1959
Elms, R. B. (Kent & Hants) b April 5, 1949
*Emburey, J. E. (Middx & W. Prov.; *CY 1984*) b Aug. 20, 1952
*Emery, R. W. G. (Auck. & Cant.) b March 28, 1915, d Dec. 18, 1982
*Emery, S. H. (NSW) b Oct. 16, 1885, d Jan. 7, 1967
*Emmett, G. M. (Glos.) b Dec. 2, 1912, d Dec. 18, 1976
*Emmett, T. (Yorks.) b Sept. 3, 1841, d June 30, 1904
*Endean, W. R. (Tvl) b May 31, 1924
*Engineer, F. M. (Bombay & Lancs.) b Feb. 25, 1938
Essop-Adam, E. A. (Zimb.) b Nov. 16, 1968
*Evans, A. J. (OUCC, Hants & Kent) b May 1, 1889, d Sept. 18, 1960
Evans, C. N. (Zimb.) b Nov. 29, 1969
Evans, D. G. L. (Glam.; Umpire) b July 27, 1933, d March 25, 1990
*Evans, E. (NSW) b March 26, 1849, d July 2, 1921
Evans, G. (OUCC, Glam. & Leics.) b Aug. 13, 1915
Evans, J. B. (Glam.) b Nov. 9, 1936
Evans, K. P. (Notts.) b Sept. 10, 1963
*Evans, T. G. (Kent; *CY 1951*) b Aug. 18, 1920
Every, T. (Glam.) b Dec. 19, 1909, d Jan. 20, 1990
Eyre, T. J. P. (Derbys.) b Oct. 17, 1939

Faber, M. J. J. (OUCC & Sussex) b Aug. 15, 1950, d Dec. 10, 1991
*Fagg, A. E. (Kent) b June 18, 1915, d Sept. 13, 1977
Fairbairn, A. (Middx) b Jan. 25, 1923
*Fairbrother, N. H. (Lancs.) b Sept. 9, 1963
*Fairfax, A. G. (NSW) b June 16, 1906, d May 17, 1955
Fairservice, C. (Kent & Middx) b Aug. 21, 1909
*Fane, F. L. (OUCC & Essex) b April 27, 1875, d Nov. 27, 1960
Fantham, W. E. (Warwicks.) b May 14, 1918
*Farnes, K. (CUCC & Essex; *CY 1939*) b July 8, 1911, d Oct. 20, 1941
*Farooq Hamid (Lahore & PIA) b March 3, 1945
*Farrer, W. S. (Border) b Dec. 8, 1936
*Farrimond, W. (Lancs.) b May 23, 1903, d Nov. 14, 1979
*Farrukh Zaman (Peshawar, NWFP, Punjab & MCB) b April 2, 1956
*Faulkner, G. A. (Tvl) b Dec. 17, 1881, d Sept. 10, 1930
*Favell, L. E. (S. Aust.) b Oct. 6, 1929, d June 14, 1987
*Fazal Mahmood (N. Ind., Punjab & Lahore; *CY 1955*) b Feb. 18, 1927
Fearnley, C. D. (Worcs.) b April 12, 1940
Featherstone, N. G. (Tvl, N. Tvl, Middx & Glam.) b Aug. 20, 1949
'Felix', N. (Wanostrocht) (Kent, Surrey & All-England) b Oct. 4, 1804, d Sept. 3, 1876
*Fellows-Smith, J. P. (OUCC, Tvl & Northants) b Feb. 3, 1932
Feltham, M. A. (Surrey & Middx) b June 26, 1963
Felton, N. A. (Som. & Northants) b Oct. 24, 1960
*Fender, P. G. H. (Sussex & Surrey; *CY 1915*) b Aug. 22, 1892, d June 15, 1985
*Ferguson, W. (T/T) b Dec. 14, 1917, d Feb. 23, 1961
*Fernandes, M. P. (BG) b Aug. 12, 1897, d May 8, 1981
Fernando, E. R. (SL) b Feb. 22, 1944
*Fernando, E. R. N. S. (SLAF) b Dec. 19, 1955
Fernando, T. L. (Colts) b Dec. 27, 1962
Fernando, U. N. K. (SSC) b March 10, 1970
Ferreira, A. M. (N. Tvl & Warwicks.) b April 13, 1955
Ferris, G. J. F. (Leics. & Leewards) b Oct. 18, 1964
**Ferris, J. J. (NSW, Glos. & S. Aust.; *CY 1889*) b May 21, 1867, d Nov. 21, 1900
*Fichardt, C. G. (OFS) b March 20, 1870, d May 30, 1923
Fiddling, K. (Yorks. & Northants) b Oct. 13, 1917, d June 19, 1992
*Fielder, A. (Kent; *CY 1907*) b July 19, 1877, d Aug. 30, 1949
*Findlay, T. M. (Comb. Is. & Windwards) b Oct. 19, 1943
Findlay, W. (OUCC & Lancs.; Sec. Surrey CCC, Sec. MCC 1926-36) b June 22, 1880, d June 19, 1953
*Fingleton, J. H. (NSW) b April 28, 1908, d Nov. 22, 1981
*Finlason, C. E. (Tvl & Griq. W.) b Feb. 19, 1860, d July 31, 1917

Finney, R. J. (Derbys.) b Aug. 2, 1960
Firth, Rev. Canon J. D'E. E. (Winchester, OUCC & Notts.; *CY 1918*) b Jan. 21, 1900, d Sept. 21, 1957
*Fisher, F. E. (Wgtn & C. Dist.) b July 28, 1924
Fisher, P. B. (OUCC, Middx & Worcs.) b Dec. 19, 1954
*Fishlock, L. B. (Surrey; *CY 1947*) b Jan. 2, 1907, d June 26, 1986
Fitton, J. D. (Lancs.) b Aug. 24, 1965
Fitzgerald, R. A. (CUCC & Middx; Sec. MCC 1863-76) b Oct. 1, 1834, d Oct. 28, 1881
*Flavell, J. A. (Worcs.; *CY 1965*) b May 15, 1929
*Fleetwood-Smith, L. O'B. (Vic.) b March 30, 1908, d March 16, 1971
Fleming, D. W. (Vic.) b April 24, 1970
Fleming, M. V. (Kent) b Dec. 12, 1964
*Fleming, S. P. (Cant.) b April 1, 1973
Fletcher, D. A. G. (Rhod. & Zimb.) b Sept. 27, 1948
Fletcher, D. G. W. (Surrey) b July 6, 1924
*Fletcher, K. W. R. (Essex; *CY 1974*) b May 20, 1944
Fletcher, S. D. (Yorks. & Lancs.) b June 8, 1964
*Floquet, C. E. (Tvl) b Nov. 3, 1884, d Nov. 22, 1963
*Flower, A. (Mash.) b April 28, 1968
*Flower, G. W. (Under-24) b Dec. 20, 1970
*Flowers, W. (Notts.) b Dec. 7, 1856, d Nov. 1, 1926
Foat, J. C. (Glos.) b Nov. 21, 1952
*Foley, H. (Wgtn) b Jan. 28, 1906, d Oct. 16, 1948
Folley, I. (Lancs. & Derbys.) b Jan. 9, 1963, d Aug. 30, 1993
Foord, C. W. (Yorks.) b June 11, 1924
Forbes, C. (Notts.) b Aug. 9, 1936
*Ford, F. G. J. (CUCC & Middx) b Dec. 14, 1866, d Feb. 7, 1940
Ford, N. M. (OUCC, Derbys. & Middx) b Nov. 18, 1906
Fordham, A. (Northants) b Nov. 9, 1964
Foreman, D. J. (W. Prov. & Sussex) b Feb. 1, 1933
*Foster, F. R. (Warwicks.; *CY 1912*) b Jan. 31, 1889, d May 3, 1958
Foster, G. N. (OUCC, Worcs. & Kent) b Oct. 16, 1884, d Aug. 11, 1971
Foster, H. K. (OUCC & Worcs.; *CY 1911*) b Oct. 30, 1873, d June 23, 1950
Foster, M. K. (Worcs.) b Jan. 1, 1889, d Dec. 3, 1940
*Foster, M. L. C. (Jam.) b May 9, 1943
*Foster, N. A. (Essex & Tvl; *CY 1988*) b May 6, 1962
Foster, P. G. (Kent) b Oct. 9, 1916, d Dec. 7, 1994
*Foster, R. E. (OUCC & Worcs.; *CY 1901*) b April 16, 1878, d May 13, 1914
*Fothergill, A. J. (Som.) b Aug. 26, 1854, d Aug. 1, 1932
Fotheringham, H. R. (Natal & Tvl) b April 4, 1953
*Fowler, G. (Lancs. & Durham) b April 20, 1957
Fowler, W. P. (Derbys., N. Dist. & Auck.) b March 13, 1959
*Francis, B. C. (NSW & Essex) b Feb. 18, 1948
Francis, D. A. (Glam.) b Nov. 29, 1953
*Francis, G. N. (B'dos) b Dec. 11, 1897, d Jan. 7, 1942
*Francis, H. H. (Glos. & W. Prov.) b May 26, 1868, d Jan. 7, 1936
Francke, F. M. (SL & Qld) b March 29, 1941
*Francois, C. M. (Griq. W.) b June 20, 1897, d May 26, 1944
*Frank, C. N. (Tvl) b Jan. 27, 1891, d Dec. 26, 1961
*Frank, W. H. B. (SA) b Nov. 23, 1872, d Feb. 16, 1945
Franklin, H. W. F. (OUCC, Surrey & Essex) b June 30, 1901, d May 25, 1985
*Franklin, T. J. (Auck.) b March 18, 1962
*Fraser, A. R. C. (Middx) b Aug. 8, 1965
*Frederick, M. C. (B'dos, Derbys. & Jam.) b May 6, 1927
*Fredericks, R. C. (†Guyana & Glam.; *CY 1974*) b Nov. 11, 1942
*Freeman, A. P. (Kent; *CY 1923*) b May 17, 1888, d Jan. 28, 1965
*Freeman, D. L. (Wgtn) b Sept. 8, 1914, d May 31, 1994
*Freeman, E. W. (S. Aust.) b July 13, 1944
*Freer, F. W. (Vic.) b Dec. 4, 1915
*French, B. N. (Notts.) b Aug. 13, 1959
Frost, G. (Notts.) b Jan. 15, 1947
Frost, M. (Surrey & Glam.) b Oct. 21, 1962
Fry, C. A. (OUCC, Hants & Northants) b Jan. 14, 1940
*Fry, C. B. (OUCC, Sussex & Hants; *CY 1895*) b April 25, 1872, d Sept. 7, 1956
*Fuller, E. R. H. (W. Prov.) b Aug. 2, 1931
*Fuller, R. L. (Jam.) b Jan. 30, 1913, d May 3, 1987
*Fullerton, G. M. (Tvl) b Dec. 8, 1922
Funston, G. K. (NE Tvl & Griq. W.) b Nov. 21, 1948
*Funston, K. J. (NE Tvl, OFS & Tvl) b Dec. 3, 1925
*Furlonge, H. A. (T/T) b June 19, 1934

Gabriel, R. S. (T/T) b June 5, 1952
*Gadkari, C. V. (M'tra & Ind. Serv.) b Feb. 3, 1928
*Gaekwad, A. D. (Baroda) b Sept. 23, 1952
*Gaekwad, D. K. (Baroda) b Oct. 27, 1928
*Gaekwad, H. G. (†M. Pradesh) b Aug. 29, 1923
Gale, R. A. (Middx) b Dec. 10, 1933

Gallian, J. E. R. (Lancs. & OUCC) b June 25, 1971
*Gallichan, N. (Wgtn) b June 3, 1906, d March 25, 1969
*Gamsy, D. (Natal) b Feb. 17, 1940
*Gandotra, A. (Delhi & Bengal) b Nov. 24, 1948
Ganguly, S. C. (Bengal) b July 8, 1966
*Gannon, J. B. (W. Aust.) b Feb. 8, 1947
*Ganteaume, A. G. (T/T) b Jan. 22, 1921
Gard, T. (Som.) b June 2, 1957
Gardner, L. R. (Leics.) b Feb. 23, 1934
Garland-Wells, H. M. (OUCC & Surrey) b Nov. 14, 1907, d May 28, 1993
Garlick, R. G. (Lancs. & Northants) b April 11, 1917, d May 16, 1988
*Garner, J. (B'dos, Som. & S. Aust.; *CY 1980*) b Dec. 16, 1952
Garnham, M. A. (Glos., Leics. & Essex) b Aug. 20, 1960
*Garrett, T. W. (NSW) b July 26, 1858, d Aug. 6, 1943
*Gaskin, B. B. MacG. (BG) b March 21, 1908, d May 1, 1979
*Gatting, M. W. (Middx; *CY 1984*) b June 6, 1957
*Gaunt, R. A. (W. Aust. & Vic.) b Feb. 26, 1934
*Gavaskar, S. M. (Bombay & Som.; *CY 1980*) b July 10, 1949
*Gay, L. H. (CUCC, Hants & Som.) b March 24, 1871, d Nov. 1, 1949
Geary, A. C. T. (Surrey) b Sept. 11, 1900, d Jan. 23, 1989
*Geary, G. (Leics.; *CY 1927*) b July 9, 1893, d March 6, 1981
*Gedye, S. G. (Auck.) b May 2, 1929
*Gehrs, D. R. A. (S. Aust.) b Nov. 29, 1880, d June 25, 1953
Ghai, R. S. (Punjab) b June 12, 1960
*Ghavri, K. D. (S'tra & Bombay) b Feb. 28, 1951
*Ghazali, M. E. Z. (M'tra & Pak. Serv.) b June 15, 1924
*Ghorpade, J. M. (Baroda) b Oct. 2, 1930, d March 29, 1978
*Ghulam Abbas (Kar., NBP & PIA) b May 1, 1947
*Ghulam Ahmed (H'bad) b July 4, 1922
Ghulam Ali (Kar. & PACO) b Sept. 8, 1966
*Gibb, P. A. (CUCC, Scotland, Yorks. & Essex) b July 11, 1913, d Dec. 7, 1977
Gibbons, H. H. (Worcs.) b Oct. 10, 1904, d Feb. 16, 1973
*Gibbs, G. L. (BG) b Dec. 27, 1925, d Feb. 21, 1979
*Gibbs, L. R. (†Guyana, S. Aust. & Warwicks.; *CY 1972*) b Sept. 29, 1934
Gibbs, P. J. K. (OUCC & Derbys.) b Aug. 17, 1944
Gibson, C. H. (Eton, CUCC & Sussex; *CY 1918*) b Aug. 23, 1900, d Dec. 31, 1976
Gibson, D. (Surrey) b May 1, 1936
Gibson, O. D. (B'dos, Border & Glam.) b March 16, 1969
Giddins, E. S. H. (Sussex), b July 20, 1971
*Giffen, G. (S. Aust.; *CY 1894*) b March 27, 1859, d Nov. 29, 1927
*Giffen, W. F. (S. Aust.) b Sept. 20, 1861, d June 29, 1949
*Gifford, N. (Worcs. & Warwicks.; *CY 1975*) b March 30, 1940
*Gilbert, D. R. (NSW, Tas. & Glos.) b Dec. 29, 1960
*Gilchrist, R. (Jam. & H'bad) b June 28, 1934
Giles, R. J. (Notts.) b Oct. 17, 1919
Gilhouley, K. (Yorks. & Notts.) b Aug. 8, 1934
Gill, A. (Notts.) b Aug. 4, 1940
*Gillespie, S. R. (Auck.) b March 2, 1957
Gilliat, R. M. C. (OUCC & Hants) b May 20, 1944
*Gilligan, A. E. R. (CUCC, Surrey & Sussex; *CY 1924*; Pres. MCC 1967-68) b Dec. 23, 1894, d Sept. 5, 1976
*Gilligan, A. H. H. (Sussex) b June 29, 1896, d May 5, 1978
Gilligan, F. W. (OUCC & Essex) b Sept. 20, 1893, d May 4, 1960
*Gilmour, G. J. (NSW) b June 26, 1951
*Gimblett, H. (Som.; *CY 1953*) b Oct. 19, 1914, d March 30, 1978
Gladstone, G. (*see* Marais, G. G.)
Gladwin, Chris (Essex & Derbys.) b May 10, 1962
*Gladwin, Cliff (Derbys.) b April 3, 1916, d April 10, 1988
*Gleeson, J. W. (NSW & E. Prov.) b March 14, 1938
*Gleeson, R. A. (E. Prov.) b Dec. 6, 1873, d Sept. 27, 1919
Glendenen, J. D. (Durham) b June 20, 1965
*Glover, G. K. (Kimberley & Griq. W.) b May 13, 1870, d Nov. 15, 1938
Glover, T. R. (OUCC) b Nov. 26, 1951
Goddard, G. F. (Scotland) b May 19, 1938
*Goddard, J. D. C. (B'dos) b April 21, 1919, d Aug. 26, 1987
*Goddard, T. L. (Natal & NE Tvl) b Aug. 1, 1931
*Goddard, T. W. J. (Glos.; *CY 1938*) b Oct. 1, 1900, d May 22, 1966
Goel, R. (Patiala & Haryana) b Sept. 29, 1942
Goldsmith, S. C. (Kent & Derbys.) b Dec. 19, 1964
Goldstein, F. S. (OUCC, Northants, Tvl & W. Prov.) b Oct. 14, 1944
*Gomes, H. A. (T/T & Middx; *CY 1985*) b July 13, 1953
*Gomez, G. E. (T/T) b Oct. 10, 1919
*Gooch, G. A. (Essex & W. Prov.; *CY 1980*) b July 23, 1953

Goodway, C. C. (Warwicks.) b July 10, 1909, d May 22, 1991
Goodwin, K. (Lancs.) b June 25, 1938
Goodwin, T. J. (Leics.) b Jan. 22, 1929
Goonatillake, F. R. M. de S. (SL) b. Aug. 15, 1951
*Goonatillake, H. M. (SL) b Aug. 16, 1952
Goonesena, G. (Ceylon, Notts., CUCC & NSW) b Feb. 16, 1931
*Gopalan, M. J. (Madras) b June 6, 1909
*Gopinath, C. D. (Madras) b March 1, 1930
*Gordon, N. (Tvl) b Aug. 6, 1911
Gore, A. C. (Eton & Army; *CY 1919*) b May 14, 1900, d June 7, 1990
*Gough, D. (Yorks.) b Sept. 18, 1970
Gould, I. J. (Middx, Auck. & Sussex) b Aug. 19, 1957
*Gover, A. R. (Surrey; *CY 1937*) b Feb. 29, 1908
*Gower, D. I. (Leics. & Hants; *CY 1979*) b April 1, 1957
Gowrie, 1st Lord (Pres. MCC 1948-49) b July 6, 1872, d May 2, 1955
Grace, Dr Alfred b May 17, 1840, d May 24, 1916
Grace, Dr Alfred H. (Glos.) b March 10, 1866, d Sept. 16, 1929
Grace, C. B. (Clifton) b March 1882, d June 6, 1938
*Grace, Dr E. M. (Glos.) b Nov. 28, 1841, d May 20, 1911
Grace, Dr Edgar M. (MCC) (son of E. M. Grace) b Oct. 6, 1886, d Nov. 24, 1974
*Grace, G. F. (Glos.) b Dec. 13, 1850, d Sept. 22, 1880
Grace, Dr Henry (Glos.) b Jan. 31, 1833, d Nov. 15, 1895
Grace, Dr H. M. (father of W. G., E. M. and G. F.) b Feb. 21, 1808, d Dec. 23, 1871
Grace, Mrs H. M. (mother of W. G., E. M. and G. F.) b July 18, 1812, d July 25, 1884
*Grace, Dr W. G. (Glos.; *CY 1896*) b July 18, 1848, d Oct. 23, 1915
Grace, W. G., jun. (CUCC & Glos.) b July 6, 1874, d March 2, 1905
Graf, S. F. (Vic., W. Aust. & Hants) b May 19, 1957
*Graham, H. (Vic. & Otago) b Nov. 22, 1870, d Feb. 7, 1911
Graham, J. N. (Kent) b May 8, 1943
*Graham, R. (W. Prov.) b Sept. 16, 1877, d April 21, 1946
*Grant, G. C. (CUCC, T/T & Rhod.) b May 9, 1907, d Oct. 26, 1978
*Grant, R. S. (CUCC & T/T) b Dec. 15, 1909, d Oct. 18, 1977
Graveney, D. A. (Glos., Som. & Durham) b Jan. 2, 1953
Graveney, J. K. (Glos.) b Dec. 16, 1924
*Graveney, T. W. (Glos., Worcs. & Qld; *CY 1953*) b June 16, 1927
Graves, P. J. (Sussex & OFS) b May 19, 1946
*Gray, A. H. (T/T, Surrey & W. Tvl) b May 23, 1963
*Gray, E. J. (Wgtn) b Nov. 18, 1954
Gray, J. R. (Hants) b May 19, 1926
Grayson, A. P. (Yorks.) b March 31, 1971
Greasley, D. G. (Northants) b Jan. 20, 1926
*Greatbatch, M. J. (C. Dist.) b Dec. 11, 1963
Green, A. M. (Sussex & OFS) b May 28, 1960
Green, D. J. (Derbys. & CUCC) b Dec. 18, 1935
Green, D. M. (OUCC, Lancs. & Glos.; *CY 1969*) b Nov. 10, 1939
*Greenhough, T. (Lancs.) b Nov. 9, 1931
*Greenidge, A. E. (B'dos) b Aug. 20, 1956
*Greenidge, C. G. (Hants & B'dos; *CY 1977*) b May 1, 1951
*Greenidge, G. A. (B'dos & Sussex) b May 26, 1948
Greensmith, W. T. (Essex) b Aug. 16, 1930
*Greenwood, A. (Yorks.) b Aug. 20, 1847, d Feb. 12, 1889
Greenwood, P. (Lancs.) b Sept. 11, 1924
Greetham, C. (Som.) b Aug. 28, 1936
*Gregory, David W. (NSW; first Australian captain) b April 15, 1845, d Aug. 4, 1919
*Gregory, E. J. (NSW) b May 29, 1839, d April 22, 1899
*Gregory, J. M. (NSW; *CY 1922*) b Aug. 14, 1895, d Aug. 7, 1973
*Gregory, R. G. (Vic.) b Feb. 28, 1916, d June 10, 1942
*Gregory, S. E. (NSW; *CY 1897*) b April 14, 1870, d August 1, 1929
*Greig, A. W. (Border, E. Prov. & Sussex; *CY 1975*) b Oct. 6, 1946
*Greig, I. A. (CUCC, Border, Sussex & Surrey) b Dec. 8, 1955
*Grell, M. G. (T/T) b Dec. 18, 1899, d Jan. 11, 1976
*Grieve, B. A. F. (Eng.) b May 28, 1864, d Nov. 19, 1917
Grieves, K. J. (NSW & Lancs.) b Aug. 27, 1925, d Jan. 3, 1992
*Grieveson, R. E. (Tvl) b Aug. 24, 1909
*Griffin, G. M. (Natal & Rhod.) b June 12, 1939
*Griffith, C. C. (B'dos; *CY 1964*) b Dec. 14, 1938
Griffith, G. ("Ben") (Surrey & Utd England XI) b Dec. 20, 1833, d May 3, 1879
*Griffith, H. C. (B'dos) b Dec. 1, 1893, d March 18, 1980
Griffith, K. (Worcs.) b Jan. 17, 1950

Griffith, M. G. (CUCC & Sussex) b Nov. 25, 1943
*Griffith, S. C. (CUCC, Surrey & Sussex; Sec. MCC 1962-74; Pres. MCC 1979-80) b June 16, 1914, d April 7, 1993
Griffiths, B. J. (Northants) b June 13, 1949
Griffiths, Rt Hon. The Lord (W. H.) (CUCC & Glam.; Pres. MCC 1990-91) b Sept. 26, 1923
*Grimmett, C. V. (Wgtn, Vic. & S. Aust.; *CY 1931*) b Dec. 25, 1891, d May 2, 1980
Grimshaw, N. (Northants) b May 5, 1911
*Groube, T. U. (Vic.) b Sept. 2, 1857, d Aug. 5, 1927
*Grout, A. T. W. (Qld) b March 30, 1927, d Nov. 9, 1968
Grover, J. N. (OUCC) b Oct. 15, 1915, d Dec. 17, 1990
Groves, M. G. M. (OUCC, Som. & W. Prov.) b Jan. 14, 1943
Grundy, J. (Notts. & Utd England XI) b March 5, 1824, d Nov. 24, 1873
*Guard, G. M. (Bombay & Guj.) b Dec. 12, 1925, d March 13, 1978
*Guest, C. E. J. (Vic. & W. Aust.) b Oct. 7, 1937
*Guha, S. (Bengal) b Jan. 31, 1946
**Guillen, S. C. (T/T & Cant.) b Sept. 24, 1924
Guise, J. L. (OUCC & Middx) b Nov. 25, 1903, d June 29, 1991
**Gul Mahomed (N. Ind., Baroda, H'bad, Punjab & Lahore) b Oct. 15, 1921, d May 8, 1992
*Gunasekera, Y. (SL) b Nov. 8, 1957
Gunawardene, A. A. W. (SSC) b March 31, 1969
*Guneratne, R. P. W. (Nomads) b Jan. 26, 1962
*Gunn, G. (Notts.; *CY 1914*) b June 13, 1879, d June 29, 1958
Gunn, G. V. (Notts.) b June 21, 1905, d Oct. 14, 1957
*Gunn, J. (Notts.; *CY 1904*) b July 19, 1876, d Aug. 21, 1963
Gunn, T. (Sussex) b Sept. 27, 1935
*Gunn, William (Notts.; *CY 1890*) b Dec. 4, 1858, d Jan. 29, 1921
*Gupte, B. P. (Bombay, Bengal & Ind. Rlwys) b Aug. 30, 1934
*Gupte, S. P. (Bombay, Bengal, Raja. & T/T) b Dec. 11, 1929
*Gursharan Singh (Punjab) b March 8, 1963
*Gurusinha, A. P. (SSC & NCC) b Sept. 16, 1966
*Guy, J. W. (C. Dist., Wgtn, Northants, Cant., Otago & N. Dist.) b Aug. 29, 1934

Haafiz Shahid (WAPDA) b May 10, 1963
Hacker, P. J. (Notts., Derbys. & OFS) b July 16, 1952
Hadlee, B. G. (Cant.) b Dec. 14, 1941
*Hadlee, D. R. (Cant.) b Jan. 6, 1948
*Hadlee, Sir R. J. (Cant., Notts. & Tas.; *CY 1982*) b July 3, 1951
*Hadlee, W. A. (Cant. & Otago) b June 4, 1915
Hafeez, A. (*see* Kardar)
*Haig, N. E. (Middx) b Dec. 12, 1887, d Oct. 27, 1966
*Haigh, S. (Yorks.; *CY 1901*) b March 19, 1871, d Feb. 27, 1921
Halfyard, D. J. (Kent & Notts.) b April 3, 1931
*Hall, A. E. (Tvl & Lancs.) b Jan. 23, 1896, d Jan. 1, 1964
*Hall, G. G. (NE Tvl & E. Prov.) b May 24, 1938, d June 26, 1987
Hall, I. W. (Derbys.) b Dec. 27, 1939
Hall, J. W. (Sussex) b March 30, 1968
Hall, Louis (Yorks.; *CY 1890*) b Nov. 1, 1852, d Nov. 19, 1915
*Hall, W. W. (B'dos, T/T & Qld) b Sept. 12, 1937
Hallam, A. W. (Lancs. & Notts.; *CY 1908*) b Nov. 12, 1869, d July 24, 1940
Hallam, M. R. (Leics.) b Sept. 10, 1931
*Halliwell, E. A. (Tvl & Middx; *CY 1905*) b Sept. 7, 1864, d Oct. 2, 1919
*Hallows, C. (Lancs.; *CY 1928*) b April 4, 1895, d Nov. 10, 1972
Hallows, J. (Lancs.; *CY 1905*) b Nov. 14, 1873, d May 20, 1910
*Halse, C. G. (Natal) b Feb. 28, 1935
*Hamence, R. A. (S. Aust.) b Nov. 25, 1915
Hamer, A. (Yorks. & Derbys.) b Dec. 8, 1916, d Nov. 3, 1993
Hammond, H. E. (Sussex) b Nov. 7, 1907, d June 16, 1985
*Hammond, J. R. (S. Aust.) b April 19, 1950
*Hammond, W. R. (Glos.; *CY 1928*) b June 19, 1903, d July 1, 1965
*Hampshire, J. H. (Yorks., Derbys. & Tas.; Umpire) b Feb. 10, 1941
Hancock, T. H. C. (Glos.) b April 20, 1972
*Hands, P. A. M. (W. Prov.) b March 18, 1890, d April 27, 1951
*Hands, R. H. M. (W. Prov.) b July 26, 1888, d April 20, 1918
*Hanif Mohammad (B'pur, Kar. & PIA; *CY 1968*) b Dec. 21, 1934
*Hanley, M. A. (Border & W. Prov.) b Nov. 10, 1918
Hanley, R. W. (E. Prov., OFS, Tvl & Northants) b Jan. 29, 1952
*Hanumant Singh (M. Pradesh & Raja.) b March 29, 1939
Harbord, W. E. (Yorks. & OUCC) b Dec. 15, 1908, d July 28, 1992
Harden, R. J. (Som. & C. Dist.) b Aug. 16, 1965

Hardie, B. R. (Scotland & Essex) b Jan. 14, 1950
*Hardikar, M. S. (Bombay) b Feb. 8, 1936
*Hardinge, H. T. W. (Kent; *CY 1915*) b Feb. 25, 1886, d May 8, 1965
*Hardstaff, J. (Notts.) b Nov. 9, 1882, d April 2, 1947
*Hardstaff, J., jun. (Notts. & Auck.; *CY 1938*) b July 3, 1911, d Jan. 1, 1990
Hardy, J. J. E. (Hants, Som., W. Prov. & Glos.) b Oct. 2, 1960
Harfield, L. (Hants) b Aug. 16, 1905, d Nov. 19, 1985
*Harford, N. S. (C. Dist. & Auck.) b Aug. 30, 1930, d March 30, 1981
*Harford, R. I. (Auck.) b May 30, 1936
Harman, R. (Surrey) b Dec. 28, 1941
*Haroon Rashid (Kar., Sind, NBP, PIA & UBL) b March 25, 1953
*Harper, R. A. (Guyana & Northants) b March 17, 1963
*Harris, 4th Lord (OUCC & Kent; Pres. MCC 1895) b Feb. 3, 1851, d March 24, 1932
*Harris, C. Z. (Cant.) b Nov. 20, 1969
Harris, David (Hants & All-England) b 1755, d May 19, 1803
Harris, M. J. (Middx, Notts., E. Prov. & Wgtn) b May 25, 1944
*Harris, P. G. Z. (Cant.) b July 18, 1927, d Dec. 1, 1991
*Harris, R. M. (Auck.) b July 27, 1933
*Harris, T. A. (Griq. W. & Tvl) b Aug. 27, 1916, d March 7, 1993
Harrison, L. (Hants) b June 8, 1922
*Harry, J. (Vic.) b Aug. 1, 1857, d Oct. 27, 1919
Hart, G. E. (Middx) b Jan. 13, 1902, d April 11, 1987
*Hart, M. N. (N. Dist.) b May 16, 1972
Hart, R. T. (C. Dist. & Wgtn) b Nov. 7, 1961
*Hartigan, G. P. D. (Border) b Dec. 30, 1884, d Jan. 7, 1955
*Hartigan, R. J. (NSW & Qld) b Dec. 12, 1879, d June 7, 1958
*Hartkopf, A. E. V. (Vic.) b Dec. 28, 1889, d May 20, 1968
*Hartland, B. R. (Cant.) b Oct. 22, 1966
Hartley, A. (Lancs.; *CY 1911*) b April 11, 1879, d Oct. 9, 1918
*Hartley, J. C. (OUCC & Sussex) b Nov. 15, 1874, d March 8, 1963
Hartley, P. J. (Warwicks. & Yorks.) b April 18, 1960
Hartley, S. N. (Yorks. & OFS) b March 18, 1956
Harvey, J. F. (Derbys.) b Sept. 27, 1939
*Harvey, M. R. (Vic.) b April 29, 1918
Harvey, P. F. (Notts.) b Jan. 15, 1923
*Harvey, R. L. (Natal) b Sept. 14, 1911
*Harvey, R. N. (Vic. & NSW; *CY 1954*) b Oct. 8, 1928
Harvey-Walker, A. J. (Derbys.) b July 21, 1944
Hasan Jamil (Kalat, Kar., Pak. Us & PIA) b July 25, 1952
*Haseeb Ahsan (Peshawar, Pak. Us, Kar. & PIA) b July 15, 1939
*Haslam, M. J. (Auck.) b Sept. 26, 1972
Hassan, B. (Notts.) b March 24, 1944
*Hassett, A. L. (Vic.; *CY 1949*) b Aug. 28, 1913, d June 16, 1993
*Hastings, B. F. (Wgtn, C. Dist. & Cant.) b March 23, 1940
*Hathorn, C. M. H. (Tvl) b April 7, 1878, d May 17, 1920
*Hathurusinghe, U. C. (TU) b Sept. 13, 1968
*Hawke, 7th Lord (CUCC & Yorks.; *CY 1909*; Pres. MCC 1914-18) b Aug. 16, 1860, d Oct. 10, 1938
*Hawke, N. J. N. (W. Aust., S. Aust. & Tas.) b June 27, 1939
Hawker, Sir Cyril (Essex; Pres. MCC 1970-71) b July 21, 1900, d Feb. 22, 1991
Hawkins, D. G. (Glos.) b May 18, 1935
*Hayden, M. L. (Qld) b Oct. 29, 1971
*Hayes, E. G. (Surrey & Leics.; *CY 1907*) b Nov. 6, 1876, d Dec. 2, 1953
*Hayes, F. C. (Lancs.) b Dec. 6, 1946
*Hayes, J. A. (Auck. & Cant.) b Jan. 11, 1927
Hayes, K. A. (OUCC & Lancs.) b Sept. 26, 1962
Haygarth, A. (Sussex; Historian) b Aug. 4, 1825, d May 1, 1903
Hayhurst, A. N. (Lancs. & Som.) b Nov. 23, 1962
*Haynes, D. L. (B'dos & Middx; *CY 1991*) b Feb. 15, 1956
Haynes, G. R. (Worcs.) b Sept. 29, 1969
Haynes, R. C. (Jam.) b Nov. 11, 1964
Haysman, M. D. (S. Aust., Leics. & N. Tvl) b April 22, 1961
Hayward, T. (Cambs. & All-England) b March 21, 1835, d July 21, 1876
*Hayward, T. W. (Surrey; *CY 1895*) b March 29, 1871, d July 19, 1939
Haywood, P. R. (Leics.) b March 30, 1947
*Hazare, V. S. (M'tra, C. Ind. & Baroda) b March 11, 1915
Hazell, H. L. (Som.) b Sept. 30, 1909, d March 31, 1990
Hazlerigg, Lord, formerly Hon. A. G. (CUCC & Leics.) b Feb. 24, 1910
*Hazlitt, G. R. (Vic. & NSW) b Sept. 4, 1888, d Oct. 30, 1915
Headley, D. W. (Middx & Kent) b Jan. 27, 1970
*Headley, G. A. (Jam.; *CY 1934*) b May 30, 1909, d Nov. 30, 1983
*Headley, R. G. A. (Worcs. & Jam.) b June 29, 1939

*Healy, I. A. (Qld; *CY 1994*) b April 30, 1964
Hearn, P. (Kent) b Nov. 18, 1925
*Hearne, Alec (Kent; *CY 1894*) b July 22, 1863, d May 16, 1952
**Hearne, Frank (Kent & W. Prov.) b Nov. 23, 1858, d July 14, 1949
*Hearne, G. A. L. (W. Prov.) b March 27, 1888, d Nov. 13, 1978
*Hearne, George G. (Kent) b July 7, 1856, d Feb. 13, 1932
*Hearne, J. T. (Middx; *CY 1892*) b May 3, 1867, d April 17, 1944
*Hearne, J. W. (Middx; *CY 1912*) b Feb. 11, 1891, d Sept. 14, 1965
Hearne, Thos. (Middx) b Sept. 4, 1826, d May 13, 1900
Hearne, Thos., jun. (Lord's Ground Superintendent) b Dec. 29, 1849, d Jan. 29, 1910
Heath, G. E. M. (Hants) b Feb. 20, 1913
Heath, M. (Hants) b March 9, 1934
Hedges, B. (Glam.) b Nov. 10, 1927
Hedges, L. P. (Tonbridge, OUCC, Kent & Glos.; *CY 1919*) b July 13, 1900, d Jan. 12, 1933
Hegg, W. K. (Lancs.) b Feb. 23, 1968
*Heine, P. S. (NE Tvl, OFS & Tvl) b June 28, 1928
*Hemmings, E. E. (Warwicks., Notts. & Sussex) b Feb. 20, 1949
Hemp, D. L. (Glam.) b Nov. 15, 1970
Hemsley, E. J. O. (Worcs.) b Sept. 1, 1943
*Henderson, M. (Wgtn) b Aug. 2, 1895, d June 17, 1970
Henderson, R. (Surrey; *CY 1890*) b March 30, 1865, d Jan. 29, 1931
Henderson, S. P. (CUCC, Worcs. & Glam.) b Sept. 24, 1958
*Hendren, E. H. (Middx; *CY 1920*) b Feb. 5, 1889, d Oct. 4, 1962
*Hendrick, M. (Derbys. & Notts.; *CY 1978*) b Oct. 22, 1948
*Hendriks, J. L. (Jam.) b Dec. 21, 1933
*Hendry, H. S. T. L. (NSW & Vic.) b May 24, 1895, d Dec. 16, 1988
*Henry, O. (W. Prov., Boland, OFS & Scotland) b Jan. 23, 1952
Hepworth, P. N. (Leics.) b May 4, 1967
Herman, O. W. (Hants) b Sept. 18, 1907, d June 24, 1987
Herman, R. S. (Middx, Border, Griq. W. & Hants) b Nov. 30, 1946
Heron, J. G. (Zimb.) b Nov. 8, 1948
*Heseltine, C. (Hants) b Nov. 26, 1869, d June 13, 1944
Hever, N. G. (Middx & Glam.) b Dec. 17, 1924, d Sept. 11, 1987
Hewett, H. T. (OUCC & Som.; *CY 1893*) b May 25, 1864, d March 4, 1921
Heyhoe-Flint, Rachael (England Women) b June 11, 1939
Heyn, P. D. (SL) b June 26, 1945
*Hibbert, P. A. (Vic.) b July 23, 1952
*Hick, G. A. (Worcs., Zimb., N. Dist. & Qld; *CY 1987*) b May 23, 1966
*Higgs, J. D. (Vic.) b July 11, 1950
*Higgs, K. (Lancs. & Leics.; *CY 1968*) b Jan. 14, 1937
Hignell, A. J. (CUCC & Glos.) b Sept. 4, 1955
*Hilditch, A. M. J. (NSW & S. Aust.) b May 20, 1956
Hill, Alan (Derbys. & OFS) b June 29, 1950
*Hill, Allen (Yorks.) b Nov. 14, 1843, d Aug. 29, 1910
*Hill, A. J. L. (CUCC & Hants) b July 26, 1871, d Sept. 6, 1950
*Hill, C. (S. Aust.; *CY 1900*) b March 18, 1877, d Sept. 5, 1945
Hill, E. (Som.) b July 9, 1923
Hill, G. (Hants) b April 15, 1913
*Hill, J. C. (Vic.) b June 25, 1923, d Aug. 11, 1974
Hill, L. W. (Glam.) b April 14, 1942
Hill, M. (Notts., Derbys & Som.) b Sept. 14, 1935
Hill, N. W. (Notts.) b Aug. 22, 1935
Hill, W. A. (Warwicks.) b April 27, 1910
Hills, R. W. (Kent) b Jan. 8, 1951
Hill-Wood, C. K. (OUCC & Derbys.) b June 5, 1907, d Sept. 21, 1988
Hilton, C. (Lancs. & Essex) b Sept. 26, 1937
Hilton, J. (Lancs. & Som.) b Dec. 29, 1930
*Hilton, M. J. (Lancs.; *CY 1957*) b Aug. 2, 1928, d July 8, 1990
*Hime, C. F. W. (Natal) b Oct. 24, 1869, d Dec. 6, 1940
*Hindlekar, D. D. (Bombay) b Jan. 1, 1909, d March 30, 1949
Hinks, S. G. (Kent & Glos.) b Oct. 12, 1960
*Hirst, G. H. (Yorks.; *CY 1901*) b Sept. 7, 1871, d May 10, 1954
*Hirwani, N. D. (M. Pradesh) b Oct. 18, 1968
*Hitch, J. W. (Surrey; *CY 1914*) b May 7, 1886, d July 7, 1965
Hitchcock, R. E. (Cant. & Warwicks.) b Nov. 28, 1929
*Hoad, E. L. G. (B'dos) b Jan. 29, 1896, d March 5, 1986
*Hoare, D. E. (W. Aust.) b Oct. 19, 1934
*Hobbs, Sir J. B. (Surrey; *CY 1909, special portrait 1926*) b Dec. 16, 1882, d Dec. 21, 1963
*Hobbs, R. N. S. (Essex & Glam.) b May 8, 1942
*Hodges, J. R. (Vic.) b Aug. 11, 1855, death unknown
Hodgkinson, G. F. (Derbys.) b Feb. 19, 1914, d Jan. 7, 1987
Hodgson, A. (Northants) b Oct. 27, 1951
Hodgson, G. D. (Glos.) b Oct. 22, 1966

Hofmeyr, M. B. (OUCC & NE Tvl) b Dec. 9, 1925
*Hogan, T. G. (W. Aust.) b Sept. 23, 1956
*Hogg, R. M. (S. Aust.) b March 5, 1951
Hogg, W. (Lancs. & Warwicks.) b July 12, 1955
*Hohns, T. V. (Qld) b Jan. 23, 1954
Holder, J. W. (Hants; Umpire) b March 19, 1945
Holder, R. I. C. (B'dos) b Dec. 22, 1967
*Holder, V. A. (B'dos, Worcs. & OFS) b Oct. 8, 1945
*Holding, M. A. (Jam., Lancs., Derbys., Tas. & Cant.; *CY 1977*) b Feb. 16, 1954
*Hole, G. B. (NSW & S. Aust.) b Jan. 6, 1931, d Feb. 14, 1990
*Holford, D. A. J. (B'dos & T/T) b April 16, 1940
*Holland, R. G. (NSW & Wgtn) b Oct. 19, 1946
*Hollies, W. E. (Warwicks.; *CY 1955*) b June 5, 1912, d April 16, 1981
Hollingdale, R. A. (Sussex) b March 6, 1906, d Aug. 1989
Hollioake, A. J. (Surrey) b Sept. 5, 1971
Holmes, Gp Capt. A. J. (Sussex) b June 30, 1899, d May 21, 1950
*Holmes, E. R. T. (OUCC & Surrey; *CY 1936*) b Aug. 21, 1905, d Aug. 16, 1960
Holmes, G. C. (Glam.) b Sept. 16, 1958
*Holmes, P. (Yorks.; *CY 1920*) b Nov. 25, 1886, d Sept. 3, 1971
Holt, A. G. (Hants) b April 8, 1911, d July 28, 1994
*Holt, J. K., jun. (Jam.) b Aug. 12, 1923
Home of the Hirsel, Lord (Middx; Pres. MCC 1966-67) b July 2, 1903
*Hone, L. (MCC) b Jan. 30, 1853, d Dec. 31, 1896
Hooker, R. W. (Middx) b Feb. 22, 1935
*Hookes, D. W. (S. Aust.) b May 3, 1955
*Hooper, C. L. (Guyana & Kent) b Dec. 15, 1966
*Hopkins, A. J. Y. (NSW) b May 3, 1874, d April 25, 1931
Hopkins, J. A. (Glam. & E. Prov.) b June 16, 1953
*Hopwood, J. L. (Lancs.) b Oct. 30, 1903, d June 15, 1985
*Horan, T. P. (Vic.) b March 8, 1854, d April 16, 1916
*Hordern, H. V. (NSW & Philadelphia) b Feb. 10, 1884, d June 17, 1938
*Hornby, A. N. (Lancs.) b Feb. 10, 1847, d Dec. 17, 1925
*Horne, P. A. (Auck.) b Jan. 21, 1960
Horner, N. F. (Yorks. & Warwicks.) b May 10, 1926
*Hornibrook, P. M. (Qld) b July 27, 1899, d Aug. 25, 1976
Horton, H. (Worcs. & Hants) b April 18, 1923
Horton, J. (Worcs.) b Aug. 12, 1916
*Horton, M. J. (Worcs. & N. Dist.) b April 21, 1934
Hossell, J. J. (Warwicks.) b May 25, 1914
*Hough, K. W. (Auck.) b Oct. 24, 1928
*Houghton, D. L. (Mash.) b June 23, 1957
*Howard, A. B. (B'dos) b Aug. 27, 1946
Howard, A. R. (Glam.) b Dec. 11, 1909, d March, 1993
Howard, B. J. (Lancs.) b May 21, 1926
Howard, K. (Lancs.) b June 29, 1941
*Howard, N. D. (Lancs.) b May 18, 1925, d May 31, 1979
Howard, Major R. (Lancs.; MCC Team Manager) b April 17, 1890, d Sept. 10, 1967
*Howarth, G. P. (Auck., Surrey & N. Dist.) b March 29, 1951
*Howarth, H. J. (Auck.) b Dec. 25, 1943
*Howell, H. (Warwicks.) b Nov. 29, 1890, d July 9, 1932
*Howell, W. P. (NSW) b Dec. 29, 1869, d July 14, 1940
Howland, C. B. (CUCC, Sussex & Kent) b Feb. 6, 1936
*Howorth, R. (Worcs.) b April 26, 1909, d April 2, 1980
*Hudson, A. C. (Natal) b March 17, 1965
Hughes, D. P. (Lancs. & Tas.; *CY 1988*) b May 13, 1947
*Hughes, K. J. (W. Aust. & Natal; *CY 1981*) b Jan. 26, 1954
*Hughes, M. G. (Vic. & Essex; *CY 1994*) b Nov. 23, 1961
Hughes, S. P. (Middx, N. Tvl & Durham) b Dec. 20, 1959
Huish, F. H. (Kent) b Nov. 15, 1869, d March 16, 1957
Hulme, J. H. A. (Middx) b Aug. 26, 1904, d Sept. 26, 1991
Human, J. H. (CUCC & Middx) b Jan. 13, 1912, d July 22, 1991
Humpage, G. W. (Warwicks. & OFS; *CY 1985*) b April 24, 1954
Humphries, D. J. (Leics. & Worcs.) b Aug. 6, 1953
*Humphries, J. (Derbys.) b May 19, 1876, d May 7, 1946
Hunt, A. V. (Scotland & Bermuda) b Oct. 1, 1910
*Hunt, W. A. (NSW) b Aug. 26, 1908, d Dec. 30, 1983
*Hunte, C. C. (B'dos; *CY 1964*) b May 9, 1932
*Hunte, E. A. C. (T/T) b Oct. 3, 1905, d June 26, 1967
Hunter, David (Yorks.) b Feb. 23, 1860, d Jan. 11, 1927
*Hunter, Joseph (Yorks.) b Aug. 3, 1855, d Jan. 4, 1891
Hurd, A. (CUCC & Essex) b Sept. 7, 1937
*Hurst, A. G. (Vic.) b July 15, 1950

Hurst, R. J. (Middx) b Dec. 29, 1933
*Hurwood, A. (Qld) b June 17, 1902, d Sept. 26, 1982
*Hussain, M. Dilawar (C. Ind. & U. Prov.) b March 19, 1907, d Aug. 26, 1967
*Hussain, N. (Essex) b March 28, 1968
*Hutchings, K. L. (Kent; *CY 1907*) b Dec. 7, 1882, d Sept. 3, 1916
Hutchinson, J. M. (Derbys.) (oldest known living county cricketer) b Nov. 29, 1896
*Hutchinson, P. (SA) b Jan. 26, 1862, d Sept. 30, 1925
*Hutton, Sir Leonard (Yorks.; *CY 1938*) b June 23, 1916, d Sept. 6, 1990
*Hutton, R. A. (CUCC, Yorks. & Tvl) b Sept. 6, 1942
*Hylton, L. G. (Jam.) b March 29, 1905, d May 17, 1955

*Ibadulla, K. (Punjab, Warwicks., Tas. & Otago) b Dec. 20, 1935
*Ibrahim, K. C. (Bombay) b Jan. 26, 1919
*Iddon, J. (Lancs.) b Jan. 8, 1902, d April 17, 1946
*Igglesden, A. P. (Kent & W. Prov.) b Oct. 8, 1964
*Ijaz Ahmed (Gujranwala, PACO, HBL & I'bad) b Sept. 20, 1968
*Ijaz Butt (Pak. Us, Punjab, Lahore, R'pindi & Multan) b March 10, 1938
*Ijaz Faqih (Kar., Sind, PWD & MCB) b March 24, 1956
*Ikin, J. T. (Lancs.) b March 7, 1918, d Sept. 15, 1984
*Illingworth, R. (Yorks. & Leics.; *CY 1960*) b June 8, 1932
*Illingworth, R. K. (Worcs. & Natal) b Aug. 23, 1963
*Ilott, M. C. (Essex) b Aug. 27, 1970
*Imran Khan (Lahore, Dawood, Worcs., OUCC, PIA, Sussex & NSW; *CY 1983*) b Nov. 25, 1952
*Imtiaz Ahmed (N. Ind., Comb. Us, NWFP, Pak. Serv., Peshawar & PAF) b Jan. 5, 1928
*Imtiaz Ali (T/T) b July 28, 1954
Inchmore, J. D. (Worcs. & N. Tvl) b Feb. 22, 1949
*Indrajitsinhji, K. S. (S'tra & Delhi) b June 15, 1937
Ingle, R. A. (Som.) b Nov. 5, 1903, d Dec. 19, 1992
Ingleby-Mackenzie, A. C. D. (Hants) b Sept. 15, 1933
Inman C. C. (Ceylon & Leics.) b Jan. 29, 1936
*Inshan Ali (T/T) b Sept. 25, 1949
*Insole, D. J. (CUCC & Essex; *CY 1956*) b April 18, 1926
*Intikhab Alam (Kar., PIA, Surrey, PWD, Sind & Punjab) b Dec. 28, 1941
*Inverarity, R. J. (W. Aust. & S. Aust.) b Jan. 31, 1944
*Inzamam-ul-Haq (Multan & UBL) b March 3, 1970
*Iqbal Qasim (Kar., Sind & NBP) b Aug. 6, 1953
Iqbal Sikandar (Karachi & PIA) b Dec. 19, 1958
*Irani, J. K. (Sind) b Aug. 18, 1923, d Feb. 25, 1982
Irani, R. C. (Lancs. & Essex) b Oct. 26, 1971
*Iredale, F. A. (NSW) b June 19, 1867, d April 15, 1926
Iremonger, J. (Notts.; *CY 1903*) b March 5, 1876, d March 25, 1956
Irfan Bhatti (R'pindi) b Sept. 28, 1964
*Ironmonger, H. (Qld & Vic.) b April 7, 1882, d June 1, 1971
*Ironside, D. E. J. (Tvl) b May 2, 1925
*Irvine, B. L. (W. Prov., Natal, Essex & Tvl) b March 9, 1944
*Israr Ali (S. Punjab, B'pur & Multan) b May 1, 1927
*Iverson, J. B. (Vic.) b July 27, 1915, d Oct. 24, 1973

*Jackman, R. D. (Surrey, W. Prov. & Rhod.; *CY 1981*) b Aug. 13, 1945
*Jackson, A. A. (NSW) b Sept. 5, 1909, d Feb. 16, 1933
Jackson, A. B. (Derbys.) b Aug. 21, 1933
*Jackson, Rt Hon. Sir F. S. (CUCC & Yorks.; *CY 1894*; Pres. MCC 1921) b Nov. 21, 1870, d March 9, 1947
Jackson, G. R. (Derbys.) b June 23, 1896, d Feb. 21, 1966
*Jackson, H. L. (Derbys.; *CY 1959*) b April 5, 1921
Jackson, John (Notts. & All-England) b May 21, 1833, d Nov. 4, 1901
Jackson, P. F. (Worcs.) b May 11, 1911
Jacques, T. A. (Yorks.) b Feb. 19, 1905
*Jadeja, A. D. (Haryana) b Feb. 1, 1971
*Jahangir Khan (N. Ind. & CUCC) b Feb. 1, 1910, d July 23, 1988
*Jai, L. P. (Bombay) b April 1, 1902, d Jan. 29, 1968
*Jaisimha, M. L. (H'bad) b March 3, 1939
Jakeman, F. (Yorks. & Northants) b Jan. 10, 1920, d May 18, 1986
*Jalal-ud-Din (PWD, Kar., IDBP & Allied Bank) b June 12, 1959
James, A. E. (Sussex) b Aug. 7, 1924
James, C. L. R. (Writer) b Jan. 4, 1901, d May 31, 1989
*James, K. C. (Wgtn & Northants) b March 12, 1904, d Aug. 21, 1976
James, K. D. (Middx, Hants & Wgtn) b March 18, 1961
James, R. M. (CUCC & Wgtn) b Oct. 2, 1934

James, S. P. (Glam., CUCC & Mash.) b Sept. 7, 1967
*James, W. R. (Mat.) b Aug. 27, 1965
*Jameson, J. A. (Warwicks.) b June 30, 1941
*Jamshedji, R. J. D. (Bombay) b Nov. 18, 1892, d April 5, 1976
*Jardine, D. R. (OUCC & Surrey; *CY 1928*) b Oct. 23, 1900, d June 18, 1958
*Jarman, B. N. (S. Aust.) b Feb. 17, 1936
Jarrett, D. W. (OUCC & CUCC) b April 19, 1952
*Jarvis, A. H. (S. Aust.) b Oct. 19, 1860, d Nov. 15, 1933
Jarvis, K. B. S. (Kent & Glos.) b April 23, 1953
*Jarvis, M. P. (Mash.) b Dec. 6, 1955
*Jarvis, P. W. (Yorks. & Sussex) b June 29, 1965
*Jarvis, T. W. (Auck. & Cant.) b July 29, 1944
*Javed Akhtar (R'pindi & Pak. Serv.) b Nov. 21, 1940
*Javed Miandad (Kar., Sind, Sussex, HBL & Glam.; *CY 1982*) b June 12, 1957
*Jayantilal, K. (H'bad) b Jan. 13, 1948
*Jayasekera, R. S. A. (SL) b Dec. 7, 1957
Jayasinghe, S. (Ceylon & Leics.) b Jan. 19, 1931
Jayasinghe, S. A. (SL) b July 15, 1955
*Jayasuriya, S. T. (CCC) b June 30, 1969
Jean-Jacques, M. (Derbys. & Hants) b July 2, 1960
Jefferies, S. T. (W. Prov., Derbys., Lancs., Hants & Boland) b Dec. 8, 1959
Jefferson, R. I. (CUCC & Surrey) b Aug. 15, 1941
*Jeganathan, S. (SL) b July 11, 1951
*Jenkins, R. O. (Worcs.; *CY 1950*) b Nov. 24, 1918
Jenkins, V. G. J. (OUCC & Glam.) b Nov. 2, 1911
*Jenner, T. J. (W. Aust. & S. Aust.) b Sept. 8, 1944
*Jennings, C. B. (S. Aust.) b June 5, 1884, d June 20, 1950
Jennings, K. F. (Som.) b Oct. 5, 1953
Jennings, R. V. (Tvl & N. Tvl) b Aug. 9, 1954
Jepson, A. (Notts.) b July 12, 1915
*Jessop, G. L. (CUCC & Glos.; *CY 1898*) b May 19, 1874, d May 11, 1955
Jesty, T. E. (Hants., Border, Griq. W., Cant., Surrey & Lancs.; *CY 1983*) b June 2, 1948
*John, V. B. (SL) b May 27, 1960
Johnson, C. (Yorks.) b Sept. 5, 1947
*Johnson, C. L. (Tvl) b 1871, d May 31, 1908
Johnson, G. W. (Kent & Tvl) b Nov. 8, 1946
*Johnson, H. H. H. (Jam.) b July 17, 1910, d June 24, 1987
Johnson, H. L. (Derbys.) b Nov. 8, 1927
*Johnson, I. W. (Vic.) b Dec. 8, 1917
Johnson, L. A. (Northants) b Aug. 12, 1936
*Johnson, L. J. (Qld) b March 18, 1919, d April 20, 1977
Johnson, P. (Notts.) b April 24, 1965
Johnson, P. D. (CUCC & Notts.) b Nov. 12, 1949
*Johnson, T. F. (T/T) b Jan. 10, 1917, d April 5, 1985
Johnston, Brian A. (Broadcaster) b June 24, 1912, d Jan. 5, 1994
*Johnston, W. A. (Vic.; *CY 1949*) b Feb. 26, 1922
Jones, A. (Glam., W. Aust., N. Tvl & Natal; *CY 1978*) b Nov. 4, 1938
Jones, A. A. (Sussex, Som., Middx, Glam., N. Tvl & OFS) b Dec. 9, 1947
*Jones, A. H. (Wgtn) b May 9, 1959
Jones, A. L. (Glam.) b June 1, 1957
Jones, A. N. (Sussex, Border & Som.) b July 22, 1961
*Jones, A. O. (Notts. & CUCC; *CY 1900*) b Aug. 16, 1872, d Dec. 21, 1914
Jones, B. J. R. (Worcs.) b Nov. 2, 1955
*Jones, C. M. (C. E. L.) (BG) b Nov. 3, 1902, d Dec. 10, 1959
*Jones, D. M. (Vic. & Durham; *CY 1990*) b March 24, 1961
*Jones, Ernest (S. Aust. & W. Aust.) b Sept. 30, 1869, d Nov. 23, 1943
Jones, E. C. (Glam.) b Dec. 14, 1912, d April 14, 1989
Jones, E. W. (Glam.) b June 25, 1942
*Jones, I. J. (Glam.) b Dec. 10, 1941
Jones, K. V. (Middx) b March 28, 1942
*Jones, P. E. (T/T) b June 6, 1917, d Nov. 20, 1991
Jones, P. H. (Kent) b June 19, 1935
*Jones, S. P. (NSW, Qld & Auck.) b Aug. 1, 1861, d July 14, 1951
Jones, W. E. (Glam.) b Oct. 31, 1916
Jordan, J. M. (Lancs.) b Feb. 7, 1932
Jorden, A. M. (CUCC & Essex) b Jan. 28, 1947
Jordon, R. C. (Vic.) b Feb. 17, 1937
*Joshi, P. G. (M'tra) b Oct. 27, 1926, d Jan. 8, 1987
Joshi, U. C. (S'tra, Ind. Rlwys, Guj. & Sussex) b Dec. 23, 1944
*Joslin, L. R. (Vic.) b Dec. 13, 1947
Jowett, D. C. P. R. (OUCC) b Jan. 24, 1931
Judd, A. K. (CUCC & Hants) b Jan. 1, 1904, d Feb. 15, 1988
Judge, P. F. (Middx, Glam. & Bengal) b May 23, 1916, d March 4, 1992
*Julian, B. P. (W. Aust.) b Aug. 10, 1970
Julian, R. (Leics.) b Aug. 23, 1936
*Julien, B. D. (T/T & Kent) b March 13, 1950
*Jumadeen, R. R. (T/T) b April 12, 1948
*Jupp, H. (Surrey) b Nov. 19, 1841, d April 8, 1889

*Jupp, V. W. C. (Sussex & Northants; *CY 1928*) b March 27, 1891, d July 9, 1960
*Jurangpathy, B. R. (CCC) b June 25, 1967

*Kabir Khan (HBFC) b April 12, 1974
*Kallicharran, A. I. (Guyana, Warwicks., Qld, Tvl & OFS; *CY 1983*) b March 21, 1949
*Kalpage, R. S. (NCC) b Feb. 19, 1970
*Kaluperuma, L. W. (SL) b May 25, 1949
*Kaluperuma, S. M. S. (SL) b Oct. 22, 1961
*Kaluwitharana, R. S. (Seb.) b Nov. 24, 1969
*Kambli, V. G. (Bombay) b Jan. 18, 1972
*Kanhai, R. B. (†Guyana, T/T, W. Aust., Warwicks. & Tas.; *CY 1964*) b Dec. 26, 1935
*Kanitkar, H. S. (M'tra) b Dec. 8, 1942
*Kapil Dev (Haryana, Northants & Worcs.; *CY 1983*) b Jan. 6, 1959
**Kardar, A. H. (formerly Abdul Hafeez) (N. Ind., OUCC, Warwicks. & Pak. Serv.) b Jan. 17, 1925
Karnain, S. H. U. (NCC & Moors) b Aug. 11, 1962
Kasprowicz, M. S. (Qld & Essex) b Feb. 10, 1972
*Keeton, W. W. (Notts.; *CY 1940*) b April 30, 1905, d Oct. 10, 1980
Keighley, W. G. (OUCC & Yorks.) b Jan. 10, 1925
*Keith, H. J. (Natal) b Oct. 25, 1927
Kelleher, H. R. A. (Surrey & Northants) b March 3, 1929
Kellett, S. A. (Yorks.) b Oct. 16, 1967
*Kelleway, C. (NSW) b April 25, 1886, d Nov. 16, 1944
Kelly, J. (Notts.) b Sept. 15, 1930
*Kelly, J. J. (NSW; *CY 1903*) b May 10, 1867, d Aug. 14, 1938
*Kelly, T. J. D. (Vic.) b May 3, 1844, d July 20, 1893
*Kempis, G. A. (Natal) b Aug. 4, 1865, d May 19, 1890
*Kendall, T. (Vic. & Tas.) b Aug. 24, 1851, d Aug. 17, 1924
Kennedy, A. (Lancs.) b Nov. 4, 1949
*Kennedy, A. S. (Hants; *CY 1933*) b Jan. 24, 1891, d Nov. 15, 1959
*Kenny, R. B. (Bombay & Bengal) b Sept. 29, 1930, d Nov. 21, 1985
*Kent, M. F. (Qld) b Nov. 23, 1953
*Kentish, E. S. M. (Jam. & OUCC) b Nov. 21, 1916
*Kenyon, D. (Worcs.; *CY 1963*) b May 15, 1924
*Kerr, J. L. (Cant.) b Dec. 28, 1910
Kerr, K. J. (Tvl & Warwicks.) b Sept. 11, 1961
*Kerr, R. B. (Qld) b June 16, 1961
Kerslake, R. C. (CUCC & Som.) b Dec. 26, 1942
Kettle, M. K. (Northants) b March 18, 1944
*Khalid Hassan (Punjab & Lahore) b July 14, 1937
*Khalid Wazir (Pak.) b April 27, 1936
*Khan Mohammad (N. Ind., Pak. Us, Som., B'pur, Sind, Kar. & Lahore) b Jan. 1, 1928
Khanna, S. C. (Delhi) b June 3, 1956
Kilborn, M. J. (OUCC) b Sept. 20, 1962
*Killick, Rev. E. T. (CUCC & Middx) b May 9, 1907, d May 18, 1953
Kilner, Norman (Yorks. & Warwicks.) b July 21, 1895, d April 28, 1979
*Kilner, Roy (Yorks.; *CY 1924*) b Oct. 17, 1890, d April 5, 1928
Kimpton, R. C. M. (OUCC & Worcs.) b Sept. 21, 1916
*King, C. L. (B'dos, Glam., Worcs. & Natal) b June 11, 1951
*King, F. McD. (B'dos) b Dec. 14, 1926, d Dec. 23, 1990
King, I. M. (Warwicks. & Essex) b Nov. 10, 1931
King, J. B. (Philadelphia) b Oct. 19, 1873, d Oct. 17, 1965
*King, J. H. (Leics.) b April 16, 1871, d Nov. 18, 1946
*King, L. A. (Jam. & Bengal) b Feb. 27, 1939
Kingsley, Sir P. G. T. (OUCC) b May 26, 1908
*Kinneir, S. P. (Warwicks.; *CY 1912*) b May 13, 1871, d Oct. 16, 1928
*Kippax, A. F. (NSW) b May 25, 1897, d Sept. 4, 1972
Kirby, D. (CUCC & Leics.) b Jan. 18, 1939
*Kirmani, S. M. H. (†Karn.) b Dec. 29, 1949
*Kirsten, G. (W. Prov.) b Nov. 23, 1967
*Kirsten, P. N. (W. Prov., Sussex, Derbys. & Border) b May 14, 1955
*Kischenchand, G. (W. Ind., Guj. & Baroda) b April 14, 1925
Kitchen, M. J. (Som.; Umpire) b Aug. 1, 1940
*Kline, L. F. (Vic.) b Sept. 29, 1934
*Knight, A. E. (Leics.; *CY 1904*) b Oct. 8, 1872, d April 25, 1946
*Knight, B. R. (Essex & Leics.) b Feb. 18, 1938
*Knight, D. J. (OUCC & Surrey; *CY 1915*) b May 12, 1894, d Jan. 5, 1960
Knight, R. D. V. (CUCC, Surrey, Glos. & Sussex; Sec. MCC 1994-) b Sept. 6, 1946
Knight, W. H. (Editor of *Wisden* 1870-79) b Nov. 29, 1812, d Aug. 16, 1879
*Knott, A. P. E. (Kent & Tas.; *CY 1970*) b April 9, 1946
Knott, C. H. (OUCC & Kent) b March 20, 1901, d June 18, 1988
Knott, C. J. (Hants) b Nov. 26, 1914
Knowles, J. (Notts.) b March 25, 1910

Knox, G. K. (Lancs.) b April 22, 1937
*Knox, N. A. (Surrey; *CY 1907*) b Oct. 10, 1884, d March 3, 1935
Kortright, C. J. (Essex) b Jan. 9, 1871, d Dec. 12, 1952
*Kotze, J. J. (Tvl & W. Prov.) b Aug. 7, 1879, d July 7, 1931
Krikken, K. M. (Derbys.) b April 9, 1969
*Kripal Singh, A. G. (Madras & H'bad) b Aug. 6, 1933, d July 23, 1987
*Krishnamurthy, P. (H'bad) b July 12, 1947
*Kuggeleijn, C. M. (N. Dist.) b May 10, 1956
*Kuiper, A. P. (W. Prov. & Derbys.) b Aug. 24, 1959
*Kulkarni, R. R. (Bombay) b Sept. 25, 1962
*Kulkarni, U. N. (Bombay) b March 7, 1942
*Kumar, V. V. (†TN) b June 22, 1935
*Kumble, A. (Karn.) b Oct. 17, 1970
*Kunderan, B. K. (Ind. Rlwys & Mysore) b Oct. 2, 1939
*Kuruppu, D. S. B. P. (BRC) b Jan. 5, 1962
*Kuruppuarachchi, A. K. (NCC) b Nov. 1, 1964
*Kuys, F. (W. Prov.) b March 21, 1870, d Sept. 12, 1953
Kynaston, R. (Middx; Sec. MCC 1846-58) b Nov. 5, 1805, d June 21, 1874

*Labrooy, G. F. (CCC) b June 7, 1964
Lacey, Sir F. E. (CUCC & Hants; Sec MCC 1898-1926) b Oct. 19, 1859, d May 26, 1946
*Laird, B. M. (W. Aust.) b Nov. 21, 1950
*Laker, J. C. (Surrey, Auck. & Essex; *CY 1952*) b Feb. 9, 1922, d April 23, 1986
*Lall Singh (S. Punjab) b Dec. 16, 1909, d Nov. 19, 1985
*Lamb, A. J. (W. Prov., Northants & OFS; *CY 1981*) b June 20, 1954
Lamb, Hon. T. M. (OUCC, Middx & Northants; Cricket Sec., TCCB 1987-) b March 24, 1953
*Lamba, R. (Delhi) b Jan. 2, 1958
*Lambert, C. B. (Guyana & N. Tvl) b Feb. 2, 1962
Lambert, G. E. E. (Glos. & Som.) b May 11, 1918, d Oct. 31, 1991
Lambert, R. H. (Ireland) b July 18, 1874, d March 24, 1956
Lambert, Wm (Surrey) b 1779, d April 19, 1851
Lampitt, S. R. (Worcs.) b July 29, 1966
*Lance, H. R. (NE Tvl & Tvl) b June 6, 1940
*Langer, J. L. (W. Aust.) b Nov. 21, 1970
Langford, B. A. (Som.) b Dec. 17, 1935
*Langley, G. R. A. (S. Aust.; *CY 1957*) b Sept. 14, 1919
*Langridge, James (Sussex; *CY 1932*) b July 10, 1906, d Sept. 10, 1966
Langridge, J. G. (John) (Sussex; *CY 1950*) b Feb. 10, 1910
Langridge, R. J. (Sussex) b April 13, 1939
*Langton, A. B. C. (Tvl) b March 2, 1912, d Nov. 27, 1942
*Lara, B. C. (T/T & Warwicks.; *CY 1995*) b May 2, 1969
*Larkins, W. (Northants, E. Prov. & Durham) b Nov. 22, 1953
*Larsen, G. R. (Wgtn) b Sept. 27, 1962
*Larter, J. D. F. (Northants) b April 24, 1940
*Larwood, H. (Notts.; *CY 1927*) b Nov. 14, 1904
*Lashley, P. D. (B'dos) b Feb. 11, 1937
Latchman, H. C. [A. H.] (Middx & Notts.) b July 26, 1943
*Latham, R. T. (Cant.) b June 12, 1961
*Lathwell, M. N. (Som.) b Dec. 26, 1971
*Laughlin, T. J. (Vic.) b Jan. 30, 1951
*Laver, F. (Vic.) b Dec. 7, 1869, d Sept. 24, 1919
*Lawrence, D. V. (Glos.) b Jan. 28, 1964
*Lawrence, G. B. (Rhod. & Natal) b March 31, 1932
Lawrence, J. (Som.) b March 29, 1914, d Dec. 10, 1988
*Lawry, W. M. (Vic.; *CY 1962*) b Feb. 11, 1937
*Lawson, G. F. (NSW & Lancs.) b Dec. 7, 1957
Leadbeater, B. (Yorks.) b Aug. 14, 1943
*Leadbeater, E. (Yorks. & Warwicks.) b Aug. 15, 1927
Leary, S. E. (Kent) b April 30, 1933, d Aug. 21, 1988
Leatherdale, D. A. (Worcs.) b Nov. 26, 1967
Lee, C. (Yorks. & Derbys.) b March 17, 1924
Lee, F. S. (Middx & Som.; Umpire) b July 24, 1905, d March 30, 1982
*Lee, H. W. (Middx) b Oct. 26, 1890, d April 21, 1981
Lee, J. W. (Middx & Som.) b Feb. 1, 1904, d June 20, 1944
Lee, P. G. (Northants & Lancs.; *CY 1976*) b Aug. 27, 1945
*Lee, P. K. (S. Aust.) b Sept. 14, 1904, d Aug. 9, 1980
*Lees, W. K. (Otago) b March 19, 1952
*Lees, W. S. (Surrey; *CY 1906*) b Dec. 25, 1875, d Sept. 10, 1924
Leese, Sir Oliver, Bt (Pres. MCC 1965-66) b Oct. 27, 1894, d Jan. 20, 1978
Lefebvre, R. P. (Holland, Som., Cant. & Glam.) b Feb. 7, 1963
*Legall, R. A. (B'dos & T/T) b Dec. 1, 1925
Legard, E. (Warwicks.) b Aug. 23, 1935
*Leggat, I. B. (C. Dist.) b June 7, 1930
*Leggat, J. G. (Cant.) b May 27, 1926, d March 8, 1973
*Legge, G. B. (OUCC & Kent) b Jan. 26, 1903, d Nov. 21, 1940
Lenham, L. J. (Sussex) b May 24, 1936

Lenham, N. J. (Sussex) b Dec. 17, 1965
*le Roux, F. L. (Tvl & E. Prov.) b Feb. 5, 1882, d Sept. 22, 1963
le Roux, G. S. (W. Prov. & Sussex) b Sept. 4, 1955
*Leslie, C. F. H. (OUCC & Middx) b Dec. 8, 1861, d Feb. 12, 1921
Lester, E. (Yorks.) b Feb. 18, 1923
Lester, G. (Leics.) b Dec. 27, 1915
Lester, Dr J. A. (Philadelphia) b Aug. 1, 1871, d Sept. 3, 1969
Lethbridge, C. (Warwicks.) b June 23, 1961
*Lever, J. K. (Essex & Natal; *CY 1979*) b Feb. 24, 1949
*Lever, P. (Lancs. & Tas.) b Sept. 17, 1940
*Leveson Gower, Sir H. D. G. (OUCC & Surrey) b May 8, 1873, d Feb. 1, 1954
*Levett, W. H. V. (Kent) b Jan. 25, 1908
Lewington, P. J. (Warwicks.) b Jan. 30, 1950
*Lewis, A. R. (CUCC & Glam.) b July 6, 1938
Lewis, C. (Kent) b July 27, 1908, d April 26, 1993
*Lewis, C. C. (Leics. & Notts.) b Feb. 14, 1968
*Lewis, D. M. (Jam.) b Feb. 21, 1946
Lewis, E. J. (Glam. & Sussex) b Jan. 31, 1942
Lewis, J. J. B. (Essex) b May 21, 1970
*Lewis, P. T. (W. Prov.) b Oct. 2, 1884, d Jan. 30, 1976
Lewis, R. V. (Hants) b Aug. 6, 1947
*Leyland, M. (Yorks.; *CY 1929*) b July 20, 1900, d Jan. 1, 1967
*Liaqat Ali (Kar., Sind, HBL & PIA) b May 21, 1955
Lightfoot, A. (Northants) b Jan. 8, 1936
*Lillee, D. K. (W. Aust., Tas. & Northants; *CY 1973*) b July 18, 1949
*Lilley, A. A. (Warwicks.; *CY 1897*) b Nov. 28, 1866, d Nov. 17, 1929
Lilley, A. W. (Essex) b May 8, 1959
Lilley, B. (Notts.) b Feb. 11, 1895, d Aug. 4, 1950
Lillywhite, Fred (Sussex; Editor of *Lillywhite's Guide to Cricketers*) b July 23, 1829, d Sept. 15, 1866
Lillywhite, F. W. ("William") (Sussex) b June 13, 1792, d Aug. 21, 1854
*Lillywhite, James, jun. (Sussex) b Feb. 23, 1842, d Oct. 25, 1929
*Lindsay, D. T. (NE Tvl, N. Tvl & Tvl) b Sept 4, 1939
*Lindsay, J. D. (Tvl & NE Tvl) b Sept. 8, 1909, d Aug. 31, 1990
*Lindsay, N. V. (Tvl & OFS) b July 30, 1886, d Feb. 2, 1976
*Lindwall, R. R. (NSW & Qld; *CY 1949*) b Oct. 3, 1921
*Ling, W. V. S. (Griq. W. & E. Prov.) b Oct. 3, 1891, d Sept. 26, 1960
*Lissette, A. F. (Auck. & N. Dist.) b Nov. 6, 1919, d Jan. 24, 1973
Lister, J. (Yorks. & Worcs.) b May 14, 1930, d Jan. 28, 1991
Lister, W. H. L. (Lancs.) b Oct. 7, 1911
Livingston, L. (NSW & Northants) b May 3, 1920
Livingstone, D. A. (Hants) b Sept. 21, 1933, d Sept. 8, 1988
*Liyanage, D. K. (Colts) b June 6, 1972
*Llewellyn, C. B. (Natal & Hants; *CY 1911*) b Sept. 26, 1876, d June 7, 1964
Llewellyn, M. J. (Glam.) b Nov. 27, 1953
Llong, N. J. (Kent) b Feb. 11, 1969
Lloyd, B. J. (Glam.) b Sept. 6, 1953
*Lloyd, C. H. (†Guyana & Lancs.; *CY 1971*) b Aug. 31, 1944
*Lloyd, D. (Lancs.) b March 18, 1947
Lloyd, G. D. (Lancs.) b July 1, 1969
*Lloyd, T. A. (Warwicks. & OFS) b Nov. 5, 1956
Lloyds, J. W. (Som., OFS & Glos.) b Nov. 17, 1954
*Loader, P. J. (Surrey and W. Aust.; *CY 1958*) b Oct. 25, 1929
Lobb, B. (Warwicks. & Som.) b Jan. 11, 1931
*Lock, G. A. R. (Surrey, Leics. & W. Aust.; *CY 1954*) b July 5, 1929
Lockwood, Ephraim (Yorks.) b April 4, 1845, d Dec. 19, 1921
*Lockwood, W. H. (Notts. & Surrey; *CY 1899*) b March 25, 1868, d April 26, 1932
Lockyer, T. (Surrey & All-England) b Nov. 1, 1826, d Dec. 22, 1869
Logan, J. D. (SA) b June 24, 1880, d Jan. 3, 1960
*Logie, A. L. (T/T) b Sept. 28, 1960
*Lohmann, G. A. (Surrey, W. Prov. & Tvl; *CY 1889*) b June 2, 1865, d Dec. 1, 1901
Lomax, J. G. (Lancs. & Som.) b May 5, 1925, d May 21, 1992
Long, A. (Surrey & Sussex) b Dec. 18, 1940
Lord, G. J. (Warwicks. & Worcs.) b April 25, 1961
Lord, Thomas (Middx; founder of Lord's) b Nov. 23, 1755, d Jan. 13, 1832
*Love, H. S. B. (NSW & Vic.) b Aug. 10, 1895, d July 22, 1969
Love, J. D. (Yorks.) b April 22, 1955
Lovell, G. B. T. (OUCC) b July 11, 1966
*Lowry, T. C. (Wgtn, CUCC & Som.) b Feb. 17, 1898, d July 20, 1976
*Lowson, F. A. (Yorks.) b July 1, 1925, d Sept. 8, 1984
*Loxton, S. J. E. (Vic.) b March 29, 1921
Loye, M. B. (Northants) b Sept. 27, 1972
*Lucas, A. P. (CUCC, Surrey, Middx & Essex) b Feb. 20, 1857, d Oct. 12, 1923
*Luckhurst, B. W. (Kent; *CY 1971*) b Feb. 5, 1939
Lumb, R. G. (Yorks.) b Feb. 27, 1950

*Lundie, E. B. (E. Prov., W. Prov. & Tvl) b March 15, 1888, d Sept. 12, 1917
Lynch, M. A. (Surrey & Guyana) b May 21, 1958
Lyon, B. H. (OUCC & Glos.; *CY 1931*) b Jan. 19, 1902, d June 22, 1970
Lyon, J. (Lancs.) b May 17, 1951
Lyon, M. D. (CUCC & Som.) b April 22, 1898, d Feb. 17, 1964
*Lyons, J. J. (S. Aust.) b May 21, 1863, d July 21, 1927
Lyons, K. J. (Glam.) b Dec. 18, 1946
*Lyttelton, Rt Hon. Alfred (CUCC & Middx; Pres. MCC 1898) b Feb. 7, 1857, d July 5, 1913
Lyttelton, Rev. Hon. C. F. (CUCC & Worcs.) b Jan. 26, 1887, d Oct. 3, 1931
Lyttelton, Hon. C. G. (CUCC) b Oct. 27, 1842, d June 9, 1922
Lyttelton, Hon. C. J. (*see* 10th Visct Cobham)

*McAlister, P. A. (Vic.) b July 11, 1869, d May 10, 1938
*Macartney, C. G. (NSW & Otago; *CY 1922*) b June 27, 1886, d Sept. 9, 1958
*Macaulay, G. G. (Yorks.; *CY 1924*) b Dec. 7, 1897, d Dec. 13, 1940
*Macaulay, M. J. (Tvl, W. Prov., OFS, NE Tvl & E. Prov.) b April 19, 1939
*MacBryan, J. C. W. (CUCC & Som.; *CY 1925*) b July 22, 1892, d July 14, 1983
*McCabe, S. J. (NSW; *CY 1935*) b July 16, 1910, d Aug. 25, 1968
*McCague, M. J. (Kent & W. Aust.) b May 24, 1969
McCanlis, M. A. (OUCC, Surrey & Glos.) b June 17, 1906, d Sept. 27, 1991
*McCarthy, C. N. (Natal & CUCC) b March 24, 1929
*McConnon, J. E. (Glam.) b June 21, 1922
*McCool, C. L. (NSW, Qld & Som.) b Dec. 9, 1916, d April 5, 1986
McCorkell, N. T. (Hants) b March 23, 1912
*McCormick, E. L. (Vic.) b May 16, 1906, d June 28, 1991
*McCosker, R. B. (NSW; *CY 1976*) b Dec. 11, 1946
McCurdy, R. J. (Vic., Derbys., S. Aust., E. Prov. & Natal) b Dec. 30, 1959
*McDermott, C. J. (Qld; *CY 1986*) b April 14, 1965
*McDonald, C. C. (Vic.) b Nov. 17, 1928
*McDonald, E. A. (Tas., Vic. & Lancs.; *CY 1922*) b Jan. 6, 1891, d July 22, 1937
*McDonnell, P. S. (Vic., NSW & Qld) b Nov. 13, 1858, d Sept. 24, 1896
McEvoy, M. S. A. (Essex & Worcs.) b Jan. 25, 1956
McEwan, K. S. (E. Prov., W. Prov., Essex & W. Aust; *CY 1978*) b July 16, 1952
*McEwan, P. E. (Cant.) b Dec. 19, 1953
McEwan, S. M. (Worcs. & Durham) b May 5, 1962
McFarlane, L. L. (Northants, Lancs. & Glam.) b Aug. 19, 1952
*McGahey, C. P. (Essex; *CY 1902*) b Feb. 12, 1871, d Jan. 10, 1935
*MacGibbon, A. R. (Cant.) b Aug. 28, 1924
*McGirr, H. M. (Wgtn) b Nov. 5, 1891, d April 14, 1964
*McGlew, D. J. (Natal; *CY 1956*) b March 11, 1929
*McGrath, G. D. (NSW) b Feb. 9, 1970
*MacGregor, G. (CUCC & Middx; *CY 1891*) b Aug. 31, 1869, d Aug. 20, 1919
*McGregor, S. N. (Otago) b Dec. 18, 1931
McHugh, F. P. (Yorks. & Glos.) b Nov. 15, 1925
*McIlwraith, J. (Vic.) b Sept. 7, 1857, d July 5, 1938
Macindoe, D. H. (OUCC) b Sept. 1, 1917, d March 3, 1986
*McIntyre, A. J. W. (Surrey; *CY 1958*) b May 14, 1918
*Mackay, K. D. (Qld) b Oct. 24, 1925, d June 13, 1982
McKechnie, B. J. (Otago) b Nov. 6, 1953
*McKenzie, G. D. (W. Aust. & Leics.; *CY 1965*) b June 24, 1941
*McKibbin, T. R. (NSW) b Dec. 10, 1870, d Dec. 15, 1939
*McKinnon, A. H. (E. Prov. & Tvl) b Aug. 20, 1932, d Dec. 2, 1983
*MacKinnon, F. A. (CUCC & Kent) b April 9, 1848, d Feb. 27, 1947
*MacLaren, A. C. (Lancs.; *CY 1895*) b Dec. 1, 1871, d Nov. 17, 1944
*McLaren, J. W. (Qld) b Dec. 24, 1887, d Nov. 17, 1921
*Maclean, J. A. (Qld) b April 27, 1946
Maclean, J. F. (Worcs. & Glos.) b March 1, 1901, d March 9, 1986
*McLean, R. A. (Natal; *CY 1961*) b July 9, 1930
MacLeay, K. H. (W. Aust. & Som.) b April 2, 1959
*McLeod, C. E. (Vic.) b Oct. 24, 1869, d Nov. 26, 1918
*McLeod, E. G. (Auck. & Wgtn) b Oct. 14, 1900, d Sept. 14, 1989
*McLeod, R. W. (Vic.) b Jan. 19, 1868, d June 14, 1907
McMahon, J. W. (Surrey & Som.) b Dec. 28, 1919
*McMahon, T. G. (Wgtn) b Nov. 8, 1929
*McMaster, J. E. P. (Eng.) b March 16, 1861, d June 7, 1929
*McMillan, B. M. (Tvl, W. Prov. & Warwicks.) b Dec. 22, 1963
*McMillan, Q. (Tvl) b June 23, 1904, d July 3, 1948
*McMorris, E. D. A. (Jam.) b April 4, 1935
*McRae, D. A. N. (Cant.) b Dec. 25, 1912, d Aug. 10, 1986

*McShane, P. G. (Vic.) b 1857, d Dec. 11, 1903
McSweeney, E. B. (C. Dist. & Wgtn) b March 8, 1957
McVicker, N. M. (Warwicks. & Leics.) b Nov. 4, 1940
*McWatt, C. A. (BG) b Feb. 1, 1922
*Madan Lal (Punjab & Delhi) b March 20, 1951
*Maddocks, L. V. (Vic. & Tas.) b May 24, 1926
*Madray, I. S. (BG) b July 2, 1934
*Madugalle, R. S. (NCC) b April 22, 1959
*Madurasinghe, A. W. R. (Kurunegala) b Jan. 30, 1961
*Maguire, J. N. (Qld, E. Prov. & Leics.) b Sept. 15, 1956
*Mahanama, R. S. (CCC) b May 31, 1966
Maher, B. J. M. (Derbys.) b Feb. 11, 1958
*Mahmood Hussain (Pak. Us, Punjab, Kar., E. Pak. & NTB) b April 2, 1932, d Dec. 25, 1991
*Mailey, A. A. (NSW) b Jan. 3, 1886, d Dec. 31, 1967
*Majid Khan (Lahore, Pak. Us, CUCC, Glam., PIA, Qld & Punjab; *CY 1970*) b Sept. 28, 1946
*Maka, E. S. (Bombay) b March 5, 1922
*Makepeace, J. W. H. (Lancs.) b Aug. 22, 1881, d Dec. 19, 1952
*Malcolm, D. E. (Derbys.; *CY 1995*) b Feb. 22, 1963
*Malhotra, A. (Haryana & Bengal) b Jan. 26, 1957
*Mallender, N. A. (Northants, Otago & Som.) b Aug. 13, 1961
*Mallett, A. A. (S. Aust.) b July 13, 1945
Mallett, A. W. H. (OUCC & Kent) b Aug. 29, 1924, d Dec. 10, 1994
*Malone, M. F. (W. Aust. & Lancs.) b Oct. 9, 1950
Malone, S. J. (Essex, Hants & Glam.) b Oct. 19, 1953
*Maninder Singh (Delhi) b June 13, 1965
*Manjrekar, S. V. (Bombay) b July 12, 1965
*Manjrekar, V. L. (Bombay, Bengal, Andhra, U. Pradesh, Raja. & M'tra) b Sept. 26, 1931, d Oct. 18, 1983
*Mankad, A. V. (Bombay) b Oct. 12, 1946
*Mankad, V. (M. H.) (W. Ind., Naw., M'tra, Guj., Bengal, Bombay & Raja.; *CY 1947*) b April 12, 1917, d Aug. 21, 1978
*Mann, A. L. (W. Aust.) b Nov. 8, 1945
*Mann, F. G. (CUCC & Middx; Pres. MCC 1984-85) b Sept. 6, 1917
*Mann, F. T. (CUCC & Middx) b March 3, 1888, d Oct. 6, 1964
Mann, J. P. (Middx) b June 13, 1919
*Mann, N. B. F. (Natal & E. Prov.) b Dec. 28, 1920, d July 31, 1952
Manning, J. S. (S. Aust. & Northants) b June 11, 1924, d May 5, 1988
*Mansell, P. N. F. (Rhod.) b March 16, 1920
*Mansoor Akhtar (Kar., UBL & Sind) b Dec. 25, 1956
Mansoor Rana (ADBP & Lahore) b Dec. 27, 1962
Mansur Ali Khan (*see* Pataudi, Mansur Ali, Nawab of)
*Mantri, M. K. (Bombay & M'tra) b Sept. 1, 1921
*Manzoor Elahi (Multan, Pak. Rlwys & IDBP) b April 15, 1963
*Maqsood Ahmed• (S. Punjab, R'pindi & Kar.) b March 26, 1925
Maqsood Rana (Lahore & NBP) b Aug. 1, 1972
*Marais, G. G. ("G. Gladstone") (Jam.) b Jan. 14, 1901, d May 19, 1978
Marie, G. V. (OUCC) b Feb. 17, 1945
*Markham, L. A. (Natal) b Sept. 12, 1924
*Marks, V. J. (OUCC, Som. & W. Aust.) b June 25, 1955
Marlar, R. G. (CUCC & Sussex) b Jan. 2, 1931
Marner, P. T. (Lancs. & Leics.) b March 31, 1936
*Marr, A. P. (NSW) b March 28, 1862, d March 15, 1940
*Marriott, C. S. (CUCC, Lancs. & Kent) b Sept. 14, 1895, d Oct. 13, 1966
Marsden, Tom (Eng.) b 1805, d Feb. 27, 1843
Marsh, F. E. (Derbys.) b July 7, 1920
*Marsh, G. R. (W. Aust.) b Dec. 31, 1958
*Marsh, R. W. (W. Aust.; *CY 1982*) b Nov. 4, 1947
Marsh, S. A. (Kent) b Jan. 27, 1961
Marshal, Alan (Qld & Surrey; *CY 1909*) b June 12, 1883, d July 23, 1915
Marshall, J. M. A. (Warwicks.) b Oct. 26, 1916
*Marshall, M. D. (B'dos, Hants & Natal; *CY 1983*) b April 18, 1958
*Marshall, N. E. (B'dos & T/T) b Feb. 27, 1924
*Marshall, R. E. (B'dos & Hants; *CY 1959*) b April 25, 1930, d Oct. 27, 1992
Martin, E. J. (Notts.) b Aug. 17, 1925
*Martin, F. (Kent; *CY 1892*) b Oct. 12, 1861, d Dec. 13, 1921
*Martin, F. R. (Jam.) b Oct. 12, 1893, d Nov. 23, 1967
Martin, J. D. (OUCC & Som.) b Dec. 23, 1941
*Martin, J. W. (NSW & S. Aust.) b July 28, 1931, d July 16, 1992
*Martin, J. W. (Kent) b Feb. 16, 1917, d Jan. 4, 1987
Martin, P. J. (Lancs.) b Nov. 15, 1968
Martin, S. H. (Worcs., Natal & Rhod.) b Jan. 11, 1909, d Feb. 1988
Martindale, D. J. R. (Notts.) b Dec 13, 1963

*Martindale, E. A. (B'dos) b Nov. 25, 1909, d March 17, 1972
*Martyn, D. R. (W. Aust.) b Oct. 21, 1971
Maru, R. J. (Middx & Hants) b Oct. 28, 1962
*Marx, W. F. E. (Tvl) b July 4, 1895, d June 2, 1974
*Mason, J. R. (Kent; *CY 1898*) b March 26, 1874, d Oct. 15, 1958
*Masood Anwar (UBL & Multan) b Dec. 12, 1967
Masood Iqbal (Lahore, Punjab U., Pak. Us & HBL) b April 17, 1952
*Massie, H. H. (NSW) b April 11, 1854, d Oct. 12, 1938
*Massie, R. A. L. (W. Aust.; *CY 1973*) b April 14, 1947
*Matheson, A. M. (Auck.) b Feb. 27, 1906, d Dec. 31, 1985
*Mathias, Wallis (Sind, Kar. & NBP) b Feb. 4, 1935, d Sept. 1, 1994
*Matthews, A. D. G. (Northants & Glam.) b May 3, 1904, d July 29, 1977
*Matthews, C. D. (W. Aust. & Lancs.) b Sept. 22, 1962
*Matthews, C. R. (W. Prov.) b Feb. 15, 1965
Matthews, C. S. (Notts.) b Oct. 17, 1931, d March 15, 1990
*Matthews, G. R. J. (NSW) b Dec. 15, 1959
*Matthews, T. J. (Vic.) b April 3, 1884, d Oct. 14, 1943
*Mattis, E. H. (Jam.) b April 11, 1957
*May, P. B. H. (CUCC & Surrey; *CY 1952*; Pres. MCC 1980-81) b Dec. 31, 1929, d Dec. 27, 1994
*May, T. B. A. (S. Aust.) b Jan. 26, 1962
Mayer, J. H. (Warwicks.) b March 2, 1902, d Sept. 6, 1981
Mayes, R. (Kent) b Oct. 7, 1921
Maynard, C. (Warwicks. & Lancs.) b April 8, 1958
*Maynard, M. P. (Glam. & N. Dist.) b March 21, 1966
*Mayne, E. R. (S. Aust. & Vic.) b July 2, 1882, d Oct. 26, 1961
*Mayne, L. C. (W. Aust.) b Jan. 23, 1942
*Mead, C. P. (Hants; *CY 1912*) b March 9, 1887, d March 26, 1958
*Mead, W. (Essex; *CY 1904*) b March 25, 1868, d March 18, 1954
Meads, E. A. (Notts.) b Aug. 17, 1916
*Meale, T. (Wgtn) b Nov. 11, 1928
*Meckiff, I. (Vic.) b Jan. 6, 1935
Medlycott, K. T. (Surrey & N. Tvl) b May 12, 1965
*Meher-Homji, K. R. (W. Ind. & Bombay) b Aug. 9, 1911, d Feb. 10, 1982
*Mehra, V. L. (E. Punjab, Ind. Rlwys & Delhi) b March 12, 1938
*Meintjes, D. J. (Tvl) b June 9, 1890, d July 17, 1979
*Melle, M. G. (Tvl & W. Prov.) b June 3, 1930
Melluish, M. E. L. (CUCC & Middx; Pres. MCC 1991-92) b June 13, 1932
*Melville, A. (OUCC, Sussex, Natal & Tvl; *CY 1948*) b May 19, 1910, d April 18, 1983
Mence, M. D. (Warwicks. & Glos.) b April 13, 1944
Mendis, G. D. (Sussex & Lancs.) b April 20, 1955
*Mendis, L. R. D. (SSC) b Aug. 25, 1952
*Mendonca, I. L. (BG) b July 13, 1934
Mercer, J. (Sussex, Glam. & Northants; *CY 1927*) b April 22, 1895, d Aug. 31, 1987
*Merchant, V. M. (Bombay; *CY 1937*) b Oct. 12, 1911, d Oct. 27, 1987
Merrick, T. A. (Leewards, Warwicks. & Kent) b June 10, 1963
*Merritt, W. E. (Cant. & Northants) b Aug. 18, 1908, d June 9, 1977
*Merry, C. A. (T/T) b Jan. 20, 1911, d April 19, 1964
Metcalfe, A. A. (Yorks. & OFS) b Dec. 25, 1963
Metson, C. P. (Middx & Glam.) b July 2, 1963
*Meuleman, K. D. (Vic. & W. Aust.) b Sept. 5, 1923
*Meuli, E. M. (C. Dist.) b Feb. 20, 1926
Meyer, B. J. (Glos.; Umpire) b Aug. 21, 1932
Meyer, R. J. O. (CUCC, Som. & W. Ind.) b March 15, 1905, d March 9, 1991
Mian Mohammad Saaed (N. Ind. Patiala & S. Punjab; Pak.'s first captain) b Aug. 31, 1910, d Aug. 23, 1979
*Middleton, J. (W. Prov.) b Sept. 30, 1865, d Dec. 23, 1913
Middleton, T. C. (Hants) b Feb. 1, 1964
**Midwinter, W. E. (Vic. & Glos.) b June 19, 1851, d Dec. 3, 1890
Mike, G. W. (Notts.) b July 14, 1966
*Milburn, B. D. (Otago) b Nov. 24, 1943
*Milburn, C. (Northants & W. Aust.; *CY 1967*) b Oct. 23, 1941, d Feb. 28, 1990
*Milkha Singh, A. G. (Madras) b Dec. 31, 1941
Miller, A. J. T. (OUCC & Middx) b May 30, 1963
*Miller, A. M. (Eng.) b Oct. 19, 1869, d June 26, 1959
*Miller, G. (Derbys., Natal & Essex) b Sept. 8, 1952
*Miller, K. R. (Vic., NSW & Notts.; *CY 1954*) b Nov. 28, 1919
*Miller, L. S. M. (C. Dist. & Wgtn) b March 31, 1923
Miller, R. (Warwicks.) b Jan. 6, 1941
*Miller, R. C. (Jam.) b Dec. 24, 1924
*Milligan, F. W. (Yorks.) b March 19, 1870, d March 31, 1900
*Millman, G. (Notts.) b Oct. 2, 1934
Millmow, J. P. (Wgtn) b Sept. 22, 1967

Millns, D. J. (Notts. & Leics.) b Feb. 27, 1965

*Mills, C. H. (Surrey, Kimberley & W. Prov.) b Nov. 26, 1867, d July 26, 1948

*Mills, J. E. (Auck.) b Sept. 3, 1905, d Dec. 11, 1972

Mills, J. M. (CUCC & Warwicks.) b July 27, 1921

Mills, J. P. C. (CUCC & Northants) b Dec. 6, 1958

Milner, J. (Essex) b Aug. 22, 1937

*Milton, C. A. (Glos.; *CY 1959*) b March 10, 1928

*Milton, W. H. (W. Prov.) b Dec. 3, 1854, d March 6, 1930

*Minnett, R. B. (NSW) b June 13, 1888, d Oct. 21, 1955

"Minshull", John (scorer of first recorded century) b *circa* 1741, d Oct. 1793

*Miran Bux (Pak. Serv., Punjab & R'pindi) b April 20, 1907, d Feb. 8, 1991

*Misson, F. M. (NSW) b Nov. 19, 1938

*Mitchell, A. (Yorks.) b Sept. 13, 1902, d Dec. 25, 1976

*Mitchell, B. (Tvl; *CY 1936*) b Jan. 8, 1909

Mitchell, C. G. (Som.) b Jan. 27, 1929

**Mitchell, F. (CUCC, Yorks. & Tvl; *CY 1902*) b Aug. 13, 1872, d Oct. 11, 1935

*Mitchell, T. B. (Derbys.) b Sept. 4, 1902

*Mitchell-Innes, N. S. (OUCC & Som.) b Sept. 7, 1914

*Modi, R. S. (Bombay) b Nov. 11, 1924

*Mohammad Aslam (N. Ind. & Pak. Rlwys) b Jan. 5, 1920

*Mohammad Farooq (Kar.) b April 8, 1938

*Mohammad Ilyas (Lahore & PIA) b March 19, 1946

*Mohammad Munaf (Sind, E. Pak., Kar. & PIA) b Nov. 2, 1935

*Mohammad Nazir (Pak. Rlwys) b March 8, 1946

*Mohsin Kamal (Lahore, Allied Bank & PNSC) b June 16, 1963

*Mohsin Khan (Pak. Rlwys, Kar., Sind, Pak. Us & HBL) b March 15, 1955

*Moin Khan (Karachi & PIA) b Sept. 23, 1971

Moin-ul-Atiq (UBL, Karachi & HBL) b Aug. 5, 1964

*Moir, A. McK. (Otago) b July 17, 1919

Moir, D. G. (Derbys. & Scotland) b April 13, 1957

*Mold, A. W. (Lancs.; *CY 1892*) b May 27, 1863, d April 29, 1921

Moles, A. J. (Warwicks. & Griq. W.) b Feb. 12, 1961

*Moloney, D. A. R. (Wgtn, Otago & Cant.) b Aug. 11, 1910, d July 15, 1942

Monckton of Brenchley, 1st Lord (Pres. MCC 1956-57) b Jan. 17, 1891, d Jan. 9, 1965

*Mongia, N. R. (Baroda) b Dec. 19, 1969

Monkhouse, G. (Surrey) b April 26, 1954

Montgomerie, R. R. (OUCC & Northants) b July 3, 1971

*Moodie, G. H. (Jam.) b Nov. 25, 1915

*Moody, T. M. (W. Aust., Warwicks. & Worcs.) b Oct. 2, 1965

*Moon, L. J. (CUCC & Middx) b Feb. 9, 1878, d Nov. 23, 1916

*Mooney, F. L. H. (Wgtn) b May 26, 1921

Moore, D. N. (OUCC & Glos.) b Sept. 26, 1910

Moore, H. I. (Notts.) b Feb. 28, 1941

Moore, R. H. (Hants) b Nov. 14, 1913

Moores, P. (Worcs., Sussex & OFS) b Dec. 18, 1962

*More, K. S. (Baroda) b Sept. 4, 1962

Morgan, D. C. (Derbys.) b Feb. 26, 1929

Morgan, M. (Notts.) b May 21, 1936

*Morgan, R. W. (Auck.) b Feb. 12, 1941

*Morkel, D. P. B. (W. Prov.) b Jan. 25, 1906, d Oct. 6, 1980

*Morley, F. (Notts.) b Dec. 16, 1850, d Sept. 28, 1884

Morley, J. D. (Sussex) b Oct. 20, 1950

*Moroney, J. (NSW) b July 24, 1917

*Morris, A. R. (NSW; *CY 1949*) b Jan. 19, 1922

*Morris, H. (Glam.) b Oct. 5, 1963

Morris, H. M. (CUCC & Essex) b April 16, 1898, d Nov. 18, 1984

*Morris, J. E. (Derbys, Griq. W. & Durham) b April 1, 1964

Morris, R. E. (OUCC) b June 8, 1967

*Morris, S. (Vic.) b June 22, 1855, d Sept. 20, 1931

*Morrison, B. D. (Wgtn) b Dec. 17, 1933

*Morrison, D. K. (Auck. & Lancs.) b Feb. 3, 1966

*Morrison, J. F. M. (C. Dist. & Wgtn) b Aug. 27, 1947

Mortensen, O. H. (Denmark & Derbys.) b Jan. 29, 1958

*Mortimore, J. B. (Glos.) b May 14, 1933

Mortlock, W. (Surrey & Utd Eng. XI) b July 18, 1832, d Jan. 23, 1884

*Moseley, E. A. (B'dos, Glam., E. Prov. & N. Tvl) b Jan. 5, 1958

Moseley, H. R. (B'dos & Som.) b May 28, 1948

*Moses, H. (NSW) b Feb. 13, 1858, d Dec. 7, 1938

*Moss, A. E. (Middx) b Nov. 14, 1930

*Moss, J. K. (Vic.) b June 29, 1947

*Motz, R. C. (Cant.; *CY 1966*) b Jan. 12, 1940

Moulding, R. P. (OUCC & Middx) b Jan. 3, 1958

*Moule, W. H. (Vic.) b Jan. 31, 1858, d Aug. 24, 1939

*Moxon, M. D. (Yorks. & Griq. W.; *CY 1993*) b May 4, 1960

*Mudassar Nazar (Lahore, Punjab, Pak. Us, HBL, PIA & UBL) b April 6, 1956
*Muddiah, V. M. (Mysore & Ind. Serv.) b June 8, 1929
*Mufasir-ul-Haq (Kar., Dacca, PWD, E. Pak. & NBP) b Aug. 16, 1944, d July 27, 1983
Mukherjee, S. P. (Bengal) b Oct. 5, 1964
Mullally, A. D. (W. Aust., Vic., Hants & Leics.) b July 12, 1969
Munasinghe, M. (SSC) b Dec. 10, 1971
Munden, V. S. (Leics.) b Jan. 2, 1928
*Munir Malik (Punjab, R'pindi, Pak. Serv. & Kar.) b July 10, 1934
*Munton, T. A. (Warwicks; *CY 1995*) b July 30, 1965
*Muralitharan, M. (TU) b April 17, 1972
**Murdoch, W. L. (NSW & Sussex) b Oct. 18, 1854, d Feb. 18, 1911
Murphy, A. J. (Lancs. & Surrey) b Aug. 6, 1962
*Murray, A. R. A. (E. Prov.) b April 30, 1922
*Murray, B. A. G. (Wgtn) b Sept. 18, 1940
*Murray, D. A. (B'dos) b Sept. 29, 1950
*Murray, D. L. (T/T, CUCC, Notts. & Warwicks.) b May 20, 1943
*Murray, J. R. (Windwards) b Jan. 20, 1968
*Murray, J. T. (Middx; *CY 1967*) b April 1, 1935
Murray-Willis, P. E. (Worcs. & Northants) b July 14, 1910, d Jan. 7, 1995
Murrell, H. R. (Kent & Middx) b Nov. 19, 1879, d Aug. 15, 1952
Murrills, T. J. (CUCC) b Dec. 22, 1953
*Musgrove, H. (Vic.) b Nov. 27, 1860, d Nov. 2, 1931
*Mushtaq Ahmed (UBL, Multan & Som.) b June 28, 1970
*Mushtaq Ali, S. (C. Ind., Guj., †M. Pradesh & U. Pradesh) b Dec. 17, 1914
*Mushtaq Mohammad (Kar., Northants & PIA; *CY 1963*) b Nov. 22, 1943
Mynn, Alfred (Kent & All-Eng.) b Jan. 19, 1807, d Oct. 31, 1861

*Nadkarni, R. G. (M'tra & Bombay) b April 4, 1932
*Nadeem Abbasi (R'pindi) b April 15, 1964
*Nadeem Ghauri (Lahore, Pak. Rlways & HBL) b Oct 12, 1962
*Nadeem Khan (Kar. & NBP) b Dec. 10, 1969
Naeem Ahmed (Kar., Pak. Us, NBP, UBL & PIA) b Sept. 20, 1952
Naeem Ahmed (Sargodha & HBL) b April 14, 1971
*Nagel, L. E. (Vic.) b March 6, 1905, d Nov. 23, 1971
*Naik, S. S. (Bombay) b Feb. 21, 1945
*Nanan, R. (T/T) b May 29, 1953
*Naoomal Jaoomal, M. (N. Ind. & Sind) b April 17, 1904, d July 18, 1980
*Narasimha Rao, M. V. (H'bad) b Aug. 11, 1954
Naseer Malik (Khairpair & NBP) b Feb. 1, 1950
*Nash, D. J. (N. Dist. & Otago) b Nov. 20, 1971
*Nash, L. J. (Tas. & Vic.) b May 2, 1910, d July 24, 1986
Nash, M. A. (Glam.) b May 9, 1945
*Nasim-ul-Ghani (Kar., Pak. Us, Dacca, E. Pak., PWD & NBP) b May 14, 1941
*Naushad Ali (Kar., E. Pak., R'pindi, Peshawar, NWFP, Punjab & Pak. Serv.) b Oct. 1, 1943
*Naved Anjum (Lahore, UBL & HBL) b July 27, 1963
*Navle, J. G. (Rajputna, C. Ind., Holkar & Gwalior) b Dec. 7, 1902, d Sept. 7, 1979
*Nayak, S. V. (Bombay) b Oct. 20, 1954
*Nayudu, Col. C. K. (C. Ind., Andhra, U. Pradesh & Holkar; *CY 1933*) b Oct. 31, 1895, d Nov. 14, 1967
*Nayudu, C. S. (C. Ind., Holkar, Baroda, Bengal, Andhra & U. Pradesh) b April 18, 1914
*Nazar Mohammad (N. Ind. & Punjab) b March 5, 1921
*Nazir Ali, S. (S. Punjab & Sussex) b June 8, 1906, d Feb. 18, 1975
Neale, P. A. (Worcs.; *CY 1989*) b June 5, 1954
*Neblett, J. M. (B'dos & BG) b Nov. 13, 1901, d March 28, 1959
Needham, A. (Surrey & Middx) b March 23, 1957
*Nel, J. D. (W. Prov.) b July 10, 1928
Nevell, W. T. (Middx, Surrey & Northants) b June 13, 1916
*Newberry, C. (Tvl) b 1889, d Aug. 1, 1916
Newell, M. (Notts.) b Feb. 25, 1965
*Newham, W. (Sussex) b Dec 12, 1860, d June 26, 1944
Newland, Richard (Sussex) b *circa* 1718, d May 29, 1791
*Newman, Sir J. (Wgtn & Cant.) b July 3, 1902
Newman, J. A. (Hants & Cant.) b Nov. 12, 1884, d Dec. 21, 1973
Newman, P. G. (Derbys.) b Jan. 10, 1959
*Newport, P. J. (Worcs., Boland & N. Tvl) b Oct. 11, 1962
*Newson, E. S. (Tvl & Rhod.) b Dec. 2, 1910, d April 24, 1988
Newstead, J. T. (Yorks.; *CY 1909*) b Sept. 8, 1877, d March 25, 1952
*Niaz Ahmed (Dacca, PWD, E. Pak. & Pak. Rlwys) b Nov. 11, 1945
Nicholas, M. C. J. (Hants) b Sept. 29, 1957
Nicholls, D. (Kent) b Dec. 8, 1943

Nicholls, R. B. (Glos.) b Dec. 4, 1933, d July 21, 1994
*Nichols, M. S. (Essex; *CY 1934*) b Oct. 6, 1900, d Jan. 26, 1961
Nicholson, A. G. (Yorks.) b June 25, 1938, d Nov. 4, 1985
*Nicholson, F. (OFS) b Sept. 17, 1909, d July 30, 1982
*Nicolson, J. F. W. (Natal & OUCC) b July 19, 1899, d Dec. 13, 1935
*Nissar, Mahomed (Patiala, S. Punjab & U. Pradesh) b Aug. 1, 1910, d March 11, 1963
*Nitschke, H. C. (S. Aust.) b April 14, 1905, d Sept. 29, 1982
Nixon, P. A. (Leics.) b Oct. 21, 1970
*Noble, M. A. (NSW; *CY 1900*) b Jan. 28, 1873, d June 22, 1940
*Noblet, G. (S. Aust.) b Sept. 14, 1916
Noon, W. M. (Northants & Notts.) b Feb. 5, 1971
*Noreiga, J. M. (T/T) b April 15, 1936
Norfolk, 16th Duke of (Pres. MCC 1957-58) b May 30, 1908, d Jan. 31, 1975
Norman, M. E. J. C. (Northants & Leics.) b Jan. 19, 1933
*Norton, N. O. (W. Prov. & Border) b May 11, 1881, d June 27, 1968
*Nothling, O. E. (NSW & Qld) b Aug. 1, 1900, d Sept. 26, 1965
*Nourse, A. D. ("Dudley") (Natal; *CY 1948*) b Nov. 12, 1910, d Aug. 14, 1981
*Nourse, A. W. ("Dave") (Natal, Tvl & W. Prov.) b Jan. 26, 1878, d July 8, 1948
Nugent, 1st Lord (Pres. MCC 1962-63) b Aug. 11, 1895, d April 27, 1973
*Nunes, R. K. (Jam.) b June 7, 1894, d July 22, 1958
*Nupen, E. P. (Tvl) b Jan. 1, 1902, d Jan. 29, 1977
*Nurse, S. M. (B'dos; *CY 1967*) b Nov. 10, 1933
Nutter, A. E. (Lancs. & Northants) b June 28, 1913
*Nyalchand, S. (W. Ind., Kathiawar, Guj. & S'tra) b Sept. 14, 1919
Nye, J. K. (Sussex) b May 23, 1914
Nyren, John (Hants) b Dec. 15, 1764, d June 28, 1837
Nyren, Richard (Hants & Sussex) b 1734, d April 25, 1797

Oakes, C. (Sussex) b Aug. 10, 1912
Oakes, J. (Sussex) b March 3, 1916
*Oakman, A. S. M. (Sussex) b April 20, 1930
Oates, T. W. (Notts.) b Aug. 9, 1875, d June 18, 1949
Oates, W. F. (Yorks. & Derbys.) b June 11, 1929
O'Brien, F. P. (Cant. & Northants) b Feb. 11, 1911, d Oct. 22, 1991
*O'Brien, L. P. J. (Vic.) b July 2, 1907
*O'Brien, Sir T. C. (OUCC & Middx) b Nov. 5, 1861, d Dec. 9, 1948
*Ochse, A. E. (Tvl) b March 11, 1870, d April 11, 1918
*Ochse, A. L. (E. Prov.) b Oct. 11, 1899, d May 6, 1949
*O'Connor, J. (Essex) b Nov. 6, 1897, d Feb. 22, 1977
*O'Connor, J. D. A. (NSW & S. Aust.) b Sept. 9, 1875, d Aug. 23, 1941
*O'Donnell, S. P. (Vic.) b Jan. 26, 1963
*Ogilvie, A. D. (Qld) b June 3, 1951
O'Gorman, T. J. G. (Derbys.) b May 15, 1967
*O'Keeffe, K. J. (NSW & Som.) b Nov. 25, 1949
*Old, C. M. (Yorks., Warwicks. & N. Tvl; *CY 1979*) b Dec. 22, 1948
*Oldfield, N. (Lancs. & Northants) b April 30, 1911
*Oldfield, W. A. (NSW; *CY 1927*) b Sept. 9, 1894, d Aug. 10, 1976
Oldham, S. (Yorks. & Derbys.) b July 26, 1948
Oldroyd, E. (Yorks.) b Oct. 1, 1888, d Dec. 27, 1964
*O'Linn, S. (Kent, W. Prov. & Tvl) b May 5, 1927
Oliver, P. R. (Warwicks.) b May 9, 1956
*O'Neill, N. C. (NSW; *CY 1962*) b Feb. 19, 1937
Ontong, R. C. (Border, Tvl, N. Tvl & Glam.) b Sept. 9, 1955
Opatha, A. R. M. (SL) b Aug. 5, 1947
Ord, J. S. (Warwicks.) b July 12, 1912
*O'Reilly, W. J. (NSW; *CY 1935*) b Dec. 20, 1905, d Oct. 6, 1992
O'Riordan, A. J. (Ireland) b July 20, 1940
Ormrod, J. A. (Worcs. & Lancs.) b Dec. 22, 1942
O'Shaughnessy, S. J. (Lancs. & Worcs.) b Sept. 9, 1961
Oslear, D. O. (Umpire) b March 3, 1929
Ostler, D. P. (Warwicks.) b July 15, 1970
*O'Sullivan, D. R. (C. Dist. & Hants) b Nov. 16, 1944
Outschoorn, L. (Worcs.) b Sept. 26, 1918, d Jan. 9, 1994
*Overton, G. W. F. (Otago) b June 8, 1919, d. Sept. 7, 1993
*Owens, M. B. (Cant.) b Nov. 11, 1969
*Owen-Smith, H. G. (W. Prov., OUCC & Middx; *CY 1930*) b Feb. 18, 1909, d Feb. 28, 1990
Owen-Thomas, D. R. (CUCC & Surrey) b Sept. 20, 1948
*Oxenham, R. K. (Qld) b July 28, 1891, d Aug. 16, 1939

*Padgett, D. E. V. (Yorks.) b July 20, 1934
*Padmore, A. L. (B'dos) b Dec. 17, 1946
Page, H. A. (Tvl & Essex) b July 3, 1962

Page, J. C. T. (Kent) b May 20, 1930, d Dec. 14, 1990
Page, M. H. (Derbys.) b June 17, 1941
*Page, M. L. (Cant.) b May 8, 1902, d Feb. 13, 1987
*Pai, A. M. (Bombay) b April 28, 1945
*Paine, G. A. E. (Middx & Warwicks.; *CY 1935*) b June 11, 1908, d March 30, 1978
*Pairaudeau, B. H. (BG & N. Dist.) b April 14, 1931
*Palairet, L. C. H. (OUCC & Som.; *CY 1893*) b May 27, 1870, d March 27, 1933
Palairet, R. C. N. (OUCC & Som.; Joint-Manager MCC in Australia 1932-33) b June 25, 1871, d Feb. 11, 1955
*Palm, A. W. (W. Prov.) b June 8, 1901, d Aug. 17, 1966
*Palmer, C. H. (Worcs. & Leics.; Pres. MCC 1978-79) b May 15, 1919
*Palmer, G. E. (Vic. & Tas.) b Feb. 22, 1859, d Aug. 22, 1910
Palmer, G. V. (Som.) b Nov. 1, 1965
*Palmer, K. E. (Som.; Umpire) b April 22, 1937
Palmer, R. (Som.) b July 12, 1942
*Pandit, C. S. (Bombay) b Sept. 30, 1961
Pardon, Charles Frederick (Editor of *Wisden* 1887-90) b March 28, 1850, d April 18, 1890
Pardon, Sydney H. (Editor of *Wisden* 1891-1925) b Sept. 23, 1855, d Nov. 20, 1925
*Parfitt, P. H. (Middx; *CY 1963*) b Dec. 8, 1936
Paris, C. G. A. (Hants; Pres. MCC 1975-76) b Aug. 20, 1911
Parish, R. J. (Aust. Administrator) b May 7, 1916
*Park, R. L. (Vic.) b July 30, 1892, d Jan. 23, 1947
*Parkar, G. A. (Bombay) b Oct. 24, 1955
*Parkar, R. D. (Bombay) b Oct. 31, 1946
Parkar, Z. (Bombay) b Nov. 22, 1957
*Parker, C. W. L. (Glos.; *CY 1923*) b Oct. 14, 1882, d July 11, 1959
*Parker, G. M. (SA) b May 27, 1899, d May 1, 1969
Parker, G. W. (CUCC & Glos.) b Feb. 11, 1912
Parker, J. F. (Surrey) b April 23, 1913, d Jan. 27, 1983
*Parker, J. M. (N. Dist. & Worcs.) b Feb. 21, 1951
*Parker, N. M. (Otago & Cant.) b Aug. 28, 1948
*Parker, P. W. G. (CUCC, Sussex, Natal & Durham) b Jan. 15, 1956
*Parkhouse, W. G. A. (Glam.) b Oct. 12, 1925
*Parkin, C. H. (Yorks. & Lancs.; *CY 1924*) b Feb. 18, 1886, d June 15, 1943
*Parkin, D. C. (E. Prov., Tvl & Griq. W.) b Feb. 18, 1870, d March 20, 1936
Parks, H. W. (Sussex) b July 18, 1906, d May 7, 1984
*Parks, J. H. (Sussex & Cant.; *CY 1938*) b May 12, 1903, d Nov. 21, 1980
*Parks, J. M. (Sussex & Som.; *CY 1968*) b Oct. 21, 1931
Parks, R. J. (Hants & Kent) b June 15, 1959
*Parore, A. C. (Auck.) b Jan. 23, 1971
Parr, F. D. (Lancs.) b June 1, 1928
Parr, George (Notts. & All-England) b May 22, 1826, d June 23, 1891
*Parry, D. R. (Comb. Is. & Leewards) b Dec. 22, 1954
*Parsana, D. D. (S'tra, Ind. Rlwys & Guj.) b Dec. 2, 1947
Parsons, A. B. D. (CUCC & Surrey) b Sept. 20, 1933
Parsons, A. E. W. (Auck. & Sussex) b Jan. 9, 1949
Parsons, G. J. (Leics., Warwicks., Boland, Griq. W. & OFS) b Oct. 17, 1959
Parsons, Canon J. H. (Warwicks.) b May 30, 1890, d Feb. 2, 1981
*Partridge, J. T. (Rhod.) b Dec. 9, 1932, d June 7, 1988
Partridge, N. E. (Malvern, CUCC & Warwicks.; *CY 1919*) b Aug. 10, 1900, d March 10, 1982
Partridge, R. J. (Northants) b Feb. 11, 1912
Parvez Mir (R'pindi, Lahore, Punjab, Pak. Us, Derbys., HBL & Glam.) b Sept. 24, 1953
*Pascoe, L. S. (NSW) b Feb. 13, 1950
Pasqual, S. P. (SL) b Oct. 15, 1961
*Passailaigue, C. C. (Jam.) b Aug. 1902, d Jan. 7, 1972
*Patankar, C. T. (Bombay) b Nov. 24, 1930
**Pataudi, Iftikhar Ali, Nawab of (OUCC, Worcs., Patiala, N. Ind. & S. Punjab; *CY 1932*) b March 16, 1910, d Jan. 5, 1952
*Pataudi, Mansur Ali, Nawab of (Sussex, OUCC, Delhi & H'bad; *CY 1968*) b Jan. 5, 1941
Patel, A. K. (S'tra) b March 6, 1957
*Patel, B. P. (Karn.) b Nov. 24, 1952
*Patel, D. N. (Worcs. & Auck.) b Oct. 25, 1958
*Patel, J. M. (Guj.) b Nov. 26, 1924, d Dec. 12, 1992
Patel, M. M. (Kent) b July 7, 1970
*Patel, R. (Baroda) b June 1, 1964
Pathmanathan, G. (OUCC, CUCC & SL) b Jan. 23, 1954
*Patiala, Maharaja of (N. Ind., Patiala & S. Punjab) b Jan. 17, 1913, d June 17, 1974
*Patil, S. M. (Bombay & M. Pradesh) b Aug. 18, 1956
*Patil, S. R. (M'tra) b Oct. 10, 1933
*Patterson, B. P. (Jam., Tas. & Lancs.) b Sept. 15, 1961

Pauline, D. B. (Surrey & Glam.) b Dec. 15, 1960
Pawson, A. G. (OUCC & Worcs.) b May 30, 1888, d Feb. 25, 1986
Pawson, H. A. (OUCC & Kent) b Aug. 22, 1921
Payn, L. W. (Natal) b May 6, 1915, d May 2, 1992
*Payne, T. R. O. (B'dos) b Feb. 13, 1957
*Paynter, E. (Lancs.; *CY 1938*) b Nov. 5, 1901, d Feb. 5, 1979
Payton, W. R. D. (Notts.) b Feb. 13, 1882, d May 2, 1943
*Peall, S. G. (MCD) b Sept. 2, 1970
Pearce, G. (Sussex) b Oct. 27, 1908, d June 16, 1986
Pearce, T. N. (Essex) b Nov. 3, 1905, d April 10, 1994
*Pearse, C. O. C. (Natal) b Oct. 10, 1884, d May 7, 1953
Pearson, D. B. (Worcs.) b March 29, 1937
*Peate, E. (Yorks.) b March 2, 1855, d March 11, 1900
Peck, I. G. (CUCC & Northants) b Oct. 18, 1957
*Peebles, I. A. R. (OUCC, Middx & Scotland; *CY 1931*) b Jan. 20, 1908, d Feb. 28, 1980
*Peel, R. (Yorks.; *CY 1889*) b Feb. 12, 1857, d Aug. 12, 1941
*Pegler, S. J. (Tvl) b July 28, 1888, d Sept. 10, 1972
*Pellew, C. E. (S. Aust.) b Sept. 21, 1893, d May 9, 1981
Penberthy, A. L. (Northants) b Sept. 1, 1969
Penn, C. (Kent) b June 19, 1963
*Penn, F. (Kent) b March 7, 1851, d Dec. 26, 1916
Penney, T. L. (Boland, Warwicks. & Mash.) b June 11, 1968
Pepper, C. G. (NSW & Aust. Serv.; Umpire) b Sept. 15, 1916, d March 24, 1993
Perera, K. G. (Mor.) b May 22, 1964
Perkins, G. C. (Northants) b June 4, 1911
Perkins, H. (CUCC & Cambs.; Sec. MCC 1876-97) b Dec. 10, 1832, d May 6, 1916
*Perks, R. T. D. (Worcs.) b Oct. 4, 1911, d Nov. 22, 1977
Perrin, P. A. (Essex; *CY 1905*) b May 26, 1876, d Nov. 20, 1945
Perryman, S. P. (Warwicks. & Worcs.) b Oct. 22, 1955
*Pervez Sajjad (Lahore, PIA & Kar.) b Aug. 30, 1942
*Petherick, P. J. (Otago & Wgtn) b Sept. 25, 1942
*Petrie, E. C. (Auck. & N. Dist.) b May 22, 1927
Petrie, R. G. (Cant.) b Aug. 23, 1967
*Phadkar, D. G. (M'tra, Bombay, Bengal & Ind. Rlwys) b Dec. 10, 1925, d March 17, 1985
Phebey, A. H. (Kent) b Oct. 1, 1924
Phelan, P. J. (Essex) b Feb. 9, 1938
*Philipson, H. (OUCC & Middx) b June 8, 1866, d Dec. 4, 1935
*Phillip, N. (Comb. Is., Windwards & Essex) b June 12, 1948
Phillips, R. B. (NSW & Qld) b May 23, 1954
*Phillips, W. B. (S. Aust.) b March 1, 1958
*Phillips, W. N. (Vic.) b Nov. 7, 1962
Phillipson, C. P. (Sussex) b Feb. 10, 1952
Phillipson, W. E. (Lancs.) b Dec. 3, 1910, d Aug. 24, 1991
*Philpott, P. I. (NSW) b Nov. 21, 1934
Piachaud, J. D. (OUCC, Hants & Ceylon) b March 1, 1937
Pick, R. A. (Notts. & Wgtn) b Nov. 19, 1963
Pickles, C. S. (Yorks.) b Jan. 30, 1966
Pickles, L. (Som.) b Sept. 17, 1932
Pienaar, R. F. (Tvl, W. Prov., N. Tvl & Kent) b July 17, 1961
Pieris, H. S. M. (SL) b Feb. 16, 1946
*Pierre, L. R. (T/T) b June 5, 1921, d April 14, 1989
Pierson, A. R. K. (Warwicks. & Leics.) b July 21, 1963
*Pigott, A. C. S. (Sussex, Wgtn & Surrey) b June 4, 1958
Pilch, Fuller (Norfolk & Kent) b March 17, 1804, d May 1, 1870
Pilling, H. (Lancs.) b Feb. 23, 1943
*Pilling, R. (Lancs.; *CY 1891*) b July 5, 1855, d March 28, 1891
Piper, K. J. (Warwicks.) b Dec. 18, 1969
*Pithey, A. J. (Rhod. & W. Prov.) b July 17, 1933
*Pithey, D. B. (Rhod., OUCC, Northants, W. Prov., Natal & Tvl) b Oct. 4, 1936
Pitman, R. W. C. (Hants) b Feb. 21, 1933
*Place, W. (Lancs.) b Dec 7, 1914
Platt, R. K. (Yorks. & Northants) b Dec. 21, 1932
*Playle, W. R. (Auck. & W. Aust.) b Dec. 1, 1938
Pleass, J. E. (Glam.) b May 21, 1923
*Plimsoll, J. B. (W. Prov. & Natal) b Oct. 27, 1917
*Pocock, B. A. (N. Dist.) b June 18, 1971
Pocock, N. E. J. (Hants) b Dec. 15, 1951
*Pocock, P. I. (Surrey & N. Tvl) b Sept. 24, 1946
Pollard, P. R. (Notts.) b Sept. 24, 1968
*Pollard, R. (Lancs.) b June 19, 1912, d Dec. 16, 1985
*Pollard, V. (C. Dist. & Cant.) b Burnley Sept. 7, 1945
Pollock, A. J. (CUCC) b April 19, 1962

*Pollock, P. M. (E. Prov.; *CY 1966*) b June 30, 1941
*Pollock, R. G. (E. Prov. & Tvl; *CY 1966*) b Feb. 27, 1944
*Ponsford, W. H. (Vic.; *CY 1935*) b Oct. 19, 1900, d April 6, 1991
Pont, K. R. (Essex) b Jan. 16, 1953
*Poole, C. J. (Notts.) b March 13, 1921
Pooley, E. (Surrey & first England tour) b Feb. 13, 1838, d July 18, 1907
*Poore, M. B. (Cant.) b June 1, 1930
*Poore, Brig-Gen. R. M. (Hants & SA; *CY 1900*) b March 20, 1866, d July 14, 1938
Pope, A. V. (Derbys.) b Aug. 15, 1909
*Pope, G. H. (Derbys.) b Jan. 27, 1911, d Oct. 29, 1993
*Pope, R. J. (NSW) b Feb. 18, 1864, d July 27, 1952
Popplewell, N. F. M. (CUCC & Som.) b Aug. 8, 1957
Portal of Hungerford, 1st Lord (Pres. MCC 1958-59) b May 21, 1893, d April 22, 1971
Porter, A. (Glam.) b March 25, 1914, d Feb. 20, 1994
Porter, G. D. (W. Aust.) b March 18, 1955
Pothecary, A. E. (Hants) b March 1, 1906, d May 21, 1991
*Pothecary, J. E. (W. Prov.) b Dec. 6, 1933
Potter, G. (Sussex) b Oct. 26, 1931
Potter, L. (Kent, Griq. W., Leics. & OFS) b Nov. 7, 1962
*Pougher, A. D. (Leics.) b April 19, 1865, d May 20, 1926
Pountain, F. R. (Sussex) b April 23, 1941
*Powell, A. W. (Griq. W.) b July 18, 1873, d Sept. 11, 1948
*Prabhakar, M. (Delhi) b April 15, 1963
Prasad, B. K. V. (Karn.) b Aug. 5, 1969
*Prasanna, E. A. S. (†Karn.) b May 22, 1940
Pratt, R. L. (Leics.) b Nov. 15, 1938
Pressdee, J. S. (Glam. & NE Tvl) b June 19, 1933
Preston, Hubert (Editor of *Wisden* 1944-51) b Dec. 16, 1868, d Aug. 6, 1960
Preston, K. C. (Essex) b Aug. 22, 1925
Preston, Norman (Editor of *Wisden* 1952-80) b March 18, 1903, d March 6, 1980
Pretlove, J. F. (CUCC & Kent) b Nov. 23, 1932
Price, D. G. (CUCC) b Feb. 7, 1965
Price, E. J. (Lancs. & Essex) b Oct. 27, 1918
*Price, J. S. E. (Middx) b July 22, 1937
*Price, W. F. F. (Middx) b April 25, 1902, d Jan. 13, 1969
Prichard, P. J. (Essex) b Jan. 7, 1965
*Prideaux, R. M. (CUCC, Kent, Northants, Sussex & OFS) b July 31, 1939
Pridgeon, A. P. (Worcs.) b Feb. 22, 1954
*Priest, M. W. (Cant.) b Aug. 12, 1961
*Prince, C. F. H. (W. Prov., Border & E. Prov.) b Sept. 11, 1874, d March 5, 1948
*Pringle, C. (Auck.) b Jan. 26, 1968
*Pringle, D. R. (CUCC & Essex) b Sept. 18, 1958
*Pringle, M. W. (W. Prov.) b June 22, 1966
Pritchard, T. L. (Wgtn, Warwicks. & Kent) b March 10, 1917
*Procter, M. J. (Glos., Natal, W. Prov., Rhod. & OFS; *CY 1970*) b Sept. 15, 1946
Prodger, J. M. (Kent) b Sept. 1, 1935
*Promnitz, H. L. E. (Border, Griq. W. & OFS) b Feb. 23, 1904, d Sept. 7, 1983
Prouton, R. O. (Hants) b March 1, 1926
Pugh, C. T. M. (Glos.) b March 13, 1937
Pullan, D. A. (Notts.) b May 1, 1944
*Pullar, G. (Lancs. & Glos.; *CY 1960*) b Aug. 1, 1935
*Puna, N. (N. Dist.) b Oct. 28, 1929
*Punjabi, P. H. (Sind & Guj.) b Sept. 20, 1921
*Pushpakumara, K. R. (SL) b July 21, 1975
*Pycroft, A. J. (Zimb.) b June 6, 1956
Pydanna, M. R. (Guyana), b Jan. 27, 1950

*Qasim Omar (Kar. & MCB) b Feb. 9, 1957
Quaife, B. W. (Warwicks. & Worcs.) b Nov. 24, 1899, d Nov. 28, 1984
*Quaife, William (W. G.) (Warwicks. & Griq. W.; *CY 1902*) b March 17, 1872, d Oct. 13, 1951
*Quinn, N. A. (Griq. W. & Tvl) b Feb. 21, 1908, d Aug. 5, 1934

*Rabone, G. O. (Wgtn & Auck.) b Nov. 6, 1921
*Rackemann, C. G. (Qld) b June 3, 1960
*Radford, N. V. (Lancs., Tvl & Worcs.; *CY 1986*) b June 7, 1957
*Radley, C. T. (Middx; *CY 1979*) b May 13, 1944
*Rae, A. F. (Jam.) b Sept. 30, 1922
Raees Mohammad (Kar.) b Dec. 24, 1932
*Rai Singh, K. (S. Punjab & Ind. Serv.) b Feb. 24, 1922
Rait Kerr, Col. R. S. (Sec. MCC 1936-52) b April 13, 1891, d April 2, 1961
Rajadurai, B. E. A. (SSC) b Aug. 24, 1965
*Rajindernath, V. (N. Ind., U. Prov., S. Punjab, Bihar & E. Punjab) b Jan. 7, 1928, d Nov. 22, 1989
*Rajinder Pal (Delhi, S. Punjab & Punjab) b Nov. 18, 1937
*Rajput, L. S. (Bombay) b Dec. 18, 1961
*Raju, S. L. V. (H'bad) b July 9, 1969
Ralph, L. H. R. (Essex) b May 22, 1920
*Ramadhin, S. (T/T & Lancs.; *CY 1951*) b May 1, 1929
*Raman, W. V. (TN) b May 23, 1965
*Ramanayake, C. P. H. (TU) b Jan. 8, 1965
*Ramaswami, C. (Madras) b June 18, 1896
*Ramchand, G. S. (Sind, Bombay & Raja.) b July 26, 1927
*Ramiz Raja (Lahore, Allied Bank, PNSC & I'bad) b July 14, 1962

*Ramji, L. (W. Ind.) b 1900, d Dec. 20, 1948
*Ramprakash, M. R. (Middx) b Sept. 5, 1969
Ramsamooj, D. (T/T & Northants) b July 5, 1932, d May 24, 1994
*Ranasinghe, A. N. (BRC) b Oct. 13, 1956
Ranasinghe, S. K. (SL) b July 4, 1962
*Ranatunga, A. (SSC) b Dec. 1, 1963
*Ranatunga, D. (SSC) b Oct. 12, 1962
Ranatunga, N. (Colts) b Jan. 22, 1966
*Ranatunga, S. (Colts & NCC) b April 25, 1969
*Ranchod, U. (Mash.) b May 17, 1969
*Randall, D. W. (Notts.; *CY 1980*) b Feb. 24, 1951
Randhir Singh (Orissa & Bihar) b Aug. 16, 1957
*Rangachari, C. R. (Madras) b April 14, 1916, d Oct. 9, 1993
*Rangnekar, K. M. (M'tra, Bombay & †M. Pradesh) b June 27, 1917, d Oct. 11, 1984
*Ranjane, V. B. (M'tra & Ind. Rlwys) b July 22, 1937
*Ranjitsinhji, K. S., afterwards H. H. the Jam Sahib of Nawanagar (CUCC & Sussex; *CY 1897*) b Sept. 10, 1872, d April 2, 1933
*Ransford, V. S. (Vic.; *CY 1910*) b March 20, 1885, d March 19, 1958
Ransom, V. J. (Hants & Surrey) b March 17, 1918
*Rashid Khan (PWD, Kar. & PIA) b Dec. 15, 1959
*Rashid Latif (Kar. & UBL) b Oct. 14, 1968
Ratcliffe, J. D. (Warwicks.) b June 19, 1969
Ratcliffe, R. M. (Lancs.) b Oct. 29, 1951
Ratnayake, N. L. K. (SSC) b Nov. 22, 1968
*Ratnayake, R. J. (NCC) b Jan. 2, 1964
*Ratnayeke, J. R. (NCC) b May 2, 1960
Rawson, P. W. E. (Zimb. & Natal) b May 25, 1957
Rayment, A. W. H. (Hants) b May 29, 1928
*Razdan, V. (Delhi) b Aug. 25, 1969
*Read, H. D. (Surrey & Essex) b Jan. 28, 1910
*Read, J. M. (Surrey; *CY 1890*) b Feb. 9, 1859, d Feb. 17, 1929
*Read, W. W. (Surrey; *CY 1893*) b Nov. 23, 1855, d Jan. 6, 1907
*Reddy, B. (TN) b Nov. 12, 1954
*Redmond, R. E. (Wgtn & Auck.) b Dec. 29, 1944
*Redpath, I. R. (Vic.) b May 11, 1941
Reed, B. L. (Hants) b Sept. 17, 1937
*Reedman, J. C. (S. Aust.) b Oct. 9, 1865, d March 25, 1924
Rees, A. (Glam.) b Feb. 17, 1938
*Reeve, D. A. (Sussex & Warwicks.) b April 2, 1963
Reeves, W. (Essex; Umpire) b Jan. 22, 1875, d March 22, 1944
*Rege, M. R. (M'tra) b March 18, 1924
*Rehman, S. F. (Punjab, Pak. Us & Lahore) b June 11, 1935
*Reid, B. A. (W. Aust.) b March 14, 1963
*Reid, J. F. (Auck.) b March 3, 1956
*Reid, J. R. (Wgtn & Otago; *CY 1959*) b June 3, 1928
*Reid, N. (W. Prov.) b Dec. 26, 1890, d June 6, 1947
Reid, R. B. (Wgtn & Auck.) b Dec. 3, 1958
Reidy, B. W. (Lancs.) b Sept. 18, 1953
*Reiffel, P. R. (Vic.) b April 19, 1966
*Relf, A. E. (Sussex & Auck.; *CY 1914*) b June 26, 1874, d March 26, 1937
*Renneburg, D. A. (NSW) b Sept. 23, 1942
*Rennie, J. A. (Mat.) b July 29, 1970
Revill, A. C. (Derbys. & Leics.) b March 27, 1923
Reynolds, B. L. (Northants) b June 10, 1932
Rhodes, A. E. G. (Derbys.) b Oct. 10, 1916, d Oct. 18, 1983
*Rhodes, H. J. (Derbys.) b July 22, 1936
*Rhodes, J. N. (Natal) b July 26, 1969
Rhodes, S. D. (Notts.) b March 24, 1910, d Jan. 7, 1989
*Rhodes, S. J. (Yorks. & Worcs.; *CY 1995*) b June 17, 1964
*Rhodes, W. (Yorks.; *CY 1899*) b Oct. 29, 1877, d July 8, 1973
Rice, C. E. B. (Tvl & Notts.; *CY 1981*) b July 23, 1949
Rice, J. M. (Hants) b Oct. 23, 1949
*Richards, A. R. (W. Prov.) b 1868, d Jan. 9, 1904
*Richards, B. A. (Natal, Glos., Hants & S. Aust.; *CY 1969*) b July 21, 1945
*Richards, C. J. (Surrey & OFS) b Aug. 10, 1958
Richards, D. L. (Chief Exec. ICC 1993-) b July 28, 1946
Richards, G. (Glam.) b Nov. 29, 1951
*Richards, I. V. A. (Comb. Is., Leewards, Som., Qld & Glam.; *CY 1977*) b March 7, 1952
*Richards, W. H. M. (SA) b Aug. 1862, d Jan. 4, 1903
*Richardson, A. J. (S. Aust.) b July 24, 1888, d Dec. 23, 1973
*Richardson, D. J. (E. Prov. & N. Tvl) b Sept. 16, 1959
*Richardson, D. W. (Worcs.) b Nov. 3, 1934
Richardson, G. W. (Derbys.) b April 26, 1938
*Richardson, P. E. (Worcs. & Kent; *CY 1957*) b July 4, 1931
*Richardson, R. B. (Leewards & Yorks.; *CY 1992*) b Jan. 12, 1962
*Richardson, T. (Surrey & Som.; *CY 1897*) b Aug. 11, 1870, d July 2, 1912
*Richardson, V. Y. (S. Aust.) b Sept. 7, 1894, d Oct. 29, 1969

*Richmond, T. L. (Notts.) b June 23, 1890, d Dec. 29, 1957
*Rickards, K. R. (Jam. & Essex) b Aug. 23, 1923
Riddington, A. (Leics.) b Dec. 22, 1911
*Ridgway, F. (Kent) b Aug. 10, 1923
*Rigg, K. E. (Vic.) b May 21, 1906
Riley, H. (Leics.) b Oct. 3, 1902, d Jan. 24, 1989
*Ring, D. T. (Vic.) b Oct. 14, 1918
Ripley, D. (Northants) b Sept. 13, 1966
Rist, F. H. (Essex) b March 30, 1914
*Ritchie, G. M. (Qld) b Jan. 23, 1960
*Rixon, S. J. (NSW) b Feb. 25, 1954
*Rizwan-uz-Zaman (Kar. & PIA) b Sept. 4, 1962
*Roach, C. A. (T/T) b March 13, 1904, d April 16, 1988
*Roberts, A. D. G. (N. Dist.) b May 6, 1947, d Oct. 26, 1989
*Roberts, A. M. E. (Comb. Is., Leewards, Hants, NSW & Leics.; *CY 1975*) b Jan. 29, 1951
Roberts, A. R. (Northants & Wgtn) b April 16, 1971
*Roberts, A. T. (Windwards) b Sept. 18, 1937
*Roberts, A. W. (Cant. & Otago) b Aug. 20, 1909, d May 13, 1978
Roberts, B. (Tvl & Derbys.) b May 30, 1962
Roberts, The Hon. Sir Denys (Pres. MCC 1989-90) b Jan. 19, 1923
Roberts, S. J. (Cant.) b March 22, 1965
Roberts, W. B. (Lancs. & Victory Tests) b Sept. 27, 1914, d Aug. 24, 1951
*Robertson, G. K. (C. Dist.) b July 15, 1960
*Robertson, J. B. (W. Prov.) b June 5, 1906, d July 5, 1985
*Robertson, J. D. (Middx; *CY 1948*) b Feb. 22, 1917
*Robertson, W. R. (Vic.) b Oct. 6, 1861, d June 24, 1938
Robertson-Glasgow, R. C. (OUCC & Som.; Writer) b July 15, 1901, d March 4, 1965
Robins, D. H. (Warwicks.) b June 26, 1914
Robins, R. V. C. (Middx) b March 13, 1935
*Robins, R. W. V. (CUCC & Middx; *CY 1930*) b June 3, 1906, d Dec. 12, 1968
Robinson, A. L. (Yorks.) b Aug. 17, 1946
Robinson, Emmott (Yorks.) b Nov. 16, 1883, d Nov. 17, 1969
Robinson, Ellis P. (Yorks. & Som.) b Aug. 10, 1911
Robinson, H. B. (OUCC & Canada) b March 3, 1919
Robinson, M. (Glam., Warwicks., H'bad & Madras) b July 16, 1921, d Aug. 8, 1994
Robinson, M. A. (Northants & Yorks.) b Nov. 23, 1966
Robinson, P. E. (Yorks. & Leics.) b Aug. 3, 1963
Robinson, P. J. (Worcs. & Som.) b Feb. 9, 1943
*Robinson, R. D. (Vic.) b June 8, 1946
*Robinson, R. H. (NSW, S. Aust. & Otago) b March 26, 1914, d Aug. 10, 1965
*Robinson, R. T. (Notts.; *CY 1986*) b Nov. 21, 1958
Robson, E. (Som.) b May 1, 1870, d May 23, 1924
Rochford, P. (Glos.) b Aug. 27, 1928, d June 18, 1992
*Rodriguez, W. V. (T/T) b June 25, 1934
Roe, B. (Som.) b Jan. 27, 1939
Roebuck, P. M. (CUCC & Som.; *CY 1988*) b March 6, 1956
Rogers, N. H. (Hants) b March 9, 1918
Rollins, A. S. (Derbys.) b Feb. 8, 1972
Romaines, P. W. (Northants, Glos. & Griq. W.) b Dec. 25, 1955
*Roope, G. R. J. (Surrey & Griq. W.) b July 12, 1946
*Root, C. F. (Derbys. & Worcs.) b April 16, 1890, d Jan. 20, 1954
*Rorke, G. F. (NSW) b June 27, 1938
*Rose, B. C. (Som.; *CY 1980*) b June 4, 1950
Rose, G. D. (Middx & Som.) b April 12, 1964
Roseberry, M. A. (Middx) b Nov. 28, 1966
*Rose-Innes, A. (Kimberley & Tvl) b Feb. 16, 1868, d Nov. 22, 1946
Ross, C. J. (Wgtn & OUCC) b June 24, 1954
Rotherham, G. A. (Rugby, CUCC, Warwicks. & Wgtn; *CY 1918*) b May 28, 1899, d Jan. 31, 1985
Rouse, S. J. (Warwicks.) b Jan. 20, 1949
Routledge, R. (Middx) b June 12, 1920
*Routledge, T. W. (W. Prov. & Tvl) b April 18, 1867, d May 9, 1927
*Rowan, A. M. B. (Tvl) b Feb. 7, 1921
*Rowan, E. A. B. (Tvl; *CY 1952*) b July 20, 1909, d April 30, 1993
*Rowe, C. G. (Wgtn & C. Dist.) b June 30, 1915
Rowe, C. J. C. (Kent & Glam.) b Nov. 11, 1951
Rowe, E. J. (Notts.) b July 21, 1920, d Dec. 17, 1989
*Rowe, G. A. (W. Prov.) b June 15, 1874, d Jan. 8, 1950
*Rowe, L. G. (Jam. & Derbys.) b Jan. 8, 1949
*Roy, A. (Bengal) b June 5, 1945
*Roy, Pankaj (Bengal) b May 31, 1928
*Roy, Pranab (Bengal) b Feb. 10, 1957
*Royle, Rev. V. P. F. A. (OUCC & Lancs.) b Jan. 29, 1854, d May 21, 1929
*Rumsey, F. E. (Worcs., Som. & Derbys.) b Dec. 4, 1935
Rundle, D. B. (W. Prov.) b Sept. 25, 1965
*Rushmere, M. W. (E. Prov.) b Jan. 7, 1965

*Russell, A. C. [C. A. G.] (Essex; *CY 1923*) b Oct. 7, 1887, d March 23, 1961
Russell, P. E. (Derbys.) b May 9, 1944
*Russell, R. C. (Glos.; *CY 1990*) b Aug. 15, 1963
Russell, S. E. J. (Middx & Glos.) b Oct. 4, 1937, d June 18, 1994
*Russell, W. E. (Middx) b July 3, 1936
Russom, N. (CUCC & Som.) b Dec. 3, 1958
Rutherford, I. A. (Worcs. & Otago) b June 30, 1957
*Rutherford, J. W. (W. Aust.) b Sept. 25, 1929
*Rutherford, K. R. (Otago) b Oct. 26, 1965
Ryan, M. (Yorks.) b June 23, 1933
*Ryder, J. (Vic.) b Aug. 8, 1889, d April 3, 1977

Saadat Ali (Lahore, UBL & HBFC) b Feb. 6, 1955
*Sadiq Mohammad (Kar., PIA, Tas., Essex, Glos. & UBL) b May 3, 1945
*Saeed Ahmed (Punjab, Pak. Us, Lahore, PIA, Kar., PWD & Sind) b Oct. 1, 1937
*Saeed Anwar (Kar., UBL & ADBP) b Sept. 6, 1968
*Saggers, R. A. (NSW) b May 15, 1917, d March 1987
Sainsbury, G. E. (Essex & Glos.) b Jan. 17, 1958
Sainsbury, P. J. (Hants; *CY 1974*) b June 13, 1934
*St Hill, E. L. (T/T) b March 9, 1904, d May 21, 1957
*St Hill, W. H. (T/T) b July 6, 1893, d 1957
Sajid Ali (Kar. & NBP) b July 1, 1963
Sajjad Akbar (Lahore, PNSC & Sargodha) b March 1, 1961
*Salah-ud-Din (Kar., PIA & Pak. Us) b Feb. 14, 1947
Sale, R., jun. (OUCC, Warwicks. & Derbys.) b Oct. 4, 1919, d Feb. 3, 1987
*Saleem Altaf (Lahore & PIA) b April 19, 1944
*Saleem Jaffer (Kar. & UBL) b Nov. 19, 1962
*Salim Malik (Lahore, HBL & Essex; *CY 1988*) b April 16, 1963
Salim Pervez (NBP) b Sept. 9, 1947
*Salim Yousuf (Sind, Kar., IDBP, Allied Bank & Customs) b Dec. 7, 1959
*Salisbury, I. D. K. (Sussex; *CY 1993*) b Jan. 21, 1970
Samaranayake, A. D. A. (SL) b Feb. 25, 1962
*Samarasekera, M. A. R. (CCC) b Aug. 5, 1961
*Samaraweera, D. P. (Colts) b. Feb. 12, 1972
Sampson, H. (Yorks. & All-England) b March 13, 1813, d March 29, 1885
*Samuelson, S. V. (Natal) b Nov. 21, 1883, d Nov. 18, 1958
*Sandham, A. (Surrey; *CY 1923*) b July 6, 1890, d April 20, 1982
*Sandhu, B. S. (Bombay) b Aug. 3, 1956
*Sardesai, D. N. (Bombay) b Aug. 8, 1940
*Sarfraz Nawaz (Lahore, Punjab, Northants, Pak. Rlwys & UBL) b Dec. 1, 1948
Sargeant, N. F. (Surrey) b Nov. 8, 1965
*Sarwate, C. T. (CP & B, M'tra, Bombay & †M. Pradesh) b June 22, 1920
*Saunders, J. V. (Vic. & Wgtn) b March 21, 1876, d Dec. 21, 1927
Savage, J. S. (Leics. & Lancs.) b March 3, 1929
Savage, R. Le Q. (OUCC & Warwicks.) b Dec. 10, 1955
Savill, L. A. (Essex) b June 30, 1935
Saville, G. J. (Essex) b Feb. 5, 1944
Saxelby, K. (Notts.) b Feb. 23, 1959
Saxelby, M. (Notts. & Durham) b Jan. 4, 1969
*Saxena, R. C. (Delhi & Bihar) b Sept. 20, 1944
Sayer, D. M. (OUCC & Kent) b Sept. 19, 1936
*Scarlett, R. O. (Jam.) b Aug. 15, 1934
*Schultz, B. N. (E. Prov.) b Aug. 26, 1970
*Schultz, S. S. (CUCC & Lancs.) b Aug. 29, 1857, d Dec. 18, 1937
*Schwarz, R. O. (Middx & Natal; *CY 1908*) b May 4, 1875, d Nov. 18, 1918
*Scott, A. P. H. (Jam.) b July 29, 1934
Scott, Christopher J. (Lancs.) b Sept. 16, 1959
Scott, Colin J. (Glos.) b May 1, 1919, d Nov. 22, 1992
Scott, C. W. (Notts. & Durham) b Jan. 23, 1964
*Scott, H. J. H. (Vic.) b Dec. 26, 1858, d Sept. 23, 1910
Scott, M. E. (Northants) b May 8, 1936
*Scott, O. C. (Jam.) b Aug. 25, 1893, d June 16, 1961
*Scott, R. H. (Cant.) b March 6, 1917
Scott, R. J. (Hants & Glos.) b Nov. 2, 1963
Scott, S. W. (Middx; *CY 1893*) b March 24, 1854, d Dec. 8, 1933
*Scott, V. J. (Auck.) b July 31, 1916, d Aug. 2, 1980
*Scotton, W. H. (Notts.) b Jan. 15, 1856, d July 9, 1893
*Sealey, B. J. (T/T) b Aug. 12, 1899, d Sept. 12, 1963
*Sealy, J. E. D. (B'dos & T/T) b Sept. 11, 1912, d Jan. 3, 1982
Seamer, J. W. (Som. & OUCC) b June 23, 1913
*Seccull, A. W. (Kimberley, W. Prov. & Tvl) b Sept. 14, 1868, d July 20, 1945
*Sekar, T. A. P. (TN) b March 28, 1955

*Selby, J. (Notts.) b July 1, 1849, d March 11, 1894
Sellers, A. B. (Yorks.; *CY 1940*) b March 5, 1907, d Feb. 20, 1981
*Sellers, R. H. D. (S. Aust.) b Aug. 20, 1940
*Selvey, M. W. W. (CUCC, Surrey, Middx, Glam. & OFS) b April 25, 1948
*Sen, P. (Bengal) b May 31, 1926, d Jan. 27, 1970
*Sen Gupta, A. K. (Ind. Serv.) b Aug. 3, 1939
*Senanayake, C. P. (CCC) b Dec. 19, 1962
*Serjeant, C. S. (W. Aust.) b Nov. 1, 1951
Seymour, James (Kent) b Oct. 25, 1879, d Sept. 30, 1930
*Seymour, M. A. (W. Prov.) b June 5, 1936
*Shackleton, D. (Hants.; *CY 1959*) b Aug. 12, 1924
*Shafiq Ahmad (Lahore, Punjab, NBP & UBL) b March 28, 1949
*Shafqat Rana (Lahore & PIA) b Aug. 10, 1943
*Shah, A. H. (Mash.) b Aug. 7, 1959
*Shahid Israr (Kar. & Sind) b March 1, 1950
*Shahid Mahboob (Kar., Quetta, R'pindi & PACO) b Aug. 25, 1962
*Shahid Mahmoud (Kar., Pak. Us & PWD) b March 17, 1939
Shahid, N. (Essex) b April 23, 1969
*Shahid Saeed (HBFC, Lahore & PACO) b Jan. 6, 1966
*Shakeel Ahmed (B'pur, HBL & I'bad) b Nov. 12, 1971
Shakil Khan (WAPDA, HBL, R'pindi & I'bad) b May 28, 1968
*Shalders, W. A. (Griq. W. & Tvl) b Feb. 12, 1880, d March 18, 1917
*Sharma, Ajay (Delhi) b April 3, 1964
*Sharma, Chetan (Haryana & Bengal) b Jan. 3, 1966
*Sharma, Gopal (U. Pradesh) b Aug. 3, 1960
*Sharma, P. (Raja.) b Jan. 5, 1948
Sharma, R. (Derbys.) b June 27, 1962
Sharma, Sanjeev (Delhi) b Aug. 25, 1965
Sharp, G. (Northants) b March 12, 1950
Sharp, H. P. H. (Middx; Middx scorer) b Oct. 6, 1917, d Jan. 15, 1995
*Sharp, J. (Lancs.) b Feb. 15, 1878, d Jan. 28, 1938
Sharp, K. (Yorks. & Griq. W.) b April 6, 1959
*Sharpe, D. (Punjab, Pak. Rlwys, Lahore & S. Aust.) b Aug. 3, 1937
*Sharpe, J. W. (Surrey & Notts.; *CY 1892*) b Dec. 9, 1866, d June 19, 1936
*Sharpe, P. J. (Yorks. & Derbys.; *CY 1963*) b Dec. 27, 1936
*Shastri, R. J. (Bombay & Glam.) b May 27, 1962
*Shaw, Alfred (Notts. & Sussex) b Aug. 29, 1842, d Jan. 16, 1907
Shaw, C. (Yorks.) b Feb. 17, 1964
Shaw, T. G. (E. Prov.) b July 5, 1959
*Sheahan, A. P. (Vic.) b Sept. 30, 1946
Sheffield, J. R. (Essex & Wgtn) b Nov. 19, 1906
*Shepherd, B. K. (W. Aust.) b April 23, 1937
Shepherd, D. J. (Glam.; *CY 1970*) b Aug. 12, 1927
Shepherd, D. R. (Glos.; Umpire) b Dec. 27, 1940
*Shepherd, J. N. (B'dos, Kent, Rhod. & Glos.; *CY 1979*) b Nov. 9, 1943
Shepherd, T. F. (Surrey) b Dec. 5, 1889, d Feb. 13, 1957
*Sheppard, Rt Rev. D. S. (Bishop of Liverpool) (CUCC & Sussex; *CY 1953*) b March 6, 1929
*Shepstone, G. H. (Tvl) b April 8, 1876, d July 3, 1940
*Sherwell, P. W. (Tvl) b Aug. 17, 1880, d April 17, 1948
*Sherwin, M. (Notts.; *CY 1891*) b Feb. 26, 1851, d July 3, 1910
*Shillingford, G. C. (Comb. Is. & Windwards) b Sept. 25, 1944
*Shillingford, I. T. (Comb. Is. & Windwards) b April 18, 1944
*Shinde, S. G. (Baroda, M'tra & Bombay) b Aug. 18, 1923, d June 22, 1955
Shine, K. J. (Hants & Middx) b Feb. 22, 1969
Shirreff, A. C. (CUCC, Hants, Kent & Som.) b Feb. 12, 1919
*Shivnarine, S. (Guyana) b May 13, 1952
*Shoaib Mohammad (Kar. & PIA) b Jan. 8, 1961
*Shodhan, R. H. (Guj. & Baroda) b Oct. 18, 1928
*Shrewsbury, Arthur (Notts.; *CY 1890*) b April 11, 1856, d May 19, 1903
*Shrimpton, M. J. F. (C. Dist. & N. Dist.) b June 23, 1940
*Shuja-ud-Din, Col. (N. Ind., Pak. Us, Pak. Serv., B'pur & R'pindi) b April 10, 1930
*Shukla, R. C. (Bihar & Delhi) b Feb. 4, 1948
*Shuter, J. (Kent & Surrey) b Feb. 9, 1855, d July 5, 1920
*Shuttleworth, K. (Lancs. & Leics.) b Nov. 13, 1944
Siddons, J. D. (Vic. & S. Aust.) b April 25, 1964
*Sidebottom, A. (Yorks. & OFS) b April 1, 1954
*Sidhu, N. S. (Punjab) b Oct. 20, 1963
*Siedle, I. J. (Natal) b Jan. 11, 1903, d Aug. 24, 1982
*Sievers, M. W. (Vic.) b April 13, 1912, d May 10, 1968
*Sikander Bakht (PWD, PIA, Sind, Kar. & UBL) b Aug. 25, 1957

Silk, D. R. W. (CUCC & Som.; Pres. MCC 1992-1994, Chairman TCCB 1994-) b Oct. 8, 1931
*Silva, S. A. R. (NCC) b Dec. 12, 1960
Simmons, J. (Lancs. & Tas.; *CY 1985*) b March 28, 1941
*Simmons, P. V. (T/T, Border & Leics.) b April 18, 1963
Simons, E. O. (W. Prov.) b March 9, 1962
*Simpson, R. B. (NSW & W. Aust.; *CY 1965*) b Feb. 3, 1936
*Simpson, R. T. (Notts. & Sind; *CY 1950*) b Feb. 27, 1920
*Simpson-Hayward, G. H. (Worcs.) b June 7, 1875, d Oct. 2, 1936
Sims, Sir Arthur (Cant.) b July 22, 1877, d April 27, 1969
*Sims, J. M. (Middx) b May 13, 1903, d April 27, 1973
*Sinclair, B. W. (Wgtn) b Oct. 23, 1936
*Sinclair, I. McK. (Cant.) b June 1, 1933
*Sinclair, J. H. (Tvl) b Oct. 16, 1876, d Feb. 23, 1913
*Sincock, D. J. (S. Aust.) b Feb. 1, 1942
*Sinfield, R. A. (Glos.) b Dec. 24, 1900, d March 17, 1988
*Singh, Charan K. (T/T) b 1938
Singh, "Robin" [R. R.] (TN) b Sept. 14, 1963
Singh, R. P. (U. Pradesh) b Jan. 6, 1963
Singh, Swaranjit (CUCC, Warwicks., E. Punjab & Bengal) b July 18, 1931
Singleton, A. P. (OUCC, Worcs. & Rhod.) b Aug. 5, 1914
*Sivaramakrishnan, L. (TN) b Dec. 31, 1965
Skelding, A. (Leics.; Umpire) b Sept. 5, 1886, d April 17, 1960
Skinner, D. A. (Derbys.) b March 22, 1920
Skinner, L. E. (Surrey & Guyana) b Sept. 7, 1950
*Slack, W. N. (Middx & Windwards) b Dec. 12, 1954, d Jan. 15, 1989
Slade, D. N. F. (Worcs.) b Aug. 24, 1940
Slade, W. D. (Glam.) b Sept. 27, 1941
*Slater, K. N. (W. Aust.) b March 12, 1935
*Slater, M. J. (NSW) b Feb. 21, 1970
*Sleep, P. R. (S. Aust.) b May 4, 1957
*Slight, J. (Vic.) b Oct. 20, 1855, d Dec. 9, 1930
Slocombe, P. A. (Som.) b Sept. 6, 1954
*Smailes, T. F. (Yorks.) b March 27, 1910, d Dec. 1, 1970
Smales, K. (Yorks. & Notts.) b Sept. 15, 1927
*Small, G. C. (Warwicks. & S. Aust.) b Oct. 18, 1961
Small, John, sen. (Hants & All-England) b April 19, 1737, d Dec. 31, 1826
*Small, J. A. (T/T) b Nov. 3, 1892, d April 26, 1958
*Small, M. A. (B'dos) b Feb. 12, 1964
Smedley, M. J. (Notts.) b Oct. 28, 1941
*Smith, A. C. (OUCC & Warwicks.; Chief Exec. TCCB 1987-) b Oct. 25, 1936
Smith, B. F. (Leics.) b April 3, 1972
*Smith, Sir C. Aubrey (CUCC, Sussex & Tvl) b July 21, 1863, d Dec. 20, 1948
*Smith, C. I. J. (Middx; *CY 1935*) b Aug. 25, 1906, d Feb. 9, 1979
*Smith, C. J. E. (Tvl) b Dec. 25, 1872, d March 27, 1947
*Smith, C. L. (Natal, Glam. & Hants; *CY 1984*) b Oct. 15, 1958
*Smith, C. W. (B'dos) b July 29, 1933
*Smith, Denis (Derbys.; *CY 1936*) b Jan. 24, 1907, d Sept. 12, 1979
*Smith, D. B. M. (Vic.) b Sept. 14, 1884, d July 29, 1963
Smith, D. H. K. (Derbys. & OFS) b June 29, 1940
*Smith, D. M. (Surrey, Worcs. & Sussex) b Jan. 9, 1956
*Smith, D. R. (Glos.) b Oct. 5, 1934
*Smith, D. V. (Sussex) b June 14, 1923
Smith, Edwin (Derbys.) b Jan. 2, 1934
*Smith, E. J. (Warwicks.) b Feb. 6, 1886, d Aug. 31, 1979
*Smith, F. B. (Cant.) b March 13, 1922
*Smith, F. W. (Tvl) No details of birth or death known
Smith, G. (Kent) b Nov. 30, 1925
Smith, G. J. (Essex) b April 2, 1935
*Smith, Harry (Glos.) b May 21, 1890, d Nov. 12, 1937
*Smith, H. D. (Otago & Cant.) b Jan. 8, 1913, d Jan. 25, 1986
Smith, I. (Glam. & Durham) b March 11, 1967
*Smith, I. D. S. (C. Dist. & Auck.) b Feb. 28, 1957
Smith, K. D. (Warwicks.) b July 9, 1956
Smith, M. J. (Middx) b Jan. 4, 1942
*Smith, M. J. K. (OUCC, Leics. & Warwicks.; *CY 1960*) b June 30, 1933
Smith, N. (Yorks. & Essex) b April 1, 1949
Smith, N. M. K. (Warwicks.) b July 27, 1967
*Smith, O. G. (Jam.; *CY 1958*) b May 5, 1933, d Sept. 9, 1959
Smith, P. A. (Warwicks.) b April 5, 1964
Smith, Ray (Essex) b Aug. 10, 1914
Smith, Roy (Som.) b April 14, 1930
*Smith, R. A. (Natal & Hants; *CY 1990*) b Sept. 13, 1963
Smith, R. C. (Leics.) b Aug. 3, 1935
*Smith, S. B. (NSW & Tvl) b Oct. 18, 1961
Smith, S. G. (T/T, Northants & Auck.; *CY 1915*) b Jan. 15, 1881, d Oct. 25, 1963
*Smith, T. P. B. (Essex; *CY 1947*) b Oct. 30, 1908, d Aug. 4, 1967
*Smith, V. I. (Natal) b Feb. 23, 1925
Smith, W. A. (Surrey) b Sept. 15, 1937

Smith, W. C. (Surrey; *CY 1911*) b Oct. 4, 1877, d July 16, 1946
*Smithson, G. A. (Yorks. & Leics.) b Nov. 1, 1926, d Sept. 6, 1970
*Snedden, C. A. (Auck.) b Jan. 7, 1918, d May 19, 1993
*Snedden, M. C. (Auck.) b Nov. 23, 1958
*Snell, R. P. (Tvl & Som.) b Sept. 12, 1968
Snellgrove, K. L. (Lancs.) b Nov. 12, 1941
*Snooke, S. D. (W. Prov. & Tvl) b Nov. 11, 1878, d April 4, 1959
*Snooke, S. J. (Border, W. Prov. & Tvl) b Feb. 1, 1881, d Aug. 14, 1966
*Snow, J. A. (Sussex; *CY 1973*) b Oct. 13, 1941
Snowden, W. (CUCC) b Sept. 27, 1952
*Sobers, Sir G. S. (B'dos, S. Aust. & Notts.; *CY 1964*) b July 28, 1936
Sohail Fazal (Lahore & HBL) b Nov. 11, 1967
*Sohoni, S. W. (M'tra, Baroda & Bombay) b March 5, 1918, d May 19, 1993
Solanky, J. W. (E. Africa & Glam.) b June 30, 1942
*Solkar, E. D. (Bombay & Sussex) b March 18, 1948
*Solomon, J. S. (BG) b Aug. 26, 1930
*Solomon, W. R. T. (Tvl & E. Prov.) b April 23, 1872, d July 12, 1964
*Sood, M. M. (Delhi) b July 6, 1939
Southern, J. W. (Hants) b Sept. 2, 1952
*Southerton, James (Surrey, Hants & Sussex) b Nov. 16, 1827, d June 16, 1880
Southerton, S. J. (Editor of *Wisden* 1934-35) b July 7, 1874, d March 12, 1935
*Sparling, J. T. (Auck.) b July 24, 1938
Speak, N. J. (Lancs.) b Nov. 21, 1966
Speight, M. P. (Sussex & Wgtn) b Oct. 24, 1967
Spencer, C. T. (Leics.) b Aug. 18, 1931
Spencer, J. (CUCC & Sussex) b Oct. 6, 1949
Spencer, T. W. (Kent) b March 22, 1914
Sperry, J. (Leics.) b March 19, 1910
*Spofforth, F. R. (NSW & Vic.) b Sept. 9, 1853, d June 4, 1926
*Spooner, R. H. (Lancs.; *CY 1905*) b Oct. 21, 1880, d Oct. 2, 1961
*Spooner, R. T. (Warwicks.) b Dec. 30, 1919
Springall, J. D. (Notts.) b Sept. 19, 1932
*Srikkanth, K. (TN) b Dec. 21, 1959
*Srinath, J. (Karn.) b Aug. 31, 1969
*Srinivasan, T. E. (TN) b Oct. 26, 1950
*Stackpole, K. R. (Vic.; *CY 1973*) b July 10, 1940
Standen, J. A. (Worcs.) b May 30, 1935
Standing, D. K. (Sussex) b Oct. 21, 1963
Stansfield-Smith, Sir Colin (CUCC & Lancs.) b Oct. 1, 1932
Stanworth, J. (Lancs.) b Sept. 30, 1960
*Stanyforth, Lt-Col. R. T. (Yorks.) b May 30, 1892, d Feb. 20, 1964
*Staples, S. J. (Notts.; *CY 1929*) b Sept. 18, 1892, d June 4, 1950
Starkie, S. (Northants) b April 4, 1926
*Statham, J. B. (Lancs.; *CY 1955*) b June 17, 1930
*Stayers, S. C. (†Guyana & Bombay) b June 9, 1937
*Steel, A. G. (CUCC & Lancs.; Pres. MCC 1902) b Sept. 24, 1858, d June 15, 1914
*Steele, D. S. (Northants & Derbys.; *CY 1976*) b Sept. 29, 1941
Steele, J. F. (Leics., Natal & Glam.) b July 23, 1946
Stemp, R. D. (Worcs. & Yorks.) b Dec. 11, 1967
Stephens, E. J. (Glos.) b March 23, 1909, d April 3, 1983
Stephenson, F. D. (B'dos, Glos., Tas., Notts., Sussex & OFS; *CY 1989*) b April 8, 1959
Stephenson, G. R. (Derbys. & Hants) b Nov. 19, 1942
Stephenson, H. H. (Surrey & All-England) b May 3, 1832, d Dec. 17, 1896
Stephenson, H. W. (Som.) b July 18, 1920
*Stephenson, J. P. (Essex & Boland) b March 14, 1965
Stephenson, Lt-Col. J. R. (Sec. MCC 1987-93) b Feb. 25, 1931
Stevens, Edward ("Lumpy") (Hants) b *circa* 1735, d Sept. 7, 1819
*Stevens, G. B. (S. Aust.) b Feb. 29, 1932
*Stevens, G. T. S. (UCS, OUCC & Middx; *CY 1918*) b Jan. 7, 1901, d Sept. 19, 1970
*Stevenson, G. B. (Yorks. & Northants) b Dec. 16, 1955
Stevenson, K. (Derbys. & Hants) b Oct. 6, 1950
Stevenson, M. H. (CUCC & Derbys.) b June 13, 1927, d Sept. 19, 1994
*Stewart, A. J. (Surrey; *CY 1993*) b April 8, 1963
Stewart, E. L. R. (Natal) b July 30, 1969
*Stewart, M. J. (Surrey; *CY 1958*) b Sept. 16, 1932
*Stewart, R. B. (SA) b Sept. 3, 1856, d Sept. 12, 1913
Stewart, R. W. (Glos. & Middx) b Feb. 28, 1945
Stewart, W. J. (Warwicks. & Northants) b Oct. 31, 1934
*Stirling, D. A. (C. Dist.) b Oct. 5, 1961
Stocks, F. W. (Notts.) b Nov. 6, 1917
*Stoddart, A. E. (Middx; *CY 1893*) b March 11, 1863, d April 3, 1915
*Stollmeyer, J. B. (T/T) b April 11, 1921, d Sept. 10, 1989
*Stollmeyer, V. H. (T/T) b Jan. 24, 1916
*Storer, W. (Derbys.; *CY 1899*) b Jan. 25, 1867, d Feb. 28, 1912
Storey, S. J. (Surrey & Sussex) b Jan. 6, 1941
Storie, A. C. (Northants, Warwicks., OFS, OUCC & Scotland) b July 25, 1965

Stott, L. W. (Auck.) b Dec. 8, 1946
Stott, W. B. (Yorks.) b July 18, 1934
Stovold, A. W. (Glos. & OFS) b March 19, 1953
*Streak, H. H. (Mat.) b March 16, 1974
*Street, G. B. (Sussex) b Dec. 6, 1889, d April 24, 1924
*Stricker, L. A. (Tvl) b May 26, 1884, d Feb. 5, 1960
Stringer, P. M. (Yorks. & Leics.) b Feb. 23, 1943
*Strudwick, H. (Surrey; *CY 1912*) b Jan. 28, 1880, d Feb. 14, 1970
*Studd, C. T. (CUCC & Middx) b Dec. 2, 1860, d July 16, 1931
*Studd, G. B. (CUCC & Middx) b Oct. 20, 1859, d Feb. 13, 1945
Studd, Sir Peter M. (CUCC) b Sept. 15, 1916
Sturt, M. O. C. (Middx) b Sept. 12, 1940
*Su'a, M. L. (N. Dist. & Auck.) b Nov. 7, 1966
*Subba Row, R. (CUCC, Surrey & Northants; *CY 1961*) b Jan. 29, 1932
*Subramanya, V. (Mysore) b July 16, 1936
*Such, P. M. (Notts., Leics. & Essex) b June 12, 1964
Sudhakar Rao, R. (Karn.) b Aug. 8, 1952
Sueter, T. (Hants & Surrey) b *circa* 1749, d Feb. 17, 1827
*Sugg, F. H. (Yorks., Derbys. & Lancs.; *CY 1890*) b Jan. 11, 1862, d May 29, 1933
Sullivan, J. (Lancs.) b Feb. 5, 1945
Sully, H. (Som. & Northants) b Nov. 1, 1939
*Sunderram, G. R. (Bombay & Raja.) b March 29, 1930
Sunnucks, P. R. (Kent) b June 22, 1916
*Surendranath, R. (Ind. Serv.) b Jan. 4, 1937
Surridge, W. S. (Surrey; *CY 1953*) b Sept. 3, 1917, d April 13, 1992
*Surti, R. F. (Guj., Raja. & Qld) b May 25, 1936
*Susskind, M. J. (CUCC, Middx & Tvl) b June 8, 1891, d July 9, 1957
*Sutcliffe, B. (Auck., Otago & N. Dist.; *CY 1950*) b Nov. 17, 1923
*Sutcliffe, H. (Yorks.; *CY 1920*) b Nov. 24, 1894, d Jan. 22, 1978
Sutcliffe, S. P. (OUCC & Warwicks.) b May 22, 1960
Sutcliffe, W. H. H. (Yorks.) b Oct. 10, 1926
Suttle, K. G. (Sussex) b Aug. 25, 1928
Swallow, I. G. (Yorks. & Som.) b Dec. 18, 1962
*Swamy, V. N. (Ind. Serv.) b May 23, 1924, d May 1, 1983
Swanton, E. W. (Middx; Writer) b Feb. 11, 1907
Swarbrook, F. W. (Derbys., Griq. W. & OFS) b Dec. 17, 1950
Swart, P. D. (Rhod., W. Prov., Glam. & Boland) b April 27, 1946
*Swetman, R. (Surrey, Notts & Glos.) b Oct. 25, 1933
Sydenham, D. A. D. (Surrey) b April 6, 1934
*Symcox, P. L. (Natal) b April 14, 1960
Symington, S. J. (Leics.) b Sept. 16, 1926

*Taber, H. B. (NSW) b April 29, 1940
*Taberer, H. M. (OUCC & Natal) b Oct. 7, 1870, d June 5, 1932
*Tahir Naqqash (Servis Ind., MCB, Punjab & Lahore) b July 6, 1959
Tait, A. (Northants & Glos.) b Dec. 27, 1953
*Talat Ali (Lahore, PIA & UBL) b May 29, 1950
*Tallon, D. (Qld; *CY 1949*) b Feb. 17, 1916, d Sept. 7, 1984
*Tamhane, N. S. (Bombay) b Aug. 4, 1931
*Tancred, A. B. (Kimberley, Griq. W. & Tvl) b Aug. 20, 1865, d Nov. 23, 1911
*Tancred, L. J. (Tvl) b Oct. 7, 1876, d July 28, 1934
*Tancred, V. M. (Tvl) b July 7, 1875, d June 3, 1904
Tanvir Mehdi (Lahore & UBL) b Nov. 7, 1972
*Tapscott, G. L. (Griq. W.) b Nov. 7, 1889, d Dec. 13, 1940
*Tapscott, L. E. (Griq. W.) b March 18, 1894, d July 7, 1934
*Tarapore, K. K. (Bombay) b Dec. 17, 1910, d June 15, 1986
Tarrant, F. A. (Vic., Middx & Patiala; *CY 1908*) b Dec. 11, 1880, d Jan. 29, 1951
Tarrant, George F. (Cambs. & All-England) b Dec. 7, 1838, d July 2, 1870
*Taslim Arif (Kar., Sind & NBP) b May 1, 1954
*Tate, F. W. (Sussex) b July 24, 1867, d Feb. 24, 1943
*Tate, M. W. (Sussex; *CY 1924*) b May 30, 1895, d May 18, 1956
*Tattersall, R. (Lancs.) b Aug. 17, 1922
*Tauseef Ahmed (PWD, UBL & Kar.) b May 10, 1958
*Tavaré, C. J. (OUCC, Kent & Som.) b Oct. 27, 1954
*Tayfield, H. J. (Natal, Rhod. & Tvl; *CY 1956*) b Jan. 30, 1929, d Feb. 25, 1994
*Taylor, A. I. (Tvl) b July 25, 1994
Taylor, B. (Essex; *CY 1972*) b June 19, 1932
*Taylor, B. R. (Cant. & Wgtn) b July 12, 1943
*Taylor, Daniel (Natal) b Jan. 9, 1887, d Jan. 24, 1957
*Taylor, D. D. (Auck. & Warwicks.) b March 2, 1923, d Dec. 5, 1980
Taylor, D. J. S. (Surrey, Som. & Griq. W.) b Nov. 12, 1942

Taylor, G. R. (Hants) b Nov. 25, 1909, d Oct. 31, 1986
*Taylor, H. W. (Natal, Tvl & W. Prov.; *CY 1925*) b May 5, 1889, d Feb. 8, 1973
*Taylor, J. M. (NSW) b Oct. 10, 1895, d May 12, 1971
*Taylor, J. O. (T/T) b Jan. 3, 1932
*Taylor, J. P. (Derbys. & Northants) b Aug. 8, 1964
*Taylor, K. (Yorks. & Auck.) b Aug. 21, 1935
Taylor, K. A. (Warwicks.) b Sept. 29, 1916
*Taylor, L. B. (Leics. & Natal) b Oct. 25, 1953
*Taylor, M. A. (NSW; *CY 1990*) b Oct 27, 1964
Taylor, M. N. S. (Notts. & Hants) b Nov. 12, 1942
Taylor, N. R. (Kent) b July 21, 1959
*Taylor, P. L. (NSW & Qld) b Aug. 22, 1956
*Taylor, R. W. (Derbys.; *CY 1977*) b July 17, 1941
Taylor, T. L. (CUCC & Yorks.; *CY 1901*) b May 25, 1878, d March 16, 1960
Taylor, W. (Notts.) b Jan. 24, 1947
Tedstone, G. A. (Warwicks. & Glos.) b Jan. 19, 1961
*Tendulkar, S. R. (Bombay & Yorks.) b April 24, 1973
Tennekoon, A. P. B. (SL) b Oct. 29, 1946
*Tennyson, 3rd Lord (Hon. L. H.) (Hants; *CY 1914*) b Nov. 7, 1889, d June 6, 1951
*Terry, V. P. (Hants) b Jan. 14, 1959
*Theunissen, N. H. (W. Prov.) b May 4, 1867, d Nov. 9, 1929
Thomas, D. J. (Surrey, N. Tvl & Glos.) b June 30, 1959
*Thomas, G. (NSW) b March 21, 1938
*Thomas, J. G. (Glam., Border, E. Prov. & Northants) b Aug. 12, 1960
Thompson, A. W. (Middx) b April 17, 1916
*Thompson, G. J. (Northants; *CY 1906*) b Oct. 27, 1877, d March 3, 1943
Thompson, J. R. (CUCC & Warwicks.) b May 10, 1918
Thompson, R. G. (Warwicks.) b Sept. 26, 1932
*Thoms, G. R. (Vic.) b March 22, 1927
*Thomson, A. L. (Vic.) b Dec. 2, 1945
*Thomson, J. R. (NSW, Qld & Middx) b Aug. 16, 1950
*Thomson, K. (Cant.) b Feb. 26, 1941
*Thomson, N. F. D. (NSW) b May 29, 1839, d Sept. 2, 1896
*Thomson, N. I. (Sussex) b Jan. 23, 1929
*Thomson, S. A. (N. Dist.) b Jan. 27, 1969
Thorne, D. A. (Warwicks & OUCC) b Dec. 12, 1964
Thornton, C. I. (CUCC, Kent & Middx) b March 20, 1850, d Dec. 10, 1929
*Thornton, P. G. (Yorks., Middx & SA) b Dec. 24, 1867, d Jan. 31, 1939
*Thorpe, G. P. (Surrey) b Aug. 1, 1969
*Thurlow, H. M. (Qld) b Jan. 10, 1903, d Dec. 3, 1975
*Tillekeratne, H. P. (NCC) b July 14, 1967
Tilly, H. W. (Middx) b May 25, 1932
Timms, B. S. V. (Hants & Warwicks.) b Dec. 17, 1940
Timms, J. E. (Northants) b Nov. 3, 1906, d May 18, 1980
Timms, W. W. (Northants) b Sept. 28, 1902, d Sept. 30, 1986
Tindall, M. (CUCC & Middx) b March 31, 1914, d July 10, 1994
Tindall, R. A. E. (Surrey) b Sept. 23, 1935
*Tindill, E. W. T. (Wgtn) b Dec. 18, 1910
Tissera, M. H. (SL) b March 23, 1939
*Titmus, F. J. (Middx, Surrey & OFS; *CY 1963*) b Nov. 24, 1932
Todd, L. J. (Kent) b June 19, 1907, d Aug. 20, 1967
Todd, P. A. (Notts. & Glam.) b March 12, 1953
Tolchard, J. G. (Leics.) b March 17, 1944
*Tolchard, R. W. (Leics.) b June 15, 1946
Tolley, C. M. (Worcs.) b Dec. 30, 1967
Tomlins, K. P. (Middx & Glos.) b Oct. 23, 1957
*Tomlinson, D. S. (Rhod. & Border) b Sept. 4, 1910, d July 11, 1993
Tompkin, M. (Leics.) b Feb. 17, 1919, d Sept. 27, 1956
Toogood, G. J. (OUCC) b Nov. 19, 1961
*Toohey, P. M. (NSW) b April 20, 1954
Tooley, C. D. M. (OUCC) b April 19, 1964
Topley, T. D. (Surrey, Essex & Griq. W.) b Feb. 25, 1964
Tordoff, G. G. (CUCC & Som.) b Dec. 6, 1929
*Toshack, E. R. H. (NSW) b Dec. 15, 1914
Townsend, A. (Warwicks.) b Aug. 26, 1921
Townsend, A. F. (Derbys.) b March 29, 1912, d Feb. 25, 1994
*Townsend, C. L. (Glos.; *CY 1899*) b Nov. 7, 1876, d Oct. 17, 1958
*Townsend, D. C. H. (OUCC) b April 20, 1912
*Townsend, L. F. (Derbys. & Auck.; *CY 1934*) b June 8, 1903, d Feb. 17, 1993
**Traicos, A. J. (Rhod. & Mash.) b May 17, 1947
*Travers, J. P. F. (S. Aust.) b Jan. 10, 1871, d Sept. 15, 1942
*Tremlett, M. F. (Som. & C. Dist.) b July 5, 1923, d July 30, 1984
Tremlett, T. M. (Hants) b July 26, 1956
*Tribe, G. E. (Vic. & Northants; *CY 1955*) b Oct. 4, 1920
*Trim, J. (BG) b Jan. 24, 1915, d Nov. 12, 1960
Trimble, G. S. (Qld) b Jan. 1, 1963
*Trimborn, P. H. J. (Natal) b May 18, 1940

**Trott, A. E. (Vic., Middx & Hawkes Bay; *CY 1899*) b Feb. 6, 1873, d July 30, 1914
*Trott, G. H. S. (Vic.; *CY 1894*) b Aug. 5, 1866, d Nov. 10, 1917
*Troup, G. B. (Auck.) b Oct. 3, 1952
*Trueman, F. S. (Yorks.; *CY 1953*) b Feb. 6, 1931
*Trumble, H. (Vic.; *CY 1897*) b May 12, 1867, d Aug. 14, 1938
*Trumble, J. W. (Vic.) b Sept. 16, 1863, d Aug. 17, 1944
Trump, H. R. J. (Som.) b Oct. 11, 1968
*Trumper, V. T. (NSW; *CY 1903*) b Nov. 2, 1877, d June 28, 1915
*Truscott, P. B. (Wgtn) b Aug. 14, 1941
*Tuckett, L. (OFS) b Feb. 6, 1919
*Tuckett, L. R. (Natal & OFS) b April 19, 1885, d April 8, 1963
*Tufnell, N. C. (CUCC & Surrey) b June 13, 1887, d Aug. 3, 1951
*Tufnell, P. C. R. (Middx) b April 29, 1966
Tuke, Sir Anthony (Pres. MCC 1982-83) b Aug. 22, 1920
Tunnicliffe, C. J. (Derbys.) b Aug. 11, 1951
Tunnicliffe, H. T. (Notts.) b March 4, 1950
Tunnicliffe, J. (Yorks.; *CY 1901*) b Aug. 26, 1866, d July 11, 1948
*Turnbull, M. J. (CUCC & Glam.; *CY 1931*) b March 16, 1906, d Aug. 5, 1944
*Turner, A. (NSW) b July 23, 1950
*Turner, C. T. B. (NSW; *CY 1889*) b Nov. 16, 1862, d Jan. 1, 1944
Turner, D. R. (Hants & W. Prov.) b Feb. 5, 1949
Turner, F. M. (Leics.) b Aug. 8, 1934
Turner, G. J. (W. Prov., N. Tvl & OUCC) b Aug. 5, 1964
*Turner, G. M. (Otago, N. Dist. & Worcs.; *CY 1971*) b May 26, 1947
Turner, R. J. (CUCC & Som.) b Nov. 25, 1967
Turner, S. (Essex & Natal) b July 18, 1943
*Twentyman-Jones, P. S. (W. Prov.) b Sept. 13, 1876, d March 8, 1954
Twining, R. H. (OUCC & Middx; Pres. MCC 1964-65) b Nov. 3, 1889, d Jan. 3, 1979
Twose, R. G. (Warwicks., N. Dist. & C. Dist.) b April 17, 1968
*Tyldesley, E. (Lancs.; *CY 1920*) b Feb. 5, 1889, d May 5, 1962
*Tyldesley, J. T. (Lancs.; *CY 1902*) b Nov. 22, 1873, d Nov. 27, 1930
*Tyldesley, R. K. (Lancs.; *CY 1925*) b March 11, 1897, d Sept. 17, 1943
*Tylecote, E. F. S. (OUCC & Kent) b June 23, 1849, d March 15, 1938
*Tyler, E. J. (Som.) b Oct. 13, 1864, d Jan. 25, 1917
*Tyson, F. H. (Northants; *CY 1956*) b June 6, 1930

Udal, S. D. (Hants) b March 18, 1969
Ufton, D. G. (Kent) b May 31, 1928
*Ulyett, G. (Yorks.) b Oct. 21, 1851, d June 18, 1898
*Umrigar, P. R. (Bombay & Guj.) b March 28, 1926
*Underwood, D. L. (Kent; *CY 1969*) b June 8, 1945
Unwin, F. St G. (Essex) b April 23, 1911, d Oct. 4, 1990

*Vaas, W. P. U. J. C. (Colts) b Jan. 27, 1975
*Valentine, A. L. (Jam.; *CY 1951*) b April 29, 1930
*Valentine, B. H. (CUCC & Kent) b Jan. 17, 1908, d Feb. 2, 1983
*Valentine, V. A. (Jam.) b April 4, 1908, d July 6, 1972
*Vance, R. H. (Wgtn) b March 31, 1955
*van der Bijl, P. G. (W. Prov. & OUCC) b Oct. 21, 1907, d Feb. 16, 1973
van der Bijl, V. A. P. (Natal, Middx & Tvl; *CY 1981*) b March 19, 1948
Van der Gucht, P. I. (Glos. & Bengal) b Nov. 2, 1911, d Dec. 15, 1993
*Van der Merwe, E. A. (Tvl) b Nov. 9, 1904, d Feb. 26, 1971
*Van der Merwe, P. L. (W. Prov. & E. Prov.) b March 14, 1937
van Geloven, J. (Yorks. & Leics.) b Jan. 4, 1934
*Van Ryneveld, C. B. (W. Prov. & OUCC) b March 19, 1928
van Zyl, C. J. P. G. (OFS & Glam.) b Oct. 1, 1961
Varachia, R. (First Pres. SA Cricket Union) b Oct. 12, 1915, d Dec. 11, 1981
Varey, D. W. (CUCC & Lancs.) b Oct. 15, 1961
*Varnals, G. D. (E. Prov., Tvl & Natal) b July 24, 1935
Vaughan, M. P. (Yorks.) b Oct. 29, 1974
*Vaughan, J. T. C. (Auck.) b Aug. 30, 1967
Vaulkhard, P. (Notts. & Derbys.) b Sept. 15, 1911
*Veivers, T. R. (Qld) b April 6, 1937
*Veletta, M. R. J. (W. Aust.) b Oct. 30, 1963
*Vengsarkar, D. B. (Bombay; *CY 1987*) b April 6, 1956
*Venkataraghavan, S. (†TN & Derbys.) b April 21, 1946
*Venkataramana, M. (TN) b April 24, 1966
*Verity, H. (Yorks.; *CY 1932*) b May 18, 1905, d July 31, 1943
*Vernon, G. F. (Middx) b June 20, 1856, d Aug. 10, 1902
Vigar, F. H. (Essex) b July 7, 1917
*Viljoen, K. G. (Griq. W., OFS & Tvl) b May 14, 1910, d Jan. 21, 1974
*Vincent, C. L. (Tvl) b Feb. 16, 1902, d Aug. 24, 1968

*Vine, J. (Sussex; *CY 1906*) b May 15, 1875, d April 25, 1946
*Vintcent, C. H. (Tvl & Griq. W.) b Sept. 2, 1866, d Sept. 28, 1943
Virgin, R. T. (Som., Northants & W. Prov.; *CY 1971*) b Aug. 26, 1939
*Viswanath, G. R. (†Karn.) b Feb. 12, 1949
*Viswanath, S. (Karn.) b Nov. 29, 1962
*Vivian, G. E. (Auck.) b Feb. 28, 1946
*Vivian, H. G. (Auck.) b Nov. 4, 1912, d Aug. 12, 1983
*Vizianagram, Maharaj Kumar of, Sir Vijay A. (U. Prov.) b Dec. 28, 1905, d Dec. 2, 1965
*Voce, W. (Notts.; *CY 1933*) b Aug. 8, 1909, d June 6, 1984
*Vogler, A. E. E. (Middx, Natal, Tvl & E. Prov.; *CY 1908*) b Nov. 28, 1876, d Aug. 9, 1946
Vonhagt, D. M. (Moors) b March 31, 1965

*Waddington, A. (Yorks.) b Feb. 4, 1893, d Oct. 28, 1959
Waddington, J. E. (Griq. W.) b Dec. 30, 1918, d Nov. 24, 1985
*Wade, H. F. (Natal) b Sept. 14, 1905, d Nov. 22, 1980
Wade, T. H. (Essex) b Nov. 24, 1910, d July 25, 1987
*Wade, W. W. (Natal) b June 18, 1914
*Wadekar, A. L. (Bombay) b April 1, 1941
*Wadsworth, K. J. (C. Dist. & Cant.) b Nov. 30, 1946, d Aug. 19, 1976
*Wainwright, E. (Yorks.; *CY 1894*) b April 8, 1865, d Oct. 28, 1919
*Waite, J. H. B. (E. Prov. & Tvl) b Jan. 19, 1930
*Waite, M. G. (S. Aust.) b Jan. 7, 1911, d Dec. 16, 1985
*Walcott, Sir C. L. (B'dos & BG; *CY 1958*) b Jan. 17, 1926
*Walcott, L. A. (B'dos) b Jan. 18, 1894, d Feb. 27, 1984
Walden, F. I. (Northants; Umpire) b March 1, 1888, d May 3, 1949
Walford, M. M. (OUCC & Som.) b Nov. 27, 1915
Walker, A. (Northants & Durham) b July 7, 1962
Walker, A. K. (NSW & Notts.) b Oct. 4, 1925
Walker, C. (Yorks. & Hants) b June 27, 1919, d Dec. 3, 1992
Walker, I. D. (Middx) b Jan. 8, 1844, d July 6, 1898
*Walker, M. H. N. (Vic.) b Sept. 12, 1948
*Walker, P. M. (Glam., Tvl & W. Prov.) b Feb. 17, 1936
Walker, V. E. (Middx) b April 20, 1837, d Jan. 3, 1906
Walker, W. (Notts.) b Nov. 24, 1892, d Dec. 3, 1991
*Wall, T. W. (S. Aust.) b May 13, 1904, d March 25, 1981
Wallace, P. A. (B'dos) b Aug. 2, 1970
*Wallace, W. M. (Auck.) b Dec. 19, 1916
Waller, A. C. (MCD) b Sept. 25, 1959
Waller, C. E. (Surrey & Sussex) b Oct. 3, 1948
*Walsh, C. A. (Jam. & Glos.; *CY 1987*) b Oct. 30, 1962
Walsh, J. E. (NSW & Leics.) b Dec. 4, 1912, d May 20, 1980
*Walter, K. A. (Tvl) b Nov. 5, 1939
*Walters, C. F. (Glam. & Worcs.; *CY 1934*) b Aug. 28, 1905, d Dec. 23, 1992
*Walters, F. H. (Vic. & NSW) b Feb. 9, 1860, d June 1, 1922
Walters, J. (Derbys.) b Aug. 7, 1949
*Walters, K. D. (NSW) b Dec. 21, 1945
Walton, A. C. (OUCC & Middx) b Sept. 26, 1933
*Waqar Hassan (Pak. Us, Punjab, Pak. Serv. & Kar.) b Sept. 12, 1932
*Waqar Younis (Multan, UBL & Surrey; *CY 1992*) b Nov. 16, 1971
*Ward, Alan (Derbys., Leics. & Border) b Aug. 10, 1947
*Ward, Albert (Yorks. & Lancs.; *CY 1890*) b Nov. 21, 1865, d Jan. 6, 1939
Ward, B. (Essex) b Feb. 28, 1944
Ward, D. (Glam.) b Aug. 30, 1934
Ward, D. M. (Surrey) b Feb. 10, 1961
*Ward, F. A. (S. Aust.) b Feb. 23, 1906, d March 25, 1974
*Ward, J. T. (Cant.) b March 11, 1937
*Ward, T. A. (Tvl) b Aug. 2, 1887, d Feb. 16, 1936
Ward, T. R. (Kent) b Jan. 18, 1968
Ward, William (MCC & Hants) b July 24, 1787, d June 30, 1849
*Wardle, J. H. (Yorks.; *CY 1954*) b Jan. 8, 1923, d July 23, 1985
*Warnapura, B. (SL) b March 1, 1953
*Warnaweera, K. P. J. (Galle) b Nov. 23, 1960
Warne, F. B. (Worcs., Vic. & Tvl) b Oct. 3, 1906, d May 29, 1994
*Warne, S. K. (Vic.; *CY 1994*) b Sept. 13, 1969
Warner, A. E. (Worcs. & Derbys.) b May 12, 1959
*Warner, Sir P. F. (OUCC & Middx; *CY 1904, special portrait 1921*; Pres. MCC 1950-51) b Oct. 2, 1873, d Jan. 30, 1963
*Warr, J. J. (CUCC & Middx; Pres. MCC 1987-88) b July 16, 1927
*Warren, A. R. (Derbys.) b April 2, 1875, d Sept. 3, 1951
*Washbrook, C. (Lancs.; *CY 1947*) b Dec. 6, 1914
*Wasim Akram (Lahore, PACO, PNSC, PIA & Lancs.; *CY 1993*) b June 3, 1966

*Wasim Bari (Kar., PIA & Sind) b March 23, 1948
Wasim Haider (Faisalabad & PIA) b June 6, 1967
*Wasim Raja (Lahore, Sargodha, Pak. Us, PIA, Punjab & NBP) b July 3, 1952
Wass, T. G. (Notts.; *CY 1908*) b Dec. 26, 1873, d Oct. 27, 1953
*Wassan, A. S. (Delhi) b March 23, 1968
Wassell, A. (Hants) b April 15, 1940
*Watkin, S. L. (Glam.; *CY 1994*) b Sept. 15, 1964
*Watkins, A. J. (Glam.) b April 21, 1922
*Watkins, J. C. (Natal) b April 10, 1923
*Watkins, J. R. (NSW) b April 16, 1943
Watkinson, M. (Lancs.) b Aug. 1, 1961
*Watson, C. (Jam. & Delhi) b July 1, 1938
Watson, F. B. (Lancs.) b Sept. 17, 1898, d Feb. 1, 1976
*Watson, G. D. (Vic., W. Aust. & NSW) b March 8, 1945
Watson, G. G. (NSW, W. Aust. & Worcs.) b Jan. 29, 1955
*Watson, W. (Yorks. & Leics.; *CY 1954*) b March 7, 1920
*Watson, W. (Auck.) b Aug. 31, 1965
*Watson, W. J. (NSW) b Jan. 31, 1931
Watson, W. K. (Border, N. Tvl, E. Prov. & Notts.) b May 21, 1955
*Watt, L. (Otago) b Sept. 17, 1924
Watts, H. E. (CUCC & Som.) b March 4, 1922, d Dec. 27, 1993
Watts, P. D. (Northants & Notts.) b March 31, 1938
Watts, P. J. (Northants) b June 16, 1940
*Waugh, M. E. (NSW & Essex; *CY 1991*) b June 2, 1965
*Waugh, S. R. (NSW & Som.; *CY 1989*) b June 2, 1965
*Wazir Ali, S. (C. Ind., S. Punjab & Patiala) b Sept. 15, 1903, d June 17, 1950
*Wazir Mohammad (B'pur & Kar.) b Dec. 22, 1929
*Webb, M. G. (Otago & Cant.) b June 22, 1947
*Webb, P. N. (Auck.) b July 14, 1957
Webb, R. J. (Otago) b Sept. 15, 1952
Webb, R. T. (Sussex) b July 11, 1922
*Webbe, A. J. (OUCC & Middx) b Jan. 16, 1855, d Feb. 19, 1941
Webster, J. (CUCC & Northants) b Oct. 28, 1917
Webster, Dr R. V. (Warwicks. & Otago) b June 10, 1939
Webster, W. H. (CUCC & Middx; Pres. MCC 1976-77) b Feb. 22, 1910, d June 19, 1986
*Weekes, E. D. (B'dos; *CY 1951*) b Feb. 26, 1925
*Weekes, K. H. (Jam.) b Jan. 24, 1912
Weekes, P. N. (Middx) b July 8, 1969
Weeks, R. T. (Warwicks.) b April 30, 1930
Weerakkody, A. P. (NCC), b Oct. 1, 1970
*Weerasinghe, C. D. U. S. (TU) b March 1, 1968
*Weir, G. L. (Auck.) b June 2, 1908
*Wellard, A. W. (Som.; *CY 1936*) b April 8, 1902, d Dec. 31, 1980
*Wellham, D. M. (NSW, Tas. & Qld) b March 13, 1959
Wellings, E. M. (OUCC & Surrey) b April 6, 1909, d Sept. 10, 1992
Wells, A. P. (Sussex & Border) b Oct. 2, 1961
Wells, B. D. (Glos. & Notts.) b July 27, 1930
Wells, C. M. (Sussex, Border, W. Prov. & Derbys.) b March 3, 1960
Wells, V. J. (Kent & Leics.) b Aug. 6, 1965
Wenman, E. G. (Kent & England) b Aug. 18, 1803, d Dec. 31, 1879
Wensley, A. F. (Sussex) b May 23, 1898, d June 17, 1970
*Wesley, C. (Natal) b Sept. 5, 1937
**Wessels, K. C. (OFS, W. Prov., N. Tvl, Sussex, Qld & E. Prov.; *CY 1995*) b Sept. 14, 1957
West, G. H. (Editor of *Wisden* 1880-86) b 1851, d Oct. 6, 1896
*Westcott, R. J. (W. Prov.) b Sept. 19, 1927
Weston, M. J. (Worcs.) b April 8, 1959
Weston, W. P. C. (Worcs.) b June 16, 1973
*Wettimuny, M. D. (SL) b June 11, 1951
*Wettimuny, S. (SL; *CY 1985*) b Aug. 12, 1956
Wettimuny, S. R. de S. (SL) b Feb. 7, 1949
*Wharton, A. (Lancs. & Leics.) b April 30, 1923, d Aug. 26, 1993
*Whatmore, D. F. (Vic.) b March 16, 1954
Wheatley, K. J. (Hants) b Jan. 20, 1946
Wheatley, O. S. (CUCC, Warwicks. & Glam.; *CY 1969*) b May 28, 1935
Whitaker, Haddon (Editor of *Wisden* 1940-43) b Aug. 30, 1908, d Jan. 5, 1982
*Whitaker, J. J. (Leics.; *CY 1987*) b May 5, 1962
Whitcombe, P. A. (OUCC & Middx) b April 23, 1923
White, A. F. T. (CUCC, Warwicks. & Worcs.) b Sept. 5, 1915, d March 16, 1993
*White, C. (Vic. & Yorks.) b Dec. 16, 1969
*White, D. J. (N. Dist.) b June 26, 1961
*White, D. W. (Hants & Glam.) b Dec. 14, 1935
White, E. C. S. (NSW) b July 14, 1913
*White, G. C. (Tvl) b Feb. 5, 1882, d Oct. 17, 1918
*White, J. C. (Som.; *CY 1929*) b Feb. 19, 1891, d May 2, 1961
White, Hon. L. R. (5th Lord Annaly) (Middx & Victory Test) b March 15, 1927, d Sept. 30, 1990

White, R. A. (Middx & Notts.; Umpire) b Oct. 6, 1936
White, R. C. (CUCC, Glos. & Tvl) b Jan. 29, 1941
*White, W. A. (B'dos) b Nov. 20, 1938
Whitehead, J. P. (Yorks. & Worcs.) b Sept. 3, 1925
Whitehouse, J. (Warwicks.) b April 8, 1949
*Whitelaw, P. E. (Auck.) b Feb. 10, 1910, d Aug. 28, 1988
Whitfield, B. J. (Natal) b March 14, 1959
Whitfield, E. W. (Surrey & Northants) b May 31, 1911
Whiting, N. H. (Worcs.) b Oct. 2, 1920
Whitington, R. S. (S. Aust. & Victory Tests; Writer) b June 30, 1912, d March 13, 1984
*Whitney, M. R. (NSW & Glos.) b Feb. 24, 1959
Whittaker, G. J. (Surrey) b May 29, 1916
Whittall, A. R. (CUCC) b March 28, 1973
*Whittall, G. J. (Mat.) b Sept. 5, 1972
Whitticase, P. (Leics.) b March 15, 1965
Whittingham, N. B. (Notts.) b Oct. 22, 1940
*Whitty, W. J. (S. Aust.) b Aug. 15, 1886, d Jan. 30, 1974
*Whysall, W. W. (Notts.; *CY 1925*) b Oct. 31, 1887, d Nov. 11, 1930
Wickremaratne, R. P. A. H. (SSC) b Feb. 21, 1971
*Wickremasinghe, A. G. D. (NCC) b Dec. 27, 1965
*Wickremasinghe, G. P. (BRC & SSC) b Aug. 14, 1971
*Wiener, J. M. (Vic.) b May 1, 1955
*Wight, C. V. (BG) b July 28, 1902, d Oct. 4, 1969
*Wight, G. L. (BG) b May 28, 1929
Wight, P. B. (BG, Som., & Cant.) b June 25, 1930
*Wijegunawardene, K. I. W. (CCC) b Nov. 23, 1964
*Wijesuriya, R. G. C. E. (Mor. & Colts) b Feb. 18, 1960
*Wijetunge, P. K. (SSC) b Aug. 6, 1971
Wild, D. J. (Northants) b Nov. 28, 1962
*Wiles, C. A. (B'dos & T/T) b Aug. 11, 1892, d Nov. 4, 1957
Wilkins, A. H. (Glam., Glos. & N. Tvl) b Aug. 22, 1953
Wilkins, C. P. (Derbys., Border, E. Prov. & Natal) b July 31, 1944
*Wilkinson, L. L. (Lancs.) b Nov. 5, 1916
Wilkinson, P. A. (Notts.) b Aug. 23, 1951
Willatt, G. L. (CUCC, Notts. & Derbys.) b May 7, 1918
*Willett, E. T. (Comb. Is. & Leewards) b May 1, 1953
Willett, M. D. (Surrey) b April 21, 1933
*Willey, P. (Northants, E. Prov. & Leics.) b Dec. 6, 1949
*Williams, A. B. (Jam.) b Nov. 21, 1949
Williams, C. C. P. (Lord Williams of Elvet) (OUCC & Essex) b Feb. 9, 1933
*Williams, D. (T/T) b Nov. 4, 1963
Williams, D. L. (Glam.) b Nov. 20, 1946
*Williams, E. A. V. (B'dos) b April 10, 1914
*Williams, N. F. (Middx, Windwards & Tas.) b July 2, 1962
Williams, R. G. (Northants) b Aug. 10, 1957
*Williams, R. J. (Natal) b April 12, 1912, d May 14, 1984
*Williams, S. C. (Leewards) b Aug. 12, 1969
Williamson, J. G. (Northants) b April 4, 1936
*Willis, R. G. D. (Surrey, Warwicks. & N. Tvl; *CY 1978*) b May 30, 1949
*Willoughby, J. T. (SA) b Nov. 7, 1874, d *circa* 1955
Willsher, E. (Kent & All-England) b Nov. 22, 1828, d Oct. 7, 1885
Wilmot, K. (Warwicks.) b April 3, 1911
Wilson, A. (Lancs.) b April 24, 1921
Wilson, A. E. (Middx & Glos.) b May 18, 1910
*Wilson, Rev. C. E. M. (CUCC & Yorks.) b May 15, 1875, d Feb. 8, 1944
*Wilson, D. (Yorks. & MCC) b Aug. 7, 1937
*Wilson, E. R. (CUCC & Yorks.) b March 25, 1879, d July 21, 1957
Wilson, J. V. (Yorks.; *CY 1961*) b Jan. 17, 1921
Wilson, J. W. (Otago) b Oct. 24, 1973
*Wilson, J. W. (Vic. & S. Aust.) b Aug. 20, 1921, d Oct. 13, 1985
Wilson, P. H. L. (Surrey, Som. & N. Tvl) b Aug. 17, 1958
Wilson, R. C. (Kent) b Feb. 18, 1928
*Wimble, C. S. (Tvl) b Jan. 9, 1864, d Jan. 28, 1930
Windows, A. R. (Glos. & CUCC) b Sept. 25, 1942
Winfield, H. M. (Notts.) b June 13, 1933
Wingfield Digby, Rev. A. R. (OUCC) b July 25, 1950
Winn, C. E. (OUCC & Sussex) b Nov. 13, 1926
*Winslow, P. L. (Sussex, Tvl & Rhod.) b May 21, 1929
Wisden, John (Sussex; founder John Wisden and Co. and *Wisden's Cricketers' Almanack*) b Sept. 5, 1826, d April 5, 1884
*Wishart, K. L. (BG) b Nov. 28, 1908, d Oct. 18, 1972
Wolton, A. V. G. (Warwicks.) b June 12, 1919, d Sept. 9, 1990
*Wood, A. (Yorks.; *CY 1939*) b Aug. 25, 1898, d April 1, 1973
*Wood, B. (Yorks., Lancs., Derbys. & E. Prov.) b Dec. 26, 1942

Wood, C. J. B. (Leics.) b Nov. 21, 1875, d June 5, 1960
Wood, D. J. (Sussex) b May 19, 1914, d March 12, 1989
*Wood, G. E. C. (CUCC & Kent) b Aug. 22, 1893, d March 18, 1971
*Wood, G. M. (W. Aust.) b Nov. 6, 1956
*Wood, H. (Kent & Surrey; *CY 1891*) b Dec. 14, 1854, d April 30, 1919
*Wood, R. (Lancs. & Vic.) b March 7, 1860, d Jan. 6, 1915
*Woodcock, A. J. (S. Aust.) b Feb. 27, 1948
Woodcock, John C. (Editor of *Wisden* 1981-86) b Aug. 7, 1926
*Woodfull, W. M. (Vic.; *CY 1927*) b Aug. 22, 1897, d Aug. 11, 1965
Woodhead, F. G. (Notts.) b Oct. 30, 1912, d May 24, 1991
Woodhouse, G. E. S. (Som.) b Feb. 15, 1924, d Jan. 19, 1988
**Woods, S. M. J. (CUCC & Som.; *CY 1889*) b April 13, 1867, d April 30, 1931
Wookey, S. M. (CUCC & OUCC) b Sept. 2, 1954
Wooler, C. R. D. (Leics. & Rhod.) b June 30, 1930
Wooller, W. (CUCC & Glam.) b Nov. 20, 1912
Woolley, C. N. (Glos. & Northants) b May 5, 1886, d Nov. 3, 1962
*Woolley, F. E. (Kent; *CY 1911*) b May 27, 1887, d Oct. 18, 1978
*Woolley, R. D. (Tas.) b Sept. 16, 1954
*Woolmer, R. A. (Kent, Natal & W. Prov.; *CY 1976*) b May 14, 1948
*Worrall, J. (Vic.) b June 21, 1861, d Nov. 17, 1937
*Worrell, Sir F. M. M. (B'dos & Jam.; *CY 1951*) b Aug. 1, 1924, d March 13, 1967
Worsley, D. R. (OUCC & Lancs.) b July 18, 1941
Worsley, Sir W. A. 4th Bt (Yorks.; Pres. MCC 1961-62) b April 5, 1890, d Dec. 4, 1973
*Worthington, T. S. (Derbys.; *CY 1937*) b Aug. 21, 1905, d Aug. 31, 1973
Wright, A. (Warwicks.) b Aug. 25, 1941
Wright, A. J. (Glos.) b July 27, 1962
*Wright, C. W. (CUCC & Notts.) b May 27, 1863, d Jan. 10, 1936
*Wright, D. V. P. (Kent; *CY 1940*) b Aug. 21, 1914
Wright, Graeme A. (Editor of *Wisden* 1987-92) b April 23, 1943
*Wright, J. G. (N. Dist., Derbys., Cant. & Auck.) b July 5, 1954
*Wright, K. J. (W. Aust. & S. Aust.) b Dec. 27, 1953
Wright, L. G. (Derbys.; *CY 1906*) b June 15, 1862, d Jan. 11, 1953
Wyatt, J. G. (Som.) b June 19, 1963
*Wyatt, R. E. S. (Warwicks. & Worcs.; *CY 1930*) b May 2, 1901
*Wynne, O. E. (Tvl & W. Prov.) b June 1, 1919, d July 13, 1975
*Wynyard, E. G. (Hants) b April 1, 1861, d Oct. 30, 1936

Yachad, M. (N. Tvl & Tvl) b Nov. 17, 1960
*Yadav, N. S. (H'bad) b Jan. 26, 1957
*Yadav, V. S. (Haryana) b March 14, 1967
*Yajurvindra Singh (M'tra & S'tra) b Aug. 1, 1952
*Yallop, G. N. (Vic.) b Oct. 7, 1952
*Yardley, B. (W. Aust.) b Sept. 5, 1947
*Yardley, N. W. D. (CUCC & Yorks.; *CY 1948*) b March 19, 1915, d Oct. 4, 1989
Yardley, T. J. (Worcs. & Northants) b Oct. 27, 1946
Yarnold, H. (Worcs.) b July 6, 1917, d Aug. 13, 1974
*Yashpal Sharma (Punjab) b Aug. 11, 1954
Yawar Saeed (Som. & Punjab) b Jan. 22, 1935
*Yograj Singh (Haryana & Punjab) b March 25, 1958
*Young, B. A. (N. Dist.) b Nov. 3, 1964
Young, D. M. (Worcs. & Glos.) b April 15, 1924, d June 18, 1993
*Young, H. I. (Essex) b Feb. 5, 1876, d Dec. 12, 1964
*Young, J. A. (Middx) b Oct. 14, 1912, d Feb. 5, 1993
*Young, R. A. (CUCC & Sussex) b Sept. 16, 1885, d July 1, 1968
*Younis Ahmed (Lahore, Kar., Surrey, PIA, S. Aust., Worcs. & Glam.) b Oct. 20, 1947
*Yuile, B. W. (C. Dist.) b Oct. 29, 1941

*Zaheer Abbas (Kar., Glos., PWD, Dawood Indust., Sind & PIA; *CY 1972*) b July 24, 1947
Zahid Ahmed (PIA, Peshawar & F'bad) b Nov. 15, 1961
*Zahid Fazal (PACO, PIA & Lahore) b Nov. 10, 1973
*Zakir Khan (Sind, Peshawar & ADBP) b April 3, 1963
Zesers, A. K. (S. Aust.) b March 11, 1967
*Zoehrer, T. J. (W. Aust.) b Sept. 25, 1961
*Zulch, J. W. (Tvl) b Jan. 2, 1886, d May 19, 1924
*Zulfiqar Ahmed (B'pur & PIA) b Nov. 22, 1926
*Zulqarnain (Pak. Rlwys, Lahore, HBFC & PACO) b May 25, 1962

PART THREE: ENGLISH CRICKET IN 1994

FEATURES OF 1994

Double-Hundreds (24)

501*	B. C. Lara†	Warwickshire v Durham at Birmingham.
294*	D. M. Ward	Surrey v Derbyshire at The Oval.
281*	J. P. Crawley§	Lancashire v Somerset at Southport.
277*	R. G. Twose	Warwickshire v Glamorgan at Birmingham.
274*	M. D. Moxon	Yorkshire v Worcestershire at Worcester.
261*	J. D. Carr	Middlesex v Gloucestershire at Lord's.
261	P. V. Simmons‡	Leicestershire v Northamptonshire at Leicester (*on county debut*).
250	J. P. Crawley§	Lancashire v Nottinghamshire at Nottingham.
236	G. A. Gooch§	Essex v Kent at Chelmsford.
235*	D. J. Bicknell	Surrey v Nottinghamshire at Nottingham.
225	M. W. Gatting§	Middlesex v Leicestershire at Leicester.
224*	M. W. Gatting§	Middlesex v England A at Lord's.
220*	C. C. Lewis	Nottinghamshire v Warwickshire at Birmingham.
215	G. A. Hick	Worcestershire v Lancashire at Manchester.
210	G. A. Gooch§	England v New Zealand (First Test) at Nottingham.
206	M. N. Lathwell	Somerset v Surrey at Bath.
205	M. Azharuddin	Derbyshire v Durham at Chesterfield.
205	G. A. Gooch§	Essex v Worcestershire at Worcester.
204	J. E. Morris	Durham v Warwickshire at Birmingham (*the first double-hundred for Durham*).
204	N. H. Fairbrother	Lancashire v Middlesex at Manchester.
203*	A. J. Moles	Warwickshire v Surrey at Guildford.
202*	A. W. Smith	Surrey v Oxford University at The Oval.
201*	M. W. Gatting§	Middlesex v Northamptonshire at Northampton.
201*	G. Kirsten	South Africans v Durham at Chester-le-Street.

† *World record.* ‡ *County record.* § *M. W. Gatting and G. A. Gooch both scored three double-hundreds; J. P. Crawley scored two.*

Five Hundreds in Successive Innings

B. C. Lara (West Indies and Warwickshire) 375 West Indies v England (Fifth Test) at St John's, 1993-94; 147 Warwickshire v Glamorgan at Birmingham, 106 and 120* v Leicestershire at Birmingham, 136 v Somerset at Taunton.

Lara extended this sequence to six hundreds in seven innings and an unprecedented seven in eight.

Three Hundreds in Successive Innings

J. D. Carr (Middlesex) 171* v Somerset at Lord's, 136 and 106* v Northamptonshire at Northampton.

G. A. Gooch (Essex and England) 210 England v New Zealand (First Test) at Nottingham, Essex 101 and 205 v Worcestershire at Worcester.

D. L. Haynes (Middlesex) 125 v Worcestershire at Lord's, 104 and 103 v Kent at Canterbury.

Hundred in Each Innings of a Match

J. D. Carr	136	106*	Middlesex v Northamptonshire at Northampton.
G. A. Gooch	101	205	Essex v Worcestershire at Worcester.
D. L. Haynes	104	103	Middlesex v Kent at Canterbury.
B. C. Lara	106	120*	Warwickshire v Leicestershire at Birmingham.
T. R. Ward	110	125	Kent v Glamorgan at Abergavenny.

Most Runs in a Day

390* B. C. Lara† .... Warwickshire v Durham at Birmingham.

† *World record.*

Fastest Authentic Hundred

K. R. Rutherford ... 71 balls (80 minutes) New Zealanders v Glamorgan at Swansea.

In contrived circumstances, M. G. N. Windows (Gloucestershire) scored 100 off 71 balls in 58 minutes against New Zealanders at Bristol.

Hundred Before Lunch

M. Azharuddin	72*-172*	Derbyshire v Durham at Chesterfield (4th day).
C. L. Hooper	103*	Kent v Essex at Chelmsford (4th day).
B. C. Lara	111*-285*	Warwickshire v Durham at Birmingham (4th day).
B. C. Lara	109*	Warwickshire v Derbyshire at Chesterfield (1st day).
M. G. N. Windows	106†	Gloucestershire v New Zealanders at Bristol (3rd day).

† *Contrived.*

Ten Sixes in an Innings

C. L. Hooper	183	Kent v Yorkshire at Maidstone.
B. C. Lara	501*	Warwickshire v Durham at Birmingham.

First to 1,000 Runs

B. C. Lara (Warwickshire) on June 6, in seven innings.

2,000 Runs

B. C. Lara (Warwickshire) on September 1.

Carrying Bat Through Completed Innings

C. W. J. Athey	169*	Sussex (319) v Kent at Tunbridge Wells.
M. R. Benson	71*	Kent (189) v Hampshire at Canterbury.
W. Larkins	158*	Durham (305) v Gloucestershire at Gateshead Fell.
V. P. Terry	141*	Hampshire (305) v Yorkshire at Leeds.

First-Wicket Partnership of 100 in Each Innings

123 171* D. J. Bicknell/A. J. Stewart, Surrey v Lancashire at Manchester.
196 126 D. P. Ostler/R. G. Twose, Warwickshire v Kent at Birmingham.

Other Notable Partnerships

First Wicket
316† G. A. Gooch/P. J. Prichard, Essex v Kent at Chelmsford.

Second Wicket
295 R. G. Twose/B. C. Lara, Warwickshire v Hampshire at Birmingham.
263 M. A. Atherton/G. A. Gooch, England v New Zealand (First Test) at Nottingham.

Third Wicket
314 B. C. Lara/T. L. Penney, Warwickshire v Durham at Birmingham.
301 G. P. Thorpe/D. M. Ward, Surrey v Derbyshire at The Oval.

Fourth Wicket
288 M. W. Gatting/J. D. Carr, Middlesex v England A at Lord's.
282* M. W. Gatting/J. D. Carr, Middlesex v Northamptonshire at Northampton.
265 G. A. Hick/T. M. Moody, Worcestershire v Lancashire at Manchester.
250 C. M. Gupte/C. J. Hollins, Oxford University v Cambridge University at Lord's.

Fifth Wicket
322*† B. C. Lara/K. J. Piper, Warwickshire v Durham at Birmingham.
253* D. J. Bicknell/A. D. Brown, Surrey v Nottinghamshire at Nottingham.

Sixth Wicket
270† J. D. Carr/P. N. Weekes, Middlesex v Gloucestershire at Lord's.
253 P. V. Simmons/P. A. Nixon, Leicestershire v Northamptonshire at Leicester.

Seventh Wicket
264 J. D. Carr/P. N. Weekes, Middlesex v Somerset at Lord's.
235 J. P. Crawley/W. K. Hegg, Lancashire v Nottinghamshire at Nottingham.

Eighth Wicket
183 D. A. Leatherdale/R. K. Illingworth, Worcestershire v Somerset at Taunton.

Ninth Wicket
170† J. C. Adams/K. P. Evans, Nottinghamshire v Somerset at Taunton.

Tenth Wicket
122 J. P. Crawley/A. A. Barnett, Lancashire v Somerset at Southport.
115 M. Watkinson/P. J. Martin, Lancashire v Sussex at Horsham.
102 R. K. Illingworth/P. Mirza, Worcestershire v Kent at Canterbury.

* *Unbroken partnership.* † *County record for that wicket.*

Twelve or More Wickets in a Match

15-147	M. J. McCague	Kent v Derbyshire at Derby.
13-147	Wasim Akram	Lancashire v Somerset at Southport.
12-102	C. A. Walsh	Gloucestershire v Nottinghamshire at Nottingham.
12-160	Mushtaq Ahmed	Somerset v Worcestershire at Taunton.
12-195	H. R. J. Trump	Somerset v Sussex at Hove.

Eight or More Wickets in an Innings

10-45	R. L. Johnson	Middlesex v Derbyshire at Derby.
9-57	D. E. Malcolm	England v South Africa (Third Test) at The Oval.
9-86	M. J. McCague	Kent v Derbyshire at Derby.
8-30	Wasim Akram......	Lancashire v Somerset at Southport.
8-30	M. Watkinson	Lancashire v Hampshire at Manchester.
8-42	A. R. K. Pierson....	Leicestershire v Warwickshire at Birmingham.
8-96	M. M. Patel........	Kent v Lancashire at Canterbury.

Hat-Tricks

D. G. Cork	Derbyshire v Kent at Derby.
P. A. J. DeFreitas..........	Derbyshire v Hampshire at Southampton.
A. Sheriyar................	Leicestershire v Durham at Durham University (2nd innings).
V. J. Wells................	Leicestershire v Durham at Durham University (1st innings).

100 Wickets

No bowler took 100 wickets. The highest aggregate was 90 by M. M. Patel (Kent).

Nine or More Wicket-Keeping Dismissals in a Match

10 ct, 1 st..	K. J. Piper	Warwickshire v Derbyshire at Chesterfield.
10 ct......	W. K. Hegg	Lancashire v Yorkshire at Leeds.
8 ct, 1 st ..	S. A. Marsh	Kent v Durham at Canterbury.
8 ct, 1 st ..	K. J. Piper	Warwickshire v Essex at Birmingham.

Six or More Wicket-Keeping Dismissals in an Innings

6 ct, 1 st ..	S. A. Marsh	Kent v Durham at Canterbury.
7 ct.......	K. J. Piper	Warwickshire v Essex at Birmingham.
6 ct, 1 st ..	K. J. Piper	Warwickshire v Derbyshire at Chesterfield.
5 ct, 1 st ..	R. J. Blakey	Yorkshire v Glamorgan at Cardiff.
6 ct.......	S. A. Marsh	Kent v South Africans at Canterbury.

Eight Catches in a Match in the Field

M. C. J. Ball	Gloucestershire v Yorkshire at Cheltenham.

Five Catches in an Innings in the Field

M. C. J. Ball	Gloucestershire v Yorkshire at Cheltenham.
R. P. Davis	Warwickshire v Somerset at Taunton.
N. V. Knight ...	Essex v Warwickshire at Birmingham.
G. I. Macmillan .	Oxford University v Durham at Oxford.

Match Double (100 Runs and 10 Wickets)

M. Watkinson	11, 117; 8-30, 3-57	Lancashire v Hampshire at Manchester.

No Byes Conceded in Total of 500 or More

A. C. Parore ...... New Zealand v England (First Test) (567-8 dec.) at Nottingham.
R. J. Turner ...... Somerset v Glamorgan (533) at Swansea.
C. W. Scott .... Durham v Hampshire (512) at Portsmouth.

Highest Innings Totals

810-4 dec.† ... Warwickshire v Durham at Birmingham.
657-7 dec. ... Warwickshire v Glamorgan at Birmingham.
625-6 dec.† ... Durham v Derbyshire at Chesterfield.
623-9 dec. ... Middlesex v Leicestershire at Leicester.
613-8 dec. ... South Africans v Sussex at Hove.
604-4 dec. ... Surrey v Nottinghamshire at Nottingham.
603-7 dec. ... Hampshire v Surrey at Southampton.
597-8 dec. ... Nottinghamshire v Warwickshire at Birmingham.
591 .... Worcestershire v Lancashire at Manchester.
589 .... Lancashire v Derbyshire at Blackpool.
570-6 dec. ... Surrey v Derbyshire at The Oval.
567-8 dec. ... England v New Zealand (First Test) at Nottingham.
567 .... Lancashire v Nottinghamshire at Nottingham.
557 .... Worcestershire v Middlesex at Lord's.
556-8 dec. ... Durham v Warwickshire at Birmingham.
556 .... Kent v Lancashire at Canterbury.
545-8 dec. ... Durham v Northamptonshire at Hartlepool.
545 .... Middlesex v Derbyshire at Derby.
541-5 dec. ... Essex v Kent at Chelmsford.
538-6 dec. ... Surrey v Durham at Darlington.
538 .... Nottinghamshire v Northamptonshire at Nottingham.
536 .... Warwickshire v Hampshire at Birmingham.
533 .... Glamorgan v Somerset at Swansea.
529 .... Northamptonshire v Derbyshire at Northampton.
525-7 dec. ... Middlesex v Essex at Uxbridge.
521 .... Lancashire v Somerset at Southport.
513-7 dec. ... Middlesex v Gloucestershire at Lord's.
512 .... Hampshire v Durham at Portsmouth.
511 .... Middlesex v Durham at Lord's.
501 .... Surrey v Leicestershire at The Oval.

† *County record.*

Highest Fourth-Innings Total

405-6 .... Essex v Worcestershire at Worcester (set 405).

Lowest Innings Totals

73 .... Oxford University v Durham at Oxford.
73 .... Worcestershire v Yorkshire at Worcester.
73† .... Derbyshire v Yorkshire at Sheffield.
83 .... Lancashire v Derbyshire at Blackpool.
84 .... Cambridge University v Kent at Cambridge.
87 .... Middlesex v Sussex at Arundel.
88 .... Surrey v Essex at Colchester.
90 .... Leicestershire v Sussex at Leicester.
95† .... Oxford University v Worcestershire at Worcester.
99† .... England v South Africa (First Test) at Lord's.

† *One man absent injured.*

Match Aggregates of 1,400 Runs

Runs-Wkts	
1,570-29	Derbyshire v Durham at Chesterfield.
1,536-27	Northamptonshire v Middlesex at Northampton.
1,527-23	Middlesex v Essex at Uxbridge.
1,480-26	Surrey v Middlesex at The Oval.
1,412-39	Sussex v Lancashire at Horsham.

70 Extras in an Innings

	b	*l-b*	*w*	*n-b*	
81	11	16	0	54	Middlesex (545) v Derbyshire at Derby.
81	21	9	1	50	Lancashire (589) v Derbyshire at Blackpool.
81	0	9	7	65	Glamorgan (533) v Somerset at Swansea.
81	5	14	4	58	Hampshire (603-7 dec.) v Surrey at Southampton.
78	28	22	2	26	Warwickshire (810-4 dec.) v Durham at Birmingham.
73	14	35	0	24	Surrey (604-4 dec.) v Nottinghamshire at Nottingham.

Under TCCB regulations, two extras were scored for every no-ball, excluding runs scored off the delivery, except in Tests. There were 20 further instances of 50 to 69 extras in an innings.

Career Aggregate Milestones†

40,000 runs	G. A. Gooch.
20,000 runs	K. J. Barnett.
10,000 runs	D. J. Bicknell, N. A. Felton, R. J. Harden, C. L. Hooper, J. P. Stephenson, A. J. Wright.
1,500 wickets	J. E. Emburey, E. E. Hemmings.
500 wickets	K. M. Curran, R. A. Harper, P. W. Jarvis, D. E. Malcolm, T. A. Munton, P. C. R. Tufnell, Waqar Younis, S. L. Watkin.

† *Achieved since September 1993.*

PETER SMITH AWARD

The Peter Smith Award, given by the Cricket Writers' Club in memory of its former chairman, for services to the presentation of cricket to the public, was won in 1994 by Brian Lara for playing the game "the way it used to be played and the way it should be played". The Award was instituted in 1992. Previous winners were David Gower and John Woodcock.

PROFESSIONALS' AWARDS, 1994

The Cricketers' Association chose Brian Lara of Warwickshire as winner of the Reg Hayter Award as Player of the Year in 1994. The John Arlott Award for Young Player of the Year went to John Crawley of Lancashire.

FIRST-CLASS AVERAGES, 1994

BATTING

(Qualification: 8 innings)

** Signifies not out.* *† Denotes a left-handed batsman.*

		M	I	NO	R	HS	100s	50s	Avge
1	J. D. Carr (*Middx*)	20	27	10	1,543	261*	6	7	90.76
2	†B. C. Lara (*Warwicks.*)	15	25	2	2,066	501*	9	3	89.82
3	M. W. Gatting (*Middx*)	19	27	3	1,671	225	6	6	69.62
4	G. A. Gooch (*Essex*)	17	29	2	1,747	236	6	5	64.70
5	C. C. Lewis (*Notts.*)	12	19	4	881	220*	2	5	58.73
6	B. M. McMillan (*South Africans*)	9	11	3	467	132	1	3	58.37
7	M. D. Moxon (*Yorks.*)	17	30	4	1,458	274*	4	6	56.07
8	S. J. Rhodes (*Worcs.*)	18	27	11	896	100*	1	5	56.00
9	G. A. Hick (*Worcs.*)	17	29	1	1,538	215	5	5	54.92
10	C. L. Hooper (*Kent*)	16	29	0	1,579	183	5	7	54.44
11	†R. G. Twose (*Warwicks.*)	18	31	5	1,411	277*	3	6	54.26
12	†G. P. Thorpe (*Surrey*)	16	25	4	1,136	190	2	7	54.09
13	M. R. Ramprakash (*Middx*)	18	26	2	1,270	135	4	6	52.91
14	A. N. Hayhurst (*Somerset*)	18	30	6	1,250	121	2	10	52.08
15	†D. J. Bicknell (*Surrey*)	18	30	4	1,354	235*	3	7	52.07
16	C. J. Hollins (*OUCC*)	8	10	2	415	131	1	2	51.87
17	P. A. Cottey (*Glam.*)	19	33	6	1,393	191	3	6	51.59
18	A. J. Moles (*Warwicks.*)	11	20	3	863	203*	1	5	50.76
19	J. P. Crawley (*Lancs.*)	20	34	3	1,570	281*	3	6	50.64
20	†N. H. Fairbrother (*Lancs.*)	12	22	2	1,002	204	4	1	50.10
21	P. N. Kirsten (*South Africans*)	10	16	5	549	130	2	1	49.90
22	R. S. M. Morris (*Hants*)	9	17	3	686	174	2	3	49.00
23	K. M. Curran (*Northants*)	15	25	5	973	114	1	8	48.65
24	†M. E. Trescothick (*Somerset*)	11	20	1	924	121	2	8	48.63
25	A. D. Brown (*Surrey*)	17	24	2	1,049	172	2	6	47.68
26	†N. V. Knight (*Essex*)	12	21	1	944	157	4	3	47.20
27	†G. Kirsten (*South Africans*)	11	19	3	751	201*	2	5	46.93
28	A. J. Stewart (*Surrey*)	16	23	3	936	142	3	4	46.80
29	M. D. Crowe (*New Zealanders*)	9	16	2	654	142	3	3	46.71
30	N. J. Speak (*Lancs.*)	19	34	6	1,304	143	3	7	46.57
31	T. M. Moody (*Worcs.*)	18	28	3	1,160	159	3	6	46.40
32	R. J. Blakey (*Yorks.*)	20	36	9	1,236	94*	0	11	45.77
33	M. C. J. Nicholas (*Hants*)	19	32	6	1,182	145	3	5	45.46
34	D. A. Leatherdale (*Worcs.*)	17	25	3	987	139	2	3	44.86
35	M. Azharuddin (*Derbys.*)	9	17	1	712	205	2	1	44.50
36	A. Fordham (*Northants*)	11	20	1	844	158	3	4	44.42
37	D. M. Ward (*Surrey*)	16	22	1	921	294*	1	5	43.85
38	N. R. Taylor (*Kent*)	16	27	3	1,049	139	3	4	43.70
39	J. E. R. Gallian (*Lancs.*)	12	20	0	874	171	2	5	43.70
40	R. A. Smith (*Hants*)	17	29	0	1,263	162	5	4	43.55
41	R. J. Bailey (*Northants*)	18	33	5	1,214	129*	3	7	43.35
42	P. Johnson (*Notts.*)	17	29	2	1,170	132	4	5	43.33
43	A. J. Lamb (*Northants*)	15	22	1	908	131	2	5	43.23
44	D. P. Ostler (*Warwicks.*)	18	29	2	1,161	186	2	6	43.00
45	R. I. Dawson (*Glos.*)	16	30	4	1,112	127*	1	7	42.76
46	T. R. Ward (*Kent*)	19	33	1	1,368	125	3	10	42.75
47	†D. L. Hemp (*Glam.*)	21	38	4	1,452	136	4	8	42.70
48	R. T. Robinson (*Notts.*)	19	31	1	1,276	182	2	10	42.53
49	†K. C. Wessels (*South Africans*)	12	18	2	679	105	1	4	42.43
50	J. E. Morris (*Durham & President's XI*)	20	35	1	1,433	204	4	6	42.14

		M	I	NO	R	HS	100s	50s	Avge
51	R. C. Irani (*Essex*)	18	29	6	965	119	2	8	41.95
52	R. J. Harden (*Somerset*)	18	31	5	1,061	131*	2	7	40.80
53	W. Larkins (*Durham & President's XI*)	16	27	3	976	158*	1	6	40.66
54	K. R. Brown (*Middx*)	20	25	9	639	102*	1	1	39.93
55	M. B. Loye (*Northants*)	15	26	3	914	132	3	5	39.73
56	M. N. Lathwell (*Somerset*)	18	32	1	1,230	206	2	9	39.67
57	†S. P. Fleming (*New Zealanders*)	9	16	1	591	151	2	1	39.40
58	V. P. Terry (*Hants*)	19	34	1	1,286	164	5	2	38.96
59	D. L. Haynes (*Middx*)	17	27	2	973	134	5	2	38.92
60	D. J. Cullinan (*South Africans*)	9	14	3	428	94	0	4	38.90
61	†P. A. Nixon (*Leics.*)	19	30	3	1,046	131	3	4	38.74
61	A. P. Grayson (*Yorks.*)	19	31	4	1,046	100	1	7	38.74
63	K. J. Barnett (*Derbys.*)	15	24	2	847	148	1	7	38.50
64	B. A. Young (*New Zealanders & President's XI*)	10	18	0	688	122	1	5	38.22
65	S. P. James (*Glam.*)	16	28	5	877	150	3	1	38.13
66	R. Q. Cake (*CUCC*)	10	18	1	647	107	1	3	38.05
67	N. E. Briers (*Leics.*)	19	35	3	1,216	154	2	5	38.00
67	T. L. Penney (*Warwicks.*)	16	24	3	798	111	1	1	38.00
69	P. J. Prichard (*Essex*)	11	17	2	569	119	3	2	37.93
70	K. R. Rutherford (*New Zealanders*)	9	17	1	603	129	2	2	37.68
71	G. Welch (*Warwicks.*)	12	15	3	446	84*	0	4	37.16
72	†D. Byas (*Yorks.*)	20	36	1	1,297	104	2	9	37.05
73	C. White (*Yorks.*)	13	20	2	663	108*	1	5	36.83
74	M. P. Vaughan (*Yorks.*)	16	30	1	1,066	117	3	3	36.75
75	J. N. Rhodes (*South Africans*)	12	16	3	477	77	0	3	36.69
76	M. A. Roseberry (*Middx*)	20	32	2	1,097	152	2	6	36.56
77	A. J. Wright (*Glos.*)	19	36	3	1,202	184*	1	7	36.42
78	V. J. Wells (*Leics.*)	16	28	4	871	87*	0	6	36.29
79	W. S. Kendall (*OUCC*)	9	10	3	253	113*	1	0	36.14
80	B. Parker (*Yorks.*)	10	18	2	578	127	1	4	36.12
81	M. P. Maynard (*Glam.*)	16	28	1	975	118	2	5	36.11
82	A. J. Hollioake (*Surrey*)	17	23	3	722	138	3	3	36.10
83	C. M. Gupte (*OUCC*)	10	17	2	541	122	2	1	36.06
84	†M. A. Butcher (*Surrey*)	12	19	2	613	134	1	3	36.05
85	M. A. Atherton (*Lancs.*)	16	27	2	899	111	2	4	35.96
86	A. Roseberry (*Glam.*)	6	8	1	249	94	0	2	35.57
87	D. J. Nash (*New Zealanders*)	8	11	6	177	56	0	1	35.40
88	†M. J. Greatbatch (*New Zealanders*)	9	18	3	528	84	0	3	35.20
89	†J. C. Adams (*Notts.*)	18	32	5	950	144*	3	2	35.18
90	W. J. Cronje (*South Africans*)	13	20	1	661	108	1	3	34.78
91	M. G. N. Windows (*Glos.*)	11	21	0	730	106	1	5	34.76
92	†R. C. Russell (*Glos.*)	19	34	8	901	85*	0	4	34.65
93	†M. Saxelby (*Durham*)	17	32	0	1,102	181	2	4	34.43
93	R. B. Richardson (*Yorks.*)	9	16	0	551	76	0	5	34.43
95	R. R. Montgomerie (*OUCC & Northants*)	19	34	3	1,062	151	2	8	34.25
96	M. Watkinson (*Lancs.*)	18	28	2	889	155	2	3	34.19
97	M. P. Speight (*Sussex*)	17	29	0	991	126	1	4	34.17
98	†P. N. Weekes (*Middx*)	16	21	2	648	117	1	2	34.10
99	G. R. Haynes (*Worcs.*)	20	32	2	1,021	141	2	4	34.03
100	S. A. Thomson (*New Zealanders*)	10	19	7	408	69	0	4	34.00
101	G. F. Archer (*Notts.*)	16	26	0	878	168	2	4	33.76
102	T. J. G. O'Gorman (*Derbys.*)	16	28	2	872	145	3	3	33.53
103	C. J. Adams (*Derbys.*)	18	32	3	969	109*	1	5	33.41
104	†A. L. Penberthy (*Northants*)	17	25	5	658	88*	0	5	32.90
105	M. W. Alleyne (*Glos.*)	20	37	1	1,184	109	2	6	32.88
106	A. W. Smith (*Surrey*)	14	21	5	524	202*	1	1	32.75

		M	I	NO	R	HS	100s	50s	Avge
107	A. R. Roberts (*Northants*)	9	12	4	261	51	0	1	32.62
108	S. A. Marsh (*Kent*)	19	31	6	807	88	0	5	32.28
109	J. A. Daley (*Durham*)	10	18	2	513	159*	1	3	32.06
110	†N. A. Folland (*Somerset*)	13	22	1	671	91	0	4	31.95
111	J. J. Whitaker (*Leics.*)	18	32	2	958	148	2	6	31.93
112	N. Hussain (*Essex*)	19	31	2	922	115*	2	5	31.79
113	D. J. Richardson (*South Africans*)	10	12	3	286	88	0	2	31.77
114	P. V. Simmons (*Leics.*)	17	30	0	953	261	1	3	31.76
115	B. F. Smith (*Leics.*)	14	23	3	628	95	0	4	31.40
116	G. R. Cowdrey (*Kent*)	10	16	1	470	114	1	2	31.33
117	B. A. Pocock (*New Zealanders*)	7	14	2	374	103*	1	2	31.16
118	N. J. Lenham (*Sussex*)	14	27	1	809	102	1	5	31.11
119	C. W. J. Athey (*Sussex*)	18	34	1	1,022	169*	2	3	30.96
120	T. S. Curtis (*Worcs.*)	18	32	1	960	180	3	1	30.96
121	†H. Morris (*Glam.*)	16	31	2	885	106	1	6	30.51
122	†W. P. C. Weston (*Worcs.*)	17	28	1	818	94	0	6	30.29
123	K. P. Evans (*Notts.*)	16	21	4	514	104	1	3	30.23
124	†P. R. Pollard (*Notts.*)	18	31	1	905	134	2	4	30.16
125	†S. Hutton (*Durham*)	14	24	2	662	101	1	3	30.09
126	N. A. Mallender (*Somerset*)	8	12	3	270	43*	0	0	30.00
127	R. J. Warren (*Northants*)	12	21	2	566	94*	0	5	29.78
128	S. R. Lampitt (*Worcs.*)	17	26	5	624	122	1	2	29.71
129	†D. M. Smith (*Sussex*)	7	14	3	326	74	0	3	29.63
130	R. J. Cunliffe (*Glos.*)	7	13	1	354	177*	1	0	29.50
131	A. P. Wells (*Sussex*)	19	35	4	909	84	0	7	29.32
132	J. W. Hall (*Sussex*)	14	27	0	789	85	0	7	29.22
133	T. Edwards (*Worcs.*)	9	11	7	116	47	0	0	29.00
134	M. V. Fleming (*Kent*)	16	29	1	810	73	0	6	28.92
135	J. J. B. Lewis (*Essex*)	16	29	3	751	109	1	4	28.88
136	M. Davies (*Glos.*)	4	8	2	173	54	0	1	28.83
137	P. A. J. DeFreitas (*Derbys.*)	14	21	2	545	108	1	3	28.68
138	R. P. Snell (*South Africans*)	8	8	3	143	94	0	1	28.60
139	G. D. Lloyd (*Lancs.*)	16	27	3	684	112	1	5	28.50
139	A. C. Parore (*New Zealanders*)	11	18	4	399	71	0	2	28.50
141	G. I. Macmillan (*OUCC & Leics.*)	10	17	3	395	69	0	3	28.21
142	F. D. Stephenson (*Sussex*)	17	28	1	752	107	1	5	27.85
143	†M. R. Benson (*Kent*)	16	28	1	737	159	1	4	27.29
144	D. P. Fulton (*Kent*)	10	16	0	433	109	1	1	27.06
145	N. F. Williams (*Middx*)	10	9	4	134	63	0	1	26.80
146	M. A. Ealham (*Kent*)	15	26	2	638	68*	0	4	26.58
147	S. D. Udal (*Hants*)	17	30	4	684	94	0	4	26.30
148	O. D. Gibson (*Glam.*)	20	31	4	710	85	0	7	26.29
149	A. S. Rollins (*Derbys.*)	16	29	2	708	97	0	6	26.22
150	T. C. Middleton (*Hants*)	13	23	3	524	102	1	1	26.20
151	S. P. Titchard (*Lancs.*)	13	21	0	549	99	0	3	26.14
152	R. D. B. Croft (*Glam.*)	19	25	2	600	80	0	2	26.08
153	P. A. Smith (*Warwicks.*)	12	17	3	363	65	0	2	25.92
154	†G. J. Parsons (*Leics.*)	16	25	6	491	70	0	2	25.84
155	J. I. Longley (*Durham*)	14	25	2	594	100*	1	5	25.82
156	†I. D. Austin (*Lancs.*)	11	16	1	386	50	0	1	25.73
157	W. M. Noon (*Notts.*)	18	30	6	617	75	0	3	25.70
158	N. M. K. Smith (*Warwicks.*)	18	21	4	435	65	0	2	25.58
159	T. H. C. Hancock (*Glos.*)	20	37	1	920	123	1	7	25.55
160	P. Moores (*Sussex*)	18	32	2	766	70*	0	4	25.53
161	A. Dale (*Glam.*)	18	29	1	711	131	2	2	25.39
162	K. M. Krikken (*Derbys.*)	15	27	10	426	85*	0	2	25.05
163	G. D. Rose (*Somerset*)	16	24	2	548	121	1	2	24.90
164	†B. C. Broad (*Glos.*)	10	20	0	496	128	1	2	24.80
165	†N. A. Felton (*Northants*)	10	19	1	445	87	0	2	24.72
166	G. W. White (*Hants*)	11	20	1	467	104	1	2	24.57

		M	I	NO	R	HS	100s	50s	Avge
167	G. D. Hodgson (*Glos.*)	9	16	1	367	113	1	1	24.46
168	R. J. Turner (*Somerset*)	18	27	5	537	104*	1	2	24.40
169	†Wasim Akram (*Lancs.*)	6	10	0	244	98	0	2	24.40
170	†S. G. Hinks (*Glos.*)	5	10	0	242	74	0	2	24.20
171	M. J. Vandrau (*Derbys.*)	13	23	5	435	66	0	1	24.16
172	D. G. Cork (*Derbys.*)	13	21	0	507	94	0	4	24.14
173	A. N. Aymes (*Hants*)	19	32	3	697	76	0	2	24.03
174	P. D. Bowler (*Derbys.*)	13	23	0	546	88	0	2	23.73
175	A. J. Dalton (*Glam.*)	6	10	2	188	51*	0	1	23.50
176	T. J. Boon (*Leics.*)	16	28	2	606	74	0	4	23.30
177	A. C. Cummins (*Durham*)	17	29	2	629	65	0	3	23.29
178	N. Shahid (*Essex*)	10	18	4	326	91	0	1	23.28
179	R. K. Illingworth (*Worcs.*)	20	25	6	438	59*	0	3	23.05
180	K. J. Piper (*Warwicks.*)	17	24	4	454	116*	1	1	22.70
181	G. F. J. Liebenberg (*South Africans*)	7	11	1	226	64*	0	2	22.60
182	C. M. Tolley (*Worcs.*)	7	11	3	180	84	0	1	22.50
183	C. W. Scott (*Durham & President's XI*)	20	33	3	670	108	2	3	22.33
184	†S. C. Ecclestone (*OUCC & Somerset*)	13	19	4	334	80*	0	1	22.26
184	A. R. K. Pierson (*Leics.*)	15	20	5	334	43*	0	0	22.26
186	D. Gough (*Yorks.*)	13	19	3	355	65	0	2	22.18
187	C. P. Metson (*Glam.*)	18	22	4	398	51	0	1	22.11
188	P. Bainbridge (*Durham*)	18	31	1	660	68	0	5	22.00
189	M. J. McCague (*Kent*)	10	16	3	285	56	0	1	21.92
190	R. P. Lefebvre (*Glam.*)	12	14	3	240	33	0	0	21.81
191	M. A. Garnham (*Essex*)	18	30	5	542	62	0	4	21.68
192	A. R. Whittall (*CUCC*)	9	11	2	193	91*	0	1	21.44
193	A. C. Hudson (*South Africans*)	12	19	1	382	116	1	1	21.22
194	B. R. Hartland (*New Zealanders*)	8	16	0	337	65	0	2	21.06
195	G. R. Larsen (*New Zealanders*)	8	12	4	168	40*	0	0	21.00
196	G. Yates (*Lancs.*)	13	20	7	272	54*	0	2	20.92
197	†K. D. James (*Hants*)	13	22	2	417	53	0	2	20.85
198	J. P. Stephenson (*Essex*)	16	27	1	535	144	1	2	20.57
199	R. L. Johnson (*Middx*)	11	13	3	205	50*	0	1	20.50
200	†D. J. Millns (*Leics.*)	19	27	10	348	64*	0	1	20.47
201	W. K. Hegg (*Lancs.*)	19	30	4	518	66	0	2	19.92
202	I. Fletcher (*Somerset*)	6	10	1	179	54*	0	2	19.88
203	D. A. Graveney (*Durham*)	13	22	6	317	65*	0	1	19.81
204	C. C. Remy (*Sussex*)	6	11	1	194	60	0	2	19.40
205	W. A. Dessaur (*Notts.*)	5	9	1	154	35	0	0	19.25
206	†J. H. Childs (*Essex*)	15	17	12	96	42*	0	0	19.20
207	†N. J. Llong (*Kent*)	7	11	0	209	44	0	0	19.00
208	J. P. Carroll (*CUCC*)	9	15	2	246	90	0	1	18.92
209	R. J. Maru (*Hants*)	9	15	4	207	38*	0	0	18.81
210	D. Ripley (*Northants*)	16	23	9	263	36*	0	0	18.78
211	M. C. J. Ball (*Glos.*)	17	28	3	468	45	0	0	18.72
212	R. P. Davis (*Warwicks.*)	12	9	2	131	35*	0	0	18.71
213	†C. E. L. Ambrose (*Northants*)	14	16	2	257	78	0	1	18.35
214	J. S. Hodgson (*CUCC*)	9	15	1	256	54	0	1	18.28
215	†M. N. Hart (*New Zealanders*)	9	11	3	146	36	0	0	18.25
216	P. J. Newport (*Worcs.*)	17	24	5	345	41	0	0	18.15
217	S. J. E. Brown (*Durham & President's XI*)	19	25	10	268	69	0	1	17.86
218	W. K. M. Benjamin (*Hants*)	9	14	1	231	54	0	2	17.76
219	†M. C. Ilott (*Essex*)	14	16	5	194	45*	0	0	17.63
220	I. D. K. Salisbury (*Sussex*)	16	25	6	331	49	0	0	17.42
221	H. R. J. Trump (*Somerset*)	14	20	4	276	45*	0	0	17.25
222	P. J. Hartley (*Yorks.*)	16	23	3	343	61	0	1	17.15
223	M. A. Feltham (*Middx*)	13	16	1	256	71	0	1	17.06

		M	I	NO	R	HS	100s	50s	Avge
224	†G. W. Jones (*CUCC*)	8	13	0	220	74	0	1	16.92
225	C. M. Wells (*Derbys.*)	11	20	2	303	42	0	0	16.83
226	D. W. Headley (*Kent*)	9	13	5	134	46*	0	0	16.75
227	S. A. Kellett (*Yorks.*)	9	16	0	266	50	0	1	16.62
228	P. W. Jarvis (*Sussex*)	17	27	6	347	70*	0	1	16.52
229	M. S. Kasprowicz (*Essex*)	17	24	4	326	44	0	0	16.30
230	P. J. Martin (*Lancs.*)	18	27	3	383	57	0	1	15.95
231	G. W. Mike (*Notts.*)	17	26	3	365	60*	0	1	15.86
232	M. Keech (*Hants*)	5	9	0	141	57	0	1	15.66
233	M. P. Bicknell (*Surrey*)	9	11	2	140	41	0	0	15.55
234	R. D. Mann (*CUCC*)	9	16	0	248	53	0	1	15.50
235	Mushtaq Ahmed (*Somerset*)	9	14	3	168	38	0	0	15.27
236	C. A. Walsh (*Glos.*)	15	24	6	274	66	0	1	15.22
237	D. E. Stanley (*CUCC*)	5	8	2	91	48	0	0	15.16
238	†R. A. Pick (*Notts.*)	16	22	7	227	65*	0	1	15.13
239	N. F. Sargeant (*Surrey*)	9	13	2	166	46	0	0	15.09
240	G. Chapple (*Lancs.*)	15	21	11	150	26*	0	0	15.00
241	A. C. S. Pigott (*Surrey*)	8	11	0	160	40	0	0	14.54
	S. J. Base (*Derbys.*)	8	12	1	160	33	0	0	14.54
243	J. E. Emburey (*Middx*)	15	19	5	203	78*	0	1	14.50
244	M. G. Field-Buss (*Notts.*)	8	9	4	72	23	0	0	14.40
245	R. C. Williams (*Glos.*)	10	14	2	171	38	0	0	14.25
	V. J. Pike (*Glos.*)	9	12	4	114	27	0	0	14.25
247	J. Ratledge (*CUCC*)	9	16	0	227	79	0	1	14.18
248	G. J. Kersey (*Surrey*)	7	11	2	127	39	0	0	14.11
249	A. R. Caddick (*Somerset*)	12	18	2	219	58*	0	1	13.68
250	A. M. Smith (*Glos.*)	12	14	2	162	29	0	0	13.50
251	F. J. Cooke (*CUCC*)	9	10	4	80	34*	0	0	13.33
252	M. A. Crawley (*Notts.*)	8	14	1	172	45	0	0	13.23
253	K. J. Shine (*Middx*)	13	8	5	39	14*	0	0	13.00
254	D. A. Reeve (*Warwicks.*)	9	10	1	116	33	0	0	12.88
255	N. M. Kendrick (*Surrey*)	7	11	2	112	25	0	0	12.44
256	†K. E. Cooper (*Glos.*)	12	16	9	84	18*	0	0	12.00
257	C. M. Pitcher (*CUCC*)	10	14	4	116	43	0	0	11.60
258	C. A. Connor (*Hants*)	15	22	3	215	25	0	0	11.31
259	P. N. Hepworth (*Leics.*)	5	10	0	113	60	0	1	11.30
260	J. C. Hallett (*Somerset*)	4	8	1	79	52	0	1	11.28
261	N. J. Haste (*CUCC*)	9	12	2	112	22	0	0	11.20
262	C. Pringle (*New Zealanders*)	8	8	0	88	24	0	0	11.00
263	T. A. Munton (*Warwicks.*)	18	17	7	106	36	0	0	10.60
264	C. E. W. Silverwood (*Yorks.*)	9	15	3	127	26	0	0	10.58
265	M. M. Patel (*Kent*)	18	27	2	256	39	0	0	10.24
266	J. Wood (*Durham*)	15	22	3	194	51	0	1	10.21
267	C. J. Townsend (*OUCC*)	10	9	3	61	22	0	0	10.16
268	R. D. Stemp (*Yorks.*)	20	28	2	263	28	0	0	10.11
269	N. V. Radford (*Worcs.*)	15	20	4	161	25	0	0	10.06
270	†J. P. Taylor (*Northants*)	13	14	7	68	26	0	0	9.71
271	M. J. Thursfield (*Hants*)	9	12	1	106	47	0	0	9.63
272	J. E. Benjamin (*Surrey*)	16	17	1	148	33*	0	0	9.25
273	S. L. Watkin (*Glam.*)	18	21	11	92	14	0	0	9.20
274	A. P. van Troost (*Somerset*)	14	18	6	108	33	0	0	9.00
275	N. G. B. Cook (*Northants*)	11	12	1	98	43*	0	0	8.90
276	J. N. B. Bovill (*Hants*)	6	9	5	35	10	0	0	8.75
277	G. C. Small (*Warwicks.*)	11	10	1	78	23	0	0	8.66
278	N. F. C. Martin (*OUCC*)	10	10	1	74	26	0	0	8.22
279	A. E. Warner (*Derbys.*)	10	15	3	96	24*	0	0	8.00
280	P. M. Such (*Essex*)	20	23	2	167	29	0	0	7.95
281	A. P. Igglesden (*Kent*)	11	16	8	61	15*	0	0	7.62
282	A. D. Mullally (*Leics.*)	14	19	4	114	23	0	0	7.60
283	M. T. Brimson (*Leics.*)	5	9	3	45	17*	0	0	7.50
284	E. E. Hemmings (*Sussex*)	14	24	12	88	14*	0	0	7.33

		M	*I*	*NO*	*R*	*HS*	*100s*	*50s*	*Avge*
285	D. E. Malcolm (*Derbys.*)	18	22	9	89	15*	0	0	6.84
286	C. E. Cuffy (*Surrey*)	12	15	8	42	10	0	0	6.00
287	A. R. C. Fraser (*Middx*)	14	15	1	80	16	0	0	5.71
288	N. G. Cowans (*Hants*)	12	15	6	51	19	0	0	5.66
289	S. J. W. Andrew (*Essex*)	6	8	1	37	11	0	0	5.28
290	E. S. H. Giddins (*Sussex*)	17	22	4	83	24	0	0	4.61
291	T. N. Wren (*Kent*)	7	11	4	31	18*	0	0	4.42
292	A. W. Maclay (*OUCC*)	9	8	4	16	6*	0	0	4.00
293	M. A. Robinson (*Yorks.*)	19	23	8	58	9	0	0	3.86
294	S. R. Barwick (*Glam.*)	12	16	6	35	8	0	0	3.50
295	J. A. Afford (*Notts.*)	15	17	6	36	10	0	0	3.27
296	J. E. Brinkley (*Worcs.*)	10	10	2	16	5	0	0	2.00
297	M. B. Owens (*New Zealanders*)	6	8	2	8	4	0	0	1.33

BOWLING

(Qualification: 10 wickets in 10 innings)

† *Denotes a left-arm bowler.*

		O	*M*	*R*	*W*	*BB*	*5W/i*	*Avge*
1	C. E. L. Ambrose (*Northants*)	540	159	1,113	77	7-44	6	14.45
2	C. A. Walsh (*Glos.*)	506	119	1,535	89	7-42	9	17.24
3	M. J. McCague (*Kent*)	341.1	67	1,084	57	9-86	5	19.01
4	I. D. Austin (*Lancs.*)	251.5	72	662	33	5-23	3	20.06
5	F. D. Stephenson (*Sussex*)	480.5	108	1,345	67	6-50	6	20.07
6	J. E. Benjamin (*Surrey*)	591.2	130	1,658	80	6-27	5	20.72
7	T. A. Munton (*Warwicks.*)	699.4	181	1,748	81	7-52	6	21.58
8	†M. M. Patel (*Kent*)	811.2	202	2,058	90	8-96	6	22.86
9	C. White (*Yorks.*)	235.2	53	761	33	5-40	2	23.06
10	S. R. Lampitt (*Worcs.*)	512.5	127	1,484	64	5-33	2	23.18
11	A. R. Caddick (*Somerset*)	372.3	71	1,186	51	6-51	3	23.25
12	C. C. Lewis (*Notts.*)	345.2	69	1,082	46	5-55	2	23.52
13	G. R. Larsen (*New Zealanders*)	226.4	73	494	21	5-24	1	23.52
14	†M. C. Ilott (*Essex*)	497.5	115	1,391	59	6-24	3	23.57
15	†Wasim Akram (*Lancs.*)	213.2	44	646	27	8-30	2	23.92
16	P. S. de Villiers (*South Africans*)	277.3	59	922	38	6-67	2	24.26
17	W. K. M. Benjamin (*Hants*)	281	97	585	24	6-46	2	24.37
18	E. S. H. Giddins (*Sussex*)	450.4	89	1,463	60	5-38	3	24.38
19	C. A. Connor (*Hants*)	574.4	131	1,764	72	7-47	2	24.50
20	D. Gough (*Yorks.*)	479.2	100	1,526	62	6-66	3	24.61
21	P. A. J. DeFreitas (*Derbys.*)	530.5	108	1,621	65	6-39	4	24.93
22	D. J. Millns (*Leics.*)	532	99	1,901	76	6-44	4	25.01
23	V. J. Wells (*Leics.*)	301.5	78	1,053	42	5-50	1	25.07
24	A. C. S. Pigott (*Surrey*)	268.3	73	737	29	6-46	1	25.41
25	P. V. Simmons (*Leics.*)	300.5	81	769	30	4-68	0	25.63
26	J. E. Emburey (*Middx*)	674	204	1,514	59	6-89	2	25.66
27	G. D. Rose (*Somerset*)	344.1	69	1,136	44	4-40	0	25.81
28	R. A. Pick (*Notts.*)	507.2	122	1,413	54	6-62	2	26.16
29	G. C. Small (*Warwicks.*)	339	79	946	36	5-46	1	26.27
30	R. L. Johnson (*Middx*)	350.4	85	1,059	40	10-45	1	26.47
31	Mushtaq Ahmed (*Somerset*)	404	114	1,196	45	7-94	4	26.57
32	G. Chapple (*Lancs.*)	458.4	110	1,474	55	6-48	4	26.80
33	A. R. C. Fraser (*Middx*)	532.5	142	1,343	50	3-16	0	26.86
34	M. W. Alleyne (*Glos.*)	351.3	68	1,103	41	5-78	1	26.90
35	R. S. Yeabsley (*OUCC*)	174.5	26	567	21	6-54	1	27.00
36	S. D. Udal (*Hants*)	678	174	1,872	69	6-79	7	27.13
37	P. L. Symcox (*South Africans*)	280.5	86	761	28	5-29	2	27.17

		O	M	R	W	BB	5W/i	Avge
38	G. Yates (*Lancs.*)	320.5	70	1,013	37	5-34	1	27.37
39	G. J. Parsons (*Leics.*)	462.3	131	1,208	44	5-34	1	27.45
40	D. W. Headley (*Kent*)	295.3	48	989	36	5-60	2	27.47
41	P. W. Trimby (*OUCC*)	243.3	48	718	26	5-84	1	27.61
42	I. D. K. Salisbury (*Sussex*)	474	143	1,336	48	6-55	3	27.83
43	P. J. Hartley (*Yorks.*)	562.1	116	1,701	61	5-89	1	27.88
44	†S. J. E. Brown (*Durham & President's XI*)	578.5	88	2,108	75	6-68	6	28.10
45	M. A. Ealham (*Kent*)	265.4	62	762	27	7-53	1	28.22
46	†P. C. R. Tufnell (*Middx*)	463.5	128	1,107	39	6-35	1	28.38
47	K. E. Cooper (*Glos.*)	418.2	98	1,095	38	4-38	0	28.81
48	V. J. Pike (*Glos.*)	199	51	578	20	6-41	1	28.90
49	M. Watkinson (*Lancs.*)	631.1	173	1,823	63	8-30	1	28.93
50	E. E. Hemmings (*Sussex*)	422	140	959	33	7-66	2	29.06
51	D. E. Malcolm (*Derbys.*)	551.3	97	2,015	69	9-57	3	29.20
52	P. J. Martin (*Lancs.*)	614.4	173	1,580	54	5-61	2	29.25
53	R. C. Irani (*Essex*)	249.4	42	834	28	4-27	0	29.78
54	D. G. Cork (*Derbys.*)	329.1	53	1,112	37	6-29	2	30.05
55	C. E. Cuffy (*Surrey*)	389.3	106	1,082	36	4-70	0	30.05
56	K. P. Evans (*Notts.*)	413.5	105	1,143	38	4-46	0	30.07
57	W. J. Cronje (*South Africans*)	159.5	45	395	13	4-47	0	30.38
58	†R. D. Stemp (*Yorks.*)	669.1	252	1,493	49	6-37	2	30.46
59	†R. K. Illingworth (*Worcs.*)	679.1	211	1,499	49	4-51	0	30.59
60	D. A. Reeve (*Warwicks.*)	144	48	308	10	2-9	0	30.80
61	M. J. Thursfield (*Hants*)	163	39	524	17	6-130	1	30.82
62	P. M. Such (*Essex*)	670	183	1,757	57	7-66	5	30.82
63	A. A. Donald (*South Africans*)	212.2	42	775	25	5-58	2	31.00
63	D. J. Nash (*New Zealanders*)	228.4	51	775	25	6-76	2	31.00
65	S. L. Watkin (*Glam.*)	613.4	140	1,708	55	6-143	2	31.05
66	M. S. Kasprowicz (*Essex*)	527.3	91	1,869	60	7-83	3	31.15
67	P. J. Newport (*Worcs.*)	516.2	103	1,654	53	4-50	0	31.20
68	†J. C. Adams (*Notts.*)	340.5	125	720	23	4-63	0	31.30
69	†T. N. Wren (*Kent*)	164.5	30	533	17	6-48	1	31.35
70	†A. M. Smith (*Glos.*)	298.3	59	1,004	32	5-40	1	31.37
71	S. R. Barwick (*Glam.*)	549.5	208	1,131	36	5-44	1	31.41
72	A. C. Cummins (*Durham*)	520.3	92	1,768	56	6-64	4	31.57
73	G. W. Mike (*Notts.*)	406.1	92	1,422	45	5-44	1	31.60
74	†J. P. Taylor (*Northants*)	333.4	56	1,141	36	5-62	1	31.69
75	†R. P. Davis (*Warwicks.*)	341	102	986	31	6-94	2	31.80
76	†J. H. Childs (*Essex*)	464.3	117	1,254	39	6-71	2	32.15
77	C. E. W. Silverwood (*Yorks.*)	249	46	883	27	4-67	0	32.70
78	R. C. Williams (*Glos.*)	245.5	46	856	26	4-28	0	32.92
79	P. A. Smith (*Warwicks.*)	182	40	594	18	3-24	0	33.00
80	J. Wood (*Durham*)	345.4	38	1,501	45	6-110	3	33.35
81	M. A. Feltham (*Middx*)	382.3	83	1,140	34	5-69	1	33.52
82	H. R. J. Trump (*Somerset*)	268.4	76	873	26	6-68	2	33.57
83	M. P. Bicknell (*Surrey*)	319.4	75	977	29	5-44	1	33.68
84	P. N. Weekes (*Middx*)	484.2	91	1,383	41	5-12	1	33.73
85	S. J. Base (*Derbys.*)	199	30	782	23	5-92	1	34.00
86	A. R. K. Pierson (*Leics.*)	500.4	131	1,267	37	8-42	1	34.24
87	†J. A. Afford (*Notts.*)	541.3	164	1,376	40	5-48	2	34.40
88	N. M. K. Smith (*Warwicks.*)	582	141	1,693	49	7-42	4	34.55
89	†K. D. James (*Hants*)	280.1	56	900	26	4-78	0	34.61
90	P. W. Jarvis (*Sussex*)	496.2	89	1,773	51	7-58	1	34.76
91	B. M. McMillan (*South Africans*)	222.4	49	662	19	4-47	0	34.84
92	R. P. Lefebvre (*Glam.*)	365.2	108	896	25	4-63	0	35.84
93	C. M. Wells (*Derbys.*)	153.3	31	469	13	4-52	0	36.07
94	N. V. Radford (*Worcs.*)	459.1	106	1,408	39	5-93	1	36.10
95	O. D. Gibson (*Glam.*)	579.5	100	2,171	60	6-64	4	36.18
96	R. G. Twose (*Warwicks.*)	190.5	41	544	15	6-28	1	36.26
97	C. L. Hooper (*Kent*)	414.1	93	1,055	29	5-52	1	36.37

		O	*M*	*R*	*W*	*BB*	*5W/i*	*Avge*
98	J. E. R. Gallian (*Lancs.*)	95	10	368	10	2-27	0	36.80
99	M. A. Robinson (*Yorks.*)	619	171	1,658	45	5-48	1	36.84
100	A. J. Hollioake (*Surrey*)	264.1	44	958	26	4-48	0	36.84
101	R. P. Snell (*South Africans*)	200.1	38	666	18	3-38	0	37.00
102	M. J. Vandrau (*Derbys.*)	290.5	63	965	26	4-53	0	37.11
103	A. L. Penberthy (*Northants*)	400.1	83	1,374	37	5-54	1	37.13
104	S. C. Ecclestone (*OUCC & Somerset*)	298.3	70	825	22	4-66	0	37.50
105	N. A. Mallender (*Somerset*)	193.4	51	602	16	3-23	0	37.62
106	N. G. Cowans (*Hants*)	349.3	93	986	26	4-76	0	37.92
107	A. P. van Troost (*Somerset*)	346.1	58	1,330	35	4-50	0	38.00
108	†A. D. Mullally (*Leics.*)	448.1	121	1,255	33	5-85	1	38.03
109	T. M. Moody (*Worcs.*)	195	48	572	15	4-24	0	38.13
110	A. P. Igglesden (*Kent*)	316.1	75	929	24	5-38	1	38.70
111	†T. G. Shaw (*South Africans*)	312.4	90	828	21	4-29	0	39.42
112	K. J. Shine (*Middx*)	332.4	76	1,156	29	4-79	0	39.86
113	†D. A. Graveney (*Durham*)	456	121	1,247	31	6-80	1	40.22
114	J. P. Stephenson (*Essex*)	332	75	1,066	26	4-74	0	41.00
115	C. Pringle (*New Zealanders*)	258	74	739	18	5-58	1	41.05
116	†R. J. Maru (*Hants*)	254.1	75	621	15	3-61	0	41.40
117	N. F. Williams (*Middx*)	326	71	1,088	26	6-49	1	41.84
118	M. A. Butcher (*Surrey*)	206.4	50	670	16	4-31	0	41.87
119	G. A. Hick (*Worcs.*)	173.2	55	462	11	3-64	0	42.00
120	†N. G. B. Cook (*Northants*)	283.3	85	715	17	3-46	0	42.05
121	A. Dale (*Glam.*)	277	65	975	23	2-7	0	42.39
122	A. E. Warner (*Derbys.*)	256	53	817	19	4-39	0	43.00
123	J. E. Brinkley (*Worcs.*)	233	40	779	18	6-98	1	43.27
124	C. R. Matthews (*South Africans*)	263.3	71	749	17	3-25	0	44.05
125	G. Welch (*Warwicks.*)	267	63	970	22	4-74	0	44.09
126	M. G. Field-Buss (*Notts.*)	245.1	71	540	12	2-23	0	45.00
127	C. M. Pitcher (*CUCC*)	258.5	56	902	20	4-37	0	45.10
128	M. C. J. Ball (*Glos.*)	325.3	78	955	21	5-69	1	45.47
129	C. J. Hollins (*OUCC*)	236.3	32	890	19	4-64	0	46.84
130	K. M. Curran (*Northants*)	423.5	86	1,463	31	4-65	0	47.19
131	†M. N. Hart (*New Zealanders*)	335.3	104	850	18	4-106	0	47.22
132	A. W. Smith (*Surrey*)	374	67	1,340	28	5-103	1	47.85
133	M. P. Vaughan (*Yorks.*)	228.3	53	678	14	4-39	0	48.42
134	J. S. Hodgson (*CUCC*)	272.3	85	732	15	4-14	0	48.80
135	A. R. Roberts (*Northants*)	242	49	870	17	3-106	0	51.17
136	R. J. Bailey (*Northants*)	166.1	33	568	11	5-59	1	51.63
137	R. D. B. Croft (*Glam.*)	715.3	154	2,166	41	5-80	1	52.82
138	†A. A. Barnett (*Lancs.*)	191.4	39	627	10	2-35	0	62.70
139	N. J. Haste (*CUCC*)	233	39	910	13	4-69	0	70.00
140	P. Bainbridge (*Durham*)	315.4	67	1,082	14	4-72	0	77.28
141	A. R. Whittall (*CUCC*)	295.3	59	1,060	11	2-34	0	96.36

The following bowlers took ten wickets but bowled in fewer than ten innings:

	O	*M*	*R*	*W*	*BB*	*5W/i*	*Avge*
K. J. Barnett (*Derbys.*)	54.2	5	173	13	5-31	1	13.30
M. B. Owens (*New Zealanders*)	127	31	424	17	5-74	1	24.94
D. M. Cousins (*Essex*)	112	21	337	13	6-35	1	25.92
J. N. B. Bovill (*Hants*)	119.4	23	421	14	5-108	1	30.07
J. G. Hughes (*Northants*)	137.2	38	428	14	5-69	1	30.57
D. J. Spencer (*Kent*)	85.5	12	347	10	4-31	0	34.70
†A. Sheriyar (*Leics.*)	98	14	400	11	4-44	0	36.36

INDIVIDUAL SCORES OF 100 AND OVER

There were 278 three-figure innings in 200 first-class matches in 1994, two more than in 1993 when 199 matches were played. Of these, 24 were double-hundreds, compared with eight in 1993. The list includes 213 hundreds hit in the County Championship, nine by the New Zealand touring team, eight by the South African touring team and 48 in other first-class games.

* *Signifies not out.*

B. C. Lara (9)
147 Warwicks. v Glam., Birmingham
106 }
120* } Warwicks. v Leics., Birmingham
136 Warwicks. v Somerset, Taunton
140 Warwicks. v Middx, Lord's
501* Warwicks. v Durham, Birmingham
197 Warwicks. v Northants, Northampton
142 Warwicks. v Derbys., Chesterfield
191 Warwicks. v Hants, Birmingham

J. D. Carr (6)
102 Middx v England A, Lord's
108* Middx v Derbys., Derby
171* Middx v Somerset, Lord's
136 }
106* } Middx v Northants, Northampton
261* Middx v Glos., Lord's

M. W. Gatting (6)
224* Middx v England A, Lord's
225 Middx v Leics., Leicester
147 Middx v Derbys., Derby
108 Middx v Essex, Uxbridge
201* Middx v Northants, Northampton
103 Middx v Surrey, The Oval

G. A. Gooch (6)
123* Essex v Hants, Southampton
236 Essex v Kent, Chelmsford
210 England v New Zealand, Nottingham
101 }
205 } Essex v Worcs., Worcester
140 Essex v Middx, Uxbridge

D. L. Haynes (5)
125 Middx v Worcs., Lord's
104 }
103 } Middx v Kent, Canterbury
123 Middx v Essex, Uxbridge
134 Middx v Glam., Lord's

G. A. Hick (5)
150 Worcs. v Glos., Worcester
101 Worcs. v Essex, Worcester
159 Worcs. v Kent, Canterbury
110 England v South Africa, Leeds
215 Worcs. v Lancs., Manchester

C. L. Hooper (5)
160 Kent v Essex, Chelmsford
136 Kent v Warwicks., Birmingham
183 Kent v Yorks., Maidstone
138 Kent v Hants, Canterbury
127 Kent v Somerset, Canterbury

R. A. Smith (5)
124 Hants v Sussex, Hove
111 Hants v Notts., Basingstoke
134 Hants v Yorks., Leeds
162 Hants v Worcs., Worcester
123 Hants v Leics., Leicester

V. P. Terry (5)
112 Hants v Oxford U., Oxford
130 Hants v Essex, Southampton
141* Hants v Yorks., Leeds
135 Hants v Surrey, Southampton
164 Hants v Durham, Portsmouth

N. H. Fairbrother (4)
136 Lancs. v Derbys., Blackpool
204 Lancs. v Middx, Manchester
103 Lancs. v Essex, Chelmsford
120 Lancs. v Glos., Manchester

D. L. Hemp (4)
127 Glam. v Warwicks., Birmingham
136 Glam. v Glos., Bristol
133 Glam. v Kent, Abergavenny
126 Glam. v South Africans, Pontypridd

P. Johnson (4)
107 Notts. v Oxford U., Oxford
101 Notts. v Durham, Nottingham
129 Notts. v Glos., Nottingham
132 Notts. v Northants, Nottingham

N. V. Knight (4)
150 Essex v Cambridge U., Cambridge
113 Essex v Warwicks., Birmingham
115 Essex v Surrey, Colchester
157 Essex v Sussex, Chelmsford

J. E. Morris (4)
204 Durham v Warwicks., Birmingham
186 Durham v Northants, Hartlepool
123* Durham v Glam., Hartlepool
149 Durham v Hants, Portsmouth

M. D. Moxon (4)
161* Yorks. v Lancs., Manchester
122 Yorks. v Kent, Maidstone
116 Yorks. v Warwicks., Scarborough
274* Yorks. v Worcs., Worcester

M. R. Ramprakash (4)
135 Middx v Durham, Lord's
131 Middx v Derbys., Derby
123* Middx v Essex, Uxbridge
124 Middx v Surrey, The Oval

J. C. Adams (3)
117* Notts. v Oxford U., Oxford
121 Notts. v Sussex, Nottingham
144* Notts. v Somerset, Taunton

R. J. Bailey (3)
113 Northants v Notts., Nottingham
129* Northants v Middx, Northampton
115 Northants v Kent, Northampton

D. J. Bicknell (3)
129 Surrey v Glos., Gloucester
190 Surrey v Durham, Darlington
235* Surrey v Notts., Nottingham

P. A. Cottey (3)
109 Glam. v Oxford U., Oxford
191 Glam. v Somerset, Swansea
142 Glam. v Leics., Cardiff

J. P. Crawley (3)
281* Lancs. v Somerset, Southport
141 Lancs. v Warwicks., Birmingham
250 Lancs. v Notts., Nottingham

M. D. Crowe (3)
102* New Zealanders v Somerset, Taunton
142 New Zealand v England, Lord's
115 New Zealand v England, Manchester

T. S. Curtis (3)
117 Worcs. v Middx, Lord's
180 Worcs. v Warwicks., Worcester
118* Worcs. v Notts., Kidderminster

A. Fordham (3)
102 Northants v Leics., Leicester
129 Northants v Glam., Northampton
158 Northants v Middx, Northampton

A. J. Hollioake (3)
123 Surrey v Worcs., The Oval
101* Surrey v Glam., Swansea
138 Surrey v Leics., The Oval

S. P. James (3)
150 Glam. v Oxford U., Oxford
138* Glam. v Cambridge U., Cambridge
116 Glam. v Worcs., Cardiff

M. B. Loye (3)
107* Northants v Worcs., Worcester
132 Northants v Yorks., Luton
113 Northants v Warwicks., Northampton

T. M. Moody (3)
108* Worcs. v Essex, Worcester
109 Worcs. v Lancs., Manchester
159 Worcs. v Durham, Worcester

M. C. J. Nicholas (3)
107 Hants v Northants, Southampton
108 Hants v Kent, Canterbury
145 Hants v Surrey, Southampton

P. A. Nixon (3)
106 Leics. v Northants, Leicester
115 Leics. v Essex, Leicester
131 Leics. v Hants, Leicester

T. J. G. O'Gorman (3)
128 Derbys. v Glam., Cardiff
143 Derbys. v New Zealanders, Derby
145 Derbys. v Lancs., Blackpool

P. J. Prichard (3)
108 Essex v Durham, Stockton-on-Tees
109 Essex v Kent, Chelmsford
119 Essex v Glos., Chelmsford

N. J. Speak (3)
105 Lancs. v Yorks., Manchester
102* Lancs. v Cambridge U., Cambridge
143 Lancs. v Yorks., Leeds

A. J. Stewart (3)
126 Surrey v Lancs., Manchester
119 England v New Zealand, Lord's
142 Surrey v Leics., The Oval

N. R. Taylor (3)
129 Kent v Cambridge U., Cambridge
139 Kent v Yorks., Maidstone
120 Kent v Somerset, Canterbury

R. G. Twose (3)
277* Warwicks. v Glam., Birmingham
142 Warwicks. v Kent, Birmingham
137 Warwicks. v Hants, Birmingham

M. P. Vaughan (3)
106* Yorks. v Oxford U., Oxford
105 Yorks. v Somerset, Bradford
117 Yorks. v Northants, Luton

T. R. Ward (3)
110 } Kent v Glam., Abergavenny
125 }
109 Kent v Surrey, The Oval

M. W. Alleyne (2)
101* Glos. v Cambridge U., Bristol
109 Glos. v Yorks., Cheltenham

G. F. Archer (2)
100 Notts. v Hants, Basingstoke
168 Notts. v Glam., Worksop

M. A. Atherton (2)
101 England v New Zealand, Nottingham
111 England v New Zealand, Manchester

C. W. J. Athey (2)
169* Sussex v Kent, Tunbridge Wells
166 Sussex v Durham, Hove

M. Azharuddin (2)
205 Derbys. v Durham, Chesterfield
109 Derbys. v Glam., Cardiff

N. E. Briers (2)
154 Leics. v Warwicks., Birmingham
147 Leics. v Middx, Leicester

A. D. Brown (2)
172 Surrey v Durham, Darlington
134* Surrey v Notts., Nottingham

D. Byas (2)
102 Yorks. v Somerset, Bradford
104 Yorks. v Lancs., Leeds

A. Dale (2)
131 Glam. v Sussex, Hove
109 Glam. v Cambridge U., Cambridge

S. P. Fleming (2)
118* New Zealanders v Middx, Lord's
151 New Zealanders v Glam., Swansea

J. E. R. Gallian (2)
171 Lancs. v Surrey, Manchester
118 Lancs. v Derbys., Blackpool

C. M. Gupte (2)
105 Oxford U. v Surrey, The Oval
122 Oxford U. v Cambridge U., Lord's

R. J. Harden (2)
103* Somerset v Hants, Taunton
131* Somerset v Worcs., Taunton

A. N. Hayhurst (2)
111* Somerset v Warwicks., Taunton
121 Somerset v Glam., Swansea

G. R. Haynes (2)
102* Worcs. v Cambridge U., Cambridge
141 Worcs. v Notts., Kidderminster

N. Hussain (2)
115* Essex v Hants, Southampton
101 Essex v Durham, Stockton-on-Tees

R. C. Irani (2)
119 Essex v Worcs., Worcester
102* Essex v Middx, Uxbridge

G. Kirsten (2)
201* South Africans v Durham, Chester-le-Street
102 South Africans v Northants, Northampton

P. N. Kirsten (2)
130 South Africans v Sussex, Hove
104 South Africa v England, Leeds

A. J. Lamb (2)
131 Northants v Hants, Southampton
114 Northants v Essex, Chelmsford

M. N. Lathwell (2)
206 Somerset v Surrey, Bath
124 Somerset v Sussex, Hove

D. A. Leatherdale (2)
138 Worcs. v Oxford U., Worcester
139 Worcs. v Somerset, Taunton

C. C. Lewis (2)
220* Notts. v Warwicks., Birmingham
108* Notts. v Middx, Nottingham

M. P. Maynard (2)
118 Glam. v Derbys., Cardiff
101 Glam. v South Africans, Pontypridd

R. R. Montgomerie (2)
101* Oxford U. v Leics., Oxford
151 Northants v Derbys., Northampton

R. S. M. Morris (2)
174 Hants v Notts., Basingstoke
101* Hants v South Africans, Southampton

D. P. Ostler (2)
149 Warwicks. v Oxford U., Oxford
186 Warwicks. v Yorks., Scarborough

P. R. Pollard (2)
110 Notts. v Northants, Nottingham
134 Notts. v Warwicks., Birmingham

R. T. Robinson (2)
182 Notts. v Essex, Ilford
134 Notts. v Worcs., Kidderminster

M. A. Roseberry (2)
119 Middx v Warwicks., Lord's
152 Middx v Durham, Lord's

K. R. Rutherford (2)
129 New Zealanders v Essex, Chelmsford
115* New Zealanders v Glam., Swansea

M. Saxelby (2)
181 Durham v Derbys., Chesterfield
131 Durham v Essex, Stockton-on-Tees

C. W. Scott (2)
108 Durham v Surrey, Darlington
107* Durham v Yorks., Durham University

G. P. Thorpe (2)
190 Surrey v Worcs., The Oval
114 Surrey v Derbys., The Oval

M. E. Trescothick (2)
121 Somerset v Surrey, Bath
115 Somerset v Glam., Swansea

M. Watkinson (2)
117 Lancs. v Hants, Manchester
155 Lancs. v Glam., Colwyn Bay

J. J. Whitaker (2)
148 Leics. v Yorks., Harrogate
107 Leics. v Durham, Durham University

The following each played one three-figure innings:

C. J. Adams, 109*, Derbys. v Surrey, The Oval.

K. J. Barnett, 148, Derbys. v Middx, Derby; M. R. Benson, 159, Kent v Glos., Cheltenham; B. C. Broad, 128, Glos. v Sussex, Bristol; K. R. Brown, 102*, Middx v Leics., Leicester; M. A. Butcher, 134, Surrey v Hants, Southampton.

R. Q. Cake, 107, Cambridge U. v Glam., Cambridge; G. R. Cowdrey, 114, Kent v South Africans, Canterbury; W. J. Cronje, 108, South Africans v Notts., Nottingham; R. J. Cunliffe, 177*, Glos. v Cambridge U., Bristol; K. M. Curran, 114, Northants v Yorks., Luton.

J. A. Daley, 159*, Durham v Hants, Portsmouth; R. I. Dawson, 127*, Glos. v Cambridge U., Bristol; P. A. J. DeFreitas, 108, Derbys. v Leics., Derby.

K. P. Evans, 104, Notts. v Sussex, Nottingham.

D. P. Fulton, 109, Kent v Cambridge U., Cambridge.

A. P. Grayson, 100, Yorks. v Worcs., Worcester.

T. H. C. Hancock, 123, Glos. v Essex, Chelmsford; G. D. Harrison, 105*, Ireland v Scotland, Glasgow; G. D. Hodgson, 113, Glos. v Warwicks., Bristol; C. J. Hollins, 131, Oxford U. v Cambridge U., Lord's; A. C. Hudson, 116, South Africans v President's XI, Scarborough; S. Hutton, 101, Durham v Northants, Hartlepool.

W. S. Kendall, 113*, Oxford U. v Surrey, The Oval.

S. R. Lampitt, 122, Worcs. v Middx, Lord's; W. Larkins, 158*, Durham v Glos., Gateshead Fell; N. J. Lenham, 102, Sussex v Lancs., Horsham; D. A. Lewis, 113*, Ireland v Scotland, Glasgow; J. J. B. Lewis, 109, Essex v Glos., Chelmsford; G. D. Lloyd, 112, Lancs. v Glos., Manchester; J. I. Longley, 100*, Durham v Derbys., Chesterfield.

B. M. McMillan, 132, South Africans v Sussex, Hove; T. C. Middleton, 102, Hants v Oxford U., Oxford; A. J. Moles, 203*, Warwicks. v Surrey, Guildford; H. Morris, 106, Glam. v Sussex, Hove.

B. Parker, 127, Yorks. v Surrey, Scarborough; B. M. W. Patterson, 114, Scotland v Ireland, Glasgow; T. L. Penney, 111, Warwicks. v Lancs., Birmingham; K. J. Piper, 116*, Warwicks. v Durham, Birmingham; B. A. Pocock, 103*, New Zealanders v Glos., Bristol.

S. J. Rhodes, 100*, Worcs. v New Zealanders, Worcester; G. D. Rose, 121, Somerset v Yorks., Bradford.

P. V. Simmons, 261, Leics. v Northants, Leicester; A. W. Smith, 202*, Surrey v Oxford U., The Oval; M. P. Speight, 126, Sussex v Hants, Hove; F. D. Stephenson, 107, Sussex v Lancs., Horsham; J. P. Stephenson, 144, Essex v Notts., Ilford; A. C. Storie, 102*, Scotland v Ireland, Glasgow.

R. J. Turner, 104*, Somerset v New Zealanders, Taunton.

M. J. Walker, 107, Kent v Surrey, The Oval; D. M. Ward, 294*, Surrey v Derbys., The Oval; P. N. Weekes, 117, Middx v Somerset, Lord's; K. C. Wessels, 105, South Africa v England, Lord's; C. White, 108*, Yorks. v Essex, Leeds: G. W. White, 104, Combined Universities v New Zealanders, Cambridge; M. G. N. Windows, 106, Glos. v New Zealanders, Bristol; A. J. Wright, 184*, Glos. v Leics., Bristol.

B. A. Young, 122, New Zealanders v Essex, Chelmsford.

TEN WICKETS IN A MATCH

There were 29 instances of bowlers taking ten or more wickets in a match in first-class cricket in 1994, one more than in 1993. The list includes 25 in the County Championship, one for the New Zealand touring team and three in other first-class matches. Two of the instances occurred in the same match, when C. E. L. Ambrose took ten wickets for Northamptonshire and C. A. Connor ten for Hampshire at Southampton.

M. M. Patel (3)
10-77, Kent v Cambridge U., Cambridge; 10-201, Kent v Lancs., Canterbury; 10-152, Kent v Durham, Canterbury.

C. A. Walsh (3)
11-143, Glos. v Somerset, Bristol; 12-102, Glos. v Notts., Nottingham; 10-160, Glos. v Yorks., Cheltenham.

C. E. L. Ambrose (2)
10-96, Northants v Derbys., Northampton; 10-88, Northants v Hants, Southampton.

C. A. Connor (2)
10-126, Hants v Northants, Southampton; 10-132, Hants v Kent, Canterbury.

T. A. Munton (2)
10-132, Warwicks. v Northants, Northampton; 10-130, Warwicks. v Essex, Birmingham.

F. D. Stephenson (2)
11-96, Sussex v Hants, Hove; 11-82, Sussex v Surrey, The Oval.

The following each took ten wickets in a match on one occasion:

I. D. Austin, 10-60, Lancs. v Middx, Manchester.
J. E. Benjamin, 10-132, Surrey v Leics., The Oval.
A. C. Cummins, 10-104, Durham v Northants, Hartlepool.
O. D. Gibson, 11-159, Glam. v Somerset, Swansea.
M. C. Ilott, 10-129, Essex v Sussex, Chelmsford.
R. L. Johnson, 11-110, Middx v Derbys., Derby.
M. J. McCague, 15-147, Kent v Derbys., Derby; D. E. Malcolm, 10-138, England v South Africa, The Oval; Mushtaq Ahmed, 12-160, Somerset v Worcs., Taunton.
D. J. Nash, 11-169, New Zealand v England, Lord's.
H. R. J. Trump, 12-195, Somerset v Sussex, Hove.
S. D. Udal, 10-163, Hants v Surrey, Southampton.
Wasim Akram, 13-147, Lancs. v Somerset, Southport; M. Watkinson, 11-87, Lancs. v Hants, Manchester.
R. S. Yeabsley, 10-104, Oxford U. v Cambridge U., Lord's.

THE NEW ZEALANDERS IN ENGLAND, 1994

New Zealand lost their 12th Test series in England and beat only Glamorgan during their programme of 12 first-class matches. But to call the enterprise a failure, as no less a judge than Sir Richard Hadlee came close to doing during the final Test at Old Trafford, would, nevertheless, be to divorce it from history both ancient and modern.

New Zealand have beaten England only four times in 65 years, all the wins coming when Hadlee himself was cutting swathes through the best batting teams everywhere. If the 1994 tour was, to some extent, the latest exercise in coming to terms with life after Hadlee – he last played for his country in 1990 – it must also be seen in the context of the temporary retirement of the steadiest of their batsmen in recent times, Andrew Jones, and of injuries to their two established fast bowlers. Chris Cairns, an all-rounder of proven Test ability, if not quite in Hadlee's exalted class, missed the trip in order to recuperate after knee surgery. Danny Morrison travelled but, because of persistent groin trouble, played only in the first one-day international. Another of the seam bowlers originally selected, Simon Doull, managed one match before being obliged to return home injured. Michael Owens replaced him but, by the end of the tour, further casualties meant Stuart Roberts of Canterbury had to be called up from English league cricket. It says much about the lack of experience and consistency in the fast bowling department that Roberts should, by taking eight wickets in 47 overs, have finished comfortably top of the averages.

No cloud is without its silver lining, however. In Dion Nash, only 22 and pleasantly ingenuous, New Zealand discovered a champion of the future. He took 17 wickets in the three Tests and at Lord's, where he surpassed any previous performance by a Kiwi bowler against England with match figures of 11 for 169, he and Martin Crowe, whose masterly batting in the last two Tests saved the tour from being a complete débâcle, all but won the day. Had Ken Rutherford, a captain whose humour and equanimity never wavered during good and mainly bad times, taken the gamble of bringing Nash back to bowl in very dim light in the dying moments of the game, the ambition of every touring side to England – victory at Lord's – might have been achieved. As it was, England held on for a draw and moved on to dominate the Third Test almost as clearly as they had the First at Trent Bridge, which they had won by an innings and 90 runs. But for rain, England would have won at Old Trafford in four days. In the event, traditional Manchester weather, another hundred by Crowe (aided, with skill and determination, by Adam Parore) and some ill-directed bowling as time ran out, combined to ensure that England won the series by no more than 1-0. Thereby justice was done; although the stronger team, England would have been flattered by a 2-0 margin.

The paradox was that New Zealand made more progress than England. A new home selection committee, under a very different chairman in Raymond Illingworth, dismantled the winter's touring party. At Old Trafford, only five players – the captain Mike Atherton, his deputy Alec Stewart, plus Angus Fraser and two insecure batsmen in Robin Smith and Graeme Hick – survived from the tour of the West Indies that had ended

THE NEW ZEALAND TOURING PARTY

[*Patrick Eagar*

Back row: G. P. Howarth (*cricket manager*), A. C. Parore, B. R. Hartland, H. T. Davis, B. A. Pocock, S. P. Fleming, S. B. Doull, D. J. Nash, M. N. Hart, B. A. Young, M. Jones (*scorer*), M. Plummer (*physiotherapist*). *Front row:* M. D. Crowe, C. Pringle, M. Sandlant (*manager*), G. R. Larsen, K. R. Rutherford (*captain*), S. A. Thomson, M. J. Greatbatch, D. K. Morrison.

barely two months before and which had included a famous and romantic victory in Bridgetown. And both Fraser and Smith were later left out of the winter touring party to Australia. Some critics looking to the long-term future were dismayed by the recall of Graham Gooch, who scored a double-century at Trent Bridge but 13 runs in his next three innings.

The rebuilding against New Zealand, was, nevertheless, half-hearted and clearly incomplete when the South African series began in July. While England were feeling their way towards a brighter future, partly by piercing the mists which had hitherto hidden Yorkshire from the gaze of the selectors, New Zealand were busy proving that, in addition to Nash and Parore, Bryan Young and Stephen Fleming both have what it takes to succeed in Test cricket. Young reached 94 at Lord's before nerves defeated him. He is a brave, compact, correct opening batsman, with a nice balance between the off and on sides and also between front and back foot. It is a pity for both himself and his country that he did not make the decision to abandon wicket-keeping earlier than he did; his true worth as a batsman has been recognised only recently.

Fleming had established himself in the last few weeks before the tour as a batsman of exciting potential. Tall and dark-haired, he shares with David Gower left-handedness, a birthday – April 1 – and the same ability to hit good balls for four. Like Gower, he is a distinctive puller of the short ball; unlike him, he is still largely an on-side player. Two hundreds in first-class matches and 170 runs in six Test innings confirmed the good impression he had made when scoring 92 in his first Test, against India, and 90 in his first one-day international. Matthew Hart and Shane Thomson may establish their Test quality too. Both were excellent in the Second Test. Hart did not take as many wickets as his beautifully poised left-arm spin threatened but, at Lord's in particular, he tied the England batsmen down and helped to create the pressure which led to their dismissal at the other end. His eventual four Test wickets from 147.3 overs cost him almost 70 runs each. Thomson, a batsman of undoubted flair, hit the ball with relish and style during his partnership with Crowe at Lord's and confirmed that he is a developing, although inexperienced, off-spinner. His batting limitations were exposed at Old Trafford, where he was distinctly unsettled by fast short-pitched bowling on a bouncy pitch.

The same, unfortunately, was true of Mark Greatbatch, who joined Fleming, Rutherford, Crowe and Young in scoring more than 500 first-class runs on the trip but could not earn a Test place until the end of the tour. He took time to recover from knee surgery, like Crowe, who played the first few matches with a palpable limp. The difference was that Crowe showed glimpses of his rare ability even before the Lord's Test, notably on his old stamping ground at Taunton. His confidence and self-esteem came surging back during his impeccable century in that match and he went on to score two Test hundreds. By contrast, Greatbatch owed his return largely to the inability of the two Blairs, Pocock and Hartland – both victims of uncertain footwork – to establish a right to go in first with Young. A broken thumb sustained in the field at Old Trafford sent Greatbatch home a disappointed man with an uncertain future.

The lack of a consistent opening pair is a frequent problem for teams which struggle in England and, since Rutherford's batting did him less than justice, New Zealand were one experienced batsman short of presenting England's bowlers with a solid challenge. In both the First and the Third

Tests, the batting was unravelled by the swing bowling of Phillip DeFreitas, whose 14th reincarnation as a Test player was by some margin his most successful. In the last match he had the support of a hostile young fast bowler in Darren Gough.

But for all the anticlimax after Lord's – the New Zealanders were held by the Combined Universities and badly beaten by Derbyshire before Old Trafford – there was no pessimism and no need for the kind of recriminations and post-mortems which have invariably followed recent tours by England. Indeed, Rutherford, who played the game as New Zealanders still do – with a smile and no attempt to bend either the laws or their spirit – made the following bullish statement at the end of the tour: "Twelve months down the line, I like to think that New Zealand will be a very, very competitive Test match unit. In one-day cricket we already are. England tours are all about development; we're disappointed to have lost the series but we're looking forward to doing well in a busy season at home."

His optimism might be vindicated if Cairns and Morrison return to full fitness and Crowe can act as elder statesman as well as prima donna batsman. Stories in the New Zealand press suggested that Crowe and the team manager, Geoff Howarth, were not seeing eye to eye. Undoubtedly there were clashes, but both were happy to give Rutherford their support.

Parore played well throughout, though his best came in the final Test when his stand of 141 with Crowe – more than three and a half hours of determined resistance between showers – saved the match. His form made watchers in the United Kingdom wonder why he had not been New Zealand's regular wicket-keeper-batsman since displacing the injured Ian Smith on the previous tour in 1990, when he was the baby of the party. He kept wicket with neatness and agility and batted with a nice mixture of solid defence and occasionally explosive attack. His penchant was for forcing strokes off the back foot, sometimes played West Indian-style against half-volleys. Already, Parore would be on the short list for wicket-keeper in a world eleven.

Nash's strong, willing, accurate fast-medium bowling was based on an excellent action, starting from close to the stumps. His efforts won him the Cornhill award as his team's man of the series and he was the bright light amid some rather dismal fast bowling. Michael Owens had some good spells at Old Trafford but the balls he bowled were seldom as impressive as his long and menacing run-up. Heath Davis was as fast and as wild as he had been when playing in Sussex two years before. Then, bowling for Bexhill against Chichester, he delivered 42 no-balls and eight wides in 14 overs. He was given every encouragement early in the tour, because of his ideal build and genuine speed, but his willingness to learn was not matched by his ability to do so.

Chris Pringle and Gavin Larsen are more experienced and both contributed much without being able to make an impact in the Tests. It was because Pringle was injured before the first match that Larsen, a medium-pacer who rarely bowls badly, at last won his Test cap, after faithful service for New Zealand in 55 one-day internationals. Even in defeat Larsen will always be glad of that Test at Nottingham. His spirit was typical of his team's: a determination to make the most of limited ability, and to enjoy the game, whatever the outcome. – Christopher Martin-Jenkins.

NEW ZEALAND TOURING PARTY

K. R. Rutherford (Otago) (*captain*), G. R. Larsen (Wellington) (*vice-captain*), M. D. Crowe (Wellington), H. T. Davis (Wellington), S. B. Doull (Northern Districts), S. P. Fleming (Canterbury), M. J. Greatbatch (Central Districts), M. N. Hart (Northern Districts), B. R. Hartland (Canterbury), D. K. Morrison (Auckland), D. J. Nash (Otago), A. C. Parore (Auckland), B. A. Pocock (Auckland), C. Pringle (Auckland), S. A. Thomson (Northern Districts), B. A. Young (Northern Districts).

M. B. Owens and S. J. Roberts (both Canterbury) joined the party after Doull and Morrison were injured. M. W. Douglas (Wellington) played in the match against Derbyshire.

Manager: M. Sandlant. *Cricket manager:* G. P. Howarth.

NEW ZEALAND TOUR RESULTS

Test matches – Played 3: Lost 1, Drawn 2.
First-class matches – Played 12: Won 1, Lost 3, Drawn 8.
Win – Glamorgan.
Losses – England, Yorkshire, Derbyshire.
Draws – England (2), Worcestershire, Somerset, Middlesex, Essex, Gloucestershire, Combined Universities.
One-day internationals – Played 1: Lost 1. Abandoned 1.
Other non first-class matches – Played 7: Won 6, Lost 1. *Wins* – England Amateur XI, Lavinia, Duchess of Norfolk's XI, Northamptonshire, Leicestershire, Ireland (2). *Loss* – Surrey.

TEST MATCH AVERAGES

ENGLAND – BATTING

	T	*I*	*NO*	*R*	*HS*	*100s*	*Avge*	*Ct*
M. A. Atherton	3	4	0	273	111	2	68.25	2
S. J. Rhodes	3	4	2	117	49	0	58.50	12
G. A. Gooch	3	4	0	223	210	1	55.75	3
A. J. Stewart	3	4	0	196	119	1	49.00	3
P. A. J. DeFreitas	3	4	1	134	69	0	44.66	1
G. A. Hick	3	4	0	133	58	0	33.25	9
C. White	3	4	0	121	51	0	30.25	3
R. A. Smith	3	4	0	120	78	0	30.00	3
A. R. C. Fraser	3	4	0	30	10	0	7.50	1

Played in three Tests: P. M. Such 4, 5*. Played in one Test: D. Gough 65; J. P. Taylor 0, 0*; D. E. Malcolm did not bat.

* *Signifies not out.*

BOWLING

	O	*M*	*R*	*W*	*BB*	*5W/i*	*Avge*
P. A. J. DeFreitas	143.3	24	451	21	5-71	1	21.47
D. Gough	47.5	7	152	6	4-47	0	25.33
C. White	62.1	15	197	6	3-18	0	32.83
A. R. C. Fraser	126	37	296	7	2-40	0	42.28
P. M. Such	123	36	264	6	2-50	0	44.00

Also bowled: G. A. Gooch 7–1–26–0; G. A. Hick 18–8–21–1; D. E. Malcolm 27.4–7–84–2; J. P. Taylor 26–6–82–2.

NEW ZEALAND – BATTING

	T	*I*	*NO*	*R*	*HS*	*100s*	*Avge*	*Ct*
M. D. Crowe	3	6	0	380	142	2	63.33	2
A. C. Parore	3	6	1	213	71	0	42.60	7
B. A. Young	3	6	0	195	94	0	32.50	3
S. A. Thomson	3	6	1	157	69	0	31.40	3
D. J. Nash	3	5	2	94	56	0	31.33	3
S. P. Fleming	3	6	0	170	54	0	28.33	1
M. N. Hart	3	5	1	99	36	0	24.75	1
K. R. Rutherford	3	6	0	96	37	0	16.00	0

Played in two Tests: M. B. Owens 2*, 4; C. Pringle 14, 0 (1 ct). Played in one Test: H. T. Davis 0*, 0*; M. J. Greatbatch 0, 21; B. R. Hartland 6, 22; G. R. Larsen 8, 2 (2 ct); B. A. Pocock 10, 2.

* *Signifies not out.*

BOWLING

	O	*M*	*R*	*W*	*BB*	*5W/i*	*Avge*
D. J. Nash	129	28	429	17	6-76	2	25.23
M. B. Owens	51	15	168	5	4-99	0	33.60
C. Pringle	78	22	201	3	1-41	0	67.00
M. N. Hart	147.3	60	278	4	1-50	0	69.50

Also bowled: H. T. Davis 21–0–93–1; G. R. Larsen 44.4–11–116–2; S. A. Thomson 79–19–163–2.

NEW ZEALAND TOUR AVERAGES – FIRST-CLASS MATCHES

BATTING

	M	*I*	*NO*	*R*	*HS*	*100s*	*Avge*	*Ct*
M. D. Crowe	9	16	2	654	142	3	46.71	6
S. P. Fleming	9	16	1	591	151	2	39.40	5
K. R. Rutherford	9	17	1	603	129	2	37.68	1
B. A. Young	9	17	0	622	122	1	36.58	11
D. J. Nash	8	11	6	177	56	0	35.40	5
M. J. Greatbatch	9	18	3	528	84	0	35.20	4
S. A. Thomson	10	19	7	408	69	0	34.00	5
B. A. Pocock	7	14	2	374	103*	1	31.16	8
A. C. Parore	11	18	4	399	71	0	28.50	21
B. R. Hartland	8	16	0	337	65	0	21.06	6
G. R. Larsen	8	12	4	168	40*	0	21.00	4
M. N. Hart	9	11	3	146	36	0	18.25	5
C. Pringle	8	8	0	88	24	0	11.00	2
S. J. Roberts	2	4	0	32	24	0	8.00	0
H. T. Davis	7	7	4	9	3*	0	3.00	2
M. B. Owens	6	8	2	8	4	0	1.33	2

Played in two matches: D. K. Morrison 10*, 0, 0* (1 ct). Played in one match: M. W. Douglas 24, 4.

* *Signifies not out.*

BOWLING

	O	*M*	*R*	*W*	*BB*	*5W/i*	*Avge*
S. J. Roberts	47.2	7	163	8	4-60	0	20.37
G. R. Larsen	226.4	73	494	21	5-24	1	23.52
M. B. Owens	127	31	424	17	5-74	1	24.94
D. J. Nash	228.4	51	775	25	6-76	2	31.00
C. Pringle	258	74	739	18	5-58	1	41.05
M. N. Hart	335.3	104	850	18	4-106	0	47.22
S. A. Thomson	247	61	633	8	2-50	0	79.12
H. T. Davis	131.4	9	719	9	3-127	0	79.88

Also bowled: M. D. Crowe 12–0–81–2; D. K. Morrison 36–6–117–4; A. C. Parore 5–0–55–0; B. A. Young 8–0–76–1.

Note: Matches in this section which were not first-class are signified by a dagger.

†ENGLAND AMATEUR XI v NEW ZEALANDERS

At Southgate, April 29. New Zealanders won by 139 runs. Toss: England Amateur XI.

The tourists seized the chance to play themselves into form. Pocock hit six fours in his hundred and Crowe made a run-a-ball fifty, though he was dropped twice and his bad knee later kept him off the field. Rutherford's innings ended abruptly when he was struck on the head by a high full toss from van Lint (who said he had intended a yorker). As in 1993 against the Australians, Steve Dean of Staffordshire was the Amateurs' best batsman, with 45; no one else reached 20 as the New Zealand bowlers shared out the wickets.

New Zealanders

B. A. Young b French 38
B. A. Pocock lbw b van Lint 109
M. D. Crowe run out 56
*K. R. Rutherford retired hurt 34
M. J. Greatbatch c Dean b Arnold 5
†A. C. Parore not out 26
G. R. Larsen not out 10
W 4, n-b 6 10

1/82 2/172 3/239 4/270 (4 wkts, 55 overs) 288

M. N. Hart, D. J. Nash, S. B. Doull and H. T. Davis did not bat.

K. R. Rutherford retired hurt at 234.

Bowling: Arnold 11–1–47–1; Aldred 10–0–60–0; French 10–0–49–1; van Lint 11–1–64–1; Evans 11–0–55–0; Hussain 2–0–13–0.

England Amateur XI

S. J. Dean c Doull b Hart 45
†S. N. V. Waterton lbw b Doull 3
*M. J. Roberts c Parore b Doull 0
M. Hussain c Young b Hart 17
D. R. Clarke c Young b Hart 12
D. Snellgrove c Young b Larsen 13
N. French c Parore b Davis 4
A. T. van Lint c Parore b Davis 4
R. A. Evans b Larsen 8
P. Aldred not out 15
K. A. Arnold c sub (C. Pringle) b Nash 5
L-b 7, w 8, n-b 8 23

1/16 2/30 3/76 4/84 5/94 6/109 7/109 8/113 9/127 (52.2 overs) 149

Bowling: Davis 11–1–37–2; Doull 11–0–37–2; Nash 8.2–2–14–1; Larsen 11–2–27–2; Hart 11–2–27–3.

Umpires: A. A. Jones and K. J. Lyons.

†LAVINIA, DUCHESS OF NORFOLK'S XI v NEW ZEALANDERS

At Arundel, May 1. New Zealanders won by 69 runs. Toss: New Zealanders.

A crowd of 7,000 saw Stephen Fleming hit an unbeaten 86 from 98 balls, with 11 fours; he added 100 for the fifth wicket with his captain, Larsen, who continued to thrive when the Duchess's team – drawn mainly from Sussex and Kent but augmented by a few old favourites – batted. Larsen took four for 17, including Randall and Matthew Fleming with successive deliveries, and the fall of six wickets for 48 effectively settled the result. The fast but erratic Davis, who had played in these parts for Sussex's Second Eleven in 1992, was less economical and bowled seven wides.

New Zealanders

B. R. Hartland c Moores b Law....... 46
B. A. Pocock c Moores b Headley..... 0
M. J. Greatbatch c Ward b Hughes ... 18
S. P. Fleming not out 86
S. A. Thomson lbw b Law 0
*G. R. Larsen c Speight b Hughes..... 48
†A. C. Parore not out 10
B 1, l-b 4, w 6, n-b 10 21

1/9 2/65 3/99 4/99 5/199 (5 wkts, 50 overs) 229

M. N. Hart, D. J. Nash, H. T. Davis and C. Pringle did not bat.

Bowling: Headley 10–2–32–1; Law 10–1–43–2; Hughes 10–0–43–2; Fleming 10–0–64–0; Patel 10–1–42–0.

Lavinia, Duchess of Norfolk's XI

P. W. G. Parker c Parore b Pringle.... 46
T. R. Ward c Fleming b Davis 29
M. P. Speight b Larsen 0
*A. P. Wells b Nash 20
D. W. Randall lbw b Larsen 0
M. V. Fleming b Larsen 0
†P. Moores c Parore b Larsen 3
D. R. Law st Parore b Hart 14
M. M. Patel st Parore b Hart......... 2
D. W. Headley c Larsen b Pringle..... 11
S. P. Hughes not not 0
L-b 13, w 18, n-b 4.......... 35

1/74 2/74 3/107 4/112 5/112 6/122 7/143 8/147 9/147 (42.5 overs) 160

Bowling: Pringle 7.5–0–26–2; Nash 8–1–29–1; Davis 7–0–42–1; Larsen 10–1–17–4; Hart 10–0–33–2.

Umpires: R. A. White and P. Willey.

†SURREY v NEW ZEALANDERS

At The Oval, May 2. Surrey won by six wickets. Toss: New Zealanders. First-team debut: G. J. Kennis. County debuts: C. E. Cuffy, A. C. S. Pigott.

Two young men, both coming in with four wickets down, played rousing innings for each side. Thomson hit 11 fours and a six while running up an unbeaten 90 from 81 balls for the New Zealanders, while Surrey all-rounder Hollioake confirmed his class with some terrific strokes – seven fours and three sixes – in 86 not out from 73 balls, after claiming two top-order wickets. Those who talked of Hollioake receiving an immediate England call-up perhaps overlooked the poor quality of the New Zealanders' bowling. Without the rock-like Ward, Surrey would have foundered well inside 55 overs; he kept going to add 146 in 22 overs with Hollioake. Several Surrey regulars took the chance of a day off, giving Pigott the chance to lead his new county on debut; he lost the toss but picked up three useful, if costly, wickets and, thanks to Ward and Hollioake, won the day.

New Zealanders

†B. A. Young c Boiling b Hollioake ... 18
B. R. Hartland c Smith b Murphy..... 11
M. D. Crowe c Smith b Hollioake..... 40
*K. R. Rutherford c Sargeant b Pigott . 11
S. P. Fleming c Kennis b Pigott....... 17
S. A. Thomson not out 90
G. R. Larsen c Sargeant b Cuffy 25
M. N. Hart b Pigott 26
D. J. Nash c Smith b Cuffy 4
C. Pringle not out 0
B 1, l-b 3, w 5, n-b 8 17

1/22 2/43 3/62 4/88 5/122 6/194 7/248 8/258 (8 wkts, 55 overs) 259

H. T. Davis did not bat.

Bowling: Cuffy 11–0–57–2; Murphy 10–1–52–1; Hollioake 6–1–19–2; Pigott 11–1–62–3; Boiling 11–0–46–0; Smith 6–0–19–0.

Surrey

M. A. Lynch lbw b Larsen........... 16
G. J. Kennis c Young b Pringle....... 7
D. M. Ward not out 88
A. D. Brown c Thomson b Larsen..... 8
A. W. Smith lbw b Thomson 35
A. J. Hollioake not out 86
L-b 6, w 7, n-b 8............ 21

1/32 2/32 3/51 4/115 (4 wkts, 54.1 overs) 261

J. Boiling, †N. F. Sargeant, *A. C. S. Pigott, A. J. Murphy and C. E. Cuffy did not bat.

Bowling: Pringle 10.1–1–52–1; Davis 4–0–18–0; Larsen 11–2–51–2; Nash 11–0–53–0; Hart 10–2–47–0; Thomson 8–0–34–1.

Umpires: J. H. Harris and P. B. Wight.

WORCESTERSHIRE v NEW ZEALANDERS

At Worcester, May 4, 5, 6. Drawn. Toss: New Zealanders.

Reciprocal declarations, following the loss of 69 overs to rain over the first two days, left the tourists needing 253 from a minimum 49 overs to win their opening first-class fixture. But a three-wicket burst from Radford shortly before tea brought down the shutters. Rutherford, at least, made his mark, with half-centuries in both innings. Yet it said little for the support he received that the first helped to save the follow-on and the second the match. The loss of Curtis in the first over of the game faced Hick with an immediate challenge to answer the doubts expressed by Ray Illingworth, chairman of the England selectors. His rapid 67, with 14 boundaries, many at the expense of the profligate Davis, was encouraging, but Rhodes provided the biggest bonus for Illingworth. He completed his seventh first-class century, from 149 balls, after adding 172 with Haynes, which all but guaranteed his selection as England wicket-keeper.

Close of play: First day, Worcestershire 265-4 (G. R. Haynes 44*, S. J. Rhodes 61*); Second day, New Zealanders 147-5 (K. R. Rutherford 59*, A. C. Parore 11*).

Worcestershire

*T. S. Curtis c Parore b Davis............... 0 – c Pocock b Pringle............ 4
W. P. C. Weston b Pringle.................. 34 – lbw b Larsen................. 4
G. A. Hick c Parore b Hart.................. 67 – c Pringle b Larsen 38
T. M. Moody b Pringle...................... 27 – not out...................... 20
G. R. Haynes c Davis b Larsen............... 82 – c Larsen b Davis 0
†S. J. Rhodes not out ....100 – c Hart b Larsen 3
P. J. Newport b Larsen...................... 0 – c Crowe b Larsen............. 0
S. R. Lampitt c Pocock b Pringle .... 0 – not out...................... 16
R. K. Illingworth not out 1
L-b 3, w 1, n-b 28.................. 32 B 5, l-b 1, n-b 12 18

1/4 2/115 3/145 4/150 5/322 6/322 7/341 (7 wkts dec.) 343 1/9 2/38 3/59 4/59 5/72 6/72 (6 wkts dec.) 103

N. V. Radford and J. E. Brinkley did not bat.

Bowling: *First Innings*—Davis 15–0–121–1; Pringle 27.5–9–64–3; Larsen 23–6–64–2; Hart 14–2–51–1; Thomson 8–0–40–0. *Second Innings*—Davis 11–2–63–1; Pringle 5–1–21–1; Larsen 5–1–13–4.

New Zealanders

B. R. Hartland c Lampitt b Radford	6	– (2) lbw b Radford	13
B. A. Pocock lbw b Brinkley	10	– (1) lbw b Radford	26
M. D. Crowe lbw b Brinkley	3	– c Hick b Radford	4
*K. R. Rutherford c Radford b Newport	84	– c Rhodes b Hick	52
M. J. Greatbatch b Lampitt	36	– not out	48
S. A. Thomson c Rhodes b Lampitt	3	– not out	5
†A. C. Parore c Radford b Newport	15		
G. R. Larsen not out	5		
M. N. Hart not out	8		
B 2, l-b 4, w 2, n-b 16	24	L-b 3, n-b 2	5
1/14 2/21 3/24 4/108 5/116 6/171 7/180	(7 wkts dec.) 194	1/33 2/46 3/49 4/137	(4 wkts) 153

C. Pringle and H. T. Davis did not bat.

Bowling: *First Innings*—Radford 21–6–46–1; Brinkley 16–4–58–2; Newport 15–3–49–2; Lampitt 8.3–2–25–2; Illingworth 3–2–4–0; Moody 2–1–6–0. *Second Innings*—Radford 11–3–39–3; Brinkley 7–0–20–0; Illingworth 3–1–12–0; Lampitt 4–0–16–0; Newport 5–0–17–0; Hick 6–0–29–1; Moody 5–0–17–0.

Umpires: R. Julian and A. G. T. Whitehead.

SOMERSET v NEW ZEALANDERS

At Taunton, May 7, 8, 9. Drawn. Toss: New Zealanders.

The tourists entered the final day on 131 for one, with Pocock and Crowe resuming a partnership of 118. However, a display of what their team manager Geoff Howarth called "inept" batting meant the New Zealanders had to follow on. Rose removed both overnight batsmen and nine wickets fell for 41 with Mushtaq Ahmed claiming five for eight in 34 balls. An opening stand of 95 in the second innings assured them of safety, however, and Crowe hit a 76-ball hundred against his old county – sparing his bad knee by hitting 16 fours and two sixes. The first two days were disrupted by rain. Batting was a struggle when Davis's extra pace removed Somerset's top three. Fletcher's half-century came at a run a ball but Turner took 150 balls to reach 50, then, as the pitch eased next day, only 47 more to complete his century.

Close of play: First day, Somerset 229-5 (A. N. Hayhurst 66*, R. J. Turner 30*); Second day, New Zealanders 131-1 (B. A. Pocock 58*, M. D. Crowe 53*).

Somerset

M. N. Lathwell c Pocock b Davis	11
I. Fletcher c Thomson b Davis	51
R. J. Harden c Greatbatch b Davis	6
N. A. Folland c Parore b Larsen	29
*A. N. Hayhurst c Pocock b Hart	84
G. D. Rose c Parore b Larsen	16
†R. J. Turner not out	104
Mushtaq Ahmed c Thomson b Hart	23
A. R. Caddick c Davis b Hart	8
A. P. van Troost not out	1
L-b 15, w 4, n-b 12	31
1/33 2/60 3/77 4/134 5/158 6/276 7/336 8/362	(8 wkts dec.) 364

H. R. J. Trump did not bat.

Bowling: Pringle 21–7–58–0; Davis 28–2–127–3; Larsen 32–10–63–2; Hart 26–7–68–3; Thomson 15–3–33–0.

New Zealanders

B. A. Young c Turner b van Troost	5	– c Caddick b Hayhurst 41
B. A. Pocock c Trump b Rose	61	– retired hurt 51
M. D. Crowe lbw b Rose	56	– not out 102
S. P. Fleming b Mushtaq Ahmed	13	– b Hayhurst 6
M. J. Greatbatch st Turner b Mushtaq Ahmed	8	– not out 44
S. A. Thomson b Mushtaq Ahmed	3	
†A. C. Parore not out	11	
*G. R. Larsen c Mushtaq Ahmed b Caddick	0	
M. N. Hart c Turner b Caddick	0	
H. T. Davis c Lathwell b Mushtaq Ahmed	0	
C. Pringle c Rose b Mushtaq Ahmed	0	
B 13, l-b 6, n-b 6	25	L-b 3 3
1/13 2/141 3/146 4/162 5/163 6/168 7/173 8/173 9/174	182	1/95 2/129 (2 wkts) 247

In the second innings B. A. Pocock retired hurt at 95-0.

Bowling: *First Innings*—Caddick 19–3–44–2; van Troost 15–4–18–1; Rose 14–2–36–2; Mushtaq Ahmed 16–2–57–5; Trump 2–1–8–0. *Second Innings*—Caddick 6–1–16–0; van Troost 5–1–13–0; Mushtaq Ahmed 11–4–38–0; Rose 6–0–22–0; Trump 16–2–76–0; Hayhurst 10–1–47–2; Lathwell 5–0–32–0.

Umpires: H. D. Bird and R. Palmer.

MIDDLESEX v NEW ZEALANDERS

At Lord's, May 12, 13, 14. Drawn. Toss: New Zealanders.

New Zealand team manager Geoff Howarth's worries about the batting – "from positions one to eleven", as he put it – were fed by another third-morning collapse, against a Middlesex attack missing four front-line bowlers. This time eight wickets went for 31 and Johnson had the New Zealanders in all kinds of trouble. However, coming together at 73 for nine, Nash and Morrison put together 28 by lunch, when rain came to their rescue. The tourists also looked shaky in the first innings: after a wet morning they slipped to 82 for five, Shine removing the first three. But Fleming, who had got off the mark with a six off Shine, batted nearly five hours for his century, supported by Parore and Larsen. Middlesex were in difficulties themselves at 62 for four, Gatting having dropped down the order, until Carr and Brown pulled them around. They declared 93 in arrears. Morrison, in his first game since injury during the Austral-Asia Cup, bowled impressively for two wickets.

Close of play: First day, New Zealanders 155-6 (S. P. Fleming 67*, G. R. Larsen 2*); Second day, New Zealanders 34-1 (B. R. Hartland 10*, M. J. Greatbatch 8*).

New Zealanders

B. A. Young c Carr b Shine	11	– (2) lbw b Johnson 12
B. R. Hartland c Brown b Shine	12	– (1) c Weekes b Shine 10
M. J. Greatbatch c Pooley b Feltham	14	– c Gatting b Johnson 16
*K. R. Rutherford c Ramprakash b Shine	0	– c Brown b Taylor 23
S. P. Fleming not out	118	– (6) c Ramprakash b Shine 5
S. A. Thomson c Brown b Feltham	5	– (5) lbw b Johnson 0
†A. C. Parore c Brown b Taylor	36	– run out 0
G. R. Larsen not out	40	– lbw b Feltham 2
M. N. Hart (did not bat)		– b Taylor 0
D. J. Nash (did not bat)		– not out 17
D. K. Morrison (did not bat)		– not out 10
L-b 6, w 1, n-b 6	13	L-b 4, n-b 2 6
1/22 2/31 3/31 4/68 5/82 6/146	(6 wkts dec.) 249	1/18 2/42 3/42 4/54 5/69 6/69 7/73 8/73 9/73 (9 wkts) 101

Bowling: *First Innings*—Shine 19–5–74–3; Johnson 16–5–36–0; Taylor 17–4–55–1; Feltham 19–8–26–2; Weekes 19–4–52–0. *Second Innings*—Shine 13–5–34–2; Johnson 16–8–35–3; Taylor 9–5–19–2; Feltham 5–2–9–1.

Middlesex

M. A. Roseberry b Morrison	5	†K. R. Brown not out	47
J. C. Pooley c Fleming b Morrison	16	L-b 9, n-b 8	17
M. R. Ramprakash c Hart b Larsen	9		—
P. N. Weekes c Fleming b Larsen	5	1/8 2/35 (4 wkts dec.)	156
J. D. Carr not out	57	3/35 4/62	

*M. W. Gatting, M. A. Feltham, R. L. Johnson, C. W. Taylor and K. J. Shine did not bat.

Bowling: Morrison 13–2–40–2; Nash 14–6–34–0; Larsen 16–5–28–2; Hart 12–2–36–0; Thomson 4–1–9–0.

Umpires: G. I. Burgess and D. R. Shepherd.

†NORTHAMPTONSHIRE v NEW ZEALANDERS

At Northampton, May 15. New Zealanders won by eight wickets. Toss: Northamptonshire.

Four days before the first international, the tourists discovered some form to complete a straightforward victory with more than ten overs to spare. They overwhelmed Northamptonshire, who were without Ambrose, Curran and Capel. The county never threatened to dominate some tidy bowling, Hart flighting the ball tantalisingly, though Penberthy and Ripley ensured respectability. The New Zealanders' fielding was sound and occasionally brilliant; Fleming made a superb one-handed running catch to dismiss Loye. The batsmen then made light work of chasing 189. Crowe, as opener, struck the ball beautifully in his 32-ball 31; Young and Parore did almost all the rest, adding 136 in 33 overs to round off an efficient display.

Northamptonshire

A. Fordham c Young b Nash	23	†D. Ripley not out	13
N. A. Felton c Rutherford b Hart	21		
R. J. Bailey b Thomson	38	B 5, l-b 6, w 2, n-b 2	15
*A. J. Lamb run out	13		—
M. B. Loye c Fleming b Pringle	18	1/38 2/75 3/105 (5 wkts, 55 overs)	188
A. L. Penberthy not out	47	4/105 5/161	

M. N. Bowen, A. R. Roberts, N. G. B. Cook and J. P. Taylor did not bat.

Bowling: Morrison 7–0–42–0; Pringle 11–3–30–1; Nash 5–1–11–1; Larsen 11–4–24–0; Hart 11–0–36–1; Thomson 10–0–34–1.

New Zealanders

†B. A. Young c Ripley b Bowen	90
M. D. Crowe c Lamb b Penberthy	31
A. C. Parore not out	60
S. A. Thomson not out	5
W 4, n-b 2	6
	—
1/51 2/187 (2 wkts, 44.3 overs)	192

G. R. Larsen, D. J. Nash, *K. R. Rutherford, S. P. Fleming, M. N. Hart, D. K. Morrison and C. Pringle did not bat.

Bowling: Taylor 8–1–32–0; Bowen 7–0–28–1; Cook 11–1–49–0; Penberthy 5–0–15–1; Bailey 7.3–0–41–0; Roberts 6–1–27–0.

Umpires: J. W. Holder and R. Julian.

†LEICESTERSHIRE v NEW ZEALANDERS

At Leicester, May 17. New Zealanders won by seven wickets. Toss: New Zealanders.

The New Zealanders' recovery continued: they rolled over Leicestershire even more easily than Northamptonshire two days earlier. Despite resting Crowe, they achieved a target of 170 with more than 21 overs to spare. On a cold and windy day, all the tourists bowled steadily – even the usually erratic Davis – and Hart excelled with three top-order wickets, including Whitaker, the only man to reach 40. Hartland and Young began their reply with 71 in 15 overs and, though the novice Brimson took two quick wickets, Parore and Fleming regained the momentum. Fleming struck Pierson for two sixes to win.

Leicestershire

P. V. Simmons c Hartland b Nash	3	A. R. K. Pierson c Parore b Davis	15
*N. E. Briers c Young b Morrison	12	M. T. Brimson not out	3
J. J. Whitaker c Morrison b Hart	43	D. J. Millns run out	0
V. J. Wells c Nash b Hart	26	L-b 12, w 5, n-b 6	23
B. F. Smith c Morrison b Hart	11		—
P. N. Hepworth c Fleming b Thomson	8	1/17 2/17 3/61 (53.3 overs)	169
†P. A. Nixon c Rutherford b Nash	22	4/94 5/101 6/123	
G. J. Parsons b Morrison	3	7/128 8/153 9/169	

Bowling: Morrison 9–2–23–2; Nash 6.3–1–28–2; Larsen 9–2–25–0; Davis 7–2–22–1; Hart 11–1–27–3; Thomson 11–1–32–1.

New Zealanders

B. R. Hartland b Pierson	38	S. P. Fleming not out	35
B. A. Young c Simmons b Brimson	36	B 8, l-b 1, w 3, n-b 2	14
†A. C. Parore not out	39		—
*K. R. Rutherford c Wells b Brimson	8	1/71 2/94 3/103 (3 wkts, 33.5 overs)	170

S. A. Thomson, G. R. Larsen, D. J. Nash, D. K. Morrison, M. N. Hart and H. T. Davis did not bat.

Bowling: Millns 4–0–23–0; Parsons 3–0–14–0; Simmons 4–0–18–0; Wells 3–0–15–0; Brimson 10–1–39–2; Pierson 9.5–1–52–1.

Umpires: B. Dudleston and T. E. Jesty.

†ENGLAND v NEW ZEALAND

First Texaco Trophy Match

At Birmingham, May 19. England won by 42 runs. Toss: New Zealand. International debuts: D. Gough, S. D. Udal.

A grey day produced a mainly grey match, coloured for England by promising debuts from fast bowler Darren Gough and off-spinner Shaun Udal, who helped bowl them to victory after New Zealand had restricted their batsmen to 224 for eight on a niggardly pitch. England left out Thorpe and DeFreitas from their 13, and Atherton once again anchored the innings with 81. But no one else passed 24 and the prospects of a big total vanished when Pringle worked his way through the middle order to take five for 45; no one had taken five wickets in a one-day international in England since the 1983 World Cup. Morrison was out of the attack by them with a strained hamstring. Gough dismissed Crowe with his sixth ball in international cricket and returned to the attack to york Young, who was trying to match Atherton's innings. Udal, bowling nice, looping off-breaks, dismissed both Parore and Rutherford and New Zealand faded away. Ray Illingworth, England's new chairman of selectors, said his team's performance was worth only seven out of ten.

Man of the Match: M. A. Atherton. *Attendance:* 17,812; *receipts* £424,135.

England

*M. A. Atherton run out	81	S. D. Udal not out	3
A. J. Stewart c Nash b Pringle	24		
R. A. Smith c Parore b Thomson	15	B 1, l-b 5, w 7	13
G. A. Gooch b Thomson	23		—
G. A. Hick b Pringle	18	1/33 (2) 2/84 (3) (8 wkts, 55 overs)	224
D. A. Reeve c Fleming b Pringle	16	3/141 (4) 4/161 (1)	
†S. J. Rhodes c Thomson b Pringle	12	5/180 (5) 6/199 (6)	
C. C. Lewis b Pringle	19	7/199 (7) 8/224 (8)	

D. Gough and A. R. C. Fraser did not bat.

Bowling: Morrison 6–0–31–0; Pringle 11–1–45–5; Nash 6–1–20–0; Larsen 10–1–43–0; Hart 11–0–45–0; Thomson 11–0–34–2.

New Zealand

B. A. Young b Gough	65	C. Pringle c Hick b Fraser	3
M. D. Crowe c Stewart b Gough	0	D. K. Morrison not out	17
†A. C. Parore b Udal	42	L-b 4, w 1	5
*K. R. Rutherford lbw b Udal	0		—
S. P. Fleming c and b Hick	17	1/2 (2) 2/78 (3) (52.5 overs)	182
S. A. Thomson c Lewis b Hick	7	3/81 (4) 4/110 (5)	
G. R. Larsen c and b Lewis	13	5/134 (1) 6/136 (6)	
D. J. Nash b Lewis	0	7/136 (8) 8/149 (7)	
M. N. Hart c Stewart b Lewis	13	9/152 (10) 10/182 (9)	

Bowling: Fraser 10–0–37–1; Gough 11–1–36–2; Udal 11–0–39–2; Reeve 4–0–15–0; Lewis 9.5–2–20–3; Hick 7–0–31–2.

Umpires: R. Palmer and N. T. Plews. Referee: C. H. Lloyd (West Indies).

†ENGLAND v NEW ZEALAND

Second Texaco Trophy Match

At Lord's, May 21, 22. Abandoned.

A full house on the Saturday at Lord's was told at 2 p.m. that play would be impossible that day. After further incessant rain, it was decided next morning to abandon the game, thus ensuring that England – on the strength of their Edgbaston win – would take the first of the year's two Texaco Trophies. This was the first time that any of England's 85 home one-day internationals had been completely abandoned, even though most are scheduled in rainy May. The only previous one-day international in England to be entirely washed out was a 1979 World Cup tie between Sri Lanka and West Indies at The Oval. Elsewhere in the south, including The Oval, Sunday League matches started on time and six England players unexpectedly represented their counties. Under the refund system, this washout was expected to cost the TCCB £700,000.

YORKSHIRE v NEW ZEALANDERS

At Leeds, May 24, 25, 26. Yorkshire won by an innings and 33 runs. Toss: New Zealanders. County debut: L. C. Weekes.

The New Zealanders, as Rutherford accepted, were outplayed in every session. Despite the efforts of Owens, who took the top four wickets in his first game since replacing the injured Doull, Yorkshire scored almost at will; Davis bowled 17 no-balls, while Blakey and White added 99 in 20 overs. White, who had already attracted Ray Illingworth's attention, continued to do well: he scored 59 in 65 balls and then picked up five wickets with some lively medium-pace, his extra bounce keeping the batsmen anxiously on the back foot. Lesroy Weekes, a 22-year-old pace bowler from the Leeward Islands under consideration as

Yorkshire's overseas player for 1995, looked quick, but lacked control. However, only Hartland, with two sturdy innings, applied himself as the tourists collapsed twice. Crowe missed the second innings with flu, but the New Zealanders seemed to lack any spirit or plan of campaign.

Close of play: First day, Yorkshire 408-5 (R. J. Blakey 84*, A. P. Grayson 20*); Second day, New Zealanders 98-1 (B. R. Hartland 60*, K. R. Rutherford 2*).

Yorkshire

*M. D. Moxon c Nash b Owens	36	A. P. Grayson not out	20
M. P. Vaughan b Owens	20		
D. Byas c and b Owens	68	B 2, l-b 17, w 1, n-b 38	58
R. B. Richardson c Crowe b Owens	63		
†R. J. Blakey not out	84	1/41 2/114 3/229 (5 wkts dec.)	408
C. White c Parore b Davis	59	4/234 5/333	

L. C. Weekes, R. D. Stemp, P. J. Hartley and M. A. Robinson did not bat.

Bowling: Owens 22–3–89–4; Pringle 26–8–87–0; Nash 23–4–106–0; Davis 20.4–1–107–1.

New Zealanders

B. R. Hartland c Stemp b White	49	– (2) c Vaughan b Hartley 60
B. A. Pocock c Richardson b Hartley	4	– (1) c sub (C. E. W. Silverwood) b White . 26
M. D. Crowe c Blakey b Hartley	1	– absent ill
*K. R. Rutherford lbw b White	33	– (3) c Hartley b Robinson 3
M. J. Greatbatch c Blakey b White	0	– (4) c Grayson b White 12
S. P. Fleming b White	10	– (5) c and b Vaughan 40
†A. C. Parore c Weekes b White	17	– (6) c Blakey b Hartley 9
D. J. Nash not out	8	– (7) c Blakey b Weekes 16
C. Pringle c Moxon b Robinson	21	– (8) c White b Weekes 12
H. T. Davis c Blakey b Weekes	2	– (9) not out 3
M. B. Owens c Blakey b Weekes	1	– (10) run out 0
B 1, l-b 4, n-b 22	27	L-b 6, w 1, n-b 14 21
1/5 2/17 3/83 4/87 5/105 6/126 7/139 8/166 9/171	173	1/70 2/100 3/102 4/160 5/164 6/177 7/195 8/200 9/202 202

Bowling: *First Innings*—Hartley 14–5–26–2; Weekes 9.4–1–43–2; Robinson 17–5–29–1; Stemp 10–2–28–0; White 15–5–42–5. *Second Innings*—Hartley 18–3–49–2; Weekes 14.4–1–92–2; White 13–5–30–2; Robinson 15–7–23–1; Vaughan 1–0–2–1.

Umpires: H. D. Bird and M. K. Reed.

ESSEX v NEW ZEALANDERS

At Chelmsford, May 28, 29, 30. Drawn. Toss: New Zealanders.

Following the humiliating defeat against Yorkshire, the tourists were content to treat this game as a net in preparation for the First Test. Though the pace was too leisurely for any chance of a result, they put up their most convincing first-class performance yet. Young and Rutherford recorded their first centuries of the tour, though Crowe twice failed to capitalise on a pitch lacking any pace. Parore, who had been struck twice by White at Headingley, took another blow, on his elbow, from his first ball from Kasprowicz. After the New Zealanders declared at lunch on the second day, Nash and Hart had Essex in some difficulty at 97 for three. But they survived to consume 126 overs in totalling 334; Irani registered 83, his highest score to date.

Close of play: First day, New Zealanders 314-3 (K. R. Rutherford 111*, S. P. Fleming 21*); Second day, Essex 175-4 (N. Hussain 53*, R. C. Irani 17*).

New Zealanders

B. A. Young b Ilott	122		
B. R. Hartland b Irani	24	(1) c Such b Stephenson	28
*K. R. Rutherford c Rollins b Kasprowicz	129		
M. D. Crowe c Kasprowicz b Irani	10	(3) lbw b Kasprowicz	14
S. P. Fleming c Stephenson b Kasprowicz	32		
S. A. Thomson not out	52	(4) not out	24
†A. C. Parore retired hurt	0	(2) c Gooch b Stephenson	20
G. R. Larsen not out	28		
M. N. Hart (did not bat)		(5) not out	6
B 2, l-b 9, n-b 20	31	B 1, l-b 1, n-b 14	16
1/70 2/261 3/287 4/343 5/347 (5 wkts dec.)	428	1/33 2/60 3/85 (3 wkts dec.)	108

D. J. Nash and H. T. Davis did not bat.

In the first innings A. C. Parore retired hurt at 347 for five.

Bowling: *First Innings*—Ilott 27–5–69–1; Kasprowicz 21–2–77–2; Such 17–4–75–0; Stephenson 16–1–63–0; Irani 21–4–66–2; Childs 22–5–55–0; Gooch 2–1–1–0; Prichard 1–0–11–0. *Second Innings*—Ilott 1–0–5–0; Kasprowicz 9–1–40–1; Irani 3–0–11–0; Stephenson 9–1–26–2; Childs 6.4–2–24–0.

Essex

*G. A. Gooch c Crowe b Nash	42
J. P. Stephenson b Nash	32
P. J. Prichard b Hart	9
N. Hussain lbw b Nash	71
J. J. B. Lewis run out	7
R. C. Irani c Fleming b Davis	83
†R. J. Rollins c Crowe b Hart	9
M. S. Kasprowicz c Nash b Larsen	28
M. C. Ilott b Hart	11
P. M. Such b Hart	24
J. H. Childs not out	1
L-b 3, n-b 14	17
1/82 2/97 3/97 4/120 5/208 6/235 7/298 8/298 9/333	334

Bowling: Davis 12–0–72–1; Nash 25–4–77–3; Larsen 21–9–39–1; Hart 44–12–106–4; Thomson 24–8–37–0.

Umpires: P. Adams and J. H. Hampshire.

ENGLAND v NEW ZEALAND

First Cornhill Test

At Nottingham, June 2, 3, 4, 5, 6. England won by an innings and 90 runs. Toss: New Zealand. Test debuts: S. J. Rhodes, C. White; H. T. Davis, G. R. Larsen.

Ray Illingworth's first Test as chairman of England's selectors ended in a crushing victory before lunch on the final day. If the opposition was inexperienced and inadequate, there could be no denying the efficiency with which England swept aside New Zealand. Illingworth's controversial start in his new role was thus given instant vindication, with Gooch and DeFreitas making triumphant returns, while Atherton scored his third century in five Tests. New Zealand's successes were of the straw-clutching variety, although wicket-keeper Parore twice batted obdurately and his gloves were commendably adhesive: he conceded no byes in 174.4 overs.

Before taking the job, Illingworth had insisted on total autonomy as a prerequisite and thus had a mandate for a revolutionary, rather than evolutionary, approach. His new broom swept aside all but five of the England team who played in the final two Tests in the Caribbean in April, including the historic victory in Barbados. Admittedly, Caddick (with a shoulder injury), Lewis (side strain) and Tufnell (personal problems, including a pending court appearance) were ruled out, as was Gough, who also succumbed to a side strain after his encouraging debut in the Birmingham one-day international. Yet Illingworth's influence was blazingly clear. As soon as he took over, he talked about a more balanced, five-man attack. Consequently, he plucked White, born in Yorkshire but raised on an Australian sheep farm, from obscurity to fill the pivotal role at No. 6. White was Illingworth's choice –

captain Atherton admitted he had scarcely seen him play – and Illingworth's alone. White's chances were limited, but he did hold two stinging catches, as well as dropping a straightforward one. With another Yorkshire player, left-arm spinner Stemp, an even more unexpected inclusion in the original 13 and Yorkshire-born Rhodes given his debut, some felt Illingworth was viewing affairs through White Rose-tinted spectacles. Stemp, along with Ilott of Essex, was omitted from the team.

Illingworth spent more than half the match in the dressing-room rather than the committee room. During the match, he removed the Rev. Andrew Wingfield Digby, the team's chaplain and spiritual adviser for the previous three years, from the TCCB budget. His explanation was typically forthright: "If any of the players need a shoulder to cry on, they're not the men to go out and stuff the Aussies next winter." Mobile telephones and (briefly, anyway) sunglasses were also banned. Fortunately, humour was not: before play on the final morning, Stewart appeared on the players' balcony with a dog collar, wraparound shades and a cellphone held to his ear. Another historic development was the appearance of West Indian Steve Bucknor, the first overseas umpire to stand in an English Test.

The match itself was played under forbidding skies – amazingly, only ten overs were lost – and was too one-sided to be gripping. The New Zealanders' form had been mostly woeful and, for once, England were overwhelming favourites. The bookies were right and the public's indifference was reflected in crowds comfortably below capacity. From 108 for five on the first afternoon, New Zealand were on the back foot. Fleming, a tall and elegant left-hander, scored his second half-century in his second Test before falling to a diving catch in the gully by White, while Parore and Hart made useful runs down the order. But apart from them, New Zealand batted hopelessly on a slow, even pitch. DeFreitas, playing his first Test for 12 months and representing his third county, Derbyshire, was the only bowler on either side to move the ball consistently. His away-swinger was in prime working order as he accounted for four of the top five.

With Morrison and Pringle unfit, New Zealand's five bowlers entered the match with just 14 Tests and 22 wickets between them. Heath Te-Ihi-O-Te-Rangi Davis's first ball in Test cricket went for four very wide wides down the leg side and Gavin Larsen, after 55 one-day internationals, finally made his debut in the five-day game. Against such a novice attack, on a decent surface, England – and especially the in-form Gooch – were almost guaranteed a huge score, and their eventual 567 was the highest total between these two teams in England.

Gooch, who had opted out of the West Indies tour, had to pledge his availability for the forthcoming trip to Australia before being picked. This he did, although his selection was by no means universally applauded. It meant the four young batsmen chosen by Atherton for the West Indian tour as the potential nucleus of England's middle order for years to come – Ramprakash, Thorpe, Maynard and Hussain – had all disappeared, and there was no place either for the highly rated Crawley. But it would have been hard for anyone to play better. Gooch's 210 was the second-highest of his 20 Test centuries. When he reached his 65th 50, he surpassed Boycott's England record of 64 and he finished the match with 1,135 runs against New Zealand, the most by an England player. Gooch was savage on anything short, of which there was plenty, and excelled with his favourite boom wide of mid-on. By comparison, Atherton's hundred was sedate, almost forgettable. The pair's partnership of 263 was their ninth century stand for England, of which seven have exceeded 150 and four 200. Smith scored 78 without looking convincing, Rhodes reached 49, including the only two sixes of the match, and DeFreitas made his second Test half-century in his 51st innings.

New Zealand's second innings was a virtual carbon copy of their first. There was another fifty, from Young this time, and again Parore and Hart provided doughty, though ultimately vain, resistance. England claimed the extra half-hour on the fourth evening, but could not separate them and were kept waiting for 90 minutes on the final morning to complete victory. DeFreitas reached 100 Test wickets when he dismissed Hartland and finished with five for 71, and nine for 165 in the match. Such, the next best bowler, wheeled away with canny variations of line and loop. The victory was totally overshadowed because, an hour's drive away in Birmingham, a chap called Lara scored 501 not out. Nevertheless, Illingworth pronounced himself "delighted" with England's performance and few could blame him. – John Etheridge.

Man of the Match: G. A. Gooch. *Attendance:* 33,032; *receipts* £626,885.

Close of play: First day, New Zealand 236-8 (M. N. Hart 28*, D. J. Nash 13*); Second day, England 277-1 (M. A. Atherton 101*, G. A. Gooch 152*); Third day, England 516-6 (S. J. Rhodes 41*, P. A. J. DeFreitas 17*); Fourth day, New Zealand 184-7 (A. C. Parore 20*, M. N. Hart 15*).

New Zealand

B. A. Young c Hick b DeFreitas	15	– (2) c Rhodes b Fraser . . . 53
B. R. Hartland c Hick b DeFreitas	6	– (1) lbw b DeFreitas . . . 22
*K. R. Rutherford lbw b DeFreitas	25	– c Atherton b Such . . . 14
M. D. Crowe c Rhodes b White	16	– lbw b DeFreitas . . . 28
S. P. Fleming c White b DeFreitas	54	– c White b Hick . . . 11
S. A. Thomson c Hick b Fraser	14	– c White b Such . . . 6
†A. C. Parore c Rhodes b Malcolm	38	– c Rhodes b DeFreitas . . . 42
G. R. Larsen c Fraser b Such	8	– c Stewart b DeFreitas . . . 2
M. N. Hart c Hick b Fraser	36	– lbw b Fraser . . . 22
D. J. Nash c Rhodes b Malcolm	19	– c Rhodes b DeFreitas . . . 5
H. T. Davis not out	0	– not out . . . 0
L-b 6, n-b 14	20	L-b 1, n-b 20 . . . 21
1/13 (2) 2/37 (1) 3/66 (4) 4/78 (3) 5/108 (6) 6/168 (5) 7/188 (7) 8/194 (8) 9/249 (9) 10/251 (10)	251	1/59 (1) 2/95 (3) 3/95 (2) 4/122 (5) 5/141 (4) 6/141 (6) 7/147 (8) 8/201 (9) 9/224 (10) 10/226 (7) 226

Bowling: *First Innings*—Malcolm 17.4–5–45–2; Fraser 21–10–40–2; DeFreitas 23–4–94–4; Such 19–7–28–1; White 13–3–38–1. *Second Innings*—Malcolm 10–2–39–0; Fraser 23–8–53–2; DeFreitas 22.3–4–71–5; Such 34–12–50–2; Hick 14–6–12–1; White 3–3–0–0.

England

*M. A. Atherton c Parore b Larsen	101
A. J. Stewart c Larsen b Davis	8
G. A. Gooch c Crowe b Thomson	210
G. A. Hick b Nash	18
R. A. Smith run out	78
C. White c Larsen b Hart	19
†S. J. Rhodes c Thomson b Nash	49
P. A. J. DeFreitas not out	51
A. R. C. Fraser c Fleming b Larsen	8
L-b 9, w 6, n-b 10	25
1/16 (2) 2/279 (1) 3/314 (4) 4/375 (3) 5/414 (6) 6/482 (5) 7/528 (7) 8/567 (9)	(8 wkts dec.) 567

P. M. Such and D. E. Malcolm did not bat.

Bowling: Davis 21–0–93–1; Nash 36–5–153–2; Larsen 44.4–11–116–2; Hart 35–7–123–1; Thomson 38–6–73–1.

Umpires: S. A. Bucknor (West Indies) and H. D. Bird.
Referee: C. H. Lloyd (West Indies).

GLAMORGAN v NEW ZEALANDERS

At Swansea, June 8, 9, 10. New Zealanders won by eight wickets. Toss: Glamorgan.

New Zealand captain Rutherford scored the season's fastest century to date, from 71 balls, to set up what was to be his team's only first-class win of the summer. They reached 306 in 66 overs, thanks to a partnership of 194 between Rutherford and Young – and despite Watkin, who conceded only one run in his first seven overs. Rutherford's first scoring stroke came off his 13th ball, but he still beat Lara's 72-ball hundred against Somerset. He retired with a strained hamstring at tea, but Thomson followed his example with a spirited fifty in 36 minutes. On an easy-paced pitch, Morris and Roseberry rescued Glamorgan from an uneasy 73 for four on the first day, with a partnership of 97. Gibson then struck a career-best 85, with four sixes, ensuring a healthy total of 361. The New Zealanders' first innings was dominated by Fleming, who struck a delightful 151, with four sixes and 21 fours. He batted for three hours and added 191 with Greatbatch, who contributed just 32.

Close of play: First day, New Zealanders 18-0 (B. A. Young 10*, B. A. Pocock 8*); Second day, Glamorgan 78-3 (D. L. Hemp 10*, P. A. Cottey 10*).

Glamorgan

S. P. James c Young b Owens	9	– c Pocock b Thomson	22
*H. Morris c Pocock b Hart	84	– (7) c Pocock b Pringle	36
A. Dale c Young b Pringle	6	– c Fleming b Thomson	17
D. L. Hemp c Young b Thomson	6	– c Young b Hart	17
P. A. Cottey c Hart b Pringle	1	– not out	90
A. Roseberry c Parore b Hart	45	– c Young b Hart	1
R. D. B. Croft b Hart	31	– (2) b Davis	6
O. D. Gibson lbw b Pringle	85	– not out	23
†C. P. Metson c Parore b Pringle	48		
S. L. Watkin not out	13		
S. Bastien b Pringle	6		
B 4, l-b 12, w 3, n-b 8	27	B 3, w 1, n-b 10	14
1/27 2/57 3/72 4/73 5/170 6/171 7/248 8/324 9/353	361	1/28 2/53 3/56 4/98 5/113 6/190	(6 wkts dec.) 226

Bowling: *First Innings*—Owens 9–3–29–1; Davis 8–1–50–0; Hart 34–5–133–3; Pringle 23.3–9–58–5; Thomson 26–8–75–1. *Second Innings*—Owens 4–1–7–0; Davis 5–0–27–1; Pringle 11.4–2–38–1; Hart 25–5–76–2; Thomson 21–5–75–2.

New Zealanders

B. A. Young c Hemp b Watkin	13	– (2) c Morris b Croft	95
B. A. Pocock c and b Bastien	17	– (1) c Morris b Watkin	3
*K. R. Rutherford c James b Bastien	24	– retired hurt	115
M. J. Greatbatch c James b Croft	34	– not out	33
S. P. Fleming c Hemp b Dale	151		
S. A. Thomson not out	14	– (5) not out	50
†A. C. Parore not out	5		
B 5, l-b 8, n-b 11	24	B 4, l-b 1, w 1, n-b 4	10
1/21 2/62 3/67 4/258 5/274	(5 wkts dec.) 282	1/7 2/229	(2 wkts) 306

C. Pringle, M. N. Hart, M. B. Owens and H. T. Davis did not bat.

In the second innings K. R. Rutherford retired hurt at 201.

Bowling: *First Innings*—Watkin 13–5–18–1; Bastien 18–4–58–2; Croft 33–9–98–1; Gibson 10–0–54–0; Dale 12–4–41–1. *Second Innings*—Watkin 18–9–31–1; Bastien 8–0–53–0; Croft 26–2–120–1; Gibson 10–0–61–0; Dale 4–0–36–0.

Umpires: B. J. Meyer and J. F. Steele.

GLOUCESTERSHIRE v NEW ZEALANDERS

At Bristol, June 11, 12, 13. Drawn. Toss: Gloucestershire.

The New Zealanders were saved from defeat only by the defiance of the ninth-wicket pair, Nash and Pringle. Set to score 360 in 68 overs, they collapsed to 174 for eight. Eventually, Morrison, whose recurrent hamstring trouble was about to end his tour, had to come in for the last 15 balls. Alleyne had revealed necessary powers of concentration in a four-hour 70 for Gloucestershire on the first day. The New Zealanders' reply contained a painstaking century by Pocock, a more enterprising innings by Young, and a positively aggressive one by Crowe. Showing little respect for Gloucestershire's modest attack, Crowe drove and pulled with masterful brilliance, taking 35 off three overs from Hancock. He faced only 53 balls and looked a certainty for the fastest hundred of the season until caught at the wicket. As it was, Windows equalled the best to date – 71 balls by Rutherford at Swansea – off a succession of occasional bowlers, including Parore, before the declaration. It was his maiden hundred, though he seemed unlikely to bask in the achievement.

Close of play: First day, New Zealanders 4-2 (B. A. Pocock 2*, B. A. Young 1*); Second day, Gloucestershire 90-3 (M. W. Alleyne 1*, M. Davies 0*).

Gloucestershire

S. G. Hinks b Morrison	0	– lbw b Morrison	7
R. J. Cunliffe c Greatbatch b Nash	7	– c Hartland b Pringle	40
T. H. C. Hancock b Pringle	20	– c Parore b Pringle	36
M. W. Alleyne b Thomson	70	– c Hartland b Young	19
R. I. Dawson c Morrison b Thomson	42	– (6) lbw b Crowe	87
M. G. N. Windows c Parore b Nash	24	– (7) c Pocock b Larsen	106
*†R. C. Russell c Parore b Larsen	31	– (8) not out	26
R. C. Williams c Larsen b Nash	38		
R. M. Wight not out	20		
M. Davies c Parore b Nash	19	– (5) c Young b Crowe	32
B 1, l-b 3, w 1, n-b 10	15	B 5, l-b 4, w 4, n-b 2	15
1/2 2/14 3/36 4/99 5/167 6/189 7/231 8/255 9/286	(9 wkts dec.) 286	1/14 2/82 3/89 4/141 5/143 6/316 7/368	(7 wkts dec.) 368

A. M. Smith did not bat.

Bowling: *First Innings*—Morrison 17–2–64–1; Nash 20.4–7–59–4; Pringle 19–3–74–1; Larsen 16–5–35–1; Thomson 20–5–50–2. *Second Innings*—Morrison 6–2–13–1; Nash 5–0–16–0; Larsen 13–2–38–1; Pringle 14–5–40–2; Thomson 11–4–40–0; Young 8–0–76–1; Crowe 12–0–81–2; Parore 5–0–55–0.

New Zealanders

B. R. Hartland lbw b Smith	0	– (2) c Cunliffe b Williams	11
B. A. Pocock not out	103	– (1) lbw b Smith	12
D. K. Morrison lbw b Smith	0	– (11) not out	0
B. A. Young c and b Williams	87	– (8) lbw b Smith	16
M. D. Crowe c Russell b Alleyne	73	– (4) b Smith	6
M. J. Greatbatch run out	2	– (3) c Hancock b Alleyne	53
S. A. Thomson not out	3	– (5) c Windows b Davies	9
†A. C. Parore (did not bat)		– (6) c Cunliffe b Wight	19
*G. R. Larsen (did not bat)		– (7) lbw b Wight	26
D. J. Nash (did not bat)		– (9) not out	24
C. Pringle (did not bat)		– (10) c Russell b Smith	24
L-b 3, w 2, n-b 22	27	B 2, l-b 6, n-b 14	22
1/0 2/3 3/167 4/257 5/259	(5 wkts dec.) 295	1/16 2/62 3/68 4/90 5/112 6/129 7/157 8/174 9/222	(9 wkts) 222

Bowling: *First Innings*—Smith 19–5–57–2; Williams 19–1–87–1; Alleyne 15–4–32–1; Davies 12.3–3–33–0; Wight 12–2–48–0; Hancock 5–2–35–0. *Second Innings*—Smith 18–6–59–4; Williams 5–1–28–1; Alleyne 9–1–29–1; Davies 20–4–55–1; Wight 16–5–43–2.

Umpires: J. W. Holder and P. Willey.

ENGLAND v NEW ZEALAND

Second Cornhill Test

At Lord's, June 16, 17, 18, 19, 20. Drawn. Toss: New Zealand.

In five days at Lord's, Ray Illingworth learned a great deal more about the task ahead of his selection panel than he did during his heady start at Trent Bridge. The innings victory in the First Test brought a bullish response from the England camp when they turned up in

London for the Second, with Atherton talking about his team "developing a ruthless streak, kicking opponents while they are down and wrapping up the series". By Monday evening, however, with their tailenders hanging on grimly in the gloom, England were relieved to escape with a draw and their 1-0 lead in the series intact.

The Test was a fascinating contest and, for the unfancied tourists, an enormously encouraging match. Just as England had dominated at Trent Bridge, so New Zealand were always in command here, but without quite getting the reward they deserved – their first ever Lord's Test victory. Their young and talented team came of age and suggested the future of New Zealand cricket was not in such bad hands after all. None of the bright lights shone more brilliantly than Nash, a boyish, enthusiastic pace bowler who was overcome with emotion by the ovation he received from the Lord's crowd. In his fifth Test, he finished with figures of 11 for 169, the best bowling return by a New Zealander against England, and with a half-century too – a double no player had achieved in a Lord's Test before – he was named Man of the Match.

Nash, bowling at a vigorous fast-medium from the Pavilion End, got extra bounce from a slow wicket; he disconcerted even the best England batsmen and made the ball move sharply, especially away from the bat. His improvement was far more significant than New Zealand's three team changes. Pocock returned as opener in place of Hartland, while Pringle and Owens beefed up the pace attack in place of Larsen and Davis. Disappointingly for them, their most experienced bowler, Morrison, was on his way home with a hamstring injury. England made just one change, the Northamptonshire left-armer Taylor coming in for his home Test debut in place of Malcolm, who made a disgruntled return to his county 24 hours before the Test began, after being told he would not be in the team. For the second time, left-arm spinner Stemp was also omitted from the final eleven. Atherton, having lost his sixth successive Test toss, switched around seven bowlers with little joy. Only when DeFreitas had the ball in his hand did the English attack look anything but bland. DeFreitas worked tirelessly for his captain and collected six wickets in the match to add to his nine in the First Test, making his latest England comeback look more permanent.

After an early wobble on the first morning, New Zealand built an impressive first-innings score over the opening two days around Crowe, who treated the Lord's crowd to a century – his 16th – of the highest calibre. Though his movement was restricted by a brace on his right knee following his recent operation, Crowe showed there are still few cleaner hitters of a ball in the world. His 142 included 20 fours and three sixes, one of which, off Fraser, made him only the second New Zealander after John Wright to pass 5,000 Test runs.

To England's frustration, they could not sweep away the New Zealand batting, even after Crowe was out at 350 for six. All the late-order batsmen made valuable contributions to a total of 476, which sorely tested England's ability to avoid the follow-on. To the astonishment of a packed Saturday crowd, they crumbled, after a powerful start by Stewart. A three-and-a-half-hour vigil by Rhodes for 32 not out kept England alive, and Rhodes and last man Such scraped past the follow-on target before Such became Nash's sixth victim. But New Zealand, with a lead of 195, were still in a position to declare an hour before the close on the fourth day, setting England to chase 407. It would have been a record fourth-innings total to win a Test had England made it but, after another bright start by Stewart and Atherton, their hopes were obliterated in Nash's second over of the last day, when he removed Atherton and Gooch.

The only objective then was survival. Despite a highly polished century from Stewart, his third in four Tests, England kept losing wickets at important times, Hick and Smith in particular struggling to assert their authority. The last hour arrived with New Zealand three wickets from victory. But Rhodes, first with Fraser, then with Taylor, blocked out time, while Such gnawed his nails on the balcony. As the poor light closed in, forcing Rutherford to withdraw Nash, who had removed five of the top six batsmen, Rhodes filibustered and fussed to eat up valuable seconds, frustrating New Zealand and earning the displeasure of the umpires. England, however, held on with two wickets to spare. Even with a £360 fine per man for slow over-rates, they must have felt they escaped lightly. – Colin Bateman.

Man of the Match: D. J. Nash. *Attendance:* 86,035; *receipts* £1,655,289.

Close of play: First day, New Zealand 316-4 (M. D. Crowe 133*, S. A. Thomson 68*); Second day, England 94-1 (M. A. Atherton 27*, G. A. Gooch 13*); Third day, England 281; Fourth day, England 56-0 (M. A. Atherton 29*, A. J. Stewart 25*).

[*Patrick Eagar*

Dion Nash on his way to 11 wickets in the Lord's Test.

New Zealand

First innings		Second innings	
B. A. Young lbw b Fraser	0	(2) c Hick b Such	94
B. A. Pocock c Smith b Such	10	(1) lbw b DeFreitas	2
*K. R. Rutherford c Stewart b DeFreitas	37	lbw b DeFreitas	0
M. D. Crowe c Smith b DeFreitas	142	b DeFreitas	9
S. P. Fleming lbw b Fraser	41	lbw b Taylor	39
S. A. Thomson run out	69	not out	38
†A. C. Parore c Rhodes b Taylor	40	not out	15
M. N. Hart b Such	25		
D. J. Nash b White	56		
C. Pringle c Hick b DeFreitas	14		
M. B. Owens not out	2		
B 3, l-b 15, w 1, n-b 21	40	L-b 4, n-b 10	14
1/0 (1) 2/39 (2) 3/67 (3) 4/138 (5) 5/318 (6) 6/350 (4) 7/391 (7) 8/397 (8) 9/434 (10) 10/476 (9)	476	1/9 (1) 2/9 (3) 3/29 (4) 4/144 (5) 5/170 (2) (5 wkts dec.)	211

Bowling: *First Innings*—Fraser 36–9–102–2; DeFreitas 35–8–102–3; Taylor 20–4–64–1; Such 30–8–84–2; White 21.1–4–84–1; Gooch 5–1–13–0; Hick 2–0–9–0. *Second Innings*—Fraser 15–0–50–0; DeFreitas 16–0–63–3; Such 25–5–55–1; White 4–1–21–0; Hick 2–2–0–0; Taylor 6–2–18–1.

England

First innings		Second innings	
*M. A. Atherton lbw b Hart	28	c Young b Nash	33
A. J. Stewart c Parore b Nash	45	c Crowe b Nash	119
G. A. Gooch lbw b Nash	13	lbw b Nash	0
R. A. Smith c and b Nash	6	c Parore b Nash	23
G. A. Hick c Young b Pringle	58	lbw b Pringle	37
C. White run out	51	c Thomson b Nash	9
†S. J. Rhodes not out	32	not out	24
P. A. J. DeFreitas c Parore b Thomson	11	lbw b Owens	3
A. R. C. Fraser c and b Nash	10	lbw b Hart	2
J. P. Taylor c Parore b Nash	0	not out	0
P. M. Such c Parore b Nash	4		
B 4, l-b 12, n-b 7	23	B 2, l-b 1, n-b 1	4
1/65 (2) 2/95 (3) 3/95 (1) 4/101 (4) 5/193 (6) 6/225 (5) 7/241 (8) 8/265 (9) 9/271 (10) 10/281 (11)	281	1/60 (1) 2/60 (3) 3/136 (4) 4/210 (5) 5/217 (2) 6/240 (6) 7/244 (8) 8/250 (9) (8 wkts)	254

Bowling: *First Innings*—Owens 7–0–34–0; Nash 25–6–76–6; Pringle 23–5–65–1; Hart 44–21–50–1; Thomson 22–8–40–1. *Second Innings*—Nash 29–8–93–5; Owens 10–3–35–1; Hart 41–23–55–1; Pringle 16–5–41–1; Thomson 12–4–27–0.

Umpires: S. A. Bucknor (West Indies) and N. T. Plews.
Referee: C. H. Lloyd (West Indies).

COMBINED UNIVERSITIES v NEW ZEALANDERS

At Cambridge, June 22, 23, 24. Drawn. Toss: New Zealanders. First-class debuts: J. N. Batty, M. T. E. Peirce.

The students had a good chance of repeating their 1990 triumph over the New Zealanders when they bowled them out twice and set out to score 133 from 50 overs. But they lost eight wickets for 80, with Larsen taking five for seven. Steer remained, however, and with Pitcher's support he began to revive their ambitions. They had added 42, only 11 short of their target, when time ran out. On the first day, the tourists totalled a merely respectable 256, before Owens removed the Universities' top four with 23 on the board. But Giles White, of Loughborough University, who had played one previous first-class match, for

Somerset against the Sri Lankans in 1991, batted five and a half hours, reaching his century while adding 153 with Steer and 86 with Hallett. That was enough for a 64-run first-innings lead. Some fine bowling from the Oxford leg-spinner Trimby ensured that the New Zealanders were dismissed for 196 the second time round.

Close of play: First day, Combined Universities 138-4 (G. W. White 40*, I. G. S. Steer 51*); Second day, New Zealanders 118-2 (B. R. Hartland 13*, G. R. Larsen 35*).

New Zealanders

B. R. Hartland c Snape b Bovill	6	– (3) c White b Trimby	25
B. A. Pocock c Steer b Bovill	21	– (1) lbw b Snape	28
*K. R. Rutherford lbw b Bovill	30	– (5) lbw b Hallett	14
M. J. Greatbatch c Trimby b Snape	68	– (2) c Snape b Trimby	37
S. P. Fleming c Peirce b Hallett	30	– (6) c Bovill b Hallett	16
S. A. Thomson c Cake b Trimby	66	– (7) lbw b Trimby	17
†B. A. Young c Montgomerie b Snape	12	– (8) c Steer b Bovill	13
G. R. Larsen c Hallett b Trimby	13	– (4) lbw b Bovill	35
S. J. Roberts c Batty b Trimby	2	– c Snape b Trimby	0
H. T. Davis lbw b Hallett	1	– not out	3
M. B. Owens not out	0	– run out	0
L-b 2, w 1, n-b 4	7	L-b 1, w 3, n-b 4	8
1/6 2/57 3/62 4/115 5/191 6/228 7/253 8/255 9/256	256	1/68 2/70 3/121 4/133 5/155 6/165 7/187 8/191 9/191	196

Bowling: *First Innings*—Bovill 15–3–51–3; Hallett 13–4–46–2; Pitcher 6–2–38–0; Snape 23–7–80–2; Trimby 17.2–4–39–3. *Second Innings*—Bovill 20–4–55–2; Hallett 18–5–43–2; Snape 13–6–39–1; Trimby 31.1–11–58–4.

Combined Universities

*R. R. Montgomerie (*Oxford*) c Young b Owens	0	– lbw b Roberts	8
M. T. E. Peirce (*Durham*) c Hartland b Owens	0	– lbw b Larsen	24
R. Q. Cake (*Cambridge*) c Hartland b Owens	3	– c Hartland b Roberts	0
J. N. Snape (*Durham*) c Greatbatch b Owens	18	– lbw b Thomson	4
G. W. White (*Loughborough*) b Roberts	104	– lbw b Larsen	1
I. G. S. Steer (*Cheltenham & Gloucester CHE*) b Larsen	67	– not out	48
†J. N. Batty (*Durham*) c Rutherford b Owens	6	– c Young b Larsen	3
J. C. Hallett (*Durham*) b Roberts	52	– c Hartland b Larsen	6
J. N. B. Bovill (*Durham*) b Roberts	7	– b Larsen	3
C. M. Pitcher (*Cambridge*) not out	12	– not out	1
P. W. Trimby (*Oxford*) b Roberts	2		
B 9, l-b 14, w 2, n-b 24	49	B 5, l-b 14, w 1, n-b 4	24
1/0 2/1 3/10 4/23 5/176 6/193 7/279 8/290 9/312	320	1/10 2/22 3/34 4/47 5/56 6/60 7/74 8/80	(8 wkts) 122

Bowling: *First Innings*—Owens 21–4–74–5; Roberts 21–5–60–4; Larsen 23–11–44–1; Davis 11–3–59–0; Thomson 22–6–60–0. *Second Innings*—Owens 5–3–12–0; Roberts 8–2–16–2; Larsen 20–10–24–5; Thomson 17–2–51–1.

Umpires: J. H. Harris and V. A. Holder.

DERBYSHIRE v NEW ZEALANDERS

At Derby, June 25, 26, 27. Derbyshire won by an innings and 18 runs. Toss: Derbyshire. First-class debut: M. E. Cassar.

Derbyshire's first victory over a touring team since they beat the South Africans in 1965 was gained in comfort, with nearly two sessions to spare. They had one previous success against the New Zealanders, in 1937. O'Gorman, dropped at slip off Nash before he scored, completed his second century in successive matches, Cork made a confident return after a month off and there was an impressive 66 on debut from Matthew Cassar, a 21-year-old Australian qualifying for England. Krikken pulled a hamstring while batting, so Rollins stepped in as wicket-keeper and Tweats held three catches as substitute. Base, back with Derbyshire on a match-contract and playing while Malcolm and DeFreitas rested, bowled particularly well. The New Zealanders were reinforced by the Wellington batsman, Mark Douglas, who was playing club cricket in the West Country. But they were hampered when Crowe retired ill after facing only two balls. Following on 214 behind, they showed no more resolution: acting-captain Larsen called the batting "spineless".

Close of play: First day, Derbyshire 349-6 (M. E. Cassar 29*, S. J. Base 3*); Second day, New Zealanders 59-1 (B. R. Hartland 34*, C. Pringle 2*).

Derbyshire

*K. J. Barnett c Owens b Roberts	6
A. S. Rollins c Parore b Nash	16
C. J. Adams c Hart b Owens	43
T. J. G. O'Gorman b Pringle	143
D. G. Cork lbw b Hart	48
M. J. Vandrau run out	31
†K. M. Krikken c Parore b Owens	35
M. E. Cassar c Greatbatch b Roberts	66
S. J. Base c Parore b Pringle	11
M. Taylor not out	2
L-b 8, w 11, n-b 4	23
1/28 2/28 3/88 4/193 5/272 6/331 7/360 8/416 9/424 (9 wkts dec.)	424

O. H. Mortensen did not bat.

In the first innings K. M. Krikken, when 7, retired hurt at 297 and resumed at 360.

Bowling: Nash 12–2–54–1; Roberts 18.2–0–87–2; Pringle 32–8–98–2; Owens 15–2–45–2; Larsen 13–3–30–0; Hart 33–11–102–1.

New Zealanders

M. J. Greatbatch c Vandrau b Base	84	(2) c Rollins b Cassar	18
B. R. Hartland b Base	0	(1) lbw b Cork	65
†A. C. Parore c sub (T. A. Tweats) b Vandrau	50	(4) c Rollins b Base	4
M. W. Douglas lbw b Mortensen	24	(5) lbw b Base	4
M. D. Crowe retired ill	5	absent ill	
M. N. Hart c sub (T. A. Tweats) b Taylor	0	lbw b Cork	33
D. J. Nash not out	14	lbw b Vandrau	4
*G. R. Larsen c sub (T. A. Tweats) b Base	0	not out	9
C. Pringle b Taylor	7	(3) b Cassar	10
S. J. Roberts c O'Gorman b Base	6	(9) c sub (D. Smit) b Vandrau	24
M. B. Owens b Taylor	1	(10) b Cassar	0
B 4, l-b 5, n-b 10	19	B 1, l-b 3, w 1, n-b 20	25
1/4 2/106 3/163 4/176 5/180 6/181 7/188 8/201 9/210	210	1/57 2/73 3/78 4/86 5/140 6/155 7/167 8/196 9/196	196

In the first innings M. D. Crowe retired ill at 172.

Bowling: *First Innings*—Mortensen 16–3–30–1; Base 16–4–58–4; Cassar 9–2–29–0; Vandrau 11–1–59–1; Taylor 11.1–6–25–3. *Second Innings*—Cork 12–1–42–2; Cassar 15.2–1–65–3; Vandrau 14–3–54–2; Base 7–0–31–2.

Umpires: J. D. Bond and T. E. Jesty.

ENGLAND v NEW ZEALAND

Third Cornhill Test

At Manchester, June 30, July 1, 2, 4, 5. Drawn. Toss: England. Test debut: D. Gough.

England duly made certain of their first home series victory since 1990. But they were denied a more emphatic 2-0 margin on the final two days by a combination of inclement weather and a fighting century from Crowe, in what he predicted would be his final appearance on English soil. Crowe began his match-saving innings late on the third afternoon, after England enforced the follow-on with a lead of 231. When he was finally caught at slip off DeFreitas for 115, nearly 70 hours later (there was again a rest day to avoid a clash with the men's final at Wimbledon), New Zealand were in sight of safety.

Winning the toss after nine successive international failures, Atherton had no hesitation in batting first. England included the off-spinner, Such, ahead of leg-spinner Salisbury on a hard surface expected to produce more bounce than turn. England also gave a Test debut to the 23-year-old Yorkshireman, Gough, dispensing with Taylor's services after just one Test. Lacking the power to extract any pace from the pitch, the limited New Zealand attack concentrated on a tight off-stump line throughout the opening day, frustrating English batsmen. Most of them paid for impatience. Atherton's superior powers of concentration allowed him to reach 96 by the close, but he was not impressed by the rashness of Stewart, Smith and Hick, which caused England to limp to 104 for four; they advanced painfully to 199 after 90 overs.

Atherton's seventh Test century was completed early on the second day, but 20 minutes later he became a third victim for Nash, the hero of Lord's, who again had good batsmen in difficulties. However, England's fortunes were revived in a dashing eighth-wicket partnership of 130 between Gough and DeFreitas, who, for once, played to his potential under pressure, while Gough answered Illingworth's call for bowlers who could put a sting in the tail. Gough's primary function, however, was that of strike bowler and he needed only five deliveries to fulfil it. Bowling short and sharp, he homed in on the gloves of the experienced Greatbatch – recalled despite a poor tour in place of the injured Pocock – and Hick at second slip accepted a gentle catch.

Suddenly there was variety and vigour in the English attack: Gough's pace and useful yorker were complemented by the outswing of DeFreitas and White's subtle change of pace. By lunch on Saturday, New Zealand were all out, with those three seamers sharing the wickets. The juggled catch which Gooch accepted off Rutherford was his 100th in Test cricket. Only Crowe, who made 70, put up real resistance, despite feeling side effects from medication for pre-Test flu. England had earlier objected to his being substituted full-time in the field.

New Zealand's second innings began with another early wicket from DeFreitas, who trapped Young lbw in his second over. By tea, at 75 for four, a finish inside three days looked possible. But the England attack ran out of steam, as Crowe, Thomson and Parore added 130 in the final session. Still, with two days remaining, their efforts seemed to be a final act of desperation.

After a rest day of uninterrupted sunshine, Manchester lived up to its sodden reputation. Only 18.5 overs were possible on the fourth day, after the morning was washed out, and England failed to take a wicket. The weather was, if anything, brighter as the final day dawned but, though play started promptly, rain intervened twice before lunch. In between the interruptions, Parore fell to an athletic gully catch by Gooch. He and Crowe had added 141, a record for New Zealand's sixth wicket against England. Finally, Crowe, who had completed his 17th Test century in four and a half hours, was taken at slip off the bowling of DeFreitas. But he had created a mood of defiance among his team-mates and Hart and Nash figured in a 21-run stand, before it rained again. Play ended at 3.20 p.m. and was abandoned an hour later. Over two innings, Crowe, almost single-handed, kept the England pace attack at bay. However, the match award went to DeFreitas, who was also England's Man of the Series, for his new all-round consistency. – Graham Otway.

Man of the Match: P. A. J. DeFreitas. *Attendance:* 41,857; *receipts* £591,492.

Men of the Series: England – P. A. J. DeFreitas; New Zealand – D. J. Nash.

Close of play: First day, England 199-4 (M. A. Atherton 96*, C. White 42*); Second day, New Zealand 84-4 (M. D. Crowe 33*, M. N. Hart 0*); Third day, New Zealand 205-5 (M. D. Crowe 65*, A. C. Parore 50*); Fourth day, New Zealand 253-5 (M. D. Crowe 94*, A. C. Parore 66*).

England

*M. A. Atherton lbw b Nash	111
A. J. Stewart c Pringle b Nash	24
G. A. Gooch c Young b Nash	0
R. A. Smith b Owens	13
G. A. Hick c Nash b Owens	20
C. White c Hart b Owens	42
†S. J. Rhodes c Parore b Nash	12
P. A. J. DeFreitas b Owens	69
D. Gough c sub (H. T. Davis) b Pringle	65
A. R. C. Fraser c Thomson b Hart	10
P. M. Such not out	5
L-b 8, w 1, n-b 2	11
1/37 (2) 2/37 (3) 3/68 (4) 4/104 (5) 5/203 (6) 6/224 (1) 7/235 (7) 8/365 (8) 9/372 (9) 10/382 (10)	382

Bowling: Nash 39–9–107–4; Owens 34–12–99–4; Pringle 39–12–95–1; Hart 27.3–9–50–1; Thomson 7–1–23–0.

New Zealand

B. A. Young c Rhodes b DeFreitas	25	– lbw b DeFreitas	8
M. J. Greatbatch c Hick b Gough	0	– c DeFreitas b White	21
*K. R. Rutherford c Gooch b DeFreitas	7	– c Rhodes b Gough	13
S. P. Fleming c Rhodes b Gough	14	– c Hick b Fraser	11
M. D. Crowe c Gooch b White	70	– c Hick b DeFreitas	115
M. N. Hart c Atherton b Gough	0	– (8) not out	16
S. A. Thomson c Rhodes b DeFreitas	9	– (6) c Smith b Gough	21
†A. C. Parore c Rhodes b White	7	– (7) c Gooch b DeFreitas	71
D. J. Nash not out	8	– not out	6
C. Pringle b White	0		
M. B. Owens c Stewart b Gough	4		
N-b 7	7	B 8, l-b 13, n-b 5	26
1/2 (2) 2/12 (3) 3/47 (4) 4/82 (1) 5/93 (6) 6/113 (7) 7/125 (8) 8/140 (5) 9/140 (10) 10/151 (11)	151	1/8 (1) 2/34 (3) 3/48 (4) 4/73 (2) 5/132 (6) 6/273 (7) 7/287 (5)	(7 wkts) 308

Bowling: *First Innings*—Fraser 12–3–17–0; Gough 16.3–2–47–4; DeFreitas 17–2–61–3; Such 5–2–8–0; White 7–1–18–3. *Second Innings*—DeFreitas 30–6–60–3; Gough 31.2–5–105–2; Fraser 19–7–34–1; White 14–3–36–1; Such 10–2–39–0; Gooch 2–0–13–0.

Umpires: S. B. Lambson (South Africa) and D. R. Shepherd.
Referee: E. D. Weekes (West Indies).

†IRELAND v NEW ZEALANDERS

At Comber, July 8. New Zealanders won by six runs. Toss: New Zealanders.

Ireland nearly caused an upset in the biggest game ever played at the well-kept pitch at Comber, just outside Belfast. Warke – who became his country's leading run-scorer when ten – and Lewis set the innings up with 103 for the third wicket. Then Benson and Narasimha Rao, the former Indian Test player, took them to 213 for four, only 21 short of the target, in the 52nd over. But Pringle thwarted their hopes as their next five wickets fell for 12 runs. The New Zealanders had batted steadily, with everyone except Young making a start, though only Fleming reached his fifty.

New Zealanders

B. R. Hartland c and b Harrison	36
B. A. Young c Millar b Cooke	2
*K. R. Rutherford c Millar b Graham	37
S. P. Fleming c Graham b Lewis	58
S. A. Thomson c Millar b Cooke	33
†A. C. Parore not out	37
G. R. Larsen c Narasimha Rao b Moore	23
L-b 3, w 3, n-b 1	7
1/12 2/74 3/92 4/158 5/185 6/233 (6 wkts, 55 overs)	233

M. N. Hart, D. J. Nash, S. J. Roberts and C. Pringle did not bat.

Bowling: Moore 10–1–56–1; Cooke 9–4–31–2; Harrison 11–2–43–1; Graham 7–0–34–1; Narasimha Rao 11–2–31–0; Lewis 7–0–35–1.

Ireland

S. J. S. Warke c Larsen b Hart	82
M. P. Rea c Young b Pringle	10
S. G. Smyth c Parore b Larsen	12
*D. A. Lewis c Rutherford b Nash	34
J. D. R. Benson c Larsen b Pringle	38
M. V. Narasimha Rao c Parore b Nash	16
G. D. Harrison c Hart b Pringle	2
S. Graham c sub (M. B. Owens) b Pringle	4
G. Cooke not out	5
E. R. Moore c Hartland b Nash	0
†R. B. Millar not out	2
B 1, l-b 13, w 7, n-b 1	22
1/21 2/49 3/152 4/154 5/213 6/214 7/219 8/219 9/225 (9 wkts, 55 overs)	227

Bowling: Nash 10–1–44–3; Pringle 11–5–27–4; Roberts 4–1–7–0; Larsen 11–1–43–1; Hart 11–2–51–1; Thomson 8–0–41–0.

Umpires: W. B. Arlow and P. L. O'Hara.

†IRELAND v NEW ZEALANDERS

At Malahide, Dublin, July 10. New Zealanders won by nine wickets. Toss: Ireland.

Rain prevented any play before the afternoon, when the New Zealanders won a 20-over match with ease. Ireland scored at more than seven an over as Rutherford gave eight bowlers, including Parore, their turn; Thomson picked up four wickets in the closing stages. But the tourists raced to 94 in eight overs before losing Parore and completed their victory with more than six overs left. Hartland was unbeaten on 80 while Benson, formerly of Leicestershire, shone for Ireland, with 41 runs and the one wicket. Conditions were bad throughout the game and it would probably have been abandoned but for the presence of the Irish President, Mary Robinson.

Ireland

J. D. R. Benson b Parore	41
S. G. Smyth b Owens	0
M. V. Narasimha Rao b Hart	17
*D. A. Lewis st Young b Parore	1
G. D. Harrison st Young b Thomson	43
S. Graham b Larsen	7
M. P. Rea c Fleming b Thomson	3
S. J. S. Warke not out	9
G. Cooke c Fleming b Thomson	2
E. R. Moore b Thomson	0
†R. B. Millar not out	1
B 2, l-b 12, w 5, n-b 3	22
1/5 2/71 3/78 4/80 5/115 6/134 7/134 8/140 9/145 (9 wkts, 20 overs)	146

Bowling: Owens 1–0–5–1; Davis 5–0–32–0; Pringle 1–0–7–0; Thomson 3–0–28–4; Fleming 1–0–11–0; Parore 4–0–16–2; Hart 3–0–22–1; Larsen 2–0–11–1.

New Zealanders

B. R. Hartland not out	80
A. C. Parore c Millar b Benson	38
†B. A. Young not out	24
L-b 2, w 4	6
1/94 (1 wkt, 13.5 overs)	148

*K. R. Rutherford, S. P. Fleming, S. A. Thomson, M. N. Hart, G. R. Larsen, C. Pringle, H. T. Davis and M. B. Owens did not bat.

Bowling: Moore 2.5–0–30–0; Cooke 3–0–26–0; Harrison 3–0–34–0; Benson 2–0–26–1; Narasimha Rao 2–0–23–0; Warke 1–0–7–0.

Umpires: L. P. Hogan and R. MacClancy.

THE SOUTH AFRICAN TOURING PARTY

[*Patrick Eagar*

Back row: C. Smith (*physiotherapist*), J. N. Rhodes, D. J. Cullinan, T. G. Shaw, A. Martyn, B. M. McMillan, P. S. de Villiers, P. L. Symcox, C. R. Matthews, G. F. J. Liebenberg, R. P. Snell, D. J. Richardson, G. Kirsten, M. J. Procter (*coach*). *Front row:* A. C. Hudson, A. A. Donald, F. Bing (*manager*), K. C. Wessels (*captain*), Goolam Rajah (*assistant manager*), W. J. Cronje, P. N. Kirsten.

THE SOUTH AFRICANS IN ENGLAND, 1994

South Africa's first Test series in England since 1965 began in triumph, when they won the First Test at Lord's in four days, vastly superior to England in every facet except spin bowling, in which the tourists chose not to compete at all. However, in the course of the two remaining Test matches, the pendulum swung from one side to the other, as seldom happens in a three-Test series. England gained the advantage during the Second Test at Headingley and used it to full effect in the Third at The Oval. Indeed, so unsettled were the South Africans on the fast pitch there that they ended in some disarray; and ultimately their complete record on paper, after losing their final one-day game against Holland, was little better than that of the New Zealanders earlier in the summer. After the tour, Mike Procter, one of the most famous names in South African cricket, was replaced as coach by the more technically-minded Englishman, Bob Woolmer, and in November Kepler Wessels gave up the captaincy. But because they took England's last two wickets in their Lord's Test, unlike New Zealand, and because they renewed official relationships so diplomatically, the South Africans' tour of 1994 can be judged an overall success.

Amid the harmony which existed between the two teams, and between the South Africans and the public (although the tourists' approach to the county games was often cautious), there was only one controversy, albeit a huge one, and it did not directly concern the tourists at all. The Lord's Test match was played in intense heat, similar to that in the West Indies where England had toured a few months before, and where they had learned a lot about reverse-swing. On the Saturday afternoon at Lord's, the England captain, Mike Atherton, was seen on television to be taking dirt from his pocket, which everyone agreed was connected with keeping the ball dry and helping it to reverse-swing. Thereafter, public opinion differed sharply during a debate which provoked newspaper editorials and phone-in programmes, and divided even those barely interested in cricket into two factions. One faction thought Atherton was cheating and that this, combined with his economy with the truth in front of the ICC referee Peter Burge, constituted a resignation issue; the other accepted his assertion that he was trying to avoid affecting the ball. It was subsequently inferred that Burge took a very dim view of Atherton's behaviour, since he fined him half his match fee at The Oval for stepping minimally out of line, by shaking his head and looking at the inside edge of his bat after being given leg-before first ball.

If the incident at Lord's was unfortunate for Atherton, coming as it did within the first year of his England captaincy, it was no less so for the South Africans. Public attention was distracted from their magnificent victory – one of only two first-class games that they won – and due credit denied them in the British media. Moreover, Procter remarked after the series that he thought the Atherton affair had had the effect of bringing the England players together, in support of their young captain.

In any event, the tourists never quite recaptured the fervent enthusiasm which they brought to the Lord's match. After 29 years away from England, a sweeping victory at the first attempt proved to be almost a cathartic experience, after which everything else was anticlimax. There may also have been a failure to redefine goals. The two previous South African parties who won Test series in England, in 1935 and 1965, had done so by one game to nil; and on their arrival Wessels and his team had spoken of a similar aim, expecting the win to come at either Headingley or The Oval, the two grounds overtly most suited to their pace bowling. The Test at Lord's was to have been a quiet reintroduction, an acclimatisation. When England capitulated after the opening day of the series, the tourists as much as anyone were taken by surprise and did not readjust their sights upwards.

More so than Atherton's handful of dust, the return of the Surrey left-hander Graham Thorpe enlivened England and started the pendulum's swing away from the tourists towards the home side. On an unexpectedly true batting pitch at Headingley, England's batsmen were labouring as usual until Thorpe came in and swiftly embarked upon a trio of scores in the seventies which lifted his side out of their hitherto defensive and unconfident approach. Now, while Atherton kept one end going, he had a partner to attack the bowling from the other, as well as to disrupt its line. Inexplicably and wrongly omitted for four Tests after two excellent innings during the West Indian tour, Thorpe was not only powerful in his pulling, which had previously been quick and sure, but in his square-cutting and straight-driving. The four South African pace bowlers – unplayable at Lord's and considered by some to be superior to the West Indian attack – suddenly became ordinary.

At Headingley, however, the South Africans still had enough steam to fight back with the tenacity that was their trademark. Apparently doomed at 105 for five in reply to 477, their later order rallied superbly under Peter Kirsten, who drew on five seasons of experience with Derbyshire to make his maiden Test hundred at the age of 39, and the large, burly all-rounder Brian McMillan, whom Atherton considered to be as good a batsman as any on the South African side. What is more, the tourists counter-attacked with aggressive strokeplay, not dogged defence. Once they had saved the follow-on, England made no more than a gesture towards winning.

Still, the cracks which had appeared in South Africa's cricket at Headingley – for instance, the uncertainty of their vice-captain Hansie Cronje against the short-pitched bowling of Darren Gough – England widened in spectacular fashion at The Oval. Pre-tour conjecture had come up with several suggestions as to what South African cricket had missed most during the years of their absence from official cricket because of apartheid, and at The Oval the answer became apparent. In their approach – tenacious spirit, buoyant morale and hard work – the tourists were like the best of Australian teams. But their batsmen shaped more like New Zealanders when confronted with the unfamiliar spectacle of a fast and bouncy pitch. Their top-order batsmen were so startled by it that they were overwhelmed.

By then the senior opening batsman, Andrew Hudson, had been dropped, his self-confidence gone, his shot selection indiscriminate. His one century of the tour was in the final game at Scarborough. But he had made 163 against West Indies in Barbados and perhaps he should have been persuaded to play at The Oval. In his absence, the half-brothers Gary and Peter Kirsten were paired as openers and could not cope with Devon Malcolm at his fastest. Earlier, on slower wickets, the left-handed Gary had demonstrated a fine cover drive and had set both of South Africa's innings in motion at Lord's; he was also a brave short leg. The tall and front-footed

Cronje at No. 3 was ever more at sea as the series went on. For a team which had two of its first three batsmen as non-contributors throughout the series, the tourists did remarkably well.

Wessels, who suffered a hairline fracture of his right forearm at Leicester, played his major innings at the most important time, on the opening day at Lord's. His fielding at first slip was safe and sound, as was his captaincy, given the limited variety in his bowling attack. Jonty Rhodes, like Thorpe, was quick to pull but at The Oval Daryll Cullinan looked a more complete batsman. In the field, at cover, Rhodes was as influential as the bowlers in making England feel boxed in at Lord's. Like his team-mates, he sparkled less thereafter, and he did not run out an England batsman until the one-day series, when England maintained their newly acquired domination. Constantly compared with Colin Bland, Rhodes was physically more flexible in the covers for being shorter, but did not have Bland's strength of throw from the boundary.

The advantages of an all-pace attack could not have been better illustrated than at Lord's. Allan Donald, used in sharp, five-over bursts, had the speed to provoke unplanned strokes from the England batsmen, on a dry surface too loose to be true. By The Oval, the drawbacks were stark, and Wessels had nowhere to turn except to the medium-pace of Cronje. Donald was found to have no change of pace – only very fast and faster – and was hit with astonishing abandon. Had Donald not recovered from an infected toe which forced him out of the attack at Headingley, the flattish off-spinner Pat Symcox would have played in the final Test. The slow left-armer Tim Shaw was tidy but predictable when bowling round the wicket, using exactly the same position in the crease and never varying his angle.

Fanie de Villiers was the most outgoing character in the party and the most popular with the public. He bowled his out-swing brilliantly from the Nursery End at Lord's but never swung the ball much again. Though similar in size and pace to Terry Alderman, he did not get so close to the stumps, or – more likely – was not allowed to by the umpires. Craig Matthews was steadiness itself as a third seamer, a taller version of Robin Jackman, who had coached him, but without enough swing, seam or pace to take wickets in quantity. McMillan was aggressive, ready to drop the ball short, but seldom made the ball leave the right-handed bat. Richard Snell, who replaced Aubrey Martyn when he went home with a back injury (depriving Wessels of the variation of a left-armer), also pitched too short, as he had when with Somerset in 1992.

Perhaps the most consistently successful member of the party was the wicket-keeper Dave Richardson (his deputy, Gerhardus Liebenberg, had only kept wicket at club level and was chosen more for his batting). By the end of the tour Richardson, a 34-year-old lawyer by profession, was one of the only two players – Donald being the other – who had played in all 17 of South Africa's Tests since their return, and well merited the distinction for his polished keeping, resolution and crisp cutting with the bat, and his cheerful demeanour.

Procter's overall objective was to make South African cricket more attacking. Thanks largely to the robust methods of McMillan and Richardson in the later order, the Test team scored at more than three runs an over in the series, when in the previous Tests since their return they had scored at only 2.28. Having aimed over the previous two years for respectability, frequently in the shape of draws, the South Africans played a more expansive game in England. It thrillingly paid off at Lord's and in their counter-attack at Headingley. For England, after their deplorable start, a drawn series – only their second at home since 1974 – was a comforting consolation. – Scyld Berry.

SOUTH AFRICAN TOURING PARTY

K. C. Wessels (Eastern Province) (*captain*), W. J. Cronje (Orange Free State) (*vice-captain*), D. J. Cullinan (Transvaal), P. S. de Villiers (Northern Transvaal), A. A. Donald (Orange Free State), A. C. Hudson (Natal), G. Kirsten (Western Province), P. N. Kirsten (Border), G. F. J. Liebenberg (Orange Free State), B. M. McMillan (Western Province), A. Martyn (Western Province), C. R. Matthews (Western Province), J. N. Rhodes (Natal), D. J. Richardson (Eastern Province), T. G. Shaw (Eastern Province), P. L. Symcox (Natal).

R. P. Snell (Transvaal) replaced Martyn, who suffered a back injury shortly after arriving in England.

Manager: F. Bing. *Assistant manager:* Goolam Rajah. *Coach:* M. J. Procter.

SOUTH AFRICAN TOUR RESULTS

Test matches – Played 3: Won 1, Lost 1, Drawn 1.
First-class matches – Played 14: Won 2, Lost 2, Drawn 10.
Wins – England, Nottinghamshire.
Losses – England, Kent.
Draws – England, Sussex, Hampshire, Gloucestershire, Durham, Northamptonshire, Leicestershire, Minor Counties, Glamorgan, President's XI.
One-day internationals – Played 2: Lost 2.
Other non first-class matches – Played 3: Won 1, Lost 1, No result 1. *Win* – Earl of Carnarvon's XI. *Loss* – President's XI. *No result* – Scotland.

TEST MATCH AVERAGES

ENGLAND – BATTING

	T	*I*	*NO*	*R*	*HS*	*100s*	*Avge*	*Ct/St*
G. P. Thorpe	2	4	1	239	79	0	79.66	2
G. A. Hick	3	6	1	304	110	1	60.80	2
A. J. Stewart	3	5	1	226	89	0	56.50	2
S. J. Rhodes	3	4	2	105	65*	0	52.50	14/2
D. Gough	3	4	2	81	42*	0	40.50	0
M. A. Atherton	3	6	0	207	99	0	34.50	1
G. A. Gooch	3	6	0	139	33	9	23.16	1
P. A. J. DeFreitas	3	4	0	73	37	0	18.25	2
J. P. Crawley	3	5	0	59	38	0	11.80	4
A. R. C. Fraser	2	3	0	10	6	0	3.33	1

Played in one Test: J. E. Benjamin 0; D. E. Malcolm 4 (1 ct); I. D. K. Salisbury 6*, 0; P. C. R. Tufnell did not bat (1 ct); C. White 10, 0.

* *Signifies not out.*

BOWLING

	O	M	R	W	BB	5W/i	Avge
D. E. Malcolm	41.3	7	138	10	9-57	1	13.80
J. E. Benjamin	28	3	80	4	4-42	0	20.00
P. C. R. Tufnell	55	21	112	4	2-31	0	28.00
A. R. C. Fraser	85.5	19	245	7	3-72	0	35.00
D. Gough	122.3	21	414	11	4-46	0	37.63
P. A. J. DeFreitas	113.3	25	358	9	4-89	0	39.77

Also bowled: G. A. Gooch 3–0–9–0; G. A. Hick 48–23–98–2; I. D. K. Salisbury 44–6–121–1; C. White 16–2–61–2.

SOUTH AFRICA – BATTING

	T	I	NO	R	HS	100s	Avge	Ct
B. M. McMillan . . .	3	5	1	264	93	0	66.00	4
K. C. Wessels	3	6	0	238	105	1	39.66	3
P. N. Kirsten	3	6	1	179	104	1	35.80	0
J. N. Rhodes	3	5	1	128	46	0	32.00	1
C. R. Matthews . . .	3	5	1	128	62*	0	32.00	0
G. Kirsten	3	6	0	190	72	0	31.66	1
D. J. Richardson . .	3	5	0	138	58	0	27.60	7
A. A. Donald	3	4	2	46	27	0	23.00	1
W. J. Cronje	3	6	1	90	38	0	18.00	2
P. S. de Villiers	3	4	1	35	14	0	11.66	0
A. C. Hudson	2	4	0	30	12	0	7.50	2

Played in one Test: D. J. Cullinan 7, 94.

* *Signifies not out.*

BOWLING

	O	M	R	W	BB	5W/i	Avge
B. M. McMillan . . .	81.2	16	267	9	3-16	0	29.66
P. S. de Villiers	123.3	27	388	12	4-62	0	32.33
A. A. Donald	89.3	15	410	12	5-74	1	34.16
C. R. Matthews . . .	125.3	35	340	8	3-25	0	42.50

Also bowled: W. J. Cronje 37–9–94–0; G. Kirsten 2–1–10–0.

SOUTH AFRICAN TOUR AVERAGES – FIRST-CLASS MATCHES

BATTING

	M	I	NO	R	HS	100s	Avge	Ct
B. M. McMillan	9	11	3	467	132	1	58.37	10
P. L. Symcox	7	5	3	104	39*	0	52.00	2
P. N. Kirsten	10	16	5	549	130	2	49.90	5
G. Kirsten	11	19	3	751	201*	2	46.93	5
K. C. Wessels	12	18	2	679	105	1	42.43	17
T. G. Shaw	9	5	3	82	66	0	41.00	4
D. J. Cullinan	9	14	3	428	94	0	38.90	5

	M	I	NO	R	HS	100s	Avge	Ct/St
J. N. Rhodes	12	16	3	477	77	0	36.69	8
C. R. Matthews	9	6	2	143	62*	0	35.75	2
W. J. Cronje	13	20	1	661	108	1	34.78	11
D. J. Richardson	10	12	3	286	88	0	31.77	23/1
R. P. Snell	8	8	3	143	94	0	28.60	0
A. A. Donald	8	6	3	68	27	0	22.66	4
G. F. J. Liebenberg	7	11	1	226	64*	0	22.60	9/3
A. C. Hudson	12	19	1	382	116	1	21.22	8
P. S. de Villiers	8	5	1	43	14	0	10.75	2

* *Signifies not out.*

BOWLING

	O	M	R	W	BB	5W/i	Avge
P. S. de Villiers	277.3	59	922	38	6-67	2	24.26
P. L. Symcox	280.5	86	761	28	5-29	2	27.17
W. J. Cronje	159.5	45	395	13	4-47	0	30.38
A. A. Donald	212.2	42	775	25	5-58	2	31.00
B. M. McMillan	222.4	49	662	19	4-47	0	34.84
R. P. Snell	200.1	38	666	18	3-38	0	37.00
T. G. Shaw	312.4	90	828	21	4-29	0	39.42
C. R. Matthews	263.3	71	749	17	3-25	0	44.05

Also bowled: G. Kirsten 22.5–5–97–0; P. N. Kirsten 18–4–76–2; J. N. Rhodes 1–0–10–0; K. C. Wessels 2–0–7–0.

Note: Matches in this section which were not first-class are signified by a dagger.

†EARL OF CARNARVON'S XI v SOUTH AFRICANS

At Highclere, June 23. South Africans won by seven wickets. Toss: Earl of Carnarvon's XI.

The South Africans played their first official match in England for 29 years amid the curiously old-fashioned atmosphere of country-house cricket. The Queen attended the exclusive gathering at Highclere Castle and 2,000 other spectators paid £25 a head, raising £30,000 for the National Playing Fields Association, with South African township cricket among the beneficiaries. However, the emphasis was on corporate hospitality, and there were complaints that the public had found it difficult to get tickets. The tourists also had problems: they arrived late because of traffic jams. Though the Earl fielded six Test players, his unexpected hero was Oxford University opener Greg Macmillan, who struck three sixes and ten fours. Gower, on his return to the crease from the commentary box, lasted only 12 balls, but Warne joined Hooper to take the total past 200. Warne was less successful when he bowled, conceding 57 in ten overs. Rhodes, with 111 from 110 balls, and Wessels put on 189 for the third wicket to ensure a comfortable victory.

Earl of Carnarvon's XI

B. C. Broad c McMillan b Matthews	4
G. I. Macmillan c Rhodes b Cronje	78
T. R. Ward st Liebenberg b Shaw	28
C. J. Adams run out	23
*D. I. Gower c Liebenberg b Cronje	7
C. L. Hooper c McMillan b de Villiers	37
M. V. Fleming lbw b Symcox	0
†S. A. Marsh c Kirsten b Cronje	4
S. K. Warne c Cronje b Matthews	22
C. A. Walsh not out	8
A. P. Igglesden run out	4
B 2, l-b 6	8
1/9 2/49 3/108 4/146 5/147 6/148 7/161 8/210 9/211 (48.2 overs)	223

Bowling: de Villiers 6.2–0–12–1; Matthews 8–0–39–2; McMillan 8–0–44–0; Shaw 10–1–36–1; Symcox 10–0–45–1; Cronje 6–0–39–3.

South Africans

G. Kirsten c Hooper b Walsh	10	D. J. Cullinan not out	2
W. J. Cronje c Marsh b Igglesden	13	W 16, n-b 4	20
*K. C. Wessels not out	68		—
J. N. Rhodes c Fleming b Walsh	111	1/24 2/28 3/217 (3 wkts, 47.2 overs)	224

T. G. Shaw, B. M. McMillan, †G. F. J. Liebenberg, P. S. de Villiers, C. R. Matthews and P. L. Symcox did not bat.

Bowling: Igglesden 10–1–51–1; Walsh 9–2–30–2; Warne 10–0–57–0; Fleming 9.2–0–43–0; Hooper 9–2–43–0.

Umpires: G. I. Burgess and G. Sharp.

KENT v SOUTH AFRICANS

At Canterbury, June 25, 26, 27. Kent won by 34 runs. Toss: Kent.

The South Africans' return to the English first-class circuit began in anticlimax, when the Saturday was washed out, and ended in defeat. It was a happier return for Cowdrey, who had been dropped in mid-May and was a last-minute inclusion when Fleming could not play. He scored the county's first hundred against the South Africans since Les Ames in 1929. Cowdrey rescued Kent from 62 for five, first in a stand of 93 with Marsh; then Headley joined him to add 110. The tourists faced one over that evening, then one ball on the final morning before they declared and Benson forfeited an innings, having agreed to set them a generous 293 in 93 overs. Headley and Igglesden had them at 64 for six until a stand of 157 between Richardson and Shaw held out the hope of safety. But after they went, Marsh's sixth catch of the innings completed Kent's first win against the South Africans since 1924.

Close of play: First day, No play; Second day, South Africans 0-0 (A. C. Hudson 0*, G. Kirsten 0*).

Kent

D. P. Fulton c Wessels b de Villiers	6	C. Penn c Richardson b Cronje	0
*M. R. Benson c Richardson b Donald	25	M. M. Patel lbw b Cronje	0
T. R. Ward lbw b de Villiers	0	A. P. Igglesden c and b Cronje	7
N. R. Taylor c Rhodes b Donald	1		
M. A. Ealham c Hudson b de Villiers	18	B 8, l-b 2, n-b 8	18
G. R. Cowdrey c Rhodes b Shaw	114		—
†S. A. Marsh c Richardson b Cronje	57	1/7 2/7 3/12 4/49 5/62	292
D. W. Headley not out	46	6/155 7/265 8/266 9/266	

Bowling: Donald 19–9–34–2; de Villiers 13–2–50–3; Matthews 19–6–36–0; Shaw 29–2–115–1; Cronje 14.5–2–47–4.

Kent forfeited their second innings.

South Africans

A. C. Hudson not out	0	– (2) b Headley	1
G. Kirsten not out	0	– (1) c Marsh b Headley	8
W. J. Cronje (did not bat)		– c Marsh b Igglesden	5
*K. C. Wessels (did not bat)		– c Marsh b Igglesden	26
D. J. Cullinan (did not bat)		– c Igglesden b Headley	0
J. N. Rhodes (did not bat)		– lbw b Penn	20
†D. J. Richardson (did not bat)		– b Patel	88
T. G. Shaw (did not bat)		– c Marsh b Headley	66
C. R. Matthews (did not bat)		– not out	15
P. S. de Villiers (did not bat)		– c Marsh b Igglesden	8
A. A. Donald (did not bat)		– c Marsh b Headley	4
		B 3, l-b 5, n-b 9	17
	—		—
(no wkt dec.)	0	1/2 2/9 3/19 4/21 5/56 6/64 7/221 8/227 9/249	258

Bowling: *First Innings*—Patel 1–1–0–0; Fulton 0.1–0–0–0. *Second Innings*—Igglesden 19–8–51–3; Headley 22.2–2–60–5; Ealham 9–3–17–0; Penn 13–4–51–1; Patel 23–4–71–1.

Umpires: H. D. Bird and K. E. Palmer.

SUSSEX v SOUTH AFRICANS

At Hove, June 29, 30, July 1. Drawn. Toss: Sussex. First-class debut: J. D. Lewry.

On only his second visit to Hove since he played for Sussex from 1976 to 1980, Wessels made few new friends when he extended the South Africans' first innings until tea on the final day. There was a further delay after the interval; the umpires had not been informed of the declaration and the pitch had not been rolled. It was flat enough already, giving the tourists plenty of batting practice as they reached 613, their highest total against an English county, beating by two a record set at Trent Bridge in 1904. But Sussex had hardly looked interested in a positive result as they moved slowly to 282 on the first day. Only Lenham fulfilled early promise. It was left to Jarvis, with a maiden fifty for Sussex, to hurry the score along on the second morning. The South Africans then had some early scares – Jason Lewry, a left-arm seamer from Goring-by-Sea, took a wicket in his second over in first-class cricket – but Peter Kirsten completed his 52nd first-class century and McMillan hit 132, with some majestic strokeplay, including 15 fours and a six. The off-spinner Symcox provided some late drama, taking five quick Sussex wickets. But Jarvis and Moores put up stiffer resistance.

Close of play: First day, Sussex 282-7 (P. W. Jarvis 32*, N. C. Phillips 2*); Second day, South Africans 312-5 (P. N. Kirsten 60*, B. M. McMillan 17*).

Sussex

C. W. J. Athey c Liebenberg b Matthews	33	– c McMillan b Symcox	25
J. W. Hall c Wessels b McMillan	48	– st Liebenberg b Symcox	12
N. J. Lenham b McMillan	76	– c Liebenberg b Snell	4
*A. P. Wells c Liebenberg b Snell	4	– (8) not out	0
M. P. Speight b Cronje	41		
†P. Moores b McMillan	15	– lbw b Symcox	18
C. C. Remy c Liebenberg b Matthews	16	– (4) c P. N. Kirsten b Symcox	10
P. W. Jarvis not out	70	– (7) not out	19
N. C. Phillips not out	37	– (5) c Wessels b Symcox	0
L-b 13, w 1, n-b 4	18	L-b 1, w 2	3
1/83 2/104 3/119 4/185 5/227 6/236 7/256 (7 wkts dec.)	358	1/28 2/42 3/52 4/52 5/53 6/91 (6 wkts)	91

J. D. Lewry and E. S. H. Giddins did not bat.

Bowling: *First Innings*—Matthews 26–8–57–2; McMillan 28–5–68–3; Symcox 36–11–102–0; Snell 19–5–65–1; Cronje 9–4–33–1; G. Kirsten 5–1–20–0. *Second Innings*—Matthews 6–2–10–0; Snell 12–3–46–1; Symcox 12–4–29–5; G. Kirsten 2.5–1–5–0.

South Africans

A. C. Hudson c Moores b Jarvis	2
G. Kirsten b Lewry	26
W. J. Cronje c Speight b Remy	94
*K. C. Wessels c and b Phillips	77
P. N. Kirsten c Remy b Phillips	130
D. J. Cullinan b Jarvis	0
B. M. McMillan c Jarvis b Wells	132
†G. F. J. Liebenberg not out	64
R. P. Snell st Moores b Remy	5
P. L. Symcox not out	37
B 5, l-b 7, n-b 34	46
1/2 2/44 3/177 4/257 5/264 6/437 7/560 8/571 (8 wkts dec.)	613

C. R. Matthews did not bat.

Bowling: Jarvis 34–4–125–2; Giddins 26–1–106–0; Phillips 36–5–127–2; Lewry 31–7–106–1; Remy 20–0–89–2; Wells 7–0–48–1.

Umpires: A. A. Jones and P. B. Wight.

HAMPSHIRE v SOUTH AFRICANS

At Southampton, July 2, 3, 4. Drawn. Toss: Hampshire. County debut: G. W. White.

The weather claimed the final morning, when Hampshire were 58 ahead after the tourists had declared with a deficit of 36, and neither side was keen to indulge in an artificial finish. Instead, Hampshire were given batting practice and the South African spinners a long work-out. Morris benefited; having been undone by Donald's hostility on the first morning, he reached his second first-class century just before the close. Terry had been the mainstay of Hampshire's first innings, scoring 75 in 67 overs. For the South Africans, Donald claimed five wickets with impressive pace on the first day, while the effervescent Rhodes dazzled in the field. Rhodes also scored an effective 77; without this and a solid half-century from Gary Kirsten, the tourists might have been embarrassed. Udal pressed his Test claims with three wickets in seven balls.

Close of play: First day, Hampshire 263-8 (A. N. Aymes 14*); Second day, Hampshire 22-0 (R. S. M. Morris 18*, V. P. Terry 4*).

Hampshire

R. S. M. Morris c Rhodes b Donald	4	– not out	101
V. P. Terry c Wessels b Snell	75	– c Kirsten b Shaw	43
R. M. F. Cox c Richardson b Donald	46	– c McMillan b Symcox	11
*M. C. J. Nicholas lbw b Snell	33		
G. W. White c Richardson b Donald	30	– (4) c Rhodes b Symcox	8
K. D. James c Hudson b Donald	42	– (5) c Wessels b Symcox	25
†A. N. Aymes not out	33	– not out	3
S. D. Udal c Wessels b Donald	0	– (6) c Symcox b Shaw	1
M. J. Thursfield c Richardson b Symcox	3		
C. A. Connor not out	15		
B 1, l-b 5, w 1, n-b 12	19	L-b 4, n-b 2	6
1/12 2/106 3/171 4/172 5/235 6/248 7/248 8/263 (8 wkts dec.)	300	1/94 2/113 3/135 4/174 5/187 (5 wkts)	198

J. N. B. Bovill did not bat.

Bowling: *First Innings*—Donald 24.5–7–58–5; McMillan 27–7–86–0; Snell 19–3–49–2; Shaw 19–4–56–0; Symcox 23–7–45–1. *Second Innings*—Donald 9–3–21–0; McMillan 2–1–6–0; Symcox 25–7–92–3; Snell 3–0–15–0; Shaw 17–2–59–2; Kirsten 1–0–1–0.

South Africans

G. Kirsten c Cox b Udal	50
A. C. Hudson c Aymes b Thursfield	27
D. J. Cullinan c Aymes b James	18
*K. C. Wessels c Udal b James	31
J. N. Rhodes c Cox b Udal	77
B. M. McMillan c White b Udal	1
†D. J. Richardson c Udal b Connor	12
R. P. Snell c White b Udal	0
P. L. Symcox c Aymes b Udal	0
T. G. Shaw not out	8
A. A. Donald not out	18
B 4, l-b 2, w 2, n-b 14	22
1/53 2/95 3/109 4/189 5/192 6/227 7/228 8/228 9/228 (9 wkts dec.)	264

Bowling: Bovill 9–2–41–0; Connor 17–3–64–1; Thursfield 13–1–44–1; Udal 27–7–63–5; James 14–4–46–2.

Umpires: H. D. Bird and R. Julian.

GLOUCESTERSHIRE v SOUTH AFRICANS

At Bristol, July 6, 7, 8. Drawn. Toss: Gloucestershire.

An unmemorable match in cricketing terms took an unpleasant turn on the final day and Russell, leading Gloucestershire in Walsh's absence, bore the brunt of the crowd's displeasure. After the South Africans declined to declare overnight, he refused to declare either and Russell himself batted for 29 overs in making six, prompting jeers while he was batting and ironic cheers when he was out, an unprecedented experience for a popular player. Gloucestershire's second innings meandered on until the close and, as the tourists came off the field, a former committee member went out and apologised. Russell, called on to explain his action by a large number of spectators who gathered in front of the pavilion, made a brief appearance, and blamed the South Africans for refusing to make a game of it and for their "lack of communication". Only 20 overs had been possible on the first day. Alleyne and Dawson batted vigilantly in both innings, against some fine bowling by de Villiers, but Russell did not declare until tea on the second day and the South Africans' acting-captain, Cronje, declared only after passing the follow-on target. They had lost their first three wickets by the fourth over, two to the left-arm seamer, Smith, in the first four balls.

Close of play: First day, Gloucestershire 43-3 (M. G. N. Windows 18*, R. I. Dawson 2*); Second day, South Africans 85-3 (K. C. Wessels 40*, P. N. Kirsten 24*).

Gloucestershire

B. C. Broad b Matthews	0	c Richardson b Cronje	3
A. J. Wright b de Villiers	9	b de Villiers	1
T. H. C. Hancock c Matthews b Shaw	10	c Wessels b Cronje	7
M. G. N. Windows c Richardson b Cronje	28	c Richardson b de Villiers	8
R. I. Dawson c Hudson b de Villiers	71	run out	42
M. W. Alleyne c Liebenberg b Shaw	75	c Kirsten b Shaw	86
*†R. C. Russell b de Villiers	31	lbw b Kirsten	6
M. C. J. Ball c Wessels b de Villiers	0	not out	26
A. M. Smith c Kirsten b de Villiers	11	not out	5
V. J. Pike not out	20		
K. E. Cooper not out	7		
B 1, l-b 3, n-b 12	16	B 11, l-b 4, n-b 2	17
1/1 2/13 3/35 4/81 5/163 6/228 7/228 8/248 9/253	(9 wkts dec.) 278	1/5 2/13 3/17 4/30 5/104 6/168 7/178	(7 wkts) 201

Bowling: *First Innings*—de Villiers 33–6–118–5; Matthews 13–3–34–1; Cronje 13–6–13–1; Shaw 27–9–45–2; Symcox 17–4–63–0; Kirsten 2–1–1–0. *Second Innings*—de Villiers 12–2–42–2; Cronje 11–4–19–2; Shaw 21–7–49–1; Symcox 15–3–46–0; Kirsten 7–2–23–1; Wessels 2–0–7–0.

South Africans

A. C. Hudson c Ball b Smith	0
G. F. J. Liebenberg c Russell b Cooper	6
*W. J. Cronje b Smith	4
K. C. Wessels lbw b Cooper	52
P. N. Kirsten c Ball b Smith	31
J. N. Rhodes not out	6
†D. J. Richardson c Ball b Cooper	1
P. L. Symcox not out	1
L-b 4, n-b 24	28
1/0 2/4 3/10 4/112 5/116 6/117	(6 wkts dec.) 129

T. G. Shaw, P. S. de Villiers and C. R. Matthews did not bat.

Bowling: Smith 18.2–1–79–3; Cooper 15–4–26–3; Pike 7–3–14–0; Ball 3–1–6–0.

Umpires: K. E. Palmer and G. Sharp.

†SCOTLAND v SOUTH AFRICANS

At Titwood, Glasgow, July 10. No result. Toss: South Africans.

Scotland approached this match with particular enthusiasm as they celebrated their election to associate membership of the International Cricket Council a few days earlier. But the weather provided a severe disappointment. Despite heavy overnight rain, the tourists were keen to start; a further downpour in the sixth over of their innings frustrated all good intentions.

South Africans

A. C. Hudson not out	2
G. Kirsten not out	3
N-b 2	2
(no wkt, 5.1 overs)	7

*W. J. Cronje, D. J. Cullinan, J. N. Rhodes, †G. F. J. Liebenberg, B. M. McMillan, P. L. Symcox, R. P. Snell, P. S. de Villiers and A. A. Donald did not bat.

Bowling: Hamilton 3–1–2–0; Hurlbatt 2.1–0–5–0.

Scotland

*A. C. Storie, I. L. Philip, B. M. W. Patterson, G. N. Reifer, G. B. J. McGurk, M. J. Smith, J. G. Williamson, G. M. Hamilton, G. P. Hurlbatt, †D. J. Haggo and K. L. P. Sheridan.

Umpires: D. Walker and A. Wood.

DURHAM v SOUTH AFRICANS

At Chester-le-Street (Ropery Lane), July 12, 13, 14. Drawn. Toss: Durham.

In very hot weather, Durham avoided an innings defeat thanks to Larkins, who defied a wrist injury suffered off the first ball of the match. The delivery by Donald – a no-ball – forced Larkins to retire and he took no further part until Durham were 190 for five in their second innings, still ten behind. He plundered nine fours in a belligerent 49 and had ensured the draw when he was seventh out. The chief feature of the match for the South Africans was a maiden double-hundred for their left-handed opener, Gary Kirsten. It showed more method than magic: he faced 306 balls and hit 25 fours and three sixes before retiring. The fact that the tourists accumulated their 428 at only 3.75 an over on a small ground testified to some accurate Durham bowling. De Villiers's consistent out-swing made him the pick of the South African attack, but Donald struggled to find his direction. This was due to be the last first-class game on the Ropery Lane ground, which was being superseded by Durham's new headquarters across town.

Close of play: First day, South Africans 99-0 (G. Kirsten 33*, A. C. Hudson 55*); Second day, Durham 34-0 (G. Fowler 15*, M. Saxelby 16*).

Durham

W. Larkins retired hurt	0	– (7) lbw b Donald	49
G. Fowler c Wessels b McMillan	68	– (1) c and b Donald	61
J. E. Morris lbw b de Villiers	2	– lbw b de Villiers	4
J. A. Daley c McMillan b de Villiers	0	– c Cronje b de Villiers	41
M. Saxelby b Donald	30	– (2) c Donald b Shaw	26
*P. Bainbridge c Shaw b de Villiers	19	– (5) c Wessels b McMillan	50
†C. W. Scott b McMillan	53	– (6) lbw b Cronje	1
J. Wood c Cronje b McMillan	0	– not out	17
D. M. Cox b de Villiers	6	– not out	26
S. J. E. Brown c G. Kirsten b McMillan	30		
S. Lugsden not out	0		
B 1, l-b 1, w 6, n-b 12	20	B 4, l-b 9, w 3, n-b 10	26
1/7 2/7 3/78 4/128 5/153 6/157 7/164 8/213 9/228	228	1/89 2/94 3/132 4/166 5/190 6/233 7/263 (7 wkts)	301

In the first innings W. Larkins retired hurt at 2.

Bowling: *First Innings*—Donald 15–3–49–1; de Villiers 20–3–80–4; Cronje 5–1–13–0; McMillan 18.2–2–47–4; Shaw 15–5–37–0. *Second Innings*—Donald 28–3–118–2; de Villiers 22–6–69–2; Shaw 19–7–49–1; McMillan 16–5–44–1; Cronje 7–3–8–1.

South Africans

G. Kirsten retired ill 201
A. C. Hudson c Scott b Brown......... 64
W. J. Cronje b Cox.................. 27
*K. C. Wessels lbw b Brown 53
P. N. Kirsten not out 42
J. N. Rhodes c Brown b Bainbridge ... 15
B. M. McMillan not out 4
L-b 5, w 7, n-b 10........... 22

1/118 2/196 3/304 4/424 (4 wkts dec.) 428

†D. J. Richardson, T. G. Shaw, P. S. de Villiers and A. A. Donald did not bat.

G. Kirsten retired ill at 399.

Bowling: Brown 25–1–97–2; Wood 30–1–110–0; Lugsden 21–5–64–0; Bainbridge 15.5–3–60–1; Cox 22–4–92–1.

Umpires: B. Dudleston and T. E. Jesty.

NORTHAMPTONSHIRE v SOUTH AFRICANS

At Northampton, July 16, 17, 18. Drawn. Toss: Northamptonshire.

The tourists were unwilling to risk defeat in the run-up to the First Test through a challenging declaration, and Northamptonshire never threatened a target of 263 in 50 overs on a pitch which yielded under three runs per over before the final afternoon. Bailey put the South Africans in, allowing Wessels, Rhodes and McMillan to score runs on the first day, and Snell then claimed the county's top three wickets in a hostile 28-ball spell. A recovery, launched when Loye and Curran added 117, restricted the South Africans' lead to 46, but with preparations for Lord's uppermost in their minds, there was little chance of a push for quick runs. Gary Kirsten completed his second century in successive matches before the game petered out.

Close of play: First day, Northamptonshire 20-0 (R. J. Warren 17*, N. A. Felton 2*); Second day, South Africans 54-1 (G. Kirsten 33*, W. J. Cronje 19*).

South Africans

G. Kirsten c Taylor b Penberthy .... 13 – (2) c Warren b Cook 102
G. F. J. Liebenberg c Ripley b Taylor .... 17 – (1) lbw b Taylor 0
W. J. Cronje c Ripley b Bowen .... 20 – c Curran b Taylor 41
*K. C. Wessels c Felton b Penberthy .... 70 – not out....................... 43
P. N. Kirsten c Penberthy b Taylor........... 9 – not out....................... 19
J. N. Rhodes c Penberthy b Snape 59
B. M. McMillan c Bailey b Curran 50
†D. J. Richardson not out.................... 21
R. P. Snell not out......................... 11
B 1, l-b 9, w 2, n-b 14 .... 26 B 2, l-b 9 11

1/27 2/36 3/70 4/100 5/174 6/236 7/271 (7 wkts dec.) 296 1/0 2/92 3/177 (3 wkts dec.) 216

P. L. Symcox and C. R. Matthews did not bat.

TAIL-ENDERS.

ALL-ROUNDERS.

ONLY ONE INSURANCE COMPANY CAN BRING YOU THE TESTS AND INSURE YOUR CAR.

Whatever your insurance needs, Cornhill has a policy to please. Motor, home, life, business or travel....you'll appreciate a quote that's as competitive as the cricket.

Ask your insurance adviser.

CORNHILL Insurance

Cornhill Insurance PLC is regulated by the Personal Investment Authority for investment business.

Test Series

Bowling: *First Innings*—Taylor 17–2–55–2; Curran 18–1–63–1; Penberthy 16–5–32–2; Bowen 14–4–53–1; Cook 20–8–38–0; Bailey 2–1–1–0; Snape 12–3–44–1. *Second Innings*—Taylor 12–3–33–2; Bowen 12–3–32–0; Bailey 10–2–26–0; Cook 11–3–25–1; Curran 4–1–25–0; Penberthy 6–0–17–0; Snape 15–4–47–0.

Northamptonshire

R. J. Warren c Rhodes b Snell	17	– c Liebenberg b Symcox	18
N. A. Felton c Rhodes b Snell	8	– st Richardson b Symcox	16
*R. J. Bailey lbw b Snell	0	– c Cronje b Symcox	46
M. B. Loye lbw b Matthews	50	– c Richardson b Snell	0
K. M. Curran c P. N. Kirsten b Cronje	81	– not out	38
J. N. Snape not out	43	– not out	11
A. L. Penberthy not out	43		
B 2, l-b 3, w 1, n-b 2	8	L-b 2	2
1/20 2/20 3/28 4/145 5/175 (5 wkts dec.)	250	1/34 2/35 3/36 4/100 (4 wkts)	131

†D. Ripley, M. N. Bowen, J. P. Taylor and N. G. B. Cook did not bat.

Bowling: *First Innings*—Snell 19–5–66–3; Matthews 22–6–67–1; McMillan 17–4–46–0; Cronje 15–7–22–1; Symcox 13–10–13–0; G. Kirsten 6–1–31–0. *Second Innings*—Matthews 6–3–6–0; McMillan 5–1–18–0; Symcox 18–6–36–3; Snell 8–0–21–1; G. Kirsten 6–1–30–0; P. N. Kirsten 2–1–8–0; Rhodes 1–0–10–0.

Umpires: A. Clarkson and D. R. Shepherd.

ENGLAND v SOUTH AFRICA

First Cornhill Test

At Lord's, July 21, 22, 23, 24. South Africa won by 356 runs. Toss: South Africa. Test debut: J. P. Crawley.

The first Test between the countries for 29 years began with the word "historic" being used to the point of monotony but ended with controversy engulfing the England captain, Mike Atherton, and threatening his future. The Atherton affair took over all discussion of the match and the genuinely historic outcome – a devastating South African victory – was all but forgotten amid the fuss.

Normally, England being bowled out for 99 on a sound wicket might have caused a great deal of anguish. However, everyone was preoccupied by the fact that Atherton, fielding on Saturday afternoon, was seen by the TV cameras taking his hand out of his pocket and rubbing it across the ball before passing it back to the bowler. He was called before the referee, Peter Burge, to explain what the official statement called his "unfamiliar action" and answer suspicions that he had broken Law 42.5 by using an artificial substance to alter the condition of the ball. Burge said he had accepted Atherton's explanation without saying what it was. But the following day, after further TV pictures were shown that looked even more sinister and England's batsmen had crumpled to a humiliating four-day defeat, Atherton admitted publicly that he had not told Burge the truth by saying that he had nothing in his pocket. In fact, he said, he had some dirt there that he picked up to keep his hands dry and prevent moisture getting on the ball while Darren Gough was trying to reverse-swing it; the second set of pictures clearly showed some of the dirt falling off it.

Ray Illingworth, the chairman of selectors, immediately fined Atherton £2,000 – half for using the dirt, though that was not a breach of any Law, and half for the lie. He hoped that would close the matter. But over the next 48 hours, there was a tidal wave of public emotion in which almost everyone from the cricket correspondent of the BBC to people who had never seen a match in their lives demanded Atherton's resignation. Illingworth and the TCCB remained staunch in their support, though. The umpires said the condition of the ball had not been changed and the South Africans made no complaint, except to grumble that their triumph had been ignored. Five days after the game ended, Atherton relieved the pressure by emerging from something close to hiding and calling a press conference at which he did not entirely explain away the pictures but stressed repeatedly that he had never cheated at cricket.

If Atherton was a cheat, he was not a very successful one. England's bowlers mostly failed, though not quite as humiliatingly as their batsmen. England had dropped both Such and Smith, who had been desperate to play against the country of his birth, and named two uncapped players in their 12: the Hampshire off-spinner Shaun Udal and the Lancashire batsman John Crawley. Udal was then left out of the team in favour of the leg-spinner Salisbury, the 12th man in the last Test against New Zealand. South Africa, concerned that both their spinners were below standard, named an attack entirely comprising right-arm seam bowlers.

The formalities included the officials being presented to Thabo Mbeki, the recently-appointed deputy president of South Africa, and reports of the almost as ritualised refusal-of-admission-to-the-pavilion: the victim was the Archbishop of Cape Town, Desmond Tutu, who was out of uniform and not wearing a jacket. On the field, the first day consisted of South Africa winning the toss and their captain, Wessels, playing an innings that epitomised his country's approach to Test cricket: unflashy but utterly determined.

Wessels spent just under five hours scoring 105. His partnerships with his fellow left-hander Gary Kirsten, whose 72 was just as deadpan though it included some high-class cutting, and Rhodes gave the South African first innings its body. At the end of the first day, the game was evenly matched at 244 for six, but it was typical of both sides that South Africa's last four wickets were able to add 116. For no obvious reason, England then collapsed before Donald's pace and de Villiers's swing; no one played a substantial innings, though Hick yet again promised flickeringly before losing his way and then his wicket.

On the third morning, England avoided the follow-on after a brief counter-attack from DeFreitas, but Donald finished off the tail to take five for 74. South Africa began consolidating their lead of 177, a task which – but for the cameras and Atherton – might have been uneventful. Though no South African batsman played a long innings, the bowlers again failed to exercise proper control, except for the occasional off-spinner Hick, who bowled 21 consecutive overs for only 27. Gough looked something close to the spearhead England had been seeking, and apparently did manage to reverse-swing the ball on the fourth morning to york Peter Kirsten and Rhodes. But the overall performance of the attack, with DeFreitas out of sorts and Fraser weary, was below par.

South Africa declared at Sunday lunchtime, setting England 456 to win, which would have been improbable in any circumstances. It is difficult to assess the extent to which England were affected by the storm gathering over the captain, who had led his team out in the morning with his hands, insouciantly and provocatively, in his pockets. Atherton and Crawley were both caught in the slips; Hick received an unkind lbw decision from umpire Randell; then Stewart, after an unusually dogged innings, was caught behind and White was out first ball. On five, Gooch had passed Viv Richards to go fourth on the list of all-time Test match run-makers. But from 74 for three, England fell away to 99 all out, a score lower than all but two in the County Championship so far. It was England's lowest only since the 46 in the Trinidad Test less than four months earlier.

The new South African flag did flutter in the closing stages, despite MCC's earlier request to the team to obey their regulations banning all flags. The match throughout was played in extreme heat and some humidity, which helped the swing bowlers and, according to Atherton, explained why he needed the dirt to dry his hands. It may also have contributed to the air of frenzy that took over when the cricket finished. – Matthew Engel.

Man of the Match: K. C. Wessels. *Attendance:* 103,198; *receipts* £2,253,275.

Close of play: First day, South Africa 244-6 (B. M. McMillan 2*, D. J. Richardson 1*); Second day, England 141-7 (I. D. K. Salisbury 3*); Third day, South Africa 195-4 (P. N. Kirsten 40*, J. N. Rhodes 23*).

South Africa

A. C. Hudson c Gooch b Gough	6	– (2) lbw b Fraser	3
G. Kirsten c DeFreitas b Hick	72	– (1) st Rhodes b Hick	44
W. J. Cronje c Crawley b Fraser	7	– c Fraser b Gough	32
*K. C. Wessels c Rhodes b Gough	105	– c Crawley b Salisbury	28
P. N. Kirsten c Rhodes b Gough	8	– b Gough	42
J. N. Rhodes b White	32	– b Gough	32
B. M. McMillan c Rhodes b Fraser	29	– not out	39
†D. J. Richardson lbw b Gough	26	– c Rhodes b Fraser	3
C. R. Matthews b White	41	– b Gough	25
P. S. de Villiers c Rhodes b Fraser	8		
A. A. Donald not out	5		
L-b 9, n-b 9	18	B 8, l-b 10, n-b 12	30
1/18 (1) 2/35 (3) 3/141 (2) 4/164 (5) 5/239 (6) 6/241 (4) 7/281 (8) 8/334 (9) 9/348 (7) 10/357 (10)	357	1/14 (2) 2/73 (3) 3/101 (1) 4/141 (4) 5/208 (6) 6/209 (5) 7/220 (8) 8/278 (9)	(8 wkts dec.) 278

Bowling: *First Innings*—DeFreitas 18–5–67–0; Gough 28–6–76–4; Salisbury 25–2–68–0; Fraser 24.5–7–72–3; Hick 10–5–22–1; White 13–2–43–2. *Second Innings*—Fraser 23–5–62–2; Gough 19.3–5–46–4; DeFreitas 14–3–43–0; Hick 24–14–38–1; Salisbury 19–4–53–1; White 3–0–18–0.

England

*M. A. Atherton c Wessels b Donald	20	– c McMillan b de Villiers	8
A. J. Stewart b Donald	12	– c Richardson b Matthews	27
J. P. Crawley c Hudson b de Villiers	9	– c Hudson b McMillan	7
G. A. Hick c Richardson b de Villiers	38	– lbw b McMillan	11
G. A. Gooch lbw b de Villiers	20	– lbw b Donald	28
C. White c Richardson b Donald	10	– c Wessels b Matthews	0
†S. J. Rhodes b McMillan	15	– not out	14
I. D. K. Salisbury not out	6	– (10) lbw b Donald	0
P. A. J. DeFreitas c Wessels b Donald	20	– (8) c G. Kirsten b Matthews	1
D. Gough c and b Donald	12	– (9) retired hurt	0
A. R. C. Fraser run out	3	– lbw b McMillan	1
B 2, l-b 5, n-b 8	15	B 1, l-b 1	2
1/19 (2) 2/41 (3) 3/68 (1) 4/107 (5) 5/119 (4) 6/136 (7) 7/141 (6) 8/161 (9) 9/176 (10) 10/180 (11)	180	1/16 (1) 2/29 (3) 3/45 (4) 4/74 (2) 5/74 (6) 6/82 (5) 7/85 (8) 8/88 (10) 9/99 (11)	99

In the second innings D. Gough retired hurt at 86.

Bowling: *First Innings*—Donald 19.3–5–74–5; de Villiers 16–5–28–3; Matthews 16–6–46–0; McMillan 10–1–25–1. *Second Innings*—Donald 12–5–29–2; de Villiers 12–4–26–1; Matthews 14–6–25–3; McMillan 6.5–2–16–3; Cronje 1–0–1–0.

Umpires: S. G. Randell (Australia) and H. D. Bird. Referee: P. J. P. Burge (Australia).

NOTTINGHAMSHIRE v SOUTH AFRICANS

At Nottingham, July 27, 28, 29. South Africans won by 134 runs. Toss: South Africans. First-class debut: L. N. P. Walker.

Fresh from their Lord's triumph, the South Africans pulled off their first win over a county on the tour. Unexpectedly, their victory was completed by the spinners, Symcox and Shaw. The groundwork, however, was a more than usually forceful display of batting. Acting-captain Cronje was the spearhead, hitting 13 fours and two sixes in three and a half hours for his first century in England, while Kirsten struck nine fours and Rhodes ten and a six in a run-a-ball 71. In contrast, Robinson made a laboured 82, spanning 257 balls and nearly five hours – but he saved Nottinghamshire from following on. Cullinan's quickfire half-century set up a target of 274 from 67 overs. Once Robinson went, his county crumbled, losing their last seven for eight runs, and all but Robinson fell to spin: Symcox finished with match figures of eight for 100. The wicket-keeper, Lindsay Walker, on his debut, was out hit wicket in both innings. The defeat completed a miserable July for Nottinghamshire, who lost six of their eight matches and won none.

Close of play: First day, Nottinghamshire 32-2 (R. T. Robinson 4*, R. T. Bates 8*); Second day, South Africans 25-1 (G. F. J. Liebenberg 11*, W. J. Cronje 3*).

South Africans

A. C. Hudson c Bates b Mike	37	– lbw b Pick	10
†G. F. J. Liebenberg lbw b Pick	0	– run out	40
*W. J. Cronje b Bates	108	– c Johnson b Pick	26
D. J. Cullinan c Johnson b Pick	12	– not out	61
P. N. Kirsten c and b Chapman	57	– not out	21
J. N. Rhodes not out	71		
B. M. McMillan lbw b Pick	15		
T. G. Shaw not out	1		
L-b 6, n-b 20	26	L-b 4, n-b 2	6
1/1 2/69 3/118 4/215 5/267 6/310 (6 wkts dec.)	327	1/13 2/59 3/95 (3 wkts dec.)	164

C. R. Matthews, P. L. Symcox and R. P. Snell did not bat.

Bowling: *First Innings*—Pick 18–3–54–3; Chapman 13.4–1–74–1; Mike 21.2–3–92–1; Dowman 5–1–23–0; Bates 15–2–52–1; Afford 5–1–26–0. *Second Innings*—Chapman 5–2–12–0; Pick 10–2–29–2; Afford 19–1–71–0; Bates 6–0–21–0; Mike 7–1–27–0.

Nottinghamshire

*R. T. Robinson c sub (D. J. Richardson) b Shaw	82	– c and b Matthews	42
W. A. Dessaur c Liebenberg b Snell	4	– c Hudson b Shaw	34
G. F. Archer c Cronje b Symcox	16	– lbw b Symcox	2
R. T. Bates c Liebenberg b Matthews	8	– (8) not out	1
P. Johnson lbw b McMillan	25	– (4) b Symcox	33
M. P. Dowman b Symcox	20	– (5) b Shaw	17
†L. N. P. Walker hit wkt b Symcox	1	– hit wkt b Symcox	0
G. W. Mike st Liebenberg b Shaw	29	– (6) c Kirsten b Shaw	3
R. A. Pick not out	12	– c McMillan b Shaw	4
R. J. Chapman c Shaw b McMillan	9	– c McMillan b Symcox	0
J. A. Afford run out	2	– c McMillan b Symcox	0
B 4, l-b 5, w 1	10	L-b 3	3
1/7 2/24 3/32 4/70 5/119 6/121 7/170 8/197 9/214	218	1/66 2/80 3/80 4/131 5/131 6/134 7/134 8/138 9/139	139

Bowling: *First Innings*—Snell 21–8–51–1; Matthews 11–5–25–1; Symcox 22–6–56–3; Shaw 28–9–58–2; McMillan 9–4–19–2. *Second Innings*—Snell 5–0–22–0; McMillan 8–2–17–0; Matthews 8–3–24–1; Shaw 22–10–29–4; Symcox 17.4–7–44–5.

Umpires: D. R. Shepherd and R. A. White.

LEICESTERSHIRE v SOUTH AFRICANS

At Leicester, July 30, 31, August 1. Drawn. Toss: South Africans. First-class debut: D. L. Maddy.

The fastest surface the tourists had encountered angered Wessels, who was hit on the forearm by his first ball on the last day, from Mullally. He decided to bat on but, after having the arm X-rayed, criticised a "stupid and sub-standard pitch" which jeopardised his players in the run-up to the Second Test. His bowlers seemed much happier with it, however. After the batsmen had run up 270 – with the help of 50 extras – Donald bowled with extreme pace and de Villiers claimed six for 67. Leicestershire lost their top six before reaching 100 but their last pair put on 38, the biggest stand of the innings. The South Africans then went for their runs and set a target of 267 in 64 overs. Though Briers and Boon opened briskly and Whitaker kept up the pace, Leicestershire were 192 for seven, but Pierson and Millns survived, helped by the bad light which forced Donald out of the attack. It was announced the following day that Cronje would join Leicestershire in 1995.

Close of play: First day, Leicestershire 74-4 (D. L. Maddy 18*, A. R. K. Pierson 7*); Second day, South Africans 51-1 (G. Kirsten 18*, W. J. Cronje 24*).

South Africans

A. C. Hudson c Pierson b Sheriyar	26	– (2) lbw b Mullally	9
G. Kirsten c Whitaker b Mullally	12	– (1) c Pierson b Millns	62
W. J. Cronje c Maddy b Mullally	30	– c Millns b Mullally	54
*K. C. Wessels c Nixon b Mullally	1	– lbw b Millns	18
D. J. Cullinan c Briers b Dakin	66	– not out	6
G. F. J. Liebenberg c Millns b Sheriyar	59	– c Smith b Pierson	1
†D. J. Richardson run out	17	– not out	2
R. P. Snell c Mullally b Pierson	7		
T. G. Shaw not out	2		
B 16, l-b 8, w 4, n-b 22	50	B 8, l-b 1, n-b 2	11
1/16 2/68 3/83 4/106 5/227 6/255 7/264 8/270 (8 wkts dec.)	270	1/10 2/113 3/151 4/154 5/159 (5 wkts dec.)	163

P. S. de Villiers and A. A. Donald did not bat.

Bowling: *First Innings*—Millns 17–3–43–0; Mullally 21–8–43–3; Sheriyar 15–3–63–2; Dakin 11–1–36–1; Pierson 17.3–2–61–1. *Second Innings*—Millns 11–2–52–2; Mullally 14–3–38–2; Sheriyar 4–0–29–0; Pierson 13–2–35–1.

Leicestershire

T. J. Boon c Richardson b de Villiers	4	– c Richardson b de Villiers	24
*N. E. Briers c Richardson b de Villiers	32	– c Cullinan b Shaw	45
J. J. Whitaker c Wessels b de Villiers	0	– c and b Shaw	59
B. F. Smith c de Villiers b Donald	7	– c Kirsten b Donald	5
D. L. Maddy c Richardson b Snell	24	– c Hudson b Donald	0
A. R. K. Pierson c Richardson b Snell	20	– (8) not out	7
†P. A. Nixon b Snell	33	– (6) c Liebenberg b Shaw	37
J. M. Dakin b de Villiers	10	– (7) c Donald b de Villiers	1
D. J. Millns c Wessels b de Villiers	2	– not out	21
A. D. Mullally c and b de Villiers	0		
A. Sheriyar not out	16		
B 8, l-b 5, w 4, n-b 2	19	B 5, l-b 8, n-b 4	17
1/13 2/19 3/38 4/67 5/91 6/96 7/111 8/123 9/129	167	1/64 2/94 3/113 4/117 5/175 6/176 7/192 (7 wkts)	216

Bowling: *First Innings*—Donald 14–2–40–1; de Villiers 20–4–67–6; Snell 15.1–4–38–3; Shaw 1–1–0–0; Cronje 7–3–9–0. *Second Innings*—Donald 13–0–45–2; de Villiers 15–3–53–2; Snell 9–0–35–0; Cronje 5–2–10–0; Shaw 22–5–60–3.

Umpires: J. C. Balderstone and K. J. Lyons.

ENGLAND v SOUTH AFRICA

Second Cornhill Test

At Leeds, August 4, 5, 6, 7, 8. Drawn. Toss: England.

It was, as Atherton remarked later, a batsman's Test. But it was also a match of revivals, first by England, as they bounced back from their defeat at Lord's, and then by the South Africans, who mounted a vigorous rearguard action to salvage a draw. It was the first drawn Test at Headingley since 1980, and the first since 1968 that occurred without the significant assistance of the weather. The bowlers of both sides, without the expected movement either in the air or off the pitch, were unable to perform well enough to achieve victory.

England were disappointed in the end, but the match did much to rehabilitate their captain's reputation, so battered at Lord's. He went out to bat to a warm reception when the game began, and returned 321 minutes later to a standing ovation, having been dismissed, for the second time in a Test in 14 months, for 99. He had justified his decision to bat first and underlined the strength of his character. Later, however, he could not resist the jibe that the century he had so nearly made would have been the best response to the gutter press. His sense of timing, so dramatically effective in the middle, had deserted him under the media spotlight.

England went in without White, whose absence with a stress fracture in the shin enabled the selectors to submit to the clamour for the left-handed Thorpe. Tufnell replaced Salisbury as the spinner; he was preferred in the final eleven to the uncapped but in-form 33-year-old Surrey seamer Joey Benjamin. South Africa were unchanged and thus again spinless. Thorpe was an immediate success. After he joined Atherton at 84 for two, his urgency, instinctive placement and crisp driving brought him 13 boundaries in his 72 (off 112 deliveries) and their partnership realised 142 in 37 overs as the South Africans' line wavered against the left-right combination. Atherton, meanwhile, was quick to punish the bowlers whenever they strayed to leg. Everything went his way until, looking for his hundred, he drove firmly but too early and the brawny McMillan – who had a hand in all four wickets on the first day – took a difficult return catch.

With Donald battling against an infected toe, which eventually forced him out of the second innings, South Africa's stereotyped swing and seam attack lacked the penetration and discipline it had at Lord's. On the second day, Stewart, annoyed at being dropped down the order so that Gooch could resume his opening partnership with Atherton, responded with 15 fours in an innings of 89. With Rhodes scoring 65 not out, Crawley 38 and most of the tailenders joining in, England were able to declare at 477 for nine – the biggest total South Africa had conceded since their return to Test cricket. England dismissed Hudson before the close and, next morning, took complete control when DeFreitas dismissed Gary Kirsten and Cronje with the third and fourth deliveries of the day. At first, only the night-watchman Richardson fought effectively and he was bowled by a shooter that suggested the Headingley pitch was becoming its old self. When Wessels was out at 105 for five, South Africa looked certain to follow on.

In fact, they recovered to within 30 of England's total after lunch on the fourth day. Much of this was due to Peter Kirsten, who at 39 years and 84 days became the sixth-oldest player to score his maiden Test century. The record-holder is Dave Nourse, 42 years and 294 days old when he scored 111 for South Africa against Australia in 1921-22; the other four were Ted Bowley, Harry Makepeace, Eric Rowan and Andy Sandham, all aged 39. Kirsten batted for almost five hours and faced 226 balls. All his experience went into maintaining vigilance and striking hard when the opportunity presented itself, and he refused to go off after Gough felled him on 50. Rhodes and McMillan gave him excellent support. The pitch never again showed the spite that accounted for Richardson, and on the fourth morning the England bowling strayed terribly against the South African tail: Matthews, who hit ten fours and a six in his 62 not out, played an especially important part.

England still had slender hopes of victory and, with Thorpe making another stylish contribution, Hick advanced fluently to his first Test century in England, with nine fours and three sixes. England declared at lunch, when they were 297 ahead with a minimum of 60 overs left to dismiss South Africa a second time. Finally, there were signs that the pitch was wearing and Gough and Tufnell both tested the batsmen. But Gary Kirsten dug in for 65 to prevent any late dramatics, and the match dribbled away with six overs remaining. – John Bishop.

Man of the Match: P. N. Kirsten. *Attendance:* 67,500; *receipts* £1,092,975.

Close of play: First day, England 268-4 (A. J. Stewart 24*, J. P. Crawley 12*); Second day, South Africa 31-1 (G. Kirsten 7*, D. J. Richardson 13*); Third day, South Africa 318-7 (B. M. McMillan 57*, C. R. Matthews 0*); Fourth day, England 144-2 (G. A. Hick 48*, G. P. Thorpe 51*).

England

First innings		Second innings	
G. A. Gooch c McMillan b de Villiers	23	c Richardson b Matthews	27
*M. A. Atherton c and b McMillan	99	c sub (D. J. Cullinan) b de Villiers	17
G. A. Hick c McMillan b de Villiers	25	lbw b McMillan	110
G. P. Thorpe c Rhodes b McMillan	72	run out	73
A. J. Stewart b McMillan	89	not out	36
J. P. Crawley lbw b Matthews	38	c Cronje b McMillan	0
†S. J. Rhodes not out	65		
P. A. J. DeFreitas b Donald	15		
D. Gough run out	27		
A. R. C. Fraser c Cronje b de Villiers	6		
B 1, l-b 5, n-b 12	18	L-b 1, n-b 3	4
1/34 (1) 2/84 (3) 3/226 (4) 4/235 (2) 5/350 (6) 6/367 (5) 7/394 (8) 8/447 (9) 9/477 (10)	(9 wkts dec.) 477	1/39 (2) 2/57 (1) 3/190 (4) 4/267 (3) 5/267 (6)	(5 wkts dec.) 267

P. C. R. Tufnell did not bat.

Bowling: *First Innings*—Donald 29–2–135–1; de Villiers 39.3–12–108–3; Matthews 39–7–97–1; McMillan 37–12–93–3; Cronje 16–3–38–0. *Second Innings*—de Villiers 25–3–98–1; McMillan 15.3–0–66–2; Matthews 24–8–53–1; G. Kirsten 2–1–10–0; Cronje 12–3–39–0.

South Africa

First innings		Second innings	
A. C. Hudson c Atherton b Gough	9	(2) c and b Tufnell	12
G. Kirsten c Rhodes b DeFreitas	7	(1) c Rhodes b DeFreitas	65
†D. J. Richardson b Fraser	48		
W. J. Cronje b DeFreitas	0	(3) not out	13
*K. C. Wessels c Crawley b Fraser	25	(4) b Tufnell	7
P. N. Kirsten c Stewart b DeFreitas	104	(5) not out	8
J. N. Rhodes c Rhodes b Gough	46		
B. M. McMillan b Tufnell	78		
C. R. Matthews not out	62		
P. S. de Villiers st Rhodes b Tufnell	13		
A. A. Donald c Crawley b DeFreitas	27		
B 8, l-b 7, n-b 13	28	B 2, l-b 2, n-b 7	11
1/13 (1) 2/31 (2) 3/31 (4) 4/91 (3) 5/105 (5) 6/199 (7) 7/314 (6) 8/391 (8) 9/410 (10) 10/447 (11)	447	1/43 (2) 2/93 (1) 3/104 (4)	(3 wkts) 116

Bowling: *First Innings*—Gough 37–3–153–2; DeFreitas 29.1–6–89–4; Fraser 31–5–92–2; Tufnell 32–13–81–2; Gooch 3–0–9–0; Hick 1–0–8–0. *Second Innings*—DeFreitas 14–3–41–1; Gough 10–5–15–0; Tufnell 23–8–31–2; Fraser 7–2–19–0; Hick 6–3–6–0.

Umpires: R. S. Dunne (New Zealand) and D. R. Shepherd.
Referee: P. J. P. Burge (Australia).

MINOR COUNTIES v SOUTH AFRICANS

At Torquay, August 10, 11, 12. Drawn. Toss: South Africans. First-class debuts: S. J. Dean, P. C. Graham, M. I. Humphries.

Simon Myles of Staffordshire held out for five overs with last man Arnold to earn a draw. Earlier, the Minor Counties had made a brave attempt to chase 270 in 52 overs: Myles had reached his fifty in 49 balls. But the spinners, Symcox and Shaw, took six wickets and three men were run out. The Minor Counties had prospered the previous day, when they took 153 runs off a limited South African attack – Cronje shared the new ball with Snell, the only front-line seamer. Cockbain declared 96 behind, as the first two mornings had been washed out, and Wessels responded by setting a target. The South African batsmen found the Minors' bowling tricky to handle on the first afternoon, but Cullinan made a lively 68 with nine fours. Myles turned the tables on Rhodes by running him out with a throw from the boundary.

Close of play: First day, South Africans 185-7 (G. F. J. Liebenberg 5*, P. L. Symcox 1*); Second day, Minor Counties 153-2 (J. R. Wileman 42*, I. Cockbain 13*).

South Africans

A. C. Hudson c Graham b Arnold	11	– (2) c Wileman b Graham	22
G. Kirsten c Humphries b Newman	1	– (1) c Graham b Arnold	10
W. J. Cronje c Humphries b Arnold	47	– c Dean b Arnold	1
*K. C. Wessels c Evans b Newman	16	– c Humphries b Graham	9
D. J. Cullinan c Myles b Scriven	68	– c Myles b Bullen	36
J. N. Rhodes run out	8	– c Wileman b Newman	33
P. N. Kirsten b Scriven	15	– not out	14
†G. F. J. Liebenberg c Bullen b Scriven	22	– c Wileman b Bullen	0
P. L. Symcox c Myles b Graham	27	– not out	39
T. G. Shaw lbw b Graham	5		
R. P. Snell not out	12		
L-b 9, n-b 8	17	L-b 1, n-b 8	9
1/5 2/17 3/42 4/119 5/154 6/164 7/183 8/224 9/232	249	1/34 2/35 3/38 4/54 5/113 6/125 7/125 (7 wkts dec.)	173

Bowling: *First Innings*—Newman 22–5–57–2; Arnold 26–6–64–2; Graham 17.3–3–44–2; Scriven 10–2–43–3; Bullen 4–0–30–0; Myles 1–0–2–0. *Second Innings*—Newman 14–4–51–1; Arnold 14–4–29–2; Graham 12–2–39–2; Scriven 1–0–11–0; Bullen 8.4–2–42–2.

Minor Counties

S. J. Dean c Cronje b Symcox	39	– c Cronje b Shaw	34
R. A. Evans c Cullinan b Snell	59	– run out	30
J. R. Wileman not out	42	– b Symcox	8
*I. Cockbain not out	13	– b Symcox	14
S. D. Myles (did not bat)		– not out	59
T. J. A. Scriven (did not bat)		– run out	8
†M. I. Humphries (did not bat)		– run out	0
P. G. Newman (did not bat)		– st Liebenberg b Shaw	8
C. K. Bullen (did not bat)		– b Symcox	2
P. C. Graham (did not bat)		– c Wessels b Symcox	0
K. A. Arnold (did not bat)		– not out	0
		B 5, l-b 3, n-b 2	10
1/59 2/121 (2 wkts dec.)	153	1/61 2/70 3/82 4/95 5/140 6/141 7/164 8/167 9/171 (9 wkts)	173

Bowling: *First Innings*—Snell 15–2–69–1; Cronje 3–1–12–0; Symcox 15–3–49–1; Shaw 13–7–23–0. *Second Innings*—Snell 5–0–24–0; Cronje 5–1–18–0; Shaw 21–8–63–2; Symcox 21–4–60–4.

Umpires: D. J. Halfyard and M. K. Reed.

GLAMORGAN v SOUTH AFRICANS

At Pontypridd, August 13, 14, 15. Drawn. Toss: Glamorgan.

The South Africans' first game at Ynysangharad Park since 1929 was well supported on three sunny days, but ended quietly. Maynard set a target of 272 from what became 58 overs. Once they lost two wickets shortly after tea, the tourists opted for batting practice before The Oval rather than entertainment. Glamorgan's first innings was dominated by

Hemp's fourth century of the season and the second by Maynard, who ended a barren spell of form and set up the declaration with a hundred at a run a ball. Hudson was even more desperate for runs but had succumbed when the South Africans lost both openers quickly on the first evening. Night-watchman Snell cashed in, falling only six short of a maiden century before lunch next day. He put on 171 with Cronje, who was later stumped by Maynard – deputising for Shaw after the wicket-keeper had two teeth knocked out by the ball.

Close of play: First day, South Africans 4-2 (R. P. Snell 0*); Second day, Glamorgan 80-4 (M. P. Maynard 30*, P. A. Cottey 6*).

Glamorgan

S. P. James c Kirsten b Snell	13	– lbw b Matthews 0
A. Dale c Hudson b Matthews	16	– c Symcox b Snell 24
D. L. Hemp c Rhodes b Cronje	126	– c Richardson b Symcox 16
*M. P. Maynard c Cullinan b Symcox	11	– c Cronje b Snell 101
P. A. Cottey c Wessels b Cronje	84	– (6) b Snell 28
A. J. Dalton not out	51	– (7) c Cullinan b Symcox 16
O. D. Gibson not out	16	– (8) c and b Shaw 2
S. L. Watkin (did not bat)		– (5) lbw b Matthews 0
R. D. B. Croft (did not bat)		– b Shaw 27
†A. D. Shaw (did not bat)		– not out 3
B 9, l-b 10, w 1	20	B 2, l-b 3 5
1/23 2/39 3/72 4/213 5/309 (5 wkts dec.)	337	1/0 2/36 3/51 4/58 5/162 6/175 7/180 8/210 9/222 (9 wkts dec.) 222

O. T. Parkin did not bat.

Bowling: *First Innings*—Matthews 15–0–94–1; Snell 18–3–59–1; Shaw 21–5–49–0; Symcox 32.1–11–63–1; Cronje 17–2–53–2. *Second Innings*—Matthews 12–0–56–2; Snell 14–1–61–3; Symcox 14–3–63–2; Shaw 17.4–6–37–2.

South Africans

A. C. Hudson c Shaw b Gibson	4	– (2) c Dale b Croft 23
G. Kirsten c Shaw b Watkin	0	– (1) not out 76
R. P. Snell c James b Croft	94	– c Dale b Gibson 8
W. J. Cronje st Maynard b Croft	78	
*K. C. Wessels not out	45	
D. J. Cullinan c Croft b Parkin	17	– (5) not out 29
J. N. Rhodes c Cottey b Parkin	37	– (4) c Shaw b Gibson 2
†D. J. Richardson not out	7	
B 1, l-b 4, w 1	6	W 2, n-b 2 4
1/4 2/4 3/175 4/192 5/223 6/272 (6 wkts dec.)	288	1/62 2/78 3/88 (3 wkts) 142

P. L. Symcox, C. R. Matthews and T. G. Shaw did not bat.

Bowling: *First Innings*—Gibson 12–4–46–1; Watkin 16–2–60–1; Parkin 20–2–56–2; Croft 34–6–102–2; Dale 4–0–19–0. *Second Innings*—Gibson 10–0–35–2; Watkin 12–2–36–0; Parkin 6–1–19–0; Croft 17–2–41–1; Dale 3–0–9–0; Hemp 2–0–2–0.

Umpires: D. J. Constant and M. J. Kitchen.

ENGLAND v SOUTH AFRICA

Third Cornhill Test

At The Oval, August 18, 19, 20, 21. England won by eight wickets. Toss: South Africa. Test debut: J. E. Benjamin.

It will always be Malcolm's Match but there was so much more to this astonishing Test than Devon Malcolm's nine for 57 in South Africa's second innings. When the game ended

19 minutes before lunch on the fourth day, only 255.2 overs had been bowled; if the bowlers had kept to the prescribed 90 overs a day, it could have finished at five o'clock on the third day. Runs came at nearly four an over; a wicket fell every 48 balls; Jonty Rhodes went to hospital after being struck on the helmet by Malcolm; Atherton and de Villiers were fined for dissent and both teams for their slow over-rates; and Malcolm delivered himself of a threat so graphic when he was hit in his turn that it has already become part of cricket folklore. The content, excitement and drama were at the level of a Superman film: value for money, even at TCCB ticket prices.

Winning the toss meant batting, but this true, fast pitch offered help to the bowlers too. Like South Africa, England had picked four seamers – introducing Benjamin and bringing back Malcolm in place of Fraser and Tufnell. Soon after Rhodes was escorted off the field, four overs beyond lunch, this attack had effectively reduced South Africa to 136 for six. The half-brothers Gary and Peter Kirsten – opening in a Test at The Oval 114 years after the Grace brothers W.G. and E.M. went out there together for England – Cronje, Wessels and Cullinan, playing in place of the out-of-form Hudson, had all been swept aside. The ball from Malcolm that struck Rhodes was fast and nasty. Rhodes ducked so low that Malcolm considered an lbw appeal. Rhodes's team-mates were worried that his epilepsy might make his condition worse. He was taken to the neurosurgery unit of Maudsley Hospital for a scan, given the all-clear but kept in overnight with concussion. Having handwritten his own lucid account of events rather than be interviewed, he did not return to bat until seven wickets fell in the second innings.

McMillan, who was also hit by Malcolm but survived to make 93 in four and a half hours, and Richardson revived South Africa with a sixth-wicket stand of 124 in 30 overs. But Benjamin, a Surrey favourite in his first Test, and DeFreitas picked up four wickets each. Once it was clear that Rhodes would not be returning yet, South Africa were all out for 332 early on the second day.

England made a traumatic start when Atherton was given lbw to his first ball, looked at his bat and shook his head repeatedly as he left: that evening he was summoned before the match referee, Peter Burge, fined half his match fee – £1,250 – and reprimanded. With Gooch also going cheaply, men of Surrey again held sway, as Thorpe made his third successive 70 and Stewart a dashing 62. But the power of Donald got rid of Hick and Crawley, who looked a year short of maturity. Just when it seemed that England had had the worst of the day, DeFreitas and Gough added 59 exhilarating runs in the final half-hour and England were only 28 behind when the innings finished next morning. That was after Gooch had called the team together in Atherton's absence and urged them to rally behind the captain. It was also after Malcolm was hit on the helmet, straight between the eyes, first ball by de Villiers. He was not hurt, only angry. He stared back at the fielders who gathered round. "You guys are going to pay for this," he was reported to have said. "You guys are history."

Malcolm turned his words into action in 99 balls, the most devastating spell by an England bowler since Jim Laker wiped out the Australians in 1956. It was the sixth-best Test analysis ever and, until Cullinan was caught off Gough, it looked as if Malcolm might join Laker by taking all ten. The Kirstens and Cronje had gone for one run and the last six wickets fell for 38, with only Cullinan, who made 94, standing firm for long. Malcolm produced a series of classic deliveries: five catches to slip and wicket-keeper from lifting balls, a bouncer hooked to long-leg, a desperately determined caught and bowled and two sets of stumps sent clattering by yorkers. He answered every question save one. Why did the selectors make him wait so long to bowl against a team who appeared alarmed by fast bowling?

England were left to make 204 and, for the first time since the Trent Bridge Test against New Zealand, Gooch showed the value of his experience. His fitness had been in doubt and Gatting had been called up as cover, but now his bold strokes inspired Atherton so that 56 came in five overs – when Gooch was bowled – 79 off ten and 107 in 16 by the close. This incisive batting settled the match and the new, mature Hick sealed England's success. He strode towards an undefeated run-a-ball 81 in the style he had so often displayed for Worcestershire. De Villiers thought he had him caught behind at 53 and expressing doubts about umpire Palmer's verdict cost him 25 per cent of his match fee. By the time his team had been fined 70 per cent of their fees for bowling 14 overs short of their target on the second day, he was left with £70 for his 31 overs, four wickets and 14 runs. England were fined 30 per cent for being six overs short. De Villiers will find it no consolation that he played in one of the great Tests. South Africa's performance was wretched compared with their win at Lord's, but England saw the victory as a rebirth, not for the first time. – Ted Corbett.

Man of the Match: D. E. Malcolm. *Attendance:* 59,705; *receipts* £1,390,551.

Men of the Series: England – D. E. Malcolm; South Africa – B. M. McMillan.

Close of play: First day, South Africa 326-8 (B. M. McMillan 91*, A. A. Donald 11*); Second day, England 281-7 (P. A. J. DeFreitas 37*, D. Gough 25*); Third day, England 107-1 (M. A. Atherton 42*, G. A. Hick 27*).

South Africa

First innings		Second innings	
G. Kirsten c Rhodes b DeFreitas	2	(2) c and b Malcolm	0
P. N. Kirsten b Malcolm	16	(1) c DeFreitas b Malcolm	1
W. J. Cronje lbw b Benjamin	38	b Malcolm	0
*K. C. Wessels lbw b Benjamin	45	c Rhodes b Malcolm	28
D. J. Cullinan c Rhodes b DeFreitas	7	c Thorpe b Gough	94
J. N. Rhodes retired hurt	8	(9) c Rhodes b Malcolm	10
B. M. McMillan c Hick b DeFreitas	93	(6) c Thorpe b Malcolm	25
†D. J. Richardson c Rhodes b Benjamin	58	(7) lbw b Malcolm	3
C. R. Matthews c Hick b Benjamin	0	(8) c Rhodes b Malcolm	0
P. S. de Villiers c Stewart b DeFreitas	14	not out	0
A. A. Donald not out	14	b Malcolm	0
B 8, l-b 10, w 1, n-b 18	37	L-b 5, n-b 9	14
1/2 (1) 2/43 (2) 3/73 (3) 4/85 (5) 5/136 (4) 6/260 (8) 7/266 (9) 8/301 (10) 9/332 (7)	332	1/0 (2) 2/1 (1) 3/1 (3) 4/73 (4) 5/137 (6) 6/143 (7) 7/143 (8) 8/175 (5) 9/175 (9) 10/175 (11)	175

In the first innings J. N. Rhodes retired hurt at 106.

Bowling: *First Innings*—DeFreitas 26.2–5–93–4; Malcolm 25–5–81–1; Gough 19–1–85–0; Benjamin 17–2–42–4; Hick 5–1–13–0. *Second Innings*—DeFreitas 12–3–25–0; Malcolm 16.3–2–57–9; Gough 9–1–39–1; Benjamin 11–1–38–0; Hick 2–0–11–0.

England

First innings		Second innings	
G. A. Gooch c Richardson b Donald	8	b Matthews	33
*M. A. Atherton lbw b de Villiers	0	c Richardson b Donald	63
G. A. Hick b Donald	39	not out	81
G. P. Thorpe b Matthews	79	not out	15
A. J. Stewart b de Villiers	62		
J. P. Crawley c Richardson b Donald	5		
†S. J. Rhodes lbw b de Villiers	11		
P. A. J. DeFreitas run out	37		
D. Gough not out	42		
J. E. Benjamin lbw b de Villiers	0		
D. E. Malcolm c sub (T. G. Shaw) b Matthews	4		
B 1, w 1, n-b 15	17	L-b 6, n-b 7	13
1/1 (2) 2/33 (1) 3/93 (3) 4/145 (4) 5/165 (6) 6/219 (7) 7/222 (5) 8/292 (8) 9/293 (10) 10/304 (11)	304	1/56 (1) 2/180 (2) (2 wkts)	205

Bowling: *First Innings*—Donald 17–2–76–3; de Villiers 19–3–62–4; Matthews 21–4–82–2; McMillan 12–1–67–0; Cronje 8–3–16–0. *Second Innings*—Donald 12–1–96–1; de Villiers 12–0–66–0; Matthews 11.3–4–37–1.

Umpires: R. S. Dunne (New Zealand) and K. E. Palmer.
Referee: P. J. P. Burge (Australia).

†ENGLAND v SOUTH AFRICA

First Texaco Trophy Match

At Birmingham, August 25. England won by six wickets. Toss: South Africa.

South Africa were unable to rouse themselves from the depression caused by their Test defeat and England won in a workmanlike fashion that was uninspiring for the crowd but encouraging for the selectors, who announced before the start that Atherton would lead the team to Australia. England had brought in several one-day specialists; Malcolm and Fraser were also in the squad but did not play in either game. The reshaped team had the same spring in its stride as at The Oval and fielded particularly well to back up solid performances from all the bowlers. South Africa's 215 was never enough on a perfectly sound pitch. The openers gave England a safe start, and Hick, maintaining the assurance of his recent Test performances, settled the game with 81 off 116 balls, driving well and pulling one huge six off Cronje. South Africa's best moment came when Jonty Rhodes, with one of his almost inhumanly elastic stop-and-throw movements at backward point, ran out Atherton.

Man of the Match: G. A. Hick. *Attendance*: 18,400; *receipts* £438,000.

South Africa

*K. C. Wessels b DeFreitas	4
G. Kirsten c DeFreitas b Lewis	30
P. N. Kirsten c Rhodes b DeFreitas	8
J. N. Rhodes c Thorpe b Cork	35
D. J. Cullinan b DeFreitas	45
W. J. Cronje b Lewis	36
†D. J. Richardson not out	20
R. P. Snell c Gough b Lewis	2
T. G. Shaw not out	17
L-b 6, w 10, n-b 2	18
1/5 (1) 2/30 (3) 3/58 (2) 4/103 (4) 5/174 (6) 6/176 (5) 7/182 (8) (7 wkts, 55 overs)	215

C. R. Matthews and P. S. de Villiers did not bat.

Bowling: DeFreitas 9–1–38–3; Gough 11–2–40–0; Lewis 8–0–32–3; Udal 11–0–34–0; Cork 11–0–46–1; Hick 5–1–19–0.

England

*M. A. Atherton run out	49
A. J. Stewart c de Villiers b Shaw	32
G. A. Hick c Shaw b Snell	81
G. P. Thorpe run out	26
N. H. Fairbrother not out	19
†S. J. Rhodes not out	0
L-b 9, w 2, n-b 1	12
1/57 (2) 2/126 (1) 3/181 (4) 4/215 (3) (4 wkts, 54 overs)	219

C. C. Lewis, P. A. J. DeFreitas, D. G. Cork, D. Gough and S. D. Udal did not bat.

Bowling: de Villiers 11–2–27–0; Matthews 11–1–42–0; Shaw 11–0–34–1; Cronje 9–0–50–0; Snell 11–0–49–1; G. Kirsten 1–0–8–0.

Umpires: J. C. Balderstone and H. D. Bird. Referee: P. J. P. Burge (Australia).

†ENGLAND v SOUTH AFRICA

Second Texaco Trophy Match

At Manchester, August 27, 28. England won by four wickets. Toss: England.

South Africa continued what appeared to be turning into a tradition, their end-of-tour collapse, while England continued their revival in a game that ended up one-sided. However, England may have been saved by rain that forced their innings into a second day when they were struggling at 80 for four. The following day – drier but miserably cold and windy – they found batting much easier; Thorpe and Rhodes took England carefully towards victory. Rhodes was in particularly imperturbable and determined form. The South

African team manager Mike Procter added to England's post-match euphoria by saying they were a good bet for the 1996 World Cup. Put in on a difficult pitch, South Africa struggled for runs, especially against DeFreitas, bowling probing in-swing against the left-handed openers. Five wickets then fell for 25 and only Cullinan and Matthews saved South Africa from humiliation. England lost their first wicket in curious fashion: Cullinan at mid-off caught Stewart but dropped the ball as he tried to throw it upwards in celebration. Commentators and spectators wondered whether he had the ball under "complete control" but Stewart walked straight off and no one on the field raised the matter.

Man of the Match: S. J. Rhodes. *Attendance:* 20,588; *receipts* £478,220.

Men of the Series: England – P. A. J. DeFreitas; South Africa – D. J. Cullinan.

Close of play: England 80-4 (26.5 overs) (G. P. Thorpe 27*, S. J. Rhodes 10*).

South Africa

G. Kirsten c Lewis b Cork	30	P. S. de Villiers not out	14
*K. C. Wessels lbw b DeFreitas	21	A. A. Donald not out	2
W. J. Cronje run out	0	L-b 6, w 4, n-b 4	14
J. N. Rhodes lbw b Cork	0		—
D. J. Cullinan run out	54	1/43 (2) 2/47 (3) (9 wkts, 55 overs)	181
B. M. McMillan st Rhodes b Udal	0	3/47 (4) 4/64 (1)	
†D. J. Richardson c Lewis b Gough	14	5/68 (6) 6/113 (7)	
T. G. Shaw b Gough	6	7/121 (8) 8/163 (9)	
C. R. Matthews b Cork	26	9/163 (5)	

Bowling: DeFreitas 11–4–12–1; Gough 10–1–39–2; Lewis 9–0–44–0; Udal 11–2–17–1; Cork 11–1–49–3; Hick 3–0–14–0.

England

*M. A. Atherton c Wessels b Matthews	19	P. A. J. DeFreitas not out	7
A. J. Stewart c Cullinan b Donald	11		
G. A. Hick lbw b Donald	0	W 4, n-b 10	14
G. P. Thorpe c Cullinan b Shaw	55		—
N. H. Fairbrother run out	3	1/27 (2) 2/28 (3) (6 wkts, 48.2 overs)	182
†S. J. Rhodes run out	56	3/42 (1) 4/60 (5)	
C. C. Lewis not out	17	5/130 (4) 6/171 (6)	

D. G. Cork, D. Gough and S. D. Udal did not bat.

Bowling: Donald 10.2–1–47–2; de Villiers 8–1–29–0; McMillan 10–1–53–0; Matthews 9–2–20–1; Shaw 11–0–33–1.

Umpires: M. J. Kitchen and K. E. Palmer. Referee: P. J. P. Burge (Australia).

†PRESIDENT'S XI v SOUTH AFRICANS

At Scarborough, August 29. President's XI won by four wickets. Toss: South Africans.

The South Africans' batting let them down again. Struggling against a West Indian pace attack, they scored barely three an over and were all out when Donald was bowled by the last ball of the innings. Only Cronje passed 25 and he hit a solitary boundary in his fifty. Though de Villiers, in particular, bowled tightly, conceding only 18 runs in ten overs, the President's XI overtook the tourists with nearly eight overs in hand.

South Africans

A. C. Hudson c Young b Benjamin	25	C. R. Matthews not out	7
G. Kirsten b Marshall	4	P. S. de Villiers b Benjamin	3
*W. J. Cronje b Benjamin	53	A. A. Donald b Benjamin	5
D. J. Cullinan run out	3	B 1, l-b 8, w 7, n-b 2	18
J. N. Rhodes b Browne	0		—
†G. F. J. Liebenberg lbw b Marshall	21	1/5 2/36 3/52 (50 overs)	151
B. M. McMillan lbw b Marshall	0	4/52 5/106 6/106	
R. P. Snell c McNamara b Browne	12	7/123 8/137 9/145	

Bowling: Marshall 10–2–28–3; Benjamin 9–0–36–4; Baptiste 10–0–19–0; Browne 10–1–22–2; Harper 6–0–25–0; McNamara 5–0–12–0.

President's XI

†B. A. Young c Rhodes b Matthews	39	P. R. Sleep not out	29
R. Chee Quee lbw b Donald	1	E. A. E. Baptiste not out	13
G. I. Foley b de Villiers	0	B 4, l-b 4, w 6, n-b 2	16
K. L. T. Arthurton lbw b de Villiers	35		—
B. E. McNamara lbw b Matthews	6	1/12 2/19 3/55 (6 wkts, 42.1 overs)	155
*R. A. Harper lbw b McMillan	16	4/64 5/93 6/130	

M. D. Marshall, K. C. G. Benjamin and B. St A. Browne did not bat.

Bowling: Donald 8–2–32–1; de Villiers 10–3–18–2; Snell 6–0–41–0; McMillan 7–0–24–1; Matthews 10–2–26–2; Rhodes 1–0–2–0; Cullinan 0.1–0–4–0.

Umpires: J. H. Hampshire and B. Leadbeater.

PRESIDENT'S XI v SOUTH AFRICANS

At Scarborough, August 31, September 1, 2. Drawn. Toss: President's XI.

Rain shortened the first day, washed out the second and, despite forfeitures, condemned the game to a draw. Harper set the South Africans to score 344 in 73 overs, but they gave up the chase with eight overs left. Hudson, at least, had the satisfaction of his only century of the tour, a three-hour innings featuring 14 fours and a five. Former Australian Test player Sleep, a regular for the President's XI, had been prevented by the declaration from extending his remarkable record of a century in his only first-class innings in 1992 and 1993; he was left on 79 not out. There were also fifties for Young, the New Zealand opener, Morris, one of four Durham players who joined the President's overseas guests, and the West Indian Arthurton.

Close of play: First day, President's XI 230-3 (K. L. T. Arthurton 48*, P. R. Sleep 27*); Second day, No play.

President's XI

B. A. Young c Cullinan b Kirsten	66	†C. W. Scott b Cronje	5
W. Larkins hit wkt b Snell	16	E. A. E. Baptiste not out	20
J. E. Morris lbw b de Villiers	57	B 2, l-b 10, n-b 10	22
K. L. T. Arthurton c Cronje b de Villiers	60		—
P. R. Sleep not out	79	1/26 2/120 3/170 (6 wkts dec.)	343
*R. A. Harper b Shaw	18	4/247 5/289 6/308	

S. J. E. Brown, M. D. Marshall and K. C. G. Benjamin did not bat.

Bowling: de Villiers 19–6–55–2; Snell 18–4–45–1; McMillan 11–2–44–0; Cronje 11–0–44–1; Shaw 20–3–99–1; Kirsten 7–0–44–1.

President's XI forfeited their second innings.

South Africans

South Africans forfeited their first innings.

A. C. Hudson c Scott b Marshall	116	B. M. McMillan not out	1
†G. F. J. Liebenberg b Marshall	17	R. P. Snell not out	6
*W. J. Cronje c Scott b Brown	36	B 3, l-b 8, n-b 16	27
D. J. Cullinan lbw b Marshall	14		—
P. N. Kirsten run out	32	1/38 2/123 3/179 (6 wkts)	270
J. N. Rhodes c Brown b Harper	21	4/214 5/254 6/263	

T. G. Shaw, P. S. de Villiers and A. A. Donald did not bat.

Bowling: Benjamin 15–4–53–0; Marshall 16–2–60–3; Brown 14–1–64–1; Harper 16–1–58–1; Baptiste 2–0–15–0; Sleep 2–0–9–0.

Umpires: J. H. Hampshire and B. Leadbeater.

BRITANNIC ASSURANCE COUNTY CHAMPIONSHIP, 1994

Warwickshire won the County Championship as the second – and by far the most important – leg of their treble in 1994. They had established themselves as the pre-eminent county of the year well before they formally wrapped up the title on September 2, the day before they went to Lord's for the NatWest final, where their dreams of winning the grand slam evaporated.

Their final margin was 42 points, the biggest since 1979. Leicestershire were second, with Nottinghamshire third a further 12 points back. This was the second year ever – the other was 1964 – that Midland counties have filled the top three positions.

There was little doubt Warwickshire would win the Championship from the moment they took over the leadership at the end of July. On August 15, Leicestershire did close the gap to nine points with a game in hand. But they promptly went down to a two-day defeat against Sussex and never threatened again.

Brian Lara's world record 501 not out came in one of the six matches Warwickshire failed to win. But he was crucial to many of their victories, by scoring his runs so quickly that the bowlers had time to get the opposition out, as well as being so good that his confidence rubbed off on his team-mates.

BRITANNIC ASSURANCE CHAMPIONSHIP

					Bonus points		
Win = 16 pts	*Played*	*Won*	*Lost*	*Drawn*	*Batting*	*Bowling*	*Points*
1 – Warwickshire (16)...	17	11	1	5	41	55	272
2 – Leicestershire (9)....	17	8	7	2	42	60	230
3 – Nottinghamshire (7) .	17	8	5	4	39	51	218
4 – Middlesex (1).......	17	7	3	7	43	57	212
5 – Northamptonshire (4)	17	8	4	5	28	53	209
6 – Essex (11)	17	7	5	5	32	63	207
7 – Surrey (6)..........	17	7	7	3	32	57	201
8 – Sussex (10).........	17	7	5	5	28	60	200
9 – Kent (8)...........	17	6	7	4	44	58	198
10 – Lancashire (13)	17	8	6	3	32	59	194*
11 – Somerset (5)........	17	7	7	3	32	47	191
12 – Gloucestershire (17) .	17	5	8	4	28	56	172†
13 { Yorkshire (12)......	17	4	6	7	38	57	159
13 { Hampshire (13).....	17	4	7	6	32	55	159†
15 – Worcestershire (2)...	17	4	6	7	42	52	158
16 – Durham (18)	17	4	10	3	32	57	153
17 – Derbyshire (15).....	17	4	9	4	25	54	143
18 – Glamorgan (3)......	17	2	8	7	29	50	111

1993 positions are shown in brackets.

* *Lancashire had 25 points deducted during the season as a penalty for a sub-standard pitch at Manchester.*

† *The totals for Gloucestershire and Hampshire include 8 points for levelling the scores in drawn games.*

At least two of Warwickshire's wins were conjured by Lara almost single-handed. He scored an outstanding century before lunch on a green wicket at Chesterfield, which every other batsman found exceptionally difficult, and his 197 made the difference at Northampton against Curtly Ambrose at his fiercest. Dermot Reeve missed nine of Warwickshire's Championship games and Tim Munton led the way, both as replacement captain and bowling spearhead. But there were enough successes for previously unregarded individuals to make it a genuine team triumph.

Leicestershire, ahead of only Gloucestershire and Durham in the pre-season betting, continued to be under-rated until the bitter end. But they drew only two matches (the second, against Warwickshire, and the last) and in between made a habit of either forcing victory, in an uncompromising style that surprised opponents and occasionally umpires, or going down heavily. Six of their eight wins came at Grace Road, usually on pitches well-crafted for their seamers.

Nottinghamshire won four of their first five games then went through a bleak period of one win in two months, before recovering to finish six points clear of an unusually bunched chasing pack. Only 21 points separated Middlesex in fourth place from Somerset in 11th, and Lancashire, who finished tenth, would have been third had they not been docked 25 points for an unsatisfactory pitch.

Middlesex, the 1993 champions, began with five draws, and were next to bottom in mid-June, by which time they had already left themselves too much to do. Northamptonshire were also slow starters before winning six of their last eight matches to finish fifth, two points ahead of Essex, who surprised themselves by winning their first three matches. They led the table for a week in early June but, while they won six games out of ten when Graham Gooch was playing, they won only one out of seven without him.

The really dominant team in the early weeks were Surrey, but they lost a vital fixture to Warwickshire at Guildford and proceeded to lose three successive matches by an innings. Eventually, they struggled to finish in seventh place, one point ahead of Sussex and three ahead of Kent, who failed to win a game until July, and on June 30 were 91 points behind Surrey.

Among the stragglers were Worcestershire, who were without a dominant fast bowler and turned out to be better-equipped for one-day cricket. Their record-breaking 15-place rise in 1993 (equalled by Warwickshire in 1994) was followed by a 13-place fall. They were clear of Durham, whose strong start of three wins in six games enabled them to avoid the wooden spoon for the first time even though they then lost seven in a row. Derbyshire were 17th, their worst showing in 20 years, but even they were 32 points clear of Glamorgan, who after their magnificent season in 1993 had an epidemic of lost form and slumped 15 positions from third to 18th. From the start of June, they were bottom after every round of matches except one.

In a generally fine summer, 111 of the 153 matches produced a result, six more than in 1993. Three games finished in two days and 30 in three, though in many cases this was a comment on the lack of fight shown by a team who were getting well beaten rather than on any inadequacy in the pitch.

Under the TCCB playing conditions, two extras were scored for every no-ball bowled whether scored off or not. Any runs scored off the bat were credited to the batsman, while byes and leg-byes were counted as no-balls, in accordance with Law 24.9, in addition to the initial penalty.

Pre-season betting (William Hill): 4-1 Middlesex; 6-1 Essex; 8-1 Surrey; 9-1 Northamptonshire and Worcestershire; 10-1 Glamorgan; 11-1 Kent and Lancashire; 14-1 Derbyshire and Somerset; 16-1 Nottinghamshire, Sussex and WARWICKSHIRE; 20-1 Yorkshire; 33-1 Hampshire; 40-1 Leicestershire; 100-1 Gloucestershire; 150-1 Durham.

Leaders: from May 9 Surrey; June 13 Essex; June 20 Surrey; August 1 onwards Warwickshire. Warwickshire became champions on September 2.

Bottom place: from May 9 Sussex and Yorkshire; May 16 Middlesex; May 23 Lancashire; May 30 Middlesex and Somerset; June 6 Glamorgan; July 4 Hampshire and Yorkshire; July 18 onwards Glamorgan.

Prize money

First (Warwickshire)	£48,500
Second (Leicestershire)	£24,250
Third (Nottinghamshire)	£14,000
Fourth (Middlesex)	£7,250
Fifth (Northamptonshire)	£3,700
Winner of each match	£600
County of the Month	£1,000
Player of the Month	£300

Scoring of Points

(*a*) For a win, 16 points plus any points scored in the first innings.

(*b*) In a tie, each side scores eight points, plus any points scored in the first innings.

(*c*) If the scores are equal in a drawn match, the side batting in the fourth innings scores eight points, plus any points scored in the first innings.

(*d*) First-innings points (awarded only for performances in the first 120 overs of each first innings and retained whatever the result of the match).

(i) A maximum of four batting points to be available: 200 to 249 runs – 1 point; 250 to 299 runs – 2 points; 300 to 349 – 3 points; 350 runs or over – 4 points.

(ii) A maximum of four bowling points to be available: 3 or 4 wickets taken – 1 point; 5 or 6 wickets taken – 2 points; 7 or 8 wickets taken – 3 points; 9 or 10 wickets taken – 4 points.

(*e*) If play starts when less than eight hours' playing time remains and a one-innings match is played, no first-innings points shall be scored. The side winning on the one innings scores 12 points.

(*f*) A county which is adjudged to have prepared a pitch unsuitable for first-class cricket shall be liable to have 25 points deducted.

(*g*) The side which has the highest aggregate of points shall be the Champion County. Should any sides in the Championship table be equal on points the side with most wins will have priority.

CHAMPION COUNTY SINCE 1864

Note: The earliest county champions were decided usually by the fewest matches lost, but in 1888 an unofficial points system was introduced. In 1890, the Championship was constituted officially. From 1977 to 1983 it was sponsored by Schweppes, and since 1984 by Britannic Assurance.

Unofficial champions	
1864	Surrey
1865	Nottinghamshire
1866	Middlesex
1867	Yorkshire
1868	Nottinghamshire
1869	Nottinghamshire Yorkshire
1870	Yorkshire
1871	Nottinghamshire
1872	Nottinghamshire
1873	Gloucestershire Nottinghamshire
1874	Gloucestershire
1875	Nottinghamshire
1876	Gloucestershire
1877	Gloucestershire
1878	Undecided
1879	Nottinghamshire Lancashire
1880	Nottinghamshire
1881	Lancashire
1882	Nottinghamshire Lancashire
1883	Nottinghamshire
1884	Nottinghamshire
1885	Nottinghamshire
1886	Nottinghamshire
1887	Surrey
1888	Surrey
1889	Surrey Lancashire Nottinghamshire
Official champions	
1890	Surrey
1891	Surrey
1892	Surrey
1893	Yorkshire
1894	Surrey
1895	Surrey
1896	Yorkshire
1897	Lancashire
1898	Yorkshire
1899	Surrey
1900	Yorkshire
1901	Yorkshire
1902	Yorkshire
1903	Middlesex
1904	Lancashire
1905	Yorkshire
1906	Kent
1907	Nottinghamshire
1908	Yorkshire
1909	Kent
1910	Kent
1911	Warwickshire
1912	Yorkshire
1913	Kent
1914	Surrey
1919	Yorkshire
1920	Middlesex
1921	Middlesex
1922	Yorkshire
1923	Yorkshire
1924	Yorkshire
1925	Yorkshire
1926	Lancashire
1927	Lancashire
1928	Lancashire
1929	Nottinghamshire
1930	Lancashire
1931	Yorkshire
1932	Yorkshire
1933	Yorkshire
1934	Lancashire
1935	Yorkshire
1936	Derbyshire
1937	Yorkshire
1938	Yorkshire
1939	Yorkshire
1946	Yorkshire
1947	Middlesex
1948	Glamorgan
1949	Middlesex Yorkshire
1950	Lancashire Surrey
1951	Warwickshire
1952	Surrey
1953	Surrey
1954	Surrey
1955	Surrey
1956	Surrey
1957	Surrey
1958	Surrey
1959	Yorkshire
1960	Yorkshire
1961	Hampshire
1962	Yorkshire
1963	Yorkshire
1964	Worcestershire
1965	Worcestershire
1966	Yorkshire
1967	Yorkshire
1968	Yorkshire
1969	Glamorgan
1970	Kent
1971	Surrey
1972	Warwickshire
1973	Hampshire
1974	Worcestershire
1975	Leicestershire
1976	Middlesex
1977	Middlesex Kent
1978	Kent
1979	Essex
1980	Middlesex
1981	Nottinghamshire
1982	Middlesex
1983	Essex
1984	Essex
1985	Middlesex
1986	Essex
1987	Nottinghamshire
1988	Worcestershire
1989	Worcestershire
1990	Middlesex
1991	Essex
1992	Essex
1993	Middlesex
1994	Warwickshire

Notes: The title has been won outright as follows: Yorkshire 31 times, Surrey 18, Nottinghamshire 14, Middlesex 11, Lancashire 8, Essex and Kent 6, Worcestershire 5, Warwickshire 4, Gloucestershire 3, Glamorgan and Hampshire 2, Derbyshire and Leicestershire 1.

Since the championship was constituted officially in 1890 it has been won outright as follows: Yorkshire 29 times, Surrey 15, Middlesex 10, Lancashire 7, Essex and Kent 6, Worcestershire 5, Nottinghamshire and Warwickshire 4, Glamorgan and Hampshire 2, Derbyshire and Leicestershire 1.

The title has been shared eight times as follows: Nottinghamshire 5, Lancashire 4, Middlesex, Surrey and Yorkshire 2, Gloucestershire and Kent 1. Only three of these instances have occurred since 1890, involving Middlesex twice, Kent, Lancashire, Surrey and Yorkshire.

Wooden Spoons: Since the major expansion of the Championship from nine teams to 14 in 1895, the counties have finished outright bottom as follows: Derbyshire, Northamptonshire and Somerset 11; Glamorgan 9; Nottinghamshire 8; Leicestershire 7; Gloucestershire, Sussex and Worcestershire 6; Hampshire 5; Warwickshire 3; Durham 2; Essex, Kent and Yorkshire 1. Lancashire, Middlesex and Surrey have never finished bottom. Leicestershire have also shared bottom place twice, once with Hampshire and once with Somerset.

BRITANNIC ASSURANCE CHAMPIONSHIP STATISTICS FOR 1994

	For			*Against*		
County	*Runs*	*Wickets*	*Avge*	*Runs*	*Wickets*	*Avge*
Derbyshire	7,550	273	27.65	8,190	240	34.12
Durham	8,121	281	28.90	8,840	224	39.46
Essex	7,658	251	30.50	8,579	272	31.54
Glamorgan	7,362	246	29.92	8,749	233	37.54
Gloucestershire	8,048	291	27.65	7,436	256	29.04
Hampshire	8,118	275	29.52	7,835	249	31.46
Kent	9,054	285	31.76	8,634	284	30.40
Lancashire	8,915	263	33.89	7,828	279	28.05
Leicestershire	8,073	263	30.69	8,205	273	30.05
Middlesex	8,469	198	42.77	9,125	270	33.79
Northamptonshire	8,438	242	34.86	8,113	247	32.84
Nottinghamshire	8,185	254	32.22	8,093	259	31.24
Somerset	8,153	261	31.23	7,501	238	31.51
Surrey	7,909	220	35.95	8,277	253	32.71
Sussex	7,700	282	27.30	7,366	274	26.88
Warwickshire	9,221	219	42.10	8,437	272	31.01
Worcestershire	8,525	249	34.23	8,814	249	35.39
Yorkshire	8,639	277	31.18	8,116	258	31.45
	148,138	4,630	31.99	148,138	4,630	31.99

COUNTY CHAMPIONSHIP – MATCH RESULTS, 1864-1994

County	*Years of Play*	*Played*	*Won*	*Lost*	*Tied*	*Drawn*
Derbyshire	1871-87; 1895-1994	2,190	541	796	1	852
Durham	1992-1994	56	8	30	0	18
Essex	1895-1994	2,153	618	618	5	912
Glamorgan	1921-1994	1,687	367	576	0	744
Gloucestershire	1870-1994	2,427	713	901	2	811
Hampshire	1864-85; 1895-1994	2,262	589	777	4	892
Kent	1864-1994	2,550	922	768	5	855
Lancashire	1865-1994	2,628	973	546	3	1,106
Leicestershire	1895-1994	2,120	465	788	1	866
Middlesex	1864-1994	2,330	868	586	5	871
Northamptonshire	1905-1994	1,887	458	661	3	765
Nottinghamshire	1864-1994	2,459	751	644	1	1,063
Somerset	1882-85; 1891-1994	2,160	507	874	3	776
Surrey	1864-1994	2,707	1,068	600	4	1,035
Sussex	1864-1994	2,599	724	892	6	977
Warwickshire	1895-1994	2,134	567	624	1	942
Worcestershire	1899-1994	2,074	515	721	2	836
Yorkshire	1864-1994	2,728	1,211	463	2	1,052
Cambridgeshire	1864-69; 1871	19	8	8	0	3
		19,585	11,873	11,873	24	7,688

Notes: Matches abandoned without a ball bowled are wholly excluded.

Counties participated in the years shown, except that there were no matches in the years 1915-18 and 1940-45; Hampshire did not play inter-county matches in 1868-69, 1871-74 and 1879; Worcestershire did not take part in the Championship in 1919.

OVERS BOWLED AND RUNS SCORED IN THE BRITANNIC ASSURANCE CHAMPIONSHIP, 1994

County	*Over-rate per hour*	*Run-rate/ 100 balls*
Derbyshire (17)	18.75	49.40
Durham (16)	18.60	51.81
Essex (6)	18.60	53.74
Glamorgan (18)	19.11	51.59
Gloucestershire (12)	19.02	47.16
Hampshire (13)	18.57	49.72
Kent (9)	19.02	57.88
Lancashire (10)	18.59	52.20
Leicestershire (2)	18.69	52.74
Middlesex (4)	18.56	60.02
Northamptonshire (5)	18.79	50.54
Nottinghamshire (3)	18.73	49.52
Somerset (11)	18.62	46.48
Surrey (7)	18.63	58.80
Sussex (8)	18.56	50.94
Warwickshire (1)	18.59	61.11
Worcestershire (15)	18.79	54.09
Yorkshire (13)	18.56	50.35
1994 average rate	18.71	52.67

1994 Championship positions are shown in brackets.

SUMMARY OF RESULTS, 1994

	Derbyshire	Durham	Essex	Glamorgan	Gloucestershire	Hampshire	Kent	Lancashire	Leicestershire	Middlesex	Northamptonshire	Nottinghamshire	Somerset	Surrey	Sussex	Warwickshire	Worcestershire	Yorkshire
Derbyshire	—	**L**	**D**	*W*	**W**	*D*	**L**	*W*	**L**	**L**	*L*	**L**	*D*	*L*	*W*	**L**	**D**	*L*
Durham	*W*	—	**L**	**W**	**W**	*D*	*L*	**L**	**L**	*L*	**W**	*L*	*L*	**L**	*L*	*D*	*D*	**L**
Essex	*D*	*W*	—	**W**	**D**	*W*	**W**	**L**	*L*	*D*	**D**	**L**	*L*	**W**	**W**	*L*	*W*	*D*
Glamorgan	**L**	*L*	*L*	—	*W*	*D*	**L**	**L**	**W**	*L*	*D*	*L*	**D**	**D**	*D*	*L*	**D**	**D**
Gloucestershire	*L*	*L*	*D*	**L**	—	*L*	**L**	*W*	**W**	*L*	**L**	*W*	**W**	**L**	**D**	**D**	*D*	**W**
Hampshire	**D**	**D**	**L**	**D**	**W**	—	*W*	*L*	*L*	**D**	**L**	**D**	*L*	**W**	*L*	*L*	*W*	*D*
Kent	*W*	**W**	*L*	*W*	*W*	**L**	—	**D**	*L*	**D**	*L*	**L**	**W**	*D*	**D**	*L*	**L**	**W**
Lancashire	**L**	*W*	*W*	*W*	**L**	**W**	*D*	—	**D**	**W**	*D*	*W*	**W**	**L**	*L*	*L*	**L**	*W*
Leicestershire	*W*	*W*	**W**	*L*	*L*	**W**	**W**	*D*	—	**L**	**W**	*L*	**W**	*L*	**L**	*D*	**W**	*L*
Middlesex	*W*	**W**	**D**	**W**	**W**	*D*	*D*	*L*	*W*	—	*L*	*D*	**W**	*W*	*L*	**D**	**D**	**D**
Northamptonshire	**W**	*L*	*D*	**D**	*W*	*W*	**W**	**D**	*L*	**W**	—	*D*	*W*	*W*	**L**	**L**	*D*	**W**
Nottinghamshire	*W*	**W**	*W*	**W**	**L**	*D*	*W*	**L**	**W**	**D**	**D**	—	*L*	**L**	**D**	*W*	*L*	*W*
Somerset	**D**	**W**	**W**	*D*	*L*	**W**	*L*	*L*	*L*	*L*	**L**	**W**	—	**W**	*W*	**L**	**W**	*D*
Surrey	**W**	*W*	*L*	*D*	*W*	*L*	**D**	*W*	**W**	**L**	**L**	*W*	*L*	—	**L**	**L**	**W**	*D*
Sussex	**L**	**W**	*L*	**D**	*D*	**W**	*D*	**W**	*W*	**W**	*W*	*D*	**L**	*W*	—	**L**	*L*	**D**
Warwickshire	*W*	**D**	**W**	**W**	*D*	**W**	**W**	**W**	**D**	*D*	*W*	**L**	*W*	*W*	*W*	—	*D*	*W*
Worcestershire	*D*	**D**	**L**	*D*	**D**	**L**	*W*	*W*	*L*	*D*	**D**	**W**	*L*	*L*	**W**	**D**	—	**L**
Yorkshire	**W**	*W*	**D**	*D*	*L*	**D**	*L*	**L**	**W**	*D*	*L*	**L**	**D**	**D**	*D*	**L**	*W*	—

Home games in bold, away games in italics. W = Won, L = Lost, D = Drawn.

COUNTY CHAMPIONSHIP – FINAL POSITIONS, 1890-1994

	Derbyshire	Essex	Glamorgan	Gloucestershire	Hampshire	Kent	Lancashire	Leicestershire	Middlesex	Northamptonshire	Nottinghamshire	Somerset	Surrey	Sussex	Warwickshire	Worcestershire	Yorkshire
1890	—	—	—	6	—	3	2	—	7	—	5	—	1	8	—	—	3
1891	—	—	—	9	—	5	2	—	3	—	4	5	1	7	—	—	8
1892	—	—	—	7	—	7	4	—	5	—	2	3	1	9	—	—	6
1893	—	—	—	9	—	4	2	—	3	—	6	8	5	7	—	—	1
1894	—	—	—	9	—	4	4	—	3	—	7	6	1	8	—	—	2
1895	5	9	—	4	10	14	2	12	6	—	12	8	1	11	6	—	3
1896	7	5	—	10	8	9	2	13	3	—	6	11	4	14	12	—	1
1897	14	3	—	5	9	12	1	13	8	—	10	11	2	6	7	—	4
1898	9	5	—	3	12	7	6	13	2	—	8	13	4	9	9	—	1
1899	15	6	—	9	10	8	4	13	2	—	10	13	1	5	7	12	3
1900	13	10	—	7	15	3	2	14	7	—	5	11	7	3	6	12	1
1901	15	10	—	14	7	7	3	12	2	—	9	12	6	4	5	11	1
1902	10	13	—	14	15	7	5	11	12	—	3	7	4	2	6	9	1
1903	12	8	—	13	14	8	4	14	1	—	5	10	11	2	7	6	3
1904	10	14	—	9	15	3	1	7	4	—	5	12	11	6	7	13	2
1905	14	12	—	8	16	6	2	5	11	13	10	15	4	3	7	8	1
1906	16	7	—	9	8	1	4	15	11	11	5	11	3	10	6	14	2
1907	16	7	—	10	12	8	6	11	5	15	1	14	4	13	9	2	2
1908	14	11	—	10	9	2	7	13	4	15	8	16	3	5	12	6	1
1909	15	14	—	16	8	1	2	13	6	7	10	11	5	4	12	8	3
1910	15	11	—	12	6	1	4	10	3	9	5	16	2	7	14	13	8
1911	14	6	—	12	11	2	4	15	3	10	8	16	5	13	1	9	7
1912	12	15	—	11	6	3	4	13	5	2	8	14	7	10	9	16	1
1913	13	15	—	9	10	1	8	14	6	4	5	16	3	7	11	12	2
1914	12	8	—	16	5	3	11	13	2	9	10	15	1	6	7	14	4
1919	9	14	—	8	7	2	5	9	13	12	3	5	4	11	15	—	1
1920	16	9	—	8	11	5	2	13	1	14	7	10	3	6	12	15	4
1921	12	15	17	7	6	4	5	11	1	13	8	10	2	9	16	14	3
1922	11	8	16	13	6	4	5	14	7	15	2	10	3	9	12	17	1
1923	10	13	16	11	7	5	3	14	8	17	2	9	4	6	12	15	1
1924	17	15	13	6	12	5	4	11	2	16	6	8	3	10	9	14	1
1925	14	7	17	10	9	5	3	12	6	11	4	15	2	13	8	16	1
1926	11	9	8	15	7	3	1	13	6	16	4	14	5	10	12	17	2
1927	5	8	15	12	13	4	1	7	9	16	2	14	6	10	11	17	3
1928	10	16	15	5	12	2	1	9	8	13	3	14	6	7	11	17	4
1929	7	12	17	4	11	8	2	9	6	13	1	15	10	4	14	16	2
1930	9	6	11	2	13	5	1	12	16	17	4	13	8	7	15	10	3
1931	7	10	15	2	12	3	6	16	11	17	5	13	8	4	9	14	1
1932	10	14	15	13	8	3	6	12	10	16	4	7	5	2	9	17	1
1933	6	4	16	10	14	3	5	17	12	13	8	11	9	2	7	15	1
1934	3	8	13	7	14	5	1	12	10	17	9	15	11	2	4	16	5
1935	2	9	13	15	16	10	4	6	3	17	5	14	11	7	8	12	1
1936	1	9	16	4	10	8	11	15	2	17	5	7	6	14	13	12	3
1937	3	6	7	4	14	12	9	16	2	17	10	13	8	5	11	15	1
1938	5	6	16	10	14	9	4	15	2	17	12	7	3	8	13	11	1
1939	9	4	13	3	15	5	6	17	2	16	12	14	8	10	11	7	1
1946	15	8	6	5	10	6	3	11	2	16	13	4	11	17	14	8	1
1947	5	11	9	2	16	4	3	14	1	17	11	11	6	9	15	7	7
1948	6	13	1	8	9	15	5	11	3	17	14	12	2	16	7	10	4
1949	15	9	8	7	16	13	11	17	1	6	11	9	5	13	4	3	1

	Derbyshire	Durham	Essex	Glamorgan	Gloucestershire	Hampshire	Kent	Lancashire	Leicestershire	Middlesex	Northamptonshire	Nottinghamshire	Somerset	Surrey	Sussex	Warwickshire	Worcestershire	Yorkshire
1950	5	—	17	11	7	12	9	1	16	14	10	15	7	1	13	4	6	3
1951	11	—	8	5	12	9	16	3	15	7	13	17	14	6	10	1	4	2
1952	4	—	10	7	9	12	15	3	6	5	8	16	17	1	13	10	14	2
1953	6	—	12	10	6	14	16	3	3	5	11	8	17	1	2	9	15	12
1954	3	—	15	4	13	14	11	10	16	7	7	5	17	1	9	6	11	2
1955	8	—	14	16	12	3	13	9	6	5	7	11	17	1	4	9	15	2
1956	12	—	11	13	3	6	16	2	17	5	4	8	15	1	9	14	9	7
1957	4	—	5	9	12	13	14	6	17	7	2	15	8	1	9	11	16	3
1958	5	—	6	15	14	2	8	7	12	10	4	17	3	1	13	16	9	11
1959	7	—	9	6	2	8	13	5	16	10	11	17	12	3	15	4	14	1
1960	5	—	6	11	8	12	10	2	17	3	9	16	14	7	4	15	13	1
1961	7	—	6	14	5	1	11	13	9	3	16	17	10	15	8	12	4	2
1962	7	—	9	14	4	10	11	16	17	13	8	15	6	5	12	3	2	1
1963	17	—	12	2	8	10	13	15	16	6	7	9	3	11	4	4	14	1
1964	12	—	10	11	17	12	7	14	16	6	3	15	8	4	9	2	1	5
1965	9	—	15	3	10	12	5	13	14	6	2	17	7	8	16	11	1	4
1966	9	—	16	14	15	11	4	12	8	12	5	17	3	7	10	6	2	1
1967	6	—	15	14	17	12	2	11	2	7	9	15	8	4	13	10	5	1
1968	8	—	14	3	16	5	2	6	9	10	13	4	12	15	17	11	7	1
1969	16	—	6	1	2	5	10	15	14	11	9	8	17	3	7	4	12	13
1970	7	—	12	2	17	10	1	3	15	16	14	11	13	5	9	7	6	4
1971	17	—	10	16	8	9	4	3	5	6	14	12	7	1	11	2	15	13
1972	17	—	5	13	3	9	2	15	6	8	4	14	11	12	16	1	7	10
1973	16	—	8	11	5	1	4	12	9	13	3	17	10	2	15	7	6	14
1974	17	—	12	16	14	2	10	8	4	6	3	15	5	7	13	9	1	11
1975	15	—	7	9	16	3	5	4	1	11	8	13	12	6	17	14	10	2
1976	15	—	6	17	3	12	14	16	4	1	2	13	7	9	10	5	11	8
1977	7	—	6	14	3	11	1	16	5	1	9	17	4	14	8	10	13	12
1978	14	—	2	13	10	8	1	12	6	3	17	7	5	16	9	11	15	4
1979	16	—	1	17	10	12	5	13	6	14	11	9	8	3	4	15	2	7
1980	9	—	8	13	7	17	16	15	10	1	12	3	5	2	4	14	11	6
1981	12	—	5	14	13	7	9	16	8	4	15	1	3	6	2	17	11	10
1982	11	—	7	16	15	3	13	12	2	1	9	4	6	5	8	17	14	10
1983	9	—	1	15	12	3	7	12	4	2	6	14	10	8	11	5	16	17
1984	12	—	1	13	17	15	5	16	4	3	11	2	7	8	6	9	10	14
1985	13	—	4	12	3	2	9	14	16	1	10	8	17	6	7	15	5	11
1986	11	—	1	17	2	6	8	15	7	12	9	4	16	3	14	12	5	10
1987	6	—	12	13	10	5	14	2	3	16	7	1	11	4	17	15	9	8
1988	14	—	3	17	10	15	2	9	8	7	12	5	11	4	16	6	1	13
1989	6	—	2	17	9	6	15	4	13	3	5	11	14	12	10	8	1	16
1990	12	—	2	8	13	3	16	6	7	1	11	13	15	9	17	5	4	10
1991	3	—	1	12	13	9	6	8	16	15	10	4	17	5	11	2	6	14
1992	5	18	1	14	10	15	2	12	8	11	3	4	9	13	7	6	17	16
1993	15	18	11	3	17	13	8	13	9	1	4	7	5	6	10	16	2	12
1994	17	16	6	18	12	13	9	10	2	4	5	3	11	7	8	1	15	13

Note: From 1969 onwards, positions have been given in accordance with the Championship regulations which state that "Should *any* sides in the table be equal on points the side with most wins will have priority".

TCCB COUNTY PITCHES TABLE OF MERIT

First-Class Matches

		Points	Matches	Average in 1994	Average in 1993
1	Somerset (12)	98	10	4.90	4.56
2	Derbyshire (6)	96	10	4.80	4.67
	Surrey (6)	96	10	4.80	4.67
4	Warwickshire (5)	76	8	4.75	4.09
5	Hampshire (5)	94	10	4.70	4.83
	Sussex (4)	94	10	4.70	4.85
7	Yorkshire (16)	103	11	4.68	4.15
8	Nottinghamshire (2)	102	11	4.64	4.89
9	Durham (8)	82	9	4.56	4.65
	Northamptonshire (14)	82	9	4.56	4.28
11	Glamorgan (13)	89	10	4.45	4.40
12	Leicestershire (11)	79	9	4.39	4.60
13	Middlesex (18)	114	13	4.38	3.91
14	Lancashire (10)	86	10	4.30	4.64
15	Gloucestershire (2)	103	12	4.29	4.89
16	Essex (15)	74	9	4.11	4.27
17	Worcestershire (1)	90	11	4.09	4.90
18	Kent (8)	78	10	3.90	4.65
	Oxford University	65	7	4.64	4.81
	Cambridge University	57	8	3.56	4.33

One-Day Matches

		Points	Matches	Average in 1994	Average in 1993
1	Nottinghamshire (3)	99	10	4.95	4.70
	Somerset (18)	99	10	4.95	3.80
3	Surrey (9)	147	15	4.90	4.45
4	Lancashire (1)	102	11	4.64	4.80
5	Hampshire (7)	101	11	4.59	4.56
6	Essex (15)	82	9	4.56	4.00
7	Durham (12)	80	9	4.44	4.20
8	Gloucestershire (4)	88	10	4.40	4.68
	Kent (6)	88	10	4.40	4.65
10	Sussex (5)	96	11	4.36	4.67
11	Derbyshire (2)	95	11	4.32	4.78
12	Warwickshire (17)	111	13	4.27	3.96
13	Yorkshire (11)	76	9	4.22	4.36
14	Leicestershire (16)	91	11	4.14	3.96
15	Glamorgan (10)	89	11	4.05	4.38
16	Northamptonshire (14)	78	10	3.90	4.04
17	Middlesex (8)	101	13	3.88	4.53
18	Worcestershire (12)	84	11	3.81	4.20
	Oxford University	8	1	4.00	—
	Cambridge University	0	0	—	—

In both tables 1993 positions are shown in brackets. Each umpire in a game marks the pitch on the following scale of merit: 6 – very good; 5 – good; 4 – above average; 3 – below average; 2 – poor; 1 – unfit.

The tables, provided by the TCCB, cover all major matches, including Tests etc., played on grounds under the county's jurisdiction. Middlesex pitches at Lord's are the responsibility of MCC.

DERBYSHIRE

President: 1994 – C. S. Elliott
1995 – G. L. Willatt
Chairman: M. A. Horton
Chairman, Cricket Committee: B. Holling
Secretary/General Manager: R. G. Taylor
Captain: K. J. Barnett
Coach: A. Hill
Head Groundsman: S. Birks
Scorer: S. W. Tacey

Derbyshire ended a dispiriting season in 17th place, their lowest in the Championship since they were bottom in 1974, and made only fleeting impressions on the one-day competitions. However, the decline on the field was balanced by an astonishing improvement in the financial state of the club. In 1993, the overdraft touched a life-threatening £480,000; by the end of last September, the deficit was cleared. Part of this was due to a legacy, ultimately £235,000, from the estate of Frank Stretton, a Derbyshire farmer. But great credit was also due to the guidance of the club chairman Mike Horton, now a member of the Test and County Cricket Board finance committee. In the autumn, the club announced a record profit of £60,956.

The hope was that Ian Bishop would resume his place as the overseas player, and he returned to Derby in April for tests to see if his back injury had cleared. Derbyshire were optimistic but Bishop, not convinced he could accomplish a full season's bowling, declined the offer. A year earlier, Bishop was injured while playing for West Indies after the start of the English season and Derbyshire were caught short. This time, they had prepared the ground with Mohammad Azharuddin, who scored 2,016 runs for them in 1991. Azharuddin stepped almost straight from airport to crease and scored a wonderful 205 against Durham but, despite some magnificent innings on Sundays, never touched those heights again. Derbyshire were irritated when India called Azharuddin back in August to prepare for a one-day competition in Sri Lanka, and they withheld a fifth of his salary to compensate for the unexpectedly early departure. They were one of the counties keenest to discuss the role of overseas players in English cricket.

A dispute about the preparation of the Chesterfield pitch for the opening match set Derbyshire's season off on a false note and their problems were compounded by injuries to important players. Kim Barnett underwent a cartilage operation in May and Dominic Cork's attempt to hobble his way to fitness, following a knee operation on his return from the England A tour to South Africa, ended with further surgery. While they were out of action, Peter Bowler struggled along with a back injury that ultimately compelled him to rest. Derbyshire already had a gap in their top batting because John Morris had joined Durham and, for the first time since 1927, nobody completed 1,000 runs. Chris Adams might have done it had five of the last six Championship days not been washed out.

The batting was never reliable – Derbyshire scored only 25 batting points, the lowest total in the Championship. Tim O'Gorman enjoyed a spectacular run of form after being recalled from a Second Eleven match at

Blackpool to play at Ilkeston in May. O'Gorman scored 658 runs in eight completed first-class innings, including centuries against Glamorgan, Lancashire and the New Zealanders, in Derbyshire's first victory over a touring team since they beat the South Africans in 1965. But when his sequence ended, the middle order became increasingly fallible. Barnett's decision to bat at about No. 5 while giving the promising Adrian Rollins a chance to open was not a success. The problems were worsened by injuries to Cork and Frank Griffith and Test demands on Phillip DeFreitas, whose performances after joining Derbyshire from Lancashire compelled attention. DeFreitas made the transition smoothly; however, Colin Wells, engaged from Sussex, found the season one long battle.

Devon Malcolm, disappointed to be omitted by England after the First Test against New Zealand, responded by taking more wickets for Derbyshire than ever before. He developed greater consistency and created Test history when he was recalled to face South Africa at The Oval. He and DeFreitas were selected to tour Australia, while Cork was a near miss after playing in two limited-overs internationals. There were signs of labour in Derbyshire's attack although Simon Base, thought to have been lost permanently to South African cricket, came back usefully, especially on Sundays. Matthew Vandrau made progress as an off-spinner but Ole Mortensen announced his retirement before the end of the summer. He was justly proud of being the first Dane to play county cricket and was a bowler in the true Derbyshire tradition of miserly seam, even if his responses to setbacks were not as phlegmatic as Les Jackson's. It will be quieter for umpires this year. He has become director of coaching in Denmark.

The best days of the season were against Lancashire. In a first-round match that provided an instant re-run of the 1993 Benson and Hedges Cup final, Derbyshire were in an apparently hopeless position until Cork, ably supported by Wells, wrenched the game round by hitting an unbeaten 64 from 34 balls. The Championship match, at Blackpool, had statisticians in high excitement. Between two of the longest innings in Championship history, DeFreitas and Malcolm hustled out Lancashire in 24 overs, but Derbyshire had only an over to spare when they won on the fourth day. They also equalled their world record, set against Middlesex earlier in July, by conceding 81 extras. The number of no-balls offered by Derbyshire throughout the season was a source of irritation to members.

Barnett admitted that too many players, including himself, failed to perform to known capacity. His re-election as captain for a 13th season was a formality, and rightly so. He later said 1995 would be his last year in charge. Such a long period in office can feel stifling to others with ambitions, and, following Morris's departure a year earlier, Bowler left for Somerset after the season, saying he no longer wanted to play under Barnett. Barnett said that if Bowler had stayed, he might have been the one looking for a move. Morris and Bowler are the only two English players to average 40 over a significant career with Derbyshire. South African batsman Daryll Cullinan was engaged as the overseas player for 1995, not least because of an intense desire to test himself in county cricket.

When they were pulled back from the brink of administrative chaos in 1993, Derbyshire won the Benson and Hedges Cup. With the club more stable than for years, they disappointed in all four competitions. The clarity of the financial planning needs to be applied to the cricket. – Gerald Mortimer.

DERBYSHIRE 1994

[*Bill Smith*

Back row: J. Brown (*youth coaching officer*), G. M. Pooley, D. J. Lovell, R. W. Sladdin, F. A. Griffith, A. S. Rollins, M. J. Vandrau, A. Richardson, A. J. Harris, M. Taylor. *Middle row:* R. G. Taylor (*secretary/general manger*), C. J. Adams, S. J. Base, P. A. J. DeFreitas, D. G. Cork, T. J. G. O'Gorman, C. M. Wells, A. Brentwood (*physiotherapist*), S. W. Tacey (*scorer*). *Front row:* K. M. Krikken, P. D. Bowler, B. J. M. Maher, K. J. Barnett (*captain*), A. Hill (*coach*), O. H. Mortensen, A. E. Warner. *Insets:* D. E. Malcolm, M. Azharuddin.

DERBYSHIRE RESULTS

All first-class matches – Played 18: Won 5, Lost 9, Drawn 4.

County Championship matches – Played 17: Won 4, Lost 9, Drawn 4.

Bonus points – Batting 25, Bowling 54.

Competition placings – Britannic Assurance County Championship, 17th; NatWest Bank Trophy, q-f; Benson and Hedges Cup, q-f; AXA Equity & Law League, 8th.

BRITANNIC ASSURANCE CHAMPIONSHIP AVERAGES

BATTING

	Birthplace	*M*	*I*	*NO*	*R*	*HS*	*Avge*
‡M. Azharuddin§	*Hyderabad, India*	9	17	1	712	205	44.50
‡K. J. Barnett	*Stoke-on-Trent*	14	23	2	841	148	40.04
‡C. J. Adams	*Whitwell*	17	31	3	926	109*	33.07
F. A. Griffith	*London*	3	5	1	123	36	30.75
‡T. J. G. O'Gorman	*Woking*	15	27	2	729	145	29.16
‡P. A. J. DeFreitas	*Scotts Head, Dominica*	8	13	1	338	108	28.16
A. S. Rollins	*Barking*	15	28	2	692	97	26.61
‡K. M. Krikken	*Bolton*	14	26	10	391	85*	24.43
M. J. Vandrau	*Epsom*	12	22	5	404	66	23.76
‡P. D. Bowler	*Plymouth*	13	23	0	546	88	23.73
‡D. G. Cork	*Newcastle-under-Lyme*	12	20	0	459	94	22.95
C. M. Wells	*Newhaven*	11	20	2	303	42	16.83
‡S. J. Base	*Maidstone*	7	11	1	149	33	14.90
‡A. E. Warner	*Birmingham*	10	15	3	96	24*	8.00
M. Taylor	*Bolton*	3	4	1	23	14*	7.66
‡D. E. Malcolm	*Kingston, Jamaica*	16	21	9	85	15*	7.08
R. W. Sladdin	*Halifax*	3	6	0	42	20	7.00

Also batted: A. J. Harris (*Ashton-under-Lyne*) (2 matches) 10, 1, 0; I. G. S. Steer (*Birmingham*) (2 matches) 27. ‡O. H. Mortensen (*Vejle, Denmark*) (1 match) did not bat.

* *Signifies not out.* ‡ *Denotes county cap.* § *Overseas player.*

The following played a total of seven three-figure innings for Derbyshire in County Championship matches – M. Azharuddin 2, T. J. G. O'Gorman 2, C. J. Adams 1, K. J. Barnett 1, P. A. J. DeFreitas 1.

BOWLING

	O	*M*	*R*	*W*	*BB*	*5W/i*	*Avge*
K. J. Barnett	54.2	5	173	13	5-31	1	13.30
P. A. J. DeFreitas	273.5	59	812	35	6-39	3	23.20
D. G. Cork	317.1	52	1,070	35	6-29	2	30.57
D. E. Malcolm	482.2	83	1,793	57	6-95	2	31.45
C. M. Wells	153.3	31	469	13	4-52	0	36.07
M. J. Vandrau	265.5	59	852	23	4-53	0	37.04
S. J. Base	176	26	693	17	5-92	1	40.76
A. E. Warner	256	53	817	19	4-39	0	43.00

Also bowled: C. J. Adams 30–3–114–3; M. Azharuddin 8–0–46–0; P. D. Bowler 1–0–17–0; F. A. Griffith 67.4–12–210–8; A. J. Harris 32–1–165–5; O. H. Mortensen 7–2–18–1; T. J. G. O'Gorman 0.5–0–8–0; A. S. Rollins 4–0–32–0; R. W. Sladdin 115–20–427–4; I. G. S. Steer 2–0–12–0; M. Taylor 71–18–180–4

Wicket-keepers: K. M. Krikken 26 ct, 2 st; A. S. Rollins 3 ct.

Leading Fielders: C. J. Adams 16; D. G. Cork 15.

DERBYSHIRE v DURHAM

At Chesterfield, April 28, 29, 30, May 1. Durham won by seven wickets. Durham 24 pts, Derbyshire 4 pts. Toss: Durham. County debuts: P. A. J. DeFreitas, C. M. Wells; J. I. Longley.

Durham made a marvellous start to their campaign to avoid a third successive wooden spoon. Two of their newcomers, Saxelby and Longley, scored maiden Championship hundreds and Morris added 90 against his old county. Saxelby's 181, from 238 balls, was Durham's highest individual innings yet. The total of 625 for six was their best, too, and the highest score at Queen's Park this century, while Sladdin's nought for 180 was the most expensive wicketless analysis in Derbyshire's history. But the innings of the match came from Azharuddin, after dogged Durham bowling enforced the follow-on. He raced to 205 from 192 balls, with six sixes, all off Graveney, and 21 fours, adding exactly 100 on the fourth morning. Of the 256 runs scored while he was in, only 33 came from his four partners. Despite his efforts, Durham passed their target of 159 with nearly 25 overs to spare. The blandness of the pitch, which produced an aggregate of 1,570 runs, bettered only four times in Championship history, caused an internal dispute; Barnett had wanted more grass left on it and ground committee chairman Ken Roe later resigned.

Close of play: First day, Durham 441-3 (S. Hutton 39*, P. Bainbridge 10*); Second day, Derbyshire 251-5 (M. Azharuddin 40*, P. A. J. DeFreitas 34*); Third day, Derbyshire 254-3 (A. S. Rollins 14*, M. Azharuddin 72*).

Durham

W. Larkins lbw b Cork	83	– c Adams b Cork	38
M. Saxelby c Krikken b Cork	181	– c Azharuddin b Malcolm	3
J. E. Morris c Adams b DeFreitas	90	– c Cork b DeFreitas	36
S. Hutton c Krikken b DeFreitas	78	– not out	33
*P. Bainbridge c Adams b DeFreitas	13	– not out	30
J. I. Longley not out	100		
A. C. Cummins c Krikken b DeFreitas	1		
†C. W. Scott not out	39		
B 2, l-b 4, w 2, n-b 32	40	L-b 2, n-b 20	22
1/169 2/359 3/393 4/445 5/521 6/531 (6 wkts dec.)	625	1/13 2/84 3/94 (3 wkts)	162

J. Wood, D. A. Graveney and S. J. E. Brown did not bat.

Bonus points – Durham 4, Derbyshire 1 (Score at 120 overs: 465-4).

Bowling: *First Innings*—Malcolm 28–3–108–0; Cork 23–3–96–2; Wells 22–6–85–0; DeFreitas 37–1–150–4; Sladdin 43.5–8–180–0. *Second Innings*—Malcolm 10–0–62–1; DeFreitas 11–1–41–1; Cork 10–1–47–1; Sladdin 1.1–0–10–0.

Derbyshire

*K. J. Barnett c Scott b Wood	69	– b Brown	11
P. D. Bowler c Hutton b Brown	28	– c Scott b Graveney	38
C. J. Adams c Graveney b Cummins	27	– c and b Brown	94
A. S. Rollins c Larkins b Brown	9	– c Scott b Brown	19
M. Azharuddin c Scott b Cummins	55	– c Morris b Bainbridge	205
C. M. Wells c Wood b Bainbridge	17	– c Larkins b Graveney	5
P. A. J. DeFreitas c Scott b Brown	52	– c Bainbridge b Graveney	8
D. G. Cork b Cummins	5	– b Cummins	20
†K. M. Krikken not out	18	– c Saxelby b Brown	1
R. W. Sladdin c Bainbridge b Wood	20	– c Hutton b Brown	0
D. E. Malcolm c Bainbridge b Graveney	9	– not out	0
B 5, l-b 4, w 1, n-b 22	32	B 4, l-b 19, w 4, n-b 14	41
1/84 2/123 3/155 4/155 5/188 6/286 7/292 8/294 9/326	341	1/17 2/149 3/169 4/305 5/327 6/383 7/425 8/441 9/441	442

Bonus points – Derbyshire 3, Durham 4.

Bowling: *First Innings*—Cummins 26–5–87–3; Wood 22–4–96–2; Brown 24–2–96–3; Bainbridge 14–4–34–1; Graveney 11.1–4–19–1. *Second Innings*—Cummins 23–4–72–1; Brown 21.5–7–93–5; Graveney 42–11–144–3; Wood 11–0–49–0; Bainbridge 16–4–61–1.

Umpires: D. J. Constant and A. A. Jones.

At Southampton, May 5, 6, 7, 9. DERBYSHIRE drew with HAMPSHIRE.

At The Oval, May 12, 13, 14, 16. DERBYSHIRE lost to SURREY by an innings and 138 runs.

DERBYSHIRE v WORCESTERSHIRE

At Derby, May 19, 20, 21, 23. Drawn. Derbyshire 4 pts, Worcestershire 7 pts. Toss: Worcestershire. Championship debut: T. Edwards.

Worcestershire finished the first day in a strong position – 24 behind with six wickets in hand – but poor weather prevented them from following it up. Missing Barnett and Cork, both absent with knee injuries, Derbyshire lacked direction or substance. Moody wrapped their innings up in only 58 overs with his best Championship figures. Krikken, twice hit on the helmet while batting, passed the wicket-keeping duties to Rollins after seven balls of Worcestershire's reply, not long before Weston retired after a similar blow from Malcolm. When two days, as well as the Sunday game, were washed out, Curtis decided to aim for an innings victory, helped by Tolley's enterprising 84, his highest score. The plan almost worked: Derbyshire were still behind when their fifth wicket fell. But Krikken and Griffith saw them to safety in miserable conditions.

Close of play: First day, Worcestershire 164-4 (C. M. Tolley 25*); Second day, No play; Third day, No play.

Derbyshire

P. D. Bowler lbw b Tolley	30	– c Edwards b Newport	46
A. S. Rollins lbw b Tolley	9	– lbw b Moody	25
C. J. Adams c Edwards b Newport	31	– c sub b Newport	0
*M. Azharuddin lbw b Tolley	6	– lbw b Tolley	4
T. J. G. O'Gorman c Edwards b Newport	10	– c Leatherdale b Brinkley	6
M. J. Vandrau c Curtis b Moody	41	– b Leatherdale	9
†K. M. Krikken lbw b Moody	22	– not out	21
F. A. Griffith c Edwards b Moody	23	– not out	30
A. E. Warner lbw b Moody	6		
A. J. Harris b Newport	0		
D. E. Malcolm not out	0		
B 4, l-b 4, n-b 2	10	B 6, l-b 8, w 3, n-b 20	37
1/36 2/51 3/75 4/91 5/93 6/156 7/167 8/175 9/184	188	1/60 2/67 3/94 4/98 5/113 6/131	(6 wkts) 178

Bonus points – Worcestershire 4.

Bowling: *First Innings*—Radford 17–3–55–0; Tolley 17–5–52–3; Newport 12–1–42–3; Brinkley 3–0–7–0; Moody 9–3–24–4. *Second Innings*—Radford 14–2–34–0; Tolley 9–0–43–1; Moody 10–1–36–1; Newport 11–1–20–2; Leatherdale 9–3–14–1; Brinkley 5–2–13–1; Illingworth 2–1–4–0.

Worcestershire

*T. S. Curtis c O'Gorman b Griffith	31	N. V. Radford lbw b Griffith	18
W. P. C. Weston retired hurt	23	J. E. Brinkley c Adams b Harris	4
G. R. Haynes c Griffith b Harris	26	†T. Edwards not out	2
T. M. Moody lbw b Harris	0		
D. A. Leatherdale c Adams b Warner	39	B 13, l-b 5, w 2, n-b 16	36
C. M. Tolley c O'Gorman b Griffith	84		—
P. J. Newport b Malcolm	18	1/67 2/67 3/110 4/164 5/189	302
R. K. Illingworth b Malcolm	21	6/249 7/286 8/298 9/302	

Bonus points – Worcestershire 3, Derbyshire 4.

W. P. C. Weston retired hurt at 25.

Bowling: Malcolm 23–7–111–2; Warner 22–6–72–1; Harris 12–1–40–3; Griffith 15–1–58–3; Vandrau 2–1–3–0.

Umpires: A. A. Jones and R. A. White.

DERBYSHIRE v NOTTINGHAMSHIRE

At Ilkeston, May 26, 27, 28, 30. Nottinghamshire won by one wicket. Nottinghamshire 19 pts, Derbyshire 5 pts. Toss: Nottinghamshire.

Nottinghamshire won through on a fluctuating final day, in which they needed 209. With Derbyshire leaning heavily on DeFreitas's bowling, the visitors were in command while Johnson was in, but were 40 short when their eighth wicket fell. Noon saw them to a tense victory, with help from Pick and Afford. Storms during the week left the pitch damp, producing what umpire Shepherd called "a nice old-fashioned game". As Derbyshire's injury list expanded – Azharuddin withdrew with a virus and Warner was hit on the head during fielding practice – O'Gorman was summoned from a second-team match at Blackpool and began a fine run of form. He steered Derbyshire to a respectable first-innings score against the accurate Pick and Adams, after Lewis had sent down six overs and retired with a side strain. Malcolm and DeFreitas bowled Nottinghamshire out for 199 and there was time for Sladdin, out for nought that morning, to complete a pair within the day as night-watchman. Another sound innings from O'Gorman left Nottinghamshire a target of 254.

Close of play: First day, Derbyshire 211-7 (T. J. G. O'Gorman 40*, F. A. Griffith 29*); Second day, Derbyshire 39-2 (A. S. Rollins 18*, F. A. Griffith 15*); Third day, Nottinghamshire 45-0 (P. R. Pollard 20*, M. A. Crawley 15*).

Derbyshire

*P. D. Bowler b Adams	33	– c Adams b Mike	6
A. S. Rollins lbw b Crawley	19	– lbw b Mike	38
C. J. Adams b Pick	31	– (5) c sub b Afford	35
C. M. Wells c Afford b Adams	7	– (7) c sub b Afford	10
P. A. J. DeFreitas lbw b Pick	0	– (8) c Archer b Mike	34
M. J. Vandrau c Lewis b Pick	1	– (9) lbw b Pick	1
T. J. G. O'Gorman not out	44	– (6) c Noon b Pick	55
†K. M. Krikken lbw b Mike	27	– (10) c Noon b Pick	0
F. A. Griffith c Adams b Pick	31	– (4) c Noon b Adams	36
R. W. Sladdin b Pick	0	– (3) lbw b Mike	0
D. E. Malcolm b Pick	10	– not out	1
B 4, l-b 15, n-b 8	27	N-b 6	6
	—		—
1/65 2/65 3/81 4/83 5/85 6/114 7/165 8/218 9/220	230	1/23 2/23 3/72 4/96 5/132 6/142 7/218 8/220 9/221	222

Bonus points – Derbyshire 1, Nottinghamshire 3 (Score at 120 overs: 214-7).

Bowling: *First Innings*—Lewis 6–0–11–0; Pick 35.4–12–62–6; Crawley 33–16–48–1; Afford 19–6–45–0; Adams 17–10–19–2; Mike 15–5–26–1. *Second Innings*—Pick 22.5–6–53–3; Mike 21–6–71–4; Adams 32–15–37–1; Afford 24–8–49–2; Crawley 11–7–12–0.

Nottinghamshire

P. R. Pollard c Bowler b Malcolm	10 – c Griffith b DeFreitas	53
M. A. Crawley b Malcolm	9 – c Rollins b DeFreitas	20
J. C. Adams c Rollins b DeFreitas	32 – c Krikken b DeFreitas	0
*R. T. Robinson c Rollins b DeFreitas	12 – c Adams b Vandrau	18
P. Johnson c O'Gorman b Malcolm	19 – lbw b Griffith	62
G. F. Archer b DeFreitas	52 – c Krikken b Griffith	3
C. C. Lewis c Krikken b Sladdin	29 – c Adams b Sladdin	19
†W. M. Noon b Wells	0 – (9) not out	26
G. W. Mike b Malcolm	24 – (8) lbw b Malcolm	5
R. A. Pick c Adams b Malcolm	2 – lbw b DeFreitas	15
J. A. Afford not out	1 – not out	1
B 2, l-b 1, n-b 6	9 L-b 11, n-b 22	33
1/17 2/38 3/68 4/73 5/90 6/137 7/138 8/187 9/190	199 1/66 2/76 3/93 4/171 5/175 6/181 7/200 8/214 9/245	(9 wkts) 255

Bonus points – Derbyshire 4.

Bowling: *First Innings*—Malcolm 24.4–7–59–5; DeFreitas 22–7–39–3; Griffith 13–4–35–0; Wells 12–2–29–1; Sladdin 9–2–34–1. *Second Innings*—Malcolm 24.3–2–91–1; DeFreitas 25–8–61–4; Sladdin 11–2–48–1; Griffith 8–3–19–2; Vandrau 8–1–25–1.

Umpires: J. C. Balderstone and D. R. Shepherd.

DERBYSHIRE v LEICESTERSHIRE

At Derby, June 9, 10, 11. Leicestershire won by seven wickets. Leicestershire 22 pts, Derbyshire 8 pts. Toss: Leicestershire.

Derbyshire lost their grip so completely that they were beaten in three days, after threatening to make Leicestershire follow on. DeFreitas had given their first innings depth with his first Championship century for four years, reaching the mark from 114 balls with 15 fours. Leicestershire were 12 short of making them bat again with their last pair together. Pierson and Millns would still have failed had Malcolm not conceded runs with such abandon. But, having achieved safety, Leicestershire took hold of the game. They took four wickets when Derbyshire batted again on Friday evening and, on the third day, captured the last six for 30. Derbyshire's bowling and fielding, with three catches dropped, were just as unreliable and Leicestershire romped to their fourth victory in five matches inside 60 overs. DeFreitas, again playing a lone hand, was awarded his county cap by Derbyshire, the third of his career; Wells was capped by Leicestershire.

Close of play: First day, Derbyshire 392; Second day, Derbyshire 97-4 (M. Azharuddin 20*, K. M. Krikken 4*).

Derbyshire

*K. J. Barnett c Nixon b Millns	4 – c Nixon b Mullally	12
P. D. Bowler c Simmons b Wells	39 – lbw b Wells	17
C. J. Adams c Briers b Millns	94 – c Parsons b Wells	16
M. Azharuddin lbw b Wells	7 – run out	39
T. J. G. O'Gorman c Nixon b Simmons	75 – lbw b Parsons	9
C. M. Wells lbw b Wells	8 – (7) run out	2
P. A. J. DeFreitas c Nixon b Simmons	108 – (8) c Simmons b Wells	0
M. J. Vandrau c Nixon b Pierson	31 – (9) not out	9
†K. M. Krikken not out	2 – (6) b Mullally	9
A. E. Warner c and b Pierson	0 – lbw b Parsons	1
D. E. Malcolm c Mullally b Pierson	0 – b Parsons	0
B 2, l-b 15, w 1, n-b 6	24 B 9, l-b 6, w 10, n-b 4	29
1/4 2/61 3/81 4/179 5/206 6/271 7/387 8/391 9/392	392 1/29 2/53 3/68 4/89 5/113 6/124 7/124 8/126 9/141	143

Bonus points – Derbyshire 4, Leicestershire 4.

Bowling: *First Innings*—Millns 19–3–91–2; Mullally 18–4–51–0; Parsons 21–0–75–0; Wells 15–3–68–3; Pierson 18.1–3–53–3; Simmons 10–1–37–2. *Second Innings*—Millns 10–2–24–0; Mullally 21–8–32–2; Wells 17–5–49–3; Parsons 9.3–4–17–3; Simmons 4–2–6–0.

Leicestershire

P. V. Simmons lbw b DeFreitas	14	– c DeFreitas b Vandrau	62
*N. E. Briers c Bowler b Warner	59	– c O'Gorman b DeFreitas	11
T. J. Boon c Adams b Malcolm	8	– c Vandrau b Malcolm	33
J. J. Whitaker c O'Gorman b Malcolm	75	– not out	79
V. J. Wells lbw b DeFreitas	13	– not out	59
B. F. Smith c Azharuddin b Malcolm	11		
†P. A. Nixon b Wells	0		
G. J. Parsons c O'Gorman b Wells	12		
A. R. K. Pierson c DeFreitas b Wells	32		
A. D. Mullally c Vandrau b Wells	11		
D. J. Millns not out	13		
L-b 2, n-b 23	25	B 3, l-b 9, n-b 8	20
1/21 2/34 3/133 4/162 5/189 6/190 7/210 8/216 9/231	273	1/57 2/97 3/147 (3 wkts)	264

Bonus points – Leicestershire 2, Derbyshire 4.

Bowling: *First Innings*—Malcolm 18–0–121–3; DeFreitas 17–4–47–2; Warner 18–7–42–1; Wells 18.5–4–61–4. *Second Innings*—DeFreitas 17–4–40–1; Malcolm 16–1–90–1; Warner 9–0–45–0; Vandrau 17.4–4–77–1.

Umpires: V. A. Holder and A. G. T. Whitehead.

At Cardiff, June 16, 17, 18, 20. DERBYSHIRE beat GLAMORGAN by eight wickets.

At Derby, June 25, 26, 27. DERBYSHIRE beat NEW ZEALANDERS by an innings and 18 runs (See New Zealand tour section).

DERBYSHIRE v MIDDLESEX

At Derby, June 30, July 1, 2. Middlesex won by an innings and 96 runs. Middlesex 23 pts, Derbyshire 5 pts. Toss: Derbyshire.

Nineteen-year-old seamer Richard Johnson became the first bowler to take all ten wickets in the Championship for 30 years, since Ian Thomson, for Sussex against Warwickshire at Worthing in 1964. In Derbyshire's second innings, Johnson captured seven for 17 in his first nine overs, rested after 12 and completed his task after tea when Taylor was caught at third slip. The opening batsman Haynes bowled the last two overs from the other end, in an attempt to ensure that Johnson took the final wicket, and had a fright when Malcolm almost played on. Although Johnson was helped by reckless batting, it was an outstanding feat by a young man in his first full season. Only one player younger than Johnson had taken ten in a first-class innings: 18-year-old Imran Adil of Bahawalpur in 1989-90. Johnson's previous best was four for 64 against Durham a week earlier – though he had attracted attention by dismissing Lara in both the Benson and Hedges Cup and the Championship. "It hasn't quite sunk in," he said afterwards. "The ball did a little bit off the seam, but it didn't really swing." Middlesex completed their third successive win, with a day to spare. Barnett had held the first innings together with an excellent century, which took him past 20,000 first-class runs. But in good batting conditions Middlesex piled on their highest total against Derbyshire. Gatting and Ramprakash, who added 202 in 44 overs, and Carr all scored hundreds. The innings of 545 also contained a world record 81 extras, 54 of them in no-balls under the two-run penalty rule. That beat the 78 conceded by Queensland against South Australia in 1991-92, which also included double no-balls, and the Championship record, 73 by Kent against Northamptonshire in 1955.

Close of play: First day, Derbyshire 313-7 (A. S. Rollins 38*); Second day, Middlesex 394-3 (M. R. Ramprakash 110*, J. D. Carr 17*).

Derbyshire

*K. J. Barnett c Brown b Johnson	148	– c Emburey b Johnson	4
M. J. Vandrau b Feltham	31	– b Johnson	0
C. J. Adams c Gatting b Shine	17	– (4) c Carr b Johnson	8
T. J. G. O'Gorman c Gatting b Emburey	39	– (3) c Emburey b Johnson	18
D. G. Cork run out	0	– c Feltham b Johnson	4
†A. S. Rollins not out	53	– c and b Johnson	2
C. M. Wells c Shine b Feltham	8	– b Johnson	32
A. E. Warner c Haynes b Emburey	0	– c Brown b Johnson	2
S. J. Base c Carr b Feltham	7	– lbw b Johnson	20
M. Taylor b Feltham	1	– c Ramprakash b Johnson	5
D. E. Malcolm c Roseberry b Feltham	4	– not out	1
L-b 17, w 1, n-b 18	36	B 2, l-b 4, w 1, n-b 2	9
1/96 2/124 3/219 4/220 5/285 6/313 7/313 8/326 9/334	344	1/4 2/9 3/30 4/34 5/35 6/36 7/43 8/93 9/104	105

Bonus points – Derbyshire 3, Middlesex 3 (Score at 120 overs: 331-8).

Bowling: *First Innings*—Johnson 20–5–65–1; Shine 17–0–93–1; Feltham 29.5–8–69–5; Emburey 30–14–43–2; Tufnell 30–9–57–0. *Second Innings*—Johnson 18.5–6–45–10; Feltham 12–4–37–0; Shine 6–2–15–0; Tufnell 2–1–2–0; Haynes 2–2–0–0.

Middlesex

D. L. Haynes c Rollins b Malcolm	46	J. E. Emburey b Wells	0
M. A. Roseberry lbw b Base	18	K. J. Shine b Cork	0
*M. W. Gatting run out	147	P. C. R. Tufnell b Wells	5
M. R. Ramprakash c sub b Malcolm	131		
J. D. Carr not out	108	B 11, l-b 16, n-b 54	81
†K. R. Brown lbw b Base	2		
M. A. Feltham b Wells	4	1/43 2/128 3/330 4/433 5/452	545
R. L. Johnson lbw b Wells	3	6/495 7/519 8/519 9/520	

Bonus points – Middlesex 4, Derbyshire 2 (Score at 120 overs: 495-6).

Bowling: Malcolm 25–4–102–2; Warner 19–4–53–0; Base 20–2–88–2; Cork 22–2–108–1; Wells 22–5–52–4; Vandrau 18–2–58–0; Taylor 10–1–57–0.

Umpires: R. Palmer and P. Willey.

At Blackpool, July 14, 15, 16, 18. DERBYSHIRE beat LANCASHIRE by three wickets.

At Northampton, July 21, 22, 23. DERBYSHIRE lost to NORTHAMPTONSHIRE by ten wickets.

DERBYSHIRE v WARWICKSHIRE

At Chesterfield, July 28, 29, 30. Warwickshire won by 139 runs. Warwickshire 22 pts, Derbyshire 4 pts. Toss: Derbyshire.

Lara ended a relatively lean run (127 in five innings) with a dazzling hundred before lunch on the first day, when 16 wickets fell on a green pitch, which mortals found extremely difficult for batting. He was dropped at slip off Malcolm when 25, then took full command. He was especially severe on Vandrau, and reached his eighth century of the season from 94 balls. Base hurried out the tail but Derbyshire were soon in trouble against Munton, who exploited the conditions admirably and finished them off with four for seven in 23 balls next morning. When Warwickshire extended their 82-run lead by reaching 190 for two, Derbyshire looked like being overwhelmed. But Barnett, dismissing Moles in his first over, took five for 31, provoking the annual thought that he should bowl his leg-spin more. Even so, Warwickshire won their sixth successive Championship victory before tea on the third day and rose to the top of the table for the first time. Piper made 11 dismissals, a county record, and was also the first player to make seven dismissals in an innings in consecutive matches.

Close of play: First day, Derbyshire 165-6 (M. J. Vandrau 7*, K. M. Krikken 3*); Second day, Derbyshire 26-1 (A. S. Rollins 17*, S. J. Base 0*).

Warwickshire

A. J. Moles c and b Base	17	– c Cork b Barnett	63
R. G. Twose hit wkt b Malcolm	5	– c Azharuddin b Base	0
B. C. Lara c Barnett b Cork	142	– lbw b Base	51
D. P. Ostler c Base b Malcolm	6	– c Rollins b Vandrau	68
T. L. Penney lbw b Wells	41	– c and b Vandrau	20
J. D. Ratcliffe lbw b Base	8	– b Barnett	3
†K. J. Piper c and b Cork	15	– c Adams b Barnett	1
G. Welch c Barnett b Base	10	– lbw b Barnett	20
N. M. K. Smith b Base	6	– c O'Gorman b Vandrau	7
D. R. Brown c O'Gorman b Base	1	– not out	3
*T. A. Munton not out	3	– c Cork b Barnett	0
N-b 26	26	B 5, l-b 6, n-b 12	23
1/13 2/51 3/64 4/224 5/239 6/250 7/270 8/270 9/273	280	1/0 2/76 3/190 4/214 5/219 6/223 7/233 8/251 9/257	259

Bonus points – Warwickshire 2, Derbyshire 4.

Bowling: *First Innings*—Malcolm 11–2–38–2; Cork 19.2–1–79–2; Base 17.5–2–92–5; Vandrau 5–0–59–0; Wells 4.4–2–12–1. *Second Innings*—Malcolm 11–2–58–0; Base 11–2–41–2; Cork 12–2–31–0; Vandrau 24–1–87–3; Barnett 12.3–2–31–5.

Derbyshire

*K. J. Barnett c Ostler b Munton	16	– (7) c Piper b Welch	13
D. G. Cork c Piper b Munton	46	– (1) c Piper b Smith	8
C. J. Adams c Piper b Twose	25	– (4) c Piper b Welch	41
T. J. G. O'Gorman run out	12	– (5) c Piper b Munton	0
M. Azharuddin c Piper b Munton	28	– (6) c Penney b Smith	36
A. S. Rollins c Penney b Twose	1	– (2) c Piper b Munton	18
M. J. Vandrau not out	18	– (9) c Piper b Smith	26
†K. M. Krikken lbw b Munton	18	– (10) not out	16
C. M. Wells c Twose b Munton	0	– (8) b Smith	24
S. J. Base c Ostler b Munton	0	– (3) st Piper b Smith	1
D. E. Malcolm c Piper b Munton	7	– b Brown	0
L-b 4, n-b 23	27	B 6, l-b 6, n-b 7	19
1/54 2/83 3/114 4/126 5/133 6/155 7/186 8/188 9/188	198	1/22 2/28 3/34 4/35 5/86 6/112 7/126 8/172 9/199	202

Bonus points – Warwickshire 4.

Bowling: *First Innings*—Munton 25.2–5–52–7; Welch 21–4–83–0; Brown 6–1–26–0; Twose 14–3–31–2; Smith 2–1–2–0. *Second Innings*—Welch 20–9–49–2; Munton 22–6–57–2; Smith 28–6–69–5; Lara 1–0–4–0; Brown 3–0–11–1.

Umpires: B. Dudleston and P. Willey.

DERBYSHIRE v GLOUCESTERSHIRE

At Chesterfield, August 4, 5, 6, 8. Derbyshire won by 155 runs. Derbyshire 21 pts, Gloucestershire 4 pts. Toss: Gloucestershire.

In conditions ideal for seam and swing, Derbyshire had to battle for runs. With the injured Azharuddin missing what was due to be his last match before returning to India, they were relieved that Walsh was also unfit, nursing a neck strain. Rollins batted steadily to give them an advantage, which was then strengthened by their four-man seam attack. Gloucestershire, apart from Wright, lacked substance and their last eight wickets fell for 89. They conceded a lead of 52, which Derbyshire built up to 418 before declaring. In the final session of the third day, Malcolm took three wickets in 11 hostile overs. Gloucestershire fought well from an apparently hopeless 67 for four overnight, but Malcolm and Cork both returned their best figures of the season to date, bowling a combined 55.5 overs to share all the wickets. Malcolm sustained his pace and Cork, after two knee operations, continued to improve his rhythm.

Close of play: First day, Derbyshire 240-8 (K. M. Krikken 5*, S. J. Base 7*); Second day, Derbyshire 92-2 (C. J. Adams 27*, S. J. Base 0*); Third day, Gloucestershire 67-4 (V. J. Pike 9*, M. W. Alleyne 8*).

Derbyshire

P. D. Bowler c Alleyne b Williams	13	– lbw b Ball	42
A. S. Rollins c Ball b Cooper	79	– c Russell b Alleyne	14
C. J. Adams c Russell b Alleyne	29	– c Windows b Ball	68
T. J. G. O'Gorman c Wright b Dawson	1	– (5) c Windows b Alleyne	22
*K. J. Barnett c Alleyne b Williams	26	– (6) not out	77
D. G. Cork c Russell b Dawson	55	– (7) hit wkt b Pike	22
M. J. Vandrau c Ball b Cooper	2	– (8) c Wright b Hancock	21
†K. M. Krikken lbw b Cooper	7	– (9) c Pike b Hancock	3
A. E. Warner run out	0	– (10) not out	24
S. J. Base b Williams	12	– (4) c Wright b Williams	31
D. E. Malcolm not out	0		
B 1, l-b 6, w 1, n-b 15	23	B 1, l-b 15, w 1, n-b 25	42
1/23 2/64 3/65 4/117 5/206 6/226 7/226 8/226 9/247	247	1/39 2/91 3/162 4/178 5/196 6/233 7/282 8/294 (8 wkts dec.)	366

Bonus points – Derbyshire 1, Gloucestershire 4.

Bowling: *First Innings*—Cooper 29.3–12–44–3; Williams 23–3–82–3; Alleyne 16–2–50–1; Dawson 18–6–38–2; Ball 2–2–0–0; Pike 6–3–26–0. *Second Innings*—Cooper 20–4–59–0; Williams 21–4–66–1; Alleyne 23–5–71–2; Dawson 4–0–20–0; Ball 36–12–84–2; Pike 15–4–34–1; Hancock 5–0–16–2.

Gloucestershire

A. J. Wright lbw b Malcolm	65	– lbw b Cork	19
M. G. N. Windows c Krikken b Base	2	– c Krikken b Malcolm	9
T. H. C. Hancock c Adams b Warner	7	– c Rollins b Malcolm	7
R. I. Dawson lbw b Base	30	– c and b Malcolm	4
M. W. Alleyne c Bowler b Malcolm	12	– (6) lbw b Cork	36
R. J. Cunliffe c Rollins b Cork	17	– (7) lbw b Cork	29
*†R. C. Russell lbw b Warner	27	– (8) c Adams b Malcolm	49
R. C. Williams c Barnett b Warner	8	– (9) lbw b Malcolm	14
M. C. J. Ball c Rollins b Warner	0	– (10) b Malcolm	41
V. J. Pike c Krikken b Cork	1	– (5) c Krikken b Cork	27
K. E. Cooper not out	4	– not out	1
L-b 6, n-b 16	22	L-b 8, w 1, n-b 18	27
1/8 2/46 3/106 4/132 5/132 6/164 7/182 8/184 9/185	195	1/16 2/32 3/50 4/50 5/114 6/139 7/162 8/199 9/254	263

Bonus points – Derbyshire 4.

Bowling: *First Innings*—Malcolm 16–1–57–2; Base 15–1–63–2; Cork 15–4–30–2; Warner 15–6–39–4. *Second Innings*—Malcolm 29.5–8–95–6; Base 9–1–39–0; Cork 26–3–81–4; Vandrau 3–2–10–0; Warner 9–1–30–0.

Umpires: J. W. Holder and B. J. Meyer.

At Eastbourne, August 11, 12, 13, 15. DERBYSHIRE beat SUSSEX by one wicket.

DERBYSHIRE v KENT

At Derby, August 18, 19, 20, 22. Kent won by 69 runs. Kent 24 pts, Derbyshire 6 pts. Toss: Kent.

A sustained performance by McCague was central to Kent's victory and his match analysis, the best of the season, helped him towards a place in England's touring team. He took 15 for 147, which beat Arthur Fielder's 14 for 95 at Maidstone in 1907 as Kent's best against Derbyshire. Kent's openers began well, scoring 97 before Cork struck with the first hat-trick of his career, dismissing Benson, Walker and Hooper. But the middle order repaired the damage so effectively that Kent still totalled 392 – including 52 extras. McCague then dominated Kent's attack even more than Cork had Derbyshire's. He kept the ball up, did not try to bowl too fast and took nine in an innings for the first time – despite a bruised foot. It was, however, overshadowed on the day by Malcolm's nine in the Oval Test match. McCague's second-innings 47 was almost as important, as the last three wickets added 96. Derbyshire, set 352, more than they have ever scored in a fourth innings, started poorly and were never able to master McCague.

Close of play: First day, Kent 387-8 (M. J. McCague 11*, M. M. Patel 4*); Second day, Derbyshire 284-9 (A. E. Warner 0*); Third day, Derbyshire 105-3 (A. S. Rollins 37*, K. J. Barnett 43*).

Kent

T. R. Ward b Warner	86	– c Barnett b Warner	15
*M. R. Benson c Krikken b Cork	24	– c Krikken b Warner	0
M. J. Walker lbw b Cork	0	– c Base b Warner	23
C. L. Hooper lbw b Cork	0	– c Base b Vandrau	82
N. J. Llong c Cork b Vandrau	10	– c Krikken b Cork	16
M. V. Fleming c Rollins b Wells	48	– lbw b Cork	2
M. A. Ealham c Bowler b Cork	64	– c Adams b Warner	30
†S. A. Marsh lbw b Cork	88	– b Vandrau	2
M. J. McCague not out	16	– lbw b Vandrau	47
M. M. Patel c Adams b Cork	4	– c and b Vandrau	15
T. N. Wren run out	0	– not out	2
B 6, l-b 14, w 5, n-b 27	52	L-b 8, w 1, n-b 4	13
1/97 2/97 3/97 4/127 5/157 6/207 7/346 8/381 9/387	392	1/5 2/24 3/61 4/143 5/145 6/146 7/151 8/203 9/226	247

Bonus points – Kent 4, Derbyshire 4.

Bowling: *First Innings*—Warner 17–5–50–1; Base 26.2–4–105–0; Wells 11–0–48–1; Cork 30–9–80–6; Vandrau 22–3–84–1; Barnett 2–0–5–0. *Second Innings*—Warner 21–2–95–4; Base 10–1–39–0; Cork 15–2–52–2; Vandrau 21–10–53–4.

Derbyshire

P. D. Bowler c Marsh b McCague	88	– c Marsh b McCague	1
A. S. Rollins c Patel b McCague	7	– c Ward b McCague	52
C. J. Adams c Hooper b McCague	4	– lbw b Wren	11
T. J. G. O'Gorman b McCague	14	– c Marsh b Wren	0
*K. J. Barnett lbw b McCague	5	– c Ward b McCague	69
D. G. Cork c Llong b McCague	56	– c Hooper b McCague	5
C. M. Wells c Hooper b Patel	36	– lbw b Wren	42
M. J. Vandrau c Ward b McCague	27	– c Benson b McCague	66
†K. M. Krikken c Llong b McCague	19	– lbw b Hooper	9
A. E. Warner not out	3	– not out	2
S. J. Base b McCague	1	– b McCague	0
B 7, l-b 17, n-b 4	28	B 12, l-b 9, w 4	25
1/37 2/41 3/93 4/99 5/197 6/206 7/252 8/283 9/284	288	1/6 2/27 3/27 4/148 5/157 6/162 7/238 8/270 9/282	282

Bonus points – Derbyshire 2, Kent 4.

Bowling: *First Innings*—McCague 25.5–4–86–9; Wren 17–4–41–0; Ealham 18–7–51–0; Fleming 9–3–19–0; Patel 25–7–46–1; Hooper 10–3–21–0. *Second Innings*—McCague 23.3–7–61–6; Wren 20–4–67–3; Ealham 9–1–43–0; Hooper 25–7–51–1; Patel 17–6–29–0; Fleming 5–2–10–0.

Umpires: M. J. Kitchen and P. B. Wight.

At Sheffield, August 30, 31, September 1, 2. DERBYSHIRE lost to YORKSHIRE by 184 runs.

DERBYSHIRE v ESSEX

At Derby, September 8, 9, 10, 12. Drawn. Derbyshire 5 pts, Essex 4 pts. Toss: Essex.

Gooch was immediately rewarded for putting Derbyshire in on a richly green pitch, as Ilott took two wickets in the first over. But from 15 for four, the home team recovered through a splendid 94 by Cork, who was then unable to bowl after straining a muscle. Nevertheless, Gooch and extras, a frequent Derbyshire failing, made the only substantial contributions when Essex batted, with Base, Malcolm and emergency seamer Adams bowling effectively. Play was first delayed on Saturday, because the bowlers' approaches were too wet, despite being covered to statutory requirements, then washed out; the same fate befell the fourth day.

Close of play: First day, Derbyshire 212-8 (A. E. Warner 12*, S. J. Base 18*); Second day, Derbyshire 52-1 (A. S. Rollins 13*, K. M. Krikken 1*); Third day, No play.

Derbyshire

P. D. Bowler lbw b Ilott	0	– c Kasprowicz b Ilott	29
A. S. Rollins run out	8	– not out	13
C. J. Adams lbw b Ilott	0		
T. J. G. O'Gorman c Knight b Kasprowicz	1		
*K. J. Barnett c Knight b Kasprowicz	38		
D. G. Cork lbw b Stephenson	94		
I. G. S. Steer lbw b Stephenson	27		
†K. M. Krikken lbw b Ilott	1	– (3) not out	1
A. E. Warner b Ilott	17		
S. J. Base not out	31		
D. E. Malcolm c Hussain b Kasprowicz	8		
L-b 10, w 2, n-b 4	16	L-b 1, n-b 8	9
1/0 2/0 3/11 4/15 5/84 6/177 7/178 8/182 9/228	241	1/51	(1 wkt) 52

Bonus points – Derbyshire 1, Essex 4.

Bowling: *First Innings*—Ilott 22–6–65–4; Kasprowicz 18.4–4–68–3; Andrew 8–0–33–0; Stephenson 14–4–51–2; Such 5–1–14–0. *Second Innings*—Ilott 7–1–25–1; Kasprowicz 7–3–23–0; Stephenson 5–3–3–0.

Essex

*G. A. Gooch c O'Gorman b Malcolm	76
N. V. Knight c Steer b Malcolm	6
P. J. Prichard c Steer b Base	14
N. Hussain c Krikken b Base	0
R. C. Irani c Bowler b Base	6
J. P. Stephenson c Krikken b Warner	9
†M. A. Garnham c Krikken b Adams	8
M. S. Kasprowicz c Barnett b Adams	4
M. C. Ilott b Base	10
S. J. W. Andrew not out	0
P. M. Such b Malcolm	6
L-b 7, n-b 34	41
1/24 2/73 3/75 4/81 5/100 6/128 7/140 8/174 9/174	180

Bonus points – Derbyshire 4.

Bowling: Warner 16–3–49–1; Malcolm 9.2–0–51–3; Base 16–1–57–4; Adams 6–1–16–2.

Umpires: J. H. Harris and B. Leadbeater.

At Taunton, September 15, 16, 17, 19. DERBYSHIRE drew with SOMERSET.

DURHAM

Patrons: Sir Donald Bradman and A. W. Austin
President: I. D. Caller
Chairman: J. D. Robson
Director of Cricket: G. Cook
Chief Executive: G. A. Wright
Captain: 1994 – P. Bainbridge
1995 – M. A. Roseberry
Head Groundsman: T. Flintoft
Scorer: B. Hunt

For Durham it was a season in which their two small steps up the Championship table failed to reflect the giant strides made by some of their young players. To finish 16th, after two years of being saddled with the wooden spoon, might have been seen as a satisfactory achievement had they not won three of their first six Championship games. That was one more victory than they managed in either of their first two seasons, but the seven successive defeats which followed left them needing to beat bottom club Glamorgan in order to appease increasingly disgruntled members.

The victory was duly achieved, courtesy of a highly responsible innings of 123 not out by John Morris, but there was still time for Durham to suffer their second two-day reverse of the season, at home to Lancashire, to maintain their record of ten defeats in each Championship season. The fact that eight of their matches failed to reach the fourth day reflected the lack of application in their batting, which was at the root of their troubles.

They slipped two places to ninth in the Sunday League and bowed out of both major one-day events as soon as they encountered first-class opposition. The NatWest defeat by Derbyshire was particularly disappointing as Durham conceded 62 in extras, with Simon Brown bowling 15 wides to provide one of the few black marks on a season in which he earned the Player of the Year award, with 74 first-class wickets for the county. Another young pace bowler who made encouraging progress was John Wood, who took 45 wickets.

Jimmy Daley and Stewart Hutton both scored their maiden first-class centuries and averaged above 30, while the famous dropped catch which allowed Brian Lara to make his record-breaking 501 was virtually the only blemish on Chris Scott's best season with bat and gloves. He had 56 victims behind the stumps and scored the first two centuries of his career. There was also a maiden century for Scott's former Nottinghamshire team-mate Mark Saxelby, who hit 181 on his Championship debut for Durham at Chesterfield. Although the more intelligent bowlers soon spotted his liking for the leg side, he was one of only two batsmen to top 1,000.

The other was Morris, whose 1,376 runs fell a shade below his usual quota at Derbyshire because of a mid-season run in which he totalled 81 in 11 innings. He was disappointing on Sundays, but he won over most of the doubting fans during his magnificent match-winning innings against Glamorgan. This was not quite the best innings of the season: Wayne Larkins's unbeaten 158 against Gloucestershire must earn that accolade. Larkins missed several games through injury and finished just short of his

1,000. But at the age of 40 his strokeplay remained as thrilling as ever and he topped the county's first-class averages with 41.73. Jon Longley, recruited from Kent, showed more inclination than others to battle it out when the going got tough, but eventually made way for Daley in the Championship side and ended the season enjoying some success as a Sunday opener.

Hopes that Anderson Cummins would blossom after his first season's experience of English cricket proved unfounded: he took three more wickets, totalling 56, at a slightly higher average of 31.57. The club were sufficiently pleased with his commitment to reach a verbal agreement that he could return in 1996. Expecting him to be in the West Indies squad to tour England in 1995, they signed a one-year replacement in Indian all-rounder Manoj Prabhakar.

At the heart of the side's failure to maintain their early promise was the loss of form suffered by new captain Phil Bainbridge. The lack of all-rounders in the club was exposed, as Bainbridge, who topped the county's batting and bowling averages in the 1993 Championship, made 660 runs at an average of 22.00 and took just 14 wickets at 77.28. It was not surprising, then, that his position as captain should be in jeopardy. However, the matter was resolved in a manner that no one outside the club saw coming. Durham called a press conference in November and announced that they had signed the 28-year-old Middlesex batsman Mike Roseberry and that he would be taking over the leadership in 1995. Since Roseberry is a Durham boy, from Houghton-le-Spring – indeed his father is on the club's Board – and made his name as an exceptionally prolific schoolboy bat in local cricket, the move was calculated to go down well with the members. Morris was appointed vice-captain and Bainbridge agreed to play on.

His predecessor as captain, David Graveney, announced his retirement at the end of the season, and was then appointed full-time secretary of the Cricketers' Association. He had always provided the fans' strongest link with the team and through his unfailing patience, charm and good humour had become something of a cult figure. His greatest cheer-leader could often be heard shouting: "Haway Davy son", despite being much younger than the 41-year-old left-arm spinner.

Graveney's departure turned the end-of-season presentation evening into an emotional occasion. He was awarded life membership, along with four other figures associated with the beginnings of first-class status: Ian Botham, Simon Hughes, Paul Parker and head groundsman Tom Flintoft. Botham's award was not unanimously well-received, especially as his autobiography had just been published, describing his move to Durham as "one of the worst mistakes I ever made". There may well have been some substance in Botham's accusations of board-room wranglings at Durham. But the directors had the enormous satisfaction of seeing their new Riverside stadium at Chester-le-Street taking shape and two Second Eleven matches were played on the ground in August. The first phase of the development, costing £2.8 million, was due for completion in February, ready to stage seven of Durham's ten home first-class matches in 1995.

With three players appearing for England Under-19 against their Indian counterparts – Melvyn Betts, Steven Lugsden and Robin Weston – and four more introduced to the first-class game – David Cox, Jason Searle, Shaun Birbeck and Darren Blenkiron – the future continues to look bright, even if it seems to be a long time coming. – Tim Wellock.

DURHAM 1994

[*Bill Smith*

Back row: J. A. Daley, A. R. Fothergill, S. J. E. Brown, G. Wigham, J. Wood, I. Smith, P. J. Berry, J. I. Longley. *Middle row:* P. Forster (*Second Eleven scorer*), S. D. Birbeck, D. M. Cox, P. J. Wilcock, P. W. Henderson, R. M. S. Weston, M. M. Betts, D. A. Blenkiron, S. Hutton, J. P. Searle, B. Hunt (*First Eleven scorer*). *Front row:* A. Walker, G. Fowler, D. A. Graveney (*vice-captain*), P. Bainbridge (*captain*), W. Larkins, J. E. Morris, C. W. Scott. *Insets:* M. Saxelby, S. Lugsden.

DURHAM RESULTS

All first-class matches – Played 19: Won 5, Lost 10, Drawn 4.

County Championship matches – Played 17: Won 4, Lost 10, Drawn 3.

Bonus points – Batting 32, Bowling 57.

Competition placings – Britannic Assurance County Championship, 16th; NatWest Bank Trophy, 2nd round; Benson and Hedges Cup, 1st round; AXA Equity & Law League, 9th.

BRITANNIC ASSURANCE CHAMPIONSHIP AVERAGES

BATTING

	Birthplace	*M*	*I*	*NO*	*R*	*HS*	*Avge*
J. E. Morris	*Crewe*	17	31	1	1,369	204	45.63
W. Larkins	*Roxton*	13	23	2	879	158*	41.85
M. Saxelby	*Worksop*	15	29	0	1,034	181	35.65
J. A. Daley	*Sunderland*	8	15	2	454	159*	34.92
S. Hutton	*Stockton-on-Tees*	13	23	2	627	101	29.85
J. I. Longley	*New Brunswick, USA*	14	25	2	594	100*	25.82
A. C. Cummins§	*Packer's Valley, Barbados*	17	29	2	629	65	23.29
C. W. Scott	*Thorpe-on-the-Hill*	17	29	3	547	108	21.03
G. Fowler	*Accrington*	3	5	0	98	60	19.60
P. Bainbridge	*Stoke-on-Trent*	16	28	1	523	67	19.37
D. A. Graveney	*Bristol*	12	21	5	306	65*	19.12
S. J. E. Brown	*Cleadon*	16	23	9	234	69	16.71
J. Wood	*Wakefield*	13	19	2	177	51	10.41
A. Walker	*Emley*	4	7	2	34	13	6.80
S. Lugsden	*Gateshead*	4	4	1	2	2	0.66

Also batted: P. J. Berry (*Saltburn*) (1 match) 3, 0; D. M. Cox (*Southall*) (2 matches) 0, 0; J. P. Searle (*Bath*) (1 match) 5*, 0*. D. A. Blenkiron (*Solihull*) (1 match) did not bat.

** Signifies not out. § Overseas player. Durham have awarded all playing staff county caps.*

The following played a total of 12 three-figure innings for Durham in County Championship matches – J. E. Morris 4, M. Saxelby 2, C. W. Scott 2, J. A. Daley 1, S. Hutton 1, W. Larkins 1, J. I. Longley 1.

BOWLING

	O	*M*	*R*	*W*	*BB*	*5W/i*	*Avge*
S. J. E. Brown	525.1	78	1,928	66	6-68	5	29.21
A. C. Cummins	520.3	92	1,768	56	6-64	4	31.57
J. Wood	303.4	34	1,367	42	6-110	3	32.54
D. A. Graveney	447	117	1,235	31	6-80	1	39.83
P. Bainbridge	291.5	62	1,004	13	4-72	0	77.23

Also bowled: P. J. Berry 15–2–58–0; D. M. Cox 52.5–7–253–0; J. A. Daley 2–0–9–0; W. Larkins 5–0–39–0; S. Lugsden 85.2–11–348–3; J. E. Morris 27.5–3–125–1; J. P. Searle 1–0–7–0; A. Walker 116–23–369–8.

Wicket-keeper: C. W. Scott 53 ct, 2 st.

Leading Fielder: P. Bainbridge 13.

At Oxford, April 13, 14, 15. DURHAM beat OXFORD UNIVERSITY by 177 runs.

At Chesterfield, April 28, 29, 30, May 1. DURHAM beat DERBYSHIRE by seven wickets.

DURHAM v ESSEX

At Stockton-on-Tees, May 5, 6, 7, 9. Essex won by ten wickets. Essex 24 pts, Durham 2 pts. Toss: Essex.

Four hours were lost to rain on the first day, but that merely ensured that the match went into four days, as Essex quite outclassed their hosts. Their commanding total was based on a solid century from Prichard and a more handsome one from Hussain. Wood removed both, lbw, in a spell of three for six in 15 balls, to claim career-best figures of six for 110, though Irani hit him for two sixes in a maiden fifty. When Durham replied, Kasprowicz's late away-swing quickly undermined their batsmen; he finished with six for 61 and they followed on, 248 behind. An innings defeat was avoided only through Saxelby, already top scorer in the first innings. Despite looking ill at ease against Such, he stood firm to make 131 – following his 181 against Derbyshire – before he was ninth out, after more than six hours.

Close of play: First day, Essex 154-2 (P. J. Prichard 50*, N. Hussain 34*); Second day, Durham 101-3 (M. Saxelby 55*, D. A. Graveney 4*); Third day, Durham 202-4 (M. Saxelby 101*, J. I. Longley 5*).

Essex

*G. A. Gooch lbw b Wood	42	– not out	13
P. J. Prichard lbw b Wood	108	– not out	21
J. J. B. Lewis lbw b Brown	10		
N. Hussain lbw b Wood	101		
N. Shahid lbw b Graveney	26		
†M. A. Garnham c Scott b Wood	0		
R. C. Irani not out	58		
M. S. Kasprowicz run out	33		
M. C. Ilott lbw b Cummins	0		
P. M. Such b Wood	2		
J. H. Childs c Larkins b Wood	0		
L-b 16, w 5, n-b 22	43	N-b 2	2
1/78 2/93 3/278 4/298 5/304 6/341 7/387 8/406 9/411	423	(no wkt)	36

Bonus points – Essex 4, Durham 2 (Score at 120 overs: 371-6).

Bowling: *First Innings*—Cummins 30–7–94–1; Brown 15–2–50–1; Bainbridge 29–9–90–0; Graveney 29–8–63–1; Wood 26.2–0–110–6. *Second Innings*—Cummins 2–0–8–0; Wood 2.1–0–20–0; Bainbridge 1–0–8–0.

Durham

W. Larkins c Gooch b Kasprowicz	1	– b Childs	23
M. Saxelby b Kasprowicz	63	– lbw b Kasprowicz	131
J. E. Morris c Gooch b Kasprowicz	18	– c and b Ilott	64
S. Hutton c Hussain b Irani	14	– lbw b Ilott	0
D. A. Graveney b Kasprowicz	12	– (10) b Kasprowicz	12
*P. Bainbridge c and b Kasprowicz	4	– (5) b Such	5
J. I. Longley lbw b Ilott	1	– (6) lbw b Ilott	7
†C. W. Scott lbw b Irani	25	– (7) c Hussain b Such	0
A. C. Cummins c Hussain b Kasprowicz	12	– (8) b Such	21
J. Wood not out	5	– (9) b Such	5
S. J. E. Brown lbw b Gooch	1	– not out	1
L-b 3, w 2, n-b 14	19	B 1, l-b 9, n-b 2	12
1/5 2/51 3/97 4/115 5/122 6/123 7/127 8/151 9/174	175	1/63 2/164 3/164 4/185 5/214 6/215 7/243 8/249 9/280	281

Bonus points – Essex 4.

Bowling: *First Innings*—Ilott 21–2–87–1; Kasprowicz 21–7–61–6; Such 7–4–7–0; Irani 8–2–17–2; Gooch 1.3–1–0–1. *Second Innings*—Kasprowicz 13.5–2–55–2; Ilott 21–5–80–3; Childs 30–9–65–1; Such 47–21–61–4; Shahid 2–0–10–0.

Umpires: J. D. Bond and J. W. Holder.

At Nottingham, May 12, 13, 14. DURHAM lost to NOTTINGHAMSHIRE by eight wickets.

DURHAM v GLOUCESTERSHIRE

At Gateshead Fell, May 19, 20, 21, 23. Durham won by 108 runs. Durham 23 pts, Gloucestershire 4 pts. Toss: Durham.

On the first day, the match was dominated by Larkins, who became the first Durham player to carry his bat in first-class cricket, contributing a magnificent 158 not out to their total of 305. The second-highest scorer was extras with 31. With Walsh unplayable in the opening overs, Larkins was almost out before scoring, but went on to complete his highest innings for Durham off 265 balls. The pitch offered bounce and some lateral movement, and Gloucestershire batted ineptly. At 129 for nine, they needed 27 to avoid the follow-on. But Durham then allowed the last pair to put on 40 and collapsed themselves to 65 for six. Then Longley demonstrated sensible application in making an unbeaten 71, and Gloucestershire were left a target of 310. With eight wickets down, Durham claimed the extra half-hour on Saturday. However, bad light forced them to wait until Monday, when they needed only 13 balls to rise to fourth place in the Championship.

Close of play: First day, Gloucestershire 52-2 (S. G. Hinks 21*, M. W. Alleyne 19*); Second day, Durham 115-6 (J. I. Longley 36*, A. C. Cummins 24*); Third day, Gloucestershire 196-8 (M. C. J. Ball 26*, K. E. Cooper 0*).

Durham

W. Larkins not out	158	– c Russell b Walsh	0
M. Saxelby c Russell b Walsh	7	– c Russell b Smith	19
J. E. Morris c Wright b Walsh	0	– b Smith	17
S. Hutton c Russell b Alleyne	19	– lbw b Cooper	4
*P. Bainbridge lbw b Walsh	3	– c Russell b Smith	0
J. I. Longley c Ball b Walsh	16	– not out	71
†C. W. Scott lbw b Ball	10	– c Alleyne b Walsh	10
A. C. Cummins c Wright b Alleyne	26	– lbw b Cooper	27
J. Wood c Russell b Walsh	8	– c Hancock b Walsh	5
D. A. Graveney b Alleyne	16	– b Smith	9
S. J. E. Brown c Broad b Alleyne	11	– b Smith	5
B 2, l-b 12, w 1, n-b 16	31	L-b 4, n-b 2	6
1/11 2/17 3/101 4/113 5/139 6/154 7/224 8/239 9/278	305	1/0 2/36 3/43 4/43 5/45 6/65 7/124 8/139 9/163	173

Bonus points – Durham 3, Gloucestershire 4.

Bowling: *First Innings*—Walsh 28–10–88–5; Cooper 17–3–45–0; Smith 16–4–50–0; Alleyne 16.3–2–70–4; Ball 12–5–38–1. *Second Innings*—Walsh 26–7–52–3; Cooper 28–8–66–2; Smith 19.5–4–40–5; Alleyne 5–0–11–0.

Gloucestershire

B. C. Broad b Cummins	0	– b Brown	10
G. D. Hodgson lbw b Brown	2	– c Scott b Cummins	0
S. G. Hinks c Longley b Brown	21	– c Larkins b Cummins	1
M. W. Alleyne c Scott b Cummins	21	– b Wood	13
A. J. Wright c Brown b Wood	16	– c Bainbridge b Wood	39
T. H. C. Hancock c and b Bainbridge	30	– lbw b Wood	61
†R. C. Russell b Wood	6	– b Wood	0
M. C. J. Ball c Wood b Brown	8	– c Longley b Brown	29
*C. A. Walsh c Longley b Wood	5	– (10) not out	11
A. M. Smith not out	26	– (9) c Morris b Wood	5
K. E. Cooper c Bainbridge b Cummins	6	– b Brown	0
B 4, l-b 7, w 7, n-b 10	28	B 1, l-b 11, w 1, n-b 19	32
1/0 2/8 3/55 4/59 5/78 6/86 7/123 8/128 9/129	169	1/3 2/11 3/19 4/51 5/148 6/149 7/150 8/168 9/196	201

Bonus points – Durham 4.

In the second innings C. A. Walsh, when 11, retired hurt at 196-8 and resumed at 196-9.

Bowling: *First Innings*—Cummins 18.3–6–59–3; Brown 20–6–49–3; Wood 14–5–30–3; Bainbridge 5–1–18–1; Graveney 1–0–2–0. *Second Innings*—Cummins 17–5–26–2; Brown 18.4–4–43–3; Wood 18–5–48–5; Bainbridge 8–1–27–0; Graveney 27–10–45–0.

Umpires: J. C. Balderstone and V. A. Holder.

At Birmingham, June 2, 3, 4, 6. DURHAM drew with WARWICKSHIRE.

DURHAM v NORTHAMPTONSHIRE

At Hartlepool, June 9, 10, 11. Durham won by an innings and 87 runs. Durham 24 pts. Toss: Durham.

Durham's third Championship win – one more than they had achieved in either of their first two seasons – took less than three days against a side missing Ambrose and Lamb through injury. The visitors twice collapsed in the face of some excellent bowling from Cummins, who took ten wickets in a match for the first time. Each of Durham's first three wickets added 100 or more, but the highlights were a high-class 186 from Morris, following his double-hundred against Warwickshire, and a diligent maiden century for Hutton. His dismissal, on 101, prompted the declaration at 545 for eight. Bailey and Loye added 116 for the third wicket before Northamptonshire lost eight wickets for 24 as the ball began to swing on the second evening, and they followed on 389 behind. Despite impressive resistance from Curran, they were again undone by Cummins, who dismissed three tailenders for no runs in ten balls.

Close of play: First day, Durham 353-2 (J. E. Morris 166*, S. Hutton 35*); Second day, Northamptonshire 8-0 (N. G. B. Cook 3*, N. A. Felton 1*).

Durham

W. Larkins lbw b Taylor	77
G. Fowler c Ripley b Curran	60
J. E. Morris c Ripley b Curran	186
S. Hutton st Ripley b Cook	101
*P. Bainbridge lbw b Bowen	27
J. I. Longley c Ripley b Penberthy	1
A. C. Cummins run out	6
†C. W. Scott run out	31
J. Wood not out	27
B 4, l-b 15, n-b 10	29
1/100 2/252 3/384 4/446 5/447 6/464 7/510 8/545	(8 wkts dec.) 545

S. J. E. Brown and S. Lugsden did not bat.

Bonus points – Durham 4 (Score at 120 overs: 380-2).

Bowling: Taylor 36–6–124–1; Curran 26–4–80–2; Bowen 25–4–83–1; Penberthy 27–6–98–1; Cook 26.3–3–86–1; Bailey 19–2–55–0.

Northamptonshire

A. Fordham c Larkins b Cummins	3	– (3) c Scott b Brown 56
N. A. Felton lbw b Brown	9	– c Scott b Wood 12
*R. J. Bailey b Bainbridge	51	– (4) c Scott b Cummins 41
M. B. Loye c Larkins b Cummins	62	– (5) b Lugsden 5
R. J. Warren lbw b Brown	11	– (6) lbw b Cummins 13
K. M. Curran c Scott b Cummins	1	– (7) not out 91
A. L. Penberthy lbw b Cummins	2	– (8) lbw b Cummins 20
†D. Ripley not out	5	– (9) c Fowler b Cummins 0
M. N. Bowen b Cummins	0	– (10) lbw b Cummins 0
N. G. B. Cook lbw b Brown	4	– (1) c Scott b Brown 5
J. P. Taylor c Bainbridge b Brown	0	– c Brown b Wood 23
L-b 2, w 2, n-b 4	8	B 4, l-b 4, w 8, n-b 20 36
1/12 2/16 3/132 4/132 5/134 6/146 7/146 8/146 9/152	156	1/17 2/43 3/117 4/135 5/141 6/158 7/238 8/242 9/242 302

Bonus points – Durham 4.

Bowling: *First Innings*—Cummins 14–5–32–5; Brown 18.1–3–49–4; Wood 9–1–31–0; Lugsden 8–1–34–0; Bainbridge 2–0–8–1. *Second Innings*—Cummins 23–4–72–5; Brown 23–5–72–2; Wood 15.2–4–57–2; Lugsden 20–2–84–1; Bainbridge 3–0–5–0; Morris 4–2–4–0.

Umpires: G. I. Burgess and J. H. Hampshire.

At Hove, June 16, 17, 18. DURHAM lost to SUSSEX by eight wickets.

At Lord's, June 23, 24, 25. DURHAM lost to MIDDLESEX by an innings and 34 runs.

DURHAM v SURREY

At Darlington, June 30, July 1, 2, 4. Surrey won by 290 runs. Surrey 21 pts, Durham 7 pts. Toss: Surrey.

A maiden century by wicket-keeper Scott, 13 years after he made his first-class debut with Nottinghamshire, earned Durham a first-innings lead of 99. But after dominating the Championship leaders for the first two days, they were battered into submission by a stand of 222 in 39 overs between Bicknell and Alistair Brown. Bicknell equalled his career-best of 190, taking 300 balls, while Brown became the first person to make three first-class centuries against Durham, hitting 172 in 152 balls. He drove five sixes off Graveney, three of them clearing the stand into the football ground and a fourth going over on the first bounce. Thorpe's declaration at 538 for six left Durham needing 440 to win. But after reaching 52 for one on Saturday evening, they lost their last nine wickets for 97 in 32 overs on a steamy final day. Pigott, with his best return yet for Surrey, completed the demolition begun by Cuffy.

Close of play: First day, Durham 108-3 (S. Hutton 11*, P. Bainbridge 23*); Second day, Surrey 90-0 (D. J. Bicknell 58*, A. W. Smith 26*); Third day, Durham 52-1 (M. Saxelby 25*, D. A. Graveney 3*).

Surrey

D. J. Bicknell b Cummins	11	– c Scott b Wood	190
A. W. Smith c Larkins b Brown	25	– b Cummins	26
*G. P. Thorpe c Scott b Bainbridge	22	– b Brown	47
D. M. Ward b Brown	24	– b Graveney	23
A. D. Brown c Saxelby b Wood	26	– c Larkins b Brown	172
A. J. Hollioake c Hutton b Brown	1	– c Longley b Brown	46
†G. J. Kersey c Scott b Graveney	39	– not out	6
A. C. S. Pigott b Wood	1		
J. Boiling not out	34		
J. E. Benjamin b Graveney	0		
C. E. Cuffy b Brown	10		
B 3, l-b 11, w 1, n-b 28	43	B 9, l-b 8, w 3, n-b 8	28
1/38 2/59 3/99 4/99 5/105 6/155 7/162 8/226 9/226	236	1/98 2/193 3/230 4/452 5/525 6/538 (6 wkts dec.)	538

Bonus points – Surrey 1, Durham 4.

Bowling: *First Innings*—Cummins 21–6–47–1; Brown 20.4–5–62–4; Wood 13–2–46–2; Bainbridge 16–5–37–1; Graveney 8–4–21–2; Morris 3–0–9–0. *Second Innings*—Cummins 26–3–102–1; Brown 25.3–2–101–3; Wood 23–4–115–1; Graveney 21–2–99–1; Bainbridge 13–2–62–0; Morris 6–0–42–0.

Durham

W. Larkins b Cuffy	49	– lbw b Benjamin	21
M. Saxelby c Kersey b Cuffy	4	– c Thorpe b Pigott	43
J. E. Morris b Benjamin	15	– (4) c Kersey b Cuffy	0
S. Hutton run out	13	– (5) lbw b Benjamin	4
*P. Bainbridge c Ward b Cuffy	34	– (6) b Cuffy	13
J. I. Longley b Pigott	51	– (7) c Hollioake b Pigott	17
A. C. Cummins c Kersey b Pigott	15	– (8) c Brown b Pigott	25
†C. W. Scott c Hollioake b Benjamin	108	– (9) c Boiling b Pigott	4
J. Wood b Pigott	0	– (10) lbw b Smith	11
D. A. Graveney c Kersey b Benjamin	29	– (3) c Kersey b Cuffy	5
S. J. E. Brown not out	2	– not out	0
L-b 9, n-b 6	15	L-b 4, n-b 2	6
1/31 2/70 3/78 4/120 5/125 6/151 7/238 8/244 9/332	335	1/37 2/54 3/54 4/65 5/86 6/91 7/125 8/134 9/141	149

Bonus points – Durham 3, Surrey 4.

Bowling: *First Innings*—Cuffy 21–3–85–3; Benjamin 31.5–10–86–3; Smith 18–3–67–0; Pigott 26–8–65–3; Hollioake 3–1–7–0; Boiling 7–3–16–0. *Second Innings*—Cuffy 15–4–39–3; Benjamin 15–3–43–2; Smith 10–3–41–1; Pigott 9–2–22–4.

Umpires: D. J. Constant and K. J. Lyons.

At Chester-le-Street, July 12, 13, 14. DURHAM drew with SOUTH AFRICANS (See South African tour section).

DURHAM v LEICESTERSHIRE

At Durham University, July 21, 22, 23. Leicestershire won by an innings and five runs. Leicestershire 24 pts, Durham 5 pts. Toss: Durham. Championship debut: A. Sheriyar.

Durham were done for in three days, thanks to two hat-tricks for the visitors. The second, by 20-year-old left-arm pace bowler Alamgir Sheriyar, making his Championship debut, wrapped up Leicestershire's victory just before tea on the third day. The first hat-trick, by Wells, wrecked Durham's first innings. This was only the second occasion two different players have taken a hat-trick in the same first-class match: the other involved Garth le Roux and Clive Rice playing for South Africa against an Australian XI at Johannesburg in 1985-86, a match recognised as first-class by *Wisden* but not currently by ICC. Sheriyar was the second player to take a hat-trick on Championship debut. The other was H. A. Sedgwick, for Yorkshire against Worcestershire at Hull in 1906. In humid conditions, Durham declined from 87 for two to 109 for seven as Wells took five for 12 in 28 balls. Brown's career-best 69 assisted a partial recovery and he then helped to reduce Leicestershire to 50 for three. But poor fielding enabled them to take command, as Whitaker and Wells put on 184. Whitaker was rarely troubled in making a fluent 107. The only serious resistance in Durham's second innings came from Daley. In his first Championship match of the season, he played some glorious strokes in making 57.

Close of play: First day, Durham 225; Second day, Leicestershire 406-9 (D. J. Millns 27*, A. Sheriyar 5*).

Durham

G. Fowler c Wells b Sheriyar	4	– c Simmons b Wells	17
W. Larkins lbw b Wells	53	– c Pierson b Wells	17
J. E. Morris c Smith b Sheriyar	4	– c Parsons b Millns	1
M. Saxelby c Nixon b Millns	53	– c Nixon b Millns	23
J. A. Daley c Nixon b Wells	0	– c Nixon b Millns	57
*P. Bainbridge c Simmons b Wells	5	– lbw b Wells	17
A. C. Cummins c Simmons b Wells	0	– c Wells b Sheriyar	29
†C. W. Scott lbw b Wells	0	– c Nixon b Sheriyar	13
D. A. Graveney not out	13	– (10) c Nixon b Sheriyar	0
S. J. E. Brown c Pierson b Millns	69	– (9) not out	2
S. Lugsden b Millns	2	– b Sheriyar	0
B 5, l-b 5, w 10, n-b 2	22	L-b 8, w 2, n-b 12	22
1/9 2/43 3/87 4/87 5/109 6/109 7/109 8/155 9/161	225	1/39 2/40 3/40 4/116 5/137 6/171 7/195 8/198 9/198	198

Bonus points – Durham 1, Leicestershire 4.

In the first innings D. A. Graveney, when 1, retired hurt at 111 and resumed at 161.

Bowling: *First Innings*—Millns 16.1–2–57–3; Sheriyar 16–4–51–2; Parsons 4–0–19–0; Wells 18–7–50–5; Pierson 16–6–29–0; Simmons 4–0–9–0. *Second Innings*—Millns 16–2–64–3; Sheriyar 14–3–44–4; Wells 13–3–39–3; Pierson 4–0–13–0; Simmons 14–3–30–0.

Leicestershire

T. J. Boon run out	8
*N. E. Briers c Scott b Brown	10
J. J. Whitaker c and b Graveney	107
P. V. Simmons c Larkins b Cummins	5
V. J. Wells b Brown	77
B. F. Smith c Saxelby b Graveney	59
†P. A. Nixon c Scott b Cummins	36
G. J. Parsons c Morris b Brown	25
A. R. K. Pierson lbw b Graveney	5
D. J. Millns not out	33
A. Sheriyar c Bainbridge b Brown	12
B 7, l-b 26, w 6, n-b 12	51
1/18 2/40 3/50 4/234 5/234 6/333 7/341 8/354 9/389	428

Bonus points – Leicestershire 4, Durham 4.

Bowling: Cummins 24–4–71–2; Brown 27–2–111–4; Lugsden 19–4–89–0; Graveney 29–5–87–3; Bainbridge 15–4–37–0.

Umpires: J. D. Bond and B. J. Meyer.

DURHAM v YORKSHIRE

At Durham University, July 28, 29, 30, August 1. Yorkshire won by 116 runs. Yorkshire 22 pts, Durham 6 pts. Toss: Yorkshire.

There were 14 balls left when White defied his sore shins to take the final wicket with his last delivery of the season. But Yorkshire's match-winner was Stemp, who turned his left-arm spinners sufficiently sharply to claim a career-best six for 37, against some dispirited batting by Durham in pursuit of 279 in 61 overs. Fear of failure provided the chief risk for two struggling sides, whose scoring-rate on the third day dropped to two an over. There were some classy strokes from the youngsters Vaughan, in a cameo 45 for Yorkshire in the first innings, and Daley, who began Durham's recovery from 38 for four with a cultured 84. His colleagues then came close to maximum batting points for the first time in seven weeks. Scott made his second century, four weeks after his first, while Blakey followed up his first-innings 94 not out with 67 to set up the declaration and Stemp's decisive performance.

Close of play: First day, Yorkshire 298-6 (R. J. Blakey 50*, M. J. Foster 15*); Second day, Durham 256-6 (C. W. Scott 66*, A. C. Cummins 14*); Third day, Yorkshire 105-5 (R. J. Blakey 29*, A. P. Grayson 3*).

Yorkshire

S. A. Kellett c Scott b Brown	30	– b Cummins	6
M. P. Vaughan b Graveney	45	– b Cummins	8
*D. Byas lbw b Walker	36	– lbw b Cummins	0
B. Parker lbw b Graveney	52	– c Scott b Graveney	32
C. White c Daley b Brown	46	– lbw b Brown	7
†R. J. Blakey not out	94	– b Graveney	67
A. P. Grayson c Scott b Brown	2	– not out	62
M. J. Foster lbw b Cummins	49	– c Morris b Graveney	4
R. D. Stemp c Graveney b Cummins	0	– c Fowler b Brown	13
C. E. W. Silverwood c Longley b Brown	18	– not out	5
M. A. Robinson lbw b Brown	5		
B 1, l-b 7, w 6, n-b 14	28	L-b 7, w 1, n-b 18	26
1/56 2/103 3/147 4/181 5/267 6/275 7/346 8/346 9/397	405	1/11 2/13 3/26 4/44 5/94 6/179 7/190 8/217 (8 wkts dec.)	230

Bonus points – Yorkshire 3, Durham 3 (Score at 120 overs: 348-8).

Bowling: *First Innings*—Cummins 31–7–89–2; Brown 33.3–3–131–5; Walker 27–9–76–1; Graveney 31–12–53–2; Bainbridge 16–5–48–0. *Second Innings*—Cummins 18–0–55–3; Walker 17–3–48–0; Graveney 40–17–64–3; Brown 18–2–48–2; Bainbridge 3–1–8–0.

Durham

G. Fowler c White b Silverwood	17	– c Kellett b Silverwood	0
J. I. Longley c Blakey b Silverwood	7	– (5) c White b Stemp	54
J. E. Morris c Robinson b White	1	– c Parker b Stemp	22
M. Saxelby c Blakey b Robinson	9	– (2) c Foster b Robinson	24
J. A. Daley c Grayson b Silverwood	84	– (4) lbw b White	23
*P. Bainbridge b Grayson	34	– c Blakey b Stemp	16
†C. W. Scott not out	107	– c Byas b Stemp	0
A. C. Cummins c Byas b Silverwood	23	– lbw b Stemp	0
D. A. Graveney b Stemp	2	– b Stemp	18
S. J. E. Brown lbw b Stemp	23	– lbw b White	0
A. Walker c Blakey b Robinson	8	– not out	0
B 8, l-b 18, n-b 16	42	B 1, l-b 2, n-b 2	5
1/13 2/14 3/36 4/38 5/101 6/231 7/267 8/276 9/342	357	1/2 2/41 3/66 4/85 5/112 6/114 7/116 8/161 9/162	162

Bonus points – Durham 3, Yorkshire 3 (Score at 120 overs: 342-8).

Bowling: *First Innings*—Silverwood 26–6–67–4; White 11–3–41–1; Robinson 31–10–72–2; Stemp 16–2–51–2; Vaughan 21–3–60–0; Grayson 9–5–10–1; Foster 8–3–23–0; Byas 3–0–7–0. *Second Innings*—Silverwood 9–1–35–1; White 13.4–1–53–2; Stemp 22–9–37–6; Robinson 6–0–17–1; Vaughan 8–2–17–0.

Umpires: J. H. Hampshire and N. T. Plews.

At Taunton, August 4, 5. DURHAM lost to SOMERSET by nine wickets.

At Canterbury, August 11, 12, 13, 15. DURHAM lost to KENT by nine wickets.

DURHAM v GLAMORGAN

At Hartlepool, August 18, 19, 20. Durham won by three wickets. Durham 21 pts, Glamorgan 5 pts. Toss: Glamorgan.

Durham ended their run of seven successive Championship defeats with a day to spare, while pushing Glamorgan ever closer towards inheriting their wooden spoon. They owed victory to a high-class unbeaten century from John Morris. After getting out to a reckless stroke in the first innings, he played with great discipline, coming in at 16 for two in pursuit of 259. Glamorgan had chosen to bat on a damp pitch and had to recover from 77 for six. But fine spin bowling by Croft led to a Durham collapse; 230 all out from 152 for two, restricting their first-innings lead to 24. Maynard then tilted the balance back with 71 off 61 balls, but Croft, who had added a useful fifty to his four wickets, turned the ball less on the final day as the pitch dried. Durham were coasting until Gibson took three wickets in four balls. Hutton repaired the damage and Morris stood firm to the end.

Close of play: First day, Durham 155-4 (P. Bainbridge 10*, S. Hutton 0*); Second day, Durham 16-1 (M. Saxelby 5*, S. J. E. Brown 8*).

Glamorgan

M. P. Maynard lbw b Brown	5	c Morris b Walker	71
*H. Morris c Scott b Cummins	9	c Scott b Cummins	3
D. L. Hemp c Scott b Brown	3	lbw b Walker	25
A. Dale c Bainbridge b Brown	17	lbw b Wood	17
P. A. Cottey b Walker	9	b Brown	40
A. J. Dalton c Bainbridge b Wood	8	b Brown	29
O. D. Gibson b Brown	46	lbw b Brown	8
R. D. B. Croft c Scott b Brown	22	c Hutton b Wood	53
†C. P. Metson not out	40	b Walker	21
S. L. Watkin c Bainbridge b Brown	8	lbw b Walker	1
S. R. Barwick lbw b Bainbridge	5	not out	0
L-b 4, w 2, n-b 28	34	L-b 2, w 2, n-b 10	14
1/5 2/21 3/29 4/54 5/54 6/77 7/136 8/151 9/163	206	1/16 2/94 3/111 4/129 5/192 6/200 7/221 8/274 9/282	282

Bonus points – Glamorgan 1, Durham 4.

Bowling: *First Innings*—Cummins 14–2–62–1; Brown 18–4–68–6; Walker 9–2–37–1; Wood 5–0–31–1; Bainbridge 0.5–0–4–1. *Second Innings*—Cummins 10–0–59–1; Brown 17–2–80–3; Walker 17–2–59–4; Wood 11.2–0–53–2; Bainbridge 12–2–29–0.

Durham

J. I. Longley lbw b Croft	52	lbw b Watkin	3
M. Saxelby lbw b Barwick	30	c Barwick b Gibson	29
J. E. Morris c Metson b Croft	57	(4) not out	123
*P. Bainbridge c Metson b Watkin	20	(5) c Dalton b Gibson	0
J. A. Daley b Barwick	1	(6) c Metson b Gibson	0
S. Hutton b Watkin	8	(7) c Metson b Gibson	40
†C. W. Scott c Morris b Croft	2	(9) not out	19
A. C. Cummins c Maynard b Gibson	8	c Croft b Gibson	13
J. Wood c Cottey b Croft	0		
S. J. E. Brown c Barwick b Gibson	33	(3) c Metson b Gibson	8
A. Walker not out	4		
B 6, l-b 6, w 3	15	B 4, l-b 12, w 5, n-b 6	27
1/54 2/123 3/152 4/155 5/175 6/176 7/181 8/187 9/211	230	1/3 2/16 3/98 4/100 5/100 6/194 7/236	(7 wkts) 262

Bonus points – Durham 1, Glamorgan 4.

Bowling: *First Innings*—Watkin 22–8–66–2; Dale 3–0–17–0; Barwick 14–5–41–2; Croft 29–6–76–4; Gibson 7–2–18–2. *Second Innings*—Gibson 20–2–88–6; Watkin 18–1–70–1; Barwick 19–6–40–0; Croft 14.5–1–48–0.

Umpires: B. Leadbeater and B. J. Meyer.

At Portsmouth, August 25, 26, 27, 29. DURHAM drew with HAMPSHIRE.

DURHAM v LANCASHIRE

At Stockton-on-Tees, September 8, 9. Lancashire won by ten wickets. Lancashire 21 pts, Durham 4 pts. Toss: Durham. First-class debut: J. P. Searle.

Though the pitch offered variable bounce on the first day, when play began an hour late following heavy rain, Durham's own undistinguished batting was the real culprit as they lost inside two days. Choosing to bat, they slipped to 58 for seven, though they recovered to 159 and then dismissed Lancashire for 202, Brown completing his sixth five-wicket haul of the season. But Durham's second innings was a shambles as they failed to muster the application to deal with Chapple's out-swing. After Martin yorked Larkins in the first over, Chapple took the next six wickets to earn career-best figures of six for 48. Durham were all out for 111 and there were no terrors in the pitch for Atherton as he steered Lancashire home.

Close of play: First day, Lancashire 154-5 (I. D. Austin 11*, M. Watkinson 41*).

Durham

W. Larkins lbw b Chapple	1	– b Martin	8
M. Saxelby b Martin	8	– lbw b Chapple	4
J. E. Morris c and b Chapple	34	– c Hegg b Chapple	7
J. A. Daley b Chapple	0	– c Crawley b Chapple	1
S. Hutton c Fairbrother b Austin	8	– c and b Chapple	11
*P. Bainbridge c Fairbrother b Austin	26	– c Austin b Chapple	11
†C. W. Scott lbw b Austin	0	– (8) b Chapple	1
A. C. Cummins c Lloyd b Austin	2	– (7) lbw b Austin	44
S. J. E. Brown c Fairbrother b Austin	22	– c Hegg b Martin	4
J. Wood run out	51	– b Austin	18
J. P. Searle not out	5	– not out	0
L-b 2	2	L-b 2	2
1/9 2/13 3/29 4/52 5/52 6/52 7/58 8/93 9/118	159	1/8 2/19 3/20 4/23 5/40 6/45 7/53 8/66 9/106	111

Bonus points – Lancashire 4.

Bowling: *First Innings*—Martin 13–5–29–1; Chapple 15–4–59–3; Austin 16–3–30–5; Watkinson 7.2–1–39–0. *Second Innings*—Martin 10–2–37–2; Chapple 16–2–48–6; Austin 6.3–1–24–2.

Lancashire

M. A. Atherton c Hutton b Wood	4	– not out	39
N. J. Speak c Larkins b Cummins	6	– not out	21
J. P. Crawley lbw b Brown	36		
N. H. Fairbrother c Hutton b Brown	19		
G. D. Lloyd c Scott b Brown	12		
I. D. Austin c Daley b Wood	26		
*M. Watkinson lbw b Brown	47		
†W. K. Hegg c Scott b Brown	2		
G. Yates not out	10		
P. J. Martin b Wood	6		
G. Chapple c Brown b Wood	4		
B 2, l-b 3, w 9, n-b 16	30	L-b 3, w 1, n-b 6	10
1/16 2/20 3/51 4/85 5/98 6/166 7/178 8/190 9/198	202	(no wkt)	70

Bonus points – Lancashire 1, Durham 4.

Bowling: *First Innings*—Cummins 12–1–49–1; Brown 19–5–56–5; Wood 13–2–67–4; Bainbridge 9–2–18–0; Searle 1–0–7–0. *Second Innings*—Brown 8–1–21–0; Wood 8–1–37–0; Bainbridge 2–2–0–0; Daley 2–0–9–0.

Umpires: H. D. Bird and V. A. Holder.

At Worcester, September 15, 16, 17, 19. DURHAM drew with WORCESTERSHIRE.

FIELDING IN 1994

(Qualification: 20 dismissals)

74 S. A. Marsh (69 ct, 5 st)
69 R. J. Blakey (65 ct, 4 st)
67 S. J. Rhodes (59 ct, 8 st)
66 K. J. Piper (61 ct, 5 st)
62 P. Moores (61 ct, 1 st)
62 P. A. Nixon (60 ct, 2 st)
61 C. P. Metson (54 ct, 7 st)
59 R. C. Russell (58 ct, 1 st)
58 C. W. Scott (56 ct, 2 st)
56 K. R. Brown (55 ct, 1 st)
52 R. J. Turner (46 ct, 6 st)
49 W. K. Hegg (46 ct, 3 st)
46 D. Ripley (40 ct, 6 st)
43 W. M. Noon (38 ct, 5 st)
40 A. N. Aymes (36 ct, 4 st)
38 M. A. Garnham (33 ct, 5 st)
34 N. Hussain
32 A. J. Wright
31 M. C. J. Ball
31 J. D. Carr
29 †T. R. Ward
28 M. W. Gatting
28 K. M. Krikken (26 ct, 2 st)
26 C. L. Hooper
25 †J. P. Crawley
25 V. P. Terry
24 D. J. Richardson (23 ct, 1 st)
23 D. Byas
23 P. V. Simmons
22 G. A. Hick
22 N. V. Knight
21 M. A. Butcher
21 A. C. Parore
21 M. A. Roseberry
21 †A. J. Stewart (20 ct, 1 st)
20 T. Edwards
20 G. I. Macmillan
20 T. M. Moody
20 M. P. Speight

† T. R. Ward took two catches and J. P. Crawley three as substitute wicket-keepers; A. J. Stewart took six catches as wicket-keeper and 14 in the field.

ESSEX

President: D. J. Insole
Chairman: D. L. Acfield
Chairman, Cricket Committee: G. J. Saville
Secretary/General Manager: P. J. Edwards
Captain: 1994 – G. A. Gooch
1995 – P. J. Prichard
Head Groundsman: S. Kerrison
Scorer: C. F. Driver

Essex did not really expect to be the force they had been in recent seasons, after the retirement of Neil Foster and Derek Pringle in 1993. Bowlers of their match-winning qualities are not replaced overnight. What was surprising was the county's failure to score runs consistently and so take some pressure off an attack which lacked the penetration of old. How one should interpret a sixth-place finish in the County Championship is open to debate. Some will argue it represented a minor achievement, given the rebuilding process. Others claim that the overall strength of all the counties leaves much to be desired. Essex certainly seemed flattered to finish just one place off the prize money, but there was nothing flattering about their one-day performances. Their embarrassing ability to snatch defeat from the jaws of victory left them 17th in the Sunday League, their lowest ever position, while they bowed out of the Benson and Hedges Cup and NatWest Trophy competitions with barely a whimper.

The stark statistic that Graham Gooch was the only batsman to score over 1,000 runs emphasises the root of Essex's problems. In nine of their 17 Championship games they failed to get more than one batting point. Against this background, the cricket committee re-engaged Mark Waugh as their overseas player in 1995 in place of Mick Kasprowicz.

After that decision was taken the problems worsened with a sudden exodus of batsmen. Nadeem Shahid thought he would have more opportunities at Surrey; more damagingly and surprisingly, Nick Knight opted to go to Warwickshire, a move that both angered and puzzled officials. The most understandable defection was that of John Stephenson who, having failed to be appointed Essex captain for 1995, chose to go to Hampshire. He has an obvious chance of replacing Mark Nicholas as captain there within a year or two. He was beaten to the Essex job by Paul Prichard, who will become the seventh post-war Essex captain.

Gooch will play on under Prichard's leadership, and the departures will make Essex even more anxious for him to carry on. Stephenson had a particularly wretched time, anyway, in 1994. He was so out of touch that he failed to pass 20 in any of his final 13 Championship innings and ended with 535 first-class runs at an average of 20.57. Nasser Hussain's return of 922 at 31.79 was also a huge disappointment after he had averaged nearly 60 and compiled seven centuries for Essex in 1993. Hussain started encouragingly with hundreds against Hampshire and Durham, but he never reached three figures again. It seemed as if he had convinced himself that, if his early form was not good enough to earn him an England call-up, nothing would. The longer the season went on, the more ill at ease he looked, on and off the field. In fairness, his close fielding was as sharp as ever. Since Prichard missed much of the season with a compound fracture of the hand, it is not surprising that Essex rarely gathered match-winning totals, particularly when Gooch was on England duty.

The Waugh move was no reflection on Kasprowicz, however. The young Australian fast bowler proved himself an enthusiastic if sometimes an erratic performer, and his bag of 60 victims for an average of 31.15 each was satisfactory, if hardly spectacular. It says much for his whole-hearted attitude that Kasprowicz turned in career-best figures of seven for 83 against Somerset within days of being informed he would not be required in 1995. His efforts were acknowledged in the award of his county cap.

Whether the runs Waugh is expected to score will cover up cracks in the bowling is open to question. Mark Ilott, despite a niggling groin injury which kept him on the sidelines for a month, finished strongly, with 59 first-class wickets at 23.57 each. However, he is prone to injury or could force his way back into the Test team, and there is no obvious back-up. Much is expected of Darren Cousins, a raw but lively right-armer, but the retention of Steve Andrew, after 150 wickets in 60 first-class matches, merely confirmed the lack of resources in the pace department, a situation partly eased by the arrival of Neil Williams from Middlesex.

Spinners John Childs and Peter Such took 90 wickets between them; Such often struggled to find his rhythm, losing his Test place as a consequence, while Childs, approaching his mid-40s, lacked his old effectiveness.

Among the batsmen, Essex continued to rely heavily on Gooch's extraordinary consistency. In 1995 he embarks upon his testimonial year and will celebrate his 42nd birthday. Age might have dulled his athleticism in the field, but his enthusiasm and hunger for runs remain. Last summer's overall first-class aggregate of 1,747 at 64.70 took him beyond 40,000 runs and his six hundreds included three doubles. Against Worcestershire in June, Gooch made 101 and 205 to become only the sixth player to score two centuries in a game five times.

Before his defection, Knight had given Essex supporters as much satisfaction as anyone. An elegant left-hander whose progress has been hindered by injuries, Knight forced his way into the side in mid-summer, finished with 944 runs at an average of 47.20, was awarded his county cap and earned selection for England A's winter tour to India. Ronnie Irani, who had moved from Old Trafford in an effort to enhance his career, did just that. He also topped 900 runs, including a maiden century against Worcestershire. His value as a medium-pace bowler was cut short by back trouble. Irani was also capped, along with Jonathan Lewis.

The Chelmsford gloom deepened in November when a Sunday tabloid splashed a story alleging that Essex and Lancashire had colluded to fix results over a weekend in August 1991 when Essex were desperate to win the Championship and Lancashire the Sunday League. It was suggested that the teams agreed to lose the game that concerned them least. The main source of the story was Don Topley, who had been released in the summer after ten years on the staff. With his cheery smile, Topley was always more popular amongst the members than in the dressing-room. Officials, who say he received generous severance pay, talked about "betrayal" and, after an investigation, said there was no evidence to support the claims. – Nigel Fuller.

ESSEX 1994

[*Bill Smith*

Back row: M. Diwan, R. J. Rollins, D. M. Cousins, D. D. J. Robinson, J. J. B. Lewis, M. G. Powell, D. W. Ayres, N. Shahid. *Middle row:* J. Davis (*physiotherapist*), N. V. Knight, P. M. Such, R. M. Pearson, S. J. W. Andrew, M. S. Kasprowicz, D. J. P. Boden, A. P. Cowan, M. C. Ilott, R. C. Irani, A. R. Butcher (*Second Eleven captain/coach*). *Front row:* M. A. Garnham, T. D. Topley, J. H. Childs, G. A. Gooch (*captain*), P. J. Prichard, J. P. Stephenson, N. Hussain.

ESSEX RESULTS

All first-class matches – Played 19: Won 7, Lost 5, Drawn 7.

County Championship matches – Played 17: Won 7, Lost 5, Drawn 5.

Bonus points – Batting 32, Bowling 63.

Competition placings – Britannic Assurance County Championship, 6th; NatWest Bank Trophy, 2nd round; Benson and Hedges Cup, q-f; AXA Equity & Law League, 17th.

BRITANNIC ASSURANCE CHAMPIONSHIP AVERAGES

BATTING

	Birthplace	*M*	*I*	*NO*	*R*	*HS*	*Avge*
‡G. A. Gooch	*Leytonstone*	10	18	2	1,343	236	83.93
‡N. V. Knight	*Watford*	11	19	1	786	157	43.66
‡R. C. Irani	*Leigh*	17	28	6	882	119	40.09
‡P. J. Prichard	*Billericay*	10	16	2	560	119	40.00
‡N. Hussain	*Madras, India*	17	29	2	789	115*	29.22
‡J. J. B. Lewis	*Isleworth*	14	26	2	688	109	28.66
‡M. A. Garnham	*Johannesburg, SA*	17	28	4	497	62	20.70
N. Shahid	*Karachi, Pakistan*	9	16	3	263	91	20.23
‡J. P. Stephenson	*Stebbing*	14	24	0	480	144	20.00
‡J. H. Childs	*Plymouth*	13	16	11	95	42*	19.00
‡M. S. Kasprowicz§	*South Brisbane, Australia*	16	23	4	298	44	15.68
‡M. C. Ilott	*Watford*	12	14	4	138	30*	13.80
‡P. M. Such	*Helensburgh*	15	19	1	125	29	6.94
S. J. W. Andrew	*London*	5	7	1	29	11	4.83
D. M. Cousins	*Cambridge*	3	5	0	24	11	4.80

Also batted: M. Diwan (*St Stephen, Canada*) (1 match) 0, 0; R. M. Pearson (*Batley*) (2 matches) 11, 7, 7; D. D. J. Robinson (*Braintree*) (1 match) 38.

* *Signifies not out.* ‡ *Denotes county cap.* § *Overseas player.*

The following played a total of 17 three-figure innings for Essex in County Championship matches – G. A. Gooch 5, N. V. Knight 3, P. J. Prichard 3, N. Hussain 2, R. C. Irani 2, J. J. B. Lewis 1, J. P. Stephenson 1.

BOWLING

	O	*M*	*R*	*W*	*BB*	*5W/i*	*Avge*
M. C. Ilott	419.3	92	1,206	52	6-24	3	23.19
P. M. Such	521	139	1,397	51	7-66	5	27.39
R. C. Irani	225.4	38	757	26	4-27	0	29.11
M. S. Kasprowicz	497.3	88	1,752	57	7-83	3	30.73
J. H. Childs	410.5	101	1,139	37	6-71	2	30.78
J. P. Stephenson	307	73	977	24	4-74	0	40.70

Also bowled: S. J. W. Andrew 123.3–24–374–7; D. M. Cousins 79.4–13–276–6; G. A. Gooch 19.3–9–24–3; N. V. Knight 11.4–0–61–1; J. J. B. Lewis 8–1–32–0; R. M. Pearson 47–12–145–2; N. Shahid 18–2–81–2.

Wicket-keeper: M. A. Garnham 31 ct, 4 st.

Leading Fielders: N. Hussain 34, N. V. Knight 22.

At Southampton, April 28, 29, 30, May 1. ESSEX beat HAMPSHIRE by eight wickets.

At Stockton-on-Tees, May 5, 6, 7, 9. ESSEX beat DURHAM by ten wickets.

ESSEX v KENT

At Chelmsford, May 12, 13, 14, 16. Essex won by four wickets. Essex 24 pts, Kent 1 pt. Toss: Kent.

On the last day, Hooper very nearly stole victory for Kent, though Essex had completely controlled the first three. After scoring a century before lunch, from 79 deliveries, Hooper was finally caught for 160 in 149 balls. He had smashed nine sixes and a pavilion window. He then scared Essex – chasing only 50 – when he and fellow-spinner Patel took the new ball and grabbed three wickets each on a pitch offering generous turn and bounce. After Kent were bowled out for only 191, Gooch and Prichard had put Essex well in front on their own. Gooch struck the tenth double-century of his career, including 28 fours and three sixes, in 332 balls, while Prichard made his fourth hundred in successive innings against Kent, and his sixth against them in five seasons. Their opening stand of 316 surpassed the county record of 270 by A. V. Avery and T. C. Dodds against Surrey in 1946. Gooch and Prichard already held Essex's all-wicket record with 403 for the second wicket against Leicestershire in 1990.

Close of play: First day, Essex 25-0 (G. A. Gooch 18*, P. J. Prichard 5*); Second day, Essex 446-3 (N. Hussain 34*, N. Shahid 10*); Third day, Kent 60-0 (D. P. Fulton 17*, M. R. Benson 34*).

Kent

D. P. Fulton c Garnham b Kasprowicz	20	– lbw b Childs	23
*M. R. Benson c Garnham b Ilott	2	– lbw b Such	38
T. R. Ward lbw b Ilott	67	– c Shahid b Such	50
C. L. Hooper c Such b Kasprowicz	0	– c Hussain b Kasprowicz	160
N. R. Taylor b Irani	47	– b Such	42
G. R. Cowdrey lbw b Ilott	0	– c Shahid b Such	4
M. V. Fleming c Garnham b Kasprowicz	22	– b Such	40
†S. A. Marsh c Gooch b Irani	19	– not out	9
D. W. Headley b Irani	2	– c Shahid b Childs	0
M. M. Patel b Irani	4	– c Hussain b Childs	4
A. P. Igglesden not out	3	– c Hussain b Childs	0
L-b 2, w 1, n-b 2	5	B 6, l-b 19, w 4	29
1/12 2/68 3/72 4/112 5/112 6/155 7/161 8/166 9/174	191	1/70 2/70 3/223 4/287 5/311 6/369 7/390 8/393 9/397	399

Bonus points – Essex 4.

Bowling: *First Innings*—Ilott 17–2–60–3; Kasprowicz 18–3–90–3; Irani 12.2–2–27–4; Such 7–3–12–0. *Second Innings*—Ilott 6–2–22–0; Kasprowicz 14–0–67–1; Such 39–8–133–5; Childs 27.4–5–127–4; Shahid 5–1–25–0.

Essex

*G. A. Gooch c Marsh b Igglesden	236	– c Marsh b Patel	37
P. J. Prichard c and b Hooper	109	– lbw b Hooper	0
J. J. B. Lewis c Headley b Patel	22	– c Fulton b Hooper	0
N. Hussain c Marsh b Headley	37	– c Patel b Hooper	6
N. Shahid not out	45	– c Benson b Patel	0
†M. A. Garnham lbw b Headley	16	– not out	4
R. C. Irani not out	30	– b Patel	0
M. S. Kasprowicz (did not bat)		– not out	1
B 4, l-b 21, w 1, n-b 20	46	B 2	2
1/316 2/366 3/421 4/451 5/487 (5 wkts dec.)	541	1/10 2/10 3/42 4/43 5/46 6/46 (6 wkts)	50

M. C. Ilott, P. M. Such and J. H. Childs did not bat.

Bonus points – Essex 4, Kent 1 (Score at 120 overs: 451-4).

Bowling: *First Innings*—Igglesden 24–1–92–1; Headley 34–5–120–2; Fleming 29–5–104–0; Patel 34–3–116–1; Hooper 21–1–84–1. *Second Innings*—Patel 7–2–29–3; Hooper 7–0–19–3.

Umpires: K. J. Lyons and B. J. Meyer.

At Leeds, May 19, 20, 21, 23. ESSEX drew with YORKSHIRE.

At Chelmsford, May 28, 29, 30. ESSEX drew with NEW ZEALANDERS (See New Zealand tour section).

ESSEX v GLOUCESTERSHIRE

At Chelmsford, June 2, 3, 4, 6. Drawn. Essex 7 pts, Gloucestershire 14 pts. Toss: Essex. County debut: R. M. Pearson.

Gloucestershire looked assured of victory when they reached the final ten overs with eight wickets in hand and only 47 runs required, but they paid the penalty for a series of undisciplined strokes. Childs reaped the rewards with a wicket in each of his last five overs, including Hancock for a career-best 123. Gloucestershire needed seven off the last over, bowled by the former Northamptonshire off-spinner Pearson, and three off the final ball. Davies scored two to give his team eight points for levelling the scores. Prichard and Lewis gathered fine, though contrasting, centuries on the opening day – Prichard reached three figures in 143 balls while Lewis took 233 – and their opponents showed little urgency in response. Less than seven overs were possible on the third day, before reciprocal declarations set Gloucestershire 280 in 71 overs and paved the way for the exciting finish.

Close of play: First day, Essex 361-8 (M. S. Kasprowicz 43*, R. M. Pearson 11*); Second day, Gloucestershire 251-7 (M. Davies 21*, A. M. Smith 13*); Third day, Gloucestershire 266-8 (M. Davies 24*, C. A. Walsh 7*).

Essex

*P. J. Prichard c Wright b Smith	119	– c Hancock b Davies	62
J. P. Stephenson c Broad b Walsh	0	– lbw b Smith	2
J. J. B. Lewis c Wright b Wight	109	– c Dawson b Davies	78
N. Hussain c Russell b Alleyne	34	– c Walsh b Davies	15
N. Shahid c Wright b Wight	13	– not out	12
R. C. Irani c Wright b Wight	0	– not out	6
†M. A. Garnham c Hancock b Walsh	6		
M. S. Kasprowicz b Walsh	43		
M. C. Ilott run out	3		
R. M. Pearson c Broad b Cooper	11		
J. H. Childs not out	0		
B 2, l-b 7, w 1, n-b 14	24	N-b 8	8
1/1 2/193 3/251 4/273 5/273 6/280 7/304 8/316 9/361	362	1/4 2/116 3/146 4/167 (4 wkts dec.)	183

Bonus points – Essex 4, Gloucestershire 4.

Bowling: *First Innings*—Walsh 22–6–43–3; Cooper 25–6–60–1; Smith 9.3–3–34–1; Alleyne 12.3–1–55–1; Wight 19–2–76–3; Davies 18–2–74–0; Hancock 3–0–11–0. *Second Innings*—Cooper 4–0–18–0; Smith 7–0–40–1; Davies 10–0–53–3; Wight 8–0–63–0; Hancock 1–0–9–0.

Gloucestershire

B. C. Broad c Hussain b Kasprowicz	34	– c Pearson b Childs	63
M. W. Alleyne c Hussain b Ilott	7	– c Hussain b Kasprowicz	1
T. H. C. Hancock c Garnham b Stephenson	2	– c Hussain b Childs	123
A. J. Wright b Pearson	47	– c Pearson b Childs	27
R. I. Dawson c Hussain b Stephenson	47	– (6) c Garnham b Childs	0
†R. C. Russell c Ilott b Childs	28	– (5) c sub b Pearson	19
R. M. Wight c Garnham b Kasprowicz	22	– (8) c Lewis b Childs	11
M. Davies not out	24	– (9) not out	3
A. M. Smith c Prichard b Kasprowicz	17		
*C. A. Walsh not out	7	– (7) c Garnham b Childs	6
K. E. Cooper (did not bat)		– (10) not out	0
L-b 13, w 2, n-b 16	31	B 6, l-b 8, n-b 12	26
1/20 2/29 3/79 4/131 5/178 6/197 7/230 8/255 (8 wkts dec.)	266	1/10 2/148 3/233 4/242 5/242 6/250 7/272 8/273 (8 wkts)	279

Bonus points – Gloucestershire 2, Essex 3.

Bowling: *First Innings*—Ilott 21.4–4–53–1; Kasprowicz 24–4–63–3; Stephenson 16–2–38–2; Childs 19–7–33–1; Pearson 27–10–54–1; Irani 4–0–12–0. *Second Innings*—Ilott 6.2–1–19–0; Kasprowicz 12.4–0–51–1; Pearson 13–1–53–1; Stephenson 6–0–26–0; Childs 24–2–71–6; Irani 9–0–45–0.

Umpires: D. J. Constant and G. Sharp.

At Worcester, June 9, 10, 11, 13. ESSEX beat WORCESTERSHIRE by four wickets.

At Cambridge, June 15, 16, 17. ESSEX drew with CAMBRIDGE UNIVERSITY.

ESSEX v NOTTINGHAMSHIRE

At Ilford, June 23, 24, 25, 27. Nottinghamshire won by two wickets. Nottinghamshire 24 pts, Essex 3 pts. Toss: Nottinghamshire.

Pollard condemned Essex to their first Championship defeat with a hair-shirted half-century, batting throughout the 62.4 overs Nottinghamshire took to reach a modest target of 167 while eight wickets fell at the other end. Robinson had fallen in the one over they faced on Saturday, but he had set up the victory by defying the home attack for the whole of the first day, striking 22 fours and one six. In response, Essex were undermined by Lewis and Afford and forced to follow on 256 behind. Stephenson's first century of the summer, spanning nearly seven hours, enabled Essex to fight back. The pitch had begun to offer turn and, when Such removed Adams and Johnson with successive deliveries soon after lunch on the final day, Nottinghamshire were a shaky 106 for five. But Pollard doggedly saw them through, to replace Essex in second place in the table.

Close of play: First day, Nottinghamshire 333-5 (R. T. Robinson 178*, W. M. Noon 27*); Second day, Essex 114-1 (J. P. Stephenson 34*, P. M. Such 6*); Third day, Nottinghamshire 1-1 (P. R. Pollard 1*, G. W. Mike 0*).

Nottinghamshire

P. R. Pollard b Cousins	0	– not out	53
*R. T. Robinson c Such b Cousins	182	– c Hussain b Ilott	0
G. F. Archer c Hussain b Irani	67	– (4) b Irani	35
J. C. Adams c Hussain b Such	25	– (5) st Garnham b Such	18
P. Johnson run out	1	– (6) c sub b Such	0
C. C. Lewis c Knight b Such	19	– (7) st Garnham b Childs	16
†W. M. Noon not out	62	– (8) c Hussain b Childs	13
K. P. Evans b Ilott	7	– (9) lbw b Such	6
G. W. Mike lbw b Ilott	0	– (3) c Cousins b Such	1
M. G. Field-Buss lbw b Irani	22	– not out	0
J. A. Afford c Hussain b Childs	0		
L-b 8, n-b 16	24	B 16, l-b 7, n-b 2	25
1/1 2/113 3/194 4/195 5/252 6/343 7/352 8/352 9/400	409	1/1 2/10 3/70 4/106 5/106 6/127 7/151 8/166	(8 wkts) 167

Bonus points – Nottinghamshire 4, Essex 3 (Score at 120 overs: 369-8).

Bowling: *First Innings*—Ilott 21–5–56–2; Cousins 21–3–65–2; Such 39–10–99–2; Stephenson 11–1–44–0; Irani 22–5–77–2; Childs 24.2–5–60–1. *Second Innings*—Ilott 4.1–1–7–1; Such 30–9–71–4; Childs 24.3–8–55–2; Irani 4–1–11–1.

Essex

*G. A. Gooch c Noon b Afford	35	– c Archer b Adams	66
J. P. Stephenson b Lewis	2	– c Adams b Evans	144
J. J. B. Lewis lbw b Lewis	6	– (4) b Field-Buss	19
N. Hussain lbw b Lewis	2	– (5) c Noon b Adams	9
R. C. Irani c Johnson b Field-Buss	61	– (7) c Johnson b Evans	32
†M. A. Garnham lbw b Mike	3	– (8) c and b Adams	62
N. V. Knight c Lewis b Afford	5	– (6) c and b Adams	39
M. C. Ilott c Archer b Afford	3	– (9) c Archer b Lewis	3
P. M. Such c Adams b Mike	12	– (3) c Noon b Evans	11
D. M. Cousins c Robinson b Afford	1	– lbw b Field-Buss	1
J. H. Childs not out	2	– not out	0
B 2, l-b 7, n-b 12	21	B 11, l-b 5, n-b 20	36
1/15 2/25 3/29 4/65 5/72 6/77 7/81 8/115 9/145	153	1/102 2/133 3/192 4/205 5/281 6/345 7/364 8/389 9/420	422

Bonus points – Nottinghamshire 4.

Bowling: *First Innings*—Lewis 11–2–56–3; Mike 12–2–54–2; Afford 17.2–8–30–4; Field-Buss 3–1–4–1. *Second Innings*—Lewis 20–2–80–1; Evans 26–6–80–3; Afford 16–3–60–0; Mike 5–0–34–0; Field-Buss 41–14–89–2; Adams 29–13–63–4.

Umpires: B. J. Meyer and P. Willey.

At Leicester, June 30, July 1, 2. ESSEX lost to LEICESTERSHIRE by an innings and 49 runs.

ESSEX v GLAMORGAN

At Southend, July 14, 15, 16, 18. Essex won by 18 runs. Essex 22 pts, Glamorgan 5 pts. Toss: Essex.

Essex clinched victory shortly before lunch on the final day when Glamorgan, 27 short of a target of 208 with five wickets in hand, lost all five in 50 deliveries for eight runs. Once Irani, brought on so that the spinners could switch ends, had trapped Metson, Glamorgan fell apart. Childs wrapped up victory: on Saturday he had taken his 500th first-class wicket for the county since joining from Gloucestershire in 1985 – a few hours after Glamorgan wicket-keeper Metson dismissed his 500th first-class victim. Run-gathering was always difficult on a slow, low pitch which offered more and more help to the spinners. Despite a sound start, Essex lost their way in the first innings, though Hussain staved off disaster. Such then undermined Glamorgan, despite determined resistance from Cottey, before a sparkling 61 from Garnham gave the Essex spinners something to defend. Morris and Gibson, promoted to No. 3 after Hemp's arm was bruised in the field, raised Glamorgan's hopes, only for them to be dashed on Monday.

Close of play: First day, Essex 260-7 (N. Hussain 71*); Second day, Glamorgan 248; Third day, Glamorgan 149-5 (R. D. B. Croft 1*, C. P. Metson 1*).

Essex

*G. A. Gooch c Cottey b Croft	53	– c James b Croft	30
J. P. Stephenson lbw b Gibson	58	– c Metson b Lefebvre	20
J. J. B. Lewis st Metson b Barwick	36	– lbw b Croft	7
N. Hussain not out	82	– c Metson b Watkin	14
N. V. Knight b Gibson	5	– c sub b Gibson	13
R. C. Irani c Maynard b Watkin	25	– c sub b Croft	4
P. M. Such lbw b Watkin	3	– (9) c Cottey b Barwick	5
†M. A. Garnham run out	0	– (7) not out	61
M. S. Kasprowicz b Watkin	2	– (8) c Cottey b Gibson	1
S. J. W. Andrew c Metson b Watkin	0	– c Gibson b Croft	7
J. H. Childs run out	0	– c Morris b Barwick	6
B 3, l-b 3, n-b 4	10	L-b 6, w 1, n-b 6	13
1/88 2/123 3/170 4/190 5/249 6/259 7/260 8/263 9/263	274	1/50 2/58 3/61 4/81 5/90 6/90 7/114 8/136 9/151	181

Bonus points – Essex 2, Glamorgan 4 (Score at 120 overs: 267-9).

Bowling: *First Innings*—Watkin 29–9–63–4; Gibson 24–8–47–2; Lefebvre 15–6–24–0; Barwick 29–10–50–1; Croft 25–4–77–1; Cottey 3–1–7–0. *Second Innings*—Watkin 14–5–25–1; Gibson 14–2–50–2; Barwick 7.4–1–15–2; Lefebvre 8–1–27–1; Croft 19–5–58–4.

Glamorgan

S. P. James c Garnham b Andrew	1	– c Hussain b Such	3
*H. Morris c Lewis b Childs	49	– c Kasprowicz b Irani	40
D. L. Hemp lbw b Such	29	– (8) c Gooch b Childs	0
M. P. Maynard b Such	35	– c Garnham b Childs	29
P. A. Cottey st Garnham b Such	54	– b Such	9
R. D. B. Croft lbw b Irani	31	– c Hussain b Childs	16
O. D. Gibson b Childs	0	– (3) st Garnham b Childs	55
R. P. Lefebvre lbw b Childs	19	– (9) lbw b Such	6
†C. P. Metson c Hussain b Such	2	– (7) lbw b Irani	15
S. L. Watkin c and b Such	2	– not out	0
S. R. Barwick not out	1	– c Knight b Childs	1
B 6, l-b 7, w 1, n-b 11	25	L-b 8, w 1, n-b 6	15
1/23 2/76 3/118 4/136 5/206 6/209 7/226 8/236 9/246	248	1/37 2/81 3/134 4/145 5/147 6/181 7/181 8/188 9/188	189

Bonus points – Glamorgan 1, Essex 4.

Bowling: *First Innings*—Kasprowicz 7–1–28–0; Andrew 16–6–31–1; Such 28–8–78–5; Stephenson 6–2–22–0; Childs 27.3–4–65–3; Irani 7–4–11–1. *Second Innings*—Kasprowicz 3–0–14–0; Andrew 2–1–1–0; Such 29–9–77–3; Childs 29.2–8–58–5; Irani 7–0–27–2; Stephenson 1–0–4–0.

Umpires: J. H. Hampshire and M. J. Kitchen.

At Birmingham, July 21, 22, 23. ESSEX lost to WARWICKSHIRE by 203 runs.

At Uxbridge, July 28, 29, 30, August 1. ESSEX drew with MIDDLESEX.

ESSEX v LANCASHIRE

At Chelmsford, August 4, 5, 6. Lancashire won by an innings and 60 runs. Lancashire 24 pts, Essex 4 pts. Toss: Essex.

Essex capitulated embarrassingly on the third afternoon. After conceding a first-innings lead of 198, they jettisoned any hope of saving the match in 11 overs, which was all Martin and Chapple needed to claim the first five wickets. Only Knight and Garnham resisted for long. Stephenson had unexpectedly decided to bat, despite humid conditions, and Lancashire quickly gained the upper hand. But Irani performed well against his former colleagues, as did Garnham, who interrupted his innings for 16 stitches after being struck above the left eye by a delivery from Martin. Later, he left the field, complaining of double vision, and on resuming was struck again by a ball from his own team-mate, Childs, which re-opened the wound, necessitating another six stitches. Meanwhile Gallian and Titchard launched Lancashire with a confident 144-run stand, before Fairbrother, taking advantage of sunnier weather and a life from Garnham's stand-in as wicket-keeper, Shahid, consolidated with his third century in successive matches.

Close of play: First day, Essex 155-8 (R. C. Irani 50*, M. A. Garnham 28*); Second day, Lancashire 264-4 (N. H. Fairbrother 60*, I. D. Austin 19*).

Essex

N. V. Knight c Hegg b Chapple	12	– c Chapple b Watkinson	53
*J. P. Stephenson c Fairbrother b Austin	20	– c Speak b Martin	1
J. J. B. Lewis c Fairbrother b Martin	4	– lbw b Chapple	1
N. Hussain lbw b Austin	18	– (6) c Titchard b Martin	0
N. Shahid c Hegg b Chapple	3	– (4) c and b Chapple	0
R. C. Irani c Fairbrother b Chapple	61	– (5) c Watkinson b Martin	12
†M. A. Garnham c Titchard b Watkinson	47	– b Yates	29
M. S. Kasprowicz c Speak b Chapple	1	– c Gallian b Yates	19
M. C. Ilott c Hegg b Martin	0	– b Yates	11
P. M. Such b Austin	6	– c Titchard b Watkinson	4
J. H. Childs not out	24	– not out	4
B 5, l-b 8, w 5, n-b 2	20	B 1, l-b 1, n-b 2	4
1/21 2/32 3/48 4/61 5/65 6/116 7/117 8/131 9/171	216	1/9 2/10 3/10 4/31 5/31 6/98 7/102 8/123 9/132	138

Bonus points – Essex 1, Lancashire 4.

In the first innings M. A. Garnham, when 20, retired hurt at 115 and resumed at 131.

Bowling: *First Innings*—Martin 17–4–44–2; Chapple 27–6–86–4; Austin 22–7–57–3; Watkinson 7.3–1–16–1. *Second Innings*—Martin 11–4–34–3; Chapple 6–4–11–2; Watkinson 9–0–42–2; Austin 4–0–17–0; Yates 5.2–0–32–3.

Lancashire

J. E. R. Gallian c Stephenson b Such	98
S. P. Titchard b Such	61
N. J. Speak b Such	5
N. H. Fairbrother b Kasprowicz	103
G. D. Lloyd c Hussain b Childs	8
I. D. Austin b Kasprowicz	38
*M. Watkinson c Knight b Childs	18
†W. K. Hegg c Irani b Such	34
G. Yates c Knight b Stephenson	12
P. J. Martin c Hussain b Childs	13
G. Chapple not out	0
B 8, l-b 6, n-b 10	24
1/144 2/154 3/213 4/228 5/304 6/333 7/355 8/377 9/408	414

Bonus points – Lancashire 4, Essex 3 (Score at 120 overs: 363-7).

Bowling: Ilott 22–5–73–0; Kasprowicz 16–1–101–2; Childs 41–13–95–3; Stephenson 18–2–65–1; Such 43.1–12–66–4.

Umpires: G. I. Burgess and R. Palmer.

ESSEX v SURREY

At Colchester, August 11, 12, 13, 15. Essex won by an innings and 87 runs. Essex 24 pts, Surrey 4 pts. Toss: Essex.

Surrey's title hopes received a severe blow in this match and they lost their last five wickets in only 28 minutes on the final day. Four of them fell to Such's off-spin in 18 balls, concluding a spell of six for eight in 25 deliveries which he began on Saturday evening. Surrey had followed on 290 behind after a lamentable display of batting – their first innings was wrapped up for 88 in 25.4 overs by Ilott and Kasprowicz, bowling unchanged. The pitch did afford generous bounce but Surrey lacked application; only Thorpe reached double figures. After the first day was all but washed out, Robinson, playing his only first-team match of the season, showed promise as he and Knight opened with 116. Knight went on to add 109 with Lewis and completed an entertaining century, while Garnham contributed an attractive fifty. Gooch missed the game with a strained hamstring. This was Essex's first Championship win without him since early June the previous year; in between they had lost five and drawn five.

Close of play: First day, Essex 14-0 (N. V. Knight 5*, D. D. J. Robinson 7*); Second day, Essex 378; Third day, Surrey 187-5 (D. J. Bicknell 70*).

Essex

N. V. Knight c Stewart b Cuffy	115
D. D. J. Robinson c Stewart b Kendrick	38
J. J. B. Lewis b Hollioake	52
N. Hussain b Hollioake	16
R. C. Irani c Butcher b Hollioake	10
†M. A. Garnham b M. P. Bicknell	55
*J. P. Stephenson c Stewart b Cuffy	20
M. S. Kasprowicz b Benjamin	10
M. C. Ilott not out	8
P. M. Such lbw b Benjamin	0
J. H. Childs c Cuffy b M. P. Bicknell	9
L-b 12, w 1, n-b 32	45
1/116 2/225 3/231 4/246 5/273 6/333 7/350 8/350 9/351	378

Bonus points – Essex 4, Surrey 4.

Bowling: Cuffy 22–3–69–2; Benjamin 24–5–62–2; M. P. Bicknell 21–5–81–2; Smith 9–1–49–0; Kendrick 15–3–51–1; Hollioake 15–3–54–3.

Surrey

D. J. Bicknell lbw b Kasprowicz	0	lbw b Such	72
M. A. Butcher c Robinson b Ilott	0	lbw b Stephenson	35
G. P. Thorpe c sub b Ilott	24	b Stephenson	5
*†A. J. Stewart b Ilott	2	c Garnham b Ilott	13
A. D. Brown c Garnham b Kasprowicz	9	c Lewis b Such	43
A. J. Hollioake lbw b Ilott	0	(7) not out	9
A. W. Smith b Kasprowicz	4	(8) c Kasprowicz b Such	4
N. M. Kendrick c Lewis b Ilott	9	(6) b Such	0
M. P. Bicknell c Lewis b Kasprowicz	0	c Lewis b Ilott	0
J. E. Benjamin lbw b Ilott	7	c Hussain b Such	1
C. E. Cuffy not out	8	c and b Such	0
L-b 13, w 2, n-b 10	25	B 2, l-b 3, n-b 16	21
1/0 2/0 3/16 4/45 5/47 6/49 7/67 8/71 9/71	88	1/66 2/82 3/108 4/187 5/187 6/194 7/198 8/202 9/203	203

Bonus points – Essex 4.

Bowling: *First Innings*—Kasprowicz 13–3–51–4; Ilott 12.4–6–24–6. *Second Innings*—Kasprowicz 12–1–44–0; Ilott 15–7–32–2; Stephenson 19–3–50–2; Irani 9–1–26–0; Such 32–14–46–6.

Umpires: H. D. Bird and A. A. Jones.

At Weston-super-Mare, August 18, 19, 20. ESSEX lost to SOMERSET by 136 runs.

ESSEX v SUSSEX

At Chelmsford, August 30, 31, September 1, 2. Essex won by seven wickets. Essex 24 pts, Sussex 5 pts. Toss: Sussex.

Knight had a dream match – awarded his county cap before the start, celebrating with a career-best 157, and learning on the final morning of his selection for England A's tour of India. Knight put on 128 with Gooch and, later, 132 with Irani, who, like Kasprowicz and Lewis, had also received his cap. But it was Gooch who had set the tempo. He struck 15 fours and a six in his 79 – and became the 15th player to reach 40,000 first-class runs when 54. Ilott, despite a spirited 73 from Speight, had undermined Sussex's first innings with six wickets and added four – his first-ever ten-wicket haul – in the second. Such was the real thorn in the visitors' side this time, however, picking up six himself to leave Essex a modest target of 106. Salisbury caused minor tremors before Knight and Irani saw them home.

Close of play: First day, Essex 34-0 (G. A. Gooch 23*, N. V. Knight 7*); Second day, Essex 367-6 (N. V. Knight 152*, M. S. Kasprowicz 3*); Third day, Sussex 187-5 (J. W. Hall 50*, F. D. Stephenson 29*).

Sussex

N. J. Lenham c Knight b Stephenson	29	– c Prichard b Ilott	4
C. W. J. Athey lbw b Ilott	15	– lbw b Ilott	0
J. W. Hall c Knight b Kasprowicz	0	– c Irani b Such	56
*A. P. Wells c Garnham b Ilott	18	– lbw b Ilott	18
M. P. Speight c Prichard b Ilott	73	– c Knight b Such	47
†P. Moores c Knight b Ilott	39	– c Irani b Such	18
F. D. Stephenson c Kasprowicz b Ilott	0	– b Such	37
P. W. Jarvis c Prichard b Such	7	– c and b Such	9
I. D. K. Salisbury not out	36	– not out	38
E. E. Hemmings c Prichard b Ilott	0	– c Knight b Such	1
E. S. H. Giddins c Gooch b Kasprowicz	3	– b Ilott	24
L-b 10, n-b 16	26	B 13, l-b 10, n-b 2	25
1/33 2/36 3/80 4/82 5/150 6/150 7/177 8/225 9/227	246	1/4 2/4 3/44 4/120 5/158 6/202 7/209 8/222 9/226	277

Bonus points – Sussex 1, Essex 4.

Bowling: *First Innings*—Ilott 22–5–72–6; Kasprowicz 15.2–4–72–2; Stephenson 15–2–54–1; Such 10–1–38–1. *Second Innings*—Ilott 26–5–57–4; Kasprowicz 11–5–19–0; Childs 25–7–62–0; Such 35–8–116–6.

Essex

*G. A. Gooch c Speight b Giddins	79	– c Wells b Salisbury	23
N. V. Knight b Giddins	157	– not out	36
P. J. Prichard b Stephenson	37	– c Hemmings b Salisbury	5
N. Hussain c Moores b Stephenson	5	– lbw b Salisbury	0
R. C. Irani b Jarvis	67	– not out	35
J. P. Stephenson c Salisbury b Giddins	0		
†M. A. Garnham c Hall b Jarvis	7		
M. S. Kasprowicz c Moores b Giddins	7		
M. C. Ilott c Moores b Jarvis	27		
P. M. Such b Giddins	13		
J. H. Childs not out	2		
B 6, l-b 4, w 1, n-b 6	17	B 5, l-b 1, w 1	7
1/128 2/214 3/220 4/352 5/353 6/364 7/371 8/384 9/416	418	1/29 2/37 3/37	(3 wkts) 106

Bonus points – Essex 4, Sussex 4.

Bowling: *First Innings*—Stephenson 18–4–70–2; Jarvis 25–3–113–3; Hemmings 27–11–63–0; Giddins 18–1–83–5; Salisbury 17–2–61–0; Athey 1–0–18–0. *Second Innings*—Jarvis 3–0–20–0; Giddins 3–2–5–0; Salisbury 11–4–41–3; Hemmings 11–2–34–0.

Umpires: G. Sharp and D. R. Shepherd.

At Derby, September 8, 9, 10, 12. ESSEX drew with DERBYSHIRE.

ESSEX v NORTHAMPTONSHIRE

At Chelmsford, September 15, 16, 17, 19. Drawn. Essex 4 pts, Northamptonshire 8 pts. Toss: Northamptonshire.

The first and final days were lost to the weather but in between Northamptonshire's dominance enabled them to leapfrog Essex in the Championship table, claiming fifth place and a share of the prize money. Lamb recorded only his second first-class century of the season, and hit Childs for three sixes, although Childs had earlier bowled nine overs for two wickets and three runs. Essex faltered against the occasional off-spin of Bailey, who took five wickets; before this match his total for 1994 was six at an average of over 80. They were well short of saving the follow-on, 207 behind with the last man in, when rain intervened. Gooch's consolation, in his last match before surrendering the captaincy, was to pass Sir Leonard Hutton as the 14th heaviest run-scorer of all time; he finished on 40,174.

Close of play: First day, No play; Second day, Northamptonshire 348-8 (A. R. Roberts 7*); Third day, Essex 197-9 (M. C. Ilott 1*, J. H. Childs 0*).

Northamptonshire

R. R. Montgomerie lbw b Childs	35
A. Fordham lbw b Kasprowicz	17
R. J. Bailey c Knight b Childs	20
R. J. Warren c Garnham b Childs	0
*A. J. Lamb c Knight b Kasprowicz	114
K. M. Curran c Prichard b Kasprowicz	62
A. L. Penberthy c Garnham b Ilott	33
†D. Ripley c Gooch b Ilott	31
A. R. Roberts c and b Childs	51
N. G. B. Cook lbw b Kasprowicz	2
J. P. Taylor not out	7
B 12, l-b 13, w 1, n-b 6	32
1/27 2/70 3/70 4/121 5/263 6/270 7/329 8/348 9/351	404

Bonus points – Northamptonshire 4, Essex 4 (Score at 120 overs: 387-9).

Bowling: Kasprowicz 24–3–92–4; Ilott 29–3–62–2; Childs 31.3–12–104–4; Such 33–8–94–0; Stephenson 8–1–27–0.

Essex

*G. A. Gooch c Ripley b Roberts	50
N. V. Knight b Bailey	15
P. J. Prichard lbw b Bailey	3
N. Hussain c Roberts b Cook	28
R. C. Irani c Lamb b Bailey	57
J. P. Stephenson c Bailey b Cook	19
†M. A. Garnham lbw b Bailey	1
M. S. Kasprowicz c Fordham b Cook	3
M. C. Ilott not out	1
P. M. Such b Bailey	0
J. H. Childs not out	0
B 12, l-b 8	20
1/38 2/46 3/101 4/115 5/176 6/181 7/188 8/197 9/197	(9 wkts) 197

Bonus points – Northamptonshire 4.

Bowling: Curran 5–0–16–0; Taylor 3–0–9–0; Cook 25–10–46–3; Bailey 22–8–59–5; Roberts 13–2–47–1.

Umpires: T. E. Jesty and A. G. T. Whitehead.

GLAMORGAN

Patron: HRH The Prince of Wales
President: W. Wooller
Chairman: F. D. Morgan
Chairman, Cricket Committee: H. D. Davies
Secretary: G. R. Stone
Cricket Secretary: M. J. Fatkin
Captain: H. Morris
Director of Coaching: A. Jones
Grounds Supervisor: L. A. Smith
Scorer: B. T. Denning

The euphoria of 1993 turned to bitter disappointment for Glamorgan as they plummeted from third to the bottom of the County Championship, a position they filled five times in the 1970s and 1980s. They finished seventh in the Sunday League, which they won in 1993, and lost in the two knock-outs to Surrey. Their defeat in the NatWest quarter-final in July effectively ended their season. Thereafter, the only objective was to climb off the bottom and Glamorgan never really threatened to do that. They had only two Championship wins – at Bristol, where Steve Barwick took nine wickets, and at Cardiff against Leicestershire.

Glamorgan had their chances to win other games, including a moral victory over Worcestershire when rain stopped them scoring the last 12 runs – but a spectacular collapse against Essex, when they failed to score 27 runs to win with five wickets standing, and a costly fielding lapse which allowed Durham to escape from 100 for five and gain an unexpected victory, were more typical and characterised Glamorgan's decline. They undoubtedly missed Viv Richards's inspiration and enthusiasm, but otherwise this was the same squad which had contributed five players to England's winter tours. Steve Watkin was the only one of the five to make an impression, and he fell back from 92 wickets to 55. Of the other tourists, Hugh Morris and Matthew Maynard failed to score 1,000 runs, while Adrian Dale and Robert Croft were both dropped following lack of form and confidence. Unlike 1993, there was a shortage of runs from the senior batsmen and Glamorgan seldom scored enough in the first innings to dictate the game.

Morris, so dependable over the past decade, was handicapped by a troublesome knee throughout the season which required surgery at the beginning of September. Organising a benefit may have contributed to his poor season, too; he managed only 885 runs at 30.51. Maynard, disillusioned after his unsuccessful West Indies tour, broke a thumb early on, and found little form apart from smashing a century against the South Africans in August. Steve James failed to secure his position as Morris's opening partner, though he rallied towards the end of the season.

There was compensation from David Hemp and Tony Cottey, the only two Glamorgan batsmen to exceed 1,000 runs. Strength of character is not the least of Cottey's virtues; on many occasions he stabilised the middle order after early wickets had fallen. A total of 1,393 runs at 51.59 reflected his best season and he thoroughly deserved his award as the county's Player of the Year. Hemp confirmed all the promise he had shown as a schoolboy when scoring hundreds for the Welsh Schools at every age level. He scored 1,452 runs in his first full season, including four centuries, and was rewarded with a place on the England A tour of India. To be compared to the young David Gower was lavish praise, but his timing and assertive strokeplay – often on slow pitches – gave pleasure to many, including the South Africans. His brilliant century against them at Pontypridd prompted the tourists to rate Hemp as the most accomplished young player they had encountered on tour.

Ottis Gibson, the Barbados all-rounder, proved an effective overseas replacement for Richards once he had adjusted to the routine of day-by-day Championship cricket. He ended a satisfactory first season with 710 runs and 60 wickets, and his destructive strokeplay – he hit both Curtly Ambrose and Courtney Walsh for enormous sixes – gained Glamorgan two Sunday League victories. Watkin's modest summer by his standards followed an unproductive tour of the West Indies, but he still led the bowling averages. Gibson's presence restricted Roland Lefebvre's Championship appearances, but the Dutch medium-pacer made valuable contributions in one-day games. Barwick bowled his off-cutters with exemplary control and created a new Glamorgan record by bowling 65.2 overs, including 29 maidens, against Somerset at Swansea. Croft's disappointing season was reflected in his figures – 41 wickets at 52.82 – but he showed signs of rediscovering form and rhythm when he returned after being dropped for two games.

Colin Metson was understandably dejected by his continued omission from England's touring teams. Season after season, Metson is highly rated by umpires and players, but is constantly overlooked by the selectors who favour inferior wicket-keepers with superior batting averages. Many of the younger players were given opportunities and showed promise in the first team. Alistair Dalton and Andrew Roseberry both achieved maiden first-class fifties while Owen Parkin showed in his only Championship game against Middlesex at Lord's that he possesses the attributes to develop into a useful opening bowler.

Overall, the players were left feeling rather shellshocked. There will be less expectation of success in 1995, but Glamorgan still possess an experienced and talented squad capable of challenging in all competitions.

The county's coaching structure continues to prosper throughout Wales, and the success of Hemp and the emergence of others is evidence of the successful organisation. Meanwhile, the club have made an offer to buy Sophia Gardens in order to update the facilities and develop the ground as their headquarters. – Edward Bevan.

GLAMORGAN 1994

[*Bill Smith*

Back row: B. S. Phelps, A. J. Dalton, R. O. Jones, G. H. J. Rees, O. T. Parkin, J. R. A. Williams, A. J. Jones, G. P. Butcher. *Middle row:* G. N. Lewis (*Second Eleven scorer*), G. R. Stone (*secretary*), J. Bishop, A. Roseberry, S. Bastien, D. L. Hemp, A. D. Shaw, S. D. Thomas, B. T. Denning (*First Eleven scorer*), D. Conway (*physiotherapist*). *Front row:* J. Derrick (*Second Eleven captain/coach*), R. P. Lefebvre, S. P. James, C. P. Metson, H. Morris (*captain*), S. R. Barwick, R. D. B. Croft, A. Dale, P. A. Cottey, A. Jones (*director of coaching*). *Insets:* O. D. Gibson, M. P. Maynard, S. L. Watkin.

GLAMORGAN RESULTS

All first-class matches – Played 21: Won 2, Lost 9, Drawn 10.

County Championship matches – Played 17: Won 2, Lost 8, Drawn 7.

Bonus points – Batting 29, Bowling 50.

Competition placings – Britannic Assurance County Championship, 18th; NatWest Bank Trophy, q-f; Benson and Hedges Cup, 1st round; AXA Equity & Law League, 7th.

BRITANNIC ASSURANCE CHAMPIONSHIP AVERAGES

BATTING

	Birthplace	*M*	*I*	*NO*	*R*	*HS*	*Avge*
‡P. A. Cottey	*Swansea*	15	25	4	1,016	191	48.38
‡D. L. Hemp	*Bermuda*	17	30	2	1,132	136	40.42
‡M. P. Maynard	*Oldham*	15	26	1	863	118	34.52
‡S. P. James	*Lydney*	12	22	4	545	116	30.27
‡H. Morris	*Cardiff*	15	29	2	765	106	28.33
A. Roseberry	*Sunderland*	4	5	1	109	65	27.25
‡R. D. B. Croft	*Morriston*	15	21	2	505	80	26.57
‡A. Dale	*Germiston, SA*	14	23	1	504	131	22.90
‡O. D. Gibson§	*Bridgetown, Barbados*	17	25	2	523	81	22.73
‡C. P. Metson	*Goffs Oak*	16	20	4	315	51	19.68
‡R. P. Lefebvre	*Rotterdam, Netherlands*	10	11	2	176	33	19.55
A. J. Dalton	*Bridgend*	3	6	0	99	44	16.50
‡S. L. Watkin	*Maesteg*	16	19	10	79	14	8.77
B. S. Phelps	*Neath*	2	4	1	18	11	6.00
‡S. R. Barwick	*Neath*	10	16	6	35	8	3.50

Also batted: S. Bastien (*Stepney*) (2 matches) 1, 0; G. P. Butcher (*Clapham*) (2 matches) 4, 41; O. T. Parkin (*Coventry*) (1 match) 2*, 0*; A. D. Shaw (*Neath*) (1 match) 1, 14.

* *Signifies not out.* ‡ *Denotes county cap.* § *Overseas player.*

The following played a total of nine three-figure innings for Glamorgan in County Championship matches – D. L. Hemp 3, P. A. Cottey 2, A. Dale 1, S. P. James 1, M. P. Maynard 1, H. Morris 1.

BOWLING

	O	*M*	*R*	*W*	*BB*	*5W/i*	*Avge*
S. L. Watkin	554.4	122	1,563	52	6-143	2	30.05
S. R. Barwick	482.5	173	1,035	34	5-44	1	30.44
O. D. Gibson	528.5	96	1,944	57	6-64	4	34.10
R. P. Lefebvre	307.2	90	777	20	4-63	0	38.85
A. Dale	221	52	781	19	2-7	0	41.10
R. D. B. Croft	528.1	117	1,568	32	5-80	1	49.00

Also bowled: S. Bastien 64.3–14–206–4; G. P. Butcher 27–5–94–0; P. A. Cottey 17.4–2–82–1; D. L. Hemp 3–0–24–0; M. P. Maynard 1–0–10–0; O. T. Parkin 28–6–95–2; B. S. Phelps 86–22–241–4.

Wicket-keepers: C. P. Metson 50 ct, 7 st; A. D. Shaw 2 ct.

Leading Fielders: M. P. Maynard 18, P. A. Cottey 15.

At Oxford, April 20, 21, 22. GLAMORGAN drew with OXFORD UNIVERSITY.

At Birmingham, April 28, 29, 30, May 1. GLAMORGAN lost to WARWICKSHIRE by an innings and 103 runs.

At Northampton, May 5, 6, 7, 9. GLAMORGAN drew with NORTHAMPTONSHIRE.

GLAMORGAN v YORKSHIRE

At Cardiff, May 12, 13, 14, 16. Drawn. Glamorgan 5 pts, Yorkshire 7 pts. Toss: Yorkshire.

The match was ruined when only 14 overs were possible on the final day. After the morning was washed out, Moxon, who had passed 15,000 runs for Yorkshire during his second innings, declared to set Glamorgan 302 in a minimum of 59 overs. But as the weather deteriorated, the game was abandoned. Play began after lunch on the first day, when Byas and Richardson rescued Yorkshire after they lost their openers for three runs. Blakey and the tailenders then consolidated, adding 103 runs for the last three wickets. Glamorgan collapsed against Stemp's left-arm spin and were in danger of following on when they lost their ninth wicket, 174 behind. But a spirited partnership of 43 between Metson and Watkin, helped by a dropped slip catch, took them to safety and their only batting point. Gough followed up his 54 with three wickets, to be rewarded on Sunday with selection for England's one-day squad.

Close of play: First day, Yorkshire 202-5 (R. J. Blakey 51*, A. P. Grayson 26*); Second day, Glamorgan 158-8 (R. P. Lefebvre 16*, C. P. Metson 7*); Third day, Yorkshire 170-3 (M. D. Moxon 88*, R. J. Blakey 9*).

Yorkshire

*M. D. Moxon lbw b Watkin	1	– not out	88
M. P. Vaughan c Maynard b Watkin	2	– c Metson b Watkin	6
D. Byas c Croft b Dale	33	– c Watkin b Dale	36
R. B. Richardson lbw b Gibson	59	– c Maynard b Croft	21
†R. J. Blakey lbw b Watkin	87	– not out	9
C. White c James b Watkin	11		
A. P. Grayson c Metson b Gibson	26		
P. J. Hartley c James b Lefebvre	22		
D. Gough b Gibson	54		
R. D. Stemp lbw b Gibson	11		
M. A. Robinson not out	1		
B 9, l-b 14, w 1, n-b 8	32	L-b 4, n-b 6	10
1/2 2/3 3/69 4/126 5/144 6/202 7/236 8/300 9/336	339	1/16 2/113 3/158 (3 wkts dec.)	170

Bonus points – Yorkshire 3, Glamorgan 4.

Bowling: *First Innings*—Gibson 26.2–6–86–4; Watkin 27–3–64–4; Lefebvre 26–12–65–1; Dale 18–5–49–1; Croft 18–5–52–0. *Second Innings*—Gibson 12–3–40–0; Watkin 12–3–20–1; Lefebvre 11–4–28–0; Croft 16–3–44–1; Dale 8–0–34–1.

Glamorgan

S. P. James lbw b Stemp	28	– not out	15
*H. Morris c Blakey b Gough	37	– not out	10
A. Dale lbw b Stemp	23		
M. P. Maynard c Byas b Stemp	10		
D. L. Hemp c Richardson b Stemp	15		
P. A. Cottey c Blakey b Hartley	3		
R. D. B. Croft st Blakey b Stemp	4		
O. D. Gibson c Blakey b Gough	0		
R. P. Lefebvre c Blakey b Gough	20		
†C. P. Metson not out	36		
S. L. Watkin c Blakey b Hartley	14		
L-b 9, w 3, n-b 6	18	L-b 1	1
1/76 2/76 3/96 4/113 5/128 6/128 7/134 8/134 9/165	208	(no wkt)	26

Bonus points – Glamorgan 1, Yorkshire 4.

Bowling: *First Innings*—Gough 20–6–57–3; Hartley 15.2–5–33–2; Robinson 11–3–44–0; White 5–1–17–0; Stemp 29–12–48–5. *Second Innings*—Gough 5–1–11–0; Hartley 6–2–12–0; Robinson 3–2–2–0.

Umpires: B. Leadbeater and R. Palmer.

At Hove, May 26, 27, 28, 30. GLAMORGAN drew with SUSSEX.

GLAMORGAN v SURREY

At Swansea, June 2, 3, 4, 6. Drawn. Glamorgan 2 pts, Surrey 4 pts. Toss: Surrey.

The unrelenting weather again wrecked any chance of a finish, with play curtailed on the first two days, only six overs bowled on the third and none on the final day. Championship leaders Surrey overcame a mid-innings stutter to gain maximum batting points, as Hollioake – who reached both his fifty and his century with sixes – and Butcher put on 116 for the sixth wicket. Benjamin reduced Glamorgan to eight for two, but James and Hemp stabilised the innings. They remained undefeated at the close and throughout what little play followed. Drizzle and sea mist persisted throughout the final day; although the captains were eager to play for bonus points, they were denied the opportunity and Glamorgan slipped to the bottom of the table.

Close of play: First day, Surrey 250-5 (A. J. Hollioake 22*, M. A. Butcher 8*); Second day, Glamorgan 57-2 (S. P. James 18*, D. L. Hemp 22*); Third day, Glamorgan 77-2 (S. P. James 19*, D. L. Hemp 41*).

Surrey

D. J. Bicknell lbw b Watkin	54
A. W. Smith c Roseberry b Lefebvre	24
*G. P. Thorpe lbw b Gibson	65
D. M. Ward b Lefebvre	35
A. D. Brown c Metson b Dale	21
A. J. Hollioake not out	101
M. A. Butcher c Metson b Watkin	62
N. M. Kendrick c Lefebvre b Watkin	22
†N. F. Sargeant c James b Watkin	5
J. E. Benjamin run out	6
C. E. Cuffy c Hemp b Croft	2
B 7, l-b 9, w 2, n-b 14	32
1/32 2/126 3/189 4/193 5/228 6/344 7/406 8/414 9/426	429

Bonus points – Surrey 4, Glamorgan 2 (Score at 120 overs: 406-6).

Bowling: Watkin 29–1–115–4; Lefebvre 32–10–74–2; Gibson 16–3–81–1; Croft 33–4–103–1; Dale 14–4–40–1.

Glamorgan

S. P. James not out	19
*H. Morris lbw b Benjamin	2
A. Dale b Benjamin	2
D. L. Hemp not out	41
L-b 9, n-b 4	13
1/6 2/8 (2 wkts)	77

P. A. Cottey, A. Roseberry, R. D. B. Croft, O. D. Gibson, R. P. Lefebvre, †C. P. Metson and S. L. Watkin did not bat.

Bowling: Cuffy 13–5–23–0; Benjamin 10–2–26–2; Butcher 4–1–10–0; Kendrick 4–2–4–0; Smith 1–0–5–0.

Umpires: D. R. Shepherd and P. Willey.

At Swansea, June 8, 9, 10. GLAMORGAN lost to NEW ZEALANDERS by eight wickets (See New Zealand tour section).

At Cambridge, June 11, 12, 13. GLAMORGAN drew with CAMBRIDGE UNIVERSITY.

GLAMORGAN v DERBYSHIRE

At Cardiff, June 16, 17, 18, 20. Derbyshire won by eight wickets. Derbyshire 23 pts, Glamorgan 7 pts. Toss: Glamorgan. First-class debut: M. Taylor.

Both teams were looking for their first win but, despite scoring 402 in their first innings, Glamorgan surrendered meekly to a Derbyshire team short of DeFreitas and Cork. Glamorgan's total was built around a century from Maynard – in his first first-class match for a month, after breaking a knuckle – and a partnership of 140 between him and Hemp. But though Watkin had the opposition struggling at 15 for two, Barnett and Azharuddin rescued them, putting on 109, and on the third day O'Gorman and Krikken frustrated Glamorgan with 145 for the eighth wicket, enabling Derbyshire to take a lead of 68 on first innings. When Glamorgan resumed, only Dale showed any resolve and Derbyshire were left with the simple target of 129. Gibson helped them on their way, with eight no-balls in four overs. He did manage to dismiss Vandrau, but Barnett and Adams, scoring at nearly seven an over, made victory certain.

Close of play: First day, Glamorgan 350-5 (P. A. Cottey 41*, R. D. B. Croft 36*); Second day, Derbyshire 292-6 (T. J. G. O'Gorman 59*, M. Taylor 3*); Third day, Glamorgan 175-7 (A. Dale 70*).

Glamorgan

S. P. James lbw b Vandrau	46	– b Malcolm	18
*H. Morris c Bowler b Malcolm	8	– b Griffith	9
A. Dale c Krikken b Warner	2	– c Vandrau b Malcolm	75
M. P. Maynard c Krikken b Vandrau	118	– c Adams b Warner	25
D. L. Hemp b Taylor	51	– lbw b Vandrau	28
P. A. Cottey b Warner	42	– b Malcolm	1
R. D. B. Croft lbw b Malcolm	36	– c Vandrau b Taylor	16
O. D. Gibson run out	28	– c Krikken b Taylor	4
†C. P. Metson c Vandrau b Malcolm	8	– not out	13
S. L. Watkin not out	13	– c O'Gorman b Griffith	2
S. Bastien b Malcolm	1	– c Bowler b Griffith	0
B 7, l-b 28, w 2, n-b 12	49	L-b 1, n-b 4	5
1/17 2/26 3/122 4/262 5/262 6/351 7/351 8/382 9/392	402	1/24 2/28 3/78 4/127 5/128 6/169 7/175 8/189 9/196	196

Bonus points – Glamorgan 4, Derbyshire 3 (Score at 120 overs: 351-7).

Bowling: *First Innings*—Malcolm 35.3–7–109–4; Warner 32–7–94–2; Griffith 18–1–66–0; Taylor 27–9–43–1; Vandrau 28–11–55–2. *Second Innings*—Malcolm 21–6–71–3; Griffith 13.4–3–32–3; Warner 11–1–30–1; Vandrau 13–0–48–1; Taylor 6–0–13–2; Barnett 1–0–1–0.

Derbyshire

First innings		Second innings	
*K. J. Barnett b Bastien	51	– not out	42
P. D. Bowler c Metson b Watkin	3		
C. J. Adams lbw b Watkin	0	– st Metson b Croft	58
M. Azharuddin c Gibson b Watkin	109		
T. J. G. O'Gorman b Dale	128	– (4) not out	2
M. J. Vandrau c Metson b Gibson	43	– (2) c Metson b Gibson	6
F. A. Griffith c Morris b Gibson	3		
M. Taylor c Metson b Watkin	3		
†K. M. Krikken not out	85		
A. E. Warner lbw b Watkin	14		
D. E. Malcolm b Watkin	2		
L-b 9, n-b 20	29	L-b 1, n-b 20	21
1/13 2/15 3/124 4/193 5/277 6/289 7/294 8/439 9/464	470	1/20 2/121 (2 wkts)	129

Bonus points – Derbyshire 4, Glamorgan 3 (Score at 120 overs: 395-7).

Bowling: *First Innings*—Watkin 31.2–3–143–6; Gibson 26–2–117–2; Bastien 30–5–87–1; Croft 33–12–67–0; Dale 14–4–47–1. *Second Innings*—Watkin 8–0–39–0; Gibson 4–0–32–1; Bastien 3.2–0–17–0; Croft 8–1–40–1.

Umpires: H. D. Bird and R. Julian.

GLAMORGAN v LANCASHIRE

At Colwyn Bay, June 23, 24, 25, 27. Lancashire won by 220 runs. Lancashire 23 pts, Glamorgan 5 pts. Toss: Lancashire.

Glamorgan's third defeat of the season was completed shortly after tea on the final day, when their batsmen were bowled out inside 51 overs by the Lancashire off-spin duo of Watkinson and Yates. They lost their last eight wickets for 54 runs. Even when Morris and Dale were putting on 84 for the second wicket, they looked unlikely to achieve a target of 386 in 80 overs. Lancashire had recovered from 96 for six, thanks chiefly to their captain, Watkinson, who struck a career-best 155 – his second century in consecutive innings – added 124 with Martin and hit six sixes off Croft. Then Chapple, deputising for Wasim Akram, took his first five-wicket haul in the Championship. Glamorgan lost eight wickets before avoiding the follow-on, which they eventually did through a half-century by Hemp and useful contributions from Lefebvre and Metson. Ninety minutes were lost to rain on the third day but Lancashire were always in control.

Close of play: First day, Lancashire 319-9 (W. K. Hegg 18*); Second day, Glamorgan 191-7 (D. L. Hemp 53*, C. P. Metson 0*); Third day, Lancashire 195-4 (N. J. Speak 14*).

Lancashire

First innings		Second innings	
S. P. Titchard c James b Watkin	0	– c Metson b Watkin	22
M. A. Atherton lbw b Lefebvre	20	– lbw b Watkin	30
J. P. Crawley c Maynard b Gibson	43	– lbw b Lefebvre	83
N. H. Fairbrother lbw b Lefebvre	1	– c Hemp b Croft	28
N. J. Speak c Morris b Croft	10	– not out	40
I. D. Austin c Metson b Watkin	2	– retired hurt	0
*M. Watkinson c Hemp b Watkin	155	– b Lefebvre	3
P. J. Martin b Gibson	37	– c Gibson b Lefebvre	2
†W. K. Hegg not out	38	– not out	27
G. Yates c Gibson b Watkin	0		
G. Chapple c Maynard b Dale	19		
B 4, l-b 12, w 2, n-b 16	34	B 6, l-b 9, w 4, n-b 10	29
1/0 2/35 3/37 4/62 5/65 6/96 7/220 8/319 9/319	359	1/63 2/66 3/159 4/195 5/199 6/209 (6 wkts dec.)	264

Bonus points – Lancashire 3, Glamorgan 4 (Score at 120 overs: 324-9).

In the second innings I. D. Austin retired hurt at 195-4.

Bowling: *First Innings*—Watkin 30–10–59–4; Gibson 29–4–91–2; Lefebvre 25–10–39–2; Barwick 31–13–38–0; Croft 24–6–91–1; Dale 4–1–25–1. *Second Innings*—Watkin 12–6–26–2; Gibson 13–2–49–0; Barwick 31.5–11–67–0; Lefebvre 21–5–64–3; Croft 9–1–43–1.

Glamorgan

S. P. James c Hegg b Chapple	12	– c Atherton b Chapple	3
*H. Morris c Speak b Chapple	52	– run out	43
A. Dale c Hegg b Chapple	11	– c Titchard b Watkinson	45
M. P. Maynard c Titchard b Chapple	0	– c Speak b Yates	26
D. L. Hemp lbw b Chapple	56	– b Watkinson	4
R. D. B. Croft c and b Austin	25	– b Watkinson	0
O. D. Gibson b Yates	3	– (8) c Fairbrother b Yates	14
R. P. Lefebvre c Austin b Yates	33	– (7) c Yates b Watkinson	23
†C. P. Metson c Atherton b Austin	36	– b Yates	1
S. L. Watkin not out	6	– not out	0
S. R. Barwick lbw b Austin	1	– c Atherton b Yates	2
B 1, l-b 2	3	L-b 4	4
1/42 2/73 3/73 4/78 5/120 6/123 7/191 8/205 9/236	238	1/5 2/89 3/111 4/121 5/123 6/131 7/161 8/162 9/163	165

Bonus points – Glamorgan 1, Lancashire 4.

Bowling: *First Innings*—Martin 27–9–57–0; Chapple 28–6–79–5; Watkinson 14–3–34–0; Austin 10.1–3–32–3; Yates 11–3–33–2. *Second Innings*—Martin 10–2–28–0; Chapple 8–2–29–1; Watkinson 21–7–73–4; Yates 11.5–4–31–4.

Umpires: K. J. Lyons and P. B. Wight.

At Bristol, June 30, July 1, 2. GLAMORGAN beat GLOUCESTERSHIRE by nine wickets.

At Southend, July 14, 15, 16, 18. GLAMORGAN lost to ESSEX by 18 runs.

GLAMORGAN v KENT

At Abergavenny, July 21, 22, 23, 25. Kent won by 94 runs. Kent 24 pts, Glamorgan 5 pts. Toss: Kent.

Glamorgan went down to their fourth Championship defeat out of five. Set a target of 473, unlikely but not impossible on this fast-scoring ground, they had lost four wickets for 147 before a partnership of 186 between Hemp and Cottey gave them an outside chance of victory. At tea, they were still together and required a further 156. But when the new ball was taken, Wren dismissed Hemp, who was quickly followed by Cottey and the tail. Kent had made the most of winning the toss, running up 373 on the first day, though their last five went quickly in the morning as Lefebvre returned his best figures for his second county. But Glamorgan collapsed from 118 for one to 181 for seven with McCague bowling fast and well; it took Gibson and Metson, adding 85 for the eighth wicket, to avert the follow-on. Their bowlers then struggled again as Ward scored his second hundred of the match, repeating his 1991 feat against Glamorgan – and Kent's ninth wicket added 69 valuable runs. On the second day, the start was delayed 20 minutes, and play extended, to accommodate a visit by the Prince of Wales, who met players and officials and sat through 16 runs and one wicket.

Close of play: First day, Kent 373-5 (C. L. Hooper 84*, M. A. Ealham 32*); Second day, Kent 60-1 (T. R. Ward 47*, N. R. Taylor 9*); Third day, Glamorgan 57-1 (H. Morris 22*, C. P. Metson 0*).

Kent

T. R. Ward lbw b Croft	110	– b Barwick	125
*M. R. Benson b Barwick	66	– c Morris b Watkin	1
N. R. Taylor c Lefebvre b Watkin	37	– c Metson b Watkin	14
C. L. Hooper lbw b Watkin	87	– lbw b Croft	30
G. R. Cowdrey c Metson b Gibson	15	– c Gibson b Barwick	39
M. V. Fleming c Croft b Barwick	2	– c Lefebvre b Croft	22
M. A. Ealham c Maynard b Lefebvre	40	– c James b Barwick	43
†S. A. Marsh c Hemp b Lefebvre	9	– run out	3
M. M. Patel b Lefebvre	5	– c James b Barwick	3
M. J. McCague not out	6	– c Morris b Croft	36
T. N. Wren c Metson b Lefebvre	0	– not out	3
B 8, l-b 5, w 8, n-b 10	31	B 2, l-b 3, n-b 6	11
1/143 2/229 3/255 4/288 5/298 6/387 7/389 8/399 9/402	408	1/5 2/77 3/132 4/196 5/239 6/239 7/246 8/249 9/318	330

Bonus points – Kent 4, Glamorgan 3 (Score at 120 overs: 399-8).

Bowling: *First Innings*—Watkin 30–6–85–2; Gibson 19–1–90–1; Lefebvre 25.2–6–63–4; Barwick 29–7–73–2; Croft 22–4–84–1. *Second Innings*—Watkin 15–5–38–2; Lefebvre 9–0–47–0; Gibson 12–0–73–0; Croft 34–5–88–3; Barwick 34.1–10–79–4.

Glamorgan

S. P. James c Marsh b Wren	13	– c Ward b Patel	30
*H. Morris c Marsh b Ealham	67	– c Ward b Patel	39
D. L. Hemp b McCague	36	– (4) c Hooper b Wren	133
M. P. Maynard c Ward b Patel	12	– (5) c Marsh b Ealham	15
P. A. Cottey c Marsh b Patel	10	– (6) c Marsh b McCague	80
R. D. B. Croft c Marsh b McCague	6	– (7) c McCague b Patel	12
O. D. Gibson c Cowdrey b Hooper	67	– (8) c Marsh b McCague	15
R. P. Lefebvre c Taylor b Patel	4	– (9) not out	13
†C. P. Metson c Patel b Ealham	17	– (3) b McCague	10
S. L. Watkin b Ealham	0	– c Benson b Patel	0
S. R. Barwick not out	0	– run out	0
L-b 6, w 4, n-b 24	34	B 3, l-b 10, n-b 18	31
1/33 2/118 3/153 4/161 5/168 6/176 7/181 8/266 9/266	266	1/56 2/72 3/117 4/147 5/333 6/335 7/361 8/363 9/375	378

Bonus points – Glamorgan 2, Kent 4.

Bowling: *First Innings*—McCague 18–1–87–2; Wren 9–1–58–1; Ealham 10–2–24–3; Patel 23–7–49–3; Fleming 2–0–21–0; Hooper 9.2–1–21–1. *Second Innings*—McCague 23.4–3–115–3; Ealham 11–0–45–1; Patel 30–6–88–4; Hooper 36–12–62–0; Wren 9–2–39–1; Fleming 3–0–16–0.

Umpires: V. A. Holder and A. G. T. Whitehead.

GLAMORGAN v SOMERSET

At Swansea, July 28, 29, 30, August 1. Drawn. Glamorgan 5 pts, Somerset 6 pts. Toss: Somerset. Championship debuts: A. J. Dalton, B. S. Phelps.

Glamorgan failed to meet the challenge of scoring 142 in 22 overs and finished on an uneasy 85 for seven. But they played more purposefully throughout than Somerset, who laboured through both innings at a run-rate rarely exceeding 2.5 an over, despite centuries from Hayhurst and Trescothick. The home attack was handicapped by an injury which prevented Watkin bowling after the first day. Barwick also missed part of Saturday, attending the birth of his daughter. In the first innings, however, he had claimed two of his county's lesser-known records, bowling 65.2 overs and 29 maidens in an innings. Glamorgan took a first-innings lead of 161, thanks mainly to the 5ft 4in Cottey, who hit a powerful career-best 191, and put on 141 in a little-and-large partnership with Gibson, who struck five sixes. Van Troost donated 28 no-balls and five wides to a total of 81 extras, which equalled the record conceded by Derbyshire twice during the season. Gibson then took his match haul to 11 for 159. But Glamorgan's hopes of victory were undone by Rose, who took three for three in ten deliveries to reduce them to 38 for five.

Close of play: First day, Somerset 257-4 (A. N. Hayhurst 105*, R. J. Turner 29*); Second day, Glamorgan 222-4 (P. A. Cottey 27*, C. P. Metson 1*); Third day, Somerset 112-3 (M. E. Trescothick 71*, H. R. J. Trump 3*).

Somerset

M. N. Lathwell c Metson b Gibson	1	– b Gibson	6
M. E. Trescothick c Metson b Gibson	0	– c Metson b Phelps	115
R. J. Harden lbw b Gibson	90	– lbw b Dale	7
I. Fletcher c Hemp b Watkin	19	– b Gibson	18
*A. N. Hayhurst c Metson b Dale	121	– (6) c Metson b Gibson	65
†R. J. Turner not out	64	– (7) c Cottey b Gibson	0
G. D. Rose c Maynard b Phelps	4	– (8) c Morris b Gibson	38
V. P. Clarke c sub b Phelps	5	– (9) c Metson b Barwick	2
J. I. D. Kerr lbw b Gibson	1	– (10) c Hemp b Gibson	4
H. R. J. Trump c Maynard b Gibson	10	– (5) b Phelps	17
A. P. van Troost st Metson b Barwick	33	– not out	0
B 5, l-b 12, w 1, n-b 6	24	B 4, l-b 12, w 2, n-b 12	30
1/2 2/3 3/43 4/186 5/296 6/306 7/314 8/319 9/339	372	1/6 2/31 3/106 4/160 5/181 6/207 7/271 8/290 9/302	302

Bonus points – Somerset 2, Glamorgan 1 (Score at 120 overs: 269-4).

Bowling: *First Innings*—Watkin 19–8–29–1; Gibson 32–9–79–5; Barwick 65.2–29–109–1; Phelps 28–5–80–2; Dale 20–3–58–1. *Second Innings*—Gibson 30.3–8–80–6; Dale 25–9–76–1; Phelps 37–14–70–2; Cottey 4–1–16–0; Barwick 19–10–44–1.

Glamorgan

A. Dale c Harden b Rose	7	– c Kerr b van Troost	5
*H. Morris lbw b Trump	25	– run out	8
D. L. Hemp c Turner b Rose	77	– b Rose	10
M. P. Maynard c Trump b Clarke	41	– b Rose	8
P. A. Cottey c Lathwell b Hayhurst	191	– (6) c and b Trump	18
†C. P. Metson c Turner b van Troost	1	– (8) not out	7
A. J. Dalton lbw b van Troost	2	– c Turner b Trump	7
O. D. Gibson run out	81	– (5) b Rose	0
B. S. Phelps c Turner b van Troost	11	– not out	4
S. R. Barwick c Hayhurst b Rose	5		
S. L. Watkin not out	11		
L-b 9, w 7, n-b 65	81	B 4, l-b 4, w 4, n-b 6	18
1/46 2/75 3/144 4/212 5/241 6/255 7/396 8/439 9/456	533	1/6 2/18 3/24 4/24 5/38 6/59 7/60	(7 wkts) 85

Bonus points – Glamorgan 4, Somerset 4 (Score at 120 overs: 518-9).

Bowling: *First Innings*—van Troost 29–3–172–3; Kerr 21–3–91–0; Rose 22–4–69–3; Trump 27–6–89–1; Clarke 20–3–93–1; Lathwell 3–0–8–0; Hayhurst 0.4–0–2–1. *Second Innings*—van Troost 8.4–1–46–1; Rose 6–0–14–3; Clarke 3–1–12–0; Trump 4–2–5–2.

Umpires: J. D. Bond and D. J. Constant.

At Lord's, August 4, 5, 6, 8. GLAMORGAN lost to MIDDLESEX by 80 runs.

At Pontypridd, August 13, 14, 15. GLAMORGAN drew with SOUTH AFRICANS (See South African tour section).

At Hartlepool, August 18, 19, 20. GLAMORGAN lost to DURHAM by three wickets.

GLAMORGAN v LEICESTERSHIRE

At Cardiff, August 25, 26, 27, 29. Glamorgan won by 150 runs. Glamorgan 22 pts, Leicestershire 5 pts. Toss: Glamorgan. Championship debut: G. P. Butcher.

Glamorgan gained their second Championship win of the season to thwart Leicestershire's attempts to close the gap on leaders Warwickshire. On the first day, Cottey rescued them from an unpromising 149 for seven with a defiant five-hour century, assisted by Metson in a partnership of 116. Leicestershire also began shakily, with Gibson removing Simmons and Wells in the 13th over. That they were only 51 adrift was due to Boon and Robinson, who made 86 in his second Championship game of the season. Hemp, reaching 50 for the 11th time in 1994 – he was rewarded with his county cap – and Metson, with his first half-century for three years, consolidated Glamorgan's advantage. After a rapid 80 from Croft, Leicestershire were set 412. But they slumped to 63 for four by the end of the third day. Despite resolute batting from Wells and Pierson, Croft completed his first five-wicket haul of the season to ensure victory before tea on Monday.

Close of play: First day, Leicestershire 24-0 (T. J. Boon 7*, N. E. Briers 4*); Second day, Glamorgan 67-3 (D. L. Hemp 28*, C. P. Metson 0*); Third day, Leicestershire 63-4 (A. R. K. Pierson 0*, V. J. Wells 1*).

Glamorgan

M. P. Maynard b Millns	27	– c Pierson b Parsons	34
*H. Morris c Nixon b Parsons	4	– c Pierson b Millns	4
D. L. Hemp c Nixon b Millns	0	– b Pierson	50
A. Dale c Wells b Millns	31	– c Nixon b Simmons	0
P. A. Cottey c Nixon b Wells	142	– (6) c Nixon b Millns	43
O. D. Gibson lbw b Brimson	12	– (7) st Nixon b Brimson	22
R. D. B. Croft lbw b Millns	0	– (8) c Robinson b Wells	80
G. P. Butcher c Nixon b Parsons	4	– (9) c Millns b Simmons	41
†C. P. Metson b Parsons	43	– (5) run out	51
S. L. Watkin not out	4	– not out	6
S. R. Barwick c Nixon b Wells	0	– not out	5
B 5, l-b 4, w 1, n-b 18	28	B 7, l-b 9, n-b 8	24
1/40 2/40 3/41 4/103 5/128 6/129 7/149 8/265 9/295	295	1/13 2/59 3/64 4/112 5/160 6/217 7/219 8/295 9/349 (9 wkts dec.)	360

Bonus points – Glamorgan 2, Leicestershire 4.

Bowling: *First Innings*—Millns 24–1–83–4; Parsons 27–10–67–3; Wells 10–4–42–2; Simmons 16–2–43–0; Brimson 17–1–42–1; Pierson 6–2–9–0. *Second Innings*—Millns 22–1–80–2; Parsons 16–1–69–1; Simmons 13–1–31–2; Pierson 17–4–54–1; Brimson 23–9–68–1; Wells 8–0–42–1.

Leicestershire

T. J. Boon run out	74	– (3) c Metson b Gibson	2
*N. E. Briers not out	36	– c Maynard b Watkin	23
J. J. Whitaker c Cottey b Watkin	0	– (4) c Morris b Croft	1
P. V. Simmons c Butcher b Gibson	0	– (1) c Cottey b Dale	22
V. J. Wells b Gibson	0	– (6) c Watkin b Croft	56
P. E. Robinson lbw b Watkin	86	– (7) c Cottey b Croft	29
†P. A. Nixon c Maynard b Watkin	11	– (8) c Metson b Barwick	34
G. J. Parsons c Metson b Gibson	1	– (9) st Metson b Croft	26
A. R. K. Pierson b Dale	2	– (5) c Maynard b Croft	26
D. J. Millns c Metson b Dale	4	– not out	2
M. T. Brimson b Barwick	0	– c Metson b Barwick	2
B 1, l-b 6, w 1, n-b 22	30	B 7, l-b 14, w 1, n-b 16	38
1/31 2/38 3/38 4/170 5/198 6/209 7/227 8/233 9/243	244	1/40 2/55 3/62 4/62 5/148 6/161 7/190 8/256 9/258	261

Bonus points – Leicestershire 1, Glamorgan 4.

In the first innings N. E. Briers, when 4, retired hurt at 24 and resumed at 198.

Bowling: *First Innings*—Gibson 18–3–72–3; Watkin 24–8–58–3; Butcher 6–1–28–0; Croft 21–6–40–0; Barwick 19.4–9–32–1; Dale 5–2–7–2. *Second Innings*—Gibson 18–6–67–1; Watkin 21–4–53–1; Dale 6–3–3–1; Croft 26–8–80–5; Butcher 10–3–24–0; Barwick 9.5–6–13–2.

Umpires: D. J. Constant and V. A. Holder.

At Worksop, August 30, 31, September 1, 2. GLAMORGAN lost to NOTTINGHAMSHIRE by an innings and 37 runs.

GLAMORGAN v WORCESTERSHIRE

At Cardiff, September 8, 9, 10, 12. Drawn. Glamorgan 4 pts, Worcestershire 3 pts. Toss: Glamorgan.

The weather denied Glamorgan a third Championship win – and their last chance to escape the bottom of the table – when they ended 12 runs short of their target of 255. The task kept growing, however, as they lost ten of what should have been 62 overs to showers; after the fourth stoppage, they needed 19 from nine deliveries. Rain had disrupted all four days and completely washed out Saturday. Worcestershire, put in on a seamers' pitch, suffered at the hands of Gibson, who took six for 64, his best performance of the season, to earn his county cap; their last five wickets fell for 44 on the second day. After reciprocal declarations, James, recalled for his first Championship game since July, completed a 140-ball century, putting on 113 with Maynard in a determined assault which almost paid off.

Close of play: First day, Worcestershire 206-5 (G. R. Haynes 10*, S. J. Rhodes 8*); Second day, Glamorgan 134-3 (M. P. Maynard 48*, P. A. Cottey 22*); Third day, No play.

Worcestershire

*T. S. Curtis c Metson b Gibson	21	– c Maynard b Cottey	45
W. P. C. Weston c Roseberry b Gibson	59	– b Lefebvre	12
G. A. Hick c Metson b Lefebvre	23		
T. M. Moody lbw b Gibson	66		
G. R. Haynes c James b Gibson	13	– (3) c Metson b Dale	1
D. A. Leatherdale c Hemp b Gibson	7	– (4) not out	54
†S. J. Rhodes c Metson b Lefebvre	34	– (5) not out	9
S. R. Lampitt c Metson b Gibson	8		
P. J. Newport c Metson b Watkin	8		
R. K. Illingworth not out	3		
N. V. Radford lbw b Watkin	1		
L-b 12, w 2, n-b 8	22	L-b 1, w 1	2
1/32 2/63 3/181 4/182 5/194 6/221 7/235 8/255 9/263	265	1/26 2/27 3/98 (3 wkts dec.)	123

Bonus points – Worcestershire 2, Glamorgan 4.

Bowling: *First Innings*—Gibson 19–2–64–6; Watkin 17.1–1–48–2; Lefebvre 29–10–67–2; Croft 5–0–30–0; Dale 6–1–44–0. *Second Innings*—Watkin 6–1–16–0; Lefebvre 8–2–11–1; Dale 5–0–25–1; Cottey 6–0–36–1; Hemp 3–0–24–0; Maynard 1–0–10–0.

Glamorgan

S. P. James c Rhodes b Lampitt	29	– st Rhodes b Illingworth	116
A. Roseberry lbw b Lampitt	16	– c Rhodes b Newport	8
D. L. Hemp c Curtis b Newport	16	– lbw b Lampitt	19
*M. P. Maynard not out	48	– c Radford b Illingworth	72
P. A. Cottey not out	22	– b Illingworth	9
O. D. Gibson (did not bat)		– not out	6
A. Dale (did not bat)		– not out	1
L-b 1, n-b 2	3	B 4, l-b 4, n-b 4	12
1/38 2/57 3/61 (3 wkts dec.)	134	1/25 2/89 3/202 4/229 5/240 (5 wkts)	243

R. D. B. Croft, R. P. Lefebvre, †C. P. Metson and S. L. Watkin did not bat.

Bonus point – Worcestershire 1.

Bowling: *First Innings*—Radford 11–2–39–0; Lampitt 15–6–48–2; Newport 11–2–31–1; Haynes 4–1–12–0; Illingworth 2–1–3–0. *Second Innings*—Newport 15–2–59–1; Radford 5–0–24–0; Haynes 3–0–12–0; Lampitt 11–1–72–1; Illingworth 17.5–1–68–3.

Umpires: G. I. Burgess and D. R. Shepherd.

At Southampton, September 15, 16, 17, 19. GLAMORGAN drew with HAMPSHIRE.

GLOUCESTERSHIRE

Patron: HRH The Princess of Wales
President: D. N. Perry
Chairman: R. W. Rossiter
Chief Executive: P. G. M. August
Captain: 1994 – C. A. Walsh
1995 – R. C. Russell
Coach: A. W. Stovold
Assistant Coach: P. W. Romaines
Head Groundsman: D. Bridle
Scorer: B. H. Jenkins

Gloucestershire, who had been desperate to retain the services of Courtney Walsh, logically and astutely gave him the captaincy. Nothing could have been more felicitous. He grew marvellously into the job, full of enthusiasm, surprising energy – ignore that seemingly languid persona – and with a gentle touch of discipline when it was needed.

Although 1994 was hardly a memorable summer for the county, the wise influence of Walsh, allied for the most part to sound tactical judgment, was always apparent. Unlike a number of fellow West Indian Test players, he seldom looked weary. He celebrated his 32nd birthday in October in India, where he took on, in addition, the leadership of his national team. During the 1994 season he often bowled quite magnificently, a tribute to stamina quite apart from sheer speed or the other penetrative assets that emanate from that lovely, effortless action. He won and nearly won matches for Gloucestershire on his own. But for an injury caused by a car accident and a brief return to the West Indies to discuss his role and responsibilities as Test captain, he would surely have taken 100 wickets. As it was, he took 89, at an average of 17.24, second only to Curtly Ambrose. His players listened to his words, and visibly doted on his deeds.

Gloucestershire lifted themselves from 17th to 12th in the table. That, in its modest way, was a reflection of emerging merits. Bob Dawson, a doughty young Devonian, was an obvious example. He went for his shots at the right times and finished top of the county's first-class batting averages. Matt Windows, small and chunky, often reaped his runs square on the off. Confidence and sagacity grew encouragingly as the season went on. Despite a hundred, away to Essex, Tim Hancock lacked consistency and fell short, by 80 runs, of his target of 1,000. He is not by nature a No. 3 and would benefit from being allowed to drop down the order, where he would be able to show more freedom, as he likes, with less guilt.

There were serious shortcomings in the higher order, leaving gaps to be plugged. Chris Broad had a wretched time of it, finally being left out when it came to Cheltenham and not returning. He was troubled persistently with a hip injury, and form remained elusive. An early hundred, at home to Sussex, followed by decent half-centuries at Worcester and Chelmsford, were no more than a deceptive prelude. He never reached 50 again. All the hopes, pragmatic and sentimental, that accompanied his return to Bristol were unrealised; and in December the club let him go. It was also miserable for Dean Hodgson, who was often out of the side and had to wait till the final match for his hundred. At least Tony Wright conquered some of the psychological demons that turned the 1993 summer for him into one of despair. Promoted to open in July, he grasped at the additional responsibilities and quietly battled his way out of trouble. His undefeated 184 against a volatile Leicestershire team was his best innings so far and contained some fluent shots of real maturity.

Next to Walsh among the bowlers, a long way behind, was Mark Alleyne, much improved at uncomplicated medium-pace. He produced career-best bowling figures at Cheltenham. Indeed, everything he did there carried a sheen. He batted superbly, with hundreds against Yorkshire in the Championship and Sunday League; he sustained that tidy assurance and added concentration, garnished with handsome drives through the off side and generally selective strokeplay, in the following fixture against Kent. After a slow start to the summer, he went past his 1,000 runs. Because of his acknowledged skills and technique, the flaws are all the more regrettable. There is surely more in his Cheltenham vein to come and be enjoyed.

Despite the disappointment of being dropped by England, Jack Russell kept wicket with vintage efficiency, taking difficult catches with deceptive ease. As a batsman, full of whims and application, he offered a number of times the backbone that his colleagues too easily lacked. When Walsh was absent, he took over as captain. It is pointless to dwell on the match with the South Africans. This meaningless contest angered the spectators who criticised Russell for not declaring to set the tourists a target. He, in turn, resented being made the scapegoat. Maybe blame should be apportioned evenly between the teams. Certainly lack of communication, a complaint of Russell's, is two-way. There was a case to dredge up something less supine for the suffering crowd. It can serve as a valuable experience for the fledgling skipper in 1995, when West Indies are touring and he will have to replace Walsh.

The prospect of a Walsh-less season filled many Gloucestershire supporters with pessimism. The club narrowly failed to sign the New Zealander Dion Nash, then switched emphasis by getting a world-class batsman, the Australian David Boon. But this coup was short-lived: Boon withdrew in November, worried about his knee. In January, Gloucestershire signed the Indian pace bowler, Javagal Srinath.

The left-arm swing of Mike Smith should never be underestimated. Vyvian Pike is a leg-spinner worth extended employment and added scope, now that he is getting the feel of county cricket. Ricardo Williams, the seamer from Haringey, is again being worked on diligently during the winter months. Martyn Ball had less success as an off-spinner, though there were his admirable slip catches and some perky batting as a bonus. But they are all going to have to work very hard in 1995. As for the one-day matches, Gloucestershire revealed no noticeable facility for them in 1994. They disappeared instantly in both the Benson and Hedges and the NatWest competitions, and did not pick up a Sunday win until well into July. – David Foot.

GLOUCESTERSHIRE 1994

[*Bill Smith*

Back row: R. C. J. Williams, K. P. Sheeraz, R. J. Cunliffe, D. R. Hewson, R. C. Williams, M. G. N. Windows. *Middle row:* B. H. Jenkins (*scorer*), M. C. J. Ball, V. J. Pike, A. M. Babington, S. G. Hinks, M. J. Cawdron, R. M. Wight, T. H. C. Hancock, R. I. Dawson, A. M. Smith, M. Davies. *Front row:* P. W. Romaines (*assistant coach*), A. J. Wright, B. C. Broad, A. W. Stovold (*coach*), R. W. Rossiter (*chairman*), P. G. M. August (*chief executive*), G. D. Hodgson, M. W. Alleyne, K. E. Cooper. *Insets:* C. A. Walsh (*captain*), R. C. Russell.

GLOUCESTERSHIRE RESULTS

All first-class matches – Played 20: Won 6, Lost 8, Drawn 6.

County Championship matches – Played 17: Won 5, Lost 8, Drawn 4.

Bonus points – Batting 28, Bowling 56.

Competition placings – Britannic Assurance County Championship, 12th; NatWest Bank Trophy, 1st round; Benson and Hedges Cup, 1st round; AXA Equity & Law League, 18th.

BRITANNIC ASSURANCE CHAMPIONSHIP AVERAGES

BATTING

	Birthplace	*M*	*I*	*NO*	*R*	*HS*	*Avge*
‡A. J. Wright	*Stevenage*	17	33	2	1,108	184*	35.74
‡R. C. Russell	*Stroud*	17	30	7	807	85*	35.08
R. I. Dawson	*Exmouth*	13	25	3	743	93	33.77
M. G. N. Windows	*Bristol*	9	17	0	564	85	33.17
M. Davies	*Neath*	3	6	2	122	54	30.50
S. G. Hinks	*Northfleet*	4	8	0	235	74	29.37
‡B. C. Broad	*Bristol*	9	18	0	493	128	27.38
T. H. C. Hancock	*Reading*	17	32	1	831	123	26.80
‡M. W. Alleyne	*Tottenham*	17	32	0	833	109	26.03
‡G. D. Hodgson	*Carlisle*	8	15	1	316	113	22.57
M. C. J. Ball	*Bristol*	15	26	2	442	45	18.41
‡C. A. Walsh§	*Kingston, Jamaica*	15	24	6	274	66	15.22
A. M. Smith	*Dewsbury*	10	12	1	146	29	13.27
R. J. Cunliffe	*Oxford*	5	10	0	130	29	13.00
R. C. Williams	*Camberwell*	8	13	2	133	34*	12.09
V. J. Pike	*Taunton*	7	11	3	94	27	11.75
K. E. Cooper	*Hucknall*	11	15	8	77	18*	11.00

Also batted: K. P. Sheeraz (*Wellington*) (1 match) 1*, 0*; R. M. Wight (*Kensington*) (1 match) 22, 11.

* *Signifies not out.* ‡ *Denotes county cap.* § *Overseas player.*

The following played a total of five three-figure innings for Gloucestershire in County Championship matches – M. W. Alleyne 1, B. C. Broad 1, T. H. C. Hancock 1, G. D. Hodgson 1, A. J. Wright 1.

BOWLING

	O	*M*	*R*	*W*	*BB*	*5W/i*	*Avge*
C. A. Walsh	506	119	1,535	89	7-42	9	17.24
M. W. Alleyne	313.3	60	1,014	37	5-78	1	27.40
K. E. Cooper	403.2	94	1,069	35	4-38	0	30.54
A. M. Smith	243.1	47	809	23	5-40	1	35.17
R. C. Williams	191.5	32	686	19	3-13	0	36.10
V. J. Pike	147.3	28	496	11	3-109	0	45.09
M. C. J. Ball	292.3	62	914	19	5-69	1	48.10

Also bowled: M. Davies 72–7–282–5; R. I. Dawson 30–9–73–2; T. H. C. Hancock 36–4–157–2; K. P. Sheeraz 15–2–34–2; R. M. Wight 27–2–139–3.

Wicket-keeper: R. C. Russell 55 ct, 1 st.

Leading Fielders: A. J. Wright 31, M. C. J. Ball 26, M. W. Alleyne 16.

GLOUCESTERSHIRE v SOMERSET

At Bristol, April 28, 29, 30, May 1. Gloucestershire won by 83 runs. Gloucestershire 21 pts, Somerset 5 pts. Toss: Gloucestershire. First-class debut: V. P. Clarke.

Gloucestershire followed their win over Somerset at the back-end of 1993 with another unexpected triumph, which was almost wholly due to the bowling of their captain Walsh. His figures of 11 for 143 reflected his enthusiasm for leadership, as well as considerable skill – and stamina after an onerous winter in the Caribbean. He achieved pace and lift on a slowish wicket. During Somerset's second innings he dismissed four of the top five for one run off 18 balls to put a target of 259 out of sight. It was a less happy start for Somerset's new captain, Hayhurst, despite his own first-innings resistance. After his departure, Folland was almost alone in standing up to Walsh's aggression. Gloucestershire had made a poor start and Caddick and Mushtaq Ahmed took four wickets each. But a back spasm prevented Caddick bowling after the first day. Of Gloucestershire's batsmen, Hinks twice batted well and Russell was dogged as ever, while Wright and Ball were run out in springtime misjudgments. Somerset were forced to recruit a club cricketer from the crowd to act as 12th man; he was forgiven when an over-eager return went for four overthrows.

Close of play: First day, Somerset 75-2 (A. N. Hayhurst 39*, N. A. Mallender 0*); Second day, Gloucestershire 135-4 (S. G. Hinks 63*, T. H. C. Hancock 2*); Third day, Somerset 128-7 (V. P. Clarke 29*, N. A. Mallender 23*).

Gloucestershire

First innings		Second innings	
B. C. Broad c Harden b Caddick	5	– c Turner b Mushtaq Ahmed	9
G. D. Hodgson lbw b Caddick	5	– lbw b Mushtaq Ahmed	28
S. G. Hinks b Mushtaq Ahmed	42	– lbw b Mallender	68
M. W. Alleyne c Lathwell b Mushtaq Ahmed	17	– b Rose	5
A. J. Wright run out	24	– c Lathwell b Mushtaq Ahmed	20
T. H. C. Hancock b Mushtaq Ahmed	33	– c Harden b Lathwell	55
†R. C. Russell b Mushtaq Ahmed	34	– not out	66
M. C. J. Ball run out	10	– c Mushtaq Ahmed b Rose	9
*C. A. Walsh c Rose b Caddick	1	– c Rose b Mushtaq Ahmed	1
A. M. Smith c Hayhurst b Caddick	16	– b van Troost	0
K. E. Cooper not out	11	– c and b van Troost	4
L-b 3, n-b 2	5	B 6, l-b 11, w 2	19
1/10 2/13 3/60 4/71 5/117 6/132 7/165 8/172 9/181	203	1/24 2/47 3/56 4/109 5/149 6/242 7/258 8/270 9/275	284

Bonus points – Gloucestershire 1, Somerset 4.

Bowling: *First Innings*—Caddick 20.1–6–40–4; Mallender 14–5–19–0; Rose 14–1–30–0; van Troost 7–2–23–0; Mushtaq Ahmed 25–4–88–4. *Second Innings*—Rose 21–8–58–2; van Troost 27.4–7–51–2; Mushtaq Ahmed 36–8–104–4; Mallender 14–6–34–1; Hayhurst 7–4–10–0; Lathwell 4–0–10–1.

Somerset

First innings		Second innings	
*A. N. Hayhurst c Ball b Cooper	49	– c Russell b Walsh	6
M. N. Lathwell c Russell b Walsh	2	– c Wright b Walsh	10
R. J. Harden c Russell b Walsh	28	– c Hancock b Walsh	0
N. A. Mallender c Ball b Cooper	15	– (9) not out	43
N. A. Folland not out	79	– (4) lbw b Cooper	24
†R. J. Turner c Russell b Walsh	16	– (5) c Russell b Walsh	0
G. D. Rose c Wright b Walsh	0	– (6) c Wright b Alleyne	31
V. P. Clarke c Broad b Smith	1	– (7) lbw b Cooper	38
Mushtaq Ahmed c Russell b Walsh	1	– (8) c Broad b Alleyne	0
A. R. Caddick c Hinks b Smith	5	– c Ball b Walsh	1
A. P. van Troost c Broad b Smith	3	– b Walsh	11
L-b 6, n-b 24	30	B 1, l-b 2, n-b 8	11
1/9 2/73 3/102 4/121 5/173 6/173 7/188 8/191 9/221	229	1/10 2/10 3/17 4/17 5/67 6/76 7/76 8/158 9/161	175

Bonus points – Somerset 1, Gloucestershire 4.

Bowling: *First Innings*—Walsh 24–6–71–5; Cooper 18–5–42–2; Smith 18.5–1–68–3; Alleyne 6–1–23–0; Ball 7–2–16–0; Hancock 2–1–3–0. *Second Innings*—Walsh 29.4–11–72–6; Cooper 30–11–51–2; Smith 8–0–17–0; Alleyne 5–1–17–2; Ball 5–0–15–0.

Umpires: H. D. Bird and B. J. Meyer.

GLOUCESTERSHIRE v SUSSEX

At Bristol, May 5, 6, 7, 9. Drawn. Gloucestershire 6 pts, Sussex 2 pts. Toss: Gloucestershire.

Broad recovered from a migraine attack to record his 50th first-class hundred and, though he did not measure it among his better ones, it had the merit of much resolve. He and Russell built a sixth-wicket partnership of 185 to face Sussex with a challenging first-innings total they had not expected: during the 29.4 overs possible on the opening day, they had reduced Gloucestershire to 65 for four. Jarvis had almost immediately accounted for Hodgson and Hinks to suggest he could be a valued asset for his new county, though Salisbury, in his first first-class appearance since the Trinidad Test, failed to find either length or confidence. Walsh claimed another five wickets to establish a 141-run lead, though on the last day there was criticism for his delayed declaration, which left Sussex needing 301 in 51 overs. Yet Walsh was not fully fit and may have feared leaving them a more tempting target. Moores equalled the Sussex record of eight catches in a match for the second time.

Close of play: First day, Gloucestershire 65-4 (B. C. Broad 13*, T. H. C. Hancock 4*); Second day, Gloucestershire 256-5 (B. C. Broad 100*, R. C. Russell 78*); Third day, Gloucestershire 39-2 (B. C. Broad 18*, M. W. Alleyne 9*).

Gloucestershire

First innings		Second innings	
B. C. Broad run out	128	c Moores b Jarvis	32
G. D. Hodgson c Moores b Jarvis	6	c Moores b Giddins	11
S. G. Hinks c Moores b Jarvis	15	c Moores b Giddins	0
M. W. Alleyne c Moores b Giddins	14	c Moores b Stephenson	9
A. J. Wright lbw b Stephenson	8	c and b Stephenson	4
T. H. C. Hancock run out	10	c Wells b Hemmings	14
†R. C. Russell c Moores b Jarvis	79	not out	38
M. C. J. Ball b Jarvis	22	b Jarvis	12
*C. A. Walsh not out	11	c Speight b Hemmings	4
A. M. Smith (did not bat)		c Athey b Hemmings	29
B 4, l-b 7, w 9, n-b 6	26	B 2, l-b 4	6
1/11 2/36 3/46 4/46 5/73 6/258 7/302 8/319	(8 wkts dec.) 319	1/22 2/22 3/39 4/53 5/74 6/74 7/89 8/94 9/159	(9 wkts dec.) 159

K. E. Cooper did not bat.

Bonus points – Gloucestershire 2, Sussex 2 (Score at 120 overs: 289-6).

In the first innings B. C. Broad, when 0, retired ill at 2 and resumed at 46-3.

Bowling: *First Innings*—Stephenson 33–14–74–1; Jarvis 32–8–78–4; Giddins 20–6–41–1; Hemmings 20–4–40–0; Salisbury 14–3–51–0; Lenham 9–0–24–0. *Second Innings*—Jarvis 19–7–48–2; Stephenson 15–4–28–2; Giddins 13–3–35–2; Hemmings 19.4–7–28–3; Salisbury 5–1–14–0.

Sussex

N. J. Lenham c Wright b Cooper	42	– c Ball b Cooper	11
C. W. J. Athey run out	8	– c Ball b Alleyne	25
D. M. Smith c Russell b Walsh	11	– not out	32
*A. P. Wells c Hodgson b Walsh	51	– not out	5
M. P. Speight c Russell b Smith	10		
†P. Moores c Russell b Walsh	1		
F. D. Stephenson c Ball b Smith	32		
I. D. K. Salisbury lbw b Smith	0		
P. W. Jarvis not out	0		
E. E. Hemmings lbw b Walsh	2		
E. S. H. Giddins b Walsh	0		
B 2, l-b 2, w 1, n-b 16	21	B 4, n-b 8	12
1/64 2/77 3/82 4/146 5/150 6/150 7/168 8/173 9/178	178	1/17 2/54	(2 wkts) 85

Bonus points – Gloucestershire 4.

In the first innings C. W. J. Athey, when 8, retired hurt at 42 and resumed at 146; D. M. Smith, when 2, retired hurt at 49 and resumed at 150-6.

Bowling: *First Innings*—Walsh 18.5–2–66–5; Cooper 16–4–43–1; Smith 14–6–31–3; Ball 12–2–34–0. *Second Innings*—Walsh 10–5–17–0; Cooper 11–2–24–1; Ball 5–1–11–0; Smith 7–2–23–0; Alleyne 4–1–6–1; Hancock 1–1–0–0.

Umpires: T. E. Jesty and B. Leadbeater.

At Worcester, May 12, 13, 14, 16. GLOUCESTERSHIRE drew with WORCESTERSHIRE.

At Gateshead Fell, May 19, 20, 21, 23. GLOUCESTERSHIRE lost to DURHAM by 108 runs.

GLOUCESTERSHIRE v SURREY

At Gloucester, May 26, 27, 28, 30. Surrey won by one wicket. Surrey 19 pts, Gloucestershire 4 pts. Toss: Surrey. First-class debut: R. J. Cunliffe.

Surrey scrambled a bye to win off the last ball in a finish that was almost indecently frenetic for the decorous setting of Archdeacon Meadow. In fact, it was a noisy match throughout. The decibel level was determined by the exuberant Surrey fielders, out to increase their lead at the top of the table; there was a quieter drama emanating from a petition, passed among the spectators, for the Gloucester fixture to stay on this King's School ground rather than the traditional Wagon Works. There was no play until the second afternoon and three declarations set Surrey 354 off 90 overs. Eight runs were still needed off the final over. Walsh's fifth ball accounted for Benjamin, but Butcher and Cuffy scampered to victory. Surrey's win had been calmly fashioned by an admirable century from Bicknell and Butcher's determination as late wickets tumbled around him. For Gloucestershire, Wright seemed to have rediscovered the form which utterly deserted him in 1993 – and took two fine catches – while the batting of Hancock and Dawson was encouraging.

Close of play: First day, No play; Second day, Gloucestershire 192-4 (A. J. Wright 47*, R. I. Dawson 18*); Third day, Gloucestershire 80-4 (A. J. Wright 26*, R. I. Dawson 2*).

Gloucestershire

B. C. Broad c Kendrick b Butcher............ 24 – c Brown b Cuffy.............. 0
R. J. Cunliffe c Sargeant b Cuffy............. 2 – c Sargeant b Cuffy............ 7
T. H. C. Hancock b Benjamin................ 75 – c Sargeant b Cuffy............ 2
M. W. Alleyne lbw b Benjamin.............. 2 – c sub b Kendrick............. 38
A. J. Wright c Brown b Benjamin............ 87 – not out...................... 35
R. I. Dawson c Kendrick b Cuffy............ 55 – not out...................... 19
†R. C. Russell c Bicknell b Benjamin......... 16
M. C. J. Ball not out........................ 27
B 2, l-b 1, w 4, n-b 24.............. 31 L-b 3, n-b 2............ 5

1/7 2/53 3/61 4/147 5/272 6/278 7/319 (7 wkts dec.) 319 1/0 2/2 3/21 4/72 (4 wkts dec.) 106

*C. A. Walsh, A. M. Smith and K. E. Cooper did not bat.

Bonus points – Gloucestershire 3, Surrey 3.

Bowling: *First Innings*—Cuffy 29–8–80–2; Benjamin 31.3–10–51–4; Butcher 22–5–96–1; Kendrick 27–6–63–0; Hollioake 9–2–26–0. *Second Innings*—Cuffy 8.3–1–16–3; Benjamin 6–2–9–0; Butcher 4–1–9–0; Hollioake 11–3–37–0; Kendrick 10–1–30–1; Stewart 1–0–2–0.

Surrey

D. J. Bicknell c Russell b Cooper............ 11 – c Wright b Cooper............129
M. A. Butcher run out...................... 22 – (7) not out................... 43
A. J. Hollioake c Ball b Cooper.............. 0 – (6) c Russell b Walsh.......... 26
G. P. Thorpe retired hurt................... 28 – (3) run out.................... 6
†N. F. Sargeant not out..................... 5 – (9) lbw b Ball................ 15
N. M. Kendrick not out..................... 0 – (8) c Wright b Cooper......... 15
*A. J. Stewart (did not bat)................. – (2) lbw b Smith.............. 44
D. M. Ward (did not bat).................... – (4) c Wright b Walsh.......... 10
A. D. Brown (did not bat)................... – (5) b Cooper................. 5
J. E. Benjamin (did not bat)................. – c Russell b Walsh............ 5
C. E. Cuffy (did not bat).................... – not out...................... 0
L-b 2, n-b 4........................ 6 B 2, l-b 9, w 3, n-b 42... 56

1/19 2/19 3/64 (3 wkts dec.) 72 1/121 2/133 3/152 4/157 5/226 6/282 7/312 8/340 9/353 (9 wkts) 354

Bonus point – Gloucestershire 1.

In the first innings G. P. Thorpe retired hurt at 72.

Bowling: *First Innings*—Walsh 7–1–36–0; Cooper 9–2–24–2; Smith 8–6–2–0; Ball 5.1–3–4–0; Alleyne 1–0–4–0. *Second Innings*—Walsh 27–4–83–3; Cooper 25–3–99–3; Smith 17–3–80–1; Ball 5–0–30–1; Alleyne 16–3–51–0.

Umpires: R. Julian and K. E. Palmer.

At Chelmsford, June 2, 3, 4, 6. GLOUCESTERSHIRE drew with ESSEX.

At Bristol, June 11, 12, 13. GLOUCESTERSHIRE drew with NEW ZEALANDERS (See New Zealand tour section).

At Nottingham, June 16, 17, 18. GLOUCESTERSHIRE beat NOTTINGHAMSHIRE by three wickets.

GLOUCESTERSHIRE v CAMBRIDGE UNIVERSITY

At Bristol, June 25, 26, 27. Gloucestershire won by 313 runs. Toss: Gloucestershire. First-class debut: V. J. Pike.

Leading Gloucestershire for the first time, against a weak University side, Alleyne celebrated with an unbeaten hundred in 95 balls. Opening bat Cunliffe had already reached a maiden century, in his seventh first-class innings, and Dawson followed up with his first hundred next day. Gloucestershire's other notable performance came from Vyvian Pike, a bridge engineer on extended summer leave from Somerset County Council. A leg-spinner who had played for Dorset, Pike took nine wickets in the match, including six for 41 in the second innings as Cambridge collapsed for 134. On the first day, the University patently missed Pitcher, at his graduation, and their attack often seemed thin and ineffective; they managed only two wickets in 130 overs, in their last match before facing Oxford.

Close of play: First day, Cambridge University 24-2 (J. Ratledge 13*, R. Q. Cake 4*); Second day, Gloucestershire 218-0 (A. J. Wright 84*, R. I. Dawson 127*).

Gloucestershire

G. D. Hodgson c Cooke b Haste	51		
R. J. Cunliffe not out	177		
T. H. C. Hancock c Cooke b Whittall	16		
*M. W. Alleyne not out	101		
A. J. Wright (did not bat)	–	(1) not out	84
R. I. Dawson (did not bat)	–	(2) not out	127
B 4, l-b 4, w 2, n-b 2	12	B 4, w 1, n-b 2	7
1/130 2/164 (2 wkts dec.)	357	(no wkt dec.)	218

†R. C. J. Williams, R. C. Williams, M. C. J. Ball, V. J. Pike and A. M. Babington did not bat.

Bowling: *First Innings*—Haste 20–4–81–1; Carroll 6–1–22–0; Whittall 26–2–136–1; Hodgson 31–7–75–0; Ratledge 7–0–35–0. *Second Innings*—Pitcher 14–1–80–0; Haste 7–1–30–0; Hodgson 8–0–69–0; Whittall 11–2–35–0.

Cambridge University

G. W. Jones c R. C. J. Williams b R. C. Williams	3	lbw b Hancock	25
R. D. Mann b R. C. Williams	0	c Cunliffe b Pike	30
J. Ratledge c Ball b Pike	25	c Ball b Pike	5
R. Q. Cake c R. C. J. Williams b Alleyne	47	c Cunliffe b Ball	8
J. P. Carroll st R. C. J. Williams b Pike	8	b Ball	0
J. S. Hodgson b Pike	0	c Dawson b Pike	10
D. E. Stanley c Wright b Alleyne	10	b R. C. Williams	9
*A. R. Whittall b R. C. Williams	8	(9) lbw b Pike	5
C. M. Pitcher c R. C. J. Williams b R. C. Williams	5	(8) lbw b Pike	5
N. J. Haste not out	1	not out	21
†F. J. Cooke c R. C. J. Williams b Babington	8	c Dawson b Pike	6
L-b 11, w 2	13	B 2, l-b 6, n-b 2	10
1/3 2/12 3/54 4/78 5/78 6/97 7/102 8/113 9/116	128	1/40 2/51 3/60 4/60 5/80 6/85 7/91 8/107 9/107	134

Bowling: *First Innings*—Babington 18.5–6–27–1; R. C. Williams 18–9–28–4; Ball 9–3–16–0; Pike 17–8–27–3; Alleyne 10–2–19–2. *Second Innings*—Babington 5–1–15–0; R. C. Williams 12–3–27–1; Hancock 6–1–15–1; Alleyne 4–1–9–0; Pike 27.3–12–41–6; Ball 21–12–19–2.

Umpires: G. I. Burgess and J. F. Steele.

GLOUCESTERSHIRE v GLAMORGAN

At Bristol, June 30, July 1, 2. Glamorgan won by nine wickets. Glamorgan 23 pts, Gloucestershire 4 pts. Toss: Glamorgan. Championship debut: V. J. Pike.

Glamorgan's first Championship win of the season was almost achieved in two days. But Russell, with a dogged, undefeated 85, and last man Pike kept them waiting until the first over of the third afternoon. The credit for the Welsh victory belonged largely to Hemp and Barwick, with bat and ball respectively. Left-hander Hemp's career-best 136 was handsome and assured, raising hopes that he might fill the formidable gap left by Richards. Yet, apart from Hemp, and Maynard, who helped him add 152, Glamorgan's highest score was 16 and the batsmen struggled against Walsh's pace and the accurate off-spin of Ball. Dropped catches did not help Gloucestershire's cause. Their batting, however, was even more fragile. Only Alleyne and Ball showed signs of holding out in the first innings, and they followed on, though there were no serious excuses in the pitch. Gloucestershire seemed quite unable to counter the old-fashioned off-cutters of Barwick, who took nine for 72 in the match.

Close of play: First day, Gloucestershire 33-0 (B. C. Broad 11*, R. J. Cunliffe 13*); Second day, Gloucestershire 166-9 (R. C. Russell 72*, V. J. Pike 8*).

Glamorgan

S. P. James c Russell b Smith	13	not out	14
*H. Morris c Dawson b Walsh	6	c Cunliffe b Walsh	5
A. Dale c Alleyne b Walsh	16		
M. P. Maynard c Broad b Ball	69		
D. L. Hemp c Smith b Ball	136	(3) not out	16
R. D. B. Croft c and b Ball	6		
O. D. Gibson c Broad b Ball	2		
R. P. Lefebvre c Alleyne b Walsh	6		
†C. P. Metson b Pike	11		
S. L. Watkin not out	7		
S. R. Barwick c Wright b Ball	0		
B 4, l-b 7, n-b 19	30	N-b 4	4
1/25 2/35 3/51 4/203 5/209 6/211 7/244 8/276 9/302	302	1/5	(1 wkt) 39

Bonus points – Glamorgan 3, Gloucestershire 4.

Bowling: *First Innings*—Walsh 20–5–68–3; Smith 16–3–66–1; Alleyne 4–0–22–0; Pike 26–5–66–1; Ball 26–2–69–5. *Second Innings*—Walsh 7–3–10–1; Smith 8–1–25–0; Ball 1.2–0–4–0.

Gloucestershire

B. C. Broad c Metson b Barwick	11	c James b Lefebvre	2
R. J. Cunliffe c Maynard b Barwick	26	c Metson b Lefebvre	11
T. H. C. Hancock c James b Barwick	0	c Hemp b Barwick	10
M. W. Alleyne c Lefebvre b Barwick	42	c Metson b Gibson	2
A. J. Wright lbw b Gibson	1	c James b Gibson	2
R. I. Dawson b Croft	1	c Maynard b Barwick	26
†R. C. Russell b Croft	2	not out	85
M. C. J. Ball c sub b Watkin	40	c Morris b Watkin	11
A. M. Smith c James b Watkin	2	c Hemp b Barwick	5
*C. A. Walsh b Watkin	5	c Croft b Barwick	6
V. J. Pike not out	1	c Hemp b Barwick	17
L-b 1, n-b 17	18	L-b 1, n-b 13	14
1/35 2/37 3/58 4/59 5/68 6/76 7/141 8/141 9/146	149	1/15 2/20 3/25 4/27 5/41 6/66 7/103 8/124 9/130	191

Bonus points – Glamorgan 4.

Bowling: *First Innings*—Watkin 18.1–5–36–3; Gibson 13–0–46–1; Croft 14–4–38–2; Barwick 20–11–28–4; Lefebvre 1–1–0–0. *Second Innings*—Gibson 17–6–45–2; Lefebvre 9–2–19–2; Barwick 28.3–14–44–5; Croft 10–1–37–0; Watkin 17–4–45–1.

Umpires: J. H. Harris and N. T. Plews.

At Bristol, July 6, 7, 8. GLOUCESTERSHIRE drew with SOUTH AFRICANS (See South African tour section).

At Portsmouth, July 14, 15, 16. GLOUCESTERSHIRE lost to HAMPSHIRE by 165 runs.

GLOUCESTERSHIRE v YORKSHIRE

At Cheltenham, July 21, 22, 23, 25. Gloucestershire won by 324 runs. Gloucestershire 22 pts, Yorkshire 5 pts. Toss: Yorkshire.

Cheltenham, ringed by rippling canvas at Festival time, lifted Gloucestershire spirits once again; Yorkshire had never before in their history lost by so many runs. The extraordinary fact was that, on the first day, Hartley and the inexperienced Silverwood made the home batsmen look ordinary and bowled them out for 291. In 26 overs before the close, Yorkshire's openers replied with a breezy 126. But next day, on an easy pitch, their batting collapsed miserably. Walsh took four wickets and Gloucestershire secured an unexpected lead of 44. Then came a fine hundred from Alleyne, and plentiful runs from several of his colleagues. An unimpressive Yorkshire side were left a daunting target of 529 and their demoralisation was compounded by the announcement that Richardson, mentally and physically exhausted, was returning to the West Indies. Blakey apart – Moxon was forced to drop down the order by a knee injury – Yorkshire could make nothing of Walsh's sustained aggression. He took ten wickets in the match for the third time in the season, assisted by the slip catching of the reliable Ball.

Close of play: First day, Yorkshire 126-0 (M. D. Moxon 43*, M. P. Vaughan 71*); Second day, Gloucestershire 228-4 (M. C. J. Ball 8*, V. J. Pike 2*); Third day, Yorkshire 154-5 (R. J. Blakey 55*, M. D. Moxon 0*).

Gloucestershire

A. J. Wright c Stemp b Hartley	7	– lbw b Stemp	85
M. G. N. Windows c Byas b Stemp	73	– lbw b Robinson	42
T. H. C. Hancock c Grayson b Hartley	5	– run out	58
R. I. Dawson c Stemp b Hartley	71	– c Byas b Stemp	27
M. W. Alleyne c Richardson b Silverwood	25	– (7) c Stemp b Vaughan	109
†R. C. Russell not out	38	– (8) c Blakey b Robinson	15
R. C. Williams c Parker b Vaughan	2	– (9) c Blakey b Vaughan	24
M. C. J. Ball c Blakey b Vaughan	24	– (5) c and b Robinson	38
*C. A. Walsh c Blakey b Silverwood	15	– (10) not out	48
V. J. Pike c Blakey b Silverwood	1	– (6) c Robinson b Stemp	4
K. E. Cooper b Hartley	9	– c Parker b Robinson	6
L-b 11, n-b 10	21	L-b 12, n-b 16	28
1/10 2/20 3/154 4/166 5/197 6/210 7/246 8/274 9/278	291	1/77 2/153 3/207 4/226 5/243 6/288 7/324 8/417 9/452	484

Bonus points – Gloucestershire 2, Yorkshire 4.

Bowling: *First Innings*—Hartley 21.3–3–77–4; Silverwood 19–5–57–3; Byas 3–1–8–0; Robinson 11–1–28–0; Stemp 18–6–48–1; Vaughan 8–1–62–2. *Second Innings*—Hartley 25–3–114–0; Silverwood 20–1–93–0; Robinson 34.1–10–92–4; Stemp 40–16–84–3; Grayson 2–1–5–0; Vaughan 18–2–84–2.

Yorkshire

*M. D. Moxon c Russell b Walsh	48	(7) c Ball b Walsh	13
M. P. Vaughan c Hancock b Alleyne	74	c Windows b Walsh	18
D. Byas c Ball b Walsh	0	(1) c Ball b Walsh	15
R. B. Richardson c Williams b Walsh	29	(3) c Alleyne b Williams	38
†R. J. Blakey c Windows b Alleyne	0	c Ball b Walsh	82
B. Parker c Dawson b Walsh	0	c Alleyne b Pike	9
A. P. Grayson c Russell b Alleyne	46	(4) c Russell b Cooper	5
P. J. Hartley c Ball b Cooper	4	b Walsh	0
R. D. Stemp c Ball b Cooper	0	c Ball b Walsh	6
C. E. W. Silverwood c Wright b Cooper	11	c Ball b Cooper	2
M. A. Robinson not out	1	not out	0
L-b 6, n-b 28	34	B 4, l-b 6, n-b 6	16
1/142 2/142 3/144 4/156 5/173 6/178 7/193 8/193 9/229	247	1/29 2/34 3/75 4/89 5/143 6/177 7/181 8/193 9/202	204

Bonus points – Yorkshire 1, Gloucestershire 4.

Bowling: *First Innings*—Walsh 17–1–75–4; Cooper 13–2–46–3; Williams 7–0–40–0; Ball 8–1–33–0; Pike 3–0–18–0; Alleyne 11.5–3–29–3. *Second Innings*—Walsh 18–4–85–6; Cooper 18–2–62–2; Williams 6–0–26–1; Alleyne 4–1–9–0; Pike 10–6–11–1; Ball 2–1–1–0.

Umpires: D. R. Shepherd and R. A. White.

GLOUCESTERSHIRE v KENT

At Cheltenham, July 28, 29, 30. Kent won by 50 runs. Kent 24 pts, Gloucestershire 6 pts. Toss: Kent.

Decorous Cheltenham witnessed a game of fluctuating excitement which finished on the third day. Gloucestershire had been set 285, an apparently unattainable dream as they lost seven wickets for 94. Then came a remarkable partnership for 127 between Alleyne, the success of the Festival, and Walsh. Alleyne followed his first-innings 96 with 80, another demonstration of composure, concentration and good-looking strokes through the off side. He also collected a career-best five for 78 at challenging medium-pace. Walsh's 66 was his highest score to date, mixing a selective approach with his more customary levity. When they finally fell to the spinners, Kent's relief was understandable. On the first day, Benson, with his only century of the season, and Ward opened with 209. There was little evidence then of how difficult the pitch would become, but Kent lost their last eight for 64. Ealham batted watchfully in the second innings, and McCague took nine wickets before Alleyne and Walsh joined forces.

Close of play: First day, Gloucestershire 32-0 (A. J. Wright 21*, M. G. N. Windows 11*); Second day, Kent 117-6 (M. A. Ealham 34*, S. A. Marsh 12*).

Kent

T. R. Ward c Cooper b Ball	98	run out	4
*M. R. Benson c Russell b Alleyne	159	c Alleyne b Walsh	2
N. R. Taylor c Ball b Williams	6	c Russell b Cooper	1
C. L. Hooper c Cooper b Alleyne	32	c Hancock b Walsh	22
G. R. Cowdrey c Windows b Alleyne	0	c Alleyne b Walsh	13
M. V. Fleming c Hancock b Walsh	1	c Alleyne b Williams	22
M. A. Ealham c Ball b Alleyne	7	not out	68
†S. A. Marsh b Walsh	13	c Windows b Walsh	20
M. J. McCague run out	16	c Russell b Cooper	3
M. M. Patel c Wright b Alleyne	0	c Russell b Williams	30
A. P. Igglesden not out	13	c Windows b Williams	0
B 4, l-b 5, w 2, n-b 4	15	L-b 4, w 2, n-b 4	10
1/209 2/220 3/296 4/296 5/297 6/315 7/330 8/330 9/330	360	1/4 2/7 3/13 4/44 5/47 6/84 7/137 8/148 9/195	195

Bonus points – Kent 4, Gloucestershire 4.

Bowling: *First Innings*—Walsh 21–6–46–2; Cooper 16–5–34–0; Williams 14–2–62–1; Pike 9–0–46–0; Alleyne 14.2–2–78–5; Ball 21–1–85–1. *Second Innings*—Walsh 22–2–82–4; Cooper 18–3–63–2; Alleyne 7–0–27–0; Williams 5.5–0–13–3; Ball 3–0–6–0.

Gloucestershire

First innings		Second innings	
A. J. Wright lbw b McCague	30	c Benson b McCague	14
M. G. N. Windows c Marsh b McCague	14	c and b Ealham	1
T. H. C. Hancock c Marsh b McCague	6	lbw b Ealham	3
R. I. Dawson c Marsh b Ealham	53	c Hooper b McCague	39
M. W. Alleyne c Benson b McCague	96	c Ward b Hooper	80
†R. C. Russell c Fleming b Ealham	8	c sub b McCague	9
R. C. Williams c Marsh b Ealham	4	run out	0
M. C. J. Ball b McCague	5	c sub b McCague	4
*C. A. Walsh c Marsh b Patel	25	st Marsh b Patel	66
V. J. Pike c Ealham b Patel	9	not out	3
K. E. Cooper not out	14	lbw b Hooper	0
B 2, l-b 5	7	B 8, l-b 7	15
1/44 2/45 3/58 4/179 5/195 6/207 7/219 8/228 9/250	271	1/14 2/16 3/46 4/70 5/88 6/88 7/94 8/221 9/233	234

Bonus points – Gloucestershire 2, Kent 4.

Bowling: *First Innings*—McCague 26–3–89–5; Igglesden 3–0–11–0; Hooper 8–1–23–0; Patel 29.5–6–92–2; Fleming 11–3–22–0; Ealham 13–2–27–3. *Second Innings*—McCague 24–8–65–4; Ealham 15–2–69–2; Patel 17–5–35–1; Hooper 9–2–23–2; Fleming 10–1–27–0.

Umpires: G. I. Burgess and R. Palmer.

At Chesterfield, August 4, 5, 6, 8. GLOUCESTERSHIRE lost to DERBYSHIRE by 155 runs.

GLOUCESTERSHIRE v NORTHAMPTONSHIRE

At Bristol, August 11, 12, 13, 15. Northamptonshire won by eight wickets. Northamptonshire 22 pts, Gloucestershire 5 pts. Toss: Gloucestershire. First-class debut: K. P. Sheeraz.

The absence of Walsh, unfit and back in the West Indies discussing his coming Test leadership duties, underlined the lack of depth in Gloucestershire's bowling. Still, the 20-year-old debutant seamer, Kamran Sheeraz, needed only three overs for his first wicket, as Fordham was caught behind. There was also encouragement for the home team from the batting: fluent strokeplay by the emergent Dawson, unlucky to miss his century, the county's only three-figure opening stand in the Championship season and, in the second innings, the discipline of Alleyne. But this was no bad return to Bristol for Curran, who had left in some disaffection. He took seven wickets and, well supported by Penberthy, got close to a hundred. The match generally lacked shape but, after some indifferent and strangely circumspect batting, the sheer fire of Ambrose, with four cheap wickets on the final day, put a Northamptonshire win firmly in sight. Montgomerie, Fordham and Bailey made sure.

Close of play: First day, Gloucestershire 269-6 (R. C. Russell 33*, R. C. Williams 3*); Second day, Northamptonshire 221-5 (K. M. Curran 53*, A. L. Penberthy 38*); Third day, Gloucestershire 152-4 (M. W. Alleyne 29*, M. Davies 1*).

Gloucestershire

A. J. Wright b Hughes	35	– b Curran	66
M. G. N. Windows c Ambrose b Roberts	77	– lbw b Curran	27
T. H. C. Hancock c Roberts b Hughes	9	– lbw b Curran	9
R. I. Dawson c Ambrose b Curran	93	– b Curran	12
M. W. Alleyne c Ripley b Ambrose	11	– lbw b Ambrose	81
R. J. Cunliffe lbw b Roberts	6	– (7) lbw b Ambrose	7
*†R. C. Russell b Ambrose	41	– (8) b Ambrose	0
R. C. Williams b Ambrose	10	– (9) c Hughes b Roberts	1
M. C. J. Ball c Bailey b Curran	6	– (10) b Ambrose	5
M. Davies c Ripley b Curran	5	– (6) c Montgomerie b Roberts	36
K. P. Sheeraz not out	1	– not out	0
L-b 1, w 1	2	B 1, l-b 7, n-b 2	10
1/110 2/112 3/126 4/169 5/186 6/264 7/283 8/284 9/293	296	1/50 2/62 3/76 4/135 5/233 6/243 7/243 8/248 9/254	254

Bonus points – Gloucestershire 2, Northamptonshire 4.

Bowling: *First Innings*—Ambrose 28–7–50–3; Curran 23–3–90–3; Hughes 16–2–63–2; Penberthy 12–5–24–0; Roberts 20–5–50–2; Bailey 5–0–18–0. *Second Innings*—Ambrose 28–8–48–4; Hughes 20–6–51–0; Penberthy 10–3–28–0; Curran 19–4–65–4; Roberts 22.1–8–50–2; Bailey 2–0–4–0.

Northamptonshire

R. R. Montgomerie c Russell b Williams	23	– b Ball	90
A. Fordham c Russell b Sheeraz	4	– c Wright b Ball	75
R. J. Bailey c Ball b Sheeraz	26	– not out	27
M. B. Loye b Alleyne	0	– not out	5
*A. J. Lamb c and b Williams	61		
K. M. Curran c Wright b Alleyne	92		
A. L. Penberthy c Russell b Williams	62		
†D. Ripley c Russell b Alleyne	1		
A. R. Roberts not out	35		
C. E. L. Ambrose c Wright b Ball	13		
J. G. Hughes c Ball b Alleyne	16		
L-b 8, n-b 8	16	L-b 1, w 1, n-b 4	6
1/14 2/52 3/55 4/94 5/148 6/262 7/271 8/296 9/315	349	1/129 2/197	(2 wkts) 203

Bonus points – Northamptonshire 2, Gloucestershire 3 (Score at 120 overs: 277-7).

Bowling: *First Innings*—Williams 35–8–82–3; Sheeraz 15–2–34–2; Alleyne 36.2–10–76–4; Ball 35–11–85–1; Davies 15–2–38–0; Dawson 3–1–6–0; Hancock 8–1–20–0. *Second Innings*—Williams 10–0–32–0; Alleyne 10–0–42–0; Ball 18–1–76–2; Davies 8–1–31–0; Hancock 3–0–21–0.

Umpires: J. H. Hampshire and N. T. Plews.

At Manchester, August 18, 19, 20, 22. GLOUCESTERSHIRE beat LANCASHIRE by two wickets.

GLOUCESTERSHIRE v LEICESTERSHIRE

At Bristol, August 30, 31, September 1, 2. Gloucestershire won by 102 runs. Gloucestershire 21 pts, Leicestershire 1 pt. Toss: Leicestershire.

As Warwickshire made certain of the Championship, Leicestershire, the only side with any chance of overtaking them, went down to their fourth defeat in five games. Their frustration was obvious throughout, especially in their bowlers' volatile appeals against Wright, who made 184 not out on the first day. It was the best score of his career and his first hundred for more than two years. He off-drove and hooked so well that it was hard to believe he had given up the captaincy in despair and dropped out of the team a year earlier. Leicestershire had started well, choosing to bowl and seizing three wickets by lunch. But then Wright put on 135 with Alleyne and 145 with Hancock. There was no play on the second day and only 42 overs on the third before contrived declarations set a target of 327 in 70 overs. Leicestershire's prospects declined and finally ended as Walsh completed his ninth five-wicket haul of the season. Nixon batted defiantly until ninth out, trying to sweep the young leg-spinner Pike.

Close of play: First day, Gloucestershire 350-4 (A. J. Wright 184*, T. H. C. Hancock 59*); Second day, No play; Third day, Leicestershire 167-3 (J. J. Whitaker 81*, V. J. Wells 25*).

Gloucestershire

A. J. Wright not out	184	– b Wells	39
M. G. N. Windows c Nixon b Millns	11	– c Nixon b Sheriyar	11
G. D. Hodgson b Millns	8	– not out	30
R. I. Dawson c Simmons b Sheriyar	5	– not out	45
M. W. Alleyne c Robinson b Mullally	38		
T. H. C. Hancock not out	59		
B 6, l-b 9, n-b 30	45	B 2, l-b 1, n-b 15	18
1/25 2/45 3/70 4/205 (4 wkts dec.)	350	1/53 2/59 (2 wkts dec.)	143

†R. C. Russell, R. C. Williams, *C. A. Walsh, M. C. J. Ball and V. J. Pike did not bat.

Bonus points – Gloucestershire 4, Leicestershire 1.

Bowling: *First Innings*—Millns 20–3–51–2; Mullally 26–8–61–1; Sheriyar 19–1–91–1; Pierson 22–4–55–0; Simmons 10–3–22–0; Wells 13–1–55–0. *Second Innings*—Sheriyar 5–0–53–1; Wells 6–1–27–1; Pierson 10–2–33–0; Mullally 8–1–27–0.

Leicestershire

P. V. Simmons c Alleyne b Walsh	2	– c Ball b Walsh	6
*N. E. Briers c Wright b Walsh	7	– c Russell b Walsh	8
T. J. Boon c Dawson b Ball	31	– c Russell b Williams	11
J. J. Whitaker not out	81	– c Russell b Williams	9
V. J. Wells not out	25	– c Windows b Ball	16
P. E. Robinson (did not bat)		– b Pike	39
†P. A. Nixon (did not bat)		– b Pike	87
A. R. K. Pierson (did not bat)		– b Walsh	16
D. J. Millns (did not bat)		– c Pike b Walsh	6
A. D. Mullally (did not bat)		– c Wright b Walsh	1
A. Sheriyar (did not bat)		– not out	0
B 3, l-b 2, n-b 16	21	B 1, l-b 11, n-b 13	25
1/4 2/15 3/96 (3 wkts dec.)	167	1/11 2/32 3/32 4/45 5/86 6/110 7/174 8/191 9/224	224

Bonus point – Gloucestershire 1.

Bowling: *First Innings*—Walsh 11–2–72–2; Williams 6–0–24–0; Pike 10–0–34–0; Alleyne 8–2–21–0; Ball 7–0–11–1. *Second Innings*—Walsh 21–8–47–5; Williams 13–5–35–2; Alleyne 7–0–39–0; Pike 15–3–55–2; Ball 13–4–36–1.

Umpires: H. D. Bird and A. G. T. Whitehead.

At Lord's, September 8, 9, 10. GLOUCESTERSHIRE lost to MIDDLESEX by an innings and 63 runs.

GLOUCESTERSHIRE v WARWICKSHIRE

At Bristol, September 15, 16, 17, 19. Drawn. Gloucestershire 4 pts, Warwickshire 4 pts. Toss: Gloucestershire.

The only play possible was on the third day. In search of improved luck, Walsh, who had not won the toss in a first-class game since May 12, successfully handed over that duty to Russell. However, despite a rapid over-rate – 46 by lunch – a solid hundred by the recently reinstated Hodgson, the sustained promise of the small and sturdy Windows and some enterprising late batting by Hancock and Ball, there was an almost tangible lack of atmosphere. Warwickshire were without Lara and Small, held back for the final title-deciding Sunday League fixture.

Close of play: First day, No play; Second day, No play; Third day, Warwickshire 24-0 (A. J. Moles 7*, R. G. Twose 12*).

Gloucestershire

A. J. Wright c Piper b Davis 27
M. G. N. Windows run out 63
G. D. Hodgson c Reeve b Davis 113
R. I. Dawson c Reeve b Davis......... 35
M. W. Alleyne c Piper b Welch........ 1
T. H. C. Hancock c Piper b Davis 70
†R. C. Russell not out................ 17
R. C. Williams c Davis b Reeve 0
M. C. J. Ball c Reeve b Davis......... 38
*C. A. Walsh c Twose b Davis 2
L-b 6 6

1/39 2/149 3/220 4/221 5/297 6/320 7/321 8/364 9/372 (9 wkts dec.) 372

A. M. Smith did not bat.

Bonus points – Gloucestershire 4, Warwickshire 4.

Bowling: Munton 11–3–34–0; Welch 13–4–36–1; Davis 41.5–12–128–6; N. M. K. Smith 26–4–102–0; P. A. Smith 4–1–11–0; Twose 8–2–17–0; Reeve 8–1–38–1.

Warwickshire

A. J. Moles not out 7
R. G. Twose not out 12
L-b 1, n-b 4................. 5

(no wkt) 24

D. P. Ostler, T. L. Penney, *D. A. Reeve, P. A. Smith, G. Welch, R. P. Davis, †K. J. Piper, N. M. K. Smith and T. A. Munton did not bat.

Bowling: Walsh 3.4–1–13–0; Smith 3–0–10–0.

Umpires: K. J. Lyons and P. B. Wight.

BIGGEST FALLS IN THE COUNTY CHAMPIONSHIP

15 places	Gloucestershire	second to 17th	1970
	Glamorgan	third to 18th	1994
14 places	Glamorgan	second to 16th	1971
	Middlesex	first to 15th	1991
13 places	Middlesex	first equal to 14th	1950
	Leicestershire	third equal to 16th	1954
	Kent	second to 15th	1989
	Worcestershire	second to 15th	1994

HAMPSHIRE

President: W. J. Weld
Chairman: D. Rich
Chairman, Cricket Committee: J. R. Gray
Chief Executive: A. F. Baker
Captain: M. C. J. Nicholas
Coach: T. M. Tremlett
Head Groundsman: N. Gray
Scorer: V. H Isaacs

It was never going to be an easy season for Hampshire – and for much of it, that seemed like an understatement. The retirement of David Gower, even the Gower who had generally underachieved in his four years with the county, and the departure of the legendary Malcolm Marshall, made it inevitable that it would be a summer of retrenchment. In fact, it was rather worse than that: Gower's departure left an upper-order gap which was hard to fill and the man brought in to succeed Marshall, Winston Benjamin, did not come off.

Hampshire's recruitment of Benjamin had raised some eyebrows; his returns often failed to match his potential in six seasons with Leicestershire. Sadly, it was the same in his first with Hampshire. Benjamin worked hard enough but it was not until his eighth Championship appearance that he finally got the return his efforts deserved and his employers expected and needed. He took five wickets in an innings against Gloucestershire, following up with a fifty, and, when he took six in the first innings of the next match, at Worcester, Hampshire believed he had broken through and their investment would reap its dividend. Instead, he fell awkwardly in the field, damaged his right shoulder and was never seen again. He had taken only 24 first-class wickets.

The bowling problems were compounded by Norman Cowans's difficulties. Hampshire had hoped that his move from Middlesex would rekindle the old fires in the former England opening bowler. Again, Cowans's attitude could not be faulted, but time had eroded his pace. Although he contained well, the penetration of earlier years was gone and his summer's work brought a meagre 26 wickets. Thus the new-ball attack which Mark Nicholas had forecast would be one of the most feared in the business collected 50 between them.

Fortunately for Nicholas, their lack of success was offset by Cardigan Connor's most successful summer in 11 years of first-class cricket. Connor's pride was hurt when he was dropped in May; when he returned, his response was to make himself irreplaceable. Armed with a previously undiscovered out-swinger, Connor took 72 first-class wickets at 24.50. Coupled with another steady season from off-spinner Shaun Udal, who was picked to tour Australia, this allowed Hampshire to finish in joint 13th place in the Championship.

That exactly matched the previous summer's placing. In the Sunday League they climbed three places to 12th and, although they went out as soon as they met first-class opposition in the NatWest Trophy, they reached the semi-final of the Benson and Hedges Cup, only to be undone as the match was dragged into the second day by the weather. Their prime bowlers – Connor, Benjamin and Udal – had one of those mornings, conceding 43 runs in three successive overs, to allow Worcestershire to canter to Lord's. Nicholas was speechless, almost tearful, with disappointment – and at that stage contemplated retirement. But by the end of the season he had put that idea on the back-burner, and pledged to spend one, if not two, more years with the county. Looking to the future, though, they signed John Stephenson, who had been passed over for the Essex captaincy. Tony Baker, the chief executive, said Stephenson had been signed "with a view" to replacing Nicholas in 1996 or 1997. He steps into a situation where there was no obviously ambitious senior professional to feel aggrieved: Paul Terry had already given up the vice-captaincy and Robin Smith, despite losing his England place in 1994, obviously still has horizons that extend beyond county cricket.

One reason for Nicholas's about-face was the emergence of several young players of genuine potential. The group was led by opening batsman Sean Morris. He signalled his breakthrough with a highly competent maiden century off Nottinghamshire at Basingstoke, reinforced that good impression with another off the South Africans, but then had his right forefinger smashed by a ball from Courtney Walsh which ended his season in mid-July. Young pace bowlers Jim Bovill and Martin Thursfield were also dogged by injury but showed enough promise to convince Nicholas they have a significant part to play in the county's future, while Giles White and, in the last two matches, Paul Whitaker suggested that in time they can give much-needed steel to a fragile upper batting order.

The other persuasive factor in Nicholas's decision to rein back his ambitions for a full-time career in the media was his own form. For the past four seasons – since he contracted malaria leading England A in Zimbabwe – runs had been elusive. Now he suddenly rediscovered the authority of old and, with Terry and Smith, was one of three batsmen to pass 1,000, making 1,182 at an impressive 45.46. Nicholas concedes that the resurrection of the Hampshire of a few years ago is not complete, but believes it drew significantly closer in the last two months of the summer. He wants to carry it nearer to fulfilment before he, like so many others, turns to journalism.

After years of discussion – and delay caused by the collapse of the property market – Hampshire announced in October that they had finally signed a lease for a new £10 million headquarters to replace Northlands Road. They have done a complex deal with various local councils and Queen's College, Oxford, owners of the 40-acre site, which is at West End, on the outskirts of Southampton close to the airport. There are plans for two pitches, for first and second team, and the county hope to be playing cricket there to greet the millennium. – Mike Neasom.

HAMPSHIRE 1994

[*Bill Smith*

Back row: J. S. Laney, G. W. White, J. N. B. Bovill, L. J. Botham, D. P. J. Flint, R. M. F. Cox. *Middle row:* R. Hayward (*assistant coach*), M. Keech, A. N. Aymes, R. S. M. Morris, S. D. Udal, M. J. Thursfield, M. Jean-Jacques, K. D. James, T. C. Middleton, T. M. Tremlett (*county coach*). *Front row:* R. J. Maru, C. A. Connor, W. K. M. Benjamin, V. P. Terry, M. C. J. Nicholas (*captain*), R. A. Smith, N. G. Cowans, M. Garaway.

HAMPSHIRE RESULTS

All first-class matches – Played 19: Won 4, Lost 7, Drawn 8.

County Championship matches – Played 17: Won 4, Lost 7, Drawn 6.

Bonus points – Batting 32, Bowling 55.

Competition placings – Britannic Assurance County Championship, 13th equal; NatWest Bank Trophy, 2nd round; Benson and Hedges Cup, s-f; AXA Equity & Law League, 12th.

BRITANNIC ASSURANCE CHAMPIONSHIP AVERAGES

BATTING

	Birthplace	*M*	*I*	*NO*	*R*	*HS*	*Avge*
‡M. C. J. Nicholas	*London*	17	30	6	1,115	145	46.45
‡R. A. Smith	*Durban, SA*	14	25	0	1,143	162	45.72
R. S. M. Morris	*Great Horwood*	8	15	2	581	174	44.69
‡V. P. Terry	*Osnabrück, W. Germany*	17	31	1	1,056	164	35.20
‡S. D. Udal	*Farnborough, Hants*	15	26	3	656	94	28.52
‡A. N. Aymes	*Southampton*	17	28	0	635	76	22.67
‡T. C. Middleton	*Winchester*	12	22	3	422	72	22.21
G. W. White	*Barnstaple*	9	16	1	324	73*	21.60
K. D. James	*Lambeth*	11	19	2	321	53	18.88
‡R. J. Maru	*Nairobi, Kenya*	9	15	4	207	38*	18.81
W. K. M. Benjamin§	*St John's, Antigua*	9	14	1	231	54	17.76
M. Keech	*Hampstead*	4	7	0	113	57	16.14
M. Jean-Jacques	*Soufrière, Dominica*	3	5	1	52	22*	13.00
J. N. B. Bovill	*High Wycombe*	4	7	5	25	10	12.50
M. J. Thursfield	*South Shields*	7	10	1	103	47	11.44
‡C. A. Connor	*The Valley, Anguilla*	13	20	1	195	25	10.26
N. G. Cowans	*Enfield St Mary, Jamaica*	12	15	6	51	19	5.66

Also batted: R. M. F. Cox (*Guildford*) (2 matches) 5, 9, 15; D. P. J. Flint (*Basingstoke*) (2 matches) 5, 3*; P. R. Whitaker (*Keighley*) (2 matches) 2, 94, 38.

* *Signifies not out.* ‡ *Denotes county cap.* § *Overseas player.*

The following played a total of 13 three-figure innings for Hampshire in County Championship matches – R. A. Smith 5, V. P. Terry 4, M. C. J. Nicholas 3, R. S. M. Morris 1.

BOWLING

	O	*M*	*R*	*W*	*BB*	*5W/i*	*Avge*
W. K. M. Benjamin	281	97	585	24	6-46	2	24.37
C. A. Connor	541	121	1,663	67	7-47	2	24.82
S. D. Udal	625	159	1,755	62	6-79	6	28.30
M. J. Thursfield	135	29	454	15	6-130	1	30.26
K. D. James	256.1	49	834	22	4-78	0	37.90
N. G. Cowans	349.3	93	986	26	4-76	0	37.92
R. J. Maru	254.1	75	621	15	3-61	0	41.40

Also bowled: J. N. B. Bovill 75.4–14–274–9; D. P. J. Flint 41–10–117–0; M. Jean-Jacques 53.1–4–242–5; M. Keech 9.3–2–39–0; M. C. J. Nicholas 4–2–7–0; P. R. Whitaker 0.1–0–4–0; G. W. White 5–1–13–0.

Wicket-keeper: A. N. Aymes 33 ct, 4 st.

Leading Fielder: V. P. Terry 22.

At Oxford, April 16, 18, 19. HAMPSHIRE drew with OXFORD UNIVERSITY.

HAMPSHIRE v ESSEX

At Southampton, April 28, 29, 30, May 1. Essex won by eight wickets. Essex 21 pts, Hampshire 7 pts. Toss: Essex. Championship debut: M. S. Kasprowicz. County debuts: W. K. M. Benjamin, N. G. Cowans; R. C. Irani.

One dropped catch turned this match. Essex, chasing a follow-on target of 172, were 97 for six when Middleton, at short leg, failed to hold a straightforward chance offered by Kasprowicz off Benjamin. Kasprowicz added 64 with Shahid and Hampshire's lead was whittled down to 78. It was Essex's second reprieve, after Hampshire failed to capitalise on a score of 251 for two. Gooch had given his bowlers first use of an unusually lively Southampton pitch, but an impressive hundred by Terry – his second in two innings – had held out the promise of a big total. Once Middleton missed his catch and then Such exploited the rough to return a career-best seven for 66, to dismiss Hampshire again for 191, Essex needed 270 at only two an over. There was a memorable last-morning joust between Gooch and Benjamin, who responded to having his first ball hit for six by Gooch the previous day by beating him nine times in his opening burst, but eventually Gooch and Hussain knocked off the runs easily.

Close of play: First day, Hampshire 282-7 (S. D. Udal 2*); Second day, Hampshire 0-0 (C. A. Connor 0*, T. C. Middleton 0*); Third day, Essex 102-2 (G. A. Gooch 57*, N. Hussain 20*).

Hampshire

T. C. Middleton c Gooch b Such	40	– (2) c Gooch b Ilott	3
V. P. Terry c Hussain b Shahid	130	– (3) lbw b Such	26
R. A. Smith lbw b Ilott	14	– (4) c Lewis b Such	25
*M. C. J. Nicholas hit wkt b Shahid	68	– (5) c Garnham b Such	26
M. Keech lbw b Ilott	10	– (6) lbw b Such	1
†A. N. Aymes c Gooch b Kasprowicz	9	– (7) c Shahid b Ilott	8
C. A. Connor c Gooch b Ilott	0	– (1) b Kasprowicz	25
S. D. Udal not out	27	– b Such	59
W. K. M. Benjamin c Garnham b Kasprowicz	0	– lbw b Such	11
M. J. Thursfield c Hussain b Kasprowicz	0	– c Shahid b Such	1
N. G. Cowans b Ilott	9	– not out	0
B 1, l-b 13	14	L-b 6	6
1/91 2/113 3/251 4/268 5/280 6/280 7/282 8/282 9/292	321	1/18 2/34 3/80 4/93 5/97 6/106 7/152 8/172 9/182	191

Bonus points – Hampshire 3, Essex 4.

Bowling: *First Innings*—Ilott 34.5–7–74–4; Kasprowicz 29–5–69–3; Irani 19–4–64–0; Gooch 3–2–1–0; Such 20–9–49–1; Childs 8–2–30–0; Shahid 5–1–20–2. *Second Innings*—Ilott 21–5–60–2; Kasprowicz 22–10–44–1; Such 28.5–9–66–7; Irani 2–1–6–0; Childs 2–0–9–0.

Essex

*G. A. Gooch b Benjamin	8	– not out	123
P. J. Prichard b Cowans	6		
J. J. B. Lewis b Connor	19	– (2) c Keech b Udal	23
N. Hussain c Aymes b Thursfield	22	– not out	115
N. Shahid b Connor	91		
†M. A. Garnham lbw b Connor	17	– (3) b Connor	0
R. C. Irani c Thursfield b Cowans	6		
M. S. Kasprowicz c Connor b Thursfield	24		
M. C. Ilott c Aymes b Benjamin	30		
P. M. Such b Benjamin	4		
J. H. Childs not out	3		
B 2, l-b 9, n-b 2	13	L-b 9	9
1/8 2/16 3/43 4/67 5/87 6/97 7/161 8/205 9/219	243	1/66 2/71	(2 wkts) 270

Bonus points – Essex 1, Hampshire 4.

Bowling: *First Innings*—Benjamin 22–4–71–3; Cowans 13–2–42–2; Connor 20.3–7–54–3; Thursfield 17–8–31–2; Udal 21–7–34–0. *Second Innings*—Benjamin 16–6–46–0; Cowans 9–3–26–0; Connor 11–0–48–1; Udal 30–4–100–1; Thursfield 6–2–26–0; Keech 2.3–0–15–0.

Umpires: K. E. Palmer and R. Palmer.

HAMPSHIRE v DERBYSHIRE

At Southampton, May 5, 6, 7, 9. Drawn. Hampshire 2 pts, Derbyshire 4 pts. Toss: Hampshire.

Contrivance could not fashion a result in a rain-ruined match, with two days lost. Yet at one stage Hampshire, who had collapsed when DeFreitas claimed the first hat-trick of his career, threatened to snatch victory. After DeFreitas transformed 57 for two into 57 for five, Smith and Udal, who hit a career-best 83, averted disaster, leading Hampshire to 271. Reciprocal declarations set Derbyshire a challenge of 315 in 69 overs. Despite lacking their captain, Barnett, who had torn a knee ligament in the field, they reached 155 for two. But Azharuddin was brilliantly caught in the deep by Terry, two more wickets fell at 158, the chase was abandoned and Hampshire were unable to strike again.

Close of play: First day, No play; Second day, Derbyshire 76-2 (C. J. Adams 20*, M. Azharuddin 28*); Third day, No play.

Hampshire

T. C. Middleton c Barnett b DeFreitas	20	– not out	40
V. P. Terry c Krikken b Malcolm	6	– c Rollins b Malcolm	10
R. S. M. Morris b Malcolm	1	– not out	49
R. A. Smith c Rollins b DeFreitas	58		
*M. C. J. Nicholas b DeFreitas	0		
†A. N. Aymes lbw b DeFreitas	0		
S. D. Udal c Bowler b Warner	83		
W. K. M. Benjamin c Cork b Mortensen	19		
M. J. Thursfield not out	23		
N. G. Cowans c Cork b Warner	0		
D. P. J. Flint c Cork b DeFreitas	5		
B 4, l-b 6, n-b 46	56	N-b 20	20
1/31 2/35 3/57 4/57 5/57 6/176 7/203 8/244 9/244	271	1/25 (1 wkt dec.)	119

Bonus points – Hampshire 2, Derbyshire 4.

Bowling: *First Innings*—Malcolm 17–4–85–2; DeFreitas 16.5–1–59–5; Warner 16–3–68–2; Cork 7–2–31–0; Mortensen 7–2–18–1. *Second Innings*—Malcolm 9–2–19–1; DeFreitas 8–0–32–0; Cork 9–0–37–0; Warner 7–0–31–0.

Derbyshire

P. D. Bowler c Aymes b Thursfield	5	– c Aymes b Udal	27
A. S. Rollins lbw b Udal	21	– run out	81
C. J. Adams not out	20	– c Flint b Udal	33
M. Azharuddin not out	28	– c Terry b Udal	12
P. A. J. DeFreitas (did not bat)		– not out	29
D. G. Cork (did not bat)		– b Udal	0
†K. M. Krikken (did not bat)		– not out	13
B 1, l-b 1	2	L-b 4	4
1/20 2/36 (2 wkts dec.)	76	1/42 2/116 3/155 4/158 5/158 (5 wkts)	199

*K. J. Barnett, A. E. Warner, D. E. Malcolm and O. H. Mortensen did not bat.

Bowling: *First Innings*—Benjamin 11–5–9–0; Cowans 11.1–5–18–0; Thursfield 7–2–16–1; Udal 12–4–30–1; Flint 1–0–1–0. *Second Innings*—Cowans 4–1–12–0; Thursfield 5–1–14–0; Udal 30.2–7–83–4; Flint 29–8–86–0.

Umpires: G. I. Burgess and B. J. Meyer.

At Hove, May 12, 13, 14, 16. HAMPSHIRE lost to SUSSEX by two wickets.

HAMPSHIRE v MIDDLESEX

At Southampton, May 19, 20, 21, 23. Drawn. Hampshire 4 pts, Middlesex 7 pts. Toss: Hampshire.

Middleton's adhesive qualities have earned their share of criticism from spectators, but they frustrated Middlesex's push for their first Championship win. He batted more than four hours for 72, when Hampshire followed on 184 behind after the third day was lost to rain. Middlesex's fortunes fluctuated in their first innings; Gatting and Ramprakash brought them round from eight for two with a partnership of 139, but Thursfield had them struggling again at 278 for eight, before Williams and Johnson put on another 92. Williams then gained the lift and movement that had eluded Hampshire's bowlers; only a solid fifty from Keech staved off total collapse. Following on, Middleton averted defeat with the support of Morris and James. Five of the Hampshire team – Cowans, James, Keech, Maru and Thursfield – were formerly on the Middlesex staff, while Middlesex included their new signing from Hampshire, Shine.

Close of play: First day, Middlesex 280-8 (R. L. Johnson 18*, N. F. Williams 2*); Second day, Hampshire 203-9 (R. J. Maru 22*, N. G. Cowans 19*); Third day, No play.

Middlesex

D. L. Haynes c Morris b Benjamin	7
M. A. Roseberry c Terry b Benjamin	0
*M. W. Gatting lbw b Cowans	51
M. R. Ramprakash c Terry b James	83
J. D. Carr c Maru b Thursfield	79
P. N. Weekes c Aymes b Thursfield	18
†K. R. Brown c Aymes b Thursfield	4
R. L. Johnson c Aymes b Thursfield	47
J. E. Emburey b Thursfield	0
N. F. Williams c Benjamin b Thursfield	63
K. J. Shine not out	12
L-b 16, w 5, n-b 2	23
1/3 2/8 3/147 4/153 5/200 6/208 7/266 8/278 9/370	387

Bonus points – Middlesex 3, Hampshire 3 (Score at 120 overs: 312-8).

Bowling: Benjamin 31–12–55–2; Cowans 28–10–46–1; Thursfield 30.3–3–130–6; James 25–4–79–1; Maru 16–4–45–0; Keech 5–2–16–0.

Hampshire

	First innings		Second innings	
R. S. M. Morris lbw b Weekes	38	– (2) lbw b Williams	44
T. C. Middleton c Brown b Williams	3	– (1) c Brown b Gatting	72
K. D. James c Weekes b Williams	0	– not out	52
V. P. Terry c Gatting b Williams	2	– lbw b Weekes	13
*M. C. J. Nicholas c Gatting b Shine	23	– not out	22
M. Keech b Emburey	57		
†A. N. Aymes lbw b Williams	13		
W. K. M. Benjamin c Brown b Williams	16		
M. J. Thursfield c Brown b Johnson	1		
R. J. Maru not out	22		
N. G. Cowans c Carr b Williams	19		
B 1, l-b 7, w 1	9	B 4, l-b 2, w 1, n-b 20	27
1/16 2/22 3/32 4/61 5/82 6/113 7/137 8/143 9/165	203	1/85 2/175 3/202	(3 wkts) 230

Bonus points – Hampshire 1, Middlesex 4.

Bowling: *First Innings*—Shine 20–4–60–1; Williams 20.3–6–49–6; Johnson 19–2–58–1; Emburey 16–3–19–1; Weekes 6–1–9–1. *Second Innings*—Williams 19–5–37–1; Shine 13–5–33–0; Emburey 29–13–64–0; Johnson 15–4–46–0; Weekes 16–3–34–1; Gatting 5–2–10–1.

Umpires: P. B. Wight and P. Willey.

At Taunton, June 2, 3, 4, 6. HAMPSHIRE lost to SOMERSET by 87 runs.

HAMPSHIRE v NOTTINGHAMSHIRE

At Basingstoke, June 9, 10, 11, 13. Drawn. Hampshire 14 pts, Nottinghamshire 5 pts. Toss: Nottinghamshire.

A pedestrian match sprang to life on the final afternoon. Hampshire required three runs off the last delivery for their first Championship win: Middleton, who had a trapped nerve in his back, and his runner Terry managed two. Hampshire earned eight points for levelling the scores. Robinson had challenged Hampshire to score 286 at a shade under five an over – in stark contrast to the previous three innings, when three an over had been the maximum. They came so close thanks to Smith, whose masterly 111 answered accusations that he was burned out. Nottinghamshire's first innings had been dominated by Archer, making the most of being missed at the wicket before scoring, and Hampshire's by Morris, who ended his search for a maiden first-class century in some style. He seemed capable of making it a double until superbly caught by Adams, low down in the covers. His 174 was the highest score for Hampshire at May's Bounty and included some lovely off-side driving.

Close of play: First day, Nottinghamshire 313-5 (W. M. Noon 44*, K. P. Evans 9*); Second day, Hampshire 159-3 (R. S. M. Morris 83*, A. N. Aymes 6*); Third day, Nottinghamshire 105-1 (R. T. Robinson 52*, G. F. Archer 31*).

Nottinghamshire

P. R. Pollard c Maru b Udal	40	– b Connor	18
*R. T. Robinson c Aymes b Benjamin	66	– c Aymes b Cowans	63
G. F. Archer b Benjamin	100	– lbw b Connor	57
J. C. Adams c Nicholas b Maru	31	– (5) c and b Connor	11
P. Johnson c Terry b Udal	5	– (4) c Maru b Cowans	1
†W. M. Noon lbw b Cowans	46	– not out	55
K. P. Evans b Connor	50	– c Aymes b Udal	13
G. W. Mike c Udal b Connor	26	– c Nicholas b Udal	1
R. A. Pick not out	34	– c sub b Maru	20
M. G. Field-Buss c Terry b Maru	7	– not out	2
J. A. Afford b Maru	9		
L-b 5, n-b 16	21	L-b 7, w 3, n-b 2	12
1/74 2/140 3/219 4/224 5/286 6/327 7/382 8/383 9/421	435	1/30 2/124 3/130 4/150 5/161 6/194 7/196 8/241 (8 wkts dec.)	253

Bonus points – Nottinghamshire 3, Hampshire 2 (Score at 120 overs: 327-6).

Bowling: *First Innings*—Benjamin 33–14–59–2; Cowans 24–10–69–1; Connor 29–7–95–2; Udal 45–8–146–2; Maru 25.4–6–61–3. *Second Innings*—Cowans 19–4–51–2; Benjamin 8–3–23–0; Connor 23–4–66–3; Udal 19–2–61–2; Maru 18–9–45–1.

Hampshire

V. P. Terry b Pick	41	– (2) b Pick	4
R. S. M. Morris c Adams b Mike	174	– (1) c Field-Buss b Mike	63
R. A. Smith lbw b Evans	16	– b Mike	111
*M. C. J. Nicholas st Noon b Field-Buss	2	– c Adams b Mike	33
†A. N. Aymes c Pick b Mike	69	– c Mike b Evans	29
S. D. Udal lbw b Evans	4	– (7) c and b Adams	5
T. C. Middleton not out	32	– (10) not out	4
R. J. Maru not out	38	– not out	22
W. K. M. Benjamin (did not bat)		– (6) c Archer b Evans	7
C. A. Connor (did not bat)		– (9) b Evans	0
L-b 10, w 1, n-b 16	27	B 1, l-b 5, w 1	7
1/89 2/131 3/144 4/304 5/309 6/339 (6 wkts dec.)	403	1/13 2/157 3/209 4/220 5/227 6/251 7/270 8/271 (8 wkts)	285

N. G. Cowans did not bat.

Bonus points – Hampshire 4, Nottinghamshire 2 (Score at 120 overs: 355-6).

Bowling: *First Innings*—Evans 29–11–75–2; Pick 25–5–94–1; Mike 26–7–83–2; Afford 22–5–84–0; Field-Buss 23.2–8–44–1; Adams 6–2–13–0. *Second Innings*—Pick 5–0–34–1; Evans 17–1–69–3; Afford 8–0–42–0; Field-Buss 15–1–61–0; Adams 7–0–33–1; Mike 8–1–40–3.

Umpires: J. H. Harris and M. J. Kitchen.

At Manchester, June 16, 17, 18, 20. HAMPSHIRE lost to LANCASHIRE by 263 runs.

At Leeds, June 23, 24, 25, 27. HAMPSHIRE drew with YORKSHIRE.

At Southampton, July 2, 3, 4. HAMPSHIRE drew with SOUTH AFRICANS (See South African tour section).

HAMPSHIRE v GLOUCESTERSHIRE

At Portsmouth, July 14, 15, 16. Hampshire won by 165 runs. Hampshire 20 pts, Gloucestershire 4 pts. Toss: Hampshire. Championship debut: G. W. White.

Hampshire's first victory of the season, and their first at home since May 1992, was completed on the third morning. Fifteen wickets fell the first day and 18 the second. The dry pitch's extra bounce sowed suspicions in the minds of all batsmen. Yet Nicholas's belief that it would ultimately turn was vindicated and Gloucestershire's second innings shattered by off-spinner Udal, who claimed his third five-wicket haul in a month on the eve of his call-up into the Test squad. Before that, pace and seam dominated. Walsh's hostility undid Hampshire's top order, with only Terry and Aymes showing the necessary application, before Cooper wrapped up the tail. Gloucestershire put up even less resistance as Benjamin finally came good, with five wickets, to earn a lead of 60. Benjamin and Udal then played the major roles in extending that advantage to 280. When Gloucestershire lost another four wickets on the second evening, it was obvious that the end would be premature.

Close of play: First day, Gloucestershire 58-5 (M. G. N. Windows 22*, M. W. Alleyne 1*); Second day, Gloucestershire 43-4 (M. C. J. Ball 5*, R. I. Dawson 0*).

Hampshire

First innings		Second innings	
R. S. M. Morris c Wright b Walsh	4	retired hurt	6
V. P. Terry c Alleyne b Walsh	47	c Wright b Walsh	9
R. A. Smith c Hancock b Smith	5	lbw b Cooper	20
*M. C. J. Nicholas c Windows b Ball	23	c Russell b Walsh	31
G. W. White lbw b Walsh	10	run out	11
†A. N. Aymes c Alleyne b Cooper	43	c Alleyne b Walsh	2
S. D. Udal c Russell b Smith	13	c Broad b Cooper	44
W. K. M. Benjamin c Hancock b Cooper	13	c Smith b Alleyne	54
R. J. Maru c Russell b Cooper	2	c Dawson b Alleyne	16
C. A. Connor c Wright b Cooper	8	c Russell b Cooper	4
J. N. B. Bovill not out	0	not out	3
L-b 6, w 2, n-b 16	24	B 1, l-b 9, w 2, n-b 8	20
1/6 2/20 3/79 4/95 5/97 6/138 7/164 8/168 9/192	192	1/35 2/70 3/74 4/78 5/134 6/156 7/197 8/215 9/220	220

Bonus points – Gloucestershire 4.

In the second innings R. S. M. Morris retired hurt at 18.

Bowling: *First Innings*—Walsh 20–7–46–3; Cooper 17.4–6–38–4; Smith 14–3–28–2; Alleyne 8–2–19–0; Ball 17–5–55–1. *Second Innings*—Walsh 17–3–60–3; Cooper 20.1–2–57–3; Smith 9–0–40–0; Alleyne 7–0–32–2; Ball 4–0–21–0.

Gloucestershire

B. C. Broad c Udal b Benjamin	2	– c Terry b Connor	15
A. J. Wright lbw b Connor	7	– c White b Udal	6
T. H. C. Hancock c Aymes b Bovill	14	– c Terry b Maru	8
M. G. N. Windows lbw b Benjamin	33	– c Terry b Udal	0
R. I. Dawson c Terry b Udal	4	– (6) b Udal	17
M. C. J. Ball c Aymes b Benjamin	0	– (5) c sub b Benjamin	25
M. W. Alleyne c Udal b Benjamin	14	– b Udal	2
†R. C. Russell c Aymes b Connor	13	– lbw b Connor	20
A. M. Smith b Benjamin	15	– c sub b Connor	4
*C. A. Walsh lbw b Connor	0	– c Smith b Udal	1
K. E. Cooper not out	18	– not out	4
B 4, l-b 2, n-b 6	12	L-b 1, n-b 12	13
1/12 2/16 3/43 4/48 5/52 6/81 7/88 8/104 9/104	132	1/23 2/35 3/35 4/43 5/68 6/71 7/90 8/105 9/106	115

Bonus points – Hampshire 4.

Bowling: *First Innings*—Benjamin 21.5–7–31–5; Connor 18–5–60–3; Bovill 6–3–12–1; Udal 8–1–23–1. *Second Innings*—Benjamin 13–3–25–1; Connor 12.5–3–41–3; Udal 19–5–46–5; Maru 3–2–2–1.

Umpires: J. D. Bond and D. J. Constant.

At Worcester, July 21, 22, 23, 25. HAMPSHIRE beat WORCESTERSHIRE by 56 runs.

HAMPSHIRE v NORTHAMPTONSHIRE

At Southampton, July 28, 29, 30, August 1. Northamptonshire won by 24 runs. Northamptonshire 20 pts, Hampshire 5 pts. Toss: Northamptonshire.

Four men dominated the match: the two captains with the bat and two West Indian pace bowlers. But Ambrose settled the issue. Connor held sway on the first day, bowling with fire and accuracy to claim seven for 47 as Northamptonshire succumbed for 164. Hampshire eased to a lead of 65, despite a career-best five for 69 from Hughes, in his first Championship match for three years. But then the initiative was wrested from them as Lamb hit a season's best 131 to set Hampshire a target of 294 in 115 overs. Nicholas rose to the challenge with a four-hour hundred, his first since 1991, but few others could master Ambrose. Bowling in short bursts because of a side strain, he returned seven for 44, improving on his best analysis for Northamptonshire for the second time in nine days. As in the previous game, against Derbyshire, he finished with ten in the match; so did the reliable Connor. Nine Northamptonshire wickets went to lbw decisions, including the top three in both innings.

Close of play: First day, Hampshire 87-4 (T. C. Middleton 24*, M. C. J. Nicholas 0*); Second day, Northamptonshire 130-3 (A. J. Lamb 57*, M. B. Loye 31*); Third day, Hampshire 12-2 (V. P. Terry 1*).

Northamptonshire

First innings		Second innings	
R. R. Montgomerie lbw b Connor	4	lbw b Cowans	22
R. J. Warren lbw b Cowans	8	lbw b Connor	7
R. J. Bailey lbw b Connor	5	lbw b Connor	9
*A. J. Lamb c Maru b Connor	9	st Aymes b Maru	131
M. B. Loye lbw b Connor	11	c Terry b Connor	48
A. L. Penberthy not out	56	lbw b Udal	7
†D. Ripley c Nicholas b James	5	lbw b Udal	20
A. R. Roberts c White b Connor	23	c Terry b Udal	30
C. E. L. Ambrose b Connor	16	c and b Udal	12
J. G. Hughes c Aymes b Connor	12	c Maru b Udal	17
N. G. B. Cook c Middleton b Maru	6	not out	43
L-b 9	9	L-b 4, n-b 8	12
1/17 2/17 3/29 4/38 5/43 6/50 7/85 8/111 9/135	164	1/10 2/28 3/57 4/163 5/191 6/222 7/281 8/291 9/295	358

Bonus points – Hampshire 4.

Bowling: *First Innings*—Cowans 16–4–41–1; Connor 26–8–47–7; James 11–4–36–1; Udal 15–4–27–0; Maru 0.5–0–4–1. *Second Innings*—Cowans 22–7–55–1; Connor 27–8–79–3; Udal 40–12–119–5; Maru 29–9–66–1; James 9–1–32–0; White 3–1–3–0.

Hampshire

First innings		Second innings	
V. P. Terry c Ambrose b Hughes	1	(2) c Ripley b Ambrose	17
T. C. Middleton c Ripley b Ambrose	24	(1) c Lamb b Ambrose	6
G. W. White c Montgomerie b Roberts	38	b Ambrose	4
R. A. Smith c Lamb b Hughes	23	lbw b Ambrose	14
R. J. Maru c Ambrose b Hughes	0	(9) c Ambrose b Penberthy	12
*M. C. J. Nicholas c Warren b Cook	53	(5) c Ripley b Penberthy	107
K. D. James not out	49	(6) c Penberthy b Ambrose	24
†A. N. Aymes b Ambrose	26	(7) c Lamb b Ambrose	31
S. D. Udal c Ripley b Ambrose	2	(8) c Cook b Roberts	12
C. A. Connor c Bailey b Hughes	8	b Ambrose	14
N. G. Cowans c Warren b Hughes	2	not out	6
L-b 3	3	B 9, l-b 9, n-b 4	22
1/1 2/54 3/83 4/83 5/88 6/174 7/207 8/209 9/226	229	1/6 2/12 3/41 4/44 5/140 6/206 7/231 8/243 9/248	269

Bonus points – Hampshire 1, Northamptonshire 4.

Bowling: *First Innings*—Ambrose 29–9–44–3; Hughes 25–8–69–5; Penberthy 20–6–29–0; Roberts 15–5–44–1; Cook 19–8–26–1; Bailey 7–3–14–0. *Second Innings*—Ambrose 28.3–11–44–7; Hughes 13–3–46–0; Penberthy 19–4–50–2; Roberts 16–5–51–1; Bailey 3–0–20–0; Cook 21–6–40–0.

Umpires: A. A. Jones and R. Julian.

At Canterbury, August 4, 5, 6, 8. HAMPSHIRE beat KENT by 18 runs.

HAMPSHIRE v SURREY

At Southampton, August 18, 19, 20, 22. Hampshire won by an innings and 68 runs. Hampshire 24 pts, Surrey 2 pts. Toss: Surrey.

Third-placed Surrey, with Stewart, Thorpe and Benjamin on Test duty, went down to their third successive thrashing by an innings. Their hopes were hit on the opening morning when Connor claimed their top three for 31. Udal took the next five, culminating with Brown, whose belligerent 78 was Surrey's only consolation. Then it was the turn of their bowlers – nine in all – to suffer. Terry, with his fourth hundred of the summer, Nicholas, with his third in four innings, the promising White and Smith all punished their lethargy and Surrey joined Derbyshire and Somerset in conceding 81 extras, before Nicholas declared at 603 for seven – Hampshire's highest total at Northlands Road in the ground's 109-year history. Butcher, with his maiden hundred, and Hollioake went some way to restoring tattered pride. But Surrey's last five wickets went down in little more than an hour on Monday. Udal found life and lift after the second new ball was taken to finish with ten for 163 as Hampshire completed their fourth win in five games.

Close of play: First day, Hampshire 164-1 (V. P. Terry 84*, G. W. White 57*); Second day, Hampshire 527-5 (M. C. J. Nicholas 120*, A. N. Aymes 55*); Third day, Surrey 323-5 (M. A. Lynch 44*, A. W. Smith 6*).

Surrey

D. J. Bicknell lbw b Connor	2	– b Maru	15
M. A. Butcher lbw b Connor	12	– c White b James	134
D. M. Ward c Aymes b Connor	0	– c Aymes b James	38
A. D. Brown c James b Udal	78	– c Udal b Maru	2
A. J. Hollioake lbw b Udal	1	– c James b Udal	65
M. A. Lynch c Maru b Udal	2	– c Cowans b Udal	60
A. W. Smith c Terry b Udal	4	– c Terry b Udal	6
†G. J. Kersey c Middleton b Udal	9	– c Middleton b Udal	1
N. M. Kendrick not out	15	– c Cowans b Connor	8
*M. P. Bicknell c Middleton b James	11	– c Cowans b Udal	29
C. E. Cuffy lbw b James	1	– not out	2
L-b 5, n-b 10	15	B 4, l-b 6, w 1, n-b 14	25
1/2 2/2 3/31 4/34 5/42 6/48 7/92 8/129 9/148	150	1/45 2/116 3/119 4/230 5/294 6/328 7/339 8/340 9/372	385

Bonus points – Hampshire 4.

Bowling: *First Innings*—Connor 19–5–49–3; Cowans 12–4–44–0; Udal 24–14–26–5; James 6.1–0–18–2; Maru 4–2–8–0. *Second Innings*—Connor 26–1–105–1; Cowans 9–3–23–0; Udal 44.1–12–137–5; Maru 26–5–82–2; James 14–4–28–2.

Hampshire

T. C. Middleton c Brown b Cuffy	0
V. P. Terry st Kersey b Smith	135
G. W. White b M. P. Bicknell	57
R. A. Smith b Hollioake	75
*M. C. J. Nicholas c Ward b Kendrick	145
K. D. James c Brown b Kendrick	14
†A. N. Aymes c Kersey b Kendrick	76
S. D. Udal not out	14
R. J. Maru not out	6
B 5, l-b 14, w 4, n-b 58	81
1/2 2/165 3/281 4/352 5/397 6/581 7/581 (7 wkts dec.)	603

C. A. Connor and N. G. Cowans did not bat.

Bonus points – Hampshire 4, Surrey 2 (Score at 120 overs: 499-5).

Bowling: Cuffy 14–3–38–1; M. P. Bicknell 23–4–92–1; Kendrick 40.3–6–159–3; Hollioake 16–4–70–1; Smith 17–0–98–1; Brown 9–0–34–0; Butcher 12–0–57–0; Lynch 10–2–35–0; D. J. Bicknell 1–0–1–0.

Umpires: V. A. Holder and P. Willey.

HAMPSHIRE v DURHAM

At Portsmouth, August 25, 26, 27, 29. Drawn. Hampshire 8 pts, Durham 6 pts. Toss: Hampshire.

Portsmouth's match in July had prompted muttering about the quality of the pitch, but three batsmen made sure there were no such noises this time. For the long-term future, it was the third whose performance was the most significant. Twenty-year-old Daley had long looked likely to be the first home-grown product to break through for the newest first-class county: here potential was finally fulfilled as he hit his maiden century – a majestic and flawless unbeaten 159 which almost gave Durham sight of a daunting target of 342 in 78 overs. He batted a shade under five hours, faced 249 balls and struck 26 fours. The other centuries came from proven performers. Terry hit 164, his fifth hundred of the season, in Hampshire's first-innings 512 while Morris countered for Durham with a pugnacious 149, his second in consecutive innings. He added 160 with Bainbridge, virtually ensuring that Durham, who had been 89 for four, would avoid the follow-on.

Close of play: First day, Hampshire 326-4 (V. P. Terry 122*, K. D. James 53*); Second day, Durham 195-4 (J. E. Morris 115*, P. Bainbridge 44*); Third day, Hampshire 129-2 (G. W. White 29*, R. A. Smith 14*).

Hampshire

First innings		Second innings	
V. P. Terry c Brown b Bainbridge	164	c Cummins b Wood	40
T. C. Middleton lbw b Brown	11	c and b Graveney	41
G. W. White c Scott b Wood	15	not out	73
R. A. Smith c Scott b Graveney	45	c Scott b Brown	22
*M. C. J. Nicholas c Morris b Wood	25	not out	30
K. D. James c Hutton b Wood	53		
†A. N. Aymes c Cummins b Wood	48		
R. J. Maru c Scott b Wood	36		
M. Jean-Jacques not out	22		
C. A. Connor c and b Graveney	18		
N. G. Cowans c Saxelby b Graveney	9		
L-b 4, w 6, n-b 56	66	B 1, l-b 2, n-b 6	9
1/39 2/60 3/151 4/188 5/326 6/382 7/454 8/465 9/486	512	1/74 2/97 3/139 (3 wkts dec.)	215

Bonus points – Hampshire 4, Durham 2 (Score at 120 overs: 449-6).

Bowling: *First Innings*—Cummins 27–1–91–0; Brown 27–3–92–1; Wood 30–0–141–5; Bainbridge 15–3–58–1; Graveney 34.5–6–126–3. *Second Innings*—Cummins 5–1–22–0; Brown 15–3–37–1; Wood 13–1–63–1; Graveney 16.3–7–35–1; Bainbridge 14–1–55–0.

Durham

First innings		Second innings	
J. I. Longley lbw b Cowans	8	c Aymes b Cowans	1
M. Saxelby c Maru b Connor	13	c Terry b Cowans	24
J. E. Morris c Aymes b James	149	b Cowans	0
J. A. Daley c White b James	3	not out	159
S. Hutton b Maru	1	c White b Cowans	33
*P. Bainbridge c Maru b James	64	st Aymes b James	27
A. C. Cummins c Maru b Cowans	65	lbw b James	7
†C. W. Scott lbw b Connor	39	run out	1
J. Wood b Connor	6		
S. J. E. Brown c Smith b Connor	15		
D. A. Graveney not out	2	(9) not out	16
B 1, l-b 8, n-b 12	21	L-b 11, n-b 6	17
1/19 2/29 3/70 4/89 5/249 6/262 7/349 8/367 9/367	386	1/1 2/1 3/56 4/142 5/247 6/257 7/258 (7 wkts)	285

Bonus points – Durham 4, Hampshire 4 (Score at 120 overs: 381-9).

Bowling: *First Innings*—Connor 32.4–6–122–4; Cowans 30–5–97–2; Jean-Jacques 0.3–0–8–0; Maru 23.3–6–43–1; James 29–7–90–3; White 2–0–10–0; Nicholas 4–2–7–0. *Second Innings*—Connor 21–5–70–0; Cowans 19.4–5–76–4; James 21–4–70–2; Maru 16–3–58–0.

Umpires: R. Palmer and D. R. Shepherd.

At Birmingham, August 30, 31, September 1, 2. HAMPSHIRE lost to WARWICKSHIRE by an innings and 95 runs.

At Leicester, September 8, 9, 10, 12. HAMPSHIRE lost to LEICESTERSHIRE by seven wickets.

HAMPSHIRE v GLAMORGAN

At Southampton, September 15, 16, 17, 19. Drawn. Hampshire 4 pts, Glamorgan 4 pts. Toss: Hampshire.

With the first and final days lost to rain and the second cut to 64 overs, it was a frustrating end to the season – except for Udal. He continued his progress towards recognition as a genuine all-rounder, with a composed career-best 94, before falling to a catch in the deep as he tried to bring up his hundred with a six. He put on 90 for the seventh wicket with Thursfield, who also reached his highest score. When Glamorgan replied, Udal added two wickets and a diving catch, which removed Roseberry after his maiden Championship fifty.

Close of play: First day, No play; Second day, Hampshire 166-5 (M. C. J. Nicholas 43*, S. D. Udal 8*); Third day, Glamorgan 197-4 (P. A. Cottey 22*, R. D. B. Croft 14*).

Hampshire

V. P. Terry c Metson b Watkin	15
P. R. Whitaker b Croft	38
G. W. White lbw b Watkin	9
R. A. Smith st Metson b Croft	29
*M. C. J. Nicholas c Maynard b Watkin	48
†A. N. Aymes b Lefebvre	15
S. D. Udal c Hemp b Barwick	94
M. J. Thursfield b Watkin	47
C. A. Connor c Roseberry b Watkin	9
J. N. B. Bovill c Maynard b Barwick	10
D. P. J. Flint not out	3
B 2, l-b 9, w 1, n-b 2	14
	—
1/38 2/60 3/74 4/107 5/140 6/191 7/281 8/291 9/328	331

Bonus points – Hampshire 3, Glamorgan 4.

Bowling: Gibson 8–2–25–0; Lefebvre 24–3–68–1; Watkin 30–3–98–5; Barwick 25.4–8–64–2; Croft 30–7–65–2.

Glamorgan

S. P. James c Aymes b Connor	16
A. Roseberry c Udal b Thursfield	65
D. L. Hemp c White b Udal	61
*M. P. Maynard b Udal	4
P. A. Cottey not out	22
R. D. B. Croft not out	14
B 2, l-b 3, n-b 10	15
	—
1/25 2/137 3/145 4/171	(4 wkts) 197

R. P. Lefebvre, †C. P. Metson, O. D. Gibson, S. L. Watkin and S. R. Barwick did not bat.

Bonus point – Hampshire 1.

Bowling: Bovill 13–2–34–0; Connor 8–2–36–1; Thursfield 8–2–28–1; Flint 11–2–30–0; Udal 13–1–64–2.

Umpires: J. C. Balderstone and G. Sharp.

KENT

Patron: HRH The Duke of Kent
President: J. G. Overy
Chairman: D. S. Kemp
Chairman, Cricket Committee: D. G. Ufton
Secretary: S. T. W. Anderson
Captain: M. R. Benson
Cricket Administrator: Ms D. F. Potter
Coach: D. H. Foster
Head Groundsman: B. A. Fitch
Scorer: J. C. Foley

Kent's supporters, perennially waiting for something to turn up, voiced even more optimism than usual at the start of the season. By the end of June, however, Kent were winless and perilously close to bottom of the Championship. When they did start winning, they could hardly stop. Starting in Maidstone Week at the beginning of July, they won six of their last ten Championship fixtures and began a surge in the Sunday League that brought them nine consecutive victories and their second successive near-miss for the title. They eventually finished third. Overall, it added up to yet another frustrating season.

The long injury list was probably the major factor. Despite the county's big squad, the loss at one time or another of Martin McCague, Alan Igglesden, Dean Headley and Duncan Spencer hampered the bowling – at one time the theory was expressed that McCague and Igglesden might really be the same person collecting two pay cheques, since it was hard to recall seeing them play together. Mark Ealham was out for a month with a groin injury and Matthew Fleming battled through the season with a bad shoulder that needed regular injections.

The batting struggled for consistency, not helped by slow pitches at Canterbury. But throughout the season Carl Hooper's role was immense with both bat and ball, and he was without doubt Kent's player of the year. He scored 1,579 first-class runs at 54.44 – apart from him, only Neil Taylor and Trevor Ward reached 1,000 – and on Sundays he was consistently brilliant. He scored 773 at 51.53, with six fifties and two hundreds, becoming the top scorer in the league for the second season running and winning £3,000.

Once again, Neil Taylor was also an important contributor to the cause, especially in that first Championship win against Yorkshire. Rarely has a player grafted so well, keeping his head as his team collapsed to 86 for five. He made 139, his highest score of the season, in six hours of deep concentration and then, in the second innings, played the perfect supporting role to Hooper. Records come and go, but Taylor is a keen follower of statistics: nobody could begrudge him passing the record of 12 hundreds at Canterbury which he shared with Frank Woolley and Colin Cowdrey, on the final Saturday of the home season at the St Lawrence Ground.

But it was the performance of Min Patel that offered most encouragement. With Richard Davis leaving for Warwickshire, he found himself the principal left-arm spinner and responded magnificently. He was the leading wicket-taker in England, with 90 at 22.86, two years after a knee injury nearly ended his career. His form attracted the attention of the England selectors, with several observers coming to monitor his progress, before the chairman Ray Illingworth himself arrived at Canterbury for a look. Although Patel missed out on the senior England tour, he earned a place in the A team touring his native India.

McCague's season fell into two halves. A shoulder injury sustained in early May sidelined him for ten weeks but, after one attempt at a comeback proved fruitless, he returned at full pelt to take a clutch of wickets, including 15 for 147 against Derbyshire, the best match figures of the season. That form won him a place on the Ashes tour. But when McCague returned, Igglesden was struck down by a back injury. Headley was used sparingly, having developed a hernia, and Spencer played his last game in June before returning early to Australia, for further diagnosis of his back trouble. Kent hope he will return.

Tim Wren was one player who benefited from the injuries afflicting the front-line bowlers and his left-arm seam added variation to the attack. After making only a handful of appearances since his debut in 1990, he burst into the season with three wickets in four balls against Yorkshire in the Sunday League. Wren was chosen ahead of the more experienced campaigners, Chris Penn and Richard Ellison, who played one first-class match between them. Ellison announced his departure, unsurprisingly, and took a job at Millfield School. Matthew Walker, a former England Under-19 captain, suggested that he could have a bright future and Julian Thompson also made his Championship debut before a shin injury ended his season early. A qualified doctor, he returned to medicine for the winter, but accepted a contract for 1995.

Kent's biggest single disappointment came in the quarter-finals of the Benson and Hedges Cup at Edgbaston. They were beaten in a controversial bowl-out after both allotted days were wiped out by rain that had seeped under the covers. They argued that play would have been possible had Warwickshire used their more comprehensive "Brumbrella", left off because of fungus on the pitch. Players and supporters were frustrated and Kent complained to the TCCB, who decided against taking action. There was a chance to take revenge, when Kent fought through to the semi-finals of the NatWest Trophy, but Warwickshire saw them off again.

The visit of the South Africans was a highlight of the year; Kent were the first county to play against Kepler Wessels and his men and the only one to beat them. Though the first day was a complete washout and only contrivance between the captains produced a result, Kent secured a morale-boosting 34-run victory, thanks to Graham Cowdrey, who regained his form with a century, and Headley, who took five for 60.

The long-term future of cricket at Maidstone was still unresolved; the local council turned down a request for £7,000 to help stage the fixture in 1995, but local business backing enabled Kent to retain the popular festival for at least another year. With Tunbridge Wells keen to stage a second week's cricket, a real threat hung over the picturesque Mote Park, on its day one of the prettiest venues in the game. – Andrew Gidley.

KENT 1994

[*Bill Smith*

Back row: M. M. Patel, S. C. Willis, N. W. Preston, J. B. D. Thompson, D. J. Spencer, M. J. Walker. *Middle row:* F. Errington (*physiotherapist*), J. C. Foley (*scorer*), T. R. Ward, D. P. Fulton, T. N. Wren, M. J. McCague, D. W. Headley, N. J. Llong, M. V. Fleming, M. A. Ealham, A. G. E. Ealham (*director of youth coaching*), D. H. Foster (*coach*). *Front row:* C. Penn, G. R. Cowdrey, C. L. Hooper, M. R. Benson (*captain*), S. A. Marsh, R. M. Ellison, N. R. Taylor, A. P. Igglesden.

KENT RESULTS

All first-class matches – Played 19: Won 8, Lost 7, Drawn 4.

County Championship matches – Played 17: Won 6, Lost 7, Drawn 4.

Bonus points – Batting 44, Bowling 58.

Competition placings – Britannic Assurance County Championship, 9th; NatWest Bank Trophy, s-f; Benson and Hedges Cup, q-f; AXA Equity & Law League, 3rd.

BRITANNIC ASSURANCE CHAMPIONSHIP AVERAGES

BATTING

	Birthplace	*M*	*I*	*NO*	*R*	*HS*	*Avge*
‡C. L. Hooper§	*Georgetown, Guyana*	16	29	0	1,579	183	54.44
‡T. R. Ward	*Farningham*	17	31	1	1,282	125	42.73
‡N. R. Taylor	*Orpington*	14	25	3	919	139	41.77
M. J. Walker	*Gravesend*	5	7	0	239	107	34.14
‡S. A. Marsh	*London*	17	29	6	732	88	31.82
‡M. R. Benson	*Shoreham*	14	26	1	699	159	27.96
‡M. V. Fleming	*Macclesfield*	15	27	0	754	73	27.92
‡M. A. Ealham	*Willesborough*	13	23	1	604	68*	27.45
‡G. R. Cowdrey	*Farnborough, Kent*	8	14	1	315	69	24.23
D. P. Fulton	*Lewisham*	8	14	0	318	50	22.71
‡M. J. McCague	*Larne*	9	15	3	265	56	22.08
‡N. J. Llong	*Ashford, Kent*	6	10	0	188	44	18.80
‡M. M. Patel	*Bombay, India*	16	25	2	245	39	10.65
D. J. Spencer	*Burnley*	4	6	1	46	13	9.20
‡D. W. Headley	*Stourbridge*	7	11	3	71	26	8.87
‡A. P. Igglesden	*Farnborough, Kent*	10	15	8	54	15*	7.71
T. N. Wren	*Folkestone*	7	11	4	31	18*	4.42

Also batted: J. B. D. Thompson (*Cape Town, SA*) (1 match) 1*, 2.

* *Signifies not out.* ‡ *Denotes county cap.* § *Overseas player.*

The following played a total of 12 three-figure innings for Kent in County Championship matches – C. L. Hooper 5, T. R. Ward 3, N. R. Taylor 2, M. R. Benson 1, M. J. Walker 1.

BOWLING

	O	*M*	*R*	*W*	*BB*	*5W/i*	*Avge*
M. J. McCague	300.1	60	953	54	9-86	5	17.64
M. M. Patel	739.2	181	1,910	79	8-96	4	24.17
M. A. Ealham	247.4	55	730	27	7-53	1	27.03
T. N. Wren	164.5	30	533	17	6-48	1	31.35
D. W. Headley	257.1	40	908	28	5-128	1	32.42
D. J. Spencer	85.5	12	347	10	4-31	0	34.70
C. L. Hooper	414.1	93	1,055	29	5-52	1	36.37
A. P. Igglesden	297.1	67	878	21	5-38	1	41.80

Also bowled: G. R. Cowdrey 0.2–0–4–0; M. V. Fleming 230.5–43–737–9; N. J. Llong 10–2–37–0; J. B. D. Thompson 33–6–120–1.

Wicket-keepers: S. A. Marsh 62 ct, 4 st; T. R. Ward 2 ct.

Leading Fielders: C. L. Hooper 26, T. R. Ward 23, D. P. Fulton 15.

At Cambridge, April 20, 21, 22. KENT beat CAMBRIDGE UNIVERSITY by 340 runs.

KENT v NOTTINGHAMSHIRE

At Canterbury, May 5, 6, 7. Nottinghamshire won by nine runs. Nottinghamshire 20 pts, Kent 4 pts. Toss: Kent. Championship debut: J. C. Adams.

Nottinghamshire won a tense match inside three days after 23 wickets fell on an eventful second day that lasted until 7.30 p.m. The pitch, relaid in 1992, caused much discussion. Unlike traditional Canterbury strips, it provided plenty of pace and bounce, delighting the seamers who claimed all but one of the wickets. Still, Kent felt they had wasted their advantage during the three hours possible on the first day, when Johnson hit out at a run a ball. His 70 was the highest innings of a low-scoring match, in which a fifth of the runs came from extras. Kent's batsmen all struggled – their first five wickets went for 47, and they conceded a lead of 60. But when Nottinghamshire resumed in mid-afternoon, they were again indebted to one main contributor, Robinson, before he became one of four batsmen out at 166. Kent were left a target of 239, far higher than anything so far in the match. Thanks to Hooper – batting down the order because of an injured thumb and wearing, unusually for him, a helmet – Kent came very close, before he was caught off Lewis in sight of home.

Close of play: First day, Nottinghamshire 167-7 (P. Johnson 69*, G. W. Mike 8*); Second day, Kent 3-0 (D. P. Fulton 1*, M. R. Benson 0*).

Nottinghamshire

P. R. Pollard c Marsh b Igglesden	1	– c sub b Igglesden	28
M. A. Crawley c Fulton b McCague	4	– c Fulton b McCague	0
J. C. Adams c Marsh b Igglesden	19	– lbw b Igglesden	5
*R. T. Robinson lbw b Headley	4	– c Marsh b Headley	52
P. Johnson lbw b Igglesden	70	– c Ealham b McCague	15
C. C. Lewis c McCague b Headley	10	– c McCague b Igglesden	23
†W. M. Noon c Llong b Igglesden	9	– c Ward b McCague	12
K. P. Evans lbw b Igglesden	0	– lbw b McCague	0
G. W. Mike b Headley	21	– b McCague	0
R. A. Pick c Hooper b Headley	3	– not out	2
J. A. Afford not out	1	– c Marsh b McCague	5
B 2, l-b 9, w 12, n-b 20	43	B 5, l-b 5, w 14, n-b 12	36
1/8 2/8 3/52 4/98 5/133 6/150 7/150 8/173 9/178	185	1/3 2/14 3/55 4/86 5/128 6/166 7/166 8/166 9/166	178

Bonus points – Kent 4.

Bowling: *First Innings*—McCague 9–2–35–1; Igglesden 16–4–38–5; Spencer 5–0–30–0; Headley 14.2–1–71–4. *Second Innings*—McCague 15.1–3–50–6; Igglesden 13–4–61–3; Spencer 1–0–7–0; Headley 14–3–39–1; Ealham 4–0–11–0.

Kent

D. P. Fulton b Lewis	5	– c Crawley b Lewis	38
*M. R. Benson c Crawley b Pick	6	– b Lewis	25
T. R. Ward c Evans b Lewis	3	– b Afford	1
C. L. Hooper c Robinson b Mike	6	– (7) c Evans b Lewis	66
N. J. Llong c Lewis b Mike	34	– (4) c Pollard b Pick	20
M. A. Ealham b Lewis	4	– (5) c Adams b Lewis	4
†S. A. Marsh c Adams b Evans	21	– (6) c Pollard b Mike	5
D. J. Spencer c Lewis b Evans	11	– run out	13
D. W. Headley not out	2	– c Adams b Lewis	2
M. J. McCague run out	7	– lbw b Pick	10
A. P. Igglesden b Mike	0	– not out	1
B 5, l-b 9, w 2, n-b 10	26	B 16, l-b 6, w 2, n-b 20	44
1/14 2/18 3/18 4/36 5/47 6/103 7/103 8/116 9/124	125	1/77 2/80 3/80 4/96 5/116 6/116 7/139 8/172 9/225	229

Bonus points – Nottinghamshire 4.

Bowling: *First Innings*—Lewis 17–5–43–3; Pick 11–5–17–1; Evans 5–1–22–2; Mike 8.3–2–29–3. *Second Innings*—Lewis 24.2–8–55–5; Pick 18–4–40–2; Evans 5–1–18–0; Mike 11–2–55–1; Afford 12–3–39–1.

Umpires: G. Sharp and P. B. Wight.

At Chelmsford, May 12, 13, 14, 16. KENT lost to ESSEX by four wickets.

KENT v LANCASHIRE

At Canterbury, May 19, 20, 21, 23. Drawn. Kent 8 pts, Lancashire 4 pts. Toss: Kent. Championship debut: N. A. Derbyshire.

This was a game for Kent's statisticians, with a crop of county records and a career-best eight for 96 from left-arm spinner Patel. Benson chose to bat and contributed the highest score of 90 to a total of 556, the highest Kent total without an individual century. Their previous record was 539 for nine declared, against Middlesex in 1928, which was also the only other Kent innings to contain six half-centuries. Kent were finally all out after lunch on the second day. Patel claimed Lancashire's top four before the close and then, after Saturday was washed out, forced Lancashire to follow on, with four wickets in 22 balls on Monday morning. At tea, Lancashire were 160 behind with four wickets down. But an unbroken stand of 147 between Lloyd and Watkinson secured the draw. Patel finished with ten wickets for the second time in the young season; this followed his 12 wickets in the match against Lancashire in 1993.

Close of play: First day, Kent 403-6 (M. V. Fleming 27*, S. A. Marsh 10*); Second day, Lancashire 171-4 (N. J. Speak 13*, M. Watkinson 33*); Third day, No play.

Kent

D. P. Fulton lbw b Watkinson 26
*M. R. Benson b Barnett 90
T. R. Ward c Speak b Watkinson 56
C. L. Hooper c Lloyd b Martin 83
N. R. Taylor b Derbyshire 54
N. J. Llong c Hegg b Barnett 44
M. V. Fleming c Crawley b Watkinson . 72
†S. A. Marsh c Titchard b Chapple 72
D. J. Spencer c Hegg b Watkinson 0
M. M. Patel b Chapple 39
A. P. Igglesden not out 0
B 6, l-b 8, w 4, n-b 2 20

1/52 2/180 3/184 4/284 5/361 6/379 7/462 8/464 9/549 — 556

Bonus points – Kent 4, Lancashire 2 (Score at 120 overs: 426-6).

Bowling: Martin 38–11–90–1; Derbyshire 21–1–107–1; Chapple 32.3–5–120–2; Watkinson 29–6–101–4; Barnett 34–2–124–2.

Lancashire

J. E. R. Gallian lbw b Patel	19	– c Fulton b Hooper 32
S. P. Titchard c Hooper b Patel	49	– b Patel 37
J. P. Crawley lbw b Patel	33	– c and b Patel 46
G. D. Lloyd c Taylor b Patel	4	– not out 93
N. J. Speak not out	57	– b Hooper 1
*M. Watkinson c Marsh b Spencer	43	– not out 62
†W. K. Hegg c Ward b Patel	26	
P. J. Martin c Ward b Patel	2	
G. Chapple c Fulton b Patel	0	
A. A. Barnett c Fulton b Patel	0	
N. A. Derbyshire b Spencer	5	
B 2, l-b 3, n-b 18	23	B 5, l-b 4, n-b 2 11
1/53 2/116 3/125 4/126 5/189 6/224 7/230 8/234 9/234	261	1/58 2/114 3/134 4/135 (4 wkts) 282

Bonus points – Lancashire 2, Kent 4.

Bowling: *First Innings*—Spencer 17.4–3–69–2; Igglesden 17–5–41–0; Fleming 6–5–4–0; Patel 38–10–96–8; Hooper 24–6–46–0. *Second Innings*—Igglesden 5–1–13–0; Patel 34–6–105–2; Hooper 22–2–83–2; Spencer 8–1–35–0; Llong 10–2–37–0.

Umpires: D. J. Constant and M. J. Kitchen.

At Leicester, May 26, 27, 28, 30. KENT lost to LEICESTERSHIRE by 139 runs.

KENT v SUSSEX

At Tunbridge Wells, June 2, 3, 4, 6. Drawn. Kent 7 pts, Sussex 5 pts. Toss: Sussex.

An unexpected declaration by Wells challenged Kent to score 221 in 25 overs and they leapt to it. Fleming was promoted to open with Ward and they put on 49 in under five overs. Hooper and Benson helped Fleming maintain the momentum: they needed 79 from eight when Stephenson had Benson caught behind, ran out Fleming and caught Fulton off Jarvis. Kent gave up the chase 69 runs short with five overs left. In the first innings, Athey carried his bat for 169, his highest score for Sussex, who reached 222 for two by tea on the first day. But Kent's bowlers struck back and Igglesden finished things off with three wickets in 11 balls in the morning. Saturday was washed out and, despite Patel, who took six Sussex wickets on Monday, only Wells's gesture made a result remotely possible.

Close of play: First day, Sussex 305-7 (C. W. J. Athey 166*, P. W. Jarvis 0*); Second day, Kent 336-6 (S. A. Marsh 26*, D. J. Spencer 10*); Third day, No play.

Sussex

C. W. J. Athey not out	169	– lbw b Patel	5
J. W. Hall c Ward b Igglesden	43	– b Spencer	4
D. M. Smith lbw b Spencer	6	– c Ward b Patel	50
*A. P. Wells c Marsh b Patel	25	– b Patel	36
M. P. Speight lbw b Patel	4	– (8) c Marsh b Patel	18
C. C. Remy c Fulton b Headley	6	– (5) c Ward b Patel	8
†P. Moores c and b Headley	11	– (6) c Hooper b Patel	68
F. D. Stephenson c Marsh b Patel	13	– (7) c Hooper b Spencer	2
P. W. Jarvis c Fulton b Igglesden	3	– not out	19
E. E. Hemmings c Hooper b Igglesden	0	– not out	5
E. S. H. Giddins c Marsh b Igglesden	8		
L-b 4, n-b 27	31	B 7, l-b 9, w 4, n-b 2	22
1/118 2/165 3/222 4/230 5/253 6/269 7/300 8/309 9/309	319	1/15 2/15 3/83 4/93 5/144 6/155 7/207 8/220 (8 wkts dec.)	237

Bonus points – Sussex 3, Kent 4.

Bowling: *First Innings*—Igglesden 22.5–6–42–4; Headley 25–5–81–2; Spencer 12–1–79–1; Fleming 12–4–34–0; Patel 29–8–65–3; Hooper 6–0–14–0. *Second Innings*—Spencer 18–3–62–2; Headley 11–2–31–0; Patel 39–9–91–6; Hooper 15–5–36–0; Fleming 1–0–1–0.

Kent

D. P. Fulton c Speight b Stephenson	0	– (6) c Stephenson b Jarvis	1
*M. R. Benson b Hemmings	55	– (4) c Moores b Stephenson	24
T. R. Ward b Jarvis	60	– (1) c Moores b Giddins	33
C. L. Hooper c Hemmings b Remy	79	– (3) b Stephenson	12
N. R. Taylor lbw b Stephenson	14	– not out	3
M. V. Fleming b Jarvis	63	– (2) run out	66
†S. A. Marsh not out	26	– not out	6
D. J. Spencer not out	10		
B 15, l-b 8, n-b 6	29	B 1, l-b 3, w 1, n-b 2	7
1/0 2/98 3/148 4/195 5/261 6/319 (6 wkts dec.)	336	1/49 2/84 3/142 4/142 5/146 (5 wkts)	152

D. W. Headley, M. M. Patel and A. P. Igglesden did not bat.

Bonus points – Kent 3, Sussex 2.

Bowling: *First Innings*—Stephenson 16–2–53–2; Giddins 13–3–39–0; Remy 16–3–54–1; Hemmings 29–5–87–1; Jarvis 24–1–80–2. *Second Innings*—Jarvis 5–1–37–1; Stephenson 9–0–62–2; Giddins 5–0–43–1; Athey 1–0–6–0.

Umpires: R. Julian and R. A. White.

KENT v MIDDLESEX

At Canterbury, June 9, 10, 11, 13. Drawn. Kent 6 pts, Middlesex 6 pts. Toss: Kent.

Two teams without a win got the result neither wanted, but the Kent coach Daryl Foster admitted his team were lucky to avoid defeat and refused to blame his side's poor form on mounting injury problems. Middlesex were favourites, at 179 for four chasing 245, until Patel and Headley came to the rescue by capturing some important wickets. The dominant figure of the match was Haynes, who followed up his 125 the last time he had batted, against Worcestershire a week earlier, with two impressive centuries – the second completed with a runner after he injured his knee in the fifties. His chief ally was Ramprakash, with whom he added 161 in 34 overs to set up a first-innings lead of 36.

Close of play: First day, Kent 236-4 (N. R. Taylor 43*, M. M. Patel 3*); Second day, Middlesex 248-3 (M. R. Ramprakash 93*, J. D. Carr 26*); Third day, Kent 146-3 (C. L. Hooper 26*, M. M. Patel 1*).

Kent

D. P. Fulton c Weekes b Emburey	35	– c and b Emburey	32
*M. R. Benson c Brown b Fraser	0	– c Brown b Fraser	4
T. R. Ward c and b Williams	52	– c Gatting b Emburey	63
C. L. Hooper c Gatting b Fraser	89	– lbw b Fraser	33
N. R. Taylor c Brown b Johnson	86	– (6) c Ramprakash b Johnson	16
M. M. Patel b Johnson	7	– (5) b Emburey	25
M. V. Fleming b Williams	46	– lbw b Williams	12
M. A. Ealham c Ramprakash b Weekes	42	– c Brown b Fraser	26
†S. A. Marsh not out	29	– c Carr b Emburey	29
D. W. Headley not out	3	– lbw b Weekes	8
A. P. Igglesden (did not bat)		– not out	1
B 13, l-b 6, n-b 10	29	L-b 12, n-b 19	31
1/0 2/55 3/131 4/229 5/244 6/317 7/353 8/403 (8 wkts dec.)	418	1/16 2/96 3/139 4/179 5/185 6/203 7/217 8/258 9/270	280

Bonus points – Kent 3, Middlesex 2 (Score at 120 overs: 335-6).

Bowling: *First Innings*—Williams 28–8–66–2; Fraser 31–5–77–2; Johnson 26–7–97–2; Emburey 38–5–105–1; Weekes 19–4–54–1. *Second Innings*—Williams 25–4–103–1; Fraser 20–10–20–3; Johnson 9–1–40–1; Emburey 24–6–48–4; Weekes 16.4–2–53–1; Ramprakash 1–0–4–0.

Middlesex

D. L. Haynes c Ward b Fleming	104	– lbw b Headley	103
M. A. Roseberry lbw b Headley	13	– run out	0
*M. W. Gatting c Hooper b Headley	5	– (4) c Fleming b Patel	16
M. R. Ramprakash c Fulton b Headley	99	– (3) b Fleming	31
J. D. Carr b Patel	64	– (8) not out	8
P. N. Weekes c Ward b Headley	48	– c Fulton b Patel	12
†K. R. Brown not out	45	– (5) c Ward b Patel	12
J. E. Emburey c Hooper b Patel	22	– (7) b Headley	2
R. L. Johnson c Hooper b Patel	8	– not out	2
N. F. Williams b Fleming	12		
A. R. C. Fraser c and b Patel	1		
B 16, l-b 12, w 1, n-b 4	33	B 4, l-b 8, n-b 6	18
1/28 2/42 3/203 4/264 5/344 6/360 7/405 8/429 9/448	454	1/4 2/85 3/130 4/152 5/179 6/194 7/195 (7 wkts)	204

Bonus points – Middlesex 4, Kent 3 (Score at 120 overs: 427-7).

Bowling: *First Innings*—Igglesden 16–0–63–0; Headley 26–2–107–4; Patel 43.3–7–118–4; Hooper 14–0–53–0; Fleming 27–5–85–2. *Second Innings*—Igglesden 14–0–60–0; Headley 11–0–51–2; Patel 14–2–56–3; Fleming 4–0–19–1; Hooper 0.4–0–6–0.

Umpires: T. E. Jesty and N. T. Plews.

At Birmingham, June 16, 17, 18, 20. KENT lost to WARWICKSHIRE by 76 runs.

At Canterbury, June 25, 26, 27. KENT beat SOUTH AFRICANS by 34 runs (See South African tour section).

KENT v YORKSHIRE

At Maidstone, June 30, July 1, 2, 4. Kent won by 175 runs. Kent 24 pts, Yorkshire 7 pts. Toss: Kent. First-class debut: G. M. Hamilton.

Neither side had won a Championship match in seven attempts, but Yorkshire looked more like breaking their duck when Kent were 86 for five before lunch on the opening day. The home team rallied through Taylor's 40th first-class century. He batted six hours for 139, with brief but dazzling support from Fleming, who hit 66 in 46 balls. In the second innings, Taylor played a supporting role to Hooper, whose blistering strokeplay brought him ten sixes, a Kent record, and 11 fours – despite a dizzy spell which forced him to retire briefly. Five of the sixes were off the unfortunate Stemp. Yorkshire were below strength with White and Gough on Test duty, and Hartley pulled out, giving Gavin Hamilton – born in Scotland but brought up in Sidcup – his debut. Their target of 454 to win was near-impossible. But Moxon scored his first Championship hundred of the season before falling to Patel, whose three for 14 in 12 balls hastened Yorkshire's demise.

Close of play: First day, Yorkshire 11-0 (M. D. Moxon 9*, M. P. Vaughan 0*); Second day, Kent 17-0 (T. R. Ward 8*, M. R. Benson 7*); Third day, Yorkshire 53-1 (M. D. Moxon 36*, D. Byas 15*).

Kent

T. R. Ward b Hamilton	23	– c Grayson b Silverwood	22
*M. R. Benson run out	4	– b Stemp	22
N. R. Taylor c Blakey b Robinson	139	– c Moxon b Hamilton	83
C. L. Hooper b Silverwood	16	– c Blakey b Robinson	183
M. A. Ealham c and b Silverwood	0	– c Grayson b Byas	21
G. R. Cowdrey c Blakey b Byas	0	– not out	47
M. V. Fleming c Blakey b Robinson	66		
†S. A. Marsh lbw b Hamilton	29		
D. W. Headley b Vaughan	26		
M. M. Patel c Moxon b Grayson	31		
A. P. Igglesden not out	15		
B 4, l-b 6, n-b 18	28	B 2, l-b 8, w 1, n-b 18	29
1/33 2/33 3/71 4/71 5/86 6/163 7/211 8/245 9/352	377	1/56 2/60 3/178 4/262 5/407 (5 wkts dec.)	407

Bonus points – Kent 4, Yorkshire 4.

In the second innings C. L. Hooper, when 38, retired ill at 112 and resumed at 178.

Bowling: *First Innings*—Silverwood 20–3–101–2; Hamilton 17–5–76–2; Robinson 26.5–4–92–2; Byas 3–1–16–1; Stemp 21–8–51–0; Grayson 7–4–7–1; Vaughan 8–2–24–1. *Second Innings*—Silverwood 18–5–63–1; Robinson 18.2–3–94–1; Hamilton 17–1–77–1; Stemp 32–10–123–1; Byas 7–2–21–1; Grayson 3–0–19–0.

Yorkshire

*M. D. Moxon c Cowdrey b Igglesden	17	– c Headley b Patel	122
M. P. Vaughan c Marsh b Headley	81	– lbw b Igglesden	2
D. Byas c Ealham b Headley	58	– lbw b Igglesden	16
R. B. Richardson c Marsh b Headley	54	– c Marsh b Headley	40
†R. J. Blakey c Marsh b Fleming	13	– c Ward b Patel	38
A. A. Metcalfe lbw b Fleming	0	– c and b Patel	0
A. P. Grayson c Marsh b Headley	22	– c Hooper b Patel	14
G. M. Hamilton c and b Hooper	48	– c Patel b Hooper	18
R. D. Stemp c Headley b Hooper	9	– c Hooper b Patel	0
C. E. W. Silverwood not out	4	– b Headley	16
M. A. Robinson b Headley	3	– not out	1
B 1, l-b 8, w 1, n-b 12	22	B 4, l-b 1, n-b 6	11
1/37 2/166 3/171 4/207 5/214 6/248 7/292 8/311 9/320	331	1/11 2/55 3/149 4/211 5/211 6/228 7/257 8/257 9/277	278

Bonus points – Yorkshire 3, Kent 4.

In the first innings R. B. Richardson, when 25, retired hurt at 205 and resumed at 248.

Bowling: *First Innings*—Igglesden 22–8–44–1; Headley 32.3–3–128–5; Fleming 13–1–36–2; Ealham 6–1–33–0; Patel 23–7–49–0; Hooper 8–0–32–2. *Second Innings*—Igglesden 20–3–74–2; Headley 22.2–6–75–2; Patel 26–7–68–5; Hooper 18–6–56–1.

Umpires: J. D. Bond and K. E. Palmer.

KENT v WORCESTERSHIRE

At Canterbury, July 14, 15, 16, 18. Worcestershire won by 140 runs. Worcestershire 21 pts, Kent 4 pts. Toss: Worcestershire. Championship debut: P. Mirza.

Chairman of selectors Ray Illingworth watched Patel, the country's leading wicket-taker, take three more wickets on the first day, as Worcestershire were dismissed for 202. He did not get an England call-up, though he was capped by the county on Saturday. But Kent never really recovered from losing Hooper to the first ball of the second morning. He became Parvaz Mirza's first Championship wicket, in a spell of three in 31 balls, and Kent made a dismal 166. Hick then punished their bowling, without both McCague and Igglesden. He was dropped on eight but went on to reach his 75th first-class century off 123 balls. Richard Illingworth and Mirza continued to frustrate the bowlers, adding 102 for the last wicket, and Kent's target was 459. They were four down by the close, but there was plenty of stubborn resistance on Monday, from Cowdrey, Marsh and last man Wren, in his first Championship game since 1990. Wren remained unbeaten after 22 overs when Worcestershire completed victory just before tea.

Close of play: First day, Kent 95-3 (C. L. Hooper 20*, G. R. Cowdrey 14*); Second day, Worcestershire 238-3 (G. A. Hick 129*, G. R. Haynes 45*); Third day, Kent 119-4 (G. R. Cowdrey 16*, M. M. Patel 1*).

Worcestershire

*T. S. Curtis c Ward b Headley	6	– lbw b Ealham	11
W. P. C. Weston lbw b Wren	0	– c Ward b Patel	24
G. A. Hick c and b Patel	46	– b Hooper	159
T. M. Moody st Marsh b Patel	27	– lbw b Headley	19
G. R. Haynes c Benson b Ealham	39	– c Marsh b Ealham	49
D. A. Leatherdale b Patel	31	– b Patel	31
†S. J. Rhodes not out	27	– c Marsh b Patel	0
S. R. Lampitt b Headley	1	– c Hooper b Patel	0
P. J. Newport c Marsh b Ealham	1	– c Cowdrey b Hooper	9
R. K. Illingworth c Marsh b Ealham	7	– not out	59
P. Mirza c Marsh b Ealham	2	– c Marsh b Wren	40
B 4, l-b 5, n-b 6	15	B 5, l-b 6, n-b 10	21
1/8 2/10 3/78 4/87 5/149 6/186 7/187 8/192 9/200	202	1/17 2/102 3/127 4/258 5/304 6/305 7/305 8/316 9/320	422

Bonus points – Worcestershire 1, Kent 4.

Bowling: *First Innings*—Headley 17–3–50–2; Wren 7–0–32–1; Fleming 7–1–17–0; Patel 27–11–55–3; Hooper 15–3–27–0; Ealham 5.4–1–12–4. *Second Innings*—Headley 12–4–30–1; Patel 42–11–106–4; Wren 19.5–6–53–1; Ealham 25–6–75–2; Fleming 20–1–65–0; Hooper 34–3–82–2.

Kent

T. R. Ward c Rhodes b Lampitt	28	– c Curtis b Newport	25
*M. R. Benson b Illingworth	20	– b Mirza	9
N. R. Taylor c Moody b Illingworth	2	– c Hick b Illingworth	40
C. L. Hooper b Mirza	20	– st Rhodes b Illingworth	11
G. R. Cowdrey c Illingworth b Mirza	18	– lbw b Illingworth	58
M. V. Fleming c Illingworth b Mirza	17	– (7) c Leatherdale b Newport	10
M. A. Ealham c Rhodes b Newport	2	– (8) c Rhodes b Illingworth	35
†S. A. Marsh st Rhodes b Illingworth	20	– (9) lbw b Lampitt	67
D. W. Headley not out	10	– (10) lbw b Newport	12
M. M. Patel b Lampitt	16	– (6) c Hick b Newport	9
T. N. Wren c Rhodes b Lampitt	0	– not out	18
L-b 6, w 1, n-b 6	13	L-b 6, n-b 18	24
1/53 2/53 3/67 4/95 5/115 6/118 7/118 8/147 9/166	166	1/21 2/66 3/95 4/104 5/133 6/155 7/203 8/232 9/267	318

Bonus points – Worcestershire 4.

Bowling: *First Innings*—Newport 15–4–37–1; Mirza 12–3–48–3; Illingworth 20–8–28–3; Lampitt 15.3–6–37–3; Hick 2–0–10–0. *Second Innings*—Mirza 16–4–39–1; Moody 7–0–39–0; Newport 26–6–100–4; Illingworth 45–20–79–4; Hick 14–1–46–0; Lampitt 3–0–9–1.

Umpires: J. C. Balderstone and P. Willey.

At Abergavenny, July 21, 22, 23, 25. KENT beat GLAMORGAN by 94 runs.

At Cheltenham, July 28, 29, 30. KENT beat GLOUCESTERSHIRE by 50 runs.

KENT v HAMPSHIRE

At Canterbury, August 4, 5, 6, 8. Hampshire won by 18 runs. Hampshire 22 pts, Kent 6 pts. Toss: Hampshire.

A gritty performance by Benson, who carried his bat for the first time, deserved to win the game. But there was little chance of that after Kent, chasing 208, collapsed from 30 without loss to 60 for six. Benson held out for nearly four hours against Connor, who claimed ten wickets for the second match running, but he could only delay Kent's defeat. Both sides struggled on a cracked pitch of irregular bounce, newly relaid, which TCCB inspector Harry Brind travelled down to look at. Smith's rapid 69 on a rain-affected first day and Nicholas's second hundred in consecutive innings helped Hampshire to a valuable 298, but Hooper produced the best batting of the match in reply. He reached 100 in 102 balls and hit one six through a pavilion window. Though Kent conceded a 25-run lead, Ealham took a career-best seven for 53 in the second innings and kept their target down.

Close of play: First day, Hampshire 136-5 (M. C. J. Nicholas 15*, A. N. Aymes 8*); Second day, Kent 214-5 (C. L. Hooper 119*, M. A. Ealham 13*); Third day, Kent 8-0 (T. R. Ward 6*, M. R. Benson 2*).

Hampshire

T. C. Middleton lbw b Igglesden	0	– c Hooper b Ealham	15
V. P. Terry c Marsh b McCague	25	– b Ealham	30
G. W. White b McCague	3	– c Marsh b McCague	2
R. A. Smith c Marsh b McCague	69	– lbw b Ealham	7
*M. C. J. Nicholas c Marsh b Patel	108	– b Ealham	12
K. D. James b Igglesden	4	– lbw b Ealham	18
†A. N. Aymes b McCague	15	– c Marsh b Ealham	29
S. D. Udal b Ealham	23	– c Benson b McCague	36
M. Jean-Jacques c Taylor b Fleming	8	– c Hooper b Ealham	0
C. A. Connor c Marsh b McCague	14	– c Ealham b McCague	20
N. G. Cowans not out	0	– not out	0
B 10, l-b 13, n-b 6	29	B 2, l-b 9, n-b 2	13
1/0 2/15 3/103 4/110 5/122 6/168 7/227 8/249 9/298	298	1/28 2/31 3/44 4/68 5/71 6/123 7/128 8/132 9/179	182

Bonus points – Hampshire 2, Kent 4.

Bowling: *First Innings*—Igglesden 24–7–94–2; McCague 29–6–89–5; Ealham 22–6–47–1; Fleming 7–1–39–1; Patel 2.5–0–6–1. *Second Innings*—Igglesden 22–7–47–0; McCague 19–4–50–3; Ealham 24–8–53–7; Patel 3–1–2–0; Fleming 8–2–19–0.

Kent

T. R. Ward c Aymes b Connor	0	– c Jean-Jacques b Connor	19
*M. R. Benson c Aymes b James	18	– not out	71
N. R. Taylor b Connor	12	– b Connor	1
C. L. Hooper c Udal b James	138	– c Aymes b Connor	2
G. R. Cowdrey lbw b James	13	– lbw b Connor	1
M. V. Fleming lbw b Connor	14	– c White b Jean-Jacques	0
M. A. Ealham run out	15	– c Udal b Jean-Jacques	2
†S. A. Marsh b Connor	7	– lbw b James	31
M. J. McCague lbw b James	9	– b Connor	22
M. M. Patel not out	17	– b Connor	6
A. P. Igglesden c Terry b Jean-Jacques	3	– b Jean-Jacques	2
L-b 3, n-b 24	27	L-b 7, w 3, n-b 22	32
1/0 2/28 3/72 4/126 5/169 6/216 7/226 8/249 9/252	273	1/30 2/38 3/40 4/49 5/56 6/60 7/108 8/165 9/186	189

Bonus points – Kent 2, Hampshire 4.

Bowling: *First Innings*—Connor 26–4–73–4; Cowans 19–4–40–0; James 17–2–78–4; Jean-Jacques 11.5–0–70–1; Udal 1–0–9–0. *Second Innings*—Connor 21–6–59–6; Cowans 9–1–25–0; Jean-Jacques 11.5–2–44–3; James 10–1–32–1; Udal 5–2–22–0.

Umpires: G. Sharp and R. A. White
(B. W. Luckhurst deputised for G. Sharp on the 4th day).

KENT v DURHAM

At Canterbury, August 11, 12, 13, 15. Kent won by nine wickets. Kent 24 pts, Durham 4 pts. Toss: Kent. Championship debut: M. J. Walker.

Kent's third Championship win in four games condemned Durham to their seventh consecutive defeat. Patel, Hooper and acting-captain Marsh were the dominant figures: Patel collected ten wickets for the third time in 1994, with an impressive repertoire of left-arm spin and flight; Hooper took eight and hit 41 in 25 balls; while Marsh made eight catches and one stumping, to follow an unbeaten 85. He and McCague, who reached a maiden fifty, put on 131 for Kent's eighth wicket, carrying them to a solid 385 after a rain-disrupted first day. Hooper, taking five wickets in a Championship innings for the first time, and Patel made Durham follow on, but Morris and Bainbridge put up more determined resistance, adding 165. Bainbridge was the only Durham batsman to fall to a seam bowler in either innings. Kent looked for a quick victory on the final morning, promoting Fleming to open. Though he was soon out, Ward and Taylor rapidly saw them to a target of 96.

Close of play: First day, Kent 173-3 (N. R. Taylor 18*, G. R. Cowdrey 30*); Second day, Durham 81-3 (M. Saxelby 45*); Third day, Durham 254-5 (S. Hutton 8*, D. A. Graveney 2*).

Kent

	First innings		Second innings	
T. R. Ward lbw b Brown	35	–	not out	47
M. J. Walker c Daley b Bainbridge	34			
N. R. Taylor c Scott b Cummins	26	–	not out	30
C. L. Hooper c Morris b Bainbridge	41			
G. R. Cowdrey c Scott b Cummins	38			
M. V. Fleming c Hutton b Bainbridge	5	–	(2) c and b Brown	11
M. A. Ealham c Scott b Bainbridge	21			
*†S. A. Marsh not out	85			
M. J. McCague st Scott b Graveney	56			
M. M. Patel st Scott b Graveney	0			
T. N. Wren c Cummins b Graveney	6			
B 3, l-b 12, w 1, n-b 22	38		L-b 4, n-b 4	8
1/75 2/81 3/132 4/182 5/189 6/203 7/240 8/371 9/371	385		1/24	(1 wkt) 96

Bonus points – Kent 4, Durham 4.

Bowling: *First Innings*—Cummins 24–6–67–2; Brown 22–1–111–1; Bainbridge 24–4–72–4; Graveney 17.3–5–66–3; Cox 13–1–54–0. *Second Innings*—Cummins 3–0–7–0; Brown 3–0–15–1; Cox 9.5–1–36–0; Graveney 9–1–34–0.

Durham

	First innings		Second innings	
J. I. Longley c Walker b Hooper	34	–	st Marsh b Hooper	24
M. Saxelby c Marsh b Hooper	62	–	c Marsh b Hooper	44
D. M. Cox c Ward b Patel	0	–	(11) c Marsh b Patel	0
J. E. Morris c Hooper b Patel	0	–	(3) c Marsh b Patel	94
*P. Bainbridge b Hooper	5	–	(4) c Marsh b Fleming	63
J. A. Daley c Marsh b Hooper	16	–	(5) c Marsh b Patel	4
S. Hutton b Patel	23	–	(6) c Ward b Patel	20
†C. W. Scott c Ward b Hooper	3	–	c Marsh b Hooper	3
A. C. Cummins not out	40	–	c Ealham b Patel	8
D. A. Graveney b Patel	1	–	(7) c Walker b Patel	9
S. J. E. Brown run out	3	–	(10) not out	0
B 4, l-b 5	9		B 4, l-b 7, w 2, n-b 2	15
1/80 2/81 3/81 4/88 5/118 6/121 7/129 8/177 9/187	196		1/69 2/72 3/237 4/237 5/250 6/272 7/275 8/279 9/284	284

Bonus points – Kent 4.

Bowling: *First Innings*—McCague 6–2–17–0; Wren 8–1–30–0; Ealham 7–0–20–0; Patel 26.5–4–68–4; Hooper 26–10–52–5. *Second Innings*—McCague 8–0–36–0; Ealham 12–2–40–0; Patel 37.5–12–84–6; Hooper 37–13–73–3; Wren 6–1–21–0; Fleming 5–1–19–1.

Umpires: B. Dudleston and J. W. Holder.

At Derby, August 18, 19, 20, 22. KENT beat DERBYSHIRE by 69 runs.

At Northampton, August 25, 26, 27. KENT lost to NORTHAMPTONSHIRE by eight wickets.

KENT v SOMERSET

At Canterbury, September 8, 9, 10, 12. Kent won by an innings and 57 runs. Kent 24 pts, Somerset 4 pts. Toss: Somerset.

Kent's sixth Championship victory was their most convincing. After rain washed out much of the first day, McCague and Wren virtually won the game with a devastating burst on the second morning. Nine wickets fell for 20 runs in 14.2 overs and Wren took a career-best six for 48. Hooper's fifth first-class century of the season took him past 1,500 runs, and he added 218 in 46 overs with Taylor. But next day it was Taylor who wrote himself into Kent's record books, when he scored his 13th hundred on the St Lawrence ground to pull ahead of Frank Woolley and Colin Cowdrey. He also completed 1,000 runs for the tenth time since his debut in 1979. Hallett's four for 59 represented his best bowling return but Somerset's batsmen, 284 behind, could not make Kent bat again. Their captain, Hayhurst, was stranded on 64 not out after three hours' batting with a sprained ankle.

Close of play: First day, Somerset 88-1 (M. N. Lathwell 38*, R. J. Harden 24*); Second day, Kent 293-3 (N. R. Taylor 76*, C. L. Hooper 121*); Third day, Somerset 111-4 (A. N. Hayhurst 17*, R. J. Turner 9*).

Somerset

M. N. Lathwell c Marsh b McCague	42	– c Marsh b McCague	52
K. A. Parsons c Marsh b Wren	16	– c Marsh b Wren	9
R. J. Harden c Marsh b McCague	24	– lbw b Wren	1
P. C. L. Holloway run out	1	– c Hooper b McCague	16
*A. N. Hayhurst c Fulton b Wren	0	– not out	64
†R. J. Turner lbw b Wren	5	– c Fulton b McCague	17
J. C. Hallett lbw b McCague	0	– lbw b Patel	10
N. A. Mallender not out	5	– c Fulton b Hooper	8
A. R. Caddick c Ward b Wren	0	– run out	20
H. R. J. Trump b Wren	0	– c Wren b Patel	6
A. P. van Troost b Wren	2	– st Marsh b Patel	1
L-b 2, w 3, n-b 8	13	B 3, l-b 13, w 7	23
1/44 2/89 3/92 4/93 5/97 6/97 7/101 8/101 9/106	108	1/32 2/34 3/79 4/94 5/134 6/172 7/187 8/217 9/226	227

Bonus points – Kent 4.

Bowling: *First Innings*—McCague 16–2–40–3; Wren 19–4–48–6; Ealham 8–2–15–0; Patel 3–1–3–0. *Second Innings*—McCague 23–4–56–3; Wren 20–4–41–2; Patel 32.1–15–58–3; Hooper 11–3–27–1; Ealham 10–3–29–0.

Kent

D. P. Fulton lbw b Mallender	1	M. J. McCague run out	7
T. R. Ward c Trump b Caddick	40	M. M. Patel lbw b Hallett	2
M. J. Walker c Parsons b Caddick	37	T. N. Wren not out	0
N. R. Taylor b van Troost	120		
C. L. Hooper c Lathwell b van Troost	127	L-b 5, w 5, n-b 24	34
*M. R. Benson b Hallett	5		——
M. A. Ealham c Lathwell b Hallett	19	1/3 2/75 3/84 4/302 5/307	392
†S. A. Marsh c van Troost b Hallett	0	6/356 7/356 8/375 9/392	

Bonus points – Kent 4, Somerset 4.

Bowling: Caddick 16–0–90–2; Mallender 14–3–61–1; van Troost 21–1–115–2; Trump 9–2–39–0; Hallett 24.2–10–59–4; Hayhurst 9–2–23–0.

Umpires: D. J. Constant and A. A. Jones.

At The Oval, September 15, 16, 17, 19. KENT drew with SURREY.

YOUNG CRICKETER OF THE YEAR

(*Elected by the Cricket Writers' Club*)

1950	R. Tattersall	1973	M. Hendrick
1951	P. B. H. May	1974	P. H. Edmonds
1952	F. S. Trueman	1975	A. Kennedy
1953	M. C. Cowdrey	1976	G. Miller
1954	P. J. Loader	1977	I. T. Botham
1955	K. F. Barrington	1978	D. I. Gower
1956	B. Taylor	1979	P. W. G. Parker
1957	M. J. Stewart	1980	G. R. Dilley
1958	A. C. D. Ingleby-Mackenzie	1981	M. W. Gatting
1959	G. Pullar	1982	N. G. Cowans
1960	D. A. Allen	1983	N. A. Foster
1961	P. H. Parfitt	1984	R. J. Bailey
1962	P. J. Sharpe	1985	D. V. Lawrence
1963	G. Boycott	1986	A. A. Metcalfe
1964	J. M. Brearley		J. J. Whitaker
1965	A. P. E. Knott	1987	R. J. Blakey
1966	D. L. Underwood	1988	M. P. Maynard
1967	A. W. Greig	1989	N. Hussain
1968	R. M. H. Cottam	1990	M. A. Atherton
1969	A. Ward	1991	M. R. Ramprakash
1970	C. M. Old	1992	I. D. K. Salisbury
1971	J. Whitehouse	1993	M. N. Lathwell
1972	D. R. Owen-Thomas	1994	J. P. Crawley

An additional award, in memory of Norman Preston, Editor of *Wisden* from 1951 to 1980, was made to C. W. J. Athey in 1980.

LANCASHIRE

Patron: HM The Queen
President: Sir Bernard Lovell
Chairman: R. Bennett
Chief Executive: J. M. Bower
Cricket Secretary: Miss R. B. FitzGibbon
Captain: M. Watkinson
Head Coach: D. Lloyd
Head Groundsman: P. Marron
Scorer: W. Davies

A patchy season, in which Lancashire finished tenth in the Championship, fourth in the Sunday League and lost in the two knockouts as soon as they came up against county opposition, had more than enough positive points to give them genuine confidence in the future. Indeed, their adherents were quick to point out that they would have been third in the Championship but for a 25-point penalty for an unfit pitch.

A reflection of Lancashire's own satisfaction was the award of caps to five players, four of them aged 25 or under and three in their first full season. Pace bowlers Peter Martin, 25 years old, and Glen Chapple, 20, both took more than 50 wickets for the first time; Australian-born Jason Gallian, 23, established himself as an opening batsman after four years qualifying; John Crawley, 22, was chosen for England; and Gary Yates, 26, played a significant part in several of Lancashire's victories. In addition, Neil Fairbrother, Mike Watkinson, Warren Hegg and Mike Atherton agreed to commit themselves to Lancashire until the end of the century.

There were hiccups, of course, the loudest coming on the weekend of the Lord's Test against South Africa, when Atherton, in his 11th Test as England's captain, was up to his neck in trouble over alleged ball-tampering. At the same time Lancashire were being penalised 25 points for preparing an unsuitable pitch for the game against Middlesex. The groundsman, Peter Marron, resigned as the Test and County Cricket Board's assistant inspector of pitches. "It would now be hypocritical of me to judge other groundsmen," he said.

Lancashire's heads could have gone down over what they considered an unjust and unjustified penalty. Instead, they responded decisively, winning the next two matches at Chelmsford and Headingley. The punishment cost the players £14,000 prize money. But the committee, which robustly defended Marron, decided to ignore the penalty when their bonus payments were calculated at the end of the season.

So there was much to gladden Lancashire hearts and start people thinking again about their first outright Championship since 1934. Lancashire won eight and lost six matches in the competition, with three victories by an innings, three by more than 200 runs and another by ten wickets inside two days. They had one of the strongest batting line-ups in the country, yet collected only 32 batting points, frequently saving their best for the second innings. Nick Speak, Crawley and Fairbrother scored over 1,000 runs and Gallian was denied only through injury; he missed seven matches. Crawley's first full season of county cricket, after three years with

Cambridge, emphasised his talent and brought him three centuries, the best of which was his 281 not out against Somerset at Southport in quite difficult conditions.

Fairbrother missed four of the first six Championship games because of injury but, once into his stride, hit the ball confidently and cleanly and looked to relish the freedom from captaincy. Watkinson, his successor, did not allow responsibility to bother him and had another satisfying all-round year, mostly now bowling off-breaks. But even more gratifying for Watkinson was the team's positive performance, for which he can take much of the credit.

Atherton's batting form was a puzzling mixture of highs for England and lows for Lancashire, as he failed to reach 1,000 in the season. He scored two centuries and a 99 and averaged 48 in Tests, but only one fifty in nine Championship matches, where a total of 333 runs gave him an average under 24. Gallian proved himself a solid opening batsman with immense powers of concentration, twice batting over eight hours, to defy Surrey – on his Championship debut – and Derbyshire. Speak again showed consistently good form, batting anywhere from opener to No. 5, Graham Lloyd disappointed in the Championship, and Steve Titchard was unable to grasp the opportunities that came his way. Hegg, in his seventh season as first-choice wicket-keeper, continued to perform admirably, although his batting has lost some of its sparkle.

Before the season started it was felt that Lancashire would have difficulties bowling out the opposition twice. Phillip DeFreitas had gone to Derbyshire and Wasim Akram would be leaving in July. His disappearance for Pakistan's tour of Sri Lanka created some disillusionment about the role of overseas players and Lancashire were leaders in the campaign to have their positions re-examined. Thankfully, Lancashire decided not to recruit an experienced opening bowler. They stood by Martin and Chapple, who responded with several outstanding displays.

In the nine matches after Wasim's departure, Martin took 36 Championship wickets and Chapple 39. Chapple fully deserved his selection, along with Gallian, for the England A trip to India. Just as pleasing was the achievement of the experienced Ian Austin, who took Wasim's place in the team and, after taking a career-best ten for 60 in the match against Middlesex, went on to claim a total of 33 inexpensive wickets and finish fourth in the national bowling averages. Off-spinner Gary Yates supplanted left-arm spinner Alex Barnett in early June, holding his place and playing his part in some encouraging performances, but Lancashire strengthened their spinning resources by signing another slow left-armer, Gary Keedy, from Yorkshire. – Brian Bearshaw.

LANCASHIRE 1994

[*Bill Smith*

Back row: N. P. Harvey, M. E. Harvey, P. J. Seal, C. Brown, J. A. L. Henderson, D. J. Shadford, A. Flintoff, R. J. Green, N. T. Wood. *Middle row:* R. Spriggs (*dressing-room attendant*), J. P. Crawley, N. A. Derbyshire, J. M. Fielding, G. Yates, S. P. Titchard, P. J. Martin, J. E. R. Gallian, G. Chapple, A. A. Barnett, D. Lloyd (*coach*). *Front row:* L. Brown (*physiotherapist*), N. J. Speak, I. D. Austin, N. H. Fairbrother, M. Watkinson (*captain*), W. K. Hegg, G. D. Lloyd, J. Stanworth, W. Davies (*scorer*). *Inset:* M. A. Atherton, Wasim Akram.

LANCASHIRE RESULTS

All first-class matches – Played 19: Won 8, Lost 7, Drawn 4.

County Championship matches – Played 17: Won 8, Lost 6, Drawn 3.

Bonus points – Batting 32, Bowling 59.

Competition placings – Britannic Assurance County Championship, 10th; NatWest Bank Trophy, 2nd round; Benson and Hedges Cup, 1st round; AXA Equity & Law League, 4th.

BRITANNIC ASSURANCE CHAMPIONSHIP AVERAGES

BATTING

	Birthplace	*M*	*I*	*NO*	*R*	*HS*	*Avge*
‡J. P. Crawley	*Maldon*	14	23	2	1,300	281*	61.90
‡N. H. Fairbrother	*Warrington*	11	20	1	939	204	49.42
‡N. J. Speak	*Manchester*	17	30	5	1,046	143	41.84
‡J. E. R. Gallian	*Sydney, Australia*	10	18	0	746	171	41.44
‡M. Watkinson	*Westhoughton*	16	26	2	831	155	34.62
‡G. D. Lloyd	*Accrington*	14	23	1	653	112	29.68
S. P. Titchard	*Warrington*	12	20	0	543	99	27.15
‡I. D. Austin	*Haslingden*	10	15	1	359	50	25.64
‡Wasim Akram§	*Lahore, Pakistan*	6	10	0	244	98	24.40
‡M. A. Atherton	*Manchester*	9	16	2	333	51	23.78
‡W. K. Hegg	*Whitefield*	17	27	4	465	66	20.21
‡G. Yates	*Ashton-under-Lyne*	12	19	6	219	54*	16.84
‡G. Chapple	*Skipton*	14	20	11	149	26*	16.55
‡P. J. Martin	*Accrington*	17	26	2	340	57	14.16
A. A. Barnett	*Malaga, Spain*	5	4	1	13	10	4.33

Also batted: N. A. Derbyshire (*Ramsbottom*) (1 match) 5; M. E. Harvey (*Burnley*) (2 matches) 2, 19, 23.

* *Signifies not out.* ‡ *Denotes county cap.* § *Overseas player.*

The following played a total of 13 three-figure innings for Lancashire in County Championship matches – N. H. Fairbrother 4, J. P. Crawley 3, J. E. R. Gallian 2, M. Watkinson 2, G. D. Lloyd 1, N. J. Speak 1.

BOWLING

	O	*M*	*R*	*W*	*BB*	*5W/i*	*Avge*
I. D. Austin	236.5	68	623	33	5-23	3	18.87
Wasim Akram	213.2	44	646	27	8-30	2	23.92
G. Chapple	421.3	99	1,380	52	6-48	4	26.53
G. Yates	294.5	65	930	34	5-34	1	27.35
M. Watkinson	563.1	162	1,639	59	8-30	1	27.77
P. J. Martin	566.4	159	1,464	51	5-61	2	28.70
J. E. R. Gallian	77	9	299	10	2-27	0	29.90

Also bowled: A. A. Barnett 124.4–20–440–7; J. P. Crawley 1–0–4–0; N. A. Derbyshire 21–1–107–1; N. H. Fairbrother 1–0–3–0; N. J. Speak 1–0–12–0.

Wicket-keepers: W. K. Hegg 42 ct, 2 st; J. P. Crawley 3 ct.

Leading Fielders: J. P. Crawley 17, N. J. Speak 16, S. P. Titchard 15.

LANCASHIRE v YORKSHIRE

Non-Championship Match

At Manchester, April 28, 29, 30, May 2. Yorkshire won by seven wickets. Toss: Lancashire.

The "friendly" Roses match, instituted in 1993 when the Championship was reduced, continued despite losing its sponsor, and Yorkshire again won handsomely, although they had the worst of the first three days. Wasim Akram, like Atherton and Richardson, did not take part, though some newspapers made repeated references to Wasim's dismissal; they meant Titchard, a mistake attributed to teething problems with the official computerised scores. With competition for batting places at Lancashire intense, Speak must have been pleased with an early century. But the first two innings were conducted at a slow pace – Yorkshire scored two runs in 11 overs during the second afternoon. Lancashire seemed to have taken control on the third evening, when Crawley and Gallian put on 154, but their desultory approach on Monday morning left Yorkshire to score 305 in 74 overs. Suddenly, Moxon stepped up a gear, reaching an unbeaten 161, and Blakey struck Barnett for six to win with three overs to spare.

Close of play: First day, Lancashire 279-6 (M. Watkinson 28*, W. K. Hegg 5*); Second day, Yorkshire 148-4 (R. J. Blakey 37*, A. P. Grayson 27*); Third day, Lancashire 159-2 (W. K. Hegg 1*, N. J. Speak 0*).

Lancashire

J. E. R. Gallian lbw b Vaughan	57	– (2) c and b Grayson	71
J. P. Crawley c Blakey b Gough	13	– (1) lbw b Stemp	77
N. J. Speak c Byas b Gough	105	– (4) c Moxon b Stemp	26
N. H. Fairbrother c Vaughan b Gough	44	– (5) not out	19
G. D. Lloyd c Blakey b Stemp	16	– (6) not out	0
S. P. Titchard lbw b Stemp	6		
*M. Watkinson c Blakey b White	47		
†W. K. Hegg c Vaughan b Gough	13	– (3) run out	12
P. J. Martin not out	43		
G. Chapple c Grayson b Stemp	1		
A. A. Barnett lbw b Gough	1		
L-b 6, n-b 2	8	B 10, l-b 2, n-b 8	20
1/13 2/135 3/224 4/233 5/245 6/252 7/291 8/346 9/351	354	1/154 2/158 3/178 4/225 (4 wkts dec.)	225

Bowling: *First Innings*—Gough 23.5–5–75–5; Robinson 20–2–65–0; White 9–1–26–1; Hartley 18–3–43–0; Stemp 39–19–59–3; Foster 7–2–28–0; Vaughan 18–4–52–1. *Second Innings*—Gough 15–4–38–0; Hartley 7–2–25–0; Foster 6–2–15–0; Stemp 18.2–3–48–2; Vaughan 11–1–38–0; Robinson 15–5–21–0; Grayson 11–4–28–1.

Yorkshire

*M. D. Moxon b Barnett	37	– not out	161
M. P. Vaughan b Martin	4	– c Titchard b Martin	49
D. Byas c Hegg b Martin	36	– run out	27
C. White c Fairbrother b Chapple	0	– c Fairbrother b Barnett	24
†R. J. Blakey lbw b Watkinson	47	– not out	40
A. P. Grayson c Fairbrother b Barnett	27		
M. J. Foster b Watkinson	30		
P. J. Hartley b Watkinson	13		
D. Gough c Barnett b Chapple	43		
R. D. Stemp lbw b Chapple	28		
M. A. Robinson not out	1		
L-b 9	9	B 1, l-b 3	4
1/5 2/71 3/72 4/89 5/148 6/182 7/189 8/202 9/258	275	1/144 2/213 3/241 (3 wkts)	305

Bowling: *First Innings*—Martin 31–11–53–2; Chapple 25.1–9–52–3; Watkinson 25–5–64–3; Barnett 47–17–87–2; Gallian 4–0–10–0. *Second Innings*—Martin 17–3–63–1; Chapple 12–2–42–0; Gallian 10–1–46–0; Barnett 20–2–100–1; Watkinson 12–0–50–0.

Umpires: V. A. Holder and R. Julian.

LANCASHIRE v SURREY

At Manchester, May 5, 6, 7, 9. Surrey won by ten wickets. Surrey 23 pts, Lancashire 4 pts. Toss: Surrey. Championship debuts: J. E. R. Gallian; C. E. Cuffy.

A century by Gallian served only to delay an otherwise effortless victory by Surrey, completed when openers Stewart and Bicknell knocked off 171 at almost four an over. The result had seemed likely after Surrey had taken full advantage of a crucial toss, reducing Lancashire to 129 for nine on a wet opening day – Barnett went first ball next morning. A juicy pitch afforded plenty of movement and Benjamin helped himself to five wickets, including Wasim Akram, whose 56-ball 50 provided the only real resistance. Stewart reached a magnificent hundred in 114 balls, in much better conditions; with able support from Ward and Brown, who hit Watkinson for five sixes, Surrey's 301 came inside two sessions. The Australian-born Gallian, his four-year residential qualification complete, resisted stoically for 500 minutes, scoring 171, the best for Lancashire on Championship debut since Jim Ricketts's 195 not out in 1867.

Close of play: First day, Lancashire 129-9 (G. Chapple 4*, A. A. Barnett 0*); Second day, Lancashire 71-2 (J. E. R. Gallian 34*, W. K. Hegg 0*); Third day, Lancashire 342.

Lancashire

First innings		Second innings	
M. A. Atherton c Thorpe b Benjamin	14	– c Brown b Cuffy	5
J. E. R. Gallian c Butcher b Benjamin	5	– c Stewart b Butcher	171
J. P. Crawley c Butcher b Cuffy	3	– c sub b Cuffy	32
N. H. Fairbrother c Butcher b Cuffy	5	– (5) b Benjamin	15
N. J. Speak c Sargeant b Butcher	11	– (6) c Hollioake b Benjamin	23
*M. Watkinson c Brown b Butcher	8	– (7) c Bicknell b Hollioake	15
Wasim Akram c and b Benjamin	50	– (8) c and b Hollioake	4
†W. K. Hegg c Boiling b Butcher	1	– (4) c Butcher b Cuffy	29
P. J. Martin c Butcher b Benjamin	9	– lbw b Cuffy	37
G. Chapple not out	4	– c Brown b Benjamin	3
A. A. Barnett c Sargeant b Benjamin	0	– not out	3
L-b 1, n-b 18	19	W 1, n-b 4	5
1/12 2/17 3/25 4/35 5/50 6/82 7/88 8/116 9/129	129	1/6 2/71 3/152 4/170 5/254 6/288 7/296 8/312 9/330	342

Bonus points – Surrey 4.

Bowling: *First Innings*—Cuffy 14–3–42–2; Benjamin 15.5–3–48–5; Butcher 10–1–32–3; Hollioake 2–0–6–0. *Second Innings*—Cuffy 41.3–19–70–4; Benjamin 32–7–87–3; Hollioake 29–3–101–2; Butcher 34–11–66–1; Brown 4–0–10–0; Stewart 1–0–8–0.

Surrey

First innings		Second innings	
D. J. Bicknell lbw b Barnett	36	– not out	67
*A. J. Stewart b Martin	126	– not out	88
G. P. Thorpe lbw b Wasim Akram	8		
D. M. Ward c Speak b Watkinson	51		
A. D. Brown b Martin	65		
A. J. Hollioake st Hegg b Watkinson	0		
M. A. Butcher c Atherton b Watkinson	0		
†N. F. Sargeant b Wasim Akram	0		
J. Boiling not out	2		
J. E. Benjamin b Wasim Akram	0		
C. E. Cuffy not out	3		
L-b 4, n-b 6	10	B 9, l-b 3, n-b 4	16
1/123 2/138 3/217 4/231 5/235 6/243 7/258 8/297 9/299 (9 wkts dec.)	301	(no wkt)	171

Bonus points – Surrey 3, Lancashire 4.

In the first innings J. Boiling, when 1, retired hurt at 278 and resumed at 299.

Bowling: *First Innings*—Wasim Akram 19–3–81–3; Martin 11.5–2–47–2; Chapple 11–5–37–0; Watkinson 14–3–86–3; Barnett 10–1–46–1. *Second Innings*—Martin 10–2–35–0; Chapple 7–2–19–0; Watkinson 11–1–37–0; Barnett 15.4–3–56–0; Gallian 2–0–12–0.

Umpires: J. H. Hampshire and K. J. Lyons.

At Cambridge, May 14, 15, 16. LANCASHIRE drew with CAMBRIDGE UNIVERSITY.

At Canterbury, May 19, 20, 21, 23. LANCASHIRE drew with KENT.

LANCASHIRE v SOMERSET

At Southport, May 26, 27, 28, 30. Lancashire won by an innings and 88 runs. Lancashire 22 pts, Somerset 3 pts. Toss: Lancashire.

Lancashire owed their first Championship win of 1994 to two outstanding performances, both of them records for the Trafalgar Road ground. The first was a magnificent 281 not out from Crawley, on a pitch that was wearing from the opening day. He batted over nine hours, faced 515 balls, and hit 30 fours and eight sixes. All the sixes came during a last-wicket stand of 122 with Barnett, who scored ten. It was the second-highest individual score for Lancashire since the war, following Fairbrother's 366 at The Oval in 1990, and their seventh highest ever. Wasim Akram countered with eight wickets for 30 – the best Championship bowling figures for Lancashire since Roy Tattersall took nine for 40 against Nottinghamshire in 1953 – when Somerset followed on, and 13 for 147 in the match, both personal bests. He was on a hat-trick three times and finished the game in half an hour on the final morning, taking the five remaining wickets in 28 balls. Somerset had now lost all eight of their matches in county competitions.

Close of play: First day, Lancashire 288-4 (J. P. Crawley 119*, W. K. Hegg 2*); Second day, Somerset 103-5 (M. N. Lathwell 45*, R. J. Turner 5*); Third day, Somerset 136-5 (R. J. Harden 46*, R. J. Turner 7*).

Lancashire

J. E. R. Gallian st Turner b Mushtaq Ahmed	53
M. A. Atherton c Parsons b Rose	17
J. P. Crawley not out	281
G. D. Lloyd lbw b Mushtaq Ahmed	4
N. J. Speak c Hayhurst b Mushtaq Ahmed	87
†W. K. Hegg c Turner b Rose	17
S. P. Titchard c Turner b Rose	0
*M. Watkinson lbw b Mushtaq Ahmed	5
Wasim Akram b Mushtaq Ahmed	23
P. J. Martin b Mushtaq Ahmed	8
A. A. Barnett c Folland b Trump	10
B 6, l-b 7, w 1, n-b 2	16
1/30 2/109 3/113 4/281 5/339 6/339 7/360 8/387 9/399	521

Bonus points – Lancashire 2, Somerset 1 (Score at 120 overs: 298-4).

Bowling: van Troost 35–10–72–0; Rose 31–8–96–3; Mushtaq Ahmed 60–17–156–6; Hayhurst 13–2–48–0; Trump 42.3–11–115–1; Parsons 4–0–21–0.

Somerset

M. N. Lathwell lbw b Wasim Akram	50 – c Lloyd b Barnett	61
N. A. Folland c Crawley b Martin	11 – c Hegg b Wasim Akram	2
R. J. Harden c Watkinson b Wasim Akram	14 – not out	51
M. E. Trescothick c Hegg b Wasim Akram	0 – c Hegg b Watkinson	7
*A. N. Hayhurst lbw b Wasim Akram	0 – c Titchard b Wasim Akram	7
K. A. Parsons c Crawley b Martin	9 – lbw b Wasim Akram	0
†R. J. Turner not out	25 – lbw b Wasim Akram	7
G. D. Rose c Hegg b Barnett	79 – b Wasim Akram	5
Mushtaq Ahmed c Titchard b Watkinson	38 – c Crawley b Wasim Akram	8
H. R. J. Trump b Martin	4 – c Hegg b Wasim Akram	0
A. P. van Troost b Wasim Akram	7 – b Wasim Akram	0
B 8, l-b 4, n-b 24	36 L-b 2, n-b 10	12
1/24 2/45 3/45 4/45 5/64 6/110 7/168 8/207 9/262	273 1/15 2/80 3/93 4/120 5/120 6/136 7/142 8/158 9/158	160

Bonus points – Somerset 2, Lancashire 4.

In the first innings R. J. Turner, when 7, retired hurt at 112 and resumed at 207.

Bowling: *First Innings*—Wasim Akram 33–5–117–5; Martin 26–9–47–3; Watkinson 23–6–67–1; Barnett 15–7–29–1; Gallian 2–1–1–0. *Second Innings*—Wasim Akram 16.4–6–30–8; Martin 6–1–26–0; Barnett 19–4–41–1; Watkinson 25–9–61–1.

Umpires: B. Leadbeater and P. Willey.

At Northampton, June 2, 3, 4, 6. LANCASHIRE drew with NORTHAMPTONSHIRE.

At Horsham, June 9, 10, 11, 13. LANCASHIRE lost to SUSSEX by 60 runs.

LANCASHIRE v HAMPSHIRE

At Manchester, June 16, 17, 18, 20. Lancashire won by 263 runs. Lancashire 20 pts, Hampshire 4 pts. Toss: Lancashire.

A notable all-round display by Watkinson, who scored 117 and took a career-best 11 wickets for 87, brought Lancashire a handsome win early on the fourth day. His first-innings eight for 30 matched his team-mate Wasim Akram's analysis three weeks earlier. Watkinson was also the first Lancashire player to get a century and ten wickets in a match since Len Hopwood in 1933. The pitch responded to spin from the opening day, when Udal took six wickets to dismiss Lancashire. Another 14 fell on the second day. But a seventh-wicket stand of 119 between Titchard, who batted five and a half hours for 99, and Watkinson, who reached his century on the third afternoon, left Hampshire to chase an improbable 426. This time Yates returned a career-best, five for 34. Gallian twisted his ankle while running in the first innings, and was run out before he had a chance to retire.

Close of play: First day, Hampshire 33-2 (K. D. James 4*, R. J. Maru 5*); Second day, Lancashire 165-6 (S. P. Titchard 63*, M. Watkinson 16*); Third day, Hampshire 124-6 (M. C. J. Nicholas 51*).

Lancashire

S. P. Titchard c Maru b Udal	26	– lbw b Connor	99
J. E. R. Gallian run out	19	– (7) lbw b Udal	4
J. P. Crawley c and b Udal	36	– b Connor	12
G. D. Lloyd b Connor	6	– lbw b Connor	4
N. J. Speak c Aymes b James	15	– lbw b Udal	12
I. D. Austin lbw b Udal	15	– b Maru	41
*M. Watkinson b Udal	11	– (8) st Aymes b Maru	117
Wasim Akram c Aymes b Maru	7	– (9) c Udal b Connor	40
P. J. Martin c Cox b Udal	4	– (2) lbw b Cowans	0
†W. K. Hegg not out	10	– c Terry b Maru	2
G. Yates lbw b Udal	13	– not out	1
B 5, l-b 7, n-b 2	14	B 5, l-b 6, n-b 6	17
1/46 2/57 3/64 4/104 5/110 6/138 7/149 8/149 9/160	176	1/1 2/29 3/37 4/62 5/122 6/136 7/255 8/341 9/347	349

Bonus points – Hampshire 4.

Bowling: *First Innings*—Cowans 10–2–32–0; Connor 16–7–26–1; Udal 30.4–7–79–6; James 10–4–19–1; Maru 11–7–8–1. *Second Innings*—Cowans 17–5–53–1; Connor 31–7–86–4; Udal 42–10–120–2; Maru 37.1–12–75–3; James 1–0–4–0.

Hampshire

V. P. Terry c Crawley b Watkinson	15	– lbw b Martin	3
R. M. F. Cox b Yates	9	– b Wasim Akram	15
K. D. James c Lloyd b Watkinson	24	– c Titchard b Watkinson	7
R. J. Maru b Watkinson	5	– (7) c Titchard b Watkinson	0
R. S. M. Morris c Titchard b Yates	5	– (8) c Speak b Yates	0
*M. C. J. Nicholas c Crawley b Watkinson	6	– (4) not out	72
M. Keech b Watkinson	18	– (5) b Yates	22
†A. N. Aymes b Watkinson	2	– (6) c Speak b Yates	0
S. D. Udal b Watkinson	0	– c sub b Yates	4
C. A. Connor not out	7	– c sub b Yates	6
N. G. Cowans b Watkinson	0	– b Watkinson	1
B 4, w 1, n-b 4	9	B 14, l-b 6, w 4, n-b 8	32
1/20 2/28 3/45 4/62 5/64 6/80 7/83 8/85 9/96	100	1/16 2/33 3/43 4/103 5/111 6/124 7/125 8/135 9/157	162

Bonus points – Lancashire 4.

Bowling: *First Innings*—Wasim Akram 19–3–36–0; Martin 7–4–9–0; Yates 13–6–21–2; Watkinson 22.3–10–30–8. *Second Innings*—Wasim Akram 10–2–35–1; Martin 10–5–11–1; Watkinson 24.3–9–57–3; Yates 13–3–34–5; Austin 3–1–5–0.

Umpires: J. W. Holder and K. E. Palmer.

At Colwyn Bay, June 23, 24, 25, 27. LANCASHIRE beat GLAMORGAN by 220 runs.

At Birmingham, June 30, July 1, 2, 4. LANCASHIRE lost to WARWICKSHIRE by six wickets.

LANCASHIRE v DERBYSHIRE

At Blackpool, July 14, 15, 16, 18. Derbyshire won by three wickets. Derbyshire 23 pts, Lancashire 2 pts. Toss: Derbyshire.

Derbyshire won with only an over to spare despite apparently having the match sewn up two days before. After batting through five sessions, they had bowled out Lancashire in 24 overs after tea on Friday, 407 behind. But second time round Lancashire applied themselves, remaining at the crease for 174.5 overs to make 589, the highest total in this country by a team following on. Atherton scored his first Championship fifty of the summer and Fairbrother his first century, while Gallian resisted for 129 overs and reached the slowest-ever Championship hundred in 453 minutes. Even the last wicket added 83 – as much as the first-innings total – and there were 81 extras, equalling the world record conceded by Derbyshire to Middlesex a fortnight earlier. Derbyshire were left 43 overs to score 183. They wobbled at 86 for four, but Azharuddin saw them within sight of victory. On the first two days it had all seemed easy for them; O'Gorman scored 145 and Rollins fell three short of a maiden century, before DeFreitas, bowling unchanged with Malcolm, returned his best analysis of the season against his old county.

Close of play: First day, Derbyshire 323-4 (T. J. G. O'Gorman 144*, A. S. Rollins 41*); Second day, Lancashire 29-0 (J. E. R. Gallian 5*, M. A. Atherton 13*); Third day, Lancashire 378-3 (J. E. R. Gallian 96*, N. J. Speak 36*).

Derbyshire

*K. J. Barnett c and b Chapple	83	– lbw b Chapple	0
D. G. Cork b Watkinson	13	– run out	30
C. J. Adams lbw b Martin	5	– c and b Watkinson	34
T. J. G. O'Gorman lbw b Martin	145	– c Lloyd b Yates	18
M. Azharuddin b Watkinson	16	– b Watkinson	48
†A. S. Rollins lbw b Gallian	97	– lbw b Gallian	14
P. A. J. DeFreitas c Chapple b Watkinson	43	– c Speak b Gallian	15
C. M. Wells b Gallian	25	– not out	14
M. J. Vandrau not out	25	– not out	2
M. Taylor not out	14		
B 1, l-b 11, n-b 12	24	L-b 2, w 5, n-b 4	11
1/36 2/41 3/160 4/185 5/328 6/402 7/447 8/448 (8 wkts dec.)	490	1/9 2/62 3/81 4/86 5/140 6/163 7/176 (7 wkts)	186

D. E. Malcolm did not bat.

Bonus points – Derbyshire 3, Lancashire 2 (Score at 120 overs: 349-5).

Bowling: *First Innings*—Martin 35–8–85–2; Chapple 29–5–94–1; Watkinson 58–26–126–3; Yates 53–14–132–0; Gallian 12–4–41–2. *Second Innings*—Martin 8–2–42–0; Chapple 3–0–26–1; Watkinson 18–2–53–2; Yates 8–1–36–1; Gallian 5–0–27–2.

Lancashire

M. A. Atherton lbw b Malcolm	6	– (2) lbw b Cork	51
J. E. R. Gallian lbw b DeFreitas	3	– (1) b DeFreitas	118
J. P. Crawley lbw b Malcolm	4	– lbw b Cork	0
N. H. Fairbrother c Azharuddin b DeFreitas	29	– c Wells b Taylor	136
N. J. Speak c Wells b Malcolm	20	– lbw b Cork	41
G. D. Lloyd lbw b DeFreitas	0	– c Cork b Vandrau	48
*M. Watkinson lbw b DeFreitas	5	– lbw b DeFreitas	0
†W. K. Hegg c O'Gorman b DeFreitas	0	– lbw b Cork	20
P. J. Martin b DeFreitas	0	– c Cork b Vandrau	20
G. Yates b Malcolm	2	– not out	54
G. Chapple not out	1	– c Cork b Vandrau	20
L-b 1, n-b 12	13	B 21, l-b 9, w 1, n-b 50	81
1/9 2/9 3/20 4/50 5/52 6/78 7/78 8/78 9/78	83	1/90 2/90 3/297 4/386 5/422 6/422 7/459 8/491 9/506	589

Bonus points – Derbyshire 4.

Bowling: *First Innings*—DeFreitas 12–4–39–6; Malcolm 12–2–43–4. *Second Innings*—Cork 35–1–135–4; DeFreitas 29–5–128–2; Malcolm 37–7–119–0; Vandrau 38.5–10–102–3; Taylor 28–8–67–1; Wells 7–2–8–0.

Umpires: B. Leadbeater and R. A. White.

LANCASHIRE v MIDDLESEX

At Manchester, July 21, 22, 23. Lancashire won by 361 runs. Lancashire 20 pts, Middlesex 4 pts. Toss: Middlesex. First-class debut: K. Marc.

Lancashire became the fourth county to be fined 25 points for a pitch "unsuitable for first-class cricket", after Essex and Nottinghamshire in 1989 and Derbyshire in 1990. Following the TCCB's announcement, Old Trafford groundsman Peter Marron resigned as the Board's assistant inspector of pitches. "I don't see how I can now sit in judgment on other groundsmen," he said. His error was to water the pitch the day before the match, failing to anticipate rain. It was damp and green at the start, and 21 wickets fell by lunch on the second day. Middlesex's seamers did not bowl well when Lancashire batted again and, with the pitch dried out by dazzling sunshine, Fairbrother scored 204, his third double-century and the highest innings for Lancashire against Middlesex. He faced 209 balls, with 21 fours and seven sixes, and hit 160 between tea and the close on the second evening. Trailing by 546, Middlesex crumpled before Austin. His first-innings figures were a career-best and, in only his third Championship match of the season, he completed his first ten-wicket haul. Lancashire videoed the action of the debutant Kervin Marc, which Middlesex said had never been questioned before. No complaint followed.

Close of play: First day, Middlesex 62-3 (J. E. Emburey 0*, M. R. Ramprakash 4*); Second day, Lancashire 414-4 (N. H. Fairbrother 198*, I. D. Austin 17*).

Lancashire

	First innings		Second innings	
J. E. R. Gallian c Carr b Gatting	29	– c Brown b Marc	20
S. P. Titchard c Roseberry b Shine	5	– c Brown b Shine	76
N. J. Speak lbw b Feltham	10	– c Gatting b Emburey	82
N. H. Fairbrother lbw b Feltham	13	– c Brown b Tufnell	204
G. D. Lloyd c Brown b Marc	20	– c Gatting b Emburey	4
I. D. Austin c Carr b Feltham	17	– c Roseberry b Tufnell	18
*M. Watkinson c Carr b Feltham	17	– c Roseberry b Emburey	29
†W. K. Hegg c Haynes b Shine	16	– lbw b Feltham	1
P. J. Martin c Haynes b Marc	2	– c Carr b Tufnell	25
G. Yates c Roseberry b Shine	4	– not out	5
G. Chapple not out	12	– not out	1
B 1, l-b 5, w 8, n-b 4	18	B 3, l-b 6, w 4, n-b 6	19
1/9 2/38 3/64 4/64 5/103 6/124 7/140 8/147 9/147	163	1/54 2/144 3/279 4/283 5/417 6/428 7/429 8/454 9/483 (9 wkts dec.)	484

Bonus points – Middlesex 4.

Bowling: *First Innings*—Shine 12.3–7–16–3; Marc 16–3–52–2; Feltham 15–2–50–4; Emburey 4–2–8–0; Gatting 7–1–31–1. *Second Innings*—Shine 19–1–100–1; Marc 13–1–81–1; Feltham 20–4–70–1; Gatting 4–0–27–0; Tufnell 41–12–126–3; Emburey 26–7–66–3; Roseberry 1–0–5–0.

Middlesex

D. L. Haynes c Hegg b Chapple	0	– b Austin	10
M. A. Roseberry lbw b Watkinson	32	– c Chapple b Gallian	42
*M. W. Gatting c Watkinson b Austin	23	– c Fairbrother b Watkinson	35
J. E. Emburey b Austin	2	– (8) b Austin	7
M. R. Ramprakash c Fairbrother b Watkinson	16	– (4) c Chapple b Martin	12
J. D. Carr lbw b Austin	0	– (5) b Austin	27
†K. R. Brown not out	12	– (6) c Austin b Martin	23
M. A. Feltham lbw b Austin	3	– (7) lbw b Chapple	10
K. Marc c Martin b Watkinson	9	– c Chapple b Austin	8
K. J. Shine c Titchard b Watkinson	0	– not out	0
P. C. R. Tufnell b Austin	0	– b Austin	5
L-b 2, n-b 2	4	B 4, l-b 2	6
1/1 2/56 3/56 4/73 5/77 6/85 7/88 8/101 9/101	101	1/11 2/69 3/101 4/101 5/151 6/151 7/166 8/180 9/180	185

Bonus points – Lancashire 4.

Bowling: *First Innings*—Martin 8–3–12–0; Chapple 9–2–38–1; Austin 12.3–5–23–5; Watkinson 11–3–26–4. *Second Innings*—Chapple 10–3–21–1; Austin 18.2–8–37–5; Watkinson 14–2–54–1; Martin 18–3–44–2; Gallian 5–0–23–1.

Umpires: J. H. Hampshire and J. W. Holder.

At Chelmsford, August 4, 5, 6. LANCASHIRE beat ESSEX by an innings and 60 runs.

At Leeds, August 11, 12, 13, 15. LANCASHIRE beat YORKSHIRE by seven wickets.

LANCASHIRE v GLOUCESTERSHIRE

At Manchester, August 18, 19, 20, 22. Gloucestershire won by two wickets. Gloucestershire 22 pts, Lancashire 4 pts. Toss: Lancashire. First-class debut: M. E. Harvey.

The pitch that four weeks earlier cost Lancashire 25 points made a successful comeback, furnishing 1,057 runs in an absorbing and fluctuating match. A Championship-best 85 from Windows gave Gloucestershire a first-innings lead of 126 on the second day, which ended early because the low sun was dazzling the batsmen. But Fairbrother, with his fourth century in five matches, and Lloyd, with his first of a hitherto undistinguished season, revived Lancashire in a stand of 231. That was precisely the figure needed by Gloucestershire to win. After another half-century from Windows, they entered the final day needing 76 with five wickets standing. The game looked Lancashire's when Gloucestershire were 200 for eight. But Walsh single-handedly knocked off the remaining 31 runs in 17 balls, hitting Watkinson for 24 in two overs; one of his three sixes broke a pavilion window. Gloucestershire had not won in Lancashire since 1965, when Tony Windows, Matthew's father, played.

Close of play: First day, Gloucestershire 139-2 (M. G. N. Windows 80*, R. I. Dawson 17*); Second day, Lancashire 140-3 (N. H. Fairbrother 47*, G. D. Lloyd 43*); Third day, Gloucestershire 155-5 (T. H. C. Hancock 2*, R. C. Russell 0*).

Lancashire

S. P. Titchard lbw b Williams	1	– b Walsh	4
M. E. Harvey c Russell b Walsh	2	– b Walsh	19
N. J. Speak c Russell b Alleyne	36	– lbw b Walsh	16
N. H. Fairbrother c Hodgson b Alleyne	42	– b Alleyne	120
G. D. Lloyd c and b Williams	23	– c Wright b Pike	112
I. D. Austin c Alleyne b Pike	22	– c Russell b Pike	7
*M. Watkinson c Russell b Walsh	9	– lbw b Alleyne	6
†W. K. Hegg lbw b Walsh	1	– lbw b Walsh	19
G. Yates not out	19	– not out	20
P. J. Martin lbw b Alleyne	0	– st Russell b Pike	5
G. Chapple c Ball b Pike	0	– b Walsh	0
L-b 3, n-b 14	17	B 4, l-b 12, n-b 12	28
1/3 2/7 3/75 4/108 5/116 6/129 7/135 8/171 9/171	172	1/8 2/39 3/54 4/285 5/299 6/306 7/314 8/346 9/353	356

Bonus points – Gloucestershire 4.

Bowling: *First Innings*—Walsh 17–7–27–3; Williams 15–4–40–2; Alleyne 13–4–28–3; Hancock 4–0–31–0; Pike 7.3–1–23–2; Ball 3–1–20–0. *Second Innings*—Walsh 26.5–1–91–5; Williams 13–3–60–0; Pike 31–6–109–3; Ball 7–2–31–0; Alleyne 17–0–49–2.

Gloucestershire

A. J. Wright c Yates b Martin	7	– lbw b Watkinson	20
M. G. N. Windows lbw b Austin	85	– c Hegg b Martin	77
G. D. Hodgson c Fairbrother b Martin	26	– b Yates	18
R. I. Dawson c Hegg b Austin	30	– c Speak b Watkinson	7
M. W. Alleyne lbw b Austin	5	– c Harvey b Martin	15
T. H. C. Hancock lbw b Austin	46	– c Speak b Watkinson	14
†R. C. Russell c Yates b Watkinson	11	– not out	19
R. C. Williams not out	34	– c Titchard b Watkinson	0
M. C. J. Ball c Fairbrother b Martin	10	– c Fairbrother b Martin	14
*C. A. Walsh c Titchard b Martin	2	– not out	31
V. J. Pike b Watkinson	18		
L-b 15, w 3, n-b 6	24	B 4, l-b 3, w 1, n-b 8	16
1/12 2/94 3/146 4/161 5/176 6/206 7/233 8/252 9/254	298	1/54 2/126 3/126 4/149 5/149 6/171 7/179 8/200	(8 wkts) 231

Bonus points – Gloucestershire 2, Lancashire 4.

Bowling: *First Innings*—Martin 23–5–53–4; Chapple 24–3–80–0; Watkinson 15.1–6–37–2; Austin 33–11–85–4; Yates 10–3–28–0. *Second Innings*—Martin 24–7–55–3; Chapple 6–0–24–0; Austin 9.5–1–40–0; Watkinson 24–8–82–4; Yates 6–0–23–1.

Umpires: B. Dudleston and A. A. Jones.

At Nottingham, August 25, 26, 27, 29. LANCASHIRE beat NOTTINGHAMSHIRE by an innings and 148 runs.

LANCASHIRE v WORCESTERSHIRE

At Manchester, August 30, 31, September 1, 2. Worcestershire won by an innings and 13 runs. Worcestershire 24 pts, Lancashire 4 pts. Toss: Worcestershire.

A partnership of 265 between Hick and Moody was the cornerstone for the highest total against Lancashire at Old Trafford since London County hit 597 in 1903. Watkinson had led Lancashire's recovery on the opening day, when the last four wickets put on 152. But Hick, whose 215 was his 77th century and his ninth over 200, broke his own record of 212 for Worcestershire against Lancashire six years before. He found a sound ally in Moody:

together they gave their team an unassailable first-innings lead of 324 – and got into gear for the NatWest final which followed. Despite their supremacy, they surprisingly accepted two offers of bad light on the second day, when Worcestershire scored 237 in 61 overs while one wicket fell. Lancashire used two substitute wicket-keepers, Crawley and Austin, for Hegg, who had a hip injury, though he made a brave fifty to delay Worcestershire on the final day.

Close of play: First day, Worcestershire 115-2 (G. A. Hick 69*, R. K. Illingworth 3*); Second day, Worcestershire 352-3 (G. A. Hick 199*, T. M. Moody 87*); Third day, Lancashire 186-4 (G. D. Lloyd 33*, I. D. Austin 20*).

Lancashire

M. A. Atherton c Rhodes b Radford	0	– c Rhodes b Illingworth	42
N. J. Speak c Rhodes b Newport	47	– c Curtis b Lampitt	33
J. P. Crawley c Rhodes b Lampitt	3	– lbw b Lampitt	0
N. H. Fairbrother c Leatherdale b Radford	0	– lbw b Hick	33
G. D. Lloyd b Lampitt	6	– c Lampitt b Hick	56
I. D. Austin c Leatherdale b Moody	41	– b Illingworth	30
*M. Watkinson c Moody b Illingworth	87	– c Leatherdale b Illingworth	4
†W. K. Hegg c Hick b Newport	34	– not out	52
G. Yates c Lampitt b Newport	2	– c Leatherdale b Hick	0
P. J. Martin c Rhodes b Lampitt	7	– c Illingworth b Newport	21
G. Chapple not out	14	– c Illingworth b Newport	1
L-b 10, n-b 16	26	B 8, l-b 3, n-b 28	39
1/0 2/11 3/16 4/33 5/107 6/115 7/208 8/218 9/250	267	1/87 2/89 3/93 4/145 5/201 6/213 7/239 8/239 9/305	311

Bonus points – Lancashire 2, Worcestershire 4.

Bowling: *First Innings*—Radford 14–4–56–2; Lampitt 11.3–0–72–3; Moody 10–1–33–1; Newport 16–2–54–3; Haynes 4–2–14–0; Illingworth 7–0–28–1. *Second Innings*—Radford 6–0–31–0; Moody 4–1–17–0; Illingworth 42–12–98–3; Newport 11.1–2–34–2; Hick 16–5–64–3; Lampitt 14–5–46–2; Weston 2–0–10–0.

Worcestershire

*T. S. Curtis c Crawley b Chapple	29
W. P. C. Weston b Chapple	9
G. A. Hick lbw b Chapple	215
R. K. Illingworth c and b Chapple	7
T. M. Moody b Martin	109
G. R. Haynes c Crawley b Martin	31
D. A. Leatherdale b Chapple	19
†S. J. Rhodes c Crawley b Martin	67
S. R. Lampitt c sub b Martin	37
P. J. Newport not out	28
N. V. Radford c Atherton b Austin	6
B 8, l-b 22, n-b 4	34
1/16 2/110 3/120 4/385 5/409 6/428 7/465 8/555 9/564	591

Bonus points – Worcestershire 4, Lancashire 2 (Score at 120 overs: 450-6).

Bowling: Martin 36–11–93–4; Chapple 31–5–149–5; Watkinson 30–6–108–0; Austin 27.3–4–104–1; Yates 22–0–107–0.

Umpires: R. Julian and P. Willey.

At Stockton-on-Tees, September 8, 9. LANCASHIRE beat DURHAM by ten wickets.

LANCASHIRE v LEICESTERSHIRE

At Manchester, September 15, 16, 17, 19. Drawn. Lancashire 8 pts, Leicestershire 5 pts. Toss: Lancashire.

Leicestershire held on as Championship runners-up, not so much through their own efforts as through the wet weather sweeping across the country. Though they lost the first day and all but an hour of the last to rain, their closest rivals, Nottinghamshire and Middlesex, had even less playing time and were unable to conjure a result. There was less conventional interference from the weather on the second day when, for the second time in four weeks, play ended early because the sun sinking behind the bowler's arm at the Stretford End was shining into the batsmen's eyes. Old Trafford is unusual among first-class grounds in having wickets pitched roughly east to west, but experienced players and members could not remember such a problem occurring until this season. Leicestershire had the worse of what play did take place, losing their first five to Chapple for 83 and then giving Lancashire's top order batting practice.

Close of play: First day, No play; Second day, Lancashire 45-1 (N. J. Speak 16*, J. P. Crawley 7*); Third day, Leicestershire 16-0 (P. V. Simmons 0*, N. E. Briers 13*).

Leicestershire

P. V. Simmons c Crawley b Chapple	18	– c Speak b Martin	28
*N. E. Briers c Hegg b Chapple	18	– not out	30
T. J. Boon lbw b Chapple	16	– not out	0
J. J. Whitaker c Martin b Chapple	4		
V. J. Wells c Barnett b Chapple	22		
P. E. Robinson st Hegg b Yates	54		
†P. A. Nixon c Hegg b Austin	0		
G. J. Parsons c Atherton b Martin	7		
A. R. K. Pierson not out	43		
D. J. Millns c Crawley b Yates	0		
A. D. Mullally c Barnett b Yates	11		
B 1, l-b 10, n-b 2	13	B 3, l-b 5, w 1	9
1/39 2/44 3/48 4/74 5/83 6/90 7/105 8/160 9/166	206	1/66	(1 wkt) 67

Bonus points – Leicestershire 1, Lancashire 4.

Bowling: *First Innings*—Martin 12–1–36–1; Chapple 21–6–58–5; Barnett 9–0–46–0; Yates 13.4–5–29–3; Austin 8–1–26–1. *Second Innings*—Martin 10–4–20–1; Chapple 7–1–24–0; Barnett 4–1–15–0.

Lancashire

S. P. Titchard c Robinson b Millns	11
N. J. Speak b Wells	70
J. P. Crawley lbw b Parsons	70
G. D. Lloyd c Mullally b Pierson	51
I. D. Austin c Mullally b Pierson	35
*M. A. Atherton not out	47
†W. K. Hegg c Briers b Wells	23
G. Yates c Simmons b Mullally	8
P. J. Martin b Wells	16
G. Chapple c Nixon b Mullally	1
B 10, l-b 8, w 4, n-b 4	26
1/26 2/164 3/176 4/257 5/260 6/301 7/316 8/357 9/358	(9 wkts dec.) 358

A. A. Barnett did not bat.

Bonus points – Lancashire 4, Leicestershire 4.

Bowling: Millns 17–3–74–1; Mullally 18.3–3–43–2; Parsons 22–6–56–1; Pierson 26–3–89–2; Simmons 13–2–42–0; Wells 16–5–36–3.

Umpires: B. Dudleston and R. Julian.

LEICESTERSHIRE

President: B. A. F. Smith
Chairman: J. M. Josephs
Chairman, Cricket Committee: P. R. Haywood
Chief Executive: A. O. Norman
Captain: N. E. Briers
Cricket Manager: J. Birkenshaw
Head Groundsman: L. Spence
Scorer: G. R. Blackburn

Leicestershire's achievement in finishing second in the Britannic Assurance Championship, their highest final placing since 1982, confounded almost every pre-season forecast. Like the champions, Warwickshire, they were a team whose collective efforts amounted to more than the sum of its parts. No individual was deemed good enough to play Test cricket, although the wicket-keeper, Paul Nixon, was chosen for the England A tour. A paucity of players of the highest calibre, however, was balanced by a clutch of those on the better side of average.

Even though they exceeded all outside expectations, the team ended up disappointed not to win the Championship. In mid-August they cut Warwickshire's lead to nine points with a game in hand. But they lost their next three matches, starting with a two-day capitulation against Sussex. None the less, considering that the county had finished in the top three only five times in 89 previous attempts, they could hardly grumble. Even in the Sunday League, they escaped the bottom five for the first time since 1983, though they achieved little in either of the knockouts.

It was possible to link advances on the field with a change of climate off it. The unhappy end of the Mike Turner era did at least conclude a period of bitter in-fighting, which inevitably affected morale. There was a widespread feeling that the former chief executive, who resigned in 1993, had not had proper acknowledgment for his achievements. However, at the annual meeting in May, the county president, Brian Smith, spoke of "disputes over policies, disputes over details and certain specific items which were handled in a manner the officers and the committee found disturbing". The meeting voted against making Turner a vice-president, or even a life member. Ironically, Turner was made an MBE in June for his services to cricket.

His successor was Tony Norman, a former brewery executive, who immediately set about increasing membership by cutting prices. The subscription went down from £47.50 to £20 and the numbers went up from about 3,000 to 4,000 – including around 750 "Gold Members" who pay more and are entitled to two tickets. Jack Birkenshaw strengthened his position as cricket manager and signed a contract lasting until 1998. After he dispensed with Winston Benjamin and signed Phil Simmons as overseas player, Birkenshaw's ruthless streak reappeared in June when he excluded four senior men – Tim Boon, James Whitaker, David Millns and the captain, Nigel Briers – from the Sunday side in favour of "some eager youngsters who want to throw themselves about and chase everything". Simmons led them to the county's best-ever Sunday total.

Individual statistics were not impressive. Only Briers scored 1,000 Championship runs. Boon, displaced by Simmons as Briers's opening partner, returned generally modest scores at No. 3, while Whitaker again failed to recapture the form which once earned him a Test cap. Ben Smith seemed to be emerging from a period of technical problems, but only slowly. Even Simmons, after rewriting the county record books with 261 on his Championship debut, fell short of expectations, averaging only 31.76, failing to record another first-class century and reaching 50 only three times more. Balancing that, however, his experience and good-humoured authority were invaluable. His accurate medium-pace also bought 30 Championship wickets and he scored 660 runs on Sundays. The South African, Hansie Cronje, will be Leicestershire's overseas player in 1995, joining his brother-in-law, Gordon Parsons, in the team, but Simmons is expected to return in 1996.

Nixon made considerable advances as a wicket-keeper-batsman. Granted his county cap after scoring a century in support of Simmons in the opening match, he made two more hundreds and became the first Leicestershire keeper to pass 1,000 first-class runs in a season since Tommy Sidwell in 1928. Even Roger Tolchard, in his long career, never got past 998. Nixon's predecessor, Phil Whitticase, having originally lost his place through injury, had to channel his energies into captaining the Second Eleven. Both Parsons and Vince Wells took more than 40 Championship wickets, while Wells scored 746 runs and was capped in June. Parsons shared a benefit in 1994 with groundsman Lol Spence, whose pitches were significantly livelier and helped the county win six of their eight home Championship games.

Of the specialist bowlers, Millns was the most impressive with a Championship haul of 68 wickets, amid signs that he might soon recapture the potency which took him to the brink of the England team in 1992. But Adrian Pierson, the off-spinner, went backwards and Alan Mullally, the leading wicket-taker in 1993, had a wretched season in which he seemed perpetually to be out of form, out of luck, or both. Slow left-armer Matthew Brimson progressed only slowly, but could now concentrate on cricket after finishing his degree. Peter Hepworth, the batsman often asked to bowl off-spin, was released. Of the players blooded in 1994, none made more impact than Alamgir Sheriyar, a left-arm pace bowler born in Birmingham of Afghan descent, who took a hat-trick on his Championship debut to wrap up Leicestershire's match against Durham; remarkably, Wells had taken a hat-trick in the first innings. More will be seen of Sheriyar, and of Darren Maddy, who scored 1,498 runs in the Second Eleven Championship, a record for the competition.

Unhappily, Leicestershire acquired a reputation for being excessively vocal in the field, even receiving a cautionary letter from the TCCB after critical comments by umpires. The club responded swiftly. Millns was warned after displaying dissent against Nottinghamshire and Mullally was suspended for a match, at a critical point in the season, after an exchange with the Sussex captain, Alan Wells. – Jon Culley.

LEICESTERSHIRE 1994

[*Bill Smith*

Back row: T. J. Mason, M. T. Brimson, V. J. Wells, P. A. Nixon, I. M. Stanger, D. L. Maddy, P. E. Robinson. *Middle row:* R. Stenner (*physiotherapist*), B. F. Smith, A. F. Haye, P. N. Hepworth, D. J. Millns, A. D. Mullally, A. R. K. Pierson, J. M. Dakin, A. Sheriyar, G. R. Blackburn (*scorer*). *Front row:* P. V. Simmons, P. Whitticase, T. J. Boon, J. M. Josephs (*chairman*), J. Birkenshaw (*manager*), B. A. F. Smith (*president*), N. E. Briers (*captain*), A. O. Norman (*chief executive*), J. J. Whitaker, G. J. Parsons.

LEICESTERSHIRE RESULTS

All first-class matches – Played 19: Won 8, Lost 7, Drawn 4.

County Championship matches – Played 17: Won 8, Lost 7, Drawn 2.

Bonus points – Batting 42, Bowling 60.

Competition placings – Britannic Assurance County Championship, 2nd; NatWest Bank Trophy, 2nd round; Benson and Hedges Cup, 1st round; AXA Equity & Law League, 10th.

BRITANNIC ASSURANCE CHAMPIONSHIP AVERAGES

BATTING

	Birthplace	*M*	*I*	*NO*	*R*	*HS*	*Avge*
P. E. Robinson	*Keighley*	5	7	0	305	86	43.57
‡P. A. Nixon	*Carlisle*	17	27	3	938	131	39.08
‡N. E. Briers	*Leicester*	17	31	2	1,042	154	35.93
‡J. J. Whitaker	*Skipton*	16	28	2	871	148	33.50
‡V. J. Wells	*Dartford*	15	26	3	746	83	32.43
B. F. Smith	*Corby*	12	20	3	541	95	31.82
‡P. V. Simmons§	*Arima, Trinidad*	17	30	0	953	261	31.76
‡G. J. Parsons	*Slough*	16	25	6	491	70	25.84
‡T. J. Boon	*Doncaster*	15	26	2	578	74	24.08
A. R. K. Pierson	*Enfield*	13	17	4	294	43*	22.61
‡D. J. Millns	*Clipstone*	17	24	8	301	64*	18.81
D. L. Maddy	*Leicester*	2	4	0	56	34	14.00
P. N. Hepworth	*Ackworth*	4	8	0	83	60	10.37
‡A. D. Mullally	*Southend-on-Sea*	13	18	4	114	23	8.14
M. T. Brimson	*Plumstead*	4	8	2	28	12	4.66

Also batted: J. M. Dakin (*Hitchin*) (1 match) 18; T. J. Mason (*Leicester*) (1 match) 3; A. Sheriyar (*Birmingham*) (2 matches) 12, 0*.

* *Signifies not out.* ‡ *Denotes county cap.* § *Overseas player.*

The following played a total of eight three-figure innings for Leicestershire in County Championship matches – P. A. Nixon 3, N. E. Briers 2, J. J. Whitaker 2, P. V. Simmons 1.

BOWLING

	O	*M*	*R*	*W*	*BB*	*5W/i*	*Avge*
V. J. Wells	285.5	74	1,001	41	5-50	1	24.41
P. V. Simmons	300.5	81	769	30	4-68	0	25.63
D. J. Millns	488	91	1,756	68	6-84	3	25.82
G. J. Parsons	462.3	131	1,208	44	5-34	1	27.45
A. R. K. Pierson	444.1	120	1,130	34	8-42	1	33.23
A. D. Mullally	413.1	110	1,174	28	5-85	1	41.92

Also bowled: M. T. Brimson 87.4–21–280–4; P. N. Hepworth 72–14–253–9; T. J. Mason 7–0–22–1; A. Sheriyar 54–8–239–8.

Wicket-keeper: P. A. Nixon 54 ct, 1 st.

Leading Fielders: P. V. Simmons 23, G. J. Parsons 17.

LEICESTERSHIRE v NORTHAMPTONSHIRE

At Leicester, April 28, 29, 30. Leicestershire won by ten wickets. Leicestershire 24 pts, Northamptonshire 3 pts. Toss: Leicestershire. First-class debut: K. J. Innes. Championship debut: P. V. Simmons.

International attention was focused on Edgbaston where the new Test record-holder Lara was beginning his Warwickshire career. But, while Lara was forced to spend the opening day in the field, his fellow-Trinidadian Simmons stole the headlines with a sensational innings to mark his arrival as Leicestershire's overseas player. He became the first player to score a double-century on Championship debut and passed not only his own highest score, 202 for Trinidad, but the 80-year-old Leicestershire record, Sam Coe's 252 not out, also against Northamptonshire. Simmons faced 354 balls in seven and a half hours and hit 34 fours and four sixes. His stand of 253 with Nixon, who made an excellent three-hour century, ended nine short of the county's sixth-wicket record. The greenish pitch was not unhelpful to the seam bowlers, but Northamptonshire were without Capel and Curran, who were injured, and Ambrose, who had failed to arrive on schedule. Leicestershire were much better equipped to take advantage and enforced the follow-on. Fordham then dug himself in to make 102, but once he was dismissed – by Simmons – offering no stroke, his team succumbed to a three-day defeat.

Close of play: First day, Leicestershire 444-5 (P. V. Simmons 247*, P. A. Nixon 105*); Second day, Northamptonshire 43-0 (A. Fordham 27*, N. A. Felton 13*).

Leicestershire

P. V. Simmons c Lamb b Bowen	261		
*N. E. Briers c Fordham b Taylor	13		
T. J. Boon c Lamb b Penberthy	10		
J. J. Whitaker c Loye b Taylor	55		
V. J. Wells c Ripley b Roberts	0		
B. F. Smith c Ripley b Taylor	0		
†P. A. Nixon c Fordham b Penberthy	106	– (2) not out	4
G. J. Parsons not out	20	– (1) not out	4
A. R. K. Pierson st Ripley b Roberts	0		
D. J. Millns st Ripley b Roberts	2		
A. D. Mullally c Fordham b Bowen	0		
B 2, l-b 5, n-b 8	15	W 1	1
1/29 2/63 3/193 4/198 5/203 6/456 7/464 8/479 9/481	482	(no wkt)	9

Bonus points – Leicestershire 4, Northamptonshire 2 (Score at 120 overs: 461-6).

Bowling: *First Innings*—Taylor 29–9–82–3; Bowen 28.4–7–90–2; Innes 10–3–33–0; Penberthy 24–3–78–2; Roberts 30–3–147–3; Bailey 11–2–45–0. *Second Innings*—Taylor 1.5–0–8–0; Bowen 1–0–1–0.

Northamptonshire

A. Fordham c Simmons b Mullally	8	– lbw b Simmons	102
N. A. Felton c Nixon b Mullally	21	– lbw b Mullally	16
R. J. Bailey c Nixon b Mullally	20	– c Simmons b Mullally	14
*A. J. Lamb c Boon b Pierson	70	– c Whitaker b Pierson	25
M. B. Loye lbw b Pierson	27	– lbw b Wells	21
A. L. Penberthy c Millns b Pierson	41	– c Nixon b Parsons	13
†D. Ripley run out	8	– not out	27
K. J. Innes b Parsons	0	– lbw b Parsons	0
A. R. Roberts lbw b Parsons	6	– c Nixon b Millns	22
M. N. Bowen c Nixon b Parsons	13	– c Nixon b Millns	0
J. P. Taylor not out	0	– b Millns	3
B 1, l-b 1, n-b 8	10	B 6, l-b 13, n-b 4	23
1/19 2/46 3/67 4/126 5/165 6/202 7/203 8/207 9/219	224	1/51 2/67 3/120 4/195 5/195 6/213 7/213 8/252 9/254	266

Bonus points – Northamptonshire 1, Leicestershire 4.

Bowling: *First Innings*—Millns 10–1–45–0; Mullally 18–4–57–3; Parsons 13.4–5–30–3; Wells 7–2–28–0; Pierson 15–3–57–3; Simmons 1–0–5–0. *Second Innings*—Mullally 22–8–56–2; Parsons 19–7–33–2; Millns 13–3–40–3; Pierson 33–10–78–1; Simmons 10–4–18–1; Wells 11–6–22–1.

Umpires: J. D. Bond and M. J. Kitchen.

At Birmingham, May 5, 6, 7, 9. LEICESTERSHIRE drew with WARWICKSHIRE.

LEICESTERSHIRE v SOMERSET

At Leicester, May 12, 13, 14, 16. Leicestershire won by five wickets. Leicestershire 23 pts, Somerset 5 pts. Toss: Somerset.

Leicestershire's second victory in three Championship games owed much to hostile seam bowling on a lively pitch, although they also achieved full batting points for a third time. Millns returned match figures of nine for 127, despite lacking full fitness; Mullally frequently beat the bat without taking a wicket. Somerset's first innings gained vital sustenance from Hayhurst, whose unbeaten 79 occupied 83 overs. When Leicestershire replied, a stand of 127 between Hepworth, called up after Boon broke a finger, and Smith provided the impetus which carried them past 400; Smith reached 95 in fine style before succumbing to Caddick's leg-cutter. Despite some magnificent play by Lathwell, Somerset began the last day only 33 ahead with effectively five wickets left – van Troost had withdrawn because of a family illness. Then Millns grabbed three wickets in four overs, including the vital one of Folland, and also ran out Turner. There was a brief scare when Leicestershire, chasing 110, slipped to 42 for four before Smith and Wells combined decisively.

Close of play: First day, Somerset 209-6 (A. N. Hayhurst 49*, H. R. J. Trump 3*); Second day, Leicestershire 236-4 (P. N. Hepworth 57*, B. F. Smith 50*); Third day, Somerset 154-4 (N. A. Folland 50*, H. R. J. Trump 1*).

Somerset

M. N. Lathwell c Nixon b Millns	11	– c Parsons b Pierson	86
I. Fletcher b Millns	12	– c and b Millns	0
R. J. Harden c Parsons b Pierson	40	– c Whitaker b Millns	5
N. A. Folland c Nixon b Wells	40	– c Nixon b Millns	91
*A. N. Hayhurst not out	79	– c Parsons b Simmons	6
†R. J. Turner c Wells b Parsons	9	– (7) run out	0
G. D. Rose c Simmons b Parsons	0	– (8) not out	8
H. R. J. Trump c Briers b Millns	21	– (6) c Parsons b Millns	13
Mushtaq Ahmed b Millns	11	– c Simmons b Millns	0
A. R. Caddick lbw b Wells	15	– c and b Simmons	7
A. P. van Troost b Wells	0	– absent	
B 6, l-b 12, w 4, n-b 28	50	B 4, l-b 2, n-b 8	14
1/28 2/29 3/121 4/171 5/202 6/202 7/246 8/268 9/288	288	1/0 2/30 3/133 4/145 5/204 6/211 7/211 8/213 9/230	230

Bonus points – Somerset 2, Leicestershire 3 (Score at 120 overs: 287-8).

Bowling: *First Innings*—Mullally 30–9–85–0; Millns 25–6–62–4; Parsons 31–11–50–2; Wells 8.5–1–25–3; Simmons 10–5–20–0; Pierson 17–8–28–1. *Second Innings*—Mullally 7–4–20–0; Millns 21–9–65–5; Parsons 15–5–37–0; Pierson 22–10–39–1; Wells 7–1–33–0; Simmons 12–5–22–2; Hepworth 1–0–8–0.

Leicestershire

P. V. Simmons c Harden b Mushtaq Ahmed	25	– c Turner b Mushtaq Ahmed	8
*N. E. Briers c Turner b Caddick	43	– lbw b Mushtaq Ahmed	24
P. N. Hepworth b van Troost	60	– c Fletcher b Caddick	5
J. J. Whitaker c Turner b Caddick	2	– b Mushtaq Ahmed	3
V. J. Wells c Trump b Mushtaq Ahmed	36	– c Harden b Caddick	20
B. F. Smith c Turner b Caddick	95	– not out	36
†P. A. Nixon run out	23	– not out	6
G. J. Parsons c Mushtaq Ahmed b Rose	38		
A. R. K. Pierson b Caddick	22		
D. J. Millns b Caddick	14		
A. D. Mullally not out	9		
B 11, l-b 7, w 2, n-b 22	42	B 6, l-b 2	8
1/74 2/91 3/97 4/140 5/267 6/293 7/340 8/357 9/398	409	1/19 2/30 3/39 4/42 5/98	(5 wkts) 110

Bonus points – Leicestershire 4, Somerset 3 (Score at 120 overs: 391-8).

Bowling: *First Innings*—Caddick 28.2–5–92–5; van Troost 21–3–87–1; Mushtaq Ahmed 40–16–91–2; Rose 19–1–73–1; Trump 15–5–48–0. *Second Innings*—Caddick 18–2–60–2; Mushtaq Ahmed 17.2–6–42–3.

Umpires: A. A. Jones and K. E. Palmer.

At Leicester, May 17. LEICESTERSHIRE lost to NEW ZEALANDERS by seven wickets (See New Zealand tour section).

At Oxford, May 18, 19, 20. LEICESTERSHIRE drew with OXFORD UNIVERSITY.

LEICESTERSHIRE v KENT

At Leicester, May 26, 27, 28, 30. Leicestershire won by 139 runs. Leicestershire 21 pts, Kent 4 pts. Toss: Kent.

A third win took Leicestershire into second place in the table. After the first day was lost to rain, Spencer, who looked particularly sharp, and Patel exploited a damp pitch. But Smith and Nixon rescued Leicestershire, enabling them to pass 200. With the exception of Hooper, Kent had nothing to counter a seam attack so noisily committed to their cause that umpire Burgess asked them to calm down. Simmons gave Leicestershire's second innings a vigorous start, while Briers played diligently to support him and then Robinson before setting Kent a target of 329 in 80 overs. After the loss of four wickets for 47, that was never a serious possibility. But Fulton and Fleming suggested the match could be saved until after tea, when Hepworth, who had bowled only 16 overs of his off-spin in the 1993 Championship, produced an inspired spell. He accounted for both of them to collect career-best figures of three for 30.

Close of play: First day, No play; Second day, Kent 69-3 (C. L. Hooper 14*, N. J. Llong 14*); Third day, Leicestershire 210-4 (P. E. Robinson 48*, B. F. Smith 6*).

Leicestershire

P. V. Simmons lbw b Spencer	36	– c Patel b Headley	42
*N. E. Briers c Ward b Headley	0	– c Hooper b Patel	82
P. N. Hepworth c Marsh b Headley	4	– c Hooper b Spencer	1
J. J. Whitaker c Marsh b Igglesden	0	– run out	7
P. E. Robinson c Marsh b Patel	6	– c Benson b Patel	78
B. F. Smith lbw b Spencer	30	– not out	37
†P. A. Nixon b Spencer	51		
G. J. Parsons b Patel	9		
A. R. K. Pierson b Patel	15		
D. J. Millns c and b Spencer	5		
A. D. Mullally not out	7		
B 9, l-b 16, w 2, n-b 14	41	B 4, l-b 22, n-b 8	34
1/12 2/34 3/35 4/55 5/77 6/124 7/145 8/186 9/195	204	1/78 2/80 3/98 4/195 5/281	(5 wkts dec.) 281

Bonus points – Leicestershire 1, Kent 4.

Bowling: *First Innings*—Igglesden 17–4–49–1; Headley 19–4–49–2; Patel 12–4–21–3; Fleming 9–2–27–0; Spencer 14.1–3–31–4; Hooper 1–0–2–0. *Second Innings*—Igglesden 17–5–35–0; Headley 19–2–76–1; Spencer 10–1–34–1; Hooper 12–2–21–0; Patel 19.2–3–68–2; Fleming 5–1–21–0.

Kent

D. P. Fulton c Millns b Mullally	7	– c Nixon b Hepworth	50
*M. R. Benson c and b Simmons	17	– c Pierson b Millns	3
T. R. Ward c Robinson b Parsons	14	– c Pierson b Parsons	4
C. L. Hooper lbw b Mullally	56	– b Parsons	9
N. J. Llong c Nixon b Mullally	15	– c Robinson b Parsons	3
M. V. Fleming c Smith b Millns	7	– c Robinson b Hepworth	46
†S. A. Marsh c Parsons b Pierson	12	– not out	36
D. J. Spencer c Robinson b Millns	12	– lbw b Pierson	0
D. W. Headley c Parsons b Millns	6	– c Simmons b Pierson	0
M. M. Patel c Whitaker b Mullally	1	– lbw b Hepworth	17
A. P. Igglesden not out	0	– c Robinson b Parsons	0
B 5, l-b 4, w 1	10	B 2, l-b 5, n-b 14	21
1/11 2/40 3/42 4/70 5/81 6/127 7/137 8/151 9/154	157	1/14 2/21 3/31 4/47 5/128 6/141 7/146 8/146 9/181	189

Bonus points – Leicestershire 4.

Bowling: *First Innings*—Millns 16.2–4–51–3; Mullally 23–11–38–4; Parsons 16–9–23–1; Simmons 12–1–28–1; Pierson 9–5–8–1. *Second Innings*—Mullally 11–2–37–0; Millns 16–5–34–1; Parsons 14.1–4–34–4; Pierson 14–5–47–2; Hepworth 11–3–30–3.

Umpires: G. I. Burgess and J. H. Harris.

At Derby, June 9, 10, 11. LEICESTERSHIRE beat DERBYSHIRE by seven wickets.

LEICESTERSHIRE v MIDDLESEX

At Leicester, June 16, 17, 18, 20. Middlesex won by ten wickets. Middlesex 23 pts, Leicestershire 4 pts. Toss: Leicestershire.

Gatting and Emburey steered the champions Middlesex to a belated first win, giving Leicestershire their first defeat. Though the pitch was the same green as the rest of the square, it was dry enough for Briers to choose to bat, and he made the 28th hundred of his career. But until Nixon's confident attack, no one else attempted to build a decent score. Gatting, however, countered with 225. He batted for seven and a half hours, striking 33 fours and two sixes, with support from Ramprakash, Carr and Brown contributing to a commanding total. Again, Mullally had no luck, but Hepworth picked up three wickets in one over. Leicestershire succumbed for 237 on the final day, with only Briers showing the necessary self-discipline. Without exaggerated help from the pitch, Emburey earned match figures of nine for 181.

Close of play: First day, Leicestershire 295-6 (P. A. Nixon 31*, G. J. Parsons 0*); Second day, Middlesex 258-3 (M. W. Gatting 106*, J. D. Carr 23*); Third day, Leicestershire 20-0 (P. V. Simmons 6*, N. E. Briers 8*).

Leicestershire

P. V. Simmons c Brown b Feltham	29	– c Feltham b Johnson	32
*N. E. Briers c Carr b Emburey	147	– c Carr b Emburey	85
T. J. Boon c Brown b Johnson	34	– lbw b Emburey	3
J. J. Whitaker b Feltham	11	– c sub b Emburey	15
B. F. Smith b Johnson	27	– c Weekes b Johnson	28
P. N. Hepworth c Brown b Johnson	5	– c Carr b Feltham	4
†P. A. Nixon c Gatting b Emburey	95	– lbw b Emburey	0
G. J. Parsons c Carr b Emburey	1	– c Ramprakash b Weekes	24
D. J. Millns c Gatting b Emburey	13	– b Feltham	21
A. D. Mullally c Brown b Emburey	23	– c Gatting b Weekes	0
M. T. Brimson not out	0	– not out	3
L-b 7, n-b 5	12	B 2, l-b 10, n-b 10	22
1/46 2/136 3/170 4/214 5/238 6/294 7/298 8/358 9/394	397	1/69 2/78 3/132 4/164 5/181 6/182 7/186 8/229 9/229	237

Bonus points – Leicestershire 3, Middlesex 3 (Score at 120 overs: 303-7).

Bowling: *First Innings*—Williams 15–3–38–0; Johnson 29–7–72–3; Feltham 40–5–131–2; Emburey 44.3–13–95–5; Weekes 25–7–54–0. *Second Innings*—Johnson 23–5–50–2; Feltham 9.3–1–19–2; Emburey 43–18–86–4; Weekes 27–4–70–2.

Middlesex

D. L. Haynes c Smith b Millns	2	– not out	8
M. A. Roseberry lbw b Parsons	19	– not out	3
*M. W. Gatting b Parsons	225		
M. R. Ramprakash c Millns b Simmons	74		
J. D. Carr b Millns	88		
†K. R. Brown not out	102		
P. N. Weekes c Parsons b Hepworth	36		
J. E. Emburey b Hepworth	1		
M. A. Feltham lbw b Hepworth	0		
R. L. Johnson c Whitaker b Brimson	31		
B 9, l-b 22, n-b 14	45	W 1	1
1/4 2/40 3/202 4/401 5/478 6/559 7/561 8/561 9/623 (9 wkts dec.)	623	(no wkt)	12

N. F. Williams did not bat.

Bonus points – Middlesex 4, Leicestershire 1 (Score at 120 overs: 445-4).

Bowling: *First Innings*—Millns 31–5–126–2; Mullally 29–6–82–0; Simmons 21–4–68–1; Parsons 31–5–93–2; Brimson 24.4–4–109–1; Hepworth 25–2–114–3. *Second Innings*—Mullally 2–0–4–0; Brimson 2–0–8–0.

Umpires: J. H. Hampshire and A. A. Jones.

At The Oval, June 23, 24, 25. LEICESTERSHIRE lost to SURREY by an innings and 50 runs.

LEICESTERSHIRE v ESSEX

At Leicester, June 30, July 1, 2. Leicestershire won by an innings and 49 runs. Leicestershire 24 pts, Essex 5 pts. Toss: Essex. First-class debuts: T. J. Mason; M. Diwan.

Leicestershire needed less than two and a half days to defeat a weakened Essex side, reduced to four capped players by injuries and Test calls. Acting-captain Stephenson was forced to retire after being struck on the hand by Millns but returned to provide the batting backbone for nearly five hours. Mullally's dreadful run of luck continued as he had Irani caught at slip off a no-ball and Stephenson dropped. Launched in tremendous style by Simmons, Leicestershire's reply reached 462, thanks chiefly to Nixon's fourth and highest first-class century and Parsons's highest score in England. Essex were 22 for two by the end of the second day and lost four more for 30 in 12 overs next morning. Irani, with 12 fours, and Childs, one short of his career-best after scoring 42 off 24 deliveries, delayed the end, but Millns and Parsons were always too lively.

Close of play: First day, Leicestershire 107-2 (P. V. Simmons 48*, J. J. Whitaker 3*); Second day, Essex 22-2 (J. J. B. Lewis 10*, N. Shahid 4*).

Essex

J. J. B. Lewis c and b Millns	0	– c Simmons b Parsons	19
*J. P. Stephenson c Mason b Millns	83	– lbw b Mullally	0
N. Shahid b Wells	13	– (4) c Nixon b Millns	7
N. Hussain c Boon b Simmons	32	– (5) c Mullally b Parsons	16
M. Diwan lbw b Simmons	0	– (6) b Millns	0
R. C. Irani c Nixon b Simmons	15	– (7) c Nixon b Millns	64
†M. A. Garnham c Simmons b Wells	39	– (8) c Mason b Wells	17
M. S. Kasprowicz c Nixon b Wells	0	– (9) c and b Wells	0
R. M. Pearson c Smith b Mason	7	– (3) c Nixon b Millns	7
D. M. Cousins c Nixon b Millns	10	– c Smith b Parsons	11
J. H. Childs not out	2	– not out	42
B 1, l-b 3, w 1, n-b 12	17	B 6, l-b 4, w 2	12
1/2 2/29 3/70 4/70 5/99 6/153 7/154 8/186 9/215	218	1/2 2/9 3/33 4/35 5/44 6/52 7/119 8/119 9/143	195

Bonus points – Essex 1, Leicestershire 4.

In the first innings J. P. Stephenson, when 3, retired hurt at 13 and resumed at 29.

Bowling: *First Innings*—Millns 17.2–5–36–3; Mullally 20–3–60–0; Wells 16–8–29–3; Parsons 12–4–34–0; Mason 7–0–22–1; Simmons 10–3–33–3. *Second Innings*—Millns 19–3–78–4; Mullally 11–6–20–1; Parsons 14.4–1–64–3; Wells 5–1–23–2.

Leicestershire

P. V. Simmons c Shahid b Irani	86
*N. E. Briers c Shahid b Kasprowicz	26
T. J. Boon c Garnham b Kasprowicz	16
J. J. Whitaker c Garnham b Irani	23
V. J. Wells c Shahid b Kasprowicz	48
B. F. Smith c Hussain b Stephenson	9
†P. A. Nixon c Irani b Cousins	115
G. J. Parsons lbw b Kasprowicz	70
T. J. Mason c Hussain b Kasprowicz	3
D. J. Millns not out	12
A. D. Mullally c Cousins b Irani	14
B 11, l-b 7, w 2, n-b 20	40
1/49 2/85 3/142 4/183 5/198 6/246 7/398 8/429 9/435	462

Bonus points – Leicestershire 4, Essex 4 (Score at 120 overs: 462-9).

Bowling: Kasprowicz 31–4–120–5; Cousins 18–3–66–1; Irani 23.2–2–99–3; Childs 16–6–45–0; Stephenson 19–5–50–1; Pearson 7–1–38–0; Shahid 6–0–26–0.

Umpires: J. C. Balderstone and T. E. Jesty.

At Harrogate, July 14, 15, 16, 18. LEICESTERSHIRE lost to YORKSHIRE by 114 runs.

At Durham University, July 21, 22, 23. LEICESTERSHIRE beat DURHAM by an innings and five runs.

At Leicester, July 30, 31, August 1. LEICESTERSHIRE drew with SOUTH AFRICANS (See South African tour section).

At Nottingham, August 4, 5, 6, 8. LEICESTERSHIRE lost to NOTTINGHAMSHIRE by six wickets.

LEICESTERSHIRE v WORCESTERSHIRE

At Leicester, August 11, 12, 13, 15. Leicestershire won by 97 runs. Leicestershire 22 pts, Worcestershire 6 pts. Toss: Worcestershire. Championship debut: D. L. Maddy.

Their seventh victory lifted Leicestershire back into second place in the Championship – without any major contribution from their specialist batsmen. But down the order Millns had an outstanding all-round game, with an unbeaten 64 – a maiden half-century and the highest score of the match – and six for 84, his best Championship figures of the season. Parsons also flourished, turning the match towards Leicestershire on the third morning, when Worcestershire lost six wickets for 73, and then making 52 despite offering two chances. He combined with Millns to add 103 for the ninth wicket, enabling Leicestershire, who had been 125 for seven, to set a target of 289 in 78 overs. This was perhaps 50 too many for Worcestershire, one man short because of a hand injury to Weston, on a pitch of variable bounce which was dusting up. But they chanced their arm and Millns, bowling with pace, aggression and control, ran through them.

Close of play: First day, Leicestershire 70-2 (T. J. Boon 9*, J. J. Whitaker 14*); Second day, Worcestershire 205-4 (G. R. Haynes 48*, R. K. Illingworth 20*); Third day, Leicestershire 230-8 (G. J. Parsons 39*, D. J. Millns 35*).

Leicestershire

P. V. Simmons c Leatherdale b Lampitt	20	– c Lampitt b Radford	0
*N. E. Briers c Moody b Newport	17	– c Rhodes b Newport	20
T. J. Boon c Hick b Lampitt	20	– c Rhodes b Lampitt	9
J. J. Whitaker b Lampitt	36	– lbw b Lampitt	0
V. J. Wells c Rhodes b Haynes	36	– lbw b Radford	13
D. L. Maddy lbw b Radford	9	– c and b Hick	34
†P. A. Nixon lbw b Newport	35	– b Newport	34
G. J. Parsons c Illingworth b Radford	24	– c Newport b Illingworth	52
A. R. K. Pierson not out	38	– c Rhodes b Lampitt	23
D. J. Millns c Illingworth b Newport	1	– not out	64
A. D. Mullally b Radford	17	– not out	5
L-b 10, n-b 20	30	B 4, l-b 15, w 2, n-b 8	29
1/45 2/45 3/98 4/113 5/148 6/166 7/203 8/250 9/252	283	1/0 2/33 3/38 4/44 5/68 6/123 7/125 8/171 9/274 (9 wkts dec.)	283

Bonus points – Leicestershire 2, Worcestershire 4.

Bowling: *First Innings*—Newport 27–3–99–3; Lampitt 30–9–81–3; Haynes 9–0–45–1; Radford 13–4–40–3; Illingworth 1–0–8–0. *Second Innings*—Radford 23–5–94–2; Lampitt 16–4–40–3; Newport 22–9–41–2; Haynes 3–0–7–0; Illingworth 14–2–45–1; Hick 20–7–37–1.

Worcestershire

*T. S. Curtis b Simmons	20	– c Nixon b Millns	8
W. P. C. Weston c Nixon b Mullally	3	– absent injured	
G. A. Hick b Parsons	39	– c Boon b Parsons	42
T. M. Moody c Pierson b Mullally	49	– c Wells b Millns	0
G. R. Haynes c Nixon b Parsons	53	– c Whitaker b Mullally	11
R. K. Illingworth c Whitaker b Millns	20	– (9) not out	1
D. A. Leatherdale c Nixon b Simmons	14	– (6) c and b Pierson	61
†S. J. Rhodes c Nixon b Parsons	34	– (2) c Maddy b Millns	9
S. R. Lampitt lbw b Parsons	14	– (7) c Maddy b Millns	19
P. J. Newport b Parsons	1	– (8) c Wells b Millns	9
N. V. Radford not out	1	– (10) c Boon b Millns	12
B 6, l-b 10, w 2, n-b 12	30	L-b 4, w 1, n-b 14	19
1/4 2/74 3/74 4/174 5/210 6/211 7/245 8/276 9/277	278	1/17 2/28 3/28 4/61 5/103 6/167 7/167 8/179 9/191	191

Bonus points – Worcestershire 2, Leicestershire 4.

Bowling: *First Innings*—Millns 18–1–81–1; Mullally 13–3–56–2; Parsons 20.3–6–34–5; Simmons 19–5–45–2; Wells 9–2–44–0; Pierson 3–2–2–0. *Second Innings*—Mullally 13–4–35–1; Millns 16.2–2–84–6; Simmons 7–1–26–0; Parsons 3–1–16–1; Pierson 12–6–26–1.

Umpires: J. D. Bond and B. J. Meyer.

LEICESTERSHIRE v SUSSEX

At Leicester, August 18, 19. Sussex won by nine wickets. Sussex 21 pts, Leicestershire 4 pts. Toss: Leicestershire.

A pitch offering irregular bounce and occasional movement off the seam could not explain Leicestershire's woeful performance. They batted badly not once but twice, capitulating inside two days when Sussex claimed the extra half-hour. Even their best period, when they reduced Sussex from 152 for two to 247 all out, was marred by poor behaviour. Neither Millns nor Vince Wells could contain his annoyance over rejected appeals and Mullally was spoken to by umpire Julian, along with his captain, after alleged abuse of Alan Wells. Leicestershire suspended Mullally for their next match. One dreadful shot after another undermined the home batsmen; they could not muster a single batting point in the first innings and did not even reach three figures in the second. Stephenson bowled cleverly and Hemmings conceded only 29 runs in 24 overs. When he had Maddy lbw, he became the 80th cricketer to take 1,500 first-class wickets, though his average was higher than any of the previous 79.

Close of play: First day, Sussex 57-1 (N. J. Lenham 29*, A. P. Wells 11*).

Leicestershire

P. V. Simmons c Athey b Giddins	18	– c Moores b Jarvis	10
*N. E. Briers c Moores b Jarvis	48	– c Speight b Stephenson	5
T. J. Boon c Moores b Jarvis	17	– c Moores b Stephenson	14
V. J. Wells c Wells b Stephenson	33	– c Lenham b Jarvis	0
B. F. Smith c Smith b Stephenson	14	– b Stephenson	12
D. L. Maddy c Stephenson b Jarvis	5	– lbw b Hemmings	8
†P. A. Nixon not out	30	– lbw b Stephenson	3
G. J. Parsons b Hemmings	9	– not out	18
D. J. Millns b Giddins	0	– c Wells b Jarvis	7
A. D. Mullally b Giddins	0	– b Salisbury	7
M. T. Brimson run out	1	– b Jarvis	2
B 1, l-b 11, w 1, n-b 4	17	B 1, l-b 2, w 1	4
1/44 2/86 3/93 4/139 5/140 6/155 7/175 8/178 9/182	192	1/15 2/15 3/25 4/37 5/50 6/52 7/56 8/72 9/81	90

Bonus points – Sussex 4.

Bowling: *First Innings*—Stephenson 15–4–27–2; Jarvis 20–3–71–3; Giddins 16–5–64–3; Hemmings 15–9–18–1. *Second Innings*—Stephenson 16–7–23–4; Jarvis 9.5–1–50–4; Hemmings 9–4–11–1; Salisbury 4–2–3–1.

Sussex

N. J. Lenham c Nixon b Mullally	51	– c Millns b Mullally	0
C. W. J. Athey c Parsons b Simmons	18		
D. M. Smith lbw b Parsons	0	– (2) not out	15
*A. P. Wells lbw b Wells	46	– (3) not out	11
M. P. Speight b Simmons	42		
†P. Moores c Smith b Millns	21		
F. D. Stephenson c Wells b Mullally	16		
P. W. Jarvis c Millns b Simmons	7		
I. D. K. Salisbury lbw b Wells	10		
E. E. Hemmings c Mullally b Millns	6		
E. S. H. Giddins not out	0		
B 8, l-b 8, n-b 14	30	B 4, l-b 1, n-b 6	11
1/36 2/106 3/152 4/189 5/193 6/207 7/227 8/235 9/243	247	1/0	(1 wkt) 37

Bonus points – Sussex 1, Leicestershire 4.

In the first innings C. W. J. Athey, when 15, retired hurt at 31 and resumed at 193.

Bowling: *First Innings*—Millns 22.3–3–79–2; Mullally 17–2–62–2; Parsons 9–2–31–1; Wells 10–2–33–2; Simmons 12–3–26–3. *Second Innings*—Mullally 4.4–1–20–1; Parsons 4–1–12–0.

Umpires: R. Julian and G. Sharp.

At Cardiff, August 25, 26, 27, 29. LEICESTERSHIRE lost to GLAMORGAN by 150 runs.

At Bristol, August 30, 31, September 1, 2. LEICESTERSHIRE lost to GLOUCESTERSHIRE by 102 runs.

LEICESTERSHIRE v HAMPSHIRE

At Leicester, September 8, 9, 10, 12. Leicestershire won by seven wickets. Leicestershire 24 pts, Hampshire 5 pts. Toss: Hampshire. First-class debut: P. R. Whitaker. Championship debut: J. M. Dakin.

After three consecutive defeats, Leicestershire defied several rain stoppages to maintain their fight for second place. Simmons ensured victory on the final day, with an ankle-high catch and two wickets to help finish off Hampshire, and a rapid 47 to make Leicestershire's target of 116 a formality. He had taken seven wickets in the match, including a Championship-best four for 68. Both Hampshire innings relied heavily on a single individual. On the first day Robin Smith, just omitted from the England tour party, scored 123, which took him past 10,000 Championship runs. His colleagues, overwhelmed by Millns, contributed 86. An assured performance by Paul Whitaker bolstered them on Saturday; a recent recruit from Derbyshire's Second Eleven, he failed by only six to become the first Hampshire player to reach a century on first-class debut. But Leicestershire had taken a 128-run lead, thanks to Nixon's third century of 1994, a career-best 131. He was the first Leicestershire wicket-keeper to score 1,000 in a season since 1928.

Close of play: First day, Leicestershire 44-2 (N. E. Briers 19*, J. J. Whitaker 4*); Second day, Leicestershire 347-9 (P. A. Nixon 130*, D. J. Millns 17*); Third day, Hampshire 152-5 (K. D. James 3*, A. N. Aymes 4*).

Hampshire

First innings		Second innings	
V. P. Terry c Nixon b Millns	7	b Millns	9
P. R. Whitaker b Millns	2	c Millns b Simmons	94
G. W. White lbw b Millns	16	c Briers b Parsons	9
R. A. Smith c Simmons b Parsons	123	b Simmons	13
*M. C. J. Nicholas c Parsons b Millns	2	c and b Pierson	10
K. D. James c and b Pierson	12	c Simmons b Pierson	12
†A. N. Aymes lbw b Simmons	3	b Millns	46
S. D. Udal c Nixon b Simmons	17	b Simmons	9
M. J. Thursfield b Simmons	8	c Parsons b Simmons	12
C. A. Connor lbw b Millns	18	b Pierson	1
J. N. B. Bovill not out	1	not out	7
L-b 3, w 1, n-b 12	16	B 1, l-b 15, w 1, n-b 4	21
1/8 2/25 3/42 4/54 5/94 6/107 7/151 8/161 9/214	225	1/28 2/68 3/95 4/128 5/144 6/174 7/196 8/210 9/221	243

Bonus points – Hampshire 1, Leicestershire 4.

Bowling: *First Innings*—Millns 17.3–5–59–5; Parsons 12–8–27–1; Wells 6–2–15–0; Pierson 24–2–76–1; Simmons 15–7–45–3. *Second Innings*—Millns 19.3–4–43–2; Parsons 10–3–17–1; Wells 6–0–29–0; Pierson 39–13–70–3; Simmons 28–9–68–4.

Leicestershire

First innings		Second innings	
P. V. Simmons lbw b Connor	18	c Aymes b Udal	47
*N. E. Briers b Bovill	22	lbw b Connor	19
T. J. Boon c Terry b Bovill	2	not out	17
J. J. Whitaker c Aymes b Connor	22	lbw b Udal	13
V. J. Wells c Nicholas b Bovill	41	not out	11
P. E. Robinson c White b Connor	13		
†P. A. Nixon c Connor b Bovill	131		
J. M. Dakin c Nicholas b Connor	18		
G. J. Parsons lbw b James	15		
A. R. K. Pierson c Udal b Bovill	27		
D. J. Millns not out	22		
B 1, l-b 13, n-b 8	22	L-b 4, n-b 6	10
1/27 2/34 3/65 4/69 5/90 6/192 7/239 8/262 9/320	353	1/64 2/78 3/98	(3 wkts) 117

Bonus points – Leicestershire 4, Hampshire 4.

Bowling: *First Innings*—Bovill 24.4–5–108–5; Connor 30–7–87–4; Thursfield 14–4–32–0; Udal 26–5–70–0; James 12–1–42–1. *Second Innings*—Connor 7–0–44–1; Bovill 5–0–21–0; Udal 11–2–25–2; Thursfield 4–0–19–0; Whitaker 0.1–0–4–0.

Umpires: J. H. Hampshire and R. A. White.

At Manchester, September 15, 16, 17, 19. LEICESTERSHIRE drew with LANCASHIRE.

MIDDLESEX

Patron: HRH The Duke of Edinburgh
President: D. C. S. Compton
Chairman: R. V. C. Robins
Chairman, Cricket Committee: R. A. Gale
Secretary: J. Hardstaff
Captain: M. W. Gatting
Coach: D. Bennett
Scorer: M. J. Smith

Fourth place in the County Championship would be seen by some counties as representing a successful season. For Middlesex, winners of eight trophies in the previous 11 years of Mike Gatting's captaincy, it was a disappointment.

There were several reasons for underperforming, principally a series of injuries that prevented the county from fielding its strongest attack. Chas Taylor had two knee operations during the year and did not make a single Championship appearance. Richard Johnson, having taken all ten wickets in the second innings at Derby, then played only one more first-class match before he, too, needed surgery on his knee. Neil Williams did not play between the middle of June and the end of August, while Philip Tufnell did not appear in the Championship until the end of June because of personal troubles.

The weather was also a factor. The first five matches were all drawn, three of them after serious interference by the weather, and Middlesex found themselves with just 25 points and only Glamorgan below them. Wins at Leicester and Derby and over Durham at Lord's raised them ten places in three weeks. But there followed two poor performances, at Arundel and Old Trafford. Four of the last six matches were won, but the title was by then out of reach.

There were some individual batting achievements, notably that of John Carr, who topped the national averages after an astonishing spell brought him 854 runs in his last seven innings for once out. The sequence began the day after a sleepless night, when he was attending the birth of his daughter, Elinor. Gatting, as always, was the mainstay of the batting. He averaged over 60 in the Championship for the fourth successive season and for the eighth time in 15 years; since 1980, Gatting has scored almost 19,000 Championship runs at an average of 61.46. Desmond Haynes made more runs than in 1993, but could not find the consistency that would have given the county a better start more frequently. Only once – against Essex at Uxbridge – did both Haynes and Mike Roseberry find form at the same time. Mark Ramprakash had a much better year, not just in quantity of runs, but in terms of confidence. He played more positively and, though he failed to regain his Test place, he was rewarded with the vice-captaincy on England A's Indian tour. In contrast, Keith Brown's batting fell away, although there can be no doubt that his wicket-keeping improved.

The real bonus was the emergence of Paul Weekes. Although he was fortunate to be dropped on six, he went on to register his maiden century against Somerset. His forthright approach, to which he has added some discretion, made him good to watch and he established himself as a regular member of the side, not only in limited-overs matches. At present, he is a batsman who bowls, but there is no reason why his off-spin cannot improve with age and experience to make him a genuine all-rounder.

It was always unlikely that John Emburey would repeat his memorable all-round feats of 1993 but he was once again the leading wicket-taker, with 59, although his batting seemed to be affected by the detached retina he suffered during the winter. While Johnson's ten for 45 at Derby may have been a one-off, there can be no doubt that he is a fast bowler of immense promise. Angus Fraser was his usual economical self, but never took more than three wickets in an innings and was originally considered too weary to be chosen for the Ashes tour. Kevin Shine began well, with four for 79 on debut for his new county against England A, but was far too wayward to be a successful opening bowler.

Performances in the three limited-overs competitions were an embarrassment. A century by Ramprakash ensured victory in the preliminary round of the Benson and Hedges Cup, but it was significant that Northamptonshire were without Curtly Ambrose. In the first round proper, the batting was far from good enough and Warwickshire won easily. The NatWest Trophy was a similar story, with Northamptonshire gaining their revenge at Uxbridge in the second round. In the Sunday League, Middlesex came 14th. While it was possible to understand Gatting's desire to shed some responsibility and encourage the younger players to cope as his career nears its end, he was little help to the side coming to the crease with the scoreboard showing 92 for five, another 84 needed from 16 overs, and the bowlers brim-full of confidence, as happened against Gloucestershire. Similarly, when batting first against Glamorgan, he appeared in the 28th over at 71 for five, far too late for Middlesex to achieve a match-winning total. While the 40-overs game has rarely been Middlesex's strongest suit, they must make a better fist of it than they did in 1994.

If 1995 is to be a more productive year, the better bowlers are going to have to stay fitter. Middlesex will be without Williams, who has moved to Essex. But they have signed as their overseas player the New Zealander Dion Nash, who will be aiming to repeat on a regular basis his stunning performance at Lord's in last year's Test match. Unexpectedly, Roseberry has also gone, to take on the captaincy of his native Durham. In theory, this will have the advantage of encouraging the substantial number of young batsmen jostling for position on the fringe of the first team, Jason Pooley being the most obvious. But with both Haynes and Roseberry gone, Middlesex will have to build a new opening partnership from scratch. It is not only Haynes's batting that will be missed: the club gained a lot from his appealing personality, positive attitude and his concern for the younger players. – Norman de Mesquita.

MIDDLESEX 1994

[*Bill Smith*

Back row: K. P. Dutch, P. Farbrace, P. N. Weekes, A. Habib, R. J. Sims. *Middle row:* S. M. Shephard (*physiotherapist*), D. Bennett (*coach*), J. C. Pooley, M. A. Feltham, J. C. Harrison, C. W. Taylor, K. Marc, K. J. Shine, R. L. Johnson, I. J. Gould (*Second Eleven coach*), A. Jones (*Second Eleven scorer*). *Front row:* M. R. Ramprakash, A. R. C. Fraser, N. F. Williams, J. D. Carr, M. W. Gatting (*captain*), J. E. Emburey, M. A. Roseberry, K. R. Brown. *Insets:* P. C. R. Tufnell, D. L. Haynes, M. J. Smith (*First Eleven scorer*).

MIDDLESEX RESULTS

All first-class matches – Played 20: Won 8, Lost 3, Drawn 9.

County Championship matches – Played 17: Won 7, Lost 3, Drawn 7.

Bonus points – Batting 43, Bowling 57.

Competition placings – Britannic Assurance County Championship, 4th; NatWest Bank Trophy, 2nd round; Benson and Hedges Cup, 1st round; AXA Equity & Law League, 14th.

BRITANNIC ASSURANCE CHAMPIONSHIP AVERAGES

BATTING

	Birthplace	*M*	*I*	*NO*	*R*	*HS*	*Avge*
‡J. D. Carr	*St John's Wood*	17	23	8	1,321	261*	88.06
‡M. W. Gatting	*Kingsbury*	17	25	2	1,389	225	60.39
‡M. R. Ramprakash	*Bushey*	17	25	2	1,261	135	54.82
‡M. A. Roseberry	*Houghton-le-Spring*	17	27	2	1,001	152	40.04
‡D. L. Haynes§	*Holders Hill, Barbados*	17	27	2	973	134	38.92
‡K. R. Brown	*Edmonton*	17	22	8	528	102*	37.71
‡P. N. Weekes	*Hackney*	13	16	0	552	117	34.50
‡N. F. Williams	*Hope Well, St Vincent*	9	8	3	132	63	26.40
K. J. Shine	*Bracknell*	10	7	5	39	14*	19.50
M. A. Feltham	*St John's Wood*	10	13	1	230	71	19.16
R. L. Johnson	*Chertsey*	9	12	2	155	47	15.50
‡J. E. Emburey	*Peckham*	14	17	4	123	26*	9.46
‡A. R. C. Fraser	*Billinge*	9	8	1	40	16	5.71
‡P. C. R. Tufnell	*Barnet*	8	6	1	14	5	2.80

Also batted: G. A. R. Harris (*Tottenham*) (2 matches) 11, 5*; K. Marc (*Mon Repos, St Lucia*) (1 match) 9, 8.

* *Signifies not out.* ‡ *Denotes county cap.* § *Overseas player.*

The following played a total of 23 three-figure innings for Middlesex in County Championship matches – J. D. Carr 5, M. W. Gatting 5, D. L. Haynes 5, M. R. Ramprakash 4, M. A. Roseberry 2, K. R. Brown 1, P. N. Weekes 1.

BOWLING

	O	*M*	*R*	*W*	*BB*	*5W/i*	*Avge*
A. R. C. Fraser	321	86	802	36	3-16	0	22.27
R. L. Johnson	299.4	68	942	36	10-45	1	26.16
J. E. Emburey	633	187	1,434	52	6-89	2	27.57
P. C. R. Tufnell	408.5	107	995	35	6-35	1	28.42
M. A. Feltham	321.3	67	989	29	5-69	1	34.10
P. N. Weekes	401.3	62	1,209	31	4-79	0	39.00
N. F. Williams	294	61	1,000	24	6-49	1	41.66
K. J. Shine	252.3	52	931	20	3-16	0	46.55

Also bowled: M. W. Gatting 26–4–97–2; G. A. R. Harris 51–11–215–1; D. L. Haynes 2–2–0–0; K. Marc 29–4–133–3; M. R. Ramprakash 2–0–6–0; M. A. Roseberry 1–0–5–0.

Wicket-keeper: K. R. Brown 48 ct, 1 st.

Leading Fielders: J. D. Carr 28, M. W. Gatting 25, M. A. Roseberry 19.

MIDDLESEX v ENGLAND A

At Lord's, April 21, 22, 23, 24. Drawn. Toss: Middlesex. First-class debut: T. A. Radford. County debut: K. J. Shine.

The sixth double-century of Mike Gatting's career saved the game after Middlesex had had to follow on. The champion county were allowed at last to use the home dressing-room at Lord's for this fixture – Middlesex were always forced out when the opposition was MCC. But their team was an unfamiliar one, with five of their Test players missing. Darren Bicknell, who had not been on the England A tour, replaced the injured Hugh Morris in the A team ahead of the out-of-form Lathwell. Bicknell scored 80 and solid performances from the lower order took their score to 357. Then Ilott followed his 45 not out with four wickets, including three in 17 balls to finish the innings. Middlesex reached safety thanks to Gatting and Carr. Their partnership added 288 in 87 overs, enabling Gatting to declare. He batted seven and a half hours to remind Ray Illingworth and his fellow-selectors of his existence, while Rhodes furthered his claims to succeed Russell with four catches and 46 runs. Crawley opened his scoring both times with a six off Shine, though on the first day he was out 35 minutes later without addition.

Close of play: First day, England A 268-7 (M. P. Bicknell 21*, M. C. Ilott 9*); Second day, Middlesex 50-2 (M. W. Gatting 27*, M. A. Feltham 7*); Third day, Middlesex 108-3 (M. W. Gatting 58*, J. D. Carr 14*).

England A

D. J. Bicknell lbw b Shine	80	– not out	13
J. P. Crawley lbw b Williams	6	– not out	33
A. Dale b Williams	35		
*A. P. Wells c Gatting b Feltham	16		
M. B. Loye c Gatting b Taylor	6		
†S. J. Rhodes b Shine	46		
R. D. B. Croft c Radford b Weekes	31		
M. P. Bicknell c Brown b Taylor	41		
M. C. Ilott not out	45		
M. J. McCague b Shine	20		
P. M. Such b Shine	9		
L-b 14, n-b 8	22	W 2	2
1/20 2/94 3/140 4/156 5/157 6/224 7/244 8/294 9/341	357		(no wkt) 48

Bowling: *First Innings*—Shine 24.1–5–79–4; Williams 27–8–72–2; Weekes 19–8–27–1; Feltham 25–4–75–1; Taylor 25–5–90–2. *Second Innings*—Shine 5–1–15–0; Williams 5–2–16–0; Taylor 3–0–10–0; Feltham 3–1–7–0.

Middlesex

M. A. Roseberry c Crawley b Ilott	5	– c Rhodes b Ilott	8
J. C. Pooley c Rhodes b M. P. Bicknell	40	– c McCague b M. P. Bicknell	8
*M. W. Gatting lbw b Dale	58	– not out	224
J. D. Carr run out	8	– (5) b Croft	102
P. N. Weekes c Rhodes b Ilott	16	– (6) not out	21
†K. R. Brown lbw b McCague	3		
T. A. Radford c Rhodes b McCague	4		
M. A. Feltham lbw b Ilott	7	– (4) lbw b Ilott	18
N. F. Williams not out	2		
C. W. Taylor b McCague	0		
K. J. Shine b Ilott	0		
B 4, l-b 4, w 1, n-b 4	13	L-b 8, w 1, n-b 4	13
1/11 2/95 3/118 4/122 5/143 6/147 7/154 8/154 9/155	156	1/11 2/29 3/70 4/358	(4 wkts dec.) 394

Bowling: *First Innings*—McCague 18–4–51–3; Ilott 18.2–9–31–4; M. P. Bicknell 10–2–24–1; Dale 7–2–26–1; Such 6–2–16–0. *Second Innings*—McCague 23–3–80–0; Ilott 32–9–80–2; M. P. Bicknell 29–6–88–1; Dale 12–1–43–0; Such 3–2–5–0; Croft 26–2–90–1.

Umpires: J. C. Balderstone and G. Sharp.

At Cambridge, April 30, May 1, 2. MIDDLESEX beat CAMBRIDGE UNIVERSITY by 78 runs.

MIDDLESEX v YORKSHIRE

At Lord's, May 5, 6, 7, 9. Drawn. Middlesex 3 pts, Yorkshire 2 pts. Toss: Middlesex.

More than half the match was lost to the weather before a declaration and two forfeitures left Middlesex needing 298 for victory in 71 overs. Gatting gave them a chance, but he was fifth out with 135 still wanted from the last 20, making the draw inevitable. There was little excitement earlier. Play did not start until 4.40 on the first day. The second morning saw nothing except what looked like a heated argument between Gatting and the groundsman about muddy patches on a nearby pitch, apparently re-seeded and not adequately covered. When play finally resumed at 2.30, Yorkshire crawled on at barely two an over. Saturday was completely washed out and Monday saw Yorkshire bat on for 28 overs – declaring three short of a third batting point.

Close of play: First day, Yorkshire 75-2 (M. D. Moxon 40*, R. B. Richardson 2*); Second day, Yorkshire 208-5 (C. White 38*, A. P. Grayson 25*); Third day, No play.

Yorkshire

*M. D. Moxon c Carr b Emburey 72
M. P. Vaughan c Emburey b Williams . 5
D. Byas c Weekes b Williams 14
R. B. Richardson c Weekes b Fraser... 10
†R. J. Blakey b Shine 14
C. White c Brown b Williams 62
A. P. Grayson b Fraser.............. 61
P. J. Hartley not out 11
D. Gough lbw b Fraser.............. 0
R. D. Stemp not out 7
B 6, l-b 16, w 1, n-b 18 41

1/20 2/50 3/88 4/133 5/135 6/266 7/280 8/280 (8 wkts dec.) 297

M. A. Robinson did not bat.

Bonus points – Yorkshire 2, Middlesex 3.

Bowling: Fraser 29–11–58–3; Shine 23–9–48–1; Williams 36–12–96–3; Emburey 19–5–32–1; Weekes 9–0–37–0; Gatting 1–0–4–0.

Yorkshire forfeited their second innings.

Middlesex

Middlesex forfeited their first innings.

D. L. Haynes c Blakey b Hartley...... 39
M. A. Roseberry lbw b Hartley 5
M. R. Ramprakash lbw b Gough...... 3
*M. W. Gatting c Grayson b Robinson. 65
J. D. Carr c Richardson b Hartley..... 14
P. N. Weekes c Blakey b Gough 32
†K. R. Brown not out 31
J. E. Emburey b Gough 0
N. F. Williams not out 3
L-b 13, w 1, n-b 18.......... 32

1/27 2/30 3/92 4/122 5/163 6/207 7/213 (7 wkts) 224

A. R. C. Fraser and K. J. Shine did not bat.

Bowling: Gough 19.4–3–74–3; Hartley 19–1–59–3; Robinson 16–4–36–1; White 8–0–28–0; Stemp 6–2–9–0; Vaughan 2–1–5–0.

Umpires: J. H. Harris and K. E. Palmer.

At Lord's, May 12, 13, 14. MIDDLESEX drew with NEW ZEALANDERS (See New Zealand tour section).

At Southampton, May 19, 20, 21, 23. MIDDLESEX drew with HAMPSHIRE.

MIDDLESEX v WARWICKSHIRE

At Lord's, May 26, 27, 28, 30. Drawn. Middlesex 5 pts, Warwickshire 5 pts. Toss: Middlesex.

After a blank first day, Gatting put Warwickshire in, to the delight of those hoping to see Lara's sixth successive first-class century. He soon made his way to the crease and, after a slow start, began to look the part. But, when he had 26, Johnson induced an edge and Brown took the catch. It was only Johnson's fourth Championship match, though he had bowled Lara in a Benson and Hedges game. Even in his short stay, Lara looked in a different class; his team-mates were less than inspired and gained only a single batting point. Middlesex fared little better, in spite of a stubborn six-and-a-half-hour century from Roseberry, and led by just 38. Lara then made amends with a scintillating 140 off 147 balls, his sixth hundred in seven innings and his tenth in 1994. Emburey dismissed him, though not before one ball had been lifted on to the south turret of the pavilion, to go with his 22 fours. Setting a target of 269 in 50 overs, Warwickshire very nearly won, thanks to Munton, who removed Gatting, Ramprakash and Roseberry in nine balls, but Middlesex just hung on.

Close of play: First day, No play; Second day, Middlesex 38-1 (M. A. Roseberry 14*, M. W. Gatting 23*); Third day, Warwickshire 90-2 (B. C. Lara 55*, T. L. Penney 8*).

Warwickshire

First innings		Second innings	
D. P. Ostler c Brown b Fraser	17	– lbw b Johnson	26
R. G. Twose b Williams	10	– lbw b Fraser	1
B. C. Lara c Brown b Johnson	26	– c and b Emburey	140
T. L. Penney lbw b Williams	43	– c Ramprakash b Fraser	11
*D. A. Reeve c Gatting b Johnson	4		
P. A. Smith c and b Johnson	24	– (5) c Gatting b Weekes	65
†K. J. Piper c Ramprakash b Williams	22	– (6) not out	32
N. M. K. Smith c Brown b Fraser	20	– (7) not out	22
R. P. Davis c Carr b Emburey	7		
G. C. Small b Williams	13		
T. A. Munton not out	5		
L-b 10, n-b 10	20	B 2, l-b 3, n-b 4	9
1/21 2/47 3/66 4/78 5/125 6/164 7/166 8/193 9/193	211	1/2 2/50 3/129 4/224 5/278 (5 wkts dec.)	306

Bonus points – Warwickshire 1, Middlesex 4.

Bowling: *First Innings*—Williams 24–4–71–4; Fraser 24–10–43–2; Johnson 22–9–45–3; Emburey 14–5–37–1; Gatting 5–1–5–0. *Second Innings*—Williams 10–0–55–0; Fraser 17–4–60–2; Johnson 17–2–64–1; Emburey 20–3–79–1; Weekes 11–1–43–1.

Middlesex

First innings		Second innings	
D. L. Haynes c and b Small	0	– (7) lbw b Munton	24
M. A. Roseberry lbw b Twose	119	– c Piper b Munton	73
*M. W. Gatting lbw b Munton	52	– lbw b Munton	18
M. R. Ramprakash c Lara b Small	37	– b Munton	0
J. D. Carr lbw b Small	0	– (1) lbw b P. A. Smith	32
P. N. Weekes c Lara b P. A. Smith	3	– (5) c Piper b P. A. Smith	29
†K. R. Brown c Piper b Small	0	– (6) b Small	46
R. L. Johnson lbw b Reeve	4	– (9) c N. M. K. Smith b Munton	0
N. F. Williams b Reeve	7	– (8) lbw b Small	10
J. E. Emburey not out	9	– not out	4
A. R. C. Fraser c Piper b Munton	3	– not out	0
B 1, l-b 10, w 2, n-b 2	15	B 3, l-b 6	9
1/0 2/77 3/156 4/156 5/163 6/174 7/185 8/201 9/246	249	1/84 2/129 3/129 4/132 5/206 6/221 7/239 8/239 9/245 (9 wkts)	245

Bonus points – Middlesex 1, Warwickshire 4.

Bowling: *First Innings*—Small 28–5–70–4; Munton 35–12–68–2; P. A. Smith 12–2–35–1; Reeve 17–4–31–2; N. M. K. Smith 3–1–15–0; Twose 5–0–19–1. *Second Innings*—Small 14–2–41–2; Munton 17–3–76–5; N. M. K. Smith 8–0–33–0; Davis 4–0–19–0; P. A. Smith 5–0–36–2; Lara 2–0–31–0.

Umpires: J. D. Bond and D. J. Constant.

MIDDLESEX v WORCESTERSHIRE

At Lord's, June 2, 3, 4, 6. Drawn. Middlesex 4 pts, Worcestershire 5 pts. Toss: Worcestershire.

Despite conceding a massive 557, Middlesex came in sight of their first Championship win of the season. Not for the first time, they found themselves playing a Championship match on the edge of the square, with a ridiculously short boundary to the Tavern and Mound Stands. Worcestershire took full advantage, Curtis making his first century of the season and Moody coming close. Next day Lampitt completed his maiden hundred and Worcestershire were finally bowled out in the 152nd over. All five bowlers had conceded more than 100. There were four stoppages that day and Saturday was rained off. To make up for lost time, Gatting declared, Worcestershire forfeited and Middlesex set out to score 349 off 80 overs. With Haynes and Ramprakash in command and only 141 needed off 33 overs, they were on course. But after they were parted, five wickets fell for 27 and Middlesex were content to hold on for a draw.

Close of play: First day, Worcestershire 398-6 (S. R. Lampitt 35*, P. J. Newport 31*); Second day, Middlesex 173-2 (M. A. Roseberry 77*, M. R. Ramprakash 45*); Third day, No play.

Worcestershire

*T. S. Curtis c Roseberry b Emburey	117
W. P. C. Weston c Roseberry b Shine	34
G. R. Haynes c Gatting b Weekes	49
T. M. Moody c Johnson b Weekes	83
D. A. Leatherdale b Emburey	14
C. M. Tolley c and b Emburey	7
S. R. Lampitt c Shine b Emburey	122
P. J. Newport c Brown b Weekes	34
R. K. Illingworth c Ramprakash b Williams	37
N. V. Radford c Roseberry b Shine	10
†T. Edwards not out	8
B 2, l-b 9, w 5, n-b 26	42
1/75 2/183 3/273 4/297 5/309 6/329 7/403 8/477 9/504	557

Bonus points – Worcestershire 4, Middlesex 3 (Score at 120 overs: 411-7).

Bowling: Williams 29–2–109–1; Johnson 25–4–118–0; Shine 24–1–109–2; Emburey 34.3–5–101–4; Weekes 39–6–109–3.

Worcestershire forfeited their second innings.

Middlesex

D. L. Haynes c Moody b Radford	1	– c Haynes b Illingworth	125
M. A. Roseberry lbw b Illingworth	97	– b Radford	11
*M. W. Gatting b Newport	35	– c Haynes b Newport	20
M. R. Ramprakash not out	59	– c Illingworth b Lampitt	61
R. L. Johnson not out	0	– (9) c Edwards b Illingworth	8
J. D. Carr (did not bat)		– c Leatherdale b Illingworth	4
†K. R. Brown (did not bat)		– not out	27
P. N. Weekes (did not bat)		– (5) c sub b Lampitt	17
J. E. Emburey (did not bat)		– (8) b Lampitt	1
N. F. Williams (did not bat)		– not out	14
L-b 14, w 1, n-b 2	17	B 6, l-b 9, w 1	16
1/2 2/70 3/205 (3 wkts dec.)	209	1/31 2/90 3/208 4/241 5/254 6/254 7/259 8/268 (8 wkts)	304

K. J. Shine did not bat.

Bonus points – Middlesex 1, Worcestershire 1.

Bowling: *First Innings*—Radford 7–0–47–1; Newport 11–4–31–1; Lampitt 8–0–41–0; Tolley 5–0–15–0; Moody 7–1–23–0; Illingworth 14.1–3–21–1; Haynes 6–2–10–0; Leatherdale 3–1–7–0. *Second Innings*—Radford 8–1–31–1; Tolley 7–1–37–0; Illingworth 30–7–75–3; Newport 14–2–61–1; Lampitt 13–1–54–3; Haynes 5–0–21–0; Moody 3–0–10–0.

Umpires: G. I. Burgess and B. Dudleston.

At Canterbury, June 9, 10, 11, 13. MIDDLESEX drew with KENT.

At Leicester, June 16, 17, 18, 20. MIDDLESEX beat LEICESTERSHIRE by ten wickets.

MIDDLESEX v DURHAM

At Lord's, June 23, 24, 25. Middlesex won by an innings and 34 runs. Middlesex 24 pts, Durham 4 pts. Toss: Middlesex.

Middlesex's second successive victory came on the third evening. Once again they won on the back of a total past 500, set up by Durham-born Roseberry, who took his aggregate in three innings against his native county to 406. Ramprakash, with his first century of the season, helped him add 179 in 52 overs and Feltham chipped in with 71. The visitors were unlucky to lose Wood, who slipped on his delivery stride, just as he had at the beginning of the NatWest Trophy tie at Uxbridge in 1992. By tea on the second day, Durham were 79 for four; Johnson had removed Saxelby and Morris in one over and Fraser dismissed Larkins in the next. They were out by lunch on Saturday and, once Johnson trapped Larkins with the second ball of the second innings, there was little likelihood of Durham surviving into the final day.

Close of play: First day, Middlesex 389-5 (M. R. Ramprakash 132*, M. A. Feltham 12*); Second day, Durham 221-7 (C. W. Scott 22*, D. A. Graveney 6*).

Middlesex

D. L. Haynes b Brown	21	J. E. Emburey not out	10
M. A. Roseberry lbw b Brown	152	A. R. C. Fraser c Scott b Brown	0
*M. W. Gatting b Graveney	23	P. N. Weekes c Scott b Brown	0
M. R. Ramprakash b Brown	135		
J. D. Carr c Scott b Morris	23	B 5, l-b 12, w 2, n-b 18	37
†K. R. Brown c Scott b Cummins	10		
M. A. Feltham c Longley b Bainbridge	71	1/25 2/95 3/274 4/340 5/372	511
R. L. Johnson c Brown b Graveney	29	6/403 7/499 8/501 9/511	

Bonus points – Middlesex 4, Durham 2 (Score at 120 overs: 413-6).

Bowling: Cummins 30–10–95–1; Brown 33.5–5–113–5; Wood 0.5–0–5–0; Bainbridge 32.1–8–116–1; Graveney 44–6–128–2; Morris 9–0–37–1.

Durham

W. Larkins c Brown b Fraser	21	– lbw b Johnson	0
M. Saxelby c Brown b Johnson	17	– c Roseberry b Fraser	13
J. E. Morris b Johnson	0	– c Feltham b Emburey	19
S. Hutton c Gatting b Emburey	43	– lbw b Feltham	15
*P. Bainbridge c Carr b Emburey	13	– b Fraser	21
J. I. Longley c Ramprakash b Fraser	22	– c Carr b Emburey	19
A. C. Cummins c Brown b Johnson	63	– lbw b Feltham	49
†C. W. Scott lbw b Johnson	47	– c Brown b Johnson	1
D. A. Graveney c Carr b Fraser	11	– lbw b Johnson	17
J. Wood b Weekes	9	– b Weekes	16
S. J. E. Brown not out	5	– not out	10
B 7, l-b 5, n-b 20	32	B 6, l-b 4, n-b 4	14
1/41 2/41 3/41 4/59 5/94 6/178 7/196 8/230 9/271	283	1/0 2/32 3/39 4/61 5/90 6/104 7/109 8/141 9/180	194

Bonus points – Durham 2, Middlesex 4.

Bowling: *First Innings*—Johnson 18.5–4–64–4; Fraser 17–3–51–3; Feltham 15–2–61–0; Emburey 34–10–77–2; Weekes 14–6–18–1. *Second Innings*—Johnson 14–3–49–3; Fraser 15–5–23–2; Feltham 14–4–55–2; Emburey 24–8–42–2; Weekes 7–0–15–1.

Umpires: R. Julian and A. G. T. Whitehead.

At Derby, June 30, July 1, 2. MIDDLESEX beat DERBYSHIRE by an innings and 96 runs.

At Arundel, July 14, 15, 16. MIDDLESEX lost to SUSSEX by 148 runs.

At Manchester, July 21, 22, 23. MIDDLESEX lost to LANCASHIRE by 361 runs.

MIDDLESEX v ESSEX

At Uxbridge, July 28, 29, 30, August 1. Drawn. Middlesex 6 pts, Essex 6 pts. Toss: Middlesex.

A batsman's pitch produced five centuries and three declarations but no result. Haynes and Roseberry shared their first century opening stand of the year and were not parted until after lunch. Then Gatting and Ramprakash both compiled their third Championship centuries of the season – Gatting in three hours and Ramprakash in six. After a slow start, Ramprakash gathered speed on the second day, smashing a six through the windscreen of his own car. Inevitably, Gooch made a hundred, but the best Essex batting came from Irani. Despite a black eye, given to him by a drunk at the ground on Friday evening, he completed a fluent century before Gooch declared 103 behind. The quest for quick runs gave Haynes's wonderful talent full scope; he reached 100 in 103 balls and struck 18 fours. Needing 381 from 92 overs, Essex rarely looked like winning, but the pitch was too good for the Middlesex spinners. Lewis defied them for three and a half hours.

Close of play: First day, Middlesex 364-5 (M. R. Ramprakash 45*, P. N. Weekes 7*); Second day, Essex 180-3 (G. A. Gooch 82*); Third day, Middlesex 175-1 (D. L. Haynes 110*, M. W. Gatting 30*).

Middlesex

D. L. Haynes c Knight b Kasprowicz	63	– c Such b Knight	123
M. A. Roseberry c Irani b Stephenson	88	– c Garnham b Childs	30
*M. W. Gatting b Kasprowicz	108	– not out	81
M. R. Ramprakash not out	123	– c Garnham b Gooch	34
J. D. Carr c Irani b Stephenson	8		
†K. R. Brown c Knight b Gooch	4		
P. N. Weekes c Garnham b Andrew	17		
M. A. Feltham c Kasprowicz b Childs	21	– (5) not out	4
J. E. Emburey not out	26		
B 2, l-b 8, w 5, n-b 52	67	L-b 1, n-b 4	5
1/140 2/227 3/318 4/342 5/351 6/394 7/441 (7 wkts dec.)	525	1/88 2/195 3/272 (3 wkts dec.)	277

K. J. Shine and P. C. R. Tufnell did not bat.

Bonus points – Middlesex 4, Essex 2 (Score at 120 overs: 418-6).

Bowling: *First Innings*—Kasprowicz 31–7–112–2; Andrew 25.3–2–114–1; Stephenson 30–7–95–2; Childs 29–4–75–1; Such 24–1–105–0; Gooch 12–6–14–1. *Second Innings*—Kasprowicz 7–1–24–0; Andrew 10–0–53–0; Childs 13–1–66–1; Such 5–0–31–0; Knight 11.4–0–61–1; Lewis 8–1–32–0; Gooch 3–0–9–1.

Essex

*G. A. Gooch b Weekes	140	– c Brown b Weekes	26
J. P. Stephenson c Gatting b Shine	8	– b Shine	0
N. V. Knight c Roseberry b Tufnell	59	– c Carr b Tufnell	32
N. Hussain lbw b Tufnell	10	– c Carr b Shine	86
J. J. B. Lewis c Brown b Shine	1	– not out	76
R. C. Irani not out	102	– lbw b Tufnell	0
†M. A. Garnham b Shine	23	– b Tufnell	8
M. S. Kasprowicz not out	36	– lbw b Emburey	44
P. M. Such (did not bat)		– not out	0
B 4, l-b 15, w 2, n-b 22	43	B 8, l-b 5, n-b 18	31
1/29 2/154 3/180 4/185 5/297 6/345	(6 wkts dec.) 422	1/5 2/60 3/84 4/204 5/205 6/219 7/302	(7 wkts) 303

S. J. W. Andrew and J. H. Childs did not bat.

Bonus points – Essex 4, Middlesex 2 (Score at 120 overs: 389-6).

Bowling: *First Innings*—Shine 25–5–93–3; Feltham 20–6–47–0; Emburey 19–2–70–0; Tufnell 44–10–125–2; Weekes 22–3–64–1; Gatting 1–0–4–0. *Second Innings*—Shine 12–2–71–2; Feltham 7–1–30–0; Tufnell 35.4–7–88–3; Weekes 13–2–35–1; Emburey 24–9–66–1.

Umpires: V. A. Holder and B. Leadbeater.

MIDDLESEX v GLAMORGAN

At Lord's, August 4, 5, 6, 8. Middlesex won by 80 runs. Middlesex 22 pts, Glamorgan 6 pts. Toss: Middlesex. First-class debut: O. T. Parkin. Championship debut: A. D. Shaw. County debut: G. A. R. Harris.

Both teams had an unfamiliar look. With Fraser and Tufnell on Test duty and other bowlers unfit, Middlesex introduced 30-year-old Gordon Harris, who played one Championship game for Leicestershire in 1986, while Glamorgan, without Watkin, Croft and Metson (missing a Championship match for the first time since joining from Middlesex in 1987) fielded Dalton, Shaw, Phelps and Parkin, who had played two Championship games between them. Perhaps Middlesex took this opposition too lightly; only Gatting punished their inexperience. Glamorgan fared little better, but Gibson made another enterprising half-century, helping them to a lead of 18. However, Haynes batted magnificently for the second successive Saturday, reaching his fifth century of the season, while Carr returned to form. Glamorgan were set 351 on the final day. A century opening partnership gave them hope but, once he had trapped Morris, Emburey exploited the wearing pitch to perfection, taking six for 89, with fellow off-spinner Weekes claiming the other four.

Close of play: First day, Middlesex 207-6 (K. R. Brown 41*, M. A. Feltham 4*); Second day, Glamorgan 273-8 (A. D. Shaw 1*, S. R. Barwick 1*); Third day, Middlesex 368-4 (J. D. Carr 78*, K. R. Brown 37*).

Middlesex

D. L. Haynes c Shaw b Gibson	20	– lbw b Barwick	134
M. A. Roseberry c Cottey b Dale	20	– run out	5
*M. W. Gatting run out	73	– b Barwick	46
M. R. Ramprakash c Cottey b Parkin	21	– c Cottey b Dale	32
J. D. Carr c Dalton b Barwick	2	– not out	78
†K. R. Brown c Shaw b Gibson	45	– not out	37
P. N. Weekes c Hemp b Parkin	7		
M. A. Feltham c Cottey b Gibson	31		
J. E. Emburey c Dalton b Barwick	0		
K. J. Shine not out	14		
G. A. R. Harris b Barwick	11		
B 2, l-b 7, w 2, n-b 12	23	B 12, l-b 8, n-b 16	36
1/42 2/42 3/79 4/92 5/181 6/203 7/233 8/242 9/242	267	1/11 2/97 3/171 4/272	(4 wkts dec.) 368

Bonus points – Middlesex 2, Glamorgan 4.

Bowling: *First Innings*—Gibson 28–7–92–3; Parkin 12–2–45–2; Dale 11–3–42–1; Barwick 21.1–4–63–3; Phelps 5–1–16–0. *Second Innings*—Gibson 21–2–87–0; Parkin 16–4–50–0; Barwick 40–11–113–2; Phelps 16–2–75–0; Dale 4–1–23–1.

Glamorgan

*H. Morris c Gatting b Feltham	20	– (2) lbw b Emburey	69
D. L. Hemp b Harris	41	– (3) c and b Emburey	28
M. P. Maynard c Emburey b Shine	39	– (4) b Weekes	3
P. A. Cottey lbw b Feltham	37	– (5) c and b Weekes	79
A. J. Dalton c Shine b Weekes	44	– (6) c Roseberry b Emburey	9
A. Dale c Emburey b Feltham	6	– (1) c Carr b Emburey	52
O. D. Gibson b Emburey	70	– b Emburey	0
†A. D. Shaw lbw b Emburey	1	– b Weekes	14
B. S. Phelps c and b Weekes	0	– b Emburey	3
S. R. Barwick b Feltham	8	– b Weekes	1
O. T. Parkin not out	2	– not out	0
B 3, l-b 7, w 1, n-b 6	17	B 1, l-b 1, n-b 10	12
1/39 2/94 3/126 4/157 5/173 6/262 7/268 8/271 9/273	285	1/119 2/126 3/131 4/199 5/221 6/221 7/256 8/263 9/269	270

Bonus points – Glamorgan 2, Middlesex 4.

Bowling: *First Innings*—Shine 10–4–35–1; Harris 16–3–61–1; Emburey 33–10–73–2; Feltham 17.3–6–51–4; Weekes 21–4–55–2. *Second Innings*—Shine 6–1–25–0; Harris 11–4–37–0; Feltham 10–1–38–0; Emburey 43–11–89–6; Weekes 30–5–79–4.

Umpires: B. Dudleston and T. E. Jesty.

MIDDLESEX v SOMERSET

At Lord's, August 11, 12, 13, 15. Middlesex won by an innings and 30 runs. Middlesex 24 pts, Somerset 4 pts. Toss: Middlesex.

This match was almost certainly decided by one dropped catch. After a blank first day, Somerset made 248 on Friday, removed both Middlesex openers for 22 by the close and reduced them to 123 for six on Saturday. Five balls before lunch, with Weekes on six, Harden put down a straightforward slip chance. When Weekes was finally out that evening, he had completed a maiden century and added 264 – seven short of the county's seventh-wicket record – with Carr, who finished on 171 not out. Though Somerset were unbeaten in their last eight Championship matches, their batting was unadventurous in the first innings and offered no resistance in the second; Middlesex won with four hours to spare. Tufnell bowled quite beautifully, taking four for 17 – in 26 overs – and eight for 58 in the match. Folland announced his retirement from county cricket at lunch on the final day.

Close of play: First day, No play; Second day, Middlesex 22-2 (M. A. Feltham 3*); Third day, Somerset 33-3 (R. J. Harden 19*, A. R. Caddick 0*).

Somerset

M. N. Lathwell c Brown b Fraser	5	– c Brown b Tufnell	13
I. Fletcher c Brown b Fraser	0	– b Fraser	0
R. J. Harden c Brown b Weekes	61	– c Brown b Shine	20
N. A. Folland c Feltham b Tufnell	27	– (6) b Shine	10
*A. N. Hayhurst c Carr b Fraser	62	– (7) lbw b Tufnell	18
†R. J. Turner not out	41	– (8) c Roseberry b Weekes	9
S. C. Ecclestone c Fraser b Weekes	8	– (9) c Gatting b Fraser	6
J. C. Hallett lbw b Tufnell	3	– (10) not out	3
A. R. Caddick lbw b Tufnell	0	– (5) lbw b Tufnell	16
H. R. J. Trump c Haynes b Weekes	11	– (4) lbw b Tufnell	0
A. P. van Troost c and b Tufnell	9	– b Fraser	2
B 4, l-b 4, w 1, n-b 12	21	B 3, l-b 3, w 1, n-b 6	13
1/6 2/17 3/87 4/140 5/194 6/204 7/209 8/209 9/232	248	1/6 2/23 3/27 4/45 5/57 6/71 7/85 8/105 9/107	110

Bonus points – Somerset 1, Middlesex 4.

Bowling: *First Innings*—Fraser 18–3–35–3; Shine 14–2–41–0; Feltham 14–3–36–0; Gatting 3–0–16–0; Tufnell 24.4–9–41–4; Weekes 24–4–71–3. *Second Innings*—Fraser 11.5–5–16–3; Shine 12–2–48–2; Tufnell 26–14–17–4; Weekes 10–3–23–1.

Middlesex

D. L. Haynes c Turner b Caddick	7	P. N. Weekes b Trump	117
M. A. Roseberry c Hayhurst b van Troost	5	A. R. C. Fraser c Hayhurst b Trump	0
M. A. Feltham c Lathwell b van Troost	34	K. J. Shine not out	0
*M. W. Gatting b Caddick	2	B 1, l-b 3, w 3, n-b 32	39
M. R. Ramprakash c Turner b Caddick	4	1/8 2/22 3/35 4/60 5/83 6/123 7/387 8/387	(8 wkts dec.) 388
J. D. Carr not out	171		
†K. R. Brown lbw b Caddick	9		

P. C. R. Tufnell did not bat.

Bonus points – Middlesex 4, Somerset 3.

Bowling: Caddick 29.4–5–84–4; van Troost 19–1–100–2; Ecclestone 8–3–13–0; Trump 23–3–103–2; Hallett 14–2–69–0; Hayhurst 5–2–8–0; Lathwell 2–0–7–0.

Umpires: R. A. White and P. B. Wight.

At Northampton, August 18, 19, 20, 22. MIDDLESEX lost to NORTHAMPTONSHIRE by six wickets.

At The Oval, August 25, 26, 27, 29. MIDDLESEX beat SURREY by two wickets.

MIDDLESEX v GLOUCESTERSHIRE

At Lord's, September 8, 9, 10. Middlesex won by an innings and 63 runs. Middlesex 24 pts, Gloucestershire 3 pts. Toss: Middlesex.

Middlesex won their fourth Championship match out of five and, as in the previous home game, Carr and Weekes set up a winning position after a modest start. Haynes, Gatting and Ramprakash were out early. The recovery started when Carr joined Roseberry but blossomed when Weekes arrived, helping Carr to add 270 in 47 overs, breaking the county's sixth-wicket record of 227 set by Clive Radley and Fred Titmus against the South Africans in 1965. Middlesex reached 500 by the close. Carr's unbeaten 261, his maiden double-hundred, took 289 balls and included 43 fours. It took his extraordinary sequence of form to 854 runs in seven innings for once out. Needing 364 to avoid the follow-on, Gloucestershire saw their chances quickly disappear when Emburey took three wickets in 14 deliveries. Before the close, Hodgson became his 1,500th first-class victim, a mark achieved only by Eddie Hemmings (three weeks earlier) among current county bowlers. The one surprise was that Gloucestershire held out until after tea on the third day. But Tufnell finished them off with a spell of five for ten in 11 overs.

Close of play: First day, Middlesex 513-7 (J. D. Carr 261*, N. F. Williams 14*); Second day, Gloucestershire 62-3 (A. J. Wright 17*, V. J. Pike 1*).

Middlesex

D. L. Haynes c Russell b Walsh	8	J. E. Emburey c Wright b Pike	16
M. A. Roseberry run out	59	N. F. Williams not out	14
*M. W. Gatting c Russell b Williams	3		
M. R. Ramprakash c Windows b Williams	2	B 4, l-b 16, w 5, n-b 18	43
J. D. Carr not out	261	1/22 2/31 3/45 4/139 5/179 6/449 7/498	(7 wkts dec.) 513
†K. R. Brown lbw b Williams	13		
P. N. Weekes c Walsh b Ball	94		

A. R. C. Fraser and P. C. R. Tufnell did not bat.

Bonus points – Middlesex 4, Gloucestershire 3.

Bowling: Walsh 17–3–54–1; Williams 23–3–124–3; Alleyne 23–6–98–0; Dawson 5–2–9–0; Pike 15–0–74–1; Hancock 6–1–36–0; Ball 21–2–98–1.

Gloucestershire

A. J. Wright c Brown b Williams	6	– c Roseberry b Tufnell	79
M. G. N. Windows b Emburey	16	– c Brown b Williams	23
G. D. Hodgson lbw b Williams	32	– c Roseberry b Emburey	5
M. W. Alleyne c Roseberry b Emburey	2	– (7) c Emburey b Tufnell	3
T. H. C. Hancock c Gatting b Emburey	0	– (8) c Brown b Tufnell	9
†R. C. Russell b Tufnell	14	– (9) c sub b Tufnell	0
R. I. Dawson c Brown b Fraser	22	– (6) c Weekes b Emburey	57
R. C. Williams lbw b Emburey	29	– (10) not out	7
M. C. J. Ball c Brown b Tufnell	45	– (11) c Roseberry b Tufnell	11
*C. A. Walsh lbw b Tufnell	5	– (4) c Brown b Tufnell	1
V. J. Pike not out	0	– (5) b Williams	13
B 8, l-b 6, n-b 14	28	B 8, l-b 21, n-b 14	43
1/19 2/41 3/43 4/43 5/64 6/101 7/117 8/189 9/198	199	1/40 2/55 3/60 4/88 5/213 6/215 7/230 8/230 9/231	251

Bonus points – Middlesex 4.

Bowling: *First Innings*—Fraser 14–7–22–1; Williams 11–5–33–2; Tufnell 26.4–6–62–3; Emburey 27–11–57–4; Weekes 3–0–11–0. *Second Innings*—Fraser 17–4–55–0; Williams 12–0–45–2; Emburey 30–10–60–2; Tufnell 28.5–13–35–6; Weekes 6–1–27–0.

Umpires: J. W. Holder and M. J. Kitchen.

At Nottingham, September 15, 16, 17, 19. MIDDLESEX drew with NOTTINGHAMSHIRE.

THE CHAMPIONS

The dates on which the County Championship has been settled since 1979 are as follows:

			Final margin
1979	Essex	August 21	77 pts
1980	Middlesex	September 2	13 pts
1981	Nottinghamshire	September 14	2 pts
1982	Middlesex	September 11	39 pts
1983	Essex	September 13	16 pts
1984	Essex	September 11	14 pts
1985	Middlesex	September 17	18 pts
1986	Essex	September 10	28 pts
1987	Nottinghamshire	September 14	4 pts
1988	Worcestershire	September 16	1 pt
1989	Worcestershire	August 31	6 pts
1990	Middlesex	September 20	31 pts
1991	Essex	September 19	13 pts
1992	Essex	September 3	41 pts
1993	Middlesex	August 30	36 pts
1994	Warwickshire	September 2	42 pts

Note: The earliest date on which the Championship has been won since it was expanded in 1895 was August 12, 1910, by Kent.

NORTHAMPTONSHIRE

Patrons: The Earl of Dalkeith and
The Earl Spencer
President: W. R. F. Chamberlain
Chairman: L. A. Wilson
Chairman, Cricket Committee: R. Wills
Chief Executive: S. P. Coverdale
Captain: A. J. Lamb
Director of Cricket: P. A. Neale
Coach: R. M. Carter
Cricket Development Officer: B. L. Reynolds
Head Groundsman: R. R. Bailey
Scorer: A. C. Kingston

Rarely in Northamptonshire's history have the performances and the personality of one cricketer dominated a season to the extent that Curtly Ambrose's did in 1994. His non-appearance at the start of the season, when chief executive Steve Coverdale was left baffled and embarrassed at the airport, left the club in turmoil and contributed significantly to a depressing start. But he did appear four days later and by the time he returned to Antigua, one match early because of a shoulder problem, he had largely redeemed himself in the eyes of team-mates and supporters with a succession of superb bowling performances, enabling the side to finish the Championship campaign with a flourish.

Ambrose's haul of 77 first-class wickets – at 14.45, comfortably on top of the national averages – was the best for the county since 1976, when Sarfraz Nawaz took 82. He collected 47 of them in seven games between mid-July and early September which brought six wins and enabled Northamptonshire to finish fifth in the table, one place lower than the previous year. The final playing record – eight victories, four defeats and five draws – was, in fact, identical to that of 1993, when the team was in contention for the title until the end of August.

This time, in contrast, salvaging pride was the principal motivation from a relatively early stage. Any lingering hopes of some consolatory silverware were extinguished when Worcestershire inflicted a narrow defeat – overcoming an inspired and inspiring Ambrose – in the quarter-finals of the NatWest Trophy. Northamptonshire had disappeared from the Benson and Hedges Cup while Ambrose was still in the Caribbean saying he "wanted a break", and could do no better than 13th in the Sunday League, trying 22 players and a bewildering number of permutations without finding a consistently successful one.

Injury and illness dogged many senior players in the course of the season. David Capel endured a variety of fitness setbacks in his benefit year and played only five times in all competitions; Alan Fordham missed six Championship matches with appendicitis; broken bones incapacitated Nigel Felton, Mal Loye and Jeremy Snape for substantial periods, and all the front-line seamers were obliged, at some point, to rest or bowl through miscellaneous aches and strains.

Of all these misfortunes, Loye's badly damaged thumb – sustained while fielding in a benefit game – was the most galling. Having confirmed the rich promise of 1993 with three centuries, each combining concentration with flair, he was ruled out for the last month, and subsequently overlooked for England's winter touring parties. Loye must surely challenge again for international recognition before long. In the meantime it was a source of deep satisfaction when, against Hampshire at Southampton in July, he was one of four county-born players in a winning Northamptonshire side, along with Russell Warren, John Hughes and Andy Roberts. Another local prospect, Kevin Innes, marked time, but two more have been taken on the staff for 1995 – opening batsman Alec Swann and all-rounder Mark Steele, son of former England hero David. Having long been regarded as the United Nations, Northamptonshire can now boast no fewer than eight home-grown cricketers on the books.

However, one of the most conspicuous recent shortcomings, the weakness in spin bowling, was again evident. Before the last match at Chelmsford, in which both Rob Bailey and Nick Cook recorded their best figures of the season, those two, plus Roberts, captured only 35 Championship wickets between them at nearly 55 runs apiece. The signing of the Indian leg-spinner, Anil Kumble, as Ambrose's replacement for one year should bolster that department, but concern persists about the effectiveness of the attack as a whole, judging by the indifferent support Ambrose received in 1994. One of the county's old boys, Neil Mallender, has rejoined from Somerset for 1995 after nine years' absence.

Tony Penberthy produced some testing spells and, like Loye, was deservedly awarded his county cap. Hughes also impressed before injury sidelined him in the closing weeks, but Paul Taylor and, to a greater degree, Kevin Curran were both well below their best with the ball, although Curran's batting prospered and he led the averages.

Notwithstanding his robust contributions in the middle order, and respectable returns from Fordham, Bailey, Loye and the captain, Allan Lamb, there were still too many erratic first-innings displays; only Derbyshire obtained fewer batting bonus points than Northamptonshire's 28, a total matched by Sussex and Gloucestershire. But encouraging signs of progress came from Richard Montgomerie, whose maiden Championship century against Derbyshire on only his third appearance in the competition secured his place for the rest of the summer, as well as Warren and, on Sundays, the flamboyant Tim Walton.

Bailey alone passed 1,000 runs, and emerged from a personal trough in the second half of the season with a magnificent innings to beat Middlesex in one of the best games seen at Northampton for some years. Felton did not play again after breaking a finger against the South Africans in July, and later announced his retirement from first-class cricket at the age of 33, terminating a career which yielded 10,242 runs over seven seasons with Somerset and six with Northamptonshire.

A year which engendered disappointment, frustration and optimism in roughly equal proportion ended with optimism dominant as David Sales, still two months short of his 17th birthday, marked his first-team debut with an assured 70 not out off 56 balls in the final Sunday League match against Essex. Northamptonshire officials, in common with those of most other counties, would dearly love to possess a comparably-talented fast bowler of the same age. – Andrew Radd.

NORTHAMPTONSHIRE 1994

[Bill Smith

Back row: J. F. Brown, J. Lewis, S. A. J. Boswell, C. J. Rika, J. G. Hughes, T. W. Harrison, D. J. Roberts. *Middle row:* R. M. Carter (*coach*), T. C. Walton, A. L. Penberthy, R. J. Warren, J. P. Taylor, M. N. Bowen, A. C. Cottam, A. R. Roberts, K. Russell (*physiotherapist*). *Front row:* N. A. Felton, D. J. Capel, N. G. B. Cook, A. J. Lamb (*captain*), R. J. Bailey, D. Ripley, A. Fordham. *Insets:* C. E. L. Ambrose, R. R. Montgomerie, K. M. Curran, M. B. Loye, J. N. Snape, K. J. Innes, I. Dawood.

NORTHAMPTONSHIRE RESULTS

All first-class matches – Played 18: Won 8, Lost 4, Drawn 6. Abandoned 1.

County Championship matches – Played 17: Won 8, Lost 4, Drawn 5.

Bonus points – Batting 28, Bowling 53.

Competition placings – Britannic Assurance County Championship, 5th; NatWest Bank Trophy, q-f; Benson and Hedges Cup, preliminary round; AXA Equity & Law League, 13th.

BRITANNIC ASSURANCE CHAMPIONSHIP AVERAGES

BATTING

	Birthplace	*M*	*I*	*NO*	*R*	*HS*	*Avge*
‡K. M. Curran	*Rusape, S. Rhodesia*	14	23	4	854	114	44.94
‡R. J. Bailey	*Biddulph*	17	31	5	1,168	129*	44.92
‡A. Fordham	*Bedford*	11	20	1	844	158	44.42
‡A. J. Lamb	*Langebaanweg, SA*	15	22	1	908	131	43.23
‡M. B. Loye	*Northampton*	13	23	3	858	132	42.90
R. R. Montgomerie	*Rugby*	8	15	2	513	151	39.46
A. R. Roberts	*Kettering*	9	12	4	261	51	32.62
R. J. Warren	*Northampton*	11	19	2	531	94*	31.23
‡A. L. Penberthy	*Troon, Cornwall*	16	24	4	615	88*	30.75
‡N. A. Felton	*Guildford*	9	17	1	421	87	26.31
‡D. Ripley	*Leeds*	15	23	9	263	36*	18.78
‡C. E. L. Ambrose§	*Swetes Village, Antigua*	14	16	2	257	78	18.35
‡J. P. Taylor	*Ashby-de-la-Zouch*	11	12	6	68	26	11.33
‡N. G. B. Cook	*Leicester*	10	12	1	98	43*	8.90
J. G. Hughes	*Wellingborough*	4	6	0	47	17	7.83
M. N. Bowen	*Redcar*	4	5	0	18	13	3.60

Also batted: ‡D. J. Capel (*Northampton*) (2 matches) 8, 6, 29; I. Dawood (*Dewsbury*) (1 match) 2*; K. J. Innes (*Wellingborough*) (1 match) 0, 0; T. C. Walton (*Low Head*) (2 matches) 5, 11.

* *Signifies not out.* ‡ *Denotes county cap.* § *Overseas player.*

The following played a total of 13 three-figure innings for Northamptonshire in County Championship matches – R. J. Bailey 3, A. Fordham 3, M. B. Loye 3, A. J. Lamb 2, K. M. Curran 1, R. R. Montgomerie 1.

BOWLING

	O	*M*	*R*	*W*	*BB*	*5W/i*	*Avge*
C. E. L. Ambrose	540	159	1,113	77	7-44	6	14.45
J. G. Hughes	137.2	38	428	14	5-69	1	30.57
J. P. Taylor	278.4	45	971	30	5-62	1	32.36
A. L. Penberthy	378.1	78	1,325	35	5-54	1	37.85
N. G. B. Cook	252.3	74	652	16	3-46	0	40.75
K. M. Curran	401.5	84	1,375	30	4-65	0	45.83
R. J. Bailey	154.1	30	541	11	5-59	1	49.18
A. R. Roberts	242	49	870	17	3-106	0	51.17

Also bowled: M. N. Bowen 87.1–14–310–5; D. J. Capel 33–7–89–0; K. J. Innes 10–3–33–0; R. R. Montgomerie 1–0–10–0; T. C. Walton 20–1–98–2.

Wicket-keepers: D. Ripley 38 ct, 6 st; R. J. Warren 8 ct.

Leading Fielders: A. J. Lamb 17, C. E. L. Ambrose 16.

At Cambridge, April 16, 17, 18. CAMBRIDGE UNIVERSITY v NORTHAMPTONSHIRE. Abandoned.

At Leicester, April 28, 29, 30. NORTHAMPTONSHIRE lost to LEICESTERSHIRE by ten wickets.

NORTHAMPTONSHIRE v GLAMORGAN

At Northampton, May 5, 6, 7, 9. Drawn. Northamptonshire 3 pts, Glamorgan 1 pt. Toss: Northamptonshire.

For the second year running, rain at lunchtime on the final day denied Northamptonshire an almost certain Championship victory over Glamorgan. There was no play on the first day, and only five overs on the third, before the weather made its decisive intervention. Glamorgan, left to chase a contrived target of 301 in 86 overs, had been reduced to 42 for five from 14 overs by Ambrose – beginning his rehabilitation after upsetting the club by failing to appear for the opening game – and Taylor. But Northamptonshire's push was then halted by a thunderstorm and further showers. Although Cottey and the adhesive Croft fell in the last of three short episodes possible after lunch, Glamorgan were able to escape. Fordham, with a second Championship century in consecutive innings, took the batting honours for Northamptonshire, hitting 21 fours in five hours, with Felton, Bailey and Lamb all playing well in support.

Close of play: First day, No play; Second day, Northamptonshire 324-4 (A. L. Penberthy 0*, D. Ripley 0*); Third day, Northamptonshire 338-4 (A. L. Penberthy 7*, D. Ripley 0*).

Northamptonshire

A. Fordham c Morris b Lefebvre	129
N. A. Felton st Metson b Croft	62
R. J. Bailey c Metson b Gibson	58
*A. J. Lamb b Dale	48
M. B. Loye retired hurt	2
A. L. Penberthy not out	7
†D. Ripley not out	0
B 12, l-b 7, w 1, n-b 12	32
1/142 2/233 3/314 4/322 (4 wkts dec.)	338

A. R. Roberts, M. N. Bowen, C. E. L. Ambrose and J. P. Taylor did not bat.

Bonus points – Northamptonshire 3, Glamorgan 1.

M. B. Loye retired hurt at 322-4.

Bowling: Gibson 23–3–73–1; Watkin 24–9–58–0; Lefebvre 25–7–59–1; Dale 14–3–57–1; Croft 32–9–72–1.

Northamptonshire forfeited their second innings.

Glamorgan

S. P. James not out	17	– c Lamb b Ambrose	8
*H. Morris not out	18	– c Felton b Taylor	0
A. Dale (did not bat)		– c Ripley b Ambrose	5
M. P. Maynard (did not bat)		– b Ambrose	6
D. L. Hemp (did not bat)		– c Loye b Taylor	1
P. A. Cottey (did not bat)		– lbw b Ambrose	8
R. D. B. Croft (did not bat)		– b Taylor	35
O. D. Gibson (did not bat)		– not out	0
R. P. Lefebvre (did not bat)		– not out	0
L-b 1, n-b 2	3	B 4, l-b 2, n-b 20	26
(no wkt dec.)	38	1/10 2/17 3/31 4/32 5/32 6/87 7/89 (7 wkts)	89

†C. P. Metson and S. L. Watkin did not bat.

Bowling: *First Innings*—Taylor 3–1–5–0; Bowen 4–1–10–0; Penberthy 3.4–0–9–0; Roberts 2–0–13–0. *Second Innings*—Ambrose 14–4–53–4; Taylor 13.4–4–30–3.

Umpires: V. A. Holder and R. A. White.

At Northampton, May 15. NORTHAMPTONSHIRE lost to NEW ZEALANDERS by eight wickets (See New Zealand tour section).

At The Oval, May 19, 20, 21, 23. NORTHAMPTONSHIRE beat SURREY by three wickets.

At Worcester, May 26, 27, 28, 30. NORTHAMPTONSHIRE drew with WORCESTERSHIRE.

NORTHAMPTONSHIRE v LANCASHIRE

At Northampton, June 2, 3, 4, 6. Drawn. Northamptonshire 4 pts, Lancashire 4 pts. Toss: Lancashire.

Responding to a seemingly generous declaration by Lamb, Lancashire fell well short of a target of 261 in 69 overs which twice appeared to be within their grasp. Gallian and Crawley shared an untroubled stand of 75 before Bailey removed both in four balls. Lloyd and Speak then took them to 154 for three with 18 overs remaining. But after Lloyd was lbw, their challenge was effectively killed off as Taylor dismissed Watkinson and Wasim Akram in one over. It was left to Martin and Chapple to prevent an unexpected home win. The captains were obliged to contrive a run-chase after rain shortened the first two days and washed out the third. Northamptonshire's first innings was built around a 112-run partnership between Curran and Penberthy. Martin achieved his first five-wicket haul in the Championship and Lancashire's reply featured a fluent 69 from Crawley between the showers. Play was also halted briefly on the final morning by a swarm of bees.

Close of play: First day, Lancashire 12-1 (J. E. R. Gallian 5*, W. K. Hegg 1*); Second day, Lancashire 190-4 (J. P. Crawley 69*, N. J. Speak 12*); Third day, No play.

Northamptonshire

	First innings		Second innings	
A. Fordham c Hegg b Wasim Akram	16	– b Barnett	20
N. A. Felton c Hegg b Martin	33	– c Crawley b Gallian	3
R. J. Bailey c Hegg b Wasim Akram	12	– not out	54
*A. J. Lamb c Lloyd b Martin	37		
M. B. Loye c Lloyd b Watkinson	39	– (4) c Lloyd b Barnett	7
K. M. Curran b Gallian	68	– (5) not out	27
A. L. Penberthy not out	79		
†D. Ripley c Gallian b Wasim Akram	3		
C. E. L. Ambrose b Martin	11		
N. G. B. Cook c Crawley b Martin	9		
J. P. Taylor c Crawley b Martin	0		
L-b 4, w 3, n-b 16	23	L-b 6, w 1, n-b 2	9
1/38 2/60 3/77 4/132 5/244 6/253 7/302 8/313 9/327	330	1/14 2/51 3/85 (3 wkts dec.)	120

Bonus points – Northamptonshire 3, Lancashire 4.

In the first innings M. B. Loye, when 18, retired hurt at 119 and resumed at 253.

Bowling: *First Innings*—Wasim Akram 23–6–71–3; Martin 19.3–4–61–5; Chapple 13–1–62–0; Barnett 12–1–48–0; Watkinson 11–0–50–1; Gallian 6–0–34–1. *Second Innings*—Martin 6–3–5–0; Chapple 6–2–8–0; Gallian 5–0–10–1; Watkinson 10–0–40–0; Barnett 6–1–35–2; Speak 1–0–12–0; Crawley 1–0–4–0.

Lancashire

J. E. R. Gallian lbw b Cook	48	– c Taylor b Bailey	29
S. P. Titchard b Taylor	6	– lbw b Ambrose	0
†W. K. Hegg c Ripley b Ambrose	16	– (8) c Ripley b Taylor	11
J. P. Crawley not out	69	– (3) b Bailey	44
G. D. Lloyd b Cook	30	– (4) lbw b Cook	52
N. J. Speak not out	12	– (5) lbw b Bailey	63
*M. Watkinson (did not bat)		– (6) b Taylor	0
Wasim Akram (did not bat)		– (7) c Penberthy b Taylor	0
P. J. Martin (did not bat)		– not out	6
G. Chapple (did not bat)		– not out	0
L-b 4, w 1, n-b 4	9	B 1, l-b 5, n-b 4	10
1/8 2/33 3/115 4/161 (4 wkts dec.)	190	1/1 2/76 3/77 4/154 5/161 6/161 7/205 8/215 (8 wkts)	215

A. A. Barnett did not bat.

Bonus point – Northamptonshire 1.

Bowling: *First Innings*—Ambrose 16–4–37–1; Taylor 13–6–16–1; Curran 17–3–50–0; Penberthy 10–2–36–0; Cook 20.3–7–47–2. *Second Innings*—Ambrose 11–2–21–1; Taylor 17–3–55–3; Curran 10–1–39–0; Penberthy 3–0–21–0; Cook 9–2–26–1; Bailey 19–6–47–3.

Umpires: J. C. Balderstone and B. J. Meyer.

At Hartlepool, June 9, 10, 11. NORTHAMPTONSHIRE lost to DURHAM by an innings and 87 runs.

NORTHAMPTONSHIRE v YORKSHIRE

At Luton, June 16, 17, 18, 20. Northamptonshire won by 160 runs. Northamptonshire 20 pts, Yorkshire 4 pts. Toss: Northamptonshire. First-class debut: R. A. Kettleborough.

Yorkshire made a gallant attempt to score a daunting 485 for victory in a little over four sessions, recording their highest-ever losing fourth-innings total in the Championship. Vaughan's third century in four first-class games, combined with a threatening innings from Richardson, offered them real hope. But once their 144-run stand had been broken there was little resistance from the remaining batsmen, although Richard Kettleborough – on his debut – played soundly for the second time in the match. An eventful opening day saw 18 wickets fall for 298 runs. Little blame could be attached to a bouncy but true pitch; Northamptonshire batted poorly – recovering from 96 for seven – while Yorkshire were undone by Ambrose, who removed Moxon, Vaughan and Richardson in 11 balls. The conditions were put in perspective as Warren, with a career-best 91, and Loye and Curran, with their fourth and first centuries for Northamptonshire respectively, built up a substantial lead, Loye batting diligently for six hours.

Close of play: First day, Yorkshire 147-8 (R. A. Kettleborough 23*, C. E. W. Silverwood 5*); Second day, Northamptonshire 304-4 (M. B. Loye 116*, K. M. Curran 48*); Third day, Yorkshire 147-2 (M. P. Vaughan 76*, R. B. Richardson 27*).

Northamptonshire

R. J. Warren c Blakey b Hartley	11	– c Richardson b Hartley	91
N. A. Felton c Richardson b Silverwood	11	– c Byas b Hartley	5
*R. J. Bailey c Robinson b Stemp	22	– b Robinson	18
M. B. Loye c Byas b Silverwood	15	– c Richardson b Silverwood	132
D. J. Capel b Robinson	8	– c Blakey b Silverwood	6
K. M. Curran lbw b Robinson	15	– c Blakey b Hartley	114
A. L. Penberthy lbw b Silverwood	2	– c Vaughan b Hartley	21
†D. Ripley not out	10	– not out	36
C. E. L. Ambrose b Hartley	31	– not out	29
M. N. Bowen b Hartley	5		
N. G. B. Cook c Blakey b Robinson	6		
L-b 1, n-b 14	15	L-b 11, w 2, n-b 16	29
1/24 2/24 3/60 4/72 5/89 6/96 7/96 8/136 9/142	151	1/17 2/57 3/178 4/191 5/356 6/413 7/418 (7 wkts dec.)	481

Bonus points – Yorkshire 4.

Bowling: *First Innings*—Hartley 21–5–39–3; Silverwood 16–4–49–3; Robinson 17.1–3–51–3; Stemp 7–2–11–1. *Second Innings*—Hartley 41–6–119–4; Silverwood 24–1–101–2; Kettleborough 6–2–18–0; Robinson 32–9–95–1; Stemp 32–12–73–0; Vaughan 30–10–55–0; Grayson 2–0–9–0.

Yorkshire

*M. D. Moxon c Ripley b Ambrose	0	– c Bowen b Penberthy	32
M. P. Vaughan c Warren b Ambrose	0	– c and b Penberthy	117
D. Byas b Penberthy	56	– b Bowen	4
R. B. Richardson c Ripley b Ambrose	0	– c Ripley b Curran	76
†R. J. Blakey c Warren b Penberthy	22	– c Curran b Ambrose	5
A. P. Grayson c Felton b Penberthy	4	– c Curran b Ambrose	3
R. A. Kettleborough not out	24	– c Ripley b Penberthy	25
P. J. Hartley b Curran	15	– c Bailey b Ambrose	4
R. D. Stemp b Curran	20	– b Penberthy	28
C. E. W. Silverwood b Ambrose	5	– c and b Bowen	10
M. A. Robinson lbw b Ambrose	0	– not out	3
L-b 2	2	L-b 8, w 1, n-b 8	17
1/0 2/1 3/1 4/46 5/68 6/93 7/110 8/140 9/148	148	1/70 2/81 3/225 4/241 5/245 6/249 7/257 8/307 9/312	324

Bonus points – Northamptonshire 4.

Bowling: *First Innings*—Ambrose 12.5–4–16–5; Curran 13–7–36–2; Capel 4–1–14–0; Penberthy 8–1–33–3; Bowen 3–0–27–0; Cook 5–3–8–0; Bailey 3–0–12–0. *Second Innings*—Ambrose 29–9–53–3; Curran 19–6–57–1; Bowen 25.3–2–99–2; Penberthy 24–7–87–4; Cook 8–1–19–0; Bailey 2–1–1–0.

Umpires: M. J. Kitchen and P. B. Wight.

NORTHAMPTONSHIRE v WARWICKSHIRE

At Northampton, June 23, 24, 25, 27. Warwickshire won by four wickets. Warwickshire 24 pts, Northamptonshire 6 pts. Toss: Warwickshire. Championship debut: G. Welch.

Lara's duel with Ambrose and his continuing absences from the field provided the main talking points of a fascinating match, won by Warwickshire with three balls to spare. Only Ambrose seriously inconvenienced Lara on the first day; he scored just 12 runs off 45 balls from his West Indies team-mate, who split his helmet when he was 170, but other bowlers escaped less lightly. Lara scored a run-a-ball 197, including three sixes and 30 fours, to equal Sir Donald Bradman's 1938-39 record of eight centuries in 11 first-class innings. It took an outstanding catch to dismiss him, Loye, at long leg, holding a hook that was going for six. Munton's match return of ten for 132 was overshadowed, but it was an outstanding effort on an unhelpful pitch. He and Graeme Welch, who took three wickets in 22 balls on Championship debut, forced Northamptonshire to follow on and then overcame stubborn second-innings resistance from Loye, who batted more than seven hours, Curran and Warren, who was stranded six short of a maiden hundred. Left to score 228 in 38 overs, Warwickshire were set on course by Ostler, with 87 in 80 balls. Although Lara – batting at No. 7 after missing more than 12 hours of fielding with a variety of reported ailments – failed, some improvised shots from Reeve settled the issue.

Close of play: First day, Warwickshire 448-9 (G. Welch 32*, T. A. Munton 24*); Second day, Northamptonshire 17-0 (D. Ripley 3*, N. A. Felton 10*); Third day, Northamptonshire 280-7 (M. B. Loye 99*, R. J. Warren 9*).

Warwickshire

First innings		Second innings	
A. J. Moles c Lamb b Penberthy	32	(6) b Ambrose	10
R. G. Twose c Ripley b Penberthy	35	b Curran	39
B. C. Lara c Loye b Taylor	197	(7) c Lamb b Cook	2
D. P. Ostler c Ripley b Taylor	17	(1) b Cook	87
T. L. Penney c Ripley b Ambrose	39	(3) c sub b Ambrose	43
P. A. Smith b Taylor	1	(4) st Ripley b Cook	4
*D. A. Reeve c Felton b Taylor	5	(5) not out	15
†K. J. Piper st Ripley b Cook	11	not out	7
N. M. K. Smith c Penberthy b Curran	28		
G. Welch not out	35		
T. A. Munton c Lamb b Ambrose	36		
B 6, l-b 14, w 1, n-b 6	27	B 1, l-b 11, w 1, n-b 10	23
1/71 2/86 3/124 4/292 5/303 6/319 7/348 8/365 9/395	463	1/107 2/168 3/190 4/191 5/208 6/213	(6 wkts) 230

Bonus points – Warwickshire 4, Northamptonshire 4.

Bowling: *First Innings*—Ambrose 27.4–10–49–2; Taylor 32–4–139–4; Curran 18–4–53–1; Penberthy 19–2–105–2; Cook 13–3–69–1; Bailey 6–0–28–0. *Second Innings*—Ambrose 13–1–56–2; Taylor 3–0–20–0; Penberthy 6–0–39–0; Curran 6–0–52–1; Cook 9.3–2–51–3.

Northamptonshire

First innings		Second innings	
R. J. Warren lbw b Munton	10	(9) not out	94
N. A. Felton c Reeve b Munton	5	c Penney b P. A. Smith	23
R. J. Bailey c Piper b Welch	54	c Piper b Munton	2
*A. J. Lamb c Penney b Welch	81	b N. M. K. Smith	22
M. B. Loye c Reeve b Welch	3	c Penney b Welch	113
K. M. Curran b P. A. Smith	23	c Piper b N. M. K. Smith	56
A. L. Penberthy c Piper b Munton	21	c Penney b Munton	19
†D. Ripley lbw b Munton	4	(1) c Piper b Munton	16
C. E. L. Ambrose lbw b Reeve	2	(11) b Munton	0
N. G. B. Cook c Piper b Munton	8	(8) c Reeve b P. A. Smith	1
J. P. Taylor not out	4	(10) c Reeve b Munton	26
B 9, l-b 4, w 5, n-b 34	52	B 7, l-b 11, w 1, n-b 32	51
1/11 2/32 3/169 4/181 5/194 6/240 7/252 8/255 9/257	267	1/43 2/43 3/48 4/83 5/205 6/249 7/256 8/341 9/423	423

Bonus points – Northamptonshire 2, Warwickshire 4.

Bowling: *First Innings*—Munton 25.1–4–53–5; Reeve 20–8–29–1; Welch 12–1–58–3; P. A. Smith 14–2–53–1; N. M. K. Smith 12–3–33–0; Twose 9–0–28–0. *Second Innings*—P. A. Smith 30–8–90–2; Munton 41.4–12–79–5; Reeve 17–8–24–0; Welch 26–8–81–1; N. M. K. Smith 51–18–118–2; Twose 10–5–13–0.

Umpires: A. A. Jones and B. Leadbeater.

At Nottingham, June 30, July 1, 2, 4. NORTHAMPTONSHIRE drew with NOTTINGHAMSHIRE.

At Northampton, July 16, 17, 18. NORTHAMPTONSHIRE drew with SOUTH AFRICANS (See South African tour section).

NORTHAMPTONSHIRE v DERBYSHIRE

At Northampton, July 21, 22, 23. Northamptonshire won by ten wickets. Northamptonshire 24 pts, Derbyshire 2 pts. Toss: Derbyshire.

Ambrose pressed home the advantage gained by Northamptonshire's batsmen on the first day, returning seven for 48, his best analysis for the county, and match figures of ten for 96; he also held four slip catches. He was involved in all ten dismissals in Derbyshire's first innings, and in four of the first six when they followed on. The early honours belonged to Montgomerie, the Oxford University captain, who batted fluently for his maiden hundred for Northamptonshire, including 24 fours, on his third Championship appearance. He shared century partnerships with Warren and Bailey, making Barnett's decision to bowl look very unfortunate. With Loye and Curran adding 115 in 22 overs, Northamptonshire achieved their highest-ever total against Derbyshire. Barnett resisted well in both innings, but although Krikken and Base put on 81 for the eighth wicket in the second to make Northamptonshire bat again, the home team needed only five balls to win, after claiming the extra half-hour.

Close of play: First day, Northamptonshire 409-4 (M. B. Loye 57*, K. M. Curran 36*); Second day, Derbyshire 196-8 (A. S. Rollins 42*, S. J. Base 13*).

Northamptonshire

R. R. Montgomerie c Cork b Base	151	– not out	8
R. J. Warren c Vandrau b Barnett	38	– not out	0
R. J. Bailey b Barnett	93		
*A. J. Lamb lbw b Barnett	11		
M. B. Loye c Rollins b Malcolm	79		
K. M. Curran c Cork b Malcolm	69		
A. L. Penberthy c Base b Vandrau	33		
†D. Ripley not out	17		
C. E. L. Ambrose c Base b Vandrau	2		
N. G. B. Cook c Cork b Vandrau	4		
J. P. Taylor c Krikken b Base	0		
B 7, l-b 13, n-b 12	32		
1/105 2/294 3/294 4/342 5/457 6/493 7/522 8/524 9/528	529	(no wkt)	8

Bonus points – Northamptonshire 4, Derbyshire 1 (Score at 120 overs: 447-4).

Bowling: *First Innings*—Malcolm 28–1–98–2; Cork 19–5–61–0; Base 31.5–8–115–2; Wells 21–6–47–0; Vandrau 32–6–97–3; Barnett 23–2–91–3. *Second Innings*—O'Gorman 0.5–0–8–0.

Derbyshire

*K. J. Barnett c Lamb b Ambrose	77	– b Ambrose	50
D. G. Cork b Ambrose	18	– c Bailey b Ambrose	13
C. J. Adams c Ripley b Ambrose	0	– retired hurt	15
T. J. G. O'Gorman b Ambrose	2	– c Ambrose b Cook	51
M. Azharuddin c Ripley b Ambrose	19	– c Curran b Taylor	43
A. S. Rollins c Curran b Ambrose	52	– lbw b Penberthy	7
C. M. Wells c Ambrose b Taylor	2	– lbw b Ambrose	24
M. J. Vandrau c Ambrose b Taylor	5	– c Lamb b Curran	7
†K. M. Krikken c Ambrose b Penberthy	15	– c Loye b Bailey	54
S. J. Base c Lamb b Ambrose	13	– c Curran b Bailey	33
D. E. Malcolm not out	4	– not out	0
B 2, l-b 2	4	B 8, l-b 16, w 1, n-b 2	27
1/33 2/33 3/43 4/107 5/126 6/137 7/147 8/180 9/202	211	1/53 2/107 3/183 4/186 5/220 6/220 7/243 8/324 9/324	324

Bonus points – Derbyshire 1, Northamptonshire 4.

In the second innings C. J. Adams retired hurt at 79.

Bowling: *First Innings*—Ambrose 19.4–5–48–7; Taylor 20–0–75–2; Penberthy 10–2–35–1; Curran 13–4–38–0; Cook 9–4–11–0; Bailey 1–1–0–0. *Second Innings*—Ambrose 19–4–48–3; Curran 19–3–76–1; Penberthy 19–8–36–1; Taylor 11–0–54–1; Bailey 12–2–41–2; Cook 21–11–45–1.

Umpires: D. J. Constant and K. J. Lyons.

At Southampton, July 28, 29, 30, August 1. NORTHAMPTONSHIRE beat HAMPSHIRE by 24 runs.

NORTHAMPTONSHIRE v SUSSEX

At Northampton, August 4, 5, 6. Sussex won by 217 runs. Sussex 22 pts, Northamptonshire 4 pts. Toss: Northamptonshire.

Sussex kept themselves in contention for the Championship after securing only their fourth win at Northampton since the last war, and their first since 1977. Left to score 400 in a day and a half, Northamptonshire capitulated in sorry fashion; Giddins and Jarvis removed the top six before Salisbury and Stephenson tidied up. Stephenson was the principal architect of victory. He passed fifty in both innings, pulling round Sussex from an uncertain 147 for five with Remy on the first day. In between, he destroyed Northamptonshire with some fiery fast bowling, aided by some irresponsible strokes, reducing them to 80 for seven. A brave last-wicket stand between Roberts and Hughes averted the follow-on, but Sussex built solidly on a lead of 129, Speight and Wells adding 146. Although Montgomerie and Loye did their best to wrest the initiative, the visitors won with a day to spare.

Close of play: First day, Sussex 256-8 (F. D. Stephenson 64*); Second day, Sussex 153-2 (M. P. Speight 70*, A. P. Wells 38*).

Sussex

N. J. Lenham c Ambrose b Roberts	42	– c Ripley b Penberthy	14
C. W. J. Athey c Bailey b Curran	42	– c Loye b Curran	20
*A. P. Wells c Loye b Ambrose	16	– (4) run out	62
M. P. Speight lbw b Ambrose	2	– (3) run out	81
C. C. Remy st Ripley b Roberts	60	– c Bailey b Hughes	2
†P. Moores c Montgomerie b Ambrose	17	– c Bailey b Penberthy	9
F. D. Stephenson c Penberthy b Hughes	64	– c Loye b Roberts	54
P. W. Jarvis c Montgomerie b Curran	0	– c Ripley b Penberthy	2
I. D. K. Salisbury lbw b Curran	0	– c and b Ambrose	14
J. D. Lewry not out	6	– not out	0
E. S. H. Giddins b Hughes	9	– c Montgomerie b Roberts	0
B 8, l-b 6, w 1	15	B 4, l-b 6, n-b 2	12
1/79 2/105 3/109 4/112 5/147 6/249 7/256 8/256 9/256	273	1/35 2/37 3/183 4/185 5/192 6/210 7/222 8/262 9/270	270

Bonus points – Sussex 2, Northamptonshire 4.

Bowling: *First Innings*—Ambrose 16–6–31–3; Hughes 21.4–7–66–2; Penberthy 12–3–37–0; Curran 22–6–70–3; Roberts 18–5–55–2. *Second Innings*—Ambrose 21–8–31–1; Hughes 13–3–51–1; Roberts 24.4–4–79–2; Curran 22–7–47–1; Penberthy 13–2–46–3; Bailey 2–1–6–0.

Northamptonshire

R. R. Montgomerie c Moores b Stephenson	29	– c Moores b Giddins	52
R. J. Warren c Moores b Lewry	0	– lbw b Giddins	16
R. J. Bailey c Moores b Stephenson	1	– c Moores b Jarvis	4
*A. J. Lamb c Giddins b Stephenson	24	– c Salisbury b Jarvis	12
M. B. Loye c Moores b Stephenson	1	– c Salisbury b Giddins	53
K. M. Curran b Jarvis	1	– c Athey b Giddins	17
A. L. Penberthy c Wells b Giddins	15	– c Athey b Salisbury	10
†D. Ripley b Giddins	7	– lbw b Salisbury	7
A. R. Roberts not out	36	– c Remy b Stephenson	1
C. E. L. Ambrose b Giddins	4	– not out	1
J. G. Hughes c Moores b Stephenson	2	– b Stephenson	0
B 5, l-b 12, w 1, n-b 6	24	B 1, l-b 6, n-b 2	9
1/2 2/3 3/57 4/66 5/67 6/67 7/80 8/110 9/114	144	1/35 2/44 3/68 4/143 5/154 6/167 7/177 8/180 9/182	182

Bonus points – Sussex 4.

Bowling: *First Innings*—Stephenson 10.1–2–22–5; Lewry 7–0–25–1; Jarvis 15–2–57–1; Giddins 12–4–23–3. *Second Innings*—Stephenson 16–5–28–2; Lewry 8–1–30–0; Jarvis 18–2–58–2; Giddins 12–3–20–4; Salisbury 11–5–39–2.

Umpires: H. D. Bird and K. E. Palmer.

At Bristol, August 11, 12, 13, 15. NORTHAMPTONSHIRE beat GLOUCESTERSHIRE by eight wickets.

NORTHAMPTONSHIRE v MIDDLESEX

At Northampton, August 18, 19, 20, 22. Northamptonshire won by six wickets. Northamptonshire 24 pts, Middlesex 6 pts. Toss: Middlesex.

Bailey, whose recent indifferent form had threatened his place, played a match-winning innings, propelling Northamptonshire to their target of 305 in 64 overs off the last possible ball of a remarkable game. He hit five sixes and 12 fours in an awesome 129 from 116 balls; the winning cover-drive off Fraser also raised his 1,000 for the season. Batsmen flourished on a benign pitch with a short boundary on the scoreboard side. The aggregate of 1,536 runs was a record for a match involving either county. Carr's two centuries brought his tally to 491 in four innings for once out; Fordham drove powerfully during his six-and-a-half-hour stay as Northamptonshire recorded their highest-ever total against Middlesex; and Gatting, with 201 not out in five hours, including one six and 31 fours, joined Gooch two months earlier as the first players since Alvin Kallicharran in 1982, and the first Englishmen since Len Hutton in 1949, to score three double-centuries in an English summer. His declaration inspired an exciting run-chase, Bailey and Curran blazing the last 84 off only 50 deliveries.

Close of play: First day, Middlesex 340-5 (J. D. Carr 132*, P. N. Weekes 33*); Second day, Northamptonshire 269-2 (A. Fordham 123*, R. J. Bailey 85*); Third day, Middlesex 150-3 (M. W. Gatting 80*, J. D. Carr 18*).

Middlesex

D. L. Haynes b Hughes	1	– lbw b Penberthy	21
M. A. Roseberry c Fordham b Curran	72	– b Ambrose	0
M. R. Ramprakash c Ripley b Curran	20	– (4) b Ambrose	25
J. D. Carr c Warren b Ambrose	136	– (5) not out	106
*M. W. Gatting c and b Ambrose	28	– (3) not out	201
†K. R. Brown c Ripley b Penberthy	42		
P. N. Weekes c Montgomerie b Hughes	50		
M. A. Feltham c and b Hughes	8		
A. R. C. Fraser lbw b Ambrose	12		
K. J. Shine not out	13		
P. C. R. Tufnell b Hughes	0		
B 4, l-b 1, w 2, n-b 9	16	B 4, l-b 5, w 2, n-b 4	15
1/1 2/41 3/114 4/208 5/291 6/344 7/371 8/372 9/393	398	1/2 2/38 3/86 (3 wkts dec.)	368

Bonus points – Middlesex 4, Northamptonshire 4.

Bowling: *First Innings*—Ambrose 25–5–73–3; Hughes 17.4–2–60–4; Curran 23–5–67–2; Penberthy 24–4–97–1; Roberts 15–2–71–0; Bailey 5–0–25–0. *Second Innings*—Ambrose 22–7–55–2; Hughes 11–7–22–0; Penberthy 20–1–80–1; Curran 12–0–77–0; Roberts 16–0–85–0; Bailey 4–0–40–0.

Northamptonshire

R. R. Montgomerie c Ramprakash b Fraser	13	– c sub b Weekes	18
A. Fordham c Brown b Fraser	158	– c Carr b Weekes	34
R. J. Warren st Brown b Tufnell	17	– c Shine b Tufnell	24
R. J. Bailey c Carr b Weekes	88	– not out	129
*A. J. Lamb not out	88	– c Ramprakash b Fraser	54
K. M. Curran c Roseberry b Fraser	13	– not out	35
A. L. Penberthy c Gatting b Tufnell	9		
†D. Ripley c Tufnell b Feltham	8		
A. R. Roberts c Gatting b Feltham	12		
C. E. L. Ambrose c and b Tufnell	7		
J. G. Hughes b Feltham	0		
B 7, l-b 22, n-b 20	49	B 5, l-b 7, n-b 2	14
1/38 2/64 3/273 4/357 5/389 6/409 7/432 8/448 9/461	462	1/37 2/70 3/133 4/224 (4 wkts)	308

Bonus points – Northamptonshire 4, Middlesex 2 (Score at 120 overs: 402-5).

Bowling: *First Innings*—Fraser 31–4–114–3; Shine 14–4–50–0; Tufnell 42–7–121–3; Feltham 25.4–5–75–3; Weekes 27–1–73–1. *Second Innings*—Fraser 12–2–58–1; Feltham 4–2–12–0; Shine 2–1–1–0; Tufnell 26–4–111–1; Weekes 19–1–112–2; Ramprakash 1–0–2–0.

Umpires: J. H. Harris and R. Palmer.

NORTHAMPTONSHIRE v KENT

At Northampton, August 25, 26, 27. Northamptonshire won by eight wickets. Northamptonshire 22 pts, Kent 4 pts. Toss: Northamptonshire. First-class debut: T. C. Walton.

Excellent seam and swing bowling, and another outstanding century from Bailey, decided the match with a day and a half to spare. It was Northamptonshire's fifth win in six matches but their first Championship victory over Kent for 17 years. The toss proved crucial; batting conditions were difficult on the first day and, apart from 103 in 22 overs from Taylor and Ealham, Kent struggled against the seamers. Bailey, who scored 115 with two sixes and 16 fours, and Warren were then instrumental in claiming a lead of 95. Although Kent shaped better in their second innings, they were eventually undermined by Ambrose. Having beaten the bat frequently without reward on the opening morning, he made inroads into the middle order and mopped up the tail with three wickets, all clean-bowled, in eight balls. Thereafter, victory was a formality. Montgomerie's fifty took him past 1,000 runs in a season for the first time.

Close of play: First day, Northamptonshire 204-5 (R. J. Warren 50*); Second day, Kent 228-7 (S. A. Marsh 26*, M. J. McCague 9*).

Kent

T. R. Ward c Warren b Taylor	3	b Curran	9
M. J. Walker b Taylor	2	c Curran b Taylor	36
N. R. Taylor not out	67	c Warren b Walton	28
C. L. Hooper c Walton b Taylor	2	c Walton b Penberthy	43
N. J. Llong c Warren b Penberthy	3	c Taylor b Ambrose	6
M. V. Fleming b Penberthy	4	lbw b Ambrose	5
M. A. Ealham c Cook b Curran	52	c Warren b Ambrose	43
*†S. A. Marsh c Ambrose b Penberthy	4	b Ambrose	31
M. J. McCague lbw b Curran	6	not out	18
M. M. Patel b Penberthy	1	b Ambrose	0
T. N. Wren c Montgomerie b Penberthy	0	b Ambrose	2
B 5, l-b 4, w 8, n-b 4	21	B 4, l-b 12, w 3, n-b 8	27
1/11 2/14 3/20 4/35 5/39 6/142 7/147 8/164 9/165	165	1/42 2/56 3/102 4/119 5/137 6/151 7/216 8/244 9/244	248

Bonus points – Northamptonshire 4.

Bowling: *First Innings*—Ambrose 14–5–22–0; Taylor 10–2–39–3; Curran 10–1–41–2; Penberthy 13.3–3–54–5. *Second Innings*—Ambrose 22.2–9–31–6; Taylor 8–0–37–1; Penberthy 16–3–65–1; Curran 17–4–47–1; Walton 10–1–52–1; Cook 1–1–0–0.

Northamptonshire

R. R. Montgomerie c Hooper b McCague	0	not out	50
A. Fordham b McCague	8	run out	70
R. J. Bailey b Patel	115	b Patel	18
*A. J. Lamb c Marsh b Fleming	16		
†R. J. Warren c Marsh b McCague	57		
N. G. B. Cook b Hooper	7		
K. M. Curran lbw b Wren	23	(4) not out	6
T. C. Walton c Wren b Fleming	5		
A. L. Penberthy b Wren	0		
C. E. L. Ambrose b McCague	5		
J. P. Taylor not out	3		
B 1, l-b 8, w 4, n-b 8	21	B 9, l-b 3	12
1/0 2/33 3/76 4/197 5/204 6/215 7/243 8/249 9/256	260	1/113 2/143	(2 wkts) 156

Bonus points – Northamptonshire 2, Kent 4.

Bowling: *First Innings*—McCague 24–7–60–4; Wren 21–2–78–2; Fleming 10.5–0–41–2; Ealham 9–1–26–0; Patel 10–2–29–1; Hooper 7–3–17–1. *Second Innings*—McCague 5–1–11–0; Wren 5–1–11–0; Ealham 6–2–21–0; Fleming 4–1–14–0; Patel 16–1–53–1; Hooper 14.1–5–34–0.

Umpires: T. E. Jesty and K. J. Lyons.

At Taunton, August 30, 31, September 1, 2. NORTHAMPTONSHIRE beat SOMERSET by two wickets.

At Chelmsford, September 15, 16, 17, 19. NORTHAMPTONSHIRE drew with ESSEX.

COUNTY MEMBERSHIP

	1984	*1993*	*1994*
Derbyshire	2,089	2,110	2,216
Durham	—	6,117	5,448
Essex	7,228	8,747	8,120
Glamorgan	3,992	10,643	13,382
Gloucestershire	2,896	3,942	4,030
Hampshire	4,580	5,070	4,950
Kent	5,181	5,101	5,416
Lancashire	10,978	13,464	13,237
Leicestershire	4,000	3,141	4,654
Middlesex	8,014	8,543	8,474
Northamptonshire	1,976	2,123	2,526
Nottinghamshire	3,780	4,552	4,362
Somerset	5,673	5,800	5,732
Surrey	5,660	5,076	5,996
Sussex	4,355	4,106	5,421
Warwickshire	5,219	7,523	8,377
Worcestershire	2,808	4,636	4,921
Yorkshire	11,000	8,139	8,184
MCC	18,000	19,549	19,812
Total	107,429	128,382	135,258

Note: The methods of recording these figures vary from county to county; e.g. corporate membership may be regarded as representing one person or more than one. The TCCB hopes to standardise these procedures.

NOTTINGHAMSHIRE

President: 1994 – C. F. Ward
Chairman: A. Wheelhouse
Chairman, Cricket Committee: A. Wheelhouse
Secretary/General Manager: B. Robson
Captain: R. T. Robinson
Senior Coach: J. A. Ormrod
Head Groundsman: R. Allsopp
Scorer: G. Stringfellow

Nottinghamshire exceeded the expectations of all but a few optimists in 1994. On the face of it, their performance, capped by third place in the Championship, was not all that remarkable for a club which has set high standards in recent times. But it was a considerable achievement given all that had happened during a winter of discontent.

At an acrimonious meeting before the season, members voiced their suspicions that they had not been told the whole truth about the departure of two managers, John Birch and Mike Hendrick, in quick succession. Shortly afterwards, Maurice Youdell was voted out as chairman by his fellow committee-members and replaced by the less abrasive Alan Wheelhouse. The club seemed to be in a bad way. The transformation that followed was largely due to the arrival of Alan Ormrod as senior coach. When they appointed him, the committee knew there was no margin for error; and they appeared to have got it spot-on.

He galvanised the undoubted playing potential, creating tremendous team spirit and a never-say-die approach. As a result, tight situations usually went Nottinghamshire's way. They won four of the first five Championship matches and, at the end of June, were up with the leaders on Sundays. The bubble then burst. A bit of heroism from David Capel robbed them of the chance to go joint-top of the Sunday League on July 3. Four days later, they tamely surrendered at Worcester in the NatWest Trophy. This was followed by heavy Championship defeats against Somerset and Surrey and, to round off the month, they were rolled over by the South Africans. In July, said captain Tim Robinson, "I wouldn't have fancied our chances against a primary school."

But it was impossible to write Nottinghamshire off. Their form returned as suddenly as it left, and they soundly beat the two sides who finished above them in the Championship, Warwickshire and Leicestershire. The innings win over Warwickshire, the champions' only defeat, was the most impressive feature of the season. Contemplating the £14,000 cheque for third place, Robinson said: "Had you offered me this in April, I would have shaken your hand."

Much of the success was due to the seam bowling, which was originally considered suspect in Chris Cairns's absence. Andy Pick's re-emergence, after two lean years, could not have been better timed, while Greg Mike finally repaid the faith shown in him. Together with Chris Lewis and Kevin Evans, they formed a menacing quartet which, on its day, was as good as any attack in the country.

The satisfaction over this was tempered by another episode of Lewis's unpredictability. After the season, he asked to leave Trent Bridge halfway through a lucrative six-year contract, saying he wanted to be nearer his girlfriend in London. This request was flatly refused, although Nottinghamshire might have been more receptive to the idea had it not been for an end-of-season flourish in which his second double-century inside 12 months – against Warwickshire – together with another hundred and three fifties gave him a harvest of 598 runs from seven Championship innings and ensured he finished top of the club's batting as well as bowling averages. What the statistics did not reveal were the occasions he exasperated officials: throwing his bat down after being run out; moaning, after being awarded his county cap, that it was long overdue; and complaining of back trouble in a television interview the day before the Surrey match, 24 hours before he mentioned it to Ormrod.

Inconsistency in the batting remained frustrating. Nottinghamshire relied heavily on Robinson and Paul Johnson, the only two to reach 1,000, who both played in their own familiar style. Robinson reverted to opening, reluctantly, while Johnson was again hampered by fitness troubles. Graeme Archer enjoyed an extended run with some impressive displays, but the two left-handers, Paul Pollard and Jimmy Adams, had mixed fortunes. Fresh from his success in the Test series against England, West Indian Adams found county cricket's daily grind a culture shock. He averaged over 100 in his first month, but barely 23 in the next four. He looked a different player on Sundays, however, scoring 674, and the development of his left-arm spin was a blessing, with Andy Afford suffering a crisis in confidence. Nottinghamshire have two more young spinners, James Hindson and Usman Afzaal, pushing for recognition. The wicket-keeping situation posed a more acute dilemma for 1995. Signing Wayne Noon from Northamptonshire turned out to have been a shrewd move as Bruce French was laid low by a viral infection after only one match. Noon seized the chance to prove his worth, particularly as a gutsy middle-order batsman.

Overall, Trent Bridge became a more harmonious place in 1994. If uncertainties surrounding Lewis's future and the fitness of Cairns, who is due to return in 1995, can be cleared up, then Ormrod's assertion that Nottinghamshire can build significantly upon that progress over the next two years may be well-founded. – Nick Lucy.

NOTTINGHAMSHIRE 1994

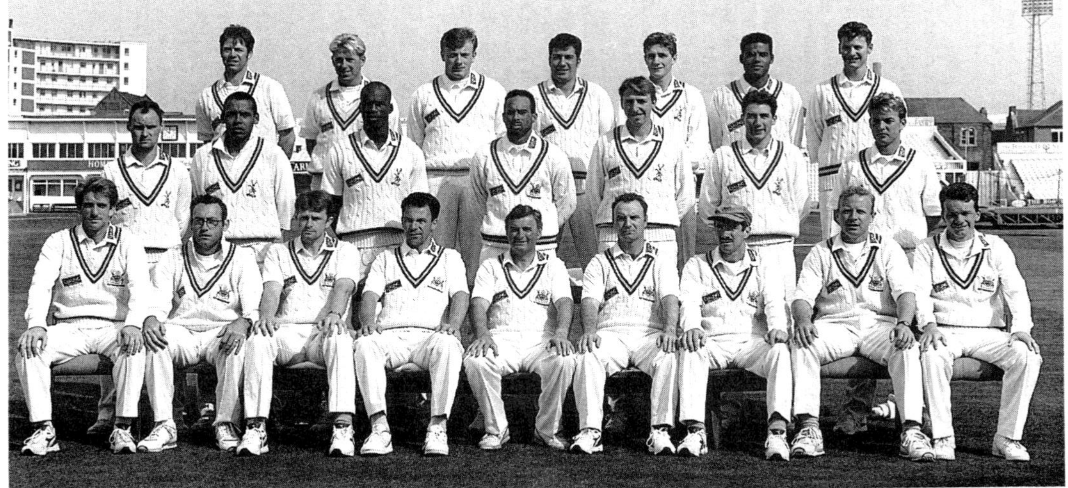

[*Bill Smith*

Back row: G. F. Archer, D. B. Pennett, R. J. Chapman, R. T. Bates, J. E. Hindson, S. A. Sylvester, M. P. Dowman. *Middle row:* M. G. Field-Buss, G. W. Mike, C. C. Lewis, J. C. Adams, M. A. Crawley, W. A. Dessaur, W. M. Noon. *Front row:* P. R. Pollard, J. A. Afford, K. P. Evans, R. T. Robinson (*captain*), J. A. Ormrod (*coach*), P. Johnson, B. N. French, R. A. Pick, M. Newell.

NOTTINGHAMSHIRE RESULTS

All first-class matches – Played 20: Won 8, Lost 6, Drawn 6.

County Championship matches – Played 17: Won 8, Lost 5, Drawn 4.

Bonus points – Batting 39, Bowling 51.

Competition placings – Britannic Assurance County Championship, 3rd; NatWest Bank Trophy, 2nd round; Benson and Hedges Cup, q-f; AXA Equity & Law League, 11th.

BRITANNIC ASSURANCE CHAMPIONSHIP AVERAGES

BATTING

	Birthplace	*M*	*I*	*NO*	*R*	*HS*	*Avge*
‡C. C. Lewis	*Georgetown, Guyana*	12	19	4	881	220*	58.73
‡R. T. Robinson	*Sutton-in-Ashfield*	16	27	1	1,148	182	44.15
‡P. Johnson	*Newark*	15	25	2	936	132	40.69
G. F. Archer	*Carlisle*	14	24	0	860	168	35.83
‡P. R. Pollard	*Nottingham*	16	28	1	863	134	31.96
‡K. P. Evans	*Calverton*	15	21	4	514	104	30.23
J. C. Adams§	*Port Maria, Jamaica*	17	30	3	781	144*	28.92
W. M. Noon	*Grimsby*	17	28	6	583	75	26.50
W. A. Dessaur	*Nottingham*	3	6	0	108	35	18.00
G. W. Mike	*Nottingham*	16	24	3	333	60*	15.85
‡R. A. Pick	*Nottingham*	13	18	6	175	65*	14.58
M. G. Field-Buss	*Mtarfa, Malta*	6	8	4	57	23	14.25
M. A. Crawley	*Newton-le-Willows*	6	11	0	129	45	11.72
‡J. A. Afford	*Crowland*	12	15	6	34	10	3.77

Also batted: R. T. Bates (*Stamford*) (1 match) 0, 6; R. J. Chapman (*Nottingham*) (1 match) 25, 2; M. P. Dowman (*Grantham*) (2 matches) 5, 31, 38; J. E. Hindson (*Huddersfield*) (4 matches) 6, 3, 11. D. B. Pennett (*Leeds*) (1 match) did not bat.

* *Signifies not out.* ‡ *Denotes county cap.* § *Overseas player.*

The following played a total of 14 three-figure innings for Nottinghamshire in County Championship matches – P. Johnson 3, J. C. Adams 2, G. F. Archer 2, C. C. Lewis 2, P. R. Pollard 2, R. T. Robinson 2, K. P. Evans 1.

BOWLING

	O	*M*	*R*	*W*	*BB*	*5W/i*	*Avge*
C. C. Lewis	345.2	69	1,082	46	5-55	2	23.52
R. A. Pick	437.2	107	1,233	46	6-62	2	26.80
G. W. Mike	377.5	88	1,303	44	5-44	1	29.61
J. C. Adams	335.5	125	699	23	4-63	0	30.39
K. P. Evans	394.5	99	1,112	36	4-46	0	30.88
J. A. Afford	466.3	141	1,187	35	5-48	2	33.91
M. G. Field-Buss	203.1	59	450	10	2-50	0	45.00

Also bowled: R. T. Bates 26–6–74–1; R. J. Chapman 17–1–80–1; M. A. Crawley 62–27–101–1; M. P. Dowman 7–1–22–0; J. E. Hindson 106–27–344–8; D. B. Pennett 3–1–9–0; P. R. Pollard 2–0–20–1; R. T. Robinson 2.1–0–31–1.

Wicket-keepers: W. M. Noon 37 ct, 5 st; J. C. Adams 2 ct.

Leading Fielders: C. C. Lewis 18, G. F. Archer 16.

At Cambridge, April 13, 14, 15. NOTTINGHAMSHIRE drew with CAMBRIDGE UNIVERSITY.

At Oxford, April 28, 29, 30. NOTTINGHAMSHIRE drew with OXFORD UNIVERSITY.

At Canterbury, May 5, 6, 7. NOTTINGHAMSHIRE beat KENT by nine runs.

NOTTINGHAMSHIRE v DURHAM

At Nottingham, May 12, 13, 14. Nottinghamshire won by eight wickets. Nottinghamshire 22 pts, Durham 5 pts. Toss: Durham.

Nottinghamshire completed their fifth straight win in all competitions on the third evening, though the day began with the game evenly poised. Durham had wiped out their first-innings deficit for the loss of one wicket and their in-form batsmen Larkins and Morris were together. But they were soon parted and left-arm spinner Afford snapped up five for 48. Adams steered Nottinghamshire to a relatively easy target of 113. On the first day Larkins, who batted for nearly four and a half hours, and the former Nottinghamshire player Saxelby gave Durham a solid start. But the spinners made the breakthrough and the seamers followed it up: nine wickets fell for 102. Nottinghamshire's first innings followed a similar pattern. After Johnson's century prepared the way for a sizeable lead, their last five wickets went for 18; Graveney returned his best figures for his third county, six for 80 on a wearing pitch.

Close of play: First day, Nottinghamshire 4-0 (P. R. Pollard 2*, M. A. Crawley 0*); Second day, Durham 64-1 (W. Larkins 30*, J. E. Morris 11*).

Durham

W. Larkins c Noon b Pick	91	– c Adams b Afford	32
M. Saxelby lbw b Field-Buss	43	– c Noon b Pick	19
J. E. Morris c Pollard b Afford	22	– c Evans b Field-Buss	46
*P. Bainbridge c Noon b Afford	2	– lbw b Lewis	0
J. I. Longley lbw b Lewis	3	– lbw b Pick	2
P. J. Berry c Noon b Evans	3	– c Lewis b Afford	0
†C. W. Scott c Crawley b Pick	13	– c Lewis b Afford	1
A. C. Cummins not out	19	– c Lewis b Afford	8
J. Wood lbw b Pick	0	– b Adams	11
D. A. Graveney c Noon b Evans	29	– c Robinson b Afford	12
S. Lugsden b Evans	0	– not out	0
B 1, l-b 4, n-b 12	17	B 7, l-b 11, n-b 6	24
1/85 2/140 3/146 4/149 5/167 6/191 7/192 8/192 9/238	242	1/35 2/77 3/78 4/102 5/103 6/107 7/119 8/140 9/142	155

Bonus points – Durham 1, Nottinghamshire 4.

Bowling: *First Innings*—Lewis 20–2–67–1; Pick 16–2–45–3; Evans 14.3–3–39–3; Afford 32–12–62–2; Field-Buss 16–9–24–1. *Second Innings*—Lewis 13–1–51–1; Pick 14–5–29–2; Afford 27.3–13–48–5; Field-Buss 9–2–9–1; Adams 1–1–0–1.

Nottinghamshire

P. R. Pollard c Bainbridge b Graveney	50	– c Scott b Cummins 13
M. A. Crawley lbw b Graveney	20	– b Lugsden 45
J. C. Adams c Berry b Graveney	60	– not out 37
*R. T. Robinson c Scott b Graveney	0	
P. Johnson b Graveney	101	
C. C. Lewis lbw b Wood	4	
†W. M. Noon lbw b Cummins	21	– (4) not out 4
K. P. Evans run out	2	
R. A. Pick c Scott b Cummins	0	
M. G. Field-Buss not out	0	
J. A. Afford c Morris b Graveney	0	
B 2, l-b 7, n-b 18	27	B 3, l-b 9, n-b 2 14
1/66 2/85 3/87 4/212 5/217 6/267 7/274 8/285 9/285	285	1/28 2/91 (2 wkts) 113

Bonus points – Nottinghamshire 2, Durham 4.

Bowling: *First Innings*—Cummins 16–2–58–2; Wood 14–1–48–1; Lugsden 18–4–58–0; Graveney 31.5–7–80–6; Berry 4–0–32–0. *Second Innings*—Cummins 7–1–19–1; Lugsden 8.2–0–15–1; Graveney 12–5–29–0; Wood 2–0–12–0; Berry 11–2–26–0.

Umpires: R. A. White and P. Willey.

NOTTINGHAMSHIRE v SUSSEX

At Nottingham, May 19, 20, 21, 23. Drawn. Nottinghamshire 5 pts, Sussex 3 pts. Toss: Nottinghamshire.

Steady drizzle wiped out Friday and Saturday and some rapid juggling was required to leave Sussex with a target of 288 in 84 overs. They appeared to be cruising to victory at 159 without loss and again at 249 for four; Athey almost reached his century. But Nottinghamshire applied the brakes well, thanks to left-arm spinners Afford and Adams, and almost seized victory when these two took four wickets in five balls. Last man Hemmings, once a Nottinghamshire spinner himself, played out the final three deliveries. Nottinghamshire's innings featured Adams's maiden Championship hundred. He batted for almost five hours, but his good work might have been wasted if Evans, who equalled his best score, had not helped him add 178 for the sixth wicket after Nottinghamshire were 142 for five.

Close of play: First day, Nottinghamshire 368-7 (G. W. Mike 22*, R. A. Pick 14*); Second day, No play; Third day, No play.

Nottinghamshire

P. R. Pollard c Smith b Hemmings	35	G. W. Mike not out	22
M. A. Crawley b Remy	19	R. A. Pick not out	14
J. C. Adams c Hall b Salisbury	121	B 3, l-b 5, w 3	11
*R. T. Robinson c Jarvis b Remy	8		
P. Johnson c Stephenson b Hemmings	31	1/31 2/84 3/93 (7 wkts dec.)	368
†W. M. Noon c Wells b Jarvis	3	4/133 5/142	
K. P. Evans c Smith b Salisbury	104	6/320 7/331	

M. G. Field-Buss and J. A. Afford did not bat.

Bonus points – Nottinghamshire 4, Sussex 3.

Bowling: Stephenson 13–2–52–0; Jarvis 27–5–117–1; Remy 17–3–67–2; Hemmings 35–11–64–2; Salisbury 18–4–60–2.

Nottinghamshire forfeited their second innings.

Sussex

C. W. J. Athey b Evans	1	– b Adams	94
J. W. Hall c Noon b Mike	6	– st Noon b Afford	56
D. M. Smith not out	38	– c Pollard b Afford	0
M. P. Speight c Crawley b Robinson	2	– c Noon b Afford	28
C. C. Remy c and b Pollard	13	– (6) c Evans b Afford	20
†P. Moores not out	17	– (7) c Pollard b Afford	15
*A. P. Wells (did not bat)		– (5) b Adams	44
F. D. Stephenson (did not bat)		– c Afford b Adams	0
I. D. K. Salisbury (did not bat)		– b Adams	0
P. W. Jarvis (did not bat)		– not out	0
E. E. Hemmings (did not bat)		– not out	0
N-b 4	4	B 5, l-b 8, n-b 8	21
1/3 2/25 3/30 4/43 (4 wkts dec.)	81	1/159 2/161 3/171 4/211 5/249 6/277 7/277 8/278 9/278 (9 wkts)	278

Bonus point – Nottinghamshire 1.

Bowling: *First Innings*—Pick 5–2–9–0; Evans 7–3–16–1; Mike 3–0–5–1; Robinson 2.1–0–31–1; Pollard 2–0–20–1. *Second Innings*—Pick 8–1–35–0; Evans 10–4–19–0; Afford 30–5–87–5; Mike 4–1–18–0; Field-Buss 9–0–26–0; Adams 23–2–80–4.

Umpires: B. Dudleston and J. H. Hampshire.

At Ilkeston, May 26, 27, 28, 30. NOTTINGHAMSHIRE beat DERBYSHIRE by one wicket.

At Middlesbrough, June 2, 3, 4. NOTTINGHAMSHIRE beat YORKSHIRE by five wickets.

At Basingstoke, June 9, 10, 11, 13. NOTTINGHAMSHIRE drew with HAMPSHIRE.

NOTTINGHAMSHIRE v GLOUCESTERSHIRE

At Nottingham, June 16, 17, 18. Gloucestershire won by three wickets. Gloucestershire 21 pts, Nottinghamshire 7 pts. Toss: Nottinghamshire.

Walsh's 12 wickets for 102 and two determined innings from Russell secured an unexpected win for Gloucestershire. Johnson, leading Nottinghamshire because Robinson was suffering from tendinitis, had answered the call of duty in grand style with a century, after his team were a precarious 86 for four. His chief ally was Mike in a seventh-wicket stand of 103. Mike then took three wickets to put Gloucestershire in danger of following on at 111 for six. But Russell led the recovery, batting more than three hours and adding 95 with Davies, who completed a maiden fifty. Nottinghamshire's collapse began when Smith claimed three victims on Friday evening. Then Walsh grabbed six for 19 in 8.3 overs next morning – five of them lbw – to dismiss Nottinghamshire for 110 and leave his team a target of 206. It was fitting that Walsh struck the winning blow after watchful contributions from Alleyne, Russell and Dawson had paved the way to victory.

Close of play: First day, Gloucestershire 6-0 (B. C. Broad 0*, R. J. Cunliffe 5*); Second day, Nottinghamshire 65-4 (P. Johnson 10*, W. M. Noon 6*).

Nottinghamshire

P. R. Pollard c Wright b Smith	19	– lbw b Smith	14
W. A. Dessaur lbw b Davies	15	– c and b Smith	4
G. F. Archer b Alleyne	23	– b Walsh	21
J. C. Adams c and b Davies	16	– lbw b Smith	0
*P. Johnson b Walsh	129	– lbw b Walsh	28
†W. M. Noon c Russell b Walsh	25	– lbw b Walsh	12
K. P. Evans c Russell b Alleyne	7	– not out	4
G. W. Mike lbw b Walsh	37	– lbw b Walsh	5
R. A. Pick c Russell b Walsh	5	– c Russell b Walsh	2
M. G. Field-Buss not out	1	– lbw b Walsh	2
J. A. Afford b Walsh	0	– lbw b Walsh	0
B 4, l-b 2, w 1, n-b 34	41	L-b 2, n-b 16	18
1/33 2/49 3/82 4/86 5/165 6/191 7/294 8/311 9/318	318	1/10 2/39 3/39 4/41 5/87 6/96 7/104 8/106 9/110	110

Bonus points – Nottinghamshire 3, Gloucestershire 4.

Bowling: *First Innings*—Walsh 17–2–60–5; Cooper 19–6–45–0; Smith 24–4–82–1; Alleyne 23–9–47–2; Davies 18–2–78–2. *Second Innings*—Walsh 16.3–4–42–7; Cooper 5–1–14–0; Smith 20–5–44–3; Davies 3–0–8–0.

Gloucestershire

B. C. Broad b Mike	24	– c and b Afford	12
R. J. Cunliffe b Pick	5	– b Pick	20
T. H. C. Hancock c and b Evans	17	– lbw b Pick	17
M. W. Alleyne lbw b Mike	36	– b Adams	33
A. J. Wright lbw b Mike	7	– c Johnson b Field-Buss	6
R. I. Dawson run out	1	– not out	43
†R. C. Russell not out	63	– c Archer b Pick	39
M. Davies lbw b Afford	54	– lbw b Field-Buss	0
A. M. Smith c Noon b Afford	0		
*C. A. Walsh b Afford	2	– (9) not out	4
K. E. Cooper c Noon b Mike	0		
L-b 6, n-b 8	14	B 12, l-b 6, w 2, n-b 14	34
1/8 2/41 3/54 4/68 5/74 6/111 7/206 8/206 9/218	223	1/21 2/57 3/64 4/74 5/129 6/201 7/204	(7 wkts) 208

Bonus points – Gloucestershire 1, Nottinghamshire 4.

Bowling: *First Innings*—Pick 16–8–38–1; Afford 16–7–43–3; Field-Buss 10–4–17–0; Evans 17–2–53–1; Mike 18–6–49–4; Adams 6–1–17–0. *Second Innings*—Pick 14–2–41–3; Mike 8–2–21–0; Afford 20–5–49–1; Field-Buss 27.5–11–50–2; Adams 20–9–29–1.

Umpires: B. Leadbeater and A. G. T. Whitehead.

At Ilford, June 23, 24, 25, 27. NOTTINGHAMSHIRE beat ESSEX by two wickets.

NOTTINGHAMSHIRE v NORTHAMPTONSHIRE

At Nottingham, June 30, July 1, 2, 4. Drawn. Nottinghamshire 6 pts, Northamptonshire 5 pts. Toss: Nottinghamshire.

An excellent batting pitch meant that the first two innings took up most of three days. Attempts to set up a finish on Monday were wrecked by rain. Nottinghamshire, who had wobbled briefly at 45 for three, eventually built a commanding total of 538, thanks to Johnson and Pollard, who revived them with a stand of 213. Johnson struck exactly 100 of his 132 in fours, in 250 minutes, while Pollard's first hundred of the season occupied five and a quarter hours. Noon took a career-best 75 off his former county and Pick also made his highest score, 65 not out, in his 12th season. Northamptonshire evaded the follow-on without difficulty. Bailey batted nearly five hours for 113, and all his colleagues reached double figures before Lamb declared 121 behind. Indeed, Northamptonshire looked the more likely winners in the early stages of their attempt to score 275 in what was 61 overs until rain intervened.

Close of play: First day, Nottinghamshire 342-5 (C. C. Lewis 51*, W. M. Noon 16*); Second day, Northamptonshire 108-1 (R. J. Warren 57*, R. J. Bailey 30*); Third day, Nottinghamshire 15-0 (P. R. Pollard 5*, R. T. Robinson 6*).

Nottinghamshire

P. R. Pollard c Capel b Cook	110	– c Ambrose b Cook	39
*R. T. Robinson b Ambrose	0	– lbw b Bailey	94
G. F. Archer b Ambrose	12		
J. C. Adams c Cook b Curran	15	– (3) b Cook	6
P. Johnson run out	132	– (4) not out	4
C. C. Lewis lbw b Ambrose	51		
†W. M. Noon run out	75		
K. P. Evans c and b Roberts	43		
G. W. Mike c Ambrose b Roberts	0		
R. A. Pick not out	65		
M. G. Field-Buss c Ambrose b Roberts	23		
B 1, l-b 6, w 1, n-b 4	12	B 1, l-b 5, n-b 4	10
1/1 2/21 3/45 4/258 5/278 6/342 7/413 8/413 9/486	538	1/113 2/147 3/153 (3 wkts dec.)	153

Bonus points – Nottinghamshire 4, Northamptonshire 2 (Score at 120 overs: 373-6).

Bowling: *First Innings*—Ambrose 35–8–77–3; Capel 26–6–65–0; Curran 32–4–134–1; Roberts 33.1–8–106–3; Cook 37–7–111–1; Bailey 9–0–38–0. *Second Innings*—Ambrose 8–3–16–0; Capel 3–0–10–0; Cook 22–4–57–2; Bailey 17.2–4–64–1.

Northamptonshire

R. J. Warren c Archer b Lewis	66	– c Archer b Lewis	15
N. A. Felton c Noon b Pick	13	– not out	43
R. J. Bailey c Pollard b Lewis	113	– not out	25
*A. J. Lamb run out	31		
M. B. Loye c Noon b Lewis	38		
K. M. Curran c Lewis b Field-Buss	40		
D. J. Capel c Pollard b Field-Buss	29		
†D. Ripley not out	30		
A. R. Roberts not out	27		
L-b 6, n-b 24	30	B 1, l-b 2, n-b 2	5
1/31 2/128 3/192 4/277 5/278 6/340 7/363 (7 wkts dec.)	417	1/23 (1 wkt)	88

C. E. L. Ambrose and N. G. B. Cook did not bat.

Bonus points – Northamptonshire 3, Nottinghamshire 2 (Score at 120 overs: 349-6).

Bowling: *First Innings*—Lewis 25–5–65–3; Evans 17–3–47–0; Pick 18–2–69–1; Mike 22–4–56–0; Field-Buss 42–9–105–2; Adams 21–5–69–0. *Second Innings*—Pick 7–2–17–0; Lewis 5–1–18–1; Field-Buss 7–0–21–0; Adams 9–1–17–0; Mike 4–1–12–0.

Umpires: G. I. Burgess and R. A. White.

At Taunton, July 14, 15, 16, 18. NOTTINGHAMSHIRE lost to SOMERSET by 111 runs.

NOTTINGHAMSHIRE v SURREY

At Nottingham, July 21, 22, 23. Surrey won by an innings and 231 runs. Surrey 23 pts, Nottinghamshire 1 pt. Toss: Nottinghamshire. First-class debut: M. P. Dowman.

Benjamin dominated the first day, Bicknell the second and Pigott the third. Not surprisingly, Surrey completed a crushing victory on Saturday evening. Benjamin imposed a stranglehold that was never relinquished, following up his career-best six for 19 against Nottinghamshire in 1993 with six for 27. Bicknell then compiled an unbeaten 235, his maiden double-century, and the longest innings ever in county cricket. Bicknell batted ten hours 38 minutes, 23 minutes longer than Arthur Shrewsbury on the same ground against Middlesex 107 years earlier. He faced 556 balls and hit 33 fours and a six, putting on 156 with Thorpe, 172 with Ward, and 253 with Brown, who cruised to 134. Nottinghamshire – whose attack was weakened when Lewis went off with a back strain – conceded 73 extras, a record for the county. Robinson, forced to retire after being hit on the forearm by Cuffy, provided the only real resistance when Nottinghamshire resumed 479 behind. The tireless Pigott finished the match off with his first six-wicket haul for Surrey. Bicknell was on the field all match, as he had been at Hove in May 1993.

Close of play: First day, Surrey 167-2 (D. J. Bicknell 58*, A. C. S. Pigott 8*); Second day, Surrey 517-4 (D. J. Bicknell 192*, A. D. Brown 95*).

Nottinghamshire

*R. T. Robinson lbw b Benjamin	14	– not out	60
W. A. Dessaur c Hollioake b Benjamin	35	– c sub b Smith	24
G. F. Archer c Kersey b Cuffy	0	– st Kersey b Smith	39
J. C. Adams c Kersey b Benjamin	0	– c and b Smith	0
M. P. Dowman b Hollioake	5	– c Thorpe b Pigott	31
C. C. Lewis b Benjamin	32	– (8) c Brown b Pigott	20
†W. M. Noon c Kersey b Benjamin	17	– (6) lbw b Pigott	36
G. W. Mike c Brown b Hollioake	0	– (7) lbw b Hollioake	0
R. T. Bates lbw b Hollioake	0	– c Kersey b Pigott	6
R. A. Pick not out	3	– c Kersey b Pigott	5
J. A. Afford b Benjamin	0	– b Pigott	4
L-b 4, w 3, n-b 12	19	B 2, l-b 10, w 1, n-b 10	23
1/25 2/26 3/31 4/46 5/90 6/119 7/120 8/120 9/124	125	1/81 2/81 3/118 4/178 5/185 6/185 7/199 8/213 9/238	248

Bonus points – Surrey 4.

In the second innings R. T. Robinson, when 39, retired hurt at 52 and resumed at 213.

Bowling: *First Innings*—Cuffy 12–2–34–1; Benjamin 15.2–5–27–6; Pigott 8–3–16–0; Hollioake 10–2–35–3; Smith 2–0–9–0. *Second Innings*—Cuffy 20–8–53–0; Benjamin 18–7–31–0; Smith 21–4–68–3; Pigott 19.2–7–46–6; Boiling 5–2–16–0; Brown 1–1–0–0; Hollioake 5–0–22–1.

Surrey

D. J. Bicknell not out	235
A. W. Smith lbw b Lewis	0
*G. P. Thorpe lbw b Adams	70
A. C. S. Pigott b Pick	11
D. M. Ward c Dessaur b Bates	81
A. D. Brown not out	134
B 14, l-b 35, n-b 24	73
1/0 2/156 3/179 4/351 (4 wkts dec.)	604

A. J. Hollioake, †G. J. Kersey, J. Boiling, J. E. Benjamin and C. E. Cuffy did not bat.

Bonus points – Surrey 3, Nottinghamshire 1 (Score at 120 overs: 323-3).

Bowling: Pick 36–6–125–1; Lewis 2–0–6–1; Mike 27–4–131–0; Afford 61–19–145–0; Bates 26–6–74–1; Adams 33–13–52–1; Dowman 7–1–22–0.

Umpires: B. Dudleston and P. B. Wight.

At Nottingham, July 27, 28, 29. NOTTINGHAMSHIRE lost to SOUTH AFRICANS by 134 runs (See South African tour section).

NOTTINGHAMSHIRE v LEICESTERSHIRE

At Nottingham, August 4, 5, 6, 8. Nottinghamshire won by six wickets. Nottinghamshire 23 pts, Leicestershire 7 pts. Toss: Leicestershire.

A dour contest in which Leicestershire held the upper hand for the first two days turned dramatically in Nottinghamshire's favour on the third afternoon. Although Leicestershire had been pegged back by Mike after being handsomely placed at 226 for three, they then reduced the home side to 179 for five. But Lewis, playing his first Championship game against his former county, hammered 95, including two sixes and 14 fours. That enabled Nottinghamshire to grasp a slender first-innings lead of 19, which soon looked decisive as Leicestershire slipped to 109 for six by the close of the third day, three of them to Afford. Despite a valiant 91 from Whitaker, Nottinghamshire were left to score only 170. Pollard and Archer did most of the work, making watchful half-centuries. Desperate for spin, Briers asked Mullally to bowl slow left-arm. It was not very slow, and the wicket-keeper put on a helmet, but it did dismiss Adams one short of victory.

Close of play: First day, Leicestershire 181-3 (T. J. Boon 43*, V. J. Wells 11*); Second day, Nottinghamshire 145-2 (G. F. Archer 31*, J. C. Adams 17*); Third day, Leicestershire 109-6 (J. J. Whitaker 49*, G. J. Parsons 0*).

Leicestershire

P. V. Simmons c and b Afford	54	– lbw b Evans	6
*N. E. Briers b Mike	58	– c Lewis b Afford	26
T. J. Boon b Mike	70	– c Noon b Pick	0
J. J. Whitaker c Lewis b Evans	11	– b Lewis	91
V. J. Wells b Afford	32	– c Archer b Adams	9
B. F. Smith lbw b Mike	5	– lbw b Afford	0
†P. A. Nixon b Afford	4	– lbw b Afford	7
G. J. Parsons not out	37	– c Archer b Afford	5
A. R. K. Pierson b Mike	0	– not out	13
D. J. Millns b Pick	26	– lbw b Lewis	0
A. D. Mullally b Pick	0	– c Noon b Adams	0
L-b 9, w 2, n-b 10	21	B 8, l-b 11, n-b 12	31
1/84 2/144 3/163 4/226 5/240 6/247 7/250 8/253 9/314	318	1/9 2/18 3/71 4/91 5/92 6/108 7/120 8/187 9/187	188

Bonus points – Leicestershire 3, Nottinghamshire 4.

Bowling: *First Innings*—Pick 20.3–2–65–2; Lewis 21–2–67–0; Evans 27–7–65–1; Afford 27–8–62–3; Mike 24–9–50–4. *Second Innings*—Pick 10–4–21–1; Evans 5–0–18–1; Afford 23–5–73–4; Lewis 9–2–22–2; Mike 3–1–8–0; Adams 22.5–11–27–2.

Nottinghamshire

P. R. Pollard c Wells b Mullally	28	– lbw b Parsons	61
*R. T. Robinson c Nixon b Mullally	55	– lbw b Pierson	6
G. F. Archer c Nixon b Wells	35	– c Smith b Wells	58
J. C. Adams b Mullally	17	– b Mullally	3
P. Johnson b Simmons	18	– not out	21
C. C. Lewis c Nixon b Parsons	95	– not out	0
†W. M. Noon b Pierson	24		
K. P. Evans c Parsons b Wells	22		
G. W. Mike b Mullally	14		
R. A. Pick b Mullally	0		
J. A. Afford not out	0		
B 9, l-b 6, n-b 14	29	B 5, l-b 9, w 1, n-b 6	21
1/91 2/92 3/148 4/154 5/179 6/233 7/278 8/305 9/307	337	1/10 2/136 3/136 4/169	(4 wkts) 170

Bonus points – Nottinghamshire 3, Leicestershire 4 (Score at 120 overs: 327-9).

Bowling: *First Innings*—Mullally 34–9–85–5; Millns 9–0–52–0; Parsons 19–6–53–1; Pierson 27–6–60–1; Wells 22–6–56–2; Simmons 13–5–16–1. *Second Innings*—Mullally 14–6–23–1; Pierson 22.1–5–70–1; Parsons 13–5–34–1; Simmons 4–1–6–0; Wells 7–2–23–1.

Umpires: K. J. Lyons and N. T. Plews.

At Birmingham, August 11, 12, 13, 15. NOTTINGHAMSHIRE beat WARWICKSHIRE by an innings and 43 runs.

At Kidderminster, August 18, 19, 20, 22. NOTTINGHAMSHIRE lost to WORCESTERSHIRE by five wickets.

NOTTINGHAMSHIRE v LANCASHIRE

At Nottingham, August 25, 26, 27, 29. Lancashire won by an innings and 148 runs. Lancashire 23 pts, Nottinghamshire 3 pts. Toss: Nottinghamshire.

The match followed a similar pattern to that against Surrey in July. Again, Nottinghamshire won the toss, paid a heavy price for poor batting – they fell away from 74 without loss – then conceded a massive total including a double-hundred. The game had seemed finely balanced, as Lancashire struggled to 245 for six. However, Crawley, omitted from the limited-overs internationals but batting for a place on the Ashes tour, was already well set. He went on to 250, the third time he had reached that score in nine months. His innings spanned seven and a half hours and contained 33 fours and two sixes. It equalled J. T. Tyldesley's 1905 record for Lancashire against Nottinghamshire. Crawley shared in a stand of 235 with Hegg as Lancashire built up a lead of 325. They had Nottinghamshire at 82 for six by the close and only an unbeaten 60 from Mike prolonged the game past lunch on the final day.

Close of play: First day, Nottinghamshire 207-8 (G. W. Mike 14*, R. J. Chapman 10*); Second day, Lancashire 265-6 (J. P. Crawley 79*, W. K. Hegg 4*); Third day, Nottinghamshire 82-6 (K. P. Evans 9*, G. W. Mike 7*).

Nottinghamshire

P. R. Pollard lbw b Chapple	44	– c Austin b Martin	3
*R. T. Robinson b Yates	42	– b Chapple	2
G. F. Archer c Hegg b Austin	9	– lbw b Chapple	0
P. Johnson c Chapple b Martin	48	– run out	34
J. C. Adams lbw b Yates	34	– c Martin b Watkinson	25
†W. M. Noon b Yates	0	– b Watkinson	0
K. P. Evans run out	0	– b Chapple	23
G. W. Mike c Hegg b Watkinson	32	– not out	60
J. E. Hindson c Speak b Yates	3	– c Crawley b Chapple	11
R. J. Chapman c Speak b Watkinson	25	– c Crawley b Watkinson	2
J. A. Afford not out	2	– c Speak b Watkinson	10
B 1, l-b 2	3	B 4, l-b 3	7
1/74 2/92 3/117 4/166 5/171 6/172 7/181 8/185 9/239	242	1/4 2/6 3/14 4/57 5/57 6/72 7/124 8/146 9/167	177

Bonus points – Nottinghamshire 1, Lancashire 3 (Score at 120 overs: 235-8).

Bowling: *First Innings*—Martin 27–8–57–1; Chapple 23–9–50–1; Watkinson 26.3–9–56–2; Austin 15–7–21–1; Yates 34–12–55–4. *Second Innings*—Martin 15–4–33–1; Chapple 21–7–64–4; Austin 7–1–27–0; Watkinson 26–15–36–4; Yates 7–3–10–0.

Lancashire

M. E. Harvey lbw b Mike	23
S. P. Titchard lbw b Mike	47
J. P. Crawley c Robinson b Hindson	250
N. J. Speak b Evans	30
G. D. Lloyd c and b Adams	18
I. D. Austin lbw b Hindson	17
*M. Watkinson b Chapman	27
†W. K. Hegg st Noon b Afford	66
G. Yates lbw b Evans	0
P. J. Martin lbw b Mike	28
G. Chapple not out	26
B 6, l-b 5, n-b 24	35
1/74 2/75 3/135 4/166 5/209 6/245 7/480 8/483 9/520	567

Bonus points – Lancashire 4, Nottinghamshire 2 (Score at 120 overs: 374-6).

Bowling: Evans 31–5–104–2; Chapman 17–1–80–1; Afford 50–13–131–1; Mike 26.3–3–101–3; Hindson 34–9–111–2; Adams 6–0–29–1.

Umpires: J. D. Bond and J. H. Harris.

NOTTINGHAMSHIRE v GLAMORGAN

At Worksop, August 30, 31, September 1, 2. Nottinghamshire won by an innings and 37 runs. Nottinghamshire 24 pts, Glamorgan 2 pts. Toss: Nottinghamshire.

The Central Avenue pitch lived up to its reputation for being at its best on the first day. On his own club ground, Archer hit a career-best 168, with 23 fours and three sixes, while Robinson just missed his hundred and Johnson and Lewis added attractive half-centuries. Showers disrupted the second day – and cost Glamorgan the services of Butcher, who slipped and broke his ankle during a rain break, trying to vault a small wall round the boundary, reportedly on his way for fish and chips. But the pitch was now showing signs of wear, and despite some defiance from Maynard and Croft, who hit three sixes into the river, Glamorgan followed on 255 behind. Briefly encouraged by Maynard and Morris, opening with a stand of 114, they were wrecked by Hindson, who took the first five wickets – his best figures in the Championship – including four for one in 21 balls. Lewis sealed Nottinghamshire's win with his sixth wicket of the match, soon after learning he had been omitted from England's touring party.

Close of play: First day, Nottinghamshire 352-4 (G. F. Archer 146*, C. C. Lewis 3*); Second day, Glamorgan 4-0 (M. P. Maynard 1*, H. Morris 3*); Third day, Glamorgan 29-0 (M. P. Maynard 8*, H. Morris 16*).

Nottinghamshire

P. R. Pollard b Dale	26
*R. T. Robinson c Metson b Gibson	99
G. F. Archer c Metson b Barwick	168
P. Johnson c Croft b Dale	51
J. C. Adams c Morris b Barwick	2
C. C. Lewis not out	68
†W. M. Noon c Hemp b Watkin	8
K. P. Evans not out	16
B 1, l-b 17, w 6, n-b 14	38
1/57 2/226 3/317 4/343 5/409 6/446 (6 wkts dec.)	476

G. W. Mike, J. E. Hindson and J. A. Afford did not bat.

Bonus points – Nottinghamshire 4, Glamorgan 1 (Score at 120 overs: 384-4).

Bowling: Gibson 20–7–79–1; Watkin 35–5–107–1; Barwick 38–8–122–2; Dale 15–4–44–2; Butcher 11–1–42–0; Croft 24–6–64–0.

Glamorgan

First innings		Second innings	
M. P. Maynard c Noon b Lewis	69	– b Hindson	58
*H. Morris c Noon b Lewis	4	– c Evans b Hindson	51
D. L. Hemp c Hindson b Mike	20	– c Afford b Hindson	10
A. Dale c Noon b Lewis	25	– c Lewis b Hindson	0
P. A. Cottey c Robinson b Afford	31	– b Lewis	43
O. D. Gibson st Noon b Afford	1	– c Robinson b Hindson	0
R. D. B. Croft st Noon b Afford	42	– run out	36
†C. P. Metson lbw b Evans	0	– lbw b Lewis	1
S. L. Watkin c Pollard b Evans	1	– c sub b Lewis	4
S. R. Barwick not out	6	– not out	0
G. P. Butcher absent injured		– absent injured	
L-b 6, n-b 16	22	B 4, l-b 3, w 1, n-b 7	15
1/13 2/50 3/115 4/142 5/153 6/170 7/179 8/185 9/221	221	1/114 2/128 3/129 4/130 5/130 6/201 7/214 8/215 9/218	218

Bonus points – Glamorgan 1, Nottinghamshire 4.

Bowling: *First Innings*—Lewis 22–4–75–3; Evans 21–3–39–2; Mike 6–1–16–1; Hindson 9–3–28–0; Afford 19.4–6–57–3. *Second Innings*—Lewis 14–4–51–3; Mike 4–0–21–0; Afford 29–9–56–0; Adams 5–2–11–0; Evans 6–2–19–0; Hindson 21–6–53–5.

Umpires: A. A. Jones and K. E. Palmer.

NOTTINGHAMSHIRE v MIDDLESEX

At Nottingham, September 15, 16, 17, 19. Drawn. Nottinghamshire 4 pts, Middlesex 3 pts. Toss: Middlesex.

Nottinghamshire, lying third, and Middlesex, fourth, were both looking for an outright win to claim the runners-up spot. But, as in 1993, the final Championship match at Trent Bridge was ruined by the weather, which washed out the first and last days as well as half the second. The one highlight was an unbeaten century from Lewis, who had scored 598 runs in his last seven Championship innings of the summer, a sequence that included a double-hundred and three other scores over fifty. The teams went into the final day hoping for a contrived finish, but the rain gave neither side a chance.

Close of play: First day, No play; Second day, Nottinghamshire 127-4 (P. Johnson 27*, G. W. Mike 4*); Third day, Middlesex 52-0 (D. L. Haynes 24*, M. A. Roseberry 23*).

Nottinghamshire

P. R. Pollard lbw b Fraser	2	M. P. Dowman b Emburey	38
*R. T. Robinson c Gatting b Emburey	37	†W. M. Noon not out	23
G. F. Archer c Brown b Johnson	19	L-b 9, w 1, n-b 28	38
P. Johnson b Fraser	48		
J. C. Adams c Carr b Williams	19	1/2 2/66 3/66	(7 wkts dec.) 350
G. W. Mike c Brown b Fraser	18	4/119 5/155	
C. C. Lewis not out	108	6/184 7/296	

K. P. Evans and D. B. Pennett did not bat.

Bonus points – Nottinghamshire 4, Middlesex 3.

Bowling: Fraser 24–5–53–3; Williams 24.3–4–102–1; Johnson 18–3–73–1; Emburey 18–7–42–2; Tufnell 25–3–71–0.

Middlesex

D. L. Haynes not out	24
M. A. Roseberry not out	23
L-b 4, w 1	5
	(no wkt) 52

*M. W. Gatting, M. R. Ramprakash, J. D. Carr, †K. R. Brown, R. L. Johnson, J. E. Emburey, A. R. C. Fraser, N. F. Williams and P. C. R. Tufnell did not bat.

Bowling: Lewis 6–3–11–0; Evans 8–3–16–0; Mike 5.3–1–12–0; Pennett 3–1–9–0.

Umpires: J. D. Bond and D. J. Constant.

SOMERSET

President: J. Luff
Chairman: R. Parsons
Chairman, Cricket Committee: B. C. Rose
Chief Executive: P. W. Anderson
Captain: A. N. Hayhurst
Director of Cricket: R. M. H. Cottam
Coach: P. J. Robinson
Head Groundsman: P. Frost
Scorer: D. A. Oldam

Once again, Somerset won nothing and failed to make a real challenge for any major prize, but there was enough success and compelling cricket to retain interest and generate future hopes.

The "if only" syndrome figured prominently in 1994. If only Somerset had displayed all through the season their form from June to mid-August, then anything would have been possible. As it was, the first few weeks were dreadful. They lost their first eight competitive matches; Andrew Caddick and Neil Mallender were soon laid low by injury; and, with Mushtaq Ahmed, perhaps jaded by his winter exertions, slow to find real form, the scene was bleak.

Then came June, and Somerset began a run of seven Championship successes (four of them without Mushtaq) in ten games; four wins in six Sunday matches; and their best limited-overs performance of the year, in the NatWest Trophy at Headingley. This was a splendid recovery, reflecting credit on all concerned, and most especially on the new captain, Andy Hayhurst, who was appointed only in January, almost, it seemed, by default. Unhappily, the last few weeks, with all-rounder Graham Rose missing several matches through injury, were more like the first month and they dropped from fifth to 11th in the Championship. Sunday League performances, although still unconvincing, enabled them to transfer the wooden spoon to Gloucestershire. But the team reserved their worst performance of the year for their largest home crowd, in the NatWest quarter-final, when Warwickshire crushed them with 35 overs to spare, Somerset showing a disturbing lack of fibre.

The discovery of the year was undoubtedly Marcus Trescothick, the 18-year-old left-handed opener born in Keynsham. Having suffered an awful first-class baptism in 1993 (14 runs in six innings), he made only seven at No. 4 against Lancashire, was promoted to open against Hampshire, dropped on two – then scored 81 and never looked back. Under-19 calls – he was named captain of the team to tour the West Indies – restricted him to 20 Championship innings, during which he scored two centuries (the first at Bath) and eight fifties, at an average of 48.63, besides some excellent one-day efforts. His safe fielding at second slip was a bonus and an equable, realistic temperament helped to suggest a bright future. After his Test match traumas in 1993, Mark Lathwell came back well with 1,230 first-class runs, and this young opening pair must be among the most attractive in the game.

Most suitably and capably, Hayhurst led the averages, with 1,250 at 52.08. Richard Harden, the most experienced batsman and regular No. 3, was something of a disappointment despite reasonable-looking figures. Nick Folland played most of the season, regularly getting into the twenties but not often further. It was a shock when he resigned in August, deciding that regular first-class cricket was not for him. His retirement was a loss to the game and to Somerset, who tended to lack sparkle after the openers had gone, which was especially damaging in one-day cricket. Simon Ecclestone and Piran Holloway showed promise, but have some way to go, and there was clearly a need for more attacking batting, which may be resolved by the signing of Peter Bowler from Derbyshire.

Despite missing six Championship games, Caddick took 51 wickets and hoped to get his shin trouble sorted out during the winter. Mallender was out for half the season, and then left for his former county, Northamptonshire, but Rose had another good year, although his Championship batting tailed off. Yet again, Andre van Troost was an infuriating combination of splendid aggression, which could rattle the best, and a wild mixture of no-balls and wides, to the despair of his many well-wishers. The loss of Mushtaq earlier than expected in July, when Pakistan demanded his return for the tour of Sri Lanka, was a heavy blow. It was the more frustrating because he had just taken 12 wickets against Worcestershire, indicating that he was recovering his standards of 1993, and it was good news that the side did not buckle on his departure.

The Championship fielding was generally good. Wicket-keeper Rob Turner, very mobile for such a big man, played in every first-class match, made catches out of half-chances and missed very little. His batting disappointed but his cap was well-deserved, as was that of off-spinner Harvey Trump, whose 12 wickets won the Sussex match, and who must be one of the best gullies in the country.

Although there were days which argued a character flaw, some encouraging results were achieved from adversity, and despite some evil weather at Taunton in May and September, crowds were good generally; weather and results at the two festivals were excellent. The county made a profit of £106,000 on the year and Philip Frost won the groundsman of the year award. The Second Eleven, well led by the former first-team wicket-keeper Neil Burns, won their Championship by a large margin, and for the first time. However, an original staff of 27 inevitably produced a strong side, which meant no room for trialists. The wide gulf between this and the Championship was recognised, sadly, with six of them, including Burns, being adjudged surplus to future requirements. With Ian Fletcher as well as Folland resigning, there will now be more room for experiment.

Finally, any remaining ugly memories of 1986 were moved further into oblivion by the graceful way Ian Botham publicly accepted honorary life membership of Somerset, with whom, he said, he spent the happiest days of his cricketing life. – Eric Hill.

SOMERSET 1994

[*Bill Smith*

Back row: N. A. Folland, I. A. Bond, P. R. Clifford, V. P. Clarke, A. P. van Troost, P. J. Bird, R. J. Turner, H. R. J. Trump. *Middle row:* P. C. L. Holloway, K. J. Parsons, M. E. Trescothick, J. I. D. Kerr, J. C. Hallett, K. A. Parsons, I. Fletcher, A. Payne. *Front row:* P. J. Robinson (*coach*), R. J. Harden, N. D. Burns, R. M. H. Cottam (*director of cricket*), C. Tate (*vice-chairman*), A. N. Hayhurst (*captain*), N. A. Mallender, M. N. Lathwell, G. D. Rose. *Insets:* Mushtaq Ahmed, A. R. Caddick.

SOMERSET RESULTS

All first-class matches – Played 18: Won 7, Lost 7, Drawn 4.

County Championship matches – Played 17: Won 7, Lost 7, Drawn 3.

Bonus points – Batting 32, Bowling 47.

Competition placings – Britannic Assurance County Championship, 11th; NatWest Bank Trophy, q-f; Benson and Hedges Cup, preliminary round; AXA Equity & Law League, 16th.

BRITANNIC ASSURANCE CHAMPIONSHIP AVERAGES

BATTING

	Birthplace	*M*	*I*	*NO*	*R*	*HS*	*Avge*
‡A. N. Hayhurst	*Manchester*	17	29	6	1,166	121	50.69
M. E. Trescothick	*Keynsham*	11	20	1	924	121	48.63
‡R. J. Harden	*Bridgwater*	17	30	5	1,055	131*	42.20
‡M. N. Lathwell	*Bletchley*	17	31	1	1,219	206	40.63
N. A. Folland	*Bristol*	12	21	1	642	91	32.10
‡N. A. Mallender	*Kirk Sandall*	8	12	3	270	43*	30.00
‡G. D. Rose	*Tottenham*	15	23	2	532	121	25.33
‡R. J. Turner	*Malvern*	17	26	4	433	64*	19.68
P. C. L. Holloway	*Helston*	4	6	0	114	50	19.00
‡H. R. J. Trump	*Taunton*	13	20	4	276	45*	17.25
I. Fletcher	*Sawbridgeworth*	5	9	1	128	54*	16.00
‡Mushtaq Ahmed§	*Sahiwal, Pakistan*	8	13	3	145	38	14.50
‡A. R. Caddick	*Christchurch, New Zealand*	11	17	2	211	58*	14.06
V. P. Clarke	*Liverpool*	2	4	0	46	38	11.50
K. A. Parsons	*Taunton*	3	5	1	38	16	9.50
A. P. van Troost	*Schiedam, Netherlands*	13	17	5	107	33	8.91
S. C. Ecclestone	*Great Dunmow*	3	5	0	42	24	8.40
J. C. Hallett	*Yeovil*	3	6	1	21	10	4.20

Also batted: P. J. Bird (*Bristol*) (2 matches) 0*, 7, 5; M. Dimond (*Taunton*) (3 matches) 25*, 9; B. T. P. Donelan (*Park Royal*) (1 match) 0; J. I. D. Kerr (*Bolton*) (1 match) 1, 4; A. Payne (*Rossendale*) (1 match) 34.

* *Signifies not out.* ‡ *Denotes county cap.* § *Overseas player.*

The following played a total of nine three-figure innings for Somerset in County Championship matches – R. J. Harden 2, A. N. Hayhurst 2, M. N. Lathwell 2, M. E. Trescothick 2, G. D. Rose 1.

BOWLING

	O	*M*	*R*	*W*	*BB*	*5W/i*	*Avge*
A. R. Caddick	347.3	67	1,126	49	6-51	3	22.97
G. D. Rose	324.1	67	1,078	42	4-40	0	25.66
Mushtaq Ahmed	377	108	1,101	40	7-94	3	27.52
H. R. J. Trump	250.4	73	789	26	6-68	2	30.34
N. A. Mallender	193.4	51	602	16	3-23	0	37.62
A. P. van Troost	326.1	53	1,299	34	4-50	0	38.20

Also bowled: P. J. Bird 44.5–9–166–0; V. P. Clarke 23–4–105–1; M. Dimond 55.3–8–216–5; B. T. P. Donelan 15–2–59–1; S. C. Ecclestone 17–4–57–0; J. C. Hallett 53.2–15–181–4; A. N. Hayhurst 77.4–23–218–7; J. I. D. Kerr 21–3–91–0; M. N. Lathwell 24–4–87–3; K. A. Parsons 4–0–21–0; A. Payne 12–2–54–0.

Wicket-keeper: R. J. Turner 44 ct, 5 st.

Leading Fielder: G. D. Rose 15.

At Bristol, April 28, 29, 30, May 1. SOMERSET lost to GLOUCESTERSHIRE by 83 runs.

At Taunton, May 7, 8, 9. SOMERSET drew with NEW ZEALANDERS (See New Zealand tour section).

At Leicester, May 12, 13, 14, 16. SOMERSET lost to LEICESTERSHIRE by five wickets.

SOMERSET v WARWICKSHIRE

At Taunton, May 19, 20, 21, 23. Warwickshire won by six wickets. Warwickshire 18 pts, Somerset 2 pts. Toss: Somerset. First-class debut: P. J. Bird.

Lara's fifth consecutive first-class hundred in the sequence he began in the Antigua Test carried Warwickshire to a remarkable victory. Reciprocal declarations after the third day was lost set them a target of 321, initially in 95 overs. But further rain interrupted their innings for two hours after lunch. Lara responded to the consequent leap in the required run-rate with a dazzling display, reaching 50 in 51 balls and 100 in 72 – the fastest century of the season to date – before he was bowled by the 94th delivery he faced for 136. Asif Din then saw Warwickshire home with 3.2 overs to spare. Lara had to bat well to make up ground with traditionalists, who had been astonished to see him take a call on a mobile phone while in the field. Somerset had recovered from early troubles through an unusually watchful Lathwell and the steady Hayhurst, who reached his century on the second day, almost half of which was washed out. Davis took five catches, all in the slips, one short of Warwickshire's record.

Close of play: First day, Somerset 255-5 (A. N. Hayhurst 76*, H. R. J. Trump 3*); Second day, Warwickshire 57-0 (D. P. Ostler 41*, R. G. Twose 13*); Third day, No play.

Somerset

M. N. Lathwell c Davis b P. A. Smith	86		
I. Fletcher c Davis b P. A. Smith	17		
R. J. Harden c Davis b P. A. Smith	0		
N. A. Folland c Piper b Davis	21		
*A. N. Hayhurst not out	111		
†R. J. Turner c Lara b Munton	40		
H. R. J. Trump c Davis b Small	15		
G. D. Rose c Lara b Munton	1	– (2) not out	13
Mushtaq Ahmed c Davis b Munton	2	– (1) not out	9
A. Payne c Munton b Davis	34		
P. J. Bird not out	0		
B 6, l-b 19, w 1, n-b 2	28		
1/36 2/36 3/76 4/149 5/249 6/272 7/295 8/299 9/349 (9 wkts dec.)	355	(no wkt dec.)	22

Bonus points – Somerset 2, Warwickshire 2 (Score at 120 overs: 284-6).

Bowling: *First Innings*—Small 36.2–6–104–1; Munton 42–17–77–3; P. A. Smith 16–7–24–3; Twose 13–1–42–0; Davis 25–9–59–2; N. M. K. Smith 15–6–24–0. *Second Innings*—Asif Din 2–0–9–0; Ostler 1.1–0–13–0.

Warwickshire

D. P. Ostler not out	41	– run out	51
R. G. Twose not out	13	– c Turner b Mushtaq Ahmed	33
B. C. Lara (did not bat)		– b Mushtaq Ahmed	136
P. A. Smith (did not bat)		– c Lathwell b Hayhurst	39
Asif Din (did not bat)		– not out	42
T. L. Penney (did not bat)		– not out	9
L-b 3	3	B 1, l-b 4, w 1, n-b 6	12
(no wkt dec.)	57	1/71 2/96 3/170 4/296 (4 wkts)	322

†K. J. Piper, N. M. K. Smith, G. C. Small, R. P. Davis and *T. A. Munton did not bat.

Bowling: *First Innings*—Bird 7–1–32–0; Payne 4–1–13–0; Mushtaq Ahmed 6–3–9–0; Rose 2–2–0–0; Trump 2–2–0–0. *Second Innings*—Rose 18.4–1–117–0; Bird 9–0–53–0; Mushtaq Ahmed 14–0–65–2; Payne 8–1–41–0; Hayhurst 4–0–41–1.

Umpires: R. Julian and K. J. Lyons.

At Southport, May 26, 27, 28, 30. SOMERSET lost to LANCASHIRE by an innings and 88 runs.

SOMERSET v HAMPSHIRE

At Taunton, June 2, 3, 4, 6. Somerset won by 87 runs. Somerset 19 pts, Hampshire 1 pt. Toss: Hampshire. First-class debut: M. Dimond.

After four successive defeats, Somerset recorded their first Championship win of the season, bowling out Hampshire following a double forfeit of innings. Van Troost ended Hampshire's sound opening by dismissing Middleton, James and Terry in the space of nine balls, before he succumbed to a hamstring injury. Mushtaq Ahmed and Mallender cleaned up, with the steady Nicholas and the blazing Benjamin offering most resistance. On a greenish pitch lacking pace, Lathwell had given Somerset a crisp start, but his partner, Trescothick, was the hero of the first day. Missed when two, he escaped single figures for the first time in his ninth first-class innings and went on to make 81. Harden and Hayhurst then took over, adding 136, with Harden edging on to his century during the 12 overs possible on the second day. No play on Saturday prefaced Hampshire's unsuccessful attempt on 333 on Monday.

Close of play: First day, Somerset 286-3 (R. J. Harden 86*, A. N. Hayhurst 47*); Second day, Somerset 332-3 (R. J. Harden 103*, A. N. Hayhurst 76*); Third day, No play.

Somerset

M. N. Lathwell c Aymes b Thursfield . . 39
M. E. Trescothick b Udal 81
R. J. Harden not out 103
N. A. Folland lbw b Cowans 15
*A. N. Hayhurst not out 76
B 3, l-b 8, w 1, n-b 6 18

1/84 2/163 3/196 (3 wkts dec.) 332

†R. J. Turner, G. D. Rose, Mushtaq Ahmed, N. A. Mallender, M. Dimond and A. P. van Troost did not bat.

Bonus points – Somerset 3, Hampshire 1.

Bowling: Benjamin 24–7–48–0; Cowans 22–2–81–1; Thursfield 23–2–83–1; James 17–4–42–0; Udal 32–10–67–1.

Somerset forfeited their second innings.

Hampshire

Hampshire forfeited their first innings.

T. C. Middleton c Turner b van Troost. 17
R. S. M. Morris c Trescothick b Mallender . 45
K. D. James b van Troost 0
V. P. Terry b van Troost 0
*M. C. J. Nicholas c Folland b Mushtaq Ahmed . 45
R. M. F. Cox lbw b Mushtaq Ahmed . . 5
†A. N. Aymes st Turner b Mushtaq Ahmed . 19
S. D. Udal lbw b Mallender 36
W. K. M. Benjamin c and b Dimond . . 36
M. J. Thursfield c Harden b Mallender . 9
N. G. Cowans not out 0
B 2, l-b 9, n-b 22 33

1/47 2/51 3/51 4/100 5/111 6/148 7/165 8/224 9/238 245

Bowling: van Troost 11–1–34–3; Mallender 13.5–5–28–3; Rose 13–0–51–0; Mushtaq Ahmed 26–7–77–3; Dimond 14–2–44–1.

Umpires: N. T. Plews and A. G. T. Whitehead.

At Bradford, June 9, 10, 11, 13. SOMERSET drew with YORKSHIRE.

SOMERSET v SURREY

At Bath, June 16, 17, 18, 20. Somerset won by 317 runs. Somerset 24 pts, Surrey 5 pts. Toss: Somerset.

A superb maiden double-century by Lathwell – Somerset's first-ever at Bath – was the foundation for a crushing victory. Ably negotiating early freshness in the pitch, Lathwell hit 33 fours. He found ideal support from Trescothick and Hayhurst, with whom he added 216. From 372 for three, however, Cuffy and Benjamin initiated a collapse of seven wickets for 56. Surrey's reply began well enough, but only Brown played a substantial innings. He hit five sixes and ten fours in 108 balls, reaching the nineties for the third time in 1994, before Rose finished Surrey off with four wickets in 22 balls. Trescothick, with his maiden hundred, and Folland enabled Somerset to extend their 140-run lead to 469. Surrey's chances of survival perished with their top three on the third evening; only Ward delayed Mallender, Mushtaq Ahmed and van Troost, backed up by some brilliant catches. Oddly, Surrey regained first place in the Championship, which they had lost during a week off.

Close of play: First day, Somerset 382-5 (R. J. Turner 1*); Second day, Somerset 17-1 (M. E. Trescothick 11*); Third day, Surrey 48-3 (D. M. Ward 15*, N. F. Sargeant 2*).

Somerset

M. N. Lathwell c Thorpe b Cuffy	206	– (3) b Smith	25
M. E. Trescothick lbw b Benjamin	36	– (1) c Butcher b Smith	121
R. J. Harden c Butcher b Benjamin	1	– (4) b Smith	17
N. A. Folland lbw b Hollioake	13	– (5) c Butcher b Smith	72
*A. N. Hayhurst lbw b Benjamin	79	– (6) not out	31
†R. J. Turner c Sargeant b Cuffy	3		
G. D. Rose c Sargeant b Benjamin	5	– c sub b Smith	25
Mushtaq Ahmed c Brown b Benjamin	6	– not out	4
N. A. Mallender not out	16	– (2) lbw b Benjamin	6
H. R. J. Trump c Hollioake b Cuffy	6		
A. P. van Troost b Pigott	4		
B 4, l-b 5, w 6, n-b 38	53	B 4, l-b 6, w 3, n-b 15	28
1/103 2/113 3/156 4/372 5/382 6/392 7/400 8/402 9/421	428	1/17 2/80 3/108 4/248 5/284 6/324 (6 wkts dec.)	329

Bonus points – Somerset 4, Surrey 3 (Score at 120 overs: 409-8).

Bowling: *First Innings*—Cuffy 32–11–72–3; Benjamin 31–6–100–5; Butcher 9–1–56–0; Pigott 17.4–1–52–1; Smith 29–4–95–0; Hollioake 10–0–41–1; Brown 1–0–3–0. *Second Innings*—Benjamin 13–1–63–1; Cuffy 12–1–49–0; Smith 33–8–103–5; Pigott 7–1–18–0; Hollioake 10–2–44–0; Butcher 7–3–19–0; Thorpe 5–0–23–0.

Surrey

D. J. Bicknell c Trump b Hayhurst	41	– b van Troost	5
M. A. Butcher c Trump b van Troost	35	– c Turner b Rose	16
*G. P. Thorpe c Trescothick b Trump	47	– c Turner b Mallender	4
D. M. Ward b Hayhurst	4	– b Mallender	59
A. D. Brown c Mushtaq Ahmed b Rose	97	– (6) c Turner b van Troost	0
A. J. Hollioake st Turner b Trump	0	– (7) c Trump b van Troost	1
A. W. Smith c Trescothick b Rose	27	– (8) not out	10
†N. F. Sargeant c Trescothick b Mallender	8	– (5) c Harden b Mushtaq Ahmed	11
A. C. S. Pigott c Lathwell b Rose	7	– c Harden b Mushtaq Ahmed	5
J. E. Benjamin c and b Rose	5	– c Hayhurst b Mushtaq Ahmed	12
C. E. Cuffy not out	0	– lbw b Mallender	7
B 4, l-b 7, w 6	17	B 3, l-b 10, w 1, n-b 8	22
1/69 2/109 3/121 4/143 5/143 6/267 7/270 8/281 9/288	288	1/10 2/18 3/40 4/87 5/88 6/106 7/124 8/131 9/145	152

Bonus points – Surrey 2, Somerset 4.

Bowling: *First Innings*—van Troost 16–4–56–1; Mallender 10–0–51–1; Mushtaq Ahmed 19–7–46–0; Trump 12–4–53–2; Rose 15.2–3–58–4; Hayhurst 6–2–13–2. *Second Innings*—van Troost 16–8–36–3; Mallender 12–4–23–3; Rose 11–6–18–1; Mushtaq Ahmed 21–6–62–3.

Umpires: V. A. Holder and T. E. Jesty.

SOMERSET v WORCESTERSHIRE

At Taunton, June 30, July 1, 2, 4. Somerset won by 53 runs. Somerset 22 pts, Worcestershire 6 pts. Toss: Somerset.

On the final evening Worcestershire were 209 for two, with Weston and Moody on course to score the 123 required from their last 27 overs, but Mushtaq Ahmed, in his last appearance before joining Pakistan's tour of Sri Lanka, turned the game. Both batsmen gave catches to Caddick in successive Mushtaq overs. After Haynes was out next over, Worcestershire began blocking, enabling the fielders to move in and Mushtaq to bowl bad balls with impunity. He bowled enough good balls to take seven for 94, 12 for 160 in the match, and give Somerset victory with seven deliveries to spare. The pitch was never totally trustworthy: Trescothick, with his fourth score over fifty in four games, and the patient Hayhurst did the hard work with the bat, then Somerset's good bowling and safe catching and Worcestershire's over-ambition reduced the visitors to 105 for seven. The first major twist occurred when Leatherdale and Illingworth added 183 in 43 overs, the highest stand of the match. After a watchful start, Leatherdale played superbly, with Illingworth a faithful ally. Somerset's lead, an unexpectedly slight 34, looked even more slender at 107 for five, but Harden found spirited partners down the order, and the challenge was eventually 332 in 76 overs.

Close of play: First day, Somerset 262-6 (A. N. Hayhurst 73*, N. A. Mallender 17*); Second day, Worcestershire 256-7 (D. A. Leatherdale 99*, R. K. Illingworth 47*); Third day, Somerset 211-6 (R. J. Harden 97*, N. A. Mallender 19*).

Somerset

M. N. Lathwell b Radford	16	– c Edwards b Tolley	7
M. E. Trescothick lbw b Leatherdale	55	– lbw b Radford	0
R. J. Harden c Edwards b Lampitt	31	– not out	131
N. A. Folland lbw b Radford	26	– c Leatherdale b Illingworth	31
*A. N. Hayhurst lbw b Moody	98	– (7) lbw b Lampitt	28
†R. J. Turner lbw b Moody	4	– (5) b Illingworth	4
G. D. Rose c Leatherdale b Tolley	22	– (6) c Tolley b Moody	7
N. A. Mallender c Moody b Lampitt	26	– c Leatherdale b Illingworth	33
Mushtaq Ahmed c Moody b Tolley	28	– not out	32
A. R. Caddick c Lampitt b Moody	11		
A. P. van Troost not out	2		
B 6, l-b 9, w 3, n-b 12	30	B 6, l-b 7, w 3, n-b 8	24
1/21 2/110 3/116 4/155 5/173 6/226 7/287 8/327 9/342	349	1/1 2/13 3/78 4/86 5/107 6/174 7/254 (7 wkts dec.)	297

Bonus points – Somerset 2, Worcestershire 3 (Score at 120 overs: 287-7).

Bowling: *First Innings*—Radford 23–7–53–2; Tolley 28–8–74–2; Moody 22–7–38–3; Illingworth 22–7–50–0; Lampitt 30–10–81–2; Leatherdale 8–1–26–1; Haynes 6–1–12–0. *Second Innings*—Radford 16–2–57–1; Tolley 15–1–56–1; Illingworth 38–17–55–3; Lampitt 21–4–58–1; Moody 12–4–20–1; Leatherdale 10.1–2–38–0.

Worcestershire

*T. S. Curtis lbw b van Troost	13 – b Caddick	12
W. P. C. Weston b Caddick	12 – c Caddick b Mushtaq Ahmed	83
A. C. H. Seymour c Trescothick b Caddick	7 – b Mushtaq Ahmed	27
T. M. Moody st Turner b Mushtaq Ahmed	13 – c Caddick b Mushtaq Ahmed	79
G. R. Haynes lbw b Mushtaq Ahmed	26 – c Turner b van Troost	2
D. A. Leatherdale c sub b Mushtaq Ahmed	139 – b Mushtaq Ahmed	13
S. R. Lampitt st Turner b Mushtaq Ahmed	0 – c Folland b Mushtaq Ahmed	28
C. M. Tolley c Rose b Caddick	0 – lbw b Caddick	5
R. K. Illingworth run out	59 – (10) c Turner b Mushtaq Ahmed	14
N. V. Radford b Mushtaq Ahmed	0 – (9) lbw b Mushtaq Ahmed	0
†T. Edwards not out	2 – not out	0
B 8, l-b 14, w 8, n-b 14	44 B 2, l-b 3, w 1, n-b 9	15
1/16 2/32 3/41 4/59 5/104 6/104 7/105 8/288 9/288	315 1/15 2/80 3/209 4/212 5/213 6/244 7/261 8/262 9/265	278

Bonus points – Worcestershire 3, Somerset 4.

Bowling: *First Innings*—van Troost 21–1–88–1; Mushtaq Ahmed 30.5–13–66–5; Mallender 21–6–56–0; Caddick 14–3–47–3; Rose 8–1–31–0; Hayhurst 1–0–5–0. *Second Innings*—van Troost 11–0–59–1; Caddick 23–5–80–2; Mushtaq Ahmed 31.5–11–94–7; Rose 3–0–15–0; Mallender 6–1–25–0.

Umpires: B. Dudleston and G. Sharp.

SOMERSET v NOTTINGHAMSHIRE

At Taunton, July 14, 15, 16, 18. Somerset won by 111 runs. Somerset 21 pts, Nottinghamshire 4 pts. Toss: Nottinghamshire.

A Somerset victory seemed likely when they set a target of 502 in just over four sessions and certain when Rose reduced Nottinghamshire to 210 for eight. But it proved less easy than that. Evans, dropped first ball, batted for 168 minutes with Adams. They added 170 for the ninth wicket, breaking a county record set in 1869, when W. McIntyre and G. Wootton put on 165 against Kent. This was the oldest surviving partnership record for any first-class county. Having lost Mallender to a groin injury, Somerset's bowlers were struggling. But Evans's dismissal signalled the end. Adams remained unbeaten on a career-best 144. The seamers had the first two innings over and done with on Taunton's usual grassy pitch early on the second afternoon. Caddick demolished Nottinghamshire, with six for 70, and only a brilliant 52 in 36 balls by Lewis kept Somerset's lead down to 89. Conditions eased as Somerset extended that by 412, building on the efforts of Trescothick and the defiant Harden and finishing with a run-a-ball flourish from Trump.

Close of play: First day, Nottinghamshire 4-0 (P. R. Pollard 1*, W. A. Dessaur 2*); Second day, Somerset 184-3 (R. J. Harden 50*, R. J. Turner 19*); Third day, Nottinghamshire 131-4 (J. C. Adams 10*, G. W. Mike 0*).

Somerset

M. N. Lathwell c Evans b Lewis	10 – c and b Lewis	26
M. E. Trescothick lbw b Evans	53 – c Archer b Lewis	59
R. J. Harden c Lewis b Evans	4 – c Evans b Pick	68
N. A. Folland b Mike	27 – c Lewis b Adams	29
*A. N. Hayhurst c Lewis b Mike	2 – (6) lbw b Pick	39
†R. J. Turner lbw b Lewis	56 – (5) lbw b Lewis	20
G. D. Rose lbw b Evans	39 – c Crawley b Pick	54
N. A. Mallender b Lewis	19 – c Crawley b Evans	36
A. R. Caddick c Adams b Lewis	3 – c Lewis b Evans	2
H. R. J. Trump not out	11 – not out	43
P. J. Bird lbw b Evans	7 – c Lewis b Pick	5
L-b 6, w 1, n-b 8	15 B 12, l-b 9, n-b 10	31
1/21 2/31 3/99 4/101 5/108 6/183 7/220 8/224 9/231	246 1/43 2/104 3/151 4/194 5/249 6/254 7/331 8/347 9/377	412

Bonus points – Somerset 1, Nottinghamshire 4.

Bowling: *First Innings*—Pick 23–3–53–0; Lewis 25–7–65–4; Mike 20–6–54–2; Evans 23.2–9–46–4; Crawley 9–2–20–0; Adams 3–1–2–0. *Second Innings*—Pick 24.2–5–100–4; Lewis 25–7–58–3; Evans 29–9–89–2; Mike 15–3–78–0; Crawley 3–2–3–0; Adams 27–12–63–1.

Nottinghamshire

P. R. Pollard c Turner b Caddick	2	– c Rose b Caddick	2
W. A. Dessaur c Turner b Caddick	11	– c Turner b Mallender	19
*R. T. Robinson c Trescothick b Caddick	15	– c Trump b Mallender	55
G. F. Archer c Turner b Rose	4	– c Harden b Trump	35
J. C. Adams c Trump b Mallender	29	– not out	144
M. A. Crawley b Caddick	1	– (7) b Rose	5
C. C. Lewis c Folland b Trump	52	– (8) c Harden b Rose	8
†W. M. Noon b Mallender	5	– (9) lbw b Rose	0
K. P. Evans not out	16	– (10) c Trescothick b Caddick	77
G. W. Mike c Trump b Caddick	15	– (6) c Turner b Rose	29
R. A. Pick c Trescothick b Caddick	0	– run out	0
L-b 3, n-b 4	7	B 1, l-b 13, n-b 2	16
1/12 2/23 3/33 4/41 5/43 6/109 7/117 8/130 9/157	157	1/8 2/55 3/108 4/131 5/174 6/198 7/210 8/210 9/380	390

Bonus points – Somerset 4.

Bowling: *First Innings*—Caddick 18.2–3–70–6; Bird 5–3–3–0; Mallender 17–6–57–2; Rose 6–1–16–1; Trump 2–1–8–1. *Second Innings*—Caddick 35–10–98–2; Mallender 12.5–3–31–2; Trump 23–7–59–1; Bird 23.5–5–78–0; Rose 21.1–3–78–4; Lathwell 5–1–32–0.

Umpires: R. Julian and R. Palmer.

At Hove, July 21, 22, 23, 25. SOMERSET beat SUSSEX by 68 runs.

At Swansea, July 28, 29, 30, August 1. SOMERSET drew with GLAMORGAN.

SOMERSET v DURHAM

At Taunton, August 4, 5. Somerset won by nine wickets. Somerset 21 pts, Durham 4 pts. Toss: Somerset. Championship debut: S. C. Ecclestone.

Durham's sixth successive Championship defeat took only two days. Though they had much the worse of a sultry, overcast opening day, when Rose and his supporting seamers had them out inside 59 overs and then Lathwell and Harden put on 104 for Somerset's second wicket, they had seemed to be recovering. Cummins took a career-best six for 64, while Morris and Saxelby, the top scorer of the first innings, quickly wiped out arrears of 63 in a sparkling stand of 92 in 19 overs. Larkins, who had not opened in the second innings because of sinus trouble, had his wrist fractured by his first ball from van Troost. But Daley's enterprise took Durham to 155 for two, in line for a handsome lead – until Caddick and van Troost cut down the last eight for 48 in 13 overs. Somerset needed 141 to win: Lathwell, with 69 from 44 balls, and Fletcher, with 54 from 63, opened with a breathtaking 104 in 13 overs. It was all over by 7.20 p.m. on the second day.

Close of play: First day, Somerset 132-3 (N. A. Folland 5*, A. N. Hayhurst 1*).

Durham

First innings		Second innings	
W. Larkins c Caddick b van Troost	17	(3) not out	6
M. Saxelby lbw b Hayhurst	42	c Trump b Caddick	48
J. E. Morris lbw b Rose	13	(1) c Turner b van Troost	49
J. A. Daley c Turner b van Troost	9	b Caddick	37
J. I. Longley c Folland b Caddick	2	c Rose b Caddick	9
*P. Bainbridge c Turner b Rose	3	c Harden b Caddick	0
†C. W. Scott lbw b Rose	0	b van Troost	6
A. C. Cummins b Rose	29	b van Troost	4
J. Wood c Turner b Hayhurst	0	c Rose b Caddick	0
S. J. E. Brown not out	4	c Turner b van Troost	1
A. Walker c Fletcher b van Troost	13	c Fletcher b Caddick	7
L-b 7, n-b 32	39	B 1, l-b 4, w 1, n-b 30	36
1/25 2/44 3/61 4/80 5/94 6/94 7/144 8/146 9/146	171	1/92 2/127 3/155 4/155 5/166 6/172 7/172 8/173 9/183	203

Bonus points – Somerset 4.

In the second innings W. Larkins, when 0, retired hurt at 92-1 and resumed at 183.

Bowling: *First Innings*—Caddick 16–2–47–1; van Troost 17.4–2–64–3; Rose 18–6–40–4; Ecclestone 3–1–8–0; Trump 1–1–0–0; Hayhurst 3–1–5–2. *Second Innings*—Caddick 17.4–5–51–6; van Troost 12–0–81–4; Rose 5–1–20–0; Ecclestone 4–0–31–0; Hayhurst 4–0–15–0.

Somerset

First innings		Second innings	
M. N. Lathwell b Cummins	67	c Scott b Wood	69
I. Fletcher b Cummins	8	not out	54
R. J. Harden c Longley b Walker	29	not out	13
N. A. Folland c Walker b Cummins	9		
*A. N. Hayhurst run out	33		
†R. J. Turner c Scott b Wood	4		
G. D. Rose b Brown	7		
S. C. Ecclestone c Bainbridge b Cummins	24		
A. R. Caddick lbw b Cummins	13		
H. R. J. Trump c Scott b Cummins	0		
A. P. van Troost not out	1		
B 8, l-b 6, w 1, n-b 24	39	L-b 1, n-b 4	5
1/13 2/117 3/131 4/140 5/176 6/192 7/224 8/224 9/233	234	1/104	(1 wkt) 141

Bonus points – Somerset 1, Durham 4.

In the first innings R. J. Turner, when 3, retired hurt at 164 and resumed at 233.

Bowling: *First Innings*—Cummins 18–3–64–6; Wood 10.2–2–59–1; Brown 18–2–56–1; Walker 16–3–35–1; Bainbridge 2–0–6–0. *Second Innings*—Cummins 5–0–38–0; Brown 4–0–35–0; Wood 6–0–47–1; Walker 3–0–14–0; Bainbridge 1.5–0–6–0.

Umpires: M. J. Kitchen and P. Willey.

At Lord's, August 11, 12, 13, 15. SOMERSET lost to MIDDLESEX by an innings and 30 runs.

SOMERSET v ESSEX

At Weston-super-Mare, August 18, 19, 20. Somerset won by 136 runs. Somerset 21 pts, Essex 4 pts. Toss: Essex.

Somerset recorded their sixth successive home win in the Championship after Essex failed to exploit an important toss. Their seamers bowled Somerset out on a green pitch for 226, a total depending heavily on Lathwell, who struck nine fours and a six, and added 57 in 15 overs with Harden, the biggest stand of the match. But this total looked far better when Essex then collapsed to 71 for eight. The last two wickets almost doubled that, as Kasprowicz, combining luck and spirit, made an unbeaten 42. Kasprowicz went on to take a career-best seven for 83. Trescothick, however, played a decisive innings of 92, while Rose and Caddick hit out to set Essex a target of 330. They had reached 66 for one when Lewis fell to a superb cover catch by Hayhurst, beginning Caddick's spell of three for 15 in 27 balls. Van Troost and Trump mopped up; only a cheerful slog of 50 in six overs from Ilott and Such delayed them until 4.22 p.m. on Saturday.

Close of play: First day, Essex 5-2 (J. J. B. Lewis 0*, N. Hussain 2*); Second day, Somerset 213-7 (G. D. Rose 31*, A. R. Caddick 27*).

Somerset

M. N. Lathwell c Hussain b Stephenson	61	– lbw b Kasprowicz	0
M. E. Trescothick b Kasprowicz	15	– c Garnham b Kasprowicz	92
R. J. Harden b Kasprowicz	18	– b Kasprowicz	13
P. C. L. Holloway c Stephenson b Ilott	28	– c Kasprowicz b Andrew	14
*A. N. Hayhurst c Garnham b Ilott	15	– c Garnham b Kasprowicz	8
†R. J. Turner b Ilott	19	– lbw b Such	16
G. D. Rose c Hussain b Ilott	9	– lbw b Kasprowicz	32
S. C. Ecclestone lbw b Stephenson	4	– lbw b Kasprowicz	0
A. R. Caddick c Knight b Stephenson	1	– c Ilott b Andrew	29
H. R. J. Trump run out	33	– c Garnham b Kasprowicz	7
A. P. van Troost not out	6	– not out	7
L-b 4, w 3, n-b 10	17	L-b 10, w 1, n-b 14	25
1/40 2/97 3/117 4/143 5/145 6/160 7/169 8/173 9/197	226	1/4 2/24 3/55 4/76 5/121 6/172 7/172 8/218 9/220	243

Bonus points – Somerset 1, Essex 4.

Bowling: *First Innings*—Kasprowicz 19.2–2–57–2; Ilott 28–8–87–4; Andrew 13–3–27–0; Stephenson 17–5–37–3; Such 5–1–14–0. *Second Innings*—Kasprowicz 27.2–2–83–7; Ilott 14–2–56–0; Stephenson 15–2–46–0; Andrew 19–5–29–2; Such 4–0–19–1.

Essex

N. V. Knight c Turner b van Troost	2	– c Hayhurst b Caddick	39
J. P. Stephenson c Rose b Caddick	1	– c Trescothick b Rose	6
J. J. B. Lewis b van Troost	3	– c Hayhurst b Caddick	18
N. Hussain c Holloway b Caddick	13	– c Rose b Trump	28
*P. J. Prichard b Rose	15	– c Turner b Caddick	7
R. C. Irani c Rose b van Troost	2	– c Turner b van Troost	19
†M. A. Garnham lbw b Rose	7	– c Turner b van Troost	0
M. S. Kasprowicz not out	42	– b Rose	10
M. C. Ilott b Rose	4	– not out	30
S. J. W. Andrew c Rose b van Troost	11	– c Rose b Trump	3
P. M. Such c Turner b Caddick	16	– c Ecclestone b Trump	29
L-b 5, n-b 19	24	N-b 4	4
1/3 2/3 3/19 4/42 5/42 6/44 7/57 8/71 9/97	140	1/29 2/66 3/69 4/85 5/108 6/108 7/128 8/132 9/143	193

Bonus points – Somerset 4.

Bowling: *First Innings*—Caddick 22.2–7–58–3; van Troost 16–3–50–4; Rose 7–1–27–3. *Second Innings*—Caddick 16–4–47–3; van Troost 15–2–61–2; Rose 15–5–39–2; Ecclestone 2–0–5–0; Hayhurst 1–0–7–0; Trump 7–2–34–3.

Umpires: J. W. Holder and K. J. Lyons.

SOMERSET v NORTHAMPTONSHIRE

At Taunton, August 30, 31, September 1, 2. Northamptonshire won by two wickets. Northamptonshire 20 pts, Somerset 3 pts. Toss: Northamptonshire. First-class debut: I. Dawood.

An abbreviated match produced a remarkable turnaround when Penberthy and Ambrose shared a stand of 145 in 31 overs after Caddick seemed to have Northamptonshire beaten at 152 for seven. Penberthy was rewarded with his cap for a Championship-best 88 from 118 balls, including a six and 14 fours; Ambrose, in ebullient mood, rode his luck to score 78 from 96, smashing two sixes and nine fours, the highest score of his career. He was out four short of victory, bringing in Dawood, whose first-class debut ended happily, although he had broken a finger keeping wicket on the first day (Warren deputised and took four catches). Rain washed out the whole of the second day and severely disrupted the first and third. Lamb asked Somerset to bat and they were 71 for three before Hayhurst and Holloway, with a maiden fifty for his new county, added 120. On the third day, Ambrose took four wickets in 15 balls – interrupted by a rain break – but the last two wickets put on 108. Two declarations left Northamptonshire to make 301 on the final day.

Close of play: First day, Somerset 151-3 (P. C. L. Holloway 26*, A. N. Hayhurst 39*); Second day, No play; Third day, Somerset 25-0 dec.

Somerset

M. N. Lathwell lbw b Ambrose	1	– not out	3
M. E. Trescothick c Taylor b Penberthy	46	– not out	18
R. J. Harden c Montgomerie b Curran	15		
P. C. L. Holloway c Warren b Penberthy	50		
*A. N. Hayhurst c Warren b Ambrose	72		
†R. J. Turner c Fordham b Ambrose	14		
G. D. Rose c Warren b Ambrose	6		
N. A. Mallender c Warren b Walton	39		
A. R. Caddick c Bailey b Ambrose	0		
H. R. J. Trump not out	45		
A. P. van Troost b Taylor	19		
B 9, l-b 19, w 5, n-b 6	39	B 4	4
1/12 2/71 3/71 4/191 5/225 6/231 7/238 8/238 9/312	346	(no wkt dec.)	25

Bonus points – Somerset 3, Northamptonshire 4.

Bowling: *First Innings*—Ambrose 29–4–59–5; Taylor 20.1–2–62–1; Curran 28–7–80–1; Penberthy 19–4–71–2; Walton 10–0–46–1. *Second Innings*—Bailey 1.5–0–11–0; Montgomerie 1–0–10–0.

Northamptonshire

R. R. Montgomerie c Rose b Caddick	9	– c and b van Troost	9
A. Fordham not out	41	– c Harden b Caddick	0
R. J. Bailey not out	18	– b Rose	42
*A. J. Lamb (did not bat)		– c Trescothick b Caddick	4
R. J. Warren (did not bat)		– c Trump b Mallender	53
K. M. Curran (did not bat)		– c Turner b Caddick	0
T. C. Walton (did not bat)		– c Rose b Caddick	11
A. L. Penberthy (did not bat)		– not out	88
C. E. L. Ambrose (did not bat)		– c Mallender b Trump	78
†I. Dawood (did not bat)		– not out	2
L-b 1, n-b 2	3	L-b 10, w 1, n-b 6	17
1/20 (1 wkt dec.)	71	1/11 2/11 3/29 4/72 5/73 6/118 7/152 8/297 (8 wkts)	304

J. P. Taylor did not bat.

Bowling: *First Innings*—Caddick 7–1–24–1; van Troost 2–0–15–0; Mallender 5–0–31–0; Rose 1–1–0–0. *Second Innings*—Caddick 25–5–92–4; van Troost 20.1–4–89–1; Mallender 16–5–62–1; Rose 5–2–10–1; Trump 8–2–41–1.

Umpires: J. C. Balderstone and D. J. Constant.

At Canterbury, September 8, 9, 10, 12. SOMERSET lost to KENT by an innings and 57 runs.

SOMERSET v DERBYSHIRE

At Taunton, September 15, 16, 17, 19. Drawn. Somerset 1 pt, Derbyshire 1 pt. Toss: Derbyshire.

Rain permitted only 71 overs, after lunch on the third day. Put in on an easy-paced pitch, Somerset were launched strongly by Trescothick and Harden. After a slow start, Harden reached his 1,000 runs for the season and just missed a hundred. Hayhurst completed a smooth half-century in the time that remained.

Close of play: First day, No play; Second day, No play; Third day, Somerset 228-4 (A. N. Hayhurst 52*, K. A. Parsons 4*).

Somerset

M. N. Lathwell b DeFreitas	10
M. E. Trescothick c Rollins b Cork	51
R. J. Harden c Wells b Malcolm	95
P. C. L. Holloway c Rollins b Cork	5
*A. N. Hayhurst not out	52
K. A. Parsons not out	4
B 4, l-b 4, w 1, n-b 2	11
1/12 2/99 3/117 4/214	(4 wkts) 228

G. D. Rose, †R. J. Turner, A. R. Caddick, H. R. J. Trump and A. P. van Troost did not bat.

Bonus points – Somerset 1, Derbyshire 1.

Bowling: DeFreitas 14–4–28–1; Base 19–4–54–0; Malcolm 13–2–43–1; Wells 7–1–31–0; Cork 15–2–50–2; Steer 2–0–12–0; Adams 1–0–2–0.

Derbyshire

P. D. Bowler, †A. S. Rollins, C. J. Adams, T. J. G. O'Gorman, *K. J. Barnett, P. A. J. DeFreitas, D. G. Cork, C. M. Wells, S. J. Base, I. G. S. Steer and D. E. Malcolm.

Umpires: J. H. Hampshire and D. R. Shepherd.

LONGEST INNINGS IN COUNTY CRICKET

Mins	*Score*	*Player*	*Match*	*Date*
638	235*	D. J. Bicknell	Surrey v Nottinghamshire at Nottingham	1994
615	267	A. Shrewsbury	Nottinghamshire v Middlesex at Nottingham	1887
606	277*	R. G. Twose	Warwickshire v Glamorgan at Birmingham	1994
598	248	T. S. Curtis	Worcestershire v Somerset at Worcester	1991
585	285	P. Holmes	Yorkshire v Nottinghamshire at Nottingham	1929
570	228*	T. S. Curtis	Worcestershire v Derbyshire at Derby	1992
566	300	R. Subba Row	Northamptonshire v Surrey at The Oval	1958
562	203*	A. J. Moles	Warwickshire v Surrey at Guildford	1994
555	216*	A. A. Metcalfe	Yorkshire v Middlesex at Leeds	1988
555	281*	J. P. Crawley	Lancashire v Somerset at Southport	1994
553	405*	G. A. Hick	Worcestershire v Somerset at Taunton	1988
540	204*	D. Brookes	Northamptonshire v Essex at Northampton	1952
540	221	T. C. Middleton	Hampshire v Surrey at Southampton	1992
530	267	A. Shrewsbury	Nottinghamshire v Sussex at Nottingham	1890
530	186*	T. S. Curtis	Worcestershire v Glamorgan at Cardiff	1991
526	214*	A. Dale	Glamorgan v Middlesex at Cardiff	1993

SURREY

Patron: HM The Queen
President: J. M. Poland
Chairman: B. G. K. Downing
Chief Executive: G. A. Woodman
Captain: A. J. Stewart
Coach: G. S. Clinton
Director of Cricket: M. J. Edwards
Head Groundsman: P. D. Brind
Scorer: 1994 – M. R. L. W. Ayers
1995 – K. Booth

To lose one's way halfway through a season may be regarded as a misfortune; to lose one's way twice in as many seasons, and on all fronts, looks like carelessness. Surrey were top of the Championship at the end of July and second at the start of August. But their supporters must have thought they had travelled back a year when their seventh victory, over Nottinghamshire, was followed in their remaining six games by four defeats – three by an innings – and two draws, consigning Surrey to the also-rans. They finished seventh, lower than the previous summer.

There was not even the consolation of a Lord's final, though Surrey reached the semi-finals in both knockouts. At least the NatWest Trophy provided a thrilling exit: a world record aggregate score after some brilliant batting in their encounter with Worcestershire. But semi-finals do not line a clouded season with silver, nor does a Sunday League finish just outside the money in sixth place.

Supporters placed the original blame on Sri Lanka. If they had not arranged a visit from Pakistan, beginning in July, then Surrey would have had Waqar Younis for the bulk of the summer – once he had recovered from his appendix operation. His presence was sorely missed by a Surrey attack which was ravaged by injuries and – with the honourable exception of Joey Benjamin – proved largely ineffectual. Martin Bicknell was an early victim, limping out in mid-May with a fractured right foot after three Championship matches. Bicknell's last first-class game until August saw Surrey's first defeat of the season – under his leadership, as Alec Stewart and Graham Thorpe were with England. By then, the vastly improved Mark Butcher was struggling with a hernia which eventually needed an operation. After nearly two months off, Butcher did re-emerge, not as a strike bowler but as an opening partner for the brilliantly consistent Darren Bicknell.

There was a manful contribution from the genial giant Cameron Cuffy, Waqar's replacement, but, solid as his performance was, his 36 wickets were a poor substitute for a world-beater. If Cuffy tours with West Indies in 1995, no doubt he will consolidate his experience and lay waste England's batting, but there was little evidence of that throughout his long, hard summer. Signing 36-year-old Tony Pigott from Sussex proved an inspired move and his tricky swing bowling eventually earned him a first-team place. Andy Smith found some turn on the Oval pitches and showed promise as an off-spinning all-rounder. He turned his maiden first-class century into a double-hundred against some accurate, if rather clubby, Oxford bowling. A lot rests on his shoulders following the sad departure of fellow off-spinner James Boiling for Durham. Not even Benjamin, ploughing his lone furrow, could save the season. Benjamin's exemplary efforts were rewarded with a well-deserved England call-up, originally for the Second Test against South Africa, though he did not play until the Third, at The Oval, where he made an admirable debut. He finished sixth in the national averages, and was chosen for the Australian tour.

So the hard work put in by an exciting batting side was for nothing. Darren Bicknell is fast becoming synonymous with consistency on another front – in being overlooked by England, despite passing 1,000 runs for a sixth consecutive year. That benchmark looks more elusive with the recent reduction in matches, so perhaps more attention should be paid to those who achieve it. Bicknell scored his maiden double-hundred, 235 not out against Nottinghamshire, but this was topped by David Ward, who made a welcome return to his best form. He did not even mind being stranded half a dozen runs short of 300 when his captain declared against Derbyshire. As in 1993, Alistair Brown and Bicknell were the only batsmen to achieve four figures for Surrey; Brown was capped and Adam Hollioake's remarkable progress continued apace. Three magnificent centuries and some exciting one-day innings, as well as 26 useful Championship wickets, reinforced Alec Stewart's confident prediction of an international career. Hollioake is a strokeplayer of the highest calibre, comfortable on both sides of the wicket, who can destroy the most experienced attack with a few telling blows.

Then there was Butcher, who reached his maiden first-class century on his return from surgery. A fine young left-hander and a clean striker of the ball, he proved he has the temperament to open the innings. Nadeem Shahid was signed from Essex and Jason Ratcliffe from Warwickshire after the season, and both could be useful assuming Thorpe and Stewart retain their Test places, especially now that Monte Lynch has moved to Gloucestershire. Shahid can also bowl leg-spin and has occasionally deputised behind the stumps. The question of wicket-keeping has still to be resolved. Stewart kept in only three late Championship matches and the specialists, Neil Sargeant and Graham Kersey, were practically inseparable on statistics.

There was an acrimonious departure from The Oval in August when Tony Murphy, who had won the NatWest quarter-final against Glamorgan with six wickets, left the club, and county cricket, after being overlooked for the semi-final.

The summer had been preceded by a troubled winter, with Stewart delaying until February his decision to carry on as captain. That helped to head off the 250 or so rebel members, who had called for a special general meeting to air their grievances over the management's handling of the club's affairs, in particular the changes on the coaching side. April brought a management reshuffle, which led to the appointment of two non-executive directors, one of them Bob Willis, the former England captain, on an executive board replacing the old management board; the unwieldy sub-committee structure was dismantled. Then came a season not much different from the last. – David Llewellyn.

SURREY 1994

[*Bill Smith*

Back row: N. F. Sargeant, M. A. Butcher, A. J. Hollioake, J. M. de la Pena, D. J. Thompson, G. J. Kennis, S. G. Kenlock, G. J. Kersey, M. R. Bainbridge. *Middle row:* G. R. Dilley (*assistant coach*), A. D. Brown, A. J. Murphy, C. E. Cuffy, J. Boiling, N. M. Kendrick, A. W. Smith, G. S. Clinton (*coach*). *Front row:* J. E. Benjamin, D. J. Bicknell, D. M. Ward, A. J. Stewart (*captain*), M. A. Lynch, M. P. Bicknell, G. P. Thorpe, A. C. S. Pigott.

SURREY RESULTS

All first-class matches – Played 18: Won 7, Lost 7, Drawn 4.

County Championship matches – Played 17: Won 7, Lost 7, Drawn 3.

Bonus points – Batting 32, Bowling 57.

Competition placings – Britannic Assurance County Championship, 7th; NatWest Bank Trophy, s-f; Benson and Hedges Cup, s-f; AXA Equity & Law League, 6th.

BRITANNIC ASSURANCE CHAMPIONSHIP AVERAGES

BATTING

	Birthplace	*M*	*I*	*NO*	*R*	*HS*	*Avge*
‡D. J. Bicknell	*Guildford*	17	28	3	1,261	235*	50.44
‡G. P. Thorpe	*Farnham*	14	21	3	897	190	49.83
‡A. D. Brown	*Beckenham*	17	24	2	1,049	172	47.68
‡D. M. Ward	*Croydon*	16	22	1	921	294*	43.85
‡A. J. Stewart	*Merton*	10	14	2	514	142	42.83
‡M. A. Lynch	*Georgetown, BG*	3	6	1	208	60	41.60
M. A. Butcher	*Croydon*	11	17	2	574	134	38.26
A. J. Hollioake	*Melbourne, Australia*	17	23	3	722	138	36.10
J. Boiling	*New Delhi, India*	5	4	2	65	34*	32.50
A. W. Smith	*Sutton*	13	19	3	291	68*	18.18
A. C. S. Pigott	*London*	8	11	0	160	40	14.54
N. M. Kendrick	*Bromley*	6	9	2	94	25	13.42
‡M. P. Bicknell	*Guildford*	8	10	2	99	38	12.37
G. J. Kersey	*Plumstead*	6	9	2	86	39	12.28
N. F. Sargeant	*Hammersmith*	8	11	2	91	27	10.11
‡J. E. Benjamin	*Christ Church, St Kitts*	15	16	1	148	33*	9.86
C. E. Cuffy§	*St Vincent*	12	15	8	42	10	6.00

Also batted: S. G. Kenlock (*Portland, Jamaica*) (1 match) did not bat.

* *Signifies not out.* ‡ *Denotes county cap.* § *Overseas player.*

The following played a total of 14 three-figure innings for Surrey in County Championship matches – D. J. Bicknell 3, A. J. Hollioake 3, A. D. Brown 2, A. J. Stewart 2, G. P. Thorpe 2, M. A. Butcher 1, D. M. Ward 1.

BOWLING

	O	*M*	*R*	*W*	*BB*	*5W/i*	*Avge*
J. E. Benjamin	563.2	127	1,578	76	6-27	5	20.76
A. C. S. Pigott	268.3	73	737	29	6-46	1	25.41
C. E. Cuffy	389.3	106	1,082	36	4-70	0	30.05
M. P. Bicknell	280.4	67	865	27	5-44	1	32.03
A. J. Hollioake	264.1	44	958	26	4-48	0	36.84
M. A. Butcher	195.4	46	637	15	4-31	0	42.46
A. W. Smith	362	66	1,283	25	5-103	1	51.32

Also bowled: D. J. Bicknell 1–0–1–0; J. Boiling 78–24–171–4; A. D. Brown 15–1–47–0; N. M. Kendrick 153.3–30–500–7; S. G. Kenlock 28–6–104–3; M. A. Lynch 10–2–35–0; A. J. Stewart 2–0–10–0; G. P. Thorpe 5–0–23–0.

Wicket-keepers: G. J. Kersey 16 ct, 2 st; N. F. Sargeant 18 ct; A. J. Stewart 6 ct, 1 st; D. M. Ward 1 ct.

Leading Fielders: M. A. Butcher 19, A. D. Brown 16.

SURREY v WORCESTERSHIRE

At The Oval, April 28, 29, 30, May 1. Surrey won by nine wickets. Surrey 24 pts, Worcestershire 5 pts. Toss: Surrey. Championship debut: J. E. Brinkley.

The match was transformed by a stand of 220 in 61 overs between Thorpe and Hollioake. They came together when Surrey were 83 for five, all taken by James Brinkley, a Scottish-born, Australian-raised fast-medium bowler in his first Championship game. But unlike Worcestershire, who had surrendered from a similar position, brought about by Butcher's career-best four for 31, Surrey went on the offensive. Hollioake's second century, in his tenth first-class innings, equalled his 123 on debut and was crammed with quality. He started 33 runs behind Thorpe but beat him to 100 by seven overs. Thorpe, more prosaic but still classy, was last out after eight hours, ten runs short of the second double-hundred of his career. Faced with a 265-run deficit, Worcestershire were unable to set much of a target. They had some consolation from wicket-keeper Rhodes, whose four catches and undefeated half-century in the first innings furthered his England claims.

Close of play: First day, Surrey 58-4 (G. P. Thorpe 26*, A. D. Brown 3*); Second day, Surrey 463-9 (G. P. Thorpe 189*, J. E. Benjamin 31*); Third day, Worcestershire 305-7 (S. R. Lampitt 20*, R. K. Illingworth 27*).

Worcestershire

*T. S. Curtis lbw b Benjamin	39	– c Butcher b Benjamin	8
W. P. C. Weston c Benjamin b Butcher	23	– c Butcher b Boiling	62
G. A. Hick c Stewart b Butcher	5	– c Brown b Butcher	26
T. M. Moody lbw b Butcher	14	– b Benjamin	60
G. R. Haynes c Hollioake b M. P. Bicknell	6	– lbw b Butcher	13
†S. J. Rhodes not out	59	– b M. P. Bicknell	17
P. J. Newport b Boiling	2	– b Hollioake	41
S. R. Lampitt c Thorpe b Butcher	22	– not out	39
R. K. Illingworth c Boiling b M. P. Bicknell	3	– c Butcher b Benjamin	31
N. V. Radford c Sargeant b M. P. Bicknell	2	– lbw b Butcher	11
J. E. Brinkley c Sargeant b M. P. Bicknell	3	– c Sargeant b Butcher	2
B 3, l-b 3, w 1, n-b 20	27	B 7, l-b 2, w 6, n-b 18	33
1/65 2/75 3/79 4/88 5/115 6/133 7/167 8/191 9/193	205	1/9 2/50 3/175 4/175 5/209 6/237 7/262 8/310 9/337	343

Bonus points – Worcestershire 1, Surrey 4.

Bowling: *First Innings*—M. P. Bicknell 21.3–8–41–4; Benjamin 23–5–69–1; Butcher 20–9–31–4; Hollioake 18–2–53–0; Boiling 7–4–5–1. *Second Innings*—M. P. Bicknell 27–8–84–1; Benjamin 30–5–87–3; Butcher 26.4–7–67–4; Hollioake 15–2–73–1; Boiling 16–5–23–1.

Surrey

D. J. Bicknell c Rhodes b Brinkley	12	– run out	24
*A. J. Stewart c Rhodes b Brinkley	3	– not out	33
G. P. Thorpe b Brinkley	190	– not out	7
D. M. Ward lbw b Brinkley	3		
J. Boiling c Rhodes b Brinkley	2		
A. D. Brown c Curtis b Brinkley	21		
A. J. Hollioake c Rhodes b Lampitt	123		
M. A. Butcher c Moody b Illingworth	6		
M. P. Bicknell c Radford b Lampitt	0		
†N. F. Sargeant lbw b Radford	27		
J. E. Benjamin not out	33		
B 1, l-b 14, w 10, n-b 25	50	L-b 2, w 1, n-b 12	15
1/6 2/25 3/33 4/47 5/83 6/303 7/320 8/327 9/391	470	1/57	(1 wkt) 79

Bonus points – Surrey 4, Worcestershire 4 (Score at 120 overs: 444-9).

Bowling: *First Innings*—Radford 26–3–84–1; Brinkley 31–5–98–6; Newport 18–2–82–0; Lampitt 16–1–69–2; Moody 15–5–52–0; Illingworth 17–3–43–1; Hick 5–0–12–0; Weston 2–0–15–0. *Second Innings*—Brinkley 9–2–33–0; Newport 7–2–15–0; Lampitt 7–0–29–0.

Umpires: A. G. T. Whitehead and P. B. Wight.

At The Oval, May 2. SURREY beat NEW ZEALANDERS by six wickets (See New Zealand tour section).

At Manchester, May 5, 6, 7, 9. SURREY beat LANCASHIRE by ten wickets.

SURREY v DERBYSHIRE

At The Oval, May 12, 13, 14, 16. Surrey won by an innings and 138 runs. Surrey 24 pts, Derbyshire 3 pts. Toss: Surrey. First-class debut: A. J. Harris.

At lunch on the second day, Ward was half a dozen paltry runs short of a triple-century and a guaranteed place in cricket history – but the next two sessions were washed out. Had Stewart known how easily Derbyshire would succumb, he might have let him bat on. Ward, however, was happy to put the team first, shared Stewart's preference for a third successive Championship victory and contented himself with 294, including five sixes and 32 fours. His partnership with Thorpe produced 301, after Stewart had been trapped by Andrew Harris's second ball in first-class cricket. Surrey took full advantage of a weak attack – DeFreitas, Cork and Mortensen were injured and flu prevented Malcolm bowling. Benjamin and Martin Bicknell were the pick of the home bowlers, though Cuffy looked good in the second innings. Only Adams showed any fight for Derbyshire; batting No. 7 because of injury, he followed his century in the Sunday match with another blistering unbeaten hundred. Of his 109, 92 came in boundaries – 17 fours and four sixes.

Close of play: First day, Derbyshire 177-6 (K. M. Krikken 8*, A. E. Warner 20*); Second day, Surrey 373-5 (D. M. Ward 216*, A. D. Brown 3*); Third day, Surrey 570-6 (D. M. Ward 294*, M. P. Bicknell 10*).

Derbyshire

P. D. Bowler c Ward b M. P. Bicknell	15	– lbw b M. P. Bicknell	5
A. S. Rollins c Sargeant b Benjamin	10	– c M. P. Bicknell b Cuffy	24
C. J. Adams c Sargeant b M. P. Bicknell	13	– (7) not out	109
*M. Azharuddin c sub b M. P. Bicknell	34	– c Ward b Benjamin	23
T. J. G. O'Gorman c Kendrick b Benjamin	44	– (3) lbw b M. P. Bicknell	2
C. M. Wells b Kendrick	11	– (5) c Sargeant b Cuffy	20
†K. M. Krikken b Cuffy	13	– (6) run out	0
A. E. Warner c Sargeant b M. P. Bicknell	20	– c Sargeant b Cuffy	7
R. W. Sladdin lbw b Benjamin	8	– c M. P. Bicknell b Benjamin	14
A. J. Harris c Sargeant b Benjamin	10	– lbw b Kendrick	1
D. E. Malcolm not out	0	– b Benjamin	10
L-b 10, n-b 20	30	L-b 1, n-b 8	9
1/21 2/36 3/43 4/103 5/130 6/146 7/177 8/192 9/208	208	1/5 2/7 3/49 4/74 5/74 6/98 7/124 8/161 9/201	224

Bonus points – Derbyshire 1, Surrey 4.

Bowling: *First Innings*—Cuffy 18.3–4–77–1; M. P. Bicknell 21–7–56–4; Benjamin 23–7–56–4; Kendrick 9–5–9–1. *Second Innings*—Cuffy 16–5–53–3; M. P. Bicknell 13–3–49–2; Hollioake 6–0–19–0; Benjamin 12.4–3–37–3; Kendrick 14–1–65–1.

Surrey

D. J. Bicknell lbw b Warner	2	A. D. Brown lbw b Warner	92
*A. J. Stewart lbw b Harris	0	M. P. Bicknell not out	10
G. P. Thorpe c sub b Harris	114	B 1, l-b 7, w 4, n-b 28	40
D. M. Ward not out	294		—
A. J. Hollioake c Bowler b Sladdin	18	1/3 2/10 3/311 (6 wkts dec.)	570
†N. F. Sargeant c Azharuddin b Sladdin	0	4/362 5/364 6/537	

N. M. Kendrick, J. E. Benjamin and C. E. Cuffy did not bat.

Bonus points – Surrey 4, Derbyshire 2 (Score at 120 overs: 510-5).

Bowling: Warner 25–2–85–2; Harris 20–0–125–2; Wells 17–0–73–0; Sladdin 50–8–155–2; Adams 12–1–61–0; Azharuddin 8–0–46–0; Bowler 1–0–17–0.

Umpires: B. Dudleston and J. H. Harris.

SURREY v NORTHAMPTONSHIRE

At The Oval, May 19, 20, 21, 23. Northamptonshire won by three wickets. Northamptonshire 20 pts, Surrey 4 pts. Toss: Surrey.

The absence of Stewart and Thorpe, on England duty, was marked by Surrey's first defeat – and Northamptonshire's first victory – in all cricket in 1994. Stand-in captain Martin Bicknell won the toss, but his decision to bat looked questionable when Ambrose collected his first five-wicket haul of the summer. Surrey were all out for 181 inside 55 overs. Some fine bowling from Benjamin kept Northamptonshire's advantage to a mere seven runs and, second time around, Ward, Brown and Hollioake made enough to suggest a challenging target. Unfortunately, rain robbed the match of the third day and the first 45 minutes of Monday. Bicknell felt obliged to declare to maintain Surrey's Championship impetus, leaving Northamptonshire to score 316 from 89 overs. Felton and Loye took them most of the way, but there were just two balls remaining when Roberts and Ripley scampered the winning run.

Close of play: First day, Northamptonshire 127-3 (R. J. Bailey 57*, A. R. Roberts 1*); Second day, Surrey 322-8 (A. J. Hollioake 66*, N. F. Sargeant 17*); Third day, No play.

Surrey

D. J. Bicknell c Ripley b Ambrose	10	– c Ripley b Taylor	3
M. A. Lynch c Lamb b Penberthy	37	– run out	46
A. W. Smith c Ripley b Ambrose	2	– run out	12
D. M. Ward c Lamb b Ambrose	32	– c and b Taylor	80
A. D. Brown c Fordham b Penberthy	18	– lbw b Penberthy	90
A. J. Hollioake c Ripley b Ambrose	1	– not out	66
M. A. Butcher not out	41	– run out	0
*M. P. Bicknell b Ambrose	4	– c Ripley b Penberthy	0
N. M. Kendrick c Penberthy b Curran	25	– c Bailey b Penberthy	0
†N. F. Sargeant c Penberthy b Curran	3	– not out	17
J. E. Benjamin c Lamb b Curran	2		
L-b 3, w 1, n-b 2	6	B 4, l-b 2, n-b 2	8
	—		—
1/16 2/28 3/77 4/89 5/103 6/103 7/107 8/145 9/167	181	1/3 2/21 3/128 4/206 5/272 6/285 7/286 8/286 (8 wkts dec.)	322

Bonus points – Northamptonshire 4.

Bowling: *First Innings*—Ambrose 18–8–38–5; Taylor 11–3–37–0; Penberthy 16–5–54–2; Curran 9.1–1–49–3. *Second Innings*—Ambrose 19–6–38–0; Taylor 18–1–85–2; Curran 7–1–34–0; Penberthy 15–1–74–3; Roberts 17–2–72–0; Bailey 3–0–13–0.

Northamptonshire

A. Fordham c Lynch b Benjamin	5	– c Sargeant b M. P. Bicknell	20
N. A. Felton c Kendrick b Hollioake	45	– c M. P. Bicknell b Benjamin	87
R. J. Bailey lbw b M. P. Bicknell	59	– lbw b Benjamin	14
*A. J. Lamb c Butcher b Benjamin	8	– c M. P. Bicknell b Benjamin	47
A. R. Roberts lbw b Hollioake	17	– (9) not out	1
M. B. Loye c Butcher b Benjamin	0	– (5) run out	66
K. M. Curran c Hollioake b M. P. Bicknell	1	– (6) c Kendrick b Hollioake	39
A. L. Penberthy lbw b Benjamin	0	– (7) c Lynch b Hollioake	4
†D. Ripley c M. P. Bicknell b Benjamin	9	– (8) not out	4
C. E. L. Ambrose lbw b Benjamin	23		
J. P. Taylor not out	0		
B 5, l-b 5, w 1, n-b 10	21	B 8, l-b 12, w 2, n-b 12	34
1/15 2/109 3/123 4/127 5/132 6/133 7/134 8/158 9/183	188	1/59 2/93 3/188 4/195 5/288 6/296 7/314 (7 wkts)	316

Bonus points – Surrey 4.

Bowling: *First Innings*—M. P. Bicknell 20–9–27–2; Benjamin 21.4–5–57–6; Butcher 10–1–33–0; Hollioake 12–3–38–2; Kendrick 9–2–23–0. *Second Innings*—M. P. Bicknell 23–4–74–1; Benjamin 21.4–4–55–3; Butcher 7–1–30–0; Kendrick 25–4–96–0; Smith 6–0–15–0; Hollioake 6–2–26–2.

Umpires: J. D. Bond and J. W. Holder.

At Gloucester, May 26, 27, 28, 30. SURREY beat GLOUCESTERSHIRE by one wicket.

At Swansea, June 2, 3, 4, 6. SURREY drew with GLAMORGAN.

SURREY v OXFORD UNIVERSITY

At The Oval, June 11, 12, 13. Drawn. Toss: Surrey. First-class debuts: S. G. Kenlock, G. J. Kennis, D. J. Thompson.

An absorbing match featured three maiden centuries: Smith of Surrey turned his into an unbeaten double-hundred, brought up with his sixth six, while the students Gupte and Kendall revealed plenty of class. Among Surrey's debutants was David Thompson, whose nickname "Lightning" seemed, at first, to indicate that he never struck in the same place twice. But his second-innings display was fast, accurate and promising and he showed few nerves as a batsman. Neither side could quite bowl the other out; Oxford declared 83 behind and, without seriously threatening a target of 268, survived 66 overs well enough. Journalist Ralph Dellor appeared briefly as a substitute during Surrey's second innings, which was also notable for its late start on the third day. When the umpires emerged, Surrey were still at the nets, mistakenly believing that play began at 11.30 a.m. as on the previous days. But they were allowed to resume four minutes behind schedule.

Close of play: First day, Surrey 397-8 (A. W. Smith 202*, A. J. Murphy 10*); Second day, Surrey 19-0 (M. A. Butcher 12*, N. M. Kendrick 5*).

Surrey

M. A. Lynch c Ecclestone b Yeabsley	30	
M. A. Butcher lbw b Yeabsley	3	(1) c sub b Ecclestone 36
A. W. Smith not out	202	(7) not out 31
N. F. Sargeant run out	29	(3) b Ecclestone 46
†G. J. Kersey c Townsend b Macmillan	32	(4) c Gupte b Ecclestone 9
G. J. Kennis c Macmillan b Trimby	23	(5) c Townsend b Trimby 18
N. M. Kendrick c and b Trimby	11	(2) c sub b Ecclestone 7
*J. Boiling c Gupte b Martin	5	(6) c Kendall b Trimby 5
D. J. Thompson st Townsend b Martin	17	(8) run out 22
A. J. Murphy not out	10	
L-b 7, w 6, n-b 22	35	B 2, l-b 3, w 1, n-b 4 10
1/29 2/52 3/121 4/206 5/273 6/305 7/329 8/367 (8 wkts dec.)	397	1/21 2/75 3/95 4/104 5/114 6/150 7/184 (7 wkts dec.) 184

S. G. Kenlock did not bat.

Bowling: *First Innings*—Ecclestone 25–3–82–0; Yeabsley 10–2–36–2; Trimby 26–3–88–2; Hollins 7–0–38–0; Martin 19–0–84–2; Macmillan 8–2–25–1; Malik 7–1–37–0. *Second Innings*—Ecclestone 14–5–66–4; Trimby 10–2–37–2; Martin 8.5–3–30–0; Hollins 5–0–30–0; Gupte 1–0–16–0.

Oxford University

*R. R. Montgomerie c Boiling b Murphy	20	lbw b Thompson 5
G. I. Macmillan b Thompson	5	c Kennis b Boiling 25
C. M. Gupte c and b Kendrick	105	c Kennis b Thompson 10
S. C. Ecclestone b Butcher	21	(5) c and b Boiling 6
W. S. Kendall b Smith	47	(4) not out 113
C. J. Hollins c Butcher b Murphy	39	lbw b Kendrick 26
H. S. Malik not out	53	b Smith 5
N. F. C. Martin not out	10	c Butcher b Smith 0
†C. J. Townsend (did not bat)		not out 6
L-b 4, n-b 10	14	B 1, l-b 2, w 5, n-b 6 14
1/6 2/38 3/88 4/192 5/246 6/270 (6 wkts dec.)	314	1/5 2/24 3/78 4/86 5/168 6/187 7/187 (7 wkts) 210

R. S. Yeabsley and P. W. Trimby did not bat.

Bowling: *First Innings*—Murphy 14–4–42–2; Thompson 13–0–86–1; Butcher 11–4–33–1; Kenlock 12–3–38–0; Kendrick 27–6–81–1; Boiling 13–5–28–0; Smith 2–1–2–1. *Second Innings*—Murphy 8–4–8–0; Thompson 14–4–37–2; Boiling 16–4–38–2; Kenlock 13–2–44–0; Smith 10–0–55–2; Kendrick 5–0–25–1.

Umpires: A. Clarkson and R. Palmer.

At Bath, June 16, 17, 18, 20. SURREY lost to SOMERSET by 317 runs.

SURREY v LEICESTERSHIRE

At The Oval, June 23, 24, 25. Surrey won by an innings and 50 runs. Surrey 24 pts, Leicestershire 5 pts. Toss: Leicestershire.

Leicestershire, who began the game in joint second place, only one point behind Surrey, were totally outclassed. Benjamin consistently got the ball to swing late away from the bat and took ten wickets in a match for the first time to become the first bowler to reach 50 Championship wickets. Leicestershire chose to bat first but conceded a 238-run advantage after magnificent centuries from both Stewart and Hollioake. Stewart's 30th first-class century was full of his customary savage shotmaking, while Hollioake's fourth delighted spectators with its range of strokeplay. Cuffy and the off-spinner Smith helped Benjamin finish off the game with a day to spare.

Close of play: First day, Surrey 104-1 (A. J. Stewart 63*, G. P. Thorpe 31*); Second day, Leicestershire 2-0 (P. V. Simmons 0*, N. E. Briers 1*).

Leicestershire

P. V. Simmons c and b Smith	39	– c sub b Cuffy	7
*N. E. Briers lbw b Cuffy	1	– c Stewart b Cuffy	4
T. J. Boon c Stewart b Benjamin	2	– lbw b Benjamin	66
J. J. Whitaker b Smith	18	– c Thorpe b Benjamin	25
V. J. Wells c Stewart b Smith	70	– b Smith	12
B. F. Smith c Stewart b Benjamin	9	– c Hollioake b Smith	18
P. N. Hepworth lbw b Benjamin	1	– c Stewart b Smith	3
†P. A. Nixon b Benjamin	58	– c Sargeant b Cuffy	12
G. J. Parsons not out	36	– c Ward b Benjamin	11
D. J. Millns b Benjamin	18	– lbw b Benjamin	13
A. D. Mullally b Benjamin	4	– not out	4
L-b 3, n-b 4	7	B 4, l-b 3, n-b 6	13
1/1 2/10 3/61 4/62 5/81 6/101 7/186 8/213 9/253	263	1/13 2/22 3/86 4/115 5/125 6/135 7/148 8/162 9/179	188

Bonus points – Leicestershire 2, Surrey 4.

Bowling: *First Innings*—Cuffy 17–7–45–1; Benjamin 23.5–2–81–6; Pigott 13–2–49–0; Smith 28–10–85–3. *Second Innings*—Benjamin 19–3–51–4; Cuffy 16–4–40–3; Smith 25–5–72–3; Pigott 5–0–18–0.

Surrey

A. W. Smith lbw b Millns	6
*A. J. Stewart b Wells	142
G. P. Thorpe c Hepworth b Parsons	64
D. M. Ward c Parsons b Mullally	21
A. D. Brown b Hepworth	20
D. J. Bicknell lbw b Simmons	59
A. J. Hollioake c and b Simmons	138
†N. F. Sargeant c Nixon b Simmons	0
A. C. S. Pigott c Wells b Hepworth	17
J. E. Benjamin c Boon b Hepworth	4
C. E. Cuffy not out	0
B 9, l-b 5, n-b 16	30
1/14 2/183 3/238 4/244 5/283 6/408 7/422 8/492 9/501	501

Bonus points – Surrey 4, Leicestershire 3 (Score at 120 overs: 476-7).

Bowling: Millns 13–3–81–1; Mullally 21–1–108–1; Wells 19–5–84–1; Parsons 27–4–75–1; Hepworth 35–9–101–3; Simmons 14.1–4–38–3.

Umpires: R. Palmer and R. A. White.

At Darlington, June 30, July 1, 2, 4. SURREY beat DURHAM by 290 runs.

SURREY v WARWICKSHIRE

At Guildford, July 14, 15, 16, 18. Warwickshire won by 256 runs. Warwickshire 21 pts, Surrey 4 pts. Toss: Surrey. Championship debut: D. R. Brown.

Warwickshire's fourth successive win put them just four points behind Championship leaders Surrey, after a game which they won through character as well as merit. Challenged to make 503, the highest fourth-innings total in Championship history, Surrey surrendered an hour and a half into the final day. In contrast, Warwickshire had recovered from 52 for five before lunch on the first morning. Lara was dismissed for two by Cuffy, who had already claimed him twice in a Red Stripe Cup match in January. But Paul Smith managed 34, despite bangs on the left elbow and right hand, and the thoroughly inexperienced Welch and Brown put on 110 for the ninth wicket. Stewart and Thorpe took Surrey to a comfortable 107 for one until Twose – bowling because of Smith's injury – dismissed both, plus Brown, within eight balls. He finished with a career-best six for 28. Doubts about the pitch were then smoothed over by Moles, who ground his way to what was believed to be the slowest double-century in Championship history, surpassing the 204 not out by Dennis

Brookes against Essex at Northampton in 1952. He batted 562 minutes and hit 29 fours in 439 balls. Acting-captain Munton's superb bowling soon had Surrey in trouble again and he collected nine wickets in the match. The game also featured 16 lbws, ten against Surrey and six against Warwickshire.

Close of play: First day, Surrey 129-6 (A. C. S. Pigott 3*, A. W. Smith 0*); Second day, Warwickshire 271-5 (A. J. Moles 140*, N. M. K. Smith 24*); Third day, Surrey 122-5 (A. D. Brown 24*, A. W. Smith 10*).

Warwickshire

First innings		Second innings	
A. J. Moles c Ward b Benjamin	5	not out	203
R. G. Twose lbw b Benjamin	5	(5) c Ward b Smith	31
B. C. Lara c Thorpe b Cuffy	2	c and b Pigott	44
D. P. Ostler b Cuffy	0	(2) c and b Benjamin	11
T. L. Penney lbw b Hollioake	8	(4) lbw b Hollioake	1
P. A. Smith lbw b Benjamin	34		
†K. J. Piper c Kersey b Cuffy	16	(9) lbw b Benjamin	0
G. Welch lbw b Pigott	59	(6) c Hollioake b Smith	0
N. M. K. Smith b Hollioake	15	(7) b Benjamin	57
D. R. Brown c Kersey b Pigott	54	(8) c Ward b Pigott	12
*T. A. Munton not out	0	(10) c Kersey b Hollioake	4
B 1, l-b 10, w 5, n-b 32	48	B 4, l-b 10, n-b 22	36
1/14 2/21 3/25 4/25 5/52 6/86 7/108 8/131 9/241	246	1/29 2/117 3/118 4/190 5/190 6/321 7/381 8/385 9/399	(9 wkts dec.) 399

Bonus points – Warwickshire 1, Surrey 4.

In the second innings N. M. K. Smith, when 33, retired hurt at 296 and resumed at 321.

Bowling: *First Innings*—Cuffy 17–3–74–3; Benjamin 18–3–79–3; Pigott 13.2–7–21–2; Hollioake 13–3–29–2; Smith 6–2–32–0. *Second Innings*—Benjamin 32–10–70–3; Cuffy 24–6–63–0; Hollioake 29.2–6–84–2; Pigott 32–9–92–2; Smith 24–5–76–2.

Surrey

First innings		Second innings	
D. J. Bicknell b Munton	0	c Piper b Welch	27
*A. J. Stewart c Piper b Twose	56	lbw b Munton	1
G. P. Thorpe c Piper b Twose	38	lbw b N. M. K. Smith	43
D. M. Ward c Ostler b Twose	17	lbw b N. M. K. Smith	4
A. D. Brown lbw b Twose	0	b Munton	29
A. J. Hollioake lbw b Twose	2	lbw b Munton	6
A. C. S. Pigott lbw b Munton	8	(9) b Munton	40
A. W. Smith lbw b Munton	4	(7) lbw b Munton	45
†G. J. Kersey not out	3	(8) c Welch b N. M. K. Smith	2
J. E. Benjamin lbw b Twose	0	st Piper b N. M. K. Smith	31
C. E. Cuffy b Munton	0	not out	2
B 2, l-b 5, n-b 8	15	B 3, l-b 11, n-b 2	16
1/0 2/107 3/112 4/112 5/116 6/129 7/140 8/141 9/142	143	1/3 2/68 3/72 4/86 5/100 6/127 7/140 8/203 9/222	246

Bonus points – Warwickshire 4.

Bowling: *First Innings*—Munton 18.5–5–41–4; Brown 4–1–22–0; Welch 7–0–39–0; N. M. K. Smith 7–4–6–0; Twose 13–3–28–6. *Second Innings*—Munton 28–6–96–5; Brown 6–1–17–0; N. M. K. Smith 33.4–13–71–4; Twose 9–3–22–0; Welch 9–3–16–1; Lara 2–0–10–0.

Umpires: K. E. Palmer and N. T. Plews.

At Nottingham, July 21, 22, 23. SURREY beat NOTTINGHAMSHIRE by an innings and 231 runs.

SURREY v SUSSEX

At The Oval, July 28, 29, 30. Sussex won by an innings and 34 runs. Sussex 22 pts, Surrey 3 pts. Toss: Sussex.

Inept batting by Surrey led to defeat by lunch on Saturday, costing them the Championship lead they had enjoyed for all but one week of the season. There was much mocking of Hall's crawl to the slowest-ever Championship fifty; his 302 minutes beat R. G. Barlow's 290 for Lancashire against Kent in 1889. But his tortoise-like 85, which finally occupied 380 minutes and 304 balls, proved crucial. Surrey set off like hares to reduce a deficit of 149 but played more like Stephenson's rabbits. They were out in just 27.3 overs, of which he bowled 14 on the way to his second 11-wicket haul of the summer. The top score was a 30-ball 34 from Sussex old boy Pigott. Thorpe hit five fours in six balls from Jarvis before his early exit, but had successfully proved his case for an England recall for the Leeds Test with a classy 71 out of a first-innings 195. Surrey's bowlers showed up their batsmen: Benjamin bowled 31 overs for 72 in sweltering conditions, while Hollioake recorded a career-best four for 48.

Close of play: First day, Sussex 40-2 (J. W. Hall 9*, A. P. Wells 4*); Second day, Sussex 344.

Surrey

D. J. Bicknell c Salisbury b Stephenson	13	– c Moores b Jarvis	14
*A. J. Stewart lbw b Stephenson	0	– c Remy b Jarvis	2
G. P. Thorpe c Hall b Stephenson	71	– c Speight b Stephenson	26
D. M. Ward c Salisbury b Stephenson	6	– lbw b Stephenson	6
A. D. Brown c Moores b Jarvis	40	– c Moores b Stephenson	2
A. J. Hollioake c Salisbury b Giddins	18	– lbw b Jarvis	5
A. W. Smith not out	16	– lbw b Giddins	8
†G. J. Kersey c Hall b Giddins	2	– c Moores b Stephenson	0
A. C. S. Pigott c Moores b Stephenson	1	– b Stephenson	34
J. E. Benjamin run out	11	– c Wells b Giddins	8
C. E. Cuffy lbw b Stephenson	1	– not out	6
B 4, l-b 4, w 4, n-b 4	16	L-b 2, n-b 2	4
1/9 2/32 3/55 4/114 5/161 6/167 7/169 8/172 9/190	195	1/8 2/19 3/28 4/46 5/55 6/55 7/55 8/97 9/105	115

Bonus points – Sussex 4.

Bowling: *First Innings*—Stephenson 22–6–50–6; Jarvis 11–2–49–1; Remy 8–0–31–0; Giddins 16–4–52–2; Salisbury 2–0–5–0. *Second Innings*—Stephenson 14–1–32–5; Jarvis 9–1–52–3; Giddins 4.3–0–29–2.

Sussex

N. J. Lenham c and b Benjamin	5
C. W. J. Athey c Brown b Pigott	20
J. W. Hall c Stewart b Hollioake	85
*A. P. Wells c Stewart b Benjamin	6
M. P. Speight c Benjamin b Smith	16
†P. Moores lbw b Hollioake	66
F. D. Stephenson c Thorpe b Cuffy	27
C. C. Remy not out	55
P. W. Jarvis c Ward b Pigott	9
I. D. K. Salisbury b Hollioake	21
E. S. H. Giddins b Hollioake	0
B 5, l-b 4, n-b 25	34
1/9 2/35 3/52 4/198 5/207 6/222 7/276 8/286 9/336	344

Bonus points – Sussex 2, Surrey 3 (Score at 120 overs: 288-8).

M. P. Speight, when 9, retired hurt at 66 and resumed at 198.

Bowling: Cuffy 27–6–60–1; Benjamin 31–10–72–2; Pigott 30–15–73–2; Hollioake 17.5–5–48–4; Smith 26–5–82–1.

Umpires: T. E. Jesty and M. J. Kitchen.

At Colchester, August 11, 12, 13, 15. SURREY lost to ESSEX by an innings and 87 runs.

At Southampton, August 18, 19, 20, 22. SURREY lost to HAMPSHIRE by an innings and 68 runs.

SURREY v MIDDLESEX

At The Oval, August 25, 26, 27, 29. Middlesex won by two wickets. Middlesex 24 pts, Surrey 6 pts. Toss: Middlesex.

Surrey's lingering title hopes were consigned to the bin after their fourth successive defeat. Middlesex did not have it easy, given a stiff target of 389 from 88 overs. Gatting, with his 82nd first-class century, and Ramprakash, just short of his second of the match, added 178 in 44. But once they were separated, wickets fell steadily, Benjamin claiming his 80th of the season. Unfortunately for Surrey, however, Carr's unprecedented run of form continued. He saw Middlesex home with two wickets and four overs to spare; by then his 593 runs from six innings (one dismissal) gave him an average second only to Lara. Surrey's batsmen gave them a promising start, with some entertaining strokeplay against a Middlesex attack which, unusually, depended on Weekes alone for spin. But Gatting was confident enough to declare 75 behind. Lynch helped Brown to set up the target with 83 in 11 overs on the last morning; he came in undefeated from his final innings after 18 seasons with Surrey.

Close of play: First day, Surrey 178-4 (D. J. Bicknell 79*, A. J. Hollioake 4*); Second day, Middlesex 190-3 (M. R. Ramprakash 48*, P. N. Weekes 5*); Third day, Surrey 230-3 (A. D. Brown 32*, M. A. Lynch 8*).

Surrey

D. J. Bicknell b Feltham	89	– c Carr b Weekes	26
M. A. Butcher lbw b Williams	2	– c sub b Weekes	70
M. A. Lynch c Brown b Feltham	27	– (5) not out	36
D. M. Ward c Brown b Shine	47	– (3) lbw b Feltham	79
A. D. Brown c Feltham b Shine	0	– (4) not out	83
A. J. Hollioake b Feltham	27		
A. W. Smith not out	68		
†G. J. Kersey c Haynes b Shine	24		
*M. P. Bicknell c sub b Feltham	38		
A. C. S. Pigott c Feltham b Weekes	30		
J. E. Benjamin c Williams b Weekes	23		
L-b 11, w 7, n-b 32	50	B 4, l-b 2, w 1, n-b 12	19
1/11 2/75 3/159 4/159 5/221 6/232 7/313 8/368 9/400	425	1/67 2/180 3/202 (3 wkts dec.)	313

Bonus points – Surrey 4, Middlesex 4.

Bowling: *First Innings*—Williams 25–6–113–1; Shine 20–2–78–3; Harris 19–4–83–0; Feltham 28–6–94–4; Weekes 8.5–1–46–2. *Second Innings*—Shine 3–0–15–0; Williams 15–2–83–0; Feltham 21–4–58–1; Weekes 28–3–117–2; Harris 5–0–34–0.

Middlesex

D. L. Haynes c Kersey b Benjamin	53	– (7) c Butcher b Benjamin	14
M. A. Roseberry c Lynch b Pigott	20	– c Butcher b Pigott	19
*M. W. Gatting c Brown b Benjamin	26	– (1) c Kersey b Pigott	103
M. R. Ramprakash b Benjamin	124	– (3) b M. P. Bicknell	90
P. N. Weekes c Lynch b Pigott	26	– (4) c Lynch b M. P. Bicknell	46
J. D. Carr not out	40	– (5) not out	62
†K. R. Brown not out	2	– (6) c Lynch b Benjamin	2
M. A. Feltham (did not bat)		– c Brown b Pigott	17
N. F. Williams (did not bat)		– c D. J. Bicknell b M. P. Bicknell	9
G. A. R. Harris (did not bat)		– not out	5
L-b 13, w 8, n-b 38	59	L-b 12, w 1, n-b 12	25
1/40 2/85 3/178 4/253 5/346 (5 wkts dec.)	350	1/40 2/218 3/238 4/285 5/304 6/326 7/357 8/373 (8 wkts)	392

K. J. Shine did not bat.

Bonus points – Middlesex 4, Surrey 2.

Bowling: *First Innings*—M. P. Bicknell 24.1–6–48–0; Pigott 23–7–54–2; Benjamin 23–6–62–3; Hollioake 5–0–43–0; Butcher 14–3–75–0; Smith 14–1–55–0. *Second Innings*—Benjamin 22–2–97–2; M. P. Bicknell 25–1–116–3; Pigott 26–2–101–3; Smith 8–1–49–0; Butcher 3–0–17–0.

Umpires: G. I. Burgess and G. Sharp.

At Scarborough, September 8, 9, 10, 12. SURREY drew with YORKSHIRE.

SURREY v KENT

At The Oval, September 15, 16, 17, 19. Drawn. Surrey 4 pts, Kent 4 pts. Toss: Surrey. Championship debut: S. G. Kenlock.

Walker's increasingly belligerent maiden first-class hundred was the highlight of a rain-ruined match. Play did not begin until 4 p.m. on the second day and was finally washed out on the last. The 20-year-old Walker started cautiously but looked ever more mature as he put on 189 with opener Ward, whose own hundred was his third of the season. Surrey's new left-arm seamer, "Mark" Kenlock, bowled positively for his three wickets but had little support. Martin Bicknell withdrew with his recurring knee injury; Stewart also left the field with a groin strain and Ward caught Ealham behind the wicket.

Close of play: First day, No play; Second day, Kent 142-2 (T. R. Ward 61*, M. J. Walker 39*); Third day, Surrey 70-1 (D. J. Bicknell 35*, G. P. Thorpe 15*).

Kent

T. R. Ward lbw b Hollioake 109
M. V. Fleming c Brown b M. P. Bicknell 17
N. R. Taylor c Hollioake b Kenlock . . . 20
M. J. Walker c Stewart b Kenlock 107
G. R. Cowdrey c Hollioake b Butcher . . 69
N. J. Llong c Butcher b Hollioake 37
M. A. Ealham c Ward b Kenlock 4
*†S. A. Marsh lbw b Butcher 47
M. J. McCague c Kenlock b Smith 6
M. M. Patel not out 9
T. N. Wren c D. J. Bicknell b Smith . . 0
L-b 14, n-b 6 20

1/26 2/56 3/245 4/266 5/343 6/352 7/402 8/431 9/432 — 445

Bonus points – Kent 4, Surrey 4.

Bowling: Benjamin 19–1–72–0; M. P. Bicknell 13–2–65–1; Kenlock 28–6–104–3; Smith 22–2–95–2; Hollioake 15–1–70–2; Butcher 9–2–25–2.

Surrey

D. J. Bicknell not out 35
M. A. Butcher c McCague b Ealham . . 20
G. P. Thorpe not out 15

1/41 (1 wkt) 70

*†A. J. Stewart, A. D. Brown, D. M. Ward, A. J. Hollioake, A. W. Smith, M. P. Bicknell, S. G. Kenlock and J. E. Benjamin did not bat.

Bowling: McCague 5–3–6–0; Wren 4–0–14–0; Patel 6–0–29–0; Ealham 5–1–17–1; Cowdrey 0.2–0–4–0.

Umpires: B. Leadbeater and N. T. Plews.

SUSSEX

President: The Duke of Richmond and Gordon
Chairman: A. M. Caffyn
Secretary: N. Bett
Captain: A. P. Wells
Manager: N. Gifford
Coach: C. E. Waller
Head Groundsman: P. Eaton
Scorer: L. V. Chandler

Sussex went into 1994 believing that a first Championship title was within their grasp at last. Expectations were high following the signing of fast bowler Paul Jarvis as "the last piece in the jigsaw" but, once again, the club could only reflect on disappointment after an eighth year passed by without a trophy.

Batting inconsistencies cost Sussex dear as they rose two places in the Championship to eighth and fared badly in one-day competition. Beaten NatWest Trophy finalists the previous year, they went out to Essex in the first round, lost to Nottinghamshire in the first round proper of the Benson and Hedges Cup and won only five Sunday League matches to finish a dismal 15th. Although they beat eventual Championship runners-up Leicestershire inside two days at Grace Road in August, to go fourth, their season effectively ended a week later when Warwickshire clinched a three-day win at Hove to make almost certain of the title. Sussex ended with seven Championship wins but might have had ten; they were only ten runs short of edging out Nottinghamshire, and lost out to Worcestershire and Derbyshire by only one wicket.

Cricket manager Norman Gifford was quick to admit his side were capable of doing a lot better and insisted that success was not far away, given the blend of youth and experience within the squad. "I was pleased by the contribution made by our bowlers, but the real disappointment was our batting in all competitions. It was one of those years when they all found it a struggle," he said. There were only five first-class centuries and no one scored 1,000 runs in the Championship. It was ironic that, after his leanest season for years, captain Alan Wells was upgraded to lead England A's tour of India. After scoring 1,000 runs in each of the previous seven seasons, Wells, in his third year as captain, was restricted to 909. He managed only one century all season and that came in the Sunday League, where he hit 618 runs.

Sussex, who had come to rely heavily on Wells's consistency, were found wanting as no one took over the mantle. Bill Athey, top-scorer with 1,600 first-class runs in 1993, scraped into four figures in the final match, against Yorkshire; Martin Speight, who missed that game through injury, was left just short and led the county's first-class averages with a modest 34.17. Despite those disappointing figures, Gifford maintained his belief in the batting's real strength, acknowledging that performances in one-day cricket were not helped by a regular shifting of the order. He was in no doubt that Sussex had one of the most balanced bowling attacks in the country. West Indian all-rounder Franklyn Stephenson was invited to take the new ball for another year after his best season yet with the county. Stephenson took 67 wickets, 26 more than the previous summer, and his 752 runs from the maximum 17 Championship games compared almost exactly with the Second Eleven record of fellow-Barbadian Vasbert Drakes who is expected to replace him in 1996.

Sussex are anxious to get the best out of 25-year-old Drakes, but he must wait another year; Stephenson says he is determined to end his Sussex career with a trophy. Bowling alongside him has done wonders for Ed Giddins, who was unlucky not to win a place on the A tour after claiming 60 wickets and a county cap on the way. The three-pronged attack of Stephenson, Giddins and Jarvis was a definite plus, and Jarvis often performed better in his first season at Sussex than figures of 51 wickets at 34.76 suggest.

Spinners Ian Salisbury and Eddie Hemmings, who took 115 first-class wickets for Sussex between them the previous season, had a joint tally of 80, but the lack of runs often gave them too little to bowl against. Salisbury, left out of the England tour to Australia, instead joined Wells on the A tour while Hemmings looked forward to his 30th season in first-class cricket. The evergreen off-spinner, who made an unsuccessful application for the coaching position at Nottinghamshire before the start of the summer, admitted that he still got a bigger kick out of playing than coaching.

The 38-year-old batsman David Smith, who played two Tests in the 1980s, had a testimonial marking his 22 years in the game. But he was restricted to only seven first-class matches in his sixth season with the county. He is due to take over the role of batting coach and Second Eleven captain, while still being registered for first-team cricket. Smith has already done much to help develop Jamie Hall and Sussex, encouraged by the strength of their Second Eleven, are keen to nurture the talents of young openers Keith Newell and Toby Peirce. Slow left-armer Jacob Dean was released, but the county signed all-rounder Alex Edwards, fast bowler James Kirtley and batsman Mark Newell on two-year contracts, all three having come up through the youth system. An important season faces all-rounders Carlos Remy and John North, yet to bridge the gap to county cricket successfully.

Chairman Alan Caffyn has told members that, for county cricket to continue in Sussex, the club must redevelop its headquarters and plans have been submitted for a £5 million transformation of the Hove County Ground. Proposals include a new multi-purpose pavilion complex at the north end of the ground, on four levels, and improvements and extensions to the east side. Many of the present buildings are over 100 years old and showing their age. The club hopes to raise more than £1 million by selling a long-term lease on the Sussex Cricketer pub, which it owns, to a brewery. – Jack Arlidge.

SUSSEX 1994

[Bill Smith

Back row: J. A. North, C. C. Remy, J. W. Dean, S. Humphries, N. C. Phillips. *Middle row:* S. Robertson (*physiotherapist*), P. W. Jarvis, J. W. Hall, J. D. Lewry, D. R. Law, E. S. H. Giddins, K. Newell, K. Greenfield, I. Waring (*youth development officer*), P. Cale (*assistant coach*). *Front row:* N. Gifford (*cricket manager*), M. P. Speight, P. Moores, N. J. Lenham, C. W. J. Athey, A. P. Wells (*captain*), D. M. Smith, I. D. K. Salisbury, F. D. Stephenson, E. E. Hemmings, C. E. Waller (*Second Eleven coach*). *Inset:* M. T. E. Peirce.

SUSSEX RESULTS

All first-class matches – Played 18: Won 7, Lost 5, Drawn 6.

County Championship matches – Played 17: Won 7, Lost 5, Drawn 5.

Bonus points – Batting 28, Bowling 60.

Competition placings – Britannic Assurance County Championship, 8th; NatWest Bank Trophy, 1st round; Benson and Hedges Cup, 1st round; AXA Equity & Law League, 15th.

BRITANNIC ASSURANCE CHAMPIONSHIP AVERAGES

BATTING

	Birthplace	*M*	*I*	*NO*	*R*	*HS*	*Avge*
‡M. P. Speight	*Walsall*	16	28	0	950	126	33.92
‡C. W. J. Athey	*Middlesbrough*	17	32	1	964	169*	31.09
‡A. P. Wells	*Newhaven*	17	32	3	889	84	30.65
‡N. J. Lenham	*Worthing*	13	25	1	729	102	30.37
‡D. M. Smith	*Balham*	7	14	3	326	74	29.63
‡J. W. Hall	*Chichester*	13	25	0	729	85	29.16
‡F. D. Stephenson§	*St James, Barbados*	17	28	1	752	107	27.85
‡P. Moores	*Macclesfield*	17	30	2	733	70*	26.17
C. C. Remy	*Castries, St Lucia*	5	9	1	168	60	21.00
‡I. D. K. Salisbury	*Northampton*	15	23	5	325	49	18.05
P. W. Jarvis	*Redcar*	16	25	4	258	44	12.28
‡E. E. Hemmings	*Leamington Spa*	14	24	12	88	14*	7.33
J. D. Lewry	*Worthing*	3	6	4	14	6*	7.00
‡E. S. H. Giddins	*Eastbourne*	16	22	4	83	24	4.61

Also batted: K. Greenfield (*Brighton*) (1 match) 35*, 26*.

* *Signifies not out.* ‡ *Denotes county cap.* § *Overseas player.*

The following played a total of five three-figure innings for Sussex in County Championship matches – C. W. J. Athey 2, N. J. Lenham 1, M. P. Speight 1, F. D. Stephenson 1.

BOWLING

	O	*M*	*R*	*W*	*BB*	*5W/i*	*Avge*
F. D. Stephenson	480.5	108	1,345	67	6-50	6	20.07
E. S. H. Giddins	424.4	88	1,357	60	5-38	3	22.61
I. D. K. Salisbury	430	137	1,215	47	6-55	3	25.85
E. E. Hemmings	422	140	959	33	7-66	2	29.06
P. W. Jarvis	462.2	85	1,648	49	7-58	1	33.63

Also bowled: C. W. J. Athey 18–1–78–1; K. Greenfield 16–1–76–0; N. J. Lenham 9–0–24–0; J. D. Lewry 65–13–209–6; C. C. Remy 41–6–152–3; A. P. Wells 7–2–27–0.

Wicket-keeper: P. Moores 60 ct.

Leading Fielders: I. D. K. Salisbury 19, M. P. Speight 19, A. P. Wells 15.

At Bristol, May 5, 6, 7, 9. SUSSEX drew with GLOUCESTERSHIRE.

SUSSEX v HAMPSHIRE

At Hove, May 12, 13, 14, 16. Sussex won by two wickets. Sussex 22 pts, Hampshire 6 pts. Toss: Sussex.

Sussex made hard work of a target of 156. From 108 for four they lost three wickets in nine balls before Moores, with the benefit of 29 off two overs from Benjamin, steadied them with a plucky 47 and Jarvis and Hemmings finished the job. The game started with a Hampshire batting crisis, which Smith relieved with a powerful 124, supplemented by a 42-ball fifty from Benjamin. Then Speight held Sussex together with a brilliant 126 off 147 balls. It took him 35 minutes to get off the mark, as Sussex limped to 73 for six, but there was no stopping him after that: he hit 16 fours and five sixes. Last man Giddins hit Udal on to the roof of the Gilligan stand. On the third day, Hampshire struggled in gloomy conditions which eventually washed out the afternoon. Stephenson claimed four for 25 and, next day, took his match figures to 11 for 96; Giddins took the last four wickets in 23 balls.

Close of play: First day, Hampshire 267-9 (W. K. M. Benjamin 51*); Second day, Hampshire 44-1 (T. C. Middleton 24*); Third day, Hampshire 112-5 (K. D. James 13*, A. N. Aymes 4*).

Hampshire

T. C. Middleton c Moores b Stephenson	0	– c Hall b Stephenson	35
V. P. Terry c Smith b Salisbury	19	– c Moores b Stephenson	15
R. S. M. Morris c Moores b Stephenson	0	– c Moores b Stephenson	14
R. A. Smith c sub b Salisbury	124	– c Moores b Stephenson	13
*M. C. J. Nicholas b Giddins	2	– c Athey b Stephenson	4
K. D. James lbw b Stephenson	4	– lbw b Stephenson	21
†A. N. Aymes lbw b Salisbury	37	– b Giddins	24
S. D. Udal c and b Stephenson	15	– not out	10
W. K. M. Benjamin c Moores b Stephenson	51	– c Speight b Giddins	2
M. J. Thursfield lbw b Salisbury	2	– lbw b Giddins	0
N. G. Cowans not out	0	– b Giddins	0
L-b 5, w 2, n-b 6	13	L-b 15, w 2, n-b 12	29
1/0 2/4 3/78 4/87 5/103 6/183 7/196 8/244 9/267	267	1/44 2/69 3/70 4/78 5/95 6/132 7/157 8/167 9/167	167

Bonus points – Hampshire 2, Sussex 4.

Bowling: *First Innings*—Stephenson 16.1–5–41–5; Jarvis 15–2–63–0; Giddins 15–2–64–1; Salisbury 28–7–90–4; Hemmings 1–0–4–0. *Second Innings*—Stephenson 24–7–55–6; Jarvis 8–2–16–0; Giddins 12.5–2–21–4; Salisbury 21–3–49–0; Hemmings 8–4–11–0.

Sussex

C. W. J. Athey lbw b Cowans	2	– c Udal b Cowans	18
J. W. Hall lbw b Cowans	5	– c Morris b Thursfield	8
D. M. Smith lbw b Cowans	15	– b James	16
*A. P. Wells c Aymes b Thursfield	5	– c Terry b Benjamin	17
M. P. Speight lbw b Udal	126	– b Cowans	15
†P. Moores b James	5	– lbw b Benjamin	47
F. D. Stephenson lbw b Benjamin	25	– lbw b Benjamin	0
I. D. K. Salisbury b Thursfield	49	– b Udal	0
P. W. Jarvis c and b Benjamin	10	– not out	19
E. E. Hemmings not out	13	– not out	6
E. S. H. Giddins b Thursfield	15		
L-b 7, n-b 2	9	B 2, l-b 7, w 1	10
1/3 2/16 3/29 4/29 5/34 6/73 7/224 8/250 9/252	279	1/29 2/49 3/49 4/70 (8 wkts) 5/108 6/108 7/109 8/139	156

Bonus points – Sussex 2, Hampshire 4.

Bowling: *First Innings*—Benjamin 21–4–49–2; Cowans 15–4–41–3; Thursfield 14.3–3–61–3; James 12–1–51–1; Udal 14–2–70–1. *Second Innings*—Benjamin 16.2–7–52–3; Cowans 10–4–29–2; Udal 12–5–20–1; Thursfield 6–2–14–1; James 9–2–32–1.

Umpires: J. C. Balderstone and V. A. Holder.

At Nottingham, May 19, 20, 21, 23. SUSSEX drew with NOTTINGHAMSHIRE.

SUSSEX v GLAMORGAN

At Hove, May 26, 27, 28, 30. Drawn. Sussex 5 pts, Glamorgan 6 pts. Toss: Sussex. Championship debut: A. Roseberry.

After torrential rain washed out the first day, Wells inserted Glamorgan, expecting the damp atmosphere to assist his bowlers. But the sun came out and Glamorgan's batsmen played themselves back into form, especially Morris and Dale, who reached his century with a six and struck 17 beautifully timed fours. Glamorgan declared with 432 on the board. But Sussex also flourished on the increasingly benign pitch. Smith led the way with 74, then Moores hit 70 in 74 balls and Sussex declared promptly on achieving their third bonus point. Giddins took three quick wickets before Morris's reciprocal declaration set Sussex 320 in 74 overs. At tea they had a chance, on 120 for two, but Wells and Speight were dismissed off successive balls and, with Hall soon following, Sussex called off the chase. Stephenson at least provided some late entertainment, with a dashing run-a-ball 71.

Close of play: First day, No play; Second day, Glamorgan 386-5 (R. D. B. Croft 13*, O. D. Gibson 0*); Third day, Glamorgan 40-0 (S. P. James 15*, H. Morris 23*).

Glamorgan

S. P. James b Giddins	44	– lbw b Giddins	20
*H. Morris c Moores b Jarvis	106	– c Salisbury b Giddins	53
A. Dale c Athey b Salisbury	131	– c Moores b Giddins	1
D. L. Hemp b Salisbury	55	– b Salisbury	42
P. A. Cottey not out	27	– not out	45
A. Roseberry b Jarvis	5	– not out	15
R. D. B. Croft not out	36		
O. D. Gibson b Stephenson	13		
L-b 10, w 3, n-b 2	15	L-b 3, w 2, n-b 6	11
1/125 2/186 3/328 4/355 5/365 6/410 (6 wkts dec.)	432	1/68 2/72 3/91 4/143 (4 wkts dec.)	187

†C. P. Metson, S. L. Watkin and S. Bastien did not bat.

Bonus points – Glamorgan 4, Sussex 2 (Score at 120 overs: 425-6).

In the first innings P. A. Cottey, when 18, retired hurt at 386 and resumed at 410.

Bowling: *First Innings*—Stephenson 29–5–73–1; Jarvis 30–7–102–2; Giddins 26–4–88–1; Salisbury 24–5–108–2; Greenfield 8–1–32–0; Athey 4–0–19–0. *Second Innings*—Wells 7–2–27–0; Athey 6–1–13–0; Giddins 12–1–45–3; Salisbury 19.3–6–55–1; Greenfield 8–0–44–0.

Sussex

C. W. J. Athey c Metson b Dale	16	– c Metson b Watkin	7
J. W. Hall lbw b Gibson	36	– c Cottey b Croft	70
D. M. Smith c Cottey b Gibson	74	– c Metson b Gibson	2
*A. P. Wells c Metson b Dale	24	– c Metson b Bastien	64
M. P. Speight c Gibson b Bastien	4	– b Bastien	0
K. Greenfield not out	35	– not out	26
†P. Moores not out	70	– c Cottey b Croft	8
F. D. Stephenson (did not bat)		– not out	71
B 2, l-b 8, w 2, n-b 29	41	L-b 8, w 2, n-b 2	12
1/50 2/87 3/138 4/160 5/197 (5 wkts dec.)	300	1/8 2/18 3/148 4/148 5/158 6/170 (6 wkts)	260

I. D. K. Salisbury, P. W. Jarvis and E. S. H. Giddins did not bat.

Bonus points – Sussex 3, Glamorgan 2.

Bowling: *First Innings*—Watkin 20–5–59–0; Bastien 16.4–4–55–1; Gibson 14–0–78–2; Dale 17–4–48–2; Croft 8.2–1–27–0; Cottey 4.4–0–23–0. *Second Innings*—Watkin 14–2–44–1; Gibson 15–2–61–1; Bastien 14.3–5–47–2; Dale 8–2–29–0; Croft 22–5–71–2.

Umpires: A. G. T. Whitehead and P. B. Wight.

At Tunbridge Wells, June 2, 3, 4, 6. SUSSEX drew with KENT.

SUSSEX v LANCASHIRE

At Horsham, June 9, 10, 11, 13. Sussex won by 60 runs. Sussex 24 pts, Lancashire 6 pts. Toss: Sussex.

A marvellous game in glorious weather ended with Sussex deservedly claiming the spoils, despite a superb display of powerful hitting from Wasim Akram. Lancashire had been set an improbable 451 on the last day and when Wasim came to the crease they were 267 for six with 23 overs left. Instead of blocking, he proceeded to pulverise the Sussex attack, striking eight sixes, to all parts of the ground, and ten fours. But, trying to reach his hundred off the 76th ball he received with another six, he was beaten by Hemmings's yorker and Sussex had won. They had always had the upper hand: Stephenson's second century for Sussex helped them to 355, and a burst of four wickets in 14 balls from Giddins reduced Lancashire to 156 for eight. But last man Martin and Watkinson pulled them around with an exciting 115-run stand which averted the follow-on. On the third day, Lenham batted with rare freedom to set up a taxing target. Then Salisbury rediscovered his form with five for 109 – despite being hit for five sixes by Wasim.

Close of play: First day, Sussex 333-7 (F. D. Stephenson 92*, I. D. K. Salisbury 18*); Second day, Lancashire 262-9 (M. Watkinson 51*, P. J. Martin 52*); Third day, Sussex 381-9 (E. E. Hemmings 3*).

Sussex

C. W. J. Athey c Hegg b Watkinson	19	– lbw b Wasim Akram	7
J. W. Hall lbw b Yates	55	– lbw b Watkinson	23
N. J. Lenham c Atherton b Watkinson	2	– lbw b Gallian	102
*A. P. Wells c Crawley b Yates	34	– c Hegg b Wasim Akram	61
M. P. Speight c Watkinson b Yates	40	– lbw b Yates	38
†P. Moores c Speak b Wasim Akram	12	– c Gallian b Yates	39
F. D. Stephenson c Watkinson b Martin	107	– c Hegg b Yates	57
P. W. Jarvis c Atherton b Gallian	44	– c Atherton b Martin	12
I. D. K. Salisbury b Watkinson	18	– c Watkinson b Martin	6
E. E. Hemmings not out	6	– not out	3
E. S. H. Giddins c Hegg b Watkinson	0		
B 4, l-b 8, w 4, n-b 2	18	B 7, l-b 13, w 1, n-b 12	33
1/49 2/51 3/105 4/140 5/161 6/185 7/292 8/333 9/351	355	1/24 2/74 3/196 4/249 5/267 6/331 7/359 8/375 9/381 (9 wkts dec.)	381

Bonus points – Sussex 4, Lancashire 4.

Bowling: *First Innings*—Wasim Akram 21–2–71–1; Martin 32–13–78–1; Gallian 15–2–42–1; Watkinson 15.2–4–40–4; Yates 31–4–112–3. *Second Innings*—Wasim Akram 19–2–84–2; Martin 20.5–4–63–2; Watkinson 21–8–43–1; Gallian 12–2–48–1; Yates 30–4–123–3.

Lancashire

M. A. Atherton c Moores b Stephenson	0 – c and b Salisbury	35
J. E. R. Gallian lbw b Jarvis	27 – c Moores b Jarvis	13
J. P. Crawley hit wkt b Stephenson	20 – c Wells b Salisbury	35
N. H. Fairbrother c Salisbury b Giddins	0 – c Athey b Hemmings	38
N. J. Speak b Giddins	62 – run out	50
G. D. Lloyd b Giddins	30 – c Speight b Salisbury	65
*M. Watkinson not out	68 – c Stephenson b Salisbury	28
Wasim Akram b Giddins	0 – b Hemmings	98
†W. K. Hegg lbw b Giddins	4 – c and b Salisbury	3
G. Yates lbw b Jarvis	9 – c Moores b Hemmings	8
P. J. Martin c and b Jarvis	57 – not out	0
L-b 7, n-b 2	9 B 8, l-b 4, w 5	17
1/0 2/22 3/40 4/84 5/147 6/152 7/152 8/156 9/171	286 1/26 2/91 3/92 4/142 5/189 6/267 7/318 8/332 9/383	390

Bonus points – Lancashire 2, Sussex 4.

Bowling: *First Innings*—Stephenson 18–3–65–2; Jarvis 23.4–7–62–3; Giddins 24–5–81–5; Hemmings 19–8–28–0; Salisbury 21–7–43–0. *Second Innings*—Stephenson 7–0–25–0; Jarvis 16–5–40–1; Giddins 14–0–84–0; Hemmings 30.1–8–120–3; Salisbury 32–11–109–5.

Umpires: J. D. Bond and D. R. Shepherd.

SUSSEX v DURHAM

At Hove, June 16, 17, 18. Sussex won by eight wickets. Sussex 24 pts, Durham 6 pts. Toss: Durham.

Salisbury and Hemmings spun Sussex to victory inside three days, helped by some reckless batting. At 147 for one, Durham had the advantage on a good pitch. But once Larkins went for 78, they capitulated alarmingly, mainly to Salisbury, in a 31-over spell from the Sea End. Athey batted Sussex into a strong position with 166. He punished the bad ball ruthlessly to hit 20 fours in a shade under six hours. Cummins bowled with great heart for five wickets, but some useful middle-order contributions helped Sussex to a lead of 133. Then Hemmings and Salisbury got to work, bowling beautifully on a pitch offering only moderate turn. With runs in the bank, they could maintain the pressure and wait for mistakes; Hemmings claimed five for 53. Sussex needed 109 and, though they lost Athey first ball, Lenham and Wells cut loose to get home with 2.5 overs of the third day to spare.

Close of play: First day, Sussex 54-0 (C. W. J. Athey 25*, J. W. Hall 15*); Second day, Durham 42-0 (W. Larkins 30*, M. Saxelby 9*).

Durham

W. Larkins c Moores b Giddins	78 – c Lenham b Salisbury	71
M. Saxelby c and b Salisbury	50 – lbw b Stephenson	9
J. E. Morris b Salisbury	28 – lbw b Hemmings	58
S. Hutton lbw b Giddins	5 – c Salisbury b Hemmings	12
J. I. Longley c and b Salisbury	9 – c Wells b Hemmings	57
A. C. Cummins c Stephenson b Athey	22 – b Salisbury	1
†C. W. Scott c Moores b Hemmings	51 – c Wells b Salisbury	0
J. Wood b Giddins	4 – (9) c Speight b Hemmings	1
*D. A. Graveney not out	7 – (8) b Jarvis	19
A. Walker c Speight b Hemmings	0 – c Athey b Hemmings	2
S. J. E. Brown c Hall b Salisbury	15 – not out	0
L-b 5, n-b 4	9 B 1, l-b 8, n-b 2	11
1/89 2/147 3/158 4/165 5/173 6/247 7/255 8/255 9/256	278 1/61 2/107 3/154 4/169 5/170 6/172 7/204 8/216 9/234	241

Bonus points – Durham 2, Sussex 4.

Bowling: *First Innings*—Stephenson 5–0–32–0; Jarvis 11–1–50–0; Salisbury 31.2–12–93–4; Hemmings 20–4–46–2; Giddins 22–6–51–3; Athey 1–0–1–1. *Second Innings*—Stephenson 12–3–23–1; Jarvis 18–2–77–1; Salisbury 26–11–64–3; Giddins 3–0–15–0; Hemmings 29.2–8–53–5.

Sussex

C. W. J. Athey c Scott b Wood	166	– b Cummins	0
J. W. Hall c Scott b Cummins	16	– c Scott b Wood	14
N. J. Lenham lbw b Brown	8	– not out	42
*A. P. Wells c Scott b Cummins	48	– not out	52
M. P. Speight lbw b Walker	49		
†P. Moores b Cummins	30		
F. D. Stephenson c Hutton b Wood	10		
P. W. Jarvis c Scott b Wood	1		
I. D. K. Salisbury not out	24		
E. E. Hemmings c Scott b Cummins	6		
E. S. H. Giddins lbw b Cummins	0		
B 3, l-b 10, w 1, n-b 39	53	W 1	1
1/61 2/74 3/183 4/312 5/328 6/358 7/363 8/387 9/411	411	1/0 2/32	(2 wkts) 109

Bonus points – Sussex 4, Durham 4.

Bowling: *First Innings*—Cummins 24–5–84–5; Brown 23–5–79–1; Walker 21–4–76–1; Graveney 26–5–57–0; Wood 19–1–102–3. *Second Innings*—Cummins 5–0–11–1; Brown 4–0–15–0; Graveney 9.1–1–49–0; Wood 3–1–10–1; Walker 6–0–24–0.

Umpires: J. H. Harris and G. Sharp.

At Worcester, June 23, 24, 25, 27. SUSSEX lost to WORCESTERSHIRE by one wicket.

At Hove, June 29, 30, July 1. SUSSEX drew with SOUTH AFRICANS (See South African tour section).

SUSSEX v MIDDLESEX

At Arundel, July 14, 15, 16. Sussex won by 148 runs. Sussex 21 pts, Middlesex 4 pts. Toss: Sussex. Championship debut: J. D. Lewry.

Just about everything went right for Sussex on their annual visit to the Castle ground. Crowds and commercial interest were up on previous years and they also bowled Middlesex out for 87 to inflict the title-holders' first Championship defeat of the season. It was an ideal start for their new left-arm swing bowler Jason Lewry, who took four for 40, including the prized wicket of Gatting for nought. Sussex's first-innings total of 228 looked inadequate on a good pitch. But next day Stephenson and Lewry reduced Middlesex to 35 for seven. It took a ninth-wicket stand of 36 between Emburey and Fraser to avoid the follow-on. Although Tufnell took three wickets just before the second-day close, Speight survived to smash a decisive 97. On a wearing pitch, a target of 380 always looked beyond Middlesex. Roseberry dug in for 76 but fell to Salisbury, who picked up six for 55.

Close of play: First day, Middlesex 23-2 (D. L. Haynes 11*, M. R. Ramprakash 8*); Second day, Sussex 196-8 (M. P. Speight 59*).

Sussex

Batsman	First innings		Second innings	
N. J. Lenham c Tufnell b Emburey	45	–	b Emburey	26
C. W. J. Athey c Johnson b Tufnell	70	–	lbw b Fraser	0
J. W. Hall c Gatting b Fraser	18	–	c Carr b Feltham	45
*A. P. Wells c Roseberry b Tufnell	7	–	c Gatting b Fraser	17
M. P. Speight c Feltham b Johnson	30	–	c Gatting b Fraser	97
†P. Moores c Ramprakash b Fraser	16	–	b Emburey	7
F. D. Stephenson c Haynes b Johnson	13	–	c Brown b Tufnell	28
I. D. K. Salisbury c Brown b Johnson	1	–	(9) c Emburey b Tufnell	0
E. E. Hemmings c Carr b Emburey	2	–	(8) c Roseberry b Tufnell	2
J. D. Lewry not out	4	–	c Carr b Tufnell	4
E. S. H. Giddins c Brown b Johnson	5	–	not out	0
B 2, l-b 9, n-b 6	17		B 6, l-b 6	12
1/93 2/135 3/151 4/155 5/186 6/204 7/208 8/217 9/219	228		1/3 2/54 3/92 4/116 5/135 6/194 7/196 8/196 9/226	238

Bonus points – Sussex 1, Middlesex 4.

Bowling: *First Innings*—Fraser 17–4–39–2; Johnson 15–1–40–4; Feltham 6–0–28–0; Tufnell 33–7–78–2; Emburey 23–9–32–2. *Second Innings*—Fraser 23.1–4–78–3; Johnson 10–5–16–0; Feltham 13–3–28–1; Emburey 16–1–43–2; Tufnell 24–5–61–4.

Middlesex

Batsman	First innings		Second innings	
D. L. Haynes run out	13	–	lbw b Stephenson	2
M. A. Roseberry lbw b Stephenson	0	–	c Moores b Salisbury	76
*M. W. Gatting c Moores b Lewry	0	–	c Moores b Stephenson	3
M. R. Ramprakash c Moores b Stephenson	8	–	c Athey b Hemmings	37
J. D. Carr lbw b Lewry	1	–	c Moores b Salisbury	9
†K. R. Brown lbw b Lewry	15	–	not out	45
M. A. Feltham b Stephenson	2	–	c Hall b Salisbury	25
R. L. Johnson b Lewry	3	–	(9) b Salisbury	20
J. E. Emburey b Stephenson	22	–	(8) c Athey b Hemmings	1
A. R. C. Fraser c Athey b Stephenson	16	–	b Salisbury	8
P. C. R. Tufnell not out	0	–	c Speight b Salisbury	4
L-b 6, w 1	7		L-b 1	1
1/1 2/3 3/26 4/27 5/27 6/30 7/35 8/50 9/86	87		1/4 2/18 3/90 4/123 5/132 6/172 7/178 8/211 9/225	231

Bonus points – Sussex 4.

Bowling: *First Innings*—Stephenson 16.1–4–25–5; Lewry 21–7–40–4; Giddins 7–4–12–0; Salisbury 2–0–4–0. *Second Innings*—Stephenson 8–1–23–2; Lewry 5–0–19–0; Giddins 14–3–34–0; Hemmings 29–7–99–2; Salisbury 17.5–2–55–6.

Umpires: K. J. Lyons and B. J. Meyer.

SUSSEX v SOMERSET

At Hove, July 21, 22, 23, 25. Somerset won by 68 runs. Somerset 23 pts, Sussex 5 pts. Toss: Somerset.

An absorbing struggle on a turning pitch swung Somerset's way because they batted better. The star turn was Lathwell. In the first innings he hit a powerful 124, going from 25 to 57 in boundaries. Later, he and Trescothick gave Somerset's second innings a great start of 166. Back on the first day, Hemmings took the first six wickets. He finished with seven for 66, but Caddick, in a career-best 58 not out, helped the last two wickets raise 82 crucial runs. Another off-spinner, Trump, soon got among the Sussex batsmen after Lenham and Athey opened with 117. At 195 for one, Somerset looked well set. Then Jarvis switched ends to take seven for 58, his best for Sussex, before he slipped on old footholds and limped off. Despite Athey's freak dismissal – pulling a ball into short-leg's armpit – Sussex looked on course for 383 at 158 for one. But Rose and Trump, whose match figures were 12 for 195, tore into the middle order and Somerset wrapped up their fourth successive win.

Close of play: First day, Somerset 277-7 (G. D. Rose 24*, A. R. Caddick 5*); Second day, Sussex 256-7 (P. W. Jarvis 0*); Third day, Sussex 26-0 (N. J. Lenham 12*, C. W. J. Athey 11*).

Somerset

First Innings		Second Innings	
M. N. Lathwell lbw b Hemmings	124	– c and b Stephenson	92
M. E. Trescothick b Hemmings	8	– c Hall b Jarvis	87
R. J. Harden c Athey b Hemmings	79	– c Moores b Jarvis	10
N. A. Folland c Moores b Hemmings	0	– c Speight b Jarvis	33
*A. N. Hayhurst c Giddins b Hemmings	19	– lbw b Jarvis	0
†R. J. Turner c Moores b Hemmings	5	– c Speight b Jarvis	19
G. D. Rose lbw b Lewry	24	– b Jarvis	2
J. C. Hallett c Moores b Giddins	5	– c Moores b Jarvis	0
A. R. Caddick not out	58	– not out	30
H. R. J. Trump b Stephenson	18	– not out	16
M. Dimond lbw b Hemmings	9		
L-b 2, w 1, n-b 8	11	B 4, l-b 3, n-b 6	13
1/17 2/190 3/190 4/230 5/237 6/252 7/272 8/278 9/324	360	1/166 2/195 3/203 4/203 5/249 6/250 7/252 8/253 (8 wkts dec.)	302

Bonus points – Somerset 3, Sussex 3 (Score at 120 overs: 301-8).

Bowling: *First Innings*—Stephenson 25–3–51–1; Jarvis 26–6–92–0; Hemmings 46.5–19–66–7; Lewry 15–3–59–1; Giddins 21–3–87–1; Athey 1–0–3–0. *Second Innings*—Stephenson 25.4–6–81–1; Lewry 9–2–36–0; Jarvis 25.2–5–58–7; Hemmings 9–2–51–0; Giddins 15–1–62–0; Athey 2–0–7–0.

Sussex

First Innings		Second Innings	
N. J. Lenham lbw b Trump	68	– b Trump	73
C. W. J. Athey c Dimond b Trump	46	– c Trescothick b Trump	40
J. W. Hall c Turner b Lathwell	59	– b Rose	54
*A. P. Wells c Turner b Rose	7	– c Trescothick b Trump	0
M. P. Speight c Turner b Caddick	0	– c Lathwell b Trump	48
†P. Moores b Trump	10	– c and b Rose	35
F. D. Stephenson c Trescothick b Lathwell	43	– c Hayhurst b Rose	5
P. W. Jarvis c Turner b Trump	18	– c Dimond b Trump	26
E. E. Hemmings b Trump	5	– c Caddick b Trump	5
J. D. Lewry not out	0	– c Trump b Rose	0
E. S. H. Giddins c Dimond b Trump	0	– not out	0
L-b 8, n-b 16	24	B 7, l-b 17, n-b 4	28
1/117 2/134 3/157 4/162 5/184 6/255 7/256 8/275 9/280	280	1/75 2/158 3/158 4/218 5/244 6/249 7/280 8/311 9/314	314

Bonus points – Sussex 2, Somerset 4.

Bowling: *First Innings*—Caddick 20–0–90–1; Dimond 13–2–36–0; Trump 32.4–16–68–6; Rose 12–3–32–1; Hallett 5–0–25–0; Lathwell 8–3–21–2. *Second Innings*—Caddick 21–4–56–0; Trump 42.3–9–127–6; Lathwell 2–0–9–0; Dimond 6–1–25–0; Hallett 10–3–28–0; Rose 15–3–45–4.

Umpires: G. I. Burgess and N. T. Plews.

At The Oval, July 28, 29, 30. SUSSEX beat SURREY by an innings and 34 runs.

At Northampton, August 4, 5, 6. SUSSEX beat NORTHAMPTONSHIRE by 217 runs.

SUSSEX v DERBYSHIRE

At Eastbourne, August 11, 12, 13, 15. Derbyshire won by one wicket. Derbyshire 20 pts, Sussex 4 pts. Toss: Sussex.

Sussex's Championship ambitions suffered a near-terminal blow at the Saffrons, with Malcolm the hero, as he was to be five days later in the Oval Test – this time, more improbably, it was as a batsman. A low-scoring game reached its climax with Derbyshire 148 for nine chasing 176, after Giddins dismissed Cork and Warner with successive balls. But Malcolm drove Stephenson for four, swung him over mid-wicket for six and then scampered the winning run with Vandrau, who made a priceless 24. Rain allowed only 15.3 overs on the first day. On the second, Sussex were quickly dismissed for 171 as DeFreitas took five for 73 but, with the pitch offering unpredictable bounce, Derbyshire fared even worse. Giddins, on his home ground, collected five for 38 as Derbyshire lost nine for 70 in 25 overs. The home team were in again before the close, to build on a lead of 48. But next day Cork, bowling unchanged, was virtually unplayable, claiming six for 29. Nevertheless, Sussex seemed assured of victory until Malcolm and Vandrau formed their match-winning alliance.

Close of play: First day, Sussex 29-1 (N. J. Lenham 12*, D. M. Smith 11*); Second day, Sussex 21-0 (N. J. Lenham 14*, C. W. J. Athey 7*); Third day, Derbyshire 94-5 (K. M. Krikken 11*, M. J. Vandrau 1*).

Sussex

N. J. Lenham lbw b DeFreitas	18	– lbw b Cork	21
C. W. J. Athey b Malcolm	3	– c Rollins b Vandrau	11
D. M. Smith c Krikken b Malcolm	63	– c Warner b Cork	4
*A. P. Wells lbw b DeFreitas	11	– c Krikken b Malcolm	11
M. P. Speight c Cork b DeFreitas	0	– b Cork	46
†P. Moores b DeFreitas	2	– lbw b Malcolm	3
F. D. Stephenson c Barnett b DeFreitas	19	– lbw b Malcolm	12
P. W. Jarvis lbw b Cork	18	– lbw b Cork	2
I. D. K. Salisbury not out	17	– c Krikken b Cork	5
E. E. Hemmings c Adams b Malcolm	1	– not out	0
E. S. H. Giddins b Malcolm	2	– b Cork	0
B 2, l-b 9, w 2, n-b 4	17	L-b 7, w 1, n-b 4	12
1/8 2/44 3/73 4/73 5/75 6/105 7/150 8/150 9/167	171	1/27 2/38 3/38 4/56 5/60 6/91 7/102 8/124 9/127	127

Bonus points – Derbyshire 4.

Bowling: *First Innings*—DeFreitas 27–5–73–5; Malcolm 15.3–4–37–4; Warner 19–6–34–0; Cork 9–3–16–1. *Second Innings*—DeFreitas 6–2–16–0; Malcolm 19–4–49–3; Vandrau 10–2–26–1; Cork 24.5–8–29–6.

Derbyshire

P. D. Bowler c Wells b Giddins	25	– c Moores b Giddins	52
A. S. Rollins lbw b Stephenson	0	– c Salisbury b Jarvis	1
C. J. Adams b Salisbury	31	– lbw b Hemmings	6
T. J. G. O'Gorman lbw b Salisbury	13	– c Speight b Hemmings	0
*K. J. Barnett c Wells b Salisbury	22	– c Smith b Salisbury	13
D. G. Cork lbw b Giddins	0	– (9) c Moores b Giddins	16
P. A. J. DeFreitas c Smith b Giddins	6	– (8) c Hemmings b Salisbury	14
M. J. Vandrau b Giddins	9	– (7) not out	24
†K. M. Krikken not out	2	– (6) lbw b Stephenson	15
A. E. Warner c Wells b Salisbury	0	– c Moores b Giddins	0
D. E. Malcolm c Stephenson b Giddins	8	– not out	15
B 2, l-b 5	7	B 12, l-b 8	20
1/15 2/53 3/70 4/85 5/94 6/102 7/110 8/113 9/114	123	1/18 2/40 3/40 4/57 5/93 6/99 7/118 8/148 9/148	(9 wkts) 176

Bonus points – Sussex 4.

Bowling: *First Innings*—Stephenson 6–0–28–1; Jarvis 5–0–20–0; Giddins 13.4–3–38–5; Salisbury 13–4–30–4; Hemmings 1–1–0–0. *Second Innings*—Stephenson 16.2–2–55–1; Jarvis 5–1–10–1; Salisbury 25–13–33–2; Giddins 16–2–38–3; Hemmings 18–9–20–2.

Umpires: J. C. Balderstone and G. I. Burgess.

At Leicester, August 18, 19. SUSSEX beat LEICESTERSHIRE by nine wickets.

SUSSEX v WARWICKSHIRE

At Hove, August 25, 26, 27. Warwickshire won by ten wickets. Warwickshire 20 pts, Sussex 4 pts. Toss: Sussex.

Warwickshire virtually secured the Championship with an efficient win – in the equivalent of two days – over Sussex, whose hopes of bridging their 38-point deficit finally crashed. Rain delayed the start for three hours and the ball moved off the seam and through the air. Only Hall, with a watchful 42, held up the Warwickshire seamers; Twose chipped in with three wickets in his fourth over. The Sussex bowlers fought back on the second day, when a crowd of nearly 3,000 saw Warwickshire slump to 67 for five. But Ostler, with a fluent fifty, and Welch, adding 30 with Small, chiselled out a precious lead of 52. Second time around, Small and Munton reduced Sussex to 32 for four. Their last chance went when Speight, who had made a determined 38, was out without further score on the third morning. Munton finished with eight in the match and Warwickshire's openers cruised to their target of 76 half an hour after lunch.

Close of play: First day, Warwickshire 9-2 (A. J. Moles 1*, K. J. Piper 4*); Second day, Sussex 107-8 (M. P. Speight 38*, E. E. Hemmings 1*).

Sussex

N. J. Lenham c Welch b Munton	10	– c Ostler b Small	1
C. W. J. Athey lbw b Twose	23	– c Lara b Small	13
J. W. Hall lbw b Smith	42	– (4) b Munton	14
*A. P. Wells c Piper b Twose	0	– (5) c Piper b Twose	12
M. P. Speight c Piper b Twose	0	– (6) c Lara b Munton	38
†P. Moores c Ostler b Small	29	– (7) lbw b Welch	0
F. D. Stephenson b Munton	1	– (3) b Munton	0
P. W. Jarvis c Piper b Munton	0	– c and b Welch	3
I. D. K. Salisbury b Small	3	– lbw b Small	13
E. E. Hemmings not out	6	– not out	14
E. S. H. Giddins lbw b Munton	0	– c Piper b Munton	7
B 1, l-b 8, n-b 8	17	L-b 1, w 5, n-b 6	12
1/13 2/59 3/61 4/61 5/102 6/103 7/107 8/120 9/125	131	1/7 2/8 3/28 4/32 5/56 6/65 7/77 8/101 9/111	127

Bonus points – Warwickshire 4.

Bowling: *First Innings*—Small 12–3–41–2; Munton 15.2–4–22–4; Twose 13–4–23–3; Welch 11–3–30–0; Smith 3–0–6–1. *Second Innings*—Small 20–7–38–3; Munton 20.4–7–52–4; Twose 6–3–11–1; Welch 7–1–25–2.

Warwickshire

A. J. Moles c Athey b Jarvis	1	– not out	44
R. P. Davis c Jarvis b Stephenson	0		
R. G. Twose b Jarvis	0	– (2) not out	34
†K. J. Piper c Salisbury b Jarvis	23		
B. C. Lara c Salisbury b Giddins	17		
D. P. Ostler c Speight b Giddins	50		
T. L. Penney b Jarvis	24		
G. Welch not out	26		
N. M. K. Smith c Speight b Giddins	2		
G. C. Small c Moores b Stephenson	13		
*T. A. Munton c Hemmings b Stephenson	3		
B 4, l-b 10, n-b 10	24	W 1	1
1/1 2/2 3/9 4/51 5/67 6/134 7/142 8/145 9/175	183	(no wkt)	79

Bonus points – Sussex 4.

Bowling: *First Innings*—Stephenson 14.2–4–50–3; Jarvis 18–4–68–4; Giddins 17–6–35–3; Hemmings 2–0–8–0; Salisbury 2–1–8–0. *Second Innings*—Stephenson 4–1–6–0; Jarvis 3–0–3–0; Salisbury 4–1–28–0; Hemmings 4–0–24–0; Giddins 2.4–0–7–0; Athey 2–0–11–0.

Umpires: N. T. Plews and R. A. White.

At Chelmsford, August 30, 31, September 1, 2. SUSSEX lost to ESSEX by seven wickets.

SUSSEX v YORKSHIRE

At Hove, September 15, 16, 17, 19. Drawn. Sussex 5 pts, Yorkshire 5 pts. Toss: Sussex. First-class debut: G. Keedy.

Another season of under-achievement for both counties ended on a suitably subdued note. Only six overs were possible on the first day – when the rest of the Championship was washed out – and none on the last. Play was abandoned with Sussex only 161 ahead and eight wickets down. On the second morning, Robinson had reduced them to 62 for four and, though a few got their eye in, only Wells, with 84, his best score of a disappointing season, went on. Moxon and Byas made a cracking response, adding 98 in 22 overs, but Giddins took four for 77 to restrict their lead to 20. Again Sussex lost four wickets cheaply. Wells and Moores rallied, both making 55, before Gough burst through with three wickets in eight balls.

Close of play: First day, Sussex 11-0 (N. J. Lenham 7*, C. W. J. Athey 2*); Second day, Yorkshire 109-2 (M. D. Moxon 57*); Third day, Sussex 181-8 (I. D. K. Salisbury 12*, E. E. Hemmings 2*).

Sussex

N. J. Lenham lbw b Robinson	14 – c Grayson b Robinson	17
C. W. J. Athey lbw b Hartley	35 – c Byas b Gough	0
J. W. Hall lbw b Robinson	4 – c Blakey b Hartley	4
*A. P. Wells lbw b Gough	84 – lbw b Gough	55
C. C. Remy c Blakey b Robinson	0 – lbw b Hartley	4
†P. Moores b Hartley	32 – b Gough	55
F. D. Stephenson b Stemp	21 – lbw b Gough	0
P. W. Jarvis lbw b Gough	5 – c Blakey b Hartley	22
I. D. K. Salisbury lbw b Robinson	14 – not out	12
E. E. Hemmings not out	0 – not out	2
E. S. H. Giddins b Gough	0	
B 1, l-b 8, n-b 8	17 L-b 1, w 1, n-b 8	10
1/33 2/59 3/61 4/62 5/131 6/172 7/185 8/226 9/226	226 1/1 2/11 3/38 4/51 5/143 6/143 7/148 8/169	(8 wkts) 181

Bonus points – Sussex 1, Yorkshire 4.

Bowling: *First Innings*—Gough 22.4–6–81–3; Hartley 21–4–72–2; Robinson 24–9–44–4; Stemp 9–4–20–1. *Second Innings*—Gough 14–2–69–4; Hartley 15–4–42–3; Robinson 16–3–54–1; Stemp 6–3–15–0.

Yorkshire

*M. D. Moxon b Giddins	66
S. A. Kellett c Moores b Stephenson	1
D. Byas run out	39
A. P. Grayson lbw b Jarvis	21
†R. J. Blakey not out	61
B. Parker b Giddins	17
P. J. Hartley c Moores b Giddins	0
D. Gough c Moores b Salisbury	5
R. D. Stemp b Giddins	5
G. Keedy lbw b Salisbury	1
M. A. Robinson c Moores b Jarvis	7
L-b 11, w 2, n-b 10	23
1/11 2/109 3/135 4/139 5/169 6/181 7/190 8/205 9/222	246

Bonus points – Yorkshire 1, Sussex 4.

Bowling: Stephenson 14–3–50–1; Jarvis 18.3–4–64–2; Giddins 23–6–77–4; Salisbury 15–3–40–2; Hemmings 3–1–4–0.

Umpires: R. Palmer and P. Willey.

BIGGEST LEAPS IN THE COUNTY CHAMPIONSHIP

15 places	Worcestershire	17th to second	1993
	Warwickshire	16th to first	1994
14 places	Gloucestershire	16th to second	1969
13 places	Warwickshire	14th to first	1911
	Worcestershire	14th to first	1964
	Gloucestershire	16th to third	1976
	Kent	14th to first equal	1977
	Surrey	16th to third	1979
	Worcestershire	15th to second	1979
	Middlesex	14th to first	1980
	Hampshire	15th to second	1985
	Lancashire	15th to second	1987

WARWICKSHIRE

President: The Earl of Aylesford
Chairman: M. J. K. Smith
Chairman, Cricket Committee: J. Whitehouse
Chief Executive: D. L. Amiss
Captain: D. A. Reeve
Director of Coaching: 1994 – R. A. Woolmer
Head Groundsman: S. J. Rouse
Scorer: A. E. Davis

Warwickshire recorded the most remarkable season by any side in the history of English county cricket. Uniquely, they won three trophies and, arguably, were only denied the fourth by the toss of a coin.

They won their fourth County Championship, their second Sunday League title and their first ever Benson and Hedges Cup. For the ninth successive time, and the 18th in the last 21 years, the NatWest Trophy went to the side batting second in the final; otherwise Warwickshire might have defeated Worcestershire to complete a clean sweep. Arguments about whether they were the best ever county team are spurious, because conditions and circumstances vary from season to season, but this record is unlikely to be equalled or beaten. The most meritorious achievement was the County Championship, in which they won 11 out of 17 matches, three more than any other county, and finally led by 42 points. Both those margins were unequalled since 1979, when Essex won 13 games to runners-up Worcestershire's seven, to lead by 77 points; but in those days 22 matches were scheduled.

Warwickshire's unforgettable season came from meticulous planning and a stroke of luck in being able to sign Brian Lara when Manoj Prabhakar withdrew because of injury. The publicity surrounding Lara's 375 against England in Antigua started a bandwagon which rolled into Edgbaston 11 days later when he scored 147 against Glamorgan, the first of what were to be six Championship hundreds in seven innings, culminating in his world record 501 not out, and nine in all. By June 6, he had scored 1,176 runs in those seven innings. Of the eight batsmen who have scored 1,000 runs by the end of May, only Bradman did it in seven, and he averaged 170.16 to Lara's 235.20.

Crucial for a good, but not outstanding county attack was Lara's scoring-rate: his 2,066 Championship runs came off 2,262 deliveries, that is five and a half runs per six balls faced. The extra time he created contributed materially to several of the wins, and his presence widened the horizons of his team-mates. The progress made by Dominic Ostler, Trevor Penney, Keith Piper, Graeme Welch and Neil Smith, together with the resurgence of Roger Twose and the solid form of Andy Moles, when he returned after injury and illness, were important factors in the self-belief of a side whose proud record in all four competitions was played 43, won 33, lost four, drew five, with one no-result. They beat all the other 17 counties at least once and only neighbours Worcestershire bettered them, with wins in the NatWest final and the Sunday League, to set against a defeat in the Benson and Hedges final – another match heavily influenced by the toss, on an unusually damp pitch – with the four-day game drawn.

Captain Dermot Reeve was one of the few players whose Championship season was moderate, with injuries limiting his appearances to eight, but Tim Munton deputised in magnificent fashion. He led Warwickshire to eight victories in nine matches and, in the middle part of the season, when Lara's form was relatively unspectacular, he held them together with a series of match-winning performances. None was more important than that against Surrey, then Championship leaders, at Guildford. There Munton's match figures of 46.5–11–137–9 ensured that a recovery from 25 for four eventually became the best win of the season. He followed up with ten for 130 against Essex and nine for 109 against Derbyshire to secure the wins which took Warwickshire to the head of the table – a position they maintained for the final seven weeks.

Reeve missed only one limited-overs match, and justified his reputation as the most effective one-day cricketer in the country. He mixed brilliant all-round improvisation with imaginative captaincy, and instilled among his players a self-belief that was often the difference between victory and defeat – especially in the NatWest semi-final against Kent.

Although 17 players appeared in the Championship, five were ever-present – Twose, Ostler, Neil Smith, Piper and Munton – and Lara and Penney missed only two matches each. With Lara leading the way, Twose and Moles averaging over 50 and Ostler, Penney and Graeme Welch over 35, the remarkable climb from 16th to top is largely explained; in 1993, nobody averaged 40 and only two over 35. Among the bowlers, Gladstone Small began well, before being hampered by injury. Off-spinner Neil Smith made considerable progress and became a match-winner in helpful conditions. Richard Davis, signed from Kent, did enough to earn his county cap – as did Penney – and the side was no longer disadvantaged on a turning pitch. Paul Smith made several positive all-round contributions and wicket-keeper Piper enjoyed his best season yet. No one from Warwickshire apart from Piper was chosen for the two England touring parties, which caused critical comment, not only from inside the county, with Munton and Twose considered especially unlucky. Twose qualified for New Zealand from April 1 this year but he can play for Warwickshire in 1995 without affecting his position; no one can make up for Lara's absence, but Twose's continued presence, and the signing of Nick Knight from Essex, will at least help.

The influence of Bob Woolmer, director of coaching, was incalculable. His fourth season at Edgbaston brought to fruition a rare ability to communicate technical advice and it was no surprise when he was given a similar appointment with the South African Test team just after the triumphant end of the season. The South Africans have agreed that Woolmer can be with Warwickshire on their pre-season tour of the Cape and for the first two months of the 1995 season.

Allan Donald's return in place of Lara in 1995 should offset any decline in the fitness of the 33-year-old Small, and further improvement can be expected from the find of the year, Welch, and Doug Brown, whose opportunities were more restricted. But Warwickshire have given themselves a very hard act to follow. – Jack Bannister.

WARWICKSHIRE 1994

[*Bill Smith*

Back row: C. E. Mulraine, M. J. Powell, A. F. Giles, D. A. Altree. *Middle row:* D. L. Amiss (*chief executive*), M. Burns, T. L. Penney, W. G. Khan, J. D. Ratcliffe, R. P. Davis, M. A. V. Bell, G. Welch, D. R. Brown, S. J. Nottingham (*physiotherapist*). *Front row:* R. N. Abberley (*coach and youth cricket organiser*), A. J. Moles, D. P. Ostler, R. A. Woolmer (*director of coaching*), T. A. Munton, D. A. Reeve (*captain*), G. C. Small, Asif Din, P. A. Smith, R. G. Twose, N. M. K. Smith, K. J. Piper. *Inset:* B. C. Lara.

WARWICKSHIRE RESULTS

All first-class matches – Played 18: Won 11, Lost 1, Drawn 6.

County Championship matches – Played 17: Won 11, Lost 1, Drawn 5.

Bonus points – Batting 41, Bowling 55.

Competition placings – Britannic Assurance County Championship, winners; NatWest Bank Trophy, finalists; Benson and Hedges Cup, winners; AXA Equity & Law League, winners.

BRITANNIC ASSURANCE CHAMPIONSHIP AVERAGES

BATTING

	Birthplace	*M*	*I*	*NO*	*R*	*HS*	*Avge*
‡B. C. Lara§	*Santa Cruz, Trinidad*	15	25	2	2,066	501*	89.82
‡R. G. Twose	*Torquay*	17	30	5	1,395	277*	55.80
‡A. J. Moles	*Solihull*	11	20	3	863	203*	50.76
‡D. P. Ostler	*Solihull*	17	28	2	1,012	186	38.92
‡T. L. Penney	*Salisbury, Rhodesia*	15	23	3	774	111	38.70
G. Welch	*Durham*	11	15	3	446	84*	37.16
‡Asif Din	*Kampala, Uganda*	3	4	1	107	42*	35.66
D. R. Brown	*Stirling*	3	6	2	113	54	28.25
‡N. M. K. Smith	*Birmingham*	17	21	4	435	65	25.58
‡K. J. Piper	*Leicester*	17	24	4	454	116*	22.70
‡P. A. Smith	*Jesmond*	11	16	2	313	65	22.35
J. D. Ratcliffe	*Solihull*	2	4	0	80	69	20.00
‡R. P. Davis	*Margate*	11	9	2	131	35*	18.71
‡D. A. Reeve	*Kowloon, Hong Kong*	8	9	1	109	33	13.62
‡T. A. Munton	*Melton Mowbray*	17	17	7	106	36	10.60
‡G. C. Small	*St George, Barbados*	11	10	1	78	23	8.66

Also batted: M. A. V. Bell (*Birmingham*) (1 match) 4*.

* *Signifies not out.* ‡ *Denotes county cap.* § *Overseas player.*

The following played a total of 16 three-figure innings for Warwickshire in County Championship matches – B. C. Lara 9, R. G. Twose 3, A. J. Moles 1, D. P. Ostler 1, T. L. Penney 1, K. J. Piper 1.

BOWLING

	O	*M*	*R*	*W*	*BB*	*5W/i*	*Avge*
T. A. Munton	693.4	177	1,745	81	7-52	6	21.54
G. C. Small	339	79	946	36	5-46	1	26.27
R. P. Davis	337	99	984	31	6-94	2	31.74
P. A. Smith	182	40	594	18	3-24	0	33.00
N. M. K. Smith	581	141	1,690	49	7-42	4	34.48
R. G. Twose	185.5	38	535	15	6-28	1	35.66
G. Welch	263	63	949	22	4-74	0	43.13

Also bowled: Asif Din 2–0–9–0; M. A. V. Bell 31–5–108–3; D. R. Brown 35–5–118–5; B. C. Lara 21–1–112–0; D. P. Ostler 1.1–0–13–0; D. A. Reeve 138–44–299–8.

Wicket-keepers: K. J. Piper 61 ct, 5 st; T. L. Penney 2 ct.

Leading Fielders: D. A. Reeve 18, R. P. Davis 15.

WARWICKSHIRE v GLAMORGAN

At Birmingham, April 28, 29, 30, May 1. Warwickshire won by an innings and 103 runs. Warwickshire 22 pts, Glamorgan 4 pts. Toss: Glamorgan. Championship debuts: B. C. Lara; O. D. Gibson.

Lara's debut dominated the match, and played a big part in Warwickshire's convincing win, even though he was outmatched statistically by the far less famous left-hander Twose. Within two days of arriving in Britain, and playing his first innings since his Test record of 375 in Antigua 11 days earlier, Lara hit 147 from 160 balls, with 104 coming in boundaries – 23 fours and two sixes. He scored his runs out of 215 in 165 minutes. Lara was particularly strong square of the wicket on either side and, such was the power and placement of his strokes, that the admiring Glamorgan fielders later realised that not one of them had ever managed a diving stop. He gave one chance, when 104, off Lefebvre, but otherwise his innings was flawless. Twose remained to reach his second Championship century that evening. Like the first, it was converted into a double; his eventual 277 was the second highest score ever made for Warwickshire. He batted for ten hours and six minutes, hitting 34 fours and a six. In 1993 his aggregate for the season was 224 at 12.44. There had been a sense of anticlimax when Glamorgan won the toss and a substantial crowd had to spend the opening day watching Lara in the field. Glamorgan's first innings was held together by a maiden hundred from yet another left-hander, Hemp, who was eighth out after scoring 127 in four and a half hours. After the visitors lost half their wickets for 158, when Hemp was 54, he played solidly and sensibly, supported by Gibson. Thanks to Lara's brilliance, Warwickshire scored a mammoth 657 for seven, equalling their previous best of 657 for six against Hampshire in 1899, at 3.73 an over. It was the highest total ever against Glamorgan; four of their bowlers conceded over 100 runs and the fifth, Watkin, 99. They resumed 292 behind and Small's first five-wicket haul since 1990 clinched a victory in a style that promised great things for the Birmingham public, who had been displaying unprecedented enthusiasm for their cricket team since the 375 had made their new signing the hottest property in the game.

Close of play: First day, Glamorgan 291-6 (D. L. Hemp 109*, O. D. Gibson 36*); Second day, Warwickshire 322-2 (R. G. Twose 104*, Asif Din 23*); Third day, Glamorgan 65-2 (S. P. James 47*, M. P. Maynard 17*).

Glamorgan

S. P. James c Asif Din b N. M. K. Smith	19	– lbw b Small	61
*H. Morris lbw b Munton	24	– b Munton	0
A. Dale c Piper b Munton	32	– c Reeve b Small	0
M. P. Maynard lbw b Reeve	5	– c P. A. Smith b Small	34
D. L. Hemp c N. M. K. Smith b Munton	127	– c Twose b Small	2
P. A. Cottey lbw b P. A. Smith	18	– c Reeve b Davis	33
R. D. B. Croft b Reeve	30	– c Davis b Munton	5
O. D. Gibson b Small	61	– c Reeve b Davis	15
R. P. Lefebvre c Twose b Munton	20	– b Davis	32
†C. P. Metson lbw b P. A. Smith	2	– c P. A. Smith b Small	0
S. L. Watkin not out	0	– not out	0
B 9, l-b 13, w 1, n-b 4	27	B 4, l-b 3	7
1/31 2/53 3/64 4/118 5/158 6/222 7/327 8/354 9/365	365	1/4 2/9 3/89 4/93 5/104 6/126 7/155 8/170 9/189	189

Bonus points – Glamorgan 3, Warwickshire 2 (Score at 120 overs: 327-6).

Bowling: *First Innings*—Small 27–6–75–1; Munton 23.4–5–57–4; N. M. K. Smith 18–3–46–1; Reeve 23–5–61–2; Davis 21–7–51–0; P. A. Smith 12–2–35–2; Lara 1–0–7–0; Twose 5–1–11–0. *Second Innings*—Small 17.3–3–46–5; Munton 21–5–73–2; P. A. Smith 2–0–14–0; Davis 12–7–24–3; N. M. K. Smith 15–4–25–0.

Warwickshire

D. P. Ostler b Gibson	42	†K. J. Piper run out	12
R. G. Twose not out	277	R. P. Davis not out	35
B. C. Lara c Maynard b Croft	147	B 7, l-b 9, w 1, n-b 14	31
Asif Din st Metson b Croft	42		
*D. A. Reeve lbw b Gibson	18	1/50 2/265 3/372 (7 wkts dec.)	657
P. A. Smith b Watkin	38	4/435 5/531	
N. M. K. Smith c Gibson b Dale	15	6/557 7/592	

G. C. Small and T. A. Munton did not bat.

Bonus points – Warwickshire 4, Glamorgan 1 (Score at 120 overs: 403-3).

Bowling: Watkin 32–7–99–1; Gibson 30–4–134–2; Croft 51–13–173–2; Lefebvre 39–11–122–0; Dale 24–3–113–1.

Umpires: J. H. Hampshire and J. W. Holder.

WARWICKSHIRE v LEICESTERSHIRE

At Birmingham, May 5, 6, 7, 9. Drawn. Warwickshire 5 pts, Leicestershire 8 pts, Toss: Warwickshire.

Lara followed his debut hundred for Warwickshire with two more – 106 and 120 not out – giving him a sequence of four in a row beginning with his 375. Although the two innings were in vivid contrast, his scoring-rate, approaching a run a ball, hardly varied, while only one of his colleagues passed 20 in either innings. Again it was his backfoot strokeplay which took the eye, with flashing square cuts and pulls leaving the fielders helpless. But otherwise Leicestershire were in charge. After the first day was all but washed out, their captain, Briers, scored 154 and Warwickshire only just avoided the follow-on after a magnificent career-best eight for 42 from the off-spinner Pierson, once on their own books. Pierson took the last eight wickets – starting with Lara – for 11 runs in 58 balls. Set 285 to win, Warwickshire were quickly in trouble against hostile bowling from Millns, but Lara steered his side to safety. Since Antigua, his phenomenal sequence had brought him 748 runs in four innings at 249.33, while his aggregate since January 1 was now 1,886.

Close of play: First day, Leicestershire 9-0 (P. V. Simmons 9*, N. E. Briers 0*); Second day, Leicestershire 356-7 (B. F. Smith 69*, A. R. K. Pierson 0*); Third day, Warwickshire 254.

Leicestershire

P. V. Simmons c Reeve b Bell	9	– c Reeve b P. A. Smith	39
*N. E. Briers c Ostler b Reeve	154	– c sub b N. M. K. Smith	22
T. J. Boon c Ostler b Small	42		
J. J. Whitaker c Reeve b Bell	25	– (3) b P. A. Smith	4
V. J. Wells c Piper b P. A. Smith	21	– (4) b N. M. K. Smith	2
B. F. Smith b Small	78	– (5) not out	25
†P. A. Nixon c Reeve b Small	7	– (6) c Piper b N. M. K. Smith	19
G. J. Parsons lbw b Bell	6	– (7) not out	11
A. R. K. Pierson not out	26		
D. J. Millns lbw b P. A. Smith	10		
A. D. Mullally c Bell b Munton	1		
B 8, l-b 6, n-b 10	24	B 3, l-b 9, w 1	13
1/11 2/100 3/162 4/212 5/320 6/341 7/348 8/378 9/402	403	1/73 2/76 3/79 4/79 5/108 (5 wkts dec.)	135

Bonus points – Leicestershire 4, Warwickshire 3 (Score at 120 overs: 396-8).

Bowling: *First Innings*—Small 27–3–77–3; Bell 26–5–89–3; Munton 27.2–6–78–1; P. A. Smith 16–2–67–2; N. M. K. Smith 13–3–35–0; Reeve 14–5–43–1. *Second Innings*—Munton 11–3–25–0; Bell 5–0–19–0; N. M. K. Smith 17–5–52–3; P. A. Smith 9–2–27–2.

Warwickshire

D. P. Ostler c Nixon b Millns	17	– lbw b Millns 14
R. G. Twose c Nixon b Parsons	51	– c Simmons b Millns 12
B. C. Lara c and b Pierson	106	– not out 120
Asif Din b Pierson	14	– (7) run out 9
*D. A. Reeve c sub b Pierson	0	– (4) c Parsons b Millns 3
P. A. Smith c sub b Pierson	13	– (5) c Whitaker b Millns 0
†K. J. Piper c sub b Pierson	0	– (6) b Pierson 8
N. M. K. Smith c Simmons b Pierson	18	– c sub b Simmons 20
G. C. Small c Millns b Pierson	5	– not out 0
M. A. V. Bell not out	4	
T. A. Munton c sub b Pierson	5	
B 14, l-b 5, n-b 2	21	B 7, l-b 3, n-b 10 20
1/27 2/129 3/201 4/201 5/206 6/210 7/229 8/238 9/247	254	1/32 2/45 3/61 4/61 5/91 6/120 7/187 (7 wkts) 206

Bonus points – Warwickshire 2, Leicestershire 4.

Bowling: *First Innings*—Mullally 20–6–55–0; Millns 13–3–52–1; Wells 6–1–29–0; Parsons 15–3–57–1; Pierson 17.5–5–42–8. *Second Innings*—Mullally 12–1–57–0; Millns 15–4–54–4; Parsons 13–4–41–0; Pierson 13–2–23–1; Simmons 3.4–1–21–1.

Umpires: B. Dudleston and D. R. Shepherd.

At Oxford, May 14, 16, 17. WARWICKSHIRE drew with OXFORD UNIVERSITY.

At Taunton, May 19, 20, 21, 23. WARWICKSHIRE beat SOMERSET by six wickets.

At Lord's, May 26, 27, 28, 30. WARWICKSHIRE drew with MIDDLESEX.

WARWICKSHIRE v DURHAM

At Birmingham, June 2, 3, 4, 6. Drawn. Warwickshire 6 pts, Durham 5 pts. Toss: Durham. First-class debut: D. M. Cox.

The astonishing record-strewn Monday, including Lara's 501 not out – the highest score in the history of first-class cricket – that concluded this game was possible only because the third day was lost to rain. Having narrowly missed joining Bradman, Fry and Procter in scoring six successive first-class hundreds, Lara became the first man to score seven in eight innings. When he ran off, the first man ever to have scored 500 runs in an innings, with one ball of the day to spare, Lara had set a string of other records. As with his five previous hundreds for Warwickshire, it was his run-rate, as well as the volume of runs, which set him apart. His 501 took six minutes under eight hours, in which he faced only 427 balls and hit 308 in boundaries – 62 fours and ten sixes. He took his staggering County Championship record to 1,176 runs from 1,175 balls in seven innings – at 235.20. Lara shared two partnerships over 300, with Penney scoring 44 out of 314, and Piper scoring a career-best 116 not out from 322 – the highest stand for Warwickshire's fifth wicket. The circumstances that allowed his assault on the record derived from Durham's own total, 556 for eight declared, injuries to two of their bowlers, Graveney and Saxelby, and a playing surface which was reported to Lord's by the umpires as too heavily in favour of batting. Bainbridge would not risk setting Warwickshire a target. The former Derbyshire batsman, Morris, reached his first century for Durham and advanced to the first double-hundred for the county, from 279 balls, helping his side to an apparently commanding position. He hit five sixes and 24 fours. Sixties from tailenders Cummins and Graveney, who put on 134 for the eighth wicket, further demonstrated the benign nature of the pitch. By the end of the

THE ROAD TO 501: LARA'S MILESTONES

FRIDAY

100 He became the first batsman in history to score seven centuries in eight first-class innings, beating the seven in nine by C. B. Fry (1901), E. Tyldesley (1926) and D. G. Bradman (four times). He had 111 by close of play.

SATURDAY

No play.

MONDAY

280 Passes the highest score by a Warwickshire batsman at Edgbaston, the 277* scored by Roger Twose 37 days earlier.

285 LUNCH – his 174 before lunch was a Warwickshire record, beating 173 by F. R. Santall v Northamptonshire at Northampton in 1933.

286 Passes the highest score by anyone on the ground, P. B. H. May's 285* for England v West Indies in 1957.

306 Passes the highest score for Warwickshire, F. R. Foster's 305* v Worcestershire at Dudley in 1914.

325 Reaches 1,000 for the season in his seventh innings, equalling Bradman in 1938.

376 Passes the highest score by a West Indian, beating his own 375, made 49 days earlier.

386 Passes the highest score by a left-hander, B. Sutcliffe's 385 for Otago v Canterbury at Christchurch in 1952-53.

418 TEA

423 His 274 from boundaries (55 fours, nine sixes) beats the 272 (68 fours) by P. A. Perrin for Essex v Derbyshire at Chesterfield in 1904.

425 Passes the highest score in English first-class cricket, 424 by A. C. MacLaren for Lancashire v Somerset at Taunton in 1895.

458 Passes the record for most runs by a batsman in a day, 345 by C. G. Macartney for the Australians v Nottinghamshire at Nottingham in 1921.

501 Passes Hanif Mohammad's 499. Becomes the highest scorer and the first man to score 500 in first-class cricket.

FIFTY AFTER FIFTY

	Mins	*Balls*	*Sixes*	*Fours*
50	97	80	—	6
100	144	138	—	14
150	201	193	—	22
200	224	220	2	30
250	246	245	5	37
300	280	278	7	44
350	319	311	8	49
400	367	350	8	53
450	430	398	9	55
501	474	427	10	62

second day, Lara had announced himself with an unbeaten 111 off 143 balls, although he made an uncertain start – bowled by a Cummins no-ball on 12 and dropped behind the wicket on 18 off Brown. Once Durham decided, after the loss of the third day, to play only for bonus points, Lara was given an open cheque to bat. He scored more boundaries before lunch than Penney managed runs – 25 fours and seven sixes to 27 runs – and his 174 runs in the 135-minute session were six short of the Championship record, 180 by K. S. Ranjitsinhji in 150 minutes for Sussex against Surrey in 1902. His first 100 had come from 138 balls; the second came from 82, the third from 58, the fourth from 72 and the fifth from 77. Between lunch and tea he scored 133, which left him needing 82 for the record. But Lara was unaware of the playing conditions by which the game had to end half an hour early, because there could be no result. Only when Piper informed him, four balls into the last over, that he had two balls left, did he blaze his final four to pass Hanif Mohammad's 499 at Karachi in 1958-59. His first reaction afterwards was, "I am not yet a complete player." The innings took Warwickshire to a club record of 810 for four, and Lara's calendar year aggregate to 2,689 from 24 innings. His 501 came seven weeks to the day after his 375 in Antigua. No one had held both individual records, Test and first-class, since Bradman more than sixty years before.

Close of play: First day, Durham 365-3 (J. E. Morris 204*, P. Bainbridge 50*); Second day, Warwickshire 210-2 (B. C. Lara 111*, T. L. Penney 17*); Third day, No play.

Durham

W. Larkins c Penney b Munton 13
M. Saxelby b Small 19
J. E. Morris c Lara b P. A. Smith 204
S. Hutton b Davis 61
*P. Bainbridge c Reeve b N. M. K. Smith . 67
J. I. Longley lbw b N. M. K. Smith . . . 24
†C. W. Scott lbw b Small 13
A. C. Cummins lbw b Twose 62
D. A. Graveney not out 65
B 2, l-b 17, w 3, n-b 6 28

1/35 2/39 3/225 4/365 5/393 6/420 7/422 8/556 (8 wkts dec.) 556

D. M. Cox and S. J. E. Brown did not bat.

Bonus points – Durham 4, Warwickshire 2 (Score at 120 overs: 393-5).

Bowling: Small 22–8–80–2; Munton 28–4–103–1; Reeve 5–2–12–0; P. A. Smith 15–5–51–1; Davis 36–12–105–1; N. M. K. Smith 32–6–97–2; Twose 9.5–1–42–1; Lara 11–1–47–0.

Warwickshire

D. P. Ostler c Scott b Cummins 8
R. G. Twose c Cox b Brown 51
B. C. Lara not out 501
T. L. Penney c Hutton b Bainbridge . . . 44
P. A. Smith lbw b Cummins 12
†K. J. Piper not out 116
B 28, l-b 22, w 2, n-b 26 78

1/8 2/123 3/437 4/488 (4 wkts dec.) 810

*D. A. Reeve, N. M. K. Smith, R. P. Davis, G. C. Small and T. A. Munton did not bat.

Bonus points – Warwickshire 4, Durham 1 (Score at 120 overs: 689-4).

Bowling: Cummins 28–1–158–2; Brown 27–1–164–1; Bainbridge 33–4–169–1; Graveney 7–1–34–0; Cox 30–5–163–0; Larkins 5–0–39–0; Morris 5.5–1–33–0.

Umpires: T. E. Jesty and P. B. Wight.

WARWICKSHIRE v KENT

At Birmingham, June 16, 17, 18, 20. Warwickshire won by 76 runs. Warwickshire 23 pts, Kent 6 pts. Toss: Warwickshire. First-innings debut: J. B. D. Thompson.

Warwickshire's third Championship win continued their unbeaten run in all competitions. It owed little to Lara, who made only 50 in two innings – the first time he had missed a century in a first-class match since the Bridgetown Test. However, Twose and Ostler opened with a stand of 196 in the first innings and 126 in the second; Ostler twice fell in sight of his first hundred at Edgbaston, underlining the success of his promotion in the absence of Moles. Twose did reach 142 but, despite a total of 417, Warwickshire's lead was kept to 58, thanks to a cultured 136 from Hooper, supported by Fleming. On the final day, Kent were asked to score 347 from 93 overs on a pitch now taking spin. With Neil Smith's off-breaks earning a career-best seven for 133, Warwickshire won in the first over of the final 20. The game provided 1,334 runs and 36 wickets; of those 21 fell to spin, including all 16 in the two teams' second innings.

Close of play: First day, Warwickshire 316-5 (D. A. Reeve 14*, K. J. Piper 9*); Second day, Kent 226-4 (C. L. Hooper 105*, M. A. Ealham 7*); Third day, Warwickshire 202-3 (T. L. Penney 12*, K. J. Piper 8*).

Warwickshire

D. P. Ostler c and b Patel	94	– c Hooper b Patel	87
R. G. Twose run out	142	– b Patel	42
B. C. Lara c Fleming b Patel	19	– b Hooper	31
T. L. Penney lbw b Ealham	20	– b Hooper	30
P. A. Smith c Fulton b Thompson	8	– (7) not out	38
*D. A. Reeve lbw b Ealham	29	– c Ward b Hooper	2
†K. J. Piper b Igglesden	16	– (5) c Fulton b Hooper	17
N. M. K. Smith c Igglesden b Ealham	24	– not out	13
R. P. Davis b Igglesden	21		
G. C. Small c Ealham b Patel	23		
T. A. Munton not out	5		
B 1, l-b 7, w 4, n-b 4	16	B 12, l-b 16	28
1/196 2/226 3/282 4/283 5/299 6/331 7/355 8/370 9/411	417	1/126 2/159 3/187 4/221 5/227 6/266 (6 wkts dec.)	288

Bonus points – Warwickshire 3, Kent 2 (Score at 120 overs: 333-6).

Bowling: *First Innings*—Igglesden 36.2–10–83–2; Thompson 25–4–89–1; Fleming 20–4–64–0; Ealham 20–6–54–3; Patel 42–12–106–3; Hooper 4–1–13–0. *Second Innings*—Igglesden 8–2–31–0; Thompson 8–2–31–0; Patel 30–6–90–2; Ealham 8–2–18–0; Fleming 3–0–13–0; Hooper 20–4–77–4.

Kent

D. P. Fulton c Piper b P. A. Smith	36	– b N. M. K. Smith	44
*M. R. Benson c Piper b Munton	1	– c sub b N. M. K. Smith	33
T. R. Ward c Piper b Small	63	– c sub b Davis	18
C. L. Hooper c and b Davis	136	– c Reeve b N. M. K. Smith	14
N. R. Taylor run out	4	– c Reeve b N. M. K. Smith	27
M. A. Ealham c Twose b Reeve	10	– (7) c Davis b N. M. K. Smith	52
M. V. Fleming c Piper b Small	73	– (6) c Penney b N. M. K. Smith	61
†S. A. Marsh c Ostler b N. M. K. Smith	8	– c Piper b Davis	4
J. B. D. Thompson not out	1	– c Penney b Davis	2
M. M. Patel b Small	0	– lbw b N. M. K. Smith	0
A. P. Igglesden b Munton	12	– not out	4
B 4, l-b 9, n-b 2	15	L-b 9, n-b 2	11
1/2 2/60 3/169 4/184 5/237 6/293 7/336 8/346 9/346	359	1/71 2/92 3/98 4/116 5/171 6/247 7/258 8/258 9/258	270

Bonus points – Kent 4, Warwickshire 4.

Bowling: *First Innings*—Small 17–4–40–3; Munton 27.4–5–80–2; P. A. Smith 6–1–13–1; N. M. K. Smith 32–7–95–1; Davis 19–3–83–1; Reeve 14–1–35–1. *Second Innings*—Small 2–0–7–0; Munton 9–0–37–0; P. A. Smith 4–1–16–0; N. M. K. Smith 31–4–133–7; Davis 27.1–7–68–3.

Umpires: J. C. Balderstone and D. R. Shepherd.

At Northampton, June 23, 24, 25, 27. WARWICKSHIRE beat NORTHAMPTONSHIRE by four wickets.

WARWICKSHIRE v LANCASHIRE

At Birmingham, June 30, July 1, 2, 4. Warwickshire won by six wickets. Warwickshire 24 pts, Lancashire 6 pts. Toss: Lancashire.

Missing Lara with a knee injury, Warwickshire completed their fifth, most satisfying, win in eight Championship games and rose to fourth place in the table. To face Lancashire's first-innings total of 392, including a superb 141 from Crawley, the third batsman to reach 1,000 runs in the season, and win with half a day to spare, spoke well of the growing confidence of their home players. Moles, in his second game of the season, shared in Warwickshire's fourth century opening stand in five innings. After he was caught, for 87, a hundred from Penney and 69 from Ratcliffe ensured a modest lead of 15, despite the hostility of Wasim Akram and Chapple, which removed their last seven wickets for 28. Then Neil Smith exploited the variable bounce in devastating fashion. His seven for 42 improved on his career-best figures for the second home match in succession. Three of his victims were bowled and two were lbw. Finally, Twose's strokeplay brought half the 180 runs Warwickshire needed to ensure victory before the threatened rain.

Close of play: First day, Lancashire 380-9 (G. Yates 29*, G. Chapple 13*); Second day, Warwickshire 350-3 (T. L. Penney 108*, J. D. Ratcliffe 44*); Third day, Warwickshire 32-0 (A. J. Moles 13*, R. G. Twose 19*).

Lancashire

First innings		Second innings	
G. D. Lloyd b Small	7	c Piper b Small	0
S. P. Titchard lbw b Munton	3	b Smith	28
J. P. Crawley c Davis b Welch	141	b Munton	54
N. H. Fairbrother c Piper b Munton	76	b Smith	12
N. J. Speak c Penney b Welch	32	c Penney b Smith	6
*M. Watkinson st Piper b Smith	40	lbw b Smith	17
Wasim Akram b Welch	0	c Ratcliffe b Smith	22
P. J. Martin b Davis	17	lbw b Smith	0
†W. K. Hegg c Ostler b Davis	0	c Ostler b Munton	2
G. Yates c Piper b Small	33	b Smith	19
G. Chapple not out	19	not out	5
L-b 8, n-b 16	24	B 9, l-b 6, w 4, n-b 10	29
1/4 2/28 3/192 4/274 5/287 6/293 7/334 8/338 9/342	392	1/0 2/100 3/108 4/114 5/137 6/150 7/150 8/161 9/187	194

Bonus points – Lancashire 4, Warwickshire 4.

Bowling: *First Innings*—Small 15.5–3–45–2; Munton 17–3–52–2; Welch 15–3–72–3; Twose 12–2–32–0; Davis 30–8–99–2; Smith 25–4–84–1. *Second Innings*—Small 5–3–7–1; Munton 26–7–62–2; Welch 10–2–44–0; Twose 4–0–16–0; Smith 20–9–42–7; Davis 1–0–8–0.

Warwickshire

First innings		Second innings	
A. J. Moles c Crawley b Yates	87	c Hegg b Chapple	25
R. G. Twose b Wasim Akram	38	b Watkinson	90
D. P. Ostler b Yates	25	c Hegg b Yates	22
T. L. Penney c Lloyd b Wasim Akram	111	not out	31
J. D. Ratcliffe c Crawley b Chapple	69	c and b Watkinson	0
†K. J. Piper c Fairbrother b Chapple	0	not out	5
G. Welch c Hegg b Wasim Akram	5		
N. M. K. Smith c Lloyd b Chapple	3		
R. P. Davis c Titchard b Wasim Akram	9		
G. C. Small c Hegg b Chapple	0		
*T. A. Munton not out	6		
B 10, l-b 20, w 2, n-b 22	54	B 5, l-b 1, n-b 4	10
1/111 2/162 3/243 4/379 5/381 6/386 7/390 8/394 9/395	407	1/75 2/122 3/171 4/171	(4 wkts) 183

Bonus points – Warwickshire 4, Lancashire 2 (Score at 120 overs: 390-6).

Bowling: *First Innings*—Wasim Akram 36.4–10–82–4; Martin 22–5–57–0; Chapple 22–5–52–4; Watkinson 25–5–88–0; Yates 24–3–98–2. *Second Innings*—Wasim Akram 16–5–39–0; Martin 5–1–21–0; Chapple 8–1–33–1; Watkinson 19.2–5–58–2; Yates 2–0–26–1.

Umpires: V. A. Holder and M. J. Kitchen.

At Guildford, July 14, 15, 16, 18. WARWICKSHIRE beat SURREY by 256 runs.

WARWICKSHIRE v ESSEX

At Birmingham, July 21, 22, 23. Warwickshire won by 203 runs. Warwickshire 24 pts, Essex 5 pts. Toss: Warwickshire.

Warwickshire's fifth successive Championship win left them just three points behind leaders Surrey. There were outstanding contributions from Munton – whose ten wickets gave him 33 in his last four matches – and Piper, who took seven catches in Essex's first innings, a Warwickshire record, though E. J. "Tiger" Smith caught four and stumped three in 1926; Piper's nine match dismissals equalled E. B. Lewis's 1949 club record. But Warwickshire's team strength was also underlined. Solid all-round batting gave them the initiative and a second-string attack offered Munton determined support; Brown, playing his second Championship game, took four wickets in five overs to help finish off Essex inside three days. On the first day, Lara, with 70 in 81 balls, became the first past 1,500 runs in the season. Smith steered the team to 361 with an attacking 65 and then Munton and Piper almost enforced the follow-on. Irani became the only bowler to dismiss Lara twice in the Championship, but Essex never had serious hopes of making their big target. Knight shone most brightly for Essex, equalling their fielding record of five catches in an innings and scoring 56 and 113. He signed for Warwickshire in October.

Close of play: First day, Essex 43-2 (N. V. Knight 22*, J. J. B. Lewis 8*); Second day, Warwickshire 156-3 (R. G. Twose 90*, R. P. Davis 5*).

Warwickshire

A. J. Moles c Knight b Irani	57	– b Irani	40
R. G. Twose c Knight b Andrew	5	– c Lewis b Childs	92
B. C. Lara c Knight b Irani	70	– lbw b Irani	9
D. P. Ostler c Knight b Irani	9	– c Hussain b Childs	11
T. L. Penney lbw b Stephenson	44	– (6) lbw b Andrew	44
†K. J. Piper b Stephenson	14	– (7) c Shahid b Kasprowicz	1
G. Welch c Knight b Childs	30	– (8) b Andrew	6
N. M. K. Smith c and b Such	65	– (9) lbw b Childs	2
D. R. Brown run out	29	– (10) not out	14
R. P. Davis not out	10	– (5) c Lewis b Childs	29
*T. A. Munton c Shahid b Kasprowicz	2	– c Kasprowicz b Such	0
L-b 5, w 1, n-b 20	26	B 4, l-b 1, w 1, n-b 14	20
1/37 2/108 3/126 4/167 5/208 6/239 7/261 8/335 9/351	361	1/100 2/116 3/141 4/164 5/217 6/220 7/240 8/249 9/267	268

Bonus points – Warwickshire 4, Essex 4.

Bowling: *First Innings*—Kasprowicz 13.2–1–62–1; Andrew 18–3–58–1; Irani 24–3–77–3; Stephenson 15–5–57–2; Such 10–1–46–1; Childs 20–6–56–1. *Second Innings*—Kasprowicz 15–0–59–1; Andrew 12–4–28–2; Such 18–1–74–1; Irani 8–3–19–2; Stephenson 6–1–20–0; Childs 19–2–63–4.

Essex

N. V. Knight c Piper b Smith	56	– c Piper b Munton 113
*J. P. Stephenson c Piper b Welch	0	– st Piper b Smith 15
P. M. Such c Piper b Welch	2	– (7) b Brown 12
J. J. B. Lewis c Piper b Smith	33	– (3) lbw b Munton 26
N. Hussain c Piper b Munton	53	– (4) lbw b Munton 11
N. Shahid lbw b Munton	4	– (5) lbw b Brown 8
R. C. Irani c Moles b Munton	18	– (6) c Lara b Brown 2
†M. A. Garnham not out	21	– lbw b Brown 2
M. S. Kasprowicz c Piper b Munton	3	– c Ostler b Smith 5
S. J. W. Andrew c Piper b Munton	4	– b Munton 4
J. H. Childs c Davis b Munton	0	– not out 1
L-b 1, n-b 20	21	L-b 2, n-b 10 12
1/16 2/22 3/104 4/129 5/134 6/178 7/193 8/203 9/207	215	1/38 2/117 3/151 4/177 5/181 6/193 7/195 8/202 9/210 211

Bonus points – Essex 1, Warwickshire 4.

Bowling: *First Innings*—Munton 23–4–89–6; Welch 11–4–38–2; Smith 21–5–64–2; Brown 7–1–17–0; Davis 6–3–6–0. *Second Innings*—Munton 21–6–41–4; Welch 8–2–26–0; Smith 23–7–57–2; Davis 22–8–60–0; Brown 9–1–25–4.

Umpires: A. A. Jones and G. Sharp.

At Chesterfield, July 28, 29, 30. WARWICKSHIRE beat DERBYSHIRE by 139 runs.

At Worcester, August 4, 5, 6, 8. WARWICKSHIRE drew with WORCESTERSHIRE.

WARWICKSHIRE v NOTTINGHAMSHIRE

At Birmingham, August 11, 12, 13, 15. Nottinghamshire won by an innings and 43 runs. Nottinghamshire 24 pts, Warwickshire 5 pts. Toss: Warwickshire.

Warwickshire's 13th Championship match brought their only defeat, and left them looking momentarily vulnerable, only nine points clear of Leicestershire, who had a game in hand. It also featured Lara's only first-class duck of the season; his average dropped below 100 for the first time. Munton put Nottinghamshire in and saw them run up 597 for eight, six fewer than Kent scored in 1992 but otherwise the highest total conceded by Warwickshire since 1928. At least Munton's 39 overs cost only 80; the others went for 493 from 127. Nottinghamshire's heroes were Pollard, with 134, and Lewis, with an unbeaten 220. A slow over-rate and bad light restricted Nottinghamshire to 268 on the first day but, once Lewis cut loose, Warwickshire were batted out of the game. His innings followed a curious pattern: he scored 13 in an hour on Friday morning, 57 in 75 minutes to lunch, 17 in an hour afterwards and then a devastating 95 to bring up his second double-hundred before tea. Meanwhile, Piper claimed his 50th dismissal of the season. He also resisted spiritedly in both innings. The promising Welch scored a career-best 84 not out and Twose a three-hour 80 when Warwickshire followed on. But Lewis completed victory with his sixth wicket of the match.

Close of play: First day, Nottinghamshire 268-4 (P. R. Pollard 117*, C. C. Lewis 20*); Second day, Warwickshire 91-3 (T. L. Penney 14*, K. J. Piper 26*); Third day, Warwickshire 134-3 (R. G. Twose 74*, T. L. Penney 24*).

Nottinghamshire

P. R. Pollard b Small	134
*R. T. Robinson c Twose b Munton	4
G. F. Archer run out	41
J. C. Adams c Twose b P. A. Smith	4
P. Johnson c Piper b Twose	63
C. C. Lewis not out	220
†W. M. Noon c Piper b Munton	33
K. P. Evans c Piper b Welch	55
G. W. Mike c Piper b Welch	6
B 10, l-b 14, w 5, n-b 8	37
1/9 2/109 3/118 4/220 5/318 6/412 7/569 8/597	(8 wkts dec.) 597

R. A. Pick and J. E. Hindson did not bat.

Bonus points – Nottinghamshire 4, Warwickshire 2 (Score at 120 overs: 385-5).

Bowling: Small 29–4–113–1; Munton 39–12–80–2; Welch 27–3–111–2; P. A. Smith 20–3–63–1; N. M. K. Smith 25–4–119–0; Twose 26–8–87–1.

Warwickshire

A. J. Moles c Hindson b Evans	15	– lbw b Lewis	14
R. G. Twose c Noon b Evans	20	– hit wkt b Lewis	80
D. P. Ostler c Noon b Mike	14	– (4) c Archer b Adams	10
T. L. Penney c Lewis b Evans	26	– (5) b Adams	33
†K. J. Piper b Pick	57	– (8) b Hindson	38
P. A. Smith c Archer b Lewis	9	– c Archer b Pick	5
B. C. Lara lbw b Mike	15	– (3) b Adams	0
G. Welch not out	84	– (7) lbw b Lewis	0
N. M. K. Smith c Noon b Lewis	38	– not out	13
G. C. Small c Noon b Mike	18	– b Pick	1
*T. A. Munton lbw b Evans	3	– b Lewis	17
B 4, l-b 7, n-b 11	22	B 6, l-b 8, n-b 8	22
1/23 2/38 3/57 4/112 5/141 6/153 7/169 8/237 9/298	321	1/58 2/59 3/85 4/151 5/151 6/155 7/181 8/203 9/212	233

Bonus points – Warwickshire 3, Nottinghamshire 4.

Bowling: *First Innings*—Pick 24–8–71–1; Evans 23–6–71–4; Mike 20–3–87–3; Lewis 16–2–61–2; Hindson 6–0–20–0. *Second Innings*—Lewis 26.1–7–86–4; Pick 14–5–41–2; Adams 29–12–41–3; Evans 6–1–22–0; Hindson 11–5–29–1.

Umpires: V. A. Holder and B. Leadbeater.

At Scarborough, August 18, 19, 20, 22. WARWICKSHIRE beat YORKSHIRE by eight wickets.

At Hove, August 25, 26, 27. WARWICKSHIRE beat SUSSEX by ten wickets.

WARWICKSHIRE v HAMPSHIRE

At Birmingham, August 30, 31, September 1, 2. Warwickshire won by an innings and 95 runs. Warwickshire 24 pts, Hampshire 6 pts. Toss: Hampshire.

Warwickshire sealed their fourth Championship title, and their first since 1972, crushing Hampshire with a session to spare. On a bare pitch, which had turned from the first day, Neil Smith and Davis took the last eight wickets, with only Nicholas showing the technique to defend against quality spin bowling. Lara scored his ninth hundred of the season – equalling Alvin Kallicharran's 1984 county record – at such a rate that the home bowlers had precious extra time to bowl Hampshire out twice. His 191, from 222 balls with 23 fours and a six, took him past 2,000 runs. It was his first hundred for five weeks and his first at Edgbaston since his 501 against Durham. He thus ended his season as he started, with a dazzling display of off-side drives, cuts and pulls, tearing Hampshire's attack to shreds. Twose's 137 was his third hundred of the season, and he put on 295 in only 61 overs with

Lara – their fourth century partnership and their second over 200. Having bowled Hampshire out for 278 on the first day, thanks to the sterling Munton and also Davis, who was later capped, Warwickshire lost 110 overs to rain over the next two days. But Munton's decision to bat on into the fourth morning was justified when Hampshire were dismissed inside 51 overs. As acting-captain, he had won eight matches out of nine and he took his total of wickets to 81, a personal best. Warwickshire's only disappointment as they set off for the following day's NatWest Trophy final, still on target for the Grand Slam, was that the England selectors continued to ignore them; only Piper appeared in the England A party announced that morning and no one on the senior Ashes tour.

Close of play: First day, Hampshire 278; Second day, Warwickshire 210-1 (R. G. Twose 84*, B. C. Lara 89*); Third day, Warwickshire 483-6 (G. Welch 43*, N. M. K. Smith 7*).

Hampshire

T. C. Middleton c Moles b Smith	18	– c Moles b Munton	2
V. P. Terry c and b Davis	71	– c Piper b Munton	36
G. W. White b Munton	30	– b Smith	18
R. A. Smith c Twose b Davis	5	– c Munton b Davis	34
*M. C. J. Nicholas c Small b Munton	2	– not out	36
K. D. James c Smith b Welch	25	– c Lara b Davis	0
†A. N. Aymes c Lara b Munton	0	– c Penney b Davis	0
S. D. Udal c Moles b Davis	64	– b Smith	1
R. J. Maru c Ostler b Small	32	– c Piper b Smith	6
C. A. Connor c Moles b Munton	21	– lbw b Smith	14
J. N. B. Bovill not out	0	– lbw b Smith	4
L-b 8, n-b 2	10	B 5, l-b 7	12
1/74 2/129 3/133 4/136 5/136 6/139 7/208 8/240 9/277	278	1/27 2/60 3/76 4/120 5/120 6/120 7/121 8/129 9/149	163

Bonus points – Hampshire 2, Warwickshire 4.

Bowling: *First Innings*—Small 20.2–7–49–1; Munton 23–5–44–4; Twose 5–1–19–0; Welch 16–6–45–1; Smith 18–5–36–1; Davis 26–7–77–3. *Second Innings*—Small 6–4–2–0; Munton 14–5–34–2; Smith 19.2–4–65–5; Davis 11–1–50–3.

Warwickshire

A. J. Moles c Aymes b Connor	24
R. G. Twose st Aymes b Udal	137
B. C. Lara c Smith b Udal	191
D. P. Ostler c Nicholas b Bovill	25
T. L. Penney b Bovill	20
G. Welch c Aymes b Connor	43
†K. J. Piper lbw b Bovill	16
N. M. K. Smith not out	29
R. P. Davis c Connor b Udal	17
G. C. Small c Udal b Connor	2
*T. A. Munton b Connor	7
B 1, l-b 10, n-b 14	25
1/54 2/349 3/384 4/403 5/434 6/474 7/484 8/519 9/521	536

Bonus points – Warwickshire 4, Hampshire 4.

Bowling: Connor 31–3–124–4; Bovill 27–4–99–3; James 19–1–86–0; Udal 28–1–142–3; Maru 14–0–74–0.

Umpires: K. J. Lyons and R. Palmer.

At Bristol, September 15, 16, 17, 19. WARWICKSHIRE drew with GLOUCESTERSHIRE.

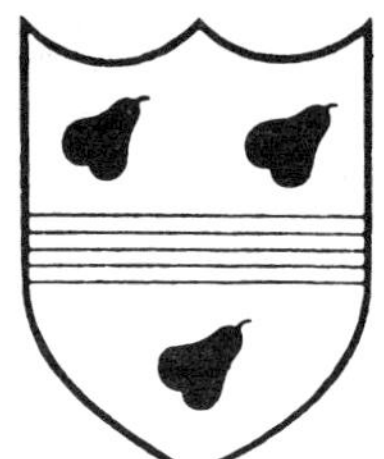

WORCESTERSHIRE

Patron: The Duke of Westminster
President: T. W. Graveney OBE
Chairman: C. D. Fearnley
Chairman, Cricket Committee: M. G. Jones
Secretary: The Rev. Michael Vockins
Captain: T. S. Curtis
Coach: D. L. Houghton
Head Groundsman: R. McLaren
Scorer: J. W. Sewter

In many respects, it could be said that Worcestershire's season went as expected. They prospered in the limited-overs game and struggled in the four-day game. One trophy, another Lord's final and second place in the Sunday League, up from 16th in 1993, exceeded their wildest hopes in one-day cricket. But in the Championship, their crash from runners-up to 15th was worse than anyone could have feared.

Their choice of overseas player had a significant influence. The previous season, they had signed young West Indian pace bowler Ken Benjamin, who shone all too briefly before succumbing to injuries. His departure left an aging attack short of a new-ball cutting edge. Though Worcestershire had several opponents on the ropes, they could rarely deliver the killer punch and recorded only four Championship victories. But the return, after a year's absence, of aggressive Australian all-rounder Tom Moody was the catalyst for a very successful one-day season, culminating in the county's first ever NatWest Trophy, after 32 years of the 60-overs competition.

That eight-wicket victory at Lord's halted Warwickshire's hopes of achieving the Grand Slam of all four domestic titles. But Worcestershire themselves were not so far off treble glory of the kind which fell to their neighbours up the M5. They were beaten by Dermot Reeve's side in the Benson and Hedges Cup final when, just as in the NatWest Trophy final eight weeks later, the toss of the coin proved decisive. Worcestershire also ran Warwickshire very close on Sundays. With four matches left, they were level on points and had a game in hand. Their fate rested in their own hands. But they threw away their advantage during a disastrous visit from Yorkshire. A Sunday League defeat preceded their dismissal for 73 on the Monday – the lowest Championship total of the season. That weekend handed the initiative back to Warwickshire in the 40-overs competition. They never relinquished it again; Worcestershire finally had to be content with the runners-up spot.

Captain Tim Curtis admitted that Worcestershire had tried to copy Glamorgan, who had demonstrated in 1993 what could be achieved in one-day cricket with a bowling attack of limited penetration. "They were successful in one-day cricket with a simple formula," he said. "They bowled their overs quickly, bowled very straight and batted aggressively. It doesn't do any harm sometimes to remind yourself of the basics – and we did those things very well for most of the time."

Moody's contribution with bat and, perhaps more decisively, ball was a major factor in Worcestershire's assault on the three limited-overs trophies.

He had bowled impressively for Western Australia in the Sheffield Shield the previous winter and became a regular fixture as the county's new-ball bowler in one-day cricket. His extra height – at 6ft 7in – and his ability to hit the deck and swing the ball in English conditions made him a difficult opponent to score against, as demonstrated by figures of 44–13–84–5 in the Benson and Hedges Cup and 52–12–141–7 in the NatWest Trophy. Moody the destructive batsman surfaced less regularly than in his previous two seasons at New Road, but he came to the fore in the semi-final and final of the NatWest Trophy and collected the Man of the Match awards in both. No one who was there will ever forget the savagery of his unbeaten 180 in the semi-final against Surrey at The Oval, when Curtis, who made 136 not out, helped him in a world record limited-overs stand of 309 in 48 overs. Even after that, Moody had to take a head-high catch on the boundary off the penultimate delivery to deny Surrey an improbable victory, as they fell only eight runs short of their 358-run target. To cap it all, Moody was the only Worcestershire player to score 1,000 Championship runs. It came as little surprise when he was voted Player of the Year.

Graeme Hick's old confidence in his technique returned as he finally came of age as a Test batsman. He scored 1,101 first-class runs for Worcestershire at 57.94 and became the youngest player, at 28 years and 19 days, to register 50 Championship centuries. The sight of Hick and Moody in tandem at full throttle was a fearsome prospect for bowlers, as Warwickshire found to their cost in the NatWest Trophy final; they shared an unbroken stand of 198 during the surge to victory. Wicket-keeper Steve Rhodes finally made the breakthrough at full international level that he deserved after five tours with England's second team. He made many telling contributions as a middle-order batsman and averaged 57.09 for the county in first-class cricket.

The biggest improvement of the season came from all-rounder Stuart Lampitt. Many of his New Road colleagues felt he deserved better than a standby spot for the England A tour of India after his fine efforts. After two disappointing seasons, Lampitt added that extra zip to his bowling to finish with 64 first-class wickets. He also contributed 624 runs at 29.71, even though he often batted at No. 8. Meanwhile, Phil Newport soldiered on manfully, despite an almost constant ankle problem, to finish with 53 wickets, while Richard Illingworth took 49. Gavin Haynes benefited from his first extended run of senior action. He scored 1,021 first-class runs. David Leatherdale made promising progress alongside him in the middle order, falling only 13 short of four figures. Both now need to find greater consistency.

But the root of Worcestershire's batting difficulties in the Championship was that there were too few significant contributions from further up the order. Curtis fell below his usual prolific standards in his benefit year, failing to reach 1,000 runs, and Hick was missing for seven matches on England duty. – John Curtis.

WORCESTERSHIRE 1994

[*Bill Smith*

Back row: K. R. Spiring, V. S. Solanki, P. Mirza, G. R. Haynes. *Middle row:* J. Smith (*physiotherapist*), D. A. Leatherdale, C. J. Eyers, A. C. H. Seymour, W. P. C. Weston, J. E. Brinkley, S. R. Lampitt, D. L. Houghton (*Second Eleven captain and coach*), T. Edwards. *Front row:* C. M. Tolley, R. K. Illingworth, N. V. Radford, S. J. Rhodes, T. S. Curtis (*captain*), D. B. D'Oliveira, G. A. Hick, P. J. Newport, T. M. Moody.

WORCESTERSHIRE RESULTS

All first-class matches – Played 20: Won 5, Lost 6, Drawn 9.

County Championship matches – Played 17: Won 4, Lost 6, Drawn 7.

Bonus points – Batting 42, Bowling 52.

Competition placings – Britannic Assurance County Championship, 15th; NatWest Bank Trophy, winners; Benson and Hedges Cup, finalists; AXA Equity & Law League, 2nd.

BRITANNIC ASSURANCE CHAMPIONSHIP AVERAGES

BATTING

	Birthplace	*M*	*I*	*NO*	*R*	*HS*	*Avge*
‡G. A. Hick	*Salisbury, Rhodesia*	10	17	0	996	215	58.58
‡S. J. Rhodes	*Bradford*	10	16	6	525	76*	52.50
‡T. M. Moody§	*Adelaide, Australia*	16	25	2	1,049	159	45.60
‡D. A. Leatherdale	*Bradford*	15	23	2	800	139	38.09
‡T. S. Curtis	*Chislehurst*	16	28	1	903	180	33.44
W. P. C. Weston	*Durham*	15	24	1	728	94	31.65
‡G. R. Haynes	*Stourbridge*	17	28	1	827	141	30.62
‡S. R. Lampitt	*Wolverhampton*	15	23	3	586	122	29.30
‡C. M. Tolley	*Kidderminster*	5	8	1	161	84	23.00
T. Edwards	*Penzance*	7	9	6	64	30*	21.33
‡R. K. Illingworth	*Bradford*	17	23	4	384	59*	20.21
‡P. J. Newport	*High Wycombe*	15	21	5	313	41	19.56
P. Mirza	*Birmingham*	2	4	1	47	40	15.66
M. J. Church	*Guildford*	3	5	0	65	38	13.00
‡N. V. Radford	*Luanshya, N. Rhodesia*	14	20	4	161	25	10.06
J. E. Brinkley	*Helensburgh*	7	9	2	16	5	2.28

Also batted: ‡D. B. D'Oliveira (*Cape Town, SA*) (1 match) 19, 48; A. C. H. Seymour (*Royston*) (2 matches) 7, 27, 31.

* *Signifies not out.* ‡ *Denotes county cap.* § *Overseas player.*

The following played a total of 13 three-figure innings for Worcestershire in County Championship matches – G. A. Hick 4, T. S. Curtis 3, T. M. Moody 3, G. R. Haynes 1, S. R. Lampitt 1, D. A. Leatherdale 1.

BOWLING

	O	*M*	*R*	*W*	*BB*	*5W/i*	*Avge*
S. R. Lampitt	498	124	1,442	60	5-33	2	24.03
R. K. Illingworth	611	184	1,401	48	4-51	0	29.18
P. J. Newport	480.2	96	1,538	51	4-50	0	30.15
N. V. Radford	427.1	97	1,323	35	5-93	1	37.80
T. M. Moody	183	46	533	14	4-24	0	38.07
J. E. Brinkley	187	32	637	10	6-98	1	63.70

Also bowled: M. J. Church 1–0–4–0; T. S. Curtis 8–1–43–0; D. B. D'Oliveira 23–2–85–2; G. R. Haynes 104.3–23–305–7; G. A. Hick 101.2–24–314–7; D. A. Leatherdale 80.1–12–278–2; P. Mirza 48–13–162–4; C. M. Tolley 118–23–413–7; W. P. C. Weston 13–4–47–0.

Wicket-keepers: S. J. Rhodes 27 ct, 6 st; T. Edwards 15 ct.

Leading Fielders: T. M. Moody 18, D. A. Leatherdale 17.

At The Oval, April 28, 29, 30, May 1. WORCESTERSHIRE lost to SURREY by nine wickets.

At Worcester, May 4, 5, 6. WORCESTERSHIRE drew with NEW ZEALANDERS (See New Zealand tour section).

At Cambridge, May 7, 8, 9. WORCESTERSHIRE drew with CAMBRIDGE UNIVERSITY.

WORCESTERSHIRE v GLOUCESTERSHIRE

At Worcester, May 12, 13, 14, 16. Drawn. Worcestershire 5 pts, Gloucestershire 7 pts. Toss: Gloucestershire.

Worcestershire's last man, Brinkley, survived the final ball of the match in conditions so murky that all five bulbs on the scoreboard's light meter had been shining since tea. The eighth wicket had fallen with 13 overs to go and Walsh bowled five overs of leg-breaks rather than provoke the umpires into leaving the field; Curtis had agreed that play should continue while it was safe. Gloucestershire paid the penalty for their turgid first-innings batting: they took ten hours to assemble 390 at 2.56 runs an over. Broad had the excuse of an injured hip: he needed pain-killers to reach his 76. The home team were more positive, thanks to Hick, who completed his 73rd century in 144 balls and went on to 150, with 20 fours and two sixes. But lumbago prevented him from fielding and he had to bat down the order when Worcestershire set off in pursuit of 265 from 54 overs.

Close of play: First day, Gloucestershire 155-4 (A. J. Wright 12*, M. C. J. Ball 0*); Second day, Worcestershire 51-2 (G. A. Hick 17*, T. M. Moody 10*); Third day, Gloucestershire 50-1 (B. C. Broad 21*, S. G. Hinks 11*).

Gloucestershire

B. C. Broad c Weston b Newport	76	– c Lampitt b Illingworth	46
G. D. Hodgson c Rhodes b Radford	18	– lbw b Radford	14
S. G. Hinks lbw b Newport	14	– c Brinkley b Newport	74
M. W. Alleyne lbw b Radford	21	– c Rhodes b Illingworth	42
A. J. Wright c Lampitt b Radford	82	– c Newport b Illingworth	7
M. C. J. Ball b Lampitt	4	– (8) not out	4
T. H. C. Hancock c Brinkley b Radford	58	– (6) st Rhodes b Illingworth	0
†R. C. Russell c Newport b Hick	46	– (7) c sub b Newport	5
*C. A. Walsh c Haynes b Lampitt	15		
A. M. Smith st Rhodes b Illingworth	27		
K. E. Cooper not out	0		
L-b 11, n-b 18	29	B 4, l-b 1, n-b 6	11
1/31 2/65 3/121 4/146 5/169 6/305 7/326 8/390 9/390	390	1/35 2/99 3/175 4/183 5/192 6/194 7/203	(7 wkts dec.) 203

Bonus points – Gloucestershire 3, Worcestershire 2 (Score at 120 overs: 301-5).

Bowling: *First Innings*—Radford 31–8–70–4; Brinkley 25–3–83–0; Moody 15–6–23–0; Newport 26–7–69–2; Illingworth 18–6–35–1; Lampitt 30–8–79–2; Weston 2–0–10–0; Hick 5.1–1–10–1. *Second Innings*—Radford 6–2–12–1; Brinkley 14–0–69–0; Illingworth 18–5–51–4; Hick 2–0–8–0; Newport 14–3–45–2; Lampitt 7–3–13–0.

Worcestershire

*T. S. Curtis lbw b Walsh	1 – b Smith	10
W. P. C. Weston lbw b Walsh	13 – c Russell b Walsh	38
G. A. Hick c Hodgson b Cooper	150 – (7) c Wright b Alleyne	6
T. M. Moody lbw b Cooper	18 – b Cooper	24
G. R. Haynes c Russell b Alleyne	25 – (3) c Hinks b Walsh	18
†S. J. Rhodes c Russell b Alleyne	42 – (5) c Russell b Smith	22
P. J. Newport lbw b Cooper	0 – (9) c Hinks b Alleyne	0
S. R. Lampitt c Ball b Walsh	5 – (6) not out	25
R. K. Illingworth not out	17 – (8) b Ball	3
N. V. Radford c and b Alleyne	5 – c Hinks b Ball	14
J. E. Brinkley not out	2 – not out	0
B 1, l-b 3, w 1, n-b 46	51	B 5, l-b 6, w 1, n-b 8 20
1/4 2/25 3/83 4/144 5/277 6/277 7/297 8/305 9/318	(9 wkts dec.) 329	1/44 2/61 3/84 4/120 5/126 6/146 7/155 8/156 9/180 (9 wkts) 180

Bonus points – Worcestershire 3, Gloucestershire 4.

Bowling: *First Innings*—Walsh 26.3–4–98–3; Cooper 28–5–78–3; Smith 15–1–69–0; Ball 7–0–36–0; Alleyne 11–3–34–3; Hancock 3–0–10–0. *Second Innings*—Cooper 16–2–57–1; Walsh 15–4–31–2; Smith 9–1–60–2; Ball 10–4–15–2; Alleyne 4–2–6–2.

Umpires: H. D. Bird and J. D. Bond.

At Derby, May 19, 20, 21, 23. WORCESTERSHIRE drew with DERBYSHIRE.

WORCESTERSHIRE v NORTHAMPTONSHIRE

At Worcester, May 26, 27, 28, 30. Drawn. Worcestershire 6 pts, Northamptonshire 4 pts. Toss: Northamptonshire.

Although the opening day was washed out, Worcestershire had the scent of victory on Saturday evening: Northamptonshire were still behind, having lost four second innings wickets. But by Monday, the weekend sun had dried out the pitch and Northamptonshire added another 219 runs for the loss of only two wickets, with Loye completing a five-hour century. Lamb even declared, setting a target of 214 in 30 overs, a luxury he could not have expected on Friday when he chose to bat and saw his team bowled out in three hours by Radford, Lampitt and Newport. Worcestershire were more circumspect than their visitors – Moody took 20 overs to reach double figures and Curtis batted 43 overs before falling one short of his first fifty of the season – but still lost five wickets the same day.

Close of play: First day, No play; Second day, Worcestershire 139-5 (D. A. Leatherdale 8*, R. K. Illingworth 4*); Third day, Northamptonshire 138-4 (M. B. Loye 9*, K. M. Curran 19*).

Northamptonshire

A. Fordham b Radford	20 – c Radford b Newport	58
N. A. Felton c Hick b Radford	0 – b Illingworth	33
R. J. Bailey c Leatherdale b Radford	3 – lbw b Radford	13
*A. J. Lamb c Rhodes b Newport	15 – c Moody b Radford	0
M. B. Loye c Moody b Radford	24 – not out	107
K. M. Curran b Newport	0 – c Hick b Radford	61
A. L. Penberthy c Moody b Newport	4 – c Lampitt b Hick	69
†D. Ripley c Hick b Lampitt	14 – not out	1
C. E. L. Ambrose b Lampitt	23	
N. G. B. Cook c Rhodes b Lampitt	3	
J. P. Taylor not out	2	
L-b 3, w 1	4	L-b 3, n-b 12 15
1/13 2/22 3/27 4/43 5/43 6/49 7/79 8/100 9/107	112	1/73 2/108 3/108 4/110 5/211 6/354 (6 wkts dec.) 357

Bonus points – Worcestershire 4.

Bowling: *First Innings*—Radford 18–5–48–4; Tolley 10–2–29–0; Lampitt 16.4–9–16–3; Newport 6–1–9–3; Leatherdale 1–0–7–0. *Second Innings*—Newport 28–4–83–1; Tolley 13–3–20–0; Moody 7–3–27–0; Lampitt 29–6–72–0; Illingworth 19–6–45–1; Radford 21–6–57–3; Hick 5–1–20–1; Leatherdale 9–1–30–0.

Worcestershire

*T. S. Curtis c Ripley b Taylor	49	– lbw b Ambrose 0
C. M. Tolley c Felton b Ambrose	11	– not out 38
G. A. Hick c Ripley b Taylor	21	– c Ripley b Ambrose 0
T. M. Moody lbw b Taylor	19	– not out 8
G. R. Haynes c Ripley b Taylor	11	
D. A. Leatherdale hit wkt b Ambrose	41	
R. K. Illingworth run out	4	
†S. J. Rhodes c Lamb b Taylor	19	
P. J. Newport c Bailey b Penberthy	2	
S. R. Lampitt c Ripley b Curran	32	
N. V. Radford not out	13	
B 4, l-b 7, w 1, n-b 22	34	B 5, l-b 2, n-b 4 11
1/21 2/48 3/113 4/114 5/133 6/145 7/184 8/194 9/218	256	1/6 2/6 (2 wkts) 57

Bonus points – Worcestershire 2, Northamptonshire 4.

Bowling: *First Innings*—Ambrose 29–9–67–2; Taylor 24–4–62–5; Curran 28.4–9–69–1; Penberthy 15–3–39–1; Cook 3–1–8–0. *Second Innings*—Ambrose 6–3–8–2; Taylor 5–0–32–0; Cook 3–1–2–0; Curran 3–0–8–0.

Umpires: R. Palmer and N. T. Plews.

At Lord's, June 2, 3, 4, 6. WORCESTERSHIRE drew with MIDDLESEX.

WORCESTERSHIRE v ESSEX

At Worcestershire, June 9, 10, 11, 13. Essex won by four wickets. Essex 22 pts, Worcestershire 8 pts. Toss: Worcestershire.

Essex moved to the top of the Championship table as Shahid scrambled the winning run from the final ball. But their total of 405 in 107 overs – the highest ever fourth-innings score to beat Worcestershire – was dominated by 205 from Gooch. It was his second century of the match, his fifth in ten innings in 1994 and his third double of the season, a feat last achieved by Alvin Kallicharran in 1982. He batted six and a quarter hours, faced 287 balls and hit a six and 24 fours, becoming the second batsman – after Lara – to reach 1,000 runs for the season. Gooch had scored twin centuries on four previous occasions. His stand of 245 in 60 overs with Irani, who completed his maiden hundred, provided the platform for the final drama; Essex started the day needing 390 and began the final session looking for 202 from 39 overs. They seemed to have lost their advantage on the third day, when they lost their last six wickets for 23 and Worcestershire ran up quick runs before declaring. Hick scored his 74th hundred – to Gooch's 110th and 111th – and his 50th in the County Championship, from 98 balls, and added 167 in 34 overs with Moody.

Close of play: First day, Worcestershire 254-6 (S. J. Rhodes 15*, S. R. Lampitt 13*); Second day, Essex 200-3 (J. J. B. Lewis 6*, R. C. Irani 8*); Third day, Essex 15-0 (G. A. Gooch 13*, J. P. Stephenson 2*).

Worcestershire

*T. S. Curtis lbw b Stephenson	13 – b Cousins	13
W. P. C. Weston c Hussain b Kasprowicz	0 – lbw b Stephenson	10
G. A. Hick c Hussain b Irani	65 – lbw b Stephenson	101
T. M. Moody c Garnham b Kasprowicz	51 – not out	108
G. R. Haynes lbw b Stephenson	55 – not out	28
D. A. Leatherdale c Hussain b Irani	4	
†S. J. Rhodes not out	76	
S. R. Lampitt c Garnham b Irani	40	
P. J. Newport c Shahid b Irani	0	
R. K. Illingworth c Garnham b Cousins	26	
J. E. Brinkley lbw b Cousins	0	
B 7, l-b 20, w 2, n-b 22	51	B 5, l-b 5, w 1, n-b 14 ... 25
1/2 2/43 3/143 4/163 5/179 6/233 7/304 8/304 9/381	381	1/21 2/43 3/210 (3 wkts dec.) 285

Bonus points – Worcestershire 4, Essex 4.

Bowling: *First Innings*—Kasprowicz 23–3–80–2; Cousins 24.4–5–78–2; Stephenson 30–11–82–2; Irani 29–6–91–4; Such 7–0–23–0. *Second Innings*—Cousins 16–2–67–1; Kasprowicz 2–0–12–0; Stephenson 21–6–95–2; Such 11–0–48–0; Irani 17–2–53–0.

Essex

*G. A. Gooch b Lampitt	101 – c Leatherdale b Newport	205
J. P. Stephenson lbw b Haynes	42 – c Haynes b Lampitt	26
P. J. Prichard retired hurt	4	
N. Hussain b Lampitt	31 – c Haynes b Lampitt	0
J. J. B. Lewis lbw b Lampitt	21 – (3) lbw b Illingworth	14
N. Shahid c Weston b Lampitt	2 – (7) not out	13
R. C. Irani not out	50 – (5) lbw b Newport	119
†M. A. Garnham lbw b Lampitt	0 – (6) c Leatherdale b Newport	5
M. S. Kasprowicz c Weston b Newport	1 – (8) not out	4
P. M. Such c Moody b Illingworth	0	
D. M. Cousins b Newport	1	
B 1, l-b 8	9	B 2, l-b 7, n-b 10 ... 19
1/105 2/184 3/187 4/239 5/251 6/251 7/259 8/261 9/262	262	1/89 2/132 3/133 4/378 5/385 6/390 (6 wkts) 405

Bonus points – Essex 2, Worcestershire 4.

In the first innings P. J. Prichard retired hurt at 119; N. Shahid, when 0, retired hurt at 187-3 and resumed at 239.

Bowling: *First Innings*—Brinkley 18–5–48–0; Moody 7–3–21–0; Lampitt 32–9–75–5; Newport 12.1–3–42–2; Haynes 7–2–28–1; Hick 1–0–7–0; Illingworth 19–6–32–1. *Second Innings*—Brinkley 17–2–64–0; Newport 22–4–96–3; Moody 6–1–23–0; Lampitt 23–1–84–2; Illingworth 25–8–66–1; Hick 5–2–21–0; Haynes 9–0–42–0.

Umpires: R. Julian and P. B. Wight.

WORCESTERSHIRE v OXFORD UNIVERSITY

At Worcester, June 17, 18, 19. Worcestershire won by 226 runs. Toss: Worcestershire. First-class debuts: P. Mirza, K. R. Spiring.

Worcestershire might have won in two days after routing Oxford for 95, 245 behind. But county officials, anxious to salvage a Father's Day barbecue scheduled for the third day's lunch interval, persuaded acting-captain Illingworth not to enforce the follow-on. On the opening morning, the leg-spinner Trimby took three wickets for seven runs as Worcestershire slipped to 90 for four. But a stand of 151 between Leatherdale and the debutant

Spiring redressed the balance. Spiring made a second fifty on Saturday, before Illingworth set an academic target of 479. Though Kendall could not bat because of a broken thumb, Oxford prolonged the game until after the barbecue, thanks to Hollins, whose 76 was his highest score yet. D'Oliveira's off-breaks earned him a career-best four for 68.

Close of play: First day, Oxford University 19-2 (C. M. Gupte 9*, C. J. Townsend 0*); Second day, Oxford University 34-2 (R. R. Montgomerie 18*, C. J. Hollins 1*).

Worcestershire

W. P. C. Weston c sub b Trimby	23	– c Townsend b Martin	29
A. C. H. Seymour c Gupte b Maclay	27	– c Malik b Trimby	87
G. R. Haynes c Martin b Trimby	10		
D. B. D'Oliveira c Townsend b Trimby	17		
D. A. Leatherdale c sub b Malik	138		
K. R. Spiring b Malik	56	– (3) c Martin b Trimby	52
C. M. Tolley c Macmillan b Malik	2	– not out	8
*R. K. Illingworth not out	53		
†T. Edwards not out	5	– (4) b Hollins	47
J. E. Brinkley (did not bat)		– (5) run out	0
P. Mirza (did not bat)		– (6) c Townsend b Trimby	0
L-b 5, n-b 4	9	N-b 10	10
1/37 2/64 3/77 4/90 5/241 6/261 7/318 (7 wkts dec.)	340	1/110 2/142 3/210 4/212 5/212 6/233 (6 wkts dec.)	233

Bowling: *First Innings*—Ecclestone 1.3–0–3–0; Maclay 20–3–59–1; Martin 9.3–4–24–0; Hollins 19–3–68–0; Trimby 28–7–92–3; Macmillan 5–0–34–0; Malik 12–0–55–3. *Second Innings*—Maclay 12–0–47–0; Trimby 15–0–79–3; Ecclestone 3–0–12–0; Hollins 7.2–1–47–1; Martin 8–1–36–1; Malik 6–1–12–0.

Oxford University

*R. R. Montgomerie c Edwards b Brinkley	7	– c Spiring b D'Oliveira	51
G. I. Macmillan c D'Oliveira b Mirza	2	– c Edwards b Brinkley	3
C. M. Gupte c and b Tolley	23	– run out	44
W. S. Kendall retired hurt	0	– absent injured	
†C. J. Townsend c Spiring b Brinkley	0	– (4) lbw b Mirza	0
S. C. Ecclestone c Tolley b Brinkley	8	– (7) not out	41
H. S. Malik b Brinkley	0	– (6) lbw b D'Oliveira	9
C. J. Hollins lbw b Mirza	33	– (5) lbw b Leatherdale	76
N. F. C. Martin c Edwards b Mirza	15	– (8) lbw b D'Oliveira	0
A. W. Maclay c Weston b Mirza	1	– (9) b D'Oliveira	2
P. W. Trimby not out	1	– (10) lbw b Illingworth	11
B 1, w 2, n-b 2	5	B 3, l-b 6, n-b 6	15
1/4 2/17 3/26 4/34 5/34 6/63 7/87 8/94 9/95	95	1/11 2/33 3/96 4/161 5/176 6/209 7/213 8/221 9/252	252

In the first innings W. S. Kendall retired hurt at 17-2; in the second innings C. M. Gupte, when 7, retired hurt at 30 and resumed at 96.

Bowling: *First Innings*—Brinkley 9–2–33–4; Mirza 11.4–1–29–4; Tolley 10–5–27–1; D'Oliveira 3–2–5–0. *Second Innings*—Brinkley 4–1–9–1; Tolley 8–2–24–0; Mirza 2–0–2–1; Leatherdale 21–6–50–1; D'Oliveira 36–13–68–4; Haynes 4–0–14–0; Illingworth 31.1–12–39–1; Weston 8–3–37–0.

Umpires: G. I. Burgess and P. Willey.

WORCESTERSHIRE v SUSSEX

At Worcester, June 23, 24, 25, 27. Worcestershire won by one wicket. Worcestershire 23 pts, Sussex 6 pts. Toss: Sussex.

A week earlier, Rhodes had saved England's bacon in the Lord's Test against New Zealand; here he played a similar role, batting 35 overs to pull off Worcestershire's first Championship win. Victory looked a formality at lunch, with 78 required and seven wickets in hand. But once Stephenson ended Hick's steady innings, he and Giddins engineered a dramatic mid-order collapse: Worcestershire lurched to 183 for seven. With six runs required, Stephenson dived for a return catch off Rhodes, only for umpire Constant to judge it a bump ball; four runs later, Illingworth was caught at silly mid-off. But Radford despatched his second ball through the covers for the winning boundary. On the first day, Stephenson and Lenham rescued Sussex from a precarious 88 for four. Salisbury bowled impressively for his five wickets in Worcestershire's first innings and, when Sussex resumed, Speight's belligerent 81 set up a lead of 235 to keep them in the contest.

Close of play: First day, Worcestershire 73-2 (W. P. C. Weston 26*, T. M. Moody 14*); Second day, Sussex 42-1 (C. W. J. Athey 20*, N. J. Lenham 14*); Third day, Worcestershire 65-1 (W. P. C. Weston 23*, G. A. Hick 17*).

Sussex

C. W. J. Athey c Rhodes b Lampitt	14	– lbw b Illingworth	57
J. W. Hall b Newport	6	– c Hick b Radford	6
N. J. Lenham b Lampitt	70	– c Rhodes b Newport	14
*A. P. Wells c Haynes b Moody	4	– c Curtis b Illingworth	38
M. P. Speight c Haynes b Moody	15	– b Lampitt	81
†P. Moores c Moody b Illingworth	41	– c Rhodes b Moody	10
F. D. Stephenson c Haynes b Hick	95	– c Illingworth b Moody	0
P. W. Jarvis c Lampitt b Radford	12	– b Lampitt	10
I. D. K. Salisbury st Rhodes b Illingworth	27	– c Moody b Lampitt	17
E. E. Hemmings lbw b Illingworth	1	– not out	2
E. S. H. Giddins not out	0	– b Lampitt	10
L-b 2, n-b 8	10	L-b 3, w 1, n-b 8	12
1/15 2/47 3/58 4/88 5/131 6/218 7/249 8/287 9/295	295	1/24 2/43 3/121 4/146 5/181 6/181 7/209 8/244 9/247	257

Bonus points – Sussex 2, Worcestershire 4.

Bowling: *First Innings*—Newport 16–2–66–1; Radford 15–5–64–1; Lampitt 18–6–35–2; Moody 11–2–42–2; Illingworth 18–6–52–3; Leatherdale 4–1–15–0; Hick 4.1–0–19–1. *Second Innings*—Newport 12–3–22–1; Radford 15–6–28–1; Illingworth 31–12–75–2; Hick 10–2–34–0; Lampitt 15.5–4–37–4; Moody 16–1–42–2; Haynes 8–2–16–0.

Worcestershire

*T. S. Curtis lbw b Giddins	26	– lbw b Stephenson	18
W. P. C. Weston c Speight b Salisbury	70	– c Salisbury b Jarvis	30
G. A. Hick c Salisbury b Giddins	1	– c Hemmings b Stephenson	73
T. M. Moody c and b Salisbury	17	– c Hall b Hemmings	28
G. R. Haynes c Wells b Salisbury	24	– lbw b Giddins	15
D. A. Leatherdale b Salisbury	40	– b Stephenson	0
†S. J. Rhodes c Speight b Hemmings	18	– not out	37
S. R. Lampitt lbw b Hemmings	57	– lbw b Giddins	0
P. J. Newport c Speight b Hemmings	35	– c Speight b Stephenson	12
R. K. Illingworth c Wells b Salisbury	5	– c Athey b Salisbury	11
N. V. Radford not out	0	– not out	4
B 8, l-b 10, n-b 6	24	L-b 7, w 1, n-b 2	10
1/42 2/44 3/91 4/149 5/154 6/201 7/223 8/290 9/313	317	1/39 2/83 3/145 4/170 5/170 6/183 7/183 8/213 9/234	(9 wkts) 238

Bonus points – Worcestershire 3, Sussex 4.

Bowling: *First Innings*—Jarvis 9–1–44–0; Stephenson 12–0–63–0; Giddins 21–7–43–2; Hemmings 28–11–70–3; Salisbury 37.2–18–79–5. *Second Innings*—Stephenson 31–10–78–4; Jarvis 13–2–49–1; Hemmings 8–5–10–1; Giddins 13–2–41–2; Salisbury 29–12–53–1.

Umpires: D. J. Constant and J. W. Holder.

At Taunton, June 30, July 1, 2, 4. WORCESTERSHIRE lost to SOMERSET by 53 runs.

At Canterbury, July 14, 15, 16, 18. WORCESTERSHIRE beat KENT by 140 runs.

WORCESTERSHIRE v HAMPSHIRE

At Worcester, July 21, 22, 23, 25. Hampshire won by 56 runs. Hampshire 21 pts, Worcestershire 4 pts. Toss: Hampshire.

Udal, a late arrival after being released from England's party at Lord's, made up for his disappointment by spinning Hampshire to victory with a second-innings haul of six for 85. His deceptive flight amply compensated for the loss of Benjamin to a shoulder injury. Nicholas had chosen to bat and, though Hampshire slipped to 67 for four, his disciplined 84 not out, supported by Aymes, eventually saw them to 228. Worcestershire were soon in worse trouble at 75 for five and the hostile Benjamin improved on his best figures for his new county for the second week running, with six for 46, although a 73-run stand by Lampitt and Leatherdale kept the deficit down to 35. Smith put his own England omission behind him with 162 – his fourth century in five Championship games – although the persevering Lampitt completed match figures of nine for 82. Worcestershire were left to score 372 though, once Curtis lost Moody, who had helped him add 94, the way was open for Udal's decisive contribution.

Close of play: First day, Worcestershire 43-2 (W. P. C. Weston 19*, T. Edwards 6*); Second day, Hampshire 197-4 (R. A. Smith 99*, R. J. Maru 0*); Third day, Worcestershire 175-3 (T. S. Curtis 78*, R. K. Illingworth 2*).

Hampshire

T. C. Middleton c Edwards b Lampitt	20	– lbw b Lampitt	19
V. P. Terry c Edwards b Radford	21	– lbw b Radford	0
G. W. White c Edwards b Newport	1	– b Lampitt	28
R. A. Smith b Newport	2	– lbw b Haynes	162
*M. C. J. Nicholas not out	84	– c Moody b Illingworth	31
†A. N. Aymes lbw b Newport	41	– (7) lbw b Lampitt	0
S. D. Udal b Newport	0	– (8) c Moody b Haynes	40
W. K. M. Benjamin c Radford b Lampitt	4	– (11) not out	1
R. J. Maru lbw b Lampitt	0	– (6) lbw b Lampitt	10
M. Jean-Jacques c Edwards b Lampitt	15	– (9) b Haynes	7
C. A. Connor lbw b Lampitt	2	– (10) c Mirza b Illingworth	6
B 2, l-b 3, w 1, n-b 32	38	B 9, l-b 3, n-b 20	32
1/45 2/46 3/54 4/67 5/167 6/175 7/186 8/190 9/218	228	1/1 2/42 3/83 4/197 5/216 6/222 7/311 8/322 9/335	336

Bonus points – Hampshire 1, Worcestershire 4.

Bowling: *First Innings*—Radford 19–3–46–1; Mirza 11–2–51–0; Newport 19–3–50–4; Lampitt 19.4–7–33–5; Illingworth 7–4–3–0; Moody 7–0–25–0; Leatherdale 4–0–15–0. *Second Innings*—Radford 19–0–66–1; Mirza 9–4–24–0; Newport 16–2–68–0; Lampitt 19–4–49–4; Moody 6–2–27–0; Illingworth 27–5–71–2; Haynes 6.3–2–19–3.

Worcestershire

*T. S. Curtis lbw b Benjamin	10	– c Terry b Connor	95
W. P. C. Weston c Aymes b Benjamin	32	– c Terry b Udal	25
G. R. Haynes lbw b Benjamin	1	– lbw b Maru	8
†T. Edwards c White b Connor	15	– (10) c Benjamin b Udal	4
T. M. Moody b Benjamin	3	– (4) c Aymes b Connor	46
D. A. Leatherdale lbw b Udal	26	– c Maru b Jean-Jacques	35
S. R. Lampitt c White b Udal	32	– lbw b Udal	1
P. J. Newport c Middleton b Benjamin	30	– not out	32
R. K. Illingworth c Maru b Udal	3	– (5) b Udal	7
N. V. Radford lbw b Benjamin	5	– (9) c Maru b Udal	25
P. Mirza not out	0	– lbw b Udal	5
L-b 3, n-b 33	36	B 4, l-b 4, n-b 24	32
1/20 2/26 3/65 4/70 5/75 6/148 7/149 8/159 9/168	193	1/51 2/75 3/169 4/202 5/210 6/212 7/254 8/295 9/307	315

Bonus points – Hampshire 4.

Bowling: *First Innings*—Benjamin 24.5–12–46–6; Connor 18–3–60–1; Jean-Jacques 12–2–53–0; Udal 10–3–31–3. *Second Innings*—Connor 37–11–105–2; Jean-Jacques 17–0–67–1; Udal 36.5–11–85–6; Maru 30–10–50–1.

Umpires: B. Leadbeater and K. E. Palmer.

WORCESTERSHIRE v WARWICKSHIRE

At Worcester, August 4, 5, 6, 8. Drawn. Worcestershire 6 pts, Warwickshire 1 pt. Toss: Worcestershire.

Warwickshire's run of six successive victories was ended by Worcestershire, the last side to defeat them in the Championship nearly 12 months earlier. But despite building a strong position Worcestershire could not force a win on the final day. On a sluggish pitch, Twose took two hours over the 12 he needed to complete 1,000 runs on a first day ravaged by bad weather. Resuming, Warwickshire lost their last seven for 87 and were then ground down by an eight-hour 180 from Curtis, who had made only 529 in 22 innings in 1994. Weston shared in a 208-run opening stand and then Leatherdale and Lampitt punished a wilting attack with 133 in 25 overs. Worcestershire declared at 473 for four and removed Twose and Ostler on the third evening. Warwickshire finally frustrated them to preserve their unbeaten record. Night-watchman Welch set the defiant tone with a career-best 66 and Moles, Penney and Lara cashed in as Moody and Illingworth rested injuries before the next day's NatWest semi-final.

Close of play: First day, Warwickshire 129-3 (D. P. Ostler 27*, T. L. Penney 0*); Second day, Worcestershire 135-0 (T. S. Curtis 61*, W. P. C. Weston 61*); Third day, Warwickshire 56-2 (A. J. Moles 15*, G. Welch 10*).

Warwickshire

First innings		Second innings	
A. J. Moles c Weston b Illingworth	39	c Leatherdale b Lampitt	67
R. G. Twose c and b Lampitt	39	lbw b Newport	14
B. C. Lara c and b Newport	5	(6) c Weston b Haynes	57
D. P. Ostler c Edwards b Newport	27	(3) lbw b Radford	7
T. L. Penney c sub b Illingworth	30	not out	84
P. A. Smith b Lampitt	6	(7) not out	17
*D. A. Reeve lbw b Lampitt	33		
†K. J. Piper c Lampitt b Illingworth	0		
N. M. K. Smith c Haynes b Newport	4		
G. Welch b Lampitt	2	(4) c Leatherdale b Newport	66
T. A. Munton not out	0		
B 2, l-b 13, n-b 16	31	B 3, l-b 7, n-b 24	34
1/62 2/71 3/124 4/130 5/141 6/193 7/193 8/204 9/211	216	1/18 2/41 3/176 4/181 5/264	(5 wkts) 346

Bonus points – Warwickshire 1, Worcestershire 4.

Bowling: *First Innings*—Radford 23–8–42–0; Moody 9–5–11–0; Newport 23–6–81–3; Lampitt 21.5–7–32–4; Illingworth 12–3–30–3; Haynes 3–1–5–0. *Second Innings*—Radford 17–2–57–1; Newport 21–6–71–2; Lampitt 14–2–59–1; Illingworth 11–3–17–0; Leatherdale 13–1–46–0; Weston 7–4–12–0; Haynes 14–5–31–1; Curtis 8–1–43–0.

Worcestershire

*T. S. Curtis c Munton b N. M. K. Smith	180
W. P. C. Weston c Reeve b N. M. K. Smith	94
A. C. H. Seymour c Penney b N. M. K. Smith	31
G. R. Haynes c Piper b N. M. K. Smith	9
D. A. Leatherdale not out	71
S. R. Lampitt not out	56
L-b 14, w 2, n-b 16	32
1/208 2/303 3/339 4/340	(4 wkts dec.) 473

T. M. Moody, P. J. Newport, R. K. Illingworth, N. V. Radford and †T. Edwards did not bat.

Bonus points – Worcestershire 2 (Score at 120 overs: 295-1).

Bowling: Munton 35–8–72–0; Welch 20–2–69–0; Reeve 20–10–26–0; P. A. Smith 17–4–59–0; N. M. K. Smith 41–6–141–4; Twose 19–0–79–0; Lara 4–0–13–0.

Umpires: J. H. Harris and A. G. T. Whitehead.

At Leicester, August 11, 12, 13, 15. WORCESTERSHIRE lost to LEICESTERSHIRE by 97 runs.

WORCESTERSHIRE v NOTTINGHAMSHIRE

At Kidderminster, August 18, 19, 20, 22. Worcestershire won by five wickets. Worcestershire 22 pts, Nottinghamshire 7 pts. Toss: Nottinghamshire. First-class debut: M. J. Church.

Worcestershire maintained their unbeaten record since first-class cricket returned to Chester Road in 1987 – six wins and two draws – thanks to contrasting centuries from Haynes and Curtis. Nottinghamshire had declared overnight, leaving them a whole day to score 362 on a flat pitch. They were soon 28 for two but Haynes, who just missed his first Championship century of 1994 in the first innings, made no mistake this time. He scored 141 in 143 balls, putting on 200 with Curtis, whose share was 49. Curtis continued to play the anchor role and he was unbeaten on 118, spanning six hours, after victory was assured by D'Oliveira's cameo 48. Lewis dominated the first three days. His 77 rescued Nottinghamshire from 178 for five and then his five for 71 earned a lead of 46. Robinson became the first Nottinghamshire player to complete 1,000 runs for the season during his composed 134.

Close of play: First day, Nottinghamshire 278-7 (C. C. Lewis 39*, G. W. Mike 1*); Second day, Worcestershire 276-8 (P. J. Newport 34*, J. E. Brinkley 5*); Third day, Nottinghamshire 315-7 (K. P. Evans 22*, G. W. Mike 9*).

Nottinghamshire

P. R. Pollard lbw b Radford	32	– lbw b Newport	17
*R. T. Robinson c Moody b Illingworth	67	– c Leatherdale b D'Oliveira	134
G. F. Archer run out	49	– c Edwards b Illingworth	22
J. C. Adams b Newport	8	– (5) b Illingworth	32
P. Johnson c Brinkley b Illingworth	4	– (4) c Moody b Newport	35
C. C. Lewis lbw b Radford	77	– c Haynes b Brinkley	30
†W. M. Noon lbw b Radford	45	– c Curtis b D'Oliveira	7
K. P. Evans c Edwards b Radford	11	– not out	22
G. W. Mike c Moody b Radford	6	– not out	9
J. E. Hindson lbw b Brinkley	6		
R. A. Pick not out	0		
L-b 17, w 2, n-b 7	26	L-b 2, w 1, n-b 4	7
1/49 2/146 3/168 4/168 5/178 6/255 7/271 8/310 9/317	331	1/42 2/79 3/138 4/247 5/247 6/254 7/299 (7 wkts dec.)	315

Bonus points – Nottinghamshire 3, Worcestershire 4.

Bowling: *First Innings*—Radford 27.1–7–93–5; Brinkley 23–4–68–1; Leatherdale 7–2–24–0; Newport 23–5–50–1; Illingworth 29–9–61–2; D'Oliveira 5–1–18–0. *Second Innings*—Radford 13–4–45–0; Brinkley 14–1–57–1; Illingworth 44–9–107–2; Newport 13–2–37–2; D'Oliveira 18–1–67–2.

Worcestershire

*T. S. Curtis lbw b Pick	0	– not out	118
M. J. Church lbw b Lewis	22	– c Pick b Lewis	0
T. M. Moody c Noon b Lewis	44	– lbw b Evans	5
G. R. Haynes c Evans b Pick	98	– lbw b Pick	141
D. A. Leatherdale c Noon b Evans	35	– c Noon b Pick	22
D. B. D'Oliveira lbw b Lewis	19	– lbw b Mike	48
P. J. Newport not out	40	– not out	9
R. K. Illingworth b Pick	0		
N. V. Radford c Noon b Lewis	7		
J. E. Brinkley c Pollard b Mike	5		
†T. Edwards c Noon b Lewis	3		
L-b 2, n-b 10	12	B 2, l-b 10, w 2, n-b 8	22
1/0 2/67 3/74 4/162 5/220 6/236 7/236 8/251 9/276	285	1/17 2/28 3/228 4/256 5/344	(5 wkts) 365

Bonus points – Worcestershire 2, Nottinghamshire 4.

Bowling: *First Innings*—Pick 20–4–58–3; Evans 19–5–48–1; Mike 19–6–61–1; Hindson 9–2–21–0; Lewis 18.5–3–71–5; Adams 11–5–24–0. *Second Innings*—Lewis 19–2–63–1; Evans 17–5–49–1; Pick 17–4–47–2; Mike 13.2–4–57–1; Hindson 16–2–82–0; Adams 15–4–55–0.

Umpires: J. H. Hampshire and T. E. Jesty.

WORCESTERSHIRE v YORKSHIRE

At Worcester, August 25, 26, 27, 29. Yorkshire won by an innings and 61 runs. Yorkshire 24 pts, Worcestershire 3 pts. Toss: Worcestershire.

Worcestershire coach David Houghton described the final two days of this match and the damaging Sunday League defeat in between as the low point of the county's season. They collapsed for 73 – the lowest Championship total of 1994 but a recovery from 11 for six, on a pitch of increasingly low bounce. They had ended Saturday with three wickets down for one run in 14 balls; Hartley bowled Weston and Brinkley with consecutive balls, struck Church's arm and forced him to retire with the hat-trick delivery and then dismissed Haynes. Robinson's five for 48 clinched Yorkshire's first win at New Road for 33 years, in just 85 minutes on Monday. Yorkshire's powerful position was established by a marathon 274 not out from Moxon, the highest post-war score for the county. He struck 40 fours from 490 balls in 535 minutes and put on 200 with Grayson, who scored his maiden century. Worcestershire's first-innings 355 relied heavily on a solid 72 from Weston and a last-wicket stand of 81 by Illingworth and Edwards.

Close of play: First day, Worcestershire 259-6 (S. R. Lampitt 27*); Second day, Yorkshire 98-2 (M. D. Moxon 53*, A. P. Grayson 0*); Third day, Worcestershire 1-3 (T. S. Curtis 1*).

Worcestershire

*T. S. Curtis c Moxon b Milburn	9	– lbw b Hartley	1
W. P. C. Weston c Hamilton b Stemp	72	– b Hartley	0
M. J. Church lbw b Milburn	38	– (4) lbw b Robinson	1
G. R. Haynes c Kellett b Robinson	35	– (5) c Grayson b Hartley	0
D. A. Leatherdale c Kellett b Hartley	47	– (6) lbw b Milburn	39
C. M. Tolley c Blakey b Hartley	16	– (7) c Moxon b Robinson	0
S. R. Lampitt c Kellett b Robinson	28	– (8) c Grayson b Robinson	5
R. K. Illingworth c Kellett b Hartley	46	– (9) b Robinson	0
N. V. Radford c Stemp b Hartley	6	– (10) lbw b Robinson	21
J. E. Brinkley c Grayson b Hartley	0	– (3) b Hartley	0
†T. Edwards not out	30	– not out	0
B 5, l-b 10, w 1, n-b 12	28	B 1, l-b 1, n-b 4	6
1/27 2/110 3/130 4/210 5/210 6/259 7/263 8/272 9/274	355	1/1 2/1 3/1 4/2 5/6 6/11 7/35 8/35 9/73	73

Bonus points – Worcestershire 2, Yorkshire 4 (Score at 120 overs: 274-9).

In the second innings M. J. Church, when 0, retired hurt at 1-2 and resumed at 1-3.

Bowling: *First Innings*—Hartley 34.5–11–89–5; Hamilton 19–4–56–0; Milburn 23–4–74–2; Robinson 33–11–73–2; Stemp 35–21–30–1; Grayson 7–2–18–0. *Second Innings*—Hartley 10–1–20–4; Stemp 1–1–0–0; Robinson 10–1–48–5; Milburn 1.2–0–3–1.

Yorkshire

*M. D. Moxon not out	274	P. J. Hartley not out	11
S. A. Kellett c Edwards b Lampitt	29		
D. Byas lbw b Illingworth	5	B 4, l-b 9, n-b 8	21
A. P. Grayson c and b Lampitt	100		—
†R. J. Blakey lbw b Haynes	14	1/79 2/98 3/298 (5 wkts dec.)	489
B. Parker c Church b Illingworth	35	4/373 5/465	

G. M. Hamilton, S. M. Milburn, R. D. Stemp and M. A. Robinson did not bat.

Bonus points – Yorkshire 4, Worcestershire 1 (Score at 120 overs: 352-3).

Bowling: Radford 20–8–50–0; Brinkley 18–5–75–0; Lampitt 29–10–76–2; Tolley 14–3–87–0; Illingworth 42–13–101–2; Leatherdale 12–0–56–0; Haynes 17–5–31–1.

Umpires: A. A. Jones and R. Julian.

At Manchester, August 30, 31, September 1, 2. WORCESTERSHIRE beat LANCASHIRE by an innings and 13 runs.

At Cardiff, September 8, 9, 10, 12. WORCESTERSHIRE drew with GLAMORGAN.

WORCESTERSHIRE v DURHAM

At Worcester, September 15, 16, 17, 19. Drawn. Worcestershire 4 pts, Durham 3 pts. Toss: Durham. First-class debut: D. A. Blenkiron.

An exhilarating performance from Moody illuminated a soggy end to the season. The first and last days were washed out and play could not begin until after tea on the second day. By the close, Moody had reached his century off 99 balls. He went on to a season's-best 159, becoming the only Worcestershire player to complete 1,000 Championship runs in 1994. An unbeaten 55 from acting-captain Rhodes shepherded his team to maximum batting points, with 351 at five an over. Durham made a solid if less spectacular response with youngsters Hutton and Daley adding an unbroken 129 before the rain returned.

Close of play: First day, No play; Second day, Worcestershire 169-3 (T. M. Moody 103*, G. R. Haynes 28*); Third day, Durham 193-2 (S. Hutton 81*, J. A. Daley 60*).

Worcestershire

W. P. C. Weston c Scott b Cummins	0	S. R. Lampitt b Wood	15
M. J. Church lbw b Brown	4	P. J. Newport not out	2
G. A. Hick b Cummins	24	L-b 14, w 2, n-b 18	34
T. M. Moody c Wood b Lugsden	159		—
G. R. Haynes c Scott b Cummins	40	1/0 2/4 3/56 (7 wkts dec.)	351
D. A. Leatherdale b Cummins	18	4/190 5/240	
*†S. J. Rhodes not out	55	6/281 7/342	

R. K. Illingworth and J. E. Brinkley did not bat.

Bonus points – Worcestershire 4, Durham 3.

Bowling: Cummins 19–3–70–4; Brown 21–3–81–1; Lugsden 12–0–68–1; Wood 14.2–0–90–1; Bainbridge 5–0–28–0.

Durham

W. Larkins c Hick b Illingworth	21
S. Hutton not out	81
J. E. Morris b Brinkley	12
J. A. Daley not out	60
L-b 3, n-b 16	19
1/48 2/64 (2 wkts)	193

*P. Bainbridge, D. A. Blenkiron, A. C. Cummins, †C. W. Scott, J. Wood, S. J. E. Brown and S. Lugsden did not bat.

Bowling: Newport 13–3–43–0; Brinkley 10–3–22–1; Lampitt 12–1–45–0; Illingworth 19–7–50–1; Hick 12–5–26–0; Church 1–0–4–0.

Umpires: M. J. Kitchen and K. E. Palmer.

COUNTY CAPS AWARDED IN 1994

Derbyshire	P. A. J. DeFreitas.
Essex	R. C. Irani, M. S. Kasprowicz, N. V. Knight, J. J. B. Lewis.
Glamorgan	O. D. Gibson, D. L. Hemp.
Kent	M. M. Patel.
Lancashire	G. Chapple, J. P. Crawley, J. E. R. Gallian, P. J. Martin, G. Yates.
Leicestershire	P. A. Nixon, P. V. Simmons, V. J. Wells.
Northamptonshire	M. B. Loye, A. L. Penberthy.
Nottinghamshire	C. C. Lewis.
Somerset	H. R. J. Trump, R. J. Turner.
Surrey	A. D. Brown.
Sussex	E. S. H. Giddins.
Warwickshire	R. P. Davis, B. C. Lara, T. L. Penney.
Worcestershire	G. R. Haynes, D. A. Leatherdale.

No caps were awarded by Gloucestershire, Hampshire, Middlesex or Yorkshire. Durham give caps to all their playing staff.

COUNTY BENEFITS AWARDED FOR 1995

Derbyshire	A. E. Warner.
Essex	G. A. Gooch (testimonial).
Glamorgan	S. R. Barwick.
Gloucestershire	G. G. M. Wiltshire (youth coach; testimonial).
Hampshire	Hampshire CCC.
Kent	S. A. Marsh.
Lancashire	N. H. Fairbrother.
Leicestershire	T. J. Boon.
Middlesex	J. E. Emburey (testimonial).
Northamptonshire	N. G. B. Cook.
Nottinghamshire	P. Johnson.
Somerset	Somerset CCC.
Surrey	Surrey CCC (150th anniversary).
Sussex	D. M. Smith (testimonial).
Warwickshire	P. A. Smith.
Worcestershire	N. V. Radford.
Yorkshire	A. A. Metcalfe.

No benefit was awarded by Durham.

YORKSHIRE

Patron: HRH The Duchess of Kent
President and Chairman: Sir Lawrence Byford
Chairman, Cricket Committee: D. B. Close
Chief Executive: C. D. Hassell
Captain: M. D. Moxon
Director of Cricket: S. Oldham
Head Groundsman: K. Boyce
Scorer: J. T. Potter

As ever, Yorkshire began the season with their confidence high and they will start 1995 the same way. But for much of the summer the county operated under a cloud of confusion. The lack of organisation and purpose was clearly reflected in the problems surrounding the overseas player.

West Indies captain Richie Richardson left early because of mental and physical exhaustion. The county had, in any case, been seeking a replacement for 1995, when West Indies tour, and despatched director of cricket Steve Oldham to South Africa during their Test series with Australia in the spring. He recommended Craig Matthews, but the committee, while extending Oldham's contract six months early, refused to back his judgment.

Matthews, it turned out, did not want to come anyway and Yorkshire suffered several rejections before they finally secured the services of Australian batsman Michael Bevan, who will also be expected to supplement the attack with his left-arm seam. Lesroy Weekes, a fast bowler from Montserrat, meanwhile, is scheduled to play second-team cricket with a view to taking over from Bevan the following year.

Yorkshire displayed some encouraging form in the opening weeks, winning three first-class friendlies by the end of May. They might well have won two of their three Championship matches too, but rain intervened in all of them. Their only defeat before June was in the Benson and Hedges Cup, where they crashed at the first hurdle. That defeat spotlighted a familiar inability to cope with pressure, when they failed to recover from 49 for three.

Subsequently, they were handicapped by Richardson's poor form and cavalier approach. And though it was encouraging that England, under Ray Illingworth, were looking Yorkshire's way, it did not help the team when it was robbed of two leading personalities in Craig White and Darren Gough. Those two also sustained injuries which seriously limited their influence, although both contributed impressively on occasions. White, indeed, developed into a formidable all-rounder by improving as a medium-pace seamer. Operating at a lively pace from a relaxed run-up, he produced the occasional delivery of extra pace and bounce which unsettled the best of batsmen. It would be reasonable to claim that White was the key member of the senior squad and the balance of the team, therefore, was badly affected when he was not available.

Yorkshire picked up only 44 points from the first eight Championship matches, a sequence which, coupled with failure in the NatWest Trophy, left them in near-despair at the bottom of the table by mid-July. Happily, they won four of the remaining nine games, but they still slipped from last year's 12th to an eventual joint 13th. Things were slightly better in the Sunday League, but they could not maintain the momentum of a serious challenge for honours, finishing fifth – an improvement of four places.

On the credit side, five players scored over 1,000 runs – Martyn Moxon, Michael Vaughan, David Byas, Richard Blakey and Paul Grayson. In the final analysis, the absence of Richardson proved a blessing in disguise: both Grayson and Bradley Parker took advantage of the situation to score steadily. Byas also had the distinction of becoming the first Yorkshire batsman to reach 700 runs in a Sunday League season. Vaughan established himself as Moxon's opening partner in his first full season, displaying an impressive range of strokes. He was prepared to take calculated risks in an attempt to dominate the bowling and, inevitably, some critics suggested that he lacked self-discipline. But, overall, Yorkshire surrendered the initiative too often and it would be a mistake to interfere too much with Vaughan. In fact, Yorkshire collectively spent a lot of time just occupying the crease and a safety-first policy brought few rewards; too often misguided theories about what a particular pitch might do shaped the team's thinking.

Peter Hartley, despite persistent problems with a suspect left knee, held the bowling together admirably and achieved a career-best return of 61 first-class wickets. Gough, however, remained the most potent strike force when pitching the ball up; in first-class cricket for Yorkshire he took a wicket every 41 balls. Mark Robinson recovered from a distinctly patchy start to take 30 wickets in the last eight Championship fixtures, no doubt inspired by the challenge for a first-team place from Chris Silverwood, who emerged as a seamer of genuine quality. Gavin Hamilton, Alex Wharf and Stuart Milburn also showed some promise, although troubled by injury, so that Yorkshire appeared to have reasonable cover in that area.

Unfortunately, the slow bowling was not so effective. Left-arm spinner Richard Stemp was called up twice by England without featuring in a Test and was selected for the A tour of India, but he was economical rather than penetrative. He was not helped by Yorkshire's decision to use Vaughan as the off-spinner, to create an extra place in the team. But Vaughan was still learning his craft and rarely looked more than tidy. Jeremy Batty, the one specialist off-spinner on the staff, found himself denied opportunity, asked for his release and signed for Somerset, while England Under-19's slow left-armer Gary Keedy refused another contract and moved to Lancashire. This situation, which left Yorkshire relying entirely on Stemp, underlined a weakness in the highly regarded Academy project run by the county at Bradford: there are simply not enough senior places available for the stream of youngsters being produced. Blakey had a moderate time behind the stumps. Though he made 69 dismissals, he fumbled quite a bit all the same. But 1,236 runs at 45.77 compensated for shortcomings.

Yorkshire undoubtedly expect to do well in 1995 – optimism is the straw which they have been clutching for many years – but they cannot really hope to become a major force until they become more professional and more determined at all levels within the club. – John Callaghan.

YORKSHIRE 1994

[*Bill Smith*

Back row: C. A. Chapman, R. A. Kettleborough, M. Broadhurst, S. M. Milburn, M. P. Vaughan, M. J. Foster, C. E. W. Silverwood, G. Keedy, A. McGrath. *Middle row:* B. Parker, C. White, A. P. Grayson, S. A. Kellett, J. D. Batty, D. Gough, R. D. Stemp, W. Morton (*physiotherapist*). *Front row:* M. A. Robinson, P. J. Hartley, A. A. Metcalfe, R. B. Richardson, M. D. Moxon (*captain*), S. Oldham (*director of cricket*), R. J. Blakey, D. Byas, D. E. V. Padgett (*club coach*).

YORKSHIRE RESULTS

All first-class matches – Played 20: Won 7, Lost 6, Drawn 7.

County Championship matches – Played 17: Won 4, Lost 6, Drawn 7.

Bonus points – Batting 38, Bowling 57.

Competition placings – Britannic Assurance County Championship, 13th equal; NatWest Bank Trophy, 2nd round; Benson and Hedges Cup, 1st round; AXA Equity & Law League, 5th.

BRITANNIC ASSURANCE CHAMPIONSHIP AVERAGES

BATTING

	Birthplace	*M*	*I*	*NO*	*R*	*HS*	*Avge*
J. D. Batty	*Bradford*	3	6	5	78	26*	78.00
‡M. D. Moxon	*Barnsley*	15	27	3	1,224	274*	51.00
‡C. White	*Morley*	7	11	2	449	108*	49.88
‡R. J. Blakey	*Huddersfield*	17	31	7	1,044	94*	43.50
A. P. Grayson	*Ripon*	16	27	3	955	100	39.79
B. Parker	*Mirfield*	9	16	2	520	127	37.14
M. P. Vaughan	*Eccles*	13	25	0	858	117	34.32
‡D. Byas	*Kilham*	17	31	0	1,050	104	33.87
‡R. B. Richardson§	*Five Islands, Antigua*	8	15	0	488	76	32.53
‡S. A. Kellett	*Mirfield*	8	14	0	258	50	18.42
G. M. Hamilton	*Broxburn*	3	4	0	70	48	17.50
‡P. J. Hartley	*Keighley*	14	22	3	330	61	17:36
M. J. Foster	*Leeds*	2	4	0	66	49	16.50
‡D. Gough	*Barnsley*	8	13	1	166	54	13.83
C. E. W. Silverwood	*Pontefract*	8	14	3	125	26	11.36
R. D. Stemp	*Birmingham*	17	26	2	235	28	9.79
‡A. A. Metcalfe	*Horsforth*	2	4	0	15	12	3.75
‡M. A. Robinson	*Hull*	16	21	7	48	7	3.42

Also batted: R. A. Kettleborough (*Sheffield*) (1 match) 24*, 25; G. Keedy (*Wakefield*) (1 match) 1; A. G. Wharf (*Bradford*) (1 match) 0, 46. S. M. Milburn (*Harrogate*) (1 match) did not bat.

* *Signifies not out.* ‡ *Denotes county cap.* § *Overseas player.*

The following played a total of ten three-figure innings for Yorkshire in County Championship matches – M. D. Moxon 3, D. Byas 2, M. P. Vaughan 2, A. P. Grayson 1, B. Parker 1, C. White 1.

BOWLING

	O	*M*	*R*	*W*	*BB*	*5W/i*	*Avge*
D. Gough	270.1	63	847	40	6-66	2	21.17
C. White	120.1	25	405	17	5-40	1	23.82
P. J. Hartley	505.1	103	1,558	57	5-89	1	27.33
R. D. Stemp	546.5	201	1,269	41	6-37	2	30.95
C. E. W. Silverwood	231	42	831	26	4-67	0	31.96
M. A. Robinson	530	149	1,443	43	5-48	1	33.55

Also bowled: J. D. Batty 77.4–18–259–6; D. Byas 16–4–52–2; M. J. Foster 15–5–41–1; A. P. Grayson 85.3–28–194–6; G. M. Hamilton 67.2–13–270–4; R. A. Kettleborough 6–2–18–0; S. M. Milburn 24.2–4–77–3; M. P. Vaughan 165.3–40–514–7; A. G. Wharf 23–4–78–1.

Wicket-keepers: R. J. Blakey 54 ct, 3 st; S. A. Kellett 1 ct.

Leading Fielders: D. Byas 21, A. P. Grayson 16.

At Manchester, April 28, 29, 30, May 2. YORKSHIRE beat LANCASHIRE by seven wickets (Non-Championship fixture).

At Lord's, May 5, 6, 7, 9. YORKSHIRE drew with MIDDLESEX.

At Cardiff, May 12, 13, 14, 16. YORKSHIRE drew with GLAMORGAN.

YORKSHIRE v ESSEX

At Leeds, May 19, 20, 21, 23. Drawn. Yorkshire 7 pts, Essex 4 pts. Toss: Yorkshire.

On the quickest pitch seen at Headingley for many years, Yorkshire were denied victory by the weather, which allowed only ten overs on Saturday, and perhaps also by Moxon's late declaration. Essex found 323 in 71 overs much too demanding and settled for a draw. An unbeaten century by White, followed by a career-best five for 40, attracted keen interest from chairman of selectors Ray Illingworth, in his search for an England all-rounder. His 108 also put Yorkshire in a strong position, though he had three escapes, two off Kasprowicz's bowling and one when he offered Stephenson a return catch. Next, Essex collapsed, struggling to cope with White's extra pace, while Silverwood, in his second first-class match, was impressively hostile. After Yorkshire finally declared, Essex were in more trouble at 49 for four, with Hussain ruled out by a back spasm. But Lewis, dropped twice on 48, and Garnham, missed on 49, organised the rearguard action.

Close of play: First day, Yorkshire 300-8 (C. White 102*, C. E. W. Silverwood 25*); Second day, Yorkshire 43-1 (M. D. Moxon 14*, D. Byas 17*); Third day, Yorkshire 74-1 (M. D. Moxon 22*, D. Byas 40*).

Yorkshire

*M. D. Moxon lbw b Stephenson	18	– c Stephenson b Irani	80
M. P. Vaughan c Garnham b Stephenson	44	– b Kasprowicz	4
D. Byas c Stephenson b Ilott	59	– c Shahid b Ilott	48
R. B. Richardson lbw b Ilott	0	– c Garnham b Irani	43
†R. J. Blakey b Ilott	7	– not out	1
C. White not out	108		
A. P. Grayson c Knight b Stephenson	10		
P. J. Hartley c Shahid b Stephenson	9		
R. D. Stemp c Garnham b Kasprowicz	1		
C. E. W. Silverwood c Such b Ilott	26		
M. A. Robinson c Hussain b Ilott	0		
L-b 11, n-b 14	25	B 4, l-b 13, n-b 10	27
1/51 2/82 3/85 4/109 5/180 6/206 7/230 8/233 9/307	307	1/8 2/97 3/193 4/203 (4 wkts dec.)	203

Bonus points – Yorkshire 3, Essex 4.

Bowling: *First Innings*—Ilott 29.5–7–89–5; Kasprowicz 30–11–75–1; Stephenson 25–9–74–4; Irani 14–2–48–0; Such 4–1–10–0. *Second Innings*—Ilott 18–3–46–1; Kasprowicz 17–1–56–1; Stephenson 10–2–37–0; Irani 7–0–47–2.

Essex

*P. J. Prichard c Grayson b White	50	– lbw b Hartley	0
J. P. Stephenson c White b Silverwood	1	– c Byas b White	3
J. J. B. Lewis b Stemp	39	– not out	52
N. Hussain c Grayson b White	5		
N. Shahid c Blakey b Silverwood	22	– (4) b White	4
N. V. Knight c Robinson b White	18	– (5) c Blakey b Hartley	11
†M. A. Garnham b Silverwood	6	– (6) not out	53
R. C. Irani c Stemp b White	21		
M. S. Kasprowicz c Grayson b Robinson	5		
M. C. Ilott not out	8		
P. M. Such b White	0		
B 2, l-b 6, w 1, n-b 4	13	L-b 5, w 1, n-b 2	8
1/18 2/72 3/82 4/117 5/134 6/143 7/167 8/176 9/179	188	1/0 2/29 3/33 4/49	(4 wkts) 131

Bonus points – Yorkshire 4.

Bowling: *First Innings*—Hartley 19–4–59–0; Silverwood 15–5–33–3; Robinson 18–6–33–1; White 13–3–40–5; Stemp 6–2–15–1. *Second Innings*—Hartley 13–7–17–2; Silverwood 11–0–43–0; Robinson 13–6–11–0; White 11–4–28–2; Stemp 10–5–13–0; Vaughan 5–1–14–0.

Umpires: G. I. Burgess and T. E. Jesty.

At Leeds, May 24, 25, 26. YORKSHIRE beat NEW ZEALANDERS by an innings and 33 runs (See New Zealand tour section).

At Oxford, May 28, 30, 31. YORKSHIRE beat OXFORD UNIVERSITY by 100 runs.

YORKSHIRE v NOTTINGHAMSHIRE

At Middlesbrough, June 2, 3, 4. Nottinghamshire won by five wickets. Nottinghamshire 20 pts, Yorkshire 4 pts. Toss: Yorkshire.

Both sides claimed that the bounce in the pitch was too steep, but the result was an absorbing contest. Already missing three senior players, Yorkshire effectively lost their captain when Moxon displaced a disc in his back; he resumed later, but could make no serious contribution. Although his direction was sometimes wayward, Mike had a career-best five for 44. Yorkshire, once 52 for five, were steadied by Kellett – until he was run out by a direct throw from Adams. Nottinghamshire's batsmen struggled, too, but Evans resisted bravely; Yorkshire bowled much too short and conceded 22 in no-balls. Makeshift opener Kellett helped Vaughan to add 65 to a slender lead, but four wickets then fell at the same score before Pick, making the ball lift and move, claimed five for 14 on the third day. Nottinghamshire required only 144, but looked vulnerable until Adams and Robinson batted sensibly to make sure of victory with a day to spare.

Close of play: First day, Nottinghamshire 31-1 (P. R. Pollard 27*, R. A. Pick 0*); Second day, Yorkshire 65-3 (D. Byas 0*).

Yorkshire

First innings		Second innings	
*M. D. Moxon c Noon b Mike	10	(9) not out	1
M. P. Vaughan c Noon b Evans	1	c Pick b Mike	43
D. Byas c Archer b Evans	11	(4) c Noon b Mike	0
S. A. Kellett run out	50	(1) lbw b Adams	19
†R. J. Blakey lbw b Pick	0	c Noon b Pick	18
A. P. Grayson c Adams b Mike	11	c Noon b Pick	11
M. J. Foster c Noon b Mike	0	c Evans b Pick	13
P. J. Hartley c Archer b Afford	39	b Evans	9
C. E. W. Silverwood c Johnson b Mike	19	(10) b Pick	0
M. A. Robinson c Evans b Mike	6	(11) b Pick	2
R. D. Stemp not out	21	(3) b Mike	0
L-b 7, n-b 6	13	L-b 3, n-b 2	5
1/6 2/28 3/28 4/52 5/52 6/129 7/133 8/133 9/156	181	1/65 2/65 3/65 4/65 5/96 6/101 7/112 8/118 9/119	121

Bonus points – Nottinghamshire 4.

In the first innings M. D. Moxon, when 10, retired hurt at 28-2 and resumed at 129-6.

Bowling: *First Innings*—Pick 18–2–40–1; Evans 21–6–62–2; Mike 18–5–44–5; Crawley 6–0–18–0; Afford 6–4–10–1. *Second Innings*—Pick 15–8–29–5; Evans 11–3–26–1; Afford 7–2–15–0; Mike 11–3–30–3; Adams 13–6–18–1.

Nottinghamshire

First innings		Second innings	
P. R. Pollard c sub b Stemp	29	c Kellett b Hartley	0
M. A. Crawley c Kellett b Stemp	4	c Foster b Hartley	2
R. A. Pick c Grayson b Hartley	5		
J. C. Adams c Hartley b Vaughan	28	(3) not out	40
*R. T. Robinson c Foster b Silverwood	21	(4) lbw b Robinson	38
P. Johnson c Byas b Silverwood	0	(5) b Hartley	16
G. F. Archer c Byas b Silverwood	0	(6) c Blakey b Silverwood	11
†W. M. Noon c Blakey b Foster	4	(7) not out	18
K. P. Evans c Stemp b Hartley	36		
G. W. Mike c Blakey b Hartley	2		
J. A. Afford not out	1		
L-b 7, n-b 22	29	B 6, l-b 2, w 4, n-b 8	20
1/28 2/37 3/39 4/92 5/92 6/92 7/105 8/127 9/136	159	1/1 2/6 3/79 4/109 5/123	(5 wkts) 145

Bonus points – Yorkshire 4.

Bowling: *First Innings*—Hartley 16.4–3–53–3; Silverwood 10–3–28–3; Stemp 20–8–34–2; Robinson 11–3–21–0; Vaughan 4–1–3–1; Foster 5–1–13–1. *Second Innings*—Hartley 16–6–36–3; Robinson 17.3–5–30–1; Silverwood 9–2–31–1; Stemp 10–2–28–0; Vaughan 2–0–7–0; Foster 2–1–5–0.

Umpires: J. W. Holder and V. A. Holder.

YORKSHIRE v SOMERSET

At Bradford, June 9, 10, 11, 13. Drawn. Yorkshire 8 pts, Somerset 7 pts. Toss: Yorkshire. County debut: B. T. P. Donelan.

Yorkshire scented their first Championship victory when Somerset were 173 for eight, 102 short of saving the follow-on. But the last two wickets added 159 and the match settled into a draw. It was marred by an incident involving Stemp, who was about to join the England squad at Lord's. Umpire Constant rejected an appeal against Lathwell because he could not see whether the ball had carried to the wicket-keeper. Stemp, at cover, expressed his opinions to Lathwell, and gestured to the dressing-room on bowling him an hour later. He was fined £500 by the TCCB for misconduct. On the first day, a partnership of 216 between Vaughan, with his first Championship century, and Byas put Yorkshire on their way to maximum batting points for the first time since May 1993. Stemp and White ensured that they added the bowling points, but Somerset were rescued by Rose, with a robust century, Mallender and Matthew Dimond, the 18-year-old who showed remarkable temperament and technique in his first innings for the county.

Close of play: First day, Yorkshire 303-5 (R. J. Blakey 36*, A. P. Grayson 4*); Second day, Somerset 195-8 (G. D. Rose 33*, N. A. Mallender 7*); Third day, Yorkshire 273-5 (C. White 71*, A. P. Grayson 34*).

Yorkshire

S. A. Kellett c Turner b Rose	14	– b Mallender	20
M. P. Vaughan run out	105	– b Rose	23
*D. Byas c Turner b Dimond	102	– lbw b Donelan	62
B. Parker lbw b Dimond	0	– lbw b Mallender	3
†R. J. Blakey c Folland b Rose	84	– c and b Hayhurst	50
C. White lbw b Mushtaq Ahmed	19	– not out	71
A. P. Grayson c Turner b Rose	45	– not out	34
P. J. Hartley c Turner b Rose	17		
R. D. Stemp c Harden b Dimond	10		
C. E. W. Silverwood not out	0		
M. A. Robinson lbw b Dimond	0		
B 9, l-b 9, n-b 10	28	L-b 2, n-b 8	10
1/27 2/243 3/243 4/244 5/283 6/378 7/409 8/418 9/424	424	1/47 2/47 3/55 4/148 5/178 (5 wkts dec.)	273

Bonus points – Yorkshire 4, Somerset 4.

Bowling: *First Innings*—Mallender 20–3–71–0; Rose 23–5–78–4; Mushtaq Ahmed 37–9–129–1; Dimond 15.3–2–73–4; Hayhurst 13–5–23–0; Donelan 8–0–32–0. *Second Innings*—Rose 12–1–63–1; Mallender 18–4–53–2; Dimond 7–1–38–0; Mushtaq Ahmed 13–1–72–0; Donelan 7–2–27–1; Hayhurst 11–5–18–1.

Somerset

M. N. Lathwell lbw b Silverwood	9	– b Stemp	29
M. E. Trescothick lbw b Stemp	54	– c Byas b Robinson	26
R. J. Harden c Blakey b Robinson	16	– not out	71
N. A. Folland c Kellett b Stemp	26	– b Hartley	56
*A. N. Hayhurst b White	26	– lbw b Hartley	0
†R. J. Turner lbw b Hartley	10	– not out	26
G. D. Rose c Byas b White	121		
B. T. P. Donelan lbw b White	0		
Mushtaq Ahmed c Parker b Stemp	6		
N. A. Mallender c Byas b Stemp	24		
M. Dimond not out	25		
B 1, l-b 2, n-b 12	15	B 4, l-b 8, w 2, n-b 2	16
1/31 2/66 3/107 4/112 5/139 6/162 7/162 8/173 9/243	332	1/60 2/64 3/154 4/154 (4 wkts)	224

Bonus points – Somerset 3, Yorkshire 4.

Bowling: *First Innings*—Hartley 22–5–80–1; Silverwood 16–2–56–1; Robinson 23–9–75–1; White 17.3–6–43–3; Stemp 28–10–67–4; Vaughan 5–2–4–0; Grayson 1–0–4–0. *Second Innings*—Hartley 14–2–33–2; Silverwood 8–3–26–0; Robinson 15–9–31–1; Stemp 28–14–57–1; White 4–1–12–0; Vaughan 18–8–47–0; Grayson 9–5–6–0.

Umpires: D. J. Constant and R. A. White.

At Luton, June 16, 17, 18, 20. YORKSHIRE lost to NORTHAMPTONSHIRE by 160 runs.

YORKSHIRE v HAMPSHIRE

At Leeds, June 23, 24, 25, 27. Drawn. Yorkshire 5 pts, Hampshire 6 pts. Toss: Hampshire.

Despite an early collapse, in which Hampshire lost five wickets for as many runs, the pitch proved easy-paced, though offering some variable bounce. Yorkshire's prospects were undermined when Terry was reprieved on 25 and went on to carry his bat for the first time, for 141. Gough, returning after injury, earned six wickets and England selection with his sustained hostility in unhelpful conditions. On the second day, Cowans and Connor punished some poor Yorkshire batting, held together by Blakey, who needed 211 balls for his 73. Smith then saved his own Test place by hurrying to 134 from 170 deliveries. Yorkshire faced a target of 374 on the final day, but soon fell behind and appeared to be heading for defeat at 144 for five. White and Grayson used up 28 overs, however, and Hartley and Gough were dropped in the tense finale, leaving both teams still without a Championship win.

Close of play: First day, Hampshire 274-6 (V. P. Terry 125*, S. D. Udal 35*); Second day, Yorkshire 236-7 (R. J. Blakey 64*, D. Gough 0*); Third day, Hampshire 325-8 (M. C. J. Nicholas 61*).

Hampshire

First innings		Second innings	
V. P. Terry not out	141	(2) c Blakey b Hartley	4
R. S. M. Morris lbw b Grayson	56	(1) b Hartley	82
K. D. James c Blakey b Grayson	0	c Byas b Gough	2
R. A. Smith c Moxon b Gough	0	c Blakey b Hartley	134
*M. C. J. Nicholas c Blakey b Gough	4	not out	61
M. Keech lbw b Gough	0	c Vaughan b Robinson	5
†A. N. Aymes c Blakey b Stemp	40	c Richardson b Gough	10
S. D. Udal c and b Gough	37	c Richardson b Grayson	7
W. K. M. Benjamin c Vaughan b Gough	7	c White b Grayson	10
C. A. Connor b Gough	0		
N. G. Cowans b Hartley	5		
B 2, l-b 5, n-b 8	15	L-b 5, w 1, n-b 4	10
1/91 2/91 3/92 4/96 5/96 6/188 7/288 8/298 9/298	305	1/6 2/11 3/225 4/242 5/258 6/290 7/303 8/325 (8 wkts dec.)	325

Bonus points – Hampshire 2, Yorkshire 3 (Score at 120 overs: 294-7).

Bowling: *First Innings*—Hartley 24.1–7–50–1; Gough 30–5–70–6; Robinson 15–6–33–0; White 7–1–24–0; Stemp 21–5–51–1; Grayson 20–7–47–2; Vaughan 7–1–23–0. *Second Innings*—Gough 20–5–57–2; Hartley 15–1–47–3; Robinson 16–3–54–1; White 15–3–59–0; Stemp 7–2–27–0; Grayson 14.3–3–43–2; Vaughan 7–1–33–0.

Yorkshire

First innings		Second innings	
*M. D. Moxon b Cowans	0	c Morris b Udal	32
M. P. Vaughan c Keech b James	36	c Nicholas b Connor	26
D. Byas b Cowans	47	c Keech b Udal	14
R. B. Richardson c Aymes b James	6	c Morris b Udal	29
†R. J. Blakey not out	73	c Keech b Cowans	34
C. White c Keech b Cowans	2	c Benjamin b Cowans	51
A. P. Grayson b Udal	36	c Keech b Connor	36
P. J. Hartley lbw b Connor	25	not out	25
D. Gough lbw b Connor	6	not out	11
R. D. Stemp c Terry b Connor	2		
M. A. Robinson c Terry b Connor	0		
B 5, l-b 15, n-b 4	24	B 4, l-b 3, n-b 10	17
1/11 2/62 3/90 4/113 5/127 6/191 7/230 8/245 9/249	257	1/45 2/76 3/79 4/144 5/144 6/219 7/260 (7 wkts)	275

Bonus points – Yorkshire 2, Hampshire 4.

Bowling: *First Innings*—Benjamin 20–8–23–0; Cowans 15–5–35–3; Connor 29–7–75–4; Udal 24–10–40–1; James 18–3–64–2. *Second Innings*—Benjamin 19–5–48–0; Cowans 15.4–3–50–2; Connor 21–5–52–2; Udal 32–10–79–3; James 16–6–31–0; Keech 2–0–8–0.

Umpires: B. Dudleston and J. H. Hampshire.

At Maidstone, June 30, July 1, 2, 4. YORKSHIRE lost to KENT by 175 runs.

YORKSHIRE v LEICESTERSHIRE

At Harrogate, July 14, 15, 16, 18. Yorkshire won by 114 runs. Yorkshire 21 pts, Leicestershire 7 pts. Toss: Yorkshire.

After two days, Leicestershire seemed well placed for a win that would have taken them to the top of the table. In fact, they ended up chasing 278 in 76 overs, and a combination of hostile pace and rash strokeplay reduced them to 68 for five. Their collapse gave Yorkshire their first Championship victory of 1994. Byas was the central figure in Yorkshire's patient first innings. Despite the general belief that the pitch would help the spinners, the seamers remained dominant. To general astonishment, Richardson wore a helmet against Simmons. After Boon was hit by a ball from Hartley, Whitaker, playing with great authority for 148, and Wells added 194. But Wells's dismissal was the first of eight for 71, with Hartley claiming three on the third morning. Yorkshire, 42 behind on first innings, then built a useful lead, with the last three wickets adding 79 vital runs. Simmons suffered a blow near the eye while fielding at short leg, and could not bat, which may have been decisive.

Close of play: First day, Yorkshire 316-8 (D. Gough 0*, R. D. Stemp 8*); Second day, Leicestershire 297-2 (J. J. Whitaker 139*, V. J. Wells 83*); Third day, Yorkshire 208-6 (R. J. Blakey 10*, P. J. Hartley 17*).

Yorkshire

*M. D. Moxon c Smith b Wells	53	– c Nixon b Millns	7
M. P. Vaughan b Parsons	5	– lbw b Parsons	22
D. Byas c Wells b Parsons	91	– lbw b Parsons	11
R. B. Richardson c Whitaker b Parsons	20	– c Simmons b Pierson	63
C. White lbw b Pierson	27	– c Smith b Pierson	45
†R. J. Blakey c Simmons b Brimson	19	– not out	46
A. P. Grayson b Wells	60	– lbw b Wells	12
P. J. Hartley b Simmons	20	– c Parsons b Millns	29
D. Gough b Parsons	4	– lbw b Wells	16
R. D. Stemp c Parsons b Millns	16	– c Nixon b Wells	21
J. D. Batty not out	3	– b Millns	21
B 1, l-b 5, w 1, n-b 6	13	B 6, l-b 12, w 4, n-b 4	26
1/14 2/128 3/168 4/197 5/223 6/261 7/304 8/308 9/321	331	1/14 2/36 3/57 4/153 5/162 6/182 7/240 8/268 9/298	319

Bonus points – Yorkshire 3, Leicestershire 4.

Bowling: *First Innings*—Millns 13.2–4–45–1; Parsons 33–10–67–4; Simmons 19–8–40–1; Wells 16–2–85–2; Pierson 25–8–63–1; Brimson 10–4–25–1. *Second Innings*—Millns 18–4–65–3; Parsons 18–6–43–2; Simmons 6–1–24–0; Wells 14–4–35–3; Pierson 32–6–106–2; Brimson 11–3–28–0.

Leicestershire

P. V. Simmons c Blakey b Hartley	10	– absent injured	
*N. E. Briers lbw b Batty	18	– c Batty b Hartley	6
T. J. Boon lbw b White	56	– (1) c Moxon b Hartley	17
J. J. Whitaker c Blakey b Hartley	148	– (3) c Blakey b Gough	6
V. J. Wells lbw b Hartley	83	– (4) c Blakey b White	11
B. F. Smith c Blakey b Hartley	1	– (5) b Stemp	47
†P. A. Nixon c Blakey b White	28	– (6) lbw b Gough	2
G. J. Parsons b Batty	1	– (7) b Hartley	29
A. R. K. Pierson b White	0	– (8) c Byas b Stemp	6
D. J. Millns not out	2	– (9) not out	13
M. T. Brimson c Blakey b Gough	8	– (10) lbw b Stemp	12
B 1, l-b 6, n-b 11	18	B 1, l-b 11, n-b 2	14
1/13 2/42 3/302 4/307 5/313 6/356 7/363 8/363 9/365	373	1/19 2/30 3/30 4/65 5/68 6/121 7/125 8/147 9/163	163

Bonus points – Leicestershire 3, Yorkshire 2 (Score at 120 overs: 331-5).

In the first innings T. J. Boon, when 35, retired hurt at 108 and resumed at 302.

Bowling: *First Innings*—Gough 30–7–81–1; Hartley 32–2–110–4; Batty 33–9–79–2; Stemp 15–7–29–0; White 9–2–28–3; Grayson 8–1–20–0; Vaughan 9–3–19–0. *Second Innings*—Hartley 14–3–51–3; Gough 13–4–30–2; White 6–0–32–1; Batty 4–0–16–0; Stemp 6.5–2–22–3.

Umpires: J. W. Holder and P. B. Wight.

At Cheltenham, July 21, 22, 23, 25. YORKSHIRE lost to GLOUCESTERSHIRE by 324 runs.

At Durham University, July 28, 29, 30, August 1. YORKSHIRE beat DURHAM by 116 runs.

YORKSHIRE v LANCASHIRE

At Leeds, August 11, 12, 13, 15. Lancashire won by seven wickets. Lancashire 24 pts, Yorkshire 5 pts. Toss: Yorkshire.

Yorkshire's decision to bat first on a rain-affected opening day proved to be a mistake. Martin, after a wayward opening burst, and Chapple made the most of the pitch's variable bounce. Yorkshire, in turn, enjoyed some success with the new ball and had Lancashire at 85 for four, but surrendered the initiative when Speak, on 23, was missed by Stemp; he went on to 143, with three sixes – off Stemp – and 18 fours. Another Lancashire batsman who exploited a reprieve was Austin, on six when Blakey failed to stump him; his fifty helped to earn a decisive lead of 190. Although Byas completed his first century at Headingley and Grayson fell only five short of his first ever, resisting stoutly as they put on 142 in 42 overs, Martin used the short delivery to good effect and kept the batsmen under pressure. He had excellent support from wicket-keeper Hegg, who collected five catches in each innings. Lancashire reached a target of 125 without any difficulty.

Close of play: First day, Yorkshire 140-4 (M. D. Moxon 62*, A. P. Grayson 9*); Second day, Lancashire 283-6 (N. J. Speak 98*, I. D. Austin 31*); Third day, Yorkshire 240-4 (D. Byas 102*, A. P. Grayson 56*).

Yorkshire

*M. D. Moxon c Watkinson b Chapple	69	– c Hegg b Chapple	15
S. A. Kellett c Hegg b Chapple	0	– c Hegg b Martin	8
D. Byas lbw b Gallian	40	– c Atherton b Watkinson	104
B. Parker c Gallian b Martin	22	– b Martin	50
†R. J. Blakey c Hegg b Austin	5	– c Hegg b Martin	0
A. P. Grayson not out	51	– c Gallian b Martin	95
G. M. Hamilton c Hegg b Chapple	1	– c Hegg b Watkinson	3
P. J. Hartley c Hegg b Chapple	0	– c Hegg b Austin	0
D. Gough c and b Martin	20	– lbw b Austin	13
R. D. Stemp c Gallian b Martin	0	– b Martin	10
M. A. Robinson c Hegg b Martin	3	– not out	6
B 1, l-b 2	3	B 2, l-b 1, w 1, n-b 6	10
1/0 2/73 3/109 4/116 5/149 6/151 7/153 8/200 9/200	214	1/19 2/34 3/128 4/128 5/270 6/274 7/275 8/297 9/299	314

Bonus points – Yorkshire 1, Lancashire 4.

Bowling: *First Innings*—Martin 23.5–3–87–4; Chapple 16–4–51–4; Austin 20–9–38–1; Gallian 7–0–17–1; Watkinson 6–1–18–0. *Second Innings*—Martin 24.4–10–68–5; Chapple 22–9–58–1; Austin 24–6–57–2; Watkinson 25–6–81–2; Gallian 6–0–44–0; Fairbrother 1–0–3–0.

Lancashire

M. A. Atherton c Hartley b Gough	21	– c Byas b Hartley	2
J. E. R. Gallian c Blakey b Robinson	8	– b Robinson	50
J. P. Crawley hit wkt b Gough	5		
N. H. Fairbrother b Hartley	30	– not out	35
N. J. Speak c Hamilton b Robinson	143	– not out	5
S. P. Titchard c Blakey b Gough	39	– (3) c Byas b Hamilton	29
*M. Watkinson c Blakey b Gough	10		
I. D. Austin c Kellett b Stemp	50		
†W. K. Hegg c Byas b Stemp	11		
P. J. Martin run out	18		
G. Chapple not out	19		
B 4, l-b 10, w 2, n-b 34	50	W 2, n-b 2	4
1/34 2/38 3/56 4/85 5/209 6/225 7/318 8/340 9/370	404	1/23 2/78 3/92 (3 wkts)	125

Bonus points – Lancashire 4, Yorkshire 4.

Bowling: *First Innings*—Gough 27–4–126–4; Hartley 25–4–94–1; Robinson 24–6–71–2; Hamilton 8–0–45–0; Stemp 25–11–53–2; Grayson 1–0–1–0. *Second Innings*—Gough 7–2–14–0; Hartley 8–1–35–1; Stemp 7–1–18–0; Robinson 10–1–42–1; Hamilton 6.2–3–16–1.

Umpires: G. Sharp and A. G. T. Whitehead.

YORKSHIRE v WARWICKSHIRE

At Scarborough, August 18, 19, 20, 22. Warwickshire won by eight wickets. Warwickshire 24 pts, Yorkshire 5 pts. Toss: Yorkshire. First-class debut: A. G. Wharf.

Warwickshire bounced back after their defeat by Nottinghamshire, with what came to seem an easy victory, though they feared running out of time on the final day. On the first day, Warwickshire bowled accurately on an easy-paced pitch of low bounce and waited for Yorkshire to get themselves out. Parker and Hartley contributed sixties but Yorkshire seemed 100 short of a reasonable total. Alex Wharf, a 19-year-old all-rounder, marked his debut by having Lara caught behind, edging a wide long hop. But Ostler scored 186 from

296 balls, and Warwickshire's lead of 149 left Yorkshire with an uphill battle. Moxon held one end firm as he completed his century on Saturday and Blakey took over his role on Monday, while Wharf made a lively 46 with a runner. But Davis exploited some slow turn for his best figures for Warwickshire. The requirement became 199 in 49 overs and Twose made light of that with an unbeaten 86.

Close of play: First day, Yorkshire 304-9 (J. D. Batty 1*, M. A. Robinson 0*); Second day, Warwickshire 346-5 (G. Welch 24*, K. J. Piper 8*); Third day, Yorkshire 201-3 (M. D. Moxon 106*, R. J. Blakey 34*).

Yorkshire

*M. D. Moxon c Welch b Munton	11	– c Munton b Small	116
M. P. Vaughan c Davis b Small	39	– b Davis	49
D. Byas c Lara b Davis	57	– c and b Davis	2
A. A. Metcalfe c Ostler b Welch	12	– c Piper b Davis	3
†R. J. Blakey c Davis b Small	23	– c Ostler b Davis	77
B. Parker c Piper b Welch	62	– b Small	8
P. J. Hartley c Welch b Smith	61	– st Piper b Davis	6
A. G. Wharf c Piper b Welch	0	– c Piper b Small	46
R. D. Stemp b Welch	20	– b Davis	0
J. D. Batty not out	6	– not out	18
M. A. Robinson lbw b Munton	1	– b Munton	1
L-b 9, w 1, n-b 8	18	B 8, l-b 9, n-b 4	21
1/42 2/52 3/90 4/138 5/175 6/269 7/269 8/293 9/303	310	1/93 2/101 3/109 4/224 5/234 6/249 7/306 8/306 9/338	347

Bonus points – Yorkshire 3, Warwickshire 4.

Bowling: *First Innings*—Munton 27.5–12–56–2; Small 18–5–52–2; Davis 15–6–53–1; Twose 5–1–15–0; Welch 21–8–74–4; Smith 18–3–51–1. *Second Innings*—Small 22–6–59–3; Munton 18.1–3–55–1; Davis 40–9–94–6; Smith 24–6–69–0; Welch 9–0–53–0.

Warwickshire

A. J. Moles b Stemp	65	– c and b Batty	48
R. G. Twose c Parker b Hartley	1	– not out	86
B. C. Lara c Blakey b Wharf	21	– c Parker b Batty	17
D. P. Ostler c and b Batty	186	– not out	40
T. L. Penney lbw b Stemp	18		
G. Welch st Blakey b Stemp	60		
†K. J. Piper b Robinson	27		
N. M. K. Smith b Batty	34		
R. P. Davis b Robinson	3		
G. C. Small c Metcalfe b Stemp	3		
*T. A. Munton not out	10		
L-b 9, n-b 22	31	L-b 3, n-b 6	9
1/15 2/44 3/235 4/267 5/325 6/393 7/403 8/408 9/419	459	1/89 2/131	(2 wkts) 200

Bonus points – Warwickshire 4, Yorkshire 2 (Score at 120 overs: 386-5).

Bowling: *First Innings*—Hartley 34–10–122–1; Wharf 23–4–78–1; Robinson 31–12–63–2; Stemp 46–11–107–4; Batty 14.4–3–59–2; Vaughan 3–0–21–0. *Second Innings*—Hartley 8–1–45–0; Robinson 7–0–24–0; Stemp 8–0–49–0; Batty 12–2–57–2; Vaughan 5.3–0–22–0.

Umpires: H. D. Bird and G. I. Burgess.

At Worcester, August 25, 26, 27, 29. YORKSHIRE beat WORCESTERSHIRE by an innings and 61 runs.

YORKSHIRE v DERBYSHIRE

At Sheffield, August 30, 31, September 1, 2. Yorkshire won by 184 runs. Yorkshire 20 pts, Derbyshire 5 pts. Toss: Yorkshire.

Yorkshire gained a remarkable victory in a game badly affected by the weather. For the second time in five days, they dismissed the opposition for 73, the lowest total of the season. Although they themselves collapsed in the first innings, losing nine wickets for 65 runs, Adams subsequently demonstrated the easy-paced nature of the pitch as he raced to 66 from 80 balls. Cork was even more robust, needing only 36 deliveries to reach 50, with ten fours and one six. With ten hours' play lost over the second and third days, both captains made positive declarations, and Derbyshire were set a target of 258 in 52 overs. But Gough and Robinson destroyed them as they slumped to 17 for six in ten. Only DeFreitas, with 27, passed six. Derbyshire were one man short – Vandrau had broken his finger – but Barnett made no excuses, firmly blaming poor batting, not the conditions, for their downfall.

Close of play: First day, Derbyshire 76-2 (C. J. Adams 56*); Second day, Derbyshire 135-5 (D. G. Cork 15*, P. A. J. DeFreitas 2*); Third day, Yorkshire 40-1 (M. D. Moxon 13*, D. Byas 9*).

Yorkshire

First innings		Second innings	
*M. D. Moxon c Bowler b Malcolm	22	– lbw b Wells	13
M. P. Vaughan lbw b Vandrau	86	– c Krikken b Cork	17
D. Byas b Vandrau	53	– c and b Wells	33
A. P. Grayson b DeFreitas	3	– c Krikken b Adams	25
†R. J. Blakey b Malcolm	12	– c Bowler b Barnett	32
B. Parker not out	26	– not out	54
S. A. Kellett lbw b Malcolm	0	– lbw b Barnett	6
D. Gough c Rollins b Vandrau	9	– b Cork	5
R. D. Stemp b Malcolm	5	– b Malcolm	18
C. E. W. Silverwood b Barnett	0	– st Krikken b Barnett	9
M. A. Robinson st Krikken b Barnett	6	– not out	0
B 2, l-b 3, n-b 8	13	L-b 6, w 2, n-b 2	10
1/71 2/170 3/175 4/175 5/192 6/196 7/209 8/218 9/221	235	1/24 2/47 3/85 4/93 5/159 6/171 7/184 8/202 9/217 (9 wkts dec.)	222

Bonus points – Yorkshire 1, Derbyshire 4.

Bowling: *First Innings*—Malcolm 22–5–63–4; Cork 16–4–49–0; DeFreitas 23–11–47–1; Vandrau 23.2–6–68–3; Barnett 3.5–1–3–2. *Second Innings*—DeFreitas 9–2–12–0; Cork 10–0–58–2; Malcolm 7–2–14–1; Adams 11–1–35–1; Wells 11–3–23–2; Rollins 4–0–32–0; Barnett 12–0–42–3.

Derbyshire

First innings		Second innings	
P. D. Bowler b Gough	0	– c Blakey b Gough	4
A. S. Rollins c Kellett b Vaughan	16	– c Blakey b Robinson	3
C. J. Adams c Grayson b Gough	66	– c Grayson b Gough	5
T. J. G. O'Gorman b Silverwood	18	– lbw b Gough	0
*K. J. Barnett c Blakey b Silverwood	10	– lbw b Robinson	1
D. G. Cork c Byas b Robinson	50	– c Grayson b Robinson	4
P. A. J. DeFreitas run out	2	– lbw b Robinson	27
C. M. Wells not out	10	– lbw b Stemp	6
†K. M. Krikken not out	14	– not out	6
D. E. Malcolm (did not bat)		– c Kellett b Gough	6
M. J. Vandrau (did not bat)		– absent injured	
L-b 6, n-b 8	14	B 2, l-b 1, n-b 8	11
1/0 2/76 3/96 4/110 5/133 6/145 7/177 (7 wkts dec.)	200	1/4 2/12 3/12 4/13 5/13 6/17 7/40 8/58 9/73	73

Bonus points – Derbyshire 1, Yorkshire 3.

Bowling: *First Innings*—Gough 20.4–5–87–2; Silverwood 10–1–48–2; Stemp 3–0–21–0; Robinson 10–4–31–1; Vaughan 3–1–7–1. *Second Innings*—Gough 11.1–3–24–4; Robinson 12–2–35–4; Stemp 3–2–4–1; Vaughan 2–1–7–0.

Umpires: G. I. Burgess and J. H. Harris.

YORKSHIRE v SURREY

At Scarborough, September 8, 9, 10, 12. Drawn. Yorkshire 8 pts, Surrey 7 pts. Toss: Yorkshire.

Heavy rain washed out the last day to end an interesting contest on one of the quicker pitches at North Marine Road. On the first day, Parker completed his maiden first-class century in 160 balls, adding 148 with Grayson. Only the persistent Pigott maintained the necessary accuracy in the Surrey attack; spinners Smith and Boiling bowled too many loose deliveries. Surrey's openers gave them a sound start, however, Darren Bicknell and Butcher putting on 159 in 50 overs. But they then collapsed, losing seven for 26 in 15 overs; Gough took five for five in 29 balls. Hollioake and Boiling averted the follow-on, with 104 for the eighth wicket. Yorkshire built carefully on a lead of 72, though Martin Bicknell picked up five wickets bowling good length and line. Grayson and Blakey made important half-centuries and appeared to have gained the advantage at the end of the third day.

Close of play: First day, Yorkshire 333-8 (B. Parker 110*); Second day, Surrey 269-7 (A. J. Hollioake 56*, J. Boiling 20*); Third day, Yorkshire 219-8 (R. J. Blakey 55*, J. D. Batty 4*).

Yorkshire

*M. D. Moxon c Stewart b Pigott	44	– lbw b M. P. Bicknell	0
S. A. Kellett c and b Smith	32	– st Stewart b Smith	43
D. Byas b Pigott	0	– lbw b M. P. Bicknell	4
A. P. Grayson c Boiling b Pigott	85	– c Thorpe b Boiling	75
†R. J. Blakey run out	2	– not out	55
B. Parker c Stewart b Smith	127	– c Butcher b Boiling	23
D. Gough c Boiling b Pigott	21	– (8) b M. P. Bicknell	2
P. J. Hartley lbw b Smith	23	– (7) c Butcher b M. P. Bicknell	0
R. D. Stemp b M. P. Bicknell	6	– lbw b M. P. Bicknell	6
J. D. Batty not out	26	– not out	4
M. A. Robinson run out	2		
L-b 9, n-b 2	11	B 1, l-b 2, n-b 4	7
1/66 2/74 3/86 4/93 5/241 6/279 7/322 8/333 9/367	379	1/0 2/4 3/117 4/123 5/181 6/182 7/188 8/200 (8 wkts)	219

Bonus points – Yorkshire 4, Surrey 4.

Bowling: *First Innings*—M. P. Bicknell 28–3–88–1; Pigott 28.1–6–85–4; Hollioake 7–0–32–0; Smith 34–7–110–3; Boiling 17–3–55–0. *Second Innings*—M. P. Bicknell 21–7–44–5; Pigott 11–3–25–0; Smith 29–5–77–1; Butcher 4–0–14–0; Boiling 26–7–56–2.

Surrey

D. J. Bicknell c Byas b Gough	79
M. A. Butcher st Blakey b Stemp	76
G. P. Thorpe c Stemp b Hartley	3
*†A. J. Stewart b Gough	4
A. D. Brown b Gough	2
D. M. Ward lbw b Gough	7
A. J. Hollioake b Robinson	68
A. W. Smith b Gough	0
J. Boiling c Blakey b Gough	27
M. P. Bicknell not out	7
A. C. S. Pigott b Hartley	6
B 10, l-b 7, w 1, n-b 10	28
1/159 2/162 3/172 4/173 5/184 6/185 7/185 8/289 9/295	307

Bonus points – Surrey 3, Yorkshire 4.

Bowling: Gough 30–10–66–6; Robinson 18–4–47–1; Hartley 14.4–2–50–2; Batty 14–4–48–0; Stemp 29–11–74–1; Grayson 2–0–5–0.

Umpires: J. C. Balderstone and J. D. Bond.

At Hove, September 15, 16, 17, 19. YORKSHIRE drew with SUSSEX.

NATWEST BANK TROPHY, 1994

Worcestershire, who narrowly lost the first Gillette Cup final in 1963, finally won cricket's premier one-day competition at the 32nd attempt in 1994. They thwarted Warwickshire's hopes of winning all four domestic competitions with a crushing eight-wicket win.

However, it was a thoroughly unsatisfactory conclusion. For the ninth successive final, victory went to the team batting second. (In that time only Middlesex, in 1989, have voluntarily batted first.) And though rough justice was done, because the positions were reversed when the same teams met two months earlier in the Benson and Hedges final, the result led to intense discussion of ways of making life fairer for teams forced to bat first in a 60-over game on a September morning.

Warwickshire were doubly disadvantaged because rain ended play on the Saturday before lunch, and they had to start their innings again 24 hours later, when conditions were just as uninviting for batsmen. There were problems too in the quarter-finals, also played in damp weather, when all four teams batting first were hustled out quickly, three of them for less than 130.

Despite the generally fine summer, the tournament was dogged by bad weather much of the way. Once again, none of the minor teams made any impact. All were beaten in the first round, and most were massacred. However, both semi-finals produced exceptional cricket and there was a particularly stunning game at The Oval. Despite scoring 357, Worcestershire had to wait until the penultimate ball before securing victory over Surrey. Their Australian all-rounder Tom Moody was Man of the Match in both the semi-final and the final.

Prize money

£31,000 for winners: WORCESTERSHIRE.
£15,500 for runners-up: WARWICKSHIRE.
£7,750 for losing semi-finalists: KENT and SURREY.
£3,875 for losing quarter-finalists: DERBYSHIRE, GLAMORGAN, NORTHAMPTONSHIRE and SOMERSET.

Man of the Match award winners received £650 in the final, £330 in the semi-finals, £280 in the quarter-finals, £170 in the second round and £140 in the first round. The prize money was increased from £80,830 in the 1993 tournament to £83,530.

FIRST ROUND

BERKSHIRE v KENT

At Finchampstead, June 21. Kent won by 143 runs. Toss: Berkshire.

Both teams recorded their highest ever totals in the competition and – through Hooper and the ex-Hampshire player, Wood – their highest individual scores; Oxley even managed Berkshire's best bowling. But Hooper's unbeaten 136 – from only 83 balls, with 13 fours and two sixes – was the match-winner. Missed on one, he added 160 at eight an over with Ward. On a damp, dark evening, Kent had to rely on slow bowling to finish the match by 8 p.m. on the first day.

Man of the Match: C. L. Hooper.

Kent

D. P. Fulton c Fusedale b Oxley 18
*M. R. Benson b Oxley 44
T. R. Ward c Loveday b Jackson 120
C. L. Hooper not out 136
N. R. Taylor c Loveday b Oxley 14
M. V. Fleming b Oxley 22
M. A. Ealham c Mercer b Oxley 1
†S. A. Marsh not out 2
B 1, l-b 6, w 4, n-b 16 27

1/28 2/107 3/267 (6 wkts, 60 overs) 384
4/312 5/366 6/375

M. M. Patel, D. W. Headley and A. P. Igglesden did not bat.

Bowling: Barrow 12–0–84–0; Oxley 12–0–87–5; Jackson 12–2–58–1; Headley 12–1–70–0; Fusedale 12–0–78–0.

Berkshire

G. E. Loveday c Patel b Ealham 25
D. A. Shaw c and b Fleming 57
J. Wood c Patel b Taylor 88
D. J. M. Mercer c Marsh b Taylor 14
G. T. Headley st Marsh b Taylor 10
N. A. Fusedale not out 32
B. S. Jackson not out 2
L-b 7, w 2, n-b 4 13

1/42 2/144 3/175 (5 wkts, 60 overs) 241
4/195 5/226

*M. L. Simmons, P. J. Oxley, †N. D. Cartmell and J. K. Barrow did not bat.

Bowling: Ealham 10–1–19–1; Hooper 10–0–20–0; Patel 12–1–44–0; Fleming 11–0–58–1; Ward 6–0–29–0; Taylor 8–0–38–3; Headley 3–0–26–0.

Umpires: D. R. Shepherd and J. F. Steele.

CAMBRIDGESHIRE v HAMPSHIRE

At March, June 21. Hampshire won by nine wickets. Toss: Hampshire.

The match was one of only two in the first round to be completed on the Tuesday, and it ended when Smith hit a six to win with nearly 29 overs to spare. Cambridgeshire had eked out their innings into the 58th over, but no one passed 17. The Man of the Match was Connor, for his four for 11; it was his first one-day award in 11 seasons at Hampshire.

Man of the Match: C. A. Connor.

Cambridgeshire

S. Mohammed c Udal b James 14
*N. T. Gadsby c Aymes b Connor 7
G. W. Ecclestone b Connor 3
N. J. Adams b Cowans 3
D. P. Norman c Keech b Connor 2
N. Mohammed c Smith b Udal 17
†M. W. C. Olley lbw b Cowans 6
A. Akhtar lbw b Udal 15
T. S. Smith c Keech b James 3
S. Turner not out 6
D. F. Ralfs b Connor 2
B 3, l-b 6, w 14, n-b 6 29

1/35 2/40 3/40 (57.1 overs) 107
4/42 5/47 6/60
7/93 8/98 9/98

Bowling: Benjamin 11–1–29–0; Cowans 12–1–21–2; Connor 11.1–5–11–4; James 12–4–14–2; Udal 10–1–20–2; Keech 1–0–3–0.

Hampshire

R. S. M. Morris not out 34
V. P. Terry lbw b Akhtar 11
R. A. Smith not out 59
B 1, l-b 3, w 2 6

1/20 (1 wkt, 31.1 overs) 110

*M. C. J. Nicholas, M. Keech, K. D. James, †A. N. Aymes, S. D. Udal, W. K. M. Benjamin, C. A. Connor and N. G. Cowans did not bat.

Bowling: Turner 9–1–29–0; Akhtar 8–1–21–1; Smith 6–1–18–0; Ralfs 7–0–28–0; Adams 1.1–0–10–0.

Umpires: A. G. T. Whitehead and P. Willey.

CHESHIRE v DURHAM

At Bowdon, June 21, 22. Durham won by five wickets. Toss: Cheshire.

After the first day and part of the second was lost, the match was reduced to 47 overs a side. Cheshire chose to bat on an uneven pitch, and Brown dismissed Hall and the former Test player Miller in his first over. Only Gray, with 51 not out on his home ground, reached double figures. Brown took five for 22, and Graveney conceded only seven runs in nine overs. Though Durham slipped to 79 for four, they won in the 34th over.

Man of the Match: S. J. E. Brown.

Cheshire

P. C. P. Simmonite b Brown	2	S. R. Renshaw c Scott b Graveney	1
A. J. Hall lbw b Brown	0	J. F. M. O'Brien b Bainbridge	7
G. Miller b Brown	0		
*I. Cockbain lbw b Brown	1	B 1, w 8, n-b 20	29
J. D. Gray not out	51		—
R. G. Hignett b Brown	0	1/0 2/0 3/10 (9 wkts, 47 overs)	107
J. D. Bean b Wood	8	4/28 5/28 6/45	
†S. Bramhall c Scott b Cummins	8	7/69 8/72 9/107	

C. Lamb did not bat.

Bowling: Cummins 10–3–25–1; Brown 10–2–22–5; Bainbridge 9–2–23–1; Wood 9–2–29–1; Graveney 9–4–7–1.

Durham

W. Larkins c Bramhall b Renshaw	34	A. C. Cummins not out	6
M. Saxelby b Renshaw	0		
J. E. Morris b Miller	25	L-b 1, w 4, n-b 6	11
J. I. Longley lbw b Miller	5		—
*P. Bainbridge not out	17	1/6 2/44 3/50 (5 wkts, 33.1 overs)	108
S. Hutton c Bean b Hignett	10	4/79 5/101	

†C. W. Scott, D. A. Graveney, J. Wood and S. J. E. Brown did not bat.

Bowling: Lamb 10–1–23–0; Renshaw 7–0–20–2; Miller 9.1–3–29–2; O'Brien 3–0–16–0; Hignett 4–0–19–1.

Umpires: K. E. Palmer and M. K. Reed.

CUMBERLAND v LEICESTERSHIRE

At Netherfield, June 21, 22. Leicestershire won by seven wickets. Toss: Leicestershire.

When play began a day late, Cumberland's openers put on 55, only for them to lose four wickets for 24. But O'Shaughnessy, formerly of Lancashire, took them to a respectable score and they removed Leicestershire's top three with 44 on the board. However, Smith and Whitaker put on 148 to win with nearly ten overs left.

Man of the Match: B. F. Smith.

Cumberland

D. J. Pearson c Briers b Parsons	30	*†S. M. Dutton not out	26
S. Sharp b Simmons	32	M. G. Scothern not out	1
S. J. O'Shaughnessy b Millns	40	B 1, l-b 10, w 3, n-b 2	16
J. D. Fitton c Nixon b Simmons	1		—
E. A. E. Baptiste c Nixon b Wells	2	1/55 2/66 3/74 (7 wkts, 60 overs)	188
D. J. Makinson lbw b Simmons	23	4/79 5/126	
D. T. Smith c Briers b Mullally	17	6/144 7/176	

R. Ellwood and M. Sharp did not bat.

Bowling: Millns 12–1–57–1; Mullally 12–2–35–1; Parsons 12–3–19–1; Wells 12–3–35–1; Simmons 12–2–31–3.

Leicestershire

P. V. Simmons c Dutton b Scothern . . . 19
*N. E. Briers c Fitton b M. Sharp 2
V. J. Wells c Fitton b Makinson 19
J. J. Whitaker not out 73
B. F. Smith not out 63
B 6, l-b 5, w 5 16

1/4 2/43 3/44 (3 wkts, 50.2 overs) 192

P. E. Robinson, P. N. Hepworth, †P. A. Nixon, G. J. Parsons, D. J. Millns and A. D. Mullally did not bat.

Bowling: Baptiste 12–5–35–0; M. Sharp 11–2–28–1; Scothern 11.2–0–58–1; Makinson 9–1–26–1; Ellwood 7–0–34–0.

Umpires: B. Dudleston and A. Clarkson.

DEVON v YORKSHIRE

At Exmouth, June 21, 22. Yorkshire won by four wickets. Toss: Devon.

Former Somerset captain Roebuck led Devon to their highest total in the competition and next day forced the closest result of the round for a minor county. Yorkshire passed their 242 with only four balls to spare. Roebuck made a vigorous 83, with ten fours, and bowled Moxon before nightfall. Two wickets early next morning left Yorkshire at 137 for five, but White redeemed some expensive bowling with an unbeaten 65 to see it through.

Man of the Match: P. M. Roebuck.

Close of play: Yorkshire 116-3 (28 overs) (R. B. Richardson 9*, R. J. Blakey 2*).

Devon

N. R. Gaywood c Blakey b Gough 20
J. G. Wyatt b White 15
S. M. Willis c White b Stemp 40
*P. M. Roebuck c Stemp b Grayson . . . 83
G. T. J. Townsend c Grayson b Robinson . 23
A. J. Pugh not out 33
K. Donohue not out 13
L-b 7, w 6, n-b 2 15

1/28 2/46 3/110 4/187 5/206 (5 wkts, 60 overs) 242

A. O. F. Le Fleming, M. C. Woodman, †C. S. Pritchard and A. W. Allin did not bat.

Bowling: Hartley 9–2–37–0; Gough 12–1–50–1; Robinson 12–1–42–1; White 5–0–25–1; Stemp 12–1–31–1; Grayson 10–0–50–1.

Yorkshire

*M. D. Moxon b Roebuck 49
M. P. Vaughan b Donohue 9
D. Byas c Donohue b Allin 36
R. B. Richardson c Wyatt b Allin 15
†R. J. Blakey b Le Fleming 13
C. White not out 65
A. P. Grayson c Wyatt b Le Fleming . . 29
P. J. Hartley not out 7
B 1, l-b 9, w 13 23

1/18 2/91 3/111 4/134 5/137 6/224 (6 wkts, 59.2 overs) 246

D. Gough, R. D. Stemp and M. A. Robinson did not bat.

Bowling: Donohue 10.2–0–58–1; Woodman 12–2–41–0; Allin 12–0–43–2; Roebuck 12–1–39–1; Le Fleming 12–1–42–2; Wyatt 1–0–13–0.

Umpires: G. I. Burgess and D. J. Halfyard.

GLAMORGAN v LINCOLNSHIRE

At Swansea, June 21, 22. Glamorgan won by 160 runs. Toss: Lincolnshire.

Though Morris fell early, James and Dale added 204 for the second wicket, enabling Glamorgan to reach 344, only one short of their one-day best. Faced with such a challenge, Lincolnshire lost wickets steadily, though they managed to take the match to its full duration after the first-day washout.

Man of the Match: S. P. James.

Glamorgan

S. P. James c Rawden b Hacker 123	R. D. B. Croft not out 2
*H. Morris c Dobbs b Hacker 4	
A. Dale c Wileman b Christmas 110	L-b 12, w 10 22
M. P. Maynard c Wileman b French . . . 75	—
O. D. Gibson run out 1	1/29 2/233 3/286 (5 wkts, 60 overs) 344
P. A. Cottey not out 7	4/288 5/340

R. P. Lefebvre, †C. P. Metson, S. L. Watkin and S. R. Barwick did not bat.

Bowling: Hacker 12–1–65–2; French 11–1–63–1; Christmas 12–1–67–1; Fletcher 9–0–61–0; Fell 12–0–51–0; Rawden 4–0–25–0.

Lincolnshire

J. R. Wileman c Maynard b Gibson . . . 14	S. D. Fletcher b Barwick 12
R. J. Evans b Watkin 15	P. J. Hacker not out 26
D. B. Storer lbw b Croft 1	†N. P. Dobbs not out 1
*M. A. Fell c Lefebvre b Croft 12	L-b 8, w 4, n-b 2 14
S. N. Warman lbw b Lefebvre 39	—
P. A. Rawden b Croft 21	1/29 2/29 3/38 (9 wkts, 60 overs) 184
N. J. French c and b Barwick 18	4/52 5/93 6/118
D. A. Christmas c Croft b Cottey 11	7/136 8/153 9/171

Bowling: Watkin 7–1–19–1; Gibson 12–2–32–1; Croft 12–4–30–3; Barwick 12–2–30–2; Lefebvre 12–1–41–1; Cottey 3–0–12–1; Morris 2–0–12–0.

Umpires: D. J. Constant and M. A. Johnson.

GLOUCESTERSHIRE v DERBYSHIRE

At Bristol, June 21, 22. Derbyshire won by three wickets. Toss: Derbyshire.

The match, one of two between first-class teams in the round, went to Derbyshire with four balls to spare. Their task seemed relatively simple at 213 for four in the 58th over, Walsh's last, but DeFreitas was run out off the fourth ball, Griffith bowled by the fifth and Warner lbw to the sixth. That left them needing 15 from two overs but, when they took 11 off Smith, Derbyshire could relax again. Earlier, Barnett put Gloucestershire in while conditions were still damp – the first day was lost altogether – and then scored his maiden hundred in the competition, after 28 matches dating back to 1979.

Man of the Match: K. J. Barnett.

Gloucestershire

B. C. Broad b Vandrau 44	R. M. Wight not out 2
A. J. Wright c Krikken b Warner 0	A. M. Smith not out 1
T. H. C. Hancock b Griffith 29	
M. W. Alleyne c Krikken b Vandrau . . 24	B 2, l-b 2, w 10, n-b 2 16
R. I. Dawson b DeFreitas 60	—
M. G. N. Windows c Bowler b Malcolm 33	1/1 2/64 3/91 (8 wkts, 60 overs) 228
†R. C. Russell c Barnett b DeFreitas . . . 10	4/147 5/205 6/210
*C. A. Walsh b Malcolm 9	7/225 8/226

K. E. Cooper did not bat.

Bowling: Warner 12–2–57–1; DeFreitas 12–2–41–2; Griffith 12–4–31–1; Malcolm 12–1–50–2; Vandrau 12–0–45–2.

Derbyshire

*K. J. Barnett not out . . . 113	A. E. Warner lbw b Walsh . . . 0
P. D. Bowler lbw b Smith . . . 9	†K. M. Krikken not out . . . 8
C. J. Adams b Cooper . . . 52	L-b 3, w 5, n-b 4 . . . 12
M. Azharuddin lbw b Cooper . . . 7	
T. J. G. O'Gorman c Russell b Alleyne . 0	1/27 2/121 3/135 (7 wkts, 59.2 overs) 229
P. A. J. DeFreitas run out . . . 28	4/147 5/214
F. A. Griffith b Walsh . . . 0	6/214 7/214

M. J. Vandrau and D. E. Malcolm did not bat.

Bowling: Cooper 12–1–30–2; Walsh 12–1–32–2; Smith 12–1–41–1; Alleyne 11.2–0–59–1; Wight 7–0–32–0; Hancock 5–0–32–0.

Umpires: T. E. Jesty and R. Julian.

LANCASHIRE v SCOTLAND

At Manchester, June 21, 22. Lancashire won by five wickets. Toss: Lancashire.

After the first day was lost, a fifty from Atherton put Lancashire on the way to a straightforward target. Reifer earned the match award for his 72, which should have enabled Scotland to look further than 178, but they lost four mid-innings wickets for 16.

Man of the Match: G. N. Reifer.

Scotland

I. L. Philip lbw b Austin . . . 9	G. P. Hurlbatt b Martin . . . 2
G. N. Reifer c Watkinson b Chapple . . 72	†D. J. Haggo not out . . . 1
G. B. J. McGurk lbw b Yates . . . 37	K. L. P. Sheridan not out . . . 1
*J. D. Love c Fairbrother b Watkinson. 11	L-b 8, w 2 . . . 10
G. Salmond run out . . . 11	
M. J. Smith run out . . . 20	1/19 2/91 3/122 (9 wkts, 60 overs) 178
J. G. Williamson b Watkinson . . . 2	4/143 5/145 6/150
G. M. Hamilton b Austin . . . 2	7/159 8/174 9/177

Bowling: Martin 12–2–33–1; Austin 12–1–29–2; Chapple 12–2–35–1; Watkinson 12–2–45–2; Yates 12–1–28–1.

Lancashire

M. A. Atherton c McGurk b Smith . . . 50	I. D. Austin not out . . . 5
N. J. Speak b Hamilton . . . 11	
J. P. Crawley c Haggo b Hurlbatt . . . 22	B 1, l-b 4, w 8, n-b 6 . . . 19
N. H. Fairbrother c Hurlbatt b Sheridan 28	
G. D. Lloyd b Hamilton . . . 19	1/13 2/43 3/106 (5 wkts, 53.3 overs) 179
*M. Watkinson not out . . . 25	4/129 5/156

†W. K. Hegg, P. J. Martin, G. Chapple and G. Yates did not bat.

Bowling: Hamilton 11–4–42–2; Hurlbatt 9–0–30–1; Williamson 11–1–40–0; Sheridan 12–4–35–1; Smith 4–1–13–1; Reifer 6.3–3–14–0.

Umpires: D. J. Dennis and J. H. Hampshire.

NORFOLK v WORCESTERSHIRE

At Lakenham, June 21, 22. Worcestershire won by 137 runs. Toss: Norfolk.

There was time only for Worcestershire's innings on the first day. With Hick and Moody dismissed cheaply – Hick by John Maynard, who got him for nought when they met in the Leeward Islands in February – Haynes seized his chance. He came within two of a maiden one-day hundred, after putting on 118 for the fourth wicket with Curtis. Next day Plumb kept Norfolk going, but 310 was way beyond their ability.

Man of the Match: G. R. Haynes.

Close of play: Worcestershire 309-8 (60 overs).

Worcestershire

*T. S. Curtis run out	78	S. R. Lampitt c Rogers b Bunting	14
A. C. H. Seymour c Crowley b Goldsmith	25	R. K. Illingworth not out	0
G. A. Hick c Goldsmith b Maynard	6	L-b 15, w 13, n-b 10	38
T. M. Moody st Crowley b Plumb	7		—
G. R. Haynes c Crowley b Cole	98	1/66 2/80 3/103 (8 wkts, 60 overs)	309
D. A. Leatherdale b Cole	7	4/221 5/232 6/264	
†S. J. Rhodes run out	36	7/305 8/309	

P. J. Newport and C. M. Tolley did not bat.

Bowling: Maynard 12–0–52–1; Cole 12–2–55–2; Goldsmith 12–2–45–1; Bunting 12–0–69–1; Plumb 12–0–73–1.

Norfolk

C. J. Rogers lbw b Moody	0	A. P. Cole not out	8
R. J. Finney c and b Moody	21	R. A. Bunting lbw b Seymour	0
S. C. Goldsmith c Hick b Haynes	8	†S. C. Crowley b Leatherdale	1
S. G. Plumb c Rhodes b Leatherdale	57	B 1, l-b 9, w 12	22
*D. R. Thomas b Hick	23		—
C. Amos b Leatherdale	21	1/0 2/34 3/42 (56.4 overs)	172
N. Fox c Curtis b Tolley	11	4/88 5/133 6/156	
J. C. Maynard c Hick b Tolley	0	7/158 8/158 9/159	

Bowling: Moody 10–1–33–2; Tolley 7–0–36–2; Haynes 7–1–9–1; Hick 12–0–34–1; Illingworth 12–3–31–0; Leatherdale 6.4–1–14–3; Seymour 2–0–5–1.

Umpires: P. Adams and B. J. Meyer.

NORTHAMPTONSHIRE v IRELAND

At Northampton, June 21, 22. Northamptonshire won by seven wickets. Toss: Northamptonshire.

Northamptonshire completed their first limited-overs victory of 1994 as Warren made an unbeaten hundred on his debut in the competition. Another successful first-timer was Narasimha Rao, the former Indian Test player, who made an unbeaten 47 in 52 balls for Ireland and later dismissed Felton and Bailey with some skilful leg-spin. Warke and Smyth put on 83 for the second wicket on the opening day, when Ambrose took one wicket for one run in five overs.

Man of the Match: R. J. Warren.

Close of play: Ireland 105-3 (43 overs) (S. G. Smyth 53*, D. A. Lewis 6*).

Ireland

S. J. S. Warke b Bailey	37	G. D. Harrison c Ambrose b Curran	15
M. P. Rea c Ripley b Ambrose	3	S. Graham not out	1
S. G. Smyth c Loye b Curran	61	L-b 6, w 3	9
J. D. R. Benson c Ambrose b Cook	3		—
*D. A. Lewis b Ambrose	6	1/5 2/88 3/93 (6 wkts, 60 overs)	182
M. V. Narasimha Rao not out	47	4/105 5/119 6/175	

†R. B. Millar, E. R. Moore and G. Cooke did not bat.

Bowling: Ambrose 12–5–17–2; Taylor 8–0–38–0; Bailey 12–4–20–1; Penberthy 7–0–27–0; Curran 10–2–35–2; Cook 11–0–39–1.

Northamptonshire

R. J. Warren not out 100
N. A. Felton lbw b Narasimha Rao . . . 37
R. J. Bailey c Moore b Narasimha Rao. 7
*A. J. Lamb st Millar b Harrison 12
M. B. Loye not out 17
L-b 5, w 3, n-b 2 10

1/85 2/95 3/125 (3 wkts, 55.1 overs) 183

K. M. Curran, A. L. Penberthy, †D. Ripley, C. E. L. Ambrose, N. G. B. Cook and J. P. Taylor did not bat.

Bowling: Moore 12–3–44–0; Cooke 12–3–48–0; Narasimha Rao 12–2–31–2; Graham 3.1–1–18–0; Harrison 12–3–22–1; Lewis 4–1–15–0.

Umpires: J. C. Balderstone and B. Leadbeater.

NORTHUMBERLAND v NOTTINGHAMSHIRE

At Jesmond, June 21, 22. Nottinghamshire won by 228 runs. Toss: Northumberland.

Nottinghamshire's 344 was their highest one-day total, Johnson fell only three short of the county's highest score in the competition, and Evans returned six wickets for ten, their best analysis. Not surprisingly, it was Nottinghamshire's biggest win by runs and the sixth biggest by any team in the tournament. Johnson shared century stands with Robinson and Lewis. Northumberland's openers reached a gallant 65 before all ten wickets fell for 51. There was no play on the first day.

Man of the Match: P. Johnson.

Nottinghamshire

P. R. Pollard c Morris b Stanley 10
*R. T. Robinson c and b Thewlis 62
J. C. Adams c Conn b Angus 1
P. Johnson b Stanley 146
C. C. Lewis run out 89
M. A. Crawley b Graham 9
G. W. Mike not out 5
L-b 4, w 8, n-b 10 22

1/36 2/43 3/155 (6 wkts, 60 overs) 344
4/276 5/315 6/344

M. G. Field-Buss, †W. M. Noon, K. P. Evans and R. A. Pick did not bat.

Bowling: Stanley 12–1–66–2; Angus 12–3–59–1; Conn 9–0–51–0; Graham 12–2–59–1; Younger 7–0–46–0; Thewlis 8–0–59–1.

Northumberland

T. W. Adcock st Noon b Crawley 28
*G. R. Morris c Noon b Pick 29
P. N. S. Dutton run out 0
M. E. Younger b Evans 6
†D. Borthwick lbw b Pick 0
O. S. Youll not out 17
M. Thewlis lbw b Evans 0
I. E. Conn c Johnson b Evans 13
G. Angus c Lewis b Evans 10
C. Stanley b Evans 0
P. C. Graham lbw b Evans 0
L-b 4, w 7, n-b 2 13

1/65 2/67 3/67 (39 overs) 116
4/67 5/75 6/75
7/104 8/116 9/116

Bowling: Lewis 6–0–20–0; Mike 6–1–13–0; Pick 7–1–25–2; Crawley 6–3–13–1; Field-Buss 7–1–31–0; Evans 7–3–10–6.

Umpires: J. D. Bond and T. G. Wilson.

OXFORDSHIRE v SOMERSET

At Aston Rowant, June 21, 22. Somerset won by 219 runs. Toss: Somerset.

Somerset completed a massive victory after lunch on the second day. Trescothick and Lathwell had opened with a stand of 156 in 30 overs, and Trescothick went on to 116, with 12 fours and a six in 124 balls, on his NatWest debut. Then Harden took charge, adding 116 with Hayhurst in the last 15 overs and reaching his own hundred just before the end. Van Troost took five wickets and Turner made four catches behind the stumps to finish off Oxfordshire in 43 overs.

Man of the Match: M. E. Trescothick.

Close of play: Oxfordshire 3-0 (2 overs) (D. C. Woods 1*, S. N. V. Waterton 2*).

Somerset

M. N. Lathwell b Evans 64
M. E. Trescothick c Jobson b Savin ...116
R. J. Harden not out 105
G. D. Rose run out 0
N. A. Folland c Savin b Garner 3
*A. N. Hayhurst not out 38
L-b 14, w 7, n-b 2 23

1/156 2/223 3/227 4/233 (4 wkts, 60 overs) 349

†R. J. Turner, Mushtaq Ahmed, N. A. Mallender, A. R. Caddick and A. P. van Troost did not bat.

Bowling: Joyner 11–1–60–0; Laudat 9–0–58–0; Savin 12–0–58–1; White 2–0–19–0; Curtis 7–1–49–0; Evans 12–0–54–1; Garner 7–0–37–1.

Oxfordshire

D. C. Woods c Turner b van Troost ... 14
†S. N. V. Waterton c Caddick b Mallender . 25
P. M. Jobson c Turner b Hayhurst 30
S. V. Laudat c Turner b van Troost.... 10
P. J. Garner b van Troost.......... 0
M. Cannons c Turner b van Troost 2
G. P. Savin c Trescothick b Mushtaq Ahmed . 23
A. White b Mushtaq Ahmed 7
S. G. Joyner b Mushtaq Ahmed....... 0
*R. A. Evans c Harden b van Troost .. 8
I. J. Curtis not out.......... 1
L-b 2, w 4, n-b 4.......... 10

1/30 2/49 3/60 4/60 5/68 6/93 7/110 8/110 9/126 (43 overs) 130

Bowling: Hayhurst 4–0–20–1; Mushtaq Ahmed 9–4–26–3; van Troost 9–1–22–5; Mallender 6–1–20–1; Caddick 8–1–17–0; Rose 6–1–23–0; Folland 1–1–0–0.

Umpires: H. D. Bird and G. Sharp.

SURREY v STAFFORDSHIRE

At The Oval, June 21, 22. Surrey won by nine wickets. Toss: Surrey.

Benjamin reduced his old county to 17 for three, but Myles helped them through the wreckage with an innings of 71. Surrey knocked off a target of 166 with ease. Their only loss was Stewart, caught immediately before the umpires took the teams off because of bad light. Resuming in the morning, Bicknell and Thorpe completed the remaining 144 runs in 30 overs.

Man of the Match: J. E. Benjamin.

Close of play: Surrey 22-1 (8.1 overs) (D. J. Bicknell 4*).

Staffordshire

S. J. Dean lbw b Benjamin.......... 2
D. Cartledge c Hollioake b Benjamin .. 1
D. A. Banks c Hollioake b Benjamin .. 5
S. D. Myles c Stewart b Pigott........ 71
P. F. Shaw b Hollioake.......... 27
*N. J. Archer lbw b Boiling.......... 12
†M. I. Humphries c Stewart b Pigott... 7
P. G. Newman not out 8
T. M. Heap b Pigott 7
R. A. Spiers not out.......... 9
L-b 7, w 5, n-b 4.......... 16

1/3 2/12 3/17 4/62 5/104 6/130 7/139 8/151 (8 wkts, 60 overs) 165

N. P. Hackett did not bat.

Bowling: Cuffy 9–1–15–0; Benjamin 12–2–26–3; Pigott 12–2–32–3; Hollioake 7–1–31–1; Boiling 12–0–23–1; Smith 8–1–31–0.

Surrey

D. J. Bicknell not out 55
*†A. J. Stewart c Archer b Hackett 17
G. P. Thorpe not out 85
L-b 1, w 6, n-b 2 9

1/22 (1 wkt, 38.4 overs) 166

D. M. Ward, A. D. Brown, A. J. Hollioake, A. W. Smith, J. Boiling, J. E. Benjamin, C. E. Cuffy and A. C. S. Pigott did not bat.

Bowling: Hackett 10–2–30–1; Newman 9.4–2–42–0; Heap 6–1–23–0; Spiers 7–0–40–0; Myles 6–0–30–0.

Umpires: A. A. Jones and R. A. White.

SUSSEX v ESSEX

At Hove, June 21, 22. Essex won by 16 runs. Toss: Sussex.

Despite an inexperienced attack, Essex bowled Sussex out, with Irani taking four wickets on his NatWest debut. Sussex had only one wicket down at 81, but then lost four for 29 in seven overs; Wells reverse swept his eighth ball to backward point. Smith, who had pulled a muscle, returned with a runner to put on 79 with Lenham, but it was too late to save Sussex. Essex just completed their innings on the first day, frequently interrupted by rain; Stephenson, who had retired with a migraine, was finally out six hours and 20 minutes after he first came to the crease. Gooch put on 77 with him and another 99 with Hussain.

Man of the Match: R. C. Irani.

Close of play: Essex 272-5 (60 overs).

Essex

*G. A. Gooch c Moores b Stephenson . 86
J. P. Stephenson b Giddins 55
N. Hussain c Moores b Salisbury 47
N. V. Knight c Moores b Stephenson . . 23
R. C. Irani b Giddins 11
J. J. B. Lewis not out 24
†M. A. Garnham not out 2
B 5, l-b 4, w 11, n-b 4 24

1/176 2/188 3/226 (5 wkts, 60 overs) 272
4/232 5/261

R. M. Pearson, M. C. Ilott, P. M. Such and D. M. Cousins did not bat.

J. P. Stephenson, when 31, retired hurt at 77 and resumed at 176.

Bowling: Stephenson 12–0–57–2; Jarvis 12–1–53–0; Salisbury 12–1–44–1; Giddins 12–1–56–2; Hemmings 12–1–53–0.

Sussex

D. M. Smith c Gooch b Irani 64
C. W. J. Athey st Garnham b Such 20
M. P. Speight run out 29
*A. P. Wells c Lewis b Pearson 1
N. J. Lenham not out 82
F. D. Stephenson b Irani 8
†P. Moores c Hussain b Irani 11
P. W. Jarvis c Gooch b Irani 1
I. D. K. Salisbury b Stephenson 0
E. E. Hemmings b Stephenson 6
E. S. H. Giddins run out 13
B 2, l-b 2, w 5, n-b 12 21

1/40 2/81 3/87 (59.2 overs) 256
4/96 5/110 6/189
7/200 8/211 9/225

D. M. Smith, when 26, retired hurt at 75 and resumed at 110.

Bowling: Ilott 11.2–2–44–0; Cousins 5–1–24–0; Such 12–1–39–1; Pearson 12–0–47–1; Stephenson 7–0–39–2; Irani 12–2–59–4.

Umpires: M. J. Kitchen and R. Palmer.

WALES MINOR COUNTIES v MIDDLESEX

At Northop Hall, June 21, 22. Middlesex won by nine wickets. Toss: Middlesex.

Wales made a dreadful start when they slumped to 69 for seven in gloomy light on the first afternoon. Resuming in better conditions, they had the minor consolation of reaching three figures. Brown made five catches and a stumping, equalling the tournament's wicket-keeping record, while Emburey conceded only five runs in 10.3 overs. It took Middlesex 17 overs to beat their target.

Man of the Match: K. R. Brown.

Close of play: Wales Minor Counties 69-7 (32 overs) (P. S. Jones 5*, A. Smith 2*).

Wales Minor Counties

C. Evans c and b Feltham	12
†A. W. Harris c Brown b Fraser	5
M. J. Newbold st Brown b Emburey	24
D. J. Chaminda c Brown b Shine	1
K. M. Bell c Brown b Shine	0
*A. C. Puddle c Brown b Feltham	5
W. G. Edwards b Johnson	5
P. S. Jones not out	26
A. Smith c Gatting b Shine	6
A. D. Griffiths c Ramprakash b Fraser	6
M. Frost c Brown b Emburey	0
L-b 2, w 6, n-b 6	14
1/16 2/27 3/30 4/30 5/40 6/62 7/66 8/89 9/103 (53.3 overs)	104

Bowling: Fraser 10–3–21–2; Feltham 12–3–23–2; Shine 12–3–31–3; Johnson 9–1–22–1; Emburey 10.3–7–5–2.

Middlesex

D. L. Haynes not out	64
M. A. Roseberry b Griffiths	36
M. R. Ramprakash not out	0
L-b 2, w 4, n-b 2	8
1/104 (1 wkt, 16.2 overs)	108

*M. W. Gatting, J. D. Carr, †K. R. Brown, M. A. Feltham, J. E. Emburey, R. L. Johnson, A. R. C. Fraser and K. J. Shine did not bat.

Bowling: Frost 5–0–28–0; Jones 3–0–30–0; Griffiths 5–0–30–1; Smith 3.2–0–18–0.

Umpires: K. J. Lyons and C. T. Spencer.

WARWICKSHIRE v BEDFORDSHIRE

At Birmingham, June 21, 22. Warwickshire won by 197 runs. Toss: Bedfordshire.

On an unpredictable pitch, Ostler and Twose shared their third century opening partnership in six days and extended it to 156 in 28 overs. But the happiest man on the field was Matthew White, a trainee architect, who bowled Lara for 23. "I was moving the ball away from the left-handers," he explained. "Lara just played down the wrong line." Next day Robinson, formerly of Surrey, held Bedfordshire together until 135 for three. But the last six wickets went for 29, their captain having left for family reasons.

Man of the Match: R. G. Twose.

Close of play: Warwickshire 361-8 (60 overs).

Warwickshire

D. P. Ostler c Sandford b Thomas	81
R. G. Twose b Bullen	110
B. C. Lara b White	23
P. A. Smith b Bullen	30
Asif Din b Bullen	24
*D. A. Reeve b Dalton	37
T. L. Penney st Sandford b Standring	18
†K. J. Piper not out	7
N. M. K. Smith c Robinson b Dalton	12
G. Welch not out	0
B 1, l-b 7, w 9, n-b 2	19
1/156 2/201 3/259 4/260 5/299 6/336 7/342 8/357 (8 wkts, 60 overs)	361

T. A. Munton did not bat.

Bowling: White 12–0–51–1; Standring 11–0–67–1; Robinson 11–0–72–0; Thomas 12–0–71–1; Dalton 4–0–34–2; Bullen 10–0–58–3.

Bedfordshire

N. S. Stanley lbw b Munton	5	†G. D. Sandford b Munton	1
R. G. Blair st Piper b N. M. K. Smith	21	M. R. White c Lara b Penney	2
D. R. Clarke b N. M. K. Smith	11	*P. D. B. Hoare absent	
J. D. Robinson b P. A. Smith	67	L-b 3, w 11, n-b 8	22
C. K. Bullen b Twose	17		—
R. N. Dalton c Piper b P. A. Smith	0	1/9 2/28 3/91 (56.3 overs)	164
P. D. Thomas lbw b Twose	4	4/135 5/135 6/141	
K. Standring not out	14	7/146 8/152 9/164	

Bowling: Munton 8–4–14–2; Welch 6–2–16–0; N. M. K. Smith 12–3–48–2; Reeve 7–2–21–0; Twose 11–1–30–2; P. A. Smith 6–1–13–2; Asif Din 5–0–11–0; Penney 1.3–0–8–1.

Umpires: J. W. Holder and P. B. Wight.

SECOND ROUND

DURHAM v DERBYSHIRE

At Darlington, July 6, 7. Derbyshire won by four wickets. Toss: Derbyshire.

With half their overs gone, Derbyshire were well placed at 119 for two in reply to 278. Rain then forced the game into a second day. Adams was yorked by the seventh ball on resumption, but Azharuddin displayed his customary elegance in making 74 not out off 73 balls, to see Derbyshire home with 11 balls remaining. He put on 109 in 19 overs with O'Gorman, whose 89 earned him the match award. Durham conceded 62 extras, with 15 wides from Brown alone, surrendering the initiative after magnificent bowling by Cummins reduced Derbyshire to 19 for two. Before that, Bainbridge forgot his dire Championship form to score 85 for Durham, who were heading for 300 until Morris fell for 67, tamely pulling a catch to square leg. Cork took three late wickets to finish with five for 43.

Man of the Match: T. J. G. O'Gorman.

Close of play: Derbyshire 119-2 (30.1 overs) (C. J. Adams 26*, T. J. G. O'Gorman 43*).

Durham

W. Larkins c Rollins b Cork	30	D. A. Graveney not out	16
M. Saxelby c Rollins b Cork	13	A. Walker b Cork	13
J. E. Morris c Adams b Vandrau	67	S. J. E. Brown b Cork	0
*P. Bainbridge b Cork	85	L-b 17, w 8, n-b 6	31
J. I. Longley lbw b Base	9		—
S. Hutton c Griffith b Vandrau	1	1/32 2/72 3/164 (60 overs)	278
A. C. Cummins c Adams b Malcolm	11	4/187 5/194 6/224	
†C. W. Scott c Griffith b DeFreitas	2	7/231 8/261 9/278	

Bowling: Base 11–0–63–1; DeFreitas 11–2–39–1; Cork 11–0–43–5; Malcolm 12–0–56–1; Griffith 6–2–24–0; Vandrau 9–1–36–2.

Derbyshire

*K. J. Barnett c Morris b Cummins	4	D. G. Cork c Hutton b Graveney	19
†A. S. Rollins c Larkins b Cummins	6	M. J. Vandrau not out	0
C. J. Adams b Bainbridge	26		
T. J. G. O'Gorman c Bainbridge b Cummins	89	L-b 20, w 21, n-b 21	62
M. Azharuddin not out	74		—
P. A. J. DeFreitas c Graveney b Cummins	0	1/10 2/19 3/121 (6 wkts, 58.1 overs)	280
		4/230 5/230 6/275	

F. A. Griffith, S. J. Base and D. E. Malcolm did not bat.

Bowling: Cummins 12–1–48–4; Brown 11.1–1–63–0; Walker 12–1–61–0; Graveney 11–2–44–1; Bainbridge 12–0–44–1.

Umpires: V. A. Holder and K. J. Lyons.

GLAMORGAN v ESSEX

At Cardiff, July 6, 7. Glamorgan won by 76 runs. Toss: Glamorgan.

Glamorgan proved superior in all departments as they strolled to their fifth successive NatWest quarter-final. Only 36.4 overs were bowled on the first day because of rain, but Glamorgan's batsmen accelerated on the second morning: Maynard and Cottey laid the foundations, taking their fourth-wicket partnership to 119, and Croft and Gibson then struck 95 in only 11 overs. Kasprowicz took all five wickets on the second day but, with a target of 317, Essex's hopes depended on Gooch. He departed in Lefebvre's third over, and once they stumbled to 88 for four, there was little doubt of the outcome. Accurate bowling from Lefebvre and Gibson, helped by excellent fielding, condemned Essex to a comprehensive defeat, though Shahid, undefeated on 85, tried his best to inject some purpose into a lethargic batting display.

Man of the Match: O. D. Gibson.

Close of play: Glamorgan 162-3 (36.4 overs) (M. P. Maynard 46*, P. A. Cottey 37*).

Glamorgan

S. P. James lbw b Cousins 18
*H. Morris c Hussain b Ilott 24
D. L. Hemp c Garnham b Ilott 6
M. P. Maynard c Stephenson b Kasprowicz . 78
P. A. Cottey c Ilott b Kasprowicz 57
R. D. B. Croft c Shahid b Kasprowicz . 50
O. D. Gibson b Kasprowicz 44
R. P. Lefebvre not out 0
†C. P. Metson c Such b Kasprowicz . . . 4
B 1, l-b 5, w 11, n-b 18 35

1/53 2/64 3/85 4/204 5/216 6/311 7/311 8/316 (8 wkts, 60 overs) 316

S. L. Watkin and S. R. Barwick did not bat.

Bowling: Ilott 12–1–43–2; Kasprowicz 12–2–60–5; Cousins 5–0–33–1; Stephenson 12–1–75–0; Irani 12–0–66–0; Such 7–0–33–0.

Essex

*G. A. Gooch lbw b Lefebvre 10
J. P. Stephenson c Metson b Lefebvre. . 19
J. J. B. Lewis c Metson b Watkin 1
N. Hussain c Metson b Gibson 26
R. C. Irani c Maynard b Gibson 30
N. Shahid not out 85
†M. A. Garnham c Metson b Croft. . . . 1
M. S. Kasprowicz c Lefebvre b Gibson. 13
M. C. Ilott c Maynard b Barwick 26
P. M. Such b Lefebvre 6
D. M. Cousins not out. 1
B 1, l-b 7, w 12, n-b 2 22

1/25 2/30 3/36 4/88 5/108 6/113 7/139 8/212 9/232 (9 wkts, 60 overs) 240

Bowling: Watkin 12–1–48–1; Lefebvre 12–3–28–3; Barwick 12–0–50–1; Croft 12–0–54–1; Gibson 9–1–34–3; Cottey 3–0–18–0.

Umpires: J. D. Bond and P. Willey.

HAMPSHIRE v KENT

At Southampton, July 6. Kent won by four wickets. Toss: Kent.

Kent made the most of their advantage when they won the toss, asking Hampshire to bat: inside 11 overs, the back of the innings had been broken as Igglesden claimed the wickets of Terry and Smith for eight runs between them. The weather was also Kent's ally; the rain that forced an 80-minute stoppage broke Hampshire's rhythm, in particular that of Morris, who had looked in prime form but was quickly dismissed on his return.

Without a masterly effort by Nicholas, supported by Aymes in a fifth-wicket partnership of 76, Hampshire would have been humiliated. As it was, a total of 187 was never likely to be defensible and Kent won with more than 13 overs to spare. Nicholas's slight consolation was the Man of the Match award.

Man of the Match: M. C. J. Nicholas.

Hampshire

R. S. M. Morris c Benson b Headley . . . 29	W. K. M. Benjamin b Headley 5
V. P. Terry c Marsh b Igglesden 1	C. A. Connor c Ealham b Fleming 5
R. A. Smith c Hooper b Igglesden 7	N. G. Cowans not out 6
*M. C. J. Nicholas c Fleming b Hooper 62	L-b 7, w 1, n-b 4 12
G. W. White b Patel 1	——
†A. N. Aymes run out 34	1/22 2/31 3/51 (59.1 overs) 187
K. D. James c Fleming b Headley 11	4/58 5/134 6/146
S. D. Udal c Marsh b Fleming 14	7/164 8/175 9/175

Bowling: Igglesden 12–3–30–2; Headley 12–1–44–3; Patel 12–3–27–1; Ealham 7–0–31–0; Hooper 12–0–37–1; Fleming 4.1–0–11–2.

Kent

T. R. Ward c Aymes b James 42	M. A. Ealham not out 18
*M. R. Benson c Aymes b Benjamin . . . 5	†S. A. Marsh not out 4
N. R. Taylor c Aymes b James 24	L-b 6, w 3, n-b 8 17
C. L. Hooper c Benjamin b James 21	——
G. R. Cowdrey c James b Udal 35	1/40 2/67 3/86 (6 wkts, 46.5 overs) 188
M. V. Fleming c Terry b Benjamin 22	4/108 5/149 6/166

D. W. Headley, M. M. Patel and A. P. Igglesden did not bat.

Bowling: Benjamin 11–2–24–2; Cowans 5–1–32–0; Connor 8.5–0–50–0; James 10–3–36–3; Udal 12–1–40–1.

Umpires: H. D. Bird and B. Dudleston.

LEICESTERSHIRE v WARWICKSHIRE

At Leicester, July 6, 7. Warwickshire won by 128 runs. Toss: Warwickshire.

Warwickshire recovered from their first defeat of the season on the Sunday with an emphatic win four days later. Although Lara hit a catch to mid-on after scoring 16, on his return after eight days off nursing a knee injury, they scored 100 in their last ten overs, chiefly through Penney and Reeve, who set a new competition record for the sixth wicket with 123, in 19 overs. Penney scored a run-a-ball 65 to claim the match award. Leicestershire gave away 48 extras and Simmons conceded almost eight an over. Repeated interruptions for rain pushed the match into a second day but Leicestershire, resuming on 133 for four next morning, surrendered their last six wickets in just 14 overs. Only Boon put up much resistance.

Man of the Match: T. L. Penney.

Close of play: Leicestershire 133-4 (33.3 overs) (T. J. Boon 38*).

Warwickshire

D. P. Ostler c Simmons b Millns 19	T. L. Penney not out 65
R. G. Twose b Simmons 40	N. M. K. Smith not out 6
B. C. Lara c Briers b Mullally 16	B 4, l-b 14, w 19, n-b 11 48
P. A. Smith c and b Parsons 50	——
Asif Din c Simmons b Millns 18	1/31 2/74 3/110 (6 wkts, 60 overs) 296
*D. A. Reeve c Smith b Mullally 34	4/162 5/162 6/285

†K. J. Piper, R. P. Davis and T. A. Munton did not bat.

Bowling: Millns 12–2–35–2; Mullally 12–3–35–2; Parsons 12–1–46–1; Wells 12–0–69–0; Simmons 11–0–87–1; Pierson 1–0–6–0.

Leicestershire

P. V. Simmons b Munton 18
*N. E. Briers lbw b Reeve 25
T. J. Boon c Ostler b N. M. K. Smith . 55
J. J. Whitaker c Penney b Davis 5
V. J. Wells b N. M. K. Smith 31
B. F. Smith c Piper b Reeve. 6
†P. A. Nixon b N. M. K. Smith 2
G. J. Parsons run out 2
A. D. Mullally b Munton 0
A. R. K. Pierson run out 0
D. J. Millns not out. 7
L-b 5, w 10, n-b 2. 17

1/33 2/64 3/74 (47.3 overs) 168
4/133 5/144 6/147
7/154 8/155 9/157

Bowling: Munton 11–1–40–2; Reeve 12–1–40–2; Davis 6–1–20–1; Twose 3–0–11–0; N. M. K. Smith 11.3–1–28–3; P. A. Smith 4–0–24–0.

Umpires: G. I. Burgess and R. A. White.

MIDDLESEX v NORTHAMPTONSHIRE

At Uxbridge, July 6. Northamptonshire won by seven wickets. Toss: Middlesex.

Lamb led Northamptonshire to a conclusive victory with six overs to spare, when he and Loye smashed 25 runs off Tufnell's final over. It had been a disastrous day for Middlesex; although they had chosen to bat, nobody but Roseberry reached 40. He batted 41 overs for 67. While 259 might have been a respectable total at Lord's, it was too little on this fast-scoring ground. Felton and Warren made a solid start and then Lamb played a dazzling innings, the highest of his four centuries in the competition. His century came off only 88 balls; in all he scored 129 off 102 balls with 13 fours and three sixes – two sixes and two fours off Tufnell in that last over. In the latter stages he needed a runner after straining a hamstring. He had admirable support from Bailey, who scored 52 as they added 163 for the third wicket.

Man of the Match: A. J. Lamb.

Middlesex

D. L. Haynes c Bailey b Cook 37
M. A. Roseberry b Ambrose. 67
*M. W. Gatting c Lamb b Taylor 11
J. D. Carr c and b Bailey 16
J. C. Pooley c Felton b Taylor 33
†K. R. Brown c Penberthy b Ambrose . 34
M. A. Feltham not out 25
R. L. Johnson not out 12
L-b 10, w 12, n-b 2. 24

1/78 2/101 3/145 (6 wkts, 60 overs) 259
4/150 5/211 6/230

J. E. Emburey, A. R. C. Fraser and P. C. R. Tufnell did not bat.

Bowling: Ambrose 12–3–26–2; Taylor 10–0–45–2; Penberthy 10–3–45–0; Curran 10–0–60–0; Cook 12–0–46–1; Bailey 6–0–27–1.

Northamptonshire

R. J. Warren c Gatting b Feltham. 36
N. A. Felton c Fraser b Emburey 20
R. J. Bailey c and b Tufnell 52
*A. J. Lamb not out 129
M. B. Loye not out 11
B 1, l-b 7, w 1, n-b 5 14

1/54 2/62 3/225 (3 wkts, 54 overs) 262

K. M. Curran, A. L. Penberthy, †D. Ripley, C. E. L. Ambrose, N. G. B. Cook and J. P. Taylor did not bat.

Bowling: Fraser 12–2–42–0; Johnson 11–1–46–0; Feltham 10–0–45–1; Emburey 10–1–50–1; Tufnell 11–0–71–1.

Umpires: M. J. Kitchen and N. T. Plews.

SURREY v LANCASHIRE

At The Oval, July 6. Surrey won by 125 runs. Toss: Lancashire.

Thorpe made sure there was no repeat of Surrey's farcical defeat by Lancashire in the previous year's Benson and Hedges Cup. His unbeaten 145, from 135 balls, was laced with class and spiced with 18 boundaries. It completed an interesting treble: career-best scores in all three one-day competitions against Lancashire. Thorpe and Ward plundered 180 runs off the wilting attack and, even after Ward was out, Hollioake scored 42 in 31 balls of mayhem, despatching Wasim Akram for a six and two fours off consecutive balls. Surrey soared past their previous highest total in any limited-overs tournament and then Cuffy emphasised their superiority by bowling superbly, dismissing Gallian, Atherton and Fairbrother in his first four overs. There was no way Lancashire could recover from 55 for six, though Wasim and Austin ran up 106 in 22 overs.

Man of the Match: G. P. Thorpe.

Surrey

D. J. Bicknell run out	33	M. P. Bicknell c Speak b Martin	7
*†A. J. Stewart c Hegg b Martin	4	A. C. S. Pigott not out	4
G. P. Thorpe not out	145	B 1, l-b 13, w 4, n-b 2	20
D. M. Ward c Crawley b Yates	87		—
A. D. Brown st Hegg b Yates	1	1/22 2/47 3/227 (6 wkts, 60 overs)	343
A. J. Hollioake c Atherton b Martin	42	4/229 5/319 6/334	

C. E. Cuffy, J. Boiling and J. E. Benjamin did not bat.

Bowling: Wasim Akram 12–1–70–0; Martin 12–0–63–3; Austin 12–1–68–0; Watkinson 6–0–46–0; Yates 12–1–61–2; Gallian 6–1–21–0.

Lancashire

M. A. Atherton b Cuffy	10	†W. K. Hegg b Benjamin	32
J. E. R. Gallian c Thorpe b Cuffy	1	P. J. Martin c Stewart b Hollioake	16
J. P. Crawley c Boiling b M. P. Bicknell	9	G. Yates not out	7
N. H. Fairbrother c Brown b Cuffy	0	B 1, l-b 3, w 1, n-b 6	11
N. J. Speak c Cuffy b Pigott	10		—
*M. Watkinson c Thorpe b Pigott	15	1/5 2/24 3/24 (49.3 overs)	218
Wasim Akram b Pigott	50	4/26 5/52 6/55	
I. D. Austin c M. P. Bicknell b Cuffy	57	7/161 8/166 9/210	

Bowling: Cuffy 11–4–43–4; M. P. Bicknell 10–2–48–1; Benjamin 10.3–1–26–1; Pigott 10–1–54–3; Boiling 7–0–38–0; Hollioake 1–0–5–1.

Umpires: J. H. Harris and R. Julian.

WORCESTERSHIRE v NOTTINGHAMSHIRE

At Worcester, July 6, 7. Worcestershire won by 89 runs. Toss: Nottinghamshire.

A convincing victory for Worcestershire was marred by acrimony over the run-out of Crawley. Standing at the non-striker's end, he believed the ball was dead when wicket-keeper Rhodes threw it back to the bowler, Illingworth, who then knocked down the wicket. Umpire Jesty gave him out, agreeing that the ball was not "finally settled in the hands of the wicket-keeper" as laid down in Law 23. Nottinghamshire were indignant, but in fact the incident had little influence on the result. By the time Crawley arrived, they were 46 for three in the 23rd over, with little prospect of overtaking Worcestershire's 263. Hick, reprieved on one during one of three short sessions on the first day, had been bowled three short of his hundred; his chief allies were Moody and Haynes, who was capped after the match. Moody later opened the bowling and conceded only 14 runs in ten overs.

Man of the Match: G. A. Hick.

Close of play: Worcestershire 36-1 (17.1 overs) (T. S. Curtis 15*, G. A. Hick 11*).

Worcestershire

*T. S. Curtis b Lewis	20	†S. J. Rhodes not out	6
W. P. C. Weston c Noon b Evans	7	S. R. Lampitt not out	16
G. A. Hick b Pick	97	B 1, l-b 8, w 6	15
T. M. Moody c Crawley b Mike	35		—
G. R. Haynes b Pick	46	1/16 2/45 3/132 (6 wkts, 60 overs)	263
D. A. Leatherdale run out	21	4/197 5/239 6/242	

R. K. Illingworth, P. J. Newport and N. V. Radford did not bat.

Bowling: Pick 11–0–45–2; Evans 10–1–24–1; Lewis 12–2–48–1; Mike 12–1–71–1; Field-Buss 6–0–31–0; Crawley 9–0–35–0.

Nottinghamshire

P. R. Pollard c Lampitt b Moody	13	G. W. Mike c Radford b Newport	3
*R. T. Robinson c Moody b Newport	5	R. A. Pick c Weston b Lampitt	10
J. C. Adams c and b Lampitt	11	M. G. Field-Buss not out	4
P. Johnson c Rhodes b Illingworth	37	B 1, l-b 2, w 6	9
M. A. Crawley run out	4		—
C. C. Lewis lbw b Haynes	23	1/11 2/24 3/46 (52.4 overs)	174
†W. M. Noon c Curtis b Lampitt	34	4/60 5/92 6/104	
K. P. Evans c and b Newport	21	7/137 8/149 9/164	

Bowling: Moody 10–4–14–1; Newport 12–0–44–3; Radford 8–1–24–0; Lampitt 7.4–1–44–3; Illingworth 9–0–25–1; Haynes 6–1–20–1.

Umpires: D. J. Constant and T. E. Jesty.

YORKSHIRE v SOMERSET

At Leeds, July 6, 7. Somerset won by three wickets. Toss: Somerset.

Hayhurst demonstrated the virtues of length and line as he claimed four wickets and brought about Yorkshire's collapse on an easy-paced pitch of generally low bounce. Byas had provided his county with a platform, but the last seven wickets fell for only 45. Rain and bad light carried the contest into a second day, when Somerset's batsmen also ran into difficulties: they were moving comfortably towards victory while Harden and Hayhurst were adding 64, in 14 overs, but Gough claimed three for six in ten balls. Somerset entered the final over, bowled by White, ten short. He struggled to achieve a consistent line and, though Turner was run out, Rose survived to hit the winning boundary with one ball to spare.

Man of the Match: A. N. Hayhurst.

Close of play: Somerset 24-0 (6 overs) (M. N. Lathwell 14*, M. E. Trescothick 10*).

Yorkshire

*M. D. Moxon c Turner b Rose	23	D. Gough lbw b Hayhurst	2
M. P. Vaughan c Lathwell b Caddick	10	C. E. W. Silverwood not out	8
D. Byas c Turner b Rose	71	M. A. Robinson run out	0
R. B. Richardson c Harden b Caddick	27	L-b 12, w 14, n-b 2	28
†R. J. Blakey c Harden b Hayhurst	18		—
C. White c Turner b Caddick	5	1/18 2/118 3/125 (59.5 overs)	215
A. P. Grayson b Hayhurst	18	4/170 5/176 6/176	
P. J. Hartley c and b Hayhurst	5	7/184 8/190 9/215	

Bowling: Caddick 12–2–28–3; van Troost 6–0–45–0; Mallender 11–2–32–0; Mushtaq Ahmed 12–3–34–0; Rose 12–1–35–2; Hayhurst 6.5–0–29–4.

Somerset

M. N. Lathwell lbw b Robinson 28
M. E. Trescothick c Blakey b Grayson . 48
R. J. Harden b Gough 64
N. A. Folland b Silverwood 18
*A. N. Hayhurst b Gough 24
G. D. Rose not out 19
Mushtaq Ahmed lbw b Gough........ 0
†R. J. Turner run out 6
N. A. Mallender not out 0
L-b 4, w 3, n-b 2............ 9

1/63 2/79 3/121 4/185 5/202 6/202 7/212 (7 wkts, 59.5 overs) 216

A. R. Caddick and A. P. van Troost did not bat.

Bowling: Gough 12–0–51–3; Hartley 12–1–43–0; Silverwood 11–2–38–1; Robinson 12–3–23–1; Grayson 7–1–25–1; White 5.5–0–32–0.

Umpires: J. C. Balderstone and A. A. Jones.

QUARTER-FINALS

DERBYSHIRE v KENT

At Derby, July 26. Kent won by five wickets. Toss: Kent.

A damp pitch, which impressed neither captain, dominated a dour contest. Only two players reached double figures in Derbyshire's innings: Cork's 62 was of particular merit, as he was suffering from a gastric virus, and Vandrau's determination took Derbyshire past 100. But a final total of 128 left their bowlers no margin of error. Ealham's accurate medium-pace earned him four for ten as he removed the lower half of the order. In turn, DeFreitas and Cork picked up two wickets each and Kent were looking shaky at 85 for five until Ealham joined Cowdrey. Despite several moral successes for the bowlers, especially Malcolm, they added 44 in 20 overs to ensure victory.

Man of the Match: M. A. Ealham.

Derbyshire

*K. J. Barnett b Igglesden 0
D. G. Cork c Taylor b McCague...... 62
C. J. Adams c Hooper b Headley 3
T. J. G. O'Gorman b Igglesden 5
M. Azharuddin c Hooper b Igglesden .. 7
P. A. J. DeFreitas b McCague........ 7
C. M. Wells c Fleming b Ealham 0
M. J. Vandrau c Hooper b Ealham 27
F. A. Griffith c Marsh b Ealham...... 8
†K. M. Krikken not out 6
D. E. Malcolm b Ealham 0
L-b 2, w 1 3

1/0 2/20 3/37 4/57 5/81 6/86 7/86 8/99 9/128 (43.5 overs) 128

Bowling: Igglesden 12–2–37–3; McCague 12–1–36–2; Headley 10–1–42–1; Hooper 1–0–1–0; Ealham 8.5–2–10–4.

Kent

T. R. Ward c Barnett b DeFreitas..... 0
*M. R. Benson b Cork 5
N. R. Taylor b DeFreitas 17
C. L. Hooper c Wells b Griffith 27
G. R. Cowdrey not out 32
M. V. Fleming b Cork 7
M. A. Ealham not out............... 26
L-b 7, w 6, n-b 2............ 15

1/0 2/20 3/28 4/77 5/85 (5 wkts, 47.3 overs) 129

†S. A. Marsh, D. W. Headley, M. J. McCague and A. P. Igglesden did not bat.

Bowling: DeFreitas 12–4–32–2; Cork 12–4–24–2; Malcolm 12–3–26–0; Griffith 3–0–18–1; Wells 8.3–2–22–0.

Umpires: J. W. Holder and K. J. Lyons.

GLAMORGAN v SURREY

At Swansea, July 26, 27. Surrey won by five wickets. Toss: Surrey.

After the first day was washed out and the pitch had sweated for two days under the covers, whoever won the toss were favourites to win the game. Surrey did and put Glamorgan in. After Cuffy had removed Morris and Dale, Murphy took six for 26 from 12 overs, his best return for Surrey in any competition. Cuffy took no more wickets, but conceded only six runs off the bat. Meanwhile Stewart, with seven catches, broke the previous tournament record of six dismissals by a wicket-keeper. Cottey and Gibson revived Glamorgan's fortunes from 61 for five with a sixth-wicket partnership of 62, but the modest total of 161 was inadequate, especially as the pitch dried out when Surrey batted. Though Bicknell was soon out, Thorpe, with an attacking half-century, and Brown, who struck a rapid 39 from 35 balls, guided Surrey to a comfortable win.

Man of the Match: A. J. Murphy.

Glamorgan

A. Dale c Stewart b Cuffy............ 17
*H. Morris c Stewart b Cuffy......... 4
D. L. Hemp c Stewart b Murphy...... 13
M. P. Maynard c Stewart b Murphy... 13
P. A. Cottey c Stewart b Murphy..... 36
R. D. B. Croft lbw b Murphy......... 0
O. D. Gibson b Murphy............. 23
R. P. Lefebvre c Brown b Hollioake... 15
†C. P. Metson c Stewart b Murphy.... 7
S. L. Watkin c Stewart b Hollioake.... 9
S. R. Barwick not out............... 0
L-b 12, w 8, n-b 4........... 24

1/25 2/33 3/53 4/58 5/61 6/123 7/124 8/137 9/153 (55.4 overs) 161

Bowling: Benjamin 10–3–32–0; Cuffy 12–6–9–2; Pigott 12–0–42–0; Murphy 12–3–26–6; Hollioake 9.4–0–40–2.

Surrey

D. J. Bicknell b Barwick............. 9
*†A. J. Stewart c Lefebvre b Gibson... 24
G. P. Thorpe c Maynard b Croft...... 56
D. M. Ward c Gibson b Dale........ 10
A. D. Brown c Maynard b Croft...... 39
A. J. Hollioake not out.............. 14
J. Boiling not out.................. 5
L-b 2, w 6................. 8

1/23 2/42 3/72 4/143 5/146 (5 wkts, 48.4 overs) 165

A. C. S. Pigott, J. E. Benjamin, C. E. Cuffy and A. J. Murphy did not bat.

Bowling: Watkin 10–2–25–0; Lefebvre 11–3–20–0; Barwick 10–3–17–1; Gibson 6–0–50–1; Dale 3–0–27–1; Croft 8.4–1–24–2.

Umpires: K. E. Palmer and G. Sharp.

SOMERSET v WARWICKSHIRE

At Taunton, July 26. Warwickshire won by eight wickets. Toss: Warwickshire.

After an hour's delay through rain, a hot sultry day made the toss vital. Somerset struggled throughout on a green pitch against the seamers, led by Small, who conceded 14 runs in seven overs, while Smith, turning the ball appreciably, produced the best figures with four for 26. The only stand of note was 33 in 15 overs between Hayhurst and Turner. In rather easier conditions, Warwickshire's openers Moles and Ostler found few problems – except against the rapid but wayward van Troost – in putting on 93 in 20 overs. Ostler was out sweeping, which brought in Lara. But after facing three balls from Trump, and hitting a six on to the pavilion roof and a three, he was lbw to his first ball from van Troost. Moles and Penney duly finished the match with nearly 36 of their 60 overs to spare.

Man of the Match: N. M. K. Smith.

Somerset

M. N. Lathwell lbw b Small	6	A. R. Caddick lbw b Munton	4
M. E. Trescothick b Small	10	H. R. J. Trump c Lara b Smith	4
R. J. Harden c Piper b Twose	9	A. P. van Troost c Piper b Smith	7
N. A. Folland c Penney b Reeve	15	L-b 3, w 13, n-b 2	18
*A. N. Hayhurst not out	29		—
†R. J. Turner c Piper b Smith	15	1/13 2/17 3/42 (50.2 overs)	124
G. D. Rose b Reeve	7	4/45 5/78 6/94	
J. I. D. Kerr c Twose b Smith	0	7/100 8/110 9/115	

Bowling: Small 7–2–14–2; Munton 11–2–30–1; Welch 10–2–25–0; Twose 2–0–8–1; Reeve 12–4–18–2; Smith 8.2–1–26–4.

Warwickshire

A. J. Moles not out	41
D. P. Ostler lbw b Trump	47
B. C. Lara lbw b van Troost	9
T. L. Penney not out	12
L-b 7, w 5, n-b 4	16
	—
1/93 2/102 (2 wkts, 24.1 overs)	125

G. Welch, R. G. Twose, *D. A. Reeve, N. M. K. Smith, †K. J. Piper, G. C. Small and T. A. Munton did not bat.

Bowling: Caddick 6–2–23–0; van Troost 7–0–44–1; Trump 6.1–2–41–1; Rose 5–1–10–0.

Umpires: V. A. Holder and B. Leadbeater.

WORCESTERSHIRE v NORTHAMPTONSHIRE

At Worcester, July 26. Worcestershire won by two wickets. Toss: Worcestershire.

This was the only quarter-final in which there was a serious danger that the toss might not prove decisive. Worcestershire's bowlers made the most of Lamb's wrong call by bowling to order, as the ball not only swung in the murk that followed an overnight storm but also jagged around off a pitch of some malevolence. Radford conceded only three runs in eight overs. Bailey and Loye batted bravely, but Newport came into the attack late in the innings and quickly took care of the tail. However, with the weather little better, Northamptonshire were given hope of defending their paltry 128 by Ambrose, who produced two spells of fast bowling of a quality and single-mindedness most often associated with his Test performances. During the second, Worcestershire collapsed from 77 for three to 96 for seven. However, Rhodes and Newport inched towards victory amid extreme tension. When Ambrose came back for his final over, with the score on 112, Rhodes blocked successfully and stayed to secure the victory. He had also made four catches and a stumping.

Man of the Match: S. J. Rhodes.

Northamptonshire

A. Fordham c Radford b Moody	0	†D. Ripley c Moody b Newport	0
R. J. Warren c and b Radford	2	N. G. B. Cook b Illingworth	1
R. J. Bailey c Rhodes b Newport	25	J. P. Taylor not out	3
*A. J. Lamb b Radford	1	B 4, l-b 4, w 1, n-b 2	11
M. B. Loye c Rhodes b Lampitt	34		—
K. M. Curran c Rhodes b Newport	26	1/0 2/6 3/12 (46.1 overs)	128
A. L. Penberthy st Rhodes b Illingworth	18	4/48 5/77 6/114	
C. E. L. Ambrose c Rhodes b Newport.	7	7/119 8/119 9/120	

Bowling: Moody 12–3–34–1; Radford 8–6–3–2; Lampitt 10–2–27–1; Newport 7.1–1–30–4; Illingworth 9–2–26–2.

Worcestershire

*T. S. Curtis lbw b Ambrose 0
A. C. H. Seymour run out. 20
G. A. Hick b Taylor 2
T. M. Moody c Curran b Ambrose 40
G. R. Haynes run out 10
D. A. Leatherdale c Ripley b Ambrose . 0
†S. J. Rhodes not out 24
S. R. Lampitt lbw b Taylor. 4
P. J. Newport c Warren b Penberthy . . 14
N. V. Radford not out. 0
B 1, l-b 5, w 3, n-b 6 15

1/1 2/11 3/57 4/77 5/83 6/86 7/96 8/128 (8 wkts, 45.1 overs) 129

R. K. Illingworth did not bat.

Bowling: Ambrose 12–4–16–3; Taylor 12–1–47–2; Curran 12–4–24–0; Penberthy 7–0–28–1; Cook 2.1–0–8–0.

Umpires: J. H. Harris and P. B. Wight.

SEMI-FINALS

SURREY v WORCESTERSHIRE

At The Oval, August 9. Worcestershire won by seven runs. Toss: Surrey.

Moody began the revels with a blistering innings and wrapped them up with a magnificent catch to win a match full of records. He and Curtis set the tone with an unbroken third-wicket stand of 309, the highest partnership for any wicket in limited-overs cricket. Moody's unbeaten 180 came from 160 deliveries, with three sixes and 25 fours; once he reached his half-century, his strokeplay went from the audacious to the outrageous. It was the highest innings for Worcestershire in any one-day competition and the highest against a first-class county in the history of this tournament. The often dour Curtis was hardly less potent, hitting 136 in 180 balls. However, Surrey seemed undaunted at the prospect of having to make the highest ever total by a side batting second. Darren Bicknell provided the anchor while first Thorpe, then Brown kept their hope alive. Later, Hollioake, who hit 60 off 36 balls, and, improbably, Benjamin hammered the score past 300. In the final over, with 22 runs required, Benjamin thrashed two enormous sixes, nailing another record – the highest aggregate of runs, 707, in a limited-overs match. He was trying for a third six when Moody stretched out his long arm to pluck the ball and the tie away from Surrey with one delivery to spare. The one man to take no pleasure from the occasion was Tony Murphy, Man of the Match in the quarter-final, who was left out by Surrey. He cleared his locker and left the club.

Man of the Match: T. M. Moody.

Worcestershire

*T. S. Curtis not out 136
A. C. H. Seymour b Pigott 10
G. A. Hick c Hollioake b Benjamin . . . 5
T. M. Moody not out. 180
L-b 8, w 2, n-b 16. 26

1/41 2/48 (2 wkts, 60 overs) 357

G. R. Haynes, D. A. Leatherdale, †S. J. Rhodes, S. R. Lampitt, P. J. Newport, R. K. Illingworth and N. V. Radford did not bat.

Bowling: Cuffy 10–0–66–0; Benjamin 12–1–72–1; Pigott 12–1–61–1; M. P. Bicknell 12–0–62–0; Boiling 10–1–48–0; Hollioake 4–0–40–0.

Surrey

D. J. Bicknell c and b Hick 89
*†A. J. Stewart c Hick b Moody 21
G. P. Thorpe run out................ 49
D. M. Ward b Radford.............. 9
A. D. Brown c Illingworth b Moody ... 52
A. J. Hollioake c and b Hick 60
M. P. Bicknell b Hick................ 2
A. C. S. Pigott b Hick............... 0
J. Boiling c Leatherdale b Radford 24
J. E. Benjamin c Moody b Lampitt 25
C. E. Cuffy not out 2
B 5, l-b 9, w 3.............. 17

1/38 2/127 3/151 (59.5 overs) 350
4/226 5/229 6/235
7/235 8/286 9/334

Bowling: Newport 6–1–31–0; Moody 8–0–43–2; Illingworth 12–1–46–0; Lampitt 8.5–0–76–1; Radford 12–1–63–2; Hick 11–0–54–4; Leatherdale 2–0–23–0.

Umpires: R. Palmer and A. G. T. Whitehead.

WARWICKSHIRE v KENT

At Birmingham, August 9. Warwickshire won by eight runs. Toss: Kent.

Warwickshire's remarkable run took them back to a Lord's final, for an unprecedented reunion with Worcestershire, whom they beat in the Benson and Hedges Cup. But it was their most improbable win of the season, resulting from some inspired captaincy and bowling by Reeve and inept tactics from Kent's middle order. After an unbeaten 105 from Moles underpinned a total of 265 – at least 20 below potential – Kent, beaten at Edgbaston in the NatWest in both 1992 and 1993, set off towards victory with a well-paced stand of 124 from Ward and Taylor. With 14 overs remaining, they needed 83, with eight wickets in hand and Hooper well set. In the search for wickets, Reeve had used up Small and Munton, leaving the closing overs to himself and Paul Smith. Stunning catches by Ostler and Piper started Kent's decline, but it did not become terminal until, with 44 needed off six overs, Ealham was caught off Reeve. Unaccountably, he failed to cross to give Hooper the strike. Hooper had already been denied much of the bowling and did not face any of the next 11 deliveries before he too fell to Reeve. He had scored 44 off only 49 balls out of 114 bowled while he was in. Reeve, improvising brilliantly, and Paul Smith, with a wholehearted performance, ensured that Kent lost a game they would have won 19 times out of 20, and a crowd of more than 10,000 cheered Warwickshire home.

Man of the Match: A. J. Moles.

Warwickshire

A. J. Moles not out 105
D. P. Ostler lbw b McCague 12
B. C. Lara c and b Ealham 29
P. A. Smith c Hooper b Ealham 5
R. G. Twose c Marsh b Headley 49
*D. A. Reeve lbw b Fleming 23
T. L. Penney c Marsh b Fleming...... 3
N. M. K. Smith c McCague b Fleming. 15
G. C. Small b McCague 1
†K. J. Piper not out................. 6
L-b 14, w 3 17

1/24 2/91 3/104 (8 wkts, 60 overs) 265
4/178 5/220 6/224
7/248 8/250

T. A. Munton did not bat.

Bowling: Wren 10–0–41–0; McCague 10–0–37–2; Headley 12–0–43–1; Ealham 10–0–47–2; Hooper 12–1–55–0; Fleming 6–0–28–3.

Kent

T. R. Ward c N. M. K. Smith b P. A. Smith . 80
*M. R. Benson b Munton 6
N. R. Taylor c Ostler b N. M. K. Smith 64
C. L. Hooper c N. M. K. Smith b Reeve 44
G. R. Cowdrey c Piper b P. A. Smith.. 1
M. V. Fleming c Piper b Munton 1
M. A. Ealham c Small b Reeve 7
†S. A. Marsh st Piper b Reeve........ 22
M. J. McCague run out.............. 1
D. W. Headley not out 7
T. N. Wren run out................. 0
B 1, l-b 12, w 9, n-b 2 24

1/12 2/136 3/183 (59.5 overs) 257
4/199 5/200 6/222
7/235 8/242 9/250

Bowling: Small 12–3–32–0; Munton 12–3–31–2; Reeve 11–0–44–3; P. A. Smith 10.5–0–66–2; N. M. K. Smith 10–0–45–1; Twose 4–0–26–0.

Umpires: J. H. Hampshire and B. J. Meyer.

FINAL

WARWICKSHIRE v WORCESTERSHIRE

At Lord's, September 3, 4. Worcestershire won by eight wickets. Toss: Worcestershire.

Warwickshire's wonderful adventure, in which they went so close to winning all four domestic titles, ended here, two days after they had secured the Championship. Instead, in what became a one-sided final through luck, keen bowling and magnificent batting, Worcestershire completed a quadruple of their own; victory meant they had won all four trophies in seven years. It was the first time they had ever won the 60-overs competition, though they were runners-up in 1963, 1966 and 1988. This was also the ninth successive final (and the 18th out of the last 21) won by the side batting second.

Warwickshire feared that their epic ambition would perish here, especially if they lost the toss and were asked to bat in damp conditions. It was worse than that. In a match carried over to the second day, after rain washed out all play after 12.25 p.m., they were required to bat on two successive moist mornings. The toss was crucial, though Worcestershire rightly pointed out that they had been equally disadvantaged in the Benson and Hedges final between the same two sides in July. The ball moved around so much on Saturday morning, especially when Newport was bowling, that even Lara needed 26 balls to get off the mark. However, Lara was still there when play was abandoned for the day, and so at 88 for three after 29 overs, with Ostler, Moles and Paul Smith all gone, Warwickshire still cherished hopes. However, conditions were just as user-friendly for Worcestershire's bowlers on Sunday. Lara, whose best form had eluded him in one-day cricket, still carried his side to a respectable total. He clipped and chipped in his wristy way so that there were seven fours and a six in his 81 – his best limited-overs score for Warwickshire. He was sixth out for 171 in the 46th over, caught at deep square leg. Neil Smith and Piper pushed the total to an eventual 223 for nine.

When Worcestershire batted, Munton bowled as well as Newport had done. But Curtis and D'Oliveira held together until the 14th over, by which time batting had become an easier business. Both were out with the score on 29. Their dismissals brought in Hick and Moody, who proceeded to share a magnificent stand of 198 off just 212 balls – the second-highest for any wicket in 32 finals. Hick, his confidence restored by his recent Test successes, his 12 fours and a six in his 93 from 101 balls. It was Moody, however, who won the Man of the Match award: earlier, he had bowled 12 overs off the reel for only 17 runs. There were ten fours and two sixes in his 88 and one six, off Paul Smith in the 40th over, went over the Grand Stand roof. Worcestershire had won emphatically, with ten overs and five balls to spare. – Paul Weaver.

Man of the Match: T. M. Moody. *Attendance:* 25,464; *receipts* £675,467.

Close of play: Warwickshire 88-3 (29 overs) (B. C. Lara 36*, R. G. Twose 20*).

Warwickshire

A. J. Moles c Rhodes b Newport	8
D. P. Ostler c Lampitt b Newport	4
B. C. Lara c Hick b Haynes	81
P. A. Smith c Haynes b Moody	13
R. G. Twose c Leatherdale b Newport	22
T. L. Penney lbw b Radford	18
*D. A. Reeve c Rhodes b Newport	13
N. M. K. Smith c Illingworth b Lampitt	20
†K. J. Piper not out	16
G. C. Small run out	5
T. A. Munton not out	0
B 1, l-b 8, w 10, n-b 4	23
	—
1/8 (2) 2/17 (1) 3/50 (4) 4/90 (5) 5/150 (6) 6/171 (3) 7/188 (7) 8/215 (8) 9/222 (10) — (9 wkts, 60 overs)	223

Bowling: Moody 12–4–17–1; Newport 12–2–38–4; Radford 12–1–45–1; Lampitt 11–1–45–1; Illingworth 6–0–35–0; Haynes 7–0–34–1.

Worcestershire

*T. S. Curtis b Reeve	11
D. B. D'Oliveira c Lara b Munton	12
G. A. Hick not out	93
T. M. Moody not out	88
L-b 6, w 11, n-b 6	23
1/29 (2) 2/29 (1) (2 wkts, 49.1 overs)	227

G. R. Haynes, D. A. Leatherdale, †S. J. Rhodes, S. R. Lampitt, P. J. Newport, R. K. Illingworth and N. V. Radford did not bat.

Bowling: Small 12–2–40–0; Munton 12–3–23–1; Reeve 6–1–30–1; P. A. Smith 7–1–54–0; Twose 5–0–36–0; N. M. K. Smith 7–0–34–0; Penney 0.1–0–4–0.

Umpires: N. T. Plews and D. R. Shepherd.

NATWEST BANK TROPHY RECORDS

(Including Gillette Cup, 1963-80)

Batting

Highest individual scores: 206, A. I. Kallicharran, Warwickshire v Oxfordshire, Birmingham, 1984; 180*, T. M. Moody, Worcestershire v Surrey, The Oval, 1994; 177, C. G. Greenidge, Hampshire v Glamorgan, Southampton, 1975; 172*, G. A. Hick, Worcestershire v Devon, Worcester, 1987; 165*, V. P. Terry, Hampshire v Berkshire, Southampton, 1985; 162*, I. V. A. Richards, Glamorgan v Oxfordshire, Swansea, 1993; 162*, C. J. Tavaré, Somerset v Devon, Torquay, 1990; 159, C. L. Smith, Hampshire v Cheshire, Chester, 1989; 158, G. D. Barlow, Middlesex v Lancashire, Lord's, 1984; 158, Zaheer Abbas, Gloucestershire v Leicestershire, Leicester, 1983; 156, D. I. Gower, Leicestershire v Derbyshire, Leicester, 1984; 155, J. J. Whitaker, Leicestershire v Wiltshire, Swindon, 1984; 154*, H. Morris, Glamorgan v Staffordshire, Cardiff, 1989; 154, P. Willey, Leicestershire v Hampshire, Leicester, 1987; 153, A. Hill, Derbyshire v Cornwall, Derby, 1986; 151*, M. P. Maynard, Glamorgan v Durham, Darlington, 1991. (93 hundreds were scored in the Gillette Cup; 154 hundreds have been scored in the NatWest Bank Trophy.)

Most runs: 2,383, G. A. Gooch; 1,964, M. W. Gatting; 1,950, D. L. Amiss.

Fastest hundred: G. D. Rose off 36 balls, Somerset v Devon, Torquay, 1990.

Most hundreds: 7, C. L. Smith; 6, G. A. Gooch; 5, D. I. Gower, I. V. A. Richards and G. M. Turner.

Highest totals (off 60 overs): 413 for four, Somerset v Devon, Torquay, 1990; 404 for three, Worcestershire v Devon, Worcester, 1987; 392 for five, Warwickshire v Oxfordshire, Birmingham, 1984; 386 for five, Essex v Wiltshire, Chelmsford, 1988; 384 for six, Kent v Berkshire, Finchampstead, 1994; 372 for five, Lancashire v Gloucestershire, Manchester, 1990; 371 for four, Hampshire v Glamorgan, Southampton, 1975; 365 for three, Derbyshire v Cornwall, Derby, 1986; 361 for eight, Essex v Cumberland, Chelmsford, 1992; 361 for eight, Warwickshire v Bedfordshire, Birmingham, 1994; 360 for two, Northamptonshire v Staffordshire, Northampton, 1990; 359 for four, Kent v Dorset, Canterbury, 1989; 357 for two, Worcestershire v Surrey, The Oval, 1994; 354 for seven, Leicestershire v Wiltshire, Swindon, 1984; 350, Surrey v Worcestershire, The Oval, 1994. *In the final:* 322 for five, Warwickshire v Sussex, Lord's, 1993.

Highest total by a minor county: 305 for nine, Durham v Glamorgan, Darlington, 1991.

Highest total by a side batting first and losing: 321 for six (60 overs), Sussex v Warwickshire, Lord's, 1993 (*in the final*).

Highest totals by a side batting second: 350 (59.5 overs), Surrey lost to Worcestershire, The Oval, 1994; 326 for nine (60 overs), Hampshire lost to Leicestershire, Leicester, 1987; 322 for five (60 overs), Warwickshire beat Sussex, Lord's, 1993 (*in the final*); 319 for nine (59.5 overs), Essex beat Lancashire, Chelmsford, 1992; 307 for five (60 overs), Hampshire beat Essex, Chelmsford, 1990; 306 for six (59.3 overs), Gloucestershire beat Leicestershire, Leicester, 1983; 305 for nine (60 overs), Durham lost to Glamorgan, Darlington, 1991.

Lowest completed totals: 39 (26.4 overs), Ireland v Sussex, Hove, 1985; 41 (20 overs), Cambridgeshire v Buckinghamshire, Cambridge, 1972; 41 (19.4 overs), Middlesex v Essex, Westcliff, 1972; 41 (36.1 overs), Shropshire v Essex, Wellington, 1974. *In the final:* 118 (60 overs), Lancashire v Kent, 1974.

Lowest total by a side batting first and winning: 98 (56.2 overs), Worcestershire v Durham, Chester-le-Street, 1968.

Shortest innings: 10.1 overs (60 for one), Worcestershire v Lancashire, Worcester, 1963.

Matches re-arranged on a reduced number of overs are excluded from the above.

Record partnerships for each wicket

248	for 1st	D. M. Smith and C. W. J. Athey, Sussex v Hampshire at Hove	1993
286	for 2nd	I. S. Anderson and A. Hill, Derbyshire v Cornwall at Derby	1986
309*	for 3rd	T. S. Curtis and T. M. Moody, Worcestershire v Surrey at The Oval	1994
234*	for 4th	D. Lloyd and C. H. Lloyd, Lancashire v Gloucestershire at Manchester	1978
166	for 5th	M. A. Lynch and G. R. J. Roope, Surrey v Durham at The Oval ..	1982
123	for 6th	D. A. Reeve and T. L. Penney, Warwickshire v Leicestershire at Leicester	1994
160*	for 7th	C. J. Richards and I. R. Payne, Surrey v Lincolnshire at Sleaford ..	1983
83	for 8th	S. N. V. Waterton and D. A. Hale, Oxfordshire v Gloucestershire at Oxford	1989
87	for 9th	M. A. Nash and A. E. Cordle, Glamorgan v Lincolnshire at Swansea	1974
81	for 10th	S. Turner and R. E. East, Essex v Yorkshire at Leeds	1982

Bowling

Most wickets: 81, G. G. Arnold; 79, J. Simmons.

Best bowling (12 overs unless stated): eight for 21 (10.1 overs), M. A. Holding, Derbyshire v Sussex, Hove, 1988; eight for 31 (11.1 overs), D. L. Underwood, Kent v Scotland, Edinburgh, 1987; seven for 15, A. L. Dixon, Kent v Surrey, The Oval, 1967; seven for 15 (9.3 overs), R. P. Lefebvre, Somerset v Devon, Torquay, 1990; seven for 19, N. V. Radford, Worcestershire v Bedfordshire, Bedford, 1991; seven for 30, P. J. Sainsbury, Hampshire v Norfolk, Southampton, 1965; seven for 32, S. P. Davis, Durham v Lancashire, Chester-le-Street, 1983; seven for 33, R. D. Jackman, Surrey v Yorkshire, Harrogate, 1970; seven for 37, N. A. Mallender, Northamptonshire v Worcestershire, Northampton, 1984.

Most economical analysis: 12–9–3–1, J. Simmons, Lancashire v Suffolk, Bury St Edmunds, 1985.

Most expensive analysis: 12–0–106–2, D. A. Gallop, Oxfordshire v Warwickshire, Birmingham, 1984.

Hat-tricks (7): J. D. F. Larter, Northamptonshire v Sussex, Northampton, 1963; D. A. D. Sydenham, Surrey v Cheshire, Hoylake, 1964; R. N. S. Hobbs, Essex v Middlesex, Lord's, 1968; N. M. McVicker, Warwickshire v Lincolnshire, Birmingham, 1971; G. S. le Roux, Sussex v Ireland, Hove, 1985; M. Jean-Jacques, Derbyshire v Nottinghamshire, Derby, 1987; J. F. M. O'Brien, Cheshire v Derbyshire, Chester, 1988.

Four wickets in five balls: D. A. D. Sydenham, Surrey v Cheshire, Hoylake, 1964.

Wicket-keeping and Fielding

Most dismissals: 66 (58 ct, 8 st), R. W. Taylor; 65 (59 ct, 6 st), A. P. E. Knott.

Most dismissals in an innings: 7 (all ct), A. J. Stewart, Surrey v Glamorgan, Swansea, 1994.

Most catches by a fielder: 26, J. Simmons; 25, G. Cook; 24, G. A. Gooch and P. J. Sharpe.

Most catches by a fielder in an innings: 4 – A. S. Brown, Gloucestershire v Middlesex, Bristol, 1963; G. Cook, Northamptonshire v Glamorgan, Northampton, 1972; C. G. Greenidge, Hampshire v Cheshire, Southampton, 1981; D. C. Jackson, Durham v Northamptonshire, Darlington, 1984; T. S. Smith, Hertfordshire v Somerset, St Albans, 1984; H. Morris, Glamorgan v Scotland, Edinburgh, 1988; C. C. Lewis, Nottinghamshire v Worcestershire, Nottingham, 1992.

Results

Largest victories in runs: Somerset by 346 runs v Devon, Torquay, 1990; Worcestershire by 299 runs v Devon, Worcester, 1987; Essex by 291 runs v Wiltshire, Chelmsford, 1988; Sussex by 244 runs v Ireland, Hove, 1985; Lancashire by 241 runs v Gloucestershire, Manchester, 1990; Nottinghamshire by 228 runs v Northumberland, Jesmond, 1994; Warwickshire by 227 runs v Oxfordshire, Birmingham, 1984; Essex by 226 runs v Oxfordshire, Chelmsford, 1985.

Victories by ten wickets (12): By Hampshire (twice), Middlesex, Northamptonshire, Surrey, Sussex, Warwickshire (twice), Yorkshire (four times).

Earliest finishes: both at 2.20 p.m. Worcestershire beat Lancashire by nine wickets at Worcester, 1963; Essex beat Middlesex by eight wickets at Westcliff, 1972.

Scores level (9): Nottinghamshire 215, Somerset 215 for nine at Taunton, 1964; Surrey 196, Sussex 196 for eight at The Oval, 1970; Somerset 287 for six, Essex 287 at Taunton, 1978; Surrey 195 for seven, Essex 195 at Chelmsford, 1980; Essex 149, Derbyshire 149 for eight at Derby, 1981; Northamptonshire 235 for nine, Derbyshire 235 for six at Lord's, 1981 (*in the final*); Middlesex 222 for nine, Somerset 222 for eight at Lord's, 1983; Hampshire 224 for eight, Essex 224 for seven at Southampton, 1985; Essex 307 for six, Hampshire 307 for five at Chelmsford, 1990. Under the rules the side which lost fewer wickets won.

WINNERS

Gillette Cup

1963 SUSSEX beat Worcestershire by 14 runs.
1964 SUSSEX beat Warwickshire by eight wickets.
1965 YORKSHIRE beat Surrey by 175 runs.
1966 WARWICKSHIRE beat Worcestershire by five wickets.
1967 KENT beat Somerset by 32 runs.
1968 WARWICKSHIRE beat Sussex by four wickets.
1969 YORKSHIRE beat Derbyshire by 69 runs.
1970 LANCASHIRE beat Sussex by six wickets.
1971 LANCASHIRE beat Kent by 24 runs.
1972 LANCASHIRE beat Warwickshire by four wickets.
1973 GLOUCESTERSHIRE beat Sussex by 40 runs.
1974 KENT beat Lancashire by four wickets.
1975 LANCASHIRE beat Middlesex by seven wickets.
1976 NORTHAMPTONSHIRE beat Lancashire by four wickets.
1977 MIDDLESEX beat Glamorgan by five wickets.
1978 SUSSEX beat Somerset by five wickets.
1979 SOMERSET beat Northamptonshire by 45 runs.
1980 MIDDLESEX beat Surrey by seven wickets.

NatWest Bank Trophy

1981 DERBYSHIRE beat Northamptonshire by losing fewer wickets with the scores level.
1982 SURREY beat Warwickshire by nine wickets.
1983 SOMERSET beat Kent by 24 runs.
1984 MIDDLESEX beat Kent by four wickets.

1985 ESSEX beat Nottinghamshire by one run.
1986 SUSSEX beat Lancashire by seven wickets.
1987 NOTTINGHAMSHIRE beat Northamptonshire by three wickets.
1988 MIDDLESEX beat Worcestershire by three wickets.
1989 WARWICKSHIRE beat Middlesex by four wickets.
1990 LANCASHIRE beat Northamptonshire by seven wickets.
1991 HAMPSHIRE beat Surrey by four wickets.
1992 NORTHAMPTONSHIRE beat Leicestershire by eight wickets.
1993 WARWICKSHIRE beat Sussex by five wickets.
1994 WORCESTERSHIRE beat Warwickshire by eight wickets.

TEAM RECORDS 1963-94

	Rounds reached				*Matches*		
	W	*F*	*SF*	*QF*	*P*	*W*	*L*
Derbyshire	1	2	3	9	61*	30	31
Durham	0	0	0	1	34	10	24
Essex	1	1	4	13	67	36	31
Glamorgan	0	1	2	12	65	33	32
Gloucestershire	1	1	5	13	65	34	31
Hampshire	1	1	8	19	82	51	31
Kent	2	5	7	14	75	45	30
Lancashire	5	8	13	17	88	61	27
Leicestershire	0	1	3	14	65	33	32
Middlesex	4	6	13	17	87	59	28
Northamptonshire	2	6	9	18	81	51	30
Nottinghamshire	1	2	3	11	67	36	31
Somerset	2	4	9	16	78	48	30
Surrey	1	4	9	19	80*	49	31
Sussex	4	8	12	17	83	55	28
Warwickshire	4	8	14	18	89	61	28
Worcestershire	1	4	10	14	74	43	31
Yorkshire	2	2	4	13	64	34	30

* Derbyshire and Surrey totals each include a bowling contest after their first-round matches were abandoned in 1991; Derbyshire lost to Hertfordshire and Surrey beat Oxfordshire.

MINOR COUNTY RECORDS

From 1964 to 1979 the previous season's top five Minor Counties were invited to take part in the competition. In 1980 these were joined by Ireland, and in 1983 the competition was expanded to embrace 13 Minor Counties, Ireland and Scotland. The number of Minor Counties dropped to 12 in 1992 when Durham attained first-class status, and 11 in 1995 when Holland were admitted to the competition.

Between 1964 and 1991 Durham qualified 21 times, including 15 years in succession from 1977-91. They reached the second round a record six times.

Including the 1995 tournament, Hertfordshire have qualified most among the other Minor Counties, 18 times, followed by Oxfordshire and Staffordshire 17, Devon 16, Berkshire, Buckinghamshire, Cambridgeshire, Cheshire and Suffolk 15, Norfolk 14, Shropshire and Wiltshire 12, Dorset 11, Bedfordshire and Lincolnshire 10, Cumberland 9, Northumberland 8, Cornwall 6, Wales Minor Counties twice and Herefordshire, who have qualified for the first time in 1995.

Only Hertfordshire have reached the quarter-finals, beating Berkshire and then Essex in 1976.

Wins by a minor county over a first-class county (8): Durham v Yorkshire (by five wickets), Harrogate, 1973; Lincolnshire v Glamorgan (by six wickets), Swansea, 1974; Hertfordshire v Essex (by 33 runs), 2nd round, Hitchin, 1976; Shropshire v Yorkshire (by 37 runs), Telford, 1984; Durham v Derbyshire (by seven wickets), Derby, 1985; Buckinghamshire v Somerset (by seven runs), High Wycombe, 1987; Cheshire v Northamptonshire (by one wicket), Chester, 1988; Hertfordshire v Derbyshire (2-1 in a bowling contest after the match was abandoned), Bishop's Stortford, 1991.

BENSON AND HEDGES CUP, 1994

Warwickshire had their first success of a brilliant season when they won the Benson and Hedges Cup final, with an easy win over Worcestershire that was helped by good fortune with the toss. This was the only competition Warwickshire had never won and left Durham, Sussex and Glamorgan as the only first-class counties never to hold the cup in its 23 seasons. Since they had won the NatWest Trophy in 1993, Warwickshire became the third county, after Lancashire in 1990 and Hampshire in 1991-92, to hold both knockout trophies simultaneously.

The triumph came despite Warwickshire winning only three matches, since they had a bye through the preliminary round and beat Kent on a bowl-out. This caused extreme bitterness amongst the losers, who protested that the game could have been played had the "Brumbrella" cover been used. It also alienated Warwickshire's most faithful supporters, who had stayed on through two fruitless days and were then refused admission to the indoor school to watch the conclusion.

Warwickshire did, however, score good away wins against strong opposition, Middlesex and Surrey, passing a Surrey total of 267 in the semi-final with Brian Lara making 70 the day after his world record 501 not out. Of the real games of cricket, all but one – Surrey's preliminary round game against Somerset – were won by the team batting second, prompting concern about the fairness of the competition.

The non-Championship teams in the competition, including Ireland for the first time, as usual made no progress, although Minor Counties gave Nottinghamshire a scare. However, two first-class counties, this time Northamptonshire and Somerset, still had to be eliminated in April, adding to the unpopularity of the all-knockout format. But by this time the counties had already decided in principle to revert to a zonal system for the preliminary stages in 1995, when the teams will again be divided into four groups before the quarter-finals.

Prize money

£31,000 for winners: WARWICKSHIRE.
£15,500 for runners-up: WORCESTERSHIRE.
£7,750 for losing semi-finalists: HAMPSHIRE and SURREY.
£3,875 for losing quarter-finalists: DERBYSHIRE, ESSEX, KENT and NOTTINGHAMSHIRE.

There was also £1,250 each for the winners of first-round matches and £925 for the winners of each preliminary match. Gold Award winners received £650 in the final, £330 in the semi-finals, £280 in the quarter-finals, £170 in the first round and £140 in the preliminary round. The prize money was increased from £93,445 in the 1993 tournament to £97,680; the total sponsorship rose from £614,032 to £622,629.

PRELIMINARY ROUND

COMBINED UNIVERSITIES v LANCASHIRE

At Oxford, April 26. Lancashire won by seven wickets. Toss: Lancashire.

Crawley, who had played nine games in the competition for Combined Universities – five as captain – returned as Lancashire's opening batsman and won the match award for his 73. He was eventually dismissed by Batty and Bovill, the Durham pairing which had already removed another former Universities captain, Gallian. Bovill's figures of two for 21 in 11 overs were the best of the match. Though none of the student batsmen failed, they had not made enough of a slow pitch which yielded the county bowlers only two wickets; Lancashire had a straightforward target of 192.

Gold Award: J. P. Crawley.

Combined Universities

*R. R. Montgomerie (*Oxford*) c Fairbrother b Yates . 52
G. I. Macmillan (*Oxford*) lbw b Watkinson . 19
I. G. S. Steer (*Cheltenham & Gloucester CHE*) run out . 43
J. N. Snape (*Durham*) not out 41
M. G. N. Windows (*Durham*) not out . . 16
L-b 11, w 9 20

1/52 2/110 3/151 (3 wkts, 55 overs) 191

S. C. Ecclestone (*Oxford*), †J. N. Batty (*Durham*), J. G. Hughes (*Sheffield Hallam*), J. N. B. Bovill (*Durham*), A. R. Whittall (*Cambridge*) and J. C. Hallett (*Durham*) did not bat.

Bowling: Wasim Akram 10–0–30–0; Martin 9–0–31–0; Watkinson 8–1–21–1; Austin 11–0–47–0; Yates 11–1–28–1; Gallian 6–0–23–0.

Lancashire

J. P. Crawley c Batty b Bovill 73
J. E. R. Gallian c Batty b Bovill 9
N. J. Speak c and b Whittall 15
N. H. Fairbrother not out 41
G. D. Lloyd not out 31
B 2, l-b 8, w 6, n-b 8 24

1/12 2/66 3/141 (3 wkts, 51.3 overs) 193

Wasim Akram, *M. Watkinson, †W. K. Hegg, P. J. Martin, G. Yates and I. D. Austin did not bat.

Bowling: Bovill 11–1–21–2; Hallett 10–1–40–0; Snape 11–2–37–0; Ecclestone 4–0–16–0; Whittall 11–3–42–1; Hughes 4.3–0–27–0.

Umpires: D. J. Constant and B. J. Meyer.

LEICESTERSHIRE v IRELAND

At Leicester, April 26. Leicestershire won by nine wickets. Toss: Ireland. County debut: P. V. Simmons.

Ireland entered their first ever Benson and Hedges match with a weakened team; some of their leading players had used all their holidays from work while contesting the ICC Trophy in Kenya. Warke, who broke his arm at the start of that tournament, returned to score 53, almost double the next highest contribution; Benson, recently released by Leicestershire, opened for his native Ireland but made only 14. The Trinidadian Phil Simmons began his county career with 64 runs, a wicket, a catch and a run-out. He was the only man dismissed, as Leicestershire eased home with nearly five overs to spare.

Gold Award: P. V. Simmons.

Ireland

J. D. R. Benson c Pierson b Parsons . . . 14
D. J. Curry b Mullally 0
S. J. S. Warke c Simmons b Millns 53
*D. A. Lewis c Briers b Simmons 27
G. D. Harrison b Pierson 6
A. R. Dunlop run out 6
A. McBrine b Millns 0
S. Graham run out 22
†P. B. Jackson not out 8
E. R. Moore c Nixon b Mullally 0
C. J. Hoey not out 2
B 4, l-b 7, w 7, n-b 4 22

1/10 2/32 3/91 (9 wkts, 55 overs) 160
4/100 5/114 6/116
7/145 8/149 9/149

Bowling: Mullally 11–5–30–2; Parsons 11–3–21–1; Millns 10–0–32–2; Wells 5–0–21–0; Simmons 7–2–29–1; Pierson 11–4–16–1.

Leicestershire

P. V. Simmons c Benson b Lewis 64
*N. E. Briers not out 70
T. J. Boon not out 19
L-b 3, w 8 11

1/105 (1 wkt, 50.1 overs) 164

J. J. Whitaker, V. J. Wells, B. F. Smith, †P. A. Nixon, G. J. Parsons, A. R. K. Pierson, D. J. Millns and A. D. Mullally did not bat.

Bowling: Moore 11–2–29–0; Harrison 9–3–22–0; Hoey 8–2–31–0; McBrine 7–0–28–0; Curry 6–1–20–0; Lewis 7–0–22–1; Benson 2.1–0–9–0.

Umpires: H. D. Bird and P. B. Wight.

MIDDLESEX v NORTHAMPTONSHIRE

At Lord's, April 26. Middlesex won by six wickets. Toss: Middlesex. First-team debut: K. J. Innes.

Both sides were without their West Indian Test stars, though the absence of Ambrose, who had controversially postponed his return, proved far more significant than that of Haynes, whose broken finger still required treatment. Asked to bat, Northamptonshire coped reasonably well with the Middlesex seamers, with Loye scoring 68 from 65 balls. But Emburey, just recovered from an eye operation, and Tufnell bowled economically and effectively, sharing six wickets for 69 in their 22 overs. Promoted to open in Haynes's place, Ramprakash made an unbeaten century and saw Middlesex home. They had started slowly, however, and needed 70 from the last ten overs; Ambrose might have made the difference.

Gold Award: M. R. Ramprakash.

Northamptonshire

A. Fordham lbw b Tufnell 38
N. A. Felton c Carr b Emburey 25
R. J. Bailey c Roseberry b Tufnell 19
*A. J. Lamb b Tufnell 25
M. B. Loye not out 68
K. M. Curran c Roseberry b Fraser 5
A. L. Penberthy b Emburey 24
M. N. Bowen b Emburey 0
†D. Ripley not out 1
L-b 11, w 12, n-b 4 27

1/67 2/80 3/121 4/136 5/154 6/230 7/230 (7 wkts, 55 overs) 232

K. J. Innes and J. P. Taylor did not bat.

Bowling: Fraser 11–3–32–1; Williams 6–0–24–0; Emburey 11–2–37–3; Johnson 9–1–45–0; Tufnell 11–1–32–3; Weekes 7–0–51–0.

Middlesex

M. A. Roseberry c Ripley b Bowen 4
M. R. Ramprakash not out 119
*M. W. Gatting c Fordham b Innes 28
J. D. Carr c Ripley b Taylor 14
P. N. Weekes b Penberthy 33
†K. R. Brown not out 15
L-b 14, w 9 23

1/16 2/80 3/140 4/192 (4 wkts, 53.5 overs) 236

J. E. Emburey, N. F. Williams, A. R. C. Fraser, P. C. R. Tufnell and R. L. Johnson did not bat.

Bowling: Bowen 10–1–39–1; Innes 6–1–25–1; Taylor 10–3–28–1; Penberthy 11–1–40–1; Curran 10.5–0–65–0; Bailey 6–0–25–0.

Umpires: J. C. Balderstone and R. Palmer.

NOTTINGHAMSHIRE v MINOR COUNTIES

At Nottingham, April 26. Nottinghamshire won by three wickets. Toss: Nottinghamshire. County debuts: J. C. Adams, W. M. Noon.

At 159 for seven, chasing a modest 192, Nottinghamshire were threatened with a humiliating defeat by the amateurs. Only Crawley and Adams, newly arrived from the West Indies, had offered much in the way of runs. But Lewis, who took 14 overs to score his first 14 runs and was almost run out on 15, suddenly swung into action, hitting 36 runs in four overs with Pick, to win with seven balls to spare. A slow pitch had enabled Nottinghamshire to tie down the Minor Counties batsmen, even if they dismissed only four. Cockbain's unbeaten 54, in 142 minutes, contained only three fours, though he and Myles accelerated convincingly.

Gold Award: I. Cockbain.

Minor Counties

S. J. Dean c Noon b Mike	13	†M. I. Humphries not out	9
M. J. Roberts c Adams b Mike	20	L-b 8, w 8, n-b 6	22
K. Sharp run out	30		—
*I. Cockbain not out	54	1/32 2/42 (4 wkts, 55 overs)	191
S. D. Myles c Pollard b Lewis	43	3/78 4/175	

R. A. Evans, K. A. Arnold, P. C. Graham, A. Smith and D. R. Thomas did not bat.

Bowling: Lewis 9–0–43–1; Pick 11–1–42–0; Mike 9–1–35–2; Afford 11–1–29–0; Field-Buss 11–0–21–0; Crawley 4–0–13–0.

Nottinghamshire

P. R. Pollard st Humphries b Smith	18	G. W. Mike c Smith b Thomas	6
M. A. Crawley c Humphries b Smith	35	R. A. Pick not out	10
J. C. Adams b Smith	40	B 1, l-b 2, w 3, n-b 4	10
P. Johnson c Cockbain b Thomas	2		—
*R. T. Robinson c Roberts b Evans	23	1/43 2/66 3/73 (7 wkts, 53.5 overs)	195
C. C. Lewis not out	48	4/113 5/131	
†W. M. Noon c Humphries b Thomas	3	6/139 7/159	

M. G. Field-Buss and J. A. Afford did not bat.

Bowling: Arnold 10–3–42–0; Graham 10–2–27–0; Smith 11–1–40–3; Thomas 9–1–36–3; Myles 3–0–14–0; Evans 10.5–1–33–1.

Umpires: V. A. Holder and A. A. Jones.

SURREY v SOMERSET

At The Oval, April 26. Surrey won by 35 runs. Toss: Surrey.

Stewart batted through 55 overs for an unbeaten 167, studded with powerful hooks and pulls. It was the highest innings for Surrey in limited-overs cricket and the fourth highest in the tournament's history. He hit one six and 18 fours in 187 balls and added 140 with Ward – whose fifty was all the brighter for his helmet, in lime green, primrose, midnight blue and scarlet. But Lathwell, who dropped Stewart on 31, almost upstaged him with his maiden century in the competition. His 120 took 136 balls, with 12 fours and two sixes. Once he and Folland were parted, however, Somerset's last eight wickets fell for 51. Martin Bicknell took four wickets, confirming his recovery after injury on the England A tour, while Butcher looked to have added a yard to his pace.

Gold Award: A. J. Stewart.

Surrey

*†A. J. Stewart not out	167	A. D. Brown not out	19
D. J. Bicknell c Turner b van Troost	8	L-b 5, w 1, n-b 4	10
G. P. Thorpe c Turner b Rose	34		—
D. M. Ward run out	50	1/9 2/105 3/245 (3 wkts, 55 overs)	288

A. J. Hollioake, M. A. Butcher, M. P. Bicknell, A. J. Murphy, J. Boiling and J. E. Benjamin did not bat.

Bowling: Caddick 11–0–62–0; van Troost 9–0–64–1; Mallender 11–0–44–0; Mushtaq Ahmed 7–0–33–0; Rose 9–1–42–1; Hayhurst 8–0–38–0.

Somerset

M. N. Lathwell b Butcher	120
*A. N. Hayhurst c Thorpe b M. P. Bicknell	7
R. J. Harden c Stewart b Butcher	34
N. A. Folland run out	38
G. D. Rose c Brown b Butcher	0
Mushtaq Ahmed c Thorpe b Murphy	3
V. P. Clarke c Hollioake b M. P. Bicknell	22
†R. J. Turner b M. P. Bicknell	6
A. P. van Troost b Murphy	5
N. A. Mallender b M. P. Bicknell	2
A. R. Caddick not out	4
L-b 9, w 1, n-b 2	12
1/10 2/98 3/202 4/202 5/207 6/222 7/242 8/243 9/248 (53.2 overs)	253

Bowling: M. P. Bicknell 10.2–0–49–4; Benjamin 10–1–54–0; Butcher 11–1–37–3; Murphy 11–0–67–2; Boiling 11–0–37–0.

Umpires: M. J. Kitchen and G. Sharp.

SUSSEX v SCOTLAND

At Hove, April 26. Sussex won by eight wickets. Toss: Scotland. County debut: P. W. Jarvis.

Sussex won at a canter, thanks to tight bowling and an unbeaten 65 from Smith. Scotland were missing three key batsmen – Reifer, Patterson and Salmond – and their total of 157 never looked adequate on a flat Hove pitch. Jarvis, on his Sussex debut, bowled a hostile opening spell, and Stephenson and Hemmings shackled the Scots so much that they did not reach 100 until the 42nd over. Former Yorkshire batsman Love held them together with 53, and hit Jarvis for a straight six. But Smith batted stylishly and shared an unbroken stand of 109 with Wells – whose seventh boundary brought up his half-century and Sussex's victory inside 41 overs.

Gold Award: D. M. Smith.

Scotland

I. L. Philip c Giddins b Jarvis	9
*A. C. Storie run out	11
G. B. J. McGurk b Salisbury	25
J. D. Love c Moores b Stephenson	53
A. B. Russell run out	6
†A. G. Davies c Moores b Stephenson	14
J. G. Williamson b Giddins	4
G. M. Hamilton not out	8
J. W. Govan not out	2
L-b 8, w 9, n-b 8	25
1/12 2/38 3/67 4/99 5/137 6/146 7/150 (7 wkts, 55 overs)	157

P. G. Duthie and M. S. Richardson did not bat.

Bowling: Jarvis 11–3–29–1; Stephenson 11–3–24–2; Giddins 11–2–29–1; Hemmings 11–1–21–0; Salisbury 9–0–41–1; Lenham 2–0–5–0.

Sussex

D. M. Smith not out	65
C. W. J. Athey c Williamson b Duthie	23
M. P. Speight b Williamson	1
*A. P. Wells not out	51
L-b 10, w 11	21
1/50 2/52 (2 wkts, 40.4 overs)	161

N. J. Lenham, †P. Moores, F. D. Stephenson, I. D. K. Salisbury, E. S. H. Giddins, P. W. Jarvis and E. E. Hemmings did not bat.

Bowling: Hamilton 9–2–27–0; Richardson 7.4–0–33–0; Williamson 7–1–24–1; Duthie 9–0–27–1; Govan 8–0–40–0.

Umpires: T. E. Jesty and A. G. T. Whitehead.

FIRST ROUND

DERBYSHIRE v LANCASHIRE

At Derby, May 10. Derbyshire won by four wickets. Toss: Derbyshire.

Cork, winner of the Gold Award in the previous season's final against Lancashire, wrenched control from them in the rematch with a remarkable 64 from 34 balls. Despite a suspect knee after surgery, he smashed 92 from 45 balls with Wells as Lancashire's bowling and fielding collapsed – Yates dropped Cork on 30. He hit seven fours and two sixes, the second, off Watkinson, giving Derbyshire victory with a ball to spare. Lancashire had failed to build on their dominance during the morning, when they reached 172 for one. Atherton, who shared stands of 86 with Gallian and 131 with Crawley, completed his first century in the competition before being stumped off a wide. Derbyshire's reply began well enough as Adams and Rollins put on 104. But good bowling by Chapple and Martin seemed to have ended their hopes; they needed 59 from the last five overs and 29 from the last two.

Gold Award: D. G. Cork.

Lancashire

J. E. R. Gallian run out 39	I. D. Austin not out 3
M. A. Atherton st Krikken b Wells 100	
J. P. Crawley b Warner 73	L-b 3, w 10, n-b 20 33
G. D. Lloyd b Warner 8	—
N. J. Speak b Cork 17	1/86 2/217 3/238 (5 wkts, 55 overs) 280
*M. Watkinson not out 7	4/258 5/268

†W. K. Hegg, P. J. Martin, G. Yates and G. Chapple did not bat.

Bowling: DeFreitas 11–2–46–0; Mortensen 11–1–50–0; Cork 11–0–67–1; Wells 11–0–57–1; Warner 11–0–57–2.

Derbyshire

P. D. Bowler lbw b Martin 0	P. A. J. DeFreitas c Hegg b Chapple . . 9
A. S. Rollins c Atherton b Chapple 70	D. G. Cork not out 64
C. J. Adams c and b Yates 34	L-b 17, w 12, n-b 2 31
*M. Azharuddin c Atherton b Yates . . . 4	—
T. J. G. O'Gorman b Austin 24	1/12 2/116 3/124 (6 wkts, 54.5 overs) 284
C. M. Wells not out 48	4/125 5/174 6/192

†K. M. Krikken, A. E. Warner and O. H. Mortensen did not bat.

Bowling: Martin 11–4–35–1; Chapple 11–1–30–2; Watkinson 8.5–0–58–0; Austin 11–1–65–1; Yates 10–0–49–2; Gallian 3–0–30–0.

Umpires: K. E. Palmer and N. T. Plews.

DURHAM v WORCESTERSHIRE

At Stockton-on-Tees, May 10. Worcestershire won by eight wickets. Toss: Durham.

Hick made a mockery of Durham's view that 200 might be a winning score on a slow pitch, steering Worcestershire home with almost ten overs to spare. Although he never looked in the slightest hurry, Hick's 104 not out came off 137 balls; he and Moody compiled an untroubled stand of 138. Worcestershire's only scare came when Curtis was bowled in the first over, but that brought in Hick. Durham's innings never broke out of the stranglehold imposed by Moody's gentle medium-pace as he opened the bowling and conceded only 22 from 11 overs off the reel. But Newport fared even better, removing both openers and returning to break the only stand of note – 57 between Bainbridge and Longley. He finished with three for 14.

Gold Award: P. J. Newport.

Durham

W. Larkins c Moody b Newport	19	D. A. Graveney not out	4
M. Saxelby c Hick b Newport	12	A. Walker not out	9
J. E. Morris c Curtis b Lampitt	23		
S. Hutton c Rhodes b Illingworth	8	B 2, l-b 11, w 7, n-b 2	22
*P. Bainbridge c Rhodes b Newport	28		
J. I. Longley b Illingworth	33	1/32 2/37 3/55 (8 wkts, 55 overs)	190
A. C. Cummins c Leatherdale b Lampitt	21	4/67 5/124 6/157	
†C. W. Scott c Rhodes b Illingworth	11	7/176 8/180	

S. J. E. Brown did not bat.

Bowling: Radford 7–1–34–0; Moody 11–4–22–0; Newport 11–4–14–3; Lampitt 11–0–27–2; Illingworth 10–0–51–3; Leatherdale 5–0–29–0.

Worcestershire

*T. S. Curtis b Cummins	0
D. B. D'Oliveira c Scott b Walker	11
G. A. Hick not out	104
T. M. Moody not out	65
L-b 2, w 7, n-b 2	11
1/1 2/53 (2 wkts, 45.4 overs)	191

G. R. Haynes, D. A. Leatherdale, †S. J. Rhodes, P. J. Newport, R. K. Illingworth, S. R. Lampitt and N. V. Radford did not bat.

Bowling: Cummins 11–0–37–1; Brown 9.4–0–47–0; Walker 6–0–20–1; Graveney 11–0–36–0; Bainbridge 8–0–49–0.

Umpires: J. H. Hampshire and J. W. Holder.

ESSEX v LEICESTERSHIRE

At Chelmsford, May 10. Essex won by eight wickets. Toss: Leicestershire.

Gooch collected his 12th century and 21st Gold Award, in his 100th Benson and Hedges Cup match, and passed 4,500 runs as Essex coasted into the quarter-finals. His unbeaten 130 spanned 153 deliveries and included 17 fours and a six; he shared a stand of 111 in 18 overs with Hussain, who hit 59 in 64 balls. Gooch was dropped by Simmons when 52, but earlier in the day the roles were reversed when he missed the West Indian without a run on the board. Simmons made good his escape to launch Leicestershire to a sound start. Once he departed, however, the innings gradually subsided.

Gold Award: G. A. Gooch.

Leicestershire

P. V. Simmons c Hussain b Topley	57	A. R. K. Pierson not out	3
*N. E. Briers c Garnham b Kasprowicz	39	D. J. Millns c Garnham b Ilott	10
J. J. Whitaker c Prichard b Irani	53	A. D. Mullally not out	0
V. J. Wells lbw b Kasprowicz	0	B 1, l-b 14, w 5, n-b 4	24
B. F. Smith lbw b Such	22		
P. E. Robinson run out	27	1/92 2/123 3/123 (9 wkts, 55 overs)	241
†P. A. Nixon b Ilott	5	4/183 5/207 6/224	
G. J. Parsons c Kasprowicz b Ilott	1	7/226 8/227 9/240	

Bowling: Ilott 11–3–28–3; Kasprowicz 11–0–52–2; Topley 11–0–46–1; Irani 11–1–61–1; Such 11–1–39–1.

Essex

*G. A. Gooch not out	130
P. J. Prichard lbw b Pierson	23
N. Hussain c and b Pierson	59
N. V. Knight not out	26
B 1, l-b 4, w 1, n-b 2	8
1/81 2/192 (2 wkts, 51.5 overs)	246

N. Shahid, †M. A. Garnham, R. C. Irani, M. S. Kasprowicz, T. D. Topley, M. C. Ilott and P. M. Such did not bat.

Bowling: Mullally 10–2–29–0; Millns 9–1–44–0; Simmons 8–0–42–0; Parsons 9.5–2–45–0; Pierson 11–0–54–2; Wells 4–0–27–0.

Umpires: V. A. Holder and D. R. Shepherd.

HAMPSHIRE v YORKSHIRE

At Southampton, May 10. Hampshire won by eight wickets. Toss: Yorkshire.

Yorkshire's hopes of moving one step along the road to Lord's were dented after only 15 overs. By then they had lost Vaughan, to his first ball, Byas and Richardson. In the event, Hampshire were challenged to score only 179. Though they lost Terry in the fifth over, they were steered relentlessly forward by Smith and Middleton, who added a decisive 102 for the second wicket. Smith was removed for an aggressive 58, but Middleton continued to adhere to the crease and, with the help of some shots from Nicholas, finished the job with four overs to spare.

Gold Award: T. C. Middleton.

Yorkshire

*M. D. Moxon c Connor b Cowans	40
M. P. Vaughan c Middleton b Cowans	0
D. Byas c Aymes b Benjamin	10
R. B. Richardson b Connor	7
†R. J. Blakey c James b Connor	40
C. White c Keech b Udal	12
A. P. Grayson not out	22
P. J. Hartley not out	19
B 2, l-b 12, w 12, n-b 2	28
1/0 2/18 3/49 4/94 5/123 6/136 (6 wkts, 55 overs)	178

M. A. Robinson, D. Gough and R. D. Stemp did not bat.

Bowling: Benjamin 11–2–26–1; Cowans 11–1–35–2; James 9–1–13–0; Connor 10–2–45–2; Udal 11–1–35–1; Keech 3–0–10–0.

Hampshire

V. P. Terry c Blakey b Robinson	10
T. C. Middleton not out	63
R. A. Smith c Blakey b Grayson	58
*M. C. J. Nicholas not out	36
L-b 5, w 8, n-b 2	15
1/16 2/118 (2 wkts, 51 overs)	182

M. Keech, †A. N. Aymes, S. D. Udal, W. K. M. Benjamin, K. D. James, C. A. Connor and N. G. Cowans did not bat.

Bowling: Gough 9–1–34–0; Hartley 9–1–31–0; Robinson 7–0–12–1; Stemp 11–2–47–0; White 3–0–10–0; Grayson 9–1–30–1; Vaughan 3–0–13–0.

Umpires: B. J. Meyer and R. Palmer.

KENT v GLOUCESTERSHIRE

At Canterbury, May 10. Kent won by four wickets. Toss: Gloucestershire.

Walsh's decision to bat first looked distinctly questionable as Gloucestershire's top three were dismissed for 16 – even though McCague dropped out of the attack after just 14 deliveries with shoulder trouble. It was only a gritty and determined fifty from Wright, supported by Russell, that kept the innings together. Kent's bowlers contributed 21 wides. Opening their reply, Benson set Kent off on a relatively comfortable journey to the quarter-finals. But it was left to Fleming to see the side through – adding an unbeaten 36 to his two wickets and a catch.

Gold Award: M. V. Fleming.

Gloucestershire

B. C. Broad lbw b Igglesden	1
G. D. Hodgson c Benson b Igglesden	3
S. G. Hinks c Fleming b Headley	4
M. W. Alleyne b Fleming	18
A. J. Wright c and b Hooper	55
T. H. C. Hancock c Hooper b Igglesden	13
†R. C. Russell c Taylor b Fleming	31
M. C. J. Ball not out	20
*C. A. Walsh c Marsh b Headley	0
A. M. Smith run out	8
K. E. Cooper not out	0
B 4, l-b 5, w 21, n-b 6	36
1/5 2/7 3/16 4/56 5/82 6/144 7/162 8/166 9/183 (9 wkts, 55 overs)	189

Bowling: McCague 2.2–0–10–0; Igglesden 11–1–26–3; Headley 10.4–0–36–2; Ealham 9–0–38–0; Fleming 11–0–39–2; Hooper 11–0–31–1.

Kent

T. R. Ward b Smith	14
*M. R. Benson c Russell b Cooper	47
N. R. Taylor lbw b Ball	30
C. L. Hooper b Walsh	4
G. R. Cowdrey c Russell b Smith	14
M. A. Ealham lbw b Ball	10
M. V. Fleming not out	36
†S. A. Marsh not out	15
L-b 6, w 7, n-b 10	23
1/28 2/84 3/96 4/122 5/132 6/150 (6 wkts, 54 overs)	193

D. W. Headley, M. J. McCague and A. P. Igglesden did not bat.

Bowling: Walsh 10–1–33–1; Cooper 11–3–19–1; Smith 11–0–40–2; Ball 11–1–32–2; Alleyne 11–1–63–0.

Umpires: G. Sharp and P. B. Wight.

MIDDLESEX v WARWICKSHIRE

At Lord's, May 10. Warwickshire won by three wickets. Toss: Warwickshire.

Once Munton had Haynes and Gatting caught behind with only 21 on the board, Middlesex were unlikely to score enough in overcast conditions. Only Ramprakash, who struggled for nearly two hours, and Carr held up Warwickshire; all five of their bowlers took wickets. The large crowd was delighted when Twose was out in the second over, which brought in Lara. Four of his first 17 balls were struck to the fence, so it was a surprise when he was bowled by his first delivery from Johnson. At 67 for four, Warwickshire were far from confident, but Reeve held them together. He did not strike a single boundary, but ensured his side a narrow success.

Gold Award: T. A. Munton.

Middlesex

D. L. Haynes c Burns b Munton	6
M. A. Roseberry c P. A. Smith b Bell	17
*M. W. Gatting c Burns b Munton	0
M. R. Ramprakash st Burns b N. M. K. Smith	42
J. D. Carr c Twose b Bell	27
P. N. Weekes c Bell b Munton	11
†K. R. Brown c Ostler b N. M. K. Smith	24
J. E. Emburey lbw b Small	0
R. L. Johnson c Penney b Reeve	1
N. F. Williams c and b N. M. K. Smith	5
A. R. C. Fraser not out	1
B 1, l-b 9, w 6	16
1/19 2/21 3/38 4/101 5/101 6/129 7/129 8/136 9/149 (54.3 overs)	150

Bowling: Small 11–3–22–1; Munton 11–3–27–3; Bell 11–1–34–2; Reeve 11–3–28–1; N. M. K. Smith 10.3–0–29–3.

Warwickshire

D. P. Ostler c Weekes b Fraser	11	N. M. K. Smith c Carr b Weekes	4
R. G. Twose b Williams	0	G. C. Small not out	5
B. C. Lara b Johnson	34	B 3, l-b 7, w 11, n-b 2	23
P. A. Smith lbw b Emburey	12		—
T. L. Penney b Weekes	39	1/4 2/32 3/67 (7 wkts, 53.2 overs)	151
*D. A. Reeve not out	23	4/67 5/137	
†M. Burns c Carr b Weekes	0	6/137 7/141	

M. A. V. Bell and T. A. Munton did not bat.

Bowling: Fraser 11–4–26–1; Williams 10.2–1–47–1; Emburey 11–4–19–1; Johnson 11–3–17–1; Weekes 10–2–32–3.

Umpires: J. H. Harris and T. E. Jesty.

NOTTINGHAMSHIRE v SUSSEX

At Nottingham, May 10. Nottinghamshire won by seven wickets. Toss: Nottinghamshire.

Coming in at an uneasy 13 for two, Robinson steered Nottinghamshire past their target of 240 with more than five overs to spare. He batted for three hours, adding 163 in 36 overs with Adams, who continued his fine start in county cricket with 86. Only Johnson's eagerness to finish the job quickly robbed Robinson of a well-deserved hundred. Earlier, Crawley, with four for 43, put the brake on Sussex's attempt to build a formidable target. He removed Wells and Lenham, who had put them into a strong position, in the same over.

Gold Award: R. T. Robinson.

Sussex

D. M. Smith st Noon b Afford	20	P. W. Jarvis not out	21
C. W. J. Athey b Afford	32	E. E. Hemmings run out	0
M. P. Speight c Mike b Afford	16		
*A. P. Wells c Pick b Crawley	51	B 1, l-b 5, w 12	18
N. J. Lenham c Evans b Crawley	44		—
K. Greenfield c Crawley b Lewis	27	1/54 2/58 3/87 (9 wkts, 55 overs)	239
F. D. Stephenson c Lewis b Crawley	4	4/171 5/177 6/185	
†P. Moores c Noon b Crawley	6	7/204 8/238 9/239	

E. S. H. Giddins did not bat.

Bowling: Lewis 8–2–33–1; Pick 11–1–53–0; Evans 8–0–34–0; Mike 7–0–36–0; Afford 11–1–34–3; Crawley 10–0–43–4.

Nottinghamshire

P. R. Pollard c Athey b Stephenson	3	P. Johnson not out	35
M. A. Crawley c Hemmings b Jarvis	1	L-b 8, w 13, n-b 4	25
J. C. Adams b Jarvis	86		—
*R. T. Robinson not out	91	1/4 2/13 3/176 (3 wkts, 49.2 overs)	241

C. C. Lewis, K. P. Evans, †W. M. Noon, G. W. Mike, R. A. Pick and J. A. Afford did not bat.

Bowling: Jarvis 9–0–34–2; Stephenson 11–0–41–1; Giddins 9.2–0–59–0; Hemmings 11–0–46–0; Lenham 9–0–53–0.

Umpires: B. Dudleston and K. J. Lyons.

SURREY v GLAMORGAN

At The Oval, May 10. Surrey won by three wickets. Toss: Surrey.

Surrey achieved their sixth victory in a fortnight. It was a year less a day since their catastrophic collapse against Lancashire, chasing the same target, 237, and they did wobble from 202 for three to 234 for seven. But Smith kept his head and his wicket, seeing them home with two balls to spare. Morris made Glamorgan's most significant contribution, with 55, but lacked support until Gibson hit a rapid 37, with five fours and a six into the pavilion. In reply, Thorpe and Darren Bicknell put on 104 and there was a vicious 25-ball blast from Brown before Smith's cool finish. Croft was the pick of the bowlers on both sides, with 11 overs of nagging off-spin.

Gold Award: D. J. Bicknell.

Glamorgan

S. P. James lbw b M. P. Bicknell...... 12
*H. Morris c Smith b Benjamin....... 55
A. Dale c Ward b Benjamin.......... 23
M. P. Maynard c Thorpe b Smith..... 19
P. A. Cottey c Thorpe b Smith....... 43
O. D. Gibson b Benjamin............ 37
R. D. B. Croft not out............... 23
R. P. Lefebvre not out.............. 6
B 1, l-b 5, w 8, n-b 4........ 18

1/15 2/61 3/91 4/158 5/170 6/216 (6 wkts, 55 overs) 236

†C. P. Metson, S. L. Watkin and S. R. Barwick did not bat.

Bowling: Cuffy 8–0–35–0; M. P. Bicknell 11–2–37–1; Benjamin 11–2–52–3; Butcher 9–0–42–0; Hollioake 5–0–26–0; Smith 11–2–38–2.

Surrey

D. J. Bicknell b Gibson............. 90
*A. J. Stewart run out............... 2
G. P. Thorpe c Morris b Croft........ 51
D. M. Ward st Metson b Croft....... 13
†A. D. Brown b Watkin.............. 38
A. J. Hollioake c Metson b Gibson.... 6
A. W. Smith not out................ 15
M. A. Butcher lbw b Lefebvre........ 5
M. P. Bicknell not out............... 2
L-b 9, w 3, n-b 6............ 18

1/4 2/108 3/142 4/202 5/212 6/215 7/234 (7 wkts, 54.4 overs) 240

J. E. Benjamin and C. E. Cuffy did not bat.

Bowling: Watkin 10–2–45–1; Lefebvre 11–0–43–1; Barwick 9–1–24–0; Gibson 8.4–0–50–2; Croft 11–2–29–2; Dale 5–0–40–0.

Umpires: G. I. Burgess and B. Leadbeater.

QUARTER-FINALS

DERBYSHIRE v WORCESTERSHIRE

At Derby, May 24. Worcestershire won by nine wickets. Toss: Worcestershire.

Although the match did not start until 2 p.m., it was easily finished in a day as Worcestershire passed Derbyshire's feeble 98 in just 18.2 overs. Still missing Barnett, who feared for his knee on the wet outfield, the title-holders batted badly and succumbed four runs below their previous low in the competition, 102 against Yorkshire in 1975. Worcestershire's bowling was consistently accurate: Moody conceded only 14 runs in 11 overs as he removed the top three batsmen. All but one of the rest were swept away in five consecutive overs from Lampitt, whose six for 26 represented his best return in any match for Worcestershire. He took the last five while just seven runs were added. Curtis and Hick cruised to victory, helped by 34 extras.

Gold Award: S. R. Lampitt.

Derbyshire

P. D. Bowler b Moody	15	†K. M. Krikken b Lampitt	0
T. J. G. O'Gorman c Radford b Moody	2	A. E. Warner not out	1
C. J. Adams b Moody	9	D. E. Malcolm c Rhodes b Lampitt	2
*M. Azharuddin lbw b Radford	5	B 2, l-b 2, w 4, n-b 4	12
C. M. Wells b Lampitt	25		—
P. A. J. DeFreitas c Rhodes b Lampitt	16	1/6 2/31 3/40 (44 overs)	98
D. G. Cork lbw b Lampitt	7	4/40 5/75 6/91	
F. A. Griffith b Lampitt	4	7/92 8/95 9/96	

Bowling: Newport 8–2–20–0; Moody 11–5–14–3; Radford 8–4–11–1; Lampitt 11–3–26–6; Leatherdale 2–0–10–0; Illingworth 4–1–13–0.

Worcestershire

*T. S. Curtis not out	25
D. B. D'Oliveira c and b DeFreitas	1
G. A. Hick not out	40
B 1, l-b 8, w 7, n-b 18	34
	—
1/7 (1 wkt, 18.2 overs)	100

T. M. Moody, C. M. Tolley, D. A. Leatherdale, †S. J. Rhodes, S. R. Lampitt, R. K. Illingworth, P. J. Newport and N. V. Radford did not bat.

Bowling: DeFreitas 4–0–29–1; Malcolm 4–1–14–0; Warner 5–0–24–0; Cork 5–0–19–0; Griffith 0.2–0–5–0.

Umpires: N. T. Plews and P. Willey.

HAMPSHIRE v ESSEX

At Southampton, May 24, 25. Hampshire won by nine wickets. Toss: Hampshire.

In a lottery of 19 overs a side, the toss assumed even greater importance than usual. The weather had claimed the first day and there were fears that a bowl-out would be necessary on the second. But the umpires decided to make a start at 4.25 p.m. and Nicholas took delight in inviting Essex to bat. Their total of 124 for three was respectable, but unlikely to trouble Hampshire, with Smith in dominant mood. He and Nicholas hurried home, sharing an unbroken stand of 114 in 13 overs. Smith hit 73 from 55 balls; one of his two sixes symbolically struck the pavilion bell to toll the visitors' exit.

Gold Award: R. A. Smith.

Essex

*G. A. Gooch c Smith b Udal	21	†M. A. Garnham not out	14
J. P. Stephenson b Cowans	47	B 1, l-b 3, w 2	6
P. J. Prichard b Udal	6		—
N. Hussain not out	30	1/44 2/53 3/89 (3 wkts, 19 overs)	124

N. V. Knight, N. Shahid, R. C. Irani, M. S. Kasprowicz, M. C. Ilott and P. M. Such did not bat.

Bowling: Benjamin 4–0–20–0; Cowans 4–0–26–1; James 1–0–9–0; Connor 4–0–28–0; Udal 4–0–17–2; Jean-Jacques 2–0–20–0.

Hampshire

R. A. Smith not out	73
V. P. Terry c and b Such	2
*M. C. J. Nicholas not out	46
L-b 2, w 4	6
	—
1/13 (1 wkt, 17.2 overs)	127

R. M. F. Cox, K. D. James, †A. N. Aymes, W. K. M. Benjamin, S. D. Udal, M. Jean-Jacques, C. A. Connor and N. G. Cowans did not bat.

Bowling: Ilott 4–0–17–0; Kasprowicz 4–0–24–0; Such 4–0–29–1; Stephenson 2.2–0–27–0; Irani 3–0–28–0.

Umpires: J. D. Bond and R. Julian.

NOTTINGHAMSHIRE v SURREY

At Nottingham, May 24, 25. Surrey won by six wickets. Toss: Surrey.

Nottinghamshire were defending an unbeaten record in 1994 but their total of 275 was not quite enough, especially with Lewis sidelined by flu. When Surrey finally began their reply, on the second day, Darren Bicknell's three-hour 109 paved the route to victory. But it was Ward who gave the run-chase its vital impetus, blasting six sixes and three fours for 73 in 57 balls, before Brown raced past the target with two sixes and a four in succession. A stylish hundred by Pollard, from 114 deliveries, had left Nottinghamshire handsomely placed and Johnson took up the charge with a 20-ball 26. But rain halted play at 195 for three in the 40th over. When it resumed 100 minutes later, Johnson was bowled and Nottinghamshire slipped to 244 for eight.

Gold Award: D. M. Ward.

Close of play: Nottinghamshire 275-8 (55 overs).

Nottinghamshire

P. R. Pollard c Ward b Butcher 104
M. A. Crawley b Smith 37
J. C. Adams lbw b Hollioake 7
P. Johnson b M. P. Bicknell 26
*R. T. Robinson c Butcher b Hollioake. 15
G. F. Archer run out 9
†W. M. Noon lbw b Benjamin 9
K. P. Evans lbw b Hollioake 8
G. W. Mike not out 15
R. A. Pick not out 16
B 1, l-b 4, w 14, n-b 10 29

1/130 2/145 3/192 4/196 5/210 6/229 7/233 8/244 (8 wkts, 55 overs) 275

J. A. Afford did not bat.

Bowling: M. P. Bicknell 11–2–31–1; Cuffy 8–1–53–0; Benjamin 11–2–44–1; Butcher 11–0–71–1; Hollioake 11–0–48–3; Smith 3–0–23–1.

Surrey

D. J. Bicknell b Afford 109
*†A. J. Stewart c Noon b Evans 11
G. P. Thorpe c Evans b Mike 24
D. M. Ward b Crawley 73
A. D. Brown not out 26
A. J. Hollioake not out 5
B 2, l-b 14, w 10, n-b 4 30

1/35 2/125 3/237 4/249 (4 wkts, 51.4 overs) 278

A. W. Smith, M. A. Butcher, M. P. Bicknell, J. E. Benjamin and C. E. Cuffy did not bat.

Bowling: Pick 9–0–39–0; Evans 8–2–50–1; Crawley 11–3–45–1; Mike 10–0–50–1; Afford 10.4–0–57–1; Adams 3–0–21–0.

Umpires: D. R. Shepherd and R. A. White.

WARWICKSHIRE v KENT

At Birmingham, May 24, 25. Warwickshire won 5-4 in a bowling contest, after the match was abandoned.

Warwickshire reached the semi-finals, but Kent complained formally to the TCCB about Edgbaston's failure to protect the pitch. Play was washed out on both days available, despite the "Brumbrella", the automated tarpaulin capable of covering the entire ground. Warwickshire chose not to use it, even though the weather forecast was dire, in an attempt to counteract the fungus fuserium, which prevents grass growth. The rain penetrated less comprehensive covers. Contrary to practice, spectators were offered refunds when the first day was abandoned. The pitch was still unfit next morning but the players rejected the idea of a move to Derby. Instead, a bowl-out was held in the indoor cricket school, five players from each side bowling two balls at a set of stumps. This aroused more controversy, as the public were kept out; the press were eventually admitted on the sponsors' insistence. Warwickshire's nominees scored one hit each; so did Kent's, until their last bowler, Llong, missed twice.

The bowlers in the deciding contest were: Warwickshire – T. A. Munton, G. C. Small, P. A. Smith, D. A. Reeve and R. P. Davis; Kent – C. L. Hooper, M. A. Ealham, D. J. Spencer, M. M. Patel and N. J. Llong.

SEMI-FINALS

SURREY v WARWICKSHIRE

At The Oval, June 7. Warwickshire won by four wickets. Toss: Warwickshire.

Spectators hurried to The Oval to see Lara, who had reached his world record 501 the previous day. But he did not bat until half past five, after leaving the field towards the end of Surrey's innings to sleep off his exhaustion. Lara still scored 70 in 73 balls, doubling his aggregate in his five previous limited-overs innings for Warwickshire. He added 93 in 20 overs with Reeve before Hollioake had the honour of knocking back his middle stump. Reeve took Warwickshire past a target of 268 and pipped Lara to the Gold Award for his captaincy, his unbeaten 46 and three wickets. Thorpe and Ward added 118 runs for Surrey's third wicket and Pigott picked up three useful wickets, but they could not save Surrey from their first one-day defeat of the season.

Gold Award: D. A. Reeve.

Surrey

D. J. Bicknell c and b Reeve	39
*†A. J. Stewart c Burns b Twose	24
G. P. Thorpe c and b N. M. K. Smith	87
D. M. Ward b N. M. K. Smith	61
A. D. Brown c Penney b N. M. K. Smith	8
A. J. Hollioake lbw b Reeve	3
M. A. Butcher c Munton b Reeve	4
A. C. S. Pigott not out	13
J. Boiling not out	9
L-b 11, w 6, n-b 2	19
1/59 2/92 3/210 4/232 5/236 6/242 7/254 (7 wkts, 55 overs)	267

J. E. Benjamin and C. E. Cuffy did not bat.

Bowling: Small 11–2–38–0; Munton 11–2–36–0; Reeve 11–0–48–3; Twose 5–0–33–1; N. M. K. Smith 8–0–54–3; P. A. Smith 9–0–47–0.

Warwickshire

D. P. Ostler b Pigott	44
†M. Burns c Thorpe b Benjamin	18
R. G. Twose c Stewart b Pigott	46
P. A. Smith lbw b Pigott	8
Asif Din c Cuffy b Boiling	19
B. C. Lara b Hollioake	70
*D. A. Reeve not out	46
T. L. Penney not out	12
L-b 3, n-b 4	7
1/28 2/106 3/117 4/120 5/158 6/251 (6 wkts, 54.1 overs)	270

N. M. K. Smith, G. C. Small and T. A. Munton did not bat.

Bowling: Cuffy 11–0–66–0; Benjamin 11–0–41–1; Butcher 3.1–0–26–0; Pigott 11–0–43–3; Hollioake 7–0–49–1; Boiling 11–1–42–1.

Umpires: D. J. Constant and B. Dudleston.

WORCESTERSHIRE v HAMPSHIRE

At Worcester, June 7, 8. Worcestershire won by three wickets. Toss: Worcestershire.

Worcestershire won through to their third Lord's final in five years, thanks to a frenetic stand of 77 in nine overs between Haynes and Leatherdale. They hit 43 in three successive overs from Udal, Connor and Benjamin. Rain and bad light halted play the previous evening, when Worcestershire required 127 from 22 overs with seven wickets left, and Hampshire's hopes rose when Connor trapped Moody leg-before. But Haynes struck 65 off 62 balls, reaching his maiden one-day fifty with successive boundaries off Udal. Hampshire's innings was interrupted for half an hour on the first morning, when a spectator collapsed and, due to the large crowd, had to be given medical attention on the field. Smith then scored his fourth century in the Benson and Hedges Cup. With Keech and Benjamin cutting loose, their final ten overs produced 87 runs. In the disappointment of defeat, the Hampshire captain Nicholas was close to tears.

Gold Award: G. R. Haynes.

Close of play: Worcestershire 118-3 (33 overs) (T. M. Moody 47*, G. R. Haynes 11*).

Hampshire

V. P. Terry c Rhodes b Newport	6	†A. N. Aymes not out	4
T. C. Middleton c Hick b Moody	17	K. D. James not out	5
R. A. Smith run out	108	L-b 7, w 3, n-b 2	12
*M. C. J. Nicholas c Curtis b Newport	37		
M. Keech c Haynes b Lampitt	37	1/21 2/53 3/122 (6 wkts, 55 overs)	244
W. K. M. Benjamin c Moody b Radford	18	4/210 5/218 6/237	

S. D. Udal, C. A. Connor and N. G. Cowans did not bat.

Bowling: Newport 11–2–35–2; Moody 11–2–17–1; Illingworth 11–0–42–0; Hick 2–0–11–0; Lampitt 11–0–67–1; Radford 7–0–39–1; Haynes 2–0–26–0.

Worcestershire

*T. S. Curtis c Middleton b Cowans	5	S. R. Lampitt not out	6
D. B. D'Oliveira c Aymes b Cowans	10	R. K. Illingworth not out	0
G. A. Hick run out	40	L-b 11, w 3, n-b 7	21
T. M. Moody lbw b Connor	56		
G. R. Haynes c Terry b Cowans	65	1/7 2/22 3/96 (7 wkts, 52.4 overs)	245
D. A. Leatherdale c Keech b Cowans	30	4/141 5/218	
†S. J. Rhodes c Nicholas b Benjamin	12	6/226 7/244	

P. J. Newport and N. V. Radford did not bat.

Bowling: Benjamin 10.4–0–55–1; Cowans 11–2–36–4; Connor 10–1–42–1; James 11–0–54–0; Udal 10–0–47–0.

Umpires: J. C. Balderstone and M. J. Kitchen.

FINAL

WARWICKSHIRE v WORCESTERSHIRE

At Lord's, July 9. Warwickshire won by six wickets. Toss: Warwickshire.

The Al Fresco Marching Jazz Band, making its debut at Lord's, provided perhaps the brightest moments of a mundane cup final. Despite a capacity 29,000 crowd and a blissful summer's day, Worcestershire failed to enjoy it. They were outgunned, outclassed and sunk virtually without trace, and many of their supporters were fleeing back up the M40 before the end. All records of this contest could be swept away from New Road in the next Severn flood.

They did have the worst of the conditions, losing the toss and batting first in the morning haze, on a pitch which had not fully dried out. The ball swung much more than it seamed and there was variation in the bounce, especially at the Pavilion end. That said, Small and Munton were a high-class double act, commanding the first 17 overs. It was English fast-medium bowling on an English morning and enabled Warwickshire to put a stranglehold on the game in which their opponents barely wriggled. Eight runs off their first over from Small, who bowled his 11 straight through because of a groin strain, were the peak of Worcestershire's effort.

Seymour inexplicably played across Munton's line in the second over and when Curtis fell to a fine catch by Piper, they were 28 for two from 11 overs. Fire was needed from Hick and Moody and when Munton did offer probably his only half-volley, Hick smashed it with relief for four. Yet Munton had the better of the duel: Hick managed only 11 runs off 46 deliveries. Worcestershire were no happier when Reeve called up his second-line attack. Twose, the Smiths and Reeve himself all seemed equally capable of penetrating a jittery order. While the batsmen's calling became almost farcical, Warwickshire's brimming confidence was exemplified by Penney's run-out of Moody, with a direct throw from square.

By 3.25 p.m. Warwickshire were embarking on the near-formality of scoring 171. Although Lara, whose presence had caused a box-office stampede, failed after some extravagant strokes, the middle order was more than adequate. Paul Smith seized the Gold Award by adding an unbeaten run-a-ball 42 to his three wickets. Warwickshire won their first Benson and Hedges Cup with more than ten overs to spare. As in the NatWest final ten months earlier, Reeve was there at the death, confirming that as a tactician, motivator and bits-and-pieces cricketer he is currently *sans pareil*. – Derek Hodgson.

Gold Award: P. A. Smith. *Attendance:* 24,910; *receipts* £674,803.

Worcestershire

*T. S. Curtis c Piper b Small	13	N. V. Radford not out	23
A. C. H. Seymour b Munton	3	P. J. Newport not out	1
G. A. Hick lbw b P. A. Smith	27	L-b 2, w 5, n-b 4	11
T. M. Moody run out	47		—
G. R. Haynes c Piper b N. M. K. Smith	22	1/10 (2) 2/28 (1) (9 wkts, 55 overs)	170
D. A. Leatherdale c Ostler b P. A. Smith	4	3/55 (3) 4/100 (5)	
†S. J. Rhodes lbw b Twose	0	5/124 (6) 6/124 (7)	
S. R. Lampitt c Penney b P. A. Smith	1	7/125 (8) 8/126 (4)	
R. K. Illingworth lbw b Reeve	18	9/168 (9)	

Bowling: Small 11–4–26–1; Munton 11–3–29–1; P. A. Smith 11–1–34–3; Reeve 9–1–38–1; N. M. K. Smith 5–0–16–1; Twose 8–1–25–1.

Warwickshire

D. P. Ostler run out	55	*D. A. Reeve not out	9
R. G. Twose run out	37	L-b 1, w 5	6
B. C. Lara c Hick b Newport	8		—
P. A. Smith not out	42	1/91 (1) 2/98 (2) (4 wkts, 44.2 overs)	172
Asif Din c Rhodes b Moody	15	3/103 (3) 4/147 (5)	

T. L. Penney, †K. J. Piper, N. M. K. Smith, G. C. Small and T. A. Munton did not bat.

Bowling: Moody 11–2–31–1; Newport 8–0–29–1; Lampitt 9.2–1–38–0; Illingworth 6–0–22–0; Radford 8–0–39–0; Hick 2–0–12–0.

Umpires: H. D. Bird and K. E. Palmer.

BENSON AND HEDGES CUP RECORDS

Batting

Highest individual scores: 198*, G. A. Gooch, Essex v Sussex, Hove, 1982; 177, S. J. Cook, Somerset v Sussex, Hove, 1990; 173*, C. G. Greenidge, Hampshire v Minor Counties (South), Amersham, 1973; 167*, A. J. Stewart, Surrey v Somerset, The Oval, 1994; 158*, B. F. Davison, Leicestershire v Warwickshire, Coventry, 1972; 155*, M. D. Crowe, Somerset v Hampshire, Southampton, 1987; 155*, R. A. Smith, Hampshire v Glamorgan, Southampton, 1989; 154*, M. J. Procter, Gloucestershire v Somerset, Taunton, 1972; 154*, C. L. Smith, Hampshire v Combined Universities, Southampton, 1990. *In the final:* 132*, I. V. A. Richards, Somerset v Surrey, 1981. (237 hundreds have been scored in the competition. The most hundreds in one season is 24 in 1991.)

Most runs: 4,607, G. A. Gooch; 2,761, C. J. Tavaré; 2,663, D. W. Randall; 2,578, M. W. Gatting; 2,557, A. J. Lamb.

Fastest hundred: M. A. Nash in 62 minutes, Glamorgan v Hampshire at Swansea, 1976.

Most hundreds: 12, G. A. Gooch; 6, W. Larkins; 5, C. G. Greenidge, A. J. Lamb and N. R. Taylor.

Highest totals: 388 for seven, Essex v Scotland, Chelmsford, 1992; 366 for four, Derbyshire v Combined Universities, Oxford, 1991; 350 for three, Essex v Oxford & Cambridge Univs, Chelmsford, 1979; 333 for four, Essex v Oxford & Cambridge Univs, Chelmsford, 1985; 331 for five, Surrey v Hampshire, The Oval, 1990; 330 for four, Lancashire v Sussex, Manchester, 1991; 327 for four, Leicestershire v Warwickshire, Coventry, 1972; 327 for two, Essex v Sussex, Hove, 1982; 325 for five, Middlesex v Leicestershire, Leicester, 1992; 321 for one, Hampshire v Minor Counties (South), Amersham, 1973; 321 for five, Somerset v Sussex, Hove, 1990. *In the final:* 290 for six, Essex v Surrey, 1979.

Highest total by a side batting second and winning: 291 for five (53.5 overs), Warwickshire v Lancashire (288 for nine), Manchester, 1981. *In the final:* 244 for six (55 overs), Yorkshire v Northamptonshire (244 for seven), 1987; 244 for seven (55 overs), Nottinghamshire v Essex (243 for seven), 1989.

Highest total by a side batting second and losing: 303 for seven (55 overs), Derbyshire v Somerset (310 for three), Taunton, 1990. *In the final:* 255 (51.4 overs), Surrey v Essex (290 for six), 1979.

Highest match aggregates: 613 for ten wickets, Somerset (310 for three) v Derbyshire (303 for seven), Taunton, 1990; 602 runs for 14 wickets, Essex (307 for four) v Warwickshire (295), Birmingham, 1991; 601 runs for 13 wickets, Somerset (307 for six) v Gloucestershire (294 for seven), Taunton, 1982; 600 runs for 16 wickets, Derbyshire (300 for six) v Northamptonshire (300), Derby, 1987.

Lowest totals: 50 in 27.2 overs, Hampshire v Yorkshire, Leeds, 1991; 56 in 26.2 overs, Leicestershire v Minor Counties, Wellington, 1982; 59 in 34 overs, Oxford & Cambridge Univs v Glamorgan, Cambridge, 1983; 61 in 26 overs, Sussex v Middlesex, Hove, 1978; 61 in 25.3 overs, Essex v Lancashire, Chelmsford, 1992; 62 in 26.5 overs, Gloucestershire v Hampshire, Bristol, 1975. *In the final:* 117 in 46.3 overs, Derbyshire v Hampshire, 1988.

Shortest completed innings: 21.4 overs (156), Surrey v Sussex, Hove, 1988.

Record partnership for each wicket

252	for 1st	V. P. Terry and C. L. Smith, Hampshire v Combined Universities at Southampton	1990
285*	for 2nd	C. G. Greenidge and D. R. Turner, Hampshire v Minor Counties (South) at Amersham	1973
269*	for 3rd	P. M. Roebuck and M. D. Crowe, Somerset v Hampshire at Southampton	1987
184*	for 4th	D. Lloyd and B. W. Reidy, Lancashire v Derbyshire at Chesterfield.	1980
160	for 5th	A. J. Lamb and D. J. Capel, Northamptonshire v Leicestershire at Northampton	1986
121	for 6th	P. A. Neale and S. J. Rhodes, Worcestershire v Yorkshire at Worcester	1988
149*	for 7th	J. D. Love and C. M. Old, Yorkshire v Scotland at Bradford	1981
109	for 8th	R. E. East and N. Smith, Essex v Northamptonshire at Chelmsford.	1977
83	for 9th	P. G. Newman and M. A. Holding, Derbyshire v Nottinghamshire at Nottingham	1985
80*	for 10th	D. L. Bairstow and M. Johnson, Yorkshire v Derbyshire at Derby	1981

Bowling

Most wickets: 147, J. K. Lever; 132, I. T. Botham.

Best bowling: seven for 12, W. W. Daniel, Middlesex v Minor Counties (East), Ipswich, 1978; seven for 22, J. R. Thomson, Middlesex v Hampshire, Lord's, 1981; seven for 32, R. G. D. Willis, Warwickshire v Yorkshire, Birmingham, 1981. *In the final:* five for 13, S. T. Jefferies, Hampshire v Derbyshire, 1988.

Hat-tricks (10): G. D. McKenzie, Leicestershire v Worcestershire, Worcester, 1972; K. Higgs, Leicestershire v Surrey in the final, Lord's, 1974; A. A. Jones, Middlesex v Essex, Lord's, 1977; M. J. Procter, Gloucestershire v Hampshire, Southampton, 1977; W. Larkins, Northamptonshire v Oxford & Cambridge Univs, Northampton, 1980; E. A. Moseley, Glamorgan v Kent, Cardiff, 1981; G. C. Small, Warwickshire v Leicestershire, Leicester, 1984; N. A. Mallender, Somerset v Combined Universities, Taunton, 1987; W. K. M. Benjamin, Leicestershire v Nottinghamshire, Leicester, 1987; A. R. C. Fraser, Middlesex v Sussex, Lord's, 1988.

Wicket-keeping and Fielding

Most dismissals: 122 (117 ct, 5 st), D. L. Bairstow.

Most dismissals in an innings: 8 (all ct), D. J. S. Taylor, Somerset v Oxford & Cambridge Univs, Taunton, 1982.

Most catches by a fielder: 62, G. A. Gooch; 54, C. J. Tavaré; 53, I. T. Botham.

Most catches by a fielder in an innings: 5, V. J. Marks, Oxford & Cambridge Univs v Kent, Oxford, 1976.

Results

Largest victories in runs: Essex by 272 runs v Scotland, Chelmsford, 1992, and by 214 runs v Oxford & Cambridge Univs, Chelmsford, 1979; Derbyshire by 206 runs v Combined Universities, Oxford, 1991; Yorkshire by 189 runs v Hampshire, Leeds, 1991; Sussex by 186 runs v Cambridge University, Hove, 1974.

Victories by ten wickets (16): By Derbyshire, Essex (twice), Glamorgan, Hampshire, Kent, Lancashire, Leicestershire (twice), Middlesex, Northamptonshire, Somerset, Warwickshire, Worcestershire, Yorkshire (twice).

Gold Awards

Most awards: 21, G. A. Gooch; 11, M. W. Gatting, T. E. Jesty and B. Wood.

WINNERS 1972-94

1972 LEICESTERSHIRE beat Yorkshire by five wickets.
1973 KENT beat Worcestershire by 39 runs.
1974 SURREY beat Leicestershire by 27 runs.
1975 LEICESTERSHIRE beat Middlesex by five wickets.
1976 KENT beat Worcestershire by 43 runs.
1977 GLOUCESTERSHIRE beat Kent by 64 runs.
1978 KENT beat Derbyshire by six wickets.
1979 ESSEX beat Surrey by 35 runs.
1980 NORTHAMPTONSHIRE beat Essex by six runs.
1981 SOMERSET beat Surrey by seven wickets.
1982 SOMERSET beat Nottinghamshire by nine wickets.
1983 MIDDLESEX beat Essex by four runs.
1984 LANCASHIRE beat Warwickshire by six wickets.
1985 LEICESTERSHIRE beat Essex by five wickets.
1986 MIDDLESEX beat Kent by two runs.
1987 YORKSHIRE beat Northamptonshire, having taken more wickets with the scores tied.
1988 HAMPSHIRE beat Derbyshire by seven wickets.
1989 NOTTINGHAMSHIRE beat Essex by three wickets.
1990 LANCASHIRE beat Worcestershire by 69 runs.
1991 WORCESTERSHIRE beat Lancashire by 65 runs.
1992 HAMPSHIRE beat Kent by 41 runs.
1993 DERBYSHIRE beat Lancashire by six runs.
1994 WARWICKSHIRE beat Worcestershire by six wickets.

WINS BY NON-CHAMPIONSHIP TEAMS

1973 OXFORD beat Northamptonshire at Northampton by two wickets.
1975 { OXFORD & CAMBRIDGE beat Worcestershire at Cambridge by 66 runs.
OXFORD & CAMBRIDGE beat Northamptonshire at Oxford by three wickets.
1976 OXFORD & CAMBRIDGE beat Yorkshire at Barnsley by seven wickets.
1980 MINOR COUNTIES beat Gloucestershire at Chippenham by three runs.
1981 MINOR COUNTIES beat Hampshire at Southampton by three runs.
1982 MINOR COUNTIES beat Leicestershire at Wellington by 131 runs.
1984 OXFORD & CAMBRIDGE beat Gloucestershire at Bristol by 27 runs.
1986 SCOTLAND beat Lancashire at Perth by three runs.
1987 MINOR COUNTIES beat Glamorgan at Oxford (Christ Church) by seven wickets.
1989 { COMBINED UNIVERSITIES beat Surrey at Cambridge by nine runs.
COMBINED UNIVERSITIES beat Worcestershire at Worcester by five wickets.
1990 { COMBINED UNIVERSITIES beat Yorkshire at Leeds by two wickets.
SCOTLAND beat Northamptonshire at Northampton by two runs.
1992 MINOR COUNTIES beat Sussex at Marlow by 19 runs.

TEAM RECORDS 1972-94

	Rounds reached				*Matches*			
	W	*F*	*SF*	*QF*	*P*	*W*	*L*	*NR*
Derbyshire	1	3	4	9	103	55	41	7
Durham	0	0	0	0	7	3	4	0
Essex	1	5	8	14	114	72	41	1
Glamorgan	0	0	1	7	95	40	51	4
Gloucestershire	1	1	2	5	95	44	48	3
Hampshire	2	2	5	12	106	57	45	4
Kent	3	6	11	15	118	74	42	2
Lancashire	2	4	8	14	113	68	39	6
Leicestershire	3	4	6	9	107	60	41	6
Middlesex	2	3	5	13	109	58	43	8
Northamptonshire	1	2	4	9	101	46	47	8
Nottinghamshire	1	2	5	12	106	63	38	5
Somerset	2	2	7	11	106	58	46	2
Surrey	1	3	7	10	108	58	46	4
Sussex	0	0	1	9	98	49	48	1
Warwickshire	1	2	6	12	106	59	42	5
Worcestershire	1	5	7	14	112	59	49	4
Yorkshire	1	2	5	8	101	52	43	6
Cambridge University	0	0	0	0	8	0	8	0
Oxford University	0	0	0	0	4	1	3	0
Oxford & Cambridge Universities	0	0	0	0	48	4	42	2
Combined Universities	0	0	0	1	27	3	23	1
Minor Counties	0	0	0	0	55	5	47	3
Minor Counties (North)	0	0	0	0	20	0	20	0
Minor Counties (South)	0	0	0	0	20	0	19	1
Minor Counties (East)	0	0	0	0	12	0	12	0
Minor Counties (West)	0	0	0	0	12	0	12	0
Scotland	0	0	0	0	54	2	49	3
Ireland	0	0	0	0	1	0	1	0

Middlesex beat Gloucestershire on the toss of a coin in their quarter-final in 1983. Derbyshire, Kent, Somerset and Warwickshire totals each include a bowling contest; Derbyshire beat Somerset and Warwickshire beat Kent when their quarter-finals, in 1993 and 1994 respectively, were abandoned.

INTERNATIONAL FLOODLIT SIXES

A floodlit six-a-side competition, involving some of the best-known international players of the past two decades, ended in farce and confusion after just one of the scheduled two days when the players' demand for immediate cash payment was not met.

A crowd estimated at "a few dozen" attended the opening day, at The Oval on September 21, to watch players such as Derek Underwood and Jeff Thomson operating a form of the game based on the successful competition in Hong Kong. *The Times* headlined its report "Rotten enterprise worthy of contempt".

[*David Munden*

Warwickshire's captain Dermot Reeve and vice-captain Tim Munton with the club's three trophies: (left to right) AXA Equity and Law League, Benson and Hedges Cup, Britannic Assurance County Championship.

AXA EQUITY & LAW LEAGUE, 1994

Warwickshire completed the third leg of their treble of domestic competitions in 1994 when they took the Sunday League for the second time, following their success in 1980.

They won the first six matches, taking a share of the lead after the fourth win on June 5, and were never again headed. They did have an uncomfortable moment after their shock defeat against Yorkshire at Scarborough on August 21, when Worcestershire ranged alongside them with a game in hand. However, Yorkshire evened things out by winning at Worcester the following week, and Warwickshire won their last three games to take the title.

Worcestershire's attack was especially well-suited to Sunday cricket, and their Australian, Tom Moody, was easily the League's most economical bowler. Kent, runners-up behind Glamorgan in 1993, were also in contention until the final week, but lost to Surrey and finished third. Before that, they had won nine consecutive matches and built largely on a sequence of six consecutive half-centuries from their West Indian all-rounder Carl Hooper, who was the leading scorer in the League for the second year running. Lancashire reverted to their old traditions of strength on Sunday, and were joint leaders with Warwickshire until mid-July, but were too inconsistent to press strongly.

Continued overleaf

AXA EQUITY & LAW LEAGUE

	M	*W*	*L*	*T*	*NR*	*Pts*	*Run-Rate*
1 – Warwickshire (10)	17	13	3	0	1	54	83.47
2 – Worcestershire (16)	17	12	4	0	1	50	77.78
3 – Kent (2)	17	12	5	0	0	48	90.31
4 – Lancashire (6)	17	11	5	0	1	46	84.66
5 – Yorkshire (9)	17	10	6	0	1	42	78.83
6 – Surrey (3)	17	9	5	0	3	42	97.99
7 – Glamorgan (1)	17	9	6	1	1	40	76.60
8 – Derbyshire (11)	17	8	7	0	2	36	86.27
9 – Durham (7)	17	6	7	1	3	32	85.89
10 – Leicestershire (14)	17	7	9	0	1	30	82.86
11 – Nottinghamshire (17)	17	6	8	0	3	30	85.91
12 – Hampshire (15)	17	7	10	0	0	28	78.14
13 – Northamptonshire (5)	17	6	9	1	1	28	81.30
14 – Middlesex (8)	17	6	10	0	1	26	80.81
15 – Sussex (4)	17	5	11	0	1	22	77.78
16 – Somerset (18)	17	5	12	0	0	20	85.09
17 – Essex (12)	17	4	11	1	1	20	73.44
18 – Gloucestershire (13)	17	4	12	0	1	18	78.70

1993 positions are shown in brackets.

When two or more counties finish with an equal number of points, the positions are decided by a) most wins, b) runs per 100 balls.

No play was possible in the following five matches: May 15 – Nottinghamshire v Durham at Nottingham; May 22 – Derbyshire v Worcestershire at Derby, Durham v Gloucestershire at Gateshead Fell, Nottinghamshire v Sussex at Nottingham, Yorkshire v Essex at Leeds.

As in the Championship, Surrey looked unbeatable at first, but lost four games out of five between mid-June and mid-July. Then they recovered to finish sixth, behind Yorkshire – equal on points but with fewer wins. Surrey recorded the highest run-rate of any county, and had an amazing win at Scarborough when they rewrote the League's records by scoring a staggering 375 for four in their 40 overs. Glamorgan, the 1993 champions, played far better cricket on Sundays than they did in the week, but this time were unable to overcome an indifferent start and finished seventh.

Somerset had another bad year in this competition, but managed to scramble off the bottom and climbed ahead of Essex, who finished in their lowest position ever, 17th, after going two months in mid-season without a win. Gloucestershire were outright bottom for the fourth time, but reported much-improved gates, mainly due to a number of home matches against nearby counties on fine Sundays.

The competition reverted to its old 40-overs format in 1994, after one unpopular year of 50-overs cricket, though the coloured clothing continued. The kit suppliers found it difficult to cope with the number of lesser-known players who turned out in the League in mid-season, and there were a number of cases of players baffling spectators by appearing with one of their club-mates' names emblazoned across their backs.

Leading run-scorers: C. L. Hooper 773 (£3,000 individual award), D. Byas 702 (£1,500); A. D. Brown 688; R. A. Smith 676; J. C. Adams 674; P. V. Simmons 660; A. P. Wells 618; M. W. Alleyne 588; D. M. Ward 581; M. R. Ramprakash 561.

Leading wicket-takers: C. A. Connor and N. M. K. Smith 26 (shared £4,500 individual award); P. J. Martin, P. J. Newport, A. Walker and V. J. Wells 25; R. P. Lefebvre and N. V. Radford 24; S. R. Lampitt 23.

Most economical bowlers (runs per over, minimum 100 overs)**:** T. M. Moody 3.04; G. J. Parsons 3.67; P. M. Such 3.72; R. P. Lefebvre 3.74; S. L. Watkin 3.75; M. A. Robinson 3.79; P. J. Newport 3.96; N. M. K. Smith 3.99.

Leading wicket-keepers: A. N. Aymes 26 (22 ct, 4 st) (£3,000 individual award); C. P. Metson 24 (19 ct, 5 st); K. M. Krikken 22 (all ct); S. J. Rhodes 21 (17 ct, 4 st); C. W. Scott 20 (16 ct, 4 st).

Leading fielders: M. W. Alleyne 14; D. A. Leatherdale 12; M. P. Maynard and D. M. Ward 10.

Prize money

£31,000 for winners: WARWICKSHIRE.
£15,500 for runners-up: WORCESTERSHIRE.
£7,750 for third place: KENT.
£3,875 for fourth place: LANCASHIRE.
£375 for the winners of each match, shared if tied or no result.

SUMMARY OF RESULTS, 1994

	Derbyshire	Durham	Essex	Glamorgan	Gloucestershire	Hampshire	Kent	Lancashire	Leicestershire	Middlesex	Northamptonshire	Nottinghamshire	Somerset	Surrey	Sussex	Warwickshire	Worcestershire	Yorkshire
Derbyshire	—	**W**	**L**	*L*	**W**	*W*	**L**	*L*	**W**	**W**	*W*	**L**	*W*	*L*	*W*	**N**	**N**	*L*
Durham	*L*	—	**W**	**L**	**N**	*W*	*L*	**L**	**N**	*W*	**T**	*N*	*W*	**L**	*W*	*L*	*L*	**W**
Essex	*W*	*L*	—	**T**	**W**	*L*	**L**	**W**	*L*	*L*	**L**	**L**	*L*	**L**	**W**	*L*	*L*	*N*
Glamorgan	**W**	*W*	*T*	—	*W*	*L*	**L**	**W**	**W**	*W*	*W*	*L*	**W**	**N**	*L*	*L*	**W**	**L**
Gloucestershire	*L*	*N*	*L*	**L**	—	*L*	**L**	*L*	**L**	*W*	**W**	*L*	**W**	**L**	**L**	**L**	*L*	**W**
Hampshire	**L**	**L**	**W**	**W**	**W**	—	*L*	*L*	*L*	**W**	**L**	**W**	*L*	**W**	*W*	*L*	*L*	*L*
Kent	*W*	**W**	*W*	*W*	*W*	**W**	—	**L**	*W*	**L**	*W*	**L**	**W**	*L*	**W**	*L*	**W**	**W**
Lancashire	**W**	*W*	*L*	*L*	**W**	**W**	*W*	—	**W**	**N**	*W*	*L*	**W**	**L**	*W*	*W*	**L**	*W*
Leicestershire	*L*	*N*	**W**	*L*	*W*	**W**	**L**	*L*	—	**W**	**L**	*W*	**W**	*W*	**L**	*L*	**L**	*L*
Middlesex	*L*	**L**	**W**	**L**	**L**	*L*	*W*	*N*	*L*	—	*W*	*W*	**W**	*L*	*L*	**L**	**W**	**L**
Northamptonshire	**L**	*T*	*W*	**L**	*L*	*W*	**L**	**L**	*W*	**L**	—	*W*	*W*	*N*	**W**	**L**	*L*	**L**
Nottinghamshire	*W*	**N**	*W*	**W**	**W**	*L*	*W*	**W**	**L**	**L**	**L**	—	*L*	**N**	**N**	*L*	*L*	*L*
Somerset	**L**	**L**	**W**	*L*	*L*	**W**	*L*	*L*	*L*	*L*	**L**	**W**	—	**W**	*L*	**L**	**L**	*W*
Surrey	**W**	*W*	*W*	*N*	*W*	*L*	**W**	*W*	**L**	**W**	**N**	*N*	*L*	—	**W**	**L**	**L**	*W*
Sussex	**L**	**L**	*L*	**W**	*W*	**L**	*L*	**L**	*W*	**W**	*L*	*N*	**W**	*L*	—	**L**	*L*	**L**
Warwickshire	*N*	**W**	**W**	**W**	*W*	**W**	**W**	**L**	**W**	*W*	*W*	**W**	*W*	*W*	*W*	—	**L**	*L*
Worcestershire	*N*	**W**	**W**	*L*	**W**	**W**	*L*	*W*	*W*	*L*	**W**	**W**	*W*	*W*	**W**	*W*	—	**L**
Yorkshire	**W**	*L*	**N**	*W*	*L*	**W**	*L*	**L**	**W**	*W*	*W*	**W**	**L**	**L**	*W*	**W**	*W*	—

Home games in bold, away games in italics. W = Won, L = Lost, T = Tied, N = No result.

DERBYSHIRE

At Southampton, May 8. DERBYSHIRE beat HAMPSHIRE by seven wickets.

At The Oval, May 15. DERBYSHIRE lost to SURREY by six wickets.

DERBYSHIRE v WORCESTERSHIRE

At Derby, May 22. No result (abandoned).

DERBYSHIRE v NOTTINGHAMSHIRE

At Ilkeston, May 29. Nottinghamshire won by seven wickets. Toss: Nottinghamshire.

A brilliant innings from Johnson, who hit three sixes and ten fours in his 90 off 64 balls, powered Nottinghamshire home with 26 deliveries remaining. Johnson and Adams added 115 in 17 overs, Adams ending the match with a six off Wells on to the roof of the press tent.

Derbyshire

*P. D. Bowler st Noon b Field-Buss	61	M. J. Vandrau b Mike	0
C. J. Adams c Noon b Pennett	16	†K. M. Krikken not out	3
M. Azharuddin lbw b Pick	52		
T. J. G. O'Gorman c Crawley b Field-Buss	8	B 3, l-b 7, w 16	26
P. A. J. DeFreitas c Pennett b Mike	33	1/28 2/125 3/157 (7 wkts, 40 overs)	227
C. M. Wells not out	16	4/157 5/202	
F. A. Griffith b Mike	12	6/224 7/224	

R. W. Sladdin and D. E. Malcolm did not bat.

Bowling: Pick 8–1–49–1; Pennett 8–0–24–1; Crawley 8–0–39–0; Mike 8–0–55–3; Field-Buss 8–0–50–2.

Nottinghamshire

P. R. Pollard c Krikken b DeFreitas	7	G. F. Archer not out	10
P. Johnson c O'Gorman b Griffith	90	L-b 12, w 2, n-b 13	27
J. C. Adams not out	72		
*R. T. Robinson c and b Wells	27	1/13 2/128 3/192 (3 wkts, 35.4 overs)	233

M. A. Crawley, D. B. Pennett, †W. M. Noon, M. G. Field-Buss, G. W. Mike and R. A. Pick did not bat.

Bowling: Malcolm 6–0–38–0; DeFreitas 7–0–28–1; Griffith 8–0–47–1; Wells 6.4–0–46–1; Vandrau 4–0–38–0; Sladdin 4–0–24–0.

Umpires: J. C. Balderstone and D. R. Shepherd.

DERBYSHIRE v LEICESTERSHIRE

At Derby, June 12. Derbyshire won by six wickets. Toss: Leicestershire.

Azharuddin took charge with Derbyshire still needing 50 off the last nine overs to pass Leicestershire's modest total. He scored 38 of the required runs in the next four overs to earn his side the points; his unbeaten 91 came from only 64 balls.

Leicestershire

P. V. Simmons b Wells	16	G. J. Parsons not out	14
*N. E. Briers c Adams b Vandrau	19	A. D. Mullally c Vandrau b Harris	1
J. J. Whitaker b DeFreitas	3	D. J. Millns not out	3
P. E. Robinson c and b Vandrau	19	L-b 5, w 2, n-b 2	9
B. F. Smith c Barnett b Griffith	36		
J. M. Dakin c Krikken b Vandrau	0	1/29 2/36 3/44 (9 wkts, 40 overs)	190
†P. A. Nixon c Bowler b Griffith	57	4/74 5/74 6/128	
P. N. Hepworth c DeFreitas b Harris	13	7/159 8/175 9/177	

Bowling: DeFreitas 8–1–28–1; Wells 4–1–19–1; Griffith 8–0–27–2; Vandrau 8–1–25–3; Harris 8–0–49–2; Barnett 4–0–37–0.

Derbyshire

*K. J. Barnett c and b Parsons	12	P. A. J. DeFreitas not out	20
P. D. Bowler lbw b Millns	8	L-b 5, w 18	23
C. J. Adams c Nixon b Simmons	28		
M. Azharuddin not out	91	1/17 2/48 (4 wkts, 35 overs)	191
T. J. G. O'Gorman b Simmons	9	3/97 4/128	

C. M. Wells, F. A. Griffith, †K. M. Krikken, A. J. Harris and M. J. Vandrau did not bat.

Bowling: Millns 6–0–31–1; Mullally 7–1–16–0; Parsons 7–0–40–1; Hepworth 4–0–26–0; Simmons 8–0–46–2; Dakin 3–0–27–0.

Umpires: V. A. Holder and A. G. T. Whitehead.

At Swansea, June 19. DERBYSHIRE lost to GLAMORGAN by five wickets.

DERBYSHIRE v MIDDLESEX

At Derby, July 3. Derbyshire won by eight wickets. Toss: Derbyshire.

Middlesex suffered two injuries on their way to defeat: Ramprakash had to be carried off with a damaged ankle sustained fielding in the covers, and Williams pulled up in his third over with hamstring trouble. Derbyshire were guided to victory by Adams and O'Gorman in an unbroken stand worth 121 in 22 overs.

Middlesex

D. L. Haynes c Rollins b Wells 5
M. A. Roseberry c Rollins b Griffith ... 27
M. R. Ramprakash c Vandrau b Malcolm . 47
*M. W. Gatting c Rollins b Malcolm .. 14
J. D. Carr not out 30
†K. R. Brown c Adams b Cork 1
M. A. Feltham c Vandrau b Wells..... 17
R. L. Johnson c Griffith b Wells 9
J. E. Emburey run out............... 6
N. F. Williams not out 2
L-b 4, w 11, n-b 2........... 17

1/8 2/62 3/98 4/108 5/110 6/133 7/157 8/167 (8 wkts, 40 overs) 175

P. C. R. Tufnell did not bat.

Bowling: Wells 8–0–55–3; Base 8–2–18–0; Griffith 8–0–46–1; Cork 8–1–19–1; Malcolm 8–0–33–2.

Derbyshire

*K. J. Barnett b Emburey............ 29
†A. S. Rollins c sub b Feltham........ 12
C. J. Adams not out 56
T. J. G. O'Gorman not out........... 63
L-b 3, w 8, n-b 6............ 17

1/25 2/56 (2 wkts, 37.4 overs) 177

M. Azharuddin, D. G. Cork, C. M. Wells, F. A. Griffith, M. J. Vandrau, S. J. Base and D. E. Malcolm did not bat.

Bowling: Johnson 7–0–29–0; Williams 2.2–0–9–0; Haynes 0.4–0–3–0; Tufnell 7–0–46–0; Feltham 6–0–25–1; Emburey 8–0–25–1; Carr 6–0–30–0; Roseberry 0.4–0–7–0.

Umpires: R. Palmer and P. Willey.

DERBYSHIRE v DURHAM

At Derby, July 10. Derbyshire won by eight wickets. Toss: Derbyshire.

DeFreitas's devastating opening spell – four wickets for nine runs in eight consecutive overs – settled the match: Durham collapsed to 29 for five, and Adams's third fifty of the season helped Derbyshire home with 13.3 overs to spare.

Durham

W. Larkins lbw b DeFreitas.......... 6
G. Fowler c Rollins b DeFreitas 0
J. E. Morris b DeFreitas............. 4
J. I. Longley run out 0
M. Saxelby b DeFreitas.............. 3
*P. Bainbridge c Rollins b Malcolm ... 29
A. C. Cummins c Azharuddin b Malcolm . 41
†C. W. Scott c Adams b Malcolm 15
D. A. Graveney not out 14
A. Walker not out 12
L-b 5, w 15 20

1/3 2/15 3/18 4/19 5/29 6/81 7/113 8/123 (8 wkts, 40 overs) 144

J. Wood did not bat.

Bowling: Wells 8–1–29–0; DeFreitas 8–3–9–4; Cork 7–0–26–0; Base 4–0–15–0; Malcolm 8–0–43–3; Griffith 5–1–17–0.

Derbyshire

*K. J. Barnett c Scott b Wood	30
†A. S. Rollins c Bainbridge b Walker	0
C. J. Adams not out	65
T. J. G. O'Gorman not out	19
B 1, l-b 13, w 6, n-b 14	34
1/3 2/83 (2 wkts, 26.3 overs)	148

M. Azharuddin, P. A. J. DeFreitas, D. G. Cork, C. M. Wells, F. A. Griffith, S. J. Base and D. E. Malcolm did not bat.

Bowling: Cummins 8–0–47–0; Walker 5–0–25–1; Bainbridge 4–0–20–0; Wood 5.3–0–31–1; Graveney 4–0–11–0.

Umpires: J. D. Bond and N. T. Plews.

At Manchester, July 17. DERBYSHIRE lost to LANCASHIRE by eight runs.

At Northampton, July 24. DERBYSHIRE beat NORTHAMPTONSHIRE on scoring-rate.

DERBYSHIRE v WARWICKSHIRE

At Chesterfield, July 31. No result. Toss: Derbyshire.

Though rain, which had already shortened the match, ended it after one innings, Warwickshire still extended their lead in the table to eight points. Twose, with 74 from 62 balls, had dominated a 68-run partnership with Penney: the stand lasted only six overs, and Penney's contribution was six.

Warwickshire

D. P. Ostler c Malcolm b Cork	10
N. M. K. Smith b Mortensen	56
B. C. Lara b Cork	11
P. A. Smith b Mortensen	21
Asif Din c Cork b Malcolm	9
R. G. Twose c Adams b Cork	74
*D. A. Reeve b Malcolm	16
T. L. Penney not out	8
D. R. Brown lbw b Cork	1
†K. J. Piper not out	8
L-b 4, w 11, n-b 10	25
1/40 2/65 3/104 4/111 5/129 6/159 7/227 8/229 (8 wkts, 36 overs)	239

T. A. Munton did not bat.

Bowling: DeFreitas 7–0–44–0; Warner 7–0–52–0; Cork 7–0–44–4; Mortensen 7–0–53–2; Malcolm 8–0–42–2.

Derbyshire

P. D. Bowler, D. G. Cork, C. J. Adams, T. J. G. O'Gorman, M. Azharuddin, P. A. J. DeFreitas, *K. J. Barnett, †K. M. Krikken, A. E. Warner, D. E. Malcolm and O. H. Mortensen.

Umpires: B. Dudleston and P. Willey.

DERBYSHIRE v GLOUCESTERSHIRE

At Chesterfield, August 7. Derbyshire won by 33 runs. Toss: Gloucestershire. First-team debuts: J. M. M. Averis, K. P. Sheeraz.

Gloucestershire suffered their ninth defeat of the season, despite a late rally from Russell and Dawson, who gamely added 52 in six overs after the visitors had reached the last ten overs still needing 108 for victory. Warner and Base had conceded only 40 runs as they shared the first 16 overs, whereas Derbyshire started briskly with 42 from six.

Derbyshire

P. D. Bowler lbw b Williams	56	*K. J. Barnett not out	50
D. G. Cork c Sheeraz b Davies	20	L-b 14, w 3, n-b 11	28
C. J. Adams c Averis b Alleyne	44		—
T. J. G. O'Gorman not out	28	1/61 2/120 3/146 (3 wkts, 40 overs)	226

A. S. Rollins, M. J. Vandrau, †K. M. Krikken, A. E. Warner, S. J. Base and D. E. Malcolm did not bat.

Bowling: Williams 5–0–35–1; Sheeraz 6–1–30–0; Davies 8–0–32–1; Ball 8–0–33–0; Averis 6–0–44–0; Alleyne 7–0–38–1.

Gloucestershire

A. J. Wright c Adams b Barnett	40	M. C. J. Ball b Cork	0
M. G. N. Windows c Barnett b Base	7	M. Davies b Cork	1
T. H. C. Hancock c O'Gorman b Warner	13	J. M. M. Averis not out	2
M. W. Alleyne c Barnett b Vandrau	39	L-b 7, w 7, n-b 6	20
R. I. Dawson lbw b Cork	38		—
*†R. C. Russell c Krikken b Malcolm	22	1/18 2/41 3/97 4/113 5/165 6/186 7/186 8/190 (8 wkts, 40 overs)	193
R. C. Williams not out	11		

K. P. Sheeraz did not bat.

Bowling: Warner 8–2–23–1; Base 8–0–17–1; Malcolm 6–0–47–1; Vandrau 8–1–51–1; Cork 8–0–35–3; Barnett 2–0–13–1.

Umpires: J. W. Holder and B. J. Meyer.

At Eastbourne, August 14. DERBYSHIRE beat SUSSEX by seven wickets.

DERBYSHIRE v KENT

At Derby, August 21. Kent won by 76 runs. Toss: Kent.

Hooper, captaining Kent for the first time, hammered 113 off 83 balls and added 164 in 21 overs with Walker to set up Kent's highest total over 40 overs and a seventh successive victory. He then rounded off an outstanding all-round effort by claiming four wickets in Derbyshire's reply. Barnett became the 13th player to reach 6,000 runs in the Sunday League.

Kent

T. R. Ward run out	35	M. A. Ealham not out	6
M. V. Fleming c Cork b Base	12	L-b 10, w 14, n-b 4	28
*C. L. Hooper c Rollins b Wells	113		—
M. J. Walker not out	69	1/44 2/80 3/244 4/289 (4 wkts, 40 overs)	295
G. R. Cowdrey b Warner	32		

†S. C. Willis, N. J. Llong, M. M. Patel, T. N. Wren and M. J. McCague did not bat.

Bowling: Base 8–0–28–1; Wells 8–0–65–1; Warner 7–0–59–1; Vandrau 5–0–35–0; Cork 8–0–52–0; Adams 4–0–46–0.

Derbyshire

P. D. Bowler c Willis b Ealham	19	M. J. Vandrau c Wren b Hooper	9
D. G. Cork run out	5	†K. M. Krikken not out	9
C. J. Adams c Walker b Ealham	38	S. J. Base c McCague b Hooper	3
T. J. G. O'Gorman b Hooper	42	B 2, l-b 10, w 8	20
*K. J. Barnett c Wren b Hooper	43		—
A. S. Rollins b Fleming	29	1/12 2/52 3/72 (34.4 overs)	219
C. M. Wells c Willis b Fleming	2	4/144 5/163 6/181	
A. E. Warner c Willis b Fleming	0	7/181 8/200 9/204	

Bowling: Wren 6–0–37–0; Ealham 6–0–32–2; Patel 4–0–41–0; McCague 5–1–17–0; Hooper 7.4–0–50–4; Fleming 6–0–30–3.

Umpires: M. J. Kitchen and P. B. Wight.

At Leeds, September 4. DERBYSHIRE lost to YORKSHIRE by four wickets.

DERBYSHIRE v ESSEX

At Derby, September 11. Essex won by two wickets. Toss: Essex.

Essex, who needed 39 from the last five overs, were taken to the brink of victory by Stephenson and Ilott, in a crucial eighth-wicket stand worth 41, and won with four balls to spare. Rain before the start reduced the match to 36 overs each.

Derbyshire

P. D. Bowler lbw b Such	17	I. G. S. Steer run out	1
D. G. Cork c Prichard b Ilott	11	†K. M. Krikken run out	15
C. J. Adams run out	27	A. E. Warner not out	27
T. J. G. O'Gorman c Prichard b Stephenson	7	L-b 11, w 10	21
*K. J. Barnett c Gooch b Cousins	34	1/24 2/48 3/67 (9 wkts, 36 overs)	170
P. A. J. DeFreitas c Ilott b Cousins	10	4/93 5/117 6/118	
C. M. Wells c Rollins b Cousins	0	7/125 8/127 9/170	

S. J. Base did not bat.

Bowling: Kasprowicz 7–0–31–0; Stephenson 7–0–40–1; Ilott 7–1–32–1; Cousins 7–0–32–3; Such 8–0–24–1.

Essex

*G. A. Gooch c Krikken b Base	20	M. C. Ilott c Krikken b Warner	24
N. V. Knight c Krikken b Base	29	P. M. Such not out	3
N. Hussain c Krikken b Base	3		
P. J. Prichard c Adams b Warner	35	L-b 1, w 15	16
R. C. Irani lbw b Cork	8		—
J. P. Stephenson not out	28	1/37 2/48 3/63 (8 wkts, 35.2 overs)	171
M. S. Kasprowicz b Wells	4	4/87 5/114 6/120	
†R. J. Rollins lbw b Wells	1	7/123 8/164	

D. M. Cousins did not bat.

Bowling: Wells 7–0–40–2; DeFreitas 8–1–26–0; Base 7–0–23–3; Cork 6.2–0–29–1; Warner 7–0–52–2.

Umpires: J. H. Harris and B. Leadbeater.

At Taunton, September 18. DERBYSHIRE beat SOMERSET by seven wickets.

DURHAM

DURHAM v ESSEX

At Stockton-on-Tees, May 8. Durham won by five wickets. Toss: Durham. County debut: A. Walker.

Longley hit the winning run off the fourth ball of the final over after a hailstorm interrupted the Essex innings and reduced the match to 35 overs per side. The former Northamptonshire seamer Walker began his Durham career with three for 19.

Essex

*G. A. Gooch c Morris b Walker 8	M. S. Kasprowicz lbw b Cummins 1
P. J. Prichard b Graveney 15	
N. V. Knight run out 5	L-b 19, w 3 22
N. Hussain not out 57	—
N. Shahid b Bainbridge 11	1/30 2/32 3/40 (7 wkts, 35 overs) 158
†M. A. Garnham b Walker 39	4/77 5/151
R. C. Irani b Walker. 0	6/151 7/158

M. C. Ilott, T. D. Topley and P. M. Such did not bat.

Bowling: Wood 8–1–38–0; Cummins 6–0–24–1; Walker 6–2–19–3; Graveney 8–1–27–1; Bainbridge 7–0–31–1.

Durham

W. Larkins c Kasprowicz b Such. 26	†C. W. Scott not out 15
M. Saxelby c Prichard b Ilott 10	
J. E. Morris c Knight b Kasprowicz . . . 37	L-b 7, w 3, n-b 2. 12
S. Hutton lbw b Ilott 18	—
*P. Bainbridge c Garnham b Irani 32	1/31 2/47 3/81 (5 wkts, 34.4 overs) 159
J. I. Longley not out 9	4/112 5/138

A. C. Cummins, J. Wood, A. Walker and D. A. Graveney did not bat.

Bowling: Kasprowicz 7.4–0–42–1; Ilott 8–1–28–2; Such 8–2–14–1; Topley 3–0–35–0; Irani 8–0–33–1.

Umpires: J. D. Bond and J. W. Holder.

At Nottingham, May 15. NOTTINGHAMSHIRE v DURHAM. No result (abandoned).

DURHAM v GLOUCESTERSHIRE

At Gateshead Fell, May 22. No result (abandoned).

At Birmingham, June 5. DURHAM lost to WARWICKSHIRE by 84 runs.

DURHAM v NORTHAMPTONSHIRE

At Hartlepool, June 12. Tied. Toss: Northamptonshire.

Needing 13 to win off the last over, and six from the final delivery, Northamptonshire levelled the scores in bizarre circumstances. Bailey holed out in the deep off Walker, only for umpire Burgess to signal a no-ball – worth two runs – for a delivery above waist-height. Bailey then scored three from the extra ball, a brilliant piece of fielding by Longley saving the boundary that would have given the visitors victory. Against his old county, Larkins scored his 13th League hundred, a record, and became the fourth man to reach 7,000 runs in the competition. Fordham, who scored his first Sunday hundred, and Curran also provided rich entertainment and the match produced an aggregate of 532 runs.

Durham

W. Larkins c Ripley b Bowen	108	J. Wood run out	2
G. Fowler c Warren b Taylor	0	†C. W. Scott not out	0
J. E. Morris b Curran	35	L-b 3, w 6, n-b 4	13
S. Hutton run out	42		—
J. I. Longley c Fordham b Curran	20	1/7 2/48 3/193 (6 wkts, 40 overs)	266
A. C. Cummins not out	46	4/199 5/252 6/263	

*D. A. Graveney, A. Walker and S. J. E. Brown did not bat.

Bowling: Taylor 8–0–58–1; Curran 8–0–44–2; Cook 8–0–38–0; Bailey 4–0–31–0; Bowen 7–0–50–1; Penberthy 5–0–42–0.

Northamptonshire

A. Fordham lbw b Wood	111	*R. J. Bailey not out	43
N. A. Felton b Cummins	8	L-b 7, w 1, n-b 2	10
M. B. Loye run out	6		—
K. M. Curran not out	88	1/16 2/31 3/190 (3 wkts, 40 overs)	266

R. J. Warren, A. L. Penberthy, †D. Ripley, M. N. Bowen, N. G. B. Cook and J. P. Taylor did not bat.

Bowling: Cummins 8–0–59–1; Brown 8–0–44–0; Wood 8–0–49–1; Graveney 8–0–40–0; Walker 8–0–67–0.

Umpires: G. I. Burgess and J. H. Hampshire.

At Hove, June 19. DURHAM beat SUSSEX by nine wickets.

At Lord's, June 26. DURHAM beat MIDDLESEX by one wicket.

DURHAM v SURREY

At Darlington, July 3. Surrey won by two runs. Toss: Durham.

After looking out of contention at 77 for six in the 20th over, Durham were revived by a stand of 107 in 17 between Cummins and Scott. But they just failed to score the 16 required off the last over.

Surrey

D. J. Bicknell lbw b Bainbridge	37	*M. P. Bicknell c and b Cummins	1
M. A. Lynch c Scott b Cummins	0	A. C. S. Pigott b Walker	6
D. M. Ward c Larkins b Bainbridge	37	L-b 1, w 5	6
A. D. Brown b Walker	44		—
A. J. Hollioake c Scott b Walker	4	1/1 2/70 3/91 (8 wkts, 40 overs)	222
A. W. Smith not out	50	4/102 5/148 6/204	
†G. J. Kersey b Walker	37	7/215 8/222	

J. Boiling and A. J. Murphy did not bat.

Bowling: Cummins 8–0–42–2; Brown 8–0–53–0; Wood 8–0–45–0; Bainbridge 8–0–38–2; Walker 8–0–43–4.

Durham

W. Larkins b Murphy 1
M. Saxelby c Ward b Pigott 36
J. E. Morris c Kersey b M. P. Bicknell . 2
J. I. Longley c Kersey b Murphy 12
*P. Bainbridge c Lynch b Pigott 10
S. Hutton c Lynch b Boiling 5
A. C. Cummins c Smith b Hollioake . . . 67
†C. W. Scott b Murphy 45
A. Walker run out 15
J. Wood not out 5
S. J. E. Brown not out 5
B 1, l-b 12, w 2, n-b 2 17

1/10 2/17 3/30 4/63 5/68 6/77 7/184 8/201 9/214 (9 wkts, 40 overs) 220

Bowling: Murphy 8–1–35–3; M. P. Bicknell 8–0–46–1; Pigott 4–1–9–2; Hollioake 8–0–51–1; Boiling 8–0–36–1; Smith 4–0–30–0.

Umpires: D. J. Constant and K. J. Lyons.

At Derby, July 10. DURHAM lost to DERBYSHIRE by eight wickets.

DURHAM v LEICESTERSHIRE

At Durham University, July 24. No result. Toss: Durham. First-team debut: A. I. Ditta.

Rain halted Leicestershire's push towards a substantial total after Simmons and Wells, whose second Sunday century of the season came off only 77 balls, had added 172 in 25 overs.

Leicestershire

P. V. Simmons lbw b Walker 88
*N. E. Briers c Scott b Cummins 1
V. J. Wells lbw b Cummins 100
J. J. Whitaker c Bainbridge b Cummins 17
B. F. Smith c Larkins b Walker 12
†P. A. Nixon b Lugsden 10
P. N. Hepworth not out 2
A. I. Ditta not out 1
B 1, l-b 4, w 6, n-b 2 13

1/15 2/187 3/205 4/217 5/233 6/238 (6 wkts, 36 overs) 244

I. M. Stanger, A. R. K. Pierson and A. Sheriyar did not bat.

Bowling: Cummins 8–0–35–3; Lugsden 8–0–55–1; Cox 4–0–24–0; Walker 7–0–37–2; Birbeck 5–0–39–0; Bainbridge 4–0–49–0.

Durham

W. Larkins, J. A. Daley, J. E. Morris, M. Saxelby, *P. Bainbridge, A. C. Cummins, †C. W. Scott, S. D. Birbeck, A. Walker, D. M. Cox and S. Lugsden.

Umpires: J. D. Bond and B. J. Meyer.

DURHAM v YORKSHIRE

At Durham University, July 31. Durham won on scoring-rate when rain ended play. Toss: Durham.

Durham secured a comfortable victory, with Larkins and Saxelby posting an opening stand of 120 in 20 overs. Though three wickets fell at the same score, they were still well ahead of the required run-rate when rain intervened.

Yorkshire

*D. Byas c Scott b Graveney 37
M. P. Vaughan c Scott b Walker 0
†R. J. Blakey lbw b Cummins 2
C. White st Scott b Graveney 39
M. J. Foster c Walker b Cox 0
P. J. Hartley run out 35
B. Parker lbw b Bainbridge 28
A. P. Grayson b Walker 0
D. Gough c Saxelby b Cummins 4
R. D. Stemp not out 14
M. A. Robinson not out 1
L-b 3, w 5, n-b 6 14

1/7 2/16 3/80 4/83 5/90 6/132 7/133 8/148 9/168 (9 wkts, 40 overs) 174

Bowling: Cummins 8–0–27–2; Walker 8–2–52–2; Birbeck 4–0–18–0; Cox 8–1–25–1; Graveney 8–1–26–2; Bainbridge 4–1–23–1.

Durham

W. Larkins c Grayson b Stemp 55
M. Saxelby c Stemp b Robinson 54
J. E. Morris c Grayson b Robinson 0
J. A. Daley not out 30
*P. Bainbridge c Grayson b Stemp 3
†C. W. Scott not out 6
B 9, l-b 6, w 2 17

1/120 2/120 3/120 4/145 (4 wkts, 31.4 overs) 165

D. A. Graveney, A. C. Cummins, A. Walker, D. M. Cox and S. D. Birbeck did not bat.

Bowling: Gough 7.4–0–21–0; Hartley 4–1–22–0; Stemp 8–2–39–2; White 2–0–16–0; Robinson 7–1–38–2; Grayson 3–1–14–0.

Umpires: J. H. Hampshire and N. T. Plews.

At Taunton, August 7. DURHAM beat SOMERSET by six wickets.

At Canterbury, August 14. DURHAM lost to KENT by 68 runs.

DURHAM v GLAMORGAN

At Hartlepool, August 21. Glamorgan won by 19 runs. Toss: Durham.

Cottey, who faced only 45 balls for his 66, built on the foundations laid by James's century. Durham fell short of a target of 242, despite an enterprising partnership of 90 in 13 overs between Cummins and Blenkiron; their captain, Bainbridge, took his 200th Sunday League wicket.

Glamorgan

S. P. James run out 102
A. Dale st Scott b Bainbridge 16
D. L. Hemp c Walker b Cummins 18
*M. P. Maynard st Scott b Graveney . . 27
P. A. Cottey not out 66
O. D. Gibson not out 5
B 2, l-b 2, w 3 7

1/44 2/87 3/139 4/219 (4 wkts, 40 overs) 241

R. D. B. Croft, †C. P. Metson, R. P. Lefebvre, G. P. Butcher and S. R. Barwick did not bat.

Bowling: Wood 5–0–29–0; Bainbridge 8–0–37–1; Cummins 8–0–53–1; Graveney 8–0–36–1; Walker 8–0–57–0; Blenkiron 3–0–25–0.

Durham

J. I. Longley lbw b Lefebvre	7	A. Walker b Barwick	6
M. Saxelby c Hemp b Gibson	1	J. Wood c Hemp b Barwick	3
J. E. Morris c Metson b Lefebvre	0	D. A. Graveney not out	1
J. A. Daley lbw b Croft	54	B 2, l-b 5, w 11, n-b 2	20
*P. Bainbridge c James b Barwick	25		
A. C. Cummins c Cottey b Lefebvre	66	1/3 2/3 3/21 (9 wkts, 40 overs)	222
D. A. Blenkiron not out	39	4/68 5/113 6/203	
†C. W. Scott b Lefebvre	0	7/204 8/211 9/219	

Bowling: Lefebvre 8–0–23–4; Gibson 8–2–38–1; Croft 8–0–42–1; Barwick 8–0–57–3; Butcher 4–0–25–0; Dale 4–0–30–0.

Umpires: B. Leadbeater and B. J. Meyer.

At Portsmouth, August 28. DURHAM beat HAMPSHIRE by ten wickets.

DURHAM v LANCASHIRE

At Stockton-on-Tees, September 11. Lancashire won by five wickets. Toss: Lancashire.

Durham struggled against Martin, collapsing from 103 for one, as he claimed five wickets for the first time in one-day competitions. An opening stand of 70 from Atherton and Speak set Lancashire on course for a straightforward win.

Durham

J. I. Longley b Martin	53	J. Wood c Yates b Martin	3
W. Larkins b Austin	26	A. Walker b Martin	9
S. Hutton b Yates	22	D. A. Graveney not out	1
J. A. Daley b Martin	6	B 4, l-b 8, w 5	17
J. E. Morris b Austin	2		
*P. Bainbridge c Hegg b Austin	11	1/55 2/103 3/114 (38 overs)	170
A. C. Cummins c Martin b Austin	10	4/115 5/118 6/143	
†C. W. Scott c Chapple b Martin	10	7/143 8/151 9/169	

Bowling: Martin 8–0–32–5; Chapple 8–1–26–0; Austin 8–0–34–4; Yates 8–0–43–1; Shadford 6–0–23–0.

Lancashire

*M. A. Atherton c Scott b Cummins	35	†W. K. Hegg not out	7
N. J. Speak c Scott b Cummins	39		
J. P. Crawley lbw b Wood	37	B 1, l-b 3, w 2, n-b 6	12
N. H. Fairbrother b Wood	25		
G. D. Lloyd c and b Cummins	6	1/70 2/81 3/127 (5 wkts, 36 overs)	172
I. D. Austin not out	11	4/146 5/158	

G. Yates, D. J. Shadford, P. J. Martin and G. Chapple did not bat.

Bowling: Bainbridge 6–1–25–0; Wood 8–2–40–2; Cummins 8–1–32–3; Graveney 8–0–35–0; Walker 6–0–36–0.

Umpires: H. D. Bird and V. A. Holder.

At Worcester, September 18. DURHAM lost to WORCESTERSHIRE by 26 runs.

ESSEX

At Stockton-on-Tees, May 8. ESSEX lost to DURHAM by five wickets.

ESSEX v KENT

At Chelmsford, May 15. Kent won by eight wickets. Toss: Essex.

Essex, restricted by tight Kent bowling, lost four wickets to run-outs, and managed only five fours in their entire innings.

Essex

*G. A. Gooch run out	29
P. J. Prichard c Fleming b Headley	0
N. V. Knight b Spencer	17
N. Hussain b Spencer	0
N. Shahid b Llong	7
J. P. Stephenson run out	6
†M. A. Garnham c Marsh b Headley	22
R. C. Irani c Llong b Headley	13
M. S. Kasprowicz run out	0
M. C. Ilott not out	10
P. M. Such run out	6
B 1, l-b 7, w 4	12
1/3 2/48 3/48 4/54 5/64 6/73 7/100 8/100 9/113 (40 overs)	122

Bowling: Igglesden 8–0–19–0; Headley 8–0–27–3; Hooper 8–0–27–0; Spencer 8–2–16–2; Llong 5–0–11–1; Fleming 3–0–14–0.

Kent

T. R. Ward c Stephenson b Kasprowicz	3
*M. R. Benson b Irani	48
C. L. Hooper not out	41
N. R. Taylor not out	17
B 2, l-b 6, w 6	14
1/30 2/93 (2 wkts, 36.3 overs)	123

N. J. Llong, G. R. Cowdrey, M. V. Fleming, †S. A. Marsh, D. W. Headley, A. P. Igglesden and D. J. Spencer did not bat.

Bowling: Kasprowicz 6–2–11–1; Ilott 5–1–19–0; Such 8–0–26–0; Irani 8–1–22–1; Stephenson 6.3–1–26–0; Shahid 3–0–11–0.

Umpires: K. J. Lyons and B. J. Meyer.

At Leeds, May 22. YORKSHIRE v ESSEX. No result (abandoned).

ESSEX v GLOUCESTERSHIRE

At Chelmsford, June 5. Essex won by 27 runs. Toss: Gloucestershire.

Essex recorded their first League win of the season. Stephenson first batted through 33 overs for 60 to hold his side together, in the face of fine fast bowling from Walsh, and then claimed two wickets in Gloucestershire's hesitant reply, which saw the top five fall within nine overs.

Essex

*P. J. Prichard c Dawson b Williams	19	M. C. Ilott run out	6
J. P. Stephenson c Russell b Walsh	60	R. M. Pearson not out	6
N. Hussain lbw b Walsh	10		
N. V. Knight c Hinks b Wight	20	L-b 4, w 2, n-b 2	8
N. Shahid b Cooper	6		—
†M. A. Garnham c Wight b Walsh	23	1/34 2/52 3/96 (9 wkts, 40 overs)	175
R. C. Irani c Wight b Walsh	0	4/114 5/119 6/121	
M. S. Kasprowicz c Russell b Smith	17	7/158 8/168 9/175	

D. M. Cousins did not bat.

Bowling: Cooper 8–0–36–1; Smith 8–1–33–1; Williams 7–0–34–1; Walsh 8–1–20–4; Wight 5–0–22–1; Alleyne 4–0–26–0.

Gloucestershire

S. G. Hinks c Garnham b Irani	18	R. M. Wight c Shahid b Stephenson	10
M. W. Alleyne c Garnham b Cousins	28	A. M. Smith run out	0
A. J. Wright b Irani	1	K. E. Cooper not out	5
T. H. C. Hancock lbw b Stephenson	0	B 3, l-b 8, w 4, n-b 4	19
R. I. Dawson c Knight b Pearson	5		—
†R. C. Russell c Hussain b Pearson	22	1/42 2/44 3/45 (39.2 overs)	148
R. C. Williams c Prichard b Ilott	31	4/63 5/65 6/93	
*C. A. Walsh c Garnham b Irani	9	7/124 8/140 9/140	

Bowling: Ilott 7–1–26–1; Kasprowicz 8–1–32–0; Irani 8–1–23–3; Stephenson 6.2–1–21–2; Cousins 5–0–16–1; Pearson 5–0–19–2.

Umpires: D. J. Constant and G. Sharp.

At Worcester, June 12. ESSEX lost to WORCESTERSHIRE by four wickets.

ESSEX v NOTTINGHAMSHIRE

At Ilford, June 26. Nottinghamshire won by seven wickets. Toss: Essex. First-team debut: M. Diwan.

Essex struggled after losing Gooch to the third ball of the match, and Johnson's 82 from 69 deliveries – Adams helping him add 103 in 21 overs – made certain of victory for the visitors.

Essex

*G. A. Gooch c Noon b Lewis	1	M. S. Kasprowicz c Pollard b Mike	7
J. P. Stephenson c Lewis b Field-Buss	49	P. M. Such not out	19
J. J. B. Lewis c Noon b Evans	23	B 1, l-b 9, w 4, n-b 6	20
N. Hussain c Evans b Field-Buss	31		—
M. Diwan run out	14	1/2 2/56 3/108 (7 wkts, 40 overs)	184
R. C. Irani run out	1	4/129 5/130	
†M. A. Garnham not out	19	6/131 7/144	

R. M. Pearson and D. M. Cousins did not bat.

Bowling: Lewis 8–0–33–1; Pennett 4–0–22–0; Evans 7–0–28–1; Mike 7–1–36–1; Field-Buss 8–0–27–2; Crawley 6–0–28–0.

Nottinghamshire

P. R. Pollard lbw b Such	10	M. A. Crawley not out	14
P. Johnson c Garnham b Stephenson	82	L-b 1, w 5, n-b 16	22
J. C. Adams not out	60		—
*R. T. Robinson b Stephenson	0	1/46 2/149 3/149 (3 wkts, 33.4 overs)	188

C. C. Lewis, G. W. Mike, †W. M. Noon, K. P. Evans, M. G. Field-Buss and D. B. Pennett did not bat.

Bowling: Kasprowicz 6–0–35–0; Such 7–1–37–1; Cousins 3–0–23–0; Pearson 5–0–29–0; Irani 8–2–29–0; Stephenson 4.4–1–34–2.

Umpires: B. J. Meyer and P. Willey.

At Leicester, July 3. ESSEX lost to LEICESTERSHIRE by 14 runs.

At Southampton, July 10. ESSEX lost to HAMPSHIRE by six wickets.

ESSEX v GLAMORGAN

At Southend, July 17. Tied. Toss: Essex.

Glamorgan's last pair, Metson and Barwick, needed ten off the final over, and scored eight from the first five balls before Barwick was run out by Knight attempting a second to win the game. Gooch's 101 off 100 deliveries was his 12th century in the competition.

Essex

*G. A. Gooch b Watkin	101	M. S. Kasprowicz b Barwick	0
J. P. Stephenson st Metson b Lefebvre	1	T. D. Topley not out	3
N. Hussain c Barwick b Croft	33	B 1, l-b 7, w 4	12
N. V. Knight c Croft b Watkin	25		—
M. A. Garnham c Metson b Barwick	13	1/12 2/122 3/157 (7 wkts, 40 overs)	214
R. C. Irani c Cottey b Lefebvre	20	4/182 5/188	
†R. J. Rollins not out	6	6/209 7/209	

R. M. Pearson and P. M. Such did not bat.

Bowling: Lefebvre 8–1–40–2; Watkin 8–0–31–2; Gibson 8–1–35–0; Barwick 8–0–49–2; Croft 7–0–41–1; Cottey 1–0–10–0.

Glamorgan

S. P. James b Kasprowicz	4	†C. P. Metson not out	14
*H. Morris st Rollins b Such	40	S. L. Watkin run out	1
M. P. Maynard b Such	19	S. R. Barwick run out	3
P. A. Cottey b Stephenson	70	L-b 7, w 8, n-b 2	17
D. L. Hemp b Pearson	3		—
O. D. Gibson b Kasprowicz	33	1/11 2/41 3/91 (40 overs)	214
R. D. B. Croft st Rollins b Stephenson	4	4/102 5/178 6/182	
R. P. Lefebvre b Irani	6	7/193 8/197 9/201	

Bowling: Stephenson 7–0–36–2; Kasprowicz 8–0–38–2; Such 8–0–32–2; Irani 6–2–35–1; Pearson 8–1–41–1; Topley 3–0–25–0.

Umpires: J. H. Hampshire and M. J. Kitchen.

At Birmingham, July 24. ESSEX lost to WARWICKSHIRE by three wickets.

At Uxbridge, July 31. ESSEX lost to MIDDLESEX by seven wickets.

ESSEX v LANCASHIRE

At Chelmsford, August 7. Essex won by five wickets. Toss: Lancashire.

Essex won for the first time in the League since June 5 with one ball to spare, lifting themselves off the bottom of the table and dealing Lancashire's title hopes a major blow. The visitors were boosted by a 159-run opening stand, in 30 overs, between Gallian and Titchard, but Stephenson led the Essex reply, and Irani – formerly with Lancashire – provided important acceleration with 33 off 29 balls.

Lancashire

J. E. R. Gallian st Rollins b Knight . . . 84
S. P. Titchard c Such b Ilott. 96
N. J. Speak c Ilott b Stephenson 26
N. H. Fairbrother c Shahid b Stephenson . 0
G. D. Lloyd not out. 2
*M. Watkinson not out 0
B 2, l-b 5, w 4, n-b 2 13

1/159 2/216 3/217 4/220 (4 wkts, 40 overs) 221

I. D. Austin, †W. K. Hegg, P. J. Martin, G. Yates and G. Chapple did not bat.

Bowling: Kasprowicz 6–1–24–0; Ilott 8–0–33–1; Stephenson 8–0–42–2; Pearson 5–0–40–0; Such 7–0–34–0; Knight 6–0–41–1.

Essex

N. V. Knight lbw b Austin. 25
*J. P. Stephenson b Watkinson 73
N. Hussain run out 38
R. C. Irani run out 33
N. Shahid c Yates b Martin 21
J. J. B. Lewis not out 21
†R. J. Rollins not out 2
L-b 4, w 5 9

1/56 2/134 3/147 4/190 5/217 (5 wkts, 39.5 overs) 222

M. S. Kasprowicz, M. C. Ilott, P. M. Such and R. M. Pearson did not bat.

Bowling: Martin 7.5–0–42–1; Chapple 8–0–50–0; Austin 5–0–18–1; Yates 8–0–47–0; Watkinson 8–1–39–1; Gallian 3–0–22–0.

Umpires: G. I. Burgess and R. Palmer.

ESSEX v SURREY

At Colchester, August 14. Surrey won by six wickets. Toss: Surrey.

Ward drove Surrey to victory with five balls remaining, hitting 91 from 71 deliveries and adding 105 in 14 overs with Hollioake. Earlier, Gooch confirmed his fitness for the Third Test against South Africa with a purposeful 63.

Essex

*G. A. Gooch c Ward b Boiling 63
J. P. Stephenson c Bicknell b Kenlock . 16
N. Hussain c Smith b Bicknell. 61
N. V. Knight b Kenlock. 23
R. C. Irani lbw b Bicknell 11
J. J. B. Lewis not out 18
†R. J. Rollins not out 9
B 1, l-b 5, w 4, n-b 6 16

1/51 2/107 3/166 4/185 5/189 (5 wkts, 38 overs) 217

P. M. Such, M. S. Kasprowicz, M. C. Ilott and D. M. Cousins did not bat.

Bowling: Bicknell 7–1–20–2; Pigott 8–0–52–0; Kenlock 8–0–44–2; Hollioake 4–0–24–0; Boiling 6–0–39–1; Butcher 5–0–32–0.

Surrey

*†A. J. Stewart c Rollins b Cousins	41	A. W. Smith not out	16
A. D. Brown c Irani b Kasprowicz	11	B 2, l-b 4, w 4	10
G. P. Thorpe b Stephenson	5		—
D. M. Ward c Rollins b Stephenson	91	1/25 2/49 (4 wkts, 37.1 overs)	219
A. J. Hollioake not out	45	3/92 4/197	

M. A. Butcher, A. C. S. Pigott, M. P. Bicknell, J. Boiling and S. G. Kenlock did not bat.

Bowling: Ilott 8–0–53–0; Kasprowicz 7–1–39–1; Stephenson 7.1–0–36–2; Such 8–0–42–0; Cousins 7–0–43–1.

Umpires: H. D. Bird and A. A. Jones.

At Weston-super-Mare, August 21. ESSEX lost to SOMERSET by 85 runs.

ESSEX v SUSSEX

At Chelmsford, September 4. Essex won by 33 runs. Toss: Sussex.

Hussain and Stephenson added 116 in 17 overs to give Essex a winning total. Only Speight, with 66 off 69 balls, successfully countered the home attack, spearheaded impressively by Ilott.

Essex

*G. A. Gooch lbw b Jarvis	11	M. C. Ilott not out	1
N. V. Knight c Moores b Stephenson	3	R. M. Pearson not out	5
N. Hussain c Greenfield b Stephenson	76		
P. J. Prichard hit wkt b Giddins	9	L-b 7, w 3, n-b 6	16
R. C. Irani lbw b Remy	6		—
J. P. Stephenson c Moores b Jarvis	68	1/13 2/21 3/53 (8 wkts, 40 overs)	207
†R. J. Rollins c Remy b Giddins	1	4/65 5/181 6/184	
M. S. Kasprowicz b Jarvis	11	7/201 8/201	

D. M. Cousins did not bat.

Bowling: Stephenson 8–0–38–2; Jarvis 8–0–42–3; Giddins 8–0–27–2; Remy 8–0–41–1; Athey 3–0–22–0; Phillips 5–0–30–0.

Sussex

C. W. J. Athey lbw b Cousins	15	P. W. Jarvis c Hussain b Ilott	9
F. D. Stephenson lbw b Kasprowicz	9	N. C. Phillips c Cousins b Ilott	6
K. Greenfield b Kasprowicz	4	E. S. H. Giddins not out	1
*A. P. Wells c Stephenson b Pearson	25	L-b 4, w 11, n-b 6	21
M. P. Speight c Prichard b Ilott	66		—
N. J. Lenham lbw b Cousins	10	1/13 2/17 3/38 (38.2 overs)	174
†P. Moores b Cousins	0	4/98 5/123 6/123	
C. C. Remy c Rollins b Ilott	8	7/151 8/160 9/172	

Bowling: Ilott 7.2–1–25–4; Kasprowicz 8–0–40–2; Stephenson 7–0–23–0; Cousins 8–1–39–3; Pearson 8–1–43–1.

Umpires: R. A. White and A. G. T. Whitehead.

At Derby, September 11. ESSEX beat DERBYSHIRE by two wickets.

ESSEX v NORTHAMPTONSHIRE

At Chelmsford, September 18. Northamptonshire won by one run. Toss: Northamptonshire. First-team debut: D. J. Sales.

David Sales, at 16 years 289 days, became the youngest player to score a half-century in the competition, hitting a remarkably assured unbeaten 70 from only 56 deliveries on his debut for Northamptonshire's first team.

Northamptonshire

R. R. Montgomerie c Rollins b Kasprowicz . 21
*A. Fordham b Stephenson. 15
T. C. Walton c Hussain b Such 34
K. M. Curran b Stephenson 9
D. J. Sales not out 70
†R. J. Warren run out. 20
A. L. Penberthy c Such b Kasprowicz. . 7
A. R. Roberts run out 20
M. N. Bowen not out 1
B 1, l-b 18, w 5, n-b 6 30

1/40 2/78 3/94 4/100 5/149 6/180 7/214 (7 wkts, 39 overs) 227

J. P. Taylor and N. G. B. Cook did not bat.

Bowling: Ilott 8–0–51–0; Kasprowicz 8–0–38–2; Cousins 8–0–51–0; Such 8–0–31–1; Stephenson 7–0–37–2.

Essex

*G. A. Gooch c Cook b Penberthy 48
N. V. Knight lbw b Curran 4
N. Hussain c and b Roberts 74
P. J. Prichard not out 65
R. C. Irani lbw b Taylor. 15
J. P. Stephenson not out 4
L-b 11, w 3, n-b 2. 16

1/13 2/86 3/193 4/222 (4 wkts, 39 overs) 226

M. S. Kasprowicz, †R. J. Rollins, M. C. Ilott, P. M. Such and D. M. Cousins did not bat.

Bowling: Taylor 8–0–53–1; Curran 8–1–30–1; Penberthy 8–1–50–1; Bowen 6–0–27–0; Walton 4–0–19–0; Cook 3–0–25–0; Roberts 2–0–11–1.

Umpires: T. E. Jesty and A. G. T. Whitehead.

GLAMORGAN

At Northampton, May 8. GLAMORGAN beat NORTHAMPTONSHIRE by four wickets.

GLAMORGAN v YORKSHIRE

At Cardiff, May 15. Yorkshire won by nine wickets. Toss: Yorkshire.

Gough celebrated his selection for England's one-day squad by joining forces with Grayson to wreck Glamorgan, who reached 95 for one but then lost nine wickets for 42 in 15 overs. It was Glamorgan's first defeat in the competition since losing to Northamptonshire on May 23, 1993.

Glamorgan

S. P. James st Blakey b Grayson 51
*H. Morris c Blakey b Gough 0
A. Dale run out 40
M. P. Maynard c Byas b Grayson 2
P. A. Cottey c Moxon b Grayson. 3
O. D. Gibson c Blakey b Robinson 5
R. D. B. Croft b Gough 8
R. P. Lefebvre b Grayson. 4
†C. P. Metson b Gough 4
S. L. Watkin b Gough. 2
S. R. Barwick not out 8
L-b 5, w 1, n-b 4. 10

1/11 2/95 3/102 4/104 5/110 6/110 7/118 8/126 9/128 (39.1 overs) 137

Bowling: Hartley 5–2–8–0; Gough 7.1–1–20–4; White 7–1–29–0; Robinson 8–0–23–1; Stemp 4–0–27–0; Grayson 8–0–25–4.

Yorkshire

*M. D. Moxon not out	55
D. Byas c Cottey b Dale	71
R. B. Richardson not out	8
B 1, l-b 4	5
1/126 (1 wkt, 36.2 overs)	139

†R. J. Blakey, C. White, A. P. Grayson, P. J. Hartley, M. J. Foster, D. Gough, R. D. Stemp and M. A. Robinson did not bat.

Bowling: Watkin 8–2–32–0; Lefebvre 6.2–1–16–0; Croft 5–0–22–0; Barwick 8–0–25–0; Gibson 5–0–20–0; Dale 4–0–19–1.

Umpires: B. Leadbeater and R. Palmer.

At Hove, May 29. GLAMORGAN lost to SUSSEX by seven wickets.

GLAMORGAN v SURREY

At Swansea, June 5. No result. Toss: Surrey.

Morris hit seven sixes and seven fours in a magnificent display, scoring an unbeaten 127 off as many balls. It was the biggest of his three League hundreds; he shared century partnerships with James and Dale, and became the second Glamorgan batsman – after Alan Jones – to reach 4,000 runs in the League. Rain ended Surrey's reply after eight overs.

Glamorgan

S. P. James lbw b Hollioake	39
*H. Morris not out	127
A. Dale not out	42
L-b 4, w 4, n-b 4	12
1/104 (1 wkt, 40 overs)	220

P. A. Cottey, D. L. Hemp, R. D. B. Croft, O. D. Gibson, R. P. Lefebvre, †C. P. Metson, S. L. Watkin and S. R. Barwick did not bat.

Bowling: Benjamin 8–0–27–0; Murphy 8–2–53–0; Butcher 4–0–33–0; Pigott 8–1–27–0; Boiling 4–0–28–0; Hollioake 8–0–48–1.

Surrey

D. J. Bicknell not out	12
A. D. Brown c Metson b Lefebvre	25
*G. P. Thorpe not out	8
L-b 1	1
1/34 (1 wkt, 8 overs)	46

D. M. Ward, A. J. Hollioake, †N. F. Sargeant, M. A. Butcher, J. Boiling, A. C. S. Pigott, J. E. Benjamin and A. J. Murphy did not bat.

Bowling: Watkin 4–0–24–0; Lefebvre 4–0–21–1.

Umpires: D. R. Shepherd and P. Willey.

GLAMORGAN v DERBYSHIRE

At Swansea, June 19. Glamorgan won by five wickets. Toss: Glamorgan.

Azharuddin's 81 not out enabled Derbyshire to reach a defensible total, but his efforts proved in vain as Morris and Maynard added 104 for Glamorgan's second wicket in 16 overs.

Derbyshire

*K. J. Barnett c Maynard b Lefebvre .. 16
P. D. Bowler st Metson b Croft 17
C. J. Adams c Barwick b Gibson 30
M. Azharuddin not out 81
T. J. G. O'Gorman b Dale 22
F. A. Griffith st Metson b Barwick 25
†K. M. Krikken not out 3
B 1, l-b 4, w 4.............. 9

1/34 2/37 3/88 4/147 5/199 (5 wkts, 39 overs) 203

A. E. Warner, M. J. Vandrau, S. J. Base and D. E. Malcolm did not bat.

Bowling: Lefebvre 8–0–38–1; Watkin 7–0–33–0; Barwick 8–0–40–1; Croft 8–0–40–1; Gibson 4–0–27–1; Dale 4–0–20–1.

Glamorgan

S. P. James c Krikken b Malcolm 18
*H. Morris c Vandrau b Malcolm 62
M. P. Maynard c Barnett b Malcolm... 65
A. Dale c Griffith b Base 10
P. A. Cottey c Vandrau b Warner 11
O. D. Gibson not out 14
R. D. B. Croft not out............... 10
L-b 6, w 6, n-b 2............ 14

1/47 2/151 3/160 4/176 5/189 (5 wkts, 38 overs) 204

R. P. Lefebvre, †C. P. Metson, S. L. Watkin and S. R. Barwick did not bat.

Bowling: Warner 8–0–28–1; Griffith 7–0–35–0; Malcolm 8–0–41–3; Vandrau 8–0–40–0; Base 7–0–54–1.

Umpires: H. D. Bird and R. Julian.

GLAMORGAN v LANCASHIRE

At Colwyn Bay, June 26. Glamorgan won by 27 runs. Toss: Lancashire.

Morris was stranded one short of another hundred, but scored exactly half his side's runs, Lefebvre then kept Lancashire in check, conceding only 15 runs in eight overs and taking three excellent catches in the deep off Barwick.

Glamorgan

S. P. James lbw b Wasim Akram 19
*H. Morris not out.................. 99
M. P. Maynard run out.............. 20
A. Dale b Watkinson................ 19
O. D. Gibson c Lloyd b Austin 9
P. A. Cottey not out 15
L-b 10, w 1, n-b 6........... 17

1/35 2/99 3/143 4/156 (4 wkts, 40 overs) 198

R. D. B. Croft, R. P. Lefebvre, †C. P. Metson, S. L. Watkin and S. R. Barwick did not bat.

Bowling: Chapple 8–1–18–0; Martin 8–0–41–0; Wasim Akram 8–0–34–1; Austin 8–0–37–1; Yates 3–0–23–0; Watkinson 5–0–35–1.

Lancashire

M. A. Atherton c Maynard b Watkin .. 1
G. D. Lloyd c Metson b Lefebvre 2
J. P. Crawley c Lefebvre b Barwick ... 36
N. H. Fairbrother c Gibson b Watkin.. 7
*M. Watkinson c Gibson b Croft 19
Wasim Akram c Lefebvre b Barwick .. 3
I. D. Austin b Barwick 27
†W. K. Hegg c Metson b Lefebvre 52
P. J. Martin c Lefebvre b Barwick 0
G. Yates not out 3
G. Chapple not out 3
L-b 10, w 6, n-b 2........... 18

1/3 2/5 3/14 4/73 5/78 6/79 7/150 8/150 9/167 (9 wkts, 40 overs) 171

Bowling: Lefebvre 8–1–15–2; Watkin 8–2–33–2; Barwick 8–0–38–4; Croft 8–0–30–1; Dale 5–1–23–0; Gibson 3–0–22–0.

Umpires: K. J. Lyons and P. B. Wight.

At Bristol, July 3. GLAMORGAN beat GLOUCESTERSHIRE by four wickets.

At Birmingham, July 12. GLAMORGAN lost to WARWICKSHIRE by four wickets.

At Southend, July 17. GLAMORGAN tied with ESSEX.

GLAMORGAN v KENT

At Ebbw Vale, July 24. Kent won by eight runs. Toss: Glamorgan.

A thunderstorm, which interrupted Kent's innings, reduced the match to 28 overs a side. Glamorgan appeared on course as Dale and Gibson shared a 50-run stand in seven overs, but 18 from the final over proved too great a task.

Kent

T. R. Ward c Metson b Lefebvre	4	*†S. A. Marsh not out	7
M. J. Walker c Metson b Barwick	5	D. W. Headley not out	1
C. L. Hooper c Lefebvre b Dale	60	L-b 3, n-b 2	5
G. R. Cowdrey c Metson b Dale	24		—
M. V. Fleming c James b Lefebvre	32	1/4 2/49 3/95 (7 wkts, 28 overs)	155
M. A. Ealham c Metson b Gibson	0	4/103 5/119	
N. J. Llong st Metson b Barwick	17	6/143 7/148	

A. P. Igglesden and T. N. Wren did not bat.

Bowling: Lefebvre 6–0–40–2; Watkin 5–0–22–0; Barwick 6–0–32–2; Gibson 8–0–30–1; Dale 3–0–28–2.

Glamorgan

S. P. James lbw b Wren	0	R. P. Lefebvre not out	3
*H. Morris c Fleming b Ealham	21	†C. P. Metson not out	5
M. P. Maynard c Ward b Wren	2	B 1, l-b 5, w 4, n-b 8	18
P. A. Cottey c Llong b Igglesden	8		—
A. Dale c Ealham b Fleming	48	1/0 2/2 3/26 (7 wkts, 28 overs)	147
R. D. B. Croft c Marsh b Igglesden	11	4/50 5/87	
O. D. Gibson b Headley	31	6/137 7/138	

S. L. Watkin and S. R. Barwick did not bat.

Bowling: Wren 7–1–22–2; Igglesden 8–0–34–2; Ealham 4–0–26–1; Headley 6–0–36–1; Fleming 3–0–23–1.

Umpires: V. A. Holder and A. G. T. Whitehead.

GLAMORGAN v SOMERSET

At Swansea, July 31. Glamorgan won by five wickets. Toss: Glamorgan.

Glamorgan triumphed with an over to spare. In a match reduced to 24 overs per side, Somerset were nevertheless bowled out inside their allocation; Gary Butcher, son of former county captain Alan, dismissed Folland with his first ball in the competition.

Somerset

M. N. Lathwell c Metson b Lefebvre .. 5
M. E. Trescothick c Cottey b Gibson .. 7
I. Fletcher c Hemp b Barwick 10
N. A. Folland c Maynard b Butcher ... 25
*G. D. Rose c Maynard b Croft 0
S. C. Ecclestone c Croft b Butcher..... 31
V. P. Clarke lbw b Croft 2
†R. J. Turner not out 9
P. J. Bird run out.................. 4
H. R. J. Trump b Barwick 1
J. I. D. Kerr run out 1
B 6, l-b 3, w 1, n-b 2 12

1/12 2/12 3/37 4/39 5/69 6/81 7/85 8/99 9/103 (23.4 overs) 107

Bowling: Lefebvre 4.4–0–18–1; Gibson 5–1–15–1; Barwick 5–0–15–2; Croft 5–0–23–2; Dale 2–0–19–0; Butcher 2–0–8–2.

Glamorgan

A. Dale c Turner b Rose............. 22
*H. Morris c Turner b Bird 13
D. L. Hemp c Fletcher b Ecclestone ... 35
M. P. Maynard c Trescothick b Trump. 4
P. A. Cottey c Turner b Clarke 6
O. D. Gibson not out 14
R. D. B. Croft not out............... 10
L-b 4, w 3 7

1/30 2/40 3/69 4/81 5/85 (5 wkts, 23 overs) 111

R. P. Lefebvre, †C. P. Metson, G. P. Butcher and S. R. Barwick did not bat.

Bowling: Bird 5–0–18–1; Kerr 3–0–11–0; Trump 5–0–17–1; Rose 3–0–25–1; Ecclestone 4–0–21–1; Clarke 3–0–15–1.

Umpires: J. D. Bond and D. J. Constant.

At Lord's, August 7. GLAMORGAN beat MIDDLESEX by seven wickets.

At Hartlepool, August 21. GLAMORGAN beat DURHAM by 19 runs.

GLAMORGAN v LEICESTERSHIRE

At Neath, August 28. Glamorgan won by 33 runs. Toss: Leicestershire. County debut: G. I. Macmillan.

Barwick claimed four for six in nine balls as Leicestershire, given a good start of 93 by Maddy and Macmillan, the Oxford Blue making his Leicestershire debut, lost all their wickets for 84 in 16 overs.

Glamorgan

S. P. James c Nixon b Dakin......... 49
*H. Morris c Maddy b Hepworth 30
D. L. Hemp c Smith b Dakin 34
M. P. Maynard c Parsons b Simmons .. 27
P. A. Cottey run out 18
O. D. Gibson not out 18
R. D. B. Croft not out............... 18
L-b 8, w 4, n-b 4............ 16

1/71 2/121 3/124 4/162 5/171 (5 wkts, 40 overs) 210

R. P. Lefebvre, †C. P. Metson, S. L. Watkin and S. R. Barwick did not bat.

Bowling: Sheriyar 8–1–44–0; Parsons 6–0–25–0; Hepworth 8–0–35–1; Wells 5–0–20–0; Dakin 8–0–37–2; Simmons 5–0–41–1.

Leicestershire

G. I. Macmillan c Gibson b Croft 46
D. L. Maddy c Lefebvre b Gibson 54
V. J. Wells c Maynard b Barwick 16
B. F. Smith c Maynard b Watkin 18
*P. V. Simmons c Metson b Gibson . . . 8
P. E. Robinson lbw b Lefebvre 18
†P. A. Nixon c Croft b Barwick 1
P. N. Hepworth c Maynard b Barwick . 1
J. M. Dakin c Morris b Barwick 6
G. J. Parsons c Gibson b Barwick 0
A. Sheriyar not out 0
L-b 7, w 2 9

1/93 2/115 3/136 4/147 5/166 6/167 7/170 8/174 9/177 (39 overs) 177

Bowling: Lefebvre 7–0–24–1; Watkin 8–0–26–1; Gibson 8–0–38–2; Croft 8–0–46–1; Barwick 8–0–36–5.

Umpires: D. J. Constant and V. A. Holder.

At Nottingham, September 4. GLAMORGAN lost to NOTTINGHAMSHIRE by eight wickets.

GLAMORGAN v WORCESTERSHIRE

At Cardiff, September 11. Glamorgan won by 29 runs. Toss: Worcestershire.

Worcestershire's hopes of winning the League were all but crushed when they collapsed in spectacular fashion against Croft, whose spell of six for six enabled him to return a final analysis of six for 20, the best figures by a Glamorgan bowler in limited-overs cricket. The visitors crumbled from 63 for no wicket to 76 for seven. Late resistance from Lampitt, Illingworth and Radford was not enough to prevent Worcestershire slipping to third place in the table, four points behind Warwickshire with one match to play.

Glamorgan

S. P. James run out 25
A. Dale c and b Moody 0
D. L. Hemp c Rhodes b Illingworth . . . 15
*M. P. Maynard c Leatherdale b Lampitt . 26
P. A. Cottey c Rhodes b Radford 29
O. D. Gibson st Rhodes b Illingworth . . 7
R. D. B. Croft not out 29
R. P. Lefebvre c Haynes b Newport . . . 16
†C. P. Metson b Radford 1
S. L. Watkin c Rhodes b Newport 4
S. R. Barwick b Newport 0
L-b 8, w 8 16

1/1 2/37 3/71 4/80 5/114 6/114 7/152 8/160 9/168 (39.5 overs) 168

Bowling: Moody 8–1–17–1; Newport 7.5–1–39–3; Illingworth 8–0–32–2; Lampitt 6–0–22–1; Hick 4–0–19–0; Radford 6–1–31–2.

Worcestershire

T. M. Moody lbw b Croft 39
*T. S. Curtis run out 25
G. A. Hick b Croft 0
G. R. Haynes lbw b Croft 0
D. A. Leatherdale c and b Croft 3
M. J. Church c Maynard b Croft 4
†S. J. Rhodes c Cottey b Croft 4
S. R. Lampitt b Lefebvre 28
R. K. Illingworth run out 15
N. V. Radford not out 14
P. J. Newport run out 0
L-b 3, w 4 7

1/63 2/63 3/63 4/64 5/70 6/75 7/76 8/110 9/139 (37.2 overs) 139

Bowling: Lefebvre 7–0–29–1; Watkin 8–0–31–0; Barwick 8–1–24–0; Croft 8–0–20–6; Cottey 2–0–15–0; Gibson 4.2–0–17–0.

Umpires: G. I. Burgess and D. R. Shepherd.

At Southampton, September 18. GLAMORGAN lost to HAMPSHIRE by seven wickets.

GLOUCESTERSHIRE

GLOUCESTERSHIRE v SUSSEX

At Bristol, May 8. Sussex won by 46 runs. Toss: Sussex.

Wells and Speight, who added 106 in 13 overs, set up victory for Sussex in a game cut to 36 overs a side by a hailstorm. Alleyne's spirited 81 off 80 balls was not enough to affect the outcome.

Sussex

D. M. Smith c Russell b Babington	25	F. D. Stephenson b Smith	1
C. W. J. Athey c Russell b Williams	2	†P. Moores not out	13
M. P. Speight c Dawson b Ball	56	L-b 2, w 4, n-b 4	10
*A. P. Wells c Alleyne b Hancock	61		—
N. J. Lenham not out	58	1/26 2/32 3/138 (6 wkts, 36 overs)	233
K. Greenfield c Alleyne b Williams	7	4/166 5/184 6/201	

E. E. Hemmings, P. W. Jarvis and E. S. H. Giddins did not bat.

Bowling: Babington 8–1–29–1; Smith 8–0–42–1; Williams 6–0–41–2; Alleyne 6–0–54–0; Ball 6–0–46–1; Hancock 2–0–19–1.

Gloucestershire

G. D. Hodgson lbw b Hemmings	29	M. C. J. Ball c Hemmings b Giddins	5
S. G. Hinks b Stephenson	0	A. M. Smith not out	1
M. W. Alleyne c Moores b Stephenson	81	A. M. Babington b Jarvis	0
A. J. Wright c Athey b Lenham	15	L-b 9, w 7	16
T. H. C. Hancock b Jarvis	16		—
*†R. C. Russell c Jarvis b Giddins	4	1/2 2/64 3/107 (35.5 overs)	187
R. I. Dawson b Jarvis	17	4/142 5/156 6/161	
R. C. Williams run out	3	7/165 8/184 9/187	

Bowling: Jarvis 7.5–0–40–3; Stephenson 8–0–38–2; Giddins 8–0–34–2; Hemmings 8–0–31–1; Greenfield 2–0–18–0; Lenham 2–0–17–1.

Umpires: T. E. Jesty and B. Leadbeater.

At Worcester, May 15. GLOUCESTERSHIRE lost to WORCESTERSHIRE by ten wickets.

At Gateshead Fell, May 22. DURHAM v GLOUCESTERSHIRE. No result (abandoned).

GLOUCESTERSHIRE v SURREY

At Gloucester, May 29. Surrey won by ten runs. Toss: Gloucestershire.

Ward, with 75 from 91 balls, paved the way for a Surrey victory which left them two points clear at the top of the table. Russell, who had just heard of his omission from England's team for the First Test against New Zealand, kept Gloucestershire in contention, hitting 70 at a run a ball.

Surrey

*†A. J. Stewart c Wright b Williams	32	A. C. S. Pigott run out	1
A. D. Brown b Cooper	0	J. Boiling not out	9
G. P. Thorpe c Hancock b Babington	6	B 1, l-b 3, w 1, n-b 12	17
D. M. Ward c Cooper b Alleyne	75		—
A. J. Hollioake c and b Alleyne	19	1/1 2/10 3/70 (7 wkts, 40 overs)	191
A. W. Smith run out	18	4/136 5/157	
M. A. Butcher not out	14	6/167 7/170	

J. E. Benjamin and A. J. Murphy did not bat.

Bowling: Cooper 7–1–19–1; Babington 7–0–39–1; Walsh 8–0–40–0; Williams 6–0–34–1; Ball 5–0–30–0; Alleyne 7–0–25–2.

Gloucestershire

S. G. Hinks lbw b Benjamin	10	K. E. Cooper b Hollioake	0
M. W. Alleyne c Stewart b Murphy	6	A. M. Babington not out	4
A. J. Wright b Benjamin	49	M. C. J. Ball not out	2
T. H. C. Hancock c Ward b Butcher	8	L-b 3	3
R. I. Dawson c Stewart b Pigott	5		—
†R. C. Russell b Hollioake	70	1/16 2/22 3/46 (9 wkts, 40 overs)	181
*C. A. Walsh b Hollioake	22	4/53 5/122 6/155	
R. C. Williams lbw b Benjamin	2	7/166 8/167 9/178	

Bowling: Benjamin 8–1–40–3; Murphy 8–1–29–1; Pigott 8–2–15–1; Butcher 7–0–35–1; Hollioake 6–0–39–3; Boiling 3–0–20–0.

Umpires: R. Julian and K. E. Palmer.

At Chelmsford, June 5. GLOUCESTERSHIRE lost to ESSEX by 27 runs.

At Nottingham, June 19. GLOUCESTERSHIRE lost to NOTTINGHAMSHIRE by 68 runs.

GLOUCESTERSHIRE v GLAMORGAN

At Bristol, July 3. Glamorgan won by four wickets. Toss: Glamorgan.

Gibson sent Gloucestershire to their fourth successive defeat with a six off the last ball, from Walsh, after openers Morris and James had built a solid platform. Gloucestershire's total owed much to a 71-run stand in 18 overs between Alleyne and Hancock.

Gloucestershire

A. J. Wright c Metson b Watkin	2	*C. A. Walsh c James b Lefebvre	30
M. G. N. Windows c Metson b Watkin	0	M. Davies b Lefebvre	2
T. H. C. Hancock c James b Gibson	43	A. M. Smith not out	1
M. W. Alleyne lbw b Cottey	49	L-b 4, w 4, n-b 8	16
R. I. Dawson lbw b Croft	11		—
†R. C. Russell c Metson b Gibson	8	1/2 2/9 3/80 (9 wkts, 40 overs)	184
R. C. Williams not out	21	4/105 5/121 6/123	
R. M. Wight run out	1	7/125 8/177 9/182	

Bowling: Watkin 7–1–26–2; Lefebvre 8–0–28–2; Barwick 7–0–24–0; Croft 8–0–49–1; Gibson 7–0–36–2; Cottey 3–0–17–1.

Glamorgan

S. P. James c and b Davies	50	R. D. B. Croft c Russell b Smith	6
*H. Morris c Russell b Wight	52	R. P. Lefebvre not out	1
M. P. Maynard st Russell b Wight	1	L-b 4, w 4, n-b 4	12
P. A. Cottey c Walsh b Davies	7		—
D. L. Hemp run out	26	1/99 2/105 3/118 (6 wkts, 40 overs)	187
O. D. Gibson not out	32	4/119 5/156 6/175	

†C. P. Metson, S. L. Watkin and S. R. Barwick did not bat.

Bowling: Williams 6–1–26–0; Walsh 8–2–32–0; Smith 7–0–30–1; Alleyne 4–0–25–0; Wight 7–0–28–2; Davies 8–1–42–2.

Umpires: J. H. Harris and N. T. Plews.

GLOUCESTERSHIRE v SOMERSET

At Bristol, July 10. Gloucestershire won by 37 runs. Toss: Gloucestershire.

Walsh bowled Rose, Turner and Caddick and ran out Payne in six balls, as Gloucestershire recorded their first win in ten one-day matches in 1994. Wright and Windows laid the foundations with an opening stand of 119, and their last ten overs brought 101 runs.

Gloucestershire

A. J. Wright c Rose b Hayhurst	50	*C. A. Walsh not out	11
M. G. N. Windows c Trump b Caddick	72	R. C. Williams not out	4
T. H. C. Hancock c Folland b Hayhurst	32	L-b 4, n-b 2	6
†R. C. Russell c Trump b Caddick	1		—
M. W. Alleyne run out	31	1/119 2/152 3/154 (6 wkts, 40 overs)	232
R. I. Dawson b Caddick	25	4/158 5/211 6/228	

R. M. Wight, A. M. Smith and M. Davies did not bat.

Bowling: Caddick 8–1–41–3; Rose 8–1–19–0; Trump 7–0–39–0; Mallender 8–0–53–0; Hayhurst 8–0–66–2; Payne 1–0–10–0.

Somerset

M. E. Trescothick c Alleyne b Williams	18	A. R. Caddick b Walsh	0
M. N. Lathwell c and b Wight	41	N. A. Mallender not out	4
R. J. Harden c Wright b Wight	31	H. R. J. Trump c and b Smith	1
N. A. Folland c Walsh b Davies	23	L-b 2, w 4, n-b 8	14
G. D. Rose b Walsh	38		—
*A. N. Hayhurst c Wright b Smith	7	1/44 2/87 3/116 (39 overs)	195
†R. J. Turner b Walsh	13	4/129 5/149 6/180	
A. Payne run out	5	7/189 8/189 9/189	

Bowling: Williams 8–0–41–1; Walsh 7–2–23–3; Smith 7–0–47–2; Wight 8–0–33–2; Davies 8–0–41–1; Alleyne 1–0–8–0.

Umpires: T. E. Jesty and D. R. Shepherd.

At Portsmouth, July 17. GLOUCESTERSHIRE lost to HAMPSHIRE by five wickets.

GLOUCESTERSHIRE v YORKSHIRE

At Cheltenham, July 24. Gloucestershire won by three wickets. Toss: Gloucestershire.

Richardson, in his last appearance for Yorkshire before returning home exhausted, struck 44 from 38 balls; he and Parker added 89 in ten overs to give Yorkshire plenty to bowl at. But Alleyne's undefeated 102, following his 109 the previous day, saw Gloucestershire home with ten balls to spare.

Yorkshire

*D. Byas c R. C. J. Williams b Hancock 48
M. P. Vaughan run out 12
†R. J. Blakey c Babington b Hancock 29
R. B. Richardson c Walsh b Babington 44
B. Parker c Alleyne b R. C. Williams 35
P. J. Hartley b Babington 20
A. P. Grayson c R. C. J. Williams b Alleyne 13
M. J. Foster run out 5
R. A. Kettleborough not out 4
C. E. W. Silverwood run out 9
M. A. Robinson c Alleyne b Walsh 1
B 1, l-b 6, w 11, n-b 22 40

1/36 2/110 3/112 4/201 5/207 6/235 7/241 8/245 9/257 (39.5 overs) 260

Bowling: R. C. Williams 8–1–43–1; Walsh 7.5–0–57–1; Babington 8–0–59–2; Alleyne 8–0–28–1; Hancock 4–0–31–2; Ball 4–0–35–0.

Gloucestershire

A. J. Wright c Hartley b Silverwood 14
M. G. N. Windows c Blakey b Silverwood 0
T. H. C. Hancock c Parker b Grayson 38
M. W. Alleyne not out 102
S. G. Hinks c Richardson b Robinson 24
R. I. Dawson c Byas b Foster 35
*C. A. Walsh c Blakey b Foster 18
R. C. Williams lbw b Hartley 0
M. C. J. Ball not out 16
L-b 8, w 2, n-b 4 14

1/1 2/22 3/74 4/115 5/196 6/236 7/241 (7 wkts, 38.2 overs) 261

†R. C. J. Williams and A. M. Babington did not bat.

Bowling: Silverwood 7–0–37–2; Hartley 7.2–0–53–1; Robinson 8–0–27–1; Kettleborough 1–0–12–0; Grayson 8–0–50–1; Foster 7–0–74–2.

Umpires: D. R. Shepherd and R. A. White.

GLOUCESTERSHIRE v KENT

At Cheltenham, July 31. Kent won by 50 runs. Toss: Gloucestershire.

Rain reduced the match to 20 overs a side, and Kent careered along at more than 11 runs an over, hitting a total of 11 sixes and 17 fours. Fleming was their most destructive batsman: his 79 came off 35 balls and included three consecutive sixes off Babington, while Hooper scored 61 off 33 balls. Gloucestershire were unable to compete.

Kent

M. V. Fleming b Williams 79
T. R. Ward b Ball 24
C. L. Hooper run out 61
M. J. Walker c Hancock b Alleyne 33
G. R. Cowdrey not out 15
M. A. Ealham not out 0
B 4, l-b 8, w 3 15

1/85 2/121 3/204 4/217 (4 wkts, 20 overs) 227

N. J. Llong, *†S. A. Marsh, D. W. Headley, M. J. McCague and T. N. Wren did not bat.

Bowling: Cooper 4–0–46–0; Williams 4–0–36–1; Babington 3–0–50–0; Ball 4–0–25–1; Alleyne 4–0–45–1; Hancock 1–0–13–0.

Gloucestershire

A. J. Wright c Walker b Llong 69
M. G. N. Windows b McCague 20
T. H. C. Hancock b McCague 0
M. W. Alleyne st Marsh b Hooper 45
R. I. Dawson c Walker b Hooper 3
*†R. C. Russell c Wren b Fleming 5
R. C. Williams not out 22
M. C. J. Ball not out 3
B 1, l-b 6, w 3 10

1/37 2/39 3/109 4/127 5/145 6/156 (6 wkts, 20 overs) 177

S. G. Hinks, K. E. Cooper and A. M. Babington did not bat.

Bowling: Wren 4–0–22–0; McCague 3–0–20–2; Hooper 4–0–45–2; Headley 4–0–38–0; Llong 3–0–29–1; Fleming 2–0–16–1.

Umpires: G. I. Burgess and R. Palmer.

At Chesterfield, August 7. GLOUCESTERSHIRE lost to DERBYSHIRE by 33 runs.

GLOUCESTERSHIRE v NORTHAMPTONSHIRE

At Bristol, August 14. Gloucestershire won by eight wickets. Toss: Gloucestershire.

Babington, who had retired from county cricket in July, but returned to help Gloucestershire in an injury crisis, bowled eight overs for only nine runs, claiming three wickets – approaching Mike Procter's county record of 8–2–6–3 against Yorkshire in 1979. Walton revived Northamptonshire from 35 for five, but their eventual total of 159 was clearly inadequate.

Northamptonshire

A. Fordham b Williams	6
M. B. Loye c and b Williams	8
†R. J. Warren c Russell b Babington	0
K. M. Curran lbw b Babington	7
T. C. Walton c Hancock b Alleyne	72
R. J. Bailey b Babington	2
A. L. Penberthy run out	15
*A. J. Lamb b Williams	18
J. G. Hughes b Ball	9
N. G. B. Cook not out	8
J. P. Taylor b Ball	1
B 2, l-b 2, w 5, n-b 4	13
1/9 2/10 3/18 4/33 5/35 6/77 7/119 8/149 9/151 (39.5 overs)	159

Bowling: Babington 8–2–9–3; Williams 8–0–33–3; Davies 4–0–19–0; Alleyne 8–0–48–1; Ball 7.5–0–26–2; Hancock 4–0–20–0.

Gloucestershire

A. J. Wright not out	61
M. G. N. Windows c Curran b Cook	41
T. H. C. Hancock b Curran	37
M. W. Alleyne not out	7
L-b 2, w 10, n-b 4	16
1/84 2/135 (2 wkts, 37 overs)	162

R. I. Dawson, *†R. C. Russell, R. C. Williams, M. C. J. Ball, S. G. Hinks, M. Davies and A. M. Babington did not bat.

Bowling: Hughes 6–0–27–0; Curran 8–0–32–1; Taylor 5–0–25–0; Penberthy 5–0–17–0; Cook 8–0–28–1; Walton 2–0–14–0; Bailey 3–0–17–0.

Umpires: J. H. Hampshire and N. T. Plews.

At Manchester, August 21. GLOUCESTERSHIRE lost to LANCASHIRE by five wickets.

GLOUCESTERSHIRE v LEICESTERSHIRE

At Moreton-in-Marsh, September 4. Leicestershire won on scoring-rate. Toss: Gloucestershire.

Rain reduced Gloucestershire's target to 225 in 35 overs after Briers, Macmillan and Wells had shone for the visitors. Briers, who hit 11 fours and batted for all but one ball of the Leicestershire innings, then held four catches.

Leicestershire

P. V. Simmons c Russell b Walsh	4	†P. A. Nixon not out	0
*N. E. Briers b Walsh	105	L-b 7, w 3, n-b 4	14
G. I. Macmillan b Williams	48		——
J. J. Whitaker b Ball	20	1/14 2/84 3/124 (4 wkts, 40 overs)	256
V. J. Wells not out	65	4/256	

T. J. Boon, A. R. K. Pierson, J. M. Dakin, G. J. Parsons and D. J. Millns did not bat.

Bowling: Walsh 6–0–32–2; Smith 8–2–44–0; Williams 8–0–44–1; Davies 8–0–43–0; Ball 7–0–58–1; Alleyne 3–0–28–0.

Gloucestershire

A. J. Wright st Nixon b Simmons	29	M. C. J. Ball b Pierson	0
M. G. N. Windows c Simmons b Wells	26	M. Davies c Simmons b Pierson	13
T. H. C. Hancock c Briers b Wells	13	A. M. Smith not out	4
M. W. Alleyne b Pierson	33	B 2, l-b 3, w 6, n-b 2	13
†R. C. Russell c Briers b Wells	8		——
R. I. Dawson c Briers b Wells	8	1/59 2/63 3/83 (31.1 overs)	155
*C. A. Walsh c Briers b Pierson	0	4/104 5/124 6/124	
R. C. Williams c Nixon b Simmons	8	7/126 8/128 9/151	

Bowling: Parsons 6–0–32–0; Millns 4–0–21–0; Simmons 6–0–22–2; Wells 8–0–46–4; Pierson 7.1–0–29–4.

Umpires: J. C. Balderstone and M. J. Kitchen.

At Lord's, September 11. GLOUCESTERSHIRE beat MIDDLESEX by 53 runs.

GLOUCESTERSHIRE v WARWICKSHIRE

At Bristol, September 18. Warwickshire won by 46 runs. Toss: Gloucestershire.

Warwickshire secured the title – and an unprecedented treble of domestic trophies – but had to stage a remarkable recovery after losing their first three wickets for as many runs. It would have been four had Walsh not dropped Penney second ball. He and Lara, in his last appearance of the season – he was not playing in the Championship match – launched the fightback with 68 in 17 overs, and Penney added another 75 with the inspirational Reeve. For Gloucestershire, only Windows and Dawson, who shared a stand of 50 in 11 overs, were able to make much headway; Small's three wickets took him to an aggregate of 200 in the competition. Warwickshire received the trophy in front of a crowd of about 4,500, mostly their own supporters.

Warwickshire

D. P. Ostler c Davies b Williams	0	R. P. Davis not out	2
N. M. K. Smith c Alleyne b Smith	0	G. C. Small not out	7
B. C. Lara c Smith b Alleyne	38		
R. G. Twose c Russell b Smith	0	L-b 11, w 6, n-b 8	25
T. L. Penney c Ball b Walsh	55		——
*D. A. Reeve c Alleyne b Walsh	50	1/1 2/1 3/3 (8 wkts, 39 overs)	183
G. Welch lbw b Walsh	0	4/71 5/146 6/146	
†K. J. Piper c Wright b Alleyne	6	7/165 8/172	

T. A. Munton did not bat.

Bowling: Williams 8–2–26–1; Smith 8–2–24–2; Walsh 7–1–24–3; Alleyne 8–0–37–2; Ball 5–0–36–0; Davies 3–0–25–0.

Gloucestershire

A. J. Wright lbw b Munton 3	R. C. Williams st Piper b Reeve 9
M. G. N. Windows b Smith 47	M. Davies not out 10
T. H. C. Hancock c Piper b Small..... 7	A. M. Smith c Munton b Smith........ 7
M. W. Alleyne c Piper b Welch....... 7	L-b 7, w 4 11
R. I. Dawson st Piper b Davis........ 29	—
†R. C. Russell lbw b Davis........... 4	1/10 2/30 3/43 (37 overs) 137
M. C. J. Ball c Smith b Small 3	4/93 5/101 6/104
*C. A. Walsh c Twose b Small........ 0	7/104 8/109 9/124

Bowling: Reeve 5–0–17–1; Munton 6–3–16–1; Small 8–2–25–3; Welch 4–1–16–1; Smith 6–0–28–2; Davis 8–0–28–2.

Umpires: K. J. Lyons and P. B. Wight.

HAMPSHIRE

HAMPSHIRE v DERBYSHIRE

At Southampton, May 8. Derbyshire won by seven wickets. Toss: Derbyshire.

Azharuddin, leading Derbyshire in the absence of the injured Barnett, guided his side to victory with 71 off 57 balls, including five sixes. He and O'Gorman shared an unbroken stand of 117 in 18 overs. Earlier, Krikken had held six catches behind the stumps in Hampshire's innings, equalling the competition record. The unusual number of overs faced by Hampshire – 38.5 – was the result of a five-ball over at the end of their innings, when a wicket fell after the time limit for 40 overs had passed, and the umpires brought the players in.

Hampshire

V. P. Terry c Krikken b Wells........ 12	K. D. James c Cork b Warner........ 15
T. C. Middleton c Krikken b DeFreitas 10	M. J. Thursfield not out 1
R. A. Smith c Krikken b Warner 64	B 1, l-b 10, w 12, n-b 18 41
*M. C. J. Nicholas c Bowler b Wells .. 0	—
M. Keech c Krikken b Warner 27	1/22 2/29 3/33 (8 wkts, 38.5 overs) 174
†A. N. Aymes c Krikken b DeFreitas.. 3	4/88 5/91 6/101
S. D. Udal c Krikken b Warner....... 1	7/149 8/174

N. G. Cowans and C. A. Connor did not bat.

Bowling: DeFreitas 7–0–32–2; Mortensen 8–1–18–0; Wells 8–1–22–2; Cork 7–0–46–0; Warner 7.5–0–33–4; Malcolm 1–0–12–0.

Derbyshire

P. D. Bowler c Aymes b Connor 16	T. J. G. O'Gorman not out........... 46
A. S. Rollins b James 9	L-b 7, w 3, n-b 2............ 12
D. G. Cork c Aymes b Connor 24	—
*M. Azharuddin not out 71	1/14 2/55 3/61 (3 wkts, 38.3 overs) 178

A. E. Warner, C. M. Wells, P. A. J. DeFreitas, †K. M. Krikken, O. H. Mortensen and D. E. Malcolm did not bat.

Bowling: Cowans 8–1–34–0; James 8–0–30–1; Thursfield 8–0–39–0; Connor 8–1–28–2; Udal 6.3–0–40–0.

Umpires: G. I. Burgess and B. J. Meyer.

At Hove, May 15. HAMPSHIRE beat SUSSEX by nine wickets.

HAMPSHIRE v MIDDLESEX

At Southampton, May 22. Hampshire won by ten wickets. Toss: Hampshire.

Terry, with three sixes and six fours, dominated a match-winning unbroken opening partnership with Middleton after Middlesex failed to recover from 79 for five, despite the efforts of Carr and Brown, who doubled the score in 13 overs together.

Middlesex

D. L. Haynes lbw b James 21
M. A. Roseberry run out 9
M. R. Ramprakash c Keech b Benjamin 3
*M. W. Gatting b Benjamin 11
J. D. Carr not out 59
P. N. Weekes c Udal b Benjamin 6
†K. R. Brown not out 35
L-b 7, w 7 14

1/31 2/37 3/38 4/66 5/79 (5 wkts, 40 overs) 158

J. E. Emburey, R. L. Johnson, M. A. Feltham and A. R. C. Fraser did not bat.

Bowling: Cowans 8–1–20–0; James 8–2–25–1; Benjamin 8–0–27–3; Connor 8–0–38–0; Udal 6–0–34–0; Keech 2–0–7–0.

Hampshire

V. P. Terry not out 91
T. C. Middleton not out 57
L-b 3, w 8 11

(no wkt, 37 overs) 159

R. A. Smith, *M. C. J. Nicholas, M. Keech, K. D. James, W. K. M. Benjamin, S. D. Udal, †A. N. Aymes, C. A. Connor and N. G. Cowans did not bat.

Bowling: Feltham 8–1–33–0; Fraser 8–2–14–0; Weekes 6–0–34–0; Emburey 7–0–40–0; Johnson 8–0–35–0.

Umpires: P. B. Wight and P. Willey.

At Taunton, June 5. HAMPSHIRE lost to SOMERSET on scoring-rate.

HAMPSHIRE v NOTTINGHAMSHIRE

At Basingstoke, June 12. Hampshire won by three wickets. Toss: Hampshire.

Benjamin propelled Hampshire to victory with 35 off just 19 balls, he and Aymes adding 53 in five overs. He hit two sixes and three fours before perishing in an attempt to win the match with another six, off Evans.

Nottinghamshire

P. R. Pollard c Nicholas b Connor 25
M. A. Crawley c Udal b Cowans 42
*P. Johnson c Morris b Udal 18
J. C. Adams c Connor b Cowans 43
G. F. Archer b Connor 49
†W. M. Noon c and b James 2
G. W. Mike b Connor 7
K. P. Evans st Aymes b Connor 0
R. A. Pick not out 17
M. G. Field-Buss not out 0
L-b 9, w 5, n-b 2 16

1/40 2/61 3/123 4/146 5/151 6/195 7/196 8/211 (8 wkts, 40 overs) 219

D. B. Pennett did not bat.

Bowling: Cowans 8–0–34–2; James 8–0–43–1; Connor 8–0–34–4; Benjamin 8–1–41–0; Udal 6–0–39–1; Keech 2–0–19–0.

Hampshire

R. S. M. Morris c Johnson b Evans	34	W. K. M. Benjamin c Pennett b Evans	35
V. P. Terry c Adams b Pennett	5	S. D. Udal not out	0
R. A. Smith b Mike	37	L-b 13, w 12, n-b 2	27
*M. C. J. Nicholas c Pick b Adams	37		—
M. Keech lbw b Mike	0	1/20 2/62 3/104 (7 wkts, 39 overs)	222
†A. N. Aymes not out	45	4/104 5/149	
K. D. James c Pollard b Pick	2	6/161 7/214	

C. A. Connor and N. G. Cowans did not bat.

Bowling: Pennett 8–0–34–1; Pick 6–0–34–1; Field-Buss 8–0–29–0; Evans 6–0–46–2; Mike 7–1–43–2; Adams 4–0–23–1.

Umpires: J. H. Harris and M. J. Kitchen.

At Manchester, June 19. HAMPSHIRE lost to LANCASHIRE by six wickets.

At Leeds, June 26. HAMPSHIRE lost to YORKSHIRE by 69 runs.

HAMPSHIRE v ESSEX

At Southampton, July 10. Hampshire won by six wickets. Toss: Hampshire.

Gooch's 99 from 98 balls lifted Essex to 142 for two, but they then collapsed, losing their last eight wickets for 41. Hampshire reached a modest target thanks mainly to Smith, though Nicholas and Cox provided more support than Gooch had enjoyed.

Essex

*G. A. Gooch c Benjamin b Udal	99	T. D. Topley c Aymes b Benjamin	0
J. P. Stephenson c Smith b Connor	15	P. M. Such run out	0
N. Hussain c Aymes b Thursfield	18	R. M. Pearson c Nicholas b Connor	7
R. C. Irani c Thursfield b Benjamin	24	W 3	3
M. Diwan c Morris b Maru	0		—
N. Shahid c Smith b Udal	14	1/19 2/81 3/142 (39.4 overs)	183
†R. J. Rollins not out	3	4/142 5/165 6/173	
M. S. Kasprowicz c Aymes b Benjamin	0	7/173 8/173 9/173	

Bowling: Benjamin 8–2–19–3; Connor 7.4–1–37–2; Thursfield 8–0–44–1; Maru 8–0–46–1; Udal 8–0–37–2.

Hampshire

R. S. M. Morris c Rollins b Kasprowicz	0	†A. N. Aymes not out	6
V. P. Terry c Hussain b Topley	8	L-b 7, w 11, n-b 8	26
R. A. Smith c Rollins b Stephenson	74		—
*M. C. J. Nicholas c Hussain b Pearson	47	1/0 2/52 (4 wkts, 39 overs)	184
R. M. F. Cox not out	23	3/123 4/166	

R. J. Maru, S. D. Udal, W. K. M. Benjamin, C. A. Connor and M. J. Thursfield did not bat.

Bowling: Kasprowicz 7–1–27–1; Stephenson 7–0–29–1; Topley 4–0–20–1; Such 8–0–40–0; Irani 5–0–37–0; Pearson 8–0–24–1.

Umpires: J. C. Balderstone and J. H. Harris.

HAMPSHIRE v GLOUCESTERSHIRE

At Portsmouth, July 17. Hampshire won by five wickets. Toss: Hampshire.

Smith, left out by the England selectors for the First Test against South Africa, vented his frustration on Gloucestershire's bowlers, hitting nine fours in 48 as Hampshire won with more than four overs to spare.

Gloucestershire

A. J. Wright c Aymes b Cowans	5	*C. A. Walsh c Aymes b James	0
M. G. N. Windows c Benjamin b Udal	48	M. Davies c Aymes b Benjamin	14
T. H. C. Hancock c Nicholas b Connor	20	A. M. Smith not out	4
M. W. Alleyne c Middleton b Udal	3	L-b 10, w 10, n-b 4	24
R. I. Dawson run out	8		—
†R. C. Russell b Benjamin	12	1/8 2/44 3/56 (39.1 overs)	149
R. C. Williams c Aymes b James	8	4/79 5/107 6/120	
R. M. Wight c sub b Cowans	3	7/127 8/127 9/128	

Bowling: Cowans 8–2–21–2; Benjamin 7.1–0–26–2; James 8–1–26–2; Connor 8–0–38–1; Udal 8–0–28–2.

Hampshire

T. C. Middleton run out	6	S. D. Udal not out	20
V. P. Terry c Alleyne b Williams	0		
R. A. Smith c Dawson b Alleyne	48	L-b 1, w 2, n-b 10	13
*M. C. J. Nicholas c Russell b Alleyne	21		—
†A. N. Aymes not out	22	1/1 2/30 3/82 (5 wkts, 35.4 overs)	152
K. D. James c Alleyne b Smith	22	4/87 5/122	

R. M. F. Cox, W. K. M. Benjamin, C. A. Connor and N. G. Cowans did not bat.

Bowling: Williams 8–2–25–1; Walsh 5.4–0–20–0; Smith 8–0–39–1; Davies 2.2–0–18–0; Alleyne 6.4–0–25–2; Wight 3–0–14–0; Hancock 2–0–10–0.

Umpires: J. D. Bond and D. J. Constant.

At Worcester, July 24. HAMPSHIRE lost to WORCESTERSHIRE by 42 runs.

HAMPSHIRE v NORTHAMPTONSHIRE

At Southampton, July 31. Northamptonshire won by six runs. Toss: Hampshire.

Terry and Smith added 98 in 14 overs to give Hampshire a strong victory chance in a match cut to 32 overs a side, and Terry batted on until the penultimate over. But once Cook removed him and James, 18 off the last over proved too formidable a task. This was Northamptonshire's first-ever Sunday League win at Southampton, and their first League win in Hampshire since 1972.

Northamptonshire

A. Fordham c Terry b Connor	21	†R. J. Warren c Aymes b Connor	5
M. B. Loye c Cowans b Maru	42	M. N. Bowen not out	2
T. C. Walton lbw b Connor	1	B 4, l-b 5, w 5	14
J. N. Snape c Connor b Udal	9		—
R. J. Bailey st Aymes b Maru	32	1/60 2/62 3/80 (8 wkts, 32 overs)	191
*A. J. Lamb c Udal b Maru	44	4/84 5/162 6/166	
A. L. Penberthy c Udal b Cowans	21	7/179 8/191	

N. G. B. Cook and J. G. Hughes did not bat.

Bowling: James 6–1–29–0; Cowans 6–0–37–1; Maru 6–0–43–3; Connor 7–0–32–3; Udal 7–0–41–1.

Hampshire

V. P. Terry c Hughes b Cook 95
R. M. F. Cox st Warren b Cook 6
R. A. Smith c Walton b Bailey 46
*M. C. J. Nicholas run out 0
M. Keech c Bailey b Snape 9
S. D. Udal b Snape 0
†A. N. Aymes not out 8
K. D. James c Bailey b Cook 2
R. J. Maru not out 6
L-b 8, w 5 13

1/32 2/130 3/130 4/158 5/159 6/170 7/173 (7 wkts, 32 overs) 185

C. A. Connor and N. G. Cowans did not bat.

Bowling: Hughes 5–0–13–0; Cook 6–0–19–3; Penberthy 7–0–44–0; Snape 7–0–38–2; Bowen 3–0–31–0; Bailey 4–0–32–1.

Umpires: A. A. Jones and R. Julian.

At Canterbury, August 7. HAMPSHIRE lost to KENT by six wickets.

HAMPSHIRE v SURREY

At Southampton, August 21. Hampshire won by seven wickets. Toss: Hampshire.

Smith's unbeaten 110 off 89 balls, his seventh League century, steered Hampshire to victory with nine balls to spare, good support coming from White who, on his Sunday debut, shared in a decisive 103-run partnership. Earlier, Smith had put on 118 with Middleton. Surrey's total was built around a hard-hitting 99 from Brown, but a late collapse saw them lose six wickets for 37. James took five wickets for the first time in the League.

Surrey

D. J. Bicknell lbw b James 40
A. D. Brown c Nicholas b James 99
D. M. Ward c Terry b Jean-Jacques . . . 35
A. J. Hollioake lbw b James 14
M. A. Butcher c and b James 4
A. W. Smith c Aymes b Jean-Jacques . . 24
†G. J. Kersey c Aymes b James 0
*M. P. Bicknell c Terry b Jean-Jacques 7
J. Boiling not out 11
N. M. Kendrick not out 1
B 1, l-b 13, w 8, n-b 4 26

1/108 2/169 3/211 4/212 5/221 6/222 7/248 8/248 (8 wkts, 39 overs) 261

A. C. S. Pigott did not bat.

Bowling: Connor 8–1–45–0; Cowans 7–1–53–0; James 8–0–42–5; Jean-Jacques 8–0–44–3; Udal 8–0–63–0.

Hampshire

T. C. Middleton c Boiling b Kendrick . . 73
V. P. Terry c Kersey b Pigott 10
R. A. Smith not out 110
*M. C. J. Nicholas c Kersey b Pigott . . 0
G. W. White not out 49
L-b 7, w 7, n-b 6 20

1/37 2/155 3/159 (3 wkts, 37.3 overs) 262

K. D. James, †A. N. Aymes, S. D. Udal, M. Jean-Jacques, C. A. Connor and N. G. Cowans did not bat.

Bowling: M. P. Bicknell 7–0–45–0; Pigott 8–1–36–2; Hollioake 7–0–56–0; Butcher 7–0–54–0; Boiling 3–0–26–0; Kendrick 5.3–0–38–1.

Umpires: V. A. Holder and P. Willey.

HAMPSHIRE v DURHAM

At Portsmouth, August 28. Durham won by ten wickets. Toss: Durham.

Durham reached their target with 32 balls to spare, Longley and Larkins securing Durham's first-ever ten-wicket victory in the competition and Hampshire's first ten-wicket defeat. Their unbroken stand of 220 was the highest ever made by an opening pair to win. It was also Durham's biggest for any wicket in any one-day tournament. Larkins scored his 14th century in the Sunday League – two more than his nearest rival, Gooch. He faced 98 deliveries and hit four sixes and 11 fours.

Hampshire

T. C. Middleton run out 2
V. P. Terry c Morris b Bainbridge 5
R. A. Smith run out 39
G. W. White run out 35
*M. C. J. Nicholas c Morris b Wood . . 45
†A. N. Aymes c Morris b Wood 54
K. D. James not out 13
R. J. Maru not out 7
B 2, l-b 5, w 6, n-b 4 17

1/5 2/35 3/86 4/100 5/197 6/200 (6 wkts, 40 overs) 217

J. N. B. Bovill, C. A. Connor and N. G. Cowans did not bat.

Bowling: Wood 8–0–34–2; Bainbridge 8–0–39–1; Brown 8–0–32–0; Walker 8–0–65–0; Cox 8–1–40–0.

Durham

J. I. Longley not out 72
W. Larkins not out 131
L-b 8, w 5, n-b 4 17

(no wkt, 34.4 overs) 220

J. E. Morris, J. A. Daley, *P. Bainbridge, S. Hutton, S. J. E. Brown, †C. W. Scott, A. Walker, J. Wood and D. M. Cox did not bat.

Bowling: Cowans 8–0–47–0; Bovill 8–0–40–0; Connor 7–0–24–0; James 5–0–35–0; Maru 6.4–0–66–0.

Umpires: R. Palmer and D. R. Shepherd.

At Birmingham, September 6. HAMPSHIRE lost to WARWICKSHIRE on scoring-rate.

At Leicester, September 11. HAMPSHIRE lost to LEICESTERSHIRE by eight runs.

HAMPSHIRE v GLAMORGAN

At Southampton, September 18. Hampshire won by seven wickets. Toss: Hampshire.

Glamorgan, the 1993 champions, ended their season on a low note as Terry, with an unbeaten 78 from 118 balls, steered Hampshire to a comfortable win.

Glamorgan

S. P. James run out 4
A. Dale c Whitaker b Connor 3
D. L. Hemp b James 13
*M. P. Maynard c Whitaker b James . . 37
P. A. Cottey lbw b Thursfield 9
O. D. Gibson c Aymes b Udal 1
R. D. B. Croft run out 0
R. P. Lefebvre c Aymes b James 25
†C. P. Metson not out 26
S. L. Watkin c Aymes b Connor 6
S. R. Barwick b Connor 5
L-b 11, w 3, n-b 2 16

1/9 2/16 3/33 4/52 5/55 6/55 7/83 8/107 9/127 (37.5 overs) 145

Bowling: Connor 7.5–1–33–3; Bovill 6–0–19–0; James 8–0–37–3; Udal 8–3–10–1; Thursfield 6–0–27–1; Whitaker 2–0–8–0.

Hampshire

V. P. Terry not out 78
P. R. Whitaker c Hemp b Watkin..... 5
R. A. Smith c Lefebvre b Croft 18
G. W. White c Dale b Lefebvre....... 23
*M. C. J. Nicholas not out........... 10
B 3, l-b 4, w 5.............. 12

1/14 2/67 3/132 (3 wkts, 36.2 overs) 146

K. D. James, †A. N. Aymes, M. J. Thursfield, S. D. Udal, C. A. Connor and J. N. B. Bovill did not bat.

Bowling: Lefebvre 8–1–19–1; Watkin 8–0–30–1; Croft 8–1–34–1; Barwick 7–0–16–0; Gibson 3–0–18–0; Dale 2–0–21–0; Hemp 0.2–0–1–0.

Umpires: J. C. Balderstone and G. Sharp.

KENT

KENT v NOTTINGHAMSHIRE

At Canterbury, May 8. Nottinghamshire won by four wickets. Toss: Nottinghamshire.

Victory over the 1993 runners-up, in a contest reduced to 37 overs per side by their slow over-rate, gave Nottinghamshire's campaign an early boost – and an early fine. Evans did most to make the result possible, claiming a Sunday-best four for 26 as Kent struggled for runs and then seeing his side home with an unbeaten 20.

Kent

T. R. Ward c Lewis b Pick 37
*M. R. Benson b Mike 12
C. L. Hooper c Adams b Evans....... 1
N. R. Taylor c Adams b Evans 1
N. J. Llong not out 41
G. R. Cowdrey c Pollard b Field-Buss.. 20
M. V. Fleming c Pick b Mike 16
†S. A. Marsh c Adams b Evans....... 2
D. W. Headley c and b Evans 1
M. J. McCague not out.............. 1
L-b 12, w 7, n-b 11.......... 30

1/56 2/58 3/58 4/67 5/114 6/151 7/158 8/160 (8 wkts, 37 overs) 162

A. P. Igglesden did not bat.

Bowling: Lewis 6–0–22–0; Pick 8–1–36–1; Evans 7–0–26–4; Mike 7–1–22–2; Crawley 4–0–20–0; Field-Buss 5–0–24–1.

Nottinghamshire

P. R. Pollard c Hooper b Headley..... 9
P. Johnson b Igglesden 12
†J. C. Adams c Llong b Headley...... 0
*R. T. Robinson b Hooper........... 43
G. F. Archer c Marsh b Igglesden..... 0
C. C. Lewis c Hooper b McCague..... 28
M. A. Crawley not out 20
K. P. Evans not out.................. 20
L-b 11, w 12, n-b 9.......... 32

1/19 2/24 3/35 4/36 5/93 6/120 (6 wkts, 35.4 overs) 164

G. W. Mike, R. A. Pick and M. G. Field-Buss did not bat.

Bowling: Igglesden 8–0–36–2; Headley 7.4–3–35–2; Fleming 3–0–19–0; McCague 8–0–32–1; Hooper 8–1–29–1; Llong 1–0–2–0.

Umpires: G. Sharp and P. B. Wight.

At Chelmsford, May 15. KENT beat ESSEX by eight wickets.

KENT v LANCASHIRE

At Canterbury, May 22. Lancashire won by eight wickets. Toss: Lancashire.

Lancashire's attack, led by the economical Martin, contained Kent, despite a brief flurry from Fleming, who hit 22 off 23 balls. Atherton's hasty journey from Lord's after the abandonment of the second one-day international against New Zealand proved a wasted one: wearing kit borrowed from a team-mate (with the name Derbyshire across his back) he departed in the third over. But Lloyd and Crawley – with his highest score in one-day competition – posted 157 in 32 overs to decide the issue.

Kent

T. R. Ward c Hegg b Martin 7
*M. R. Benson c Atherton b Gallian ... 22
C. L. Hooper lbw b Martin 1
N. R. Taylor b Gallian 36
N. J. Llong c Watkinson b Yates...... 13
M. V. Fleming b Wasim Akram 22
M. A. Ealham b Martin 14
†S. A. Marsh not out................ 24
D. J. Spencer b Austin 6
D. W. Headley b Wasim Akram 1
A. P. Igglesden not out 3
L-b 7, w 3, n-b 7............ 17

1/14 2/22 3/50 4/79 5/94 6/111 7/134 8/146 9/151 (9 wkts, 40 overs) 166

Bowling: Martin 8–3–15–3; Wasim Akram 8–0–36–2; Austin 8–0–35–1; Watkinson 7–0–36–0; Gallian 6–0–20–2; Yates 3–0–17–1.

Lancashire

M. A. Atherton c Marsh b Igglesden... 2
G. D. Lloyd not out................. 55
J. P. Crawley lbw b Ealham.......... 91
J. E. R. Gallian not out 6
B 4, l-b 3, w 7, n-b 2 16

1/2 2/159 (2 wkts, 36.5 overs) 170

N. J. Speak, *M. Watkinson, Wasim Akram, I. D. Austin, †W. K. Hegg, G. Yates and P. J. Martin did not bat.

Bowling: Igglesden 8–1–20–1; Headley 4–1–13–0; Spencer 6–0–18–0; Ealham 6.5–0–44–1; Hooper 8–0–38–0; Fleming 4–0–30–0.

Umpires: D. J. Constant and M. J. Kitchen.

At Leicester, May 29. KENT beat LEICESTERSHIRE by 60 runs.

KENT v SUSSEX

At Tunbridge Wells, June 5. Kent won by five wickets. Toss: Sussex.

Hooper, with two sixes and seven fours, shared a decisive partnership of 73 in 11 overs with Taylor. Giddins bowled well for four for 23, his best League figures, and refused to concede defeat without a struggle, but Kent reached their target with 13 balls to spare.

Sussex

D. M. Smith b Hooper 36
K. Greenfield c Taylor b Spencer...... 28
*A. P. Wells c and b Fleming 63
N. J. Lenham b Fleming............. 8
F. D. Stephenson b Headley.......... 25
†P. Moores c Taylor b Fleming 10
J. A. North b Headley 3
C. C. Remy not out................. 5
B 1, l-b 12, w 13, n-b 4 30

1/68 2/93 3/121 4/178 5/199 6/199 7/208 (7 wkts, 40 overs) 208

E. E. Hemmings, P. W. Jarvis and E. S. H. Giddins did not bat.

Bowling: Igglesden 6–0–26–0; Headley 8–0–55–2; Hooper 8–0–32–1; Spencer 8–0–26–1; Ealham 5–0–31–0; Fleming 5–0–25–3.

Kent

T. R. Ward c Moores b Giddins	29	M. A. Ealham not out	9
*M. R. Benson c North b Hemmings	46		
C. L. Hooper c Lenham b Giddins	74	L-b 8, w 6, n-b 6	20
N. R. Taylor b Giddins	33		—
N. J. Llong not out	1	1/50 2/127 3/200 (5 wkts, 37.5 overs)	212
M. V. Fleming lbw b Giddins	0	4/203 5/203	

†S. A. Marsh, D. J. Spencer, D. W. Headley and A. P. Igglesden did not bat.

Bowling: Jarvis 8–1–40–0; Stephenson 7.5–0–51–0; Giddins 7–0–23–4; Remy 6–0–40–0; Hemmings 8–0–37–1; Greenfield 1–0–13–0.

Umpires: R. Julian and R. A. White.

KENT v MIDDLESEX

At Canterbury, June 12. Middlesex won by 11 runs. Toss: Kent.

The Middlesex spinners, Emburey and Weekes, sapped Kent's strength as they declined from a useful 97 for one. The visitors' total owed much to Roseberry, who opened the innings and was run out off the last ball, with support coming from Ramprakash and Brown.

Middlesex

D. L. Haynes c Taylor b Headley	13	M. A. Feltham not out	4
M. A. Roseberry run out	105		
M. R. Ramprakash c Marsh b Ealham	41	L-b 1, w 5, n-b 4	10
*M. W. Gatting c Fleming b Hooper	5		—
†K. R. Brown c Ealham b Headley	32	1/34 2/116 3/130 (7 wkts, 40 overs)	213
J. D. Carr c Benson b Fleming	0	4/200 5/205	
P. N. Weekes c Benson b Headley	3	6/208 7/213	

J. E. Emburey, R. L. Johnson and A. R. C. Fraser did not bat.

Bowling: Igglesden 8–2–21–0; Headley 8–0–54–3; Spencer 4–0–28–0; Ealham 6–0–38–1; Hooper 8–0–42–1; Fleming 6–0–29–1.

Kent

T. R. Ward c Roseberry b Feltham	32	D. J. Spencer c Roseberry b Emburey	12
*M. R. Benson b Johnson	47	D. W. Headley c Fraser b Johnson	1
C. L. Hooper c Feltham b Johnson	24	A. P. Igglesden not out	1
N. R. Taylor c Haynes b Weekes	1	L-b 3, w 2, n-b 4	9
N. J. Llong b Emburey	6		—
M. V. Fleming b Weekes	27	1/50 2/97 3/106 (38.5 overs)	202
M. A. Ealham c Carr b Weekes	14	4/116 5/125 6/158	
†S. A. Marsh run out	28	7/160 8/192 9/201	

Bowling: Feltham 8–0–44–1; Fraser 7–0–38–0; Emburey 8–0–46–2; Johnson 8–0–34–3; Weekes 8–0–37–3.

Umpires: T. E. Jesty and N. T. Plews.

At Birmingham, June 19. KENT lost to WARWICKSHIRE by six wickets.

KENT v YORKSHIRE

At Maidstone, July 3. Kent won by eight wickets. Toss: Yorkshire.

Wren, despite a dislocated finger, bowled Byas, Metcalfe and Richardson in four balls to hamper Yorkshire's progress. Then Ward, with 59 off 57 deliveries, and Hooper led Kent's successful chase.

Yorkshire

*M. D. Moxon b Igglesden 4
D. Byas b Wren 13
A. A. Metcalfe b Wren 10
R. B. Richardson b Wren 0
†R. J. Blakey lbw b Ealham 9
A. P. Grayson b Fleming 55
P. J. Hartley c Ward b Fleming 35
M. J. Foster b Fleming 9
G. M. Hamilton not out 16
C. E. W. Silverwood not out 1
L-b 8, w 5 13

1/8 2/32 3/32 (8 wkts, 40 overs) 165
4/36 5/54 6/134
7/141 8/161

M. A. Robinson did not bat.

Bowling: Igglesden 8–0–29–1; Wren 6–1–29–3; Ealham 6–2–14–1; Thompson 6–1–18–0; Hooper 8–0–35–0; Fleming 6–0–32–3.

Kent

T. R. Ward c Blakey b Hartley 59
*M. R. Benson c Moxon b Robinson . . . 7
C. L. Hooper not out 52
N. R. Taylor not out 25
L-b 11, w 4, n-b 8 23

1/50 2/106 (2 wkts, 28.3 overs) 166

G. R. Cowdrey, M. V. Fleming, M. A. Ealham, †S. A. Marsh, J. B. D. Thompson, T. N. Wren and A. P. Igglesden did not bat.

Bowling: Hartley 5–1–39–1; Silverwood 6.3–0–38–0; Robinson 7–0–21–1; Hamilton 6–0–37–0; Foster 2–0–8–0; Grayson 2–0–12–0.

Umpires: J. D. Bond and K. E. Palmer.

KENT v WORCESTERSHIRE

At Canterbury, July 17. Kent won by four wickets. Toss: Kent.

Fleming masterminded Kent's victory, capturing four wickets in 13 balls and then hitting 39 in a crucial fifth-wicket stand of 60 with Ealham. McCague also took four wickets – both he and Fleming returned Sunday-best figures – as Worcestershire's last eight wickets fell for 39.

Worcestershire

T. M. Moody lbw b Wren 17
*T. S. Curtis lbw b McCague 15
G. A. Hick c Marsh b Fleming 48
G. R. Haynes c Patel b Fleming 13
D. A. Leatherdale c Marsh b Fleming . . 0
†S. J. Rhodes c and b McCague 14
S. R. Lampitt c Marsh b Fleming 2
N. V. Radford run out 14
R. K. Illingworth b McCague 3
P. J. Newport not out 0
P. Mirza lbw b McCague 0
B 1, l-b 11, w 6 18

1/32 2/60 3/105 (36.5 overs) 144
4/106 5/109 6/113
7/140 8/143 9/144

Bowling: Wren 8–1–21–1; Ealham 6–1–17–0; McCague 6.5–0–19–4; Patel 2–0–10–0; Hooper 8–0–29–0; Fleming 6–0–36–4.

Kent

T. R. Ward c Haynes b Newport 4
M. J. Walker lbw b Newport 19
C. L. Hooper c and b Moody 1
G. R. Cowdrey c Rhodes b Radford . . . 12
M. V. Fleming b Haynes 39
M. A. Ealham b Radford 34
N. J. Llong not out 15
*†S. A. Marsh not out 10
L-b 7, w 4 11

1/6 2/27 3/31 (6 wkts, 39.2 overs) 145
4/47 5/107 6/124

M. M. Patel, M. J. McCague and T. N. Wren did not bat.

Bowling: Moody 8–1–14–1; Newport 8–1–28–2; Radford 8–1–13–2; Lampitt 4.2–0–24–0; Illingworth 4–0–21–0; Mirza 2–0–16–0; Haynes 5–0–22–1.

Umpires: J. C. Balderstone and P. Willey.

At Ebbw Vale, July 24. KENT beat GLAMORGAN by eight runs.

At Cheltenham, July 31. KENT beat GLOUCESTERSHIRE by 50 runs.

KENT v HAMPSHIRE

At Canterbury, August 7. Kent won by six wickets. Toss: Kent.

Kent made it five wins in a row, Hooper and Fleming setting them on course with 82 in 15 overs for the second wicket. Terry, when 14, reached 5,000 runs in the competition.

Hampshire

V. P. Terry lbw b Ealham	21	K. D. James b McCague	12
T. C. Middleton b Headley	65	M. Jean-Jacques not out	4
R. A. Smith c Llong b Hooper	13	L-b 3, w 5, n-b 2	10
*M. C. J. Nicholas c Marsh b Fleming	8		—
M. Keech run out	11	1/48 2/77 3/88 (7 wkts, 40 overs)	169
†A. N. Aymes not out	24	4/107 5/138	
S. D. Udal b Headley	1	6/140 7/161	

C. A. Connor and N. G. Cowans did not bat.

Bowling: Wren 8–1–22–0; McCague 8–0–36–1; Ealham 6–0–31–1; Hooper 8–0–29–1; Fleming 4–0–13–1; Headley 6–0–35–2.

Kent

T. R. Ward c Aymes b Cowans	4	M. A. Ealham not out	7
M. V. Fleming b Connor	37	L-b 12, w 8, n-b 6	26
C. L. Hooper c Nicholas b Jean-Jacques	56		—
M. J. Walker c Terry b James	20	1/11 2/93 (4 wkts, 36 overs)	170
G. R. Cowdrey not out	20	3/138 4/149	

N. J. Llong, *†S. A. Marsh, D. W. Headley, M. J. McCague and T. N. Wren did not bat.

Bowling: Cowans 6–1–19–1; Jean-Jacques 8–0–45–1; Connor 8–1–28–1; James 6–0–43–1; Udal 8–1–23–0.

Umpires: G. Sharp and R. A. White.

KENT v DURHAM

At Canterbury, August 14. Kent won by 68 runs. Toss: Durham.

Kent maintained their challenge for honours with Hooper and Fleming sharing another important second-wicket stand, this time 154 in 24 overs. Durham then struggled after a poor start, despite Daley's unbeaten 98 from 118 balls.

Kent

T. R. Ward b Cummins	10	N. J. Llong not out	31
M. V. Fleming c Walker b Graveney	68	*†S. A. Marsh not out	7
C. L. Hooper c Birbeck b Cummins	77	B 4, l-b 11, w 4, n-b 6	25
M. J. Walker st Scott b Graveney	20		—
G. R. Cowdrey c Morris b Graveney	13	1/14 2/168 3/193 (6 wkts, 40 overs)	264
M. A. Ealham c Scott b Walker	13	4/209 5/209 6/243	

M. J. McCague, M. M. Patel and T. N. Wren did not bat.

Bowling: Cummins 8–0–56–2; Walker 8–0–43–1; Birbeck 8–0–43–0; Graveney 8–1–49–3; Bainbridge 8–0–58–0.

Durham

J. I. Longley b McCague	20	A. Walker c Ward b Llong	6
M. Saxelby b Ealham	1	*P. Bainbridge not out	9
J. E. Morris b Ealham	0		
J. A. Daley not out	98	L-b 10, w 7	17
S. Hutton lbw b McCague	0		——
A. C. Cummins c Marsh b McCague	18	1/5 2/5 3/51 (8 wkts, 40 overs)	196
†C. W. Scott c Marsh b Patel	18	4/51 5/77 6/105	
S. D. Birbeck c Walker b Llong	9	7/167 8/177	

D. A. Graveney did not bat.

Bowling: Wren 5–0–15–0; Ealham 8–0–52–2; McCague 5–0–20–3; Patel 8–0–25–1; Hooper 7–0–37–0; Fleming 3–0–12–0; Llong 4–0–25–2.

Umpires: B. Dudleston and J. W. Holder.

At Derby, August 21. KENT beat DERBYSHIRE by 76 runs.

At Northampton, August 28. KENT beat NORTHAMPTONSHIRE by 40 runs.

KENT v SOMERSET

At Canterbury, September 11. Kent won by 66 runs. Toss: Somerset.

Kent successfully defended a modest-looking total of 172, thanks largely to fine bowling from McCague and Hooper, as Somerset were dismissed for 106. The result – Kent's ninth successive victory – left them two points behind leaders Warwickshire going into the final round of matches. Before the game, groundsman Brian Fitch was injured when a gust of wind blew one of the covers several yards into the air with him clinging on to it. He fell on to the wicket and had to be stretchered off; play was delayed 15 minutes.

Kent

T. R. Ward c Hallett b Trump	46	M. J. McCague b Mallender	7
M. V. Fleming run out	3	M. M. Patel b Hayhurst	1
C. L. Hooper c Turner b Ecclestone	2	T. N. Wren not out	5
M. J. Walker b Ecclestone	8	L-b 7, w 5	12
G. R. Cowdrey b Caddick	24		——
N. J. Llong b Mallender	55	1/23 2/26 3/49 (39.2 overs)	172
M. A. Ealham lbw b Hayhurst	9	4/78 5/92 6/143	
*†S. A. Marsh lbw b Caddick	0	7/144 8/158 9/159	

Bowling: Mallender 7.2–0–38–2; Ecclestone 8–1–33–2; Trump 6–1–23–1; Caddick 8–2–17–2; Hallett 5–0–39–0; Hayhurst 5–0–15–2.

Somerset

M. N. Lathwell c Llong b Ealham	7	J. C. Hallett c and b Hooper	5
K. A. Parsons c Marsh b Fleming	18	A. R. Caddick c Hooper b McCague	7
R. J. Harden b Ealham	0	H. R. J. Trump st Marsh b Patel	6
P. C. L. Holloway c Marsh b McCague	15	L-b 3, w 3	6
*A. N. Hayhurst b McCague	11		——
S. C. Ecclestone b Hooper	7	1/13 2/14 3/39 (39.2 overs)	106
†R. J. Turner c Marsh b McCague	5	4/52 5/55 6/63	
N. A. Mallender not out	19	7/71 8/82 9/93	

Bowling: Wren 8–1–20–0; Ealham 5–0–11–2; Fleming 7–0–28–1; McCague 8–0–25–4; Hooper 8–3–10–2; Patel 3.2–0–9–1.

Umpires: D. J. Constant and A. A. Jones.

At The Oval, September 18. KENT lost to SURREY by 24 runs.

LANCASHIRE

LANCASHIRE v SURREY

At Manchester, May 8. Surrey won by one run. Toss: Lancashire.

Lancashire were apparently cruising to victory at 164 for two in the 37th over, Lloyd and Fairbrother having added 140. But they lost their way when Fairbrother retired with a hamstring strain. The next three wickets fell for three runs and they failed to score the 13 required from the final over.

Surrey

A. D. Brown c Hegg b Martin	18	M. P. Bicknell c Austin b Gallian	9
*A. J. Stewart c Atherton b Yates	40	†N. F. Sargeant not out	11
G. P. Thorpe c Hegg b Wasim Akram	10	L-b 1, w 6	7
D. M. Ward run out	39		—
A. J. Hollioake lbw b Yates	0	1/31 2/68 3/77 (7 wkts, 40 overs)	179
A. W. Smith c Fairbrother b Martin	28	4/77 5/135	
M. A. Butcher not out	17	6/150 7/166	

A. J. Murphy and J. E. Benjamin did not bat.

Bowling: Austin 8–0–31–0; Martin 8–0–36–2; Wasim Akram 5.2–0–31–1; Watkinson 8–0–24–0; Yates 5–0–29–2; Gallian 5.4–0–27–1.

Lancashire

M. A. Atherton c Thorpe b Bicknell	12	I. D. Austin not out	9
G. D. Lloyd run out	77	†W. K. Hegg not out	1
J. P. Crawley run out	1	B 4, l-b 8, w 4, n-b 2	18
N. H. Fairbrother retired hurt	59		—
*M. Watkinson run out	0	1/21 2/24 (6 wkts, 40 overs)	178
J. E. R. Gallian c Bicknell b Hollioake	1	3/164 4/167	
Wasim Akram run out	0	5/167 6/176	

G. Yates and P. J. Martin did not bat.

N. H. Fairbrother retired hurt at 164-2.

Bowling: Bicknell 8–1–18–1; Benjamin 8–1–31–0; Butcher 7–0–37–0; Smith 3–0–17–0; Murphy 8–0–41–0; Hollioake 6–0–22–1.

Umpires: J. H. Hampshire and K. J. Lyons.

At Canterbury, May 22. LANCASHIRE beat KENT by eight wickets.

LANCASHIRE v SOMERSET

At Manchester, May 29. Lancashire won by 15 runs. Toss: Somerset.

Crawley celebrated the award of his county cap – Martin was likewise honoured before the start – by top-scoring for Lancashire in a match reduced to 31 overs a side. Somerset fell short despite a defiant innings from Rose, whose 68 came from only 49 balls.

Lancashire

M. A. Atherton c Clarke b Bird....... 5
G. D. Lloyd c Clarke b Rose.......... 28
J. P. Crawley c Harden b Payne...... 60
J. E. R. Gallian c Mushtaq Ahmed b Hayhurst. 44
Wasim Akram c Bird b Payne......... 7
N. J. Speak c Lathwell b Rose......... 16
*M. Watkinson c Folland b Payne..... 14
I. D. Austin c Bird b Payne........... 4
†W. K. Hegg not out................. 13
P. J. Martin c Hayhurst b Rose....... 2
B 1, l-b 3, w 8, n-b 2........ 14

1/22 2/56 3/133 4/150 5/165 6/186 7/191 8/193 9/207 (9 wkts, 31 overs) 207

G. Yates did not bat.

Bowling: van Troost 5–0–37–0; Bird 3–0–23–1; Mushtaq Ahmed 7–0–39–0; Rose 6–0–30–3; Hayhurst 6–0–37–1; Payne 4–0–37–4.

Somerset

M. N. Lathwell c Hegg b Yates....... 24
N. A. Folland b Wasim Akram....... 19
R. J. Harden c Speak b Gallian....... 27
G. D. Rose run out.................. 68
V. P. Clarke c Atherton b Gallian..... 4
*A. N. Hayhurst not out............. 23
A. Payne b Wasim Akram............ 4
†P. C. L. Holloway not out............ 3
B 1, l-b 11, w 4, n-b 4....... 20

1/47 2/49 3/152 4/157 5/157 6/181 (6 wkts, 31 overs) 192

Mushtaq Ahmed, A. P. van Troost and P. J. Bird did not bat.

Bowling: Martin 6–1–26–0; Austin 6–0–36–0; Yates 6–0–29–1; Wasim Akram 7–0–34–2; Watkinson 4–0–45–0; Gallian 2–0–10–2.

Umpires: B. Leadbeater and P. Willey.

At Northampton, June 5. LANCASHIRE beat NORTHAMPTONSHIRE by eight runs.

At Horsham, June 12. LANCASHIRE beat SUSSEX by seven wickets.

LANCASHIRE v HAMPSHIRE

At Manchester, June 19. Lancashire won by six wickets. Toss: Lancashire.

Rain reduced the game to 27 overs a side, and Lancashire reached their fifth consecutive win with 16 balls remaining after Fairbrother provided the necessary impetus with 32 off 34 balls.

Hampshire

R. S. M. Morris c Chapple b Martin... 6
V. P. Terry c Hegg b Chapple........ 25
R. M. F. Cox lbw b Chapple......... 7
*M. C. J. Nicholas not out........... 33
M. Keech c Crawley b Chapple....... 17
†A. N. Aymes c Hegg b Austin....... 2
K. D. James c Yates b Austin........ 3
S. D. Udal c Watkinson b Martin..... 9
C. A. Connor b Wasim Akram....... 1
M. J. Thursfield not out............. 0
B 4, w 4, n-b 2............. 10

1/22 2/44 3/49 4/69 5/75 6/87 7/103 8/111 (8 wkts, 27 overs) 113

N. G. Cowans did not bat.

Bowling: Martin 5–0–15–2; Austin 5–0–17–2; Wasim Akram 6–0–35–1; Chapple 6–0–29–3; Watkinson 5–0–13–0.

Lancashire

G. D. Lloyd b James	15	Wasim Akram not out	11
N. J. Speak lbw b Connor	12	L-b 5, w 6	11
J. P. Crawley c Aymes b James	6		—
N. H. Fairbrother c James b Cowans	32	1/34 2/34 (4 wkts, 24.2 overs)	115
*M. Watkinson not out	28	3/51 4/97	

I. D. Austin, †W. K. Hegg, G. Yates, P. J. Martin and G. Chapple did not bat.

Bowling: Cowans 6–0–16–1; Thursfield 5–0–28–0; Connor 6–0–16–1; James 5–0–27–2; Udal 2–0–18–0; Keech 0.2–0–5–0.

Umpires: J. W. Holder and K. E. Palmer.

At Colwyn Bay, June 26. LANCASHIRE lost to GLAMORGAN by 27 runs.

At Birmingham, July 3. LANCASHIRE beat WARWICKSHIRE by 93 runs.

LANCASHIRE v DERBYSHIRE

At Manchester, July 17. Lancashire won by eight runs. Toss: Lancashire.

Crawley marked his England call-up for the First Test against South Africa with 64 for Lancashire. Atherton, the England captain, was forced to leave the field for treatment on a back injury. Wells and Griffith added 55 to resurrect Derbyshire's hopes after slumping to 148 for eight, but Lancashire held on.

Lancashire

M. A. Atherton c Cork b Wells	25	†W. K. Hegg not out	6
J. E. R. Gallian c Rollins b DeFreitas	5		
J. P. Crawley run out	64	B 2, l-b 4, w 5, n-b 2	13
N. H. Fairbrother c Adams b Griffith	51		—
G. D. Lloyd run out	20	1/7 2/55 3/134 (6 wkts, 40 overs)	211
*M. Watkinson c Rollins b Malcolm	27	4/153 5/198 6/211	

I. D. Austin, P. J. Martin, G. Yates and G. Chapple did not bat.

Bowling: DeFreitas 8–0–28–1; Wells 8–0–26–1; Malcolm 8–0–39–1; Vandrau 5–0–37–0; Cork 6–0–42–0; Griffith 5–0–33–1.

Derbyshire

*K. J. Barnett run out	31	M. J. Vandrau c Martin b Chapple	10
D. G. Cork c Austin b Yates	49	F. A. Griffith c Gallian b Martin	31
C. J. Adams c Hegg b Austin	0		
T. J. G. O'Gorman b Yates	4	L-b 5, w 1	6
M. Azharuddin c Hegg b Gallian	17		—
P. A. J. DeFreitas c Fairbrother b Yates	16	1/74 2/74 3/86 (9 wkts, 40 overs)	203
†A. S. Rollins c Hegg b Gallian	11	4/89 5/110 6/128	
C. M. Wells not out	28	7/133 8/148 9/203	

D. E. Malcolm did not bat.

Bowling: Chapple 7–1–23–1; Martin 8–1–49–1; Austin 8–0–40–1; Watkinson 4–0–27–0; Yates 8–0–35–3; Gallian 5–0–24–2.

Umpires: B. Leadbeater and R. A. White.

LANCASHIRE v MIDDLESEX

At Manchester, July 24. No result. Toss: Middlesex. County debut: R. S. Yeabsley.
A downpour ended play in the 13th over.

Lancashire

J. E. R. Gallian c and b Feltham	21
S. P. Titchard not out	19
N. J. Speak not out	5
W 3	3
1/32 (1 wkt, 12.1 overs)	48

G. D. Lloyd, N. H. Fairbrother, *M. Watkinson, I. D. Austin, †W. K. Hegg, P. J. Martin, G. Yates and G. Chapple did not bat.

Bowling: Shine 6.1–0–18–0; Feltham 5–0–26–1; Yeabsley 1–0–4–0.

Middlesex

D. L. Haynes, J. C. Pooley, M. R. Ramprakash, *M. W. Gatting, †K. R. Brown, M. A. Roseberry, P. N. Weekes, M. A. Feltham, K. J. Shine, R. S. Yeabsley and P. C. R. Tufnell.

Umpires: J. H. Hampshire and J. W. Holder.

At Chelmsford, August 7. LANCASHIRE lost to ESSEX by five wickets.

At Leeds, August 14. LANCASHIRE beat YORKSHIRE by 43 runs.

LANCASHIRE v GLOUCESTERSHIRE

At Manchester, August 21. Lancashire won by five wickets. Toss: Gloucestershire. First-team debut: D. J. Shadford.

Alleyne's run-a-ball 83 helped Gloucestershire to respectability, but Fairbrother and Lloyd pushed Lancashire towards their target with a stand of 54 in nine overs.

Gloucestershire

A. J. Wright b Watkinson	39
M. G. N. Windows c Fairbrother b Martin	15
T. H. C. Hancock c Shadford b Watkinson	2
M. W. Alleyne not out	83
R. I. Dawson c Watkinson b Yates	2
S. G. Hinks c Martin b Yates	31
†R. C. Russell c Titchard b Martin	13
R. C. Williams run out	8
*C. A. Walsh run out	0
L-b 1, w 4	5
1/25 2/30 3/99 4/104 5/163 6/178 7/198 8/198 (8 wkts, 40 overs)	198

M. C. J. Ball and M. Davies did not bat.

Bowling: Chapple 8–0–22–0; Martin 8–0–52–2; Watkinson 8–0–28–2; Austin 8–0–44–0; Yates 8–0–51–2.

Lancashire

S. P. Titchard c Wright b Walsh 1
I. D. Austin c Alleyne b Davies 22
N. J. Speak c Hancock b Davies 34
N. H. Fairbrother b Walsh 63
G. D. Lloyd not out 44
*M. Watkinson c Ball b Walsh 10
†W. K. Hegg not out 12
L-b 7, w 4, n-b 2 13

1/2 2/41 3/101 4/155 5/172 (5 wkts, 38.4 overs) 199

D. J. Shadford, P. J. Martin, G. Yates and G. Chapple did not bat.

Bowling: Williams 8–0–40–0; Walsh 7.4–3–28–3; Alleyne 8–1–45–0; Davies 8–0–42–2; Ball 6–0–27–0; Hancock 1–0–10–0.

Umpires: B. Dudleston and A. A. Jones.

At Nottingham, August 28. LANCASHIRE lost to NOTTINGHAMSHIRE by eight wickets.

LANCASHIRE v WORCESTERSHIRE

At Manchester, September 6 (Tuesday). Worcestershire won by nine wickets. Toss: Worcestershire.

Moody and Hick, the heroes of Worcestershire's NatWest Trophy triumph two days earlier, earned their side victory again. Rain revised the target to 135 in 30 overs. They added an unbroken 102, steering Worcestershire home with more than four overs to spare. The result ended Lancashire's last hopes of the Sunday title while maintaining Worcestershire's.

Lancashire

M. A. Atherton b Newport 5
N. J. Speak c Rhodes b Radford 27
J. P. Crawley run out 4
N. H. Fairbrother c Leatherdale b Haynes . 37
G. D. Lloyd c Church b Illingworth ... 25
*M. Watkinson not out 35
I. D. Austin c Rhodes b Radford 11
†W. K. Hegg c Rhodes b Radford 1
L-b 3 3

1/17 2/22 3/56 4/98 5/101 6/133 7/148 (7 wkts, 33 overs) 148

G. Yates, P. J. Martin and G. Chapple did not bat.

Bowling: Moody 8–0–28–0; Newport 6–1–17–1; Radford 7–1–40–3; Lampitt 5–0–35–0; Illingworth 5–0–13–1; Haynes 2–0–12–1.

Worcestershire

T. M. Moody not out 55
*T. S. Curtis c Hegg b Chapple 15
G. A. Hick not out 63
L-b 4 4

1/35 (1 wkt, 25.4 overs) 137

G. R. Haynes, D. A. Leatherdale, M. J. Church, †S. J. Rhodes, S. R. Lampitt, N. V. Radford, R. K. Illingworth and P. J. Newport did not bat.

Bowling: Chapple 8–0–38–1; Martin 8–1–31–0; Austin 3–0–20–0; Watkinson 4.4–0–27–0; Yates 2–0–17–0.

Umpires: J. D. Bond and G. Sharp.

At Stockton-on-Tees, September 11. LANCASHIRE beat DURHAM by five wickets.

LANCASHIRE v LEICESTERSHIRE

At Manchester, September 18. Lancashire won by 47 runs. Toss: Leicestershire.

Lancashire secured fourth place in the final table thanks to Watkinson who, despite a broken thumb, produced a telling bowling performance. His four victims included Simmons, whose departure effectively ended Leicestershire's challenge. Yates and Chapple were capped before the game.

Lancashire

M. A. Atherton c and b Pierson....... 40
N. J. Speak c Macmillan b Dakin..... 7
J. P. Crawley c Robinson b Simmons.. 39
N. H. Fairbrother b Dakin........... 49
G. D. Lloyd c Dakin b Wells......... 14
I. D. Austin c Dakin b Wells......... 2
*M. Watkinson c Parsons b Simmons.. 12
†W. K. Hegg c Robinson b Wells..... 21
G. Yates run out.................... 7
P. J. Martin not out................. 8
G. Chapple not out.................. 1
B 2, l-b 5, w 3.............. 10

1/24 2/78 3/109 4/140 5/149 6/170 7/174 8/201 9/204 (9 wkts, 40 overs) 210

Bowling: Parsons 8–0–16–0; Dakin 8–0–46–2; Wells 8–0–47–3; Pierson 8–0–48–1; Simmons 8–0–46–2.

Leicestershire

P. V. Simmons c Lloyd b Watkinson... 44
*N. E. Briers b Martin.............. 8
G. I. Macmillan c Fairbrother b Watkinson. 11
P. E. Robinson b Yates.............. 11
V. J. Wells c Hegg b Watkinson...... 5
B. F. Smith b Chapple............... 28
D. L. Maddy c Lloyd b Yates......... 14
†P. A. Nixon c Crawley b Austin..... 15
J. M. Dakin b Watkinson............ 3
G. J. Parsons c Atherton b Martin.... 4
A. R. K. Pierson not out............. 3
L-b 7, w 6, n-b 4............ 17

1/29 2/54 3/79 4/85 5/89 6/117 7/140 8/153 9/153 (36.5 overs) 163

Bowling: Martin 6.5–0–26–2; Chapple 8–0–34–1; Austin 6–0–26–1; Watkinson 8–0–34–4; Yates 8–1–36–2.

Umpires: B. Dudleston and R. Julian.

LEICESTERSHIRE

At Birmingham, May 8. LEICESTERSHIRE lost to WARWICKSHIRE by 22 runs.

LEICESTERSHIRE v SOMERSET

At Leicester, May 15. Leicestershire won by eight wickets. Toss: Leicestershire.

Simmons hit ten fours in a sparkling innings of 72, setting up a victory with nearly four overs to spare, after Millns had held Somerset in check, conceding only 11 runs in eight overs.

Somerset

M. N. Lathwell b Millns............. 12
N. A. Folland lbw b Millns.......... 2
R. J. Harden c Nixon b Wells........ 8
G. D. Rose b Simmons............... 36
*A. N. Hayhurst lbw b Wells......... 23
V. P. Clarke run out................ 26
A. Payne not out................... 32
Mushtaq Ahmed b Parsons........... 11
†R. J. Turner not out............... 5
B 4, l-b 5, w 4.............. 13

1/16 2/19 3/41 4/76 5/120 6/120 7/138 (7 wkts, 40 overs) 168

A. R. Caddick and H. R. J. Trump did not bat.

Bowling: Parsons 8–1–33–1; Millns 8–0–11–2; Wells 8–0–40–2; Pierson 8–0–36–0; Simmons 8–0–39–1.

Leicestershire

P. V. Simmons c Harden b Hayhurst .. 72
V. J. Wells b Mushtaq Ahmed 23
J. J. Whitaker not out 44
B. F. Smith not out 18
L-b 4, w 7, n-b 2............ 13

1/71 2/131 (2 wkts, 36.1 overs) 170

P. E. Robinson, *N. E. Briers, †P. A. Nixon, J. M. Dakin, G. J. Parsons, A. R. K. Pierson and D. J. Millns did not bat.

Bowling: Caddick 7–1–30–0; Rose 8–1–21–0; Payne 4.1–0–32–0; Mushtaq Ahmed 6–0–39–1; Trump 4–0–13–0; Clarke 4–0–24–0; Hayhurst 3–0–7–1.

Umpires: A. A. Jones and K. E. Palmer.

LEICESTERSHIRE v KENT

At Leicester, May 29. Kent won by 60 runs. Toss: Leicestershire.

Hooper's off-spin killed off Leicestershire, claiming four wickets as they replied to Kent's substantial total of 254, which owed much to openers Ward – who scored 50 out of 61 – and Benson. Leicestershire at least achieved respectability, through a ninth-wicket stand of 63 between Mullally and Pierson.

Kent

T. R. Ward c Simmons b Parsons 50
*M. R. Benson run out 74
C. L. Hooper b Dakin................ 33
M. V. Fleming c Robinson b Dakin ... 35
N. R. Taylor b Mullally 3
N. J. Llong not out 18
M. A. Ealham c Simmons b Mullally .. 14
†S. A. Marsh not out................ 9
B 3, l-b 7, w 8.............. 18

1/61 2/141 3/184 (6 wkts, 40 overs) 254
4/191 5/214 6/232

D. J. Spencer, D. W. Headley and A. P. Igglesden did not bat.

Bowling: Mullally 8–0–43–2; Millns 6–0–44–0; Simmons 8–0–51–0; Parsons 8–1–32–1; Pierson 6–0–43–0; Dakin 4–0–31–2.

Leicestershire

P. V. Simmons b Igglesden........... 9
J. J. Whitaker b Headley 2
B. F. Smith c Hooper b Igglesden 9
P. E. Robinson c Fleming b Spencer... 31
J. M. Dakin c Headley b Hooper...... 14
*N. E. Briers b Hooper.............. 10
†P. A. Nixon c Ward b Hooper....... 14
G. J. Parsons c Igglesden b Hooper.... 1
A. R. K. Pierson not out............. 29
A. D. Mullally run out............... 38
D. J. Millns c Marsh b Igglesden...... 2
B 1, l-b 20, w 8, n-b 6 35

1/13 2/15 3/48 (37.2 overs) 194
4/71 5/92 6/92
7/102 8/124 9/187

Bowling: Igglesden 6.2–0–22–3; Headley 5–1–16–1; Spencer 7–0–42–1; Hooper 8–0–37–4; Ealham 7–0–31–0; Fleming 4–0–25–0.

Umpires: G. I. Burgess and J. H. Harris.

At Derby, June 12. LEICESTERSHIRE lost to DERBYSHIRE by six wickets.

LEICESTERSHIRE v MIDDLESEX

At Leicester, June 19. Leicestershire won by 61 runs. Toss: Leicestershire. First-team debut: I. M. Stanger.

Leicestershire sprang a surprise by omitting four senior players, including captain Briers and vice-captain Whitaker, and then amassed their first-ever total over 300 in the Sunday League. Simmons, in charge for the day, hit five sixes and 16 fours in a spectacular 106-ball 140. He and Wells, whose 101 came from 90 balls, added 241 for the second wicket, a Leicestershire record for any wicket in the competition. Middlesex's best effort in a forlorn reply came from Feltham, a run-a-ball 75.

Leicestershire

*P. V. Simmons c Shine b Feltham 140
P. N. Hepworth b Shine 2
V. J. Wells c Johnson b Emburey 101
P. E. Robinson b Weekes 25
B. F. Smith run out 4
J. M. Dakin c Roseberry b Johnson . . . 8
†P. A. Nixon not out. 4
A. D. Mullally b Weekes 0
D. L. Maddy not out 3
B 2, l-b 8, w 4 14

1/9 2/250 3/265 4/286 5/292 6/295 7/296 (7 wkts, 40 overs) 301

I. M. Stanger and G. J. Parsons did not bat.

Bowling: Shine 8–1–53–1; Feltham 8–0–41–1; Emburey 8–0–33–1; Johnson 8–0–70–1; Weekes 8–0–94–2.

Middlesex

D. L. Haynes c Mullally b Stanger. 40
M. A. Roseberry c Nixon b Mullally . . . 12
M. R. Ramprakash c Robinson b Parsons . 48
†K. R. Brown st Nixon b Parsons 4
*J. D. Carr st Nixon b Hepworth 16
J. C. Harrison lbw b Parsons 2
M. A. Feltham c Smith b Mullally. 75
R. L. Johnson lbw b Parsons 6
J. E. Emburey c Dakin b Wells 16
P. N. Weekes c Stanger b Wells 3
K. J. Shine not out 1
B 1, l-b 10, w 2, n-b 4 17

1/33 2/66 3/80 4/122 5/125 6/146 7/164 8/222 9/237 (34.5 overs) 240

Bowling: Mullally 7.5–0–32–2; Stanger 8–0–54–1; Parsons 8–0–50–4; Hepworth 7–0–59–1; Dakin 2–0–25–0; Wells 2–0–9–2.

Umpires: J. H. Hampshire and A. A. Jones.

At The Oval, June 26. LEICESTERSHIRE beat SURREY by 122 runs.

LEICESTERSHIRE v ESSEX

At Leicester, July 3. Leicestershire won by 14 runs. Toss: Leicestershire.

Simmons turned in an inspired all-round performance – 51 runs and four for 19 – as Leicestershire recorded their third successive victory, all under his captaincy. Mullally conceded only nine runs in seven overs, and wicket-keeper Nixon's six catches equalled the League record.

Leicestershire

*P. V. Simmons b Irani 51
P. N. Hepworth lbw b Topley 5
V. J. Wells c and b Stephenson 5
B. F. Smith c and b Topley 11
P. E. Robinson run out 29
†P. A. Nixon c Topley b Pearson 17
D. L. Maddy c Topley b Pearson. 6
J. M. Dakin b Pearson 2
G. J. Parsons c Garnham b Cousins . . . 3
A. D. Mullally not out. 7
I. M. Stanger c Garnham b Cousins . . . 1
L-b 10, w 4, n-b 10. 24

1/55 2/62 3/85 4/89 5/135 6/136 7/141 8/149 9/158 (33.5 overs) 161

Bowling: Kasprowicz 2–0–17–0; Stephenson 6–0–17–1; Topley 7–0–45–2; Irani 5.1–0–22–1; Pearson 8–0–33–3; Cousins 5.4–0–17–2.

Essex

J. J. B. Lewis c Nixon b Mullally	0	T. D. Topley b Simmons	6
*J. P. Stephenson c Nixon b Parsons	0	R. M. Pearson not out	3
R. C. Irani lbw b Mullally	15	D. M. Cousins c Nixon b Simmons	2
N. Hussain c Parsons b Stanger	23	L-b 3, w 6	9
M. Diwan c Nixon b Parsons	10		—
N. Shahid c Nixon b Mullally	41	1/0 2/8 3/34 (39 overs)	147
†M. A. Garnham c Nixon b Simmons	29	4/48 5/75 6/123	
M. S. Kasprowicz lbw b Simmons	9	7/135 8/141 9/143	

Bowling: Mullally 7–3–9–3; Parsons 8–0–32–2; Wells 6–1–19–0; Stanger 8–0–37–1; Hepworth 6–0–28–0; Simmons 4–0–19–4.

Umpires: J. C. Balderstone and T. E. Jesty.

LEICESTERSHIRE v NORTHAMPTONSHIRE

At Leicester, July 10. Northamptonshire won by eight runs. Toss: Northamptonshire. First-team debut: A. F. Haye.

A Leicestershire victory seemed certain at 201 for five, needing ten from three overs. But they lost their last five wickets for one run in 12 balls. Penberthy and Snape earlier boosted Northamptonshire with a fifth-wicket stand of 61 in eight overs.

Northamptonshire

M. B. Loye run out	30	J. N. Snape not out	31
*R. J. Bailey c Simmons b Stanger	46	B 4, l-b 14, w 6, n-b 6	30
T. C. Walton c and b Pierson	10		—
K. M. Curran c Maddy b Wells	36	1/51 2/77 (4 wkts, 40 overs)	210
A. L. Penberthy not out	27	3/141 4/149	

K. J. Innes, C. E. L. Ambrose, †D. Ripley, N. G. B. Cook and M. N. Bowen did not bat.

Bowling: Mullally 8–1–41–0; Wells 8–0–42–1; Pierson 8–0–20–1; Simmons 7–0–32–0; Stanger 8–0–48–1; Hepworth 1–0–9–0.

Leicestershire

*P. V. Simmons b Ambrose	4	A. F. Haye c Curran b Bailey	0
D. L. Maddy b Penberthy	25	A. R. K. Pierson run out	1
V. J. Wells c Ambrose b Penberthy	13	I. M. Stanger not out	0
B. F. Smith b Bailey	33	L-b 9, w 4	13
†P. A. Nixon c Walton b Ambrose	60		—
P. N. Hepworth c Ambrose b Penberthy	49	1/6 2/41 3/52 (39.1 overs)	202
J. M. Dakin c Innes b Ambrose	4	4/102 5/194 6/201	
A. D. Mullally st Ripley b Bailey	0	7/201 8/201 9/202	

Bowling: Bowen 4–0–22–0; Ambrose 8–1–24–3; Penberthy 8–0–48–3; Curran 7.1–0–40–0; Bailey 7–0–33–3; Cook 5–0–26–0.

Umpires: D. J. Constant and A. G. T. Whitehead.

At Scarborough, July 17. LEICESTERSHIRE lost to YORKSHIRE by five wickets.

At Durham University, July 24. DURHAM v LEICESTERSHIRE. No result.

At Nottingham, August 7. LEICESTERSHIRE beat NOTTINGHAMSHIRE by 26 runs.

LEICESTERSHIRE v WORCESTERSHIRE

At Leicester, August 14. Worcestershire won by two runs. Toss: Worcestershire.

Curtis and Hick, with the bat, and Lampitt and Illingworth, with the ball, engineered a narrow victory which kept Worcestershire in second place, four points behind Warwickshire. Pierson needed three from the final ball, but was caught in the deep.

Worcestershire

T. M. Moody lbw b Parsons 16
*T. S. Curtis c Maddy b Hepworth 52
G. A. Hick c Stanger b Hepworth 65
G. R. Haynes c Smith b Hepworth 10
D. A. Leatherdale c Robinson b Stanger 2
D. B. D'Oliveira b Hepworth 9
†S. J. Rhodes lbw b Hepworth 9
S. R. Lampitt c Maddy b Pierson 16
N. V. Radford not out 5
R. K. Illingworth not out 0
B 10, l-b 7, w 2 19

1/26 2/125 3/143 (8 wkts, 40 overs) 203
4/151 5/161 6/174
7/184 8/199

P. J. Newport did not bat.

Bowling: Parsons 8–0–24–1; Stanger 7–0–42–1; Wells 5–0–22–0; Pierson 7–0–28–1; Simmons 5–0–19–0; Hepworth 8–0–51–5.

Leicestershire

*P. V. Simmons c Rhodes b Moody ... 11
D. L. Maddy b Illingworth 53
V. J. Wells c Rhodes b Moody 0
B. F. Smith c Radford b Lampitt 56
P. E. Robinson c D'Oliveira b Lampitt . 7
†P. A. Nixon c Haynes b Lampitt 3
P. N. Hepworth run out 32
J. M. Dakin b Lampitt 9
G. J. Parsons not out 25
A. R. K. Pierson c Haynes b Newport . 0
L-b 2, w 3 5

1/13 2/14 3/93 (9 wkts, 40 overs) 201
4/108 5/116 6/136
7/151 8/201 9/201

I. M. Stanger did not bat.

Bowling: Moody 8–0–52–2; Newport 5–0–27–1; Hick 5–0–44–0; Radford 6–0–34–0; Illingworth 8–1–17–1; Lampitt 8–1–25–4.

Umpires: J. D. Bond and B. J. Meyer.

LEICESTERSHIRE v SUSSEX

At Leicester, August 21. Sussex won by 42 runs. Toss: Sussex.

Chasing 206, Leicestershire never recovered from losing their first four wickets in the space of ten deliveries, as they stumbled from 21 to 22, despite late flourishes from Dakin and Parsons.

Sussex

K. Greenfield c Maddy b Hepworth ... 31
C. W. J. Athey c Simmons b Hepworth 25
F. D. Stephenson c Smith b Parsons ... 9
*A. P. Wells b Mullally 51
M. P. Speight b Simmons 7
†P. Moores b Simmons 5
J. A. North st Nixon b Wells 3
C. C. Remy c Stanger b Mullally 9
P. W. Jarvis c Wells b Hepworth 15
I. D. K. Salisbury not out 13
E. S. H. Giddins not out 0
B 4, l-b 9, w 4, n-b 20 37

1/69 2/77 3/88 (9 wkts, 40 overs) 205
4/121 5/129 6/140
7/172 8/181 9/195

Bowling: Mullally 8–1–45–2; Stanger 5–0–35–0; Parsons 8–0–25–1; Hepworth 8–0–47–3; Wells 7–0–26–1; Simmons 4–0–14–2.

Leicestershire

*P. V. Simmons b Giddins	13	G. J. Parsons b Giddins	29
D. L. Maddy c Moores b Jarvis	4	I. M. Stanger c and b Remy	6
V. J. Wells run out	0	A. D. Mullally not out	2
B. F. Smith lbw b Jarvis	0	L-b 6, w 16, n-b 4	26
†P. A. Nixon c and b Remy	14		—
P. E. Robinson b Salisbury	19	1/21 2/21 3/21 (37 overs)	163
P. N. Hepworth lbw b Remy	9	4/22 5/49 6/64	
J. M. Dakin c Wells b Remy	41	7/90 8/133 9/158	

Bowling: Stephenson 8–0–30–0; Jarvis 6–0–18–2; Giddins 7–1–32–2; Salisbury 8–0–34–1; Remy 8–0–43–4.

Umpires: R. Julian and G. Sharp.

At Neath, August 28. LEICESTERSHIRE lost to GLAMORGAN by 33 runs.

At Moreton-in-Marsh, September 4. LEICESTERSHIRE beat GLOUCESTERSHIRE on scoring-rate.

LEICESTERSHIRE v HAMPSHIRE

At Leicester, September 11. Leicestershire won by eight runs. Toss: Hampshire.

Pierson's accurate off-spin thwarted Hampshire's run-chase after Leicestershire, spearheaded by Wells, had rallied from the depths of 58 for five.

Leicestershire

P. V. Simmons lbw b Connor	0	J. M. Dakin c Aymes b Bovill	5
*N. E. Briers b Connor	4	G. J. Parsons c Smith b Bovill	14
G. I. Macmillan c Aymes b Connor	8	A. R. K. Pierson not out	7
J. J. Whitaker c Whitaker b James	12	L-b 2, w 4, n-b 2	8
V. J. Wells c Smith b Thursfield	44		—
B. F. Smith c Aymes b James	11	1/4 2/13 3/16 (39.3 overs)	156
D. L. Maddy c Smith b Thursfield	21	4/42 5/58 6/99	
†P. A. Nixon st Aymes b Thursfield	22	7/118 8/135 9/135	

Bowling: Connor 8–1–20–3; Bovill 7.3–2–25–2; Thursfield 8–0–31–3; James 8–0–27–2; Udal 8–0–51–0.

Hampshire

T. C. Middleton c Nixon b Parsons	41	M. J. Thursfield lbw b Dakin	1
P. R. Whitaker b Dakin	7	C. A. Connor c Pierson b Wells	2
R. A. Smith c Nixon b Dakin	13	J. N. B. Bovill b Simmons	1
G. W. White b Wells	1	L-b 11, w 10	21
*M. C. J. Nicholas c Maddy b Pierson	8		—
†A. N. Aymes b Pierson	7	1/11 2/34 3/44 (39.4 overs)	148
K. D. James not out	39	4/72 5/89 6/97	
S. D. Udal c and b Pierson	7	7/114 8/117 9/128	

Bowling: Parsons 8–2–20–1; Dakin 8–0–32–3; Wells 8–2–37–2; Simmons 7.4–1–27–1; Pierson 8–0–21–3.

Umpires: J. H. Hampshire and R. A. White.

At Manchester, September 18. LEICESTERSHIRE lost to LANCASHIRE by 47 runs.

MIDDLESEX

MIDDLESEX v YORKSHIRE

At Lord's, May 8. Yorkshire won by six wickets. Toss: Yorkshire.

White's run-a-ball half-century, including two sixes and five fours, guided Yorkshire to a modest target of 158 with 15 deliveries remaining.

Middlesex

D. L. Haynes b Stemp	32
M. R. Ramprakash b Gough	4
*M. W. Gatting b Stemp	51
J. D. Carr lbw b White	12
P. N. Weekes b Stemp	9
†K. R. Brown c Moxon b Hartley	15
J. E. Emburey b White	1
R. L. Johnson b Gough	14
N. F. Williams c Blakey b Hartley	0
A. R. C. Fraser not out	3
C. W. Taylor not out	2
B 1, w 5, n-b 8	14
1/6 2/79 3/102 4/122 5/122 6/125 7/152 8/152 9/153 (9 wkts, 40 overs)	157

Bowling: Hartley 8–1–28–2; Gough 8–1–24–2; White 8–0–39–2; Robinson 8–0–34–0; Stemp 8–0–31–3.

Yorkshire

*M. D. Moxon c Brown b Fraser	16
D. Byas b Fraser	16
R. B. Richardson c Williams b Fraser	38
†R. J. Blakey lbw b Johnson	10
C. White not out	54
A. P. Grayson not out	12
B 4, l-b 3, w 5	12
1/19 2/32 3/71 4/108 (4 wkts, 37.3 overs)	158

M. J. Foster, M. A. Robinson, D. Gough, P. J. Hartley and R. D. Stemp did not bat.

Bowling: Williams 8–3–23–0; Fraser 8–0–31–3; Taylor 3–0–21–0; Emburey 7.3–0–24–0; Johnson 7–1–36–1; Weekes 4–0–16–0.

Umpires: J. H. Harris and K. E. Palmer.

At Southampton, May 22. MIDDLESEX lost to HAMPSHIRE by ten wickets.

MIDDLESEX v WARWICKSHIRE

At Lord's, May 29. Warwickshire won by three wickets. Toss: Warwickshire.

Warwickshire survived the loss of Lara, leg-before to Feltham first ball, to win with an over to spare. Haynes shone for Middlesex, top-scoring and holding two fine catches in the deep.

Middlesex

D. L. Haynes c Ostler b N. M. K. Smith	31
M. A. Roseberry b Small	10
M. R. Ramprakash c Ostler b P. A. Smith	24
*M. W. Gatting c and b N. M. K. Smith	3
†K. R. Brown c Burns b Munton	24
J. D. Carr b Small	13
P. N. Weekes not out	25
M. A. Feltham c sub b P. A. Smith	8
R. L. Johnson not out	7
B 1, l-b 7, w 2	10
1/27 2/47 3/58 4/80 5/105 6/114 7/138 (7 wkts, 38 overs)	155

N. F. Williams and A. R. C. Fraser did not bat.

Bowling: Reeve 4–0–9–0; Munton 7–0–37–1; Small 8–0–42–2; N. M. K. Smith 7–0–23–2; Twose 4–0–18–0; P. A. Smith 8–1–18–2.

Warwickshire

D. P. Ostler b Johnson	42	*D. A. Reeve st Brown b Weekes	2
†M. Burns c Roseberry b Williams	6	N. M. K. Smith not out	3
B. C. Lara lbw b Feltham	0	L-b 2, w 6	8
P. A. Smith c Haynes b Fraser	44		
Asif Din c Haynes b Feltham	14	1/15 2/15 3/72 (7 wkts, 37 overs)	156
R. G. Twose run out	18	4/102 5/117	
T. L. Penney not out	19	6/143 7/147	

G. C. Small and T. A. Munton did not bat.

Bowling: Williams 8–2–20–1; Feltham 7–0–41–2; Fraser 7–0–29–1; Johnson 7–1–38–1; Weekes 8–1–26–1.

Umpires: J. D. Bond and D. J. Constant.

MIDDLESEX v WORCESTERSHIRE

At Lord's, June 5. Middlesex won by 21 runs. Toss: Worcestershire.

Ramprakash and Brown added 99 for the fifth wicket in 15 overs for Middlesex, and Worcestershire then subsided to Johnson, who sent back D'Oliveira, Illingworth and Radford in four balls; five wickets fell for 19 runs.

Middlesex

D. L. Haynes c Radford b Newport	9	P. N. Weekes run out	0
M. A. Roseberry c Leatherdale b Radford	13	M. A. Feltham not out	0
M. R. Ramprakash c Tolley b Lampitt	80	L-b 5, w 5, n-b 2	12
*M. W. Gatting c Leatherdale b Lampitt	9		
J. D. Carr b Lampitt	7	1/20 2/30 3/57 (6 wkts, 40 overs)	174
†K. R. Brown not out	44	4/74 5/173 6/173	

J. E. Emburey, N. F. Williams and R. L. Johnson did not bat.

Bowling: Newport 8–0–43–1; Moody 8–0–29–0; Radford 8–2–32–1; Lampitt 8–0–37–3; Illingworth 8–0–28–0.

Worcestershire

T. M. Moody b Williams	31	N. V. Radford lbw b Johnson	0
*T. S. Curtis b Feltham	11	P. J. Newport c Roseberry b Feltham	17
G. R. Haynes run out	17	†T. Edwards not out	1
D. A. Leatherdale b Weekes	18	L-b 19, w 3	22
D. B. D'Oliveira b Johnson	16		
S. R. Lampitt b Feltham	19	1/37 2/71 3/84 (39 overs)	153
C. M. Tolley run out	1	4/101 5/113 6/116	
R. K. Illingworth c Brown b Johnson	0	7/120 8/120 9/152	

Bowling: Williams 8–1–27–1; Johnson 8–1–32–3; Feltham 8–1–28–3; Emburey 8–1–28–0; Weekes 7–1–19–1.

Umpires: G. I. Burgess and B. Dudleston.

At Canterbury, June 12. MIDDLESEX beat KENT by 11 runs.

At Leicester, June 19. MIDDLESEX lost to LEICESTERSHIRE by 61 runs.

MIDDLESEX v DURHAM

At Lord's, June 26. Durham won by one wicket. Toss: Durham.

Having been the pick of the Durham bowlers, with three wickets, Walker then clinched a narrow victory by hitting the third ball of the final over for six, and scoring the winning run off the next delivery. Ramprakash and Carr added 71 for Middlesex's fourth wicket in just eight overs. Tufnell returned to the team for his first match since April 26.

Middlesex

D. L. Haynes lbw b Bainbridge	52	M. A. Feltham c Scott b Walker	5
M. A. Roseberry c Scott b Brown	14	R. L. Johnson not out	2
M. R. Ramprakash lbw b Walker	97	L-b 11, w 1, n-b 2	14
*M. W. Gatting b Walker	16		—
J. D. Carr b Bainbridge	33	1/18 2/107 3/150 (6 wkts, 40 overs)	249
†K. R. Brown not out	16	4/221 5/228 6/236	

A. R. C. Fraser, P. C. R. Tufnell and K. J. Shine did not bat.

Bowling: Cummins 8–0–52–0; Brown 8–0–61–1; Graveney 8–0–34–0; Walker 8–0–49–3; Bainbridge 8–0–42–2.

Durham

W. Larkins c Haynes b Shine	38	D. A. Graveney c Brown b Shine	9
M. Saxelby c Brown b Feltham	54	A. Walker not out	12
J. E. Morris lbw b Fraser	10	S. J. E. Brown not out	0
J. I. Longley c Roseberry b Tufnell	18	B 4, l-b 5, w 1, n-b 10	20
S. Hutton c Fraser b Tufnell	33		—
*P. Bainbridge c Brown b Johnson	21	1/55 2/81 3/118 (9 wkts, 39.4 overs)	250
A. C. Cummins c Johnson b Feltham	32	4/158 5/172 6/203	
†C. W. Scott run out	3	7/207 8/228 9/238	

Bowling: Fraser 8–1–43–1; Johnson 8–0–55–1; Shine 7.4–0–73–2; Feltham 8–0–34–2; Tufnell 8–0–36–2.

Umpires: R. Julian and A. G. T. Whitehead.

At Derby, July 3. MIDDLESEX lost to DERBYSHIRE by eight wickets.

At Arundel, July 17. MIDDLESEX lost to SUSSEX by 17 runs.

At Manchester, July 24. LANCASHIRE v MIDDLESEX. No result.

MIDDLESEX v ESSEX

At Uxbridge, July 31. Middlesex won by seven wickets. Toss: Middlesex.

Bottom-placed Essex collapsed in spectacular fashion after a 60-run opening stand between Gooch and Stephenson, losing their last seven wickets for 20 runs in six overs. Yeabsley – who had taken ten wickets for Oxford in the University Match – claimed five in his second game for Middlesex.

Essex

*G. A. Gooch b Tufnell	33	P. M. Such c Tufnell b Yeabsley	0
J. P. Stephenson c Gatting b Yeabsley	26	R. M. Pearson not out	2
N. Hussain c Haynes b Yeabsley	30	D. M. Cousins c Brown b Yeabsley	1
N. V. Knight st Brown b Tufnell	1	B 1, l-b 3, w 7	11
M. A. Garnham run out	16		—
R. C. Irani c Gatting b Weekes	8	1/60 2/74 3/79 (31 overs)	135
†R. J. Rollins c Ramprakash b Weekes	5	4/115 5/120 6/128	
M. S. Kasprowicz lbw b Yeabsley	2	7/132 8/132 9/134	

Bowling: Feltham 5–0–22–0; Shine 5–0–30–0; Tufnell 8–0–25–2; Yeabsley 8–1–32–5; Weekes 5–0–22–2.

Middlesex

D. L. Haynes lbw b Such	41	†K. R. Brown not out	1
M. A. Roseberry b Such	29		
M. R. Ramprakash c Kasprowicz b Cousins	30	B 4, l-b 4, w 13, n-b 6	27
			—
J. C. Pooley not out	8	1/69 2/83 3/134 (3 wkts, 29.5 overs)	136

*M. W. Gatting, P. N. Weekes, K. J. Shine, M. A. Feltham, R. S. Yeabsley and P. C. R. Tufnell did not bat.

Bowling: Kasprowicz 3–0–12–0; Cousins 7.5–0–41–1; Such 8–0–27–2; Stephenson 7–0–32–0; Pearson 4–0–16–0.

Umpires: V. A. Holder and B. Leadbeater.

MIDDLESEX v GLAMORGAN

At Lord's, August 7. Glamorgan won by seven wickets. Toss: Glamorgan.

Brown and Gatting pulled Middlesex out of trouble at 71 for five, adding 79 in 12 overs, but Glamorgan were always in charge as Hemp and Maynard put on 97 for the third wicket.

Middlesex

M. A. Roseberry b Gibson	9	*M. W. Gatting not out	41
J. C. Pooley lbw b Lefebvre	1		
M. R. Ramprakash lbw b Croft	7	B 3, l-b 2, w 1, n-b 3	9
A. Habib run out	11		—
P. N. Weekes b Barwick	20	1/5 2/13 3/25 (5 wkts, 40 overs)	150
†K. R. Brown not out	52	4/35 5/71	

J. E. Emburey, R. S. Yeabsley, G. A. R. Harris and K. J. Shine did not bat.

Bowling: Lefebvre 8–1–20–1; Gibson 8–0–32–1; Croft 8–0–26–1; Barwick 8–2–17–1; Dale 4–0–17–0; Butcher 4–0–33–0.

Glamorgan

A. Dale c sub b Shine	6	P. A. Cottey not out	0
*H. Morris c Brown b Harris	22	B 1, l-b 4, w 4, n-b 4	13
D. L. Hemp b Shine	73		—
M. P. Maynard not out	38	1/12 2/51 3/148 (3 wkts, 37.1 overs)	152

R. D. B. Croft, O. D. Gibson, †A. D. Shaw, R. P. Lefebvre, G. P. Butcher and S. R. Barwick did not bat.

Bowling: Shine 7–0–23–2; Yeabsley 8–0–40–0; Harris 8–0–28–1; Emburey 8–1–21–0; Weekes 6.1–0–35–0.

Umpires: B. Dudleston and T. E. Jesty.

MIDDLESEX v SOMERSET

At Lord's, August 14. Middlesex won by eight wickets. Toss: Somerset.

Somerset made sluggish progress, their innings containing just one six and six fours, and Middlesex's advantage was pressed home by Roseberry and Pooley with a 112-run opening stand.

Somerset

I. Fletcher c Carr b Shine 4
*A. N. Hayhurst c Brown b Weekes . . . 49
P. C. L. Holloway c Weekes b Tufnell . 29
M. N. Lathwell run out 2
S. C. Ecclestone c Ramprakash b Tufnell . 22
V. P. Clarke c Ramprakash b Tufnell . . 0
†R. J. Turner not out 29
J. C. Hallett run out 16
J. I. D. Kerr not out 1
L-b 5, w 2 7

1/21 2/71 3/79 4/106 5/106 6/111 7/150 (7 wkts, 40 overs) 159

H. R. J. Trump and P. J. Bird did not bat.

Bowling: Fraser 7–2–18–0; Shine 8–1–26–1; Feltham 5–0–15–0; Tufnell 8–0–28–3; Weekes 8–0–46–1; Ramprakash 4–0–21–0.

Middlesex

M. A. Roseberry lbw b Hallett 50
J. C. Pooley b Hallett 59
M. R. Ramprakash not out 29
J. D. Carr not out 18
L-b 2, w 3 5

1/112 2/119 (2 wkts, 34.5 overs) 161

*M. W. Gatting, †K. R. Brown, P. N. Weekes, M. A. Feltham, A. R. C. Fraser, K. J. Shine and P. C. R. Tufnell did not bat.

Bowling: Bird 8–1–25–0; Kerr 4–0–23–0; Trump 7.5–0–32–0; Ecclestone 3–0–20–0; Hallett 7–0–40–2; Clarke 5–0–19–0.

Umpires: R. A. White and P. B. Wight.

At Northampton, August 21. MIDDLESEX beat NORTHAMPTONSHIRE by 34 runs.

At The Oval, August 28. MIDDLESEX lost to SURREY by seven wickets.

MIDDLESEX v GLOUCESTERSHIRE

At Lord's, September 11. Gloucestershire won by 53 runs. Toss: Middlesex.

Windows and Dawson helped Gloucestershire recover from a poor start, adding 90 for the fourth wicket. Middlesex then came unstuck against the spin of Davies and Ball.

Gloucestershire

A. J. Wright b Fraser 1
M. G. N. Windows b Weekes 69
T. H. C. Hancock b Williams 7
M. W. Alleyne b Williams 1
R. I. Dawson c Tufnell b Johnson 45
†R. C. Russell run out 2
M. C. J. Ball c Pooley b Fraser 24
R. C. Williams not out 9
*C. A. Walsh not out 2
B 4, l-b 1, w 2, n-b 8 15

1/1 2/22 3/24 4/114 5/123 6/145 7/172 (7 wkts, 40 overs) 175

M. Davies and A. M. Smith did not bat.

Bowling: Williams 8–1–17–2; Fraser 8–2–23–2; Johnson 8–0–50–1; Tufnell 8–0–38–0; Weekes 8–0–42–1.

Middlesex

M. A. Roseberry b Walsh	13	N. F. Williams c Ball b Davies	0
J. C. Pooley c Alleyne b Williams	0	A. R. C. Fraser not out	11
M. R. Ramprakash c Wright b Davies	39	P. C. R. Tufnell b Ball	1
J. D. Carr c Wright b Smith	18	L-b 2, w 5, n-b 2	9
P. N. Weekes c Alleyne b Williams	22		—
†K. R. Brown run out	8	1/13 2/25 3/65 (33.2 overs)	122
*M. W. Gatting run out	1	4/75 5/92 6/99	
R. L. Johnson c Hancock b Ball	0	7/103 8/105 9/120	

Bowling: Williams 8–1–36–2; Walsh 6–1–14–1; Smith 5–0–21–1; Davies 8–1–23–2; Ball 6.2–0–26–2.

Umpires: J. W. Holder and M. J. Kitchen.

At Nottingham, September 18. MIDDLESEX beat NOTTINGHAMSHIRE by six wickets.

NORTHAMPTONSHIRE

NORTHAMPTONSHIRE v GLAMORGAN

At Northampton, May 8. Glamorgan won by four wickets. Toss: Northamptonshire.

Glamorgan opened their title defence with a win, despite collapsing from 109 for two to 124 for six. Their nerves were settled by Gibson, who drove Ambrose for a magnificent straight six to clinch victory. Earlier, Watkin, with three wickets in ten balls, had demolished Northamptonshire's top order.

Northamptonshire

A. Fordham c Metson b Lefebvre	2	C. E. L. Ambrose st Metson b Dale	3
M. B. Loye lbw b Watkin	10	M. N. Bowen not out	17
R. J. Bailey c Metson b Watkin	5		
*A. J. Lamb c Metson b Watkin	4	L-b 7, w 5, n-b 2	14
R. J. Warren c Dale b Croft	8		—
A. L. Penberthy not out	69	1/14 2/14 3/19 (8 wkts, 40 overs)	148
J. N. Snape b Croft	3	4/24 5/52 6/59	
†D. Ripley c Maynard b Dale	13	7/90 8/98	

J. P. Taylor did not bat.

Bowling: Lefebvre 8–1–28–1; Watkin 8–1–19–3; Barwick 8–1–41–0; Gibson 3–0–13–0; Croft 7–1–19–2; Dale 6–0–21–2.

Glamorgan

S. P. James c Ripley b Penberthy	14	O. D. Gibson not out	11
*H. Morris c Warren b Penberthy	7	R. P. Lefebvre not out	15
M. P. Maynard lbw b Bailey	54	L-b 6, w 10, n-b 8	24
A. Dale b Bowen	22		—
P. A. Cottey lbw b Bailey	4	1/34 2/39 3/109 (6 wkts, 38.1 overs)	151
R. D. B. Croft run out	0	4/120 5/124 6/124	

†C. P. Metson, S. L. Watkin and S. R. Barwick did not bat.

Bowling: Ambrose 7.1–3–25–0; Bowen 8–0–28–1; Penberthy 6–0–24–2; Taylor 7–1–36–0; Snape 4–0–18–0; Bailey 6–1–14–2.

Umpires: V. A. Holder and R. A. White.

At The Oval, May 22. SURREY v NORTHAMPTONSHIRE. No result.

At Worcester, May 29. NORTHAMPTONSHIRE lost to WORCESTERSHIRE by 18 runs.

NORTHAMPTONSHIRE v LANCASHIRE

At Northampton, June 5. Lancashire won by eight runs. Toss: Northamptonshire.

Wasim Akram, with 33 off 21 balls, a League-best five-wicket haul, and two catches, thwarted Lamb's bid for victory. The Northamptonshire captain hit 78 from 102 deliveries, scoring the last 23 with a runner after pulling a hamstring. Loye was awarded his county cap in the interval, moments after colliding with an advertising board and leaving the field dazed.

Lancashire

G. D. Lloyd c Cook b Taylor	10
J. E. R. Gallian c Ripley b Ambrose	12
J. P. Crawley c Felton b Ambrose	0
N. H. Fairbrother b Bailey	38
N. J. Speak lbw b Ambrose	28
Wasim Akram lbw b Cook	33
*M. Watkinson c Penberthy b Taylor	30
I. D. Austin c Cook b Taylor	12
†W. K. Hegg not out	3
P. J. Martin b Ambrose	4
G. Yates not out	2
B 1, l-b 11, w 7	19
1/22 2/22 3/38 4/93 5/120 6/148 7/182 8/182 9/187 (9 wkts, 39 overs)	191

Bowling: Ambrose 8–3–20–4; Curran 7–1–37–0; Penberthy 6–0–24–0; Taylor 7–1–30–3; Cook 7–0–52–1; Bailey 4–0–16–1.

Northamptonshire

A. Fordham lbw b Wasim Akram	0
N. A. Felton b Martin	7
*A. J. Lamb b Martin	78
K. M. Curran c Wasim Akram b Gallian	37
M. B. Loye b Wasim Akram	12
A. L. Penberthy c Hegg b Austin	3
R. J. Bailey c Wasim Akram b Watkinson	6
†D. Ripley lbw b Wasim Akram	8
C. E. L. Ambrose c Lloyd b Wasim Akram	9
N. G. B. Cook b Wasim Akram	1
J. P. Taylor not out	0
L-b 8, w 12, n-b 2	22
1/4 2/27 3/92 4/118 5/131 6/146 7/169 8/179 9/183 (38.3 overs)	183

Bowling: Wasim Akram 7.3–0–41–5; Martin 8–0–37–2; Watkinson 8–1–28–1; Austin 8–0–31–1; Gallian 4–0–20–1; Yates 3–0–18–0.

Umpires: J. C. Balderstone and B. J. Meyer.

At Hartlepool, June 12. NORTHAMPTONSHIRE tied with DURHAM.

NORTHAMPTONSHIRE v YORKSHIRE

At Luton, June 19. Yorkshire won by ten runs. Toss: Northamptonshire.

Most attention centred on Gough's return after a month-long absence with a side strain: he took two for 35, and Northamptonshire were soon in trouble. Last man Cook scored 21 off ten balls to make the result closer than had seemed likely. Umpire Peter Wight was unable to take the field for Northamptonshire's innings after being struck by a straight-drive from Richardson; Mervyn Kitchen stood at both ends, with Roy Wills, chairman of Northamptonshire's cricket committee, at square leg.

Yorkshire

*M. D. Moxon c Warren b Innes	45	A. P. Grayson not out	9
D. Byas c Cook b Bowen	22		
A. A. Metcalfe c Ripley b Penberthy	2	L-b 7, w 10, n-b 2	19
R. B. Richardson c Warren b Curran	55		—
†R. J. Blakey c Cook b Penberthy	20	1/55 2/59 3/106 (6 wkts, 40 overs)	204
P. J. Hartley c Bailey b Penberthy	32	4/157 5/169 6/204	

M. J. Foster, D. Gough, C. E. W. Silverwood and M. A. Robinson did not bat.

Bowling: Ambrose 7–0–21–0; Curran 4–0–31–1; Bowen 8–0–36–1; Penberthy 7–0–49–3; Cook 8–0–25–0; Innes 6–0–35–1.

Northamptonshire

N. A. Felton c Blakey b Gough	17	K. J. Innes run out	5
R. J. Warren lbw b Hartley	0	M. N. Bowen b Gough	2
M. B. Loye lbw b Hartley	9	N. G. B. Cook not out	21
K. M. Curran c Foster b Silverwood	20	L-b 6, w 7, n-b 2	15
*R. J. Bailey c Foster b Silverwood	58		—
A. L. Penberthy c Moxon b Grayson	4	1/2 2/30 3/30 (39.4 overs)	194
†D. Ripley b Robinson	21	4/85 5/90 6/122	
C. E. L. Ambrose run out	22	7/162 8/167 9/170	

Bowling: Hartley 8–0–41–2; Gough 7.4–0–35–2; Robinson 8–0–43–1; Silverwood 8–0–32–2; Grayson 8–1–37–1.

Umpires: M. J. Kitchen and P. B. Wight.

NORTHAMPTONSHIRE v WARWICKSHIRE

At Northampton, June 26. Warwickshire won by 114 runs. Toss: Warwickshire. First-team debut: I. Dawood.

Having persuaded Lara, who wanted to rest a sore knee, to play at the last minute, Warwickshire easily completed their sixth straight win, opening up a two-point lead at the top of the table. Lara and Ostler added 96 in 16 overs, although Lara received a blow near his left eye as he miscued a sweep at Roberts. He hit the next ball for six, and attempted another big hit off the following delivery, only to be brilliantly caught by Montgomerie in the deep.

Warwickshire

D. P. Ostler c Curran b Roberts	78	R. G. Twose not out	18
†M. Burns c Curran b Taylor	2	N. M. K. Smith not out	11
B. C. Lara c Montgomerie b Roberts	34	B 4, l-b 4, w 7, n-b 2	17
P. A. Smith run out	28		—
Asif Din b Curran	21	1/20 2/116 3/130 (6 wkts, 40 overs)	218
*D. A. Reeve lbw b Curran	9	4/161 5/179 6/192	

G. C. Small, T. A. Munton and R. P. Davis did not bat.

Bowling: Curran 8–0–36–2; Taylor 8–0–39–1; Ambrose 8–0–39–0; Cook 8–1–42–0; Roberts 6–0–40–2; Bailey 2–0–14–0.

Northamptonshire

R. R. Montgomerie lbw b Munton 1	C. E. L. Ambrose c Lara b Davis 2
N. A. Felton c Small b Reeve 1	N. G. B. Cook c Lara b Davis........ 0
M. B. Loye c Burns b Small 16	J. P. Taylor not out 11
K. M. Curran c Twose b N. M. K. Smith . 5	B 3, l-b 10, w 6............. 19
*R. J. Bailey c sub b Davis 44	
A. L. Penberthy c and b N. M. K. Smith 3	1/2 2/9 3/26 (33.2 overs) 104
A. R. Roberts c Burns b N. M. K. Smith 0	4/31 5/42 6/42
†I. Dawood st Burns b N. M. K. Smith. 2	7/48 8/63 9/69

Bowling: Reeve 6–2–13–1; Munton 6–2–9–1; N. M. K. Smith 8–2–19–4; Small 4–0–9–1; Davis 6.2–0–19–3; Asif Din 3–0–22–0.

Umpires: A. A. Jones and B. Leadbeater.

At Nottingham, July 3. NORTHAMPTONSHIRE beat NOTTINGHAMSHIRE by one wicket.

At Leicester, July 10. NORTHAMPTONSHIRE beat LEICESTERSHIRE by eight runs.

NORTHAMPTONSHIRE v DERBYSHIRE

At Northampton, July 24. Derbyshire won on scoring-rate when rain ended play. Toss: Northamptonshire.

Azharuddin's maiden century in the Sunday League included eight sixes, his runs coming off just 81 balls, and he added 142 in 19 overs with Rollins. Northamptonshire were well behind the clock when a thunderstorm ended the match.

Derbyshire

*K. J. Barnett c Snape b Penberthy.... 33	C. M. Wells not out................. 3
D. G. Cork b Penberthy 41	L-b 6, w 2 8
M. Azharuddin not out 111	
T. J. G. O'Gorman c Bailey b Snape... 2	1/75 2/77 (4 wkts, 40 overs) 233
A. S. Rollins c Bailey b Ambrose...... 35	3/87 4/229

†K. M. Krikken, F. A. Griffith, M. J. Vandrau, S. J. Base and A. E. Warner did not bat.

Bowling: Innes 7–1–55–0; Ambrose 8–0–33–1; Cook 6–0–35–0; Penberthy 8–0–47–2; Bailey 8–0–36–0; Snape 3–0–21–1.

Northamptonshire

A. Fordham c Rollins b Base 31	J. N. Snape not out 16
R. J. Warren c Krikken b Warner..... 6	
M. B. Loye c Krikken b Cork 10	B 1, l-b 6, w 4.............. 11
*A. J. Lamb c Krikken b Griffith 21	
R. J. Bailey not out 36	1/14 2/40 3/58 (5 wkts, 30 overs) 140
A. L. Penberthy c Krikken b Griffith .. 9	4/80 5/92

K. J. Innes, †D. Ripley, N. G. B. Cook and C. E. L. Ambrose did not bat.

Bowling: Wells 8–1–23–0; Warner 5–0–17–1; Cork 6–1–22–1; Base 6–0–30–1; Griffith 5–0–41–2.

Umpires: D. J. Constant and K. J. Lyons.

At Southampton, July 31. NORTHAMPTONSHIRE beat HAMPSHIRE by six runs.

NORTHAMPTONSHIRE v SUSSEX

At Northampton, August 7. Northamptonshire won by six wickets. Toss: Northamptonshire.

Batsmen on both sides struggled for runs on a relaid pitch, being used for the first time. Sussex were contained by Ambrose and Cook, who conceded only 32 in 16 overs between them, before a half-century by Warren decided the result.

Sussex

D. M. Smith c Walton b Taylor....... 29
C. C. Remy c Penberthy b Curran..... 0
K. Greenfield b Penberthy 31
M. P. Speight c Walton b Penberthy... 5
*C. W. J. Athey run out 24
J. A. North c Lamb b Walton 7
†P. Moores not out 18
P. W. Jarvis st Ripley b Cook 2
I. D. K. Salisbury not out 8
B 2, l-b 19, w 7 28

1/1 2/48 3/68 4/79 5/110 6/120 7/124 (7 wkts, 40 overs) 152

J. D. Lewry and E. S. H. Giddins did not bat.

Bowling: Curran 7–1–29–1; Ambrose 8–3–14–0; Taylor 6–0–31–1; Penberthy 5–2–17–2; Walton 6–0–22–1; Cook 8–0–18–1.

Northamptonshire

A. Fordham c Athey b Salisbury 26
M. B. Loye b Jarvis................. 14
R. J. Warren c Smith b Lewry........ 55
K. M. Curran b Salisbury............ 20
T. C. Walton not out................ 6
*A. J. Lamb not out 6
B 2, l-b 5, w 18, n-b 4 29

1/24 2/92 3/135 4/143 (4 wkts, 38.1 overs) 156

†D. Ripley, A. L. Penberthy, C. E. L. Ambrose, N. G. B. Cook and J. P. Taylor did not bat.

Bowling: Jarvis 8–0–26–1; Giddins 5–0–33–0; Remy 5–1–15–0; Lewry 8–1–24–1; North 4.1–0–27–0; Salisbury 8–0–24–2.

Umpires: H. D. Bird and K. E. Palmer.

At Bristol, August 14. NORTHAMPTONSHIRE lost to GLOUCESTERSHIRE by eight wickets.

NORTHAMPTONSHIRE v MIDDLESEX

At Northampton, August 21. Middlesex won by 34 runs. Toss: Northamptonshire.

Ramprakash starred in Middlesex's innings, facing only 68 balls for his 73. Gordon Harris then demolished Northamptonshire. He had been recruited a few weeks earlier during an injury crisis, eight years after his only first-class match, for Leicestershire. Lamb's gallant 69 from 46 deliveries proved in vain.

Middlesex

D. L. Haynes c Curran b Innes 34
J. C. Pooley b Penberthy 77
M. R. Ramprakash b Penberthy 73
†K. R. Brown c Ripley b Walton...... 24
J. D. Carr not out 32
P. N. Weekes not out 13
L-b 5, w 9, n-b 2............ 16

1/72 2/146 3/207 4/233 (4 wkts, 40 overs) 269

*M. W. Gatting, M. A. Feltham, G. A. R. Harris, P. C. R. Tufnell and K. J. Shine did not bat.

Bowling: Curran 8–0–43–0; Taylor 8–1–47–0; Penberthy 8–0–67–2; Innes 7–0–53–1; Cook 4–0–36–0; Walton 5–0–18–1.

Northamptonshire

A. Fordham b Shine	14	†D. Ripley b Harris	1
A. L. Penberthy c Brown b Harris	2	J. P. Taylor c Brown b Harris	0
R. J. Warren c Gatting b Harris	0	N. G. B. Cook not out	0
K. M. Curran c Weekes b Feltham	30	B 1, l-b 14, w 12, n-b 8	35
T. C. Walton b Feltham	54		—
R. J. Bailey c Gatting b Tufnell	27	1/15 2/20 3/24 (38.1 overs)	235
*A. J. Lamb b Tufnell	69	4/125 5/130 6/211	
K. J. Innes c Brown b Harris	3	7/219 8/221 9/235	

Bowling: Harris 7.1–1–26–5; Shine 8–0–60–1; Tufnell 8–0–42–2; Feltham 8–0–54–2; Weekes 7–0–38–0.

Umpires: J. H. Harris and R. Palmer.

NORTHAMPTONSHIRE v KENT

At Northampton, August 28. Kent won by 40 runs. Toss: Northamptonshire.

Hooper passed fifty for the sixth successive League innings, equalling Barry Richards's sequence in 1976 and Dean Jones's in 1992, and went on to a brilliant 122 – his second successive century – off 112 balls, including three sixes off Taylor in the space of four deliveries. He and Cowdrey led a ferocious assault during their stand of 143 and, although they were separated, Kent added 109 in the last ten overs, only Ambrose escaping the carnage. Kent climbed into second place, two points behind Warwickshire.

Kent

T. R. Ward b Ambrose	9	N. J. Llong not out	10
M. V. Fleming c Cook b Ambrose	0	*†S. A. Marsh not out	1
C. L. Hooper c Warren b Ambrose	122	L-b 7, w 8	15
M. J. Walker c Warren b Ambrose	6		—
G. R. Cowdrey b Cook	82	1/8 2/11 3/21 (6 wkts, 40 overs)	273
M. A. Ealham c Cook b Bailey	28	4/164 5/226 6/269	

M. M. Patel, T. N. Wren and M. J. McCague did not bat.

Bowling: Curran 8–1–61–0; Ambrose 8–1–20–4; Walton 2–0–16–0; Bowen 3–0–37–0; Taylor 8–0–59–0; Cook 8–0–46–1; Bailey 3–0–27–1.

Northamptonshire

R. R. Montgomerie c Cowdrey b McCague	40	M. N. Bowen not out	27
A. Fordham b Ealham	9	N. G. B. Cook c Ward b Patel	3
R. J. Bailey c Ealham b Wren	1	J. P. Taylor not out	0
K. M. Curran st Marsh b Hooper	33	L-b 7, w 9	16
T. C. Walton c Ward b Patel	57		—
†R. J. Warren c Wren b Fleming	4	1/16 2/28 3/88 (9 wkts, 40 overs)	233
*A. J. Lamb b Hooper	25	4/90 5/100 6/153	
C. E. L. Ambrose c Fleming b Patel	18	7/194 8/211 9/232	

Bowling: Wren 8–0–52–1; Ealham 8–1–23–1; McCague 5–0–20–1; Hooper 8–0–47–2; Fleming 7–1–34–1; Patel 4–0–50–3.

Umpires: T. E. Jesty and K. J. Lyons.

At Taunton, September 4. NORTHAMPTONSHIRE beat SOMERSET by seven wickets.

At Chelmsford, September 18. NORTHAMPTONSHIRE beat ESSEX by one run.

NOTTINGHAMSHIRE

At Canterbury, May 8. NOTTINGHAMSHIRE beat KENT by four wickets.

NOTTINGHAMSHIRE v DURHAM

At Nottingham, May 15. No result (abandoned).

NOTTINGHAMSHIRE v SUSSEX

At Nottingham, May 22. No result (abandoned).

At Ilkeston, May 29. NOTTINGHAMSHIRE beat DERBYSHIRE by seven wickets.

At Leeds, June 5. NOTTINGHAMSHIRE lost to YORKSHIRE by seven wickets.

At Basingstoke, June 12. NOTTINGHAMSHIRE lost to HAMPSHIRE by three wickets.

NOTTINGHAMSHIRE v GLOUCESTERSHIRE

At Nottingham, June 19. Nottinghamshire won by 68 runs. Toss: Gloucestershire.

Nottinghamshire's winning total was built around Johnson's aggressive 67 off 41 balls, plus solid contributions from Pollard – he and Johnson posted an opening stand of 103 – and Adams.

Nottinghamshire

P. R. Pollard b Alleyne 29
*P. Johnson c Alleyne b Walsh 67
J. C. Adams run out 70
G. F. Archer c Smith b Williams...... 7
M. A. Crawley c Windows b Cooper... 19
C. C. Lewis c Hancock b Williams 26
G. W. Mike run out 1
†W. M. Noon lbw b Williams 0
K. P. Evans not out................. 13
M. G. Field-Buss not out 0
B 1, l-b 2, w 2, n-b 11 16

1/103 2/106 3/124 (8 wkts, 39 overs) 248
4/159 5/212 6/220
7/220 8/246

D. B. Pennett did not bat.

Bowling: Cooper 8–1–55–1; Smith 7–0–55–0; Walsh 8–0–44–1; Alleyne 8–0–37–1; Williams 8–0–54–3.

Gloucestershire

G. D. Hodgson lbw b Lewis.......... 3
M. G. N. Windows c Pollard b Lewis.. 2
T. H. C. Hancock lbw b Evans 10
M. W. Alleyne c Archer b Field-Buss .. 33
A. J. Wright run out 16
R. I. Dawson b Pennett 35
†R. C. Russell b Evans 25
*C. A. Walsh b Mike 20
R. C. Williams b Pennett 3
A. M. Smith c Mike b Lewis 7
K. E. Cooper not out................ 0
L-b 6, w 2, n-b 18........... 26

1/6 2/17 3/32 (34.1 overs) 180
4/72 5/83 6/148
7/160 8/168 9/180

Bowling: Pennett 8–1–26–2; Lewis 7–1–29–3; Mike 7.1–0–36–1; Evans 6–0–33–2; Field-Buss 6–0–50–1.

Umpires: B. Leadbeater and A. G. T. Whitehead.

At Ilford, June 26. NOTTINGHAMSHIRE beat ESSEX by seven wickets.

NOTTINGHAMSHIRE v NORTHAMPTONSHIRE

At Nottingham, July 3. Northamptonshire won by one wicket. Toss: Northamptonshire.

Northamptonshire registered their first Sunday League win of the season in their eighth match, thanks to Capel, who struck the last possible delivery for four. Capel was batting at No. 9 with a runner, after breaking down with a knee injury while bowling, but hit 29 off only 12 balls. Lewis, with 53 from 40 balls, gave Nottinghamshire's innings late momentum.

Nottinghamshire

P. R. Pollard lbw b Taylor	30
P. Johnson c Ripley b Capel	1
J. C. Adams c Bailey b Cook	66
*R. T. Robinson c Ambrose b Cook	13
M. A. Crawley c Ripley b Bailey	17
C. C. Lewis not out	53
†W. M. Noon run out	6
K. P. Evans not out	17
B 2, l-b 10, w 14, n-b 2	28
1/6 2/49 3/112 4/149 5/155 6/165 (6 wkts, 40 overs)	231

G. W. Mike, R. T. Bates and D. B. Pennett did not bat.

Bowling: Capel 2.5–0–20–1; Ambrose 8–1–34–0; Bailey 6.1–0–33–1; Penberthy 8–1–40–0; Taylor 7–0–57–1; Cook 8–0–35–2.

Northamptonshire

*A. J. Lamb c Noon b Lewis	13
M. B. Loye c Pollard b Crawley	64
T. C. Walton c and b Evans	27
K. M. Curran b Mike	11
R. J. Bailey c Noon b Mike	6
A. L. Penberthy c Mike b Pennett	6
C. E. L. Ambrose b Mike	37
†D. Ripley run out	11
D. J. Capel not out	29
N. G. B. Cook c Noon b Mike	0
J. P. Taylor not out	5
L-b 10, w 7, n-b 6	23
1/30 2/83 3/124 4/132 5/140 6/151 7/189 8/207 9/207 (9 wkts, 40 overs)	232

Bowling: Lewis 7–0–55–1; Pennett 5–0–31–1; Evans 8–0–41–1; Mike 8–0–41–4; Bates 5–1–29–0; Crawley 7–0–25–1.

Umpires: G. I. Burgess and R. A. White.

At Taunton, July 17. NOTTINGHAMSHIRE lost to SOMERSET by 126 runs.

NOTTINGHAMSHIRE v SURREY

At Nottingham, July 24. No result. Toss: Surrey.

Rain deprived Surrey of a likely victory; racing along at 8.75 an over, they were well ahead of the required scoring-rate when a storm broke over the ground before the 20 overs necessary to achieve a result. Adams, with an unbeaten 93, his fifth successive Sunday half-century for Nottinghamshire, and Darren Bicknell and Brown, with fifties for Surrey, took the batting honours. Adams also kept wicket, after Noon was struck on the helmet by a ball from Pigott while batting.

Nottinghamshire

M. P. Dowman c Smith b Kenlock 11
*P. Johnson c Kersey b Pigott 3
J. C. Adams not out 93
G. F. Archer c Pigott b Boiling 41
M. A. Crawley c Kersey b Kenlock.... 30
†W. M. Noon retired hurt 5
G. W. Mike c Kenlock b Pigott....... 1
K. P. Evans not out.................. 18
B 1, l-b 9, w 5, n-b 6 21

1/10 2/30 3/124 4/185 5/196 (5 wkts, 40 overs) 223

R. A. Pick, M. G. Field-Buss and D. B. Pennett did not bat.

W. M. Noon retired hurt at 194.

Bowling: Murphy 8–0–39–0; Pigott 8–0–41–2; Kenlock 8–1–39–2; Hollioake 8–0–45–0; Boiling 8–0–49–1.

Surrey

D. J. Bicknell not out 61
A. D. Brown c Crawley b Field-Buss... 55
D. M. Ward not out 9
L-b 3, w 9, n-b 6............ 18

1/108 (1 wkt, 16.2 overs) 143

*G. P. Thorpe, A. J. Hollioake, A. W. Smith, †G. J. Kersey, S. G. Kenlock, A. C. S. Pigott, J. Boiling and A. J. Murphy did not bat.

Bowling: Pennett 2–0–18–0; Pick 6–0–47–0; Evans 3–0–29–0; Crawley 2–0–13–0; Field-Buss 2–0–16–1; Mike 1.2–0–17–0.

Umpires: B. Dudleston and P. B. Wight.

NOTTINGHAMSHIRE v LEICESTERSHIRE

At Nottingham, August 7. Leicestershire won by 26 runs. Toss: Leicestershire.

Nixon scored a Sunday-best 72 after coming in at 36 for four, giving Leicestershire's bowlers something to defend, and they rose to the task well. Nottinghamshire slumped from 93 for one to 103 for six, losing five wickets for ten runs in 43 balls.

Leicestershire

*P. V. Simmons b Pick.............. 16
D. L. Maddy c Noon b Evans 6
V. J. Wells c Dowman b Pick 1
B. F. Smith c Noon b Evans 3
P. E. Robinson c Johnson b Mike 22
†P. A. Nixon b Lewis 72
P. N. Hepworth c Pick b Mike 11
G. J. Parsons st Noon b Adams....... 3
A. R. K. Pierson b Lewis 4
A. D. Mullally b Pick 4
I. M. Stanger not out................ 0
L-b 15, w 11 26

1/14 2/27 3/30 4/36 5/116 6/140 7/146 8/163 9/164 (36.3 overs) 168

Bowling: Evans 8–1–13–2; Pick 5.3–0–24–3; Mike 8–0–35–2; Lewis 6–0–30–2; Crawley 3–0–25–0; Adams 6–1–26–1.

Nottinghamshire

P. R. Pollard c Maddy b Wells 53
P. Johnson c Maddy b Stanger........ 19
J. C. Adams c Pierson b Mullally 21
*R. T. Robinson b Parsons........... 0
M. P. Dowman b Mullally 0
C. C. Lewis c Robinson b Wells 0
M. A. Crawley c Robinson b Wells.... 10
†W. M. Noon lbw b Simmons 17
G. W. Mike b Wells 0
K. P. Evans not out.................. 2
R. A. Pick c and b Mullally 6
L-b 11, w 3 14

1/33 2/93 3/101 4/102 5/103 6/103 7/130 8/130 9/135 (38.3 overs) 142

Bowling: Mullally 7.3–0–29–3; Stanger 6–0–24–1; Parsons 8–1–14–1; Wells 8–2–31–4; Pierson 4–0–18–0; Simmons 5–0–15–1.

Umpires: K. J. Lyons and N. T. Plews.

At Birmingham, August 14. NOTTINGHAMSHIRE lost to WARWICKSHIRE by 72 runs.

At Worcester, August 21. NOTTINGHAMSHIRE lost to WORCESTERSHIRE by 21 runs.

NOTTINGHAMSHIRE v LANCASHIRE

At Nottingham, August 28. Nottinghamshire won by eight wickets. Toss: Lancashire.

Lancashire's title aspirations were badly hit by this defeat, while Nottinghamshire recorded their first League win since June 26. Robinson's unbeaten century, a competition-best 119 off 120 balls, backed up by Johnson, guided the home side to a challenging target of 227 with three balls to spare.

Lancashire

I. D. Austin c Johnson b Evans	13
S. P. Titchard st Noon b Hindson	36
J. P. Crawley b Chapman	66
G. D. Lloyd b Chapman	27
N. J. Speak b Evans	19
*M. Watkinson not out	35
†W. K. Hegg c Robinson b Pennett	2
G. Yates b Pennett	14
L-b 7, w 5, n-b 2	14
1/18 2/93 3/143 4/164 5/208 6/211 7/226 (7 wkts, 39 overs)	226

P. J. Martin, G. Chapple and D. J. Shadford did not bat.

Bowling: Chapman 8–0–44–2; Evans 7–1–29–2; Mike 7–0–46–0; Pennett 5–0–39–2; Hindson 8–0–38–1; Dowman 4–0–23–0.

Nottinghamshire

*R. T. Robinson not out	119
M. P. Dowman c Yates b Watkinson	17
P. Johnson b Watkinson	54
J. C. Adams not out	17
B 5, l-b 8, w 7	20
1/87 2/191 (2 wkts, 38.3 overs)	227

P. R. Pollard, †W. M. Noon, K. P. Evans, G. W. Mike, R. J. Chapman, J. E. Hindson and D. B. Pennett did not bat.

Bowling: Martin 8–0–28–0; Chapple 7–0–40–0; Austin 7.3–0–53–0; Watkinson 8–0–36–2; Yates 6–0–38–0; Shadford 2–0–19–0.

Umpires: J. D. Bond and J. H. Harris.

NOTTINGHAMSHIRE v GLAMORGAN

At Nottingham, September 4. Nottinghamshire won by eight wickets. Toss: Glamorgan.

Evans dismissed Lefebvre, Metson and Watkin with the last three balls of his spell to become only the second Nottinghamshire bowler (after Kevin Saxelby in 1987) to perform a hat-trick in the competition. Rain reduced Nottinghamshire's target to 138 in 31 overs, and they reached it with two overs remaining.

Glamorgan

S. P. James run out 17
A. Dale b Adams.................... 61
D. L. Hemp c Evans b Bates 32
*M. P. Maynard b Adams 8
P. A. Cottey b Evans 8
O. D. Gibson not out 19
R. D. B. Croft b Evans.............. 6
R. P. Lefebvre b Evans.............. 9
†C. P. Metson b Evans 0
S. L. Watkin b Evans 0
S. R. Barwick not out 1
B 1, l-b 6, w 2, n-b 8 17

1/50 2/116 3/124 (9 wkts, 40 overs) 178
4/137 5/147 6/161
7/173 8/173 9/173

Bowling: Chapman 4–0–24–0; Evans 8–0–29–5; Mike 4–0–21–0; Bates 8–1–33–1; Hindson 8–0–38–0; Adams 8–0–26–2.

Nottinghamshire

*R. T. Robinson c Metson b Lefebvre . 2
M. P. Dowman not out.............. 52
J. C. Adams c Maynard b Gibson..... 65
P. Johnson not out.................. 13
L-b 2, w 2, n-b 2............ 6

1/3 2/118 (2 wkts, 29 overs) 138

P. R. Pollard, R. T. Bates, †W. M. Noon, K. P. Evans, G. W. Mike, R. J. Chapman and J. E. Hindson did not bat.

Bowling: Lefebvre 7–0–29–1; Watkin 8–0–28–0; Barwick 7–0–31–0; Croft 2–0–17–0; Gibson 5–0–31–1.

Umpires: K. E. Palmer and P. Willey.

NOTTINGHAMSHIRE v MIDDLESEX

At Nottingham, September 18. Middlesex won by six wickets. Toss: Middlesex.

Middlesex, after a tight bowling display, were set on course for victory by Weekes, who hit 50 off 56 balls, and Pooley, with 55 off 69, in an opening stand of 106. Mike was out handled the ball in an incident reminiscent of Gooch's dismissal in the Old Trafford Test the previous year: he gloved away a ball that was dropping on to his stumps.

Nottinghamshire

*R. T. Robinson lbw b Weekes 44
M. P. Dowman b Fraser.............. 0
J. C. Adams c Carr b Williams 0
P. Johnson c Williams b Johnson...... 27
P. R. Pollard c Roseberry b Johnson... 46
†W. M. Noon st Brown b Tufnell 7
K. P. Evans not out................. 25
G. W. Mike handled the ball 0
J. E. Hindson run out 21
L-b 4, w 4, n-b 2............ 10

1/2 2/3 3/73 (8 wkts, 40 overs) 180
4/93 5/120 6/144
7/144 8/180

R. J. Chapman and D. B. Pennett did not bat.

Bowling: Fraser 8–1–30–1; Williams 8–1–27–1; Johnson 8–0–43–2; Weekes 8–0–37–1; Tufnell 8–0–39–1.

Middlesex

P. N. Weekes b Mike 50
J. C. Pooley b Mike................. 55
M. R. Ramprakash b Adams 3
M. A. Roseberry run out............. 14
J. D. Carr not out 18
†K. R. Brown not out 32
L-b 4, w 8 12

1/106 2/111 (4 wkts, 38.3 overs) 184
3/117 4/138

*M. W. Gatting, R. L. Johnson, N. F. Williams, A. R. C. Fraser and P. C. R. Tufnell did not bat.

Bowling: Evans 8–0–32–0; Chapman 5.3–0–30–0; Hindson 2–0–17–0; Mike 8–1–47–2; Pennett 7–0–35–0; Adams 8–0–19–1.

Umpires: J. D. Bond and D. J. Constant.

SOMERSET

At Leicester, May 15. SOMERSET lost to LEICESTERSHIRE by eight wickets.

SOMERSET v WARWICKSHIRE

At Taunton, May 22. Warwickshire won by five wickets. Toss: Warwickshire. County debut: P. C. L. Holloway.

Rain reduced the match to 20 overs a side, and Warwickshire took the points thanks to Reeve, who hit Mushtaq Ahmed for two sixes in three balls, and Paul Smith. The late start gave Reeve time to drive down from Lord's, after the one-day international there was washed out. When Warwickshire batted, Bird dismissed Lara to claim an illustrious first wicket for the county.

Somerset

N. A. Folland b Twose	11
A. Payne c Burns b Reeve	3
M. N. Lathwell c Burns b P. A. Smith	31
G. D. Rose c Asif Din b Twose	3
V. P. Clarke run out	3
†P. C. L. Holloway c Reeve b P. A. Smith	14
*A. N. Hayhurst c and b P. A. Smith	28
Mushtaq Ahmed not out	0
R. J. Harden not out	1
B 1, l-b 7, w 3	11
1/5 2/29 3/37 4/47 5/57 6/103 7/103 (7 wkts, 20 overs)	105

H. R. J. Trump and P. J. Bird did not bat.

Bowling: Reeve 4–0–16–1; Munton 4–1–31–0; Small 4–1–8–0; Twose 4–0–24–2; P. A. Smith 4–0–18–3.

Warwickshire

†M. Burns c Payne b Rose	9
B. C. Lara b Bird	11
D. P. Ostler c Trump b Rose	2
P. A. Smith c Lathwell b Clarke	41
*D. A. Reeve run out	25
Asif Din not out	8
R. G. Twose not out	6
L-b 4	4
1/14 2/19 3/24 4/79 5/94 (5 wkts, 19.2 overs)	106

N. M. K. Smith, T. L. Penney, G. C. Small and T. A. Munton did not bat.

Bowling: Rose 4–0–12–2; Bird 4–0–22–1; Mushtaq Ahmed 3–0–23–0; Payne 4–0–16–0; Hayhurst 3–0–14–0; Clarke 1.2–0–15–1.

Umpires: R. Julian and K. J. Lyons.

At Manchester, May 29. SOMERSET lost to LANCASHIRE by 15 runs.

SOMERSET v HAMPSHIRE

At Taunton, June 5. Somerset won on scoring-rate. Toss: Somerset.

Somerset scored their first win of the season in any competition: Mallender, who had received £1,000 from a benefit collection, cut through Hampshire's middle order as the visitors chased a revised target of 199 in 36 overs. Benjamin was warned for excessive use of the bouncer against Trescothick.

Somerset

M. N. Lathwell c Cox b Cowans 55
M. E. Trescothick hit wkt b Udal 45
R. J. Harden c Nicholas b Udal 13
G. D. Rose c Cox b James 5
*A. N. Hayhurst c Aymes b Connor . . . 14
N. A. Folland b Benjamin 34
†R. J. Turner c Terry b Connor 21
Mushtaq Ahmed run out 0
A. P. van Troost not out 9
N. A. Mallender not out 4
L-b 9, w 2, n-b 10 21

1/80 2/110 3/131 4/135 5/169 6/197 7/197 8/215 (8 wkts, 40 overs) 221

H. R. J. Trump did not bat.

Bowling: James 8–0–36–1; Cowans 8–0–30–1; Benjamin 8–0–52–1; Connor 8–0–49–2; Udal 8–0–45–2.

Hampshire

V. P. Terry b van Troost 0
T. C. Middleton c Trescothick b Mushtaq Ahmed . 62
R. M. F. Cox c Turner b van Troost . . . 3
*M. C. J. Nicholas c Hayhurst b Mallender . 25
M. Keech lbw b Mallender 1
K. D. James c Trescothick b Mallender 2
S. D. Udal b Mushtaq Ahmed 6
W. K. M. Benjamin b Mallender 4
†A. N. Aymes run out 39
C. A. Connor not out 17
N. G. Cowans c Rose b van Troost 0
B 1, l-b 10, w 11 22

1/1 2/9 3/52 4/55 5/60 6/79 7/87 8/162 9/181 (35.1 overs) 181

Bowling: van Troost 6.1–0–21–3; Rose 8–0–47–0; Trump 6–0–23–0; Mallender 8–0–38–4; Mushtaq Ahmed 7–0–41–2.

Umpires: N. T. Plews and A. G. T. Whitehead.

At Leeds, June 12. SOMERSET beat YORKSHIRE by two runs.

SOMERSET v SURREY

At Bath, June 19. Somerset won by 18 runs. Toss: Surrey.

Rose was Somerset's all-round hero: he hit 62, adding 105 for the fourth wicket with Folland, and then claimed four for 35 as Surrey declined from 159 for two.

Somerset

M. N. Lathwell c Ward b Boiling 21
M. E. Trescothick c Sargeant b Boiling . 37
R. J. Harden c and b Boiling 12
N. A. Folland c Thorpe b Pigott 75
G. D. Rose c Bicknell b Benjamin 62
*A. N. Hayhurst c Ward b Murphy . . . 10
Mushtaq Ahmed not out 12
†R. J. Turner not out 1
L-b 5, w 4 9

1/50 2/66 3/95 4/200 5/224 6/229 (6 wkts, 40 overs) 239

N. A. Mallender, H. R. J. Trump and M. Dimond did not bat.

Bowling: Benjamin 8–1–43–1; Murphy 8–0–51–1; Pigott 8–1–37–1; Boiling 8–0–33–3; Smith 2–0–18–0; Hollioake 6–0–52–0.

Surrey

D. J. Bicknell b Mushtaq Ahmed 36
A. D. Brown c Turner b Rose 29
*G. P. Thorpe lbw b Hayhurst 45
D. M. Ward c Trump b Rose 54
A. J. Hollioake c Folland b Rose 14
A. W. Smith c Folland b Rose 12
†N. F. Sargeant b Mallender 3
A. C. S. Pigott not out 11
J. Boiling b Mallender 0
J. E. Benjamin c Harden b Mallender . . 3
A. J. Murphy not out 1
L-b 9, w 4 13

1/44 2/72 3/159 4/189 5/191 6/204 7/207 8/207 9/217 (9 wkts, 40 overs) 221

Bowling: Rose 8–0–35–4; Dimond 4–0–33–0; Mushtaq Ahmed 8–0–30–1; Trump 5–0–35–0; Hayhurst 7–0–38–1; Mallender 8–0–41–3.

Umpires: V. A. Holder and T. E. Jesty.

SOMERSET v WORCESTERSHIRE

At Taunton, July 3. Worcestershire won by five wickets. Toss: Somerset.

Radford, coming in with 31 needed off three overs, blasted Worcestershire to victory with 23 from only 13 deliveries. He hit a towering six off Rose, who had earlier bolstered Somerset with a brisk 66-ball 69.

Somerset

M. E. Trescothick c Edwards b Moody . 2
M. N. Lathwell c Edwards b Moody . . . 13
R. J. Harden b Lampitt 59
N. A. Folland c Seymour b Moody 9
G. D. Rose run out 69
*A. N. Hayhurst c Leatherdale b Illingworth . 15
Mushtaq Ahmed b Leatherdale 2
N. A. Mallender run out 9
A. P. van Troost not out 2
†R. J. Turner run out 1
L-b 5, w 4, n-b 4 13

1/8 2/35 3/51 4/141 5/170 6/182 7/182 8/193 9/194 (9 wkts, 40 overs) 194

H. R. J. Trump did not bat.

Bowling: Newport 8–0–40–0; Moody 8–0–18–3; Lampitt 6–0–39–1; Illingworth 8–0–34–1; Radford 6–0–38–0; Leatherdale 4–0–20–1.

Worcestershire

*T. S. Curtis c Turner b Mallender 55
A. C. H. Seymour b Trump 15
T. M. Moody c Harden b Mushtaq Ahmed . 14
G. R. Haynes c Turner b Mallender . . . 1
D. A. Leatherdale c Turner b Rose 36
S. R. Lampitt not out 35
N. V. Radford not out 23
L-b 9, w 5, n-b 2 16

1/34 2/69 3/75 4/95 5/164 (5 wkts, 39.5 overs) 195

C. M. Tolley, R. K. Illingworth, P. J. Newport and †T. Edwards did not bat.

Bowling: van Troost 6–0–34–0; Rose 5–0–23–1; Trump 8–0–31–1; Mushtaq Ahmed 8–0–27–1; Mallender 8–0–33–2; Hayhurst 4.5–0–38–0.

Umpires: B. Dudleston and G. Sharp.

At Bristol, July 10. SOMERSET lost to GLOUCESTERSHIRE by 37 runs.

SOMERSET v NOTTINGHAMSHIRE

At Taunton, July 17. Somerset won by 126 runs. Toss: Somerset. County debut: S. C. Ecclestone.

Somerset amassed 319, their highest-ever limited-overs score at Taunton, with Lathwell hitting two sixes and 15 fours in his maiden Sunday League century. He scored 117 from only 87 balls, and Rose powered his way to an unbeaten 61 off just 32. Nottinghamshire, in dire straits at 35 for five in reply, were steered to respectability by Adams.

Somerset

M. N. Lathwell c Robinson b Evans . . . 117
M. E. Trescothick c Field-Buss b Pick . 34
R. J. Harden hit wkt b Crawley 24
N. A. Folland c Crawley b Pick 61
G. D. Rose not out 61
S. C. Ecclestone not out 13
B 1, l-b 4, w 2, n-b 2 9

1/83 2/163 3/199 4/282 (4 wkts, 40 overs) 319

†R. J. Turner, A. R. Caddick, *N. A. Mallender, H. R. J. Trump and A. P. van Troost did not bat.

Bowling: Lewis 8–0–61–0; Evans 6–0–53–1; Pick 7–0–48–2; Field-Buss 5–0–55–0; Crawley 8–0–38–1; Mike 6–0–59–0.

Nottinghamshire

P. R. Pollard b Rose 11
*R. T. Robinson c Turner b van Troost 6
J. C. Adams c Rose b Ecclestone 86
G. F. Archer c Turner b van Troost . . . 0
C. C. Lewis c Turner b van Troost 5
M. A. Crawley c Turner b van Troost . . 2
†W. M. Noon c Lathwell b Ecclestone . 27
K. P. Evans b Mallender 10
G. W. Mike not out 23
R. A. Pick c Harden b Ecclestone 4
M. G. Field-Buss not out 2
L-b 6, w 7, n-b 4 17

1/10 2/20 3/21 4/31 5/35 6/103 7/149 8/168 9/184 (9 wkts, 40 overs) 193

Bowling: Rose 8–0–29–1; van Troost 8–1–23–4; Caddick 4–0–23–0; Ecclestone 7–0–41–3; Mallender 5–0–38–1; Trump 8–0–33–0.

Umpires: R. Julian and R. Palmer.

At Hove, July 24. SOMERSET lost to SUSSEX by seven wickets.

At Swansea, July 31. SOMERSET lost to GLAMORGAN by five wickets.

SOMERSET v DURHAM

At Taunton, August 7. Durham won by six wickets. Toss: Somerset.

Cummins achieved victory for Durham with an undefeated 46 from 20 balls, including three sixes and four fours, after Longley and Saxelby set up the innings. Somerset had slumped to 38 for four but Rose, who faced 99 deliveries, and Ecclestone retrieved the situation with a stand of 138.

Somerset

M. N. Lathwell b Walker 4
M. E. Trescothick c Cummins b Birbeck 23
*A. N. Hayhurst lbw b Walker 2
I. Fletcher lbw b Walker 1
G. D. Rose not out 91
S. C. Ecclestone c Scott b Brown 66
V. P. Clarke b Cummins 17
†R. J. Turner not out 6
L-b 9, w 12, n-b 2 23

1/4 2/16 3/22 4/38 5/176 6/218 (6 wkts, 40 overs) 233

J. I. D. Kerr, H. R. J. Trump and P. J. Bird did not bat.

Bowling: Walker 8–1–30–3; Cummins 8–1–40–1; Birbeck 7–0–47–1; Brown 6.4–0–57–1; Graveney 5–0–26–0; Bainbridge 5.2–0–24–0.

Durham

J. I. Longley c Fletcher b Kerr	88	A. Walker not out	4
M. Saxelby c Trump b Kerr	52	L-b 10, w 9	19
J. E. Morris c Fletcher b Trump	1		—
J. A. Daley c Trescothick b Hayhurst	24	1/93 2/95 (4 wkts, 39.2 overs)	234
A. C. Cummins not out	46	3/157 4/211	

*P. Bainbridge, †C. W. Scott, D. A. Graveney, S. D. Birbeck and S. J. E. Brown did not bat.

Bowling: Bird 8–0–41–0; Clarke 4–0–27–0; Rose 8–0–36–0; Trump 8–0–24–1; Kerr 6.2–0–45–2; Hayhurst 5–0–51–1.

Umpires: M. J. Kitchen and P. Willey.

At Lord's, August 14. SOMERSET lost to MIDDLESEX by eight wickets.

SOMERSET v ESSEX

At Weston-super-Mare, August 21. Somerset won by 85 runs. Toss: Essex.

Somerset ended a run of four defeats thanks to the bowling of Trump and Ecclestone, who took seven wickets between them as they worked through Essex after a 53-run opening stand.

Somerset

M. N. Lathwell c Hussain b Ilott	5	A. R. Caddick c Hussain b Ilott	0
M. E. Trescothick c Irani b Such	60	H. R. J. Trump not out	0
R. J. Harden c Rollins b Cousins	11		
P. C. L. Holloway c Lewis b Cousins	22	B 2, l-b 11, w 2, n-b 4	19
G. D. Rose lbw b Cousins	4		—
S. C. Ecclestone b Kasprowicz	14	1/15 2/53 3/96 (8 wkts, 40 overs)	204
*A. N. Hayhurst c Stephenson b Ilott	38	4/108 5/113 6/140	
†R. J. Turner not out	31	7/200 8/203	

A. P. van Troost did not bat.

Bowling: Kasprowicz 8–0–46–1; Ilott 8–0–36–3; Cousins 8–1–48–3; Stephenson 8–0–38–0; Such 8–0–23–1.

Essex

N. V. Knight b Trump	22	M. C. Ilott b Ecclestone	2
J. P. Stephenson lbw b Trump	26	P. M. Such b Rose	0
N. Hussain c Trump b Ecclestone	16	D. M. Cousins not out	0
*P. J. Prichard b Trump	11	L-b 5, w 6, n-b 2	13
J. J. B. Lewis c Turner b Rose	8		—
R. C. Irani c Harden b Ecclestone	13	1/53 2/54 3/83 (32.1 overs)	119
†R. J. Rollins run out	0	4/85 5/98 6/98	
M. S. Kasprowicz c Trump b Ecclestone	8	7/111 8/119 9/119	

Bowling: van Troost 5–0–21–0; Caddick 8–0–31–0; Trump 8–3–19–3; Ecclestone 8–0–31–4; Rose 3.1–0–12–2.

Umpires: J. W. Holder and K. J. Lyons.

SOMERSET v NORTHAMPTONSHIRE

At Taunton, September 4. Northamptonshire won by seven wickets. Toss: Northamptonshire.

Bailey, with an unbeaten 94 from 99 balls, and Montgomerie added 128 for Northamptonshire's second wicket. Victory was almost certain when Curran joined Bailey to put on another 68. Somerset failed to capitalise on a fine innings from Lathwell, declining from 157 for one in the 29th over.

Somerset

M. N. Lathwell c Curran b Walton 83
M. E. Trescothick c Warren b Penberthy 35
R. J. Harden c Walton b Bailey 31
P. C. L. Holloway b Bailey 0
S. C. Ecclestone c Walton b Curran ... 21
*A. N. Hayhurst c Innes b Curran 20
†R. J. Turner not out 11
J. I. D. Kerr c Lamb b Curran 3
A. P. van Troost not out 1
B 1, l-b 8, n-b 14 23

1/64 2/157 3/157 4/167 5/210 6/211 7/225 (7 wkts, 40 overs) 228

N. A. Mallender and H. R. J. Trump did not bat.

Bowling: Bowen 4–0–25–0; Curran 6–1–26–3; Penberthy 5–0–27–1; Innes 6–0–44–0; Cook 8–0–36–0; Bailey 8–0–42–2; Walton 3–0–19–1.

Northamptonshire

R. R. Montgomerie c Harden b Ecclestone . 74
A. Fordham lbw b Kerr 7
R. J. Bailey not out 94
K. M. Curran run out 35
T. C. Walton not out 6
L-b 5, w 4, n-b 6 15

1/13 2/141 3/209 (3 wkts, 39.2 overs) 231

*A. J. Lamb, †R. J. Warren, K. J. Innes, M. N. Bowen, N. G. B. Cook and A. L. Penberthy did not bat.

Bowling: van Troost 8–0–48–0; Kerr 8–0–43–1; Mallender 8–0–46–0; Trump 8–0–36–0; Ecclestone 7.2–0–53–1.

Umpires: V. A. Holder and P. B. Wight.

At Canterbury, September 11. SOMERSET lost to KENT by 66 runs.

SOMERSET v DERBYSHIRE

At Taunton, September 18. Derbyshire won by seven wickets. Toss: Somerset.

Bowler and Barnett settled the outcome with an unbroken fourth-wicket stand of 103, which was dominated by Barnett's forceful 50-ball innings.

Somerset

M. N. Lathwell c Base b Wells 0
M. E. Trescothick b Wells 17
R. J. Harden c Adams b Base 57
P. C. L. Holloway c Krikken b Warner. 7
G. D. Rose c Krikken b Warner 1
S. C. Ecclestone c Steer b DeFreitas ... 44
*A. N. Hayhurst not out 31
†R. J. Turner c Cork b Base 9
N. A. Mallender b Base 6
A. R. Caddick not out 1
L-b 2, w 7, n-b 8 17

1/0 2/40 3/71 4/76 5/112 6/148 7/166 8/181 (8 wkts, 40 overs) 190

H. R. J. Trump did not bat.

Bowling: Wells 8–1–26–2; DeFreitas 8–0–37–1; Warner 8–0–46–2; Base 8–0–31–3; Cork 8–0–48–0.

Derbyshire

D. G. Cork c Hayhurst b Rose	11	*K. J. Barnett not out	56
P. D. Bowler not out	66	L-b 13, w 6, n-b 4	23
C. J. Adams c Turner b Caddick	23		—
T. J. G. O'Gorman c Turner b Trump	12	1/15 2/52 3/88 (3 wkts, 38.3 overs)	191

†K. M. Krikken, C. M. Wells, P. A. J. DeFreitas, A. E. Warner, S. J. Base and I. G. S. Steer did not bat.

Bowling: Ecclestone 8–0–39–0; Rose 8–2–19–1; Caddick 8–0–34–1; Trump 7.3–0–37–1; Mallender 7–0–49–0.

Umpires: J. H. Hampshire and D. R. Shepherd.

SURREY

At Manchester, May 8. SURREY beat LANCASHIRE by one run.

SURREY v DERBYSHIRE

At The Oval, May 15. Surrey won by six wickets. Toss: Surrey.

An unbeaten 119 off 86 balls by Adams was eclipsed as Surrey were driven to victory by Stewart and Thorpe, who added 134 in 18 overs. Brown, who was capped before the match, set the tone for the run-chase with 32 from only 20 deliveries, including six fours.

Derbyshire

*P. D. Bowler c and b Butcher	67	T. J. G. O'Gorman not out	4
A. S. Rollins b Butcher	26	B 5, l-b 5, n-b 8	18
C. J. Adams not out	119		—
M. Azharuddin c Ward b Murphy	13	1/49 2/162 3/228 (3 wkts, 40 overs)	247

C. M. Wells, A. E. Warner, P. A. J. DeFreitas, †K. M. Krikken, O. H. Mortensen and D. E. Malcolm did not bat.

Bowling: Bicknell 8–1–37–0; Murphy 8–1–42–1; Pigott 8–0–32–0; Butcher 5–0–47–2; Smith 8–0–45–0; Hollioake 3–0–34–0.

Surrey

*A. J. Stewart lbw b DeFreitas	92	A. W. Smith not out	8
A. D. Brown c DeFreitas b Malcolm	32	L-b 4, w 4, n-b 7	15
G. P. Thorpe c Bowler b Malcolm	60		—
D. M. Ward c Rollins b Wells	35	1/48 2/182 (4 wkts, 36.1 overs)	253
A. J. Hollioake not out	11	3/195 4/242	

M. A. Butcher, M. P. Bicknell, †N. F. Sargeant, A. J. Murphy and A. C. S. Pigott did not bat.

Bowling: DeFreitas 8–0–36–1; Mortensen 6–0–51–0; Malcolm 8–0–63–2; Warner 8–1–37–0; Wells 6.1–0–62–1.

Umpires: B. Dudleston and J. H. Harris.

SURREY v NORTHAMPTONSHIRE

At The Oval, May 22. No result. Toss: Surrey.

Surrey were denied an almost certain victory by rain, which first intervened after Martin Bicknell had demolished Northamptonshire's batting. Resuming at 40 for five, with the innings now reduced to 29 overs, Northamptonshire were spared further misery by a final downpour. Lamb flew down to the match by helicopter after acting as godparent at the christening of Earl Spencer's son; Stewart crossed the Thames after the one-day international at Lord's was abandoned.

Northamptonshire

A. Fordham c Stewart b Bicknell	6	†D. Ripley not out	4
M. B. Loye b Bicknell	1		
R. J. Bailey c Lynch b Bicknell	0	L-b 2, w 11	13
*A. J. Lamb lbw b Bicknell	6		—
A. L. Penberthy c Thorpe b Pigott	15	1/8 2/9 3/10 (7 wkts, 22.3 overs)	53
D. J. Capel lbw b Bicknell	0	4/21 5/21	
K. M. Curran c Stewart b Butcher	8	6/44 7/53	

C. E. L. Ambrose, N. G. B. Cook and J. P. Taylor did not bat.

Bowling: Bicknell 8–3–12–5; Murphy 5–2–11–0; Butcher 6–0–20–1; Pigott 3.3–0–8–1.

Surrey

*†A. J. Stewart, A. D. Brown, G. P. Thorpe, D. M. Ward, A. J. Hollioake, M. A. Butcher, M. P. Bicknell, A. W. Smith, M. A. Lynch, A. J. Murphy and A. C. S. Pigott.

Umpires: J. D. Bond and J. W. Holder.

At Gloucester, May 29. SURREY beat GLOUCESTERSHIRE by ten runs.

At Swansea, June 5. GLAMORGAN v SURREY. No result.

At Bath, June 19. SURREY lost to SOMERSET by 18 runs.

SURREY v LEICESTERSHIRE

At The Oval, June 26. Leicestershire won by 122 runs. Toss: Surrey. County debut: J. M. de la Pena.

Wells, having scored his maiden century in the competition the previous week, now put in his best limited-overs performance with the ball. He destroyed Surrey, taking five for ten after Simmons, with 72 off 63 balls, led the visitors to an imposing 263. Mullally provided late impetus with an assault that included three sixes and three fours.

Leicestershire

P. N. Hepworth b Pigott	15	G. J. Parsons c Stewart b Hollioake	2
*P. V. Simmons c Pigott b Smith	72	A. D. Mullally b Pigott	37
V. J. Wells c and b Smith	35	I. M. Stanger b Pigott	0
B. F. Smith lbw b Hollioake	46	L-b 5, w 3, n-b 2	10
P. E. Robinson not out	39		—
†P. A. Nixon b Boiling	2	1/31 2/124 3/131 (37.5 overs)	263
D. L. Maddy run out	1	4/199 5/206 6/207	
J. M. Dakin lbw b Boiling	4	7/215 8/218 9/263	

Bowling: de la Pena 3–0–34–0; Benjamin 8–1–44–0; Pigott 7.5–0–48–3; Boiling 8–0–51–2; Hollioake 8–0–53–2; Smith 3–0–28–2.

Surrey

A. D. Brown b Mullally	8	J. Boiling c Parsons b Dakin	16
*†A. J. Stewart b Wells	36	J. E. Benjamin c Dakin b Stanger	7
G. P. Thorpe c Stanger b Wells	23	J. M. de la Pena not out	0
D. M. Ward c Maddy b Stanger	6	L-b 6, w 8, n-b 2	16
A. J. Hollioake c Smith b Stanger	27		—
D. J. Bicknell c Robinson b Wells	0	1/17 2/72 3/77 (29.3 overs)	141
A. W. Smith b Wells	0	4/84 5/94 6/95	
A. C. S. Pigott c Simmons b Wells	2	7/102 8/124 9/134	

Bowling: Mullally 7–0–55–1; Parsons 6–0–26–0; Wells 6–2–10–5; Simmons 2–0–10–0; Stanger 8–0–34–3; Dakin 0.3–0–0–1.

Umpires: R. Palmer and R. A. White.

At Darlington, July 3. SURREY beat DURHAM by two runs.

SURREY v WORCESTERSHIRE

At The Oval, July 12 (Tuesday). Worcestershire won by nine wickets. Toss: Surrey.

Worcestershire recovered strongly from their defeat in the Benson and Hedges Cup final three days earlier; openers Moody and Curtis took them within three runs of their 222-run target before being parted. The win lifted Worcestershire to second place in the table, two points behind Warwickshire. Surrey staged a partial recovery from 40 for four with Darren Bicknell and Ward adding 157.

Surrey

*†A. J. Stewart c Rhodes b Moody	20	M. P. Bicknell b Illingworth	5
A. D. Brown b Mirza	1	A. C. S. Pigott not out	4
G. P. Thorpe c and b Newport	9	B 2, l-b 7, w 13, n-b 2	24
D. M. Ward b Mirza	63		—
A. J. Hollioake c Rhodes b Newport	0	1/5 2/38 3/40 (6 wkts, 40 overs)	221
D. J. Bicknell not out	95	4/40 5/197 6/214	

A. J. Murphy, J. Boiling and J. E. Benjamin did not bat.

Bowling: Moody 8–0–27–1; Mirza 7–0–41–2; Newport 8–1–40–2; Illingworth 8–0–52–1; Radford 5–0–19–0; Haynes 2–0–13–0; Hick 2–0–20–0.

Worcestershire

T. M. Moody c Benjamin b Murphy	107
*T. S. Curtis not out	99
G. A. Hick not out	4
L-b 2, w 3, n-b 8	13
	—
1/219 (1 wkt, 36.3 overs)	223

P. Mirza, D. A. Leatherdale, †S. J. Rhodes, G. R. Haynes, S. R. Lampitt, R. K. Illingworth, N. V. Radford and P. J. Newport did not bat.

Bowling: M. P. Bicknell 6–0–33–0; Benjamin 7–1–49–0; Murphy 3.3–0–20–1; Pigott 7–1–27–0; Boiling 5–0–43–0; Hollioake 8–0–49–0.

Umpires: M. J. Kitchen and B. J. Meyer.

SURREY v WARWICKSHIRE

At Guildford, July 17. Warwickshire won by 13 runs. Toss: Warwickshire.

Warwickshire's eighth victory in nine Sunday games was set up by Twose with a brilliant unbeaten 96 off 67 balls, featuring seven sixes. He took 23 off the last over of the innings, bowled by Hollioake, and Surrey's challenge wilted once the third-wicket stand of 110 between Brown and Ward was broken.

Warwickshire

D. P. Ostler c Smith b Boiling 55
N. M. K. Smith c and b Pigott 3
B. C. Lara c Stewart b Murphy 0
Asif Din c Lynch b Hollioake 17
R. G. Twose not out 96
*D. A. Reeve c Boiling b Kendrick 3
T. L. Penney c Pigott b Kendrick 26
G. Welch b Pigott 26
†K. J. Piper not out 13
L-b 3, w 3, n-b 4 10

1/14 2/18 3/66 4/82 5/93 6/137 7/188 (7 wkts, 40 overs) 249

G. C. Small and T. A. Munton did not bat.

Bowling: Pigott 8–0–38–2; Murphy 7–0–38–1; Hollioake 8–0–66–1; Boiling 8–1–39–1; Kendrick 7–0–48–2; Smith 2–0–17–0.

Surrey

D. J. Bicknell run out 3
A. D. Brown c Welch b Smith 69
*†A. J. Stewart b Munton 0
D. M. Ward run out 63
M. A. Lynch lbw b Twose 0
A. J. Hollioake c Ostler b Welch 26
A. W. Smith c Welch b Reeve 14
A. C. S. Pigott c Ostler b Small 15
N. M. Kendrick not out 13
J. Boiling not out 16
B 3, l-b 7, w 3, n-b 4 17

1/6 2/9 3/119 4/121 5/163 6/180 7/201 8/206 (8 wkts, 40 overs) 236

A. J. Murphy did not bat.

Bowling: Reeve 8–0–39–1; Munton 7–0–39–1; Smith 8–0–29–1; Small 6–0–54–1; Twose 8–0–40–1; Welch 3–0–25–1.

Umpires: K. E. Palmer and N. T. Plews.

At Nottingham, July 24. NOTTINGHAMSHIRE v SURREY. No result.

SURREY v SUSSEX

At The Oval, July 31. Surrey won by six wickets. Toss: Surrey.

Surrey, ailing at 49 for three, were rescued by Hollioake, who struck eight fours in his run-a-ball 72, adding 72 in eight overs with Smith to pass the Sussex total.

Sussex

D. M. Smith c Kersey b M. P. Bicknell 13
M. P. Speight c Hollioake b M. P. Bicknell . 4
F. D. Stephenson c M. P. Bicknell b Hollioake . 35
*A. P. Wells c Ward b Boiling 38
C. W. J. Athey c Thorpe b Kenlock . . . 12
K. Greenfield c Boiling b Murphy 10
†P. Moores not out 41
C. C. Remy c Boiling b Murphy 0
I. D. K. Salisbury not out 4
B 1, l-b 11, w 12, n-b 4 28

1/26 2/26 3/80 4/116 5/122 6/138 7/138 (7 wkts, 40 overs) 185

J. D. Lewry and E. S. H. Giddins did not bat.

Bowling: M. P. Bicknell 8–0–41–2; Murphy 7–0–32–2; Kenlock 8–1–27–1; Hollioake 8–0–40–1; Boiling 8–0–30–1; Smith 1–0–3–0.

Surrey

D. J. Bicknell b Remy	19	A. W. Smith not out	32
A. D. Brown c Greenfield b Giddins	13	B 4, l-b 4, w 3, n-b 6	17
G. P. Thorpe c Moores b Giddins	3		—
D. M. Ward c Athey b Lewry	33	1/23 2/28 (4 wkts, 38.1 overs)	189
A. J. Hollioake not out	72	3/49 4/117	

†G. J. Kersey, S. G. Kenlock, *M. P. Bicknell, J. Boiling and A. J. Murphy did not bat.

Bowling: Giddins 7.1–0–48–2; Stephenson 7–1–28–0; Remy 8–0–33–1; Lewry 8–2–21–1; Salisbury 8–0–51–0.

Umpires: T. E. Jesty and M. J. Kitchen.

At Colchester, August 14. SURREY beat ESSEX by six wickets.

At Southampton, August 21. SURREY lost to HAMPSHIRE by seven wickets.

SURREY v MIDDLESEX

At The Oval, August 28. Surrey won by seven wickets. Toss: Surrey.

Brown's match-winning innings – 142 not out from 122 balls, with two sixes and 13 fours – was the highest for Surrey in the Sunday League. It outshone Roseberry's excellent century for Middlesex; his unbeaten 119 came from 116 balls with four sixes and five fours.

Middlesex

M. A. Roseberry not out	119	†K. R. Brown not out	39
J. C. Pooley b Boiling	28	L-b 6, w 3, n-b 10	19
M. R. Ramprakash b Pigott	3		—
P. N. Weekes lbw b Boiling	36	1/60 2/67 (4 wkts, 40 overs)	261
J. D. Carr b Hollioake	17	3/129 4/190	

*M. W. Gatting, M. A. Feltham, G. A. R. Harris, P. C. R. Tufnell and K. J. Shine did not bat.

Bowling: Cuffy 6–0–43–0; M. P. Bicknell 8–0–56–0; Pigott 8–0–43–1; Boiling 8–0–30–2; Butcher 4–0–37–0; Smith 2–0–17–0; Hollioake 4–0–29–1.

Surrey

D. J. Bicknell c Gatting b Tufnell	57	M. A. Butcher not out	6
A. D. Brown not out	142	L-b 5, w 8, n-b 6	19
D. M. Ward c and b Weekes	11		—
A. J. Hollioake c Carr b Gatting	27	1/136 2/165 3/246 (3 wkts, 37.2 overs)	262

A. W. Smith, †G. J. Kersey, *M. P. Bicknell, J. Boiling, A. C. S. Pigott and C. E. Cuffy did not bat.

Bowling: Shine 1–0–20–0; Harris 6–0–47–0; Feltham 8–0–52–0; Tufnell 8–0–35–1; Gatting 6.2–0–58–1; Weekes 8–0–45–1.

Umpires: G. I. Burgess and G. Sharp.

At Scarborough, September 11. SURREY beat YORKSHIRE by 205 runs.

SURREY v KENT

At The Oval, September 18. Surrey won by 24 runs. Toss: Kent.

Kent had to settle for third place in the final table as Surrey ended the visitors' run of nine consecutive victories. Surrey were indebted to Darren Bicknell and Thorpe, who added 115 in 22 overs. For Kent, the departure of Fleming proved a turning point as the remaining batsmen struggled. Amid some emotion from his team-mates, Boiling took three for 27 on his final appearance for Surrey before joining Durham.

Surrey

D. J. Bicknell b Fleming	79
A. D. Brown c Fleming b Wren	9
G. P. Thorpe c Cowdrey b Hooper	60
D. M. Ward lbw b Fleming	3
A. J. Hollioake b Patel	11
*†A. J. Stewart b McCague	12
M. A. Butcher run out	5
J. Boiling c Marsh b McCague	0
A. C. S. Pigott not out	6
J. E. Benjamin not out	1
B 1, l-b 8, w 10	19
1/16 2/131 3/140 4/172 5/184 6/195 7/195 8/200 (8 wkts, 40 overs)	205

S. G. Kenlock did not bat.

Bowling: Wren 5–0–32–1; Ealham 5–0–20–0; Hooper 8–1–30–1; McCague 7–0–34–2; Patel 8–0–56–1; Fleming 7–1–24–2.

Kent

T. R. Ward c Ward b Pigott	19
M. V. Fleming c Thorpe b Benjamin	65
C. L. Hooper c Brown b Boiling	30
M. J. Walker c Ward b Boiling	7
G. R. Cowdrey c Thorpe b Hollioake	24
N. J. Llong st Stewart b Boiling	3
M. A. Ealham run out	1
*†S. A. Marsh b Kenlock	13
M. J. McCague c and b Hollioake	5
M. M. Patel c Bicknell b Hollioake	5
T. N. Wren not out	0
L-b 5, w 4	9
1/31 2/122 3/123 4/137 5/141 6/143 7/169 8/175 9/179 (37.4 overs)	181

Bowling: Benjamin 8–0–22–1; Pigott 8–0–36–1; Butcher 2–0–18–0; Kenlock 5–0–31–1; Boiling 8–1–27–3; Hollioake 6.4–0–42–3.

Umpires: B. Leadbeater and N. T. Plews.

SUSSEX

At Bristol, May 8. SUSSEX beat GLOUCESTERSHIRE by 46 runs.

SUSSEX v HAMPSHIRE

At Hove, May 15. Hampshire won by nine wickets. Toss: Sussex.

Rain early in their innings left Hampshire to chase a revised target of 150 in 37 overs. They achieved it with ease, thanks to an unbroken stand of 139 between Terry and Smith. Sussex had slipped from 123 for two, losing seven wickets for 35 runs, mainly to the spinners.

Sussex

K. Greenfield c Terry b Udal 61
C. W. J. Athey c Benjamin b Maru 11
M. P. Speight st Aymes b Maru 13
*A. P. Wells lbw b Udal 33
F. D. Stephenson run out 11
J. A. North run out 0
†P. Moores lbw b Maru 0
C. C. Remy c Udal b Connor 11
I. D. K. Salisbury not out 8
P. W. Jarvis run out 2
E. S. H. Giddins not out 1
B 1, l-b 7, w 1, n-b 2 11

1/32 2/59 3/123 4/128 5/129 6/130 7/145 8/151 9/158 (9 wkts, 40 overs) 162

Bowling: James 6–1–18–0; Connor 8–1–24–1; Maru 8–0–33–3; Benjamin 8–1–36–0; Udal 8–1–31–2; Keech 2–0–12–0.

Hampshire

V. P. Terry not out 52
T. C. Middleton lbw b Jarvis 6
R. A. Smith not out 82
B 3, l-b 1, w 6 10

1/11 (1 wkt, 30.4 overs) 150

*M. C. J. Nicholas, M. Keech, K. D. James, †A. N. Aymes, S. D. Udal, W. K. M. Benjamin, R. J. Maru and C. A. Connor did not bat.

Bowling: Jarvis 5–1–11–1; Remy 8–1–33–0; Stephenson 8–2–28–0; Salisbury 4–0–34–0; Giddins 5–0–34–0; Athey 0.4–0–6–0.

Umpires: J. C. Balderstone and V. A. Holder.

At Nottingham, May 22. NOTTINGHAMSHIRE v SUSSEX. No result (abandoned).

SUSSEX v GLAMORGAN

At Hove, May 29. Sussex won by seven wickets. Toss: Glamorgan.

Two stoppages for rain reduced the Sussex target to 115 in 33 overs, and an opening stand of 67 in 13 overs between Smith and Greenfield made that a straightforward task, duly achieved with more than five overs to spare.

Glamorgan

S. P. James c Stephenson b Giddins . . . 19
*H. Morris c Speight b Remy 15
A. Dale c Moores b Hemmings 15
P. A. Cottey c and b Hemmings 16
D. L. Hemp c and b Hemmings 3
R. D. B. Croft b Giddins 23
O. D. Gibson c Wells b Stephenson 2
R. P. Lefebvre c Stephenson b Jarvis . . 15
†C. P. Metson b Giddins 8
S. L. Watkin not out 2
L-b 8, w 11, n-b 2 21

1/37 2/63 3/65 4/70 5/92 6/97 7/122 8/131 9/139 (9 wkts, 40 overs) 139

S. R. Barwick did not bat.

Bowling: Stephenson 8–2–21–1; Giddins 8–1–28–3; Jarvis 8–1–32–1; Remy 8–0–27–1; Hemmings 8–2–23–3.

Sussex

D. M. Smith c Hemp b Gibson 43
K. Greenfield b Gibson 27
*A. P. Wells not out 21
M. P. Speight c Metson b Croft 2
N. J. Lenham not out 21
L-b 2, n-b 2 4

1/67 2/80 3/86 (3 wkts, 27.4 overs) 118

F. D. Stephenson, †P. Moores, C. C. Remy, E. E. Hemmings, P. W. Jarvis and E. S. H. Giddins did not bat.

Bowling: Gibson 6–0–35–2; Watkin 6–1–18–0; Lefebvre 3–0–22–0; Barwick 8–0–20–0; Croft 4.4–0–21–1.

Umpires: A. G. T. Whitehead and P. B. Wight.

At Tunbridge Wells, June 5. SUSSEX lost to KENT by five wickets.

SUSSEX v LANCASHIRE

At Horsham, June 12. Lancashire won by seven wickets. Toss: Lancashire. First-team debut: J. D. Lewry.

Lancashire won with 15 balls to spare thanks to Atherton, who faced 102 deliveries for his century, hitting 13 fours. He and Gallian finished the match with an unbroken stand of 121. Earlier, Hall had led the way for Sussex with 69 from 75 balls, though the later order failed to cash in.

Sussex

K. Greenfield c Crawley b Wasim Akram . 19
J. W. Hall lbw b Gallian 69
*A. P. Wells lbw b Yates 33
M. P. Speight b Austin 45
F. D. Stephenson b Wasim Akram 26
†P. Moores b Wasim Akram 8
J. A. North run out 4
P. W. Jarvis lbw b Martin 6
C. C. Remy c Crawley b Martin 0
J. D. Lewry not out 1
L-b 7, w 9, n-b 2. 18

1/62 2/119 3/145 4/203 5/213 6/220 7/223 8/228 9/229 (9 wkts, 40 overs) 229

E. S. H. Giddins did not bat.

Bowling: Martin 7–1–32–2; Austin 8–1–36–1; Watkinson 2–0–14–0; Wasim Akram 8–1–47–3; Yates 8–0–44–1; Gallian 7–0–49–1.

Lancashire

M. A. Atherton not out 101
G. D. Lloyd c Jarvis b Stephenson 12
J. P. Crawley c Lewry b Jarvis 10
N. H. Fairbrother c Moores b Remy . . . 33
J. E. R. Gallian not out 58
L-b 5, w 11, n-b 2. 18

1/30 2/60 3/111 (3 wkts, 37.3 overs) 232

Wasim Akram, *M. Watkinson, I. D. Austin, †W. K. Hegg, G. Yates and P. J. Martin did not bat.

Bowling: Lewry 6.3–0–49–0; Stephenson 8–0–40–1; Jarvis 6–0–23–1; Giddins 7–0–42–0; Remy 8–0–51–1; Greenfield 2–0–22–0.

Umpires: J. D. Bond and D. R. Shepherd.

SUSSEX v DURHAM

At Hove, June 19. Durham won by nine wickets. Toss: Durham.

An undefeated second-wicket stand of 142 between Saxelby and Morris secured a comfortable victory for the visitors with 7.3 overs remaining.

Sussex

K. Greenfield b Brown 15
J. W. Hall lbw b Bainbridge.......... 33
*A. P. Wells c Saxelby b Bainbridge ... 35
M. P. Speight c Larkins b Bainbridge .. 10
N. J. Lenham run out 18
F. D. Stephenson c Graveney b Brown . 12
†P. Moores c Longley b Bainbridge.... 22
P. W. Jarvis b Walker............... 15
I. D. K. Salisbury c Saxelby b Cummins 12
E. E. Hemmings not out 6
E. S. H. Giddins b Walker 2
L-b 5, w 3 8

1/33 2/80 3/94 4/102 5/128 6/130 7/159 8/180 9/182 (39.5 overs) 188

Bowling: Cummins 8–0–38–1; Brown 8–2–35–2; Walker 7.5–0–40–2; Graveney 8–0–38–0; Bainbridge 8–0–32–4.

Durham

W. Larkins c Speight b Giddins....... 30
M. Saxelby not out 79
J. E. Morris not out................. 77
L-b 2, n-b 2 4

1/48 (1 wkt, 32.3 overs) 190

*P. Bainbridge, S. Hutton, J. I. Longley, A. C. Cummins, A. Walker, †C. W. Scott, D. A. Graveney and S. J. E. Brown did not bat.

Bowling: Stephenson 7.3–0–32–0; Jarvis 6–0–36–0; Hemmings 8–0–36–0; Giddins 3–0–28–1; Salisbury 7–0–47–0; Greenfield 1–0–9–0.

Umpires: J. H. Harris and G. Sharp.

At Worcester, June 26. SUSSEX lost to WORCESTERSHIRE by 97 runs.

SUSSEX v MIDDLESEX

At Arundel, July 17. Sussex won by 17 runs. Toss: Middlesex.

Wells scored his first 27 runs in singles, taking 54 balls, before accelerating with 76 off the next 47 balls faced. He added 116 with Greenfield, helping to condemn Middlesex to a fourth successive defeat.

Sussex

J. W. Hall c Weekes b Johnson 14
M. P. Speight b Fraser 18
F. D. Stephenson c Feltham b Weekes . 36
*A. P. Wells st Brown b Weekes 103
C. W. J. Athey b Tufnell 4
K. Greenfield not out 42
†P. Moores not out 1
B 1, l-b 3, w 3.............. 7

1/31 2/39 3/94 4/104 5/220 (5 wkts, 40 overs) 225

I. D. K. Salisbury, C. C. Remy, J. D. Lewry and E. S. H. Giddins did not bat.

Bowling: Fraser 8–1–36–1; Johnson 8–0–36–1; Feltham 8–0–62–0; Tufnell 8–0–30–1; Weekes 8–0–57–2.

Middlesex

D. L. Haynes c and b Salisbury 42
J. C. Pooley lbw b Stephenson 0
M. R. Ramprakash b Athey 33
*M. W. Gatting run out 29
†K. R. Brown c Hall b Lewry 28
J. D. Carr c Wells b Lewry 18
P. N. Weekes b Stephenson 22
M. A. Feltham b Stephenson 9
R. L. Johnson not out 14
A. R. C. Fraser b Stephenson......... 0
P. C. R. Tufnell b Giddins 1
L-b 7, w 3, n-b 2............ 12

1/1 2/79 3/83 4/132 5/147 6/161 7/190 8/201 9/201 (39.5 overs) 208

Bowling: Stephenson 8–0–24–4; Giddins 7.5–1–41–1; Remy 6–0–43–0; Lewry 7–0–43–2; Salisbury 8–0–38–1; Athey 3–0–12–1.

Umpires: K. J. Lyons and B. J. Meyer.

SUSSEX v SOMERSET

At Hove, July 24. Sussex won by seven wickets. Toss: Sussex.

Somerset's disappointing total of 157 was easily overhauled, with Smith, who faced 74 balls, and Greenfield sharing an unbroken stand of 71 in 14 overs; they completed victory with more than eight overs in hand.

Somerset

M. N. Lathwell c Moores b Stephenson. 9
M. E. Trescothick c Stephenson b Remy 18
R. J. Harden b Phillips 22
N. A. Folland c Stephenson b Phillips . 21
*A. N. Hayhurst c Giddins b Stephenson . 21
†R. J. Turner not out 37
J. C. Hallett c Wells b Stephenson 16
J. I. D. Kerr not out 1
L-b 3, w 3, n-b 6 12

1/20 2/40 3/63 4/89 5/111 6/155 (6 wkts, 40 overs) 157

M. Dimond, H. R. J. Trump and A. P. van Troost did not bat.

Bowling: Stephenson 8–0–34–3; Giddins 8–1–45–0; Remy 8–0–29–1; North 8–0–27–0; Phillips 8–2–19–2.

Sussex

D. M. Smith not out 55
M. P. Speight lbw b van Troost 2
F. D. Stephenson b Kerr 46
C. W. J. Athey c and b Trump 2
K. Greenfield not out 31
B 5, l-b 2, w 7, n-b 8 22

1/4 2/81 3/87 (3 wkts, 31.5 overs) 158

*A. P. Wells, †P. Moores, C. C. Remy, J. A. North, N. C. Phillips and E. S. H. Giddins did not bat.

Bowling: van Troost 6–0–29–1; Dimond 4–0–31–0; Trump 8–0–31–1; Kerr 8–2–36–1; Hayhurst 3–0–10–0; Hallett 2.5–0–14–0.

Umpires: G. I. Burgess and N. T. Plews.

At The Oval, July 31. SUSSEX lost to SURREY by six wickets.

At Northampton, August 7. SUSSEX lost to NORTHAMPTONSHIRE by six wickets.

SUSSEX v DERBYSHIRE

At Eastbourne, August 14. Derbyshire won by seven wickets. Toss: Derbyshire. First-team debut: A. D. Edwards.

Cork was Derbyshire's mainstay in both departments, containing Sussex with a tight bowling spell and then scoring 66 off 68 balls to clinch victory.

Sussex

D. M. Smith c Krikken b Warner	10	J. A. North lbw b Malcolm	0
C. C. Remy c Barnett b Warner	14	†P. Moores not out	12
M. P. Speight c O'Gorman b Base	7	B 4, l-b 5, w 9, n-b 4	22
K. Greenfield b Cork	5		—
C. W. J. Athey not out	58	1/26 2/29 3/38 (6 wkts, 40 overs)	152
*A. P. Wells b Malcolm	24	4/48 5/102 6/102	

A. D. Edwards, J. D. Lewry and N. C. Phillips did not bat.

Bowling: DeFreitas 8–1–27–0; Warner 8–0–40–2; Base 8–1–38–1; Cork 8–0–18–1; Malcolm 8–1–20–2.

Derbyshire

P. D. Bowler c Moores b Remy	16	*K. J. Barnett not out	10
D. G. Cork run out	66	L-b 3, w 9, n-b 2	14
C. J. Adams c Remy b Phillips	22		—
T. J. G. O'Gorman not out	28	1/62 2/105 3/124 (3 wkts, 34.4 overs)	156

A. S. Rollins, P. A. J. DeFreitas, †K. M. Krikken, A. E. Warner, S. J. Base and D. E. Malcolm did not bat.

Bowling: Edwards 5–1–24–0; Lewry 4–0–22–0; Remy 3–0–22–1; Athey 4.4–0–22–0; Phillips 8–0–31–1; North 8–1–26–0; Greenfield 2–0–6–0.

Umpires: J. C. Balderstone and G. I. Burgess.

At Leicester, August 21. SUSSEX beat LEICESTERSHIRE by 42 runs.

SUSSEX v WARWICKSHIRE

At Hove, August 28. Warwickshire won by five wickets. Toss: Warwickshire.

Still chasing the Grand Slam, Warwickshire restricted the home side's batsmen effectively, and were then guided to their target by Ostler with an unbeaten 84 including 11 fours. Joint leaders Worcestershire's simultaneous defeat by Yorkshire saw Warwickshire pull ahead of them by four points, while maintaining a two-point lead over Kent, who beat Northamptonshire.

Sussex

K. Greenfield c Penney b Reeve	4	P. W. Jarvis not out	7
C. W. J. Athey b Welch	30	I. D. K. Salisbury not out	2
F. D. Stephenson c Moles b Reeve	16		
*A. P. Wells c Twose b P. A. Smith	60	B 1, l-b 10, w 6, n-b 2	19
M. P. Speight c N. M. K. Smith b Welch	7		—
†P. Moores run out	2	1/12 2/35 3/94 (7 wkts, 39 overs)	157
C. C. Remy run out	10	4/115 5/124 6/139 7/153	

N. C. Phillips and E. S. H. Giddins did not bat.

Bowling: Reeve 8–1–16–2; Munton 7–1–30–0; N. M. K. Smith 4–0–21–0; Welch 8–0–30–2; P. A. Smith 8–2–35–1; Twose 4–0–14–0.

Warwickshire

D. P. Ostler not out	84	T. L. Penney not out	10
N. M. K. Smith c Speight b Giddins	15		
A. J. Moles b Athey	31	L-b 4, w 6	10
R. G. Twose c Giddins b Athey	1		—
P. A. Smith b Remy	0	1/42 2/98 3/115 (5 wkts, 35 overs)	161
*D. A. Reeve b Stephenson	10	4/119 5/140	

G. Welch, †K. J. Piper, R. P. Davis and T. A. Munton did not bat.

Bowling: Stephenson 7–1–37–1; Jarvis 6–0–25–0; Giddins 6–1–25–1; Salisbury 3–0–23–0; Remy 8–0–20–1; Athey 5–0–27–2.

Umpires: N. T. Plews and R. A. White.

At Chelmsford, September 4. SUSSEX lost to ESSEX by 33 runs.

SUSSEX v YORKSHIRE

At Hove, September 18. Yorkshire won by 37 runs. Toss: Sussex. County debut: M. T. E. Peirce.

Byas set a new Yorkshire record of 702 runs in a season, surpassing John Hampshire's 684 in 1976. Gough then turned in a devastating bowling performance. On his 24th birthday, he took five wickets, for the first time in any one-day competition, for just 13 runs, while Sussex lost their last six wickets for 29.

Yorkshire

*M. D. Moxon c Peirce b Jarvis	21	P. J. Hartley c Stephenson b Giddins	2
D. Byas b Remy	54	D. Gough not out	13
†R. J. Blakey b Remy	18	L-b 5, w 6, n-b 2	13
B. Parker run out	36		—
A. P. Grayson c Peirce b Remy	2	1/37 2/82 3/111 (6 wkts, 40 overs)	214
A. A. Metcalfe not out	55	4/117 5/164 6/189	

G. M. Hamilton, R. D. Stemp and M. A. Robinson did not bat.

Bowling: Stephenson 8–0–37–0; Giddins 7–1–44–1; Jarvis 7–0–37–1; Remy 8–0–30–3; Newell 4–0–25–0; Phillips 6–0–36–0.

Sussex

N. J. Lenham c Grayson b Gough	3	P. W. Jarvis b Gough	5
K. Newell lbw b Robinson	10	N. C. Phillips not out	5
M. T. E. Peirce b Robinson	6	E. S. H. Giddins b Gough	0
*A. P. Wells c Hartley b Hamilton	64	B 4, l-b 8, w 4	16
K. Greenfield c Hartley b Grayson	35		—
†P. Moores b Gough	23	1/10 2/18 3/25 (39.3 overs)	177
F. D. Stephenson c Byas b Hartley	10	4/108 5/148 6/155	
C. C. Remy b Gough	0	7/155 8/166 9/172	

Bowling: Hartley 8–0–35–1; Gough 7.3–1–13–5; Robinson 8–1–21–2; Hamilton 6–0–30–1; Stemp 5–0–29–0; Grayson 5–0–37–1.

Umpires: R. Palmer and P. Willey.

WARWICKSHIRE

WARWICKSHIRE v LEICESTERSHIRE

At Birmingham, May 8. Warwickshire won by 22 runs. Toss: Warwickshire.

Bell claimed five for six in 18 balls to undermine Leicestershire's run-chase. For Warwickshire, Reeve and Asif Din had added an unbroken 129 for the fifth wicket, rallying the home side from 44 for four.

Warwickshire

D. P. Ostler b Parsons . . . 9	*D. A. Reeve not out . . . 65
R. G. Twose c Hepworth b Parsons . . . 10	B 7, l-b 2, w 2 . . . 11
B. C. Lara b Wells . . . 19	—
P. A. Smith c Hepworth b Parsons . . . 5	1/18 2/26 (4 wkts, 40 overs) 173
Asif Din not out . . . 54	3/36 4/44

†M. Burns, N. M. K. Smith, M. A. V. Bell, G. C. Small and T. A. Munton did not bat.

Bowling: Mullally 8–0–32–0; Parsons 8–0–31–3; Wells 8–0–32–1; Simmons 8–1–40–0; Pierson 8–2–29–0.

Leicestershire

P. V. Simmons c Burns b Munton . . . 27	G. J. Parsons b Bell . . . 0
V. J. Wells c and b Munton . . . 6	A. R. K. Pierson not out . . . 11
J. J. Whitaker b Bell . . . 33	A. D. Mullally run out . . . 12
B. F. Smith lbw b Small . . . 3	L-b 8, w 7 . . . 15
*N. E. Briers c Burns b Bell . . . 24	—
†P. A. Nixon c Burns b Bell . . . 8	1/29 2/34 3/37 (39.3 overs) 151
P. N. Hepworth c and b P. A. Smith . . 12	4/94 5/106 6/110
J. M. Dakin b Bell . . . 0	7/110 8/111 9/131

Bowling: Reeve 5.3–0–40–0; Munton 8–1–15–2; Small 7–2–19–1; N. M. K. Smith 8–1–34–0; Bell 8–0–19–5; P. A. Smith 3–0–16–1.

Umpires: B. Dudleston and D. R. Shepherd.

At Taunton, May 22. WARWICKSHIRE beat SOMERSET by five wickets.

At Lord's, May 29. WARWICKSHIRE beat MIDDLESEX by three wickets.

WARWICKSHIRE v DURHAM

At Birmingham, June 5. Warwickshire won by 84 runs. Toss: Warwickshire.

Ostler's 83 off 94 balls, with two sixes and nine fours, was the major contribution for Warwickshire, and Durham never recovered from the loss of Larkins and Morris in Munton's opening over. Warwickshire joined Surrey at the top of the table.

Warwickshire

D. P. Ostler c Bainbridge b Cummins . . 83	N. M. K. Smith b Cummins . . . 11
†M. Burns c Cummins b Graveney . . . 37	R. P. Davis b Walker . . . 5
B. C. Lara c Walker b Graveney . . . 6	B 1, l-b 4, w 4, n-b 2 . . . 11
P. A. Smith b Walker . . . 2	—
Asif Din lbw b Cummins . . . 27	1/60 2/71 3/74 (8 wkts, 40 overs) 236
R. G. Twose c Scott b Walker . . . 27	4/165 5/168 6/204
T. L. Penney not out . . . 27	7/225 8/236

G. C. Small and *T. A. Munton did not bat.

Bowling: Cummins 8–1–40–3; Wood 8–0–48–0; Graveney 8–0–32–2; Walker 8–0–51–3; Bainbridge 6–0–41–0; Birbeck 2–0–19–0.

Durham

W. Larkins c Lara b Munton 0	J. Wood lbw b Twose 3
M. Saxelby c Twose b Davis 39	D. A. Graveney not out 25
J. E. Morris c Burns b Munton 2	A. Walker c Davis b P. A. Smith 4
J. I. Longley lbw b N. M. K. Smith ... 12	
*P. Bainbridge c Lara b N. M. K. Smith 29	B 1, l-b 1, w 2.............. 4
A. C. Cummins c Lara b Davis 8	—
S. D. Birbeck st Burns b N. M. K. Smith . 0	1/0 2/2 3/42 (39.2 overs) 152
†C. W. Scott b P. A. Smith 26	4/81 5/85 6/87 7/91 8/104 9/144

Bowling: Munton 8–0–28–2; Twose 6.4–0–29–1; Small 3.2–0–19–0; N. M. K. Smith 8–2–27–3; Davis 8–1–25–2; P. A. Smith 5.2–0–22–2.

Umpires: T. E. Jesty and P. B. Wight.

WARWICKSHIRE v KENT

At Birmingham, June 19. Warwickshire won by six wickets. Toss: Warwickshire.

After four Sunday failures, Lara boosted Warwickshire with his maiden half-century in the competition, scoring 63 off 64 balls. Asif Din, who hit 86 in 79 balls, wrapped up the match in an unbroken stand of 96 with Reeve.

Kent

T. R. Ward c Burns b Small.......... 63	†S. A. Marsh not out................ 24
*M. R. Benson c Burns b Munton 0	J. B. D. Thompson not out........... 3
C. L. Hooper lbw b Small............ 25	
N. R. Taylor run out................ 27	L-b 8, w 6 14
N. J. Llong c Penney b N. M. K. Smith 1	—
M. V. Fleming b N. M. K. Smith 23	1/13 2/84 3/111 (7 wkts, 40 overs) 210
M. A. Ealham c P. A. Smith b N. M. K. Smith . 30	4/113 5/133 6/157 7/200

D. W. Headley and A. P. Igglesden did not bat.

Bowling: Reeve 6–0–29–0; Munton 8–0–54–1; Small 8–0–35–2; P. A. Smith 8–0–35–0; N. M. K. Smith 8–1–34–3; Twose 2–0–15–0.

Warwickshire

D. P. Ostler lbw b Igglesden.......... 2	*D. A. Reeve not out 26
†M. Burns b Headley................ 14	B 1, l-b 9, n-b 2 12
B. C. Lara c Benson b Hooper........ 63	—
P. A. Smith c Headley b Ealham...... 8	1/15 2/27 (4 wkts, 38.1 overs) 211
Asif Din not out.................... 86	3/66 4/115

R. G. Twose, T. L. Penney, N. M. K. Smith, G. C. Small and T. A. Munton did not bat.

Bowling: Headley 8–0–33–1; Igglesden 8–2–37–1; Thompson 4–0–27–0; Ealham 7.1–0–42–1; Fleming 3–0–21–0; Hooper 8–0–41–1.

Umpires: J. C. Balderstone and D. R. Shepherd.

At Northampton, June 26. WARWICKSHIRE beat NORTHAMPTONSHIRE by 114 runs.

WARWICKSHIRE v LANCASHIRE

At Birmingham, July 3. Lancashire won by 93 runs. Toss: Lancashire.

Warwickshire suffered their first defeat of the season in any competition, losing their 23-match unbeaten record stretching back to their Championship defeat by Worcestershire on August 30, 1993. Fairbrother, with 70 off 103 balls, helped Lancashire recover from a disastrous start – Lloyd and Crawley out in Munton's first over – despite Reeve bowling so tightly that he conceded only nine in his eight overs. Warwickshire then crumbled against Yates's off-spin. The win brought Lancashire level on points with Warwickshire at the top of the table.

Lancashire

G. D. Lloyd c Reeve b Munton 0
S. P. Titchard st Burns b N. M. K. Smith . 37
J. P. Crawley b Munton 0
N. H. Fairbrother b Welch........... 70
N. J. Speak c Twose b P. A. Smith.... 33
*M. Watkinson c Davis b Munton 18
Wasim Akram b P. A. Smith 3
†W. K. Hegg not out................ 28
P. J. Martin not out................ 0
B 1, l-b 7, w 3, n-b 4 15

1/3 2/3 3/92 4/144 5/170 6/171 7/179 (7 wkts, 40 overs) 204

G. Yates and G. Chapple did not bat.

Bowling: Reeve 8–3–9–0; Munton 8–0–57–3; P. A. Smith 6–0–42–2; N. M. K. Smith 8–2–22–1; Davis 4–0–30–0; Welch 6–0–36–1.

Warwickshire

D. P. Ostler c Hegg b Watkinson 22
†M. Burns c Yates b Chapple......... 0
R. G. Twose c and b Yates 21
P. A. Smith b Yates 4
Asif Din lbw b Chapple 3
T. L. Penney b Yates 26
*D. A. Reeve run out 13
N. M. K. Smith c Lloyd b Wasim Akram . 1
G. Welch lbw b Wasim Akram 5
R. P. Davis c Hegg b Yates 5
T. A. Munton not out 1
B 1, l-b 6, w 3.............. 10

1/2 2/40 3/53 4/58 5/60 6/94 7/97 8/104 9/110 (29.4 overs) 111

Bowling: Chapple 6–1–29–2; Martin 5–0–16–0; Watkinson 6–0–10–1; Wasim Akram 5–1–15–2; Yates 7.4–0–34–4.

Umpires: V. A. Holder and M. J. Kitchen.

WARWICKSHIRE v GLAMORGAN

At Birmingham, July 12 (Tuesday). Warwickshire won by four wickets. Toss: Glamorgan.

Paul Smith followed his Gold Award in the Benson and Hedges Cup final three days earlier with another notable all-round return. He claimed five for 38 as Glamorgan collapsed from 104 for one, and made useful runs after Warwickshire had slipped to 45 for four in reply. Reeve – latterly needing a runner – and Twose settled the issue with a decisive 56-run stand.

Glamorgan

S. P. James run out 41
*H. Morris b P. A. Smith............ 42
M. P. Maynard b P. A. Smith 19
P. A. Cottey b N. M. K. Smith 18
D. L. Hemp c Twose b P. A. Smith ... 1
O. D. Gibson lbw b P. A. Smith 5
R. D. B. Croft c Piper b P. A. Smith .. 0
R. P. Lefebvre st Piper b N. M. K. Smith . 8
†C. P. Metson run out............... 2
S. L. Watkin lbw b N. M. K. Smith ... 2
S. R. Barwick not out 0
B 4, l-b 11, w 2............. 17

1/64 2/104 3/115 4/120 5/126 6/126 7/139 8/148 9/148 (38.3 overs) 155

Bowling: Reeve 7–0–19–0; Munton 8–2–18–0; Small 8–0–37–0; P. A. Smith 8–1–38–5; N. M. K. Smith 7.3–0–28–3.

Warwickshire

D. P. Ostler c Hemp b Lefebvre	11	R. G. Twose b Barwick	28
N. M. K. Smith c Croft b Lefebvre	10	T. L. Penney not out	12
B. C. Lara b Lefebvre	1	L-b 5, w 4	9
P. A. Smith c Morris b Croft	27		
Asif Din lbw b Croft	6	1/25 2/25 3/31 (6 wkts, 38.3 overs)	156
*D. A. Reeve not out	52	4/45 5/81 6/137	

†K. J. Piper, G. C. Small and T. A. Munton did not bat.

Bowling: Watkin 8–0–26–0; Lefebvre 8–0–28–3; Barwick 8–0–18–1; Croft 7–0–40–2; Gibson 7.3–1–39–0.

Umpires: J. H. Hampshire and R. Palmer.

At Guildford, July 17. WARWICKSHIRE beat SURREY by 13 runs.

WARWICKSHIRE v ESSEX

At Birmingham, July 24. Warwickshire won by three wickets. Toss: Warwickshire.

Warwickshire's victory took them six points clear at the top of the table. Paul Smith again played a key role, bowling tidily and ushering his side to the brink of another win with 45 from 55 balls. Cousins, however, gave Warwickshire a scare by taking three for three in nine deliveries.

Essex

N. V. Knight c Piper b P. A. Smith	40	R. M. Pearson not out	0
*J. P. Stephenson c Piper b Reeve	14	D. M. Cousins c Penney b N. M. K. Smith	0
N. Hussain c Asif Din b P. A. Smith	31		
R. C. Irani run out	11		
†M. A. Garnham c Penney b Munton	11	B 1, l-b 6, w 8, n-b 2	17
N. Shahid c Piper b Munton	13		
M. Diwan c Twose b N. M. K. Smith	7	1/36 2/86 3/102 (35.4 overs)	147
M. S. Kasprowicz run out	2	4/112 5/129 6/138	
P. M. Such b N. M. K. Smith	1	7/143 8/147 9/147	

Bowling: Reeve 6–1–24–1; Munton 8–1–34–2; Small 6–1–20–0; P. A. Smith 8–0–34–2; N. M. K. Smith 7.4–0–28–3.

Warwickshire

D. P. Ostler b Stephenson	21	*D. A. Reeve lbw b Cousins	0
N. M. K. Smith c Garnham b Irani	11	†K. J. Piper not out	0
B. C. Lara lbw b Such	13	B 1, l-b 5, w 2, n-b 10	18
P. A. Smith run out	45		
Asif Din c Garnham b Cousins	20	1/30 2/40 3/58 (7 wkts, 34.2 overs)	148
R. G. Twose c Hussain b Cousins	14	4/118 5/135	
T. L. Penney not out	6	6/146 7/146	

G. C. Small and T. A. Munton did not bat.

Bowling: Irani 5–0–25–1; Stephenson 8–0–34–1; Such 8–1–25–1; Kasprowicz 3–0–26–0; Cousins 6–1–18–3; Pearson 4.2–0–14–0.

Umpires: A. A. Jones and G. Sharp.

At Chesterfield, July 31. DERBYSHIRE v WARWICKSHIRE. No result.

WARWICKSHIRE v WORCESTERSHIRE

At Birmingham, August 7. Worcestershire won by three runs. Toss: Warwickshire.

Edgbaston's largest Sunday League crowd since Warwickshire won the title in 1980 – 10,500 – boosted Asif Din's benefit but saw Worcestershire close the gap on their neighbours to four points, with a game in hand. Warwickshire looked strong favourites as openers Ostler and Neil Smith began the run-chase with 105 in 14 overs. But two collapses left them needing eight to win off the last over from Leatherdale, and they could only score four, while losing Piper.

Worcestershire

T. M. Moody lbw b Munton 0
*T. S. Curtis c Piper b Reeve 6
A. C. H. Seymour c Piper b Small 29
G. R. Haynes c N. M. K. Smith b Munton . 76
D. A. Leatherdale c Munton b Small ... 6
S. R. Lampitt lbw b Twose 13
D. B. D'Oliveira b Twose 27
N. V. Radford b Twose 0
R. K. Illingworth not out 1
B 1, l-b 7, w 12, n-b 4 24

1/2 2/15 3/67 4/94 5/124 6/180 7/180 8/182 (8 wkts, 38 overs) 182

P. J. Newport and †T. Edwards did not bat.

Bowling: Reeve 8–1–14–1; Munton 8–0–32–2; Small 8–0–30–2; N. M. K. Smith 3–0–15–0; P. A. Smith 6–0–47–0; Twose 5–0–36–3.

Warwickshire

D. P. Ostler c Seymour b Radford 42
N. M. K. Smith c Seymour b Radford . 47
B. C. Lara c Moody b Lampitt 37
P. A. Smith b Radford 7
Asif Din run out 0
R. G. Twose b Radford 1
*D. A. Reeve c Newport b Leatherdale. 18
T. L. Penney not out 7
†K. J. Piper b Leatherdale 0
G. C. Small not out 1
B 4, l-b 3, w 4, n-b 8 19

1/105 2/105 3/120 4/120 5/129 6/167 7/175 8/178 (8 wkts, 38 overs) 179

T. A. Munton did not bat.

Bowling: Newport 8–0–39–0; Haynes 2–0–18–0; Illingworth 8–4–25–0; Lampitt 7–0–39–1; Radford 8–0–36–4; Leatherdale 5–1–15–2.

Umpires: J. H. Harris and A. G. T. Whitehead.

WARWICKSHIRE v NOTTINGHAMSHIRE

At Birmingham, August 14. Warwickshire won by 72 runs. Toss: Nottinghamshire.

Lara, with three sixes (one on to the pavilion roof) and five fours in a 72-ball innings, added 121 in 18 overs with Twose to build on another good start from Ostler and Neil Smith. Warwickshire eventually registered their highest total in the competition at Edgbaston, and retained their four-point lead. Robinson's consolation was that he passed 5,000 runs in the competition.

Warwickshire

D. P. Ostler c Crawley b Adams 59
N. M. K. Smith run out 33
B. C. Lara b Chapman 75
R. G. Twose c Field-Buss b Lewis 44
P. A. Smith b Mike 15
*D. A. Reeve c Lewis b Crawley 29
T. L. Penney not out 7
†K. J. Piper not out 0
B 8, l-b 6, w 12, n-b 6 32

1/92 2/105 3/226 4/245 5/274 6/288 (6 wkts, 40 overs) 294

R. P. Davis, G. C. Small and T. A. Munton did not bat.

Bowling: Mike 6–0–50–1; Lewis 8–0–56–1; Field-Buss 5–0–51–0; Adams 8–1–35–1; Chapman 8–0–39–1; Crawley 5–0–49–1.

Nottinghamshire

P. R. Pollard c Piper b Reeve 3
*R. T. Robinson st Piper b N. M. K. Smith . 76
J. C. Adams c N. M. K. Smith b Reeve 9
P. Johnson c Piper b Small 45
C. C. Lewis c P. A. Smith b Davis 3
G. F. Archer run out 7
M. A. Crawley c Davis b N. M. K. Smith . 36
†W. M. Noon lbw b P. A. Smith 2
G. W. Mike not out 29
M. G. Field-Buss c Small b N. M. K. Smith . 3
R. J. Chapman not out 2
L-b 3, w 4 7

1/14 2/35 3/106 4/117 5/134 6/182 7/185 8/191 9/200 (9 wkts, 40 overs) 222

Bowling: Reeve 6–0–22–2; Munton 8–0–36–0; Davis 8–0–44–1; Small 4–0–33–1; N. M. K. Smith 8–0–47–3; P. A. Smith 6–0–37–1.

Umpires: V. A. Holder and B. Leadbeater.

At Scarborough, August 21. WARWICKSHIRE lost to YORKSHIRE by 54 runs.

At Hove, August 28. WARWICKSHIRE beat SUSSEX by five wickets.

WARWICKSHIRE v HAMPSHIRE

At Birmingham, September 6 (Tuesday). Warwickshire won on scoring-rate when rain ended play. Toss: Hampshire.

Lara's last innings of the season at Edgbaston – a run-a-ball 56, his fifth one-day fifty for the county – helped Warwickshire to an important victory in their pursuit of the treble after their NatWest Trophy setback. They were nine runs ahead of what they needed to win on scoring-rate when rain washed out the match, Reeve and Penney sharing an unbroken stand of 51 in nine overs.

Hampshire

R. A. Smith c Lara b Welch 68
T. C. Middleton b Small 12
G. W. White b Davis 22
V. P. Terry c Welch b Davis 6
*M. C. J. Nicholas not out 41
†A. N. Aymes not out 26
L-b 11, w 3, n-b 8 22

1/40 2/89 3/115 4/123 (4 wkts, 40 overs) 197

K. D. James, S. D. Udal, J. N. B. Bovill, C. A. Connor and M. J. Thursfield did not bat.

Bowling: Reeve 2–0–16–0; Munton 8–0–38–0; Small 8–1–29–1; Smith 4–0–19–0; Welch 8–0–32–1; Davis 8–0–29–2; Twose 2–0–23–0.

Warwickshire

D. P. Ostler c Aymes b James 4
N. M. K. Smith c Nicholas b James . . . 9
B. C. Lara b Thursfield 56
R. G. Twose run out 14
T. L. Penney not out 26
*D. A. Reeve not out 19
B 3, l-b 5, w 7, n-b 4 19

1/5 2/28 3/74 4/96 (4 wkts, 28 overs) 147

R. P. Davis, G. Welch, †K. J. Piper, G. C. Small and T. A. Munton did not bat.

Bowling: James 4–1–20–2; Bovill 6–0–33–0; Connor 6–0–33–0; Thursfield 6–0–18–1; Udal 6–0–35–0.

Umpires: H. D. Bird and J. H. Harris.

At Bristol, September 18. WARWICKSHIRE beat GLOUCESTERSHIRE by 46 runs.

WORCESTERSHIRE

WORCESTERSHIRE v GLOUCESTERSHIRE

At Worcester, May 15. Worcestershire won by ten wickets. Toss: Worcestershire.

Worcestershire powered to the most emphatic of victories with exactly 100 balls to spare. It was their fourth ten-wicket win in the League, more than any other county. Moody, who faced 67 deliveries, hit 60 in boundaries and finished the match with a six off Ball.

Gloucestershire

G. D. Hodgson lbw b Moody	10
S. G. Hinks c and b Radford	12
M. W. Alleyne c Hick b Illingworth	40
A. J. Wright c Rhodes b Moody	0
T. H. C. Hancock c Rhodes b Lampitt	7
R. I. Dawson b Lampitt	2
M. C. J. Ball not out	28
*C. A. Walsh b Newport	9
†R. C. J. Williams not out	13
L-b 8, w 4, n-b 2	14
1/16 2/41 3/42 4/60 5/62 6/94 7/109 (7 wkts, 40 overs)	135

A. M. Smith and A. M. Babington did not bat.

Bowling: Newport 8–0–22–1; Moody 8–1–20–2; Radford 8–0–28–1; Lampitt 8–0–25–2; Illingworth 6–1–23–1; Leatherdale 2–0–9–0.

Worcestershire

T. M. Moody not out	78
*T. S. Curtis not out	46
L-b 1, w 2, n-b 14	17
(no wkt, 23.2 overs)	141

D. B. D'Oliveira, G. A. Hick, G. R. Haynes, †S. J. Rhodes, P. J. Newport, S. R. Lampitt, R. K. Illingworth, N. V. Radford and D. A. Leatherdale did not bat.

Bowling: Babington 7–0–46–0; Walsh 4–0–19–0; Smith 3–0–19–0; Alleyne 4–0–28–0; Ball 4.2–0–26–0; Hancock 1–0–2–0.

Umpires: H. D. Bird and J. D. Bond.

At Derby, May 22. DERBYSHIRE v WORCESTERSHIRE. No result (abandoned).

WORCESTERSHIRE v NORTHAMPTONSHIRE

At Worcester, May 29. Worcestershire won by 18 runs. Toss: Northamptonshire.

Curran's undefeated 75 off 106 balls was not enough to deny Worcestershire. Hick and Moody opened the bowling and Newport and Lampitt kept down the visitors as they looked to score 75 off the last ten overs.

Worcestershire

T. M. Moody c Ripley b Taylor	15
*T. S. Curtis b Curran	5
G. A. Hick c Curran b Capel	36
G. R. Haynes run out	43
D. A. Leatherdale b Ambrose	41
D. B. D'Oliveira c Ripley b Taylor	0
†S. J. Rhodes c Ambrose b Cook	2
S. R. Lampitt not out	19
R. K. Illingworth run out	2
N. V. Radford not out	4
L-b 6, w 1, n-b 4	11
1/20 2/24 3/85 4/134 5/134 6/137 7/168 8/171 (8 wkts, 40 overs)	178

P. J. Newport did not bat.

Bowling: Ambrose 8–1–34–1; Curran 6–1–14–1; Taylor 8–0–35–2; Capel 7–0–34–1; Penberthy 6–0–36–0; Cook 5–0–19–1.

Northamptonshire

A. Fordham c Haynes b Moody 14	†D. Ripley b Lampitt 7
M. B. Loye run out 3	C. E. L. Ambrose not out 1
*A. J. Lamb c Rhodes b Newport 20	L-b 6 6
K. M. Curran not out 75	
R. J. Bailey c Curtis b Newport 21	1/8 2/23 3/53 (7 wkts, 40 overs) 160
D. J. Capel c and b Radford 13	4/113 5/139
A. L. Penberthy c Illingworth b Lampitt 0	6/145 7/158

N. G. B. Cook and J. P. Taylor did not bat.

Bowling: Moody 7–2–17–1; Hick 8–0–26–0; Lampitt 8–0–34–2; Newport 8–1–21–2; Illingworth 4–0–24–0; Radford 5–0–32–1.

Umpires: R. Palmer and N. T. Plews.

At Lord's, June 5. WORCESTERSHIRE lost to MIDDLESEX by 21 runs.

WORCESTERSHIRE v ESSEX

At Worcester, June 12. Worcestershire won by four wickets. Toss: Worcestershire.

In a game dominated by the bowlers, Knight's diligent innings prevented a total Essex collapse, but Worcestershire claimed victory thanks to Moody, who provided an explosive start with 28 off 21 balls, and Haynes.

Essex

*G. A. Gooch c Rhodes b Newport 2	P. M. Such c Curtis b Tolley 0
J. P. Stephenson c Rhodes b Moody 5	S. J. W. Andrew c Leatherdale b Newport 4
N. V. Knight not out 61	
N. Hussain c Curtis b Moody 3	D. M. Cousins c Curtis b Lampitt 6
J. J. B. Lewis c and b Newport 0	W 1, n-b 2 3
†M. A. Garnham c Leatherdale b Illingworth 14	1/3 2/11 3/21 (39.4 overs) 119
R. C. Irani st Rhodes b Illingworth 7	4/22 5/55 6/67
T. D. Topley c Rhodes b Lampitt 14	7/102 8/103 9/108

Bowling: Newport 8–1–21–3; Moody 8–0–24–2; Lampitt 7.4–0–24–2; Illingworth 8–0–26–2; Tolley 8–1–24–1.

Worcestershire

T. M. Moody lbw b Stephenson 28	†S. J. Rhodes not out 7
A. C. H. Seymour c Stephenson b Cousins 4	S. R. Lampitt not out 15
G. A. Hick c Garnham b Stephenson 11	L-b 2, w 6, n-b 2 10
G. R. Haynes b Irani 30	
D. A. Leatherdale c Knight b Irani 12	1/38 2/38 3/60 (6 wkts, 33.1 overs) 122
*T. S. Curtis lbw b Irani 5	4/82 5/94 6/102

P. J. Newport, R. K. Illingworth and C. M. Tolley did not bat.

Bowling: Andrew 3–1–23–0; Cousins 8–2–23–1; Stephenson 8–0–31–2; Irani 8–0–22–3; Such 6–0–17–0; Topley 0.1–0–4–0.

Umpires: R. Julian and P. B. Wight.

WORCESTERSHIRE v SUSSEX

At Worcester, June 26. Worcestershire won by 97 runs. Toss: Worcestershire.

Hick hit a six and 12 fours in his 88-ball century, contributing 96 to a second-wicket stand of 141 with Seymour. Nicky Phillips took a wicket with his third ball for Sussex, Parvaz Mirza doing likewise for Worcestershire; both were making their first appearances for their counties in competitive cricket.

Worcestershire

T. M. Moody c Moores b Phillips 27
A. C. H. Seymour c Wells b Salisbury.. 57
G. A. Hick c Stephenson b Giddins ...103
G. R. Haynes c Greenfield b Jarvis.... 13
D. A. Leatherdale not out............ 25
†S. J. Rhodes not out 3
B 2, l-b 4, w 6, n-b 2 14

1/50 2/191 3/203 4/221 (4 wkts, 40 overs) 242

*T. S. Curtis, S. R. Lampitt, R. K. Illingworth, P. Mirza and N. V. Radford did not bat.

Bowling: Jarvis 8–0–51–1; Stephenson 8–0–25–0; Giddins 8–0–38–1; Phillips 6–0–38–1; Salisbury 6–0–49–1; Greenfield 4–0–35–0.

Sussex

J. W. Hall b Mirza 4
M. P. Speight b Radford............. 57
F. D. Stephenson c Curtis b Moody ... 1
*A. P. Wells c Leatherdale b Moody... 7
N. J. Lenham c and b Lampitt 2
K. Greenfield c Curtis b Illingworth ... 22
†P. Moores st Rhodes b Illingworth.... 9
P. W. Jarvis c Hick b Illingworth 17
I. D. K. Salisbury lbw b Illingworth ... 2
N. C. Phillips not out 11
E. S. H. Giddins b Leatherdale 1
B 4, l-b 7, w 1.............. 12

1/5 2/8 3/36 4/40 5/88 6/105 7/113 8/120 9/143 (36.3 overs) 145

Bowling: Moody 8–0–24–2; Mirza 8–1–25–1; Lampitt 4–2–19–1; Radford 6–0–37–1; Illingworth 8–0–23–4; Haynes 2–0–4–0; Leatherdale 0.3–0–2–1.

Umpires: D. J. Constant and J. W. Holder.

At Taunton, July 3. WORCESTERSHIRE beat SOMERSET by five wickets.

At The Oval, July 12. WORCESTERSHIRE beat SURREY by nine wickets.

At Canterbury, July 17. WORCESTERSHIRE lost to KENT by four wickets.

WORCESTERSHIRE v HAMPSHIRE

At Worcester, July 24. Worcestershire won by 42 runs. Toss: Hampshire.

Rain reduced the match to 38 overs per side, and Worcestershire's total was built around a third-wicket stand of 155 in 28 overs between Curtis and Haynes. Hampshire, 11 for three at the start of their reply, finished well short despite spirited innings from Aymes and Udal.

Worcestershire

*T. S. Curtis c Middleton b Cowans ... 69
A. C. H. Seymour c Nicholas b Jean-Jacques . 6
T. M. Moody b Cowans 0
G. R. Haynes c Middleton b Connor... 83
N. V. Radford not out............... 11
D. A. Leatherdale c Cowans b Connor . 9
S. R. Lampitt not out 0
L-b 13, w 6, n-b 4........... 23

1/18 2/19 3/174 4/182 5/199 (5 wkts, 38 overs) 201

†D. B. D'Oliveira, R. K. Illingworth, P. J. Newport and C. M. Tolley did not bat.

Bowling: Cowans 8–0–38–2; Jean-Jacques 8–0–33–1; James 8–0–39–0; Connor 8–0–39–2; Udal 6–0–39–0.

Hampshire

T. C. Middleton c D'Oliveira b Newport	0	C. A. Connor c Leatherdale b Illingworth	2
V. P. Terry b Moody	4	N. G. Cowans not out	1
R. A. Smith c Newport b Radford	45		
*M. C. J. Nicholas b Newport	1		
R. M. F. Cox run out	7	B 2, l-b 9, w 10	21
†A. N. Aymes run out	32		
K. D. James c Newport b Haynes	3	1/5 2/6 3/11 (36.2 overs)	159
S. D. Udal b Newport	35	4/47 5/71 6/89	
M. Jean-Jacques run out	8	7/144 8/151 9/158	

Bowling: Moody 8–0–35–1; Newport 8–0–21–3; Lampitt 6.2–2–13–0; Radford 8–0–44–1; Haynes 2–0–10–1; Illingworth 4–0–25–1.

Umpires: B. Leadbeater and R. Palmer.

At Birmingham, August 7. WORCESTERSHIRE beat WARWICKSHIRE by three runs.

At Leicester, August 14. WORCESTERSHIRE beat LEICESTERSHIRE by two runs.

WORCESTERSHIRE v NOTTINGHAMSHIRE

At Worcester, August 21. Worcestershire won by 21 runs. Toss: Worcestershire.

This victory, coupled with Warwickshire's defeat against Yorkshire, brought Worcestershire level on 42 points with their Midland rivals at the top of the table. They successfully defended a modest total on a slow pitch, although Lewis, who was dropped on nought, threatened with 75 from 85 balls before becoming ninth man out, to a stunning catch by Church.

Worcestershire

T. M. Moody lbw b Mike	20	R. K. Illingworth c Hindson b Bates	10
*T. S. Curtis lbw b Hindson	37	P. J. Newport not out	5
M. J. Church b Hindson	18	†T. Edwards not out	3
G. R. Haynes b Hindson	7	B 1, l-b 10, w 3, n-b 6	20
D. A. Leatherdale lbw b Lewis	22		
D. B. D'Oliveira c Adams b Hindson	6	1/60 2/76 3/91 (9 wkts, 40 overs)	169
S. R. Lampitt c Crawley b Bates	21	4/94 5/102 6/143	
N. V. Radford lbw b Lewis	0	7/143 8/157 9/165	

Bowling: Lewis 7–0–31–2; Chapman 4–0–19–0; Mike 5–0–15–1; Bates 8–0–34–2; Hindson 8–0–19–4; Adams 8–0–40–0.

Nottinghamshire

P. R. Pollard c Curtis b Newport	4	R. T. Bates b Illingworth	16
*R. T. Robinson c Edwards b Newport	3	J. E. Hindson not out	3
J. C. Adams lbw b Radford	25	R. J. Chapman lbw b Radford	0
C. C. Lewis c Church b Lampitt	75	B 1, l-b 6, w 4	11
M. A. Crawley c Edwards b Radford	0		
M. P. Dowman c Edwards b Lampitt	6	1/9 2/10 3/54 (36.3 overs)	148
†W. M. Noon c Edwards b Lampitt	5	4/54 5/71 6/93	
G. W. Mike lbw b Lampitt	0	7/95 8/141 9/146	

Bowling: Newport 8–0–29–2; Moody 8–2–18–0; Illingworth 8–0–29–1; Radford 6.3–0–43–3; Lampitt 6–1–22–4.

Umpires: J. H. Hampshire and T. E. Jesty.

WORCESTERSHIRE v YORKSHIRE

At Worcester, August 28. Yorkshire won by 19 runs. Toss: Worcestershire.

Having beaten Warwickshire the previous week, Yorkshire upset Worcestershire's title challenge. It was their first home defeat in limited-overs cricket in 1994 and came despite a determined eighth-wicket stand of 79 in 13 overs between Curtis and Illingworth. Moody had been out first ball and Worcestershire had plunged to 55 for seven. Metcalfe played the key innings for Yorkshire, striking an undefeated 41 from 32 balls.

Yorkshire

*M. D. Moxon c Lampitt b Illingworth. 14
D. Byas c Moody b Radford.......... 34
†R. J. Blakey lbw b Radford 27
B. Parker c Curtis b Illingworth....... 29
A. P. Grayson c Leatherdale b Lampitt. 14
A. A. Metcalfe not out 41
P. J. Hartley c Leatherdale b Newport . 0
G. M. Hamilton not out 14
L-b 9, w 2, n-b 4............ 15

1/44 2/84 3/86 (6 wkts, 39 overs) 188
4/110 5/149 6/149

C. E. W. Silverwood, R. D. Stemp and M. A. Robinson did not bat.

Bowling: Newport 8–0–45–1; Moody 8–3–18–0; Illingworth 8–0–35–2; Radford 7–0–32–2; Lampitt 8–0–49–1.

Worcestershire

T. M. Moody lbw b Hartley 0
*T. S. Curtis not out 81
M. J. Church c and b Silverwood 2
G. R. Haynes lbw b Silverwood....... 0
D. A. Leatherdale lbw b Hartley 3
D. B. D'Oliveira c Blakey b Hamilton.. 10
S. R. Lampitt lbw b Robinson 6
N. V. Radford c Grayson b Hamilton.. 6
R. K. Illingworth b Stemp 31
P. J. Newport c Blakey b Silverwood .. 1
†T. Edwards not out 16
B 1, l-b 5, w 3, n-b 4 13

1/0 2/5 3/5 (9 wkts, 39 overs) 169
4/16 5/34 6/46
7/55 8/134 9/136

Bowling: Hartley 8–1–21–2; Silverwood 8–1–29–3; Robinson 8–1–27–1; Hamilton 8–0–44–2; Grayson 2–0–13–0; Stemp 5–0–29–1.

Umpires: A. A. Jones and R. Julian.

At Manchester, September 6. WORCESTERSHIRE beat LANCASHIRE by nine wickets.

At Cardiff, September 11. WORCESTERSHIRE lost to GLAMORGAN by 29 runs.

WORCESTERSHIRE v DURHAM

At Worcester, September 18. Worcestershire won by 26 runs. Toss: Durham.

Worcestershire's victory earned them second place. It was achieved with another efficient bowling performance – Radford's three wickets took him past a League aggregate of 200. Earlier, Rhodes and Lampitt gave their innings a vital late boost, adding 66 in the last nine overs. Graveney, on his final appearance before retirement, led out the Durham team.

Worcestershire

T. M. Moody c Daley b Bainbridge	1	S. R. Lampitt run out	23
*T. S. Curtis c Larkins b Wood	0	N. V. Radford not out	1
G. A. Hick c Scott b Bainbridge	26	L-b 8, w 8, n-b 2	18
G. R. Haynes lbw b Walker	13		—
D. A. Leatherdale c Scott b Graveney	31	1/1 2/3 3/34 (7 wkts, 40 overs)	172
M. J. Church c Scott b Wood	13	4/70 5/88	
†S. J. Rhodes not out	46	6/105 7/171	

P. J. Newport and R. K. Illingworth did not bat.

Bowling: Wood 8–2–26–2; Bainbridge 8–1–34–2; Cummins 8–1–26–0; Walker 8–0–44–1; Graveney 8–0–34–1.

Durham

J. I. Longley st Rhodes b Illingworth	31	J. Wood c Moody b Newport	28
W. Larkins lbw b Moody	0	A. Walker c Lampitt b Radford	7
S. Hutton c Leatherdale b Newport	1	D. A. Graveney not out	4
J. A. Daley run out	6	L-b 7, w 4	11
J. E. Morris c Illingworth b Radford	19		—
*P. Bainbridge c Church b Radford	27	1/0 2/3 3/31 (37.3 overs)	146
A. C. Cummins c Haynes b Lampitt	3	4/44 5/88 6/95	
†C. W. Scott b Newport	9	7/95 8/127 9/140	

Bowling: Newport 7.3–2–21–3; Moody 8–1–21–1; Illingworth 8–0–37–1; Lampitt 7–1–28–1; Radford 7–0–32–3.

Umpires: M. J. Kitchen and K. E. Palmer.

YORKSHIRE

At Lord's, May 8. YORKSHIRE beat MIDDLESEX by six wickets.

At Cardiff, May 15. YORKSHIRE beat GLAMORGAN by nine wickets.

YORKSHIRE v ESSEX

At Leeds, May 22. No result (abandoned).

YORKSHIRE v NOTTINGHAMSHIRE

At Leeds, June 5. Yorkshire won by seven wickets. Toss: Yorkshire. First-team debut: R. A. Kettleborough.

Byas, Yorkshire's acting-captain, guided his side to victory with an unbeaten 101 from 124 balls, including two sixes and 11 fours; he and Kellett put on 129. In an odd sort of hat-trick, Nottinghamshire had lost Crawley and Mike, both run out, and Noon, leg-before, in successive deliveries near the end of their innings. Later, Crawley dislocated a finger while bowling his first over.

Nottinghamshire

P. R. Pollard c Grayson b Kettleborough	47	†W. M. Noon lbw b Hartley	0
P. Johnson c Blakey b Silverwood	5	K. P. Evans not out	3
J. C. Adams b Silverwood	47	B 1, l-b 2, w 1, n-b 4	8
*R. T. Robinson not out	48		—
G. F. Archer c Blakey b Silverwood	0	1/9 2/74 3/119 (7 wkts, 40 overs)	190
M. A. Crawley run out	32	4/119 5/180	
G. W. Mike run out	0	6/180 7/180	

M. G. Field-Buss and R. A. Pick did not bat.

Bowling: Silverwood 8–0–32–3; Hartley 8–1–37–1; Robinson 5–0–24–0; Grayson 7–0–35–0; Kettleborough 4–0–17–1; Foster 8–0–42–0.

Yorkshire

*D. Byas not out	101	M. J. Foster not out	2
M. P. Vaughan run out	7	L-b 19, w 5	24
†R. J. Blakey c Noon b Mike	0		—
S. A. Kellett run out	58	1/26 2/45 3/174 (3 wkts, 38 overs)	192

B. Parker, R. A. Kettleborough, A. P. Grayson, P. J. Hartley, C. E. W. Silverwood and M. A. Robinson did not bat.

Bowling: Evans 7–1–22–0; Pick 8–0–54–0; Mike 7–1–32–1; Crawley 0.4–0–4–0; Adams 7.2–0–30–0; Field-Buss 8–1–31–0.

Umpires: J. W. Holder and V. A. Holder.

YORKSHIRE v SOMERSET

At Leeds, June 12. Somerset won by two runs. Toss: Yorkshire.

Yorkshire just failed to score 13 for victory off the final over, from Hayhurst, after Byas had established a strong position with a run-a-ball 58. Mallender turned the match Somerset's way with a burst of three quick wickets.

Somerset

M. N. Lathwell st Blakey b Robinson	43	Mushtaq Ahmed not out	4
M. E. Trescothick run out	74		
R. J. Harden c Byas b Silverwood	35	L-b 3, w 4, n-b 2	9
G. D. Rose c Foster b Grayson	15		—
N. A. Folland b Grayson	29	1/87 2/156 3/159 (5 wkts, 40 overs)	226
*A. N. Hayhurst not out	17	4/196 5/208	

†R. J. Turner, A. P. van Troost, N. A. Mallender and M. Dimond did not bat.

Bowling: Silverwood 8–1–38–1; Hartley 8–0–56–0; Robinson 8–0–30–1; White 6–0–35–0; Grayson 8–0–44–2; Foster 2–0–20–0.

Yorkshire

*D. Byas c Hayhurst b Mushtaq Ahmed	58	P. J. Hartley not out	40
S. A. Kellett b van Troost	16	C. E. W. Silverwood not out	6
R. B. Richardson b Hayhurst	16		
†R. J. Blakey lbw b Mallender	9	L-b 4, w 7, n-b 2	13
C. White lbw b Mallender	34		—
M. J. Foster b Mallender	4	1/52 2/91 3/103 (8 wkts, 40 overs)	224
A. P. Grayson lbw b Mallender	0	4/118 5/126 6/126	
R. A. Kettleborough lbw b Hayhurst	28	7/162 8/202	

M. A. Robinson did not bat.

Bowling: van Troost 8–0–45–1; Rose 6–0–48–0; Mushtaq Ahmed 8–0–26–1; Hayhurst 8–0–44–2; Mallender 8–0–45–4; Dimond 2–0–12–0.

Umpires: D. J. Constant and R. A. White.

At Luton, June 19. YORKSHIRE beat NORTHAMPTONSHIRE by ten runs.

YORKSHIRE v HAMPSHIRE

At Leeds, June 26. Yorkshire won by 69 runs. Toss: Yorkshire.

Blakey built on a solid start from Moxon on a pitch that kept low. The Yorkshire attack, with Robinson outstanding, then kept Hampshire in check.

Yorkshire

*M. D. Moxon c Terry b Udal	58
D. Byas b Benjamin	30
A. A. Metcalfe c Connor b Udal	25
R. B. Richardson b Benjamin	3
†R. J. Blakey not out	38
C. White b Benjamin	27
P. J. Hartley b Connor	1
A. P. Grayson not out	2
L-b 3, w 4	7
1/53 2/116 3/119 4/123 5/179 6/182 (6 wkts, 40 overs)	191

D. Gough, C. E. W. Silverwood and M. A. Robinson did not bat.

Bowling: James 8–0–31–0; Cowans 8–1–45–0; Connor 8–0–49–1; Benjamin 8–0–26–3; Udal 8–0–37–2.

Hampshire

V. P. Terry lbw b Silverwood	16
R. S. M. Morris run out	15
R. A. Smith b Robinson	19
*M. C. J. Nicholas b Hartley	9
M. Keech c Grayson b White	15
†A. N. Aymes not out	21
W. K. M. Benjamin b White	0
K. D. James c Moxon b Silverwood	9
S. D. Udal b Grayson	4
C. A. Connor b White	1
N. G. Cowans b Gough	0
B 1, l-b 8, w 4	13
1/33 2/46 3/62 4/71 5/94 6/94 7/107 8/114 9/121 (37.3 overs)	122

Bowling: Hartley 6–0–18–1; Gough 6.3–0–18–1; Robinson 8–1–17–1; Silverwood 8–0–33–2; White 8–1–25–3; Grayson 1–0–2–1.

Umpires: B. Dudleston and J. H. Hampshire.

At Maidstone, July 3. YORKSHIRE lost to KENT by eight wickets.

YORKSHIRE v LEICESTERSHIRE

At Scarborough, July 17. Yorkshire won by five wickets. Toss: Yorkshire.

Richardson settled the result with 39 from 26 deliveries, striking four to win off the last ball. Simmons again prospered for Leicestershire before Robinson restricted the visitors' progress.

Leicestershire

*P. V. Simmons b Hartley	85
D. L. Maddy lbw b Robinson	26
V. J. Wells c Gough b Robinson	8
J. J. Whitaker lbw b Robinson	2
B. F. Smith run out	10
†P. A. Nixon c Byas b White	19
P. N. Hepworth c Blakey b Silverwood	1
A. D. Mullally b Silverwood	0
G. J. Parsons not out	14
A. R. K. Pierson b White	0
I. M. Stanger not out	3
B 1, l-b 6, w 5, n-b 2	14
1/56 2/80 3/90 4/116 5/150 6/153 7/153 8/169 9/176 (9 wkts, 40 overs)	182

Bowling: Hartley 8–0–33–1; Gough 8–1–38–0; Robinson 8–0–28–3; Silverwood 5–1–21–2; White 7–0–32–2; Grayson 4–0–23–0.

Yorkshire

*M. D. Moxon b Pierson	16	B. Parker not out	0
D. Byas run out	63		
†R. J. Blakey lbw b Simmons	41	B 1, l-b 9, w 7, n-b 2	19
R. B. Richardson not out	39		—
C. White run out	8	1/29 2/123 3/154 (5 wkts, 40 overs)	186
P. J. Hartley run out	0	4/178 5/182	

A. P. Grayson, D. Gough, C. E. W. Silverwood and M. A. Robinson did not bat.

Bowling: Mullally 8–0–34–0; Parsons 8–0–15–0; Pierson 8–0–30–1; Stanger 4–0–20–0; Wells 8–0–54–0; Simmons 4–0–23–1.

Umpires: J. W. Holder and P. B. Wight.

At Cheltenham, July 24. YORKSHIRE lost to GLOUCESTERSHIRE by three wickets.

At Durham University, July 31. YORKSHIRE lost to DURHAM on scoring-rate.

YORKSHIRE v LANCASHIRE

At Leeds, August 14. Lancashire won by 43 runs. Toss: Yorkshire.

The architects of Lancashire's Roses victory were Fairbrother, with an unbeaten 58 from 65 balls, and Martin, who took three for ten in his eight overs. Metcalfe played a lone hand in Yorkshire's disappointing batting effort on a pitch of variable bounce.

Lancashire

M. A. Atherton b Stemp	38	I. D. Austin lbw b Hartley	9
J. E. R. Gallian b Stemp	29	†W. K. Hegg not out	18
N. J. Speak run out	5	L-b 4, w 5	9
N. H. Fairbrother not out	58		—
G. D. Lloyd run out	14	1/63 2/70 3/84 (6 wkts, 40 overs)	183
*M. Watkinson c and b Grayson	3	4/131 5/140 6/153	

P. J. Martin, G. Yates and G. Chapple did not bat.

Bowling: Hartley 7–1–26–1; Gough 8–0–37–0; Foster 3–0–17–0; Robinson 6–0–30–0; Stemp 8–0–30–2; Grayson 8–0–39–1.

Yorkshire

*M. D. Moxon lbw b Chapple	10	D. Gough c Austin b Martin	9
D. Byas c Hegg b Martin	0	R. D. Stemp b Martin	2
†R. J. Blakey lbw b Austin	10	M. A. Robinson not out	0
B. Parker c Atherton b Austin	4	L-b 6, w 2	8
A. P. Grayson lbw b Yates	14		—
A. A. Metcalfe not out	65	1/10 2/12 3/25 (9 wkts, 40 overs)	140
M. J. Foster b Yates	6	4/33 5/71 6/81	
P. J. Hartley c Watkinson b Chapple	12	7/111 8/133 9/140	

Bowling: Chapple 8–2–20–2; Martin 8–4–10–3; Austin 8–0–30–2; Yates 8–0–30–2; Watkinson 8–0–44–0.

Umpires: G. Sharp and A. G. T. Whitehead.

YORKSHIRE v WARWICKSHIRE

At Scarborough, August 21. Yorkshire won by 54 runs. Toss: Yorkshire.

An inexperienced Yorkshire attack, containing two 19-year-olds in Wharf and Hamilton, reduced League leaders Warwickshire to 67 for six. Although Reeve tried to turn the innings around, his side, with Lara resting an injured knee, was well beaten. Blakey and Hartley gave the Yorkshire innings a significant late push, piling on 57 in the last six overs.

Yorkshire

*M. D. Moxon c Piper b N. M. K. Smith . 40
D. Byas c Munton b Welch 55
†R. J. Blakey not out 55
B. Parker c Moles b P. A. Smith 22
P. J. Hartley not out 28
B 1, l-b 3, w 5 9

1/88 2/112 3/152 (3 wkts, 40 overs) 209

A. A. Metcalfe, A. P. Grayson, A. G. Wharf, G. M. Hamilton, R. D. Stemp and M. A. Robinson did not bat.

Bowling: Reeve 8–0–45–0; Munton 8–1–27–0; Small 4–0–37–0; Welch 8–0–24–1; N. M. K. Smith 8–0–38–1; P. A. Smith 4–0–34–1.

Warwickshire

D. P. Ostler c Blakey b Hartley 6
N. M. K. Smith b Wharf 1
A. J. Moles c Blakey b Hartley 20
R. G. Twose c Wharf b Robinson 25
P. A. Smith lbw b Robinson. 5
*D. A. Reeve lbw b Hamilton 41
T. L. Penney lbw b Hamilton. 0
G. Welch c Metcalfe b Wharf 26
†K. J. Piper b Stemp. 4
G. C. Small b Wharf. 7
T. A. Munton not out 15
L-b 1, w 1, n-b 3. 5

1/2 2/26 3/31 4/48 5/67 6/67 7/102 8/106 9/119 (33.1 overs) 155

Bowling: Hartley 7–0–32–2; Wharf 8–2–39–3; Robinson 6–2–20–2; Hamilton 6.1–0–27–2; Stemp 6–0–36–1.

Umpires: H. D. Bird and G. I. Burgess.

At Worcester, August 28. YORKSHIRE beat WORCESTERSHIRE by 19 runs.

YORKSHIRE v DERBYSHIRE

At Leeds, September 4. Yorkshire won by four wickets. Toss: Yorkshire.

Byas passed 600 runs for the season in the League during his unbeaten 87. He steered Yorkshire to victory with ten balls to spare, surviving a fine spell from Base and adding 59 in 11 overs with Metcalfe, who made 17.

Derbyshire

P. D. Bowler c Parker b Hamilton. 11
D. G. Cork lbw b Stemp. 48
C. J. Adams lbw b Stemp 17
T. J. G. O'Gorman c Blakey b Hamilton 15
*K. J. Barnett not out 35
P. A. J. DeFreitas not out. 26
B 1, l-b 4, w 3 8

1/25 2/66 3/94 4/97 (4 wkts, 40 overs) 160

C. M. Wells, A. E. Warner, S. J. Base, †K. M. Krikken and D. E. Malcolm did not bat.

Bowling: Hartley 8–0–31–0; Gough 8–1–41–0; Hamilton 8–0–29–2; Robinson 8–0–25–0; Stemp 8–0–29–2.

Yorkshire

*M. D. Moxon c Adams b Base	15
D. Byas not out	87
†R. J. Blakey c Cork b Base	7
B. Parker b Base	3
A. P. Grayson run out	2
A. A. Metcalfe c Krikken b Warner	17
P. J. Hartley b Warner	4
D. Gough not out	9
B 1, l-b 9, w 6, n-b 2	18
1/39 2/47 3/53 4/56 5/115 6/127 (6 wkts, 38.2 overs)	162

R. D. Stemp, G. M. Hamilton and M. A. Robinson did not bat.

Bowling: Wells 6–0–18–0; DeFreitas 6–0–19–0; Base 8–0–20–3; Cork 7–0–31–0; Malcolm 6.2–0–41–0; Warner 5–0–23–2.

Umpires: J. W. Holder and T. E. Jesty.

YORKSHIRE v SURREY

At Scarborough, September 11. Surrey won by 205 runs. Toss: Yorkshire.

Surrey posted a new record for the highest total in the competition, eclipsing Somerset's 360 for three against Glamorgan at Neath in 1990. Brown, who scored 133 from 84 balls, with five sixes and 13 fours, and Thorpe, with 102 not out in 81 balls, including three sixes and eight fours, added 160 before Hollioake weighed in with a blistering 59 from just 19 deliveries – despite a groin strain. He reached 50 in 15 balls, beating Graham Rose's record of 16 in the Neath match. Surrey struck 18 sixes in all, equalling Derbyshire's record against Worcestershire at Knypersley in 1985. Only Somerset, who beat Glamorgan by 220 in the match four years earlier, had recorded a heavier victory in runs.

Surrey

D. J. Bicknell lbw b Robinson	20
A. D. Brown b Grayson	133
G. P. Thorpe not out	102
D. M. Ward b Hamilton	27
A. J. Hollioake c Robinson b Gough	59
A. C. S. Pigott not out	14
B 2, l-b 4, w 12, n-b 2	20
1/79 2/239 3/280 4/358 (4 wkts, 40 overs)	375

*†A. J. Stewart, S. G. Kenlock, M. P. Bicknell, J. Boiling and J. E. Benjamin did not bat.

Bowling: Hartley 8–2–61–0; Gough 8–0–62–1; Robinson 8–1–43–1; Hamilton 6–0–75–1; Stemp 6–0–71–0; Grayson 3–0–39–1; Byas 1–0–18–0.

Yorkshire

*M. D. Moxon b M. P. Bicknell	37
D. Byas c D. J. Bicknell b M. P. Bicknell	13
†R. J. Blakey c Boiling b Kenlock	39
B. Parker c Kenlock b M. P. Bicknell	7
A. P. Grayson c Boiling b Pigott	0
A. A. Metcalfe c Stewart b Kenlock	15
P. J. Hartley c M. P. Bicknell b Kenlock	4
D. Gough c Ward b Kenlock	39
G. M. Hamilton run out	11
R. D. Stemp c Kenlock b M. P. Bicknell	1
M. A. Robinson not out	0
L-b 3, w 1	4
1/44 2/59 3/69 4/69 5/106 6/118 7/119 8/139 9/164 (28.2 overs)	170

Bowling: Benjamin 5–0–27–0; M. P. Bicknell 7–0–50–4; Pigott 5–1–29–1; Kenlock 7.2–1–30–4; Boiling 4–0–31–0.

Umpires: J. C. Balderstone and J. D. Bond.

At Hove, September 18. YORKSHIRE beat SUSSEX by 37 runs.

SUNDAY LEAGUE RECORDS

Batting

Highest individual score: 176, G. A. Gooch, Essex v Glamorgan, Southend, 1983.

Most runs: 7,906, G. A. Gooch; 7,378, W. Larkins; 7,062, D. W. Randall; 7,040, D. L. Amiss; 6,935, C. W. J. Athey; 6,650, C. T. Radley; 6,639, D. R. Turner; 6,506, P. Willey; 6,344, C. G. Greenidge; 6,265, C. E. B. Rice; 6,144, G. M. Turner; 6,130, K. J. Barnett; 6,121, C. J. Tavaré.

Most runs in a season: 917, T. M. Moody, Worcestershire, 1991.

Most hundreds: 14, W. Larkins; 12, G. A. Gooch; 11, C. G. Greenidge; 9, K. S. McEwan and B. A. Richards. 485 hundreds have been scored in the League. The most in one season is 40 in 1990.

Most sixes in an innings: 13, I. T. Botham, Somerset v Northamptonshire, Wellingborough School, 1986.

Most sixes by a team in an innings: 18, Derbyshire v Worcestershire, Knypersley, 1985 and Surrey v Yorkshire, Scarborough, 1994.

Most sixes in a season: 26, I. V. A. Richards, Somerset, 1977.

Highest total: 375 for four, Surrey v Yorkshire, Scarborough, 1994.

Highest total by a side batting second: 317 for six, Surrey v Nottinghamshire, The Oval, 1993 (50-overs match).

Highest match aggregate: 631 for 13 wickets, Nottinghamshire (314 for seven) v Surrey (317 for six), The Oval, 1993 (50-overs match).

Lowest total: 23 (19.4 overs), Middlesex v Yorkshire, Leeds, 1974.

Shortest completed innings: 16 overs (59), Northamptonshire v Middlesex, Tring, 1974.

Shortest match: 2 hr 13 min (40.3 overs), Essex v Northamptonshire, Ilford, 1971.

Record partnerships for each wicket

239	for 1st	G. A. Gooch and B. R. Hardie, Essex v Nottinghamshire at Nottingham	1985
273	for 2nd	G. A. Gooch and K. S. McEwan, Essex v Nottinghamshire at Nottingham	1983
223	for 3rd	S. J. Cook and G. D. Rose, Somerset v Glamorgan at Neath	1990
219	for 4th	C. G. Greenidge and C. L. Smith, Hampshire v Surrey at Southampton	1987
190	for 5th	R. J. Blakey and M. J. Foster, Yorkshire v Leicestershire at Leicester	1993
124*	for 6th	J. J. Whitaker and P. A. Nixon, Leicestershire v Surrey at The Oval	1992
132	for 7th	K. R. Brown and N. F. Williams, Middlesex v Somerset at Lord's	1988
110*	for 8th	C. L. Cairns and B. N. French, Nottinghamshire v Surrey at The Oval	1993
105	for 9th	D. G. Moir and R. W. Taylor, Derbyshire v Kent at Derby	1984
57	for 10th	D. A. Graveney and J. B. Mortimore, Gloucestershire v Lancashire at Tewkesbury	1973

Bowling

Most wickets: 386, J. K. Lever; 346, D. L. Underwood; 333, J. E. Emburey; 307, J. Simmons; 303, S. Turner; 284, N. Gifford; 281, E. E. Hemmings; 267, J. N. Shepherd; 256, I. T. Botham; 250, A. C. S. Pigott; 249, T. E. Jesty; 234, R. D. Jackman and P. Willey.

Most wickets in a season: 34, R. J. Clapp, Somerset, 1974, and C. E. B. Rice, Nottinghamshire, 1986.

Best bowling: eight for 26, K. D. Boyce, Essex v Lancashire, Manchester, 1971; seven for 15, R. A. Hutton, Yorkshire v Worcestershire, Leeds, 1969; seven for 39, A. Hodgson, Northamptonshire v Somerset, Northampton, 1976; seven for 41, A. N. Jones, Sussex v Nottinghamshire, Nottingham, 1986; six for six, R. W. Hooker, Middlesex v Surrey, Lord's, 1969; six for seven, M. Hendrick, Derbyshire v Nottinghamshire, Nottingham, 1972; six for nine, N. G. Cowans, Middlesex v Lancashire, Lord's, 1991.

Most economical analysis: 8–8–0–0, B. A. Langford, Somerset v Essex, Yeovil, 1969.

Most expensive analyses: 8–0–96–1, D. G. Cork, Derbyshire v Nottinghamshire, Nottingham, 1993; 8–0–94–2, P. N. Weekes, Middlesex v Leicestershire, Leicester, 1994; 7.5–0–89–3, G. Miller, Derbyshire v Gloucestershire, Gloucester, 1984; 8–0–88–1, E. E. Hemmings, Nottinghamshire v Somerset, Nottingham, 1983.

Hat-tricks (24): A. Ward, Derbyshire v Sussex, Derby, 1970; R. Palmer, Somerset v Gloucestershire, Bristol, 1970; K. D. Boyce, Essex v Somerset, Westcliff, 1971; G. D. McKenzie, Leicestershire v Essex, Leicester, 1972; R. G. D. Willis, Warwickshire v Yorkshire, Birmingham, 1973; W. Blenkiron, Warwickshire v Derbyshire, Buxton, 1974; A. Buss, Sussex v Worcestershire, Hastings, 1974; J. M. Rice, Hampshire v Northamptonshire, Southampton, 1975; M. A. Nash, Glamorgan v Worcestershire, Worcester, 1975; A. Hodgson, Northamptonshire v Somerset, Northampton, 1976; A. E. Cordle, Glamorgan v Hampshire, Portsmouth, 1979; C. J. Tunnicliffe, Derbyshire v Worcestershire, Derby, 1979; M. D. Marshall, Hampshire v Surrey, Southampton, 1981; I. V. A. Richards, Somerset v Essex, Chelmsford, 1982; P. W. Jarvis, Yorkshire v Derbyshire, Derby, 1982; R. M. Ellison, Kent v Hampshire, Canterbury, 1983; G. C. Holmes, Glamorgan v Nottinghamshire, Ebbw Vale, 1987; K. Saxelby, Nottinghamshire v Worcestershire, Nottingham, 1987; K. M. Curran, Gloucestershire v Warwickshire, Birmingham, 1989; M. P. Bicknell, Surrey v Derbyshire, The Oval, 1992; M. J. McCague, Kent v Glamorgan, Swansea, 1992; A. Dale, Glamorgan v Durham, Colwyn Bay, 1993; R. K. Illingworth, Worcestershire v Sussex, Hove, 1993; K. P. Evans, Nottinghamshire v Glamorgan, Nottingham, 1994.

Four wickets in four balls: A. Ward, Derbyshire v Sussex, Derby, 1970.

Wicket-keeping and Fielding

Most dismissals: 257 (234 ct, 23 st), D. L. Bairstow; 236 (187 ct, 49 st), R. W. Taylor; 223 (184 ct, 39 st), E. W. Jones.

Most dismissals in a season: 29 (26 ct, 3 st), S. J. Rhodes, Worcestershire, 1988.

Most dismissals in an innings: 7 (6 ct, 1 st), R. W. Taylor, Derbyshire v Lancashire, Manchester, 1975.

Most catches in an innings: 6, K. Goodwin, Lancashire v Worcestershire, Worcester, 1969; R. W. Taylor, Derbyshire v Lancashire, Manchester, 1975; K. M. Krikken, Derbyshire v Hampshire, Southampton, 1994; and P. A. Nixon, Leicestershire v Essex, Leicester, 1994.

Most stumpings in an innings: 4, S. J. Rhodes, Worcestershire v Warwickshire, Birmingham, 1986 and N. D. Burns, Somerset v Kent, Taunton, 1991.

Most catches by a fielder: 101, J. F. Steele; 100, V. P. Terry; 97, D. P. Hughes; 94, G. Cook; 93†, C. W. J. Athey; 91, C. T. Radley.

† C. W. J. Athey has also taken two catches as a wicket-keeper.

Most catches by a fielder in a season: 16, J. M. Rice, Hampshire, 1978.

Most catches by a fielder in an innings: 5, J. M. Rice, Hampshire v Warwickshire, Southampton, 1978.

Results

Largest victory in runs: Somerset by 220 runs v Glamorgan, Neath, 1990.

Victories by ten wickets (27): By Derbyshire, Durham, Essex (three times), Glamorgan (twice), Hampshire (twice), Leicestershire (twice), Middlesex (twice), Northamptonshire, Nottinghamshire, Somerset (twice), Surrey (twice), Warwickshire, Worcestershire (four times) and Yorkshire (three times). This does not include those matches in which the side batting second was set a reduced target but does include matches where both sides faced a reduced number of overs.

Ties: There have been 39 tied matches. Lancashire and Worcestershire have each tied eight times.

CHAMPIONS 1969-94

John Player's County League
1969 Lancashire
John Player League
1970 Lancashire
1971 Worcestershire
1972 Kent
1973 Kent
1974 Leicestershire
1975 Hampshire
1976 Kent
1977 Leicestershire
1978 Hampshire
1979 Somerset
1980 Warwickshire
1981 Essex
1982 Sussex
1983 Yorkshire
John Player Special League
1984 Essex
1985 Essex
1986 Hampshire
Refuge Assurance League
1987 Worcestershire
1988 Worcestershire
1989 Lancashire
1990 Derbyshire
1991 Nottinghamshire
Sunday League
1992 Middlesex
AXA Equity & Law League
1993 Glamorgan
1994 Warwickshire

MATCH RESULTS 1969-94

			Matches				*League positions*	
	P	*W*	*L*	*T*	*NR*	*1st*	*2nd*	*3rd*
Derbyshire	419	180	197	2	40	1	0	1
Durham	51	21	21	1	8	0	0	0
Essex	419	220	156	6	37	3	5*	3
Glamorgan	419	146	225	4	44	1	0	0
Gloucestershire	419	145	222	4	48	0	1	1
Hampshire	419	211	167	6	35	3	1	3
Kent	419	224	149	5	41	3	3	4
Lancashire	419	209	154	8	48	3	2	2
Leicestershire	419	178	187	2	52	2	2*	2
Middlesex	419	194	175	6	44	1	1	3
Northamptonshire	419	160	212	4	43	0	0	1
Nottinghamshire	419	173	205	3	38	1	2	1
Somerset	419	198	178	2	41	1	6*	0
Surrey	419	184	186	4	45	0	0	1
Sussex	419	183	187	5	44	1	2*	1
Warwickshire	419	167	199	6	47	2	0	1
Worcestershire	419	203	173	8	35	3	3	1
Yorkshire	419	184	187	2	46	1	1	0

* *Includes one shared 2nd place in 1976.*

OXFORD UNIVERSITY 1994

[*Bill Smith*

Back row: L. J. Lenham (*coach*), I. J. Sutcliffe, P. W. Trimby, N. F. C. Martin, G. I. Macmillan, A. W. Maclay, H. S. Malik, C. J. Hollins, G. S. Gordon (*scorer*). *Front row:* C. J. Townsend, S. C. Ecclestone, R. R. Montgomerie (*captain*), R. S. Yeabsley, C. M. Gupte.

THE UNIVERSITIES IN 1994

OXFORD

President: C. A. Fry (Trinity)
Hon. Treasurer: Dr S. R. Porter (Nuffield College)

Captain: R. R. Montgomerie (Rugby and Worcester)
Secretary: R. S. Yeabsley (Haberdashers' Aske's, Elstree and Keble)

Captain for 1995: G. I. Macmillan (Guildford CS, Charterhouse, University of Southampton and Keble)
Secretary: W. S. Kendall (Bradfield College and Keble)

It would have been unreasonable to expect Oxford University to equal the achievements of 1993, when they won two first-class matches and drew the remainder. The new captain, Richard Montgomerie, had only Richard Yeabsley from the previous season's successful quartet of seamers. Yeabsley missed the first three matches with a fractured finger, while leg-spinner Patrick Trimby disappeared after the first two to prepare for his finals, returning for the three away games. In the event, six players made their first-class debuts in the first eight days and a heavy defeat by Durham in an opening match badly affected by rain was not unexpected. The newcomers quickly adapted to senior cricket and Oxford's only other home defeat was by Yorkshire. Ironically, they were the only county Oxford bowled out and the university replied with a partnership of 148, their highest at The Parks all season. But they were let down by the middle order in the second innings. At Lord's, they had high hopes of a second successive win over Cambridge, only to be thwarted by a rearguard action.

The main strength was the batting. In Montgomerie and Gregor Macmillan, who was elected captain for 1995, Oxford had a most reliable pair of openers. Chinmay Gupte at No. 3 also had a successful season. He figured with Montgomerie in the stand against Yorkshire and hit two centuries, one against Cambridge, in the last three matches. Two new recruits, Simon Ecclestone, who led Durham University in 1993, and Chris Hollins, emerged as outstanding all-rounders, though Ecclestone was troubled by a knee injury. Hollins crowned the season, in which he averaged over 50, with a magnificent hundred in the Varsity Match. Another century-maker, Will Kendall, was unlucky to miss the match at Lord's after fracturing a finger against Worcestershire. The only disappointment was Andrew Ridley, the second Bradman Scholar, who took most of the season to adjust to English pitches but hit a double-century for the Authentics against Cambridge University Crusaders. He is certain to be a serious contender in 1995.

Once Yeabsley returned, Oxford had a well-balanced attack, complemented by Ecclestone and Alasdair Maclay. It lacked the pace of 1993, but everyone had a decent share of the wickets and Yeabsley took ten against Cambridge. Overall, Oxford took more first-class wickets than they conceded and the many individual performances did not go unnoticed, with six players going to counties after the Varsity Match: Macmillan (Leicestershire), Ecclestone (Somerset), Trimby (Warwickshire), Yeabsley

(Middlesex), Kendall (Hampshire) and Montgomerie, who established himself as Northamptonshire's regular opener.

Fielding was of a consistently high standard. Oxford were fortunate to have several specialists – none better than Macmillan at slip. He took 20 catches and the tidy wicket-keeper Chris Townsend made 13 with four stumpings. Coach Les Lenham continued to play a major role in every aspect of Oxford's game, and head groundsman Richard Sula again produced excellent pitches, never easy in a wet spring. – Paton Fenton.

OXFORD UNIVERSITY RESULTS

First-class matches – Played 10: Lost 3, Drawn 7.

FIRST-CLASS AVERAGES

BATTING AND FIELDING

	Birthplace	*M*	*I*	*NO*	*R*	*HS*	*Avge*	*Ct/St*
C. J. Hollins	*Bromley*	8	10	2	415	131	51.87	6
W. S. Kendall	*Wimbledon*	9	10	3	253	113*	36.14	8
C. M. Gupte	*Poona, India*	10	17	2	541	122	36.06	7
R. R. Montgomerie	*Rugby*	10	17	1	541	101*	33.81	3
S. C. Ecclestone	*Great Dunmow*	10	14	4	292	80*	29.20	2
G. I. Macmillan	*Guildford*	10	17	3	395	69	28.21	20
A. C. Ridley	*Sydney, Australia*	3	4	1	65	36*	21.66	0
H. S. Malik	*Sargodha, Pakistan*	5	7	1	110	53*	18.33	3
C. J. Townsend	*Wokingham*	10	9	3	61	22	10.16	13/4
N. F. C. Martin	*Birmingham*	10	10	1	74	26	8.22	5
P. W. Trimby	*Shrewsbury*	5	5	2	21	11	7.00	2
I. J. Sutcliffe	*Leeds*	5	4	1	18	8*	6.00	2
A. W. Maclay	*Salisbury*	9	8	4	16	6*	4.00	0

Also batted: R. S. Yeabsley (*St Albans*) (6 matches) 0, 52*, 1 (5 ct).

* *Signifies not out.*

The following played a total of five three-figure innings for Oxford University – C. M. Gupte 2, C. J. Hollins 1, W. S. Kendall 1, R. R. Montgomerie 1.

BOWLING

	O	*M*	*R*	*W*	*BB*	*5W/i*	*Avge*
R. S. Yeabsley	174.5	26	567	21	6-54	1	27.00
P. W. Trimby	195	33	621	19	5-84	1	32.68
H. S. Malik	68	14	241	7	3-10	0	34.42
S. C. Ecclestone	281.3	66	768	22	4-66	0	34.90
G. I. Macmillan	94	17	324	7	1-15	0	46.28
C. J. Hollins	236.3	32	890	19	4-64	0	46.84
N. F. C. Martin	144.4	27	480	7	2-84	0	68.57
A. W. Maclay	204.4	35	669	9	3-30	0	74.33

Also bowled: C. M. Gupte 1–0–16–0; R. R. Montgomerie 3–0–18–0.

Note: Matches in this section which were not first-class are signified by a dagger.

†At Oxford, April 12. No result. Northamptonshire batted first by mutual agreement. Northamptonshire 39 for no wkt (12 overs) v Oxford University.

OXFORD UNIVERSITY v DURHAM

At Oxford, April 13, 14, 15. Durham won by 177 runs. Toss: Durham. First-class debuts: S. C. Ecclestone, W. S. Kendall, N. F. C. Martin, A. C. Ridley; S. D. Birbeck. County debuts: J. E. Morris, M. Saxelby.

Oxford, fielding four players new to first-class cricket, lost their first match against county opposition since Hampshire beat them nearly two years before. Rain played havoc, cutting more than seven hours over the three days; when play resumed at 2 p.m. on the last day, Oxford declared and Durham forfeited their second innings. That left the university needing 251 in 220 minutes. With left-arm seamer Brown taking five for eight in 9.3 overs, they were skittled for 73. Durham's 270 for nine declared owed much to Bainbridge, their new captain, and Scott; they put on 111 after half the side was out for 113. Leg-spinner Trimby took five wickets for the first time and Macmillan held five slip catches.

Close of play: First day, Durham 193-5 (P. Bainbridge 57*, C. W. Scott 26*); Second day, Oxford University 20-1 (G. I. Macmillan 6*, C. M. Gupte 8*).

Durham

W. Larkins b Trimby	32
M. Saxelby c Macmillan b Trimby	12
J. E. Morris c Macmillan b Maclay	1
S. Hutton c Malik b Trimby	35
J. A. Daley c Macmillan b Trimby	18
*P. Bainbridge c Macmillan b Ecclestone	68
†C. W. Scott c Macmillan b Trimby	64
J. Wood c Kendall b Ecclestone	0
S. D. Birbeck c Ecclestone b Macmillan	6
D. A. Graveney not out	11
S. J. E. Brown not out	4
L-b 7, n-b 12	19
1/23 2/24 3/56 4/94 5/113 6/224 7/224 8/253 9/257 (9 wkts dec.)	270

Bowling: Ecclestone 14–6–25–2; Maclay 24–9–65–1; Trimby 33–5–84–5; Martin 13–5–30–0; Macmillan 12–2–25–1; Malik 12–4–34–0.

Durham forfeited their second innings.

Oxford University

*R. R. Montgomerie lbw b Brown	6	–	c Birbeck b Brown	0
G. I. Macmillan not out	6	–	lbw b Wood	2
C. M. Gupte not out	8	–	c Larkins b Brown	7
A. C. Ridley (did not bat)		–	lbw b Birbeck	20
W. S. Kendall (did not bat)		–	b Wood	0
S. C. Ecclestone (did not bat)		–	lbw b Birbeck	0
H. S. Malik (did not bat)		–	b Brown	27
N. F. C. Martin (did not bat)		–	lbw b Wood	1
†C. J. Townsend (did not bat)		–	lbw b Brown	8
A. W. Maclay (did not bat)		–	not out	0
P. W. Trimby (did not bat)		–	b Brown	0
			B 5, l-b 2, w 1	8
1/6 (1 wkt dec.)	20		1/2 2/10 3/22 4/24 5/25 6/38 7/39 8/71 9/72	73

Bowling: *First Innings*—Brown 5.1–2–11–1; Wood 4–0–9–0; Birbeck 1–1–0–0. *Second Innings*—Brown 9.3–6–8–5; Wood 8–3–15–3; Birbeck 6–1–13–2; Bainbridge 8–2–18–0; Graveney 9–4–12–0.

Umpires: D. J. Constant and J. F. Steele.

OXFORD UNIVERSITY v HAMPSHIRE

At Oxford, April 16, 18, 19. Drawn. Toss: Hampshire. County debut: M. Keech.

Terry and Middleton opened for Hampshire with a partnership of 189, after rain washed out the first day and the captains agreed to start the second 30 minutes early. Terry hit two sixes and 14 fours in the first century of the season and Middleton followed at a slower pace before falling to Trimby. The remaining batsmen struggled against steady spin bowling; Trimby deceived both Nicholas and Keech (formerly of Middlesex) with googlies. In reply, Montgomerie and Macmillan put on 70 for the first wicket. But Montgomerie's dismissal for 50 signalled an alarming collapse. Five wickets fell for 15 and only Martin and Gupte enabled Oxford to hold out until shortly before tea. Nicholas waived the follow-on to give his middle and lower order batting practice, though they hardly took advantage; off-spinner Malik took a career-best three for ten.

Close of play: First day, No play; Second day, Oxford University 24-0 (R. R. Montgomerie 18*, G. I. Macmillan 6*).

Hampshire

T. C. Middleton c Montgomerie b Trimby	102		
V. P. Terry c Martin b Malik	112		
K. D. James c and b Macmillan	29		
*M. C. J. Nicholas lbw b Trimby	34		
R. M. F. Cox b Maclay	8	(3) not out	20
M. Keech b Trimby	12	(1) c and b Malik	16
†A. N. Aymes not out	15	(2) b Martin	11
S. D. Udal not out	21	(4) st Townsend b Malik	6
M. J. Thursfield (did not bat)	–	(5) b Malik	0
C. A. Connor (did not bat)	–	(6) not out	5
L-b 5, w 3, n-b 12	20	W 1, n-b 2	3
1/189 2/252 3/263 4/287 5/306 6/315 (6 wkts dec.)	353	1/25 2/43 3/51 4/53 (4 wkts dec.)	61

D. P. J. Flint did not bat.

Bowling: *First Innings*—Ecclestone 19–3–42–0; Maclay 15.2–1–64–1; Trimby 35–6–102–3; Martin 6–0–23–0; Malik 24–5–89–1; Macmillan 8–3–28–1. *Second Innings*—Maclay 6–2–19–0; Martin 7–2–21–1; Malik 6–3–10–3; Trimby 5–2–11–0.

Oxford University

*R. R. Montgomerie c Middleton b Udal	50
G. I. Macmillan c and b Udal	23
A. C. Ridley c Terry b Connor	1
W. S. Kendall c Terry b Connor	1
S. C. Ecclestone c Middleton b Flint	19
H. S. Malik c Terry b Thursfield	3
N. F. C. Martin b Connor	26
C. M. Gupte c Middleton b James	21
†C. J. Townsend lbw b James	0
A. W. Maclay b Connor	0
P. W. Trimby not out	5
B 3, l-b 10	13
1/70 2/71 3/77 4/77 5/85 6/109 7/140 8/144 9/157	162

Bowling: Connor 16.4–7–37–4; Thursfield 15–9–26–1; Udal 26–8–54–2; James 10–3–20–2; Flint 8–3–12–1.

Umpires: B. Dudleston and J. F. Steele.

OXFORD UNIVERSITY v GLAMORGAN

At Oxford, April 20, 21, 22. Drawn. Toss: Oxford University. First-class debuts: C. J. Hollins, I. J. Sutcliffe; G. P. Butcher, A. J. Dalton. County debut: O. D. Gibson.

The game petered out after Glamorgan's acting-captain, Metson, made the third declaration, setting Oxford an unlikely 310 in two and a half hours. But there had been plenty of good batting before that. For the second match running, both county openers made centuries. Cottey was first to the mark before he was stumped, giving Chris Hollins, son of England footballer John Hollins, his first first-class wicket; James, who put on 197 with Cottey and 125 with Hemp, followed up with 150. But Hollins persevered with his off-spin to pick up Hemp and Gibson in one over. Glamorgan declared in the morning, whereupon Montgomerie and Macmillan opened with 126, the highest first-wicket stand for either Oxford or Cambridge since 1983. Montgomerie also declared at the overnight score, 98 behind; Gibson then made up for his first-innings duck with 61, while Hemp completed a second fifty.

Close of play: First day, Glamorgan 355-5 (A. J. Dalton 21*, R. P. Lefebvre 4*); Second day, Oxford University 257-9 (C. J. Townsend 7*, A. W. Maclay 6*).

Glamorgan

First innings		Second innings	
S. P. James st Townsend b Macmillan	150		
P. A. Cottey st Townsend b Hollins	109	(5) c Macmillan b Ecclestone	1
D. L. Hemp c Townsend b Hollins	51	(4) not out	50
A. J. Dalton not out	21		
O. D. Gibson c Macmillan b Hollins	0	(3) c Macmillan b Ecclestone	61
G. P. Butcher c Townsend b Ecclestone	5		
R. P. Lefebvre not out	4	(2) c Hollins b Martin	28
*†C. P. Metson (did not bat)		(1) c Kendall b Maclay	35
S. D. Thomas (did not bat)		(6) not out	15
B 1, l-b 6, w 6, n-b 2	15	L-b 4, w 1, n-b 16	21
1/197 2/322 3/322 4/322 5/345 (5 wkts dec.)	355	1/47 2/97 3/160 4/166 (4 wkts dec.)	211

S. Bastien and S. R. Barwick did not bat.

Bowling: *First Innings*—Ecclestone 26–6–61–1; Maclay 22–6–48–0; Hollins 28–3–105–3; Martin 17–1–58–0; Montgomerie 3–0–18–0; Macmillan 13–0–58–1. *Second Innings*—Ecclestone 18–3–43–2; Maclay 15–1–66–1; Martin 7.2–0–35–1; Hollins 15–0–63–0.

Oxford University

First innings		Second innings	
*R. R. Montgomerie c Dalton b Barwick	80	c James b Thomas	3
G. I. Macmillan c Barwick b Lefebvre	50	not out	44
C. M. Gupte c Metson b Lefebvre	0	c Butcher b Bastien	19
A. C. Ridley lbw b Lefebvre	8	not out	36
W. S. Kendall c Metson b Butcher	25		
S. C. Ecclestone c Lefebvre b Butcher	26		
I. J. Sutcliffe c Dalton b Barwick	1		
N. F. C. Martin c Metson b Thomas	12		
C. J. Hollins c Metson b Thomas	19		
†C. J. Townsend not out	7		
A. W. Maclay not out	6		
L-b 11, w 2, n-b 10	23	B 4, l-b 1, w 1, n-b 2	8
1/126 2/126 3/149 4/167 5/198 6/205 7/215 8/234 9/247 (9 wkts dec.)	257	1/3 2/29 (2 wkts)	110

Bowling: *First Innings*—Gibson 9–0–31–0; Bastien 19–9–27–0; Thomas 21–2–80–2; Lefebvre 23–5–48–3; Barwick 22–12–24–2; Butcher 7–0–36–2. *Second Innings*—Bastien 9–3–12–1; Thomas 9–1–28–1; Lefebvre 6–3–13–0; Barwick 8–2–26–0; Butcher 3–0–18–0; Cottey 1–0–8–0.

Umpires: J. W. Holder and M. J. Kitchen.

OXFORD UNIVERSITY v NOTTINGHAMSHIRE

At Oxford, April 28, 29, 30. Drawn. Toss: Oxford University. First-class debut: D. J. Pipes.

Nottinghamshire's batting was dominated by Adams, on his first-class debut for the county, and Johnson. In the first innings, Adams hit an unbeaten 117, following a punishing 69 by Johnson; in the second, Johnson made his century and Adams, still undefeated, another fifty. Oxford had made a spirited reply to Nottinghamshire's 252 for eight, despite losing Macmillan to Sylvester's first ball. Montgomerie and Gupte added 98 for the second wicket and then Ecclestone and Kendall put on 130 before their captain called them in at 238 for three. But any hopes of repeating their victory in 1993 were killed when Robinson's over-cautious declaration left Oxford to score 293 in 190 minutes.

Close of play: First day, Oxford University 17-1 (R. R. Montgomerie 9*, C. M. Gupte 8*); Second day, Nottinghamshire 76-2 (M. A. Crawley 23*, P. Johnson 38*).

Nottinghamshire

P. R. Pollard run out	19	– lbw b Ecclestone	10
M. A. Crawley c Townsend b Ecclestone	4	– c Macmillan b Yeabsley	24
J. C. Adams not out	117	– (6) not out	52
P. Johnson lbw b Ecclestone	69	– c Sutcliffe b Maclay	107
*R. T. Robinson c Townsend b Ecclestone	0	– (3) c Montgomerie b Ecclestone	4
†W. M. Noon c Yeabsley b Hollins	7	– (5) c Macmillan b Maclay	27
D. J. Pipes b Hollins	1	– (8) not out	11
R. A. Pick c Macmillan b Hollins	0	– (7) c Sutcliffe b Hollins	36
M. G. Field-Buss lbw b Hollins	15		
S. A. Sylvester not out	6		
B 1, l-b 3, w 2, n-b 8	14	L-b 2, w 1, n-b 4	7
1/13 2/30 3/128 4/128 5/173 6/187 7/187 8/227 (8 wkts dec.)	252	1/15 2/23 3/78 4/174 5/184 6/237 (6 wkts dec.)	278

J. A. Afford did not bat.

Bowling: *First Innings*—Yeabsley 24–0–66–0; Ecclestone 23–6–51–3; Martin 5–1–12–0; Maclay 16–2–55–0; Hollins 22.1–3–64–4. *Second Innings*—Yeabsley 18–3–82–1; Ecclestone 18–3–59–2; Maclay 13–0–58–2; Hollins 17–2–77–1.

Oxford University

*R. R. Montgomerie c Noon b Afford	53	– c Adams b Pick	7
G. I. Macmillan c Pick b Sylvester	0	– b Afford	40
C. M. Gupte b Pick	46	– not out	39
S. C. Ecclestone not out	80		
W. S. Kendall not out	42		
I. J. Sutcliffe (did not bat)		– (4) not out	8
B 5, l-b 8, n-b 4	17	L-b 2, w 1, n-b 6	9
1/2 2/100 3/108 (3 wkts dec.)	238	1/29 2/76 (2 wkts)	103

N. F. C. Martin, C. J. Hollins, R. S. Yeabsley, †C. J. Townsend and A. W. Maclay did not bat.

Bowling: *First Innings*—Pick 21–4–48–1; Sylvester 17–3–38–1; Afford 19–8–46–1; Field-Buss 16–4–43–0; Crawley 7–3–16–0; Adams 5–0–21–0; Pipes 4–0–13–0. *Second Innings*—Pick 6–2–13–1; Sylvester 5–0–19–0; Field-Buss 12–2–24–0; Afford 16–5–24–1; Crawley 8–3–15–0; Pipes 4–3–6–0.

Umpires: J. H. Harris and D. R. Shepherd.

†At Oxford, May 4. Oxford University won by seven wickets. Toss: Bedfordshire. Bedfordshire 172 for five (48 overs) (N. A. Stanley 57); Oxford University 176 for three (47.1 overs) (I. J. Sutcliffe 75 not out, C. J. Hollins 40 not out).

†At Oxford, May 6. Oxford University won by eight runs. Toss: Oxford University. Oxford University 189 (53.5 overs) (I. J. Sutcliffe 44, A. C. Ridley 38; K. Jahangir three for 43); Hertfordshire 181 for eight (55 overs) (M. R. Gouldstone 46, R. Premadasa 32).

†At Oxford, May 9. Oxford University won by five wickets. Toss: Oxford University. Berkshire 235 for six (55 overs) (D. A. Shaw 118, M. L. Simmons 43); Oxford University 239 for five (53.2 overs) (I. J. Sutcliffe 62, C. M. Gupte 47, W. S. Kendall 35).

†At Oxford, May 13. Oxford University won by eight wickets. Toss: Oxfordshire. Oxfordshire 181 for seven (55 overs) (S. N. V. Waterton 44, J. S. Hartley 32); Oxford University 185 for two (53 overs) (R. R. Montgomerie 55, G. I. Macmillan 39, C. M. Gupte 52 not out).

OXFORDSHIRE UNIVERSITY v WARWICKSHIRE

At Oxford, May 14, 16, 17. Drawn. Toss: Warwickshire. First-class debut: G. Welch.

Rain washed out more than half the match. After Twose went cheaply, Ostler hit 149 and Paul Smith had time to complete an unbeaten fifty before Reeve declared at 303 for five on the second day. Torrential overnight rain, which flooded the square, ruined any chances of play on the third day.

Close of play: First day, Warwickshire 175-3 (D. P. Ostler 119*, P. A. Smith 5*); Second day, Oxford University 47-2 (G. I. Macmillan 16*, S. C. Ecclestone 5*).

Warwickshire

D. P. Ostler c and b Yeabsley 149
R. G. Twose c Townsend b Ecclestone 16
T. L. Penney c Montgomerie b Ecclestone . 24
*D. A. Reeve c Yeabsley b Hollins 7
P. A. Smith not out 50
J. D. Ratcliffe c Townsend b Hollins . . . 7
†M. Burns not out 36
L-b 2, w 1, n-b 11 14

1/34 2/118 3/147 4/213 5/235 (5 wkts dec.) 303

R. P. Davis, N. M. K. Smith, T. A. Munton and G. Welch did not bat.

Bowling: Ecclestone 27–6–87–2; Maclay 9–2–31–0; Yeabsley 17–1–52–1; Hollins 25–2–87–2; Martin 11–2–44–0.

Oxford University

*R. R. Montgomerie lbw b Reeve 16
G. I. Macmillan not out 16
C. M. Gupte lbw b Reeve 4
S. C. Ecclestone not out 5
N-b 6 6

1/26 2/30 (2 wkts) 47

W. S. Kendall, I. J. Sutcliffe, N. F. C. Martin, C. J. Hollins, R. S. Yeabsley, †C. J. Townsend and A. W. Maclay did not bat.

Bowling: Munton 6–4–3–0; Welch 4–0–21–0; Davis 4–3–2–0; Reeve 6–4–9–2; Twose 5–3–9–0; N. M. K. Smith 1–0–3–0.

Umpires: R. Julian and M. K. Reed.

OXFORD UNIVERSITY v LEICESTERSHIRE

At Oxford, May 18, 19, 20. Drawn. Toss: Oxford University. First-class debut: A. Sheriyar. County debut: B. C. Fourie.

Left most of the final day to chase a nominal 330, Montgomerie and Macmillan ensured the draw with their second three-figure stand in a month. Montgomerie went on to Oxford's first century of the season. The day before, however, Millns dismissed both with seven runs on the board; he added another four wickets and South African Brenden Fourie three as the students slumped to 76 for nine. Their eventual 139 owed everything to a last-wicket stand in which Hollins made his maiden fifty, in his second first-class innings, while Maclay contributed a single. Though Oxford still trailed by 164, Briers did not enforce the follow-on. In Leicestershire's first innings, he and Hepworth opened soundly but without sparkle against Ecclestone's steady seam and Hollins's off-spin. The best batting came from Smith, with 75, who added 90 for the fifth wicket with Nixon.

Close of play: First day, Oxford University 1-0 (R. R. Montgomerie 0*, G. I. Macmillan 1*); Second day, Leicestershire 129-2 (N. E. Briers 36*, V. J. Wells 70*).

Leicestershire

P. N. Hepworth c Martin b Yeabsley	20	– b Ecclestone	10
*N. E. Briers c Kendall b Hollins	46	– not out	51
J. J. Whitaker c Yeabsley b Hollins	18	– c Gupte b Martin	10
V. J. Wells c Kendall b Macmillan	38	– not out	87
B. F. Smith c Kendall b Yeabsley	75		
†P. A. Nixon lbw b Ecclestone	38		
A. R. K. Pierson c Macmillan b Hollins	13		
D. J. Millns not out	24		
M. T. Brimson not out	17		
B 1, l-b 3, n-b 10	14	B 1, l-b 2, n-b 4	7
1/56 2/92 3/109 4/155 5/245 6/249 7/272 (7 wkts dec.)	303	1/10 2/40 (2 wkts dec.)	165

B. C. Fourie and A. Sheriyar did not bat.

Bowling: *First Innings*—Ecclestone 24–10–56–1; Maclay 10–0–43–0; Yeabsley 15–2–41–2; Hollins 26–6–90–3; Macmillan 11–2–38–1; Martin 9–2–31–0. *Second Innings*—Ecclestone 6–1–21–1; Hollins 13–4–32–0; Yeabsley 10–0–48–0; Martin 10–1–29–1; Maclay 7.2–1–32–0.

Oxford University

*R. R. Montgomerie c Nixon b Millns	4	– not out	101
G. I. Macmillan c Nixon b Millns	3	– c Wells b Brimson	64
C. M. Gupte lbw b Fourie	12	– c Nixon b Fourie	9
S. C. Ecclestone c Pierson b Fourie	31	– st Nixon b Pierson	18
W. S. Kendall b Fourie	3	– b Sheriyar	13
I. J. Sutcliffe lbw b Millns	5		
C. J. Hollins c and b Wells	68	– (6) not out	13
N. F. C. Martin lbw b Millns	0		
R. S. Yeabsley c Nixon b Millns	0		
†C. J. Townsend c Nixon b Millns	0		
A. W. Maclay not out	1		
B 1, l-b 7, n-b 4	12	B 6, l-b 2, w 1, n-b 2	11
1/6 2/7 3/41 4/57 5/64 6/72 7/72 8/72 9/76	139	1/118 2/141 3/172 4/197 (4 wkts)	229

Bowling: *First Innings*—Sheriyar 13–3–34–0; Fourie 8–1–19–3; Millns 13–3–44–6; Wells 11–4–22–1; Brimson 9–3–12–0. *Second Innings*—Millns 3–0–6–0; Sheriyar 12–0–35–1; Fourie 20–1–54–1; Pierson 26–7–41–1; Brimson 24.3–7–55–1; Wells 5–0–30–0.

Umpires: B. Leadbeater and K. E. Palmer.

†At Oxford, May 23. No result. Toss: Oxford University. Oxford University 253 for five (55 overs) (W. S. Kendall 66, I. J. Sutcliffe 100 not out, R. S. Yeabsley 31); Royal Navy 109 for five (40 overs) (C. Hobson 35 not out).

OXFORD UNIVERSITY v YORKSHIRE

At Oxford, May 28, 30, 31. Yorkshire won by 100 runs. Toss: Yorkshire.

Oxford's last first-class match at The Parks ended, like the first, in defeat. Challenged to score 267 in 205 minutes, Montgomerie and Macmillan set off with 60. But some good spin bowling by Vaughan and Stemp reduced Oxford to 92 for eight. Yorkshire were delayed by Yeabsley and Townsend, who added 66. But once Townsend went, last man Maclay soon followed and Yeabsley was left with an unbeaten maiden fifty. Yorkshire's batsmen had struggled against the students' seam attack, with only acting-captain Byas and Foster reaching half-centuries. They were the first county Oxford had bowled out in 1994 and their bowlers were soon made to look ordinary by Montgomerie and Gupte, whose 148 for the second wicket was Oxford's highest partnership of the season to date. It ended when Gupte was caught for a career-best 72 and Montgomerie later declared 42 behind. Yorkshire's second innings was dominated by Vaughan, who completed a maiden century.

Close of play: First day, Oxford University 40-1 (R. R. Montgomerie 12*, C. M. Gupte 4*); Second day, Yorkshire 102-3 (M. P. Vaughan 56*, B. Parker 0*).

Yorkshire

S. A. Kellett c Townsend b Ecclestone	6	– b Yeabsley	2
M. P. Vaughan c Kendall b Macmillan	29	– not out	106
A. P. Grayson c Macmillan b Martin	7	– c and b Hollins	37
†R. J. Blakey lbw b Hollins	19	– c and b Hollins	2
*D. Byas c Kendall b Yeabsley	71	– (6) not out	45
B. Parker b Yeabsley	34	– (5) run out	24
M. J. Foster not out	63		
R. D. Stemp c Gupte b Yeabsley	0		
M. Broadhurst b Ecclestone	6		
C. E. W. Silverwood c Gupte b Yeabsley	2		
M. A. Robinson c Yeabsley b Hollins	9		
B 1, l-b 2, w 5	8	L-b 2, w 2, n-b 4	8
1/19 2/41 3/55 4/91 5/169 6/176 7/178 8/195 9/212	254	1/8 2/96 3/100 4/136 (4 wkts dec.)	224

Bowling: *First Innings*—Ecclestone 29–7–67–2; Yeabsley 20–3–75–4; Martin 14–5–23–1; Macmillan 10–2–15–1; Hollins 11–0–62–2; Maclay 6–3–9–0. *Second Innings*—Yeabsley 17–1–63–1; Ecclestone 12–1–39–0; Maclay 5–1–21–0; Hollins 9–2–29–2; Macmillan 12–0–70–0.

Oxford University

*R. R. Montgomerie lbw b Grayson	80	– c Blakey b Silverwood	25
G. I. Macmillan c Byas b Broadhurst	15	– c Foster b Stemp	28
C. M. Gupte c Silverwood b Vaughan	72	– b Stemp	0
S. C. Ecclestone not out	19	– c and b Vaughan	5
C. J. Hollins not out	6	– st Blakey b Vaughan	4
W. S. Kendall (did not bat)		– c Stemp b Vaughan	9
I. J. Sutcliffe (did not bat)		– c Foster b Vaughan	4
N. F. C. Martin (did not bat)		– b Stemp	3
R. S. Yeabsley (did not bat)		– not out	52
†C. J. Townsend (did not bat)		– c Blakey b Foster	22
A. W. Maclay (did not bat)		– lbw b Foster	0
L-b 2, w 2, n-b 16	20	B 2, l-b 2, n-b 10	14
1/28 2/176 3/192 (3 wkts dec.)	212	1/60 2/63 3/66 4/71 5/82 6/85 7/88 8/92 9/158	166

Bowling: *First Innings*—Broadhurst 8–0–45–1; Silverwood 13–2–45–0; Robinson 11–2–23–0; Stemp 25–15–39–0; Vaughan 17–3–33–1; Foster 6–2–12–0; Grayson 5–1–13–1. *Second Innings*—Broadhurst 3–0–7–0; Robinson 11–1–54–0; Stemp 30–12–50–3; Silverwood 5–2–7–1; Vaughan 16–5–39–4; Grayson 2–1–1–0; Foster 3.5–1–4–2.

Umpires: K. J. Lyons and G. Sharp.

†At Oxford, June 1, 2, 3. Drawn. Toss: Oxford University. Oxford University 340 for seven dec. (M. Jarrett 59, I. J. Sutcliffe 92, H. S. Malik 84, W. S. Kendall 47) and 201 for five dec. (G. I. Macmillan 37, C. J. Hollins 30, J. Ricketts 49, R. S. Yeabsley 52); Combined Services 211 (Capt. P. S. Germain 72 not out; A. W. Maclay four for 52, J. Ricketts three for 55) and 43 for no wkt.

†At Oxford, June 7, 8, 9. Oxford University won by six wickets. Toss: Oxford University. MCC 286 for four dec. (C. J. Rogers 52, D. A. Thorne 36, J. F. Venter 106 not out, G. V. Palmer 60) and 218 for four dec. (C. J. Rogers 49, A. P. Tarrant 66, D. A. Thorne 35 not out; C. J. Hollins three for 59); Oxford University 253 for three dec. (C. M. Gupte 46, G. I. Macmillan 128 not out, C. J. Hollins 50 not out) and 253 for four (G. I. Macmillan 152, N. F. C. Martin 77; K. C. Williams three for 42).

At The Oval, June 11, 12, 13. OXFORD UNIVERSITY drew with SURREY.

†At Oxford, June 15. Oxford University won by 61 runs. Toss: Oxford University. Oxford University 227 for six (55 overs) (R. R. Montgomerie 67, C. M. Gupte 54, H. S. Malik 30 not out; P. Harrison three for 37); Midlands Club Cricket Conference 166 (52.5 overs) (J. Waterhouse 54; H. S. Malik six for 28).

At Worcester, June 17, 18, 19. OXFORD UNIVERSITY lost to WORCESTERSHIRE by 226 runs.

†At Oxford, June 27. Tied. Toss: Oxford University. Oxford University 233 for seven dec. (R. R. Montgomerie 124; E. S. Brookes four for 76); Wiltshire 233 for seven (R. J. Greatorex 38, C. I. Maplesden 86; R. S. Yeabsley three for 64).

At Lord's, June 29, 30, July 1. OXFORD UNIVERSITY drew with CAMBRIDGE UNIVERSITY.

CAMBRIDGE

President: Professor A. D. Buckingham (Pembroke)

Captain: A. R. Whittall (Falcon College, Zimbabwe and Trinity)
Secretary: R. Q. Cake (KCS, Wimbledon and St John's)

Captain for 1995: A. R. Whittall (Falcon College, Zimbabwe and Trinity)
Secretary: J. Ratledge (Bolton GS and St John's)

For the first time in several seasons, Cambridge had no experienced players to call upon. Without an Atherton or a Crawley, it was always going to be a difficult year for captain Andy Whittall and his players. And so it turned out, with only the captain's heroism at Lord's preventing a second successive defeat by Oxford.

Though Whittall's first-innings 40, equalling his best score made in the same fixture the previous year, was not enough to avert the follow-on, a defiant, and often aggressive unbeaten 91 in the second enabled his side to avoid defeat. But Cambridge had been hoping that Whittall would be able to bear the brunt of the bowling with his off-spin. However, the ability of his debut year, which had impressed several seasoned watchers, had deserted him and the pressures of captaining a young and inexperienced team took its toll on his own form. Despite his personal difficulties, Whittall bowled the most overs – 295 – and claimed 11 wickets. The other

CAMBRIDGE UNIVERSITY 1994

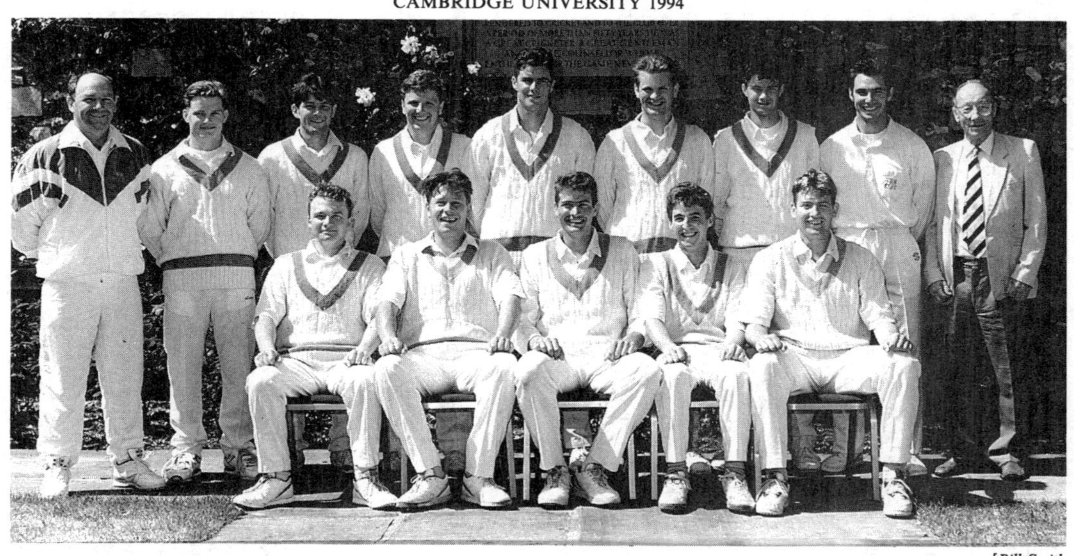

[*Bill Smith*

Back row: G. J. Saville (*coach*), J. Ratledge, F. J. Cooke, J. S. Hodgson, D. E. Stanley, N. J. Haste, R. D. Mann, E. J. How, A. R. May (*scorer*).
Front row: G. W. Jones, C. M. Pitcher, A. R. Whittall (*captain*), R. Q. Cake, J. P. Carroll.

48 which fell to bowlers were shared out between only three players: appropriately named seamers, Chris Pitcher and Nick Haste, plus off-spinner James Hodgson. Pitcher, in particular, bowled with great spirit for his 20 wickets, while Hodgson, who took 15 in 272 overs, caused most comment by his habit of putting a sweater on to bowl and then returning it to the umpire at the end of the over. He was the side's most economical bowler by far, conceding only 2.68 an over.

The shortage of reliable batsmen was the cause of most of Cambridge's difficulties, with a great burden placed upon the relatively inexperienced Russell Cake. He did not disappoint, scoring 644 runs in nine matches at 42.93, including the university's only century of the term, against Glamorgan. He played for Surrey's Second Eleven on a summer contract. The next-highest run-maker was Hodgson, with just 256 runs at a fraction over 18. It said much about the brittle batting that Whittall, thanks to the effort at Lord's, was second in the Cambridge averages with 193 runs at 21.44. Such was the shortage of talent available that captain and coach Graham Saville quickly decided that there was little to choose from. Only 13 players were used all term, with nine playing in all nine first-class games.

Much had been made of the declining standard of pitches at Fenner's in previous seasons, but this problem was arrested in 1994, with the promise of further improvement to come following the decision to re-lay the entire square bit by bit, starting in the winter of 1994-95. The wet weather in April did not help groundsman Tony Pocock – the first match was ruined and the second abandoned without a ball bowled – David Hallett.

CAMBRIDGE UNIVERSITY RESULTS

First-class matches – Played 9: Lost 3, Drawn 6. Abandoned 1.

FIRST-CLASS AVERAGES

BATTING AND FIELDING

	Birthplace	*M*	*I*	*NO*	*R*	*HS*	*Avge*	*Ct/St*
R. Q. Cake	*Chertsey*	9	16	1	644	107	42.93	3
A. R. Whittall	*Mutare, Zimbabwe*	9	11	2	193	91*	21.44	3
J. P. Carroll	*Bebington*	9	15	2	246	90	18.92	2
J. S. Hodgson	*Guildford*	9	15	1	256	54	18.28	8
G. W. Jones	*Birmingham*	8	13	0	220	74	16.92	0
R. D. Mann	*Middlesbrough*	9	16	0	248	53	15.50	2
D. E. Stanley	*Bromley*	5	8	2	91	48	15.16	2
J. Ratledge	*Preston*	9	16	0	227	79	14.18	1
F. J. Cooke.	*Birmingham*	9	10	4	80	34*	13.33	9/1
N. J. Haste.	*Northampton*	9	12	2	112	22	11.20	2
C. M. Pitcher	*Croydon*	9	12	2	103	43	10.30	4
M. C. Bashforth. . . .	*Sydney, Australia*	3	5	3	13	9*	6.50	1

Also batted: M. A. T. Hall (*Windsor*) (2 matches) 4, 1.

* *Signifies not out.*

R. Q. Cake played the only three-figure innings for Cambridge University.

BOWLING

	O	*M*	*R*	*W*	*BB*	*5W/i*	*Avge*
C. M. Pitcher	252.5	54	864	20	4-37	0	43.20
J. S. Hodgson	272.3	85	732	15	4-14	0	48.80
N. J. Haste	233	39	910	13	4-69	0	70.00
A. R. Whittall....	295.3	59	1,060	11	2-34	0	96.36

Also bowled: M. C. Bashforth 28–9–108–0; J. P. Carroll 6–1–22–0; M. A. T. Hall 2–0–2–0; J. Ratledge 16–0–66–0.

Note: Matches in this section which were not first-class are signified by a dagger.

†At Cambridge, April 7, 8. Cambridge University v Loughborough University. Abandoned.

†At Cambridge, April 9, 10. Cambridge University v Durham University. Abandoned.

CAMBRIDGE UNIVERSITY v NOTTINGHAMSHIRE

At Cambridge, April 13, 14, 15. Drawn. Toss: Nottinghamshire. First-class debuts: M. C. Bashforth, F. J. Cooke, J. S. Hodgson, R. D. Mann, J. Ratledge.

Play was possible only on the first day and for two minutes on the second before the game was abandoned because of heavy rain. Unusually, Nottinghamshire forsook the chance of some early season batting practice by electing to field. Conditions were damp and chilly as Cambridge, having enjoyed an opening partnership of 41, then subsided for 144 in 77 overs. The county lost Pollard in the ninth over and reached 36 for one at the close; Crawley added just two runs to that from two balls on the second morning before rain and hail swept the ground.

Close of play: First day, Nottinghamshire 36-1 (M. A. Crawley 13*, W. A. Dessaur 8*); Second day, Nottinghamshire 38-1 (M. A. Crawley 15*, W. A. Dessaur 8*).

Cambridge University

G. W. Jones c Dessaur b Pick	35
R. Q. Cake c Crawley b Chapman	21
J. Ratledge c French b Afford	6
J. S. Hodgson c Robinson b Afford	0
J. P. Carroll c Pollard b Afford	17
R. D. Mann c French b Field-Buss	17
C. M. Pitcher c Evans b Chapman	0
*A. R. Whittall c Archer b Field-Buss	0
N. J. Haste b Evans	3
†F. J. Cooke lbw b Evans	24
M. C. Bashforth not out	9
B 6, l-b 5, w 1	12
1/41 2/59 3/67 4/67 5/96 6/97 7/100 8/109 9/111	144

Bowling: Pick 15–4–36–1; Evans 19–6–31–2; Chapman 13–6–21–2; Afford 16–8–22–3; Field-Buss 14–6–23–2.

Nottinghamshire

P. R. Pollard lbw b Pitcher	13
M. A. Crawley not out	15
W. A. Dessaur not out	8
L-b 2	2
1/24	(1 wkt) 38

*R. T. Robinson, G. F. Archer, K. P. Evans, †B. N. French, M. G. Field-Buss, R. A. Pick, R. J. Chapman and J. A. Afford did not bat.

Bowling: Pitcher 9–2–21–1; Haste 6.2–1–14–0; Whittall 2–1–1–0.

Umpires: H. D. Bird and T. E. Jesty.

CAMBRIDGE UNIVERSITY v NORTHAMPTONSHIRE

At Cambridge, April 16, 17, 18. Abandoned without a ball bowled.

CAMBRIDGE UNIVERSITY v KENT

At Cambridge, April 20, 21, 22. Kent won by 340 runs. Toss: Cambridge University.

Cambridge were taken apart by Patel, who claimed five in their first-innings 84 and then bowled unchanged throughout their second attempt to finish with ten for 77. Though Kent had preferred batting practice to enforcing the follow-on, the University might have gone even more cheaply the second time had Whittall not steered them from 77 for seven to 122. On the first day, Fulton completed a maiden century in 250 minutes, hitting ten fours from 214 balls, after he and Ward set a brisk tempo with 144 in 40 overs. Taylor added another century before the close. For Cambridge, Pitcher took seven of the ten county wickets to fall; he even instigated a mini-collapse after tea on the second day, when three went in nine balls.

Close of play: First day, Kent 363-3 (N. R. Taylor 107*, G. R. Cowdrey 26*); Second day, Kent 64-3 (M. V. Fleming 16*, D. W. Headley 6*).

Kent

D. P. Fulton hit wkt b Hodgson	109		
T. R. Ward b Haste	86		
N. J. Llong c Bashforth b Pitcher	21		
N. R. Taylor b Pitcher	129		
G. R. Cowdrey c Cooke b Pitcher	41		
M. V. Fleming not out	26	(4) b Pitcher	30
M. A. Ealham not out	13	(3) b Whittall	3
†S. A. Marsh (did not bat)	–	(1) c Carroll b Pitcher	18
*M. R. Benson (did not bat)	–	(2) b Pitcher	13
D. W. Headley (did not bat)	–	(5) not out	17
M. M. Patel (did not bat)	–	(6) c Hodgson b Pitcher	11
B 5, l-b 12, w 2, n-b 2	21	L-b 6, n-b 2	8
1/144 2/183 3/260 4/387 5/412 (5 wkts dec.)	446	1/36 2/39 3/39 4/84 5/100 (5 wkts dec.)	100

Bowling: *First Innings*—Pitcher 36–6–123–3; Haste 24–3–112–1; Whittall 31–8–94–0; Bashforth 12–5–48–0; Hodgson 24–11–52–1. *Second Innings*—Pitcher 12.5–1–37–4; Whittall 13–3–21–1; Haste 5–0–36–0.

Cambridge University

G. W. Jones c Marsh b Llong	5	– c Taylor b Patel	8
R. Q. Cake lbw b Headley	0	– c Fulton b Llong	26
J. Ratledge run out	4	– c Ward b Llong	3
J. S. Hodgson c and b Patel	16	– st Marsh b Patel	3
J. P. Carroll c Benson b Patel	19	– c Benson b Patel	0
R. D. Mann c Ward b Headley	17	– c Fulton b Patel	18
N. J. Haste c Ward b Patel	10	– c Ward b Llong	20
C. M. Pitcher c Cowdrey b Patel	6	– lbw b Llong	0
*A. R. Whittall c Headley b Patel	3	– c and b Patel	34
†F. J. Cooke not out	0	– c Ealham b Llong	4
M. C. Bashforth b Headley	0	– not out	0
B 1, l-b 3	4	B 2, l-b 2, n-b 2	6
1/1 2/10 3/11 4/47 5/48 6/66 7/78 8/84 9/84	84	1/19 2/24 3/41 4/41 5/43 6/77 7/77 8/113 9/120	122

Bowling: *First Innings*—Headley 11–5–10–3; Ealham 9–4–15–0; Fleming 9–5–9–0; Llong 9–3–13–1; Patel 21–7–33–5. *Second Innings*—Headley 5–1–11–0; Patel 27–9–44–5; Llong 22.3–6–63–5.

Umpires: J. H. Hampshire and M. K. Reed.

CAMBRIDGE UNIVERSITY v MIDDLESEX

At Cambridge, April 30, May 1, 2. Middlesex won by 78 runs. Toss: Middlesex. First-class debut: J. C. Harrison.

For once the University had a county rattled, with Middlesex wobbling from 95 for one to 122 for six against spirited bowling by Pitcher and Hodgson. But Middlesex were rescued by unbeaten fifties from Johnson, whose previous first-class aggregate was nine in three innings, and Carr. Cambridge started brightly but lost their last nine wickets for 59; Weekes took five for the first time and conceded only 12 runs in 14.1 overs. He and Emburey then shared an unbroken partnership of 88 for Middlesex's third wicket, before Carr invited Cambridge to score 300 in four hours plus 20 overs. Although the target was never in sight, they seemed quite capable of saving the game at 201 for six, with Carroll batting soundly. But they folded against the spinners again. Carroll was last out, caught on the boundary to give Weekes his ninth wicket.

Close of play: First day, Cambridge University 5-1 (R. Q. Cake 1*); Second day, Middlesex 101-2 (J. E. Emburey 41*, P. N. Weekes 15*).

Middlesex

M. A. Roseberry b Hodgson	40	– (2) c Ratledge b Whittall	38
J. C. Pooley c Mann b Haste	13		
†K. R. Brown c Cake b Hodgson	61		
J. E. Emburey b Pitcher	2	– (3) not out	78
J. C. Harrison lbw b Pitcher	0	– (1) c Hodgson b Pitcher	4
M. A. Feltham c and b Hodgson	1		
R. L. Johnson not out	50		
P. N. Weekes c Hodgson b Haste	15	– (4) not out	39
*J. D. Carr not out	55		
B 5, l-b 8, w 1, n-b 6	20	L-b 4	4
1/22 2/95 3/106 4/112 5/119 6/122 7/151 (7 wkts dec.)	257	1/8 2/75 (2 wkts dec.)	163

K. J. Shine and C. W. Taylor did not bat.

Bowling: *First Innings*—Pitcher 19–7–33–2; Haste 19–3–63–2; Whittall 25–4–77–0; Bashforth 10–2–32–0; Hodgson 16.3–6–39–3. *Second Innings*—Pitcher 14–5–42–1; Haste 11–4–23–0; Bashforth 6–2–28–0; Whittall 19–8–41–1; Hodgson 6–0–25–0.

Cambridge University

G. W. Jones lbw b Taylor	4	– b Feltham	3
R. Q. Cake lbw b Weekes	40	– b Weekes	24
J. Ratledge b Emburey	23	– c Brown b Emburey	21
J. S. Hodgson b Emburey	0	– c Brown b Johnson	26
J. P. Carroll c Carr b Emburey	13	– c Carr b Weekes	90
R. D. Mann lbw b Weekes	8	– c Harrison b Weekes	13
N. J. Haste c Pooley b Weekes	11	– c Johnson b Weekes	3
*A. R. Whittall b Weekes	1	– (9) c Taylor b Emburey	1
C. M. Pitcher c Weekes b Taylor	9	– (8) c Harrison b Emburey	24
†F. J. Cooke not out	0	– c Roseberry b Emburey	0
M. C. Bashforth c Roseberry b Weekes	4	– not out	0
B 2, l-b 6	8	B 5, l-b 8, w 3	16
1/5 2/62 3/70 4/70 5/93 6/98 7/106 8/111 9/117	121	1/17 2/52 3/52 4/98 5/133 6/137 7/201 8/205 9/213	221

Bowling: *First Innings*—Shine 14–6–19–0; Taylor 17–6–29–2; Emburey 16–8–21–3; Feltham 4–0–16–0; Johnson 7–1–16–0; Weekes 14.1–7–12–5. *Second Innings*—Feltham 5–1–18–1; Shine 5–2–4–0; Weekes 30.4–10–83–4; Emburey 25–9–59–4; Taylor 8–2–14–0; Johnson 12–3–30–1.

Umpires: P. Adams and K. J. Lyons.

CAMBRIDGE UNIVERSITY v WORCESTERSHIRE

At Cambridge, May 7, 8, 9. Drawn. Toss: Worcestershire. First-class debut: M. A. T. Hall.

The first day was limited by rain to one session, in which D'Oliveira played a dominant innings of 61. Worcestershire batted on, allowing Haynes to complete an unbeaten hundred from 180 balls, with two sixes and eight fours, and he and Leatherdale added 115 for the fourth wicket. But Cambridge's batsmen put up a decent fight: Mann, promoted to open after Jones injured his back in the field, made a maiden fifty and Hodgson a career-best 41, and they edged past 200 despite being one man short. Worcestershire batted out the remainder of the match.

Close of play: First day, Worcestershire 115-2 (G. R. Haynes 13*, T. M. Moody 1*); Second day, Cambridge University 127-3 (J. S. Hodgson 11*, J. P. Carroll 7*).

Worcestershire

*T. S. Curtis c Hodgson b Whittall	25	– b Pitcher	28
D. B. D'Oliveira b Whittall	61	– b Pitcher	11
G. R. Haynes not out	102		
T. M. Moody c Mann b Haste	64		
D. A. Leatherdale not out	49		
P. J. Newport (did not bat)		– (3) c Cooke b Hodgson	32
S. R. Lampitt (did not bat)		– (4) not out	22
C. M. Tolley (did not bat)		– (5) not out	9
B 4, l-b 11, n-b 8	23	B 2, l-b 3, w 1	6
1/91 2/112 3/209	(3 wkts dec.) 324	1/15 2/53 3/89	(3 wkts dec.) 108

R. K. Illingworth, †T. Edwards and J. E. Brinkley did not bat.

Bowling: *First Innings*—Pitcher 17–3–55–0; Haste 18–1–93–1; Hodgson 23–5–68–0; Whittall 24.4–7–93–2. *Second Innings*—Pitcher 12–4–31–2; Hodgson 26–16–25–1; Haste 6–4–11–0; Whittall 8–2–27–0; Ratledge 3–0–7–0; Hall 2–0–2–0.

Cambridge University

R. D. Mann c Moody b Leatherdale	53	C. M. Pitcher c Moody b Lampitt	0
R. Q. Cake c Haynes b D'Oliveira	21	†F. J. Cooke c Edwards b Lampitt	2
J. Ratledge c Edwards b Leatherdale	18	G. W. Jones absent injured	
J. S. Hodgson c Haynes b Moody	41		
J. P. Carroll run out	21	B 4, l-b 16, w 1, n-b 8	29
M. A. T. Hall lbw b Brinkley	4		—
N. J. Haste run out	5	1/50 2/103 3/104 4/175 5/179	203
*A. R. Whittall not out	9	6/189 7/197 8/197 9/203	

Bowling: Newport 16–4–50–0; Tolley 12–6–22–0; Brinkley 10–1–22–1; Illingworth 31–12–43–0; D'Oliveira 12–5–18–1; Leatherdale 7–4–11–2; Moody 5–1–16–1; Lampitt 2.2–1–1–2.

Umpires: A. A. Jones and M. K. Reed.

†At Cambridge, May 10. Cambridge University won by four wickets. Toss: Cambridgeshire. Cambridgeshire 157 for nine (55 overs) (Saleem Mohammed 55, M. A. Burton 50 not out; M. C. Bashforth five for 19, E. J. How three for 47); Cambridge University 161 for six (54.4 overs) (D. E. Stanley 82).

†At Cambridge, May 11, 12, 13. MCC won by 33 runs. Toss: MCC. MCC 199 (J. Foster 30, A. M. Brown 37, G. Miller 44; A. R. Whittall three for 74, J. S. Hodgson three for 41) and 277 for six dec. (A. M. Brown 100 retired hurt, A. M. Bredin 34, K. P. T. Thomas 50 not out, D. P. Hughes 47 not out; J. Ratledge three for 46); Cambridge University 255 for six dec. (R. Q. Cake 179 not out) and 188 (R. Q. Cake 42, J. S. Hodgson 77; K. C. Williams four for 56).

CAMBRIDGE UNIVERSITY v LANCASHIRE

At Cambridge, May 14, 15, 16. Drawn. Toss: Lancashire. First-class debuts: D. E. Stanley; N. A. Derbyshire, J. M. Fielding.

Two former Cambridge captains batted aggressively for Lancashire but fell short of centuries. Atherton made 86 out of 131 and Crawley 81 out of 141. But Speak, who partnered both, advanced more cautiously to 102 from 268 balls, out of a total of 293. Lancashire promptly declared and Cambridge replied with their best batting of the term. Ratledge, who had played for the county's Second Eleven in 1993, joined Cake in adding 154 in 47 overs and Whittall was afforded the luxury of a declaration for the first time. Lancashire juggled their order and were reduced to 83 for five, but Yates led a recovery. A target of 268 in 65 overs was never an option for the University, though Cake celebrated his 21st birthday with his second seventy of the match.

Close of play: First day, Lancashire 185-1 (N. J. Speak 54*, J. P. Crawley 30*); Second day, Lancashire 25-1 (M. Watkinson 6*, W. K. Hegg 5*).

Lancashire

M. A. Atherton st Cooke b Hodgson	86		
N. J. Speak not out	102	– (7) c and b Pitcher	25
J. P. Crawley c Pitcher b Whittall	81	– (6) c Haste b Hodgson	1
G. D. Lloyd not out	3	– (1) c Cooke b Pitcher	12
*M. Watkinson (did not bat)		– (2) c Cake b Haste	11
†W. K. Hegg (did not bat)		– (3) b Hodgson	28
I. D. Austin (did not bat)		– (4) c Hodgson b Whittall	27
G. Yates (did not bat)		– (5) not out	53
J. M. Fielding (did not bat)		– (8) not out	27
B 1, l-b 6, n-b 14	21	B 8, l-b 8, w 1	17
	—		—
1/131 2/272 (2 wkts dec.)	293	1/19 2/33 3/82 4/82 5/83 6/160 (6 wkts dec.)	201

J. E. R. Gallian and N. A. Derbyshire did not bat.

Bowling: *First Innings*—Pitcher 21–3–81–0; Haste 17–2–71–0; Whittall 27.5–5–95–1; Hodgson 19–11–39–1. *Second Innings*—Pitcher 16–5–46–2; Haste 14.3–2–62–1; Whittall 10–0–40–1; Hodgson 11–2–37–2.

Cambridge University

R. D. Mann c Hegg b Derbyshire	4	– c Hegg b Yates	17
R. Q. Cake c Lloyd b Yates	77	– not out	70
J. Ratledge c Hegg b Watkinson	79	– c Watkinson b Fielding	6
J. S. Hodgson c Atherton b Yates	34	– not out	12
J. P. Carroll st Hegg b Fielding	14		
M. A. T. Hall run out	1		
D. E. Stanley not out	0		
B 2, l-b 7, w 1, n-b 8	18	B 2, l-b 5, n-b 6	13
1/4 2/158 3/189 4/222 5/226 6/227 (6 wkts dec.)	227	1/49 2/64 (2 wkts)	118

*A. R. Whittall, C. M. Pitcher, N. J. Haste and †F. J. Cooke did not bat.

Bowling: *First Innings*—Derbyshire 16–3–48–1; Watkinson 17–2–43–1; Austin 10–3–27–0; Fielding 10.4–3–38–1; Yates 13–2–49–2; Gallian 4–0–13–0. *Second Innings*—Derbyshire 7–1–13–0; Watkinson 14–4–27–0; Yates 13–3–34–1; Austin 5–1–12–0; Fielding 9–3–15–1; Atherton 7–2–10–0.

Umpires: N. T. Plews and G. Sharp.

†At Cambridge, May 22. Cambridge University v Cryptics. Abandoned.

†At Cambridge, June 4. Drawn. Toss: Quidnuncs. Cambridge University 49 for one v Quidnuncs.

†At Cambridge, June 5. Drawn. Toss: Cambridge University. Cambridge University 185 for eight dec. (G. W. Jones 82); Free Foresters 161 for nine (C. J. C. Rowe 41, R. Mason 45; J. S. Hodgson five for 37).

†At Arundel, June 9. Lavinia, Duchess of Norfolk's XI won by eight wickets. Toss: Cambridge University. Cambridge University 196 for six dec. (G. W. Jones 32, J. Ratledge 114; D. R. Law three for 35); Lavinia, Duchess of Norfolk's XI 200 for two (J. Hardy 30, S. Savant 38 not out, C. K. Bullen 104 not out).

†At Arundel, June 14. Club Cricket Conference won by nine wickets. Toss: Cambridge University. Cambridge University 101 (43.1 overs); Club Cricket Conference 105 for one (25.4 overs) (B. Debenham 48 not out, B. Moore 34).

CAMBRIDGE UNIVERSITY v GLAMORGAN

At Cambridge, June 11, 12, 13. Drawn. Toss: Glamorgan. First-class debut: A. D. Shaw.

The batsmen were on top for most of the game. James and Dale kicked off with 171 from 57 overs: Dale reached his century in three hours, but James, back at his former university, took almost five. He had already scored 150 against Oxford in April. After Glamorgan declared at 307 for two, Cake survived two chances to reach his first hundred for

Cambridge with a six; he also hit 11 fours in four and a half hours. With Carroll helping him to add 100 and Stanley 97, the University were able to declare at 244. Roseberry narrowly failed to become the fourth century-maker of the match as Glamorgan set Cambridge 261 in 140 minutes and 20 overs. Cake completed his fourth successive score of 50 or more as they batted out time.

Close of play: First day, Cambridge University 19-1 (G. W. Jones 9*); Second day, Glamorgan 29-0 (A. Roseberry 16*, P. A. Cottey 12*).

Glamorgan

S. P. James not out	138		
A. Dale c Cooke b Whittall	109		
D. L. Hemp b Haste	48	– (5) not out	6
P. A. Cottey not out	5	– (2) b Haste	59
A. Roseberry (did not bat)		– (1) b Haste	94
A. J. Dalton (did not bat)		– (3) c Cooke b Haste	1
R. P. Lefebvre (did not bat)		– (4) c Stanley b Haste	32
B 2, l-b 5	7	L-b 3, w 2	5
1/171 2/282 (2 wkts dec.)	307	1/105 2/109 3/178 4/197 (4 wkts dec.)	197

R. D. B. Croft, †A. D. Shaw, S. Bastien and *S. R. Barwick did not bat.

Bowling: *First Innings*—Pitcher 20–8–39–0; Haste 18.3–1–74–1; Whittall 28–5–106–1; Hodgson 21–2–81–0. *Second Innings*—Haste 15.4–1–69–4; Pitcher 9–2–41–0; Whittall 9–1–36–0; Hodgson 15–1–48–0.

Cambridge University

G. W. Jones c Shaw b Lefebvre	9	– c and b Croft	22
R. D. Mann run out	8	– b Lefebvre	0
R. Q. Cake c Bastien b Croft	107	– (4) c Dale b Croft	66
J. P. Carroll run out	48	– (5) not out	3
J. Ratledge lbw b Dale	0	– (3) c James b Bastien	5
J. S. Hodgson c James b Dale	0		
D. E. Stanley c Hemp b Cottey	48		
N. J. Haste run out	2		
C. M. Pitcher not out	11		
B 3, l-b 7, w 1	11	B 4, l-b 4	8
1/19 2/20 3/120 4/121 5/121 6/218 7/232 8/244 (8 wkts dec.)	244	1/0 2/5 3/100 4/104 (4 wkts)	104

*A. R. Whittall and †F. J. Cooke did not bat.

Bowling: *First Innings*—Bastien 12–4–25–0; Lefebvre 22–7–49–1; Croft 37–11–100–1; Barwick 22–11–30–0; Dale 10–4–14–2; Cottey 6–1–16–1. *Second Innings*—Bastien 8–6–3–1; Lefebvre 7–3–9–1; Dale 4–2–6–0; Barwick 15–10–16–0; Croft 14.2–5–47–2; Hemp 3–0–15–0.

Umpires: J. C. Balderstone and B. Dudleston.

CAMBRIDGE UNIVERSITY v ESSEX

At Cambridge, June 15, 16, 17. Drawn. Toss: Cambridge University.

Essex ran up 323 at four an over on the first day, with Knight making his highest score yet, 150 from 216 balls with 22 fours in a little under five hours. In reply, Jones scored 74, his maiden half-century, but only Cake offered much support; the other nine batsmen made 42 between them and Cousins took a career-best six for 35. But a Cambridge bowler, the off-spinner Hodgson, tied down Essex in their second innings, giving away only 14 runs in

19 overs, 12 of which were maidens. He also took four wickets, including Knight for eight. Garnham retired with a back injury and played no further part, but Stephenson took three fine slip catches after setting the University a target of 275 in 200 minutes plus 20 overs. They easily saved the game.

Close of play: First day, Cambridge University 19-0 (G. W. Jones 7*, R. D. Mann 3*); Second day, Essex 79-1 (N. Shahid 32*, M. A. Garnham 0*).

Essex

N. V. Knight c Carroll b Hodgson	150	(5) c and b Hodgson	8
*J. P. Stephenson c Cooke b Pitcher	10	(6) not out	13
†M. A. Garnham lbw b Hodgson	44	retired hurt	1
N. Hussain c Cooke b Pitcher	62		
N. Shahid not out	30	(2) c Pitcher b Hodgson	33
J. J. B. Lewis not out	14	(1) c Pitcher b Hodgson	42
T. D. Topley (did not bat)		(4) c Whittall b Hodgson	2
R. M. Pearson (did not bat)		(7) c Haste b Whittall	20
S. J. W. Andrew (did not bat)		(8) lbw b Whittall	8
B 8, l-b 3, n-b 2	13	B 5	5
1/39 2/113 3/221 4/301 (4 wkts dec.)	323	1/68 2/81 3/90 4/95 5/120 6/132 (6 wkts dec.)	132

D. M. Cousins and J. H. Childs did not bat.

In the second innings M. A. Garnham retired hurt at 81.

Bowling: *First Innings*—Pitcher 19–2–86–2; Haste 22–8–50–0; Whittall 19–2–101–0; Hodgson 21–5–75–2. *Second Innings*—Pitcher 14–3–54–0; Haste 6–2–25–0; Hodgson 19–12–14–4; Whittall 9–3–34–2.

Cambridge University

G. W. Jones lbw b Shahid	74	b Andrew	9
R. D. Mann c Garnham b Cousins	10	c Stephenson b Pearson	15
J. Ratledge st Garnham b Childs	11	c Stephenson b Topley	21
R. Q. Cake c Garnham b Cousins	42	c Stephenson b Childs	41
J. P. Carroll c Stephenson b Pearson	0	(7) not out	6
J. S. Hodgson lbw b Cousins	8	(5) lbw b Cousins	23
D. E. Stanley lbw b Cousins	6	(6) not out	9
N. J. Haste lbw b Andrew	4		
C. M. Pitcher b Cousins	0		
†F. J. Cooke not out	2		
*A. R. Whittall lbw b Cousins	1		
L-b 8, w 1, n-b 14	23	B 7, l-b 8, w 1, n-b 4	20
1/39 2/70 3/137 4/140 5/166 6/167 7/178 8/178 9/180	181	1/17 2/49 3/57 4/119 5/129 (5 wkts)	144

Bowling: *First Innings*—Andrew 14–4–29–1; Cousins 18.2–3–35–6; Childs 14–5–20–1; Topley 7–1–25–0; Pearson 14–4–39–1; Shahid 12–4–25–1. *Second Innings*—Andrew 13–5–22–1; Cousins 14–5–26–1; Pearson 13–3–42–1; Topley 9–2–22–1; Childs 11–4–16–1; Hussain 1–0–1–0.

Umpires: J. D. Bond and R. A. White.

†At Aldershot, June 18, 19, 20. Combined Services won by five wickets. Toss: Cambridge University. Cambridge University 285 for seven dec. (R. D. Mann 79, R. Q. Cake 103 not out; AEM J. Mann three for 76) and 199 for four dec. (J. Ratledge 97, J. S. Hodgson 32); Combined Services 179 (SAC R. Beeston 53, Capt. P. S. Germain 41; N. J. Haste three for 39, A. R. Whittall five for 68) and 308 for five (Capt. R. J. Greatorex 75, Lt C. H. G. St George 34, Capt. D. R. E. O'Kelly 39, Sgt N. Palmer 48, Capt. P. S. Germain 55 not out, Lt P. H. G. Moore 33 not out; J. S. Hodgson three for 84).

At Bristol, June 25, 26, 27. CAMBRIDGE UNIVERSITY lost to GLOUCESTERSHIRE by 313 runs.

THE UNIVERSITY MATCH, 1994

OXFORD UNIVERSITY v CAMBRIDGE UNIVERSITY

At Lord's, June 29, 30, July 1. Drawn. Toss: Oxford University.

When Cambridge followed on, 200 behind, and were reduced to 27 for four before lunch on the final day, this match looked like a replay of Oxford's triumph the previous year. But the Cambridge captain, Whittall, held out for a draw and almost reached a maiden hundred in the process. Oxford had to be satisfied with centuries for Gupte and Hollins and a ten-wicket return for Yeabsley. On the first morning, Oxford's openers put on 104 before Macmillan was out to the penultimate ball. The rest of the day belonged to Gupte and Hollins, who added 231 for the fourth wicket by the close, including Gupte's second first-class century and Hollins's first. Next morning, they took the stand to 250 and the score to 398 for three, but six wickets fell in 11 overs in the chase for quick runs. Although Ecclestone was limited to four overs by a back injury, Yeabsley soon had Cambridge on the run. Only the last-wicket pair, Pitcher and Cooke, dragged the total past 200. In fact they reached 253, their biggest total of the season, before Pitcher gave Yeabsley his sixth wicket at the start of the final day. Nothing seemed to have changed in the second innings, as Yeabsley swept up another three wickets in 14 balls, including Ratledge, suffering from colitis, for a king pair. But as the bowlers tired – the leg-spinner, Trimby, was further handicapped by swollen feet – Hodgson dug in for a three-hour fifty, while Whittall went on the offensive. He hit 13 fours and two sixes in two and a half hours, and was still unbeaten when stumps were drawn.

Close of play: First day, Oxford University 379-3 (C. M. Gupte 116*, C. J. Hollins 119*); Second day, Cambridge University 252-9 (C. M. Pitcher 43*, F. J. Cooke 33*).

Oxford University

*R. R. Montgomerie (*Rugby and Worcester*) lbw b Whittall . 33
G. I. Macmillan (*Charterhouse, Soton U. and Keble*) c Whittall b Hodgson . 69
C. M. Gupte (*John Lyon and Pembroke*) run out . 122
S. C. Ecclestone (*Bryanston, Durham U. and Keble*) c Whittall b Haste . 13
C. J. Hollins (*Tonbridge, Durham U. and Keble*) c Hodgson b Haste . 131
H. S. Malik (*KCS, Wimbledon and Keble*) c Cake b Pitcher . 13
R. S. Yeabsley (*Haberdashers' Aske's, Elstree and Keble*) run out . 1
N. F. C. Martin (*King Edward's, Birmingham and Keble*) lbw b Pitcher . 7
†C. J. Townsend (*Dean Close and Brasenose*) not out . 18
P. W. Trimby (*Shrewsbury and Worcester*) c Stanley b Pitcher . 4
A. W. Maclay (*Winchester and St Edmund Hall*) not out . 6

B 3, l-b 27, w 6 36

1/104 2/118 3/148 4/398 5/399 6/405 7/418 8/420 9/436 (9 wkts dec.) 453

Bowling: Pitcher 20–2–95–3; Haste 23–2–96–2; Whittall 33–6–123–1; Hodgson 32–7–85–1; Ratledge 6–0–24–0.

Cambridge University

Batsman	First innings		Second innings	
G. W. Jones (*King's, Chester and Gonville & Caius*)	c Martin b Yeabsley	21	lbw b Yeabsley	2
R. D. Mann (*Wellingborough and St John's*)	c Hollins b Yeabsley	31	c Hollins b Yeabsley	7
J. Ratledge (*Bolton GS and St John's*)	c Macmillan b Yeabsley	0	lbw b Yeabsley	0
R. Q. Cake (*KCS, Wimbledon and St John's*)	c Macmillan b Maclay	27	c Gupte b Hollins	27
J. P. Carroll (*Rendcomb and Homerton*)	lbw b Trimby	2	b Ecclestone	5
J. S. Hodgson (*Wellington C., Durham U. and Hughes Hall*)	c Townsend b Yeabsley	29	b Yeabsley	54
D. E. Stanley (*Abingdon and Gonville & Caius*)	lbw b Maclay	0	b Macmillan	9
*A. R. Whittall (*Falcon, Zimbabwe and Trinity*)	c Hollins b Maclay	40	not out	91
N. J. Haste (*Wellingborough and Pembroke*)	c Macmillan b Yeabsley	10	c Trimby b Ecclestone	22
C. M. Pitcher (*St Edward's, Oxford and Selwyn*)	c Macmillan b Yeabsley	43	not out	0
†F. J. Cooke (*Millfield and Fitzwilliam*)	not out	34		
	L-b 8, n-b 8	16	B 7, l-b 10, w 1, n-b 8	26
1/44 2/44 3/69 4/80 5/94 6/94 7/140 8/171 9/186		253	1/14 2/14 3/21 4/27 5/83 6/105 7/170 8/229	(8 wkts) 243

Bowling: *First Innings*—Ecclestone 4–0–23–0; Yeabsley 22.5–7–54–6; Trimby 30–5–91–1; Maclay 13–2–30–3; Hollins 8–1–34–0; Macmillan 5–2–9–0; Malik 1–0–4–0. *Second Innings*—Yeabsley 21–7–50–4; Maclay 11–2–22–0; Hollins 24–5–64–1; Ecclestone 18–6–31–2; Trimby 13–3–37–0; Macmillan 10–4–22–1.

Umpires: J. W. Holder and B. Leadbeater.

OXFORD v CAMBRIDGE, NOTES

Since the war Cambridge have won nine times (1949, 1953, 1957, 1958, 1972, 1979, 1982, 1986 and 1992) and Oxford eight (1946, 1948, 1951, 1959, 1966, 1976, 1984 and 1993). All other matches have been drawn; the 1988 fixture was abandoned without a ball being bowled.

Ninety-eight three-figure innings have been played in the University matches. For the fullest lists see the 1940 and 1993 *Wisdens*. There have been three double-centuries for Cambridge (211 by G. Goonesena in 1957, 201 by A. Ratcliffe in 1931 and 200 by Majid Khan in 1970) and two for Oxford (238* by Nawab of Pataudi, sen. in 1931 and 201* by M. J. K. Smith in 1954). Ratcliffe's score was a record for the match for only one day, before being beaten by Pataudi's. M. J. K. Smith and R. J. Boyd-Moss (Cambridge) are the only players to score three hundreds.

The highest totals in the fixture are 503 in 1900, 457 in 1947, 453 for eight in 1931 and 453 for nine in 1994, all by Oxford. Cambridge's highest is 432 for nine in 1936. The lowest totals are 32 by Oxford in 1878 and 39 by Cambridge in 1858.

F. C. Cobden, in the Oxford v Cambridge match in 1870, performed the hat-trick by taking the last three wickets and won an extraordinary game for Cambridge by two runs. The feat is without parallel in first-class cricket. Other hat-tricks, all for Cambridge, have been credited to A. G. Steel (1879), P. H. Morton (1880), J. F. Ireland (1911) and R. G. H. Lowe (1926). S. E. Butler, in the 1871 match, took all the wickets in the Cambridge first innings.

D. W. Jarrett (Oxford 1975, Cambridge 1976), S. M. Wookey (Cambridge 1975-76, Oxford 1978) and G. Pathmanathan (Oxford 1975-78, Cambridge 1983) are alone in gaining cricket Blues for both Universities.

A full list of Blues from 1837 may be found in Wisdens *published between 1923 and 1939. The lists thereafter were curtailed:* Wisdens *from 1948 to 1972 list Blues since 1880; from 1973 to 1983 since 1919; from 1984 to 1992 since 1946.*

THE COMMERCIAL UNION UAU CHAMPIONSHIP, 1994

By GRENVILLE HOLLAND

In June 1994, the curtain came down on UAU cricket. The Universities Athletic Union came into being shortly after the First World War to provide sport for a handful of provincial universities. As their number grew, so did the UAU, but, when the polytechnics took on university status in the early 1990s, that original handful had become a prodigious family. To meet this increased demand, in 1994 the UAU merged with the British Universities Sports Federation (BUSF) to form a single national athletic union, the British Universities Sports Association (BUSA). From 1995, all university cricket – apart from Oxford and Cambridge – will be administered by BUSA.

The new organisation inherited a competition in which too many universities faced too many fixtures in the short summer term, which made inappropriate use of the limited funds available and which offered some universities little genuinely competitive cricket until its final stages. BUSA's response was swift and welcome. In the autumn, they canvassed opinion and recommended that, from 1995, "First Elevens will only be accepted for the senior championship if their institution is entering two cricket teams or if the performance of their single team in last year's championship merits a single slot." This proposed innovation was expected to restrict the senior championship to around 65 teams, reducing to 32 in the first knockout round.

The 1994 season, beginning in April, thus saw the last great university stampede. By June 12, there were eight survivors: in the northern half, Durham, Edinburgh, Hull and Newcastle, and in the southern half, Brighton, Kent, Oxford and Swansea. Durham fell at the very first and very last hurdles; in between they won everything with ease. They had not lost a league match at the Racecourse ground for over 30 years, but Newcastle deservedly demolished that record on April 27. They notched up 239 for seven in 60 overs and Durham were 32 runs short when their last wicket fell. Thereafter, Durham swept all before them in the north-eastern division. Against Sunderland, they piled up 429, with 129 from Brett Hames and 94 from Jim Williams, and won by 310. The captain, Alex Richards, scored successive centuries to inspire victories over Northumbria and Teesside.

Newcastle also won their remaining group games to head the division, and both qualified for the knockout stage. There, Durham passed straight through to the second round when Bedford had to scratch. Their first real opponents were Nottingham Trent, who had beaten Loughborough by seven wickets, through an undefeated 111 by Glendenning, a week earlier. But they succumbed by 152 runs against Durham, for whom Jeremy Snape batted superbly, making 150 out of 318. In the quarter-final, Newcastle returned to the Racecourse, hoping to repeat their league victory. This time, however, Richards scored 148 not out in Durham's 343 for seven, before James Bovill's hostile pace took the heart out of Newcastle; they were all out for 59, with Bovill claiming five for 40.

Kent continued their recent run of success, beating Greenwich and Sussex in the south-east league. Their first knockout opponents were Royal Holloway and Bedford, who carefully built a total of 152 for four; Kent struggled to overtake them, losing seven wickets, and owed much to 68 from the experienced Rob Archer. West London Institute proved less difficult after Joe Owen took seven for 34 to dismiss them for 134. A walkover against East Anglia took Kent into a quarter-final with Brighton, who made a spectacular rise in 1994. In the southern league, they overwhelmed Surrey by 154 runs, thanks to 161 not out from Glyn Treagus, and Ian Duggan helped them to another comfortable win over Sussex. In the second knockout round, Brighton managed only 112 on a poor pitch, but bowled out Kingston for 64, with six for 24 from Jason Whitiker. Next, they coasted to a nine-wicket win over Reading. Their quarter-final with Kent went to the last over. Brighton reached 243 for four in 60 overs, with Treagus falling for 99; Kent required 100 from their last ten and scraped through to their fourth successive semi-final with one ball and two wickets to spare. Brighton's left-arm spinner Neil Garrett took seven for 62.

Kent's semi-final opponents were Swansea, the 1988 champions, who had easily led the South Wales division. They defeated both Cardiff Institute and Cardiff University by seven wickets. Against Glamorgan University, their captain, James Langworth, and David Bowen shared an opening stand of 187 in 30 overs, out of 301 for six, before Scott Moffat, with six for 26, completed a 180-run win. In the knockout, visitors Southampton lost by 181; they were dismissed for 84, with Andy Law returning five for 14 in his 12 overs, after Gul Khan scored 130 not out. Bristol offered a little more resistance, scoring 164, but Swansea sailed through to the last eight by five wickets.

Oxford University, like Cambridge, had always declined to be distracted from their first-class programme by the UAU championship. But in 1994, Oxford broke with tradition, to provide their Second Eleven with some competitive cricket. They won their south Midlands group and beat Exeter away and Keele at home in the knockout. But their real test came when they travelled to meet Swansea. Half-centuries from Moffat and Bowen set them a target of 239 and they were all out 46 runs short; Law and Morris bowled skilfully for four wickets apiece.

Edinburgh became the first of the Scottish universities – who did not enter until 1993 – to reach the last four, beating Liverpool and Hull in the knockout rounds. But they arrived an hour late for the semi-final and forfeited the toss. Durham made 248 on an uneven pitch, with Snape contributing 67 and then following up with five for 44. Edinburgh's total of 120 leant heavily on wicket-keeper Rigby. Meanwhile, at Southgate, Kent made a determined attempt on a target of 233, with Joe Grigg batting forcefully for 69, but Law took six for 71 and they were dismissed with two overs to spare.

SEMI-FINALS

At Liverpool, June 20. Durham won by 128 runs. Toss: Durham. Durham 248 for five (55 overs) (M. T. E. Peirce 55, J. N. Snape 67); Edinburgh 120 (49 overs) (J. Rigby 68 not out; J. N. Snape five for 44).

At Southgate, June 20. Swansea won by 23 runs. Toss: Swansea. Swansea 232 (60 overs) (D. M. Bowen 40, S. P. Moffat 60); Kent 209 (58 overs) (J. Grigg 69; A. R. Law six for 71).

FINAL

DURHAM v SWANSEA

At Luton Town CC, June 27. Swansea won by 67 runs. Toss: Swansea.

Durham's hopes of a fifth consecutive UAU title were dashed when their middle order succumbed to the medium-pacer, Nick Davies. They started well after Langworth elected to bat on a fast, true pitch offering some bounce. But he struggled against Richard Ballinger and Bovill and, when his painstaking innings ended, Swansea were 23 for two from 15 overs. That was 47 for three when the frustrated Moffat mistimed a pull to mid-off. If the slips had held some easy chances, Swansea's situation would have become almost irretrievable. Durham retained the initiative when Jerome Connor and Andrew Varley – caught by the diving Snape at gully – fell either side of lunch. But Alastair Richardson tired and grew wayward, Robin Jones's off-spin was too gentle and Ballinger and Bovill never returned. Joining forces at 93 for five, Grant Humphries and Duncan Verry nearly doubled Swansea's score in less than 20 overs. Although a target of 203 was not insurmountable, Durham began anxiously, losing Toby Peirce and Snape to Davies while reaching 23. Williams and Richards carefully restored equilibrium but, in the first two overs after tea, Richards swept uppishly to fine leg and Williams drove to mid-off. Davies immediately returned and, sustained by excellent fielding, removed four batsmen in rapid succession. Durham collapsed for 135, a swift and unexpected demise; Swansea had taken the final UAU title in style.

Swansea

*†J. M. Langworth b Ballinger	6
D. M. Bowen b Bovill	4
S. P. Moffat c Bovill b Richardson	19
J. M. Connor b Richardson	31
G. M. Humphries c Bovill b Jones	61
A. E. Varley c Snape b Richardson	1
D. J. Verry not out	53
N. M. Davies b Snape	0
M. T. Madurasinghe not out	7
B 1, l-b 7, w 1, n-b 11	20
1/5 2/23 3/47 4/90 5/93 6/180 7/180 (7 wkts, 60 overs)	202

A. R. Law and P. J. Morris did not bat.

Bowling: Ballinger 10–3–13–1; Bovill 11–3–27–1; Snape 20–3–58–1; Richardson 12–1–58–3; Jones 7–0–38–1.

Durham

J. R. A. Williams c Madurasinghe b Morris	55
M. T. E. Peirce lbw b Davies	6
J. N. Snape c Connor b Davies	2
*A. C. Richards c Morris b Moffat	22
P. J. Deakin c Langworth b Davies	15
R. O. Jones c Langworth b Davies	12
P. A. Bhatia c Langworth b Davies	0
†T. E. Smethers c Madurasinghe b Moffat	12
R. J. Ballinger c and b Davies	0
J. N. B. Bovill c Davies b Law	4
A. W. Richardson not out	4
L-b 3	3
1/11 2/23 3/88 4/92 5/110 6/114 7/117 8/117 9/127 (51.2 overs)	135

Bowling: Davies 13–3–27–6; Law 12–2–29–1; Connor 4–0–20–0; Moffat 15.2–4–33–2; Morris 7–0–23–1.

Umpires: K. Hopley and C. Puckett.

WINNERS 1927-94

1927	Manchester	1955	Birmingham	1975	Loughborough Colls.
1928	Manchester	1956	Null and void	1976	Loughborough
1929	Nottingham	1957	Loughborough Colls.	1977	Durham
1930	Sheffield	1958	Null and void	1978	Manchester
1931	Liverpool	1959	Liverpool	1979	Manchester
1932	Manchester	1960	Loughborough Colls.	1980	Exeter
1933	Manchester	1961	Loughborough Colls.	1981	Durham
1934	Leeds	1962	Manchester	1982	Exeter
1935	Sheffield	1963	Loughborough Colls.	1983	Exeter
1936	Sheffield	1964	Loughborough Colls.	1984	Bristol
1937	Nottingham	1965	Hull	1985	Birmingham
1938	Durham	1966	Newcastle / Southampton	1986	Durham
1939	Durham			1987	Durham
1946	Not completed	1967	Manchester	1988	Swansea
1947	Sheffield	1968	Southampton	1989	Loughborough
1948	Leeds	1969	Southampton	1990	Durham
1949	Leeds	1970	Southampton	1991	Durham
1950	Manchester	1971	Loughborough Colls.	1992	Durham
1951	Manchester	1972	Durham	1993	Durham
1952	Loughborough Colls.	1973	Leicester / Loughborough Colls.	1994	Swansea
1953	Durham				
1954	Manchester	1974	Durham		

UMPIRES FOR 1995

FIRST-CLASS UMPIRES

J. C. Balderstone, H. D. Bird, J. D. Bond, G. I. Burgess, D. J. Constant, B. Dudleston, J. H. Hampshire, J. H. Harris, J. W. Holder, V. A. Holder, T. E. Jesty, A. A. Jones, R. Julian, M. J. Kitchen, B. Leadbeater, K. J. Lyons, B. J. Meyer, K. E. Palmer, R. Palmer, N. T. Plews, G. Sharp, D. R. Shepherd, R. A. White, A. G. T. Whitehead, P. B. Wight and P. Willey. *Reserves:* P. Adams, A. Clarkson, M. J. Harris, M. K. Reed and J. F. Steele.

MINOR COUNTIES UMPIRES

P. Adams, K. Bray, P. Brown, D. L. Burden, R. K. Curtis, D. J. Halfyard, M. A. Johnson, B. Knight, S. W. Kuhlmann, G. I. McLean, M. P. Moran, D. Norton, C. T. Puckett, G. P. Randall-Johnson, J. G. Reed, M. K. Reed, K. S. Shenton, C. Smith, C. T. Spencer, G. A. Stickley, C. Stone, J. M. Tythcott, G. Williams, T. G. Wilson and R. Wood. *Reserves:* A. R. Bundy, A. Carter, S. P. Chitty, A. R. Clark, K. Coburn, J. A. Gurney, A. J. Hardy, C. S. Kelly, P. W. Kingston-Davey, R. E. Lawson, D. Lea, G. Lowden, P. R. Mitchell, G. B. Smith, M. D. Smith, W. E. Smith, K. G. Sutherland, T. J. White, B. H. Willey and N. J. Williams.

OTHER FIRST-CLASS MATCH, 1994

SCOTLAND v IRELAND

At Hamilton Crescent, Glasgow, June 11, 12, 13. Drawn. Toss: Ireland. First-class debuts: J. G. Williamson; G. Cooke, R. B. Millar.

Only 13 wickets fell over three days on a superb Hamilton Crescent pitch, and a draw was almost pre-ordained. Scotland made little attempt to pursue 319 in 63 overs after losing Philip and Patterson early and the game was called off during the final hour. Warke had celebrated his 92nd Irish cap – a record – with an opening stand of 103 with Rea, and Smyth contributed 70, enabling Ireland to declare at 316 after 100 overs. But Storie and Patterson scored centuries as they put on 188 for Scotland's second wicket before declaring 37 behind. Ireland continued to score steadily, with both Lewis and Harrison making hundreds. Harrison's, which included 14 fours and two sixes, was his first for his country and their unbroken partnership of 224 equalled Ireland's best for any wicket. The final day was also remarkable for the spectacle of Philip bowling slow left-arm lobs.

Close of play: First day, Scotland 29-0 (I. L. Philip 18*, A. C. Storie 8*); Second day, Ireland 60-3 (D. A. Lewis 9*, G. D. Harrison 1*).

Ireland

S. J. S. Warke c Philip b Sheridan	60	– c Orr b Richardson 13
M. P. Rea run out	49	– b Sheridan 27
S. G. Smyth c Patterson b Hamilton	70	
*D. A. Lewis lbw b Storie	39	– (3) not out 113
N. G. Doak not out	27	– (4) b Richardson 4
G. D. Harrison c Philip b Govan	43	– (5) not out 105
S. Graham not out	2	
B 5, l-b 9, w 2, n-b 10	26	B 2, l-b 5, w 2, n-b 10 19
1/103 2/138 3/216 4/237 5/301 (5 wkts dec.)	316	1/35 2/49 3/57 (3 wkts dec.) 281

†R. B. Millar, E. R. Moore, C. J. Hoey and G. Cooke did not bat.

Bowling: *First Innings*—Hamilton 20–2–70–1; Richardson 14–2–53–0; Williamson 18–4–38–0; Govan 15–3–57–1; Sheridan 25–7–62–1; Storie 8–2–22–1. *Second Innings*—Hamilton 13–5–24–0; Richardson 10–1–41–2; Williamson 9–1–39–0; Sheridan 24–12–34–1; Govan 18–3–80–0; Storie 4–0–9–0; Philip 5–0–47–0.

Scotland

I. L. Philip c Millar b Cooke	22	– c Doak b Cooke 10
*A. C. Storie not out	102	– not out 64
B. M. W. Patterson c Millar b Lewis	114	– b Graham 22
G. B. J. McGurk not out	11	– run out 34
G. Salmond (did not bat)		– not out 28
B 5, l-b 1, w 10, n-b 14	30	L-b 2, w 1, n-b 8 11
1/44 2/232 (2 wkts dec.)	279	1/19 2/63 3/130 (3 wkts) 169

†D. A. Orr, J. G. Williamson, J. W. Govan, K. L. P. Sheridan, G. M. Hamilton and M. S. Richardson did not bat.

Bowling: *First Innings*—Moore 21.1–4–67–0; Cooke 15–5–39–1; Hoey 13–0–47–0; Lewis 6–1–27–1; Graham 14–2–35–0; Harrison 16–2–45–0; Warke 5–1–13–0. *Second Innings*—Moore 13–2–48–0; Cooke 8–1–26–1; Graham 5–1–8–1; Harrison 11–2–39–0; Hoey 11–2–32–0; Smyth 1–0–14–0.

Umpires: J. Breslin and L. A. Redford.

MCC MATCHES IN 1994

A charming ceremony took place during England's tour of the West Indies in early 1994. On a bleached, bone-hard ground in a Barbadian village, where many West Indian Test players learned their cricket, the President of MCC, Dennis Silk, formally challenged Holder's Hill CC to a match. Thus, in September, Holder's Hill, managed by Sir Garfield Sobers and captained by Desmond Haynes, became the first overseas village team to play at Lord's.

In a Caribbean carnival atmosphere, enhanced by steel bands and rum punch, MCC elected to bat. Mike Roseberry, with an aggressive 70, provided the backbone of the innings, while a final flourish from Peter Moores and Phillip DeFreitas enabled the club to reach 220 from their 50 overs. Openers Philo Wallace and Adrian Griffith set about the chase with some delightful strokes all round the wicket, raising 82 before they were parted. But, after that, Holder's Hill fell away in the face of some brilliant seam bowling by John Stephenson, then with Essex, who earned the match award for his five for 45. MCC won by 35 runs.

There was an exciting match in July at Dean Park in Bournemouth – the ground abandoned by Hampshire after 1992 – when MCC lost to Dorset by three wickets in the final over. Paul Romaines scored a magnificent unbeaten 153 and MCC declared at 240 for six. But Dorset paced their reply perfectly, Giles Reynolds leading them to victory with a well-struck 97.

MCC played a record 220 schools during the season, a pleasing result of their policy of encouraging schools cricket. One of the highlights was the appearance of West Indian umpire Steve Bucknor, who stood in the club's tied game with Wellington College, on a weekend off between Tests in June. He then volunteered to stand in an Under-14 six-a-side house match.

Of their 343 scheduled games against all teams, MCC won 127, lost 48, drew 129 and tied two, with 37 games abandoned. – John Jameson.

Note: Matches in this section were not first-class.

At Lord's, May 4. MCC Young Cricketers won by four wickets. Toss: MCC. MCC 172 for three dec. (J. E. M. Nicolson 78, J. R. Wood 51 not out); MCC Young Cricketers 175 for six (N. Pratt 64; D. A. Graveney three for 29).

At Cambridge, May 11, 12, 13. MCC beat CAMBRIDGE UNIVERSITY by 33 runs (See The Universities in 1994).

At Shenley Park, May 17. Hertfordshire v MCC. Abandoned.

At Gidea Park & Romford CC, May 18. Club Cricket Conference v MCC. Abandoned.

At Wormsley, May 29. Drawn. Toss: MCC. MCC 210 for five dec. (L. Potter 88, C. K. Bullen 53, R. D. V. Knight 42 not out); J. Paul Getty's XI 208 for nine (M. J. Church 49, S. D. Udal 42; L. Potter three for 31).

At Beaconsfield CC, June 7. Drawn. Toss: MCC. MCC 229 for three dec. (M. E. Gear 87, R. P. Merriman 100 not out); National Association of Young Cricketers 181 for seven (P. G. Hudson 52, D. Taylor 78; L. Potter four for 48).

At Oxford, June 7, 8, 9. MCC lost to OXFORD UNIVERSITY by six wickets (See The Universities in 1994).

At Durham, June 13, 14. Drawn. Toss: MCC. MCC 228 for seven dec. (P. W. Romaines 33, J. F. Venter 37; A. W. Richardson three for 43, P. J. Deakin three for 53) and 254 for seven dec. (P. W. Romaines 102, C. F. B. P. Rudd 37 not out; J. N. Snape three for 52); Durham University 233 for seven dec. (M. T. E. Peirce 49, J. N. Snape 58, P. J. Deakin 36, P. A. Bhatia 44 not out; J. F. Venter four for 64) and 214 for seven (B. Hames 68, A. C. Richards 48; C. F. B. P. Rudd three for 41).

At Clontarf, Dublin, June 25, 26, 27. MCC won by 107 runs. Toss: Ireland. MCC 331 for eight dec. (M. S. A. McEvoy 60, D. A. Thorne 64, G. J. Toogood 63, D. C. Briance 59, R. J. Parks 32, Extras 35; E. R. Moore three for 62) and 215 for five dec. (P. W. G. Parker 80, M. S. A. McEvoy 61); Ireland 250 (S. J. S. Warke 51, M. P. Rea 44, S. Graham 55; S. V. Aldis four for 69, C. R. Trembath three for 60) and 189 (M. P. Rea 79; S. V. Aldis four for 36).

At Arundel, July 3. Drawn. Toss: Lavinia, Duchess of Norfolk's XI. Lavinia, Duchess of Norfolk's XI 289 for four dec. (S. M. Lynch 154 not out, C. J. Rika 86); MCC 287 for six (K. Greenfield 101, A. J. Goldsmith 42, P. Bedford 86 not out; J. Brown three for 111).

At Dean Park, Bournemouth, July 8. Dorset won by three wickets. Toss: MCC. MCC 240 for six dec. (P. W. Romaines 153 not out; S. Walbridge four for 54); Dorset 244 for seven (T. W. Richings 30, G. V. Palmer 33, G. D. Reynolds 97 not out; K. C. Williams three for 53).

At Lord's, July 12. MCC drew with MCC SCHOOLS (See Schools Cricket in 1994).

At Roehampton, July 15. Drawn. Toss: Bank of England. MCC 241 for four dec. (A. J. T. Miller 64, N. J. C. Gandon 43, J. R. Wood 40 not out, K. C. Williams 42 not out); Bank of England 197 for nine (S. P. Henderson 73, S. Hodge 52; S. D. Weale three for 55).

At Aldershot, August 11. Combined Services v MCC. Abandoned.

At Harborne CC, August 11. Midlands Club Cricket Conference v MCC. Abandoned.

At Lord's, August 17, 18. Drawn. Toss: MCC. Scotland 205 for five dec. (M. J. Smith 100 not out; O. H. Mortensen four for 62) and 203 for seven dec. (G. B. J. McGurk 34, G. N. Reifer 73 not out); MCC 153 for seven dec. (K. C. Williams 70 not out; D. Cowan five for 45) and 253 for six (G. J. Toogood 30, J. R. Wood 64, C. F. B. P. Rudd 65, P. J. Mir 57 not out).

At Caythorpe CC, August 17. Drawn. Toss: MCC. MCC 175 for eight dec. (R. P. Merriman 43, H. Cartwright 36 not out; M. Carey three for 66); National Association of Young Cricketers 175 for seven (P. G. Hudson 86, I. Cheesewright 30; P. A. W. Heseltine three for 72).

At Lord's, September 6. MCC won by 35 runs. Toss: MCC. MCC 220 for eight (50 overs) (M. A. Roseberry 70, D. M. Ward 31, P. Moores 30); Holder's Hill CC 185 (45.2 overs) (P. A. Wallace 39, A. F. G. Griffith 68; J. P. Stephenson five for 45).

OTHER MATCHES, 1994

Note: Matches in this section were not first-class.

At Uxbridge, April 19, 20, 21, 22. England Under-19 won by 102 runs. Toss: England Under-19. England Under-19 318 (C. J. Schofield 73, M. E. Trescothick 63, D. R. Law 36, Extras 58; K. Marc three for 51, R. J. Burroughs three for 48) and 251 (C. J. Schofield 57, I. J. Mason 34, Extras 40; A. A. Choudry three for 45, R. J. Burroughs three for 52); Middlesex Second XI 236 (A. Habib 68, R. J. Sims 56; D. R. Law four for 83, G. Keedy three for 31) and 231 (J. C. Harrison 30, O. A. Shah 53, P. Farbrace 46, S. K. Mohammed 30; D. R. Law six for 46).

At Oxford, April 23. Combined Universities v Gloucestershire. Abandoned.

At Christ Church, Oxford, April 24. Kent won by 21 runs. Toss: Kent. Kent 231 (54.2 overs) (M. R. Benson 30, M. V. Fleming 31, T. R. Ward 42, S. A. Marsh 33; J. N. B. Bovill three for 23, J. N. Snape three for 56); Combined Universities 210 for six (55 overs) (R. R. Montgomerie 32, G. I. Macmillan 71, G. W. White 33 not out, Extras 38; M. V. Fleming three for 36).

At Manchester, May 1. Yorkshire won by 39 runs. Toss: Lancashire. Yorkshire 169 for seven (40 overs) (R. J. Blakey 45, C. White 50 not out; G. Chapple three for 42); Lancashire 130 (36.4 overs) (M. Watkinson 38; C. White five for 12).

COSTCUTTER CUP

A 55-over competition contested by Yorkshire and three other invited counties.

At Harrogate, July 11. Gloucestershire won by six wickets. Toss: Nottinghamshire. Nottinghamshire 233 for eight (55 overs) (M. A. Crawley 40, C. C. Lewis 33, W. M. Noon 60 not out); Gloucestershire 236 for four (52.1 overs) (T. H. C. Hancock 129 not out, R. C. Russell 47 not out; R. T. Bates three for 36).

At Harrogate, July 12. Sussex won by three wickets. Toss: Yorkshire. Yorkshire 193 for seven (55 overs) (M. P. Vaughan 35, R. J. Blakey 55 not out, Extras 38); Sussex 197 for seven (54 overs) (C. W. J. Athey 71; M. A. Robinson three for 29).

At Harrogate, July 13. **Final:** Gloucestershire won by two wickets. Toss: Sussex. Sussex 218 for nine (55 overs) (N. J. Lenham 44, C. W. J. Athey 36, A. P. Wells 42); Gloucestershire 220 for eight (54.2 overs) (T. H. C. Hancock 38, R. C. Williams 43 not out, Extras 33).

NORTHERN ELECTRIC TROPHY

At Scarborough, September 3. Durham won by 12 runs. Toss: Durham. Durham 222 for eight (50 overs) (S. Hutton 68, J. A. Daley 57, P. Bainbridge 44; D. Gough four for 29); Yorkshire 210 (50 overs) (B. Parker 46, D. Byas 53; J. Wood four for 32, A. Walker three for 45).

JOSHUA TETLEY FESTIVAL TROPHY

A 50-over competition contested by Yorkshire and three other invited counties.

At Scarborough, September 5. Durham won by three wickets. Toss: Lancashire. Lancashire 234 for seven (50 overs) (S. P. Titchard 36, N. H. Fairbrother 60, G. D. Lloyd 47 not out; A. C. Cummins three for 47); Durham 237 for seven (48.3 overs) (J. E. Morris 124; G. Yates five for 28).

At Scarborough, September 6. Yorkshire won by three wickets. Toss: Gloucestershire. Gloucestershire 196 (49.1 overs) (M. W. Alleyne 41, R. I. Dawson 32); Yorkshire 199 for seven (47.5 overs) (R. J. Blakey 52, A. P. Grayson 52).

At Scarborough, September 7. **Final:** Yorkshire won by three wickets. Toss: Durham. Durham 282 for nine (50 overs) (W. Larkins 37, S. Hutton 57, J. E. Morris 83, A. C. Cummins 47; L. C. Weekes three for 58); Yorkshire 283 for seven (49.4 overs) (M. D. Moxon 52, S. A. Kellett 130).

I ZINGARI RESULTS, 1994

Matches 25: Won 8, Lost 8, Drawn 9. Abandoned 2.

May 3	Eton College	Drawn
May 8	Hampshire Hogs	Drawn
May 14	Royal Artillery	Drawn
May 15	Staff College	Won by 164 runs
May 21	Eton Ramblers	Abandoned
May 28	Royal Armoured Corps	Won by 106 runs
June 2	Harrow School	Drawn
June 5	Earl of Carnarvon's XI	Abandoned
June 12	Sandhurst Wanderers	Won by 30 runs
June 18	Guards CC	Lost by four wickets
June 18	Charterhouse	Lost by 102 runs
June 25	Rickling Green CC	Lost by 41 runs
June 26	J. Paul Getty's XI	Lost by seven wickets
June 29	Winchester College	Lost by seven wickets
July 3	Hagley CC	Lost by three wickets
July 8	I Zingari (Australia)	Won by 51 runs
July 9	Green Jackets Club	Won by 63 runs
July 16	Gentlemen of Leicestershire	Won by three wickets
July 17	Sir John Starkey's XI	Drawn
July 23	Hurlingham CC	Drawn
July 24	Lavinia, Duchess of Norfolk's XI	Drawn
July 30	Lord Kingsdown's XI	Drawn
July 31	Band of Brothers	Won by three wickets
August 6, 7	South Wales Hunts XI	Drawn
August 14	Captain R. H. Hawkins's XI	Lost by six wickets
August 21	Royal Navy CC	Lost by five wickets
September 4	J. H. Pawle's XI	Won by four wickets

THE MINOR COUNTIES IN 1994

By MICHAEL BERRY and ROBERT BROOKE

For the third time in four seasons, both Minor Counties trophies were won by the same county. On this occasion it was not Staffordshire, double-winners twice in the previous three seasons, but **Devon** who landed both the Championship and knockout cup. The key to their success was the tactical leadership of Peter Roebuck, the former Somerset captain. His thoughtful captaincy inspired a Devon side which had been beaten by Staffordshire in both the 1991 knockout cup final and the 1992 Championship play-off. Roebuck also led by example on the field, principally with the ball. His 44 wickets won him the Frank Edwards Bowling Trophy, and included a devastating second-innings return of nine for 12 that set up victory over Oxfordshire, who were bowled out for just 40 in their second innings, the lowest Championship total of the season. Nick Gaywood (814) and Julian Wyatt (665) piled up the runs, and both Steve Willis and debutant Gareth Townsend finished on exactly 500 for the season. Keith Donohue's 26 victims helped Devon win four of their nine divisional matches. Getting one more bonus point than Cambridgeshire in the final brought them the title for the first time since 1978, and only the second time in their history.

Runners-up to Devon in the Western Division were **Herefordshire**, in only their third season in the competition, who were unbeaten in the Championship. Herefordshire also won four of their nine games, one of which saw them pursue a target of 335 in 70 overs to

MINOR COUNTIES CHAMPIONSHIP, 1994

Champions: Devon.

Eastern Division	*M*	*W*	*L*	*D*	*NR*	*Bonus Points* *Batting*	*Bowling*	*Total Points*
Cambridgeshire^NW	9	4	0	5	0	23	21	108
Cumberland^NW	9	3	2	4	0	21	24	93
Staffordshire^NW	9	2	1	6	0	30	27	89
Suffolk^NW	9	2	1	6	0	23	19	82
Norfolk^NW	9	2	0	7	0	25	22	79
Lincolnshire	9	2	1	6	0	22	22	76
Buckinghamshire	9	1	3	4	1	19	22	70
Northumberland	9	2	4	3	0	17	14	63
Bedfordshire	9	1	2	6	0	18	21	55
Hertfordshire	9	1	6	1	1	9	12	42

Western Division	*M*	*W*	*L*	*D*	*NR*	*Bonus Points* *Batting*	*Bowling*	*Total Points*
Devon^NW	9	4	1	4	0	16	28	108
Herefordshire^NW	9	4	0	5	0	22	14	100
Cheshire^NW	9	3	1	4	1	25	21	99
Berkshire^NW	9	3	3	3	0	21	25	94
Cornwall^NW	9	3	3	3	0	19	24	91
Dorset^NW	9	2	3	3	1	14	27	78
Shropshire	9	2	4	3	0	17	27	76
Wiltshire	9	1	1	7	0	23	19	58
Oxfordshire	9	0	3	6	0	16	21	37
Wales	9	0	3	6	0	12	21	33

The totals for Suffolk and Buckinghamshire include 8 points for batting last in a match drawn with the scores level.

Win = 16 pts. No result (including abandoned games) = 5 pts.
^NW *Denotes qualified for NatWest Bank Trophy in 1995.*

beat Cornwall by six wickets with 14 balls to spare, and they would have overhauled Devon at the top had they won their final fixture with Wiltshire. However, rain washed the match out with Herefordshire in a strong position. Harshad Patel, who returned after a 12-month lay-off owing to a back injury, made 747 runs and both Alvin Kallicharran (725) and Martin Weston (643) also scored freely. Mike Bailey, an off-spinner, took 17 wickets.

Cheshire, Western Division winners in 1993, had another successful summer to finish third. In his final season in Minor Counties cricket, Geoff Miller took 32 wickets, including 11 for 73 in the win over Wales, and topped the batting averages. No batsman passed 500 runs and Ian Cockbain, the captain, made only 283 in seven matches (including 111 not out against Wales) before his season ended prematurely when he dislocated a shoulder against Oxfordshire. The early-season defeat of Cornwall featured a spectacular over from David Toseland that was plundered for 31 runs, 29 off the bat of Cheshire's big-hitting John Bean.

Berkshire could have claimed the regional title had they beaten Cheshire in the last match of the season, but after a bizarre pre-lunch session in which they bowled 74 overs in two hours (47 and 27) in order to avoid a £500 fine for falling below the stipulated over-rate of 17.5 an hour during the season, they were beaten by 12 runs. David Mercer's 831 runs at 69.25 won him the Wilfred Rhodes batting trophy and Gary Loveday also enjoyed another abundant season with 676. Spin bowlers David Hartley (34), Neil Fusedale (29) and Peter Lewington (26) shared 89 wickets. Lewington, who established a new Berkshire career record when he took his 584th victim against Wales, announced his retirement as soon as his total reached 600. He had started his farewell season with match figures of nine for 80 as Berkshire defeated close rivals Oxfordshire for the first time since 1977.

The biggest improvement of the Western Division programme came from **Cornwall**, where the imported talents of Mark Briers (from Durham) and Laurie Potter (Leicestershire) proved decisive in a dramatic revival. The county who had turned the acquisition of wooden spoons into an art form (nine in 11 years) beat Berkshire to record their first Championship win since 1991 and also got the better of Shropshire and Wiltshire, the latter succumbing by ten wickets by mid-afternoon on the second day. Potter made 309 runs in five matches while Briers, who played seven games, scored 352 runs and took 31 wickets with his leg-breaks. Cornwall, led by Godfrey Furse, who had taken over the captaincy from Graham Watts, were also well served by a handful of home-grown players, notably Gary Thomas (648 runs) and Steve Williams (465). They also blooded a promising new wicket-keeper in Andrew Snell.

Richard Scott returned to the **Dorset** ranks from Gloucestershire to score 403 runs in eight matches. Giles Reynolds, the Dorset captain, made 559, while 529 came from Graeme Calway, who has now emigrated to South Africa. Both Calway (127) and Scott (118 not out) scored centuries when Dorset piled up the biggest total of the season in making 463 in the drawn game with Wiltshire. Julian Shackleton (28 wickets), Alan Willows (26) and Paul Garlick (24) ensured that Dorset picked up 27 bowling bonus points, a tally bettered only by the eventual champions, Devon.

Shropshire again missed out on a NatWest Trophy place after a miserable start to the season. Brittle batting contributed to three straight defeats in the Championship and knockout cup before they recovered to record victories over Devon and Oxfordshire. Kevin Sharp (622 runs) and Tony Parton (608) helped stabilise the batting, while Adam Byram (31 wickets), Marcus Marvell, Mark Davies and Andy Johnson all had memorable moments. Slow left-armers Byram (against Herefordshire) and Marvell (against Wales) both performed the hat-trick, but the best and worst days of Shropshire's season came in the same fixture against Cheshire at New Brighton. Dismissed for 57 on a green pitch in the first innings, they fought back to amass 404 on the second day, Davies (172) and Johnson (145) establishing a Minor Counties record fifth-wicket partnership of 289. In doing so, Davies, the captain, also created a record individual score for the county.

Wiltshire beat Shropshire by 15 runs in their second match, but failed to win again. Mid-season availability problems became a handicap and, having lost the services of Lawrence Smith before the season started, Wiltshire owed much to the runs of Steve Perrin (659) and Rob Savage (576). But the Wiltshire bowlers, so impressive in the demolition of Shropshire, never lived up to their early performance.

Oxfordshire, under the captaincy of Rupert Evans, had a season to forget. They failed to win a single Championship match for the first time since 1985, saw former skipper Phil Garner retire during the summer after 13 years with the county, and only just avoided the wooden spoon. As always, Stuart Waterton was a consistent run-scorer, with 762, and Tim Lester, who has now taken up a teaching post in Australia, bowed out with two unbeaten centuries against Shropshire, after 78 previous appearances without one. Evans (29 wickets) and Ian Curtis (25) again shouldered the bulk of the Oxfordshire bowling.

After positive signs of progress in 1993, **Wales** dropped back to bottom spot. Their season began inauspiciously against Herefordshire, when, needing 12 to win off two overs with four wickets in hand, they lost by three runs. The season in general was also an anticlimax, although Stefan Jones performed admirably with bat and ball, and Andy Puddle, their captain, scored 465 runs.

Cambridgeshire triumphed at the head of the Eastern Division table, ahead of Cumberland, whom they beat by eight wickets, and Staffordshire. When Stuart Turner hoisted the last ball of their final fixture with Buckinghamshire for a winning six, they had won three of their final four matches. They won four in all and were unbeaten, their last-wicket pair having blocked out 7.5 overs to deny Norfolk victory at Lakenham. Nigel Gadsby, their captain, scored 661 runs and Saleem Mohammed, who had followed his brother Nadeem into the side, backed him up with 465. Turner (27 wickets) and Dominic Ralfs (23) were effective opening bowlers.

Cumberland's season was notable for the baptism into Minor Counties cricket of Marcus Sharp, a 6ft 7in pace bowler previously with Lancashire, who had been recommended by David Lloyd. Sharp took 34 wickets in seven appearances, including match figures of nine for 88 on his debut against Suffolk. Mike Scothern gave Sharp excellent support with the ball to claim 33 wickets, and David Makinson, normally a bowler who can bat, became a batsman who can bowl by scoring 507 runs, a figure that included an innings of 102 not out against Suffolk.

After their three years as Minor Counties champions, **Staffordshire's** run of non-stop success finally came to an end. Despite an early exit from the knockout cup against Herefordshire, Staffordshire were in contention for the Championship until a last-match defeat by Bedfordshire. The Staffordshire batting was as strong as ever with eight players averaging 35 or more. One of them, the newcomer Kaushik Patel, brother of New Zealand Test all-rounder Dipak, made 145 not out to steer Staffordshire to victory over Buckinghamshire. Steve Dean (644 runs) and David Cartledge (592) excelled with the bat and Paul Newman took 35 wickets. But Staffordshire lacked back-up bowling, even though Lee Slater made an eye-catching debut with match figures of ten for 90 in the demolition of Hertfordshire.

Suffolk and Norfolk both won places in the NatWest Trophy on the strength of a couple of wins apiece. **Suffolk**, with new captain Phil Caley at the helm, languished near the bottom at the half-way stage of the season but then conjured up victories over Northumberland and Hertfordshire, as well as gaining an extra eight points as the side batting last when the fixture with Cambridgeshire was drawn with the scores level. Derek Randall, the former England batsman, who had signed a two-year contract with the county, compiled a maiden Minor Counties century in the final game with Norfolk to boost his total of runs to 597. Andrew Golding, a slow left-armer, bowled more than 365 overs in nine games to take 49 wickets, and Danny Carter, blooded for the first time, ended with 24 from five appearances.

Norfolk had only 19 points from their first four matches, but the last five brought a further 60, including comprehensive back-to-back wins over Hertfordshire and Northumberland at Lakenham. Hertfordshire were humbled by ten wickets, with Carl Rogers scoring 81 not out and 63 not out on the way to collecting 775 runs. Rodney Bunting helped set up a massive 246-run victory over Northumberland with a match return of nine for 51. Bunting proved to be the best new-ball bowler in the Championship with 44 wickets, while Steve Plumb's all-round talents brought him 561 runs and 28 wickets.

Prolific opening batsmen Jonathan Wileman and Russell Evans dominated **Lincolnshire's** season with a series of headline-writing feats. They feasted on the unsuspecting Northumberland bowlers at the start of the season with a remarkable sequence of three unbeaten double-century partnerships. In the knockout cup they scored 253 in 50.4 overs, and then, in a historic ten-wicket win at Grimsby, they put on 279 in 47 overs and 205 in 41 as Lincolnshire became the first Minor Counties side to win a Championship game without losing a wicket. They went on to reach the final of the MCC Trophy, losing at Lord's for the second time in five years, and Wileman won himself a second chance at Nottinghamshire by ending the season as the leading run-scorer in the Championship with 863 runs, a total that contained four centuries. Mark Fell, their new captain, accrued 620 runs and Steve Bradford, an unsung slow left-armer, had a vintage summer with the ball, his 55 victims (from 392 overs) making him the Championship's most successful wicket-taker.

Andy Clarke, the former Sussex leg-spinner, proved excellent value for **Buckinghamshire**. Clarke, who took up a teaching post in the county, took eight for 68 against Cambridgeshire and finished with 48 victims. Tim Scriven, the new captain, finished with 21 wickets, but only Malcolm Roberts did himself total justice with the bat with 575 runs. Buckinghamshire also benefited from the new ruling to award eight points to teams batting last in games that finish as a draw with the scores level. Chasing 280 to beat Lincolnshire at Slough, they reached 279 for seven.

Northumberland flattered to deceive when they beat Cheshire in the preliminary round of the knockout cup and defeated both Hertfordshire and Buckinghamshire in the first two Championship matches. Thereafter it was all downhill, and they lost their last three matches, the turning point of their summer being the ten-wicket defeat in the knockout cup by Lincolnshire. Graeme Morris, their captain, missed three Championship matches, although he still topped their batting averages. Tim Adcock (464 runs) and Craig Stanley (20 wickets) were the other major individual successes. In the victory over Hertfordshire, Peter Graham, later called up by the Minor Counties representative side, passed 300 Championship wickets.

Bedfordshire, after an upturn in fortunes in 1993, struggled to live up to the previous year's improvement, although they did manage to beat Staffordshire, thanks to veteran Ray Swann's 107, and lost by only one run to Cumberland. In the match against Buckinghamshire, Swann opened the batting with his son, Alec. The batting was headed by Neil Stanley (509) and Chris Bullen, whose 150 against Suffolk was the highest score by a Bedfordshire player for more than 30 years, while six different players scored centuries. One of these was Jonathan Robinson, who also topped the bowling averages with 24 wickets.

Hertfordshire, who finished bottom of the Eastern Division for the first time after six defeats in nine games, were rebuilding, and the decision of Andy Needham to quit Minor Counties cricket midway through the season deprived them of their most influential player. Several newcomers showed promise, with Richard Jerome, an off-spinner, returning an analysis of 5.3–4–1–4 in their sole win, over Bedfordshire, who collapsed from 65 for four to 77 all out. Hertfordshire also made a magnificent attempt to score 337 for victory over Northumberland at Jesmond, finally losing by nine runs.

CHAMPIONSHIP FINAL

CAMBRIDGESHIRE v DEVON

At Worcester, September 11, 12. Drawn. Cambridgeshire 2 pts, Devon 3 pts. Toss: Devon.

Devon took the 1994 Minor Counties title by virtue of having gained more bonus points when the inaugural two-day final ended in a weather-disrupted draw. The ill-conceived ruling, whereby first-innings bonus points became decisive in the event of a drawn game, always pointed to a second-day deadlock, and the intervention of rain only exaggerated the loophole in a ruling that will be modified for 1995. The one incident that turned the balance towards Devon was when Ecclestone dropped Roebuck at point off the bowling of Turner on the first day. Roebuck went on to score a vital 33 not out, which secured an all-important batting point. A second half-century from Gadsby allowed Cambridgeshire to set Devon a target of 169 in two hours, but rain, which had delayed the second day's play by nearly four hours, prevented them from replying.

Cambridgeshire

Saleem Mohammed c Roebuck b Le Fleming	1	– c Folland b Donohue	31
*N. T. Gadsby b Allin	62	– not out	60
G. W. Ecclestone c Wyatt b Roebuck	18	– lbw b Donohue	32
Nadeem Mohammed c Boase b Roebuck	0		
N. J. Adams b Allin	39	– run out	8
D. P. Norman b Allin	4		
†S. L. Williams not out	16	– (4) lbw b Roebuck	29
S. Turner not out	6		
L-b 6, w 1	7	L-b 5	5
1/1 2/36 3/40 4/124 5/129 6/132 (6 wkts dec.)	153	1/51 2/105 3/144 4/165 (4 wkts dec.)	165

T. S. Smith, Ajaz Akhtar and D. F. Ralfs did not bat.

Bowling: *First Innings*—Donohue 12–2–37–0; Le Fleming 4–1–6–1; Roebuck 15–6–33–2; Allin 14.2–1–54–3; Woodman 4–0–17–0. *Second Innings*—Donohue 10–0–48–2; Le Fleming 5–1–18–0; Roebuck 6–1–26–1; Allin 5–2–25–0; Woodman 11–3–43–0.

Devon

N. R. Gaywood c Gadsby b Ralfs	4
J. G. Wyatt run out	39
N. A. Folland c Ecclestone b Smith	18
S. M. Willis not out	29
G. T. J. Townsend lbw b Smith	17
*P. M. Roebuck not out	33
L-b 8, n-b 2	10
1/5 2/66 3/74 4/99 (4 wkts dec.)	150

K. Donohue, A. O. F. Le Fleming, †D. K. Boase, M. C. Woodman and A. W. Allin did not bat.

Bowling: Turner 14–4–45–0; Ralfs 7–1–22–1; Ajaz Akhtar 10–2–33–0; Smith 15.3–4–42–2.

Umpires: P. Adams and R. K. Curtis.

MCC TROPHY FINAL

DEVON v LINCOLNSHIRE

At Lord's, August 24. Devon won by 18 runs. Toss: Lincolnshire.

A century before lunch by Gaywood, a left-hander who produced a sumptuous exhibition of clean hitting, laid the foundations for Devon to take the knockout cup for the second time in three years. He was particularly productive through extra cover, and his only scare came as he scampered through to 100. Roebuck hit a cameo half-century and Townsend and Willis picked up the tempo as 60 came off the final five overs. At 70 for four in the 27th over, Lincolnshire looked set to be swamped. But Fell and Gillett were the architects of a brave recovery with a fifth-wicket stand of 93, and some lusty hitting from Christmas and Fletcher kept them in contention until the latter holed out to backward point.

Devon

N. R. Gaywood lbw b Fletcher	106
J. G. Wyatt c and b Bradford	24
*P. M. Roebuck c French b Fell	54
G. T. J. Townsend b French	29
S. M. Willis b Christmas	27
J. K. Tierney not out	7
K. Donohue not out	2
B 2, l-b 19, w 5, n-b 6	32
1/90 2/193 3/201 4/269 5/275 (5 wkts, 55 overs)	281

†D. K. Boase, A. O. F. Le Fleming, A. C. Cottam and A. W. Allin did not bat.

Bowling: Fletcher 9–0–48–1; French 9–1–48–1; Wileman 5–0–27–0; Christmas 10–0–47–1; Bradford 11–0–51–1; Fell 11–1–39–1.

Lincolnshire

J. R. Wileman c and b Cottam 10	S. D. Fletcher c Cottam b Le Fleming . 25
R. J. Evans b Donohue 14	S. A. Bradford not out 9
P. J. Heseltine lbw b Donohue 0	†N. P. Dobbs c Boase b Donohue 0
S. N. Warman c Cottam b Allin 23	
*M. A. Fell c Gaywood b Roebuck 73	B 2, l-b 17, w 7 26
D. E. Gillett c and b Roebuck 53	
N. French c Cottam b Tierney 7	1/16 2/16 3/40 (53.3 overs) 263
D. A. Christmas c Roebuck	4/70 5/163 6/191
b Le Fleming . 23	7/193 8/232 9/257

Bowling: Le Fleming 9–0–62–2; Donohue 10.3–3–45–3; Cottam 8–1–31–1; Allin 11–3–26–1; Roebuck 11–0–50–2; Tierney 4–0–30–1.

Umpires: S. W. Kuhlmann and C. Smith.

*In the averages that follow, * against a score signifies not out.*

LEADING AVERAGES

Qualification: Average 30

Batting: 6 innings; bowling 10 innings

BEDFORDSHIRE

Matches 9: Won – Staffordshire. Lost – Cumberland, Hertfordshire. Drawn – Buckinghamshire, Cambridgeshire, Lincolnshire, Norfolk, Northumberland, Suffolk.

Batting

	M	*I*	*NO*	*R*	*HS*	*100s*	*50s*	*Avge*
C. K. Bullen	9	16	4	520	150*	1	2	43.33
N. A. Stanley	7	14	1	509	112*	2	2	39.15
D. R. Clarke	5	10	1	333	133*	1	0	37.00
P. D. B. Hoare	7	13	2	388	103*	1	1	35.27
J. D. Robinson	7	14	2	414	100*	1	1	34.50

Bowling

	O	*M*	*R*	*W*	*BB*	*5W/i*	*Avge*
J. D. Robinson	129	25	525	24	7-67	1	21.87
R. N. Dalton	137.3	26	498	21	6-41	2	23.71

BERKSHIRE

Matches 9: Won – Dorset, Oxfordshire, Shropshire. Lost – Cheshire, Cornwall, Herefordshire. Drawn – Devon, Wales, Wiltshire.

Batting

	M	*I*	*NO*	*R*	*HS*	*100s*	*50s*	*Avge*
D. J. M. Mercer	9	17	5	831	119*	2	6	69.25
G. E. Loveday	8	16	2	676	111*	2	4	48.28
J. Hodgson	7	14	4	395	101*	1	2	39.50
N. J. D. Cartmell	5	8	2	224	78	0	1	37.33

Bowling

	O	M	R	W	BB	5W/i	Avge
P. J. Lewington	195.4	59	488	26	6-53	3	18.76
N. A. Fusedale	222.4	58	748	29	4-31	0	25.79
D. J. B. Hartley	238	36	944	34	6-49	3	27.76
D. J. Foster	99.3	14	445	15	7-48	1	29.66

BUCKINGHAMSHIRE

Matches 9: Won – Cumberland. Lost – Cambridgeshire, Northumberland, Staffordshire. Drawn – Bedfordshire, Lincolnshire, Norfolk, Suffolk. No result – Hertfordshire.

Batting

	M	I	NO	R	HS	100s	50s	Avge
B. S. Percy	6	9	1	390	105	1	1	48.75
M. J. Roberts	7	13	1	575	111*	1	5	47.91
T. J. Barry	6	8	2	237	63*	0	1	39.50
R. R. Baigent	6	11	1	392	100	1	2	39.20
S. G. Lynch	4	8	4	137	49*	0	0	34.25
T. P. Russell	9	10	5	167	40	0	0	33.40
S. M. Shearman	7	14	3	350	67*	0	3	31.81

Bowling

	O	M	R	W	BB	5W/i	Avge
A. R. Clarke	346.5	68	1,270	48	8-68	2	26.45

CAMBRIDGESHIRE

Matches 10: Won – Buckinghamshire, Cumberland, Hertfordshire, Lincolnshire. Drawn – Bedfordshire, Devon (Championship final), Norfolk, Northumberland, Staffordshire, Suffolk.

Batting

	M	I	NO	R	HS	100s	50s	Avge
N. T. Gadsby	10	20	6	661	92*	0	7	47.21
B. Roberts	6	11	2	391	101*	1	3	43.44
G. W. Ecclestone	7	12	2	409	86*	0	3	40.90

Bowling

	O	M	R	W	BB	5W/i	Avge
S. Turner	207.5	60	594	27	5-31	2	22.00
D. F. Ralfs	256.2	70	687	23	4-23	0	29.86

CHESHIRE

Matches 9: Won – Berkshire, Cornwall, Wales. Lost – Devon. Drawn – Herefordshire, Oxfordshire, Shropshire, Wiltshire. No result – Dorset.

Batting

	M	I	NO	R	HS	100s	50s	Avge
G. Miller	9	8	2	404	90	0	5	67.33
P. R. J. Bryson	5	9	2	416	85	0	5	59.42
R. G. Hignett	9	15	2	429	61	0	3	33.00
S. T. Crawley	7	11	0	332	102	1	2	30.18

Bowling

	O	*M*	*R*	*W*	*BB*	*5W/i*	*Avge*
G. Miller	181.2	44	518	32	6-53	4	16.18
E. S. Garnett	91.2	23	341	13	5-60	1	26.23

CORNWALL

Matches 9: Won – Berkshire, Shropshire, Wiltshire. Lost – Cheshire, Dorset, Herefordshire. Drawn – Devon, Oxfordshire, Wales.

Batting

	M	*I*	*NO*	*R*	*HS*	*100s*	*50s*	*Avge*
L. Potter	5	9	2	309	85	0	3	44.14
G. M. Thomas	9	16	1	648	164	2	3	43.20
M. P. Briers	7	12	3	352	61	0	3	39.11
S. M. Williams	8	15	3	465	140*	1	2	38.75
C. C. Lovell	6	9	3	214	47*	0	0	35.66

Bowling

	O	*M*	*R*	*W*	*BB*	*5W/i*	*Avge*
M. P. Briers	201.3	24	764	31	5-43	1	24.64

CUMBERLAND

Matches 9: Won – Bedfordshire, Northumberland, Suffolk. Lost – Buckinghamshire, Cambridgeshire. Drawn – Hertfordshire, Lincolnshire, Norfolk, Staffordshire.

Batting

	M	*I*	*NO*	*R*	*HS*	*100s*	*50s*	*Avge*
D. J. Makinson	9	12	2	507	102*	1	3	50.70
S. Sharp	4	8	1	293	96	0	3	41.85
D. Patel	8	15	2	448	120*	1	3	34.46

Bowling

	O	*M*	*R*	*W*	*BB*	*5W/i*	*Avge*
M. A. Sharp	187.2	39	626	34	6-36	3	18.41
A. R. Wilson	80.1	27	233	10	6-39	1	23.30
M. G. Scothern	225.3	45	788	33	6-53	3	23.87

DEVON

Matches 10: Won – Cheshire, Dorset, Oxfordshire, Wales. Lost – Shropshire. Drawn – Berkshire, Cambridgeshire (Championship final), Cornwall, Herefordshire, Wiltshire.

Batting

	M	*I*	*NO*	*R*	*HS*	*100s*	*50s*	*Avge*
N. R. Gaywood	10	18	4	814	139*	2	2	58.14
G. T. J. Townsend	10	15	6	500	65	0	4	55.55
P. M. Roebuck	10	13	5	342	81*	0	2	42.75
S. M. Willis	10	17	5	500	82*	0	3	41.66
J. G. Wyatt	10	18	1	665	123	1	4	39.11

Bowling

	O	M	R	W	BB	5W/i	Avge
P. M. Roebuck	286.1	103	554	44	9-12	3	12.59
A. O. F. Le Fleming	126	39	306	16	3-26	0	19.12
K. Donohue	189.3	41	563	26	4-36	0	21.65
M. C. Woodman	150	29	501	18	3-25	0	27.83

DORSET

Matches 9: Won – Cornwall, Shropshire. Lost – Berkshire, Devon, Herefordshire. Drawn – Oxfordshire, Wales, Wiltshire. No result – Cheshire.

Batting

	M	I	NO	R	HS	100s	50s	Avge
G. D. Reynolds	9	16	4	559	95*	0	4	46.58
R. J. Scott	8	14	2	403	118*	1	2	33.58
G. S. Calway	9	16	0	529	127	2	3	33.06
A. Willows	9	15	5	323	59*	0	2	32.30

Bowling

	O	M	R	W	BB	5W/i	Avge
J. H. Shackleton	212.5	81	428	28	5-25	2	15.28
A. Willows	185	41	547	26	4-28	0	21.03
R. A. Pyman	98	25	298	13	5-16	1	22.92
P. L. Garlick	189.5	35	650	24	5-40	1	27.08

HEREFORDSHIRE

Matches 9: Won – Berkshire, Cornwall, Dorset, Wales. Drawn – Cheshire, Devon, Oxfordshire, Shropshire, Wiltshire.

Batting

	M	I	NO	R	HS	100s	50s	Avge
A. I. Kallicharran	9	16	5	725	100	1	7	65.90
S. M. Brogan	4	8	3	306	103*	1	1	61.20
M. J. Weston	6	12	1	643	143	2	5	58.45
H. V. Patel	9	18	2	747	116	1	5	46.68
R. P. Skyrme	7	11	1	421	124	1	3	42.10
R. Hall	6	12	4	277	70*	0	3	34.62
S. R. Bevins	5	7	4	94	27*	0	0	31.33

Bowling

No bowler took ten wickets at an average of 30 or less. The leading bowler was M. J. Bailey 147.2–26–518–17–6/78–1–30.47.

HERTFORDSHIRE

Matches 9: Won – Bedfordshire. Lost – Cambridgeshire, Lincolnshire, Norfolk, Northumberland, Staffordshire, Suffolk. Drawn – Cumberland. No result – Buckinghamshire.

Batting

	M	I	NO	R	HS	100s	50s	Avge
M. C. G. Wright	4	6	1	170	65	0	1	34.00
M. R. Gouldstone	9	16	2	434	100*	1	2	31.00
R. S. Jerome	5	9	3	181	50*	0	1	30.16

Bowling

	O	M	R	W	BB	5W/i	Avge
D. Surridge	145.5	27	437	20	5-36	2	21.85

LINCOLNSHIRE

Matches 9: Won – Hertfordshire, Northumberland. Lost – Cambridgeshire. Drawn – Bedfordshire, Buckinghamshire, Cumberland, Norfolk, Staffordshire, Suffolk.

Batting

	M	I	NO	R	HS	100s	50s	Avge
R. J. Evans	6	11	3	553	115*	1	5	69.12
J. R. Wileman	9	18	5	863	142*	4	1	66.38
S. N. Warman	8	10	3	450	94	0	5	64.28
M. A. Fell	9	15	4	620	126	2	3	56.36
D. A. Christmas	9	9	6	131	38*	0	0	43.66
P. J. Heseltine	6	10	2	284	55	0	2	35.50
D. E. Gillett	5	10	1	271	62	0	2	30.11

Bowling

	O	M	R	W	BB	5W/i	Avge
S. A. Bradford	392	99	1,271	55	7-103	6	23.10

NORFOLK

Matches 9: Won – Hertfordshire, Northumberland. Drawn – Bedfordshire, Buckinghamshire, Cambridgeshire, Cumberland, Lincolnshire, Staffordshire, Suffolk.

Batting

	M	I	NO	R	HS	100s	50s	Avge
D. R. Thomas	9	15	9	461	75*	0	1	76.83
C. J. Rogers	9	17	2	775	116	2	5	51.66
S. G. Plumb	9	17	2	561	91	0	3	37.40
S. C. Goldsmith	9	16	0	537	94	0	5	33.56

Bowling

	O	M	R	W	BB	5W/i	Avge
R. A. Bunting	234	53	851	44	5-35	2	19.34
A. P. Cole	60.5	12	196	10	4-6	0	19.60
S. G. Plumb	232.1	61	614	28	6-58	2	21.92
D. R. Thomas	163	43	398	17	4-36	0	23.41
S. C. Goldsmith	128	28	382	13	3-38	0	29.38

NORTHUMBERLAND

Matches 9: Won – Buckinghamshire, Hertfordshire. Lost – Cumberland, Lincolnshire, Norfolk, Suffolk. Drawn – Bedfordshire, Cambridgeshire, Staffordshire.

Batting

	M	*I*	*NO*	*R*	*HS*	*100s*	*50s*	*Avge*
G. R. Morris	6	12	3	347	91	0	3	38.55
G. Hallam	7	14	5	339	80*	0	3	37.66
O. S. Youll	6	11	1	309	103	1	0	30.90

Bowling

	O	*M*	*R*	*W*	*BB*	*5W/i*	*Avge*
P. C. Graham	91.1	16	273	12	5-43	1	22.75
C. Stanley	150.5	24	538	20	4-82	0	26.90

OXFORDSHIRE

Matches 9: Lost – Berkshire, Devon, Shropshire. Drawn – Cheshire, Cornwall, Dorset, Herefordshire, Wales, Wiltshire.

Batting

	M	*I*	*NO*	*R*	*HS*	*100s*	*50s*	*Avge*
D. C. Woods	5	9	5	257	72*	0	2	64.25
T. A. Lester	9	16	6	579	100*	2	3	57.90
S. N. V. Waterton	9	18	3	762	140*	2	4	50.80
S. V. Laudat	5	9	0	273	86	0	2	30.33

Bowling

	O	*M*	*R*	*W*	*BB*	*5W/i*	*Avge*
K. A. Arnold	87.2	13	308	14	3-15	0	22.00
A. Jones	84.4	14	294	12	4-50	0	24.50
R. A. Evans	316.5	63	823	29	5-64	1	28.37

SHROPSHIRE

Matches 9: Won – Devon, Oxfordshire. Lost – Berkshire, Cornwall, Dorset, Wiltshire. Drawn – Cheshire, Herefordshire, Wales.

Batting

	M	*I*	*NO*	*R*	*HS*	*100s*	*50s*	*Avge*
K. Sharp	9	17	2	622	119*	2	2	41.46
T. Parton	9	17	2	608	116	2	1	40.53
M. R. Davies	9	15	3	434	172	1	1	36.16
P. M. Blakeley	7	13	6	221	34	0	0	31.57

Bowling

	O	*M*	*R*	*W*	*BB*	*5W/i*	*Avge*
A. B. Byram	191	33	713	31	5-49	2	23.00
M. J. Marvell	111.2	14	483	21	6-59	2	23.00
P. M. Blakeley	113.1	19	376	16	3-23	0	23.50
A. S. Barnard	171	40	495	19	5-51	1	26.05

STAFFORDSHIRE

Matches 9: Won – Buckinghamshire, Hertfordshire. Lost – Bedfordshire. Drawn – Cambridgeshire, Cumberland, Lincolnshire, Norfolk, Northumberland, Suffolk.

Batting

	M	*I*	*NO*	*R*	*HS*	*100s*	*50s*	*Avge*
N. J. Archer	8	9	6	262	76*	0	1	87.33
S. D. Myles	5	9	3	354	79	0	4	59.00
K. N. Patel	5	10	3	392	145*	1	1	56.00
J. A. Waterhouse	7	13	4	423	63	0	4	47.00
P. F. Shaw	9	15	5	414	64*	0	3	41.40
T. M. Heap	9	8	5	114	50	0	1	38.00
D. Cartledge	9	18	2	592	113*	2	2	37.00
S. J. Dean	9	18	0	644	67	0	7	35.77

Bowling

	O	*M*	*R*	*W*	*BB*	*5W/i*	*Avge*
L. J. Slater	60.4	11	202	13	5-42	2	15.53
J. Brown	122	25	370	14	3-39	0	26.42
P. G. Newman	315.3	60	940	35	5-61	1	26.85

SUFFOLK

Matches 9: Won – Hertfordshire, Northumberland. Lost – Cumberland. Drawn – Bedfordshire, Buckinghamshire, Cambridgeshire, Lincolnshire, Norfolk, Staffordshire.

Batting

	M	*I*	*NO*	*R*	*HS*	*100s*	*50s*	*Avge*
I. D. Graham	4	6	2	191	72*	0	2	47.75
P. J. Caley	9	15	6	414	79	0	3	46.00
D. W. Randall	7	14	0	597	112	1	5	42.64
J. L. Clinch	7	14	3	331	84	0	1	30.09

Bowling

	O	*M*	*R*	*W*	*BB*	*5W/i*	*Avge*
D. M. Carter	109	14	384	24	6-47	2	16.00
A. K. Golding	365.5	71	1,160	49	8-82	4	23.67

WALES MINOR COUNTIES

Matches 9: Lost – Cheshire, Devon, Herefordshire. Drawn – Berkshire, Cornwall, Dorset, Oxfordshire, Shropshire, Wiltshire.

Batting

	M	*I*	*NO*	*R*	*HS*	*100s*	*50s*	*Avge*
G. Edwards	3	6	2	140	36	0	0	35.00
P. S. Jones	8	14	5	280	64*	0	2	31.11
A. C. Puddle	9	18	3	465	100*	1	1	31.00
M. J. Newbold	8	16	3	403	87	0	2	31.00

Bowling

	O	M	R	W	BB	5W/i	Avge
J. P. J. Sylvester	97	14	370	16	5-63	1	23.12

WILTSHIRE

Matches 9: Won – Shropshire. Lost – Cornwall. Drawn – Berkshire, Cheshire, Devon, Dorset, Herefordshire, Oxfordshire, Wales.

Batting

	M	I	NO	R	HS	100s	50s	Avge
S. M. Perrin.........	8	15	2	659	123*	1	5	50.69
R. R. Savage	8	15	2	576	120*	2	3	44.30
G. Sheppard.........	8	12	6	182	63*	0	1	30.33

Bowling

No bowler took ten wickets at an average of 30 or less. The leading bowler was P. D. North 127–29–387–11–5/55–1–35.18.

THE MINOR COUNTIES CHAMPIONS

1895	Norfolk / Durham / Worcestershire	1927	Staffordshire	1965	Somerset II
		1928	Berkshire	1966	Lincolnshire
		1929	Oxfordshire	1967	Cheshire
1896	Worcestershire	1930	Durham	1968	Yorkshire II
1897	Worcestershire	1931	Leicestershire II	1969	Buckinghamshire
1898	Worcestershire	1932	Buckinghamshire	1970	Bedfordshire
1899	Northamptonshire / Buckinghamshire	1933	Undecided	1971	Yorkshire II
		1934	Lancashire II	1972	Bedfordshire
1900	Glamorgan / Durham / Northamptonshire	1935	Middlesex II	1973	Shropshire
		1936	Hertfordshire	1974	Oxfordshire
		1937	Lancashire II	1975	Hertfordshire
1901	Durham	1938	Buckinghamshire	1976	Durham
1902	Wiltshire	1939	Surrey II	1977	Suffolk
1903	Northamptonshire	1946	Suffolk	1978	Devon
1904	Northamptonshire	1947	Yorkshire II	1979	Suffolk
1905	Norfolk	1948	Lancashire II	1980	Durham
1906	Staffordshire	1949	Lancashire II	1981	Durham
1907	Lancashire II	1950	Surrey II	1982	Oxfordshire
1908	Staffordshire	1951	Kent II	1983	Hertfordshire
1909	Wiltshire	1952	Buckinghamshire	1984	Durham
1910	Norfolk	1953	Berkshire	1985	Cheshire
1911	Staffordshire	1954	Surrey II	1986	Cumberland
1912	In abeyance	1955	Surrey II	1987	Buckinghamshire
1913	Norfolk	1956	Kent II	1988	Cheshire
1914	Staffordshire†	1957	Yorkshire II	1989	Oxfordshire
1920	Staffordshire	1958	Yorkshire II	1990	Hertfordshire
1921	Staffordshire	1959	Warwickshire II	1991	Staffordshire
1922	Buckinghamshire	1960	Lancashire II	1992	Staffordshire
1923	Buckinghamshire	1961	Somerset II	1993	Staffordshire
1924	Berkshire	1962	Warwickshire II	1994	Devon
1925	Buckinghamshire	1963	Cambridgeshire		
1926	Durham	1964	Lancashire II		

† *Disputed. Some sources claim the Championship was never decided.*

RAPID CRICKETLINE SECOND ELEVEN CHAMPIONSHIP, 1994

Somerset were runaway champions, finishing a massive 61 points ahead of their nearest rivals, Yorkshire, who just pipped Kent for second place. It was the first time Somerset had won the title, and they looked likely winners from early on as they swept through the season with ten wins, leaving Derbyshire and Durham as the only counties never to have won the Championship. Yorkshire could find consolation in becoming the first county to win the Bain Clarkson Trophy twice, with a convincing win over Leicestershire in the final. Somerset were disappointing in that competition, finishing fifth in their zone.

It was a vintage year for batsmen, 11 of whom passed 1,000 runs – nine more than in 1993 and one more than the record set in the batsman's summer of 1990. Another record fell to Darren Maddy of Leicestershire, who was named Rapid Cricketline Second Eleven Player of the Year. His aggregate of 1,498 runs in 29 innings beat the Ceylonese Stanley Jayasinghe's 1,485 in 32 for the same county 33 years earlier. The next most prolific were Matthew Walker of Kent, with 1,269 in 27 innings, and Jason Ratcliffe of Warwickshire, whose 1,219 came in 30 innings. Maddy was alone in scoring five centuries, while Walker was one of another six with four, and there were six double-hundreds. The highest, Paul Pollard's 277 not out for Nottinghamshire against Gloucestershire, was a record for the competition, four more than the previous best by Richard Blakey for Yorkshire in 1986. Pollard's innings dominated an unbroken third-wicket partnership of 387 with Mathew Dowman (134 not out), which was also a competition record, surpassing the 385 compiled for Worcestershire by Martin Weston and Graeme Hick in 1984. An unbeaten double-century by Worcestershire's Philip Weston contributed to his average of 139.66 for 419 runs in four innings and Giles White of Hampshire averaged 109.50 for his 438 runs in eight innings. There were no three-figure averages among those who passed 500 runs, the highest being Graeme Archer, whose 590 runs for Nottinghamshire came at 84.28, and Dean Hodgson, who averaged 75.27 in scoring 828 for Gloucestershire.

Continued over

SECOND ELEVEN CHAMPIONSHIP, 1994

					Bonus points		
Win = 16 points	*M*	*W*	*L*	*D*	*Batting*	*Bowling*	*Points*
1 – Somerset (9)	17	10	3	4	44	47	251
2 – Yorkshire (3)	17	6	2	9	50	44	190
3 – Kent (11)	17	6	2	9	44	49	189
4 – Leicestershire (13)	17	5	2	10	54	49	183
5 – Northamptonshire (12)	17	3	4	10	53	50	159
6 – Gloucestershire (4)	17	4	3	10	43	50	157
7 – Durham (14)	17	4	5	8	40	49	149
8 – Worcestershire (16)	17	3	3	11	55	46	149
9 – Sussex (8)	17	3	1	13	48	49	145
10 – Middlesex (1)	17	3	6	8	42	54	144
11 – Surrey (6)	17	3	4	10	39	46	133
12 – Essex (7)	17	3	5	9	34	50	132
13 – Hampshire (10)	17	2	5	10	46	51	129
14 – Warwickshire (15)	17	1	2	14	55	52	123
15 – Lancashire (2)	17	2	3	12	38	50	120
16 – Derbyshire (17)	17	2	4	11	36	48	116
17 – Glamorgan (18)	17	2	3	12	41	40	113
18 – Nottinghamshire (5)	17	0	5	12	46	45	91

1993 positions are shown in brackets.

The total for Northamptonshire includes 8 points for batting second in a match drawn with the scores level. The total for Durham includes 12 points for a win in a one-innings match.

Not surprisingly, the bowlers often struggled, and only four took 50 wickets. Sussex's Barbadian seam bowler, Vasbert Drakes, was alone in passing 60, with a county record of 65, while the slow left-armer, Alex Barnett of Lancashire, continued to make his mark in the competition with 58. He worked hard for his wickets, sending down a phenomenal 617 overs, compared with Drakes's 405.2. In fact, no one else bowled 500, the next most being 476.3 of off-spin for Yorkshire by Jeremy Batty, who was rewarded with 51 wickets. Among bowlers taking 20 wickets, the best average belonged to the Essex slow left-armer Courtney Ricketts, whose 25 wickets cost 15.52 apiece, and Somerset's Vince Clarke, whose leg-spin brought him 41 at 16.68. The season's best return was eight for 41 for Leicestershire by the young off-spinner, Tim Mason.

Drakes was also the leading all-rounder, with 751 runs in addition to his 65 wickets in 14 matches. Mark Garaway of Hampshire was the leading wicket-keeper with 46 dismissals. He was one of six players who appeared in all 17 of their county's matches.

After winning two of their first three matches, **Derbyshire** won no more and again finished near the bottom of the table. There was satisfaction, though, in their policy of introducing as many trialists as possible, which saw 49 players involved – more than any other county. They concentrated on local players and signed two – Johnny Owen, a top-order batsman, and Paul Aldred, a swing bowler. Another exciting new signing was 21-year-old Matthew Cassar, an economical fast bowler and top-order batsman, who scored the most runs, 694, and took by far the most wickets, 46, including seven for 68 against Somerset.

Durham's climb back to the middle of the table owed more to steady all-round contributions than to outstanding individual performances. Darren Blenkiron and Peter Wilcock – both consistent rather than spectacular – were alone in accumulating 600 runs, with six fifties apiece and a century for Blenkiron. Robin Weston followed his maiden century against Derbyshire with another against Surrey. The majority of the wickets were shared by Shaun Birbeck, bowling medium pace, and two spinners – left-armer David Cox and Jason Searle, an off-spinner. Colin Campbell came in for the last match against Essex and took six for 40.

Consistency was lacking in **Essex**, whose batting was particularly vulnerable and left them with the fewest batting points. However, Darren Robinson passed 1,000 runs, with two hundreds and seven fifties, and there were some impressive individual scores: Nick Knight made 211 not out against Northamptonshire, Muneeb Diwan scored 196 against Sussex in the same innings that Steve Andrew reached his maiden century, and Robert Rollins, the wicket-keeper, made 151 not out against Worcestershire. Off-spinner Richard Pearson was the leading wicket-taker with 46, while Darren Cousins confirmed his recovery from major surgery with 32.

Glamorgan moved up one place from the bottom of the table and were encouraged to see several players successfully progressing to the first team. There were some useful batting performances, notably from Andrew Roseberry and Alistair Dalton, who was named the county's Second Eleven Player of the Year. Gary Butcher and Jamie Bishop were also consistent, and Adrian Shaw, the wicket-keeper, hit a maiden hundred against Hampshire. Left-arm spinner Stuart Phelps and Owen Parkin, at medium pace, were alone in taking 20 wickets and with Parkin, Steve Bastien and Darren Thomas all injured at times, the bowling was a weakness. Simon Moore, a pace bowler who played in only two matches, made his mark with a return of eight for 66 against Lancashire.

The most satisfying of **Gloucestershire's** four wins was a first victory over Yorkshire – by an innings at Bradford – in which opening batsman Dean Hodgson made 194 not out. He scored another three centuries, including 104 and 111 not out against Glamorgan, his second instance of two in a match in the Championship. It was disappointing that no newcomers made appreciable progress. Five bowlers passed 20 wickets, pace bowler Pashah Sheeraz and Vyvian Pike, a leg-spinner, doing so for the first time. The most incisive was Andy Babington, who took 36 before retiring in July, including seven for 30 (match figures of 11 for 131) against Middlesex to dismiss them for 58. Muhammad Akram, on trial as a fast bowler, took six for 66 against Essex, and Ricardo Williams took his career tally to a county record 155, before being promoted to the first team.

Hampshire slipped down three places. Of their 41 players, Paul Whitaker, the left-hander formerly with Derbyshire, was the outstanding batsman with 1,147 runs. His maiden century in the competition came against Somerset and was followed by three more, including a county record 211 against Middlesex. The next most prolific was Rupert Cox, whose 667 runs included six fifties, while Giles White, formerly with Somerset, headed the averages with 438 in four matches. Martin Jean-Jacques and the left-arm spinner, Darren Flint, bore the brunt of the bowling, sharing 63 wickets. No one else took 20, but James Bovill had 16 from only 78 overs, including six for 69 against Middlesex.

Kent's consistency took them to third place. Theirs was the most settled side, featuring just 23 players, of whom Richard Ellison played in all the matches. The strong batting was headed by Matthew Walker, whose 1,269 runs included four hundreds. Nigel Llong, another left-hander, also made four, including 250 against Worcestershire. There were 13 centuries in all, including a first for Grant Sheen against Lancashire and two for David Fulton. Eddie Stanford, a left-arm spinner in his first full season, took 55 wickets, including six for 43 against Nottinghamshire, and was rewarded with a contract for 1995. Of the other five to take 20 wickets, fast bowler Julian Thompson was the most economical, while Duncan Spencer, making a rare appearance, destroyed Somerset with seven for 47.

Although **Lancashire**, runners-up in 1993, finished near the foot of the table, they were encouraged by the introduction of some young and promising players in a side whose average age was under 20. Mark Harvey forced his way into the first team, along with Darren Shadford, who showed surprising maturity in his first full season and scored the most runs. He was closely followed by Nathan Wood and Richard Green, also in his first full season. Ian Austin scored two centuries in the match against Glamorgan. Part way through the season, John Stanworth handed over the captaincy to Alex Barnett, who bowled his left-arm spin tirelessly.

Leicestershire shot up to fourth place in the Championship, as well as being runners-up in the Bain Clarkson Trophy. Two batsmen stood out, both Darren Maddy and the experienced Phil Robinson passing 1,000 runs. Maddy's Championship record of 1,498 runs included five hundreds, the biggest being 170 against Essex, and seven fifties. Robinson, who topped the averages, had three hundreds and seven fifties in his 1,037 runs. Jonathan Dakin, a left-handed batsman and right-arm medium-pace bowler, was the outstanding all-rounder with 772 runs and 34 wickets, including six for 35 against Northamptonshire. Matthew Brimson bowled 469 overs of left-arm spin to take 45 wickets, and off-spinner Tim Mason's 35 featured eight for 41 in an innings (13 for 77 in the match) against Durham.

Champions in 1993, **Middlesex** slid to tenth place, losing more matches than any other county. The batting, their mainstay for several seasons, faltered, with only the ever-present Jason Pooley passing 600 runs. He did so in style, scoring 1,076 with four hundreds, including 123 not out (carrying his bat) and 126 in the match against Hampshire. Although the bowling was considered disappointing, their 54 bowling bonus points were more than any other county managed. The most wickets fell to Kervin Marc, bowling medium-fast, who began well but found the season wearing and proved to be expensive. Off-spinner Keith Dutch had an unproductive season, although Oxford Blue Richard Yeabsley bowled steadily at medium pace, and promise was shown by slow left-armer Umar Rashid and Amer Khan, a leg-spinner who came in at the end of the season. Two young batsmen caught the eye: 16-year-old David Nash, a wicket-keeper-batsman, and 15-year-old Owais Shah.

A successful season for **Northamptonshire** saw them move up to fifth place in the Championship, as well as reaching the one-day semi-final. Tim Walton and Tom Harrison both passed 800 runs, while Russell Warren had 655 in seven matches. Walton scored a career-best 181 against Middlesex. David Sales, just 16, showed immense promise during his limited appearances and scored 166 against Nottinghamshire before making his first-team debut. Mark Bowen was again the leading wicket-taker and there were some impressive performances from fast bowler Scott Boswell and the off-spinner, Jason Brown.

Although it was a disappointing season for **Nottinghamshire**, who plummeted to the bottom of the table, there were some notable individual performances. In a generally inexperienced batting line-up, the Australian Lyndsay Walker was the most consistent. He scored two centuries, while there were three from Graeme Archer, whose excellent start earned him a place in the first team. Mathew Dowman and Wayne Dessaur scored the most runs, but it was Paul Pollard who played the innings of the season: the Championship record 277 not out against Gloucestershire. Most wickets fell to the spinners, with 43 each for the left-armer, James Hindson, and off-spinner Richard Bates, who also took 19 catches.

Somerset won their first Second Eleven Championship title by a huge margin, beating ten counties in the process. Their success came from a good all-round team effort, involving 33 players. Keith Parsons was again the leading batsman, passing 1,000 runs for the first time. His identical twin, Kevin, could not maintain the standards he set the previous season and was not retained, but made his mark when given out handled the ball against Lancashire. With a mixture of seam and leg-spin, Vince Clarke – Liverpool-born, Australian-bred – had the knack of taking vital wickets. He collected 41 in all to go with his 581 runs, and underlined his all-round ability with a maiden century against Worcestershire and the side's best innings return, seven for 32 against Middlesex. Pace bowler Paul Bird was close behind with 39 wickets, including match figures of ten for 90 against Sussex. The side was well led by Neil Burns, who had a sound season behind the stumps and totalled 938 with the bat, but was still not retained for 1995.

Surrey continued their downward slide to 11th. The 36-year-old Monte Lynch scored 1,072 runs, but otherwise only Graham Kersey passed 600. Kersey's 769 featured four hundreds, including 151 not out against Durham. There was a maiden century in that match for Neil Kendrick, who made a significant all-round contribution with 571 runs and 32 wickets, including seven for 64 against Essex. Jason de la Pena, the pace bowler who joined Surrey from Gloucestershire, took 33 wickets but, like Kendrick, he was expensive. The most impressive bowling performance of the season came from Richard Nowell, who took seven for 13 in the second innings (11 for 72 in the match) against Northamptonshire.

Sussex, beaten only once, felt they might have won more than three had the weather not ruined their last seven games. The outstanding player was the Barbadian Vasbert Drakes, unable to play in the County Championship because of the presence of Franklyn Stephenson and probably the fastest bowler in the Second Eleven Championship. As well as being the leading wicket-taker in second-team cricket, he scored 751 runs, with seven fifties – second in Sussex only to Keith Newell's 817. After a slow start, Newell began to fulfil his earlier promise, hitting more than 600 runs in his last six matches, while Toby Peirce made his presence felt after coming down from university in July. Newell's younger brother, Mark, and James Kirtley were seen as fine prospects with bat and ball respectively and both were rewarded with contracts for 1995. Following Drakes in the bowling averages was Jason Lewry, a fast left-arm bowler, who made his first-team debut. The wicket-keeper, Shaun Humphries, again played in all 17 matches, as did John North, who scored 748 runs.

Warwickshire's record of more drawn matches than any other county and fewer wins than all but Nottinghamshire does not reflect their attempt always to play positive cricket. They were restricted by call-ups to the first team, who were going for the Grand Slam, and the intervention of rain on 26 of 51 days. In a strong batting side, which earned the most bonus points (equal with Worcestershire), both Jason Ratcliffe and the left-handed Wasim Khan passed 1,000 runs. Although way ahead of the rest, these two were well supported by Michael Powell, who scored 677 runs in his first full season, and Doug Brown, the Scottish all-rounder, who was back to full fitness after two years of injury. As well as scoring 540 runs, Brown shared the bowling honours with left-arm spinner Ashley Giles. There were promising performances from several of the younger bowlers, especially the left-armer Darren Altree.

Worcestershire were another strong batting side and shared the most batting points with Warwickshire as they moved up eight places to the middle of the table. Their positive attitude was rewarded when they won the first three games, but thereafter they were often frustrated. Reuben Spiring, Adam Seymour and the Zimbabwean coach, David Houghton, all passed 800 runs, with Chris Tolley close behind. There were some significant individual scores, notably Philip Weston's unbeaten 200 against Hampshire – followed by 110 in the second innings – Spiring's 166 not out and Tolley's 164 against Surrey and Seymour's 160 not out against Somerset. Only Parvaz Mirza passed 25 wickets and his 30, the fruit of 306 overs, were expensive.

Yorkshire, another side whose strength lay in the batting, were runners-up in the Second Eleven Championship and winners of the one-day competition. Having narrowly missed the mark in 1993, Ashley Metcalfe passed 1,000 runs, while 18-year-old Anthony McGrath scored 815 in ten fewer innings. His three hundreds included 218 not out against Surrey and he shared in three century opening partnerships with Chris Schofield. The highest of these was 219 against Kent, and featured Schofield's maiden century. Another came in the match against Somerset, which was also memorable for Metcalfe's 109 and 136 not out and Jeremy Batty's match return of ten for 118. Batty also took seven for 71 against Hampshire and was by far the best bowler in an attack that gained the second-fewest bonus points. With 51 wickets, he was one of only four to pass 50 in the Championship. Of the 26 players used during the season, 11 came from the Cricket Academy. Colin Chapman, the wicket-keeper, played in all the matches for the second successive season.

*In the averages that follow, * against a score signifies not out, * against a name signifies the captain and † signifies a wicket-keeper.*

DERBYSHIRE SECOND ELEVEN

Matches 17: Won – Essex, Lancashire. Lost – Glamorgan, Kent, Leicestershire, Somerset. Drawn – Durham, Gloucestershire, Hampshire, Middlesex, Northamptonshire, Nottinghamshire, Surrey, Sussex, Warwickshire, Worcestershire, Yorkshire.

Batting Averages

	M	*I*	*NO*	*R*	*HS*	*100s*	*Avge*
P. D. Bowler	2	3	0	231	139	1	77.00
C. M. Wells	2	4	0	283	135	1	70.75
T. J. G. O'Gorman	3	6	2	280	114*	1	70.00
M. J. Vandrau	4	8	0	503	171	2	62.87
A. C. H. Seymour	2	4	2	122	67	0	61.00
S. J. Base	4	7	3	183	48	0	45.75
J. E. Owen	4	6	1	227	100*	1	45.40
*†B. J. M. Maher	11	10	6	168	44	0	42.00
M. E. Cassar	12	20	3	694	100	1	40.82
D. J. Lovell	7	14	1	493	142	1	37.92
I. G. S. Steer	7	11	0	386	85	0	35.09
T. A. Tweats	4	8	1	239	131	1	34.14
M. R. May	5	10	1	286	61	0	31.77
A. D. Bairstow	2	3	1	62	47	0	31.00
A. S. Rollins	3	5	1	120	93	0	30.00
M. Hood	2	3	0	78	33	0	26.00
†G. M. Pooley	12	21	1	469	61*	0	23.45
P. Aldred	9	12	3	190	37*	0	21.11
G. R. Hill	6	11	0	228	73	0	20.72
J. N. Batty	4	7	0	138	77	0	19.71
J. D. Cokayne	2	4	1	54	34	0	18.00
S. J. Lacey	5	9	1	127	69	0	15.87
A. J. Harris	12	17	6	140	29*	0	12.72
R. W. Sladdin	11	18	3	180	52	0	12.00
M. Taylor	13	16	6	107	30	0	10.70
A. W. Richardson	4	7	0	72	30	0	10.28
A. Richardson	9	8	3	25	11	0	5.00

Played in three matches: S. O. Moore 0, 2. Played in two matches: K. J. Dean 0, 10*, 5; F. A. Griffith 4, 1, 10; O. Mathias 4, 18, 5, 7. Played in one match: A. A. Choudry 4; D. G. Cork 59; G. W. Deane 1, 10*; M. Diwan 48, 14*; R. J. Fisher 5, 7; B. A. Hames 69*; K. Hunter 5, 11; R. O. Jones 16; J. C. Maynard 2; C. M. Patel 22*; S. Platt 6, 25; D. Spasic 58, 23; P. G. T. Davies, M. J. Deane, Mohammad Amjad, O. H. Mortensen, I. M. Stanger and D. R. Womble did not bat.

Note: In the match v Sussex at Horsham I. G. S. Steer, called up for a first-team match, was replaced by B. A. Hames.

Bowling Averages

	O	M	R	W	BB	Avge
D. G. Cork	23.1	8	66	5	4-38	13.20
M. E. Cassar	303.1	59	981	46	7-68	21.32
K. J. Dean	42	3	161	6	3-58	26.83
A. J. Harris	250.4	46	888	28	4-18	31.71
A. Richardson	167.3	33	549	17	3-17	32.29
P. Aldred	188	29	612	18	4-74	34.00
S. O. Moore	45.3	7	197	5	2-36	39.40
I. G. S. Steer	76	23	204	5	2-46	40.80
M. Taylor	271.4	62	1,021	25	4-67	40.84
S. J. Base	95.5	10	360	7	4-78	51.42
A. W. Richardson	64	5	327	6	2-35	54.50
R. W. Sladdin	268.2	89	836	15	5-98	55.73

Also bowled: A. A. Choudry 16.2–5–60–0; M. J. Deane 14–2–57–0; F. A. Griffith 31–8–87–2; G. R. Hill 1–0–1–0; K. Hunter 8–2–30–1; R. O. Jones 24–1–71–1; S. J. Lacey 82–16–310–3; D. J. Lovell 5–0–25–0; B. J. M. Maher 8–1–28–1; J. C. Maynard 19–1–75–2; Mohammad Amjad 20–3–89–3; O. H. Mortensen 19.1–3–55–0; C. M. Patel 23–2–126–1; G. M. Pooley 1–0–6–0; A. S. Rollins 14–1–71–1; A. C. H. Seymour 7–1–30–0; D. Spasic 26–3–95–2; I. M. Stanger 17–1–73–2; T. A. Tweats 7–1–30–0; M. J. Vandrau 58.2–18–160–3; C. M. Wells 33.1–3–134–2; D. R. Womble 18–3–54–1.

DURHAM SECOND ELEVEN

Matches 17: Won – Essex, Gloucestershire, Lancashire, Worcestershire. Lost – Leicestershire, Northamptonshire, Somerset, Surrey, Sussex. Drawn – Derbyshire, Glamorgan, Hampshire, Kent, Middlesex, Nottinghamshire, Warwickshire, Yorkshire.

Batting Averages

	M	I	NO	R	HS	100s	Avge
G. Fowler	7	11	2	503	161	2	55.88
I. Smith	10	18	3	545	88	0	36.33
D. A. Blenkiron	15	25	3	780	110	1	35.45
R. M. S. Weston	8	14	1	459	140	2	35.30
J. A. Daley	10	17	0	591	106	1	34.76
J. I. Longley	3	5	0	152	77	0	30.40
S. Hutton	7	12	1	327	67	0	29.72
†A. R. Fothergill	12	17	6	302	60	0	27.45
P. J. Berry	5	6	0	146	54	0	24.33
S. D. Birbeck	13	18	4	334	81*	0	23.85
P. J. Wilcock	16	29	1	667	75	0	23.82
D. Williamson	4	8	2	125	34*	0	20.83
J. Wood	3	3	0	56	39	0	18.66
†D. G. C. Ligertwood	5	9	1	148	57*	0	18.50
N. J. Trainor	5	9	0	146	48	0	16.22
D. M. Cox	11	12	3	142	40	0	15.77
P. W. Henderson	2	3	1	30	17	0	15.00
A. Walker	5	5	0	67	35	0	13.40
M. M. Betts	9	11	4	86	19*	0	12.28
J. P. Searle	13	14	7	72	17*	0	10.28
K. Thomson	4	4	0	38	24	0	9.50
S. Lugsden	6	6	2	36	15*	0	9.00

Played in two matches: A. Jones 3, 0*, 0*; F. A. Rose 47, 33. Played in one match: A. Agrawalla 20, 7*; P. Bainbridge 73, 5; C. Campbell 1; D. Gormley 86; N. Killeen 39*, 13*; S. T. Knox 11, 1; D. M. Lane 46, 19; G. R. Mason 21, 8; M. Saxelby 39, 12; G. Wigham 2, 1.

Bowling Averages

	O	*M*	*R*	*W*	*BB*	*Avge*
C. Campbell	32	6	86	9	6-40	9.55
S. D. Birbeck	240	54	719	34	5-71	21.14
A. Walker	144.2	44	350	16	5-33	21.87
D. M. Cox	361.4	134	893	39	5-32	22.89
D. Williamson	93	25	290	11	4-93	26.36
J. P. Searle	299.2	74	889	27	6-100	32.92
S. Lugsden	156.3	35	448	13	3-44	34.46
K. Thomson	57	18	175	5	3-37	35.50
J. Wood	63	6	284	8	3-52	35.55
F. A. Rose	55	14	145	4	3-72	36.25
M. M. Betts	188.3	29	813	21	5-85	38.71
D. A. Blenkiron	109	28	331	7	2-32	47.28
P. J. Berry	108	24	348	4	2-58	87.00

Also bowled: A. Agrawalla 9–0–101–1; P. Bainbridge 34–11–96–2; G. Fowler 2.2–0–12–0; D. Gormley 3–2–1–0; P. W. Henderson 33–4–147–1; A. Jones 48–5–155–1; N. Killeen 25–6–83–3; D. M. Lane 5–2–8–1; G. R. Mason 13–0–85–2; I. Smith 40–3–180–1; R. M. S. Weston 11.2–3–41–0; G. Wigham 2–1–2–0; P. J. Wilcock 2–0–5–0.

ESSEX SECOND ELEVEN

Matches 17: Won – Kent, Middlesex, Worcestershire. Lost – Derbyshire, Durham, Gloucestershire, Somerset, Yorkshire. Drawn – Glamorgan, Hampshire, Lancashire, Leicestershire, Northamptonshire, Nottinghamshire, Surrey, Sussex, Warwickshire.

Batting Averages

	M	*I*	*NO*	*R*	*HS*	*100s*	*Avge*
N. V. Knight	2	4	1	246	211*	1	82.00
*A. R. Butcher	7	10	6	232	74*	0	58.00
J. J. B. Lewis	3	5	2	135	67*	0	45.00
D. D. J. Robinson	16	30	1	1,082	120	2	37.31
N. Pratt	2	4	1	107	72*	0	35.66
M. Diwan	14	25	1	828	196	2	34.50
G. A. Khan	11	19	1	548	106*	1	30.44
S. J. W. Andrew	10	13	5	228	100*	1	28.50
†R. J. Rollins	16	29	4	691	151*	1	27.64
C. I. O. Ricketts	8	12	1	283	56*	0	25.72
N. Shahid	11	19	1	426	100*	1	23.66
M. G. Powell	7	12	2	199	46	0	19.90
R. M. Pearson	13	19	4	273	44*	0	18.20
A. J. E. Hibbert	6	10	0	171	47	0	17.10
D. M. Cousins	13	15	7	125	22	0	15.62
D. J. P. Boden	13	21	1	293	91*	0	14.65
T. D. Topley	9	14	1	161	35	0	12.38
D. W. Ayres	6	7	3	33	15	0	8.25

Played in two matches: I. J. Harvey 21*, 17. Played in one match: N. C. Adams 0, 9; C. Atkins 4; I. N. Blanchett 2, 1; A. C. Churchill 6, 19; A. P. Cole 15, 0; G. J. Fogarty 4, 10; C. J. A. Goodwin 4, 1; M. C. Ilott 10, 1; D. G. C. Ligertwood 77, 5; P. J. Prichard 24, 10; G. M. Roberts 26, 6; M. J. Saggers 2; C. Stanley 2, 0*; J. P. Stephenson 0; P. Thompson 10; A. D. Brown, J. H. Childs and D. Follett did not bat.

Bowling Averages

	O	M	R	W	BB	Avge
M. C. Ilott	26	5	75	6	6-48	12.50
C. Stanley	25	9	60	4	2-29	15.00
C. I. O. Ricketts	189.2	67	388	25	5-31	15.52
J. H. Childs	33	15	66	4	2-21	16.50
P. Thompson	33	8	92	5	5-43	18.40
S. J. W. Andrew	226.4	41	639	26	3-8	24.57
N. Shahid	99.1	26	278	11	5-45	25.27
I. J. Harvey	28.5	5	103	4	3-16	25.75
R. M. Pearson	474.1	130	1,188	46	6-71	25.82
D. M. Cousins	315.2	72	981	32	4-36	30.65
D. J. P. Boden	237.3	51	899	27	4-47	33.29
D. W. Ayres	69.5	18	263	7	3-35	37.57
M. G. Powell	180.4	41	572	10	4-147	57.20
T. D. Topley	163	34	616	6	2-54	102.66

Also bowled: C. Atkins 31–9–108–2; I. N. Blanchett 18–2–75–0; A. C. Churchill 3–1–7–0; A. P. Cole 10–1–24–0; G. J. Fogarty 1–0–5–0; D. Follett 19.1–3–78–3; C. J. A. Goodwin 19–4–53–3; N. Pratt 3–1–2–0; G. M. Roberts 48–13–140–2; D. D. J. Robinson 3–1–6–0; R. J. Rollins 0.3–0–10–0; M. J. Saggers 11–2–37–1; J. P. Stephenson 21–5–57–2.

GLAMORGAN SECOND ELEVEN

Matches 17: Won – Derbyshire, Somerset. Lost – Kent, Lancashire, Yorkshire. Drawn – Durham, Essex, Gloucestershire, Hampshire, Leicestershire, Middlesex, Northamptonshire, Nottinghamshire, Surrey, Sussex, Warwickshire, Worcestershire.

Batting Averages

	M	I	NO	R	HS	100s	Avge
J. P. J. Sylvester	3	6	0	317	110	1	52.83
A. J. Dalton	10	15	0	676	103	1	45.06
A. Roseberry	12	21	0	794	125	1	37.80
G. P. Butcher	14	25	6	685	77	0	36.05
J. Bishop	13	22	0	691	135	1	31.40
*J. Derrick	14	18	8	287	39*	0	28.70
J. R. A. Williams	9	15	0	420	64	0	28.00
G. H. J. Rees	16	23	4	519	67*	0	27.31
R. O. Jones	8	11	1	225	48	0	22.50
S. P. James	4	6	0	133	80	0	22.16
A. J. Jones	8	13	2	210	67*	0	19.09
†A. D. Shaw	14	18	4	244	100*	1	17.42
B. S. Phelps	13	18	4	212	39*	0	15.14
S. D. Thomas	11	12	0	147	50	0	12.25
O. T. Parkin	8	7	2	17	6	0	3.40
D. J. Worrad	4	6	2	10	6*	0	2.50

Played in four matches: S. R. Barwick 2, 1, 5. Played in three matches: S. Bastien 2, 5; A. P. Davies 31, 22*, 1; R. P. Lefebvre 4, 15, 16. Played in two matches: R. D. B. Croft 88, 38*, 43; G. J. M. Edwards 0*; A. W. Evans 5, 32*; S. O. Moore 0*. Played in one match: C. Feltham 1*; P. J. Nicholson 17; N. J. Wood 0, 13*; B. Zuiderent 30, 3; D. A. Cosker, R. E. Evans and P. S. Jones did not bat.

Note: In the match v Surrey at The Oval O. T. Parkin and A. D. Shaw, called up for a first-team match, were replaced by J. Derrick and G. H. J. Rees.

Bowling Averages

	O	*M*	*R*	*W*	*BB*	*Avge*
S. O. Moore	50	14	150	8	8-66	18.75
O. T. Parkin	189	41	556	24	5-59	23.16
N. J. Wood	37	11	148	6	4-73	24.66
R. P. Lefebvre	72	18	215	6	3-51	35.83
R. D. B. Croft	73.2	16	221	6	4-126	36.83
B. S. Phelps	397.4	109	1,210	30	5-34	40.33
J. Derrick	185.5	50	577	14	4-63	41.21
S. Bastien	84.2	17	248	5	3-125	49.60
G. P. Butcher	236.4	50	847	16	5-86	52.93
S. D. Thomas	235	29	861	16	4-46	53.81
D. J. Worrad	78.5	11	364	6	2-58	60.66
R. O. Jones	171.2	28	579	8	2-119	72.37

Also bowled: S. R. Barwick 115.3–33–274–2; D. A. Cosker 16–6–46–2; A. J. Dalton 1–1–0–0; A. P. Davies 34.5–7–87–2; G. J. M. Edwards 17.3–5–53–3; C. Feltham 45–7–136–3; P. S. Jones 16–5–29–2; J. P. J. Sylvester 28–2–129–4.

GLOUCESTERSHIRE SECOND ELEVEN

Matches 17: Won – Essex, Middlesex, Northamptonshire, Yorkshire. Lost – Durham, Surrey, Worcestershire. Drawn – Derbyshire, Glamorgan, Hampshire, Kent, Lancashire, Leicestershire, Nottinghamshire, Somerset, Sussex, Warwickshire.

Batting Averages

	M	*I*	*NO*	*R*	*HS*	*100s*	*Avge*
G. D. Hodgson	8	15	4	828	194*	4	75.27
S. G. Hinks	8	14	2	638	148	3	53.16
A. J. Wright	2	4	0	193	73	0	48.25
R. C. Williams	8	13	2	418	125	1	38.00
J. M. M. Averis	4	5	3	75	28*	0	37.50
R. J. Cunliffe	14	22	2	700	139	1	35.00
J. Shepherd	3	5	0	171	52	0	34.20
T. H. C. Hancock	3	5	0	169	112	1	33.80
R. I. Dawson	4	5	0	167	60	0	33.40
†R. C. J. Williams	16	22	3	577	95	0	30.36
D. R. Hewson	16	25	2	677	83*	0	29.43
Z. A. Sher	2	4	1	84	32	0	28.00
R. M. Wight	10	15	1	378	108	1	27.00
M. W. Alleyne	2	4	0	107	50	0	26.75
K. P. Sheeraz	15	16	6	192	49	0	19.20
M. Davies	12	16	5	172	36	0	15.63
M. J. Cawdron	15	19	2	218	47	0	12.82
N. Davey	5	6	0	67	22	0	11.16
A. M. Babington	8	9	4	41	16	0	8.20
V. J. Pike	8	9	2	55	28	0	7.85

Played in three matches: Muhammad Akram 1, 9, 31*; A. M. Smith 4, 6. Played in two matches: M. C. J. Ball 28, 0, 21*; †P. J. Nicholson 2; T. R. Samuels 28; M. J. Tamplin 5, 2, 11; B. L. Worrad 2*, 2. Played in one match: J. M. Fielding 0; D. E. A. Lawrence 5, 2; J. P. J. Sylvester 6, 1*; J. G. Whitby-Coles 1*; M. G. N. Windows 20, 22; K. E. Cooper, S. G. Joyner and M. J. O'Sullivan did not bat.

Bowling Averages

	O	*M*	*R*	*W*	*BB*	*Avge*
A. M. Smith	24.5	6	59	6	5-24	9.83
Muhammad Akram	99.2	21	265	16	6-66	16.56
A. M. Babington	227.5	41	783	36	7-30	21.75
R. M. Wight	192.3	45	561	23	5-15	24.39
R. C. Williams	185.2	45	520	21	4-39	24.76
V. J. Pike	247.4	67	695	28	4-48	24.82
M. J. Cawdron	206.3	53	556	18	5-24	30.88
K. P. Sheeraz	327.1	82	918	23	5-28	39.91
M. Davies	283	79	789	19	5-34	41.52

Also bowled: M. W. Alleyne 43–14–131–4; J. M. M. Averis 44–9–159–3; M. C. J. Ball 67–22–173–5; R. I. Dawson 2–2–0–1; J. M. Fielding 6–3–6–0; T. H. C. Hancock 5–0–34–0; S. G. Joyner 25–1–94–4; M. J. O'Sullivan 31–7–109–2; T. R. Samuels 54–7–112–3; Z. A. Sher 10–1–21–0; J. G. Whitby-Coles 6–1–25–1.

HAMPSHIRE SECOND ELEVEN

Matches 17: Won – Nottinghamshire, Warwickshire. Lost – Kent, Leicestershire, Somerset, Sussex, Worcestershire. Drawn – Derbyshire, Durham, Essex, Glamorgan, Gloucestershire, Lancashire, Middlesex, Northamptonshire, Surrey, Yorkshire.

Batting Averages

	M	*I*	*NO*	*R*	*HS*	*100s*	*Avge*
G. W. White	4	8	4	438	129*	1	109.50
M. Brink	3	5	1	288	139	1	72.00
P. R. Whitaker	14	22	2	1,147	211	4	57.35
K. D. James	4	8	2	299	120*	1	49.83
J. S. Laney	11	19	2	591	91	0	34.76
R. M. F. Cox	13	23	1	667	76	0	30.31
S. C. Janes	6	10	0	302	115	1	30.20
G. R. Treagus	6	9	3	174	35	0	29.00
M. Keech	10	19	2	474	116	1	27.88
†M. Garaway	17	26	5	519	53	0	24.71
R. J. Maru	4	6	0	119	54	0	19.83
L. J. Botham	6	9	0	157	35	0	17.44
M. Jean-Jacques	13	16	1	260	79	0	17.33
T. C. Middleton	4	8	0	118	34	0	14.75
Imtiaz Ahmed	4	8	0	88	30	0	11.00
D. B. Goldstraw	7	7	4	33	18*	0	11.00
R. R. Dibden	9	8	2	62	20*	0	10.33
C. E. Sketchley	4	7	2	40	16	0	8.00
D. P. J. Flint	15	16	6	59	25	0	5.90

Played in four matches: M. J. Thursfield 135, 29. Played in three matches: M. W. Handman 3, 6, 10, 0; I. J. Harvey 34, 33, 6. Played in two matches: J. E. Allen 3*, 4*, 4*, 0; J. N. B. Bovill 0, 0; C. A. Connor 16, 31*, 9; W. S. Kendall 5, 11, 34, 59. Played in one match: C. S. Atkins 9; R. J. Baggs 0; C. E. Dagnall 4; N. Davey 26, 5; J. W. Dike 8, 24; P. N. Gover 23, 0; R. A. C. Jerman 5; B. McCreesh 26; R. I. McKinlay 10, 4; R. T. P. Miller 16, 4; L. Savident 6, 3; J. L. Taylor 0, 34; D. M. Thomas 4, 8; U. D. Valjee 3, 28; C. J. Chandler did not bat.

Bowling Averages

	O	*M*	*R*	*W*	*BB*	*Avge*
J. N. B. Bovill	77.1	19	250	16	6-69	15.62
M. J. Thursfield	87.1	22	225	12	5-50	18.75
M. W. Handman	37.3	8	99	5	2-22	19.80
C. E. Sketchley	126	32	384	13	5-96	29.53
R. J. Maru	155	59	407	13	4-46	31.30
K. D. James	90	25	232	7	3-52	33.14
D. B. Goldstraw	166.4	30	603	18	5-21	33.50
J. E. Allen	31	3	165	4	2-57	41.25
M. Jean-Jacques	383	100	1,243	30	5-54	41.43
D. P. J. Flint	433.2	104	1,431	33	5-63	43.36
R. R. Dibden	179	41	699	15	4-59	46.60
L. J. Botham	101	12	432	9	3-51	48.00
P. R. Whitaker	115.4	15	473	9	3-72	52.55

Also bowled: C. S. Atkins 42–16–132–4; C. J. Chandler 5–2–8–0; R. M. F. Cox 2–0–20–0; C. A. Connor 49.1–11–121–3; C. E. Dagnall 22–4–102–3; J. W. Dike 17–1–74–3; I. J. Harvey 36–5–170–3; Imtiaz Ahmed 6–1–29–0; M. Keech 31–7–112–1; W. S. Kendall 2–0–21–1; J. S. Laney 3.1–1–20–0; R. T. P. Miller 5–1–22–1; L. Savident 6–0–39–0; D. M. Thomas 9–2–26–1; G. W. White 8–3–32–1.

KENT SECOND ELEVEN

Matches 17: Won – Derbyshire, Glamorgan, Hampshire, Middlesex, Nottinghamshire, Somerset. Lost – Essex, Yorkshire. Drawn – Durham, Gloucestershire, Lancashire, Leicestershire, Northamptonshire, Surrey, Sussex, Warwickshire, Worcestershire.

Batting Averages

	M	*I*	*NO*	*R*	*HS*	*100s*	*Avge*
D. J. Spencer	2	3	1	142	80*	0	71.00
M. A. Ealham	2	4	1	206	71	0	68.66
N. R. Taylor	2	3	0	197	99	0	65.66
M. V. Fleming	2	3	0	182	117	1	60.66
D. P. Fulton	8	15	2	718	127*	2	55.23
M. J. Walker	14	27	3	1,269	130*	4	52.87
N. J. Llong	10	18	1	886	250	4	52.11
G. R. Cowdrey	9	15	1	603	178*	1	43.07
S. Ahmed	7	10	2	246	69*	0	30.75
*R. M. Ellison	17	28	7	636	74	0	30.28
†S. C. Willis	16	24	4	563	72	0	28.15
G. J. J. Sheen	13	24	3	526	122	1	25.04
N. W. Preston	15	16	4	291	57	0	24.25
J. B. D. Thompson	9	13	1	278	50*	0	23.16
*C. Penn	15	14	1	280	86	0	21.53
M. J. McCague	5	7	0	117	59	0	16.71
E. J. Stanford	16	14	10	34	11	0	8.50
B. J. Phillips	8	9	2	57	22	0	8.14
T. N. Wren	12	13	1	74	18	0	6.16

Played in two matches: M. R. Fletcher 6, 3. Played in one match: W. J. House 23*, 20*; M. M. Patel 23; N. C. Price 2.

Bowling Averages

	O	*M*	*R*	*W*	*BB*	*Avge*
M. M. Patel	32	13	56	5	4-29	11.20
D. J. Spencer	26.5	1	91	7	7-47	13.00
J. B. D. Thompson	164.4	38	439	22	5-19	19.95
M. A. Ealham	30.3	7	84	4	2-17	21.00
G. J. J. Sheen	138	30	447	21	4-58	21.28

	O	M	R	W	BB	Avge
E. J. Stanford	456.5	110	1,267	55	6-43	23.03
M. J. McCague	55	12	164	6	3-36	27.33
N. W. Preston	229.4	51	656	23	4-41	28.52
T. N. Wren	268.4	69	779	23	3-29	33.86
C. Penn	222	56	559	16	3-33	34.93
R. M. Ellison	240	58	660	18	5-28	36.66
N. J. Llong	285.3	51	886	22	5-56	40.27

Also bowled: G. R. Cowdrey 11.5–1–49–1; M. V. Fleming 27–3–91–2; M. R. Fletcher 10–3–22–0; B. J. Phillips 34–2–140–2; M. J. Walker 1–0–2–0.

LANCASHIRE SECOND ELEVEN

Matches 17: Won – Glamorgan, Yorkshire. Lost – Derbyshire, Durham, Northamptonshire. Drawn – Essex, Gloucestershire, Hampshire, Kent, Leicestershire, Middlesex, Nottinghamshire, Somerset, Surrey, Sussex, Warwickshire, Worcestershire.

Batting Averages

	M	I	NO	R	HS	100s	Avge
I. D. Austin	4	8	2	468	178	2	78.00
G. Chapple	2	4	1	167	51	0	55.66
D. J. Shadford	14	23	8	777	106*	2	51.80
S. P. Titchard	6	11	1	454	109	1	45.40
M. E. Harvey	8	13	2	457	120*	1	41.54
A. Flintoff	4	5	1	159	109*	1	39.75
P. C. McKeown	3	3	0	110	94	0	36.66
N. T. Wood	13	23	2	743	88	0	35.38
*J. Stanworth	6	5	3	65	52*	0	32.50
R. J. Green	16	28	3	725	103	1	29.00
G. Yates	2	4	1	80	59*	0	26.66
J. M. Fielding	11	16	2	307	94*	0	21.92
L. J. Marland	6	8	1	137	37	0	19.57
C. Brown	16	15	7	127	23	0	15.87
A. A. Barnett	14	19	4	222	46*	0	14.80
S. E. Dearden	4	5	0	73	33	0	14.60
M. S. Ramsbottom	5	8	1	99	35	0	14.14
†N. P. Harvey	16	19	2	215	40	0	12.64
A. D. Mawson	2	4	0	49	30	0	12.25
J. Ratledge	3	5	0	46	20	0	9.20
N. A. Derbyshire	14	13	4	67	38	0	7.44
P. J. Seal	9	5	1	22	10	0	5.50

Played in one match: P. J. Berry 108, 21; J. R. Byrne 4*, 3; A. J. Crozier 3; C. E. Dagnall 7; C. Duxbury 14, 13*; J. E. R. Gallian 29, 26; G. D. Lloyd 161, 94; P. J. Martin 95, 22; †J. R. Moyes 15*, 0*; N. J. Speak 0.

Note: In the match v Middlesex at Haslingden S. P. Titchard, called up for a first-team match, was replaced by S. E. Dearden.

Bowling Averages

	O	M	R	W	BB	Avge
G. Yates	79.5	29	188	10	5-47	18.80
R. J. Green	69	17	216	10	5-64	21.60
A. A. Barnett	617	216	1,414	58	6-75	24.37
I. D. Austin	79	28	165	6	3-21	27.50
G. Chapple	57	8	174	6	5-75	29.00
C. Brown	340	94	1,046	30	5-48	34.86
N. A. Derbyshire	285.4	55	1,077	25	4-33	43.08
D. J. Shadford	208.2	42	766	16	4-49	47.87
S. E. Dearden	92	9	393	7	2-29	56.14
J. M. Fielding	250.4	62	774	10	3-79	77.40

Also bowled: J. R. Byrne 27–6–97–3; C. E. Dagnall 4–0–20–0; C. Duxbury 8–0–24–0; A. Flintoff 3–0–8–0; J. E. R. Gallian 17–4–23–3; P. J. Martin 22–12–36–5; P. J. Seal 106–28–354–3.

LEICESTERSHIRE SECOND ELEVEN

Matches 17: Won – Derbyshire, Durham, Hampshire, Northamptonshire, Surrey. Lost – Somerset, Worcestershire. Drawn – Essex, Glamorgan, Gloucestershire, Kent, Lancashire, Middlesex, Nottinghamshire, Sussex, Warwickshire, Yorkshire.

Batting Averages

	M	*I*	*NO*	*R*	*HS*	*100s*	*Avge*
P. E. Robinson	12	23	8	1,037	125*	3	69.13
T. J. Boon	2	4	1	203	60*	0	67.66
B. F. Smith	4	6	1	324	100	1	64.80
D. L. Maddy	16	29	2	1,498	170	5	55.48
P. N. Hepworth	8	13	1	602	169*	2	50.16
I. J. Sutcliffe	6	9	1	346	88	0	43.25
A. I. Ditta	14	20	7	525	62	0	40.38
J. M. Dakin	15	23	3	772	125*	2	38.60
S. J. Bartle	9	15	2	480	81	0	36.92
G. I. Macmillan	8	14	0	468	146	2	33.42
N. A. Stanley	6	9	1	233	102*	1	29.12
*†P. Whitticase	14	17	5	329	65*	0	27.41
D. A. Turner	5	7	3	102	59*	0	25.50
M. T. Brimson	13	12	6	135	50	0	22.50
T. J. Mason	11	8	2	111	29	0	18.50
I. M. Stanger	11	8	3	80	31*	0	16.00
C. J. Griffiths	3	3	0	38	18	0	12.66
A. F. Haye	9	13	0	161	36	0	12.38
A. Sheriyar	11	6	2	26	9	0	6.50

Played in one match: C. S. Atkins 36; A. S. Christmas 5; C. D. Crowe 1, 86; C. D. Durant 0; D. J. Millns 1; A. R. K. Pierson 13; P. A. Rawden 3; J. F. Venter 37, 54*; P. Aldred and A. D. Mullally did not bat.

Bowling Averages

	O	*M*	*R*	*W*	*BB*	*Avge*
A. D. Mullally	24	5	86	5	5-86	17.20
T. J. Mason	264.5	95	638	35	8-41	18.22
C. S. Atkins	35	8	111	5	3-50	22.20
J. M. Dakin	276.3	69	785	34	6-35	23.08
M. T. Brimson	468.1	143	1,215	45	6-69	27.00
A. I. Ditta	213	57	686	25	3-26	27.44
A. Sheriyar	261.3	67	784	25	4-39	31.36
D. A. Turner	123	37	338	9	3-40	37.55
S. J. Bartle	93	27	277	7	3-13	39.57
I. M. Stanger	247.2	70	715	17	3-39	42.05
P. N. Hepworth	64	21	202	4	2-30	50.50

Also bowled: P. Aldred 30–5–98–1; T. J. Boon 2.4–0–8–0; A. S. Christmas 20–3–96–1; C. D. Crowe 35–13–74–3; C. J. Griffiths 25–11–60–3; A. F. Haye 83–12–323–3; G. I. Macmillan 24.4–5–84–3; D. L. Maddy 28–5–100–0; D. J. Millns 31–7–83–3; A. R. K. Pierson 9–0–46–0; P. A. Rawden 27–0–107–1; P. E. Robinson 1–0–9–0; J. F. Venter 42–11–126–2.

MIDDLESEX SECOND ELEVEN

Matches 17: Won – Nottinghamshire, Surrey, Worcestershire. Lost – Essex, Gloucestershire, Kent, Northamptonshire, Somerset, Yorkshire. Drawn – Derbyshire, Durham, Glamorgan, Hampshire, Lancashire, Leicestershire, Sussex, Warwickshire.

Batting Averages

	M	*I*	*NO*	*R*	*HS*	*100s*	*Avge*
P. N. Weekes	4	6	0	325	115	1	54.16
*J. C. Pooley	17	29	5	1,076	172	4	44.83
†D. C. Nash	4	6	1	219	77	0	43.80
K. J. Shine	5	5	3	70	25*	0	35.00
R. S. Yeabsley	7	11	4	233	51*	0	33.28
M. A. Feltham	3	4	1	97	71	0	32.33
R. J. Sims	12	20	0	554	79	0	27.70
†P. Farbrace	14	20	1	523	111*	1	27.52
T. A. Radford	12	22	3	501	99*	0	26.36
A. Habib	14	24	3	535	65	0	25.47
R. J. Ballinger	5	6	2	82	25*	0	20.50
K. G. Sedgbeer	2	4	0	81	41	0	20.25
U. Rashid	7	9	1	159	41	0	19.87
J. C. Harrison	14	23	2	410	83*	0	19.52
K. P. Dutch	11	15	2	243	64	0	18.69
R. Rao	4	6	1	85	50	0	17.00
O. A. Shah	4	7	0	105	37	0	15.00
J. P. Hewitt	4	4	1	38	24*	0	12.66
*I. J. Gould	5	7	2	48	19	0	9.60
K. Marc	15	16	3	117	19	0	9.00
S. Patel	2	4	0	14	14	0	3.50

Played in four matches: C. W. Taylor 12, 0. Played in three matches: R. L. Johnson 76, 5*, 81. Played in two matches: R. A. Fay 35* 2, 2; A. A. Khan 0, 0; J. Mallett 0*, 4*; N. F. Williams 2, 0. Played in one match: W. R. Addison 4, 5; †J. Bahl 2; M. D. Broom 6, 0; R. J. Burroughs 5; †N. D. J. Cartmell 16, 20; A. G. J. Fraser 0, 51*; C. J. Knapman 11; M. A. Roseberry 44*, 9; P. C. R. Tufnell did not bat.

Note: Owing to first-team calls J. C. Pooley was replaced by I. J. Gould in the match v Surrey at Harrow and N. F. Williams was replaced by J. P. Hewitt in the match v Hampshire at Southampton.

Bowling Averages

	O	*M*	*R*	*W*	*BB*	*Avge*
K. J. Shine	120.5	30	341	16	3-42	21.31
R. J. Ballinger	88.1	15	281	13	5-29	21.61
J. P. Hewitt	61.3	8	274	12	6-80	22.83
R. S. Yeabsley	163.3	32	586	23	5-76	25.47
U. Rashid	239.5	88	559	18	6-21	31.05
K. P. Dutch	347	93	949	29	4-77	32.72
S. Patel	42.5	3	188	5	3-78	37.60
P. N. Weekes	157.2	42	453	12	3-62	37.75
K. Marc	346.1	49	1,245	32	6-56	38.90
C. W. Taylor	97	20	283	6	2-41	47.16

Also bowled: W. R. Addison 22–4–94–3; R. J. Burroughs 25–5–64–0; R. A. Fay 52–7–142–2; M. A. Feltham 75–19–142–7; I. J. Gould 20–1–104–2; A. Habib 26.5–2–125–3; J. C. Harrison 78–15–263–3; R. L. Johnson 53.3–10–132–3; A. A. Khan 79–26–180–8; C. J. Knapman 22–5–71–1; J. Mallett 21–0–84–2; R. Rao 42.3–7–133–1; K. G. Sedgbeer 29–9–85–2; P. C. R. Tufnell 21–2–71–2; N. F. Williams 29.5–4–108–1.

NORTHAMPTONSHIRE SECOND ELEVEN

Matches 17: Won – Durham, Lancashire, Middlesex. Lost – Gloucestershire, Leicestershire, Surrey, Yorkshire. Drawn – Derbyshire, Essex, Glamorgan, Hampshire, Kent, Nottinghamshire, Somerset, Sussex, Warwickshire, Worcestershire.

Batting Averages

	M	*I*	*NO*	*R*	*HS*	*100s*	*Avge*
J. N. Snape	4	6	1	375	176	2	75.00
D. J. Sales	5	8	2	389	166	1	64.83
R. J. Warren	7	13	1	655	141*	2	54.58
T. C. Walton	13	22	3	820	181	1	43.15
T. W. Harrison	12	21	0	823	130	2	39.19
R. R. Montgomerie	4	7	0	240	119	1	34.28
D. J. Capel	4	7	1	198	65	0	33.00
A. R. Roberts	8	14	0	445	77	0	31.78
K. J. Innes	10	15	2	372	106	1	28.61
†I. Dawood	9	11	3	207	82	0	25.87
M. N. Bowen	12	12	2	253	56	0	25.30
J. P. Taylor	3	5	2	74	40	0	24.66
C. J. Rika	12	17	1	379	57	0	23.68
D. J. Roberts	6	11	3	152	29*	0	19.00
*R. M. Carter	11	10	4	110	43*	0	18.33
A. C. Cottam	13	13	4	150	30*	0	16.66
J. G. Hughes	5	8	3	79	50*	0	15.80
J. F. Brown	11	8	4	47	18	0	11.75
J. D. Wells	6	10	1	104	53	0	11.55
S. A. J. Boswell	9	7	0	46	18	0	6.57

Played in three matches: †C. Nevin 18, 0. Played in two matches: C. S. Atkins 34; †T. M. B. Bailey 64, 13, 6*; N. G. B. Cook 16, 62*, 0; S. Elworthy 31, 1, 37, 2; A. Fordham 22*, 64, 9; J. Lewis 7*, 4*, 0; A. J. Swann 86, 36, 61. Played in one match: K. M. Curran 52, 25; N. A. Felton 1, 23; G. Herbert 3, 5; S. J. Renshaw 23; †D. Ripley, 50, 1*; T. J. Roberts did not bat.

Bowling Averages

	O	*M*	*R*	*W*	*BB*	*Avge*
N. G. B. Cook	56	35	72	9	6-10	8.00
K. M. Curran	21	5	38	4	3-30	9.50
C. S. Atkins	28.5	12	64	5	3-22	12.80
D. J. Capel	58.5	13	173	11	4-49	15.72
K. J. Innes	144	33	482	19	3-49	25.36
J. D. Wells	52.3	13	158	6	4-33	26.33
M. N. Bowen	308.3	73	898	32	4-64	28.06
J. G. Hughes	123	22	419	14	5-66	29.92
J. P. Taylor	99.5	16	321	9	4-40	35.66
S. A. J. Boswell	168.2	25	671	17	4-34	39.47
S. Elworthy	64	10	241	6	3-92	40.16
J. F. Brown	266.1	80	847	21	3-17	40.33
T. C. Walton	171.2	24	773	17	3-37	45.47
T. W. Harrison	55.1	9	184	4	2-22	46.00
A. C. Cottam	215	58	668	13	2-50	51.38
C. J. Rika	65.4	3	313	6	1-1	52.16
A. R. Roberts	205.5	37	725	13	3-25	55.76

Also bowled: J. Lewis 43–7–117–3; S. J. Renshaw 19–1–110–0; J. N. Snape 53–15–158–3.

NOTTINGHAMSHIRE SECOND ELEVEN

Matches 17: Lost – Hampshire, Kent, Middlesex, Somerset, Warwickshire. Drawn – Derbyshire, Durham, Essex, Glamorgan, Gloucestershire, Lancashire, Leicestershire, Northamptonshire, Surrey, Sussex, Worcestershire, Yorkshire.

Batting Averages

	M	*I*	*NO*	*R*	*HS*	*100s*	*Avge*
G. F. Archer	5	9	2	590	146*	3	84.28
M. A. Crawley	6	11	1	529	139*	1	52.90
†L. N. Walker	13	22	5	800	116	2	47.05
*M. Newell	14	18	3	635	80	0	42.33
M. P. Dowman	14	25	2	890	140	2	38.69
W. A. Dessaur	13	24	0	835	124	2	34.79
†B. N. French	3	5	1	124	53	0	31.00
J. A. Afford	7	8	6	60	31	0	30.00
R. W. J. Howitt	2	4	1	81	30	0	27.00
N. A. Gie	2	4	0	100	74	0	25.00
J. E. Hindson	14	23	3	389	55	0	19.45
D. B. Pennett	13	17	6	203	37*	0	18.45
U. Afzaal	10	14	1	186	40*	0	14.30
R. J. Chapman	16	17	5	170	37	0	14.16
R. T. Bates	15	23	1	268	48	0	12.18
G. W. Mike	4	7	1	66	22	0	11.00
M. G. Field-Buss	4	6	1	55	33	0	11.00
S. A. Sylvester	9	11	2	97	31	0	10.77

Played in two matches: C. Banton 121*, 69, 49; M. Broadhurst 1; R. A. Pick 28, 1, 98; P. R. Pollard 9, 100*, 277*; G. E. Welton 12, 3. Played in one match: K. Afzaal 57, 3*; N. Armstrong 4*; J. N. Batty 7, 0; J. Bennett 27, 6*; C. Dagnall 3; C. Durrant 14, 3; K. P. Evans 59, 4; C. C. Lewis 97*, 23; A. McKinlay 0; L. J. Marland 28, 0; R. T. Robinson 119; D. B. Storer 12, 2; P. Trend did not bat.

Bowling Averages

	O	*M*	*R*	*W*	*BB*	*Avge*
K. P. Evans	26	13	39	5	3-4	7.80
R. A. Pick	21	2	68	4	2-25	17.00
J. A. Afford	183.3	42	532	24	6-66	22.16
J. E. Hindson	395	103	1,136	43	6-81	26.41
R. T. Bates	419.2	96	1,218	43	6-225	28.32
M. G. Field-Buss	78.4	13	249	8	4-74	31.12
U. Afzaal	205.5	55	595	13	2-28	45.76
R. J. Chapman	256.1	50	1,017	19	2-22	53.52
S. A. Sylvester	148.1	25	545	8	4-47	68.12
D. B. Pennett	161.3	28	674	8	2-32	84.25

Also bowled: N. Armstrong 7–0–36–1; M. Broadhurst 26.1–1–150–3; M. A. Crawley 35.3–16–76–2; C. Dagnall 12–2–43–1; W. A. Dessaur 7.3–1–68–0; M. P. Dowman 42–7–135–1; C. C. Lewis 8–1–33–0; G. W. Mike 77–20–228–2.

SOMERSET SECOND ELEVEN

Matches 17: Won – Derbyshire, Durham, Essex, Hampshire, Leicestershire, Middlesex, Nottinghamshire, Surrey, Sussex, Warwickshire. Lost – Glamorgan, Kent, Yorkshire. Drawn – Gloucestershire, Lancashire, Northamptonshire, Worcestershire.

Batting Averages

	M	*I*	*NO*	*R*	*HS*	*100s*	*Avge*
S. C. Ecclestone	3	4	2	151	66	0	75.50
M. E. Trescothick	4	6	1	321	132	1	64.20
K. A. Parsons	14	23	2	1,117	169	2	53.19
I. Fletcher	10	19	3	781	149*	2	48.81
P. C. L. Holloway	15	23	4	890	145	1	46.84
*†N. D. Burns	16	25	4	938	165*	2	44.66
V. P. Clarke	13	20	3	581	101*	1	34.17

	M	*I*	*NO*	*R*	*HS*	*100s*	*Avge*
J. I. D. Kerr	7	9	2	220	107*	1	31.42
K. J. Parsons	15	22	2	484	95	0	24.20
B. T. P. Donelan	9	8	1	139	61*	0	19.85
J. C. Hallett	7	9	2	138	41	0	19.71
P. R. Clifford	4	3	1	35	28*	0	17.50
A. Payne	14	19	3	258	72*	0	16.12
I. A. Bond	10	9	3	96	38*	0	16.00
H. R. J. Trump	3	4	1	46	32	0	15.33
P. J. Bird	12	12	4	101	39	0	12.62
M. Dimond	7	8	3	24	10*	0	4.80

Played in five matches: R. J. Harding 0*, 6. Played in two matches: T. W. J. Farley 0*, 0*; N. A. Mallender 20, 31*, 5*; K. G. Sedgbeer 89; S. M. Trego 2. Played in one match: J. R. Dalwood 13; N. A. Folland 106*; †S. P. Griffiths 28; D. Lye 21; A. Mohammed 0; G. D. Rose 8; B. R. K. Staunton 0, 3; P. C. Turner 4*; A. P. van Troost 14; N. L. Cutler and P. J. Robinson did not bat.

Bowling Averages

	O	*M*	*R*	*W*	*BB*	*Avge*
V. P. Clarke	232	56	684	41	7-32	16.68
N. A. Mallender	54	9	119	7	3-46	17.00
J. I. D. Kerr	67.2	9	219	11	3-30	19.90
A. Payne	216.3	49	650	31	5-39	20.96
M. Dimond	122.4	20	420	19	4-26	22.10
P. J. Bird	305.4	76	894	39	6-41	22.92
H. R. J. Trump	144.1	48	344	11	4-83	31.27
K. A. Parsons	68	18	196	6	2-30	32.66
J. C. Hallett	155.5	29	447	12	3-39	37.25
R. J. Harding	89.1	18	298	8	2-15	37.25
B. T. P. Donelan	136	20	655	10	4-99	65.50
I. A. Bond	152.5	18	578	8	2-21	72.25

Also bowled: P. R. Clifford 83–16–288–3; N. L. Cutler 23–2–87–2; S. C. Ecclestone 18.3–2–62–1; T. W. J. Farley 15–2–57–4; A. Mohammed 16–3–47–3; K. J. Parsons 7–0–52–2; G. D. Rose 10–3–11–1; K. G. Sedgbeer 10–2–43–0; S. M. Trego 6–0–30–0; M. E. Trescothick 16–4–40–3; P. C. Turner 24–8–66–3; A. P. van Troost 22–4–84–1.

SURREY SECOND ELEVEN

Matches 17: Won – Durham, Gloucestershire, Northamptonshire. Lost – Leicestershire, Middlesex, Somerset, Sussex. Drawn – Derbyshire, Essex, Glamorgan, Hampshire, Kent, Lancashire, Nottinghamshire, Warwickshire, Worcestershire, Yorkshire.

Batting Averages

	M	*I*	*NO*	*R*	*HS*	*100s*	*Avge*
†G. J. Kersey	12	17	5	769	151*	4	64.08
A. C. S. Pigott	3	3	2	62	39*	0	62.00
A. Tarrant	2	4	0	245	99	0	61.25
M. A. Butcher	5	7	2	292	83	0	58.40
A. W. Smith	5	7	2	284	137*	1	56.80
M. P. Bicknell	2	3	1	111	101*	1	55.50
K. T. Medlycott	7	12	5	369	106	1	52.71
M. A. Lynch	13	22	1	1,072	164	2	51.04
N. M. Kendrick	11	17	2	571	101	1	38.06
J. Wileman	3	5	1	149	47	0	37.25
S. J. Cooper	4	5	1	148	48	0	37.00
J. Boiling	8	7	2	157	70*	0	31.40

	M	I	NO	R	HS	100s	Avge
S. G. Kenlock	11	4	2	55	35*	0	27.50
R. Q. Cake	8	13	0	287	100	1	22.07
M. R. Bainbridge	15	23	1	451	84	0	20.50
G. J. Kennis	15	25	1	450	67	0	18.75
S. J. Pawson	7	10	4	98	26	0	16.33
A. J. Murphy	3	4	2	32	14*	0	16.00
†N. F. Sargeant	11	17	2	223	62	0	14.86
R. W. Nowell	8	13	3	129	43*	0	12.90
D. J. Thompson	10	8	1	85	60	0	12.14
B. Hollioake	3	4	2	23	14*	0	11.50
J. M. de la Pena	12	10	4	33	13*	0	5.50

Played in two matches: P. Thomas 2. Played in one match: D. Dyer 15, 0; M. Hodgson 16, 2; J. Powell 18, 4; M. R. Powell 5, 0; C. I. O. Ricketts 2*, 0; O. M. Slipper 57, 40; D. J. Tomlinson 11, 0; A. Tudor 41*; A. N. Muggleton did not bat.

Note: Owing to first-team calls, J. Boiling was replaced by N. M. Kendrick in the match v Nottinghamshire at Oxted and A. J. Murphy was replaced by S. G. Kenlock in the match v Middlesex at Harrow.

Bowling Averages

	O	M	R	W	BB	Avge
R. W. Nowell	114.5	38	288	17	7-13	16.94
A. J. Murphy	75	19	234	12	4-52	19.50
A. C. S. Pigott	57	20	120	6	2-26	20.00
S. G. Kenlock	264.2	71	681	27	5-35	25.22
J. Boiling	177.2	45	467	15	3-110	31.13
N. M. Kendrick	398	106	1,060	32	7-64	33.12
J. M. de la Pena	268.5	27	1,170	33	4-54	35.45
M. R. Bainbridge	143.5	35	468	13	4-59	36.00
S. J. Pawson	107	16	408	10	4-48	40.80
A. W. Smith	94.3	20	331	8	5-95	41.37
G. J. Kennis	73.2	11	269	6	2-24	44.83
D. J. Thompson	234.2	39	854	14	4-86	61.00

Also bowled: M. P. Bicknell 38.3–5–139–2; M. A. Butcher 28–4–88–0; B. Hollioake 26–5–121–1; G. J. Kersey 3–0–26–1; M. A. Lynch 31.5–5–92–3; K. T. Medlycott 63.3–11–191–1; J. Powell 6–1–19–0; M. R. Powell 15–2–60–0; N. F. Sargeant 1–0–5–0; P. Thomas 28–0–155–3; D. J. Tomlinson 11–1–43–0; A. Tudor 9–2–39–2; J. Wileman 10–3–29–2.

SUSSEX SECOND ELEVEN

Matches 17: Won – Durham, Hampshire, Surrey. Lost – Somerset. Drawn – Derbyshire, Essex, Glamorgan, Gloucestershire, Kent, Lancashire, Leicestershire, Middlesex, Northamptonshire, Nottinghamshire, Warwickshire, Worcestershire, Yorkshire.

Batting Averages

	M	I	NO	R	HS	100s	Avge
N. J. Lenham	3	5	0	310	84	0	62.00
M. T. E. Peirce	8	14	4	445	89*	0	44.50
J. W. Hall	3	4	0	175	137	1	43.75
G. Norris	5	10	1	335	118	1	37.22
C. C. Remy	7	12	0	413	99	0	34.41
V. C. Drakes	14	24	2	751	90	0	34.13
M. Newell	8	12	3	301	81*	0	33.44
K. Newell	16	29	3	817	159	2	31.42
J. A. North	17	26	2	748	124	1	31.16
D. M. Smith	3	4	0	124	81	0	31.00
*K. Greenfield	13	20	2	548	159*	1	30.44
D. R. Law	13	18	2	347	49	0	21.68

	M	*I*	*NO*	*R*	*HS*	*100s*	*Avge*
A. D. Edwards	4	5	2	60	30	0	20.00
N. C. Phillips	15	21	8	228	41*	0	17.53
J. W. Dean	10	15	3	201	28	0	16.75
†S. Humphries	17	17	6	175	51	0	15.90
R. J. Kirtley	5	3	2	9	6*	0	9.00
J. D. Lewry	12	8	2	47	20	0	7.83
R. C. Thelwell	2	4	1	15	13	0	5.00

Played in two matches: J. D. Chaplin 1, 13*; R. S. C. Martin-Jenkins 0. Played in one match: C. W. J. Athey 122; P. G. Hudson 0, 3; B. Poots 20*, 16*; N. Pratt 61; A. P. Wells 32; J. P. Pyemont, M. R. Strong and C. E. Waller did not bat.

Bowling Averages

	O	*M*	*R*	*W*	*BB*	*Avge*
V. C. Drakes	405.2	87	1,150	65	8-59	17.69
J. D. Lewry	309.1	65	853	33	6-73	25.84
J. D. Chaplin	45	9	117	4	3-24	29.25
R. J. Kirtley	89.2	11	309	10	3-8	30.90
K. Newell	76.4	18	241	7	3-34	34.42
C. C. Remy	109.5	16	443	11	3-53	40.27
J. A. North	142.1	19	497	12	2-24	41.41
J. W. Dean	198	55	517	12	2-27	43.08
D. R. Law	198.4	42	652	15	4-44	43.46
N. C. Phillips	340.5	82	987	20	3-38	49.35

Also bowled: A. D. Edwards 51–13–144–3; K. Greenfield 77.4–22–247–3; N. J. Lenham 12–4–46–0; R. S. C. Martin-Jenkins 19.3–3–55–2; M. Newell 2–0–28–0; M. T. E. Peirce 34–5–120–2; B. Poots 6–1–18–1; N. Pratt 3–0–23–0; M. R. Strong 8–0–37–0; C. E. Waller 11–3–54–0.

WARWICKSHIRE SECOND ELEVEN

Matches 17: Won – Nottinghamshire. Lost – Hampshire, Somerset. Drawn – Derbyshire, Durham, Essex, Glamorgan, Gloucestershire, Kent, Lancashire, Leicestershire, Middlesex, Northamptonshire, Surrey, Sussex, Worcestershire, Yorkshire.

Batting Averages

	M	*I*	*NO*	*R*	*HS*	*100s*	*Avge*
A. J. Moles	3	6	0	477	164	2	79.50
J. D. Ratcliffe	16	30	8	1,219	192*	2	55.40
D. R. Brown	12	15	5	540	110*	1	54.00
S. Vestergaard	5	4	2	99	44	0	49.50
M. J. Powell	13	21	6	677	167*	1	45.13
A. Singh	2	3	0	135	126	1	45.00
G. D. Yates	2	3	0	125	73	0	41.66
G. Welch	7	10	2	328	169	1	41.00
T. L. Penney	2	3	0	121	111	1	40.33
W. G. Khan	16	31	4	1,068	140*	1	39.55
R. P. Davis	6	8	2	196	43	0	32.66
A. F. Giles	16	22	5	469	72	0	27.58
†M. Burns	15	26	4	603	77	0	27.40
C. E. Mulraine	12	20	2	452	77*	0	25.11
M. A. Sheikh	12	13	3	161	39*	0	16.10
M. A. Wagh	2	3	0	43	25	0	14.33
†A. Frost	6	5	0	40	20	0	8.00
P. W. Trimby	7	2	1	4	4*	0	4.00

Played in 12 matches: D. A. Altree 5*, 0*, 0*, 0*, 0*, 0*. Played in three matches: B. T. P. Donelan 1. Played in two matches: Asif Din 27, 33; M. A. V. Bell 28; D. Brock 5*; D. R. Maynard 7; P. A. Smith 38, 34; D. Follett did not bat. Played in one match: D. P. Ostler 20, 30*; †S. Platt 9*; D. A. Reeve 90; N. M. K. Smith 0; D. Williamson 58; S. McDonald did not bat.

Bowling Averages

	O	*M*	*R*	*W*	*BB*	*Avge*
P. A. Smith	37.2	7	131	7	4-61	18.71
M. J. Powell	34.3	8	91	4	2-29	22.75
M. A. V. Bell	55	13	184	8	4-43	23.00
M. A. Sheikh	231.4	63	576	24	4-52	24.00
R. P. Davis	211.2	65	540	21	5-85	25.71
D. R. Brown	284.2	53	1,002	34	5-71	29.47
S. McDonald	50	17	151	5	4-71	30.20
A. F. Giles	454.2	111	1,291	41	4-64	31.48
S. Vestergaard	95.4	24	285	9	2-27	31.66
G. Welch	171.4	34	644	19	5-52	33.89
D. A. Altree	262.3	47	853	22	3-23	38.77
D. R. Maynard	44	8	164	4	2-66	41.00
D. Brock	42	5	177	4	2-25	44.25
B. T. P. Donelan	57	12	212	4	2-55	53.00
P. W. Trimby	149.2	29	506	9	3-115	56.22

Also bowled: Asif Din 4–0–11–0; M. Burns 20–7–48–2; D. Follett 31–2–160–0; W. G. Khan 17–0–128–1; C. E. Mulraine 5–1–53–1; T. L. Penney 2–0–14–0; J. D. Ratcliffe 63–16–221–3; D. A. Reeve 9–4–13–1; N. M. K. Smith 25–8–51–1; M. A. Wagh 1–1–0–0; D. Williamson 3–0–11–0; G. D. Yates 11–1–35–1.

WORCESTERSHIRE SECOND ELEVEN

Matches 17: Won – Gloucestershire, Hampshire, Leicestershire. Lost – Durham, Essex, Middlesex. Drawn – Derbyshire, Glamorgan, Kent, Lancashire, Northamptonshire, Nottinghamshire, Somerset, Surrey, Sussex, Warwickshire, Yorkshire.

Batting Averages

	M	*I*	*NO*	*R*	*HS*	*100s*	*Avge*
W. P. C. Weston	2	4	1	419	200*	2	139.66
*†D. L. Houghton	14	15	1	820	136	2	58.57
A. C. H. Seymour	10	18	2	834	160*	3	52.12
C. M. Tolley	11	18	2	796	164	2	49.75
K. R. Spiring	14	23	3	900	166*	2	45.00
I. R. J. McLaren	7	10	3	301	84*	0	43.00
P. C. McKeown	2	4	0	149	80	0	37.25
M. I. Bradford	6	10	1	318	86	0	35.33
S. W. K. Ellis	6	9	1	280	89	0	35.00
†D. G. C. Ligertwood	2	4	1	99	43	0	33.00
V. S. Solanki	10	18	1	545	112	1	32.05
C. J. Eyers	16	18	5	395	60	0	30.38
M. J. Church	9	14	0	374	95	0	26.71
D. B. D'Oliveira	12	18	2	354	85	0	22.12
J. E. Brinkley	6	4	1	57	34	0	19.00
C. W. Boroughs	7	11	1	178	61	0	17.80
†T. Edwards	9	5	3	30	23*	0	15.00
B. E. A. Preece	10	10	5	43	22*	0	8.60
P. Mirza	14	11	2	76	28	0	8.44

Played in three matches: B. M. McCorkhill 7, 0, 9*. Played in two matches: †M. R. Gill 15*, 7, 4; J. T. Ralph 4*, 5, 5. Played in one match: S. E. Brinkley 1, 1; A. Farooque 33, 4*; D. A. Leatherdale 96, 86*; †C. J. McDonald 6*, 16*; D. R. McDonnell 1, 50; †P. J. Nicholson 10, 5; G. F. Shephard 43; P. A. Swainson 1; †N. Workman 4*, 0*; A. Wylie 0*; D. Brewer, D. Follett and T. Saddique did not bat.

Bowling Averages

	O	*M*	*R*	*W*	*BB*	*Avge*
D. A. Leatherdale	15	4	24	5	5-24	4.80
D. Follett	13	2	48	5	5-48	9.60
J. E. Brinkley	153.2	40	394	18	4-30	21.88
B. E. A. Preece	182	41	516	20	4-36	25.80
S. W. K. Ellis	149	30	555	20	6-45	27.75
I. R. J. McLaren	203.2	40	601	20	4-45	30.05
W. P. C. Weston	29.3	3	132	4	3-61	33.00
V. S. Solanki	190.1	36	606	18	4-51	33.66
P. Mirza	305.5	63	1,029	30	7-71	34.30
A. C. H. Seymour	48.5	9	175	5	2-42	35.00
D. B. D'Oliveira	285.5	67	832	23	5-62	36.17
C. M. Tolley	262.2	51	908	22	3-38	41.27
C. J. Eyers	233.4	36	916	20	4-81	45.80
B. M. McCorkhill	34	10	101	2	1-3	50.50
M. I. Bradford	91.3	20	293	4	3-42	73.25

Also bowled: C. W. Boroughs 3–0–20–0; D. Brewer 18–1–59–2; M. J. Church 12–4–40–1; A. Farooque 7–0–32–0; J. T. Ralph 29–6–90–0; T. Saddique 31–5–172–3; G. F. Shephard 7–1–18–1; K. R. Spiring 5–0–18–0; A. Wylie 17–4–70–0.

YORKSHIRE SECOND ELEVEN

Matches 17: Won – Essex, Glamorgan, Kent, Middlesex, Northamptonshire, Somerset. Lost – Gloucestershire, Lancashire. Drawn – Derbyshire, Durham, Hampshire, Leicestershire, Nottinghamshire, Surrey, Sussex, Warwickshire, Worcestershire.

Batting Averages

	M	*I*	*NO*	*R*	*HS*	*100s*	*Avge*
A. McGrath	9	16	3	815	218*	3	62.69
*A. A. Metcalfe	15	26	6	1,043	136*	2	52.15
S. A. Kellett	8	15	1	675	128*	2	48.21
B. Parker	10	17	0	720	126	1	42.35
J. D. Batty	13	13	5	281	59	0	35.12
C. J. Schofield	12	20	3	596	105	1	35.05
J. Middlebrook	2	3	0	102	62	0	34.00
†C. A. Chapman	17	25	2	765	77	0	33.26
A. P. Grayson	2	4	0	124	73	0	31.00
R. A. Kettleborough	16	28	3	714	97	0	28.56
M. J. Foster	14	21	3	507	80	0	28.16
A. G. Wharf	3	5	2	78	28*	0	26.00
L. C. Weekes	7	7	2	115	43	0	23.00
G. M. Hamilton	7	10	4	118	25*	0	19.66
D. M. Hamilton	5	8	4	77	17*	0	19.25
A. C. Morris	6	9	1	139	47	0	17.37
G. Keedy	13	10	4	80	21	0	13.33
R. Robinson	2	4	1	40	23	0	13.33
I. D. Fisher	4	4	3	10	8*	0	10.00
S. M. Milburn	11	8	2	56	31*	0	9.33
M. Broadhurst	5	4	1	17	11	0	5.66

Played in two matches: C. E. W. Silverwood did not bat. Played in one match: J. W. Hood 37, 20; R. D. Stemp 36, 4; M. Wood 38*, 11; P. M. Hutchison did not bat.

Bowling Averages

	O	*M*	*R*	*W*	*BB*	*Avge*
J. D. Batty	476.3	127	1,324	51	7-71	25.96
L. C. Weekes	181.1	28	673	24	5-93	28.04
G. M. Hamilton	142.3	22	580	20	5-90	29.00
G. Keedy	414	136	1,060	33	5-71	32.12
I. D. Fisher	109.2	31	329	10	5-57	32.90
M. J. Foster	227	44	788	22	3-50	35.81
A. G. Wharf	77.5	9	294	8	4-65	36.75
D. M. Hamilton	83.5	20	221	6	3-32	36.83
S. M. Milburn	239.5	40	864	21	3-26	41.14
R. A. Kettleborough	100.5	17	379	7	2-32	54.14
M. Broadhurst	73	10	305	5	3-45	61.00

Also bowled: A. P. Grayson 24–2–115–2; P. M. Hutchison 16–2–67–1; S. A. Kellett 2–0–3–1; A. McGrath 20–6–43–0; J. Middlebrook 10–2–32–1; A. C. Morris 14–2–57–1; R. Robinson 7–3–21–1; C. J. Schofield 1–0–13–0; C. E. W. Silverwood 45–7–161–3; R. D. Stemp 41–12–158–1.

SECOND ELEVEN CHAMPIONS

1959	Gloucestershire	1972	Nottinghamshire	1985	Nottinghamshire
1960	Northamptonshire	1973	Essex	1986	Lancashire
1961	Kent	1974	Middlesex	1987	Kent / Yorkshire
1962	Worcestershire	1975	Surrey	1988	Surrey
1963	Worcestershire	1976	Kent	1989	Middlesex
1964	Lancashire	1977	Yorkshire	1990	Sussex
1965	Glamorgan	1978	Sussex	1991	Yorkshire
1966	Surrey	1979	Warwickshire	1992	Surrey
1967	Hampshire	1980	Glamorgan	1993	Middlesex
1968	Surrey	1981	Hampshire	1994	Somerset
1969	Kent	1982	Worcestershire		
1970	Kent	1983	Leicestershire		
1971	Hampshire	1984	Yorkshire		

BAIN CLARKSON TROPHY, 1994

Counties are restricted to players qualified for England and for competitive county cricket, only two of whom may be capped players. The matches are of 55 overs per side.

North Zone	*P*	*W*	*L*	*NR*	*Points*	*Runs/100b*
Yorkshire	10	7	3	0	14	81.63
Leicestershire	10	7	3	0	14	73.24
Durham	10	6	3	1	13	69.31
Nottinghamshire	10	4	5	1	9	70.83
Derbyshire	10	4	6	0	8	58.08
Lancashire	10	1	9	0	2	64.48

South-West Zone	*P*	*W*	*L*	*NR*	*Points*	*Runs/100b*
Gloucestershire	10	6	2	2	14	63.34
Warwickshire	10	5	4	1	11	77.37
Hampshire	10	5	4	1	11	63.70
Glamorgan	10	4	4	2	10	59.56
Somerset	10	4	5	1	9	78.26
Worcestershire	10	2	7	1	5	57.16

South-East Zone	*P*	*W*	*L*	*NR*	*Points*	*Runs/100b*
Northamptonshire	12	8	4	0	16	72.50
Middlesex	12	7	5	0	14	79.30
Surrey	12	7	5	0	14	72.52
Kent	12	6	5	1	13	67.24
Sussex	12	6	6	0	12	70.34
Essex	12	5	7	0	10	65.94
MCC Young Cricketers	12	2	9	1	5	68.95

Note: Leicestershire qualified for the semi-final as the best runners-up.

SEMI-FINALS

At Bristol, August 18. Leicestershire won by 48 runs. Toss: Gloucestershire. Leicestershire 244 for eight (P. N. Hepworth 59, P. E. Robinson 50, A. F. Haye 45); Gloucestershire 196 (47.5 overs) (R. C. J. Williams 55, N. Davey 40; I. M. Stanger four for 36).

At Leeds, August 19. Yorkshire won by six wickets. Toss: Yorkshire. Northamptonshire 113 (36.4 overs) (I. Dawood 32 not out; G. Keedy three for 31); Yorkshire 117 for four (38.4 overs) (C. J. Schofield 42).

FINAL

LEICESTERSHIRE v YORKSHIRE

At Leeds, September 5. Yorkshire won by six wickets. Toss: Leicestershire.
Man of the Match: A. A. Metcalfe.

Leicestershire

D. L. Maddy c Parker b Hamilton 8
P. N. Hepworth c Foster b Hamilton .. 69
B. F. Smith c Milburn b Keedy 27
P. E. Robinson c Chapman b Batty.... 13
S. J. Bartle c and b Keedy 3
J. M. Dakin b Foster................ 18
A. I. Ditta b Milburn 0
*†P. Whitticase not out.............. 26
T. J. Mason lbw b Milburn 2
I. M. Stanger not out................ 15
B 1, l-b 5, w 5.............. 11

1/18 2/70 3/91 4/108 5/147 6/147 7/147 8/156 (8 wkts, 55 overs) 192

A. Sheriyar did not bat.

Bowling: Hamilton 11–2–41–2; Milburn 10–2–30–2; Foster 6–0–19–1; Kettleborough 6–1–20–0; Batty 11–1–40–1; Keedy 11–1–36–2.

Yorkshire

*A. A. Metcalfe b Stanger 93
C. J. Schofield c Mason b Bartle 38
R. A. Kettleborough c Robinson b Bartle . 18
B. Parker not out................... 7
A. C. Morris run out................ 1
†C. A. Chapman not out............. 4
L-b 11, w 7, n-b 14.......... 32

1/113 2/179 3/180 4/184 (4 wkts, 52.1 overs) 193

M. J. Foster, J. D. Batty, G. M. Hamilton, S. M. Milburn and G. Keedy did not bat.

Bowling: Sheriyar 3–0–15–0; Stanger 9–4–21–1; Dakin 11–0–44–0; Ditta 10.1–1–31–0; Mason 6–2–16–0; Hepworth 2–0–13–0; Bartle 11–1–42–2.

Umpires: G. I. Burgess and B. Dudleston.

WINNERS 1986-94

1986	Northamptonshire	1989	Middlesex	1992	Surrey
1987	Derbyshire	1990	Lancashire	1993	Leicestershire
1988	Yorkshire	1991	Nottinghamshire	1994	Yorkshire

THE LANCASHIRE LEAGUES, 1994

By CHRIS ASPIN

The two major Lancashire competitions went to the final afternoon before being settled. Nelson were Lancashire League champions for the first time since 1986, though Bacup fought them right to the line; meanwhile, the Central Lancashire League title went to Radcliffe, when they beat Oldham in their last match. Haslingden regained the Jennings Worsley Cup, the Lancashire League's knockout, by beating Todmorden while the Lees Wood Cup went to Littleborough, who defeated Rochdale.

Of the four winning clubs, all but Littleborough had Australian professionals, but the future recruitment of top-flight Australians was in serious doubt when their Board recalled three pros – Michael Bevan from Rawtenstall, Jo Angel from Burnley and Damien Fleming from Enfield – in late July to train for the tour of Sri Lanka and Pakistan. Their clubs had to find substitute professionals for the last eight matches.

Joe Scuderi of South Australia remained to spearhead Nelson's campaign. In his fourth season at the club, he hit the highest innings of the season, an unbeaten 175 against Todmorden. But the most successful pro in the Lancashire League was West Indian Roger Harper, who scored more runs – 1,465 – and took more wickets – 92, in 501 overs – than anyone else. In his sixth year with Bacup, he almost secured them the title and just missed the club record of 1,518, set by Everton Weekes in 1951.

Bacup were frustrated at the last by Church, for whom Western Australian Mark Atkinson, without a five-wicket haul all season, suddenly produced a spell of five for none – including a hat-trick – in seven balls. His final figures were eight for 62. Rishton's Peter Sleep, the former Australian Test player, headed the batting averages with 1,432 at 84.23 and also took 72 wickets. He was punished heavily at Rawtenstall, taking one for 100 as Peter Wood and Bevan shared an unbroken second-wicket stand of 239. But rain reduced Rishton's target from 269 to 223 and Sleep scored 83 not out to secure victory by seven wickets.

Amateur Michael Ingham of Haslingden became only the sixth player in 102 years of the Lancashire League to score 10,000 runs when he reached 16 at Ramsbottom. Ten runs later, he was given out hit the ball twice. The West Indian Test player, Keith Arthurton, caused some surprise by making the appeal; nobody could remember such a dismissal occurring before in the history of the League. David Pearson of East Lancashire made 1,012 to join an exclusive band of five amateurs who have reached four figures in a season; and Gary Barker scored 897 for Enfield, passing his own club record of 888 set three years before. The leading amateur wicket-taker was Nick Riley of Ramsbottom, with 62 at 21.40; Ramsbottom wicket-keeper Jack Simpson equalled the League record with 53 dismissals.

In the Central Lancashire League, Radcliffe edged ahead of Werneth to take their first championship since 1971, with the help of Australian Geoff Foley, who headed the batting averages with 1,594 at 69.30 and scored a match-winning century in the decisive final game. Second-placed Werneth made a remarkable rise from next to bottom in 1993; their hero was John Punchard, newly arrived from Royton. He narrowly outstripped professional Steve O'Shaughnessy with 1,184 runs at 42.28 and 65 wickets at 19.93, both amateur records for the club. Against Crompton, he scored 143 not out and took five for 35, and he celebrated his 37th birthday with 101, six for 36 and two catches against Heywood.

Two other amateurs reached four figures, both Australians: Dean Temple of Stand made 1,270 and Justin Gale of Ashton 1,190. The most successful amateur bowlers were Craig Hopkinson of Royton with 82 and Rick Blackman of Unsworth with 80. Kelvin Williams, the Unsworth professional, returned nine for 17 against Stand, and Milnrow spinner Nigel Doyle, coming on first change against Royton, took five for none in his first five overs, finishing with six for 35. Royton and Middleton tied both their League matches, scoring 148 each in the first encounter and 149 in the second.

MARSDEN BS LANCASHIRE LEAGUE

	P	*W*	*L*	*NR*	*Bonus Pts*	*Pts*	*Professional*	*Runs*	*Avge*	*Wkts*	*Avge*
Nelson	26	20	6	0	12	92	J. C. Scuderi	1,114	65.52	61	13.70
Bacup	26	18	7	1	11	84	R. A. Harper	1,465	77.10	92	12.31
Haslingden	26	18	7	1	7	80	B. E. McNamara	1,066	50.76	82	13.80
East Lancs.	26	17	8	1	8	77	A. C. Dawson	550	28.94	50	24.46
Burnley	26	16	10	0	7	71	J. Angel	235	23.50	53	14.03
Ramsbottom	26	15	10	1	7	68	K. L. T. Arthurton	849	40.42	48	18.54
Church	26	14	11	1	6	63	M. P. Atkinson	811	45.05	46	25.50
Todmorden	26	12	13	1	7	56	S. Williams	609	26.47	76	19.53
Enfield	26	10	15	1	7	48	D. W. Fleming	467	33.35	47	16.40
Rishton	26	11	14	1	3	48	P. R. Sleep	1,432	84.23	72	22.00
Rawtenstall	26	8	17	1	10	43	M. G. Bevan	756	68.72	43	18.20
Colne	26	8	17	1	2	35	C. Killen	677	32.23	61	20.01
Lowerhouse	26	5	20	1	5	26	C. Light	1,002	45.54	33	34.18
Accrington	26	4	21	1	2	19	S. L. Campbell	481	21.86	13	51.84

Note: Four points awarded for a win; one point for a no-result; one point for bowling out the opposition.

CENTRAL LANCASHIRE LEAGUE

	P	*OW*	*LW*	*L*	*D*	*Pts*	*Professional*	*Runs*	*Avge*	*Wkts*	*Avge*
Radcliffe	30	11	9	7	3	97	G. I. Foley	1,594	69.30	55	15.05
Werneth	30	9	11	7	3	95	S. J. O'Shaughnessy	1,076	43.04	62	22.00
Rochdale	30	5	13	6	6	89	N. C. Johnson	1,243	54.04	81	17.19
Littleborough	30	7	8	7	8	83	J. D. Fitton	1,474	61.41	47	19.72
Norden	30	8	6	8	8	80	A. L. Logie	1,711	65.80	80	18.75
Walsden	30	8	5	10	7	74	A. J. Bichel	1,124	44.96	93	20.68
Stand	30	10	3	12	5	73*	M. Warden	673	32.04	111	14.65
Milnrow	30	8	6	12	4	72	J. Kirton	748	26.71	52	26.86
Unsworth	30	6	8	11	5	72	K. Williams	1,028	44.69	78	17.28
Ashton	30	9	4	13	4	69	B. Roberts	887	32.85	43	20.32
Middleton	30	5	8	12	5	69†	M. Handman	627	28.50	35	26.82
Royton	30	9	2	15	4	63†	J. Grant	323	13.45	83	18.13
Heywood	30	6	5	14	5	60	A. Badenhorst	535	22.29	65	15.13
Oldham	30	3	3	19	5	38*	S. Bell	124	6.52	42	23.61
Crompton	30	2	1	24	3	20	T. Whittle	506	16.86	29	32.55
Stockport	30	1	2	24	3	19	S. Vincent	452	16.74	12	36.41

* Includes three points for a tie. † Includes six points for two ties.

Notes: Five points awarded for an outright win; four points for a limited win; two points for a draw. A team achieves an outright win by bowling out the opposition. Averages include cup games.

LEAGUE CRICKET IN ENGLAND AND WALES, 1994

By GEOFFREY DEAN

While Warwickshire were making easy work of the County Championship, the battle to decide their local league was the most exciting for many years. Seven of the 12 teams in the Birmingham League were almost neck and neck with five weeks to go. By a quirk of the fixture list, the four leading teams were playing each other on the final Saturday, and each had a chance of the title.

Provided there was a definite result, the Championship had to go to the winners of the game between Walsall and Wolverhampton. On a very difficult wicket at Walsall, a captain's innings of 45 by Nick Archer helped the home team to 139. Wolverhampton were soon reduced to 34 for six. They recovered, thanks to 54 from Andy Williams, and when John Turner came in and hit three sixes in an over, there was a chance that Wolverhampton might win. However, the England Amateur fast bowler, Keith Arnold, had figures of seven for 37 and Walsall edged home by 14 runs.

The phone lines were running hot between this ground and West Bromwich down the road, just in case neither side won, in which case West Bromwich Dartmouth or Old Hill could have been champions. David Houghton, the former Zimbabwe captain, made a match-winning 74 for Dartmouth and they squeezed into second place; they also won the League Cup for the fifth time in six years. There was some cause for pride for all the clubs in the League: when Warwickshire and Worcestershire played each other in the NatWest final, 19 of the 22 players had Birmingham League experience.

In this League and elsewhere, it was a batsman's year, with batting records being broken in the sunshine up and down the country. One of the most remarkable performances came from Reading's Aftab Habib, who scored 1,078 runs at the astonishing average of 154. It was the first time a batsman had passed 1,000 runs for the season in the Thames Valley League. Similarly, no one had managed the feat in the Middlesex League until Lee Deller of South Hampstead totalled 1,002. In the Northants County League, Horton House's Jeremy Goode became the first to score four hundreds in a season, also hitting a 99 in his aggregate of 1,029. He might have beaten the league record of 1,122 but was out for a single in his final innings.

Habib's runs did not win Reading the Championship. They finished third behind Finchampstead and Boyne Hill who swapped places on the final Saturday of the season to make Finchampstead champions for the first time. Boyne Hill needed to beat Wokingham to clinch the title, but they could take only four opposition wickets. Finchampstead, however, dismissed Marlow for 112 to win by 83 runs, with 44-year-old Peter Lewington – who first played for the club 30 years earlier, before joining Warwickshire – taking four for 15.

Deller's South Hampstead did not feature in the running for the Middlesex League either. When the final round of fixtures began, all that leaders Richmond needed, as it turned out, was a winning draw at home to Stanmore. But they had the misfortune to run into Angus Fraser in unhappy mood the day after his omission from England's Ashes party to Australia. There was rain about – indeed just down the road at Lord's there was no play after lunch in the NatWest Final – and conditions at Richmond were poor, but when they heard that their challengers Finchley were making a start against Brondesbury, the leaders decided they had to play. Fraser took four for 32 from 14 overs as Richmond were restricted to 156 for eight. They then went out to field in rain throughout and, handicapped by a wet ball, were beaten by eight wickets. Finchley, meanwhile, got in just enough play to gain a winning draw, which gave them their third successive title. No other matches were even started in the Middlesex League that day.

Fraser was one of several current Test players to make unpaid appearances in league cricket during the summer, although he was the only one to finish on the winning side as club players raised their game to thwart them. Nottinghamshire's Chris Lewis returned to London one weekend to play for Wembley, the club he represented as a youth, against Finchley. Lewis, down to bat at No. 3, had a long wait as the opening pair put on 190. He hit a quick 35 before taking three wickets in a drawn game. In the Western League, Australia's Shane Warne turned out for his old club in Bristol, Imperial, in an away game against St Fagans of South Wales. He took four for 61 from 21 overs and was hit for three sixes by a PE teacher from Merthyr Tydfil, Adam Rosser, who, after Warne had demolished England at Brisbane, suggested that the Test batsmen might try his method: "I just decided to plonk my left foot down the wicket, close my eyes and have a swing." Warne was on the losing team that day. So was Allan Donald, South Africa's spearhead, when he played for a relative's club, Overstone, in the Northants County League against County Colts, a side mainly comprising Northamptonshire second-teamers. Donald forced one batsman to retire hurt but bowled only nine overs before Colts reached a small target.

Another batting record fell in the Western League, thanks partially to the generosity of Malmesbury on the wet last Saturday of the season. Swindon's naturalised Australian, Brett Johnson, needed another 32 from his final innings to beat the league record of 1,208, set by New Zealander Matthew Horne in 1990. Malmesbury fielded long enough for Johnson to make an unbeaten 47 out of 76 for one, at which point the game was abandoned. The Swindon captain's 1,224 runs came at an average of 94 and he was dismissed only three times for under 50. Bath were crowned champions for the first time since 1974. In the neighbouring South Wales Association, Ynysygerwn won their first title for six years. Elsewhere in the Principality, a six-year monopoly of the West Wales Club Conference by Aberystwyth was ended by Lampeter, who were beaten only once on their way to a second Championship. Cardiff won the premier knockout competition, the Welsh Cup, for the first time in ten years.

Spencer, based in Wandsworth, became the ninth different winners of the Surrey Championship in the last nine years. Newly promoted from the second division, they won ten out of 16 games completed – no mean achievement in non-limited-overs cricket – to take their first title. Courtney Ricketts played a key part with 420 runs and 31 wickets. Wimbledon were condemned to runners-up spot for the second successive year after heavy defeats in August by Sunbury and 1993 champions Esher. Honor Oak were helped into third place by Steve Cooper's 882 runs and 20 wickets. At the other end of the table, Bombay's Ranji Trophy batsman, Zubin Bharucha, scored 1,042 but failed to save Reigate Priory from relegation.

The Southern League maintained a similar record, eight winners in eight years. United Services' first Championship was based on all-round contributions – no one made a hundred all season. Bromley's three-year reign as Kent League champions was ended by St Lawrence, who went top at the start of July and were never shifted. Mark Alexander averaged 83 for Bromley, joint runners-up with Folkestone, but received a club ban for abusing an umpire in a cup match in the *Evening Standard* knockout. The Kent League witnessed one of the outstanding bowling performances of the season when seamer Nick Preston took five wickets in successive balls for Sevenoaks Vine against Midland Bank. That same August day, Alex Tait of Gore Court took the first nine Dover wickets for 55 but was thwarted by the last pair who held on for a draw. Tait finished with 51 victims, eight more than 50-year-old Geoff Burton of Bexley. An altogether younger campaigner, Vaughan Williams, 16, averaged 59 for Holmesdale. As so often, though, this was not too encouraging for English cricket: Williams is Australian. Chichester won the Sussex League for the third successive year, ahead of Hastings and Brighton & Hove. The Hastings captain, Jason Finch, paid the penalty for dissent at an umpire's decision by being suspended for two crucial late-season matches. Bognor won their fourth consecutive wooden spoon.

There was an astonishing performance with the ball in the Essex League. With 16 overs of the match remaining between Westcliff and Old Brentwoods, only one wicket had fallen all day. Up stepped Mike Davill, a 46-year-old medium-pacer, to take all ten Old Brentwood wickets for 46 runs. The best innings of the season, and indeed the highest in the history of the Essex League, came from Mark Powell, of Leigh-on-Sea, who hit 172 not out against Orsett and Thurrock. Another league batting record went in the Durham County League where John Pollard of Evenwood made an unbeaten 212. Champions Kimblesworth were indebted to Dennison Thomas, who did the double of 1,000 runs and 100 wickets. Another West Indian, Dawnley Joseph, made 1,551 runs for Redcar before injury cut short his season in the North Yorkshire & South Durham League, where Middlesbrough retained their title. Elsewhere in the north-east, the Australian Steve Russell hit six hundreds, and averaged 92, as well as taking 92 wickets at 11 to mastermind Sacriston's Tyneside Senior League title. In the Northumberland County League, Ashington's Ian Conn became the first amateur in the League's history to take ten wickets, for 35 runs against Blyth.

In Yorkshire, Sheffield Collegiate were crowned Yorkshire League champions for the fourth time in five years, while East Bierley retained their Bradford League title, thanks largely to David Jay's 71 wickets at 12 and to heavy scoring from three batsmen, the McGrath brothers, Dermot and Anthony, and Steve Maher, all of whom totalled more than 700 runs. Chris Pickles of Spen Victoria and Ian Priestley of Pudsey St Lawrence each passed 1,000. Horsforth Hall Park won the Airedale & Wharfedale League for the first time in 26 years while Meltham, with former Yorkshire spinners Paul Booth and Ian Swallow to the fore, achieved a Huddersfield League and Sykes Cup double for the first time. Esholt of the Leeds League also did the double, though they did it the hard way because they actually tied three games on their way to the Hepworth Cup. In the final against Woodhouse, both Tahir Mahmood and Woodhouse's West Indian Test batsman Stuart Williams hit 127. In 91 previous finals, only three centuries had been scored, though the Test selector Brian Bolus, then 16, did make 99 for Whitkirk in 1950.

Gomersal's win in the Central Yorkshire League was remarkable. They were docked 12 points, reduced to six on appeal, for picking a player required by a league representative side on the same day. To win the League, they needed three Thornhill wickets from the last seven balls to pick up the extra points for bowling out the opposition: they took them in three.

Among the record-breakers in the north were Phil Jeffery, Beckwithshaw's Australian opener, who beat the 55-year-old Airedale & Wharfedale record aggregate as early as July 23; Terry Hunte of Kendal in the Northern League, who passed Bill Alley's total of 1,345 runs, set in 1953; Alan Sippy of Furness, who became the first man in the North Lancashire to pass 2,000; Mudassar Nazar of Bolton, the former Pakistan Test player, and Ian Wrigglesworth of Clitheroe, who beat League records in the Manchester Association and the Ribblesdale and helped their teams to the title; and Hylton Ackerman, son of Northamptonshire's South African big-hitter, who went past Barry Wood's record aggregate in the Saddleworth League.

Up and down the country, even in quiet places like Carmarthen, leagues announced new measures to deal with the increasing problems of on-field dissent and indiscipline. League cricket continued to thrive, though the extent to which the best performances came from overseas players remained discouraging. Denton, members of the country's newest big league, the Lancashire County, had hoped to make a publicity splash by engaging Viv Richards. He chose not to play in the end, but Denton won the league anyway, with the West Indian fast bowler Kenny Benjamin as their professional; Malcolm Marshall is due to play for them in 1995.

LEAGUE WINNERS, 1994

League	*Winners*	*League*	*Winners*
Airedale & Wharfedale	Horsforth Hall Park	**Midland Club Championship**	Kings Heath
Bassetlaw	Farnsfield	**Midland Combined Counties**	Highway
Birmingham	Walsall	**Northants County**	Old Northamptonians
Bolton	Farnworth Social Circle	**Northern**	Kendal
	Walkden	**North Lancashire**	Millom
Bradford	East Bierley	**North Staffs. & South Cheshire**	Audley
Central	Loughborough	**Northumberland County**	Tynedale
Central Yorkshire	Gomersal	**North Wales**	Northop Hall
Cherwell	Leighton Buzzard	**North Yorks. & South Durham**	Middlesbrough
Cheshire County	Widnes	**Notts. Alliance**	Kimberley Institute
Cornwall	St Austell	**Ribblesdale**	Clitheroe
Derbyshire County	Ilkeston Rutland	**Saddleworth**	Heyside
Devon	Exmouth	**Somerset**	Taunton St Andrews
Dorset	Bournemouth	**Southern**	United Services
Durham County	Kimblesworth	**South Thames**	Sidcup
Durham Senior	Eppleton	**South Wales Association**	Ynysygerwn
Essex	Woodford Wells	**Surrey Championship**	Spencer
Hertfordshire	St Albans	**Sussex**	Chichester
Huddersfield	Meltham	**Thames Valley**	Finchampstead
Kent	St Lawrence	**Three Counties**	Chepstow
Lancashire County	Denton	**Two Counties (Suffolk/Essex)**	Bury St Edmunds
Leeds	Esholt	**Tyneside Senior**	Sacriston
Liverpool Competition	Chester	**Western**	Bath
Manchester Association	Bolton	**West Wales Club Conference**	Lampeter
Middlesex	Finchley	**Yorkshire**	Sheffield Collegiate

Note: To avoid confusion traditional League names have been given in this list and sponsors' names omitted.

NATIONAL CLUB CHAMPIONSHIP, 1994

Chorley of the Northern League became only the second Lancashire club to win the National Club Championship since its inauguration in 1969 – following Blackpool in 1990 – when they beat Ealing of the Middlesex League by five wickets. Chorley who, under the rules of the competition, were without their Australian professional Stewart Oliver, reached the final with a sequence of straightforward wins over powerful clubs: Wigan, Blackpool, Coventry and North Warwickshire, and then the Cheshire team Grappenhall, whom they beat in the semi-finals by seven wickets. Ealing beat Bromley in the quarter-finals and then scored a six-wicket win over fancied Kidderminster.

The 1993 winners Old Hill had gone out to Coventry and North Warwickshire in the last 16; Old Hill needed three to win off the last ball but could manage only two. One of the shocks of the tournament came when two-time champions Teddington were bowled out for just 39 by the Essex club Fives and Heronians and went down by ten wickets.

The future of the competition was threatened during the winter by a possible boycott from teams affiliated to the Club Cricket Conference, which is strongest in London and the Home Counties. This followed a change of rules by the National Cricket Association, which would allow semi-professionals (i.e. those whose main income does not come from playing) to take part, provided they are eligible for England. "The change is designed to recognise the cricket culture and traditions that exist in all parts of the country," said Terry Bates of the NCA. Representatives of clubs in the south-east, where very few players receive payment, said the change was unfair on them and would open the door to professionalism in their leagues. – Russell Grant.

FINAL

CHORLEY v EALING

At Lord's, August 26. Chorley won by five wickets. Toss: Chorley.

Chorley won the final with only three balls to spare, despite being in a seemingly commanding position after Bannister and Fazackerley put on 109 for the first wicket. Seven bowlers all struggled and Ealing put down several catches, but it was still halfway through the 45th over before the Chorley captain Horridge shepherded his team to safety. Ealing had made 235 for nine. In contrast, they lost both their openers quickly and were rescued by the middle order, before five wickets tumbled for 27.

Ealing

*M. S. Ahluwalia b Catterall 16
S. R. A. Western c Fazackerley b Purnell . 12
R. M. Pepper b Bannister 69
P. E. Wellings run out 47
K. Dandeniya c Bannister b Deakin . . . 57
U. Rashid c and b Purnell 5
†M. I. Ingram st Senior b Deakin 3
S. P. H. Gane c Deakin b Purnell 0
A. L. Price lbw b Deakin 10
P. Malik not out 0
B 3, l-b 4, w 9 16

1/18 2/58 3/139 4/176 5/208 6/216 7/220 8/234 9/235 (9 wkts, 45 overs) 235

B. R. Lemmon did not bat.

Bowling: Critchley 9–0–45–0; Purnell 8–0–27–3; Catterall 6–0–46–1; Eccleshare 9–1–15–0; Deakin 8–0–65–3; Bannister 5–0–30–1.

Chorley

N. Bannister c Ingram b Rashid	41	M. Richardson not out	5
J. Fazackerley c Pepper b Rashid	70		
*R. Horridge not out	42	B 3, l-b 12, w 6, n-b 2	23
N. Heaton b Price	24		—
†N. Senior c Gane b Lemmon	30	1/109 2/122 3/170 (5 wkts, 44.3 overs)	236
P. Deakin run out	1	4/218 5/228	

R. Purnell, D. Catterall, M. Critchley and K. Eccleshare did not bat.

Bowling: Gane 9–1–41–0; Malik 3–1–11–0; Rashid 9–0–36–2; Lemmon 8.3–0–43–1; Wellings 3–0–21–0; Price 8–0–45–1; Dandeniya 4–0–24–0.

Umpires: P. R. Mitchell and C. W. Powell.

WINNERS 1969-94

1969	Hampstead	1978	Cheltenham	1987	Old Hill
1970	Cheltenham	1979	Scarborough	1988	Enfield
1971	Blackheath	1980	Moseley	1989	Teddington
1972	Scarborough	1981	Scarborough	1990	Blackpool
1973	Wolverhampton	1982	Scarborough	1991	Teddington
1974	Sunbury	1983	Shrewsbury	1992	Optimists
1975	York	1984	Old Hill	1993	Old Hill
1976	Scarborough	1985	Old Hill	1994	Chorley
1977	Southgate	1986	Stourbridge		

NATIONAL VILLAGE CRICKET CHAMPIONSHIP, 1994

Three of the eight quarter-finalists in the 23rd National Village Championship had reached the final at Lord's before. But experience counted for nothing this time: Freuchie, Frocester and Goatacre all lost, Goatacre off the last ball of the match. The fourth losing quarter-finalists, Bardon Hill, failed in their bid to hit the last ball for a six that would have given them victory. Their conquerors were Elvaston, representatives of a small village on the outskirts of Derby and members of the Central Derbyshire League. They went on to score a 30-run win over the Yorkshire team Bardsey in the semi-final and then beat Werrington, from Cornwall, in a one-sided final to become the second Derbyshire team to take the title, after Quarndon in 1983. Werrington reached the final after a four-wicket win over Botany Bay from Hertfordshire.

The 1993 champions Kington were dramatically knocked out of the tournament in the third round by Chaddesley Corbett, who had lost fewer wickets in a game with the scores tied. In Somerset, Barrington's chairman was justifiably upset when a six hit by a Kilve player not only won the game but went through his windscreen. During Addingham's fourth round match against Old Sharlston in Yorkshire, the ball was stolen by a cow in the next field. The competition, organised by *The Cricketer*, will be sponsored from next season by Alliance & Leicester Giro. – Amanda Ripley.

FINAL

ELVASTON v WERRINGTON

At Lord's, August 28. Elvaston won by 55 runs. Toss: Werrington.

Paul Birch, 21, became the second player to score a hundred in the village final, following Kevin Iles of Goatacre in 1990. Birch's 101 was an undoubted match-winner for Elvaston. He thrived on the shortness of both the bowling and the Tavern boundary. But he had a couple of narrow squeaks: he was dropped at cover on 83 and was still two short of his century with two balls of the innings remaining. He turned blind for a second run and only just beat a misdirected throw from the square-leg boundary. Birch dominated an innings of 227 for five, a total surpassed in the final only in Iles's match; 109 of the runs came in the last ten overs, and Werrington were never in the hunt. They lost the first six batsmen for 83, two of them to Birch himself, before Richard Parish and Geoff Stanbury made their score respectable.

Elvaston

*S. M. Thompson c Dennis b Stanbury . 17
R. Bostock c Cobbledick b Johns 14
P. E. Birch not out 101
S. Chester run out 16
R. A. Torry lbw b Parish 37
S. R. Murray b Stanbury 31
S. J. Schofield not out 1
L-b 7, w 3 10

1/30 2/51 3/97 4/176 5/217 (5 wkts, 40 overs) 227

S. Plant, M. White, †P. J. Dolman and P. D. Thomason did not bat.

Bowling: Johns 9–0–45–1; Parish 8–0–54–1; Moore 9–0–40–0; Stanbury 5–0–47–2; Cobbledick 9–0–34–0.

Werrington

*N. J. Dennis c Bostock b Thomason . . 17
L. P. Bailey b Thomason 12
C. J. Walters c and b Birch 16
D. A. J. Taylor b Thompson 24
†G. S. Hutchings b Birch 3
S. S. Martin lbw b Thompson 0
R. J. Parish b Thompson 30
G. C. Stanbury not out 40
D. A. Johns b Murray 0
K. R. Moore b Murray 4
C. R. Cobbledick not out 15
B 2, l-b 4, w 4, n-b 1 11

1/16 2/30 3/69 4/77 5/77 6/83 7/131 8/133 9/149 (9 wkts, 40 overs) 172

Bowling: Murray 9–2–34–2; Thomason 6–1–28–2; Plant 4–0–20–0; Birch 9–1–36–2; Thompson 9–0–33–3; White 3–0–15–0.

Umpires: T. H. Duckett and B. Wilson.

WINNERS 1972-94

1972 Troon (Cornwall)
1973 Troon (Cornwall)
1974 Bomarsund (Northumberland)
1975 Gowerton (Glamorgan)
1976 Troon (Cornwall)
1977 Cookley (Worcestershire)
1978 Linton Park (Kent)
1979 East Bierley (Yorkshire)
1980 Marchwiel (Clwyd)
1981 St Fagans (Glamorgan)
1982 St Fagans (Glamorgan)
1983 Quarndon (Derbyshire)
1984 Marchwiel (Clwyd)
1985 Freuchie (Fife)
1986 Forge Valley (Yorkshire)
1987 Longparish (Hampshire)
1988 Goatacre (Wiltshire)
1989 Toft (Cheshire)
1990 Goatacre (Wiltshire)
1991 St Fagans (Glamorgan)
1992 Hursley Park (Hampshire)
1993 Kington (Herefordshire)
1994 Elvaston (Derbyshire)

IRISH CRICKET IN 1994

By DEREK SCOTT

Ireland, elected Associate Members of the International Cricket Council in 1993, had their baptism in the ICC Trophy in Nairobi in February. It was a great experience, but bad luck dogged the team from the start and, in great heat, they played below their potential. Realistically, though, they achieved their objective by finishing in the top eight.

Many of their players used up all their work leave for the Nairobi trip, so 21 different people had to be used for the eight matches in the home season, eight of whom played only one match each. There were respectable performances in the two UK knockout tournaments, but the big disappointment was defeat by just six runs against the New Zealanders in a 55-over match at Comber. "We did not win it, you lost it," said one of the visitors.

During the season, Stephen Warke won his 100th cap and scored his 4,000th run, the first player to reach either landmark for Ireland. Garfield Harrison scored his maiden century in the drawn game against Scotland, which was played on the superb Hamilton Crescent pitch in Glasgow. He was appointed Cricket Development Officer for Northern Ireland. The new captain, Alan Lewis, also scored a century against Scotland and averaged over 40, as did Narasimha Rao and Michael Rea. The bowling is better left unrecorded, the average runs per wicket against the team being 48.53.

The domestic titles were shared around all over the country. Pride of place must go to Limavady in the North-West, who won their local league for the first time since 1976 at the last gasp, having previously been victorious in the Irish Senior Cup. In winning the league they deprived Donemana of a tenth successive title. Limavady's great star was Desmond Curry, a Donemana man, who scored centuries in both the semi-final and final of the Cup. Another North-West club, Strabane, were the beaten finalists.

Ardmore, in their 99th year, won their first senior title, taking home the North-West Cup by beating Eglinton in a two-innings final. In the Northern Union, Lisburn and North Down played a tied two-innings final and shared the Cup, the last Lisburn wicket falling on the last ball of the match. Ten years after their previous title, Downpatrick won the Northern League for the sixth time. Their captain Jim Patterson and professional Wasim Haider were mainly responsible.

The Munster Cup Final had an aggregate of 138 runs in 76.3 overs, with Limerick beating Cork County by 71 to 67. Church of Ireland retained the Munster Senior League by dint of the all-round contribution of Steve Alleyne, whose brother Mark plays for Gloucestershire. In Dublin, YMCA won their seventh Cup in 11 seasons, beating Malahide by one wicket in the final. The last pair successfully negotiated the 24 runs required to win. Pembroke, with a young team, won the League for the first time in 21 years. The all-round play of Stuart McCready was a big factor. The "overs" league, run in August, was won by Clontarf, who are experts at this form of cricket. Andre Botha from South Africa had a great season for Clontarf with 733 runs and 42 wickets. Uniquely, North-West won the Allied Irish Bank Senior Interprovincial Championship for the third successive year, during which time they have remained unbeaten. They were a powerful team and their host of internationals – Curry, Rao, Stephen Smyth, David Cooke and Junior McBrine – all did well.

SCOTTISH CRICKET IN 1994

By J. WATSON BLAIR

Scotland was at last admitted as an associate member of the International Cricket Council in July, thus opening the door for competition in world cricket. It will be 1998 before the Scots get the chance to compete in an ICC Trophy, the preliminary competition of the World Cup. But to compete at the highest level, some reorganisation will be necessary, and the Scottish Cricket Union will require the fullest support of everyone interested in cricket, particularly the administrators of the many competitions.

The greatest success on the field came at home in the Triple Crown competition, when Scotland beat the England Amateur XI in a thrilling finish to take the trophy by a fraction of a point. Alastair Storie's excellent 116 was a fine reply to critics of his earlier performances. Much of Scotland's cricket otherwise was enjoyable rather than successful. The pre-season tour of Zimbabwe fell short of expectations, although it did provide much-needed experience. Later, the team took part in a quadrangular tournament in The Netherlands with the Dutch and Danish national teams and a Dutch Under-23 XI. The Scots were hampered by limited experience of the matting wickets.

The biggest disappointment came in July when the South Africans visited Scotland for the first time since 1951. The match then was ruined by rain. In 1994 it was even worse and only 31 balls were bowled, representing disappointment to the spectators and a heavy financial loss to the SCU.

There was some optimism that the Scots might improve their performances in the English knockout competitions in 1995. The decision to revert to group matches instead of straight knockouts in the Benson and Hedges was warmly welcomed. And the SCU announced that it was hoping to sign Malcolm Marshall, the former Test fast bowler, as the overseas professional.

On the domestic scene the North District emerged as winners of the Royal Bank Area Championship, while the Whyte & Mackay Scottish Cup was won by Forfarshire, winners in 1968. The beaten finalists, Poloc, were also previous winners in 1984. In the many leagues throughout Scotland, some of the results were surprising: the titles changed hands in all three of the major competitions. Strathmore County, after challenging for several years, won the Caledonian 80/- County Championship with Aberdeenshire close behind. For the first time since 1961, the D. M. Hall Western Union Championship was won by Ayr, with Ferguslie in second place. Heriot's Former Pupils, seven times winners between 1977 and 1983, broke the recent grip on the title by Grange, by triumphing in the Ryden East League. They were closely followed by Stenhousemuir.

Winners of other Scottish Leagues

Dukes Strathmore Union: Gordonians; **Edinburgh Woollen Mill Border League:** Kelso; **Macallan North of Scotland League:** Buckie; **Glasgow & District League:** Hillhead High School Former Pupils.

THE TRIPLE CROWN TOURNAMENT, 1994

By GARETH A. DAVIES

The second Triple Crown Tournament was settled by the very last ball when the hosts, Scotland, dismissed England with the scores level. That meant a Scottish victory, as they had lost fewer wickets, and they edged out England by a fraction of a point in a complicated piece of arithmetic that decided the final table.

The England team – an Amateur XI drawn from the Minor Counties – were favourites to retain their title; they beat Ireland, by nine wickets through an undefeated 130 from Steve Dean, and then Wales. Scotland lost their opening game with Wales, whose captain, Andy Puddle, led with a delightful 76, but rallied against Ireland, with Alastair Storie finding form. Storie was also dominant against England, scoring 116. Coincidentally, England wicket-keeper Stuart Waterton also made 116 before falling to the third ball of the last over, with eight runs required. Richard Ellwood hit a six, but was run out next ball and the final delivery yielded only one.

Ireland, the hosts in 1995, did not win until their last match, against Wales. Stephen Warke, who made 95, became their first player to score 4,000 runs, in his 100th representative match, and enabled them to rise fractionally above Wales in the final table.

Results

At Hamilton Crescent, Glasgow, July 20. England Amateur XI won by nine wickets. Toss: Ireland. Ireland 212 for six (55 overs) (D. A. Lewis 57, J. D. R. Benson 51, M. V. Narasimha Rao 38 not out); England Amateur XI 213 for one (47.5 overs) (S. J. Dean 130 not out, S. N. V. Waterton 37, M. J. Roberts 37 not out).

At Titwood, Glasgow, July 20. Wales won by five wickets. Toss: Wales. Scotland 213 for seven (55 overs) (I. L. Philip 52, B. M. W. Patterson 89; A. D. Griffiths three for 33); Wales 217 for five (52.1 overs) (M. J. Newbold 80 not out, A. C. Puddle 76).

At Glenpark, Greenock, July 21. England Amateur XI won by three wickets. Toss: England Amateur XI. Wales 158 for eight (35 overs) (N. Lloyd 30; P. G. Roshier three for 24); England Amateur XI 160 for seven (34.1 overs) (M. Hussain 34; A. Smith four for 23).

At Raeburn Place, Edinburgh, July 21. Scotland won by 34 runs. Toss: Ireland. Scotland 198 for eight (46 overs) (A. C. Storie 67, B. M. W. Patterson 44; E. R. Moore three for 39); Ireland 164 (42.5 overs) (S. J. S. Warke 55).

At Titwood, Glasgow, July 22. Ireland won by 15 runs. Toss: Ireland. Ireland 311 for five (55 overs) (S. J. S. Warke 95, M. P. Rea 87, S. G. Smyth 43, J. D. R. Benson 52); Wales 296 (54.1 overs) (M. Tamplin 57, K. M. Bell 66; S. Graham four for 49).

At Hamilton Crescent, Glasgow, July 22. Scotland won by virtue of losing fewer wickets. Toss: Scotland. Scotland 239 for seven (55 overs) (I. L. Philip 55, A. C. Storie 116; P. G. Roshier three for 46); England Amateur XI 239 (55 overs) (S. N. V. Waterton 116, D. Clarke 42; D. Cowan four for 41).

FINAL TABLE

	Played	Won	Lost	Points	Avge
Scotland	3	2	1	4	0.799
England Amateur XI	3	2	1	4	0.788
Ireland	3	1	2	2	0.685
Wales	3	1	2	2	0.624

The average was obtained by dividing teams' scoring-rate (runs scored divided by wickets lost) by their strike-rate (balls bowled divided by wickets taken).

CAREER FIGURES

Players retiring from county cricket or not retained

BATTING

	M	I	NO	R	HS	100s	Avge	1,000r/season
A. M. Babington	95	101	40	515	58	0	8.44	0
S. Bastien	54	41	18	182	36*	0	7.91	0
P. J. Berry	26	38	13	516	76	0	20.64	0
D. J. P. Boden	4	3	0	10	5	0	3.33	0
B. C. Broad	340	613	38	21,892	227*	50	38.07	11
N. D. Burns	156	234	52	5,349	166	5	29.39	0
V. P. Clarke	2	4	0	46	38	0	11.50	0
R. M. F. Cox	19	29	4	605	104*	1	24.20	0
M. A. Crawley	80	126	22	3,378	160*	8	32.48	1
M. Diwan	1	2	0	0	0	0	0.00	0
D. B. D'Oliveira	232	362	22	9,445	237	10	27.77	4
B. T. P. Donelan	53	66	21	1,105	68*	0	24.55	0
R. M. Ellison	207	284	72	5,046	108	1	23.80	0
N. A. Felton	211	361	21	10,242	173*	15	30.12	5
J. M. Fielding	1	1	1	27	27*	0	—	0
I. Fletcher	14	22	3	460	65*	0	24.21	0
N. A. Folland	32	56	5	1,755	108*	2	34.41	0
A. R. Fothergill	12	17	1	127	29	0	7.93	0
G. Fowler	292	495	27	16,663	226	36	35.60	8
D. A. Graveney	457	580	178	7,107	119	2	17.67	0
P. W. Henderson	5	7	0	119	46	0	17.00	0
P. N. Hepworth	59	98	8	2,113	129	3	23.47	1
S. G. Hinks	182	319	19	8,715	234	11	29.05	3
M. Jean-Jacques	60	74	17	681	73	0	11.94	0
O. H. Mortensen	157	173	94	709	74*	0	8.97	0
A. J. Murphy	84	86	39	323	38	0	6.87	0
A. Payne	4	4	2	124	51*	0	62.00	0
C. Penn	128	146	36	2,048	115	1	18.61	0
A. W. Richardson	2	3	0	14	9	0	4.66	0
A. C. H. Seymour	36	62	5	1,699	157	2	29.80	0
R. W. Sladdin	33	42	9	372	51*	0	11.27	0
D. M. Smith	319	513	91	15,265	213	28	36.17	7
I. Smith	81	111	14	2,350	116	4	24.22	0
T. D. Topley	120	138	29	1,693	66	0	15.53	0
R. M. Wight	19	31	5	593	62*	0	22.80	0

* *Signifies not out.*

Continued overleaf

BOWLING AND FIELDING

	R	*W*	*BB*	*Avge*	*5W/i*	*10W/m*	*Ct/St*
A. M. Babington . .	7,587	208	8-107	36.47	3	0	32
S. Bastien	4,672	123	6-52	37.98	7	1	7
P. J. Berry	1,756	39	7-113	45.02	1	1	10
D. J. P. Boden	284	7	4-11	40.57	—	—	2
B. C. Broad	1,037	16	2-14	64.81	—	—	189
N. D. Burns	8	0	—	—	—	—	316/32
V. P. Clarke	105	1	1-93	105.00	—	—	0
R. M. F. Cox	1	0	—	—	—	—	11
M. A. Crawley	2,985	64	6-92	46.64	1	0	67
M. Diwan	—	—	—	—	—	—	0
D. B. D'Oliveira . .	2,111	50	4-68	42.22	—	—	203
B. T. P. Donelan . .	4,627	106	6-62	43.65	4	1	14
R. M. Ellison	13,773	475	7-33	28.99	18	2	86
N. A. Felton	345	2	1-48	172.50	—	—	122
J. M. Fielding	53	2	1-15	26.50	—	—	0
I. Fletcher	—	—	—	—	—	—	4
N. A. Folland	—	—	—	—	—	—	20
A. R. Fothergill . . .	—	—	—	—	—	—	16/3
G. Fowler	366	10	2-34	36.60	—	—	152/5
D. A. Graveney . . .	29,867	981	8-85	30.44	40	7	241
P. W. Henderson . .	405	10	3-59	40.50	—	—	1
P. N. Hepworth . . .	1,269	30	3-30	42.30	—	—	31
S. G. Hinks	383	8	2-18	47.87	—	—	114
M. Jean-Jacques . . .	4,514	124	8-77	36.40	2	1	15
O. H. Mortensen . .	10,364	434	6-27	23.88	16	1	47
A. J. Murphy	7,934	208	6-97	38.14	6	0	17
A. Payne	187	5	2-15	37.40	—	—	2
C. Penn	9,840	296	7-70	33.24	12	0	56
A. W. Richardson .	112	2	2-38	56.00	—	—	0
A. C. H. Seymour .	27	0	—	—	—	—	17
R. W. Sladdin	3,805	93	6-58	40.91	2	0	14
D. M. Smith	1,574	30	3-40	52.46	—	—	204
I. Smith	2,801	62	3-48	45.17	—	—	35
T. D. Topley	10,147	367	7-75	27.64	15	2	70
R. M. Wight	1,456	33	3-65	44.12	—	—	11

HONOURS' LIST, 1994-95

In 1994-95, the following were decorated for their services to cricket:

New Year's Honours, 1994: H. T. Brind (Surrey groundsman and TCCB inspector of pitches) MBE, J. R. Murray (West Indies) MBE (Grenada list), B. A. Hosking (services to New Zealand cricket and electric power industry) OBE, I. D. S. Smith (New Zealand) MBE, K. Smithies (England women's captain) OBE, Lt-Col. J. R. Stephenson (retiring secretary of MCC) CBE, E. W. Swanton (cricket writer) CBE, M. A. Youdell (Nottinghamshire chairman – services to youth clubs) MBE.

Queen's Birthday Honours: T. E. Bailey (England) CBE, T. M. B. Rice (services to arts, particularly music, and sport) Knight Bachelor, I. V. A. Richards (West Indies) OBE, J. Sokell (Wombwell Cricket Lovers' Society – services to cricket in Yorkshire) MBE, F. M. Turner (former Leicestershire chief executive – services to cricket in Leicestershire) MBE.

New Year's Honours, 1995: M. J. Hopkins (designer of Mound Stand at Lord's – services to architecture) Knight Bachelor, D. O. Neely (chairman of New Zealand selectors – services to cricket) MBE, D. R. W. Silk (TCCB chairman, former MCC president – services to cricket and education) CBE.

INDIA UNDER-19 IN ENGLAND, 1994

By GERALD HOWAT

It was an experienced India Under-19 side which arrived in England in July 1994. Twelve of the 16-strong party had already played first-class cricket (compared to nine of England's 16), some in the Ranji Trophy final. The cricket manager, former Test batsman Sandeep Patil, declared that his team had come to learn and to play positive cricket. No doubt they did learn, especially from their defeats in the two one-day internationals, which England won by a canter. But they were not always positive. Having won the First "Test" at Taunton with some convincing batting and bowling, the tourists adopted a negative approach in the two remaining games of the series, with their first innings dragging on into the fourth day, and only drew the games to win the series. Their predecessors in 1981 – who included Ravi Shastri and Navjot Sidhu – had not won any of their international games, so the Indians must have been well pleased. They were unbeaten in their minor matches, winning six and drawing two.

The side could bat down the order; indeed, their lowest completed innings in the Tests was 393. Yet no one player emerged as outstanding. Amol Muzumdar, perhaps burdened by the expectations generated by his record score on first-class debut, 260 for Bombay earlier in the year, never established himself. There were parallels between him and the West Indian, Shivnarine Chanderpaul, who toured in 1993. Both are slightly built and elegant players, and good timers of the ball. Chanderpaul scored heavily and went on to win full Test selection within a few months; Muzumdar easily topped 500 runs overall, but made only 87 of them in the three Tests. Vangipurappy Laxman, who could cut late and drive strongly, averaged nearly 70. The Kumars, Arun and Tarun (not related), were usually reliable, and opener Jitender Singh scored 172 in the Second Test, an essay in concentration and technique. There were two wicket-keepers of equal ability, each of whom won Test selection and both of whom could bat well: Pankaj Dharmani and Milap Mewada.

First impressions suggested that this was a team of spin bowlers. They dominated the early matches and Balaji Rao, the leg-spin and googly bowler, took wickets in virtually every game, finishing with 32 at just over 21. The left-arm spinner, Rahul Sanghvi, a pupil of Bishen Bedi, took 15 and Sridharan Sriram, another left-armer, bowled tidily in the Tests. All of them, however, found it difficult to bowl to left-handers – a point underlined at Edgbaston in the Third Test, when Marcus Trescothick of Somerset made a double-century, and two other left-handers backed him up with fifties – out of a total of 381. The two seamers came into their own when the Test series began. Iqbal Siddiqui, though not matching the speed of his English counterparts, could muster some pace. He was used sparingly outside the Tests; but he took 18 wickets in the three games at 24.00, and was voted India's player of the series. His partner, Mohammad Saif, was more military medium but sustained a good line just outside the off-stump, often to a seven-two field. Amit Sharma of Punjab, who led the team, could do nothing right until the First Test, but there made the century which ensured India's success. As an off-spinner, he bowled economically without taking many wickets. His leadership on the field was alert, and he commanded the respect of his players.

India's various English opponents could also take some pleasure from their own performances. Openers Trescothick and Michael Vaughan, the captain, easily dominated the international team. Among the younger players who impressed the visitors was the Kanpur-born Birmingham-bred schoolboy, Anurag Singh, who made two centuries against them, for ESCA and a Development of Excellence XI, and was selected for England in the last two Tests. The weather was generally excellent and the atmosphere of the tour thoroughly enjoyable; some of the Indians are bound to be seen on English cricket fields again. There was some disquiet among the counties that players who were already in their Championship sides like Trescothick and Vaughan should be taken away for what some coaches regarded as an inferior form of cricket. This was vigorously contested by National Cricket Association officials, who insisted that young players benefited from a range of cricket and particularly from the experience of international competition.

TOUR PARTY

Amit Sharma (Punjab) (*captain*), A. A. Muzumdar (Bombay) (*vice-captain*), P. Dharmani (Punjab), Iqbal Siddiqui (Maharashtra), Jaswinder Singh (Railways), Javed Zaman (Assam), Jitender Singh (Haryana), H. Kanitkar (Maharashtra), J. Arun Kumar (Karnataka), Tarun Kumar (Bihar), V. V. S. Laxman (Hyderabad), M. Mewada (Baroda), Mohammad Saif (Madhya Pradesh), B. Rao (Tamil Nadu), R. Sanghvi (Delhi), S. Sriram (Tamil Nadu).

Manager: G. Dasgupta. *Cricket manager:* S. M. Patil.

RESULTS

Matches – Played 13: Won 7, Lost 2, Drawn 4.

Note: Matches in this section were not first-class.

At Wellington College, July 30. India Under-19 won by 62 runs. Toss: India Under-19. India Under-19 290 for two (55 overs) (J. Arun Kumar 124 retired hurt, Tarun Kumar 94, A. A. Muzumdar 38 not out); ESCA Under-19 228 for nine (55 overs) (A. D. Bairstow 36, A. J. Swann 32, A. Singh 100; B. Rao five for 52).

At Wellington College, July 31. India Under-19 won by five wickets. Toss: National Association of Young Cricketers. National Association of Young Cricketers 170 (54.5 overs) (D. Dyer 40; B. Rao three for 42); India Under-19 171 for five (52.5 overs) (V. V. S. Laxman 84 not out).

At Wellington College, August 2. India Under-19 won by 139 runs. Toss: India Under-19. India Under-19 266 for two (55 overs) (Jitender Singh 84, A. A. Muzumdar 101 not out, V. V. S. Laxman 54 not out); League Cricket Conference Under-25 127 (42.2 overs) (N. Bannister 40, A. McDowell 37; B. Rao five for 28).

At Cardiff, August 4. First one-day international: England Under-19 won by four wickets. Toss: England Under-19. India Under-19 139 (49.4 overs); England Under-19 143 for six (33.3 overs) (M. E. Trescothick 38, V. S. Solanki 30).

At Bristol, August 6. Second one-day international: England Under-19 won by ten wickets. Toss: India Under-19. India Under-19 186 for nine (55 overs) (Tarun Kumar 40, P. Dharmani 43 not out); England Under-19 187 for no wkt (36.1 overs) (M. E. Trescothick 84 not out, M. P. Vaughan 98 not out).

At Weston-super-Mare, August 7, 8, 9. India Under-19 won by seven wickets. Toss: India Under-19. Southern Development of Excellence XI 132 (M. J. Cawdron 39; Iqbal Siddiqui five for 45) and 204 (M. J. Cawdron 82; S. Sriram five for 40); India Under-19 178 for six dec. (V. V. S. Laxman 102 not out; A. D. Edwards three for 47) and 161 for three (A. A. Muzumdar 73 not out, P. Dharmani 73).

ENGLAND UNDER-19 v INDIA UNDER-19

First "Test" Match

At Taunton, August 11, 12, 13, 14. India Under-19 won by nine wickets. Toss: England Under-19.

England's defeat was predictable once they collapsed inside 53 overs, after India scored an imposing 430. Despite a fight-back on the third day, they set a target of 161. India took only 43.2 overs, with Muzumdar making a stylish half-century. After losing three quick wickets on a damp first morning, India had established their mastery through a partnership of 205 between Laxman and Amit Sharma. Both made hundreds, and Dharmani and the tail added 139 on the second day. When England batted, the seamers struck at once, sending back both openers at two. While the Indian spinners bowled well, it was Siddiqui, finding some pace from a grassy pitch, who picked up five wickets. England followed on 251 behind. Trescothick scored quickly and a 194-run stand between two of the seven players in the side with Yorkshire connections, captain Vaughan, who made 162, and Schofield, was an all-wicket record for England at this level. But they surrendered tamely on the final morning.

Close of play: First day, India Under-19 291-7 (P. Dharmani 24*, Iqbal Siddiqui 1*); Second day, England Under-19 11-0 (M. E. Trescothick 10*, M. P. Vaughan 0*); Third day, England Under-19 403-7.

India Under-19

Jitender Singh c Dawood b Silverwood	13	– not out	61
J. Arun Kumar c Dawood b Lugsden	0	– c Vaughan b Keedy	38
A. A. Muzumdar c Dawood b Betts	14	– not out	53
V. V. S. Laxman c Trescothick b Betts	119		
*Amit Sharma b Innes	105		
†P. Dharmani run out	84		
S. Sriram lbw b Innes	0		
Mohammad Saif c Dawood b Lugsden	8		
Iqbal Siddiqui c Vaughan b Silverwood	22		
B. Rao not out	39		
R. Sanghvi not out	8		
B 4, l-b 5, w 1, n-b 8	18	B 5, l-b 1, n-b 4	10
1/0 2/27 3/27 4/232 5/269 6/269 7/278 8/369 9/392 (9 wkts dec.)	430	1/62 (1 wkt)	162

Bowling: *First Innings*—Silverwood 29–10–79–2; Lugsden 32–4–124–2; Innes 15–4–34–2; Betts 20–9–54–2; Morris 12–2–41–0; Keedy 18–4–62–0; Vaughan 4–0–27–0. *Second Innings*—Silverwood 6–0–32–0; Betts 4–0–25–0; Lugsden 10–2–33–0; Keedy 13–6–23–1; Morris 4–0–13–0; Innes 6.2–0–30–0.

England Under-19

M. E. Trescothick c Dharmani b Iqbal Siddiqui	1	– b Rao 73
*M. P. Vaughan b Mohammad Saif	1	– c J. Arun Kumar b Iqbal Siddiqui 162
A. McGrath c Dharmani b Iqbal Siddiqui	10	– lbw b Rao 3
C. J. Schofield c Sriram b Iqbal Siddiqui	32	– c Jitender Singh b Iqbal Siddiqui 92
A. C. Morris c Amit Sharma b Rao	52	– c Muzumdar b Mohammad Saif 6
K. J. Innes c Dharmani b Rao	50	– c Dharmani b Mohammad Saif 1
†I. Dawood lbw b Iqbal Siddiqui	2	– lbw b Sriram 36
C. E. W. Silverwood c Dharmani b Iqbal Siddiqui	2	– b Iqbal Siddiqui 15
M. M. Betts b Rao	2	– not out 5
G. Keedy c Laxman b Sharma	16	– c Sriram b Iqbal Siddiqui 0
S. Lugsden not out	0	– b Rao 0
L-b 6, w 3, n-b 2	11	B 4, l-b 6, w 6, n-b 2 18
1/2 2/2 3/16 4/52 5/104 6/112 7/124 8/139 9/179	179	1/112 2/132 3/326 4/344 5/348 6/356 7/394 8/410 9/410 411

Bowling: *First Innings*—Iqbal Siddiqui 17–2–75–5; Mohammad Saif 6–1–31–1; Sanghvi 17–6–26–0; Rao 8.5–1–34–3; Amit Sharma 2–1–4–1; Sriram 2–0–3–0. *Second Innings*—Iqbal Siddiqui 21–3–88–4; Mohammad Saif 15–1–46–2; Sanghvi 27–7–56–0; Amit Sharma 8–0–46–0; Rao 34–7–99–3; Laxman 7–2–22–0; Sriram 15–2–44–1.

Umpires: J. H. Harris and P. Willey.

At Shenley, August 16, 17, 18. India Under-19 won by 113 runs. Toss: India Under-19. India Under-19 185 for six dec. (S. Sriram 38 not out, M. Mewada 35; S. D. Thomas three for 58) and 276 for two dec. (J. Arun Kumar 75, M. Mewada 78, H. Kanitkar 61 not out, A. A. Muzumdar 51 not out); Development of Excellence XI 203 for three dec. (A. Singh 102 not out, D. J. Sales 50, M. Powell 37) and 145 (S. D. Thomas 46 not out, D. Thomson 36; Iqbal Siddiqui three for 34, V. V. S. Laxman three for six).

At Oundle, August 20, 21, 22. India Under-19 won by six wickets. Toss: Northern Development of Excellence XI. Northern Development of Excellence XI 305 for eight dec. (N. T. Wood 87 not out, A. D. Bairstow 37, A. Flintoff 64; Mohammad Saif three for 37) and 164 for seven dec. (P. C. McKeown 49, A. Flintoff 38); India Under-19 157 for nine dec. (M. Mewada 43; N. Killeen four for 38) and 315 for four (Jitender Singh 50, M. Mewada 79, Tarun Kumar 75, Amit Sharma 54).

ENGLAND UNDER-19 v INDIA UNDER-19

Second "Test" Match

At Leeds, August 24, 25, 26, 27. Drawn. Toss: India Under-19.

The match was condemned to a draw when the two first innings were not completed until 12.15 on the fourth day. Sharma seemed to have justified his decision to make England bat when Siddiqui and Mohammad Saif reduced them to 204 for seven on the first day, but next morning a ninth-wicket partnership of 119 between Dawood – who reached his century – and Keedy took England to 348. Jitender Singh dominated India's reply with 172, taking up 636 minutes. No attempt was made to force the pace, which dropped to 2.29 an over on the third day; Mewada and Sriram batted for three hours each. England's bowlers conceded 84 extras. On what had become a docile pitch, Trescothick made an entertaining and carefree 140, with 20 fours and three sixes, on the final afternoon.

Close of play: First day, England Under-19 204-7 (I. Dawood 13*, M. M. Betts 1*); Second day, India Under-19 150-2 (Jitender Singh 51*, V. V. S. Laxman 22*); Third day, India Under-19 393-6 (Jitender Singh 161*, S. Sriram 39*).

England Under-19

	First Innings		Second Innings	
M. E. Trescothick	c Rao b Iqbal Siddiqui	22	c Dharmani b Sriram	140
*M. P. Vaughan	c Amit Sharma b Mohammad Saif	77	c Mewada b Mohammad Saif	15
A. Singh	lbw b Iqbal Siddiqui	3	b Rao	35
C. J. Schofield	c Iqbal Siddiqui b Mohammad Saif	31	c Dharmani b Rao	2
A. C. Morris	b Mohammad Saif	1	c Rao b Jitender Singh	51
K. J. Innes	c and b Mohammad Saif	16	c Sriram b Dharmani	27
A. D. Edwards	c Jitender Singh b Iqbal Siddiqui	21	not out	3
†I. Dawood	c Laxman b Iqbal Siddiqui	111	not out	0
M. M. Betts	c Mewada b Laxman	4		
G. Keedy	c Laxman b Mohammad Saif	33		
S. Lugsden	not out	0		
	B 3, l-b 16, w 8, n-b 2	29	B 2, l-b 14, w 3, n-b 2	21
	1/34 2/60 3/137 4/142 5/153 6/187 7/202 8/229 9/348	348	1/57 2/208 3/208 4/217 5/281 6/294 (6 wkts dec.)	294

Bowling: *First Innings*—Iqbal Siddiqui 32.1–7–124–4; Mohammad Saif 36–8–128–5; Laxman 9–4–20–1; Sriram 7–1–14–0; Rao 10–1–39–0; Amit Sharma 2–0–4–0. *Second Innings*—Iqbal Siddiqui 6–0–45–0; Mohammad Saif 9–0–32–1; Laxman 4–0–22–0; Sriram 15–5–46–1; Rao 16–2–59–2; Amit Sharma 2–0–25–0; Muzumdar 2–0–13–0; Jitender Singh 4–0–13–1; Dharmani 1.5–0–12–1; Tarun Kumar 2–0–11–0.

India Under-19

Tarun Kumar	b Trescothick	45
Jitender Singh	c Lugsden b Morris	172
A. A. Muzumdar	lbw b Edwards	2
V. V. S. Laxman	c Trescothick b Betts	28
*Amit Sharma	c Dawood b Betts	0
P. Dharmani	lbw b Morris	15
†M. Mewada	lbw b Morris	36
S. Sriram	c Keedy b Trescothick	51
Mohammad Saif	c Innes b Lugsden	21
Iqbal Siddiqui	b Betts	16
B. Rao	not out	9
	B 19, l-b 26, w 1, n-b 38	84
	1/87 2/94 3/156 4/156 5/180 6/300 7/414 8/432 9/455	479

Bowling: Betts 22.5–4–118–3; Lugsden 32–10–75–1; Edwards 25–9–41–1; Innes 5.1–1–10–0; Morris 25.5–8–44–3; Trescothick 21–7–51–2; Keedy 34–13–57–0; Vaughan 15–2–38–0.

Umpires: B. Leadbeater and B. J. Meyer.

At Sleaford, August 30, 31, September 1. Drawn. Toss: MCC Young Cricketers. MCC Young Cricketers 265 (R. Rao 60, M. Newell 84, A. Tudor 58; R. Sanghvi four for 70, H. Kanitkar three for 67) and 36 for two; India Under-19 207 for three dec. (J. Arun Kumar 70, H. Kanitkar 46 not out, P. Dharmani 48 not out).

At Old Hill, September 4, 5, 6. Drawn. Toss: India Under-19. India Under-19 261 for eight dec. (Jitender Singh 41, V. V. S. Laxman 88, P. Dharmani 58; N. Killeen three for 39) and 265 for six dec. (J. Arun Kumar 126, Jitender Singh 53; R. W. Nowell three for 64); England Under-18 261 for four dec. (O. H. Shah 104, V. S. Solanki 47, M. A. Wagh 36 not out) and 212 for eight (D. J. Sales 60, V. S. Solanki 46, O. H. Shah 43; R. Sanghvi three for 75, S. Sriram five for 41).

ENGLAND UNDER-19 v INDIA UNDER-19

Third "Test" Match

At Birmingham, September 8, 9, 10, 11. Drawn. Toss: India Under-19.

As at Headingley, India's first innings dragged into the fourth day, and the draw ensured them a 1-0 series win. In mitigation, rain had restricted the first day to 13.4 overs, during which England, in the first twist of a fluctuating game, collapsed to 27 for five. But Trescothick and Morris redeemed the situation, adding 141. Trescothick went on to 206 from 233 balls; he and Morris, and later Thomas, all left-handers, posed problems for the Indian spinners. England eventually totalled 381, and had hopes of levelling the series when India were 89 for five. Thereafter, Dharmani scored 178, the highest innings of the tour, with 26 fours and one six, guiding India to a first-innings lead of 12. He finally fell to Thomas, the most effective of the English seamers. In the last session Vaughan became the second highest scorer in England Under-19 cricket, with 776 runs.

Close of play: First day, England Under-19 27-5 (M. E. Trescothick 11*); Second day, India Under-19 56-1 (Jitender Singh 19*, A. A. Muzumdar 6*); Third day, India Under-19 266-7 (P. Dharmani 110*).

England Under-19

First innings		Second innings	
*M. P. Vaughan c Mohammad Saif	6	c Muzumdar b Iqbal Siddiqui	40
M. E. Trescothick st Dharmani b Sanghvi	206	run out	25
A. McGrath lbw b Mohammad Saif	1	lbw b Iqbal Siddiqui	5
C. J. Schofield c J. Arun Kumar b Iqbal Siddiqui	3	not out	23
M. M. Betts lbw b Iqbal Siddiqui	0		
A. Singh c Sriram b Mohammad Saif	3		
A. C. Morris lbw b Amit Sharma	54	(5) c Rao b Iqbal Siddiqui	5
A. D. Edwards b Sanghvi	37	(6) not out	23
†I. Dawood b Sanghvi	0		
S. D. Thomas c Iqbal Siddiqui b Amit Sharma	54		
G. Keedy not out	4		
B 4, l-b 5, w 2, n-b 2	13	B 4, l-b 3	7
1/6 2/8 3/14 4/14 5/27 6/168 7/277 8/283 9/341	381	1/51 2/62 3/75 4/85 (4 wkts dec.)	128

Bowling: *First Innings*—Iqbal Siddiqui 15–4–54–2; Mohammad Saif 28–4–120–3; Sriram 11–3–36–0; Sanghvi 14–1–70–3; Rao 6–0–36–0; Amit Sharma 6.5–1–38–2; Laxman 4–1–18–0. *Second Innings*—Iqbal Siddiqui 13–2–46–3; Mohammad Saif 10–1–43–0; Sanghvi 5–0–15–0; Laxman 3–0–7–0; Sriram 3–2–4–0; Amit Sharma 1–0–1–0; Muzumdar 1–0–2–0; J. Arun Kumar 1–0–3–0.

India Under-19

Jitender Singh run out	24
J. Arun Kumar c Dawood b Edwards	14
A. A. Muzumdar c Vaughan b Thomas	18
V. V. S. Laxman c Trescothick b Morris	4
*Amit Sharma lbw b Morris	8
†P. Dharmani c Schofield b Thomas	178
S. Sriram c Dawood b Thomas	34
Mohammad Saif c Trescothick b Betts	18
Iqbal Siddiqui c McGrath b Thomas	21
B. Rao st Dawood b Keedy	17
R. Sanghvi not out	0
B 11, l-b 3, w 5, n-b 38	57
1/44 2/65 3/78 4/86 5/89 6/160 7/266 8/310 9/369	393

Bowling: Betts 19–4–92–1; Thomas 38.5–7–81–4; Morris 26–9–56–2; Edwards 26–10–58–1; Keedy 32–8–65–1; Trescothick 4–2–5–0; Vaughan 7–0–22–0.

Umpires: B. Dudleston and K. E. Palmer.

NAYC UNDER-19 COUNTY FESTIVALS, 1994

By PHILIP HOARE

Yorkshire claimed their second Under-19 title in three years after winning a tense and exciting match against Durham – who were also losing finalists in 1993 – by two runs. A relatively young team, Yorkshire emerged as a strong force during the Cambridge festival, where they won the Norman Yardley Trophy. Their strength was in bowling to their field placings, which reflected well on the maturity of their captain, John Randerson.

They met Cheshire in the area final, a match reduced to 49 overs a side after rain. Cheshire soon regretted choosing to bat on a damp pitch; they were reduced to 88 for nine, though the last wicket added 32. Off-spinner James Middlebrook took four for 31. Once the roller had reduced the potency of the spin in the wicket, Lee Baxter – defying a chipped bone in his elbow – and Randerson swept home without being parted. Durham won the Tom Orford Trophy at the Oxford festival for the second year running, defeating Worcestershire in the final. Neil Killeen returned five for 38 as Worcestershire succumbed for 111; only the captain, James Ralph, passed 20. Nick Trainor and Stephen Meek ensured that Durham passed their target inside 38 overs.

Among the other teams at Oxford, there were several outstanding performances. Anurag Singh of Warwickshire made 117 against Berkshire and 112 against Cornwall, while Chris Tetley took five for 63 against Buckinghamshire and six for 28 against Somerset to help Worcestershire through to the final against Durham. The highest score of the two festivals came at Cambridge, where Carl Crowe made an unbeaten 157 for Leicestershire against Suffolk, followed by two fifties, including 74 against Yorkshire. Ian Blanchett had a splendid match for Norfolk against Cambridgeshire, making 130 not out and taking five for 61.

In all, 34 first-class and minor counties sent nearly 400 youngsters to the two festivals, staged over one week in Oxford and Cambridge and supported by the TCCB, NCA and Lord's Taverners. They enjoyed better weather than usual, and firm pitches, thanks in part to improved covering. The only serious disruption was at Cambridge on Thursday, when the area semi-finals – Cheshire v Sussex and Surrey v Yorkshire – were rained off after four and six overs respectively. This meant that the area finalists had to be selected on bonus points; Cheshire crept through one point ahead of Surrey, with both unbeaten.

Surrey won the Hilda Overy Championship, which encompassed the festival as well as other matches played during the summer. They won all seven of the games they played for a points average of 22.85. Durham's final defeat by Yorkshire cost them this title, too; they won their other eight matches with maximum bonus points, and finished just behind Surrey on 22.00. The 1995 Championship will incorporate a series of two-day fixtures to be played by eight of the first-class counties; Essex, Hampshire, Middlesex and Surrey are pulling out of the festivals to concentrate on the two-day games.

AREA FINALS

At Clare College, Cambridge, August 12. Yorkshire won by ten wickets. Toss: Cheshire. Cheshire 120 (34.1 overs) (D. M. Lane three for 15, J. D. Middlebrook four for 31); Yorkshire 123 for no wkt (32.3 overs) (L. D. Baxter 67 not out, J. Randerson 52 not out).

At Jesus College, Oxford, August 12. Durham won by eight wickets. Toss: Worcestershire. Worcestershire 111 (35.3 overs) (J. Ralph 36; N. Killeen five for 38); Durham 114 for two (37.3 overs) (N. J. Trainor 48, S. K. Meek 32 not out).

FINAL

DURHAM v YORKSHIRE

At Fenner's, Cambridge, August 14. Yorkshire won by two runs. Toss: Yorkshire.

The best finish in an Under-19 final for some years saw Durham needing four to win from the final ball. But they managed only a single. It had been a fine fight-back by Durham, who were subdued until tea, when they wanted 169 from the remaining 32 overs. The gathering cloud cover seemed to tilt the balance even further towards Yorkshire's bowlers. But Nick Trainor, with 75, captain Quentin Hughes and the lower order batted aggressively, forcing the fielders out towards the boundaries, and almost pulled off victory. Yorkshire had scored 239 in their 60 overs, and had looked likely to make more. It was a warm and sunny day, and Ian Cheesewright ran up 102, with some stylish and firmly-struck shots on the on-side, supported by John Randerson and Paul Winrow. But Durham's seam attack tightened its grip in the last ten overs; Neil Killeen returned four for 48, beginning a fine all-round performance.

Yorkshire

L. D. Baxter b Killeen	0	J. D. Middlebrook not out	8
*J. Randerson c Hawthorne b Jones	23	†M. W. Garside not out	4
I. Cheesewright run out	102		
D. Ellis b Hubber	17	B 3, l-b 10, w 9, n-b 1	23
C. D. J. Bailey b Hubber	6		
P. R. Winrow c Williamson b Killeen	36	1/0 2/73 3/137 (8 wkts, 60 overs)	239
R. L. Burton b Killeen	9	4/151 5/191 6/213	
D. M. Lane c McDonald b Killeen	11	7/213 8/224	

D. J. Stephenson did not bat.

Bowling: Killeen 12–2–48–4; Campbell 10–2–39–0; Jones 6–0–29–1; Williamson 6–0–20–0; Hubber 13–3–43–2; Hughes 13–0–47–0.

Durham

N. J. Trainor run out	75	A. McDonald b Winrow	4
R. A. Hawthorne b Lane	1	H. Hubber not out	5
†W. Ritzema lbw b Lane	1	C. L. Campbell not out	5
S. K. Meek c Baxter b Middlebrook	21	B 5, l-b 5, w 17, n-b 1	28
D. Williamson b Middlebrook	9		
*Q. J. Hughes c and b Winrow	36	1/10 2/26 3/71 (9 wkts, 60 overs)	237
I. Jones b Stephenson	21	4/89 5/135 6/166	
N. Killeen run out	31	7/213 8/225 9/228	

Bowling: Lane 10–3–38–2; Stephenson 10–2–49–1; Burton 7–1–14–0; Middlebrook 15–2–64–2; Baxter 10–2–22–0; Winrow 8–0–40–2.

Umpires: T. E. Jesty and R. Palmer.

PAST WINNERS

1986	Lancashire	1989	Warwickshire	1992	Yorkshire
1987	Yorkshire	1990	Essex	1993	Lancashire
1988	Warwickshire	1991	Middlesex	1994	Yorkshire

SCHOOLS CRICKET IN 1994

Schools cricket in the British Isles, especially in the south of England, suffered from a series of wet Saturdays in April and May, with match after match abandoned, and exams in June made their usual demands on players. The long, dry spell which will be entrenched in the memory of cricket-lovers began as the summer term was ending, so that the festivals, at least, enjoyed the panorama of blue skies and white marquees. It follows that school sides found it difficult to become established in the few weeks available to them. Because of examinations and the early departure of school-leavers, younger players, often only 14, who came into the first eleven in mid-term, made more appearances than their seniors had done. So many schools now report having a young eleven that it has ceased to be a novelty. These young cricketers do not lack enthusiasm, but while their obvious enjoyment is pervasive and infectious, standards are inevitably lowered.

To a varying degree, the schools whose records appear in the following pages all offer sound coaching to their players. There are staff with NCA coaching qualifications and experience in playing at county, university or club level, and in many cases the services of a professional gilds the lily. Their teams play on favourable wickets on which 450 runs in a match are not uncommon, half-centuries abound, and the top three or four batsmen will win plaudits for their technique. Bowlers, however, can find difficulty in dismissing sides. Those of genuine pace are rare, though there are plenty of medium-paced seamers displaying the virtues of line and length. There is a high proportion of spinners, often drawn from younger players not afraid to attack and give the ball a high trajectory. They are the beneficiaries of conventional cricket, rather than the scapegoats of the limited-overs game. As long as schools are ready to make equitable declarations, the conventional game must be the flagship of first eleven cricket at school level, and the experience of the 1994 season suggests most schools interpret their role sensibly. There remain a few who retain a negative attitude, determined not to lose whatever the price: names are known on the circuit.

Boys who wish to play in July and August can find a great deal of cricket is available through clubs and the county associations. Most prestigious in the Schools' seasonal calendar is the annual MCC Oxford and Lord's Festival, where among those watching in 1994 were Micky Stewart, the NCA Director of Coaching and Excellence, and Graham Saville, the England Under-19 manager. The Festival, unlike its three immediate predecessors, was played in mostly glorious weather and in a heat wave, although the first day was interrupted by rain. At the end of seven days' cricket, those who had survived to the end, and passed through the various stages of selection, had endured – and, one hopes, enjoyed – a marathon exercise.

Of the boys chosen by the Headmasters' Conference (HMC) and English Schools Cricket Association (ESCA) selectors, there was a large number of able batsmen. Among those who got no further than the Oxford "prelims" were David Lawrence (Cheltenham), Christopher Walsh (Tonbridge) and Michael Sutliff (Wyggeston & Queen Elizabeth I SFC). Spinners included Gareth Batty (Bingley GS), while Christopher McDonald (De La Salle,

Lancashire) kept wicket well. The three bowlers of any pace at Oxford all appeared at Lord's.

After a particularly entertaining final trial at Christ Church ground, Oxford, the HMC and ESCA selectors invited a squad to play in at least one match at Lord's. To their ranks were added three others from the Oxford Festival, selected independently by the National Association of Young Cricketers (NAYC) for their match against the MCC Schools. The possible overlap in selection can be a source of confusion, not to say occasional irritation to the organisers. What is more important is that the following 16 boys from those at Oxford played cricket at the game's headquarters: Richard Baggs, Andrew Bairstow, Dean Cosker, Michael Davies, Orlando Le Fleming, Ian Gompertz, Barry Hyam, Neil Killeen, Patrick McKeown, Lee Marland, Robin Martin-Jenkins, Paul Mitchell, Wayne Ritzema, Anurag Singh, Alec Swann and James Taylor. Their schools may be found in the scorecards that follow. – Gerald Howat.

HMC SOUTHERN SCHOOLS v HMC NORTHERN SCHOOLS

At Wadham College, Oxford, July 8, 9. HMC Southern Schools won by one wicket.

Southern Schools snatched an unlikely victory with one ball to spare after Northern Schools had mostly dominated. The shortened first day featured vigorous innings from Bairstow and McKeown, followed by a sound knock from Lawrence, and on the second day, Ritzema's neatly made century enabled Marland to set a target of 241. Southern Schools were 129 for six when the last 20 overs began and 161 for six ten overs later, but then Ford launched an assault on the bowling, going swiftly from 50 to 93 before being well caught by Bairstow, and Goodwin settled matters by hitting Le Fleming for 12 off the first five balls of the final over. Southern Schools bowled steadily but without much penetration, while the pick of Northern Schools' bowlers were Martin-Jenkins and Davies. The fielding was excellent throughout.

HMC Northern Schools

First innings		Second innings	
*L. J. Marland (*Manchester GS*) c Durant b Diment	11	(3) c Walsh b Bates	10
A. D. Bairstow (*Woodhouse Grove*) c Bates b Goodwin	66		
C. Clark (*Durham*) c and b Goodwin	33	(6) not out	4
P. C. McKeown (*Rossall*) not out	78		
J. M. Edington (*Sedbergh*) c Ford b Diment	14	c Ford b Diment	9
R. S. C. Martin-Jenkins (*Radley*) not out	16	(4) c Gompertz b Bates	10
†W. Ritzema (*Durham*) (did not bat)		(1) run out	103
J. R. Carpenter (*Birkenhead*) (did not bat)		(2) c Singh b Gompertz	33
A. O. F. Le Fleming (*Exeter*) (did not bat)		(7) c and b Bates	6
Extras	4	Extras	12
1/16 2/89 3/140 4/175 (4 wkts dec.)	222	1/71 2/86 3/110 4/176 5/177 6/187 (6 wkts dec.)	187

M. K. Davies (*Loughborough GS*) and A. B. Birley (*Birkenhead*) did not bat.

Bowling: *First Innings*—Diment 16–3–56–2; Gompertz 14–1–68–0; Goodwin 12–3–52–2; Bates 8–0–44–0. *Second Innings*—Diment 12–2–25–1; Gompertz 11–2–46–1; Dyer 5–1–18–0; Bates 22–10–55–3; Goodwin 11–4–32–0.

HMC Southern Schools

Batsman	First innings		Second innings	
C. D. Walsh (*Tonbridge*)	c Clark b Birley	9	c Martin-Jenkins b Le Fleming	0
D. E. A. Lawrence (*Cheltenham*)	run out	77	(8) c and b Davies	16
*P. M. Mitchell (*Millfield*)	run out	16	(2) b Birley	0
A. Singh (*King Edward's, Birmingham*)	c Ritzema b Davies	21	b Davies	63
J. A. Ford (*Tonbridge*)	c Ritzema b Davies	12	c Bairstow b Martin-Jenkins	93
I. Gompertz (*Blundell's*)	b Davies	14	c Edington b Carpenter	7
J. J. Bates (*Hurstpierpoint*)	c Marland b Martin-Jenkins	8	c Bairstow b Le Fleming	8
D. O. Dyer (*Trinity*)	run out	1	(3) c Clark b Davies	21
†C. D. Durant (*Oakham*)	st Ritzema b Birley	3	(10) not out	0
S. H. Diment (*King's, Taunton*)	not out	0	(9) run out	16
G. Goodwin (*Felsted*)	b Martin-Jenkins	0	not out	12
	Extras	8	Extras	9
1/9 2/37 3/72 4/94 5/114 6/146 7/149 8/165 9/166		169	1/0 2/0 3/52 4/101 5/108 6/118 7/164 8/233 9/233	(9 wkts) 245

Bowling: *First Innings*—Le Fleming 12–2–40–0; Birley 9–3–28–2; Carpenter 9–0–37–0; Martin-Jenkins 9–0–41–2; Davies 10–2–19–3. *Second Innings*—Le Fleming 12.5–2–83–2; Birley 8–1–26–1; Davies 24–7–76–3; Martin-Jenkins 11–2–32–1; Carpenter 8–3–22–1.

ESCA NORTH v ESCA SOUTH

At St Edward's School, Oxford, July 8, 9. Drawn.

Their superior bowling gave the North the upper hand for most of the match. Their first three batsmen, Trainor, Sutliff and Swann, performed well in both innings, with only Cosker bowling accurately enough to keep them in check. However, when the South batted, Killeen twice caused early damage and his pace was a constant threat. Taylor and Hyam batted sensibly in the first innings and Baggs was commanding in the second to give the South a hint of victory, but there was not enough support. Both sides were sharp in the field, with the wicket-keeping of Hyam particularly good.

ESCA North

Batsman	First innings		Second innings	
*N. J. Trainor (*St Edward Campion; Durham*)	c Hudson b Cosker	43	(7) c Dickinson b Cosker	35
M. D. R. Sutliff (*Wyggeston & QE I SFC; Leics.*)	retired	57	(6) retired	59
A. J. Swann (*Sponne; Northants*)	st Taylor b Byrne	26	(1) retired	61
M. Roberts (*Hymers; Humberside*)	c Taylor b Byrne	2	c Baggs b Pattison	2
T. W. Roberts (*Bishop Stopford; Northants*)	not out	10	(3) c Taylor b Pattison	14
B. Leigh (*Thomas Rotherham; Yorks.*)	not out	6	(2) c Cosker b Whalley	19
G. Thorpe (*N. Warwicks. CAT; Warwicks.*)	(did not bat)	–	(5) c Dickinson b Cosker	21
†C. J. McDonald (*De La Salle; Lancs.*)	(did not bat)	–	c and b Cosker	1
I. A. Radford (*Dartford HS; Warwicks.*)	(did not bat)	–	c Hyam b Pattison	10
G. J. Batty (*Bingley GS; Yorks.*)	(did not bat)	–	not out	3
N. Killeen (*Derwentside; Durham*)	(did not bat)	–	b Cosker	3
	Extras	17	Extras	12
1/83 2/135 3/144 4/147		(4 wkts dec.) 161	1/54 2/94 3/99 4/104 5/144 6/200 7/227 8/240	(8 wkts dec.) 240

Bowling: *First Innings*—Dickinson 7–0–32–0; Whalley 6–2–14–0; Pattison 12–4–42–0; Hudson 4–1–17–0; Cosker 14–9–27–1; Byrne 7–0–16–2. *Second Innings*—Dickinson 5–0–30–0; List 6–1–12–0; Whalley 8–1–20–1; Cosker 25–10–61–4; Bainbridge 5–2–27–0; Pattison 11–3–39–3; Byrne 7–2–25–0; Hudson 5–0–16–0.

ESCA South

P. C. Bainbridge (*Richmond; Surrey*) b Killeen	0	– b Killeen	4
†J. L. Taylor (*Itchen; Hants*) run out	45	– (6) st McDonald b Thorpe	18
L. R. J. List (*Abingdon; Oxon.*) c Trainor b Killeen	4	– c and b Batty	23
*R. J. Baggs (*Clyst Vale; Devon*) c McDonald b Killeen	19	– c Sutliff b Trainor	93
S. P. Byrne (*London Oratory; London*) c M. Roberts b Radford	13	– c Swann b Trainor	13
†B. J. Hyam (*Havering SFC; Essex*) b Batty	37	– (8) not out	7
P. G. Hudson (*Collyers; Sussex*) st McDonald b Trainor	22	– (2) lbw b Radford	6
L. J. Pattison (*Salesian C.; Hants*) not out	22	– (9) b Radford	1
D. A. Cosker (*Millfield; Somerset*) lbw b T. W. Roberts	0	– (10) not out	2
G. Whalley (*Pate's GS; Glos.*) c Swann b T. W. Roberts	0		
P. M. Dickinson (*Farnham; Surrey*) not out	1	– (7) c Killeen b Trainor	7
Extras	19	Extras	12
1/0 2/4 3/33 4/53 5/121 6/138 7/175 8/176 9/176 (9 wkts dec.)	182	1/10 2/11 3/62 4/94 5/137 6/170 7/176 8/178 (8 wkts)	186

Bowling: *First Innings*—Killeen 7–1–25–3; Radford 8–2–26–1; Thorpe 8–2–24–0; Batty 9–1–36–1; M. Roberts 6–0–28–0; Trainor 7–2–20–1; T. W. Roberts 4–0–10–2. *Second Innings*—Killeen 12–4–23–1; Radford 7–3–13–2; Thorpe 18–2–74–1; Batty 10–1–36–1; Trainor 12–2–32–3.

At St Edward's School, Oxford, July 10. L. J. Marland's XI won by 111 runs. L. J. Marland's XI 276 for four dec. (L. J. Marland 67 retired, P. C. Bainbridge 59 retired, P. C. McKeown 54 retired); N. J. Trainor's XI 165 (J. M. Edington 72; N. Killeen five for 27, G. Goodwin three for 41).

At St John's College, Oxford, July 10. Drawn. A. D. Bairstow's XI 234 for four dec. (C. D. Walsh 58 retired, R. J. Baggs 58 retired); P. M. Mitchell's XI 205 for seven (P. M. Mitchell 56 retired, J. L. Taylor 46, A. Singh 43).

At Christ Church, Oxford, July 11. MCC Schools West won by seven wickets in a 12-a-side match. MCC Schools East 219 for nine dec. (M. D. R. Sutliff 48, P. M. Mitchell 73, Extras 40; D. A. Cosker five for 52); MCC Schools West 223 for four (A. J. Swann 47, R. J. Baggs 75 not out, J. L. Taylor 52 not out).

MCC v MCC SCHOOLS

At Lord's, July 12. Drawn. Toss: MCC Schools.

MCC, led by the former Lancashire spinner, Jack Simmons, put on 123 for the first wicket, with Stewart, an Eastbourne College housemaster, making a half-century on his debut at Lord's. Lynch, a New Zealand Under-19 player, tested the covers with some powerful driving and, once past his century, took 20 off an over. In very hot conditions, the Schools' bowlers stuck manfully to their task, until a declaration after 54 overs set an interesting challenge. The Schools made a sound start through a second-wicket partnership of 112 between Mitchell and Swann, with Singh sustaining the momentum. However, with 125 needed in the last hour, the experienced spinners, Simmons and Potter, took control. Despite an effective 43 by Martin-Jenkins and a final flurry by Le Fleming, the Schools ended five runs short with the last pair together.

MCC

S. M. Lynch st Hyam b Cosker 128
D. A. Stewart c sub b Cosker......... 59
L. Potter c Hyam b Swann........... 27
P. J. Mir not out.................... 39
S. M. Clements not out.............. 11
B 4, l-b 11, w 3............. 18

1/123 2/186 3/266 (3 wkts dec.) 282

†S. J. Young, P. A. Veness, S. P. Hughes, *J. Simmons, K. Staple and M. G. Boocock did not bat.

Bowling: Killeen 8–1–21–0; Le Fleming 9–1–38–0; Martin-Jenkins 10–1–36–0; Cosker 22–0–122–2; Swann 5–1–50–1.

MCC Schools

*A. D. Bairstow c Potter b Staple 6
A. J. Swann c sub b Potter........... 70
P. M. Mitchell run out 61
A. Singh st Young b Potter........... 26
R. J. Baggs lbw b Potter............. 5
R. S. C. Martin-Jenkins lbw b Simmons 43
†B. J. Hyam c Veness b Simmons 21
A. O. F. Le Fleming not out.......... 23
M. K. Davies b Simmons 0
N. Killeen st Young b Simmons....... 0
D. A. Cosker not out................ 3
B 6, l-b 14................. 20

1/10 2/122 3/157 4/163 5/194 6/234 7/249 8/249 9/271 (9 wkts) 278

Bowling: Staple 6–0–16–1; Hughes 7–0–26–0; Boocock 12–2–55–0; Simmons 8–0–38–4; Veness 8–0–32–0; Mir 7–1–17–0; Potter 13–2–74–3.

Umpires: K. Bray and G. A. Plow.

MCC SCHOOLS v NATIONAL ASSOCIATION OF YOUNG CRICKETERS

At Lord's, July 13. NAYC won by four wickets. Toss: MCC Schools.

Heavy thunderstorms, following a long spell of sultry heat which had hardened the ground, delayed the start until the afternoon, when a 35-overs match was played. On a lively wicket the NAYC opening bowlers, Harvey and Burroughs, were too sharp for MCC Schools, who were in some trouble at 26 for three. However, the 1994 MCC Oxford Festival was noticeable for its array of batsmen, and the left-handed Baggs played attackingly while Singh confirmed that he is one of the most promising schoolboys in the country, leaning into the ball with a textbook cover drive. His running between the wickets with McKeown was an education. When NAYC replied, James Taylor of Hampshire batted with vigour and, for the second evening running, Le Fleming, who has won selection for Devon as a medium-fast bowler, featured in a late chase, spoiling Swann's analysis as his 38 took NAYC to victory with three balls to spare.

MCC Schools

A. J. Swann c Treagus b Burroughs.... 9
*A. D. Bairstow c Gompertz b Harvey . 0
P. M. Mitchell c Le Fleming b Harvey . 2
A. Singh c Le Fleming b Harvey...... 82
R. J. Baggs run out 21
P. C. McKeown c Gompertz b Harvey . 36
R. S. C. Martin-Jenkins not out....... 16
†W. Ritzema not out................ 2
L-b 3, w 4................. 7

1/0 2/13 3/26 4/76 5/153 6/164 (6 wkts, 35 overs) 175

M. K. Davies, D. A. Cosker and N. Killeen did not bat.

Bowling: Harvey 8–0–42–4; Burroughs 8–1–34–1; Gompertz 7–0–46–0; Le Fleming 5–1–18–0; Lacey 7–0–32–0.

National Association of Young Cricketers

P. G. Hudson b Swann	28
G. R. Treagus c Ritzema b Swann	19
L. J. Marland run out	6
D. Taylor lbw b Swann	21
J. L. Taylor b Swann	23
A. O. F. Le Fleming c Swann b Davies	38
*S. J. Lacey not out	19
I. Gompertz not out	8
B 4, l-b 9, w 1	14
1/45 2/56 3/72 4/98 5/112 6/154 (6 wkts, 34.3 overs)	176

I. Harvey, R. Burroughs and †B. J. Hyam did not bat.

Bowling: Killeen 7.3–0–41–0; Martin-Jenkins 6–1–12–0; Cosker 1–0–6–0; Swann 9–0–61–4; Davies 11–0–43–1.

Umpires: T. H. Duckett and R. Johnson.

The National Cricket Association selected the following to play for NCA Young Cricketers against Combined Services: *A. D. Bairstow (Yorks.), G. R. Treagus (Hants), A. J. Swann (Northants), A. Singh (Warwickshire), R. J. Baggs (Devon), I. Gompertz (Devon), †B. J. Hyam (Essex), R. S. C. Martin-Jenkins (Sussex), R. Dibden (Hants), A. O. F. Le Fleming (Devon) and I. Harvey (Essex).

At Lord's, July 14. Drawn. Toss: Combined Services. NCA Young Cricketers 263 for two dec. (G. R. Treagus 70, A. J. Swann 80 not out, A. Singh 46 not out); Combined Services 204 for six (Lt C. St George 66 not out, Flt Lt A. W. J. Spiller 40; I. Gompertz three for 49).

At Pontarddulais, July 18, 19, 20. Drawn. Irish Schools 302 for three dec. (M. Jones 55, P. Arnold 81, K. McCallan 81 not out, A. Patterson 34, R. O'Reilly 30 not out) and 174 for eight dec. (G. Molins 48); Welsh Schools 207 (P. A. J. Richards 44, Adrian J. Harries 50, B. Worrad 53; D. McCann three for 34) and 114 for four (A. Evans 65 not out).

At Wolverhampton CC, July 21, 22. Drawn. Irish Schools 176 for seven dec. (P. Arnold 51; D. A. Cosker three for 58) and 240 for seven dec. (K. McCallan 62, R. O'Reilly 70; R. S. C. Martin-Jenkins three for 47); English Schools 219 for five dec. (A. J. Swann 49) and 110 for five (A. Singh 58; Butler three for 55).

At Broughty Ferry, July 26, 27. Welsh Schools won by 53 runs. Welsh Schools 349 for three dec. (D. Teague 33, A. Evans 130, Andrew Harries 109 not out, P. A. J. Richards 39 not out) and 223 for eight dec. (D. Teague 53, A. Evans 68; K. Stott three for 61); Scotland Young Cricketers 204 (D. Lockhart 58, A. Burgess 34, J. Kerr 38; A. P. Davies six for 70, Andrew Harries three for 52) and 315 (D. Lockhart 106, D. Parsons 56, A. Burgess 77; A. P. Davies three for 85, Andrew Harries six for 100).

At Neath, August 1, 2. Drawn. English Schools 222 (A. D. Bairstow 53, B. J. Hyam 54; A. P. Davies four for 63) and 39 for no wkt; Welsh Schools 148 for seven dec.

At Moseley CC, August 4, 5. English Schools won by nine wickets. Scotland Young Cricketers 99 (A. O. F. Le Fleming five for 49, R. S. C. Martin-Jenkins four for 39) and 181 (D. Parsons 58; A. O. F. Le Fleming three for 27, G. Thorpe three for 62); English Schools 146 for seven dec. (P. C. McKeown 67) and 137 for one (A. J. Swann 55 not out).

ETON v HARROW

At Lord's, June 28. Drawn. Toss: Eton.

An uninspiring game suddenly came alive in the closing stages. Chasing 236 in what became 46 overs, Eton had lost the previous year's centurion, Machin, for nought and reached only 51 by the 23rd. Then Fulton and Hardy let rip and the next 23 overs yielded 179. With eight left they needed 60 and had nine wickets in hand. But Rayner bowled Hardy and Duberly with consecutive deliveries and, after Roundell had removed Lightfoot, finally dismissed Fulton for 112. He had hit three sixes and 11 fours from 138 balls. Nine runs were required from Roundell's last over; for a wild moment, when two wickets fell off the first two deliveries, any result seemed possible. But both sides had shot their bolt and the game was drawn. Despite asking Harrow to bat, Lightfoot and his spin attack never quite exerted their control of the previous year, though they conceded under two an over before lunch. Growing more aggressive, the left-handed Chittenden brought up the 100 with a six; first he, then Roundell, looked likely to score the third successive century in this fixture. But with both falling short, the honours went to the 16-year-old Fulton.

Harrow

J. P. Litherland run out	11	†R. M. W. Norris not out	7
S. D. G. Engelen c Hardy b Lightfoot	14	W. A. T. Gillions not out	0
M. C. R. Crawford c Jafri b Duberly	1	L-b 3, w 3, n-b 5	11
O. H. Chittenden c Duberly b Steel	96		—
S. F. Roundell b Steel	89	1/26 2/30 3/41 (6 wkts dec.)	235
M. S. Rayner run out	6	4/201 5/226 6/228	

*P. A. J. Montgomery, M. G. Hatcher and R. D. C. R. Pollock-Hill did not bat.

Bowling: Bruce 19–4–68–0; Dunlop 12–3–20–0; Duberly 15–2–45–1; Lightfoot 24–5–62–1; Jafri 4–1–11–0; Fraser 2–0–11–0; Steel 5–1–15–2.

Eton

J. C. S. Hardy b Rayner	75	C. E. Steel c and b Roundell	0
H. V. Machin lbw b Rayner	0	A. F. Jafri not out	2
J. A. G. Fulton b Rayner	112	L-b 4, w 8, n-b 9	21
H. G. Duberly b Rayner	0		—
*C. G. R. Lightfoot b Roundell	5	1/6 2/176 3/176 (7 wkts)	230
T. O. M. Fraser not out	15	4/191 5/226	
†G. W. Deedes run out	0	6/227 7/227	

R. J. Dunlop and R. W. J. Bruce did not bat.

Bowling: Rayner 14–2–47–4; Hatcher 6–0–46–0; Roundell 14–0–82–2; Gillions 5–2–9–0; Pollock-Hill 5–1–18–0; Montgomery 2–0–24–0.

Umpires: P. T. Newman and R. Wood.

Of the 159 matches played between the two schools since 1805, Eton have won 52, Harrow 44 and 63 have been drawn. Matches during the two world wars are excluded from the reckoning. The fixture was reduced from a two-day two-innings-a-side match to one day in 1982. Forty-eight centuries have been scored, the highest being 183 by D. C. Boles of Eton in 1904; M. C. Bird of Harrow is the only batsman to have made two hundreds in a match, in 1907. The highest score since the First World War is 161 not out by M. K. Fosh of Harrow in 1975, Harrow's last victory. Since then Eton have won in 1977, 1985, 1990 and 1991; all other games have been drawn. A full list of centuries since 1918 and results from 1950 can be found in Wisdens *prior to 1994.*

HIGHLIGHTS FROM THE SCHOOLS

The dismal weather at the beginning of the summer caused many games to be cancelled or curtailed, affecting the results of batsmen and bowlers alike. Gordonstoun in Morayshire was an exception, reporting the best May in years. From the schools whose results are recorded here, only three batsmen reached 1,000 runs, the same as in the poor summer of 1991. P. A. Sogbodjor of Christ's College, Finchley, was by far the most prolific with 1,332 at 70.10, followed by W. Ritzema of Durham (1,038 at 57.66) and C. Jones of Victoria College, Jersey (1,019 at 72.78). Sogbodjor had the advantage of playing more innings than anyone else (26), while Ritzema and Jones had 21 and 20 respectively. Of those who passed 500, four batsmen recorded three-figure averages. The highest of these was that of I. Gompertz of Blundell's, whose 875 from 14 innings came at an average of 125.00; the others were O. M. Slipper of St Edward's, Oxford, with 558 runs at 111.60 and R. W. Nowell of Trinity, with 737 at 105.28, who both had ten innings, followed by O. A. Shah of Isleworth & Syon, whose 510 runs at 102.00 came from eight innings. There were 18 scores of 150 or more, but Sogbodjor was alone in going on to a double-century with 206 not out. His five hundreds were also the most, while seven batsmen made four.

If the batting records were less spectacular than in 1993, the bowling suffered even more. No bowler took 60 wickets and only three collected 50, two fewer than in 1991, which provided the worst record for many years. The three were L. J. Botham of Rossall, with 54 at 10.00 off 230 overs, M. G. J. Walker of Barnard Castle, whose 51 off 287.3 overs cost 16.13 apiece, and A. G. Levenger of Solihull, who bowled 228 overs for his 50 at 14.88. Another seven bowlers took 45 wickets or more, all requiring at least 200 overs to do so. Seven boys sent down more than 250 overs, with J. R. Burrans, a spinner from Pocklington (314), alone in bowling 300.

The only bowler to pass 30 wickets with a single-figure average was A. B. Birley of Birkenhead, whose 40 cost just 7.77 apiece. The best innings return was nine for 45 by G. Henderson of St George's, Weybridge, and there were eight instances of eight-wicket returns. Five hat-tricks were reported: from T. J. Allen of Campbell College, B. Lockwood of Clifton College, S. J. Speller of St John's, Leatherhead, N. P. Sproule of St Lawrence College, Ramsgate and J. M. Palmer of Lord Wandsworth College. This last hat-trick was remarkable for being all stumped – by the reserve wicket-keeper, C. J. Walker.

In terms of aggregates, the leading all-rounders were J. W. Hatch of Barnard Castle, with 910 runs at 45.50 and 47 wickets at 15.06, C. G. Taylor of Colston's Collegiate, who had 917 runs at 61.13 and 40 wickets at 15.00, and Botham, who hit 774 runs at 70.36 in addition to his 54 wickets at 10.00. In terms of averages, four boys stood out, doing better than 70 with the bat and 12 with the ball: Nowell (737 runs at 105.28, 29 wickets at 10.65), D. Sales of Caterham (830 runs at 83.00, 34 wickets at 11.23), Botham (as above) and S. C. B. Tomlinson of The Oratory (564 runs at 70.50, 35 wickets at 10.40). The Cricket Society's Wetherall Award went to Nowell, who was honoured for a second time, having shared the 1992 award with D. Spencer of Kingston GS.

Twenty-seven schools won more than half their matches, and of these Isleworth & Syon won 75 per cent, King's College School, Wimbledon won 73 per cent and Tonbridge 71 per cent. Isleworth & Syon and Tonbridge were unbeaten, as were ten other schools. Of these Bryanston and Queen Elizabeth GS, Wakefield, also won more than half their matches, but some had an alarmingly high percentage of draws, the most extreme being St Peter's, York, who drew 17 of their 21 encounters. Harrow, another side with a high preponderance of draws, had the unenviable record of no wins. Again several schools expressed their frustration at the negative attitude of some opposing sides, while many were proud of their positive approach.

The Sir Garfield Sobers International Schools' Cricket Tournament took place in Barbados in July and August, unfortunately clashing with the MCC Oxford and Lord's Festival. Of the four British schools which participated in 1994 – Bradfield, Dr Challoner's GS, The Leys and Merchiston Castle – Dr Challoner's did best in taking 11th place. The tournament has featured some notable players in the eight years it has been held: in 1987 it was Brian Lara, playing for the Fatima College, who made the headlines.

Details of records broken, other outstanding performances and interesting features of the season may be found in the returns from the schools which follow.

THE SCHOOLS

(Qualification: Batting 150 runs; Bowling 15 wickets)

* *On name indicates captain.* * *On figures indicates not out.*

Note: The line for batting reads Innings–Not Outs–Runs–Highest Score–100s–Average; that for bowling reads Overs–Maidens–Runs–Wickets–Best Bowling–Average.

ABINGDON SCHOOL

Played 14: Won 3, Lost 1, Drawn 10. Abandoned 2

Master i/c: A. M. Broadbent

Wins v: Magdalen College S.; A. M. Broadbent's XI; UCS, Hampstead.

Batting—T. C. B. Pollard 14–1–520–121*–2–40.00; L. R. J. List 12–1–364–88–0–33.09; R. J. Finch 11–1–204–53*–0–20.40; J. R. V. Dolleymore 13–2–220–86–0–20.00.

Bowling—*B. M. Fuggles 79.4–25–248–15–4/17–16.53; D. A. Melin 141.2–22–582–22–4/34–26.45.

AMPLEFORTH COLLEGE

Played 16: Won 4, Lost 6, Drawn 6. Abandoned 1

Master i/c: G. D. Thurman Cricket professional: D. Wilson

Wins v: Sedbergh; OACC; Saints; Dulwich C.

Batting—H. R. Lucas 16–3–532–102*–2–40.92; J. J. Hobbs 16–2–518–115*–1–37.00; H. P. Hickman 16–1–373–73*–0–24.86; A. D. Codrington 14–0–275–59–0–19.64; A. A. Richter 14–1–155–66–0–11.92.

Bowling—P. Wilkie 188.4–47–556–30–6/22–18.53; T. E. Pinsent 134–23–452–23–5/19–19.65; D. A. Johnston-Stewart 162.2–23–644–23–4/27–28.00; A. H. Robinson 190.2–26–800–26–6/48–30.76.

ARDINGLY COLLEGE

Played 20: Won 8, Lost 6, Drawn 6

Master i/c: R. A. F. King Cricket professional: S. Sawant

Wins v: Old Ardinians; Brighton; Reigate GS; Worth; Headmaster's XI; St Paul's, Brisbane; XL Club; Cranleigh.

Batting—G. I. Best 20–1–556–83–0–29.26; B. A. Hubbard 18–1–472–88–0–27.76; J. A. Hubbard 18–1–466–83–0–27.41; J. R. Virgo 18–3–385–87*–0–25.66; G. M. Turner 11–2–176–30–0–19.55; J. R. Andrews 14–5–161–25*–0–17.88; A. D. H. Spencer 19–1–302–53–0–16.77.

Bowling—B. A. Hubbard 169.4–58–445–31–6/14–14.35; *A. E. Warren 170.4–29–666–26–6/74–25.61; R. E. J. Watts 116.4–19–424–15–4/17–28.26.

ASHVILLE COLLEGE

Played 18: Won 5, Lost 3, Drawn 10. Abandoned 2

Master i/c: S. Herrington

Wins v: Belfast RA; Bury GS; Silcoates; XL Club; Craven Gents.

Batting—S. Kay 13–3–396–65–0–39.60; J. Haigh-Lumby 17–4–362–67*–0–27.84; J. Cousen 18–0–498–67–0–27.66; R. Rawlings 12–0–253–59–0–21.08.

Bowling—G. Parker 170–41–503–35–5/9–14.37; R. Smart 151–25–560–24–5/29–23.33.

BABLAKE SCHOOL

Played 14: Won 3, Lost 9, Drawn 2. Abandoned 1

Master i/c: B. J. Sutton

Stuart Smyth, who headed the batting averages, represented Warwickshire Under-19.

Wins v: King Edward's, Five Ways; King Edward's, Nuneaton; Bishop Vesey's GS.

Batting—S. N. Smyth 13–2–633–136*–2–57.54; *C. J. Gardiner 14–1–408–125–1–31.38; S. Tearne 14–2–179–38–0–14.91; M. G. Bull 12–0–165–29–0–13.75.

Bowling—R. M. G. Sutton 93.1–10–389–18–5/15–21.61.

BANCROFT'S SCHOOL

Played 23: Won 9, Lost 8, Drawn 6. Abandoned 4

Master i/c: J. G. Bromfield Cricket professional: J. K. Lever

A record of just six draws in 23 matches is testament to the positive approach of Bancroft's under the captaincy of Peter Vohmann, whose batting experience was also crucial. A significant all-round contribution was made by Asif Khan, a slow left-arm bowler and right-handed batsman who headed the bowling and whose 104 against MCC was a highlight. Stuart Greenhill emerged as another strong all-rounder, batting left-handed and bowling right-arm medium. The season was preceded in December by a successful tour to South Africa.

Wins v: St Joseph's; Langa CC; Chigwell; Enfield GS; Aylesbury GS; J. G. Bromfield's XI; Royal Anglian Regiment; XL Club; Old Bancroftians.

Batting—S. M. Greenhill 17–5–476–94*–0–39.66; P. M. Eacott 19–5–419–66–0–29.92; *P. T. Vohmann 20–1–554–82–0–29.15; A. A. Khan 19–1–520–104–1–28.88; J. R. Davey 14–3–201–56*–0–18.27; P. D. Baker 19–0–289–47–0–15.21.

Bowling—A. A. Khan 245.5–40–784–35–7/69–22.40; S. M. Greenhill 129.4–26–399–17–4/23–23.47; E. D. Mann 205.1–27–677–25–4/31–27.08; P. D Baker 141.2–29–452–15–4/33–30.13.

BANGOR GRAMMAR SCHOOL

Played 25: Won 17, Lost 4, Drawn 4. Abandoned 3

Master i/c: C. C. J. Harte

In a side whose positive approach was rewarded by excellent results, Ross Cunningham led from the front with both bat and ball. Mark English and Matthew Scott were a prolific opening pair, whose stand of 206 against Cheadle Hulme was a school record for any wicket.

Wins v: Arnold; Ballyclare HS; Ballymena Acad.; Campbell C.; Cheadle Hulme; Donaghadee CC; Down HS; RS, Dungannon; Foyle and Londonderry C. (twice); Friends, Lisburn (twice); Limavady GS; Lurgan C.; Royal Belfast AI; The Staff; Sullivan US.

Batting—M. T. C. English 23–6–827–118*–2–48.64; M. N. Scott 24–5–694–93–0–36.52; B. J. Cunningham 18–4–410–86–0–29.28; *R. C. Cunningham 23–5–473–54*–0–26.27; A. M. Hopper 16–2–294–84–0–21.00; M. J. Williamson 15–5–170–58–0–17.00; K. M. Miskelly 15–3–176–56–0–14.66.

Bowling—C. M. Kennedy 137–22–476–43–6/19–11.06; R. C. Cunningham 159.5–34–511–40–4/8–12.77; M. J. Williamson 202.4–48–574–39–5/13–14.71; S. J. Larmour 98–22–278–18–3/11–15.44; M. R. Cheevers 106.1–20–351–21–3/13–16.71.

BARNARD CASTLE SCHOOL

Played 22: Won 11, Lost 5, Drawn 6

Master i/c: C. P. Johnson

A young XI developed into an eager and promising side who won half their matches. The captain, Jodie Hatch, set new school records with his aggregate of 910 and his innings of 185 not out against UCS, Hampstead. He also took 47 wickets, while 51 fell to Martin Walker, these two featuring in a formidable attack with Jonathan Benson and Hatch's younger brother, Nicky. Two teams from Australia and one from South Africa were welcomed during the season.

Wins v: A. W. Hutchinson's XI; Silcoates; Woodbridge; Pocklington; Dame Allan's; King Edward VII, Lytham; St Bees; Yarra Valley Anglican S, Victoria; UCS, Hampstead; MCC; Scotch C., Melbourne.

Batting—*J. W. Hatch 22–2–910–185*–2–45.50; J. Benson 20–4–472–74–0–29.50; M. G. J. Walker 21–3–406–51–0–22.55; A. Taylor 17–3–265–46–0–18.92; L. A. J. Haslam 15–4–182–56*–0–16.54; N. G. Hatch 20–2–180–32–0–10.00.

Bowling—J. Benson 133.2–31–367–35–6/24–10.48; J. W. Hatch 278.1–75–708–47–6/83–15.06; M. G. J. Walker 287.3–51–823–51–7/26–16.13; N. G. Hatch 146.5–27–425–26–4/19–16.34.

BEDFORD SCHOOL

Played 16: Won 6, Lost 3, Drawn 7. Abandoned 2

Master i/c: D. W. Jarrett Cricket professional: R. G. Caple

Unbeaten by schools, Bedford won six of their last eight games, three in exciting run-chases at the end-of-term festival. The captain, Toby Bailey, scored the most runs and kept wicket superbly, a fine understanding with the bowlers resulting in a dozen leg-side stumpings. Although Marc Snell had a disappointing season by his standards, he played the side's biggest innings — 151 not out against The Leys. He went on to captain England Under-16, while Bailey played for Bedfordshire and Northamptonshire Second XI.

Wins v: Oundle; Kearsney C., Natal; St Paul's, Brisbane; Stowe; Old Bedfordians; Wellington C.

Batting—B. S. Cheema 16–3–594–123–2–45.69; A. S. L. Cole 15–2–538–114–1–41.38; B. J. Smith 14–7–277–62–0–39.57; *T. M. B. Bailey 17–1–625–121–1–39.06; M. J. Oliver 13–6–224–59*–0–32.00; M. E. Snell 18–2–486–151*–1–30.37; J. G. Doyle 13–1–198–57*–0–16.50.

Bowling—A. C. Snowdon 199–27–764–30–5/74–25.46.

BEDFORD MODERN SCHOOL

Played 20: Won 4, Lost 3, Drawn 13. Abandoned 2

Master i/c: N. J. Chinneck

A highlight was the match against Watford GS, in which I. R. Chadwick (105) and B. J. Young (112 not out) provided the first instance for more than a decade of two centuries in one innings. M. J. Brownridge made a useful all-round contribution and promise for the future came in the appearance of the Under-15 side in the Lord's Taverners semi-finals.

Wins v: Christ's C., Cambridge; St Albans; Old Boys; Berkhamsted.

Batting—B. J. Young 20–4–838–117–2–52.37; I. R. Chadwick 19–1–660–105–1–36.66; *M. J. Brownridge 17–2–487–76–0–32.46; A. G. Brown 19–3–513–101*–1–32.06; S. J. Robinson 14–6–160–29*–0–20.00.

Bowling—S. J. Robinson 89.2–13–341–16–4/15–21.31; M. J. Brownridge 212.3–35–715–26–5/60–27.50; D. C. Rolton 164–24–687–23–4/29–29.86; J. C. P. Woods 191.4–28–743–20–3/62–37.15.

BEECHEN CLIFF SCHOOL

Played 13: Won 2, Lost 2, Drawn 9. Abandoned 2

Master i/c: K. J. L. Mabe Cricket professional: P. J. Colbourne

Ben Staunton, who played for Somerset Second XI, provided highlights with an aggressive 147 not out against King Edward's, Bath, followed later in the season by 102 against MCC. Mark Prentice made a consistent and significant all-round contribution.

Wins v: Queen Elizabeth's Hospital; Rutlish.

Batting—B. R. K. Staunton 9–1–422–147*–2–52.75; S. L. Kembery 10–0–297–70–0–29.70; M. J. Prentice 11–0–304–84–0–27.63.

Bowling—M. J. Prentice 163–42–405–25–7/29–16.20.

BERKHAMSTED SCHOOL

Played 13: Won 5, Lost 5, Drawn 3. Abandoned 3

Master i/c: J. G. Tolchard Cricket professional: M. Herring

N. A. Wolstenholme completed his career in the XI with the best batting record ever compiled for the school: in four years he scored a total of 2,284 runs at 44.78, including seven hundreds.

Wins v: Aldenham; Monmouth; Framlingham; Old Berkhamstedians; Gentlemen of Hertfordshire.

Batting—*N. A. Wolstenholme 13–2–709–140–4–64.45; R. D. Mackintosh 12–1–398–84–0–36.18; E. N. Tolchard 13–2–239–56–0–21.72.

Bowling—E. J. Clarke 102–14–373–15–4/44–24.86; S. M. Dev 153–27–572–17–4/51–33.64.

BETHANY SCHOOL

Played 10: Won 4, Lost 3, Drawn 3. Abandoned 1

Master i/c: P. Norgrove Cricket professional: G. Campbell

Wins v: Oakwood Park GS; Old Boys; Rochester Clergy; PTA XI.

Batting—*A. Owen 9–1–320–60–0–40.00; F. Sadigeen 10–1–338–70–0–37.55.

Bowling—F. Sadigeen 104–6–339–23–6/16–14.73.

BIRKENHEAD SCHOOL

Played 17: Won 7, Lost 0, Drawn 10

Master i/c: P. A. Whittel

Wins v: Ellesmere; Ormskirk GS; St David's; Liverpool C.; King's, Chester; Foyle and Londonderry C.; Old Boys.

Batting—*J. R. Carpenter 12–1–781–142*–3–71.00; E. J. Clarke 11–1–344–75*–0–34.40; Z. R. Feather 9–1–222–57–0–27.75; E. J. N. Roberts 15–0–402–68–0–26.80; S. J. Carpenter 17–2–333–44–0–22.20.

Bowling—B. C. Attwood 60.5–20–136–19–7/26–7.15; A. B. Birley 164.5–58–311–40–8/30–7.77; J. R. Carpenter 150–46–356–22–4/46–16.18; Z. R. Feather 105–33–271–15–2/15–18.06.

BISHOP'S STORTFORD COLLEGE

Played 19: Won 9, Lost 2, Drawn 7, Tied 1. Abandoned 5

Master i/c: D. A. Hopper Cricket professional: C. S. Bannister

In their 125th anniversary year, a young side equalled the record of nine victories for the third successive season; the most satisfying were by ten wickets over Uppingham and Chigwell, the latter being bowled out for 39. Their positive approach brought several exciting close finishes, including a tie with Oakham and a drawn match against Bromsgrove where the scores finished level. Their strength lay in the bowling – headed by Andrew Bruce (fast-medium), who took five in an innings four times, and Mick Bashford (slow left-arm) who twice took seven in an innings – supported by fielding which was often electric. Hard practice in this department was rewarded with 12 run-outs from direct hits. Sam Fishpool's unbeaten 122 was the side's only century and brought success in the run-chase against Framlingham.

Wins v: Uppingham; Aldenham; Framlingham; Bishop's Stortford HS; Chigwell; The Leys; The Perse; Gresham's; Stamford.

Batting—J. J. Mew 14–5–368–62*–0–40.88; J. D. Lamb 17–1–581–79–0–36.31; S. J. C. Fishpool 20–3–598–122*–1–35.17; C. J. Thorogood 17–2–386–69–0–25.73; M. Bashford 12–2–209–83–0–20.90; L. P. Westell 15–3–209–43–0–17.41.

Bowling—A. J. Bruce 211.3–38–619–41–5/22–15.09; M. Bashford 266.5–92–598–39–7/30–15.33; *T. E. Laverack 222.5–60–579–24–5/17–24.12; L. P. Westell 112.1–23–439–18–4/23–24.38.

BLOXHAM SCHOOL

Played 12: Won 4, Lost 0, Drawn 8. Abandoned 4

Master i/c: C. N. Boyns

Wins v: South Oxfordshire Amateurs; Banbury CC; Rendcomb; Old Bloxhamists.

Batting—*A. Leonard 9–6–175–35*–0–58.33; M. B. Palmer 12–3–441–102*–1–49.00; A. R. Hurst 11–1–301–63–0–30.10; M. G. Hicks 10–1–233–91*–0–25.88; I. A. R. Adams 8–1–173–65–0–24.71; R. S. Tarrant 12–0–234–37–0–19.50.

Bowling—I. A. R. Adams 126.3–29–385–30–5/11–12.83.

BLUNDELL'S SCHOOL

Played 15: Won 4, Lost 7, Drawn 4. Abandoned 1

Master i/c: T. H. C. Noon — Cricket professional: R. Harriott

The outstanding player was Ian Gompertz, who completed his fifth season in the XI. His 875 runs included 122 not out against MCC, 115 against Canford, 102 not out against Plymouth College, and 158 not out against Ampleforth. In the Plymouth game he shared in a double-century partnership with James Lewis and completed an excellent game with a return of seven for 68. He played for English Schools and NAYC.

Wins v: Downside; King's, Bruton; Devon Dumplings; Plymouth C.

Batting—*I. Gompertz 14–7–875–158*–4–125.00; G. D. S. Vaughan 11–1–229–78*–0–22.90; E. D. Dorey 14–2–247–53*–0–20.58; P. S. Palmer 11–2–151–73*–0–16.77; J. Lewis 14–1–207–77*–0–15.92.

Bowling—I. Gompertz 159.4–37–531–36–7/68–14.75; T. Blair 148–28–498–20–3/35–24.90; T. Rowson 110.1–12–433–17–3/59–25.47.

BRADFIELD COLLEGE

Played 14: Won 3, Lost 1, Drawn 10

Master i/c: F. R. Dethridge — Cricket professional: J. F. Harvey

Wins v: Wellington C.; Berkshire Under-19; R. Dellor's XI.

Batting—R Perkins 15–2–604–118*–1–46.46; C. Williams 15–0–386–72–0–25.73; H. G. Austen-Brown 13–3–197–54–0–19.70; *T. P. Dellor 14–1–248–59–0–19.07.

Bowling—H. Forbes 91–18–325–16–4/28–20.31; E. J. Kendall 198–35–572–21–5/41–27.23.

BRADFORD GRAMMAR SCHOOL

Played 21: Won 7, Lost 3, Drawn 11. Abandoned 1

Master i/c: A. G. Smith

In a strong batting side, in which six centuries were shared by four batsmen, Matthew Anderson broke his own school record of the previous season with 988 runs. His opening partnership with Simon Davies was one of the team's strengths, with strong support from D. J. Groom, who scored seven fifties. Lack of penetration left the side with 11 draws, while the three defeats followed generous declarations.

Wins v: Silcoates; Halifax Nomads; Parents' XI; Old Boys; William Hulme GS; Craven Gentlemen; MCC.

Batting—D. J. Groom 18–7–739–92–0–67.18; *M. J. Anderson 19–3–988–120–2–61.75; S. E. P. Davies 19–3–875–138*–2–54.68; D. C. Illingworth 14–7–232–100*–1–33.14; A. J. Myers 19–3–444–102*–1–27.75; D. J. Greaves 13–2–190–57–0–17.27.

Bowling—A. J. Myers 168–54–418–19–4/27–22.00; G. S. Kinvig 179–38–581–22–4/31–26.40; R. E. Walker 112–17–540–20–5/21–27.00; J. R. Crabtree 128.1–21–471–15–2/23–31.40; J. R. Cockcroft 165.3–26–714–17–3/47–42.00.

BRENTWOOD SCHOOL

Played 19: Won 8, Lost 4, Drawn 7. Abandoned 2

Master i/c: B. R. Hardie

Wins v: Chigwell; Bancroft's; Sevenoaks; Old Brentwoods (twice); Royal Anglian; Barcelona CC (twice).

Batting—A. K. Amin 11–2–329–101*–1–36.55; *B. Weller 12–1–341–80*–0–31.00; N. D. E. Boyce 8–2–169–71–0–28.16; P. D. A. Jones 13–3–276–103*–1–27.60; B. J. Tappin 10–1–245–86–0–27.22; J. E. P. Crapnell 11–4–166–58*–0–23.71; T. M. Witney 12–1–256–54–0–23.27; O. M. Watkins 14–1–165–37–0–12.69.

Bowling—J. E. P. Crapnell 117.1–19–399–16–4/16–24.93; N. D. E. Boyce 187.4–29–672–25–4/70–26.88; I. T. Belchamber 167–24–630–23–3/15–27.39.

BRIGHTON COLLEGE

Played 15: Won 1, Lost 7, Drawn 7. Abandoned 1

Master i/c: J. Spencer — Cricket professional: J. D. Morley

Edward Hart led the side by example with both bat and ball. The vice-captain, Clare Connor, stood up well to the opening bowlers after being promoted to open, and played for England Women Under-19. A tour of Zimbabwe was planned for October.

Win v: Ipswich.

Batting—*E. S. Hart 16–2–617–118–2–44.07; G. B. F. Hudson 16–0–331–80–0–20.68; Miss C. J. Connor 14–1–183–27–0–14.07; J. B. Holt 16–0–196–39–0–12.25; S. E. Green 16–0–163–52–0–10.18.

Bowling—E. S. Hart 187.5–55–502–27–7/81–18.59; G. B. F. Hudson 154.5–25–500–20–3/27–25.00.

BRISTOL GRAMMAR SCHOOL

Played 17: Won 5, Lost 4, Drawn 8. Abandoned 1

Masters i/c: K. Blackburn and D. Crawford

Against the XL Club, 16-year-old Anthony Richardson scored the XI's first century for two years.

Wins v: Queen Elizabeth's Hospital; Wellington; Old Bristolians; Westminster C., Adelaide; XL Club.

Batting—M. Sutherland 15–1–498–97–0–35.57; A. Richardson 13–3–335–107*–1–33.50; J. Barnes 14–5–285–81*–0–31.66; J. Tyler 10–2–253–89*–0–31.62; *G. Axson 16–1–397–77–0–26.46; T. Button 11–2–225–65–0–25.00; A. Mitchell 11–2–150–43–0–16.66.

Bowling—M. Batchelor 93.1–18–336–20–5/17–16.80; J. J. Goodall 105–20–378–17–4/15–22.23; A. Mitchell 192–37–684–28–6/67–24.42.

BRYANSTON SCHOOL

Played 13: Won 8, Lost 0, Drawn 5. Abandoned 3

Master i/c: T. J. Hill

Pre-season coaching by R. J. Maru bore fruit in an unbeaten season in which eight of 13 matches were won. The side owed much to swing bowler Tom Brunner, a 16-year-old already in his third season, who took five wickets on five occasions. MCC were beaten by two wickets when James Hallett came in to face the last ball and hit it for six, and the season finished with an enjoyable tour of The Netherlands, in which two 50-overs matches on matting were won and two lost.

Wins v: XL Club; Clayesmore; Prior Park; Winchester; MCC; Portsmouth GS; Dorset Rangers; Milton Abbey.

Batting—P. J. Brenchley 11–4–322–101*–1–46.00; *R. J. Wagstaffe 13–1–550–91*–0–45.83; T. C. Z. Lamb 11–0–433–131–1–39.36; R. J. Hannon 11–1–256–110–1–25.60; E. O. G. Hunt 10–2–163–46–0–20.37; J. O. Cooke 12–2–181–38–0–18.10.

Bowling—T. P. W. Brunner 132.5–25–349–34–6/37–10.26; M. W. Davis 86.4–9–383–17–3/24–22.52.

CAMPBELL COLLEGE

Played 20: Won 4, Lost 5, Drawn 11

Master i/c: E. T. Cooke

R. H. Lucas took his career record to 1,675 runs at 28.38 and 113 wickets at 12.55 in his four years in the XI.

Wins v: Larne GS; BRA Second XI; Foyle C.; Down HS.

Batting—*R. H. Lucas 18–4–612–74*–0–43.71; S. R. J. Flanagan 12–1–212–76–0–19.27; J. H. S. Montgomery 18–3–289–59–0–19.26; R. K. Long 13–3–192–29–0–19.20; S. D. Hughes 18–2–301–51*–0–18.81.

Bowling—S. D. Hughes 118–23–325–23–5/28–14.13; R. K. Long 111–24–357–25–5/59–14.28; N. J. Boomer 90–17–289–15–2/6–19.26; S. R. J. Flanagan 137–31–315–16–4/25–19.68; T. J. Allen 111–11–435–20–5/1–21.75.

CANFORD SCHOOL

Played 12: Won 5, Lost 2, Drawn 5. Abandoned 4

Master i/c: S. J. Turrill Cricket professional: J. J. E. Hardy

In his fifth season in the XI, Graham Herring led by example as some strong sides were beaten, including Sherborne for the first time in eight years.

Wins v: Downside; King Edward VI, Southampton; Sherborne; Taunton; Cygnets.

Batting—*G. P. A. Herring 13–3–481–80–0–48.10; S. J. Neal 10–2–338–112*–1–42.25; T. W. Cutler 10–0–334–108–1–33.40; N. J. Makin 11–0–326–67–0–29.63; A. C. Major 11–3–184–61–0–23.00.

Bowling—T. W. Cutler 177.1–37–512–25–6/38–20.48; A. C. Major 204.3–33–754–23–4/82–32.78.

CATERHAM SCHOOL

Played 14: Won 9, Lost 1, Drawn 4

Master i/c: A. G. Tapp Cricket professional: W. Raja

The outstanding all-rounder was 16-year-old David Sales, an attacking batsman and medium-pace bowler. He played for England Under-18 and the Development of Excellence XI, made his first-team debut for Northamptonshire at the end of the season, and was selected for the England Under-19 tour to the West Indies.

Wins v: Kingston GS; Tiffin; St Dunstan's; Surrey YC; Whitgift; Eldoraigne, South Africa; Old Boys; Elizabeth C.; Yarra Valley GS, Australia.

Batting—D. J. Sales 14–4–830–159–2–83.00; A. Patel 12–2–304–63–0–30.40; S. Haydock 12–0–305–98–0–25.41; J. Winter 14–2–228–78*–0–19.00.

Bowling—D. J. Sales 134.1–35–382–34–5/12–11.23; W. McKeran 163.2–44–487–32–6/17–15.21; K. Barton 146–62–414–23–5/37–18.00.

CHELTENHAM COLLEGE

Played 16: Won 5, Lost 2, Drawn 9. Abandoned 3

Master i/c: M. W. Stovold Cricket professional: M. D. Briers

Five wins, including the final of the Chesterton Cup over King's, Worcester, was a respectable tally for an inexperienced side. The captain, David Lawrence, was the leading batsman, while B. R. Passenger bowled fast but without luck.

Wins v: Dean Close; Rendcomb; Hereford Cathedral S.; Malvern; King's, Worcester.

Batting—*D. E. A. Lawrence 15–1–638–105–2–45.57; W. B. Hale 16–4–409–110*–1–34.08; W. F. A. Chambers 10–3–227–57*–0–32.42; T. D. Beim 13–2–287–78–0–26.09; T. E. Lacey 12–2–231–51*–0–23.10; T. R. O. Jones 16–0–335–65–0–20.93; M. S. Inglis 13–3–169–39*–0–16.90.

Bowling—W. F. A. Chambers 72–13–229–17–5/35–13.47; D. E. A. Lawrence 111–21–360–17–4/21–21.17; B. R. Passenger 179–28–549–19–5/19–28.89.

CHIGWELL SCHOOL

Played 15: Won 1, Lost 9, Drawn 5

Master i/c: D. N. Morrison

Win v: St Edmund's, Ware.

Batting—M. Ali 13–2–371–73–0–33.72; K. Choudhary 10–3–231–58–0–33.00; T. Jolly 15–0–338–97–0–22.53.

Bowling—G. Plowright 102.1–18–479–20–4/22–23.95.

CHRIST COLLEGE, BRECON

Played 12: Won 4, Lost 2, Drawn 6. Abandoned 4

Master i/c: C. W. Kleiser Cricket professional: S. Barwick

A considerable impact was made by the school's first cricket scholar, Andrew Davies, who also played for Welsh Schools and Glamorgan Second XI. A left-hander whose considerable ability allowed others to blossom and gain in confidence, he bowled superbly to dismiss both Llandovery and Wellington and scored 169 not out as Malvern A were beaten by more than 200 runs. Richard Thomas at last fulfilled his potential and Tom Harbottle proved a useful grafting opening bat.

Wins v: St David's UC, Lampeter; Malvern A XI; Llandovery; Wellington S.

Batting—A. P. Davies 12–3–612–169*–2–68.00; R. T. Thomas 10–2–333–82*–0–41.62; T. Harbottle 8–0–235–47–0–29.37.

Bowling—A. P. Davies 144.5–44–284–28–7/26–10.14; *D. Bartlett 95.5–21–281–15–6/24–18.73.

CHRIST'S COLLEGE, FINCHLEY

Played 28: Won 15, Lost 10, Drawn 3

Master i/c: S. S. Goldsmith

In a side which achieved a record number of wins for this century, the captain, Peter Sogbodjor, was outstanding. He scored 1,332 runs in exhilarating fashion, beating his own record of 1,102 set the previous season. His five centuries included a school record 206 not out against Brondesbury CC, as well as 139 against Mill Hill, 121 not out against St Ignatius College, 104 not out against Enfield GS and 102 not out against Barclays Bank. In his 97 appearances for the first XI, which beat by one the previous best achieved by F. C. Cousins (1880-83), he totalled 3,688 runs and nine centuries, beating the previous records of 1,977 and four respectively. He was also a fine fielder, breaking the 100-year-old record with his career tally of 41 catches and, having taken over as wicket-keeper in 1993, set a new standard with 57 dismissals in all, including 13 stumpings in a season in 1993.

Wins v: S. S. Goldsmith's XI; St Ignatius (twice); Enfield GS; Mill Hill S.; Brondesbury CC; Woodhouse SFC; Barclays Bank (London); Gentlemen of Hertfordshire; East Barnet S.; Weavers; Old Hendonians; Staff XI; Middlesex Teachers XI; Gentlemen of Finchley.

Batting—*P. A. Sogbodjor 26–7–1,332–206*–5–70.10; G. J. Morjaria 22–8–597–83*–0–42.64; E. J. R. Gallagher 17–4–497–110*–2–38.23; M. H. Cable 23–3–242–48*–0–12.10; N. Symonds 21–0–206–46–0–9.80; R. R. Persad 21–1–160–24–0–8.00.

Bowling—T. Patel 84–20–310–18–4/25–17.22; G. J. Morjaria 173.3–39–546–31–5/12–17.61; N. Symonds 148.3–15–651–32–6/30–20.34; M. H. Cable 127.3–15–574–22–6/22–26.09.

CHRIST'S HOSPITAL

Played 14: Won 4, Lost 8, Drawn 2. Abandoned 4

Master i/c: H. Holdsworth Cricket professionals: K. G. Suttle and P. J. Graves

It was not until they encountered the hard wickets during the end-of-term cricket week that the side began to fulfil their potential.

Wins v: Worth; Pioneers CC; Brighton; St Edmund's, Ware.

Batting—A. M. Buset 12–1–363–98–0–33.00; *J. A. Cordner 13–2–329–61–0–29.90; T. A. Smith 12–2–189–62–0–18.90; N. J. Codd 14–0–207–41–0–14.78; J. R. J. Edwards 13–0–179–55–0–13.76.

Bowling—A. H. Meredith-Jones 110–13–427–22–5/12–19.40; B. E. Bickley 169–40–525–26–5/75–20.19; J. M. Sheppy 125.5–21–447–21–4/40–21.28; J. P. Cheesmur 100–26–365–17–4/77–21.47; J. A. Cordner 148–21–500–18–4/21–27.77.

CLAYESMORE SCHOOL

Played 12: Won 7, Lost 2, Drawn 3

Masters i/c: R. J. Hammond and R. J. Denning

M. Swarbrick's 133 not out against Abbotsholme was a record for the school. The most successful bowler was 14-year-old T. C. Hicks, son of the former Cambridge University hockey captain who coached the XI.

Wins v: Allhallows; Dorset Rangers; Canford II; Poole GS; Embley Park; XL Club; Bearwood.

Batting—*M. Swarbrick 12–4–655–133*–2–81.87; A. M. Philp 9–2–236–82*–0–33.71; R. Gulliver 12–0–372–78–0–31.00; T. C. Hicks 12–2–256–65–0–25.60.

Bowling—A. M. Philp 108–25–249–26–7/26–9.57; T. C. Hicks 144–27–420–32–6/18–13.12; K. R. Balmforth 98–18–319–17–4/46–18.76.

CLIFTON COLLEGE

Played 18: Won 4, Lost 6, Drawn 8. Abandoned 4

Master i/c: D. C. Henderson Cricket professional: F. J. Andrew

A highlight was the performance against Felsted of Ben Lockwood, whose first five overs brought him seven for four, including a hat-trick. David England headed the batting, supported by the South African Donald Gibson and Rupert Swetman, son of the former England wicket-keeper Roy Swetman. The side also featured Jody Kitchen, son of the former Somerset player and Test umpire Mervyn Kitchen.

Wins v: King's, Taunton; Monmouth; Felsted; Eastbourne.

Batting—*D. J. R. England 17–1–660–113–1–41.25; D. Gibson 13–3–392–133–1–39.20; A. J. C. Turner 13–0–350–59–0–26.92; R. W. Swetman 18–0–408–94–0–22.66; J. Kitchen 15–1–225–51–0–16.07; D. A. Kirtley 17–2–233–86–0–15.53; D. R. Grewcock 14–2–162–55–0–13.50.

Bowling—A. J. G. Wadsworth 176.4–42–491–30–5/24–16.36; B. Lockwood 195–60–508–28–7/14–18.14; A. J. C. Turner 104.5–15–340–15–5/47–22.66.

COLFE'S SCHOOL

Played 13: Won 2, Lost 4, Drawn 7. Abandoned 3

Master i/c: D. P. H. Meadows

Wins v: XL Club; Staff XI.

Batting—R. Key 10–3–410–92*–0–58.57; *P. Thompson 11–1–326–120–1–32.60; M. Groves 10–1–218–95–0–24.22; A. Wix 12–1–177–52–0–16.09.

Bowling—R. Cox 124.1–13–493–16–4/29–30.81.

COLSTON'S COLLEGIATE SCHOOL

Played 18: Won 9, Lost 1, Drawn 8. Abandoned 3

Masters i/c: M. P. B. Tayler and A. J. Palmer

The outstanding player was Christopher Taylor, who took 40 wickets with his off-spin and scored 900 runs for the second successive season, setting a new record with 917. He scored 161 against MCC, 108 not out against Balliol College and 136 against the Old Boys. Centuries also came from the brothers Duncan and Alistair Bell as the side equalled their record nine wins of 1993, but with fewer losses. The only defeat was at the hands of Hutton GS, despite the endeavours of Duncan Bell, who took eight for 32.

Wins v: King's, Gloucester; King Edward's, Bath; Clifton C.; Wellington; XL Club; Master of the Society of Merchant Venturers' XI; Beechen Cliff; MCC; Old Boys.

Batting—C. G. Taylor 17–2–917–161–3–61.13; A. J. C. Bell 14–1–556–106–1–42.76; *D. S. C. Bell 17–4–510–118–1–39.23; Q. J. Waraich 17–2–501–100*–1–33.40; C. J. Aust 11–4–221–48–0–31.57.

Bowling—D. S. C. Bell 102.5–29–351–27–8/32–13.00; C. G. Taylor 193.3–53–600–40–7/12–15.00; M. R. James 129.3–23–445–23–4/13–19.34.

CRANBROOK SCHOOL

Played 17: Won 3, Lost 3, Drawn 11. Abandoned 6

Master i/c: A. J. Presnell

Wins v: Simon Langton; Shebbear (twice).

Batting—N. Byrom 16–2–450–90–0–32.14; K. Jarrett 16–1–471–88–0–31.40; N. Pink 16–0–317–50–0–19.81.

Bowling—F. Devlin 113–32–296–24–7/25–12.33; D. Guy 140.3–36–426–25–4/24–17.04.

CRANLEIGH SCHOOL

Played 14: Won 7, Lost 4, Drawn 3. Abandoned 6

Master i/c: D. C. Williams

In a young side whose batting tended to be fragile, D. E. M. G. Copleston and G. A. M. Brown were the most reliable. The bowling was stronger, headed by T. W. P. Evans despite his not being fully fit, while S. A. M. Clyde proved to be a thoughtful slow bowler and A. N. Price bowled some tight left-arm spin. They were superbly backed up by the captain, A. Riva, whose outstanding wicket-keeping made up for his disappointing batting.

Wins v: St Paul's; Brighton; St John's; Loretto; Cryptics; XL Club; Cranleigh CC.

Batting—D. E. M. G. Copleston 15–3–356–91*–0–29.66; G. A. M. Brown 15–2–307–51–0–23.61; *A. Riva 15–2–262–112*–1–20.15; A. N. Price 16–1–246–71*–0–16.40; M. D. Colgate 15–1–180–65*–0–12.85.

Bowling—T. W. P. Evans 144.5–39–391–24–5/19–16.29; S. A. M. Clyde 129.3–30–363–17–6/54–21.35; A. N. Price 145.2–39–406–18–3/21–22.55; A. G. Hillier 105.2–23–385–17–5/62–22.64.

CULFORD SCHOOL

Played 13: Won 3, Lost 7, Drawn 2, Tied 1. Abandoned 1

Master i/c: R. P. Shepperson

Highlights of a season which featured much positive cricket included the first ever match against MCC, the visit of Trinity GS from Australia and a thrilling victory over the XL Club. The left-arm opening bowler, George Ornbo, who is expected to return for another year, took his tally for the XI to a school record of 50. The young all-rounder, Matthew Grinham, enjoyed an excellent debut season.

Wins v: Woodbridge; Pimpernel CC; XL Club.

Batting—M. J. Grinham 12–2–320–89–0–32.00; *J. J. W. Sallis 13–1–365–92*–0–30.41; B. Backhouse 13–2–300–59–0–27.27; B. R. Lindley 12–0–214–77–0–17.83.

Bowling—G. A. Ornbo 110–31–229–25–5/49–9.16; M. J. Grinham 125–31–350–22–5/23–15.90.

DAME ALLAN'S SCHOOL

Played 10: Won 6, Lost 3, Drawn 1

Master i/c: J. Benn

Wins v: St Cuthbert's; RGS, Newcastle; King's, Tynemouth; Morpeth; Northumberland CCC Club & Ground; Ballymena Acad.

Batting—M. A. F. Hynd 9–3–281–58*–0–46.83.

Bowling—A. R. Robson 64–11–182–15–5/36–12.13.

DARTFORD GRAMMAR SCHOOL

Played 12: Won 4, Lost 5, Drawn 3. Abandoned 3

Masters i/c: C. J. Plummer and G. T. Prout

Wins v: Oakwood Park GS; Staff XI; St George's; Judd.

Batting—*D. M. Rye 9–2–283–71*–0–40.42; K. Newman 8–3–151–38*–0–30.20; K. M. Ring 10–1–270–87–0–30.00; J. Scott 8–0–160–77–0–20.00; S. J. Pollard 11–0–215–69–0–19.54.

Bowling—L. P. Jeffs 105–7–354–17–4/39–20.82.

DAUNTSEY'S SCHOOL

Played 12: Won 4, Lost 0, Drawn 8. Abandoned 2

Master i/c: D. C. R. Baker Cricket professional: P. K. Knowles

Wins v: Tenterden; Wendywood; Old Dauntseians; D. C. R. Baker's XI.

Batting—A. Darbyshire 11–4–333–76–0–47.57; D. Nethercott 11–0–345–52–0–31.36; *J. Gaiger 11–1–312–110*–1–31.20; D. Bell 8–2–174–41*–0–29.00; O. Lawson 10–1–217–107*–1–24.11; M. Gauguier 9–2–160–60–0–22.85.

Bowling—A. Darbyshire 149–41–392–34–7/83–11.52; D. Hagelthorn 102.4–33–308–16–5/40–19.25.

DEAN CLOSE SCHOOL

Played 13: Won 2, Lost 4, Drawn 7. Abandoned 3

Master i/c: C. M. Kenyon Cricket professional: S. Hansford

Failure of both batting and bowling brought disappointing results, although with eight of the XI expected to return in 1995, there is optimism for the future. The season was followed by a tour to Zimbabwe.

Wins v: Dean Close Common Room; Barton Peveril C.

Batting—*L. M. Simmonds 12–0–344–58–0–28.66; T. N. Johnson 12–1–307–100*–1–27.90; N. G. A. Miller 11–1–251–60*–0–25.10; A. J. Thompson 11–0–212–65–0–19.27; R. W. J. Chubb 10–1–157–42–0–17.44; D. T. Gilroy 11–1–171–56*–0–17.10.

Bowling—No bowler took 15 wickets. The leading bowler was S. H. Kenworthy 53.4–8–160–13–4/18–12.30.

DENSTONE COLLEGE

Played 20: Won 8, Lost 1, Drawn 11. Abandoned 3

Master i/c: A. N. James

Denstone enjoyed another excellent season in which, again, they were never bowled out. For the second year running, there was a new record aggregate of runs – this time from 16-year-old R. W. J. Howitt, whose 918 included a century, a 99 and seven other fifties. A total of 21 half-centuries helped the side to compile ten century partnerships, three of which passed 150 and the best of which was 171 for the third wicket between Howitt and M. P. Tweddle against Old Swinford Hospital. Howitt went on to play for Nottinghamshire Second XI.

Wins v: Staffordshire Gentlemen; Ellesmere C.; Old Swinford Hospital; King's, Macclesfield; Trent; Abbot Beyne; Bishop Vesey's; King Edward's, Aston.

Batting—R. W. J. Howitt 17–3–918–104*–1–65.57; *D. M. Campion 17–3–498–87–0–35.57; A. T. Griffin 13–5–268–114–1–33.50; R. J. Davies 18–1–462–92–0–27.17; D. J. O'Keefe 15–3–313–54*–0–26.08; M. P. Tweddle 17–6–236–75*–0–21.45.

Bowling—A. T. Griffin 127–26–371–21–4/16–17.66; J. A. J. Cure 171.2–22–624–34–5/56–18.35; J. M. R. Hudson 95–12–382–16–5/41–23.87; R. E. Wheatman 144–36–454–16–3/47–28.37.

DOVER COLLEGE

Played 12: Won 3, Lost 7, Drawn 2. Abandoned 1

Master i/c: D. C. Butler

Although the bowling and fielding were sound, brittle batting was a handicap. A highlight was a sixth-wicket partnership of 96 in 55 minutes between Brenton Amedee (38) and Matthew Telford (77) in the successful pursuit of 206 against King's, Rochester.

Wins v: King's, Rochester; XL Club; Staff XI.

Batting—*B. C. Amedee 10–1–177–38–0–19.66; R. J. P. Chappell 10–0–195–38–0–19.50.

Bowling—R. J. P. Chappell 114.1–18–386–17–4/53–22.70; B. C. Amedee 130.5–22–418–17–5/49–24.58.

DOWNSIDE SCHOOL

Played 15: Won 1, Lost 8, Drawn 6

Master i/c: K. J. Burke Cricket professional: B. Bing

Win v: Lancaster GS.

Batting—I. W. Kirkpatrick 11–3–198–47–0–24.75; *A. D. Graham 14–0–271–65–0–19.35; C. P. Reid 14–0–229–64–0–16.35; J. W. J. Hynes 14–0–221–47–0–15.78; H. D. Vyvyan 12–1–167–36*–0–15.18.

Bowling—J. W. J. Hynes 162–45–468–19–4/52–24.63; C. P. Reid 175.5–36–567–22–6/15–25.77.

DUKE OF YORK'S ROYAL MILITARY SCHOOL

Played 12: Won 6, Lost 2, Drawn 4. Abandoned 5

Master i/c: S. Salisbury Cricket professional: I. J. Hansen

In recording their most successful season for 20 years, the side owed much to Russell Martindale's all-round talent and in particular his seam bowling: his return of seven for three was crucial in the dismissal of St Augustine's for eight runs. He was ably supported by medium-pacers Tim Goodridge and brothers Edward and John Budd.

Wins v: Dover C.; Bethany; St Augustine's; Maidstone GS; Sutton Valence; Headmaster's XI.

Batting—R. J. J. Martindale 8–3–199–70*–0–39.80; C. M. G. Pollock 12–4–228–51–0–28.50; *E. J. Budd 11–2–238–66*–0–26.44.

Bowling—T. H. Goodridge 60.2–18–183–23–6/26–7.95; J. D. Budd 65–13–208–17–5/20–12.23; R. J. J. Martindale 150–41–380–27–7/3–14.07.

DURHAM SCHOOL

Played 22: Won 10, Lost 1, Drawn 11. Abandoned 3

Master i/c: N. J. Willings Cricket professional: M. Hirsch

In another excellent season, Durham recorded ten wins and would have had more but for the frustratingly negative approach of some opponents. In a strong side, captained by Chris Clark, five batsmen scored 500 runs and five bowlers took 20 wickets. As well as effecting a school record 39 victims behind the stumps, Wayne Ritzema scored 1,000 runs for the second successive season, with hundreds against Pocklington (113), Durham Pilgrims (101 not out), Queen Elizabeth's Hospital (155 not out) and the visiting South African side, Kearsney College, in a two-day game (107). He finished his career in the XI with 2,730 runs to his name and played for English Schools, MCC Schools and Durham Under-19. There were four partnerships of more than 200 and a fifth-wicket record of 191 against Kearsney College between Ritzema and Ben Cosbie-Ross, who scored a maiden century. John Windows was the outstanding all-rounder, with 705 runs, 34 wickets and eight catches.

Wins v: Ampleforth; MCC; Sedbergh; Dame Allan's; RGS, Newcastle; Eglingham CC; Barnard Castle; XL Club; St Bees; Queen Elizabeth's Hospital.

Batting—W. Ritzema 21–3–1,038–155*–4–57.66; *C. Clark 18–4–734–95–0–52.42; W. Halford 8–4–176–102–1–44.00; B. Cosbie-Ross 18–5–521–103*–1–40.07; J. B. Windows 22–4–705–144–1–39.16; M. Coates 21–1–504–80–0–25.20; E. Cleland 14–3–209–60–0–19.00.

Bowling—R. McLaren 74–18–240–25–5/5–9.60; O. Jaber 83.3–17–301–22–7/26–13.68; J. B. Windows 186.3–49–611–34–5/22–17.97; C. Clark 92–25–290–15–4/49–19.33; J. Bailey 188.4–42–592–29–5/20–20.41; M. Coates 236–70–758–25–5/44–30.32.

EASTBOURNE COLLEGE

Played 15: Won 7, Lost 7, Drawn 1. Abandoned 4

Master i/c: N. L. Wheeler Cricket professional: J. N. Shepherd

The season started with a flourish as five opponents were bowled out and easily beaten, but injury, examinations and holiday jobs took their toll and a one-run loss to Epsom was followed by a miserable end-of-season festival at Felsted. There was some bright, adventurous batting, but the bowlers seemed to find the season too long for them.

Wins v: Christ's Hospital; Lancing; Ardingly; Worth; St John's, Leatherhead; Old Eastbournians; Seaford.

Batting—T. J. White 14–3–407–102–1–37.00; *A. J. H. Bogdanovski 14–3–357–99–0–32.45; R. F. Marchant 12–1–317–74–0–28.81; M. S. M. Justice 12–1–206–56*–0–18.72; C. J. H. Baker 9–0–165–49–0–18.33; C. J. Dyer 12–2–156–33–0–15.60.

Bowling—T. Mills 64–4–260–18–4/14–14.44; C. J. A. Dawson 177–43–537–26–5/41–20.65; C. J. Dyer 117–14–520–20–5/38–26.00.

THE EDINBURGH ACADEMY

Played 19: Won 10, Lost 2, Drawn 7

Master i/c: G. R. Bowe

Wins v: Edinburgh Academicals; Glenalmond; D. W. J. Moffat's XI; XL Club; Kelvinside Acad.; Loretto; Fettes; Academicals; Brighton C.; King's, Macclesfield.

Batting—J. S. D. Moffat 17–3–614–96*–0–43.85; D. A. T. G. Rutherford 20–2–464–55*–0–25.77; A. S. Eaton 19–4–334–75*–0–22.26; G. B. MacLeod 19–1–385–45–0–21.38; J. P. L. Boyd 16–7–190–59–0–21.11; *M. D. Fairweather 18–1–243–35–0–14.29; I. A. Hathorn 16–2–163–26*–0–11.64.

Bowling—L. L. Moodley 199–41–627–44–6/24–14.25; A. S. Eaton 239–49–743–44–5/34–16.88; M. D. Fairweather 128–39–353–20–4/13–17.65; J. S. D. Moffat 151–42–347–16–3/61–21.68.

ELIZABETH COLLEGE, GUERNSEY

Played 19: Won 3, Lost 6, Drawn 10. Abandoned 5

Master i/c: M. E. Kinder

In a season of rebuilding, much depended on the captain, Simon Beck, whose 741 runs took his career aggregate to 2,081 in five seasons. The bowling and fielding were disappointing, but with most of the side expected to return in 1995, the future looks brighter.

Wins v: Guernsey CA; Guernsey Police; Elizabeth C. Second XI.

Batting—*S. A. Beck 19–2–741–115–1–43.58; M. C. Stokes 19–1–587–99–0–32.61; J. Arnold 17–1–404–108–1–25.25; P. W. Oliver 13–1–198–37*–0–16.50; O. T. Brock 17–2–195–28–0–13.00; S. J. Fooks 15–1–176–49*–0–12.57.

Bowling—J. A. Barrett 127–17–554–20–4/22–27.70.

ELLESMERE COLLEGE

Played 17: Won 2, Lost 6, Drawn 9. Abandoned 1

Master i/c: E. Marsh Cricket professional: R. G. Mapp

Wins v: Liverpool C.; Frankton CC.

Batting—*J. H. Nunn 14–4–218–36–0–21.80; C. N. C. Hill 17–5–258–37–0–21.50; T. F. Stewart 14–1–275–56–0–21.15; O. M. Dunk 16–4–249–59*–0–20.75; J. P. Terry 17–0–264–34–0–15.52; K. T. O'Shea 14–0–156–39–0–11.14.

Bowling—P. R. Harper 148–44–445–24–5/32–18.54; J. R. C. Maddocks 161–30–501–19–4/18–26.36; T. F. Stewart 170–21–615–22–3/29–27.95.

ELTHAM COLLEGE

Played 20: Won 4, Lost 7, Drawn 9. Abandoned 1

Masters i/c: P. McCartney and B. Withecombe Cricket professionals: R. Hills and R. Winup

The total of 277 for six against Colfe's was a new school record, passing by 22 the previous best set in 1980.

Wins v: Old Elthamians; Gravesend GS; St Olave's; Langley Park.

Batting—J. M. Bensted 18–4–422–115–1–30.14; P. S. Pay 11–0–297–69–0–27.00; B. P. Dell 19–2–437–133–1–25.70; T. B. Beames 15–4–226–56*–0–20.54; *B. P. Cartwright 14–3–224–55–0–20.36; D. J. Hadley 16–2–247–63–0–17.64; D. Harris 14–0–183–28–0–13.07.

Bowling—J. M. Bensted 117.1–14–417–26–5/18–16.03; B. P. Cartwright 186–43–576–35–5/2–16.45; T. B. Beames 200.1–38–657–31–4/28–21.19; P. S. Attreed 95–13–367–15–5/47–24.46.

EMANUEL SCHOOL

Played 15: Won 6, Lost 5, Drawn 4. Abandoned 4

Master i/c: J. R. Cremer Cricket professional: J. R. Cremer

Emanuel were runners-up in the Under-19 London Cup and semi-finalists in the Under-19 Surrey Cup.

Wins v: Tiffin; KCS, Wimbledon; RGS, Reigate; John Fisher; Westminster City; Haberdashers' Hatcham & Aske's.

Batting—T. S. Seaton 14–3–818–161–3–74.36; *D. A. Darriba 14–4–389–66*–0–38.90; P. S. Seaton 8–2–165–68–0–27.50; N. Chetram 8–2–159–67*–0–26.50; G. Mustoe 12–0–171–41–0–14.25; S. Dillsworth 13–2–155–32–0–14.09.

Bowling—D. A. Darriba 133.3–34–348–30–7/31–11.60; C. Hicks 90.2–30–264–20–5/25–13.20; T. Seaton 130.5–31–380–21–4/35–18.09; S. Dillsworth 122–33–332–15–4/9–22.13.

ENFIELD GRAMMAR SCHOOL

Played 24: Won 6, Lost 6, Drawn 12. Abandoned 2

Master i/c: J. J. Conroy

Fifteen-year-old Aaron Laraman made a significant contribution with 791 runs and 28 wickets.

Wins v: Bishop's Stortford HS; RGS, Colchester; Old Boys; Owens; Queen Elizabeth, Barnet; Verulam.

Batting—A. Laraman 17–4–791–101–2–60.84; P. Honnor 22–1–588–103–1–28.00; M. Nicholls 17–1–378–71*–0–23.62; R. Baker 9–1–184–53–0–23.00; T. Atkins 15–4–222–72–0–20.18; D. Evans 20–4–310–66–0–19.37; *J. Mitchell 19–5–211–27–0–15.07; M. Bowen 17–1–221–58–0–13.81.

Bowling—R. Baker 78–12–271–17–4/13–15.94; M. Nicholls 214–26–656–31–4/30–21.16; J. Mitchell 234.1–24–855–36–6/40–23.75; A. Laraman 166–25–723–28–4/34–25.82.

EPSOM COLLEGE

Played 6: Won 2, Lost 1, Drawn 3. Abandoned 1

Master i/c: M. D. Hobbs

A highlight was the dismissal of Lancing for 46 by N. S. F. Wherry (four for 24) and L. J. Webster (six for 17).

Wins v: Lancing; Eastbourne C.

Batting—N. S. F. Wherry 6–2–168–70*–0–42.00; *R. E. Arthur 6–0–242–88–0–40.33; J. E. Harris 7–0–209–71–0–29.85.

Bowling—No bowler took 15 wickets.

ETON COLLEGE

Played 13: Won 2, Lost 5, Drawn 6. Abandoned 4

Master i/c: J. A. Claughton Cricket professional: J. M. Rice

Eton suffered their most disappointing season for many years, in which St Edward's, Oxford, inflicted the first defeat by a school since 1990. The younger players prospered, with James Fulton, a left-hander, scoring two hundreds and the Under-15 side beating King's, Macclesfield, to win the Lord's Taverners Trophy for the first time.

Wins v: Winchester; Eton Ramblers.

Batting—J. A. G. Fulton 12–1–471–112–2–42.81; H. V. Machin 12–0–377–80–0–31.41; *C. G. R. Lightfoot 11–5–157–27*–0–26.16; H. G. Duberly 11–3–186–48*–0–23.25; J. C. S. Hardy 12–0–258–75–0–21.50.

Bowling—C. G. R. Lightfoot 164.4–37–475–20–3/22–23.75.

EXETER SCHOOL

Played 19: Won 10, Lost 5, Drawn 4. Abandoned 2

Master i/c: M. C. Wilcock

Orlando Le Fleming, who headed both averages, played for English Schools, MCC Schools, NAYC, NCA Young Cricketers, the Development of Excellence XI and Devon. Fifteen-year-old Patrick Drought, coming into the side at the end of the season, scored 131 runs in his three innings.

Wins v: Exeter St James; Blundell's; Kelly C.; Taunton; Exeter CC; Queen's, Taunton; Wells Cathedral S.; Headmaster's XI; Hereford Cathedral S.; The Chase.

Batting—*A. O. F. Le Fleming 11–3–452–133*–1–56.50; T. A. Sowman 14–5–305–59*–0–33.88; R. J. Smith 12–2–301–78*–0–30.10; J. D. Evennett 14–4–285–61–0–28.50; M. H. Price 15–2–348–68–0–26.76; J. P. Janion 14–3–227–54–0–20.63; W. C. Cruft 14–0–255–51–0–18.21.

Bowling—A. O. F. Le Fleming 83.2–28–188–19–5/8–9.89; M. J. Porter 147.3–31–559–40–7/37–13.97; J. D. Evennett 182.1–38–563–38–8/30–14.81; M. H. Price 127.2–21–469–24–4/18–19.54.

FETTES COLLEGE

Played 13: Won 3, Lost 8, Drawn 2

Master i/c: C. H. Carruthers Cricket professional: J. van Geloven

Wins v: Kelvinside Acad.; George Watson's; Stewart's Melville.

Batting—I. E. G. Forbes 12–1–252–68–0–22.90; A. I. F. Nelson 14–1–285–78*–0–21.92; T. F. White 12–2–203–52*–0–20.30.

Bowling—T. F. White 138.1–39–342–20–5/65–17.10; I. E. G. Forbes 182.4–41–559–24–4/18–23.29.

FOREST SCHOOL

Played 19: Won 10, Lost 2, Drawn 7. Abandoned 3

Master i/c: S. Turner

Ten wins were the best in recorded history for the school. A highlight was the bowling of D. Ducat, whose 43 wickets included four for nought in an over.

Wins v: Chigwell; St Dunstan's; Brentwood; Ilford CHS; Incogniti; Enfield; Essex Schools Under-19; Culford; Bancroft's; Southend HS.

Batting—S. Moss 18–4–661–113*–1–47.21; G. Kilby 14–1–385–55–0–29.61; J. McKay 16–2–380–59*–0–27.14; W. Rogers 15–4–259–58–0–23.54; *N. Sims 18–2–350–118*–1–21.87.

Bowling—D. Ducat 192.5–36–667–43–6/37–15.51; W. Rogers 158.3–33–482–30–6/64–16.06; J. McKay 93.1–22–316–17–4/16–18.58; S. Oliver 226.5–79–513–27–3/23–19.00.

FRAMLINGHAM COLLEGE

Played 14: Won 4, Lost 4, Drawn 6. Abandoned 2

Master i/c: P. J. Hayes Cricket professional: C. Rutterford

Wins v: Norwich; Monmouth; Royal Anglian Regiment; Winchester.

Batting—J. H. Phillips 14–3–466–104–1–42.36; J. H. Pearl 13–4–368–86*–0–40.88; W. D. Buck 11–0–239–55–0–21.72; C. J. Clementson 13–3–181–51–0–18.10; J. A. Misick 13–1–215–45–0–17.91; *J. R. Roberts 11–0–161–25–0–14.63.

Bowling—W. D. Buck 181.2–41–618–22–5/62–28.09.

GIGGLESWICK SCHOOL

Played 13: Won 3, Lost 2, Drawn 8. Abandoned 1

Master i/c: C. Green Cricket professional: S. A. Pearce

Wins v: St Bees; XL Club; Old Giggleswickians.

Batting—C. J. Shorrock 11–4–220–50*–0–31.42; *S. J. Nesbitt 12–1–318–100*–1–28.90; J. A. E. Caton 12–0–228–57–0–19.00.

Bowling—S. J. Nesbitt 148–34–441–28–5/21–15.75; J. B. Savage 192–45–499–24–4/17–20.79.

THE GLASGOW ACADEMY

Played 12: Won 4, Lost 0, Drawn 8

Master i/c: A. G. Lyall Cricket professional: V. Hariharan

Euan Stubbs and Suhail Riaz played for Scotland Under-16 and Under-15 respectively.

Wins v: Kelvinside Acad.; Morrison's Acad.; George Heriot's; XL Club.

Batting—*A. C. Lindsay 11–1–368–91–0–36.80; R. I. Higgins 11–4–175–48*–0–25.00; E. Stubbs 9–1–165–41–0–20.62; R. Patel 11–2–173–42*–0–19.22.

Bowling—R. Munday 59–13–185–17–6/46–10.88; G. Cross 116–16–397–29–6/39–13.68; A. C. Lindsay 103–30–251–17–5/44–14.76; R. I. Higgins 111–24–361–17–4/6–21.23.

GLENALMOND

Played 13: Won 3, Lost 1, Drawn 9

Master i/c: J. D. Bassett

In an improved season, Glenalmond competed effectively on the Scottish circuit and were particularly encouraged to measure themselves against English schools opposition in closely fought draws against Sedbergh and King's, Ely.

Wins v: Merchiston; Fettes; XL Club.

Batting—T. M. Stevenson 12-6-167-37-0-27.83; A. D. M. Gully 14-2-281-70*-0-23.41; J. R. Hammond-Chambers 12-1-245-52-0-22.27; A. E. Mackintosh-Walker 13-2-232-55-0-21.09; A. R. D. Croall 13-0-271-72-0-20.84; M. W. Craig 12-0-227-41-0-18.91.

Bowling—A. K. P. Young 150.2-37-399-28-6/35-14.25; A. D. M. Gully 149-32-465-22-5/42-21.13.

GORDONSTOUN SCHOOL

Played 8: Won 5, Lost 1, Drawn 1, Tied 1

Master i/c: C. J. Barton

In a magnificent summer, which included the driest May in Morayshire for 30 years, the cricket matched the weather, with some positive and exciting matches. Highlights were the victory over MCC and the successful pursuit of 312 for no loss against Old Gordonstounians.

Wins v: Robert Gordon's; Elgin CC; MCC; Old Gordonstounians; C. J. Barton's XI.

Batting—S. A. B. MacDonald 7-2-326-114-1-65.20; A. H. B. Fraser-Tytler 7-2-292-132*-1-58.40; *S. A. Walton 8-1-323-160*-1-46.14.

Bowling—J. L. Shrago 94.2-15-385-22-6/34-17.50; M. C. Hepburn 111-27-413-21-6/12-19.66.

GRESHAM'S SCHOOL

Played 19: Won 6, Lost 6, Drawn 7. Abandoned 1

Master i/c: A. M. Ponder

Both batting and bowling records fell at Gresham's: Alastair Ponder's aggregate of 716 was the highest ever for the school, and Jeremy Mobbs became the most successful bowler with 48 wickets. His seven for 88 against Oundle and Ollie Morgan's 140 against Bromsgrove were particularly memorable.

Wins v: Wisbech GS; Culford; The Perse; West Norfolk CC; King Edward VII; Royal Anglian Regiment.

Batting—*A. R. Ponder 19-4-716-121*-1-47.73; O. Morgan 15-0-442-140-1-29.46; N. Hood 17-0-373-55-0-21.94; T. Hood 15-1-301-59-0-21.50; J. Wyatt 16-3-221-44*-0-17.00; J. Cuff 13-1-150-31-0-12.50.

Bowling—J. Mobbs 244.5-59-770-48-7/88-16.04; J. Woodwark 131.3-20-467-22-4/18-21.22; M. McHale 170.5-28-585-25-7/47-23.40; P. Webster 144-23-492-16-5/54-30.75.

HABERDASHERS' ASKE'S SCHOOL

Played 18: Won 7, Lost 1, Drawn 10. Abandoned 2

Masters i/c: S. D. Charlwood and D. I. Yeabsley

Good team spirit and significant contributions from everyone resulted in a better season than had been expected. Highlights were successful run-chases on consecutive days against Bedford Modern and Old Haberdashers, followed by an excellent victory on tour over a strong Devon Under-16 side.

Wins v: Bancroft's; Watford GS; Enfield GS; Bedford Modern; Old Haberdashers; Devon U-16; Budleigh Salterton CC.

Batting—A. E. Plaskow 15–7–502–88–0–62.75; N. J. Fielden 17–3–551–78–0–39.35; A. R. Lock 12–1–241–64–0–21.90; B. Ashworth 12–2–178–34–0–17.80; *S. F. Byrne 15–2–219–43–0–16.84; S. Shah 14–3–173–30–0–15.72; J. Bilimoria 16–2–216–53–0–15.42.

Bowling—A. E. Plaskow 77.3–9–354–19–6/57–18.63; P. R. Samuels 166–26–487–25–4/23–19.48; S. R. Sher 164.2–41–459–23–4/27–19.95; H. Saegusa 156.4–46–414–20–6/46–20.70; N. J. Fielden 169.1–33–548–24–4/28–22.83.

HAILEYBURY

Played 14: Won 3, Lost 1, Drawn 10. Abandoned 4

Master i/c: M. S. Seymour Cricket professional: P. M. Ellis

The side responded with enthusiasm to the coaching of Graham Barlow, whose impact was considerable. Robert Walker was an exemplary captain, making intelligent use of his bowlers and always ready to capitalise on promising situations. The positive approach that continued to characterise the Haileybury XI resulted in some close finishes, notably against Felsted (won by three runs) and Sherborne (lost by two wickets).

Wins v: Privateers; Dulwich; Felsted.

Batting—P. D. Stafford 13–0–481–99–0–37.00; N. D. Hughes 13–2–355–88*–0–32.27; J. E. L. Dahl 10–3–176–50–0–25.14; *R. E. Walker 13–0–301–75–0–23.15; D. A. Cruickshank 12–0–256–72–0–21.33; M. O. Elmes 9–0–173–62–0–19.22; S. M. Osman 13–2–186–57–0–16.90.

Bowling—D. W. Stahl 128–38–374–25–4/20–14.96; N. D. Hughes 105–22–289–17–4/9–17.00; B. R. J. Macaulay 142–31–431–18–5/30–23.94.

HAMPTON SCHOOL

Played 20: Won 3, Lost 6, Drawn 11. Abandoned 1

Master i/c: A. J. Cook Cricket professional: P. Farbrace

Wins v: Watford; Headmaster's XI; Old Hamptonians.

Batting—*M. P. Hall 16–2–772–110*–1–55.14; A. S. Barnes 14–3–425–86–0–38.63; T. J. Green 15–3–258–35–0–21.50; M. J. Templeman 15–1–273–57–0–19.50; C. J. H. S. Clark 16–0–201–47–0–12.56.

Bowling—P. J. Frost 121.5–30–334–20–4/28–16.70; T. J. Green 216.4–49–670–35–7/46–19.14; N. T. Barnes 172.4–26–570–24–4/41–23.75; E. Holdsworth 124–18–533–20–6/67–26.65.

HARROW SCHOOL

Played 12: Won 0, Lost 1, Drawn 11. Abandoned 4

Master i/c: W. Snowden Cricket professional: R. K. Sethi

Harrow failed to win a game but lost only to Felsted. The high number of draws was due to the wet weather and lack of bowling support for Simon Roundell and Mark Rayner. While Justin Litherland was the leading batsman, the outstanding partnership – 160 for the fourth wicket – was compiled by Oliver Chittenden and Roundell against Eton at Lord's.

Batting—J. P. Litherland 11–1–454–101*–1–45.40; S. F. Roundell 11–2–288–89–0–32.00; M. C. R. Crawford 11–1–230–45–0–23.00; O. H. Chittenden 10–0–218–96–0–21.80; S. D. G. Engelen 11–0–214–36–0–19.45.

Bowling—S. F. Roundell 94.2–17–339–20–4/24–16.95; M. S. Rayner 139–31–410–22–4/31–18.63.

THE HARVEY GRAMMAR SCHOOL

Played 19: Won 8, Lost 4, Drawn 7. Abandoned 3

Master i/c: P. J. Harding

The side, which lost only one schools match, regained the Kent County Cup when they beat Simon Langton GS in the final.

Wins v: Maidstone GS; Erith; Leigh CC; XL Club; Tunbridge Wells GS; Simon Langton GS; Wootton Courtenay CC; Watchet CC.

Batting—D. E. Johnson 16–5–422–68–0–38.36; J. Hughes 18–2–457–60–0–28.56; D. Fletcher 16–3–346–120*–1–26.61; D. Himsworth 15–4–281–67*–0–25.54; *L. Stone 14–4–235–58–0–23.50; J. Smith 14–1–285–107–1–21.92.

Bowling—L. Stone 185–60–393–35–6/7–11.22; S. Wood 121.3–32–343–28–5/21–12.25; M. Bristow 126–25–348–24–3/7–14.50.

HEREFORD CATHEDRAL SCHOOL

Played 16: Won 4, Lost 2, Drawn 10. Abandoned 1

Master i/c: A. Connop

Wins v: Llandovery C.; Wrekin; XL Club; Gentlemen of Herefordshire.

Batting—B. J. Albright 15–3–549–100*–1–45.75; *D. F. Kings 12–2–440–75*–0–44.00; S. J. Price 11–4–306–94–0–43.71; J. Andrews 13–1–290–46–0–24.16; T. I. Hall 13–4–216–57–0–24.00.

Bowling—G. P. Holland 116.5–20–409–20–3/15–20.45; J. Butlin 137.5–31–436–21–6/98–20.76.

HIGHGATE SCHOOL

Played 13: Won 4, Lost 2, Drawn 7. Abandoned 3

Masters i/c: R. G. W. Marsh and R. J. Davis Cricket professional: R. E. Jones

A young side, which featured the O'Brien brothers, Matthew (M. A. P.) and Michael (M. A. J.), were pleased to number the Masters' Common Room among their victims for the first time since 1959.

Wins v: Christ's College; Hendon; Masters' Common Room; North London Police.

Batting—S. M. Khan 12–6–319–82*–0–53.16; R. H. Beenstock 10–3–337–105*–1–48.14; M. A. P. O'Brien 8–0–226–55–0–28.25; G. R. Saade 8–2–166–67–0–27.66; S. D. Philipson 8–0–220–56–0–27.50; M. A. J. O'Brien 10–0–223–70–0–22.30; *T. O. Jenkins 11–0–234–102–1–21.27.

Bowling—C. J. P. Thomas 113–23–299–16–4/52–18.68; G. R. Saade 115–21–286–15–4/48–19.06; C. T. Millward 154–26–567–20–5/70–28.35.

HURSTPIERPOINT COLLEGE

Played 15: Won 7, Lost 2, Drawn 6. Abandoned 4

Master i/c: M. E. Allbrook Cricket professional: D. J. Semmence

Highlights in a successful season were the 170-run defeat of Eastbourne in the final of the Langdale Trophy and the match against Seaford College, who were beaten before lunch (Seaford 39, Hurstpierpoint 40 for one). The captain, Justin Bates, led by example with 580 runs and 25 wickets (off-spin) and was well supported by the wicket-keeper Simon May and opening bowler James Paterson.

Wins v: Ardingly (twice); Seaford; Christ's Hospital; Eastbourne; Brighton; Lancing.

Batting—*J. J. Bates 14–3–580–129–3–52.72; S. P. May 11–2–318–101*–1–35.33; N. J. Jenkin 14–3–311–56–0–28.27; J. E. R. Paterson 13–4–174–37*–0–19.33; J. E. Riddy 14–0–229–66–0–16.35.

Bowling—J. E. R. Paterson 134.1–30–334–27–5/38–12.37; J. J. Bates 137.4–44–322–25–6/27–12.88; L. J. Atkins 123–28–311–20–4/50–15.55; J. C. A. Catterall 77.5–11–317–19–3/23–16.68.

IPSWICH SCHOOL

Played 15: Won 2, Lost 5, Drawn 8. Abandoned 4

Master i/c: A. K. Golding Cricket professional: R. E. East

Wins v: King's, Macclesfield; Edinburgh Acad.

Batting—S. Henwood 15–1–527–100*–1–37.64; G. McCartney 15–2–333–100*–1–25.61; *J. East 15–1–271–56*–0–19.35; J. Lear 11–0–193–39–0–17.54; C. Robinson 13–1–191–34–0–15.91; J. Collins 14–1–192–43–0–14.76.

Bowling—J. East 239–28–519–33–5/45–15.72; C. Robinson 174–39–654–20–4/53–32.70.

ISLEWORTH & SYON SCHOOL

Played 16: Won 12, Lost 0, Drawn 4. Abandoned 1

Master i/c: B. A. Goldsby

Unbeaten, the side won 12 of their 16 matches and took the Middlesex Schools' County Cup – both achievements for the first time. Fifteen-year-old Owais Shah was again outstanding as he averaged 102 in his eight innings. He played for Middlesex Second XI as well as representing England Under-17 and Under-18, for whom he scored a century against the touring Indian Under-19 side, before being selected to tour the West Indies with England Under-19.

Wins v: Hampton XI; St James; Halliford; St Mark's; Ealing C.; Latymer; John Lyon; Latymer Upper; Weald C.; Christ's C.; Old Isleworthians; Heathlands.

Batting—O. A. Shah 8–3–510–119–2–102.00; *B. M. Goldsby 13–8–307–91*–0–61.40; M. A. Khan 11–7–183–52–0–45.75; W. S. Bokhari 10–4–256–55*–0–42.66; A. A. Khan 10–2–247–70–0–30.87; N. S. Ahmed 11–0–240–60–0–21.81.

Bowling—B. M. Goldsby 142.3–35–454–37–5/57–12.27; W. S. Bokhari 100.1–14–368–24–6/49–15.33.

THE JOHN LYON SCHOOL

Played 19: Won 6, Lost 4, Drawn 9. Abandoned 1

Master i/c: I. R. Parker Cricket professional: A. R. G. Fraser

Wins v: Middlesex Colts; Drayton; Teddington; Richmond; Queen Elizabeth's, Barnet; Christ's C.

Batting—R. A. Holgate 19–5–690–95–0–49.28; N. B. Patel 14–1–358–106*–1–27.53; M. C. Ball 17–2–364–55*–0–24.26; K. S. Merali 15–2–176–39–0–13.53; J. P. Welch 13–0–157–54–0–12.07.

Bowling—J. P. Welch 168.4–41–442–30–5/12–14.73; N. B. Patel 140.4–29–393–20–5/63–19.65; K. S. Merali 138.5–19–454–20–3/21–22.70.

KELLY COLLEGE

Played 11: Won 3, Lost 3, Drawn 5

Master i/c: G. C. L. Cooper

Wins v: Devon Dumplings; Richard Huish; Grenville.

Batting—*D. S. Edwards 11–2–499–108*–2–55.44; J. L. Roué 11–1–420–102–1–42.00; R. G. Goldring 10–1–296–80–0–32.88.

Bowling—T. Doubell 88.3–16–312–23–5/15–13.56.

KIMBOLTON SCHOOL

Played 22: Won 11, Lost 1, Drawn 10. Abandoned 2

Master i/c: R. P. Merriman Cricket professional: M. E. Latham

Kimbolton's most successful season ever saw them win 11 matches, losing only once, and winning the Inter-Schools Festival. Bradley Robinson, with 911 runs, and Paul Pippard, with 701, were particularly prolific and set a record third-wicket partnership of 194 unbroken. Robinson scored an unbeaten century against the New South Wales Antipodeans, while Dominic Ford did so at the expense of Berkhamsted in a record total of 307 for five. Rupesh Kanani and Jeremy Follett led an effective seam attack, while Pippard was the dominant spinner.

Wins v: R. P. Merriman's XI; Leicestershire Gentlemen; Bedford Modern; XL Club; Old Kimboltonians; Antipodeans, New South Wales; Wisbech GS; The Perse; Berkhamsted; Framlingham; Winchester.

Batting—B. I. Robinson 21–4–911–104*–1–53.58; P. S. Pippard 18–4–701–95*–0–50.07; *J. P. Latham 17–7–374–44–0–37.40; D. R. Ford 19–3–459–109*–1–28.68; A. J. Scott 19–4–361–80*–0–24.06; R. K. Kanani 18–3–321–65–0–21.40.

Bowling—J. C. R. Follett 195.3–45–673–32–6/22–21.03; J. P. Latham 213.5–45–637–24–4/75–26.54; R. K. Kanani 212.1–27–890–33–4/40–26.96; R. A. Beadles 149–22–565–19–3/40–29.73.

KING EDWARD VI COLLEGE, STOURBRIDGE

Played 11: Won 1, Lost 7, Drawn 3. Abandoned 1

Master i/c: R. A. Williams

Win v: XL Club.

Batting—R. T. Crowley 9–0–312–96–0–34.66; *M. J. Porter 9–1–294–91*–0–36.75.

Bowling—No bowler took 15 wickets. The leading bowler was A. J. Turner 68–4–364–14–4/46–26.00.

KING EDWARD VI SCHOOL, SOUTHAMPTON

Played 21: Won 6, Lost 5, Drawn 10. Abandoned 4

Master i/c: R. J. Putt

In a season when four batsmen passed 500 runs, the averages were headed by the 1993 England Under-14 captain, John Claughton, nephew of J. A. Claughton, formerly of Warwickshire and Oxford University and currently in charge of cricket at Eton.

Wins v: Brockenhurst C.; Queen Mary's; Peter Symonds; The Staff; Farnborough C.; Taunton's.

Batting—J. A. Claughton 13–2–510–104*–1–46.36; T. R. Osman 19–2–569–92–0–33.47; *M. Holden 21–1–617–101*–1–30.85; M. W. Masters 19–0–558–83–0–29.36; C. F. Craft 20–3–316–66–0–18.58; M. R. Vallance 16–2–257–36–0–18.35.

Bowling—S. R. G. Francis 141–40–364–31–4/21–11.74; A. T. Hill 104.1–11–474–23–5/58–20.60; S. J. Andrews 189.5–37–619–26–4/29–23.80; D. R. Baxendale 185–34–636–19–3/42–33.47.

KING EDWARD VII SCHOOL, LYTHAM

Played 19: Won 9, Lost 4, Drawn 6. Abandoned 1

Master i/c: A. M. Weston

The side developed well to achieve a record nine wins. They were admirably captained by D. J. Tomlinson, who made a major all-round contribution with 623 runs and 46 wickets. Two young batsmen, J. A. Kok and M. R. Moore, showed promise with the bat.

Wins v: QEGS, Blackburn; Burnley Habergham; King William's, IOM; Stockport GS; St Mary's, Crosby; Lidunians; Kirkham; Latymer Upper; Woodbridge.

Batting—*D. J. Tomlinson 19–2–623–75*–0–36.64; J. A. Kok 8–1–246–94–0–35.14; M. R. Moore 19–0–538–63–0–28.31; R. J. Macauley 17–1–300–55–0–18.75; R. B. Postlethwaite 17–4–195–46–0–15.00.

Bowling—C. J. Scott 68.1–12–225–17–6/17–13.23; D. J. Tomlinson 241–55–730–46–5/24–15.86; R. J. Thomas 158.1–19–647–28–6/64–23.10.

KING EDWARD'S SCHOOL, BIRMINGHAM

Played 24: Won 13, Lost 3, Drawn 8. Abandoned 2

Master i/c: M. D. Stead — Cricket professional: J. Huband

Anurag Singh and Mark Wagh both passed 800 runs, with four and two centuries respectively. They both played for Warwickshire Second XI, Wagh also played for NAYC and England Under-18, and Singh represented MCC Schools, NCA Young Cricketers and the Development of Excellence XI.

Wins v: King Edward's, Stourbridge; Denstone; King Henry VIII, Coventry; Solihull; Shrewsbury; Warwick; King's, Worcester; Loughborough GS; Malvern; Wolverhampton GS; Kestrels; King Edward's, Aston; XL Club.

Batting—M. A. Wagh 16–6–831–111*–2–83.10; *A. Singh 14–3–875–146*–4–79.54; T. Robinson 22–5–670–101*–1–39.41; A. P. Blaikley 20–2–545–69–0–30.27; A. R. Chitre 16–4–288–58*–0–24.00; M. S. Kazi 15–5–189–75–0–18.90; S. K. Mallela 11–1–175–40–0–17.50.

Bowling—A. P. Blaikley 74–13–250–17–5/8–14.70; M. A. Wagh 249.5–52–824–35–5/20–23.54; S. Y. Khan 173.4–21–629–24–3/17–26.20; A. Singh 114.1–23–408–15–6/26–27.20; M. C. J. Royle 144–21–588–20–4/13–29.40; M. S. Kazi 125–14–539–16–5/43–33.68.

KING HENRY VIII SCHOOL, COVENTRY

Played 16: Won 5, Lost 3, Drawn 8. Abandoned 1

Master i/c: A. M. Parker

Wins v: King Edward's, Stourbridge; Old Swinford Hospital S.; Bablake; XL Club; King Edward's, Aston.

Batting—*J. D. Ham 15–3–567–84–0–47.25; T. A. Oldham 16–3–383–69*–0–29.46; A. Senghera 11–3–228–74*–0–28.50; R. Blundell 15–3–312–64*–0–26.00; S. White 11–4–167–51*–0–23.85; K. Knights 13–0–156–50–0–12.00.

Bowling—K. Knights 122–32–395–25–7/31–15.80; R. Blundell 120.5–27–384–23–4/34–16.69; R. Quinn 113–23–340–16–4/25–21.25.

KING'S COLLEGE, TAUNTON

Played 15: Won 3, Lost 4, Drawn 8. Abandoned 1

Master i/c: R. J. R. Yeates Cricket professional: D. Breakwell

With many players making a contribution, it was a promising season – especially for N. R. Boulton, who is expected to be in the XI for another four years.

Wins v: Wellington; Monmouth; Blundell's.

Batting—C. J. D. Ross 7–3–171–66–0–42.75; A. T. Dart 14–0–575–94–0–41.07; N. R. Boulton 14–0–552–144–1–39.42; B. W. Hiles 11–1–324–73–0–32.40; S. H. Diment 12–2–272–49–0–27.20; P. J. R. Chappell 12–4–193–60–0–24.12; *M. J. Wrout 13–1–279–60–0–23.25.

Bowling—S. H. Diment 234–44–723–33–6/32–21.90; T. W. J. Farley 123.5–21–426–18–6/33–23.66; D. J. Bostock 117–27–388–16–5/31–24.25.

KING'S COLLEGE SCHOOL, WIMBLEDON

Played 22: Won 16, Lost 3, Drawn 3. Abandoned 1

Master i/c: G. C. McGinn Cricket professional: L. J. Moody

It was another outstanding year, in which 16 of 22 matches were won, nine consecutively. David Gorrod led by example with both bat and ball and scored his maiden century to secure victory over Elizabeth College, Guernsey. The season culminated in a successful tour to Antigua and St Lucia, where four of six matches were won, including that against Antigua Under-19.

Wins v: Wimbledon CC; Tiffin; Sutton HS; Kingston GS; Archbishop Tennison; UCS Hampstead; Strode C.; KCS Old Boys; King's, Canterbury; City of London; Surrey YC; Elizabeth C., Guernsey; Antigua U-19; Antigua Schools U-18; Clendon GS, St Lucia; St Lucia Northern Schools.

Batting—*D. E. Gorrod 22–2–724–111*–1–36.20; P. J. D. Redwood 22–3–669–127*–1–35.21; R. Sleigh 22–1–666–98*–0–31.71; S. A. L. Pervez 19–6–351–55*–0–27.00; L. A. Whitaker 15–2–292–75*–0–22.46; O. B. Gobat 16–4–269–50*–0–22.41.

Bowling—S. M. Sheikh 116.1–18–372–26–6/29–14.30; M. J. M. Costello 212–39–689–47–4/20–14.65; D. E. Gorrod 203.5–36–593–37–4/19–16.02; O. B. Gobat 152.4–23–484–30–5/34–16.13.

KING'S SCHOOL, BRUTON

Played 12: Won 5, Lost 3, Drawn 4. Abandoned 4

Master i/c: P. Platts-Martin Cricket professional: N. J. Lockhart

Highlights were the eight-wicket win over Sherborne and the fine all-round performances of Oliver Fowlston, who shared with James Rooke in a third-wicket stand of 221 in 27.3 overs against Monkton Combe.

Wins v: MCC; Headmaster's XI; Sherborne; Old Boys; Downside.

Batting—*O. R. Fowlston 12–2–570–123–2–57.00; J. E. K. Rooke 12–3–297–102*–1–33.00; J. A. Weir 12–1–313–61–0–28.45; C. B. Higgins 10–1–161–48–0–17.88.

Bowling—O. R. Fowlston 141.1–40–421–25–6/45–16.84; J. P. Thomas 142.3–30–387–20–4/47–19.35.

THE KING'S SCHOOL, CANTERBURY

Played 11: Won 2, Lost 2, Drawn 7. Abandoned 3

Master i/c: A. W. Dyer Cricket professional: A. G. E. Ealham

The match against the Band of Brothers was a particularly memorable one for Chris North, a colt: batting at No. 4, he scored 96 and then took seven for 39 with his leg-spin.

Wins v: Dover C.; Sutton Valence.

Batting—Q. Wiseman 9–2–264–68*–0–37.71; J. W. Lewis-Jones 10–1–317–97–0–35.22; C. M. North 9–0–248–96–0–27.55.

Bowling—C. M. North 105.2–17–367–23–7/39–15.95; A. R. Wilson 144.1–34–425–22–4/25–19.31.

THE KING'S SCHOOL, CHESTER

Played 18: Won 10, Lost 5, Drawn 3. Abandoned 1

Master i/c: K. H. Mellor

Wins v: Sandbach; Oswestry; St David's; Wolverhampton GS; Coleraine; XL Club; MCC; Liverpool C.; Aldenham; OKS.

Batting—R. J. Falconer 17–5–692–96–0–57.66; P. R. T. Brotherhood 16–2–386–96*–0–27.57; D. E. Atkin 15–4–302–79*–0–27.45; S. J. McCormick 14–1–254–60*–0–19.53; C. J. Evans 17–0–317–78–0–18.64; K. J. Ollier 17–1–298–63–0–18.62; I. D. Tatt 14–4–186–54*–0–18.60.

Bowling—D. E. Atkin 183–62–451–40–7/29–11.27; B. K. Smith 107–22–374–23–5/33–16.26; A. J. Douglas 150–39–460–24–3/9–19.16; J. N. A. Cornelius 160–30–555–23–4/24–24.13.

THE KING'S SCHOOL, ELY

Played 17: Won 5, Lost 2, Drawn 10. Abandoned 3

Masters i/c: C. J. Limb and W. S. Marshall Cricket professional: T. G. A. Morley

Undefeated by schools, the side retained the Cambridgeshire Schools Under-19 Cup.

Wins v: King Edward VII HS, King's Lynn; Newport FGS; King's, Peterborough; Wisbech GS; Enzymes.

Batting—M. C. Parker 14–3–505–94–0–45.90; C. W. Kisby 14–3–260–56*–0–23.63; I. P. N. Haigh 14–2–209–36–0–17.41; C. D. Marshall 15–1–241–39–0–17.21; D. J. Nye 15–0–228–38–0–15.20; D. J. Parker 12–1–162–49*–0–14.72.

Bowling—C. W. Kisby 61.5–7–223–18–4/10–12.38; D. J. Parker 103.5–17–301–24–5/45–12.54; M. C. Parker 113–24–343–17–4/40–20.17.

THE KING'S SCHOOL, MACCLESFIELD

Played 22: Won 7, Lost 4, Drawn 11

Master i/c: D. M. Harbord Cricket professional: S. Moores

An inexperienced side did well to record seven victories, five of which were achieved when batting second. Opening batsmen Andrew Bones and Stephen Mitchell put on 203 against Arnold School and 228 against King's, Chester, who were beaten by ten wickets. Bones and his brother Robin, the captain, both passed 500 runs.

Wins v: Bury GS; Arnold; King's, Chester; Staff XI; Newcastle-Under-Lyme; Hull U.; Brighton.

Batting—A. S. Bones 19–2–686–129*–1–40.35; *R. J. Bones 19–5–564–73*–0–40.28; S. D. Gatie 13–3–332–108*–1–33.20; S. R. Mitchell 19–3–471–126*–1–29.43; M. J. Patterson 11–3–163–33*–0–20.37; J. Farshchi 15–2–227–42–0–17.46.

Bowling—P. M. Daniels 207–39–693–26–4/42–26.65; J. Farshchi 194–24–890–31–4/22–28.70; N. M. Mason 172–19–686–23–3/26–29.82; A. J. Wheeler 149–28–511–17–5/60–30.05.

KING'S SCHOOL, WORCESTER

Played 22: Won 8, Lost 6, Drawn 8. Abandoned 1

Master i/c: D. P. Iddon

Tom Bawden bowled genuinely fast on occasions, his 44 wickets taking his tally for four years in the XI to 130.

Wins v: Dean Close; Monmouth; RGS, Worcester; Worcestershire CCC Club and Ground; XL Club; Victoria C.; Reigate; Victoriana XI.

Batting—A. Fiaz 22–3–834–101*–1–43.89; L. R. Chivers 14–3–396–80–0–36.00; C. W. Gough 22–1–555–135–1–26.42; E. M. Oliver 12–2–255–39*–0–25.50; S. R. Thomas 12–2–211–52*–0–21.10; *T. P. Bawden 16–3–255–85–0–19.61; T. A. Morris 20–0–277–51–0–13.85.

Bowling—T. P. Bawden 242.4–52–769–44–7/48–17.47; C. W. Gough 106.2–21–434–22–4/23–19.72; M. Rowan 174.3–34–570–20–4/29–28.50.

KING WILLIAM'S COLLEGE

Played 11: Won 2, Lost 4, Drawn 5

Master i/c: A. Maree Cricket professional: D. Mark

Wins v: St Ambrose; Aldenham.

Batting—G. White 11–2–529–114–2–58.77.

Bowling—G. White 100–32–258–23–7/38–11.21.

KINGSTON GRAMMAR SCHOOL

Played 15: Won 3, Lost 7, Drawn 5. Abandoned 4

Master i/c: J. A. Royce Cricket professional: C. Mutucumarawa

Wins v: Sutton GS; Teddington CC; Hampton Wick Royal CC.

Batting—C. W. Ross 11–0–293–65–0–26.63; D. J. S. Roberts 14–1–334–112–1–25.69; *C. J. Lipscomb 14–2–274–65–0–22.83; L. D. Garrard 11–1–155–63*–0–15.50; S. Lyon 14–1–177–60–0–13.61.

Bowling—P. W. Anderson 113.5–1–516–18–6/52–28.66; S. Lyon 135.4–15–525–18–6/65–29.16.

LANGLEY PARK SCHOOL

Played 9: Won 3, Lost 3, Drawn 3

Master i/c: C. H. Williams

Wins v: Royal Russell; St Columba; Maidstone GS.

Batting—*J. Evans 9–3–370–121*–1–61.66; G. Butler 7–1–168–39–0–28.00; G. Smith 8–0–166–87–0–20.75.

Bowling—D. Montefusco 71.2–12–207–15–6/34–13.80.

LATYMER UPPER SCHOOL

Played 18: Won 2, Lost 5, Drawn 11. Abandoned 1

Master i/c: G. W. L. Bearman Cricket professional: K. L. Mayers

Wins v: Lord Williams's; New South Wales U-18 Select XI.

Batting—M. H. Pryor 18–2–550–97–0–34.37; *L. G. Buchanan 18–3–276–49*–0–18.40; J. E. Woolard 17–3–237–53*–0–16.92; J. D. Hall 16–0–210–36–0–13.12; J. C. Hedges 14–1–163–52–0–12.53; A. Thein 18–0–185–50–0–10.27.

Bowling—M. H. Pryor 169–39–385–29–4/20–13.27.

LEEDS GRAMMAR SCHOOL

Played 14: Won 2, Lost 1, Drawn 11. Abandoned 1

Master i/c: R. Hill

Although they were undefeated by schools, the team's bowling was not penetrative enough to force victory from promising positions.

Wins v: Pocklington; Past XI.

Batting—J. S. Wood 15–1–507–102*–1–36.21; O. T. Robertson 13–1–408–83–0–34.00; T. C. N. Golby 13–5–261–85–0–32.62; D. L. Peters 9–0–156–34–0–17.33; M. N. Richmond 13–0–225–61–0–17.30; B. Patel 12–0–185–52–0–15.41; P. J. Miller 12–2–150–30–0–15.00.

Bowling—D. P. Butler 124–5–427–21–5/55–20.33; B. Williams 137–26–383–17–3/25–22.52; *T. E. Limbert 171–31–610–25–4/42–24.40.

LEIGHTON PARK SCHOOL

Played 7: Won 3, Lost 1, Drawn 3. Abandoned 3

Master i/c: M. J. Morris

Characterised by enthusiasm and competitiveness, the side were well led by Dan Paton in an enjoyable and successful season. Tom Rose was a fine prospect and with Nick Torry against Bearwood put on 166 for the first wicket, which is believed to be a school record.

Wins v: Reading Blue Coats; Michael Beer's XI; Old Leightonians.

Batting—T. W. M. Rose 6–1–275–95*–0–55.00; N. J. Torry 7–1–190–100*–1–31.66.

Bowling—*D. T. Paton 98.3–13–359–15–4/48–23.93.

LLANDOVERY COLLEGE

Played 11: Won 4, Lost 3, Drawn 4

Master i/c: T. G. Marks

The all-rounder Shaun Howells was ably supported in both departments by Edward Evans, who bowled accurately and batted aggressively. A highlight was the 119-run win over Ruthin, in which Howells made a half-century and took five wickets.

Wins v: Dyfed Schools U-15; Llandovery CC; Ruthin; Gowerton President's XI.

Batting—S. C. Howells 8–3–294–75*–0–58.80; E. Evans 8–3–224–66*–0–44.80; R. T. Davies 11–2–254–54*–0–28.22; *G. A. Watts 8–1–183–46*–0–26.14.

Bowling—E. Evans 83–14–213–22–6/46–9.68; S. C. Howells 90–25–241–20–6/34–12.05.

LORD WANDSWORTH COLLEGE

Played 14: Won 4, Lost 2, Drawn 8. Abandoned 3

Master i/c: M. C. Russell

In a season featuring a fine team performance, the captain, David Thomas, led by example to dominate the averages. A highlight was his 121 against Reed's, when he reached his century from 58 balls. Mark Palmer was an excellent spinner and against St Bartholomew's, Newbury, took a hat-trick, all stumped by stand-in wicket-keeper Colin Walker – a feat achieved only once in first-class cricket, by W. H. Brain off C. L. Townsend in 1893. Walker, in his first season, proved to be a talented batsman, while with the ball Richard Morgan was an effective foil to Thomas, swinging the ball and finding edges.

Wins v: 12 Star, Brussels; Shiplake; KES, Witley; Reed's.

Batting—*D. M. Thomas 13–4–598–121–2–66.44; J. M. Palmer 10–3–233–52*–0–33.28; C. J. Walker 12–4–228–60*–0–28.50; S. J. Butler 12–2–254–65–0–25.40; D. I. Holman 10–2–154–45*–0–19.25.

Bowling—D. M. Thomas 154.2–47–344–31–5/20–11.09; J. M. Palmer 89.4–16–410–26–5/12–15.76; R. A. G. R. Morgan 129.4–21–489–22–6/15–22.22.

LORD WILLIAMS'S SCHOOL

Played 12: Won 2, Lost 4, Drawn 6

Master i/c: J. E. Fulkes

A young side gained useful experience. Daniel Bennett's 102 not out against Magdalen College School was the XI's first century for three years.

Wins v: Rycotewood C.; Royal Latin S.

Batting—D. Bennett 10–1–236–102*–1–26.22; S. Whittam 11–3–188–48*–0–23.50.

Bowling—A. Lewis 98.1–17–346–20–4/31–17.30; S. Whittam 78–6–392–15–4/26–26.13.

LORETTO SCHOOL

Played 18: Won 6, Lost 6, Drawn 6. Abandoned 2

Master i/c: R. P. Whait

Wins v: Strathallan; Kelvinside Acad.; Fettes; Ardingly; Scottish Wayfarers; Old Lorettonians.

Batting—A. G. Shaw 14–5–428–86–0–47.55; R. A. G. Grant 17–1–385–60*–0–24.06; *R. S. F. Steenberg 16–4–279–56–0–23.25; A. G. Fleming-Brown 13–0–293–66–0–22.53.

Bowling—A. G. Shaw 223.4–42–553–36–7/28–15.36; R. A. G. Grant 89.3–7–306–18–7/55–17.00; S. J. Murray 125.4–31–329–15–4/47–21.93; P. J. Middlemiss 133–27–498–18–4/34–27.66.

LOUGHBOROUGH GRAMMAR SCHOOL

Played 17: Won 5, Lost 2, Drawn 10. Abandoned 3

Master i/c: J. S. Weitzel

Two days after beating MCC with a total of 268 for eight – their second-highest to win a match batting second – the side compiled a record total of 296 for three, batting first against the Old Boys. Left-arm spinner Michael Davies played for English Schools and MCC Schools.

Wins v: Bablake; RGS, Worcester; Warwick; Antipodeans, New South Wales; MCC.

Batting—D. P. Reddyhough 11–3–327–92–0–40.87; R. G. H. Widdowson 17–3–560–107*–1–40.00; J. F. C. Young 16–1–503–109–2–33.53; R. A. J. Parkin 16–2–430–99–0–30.71; M. K. Davies 14–2–285–70–0–23.75; A. Fenn 9–2–155–53–0–22.14.

Bowling—M. K. Davies 216–48–632–34–5/49–18.58; M. J. Simpson 136–23–564–20–4/24–28.20.

MAGDALEN COLLEGE SCHOOL

Played 18: Won 5, Lost 1, Drawn 12. Abandoned 4

Master i/c: P. Askew

Wins v: RGS, High Wycombe; King Edward VI, Southampton; South Oxfordshire Amateurs; Pocklington; Chigwell.

Batting—*W. W. Hopkin 17–2–457–83*–0–30.46; P. J. Denning 16–4–343–64–0–28.58; A. J. Stiff 18–3–428–78–0–28.53; S. M. Ison 16–0–425–102–1–26.56; A. Booth 16–3–330–48–0–25.38; S. R. Sharpe 19–3–382–57–0–23.87; D. D. Harris 15–2–178–39–0–13.69.

Bowling—S. R. Sharpe 119–16–449–22–5/21–20.40; B. Bradshaw 110–20–350–17–5/38–20.58; N. J. Carlsen 150–29–510–21–5/40–24.28; A. Booth 221–21–976–35–6/53–27.88.

MALVERN COLLEGE

Played 7: Won 3, Lost 1, Drawn 3. Abandoned 4

Master i/c: A. J. Murtagh Cricket professional: R. W. Tolchard

The wicket-keeper was Dan Walker, son of the Glamorgan and England all-rounder, P. M. Walker.

Wins v: Warwick; Monmouth; Exeter.

Batting—*J. Robbins 17–5–519–100*–1–43.25; J. Morgan 15–2–392–87–0–30.15; G. Franklin 14–2–313–85–0–26.08; S. Varney 14–3–283–53–0–25.72; S. Peachey 13–0–278–50–0–21.38; J. Horton 15–0–313–58–0–20.86.

Bowling—S. Peachey 110–25–311–17–5/36–18.29; W. Gilroy 136–26–435–21–4/35–20.71; G. Franklin 170–35–555–20–6/44–27.75.

MANCHESTER GRAMMAR SCHOOL

Played 22: Won 6, Lost 4, Drawn 12

Master i/c: D. Moss

Despite suffering surprisingly little interference from the weather, the experienced XI had a less successful season than had been expected. They began with the school's first overseas tour to Barbados in December and finished with an equally enjoyable end-of-term international festival at Tonbridge School. The batting was again strong, with seven batsmen scoring fifties and two centuries each from Lee Marland and Mark Chilton. Robert Salisbury's unorthodox style produced some quick middle-order runs and Stephen Hall took over as Marland's opening partner after Scott Richardson was injured. The emergence of left-arm seamer John O'Loughlin added to the options in that department, but the spin attack was less impressive. Marland went on to play for NAYC and Lancashire and Nottinghamshire Second XIs.

Wins v: Bolton S.; Liverpool C.; King Edward VII, Lytham; St Ambrose; Pocklington; Worksop C.

Batting—M. J. Chilton 19–5–824–107*–2–58.85; *L. J. Marland 18–4–776–122–2–55.42; S. A. Richardson 11–2–387–98*–0–43.00; R. J. Salisbury 15–7–334–71–0–41.75; S. R. Hall 12–0–287–65–0–23.91; P. D. Knott 19–3–328–57–0–20.50; D. S. Marks 16–4–233–45–0–19.41.

Bowling—J. A. O'Loughlin 157–41–436–26–5/11–16.76; C. W. Fogg 111.5–26–328–17–3/22–19.29; D. S. Marks 89.4–18–324–16–4/4–20.25; R. M. Bipul 125.1–28–357–17–3/30–21.00; M. J. Chilton 171.1–36–521–23–3/14–22.65; L. J. Marland 181–42–566–21–3/20–26.95.

MARLBOROUGH COLLEGE

Played 12: Won 2, Lost 2, Drawn 8. Abandoned 4

Master i/c: R. B. Pick Cricket professional: R. M. Ratcliffe

More than half the scheduled matches were affected by the weather, with no match completed in May. A highlight was a century off 73 balls against Rugby by Lee Ratcliffe, son of R. M. Ratcliffe of Lancashire, who showed exceptional form with both bat and ball and was selected for England Under-17. Tom and Seth Holmes were the first brothers since 1968 to appear together in the XI.

Wins v: Romany; XL Club.

Batting—L. J. Ratcliffe 13–2–650–133*–4–59.09; G. Murgai 11–2–323–91–0–35.88; U. B. Singh 10–3–216–118*–1–30.85; A. M. Wade 10–1–242–105*–1–26.88; *C. A. Gough 9–0–168–79–0–18.66.

Bowling—L. J. Ratcliffe 175.4–42–422–23–5/37–18.34; G. Murgai 68–9–281–15–5/12–18.73.

MERCHANT TAYLORS' SCHOOL, CROSBY

Played 18: Won 4, Lost 1, Drawn 13. Abandoned 1

Master i/c: Rev. D. A. Smith Cricket professional: G. Dros

It was a season of post-war records for the side, whose top five batsmen all scored more than 300 runs for the first time since 1932. The opening partnership of 209 against St Mary's, Crosby, between Guy Edwards (129) and Matthew Wilson (76 not out) beat all existing records for any wicket. There were three other century partnerships, the total of four being the most since 1933. Edwards went on to make three more centuries in succession (all unbeaten), which was almost certainly a first for the school. He hit 101 not out against the XL Club, 105 not out against Scotch College, Melbourne, and 100 not out against Hulme GS. The bowling was headed by Philip Janson in his last year with the XI.

Wins v: Liverpool C.; Northern Nomads; XL Club; Hulme GS.

Batting—*G. A. Edwards 16-4-630-129-4-52.50; N. C. Delaney 14-3-410-70-0-37.27; T. M. Wilson 17-5-334-76*-0-27.83; G. R. Ball 14-3-304-69-0-27.63; S. B. Howard 16-2-380-72*-0-27.14.

Bowling—P. H. Janson 163-45-448-34-6/29-13.17; N. C. Delaney 144-40-371-20-3/27-18.55.

MERCHANT TAYLORS' SCHOOL, NORTHWOOD

Played 21: Won 9, Lost 1, Drawn 11. Abandoned 2

Master i/c: W. M. B. Ritchie Cricket professional: H. C. Latchman

Unbeaten by schools, the young XI lost only to MCC and won nine matches. Two players were outstanding: opening bat Daniel Grundy scored nearly twice as many runs as the next batsman, while the lively medium pace of Paul Harris brought him 43 wickets, more than twice as many as anyone else. Others showed promise, including Amritt Latchman, a left-handed batsman and leg-spin bowler, who is the son of H. C. Latchman of Middlesex and Nottinghamshire. A tour to Malaysia was planned for 1995.

Wins v: Latymer Upper; St John's C., Oxford; Highgate; Felsted; Dulwich; Berkhamsted; Westminster; Loretto; Ardingly.

Batting—D. J. Grundy 18-4-793-114*-2-56.64; E. N. Lamb 9-4-229-48*-0-45.80; P. D. C. Wise 10-2-320-62-0-40.00; P. V. Harris 15-6-337-86*-0-37.44; A. C. Thorpe 18-5-411-80-0-31.61; A. Latchman 13-3-267-67-0-26.70; *P. Parekh 20-2-276-90-0-15.33.

Bowling—P. V. Harris 204-49-521-43-7/26-12.11; A. Latchman 125.4-29-358-21-4/16-17.04; N. P. Sapra 131-39-334-18-4/27-18.55.

MERCHISTON CASTLE SCHOOL

Played 16: Won 8, Lost 6, Drawn 2

Master i/c: C. W. Swan

Wins v: Dollar Acad.; Merchistonians; Dundee HS; Strathallan; RGS, Newcastle; Edinburgh Acad.; Fettes; South District U-16.

Batting—A. J. Scott 15-5-440-90*-0-44.00; J. N. Mackley 15-3-366-76*-0-30.50; G. F. A. Milligan 11-4-173-52*-0-24.71; D. B. Finlay 11-0-254-64-0-23.09; G. M. English 14-1-277-52*-0-21.30; C. M. R. Tulloch 14-2-219-69-0-18.25.

Bowling—E. J. W. Weston 67-16-182-16-6/20-11.37; A. P. Paterson 161-39-383-32-5/14-11.96; G. F. A. Milligan 142-37-376-23-4/19-16.34; E. J. Mackie 166-49-426-22-5/22-19.36; J. G. D. Gordon 109-18-346-15-3/26-23.06.

MILL HILL SCHOOL

Played 17: Won 6, Lost 4, Drawn 7

Master i/c: S. T. Plummer Cricket professional: I. J. F. Hutchinson

Wins v: Millers CC; Queen Elizabeth, Barnet; Old Millhillians; UCS, Hampstead; Queen's, Taunton; Enfield GS.

Batting—J. L. Goldberg 17–3–488–90–0–34.85; D. L. Goodwin 18–1–565–113*–2–33.23; S. A. Selwood 15–3–382–95–0–31.83; T. P. Russell 10–1–166–44–0–18.44; S. Sandhu 12–0–189–27–0–15.75.

Bowling—A. M. Akram 143–34–411–30–8/28–13.70; S. A. Selwood 86–19–286–18–5/38–15.88; R. J. Peach 99–22–332–17–7/35–19.52; L. J. Baldwin 157–23–570–21–4/41–27.14.

MILLFIELD SCHOOL

Played 13: Won 7, Lost 1, Drawn 5. Abandoned 2

Master i/c: A. D. Curtis Cricket professional: G. C. Wilson

A winter tour to Sri Lanka preceded a successful season. Paul Mitchell, who has represented Young Zimbabwe, scored three centuries and played for English Schools and MCC Schools, as did Dean Cosker, who also played for Somerset Second XI. Left-arm spinner Ben McCorkill took the most wickets, passing 40 for the second season, and played for England Under-17, while Kevin Barrett and the wicket-keeper, Richard Evans, represented Welsh Schools.

Wins v: Exeter U.; King's, Taunton; Downside; Free Foresters; Monmouth; XL Club; Gloucester CCC II.

Batting—*P. M. Mitchell 16–3–686–124*–3–52.76; L. Sutton 16–3–605–177*–1–46.53; J. P. Hart 13–4–398–65*–0–44.22; K. A. O. Barrett 16–4–378–50*–0–31.50; T. D. Martin 10–1–196–61–0–21.77.

Bowling—D. A. Cosker 217.5–69–559–34–4/24–16.44; B. M. McCorkill 272.1–76–786–41–5/10–19.17; J. P. Hart 166.4–29–558–16–4/32–34.87.

MILTON ABBEY SCHOOL

Played 8: Won 5, Lost 2, Drawn 1. Abandoned 1

Master i/c: P. W. Wood

Wins v: Poole GS; XL Club; Agrarians; Allhallows; P. Salmon's XI.

Batting—*N. K. G. Tomlin 8–0–192–50–0–24.00; F. Gibson 8–1–151–48–0–21.57.

Bowling—J. N. Butler 102.3–24–249–26–5/15–9.57; G. Fox 69.3–13–238–18–5/40–13.22.

MONMOUTH SCHOOL

Played 19: Won 3, Lost 8, Drawn 8. Abandoned 3

Master i/c: D. H. Messenger Cricket professional: G. I. Burgess

A hitherto undistinguished season blossomed at the Winchester Festival, where a record total of 315 for seven inflicted on Kimbolton their only defeat of the season. The foundation of this innings was an opening partnership of 166 between Jonathan Hughes (93) and the captain, Huw Sullivan (66). Hughes, the wicket-keeper, took his tally of victims in two seasons to 59 and opening bowler Paul Davies completed five years in the XI with 99 wickets to his name. His opening partner, Ben Morgan, played for England Under-17.

Wins v: Gloucester Gypsies; Kimbolton; Winchester.

Batting—J. T. Goodwin 18–3–546–76–0–36.40; J. N. Hern 18–3–535–84–0–35.66; M. M. Brogan 11–0–338–83–0–30.72; J. A. Hughes 18–0–498–93–0–27.66; I. J. Plumley 14–4–243–43–0–24.30; *H. R. Sullivan 12–1–166–66–0–15.09.

Bowling—B. M. Morgan 179.3–44–512–21–4/44–24.38; P. W. Davies 146–25–442–18–3/11–24.55; I. J. Plumley 137.2–28–505–18–4/32–28.05.

NEWCASTLE-UNDER-LYME SCHOOL

Played 16: Won 5, Lost 5, Drawn 6. Abandoned 1

Master i/c: S. A. Robson Cricket professional: T. Fielding

A young side had a mixed season in which they lost a record five times. However, the batting of P. D. A. Turner was a revelation and his spectacular contributions were a major factor in the five victories. Against Tettenhall College, he scored 108 not out and with A. D. Sims (25 not out) put on a record 114 unbroken for the seventh wicket. In beating Wolverhampton GS he scored 82 of the last 129 runs off the final 11 overs and his 113 not out against Mount St Mary's included eight sixes and 12 fours, his second fifty coming from just 11 scoring strokes. Although the bowling was sometimes wayward, the catching was reliable.

Wins v: Bishop Vesey's GS; Tettenhall C.; Wolverhampton GS; Mount St Mary's; Sandbach S.

Batting—P. D. A. Turner 15–5–627–113*–2–62.70; *R. J. Pointon 12–2–241–60*–0–24.10.

Bowling—J. R. Voce 108–27–326–16–5/14–20.37; C. D. Moss 159–27–610–18–6/36–33.88.

NOTTINGHAM HIGH SCHOOL

Played 16: Won 2, Lost 3, Drawn 11. Abandoned 1

Master i/c: J. Lamb Cricket professional: K. Poole

Highlights were the batting of David Smit – brother of the England women's wicket-keeper – who scored nearly twice as many runs as the next batsman, and a maiden century by 14-year-old Andrew Hunt, who averaged 100.50 in his five innings.

Wins v: Bishop Vesey's GS; Forest Amateurs.

Batting—A. J. Hunt 5–3–201–115*–1–100.50; *D. Smit 13–2–633–157*–2–57.54; J. L. Rayner 12–4–319–56–0–39.87; M. A. Fletcher 9–5–152–45*–0–38.00; P. M. Dunn 11–0–292–100–1–26.54; C. J. Freeston 12–2–258–51–0–25.80; T. W. B. Coupe 12–1–239–61–0–21.72.

Bowling—A. R. Carden 141.5–32–406–26–6/21–15.61.

OAKHAM SCHOOL

Played 18: Won 6, Lost 0, Drawn 11, Tied 1

Master i/c: J. Wills Cricket professional: D. S. Steele

Unbeaten, and victorious in a third of their matches, Oakham owed much to the captain, James Bull, who headed the averages. He ended his career in the XI with 2,224 runs and 84 wickets, while Cristian Durant, who continued to excel behind the stumps, set a new career record of 73 dismissals.

Wins v: Worksop; Bromsgrove; Stamford; Ratcliffe; Lincolnshire Gentlemen; MCC.

Batting—*J. J. Bull 16–2–699–101*–1–49.92; R. A. E. Martin 12–3–319–67–0–35.44; C. D. Durant 13–4–287–76*–0–31.88; A. M. James 12–6–181–37*–0–30.16; S. H. Greenwood 11–0–311–58–0–28.27; M. R. K. Bailey 13–1–256–52–0–21.33.

Bowling—J. J. Bull 170.3–46–427–30–7/53–14.23; A. M. James 202.1–48–549–38–6/39–14.44; O. J. C. Marshall 141–38–404–16–4/27–25.25.

THE ORATORY SCHOOL

Played 16: Won 9, Lost 1, Drawn 6. Abandoned 4

Master i/c: P. L. Tomlinson Cricket professional: J. B. K. Howell

Playing positive cricket, the XI won nine matches and were only a wicket away from victory in three of the draws. James Tomlinson was an excellent captain, while his younger brother, Steven, headed the averages with 564 runs and 35 wickets.

Wins v: Pangbourne; Headmaster's Invitation XI; Reading; Leighton Park; Cokethorpe; RGS, High Wycombe; South Oxfordshire Amateurs; XL Club; Berkshire Gentlemen.

Batting—S. C. B. Tomlinson 13–5–564–85*–0–70.50; *J. P. S. Tomlinson 10–2–386–68*–0–48.25; J. P. C. Stebbings 13–3–352–100–1–35.20; J. A. D. Urquhart 10–3–194–55–0–27.71; D. H. Orchard 12–1–157–42–0–14.27.

Bowling—S. C. B. Tomlinson 146.2–42–364–35–6/12–10.40; T. G. Limburn 95–13–323–22–4/31–14.68; D. H. Orchard 84–15–282–18–4/25–15.66.

OUNDLE SCHOOL

Played 18: Won 11, Lost 2, Drawn 5. Abandoned 2

Master i/c: J. R. Wake Cricket professional: T. Howorth

Sound all-round contributions and an excellent team spirit brought 11 victories, which equalled the record set the previous year, although the wet May meant that fewer matches were played in 1994. Especially satisfying were the wins over strong South African representative sides and the Antipodeans in the annual International Cricket Festival. The side's willingness to risk defeat in pursuit of victory led to several thrilling run-chases ending positively in the final over. James Samworth scored the most runs and headed the batting averages, while Christo Daniels topped the bowling averages. The most wickets, however, fell to Harry Preston, who received the George Gilroy Memorial Cup, presented in memory of the previous season's leading bowler, who tragically died in Australia earlier in the year.

Wins v: Repton; MCC; Free Foresters; Wellingborough; Gresham's; St Edward's; XL Club; Oundle Rovers; Antipodeans, New South Wales; Andrew Rabie, Eastern Province; Paarl, Western Province.

Batting—J. P. Samworth 14–2–592–123*–2–49.33; J. D. Pilch 11–6–193–59*–0–38.60; *A. M. Macleod-Smith 13–1–376–94*–0–31.33; C. R. Wilson 14–0–338–109–1–24.14; J. C. Thomas 13–3–241–50*–0–24.10; E. P. Reynolds 16–0–377–80–0–23.56; B. J. Colbeck 12–2–208–57–0–20.80; B. B. Briggs 13–3–206–39–0–20.60.

Bowling—C. G. M. Daniels 136.5–33–394–23–6/26–17.13; T. J. Rayden 97–30–312–17–5/19–18.35; H. C. Preston 212.1–53–484–26–4/54–18.61; B. J. Colbeck 146.5–29–488–18–4/88–27.11.

THE PERSE SCHOOL

Played 16: Won 4, Lost 4, Drawn 8. Abandoned 1

Master i/c: A. C. Porter Cricket professional: D. C. Collard

Wins v: Chigwell; Royal Hospital S.; Old Perseans; Hills Road SFC.

Batting—A. P. Gibson 14–3–402–86*–0–36.54; *T. J. Sheppard 16–1–464–94–0–30.93; E. R. Walker 16–0–424–72–0–26.50; P. Horsley 15–0–350–72–0–23.33; P. Siddle 14–2–254–42–0–21.16.

Bowling—J. Mayer 181.2–32–563–39–5/52–14.43; B. H. Brooks 101.2–14–332–16–5/56–20.75.

PLYMOUTH COLLEGE

Played 14: Won 3, Lost 6, Drawn 5. Abandoned 5

Master i/c: T. J. Stevens

Wins v: Philanthropists; Plymouth CC; XL Club.

Batting—J. Fabian 13–4–536–106–2–59.55; *E. James 11–2–232–93*–0–25.77; J. Conaghan 14–3–282–86*–0–25.63; R. Moist 10–0–227–84–0–22.70; T. Holme 12–0–157–58–0–13.08.

Bowling—E. James 122.1–34–387–19–5/31–20.36; P. Trinder 86.3–9–391–18–5/49–21.72; G. Brooks 95–12–411–17–4/44–24.17.

POCKLINGTON SCHOOL

Played 25: Won 5, Lost 8, Drawn 12

Master i/c: D. Nuttall

A young side developed excitingly under the challenging captaincy of Daniel Clappison. He and his opening partner, Robert Milne, both passed 500 runs, but the most prolific batsman was Matthew Stacey with 886. Two spinners, Jon Burrans and Gavin Stewart, bore the brunt of the bowling, sending down 531 overs between them and sharing 80 wickets.

Wins v: Ampleforth; Sedbergh; Chigwell; Wellingborough; Londesborough Park.

Batting—M. B. Stacey 18–2–886–137–2–55.37; G. J. T. Stewart 14–5–251–95*–0–27.88; P. R. Mouncey 17–3–390–118–1–27.85; R. S. Milne 23–1–528–77–0–24.00; *D. Clappison 23–1–506–87*–0–23.00; C. R. Wood 18–1–387–81–0–22.76; G. Johnson 17–5–163–39*–0–13.58.

Bowling—G. J. T. Stewart 217–29–785–35–5/37–22.42; J. R. Burrans 314–45–1,130–45–5/85–25.11.

PORTSMOUTH GRAMMAR SCHOOL

Played 12: Won 2, Lost 5, Drawn 5. Abandoned 3

Master i/c: G. D. Payne Cricket professional: R. J. Parks

Wins v: King Edward VI, Southampton; MCC.

Batting—S. A. Hamilton 6–1–167–53*–0–33.40; J. C. E. Moon 11–2–260–59–0–28.88; J. F. Gannon 11–0–306–79–0–27.81; *J. S. Greer 10–0–235–79–0–23.50; R. Burgess 9–1–178–63–0–22.25.

Bowling—M. W. Haines 89–20–262–16–3/21–16.37; J. R. Scott 110–23–269–15–3/20–17.93; M. Bulbeck 120.5–24–411–19–5/36–21.63.

PRIOR PARK COLLEGE

Played 13: Won 2, Lost 4, Drawn 7. Abandoned 3

Master i/c: D. R. Holland

Frustrated by the weather, the side felt they had not fulfilled their potential. Highlights were the six-wicket win at Downside and a maiden century against the XL Club by 15-year-old Tony Atkins.

Wins v: Wells Cathedral S.; Downside.

Batting—A. Atkins 13–2–340–122–1–30.90; L. Dokic 10–1–236–63–0–26.22; *I. Okoli 13–0–308–97–0–23.69; S. Yang 12–2–229–43–0–22.90; B. Brodie 12–1–246–52–0–22.36.

Bowling—L. Dokic 108–19–384–25–5/51–15.36.

QUEEN ELIZABETH GRAMMAR SCHOOL, WAKEFIELD

Played 12: Won 8, Lost 0, Drawn 4. Abandoned 3

Master i/c: T. Barker

Undefeated, the XI won a record eight of their 12 matches.

Wins v: MCC; Bradford GS; Woodhouse Grove; RGS, Lancaster; William Hulme GS; Ashville; Ermysteds GS; Old Boys XI.

Batting—A. M. R. Birkby 11–4–494–116*–1–70.57; G. R. J. Dawson 11–2–454–153–1–50.44; D. J. Bousfield 8–2–171–60*–0–28.50; R. M. Wade 9–2–190–49–0–27.14; G. A. Daniels 12–0–211–40–0–17.58.

Bowling—R. A. Hughes 141.2–28–454–27–6/9–16.81; G. A. Daniels 96–15–363–19–3/34–19.10.

QUEEN ELIZABETH'S HOSPITAL

Played 12: Won 4, Lost 4, Drawn 4

Masters i/c: M. S. E. Broadley and P. J. Kirby

As the more experienced players led by example, some of the younger players made their mark and showed much promise. The fielding was of a particularly high standard.

Wins v: Bristol Cathedral S.; West Buckland S.; Queen's, Taunton; Hutton GS.

Batting—I. K. Ross 11–1–316–109*–1–31.60; N. Varshney 10–1–260–91–0–28.88; *N. C. Abbott 11–3–188–37–0–23.50.

Bowling—N. Patel 79–14–291–22–5/40–13.22; J. M. Buck 87.1–12–298–16–4/10–18.62; A. P. Morris 107.5–20–331–15–4/18–22.06.

QUEEN'S COLLEGE, TAUNTON

Played 13: Won 2, Lost 5, Drawn 6

Master i/c: J. W. Davies

An inability to defend substantial totals was a major factor in the five defeats. The season finished on a high note, when a fine century from the captain, Graham Lewis, helped to bring victory over Taunton.

Wins v: Wycliffe; Taunton S.

Batting—*G. Lewis 10–1–369–109–1–41.00; H. Bowden 12–1–357–67–0–32.45; T. Hobden 9–0–217–97–0–24.11; G. Stotesbury 12–1–255–74–0–23.18; P. Burke 13–2–219–74*–0–19.90.

Bowling—G. Lewis 108–15–389–21–5/35–18.52; P. Burke 101–17–408–17–5/19–24.00; S. Pratt 153–26–582–18–5/68–32.33.

RADLEY COLLEGE

Played 14: Won 5, Lost 1, Drawn 8. Abandoned 4

Master i/c: W. J. Wesson Cricket professionals: A. G. Robinson and A. R. Wagner

Robin Martin-Jenkins was the leading all-rounder, heading both averages and going on to play for English Schools, MCC Schools and Sussex Second XI. He featured in two significant second-wicket partnerships, scoring 105 not out when he and the left-handed Andrew Strauss (91) put on 185 against Bradfield, and making 139 when adding 189 against Shrewsbury with the under-19 polo international, Malcolm Borwick (60). Ben Hutton, another left-hander and son of Richard and grandson of Sir Leonard, was a regular in the side, while 15-year-old Charlie Pragnell was a promising leg-spinner.

Wins v: Marlborough; Winchester; Eton; Shrewsbury; W. J. Wesson's XI.

Batting—*R. S. C. Martin-Jenkins 13–3–620–139–3–62.00; M. R. Bellhouse 13–7–371–73*–0–61.83; A. J. Strauss 14–1–575–91*–0–44.23; M. P. Borwick 12–1–291–60–0–26.45; B. L. Hutton 14–0–352–62–0–25.14.

Bowling—R. S. C. Martin-Jenkins 171–51–416–32–4/31–13.00; C. W. G. Goldsmith 146.3–34–353–24–4/38–14.70; C. E. Pragnell 87–16–286–15–3/38–19.06.

RATCLIFFE COLLEGE

Played 9: Won 1, Lost 2, Drawn 6. Abandoned 3

Master i/c: R. M. Hughes

Win v: Emeriti CC.

Batting—I. Usman 7–0–233–72–0–33.28; *E. W. Davies 9–2–169–65*–0–24.14.

Bowling—J. Peris 110.3–8–478–17–4/92–28.11.

READING SCHOOL

Played 13: Won 6, Lost 6, Drawn 1. Abandoned 1

Master i/c: S. A. Stevenson

Wins v: Lord Williams's; Douai; Shiplake; Forest; Bearwood; Old Readingensians.

Batting—D. J. Airey 11–4–331–80–0–47.28; S. D. Patel 10–2–254–81–0–31.75; R. B. Boot 9–1–234–87–0–29.25; T. Ahmed 11–1–179–48*–0–17.90; J. D. Martin 13–1–208–42*–0–17.33.

Bowling—S. D. Patel 152.4–46–432–28–5/30–15.42; R. Pilkington 112–27–312–18–4/7–17.33; S. J. Leitch 131–17–459–26–4/49–17.65.

REED'S SCHOOL

Played 10: Won 1, Lost 5, Drawn 4

Master i/c: G. D. Adeney

A young and inexperienced side showed real resolve and were rewarded with victory over a strong Tiffin side, successfully chasing 194 runs in 50 minutes and 20 overs.

Win v: Tiffin.

Batting—R. Hilton 8–1–175–73–0–25.00; A. Klimcke 9–1–198–59*–0–24.75; R. Cook 9–2–151–48–0–21.57; *R. Webster 9–1–155–38–0–19.37; C. Hugall 10–1–159–45–0–17.66.

Bowling—R. Hilton 84.3–4–423–16–3/32–26.43.

REIGATE GRAMMAR SCHOOL

Played 21: Won 3, Lost 10, Drawn 8. Abandoned 3

Master i/c: D. C. R. Jones — Cricket professional: H. Newton

It was another disappointing season, in which no school was beaten and a record ten defeats were suffered. The captain, D. C. Sainsbury, made up for poor bowling form with 513 runs, and on tour in Jersey set a fourth-wicket record of 183 unbroken with the leading bowler, J. J. Hylton, who made 100 not out. Opening batsman R. J. C. Lowe frequently held the fragile batting together and scored a century against the XL Club.

Wins v: XL Club; Common Room XI; Turville CC.

Batting—R. J. C. Lowe 22–0–668–104–1–30.36; *D. C. Sainsbury 19–2–513–79*–0–30.17; J. J. Hylton 16–3–307–100*–1–23.61; S. N. Teasdale 21–1–397–75–0–19.85; D. C. Jackson 11–1–193–43–0–19.30; R. J. Callcut 20–1–296–58–0–15.57; P. W. Sainsbury 14–0–212–43–0–15.14.

Bowling—J. J. Hylton 162.3–30–518–26–4/19–19.92; O. R. Mirza 115–19–422–20–5/66–21.10; G. J. M. Watkins 144.2–35–458–15–4/42–30.53; T. A. A. Khan 164–30–523–16–3/19–32.68.

RENDCOMB COLLEGE

Played 16: Won 4, Lost 8, Drawn 4

Master i/c: C. Burden Cricket professional: D. Essenhigh

A highlight was a four-match tour to Barbados.

Wins v: King's, Gloucester; New College, Swindon; Pate's GS; Grantley Adams Memorial S., Barbados.

Batting—C. E. Lawton 12–4–250–54*–0–31.25; *I. Kwelagobe 12–2–228–56–0–22.80; F. G. E. Barton 15–2–280–56–0–21.53; F. B. Ingham 11–3–153–52–0–19.12; C. E. Jarrett 13–1–158–48–0–13.16.

Bowling—I. Kwelagobe 112.4–13–413–27–4/21–15.29; C. E. Lawton 120–16–419–26–6/21–16.11; P. D. Boydell 81.2–6–334–15–5/41–22.26.

REPTON SCHOOL

Played 18: Won 4, Lost 2, Drawn 12

Master i/c: M. Stones Cricket professional: M. K. Kettle

Wins v: Cheltenham; King Edward's, Birmingham; Repton Pilgrims; Friars CC.

Batting—S. A. Twigg 14–2–549–131*–2–45.75; J. G. R. Cook 11–2–316–76–0–35.11; J. F. Sheard 14–0–412–65–0–29.42; N. D. Tomlinson 10–3–191–54*–0–27.28; D. J. O'Gram 12–2–216–77–0–21.60; *J. W. S. Piper 12–2–168–54*–0–16.80.

Bowling—J. R. Webster 136–17–490–22–4/31–22.27; J. F. Sheard 151–24–480–21–4/23–22.85; J. W. S. Piper 175–34–570–23–5/34–24.78.

RICHARD HUISH COLLEGE

Played 7: Won 2, Lost 1, Drawn 4. Abandoned 3

Master i/c: W. J. Maidlow

The weather permitted only seven matches to be played at a time when the future of cricket at the college was under threat. A highlight was an innings of 110 by Steven Jenkins against the Royal Naval College, Dartmouth. Matthew Dimond made his County Championship debut for Somerset in June and was selected for the England Under-19 tour to the West Indies.

Wins v: Exeter S.; Royal Naval College, Dartmouth.

Batting—No player scored 150 runs. The leading batsmen were M. Dimond 4–0–129–56–0–32.25; D. Hewitt 5–0–129–59–0–25.80.

Bowling—No bowler took 15 wickets. The leading bowler was D. Hewitt 60.4–12–180–11–3/38–16.36.

ROSSALL SCHOOL

Played 20: Won 10, Lost 3, Drawn 7

Master i/c: P. Philpott

The successful Rossall side was captained by 16-year-old Liam Botham (son of Ian), who had another outstanding all-round season with 774 runs and 54 wickets with impressive averages. He played for Hampshire Second XI.

Wins v: King Edward's, Lytham; St Bees; RGS, Lancaster; Arnold; Stonyhurst; Sedbergh; King's, Macclesfield; Old Rossallians; Knockturnes Club; Loretto.

Batting—*L. J. Botham 17-6-774-114*-2-70.36; P. C. McKeown 15-2-774-104*-1-59.53; J. E. G. Birch 19-4-596-103*-1-39.73; S. N. C. Roberts 12-2-251-67-0-25.10; B. E. P. Shaw 12-1-215-47-0-19.54; A. J. Greenwood 13-3-170-49-0-17.00; C. M. Hill 18-1-249-47*-0-14.64.

Bowling—L. J. Botham 230-74-540-54-6/36-10.00; C. L. Simpson 166-50-415-31-4/42-13.38; M. J. Dewhurst 119-27-394-20-6/30-19.70; O. D. J. Wadsworth 178-55-472-15-3/43-31.46.

THE ROYAL GRAMMAR SCHOOL, GUILDFORD

Played 15: Won 8, Lost 3, Drawn 4. Abandoned 2

Master i/c: S. B. R. Shore

In the best season for some years, the batting was dominated by Ben Fraser, whose three hundreds in a sequence of eight innings were a school record. The all-round bowling was excellent and the fielding improved as a strong team spirit developed.

Wins v: Portsmouth; Emanuel; Wallington; Reed's; Eltham; Kingston GS; RGS, Colchester; RGS, High Wycombe.

Batting—B. J. Fraser 14-1-595-114-3-45.76; R. C. Kitzinger 14-0-276-50-0-19.71; T. W. Grafton 15-3-220-60*-0-18.33; G. E. Newman 11-0-176-45-0-16.00; *D. J. Honey 15-2-185-37-0-14.23.

Bowling—T. W. Grafton 103.2-15-371-26-4/18-14.26; B. R. Morgan 86.2-16-261-17-4/25-15.35; B. J. Fraser 85.3-13-326-18-6/52-18.11; R. J. Kitzinger 164.1-41-489-26-3/21-18.80; D. J. Honey 150.4-31-473-18-4/65-26.27.

THE ROYAL GRAMMAR SCHOOL, NEWCASTLE

Played 18: Won 9, Lost 5, Drawn 4

Master i/c: D. W. Smith

Wins v: RGS, Worcester; RGS, Guildford; QEGS, Hexham; King's, Tynemouth (twice); Ashington; Penrith; Barnard Castle; Yarm School.

Batting—B. A. Jones-Lee 18-3-548-85*-0-36.53; C. E. G. Ryan 15-3-327-55*-0-27.25; I. B. Park 15-2-243-71*-0-18.69; *M. J. Smalley 14-0-201-44-0-14.35; S. M. Stoker 14-1-168-49-0-12.92; C. P. Mordue 15-2-162-45-0-12.46.

Bowling—M. J. Smalley 182.5-53-381-33-6/15-11.54; C. E. G. Ryan 211-49-532-46-6/52-11.56; J. C. Dresser 100-19-305-19-4/13-16.05.

THE ROYAL GRAMMAR SCHOOL, WORCESTER

Played 23: Won 7, Lost 6, Drawn 10. Abandoned 1

Master i/c: B. M. Rees Cricket professional: M. J. Horton

Following the departure of ten of the previous season's successful side, the school had an ordinary season. B. C. M. Taylor took 40 wickets and won the *Daily Telegraph* Midlands bowling award, while E. Sellwood looked a promising off-spinner.

Wins v: Rendcomb; Old Swinford Hospital; XL Club; Bromsgrove; RGS, Guildford; RGS, High Wycombe; RGS, Colchester.

Batting—N. C. Fletcher 22–0–732–98–0–33.27; *M. R. G. Prudham 23–1–679–132*–1–30.86; J. C. W. Young 19–0–568–93–0–29.89; D. T. Fidoe 21–4–460–73–0–27.05; J. E. K. Schofield 6–0–150–78–0–25.00; R. A. Brookes 16–5–228–38–0–20.72; M. J. Sellek 16–3–252–46*–0–19.38; E. Sellwood 17–1–271–47–0–16.93; R. D. Davies 15–3–167–30*–0–13.91.

Bowling—B. C. M. Taylor 227.1–51–768–40–5/36–19.20; E. Sellwood 263.4–75–619–31–7/73–19.96; M. J. Sellek 210.2–44–599–28–6/24–21.39.

RUGBY SCHOOL

Played 15: Won 4, Lost 3, Drawn 8. Abandoned 1

Master i/c: K. Siviter Cricket professional: W. J. Stewart

Wins v: Oundle; Stowe; Malvern; Old Rugbeians.

Batting—E. J. Lowe 15–4–733–113*–3–66.63; *C. J. C. Robards 14–2–577–108–1–48.08; J. A. Roper 13–4–326–64*–0–36.22; S. J. T. Parry 13–2–345–79–0–31.36; J. D. B. Lloyd 15–0–289–58–0–19.26; M. J. Howe 12–2–188–43*–0–18.80.

Bowling—J. A. Froome 158.2–40–545–22–3/18–24.77; M. J. Howe 159–25–673–25–5/57–26.92.

RYDAL SCHOOL

Played 13: Won 3, Lost 3, Drawn 7

Master i/c: M. T. Leach Cricket professional: R. W. C. Pitman

Matthew Bennett, who captained the school at both cricket and rugby, was the leading all-rounder in a young side. A bonus was the contribution of Sam Scrutton, who came to the sixth form from St David's, Llandudno.

Wins v: St David's; Old Rydalians; Ellesmere.

Batting—S. Scrutton 10–3–298–78*–0–42.57; *M. H. Bennett 13–2–426–73–0–38.72; H. G. Williams 9–2–161–66*–0–23.00; D. S. Hanlon 10–0–181–50–0–18.10.

Bowling—J. W. B. Martin 181–44–487–33–6/14–14.75; M. H. Bennett 141.4–32–320–18–3/15–17.77.

ST DUNSTAN'S COLLEGE

Played 12: Won 3, Lost 3, Drawn 6. Abandoned 2

Master i/c: O. T. Price Cricket professional: G. S. Clinton

A hard-working young side were coached during the season by former England wicket-keeper Bob Taylor and the England bowler, Angus Fraser. Joe Jacoby played the side's only three-figure innings in the high-scoring draw with Sevenoaks and Chris Beales was an adventurous captain.

Wins v: Colfe's; Bancroft's; XL Club.

Batting—J. E. M. Jacoby 14–4–484–114–1–48.40; L. Speed 14–1–346–78–0–26.61; N. V. Kirby 13–2–203–51*–0–18.45; *C. J. Beales 12–0–150–26–0–12.50.

Bowling—D. K. Farley 83–18–260–15–3/31–17.33; J. C. Welch 73.3–9–292–16–4/39–18.25.

ST EDWARD'S SCHOOL, OXFORD

Played 12: Won 7, Lost 1, Drawn 4. Abandoned 2

Master i/c: D. Drake-Brockman Cricket professional: G. V. Palmer

The season was the most successful since the war, equalling that of the 1943 XI in which John Woodcock played. Oliver Slipper's batting average of 111.60 was the best since 1928; his 558 runs in ten innings featured five unbeaten fifties, including 100 not out against Eton and 107 not out against Abingdon. He went on to play for Surrey Second XI. The accurate seam attack of Nicholas Prior, John Blythe and Nicholas Obolensky was well supported in the field.

Wins v: Cryptics; RGS, High Wycombe; Eton; MCC; St Edward's Martyrs; Abingdon; Cheltenham.

Batting—*O. M. Slipper 10–5–558–107*–2–111.60; R. P. Matthews 7–1–174–84–0–29.00; G. S. Peddy 9–2–193–47*–0–27.57; A. S. Peebles 9–3–157–68*–0–26.16.

Bowling—J. N. St J. Blythe 106–33–229–17–4/23–13.47; N. G. L. Prior 173–52–428–26–5/40–16.46; N. Obolensky 138.3–32–327–17–5/36–19.23.

ST GEORGE'S COLLEGE, WEYBRIDGE

Played 12: Won 3, Lost 1, Drawn 8. Abandoned 2

Master i/c: D. G. Ottley

Giles Henderson, who headed the bowling averages, took nine for 45 against Kingston GS.

Wins v: Hampton; Tiffin; Kingston GS.

Batting—*N. Hoyle 11–1–376–77–0–37.60; A. Watts 11–1–332–108*–1–33.20; P. Alston 10–2–242–100–1–30.25; C. Fletcher 11–2–242–57–0–26.88; L. Fernando 9–2–154–52*–0–22.00; G. Henderson 12–0–261–70–0–21.75; J. Stephens 10–1–152–33–0–16.88.

Bowling—G. Henderson 157.2–54–476–30–9/45–15.86; C. Fletcher 109.4–26–341–16–5/19–21.31; N. Hoyle 171.5–46–542–22–5/48–24.63.

ST JOHN'S SCHOOL, LEATHERHEAD

Played 11: Won 2, Lost 3, Drawn 6. Abandoned 3

Master i/c: A. B. Gale Cricket professional: E. Shepperd

A highlight in an unspectacular year was Simon Speller's hat-trick against Cranleigh, although it did not save the school from defeat.

Wins v: Reigate GS; Headmaster's XI.

Batting—H. F. Keeys 10–3–183–70*–0–26.14; R. B. Vosser 10–1–210–77*–0–23.33; *S. J. Speller 10–0–173–52–0–17.30; T. E. Goodyer 10–0–150–49–0–15.00.

Bowling—C. D. Griffith 92–19–305–17–5/21–17.94; S. J. Speller 95–16–299–15–4/53–19.93; P. D. Tyler 119.5–26–386–17–3/7–22.70.

ST JOSEPH'S COLLEGE, IPSWICH

Played 18: Won 7, Lost 4, Drawn 7

Master i/c: A. C. Rutherford Cricket professional: J. Pugh

Aaron Brown's school record of 738 runs included 109 off 33 deliveries against Browns CC.

Wins v: Gentlemen of Suffolk; Essex U.; Ipswich & East Suffolk CC; Colchester SFC; East Bergholt; Royal Hospital S.; Browns CC.

Batting—*A. Brown 17–1–738–127–3–46.12; E. Manning 16–2–553–72–0–39.50; P. King 14–3–369–82–0–33.54; J. Townrow 18–1–388–78–0–22.82; D. Potter 10–1–172–62–0–19.11.

Bowling—C. Jack 110.2–13–414–25–5/46–16.56; A. Brown 152.4–23–512–30–4/28–17.06; P. King 84–19–285–16–5/24–17.81; J. Townrow 104.5–11–369–20–7/55–18.45; J. Payne 123.2–18–447–22–4/32–20.31.

ST LAWRENCE COLLEGE, RAMSGATE

Played 13: Won 8, Lost 1, Drawn 4. Abandoned 3

Master i/c: N. O. S. Jones Cricket professional: A. P. E. Knott

A young side, who fielded particularly well, enjoyed a successful season under the captaincy of the Kent Under-16 wicket-keeper, Benedict Swindells, and gained confidence from the coaching of Alan Knott. Their last match, against Gravesend GS, was particularly memorable: Nick Sproule, a leg-spinner who also headed the batting averages, took a hat-trick and Kevin Thickitt, who took the most wickets as well as scoring the most runs, made 137 not out.

Wins v: Sir Roger Manwood's; Chatham House; St Augustine's; King's, Rochester; Harbledown CC; Old Lawrentians; Harvey GS; Gravesend GS.

Batting—N. P. Sproule 10–6–189–57*–0–47.25; *B. C. Swindells 11–2–348–103*–1–38.66; K. Thickitt 11–1–352–137*–1–35.20; G. A. P. Grinsted 8–2–205–50*–0–34.16; A. J. Boaler 11–2–270–60*–0–30.00.

Bowling—K. Thickitt 124.3–34–327–26–6/58–12.57; R. A. Hicks 84.1–17–250–17–5/28–14.70; N. P. Sproule 77.1–9–302–19–6/35–15.89.

ST PAUL'S SCHOOL

Played 14: Won 5, Lost 2, Drawn 7. Abandoned 2

Master i/c: G. Hughes Cricket professional: M. Heath

Wins v: Lords and Commons; Highgate; The Masters; Fettes; The Leys.

Batting—F. A. Badat 13–4–653–145*–2–72.55; *T. B. Peters 12–5–487–100*–1–69.57; A. J. Baldock 13–0–474–88–0–36.46; J. F. A. Poulet 13–1–372–100*–1–31.00; D. S. Hyman 10–1–159–60–0–17.66.

Bowling—T. B. Peters 178.2–47–447–24–4/40–18.62; J. Sherjan 175–60–491–23–3/3–21.34; J. S. Grant 117.2–26–361–16–4/14–22.56.

ST PETER'S SCHOOL, YORK

Played 21: Won 4, Lost 0, Drawn 17

Master i/c: D. Kirby Cricket professional: K. F. Mohan

The unbeaten side drew as many as 17 matches, although many were close and exciting. Their strength lay in the depth of batting and excellent fielding, while the bowlers struggled on the easy home batting pitches. However, the varied attack persevered and Nick Ogden collected 35 wickets to set alongside his 433 runs.

Wins v: Loretto; Rossall; Yarra Valley HS, Melbourne; XL Club.

Batting—T. J. Archer 21–5–523–81*–0–32.68; A. L. T. Kay 17–2–469–79–0–31.26; N. J. Ogden 20–4–433–92–0–27.06; M. S. Bradley 19–1–485–78–0–26.94; P. C. Taylor 16–2–307–96–0–21.92; *T. W. F. Cockcroft 15–0–325–74–0–21.66.

Bowling—M. S. Bradley 199.1–53–512–23–3/24–22.26; N. J. Ogden 221.3–38–790–35–5/52–22.57; P. T. Batty 157.3–35–403–16–4/39–25.18.

SEDBERGH SCHOOL

Played 14: Won 2, Lost 4, Drawn 8. Abandoned 2

Master i/c: N. A. Rollings Cricket professional: T. Hunte

The batting of James Edington was a highlight in an otherwise unremarkable season. His aggregate of 828 runs was a school record, as were his four centuries, which took his tally to seven in his three years.

Wins v: Woodridge College, South Africa; N. A. Rollings's XI.

Batting—J. M. Edington 16–4–828–137*–4–69.00; B. J. D. Heap 12–2–342–82–0–34.20; *T. C. M. Barraclough 10–3–184–58*–0–26.28; D. C. Croft 15–2–325–75*–0–25.00; P. J. Jameson 12–1–227–105*–1–20.63.

Bowling—M. A. Biker 114–17–344–17–3/43–20.23; M. W. Farnsworth 135–38–373–17–5/45–21.94.

SEVENOAKS SCHOOL

Played 15: Won 4, Lost 3, Drawn 8. Abandoned 4

Master i/c: I. J. B. Walker Cricket professional: C. J. Tavaré

Wins v: MCC; Woodhouse Grove; Skinners'; Knockholt CC.

Batting—*W. J. House 11–1–518–121*–2–51.80; A. D. M. Wright 13–0–369–81–0–28.38; N. Shirreff 12–4–215–94*–0–26.87; T. M. Briggs 12–3–233–65–0–25.88; N. J. P. Reason 9–1–157–32–0–19.62.

Bowling—M. Abbas Khan 43.5–10–149–17–5/20–8.76; W. J. House 100–35–226–15–4/5–15.06.

SHEBBEAR COLLEGE

Played 16: Won 7, Lost 3, Drawn 6

Master i/c: A. Bryan

Chris Knapman's return of eight for four against Grenville College was a highlight for the XI, who lost only to Cranbrook in schools matches.

Wins v: Blundell's Second XI; Exeter S.; Gravesend GS (twice); Grenville C.; Old Shebbeareans; Linton Park.

Batting—*P. Lockyer 14–2–532–82–0–44.33; M. Rayson 11–5–174–31*–0–29.00; M. Heal 14–4–269–61–0–26.90; C. Knapman 14–3–211–50–0–19.18; W. Coates 14–3–181–39–0–16.45; J. Armstrong 15–3–164–40*–0–13.66.

Bowling—C. Knapman 176–63–379–34–8/4–11.14; P. Lockyer 112–29–292–17–4/17–17.17; W. Coates 79–12–296–16–5/36–18.50.

SHERBORNE SCHOOL

Played 11: Won 4, Lost 5, Drawn 2. Abandoned 2

Master i/c: M. D. Nurton Cricket professional: A. Willows

Wins v: Haileybury; Blundell's; Clifton; Sherborne Town.

Batting—W. G. Hargrove 12–3–251–58*–0–27.88; T. J. Percival 13–1–314–62–0–26.16; N. P. C. Hyde 12–0–289–50–0–24.08; J. N. Butler 12–1–228–50–0–20.72; E. A. Bellew 12–2–184–78–0–18.40.

Bowling—A. D. Nurton 153.1–40–391–20–6/14–19.55; N. P. C. Hyde 116.5–31–321–16–5/29–20.06; P. C. H. Harvey 88–13–340–15–5/54–22.66; B. T. Bishop 149.1–30–428–18–3/26–23.77.

SHREWSBURY SCHOOL

Played 18: Won 3, Lost 4, Drawn 11

Master i/c: S. M. Holroyd Cricket professionals: A. P. Pridgeon and P. H. Bromley

Wins v: Eton; Old Swinford Hospital; Ellesmere.

Batting—S. W. K. Ellis 18–3–782–114*–2–52.13; I. J. W. McCarter 16–1–526–93–0–35.06; I. S. Dhariwal 13–6–178–24–0–25.42; N. J. B. Green 16–3–310–76–0–23.84; J. D. W. Cox 17–1–358–63–0–22.37; C. J. Clarke 19–2–336–100–1–19.76; D. J. Umpleby 15–5–182–38–0–18.20; M. A. Randall 12–1–152–24–0–13.81.

Bowling—J. P. Elcock 211–27–735–30–6/77–24.50; I. J. W. McCarter 180–15–633–25–6/27–25.32; S. W. K. Ellis 244–43–731–26–4/36–28.11; I. S. Dhariwal 184–29–654–15–3/38–43.60.

SIMON LANGTON GRAMMAR SCHOOL

Played 18: Won 12, Lost 3, Drawn 3

Master i/c: R. H. Green

It was another successful season, in which the side won the Kent Schools Under-19 League again and were runners-up in the Lemon Cup.

Wins v: Gravesend GS; Chatham GS; Rochester Maths; Norton Knatchbull; Chatham House; Borden GS; Judd; Dartford GS; Chislehurst & Sidcup GS; Old Langtonians; Simon Langton Staff; Eltham C.

Batting—D. Mathews 15–2–485–150*–1–37.30; *B. Ralph 14–4–301–68*–0–30.10; E. Roberts 17–1–471–82–0–29.43; S. Tophill 8–2–162–39*–0–27.00; R. White 14–2–247–53–0–20.58; R. Marsh 11–1–171–62–0–17.10; S. Fletcher 15–1–236–60–0–16.85.

Bowling—R. Marsh 144.3–28–425–39–5/18–10.89; S. Tophill 79–19–230–20–7/29–11.50; M. Bridger 142.4–28–454–27–5/31–16.81.

SOLIHULL SCHOOL

Played 21: Won 8, Lost 5, Drawn 8

Master i/c: D. J. Dunn Cricket professional: S. P. Perryman

The opening partnership of 232 between G. R. Weston (81) and S. J. Legg (134 not out) against Newcastle HS was a record for the school, who won the Warwickshire Under-19 Cup.

Wins v: Wolverhampton GS; King Edward's, Aston; Solihull SFC; Joseph Chamberlain C.; King's, Worcester; Newcastle HS; Aylesbury GS; North Warwickshire C.

Batting—*S. J. Legg 16–5–837–159*–3–76.09; C. R. Briggs 17–1–514–83–0–32.12; W. L. Speer 16–2–345–56–0–24.64; E. J. Dawes 12–3–208–46–0–23.11; G. R. Weston 16–2–318–81–0–22.71; T. E. Whitelock 15–6–152–52–0–16.88; N. J. Mortimer 14–2–155–53–0–12.91.

Bowling—A. G. Levenger 228–48–744–50–8/50–14.88; J. M. Legg 185–45–567–29–5/10–19.55; W. L. Speer 145–22–523–23–3/18–22.73.

SOUTH CRAVEN SCHOOL

Played 8: Won 4, Lost 1, Drawn 2, Tied 1. Abandoned 2

Master i/c: D. M. Birks

In their best season to date, which included a first fixture with MCC, the side won half of their eight matches. They owed much to Mark Chapman, whose aggregate was a school record and included the first century for the XI.

Wins v: Ermysted's GS; Batley GS; Army Apprentices (Harrogate); Scarborough SFC.

Batting—M. Chapman 8–2–334–109*–1–55.66; N. Spragg 8–0–289–93–0–36.12.

Bowling—No bowler took 15 wickets. The leading bowlers were M. Chapman and A. Emmott, who took nine each.

STAMFORD SCHOOL

Played 11: Won 3, Lost 3, Drawn 5. Abandoned 5

Master i/c: P. D. McKeown

Wins v: Queen Elizabeth HS, Gainsborough; XL Club; Staff XI.

Batting—D. C. Woolf 7–3–173–35–0–43.25; L. H. Jackson 13–1–388–128–1–32.33; S. E. G. Fuller 14–4–312–56*–0–31.20; R. J. H. Thorley 9–2–154–66*–0–22.00; S. A. P. Todd 11–1–216–58*–0–21.60; T. E. Smith 14–0–207–45–0–14.78.

Bowling—No bowler took 15 wickets. The leading bowler was L. H. Jackson 101–13–427–14–4/26–30.50.

STOCKPORT GRAMMAR SCHOOL

Played 11: Won 2, Lost 3, Drawn 6. Abandoned 1

Master i/c: S. Teasdale Cricket professional: D. J. Makinson

Wins v: King's, Chester; Arnold.

Batting—T. W. Clarke 11–2–388–97–0–43.11; N. D. Hayes 8–0–242–108–1–30.25; N. S. Thompson 11–1–237–63*–0–23.70; B. Wren 9–1–150–54*–0–18.75.

Bowling—C. Pimlott 70.2–9–205–20–4/15–10.25; N. S. Thompson 116–17–360–28–8/51–12.85.

STOWE SCHOOL

Played 11: Won 1, Lost 5, Drawn 5. Abandoned 1

Master i/c: M. J. Harris

Win v: Free Foresters.

Batting—P. R. Denning 9–0–369–108–1–41.00; M. M. G. Smith 5–1–160–103–1–40.00; P. A. McSweeney 10–1–305–73*–0–33.88; G. I. Smith-Walker 8–1–165–102–1–23.57; A. Carling 11–1–223–74*–0–22.30; S. N. R. Gerard 11–1–186–62–0–18.60.

Bowling—E. J. Rogers 102–22–438–16–3/26–27.37.

STRATHALLAN SCHOOL

Played 15: Won 5, Lost 2, Drawn 8. Abandoned 1

Master i/c: R. J. W. Proctor

With reliable openers in Duncan Forbes and the Scotland Under-19 representative, Dougal Fergusson, the batting had a sound basis and the young side was bowled out only once. Their own attack often struggled, although at the end of the season an effective opening partnership emerged, supported by three spinners.

Wins v: Lomond S.; Dollar Acad.; Scottish Wayfarers; West District Under-19; Perth Northern.

Batting—D. G. O. Fergusson 14–2–570–86–0–47.50; D. G. Forbes 12–0–362–63–0–30.16; R. J. D. Barr 10–2–207–55–0–25.87; G. J. McKendry 10–3–174–35–0–24.85; *A. Jeffery 12–3–182–29–0–20.22; B. S. Ward 12–2–201–41*–0–20.10.

Bowling—A. J. Y. Duncan 57.4–14–182–16–5/54–11.37; P. J. Watson 187.3–45–522–27–7/60–19.33; D. R. G. Elder 108–12–358–16–4/50–22.37.

TAUNTON SCHOOL

Played 11: Won 1, Lost 4, Drawn 6. Abandoned 2

Master i/c: D. Baty Cricket professional: A. Kennedy

Win v: King's, Bruton.

Batting—T. M. Phillips 10–0–249–72–0–24.90; T. J. Bradnock 8–0–181–41–0–22.62; R. H. Wickes 10–0–164–60–0–16.40.

Bowling—J. Ord 161.5–37–453–25–6/63–18.12; T. M. Phillips 124.3–26–383–19–4/21–20.15.

TIFFIN SCHOOL

Played 17: Won 5, Lost 8, Drawn 4. Abandoned 1

Master i/c: M. J. Williams

Wins v: St Benedict's; Reigate; Old Tiffinians; Elizabeth C., Guernsey; John Fisher.

Batting—R. C. Ward 16–2–553–121*–2–39.50; B. W. O'Connell 7–1–186–79*–0–31.00; A. D. Nutt 16–3–400–71*–0–30.76; S. M. Pashley 15–0–321–49–0–21.40; *O. W. Burley 13–2–228–55–0–20.72; M. C. Anstey 13–0–183–65–0–14.07.

Bowling—M. E. Bennett 195–40–627–21–7/44–29.85; M. J. Hooke 136.5–13–578–19–5/68–30.42.

TONBRIDGE SCHOOL

Played 17: Won 12, Lost 0, Drawn 5. Abandoned 2

Master i/c: P. B. Taylor Cricket professional: C. Stone

Undefeated, the XI won 12 of the 14 matches completed, mostly by large margins. The opening batsmen, Christopher Walsh and Edward Smith, scored two centuries apiece as they averaged 92.30 and 90 respectively, both of which surpassed the previous record. Averaging 93.10 as a partnership, they shared five century stands. Walsh, with 105 not out, and Christopher Charlton (109*) put on 222 unbroken for the second wicket against the Band of Brothers. The season ended with six consecutive victories in two festivals, including the International Schools Festival, with teams from Australia and South Africa, which the school hosted. The last fixture of the season, a tight three-wicket win over Maritzburg College from Natal, was a particularly fine match.

Wins v: Tonbridge CC; Lancing; Free Foresters; Band of Brothers; Wellington C.; Eton; Clifton; Eastbourne; Felsted; Manchester GS; West Torrens, Adelaide; Maritzburg C., Natal.

Batting—C. D. Walsh 15-5-923-126*-2-92.30; E. T. Smith 11-3-720-150*-2-90.00; C. S. Charlton 13-5-423-109*-1-52.87; *J. A. Ford 13-4-406-124-1-45.11; W. M. Fyfe 7-1-209-59-0-34.83.

Bowling—W. M. Fyfe 156.3-26-471-36-6/42-13.08; T. J. Rice-Oxley 132.1-33-336-23-5/12-14.60; C. S. Charlton 176.5-47-467-29-6/22-16.10; J. A. Ford 110-26-306-15-3/24-20.40.

TRENT COLLEGE

Played 20: Won 5, Lost 2, Drawn 12, Tied 1

Master i/c: T. P. Woods Cricket professional: G. Miller

Noel Gie, son of Clive Gie of Western Province and Natal, compiled a record aggregate of 857.

Wins v: Nottinghamshire U-17; XL Club; Friars; Trinity GS, Melbourne; Headmaster's XI.

Batting—*N. A. Gie 20-5-857-131*-3-57.13; A. M. Lock 19-1-598-76-0-33.22; B. L. Spendlove 13-2-329-80-0-29.90; T. W. Hancock 17-2-397-55*-0-26.46; A. C. Garratt 11-3-187-60-0-23.37; N. J. Brown 14-4-199-54*-0-19.90; M. L. White 10-2-158-40-0-19.75; K. G. Reesby 13-2-183-39-0-16.63.

Bowling—T. W. Hancock 139.3-40-373-23-5/26-16.21; B. S. Morrison 127-26-303-17-5/23-17.82; J. M. Cottrill 133-28-378-20-5/73-18.90; M. L. White 181.5-39-547-24-4/20-22.79; M. J. Hartley 151.5-34-426-18-4/32-23.66.

TRINITY SCHOOL

Played 16: Won 8, Lost 0, Drawn 8. Abandoned 3

Masters i/c: I. W. Cheyne and B. Widger

Unbeaten for the second time in three years, Trinity won half their matches. Joint-captains Richard Nowell and David Dyer again dominated with bat and ball, Nowell becoming the first player to average over 100 with the bat. Nowell's five years in the XI brought him 4,250 runs and 232 wickets, both records, while Dyer left with 2,464 runs and 129 wickets. Nowell joined Surrey on a cricket scholarship and played for the county Second XI, England Under-18 and Development of Excellence XI. A. J. T. Clark opened the bowling with considerable success and, although his batting opportunities were limited, he performed well when required and scored a fine century against MCC. The 208-run victory over King's, Rochester, featured a hundred before lunch by the opening batsman-wicket-keeper Sheran de Silva, a nephew of the Sri Lankan Test batsman, P. A. de Silva. Both he and Clark are expected to return in 1995.

Wins v: King's, Rochester; Wallington CGS; Colfe's; Langley Park; Hampton; Whitgift; Caterham; Old Mid-Whitgiftians.

Batting—*R. W. Nowell 10–3–737–146–2–105.28; *D. O. Dyer 14–3–756–152*–2–68.72; A. J. T. Clark 7–3–273–109–1–68.25; S. N. De Silva 14–1–426–112–1–32.76; D. O. Robinson 10–2–178–67–0–22.25; G. Chuter 11–2–178–80–0–19.77.

Bowling—R. W. Nowell 144.3–52–309–29–6/18–10.65; A. J. T. Clark 179.3–67–384–31–5/38–12.38; D. O. Dyer 184.4–43–606–25–4/79–24.24.

TRURO SCHOOL

Played 11: Won 2, Lost 3, Drawn 6. Abandoned 3

Master i/c: D. M. Phillips

A young XI played with determination against older and more experienced sides. Highlights were a first fixture against MCC and the one-run victory over Bristol GS, which was achieved with a wicket off the last possible ball.

Wins v: Old Boys; Bristol GS.

Batting—R. C. Harmer 10–4–194–63*–0–32.33; T. G. Sharp 10–1–258–70*–0–28.66; A. W. R. Lear 11–0–278–62–0–25.27.

Bowling—C. E. Shreck 102.5–21–267–22–4/3–12.13.

UNIVERSITY COLLEGE SCHOOL

Played 17: Won 4, Lost 5, Drawn 8. Abandoned 1

Master i/c: S. M. Bloomfield Cricket professional: W. G. Jones

Wins v: Aldenham; Barnard Castle; Woodbridge; King Edward VII, Lytham.

Batting—B. J. Marshall 13–3–279–53*–0–27.90; A. J. Renton 12–2–257–41–0–25.70; J. D. Buck 16–3–332–58–0–25.53; S. Lawrence 12–1–235–49–0–21.36; G. M. J. Taylor 10–2–162–45*–0–20.25; J. A. Cymerman 13–2–190–39*–0–17.27; *F. J. Renton 16–0–228–36–0–14.25.

Bowling—A. J. Renton 137.2–36–323–27–5/33–11.96; G. M. J. Taylor 214.5–54–571–32–7/55–17.84; S. Lawrence 193.3–44–571–18–5/24–31.72.

UPPINGHAM SCHOOL

Played 17: Won 4, Lost 4, Drawn 9. Abandoned 2

Master i/c: I. E. W. Sanders Cricket professional: M. R. Hallam

Rain frustrated Ed Hill in his pursuit of 1,000 runs, leaving him stranded two short on 144 not out against Blundell's in the last match. However, he was already 138 ahead of the school record, set the previous season by J. N. Beaumont.

Wins v: Old Uppinghamians; Rugby; Ampleforth; Canford.

Batting—*E. W. R. Hill 17–3–998–144*–3–71.28; S. C. Debenham 9–4–202–74–0–40.40; J. M. T. Hunter 15–2–437–67–0–33.61; B. P. Aspell 17–2–470–70–0–31.33; A. D. J. Dawe 16–0–422–64–0–26.37; N. C. Milbank 15–1–354–63–0–25.28; R. R. J. Buchanan 11–4–175–53*–0–25.00.

Bowling—R. R. J. Buchanan 144.1–27–450–20–5/44–22.50; S. C. Debenham 213.4–38–817–16–5/48–51.06.

VICTORIA COLLEGE, JERSEY

Played 22: Won 10, Lost 3, Drawn 9.

Master i/c: D. A. R. Ferguson

Two players dominated. The captain, Chris Jones, scored 1,019 runs and took 32 wickets, while Stuart Ramskill passed 500 runs and took 47 wickets, which brought his total in five seasons to a school record of 203.

Wins v: Clifton (twice); Sporting CF; Reigate; Sussex O-50; Portsmouth GS; R. E. S. Young's XI; Jersey Island CC; Abbotsholme; Bearwood.

Batting—*C. Jones 20–6–1,019–109*–2–72.78; S. A. Ramskill 17–5–583–99*–0–48.58; C. J. D. O'Brien 20–0–512–46–0–25.60; C. N. A. Gothard 21–0–456–82–0–21.71; R. A. Skilton 20–1–359–79–0–18.89.

Bowling—S. A. Ramskill 236–49–882–47–7/37–18.76; C. Jones 215–53–615–32–7/47–19.21; C. N. A. Gothard 245–52–789–34–5/28–23.20.

WARWICK SCHOOL

Played 14: Won 1, Lost 7, Drawn 6.

Master i/c: D. C. Elstone

Win v: Bablake

Batting—H. Munton 14–2–577–134*–1–48.08; S. Kelley 14–0–298–59–0–21.28; D. Kenny 13–1–210–94–0–17.50; J. Harcourt 13–0–225–64–0–17.30.

Bowling—T. Tyler 110–20–397–15–4/35–26.46; E. Rushton 139.5–22–532–16–2/28–33.25; D. Kenny 163.1–26–685–16–4/63–42.81.

WATFORD GRAMMAR SCHOOL

Played 14: Won 3, Lost 4, Drawn 7. Abandoned 2

Master i/c: W. L. Miller

In a season of rebuilding, cancellations left the side without a match for a month after the first four, and the fifth game brought the unwelcome record of 67 extras conceded. The captain, Ian Mulholland, did well to pull the side together then, and they won two of the last three matches. The promising James Phang, a left-hander, carried his bat in the first match and was unlucky to be out for 97 in his last innings. Once he had sorted out his run-up, Farouk Khan bowled his left-arm deliveries tirelessly and well.

Wins v: Dr Challoner's GS; Enfield GS; RGS, High Wycombe.

Batting—J. C. K. Phang 11–1–284–97–0–28.40; *I. Mulholland 13–2–250–74–0–22.72; M. E. Smith 14–0–306–60–0–21.85; J. E. Forage 12–1–237–49–0–21.54; I. D. Southern 13–2–214–54*–0–19.45.

Bowling—F. Butt 115–26–333–15–5/21–22.20; F. M. Khan 169.2–32–524–20–5/54–26.20.

WELLINGBOROUGH SCHOOL

Played 17: Won 3, Lost 2, Drawn 12. Abandoned 2

Master i/c: M. H. Askham — Cricket professional: J. C. J. Dye

The slow left-arm bowling of 14-year-old Kristopher Saville augured well for the future.

Wins v: Ratcliffe; XL Club; Chigwell.

Batting—K. G. Potter 17–1–550–104*–1–34.37; S. L. Shah 17–2–426–108*–1–28.40; K. P. Wildman 14–2–290–76–0–24.16; A. L. Taylor 12–1–193–48–0–17.54; *J. R. E. Wilson 16–3–176–38–0–13.53.

Bowling—M. J. Banner 123–4–533–25–5/34–21.32; K. G. Potter 144.5–20–462–20–4/47–23.10; K. M. C. Saville 169–23–607–26–5/27–23.34.

WELLINGTON COLLEGE

Played 16: Won 4, Lost 5, Drawn 6, Tied 1. Abandoned 2

Masters i/c: C. M. S. Potter and R. I. H. B. Dyer Cricket professional: P. J. Lewington

A young side learned much and enjoyed their season. Although their off-spinner, Robert Bridge, sent down as many as 157 overs, he was hampered by the wetness of the ball and failed to take 15 wickets.

Wins v: Royal Logistics Corps; Free Foresters; Winchester; Stowe.

Batting—*H. J. Bishop 14–4–329–56*–0–32.90; A. C. Northey 16–2–436–101*–1–31.14; D. C. M. Neville 14–2–321–56–0–26.75; C. P. R. Hodgson 17–3–369–71–0–26.35; E. M. G. Britton 17–0–370–53–0–21.76; J. D. J. Brownrigg 14–1–252–59–0–19.38.

Bowling—R. H. White 102.3–22–350–20–6/49–17.50; H. J. Bishop 167.1–33–414–19–4/20–21.78; C. P. R. Hodgson 157.4–36–488–21–5/82–23.23.

WELLINGTON SCHOOL

Played 17: Won 9, Lost 6, Drawn 2. Abandoned 2

Master i/c: P. M. Pearce

For their record nine wins, the side played positively under the captaincy of Dan McKinnon, an outstanding fielder. A significant contribution was made by Graham Scott, whose 851 runs, three hundreds and average of 60.78 were all school records.

Wins v: Wells Cathedral S.; Mallards; Queen Elizabeth's Hospital; Plymouth C.; Queen's, Taunton; Kelly C.; E. M. Wesson's XI; Broad Clyst CC; Torquay CC.

Batting—G. Scott 17–3–851–135*–3–60.78; R. Cooper 15–2–469–91–0–36.07; A. Fulker 17–3–319–51–0–22.78.

Bowling—A. Fulker 167.5–14–663–43–8/44–15.41; D. Hewitt 163–32–580–20–3/16–29.00; M. Coleman 127–20–509–16–5/59–31.81.

WELLS CATHEDRAL SCHOOL

Played 13: Won 4, Lost 6, Drawn 3. Abandoned 1

Master i/c: M. Stringer

Wins v: Blue School, Wells; Somerset Stragglers; Queen's, Taunton; Old Wellensians.

Batting—J. Pym 14–1–497–88*–0–38.23; J. Stone 14–2–424–106–1–35.33; E. Hoskins 13–1–258–87–0–21.50; R. Bates 11–0–210–81–0–19.09; C. Wheen 11–0–169–44–0–15.36.

Bowling—J. Stone 94.2–16–348–23–5/51–15.13; E. Hay 65.3–6–373–22–4/8–16.95; M. Ferguson 86–8–409–18–6/15–22.72.

WHITGIFT SCHOOL

Played 15: Won 7, Lost 4, Drawn 4. Abandoned 2

Master i/c: P. C. Fladgate

A young side, who achieved positive results in all but four games, gained in confidence throughout the season. The captain, Chris Catling, headed the batting and scored his first century for the school in his last innings. The side's other century came from the all-rounder, Stephen Lampkin, against Reigate, while the most successful bowler was an off-spinner, Gareth Tucker. The under-15 player, James Furner, made a promising start in the XI.

Wins v: Honesti; Christ's Hospital; St George's, Weybridge; Reigate; OWA; Randburg HS, South Africa; Domini.

Batting—J. P. Furner 6-2-198-47*-0-49.50; *C. E. Catling 13-3-493-106*-1-49.30; S. P. O. Lampkin 9-1-308-120-1-38.50; G. K. Spring 12-3-177-58-0-19.66; A. W. J. Middleton 14-1-196-66-0-15.07.

Bowling—G. A. J. Tucker 153.5-45-394-28-4/14-14.07; A. A. Chmielowski 131-30-349-19-4/53-18.36; G. K. Spring 171.4-55-432-23-6/13-18.78; S. P. O. Lampkin 113-24-312-16-4/15-19.50.

WINCHESTER COLLEGE

Played 18: Won 6, Lost 8, Drawn 4. Abandoned 3

Master i/c: K. N. Foyle Cricket professional: I. C. D. Stuart

A good all-round team performance brought respectable results, despite the lack of consistent individual run-scoring. Edward Craig, one of several promising colts, scored the side's only century.

Wins v: PGS; Royal Green Jackets; Lord Wandsworth; I Zingari; Old Wykehamists; Berkhamsted.

Batting—N. A. Clark 17-3-480-65-0-34.28; S. J. Hollis 15-6-260-35*-0-28.88; E. D. C. Craig 12-0-326-112-1-27.16; *C. F. P. Villiers 16-1-395-69-0-26.33; J. D. Adams 16-1-348-75-0-23.20; G. C. Close-Brooks 17-2-258-52-0-17.20; S. C. Kent 15-2-186-49-0-14.30.

Bowling—T. D. S. Rathbone 168.4-28-495-26-4/32-19.03; M. H. Witcomb 112-21-370-16-5/42-23.12; G. C. Close-Brooks 263.5-45-800-30-4/52-26.66; G. W. Phillips 165.5-34-548-16-3/52-34.25.

WOODBRIDGE SCHOOL

Played 16: Won 1, Lost 6, Drawn 9. Abandoned 2

Master i/c: Rev. M. E. Percival

Win v: Norwich S.

Batting—G. A. Haggart 11-3-286-84-0-35.75; T. E. Percival 14-2-397-72-0-33.08; *B. D. Harper 14-1-394-102-1-30.30; J. E. Guest 14-1-217-39-0-16.69.

Bowling—G. A. Haggart 93.2-18-310-15-4/56-20.66; T. E. Percival 97-17-439-19-4/11-23.10; J. E. Canham 163-28-582-18-6/41-32.33.

WOODHOUSE GROVE SCHOOL

Played 15: Won 6, Lost 2, Drawn 7. Abandoned 3

Master i/c: R. I. Frost Cricket professional: A. Botha

Three senior boys dominated. Andrew Bairstow, son of the former Yorkshire and England wicket-keeper, scored three centuries in his 938 runs, which comfortably passed the previous record of 687, set in 1985 by Bruce Percy of Buckinghamshire. He represented English Schools and NAYC, captained MCC Schools and NCA Young Cricketers at Lord's, and played for Derbyshire Second XI. Anthony Cadman passed 500 runs, took 22 wickets and was outstanding in the field, while Ned Taylor hit 411 runs and was the leading bowler with 29 wickets, sending down a mixture of seam and swing.

Wins v: Eastbourne; Barnard Castle; Old Grovians; XL Club; Hawks CC; Headmaster's XI.

Batting—A. D. Bairstow 15–2–938–166*–3–72.15; N. B. Taylor 15–6–411–57*–0–45.66; A. M. Cadman 15–3–539–104–1–44.91; D. T. Brier 12–4–224–42*–0–28.00.

Bowling—A. M. Cadman 100.5–16–333–22–5/23–15.13; N. B. Taylor 173.1–50–453–29–6/33–15.62; R. D. Graves 149–42–378–19–4/22–19.89; A. R. Rowan 86.1–14–351–16–6/35–21.93.

WORKSOP COLLEGE

Played 16: Won 5, Lost 2, Drawn 9.

Master i/c: C. G. Paton Cricket professional: A. Kettleborough

The season was notable for the presence in the side of three Wilkinsons, of whom identical twins Laurence and Fergus opened the bowling with economical right-arm and left-arm medium-pace respectively. Richard Wilkinson (no relation), a right-handed batsman and off-spin bowler who has represented England at Under-15 and Under-17 levels, signed a one-year contract with the Yorkshire Cricket Academy.

Wins v: Repton; XL Club; Old Worksopians; Notts. Cross Arrows; Dinnington.

Batting—R. Wilkinson 15–0–617–147–2–41.13; C. R. Ireland 16–0–541–112–1–33.81; L. F. H. Wilkinson 16–5–346–59–0–31.45; F. W. H. Wilkinson 12–5–196–44*–0–28.00; *I. P. Jenkinson 13–1–310–57–0–25.83; D. J. Smith 16–3–244–41–0–18.76.

Bowling—C. E. Dews 68–14–214–16–4/22–13.37; L. F. H. Wilkinson 128–41–282–17–3/16–16.58; R. Wilkinson 116–32–321–15–5/34–21.40; J. W. Ireland 118.1–29–350–15–5/18–23.33.

WREKIN COLLEGE

Played 13: Won 4, Lost 1, Drawn 8. Abandoned 1

Master i/c: M. de Weymarn Cricket professional: D. A. Banks

Wins v: Liverpool C.; Oswestry S.; King's, Worcester; Sundowners.

Batting—*R. P. L. Burton 11–2–601–97–0–66.77; L. M. Preston 12–0–388–59–0–32.33; J. W. Marshall 12–0–279–50–0–23.25.

Bowling—I. W. McArthur 87–13–308–17–4/6–18.11; B. J. Morley 115–18–388–15–3/32–25.86; M. D. Attwood 164–28–515–16–3/60–32.18.

WYGGESTON & QUEEN ELIZABETH I SIXTH FORM COLLEGE

Played 10: Won 6, Lost 0, Drawn 4. Abandoned 2

Master i/c: G. G. Wells

The unbeaten side won six of their ten matches and took the Leicestershire Under-19 Cup for the first time since 1988. Their success was due to a powerful batting line-up, led by Michael Sutliff, a left-hander who played for English Schools, and Sundip Patel, whose aggregate of 498 was the highest since 1970. Michael Sutliff (M. D. R.) was joined by his brother Martin (M. J. C.) in an unbroken second-wicket partnership of 132 against Lawrence Sheriff GS.

Wins v: High Pavement; King Edward VI, Stourbridge; Countesthorpe C.; Lutterworth GS; Lawrence Sheriff GS; Groby C.

Batting—S. Patel 9–1–498–115–2–62.25; *M. D. R. Sutliff 6–1–241–97–0–48.20; B. Thankey 7–3–188–68–0–47.00; R. J. Green 9–2–185–60–0–26.42; M. J. C. Sutliff 7–1–150–57–0–25.00.

Bowling—No bowler took 15 wickets. The leading bowler was R. J. Green 55–11–185–11–3/6–16.81.

GIRLS' SCHOOLS

DENSTONE COLLEGE

Played 8: Won 7, Lost 1, Drawn 0

Mistress i/c: J. Morris

Wins v: Charterhouse; Ardingly; Bromsgrove; Wrekin; Rydal; Malvern; Newcastle HS.

Batting—C. Chell 8–5–150–47*–0–50.00; O. Simons 5–1–171–56*–0–42.75.

Bowling—E. Pattison 60.3–10–142–22–7/18–6.45; O. Simons 53–10–135–17–4/16–7.94.

ROEDEAN SCHOOL

Played 12: Won 5, Lost 7, Drawn 0. Abandoned 2

Staff i/c: A. S. England and A. F. Romanov

Georgina Baker and Sarah Constantine set a new post-war record of 86 for the first wicket against Moira House, only for Constantine and Elizabeth Hamilton to break it again with 90 unbeaten against Brighton and Hove LCC.

Wins v: Ardingly; Brighton & Hove LCC; Charterhouse; Fathers' XI; Moira House.

Batting—G. M. Baker 8–0–159–51–0–19.87.

Bowling—E. L. Hamilton 33–0–132–16–4/11–8.25; *S. Halim 70.3–10–268–21–6/19–12.76.

YOUTH CRICKET

UNDER-15 CRICKET

The Midlands won the Bunbury ESCA Festival for English regional under-15 teams, staged in Northumberland from July 25-27. They beat two of their three opponents, North and South, and had the better of a draw against the fourth team in the tournament, West.

In hot weather, batsmen dominated the tournament but no one scored a century. The most prolific batsman was Gareth Jenkins from Essex who scored 84, 70 and 54 and won the Neil Lloyd Trophy as the best batsman of the week.

After a two-day representative game at Jesmond in which ESCA beat the ESCA President's Headmasters' Conference XI by eight wickets, a 14-strong England party was selected, comprising Paul Franks (Nottinghamshire) (*captain*), Matthew Boyden (Norfolk), Andrew Edwards (Somerset), Graham Edwards (Cornwall), Jamie Grove (Suffolk), Gareth Jenkins (Essex), David Lye (Devon), Zac Morris (Yorkshire), Simon North (Lancashire), Stephen Peters (Essex), Jonathan Powell (Essex), Graham Smith (Hertfordshire), Graham Swann (Northamptonshire) and James Troughton (Warwickshire).

This squad played the other home countries and remained unbeaten. Their fixture with Wales was rained off but they beat Scotland's Under-16 by 48 runs, thanks to an unbeaten 125 from Peters and five for 19 from off-spinner Powell, who took 12 wickets in three matches. England also beat Ireland, by eight wickets, with Jenkins scoring 124 not out.

High Wycombe of Buckinghamshire won the Sun Life of Canada Under-15 Club Championship finals, beating Caythorpe of Nottinghamshire by eight wickets with two balls remaining in the final at May's Bounty, Basingstoke. High Wycombe beat Mildenhall (Suffolk) in one semi-final while Caythorpe beat Taunton. A total of 1,184 clubs from 37 counties took part in the competition.

The Lord's Taverners/*Cricketer* Colts Trophy for Schools was won by Eton College.

UNDER-13 CRICKET

Little Houghton of Northamptonshire took the 1994 Ken Barrington Cup as winners of the NatWest Bank Under-13 Club Championship. They won six games out of seven in the round-robin finals at Sherborne School in Dorset, finishing clear of Horsham (Sussex), North Warwick (Warwickshire), Baildon (Yorkshire), Tynemouth (Northumberland), Gidea Park & Romford (Essex) and Exmouth (Devon).

The winners, with an almost identical team, had finished level on points at the head of the table in 1993, but lost the title on run-rate to Cheltenham. Little Houghton do not have a ground of their own and had to play all their matches away. The winning team was: Mark Powell (*captain*), Guy Anderson, Iain Cameron, Tom Dann, Ben Frazer, Richard Kaufman, Kelvin Locke and Anthony Romaine.

Michael Woods of Exmouth was named Best Batsman of the finals and Carl Eyden of North Warwick was Best Bowler. A total of 1,180 teams took part. They each comprise eight players who bat in pairs for five overs, conceding eight runs every time they lose a wicket.

UNDER-11 CRICKET

Headfield Junior School from Dewsbury, Yorkshire won the Wrigley Softball Cricket finals at Edgbaston on July 18, beating St Edwards Royal Free School, Windsor, by 11 runs.

The tournament, founded in 1981, involved almost 30,000 boys and girls aged under 11 from 3,000 schools all over Britain. Sixteen teams contested the finals including Crynallt School, Neath, one of whose players, Richard Young, took a clean-bowled hat-trick.

Each team has eight players and 12 overs per innings – they start with 200 runs and forfeit six every time a wicket falls; pairs of batsmen stay in for three overs regardless of how many times they are out. The game lasts only an hour and can be played on any surface, including a playground or car park, and is thus well-suited to inner-city schools. Trevor Bailey, who started the Wrigley tournament, points out that Gary Sobers learned the game playing with a tennis ball.

The winning squad, all boys and all born in Yorkshire, comprised Luqman Adam (*captain*), Akber Valli, Irfan Qureshi, Muhammed Saeed, Nasir Hussain, Shohaib Shafaq, Zuber Patel, Huzafa Patel and Sadiq Darwan. In their semi-final they won a Roses match by just one run against another all-Asian team, Deepdale School from Preston.

WOMEN'S CRICKET, 1994

By CAROL SALMON

English women's cricket saw significant changes on and off the field, as administrators and players alike attempted to build on England's World Cup victory in 1993. There were several changes of personnel, with Sharon Bayton of Surrey being elected chairman of the Women's Cricket Association, in succession to Cathy Mowat of Middlesex, and Norma Izard of Kent, who managed the World Cup campaign, taking over as president after Audrey Collins retired. Collins, awarded an OBE in 1988 for her services to cricket, was the WCA's president for 12 years, the longest-serving ever, but she had worked for a full 49 in the administration of the game. Her playing career was blighted by the Second World War, which restricted her to just one appearance for England.

The administrative headquarters moved from Headingley to Edgbaston and, in an attempt to increase the number of clubs joining the association, affiliation fees were slashed. Instead, clubs were asked to pay entry fees to take part in the various competitions. New age-group competitions were introduced and a stronger emphasis placed on development, particularly in areas where the women's game is not strong. The association appointed a new coach for the senior England team – John Bown, an NCA senior staff coach and Derbyshire club cricketer who had helped to coach England during the World Cup. He replaced the association's first coach, Ruth Prideaux, who retired, and former international Enid Bakewell was appointed Under-21 coach. The top priority for the new hierarchy was England's defence of the European Cup, in Dublin in July 1995. After that, England tour India in January 1996 and then entertain New Zealand in a three-Test series a few months later.

At the domestic level, Yorkshire and The North continued to dominate the women's game. At Cambridge in August, Yorkshire met East Midlands in the area championship final for the fifth year running, and won their third successive title. A few weeks later, The North repeated their clean sweep the previous year at the territorial tournament in Oxford. Middle-order batsman Debra Maybury played a vital role in both winning teams, scoring 68 for Yorkshire in the area final and the only century in the territorial tournament. On the fringe of the World Cup squad in 1993, she could be a key player for England in future.

Surprisingly, the northern stranglehold was broken when it came to the club competitions. Wakefield, who had won both in 1993, were eliminated in the third round of the National Club Knockout by Newark & Sherwood, from Nottinghamshire, led by England captain Karen Smithies. Newark & Sherwood reached the final, staged in Oxford, for the first time, as did Shepperton. The outcome could hardly have been closer; after rain reduced the match to 20 overs a side, Newark & Sherwood levelled the scores on 118, thanks to England Under-19 captain Ella Donnison who scored 59, and claimed victory through having lost fewer wickets. Wakefield did push through to the Premier League final in Staffordshire, but lost a low-scoring game to Surrey club Redoutables, for whom England opener Janette Brittin made an unbeaten 55.

Note: Matches in this section were not first-class.

AREA CHAMPIONSHIP

At Cambridge, August 2. **Semi-final:** Yorkshire won by seven wickets. Toss: Yorkshire. East Anglia 60 (30.5 overs) (J. van Noortwijk three for six, M. Reynard three for 21); Yorkshire 62 for three (14.2 overs) (D. Maybury 42).

At Cambridge, August 2. **Semi-final:** East Midlands won by 20 runs. Toss: Surrey. East Midlands 223 for eight (55 overs) (J. Smit 54, K. Lowe 52, K. Smithies 42; C. Barrs three for 59); Surrey 203 (53.3 overs) (R. Lupton 66, J. A. Brittin 59; J. M. Chamberlain three for 54).

At Cambridge, August 3. **Final:** Yorkshire won by 110 runs. Toss: East Midlands. Yorkshire 233 (54.1 overs) (D. Maybury 68, S. Metcalfe 48, A. Elder 50; G. Morris four for 49); East Midlands 123 (38.2 overs) (E. Donnison 39; N. Holt three for 32, J. Tedstone four for five).

TERRITORIAL TOURNAMENT

At Oxford, August 27. The North won by 46 runs. Toss: The North. The North 189 (55 overs) (S. Metcalfe 55); The East 143 (50.3 overs) (N. Holt three for 24).

At Oxford, August 27. The Mid-West won by one wicket. Toss: The Mid-West. The South 175 (54.1 overs); The Mid-West 177 for nine (54.5 overs) (J. Smit 74, B. A. Daniels 51; R. Heggs four for 23).

At Oxford, August 28. The East won by 55 runs. Toss: The East. The East 166 for nine (55 overs) (A. Bainbridge 43; R. Heggs three for 23); The South 111 (53.2 overs) (C. Barrs 31; C. Moat four for 20).

At Oxford, August 28. The North won by 76 runs. Toss: The North. The North 214 for eight (55 overs) (D. Maybury 48, J. Tedstone 49); The Mid-West 138 for nine (55 overs) (H. Clark 40 not out; C. E. Taylor three for 19).

At Oxford, August 29. The East won by 46 runs. Toss: The East. The East 190 (54.1 overs) (A. Godliman 59, D. Stock 42; S. Redfern three for 37); The Mid-West 144 (42.4 overs) (J. Smit 60; C. Whichcord three for 34, D. Stock three for 18).

At Oxford, August 29. The North won by 77 runs. Toss: The North. The North 201 for six (55 overs) (D. Maybury 109, L. Burnley 34); The South 124 (39.2 overs) (M. Reynard three for five).

NATIONAL CLUB KNOCKOUT FINAL

At Christ Church, Oxford, September 3. Newark & Sherwood won by virtue of losing fewer wickets. Toss: Newark & Sherwood. Shepperton 118 for six (20 overs) (N. Sherriff 37); Newark & Sherwood 118 for two (20 overs) (E. Donnison 59).

PREMIER LEAGUE FINAL

At Meir Heath, Staffordshire, September 18. Redoutables won by seven wickets. Toss: Redoutables. Wakefield 113 for nine (50 overs) (P. Lovell three for 16); Redoutables 114 for three (39 overs) (J. A. Brittin 55 not out).

PART FOUR: OVERSEAS CRICKET IN 1993-94

FEATURES OF 1993-94

Double-Hundreds (34)

375†	B. C. Lara	West Indies v England (Fifth Test) at St John's.
366‡	M. V. Sridhar	Hyderabad v Andhra at Secunderabad.
337*†	D. J. Cullinan	Transvaal v Northern Transvaal at Johannesburg.
307*	T. N. Lazard	Boland v Western Province at Worcester.
286	J. P. Crawley	England A v Eastern Province at Port Elizabeth.
271	P. N. Kirsten	Border v Northern Transvaal at East London.
268	G. S. Blewett	South Australia v Victoria at Melbourne.
267	Shahid Nawaz	Faisalabad v Lahore at Lahore.
264	A. D. Jadeja	North Zone v Central Zone at Baroda.
260§	A. A. Muzumdar	Bombay v Haryana at Faridabad.
251	W. J. Cronje	Orange Free State v Australians at Bloemfontein.
250	Vikram Rathore	Punjab v Jammu and Kashmir at Mohali.
235*	Ajay Sharma	Delhi v Himachal Pradesh at Una.
233	J. L. Langer	Western Australia v Tasmania at Perth.
229	Shahid Saeed	Lahore v Faisalabad at Lahore.
225	S. S. Sugwekar	Maharashtra v Orissa at Pune.
222	P. A. de Silva	Nondescripts CC v Sinhalese SC at Colombo (Maitland Place, NCC).
218	P. K. Amre	Rajasthan v Madhya Pradesh at Udaipur.
217	Asif Din	Warwickshire v Mashonaland XI at Harare.
215	W. R. James	Matabeleland v Mashonaland Country Districts at Bulawayo.
215	Yusuf Ali Khan	Railways v Uttar Pradesh at Delhi.
214	G. S. Blewett	South Australia v Tasmania at Adelaide.
214	C. B. Lambert	Northern Transvaal v Transvaal at Johannesburg.
211‡	V. Jaisimha	Hyderabad v Andhra at Secunderabad.
208	S. J. Kalyani	Bengal v Tripura at Calcutta.
207*‡	N. David	Hyderabad v Andhra at Secunderabad.
206	B. C. Lara	Trinidad v Jamaica at Port-of-Spain.
203*	M. G. Bevan	New South Wales v Western Australia at Sydney.
202*	Mahmood Hamid	Karachi Whites v Lahore at Karachi.
202	M. H. Austen	Wellington v Central Districts at Wanganui.
200*	Aamer Malik	Lahore v Sargodha at Sargodha.
200*	Saurav C. Ganguly	Bengal v Tripura at Calcutta.
200	D. S. Lehmann	South Australia v Western Australia at Adelaide.
200	Shakeel Ahmed	Habib Bank v PNSC at Lahore.

† *National record.* ‡ *In the same innings.* § *On debut.*

Note: B. C. Lara and G. S. Blewett both scored two double-hundreds.

Hundred on First-Class Debut

260†	A. A. Muzumdar	Bombay v Haryana at Faridabad.
133*	R. J. Davison	New South Wales v Tasmania at Sydney.
132	A. V. Kale	Maharashtra v Baroda at Pune.
108	R. Sanghi	Rajasthan v Madhya Pradesh at Udaipur.
103	C. Wait	Eastern Province B v Western Province B at Goodwood.

† *World record.*

Three Hundreds in Successive Innings

S. S. Bhave (Maharashtra)	111 v Baroda at Pune, 180 v Saurashtra at Pune, 129 v Vidarbha at Nagpur.
Saurav C. Ganguly (Bengal)......	200* v Tripura at Calcutta, 148 and 100* v Assam at Calcutta.
M. L. Hayden (Queensland) (2) ...	173* v New South Wales at Brisbane, 165 and 116 v South Australia at Adelaide.
	121* v Tasmania at Brisbane, 126 and 155 v Victoria at Brisbane.
D. M. Jones (Victoria)	155 v New South Wales at Sydney, 145 and 152* v South Australia at Melbourne.
Mahmood Hamid (Karachi Whites)	202* v Lahore at Karachi, 102 v Bahawalpur at Karachi, 157 v Islamabad at Karachi.
Ajay Sharma (Delhi)............	151 North Zone v Central Zone at Baroda, 110 North Zone v West Zone at Baroda, 235* v Himachal Pradesh at Una.
S. S. Sugwekar (Maharashtra)	106 and 106* v Vidarbha at Nagpur, 225 v Orissa at Pune.

Hundred in Each Innings of a Match

R. Bittoo	103	150	Himachal Pradesh v Jammu and Kashmir at Una.
W. J. Cronje	150	107	Orange Free State v Natal at Bloemfontein.
Saurav C. Ganguly ..	148	100*	Bengal v Assam at Calcutta.
M. L. Hayden (2) ...	165	116	Queensland v South Australia at Adelaide.
	126	155	Queensland v Victoria at Brisbane.
D. F. Hills.........	114	126	Tasmania v South Australia at Adelaide.
D. M. Jones	145	152*	Victoria v South Australia at Melbourne.
P. C. Nobes........	140	106	South Australia v Queensland at Adelaide.
A. J. Stewart	118	143	England v West Indies (Fourth Test) at Bridgetown.
S. S. Sugwekar	106	106*	Maharashtra v Vidarbha at Nagpur.

Hundred Before Lunch

Saurav C. Ganguly ..	93* to 200*	Bengal v Tripura at Calcutta (2nd day).

Carrying Bat Through Completed Innings

S. S. Bhave	28*	West Zone (103) v East Zone at Surat.
M. H. Dekker	68*	Zimbabwe (187) v Pakistan (Second Test) at Rawalpindi.
M. L. Hayden	173*	Queensland (281) v New South Wales at Brisbane.
Ajay Mehra	152*	Punjab (349) v Baroda at Baroda.
Mohammad Nawaz .	140*	Sargodha (262) v Faisalabad at Faisalabad.
V. Yadav	80*	Rajasthan (208) v Vidarbha at Alwar.

* *Not out.*

First-Wicket Partnership of 100 in Each Innings

183 243 T. J. Barsby/M. L. Hayden, Queensland v South Australia at Adelaide.

Other Notable Partnerships

First Wicket
325* H. A. Kinikar/S. S. Bhave, Maharashtra v Saurashtra at Pune.
316 M. H. Austen/R. T. Hart, Wellington v Central Districts at Wanganui.

Second Wicket
342 Shakeel Ahmed/Idrees Baig, Habib Bank v PNSC at Lahore.
317* R. G. Twose/Asif Din, Warwickshire v Mashonaland XI at Harare.
311* W. N. Phillips/D. M. Jones, Victoria v South Australia at Melbourne.
308† C. B. Lambert/J. J. Strydom, Northern Transvaal v Transvaal at Johannesburg.

Third Wicket
360† T. N. Lazard/J. B. Commins, Boland v Western Province at Worcester.
340 Bantoo Singh/Ajay Sharma, Delhi v Himachal Pradesh at Una.
334 S. J. Kalyani/Saurav C. Ganguly, Bengal v Tripura at Calcutta.
319 A. D. Jadeja/Ajay Sharma, North Zone v Central Zone at Baroda.
310 Shahid Saeed/Zahid Fazal, Lahore v Faisalabad at Lahore.
303 M. A. Atherton/R. A. Smith, England v West Indies (Fifth Test) at St John's.
290 D. F. Hills/R. T. Ponting, Tasmania v South Australia at Adelaide.
286 G. S. Blewett/D. S. Lehmann, South Australia v Tasmania at Hobart.
271 G. R. Marsh/D. R. Martyn, Western Australia v New South Wales at Perth.
261 J. P. Crawley/A. P. Wells, England A v Eastern Province at Port Elizabeth.

Fourth Wicket
344‡ M. V. Sridhar/V. Jaisimha, Hyderabad v Andhra at Secunderabad.
318 J. A. Brayshaw/D. S. Lehmann, South Australia v Western Australia at Adelaide.
311 Shahid Nawaz/Ijaz Ahmed, Faisalabad v Lahore at Lahore.
283 D. J. Cullinan/S. J. Cook, Transvaal v Northern Transvaal at Johannesburg.
277 J. D. Siddons/D. S. Lehmann, South Australia v Tasmania at Hobart.

Fifth Wicket
326‡ M. V. Sridhar/N. David, Hyderabad v Andhra at Secunderabad.
258 Salim Malik/Inzamam-ul-Haq, Pakistan v New Zealand (Second Test) at Wellington.
231 Ijaz Ahmed/Naseer Ahmed, Railways v HBFC at Multan.
227 S. V. Manjrekar/S. S. Dighe, Bombay v Baroda at Baroda.

Sixth Wicket
225* Manzoor Akhtar/Mohammad Javed, Karachi Blues v Sargodha at Sargodha.

Seventh Wicket
259 R. J. Shastri/S. V. Bahatule, Bombay v Karnataka at Bangalore.
251 J. J. Martin/K. S. More, Baroda v Gujarat at Baroda.
230 K. S. Chavan/M. S. Narula, Baroda v Punjab at Baroda.
227 S. M. H. Kirmani/S. Joshi, Karnataka v Bombay at Bangalore.

Eighth Wicket
249*† Shaukat Mirza/Akram Raza, Habib Bank v PNSC at Lahore.

Ninth Wicket
207† Mahmood Hamid/Athar Laeeq, Karachi Whites v Lahore at Karachi.

Tenth Wicket
127 Sanjay Sharma/Arun Sharma, Jammu and Kashmir v Himachal Pradesh at Una.
105 L. Sagara/M. Vellavarayan, Colombo CC v Nondescripts CC at Colombo (PSS).

* *Unbroken partnership.* † *National record for that wicket.* ‡ *Same innings.*

Twelve or More Wickets in a Match

15-140 P. Jain .... Haryana v Himachal Pradesh at Bhiwani.
14-79 M. Munasinghe........... Western Province (North) v Central Province at Colombo (Braybrook Place).
14-94 K. N. A. Padmanabhan.... Kerala v Andhra at Kottayam.

14-103	Naved Anjum	Habib Bank v United Bank at Rawalpindi.
14-119	C. Pringle	Auckland v Otago at Dunedin.
13-113	S. Silva	Western Province (South) v Central Province at Colombo (Maitland Crescent).
13-135	Waqar Younis	Pakistan v Zimbabwe (First Test) at Karachi.
12-76	B. Vij	Punjab v Himachal Pradesh at Mohali.
12-95	C. E. Eksteen	Transvaal v Western Province at Cape Town.
12-128	S. K. Warne	Australia v South Africa (Second Test) at Sydney.
12-162	M. V. Rao	Services v Punjab at Mohali.
12-183	Jasbir Singh	Uttar Pradesh v Madhya Pradesh at Bhilai.

Eight or More Wickets in an Innings

9-38	M. Munasinghe	Western Province (North) v Central Province at Colombo (Braybrook Place).
9-56	Naved Anjum	Habib Bank v United Bank at Rawalpindi.
8-51	R. Dhanraj	Trinidad v Barbados at Port-of-Spain.
8-51	Nadeem Ghauri	Habib Bank v National Bank at Gujranwala.
8-52	N. D. Hirwani	Madhya Pradesh v Vidarbha at Nagpur.
8-55	D. Johnson	Karnataka v Assam at Bangalore.
8-57	K. N. A. Padmanabhan	Kerala v Andhra at Kottayam.
8-61	P. V. Gandhe	Vidarbha v Rajasthan at Alwar.
8-66	N. D. Hirwani	Madhya Pradesh v Railways at Gwalior.
8-67	P. Jain	Haryana v Himachal Pradesh at Bhiwani.
8-75	A. R. C. Fraser	England v West Indies (Fourth Test) at Bridgetown.
8-104	Ayaz Jilani	Islamabad v Rawalpindi at Rawalpindi.
8-114	Mohammad Zahid	PACO v Habib Bank at Lahore.
8-123	Shahid Ali Khan	HBFC v PACO at Lahore.
8-125	Jasbir Singh	Uttar Pradesh v Madhya Pradesh at Bhilai.

Note: N. D. Hirwani took eight wickets twice.

Hat-Tricks

Arshad Ayub	Hyderabad v Kerala at Kottayam.
P. V. Gandhe	Vidarbha v Rajasthan at Alwar.
S. Sensharma	Bengal v Delhi at Calcutta.
Shahid Ali Khan	HBFC v PACO at Lahore.

Most Overs Bowled in a Match

101-19-276-5	Sushil Kumar	Orissa v Maharashtra at Pune.

Most Overs Bowled in an Innings

78-21-164-5	Nadeem Khan	National Bank v PIA at Hyderabad.
78-12-231-2	Sushil Kumar	Orissa v Maharashtra at Pune.

Nine or More Wicket-Keeping Dismissals in a Match

10 ct, 1 st	I. A. Healy	Australians v Northern Transvaal at Verwoerdburg.
10 ct	H. M. de Vos	Western Transvaal v Eastern Transvaal at Potchefstroom.
10 ct	N. R. Mongia	Rest of India v Punjab at Ludhiana.
6 ct, 3 st	M. O. Johnston	Transvaal B v Natal B at Durban.
9 ct	Rashid Latif	Pakistan v New Zealand (First Test) at Auckland.
9 ct	S. J. Rhodes	England A v Transvaal at Johannesburg.
8 ct, 1 st	A. Vaidya	Karnataka v Assam at Bangalore.

Six or More Wicket-Keeping Dismissals in an Innings

7 ct	H. M. de Vos	Western Transvaal v Eastern Transvaal at Potchefstroom.
7 ct	P. Kirsten	Griqualand West v Western Transvaal at Potchefstroom.
5 ct, 1 st ..	P. B. Dassanayake	Sri Lanka Board XI v South Africans at Galle.
5 ct, 1 st ..	I. A. Healy	Australians v Northern Transvaal at Verwoerdburg.
5 ct, 1 st ..	R. D. Jacobs	Leeward Islands v Jamaica at Kingston.
4 ct, 2 st ..	M. O. Johnston	Transvaal B v Natal B at Durban.
6 ct	N. R. Mongia	Rest of India v Punjab at Ludhiana.
6 ct	B. Ngondo	Mashonaland Under-24 v Mashonaland Country Districts at Harare.
6 ct	Pervez-ul-Hasan	PNSC v PACO at Hyderabad.

Five Catches in an Innings in the Field

R. S. Dravid .... Karnataka v Goa at Bangalore.
T. O. Powell .... Jamaica v Trinidad at Port-of-Spain.

Match Double (100 Runs and 10 Wickets)

R. A. Harper....... 79, 27; 5-61, 5-38 Guyana v Leeward Islands at Berbice.

Wicket-Keeper's Double (100 Runs and 10 Dismissals)

H. M. de Vos	50*, 95; 10 ct	Western Transvaal v Eastern Transvaal at Potchefstroom.
N. R. Mongia	100*, 10 ct	Rest of India v Punjab at Ludhiana.

No Byes Conceded in Total of 500 or More

P. B. Dassanayake .. Sri Lanka v India (First Test) (511) at Lucknow.
R. C. Russell....... England v West Indies (Fifth Test) (593-5 dec.) at St John's.

Highest Innings Totals

944-6 dec.†... Hyderabad v Andhra at Secunderabad.
744-7 .... Habib Bank v PNSC at Lahore.
718 .... Bombay v Haryana at Faridabad.
708-9 dec. ... North Zone v Central Zone at Baroda.
645-9 dec. ... Maharashtra v Orissa at Pune.
607-6 dec. ... Australia v New Zealand (Third Test) at Brisbane.
602-9 dec. ... Transvaal v Northern Transvaal at Johannesburg.

† *National record.*

Lowest Innings Totals

31 ...... Kurunegala Youth CC v Sinhalese SC at Colombo (Maitland Place, SCC) (two men absent).
44 ...... Tripura v Bihar at Agartala (2nd innings).
46 ...... England v West Indies (Third Test) at Port-of-Spain.
56 ...... Western Province (South) v North Western Province at Kurunegala.

62 ...... Tripura v Bihar at Agartala (1st innings).
64 ...... North Western Province v Western Province (City) at Kurunegala.
65 ...... Kerala v Hyderabad at Kottayam.
67 ...... Eastern Province v Northern Transvaal at Verwoerdburg.
69 ...... Southern Province v Western Province (North) at Matara.
75 ...... Mashonaland v Mashonaland Under-24 at Harare.
75 ...... Maharashtra v Bombay at Thane.
75 ...... PNSC v PACO at Hyderabad.
80 ...... East Zone v South Zone at Rajkot.

50 Extras in an Innings

	b	*l-b*	*w*	*n-b*	
63	12	11	17	23	North Western Province (324) v Central Province at Kurunegala.
59	9	17	7	26	Western Province (City) (377) v Southern Province at Galle.
58	6	14	8	30	Auckland (322-4 dec.) v Wellington at Auckland.
58	11	13	7	27	Nondescripts CC (343) v Colombo CC at Colombo (PSS).
56	22	17	1	16	ADBP (456) v National Bank at Faisalabad.
55	0	6	0	49†	Western Australia (373) v Queensland at Perth.
54	31	14	7	2	Orissa (396) v Assam at Berhampur.
53	7	26	13	7	Northern Transvaal (517-8 dec.) v Transvaal at Johannesburg.
53	14	16	1	22†	Western Australia (503-8 dec.) v New South Wales at Perth.
52	9	20	0	23	England (593) v West Indies (Fifth Test) at St John's.
52	6	15	1	30	Western Province City v Western Province North at Matura.
50	8	6	0	36	England (394-7 dec.) v West Indies (Fourth Test) at Bridgetown.

† *Under Australian Cricket Board playing conditions, two extras were scored for every no-ball, excluding runs scored off the delivery.*

ENGLAND IN THE WEST INDIES, 1993-94

By ALAN LEE

When England headed for the Caribbean in January 1994, many people might have predicted that the series would end in a 3-1 win for the West Indies. And that, three months later, was how things turned out. So everything went to plan? Well, hardly. Modern tours seldom seem to run along humdrum straight lines but this one broke all the rules of logic and expectation. It was a tour of exhausting extremes, on which despair gave way to triumph at impossibly short notice and soaring personal achievement attended every game in the series and, it sometimes seemed, every day. Some of the performances – like Curtly Ambrose's amazing bowling to turn the Port-of-Spain Test, the heroic deeds from Alec Stewart and Angus Fraser to give England an improbable, indeed almost unthinkable, win in Bridgetown and, above all, Brian Lara's world Test record 375 in Antigua – will be remembered as long as the game is played.

In the final analysis, it was a disappointment for England because, with only a handful of exceptions, the selected players made no obvious progress and, as a unit, they made no impression on the supremacy that West Indies have paraded for so long. But disappointing did not mean dull, nor did the eventual outcome begin to measure up to the misery for England that threatened in the stunned hours and days following the nadir of 46 all out in Trinidad. That was quite some way to lose a match which ought to have been won, and a series which, at that stage, appeared to be heading inexorably towards a West Indian clean sweep.

In this context, England's subsequent victory in Barbados, where no visiting Test side had won for 59 years, was a monumental feat, fit to stand alongside the greatest of all Test wins. Here was a team which had suffered humiliating disillusionment and all the accompanying torture from within and without, but recovered to defeat the world's strongest side in their acknowledged fortress. If Mike Atherton never achieved anything else as England captain, he could forever be proud of that.

But Atherton seemed likely to achieve plenty more. Only the following week, he was cajoling his weary players to one final effort of defiance when faced by a West Indian total approaching 600, including Lara's world record. Atherton made 135 himself, with the resilience he had maintained throughout the tour and, against all likelihood, England ended the series with honour intact and heads held high. Quite how much of this can be attributed to the captain can never accurately be measured; suffice to say that a weaker man than Atherton could not possibly have returned home from what remained an emphatic defeat with his reputation enhanced.

In retrospect, the most baffling aspect of it all was that, not 12 months earlier, Atherton had been unsure of even a place in the England side; in India the previous winter he was conspicuously excluded from all plans. At that stage, the thought that he would inherit the captaincy before the end of summer was a fanciful one: if Graham Gooch was about to go then Stewart was well-established as his deputy – and Mike Gatting waited in the wings.

The shift of mood that swept Atherton into power did an immeasurable service to English cricket. This means no disrespect to Stewart, because his role on tour would have been vital even if he had not flourished with the bat. But Atherton, surprising many who had mistaken his reserved nature for weakness, offered a strength of character rare in one so young. He was able to rise above the petty problems which afflict any tour without ever distancing himself from his players. He was loyal without pandering to inadequacy, opinionated without being intransigent. Tactically, the harsh could call him negative at times but, with the resources available, no blame could be attached. Then there was his batting. Like Gooch before him, and like Allan Border in Australia, the additional responsibility was no impediment, much more an inspiration. Atherton knew his resolve would be specifically tested by West Indian fast bowlers who make it their business to undermine a new opposition captain. They set about him in Jamaica, during the First Test, when Atherton was subjected to as harrowing a spell of legitimate short-pitched bowling as I have seen. But he did not weaken under the assault; the ultimate mark of respect was that it was never tried again. Atherton went on to make 510 runs in the five Tests, more than anyone bar Lara, and with Stewart scoring 477 and both men averaging above 50, the new opening pair was demonstrably England's greatest single advance of the tour.

While Atherton's batting shouted defiance as it proceeded in a correct and measured fashion, Stewart thrived as a shotmaker of great fluency. There were times when Courtney Walsh, in particular, was quite unable to bowl to him and, on pitches when the bounce was relatively even (a rarity in the Caribbean), Stewart's favoured pull was irrepressible. He became, in Barbados, the first Englishman ever to make centuries in each innings of a Test against West Indies. Like Atherton, he returned with his stature greatly increased.

This could be said of precious few others in the party, which was responsible for the noticeable stress suffered by the team manager, Keith Fletcher. Nobody looked more shattered by the débâcle in Trinidad, nor more depressed by the feeble surrender to a scratch team in Grenada which followed. At that point, England had lost seven consecutive overseas Tests since Fletcher became manager. With Raymond Illingworth appointed during the tour as a deliberately high-profile chairman of selectors – rather than tour manager M. J. K. Smith – the theory that his position was becoming untenable gathered strength. Fletcher, however, is not only a likeable man but a quietly diligent one; his unseen work with individual players, making them think lucidly about their game and teaching them to feel good about it, deserved appreciation. Barbados was as much a tonic to him as to anybody.

The greatest single failure among the party was probably Robin Smith, though this judgment must be influenced by the fact that he began the tour burdened by so many hopes and expectations. He was, unarguably, the most accomplished player of fast bowling in the side and his role as the foundation of the batting was taken as read. He was a banker, but like so many odds-on favourites, he failed to deliver. His technique developed an alarming blip, his bat coming down crookedly from the direction of second slip, and his confidence nose-dived. He was confessing that his tour had been a "disaster" even after making 175 in the last Test in Antigua and, when Fletcher publicly warned that Smith was being distracted by commercial activities, he was voicing a common concern.

Like Smith, Graeme Hick averaged 35 in the Tests. But he failed to build on his 96 in the second innings of the First Test, which had all the makings of a career breakthrough. He was not even home before Illingworth was talking ominously of time running out for him. Among the fringe batsmen Graham Thorpe made much the most progress, though he, too, had to cure technical problems before batting with authority late in the tour. Mark Ramprakash continued to look the part without offering any evidence that he has the temperament for this level, and neither Matthew Maynard nor Nasser Hussain advanced their claims for further attention, or justified their original selection ahead of older batsmen like Mike Gatting, David Gower (who retired after his omission) and Allan Lamb.

More worrying, in the longer term, was the bowling, which exhibited the legacies of the "soft" domestic cricket that Fletcher, like his predecessor Micky Stewart, was fond of castigating. Fraser bowled heroically once his fitness and rhythm were in tune but, critically, he did not once play a Test match with Devon Malcolm. The liaison of pace and perseverance is mutually beneficial and the knee injury which obliged Malcolm to return home for treatment in mid-tour was a grievous blow to England. He recovered sufficiently to rejoin the party but was not risked in the remaining Tests.

To some degree, the inadequacy of the bowling was self-inflicted, for the best use was never made of Phil Tufnell. Whenever he played, he was able to contain more effectively than any of the seam bowlers, buying wickets at the other end. Yet it was not until the last two Tests that he was given his chance, when previously he should have played as well as, if not instead of, Ian Salisbury. Much of the seam bowling was depressingly poor, betraying an inability to adapt to the different demands of overseas pitches. Andy Caddick, in patches, was the best and Fletcher insisted that, properly focused, he could be a high-quality Test bowler for years to come.

West Indies have never been short of this commodity these past 20 years, but there were signs that they are not quite so well provided for as of old. Ambrose was magnificent. He was deservedly named man of the series, not only for taking 26 wickets at 19.96 apiece and deciding the Trinidad Test single-handed, but for the more profound truth that West Indies now look to him whenever they need wickets. In the past, any one of four could notionally be thought the spearhead bowler; now, Ambrose carried the load alone, supported by capable, skilful but seldom devastating seamers, of whom Kenny Benjamin, with 22 wickets, did particularly well.

There was even talk of an increasing dependence on spin in the Caribbean, borne out by figures in the Red Stripe Cup but not, so far, carried into the Test arena. Spin is still used primarily to give the fast bowlers a rest and cure any shortfall in over-rate. When a young leg-break bowler was included, he was a great success – but with the bat rather than the ball. Shivnarine Chanderpaul, still in his teens and a product of extensive coaching on a Georgetown pitch cut out especially for him when his talent was identified and his schooling terminated early, made a half-century in each of his first four Tests, batting with startling maturity. He does not have the flair or range of his fellow left-hander Lara, but he could be the glue in the West Indian middle order for many years. Another influential figure was Adams who, with Arthurton, completed a run of four left-handers from No. 3 to 6 in the last four Tests.

It was a brave move to choose Chanderpaul, and not only because of his youth and inexperience. The omission of Phil Simmons brought hysterical protests in Trinidad, where the feeling persists that their players are discriminated against in selection. This is a legacy of the inter-island jealousies which once divided West Indian cricket but have largely been overcome, thanks to a succession of wise men at the helm. Richie Richardson, the present captain, is among this number. Though growing exhaustion affected his form, and his strategy, especially upon winning the toss, sometimes seemed bizarre, he played a full part in ensuring this series was free of acrimony. The tour's most bitter moment, when Walsh released a barrage at the notoriously inept England No. 11, Malcolm, on the fourth day of the First Test, took place when he was off the field with a headache. Nothing similar occurred again. The matches were, indeed, played virtually throughout in a fine spirit, which says a good deal for both captains.

ENGLAND TOURING PARTY

M. A. Atherton (Lancashire) (*captain*), A. J. Stewart (Surrey) (*vice-captain*), A. R. Caddick (Somerset), A. R. C. Fraser (Middlesex), G. A. Hick (Worcestershire), N. Hussain (Essex), A. P. Igglesden (Kent), C. C. Lewis (Nottinghamshire), D. E. Malcolm (Derbyshire), M. P. Maynard (Glamorgan), M. R. Ramprakash (Middlesex), R. C. Russell (Gloucestershire), I. D. K. Salisbury (Sussex), R. A. Smith (Hampshire), G. P. Thorpe (Surrey), P. C. R. Tufnell (Middlesex), S. L. Watkin (Glamorgan).

Tour manager: M. J. K. Smith. *Team manager:* K. W. R. Fletcher. *Scorer:* A. E. Davis (Warwickshire). *Physiotherapist:* D. G. Roberts (Worcestershire).

ENGLAND TOUR RESULTS

Test matches – Played 5: Won 1, Lost 3, Drawn 1.
First-class matches – Played 9: Won 2, Lost 4, Drawn 3.
Wins – West Indies, Leeward Islands.
Losses – West Indies (3), West Indies Board XI.
Draws – West Indies, Barbados, West Indies Board President's XI.
One-day internationals – Played 5: Won 2, Lost 3.
Other non first-class matches – Played 2: Won 1, Drawn 1. *Win* – Antiguan XI. *Draw* – St Kitts & Nevis.

TEST MATCH AVERAGES

WEST INDIES – BATTING

	T	*I*	*NO*	*R*	*HS*	*100s*	*Avge*	*Ct*
B. C. Lara	5	8	0	798	375	2	99.75	9
J. C. Adams	5	7	1	374	137	1	62.33	8
S. Chanderpaul	4	6	1	288	77	0	57.60	3
K. L. T. Arthurton	5	7	0	273	126	1	39.00	1
D. L. Haynes	4	7	1	217	63	0	36.16	0
R. B. Richardson	4	7	1	163	63	0	27.16	4
W. K. M. Benjamin	5	6	0	138	44	0	23.00	3
P. V. Simmons	2	4	1	50	22*	0	16.66	0
J. R. Murray	5	6	1	80	34	0	16.00	13
C. E. L. Ambrose	5	6	0	91	44	0	15.16	1
K. C. G. Benjamin	5	6	2	58	43*	0	14.50	0
C. A. Walsh	5	6	2	42	18*	0	10.50	1

Played in one Test: S. C. Williams 3, 21*.

* *Signifies not out.*

BOWLING

	O	*M*	*R*	*W*	*BB*	*5W/i*	*Avge*
C. E. L. Ambrose	224.2	59	519	26	6-24	2	19.96
K. C. G. Benjamin	181.5	38	566	22	6-66	1	25.72
C. A. Walsh	227.2	44	646	19	5-94	1	34.00
W. K. M. Benjamin	190.2	48	498	12	3-56	0	41.50

Also bowled: J. C. Adams 49.5–8–173–4; K. L. T. Arthurton 5–1–9–0; S. Chanderpaul 65–10–209–1; P. V. Simmons 3–1–4–0.

ENGLAND – BATTING

	T	*I*	*NO*	*R*	*HS*	*100s*	*Avge*	*Ct*
M. A. Atherton	5	9	0	510	144	2	56.66	3
A. J. Stewart	5	9	0	477	143	2	53.00	2
R. A. Smith	5	9	0	320	175	1	35.55	1
G. A. Hick	5	9	0	316	96	0	35.11	3
G. P. Thorpe	5	9	0	239	86	0	26.55	7
R. C. Russell	5	9	1	195	62	0	24.37	10
C. C. Lewis	5	9	1	170	75*	0	21.25	2
I. D. K. Salisbury	2	4	0	63	36	0	15.75	1
A. R. Caddick	4	6	1	69	29*	0	13.80	2
M. R. Ramprakash	4	7	0	73	23	0	10.42	2
A. R. C. Fraser	4	6	3	11	8*	0	3.66	2
A. P. Igglesden	2	4	2	4	3*	0	2.00	0

Played in two Tests: P. C. R. Tufnell 0*, 0 (2 ct). Played in one Test: D. E. Malcolm 6, 18; M. P. Maynard 35, 0 (1 ct).

* *Signifies not out.*

BOWLING

	O	*M*	*R*	*W*	*BB*	*5W/i*	*Avge*
A. R. C. Fraser	168.5	39	443	16	8-75	1	27.68
A. R. Caddick	170.2	30	545	18	6-65	2	30.27
I. D. K. Salisbury	68	9	276	7	4-163	0	39.42
C. C. Lewis	168.3	18	553	14	4-61	0	39.50

Also bowled: G. A. Hick 77–14–198–2; A. P. Igglesden 55.3–8–183–3; D. E. Malcolm 28–4–132–3; M. R. Ramprakash 20–3–48–0; A. J. Stewart 3.2–0–13–0; G. P. Thorpe 2–1–1–0; P. C. R. Tufnell 113–36–291–4.

ENGLAND TOUR AVERAGES – FIRST-CLASS MATCHES

BATTING

	M	*I*	*NO*	*R*	*HS*	*100s*	*Avge*	*Ct/St*
M. A. Atherton	7	12	0	704	144	3	58.66	4
A. J. Stewart	7	12	0	590	143	2	49.16	5
N. Hussain	3	5	2	144	103*	1	48.00	3
M. R. Ramprakash	8	14	2	457	154*	1	38.08	5
G. A. Hick	8	14	1	480	96	0	36.92	5
R. A. Smith	8	15	1	491	175	1	35.07	4
R. C. Russell	8	12	2	268	62	0	26.80	17/1
G. P. Thorpe	9	14	0	370	86	0	26.42	9
M. P. Maynard	4	6	1	103	40*	0	20.60	3

	M	*I*	*NO*	*R*	*HS*	*100s*	*Avge*	*Ct*
C. C. Lewis	7	10	1	176	75*	0	19.55	4
A. R. Caddick	6	7	1	105	36	0	17.50	3
I. D. K. Salisbury	4	5	0	66	36	0	13.20	4
A. R. C. Fraser	6	7	3	20	9	0	5.00	2
D. E. Malcolm	3	5	0	24	18	0	4.80	0
P. C. R. Tufnell	4	5	3	6	5*	0	3.00	3
A. P. Igglesden	4	7	3	8	3*	0	2.00	0

Played in three matches: S. L. Watkin 5*, 19, 0.

* *Signifies not out.*

BOWLING

	O	*M*	*R*	*W*	*BB*	*5W/i*	*Avge*
A. R. C. Fraser	205.5	51	539	20	8-75	1	26.95
I. D. K. Salisbury	145	29	462	17	4-59	0	27.17
A. R. Caddick	231.2	43	746	25	6-65	2	29.84
D. E. Malcolm	91	8	444	14	7-134	1	31.71
C. C. Lewis	190	22	614	19	4-61	0	32.31
S. L. Watkin	69	13	235	5	2-43	0	47.00
A. P. Igglesden	113.3	16	403	8	2-13	0	50.37
P. C. R. Tufnell	212.3	61	554	10	4-87	0	55.40

Also bowled: G. A. Hick 116–20–310–4; M. R. Ramprakash 21.2–3–50–1; A. J. Stewart 3.2–0–13–0; G. P. Thorpe 4–1–6–0.

Note: Matches in this section which were not first-class are signified by a dagger.

†At St John's, Antigua, January 23, 24, 25, 26. England XI won by 203 runs. Toss: England XI. England XI 419 (M. A. Atherton 108, A. J. Stewart 100 retired hurt, A. R. Caddick 77, S. L. Watkin 45, Extras 43; H. A. G. Anthony four for 130) and 265 for three dec. (G. P. Thorpe 80, G. A. Hick 111, R. A. Smith 34 not out); Antiguan XI 360 (E. Waldron 43, D. R. E. Joseph 44, A. Walsh 39, M. V. Simon 129, H. A. G. Anthony 46; A. R. Caddick five for 106, I. D. K. Salisbury three for 105) and 121 (E. Waldron 39, M. V. Simon 38; S. L. Watkin four for 32, I. D. K. Salisbury four for ten).

†At Basseterre, St Kitts, January 29, 30, 31. Drawn. Toss: England XI. England XI 308 for six dec. (A. J. Stewart 67, M. R. Ramprakash 136, R. A. Smith 71; J. C. Maynard three for 91) and 184 for seven dec. (C. C. Lewis 65; R. Powell three for 39); St Kitts & Nevis 258 (M. Liburd 36, B. Thompson 32, H. W. Williams 53, R. Powell 35, Extras 43; A. R. C. Fraser three for 39, P. C. R. Tufnell three for 58) and 22 for four.

LEEWARD ISLANDS v ENGLAND XI

At St John's, Antigua, February 3, 4, 5, 6. England XI won by seven wickets. Toss: Leeward Islands.

This was not representative of the Leeward Islands side about to win the Red Stripe Cup but, even omitting all five of their Test players, they presented England with their first serious opposition. It was a test passed with distinction: England dominated the game, twice bowling out the Islands for under 200 and winning with almost two sessions in hand. No one contributed more than Caddick, who extracted steep bounce and maintained a tight line. He deserved better than three wickets in each innings, not to mention the sore right shin which kept him out of the build-up to the First Test. Salisbury's leg-spin was also impressive; on the third afternoon, he took three of the first four wickets in the Leewards' second innings, effectively deciding the match. Atherton and Ramprakash opened with 105, but uncertainty surrounding the middle order was evident during a collapse to 226 for eight, salvaged by a doughty 56 from Russell. Needing only 43 in their second innings, England lost three wickets for 20 before order was restored.

Close of play: First day, England XI 19-0 (M. A. Atherton 8*, M. R. Ramprakash 5*); Second day, England XI 231-8 (R. C. Russell 19*, A. R. Caddick 2*); Third day, Leeward Islands 129-8 (W. D. Phillip 8*, V. A. Walsh 1*).

Leeward Islands

*S. C. Williams c Russell b Lewis	10	– c Caddick b Salisbury	24
L. A. Harrigan c Atherton b Caddick	0	– c Maynard b Salisbury	12
C. W. Walwyn c Russell b Caddick	65	– c Ramprakash b Watkin	30
H. W. Williams c Lewis b Watkin	14	– lbw b Caddick	25
†R. D. Jacobs run out	27	– (6) c Hussain b Hick	5
D. R. E. Joseph st Russell b Salisbury	18	– (5) c Lewis b Salisbury	2
H. A. G. Anthony lbw b Salisbury	9	– b Caddick	8
L. C. Weekes b Caddick	9	– c Hussain b Salisbury	1
W. D. Phillip c Salisbury b Lewis	9	– not out	31
V. A. Walsh not out	7	– lbw b Caddick	5
J. C. Maynard lbw b Lewis	0	– lbw b Lewis	14
L-b 6, n-b 7	13	L-b 3, n-b 13	16
1/3 2/28 3/70 4/119 5/124 6/145 7/158 8/160 9/181	181	1/35 2/61 3/83 4/86 5/94 6/113 7/118 8/120 9/139	173

Bowling: *First Innings*—Caddick 22–6–62–3; Watkin 16–7–33–1; Lewis 9.5–2–21–3; Salisbury 18–6–49–2; Hick 7–2–10–0. *Second Innings*—Caddick 19–6–32–3; Watkin 12–2–30–1; Lewis 4.4–0–29–1; Salisbury 28–7–59–4; Hick 5–0–20–1.

England XI

*M. A. Atherton c Phillip b Weekes	77	– b Walsh	9
M. R. Ramprakash lbw b Anthony	41	– c Phillip b Maynard	4
G. P. Thorpe c Jacobs b Maynard	11	– c and b Walsh	4
G. A. Hick c Jacobs b Maynard	0	– not out	11
N. Hussain c Jacobs b Weekes	14	– not out	15
M. P. Maynard lbw b Walsh	25		
†R. C. Russell c S. C. Williams b Phillip	56		
C. C. Lewis b Phillip	6		
I. D. K. Salisbury lbw b Anthony	3		
A. R. Caddick c Phillip b Anthony	36		
S. L. Watkin not out	5		
B 5, l-b 8, w 8, n-b 17	38	L-b 1	1
1/105 2/127 3/128 4/156 5/169 6/201 7/216 8/226 9/296	312	1/12 2/16 3/20	(3 wkts) 44

Bowling: *First Innings*—Walsh 25–3–90–1; Weekes 20–5–44–2; Phillip 30.4–10–49–2; Maynard 18–2–65–2; Anthony 24–8–51–3. *Second Innings*—Walsh 5–0–23–2; Maynard 4–0–16–1; Phillip 0.4–0–4–0.

Umpires: J. Stevens and P. C. White.

BARBADOS v ENGLAND XI

At Bridgetown, February 10, 11, 12, 13. Drawn. Toss: Barbados.

There was no prospect of a positive result once the two first innings had occupied three complete days, and inertia was not England's sole frustration. Fraser had two bones in his left hand broken while batting and was ruled out for at least a week, an unwanted addition to England's worries. Their fielding also gave cause for concern, especially during a crazy hour on the second day when the Barbados last-wicket pair were dropped five times – all off Malcolm, depriving him of an eighth wicket for a career-best analysis. Paradoxically, the most impressive England bowler was Tufnell, who took no wickets in the first innings. Holder and Campbell batted attractively for Barbados but, after they carried on into the second afternoon, Atherton did not rush England's reply. His own reassuring century took almost six hours. Against some brisk swing bowling from Gibson, England lost their last seven wickets for 56, but there was time only for a token Barbados declaration.

Close of play: First day, Barbados 289-6 (V. C. Drakes 2*); Second day, England XI 144-2 (M. A. Atherton 71*, A. R. C. Fraser 6*); Third day, England XI 302.

Barbados

D. L. Haynes c Thorpe b Malcolm	6	– b Igglesden	2
P. A. Wallace c Ramprakash b Malcolm	57	– lbw b Igglesden	7
S. L. Campbell b Malcolm	83	– c Russell b Tufnell	54
*R. I. C. Holder lbw b Malcolm	85	– c Stewart b Hick	43
L. K. Puckerin c Smith b Malcolm	6	– lbw b Tufnell	11
†C. O. Browne c Thorpe b Igglesden	41	– not out	25
V. C. Drakes c Russell b Malcolm	2	– not out	34
O. D. Gibson b Malcolm	3		
W. E. Reid c Tufnell b Igglesden	3		
S. M. Skeete c Russell b Fraser	34		
D. R. Maynard not out	17		
L-b 1, n-b 10	11	B 5, l-b 3, n-b 8	16
1/14 2/96 3/179 4/187 5/285 6/289 7/292 8/295 9/299	348	1/3 2/22 3/99 4/129 5/130 (5 wkts dec.)	192

Bowling: *First Innings*—Malcolm 26–1–134–7; Igglesden 20–4–71–2; Fraser 19–4–62–1; Tufnell 31–6–62–0; Hick 6–1–18–0. *Second Innings*—Malcolm 13–1–67–0; Igglesden 7–1–13–2; Tufnell 24–7–51–2; Hick 16–3–48–1; Thorpe 2–0–5–0.

England XI

*M. A. Atherton b Reid	108		
A. J. Stewart b Drakes	47		
M. R. Ramprakash c Browne b Gibson	6	– (2) not out	21
A. R. C. Fraser c Browne b Maynard	9		
R. A. Smith lbw b Reid	59	– (1) not out	25
G. A. Hick c Campbell b Gibson	20		
G. P. Thorpe c Campbell b Drakes	16		
†R. C. Russell lbw b Gibson	6		
A. P. Igglesden c Browne b Gibson	3		
P. C. R. Tufnell not out	0		
D. E. Malcolm b Gibson	0		
B 1, l-b 1, w 3, n-b 23	28	N-b 2	2
1/87 2/128 3/149 4/246 5/268 6/276 7/288 8/302 9/302	302	(no wkt)	48

Bowling: *First Innings*—Gibson 32.1–11–87–5; Skeete 4–1–20–0; Drakes 28–2–92–2; Maynard 18.2–4–52–1; Reid 22–5–49–2. *Second Innings*—Gibson 6–1–12–0; Maynard 5–2–16–0; Reid 7–3–11–0; Haynes 3–1–6–0; Campbell 2–1–3–0.

Umpires: D. Holder and H. Moore.

†WEST INDIES v ENGLAND

First One-Day International

At Bridgetown, February 16. England won by 61 runs. Toss: England.

England comfortably defended what seemed an inadequate total, but this was not so much a victory for them as a surrender by West Indies. Complacency had marked the home team's preparations, with four players, the captain included, failing to arrive for eve-of-match practice, and this attitude translated to their batting. All the main batsmen were out to rash attacking strokes and, by the time Adams showed a more rational approach, it was all too late. England's fifth consecutive one-day win over West Indies was launched by a fine innings from Atherton. Playing, remarkably, only his 11th limited-overs international and his first since he was named Man of the Series against West Indies in 1991, he batted through 46 overs, compensating for low scores by the rest of the top four and allowing Hick and Maynard the freedom to carry the total past 200.

Man of the Match: M. A. Atherton.

England

*M. A. Atherton c Richardson b Cummins . 86	C. C. Lewis not out 6
†A. J. Stewart c Lara b Benjamin 11	B 4, l-b 7, n-b 3 14
G. P. Thorpe c Adams b Benjamin 4	—
R. A. Smith c and b Harper 12	1/35 (2) 2/45 (3) (5 wkts, 50 overs) 202
G. A. Hick c Simmons b Cummins 47	3/73 (4) 4/166 (1)
M. P. Maynard not out 22	5/176 (5)

S. L. Watkin, A. P. Igglesden, P. C. R. Tufnell and D. E. Malcolm did not bat.

Bowling: Ambrose 10–2–35–0; Walsh 10–0–42–0; Benjamin 10–2–38–2; Cummins 10–1–28–2; Harper 10–0–48–1.

West Indies

D. L. Haynes c Malcolm b Igglesden . . . 17	C. E. L. Ambrose c Smith b Malcolm . . 10
B. C. Lara c Igglesden b Malcolm 9	C. A. Walsh not out 1
*R. B. Richardson c Maynard b Lewis . 12	B 1, l-b 10, w 11 22
K. L. T. Arthurton b Lewis 6	—
P. V. Simmons b Lewis 0	1/17 (2) 2/43 (1) (40.4 overs) 141
†J. C. Adams c Thorpe b Igglesden 29	3/48 (3) 4/48 (5)
R. A. Harper lbw b Watkin 11	5/55 (4) 6/82 (7)
A. C. Cummins c Thorpe b Malcolm . . 24	7/121 (6) 8/122 (9)
W. K. M. Benjamin c Thorpe b Tufnell 0	9/136 (8) 10/141 (10)

Bowling: Malcolm 8.4–1–41–3; Watkin 8–1–27–1; Lewis 8–2–18–3; Igglesden 8–2–12–2; Tufnell 8–0–32–1.

Umpires: L. H. Barker and C. R. Duncan.

WEST INDIES v ENGLAND

First Test Match

At Kingston, February 19, 20, 21, 23, 24. West Indies won by eight wickets. Toss: England.

The momentous victory here in February 1990 had sustained English optimism at the start of this series but Sabina Park was not now so accommodating. England were always in trouble after squandering a century opening stand by losing seven wickets for 73 on the first afternoon. Although there was a flurry of excitement as West Indies stumbled to 23 for three, their middle order proved decisively more resilient. The match was as good as over when England, trailing by 173, collapsed to 63 for four on the third evening. But the quality of Walsh's fast bowling in that session was later compromised by an unwarranted and unpunished intimidation of the England No. 11, Malcolm. In allowing such cynical bowling, directed at the body and latterly from round the wicket, to pass unchecked, the Zimbabwean umpire, Ian Robinson, may have undermined confidence in the new ICC panel of independent umpires.

England decided to counter the predictable battery of West Indian fast bowlers with four seamers of their own, the same strategy they had employed here four years earlier. Omitted, along with the unlucky Tufnell, was his Middlesex colleague, Ramprakash, so Thorpe was asked to bat at No. 3, ahead of the more experienced Smith and Hick. Atherton won a valuable toss and, midway through the first afternoon, England were in tranquil waters at 121 without loss. As so often with West Indian pace, the storm gathered dramatically and without warning: three wickets fell for 13 runs. Kenny Benjamin had both openers caught behind and, when Smith, of whom much was expected, was bowled by Walsh pushing down the wrong line, the previously subdued crowd transformed the atmosphere. Benjamin finished with six for 66, easily his best Test figures, and England fell at least 100 short of a competitive total.

When Haynes, Simmons and Richardson, all showing signs of rustiness, were banished by Caddick and a fired-up Malcolm, England briefly hoped Kingston history might repeat itself. Thereafter, however, the bowling lacked the consistency or penetration to trouble players as good as Lara, Arthurton and Adams. The three left-handers amassed 304 between them. Although Arthurton alone reached a century, Lara played strokes well worth the price of admission in his 83, and Adams provided the solidity among the shotmakers which West Indies had lacked since the retirement of Logie. He was finally stranded on 95 not out.

The England openers were batting as comfortably as they had done in the first innings until Stewart was run out attempting a third run, whereupon Walsh discernibly changed gear. In the second half of an unbroken two-hour spell he bowled harrowingly fast and short to dismiss Atherton and Smith – both caught by Adams, who equalled the West Indian record of six catches in a Test. When Maynard went too, England were virtually finished. But Hick, arriving at the height of the battle, won many admirers with an innings of 96, obliging West Indies to bat again and taking the game ten minutes into its fifth day. Hick, who had totalled only 75 runs in seven innings against West Indies in 1991, batted for 310 minutes before being sharply caught at slip by the substitute, Harper. A last-wicket stand of 39 further frustrated West Indies, provoking the unedifying assault by Walsh against Malcolm who, despite a Test-best 18, remained one of the most inept batsmen in international cricket. English morale suffered another blow when Malcolm flew home a few days later, for an operation on a knee injury quite unrelated to the body blows he had taken.

Man of the Match: J. C. Adams.

Close of play: First day, England 209-7 (M. P. Maynard 24*, A. R. Caddick 3*); Second day, West Indies 238-4 (K. L. T. Arthurton 113*, J. C. Adams 21*); Third day, England 80-4 (G. A. Hick 24*, R. C. Russell 6*); Fourth day, West Indies 87-2 (D. L. Haynes 40*).

England

*M. A. Atherton c Murray b K. C. G. Benjamin	55	– c Adams b Walsh	28
A. J. Stewart c Murray b K. C. G. Benjamin	70	– run out	19
G. P. Thorpe b K. C. G. Benjamin	16	– (7) b W. K. M. Benjamin	14
R. A. Smith b Walsh	0	– (3) c Adams b Walsh	2
G. A. Hick b Adams	23	– (4) c sub (R. A. Harper) b K. C. G. Benjamin	96
M. P. Maynard lbw b K. C. G. Benjamin	35	– (5) c Murray b W. K. M. Benjamin	0
†R. C. Russell lbw b K. C. G. Benjamin	0	– (6) c Adams b W. K. M. Benjamin	32
C. C. Lewis c Adams b Ambrose	8	– lbw b Ambrose	21
A. R. Caddick c Adams b K. C. G. Benjamin	3	– not out	29
A. P. Igglesden not out	3	– c Adams b K. C. G. Benjamin	0
D. E. Malcolm run out	6	– b Walsh	18
B 2, l-b 5, w 4, n-b 4	15	B 1, l-b 3, w 2, n-b 2	8
1/121 (2) 2/133 (1) 3/134 (4) 4/172 (5) 5/172 (3) 6/172 (7) 7/194 (8) 8/209 (9) 9/227 (6) 10/234 (11)	234	1/34 (2) 2/39 (3) 3/58 (1) 4/63 (5) 5/126 (6) 6/155 (7) 7/213 (8) 8/226 (4) 9/228 (10) 10/267 (11)	267

Bowling: *First Innings*—Ambrose 22–8–46–1; Walsh 23–6–41–1; K. C. G. Benjamin 24–7–66–6; W. K. M. Benjamin 19.1–7–43–0; Adams 10–1–31–1. *Second Innings*—Ambrose 24–4–67–1; Walsh 24.5–6–67–3; W. K. M. Benjamin 20–3–56–3; K. C. G. Benjamin 18–2–60–2; Adams 2–0–9–0; Simmons 3–1–4–0.

West Indies

D. L. Haynes c Thorpe b Malcolm	4	– not out	43
P. V. Simmons c Russell b Caddick	8	– lbw b Igglesden	12
*R. B. Richardson c Maynard b Malcolm	5	– (4) not out	4
B. C. Lara b Hick	83	– (3) b Caddick	28
K. L. T. Arthurton c Lewis b Malcolm	126		
J. C. Adams not out	95		
†J. R. Murray lbw b Igglesden	34		
W. K. M. Benjamin b Caddick	38		
C. E. L. Ambrose b Caddick	0		
K. C. G. Benjamin b Lewis	0		
C. A. Walsh lbw b Lewis	0		
L-b 10, w 1, n-b 3	14	B 5, l-b 3	8
1/12 (1) 2/12 (2) 3/23 (3) 4/167 (4) 5/256 (5) 6/319 (7) 7/389 (8) 8/389 (9) 9/390 (10) 10/407 (11)	407	1/38 (2) 2/87 (3)	(2 wkts) 95

Bowling: *First Innings*—Malcolm 23–3–113–3; Caddick 29–5–94–3; Lewis 26–4–82–2; Igglesden 24–5–53–1; Hick 21–4–55–1. *Second Innings*—Malcolm 5–1–19–0; Caddick 6–1–19–1; Lewis 3–0–6–0; Igglesden 7–0–36–1; Hick 3–1–2–0; Stewart 2.2–0–5–0.

Umpires: I. D. Robinson (Zimbabwe) and S. A. Bucknor. Referee: S. M. Gavaskar (India).

†WEST INDIES v ENGLAND

Second One-Day International

At Kingston, February 26. West Indies won by three wickets, their target having been revised to 238 from 47 overs. Toss: West Indies.

Played throughout amid a near-deafening din from a capacity crowd, this was a competitive game in which the weather may have been decisive. A shower, when England were marginally on top, reduced West Indies' target from 96 in 14 overs to 80 in 11. Marshalled by local hero Adams, West Indies won with seven balls in hand, having taken 16 from the 43rd over, bowled by Igglesden, whose previous six overs cost only 13. England's top-order batsmen had done their work well, following up another century opening stand with substantial innings from Smith and Hick. They did not make the most of the last overs, however, and, though Walsh sprained his ankle, West Indies could even get through 11 overs from Simmons and Arthurton without undue punishment. Haynes, back near to his best, set up the run-chase and England's bowling again looked uninspired under pressure.

Man of the Match: J. C. Adams.

England

*M. A. Atherton c Arthurton b Harper . 46
†A. J. Stewart run out 66
R. A. Smith c Harper b K. C. G. Benjamin . 56
G. A. Hick c Cummins b Arthurton . . . 31
M. P. Maynard b Cummins 22
N. Hussain c Richardson b Cummins . . 10
C. C. Lewis b K. C. G. Benjamin 0
S. L. Watkin b K. C. G. Benjamin 0
A. P. Igglesden not out 2
P. C. R. Tufnell not out 2
L-b 9, w 7, n-b 2 18

1/112 (2) 2/128 (1) 3/209 (4) 4/214 (3) 5/247 (6) 6/248 (7) 7/248 (8) 8/249 (5) — (8 wkts, 50 overs) 253

A. R. C. Fraser did not bat.

Bowling: Walsh 5–1–26–0; K. C. G. Benjamin 10–1–44–3; Cummins 8–1–42–2; W. K. M. Benjamin 8–0–33–0; Harper 8–0–45–1; Simmons 7–0–32–0; Arthurton 4–0–22–1.

West Indies

D. L. Haynes c and b Hick 53
B. C. Lara lbw b Watkin 8
P. V. Simmons b Fraser 39
K. L. T. Arthurton st Stewart b Hick . . 12
*R. B. Richardson c Fraser b Watkin . . 32
†J. C. Adams not out 52
R. A. Harper lbw b Watkin 0
A. C. Cummins c Smith b Watkin. 16
W. K. M. Benjamin not out 9
B 3, l-b 7, w 6, n-b 3 19

1/13 (2) 2/111 (1) 3/128 (3) 4/130 (4) 5/186 (5) 6/186 (7) 7/223 (8) — (7 wkts, 45.5 overs) 240

K. C. G. Benjamin and C. A. Walsh did not bat.

Bowling: Igglesden 7–1–29–0; Watkin 9.5–1–49–4; Fraser 9–0–50–1; Lewis 9–0–48–0; Tufnell 4–0–22–0; Hick 7–0–32–2.

Umpires: L. H. Barker and S. A. Bucknor.

†WEST INDIES v ENGLAND

Third One-Day International

At St Vincent, March 2. West Indies won by 165 runs. Toss: England.

From the moment when Atherton so misread the pitch that he chose to field, this was a dire day for England. They bowled appallingly and batted utterly without spirit on the way to their heaviest defeat in any one-day international – another shattering blow to already shaky morale. But, on a blissful day at the Caribbean's most scenic ground, credit was due to West Indies for cricket of imposing superiority. Their batting was often breathtaking, especially that of Lara, who made 60 from 41 balls, and Richardson, whose 52 came from 26 balls in the late acceleration to what was easily a record score by any country in a one-day international against England. The bowlers then did their simpler job so professionally that, Hick apart, not one England batsman threatened an innings. Atherton, having erroneously dropped himself down the order on the theory that Lewis might make a brisker start, cut a sorry figure, left helpless by the early collapse.

Man of the Match: D. L. Haynes.

West Indies

D. L. Haynes c Lewis b Tufnell	83
P. V. Simmons c Hussain b Tufnell	63
B. C. Lara c Stewart b Fraser	60
K. L. T. Arthurton c Smith b Watkin	28
*R. B. Richardson not out	52
†J. C. Adams c Smith b Watkin	6
R. A. Harper run out	15
A. C. Cummins not out	0
L-b 4, w 2	6
1/145 (2) 2/156 (1) 3/230 (3) 4/242 (4) 5/256 (6) 6/300 (7) (6 wkts, 50 overs)	313

W. K. M. Benjamin, C. E. L. Ambrose and K. C. G. Benjamin did not bat.

Bowling: Igglesden 10–1–65–0; Watkin 9–0–61–2; Lewis 9–0–67–0; Fraser 10–1–46–1; Hick 3–0–18–0; Tufnell 9–0–52–2.

England

C. C. Lewis lbw b Cummins	2
†A. J. Stewart c Adams b K. C. G. Benjamin	13
R. A. Smith b Ambrose	18
G. A. Hick c Cummins b Harper	32
M. P. Maynard c Simmons b Cummins	6
N. Hussain c and b Harper	16
*M. A. Atherton not out	19
S. L. Watkin c Lara b Arthurton	4
A. P. Igglesden c Ambrose b Lara	18
A. R. C. Fraser st Adams b Lara	1
P. C. R. Tufnell not out	0
B 1, l-b 12, w 6	19
1/7 (1) 2/24 (2) 3/41 (3) 4/64 (5) 5/98 (6) 6/105 (4) 7/119 (8) 8/144 (9) 9/148 (10) (9 wkts, 50 overs)	148

Bowling: K. C. G. Benjamin 6–0–21–1; Cummins 8–1–22–2; W. K. M. Benjamin 5–1–15–0; Ambrose 6–2–13–1; Simmons 7–1–18–0; Harper 10–0–29–2; Arthurton 6–1–12–1; Lara 2–0–5–2.

Umpires: L. H. Barker and G. T. Johnson.

†WEST INDIES v ENGLAND

Fourth One-Day International

At Port-of-Spain, March 5. West Indies won by 15 runs, England's target having been revised to 209 from 36 overs. Toss: England.

Everything fell in England's favour in this match, but still the result went against them. Winning the toss on a pitch damp and uneven enough to make life unpleasant for the batsmen, they bowled without discipline to concede almost six runs an over. Yet they received the lifeline of a substantially reduced target after rain ended West Indies' innings. Needing 209 from 36 overs, they were on course as long as Atherton and Smith were together. But a familiar collapse ensued, in an unfamiliar manner, against the off-spin of Harper. For West Indies, Haynes made the 17th one-day international century of his long career and batted through all but two overs of the innings, though never more destructively than in the initial hour, when England conceded any right to victory in this match or the series.

Man of the Match: D. L. Haynes.

West Indies

D. L. Haynes b Lewis	115
P. V. Simmons c Hick b Lewis	16
B. C. Lara lbw b Fraser	19
K. L. T. Arthurton c Stewart b Fraser	0
*R. B. Richardson c Ramprakash b Caddick	13
†J. C. Adams c Caddick b Fraser	40
R. A. Harper b Lewis	23
A. C. Cummins not out	13
W. K. M. Benjamin not out	0
B 4, l-b 4, w 13, n-b 5	26
1/45 (2) 2/75 (3) 3/75 (4) 4/98 (5) 5/222 (6) 6/238 (1) 7/265 (7) (7 wkts, 45.4 overs)	265

C. E. L. Ambrose and K. C. G. Benjamin did not bat.

Bowling: Igglesden 3–0–16–0; Caddick 10–0–60–1; Fraser 10–0–31–3; Lewis 9.4–1–59–3; Salisbury 9–0–58–0; Hick 4–0–33–0.

England

*M. A. Atherton b K. C. G. Benjamin	41
†A. J. Stewart b K. C. G. Benjamin	2
R. A. Smith b Harper	45
G. A. Hick c and b Harper	10
M. P. Maynard b Harper	8
M. R. Ramprakash b Ambrose	31
C. C. Lewis c Lara b Harper	4
A. R. Caddick not out	20
I. D. K. Salisbury b Cummins	5
A. P. Igglesden run out	0
A. R. C. Fraser not out	4
B 1, l-b 9, w 11, n-b 2	23
1/23 (2) 2/86 (1) 3/110 (3) 4/121 (4) 5/130 (5) 6/145 (7) 7/177 (6) 8/184 (9) 9/184 (10) (9 wkts, 36 overs)	193

Bowling: K. C. G. Benjamin 8–0–37–2; Cummins 6–0–34–1; Ambrose 8–0–34–1; W. K. M. Benjamin 7–0–38–0; Harper 7–0–40–4.

Umpires: S. A. Bucknor and C. E. Cumberbatch.

†WEST INDIES v ENGLAND

Fifth One-Day International

At Port-of-Spain, March 6. England won by five wickets, their target having been revised to 201 from 40 overs. Toss: West Indies.

With the series already decided, this was a hollow occasion to which West Indies contributed by resting both Haynes and Ambrose. England reduced the margin to 3-2, but their cricket was impressive only by comparison with their previous two games, although Lewis bowled better than at any stage of the tour and Salisbury's leg-spin genuinely troubled good batsmen. A rumbustious 84 by Simmons ensured a useful total of 250, but rain in the early stages of England's reply reduced the requirement to 201 from 40 overs. Stewart, with some vivid strokeplay, scored 53 from 38 balls in his rush to ensure England would be up with the asking-rate if further rain fell. After he was bowled in the 13th over, Atherton and Hick saw them home with something to spare.

Man of the Match: A. J. Stewart.

West Indies

P. V. Simmons b Salisbury	84
†J. C. Adams c Atherton b Salisbury	23
B. C. Lara c Stewart b Caddick	16
K. L. T. Arthurton c Ramprakash b Lewis	17
*R. B. Richardson c Stewart b Salisbury	15
R. I. C. Holder run out	26
R. A. Harper c and b Lewis	37
A. C. Cummins c Smith b Lewis	11
W. K. M. Benjamin c Ramprakash b Lewis	8
K. C. G. Benjamin not out	0
B 1, l-b 10, w 1, n-b 1	13
1/89 (2) 2/126 (1) 3/135 (3) 4/164 (5) 5/164 (4) 6/230 (7) 7/232 (6) 8/248 (8) 9/250 (9) (9 wkts, 50 overs)	250

C. A. Walsh did not bat.

Bowling: Fraser 10–2–41–0; Watkin 10–0–56–0; Lewis 10–0–35–4; Caddick 10–2–66–1; Salisbury 10–0–41–3.

England

*M. A. Atherton b K. C. G. Benjamin	51
†A. J. Stewart b Cummins	53
R. A. Smith lbw b Cummins	4
G. A. Hick not out	47
M. P. Maynard c Adams b K. C. G. Benjamin	1
M. R. Ramprakash c Adams b Walsh	10
C. C. Lewis not out	16
B 2, l-b 9, w 4, n-b 4	19
1/62 (2) 2/83 (3) 3/151 (1) 4/156 (5) 5/174 (6) (5 wkts, 36.4 overs)	201

A. R. Caddick, I. D. K. Salisbury, S. L. Watkin and A. R. C. Fraser did not bat.

Bowling: W. K. M. Benjamin 8–1–33–0; Walsh 10–0–58–1; Cummins 7.4–0–36–2; K. C. G. Benjamin 9–0–55–2; Harper 2–0–8–0.

Umpires: S. A. Bucknor and C. E. Cumberbatch.

WEST INDIES BOARD PRESIDENT'S XI v ENGLAND XI

At Georgetown, March 10, 11, 12, 13. Drawn. Toss: England XI.

With most of the regional teams no longer enthusiastic about fixtures against touring sides, this was as competitive as England's programme outside the internationals was to get, the President's XI being a shadow West Indian side. It could be argued, therefore, that England squandered the chance of a Test match rehearsal by choosing all their young batsmen and all four fit seam bowlers, plain indication that they were unsure of their best team. Atherton and Stewart both rested, with Smith taking over the captaincy. Traditional Georgetown rain, which prevented any play on the second day and until after lunch on the third, ruined the match anyway. Although Ramprakash – on his first visit to his father's native Guyana – and Hussain made centuries, England completed the four days no closer to a strategy for the next Test than they had been following their defeat in Kingston.

Close of play: First day, England XI 308-2 (M. R. Ramprakash 154*, M. P. Maynard 40*); Second day, No play; Third day, West Indies Board President's XI 181-7 (K. A. Wong 9*, R. Dhanraj 1*).

England XI

*R. A. Smith c Semple b Browne	8	– c Semple b Perry 43
M. R. Ramprakash not out	154	
G. P. Thorpe b Dhanraj	84	
M. P. Maynard not out	40	
N. Hussain (did not bat)		– (2) not out 103
†R. C. Russell (did not bat)		– (3) not out 11
B 2, l-b 3, n-b 17	22	L-b 4, n-b 9 13
1/44 2/202 (2 wkts dec.)	308	1/121 (1 wkt dec.) 170

C. C. Lewis, I. D. K. Salisbury, A. R. Caddick, S. L. Watkin and A. R. C. Fraser did not bat.

Bowling: *First Innings*—Cuffy 17–4–46–0; Browne 17–3–59–1; Perry 17–1–54–0; Dhanraj 27–3–101–1; Hooper 14–5–32–0; Chanderpaul 4–0–11–0. *Second Innings*—Cuffy 8–1–28–0; Browne 6–1–30–0; Hooper 11–1–48–0; Perry 14–3–22–1; Dhanraj 9.5–0–37–0; Chanderpaul 1–0–1–0.

West Indies Board President's XI

D. A. Joseph c Salisbury b Lewis	7	– c Maynard b Salisbury	45
R. G. Samuels lbw b Caddick	12	– b Fraser	56
K. F. Semple c Russell b Salisbury	76	– not out	29
*C. L. Hooper lbw b Fraser	7		
S. Chanderpaul c Smith b Salisbury	3	– (4) c Russell b Ramprakash	28
K. Mason b Fraser	29		
N. O. Perry c and b Salisbury	32		
†K. A. Wong not out	9		
R. Dhanraj not out	1		
B 1, l-b 2, n-b 2	5	L-b 8, n-b 4	12
1/15 2/26 3/37 4/48 5/139 6/143 7/180 (7 wkts dec.)	181	1/78 2/132 3/170 (3 wkts)	170

C. E. Cuffy and B. St A. Browne did not bat.

Bowling: *First Innings*—Lewis 7–2–11–1; Caddick 12–1–61–1; Fraser 10–4–18–2; Salisbury 21–6–52–3; Watkin 10–1–36–0. *Second Innings*—Caddick 8–0–46–0; Watkin 11–0–72–0; Fraser 8–4–16–1; Salisbury 10–1–26–1; Ramprakash 1.2–0–2–1.

Umpires: L. H. Barker and E. Nicholls.

WEST INDIES v ENGLAND

Second Test Match

At Georgetown, March 17, 18, 19, 20, 22. West Indies won by an innings and 44 runs. Toss: West Indies. Test debut: S. Chanderpaul.

The superiority of West Indies was overwhelming, during a game they were able to win in comfort despite donating first use of the pitch to a grateful England. Atherton's impressive 144 ensured the gift was not entirely spurned. But a total of 322 was plainly insufficient and West Indies, inspired by an irrepressible Lara, dictated the match from that point. They won midway through the final day, immediately prompting talk of a clean sweep of the five Tests.

Both teams made late, contentious selections. West Indies omitted Simmons, after 16 consecutive caps, and included the Guyanese teenager, Chanderpaul, as much for his leg-breaks as his left-handed batting. England decided against a second spinner, choosing only Salisbury, though he seemed to be there more through mistrust of the seamers rather than any belief that it was the correct policy.

Richardson's curious decision to bowl was almost vindicated when Walsh took wickets in each of his first two overs. England's best passage of the match then carried them to 245 for three before their last seven wickets fell for 77. Smith, missed at slip by Lara off Winston Benjamin when 27, imposed himself for the first time; his stand of 171 with Atherton was a third-wicket record for any Test at Bourda. Atherton, playing with imperious command, added a further 72 with Hick. On a slow pitch, inclined to keep low, the West Indian bowlers seemed to have been subdued. This assumption is always dangerous, however: Ambrose roused himself after a lethargic few weeks and struck the critical blows of the match. He removed Hick, Thorpe and finally Atherton, who had batted eight minutes short of seven hours for the highest score on the ground by an Englishman since Sir Leonard Hutton's 169 in 1953-54. Due to Guyana government policy, and rain in 1989-90, England had not played a Test on the ground at all for 20 years.

Half the second day remained when West Indies began batting, and it was soon evident that England would struggle to bowl them out. After Richardson had made a modest success of his role as stand-in opener, Haynes and Lara took 89 off the day's last 20 overs. With the prospect of something special from Lara, not to mention their own Chanderpaul, the Saturday crowd was massed and exuberant, compared with some thin attendances on other days. They were not disappointed. After Salisbury had taken two early wickets, Lara's control was hypnotic, his timing and placement stunning. Undone, at length, by a minor misjudgment when hitting through mid-wicket, he had batted only 257 minutes, hit 112 in boundaries and exerted such a spell over the day that England were grateful to remove him for as little as 167. Adams, his foil in a fourth-wicket stand of 112, now assumed the senior role, advancing in his quiet, understated way to the maiden Test hundred he had missed at Kingston while, to the noisy delight of the stands, trees and other vantage points, Chanderpaul made a debut half-century of wristy elegance.

England's four main bowlers were powerless against the assault: the recruitment of Hick and Ramprakash for 35 overs of part-time spin told its own story. After five sessions in the field, the tourists faced a deficit of 234 and needed further heroics if the contest was to be extended. When Atherton was out to Ambrose's fourth ball – a beauty which brought him his 200th Test wicket – and Ramprakash failed again, the die was cast. Stewart batted fluently, if at times fortunately, but Smith and Hick, who was struck painfully on the elbow and bowled next ball, were swept away before the close of the fourth day. Realistically, only rain could alter the outcome by then. Lewis and Salisbury did their best, with two hours' resistance for the eighth wicket. But once the patience and perseverance of the bowling broke their partnership, the last two wickets followed inside two overs, giving Kenny Benjamin seven in the match to Ambrose's eight.

Man of the Match: B. C. Lara.

Close of play: First day, England 258-5 (M. A. Atherton 131*, I. D. K. Salisbury 2*); Second day, West Indies 152-1 (D. L. Haynes 53*, B. C. Lara 57*); Third day, West Indies 487-6 (J. C. Adams 102*, W. K. M. Benjamin 37*); Fourth day, England 119-4 (A. J. Stewart 72*, G. P. Thorpe 10*).

England

First innings		Second innings	
*M. A. Atherton c Murray b Ambrose	144	– b Ambrose	0
A. J. Stewart b Walsh	0	– b K. C. G. Benjamin	79
M. R. Ramprakash lbw b Walsh	2	– b Ambrose	5
R. A. Smith c Lara b K. C. G. Benjamin	84	– c Richardson b Ambrose	24
G. A. Hick c Richardson b Ambrose	33	– b K. C. G. Benjamin	5
G. P. Thorpe b Ambrose	0	– b Walsh	20
I. D. K. Salisbury lbw b W. K. M. Benjamin	8	– (9) b Walsh	19
†R. C. Russell c Richardson b Ambrose	13	– (7) c Murray b Ambrose	6
C. C. Lewis c Richardson b K. C. G. Benjamin	17	– (8) c Adams b K. C. G. Benjamin	24
A. R. C. Fraser not out	0	– b K. C. G. Benjamin	0
A. P. Igglesden b K. C. G. Benjamin	0	– not out	1
L-b 14, n-b 7	21	B 2, l-b 2, w 1, n-b 2	7
1/0 (2) 2/2 (3) 3/173 (4) 4/245 (5) 5/253 (6) 6/276 (1) 7/281 (7) 8/322 (8) 9/322 (9) 10/322 (11)	322	1/0 (1) 2/30 (3) 3/91 (4) 4/96 (5) 5/129 (2) 6/140 (6) 7/150 (7) 8/185 (8) 9/186 (10) 10/190 (9)	190

Bowling: *First Innings*—Ambrose 30–8–58–4; Walsh 26–7–69–2; K. C. G. Benjamin 23.5–5–60–3; W. K. M. Benjamin 26–9–62–1; Adams 3–1–10–0; Chanderpaul 16–2–49–0. *Second Innings*—Ambrose 23–5–37–4; Walsh 25–4–71–2; W. K. M. Benjamin 16–4–44–0; K. C. G. Benjamin 19–6–34–4; Adams 2–2–0–0.

West Indies

D. L. Haynes c Russell b Salisbury	63
*R. B. Richardson c Lewis b Fraser	35
B. C. Lara c Atherton b Lewis	167
K. L. T. Arthurton c Thorpe b Salisbury	5
J. C. Adams lbw b Igglesden	137
S. Chanderpaul b Salisbury	62
†J. R. Murray lbw b Salisbury	0
W. K. M. Benjamin b Fraser	44
C. E. L. Ambrose c Russell b Lewis	10
K. C. G. Benjamin c Russell b Lewis	1
C. A. Walsh not out	10
B 2, l-b 6, w 1, n-b 13	22
1/63 (2) 2/177 (1) 3/203 (4) 4/315 (3) 5/441 (6) 6/441 (7) 7/505 (8) 8/520 (9) 9/532 (10) 10/556 (5)	556

[Graham Morris

Curtly Ambrose celebrates yet another wicket in England's Port-of-Spain débâcle – Graham Thorpe bowled for three.

Bowling: Lewis 28–1–110–3; Igglesden 24.3–3–94–1; Fraser 29–5–85–2; Salisbury 37–4–163–4; Hick 20–1–61–0; Ramprakash 15–1–35–0.

Umpires: S. Venkataraghavan (India) and C. R. Duncan.
Referee: J. R. Reid (New Zealand).

WEST INDIES v ENGLAND

Third Test Match

At Port-of-Spain, March 25, 26, 27, 29, 30. West Indies won by 147 runs. Toss: West Indies.

The fourth day of this match witnessed an astonishing transformation: when it began England were enviably placed for a victory which would have kept the series alive; by the end they were threatened by their lowest score in history. Eventually, by a single run, they avoided the ultimate indignity of equalling the 45 all out recorded at Sydney, 107 years earlier, but the England side of 1887 actually won. The 1994 side lost both match and series during a staggering collapse to fast bowling of the highest calibre from Ambrose, who finished with six for 24 in the innings and 11 for 84 in the match.

West Indies, retaining the team that won in Georgetown, again won the toss and Richardson once more did the unexpected by choosing to bat first. The pitch looked mottled and rough and lived up to its reputation of being at its most mischievous on the first day but, thanks chiefly to a highly disciplined innings of 63 in 260 minutes from Richardson himself, West Indies reached 158 for one before six wickets fell for 54 during the evening session. England, whose only change had been to replace Igglesden with Caddick, removed both openers through the leg-spin of Salisbury, but Lewis, operating accurately from around the wicket, then dismissed three of the left-handers at little cost. The remaining West Indies wickets fell rapidly at the start of the second day, which ended with England only 16 runs behind, with five wickets standing. Atherton played another assiduous innings but batting conditions were still not easy; it was puzzling to see West Indies lapse into a period of lethargic, defensive cricket until they could take the new ball late in the day. An invaluable sixth-wicket stand of 82 between Thorpe and Russell was completed on the third morning before Ambrose broke through in a spell of three for 18 from 26 balls. Salisbury, however, played with spirit to add 34 for the tenth wicket with Fraser: England's lead of 76 was their first first-innings advantage in the Caribbean since the corresponding Test of 1989-90.

Caddick now justified his inclusion with two important wickets as West Indies shakily wiped out the arrears. Richardson and Lara were both out to injudicious attacking strokes, Lara through a spectacular diving catch at mid-off by Salisbury, and Haynes was bowled by Lewis with the deficit still 25. Arthurton and Adams rebuilt carefully but their work was sacrificed in the closing overs; Arthurton was caught off a rash pull and Adams, unable to resist a high full toss from Salisbury, was unlucky enough to hit it directly into the forearm of Smith, at short leg, and see Russell catch the rebound. England spent the rest day contemplating victory. However, when they resumed, West Indies were blessed with two dropped catches by the usually reliable Hick, at slip. Chanderpaul was the man reprieved, when four and 29, and with forthright support from Winston Benjamin, he stretched the advantage against some stray and increasingly dispirited England bowling before giving Caddick his sixth wicket. Shortly afterwards West Indies were all out 193 ahead.

Thus England were facing a target at least 70 runs bigger than it should have been. Furthermore, a rain break meant that only 15 overs of the day remained. This was crucial, because Ambrose was able to give his all and England knew they would have to face him again next morning. He supplied one of the most devastating spells of even his career. Atherton, half forward, was leg-before to the first ball of the innings and Ramprakash, nervily calling a second run to long leg, run out off the fifth. Smith and Hick, confidence low, were swept aside and when Stewart, the one batsman to get a start, lost his off stump, it was 26 for five. Walsh, almost the Lock to Ambrose's Laker, took a wicket at last when Salisbury was caught at slip. But Ambrose, rampaging in as if on springs, added Russell and Thorpe to his collection before play ended with England a mortifying 40 for eight, all hope lost. The game lasted only 17 minutes on the final morning, Walsh claiming the last two wickets. As Ambrose was carried shoulder-high from the ground, the great calypsonian Lord Kitchener serenaded his success outside the dressing-room. For England, a match which had promised much for three days had ended in utter humiliation.

Man of the Match: C. E. L. Ambrose.

Close of play: First day, West Indies 227-7 (J. R. Murray 22*, C. E. L. Ambrose 5*); Second day, England 236-5 (G. P. Thorpe 64*, R. C. Russell 17*); Third day, West Indies 143-5 (S. Chanderpaul 1*); Fourth day, England 40-8 (C. C. Lewis 1*).

West Indies

D. L. Haynes b Salisbury	38	– b Lewis	19
*R. B. Richardson lbw b Salisbury	63	– c and b Caddick	3
B. C. Lara lbw b Lewis	43	– c Salisbury b Caddick	12
K. L. T. Arthurton lbw b Lewis	1	– c Stewart b Caddick	42
J. C. Adams c Smith b Lewis	2	– c Russell b Salisbury	43
S. Chanderpaul b Fraser	19	– c Fraser b Caddick	50
†J. R. Murray not out	27	– c Russell b Caddick	14
W. K. M. Benjamin b Fraser	10	– c Fraser b Lewis	35
C. E. L. Ambrose c Thorpe b Fraser	13	– b Caddick	12
K. C. G. Benjamin b Fraser	9	– not out	5
C. A. Walsh lbw b Lewis	0	– lbw b Lewis	1
B 1, l-b 13, w 1, n-b 12	27	B 8, l-b 13, n-b 12	33
1/66 (1) 2/158 (2) 3/158 (3) 4/163 (5) 5/164 (4) 6/201 (6) 7/212 (8) 8/241 (9) 9/251 (10) 10/252 (11)	252	1/15 (2) 2/37 (3) 3/51 (1) 4/131 (4) 5/143 (5) 6/167 (7) 7/227 (8) 8/247 (9) 9/267 (6) 10/269 (11)	269

Bowling: *First Innings*—Fraser 24–9–49–4; Caddick 19–5–43–0; Lewis 25.2–3–61–4; Salisbury 22–4–72–2; Ramprakash 2–1–8–0; Hick 3–1–5–0. *Second Innings*—Fraser 25–6–71–0; Caddick 26–5–65–6; Lewis 27.5–6–71–3; Salisbury 9–1–41–1.

England

*M. A. Atherton c Murray b W. K. M. Benjamin	48	– lbw b Ambrose	0
A. J. Stewart b Ambrose	6	– b Ambrose	18
M. R. Ramprakash c and b W. K. M. Benjamin	23	– run out	1
R. A. Smith lbw b Ambrose	12	– b Ambrose	0
G. A. Hick lbw b Walsh	40	– c Murray b Ambrose	6
G. P. Thorpe c Lara b Ambrose	86	– b Ambrose	3
†R. C. Russell b Ambrose	23	– (8) c sub (P. V. Simmons) b Ambrose	4
C. C. Lewis b Ambrose	9	– (9) c W. K. M. Benjamin b Walsh	6
I. D. K. Salisbury c Lara b Walsh	36	– (7) c Lara b Walsh	0
A. R. Caddick c Lara b W. K. M. Benjamin	6	– c Lara b Walsh	1
A. R. C. Fraser not out	8	– not out	0
B 10, l-b 9, w 1, n-b 11	31	L-b 6, n-b 1	7
1/16 (2) 2/82 (3) 3/87 (1) 4/115 (4) 5/167 (5) 6/249 (7) 7/273 (8) 8/281 (6) 9/294 (10) 10/328 (9)	328	1/0 (1) 2/1 (3) 3/5 (4) 4/21 (5) 5/26 (2) 6/27 (7) 7/37 (8) 8/40 (6) 9/45 (10) 10/46 (9)	46

Bowling: *First Innings*—Ambrose 29–6–60–5; Walsh 27.2–3–77–2; K. C. G. Benjamin 20–5–70–0; W. K. M. Benjamin 24–3–66–3; Adams 4–0–18–0; Chanderpaul 5–0–13–0; Arthurton 3–0–5–0. *Second Innings*—Ambrose 10–1–24–6; Walsh 9.1–1–16–3.

Umpires: S. Venkataraghavan (India) and S. A. Bucknor.
Referee: J. R. Reid (New Zealand).

WEST INDIES BOARD XI v ENGLAND XI

At St George's, Grenada, April 2, 3, 4, 5. West Indies Board XI won by eight wickets. Toss: West Indies Board XI.

It was at the end of this match, as Williams struck five consecutive fours off Tufnell to inflict a dispiritingly severe defeat, that the England tour touched its nadir. The persistent plagues on their ambitions – batting collapses, bowling inadequacies, dropped catches and untimely ailments – were all in evidence. On the third afternoon, at 140 for one and leading by 146, England had seemed in no danger. But the locally-born leg-spinner, Rawl Lewis, took four for 12 in a 12-over spell to humiliate them. Seven wickets fell for ten as tour manager Mike Smith unsuccessfully attempted to summon Thorpe from his hotel sick bed. The Board side, comprising fringe Test candidates, scored the required 172 next morning, Williams completing his century with the winning stroke. Lewis had also taken five wickets in the first innings as England surrendered another strong position of 206 for one. Although Malcolm, back after his trip home for knee surgery, took four wickets, they were hollow successes within a performance roundly criticised by Atherton – who fielded as a substitute – and the rest of the tour management.

Close of play: First day, England XI 281-4 (G. P. Thorpe 11*, S. L. Watkin 3*); Second day, West Indies Board XI 260-5 (R. I. C. Holder 108*, C. O. Browne 18*); Third day, West Indies Board XI 47-0 (S. C. Williams 19*, P. A. Wallace 28*).

England XI

*†A. J. Stewart c Gibson b Lewis	65	– (6) c Jacobs b Lewis	1
M. R. Ramprakash c Wallace b Gibson	91	– c Jacobs b Gibson	67
G. A. Hick lbw b Antoine	59	– c Wallace b Lewis	74
R. A. Smith c Browne b Lewis	36	– (1) lbw b Cummins	0
G. P. Thorpe c Campbell b Cummins	16	– absent ill	
S. L. Watkin c Wallace b Lewis	19	– (7) c Wallace b Lewis	0
N. Hussain b Lewis	6	– (5) c Lewis b Gibson	6
M. P. Maynard c Williams b Cummins	2	– (4) c Browne b Lewis	1
A. P. Igglesden st Browne b Lewis	1	– not out	0
P. C. R. Tufnell not out	5	– (8) run out	1
D. E. Malcolm b Cummins	0	– (10) b Gibson	0
L-b 5, n-b 14	19	L-b 6, n-b 9	15
1/99 2/206 3/257 4/277 5/301 6/308 7/313 8/313 9/316	319	1/0 2/140 3/155 4/159 5/162 6/162 7/164 8/164 9/165	165

Bowling: *First Innings*—Cummins 21.5–0–82–3; Gibson 18–1–65–1; Antoine 15–1–54–1; Lewis 33–6–95–5; Simmons 6–1–18–0. *Second Innings*—Cummins 9–1–33–1; Antoine 8–0–41–0; Gibson 16–7–22–3; Lewis 20–7–51–4; Simmons 5–0–12–0.

West Indies Board XI

P. V. Simmons b Malcolm	18	– (3) c Stewart b Igglesden	19
S. C. Williams c Stewart b Watkin	30	– (1) not out	102
P. A. Wallace c Hick b Watkin	25	– (2) c Smith b Watkin	40
*R. I. C. Holder c Hussain b Tufnell	116		
S. L. Campbell c sub (M. A. Atherton) b Tufnell	5	– (4) not out	5
R. D. Jacobs b Tufnell	41		
†C. O. Browne c Ramprakash b Malcolm	30		
A. C. Cummins c Hick b Malcolm	1		
O. D. Gibson c sub (I. D. K. Salisbury) b Malcolm	0		
R. N. Lewis not out	15		
E. C. Antoine lbw b Tufnell	16		
B 1, l-b 1, n-b 14	16	B 6	6
1/40 2/62 3/100 4/121 5/174 6/271 7/273 8/273 9/286	313	1/81 2/130	(2 wkts) 172

Bowling: *First Innings*—Malcolm 18–2–81–4; Igglesden 23–3–84–0; Tufnell 29.4–7–87–4; Watkin 12–1–43–2; Hick 5–0–16–0. *Second Innings*—Malcolm 6–0–30–0; Igglesden 8–0–52–1; Tufnell 14.5–5–63–0; Watkin 8–2–21–1.

Umpires: D. Holder and G. T. Johnson (I. Lord deputised for D. Holder on the 3rd day).

WEST INDIES v ENGLAND

Fourth Test Match

At Bridgetown, April 8, 9, 10, 12, 13. England won by 208 runs. Toss: West Indies.

Cricket's aptitude for producing the inexplicable has seldom been so convincingly demonstrated. England arrived at the supposedly impregnable bastion of West Indian cricket with their form and confidence rock-bottom. Even team manager Keith Fletcher admitted a draw would have been considered a triumph: West Indies had won their last 12 Tests on the ground. To win, and win handsomely, becoming the first visiting Test team to succeed at Bridgetown since R. E. S. Wyatt's England team 59 years earlier, and only the second ever, beggared belief. And yet it was no fluke. England dictated the game and won on merit, eight minutes after the scheduled tea interval on the final day. Each of the five days had attracted capacity crowds, swelled by about 6,000 holidaying England supporters, creating a unique and strangely bipartisan atmosphere for a Caribbean Test.

West Indies fielded the same team who won in Georgetown and Port-of-Spain, but England substituted Tufnell for Salisbury. Richardson again won the toss and followed Barbados tradition, if not logic, by bowling first. The pitch was truer and faster than any encountered thus far and Atherton and Stewart profited with a first-wicket stand of 171, one short of the England record on the ground. The scoring-rate was brisk and their command such that it came as a surprise when Atherton fell for 85. Stewart proceeded to a chanceless century, on his 31st birthday, in 293 minutes, but the loss of four wickets in the final session, prolonged by the slow over-rate until cut off by bad light, undermined England's control.

It seemed the familiar pattern had been restored on the second day, when four wickets from Ambrose, at a personal cost of 24, restricted the total to 355. But the West Indian reply was quickly in trouble, despite Haynes surviving a controversial run-out appeal when he eased up, believing his shot had crossed the boundary. Haynes later retired hurt, struck on the finger by Lewis, initiating a disastrous period for West Indies. In his eighth over with the new ball, Fraser dismissed Richardson and Arthurton and, after Lara had seen a lavish drive superbly caught at cover by the substitute, Hussain, he returned for a crucial evening spell which brought him four for one in 17 balls. It was easily his most effective and impressive bowling since his prolonged pelvic injury and, with Tufnell containing skilfully at the other end, West Indies were 205 for eight when Ambrose became a seventh victim for Fraser on the third morning. Chanderpaul's remarkable temperament was again in evidence as he batted five hours in company with the tail, who eventually carried the side past 300. The last three wickets added 170 but Fraser still achieved figures of eight for 75, the best by an Englishman against West Indies, and the best for England since Bob Willis took eight for 43 against Australia at Headingley in 1981.

The lead of 51 was precarious, however, when Walsh quickly dismissed Atherton and Ramprakash. With Smith failing once more, England were tottering until Hick joined Stewart and, with the aid of a generous supply of no-balls, added 92 before the close of the third day – delayed, like the previous two, by a desultory over-rate which was to produce a heavy fine for the West Indians. The first session of the fourth day was a critical one. Having survived it for the loss of one more wicket – Hick – they were well-placed. Stewart, who scored only 13 in the two hours to lunch, then advanced rapidly to his second century of the match, the first England player to achieve the feat against West Indies. If his second innings lacked the fluency of his first, it surpassed it for application; he had been batting almost eight hours when he played on, wearily, for the second time in the game. His stand of 150 with Thorpe was a record for England's fifth wicket against West Indies.

Thorpe's breezy 84, made in 188 minutes, permitted Atherton the unaccustomed luxury of a declaration and West Indies, set an improbable 446, 40 more than had ever been made to win a Test, were 47 for two at the close, the retirement of Richardson with a hamstring strain adding to their woes. If Russell had not missed a stumping with Lara on strike, England might have thought they were nearly home; as it was, they had to wait 75 minutes on the fifth morning before, crucially, he mishooked Caddick to mid-on where Tufnell took an impressive catch. With Haynes batting down the order with his damaged finger, the rest was not far short of a procession. Last man Walsh hit Tufnell for three defiant sixes in an over, but two balls later Ambrose was bowled and angrily swatted down his stumps, an act which cost him a £1,000 fine from the referee. This passed unnoticed by most of the England supporters, who were already on the field celebrating.

Man of the Match: A. J. Stewart.

Close of play: First day, England 299-5 (G. A. Hick 26*, R. C. Russell 3*); Second day, West Indies 188-7 (S. Chanderpaul 31*, C. E. L. Ambrose 35*); Third day, England 171-3 (A. J. Stewart 62*, G. A. Hick 52*); Fourth day, West Indies 47-2 (B. C. Lara 10*, K. L. T. Arthurton 0*).

England

First innings		Second innings	
*M. A. Atherton c Lara b K. C. G. Benjamin	85	c Lara b Walsh	15
A. J. Stewart b W. K. M. Benjamin	118	b Walsh	143
M. R. Ramprakash c Murray b W. K. M. Benjamin	20	c Chanderpaul b Walsh	3
R. A. Smith c Murray b W. K. M. Benjamin	10	lbw b K. C. G. Benjamin	13
G. A. Hick c Murray b Ambrose	34	c Lara b Walsh	59
G. P. Thorpe c sub (P. V. Simmons) b K. C. G. Benjamin	7	c Arthurton b Walsh	84
†R. C. Russell c Chanderpaul b Ambrose	38	not out	17
C. C. Lewis c Murray b Ambrose	0	c Walsh b Adams	10
A. R. Caddick b Ambrose	8		
A. R. C. Fraser c Chanderpaul b Walsh	3		
P. C. R. Tufnell not out	0		
L-b 8, n-b 24	32	B 8, l-b 6, n-b 36	50
1/171 (1) 2/223 (3) 3/242 (4) 4/265 (2) 5/290 (6) 6/307 (5) 7/307 (8) 8/327 (9) 9/351 (10) 10/355 (7)	355	1/33 (1) 2/43 (3) 3/79 (4) 4/194 (5) 5/344 (2) 6/382 (6) 7/394 (8) (7 wkts dec.)	394

Bowling: *First Innings*—Ambrose 24.2–5–86–4; Walsh 24–3–88–1; W. K. M. Benjamin 22–4–76–3; K. C. G. Benjamin 20–5–74–2; Chanderpaul 10–4–23–0. *Second Innings*—Ambrose 22–4–75–0; Walsh 28–5–94–5; W. K. M. Benjamin 22–3–58–0; K. C. G. Benjamin 20–1–92–1; Chanderpaul 10–3–30–0; Adams 6.5–0–31–1.

West Indies

First innings		Second innings	
D. L. Haynes c Atherton b Fraser	35	(8) c Thorpe b Tufnell	15
*R. B. Richardson c Atherton b Fraser	20	(1) c Ramprakash b Caddick	33
B. C. Lara c sub (N. Hussain) b Lewis	26	c Tufnell b Caddick	64
K. L. T. Arthurton c Russell b Fraser	0	(5) b Tufnell	52
J. C. Adams c Thorpe b Fraser	26	(2) c Russell b Caddick	12
S. Chanderpaul c Ramprakash b Tufnell	77	c sub (N. Hussain) b Hick	5
†J. R. Murray c Thorpe b Fraser	0	c Thorpe b Caddick	5
W. K. M. Benjamin c Hick b Fraser	8	(9) c Stewart b Tufnell	3
C. E. L. Ambrose c Hick b Fraser	44	(10) b Lewis	12
K. C. G. Benjamin not out	43	(4) c Hick b Caddick	0
C. A. Walsh c Tufnell b Fraser	13	not out	18
L-b 1, n-b 11	12	B 1, l-b 7, n-b 10	18
1/55 (2) 2/55 (4) 3/95 (3) 4/126 (5) 5/126 (1) 6/126 (7) 7/134 (8) 8/205 (9) 9/263 (6) 10/304 (11)	304	1/43 (2) 2/43 (4) 3/128 (3) 4/150 (6) 5/164 (5) 6/179 (7) 7/195 (1) 8/199 (9) 9/216 (8) 10/237 (10)	237

In the first innings D. L. Haynes, when 35, retired hurt at 51 and resumed at 126-4. In the second innings R. B. Richardson, when 18, retired hurt at 32 and resumed at 150.

Bowling: *First Innings*—Fraser 28.5–7–75–8; Caddick 24–2–92–0; Lewis 17–2–60–1; Tufnell 32–12–76–1. *Second Innings*—Fraser 17–7–40–0; Caddick 17–3–63–5; Tufnell 36–12–100–3; Lewis 8.2–1–23–1; Hick 4–2–3–1.

Umpires: D. B. Hair (Australia) and L. H. Barker. Referee: J. R. Reid (New Zealand).

WEST INDIES v ENGLAND

Fifth Test Match

At St John's, Antigua, April 16, 17, 18, 20, 21. Drawn. Toss: West Indies. Test debut: S. C. Williams.

A contest which scarcely progressed beyond its first innings, tied at 593 runs each, nevertheless earned an eternal place in cricket history by dint of an innings of 375 by Brian Lara, beating by ten runs the record individual score in Test cricket, created 36 years earlier by Sir Garfield Sobers. Lara broke the record from the 530th ball he faced, having batted for the equivalent of more than two days. He had not given a single chance and, until tension and fatigue almost overcame him in the home straight, scarcely made a mistake. Sobers himself came onto the field to shake Lara's hand in the chaotic moments which followed an exultantly pulled four from a short ball by Lewis. It was only Lara's third Test century but the previous two had been 277 and 167, confirming his appetite for the long innings. After the 277 he said he had been thinking of the record. Having achieved it this time, Lara went to Trinidad for a triumphal homecoming before leaving to play county cricket for Warwickshire.

One of the most remarkable aspects of the innings was that it was born out of the adversity of 12 for two, West Indies' makeshift opening pair having lasted barely half an hour on the first morning. Another was that the record, or at least a threat to the old record, looked inevitable by the time Lara had made 50, such was his obvious determination and his absolute mastery of England's bowlers on an utterly inoffensive pitch, only partially offset by a turgidly slow outfield which turned many fours into twos.

With both Richardson, the captain, and his deputy Haynes injured, West Indies gave Stuart Williams his Test debut and recalled Simmons. They were led for the first time by Walsh, against an unchanged and newly confident England. The tourists' buoyancy lasted only as long as it took Lara to make 164 not out on the opening day. A third-wicket stand of 179 with Adams was followed by one of 183 for the fourth with Arthurton, whose contribution was only 47. The biggest stand, 219 with Chanderpaul, was also the longest, extending through four rain interruptions, none of which could disturb Lara, on the second afternoon, and into the momentous third morning, which Lara commenced on 320.

Until this point, Lara had never looked likely to get out but, as the remaining milestones to the record were ticked off and the enormity of it all combined with his natural weariness, he needed shepherding through the final stages by the impressively mature Chanderpaul. He reached 365, the famed Sobers figure, with a cover-driven four off Caddick which had the capacity crowd on its feet, then composed himself once again for the historic pull off Lewis and the inevitable pitch invasion ensued. When Lara fell to a tired drive, with the declaration due, he had batted 766 minutes, faced 538 balls and hit 45 fours. Chanderpaul scored an unbeaten 75, his fourth half-century in his first four Tests, and all England could aspire to was the not inconsiderable task of batting out time.

This they achieved in some comfort, Atherton batting with great authority after being dropped on 46 and Smith profiting from two "dismissals" off no-balls from Walsh to make an overdue century. Eventually, Smith was treating the bowling with such disdain that the new record did not look entirely safe. But he was still 200 short when the stand of 303, a third-wicket record for England against West Indies, was ended. It was the first time since 1976 at Headingley that two England batsmen had made centuries in the same Test innings against West Indies, and Atherton's 135 in 535 minutes meant that he had batted for more than 28 hours in the series. The performance of Atherton and Smith also guaranteed only the fourth draw in the last 29 Tests between these teams. Once Russell and Lewis had added half-centuries and the scores had finished uncannily level on first innings, only 34 overs remained. Of these, 24 were played out to end a game of total stalemate but glittering memories.

Man of the Match: B. C. Lara. *Man of the Series:* C. E. L. Ambrose.

Close of play: First day, West Indies 274-3 (B. C. Lara 164*, K. L. T. Arthurton 25*); Second day, West Indies 502-4 (B. C. Lara 320*, S. Chanderpaul 41*); Third day, England 185-2 (M. A. Atherton 63*, R. A. Smith 68*); Fourth day, England 442-6 (R. C. Russell 18*, C. C. Lewis 12*).

West Indies

	First innings		Second innings
P. V. Simmons lbw b Caddick	8	– not out	22
S. C. Williams c Caddick b Fraser	3	– not out	21
B. C. Lara c Russell b Caddick	375		
J. C. Adams c sub (N. Hussain) b Fraser	59		
K. L. T. Arthurton c Russell b Caddick	47		
S. Chanderpaul not out	75		
L-b 3, n-b 23	26		
1/11 (2) 2/12 (1) 3/191 (4) 4/374 (5) 5/593 (3)	(5 wkts dec.) 593		(no wkt) 43

†J. R. Murray, W. K. M. Benjamin, C. E. L. Ambrose, K. C. G. Benjamin and *C. A. Walsh did not bat.

Bowling: *First Innings*—Fraser 43–4–121–2; Caddick 47.2–8–158–3; Tufnell 39–8–110–0; Lewis 33–1–140–0; Hick 18–3–61–0. *Second Innings*—Fraser 2–1–2–0; Caddick 2–1–11–0; Tufnell 6–4–5–0; Hick 8–2–11–0; Ramprakash 3–1–5–0; Thorpe 2–1–1–0; Stewart 1–0–8–0.

England

*M. A. Atherton c Murray b Ambrose	135
A. J. Stewart c Ambrose b K. C. G. Benjamin	24
M. R. Ramprakash lbw b K. C. G. Benjamin	19
R. A. Smith lbw b K. C. G. Benjamin	175
G. A. Hick b K. C. G. Benjamin	20
G. P. Thorpe c Adams b Chanderpaul	9
†R. C. Russell c Murray b W. K. M. Benjamin	62
C. C. Lewis not out	75
A. R. Caddick c W. K. M. Benjamin b Adams	22
A. R. C. Fraser b Adams	0
P. C. R. Tufnell lbw b W. K. M. Benjamin	0
B 9, l-b 20, n-b 23	52
1/40 (2) 2/70 (3) 3/373 (4) 4/393 (1) 5/401 (5) 6/417 (6) 7/535 (7) 8/585 (9) 9/589 (10) 10/593 (11)	593

Bowling: Ambrose 40–18–66–1; Walsh 40–9–123–0; W. K. M. Benjamin 41.1–15–93–2; K. C. G. Benjamin 37–7–110–4; Chanderpaul 24–1–94–1; Adams 22–4–74–2; Arthurton 2–1–4–0.

Umpires: D. B. Hair (Australia) and S. A. Bucknor. Referee: J. R. Reid (New Zealand).

ENGLAND A IN SOUTH AFRICA, 1993-94

By GLENN MOORE

The true measure of the fifth England A tour, the progress of the players involved, can only be judged in time. In itself, the first official English tour of South Africa for 29 years was unreservedly successful. Both the results – the team began with eight straight wins – and performances were impressive and the side conducted itself admirably on and off the field.

The tour was given the best possible chance, being well-scheduled, thoughtfully selected and intelligently led, with both management and senior professionals proving excellent choices. There were several outstanding tourists, notably John Crawley, who made 779 first-class runs at 64.91, including a career-best 286, and Mark Ilott, who took 37 wickets at 14.18. Steve Rhodes, on his fourth trip with England A, deservedly won the Player of the Tour award for a contribution that went far beyond his 33 dismissals and 293 runs at 41.85. Of the younger players, Malachy Loye and Darren Gough progressed rapidly, while the experienced Alan Wells and Peter Such showed no signs of dwelling on the disappointment of their exclusion from the senior tour to the Caribbean.

Apart from the unfortunate Martin Bicknell, whose tour was first disrupted, then cut short by rib muscle and back injuries, only Mark Lathwell will wish to forget the trip. Lathwell, an unhappy traveller at the best of times, became locked into a spiral of low confidence and poor form after a misleadingly promising start. In 13 first-class innings he reached double figures only five times. He was subsequently omitted from the April reunion match against champion county Middlesex.

With most matches being played on unresponsive pitches, team manager Phil Neale, in his first representative role, and captain Hugh Morris developed a policy of disciplined, high-pressure cricket involving tight bowling to primarily defensive fields. There were spells of incisive attacking bowling, notably from Ilott and, when conditions suited, from Martin McCague, returning after an operation for a stress fracture, but batsmen were usually squeezed into giving their wicket away. Not that the side were boring – they always looked to win matches and, as the unofficial Test beckoned, surprised locals by spurning the opportunity of batting practice against Border to go for what would have been their fifth win in the seven matches against provincial sides.

Much had been heard about the strength of South African domestic cricket; the reality was disappointing. Apart from Natal, for whom several players performed above expectations, only Orange Free State, breaking off from a successful defence of the Castle Cup, were the tourists' equals. The four sides defeated, Transvaal, Eastern Province, Western Province and Northern Transvaal, were all heavily beaten – only Eastern Province managed to take play into the fourth day. All six one-day games were won and, when they arrived in Durban backed by eight successive victories, it seemed possible that the tourists would win every match. Such thoughts were rudely ended as a young Natal side, led by West Indian Malcolm Marshall, crushed them by an innings with enough ease to raise questions about their character. The following games, against Northern Transvaal's strong pace attack on a volatile wicket, and Orange Free State, where

England A successfully batted out the final day for a draw, largely answered them to Neale's satisfaction.

Such was the team's progress that their final opponents, South Africa A, were selected on merit rather than, as originally intended, on potential. Thus Jimmy Cook, at 40, made an appearance. The match itself was a disappointment, with a flat pitch and negative cricket from both sides. While England were anxious not to spoil their tour record, several South Africans regarded the match as a Test trial. Consequently the game, despite being played over five days, was always destined for a draw – though that should not obscure some good performances, notably from Wells.

If there was one area of prolonged concern, it was in the fielding. In eight first-class matches 35 chances were missed and the ground fielding was no better. With practice, there was some improvement, but the disparity with the consistently high standards of South African fielding made the weaknesses all the more noticeable.

But ultimately the trip was about more than cricket. Touring cricketers normally lead a cloistered life of airports, hotels, nets and matches. This party was privileged to be able to play a part, however small, in the transformation of South Africa from an apartheid society to a multi-racial democracy. The opening match of the tour at Alexandra, north of Johannesburg, on an artificial pitch subsidised by British money on the outskirts of one of South Africa's most volatile and deprived areas, set the tone. Several non-white players drawn from the development programme, notably pace bowler Walter Masemola and Geoffrey Toyana, captain for the day, joined three internationals – Mark Rushmere, Clive Eksteen and Mandy Yachad – in a Transvaal Invitation XI. Though England A won without much difficulty, it was one of those rare occasions when taking part really was more important. Visits to two other townships, Zwide and Langa, followed and were beneficial to all. Seeing the squalor of life in such places put much in perspective for the players, while their presence raised the residents' esteem and rewarded those working to promote cricket and racial harmony there.

ENGLAND A TOURING PARTY

H. Morris (Glamorgan) (*captain*), A. P. Wells (Sussex) (*vice-captain*), M. P. Bicknell (Surrey), D. G. Cork (Derbyshire), J. P. Crawley (Lancashire), R. D. B. Croft (Glamorgan), A. Dale (Glamorgan), D. Gough (Yorkshire), M. C. Ilott (Essex), M. N. Lathwell (Somerset), M. B. Loye (Northamptonshire), M. J. McCague (Kent), S. J. Rhodes (Worcestershire), P. M. Such (Essex).

J. P. Taylor (Northamptonshire) joined the party after Bicknell flew home with injuries; Cork also returned because of family illness.

Tour manager: R. M. Bennett. *Team manager*: P. A. Neale (Northamptonshire). *Physiotherapist:* W. P. Morton (Yorkshire).

ENGLAND A TOUR RESULTS

First-class matches – Played 8: Won 4, Lost 1, Drawn 3.
Wins – Transvaal, Eastern Province, Western Province, Northern Transvaal.
Loss – Natal.
Draws – Orange Free State, Border, South Africa A.
Non first-class matches – Played 6: Won 6. *Wins* – Transvaal Invitation XI, Western Transvaal, Eastern Transvaal, Eastern Province Invitation XI, Western Province Invitation XI, Griqualand West.

ENGLAND A AVERAGES – FIRST-CLASS MATCHES

BATTING

	M	*I*	*NO*	*R*	*HS*	*100s*	*Avge*	*Ct/St*
J. P. Crawley	8	13	1	779	286	2	64.91	4
A. P. Wells	8	14	3	593	130	2	53.90	9
S. J. Rhodes	8	11	4	293	108	1	41.85	30/3
M. B. Loye	8	12	1	439	71	0	39.90	5
H. Morris	8	14	1	402	79	0	30.92	8
R. D. B. Croft	5	4	1	69	32*	0	23.00	3
A. Dale	7	11	2	196	64	0	21.77	1
D. Gough	5	6	2	75	24	0	18.75	2
M. N. Lathwell	7	13	1	215	83	0	17.91	8
M. C. Ilott	6	5	1	40	18*	0	10.00	2
P. M. Such	6	6	2	25	12*	0	6.25	2
M. J. McCague	5	5	0	31	14	0	6.20	3

Played in four matches: D. G. Cork 9, 16, 7 (2 ct). Played in two matches: J. P. Taylor 11, 0, 1 (2 ct). Played in one match: M. P. Bicknell 5*, 22.

* *Signifies not out.*

BOWLING

	O	*M*	*R*	*W*	*BB*	*5W/i*	*Avge*
M. C. Ilott	229.1	60	525	37	6-61	2	14.18
D. G. Cork	129.1	34	333	17	4-50	0	19.58
D. Gough	192.1	34	589	23	5-81	1	25.60
R. D. B. Croft	177	52	397	14	5-41	1	28.35
M. J. McCague	150	32	434	15	4-84	0	28.93
A. Dale	120	24	333	11	3-34	0	30.27
P. M. Such	272.3	76	623	19	4-51	0	32.78
J. P. Taylor	62	8	205	5	2-65	0	41.00

Also bowled: M. P. Bicknell 4–2–4–0.

Note: Matches in this section which were not first-class are signified by a dagger.

†At Alexandra, December 4. England A won by 43 runs. Toss: England A. England A 121 (43.2 overs) (M. B. Loye 38; W. Masemola three for 25, C. E. Eksteen three for 29); Transvaal Invitation XI 78 (38.3 overs) (D. G. Cork six for nine).

†At Potchefstroom, December 6. England A won by 82 runs. Toss: Western Transvaal. England A 260 for six (50 overs) (H. Morris 55, J. P. Crawley 88, A. P. Wells 61); Western Transvaal 178 for seven (50 overs) (H. M. de Vos 43, A. J. van Deventer 52).

†At Springs, December 8. England A won by 77 runs. Toss: Eastern Transvaal. England A 281 for six (50 overs) (M. N. Lathwell 133, M. B. Loye 41, A. P. Wells 37 not out); Eastern Transvaal 204 for three (50 overs) (W. R. Radford 39, A. Norris 55, S. M. Skeete 77).

TRANSVAAL v ENGLAND A

At Johannesburg, December 10, 11, 12. England A won by nine wickets. Toss: Transvaal.

Despite having only four fit players on the third morning, England A emerged with a comfortable victory – with more than a day to spare – and a vibrant team spirit. Ilott played the outstanding role, taking six for 61 in Transvaal's second innings, but it was an all-round performance which saw the whole party, down to the coach and physiotherapist, take the field. After good seam bowling had dismissed Transvaal cheaply on a good pitch, Lathwell batted England A into a strong position, with an attacking 83, only to become the first of seven players affected by gastro-enteritis. The third morning was abandoned, because the tourists could not field 11 players, but, mindful of a patient 1,000-strong crowd, England A resumed after lunch, using five substitute fielders including coach Phil Neale and physio Wayne Morton, who had played only a couple of club matches. Three hours later they had won, Transvaal having collapsed against Ilott, who took three wickets in an over, to leave England A needing only 69 for victory. The only healthy batsmen got the runs.

Close of play: First day, England A 146-3 (M. N. Lathwell 77*, M. C. Ilott 0*); Second day, Transvaal 100-2 (M. D. Haysman 43*, M. W. Rushmere 23*).

Transvaal

First innings		Second innings	
M. Yachad c Rhodes b Ilott	4	c Lathwell b Ilott	9
B. M. White lbw b Gough	6	lbw b Cork	11
M. D. Haysman c Rhodes b Ilott	52	c Rhodes b Gough	52
M. W. Rushmere lbw b Dale	12	not out	64
*S. J. Cook c Lathwell b Dale	4	c Rhodes b Ilott	9
D. R. Laing run out	31	c Wells b Ilott	0
†N. Pothas c Morris b Cork	8	lbw b Ilott	2
S. Jacobs c Rhodes b Cork	0	c Rhodes b Ilott	2
C. E. Eksteen c Morris b Dale	16	c Rhodes b Ilott	4
S. D. Jack not out	15	c Rhodes b Such	24
M. R. Hobson c Rhodes b Gough	0	b Such	0
L-b 3, n-b 10	13	L-b 16, w 2, n-b 5	23
1/8 2/14 3/39 4/48 5/118 6/119 7/119 8/136 9/160	161	1/15 2/46 3/114 4/131 5/131 6/133 7/143 8/157 9/200	200

Bowling: *First Innings*—Ilott 14–2–32–2; Gough 10.3–5–27–2; Cork 16–0–60–2; Dale 11–1–34–3; Such 2–0–5–0. *Second Innings*—Ilott 26–5–61–6; Gough 14–2–53–1; Such 15.3–4–43–2; Cork 10–5–13–1; Dale 6–2–14–0.

England A

First innings		Second innings	
M. N. Lathwell c Pothas b Jack	83	c Hobson b Jack	0
*H. Morris c White b Jack	7		
J. P. Crawley run out	44		
A. P. Wells lbw b Hobson	7	(3) not out	27
M. C. Ilott c Pothas b Jack	5		
M. B. Loye c Pothas b Hobson	19		
A. Dale b Hobson	43		
†S. J. Rhodes b Hobson	45	(2) not out	33
D. G. Cork lbw b White	9		
D. Gough not out	9		
P. M. Such c Pothas b White	0		
B 5, l-b 8, n-b 9	22	B 4, w 4, n-b 1	9
1/9 2/111 3/141 4/156 5/167 6/188 7/275 8/276 9/291	293	1/0	(1 wkt) 69

Bowling: *First Innings*—Jack 21–1–76–3; Hobson 23–1–76–4; Jacobs 27–11–45–0; Laing 12–2–36–0; Eksteen 27–11–43–0; White 2.5–1–4–2. *Second Innings*—Jack 6–1–17–1; Hobson 5–0–30–0; Eksteen 3–1–6–0; Jacobs 2.3–0–12–0.

Umpires: R. E. Koertzen and C. J. Mitchley.

†At Zwide, December 15. England A won by 103 runs. Toss: England A. England A 189 for seven (45 overs) (J. P. Crawley 58, A. Dale 39; C. Wait four for 34, including a hat-trick); Eastern Province Invitation XI 86 (33.2 overs) (M. J. McCague three for 27, A. Dale three for 11).

EASTERN PROVINCE v ENGLAND A

At Port Elizabeth, December 17, 18, 19, 20. England A won by an innings and 70 runs. Toss: Eastern Province.

A massive 286 from Crawley set England A up for a crushing victory against a poor Eastern Province side. Though made on a docile pitch against weak bowling – Baptiste apart – Crawley's innings showed style and concentration which announced him as an outstanding prospect. His maiden double-hundred, the highest innings in 104 years of first-class cricket at St George's, took 17 minutes short of ten hours and featured 36 fours and four sixes in 468 balls. Wells helped him add 261 for the third wicket. It made Baptiste's decision to put England A in appear quite ridiculous. The exhausted Province side, shorn of their international players, collapsed twice to lose midway through the fourth day. Only Grant Morgan – whose first-class debut attracted some attention as he was replacing a player attending his tribal initiation ceremony – showed genuine resistance, batting undefeated for four hours, while Botha and Baptiste profited from another loose fielding performance to reach half-centuries. On the first morning, play had been halted for 45 minutes because one of the revolving sightscreens was stuck.

Close of play: First day, England A 310-2 (J. P. Crawley 150*, A. P. Wells 51*); Second day, Eastern Province 127-8 (G. Morgan 10*, R. A. Lyle 2*); Third day, Eastern Province 185-4 (A. Botha 52*, E. A. E. Baptiste 58*).

England A

M. N. Lathwell c Pope b Baptiste	5
*H. Morris c Huckle b Shaw	79
J. P. Crawley c and b Lyle	286
A. P. Wells c Lyle b Huckle	126
M. B. Loye c and b Shaw	7
†S. J. Rhodes not out	27
B 9, l-b 11, w 7, n-b 9	36
1/24 2/177 3/438 4/473 5/566 (5 wkts dec.)	566

R. D. B. Croft, D. G. Cork, M. J. McCague, M. C. Ilott and P. M. Such did not bat.

Bowling: Lyle 27.2–4–101–1; Baptiste 25–7–60–1; Roe 20–3–84–0; Huckle 49–9–166–1; Shaw 39–8–135–2.

Eastern Province

P. G. Amm c Crawley b Ilott	20	– (2) c Ilott b Croft	23
M. C. Venter lbw b Cork	31	– (1) lbw b Cork	10
A. Botha lbw b Cork	7	– lbw b Ilott	74
L. J. Koen st Rhodes b Croft	20	– c Rhodes b Cork	0
S. C. Pope c Rhodes b Croft	3	– c Rhodes b McCague	31
*E. A. E. Baptiste lbw b Cork	1	– c Rhodes b McCague	58
T. G. Shaw lbw b Croft	4	– c Crawley b Such	42
†G. Morgan not out	60	– not out	26
A. G. Huckle b McCague	5	– (10) run out	8
R. A. Lyle b Croft	11	– (9) lbw b Such	7
G. Roe c Lathwell b Croft	0	– c Rhodes b Ilott	0
B 1, l-b 13, w 1, n-b 15	30	B 5, l-b 8, w 2, n-b 10	25
1/58 2/70 3/76 4/99 5/101 6/107 7/107 8/125 9/178	192	1/34 2/36 3/36 4/84 5/186 6/228 7/274 8/282 9/304	304

Bowling: *First Innings*—McCague 9–4–32–1; Ilott 12–3–35–1; Cork 16–3–47–3; Croft 16–6–41–5; Such 7–1–23–0. *Second Innings*—McCague 27–8–74–2; Ilott 27.4–6–65–2; Croft 20–7–40–1; Cork 20–6–58–2; Such 23–5–54–2.

Umpires: R. E. Koertzen and R. A. Noble.

†At Langa, December 23. England A won by 19 runs. Toss: England A. England A 170 for nine (45 overs) (A. P. Wells 65; M. A. Meyer four for 25); Western Province Invitation XI 151 for seven (45 overs) (H. D. Ackerman 68; D. Gough three for 32).

WESTERN PROVINCE v ENGLAND A

At Cape Town, December 26, 27, 28. England A won by ten wickets. Toss: Western Province.

A strong all-round performance gained England A their eighth successive win and an extra day off on the Cape beaches. After a solid start, Western Province, then the leaders of the domestic Castle Cup, lost all ten first-innings wickets for 114. Only opener Jordaan resisted, surviving for four hours, as Ilott, Cork and Gough took three wickets each – Cork inside two overs. After patient batting from Dale and Loye had earned England A a 144-run lead, the same three collected another nine second-innings wickets. Herschelle Gibbs, a 19-year-old who had represented South Africa at junior level in cricket, football and rugby union, provided the staunchest batting before becoming one of Gough's seven victims in the match.

Close of play: First day, England A 74-2 (J. P. Crawley 29*, A. P. Wells 12*); Second day, England A 321.

Western Province

S. G. Koenig c Loye b Ilott	26	– lbw b Cork	33
D. Jordaan c Rhodes b Cork	65	– lbw b Gough	13
C. A. Best lbw b Ilott	0	– c Croft b Gough	1
H. H. Gibbs b Cork	20	– c Rhodes b Gough	43
A. P. Kuiper b Cork	0	– st Rhodes b Croft	5
*E. O. Simons lbw b Gough	7	– c Rhodes b Ilott	22
A. C. Dawson not out	25	– c Wells b Gough	3
†R. J. Ryall c Lathwell b Ilott	2	– not out	24
M. W. Pringle c Loye b Gough	7	– lbw b Cork	1
A. Martyn b Croft	8	– c Dale b Ilott	13
D. MacHelm b Gough	0	– c Crawley b Ilott	1
L-b 5, w 1, n-b 11	17	B 4, l-b 11, w 2, n-b 2	19
1/63 2/65 3/118 4/118 5/124 6/146 7/152 8/159 9/176	177	1/29 2/35 3/64 4/75 5/117 6/124 7/142 8/143 9/165	178

Bowling: *First Innings*—Ilott 19–3–42–3; Gough 17.5–2–47–3; Cork 15–1–52–3; Dale 7–3–7–0; Croft 21–8–24–1. *Second Innings*—Ilott 21–7–26–3; Gough 21–3–57–4; Dale 3–0–15–0; Cork 16–6–36–2; Croft 14–5–29–1.

England A

M. N. Lathwell lbw b Martyn	8	– not out	22
*H. Morris c Ryall b Simons	19	– not out	12
J. P. Crawley c Koenig b Dawson	51		
A. P. Wells c Ryall b Martyn	24		
M. B. Loye c Ryall b Simons	68		
A. Dale b Dawson	64		
†S. J. Rhodes lbw b Dawson	21		
R. D. B. Croft b Dawson	0		
D. G. Cork c Koenig b Dawson	16		
D. Gough b MacHelm	12		
M. C. Ilott not out	18		
B 1, l-b 6, w 1, n-b 12	20	W 1	1
1/9 2/37 3/94 4/116 5/228 6/273 7/273 8/276 9/292	321	(no wkt)	35

Bowling: *First Innings*—Pringle 23–2–57–0; Martyn 24–5–81–2; Simons 23–5–53–2; Dawson 18–6–42–5; MacHelm 17.1–7–39–1; Kuiper 14–2–40–0; Best 2–0–2–0. *Second Innings*—Pringle 5.5–1–12–0; Dawson 5–0–23–0.

Umpires: R. Brooks and C. J. Mitchley.

NATAL v ENGLAND A

At Durban, January 1, 2, 3, 4. Natal won by an innings and 57 runs. Toss: England A.

Having won the toss for the first time in four first-class matches, Morris inexplicably asked Natal to bat. Four hours later Natal were 192 without loss and Bicknell was preparing to return to England, having broken down after just four overs with a back spasm. It was the prelude to a comprehensive defeat by a relatively inexperienced side. Three Natal batsmen, including the promising 19-year-old Dale Benkenstein, just fell short of centuries, and Marshall was able to declare on 458 at tea on the second day. By then off-spinner Such had bowled 60 overs. England lost two wickets that night and, batting poorly all through the order, were dismissed 342 behind. Better performances from Crawley and Loye and brave resistance from Bicknell – who batted in pain for 88 minutes with Lathwell as his runner – could not extend play past the mid-point of the final day.

Close of play: First day, Natal 296-6 (D. M. Benkenstein 40*, U. H. Goedeke 0*); Second day, England A 43-2 (H. Morris 13*, A. P. Wells 14*); Third day, England A 183-3 (J. P. Crawley 68*, M. B. Loye 27*).

Natal

C. R. B. Armstrong c Wells b Such	97
D. J. Watson c Gough b McCague	87
N. E. Wright c Rhodes b Gough	9
M. L. Bruyns c Morris b Such	6
N. C. Johnson b McCague	22
D. M. Benkenstein c Morris b Dale	95
D. N. Crookes lbw b Such	16
†U. H. Goedeke lbw b Dale	28
S. M. Pollock c Rhodes b Dale	39
L. Klusener not out	20
*M. D. Marshall not out	14
B 9, l-b 9, n-b 7	25
1/192 2/200 3/214 4/222 5/265 6/292 7/364 8/418 9/429 (9 wkts dec.)	458

Bowling: McCague 30–8–77–2; Bicknell 4–2–4–0; Gough 31.5–2–134–1; Dale 34–8–95–3; Such 60–15–130–3.

England A

M. N. Lathwell b Klusener	2	– c Bruyns b Crookes	36
*H. Morris c Goedeke b Crookes	16	– c Benkenstein b Pollock	25
J. P. Crawley c Johnson b Klusener	12	– c Watson b Benkenstein	81
A. P. Wells lbw b Pollock	17	– c Watson b Crookes	20
M. B. Loye b Klusener	11	– c Goedeke b Crookes	68
A. Dale c Goedeke b Pollock	13	– c and b Klusener	2
†S. J. Rhodes c Johnson b Crookes	3	– c Goedeke b Klusener	13
D. Gough c Watson b Crookes	24	– (9) not out	2
M. J. McCague b Pollock	1	– (10) c Goedeke b Klusener	0
M. P. Bicknell not out	5	– (8) b Crookes	22
P. M. Such c Johnson b Crookes	4	– c Wright b Klusener	2
B 4, l-b 3, n-b 1	8	B 6, l-b 6, n-b 2	14
1/3 2/17 3/49 4/49 5/64 6/67 7/97 8/105 9/105	116	1/62 2/70 3/104 4/204 5/218 6/242 7/275 8/282 9/283	285

Bowling: *First Innings*—Marshall 7–4–4–0; Klusener 18–6–37–3; Pollock 18–8–33–3; Crookes 26.2–9–35–4. *Second Innings*—Marshall 28–9–53–0; Klusener 21.5–2–61–4; Crookes 46–10–103–4; Pollock 15–4–37–1; Benkenstein 10–3–19–1.

Umpires: W. Diedricks and D. L. Orchard.

NORTHERN TRANSVAAL v ENGLAND A

At Verwoerdburg, January 7, 8, 9. England A won by eight wickets. Toss: Northern Transvaal.

After the defeat at Durban, the tour management regarded this match as an examination of their batsmen's mental strength: did they have it in them to build innings of Test quality and length? Instead, a difficult, often dangerous pitch turned it into a test of their courage. With Morris setting a captain's example, they passed with distinction to win early on the third day. Ilott, bowling beautifully again, and a genuinely quick McCague ensured that Northern Transvaal were dismissed inside 72 overs – Cork bowled equally impressively but with no luck. Opener Sommerville was ninth out. Morris, batting for three and a half hours, steered England A to a 67-run lead which, when the home team were 49 for six, looked enough for an innings win. But Elworthy, batting as well as he had bowled, and Bryson, slogging 44 in 40 balls, put on 74 in 12 overs to set a target of 96. However, Northern Transvaal's chance went when Lambert dropped Wells on two.

Close of play: First day, England A 81-4 (H. Morris 29*, M. B. Loye 2*); Second day, England A 5-0 (M. N. Lathwell 4*, H. Morris 0*).

Northern Transvaal

C. B. Lambert hit wkt b McCague	1 – c Croft b Ilott	4
B. J. Sommerville c Rhodes b McCague	60 – c Croft b Dale	13
R. F. Pienaar c Cork b Ilott	1 – c Rhodes b Cork	22
M. J. R. Rindel c McCague b Ilott	4 – lbw b Cork	2
†K. J. Rule lbw b Ilott	1 – b Ilott	1
*J. J. Strydom b Dale	12 – c Wells b Ilott	0
D. J. van Zyl c Rhodes b McCague	4 – c Crawley b McCague	17
S. Elworthy c Wells b Croft	24 – lbw b Dale	37
R. E. Bryson run out	0 – c Lathwell b Cork	44
T. Bosch c Cork b Ilott	13 – not out	4
C. van Noordwyk not out	6 – c Lathwell b Cork	5
B 4, l-b 5, w 3	12 B 1, l-b 3, w 1, n-b 8	13
1/7 2/11 3/17 4/24 5/48 6/61 7/101 8/101 9/120	138 1/10 2/37 3/48 4/49 5/49 6/49 7/75 8/149 9/157	162

Bowling: *First Innings*—McCague 18–4–34–3; Ilott 19.1–8–32–4; Cork 18–9–17–0; Dale 4–0–15–1; Croft 12–2–31–1. *Second Innings*—McCague 11–1–37–1; Ilott 14–3–64–3; Cork 18.1–4–50–4; Dale 7–3–7–2.

England A

M. N. Lathwell b Elworthy	5 – b Elworthy	21
*H. Morris b Bosch	57 – c Sommerville b Elworthy	14
J. P. Crawley c Sommerville b Elworthy	16 – not out	26
A. Dale c Pienaar b Elworthy	11	
M. C. Ilott c Lambert b Bosch	3	
M. B. Loye lbw b Bosch	40	
A. P. Wells c Rule b Pienaar	11 – (4) not out	31
†S. J. Rhodes not out	18	
R. D. B. Croft run out	8	
D. G. Cork c Sommerville b Elworthy	7	
M. J. McCague b Bryson	3	
B 8, l-b 9, w 1, n-b 8	26 B 1, l-b 1, n-b 2	4
1/5 2/58 3/76 4/79 5/142 6/155 7/165 8/194 9/202	205 1/32 2/37	(2 wkts) 96

Bowling: *First Innings*—Bryson 15.4–3–53–1; Elworthy 25–8–55–4; van Noordwyk 14–1–34–0; Bosch 13–5–31–3; Pienaar 3–0–15–1. *Second Innings*—Elworthy 8–2–25–2; Bryson 4–0–19–0; van Noordwyk 7–1–23–0; Bosch 4–0–27–0.

Umpires: S. B. Lambson and S. F. Marais.

†At Kimberley, January 12. England A won by 82 runs. Toss: Griqualand West. England A 216 (49.4 overs) (R. D. B. Croft 51, D. G. Cork 47; J. E. Johnson five for 33, B. E. van der Vyfer three for 34); Griqualand West 134 for eight (50 overs) (F. C. Brooker 30, F. Viljoen 44).

ORANGE FREE STATE v ENGLAND A

At Bloemfontein, January 14, 15, 16, 17. Drawn. Toss: Orange Free State.

A century of great concentration by Crawley saved England A from defeat against the Castle Cup champions. For three days the match looked like a repeat of Durban, with England batting poorly in response to a daunting total. This time, however, they showed reserves of character and aptitude. Forceful bowling in fierce heat by McCague prevented Orange Free State's first innings, once 249 for three, from passing 400. But only Wells put up a fight as England A were dismissed inside 80 overs. Stephenson declined to force the follow-on, then delayed his declaration as Arthur scored the only century conceded by England A throughout the trip, finally setting a target of 453. The tourists lost Lathwell and night-watchman Taylor in the last five balls of the third day, but Crawley's four-and-a-half-hour 128 secured the draw. Orange Free State were less than enthused, as they thought they had dismissed him early in both innings; umpire Wilson twice refused to give him out.

Close of play: First day, Orange Free State 344-9 (B. T. Player 10*, H. C. Bakkes 1*); Second day, Orange Free State 28-0 (J. M. Arthur 8*, G. F. J. Liebenberg 16*); Third day, England A 59-2 (H. Morris 25*).

Orange Free State

J. M. Arthur c and b McCague	9	– c Rhodes b Taylor	106
G. F. J. Liebenberg lbw b Taylor	82	– lbw b Gough	21
P. J. R. Steyn st Rhodes b Dale	80	– (6) c Loye b Such	11
L. J. Wilkinson b McCague	43	– c Gough b Dale	0
J. F. Venter lbw b McCague	27	– (3) c Morris b Such	33
C. F. Craven b Gough	28	– (5) c Lathwell b Gough	37
†P. J. L. Radley b Gough	4	– (9) not out	12
N. Boje c McCague b Such	1	– (10) b Taylor	0
*F. D. Stephenson c Rhodes b McCague	46	– (7) b Such	2
B. T. Player not out	29	– (8) run out	9
H. C. Bakkes c Rhodes b Gough	7	– not out	21
L-b 6, w 2, n-b 6	14	B 2, l-b 1, n-b 7	10
1/13 2/143 3/190 4/249 5/252 6/269 7/279 8/309 9/343	370	1/34 2/117 3/120 4/182 5/202 6/217 7/227 8/228 9/230 (9 wkts dec.)	262

Bowling: *First Innings*—McCague 25–4–84–4; Gough 28.5–5–77–3; Taylor 23–2–81–1; Such 23–4–73–1; Dale 13–2–49–1. *Second Innings*—McCague 9–0–26–0; Gough 17–2–49–2; Such 35–5–88–3; Taylor 19–2–65–2; Dale 7–0–31–1.

England A

M. N. Lathwell b Stephenson	0	– b Boje	29
*H. Morris b Bakkes	2	– lbw b Boje	64
J. P. Crawley c Radley b Player	31	– (4) c Radley b Player	128
A. P. Wells c Venter b Stephenson	53	– (5) run out	46
M. B. Loye st Radley b Venter	11	– (6) not out	26
A. Dale c Stephenson b Bakkes	20	– (7) not out	15
†S. J. Rhodes b Venter	3		
D. Gough c Radley b Craven	15		
J. P. Taylor lbw b Stephenson	11	– (3) b Boje	0
M. J. McCague c Liebenberg b Craven	14		
P. M. Such not out	12		
B 1, l-b 4, w 1, n-b 2	8	B 4, l-b 5, n-b 4	13
1/0 2/4 3/71 4/94 5/98 6/102 7/131 8/142 9/152	180	1/59 2/59 3/155 4/259 5/282 (5 wkts)	321

Bowling: *First Innings*—Stephenson 15–4–48–3; Bakkes 16–4–32–2; Craven 13.3–2–35–2; Player 17–5–22–1; Venter 6–0–23–2; Boje 12–5–15–0. *Second Innings*—Stephenson 16–2–46–0; Bakkes 22–5–64–0; Venter 26–6–79–0; Player 15–4–34–1; Boje 35–7–89–3; Steyn 1–1–0–0.

Umpires: C. J. Mitchley and W. J. Wilson.

BORDER v ENGLAND A

At East London, January 21, 22, 23, 24. Drawn. Toss: England A.

Rain – the first to affect play to any degree during the tour – and late resistance by the Border tail prevented England A from gaining a deserved victory. A first representative century from Rhodes, who added 131 with Loye over 64 overs, enabled the tourists to overcome a poor start, then Ilott once again bowled them to a strong position. After the final morning was lost to the weather, Morris set Border 296 to win. Such's best bowling of the tour took his team to the brink of victory, but the last pair survived 29 balls to draw. Cork was replaced by McCague after the first day's play – in which he had taken no part – so that he could return to England because of a family illness.

Close of play: First day, England A 229-6 (S. J. Rhodes 59*, R. D. B. Croft 2*); Second day, Border 125-4 (P. C. Strydom 16*, F. J. C. Cronje 3*); Third day, England A 175-5 (S. J. Rhodes 15*).

England A

J. P. Crawley c Cronje b Badenhorst	49	– b Fourie	14
*H. Morris run out	15	– c Palframan b Fourie	55
A. Dale b Fourie	12	– b Botha	11
A. P. Wells lbw b Fourie	10	– c Stonier b Fourie	46
M. B. Loye b Howell	71	– lbw b Cronje	23
†S. J. Rhodes c Stonier b Botha	108	– not out	15
J. P. Taylor c Palframan b Badenhorst	1		
R. D. B. Croft b Howell	29		
M. C. Ilott run out	0		
M. J. McCague c Bauermeister b Howell	13		
P. M. Such not out	2		
B 2, l-b 3, w 4, n-b 1	10	B 6, l-b 4, n-b 1	11
1/35 2/59 3/75 4/93 5/224 6/227 7/285 8/296 9/308	320	1/17 2/54 3/120 4/137 5/175 (5 wkts dec.)	175

Bowling: *First Innings*—Fourie 21–2–84–2; Badenhorst 27–3–92–2; Botha 24–10–36–1; Howell 39–21–49–3; Strydom 2–0–5–0; Bauermeister 19–5–31–0; Cronje 7–3–18–0. *Second Innings*—Badenhorst 9–0–21–0; Howell 11–1–43–0; Fourie 21–4–59–3; Bauermeister 9–3–16–0; Botha 8–3–14–1; Cronje 4–0–12–1.

Border

M. P. Stonier c Rhodes b Taylor	8	– c Taylor b Croft	48
A. G. Lawson c Ilott b Croft	23	– c Morris b McCague	0
B. M. Osborne run out	50	– c Wells b Taylor	22
P. J. Botha c Morris b Ilott	16	– c Wells b Such	36
P. C. Strydom lbw b Such	26	– b Such	17
F. J. C. Cronje b McCague	16	– (7) c Loye b Croft	13
†S. J. Palframan c Taylor b Such	3	– (8) c Rhodes b Ilott	25
K. G. Bauermeister b Croft	23	– (6) b Such	2
*I. L. Howell not out	21	– lbw b Such	7
B. C. Fourie c Rhodes b Ilott	2	– not out	7
A. Badenhorst c Rhodes b Ilott	0	– not out	8
B 1, l-b 4, w 1, n-b 6	12	L-b 2, w 2	4
1/12 2/88 3/91 4/114 5/145 6/149 7/160 8/180 9/200	200	1/10 2/48 3/97 4/127 5/127 6/130 7/164 8/172 9/180 (9 wkts)	189

Bowling: *First Innings*—McCague 12–2–48–1; Ilott 12.5–3–30–3; Taylor 15–3–36–1; Croft 29–10–43–2; Such 23–11–38–2. *Second Innings*—McCague 9–1–22–1; Ilott 9–3–24–1; Such 31–13–51–4; Taylor 5–1–23–1; Croft 23–4–67–2.

Umpires: E. H. Baillie and K. E. Liebenberg.

SOUTH AFRICA A v ENGLAND A

Unofficial Test

At Port Elizabeth, January 27, 28, 29, 30, 31. Drawn. Toss: South Africa A.

A disappointingly slow, lifeless pitch – the one on which England A had amassed 566 for five earlier in the tour – effectively prevented any result, despite five cloudless days. On seeing the wicket, England omitted McCague and, Cork having departed, included a sixth specialist batsman, the out-of-form Lathwell. After Morris lost his sixth toss in eight first-class matches, Simons and Liebenberg made the most of the conditions, Simons batting himself into the national squad for the imminent visit of Australia and Liebenberg earning a place on the later tour of England. Tight bowling, notably from Such and Ilott, prevented South Africa A from scoring quickly or heavily enough to control the match, however, although home spirits were lifted when Lathwell went fourth ball on the second evening. At 63 for three England A were vulnerable but Wells, whose century against Eastern Province had been overshadowed by Crawley's 286, batted with great determination for five and a half hours, adding 171 with Loye, before falling to a poor leg-before decision. Resuming after lunch on the fourth day, South Africa A proved unable to accelerate without losing wickets. Ilott finished them off with four for eight in 19 balls, after Gough made the initial inroads. England A were left with a target of 250 in 65 overs but the early loss of wickets meant this was never considered; Wells and Loye again saw their team to safety.

Close of play: First day, South Africa A 173-4 (A. P. Kuiper 7*, E. O. Simons 5*); Second day, England A 54-2 (H. Morris 17*, M. C. Ilott 1*); Third day, England A 269-7 (S. J. Rhodes 0*); Fourth day, South Africa A 156-3 (P. J. R. Steyn 54*, A. P. Kuiper 27*).

South Africa A

J. M. Arthur b Such	37	– c Lathwell b Gough	7
G. F. J. Liebenberg lbw b Gough	79	– c Wells b Gough	18
P. J. R. Steyn run out	23	– c Such b Ilott	69
*S. J. Cook c Morris b Ilott	15	– b Gough	48
A. P. Kuiper lbw b Ilott	12	– c Loye b Gough	45
E. O. Simons lbw b Croft	88	– lbw b Ilott	7
†S. J. Palframan lbw b Ilott	4	– c Such b Ilott	0
D. N. Crookes c Wells b Such	41	– lbw b Gough	7
C. E. Eksteen c Rhodes b Ilott	14	– (10) b Ilott	2
M. W. Pringle lbw b Gough	33	– (9) not out	10
A. Martyn not out	0	– b Ilott	0
L-b 5, n-b 6	11	B 2, l-b 6	8
1/87 (1) 2/144 (3) 3/145 (2) 4/165 (4) 5/191 (5) 6/197 (7) 7/269 (8) 8/305 (9) 9/357 (6) 10/357 (10)	357	1/21 (1) 2/26 (2) 3/112 (4) 4/181 (3) 5/193 (5) 6/196 (7) 7/205 (8) 8/207 (6) 9/221 (10) 10/221 (11)	221

Bowling: *First Innings*—Ilott 34–11–71–4; Gough 28.1–9–64–2; Croft 33–7–94–1; Dale 15–2–35–0; Such 43–17–88–2. *Second Innings*—Ilott 20.3–6–43–5; Gough 23–4–81–5; Dale 13–3–31–0; Such 10–1–30–0; Croft 9–3–28–0.

England A

M. N. Lathwell c Palframan b Pringle	0	– lbw b Martyn	4
*H. Morris c Kuiper b Eksteen	21	– b Martyn	16
J. P. Crawley lbw b Simons	29	– c Cook b Pringle	12
M. C. Ilott c Cook b Martyn	14		
A. P. Wells lbw b Kuiper	130	– (4) not out	45
M. B. Loye lbw b Kuiper	51	– (5) c Simons b Martyn	44
A. Dale c Crookes b Eksteen	5	– (6) not out	0
†S. J. Rhodes c and b Martyn	7		
R. D. B. Croft not out	32		
D. Gough c Palframan b Pringle	13		
P. M. Such c Martyn b Crookes	5		
B 5, l-b 10, w 2, n-b 5	22	B 1, l-b 2, n-b 2	5
1/4 (1) 2/49 (3) 3/63 (2) 4/92 (4) 5/263 (6) 6/268 (7) 7/269 (5) 8/287 (8) 9/317 (10) 10/329 (11)	329	1/15 (1) 2/24 (2) 3/43 (3) 4/124 (5)	(4 wkts) 126

Bowling: *First Innings*—Pringle 23–3–72–2; Martyn 29–7–72–2; Simons 26–11–40–1; Eksteen 41–21–48–2; Crookes 21.5–7–61–1; Kuiper 7–0–21–2. *Second Innings*—Pringle 8–1–17–1; Martyn 15–6–23–3; Eksteen 19–8–28–0; Simons 5–0–16–0; Crookes 9–0–27–0; Kuiper 4–1–12–0.

Umpires: S. B. Lambson and C. J. Mitchley.

ENGLAND UNDER-19 IN SRI LANKA, 1993-94

England Under-19 toured Sri Lanka in December and January 1993-94, playing 11 games. They won two, lost four and drew five. Sri Lanka Under-19 took the three-match "Test" series 1-0 thanks to their victory in the second match at Galle after a draw at Colombo; the final game at Kandy was severely disrupted by rain. Sri Lanka Under-19 won the one-day series 2-1. England also played two three-day games against local opposition, both drawn, two two-day games, one won and one drawn, and lost another one-day game.

The party of 15 originally named for the tour was: M. P. Vaughan (Yorkshire) (*captain*), G. P. Butcher (Glamorgan), I. Dawood (Yorkshire), J. A. L. Henderson (Lancashire), K. J. Innes (Northamptonshire), R. L. Johnson (Middlesex), G. Keedy (Yorkshire), D. R. Law (Sussex), T. J. Mason (Leicestershire), M. J. Powell (Warwickshire), C. J. Schofield (Yorkshire), S. D. Thomas (Glamorgan), M. E. Trescothick (Somerset), R. M. S. Weston (Durham), N. T. Wood (Lancashire). M. M. Betts (Durham) replaced Henderson, who withdrew because of a back operation.

Manager: J. R. T. Barclay. *Coach:* G. J. Saville.

First Under-19 "Test": At Colombo, January 4, 5, 6, 7. Drawn. Toss: England Under-19. England Under-19 287 (N. T. Wood 53, M. P. Vaughan 99, K. J. Innes 38; M. Jayawardene three for 63, T. Samaraweera three for 42) and 145 (M. P. Vaughan 47; S. Silva four for 47, T. Samaraweera five for 35); Sri Lanka Under-19 351 for nine dec. (M. Jayawardene 108, P. Harmer 31, S. Warusamana 63 not out) and 16 for no wkt.

Second Under-19 "Test": At Galle, January 14, 15, 16, 17. Sri Lanka Under-19 won by 117 runs. Toss: Sri Lanka Under-19. Sri Lanka Under-19 182 (M. Jayawardene 43, S. Silva 42; R. L. Johnson three for 28, G. Keedy three for 30) and 234 (A. Gunawardene 71, S. Warusamana 57; M. M. Betts four for 52, R. L. Johnson three for 57); England Under-19 150 (C. J. Schofield 48 not out; S. Wijenayake three for 36, T. Samaraweera five for 47) and 149 (S. Wijenayake three for 25, S. Silva three for 37).

Third Under-19 "Test": At Kandy, January 20, 21, 22, 23. Drawn. Toss: England Under-19. England Under-19 168 for five (R. M. S. Weston 33, K. J. Innes 35 not out) v Sri Lanka Under-19.

THE INDIANS IN SRI LANKA, 1993-94

By R. MOHAN

India's first victory in an overseas Test, let alone series, since the defeat of England in 1986 may have been a while coming, but beating their neighbours on Sri Lankan soil gave the players enormous satisfaction. However, success was accompanied by acrimony. Throughout the series, the referee, Peter Burge, was kept busy with complaints over the umpiring from the Indians, who believed they had to take many more than the 20 wickets usually required to win a Test.

The controversy was at its height during the Second Test, when the Indians accused umpires Ponnadurai and Anandappa of palpably biased decision-making. Burge could do little other than send his observations back to headquarters, but at the behest of ICC he did call for a meeting mid-Test between the contestants to cool them down. India's delight in their eventual victory helped to restore normal relations between the two sides, which had been bitterly strained by the midfield exchanges.

The Sri Lankans have always possessed a formidable home record – particularly against neighbours India and Pakistan – based on their determination not to lose on their island, but this Indian team proved superior on most counts, even if it did not earn regular marks for diplomacy. India's once dismal Test fortunes – and those of their captain, Mohammad Azharuddin – had been turned around so completely by their 3-0 success over England a few months earlier that the team was brimming with confidence. The batting established a dominance it had rarely achieved on foreign soil, thanks to the brilliance of Vinod Kambli, who made two Test centuries, and Sachin Tendulkar, while the obdurate openers Navjot Sidhu and Manoj Prabhakar anchored the innings. In contrast, the Sri Lankans seemed out of touch, despite their recent successes against England. Only the senior batsmen, Arjuna Ranatunga and Aravinda de Silva, prospered in the decisive Second Test against the guileful leg-breaks and top-spin of Anil Kumble. Kumble and the all-rounder Prabhakar took the bowling honours, sharing 25 wickets of the 39 Sri Lankan wickets to fall.

Sri Lanka were under pressure even in the 49 minutes of the First Test that were possible in rainy Kandy, one of the biggest washouts in history. But they found their feet in time to stave off what might have been a second successive defeat in the final Test, through centuries from de Silva and Roshan Mahanama. They took the limited-overs series by the odd match in three, after each team won a game against the run of play and Sri Lanka claimed the decider in the final over. The compelling attractions of limited-overs cricket, from the spectators' point of view at least, were stressed once again. What was surprising was the pathetic turnout at the two Tests in Colombo. Even the match at the Sinhalese Sports Club, with its history of international cricket, was so sparsely attended that, despite the sponsorship available, the future of Test cricket in the island must be under dire threat.

INDIAN TOURING PARTY

M. Azharuddin (Hyderabad) (*captain*), S. R. Tendulkar (Bombay) (*vice-captain*), P. K. Amre (Rajasthan), S. A. Ankola (Bombay), R. K. Chauhan (Madhya Pradesh), V. G. Kambli (Bombay), Kapil Dev (Haryana), A. Kumble (Karnataka), K. S. More (Baroda), M. Prabhakar (Delhi), S. L. V. Raju (Hyderabad), W. V. Raman (Tamil Nadu), Ajay Sharma (Delhi), N. S. Sidhu (Punjab), J. Srinath (Karnataka), V. S. Yadav (Haryana).

Tour manager: Group Capt. G. S. Shaktawat. *Cricket manager:* A. L. Wadekar.

INDIAN TOUR RESULTS

Test matches – Played 3: Won 1, Drawn 2.
First-class matches – Played 4: Won 1, Drawn 3.
Win – Sri Lanka.
Draws – Sri Lanka (2), Sri Lankan Board President's XI.
One-day internationals – Played 3: Won 1, Lost 2.

TEST MATCH AVERAGES

SRI LANKA – BATTING

	T	*I*	*NO*	*R*	*HS*	*100s*	*Avge*	*Ct*
P. A. de Silva	3	5	0	266	148	1	53.20	0
H. P. Tillekeratne	3	4	0	167	86	0	41.75	4
R. S. Mahanama	3	5	0	188	151	1	37.60	2
A. P. Gurusinha	3	5	1	144	56	0	36.00	0
A. Ranatunga	3	5	1	131	88	0	32.75	1
K. P. J. Warnaweera	3	3	2	23	20	0	23.00	0
U. C. Hathurusinghe	3	5	0	112	43	0	22.40	0
G. P. Wickremasinghe	2	3	1	15	11*	0	7.50	1

Played in two Tests: A. M. de Silva 0, 1 (3 ct); D. K. Liyanage 2, 8; M. Muralitharan 7 (1 ct). Played in one Test: S. T. Jayasuriya 0, 31* (2 ct); R. S. Kalpage 1, 5 (1 ct); R. S. Kaluwitharana 40 (2 ct); C. P. H. Ramanayake did not bat.

* *Signifies not out.*

BOWLING

	O	*M*	*R*	*W*	*BB*	*5W/i*	*Avge*
M. Muralitharan	47.1	12	136	4	4-136	0	34.00
G. P. Wickremasinghe	87	18	236	6	3-83	0	39.33
K. P. J. Warnaweera	63.1	4	248	6	3-76	0	41.33
R. S. Kalpage	46	4	131	3	2-97	0	43.66
U. C. Hathurusinghe	49	9	136	3	1-35	0	45.33

Also bowled: P. A. de Silva 7–0–17–0; A. P. Gurusinha 34–3–100–2; S. T. Jayasuriya 8–2–30–0; D. K. Liyanage 29–5–95–0; A. Ranatunga 6–3–7–0.

INDIA - BATTING

	T	*I*	*NO*	*R*	*HS*	*100s*	*Avge*	*Ct*
S. R. Tendulkar....	3	3	1	203	104*	1	101.50	3
V. G. Kambli	3	3	0	249	125	2	83.00	1
N. S. Sidhu	3	3	0	225	104	1	75.00	0
M. Prabhakar	3	3	0	154	95	0	51.33	0
M. Azharuddin	3	3	0	97	50	0	32.33	4
P. K. Amre	3	3	1	57	21	0	28.50	3

Played in three Tests: R. K. Chauhan 2, 15* (2 ct); Kapil Dev 35, 27 (1 ct); A. Kumble 1, 9 (3 ct); K. S. More 4, 4 (5 ct). Played in two Tests: J. Srinath 0* (1 ct). Played in one Test: S. L. V. Raju 1 (1 ct).

* *Signifies not out.*

BOWLING

	O	*M*	*R*	*W*	*BB*	*5W/i*	*Avge*
M. Prabhakar	91.5	31	223	12	3-43	0	18.58
J. Srinath	33	8	78	3	2-42	0	26.00
A. Kumble	140.3	36	375	13	5-87	1	28.84
Kapil Dev........	93.1	39	159	5	2-34	0	31.80
R. K. Chauhan....	93	31	197	4	3-59	0	49.25

Also bowled: S. L. V. Raju 52–10–121–2; S. R. Tendulkar 3–0–4–0.

Note: Matches in this section which were not first-class are signified by a dagger.

SRI LANKAN BOARD PRESIDENT'S XI v INDIANS

At Kurunegala, July 12, 13, 14. Drawn. Toss: Indians.

A chartered Russian helicopter, once used by Soviet leader Mikhail Gorbachev, flew the Indians each day from Colombo to the Welagedera Stadium. Huge crowds saw the Indian batsmen begin their tour on a positive note on a slow pitch; captain Azharuddin reached his hundred while an unbroken seventh-wicket stand of 89 between More and Kumble carried the total to 342 in a day. Azharuddin declared overnight and his spinners reduced the home side to 97 for four. But a 192-run partnership between Tillekeratne and Jayasuriya – who hit 21 fours and a six – enabled the President's XI not only to take the lead but to bat well into the third day. There was time for Sidhu and Amre to knock off the deficit while compiling unbeaten fifties.

Close of play: First day, Indians 342-6 (K. S. More 60*, A. Kumble 44*); Second day, Sri Lankan Board President's XI 289-5 (S. T. Jayasuriya 111*, K. R. Pushpakumara 0*).

Indians

M. Prabhakar c Kaluwitharana b Hathurusinghe	53		
N. S. Sidhu c Hathurusinghe b Pushpakumara..	0	– not out......................	66
V. G. Kambli c Jayasuriya b Weerakkody	17	– (1) c Wijetunge b Pushpakumara	10
S. R. Tendulkar c Mendis b Wijetunge	35		
*M. Azharuddin c Samaraweera b Kalpage	100		
P. K. Amre lbw b Kalpage..................	11	– (3) not out..................	70
†K. S. More not out	60		
A. Kumble not out.........................	44		
B 5, l-b 5, w 2, n-b 10	22	L-b 1, n-b 1	2
1/3 2/30 3/83 4/153 5/198 6/253 (6 wkts dec.)	342	1/13 (1 wkt)	148

S. L. V. Raju, S. A. Ankola and J. Srinath did not bat.

Bowling: *First Innings*—Weerakkody 15–3–57–1; Pushpakumara 19–1–98–1; Hathurusinghe 8–1–28–1; Wijetunge 15–5–51–1; Kalpage 25–1–77–2; Jayasuriya 8–0–21–0. *Second Innings*—Weerakkody 7–1–19–0; Pushpakumara 8–1–30–1; Wijetunge 15–3–50–0; Kalpage 13–3–42–0; Jayasuriya 2–0–6–0.

Sri Lankan Board President's XI

U. C. Hathurusinghe c More b Raju . . . 36
D. P. Samaraweera b Raju 18
C. Mendis c Kambli b Raju 13
M. S. Atapattu lbw b Kumble 2
*H. P. Tillekeratne c Srinath b Kambli . 101
S. T. Jayasuriya c Kambli b Raju 151
K. R. Pushpakumara c More b Prabhakar . 0
†R. S. Kaluwitharana lbw b Prabhakar . 1
R. S. Kalpage not out 69
A. P. Weerakkody c Sidhu b Tendulkar 12
P. K. Wijetunge c Azharuddin b Kumble . 0

L-b 3, w 2, n-b 7 12

1/53 2/62 3/69 4/97 5/289 6/289 7/298 8/376 9/412 415

Bowling: Prabhakar 11–1–29–2; Srinath 18–1–61–0; Raju 38–9–101–4; Ankola 19–4–50–0; Kumble 37.3–5–142–2; Kambli 4–0–19–1; Tendulkar 2–0–10–1.

Umpires: L. V. Jayasundara and M. M. Mendis.

SRI LANKA v INDIA

First Test Match

At Kandy, July 17, 18, 19, 21, 22. Drawn. Toss: India.

Rain in the central hills of Sri Lanka made this the shortest-ever Test (excluding those completely abandoned). Only 12 overs – 49 minutes of play – were possible, on the second day, compared to 17.2 overs in 50 minutes at Nottingham in 1926; ironically, the rest day was the sunniest of the week, but the Sri Lankan board said there was no provision in the playing conditions to make use of it. In the brief interlude of cricket, Sri Lanka were put in and reached 24 for three. Kapil Dev, playing his 125th Test to equal Sunil Gavaskar's record for India, picked up one wicket and Prabhakar two, in wet conditions ideal for swing and seam bowling.

Close of play: First day, No play; Second day, Sri Lanka 24-3 (A. P. Gurusinha 10*, A. Ranatunga 7*); Third day, No play; Fourth day, No play.

Sri Lanka

R. S. Mahanama c More b Kapil Dev . 0
U. C. Hathurusinghe c Kumble b Prabhakar . 4
A. P. Gurusinha not out 10
P. A. de Silva c Kumble b Prabhakar . . 1
*A. Ranatunga not out 7

L-b 1, n-b 1 2

1/0 (1) 2/6 (2) 3/8 (4) (3 wkts) 24

H. P. Tillekeratne, †A. M. de Silva, C. P. H. Ramanayake, K. P. J. Warnaweera, D. K. Liyanage and M. Muralitharan did not bat.

Bowling: Kapil Dev 5–1–10–1; Prabhakar 6–1–13–2; Srinath 1–1–0–0.

India

M. Prabhakar, N. S. Sidhu, V. G. Kambli, S. R. Tendulkar, *M. Azharuddin, P. K. Amre, Kapil Dev, †K. S. More, A. Kumble, R. K. Chauhan and J. Srinath.

Umpires: K. T. Francis and T. M. Samarasinghe. Referee: P. J. P. Burge (Australia).

†SRI LANKA v INDIA

First One-Day International

At Khettarama Stadium, Colombo, July 25. India won by one run. Toss: Sri Lanka.

India squeezed home with a run to spare, bowling Sri Lanka out with the second ball of the final over. The home team seemed to have taken control of the game after breaking an opening partnership of 77 between Sidhu and Prabhakar. But Azharuddin kept the innings together, with 53 in 57 balls, despite losing partners at regular intervals. Sri Lanka were still in the driver's seat as Aravinda de Silva and Hathurusinghe added 115 for the third wicket. They reached the final over needing five, though a flurry of wickets meant they were down to their last pair. Kalpage hit the first ball to mid-wicket and ran three, leaving Wickremasinghe on strike. A swinging yorker from Prabhakar bowled him.

Man of the Match: M. Azharuddin.

India

M. Prabhakar c and b Gurusinha 39
N. S. Sidhu b Kalpage 39
V. G. Kambli b Kalpage 9
*M. Azharuddin c Hathurusinghe b Ramanayake . 53
S. R. Tendulkar c Gurusinha b Jayasuriya . 21
P. K. Amre b Kalpage 7
Kapil Dev c Tillekeratne b Wickremasinghe . 27
†V. S. Yadav c Kalpage b Ramanayake . 6
A. Kumble not out 0
L-b 1, w 5, n-b 5 11

1/77 2/92 3/97 4/139 5/148 6/200 7/210 8/212 (8 wkts, 50 overs) 212

R. K. Chauhan and J. Srinath did not bat.

Bowling: Ramanayake 10–0–50–2; Wickremasinghe 9–0–41–1; Hathurusinghe 4–0–24–0; Gurusinha 7–0–21–1; Jayasuriya 10–0–33–1; Kalpage 10–0–42–3.

Sri Lanka

R. S. Mahanama st Yadav b Kumble . 24
U. C. Hathurusinghe lbw b Chauhan . . 64
A. P. Gurusinha c Kapil Dev b Kumble 0
P. A. de Silva c Amre b Srinath 62
*A. Ranatunga lbw b Chauhan 2
H. P. Tillekeratne c Kambli b Prabhakar . 5
S. T. Jayasuriya c Amre b Kapil Dev . . 17
R. S. Kalpage not out 9
†A. M. de Silva run out 4
C. P. H. Ramanayake b Srinath 0
G. P. Wickremasinghe b Prabhakar . . . 0
L-b 5, w 15, n-b 4 24

1/46 2/46 3/161 4/172 5/173 6/186 7/196 8/207 9/208 (49.2 overs) 211

Bowling: Kapil Dev 10–3–29–1; Prabhakar 9.2–0–50–2; Srinath 10–0–64–2; Kumble 10–2–22–2; Chauhan 10–0–41–2.

Umpires: K. T. Francis and T. M. Samarasinghe.

SRI LANKA v INDIA

Second Test Match

At Sinhalese Sports Club, Colombo, July 27, 28, 29, 31, August 1. India won by 235 runs. Toss: India. Test debut: R. S. Kalpage.

India's first win on Sri Lankan soil, and their first in 27 overseas Tests since beating England at Leeds in 1986, came late on the final day. Clinging on after being set an improbable 472 in nine hours, Sri Lanka were doing well enough on the final morning as Aravinda de Silva led them to 180 for three. But the new ball proved the last straw. Prabhakar struck twice in five deliveries and they collapsed to 198 for seven. De Silva – who had become the second Sri Lankan to score 2,000 Test runs in the first innings – threw away his wicket in frustration, after a patient six-hour 93, and soon India had ended an away sequence of ten defeats and 16 draws.

Their victory was clouded by rancour over a series of umpiring decisions. The Indians insisted that time and again their own batsmen were given out in doubtful circumstances – notably Kapil Dev, who celebrated his new status as the second-most-capped player in Test history by racing to 35 in 28 balls, only to be judged lbw to a delivery that seemed to be well clear of his stumps – while the Sri Lankans received the benefit of the doubt. But India did not help their case by over-demonstrative appealing – sledging, according to the Sri Lankans – or by Kambli's tearful reluctance to leave the crease when he hoped to score a fourth hundred in consecutive Test innings.

Batting first on a green-looking pitch which played fast and true, India were steered to a total of 366 thanks to Kambli's third century on the trot, following his 224 against England and 227 against Zimbabwe. But he fell early on the second morning and, after the last five Indian wickets had tumbled for 14, Sri Lanka were helped to the sound position of 200 for four by the close. Ranatunga dominated a century stand with Tillekeratne, but he added only six on the third day, when Kumble set up an Indian first-innings lead of 112. Sidhu and Prabhakar extended this by 171 – the highest opening partnership for India since Sunil Gavaskar and Kris Srikkanth put on 200 against Pakistan at Madras in 1986-87. Prabhakar equalled his highest Test score of 95 and next day Sidhu advanced to his fourth Test century, while Tendulkar, with his sixth, gave India the thrust towards the declaration. Kumble kept the Sri Lankan batsmen on a leash while the seamers worked away, but at first the home team seemed capable of achieving the draw. In the event they lost not only the match but 45 per cent of their fees for a dreadfully slow over-rate.

Man of the Match: M. Prabhakar.

Close of play: First day, India 300-4 (V. G. Kambli 119*, P. K. Amre 6*); Second day, Sri Lanka 200-4 (A. Ranatunga 82*, H. P. Tillekeratne 23*); Third day, India 205-2 (N. S. Sidhu 85*, S. R. Tendulkar 13*); Fourth day, Sri Lanka 86-2 (A. P. Gurusinha 19*, P. A. de Silva 10*).

India

First innings		Second innings	
M. Prabhakar lbw b Gurusinha	4	c Tillekeratne b Kalpage	95
N. S. Sidhu c Tillekeratne b Warnaweera	82	c A. M. de Silva b Hathurusinghe	104
V. G. Kambli c Mahanama b Hathurusinghe	125	c A. M. de Silva b Warnaweera	4
S. R. Tendulkar c Tillekeratne b Kalpage	28	not out	104
*M. Azharuddin lbw b Wickremasinghe	26	c Tillekeratne b Kalpage	21
P. K. Amre c Kalpage b Warnaweera	21	not out	15
Kapil Dev lbw b Gurusinha	35		
†K. S. More c Mahanama b Warnaweera	4		
A. Kumble lbw b Wickremasinghe	1		
R. K. Chauhan c A. M. de Silva b Wickremasinghe	2		
J. Srinath not out	0		
B 9, l-b 3, w 10, n-b 16	38	B 5, l-b 1, w 2, n-b 8	16
1/25 (1) 2/151 (2) 3/219 (4) 4/282 (5) 5/311 (3) 6/352 (7) 7/362 (6) 8/363 (9) 9/366 (10) 10/366 (8)	366	1/171 (1) 2/176 (3) 3/263 (2) 4/316 (4) (4 wkts dec.)	359

Bowling: *First Innings*—Liyanage 19–3–64–0; Wickremasinghe 27–6–83–3; Hathurusinghe 17–2–48–1; Gurusinha 16–2–49–2; Warnaweera 20.1–1–76–3; Kalpage 8–1–34–1. *Second Innings*—Wickremasinghe 22–4–58–0; Liyanage 10–2–31–0; Warnaweera 20–1–86–1; Gurusinha 7–0–24–0; Hathurusinghe 12–1–35–1; Kalpage 38–3–97–2; Ranatunga 2–1–5–0; P. A. de Silva 7–0–17–0.

Sri Lanka

R. S. Mahanama c More b Prabhakar	22	– lbw b Kapil Dev	9
U. C. Hathurusinghe b Kumble	37	– c Azharuddin b Prabhakar	43
A. P. Gurusinha lbw b Prabhakar	4	– c Chauhan b Kumble	39
P. A. de Silva c Azharuddin b Kumble	22	– c Azharuddin b Kumble	93
*A. Ranatunga c Srinath b Kumble	88	– c More b Prabhakar	14
H. P. Tillekeratne c More b Srinath	28	– c sub (W. V. Raman) b Prabhakar	2
†A. M. de Silva c Amre b Kumble	0	– b Kapil Dev	1
R. S. Kalpage c More b Srinath	1	– c Amre b Srinath	5
D. K. Liyanage lbw b Kumble	2	– c Azharuddin b Chauhan	8
G. P. Wickremasinghe not out	11	– lbw b Kumble	4
K. P. J. Warnaweera b Prabhakar	20	– not out	2
B 9, l-b 5, w 4, n-b 1	19	B 6, l-b 6, w 3, n-b 1	16
1/48 (1) 2/60 (3) 3/85 (2) 4/96 (4) 5/207 (5) 6/208 (7) 7/209 (8) 8/218 (6) 9/218 (9) 10/254 (11)	254	1/44 (1) 2/59 (2) 3/127 (3) 4/180 (5) 5/182 (6) 6/191 (7) 7/198 (8) 8/221 (4) 9/229 (9) 10/236 (10)	236

Bowling: *First Innings*—Kapil Dev 11–4–26–0; Prabhakar 15.5–5–43–3; Srinath 17–5–42–2; Kumble 24–3–87–5; Chauhan 10–1–42–0. *Second Innings*—Kapil Dev 26–13–34–2; Prabhakar 18–4–49–3; Srinath 15–2–36–1; Kumble 38.1–14–85–3; Chauhan 24–18–20–1.

Umpires: I. Anandappa and S. Ponnadurai. Referee: P. J. P. Burge (Australia).

SRI LANKA v INDIA

Third Test Match

At P. Saravanamuttu Stadium, Colombo, August 4, 5, 6, 8, 9. Drawn. Toss: Sri Lanka.

A splendidly crafted 148 by de Silva gave Sri Lanka every chance of building up a big first-innings total on a pitch which played better than its motley look suggested. It was his sixth Test hundred, but his first at home; he reached his century with a six and, in all, hit 17 fours and two sixes in six and a half hours. However, Sri Lanka left themselves vulnerable by going on to make only 351, despite a fifty from Tillekeratne. The Indian openers made another useful start, of 86, and old schoolmates Kambli and Tendulkar again batted positively with 162 in 204 minutes. The in-form Kambli cracked his fourth century – 120 in five and a quarter hours – in his last five Tests (including Kandy, where he did not get to bat) and Azharuddin made his first Test fifty in two tours of Sri Lanka. Then, on the fourth day, off-spinner Muralitharan took four of India's last five wickets to make sure that the lead was a marginal 95.

The only threat of defeat for Sri Lanka lay in a batting collapse, which Mahanama precluded with a classy innings of 151, with 19 fours, in 520 minutes. There was a brief glimmer of hope for the Indians when three quick wickets on the final morning reduced Sri Lanka to 157 for four. But Mahanama and Tillekeratne, who needed a runner after injuring his knee, added 132 to steer the home team to safety.

The bad feeling which plagued the previous Test persisted, especially when the umpires paid close attention to what they feared were scuff marks on a ball being used by Prabhakar. But Tendulkar, leading the team for the first time after fever kept Azharuddin off the field in the closing stages, did his best to maintain calm. Kapil Dev, still seeking the seven wickets he needed to head the list of Test wicket-takers, did notch up another landmark: on the fourth day he passed Lance Gibbs's record of 27,115 deliveries in Test cricket.

Man of the Match: R. S. Mahanama.

Men of the Series: Sri Lanka – P. A. de Silva; India – M. Prabhakar.

Close of play: First day, Sri Lanka 226-4 (P. A. de Silva 118*, H. P. Tillekeratne 14*); Second day, India 84-0 (M. Prabhakar 37*, N. S. Sidhu 39*); Third day, India 384-5 (M. Azharuddin 47*, A. Kumble 0*); Fourth day, Sri Lanka 132-1 (R. S. Mahanama 67*, A. P. Gurusinha 34*).

Sri Lanka

	First innings		Second innings	
R. S. Mahanama lbw b Prabhakar	6	– c Chauhan b Prabhakar	151
U. C. Hathurusinghe c Amre b Kapil Dev	6	– c sub (W. V. Raman) b Raju	22
A. P. Gurusinha c Tendulkar b Kumble	56	– c sub (W. V. Raman) b Kumble	35
P. A. de Silva c Raju b Kumble	148	– c Kambli b Kumble	2
*A. Ranatunga c Kapil Dev b Raju	9	– c Tendulkar b Prabhakar	13
H. P. Tillekeratne b Chauhan	51	– c and b Kumble	86
S. T. Jayasuriya lbw b Chauhan	0	– not out	31
†R. S. Kaluwitharana b Prabhakar	40		
G. P. Wickremasinghe c Tendulkar b Chauhan	0		
M. Muralitharan b Kapil Dev	7		
K. P. J. Warnaweera not out	1		
B 3, l-b 20, w 1, n-b 3	27	B 6, l-b 4, w 1, n-b 1	12
1/13 (2) 2/29 (1) 3/165 (3) 4/182 (5) 5/281 (4) 6/286 (6) 7/309 (7) 8/309 (9) 9/347 (8) 10/351 (10)	351	1/75 (2) 2/142 (3) 3/144 (4) 4/157 (5) 5/289 (1) 6/352 (6)	(6 wkts) 352

Bowling: *First Innings*—Kapil Dev 27.1–10–56–2; Prabhakar 21–7–59–2; Raju 25–5–55–1; Tendulkar 3–0–4–0; Kumble 40–12–95–2; Chauhan 26–7–59–3. *Second Innings*—Kapil Dev 24–11–33–0; Prabhakar 31–14–59–2; Kumble 38.2–7–108–3; Raju 27–5–66–1; Chauhan 33–5–76–0.

India

M. Prabhakar c Jayasuriya b Wickremasinghe	55
N. S. Sidhu c Kaluwitharana b Wickremasinghe	39
V. G. Kambli lbw b Warnaweera	120
S. R. Tendulkar c Ranatunga b Hathurusinghe	71
*M. Azharuddin c Wickremasinghe b Muralitharan	50
P. K. Amre c Kaluwitharana b Wickremasinghe	21
A. Kumble b Muralitharan	9
Kapil Dev lbw b Warnaweera	27
†K. S. More c and b Muralitharan	4
R. K. Chauhan not out	15
S. L. V. Raju c Jayasuriya b Muralitharan	1
B 5, l-b 12, w 1, n-b 16	34
1/86 (2) 2/109 (1) 3/271 (4) 4/334 (3) 5/384 (6) 6/388 (5) 7/397 (7) 8/409 (9) 9/437 (8) 10/446 (11)	446

Bowling: Wickremasinghe 38–8–95–3; Gurusinha 11–1–27–0; Warnaweera 23–2–86–2; Hathurusinghe 20–6–53–1; Ranatunga 4–2–2–0; Muralitharan 47.1–12–136–4; Jayasuriya 8–2–30–0.

Umpires: B. C. Cooray and P. Manuel. Referee: P. J. P. Burge (Australia).

†SRI LANKA v INDIA

Second One-Day International

At Khettarama Stadium, Colombo, August 12 (day/night). Sri Lanka won by eight runs. Toss: India.

The first floodlit match between the two countries drew the biggest crowd of the tour, thought to be about 40,000. As in the earlier game at Khettarama, a team apparently coasting to victory was bowled out in the final over. This time it was India. Despite ten wides by Kapil Dev, the Indians had restricted Sri Lanka's middle order until Ranatunga's run-a-ball 50 and Kalpage lifted the momentum. Though Sidhu went second ball, a target of 4.1 an over seemed the simplest thing as Prabhakar and Azharuddin put on 136. An over-ambitious shot by Azharuddin ended that stand, but India needed only 30 runs from eight overs with seven wickets in hand when Prabhakar holed out. The batting immediately plunged into disarray, and occasional off-spinner de Silva finished the job with four balls remaining.

Man of the Match: A. Ranatunga.

Sri Lanka

A. P. Gurusinha c Chauhan b Prabhakar	9	†R. S. Kaluwitharana run out	9
U. C. Hathurusinghe run out	38	R. S. Kalpage not out	17
H. P. Tillekeratne lbw b Chauhan	23	G. P. Wickremasinghe not out	1
P. A. de Silva c Azharuddin b Kapil Dev	16	B 1, l-b 8, w 13, n-b 2	24
*A. Ranatunga c Tendulkar b Prabhakar	50	1/27 2/82 3/103 4/109 5/142 6/158 7/202	(7 wkts, 50 overs) 204
S. T. Jayasuriya lbw b Chauhan	17		

C. P. H. Ramanayake and M. Muralitharan did not bat.

Bowling: Kapil Dev 10–1–36–1; Prabhakar 8–1–33–2; Srinath 8–1–34–0; Tendulkar 6–1–20–0; Chauhan 9–0–37–2; Kumble 9–0–35–0.

India

M. Prabhakar c Kalpage b Jayasuriya	86	†V. S. Yadav b Kalpage	1
N. S. Sidhu c Tillekeratne b Wickremasinghe	0	A. Kumble lbw b de Silva	10
V. G. Kambli lbw b Wickremasinghe	7	R. K. Chauhan c and b Kalpage	4
*M. Azharuddin c Gurusinha b Wickremasinghe	62	J. Srinath not out	0
S. R. Tendulkar run out	15	L-b 6, w 4	10
P. K. Amre b Muralitharan	1	1/0 2/16 3/152 4/175 5/178 6/179 7/180 8/189 9/196	(49.2 overs) 196
Kapil Dev lbw b Jayasuriya	0		

Bowling: Ramanayake 7–2–23–0; Wickremasinghe 8–0–34–3; Gurusinha 2–0–10–0; Hathurusinghe 5–1–14–0; Muralitharan 10–0–38–1; Jayasuriya 10–0–45–2; Kalpage 6–0–22–2; de Silva 1.2–0–4–1.

Umpires: B. C. Cooray and D. N. Pathirana.

†SRI LANKA v INDIA

Third One-Day International

At Moratuwa, August 14. Sri Lanka won by four wickets. Toss: India.

Sri Lanka were more convincing winners than the last-over finish suggested. Mahanama maintained his form of the Third Test and made 92, helped by a runner, until cramp and the inflamed toe that kept him out of the previous game caused him such pain that he had to be carried off. Though there were some nervous moments as three wickets fell, Sri Lanka won the match and the series. Azharuddin had carried the Indian innings with his third half-century of the series; his 85 made him India's top limited-overs run-scorer, with 4,114 to Kris Srikkanth's 4,092. But he had little support and Sri Lanka's target was a modest 228 on an easy pitch.

Man of the Match: R. S. Mahanama.

India

M. Prabhakar c Gurusinha b Wickremasinghe	17	Kapil Dev c de Silva b Ramanayake	4
N. S. Sidhu c Kalpage b Wickremasinghe	7	†V. S. Yadav run out	27
V. G. Kambli c Mahanama b Muralitharan	19	A. Kumble not out	4
*M. Azharuddin c Jayasuriya b Ramanayake	85	R. K. Chauhan b Wickremasinghe	0
S. R. Tendulkar c Muralitharan b Jayasuriya	25	J. Srinath not out	5
Ajay Sharma st Kaluwitharana b Jayasuriya	20	L-b 8, w 3, n-b 3	14
		1/22 2/43 3/65 4/112 5/165 6/181 7/217 8/218 9/219	(9 wkts, 50 overs) 227

Bowling: Ramanayake 10–1–42–2; Wickremasinghe 10–1–54–3; Hathurusinghe 3–0–12–0; Gurusinha 2–0–7–0; Muralitharan 5–1–21–1; Jayasuriya 10–1–38–2; Kalpage 10–0–45–0.

Sri Lanka

R. S. Mahanama retired hurt	92	R. S. Kalpage not out	5
U. C. Hathurusinghe c Kambli b Prabhakar	12	C. P. H. Ramanayake not out	4
A. P. Gurusinha run out	43		
P. A. de Silva b Chauhan	30	L-b 15, w 5	20
*A. Ranatunga c Kumble b Prabhakar	22		
S. T. Jayasuriya lbw b Prabhakar	2	1/27 2/112 3/178 4/216 5/217 6/222 (6 wkts, 49.3 overs)	231
†R. S. Kaluwitharana c Kapil Dev b Srinath	1		

G. P. Wickremasinghe and M. Muralitharan did not bat.

R. S. Mahanama retired hurt at 213.

Bowling: Kapil Dev 7–1–22–0; Prabhakar 9–1–38–3; Srinath 9.3–1–46–1; Tendulkar 4–0–15–0; Chauhan 10–0–39–1; Kumble 7–0–37–0; Ajay Sharma 3–0–19–0.

Umpires: B. C. Cooray and P. Manuel.

FUTURE TOURS

1995	West Indians to England	1996	Indians to England Pakistanis to England
1995-96	Sri Lankans to Pakistan* England to South Africa New Zealanders to India* Pakistanis to Australia* West Indians to Australia Sri Lankans to Australia Zimbabweans to New Zealand WORLD CUP (*in India, Pakistan and Sri Lanka, February/March 1996*) New Zealanders to the West Indies*	1996-97	Australians to Sri Lanka* Australians to India* England to Pakistan* England to Sri Lanka* West Indians to Australia New Zealanders to India Pakistanis to Australia England to New Zealand Australians to New Zealand Indians to the West Indies
		1997	Australians to England

* *Signifies unconfirmed.*

THE SOUTH AFRICANS IN SRI LANKA, 1993-94

By COLIN BRYDEN

The first tour of Sri Lanka by a South African team produced a satisfying result for the visitors. The series was decided in the Second Test, which they won by an innings and 208 runs. This was the biggest winning margin in South Africa's history and Sri Lanka's heaviest defeat. In view of the difficulties experienced in Sri Lanka by other visitors – Australia, New Zealand and England – in the preceding year, it provided further evidence that the South Africans were rapidly establishing themselves as a competent team at Test level.

The victory confirmed the belief of the South African captain, Kepler Wessels, that his team's strength lay in fast bowling, even in generally unhelpful circumstances. It came after South Africa had narrowly avoided defeat in the First Test at Moratuwa. There the tour selectors had been persuaded by a bare, seemingly under-prepared pitch to pick both their spin bowlers as well as all six of the specialist batsmen on tour. Although this left Allan Donald and Brett Schultz to carry the pace banner on their own, they took nine of the wickets in the first innings and always looked more likely to strike than the spinners, Pat Symcox and Clive Eksteen, both playing in their first Test. A remarkable unbeaten century by Jonty Rhodes, who had given no previous indication on tour that he could cope with the local spin bowlers, enabled South Africa to escape from a dire situation. After that, Brian McMillan and Richard Snell returned to give Wessels a four-pronged pace attack; 40-year-old Jimmy Cook was the batsman who made way, and a long-awaited Test career seemed to be over after just three matches.

The South Africans, who had attended two three-day training camps in Durban, the hottest and most humid of South Africa's cities, coped well with the Sri Lankan climate as well as the slow pitches. Discipline was the watchword in the batting, while the pace of Schultz and Donald was always a little too much for the Sri Lankans. They extracted enough bounce to make batting uncomfortable and Schultz, on his first tour, was easily the most impressive bowler in the series. A strongly-built left-armer who bowled with palpable aggression, he took 20 wickets at 16.30 in three Tests. All South Africa's top-order batsmen performed satisfactorily, with Rhodes and Daryll Cullinan scoring maiden Test centuries and Hansie Cronje his second. Both openers, Wessels and Andrew Hudson, reached the nineties and they shared two century opening partnerships. South Africa's catching was the only disappointment: more than a dozen chances were spilled during the series.

The Sri Lankan batting was generally disappointing, although their two most experienced players, Arjuna Ranatunga and Aravinda de Silva, were consistent. After a promising match in Moratuwa, Hashan Tillekeratne struggled against the fast bowlers. The opening batsmen, Roshan Mahanama and Chandika Hathurusinghe, were usually overwhelmed by Schultz and Donald. But Ranatunga said it was unlikely that any other batsmen in the country would cope better. On the limited evidence of two warm-up matches, he may well have been correct. If the Board XIs assembled for these games were an indication of the next level of Sri Lankan talent, there is not a great deal of depth.

The off-spinner, Muttiah Muralitharan, was the only bowler who regularly troubled the South African batsmen. He turned the ball prodigiously although, lacking variation, he seldom threatened to run through the batting order. With the South Africans making liberal use of their pads, there were long periods of stalemate when he was bowling. But the non-selection of Jayananda Warnaweera, whose action had been the subject of some controversy, left him without a partner of similar menace. The new-ball bowlers, Pramodya Wickremasinghe and Champaka Ramanayake, lacked real pace. For a batsman of such panache, Ranatunga proved surprisingly cautious as a captain, particularly in the Third Test when he and de Silva batted exceedingly slowly even though a more aggressive approach might have saved the series.

For the first time in Sri Lanka, an independent umpire, Brian Aldridge of New Zealand, stood in the Tests. Ironically, he made more contentious decisions than the home officials. Despite agreement in principle before the tour, video replays were not used; the Sri Lankan board decided that technical facilities were not good enough. Crowds were disappointing at the Tests – perhaps because the board allowed live TV coverage – but for the limited-overs internationals, shown live during the first innings and after a time-lag in the second, the grounds were packed.

SOUTH AFRICAN TOURING PARTY

K. C. Wessels (Eastern Province) (*captain*), W. J. Cronje (Orange Free State) (*vice-captain*), S. J. Cook (Transvaal), D. J. Cullinan (Transvaal), P. S. de Villiers (Northern Transvaal), A. A. Donald (Orange Free State), C. E. Eksteen (Transvaal), A. C. Hudson (Natal), B. M. McMillan (Western Province), S. J. Palframan (Border), J. N. Rhodes (Natal), D. J. Richardson (Eastern Province), B. N. Schultz (Eastern Province), R. P. Snell (Transvaal), P. L. Symcox (Natal).

Tour manager: C. Docrat. *Cricket manager:* M. J. Procter.

SOUTH AFRICAN TOUR RESULTS

Test matches – Played 3: Won 1, Drawn 2.
First-class matches – Played 5: Won 2, Drawn 3.
Wins – Sri Lanka, Sri Lankan Board XI.
Draws – Sri Lanka (2), Sri Lankan Board President's XI.
One-day internationals – Played 3: Won 1, Lost 1, No result 1.

TEST MATCH AVERAGES

SRI LANKA – BATTING

	T	*I*	*NO*	*R*	*HS*	*100s*	*Avge*	*Ct*
A. Ranatunga	3	5	0	250	131	1	50.00	0
P. A. de Silva	3	5	0	235	82	0	47.00	2
H. P. Tillekeratne	3	5	1	180	92	0	45.00	6
S. T. Jayasuriya	2	3	0	125	65	0	41.66	2
R. S. Mahanama	3	5	0	102	53	0	20.40	2

	T	I	NO	R	HS	100s	Avge	Ct/St
G. P. Wickremasinghe	2	3	0	49	21	0	16.33	2
M. Muralitharan	3	3	2	16	14*	0	16.00	1
U. C. Hathurusinghe	3	5	0	45	34	0	9.00	1
P. B. Dassanayake	3	4	0	25	10	0	6.25	2/4
H. D. P. K. Dharmasena	2	3	0	12	5	0	4.00	0
C. P. H. Ramanayake	2	3	2	3	3*	0	3.00	1

Played in one Test: A. P. Gurusinha 26, 27 (1 ct); R. S. Kalpage 42, 0*; D. K. Liyanage 0; P. K. Wijetunge 10, 0.

* *Signifies not out.*

BOWLING

	O	M	R	W	BB	5W/i	Avge
U. C. Hathurusinghe	34	17	48	3	1-7	0	16.00
P. A. de Silva	35	5	89	5	3-39	0	17.80
M. Muralitharan	174.1	47	356	16	5-101	2	22.25
C. P. H. Ramanayake	55	10	164	4	3-75	0	41.00
G. P. Wickremasinghe	72	16	228	5	2-58	0	45.60

Also bowled: H. D. P. K. Dharmasena 91–25–199–2; A. P. Gurusinha 3–0–3–0; S. T. Jayasuriya 17–3–73–1; R. S. Kalpage 25.5–8–44–1; D. K. Liyanage 25–5–75–1; A. Ranatunga 2–0–6–0; H. P. Tillekeratne 2–0–5–0; P. K. Wijetunge 52–5–118–2.

SOUTH AFRICA – BATTING

	T	I	NO	R	HS	100s	Avge	Ct
W. J. Cronje	3	5	1	237	122	1	59.25	3
D. J. Cullinan	3	5	0	237	102	1	47.40	1
A. C. Hudson	3	5	0	202	90	0	40.40	1
K. C. Wessels	3	5	0	188	92	0	37.60	1
P. L. Symcox	3	4	0	149	50	0	37.25	0
J. N. Rhodes	3	5	1	145	101*	1	36.25	2
D. J. Richardson	3	4	0	79	62	0	19.75	17
A. A. Donald	3	3	2	5	4*	0	5.00	2
B. N. Schultz	3	3	0	6	6	0	2.00	0
B. M. McMillan	2	3	1	2	2	0	1.00	2

Played in two Tests: R. P. Snell 48, 13*. Played in one Test: S. J. Cook 7, 24; C. E. Eksteen 1, 4*.

* *Signifies not out.*

BOWLING

	O	M	R	W	BB	5W/i	Avge
B. N. Schultz	124.1	35	326	20	5-48	2	16.30
A. A. Donald	102	33	232	12	5-69	1	19.33
R. P. Snell	56	15	133	5	3-32	0	26.60
P. L. Symcox	70	12	230	4	3-75	0	57.50

Also bowled: W. J. Cronje 34–16–59–1; C. E. Eksteen 23–6–78–0; B. M. McMillan 43–9–113–2.

SOUTH AFRICAN AVERAGES – FIRST-CLASS MATCHES

BATTING

	M	*I*	*NO*	*R*	*HS*	*100s*	*Avge*	*Ct*
P. L. Symcox	4	5	1	226	77*	0	56.50	0
W. J. Cronje	5	8	2	330	122	1	55.00	5
D. J. Cullinan	5	8	0	347	102	1	43.37	5
A. C. Hudson	5	8	0	324	91	0	40.50	5
R. P. Snell	3	3	1	81	48	0	40.50	0
K. C. Wessels	5	8	0	298	92	0	37.25	2
S. J. Cook	3	5	1	121	88	0	30.25	1
J. N. Rhodes	5	8	1	205	101*	1	29.28	3
D. J. Richardson	4	5	0	82	62	0	16.40	20
B. M. McMillan	3	4	1	45	43	0	15.00	3
C. E. Eksteen	3	3	1	6	4*	0	3.00	2
A. A. Donald	4	4	2	5	4*	0	2.50	3
B. N. Schultz	4	4	1	6	6	0	2.00	0

Played in one match: P. S. de Villiers 6; S. J. Palframan 10 (3 ct).

* *Signifies not out.*

BOWLING

	O	*M*	*R*	*W*	*BB*	*5W/i*	*Avge*
P. S. de Villiers	30.4	8	68	5	5-68	1	13.60
B. N. Schultz	153.1	44	382	27	5-48	2	14.14
R. P. Snell	83	22	208	9	4-75	0	23.11
C. E. Eksteen	65.4	22	213	9	4-28	0	23.66
A. A. Donald	128	38	310	13	5-69	1	23.84
B. M. McMillan	60.4	13	154	6	3-30	0	25.66
P. L. Symcox	95	21	301	4	3-75	0	75.25

Also bowled: W. J. Cronje 45–20–75–1.

Note: Matches in this section which were not first-class are signified by a dagger.

SRI LANKAN BOARD XI v SOUTH AFRICANS

At Galle, August 13, 14, 15. South Africans won by an innings and 13 runs. Toss: Sri Lankan Board XI.

The South Africans established the platform for a comfortable win when Schultz wrecked the home team's innings on the first morning. After conceding one run in his first four overs, he switched ends and took four for ten in his next six. Another fiery performance in the second innings ensured his place in the Test side. The South African batting was less impressive, although Cullinan and Cook put on 170 in 152 minutes for the fourth wicket. The left-handed Wickremaratne played some attractive shots for the Board XI, while their wicket-keeper, Dassanayake, claimed six victims without conceding any extras. But the tourists won before lunch on the third day.

Close of play: First day, South Africans 159-3 (D. J. Cullinan 64*, S. J. Cook 42*); Second day, Sri Lankan Board XI 130-6 (P. B. Dassanayake 7*, P. K. Wijetunge 8*).

Sri Lankan Board XI

*C. Mendis c Cullinan b McMillan	14	– c and b Eksteen 32
D. P. Samaraweera c Wessels b Schultz	11	– c Hudson b Schultz 12
N. Nawaz b Schultz	0	– c Donald b McMillan 7
M. S. Atapattu c Hudson b Schultz	1	– b Eksteen 9
R. P. A. H. Wickremaratne c Cronje b Eksteen	31	– c Hudson b Eksteen 29
S. Jayantha c Cullinan b Schultz	1	– c Richardson b McMillan 22
†P. B. Dassanayake c Hudson b Eksteen	2	– c McMillan b Schultz 7
D. K. Liyanage c Cronje b Eksteen	10	– (9) c Cullinan b Schultz 0
U. D. U. Chandana c Eksteen b Donald	3	– (10) c Richardson b McMillan 32
P. K. Wijetunge b Eksteen	3	– (8) c Richardson b Eksteen 22
K. R. Pushpakumara not out	5	– not out 0
B 2, l-b 3, w 2, n-b 2	9	L-b 6, w 1, n-b 3 10
1/25 2/25 3/29 4/29 5/32 6/45 7/58 8/66 9/82	90	1/14 2/34 3/51 4/91 5/92 6/117 7/130 8/130 9/176 182

Bowling: *First Innings*—Donald 12–3–28–1; Schultz 13–6–18–4; McMillan 6–2–11–1; Eksteen 8.4–2–28–4. *Second Innings*—Donald 14–2–50–0; Schultz 16–3–38–3; McMillan 11.4–2–30–3; Eksteen 21–11–55–4; Cronje 1–0–3–0.

South Africans

*K. C. Wessels lbw b Pushpakumara	31
A. C. Hudson c Dassanayake b Liyanage	0
W. J. Cronje c Dassanayake b Liyanage	15
D. J. Cullinan b Atapattu b Jayantha	92
S. J. Cook c Dassanayake b Chandana	88
J. N. Rhodes c Dassanayake b Chandana	1
B. M. McMillan st Dassanayake b Wijetunge	43
†D. J. Richardson c Nawaz b Pushpakumara	3
C. E. Eksteen c Dassanayake b Chandana	1
A. A. Donald c sub (R. P. Arnold) b Wijetunge	0
B. N. Schultz not out	0
W 2, n-b 9	11
1/2 2/33 3/51 4/221 5/228 6/241 7/262 8/285 9/285	285

Bowling: Liyanage 21–4–65–2; Pushpakumara 20–2–75–2; Wijetunge 20.3–2–65–2; Chandana 17–3–59–3; Jayantha 8–1–21–1.

Umpires: L. V. Jayasundara and T. Kudahetti.

SRI LANKAN BOARD PRESIDENT'S XI v SOUTH AFRICANS

At Kurunegala, August 18, 19, 20. Drawn. Toss: South Africans.

A good batting pitch provided worthwhile practice against a much stronger side than the South Africans had faced in Galle. Hudson, Wessels, Cronje, Rhodes and Symcox all spent enough time at the crease to acquaint themselves with Sri Lankan conditions, though none could master Dharmasena, who took five wickets bowling off-spin at a brisk pace. Samaraweera made a patient 72 for the President's XI while the left-handers Wickremaratne and Jayasuriya displayed some handsome strokes. The South African opening bowlers, Snell and de Villiers, stuck to their task in hot weather on an unresponsive pitch and were rewarded when the tail crumbled, giving the tourists first-innings lead.

Close of play: First day, South Africans 303-7 (P. L. Symcox 53*, S. J. Palframan 10*); Second day, Sri Lankan Board President's XI 262-5 (S. T. Jayasuriya 54*, U. D. U. Chandana 25*).

South Africans

A. C. Hudson lbw b Jayasuriya	91	– (2) lbw b Liyanage	31
*K. C. Wessels c Tillekeratne b Dharmasena	62	– (1) c Fernando b Liyanage	17
W. J. Cronje c and b Anurasiri	40	– (5) not out	38
D. J. Cullinan c Samaraweera b Dharmasena	1	– b Liyanage	17
S. J. Cook lbw b Dharmasena	0	– (6) not out	2
J. N. Rhodes c Samaraweera b Dharmasena	9	– (3) c Samaraweera b Anurasiri	50
R. P. Snell b Pushpakumara	20		
P. L. Symcox not out	77		
†S. J. Palframan c Wickremaratne b Pushpakumara	10		
P. S. de Villiers lbw b Dharmasena	6		
B 5, l-b 9, w 2, n-b 1	17	L-b 1	1
1/162 2/166 3/167 4/167 5/181 6/208 7/271 8/311 9/333 (9 wkts dec.)	333	1/34 2/59 3/83 4/153 (4 wkts)	156

C. E. Eksteen did not bat.

Bowling: *First Innings*—Liyanage 10–0–39–0; Pushpakumara 15–0–80–2; Dharmasena 35–9–91–5; Anurasiri 33–7–77–1; Chandana 4–0–20–0; Jayasuriya 6–1–12–1; Tillekeratne 1–1–0–0. *Second Innings*—Liyanage 14–5–29–3; Pushpakumara 11–1–57–0; Anurasiri 19–2–53–1; Dharmasena 8–4–16–0; Tillekeratne 1–1–0–0.

Sri Lankan Board President's XI

C. Mendis c Palframan b de Villiers	5
D. P. Samaraweera c Palframan b de Villiers	72
*H. P. Tillekeratne b Snell	3
R. P. A. H. Wickremaratne c Cullinan b Eksteen	82
S. T. Jayasuriya c Rhodes b Snell	54
†U. N. K. Fernando lbw b Snell	11
U. D. U. Chandana c Cook b Snell	37
D. K. Liyanage b de Villiers	7
H. D. P. K. Dharmasena lbw b de Villiers	1
S. D. Anurasiri not out	2
K. R. Pushpakumara c Palframan b de Villiers	0
B 6, l-b 6, n-b 5	17
1/12 2/23 3/160 4/182 5/223 6/262 7/285 8/288 9/291	291

Bowling: Snell 27–7–75–4; de Villiers 30.4–8–68–5; Cronje 10–4–13–0; Symcox 25–9–71–0; Eksteen 13–3–52–1.

Umpires: M. M. Mendis and E. K. G. Wijewardene.

†SRI LANKA v SOUTH AFRICA

First One-Day International

At Kandy, August 22. No result. Toss: South Africa. International debut: P. L. Symcox.

The opening international was spoiled by rain, which reduced it to 46 overs before the teams could make a start. After another interruption rain ended the Sri Lankan innings prematurely. Further showers revised South Africa's target repeatedly, before rain finally concluded proceedings after only 14 overs. Mahanama and Hathurusinghe had benefited from some wayward bowling to put on 110 for the first wicket before some tight off-spin from Symcox slowed the scoring. South Africa's batting looked even more uncertain against the sharp off-spin of Muralitharan.

Sri Lanka

R. S. Mahanama run out	49	A. P. Gurusinha not out	22
U. C. Hathurusinghe c Cullinan b Symcox	51	†R. S. Kaluwitharana not out	1
P. A. de Silva c Rhodes b Symcox	2	L-b 7, w 15	22
*A. Ranatunga c Snell b Donald	29	1/110 2/116 3/121 (5 wkts, 41.3 overs)	179
S. T. Jayasuriya run out	3	4/127 5/171	

H. P. Tillekeratne, R. S. Kalpage, G. P. Wickremasinghe and M. Muralitharan did not bat.

Bowling: Donald 7–0–23–1; de Villiers 5–0–23–0; Snell 6.3–0–33–0; McMillan 5–0–33–0; Symcox 9–1–28–2; Cronje 9–0–32–0.

South Africa

A. C. Hudson b de Silva	6	B. M. McMillan not out	3
*K. C. Wessels c Ranatunga b de Silva	4		
W. J. Cronje c Mahanama b Muralitharan	22	B 3, l-b 2, w 4	9
D. J. Cullinan b Muralitharan	0	1/9 2/26 (4 wkts, 14 overs)	52
J. N. Rhodes not out	8	3/39 4/40	

†D. J. Richardson, R. P. Snell, P. L. Symcox, P. S. de Villiers and A. A. Donald did not bat.

Bowling: Wickremasinghe 3–1–6–0; de Silva 5–0–23–2; Kalpage 1–0–3–0; Muralitharan 3–0–6–2; Jayasuriya 2–0–9–0.

Umpires: B. C. Cooray and P. Manuel.

SRI LANKA v SOUTH AFRICA

First Test Match

At Moratuwa, August 25, 26, 28, 29, 30. Drawn. Toss: Sri Lanka. Test debuts: P. B. Dassanayake, P. K. Wijetunge; C. E. Eksteen, P. L. Symcox.

Sri Lanka seemed to have their inaugural Test with South Africa sewn up on the final afternoon, when the tourists slipped to 138 for six – still 226 behind – with three hours left. But Rhodes transcended his earlier unconvincing form to play the innings of his life. With staunch support from the tail, only one more wicket fell and Rhodes reached his maiden Test hundred just before the end.

Inspecting the pitch the day before the match, the South Africans had assumed an under-prepared surface would assist spin. They gave first caps to both their slow bowlers, Symcox and Eksteen, and left out the all-rounder, McMillan. Sri Lanka, who introduced the wicket-keeper Dassanayake and left-arm spinner Wijetunge, won what seemed to be a good toss. But Donald dismissed Hathurusinghe for one, the first of a distressing sequence of low scores for him, and pace continually troubled the Sri Lankans, though Mahanama batted capably, Ranatunga adventurously and Tillekeratne soundly, until he played across a full-pitched in-swinger from Schultz on 92.

South Africa also had problems with seam, despite their earlier fears of spin. After a solid start, they foundered against the second new ball, losing three wickets in three overs. Clean hitting by Symcox partially rescued the innings. After he also claimed two wickets in his first over of the evening, Sri Lanka finished the day with an overall lead of 90. Both Donald and Schultz struck next morning but the most attractive batting of the match, a partnership of 121 in 103 minutes between de Silva and Ranatunga, put Sri Lanka on top. Ranatunga went on to 131, his fourth Test century, including 18 fours and a six. He eventually became the first Sri Lankan to score 2,500 Test runs – though television replays suggested he should have been caught and bowled by Cronje when 58.

Shortly after he was out, Ranatunga declared, setting South Africa a target of 365 from a minimum 115 overs. That was never likely to be achieved, with the ball keeping low and turning appreciably. Once Hudson and Cronje were out cheaply and Wessels followed early on the final day, survival was South Africa's aim. Though Cook and Cullinan each batted resolutely for more than two hours, Sri Lanka scented victory with six down. But Rhodes countered the spinners with nimble footwork and pad play, supported by Symcox for 76 minutes and then Eksteen, who defended solidly for an hour and a half. Rhodes was still unbeaten after four and a quarter hours and 101 runs, including 14 fours and a six.

Man of the Match: A. Ranatunga.

Close of play: First day, Sri Lanka 241-5 (H. P. Tillekeratne 37*, R. S. Kalpage 39*); Second day, South Africa 81-0 (K. C. Wessels 39*, A. C. Hudson 39*); Third day, Sri Lanka 26-2 (U. C. Hathurusinghe 6*, A. P. Gurusinha 0*); Fourth day, South Africa 25-2 (K. C. Wessels 9*, D. J. Cullinan 4*).

Sri Lanka

First innings		Second innings	
R. S. Mahanama b Schultz	53	lbw b Symcox	17
U. C. Hathurusinghe c Richardson b Donald	1	b Donald	9
A. P. Gurusinha c Richardson b Donald	26	(4) b Schultz	27
P. A. de Silva c Wessels b Schultz	27	(5) c Richardson b Symcox	68
*A. Ranatunga c Richardson b Donald	44	(6) b Schultz	131
H. P. Tillekeratne lbw b Schultz	92	(7) not out	33
R. S. Kalpage c Richardson b Cronje	42	(8) not out	0
†P. B. Dassanayake b Schultz	7		
P. K. Wijetunge b Donald	10	(3) c Hudson b Symcox	0
G. P. Wickremasinghe c Rhodes b Donald	11		
M. Muralitharan not out	2		
L-b 11, w 1, n-b 4	16	B 3, l-b 6, n-b 6	15
1/5 (2) 2/77 (3) 3/100 (1) 4/157 (5) 5/168 (4) 6/258 (7) 7/273 (8) 8/285 (9) 9/313 (10) 10/331 (6)	331	1/26 (1) 2/26 (3) 3/34 (2) 4/75 (4) 5/196 (5) 6/299 (6) (6 wkts dec.)	300

Bowling: *First Innings*—Donald 28–5–69–5; Schultz 31.2–12–75–4; Eksteen 14–4–44–0; Cronje 26–14–32–1; Symcox 28–3–100–0. *Second Innings*—Donald 22–5–73–1; Schultz 20–2–82–2; Cronje 8–2–27–0; Symcox 21–2–75–3; Eksteen 9–2–34–0.

South Africa

First innings		Second innings	
*K. C. Wessels c Tillekeratne b Muralitharan	47	(2) c Wickremasinghe b Muralitharan	16
A. C. Hudson c Gurusinha b Wijetunge	90	(1) c Dassanayake b Hathurusinghe	4
W. J. Cronje b Muralitharan	17	c sub (S. T. Jayasuriya) b Wickremasinghe	1
D. J. Cullinan lbw b Hathurusinghe	33	lbw b Wickremasinghe	46
S. J. Cook b Wickremasinghe	7	c Tillekeratne b Wijetunge	24
J. N. Rhodes c Tillekeratne b Muralitharan	8	not out	101
†D. J. Richardson c and b Wickremasinghe	2	c Tillekeratne b de Silva	4
P. L. Symcox c Mahanama b Muralitharan	48	c Hathurusinghe b de Silva	21
C. E. Eksteen b Muralitharan	1	not out	4
A. A. Donald not out	0		
B. N. Schultz lbw b Kalpage	0		
L-b 4, w 1, n-b 9	14	B 10, l-b 4, w 1, n-b 15	30
1/104 (1) 2/152 (3) 3/179 (2) 4/203 (5) 5/203 (4) 6/206 (7) 7/240 (6) 8/262 (9) 9/267 (8) 10/267 (11)	267	1/13 (1) 2/15 (3) 3/47 (2) 4/92 (4) 5/126 (5) 6/138 (7) 7/199 (8) (7 wkts)	251

Bowling: *First Innings*—Wickremasinghe 19–4–58–2; Gurusinha 3–0–3–0; Kalpage 17.5–6–23–1; Wijetunge 29–2–58–1; Muralitharan 39–8–104–5; de Silva 1–0–3–0; Hathurusinghe 4–0–14–1. *Second Innings*—Wickremasinghe 22–6–59–2; Hathurusinghe 9–5–9–1; Muralitharan 31–11–48–1; Wijetunge 23–3–60–1; Kalpage 8–2–21–0; de Silva 17–3–35–2; Tillekeratne 2–0–5–0.

Umpires: B. L. Aldridge (New Zealand) and K. T. Francis.
Referee: J. R. Reid (New Zealand).

†SRI LANKA v SOUTH AFRICA

Second One-Day International

At Khettarama Stadium, Colombo, September 2 (day/night). South Africa won by 124 runs. Toss: South Africa.

History favoured the team batting first in floodlit matches at Khettarama, and South Africa duly recorded their biggest victory by runs in limited-overs internationals. Sri Lanka collapsed as the humidity and early evening dew enabled the pace attack to swing the white balls and extract sideways movement from the pitch. Sixteen wides in a total of 98 were an indication of the extent of that swing rather than an indictment of the bowlers' accuracy. Earlier, South Africa had batted solidly without fully mastering the bowling. McMillan scored a rapid 35 and the tailenders Symcox and Snell hit judiciously as 43 runs came off the last five overs. McMillan followed up with three cheap wickets as well as three slip catches.

Man of the Match: B. M. McMillan.

South Africa

Batsman	Runs
*K. C. Wessels c Tillekeratne b Jayasuriya	28
A. C. Hudson c Mahanama b Ranatunga	48
D. J. Cullinan st Dassanayake b Jayasuriya	5
J. N. Rhodes c Mahanama b Kalpage	43
S. J. Cook c Dassanayake b Wickremasinghe	15
B. M. McMillan c Tillekeratne b Jayasuriya	35
P. L. Symcox c Mahanama b Jayasuriya	12
R. P. Snell not out	12
†D. J. Richardson not out	1
L-b 12, w 8, n-b 3	23
1/90 2/92 3/102 4/138 5/174 6/198 7/214 (7 wkts, 50 overs)	222

P. S. de Villiers and A. A. Donald did not bat.

Bowling: Wickremasinghe 7–0–28–1; Hathurusinghe 3–0–14–0; de Silva 4–1–14–0; Kalpage 10–1–42–1; Muralitharan 6–0–28–0; Jayasuriya 10–0–53–4; Ranatunga 10–1–31–1.

Sri Lanka

Batsman	Runs
R. S. Mahanama c Richardson b de Villiers	11
U. C. Hathurusinghe c McMillan b Donald	10
S. T. Jayasuriya lbw b McMillan	3
P. A. de Silva c Richardson b McMillan	8
*A. Ranatunga c de Villiers b McMillan	6
A. P. Gurusinha c McMillan b Snell	1
H. P. Tillekeratne c Richardson b de Villiers	20
R. S. Kalpage c Richardson b Symcox	0
†P. B. Dassanayake c McMillan b Donald	11
G. P. Wickremasinghe b de Villiers	4
M. Muralitharan not out	0
L-b 7, w 16, n-b 1	24
1/24 2/24 3/34 4/39 5/43 6/52 7/60 8/92 9/92 (34 overs)	98

Bowling: Donald 7–1–18–2; de Villiers 10–4–15–3; Snell 5–0–15–1; McMillan 5–1–12–3; Symcox 5–0–20–1; Wessels 2–0–11–0.

Umpires: D. N. Pathirana and T. M. Samarasinghe.

†SRI LANKA v SOUTH AFRICA

Third One-Day International

At Khettarama Stadium, Colombo, September 4 (day/night). Sri Lanka won by 44 runs. Toss: Sri Lanka. International debut: R. P. A. H. Wickremaratne.

For the second time in 48 hours the toss proved crucial: South Africa collapsed almost as spectacularly as Sri Lanka had done two nights before. The main damage was done by Ramanayake who, on his recall to the side, swung the ball prodigiously and took three of the first four wickets. After he had ripped the heart out of the innings the tourists were 103 for nine and poised for their lowest one-day total before Snell and de Villiers added 51, a South African last-wicket record. For Sri Lanka, de Silva played the anchor role with only one four in his unbeaten 61. With a large playing surface and a spongy outfield, Khettarama yielded only 20 fours in four innings.

Man of the Match: C. P. H. Ramanayake.

Sri Lanka

Batsman	Runs
R. S. Mahanama st Richardson b Symcox	41
U. C. Hathurusinghe c Richardson b Donald	2
H. P. Tillekeratne c Richardson b McMillan	15
P. A. de Silva not out	61
*A. Ranatunga c Donald b Snell	30
S. T. Jayasuriya b Donald	5
R. P. A. H. Wickremaratne st Richardson b Symcox	1
R. S. Kalpage c and b Snell	9
†P. B. Dassanayake run out	14
G. P. Wickremasinghe b de Villiers	0
B 1, l-b 5, w 14	20
1/7 2/53 3/73 4/127 5/136 6/141 7/156 8/191 9/198 (9 wkts, 50 overs)	198

C. P. H. Ramanayake did not bat.

Bowling: Donald 10–0–35–2; de Villiers 10–1–31–1; Snell 10–0–52–2; McMillan 10–0–41–1; Symcox 10–1–33–2.

South Africa

Batsman	Runs
A. C. Hudson c Dassanayake b Wickremasinghe	1
*K. C. Wessels lbw b Ramanayake	16
W. J. Cronje c Dassanayake b Ramanayake	2
D. J. Cullinan b Ramanayake	3
J. N. Rhodes b Kalpage	27
B. M. McMillan c Mahanama b Hathurusinghe	7
†D. J. Richardson run out	5
P. L. Symcox c Kalpage b Hathurusinghe	3
R. P. Snell c Kalpage b Ramanayake	51
A. A. Donald b Kalpage	0
P. S. de Villiers not out	12
L-b 3, w 19, n-b 5	27
1/2 2/10 3/18 4/38 5/56 6/72 7/77 8/101 9/103 (46.1 overs)	154

Bowling: Ramanayake 8.1–0–17–4; Wickremasinghe 6–2–24–1; Hathurusinghe 10–2–18–2; Ranatunga 6–0–24–0; Kalpage 10–0–36–2; Jayasuriya 6–0–32–0.

Umpires: K. T. Francis and P. Manuel.

SRI LANKA v SOUTH AFRICA

Second Test Match

At Sinhalese Sports Club, Colombo, September 6, 7, 8, 10. South Africa won by an innings and 208 runs. Toss: Sri Lanka. Test debut: H. D. P. K. Dharmasena.

This match provided South Africa's biggest Test win and Sri Lanka's heaviest defeat; it was completed before lunch on the fourth day as the Sri Lankan batsmen were overwhelmed by pace. Schultz, in his fourth Test, took nine wickets for 106 on a pitch with more bounce than any other in Sri Lanka, although by most standards it was ideal for batting. South Africa returned to a pace-oriented attack, adding McMillan and Snell at the expense of batsman Cook and spinner Eksteen; Sri Lanka also included an extra pace bowler, Ramanayake, and brought in Dharmasena, who bowls off-cutters, for the slow left-armer Wijetunge.

With Donald restricted to 12 overs by a minor tendinitis problem in his left knee, Schultz made the most of his chance and had all the batsmen in difficulty. He should have had both openers (both were dropped by Cullinan at slip) even before Mahanama was caught behind in the sixth over. Though Hathurusinghe survived for almost three hours and de Silva and Jayasuriya batted attractively, Sri Lanka were all out shortly after tea, with Schultz taking five wickets in a Test innings for the first time.

South Africa's grip tightened on the second day, with Wessels and Hudson taking their opening partnership to 137 before Hudson was dismissed in the 60th over. Wessels seemed set for a hundred until he misjudged Muralitharan's flight, but Cronje and Cullinan continued relentlessly as South Africa reached 280 for two, already 112 ahead, on the second day. Unshaken by the loss of three partners in seven overs next morning, Cronje completed his second Test hundred just after lunch. He eventually fell for 122, but Symcox and Snell then provided the most aggressive batting of the match. They took full advantage of tiring bowlers to put on 79 in 71 minutes for the eighth wicket. In the circumstances, Muralitharan's second five-wicket haul of the series, conceding fewer than two runs an over in a 54-over stint, represented outstanding bowling.

Resuming 327 behind, Sri Lanka began their second innings disastrously. They lost both openers in the first three overs and went into the rest day at a hopeless 49 for four. Their two most experienced batsmen, de Silva and Ranatunga, were still at the crease, but Ranatunga was out to Schultz without addition on the fourth morning and de Silva went to Donald 20 minutes later. The rest was a formality. Wickremasinghe briefly lifted Sri Lankan spirits by hitting two sixes off Snell before being caught on the square leg boundary attempting a third.

Man of the Match: B. N. Schultz.

Close of play: First day, South Africa 48-0 (K. C. Wessels 19*, A. C. Hudson 19*); Second day, South Africa 280-2 (W. J. Cronje 54*, D. J. Cullinan 52*); Third day, Sri Lanka 49-4 (P. A. de Silva 22*, A. Ranatunga 14*).

Sri Lanka

R. S. Mahanama c Richardson b Schultz	7	– b Schultz	0
U. C. Hathurusinghe c McMillan b Donald	34	– c Cronje b Donald	0
H. P. Tillekeratne c Cronje b McMillan	9	– c Richardson b Snell	9
P. A. de Silva c Richardson b Schultz	34	– c and b Donald	24
*A. Ranatunga c Cullinan b Snell	11	– (6) c Richardson b Schultz	14
S. T. Jayasuriya b Schultz	44	– (7) b Schultz	16
†P. B. Dassanayake c Richardson b Donald	0	– (8) c Richardson b Snell	10
H. D. P. K. Dharmasena c Richardson b Schultz	5	– (9) c Richardson b Schultz	2
C. P. H. Ramanayake not out	3	– (5) lbw b McMillan	0
G. P. Wickremasinghe b Schultz	17	– c Donald b Snell	21
M. Muralitharan c Rhodes b Snell	0	– not out	14
L-b 3, n-b 1	4	L-b 4, n-b 5	9
1/7 (1) 2/27 (3) 3/72 (4) 4/85 (5) 5/117 (2) 6/119 (7) 7/145 (8) 8/147 (6) 9/167 (10) 10/168 (11)	168	1/1 (1) 2/1 (2) 3/30 (3) 4/31 (5) 5/49 (6) 6/54 (4) 7/69 (7) 8/76 (9) 9/101 (10) 10/119 (8)	119

Bowling: *First Innings*—Donald 12–4–22–2; Schultz 20–8–48–5; Snell 19–3–57–2; McMillan 9–1–38–1; Symcox 2–2–0–0. *Second Innings*—Donald 10–7–6–2; Schultz 16–4–58–4; Snell 12–4–32–3; McMillan 4–0–11–1; Symcox 1–0–8–0.

South Africa

*K. C. Wessels c Dassanayake b Muralitharan	92
A. C. Hudson lbw b Wickremasinghe	58
W. J. Cronje b de Silva	122
D. J. Cullinan c and b Muralitharan	52
J. N. Rhodes run out	10
B. M. McMillan b Muralitharan	0
†D. J. Richardson c Jayasuriya b Muralitharan	11
P. L. Symcox st Dassanayake b de Silva	50
R. P. Snell st Dassanayake b de Silva	48
A. A. Donald not out	4
B. N. Schultz st Dassanayake b Muralitharan	6
B 5, l-b 20, w 1, n-b 16	42
1/137 (2) 2/179 (1) 3/284 (4) 4/306 (5) 5/307 (6) 6/333 (7) 7/401 (3) 8/480 (8) 9/487 (9) 10/495 (11)	495

Bowling: Ramanayake 20–5–63–0; Wickremasinghe 31–6–111–1; Hathurusinghe 7–4–12–0; Dharmasena 45–12–91–0; Muralitharan 54–17–101–5; Jayasuriya 9–1–47–0; de Silva 13–1–39–3; Ranatunga 2–0–6–0.

Umpires: B. L. Aldridge (New Zealand) and T. M. Samarasinghe.
Referee: J. R. Reid (New Zealand).

SRI LANKA v SOUTH AFRICA

Third Test Match

At P. Saravanamuttu Stadium, Colombo, September 14, 15, 16, 18, 19. Drawn. Toss: South Africa.

The final day of the series was abandoned after heavy overnight rain soaked the ground. But Sri Lanka had probably forfeited their chance of drawing level already, thanks to their negative batting on the third day, when they added only 128 in 72.5 overs.

Needing no more than a draw to win the series, South Africa had every reason for confidence when Wessels decided to bat on another slow pitch. They took the score cautiously to 51 before Hudson prodded a catch to short leg off Dharmasena; Wessels was bowled by an in-swinger from Liyanage (who had replaced fellow-seamer Wickremasinghe) four balls later. There were more alarms when Cronje, Rhodes and McMillan were out in quick succession in mid-afternoon, reducing South Africa to 128 for five. But Cullinan and Richardson batted sensibly, both reaching their highest Test scores by the close. Though Richardson mistimed a drive to mid-on early next morning, Cullinan moved smoothly and patiently towards his maiden Test century, alternating sound defence with sweetly timed drives, pulls and cuts. He slashed wildly at Liyanage on 98, edging a difficult low chance to the wicket-keeper, then drove firmly past mid-off for his 17th boundary before lofting a simple catch off the occasional left-arm spin of Jayasuriya; Cullinan had batted for just short of six hours. South Africa's eventual 316 was not as imposing as they would have wished: Muralitharan bowled impressively again to take his haul of wickets to 15 in four innings.

Sri Lanka made another poor start, as Hathurusinghe fell to Donald for the seventh time in succession. The experiment of moving Dassanayake to No. 3 was partially successful, as he batted for more than an hour before being run out by Rhodes, who made an astounding diving stop at cover, but runs had been slowly earned. After Mahanama was caught at second slip, de Silva and Ranatunga posted fifty in almost even time, reaching 117 for three that night. But their tactics were difficult to understand on the third day. In complete contrast to the previous evening, de Silva and Ranatunga added only 36 runs in 27.4 overs before lunch. Tillekeratne continued the slow accumulation and, although Jayasuriya showed more enterprise, Sri Lanka were only 245 for five by the close of play. Jayasuriya continued to attack on the fourth morning and his 65 came off 92 balls with nine boundaries – compared with 263 balls and 384 minutes for de Silva's 82.

After declaring 20 behind, Sri Lanka entertained brief hopes; Wessels was out in the sixth over and Hudson and Cullinan were dismissed soon after tea. Cronje batted soundly, however, supported by Rhodes. They put on 94 for the fourth wicket before Rhodes was bowled by a leg-break from Muralitharan – a rare venture into variation for the bowler.

Man of the Match: D. J. Cullinan.

Close of play: First day, South Africa 231-5 (D. J. Cullinan 85*, D. J. Richardson 51*); Second day, Sri Lanka 117-3 (P. A. de Silva 44*, A. Ranatunga 30*); Third day, Sri Lanka 245-5 (H. P. Tillekeratne 29*, S. T. Jayasuriya 35*); Fourth day, South Africa 159-4 (W. J. Cronje 73*, B. M. McMillan 0*).

South Africa

A. C. Hudson c Tillekeratne b Dharmasena .... 22 – (2) b Ramanayake 28
*K. C. Wessels b Liyanage .... 26 – (1) c Mahanama b Hathurusinghe 7
W. J. Cronje b Ramanayake.................. 24 – not out...................... 73
D. J. Cullinan c Ramanayake b Jayasuriya.....102 – c sub (D. P. Samaraweera)
b Dharmasena . 4
J. N. Rhodes st Dassanayake b Muralitharan... 7 – b Muralitharan............... 19
B. M. McMillan c Jayasuriya b Muralitharan... 2 – not out...................... 0
†D. J. Richardson c de Silva b Muralitharan ... 62
P. L. Symcox c Tillekeratne b Ramanayake 30
R. P. Snell not out 13
A. A. Donald lbw b Ramanayake 1
B. N. Schultz c de Silva b Muralitharan 0
B 6, l-b 10, n-b 11.................. 27 B 4, l-b 17, n-b 7 28

1/51 (1) 2/53 (2) 3/96 (3) 4/108 (5) 316 1/11 (1) 2/58 (2) (4 wkts) 159
5/128 (6) 6/250 (7) 7/281 (4) 3/65 (4) 4/159 (5)
8/311 (8) 9/315 (10) 10/316 (11)

Bowling: *First Innings*—Ramanayake 25–4–75–3; Liyanage 21–4–58–1; Hathurusinghe 6–4–6–0; Dharmasena 28–5–79–1; Muralitharan 35.1–8–64–4; de Silva 1–0–9–0; Jayasuriya 5–1–9–1. *Second Innings*—Ramanayake 10–1–26–1; Hathurusinghe 8–4–7–1; Liyanage 4–1–17–0; Muralitharan 15–3–39–1; Dharmasena 18–8–29–1; Jayasuriya 3–1–17–0; de Silva 3–1–3–0.

Sri Lanka

R. S. Mahanama c McMillan b Schultz. 25
U. C. Hathurusinghe c Richardson
b Donald . 1
†P. B. Dassanayake run out 8
P. A. de Silva lbw b Symcox 82
*A. Ranatunga c Richardson
b Schultz . 50
H. P. Tillekeratne c Richardson
b Schultz . 37
S. T. Jayasuriya c Cronje b Schultz 65
H. D. P. K. Dharmasena
c Richardson b Schultz . 5
D. K. Liyanage b Donald 0
C. P. H. Ramanayake not out 0
B 7, l-b 9, n-b 7 23

1/1 (2) 2/27 (3) 3/55 (1) (9 wkts dec.) 296
4/156 (5) 5/202 (4)
6/263 (6) 7/273 (8)
8/294 (9) 9/296 (7)

M. Muralitharan did not bat.

Bowling: Donald 30–12–62–2; Schultz 36.5–9–63–5; McMillan 30–8–64–0; Snell 25–8–44–0; Symcox 18–5–47–1.

Umpires: B. L. Aldridge (New Zealand) and B. C. Cooray.
Referee: J. R. Reid (New Zealand).

THE NEW ZEALANDERS IN AUSTRALIA, 1993-94

By GREG BAUM

Played before sparse crowds in three of Australia's Test outposts, this series unfortunately fulfilled all its expectations. It was low-key, one-sided, lacking in authentic drama and unable to rise above the perception that it was merely a warm-up for the season's main event.

Martin Crowe had a wry smile when he announced New Zealand as "first among the touring teams". He well knew it was the chronological rather than the absolute truth, and that the Kiwis could not compare with South Africa in their ability to capture Australia's imagination, nor, as it transpired, their wickets. New Zealand were out of season, out of form, lacking in experience and soon to run out of luck as well. They were further disadvantaged when they were pitched headlong into the most alien environment in the country: the fast and high-bouncing WACA ground in Perth.

As if those were not obstacles enough, Crowe's bothersome right knee broke down altogether during the First Test and he was forced to go home for surgery and a prolonged convalescence. Although Ken Rutherford proved an able replacement as captain, astute on the field and forthright off it, his most profound handicap was the loss of Crowe's batting. Willie Watson and Chris Cairns also broke down and the curse of injuries continued to plague New Zealand: by the end of the World Series, in which they blew a good chance of reaching the final, 21 players had been rotated through a nominal squad of 14. The teams for the Second and Third Tests boasted less international experience than the state teams of Queensland and New South Wales.

Against this bleak backdrop, the very least New Zealand needed was to play to the best of their ability; sadly, they did not. There was some initial trepidation in Australia, not only about the possibility of post-Ashes complacency, but because the New Zealanders have a long history of underdoggedness in these encounters, as important to them as the Ashes are to Australia. That spirit momentarily asserted itself in the First Test, but departed with Crowe. Thereafter, the Kiwis' essential frailty could not be disguised. In the Second Test at Hobart, New Zealand suffered their heaviest ever Test defeat and they were crushed again by an innings in the Third Test in Brisbane and meekly surrendered the Trans-Tasman Trophy.

Post-Hadlee, New Zealand's attack had developed an unhealthy dependence on Danny Morrison. Although at first he was full of vitality, he was miserably let down by his fieldsmen, who contrived to drop 13 catches in the Tests. Morrison took only one wicket after the first day of the series – a caught-and-bowled – and his final figures were a scarcely credible three for 422. Soon afterwards, he returned to New Zealand to nurse an injured knee and a broken heart. New Zealand's other senior bowlers, Cairns and Dipak Patel, were also hindered by injury, no one else stepped forward and, in the Third Test, five bowlers conceded more than 100 runs in Australia's only innings, the second such occurrence in Test history.

New Zealand's batting was equally lightweight. Andrew Jones was typically resilient and Rutherford at least had the courage of his attacking convictions. But Mark Greatbatch had a horrid series, falling to Craig McDermott five times in six innings for a total of 67 runs, and there was no authentic batting below No. 5. By the Third Test, when Greatbatch was eased down the order away from the new ball, New Zealand's opening batsmen were a pair of rookies, one of them the converted wicket-keeper Bryan Young.

Since their Ashes triumph, Australia had lost Merv Hughes, who was undergoing exhaustive rehabilitation from knee surgery, but had regained McDermott. Glenn McGrath joined Paul Reiffel as back-up. New Zealand's batsmen were no more conversant with Shane Warne's leg-spin than they had been earlier in the year and his 18 wickets eclipsed the Australian record against New Zealand (17, shared by himself and McDermott). Tim May joined him in the Second Test in a spinners' smorgasbord of 16 wickets. Australia's batting was rarely challenged after the first day of the series and ran riot, Nos. 1 to 7 in the order each making a century and averaging better than 50. If suspicions lingered about Australia's vulnerability to pressure, New Zealand were not the team to probe them.

The spirit between the sides was good, for the teams were too far apart for friction. Jones was censured by referee Venkataraghavan in Perth for obvious dissent in throwing the ball to the ground when an appeal for a catch against Mark Taylor was denied. Rutherford forgave the Australians their intermittent and sometimes gratuitous sledging, saying he wished his own team would play with such vigour. He also said he feared that in cricket's emerging new order, New Zealand would find themselves in an unofficial second division. As the Third Test neared its inexorable conclusion, Australian and New Zealand officials were finalising what amounted to a rescue package, whereby Australia would lend coaches and technology to their struggling neighbours. But despite New Zealand's claim that the Australians were their most popular and therefore most profitable touring team, Australia's philanthropy did not extend to a pledge of more frequent visits. Rather, it was announced that New Zealand had been jostled aside by South Africa for a permanent place in Australia's four-year cycle, and it seemed certain that the trans-Tasman neighbours would play even less often in future.

The most disappointing aspect of the series was that the Australian public recognised it for the bland offering it was and stayed resolutely away. Even Hobart, so anxious for so long for a second opportunity to host a Test, saw its match outdrawn by a local cultural festival. The aggregate attendance of the three Tests was almost exceeded by the first one-day international of the summer, between Australia and South Africa, in Melbourne two days later. The main event was about to begin.

NEW ZEALAND TOURING PARTY

M. D. Crowe (Wellington) (*captain*), K. R. Rutherford (Otago) (*vice-captain*), T. E. Blain (Central Districts), C. L. Cairns (Canterbury), S. B. Doull (Northern Districts), M. J. Greatbatch (Central Districts), M. J. Haslam (Auckland), A. H. Jones (Wellington), D. K. Morrison (Auckland), D. N. Patel (Auckland), B. A. Pocock (Northern Districts), M. L. Su'a (Auckland), W. Watson (Auckland), B. A. Young (Northern Districts).

R. P. de Groen and D. J. White (both of Northern Districts) and C. Z. Harris (Canterbury) joined the party during the tour as cover for Crowe, Greatbatch and Watson.

Manager: M. Sandlant. *Coach:* G. P. Howarth.

NEW ZEALAND TOUR RESULTS

Test matches – Played 3: Lost 2, Drawn 1.
First-class matches – Played 7: Won 2, Lost 3, Drawn 2.
Wins – New South Wales, South Australia.
Losses – Australia (2), Western Australia.
Draws – Australia, Tasmania.
One-day internationals – Played 8: Won 3, Lost 4, No result 1. *Wins* – Australia, South Africa (2). *Losses* – Australia (3), South Africa. *No result* – South Africa.
Other non first-class matches – Played 2: Lost 2. *Losses* – ACB Chairman's XI, Australian Cricket Academy.

TEST MATCH AVERAGES

AUSTRALIA – BATTING

	T	*I*	*NO*	*R*	*HS*	*100s*	*Avge*	*Ct/St*
S. R. Waugh	3	3	2	216	147*	1	216.00	1
M. A. Taylor	3	4	1	286	142*	1	95.33	5
D. C. Boon	3	4	1	262	106	1	87.33	3
M. J. Slater	3	4	0	305	168	1	76.25	0
M. E. Waugh....	3	3	0	215	111	1	71.66	3
I. A. Healy......	3	3	1	129	113*	1	64.50	13/1
A. R. Border	3	3	0	181	105	1	60.33	3

Played in three Tests: C. J. McDermott 35; S. K. Warne 11, 74* (4 ct). Played in two Tests: G. D. McGrath 0; P. R. Reiffel 51, 23*; T. B. A. May did not bat (2 ct).

* *Signifies not out.*

BOWLING

	O	*M*	*R*	*W*	*BB*	*5W/i*	*Avge*
S. K. Warne	151.3	49	305	18	6-31	1	16.94
M. E. Waugh.......	48	18	94	5	1-7	0	18.80
T. B. A. May.......	93.3	33	202	9	5-65	1	22.44
C. J. McDermott....	133	39	340	12	4-39	0	28.33
G. D. McGrath.....	96	26	253	6	3-66	0	42.16

Also bowled: A. R. Border 2–2–0–0; P. R Reiffel 48–6–141–2; S. R. Waugh 18–3–41–1.

NEW ZEALAND – BATTING

	T	*I*	*NO*	*R*	*HS*	*100s*	*Avge*	*Ct*
A. H. Jones	3	6	0	324	143	1	54.00	3
K. R. Rutherford....	3	6	0	250	86	0	41.66	2
T. E. Blain.........	3	5	1	165	42*	0	41.25	4
C. L. Cairns........	2	3	0	99	78	0	33.00	0
B. A. Pocock	3	6	0	97	34	0	16.16	1
D. N. Patel	3	6	1	76	20	0	15.20	3
M. L. Su'a	2	3	1	25	14*	0	12.50	0
M. J. Greatbatch....	3	6	0	67	35	0	11.16	1
S. B. Doull.........	2	4	0	35	24	0	8.75	2
R. P. de Groen	2	4	2	12	6	0	6.00	0
D. K. Morrison	3	5	1	20	20*	0	5.00	2

Played in one Test: M. D. Crowe 42, 31*; C. Z. Harris 0, 4; W. Watson 0*; B. A. Young 38, 53.

* *Signifies not out.*

BOWLING

	O	*M*	*R*	*W*	*BB*	*5W/i*	*Avge*
C. L. Cairns	65	11	253	5	4-113	0	50.60
S. B. Doull........	54	5	204	3	2-105	0	68.00
R. P. de Groen	82	23	233	3	2-113	0	77.66
M. L. Su'a........	63.5	5	245	3	2-72	0	81.66
D. N. Patel	103	11	384	4	1-37	0	96.00
D. K. Morrison....	126	16	422	3	2-113	0	140.66

Also bowled: C. Z. Harris 2–0–18–0; A. H. Jones 2–0–6–0; B. A. Pocock 2–0–10–0; W. Watson 24–11–52–1.

NEW ZEALAND AVERAGES – FIRST-CLASS MATCHES

BATTING

	M	*I*	*NO*	*R*	*HS*	*100s*	*Avge*	*Ct/St*
A. H. Jones	6	12	0	610	143	1	50.83	3
K. R. Rutherford....	7	13	0	528	86	0	40.61	10
T. E. Blain.........	7	12	5	280	45*	0	40.00	14/1
M. D. Crowe	4	8	1	238	105	1	34.00	3
C. L. Cairns........	4	7	0	215	78	0	30.71	2
M. J. Greatbatch....	5	9	0	216	65	0	24.00	2
B. A. Young........	4	8	0	185	53	0	23.12	4
D. K. Morrison	5	9	4	109	46*	0	21.80	2
M. L. Su'a	6	10	2	162	56	0	20.25	0
B. A. Pocock	7	14	0	259	60	0	18.50	6
D. N. Patel	6	12	2	158	50	0	15.80	6
C. Z. Harris........	2	4	2	20	15*	0	10.00	0
R. P. de Groen	3	4	2	12	6	0	6.00	1
S. B. Doull.........	5	7	0	36	24	0	5.14	3

Played in three matches: W. Watson 4, 0* (1 ct). Played in two matches: M. J. Haslam did not bat. Played in one match: D. J. White 1*, 14*.

* *Signifies not out.*

BOWLING

	O	*M*	*R*	*W*	*BB*	*5W/i*	*Avge*
S. B. Doull........	137.4	16	485	16	6-55	1	30.31
R. P. de Groen	123	40	313	8	3-50	0	39.12
C. L. Cairns	126	19	484	11	5-105	1	44.00
M. L. Su'a........	178.4	23	620	14	4-84	0	44.28
W. Watson	93	29	231	5	2-51	0	46.20
D. N. Patel	179	23	663	14	6-87	1	47.35
D. K. Morrison....	192	28	614	11	6-54	1	55.81

Also bowled: C. Z. Harris 6–2–33–0; M. J. Haslam 57–8–149–4; A. H. Jones 8–0–32–0; B. A. Pocock 7–1–27–0.

Note: Matches in this section which were not first-class are signified by a dagger.

†At Lilac Hill, October 19. ACB Chairman's XI won by six wickets. New Zealanders batted first by mutual agreement. New Zealanders 189 (47.4 overs) (B. A. Pocock 68, W. Watson 57 not out); ACB Chairman's XI 192 for four (43.2 overs) (M. R. J. Veletta 31, D. R. Martyn 80 not out; D. N. Patel three for 37).

WESTERN AUSTRALIA v NEW ZEALANDERS

At Perth, October 21, 22, 23, 24. Western Australia won by an innings and nine runs. Toss: Western Australia.

Western Australia ambushed a still-disoriented New Zealand and thrashed them, maintaining the state's traditional ascendancy over touring teams. Worse, Greatbatch suffered a broken finger, ruling himself out until the First Test. The tall pace bowler Angel, who had played against West Indies in the Test on this ground the previous summer, was the destroyer. Maintaining a fuller length than before, he took five for 32 in the New Zealanders' first innings of 149 and five for 108 in their improved second effort of 350. By then he was bowling despite a broken bone in his hand, which almost certainly cost him a Test place. Moody thundered a century for Western Australia, who set up a massive lead of 359. Makeshift openers Rutherford and Jones, and Patel, all reached 50 in New Zealand's vain attempt to save the match.

Close of play: First day, Western Australia 64-2 (J. L. Langer 28*, B. P. Julian 6*); Second day, Western Australia 376-6 (M. R. J. Veletta 10*, T. J. Zoehrer 9*); Third day, New Zealanders 155-2 (A. H. Jones 61*, D. N. Patel 32*).

New Zealanders

M. J. Greatbatch c Julian b Angel	20	– absent injured	
B. A. Pocock c Moody b Angel	1	– (5) c Veletta b Angel	31
A. H. Jones c Julian b Moody	47	– (2) run out	67
*M. D. Crowe c Zoehrer b Atkinson	18	– (3) c Veletta b Angel	8
K. R. Rutherford c Martyn b Angel	1	– (1) c Martyn b Angel	51
D. N. Patel c Zoehrer b Julian	8	– (4) lbw b Angel	50
C. L. Cairns c McPhee b Atkinson	22	– (6) c Langer b Atkinson	36
†T. E. Blain not out	19	– (7) c Julian b Angel	13
S. B. Doull c Zoehrer b Angel	1	– (8) lbw b Atkinson	0
M. L. Su'a c Zoehrer b Atkinson	0	– (9) lbw b Stewart	39
D. K. Morrison c Veletta b Angel	4	– (10) not out	46
L-b 3, n-b 5	8	B 1, l-b 4, w 4	9
1/20 2/24 3/73 4/83 5/99 6/116 7/130 8/141 9/142	149	1/78 2/92 3/162 4/189 5/232 6/258 7/260 8/266 9/350	350

Bowling: *First Innings*—Angel 20.1–7–32–5; Atkinson 18–4–46–3; Moody 9–5–8–1; Julian 14–5–38–1; Stewart 15–5–22–0. *Second Innings*—Angel 34–7–108–5; Atkinson 22–6–61–2; Julian 29–7–81–0; Moody 11–4–16–0; Stewart 22.4–3–70–1; Zoehrer 7–2–9–0.

Western Australia

M. W. McPhee c Patel b Doull	7
*G. R. Marsh b Cairns	16
J. L. Langer c Blain b Patel	61
B. P. Julian c Blain b Su'a	59
D. R. Martyn b Morrison	80
T. M. Moody b Su'a	110
M. R. J. Veletta lbw b Su'a	11
†T. J. Zoehrer c Blain b Morrison	83
M. P. Atkinson c and b Doull	39
J. Angel not out	8
J. Stewart c Cairns b Su'a	6
B 1, l-b 8, n-b 19	28
1/27 2/51 3/135 4/164 5/349 6/359 7/386 8/473 9/497	508

Bowling: Morrison 31–5–88–2; Cairns 23–2–105–1; Doull 23–3–98–2; Su'a 31.5–4–84–4; Patel 24–3–105–1; Jones 3–0–19–0.

Umpires: R. J. Evans and T. A. Prue.

†At North Sydney, October 27. Australian Cricket Academy won by 110 runs. Toss: Australian Cricket Academy. Australian Cricket Academy 241 (49.1 overs) (J. Arnberger 79, J. Maher 46, M. J. Di Venuto 45, D. A. Fitzgerald 32; C. L. Cairns four for 39); New Zealanders 131 (42.2 overs) (T. E. Blain 40).

NEW SOUTH WALES v NEW ZEALANDERS

At Newcastle, October 29, 30, 31, November 1. New Zealanders won by three wickets. Toss: New South Wales.

Winless in three matches, the New Zealanders at last happened upon some form. The Waugh twins and Bevan sped New South Wales to 218 for three, but Patel avenged himself for the three sixes Bevan hit off him, taking six consecutive wickets. New South Wales were already missing Holdsworth and, after Taylor declared in the morning, lost Whitney to a knee injury, which was to force his retirement. None the less, they bowled out the New Zealanders for 163, only Rutherford reaching 50. The tourists retaliated by bowling them out for 109: Morrison despatched four of Australia's top six in a six-over burst and Patel took his match tally to nine. Chasing 246, New Zealand were a precarious 167 for six at the close. But injury forced off-spinner Matthews out of the home attack and Blain piloted the tourists to a morale-boosting win on the stroke of lunch.

Close of play: First day, New South Wales 299-8 (G. R. J. Matthews 31*, G. D. McGrath 3*); Second day, New South Wales 61-4 (M. G. Bevan 4*, G. R. J. Matthews 3*); Third day, New Zealanders 167-6 (T. E. Blain 5*, M. L. Su'a 0*).

New South Wales

*M. A. Taylor b Doull	26	– (2) c Pocock b Morrison	30
M. J. Slater c Young b Doull	16	– (1) c Blain b Morrison	19
S. R. Waugh lbw b Patel	88	– lbw b Morrison	4
M. E. Waugh c Pocock b Patel	63	– b Morrison	1
M. G. Bevan c Crowe b Patel	55	– c Pocock b Patel	17
G. R. J. Matthews not out	31	– c Crowe b Morrison	7
B. E. McNamara c and b Patel	9	– c Crowe b Patel	7
†P. A. Emery c Rutherford b Patel	0	– c Rutherford b Patel	2
P. J. S. Alley st Blain b Patel	3	– b Morrison	19
G. D. McGrath not out	3	– not out	0
M. R. Whitney (did not bat)		– absent injured	
L-b 3, n-b 2	5	L-b 3	3
1/43 2/50 3/169 4/218 5/267 6/283 7/285 8/293 (8 wkts dec.)	299	1/24 2/36 3/44 4/55 5/69 6/82 7/88 8/91 9/109	109

Bowling: *First Innings*—Morrison 18–3–50–0; Su'a 13–1–41–0; Watson 14–4–44–0; Doull 23–3–74–2, Patel 23–2–87–6. *Second Innings*—Morrison 17–4–54–6; Watson 6–2–17–0; Patel 10–2–35–3.

New Zealanders

B. A. Pocock run out	39	– (2) lbw b McGrath	0
B. A. Young c M. E. Waugh b Whitney	0	– (1) c Taylor b M. E. Waugh	43
A. H. Jones lbw b McGrath	1	– c Emery b Matthews	44
*M. D. Crowe c Emery b McNamara	12	– c Slater b McGrath	15
K. R. Rutherford c McGrath b Matthews	65	– c Emery b McNamara	47
D. N. Patel b Matthews	9	– b Matthews	5
†T. E. Blain c Bevan b Matthews	6	– not out	45
M. L. Su'a c Slater b McNamara	7	– c Alley b McNamara	12
D. K. Morrison not out	13	– not out	26
S. B. Doull c sub (R. Chee Quee) b McNamara	0		
W. Watson b Matthews	4		
L-b 1, w 1, n-b 5	7	B 1, l-b 4, n-b 5	10
1/0 2/2 3/19 4/110 5/133 6/136 7/139 8/154 9/154	163	1/10 2/72 3/106 4/106 5/127 6/167 7/200 (7 wkts)	247

Bowling: *First Innings*—McGrath 18–8–26–1; Whitney 6–4–4–1; McNamara 14–5–29–3; Alley 9–2–43–0; M. E. Waugh 2–0–2–0; Matthews 15.5–4–52–4; S. R. Waugh 5–1–6–0. *Second Innings*—McGrath 24.2–6–53–2; Alley 24–4–62–0; M. E. Waugh 13.5–6–20–1; McNamara 16–6–37–2; Matthews 28.1–5–67–2; Bevan 1–0–3–0.

Umpires: D. B. Hair and I. S. Thomas.

TASMANIA v NEW ZEALANDERS

At Launceston, November 4, 5, 6, 7. Drawn. Toss: New Zealanders.

On a lively pitch, Cairns tore through Tasmania's batting, including home town hero Boon in his only first-class appearance for his state all season. But all-rounder Shaun Young and wicket-keeper Atkinson scratched up a working score. For New Zealand, Bryan Young made a duck and Jones was run out – both for the third time on the tour – while Crowe fell to a crude slog before he declared 91 behind. Despite 54 from the precocious Ponting, Tasmania rambled along at less than three runs an over until they were emboldened to declare, challenging New Zealand to score 299 from the final two sessions. After a faltering start, Crowe and Jones went in pursuit; Crowe, dropped at 17 and 46, proceeded by progressively smoother strokes to the century that announced his return to form. But when he and Jones fell, the match settled into a draw.

Close of play: First day, Tasmania 207-6 (S. Young 47*, M. N. Atkinson 29*); Second day, New Zealanders 152-5 (C. L. Cairns 29*, T. E. Blain 2*); Third day, Tasmania 184-4 (D. J. Buckingham 43*, R. J. Tucker 2*).

Tasmania

D. F. Hills lbw b Su'a	27	– lbw b Haslam	26
N. C. P. Courtney c Blain b Cairns	20	– c Cairns b Haslam	31
*D. C. Boon c Young b Cairns	2	– c Rutherford b Su'a	21
R. T. Ponting c Pocock b Watson	15	– c Pocock b Watson	54
D. J. Buckingham lbw b Cairns	18	– c Watson b Haslam	47
R. J. Tucker c sub (D. K. Morrison) b Watson	36	– b Watson	6
S. Young c Blain b Su'a	77	– not out	12
†M. N. Atkinson c Rutherford b Cairns	69	– not out	3
C. D. Matthews c Blain b Cairns	21		
S. Herzberg not out	5		
T. J. Cooley not out	1		
N-b 15	15	L-b 3, n-b 4	7
1/29 2/36 3/66 4/68 5/110 6/133 7/275 8/279 9/300 (9 wkts dec.)	306	1/61 2/61 3/110 4/177 5/189 6/199 (6 wkts dec.)	207

Bowling: *First Innings*—Cairns 32–4–105–5; Su'a 25–6–70–2; Watson 24–4–67–2; Haslam 16–2–55–0; Pocock 3–1–9–0. *Second Innings*—Cairns 6–2–21–0; Su'a 12–1–53–1; Watson 25–8–51–2; Pocock 2–0–8–0; Haslam 24–4–64–3; Jones 3–0–7–0.

New Zealanders

B. A. Young c Atkinson b Cooley	0	– (2) c Hills b Herzberg	3
B. A. Pocock c Atkinson b Matthews	15	– (1) c Courtney b Herzberg	13
A. H. Jones run out	67	– c Ponting b Cooley	60
*M. D. Crowe c Young b Matthews	7	– b Tucker	105
K. R. Rutherford c Ponting b Herzberg	21	– c Atkinson b Cooley	17
C. L. Cairns c Atkinson b Herzberg	48	– c Atkinson b Matthews	10
†T. E. Blain not out	18	– c Ponting b Matthews	13
M. L. Su'a c Courtney b Young	22	– (9) not out	1
D. J. White not out	1	– (8) not out	14
B 2, l-b 9, w 1, n-b 4	16	L-b 7, w 1, n-b 3	11
1/0 2/38 3/53 4/99 5/149 6/176 7/211 (7 wkts dec.)	215	1/16 2/29 3/188 4/206 5/206 6/221 7/236 (7 wkts)	247

W. Watson and M. J. Haslam did not bat.

Bowling: *First Innings*—Cooley 25–6–61–1; Matthews 19–6–37–2; Young 17–7–33–1; Herzberg 25–6–63–2; Tucker 5–1–10–0. *Second Innings*—Cooley 13–4–33–2; Matthews 14–2–43–2; Young 14–3–42–0; Herzberg 25–5–79–2; Tucker 9–1–34–1; Buckingham 2–0–8–0; Boon 1–0–1–0.

Umpires: T. R. Hogarth and S. G. Randell.

AUSTRALIA v NEW ZEALAND

First Test Match

At Perth, November 12, 13, 14, 15, 16. Drawn. Toss: New Zealand. Test debuts: G. D. McGrath; B. A. Pocock.

The first two days of this Test were a dying echo of past New Zealand heroics, but by the third a note of Australian mastery was rising, and it would resound through the series. Only Australia's unaccountable dithering on the fourth day prevented a clean sweep beginning here.

Unseasonal rain delayed the match by an hour and caused the pitch to sweat profusely under its covers. Morrison and Cairns seized the chance to rip through Australia's top order, Morrison claiming Border for the seventh time in Tests and Cairns sending back Boon for his second successive Test match golden duck. Only Taylor stood firm. Next morning, as pitch and attack mellowed, Healy stroked his second Test – and first-class – century. It was doubly satisfying for him: he had been jeered 12 months earlier by the parochial Western Australian crowd, who thought Zoehrer should have replaced him in a one-day international. With support from Reiffel and McDermott, he lifted Australia to 398.

Jones marshalled New Zealand's reply with 143, his seventh Test century, Cairns hit a rollicking 78, and by the fourth morning New Zealand had established a slender lead. It was not until the second new ball that McDermott took his second wicket, his 200th in Tests – having been stuck on 198 since March – and Warne was tamed to such an extent that Cairns, fooled by a flipper, was his only wicket, and his first in three first-class matches at the WACA.

Morrison bowled superbly when the Australian openers resumed, both groping blindly for his out-swinger, but he had wretched luck. He lacked support, for Watson had torn a hamstring while batting and Cairns had a bruised heel. The modest off-spinner Patel shared the new ball and bowled almost throughout. Slowly, Slater rediscovered his footwork and confidence, then took three boundaries from Cairns's only over and moved energetically to 99, whereupon he glanced Patel to wicket-keeper Blain. He had lost a century but saved his Test place.

Taylor, as blessed as Morrison was cursed, might have been lbw at three, and caught twice before he was 20. But with the pitch now benign, he advanced methodically to 142 not out, the 11th of his Test centuries, each on a different ground, against six different opponents. He shared a long and sometimes lackadaisical partnership with Boon, who passed 1,000 Test runs in the calendar year. Although Australia's lead grew beyond 300, Border delayed his declaration until just before lunch on the final day.

The pitch remained mild and, despite losing Greatbatch to a leg-side catch first ball, New Zealand batted the day out. Pocock extended his time at the crease in his maiden Test to almost five hours, while the brave Crowe hobbled between the wickets and winced with every shot to see the job through before flying back to Auckland. He would have grimaced more had he known what was about to befall his team.

Man of the Match: A. H. Jones. *Attendance:* 26,484.

Close of play: First day, Australia 229-6 (I. A. Healy 30*, P. R. Reiffel 16*); Second day, New Zealand 123-2 (A. H. Jones 62*, M. D. Crowe 2*); Third day, New Zealand 390-6 (C. L. Cairns 66*, T. E. Blain 35*); Fourth day, Australia 218-1 (M. A. Taylor 94*, D. C. Boon 15*).

Australia

M. A. Taylor b Cairns	64	– (2) not out	142
M. J. Slater c Patel b Cairns	10	– (1) c Blain b Patel	99
D. C. Boon c Rutherford b Cairns	0	– not out	67
M. E. Waugh lbw b Morrison	36		
*A. R. Border c Rutherford b Morrison	16		
S. R. Waugh c Blain b Patel	44		
†I. A. Healy not out	113		
P. R. Reiffel c Jones b Watson	51		
S. K. Warne c Patel b Cairns	11		
C. J. McDermott b Su'a	35		
G. D. McGrath lbw b Su'a	0		
B 4, l-b 7, n-b 7	18	L-b 6, n-b 9	15
1/37 (2) 2/37 (3) 3/100 (4) 4/129 (5) 5/164 (1) 6/198 (6) 7/291 (8) 8/329 (9) 9/398 (10) 10/398 (11)	398	1/198 (1) (1 wkt dec.)	323

Bowling: *First Innings*—Morrison 35–4–113–2; Cairns 28–4–113–4; Watson 24–11–52–1; Su'a 19.5–2–72–2; Patel 8–0–37–1. *Second Innings*—Morrison 25–5–80–0; Patel 39–4–144–1; Cairns 1–0–12–0; Su'a 20–0–71–0; Pocock 2–0–10–0.

New Zealand

M. J. Greatbatch c Healy b McGrath	18	– c Healy b McDermott	0
B. A. Pocock c Boon b McDermott	34	– c Healy b McGrath	28
A. H. Jones c Healy b M. E. Waugh	143	– lbw b M. E. Waugh	45
*M. D. Crowe c Taylor b Reiffel	42	– not out	31
K. R. Rutherford c Healy b McDermott	17	– lbw b S. R. Waugh	39
D. N. Patel c S. R. Waugh b Reiffel	20	– not out	18
C. L. Cairns b Warne	78		
†T. E. Blain lbw b McDermott	36		
M. L. Su'a not out	14		
D. K. Morrison lbw b McGrath	0		
W. Watson not out	0		
B 1, l-b 6, n-b 10	17	L-b 1, n-b 4	5
1/25 (1) 2/100 (2) 3/199 (4) 4/239 (5) 5/275 (3) 6/292 (6) 7/394 (8) 8/413 (7) 9/418 (10) (9 wkts dec.)	419	1/0 (1) 2/66 (3) 3/85 (2) 4/145 (5) (4 wkts)	166

Bowling: *First Innings*—McDermott 40–10–127–3; McGrath 39–12–92–2; Reiffel 24–2–75–2; Warne 37.1–6–90–1; M. E. Waugh 13–5–18–1; S. R. Waugh 4–0–10–0; Border 2–2–0–0. *Second Innings*—McDermott 13–3–40–1; McGrath 16–6–50–1; Reiffel 7–2–25–0; M. E. Waugh 6–4–17–1; Warne 13–6–23–0; S. R. Waugh 7–2–10–1.

Umpires: D. B. Hair and A. J. McQuillan. Referee: S. Venkataraghavan (India).

SOUTH AUSTRALIA v NEW ZEALANDERS

At Adelaide, November 19, 20, 21, 22. New Zealanders won by seven wickets. Toss: South Australia.

Rain delayed the match by three hours, softening the usually hard pitch and helping the tourists' new captain, Rutherford, make a winning start. South Australia, a powerful batting team then leading the Sheffield Shield table, were shot out in three and a half hours; Doull cut the ball about for six wickets, ably assisted by de Groen, who had flown in the previous day. There were runs at last for Greatbatch and Young, together with a breezy fifty from night-watchman Su'a and another from Rutherford, who declared with an overnight lead of 118. Doull and de Groen again made deep inroads into South Australia's batting, though they were stalled by Brayshaw's 94, and the New Zealanders were left needing 143 to win at less than three an over. Greatbatch's second thumping half-century and a 131-run opening stand with Pocock guaranteed victory, momentarily delayed by the unfortunate Young's fourth duck on tour.

Close of play: First day, New Zealanders 8-1 (M. J. Greatbatch 0*, M. L. Su'a 4*); Second day, New Zealanders 276-6 (C. Z. Harris 15*, T. E. Blain 1*); Third day, South Australia 247-7 (D. A. Reeves 35*, T. B. A. May 13*).

South Australia

G. R. Blewett c Blain b Doull	47	– c Rutherford b Haslam 49
P. C. Nobes c Rutherford b Su'a	0	– lbw b Su'a 17
J. A. Brayshaw b Doull	16	– b Doull 94
*D. S. Lehmann c Blain b Doull	6	– b Su'a 16
D. S. Webber c Young b de Groen	3	– lbw b Doull 10
†T. J. Nielsen c Greatbatch b de Groen	17	– lbw b de Groen 8
J. C. Scuderi c de Groen b Doull	51	– lbw b de Groen 0
D. A. Reeves c Blain b Doull	5	– not out 40
T. B. A. May c Young b Su'a	3	– c Rutherford b de Groen 13
B. N. Wigney c Rutherford b Doull	0	– c Patel b Doull 7
P. E. McIntyre not out	3	
L-b 2, w 2, n-b 3	7	L-b 3, n-b 3 6
1/3 2/23 3/33 4/36 5/92 6/96 7/115 8/126 9/129	158	1/48 2/86 3/110 4/144 5/175 6/175 7/214 8/247 9/260 (9 wkts dec.) 260

Bowling: *First Innings*—Su'a 12–2–56–2; de Groen 17–7–30–2; Doull 17.5–1–55–6; Harris 4–2–15–0. *Second Innings*—Su'a 21–4–71–2; de Groen 24–10–50–3; Doull 19.5–4–54–3; Haslam 17–2–30–1; Patel 19–5–52–0.

New Zealanders

B. A. Pocock b Scuderi	3	– (2) c May b Nielsen 60
M. J. Greatbatch c Webber b Reeves	65	– (1) c Brayshaw b Wigney 64
M. L. Su'a c Brayshaw b Reeves	56	
B. A. Young c Nielsen b Scuderi	48	– (3) lbw b Wigney 0
*K. R. Rutherford c and b Reeves	76	
C. Z. Harris not out	15	– (5) not out 1
D. N. Patel b Reeves	0	– (4) not out 10
†T. E. Blain not out	1	
L-b 7, n-b 5	12	L-b 7, w 1 8
1/3 2/121 3/128 4/245 5/272 6/275	(6 wkts dec.) 276	1/131 2/131 3/135 (3 wkts) 143

R. P. de Groen, S. B. Doull and M. J. Haslam did not bat.

Bowling: *First Innings*—Wigney 22–4–58–0; Scuderi 21–7–55–2; Reeves 19–2–62–4; Blewett 12–2–35–0; May 19–7–37–0; Lehmann 4–0–22–0. *Second Innings*—Reeves 6–1–19–0; Scuderi 8–0–24–0; May 17–3–49–0; Wigney 10–3–24–2; McIntyre 8–3–11–0; Lehmann 3–1–4–0; Nielsen 3.5–2–5–1.

Umpires: S. J. Davis, D. J. Harper and R. B. Woods.

AUSTRALIA v NEW ZEALAND

Second Test Match

At Hobart, November 26, 27, 28, 29. Australia won by an innings and 222 runs. Toss: Australia. Test debut: R. P. de Groen.

Having waited patiently for four years for the chance to host a second Test, Hobart witnessed a match so one-sided that even New Zealand captain Rutherford judged it scarcely worthy of the status. Spinners Warne and May combined for 16 wickets to deliver New Zealand's heaviest Test defeat and Australia's fourth most emphatic win. It was all over in less than 20 hours.

New Zealand began literally on the wrong foot when the all-rounder Cairns insisted at breakfast that his bruised left heel was too sore for him to play even as a specialist batsman. This left New Zealand with one world-class bowler and a very long tail indeed. Next, they lost the toss and had to field on an unusually sticky Hobart day. Within the first hour they had dropped the first two of seven squandered chances: Morrison, of course, suffered most. Australia's batsmen had a feast and by tea next day had plundered 544 for six, whereupon Border folded up his napkin and declared. There were three centuries: Slater contributed a rousing 168 in five and a half hours with 17 boundaries, though not before he almost ran himself out for a second consecutive 99. Boon's first Test century in Tasmania, the state for which he is an advert around the world, made him the fifth Australian to surpass 6,000 Test runs. Next morning, it was Mark Waugh's turn, as he raced from 18 overnight to raise 100 with a scorching cover drive off the last ball before lunch. Border was dropped off Morrison at three and caught and bowled by him for 60 – the story of the series in cameo.

New Zealand went in just before 4 p.m. on the second day and in less than ten playing hours were all out twice – each time for 161, and still 23 runs shy of the original follow-on target. Both innings had the same pattern. McDermott began by dismissing Greatbatch, Mark Waugh took a high-order wicket and Warne and May rolled up the rest like an old carpet. May, mostly through his heavily disguised arm-ball, took five wickets in an innings for the third time in Tests, all in 1993. Warne reciprocated with six for 31, giving him 63 Test wickets in a calendar year – already more than any spinner in history. Of the batsmen, Jones made a fight of the first innings, but by the second was mentally exhausted and hooked a bouncer directly to square leg. Rutherford boldly took the fight to Warne and was rewarded with a fluent second-innings 55 until he was bowled behind his legs trying to sweep. New Zealand's most combative player was Blain, who kept a straight bat and a cool head. On the way to 40 in the first innings he smacked May for four boundaries in a single over, as if to signal to the cowering dressing-room that the devils were as much in their own minds as in the pitch or the attack. But the gesture was lost on a team already mentally defeated.

Man of the Match: M. E. Waugh. *Attendance:* 13,220

Close of play: First day, Australia 329-2 (D. C. Boon 105*, M. E. Waugh 18*); Second day, New Zealand 81-2 (A. H. Jones 34*, K. R. Rutherford 15*); Third day, New Zealand 127-5 (C. Z. Harris 4*, T. E. Blain 9*).

Australia

M. A. Taylor c Jones b Su'a	27
M. J. Slater c Morrison b Patel	168
D. C. Boon c Jones b Doull	106
M. E. Waugh c Doull b de Groen	111
*A. R. Border c and b Morrison	60
S. R. Waugh not out	25
†I. A. Healy c Doull b de Groen	1
P. R. Reiffel not out	23
B 7, l-b 2, n-b 14	23
1/65 (1) 2/300 (2) 3/335 (3) 4/485 (4) 5/501 (5) 6/502 (7)	(6 wkts dec.) 544

S. K. Warne, C. J. McDermott and T. B. A. May did not bat.

Bowling: Morrison 33-4-125-1; Su'a 24–3–102–1; Doull 21–0–99–1; de Groen 36–9–113–2; Patel 23–3–78–1; Harris 2–0–18–0.

New Zealand

M. J. Greatbatch c May b McDermott	12	– c M. E. Waugh b McDermott	0
B. A. Pocock lbw b M. E. Waugh	9	– st Healy b Warne	15
A. H. Jones c Healy b May	47	– c Border b M. E. Waugh	18
*K. R. Rutherford c Taylor b May	17	– b Warne	55
D. N. Patel c Taylor b Warne	18	– lbw b May	16
C. Z. Harris c M. E. Waugh b May	0	– b May	4
†T. E. Blain c Warne b May	40	– c and b Warne	29
M. L. Su'a c Taylor b Warne	6	– b Warne	5
D. K. Morrison c M. E. Waugh b May	0	– b Warne	0
S. B. Doull lbw b Warne	0	– c May b Warne	1
R. P. de Groen not out	0	– not out	3
B 2, l-b 1, n-b 9	12	B 2, l-b 5, n-b 8	15
1/15 (1) 2/47 (2) 3/84 (4) 4/105 (3) 5/107 (6) 6/117 (5) 7/137 (8) 8/138 (9) 9/139 (10) 10/161 (7)	161	1/1 (1) 2/29 (3) 3/84 (2) 4/103 (4) 5/111 (5) 6/133 (6) 7/149 (8) 8/149 (9) 9/158 (7) 10/161 (10)	161

Bowling: *First Innings*—McDermott 15–3–29–1; Reiffel 5–1–13–0; S. R. Waugh 4–1–8–0; M. E. Waugh 9–4–7–1; May 31.3–10–65–5; Warne 18–5–36–3. *Second Innings*—McDermott 17–8–42–1; Reiffel 12–1–28–0; M. E. Waugh 4–0–8–1; May 25–13–45–2; Warne 19.5–9–31–6.

Umpires: D. B. Hair and W. P. Sheahan. Referee: S. Venkataraghavan (India).

AUSTRALIA v NEW ZEALAND

Third Test Match

At Brisbane, December 3, 4, 5, 6, 7. Australia won by an innings and 96 runs. Toss: New Zealand. Test debut: B. A. Young.

As this was Allan Border's 150th Test match, as it was played on his adopted home ground, as it featured his 27th century (his last before retiring), and as Australia again won handsomely, this became a kind of impromptu Border benefit. New Zealand had brought him despair in his first full season as captain, eight years before, but this shattered and sorry team offered no more than a guard of honour.

New Zealand regained Cairns from injury and brought in erstwhile wicket-keeper Young as opener – overlooking his four ducks on tour – to shield Greatbatch from McDermott. After doubts about Warne's sore spinning finger were resolved, Australia's only change was to bring in McGrath for Reiffel. Batting first on a steamy Brisbane morning, New Zealand began with renewed determination; Young resisted for more than three hours and Jones contributed a vigorous 56. But once Warne's flipper had burrowed beneath his shocked defences and McDermott had nipped Rutherford and Greatbatch in the bud, only the dauntless Blain salvaged respectability. Morrison made his fourth consecutive Test duck as Warne and McDermott collected four wickets each and Healy gathered in five catches to displace Wally Grout in second place behind Rod Marsh among Australian wicket-keepers. Finally, Border took his 150th Test catch, a new landmark for a fielder.

When Australia batted, New Zealand paid dearly for three more dropped catches. Taylor, Boon and Mark Waugh each had a century at his mercy until boredom undermined concentration. But Border and Steve Waugh put their hard heads together to compile a fifth-wicket partnership of 159. Border rediscovered his lost cut shot and profited to reach 100 in the youthful time of just over four hours; the prolonged flourish of his bat to the ecstatic crowd seemed to say "farewell" as much as "thank you". He was out soon after that, whereupon the sky became apocalyptically stormy, but Waugh and Warne, sensing no danger from either the elements or the opposition, twice refused to go off. Waugh's tightened technique took him to his sixth Test century. Next day the pair batted on blithely to a declaration at lunch; Warne had 74, his highest first-class score, and Australia 607, their highest ever against New Zealand and their third total beyond 600 in 1993. Five demoralised New Zealand bowlers conceded at least a century of runs.

Young bolstered New Zealand's second innings with a poised half-century, but Warne, after having Jones caught at mid-wicket from a limp pull, bowled Young with a ball that spun prodigiously around his outstretched front pad. Like Gatting and Gooch before him, Young had discovered that elementary defence was not enough. Rain delayed Australia, but not unduly. On the final morning, McGrath bowled Blain through his gate, Warne bowled Patel through his legs and the last thread of resistance was snapped when Rutherford hooked McGrath deep to the ubiquitous Warne and departed for 86. New Zealand had surrendered their most prized cricket possession, the Trans-Tasman Trophy, with scarcely a squawk.

Man of the Match: S. K. Warne. *Man of the Series:* S. K. Warne.

Attendance: 24,666.

Close of play: First day, New Zealand 208-9 (T. E. Blain 20*, R. P. de Groen 1*); Second day, Australia 241-3 (D. C. Boon 72*, A. R. Border 5*); Third day, Australia 533-6 (S. R. Waugh 113*, S. K. Warne 37*); Fourth day, New Zealand 158-5 (K. R. Rutherford 40*, T. E. Blain 7*).

New Zealand

First innings		Second innings	
B. A. Pocock c Healy b McDermott	0	(2) c Healy b McDermott	11
B. A. Young c Healy b M. E. Waugh	38	(1) b Warne	53
A. H. Jones b Warne	56	c Border b Warne	15
*K. R. Rutherford c Boon b McDermott	36	c Warne b McGrath	86
M. J. Greatbatch c Healy b McDermott	35	lbw b McDermott	2
C. L. Cairns c and b Warne	5	c Healy b McGrath	16
D. N. Patel c Boon b May	1	(8) b Warne	3
†T. E. Blain not out	42	(7) b McGrath	18
D. K. Morrison c Healy b Warne	0	not out	20
S. B. Doull c Healy b McDermott	10	c Taylor b Warne	24
R. P. de Groen c Border b Warne	3	b May	6
B 2, l-b 3, n-b 2	7	B 7, l-b 12, n-b 5	24
1/2 (1) 2/96 (3) 3/98 (2) 4/167 (4) 5/170 (5) 6/174 (7) 7/174 (6) 8/178 (9) 9/193 (10) 10/233 (11)	233	1/34 (2) 2/80 (3) 3/81 (1) 4/84 (5) 5/138 (6) 6/187 (7) 7/218 (8) 8/230 (4) 9/265 (10) 10/278 (11)	278

Bowling: *First Innings*—McDermott 23–11–39–4; McGrath 20–7–45–0; S. R. Waugh 3–0–13–0; M. E. Waugh 10–4–14–1; May 21–7–51–1; Warne 28.3–12–66–4. *Second Innings*—McDermott 25–4–63–2; McGrath 21–1–66–3; May 16–3–41–1; Warne 35–11–59–4; M. E. Waugh 6–1–30–0.

Australia

M. J. Slater c Blain b Patel	28
M. A. Taylor c Pocock b Doull	53
D. C. Boon c Blain b Doull	89
M. E. Waugh c Greatbatch b Cairns	68
*A. R. Border c Patel b de Groen	105
S. R. Waugh not out	147
†I. A. Healy run out	15
S. K. Warne not out	74
B 6, l-b 13, n-b 9	28
1/80 (1) 2/102 (2) 3/227 (4) 4/277 (3) 5/436 (5) 6/465 (7)	(6 wkts dec.) 607

C. J. McDermott, T. B. A. May and G. D. McGrath did not bat.

Bowling: Morrison 33–3–104–0; Cairns 36–7–128–1; Doull 33–5–105–2; de Groen 46–14–120–1; Patel 33–4–125–1; Jones 2–0–6–0.

Umpires: P. D. Parker and S. G. Randell. Referee: S. Venkataraghavan (India).

New Zealand's matches v Australia and South Africa in the Benson and Hedges World Series (December 11–January 19) may be found in that section.

THE ZIMBABWEANS IN PAKISTAN, 1993-94

By QAMAR AHMED

Pakistan won their first-ever Test series against Zimbabwe 2-0, with a clean sweep in the one-day series. But the tour was less one-sided than this summary suggests. Zimbabwe, who had played their first Test barely a year earlier, came close to pulling off an upset in the Second Test at Rawalpindi. There they reached 135 for one in pursuit of 240 to win before they were devastated by Waqar Younis and Wasim Akram and lost by 52 runs. This settled the series, as Pakistan had already won the First Test at Karachi.

The tour was hastily arranged when Pakistan cancelled another series with India and also dropped out of the Hero Cup in Bengal because of political worries. It enabled Pakistan to play their first home series for two years, before setting off for New Zealand, while the Zimbabweans, who had travelled to India for the Hero Cup, were delighted to continue their Test education. "We have discovered that we can now stand the pressure of a three-Test tour," said their captain, Andy Flower.

Though the tourists failed to win any of their seven matches during their month in Pakistan, they left a lasting impression on the cricketing public. Their fielding was excellent and their bowlers ably exploited helpful conditions to keep Pakistan's scoring down. At Rawalpindi, Zimbabwe twice dismissed their hosts for under 250; in the final Test at Lahore they bowled them out for a paltry 147.

Though the inexperienced batting often let them down, Alistair Campbell and Mark Dekker won general admiration for the way they braved Pakistan's pace attack. Campbell, the tourists' man of the series, scored 205 – more than anyone on either side – at 41.00 in the Tests and Dekker, who carried his bat through the Rawalpindi collapse, averaged 35.75. Andy Flower, Zimbabwe's new captain, scored 158 at 39.50. The medium-pacers, Eddo Brandes, David Brain, Heath Streak and John Rennie, bowled steadily and intelligently.

Wasim and Waqar proved to be the major difference between the two teams. Waqar, who led Pakistan in the First Test because of the wrist injury Wasim had suffered in Sharjah, collected 27 wickets at 13.81. He bowled in five innings and took five or more wickets in four of them. On his return, Wasim picked up 11 wickets at 18.45 in the last two Tests, while newcomer Ashfaq Ahmed made a promising debut.

But Pakistan had little to boast about as far as their batting was concerned. Despite the experience of players like Javed Miandad and Shoaib Mohammad, who returned to Test cricket for the first time since the 1992 tour of England, not one of them could score a century, either in the Tests or in the one-day internationals – a testimony to Zimbabwe's ever-improving performance. Shoaib came closest, with 81 in the First Test in Karachi, but it was the reliable and gutsy left-hander, Asif Mujtaba, who headed the averages, scoring 184 runs in six innings, including three fifties. Rashid Latif put in a fine all-round performance with 169 runs and seven catches behind the stumps – five of them in the last Test. But had Zimbabwe possessed a little more experience, Pakistan might have been severely embarrassed by their first-time visitors. Despite the scoreline, Zimbabwe had greater cause for satisfaction.

ZIMBABWEAN TOURING PARTY

A. Flower (Mashonaland) (*captain*), D. L. Houghton (Mashonaland) (*vice-captain*), D. H. Brain (Mashonaland), E. A. Brandes, G. K. Bruk-Jackson (Mashonaland Country Districts), A. D. R. Campbell (Mashonaland Country Districts), M. H. Dekker (Matabeleland), G. W. Flower (Mashonaland Under-24), W. R. James (Matabeleland), S. G. Peall (Mashonaland Country Districts), U. Ranchod (Mashonaland), J. A. Rennie (Matabeleland), P. A. Strang (Mashonaland Country Districts), H. H. Streak (Matabeleland), G. J. Whittall (Matabeleland).

Manager: M. A. Meman. *Coach:* J. H. Hampshire.

ZIMBABWEAN TOURING RESULTS

Test matches – Played 3: Lost 2, Drawn 1.
First-class matches – Played 4: Lost 2, Drawn 2.
Losses – Pakistan (2).
Draws – Pakistan, Bank of Khyber XI.
One-day internationals – Played 3: Lost 3.

TEST MATCH AVERAGES

PAKISTAN – BATTING

	T	*I*	*NO*	*R*	*HS*	*100s*	*Avge*	*Ct*
Asif Mujtaba	3	6	3	184	65*	0	61.33	2
Rashid Latif	3	4	1	169	68*	0	56.33	7
Shoaib Mohammad	3	5	1	179	81	0	44.75	1
Inzamam-ul-Haq	3	5	1	163	57*	0	40.75	7
Javed Miandad	3	5	0	143	70	0	28.60	0
Basit Ali	3	5	0	143	40	0	28.60	1
Aamir Sohail	3	6	0	143	63	0	23.83	4
Wasim Akram	2	3	1	42	16*	0	21.00	1
Waqar Younis	3	4	0	37	17	0	9.25	0
Ata-ur-Rehman	3	3	0	10	10	0	3.33	1

Played in two Tests: Mushtaq Ahmed 18, 1. Played in one Test: Ashfaq Ahmed 0, 1*; Tauseef Ahmed 21*.

* *Signifies not out.*

BOWLING

	O	*M*	*R*	*W*	*BB*	*5W/i*	*Avge*
Waqar Younis	130.4	31	373	27	7-91	4	13.81
Wasim Akram	76.2	14	203	11	5-65	1	18.45
Ata-ur-Rehman	66	22	134	6	2-20	0	22.33
Mushtaq Ahmed	61	19	126	3	2-24	0	42.00

Also bowled: Aamir Sohail 6–0–25–0; Ashfaq Ahmed 23–9–53–2; Asif Mujtaba 3–2–1–0; Shoaib Mohammad 5–1–17–0; Tauseef Ahmed 29–9–62–0.

ZIMBABWE – BATTING

	T	I	NO	R	HS	100s	Avge	Ct
A. D. R. Campbell	3	5	0	205	75	0	41.00	3
A. Flower	3	5	1	158	63	0	39.50	7
M. H. Dekker	3	5	1	143	68*	0	35.75	1
D. L. Houghton	3	5	0	123	50	0	24.60	3
G. W. Flower	3	5	0	79	30	0	15.80	0
D. H. Brain	2	3	0	46	28	0	15.33	0
G. J. Whittall	3	5	0	66	33	0	13.20	0
E. A. Brandes	3	5	1	45	18	0	11.25	2
G. K. Bruk-Jackson	2	4	0	39	31	0	9.75	0
S. G. Peall	2	4	1	21	11*	0	7.00	1
H. H. Streak	3	5	1	21	19*	0	5.25	1
J. A. Rennie	2	3	0	5	3	0	1.66	0

Played in one Test: W. R. James 8 (3 ct).

** Signifies not out.*

BOWLING

	O	M	R	W	BB	5W/i	Avge
D. H. Brain	95	24	184	12	5-42	1	15.33
E. A. Brandes	141	26	394	13	3-45	0	30.30
H. H. Streak	110.5	22	284	8	5-56	1	35.50
J. A. Rennie	59.4	15	171	3	2-22	0	57.00

Also bowled: A. D. R. Campbell 1–0–3–0; A. Flower 0.1–0–0–0; G. W. Flower 20–4–36–1; S. G. Peall 55–17–111–2; G. J. Whittall 43.5–15–92–1.

Note: Matches in this section which were not first-class are signified by a dagger.

BANK OF KHYBER XI v ZIMBABWEANS

At Peshawar, November 26, 27, 28. Drawn. Toss: Zimbabweans.

The batsmen beat the bowlers hands down in this warm-up match, with 659 runs scored to seven wickets taken. Against an inexperienced attack, not helped by poor fielding or wicket-keeper Tahir Rashid's lapses, the Zimbabweans piled up 405 runs over a day and a half. Campbell took charge after three wickets fell before lunch, in partnership first with Houghton and then with Andy Flower. The scoring-rate speeded up on the second morning, when they added 126 in two hours. Both Campbell, who hit 17 fours, and Flower, with 14, made centuries before retiring, and the declaration came 50 minutes after lunch. The home team batted for the rest of the match, losing only two wickets to the bowlers, though captain Shoaib Mohammad retired after reaching a six-hour century.

Close of play: First day, Zimbabweans 212-4 (A. D. R. Campbell 82*, A. Flower 27*); Second day, Bank of Khyber XI 59-0 (Shakeel Ahmed 30*, Shoaib Mohammad 15*).

Zimbabweans

G. W. Flower b Kabir Khan 23
M. H. Dekker lbw b Ashfaq Ahmed ... 20
†W. R. James c Tahir Rashid b Kabir Khan . 1
A. D. R. Campbell retired ill 135
D. L. Houghton b Mohammad Asif.... 34
*A. Flower retired hurt 103
G. J. Whittall not out 19
G. K. Bruk-Jackson c Ashfaq Ahmed b Mohammad Asif . 2
S. G. Peall not out 26
B 11, l-b 11, w 1, n-b 19 42

1/49 2/50 3/67 4/137 5/363 (5 wkts dec.) 405

D. H. Brain and J. A. Rennie did not bat.

A. D. R. Campbell retired ill and A. Flower retired hurt at 338.

Bowling: Irfan Bhatti 17–3–54–0; Ashfaq Ahmed 30–4–104–1; Kabir Khan 22–6–48–2; Mohammad Asif 37–8–92–2; Shoaib Mohammad 2–0–13–0; Shahid Hussain 22–5–70–0; Ijaz Ahmed 1–0–2–0.

Bank of Khyber XI

Shakeel Ahmed c and b Whittall	50	Ijaz Ahmed not out	1
*Shoaib Mohammad retired out	101	B 5, l-b 6, w 2, n-b 7	20
Atif Rauf b Peall	32		—
Shahid Javed not out	50	1/89 2/158 3/251 (3 wkts)	254

†Tahir Rashid, Irfan Bhatti, Mohammad Asif, Ashfaq Ahmed, Kabir Khan and Shahid Hussain did not bat.

Bowling: Brain 19–6–64–0; Rennie 22.5–10–56–0; Whittall 17–4–31–1; Peall 25–6–42–1; A. Flower 6.1–1–9–0; Dekker 10–2–22–0; Campbell 4–0–19–0.

Umpires: Mian Said Shah and Mohammad Iqbal.

PAKISTAN v ZIMBABWE

First Test Match

At Defence Stadium, Karachi, December 1, 2, 3, 5, 6. Pakistan won by 131 runs. Toss: Pakistan. Test debuts: G. K. Bruk-Jackson, M. H. Dekker, S. G. Peall, J. A. Rennie, H. H. Streak, G. J. Whittall.

Pakistan abandoned Karachi's National Stadium, where they had remained unbeaten in 30 Tests, for the smaller Defence Stadium, which became the 70th Test ground. It did not change their luck. It was an unfamiliar game in other respects: this was the first Test between the two sides, both captains were leading their teams for the first time and Zimbabwe fielded six debutants. Waqar Younis, deputising for the injured Wasim Akram, became Pakistan's youngest Test captain at 22 years and 15 days, beating Javed Miandad by 245 days. Not surprisingly, Andy Flower was also the youngest man to lead his country, at 25; his only predecessor, the 36-year-old Houghton, remained in the team.

It was to be Waqar's match, however. He returned his best-ever Test figures of 13 for 135, five bowled and seven lbw, to set up a 131-run win. Zimbabwe did well to hold out until the end of the final day. Earlier, their sensible bowling, backed up by some impressive fielding, meant that Pakistan could not score as freely as they would have liked. On the first day they batted for 75 overs, losing only two wickets but falling short of 200. Aamir Sohail was bowled by Peall, in his first over, for 63, but the tone was set by Shoaib Mohammad's cautious 71. The next day dragged on slothfully while Pakistan scored 191 runs. The new ball was taken in the second over and helped Rennie to his first Test wicket, Shoaib for 81. Miandad was the next to go, lbw to Brandes for 70. Rashid Latif stepped up the pace slightly and Pakistan declared 25 minutes into the third day.

Zimbabwe batted bravely against the fire and fury of Waqar to reach 179 for four by the close. Though Waqar removed both openers without much cost, Campbell scored his third Test fifty, including seven fours, and Houghton almost added another. Andy Flower's 63 seemed to be setting up a very respectable total. But they crashed from 280 for five to 289 all out, with Waqar dismissing four men in 15 balls to finish with seven for 91.

In their second innings Pakistan gathered runs much more quickly, and the declaration set Zimbabwe to score 266 from 68 overs. The early loss of Dekker and Campbell forced them onto the defensive before Waqar inspired another collapse, six wickets for 31 runs reducing them to a humiliating 92 for eight. Though the end seemed inevitable, Streak and Brandes made the bowlers fight for the last two wickets, holding out for more than an hour. But once Waqar had broken through he trapped the last man, Rennie, with just over five overs to spare.

Man of the Match: Waqar Younis.

Close of play: First day, Pakistan 197-2 (Shoaib Mohammad 71*, Javed Miandad 37*); Second day, Pakistan 388-8 (Rashid Latif 52*, Tauseef Ahmed 8*); Third day, Zimbabwe 179-4 (A. Flower 21*, G. J. Whittall 12*); Fourth day, Pakistan 111-3 (Inzamam-ul-Haq 47*, Asif Mujtaba 2*).

Pakistan

First innings		Second innings	
Aamir Sohail b Peall	63	– run out	29
Shoaib Mohammad c A. Flower b Rennie	81		
Inzamam-ul-Haq c A. Flower b Brandes	21	– (2) not out	57
Javed Miandad lbw b Brandes	70	– run out	12
Basit Ali c A. Flower b Whittall	36	– (3) c and b Brandes	13
Asif Mujtaba c Dekker b Brandes	4	– (5) not out	10
†Rashid Latif not out	68		
*Waqar Younis c Peall b G. W. Flower	13		
Mushtaq Ahmed c A. Flower b Peall	18		
Tauseef Ahmed not out	21		
B 14, l-b 13, n-b 1	28	B 6, l-b 2, w 1, n-b 1	10
1/95 (1) 2/134 (3) 3/217 (2) 4/268 (4) 5/280 (6) 6/305 (5) 7/332 (8) 8/363 (9)	(8 wkts dec.) 423	1/47 (1) 2/76 (3) 3/108 (4)	(3 wkts dec.) 131

Ata-ur-Rehman did not bat.

Bowling: *First Innings*—Brandes 35–4–106–3; Streak 29–6–77–0; Rennie 32–6–90–1; Whittall 12–4–26–1; Peall 41–10–89–2; G. W. Flower 6–2–8–1. *Second Innings*—Brandes 13–0–59–1; Rennie 3–0–24–0; Streak 10–1–40–0.

Zimbabwe

First innings		Second innings	
G. W. Flower b Waqar Younis	24	– b Ata-ur-Rehman	25
M. H. Dekker lbw b Waqar Younis	5	– lbw b Waqar Younis	0
A. D. R. Campbell lbw b Mushtaq Ahmed	53	– c Inzamam-ul-Haq b Mushtaq Ahmed	8
D. L. Houghton lbw b Waqar Younis	46	– lbw b Waqar Younis	18
*†A. Flower lbw b Ata-ur-Rehman	63	– c Inzamam-ul-Haq b Mushtaq Ahmed	21
G. J. Whittall run out	33	– b Ata-ur-Rehman	2
G. K. Bruk-Jackson b Waqar Younis	31	– lbw b Waqar Younis	4
S. G. Peall c Aamir Sohail b Waqar Younis	0	– b Waqar Younis	0
H. H. Streak b Waqar Younis	0	– not out	19
E. A. Brandes not out	0	– b Waqar Younis	17
J. A. Rennie lbw b Waqar Younis	3	– lbw b Waqar Younis	0
B 5, l-b 24, w 1, n-b 1	31	B 12, l-b 5, n-b 3	20
1/16 (2) 2/71 (1) 3/132 (3) 4/153 (4) 5/230 (6) 6/280 (5) 7/284 (7) 8/284 (9) 9/285 (8) 10/289 (11)	289	1/1 (2) 2/17 (3) 3/61 (4) 4/63 (1) 5/65 (6) 6/78 (7) 7/80 (8) 8/92 (5) 9/130 (10) 10/134 (11)	134

Bowling: *First Innings*—Waqar Younis 34.1–8–91–7; Ata-ur-Rehman 15–5–28–1; Mushtaq Ahmed 39–11–89–1; Tauseef Ahmed 23–7–49–0; Shoaib Mohammad 1–0–1–0; Aamir Sohail 1–0–1–0; Asif Mujtaba 3–2–1–0. *Second Innings*—Waqar Younis 21.5–7–44–6; Ata-ur-Rehman 16–6–20–2; Mushtaq Ahmed 17–7–24–2; Tauseef Ahmed 6–2–13–0; Aamir Sohail 2–0–16–0.

Umpires: Mahboob Shah and Shakeel Khan. Referee: R. S. Madugalle (Sri Lanka).

PAKISTAN v ZIMBABWE

Second Test Match

At Rawalpindi Cricket Stadium, Rawalpindi, December 9, 10, 11, 13, 14. Pakistan won by 52 runs. Toss: Zimbabwe. Test debut: Ashfaq Ahmed.

But for a collapse of nine wickets for 52 on the final day, Zimbabwe might have won their first-ever Test victory and levelled the series. Set 240 to win, they cruised to 135 for one, thanks to Dekker and Campbell. Once Campbell went, however, Waqar Younis and

Wasim Akram ripped through their batting, Zimbabwe were all out for 187 and the series was Pakistan's. Dekker remained unbeaten after 289 minutes, the first Zimbabwean to carry his bat in a Test.

A seaming pitch at Rawalpindi Cricket Stadium, which superseded the Pindi Club and became the 71st Test ground, produced a low-scoring match. Pakistan dropped their two spinners as Wasim returned after a wrist injury; his seven for 133, combined with Waqar's nine for 138, secured his first win in four Tests as captain. Zimbabwe retained off-spinner Peall, who hardly bowled, and switched one medium-pacer, Brain, for another, Rennie. All Flower's seamers performed extremely well to contain Pakistan's unpredictable line-up. On the first day, only 185 runs came from 75 overs, and that owed much to Asif Mujtaba and Rashid Latif, who added 54 for the sixth wicket before the close. But though Mujtaba reached an unbeaten and disciplined fifty, Pakistan were dismissed for 245 after lunch next day. Brandes, Brain and Streak shared the wickets, with Brain taking four for 41 in 32 overs.

Zimbabwe reached 129 for four by the close, which might have been more had Campbell not fallen to a dubious – and unpopular – lbw decision by umpire Javed Akhtar. In 69 minutes, he had scored a swashbuckling 63 from 55 balls, with 11 fours and a six, and added 102 with Dekker. On the third day, they passed 200, with only one more wicket down, before losing three for one run. Their eventual lead was nine. But they followed up that slight advantage with three Pakistani wickets for 40 that night, which became five for 58 next morning. Pakistan escaped from this precarious position through some uncharacteristic fielding lapses by Zimbabwe and another steady fifty from Mujtaba, who added 74 with Basit Ali and 77 with Latif. They reached 248 on the last morning, Streak finishing with eight for 114 in his second Test.

Zimbabwe had 67 overs to score 240 and, though the first ball completed a pair for Grant Flower, a sporting crowd of 15,000 chanted their praises as Dekker and Campbell added 135 in three hours. But when Campbell was caught off Ata-ur-Rehman – after hitting ten fours and a six – Zimbabwe went to pieces. Wasim and Waqar split the last eight wickets. Only one more batsman, Peall, reached double figures before he gave Inzamam-ul-Haq his fifth catch of the match with 4.4 overs to spare. "We had an opportunity to create history," said Zimbabwe coach John Hampshire, "but then it isn't easy to bat against Wasim and Waqar."

Man of the Match: Waqar Younis.

Close of play: First day, Pakistan 185-5 (Asif Mujtaba 25*, Rashid Latif 32*); Second day, Zimbabwe 129-4 (M. H. Dekker 37*, H. H. Streak 0*); Third day, Pakistan 40-3 (Inzamam-ul-Haq 9*, Javed Miandad 1*); Fourth day, Pakistan 221-8 (Wasim Akram 5*, Waqar Younis 1*).

Pakistan

Aamir Sohail c Houghton b Streak	8	– lbw b Streak	9
Shoaib Mohammad lbw b Brain	18	– c A. Flower b Streak	13
Inzamam-ul-Haq b Brain	38	– b Brandes	14
Javed Miandad b Streak	20	– (5) b Streak	10
Basit Ali c Streak b Brandes	25	– (6) lbw b Brandes	40
Asif Mujtaba not out	54	– (7) c A. Flower b Brain	51
†Rashid Latif lbw b Brain	33	– (8) c Houghton b Streak	61
*Wasim Akram c Campbell b Brandes	11	– (9) lbw b Brandes	15
Waqar Younis lbw b Brandes	7	– (10) c Campbell b Streak	17
Ata-ur-Rehman lbw b Brain	10	– (4) lbw b Brain	0
Ashfaq Ahmed c A. Flower b Streak	0	– not out	1
B 4, l-b 12, w 2, n-b 3	21	B 1, l-b 11, w 3, n-b 2	17
1/29 (2) 2/33 (1) 3/99 (4) 4/101 (3) 5/131 (5) 6/187 (7) 7/209 (8) 8/225 (9) 9/241 (10) 10/245 (11)	245	1/25 (1) 2/38 (2) 3/39 (4) 4/54 (3) 5/58 (5) 6/132 (6) 7/209 (7) 8/219 (8) 9/240 (9) 10/248 (10)	248

Bowling: *First Innings*—Brandes 32–5–82–3; Brain 32–9–41–4; Streak 23.2–5–58–3; Whittall 17–6–39–0; Peall 6–3–9–0. *Second Innings*—Brandes 31–9–71–3; Brain 34–6–73–2; Streak 20.3–3–56–5; Peall 8–4–13–0; Whittall 4–1–10–0; G. W. Flower 4–0–13–0.

Zimbabwe

G. W. Flower c Inzamam-ul-Haq b Wasim Akram	0	– b Wasim Akram	0
M. H. Dekker c Inzamam-ul-Haq b Waqar Younis	68	– not out	68
A. D. R. Campbell lbw b Ata-ur-Rehman	63	– c Aamir Sohail b Ata-ur-Rehman	75
D. L. Houghton c Asif Mujtaba b Ashfaq Ahmed	5	– lbw b Waqar Younis	4
*†A. Flower c Wasim Akram b Waqar Younis	12	– c Rashid Latif b Waqar Younis	0
H. H. Streak c Inzamam-ul-Haq b Waqar Younis	2	– (8) b Waqar Younis	0
G. J. Whittall c Inzamam-ul-Haq b Ashfaq Ahmed	29	– (6) lbw b Wasim Akram	0
G. K. Bruk-Jackson c Aamir Sohail b Waqar Younis	0	– (7) c Rashid Latif b Wasim Akram	4
D. H. Brain c Ata-ur-Rehman b Waqar Younis	16	– b Waqar Younis	2
E. A. Brandes c Basit Ali b Wasim Akram	18	– lbw b Wasim Akram	1
S. G. Peall not out	11	– c Inzamam-ul-Haq b Wasim Akram	10
B 9, l-b 10, w 1, n-b 10	30	B 1, l-b 11, w 1, n-b 10	23
1/0 (1) 2/102 (3) 3/110 (4) 4/126 (5) 5/131 (6) 6/203 (7) 7/203 (2) 8/204 (8) 9/225 (9) 10/254 (10)	254	1/0 (1) 2/135 (3) 3/140 (4) 4/144 (5) 5/147 (6) 6/152 (7) 7/153 (8) 8/164 (9) 9/168 (10) 10/187 (11)	187

Bowling: *First Innings*—Wasim Akram 21–4–68–2; Waqar Younis 19–3–88–5; Ata-ur-Rehman 14–4–40–1; Ashfaq Ahmed 17–8–31–2; Aamir Sohail 3–0–8–0. *Second Innings*—Wasim Akram 23.2–3–65–5; Waqar Younis 21–4–50–4; Ata-ur-Rehman 8–1–22–1; Ashfaq Ahmed 6–1–22–0; Shoaib Mohammad 4–1–16–0.

Umpires: Javed Akhtar and Shakoor Rana. Referee: R. S. Madugalle (Sri Lanka).

PAKISTAN v ZIMBABWE

Third Test Match

At Lahore, December 16, 17, 18, 20, 21. Drawn. Toss: Zimbabwe. Test debut: W. R. James.

The final Test was ruined by fog and bad light, which kept the players off the field for just over eight hours. But a result might have been possible had the umpires and teams been more anxious to get on. The light was not always as bad as the umpires seemed to believe and, on the final day, Pakistan's batting was completely aimless. Even Zimbabwe, who were in the stronger position, showed no signs of urgency.

The hero of the first day and, as things turned out, the match, was the medium-pacer Brain, who took five wickets for 42 as Pakistan were all out for 147 within 52 overs after being asked to bat. In his first over, Brain had Aamir Sohail caught in the gully. Shoaib Mohammad and Inzamam-ul-Haq began to repair the damage but were dismissed within four balls and Pakistan went into lunch tottering at 60 for three. Javed Miandad and Basit Ali managed 53 for the fourth wicket but Brain then removed Basit, the normally reliable Asif Mujtaba without scoring, and Miandad himself after two hours. The rest put up little resistance.

Next day the mist descended, cutting 105 minutes from the morning and 25 in the evening. Zimbabwe advanced from 15 to 110, losing Dekker, Campbell and Grant Flower, all caught by Rashid Latif behind the wicket. Flower survived a blow on the helmet from Waqar Younis to make a painful, three-hour 30. A further 11 runs came in the 21 minutes possible on the third day. There was another late start after the rest day, even though it was sunny, and Zimbabwe lost four more wickets in taking the lead, but their captain, Andy Flower, batted for two and a half hours to take them to 230, with support from the tail. Waqar Younis wrapped up the innings with his 16th analysis of five or more wickets in 26 Tests.

Trailing by 83 runs, Pakistan reached 37 without loss overnight. After a further 45 minutes were lost on the final morning, Brain dismissed Sohail for the second time in the match, the signal for Pakistan to bat out the day. Shoaib and Mujtaba shared an unbroken stand of 118: Shoaib made a tortuous 53 in 315 minutes – one of the slowest fifties in Test history – and Mujtaba reached his own half-century at twice his partner's rate. Brain's brave first-day effort was all but forgotten as the Test ended in stalemate.

Man of the Match: D. H. Brain.

Men of the Series: Pakistan – Waqar Younis; Zimbabwe – A. D. R. Campbell.

Close of play: First day, Zimbabwe 15-0 (G. W. Flower 10*, M. H. Dekker 2*); Second day, Zimbabwe 110-3 (D. L. Houghton 47*, A. Flower 10*); Third day, Zimbabwe 121-3 (D. L. Houghton 50*, A. Flower 15*); Fourth day, Pakistan 37-0 (Aamir Sohail 19*, Shoaib Mohammad 8*).

Pakistan

First innings		Second innings	
Aamir Sohail c Campbell b Brain	2	– c James b Brain	32
Shoaib Mohammad c Brandes b Rennie	14	– not out	53
Inzamam-ul-Haq b Brandes	33		
Javed Miandad lbw b Brain	31		
Basit Ali b Brain	29		
Asif Mujtaba c James b Brain	0	– (3) not out	65
†Rashid Latif c Houghton b Brandes	7		
*Wasim Akram not out	16		
Waqar Younis b Brain	0		
Mushtaq Ahmed b Brandes	1		
Ata-ur-Rehman c James b Rennie	0		
B 4, l-b 6, n-b 4	14	B 7, l-b 13, w 1, n-b 3	24
1/3 (1) 2/50 (2) 3/54 (3) 4/107 (5) 5/111 (6) 6/130 (4) 7/130 (7) 8/135 (9) 9/140 (10) 10/147 (11)	147	1/56 (1)	(1 wkt) 174

Bowling: *First Innings*—Brandes 14–3–45–3; Brain 15–3–42–5; Streak 12–3–28–0; Rennie 10.4–3–22–2. *Second Innings*—Brandes 16–5–31–0; Brain 14–6–28–1; Streak 16–4–216–4–25–0; Rennie 14–6–35–0; G. W. Flower 10–2–15–0; Whittall 10.5–4–17–0; Campbell 1–0–3–0; A. Flower 0.1–0–0–0.

Zimbabwe

G. W. Flower c Rashid Latif b Ata-ur-Rehman	30
M. H. Dekker c Rashid Latif b Wasim Akram	2
A. D. R. Campbell c Rashid Latif b Waqar Younis	6
D. L. Houghton c Rashid Latif b Waqar Younis	50
*A. Flower not out	62
G. J. Whittall c Asif Mujtaba b Wasim Akram	2
†W. R. James c Shoaib Mohammad b Waqar Younis	8
H. H. Streak b Waqar Younis	0
D. H. Brain c Aamir Sohail b Wasim Akram	28
E. A. Brandes lbw b Wasim Akram	9
J. A. Rennie c Rashid Latif b Waqar Younis	2
B 10, l-b 13, w 1, n-b 7	31
1/17 (2) 2/35 (3) 3/88 (1) 4/121 (4) 5/126 (6) 6/141 (7) 7/141 (8) 8/187 (9) 9/215 (10) 10/230 (11)	230

Bowling: Wasim Akram 32–7–70–4; Waqar Younis 34.4–9–100–5; Ata-ur-Rehman 13–6–24–1; Mushtaq Ahmed 5–1–13–0.

Umpires: Athar Zaidi and Khizar Hayat. Referee: R. S. Madugalle (Sri Lanka).

†PAKISTAN v ZIMBABWE

First One-Day International

At National Stadium, Karachi, December 24. Pakistan won by seven wickets. Toss: Pakistan.

Returning to their traditional venue in Karachi, Pakistan won with 6.1 overs to spare. Wasim Akram set up their victory with five wickets for 15, his best figures in one-day internationals; he had Zimbabwe's captain, Andy Flower, caught behind off the first ball of the match. Only Houghton and Dekker, who added 70 for the fourth wicket, offered much resistance as Zimbabwe were bowled out in 38 of the allotted 40 overs. Opener Saeed Anwar dominated Pakistan's reply with 68 from 61 balls, though he was dropped by Andy Flower off Brandes's second ball. A crowd of 22,000 enjoyed every moment as he took the tourists' attack apart; he hit seven fours and Pakistan needed only 18 more when he was bowled by Streak.

Man of the Match: Wasim Akram.

Zimbabwe

*†A. Flower c Rashid Latif b Wasim Akram	0
G. W. Flower b Aqib Javed	6
A. D. R. Campbell b Wasim Akram	8
D. L. Houghton c Basit Ali b Salim Malik	52
M. H. Dekker run out	33
G. J. Whittall run out	18
D. H. Brain b Aqib Javed	4
E. A. Brandes lbw b Wasim Akram	2
S. G. Peall b Wasim Akram	0
H. H. Streak c Javed Miandad b Wasim Akram	2
J. A. Rennie not out	3
B 1, l-b 9, w 3, n-b 2	15
1/0 2/19 3/22 4/92 5/117 6/128 7/131 8/131 9/139 (38 overs)	143

Bowling: Wasim Akram 7–1–15–5; Aqib Javed 8–1–21–2; Waqar Younis 7–0–43–0; Mushtaq Ahmed 8–1–21–0; Salim Malik 5–0–19–1; Asif Mujtaba 3–0–14–0.

Pakistan

Saeed Anwar b Streak	68
Asif Mujtaba b Brain	11
Inzamam-ul-Haq b Streak	12
Basit Ali not out	41
†Rashid Latif not out	10
L-b 2, w 2, n-b 1	5
1/18 2/48 3/126 (3 wkts, 33.5 overs)	147

Javed Miandad, Salim Malik, *Wasim Akram, Waqar Younis, Mushtaq Ahmed and Aqib Javed did not bat.

Bowling: Brandes 5–0–31–0; Brain 7–0–30–1; Peall 7–1–30–0; Streak 8–2–15–2; Rennie 6–0–32–0; Dekker 0.5–0–7–0.

Umpires: Amanullah Khan and Feroz Butt.

†PAKISTAN v ZIMBABWE

Second One-Day International

At Rawalpindi Cricket Stadium, Rawalpindi, December 25. Pakistan won by six wickets. Toss: Pakistan.

Pakistan claimed the series with their second win in two days, though they did not reach their target of 196 until the final over. Saeed Anwar and Asif Mujtaba gave them a comfortable start, with 88 for the first wicket. Dekker bowled Anwar and Basit Ali in quick succession but Mujtaba, dropped by Dekker on 45, proceeded serenely until he was out in the penultimate over with eight required. Zimbabwe had owed much of their 195 to Campbell and Houghton, who put on 102 for the third wicket; Campbell made 74 and Houghton, with a 49-ball fifty, became the first Zimbabwean to score 1,000 runs in one-day internationals.

Man of the Match: Asif Mujtaba.

Zimbabwe

*A. Flower lbw b Wasim Akram 14	G. J. Whittall not out 3
M. H. Dekker b Aamir Nazir 23	
A. D. R. Campbell b Wasim Akram . . . 74	
D. L. Houghton c Basit Ali b Waqar Younis . 58	L-b 12, w 9, n-b 2 23
D. H. Brain c Asif Mujtaba b Waqar Younis . 0	1/30 2/87 3/189 4/190 5/195 (5 wkts, 40 overs) 195

G. W. Flower, †W. R. James, E. A. Brandes, H. H. Streak and J. A. Rennie did not bat.

Bowling: Wasim Akram 8–0–32–2; Aamir Nazir 8–0–30–1; Aqib Javed 8–0–31–0; Waqar Younis 8–0–46–2; Salim Malik 7–0–37–0; Asif Mujtaba 1–0–7–0.

Pakistan

Saeed Anwar b Dekker 45	*Wasim Akram not out 6
Asif Mujtaba c Whittall b Streak 61	B 1, l-b 7, w 8 16
Basit Ali b Dekker 5	
Javed Miandad c Rennie b Brandes . . . 19	1/88 2/98 3/121 4/188 (4 wkts, 39.4 overs) 196
Inzamam-ul-Haq not out 44	

Salim Malik, †Rashid Latif, Waqar Younis, Aqib Javed and Aamir Nazir did not bat.

Bowling: Brandes 8–1–40–1; Brain 7–1–30–0; Rennie 7.4–0–38–0; Streak 7–0–31–1; G. W. Flower 3–0–15–0; Dekker 4–0–16–2; Campbell 2–0–9–0; A. Flower 1–0–9–0.

Umpires: Khalid Aziz and Siddiq Khan.

†PAKISTAN v ZIMBABWE

Third One-Day International

At Lahore, December 27. Pakistan won by 75 runs. Toss: Pakistan. International debut: Irfan Bhatti.

Pakistan completed a clean sweep in the one-day series when they dismissed Zimbabwe for 141. The tourists' pursuit of 217 in 40 overs began badly when 25-year-old medium-pacer Irfan Bhatti, making his international debut, dismissed both openers on 21. Campbell and Houghton tried to rally Zimbabwe but, once leg-spinner Mushtaq Ahmed removed them, the rest offered little defiance; occasional bowler Salim Malik picked up three for 22. Pakistan had been in the same precarious position, 61 for three, but they recovered through an entertaining stand of 127 between Inzamam-ul-Haq and Javed Miandad. Inzamam hit nine fours in an unbeaten 80 from 94 balls and Miandad made his 50th half-century – excluding his eight hundreds – in 228 limited-overs internationals.

Man of the Match: Inzamam-ul-Haq.

Pakistan

Saeed Anwar c James b Brandes 25	*Wasim Akram not out 17
Asif Mujtaba c James b Rennie 12	B 1, l-b 3, w 10, n-b 4 18
Inzamam-ul-Haq not out 80	
Basit Ali b Streak 9	1/41 2/42 3/61 4/188 (4 wkts, 40 overs) 216
Javed Miandad lbw b Streak 55	

Salim Malik, †Rashid Latif, Mushtaq Ahmed, Aqib Javed and Irfan Bhatti did not bat.

Bowling: Brandes 8–0–44–1; Brain 6–0–33–0; Rennie 8–0–53–1; Streak 8–0–32–2; Dekker 5–0–27–0; Whittall 4–0–18–0; Campbell 1–0–5–0.

Zimbabwe

*A. Flower c Aqib Javed b Irfan Bhatti 15
M. H. Dekker c Mushtaq Ahmed b Irfan Bhatti . 4
A. D. R. Campbell st Rashid Latif b Mushtaq Ahmed . 26
D. L. Houghton lbw b Mushtaq Ahmed 9
G. J. Whittall c Rashid Latif b Mushtaq Ahmed . 7
G. K. Bruk-Jackson st Rashid Latif b Salim Malik . 12
†W. R. James not out 14
D. H. Brain c and b Salim Malik 1
E. A. Brandes c Irfan Bhatti b Salim Malik . 7
H. H. Streak c Asif Mujtaba b Basit Ali 7
J. A. Rennie not out 12

B 4, l-b 9, w 11, n-b 3 27

1/21 2/21 3/61 4/66 5/79 6/88 7/91 8/101 9/117 (9 wkts, 40 overs) 141

Bowling: Wasim Akram 5–0–29–0; Irfan Bhatti 8–0–22–2; Aqib Javed 4–0–8–0; Mushtaq Ahmed 8–1–19–3; Salim Malik 8–1–22–3; Asif Mujtaba 4–0–11–0; Basit Ali 3–0–17–1.

Umpires: Iftikhar Malik and Ikram Rabbani.

ICC CODE OF CONDUCT – BREACHES AND PENALTIES IN 1993-94

V. G. Kambli India v Sri Lanka, 2nd Test at Colombo.
Dissent at dismissal. Severely reprimanded by P. J. P. Burge.

A. H. Jones New Zealand v Australia, 1st Test at Perth.
Dissent at disallowed appeal. Severely reprimanded by S. Venkataraghavan.

P. N. Kirsten South Africa v Australia, 3rd Test at Adelaide.
Dissent at team-mates' dismissals. Fined 25 per cent of match fee by J. L. Hendricks.
Dissent at dismissal. Fined 40 per cent of match fee by J. L. Hendricks.

M. G. Hughes Australia v South Africa, 1st Test at Johannesburg.
Abuse of batsman. Fined 10 per cent of match fee by D. B. Carr.

S. K. Warne Australia v South Africa, 1st Test at Johannesburg.
Abuse of batsman. Fined 10 per cent of match fee by D. B. Carr.

C. E. L. Ambrose West Indies v England, 4th Test at Bridgetown.
Demolished stumps when dismissed. Fined $US1,500 by J. R. Reid.

N. R. Mongia India v Australia, Austral-Asia Cup at Sharjah.
Dissent at disallowed appeal. Fined $US750 and suspended for one match by A. M. Ebrahim.

D. J. Nash New Zealand v Pakistan, Austral-Asia Cup at Sharjah.
Abuse of batsman. Fined $US350 by A. M. Ebrahim.

M. A. Atherton England v South Africa, 3rd Test at The Oval.
Dissent at dismissal. Fined 50 per cent of match fee by P. J. P. Burge.

P. S. de Villiers South Africa v England, 3rd Test at The Oval.
Dissent at disallowed appeal. Fined 25 per cent of match fee by P. J. P. Burge.

THE WEST INDIANS IN SRI LANKA, 1993-94

By DICKY RUTNAGUR

If ever a cricket tour proved a non-event, it was West Indies' whistle-stop visit to Sri Lanka, which featured the first-ever Test between the two. The tour was savaged by bad weather: only one of its five fixtures ran its full course. The Test match, which was riveting while it lasted, had less than 12 hours' play. The only other first-class match, at Galle, was even more abbreviated. Rain prevented a finish to the first one-day international and the third was turned into a 23-over match.

The Test match, very poorly attended, suffered from being staged in Moratuwa, 12 miles from Colombo, at the Tyronne Fernando Stadium, the most poorly appointed of the four venues in Greater Colombo. The stadium is named after the President of the Sri Lankan cricket board, who also happens to be a cabinet minister and MP for Moratuwa. The three one-day internationals were all favoured with venues in the city itself.

The most relevant shortcoming of the Moratuwa ground, laid on old pasture-land, was its inadequate drainage. This deficiency was emphasised more than once during the Test. After the first day's play was abandoned, the touring team went directly to the Sinhalese Sports Club ground in Colombo and had an extensive outdoor practice. They said afterwards that very nearly a full day's play would have been possible there. Again, on the last day, when not a ball was bowled despite bright sunshine, cricket was played all over Colombo in perfect conditions.

Considering how passionately Sri Lanka clamoured for Test status and, later, bemoaned the absence of incoming tours – due to political troubles – which held back their standards, it was jarring to observe how little they valued Test cricket. In fact, when the tour was first projected, it included a three-Test series. It was rearranged and shortened to accommodate the Hero Cup, a limited-overs competition in India in which both teams took part.

Judging by the tension between the sides in the only match played in its entirety, a longer or less disrupted tour could have been unpleasant. While Sri Lanka were successfully chasing runs under the floodlights of the Khettarama Stadium, the West Indians claimed that the captain, Ranatunga, when non-striker, prompted the umpires. Matters were brought to a head when Ranatunga, in a clear violation of the spirit of the game, took a run after a return from the field was deflected off his leg.

WEST INDIAN TOURING PARTY

R. B. Richardson (Leeward Islands) (*captain*), D. L. Haynes (Barbados) (*vice-captain*), J. C. Adams (Jamaica), C. E. L. Ambrose (Leeward Islands), K. L. T. Arthurton (Leeward Islands), K. C. G. Benjamin (Leeward Islands), W. K. M. Benjamin (Leeward Islands), A. C. Cummins (Barbados), R. A. Harper (Guyana), R. I. C. Holder (Barbados), C. L. Hooper (Guyana), B. C. Lara (Trinidad & Tobago), J. R. Murray (Windward Islands), P. V. Simmons (Trinidad & Tobago), C. A. Walsh (Jamaica).

Manager: D. A. J. Holford. *Cricket manager:* R. B. Kanhai.

WEST INDIAN TOUR RESULTS

Test match – Played 1: Drawn 1.
First-class matches – Played 2: Drawn 2.
Draws – Sri Lanka, Sri Lankan Board President's XI.
One-day internationals – Played 3: Won 1, Lost 1, No result 1.

Note: Matches in this section which were not first-class are signified by a dagger.

†SRI LANKA v WEST INDIES

First One-Day International

At P. Saravanamuttu Stadium, Colombo, December 1. No result. Toss: West Indies.

The ravages of overnight rain trimmed the game to 39 overs a side and dark clouds, which heralded another furious thunderstorm, brought about a premature finish. An indiscreet bouncer from Kenny Benjamin induced the umpires to offer the beleaguered Sri Lankan batsmen the light; they readily accepted, having been kept down to 16 runs in the first ten overs by the accuracy of Ambrose and Walsh, while losing the wicket of de Silva. Jayasuriya had been forced to retire with cramp. West Indies also found runs hard to get on a slow pitch. Lara was the exception: his drives and clips off the legs raced to the boundary despite an extremely heavy outfield; he hit eight fours in 118 balls.

West Indies

B. C. Lara c and b Jayasuriya 89
P. V. Simmons c Kalpage b Ratnayake. 11
*R. B. Richardson b Anurasiri 21
K. L. T. Arthurton not out 37
C. L. Hooper not out 13
L-b 15, w 9, n-b 2 26

1/33 2/121 3/154 (3 wkts, 39 overs) 197

J. C. Adams, R. A. Harper, †J. R. Murray, K. C. G. Benjamin, C. A. Walsh and C. E. L. Ambrose did not bat.

Bowling: Wickremasinghe 7–1–22–0; Ratnayake 7–1–37–1; Kalpage 8–0–37–0; Ranatunga 1–0–10–0; Anurasuri 8–1–26–1; Jayasuriya 7–1–40–1; de Silva 1–0–10–0.

Sri Lanka

R. S. Mahanama not out 10
S. T. Jayasuriya retired hurt 4
P. A. de Silva c Simmons b Walsh 2
*A. Ranatunga not out 11
L-b 6, w 1, n-b 1 8

1/16 (1 wkt, 12.1 overs) 35

H. P. Tillekeratne, R. P. A. H. Wickremaratne, R. S. Kalpage, †R. S. Kaluwitharana, R. J. Ratnayake, G. P. Wickremasinghe and S. D. Anurasiri did not bat.

S. T. Jayasuriya retired hurt at 13.

Bowling: Ambrose 5–2–4–0; Walsh 5–1–10–1; Benjamin 1.1–0–5–0; Hooper 1–0–10–0.

Umpires: B. C. Cooray and P. Manuel.

SRI LANKAN BOARD PRESIDENT'S XI v WEST INDIANS

At Galle, December 3, 4, 5. Drawn. Toss: West Indians.

Less than seven hours' play was possible, the last day being washed out. The West Indians used the game for batting practice. Hooper's innings was the highlight: his 89 included ten fours and three sixes. Chaminda Waas, a 19-year-old left-arm pace bowler, showed impressive stamina and control.

Close of play: First day, West Indians 93-1 (P. V. Simmons 30*, C. L. Hooper 53*); Second day, West Indians 278-6 (R. I. C. Holder 72*, J. R. Murray 0*).

West Indians

*D. L. Haynes c Wickremaratne b Vaas 10	R. A. Harper c Dassanayake b Hathurusinghe . 57
P. V. Simmons c Wickremaratne b Ratnayake . 31	†J. R. Murray not out 0
C. L. Hooper lbw b Gurusinha. 89	
J. C. Adams c Dassanayake b Gurusinha . 4	B 3, l-b 1, n-b 6 10
R. I. C. Holder not out 71	
K. L. T. Arthurton c Wickremaratne b Wijetunge . 7	1/14 2/97 3/127 4/139 5/165 6/279 (6 wkts) 279

W. K. M. Benjamin, A. C. Cummins and K. C. G. Benjamin did not bat.

Bowling: Vaas 24–13–35–1; Ratnayake 15–7–16–1; Gurusinha 13–6–26–2; Wijetunge 25–1–100–1; Hathurusinghe 6.5–2–26–1; Chandana 16–2–45–0; Atapattu 6–0–27–0.

Sri Lankan Board President's XI

U. C. Hathurusinghe, D. P. Samaraweera, A. P. Gurusinha, M. S. Atapattu, †P. B. Dassanayake, R. P. A. H. Wickremaratne, U. D. U. Chandana, *R. J. Ratnayake, S. Jayantha, P. K. Wijetunge and W. P. U. J. C. Vaas.

Umpires: L. V. Jayasundara and W. A. U. Wickremasinghe.

SRI LANKA v WEST INDIES

Test Match

At Moratuwa, December 9, 10, 11, 12, 13. Drawn. Toss: Sri Lanka. Test debut: D. P. Samaraweera.

The first-ever Test between the two countries was wrecked by the weather. Only 11½ hours' play was possible and there would have been less had the teams not agreed to forego the rest day after the scheduled first day was lost. The irony was that not a drop of rain fell during the hours of play and yet a full six hours was possible only on the second day. Not a ball was bowled on days four and five.

However, what little cricket the weather allowed was enthralling and eventful, and the low-scoring match was evenly poised when the last ball was bowled. The tone was set by a bald, turning pitch; West Indies, for the first time in five years, played two front-line spinners, Harper joining Hooper, as in the Sydney Test in 1988-89. Sri Lanka included four spinners and only one specialist seamer – Ranatunga had to share the new ball with Wickremasinghe.

The reading of the pitch proved accurate. The Sri Lankan spinners shared all ten wickets, with off-spinner Muralitharan claiming four. The West Indian pair were less successful, with only a wicket apiece among the three Sri Lanka lost in scoring 66 on the rescheduled opening day. They threatened on the second too, but were contained by the expertise, involving a fair measure of pad-play, of de Silva and Ranatunga. De Silva scored a brave 53, in 143 minutes, despite a badly swollen finger after his right hand was struck by a ball from Walsh that lifted abruptly from a length. So precise was his judgment of which balls to leave outside off stump that it seemed unjust when he played on trying to take his bat away from a short one from Benjamin, whose next delivery made Jayasuriya pay the penalty for aiming across the line. When a superb ball from Walsh cut away to find Ranatunga's edge, Sri Lanka were 130 for six. They recovered thanks to a defiant seventh-wicket stand between Kalpage and wicket-keeper Dassanayake. Once they were parted, Ambrose effortlessly demolished the tail, though earlier he had looked innocuous compared to Benjamin, who bowled tirelessly and extracted pace and bounce from an utterly dead pitch.

West Indies then took a slender 14-run lead, despite losing four for 84, owing everything to a fifth-wicket partnership between Richardson and Hooper. Richardson played circumspectly for 203 minutes, and Hooper, using his feet to combat the turning ball, batted in commanding fashion until he had almost run out of partners; the last six wickets went down for 36 runs. Richardson's dismissal, which started the collapse, was a curious one. Charging down the pitch to Kalpage, he was stumped by some distance, as the TV replay confirmed. Umpire Samarasinghe, at square leg, turned the appeal down, however, only for umpire Francis to rule the dismayed batsman caught behind.

Close of play: First day, Sri Lanka 66-3 (P. A. de Silva 29*, A. Ranatunga 6*); Second day, West Indies 99-4 (R. B. Richardson 26*, C. L. Hooper 9*); Third day, Sri Lanka 43-2 (H. P. Tillekeratne 9*, P. A. de Silva 15*); Fourth day, No play.

Sri Lanka

	First innings		Second innings	
R. S. Mahanama c Murray b Benjamin	11	– c Simmons b Benjamin		11
D. P. Samaraweera c Harper b Hooper	16	– run out		5
H. P. Tillekeratne c Lara b Harper	0	– not out		9
P. A. de Silva b Benjamin	53	– not out		15
*A. Ranatunga c Lara b Walsh	31			
S. T. Jayasuriya lbw b Benjamin	0			
R. S. Kalpage c Richardson b Ambrose	39			
†P. B. Dassanayake c Murray b Benjamin	18			
G. P. Wickremasinghe c Lara b Ambrose	0			
S. D. Anurasiri b Ambrose	1			
M. Muralitharan not out	1			
B 1, l-b 9, n-b 10	20	L-b 2, n-b 1		3
1/18 (1) 2/20 (3) 3/57 (2) 4/106 (4) 5/106 (6) 6/130 (5) 7/181 (8) 8/182 (9) 9/188 (7) 10/190 (10)	190	1/17 (1) 2/18 (2)	(2 wkts)	43

Bowling: *First Innings*—Ambrose 12.2–5–14–3; Walsh 21–6–40–1; Harper 24–12–36–1; Hooper 20–5–44–1; Benjamin 20–8–46–4; Arthurton 1–1–0–0. *Second Innings*—Ambrose 6–2–13–0; Walsh 9.1–4–20–0; Benjamin 6–5–5–1; Harper 1–0–3–0.

West Indies

D. L. Haynes lbw b Anurasiri	20
P. V. Simmons c Dassanayake b Kalpage	17
*R. B. Richardson c Dassanayake b Kalpage	51
B. C. Lara c Dassanayake b Muralitharan	18
K. L. T. Arthurton c Jayasuriya b Anurasiri	0
C. L. Hooper c Samaraweera b Muralitharan	62
R. A. Harper lbw b Jayasuriya	3
†J. R. Murray lbw b Anurasiri	7
W. K. M. Benjamin b Muralitharan	2
C. E. L. Ambrose not out	7
C. A. Walsh c Kalpage b Muralitharan	0
B 4, l-b 1, n-b 12	17
1/42 (1) 2/42 (2) 3/78 (4) 4/84 (5) 5/168 (3) 6/178 (7) 7/191 (8) 8/191 (6) 9/204 (9) 10/204 (11)	204

Bowling: Wickremasinghe 11–0–35–0; Ranatunga 4–1–6–0; Anurasiri 35–6–77–3; Kalpage 10–2–27–2; Muralitharan 15.5–4–47–4; Jayasuriya 3–0–7–1.

Umpires: K. T. Francis and T. M. Samarasinghe. Referee: Zaheer Abbas (Pakistan).

†SRI LANKA v WEST INDIES

Second One-Day International

At Khettarama Stadium, Colombo, December 16 (day/night). Sri Lanka won by three wickets. Toss: West Indies.

Sri Lanka pulled off only their second win in 18 limited-overs matches against West Indies with five balls to spare. A brave recovery was shaped by their captain, Ranatunga, who, after an unglamorous innings, improbably savaged Ambrose for 12 runs in the penultimate over to level the scores. Sri Lanka entered the last nine overs needing only 50. Then Cummins, moving the ball menacingly in the night air, took three wickets in two overs. Bowling under the floodlights proved a mixed blessing, however; the ball often swung too much, and West Indies gave away 18 wides. Earlier, Haynes and Lara made a rollicking start, with 128 from 26 overs, but the later batsmen were bogged down by the spinners.

Man of the Match: A. Ranatunga.

West Indies

D. L. Haynes c and b Anurasiri....... 51
B. C. Lara c Mahanama b Jayasuriya .. 65
P. V. Simmons c Wickremasinghe b Kalpage . 10
K. L. T. Arthurton not out........... 50
*R. B. Richardson b Kalpage......... 15
C. L. Hooper c Tillekeratne b Kalpage . 4
A. C. Cummins run out 1
†J. C. Adams lbw b Kalpage......... 0
W. K. M. Benjamin b Liyanage....... 11
C. E. L. Ambrose not out............ 2
L-b 9, w 9, n-b 2............ 20

1/128 2/136 3/155 4/184 5/194 6/195 7/195 8/223 (8 wkts, 49 overs) 229

C. A. Walsh did not bat.

Bowling: Wickremasinghe 8–0–40–0; Liyanage 8–0–36–1; Kalpage 10–0–45–4; Anurasiri 10–0–32–1; Ranatunga 2–0–16–0; Jayasuriya 10–0–41–1; de Silva 1–0–10–0.

Sri Lanka

R. S. Mahanama c Lara b Cummins... 18
S. T. Jayasuriya c Adams b Walsh 11
H. P. Tillekeratne b Hooper.......... 26
P. A. de Silva c Hooper b Cummins ... 51
*A. Ranatunga not out 66
R. S. Kalpage lbw b Cummins........ 1
†R. S. Kaluwitharana lbw b Cummins . 2
R. P. A. H. Wickremaratne b Ambrose 3
D. K. Liyanage not out.............. 11
B 4, l-b 9, w 18, n-b 10 41

1/26 2/40 3/120 4/180 5/187 6/189 7/208 (7 wkts, 48.1 overs) 230

G. P. Wickremasinghe and S. D. Anurasiri did not bat.

Bowling: Ambrose 9–0–49–1; Walsh 8.1–1–31–1; Cummins 10–0–33–4; Benjamin 10–0–50–0; Hooper 7–0–33–1; Arthurton 4–0–21–0.

Umpires: B. C. Cooray and K. T. Francis.

†SRI LANKA v WEST INDIES

Third One-Day International

At Sinhalese Sports Club, Colombo, December 18. West Indies won by six wickets. Toss: West Indies.

Heavy rain reduced the final contest to 25 overs a side – further curtailed by West Indies' inability to complete their quota in time. The pitch had sweated profusely and offered ample movement which Walsh exploited to capture the first three wickets and, though de Silva batted sensibly, Sri Lanka failed to recover. West Indies were cruising at first but the spinners put on enough pressure to raise the asking-rate to 35 in five overs. However, Arthurton struck a gigantic six over extra cover to ease the pressure and put West Indies on course for victory.

Man of the Match: K. L. T. Arthurton. *Man of the Series:* B. C. Lara.

Sri Lanka

R. S. Mahanama c Richardson b Walsh 10
S. T. Jayasuriya c Arthurton b Walsh .. 1
H. P. Tillekeratne b Walsh........... 6
P. A. de Silva c Ambrose b Simmons .. 34
*A. Ranatunga c Adams b Simmons ... 7
R. S. Kalpage not out 26
†R. S. Kaluwitharana not out......... 6
B 1, l-b 6, w 5, n-b 1 13

1/2 2/14 3/25 4/49 5/82 (5 wkts, 23 overs) 103

D. P. Samaraweera, D. K. Liyanage, G. P. Wickremasinghe and S. D. Anurasiri did not bat.

Bowling: Ambrose 5–2–12–0; Walsh 5–0–24–3; Benjamin 4–0–21–0; Cummins 4–0–15–0; Simmons 5–0–24–2.

West Indies

D. L. Haynes c Jayasuriya b Anurasiri	23	K. L. T. Arthurton not out	24
B. C. Lara b Jayasuriya	29		
*R. B. Richardson c Samaraweera b Jayasuriya	2	L-b 5, w 4, n-b 1	10
C. L. Hooper run out	4	1/42 2/58 (4 wkts, 22.1 overs)	107
P. V. Simmons not out	15	3/65 4/67	

†J. C. Adams, A. C. Cummins, W. K. M. Benjamin, C. E. L. Ambrose and C. A. Walsh did not bat.

Bowling: Wickremasinghe 4.1–0–20–0; Liyanage 3–1–16–0; Anurasiri 5–0–17–1; Kalpage 5–0–21–0; Jayasuriya 5–0–28–2.

Umpires: D. N. Pathirana and T. M. Samarasinghe.

THE COOPERS & LYBRAND RATINGS

Introduced in 1987, the Coopers & Lybrand Ratings (formerly the Deloitte Ratings) rank Test cricketers on a scale up to 1,000 according to their performances in Test matches. The ratings are calculated by computer and take into account playing conditions, the quality of the opposition and the result of the matches. A player cannot get a full rating until he has played 20 innings or taken 50 wickets in Tests.

The leading 30 batsmen and bowlers in the Ratings after the 1993-94 series between Sri Lanka and Pakistan which ended on August 28 were:

	Batsmen	*Rating*		*Bowlers*	*Rating*
1.	B. C. Lara (*WI*)	871	1.	Waqar Younis (*Pak.*)	904
2.	S. R. Tendulkar (*Ind.*)	762	2.	C. E. L. Ambrose (*WI*)	903
3.	D. C. Boon (*Aus.*)	749	3.	S. K. Warne (*Aus.*)	876
4.	D. L. Haynes (*WI*)	734	4.	A. Kumble (*Ind.*)	861
5.	Inzamam-ul-Haq (*Pak.*)	718	5.	Wasim Akram (*Pak.*)	791
6.	S. R. Waugh (*Aus.*)	717	6.	A. A. Donald (*SA*)	713
7.	A. J. Stewart (*Eng.*)	709	7.	C. J. McDermott (*Aus.*)	634
8.	R. B. Richardson (*WI*)	698	8.	M. G. Hughes (*Aus.*)	631
9.	V. G. Kambli (*Ind.*)	689*	9.	A. R. C. Fraser (*Eng.*)	611
10.	G. A. Gooch (*Eng.*)	682	10.	P. A. J. DeFreitas (*Eng.*)	602
11.	M. D. Crowe (*NZ*)	681	11.	Kapil Dev (*Ind.*)	595
12.	M. A. Atherton (*Eng.*)	668	12.	W. K. M. Benjamin (*WI*)	592
13.	M. A. Azharuddin (*Ind.*)	666	13.	S. L. V. Raju (*Ind.*)	581
14.	N. S. Sidhu (*Ind.*)	654	14.	C. A. Walsh (*WI*)	571
15.	M. J. Slater (*Aus.*)	651	15.	M. Prabhakar (*Ind.*)	553
16.	Salim Malik (*Pak.*)	644	16.	M. Muralitharan (*SL*)	551
17.	G. P. Thorpe (*Eng.*)	643*	17.	K. C. G. Benjamin (*WI*)	522†
18.	G. A. Hick (*Eng.*)	639	18.	T. B. A. May (*Aus.*)	520
19.	H. P. Tillekeratne (*SL*)	618	19.	D. E. Malcolm (*Eng.*)	519
20.	M. A. Taylor (*Aus.*)	612	20.	D. K. Morrison (*NZ*)	506
21.	M. E. Waugh (*Aus.*)	611	21.	C. R. Matthews (*SA*)	486†
22.	Shoaib Mohammad (*Pak.*)	609	22.	P. R. Reiffel (*Aus.*)	483†
23.	J. N. Rhodes (*SA*)	591	23.	K. P. J. Warnaweera (*SL*)	468†
24.	A. C. Hudson (*SA*)	590	24.	P. S. de Villiers (*SA*)	459†
25.	K. C. Wessels (*SA*)	577	25.	R. K. Chauhan (*Ind.*)	429†
26.	Basit Ali (*Pak.*)	574*	26.	B. M. McMillan (*SA*)	408†
27.	Javed Miandad (*Pak.*)	570	27.	Mushtaq Ahmed (*Pak.*)	401†
28.	P. A. de Silva (*SL*)	569	28.	P. C. R. Tufnell (*Eng.*)	394
29.	W. J. Cronje (*SA*)	566	29.	S. R. Waugh (*Aus.*)	388
30.	B. A. Young (*NZ*)	555*	30.	D. J. Nash (*NZ*)	378†

* *Signifies the batsman has played fewer than 20 Test innings.*

† *Signifies the bowler has taken fewer than 50 wickets.*

THE SOUTH AFRICANS IN AUSTRALIA, 1993-94

By STEVEN LYNCH

The success of South Africa's first tour of Australia for 30 years was assured at Sydney, when a young side – temporarily under the direction of Hansie Cronje, after an injury to the captain Kepler Wessels – pulled off a remarkable victory, dismissing Australia for 111 to win the Second Test by the slender margin of five runs.

That Sydney triumph had looked most unlikely from the first day, when South Africa slid to 169 all out, with Shane Warne taking seven wickets. On an indifferent pitch, Australia's 292 seemed to have insured them against defeat, and when South Africa were 110 for five a premature end was in sight. However, Jonty Rhodes organised the later order to stretch the lead into three figures. Australia's hopes of victory with a day to spare were dashed by the lively Fanie de Villiers, who reduced the home side to 63 for four that night. Next morning, Australia soon lost Allan Border, and from then on a crowd of around 12,000 – admitted free – held its collective breath as Australia inched towards the target. All looked lost at 75 for eight, but then Craig McDermott played a forthright innings – until last man Glenn McGrath popped a return catch to de Villiers, who took ten for 123 in the match, to ignite South African celebrations from Sydney to Soweto. Australian batsmen are supposed to be superstitious about 87 rather than "Nelson", but 111 had become the unlucky number of Australian cricket, with this collapse joining those against England at Melbourne and Adelaide in 1954-55, Sydney in 1978-79, and Headingley in 1981.

The euphoria of the historic Sydney victory outweighed an anticlimactic end to the tour, defeat in the one-day World Series finals being followed by a comprehensive reverse in the Adelaide Test. Despite this, the Test series was shared, mirroring the performance of South Africa's last two touring teams in Australia, in 1952-53 and 1963-64; the First Test had been ruined by unseasonal weather, which allowed little more than four hours' play over the first three days at Melbourne.

Wessels, returning to the country for which he played 24 Tests in the 1980s, was a reliable batting bulwark, although his effectiveness was reduced first by an old knee injury, and then, in the Sydney Test, a broken finger. His stirring response to the second injury was to promote himself two places in the batting order. His vice-captain, Cronje – at 24 the youngest player in the party – played several impressive innings and showed signs of maturing into a genuine Test No. 3. His form dropped off after he assumed the captaincy on Wessels's return home, and it was with some relief that he handed back the reins when the teams reconvened in South Africa – another month, another Test series.

Although opener Andrew Hudson was solid, South Africa had some problems with their middle-order batting. Daryll Cullinan – fresh from a record score of 337 not out at home – made a century against Queensland, but disappointed in the Tests, where he regularly failed to spot Warne's well-disguised flipper. Dave Callaghan was given few opportunities outside the one-day matches. When all-rounder Brian McMillan – another who struggled in vain to work out the wiles of Warne – injured his knee, the reinforcement was Western Province opener Gary Kirsten. A left-hander with a penchant for the cut, he looked limited at first but, given the encouragement of a regular place, blossomed, scoring South Africa's only century of the one-day series in the first final.

The Kirsten family completed a double after Wessels's injury, when Peter, Gary's 38-year-old half-brother, was summoned as an experienced replacement. He had an eventful time: he scored 97 in his first match, using a runner after injuring a hamstring, and later had his cheekbone broken by a McGrath bouncer. After plastic surgery, he returned just five days later for the one-day finals, which South Africa reached after some spirited efforts in their later matches. Then, in the Third Test, he was fined twice for dissent. But, overall, people thought South Africa needed a few more Kirstens. Rhodes overcame a broken finger to play some important innings, none more so than his rearguard 76 at Sydney, and his fielding was magnificent. The side's ground fielding, indeed, was good to watch, although an inordinate number of slip catches went down in the Tests, many of them through the hands of the luckless Cullinan.

Such is South Africa's current strength in fast bowling that they were able to shrug off the absence of injured left-armer Brett Schultz, who had topped the averages on the preceding Sri Lankan tour. The surprise was de Villiers, who had an undistinguished season with Kent in 1990. In Australia he proved the steadiest bowler at the death in the one-day games, and crowned his trip with ten wickets in the epic Sydney Test. Donald let rip at times – probably his fastest spell came in the rain-ruined First Test – but showed signs of being overbowled. The inconsistent Richard Snell – another with one indifferent county season (with Somerset) behind him – bowled well when the mood took him. Medium-pacer Craig Matthews bowled some tight spells, and looked likely to prosper on English pitches. Neither of the spinners looked genuinely Test-class. Dave Rundle had little opportunity – although he took four for 42 on his international debut – while his fellow off-spinner Pat Symcox, for all his bullish appealing, seemed unlikely to trouble good batsmen on good pitches. A big man with a prancing action, Symcox did contribute a long, steady spell at Sydney, and it should perhaps be borne in mind that Australia's off-spinner, Tim May, toiled through 107 overs in the Tests before taking a wicket. The wicket-keeping was in the safe hands of Dave Richardson; his ability left little scope for his deputy, Errol Stewart.

The South Africans showed that they had come to terms with the demands of Test cricket. When all their fast bowlers are fit – and when the batsmen do not have to face a bowler of the calibre of Warne – they will prove doughty opponents for any of the Test-playing nations. The Australians did not learn a great deal from the series. Warne was the pick of the bowlers but, in the absence of the injured Hughes, the pace attack looked limited, despite the raw promise of McGrath. Mark Taylor's 170 at Melbourne answered those critics anxious to find a place, at his expense, for the prolific Queenslander Matthew Hayden, while Michael Slater continued to show signs of genius, interspersed with some across-the-line hitting. Border, David Boon and Mark Waugh were all relatively quiet, but Steve Waugh – unfit for the first two Tests – returned to the fold with a scintillating 164 (and four for 26) at Adelaide, a one-off performance which, oddly, earned him the Man of the Series award.

SOUTH AFRICAN TOURING PARTY

K. C. Wessels (Eastern Province) (*captain*), W. J. Cronje (Orange Free State) (*vice-captain*), D. J. Callaghan (Eastern Province), D. J. Cullinan (Transvaal), P. S. de Villiers (Northern Transvaal), A. A. Donald (Orange Free State), A. C. Hudson (Natal), B. M. McMillan (Western Province), C. R. Matthews (Western Province), J. N. Rhodes (Natal), D. J. Richardson (Eastern Province), D. B. Rundle (Western Province), R. P. Snell (Transvaal), E. L. R. Stewart (Natal), P. L. Symcox (Natal).

G. Kirsten (Western Province) joined the tour as cover when McMillan was injured; P. N. Kirsten (Border) replaced Wessels after the Sydney Test.

Manager: R. Muzzell. *Coach:* M. J. Procter.

TOUR RESULTS

Test matches – Played 3: Won 1, Lost 1, Drawn 1.
First-class matches – Played 5: Won 1, Lost 2, Drawn 2.
Win – Australia.
Losses – Australia, Victoria.
Draws – Australia, Queensland.
One-day internationals – Played 11: Won 4, Lost 6, No result 1. *Wins* – Australia (3), New Zealand. *Losses* – Australia (4), New Zealand (2). *No result* – New Zealand.
Other non first-class match – Lost v Prime Minister's XI.

TEST MATCH AVERAGES

AUSTRALIA – BATTING

	T	*I*	*NO*	*R*	*HS*	*100s*	*Avge*	*Ct/St*
M. A. Taylor	3	5	0	304	170	1	60.80	4
M. J. Slater	3	5	0	185	92	0	37.00	0
D. C. Boon	3	5	0	156	50	0	31.20	1
A. R. Border	3	5	0	146	84	0	29.20	1
D. R. Martyn	2	3	0	73	59	0	24.33	0
M. E. Waugh	3	5	0	116	84	0	23.20	4
I. A. Healy	3	5	2	41	19	0	13.66	6/1
S. K. Warne	3	4	1	16	11	0	5.33	2

Played in three Tests: C. J. McDermott 6, 29*; T. B. A. May 8*, 0 (1 ct). Played in two Tests: P. R. Reiffel 32*, 2* (1 ct). Played in one Test: G. D. McGrath 9, 1; S. R. Waugh 164, 1 (1 ct).

* *Signifies not out.*

BOWLING

	O	*M*	*R*	*W*	*BB*	*5W/i*	*Avge*
S. R. Waugh	24	10	30	4	4-26	0	7.50
S. K. Warne	175.1	63	307	18	7-56	2	17.05
C. J. McDermott	115.1	33	246	14	4-33	0	17.57

Also bowled: A. R. Border 7–4–9–0; G. D. McGrath 33–8–62–2; T. B. A. May 117–41–228–2; P. R. Reiffel 47–12–106–1; M. E. Waugh 18–6–30–1.

SOUTH AFRICA – BATTING

	T	*I*	*NO*	*R*	*HS*	*100s*	*Avge*	*Ct*
K. C. Wessels	2	3	1	84	63*	0	42.00	0
J. N. Rhodes	3	5	2	124	76*	0	41.33	3
A. C. Hudson	3	5	1	157	90	0	39.25	2
G. Kirsten	3	5	0	174	67	0	34.80	2
W. J. Cronje	3	5	0	153	71	0	30.60	1
P. S. de Villiers	3	4	0	54	30	0	13.50	2
D. J. Richardson	3	4	0	44	24	0	11.00	10
A. A. Donald	3	4	3	11	10	0	11.00	0
D. J. Cullinan	3	5	0	26	10	0	5.20	0

Played in two Tests: C. R. Matthews 0, 4; P. L. Symcox 7, 4. Played in one Test: P. N. Kirsten 79, 42; B. M. McMillan 2, 4; R. P. Snell 10, 1 (1 ct).

* *Signifies not out.*

BOWLING

	O	*M*	*R*	*W*	*BB*	*5W/i*	*Avge*
P. S. de Villiers	132.3	37	311	11	6-43	1	28.27
A. A. Donald	127.2	26	373	13	4-83	0	28.69
B. M. McMillan	41	3	122	4	3-89	0	30.50
P. L. Symcox	72.5	17	153	4	2-49	0	38.25
C. R. Matthews	58	21	121	3	3-68	0	40.33

Also bowled: W. J. Cronje 28–8–66–0; G. Kirsten 23–8–62–1; P. N. Kirsten 4–0–17–0; R. P. Snell 31–9–82–2.

SOUTH AFRICAN AVERAGES – FIRST-CLASS MATCHES

BATTING

	M	*I*	*NO*	*R*	*HS*	*100s*	*Avge*	*Ct/St*
A. C. Hudson	4	7	1	273	105	1	45.50	2
W. J. Cronje	5	9	0	357	145	1	39.66	2
J. N. Rhodes	4	7	2	191	76*	0	38.20	3
G. Kirsten	4	7	0	207	67	0	29.57	2
K. C. Wessels	4	7	1	164	63*	0	27.33	2
C. R. Matthews	4	5	2	61	42*	0	20.33	0
D. J. Cullinan	4	7	0	139	113	1	19.85	0
D. B. Rundle	2	4	1	52	29	0	17.33	2
D. J. Callaghan	2	4	1	52	24*	0	17.33	3
B. M. McMillan	2	4	0	67	55	0	16.75	1
P. S. de Villiers	4	5	1	56	30	0	14.00	2
D. J. Richardson	4	6	0	77	26	0	12.83	13/2
P. L. Symcox	3	4	0	44	18	0	11.00	1
R. P. Snell	2	4	0	42	16	0	10.50	1
A. A. Donald	5	6	3	22	10	0	7.33	0

Played in one match: P. N. Kirsten 79, 42; E. L. R. Stewart 7, 6 (3 ct).

* *Signifies not out.*

BOWLING

	O	*M*	*R*	*W*	*BB*	*5W/i*	*Avge*
B. M. McMillan....	53.1	5	148	7	3-26	0	21.14
P. S. de Villiers	169.4	44	398	16	6-43	1	24.87
C. R. Matthews....	112	33	257	8	3-68	0	32.12
A. A. Donald......	193.1	39	552	17	4-83	0	32.47
D. B. Rundle	66	13	180	5	3-51	0	36.00
P. L. Symcox	92.5	21	209	5	2-49	0	41.80

Also bowled: D. J. Callaghan 7–1–20–1; W. J. Cronje 38–10–96–0; G. Kirsten 32–8–99–3; P. N. Kirsten 4–0–17–0; R. P. Snell 61–13–168–3.

Note: Matches in this section which were not first-class are signified by a dagger.

†At Canberra, December 2. Prime Minister's XI won by four runs. Toss: Prime Minister's XI 156 for eight (42 overs) (M. L. Hayden 42, R. T. Ponting 36; P. L. Symcox three for 23); South Africans 152 (42 overs) (W. J. Cronje 60).

VICTORIA v SOUTH AFRICANS

At Melbourne, December 4, 5, 6, 7. Victoria won by six wickets. Toss: Victoria.

The South Africans' first first-class match in Australia for 30 years brought defeat against Victoria, for whom fast-medium bowler Fleming and 19-year-old leg-spinner Howard had decisive spells. The tourists also lost McMillan who, after top-scoring with 55 in their first innings, was on a hat-trick when he tore a knee ligament. He slipped on the treacherous run-ups, which, like the rest of the outfield, were in a sorry state after recent pop concerts by U2 and Madonna. McMillan needed surgery and missed the first two Tests. The ninth-wicket pair, Matthews and Rundle, had contributed the South Africans' highest stand and Victoria too were indebted to an unbeaten ninth-wicket stand of 101 between Fleming and Howard – after they had lost five wickets for 11 runs. Only Rhodes, with 59, made much of Howard's leg-spin second time around. Next morning Victoria needed only 33.1 overs to score 110 for victory.

Close of play: First day, Victoria 5-0 (W. N. Phillips 4*, D. J. Ramshaw 1*); Second day, Victoria 260-8 (D. W. Fleming 29*, C. Howard 8*); Third day, South Africans 168-9 (D. B. Rundle 14*).

South Africans

*K. C. Wessels c Dodemaide b Fleming	16	– (2) c Berry b Fleming	32
W. J. Cronje b Cook	41	– (1) run out	3
B. M. McMillan b Fleming	55	– (10) c Berry b Howard	6
J. N. Rhodes c Jones b Fleming	8	– (3) c and b Howard	59
D. J. Callaghan c Berry b Howard	20	– (4) c Herman b Hodge	8
†E. L. R. Stewart c Ayres b Cook	7	– (5) lbw b Howard	6
P. L. Symcox b Fleming	15	– (6) b Howard	18
R. P. Snell c Berry b Fleming	16	– (7) b Dodemaide	15
D. B. Rundle c Berry b Dodemaide	29	– (8) not out	14
C. R. Matthews not out	42	– (9) b Fleming	2
A. A. Donald b Fleming	6	– c Ramshaw b Howard	5
B 2, l-b 4	6	B 4, l-b 5, n-b 1	10
1/39 2/87 3/101 4/128 5/140 6/156 7/178 8/185 9/249	261	1/3 2/59 3/90 4/97 5/130 6/131 7/145 8/147 9/168	178

Bowling: *First Innings*—Cook 15–3–43–2; Fleming 28–4–86–6; Dodemaide 15–3–47–1; Howard 32–10–79–1. *Second Innings*—Cook 11–1–36–0; Fleming 18–8–31–2; Dodemaide 12–4–34–1; Howard 24.5–9–42–5; Herman 8–2–24–0; Hodge 2–0–2–1.

Victoria

W. N. Phillips c Stewart b Snell	7	– (2) b Matthews 4
D. J. Ramshaw c sub (A. C. Hudson) b McMillan	71	– (1) c Rundle b Donald 41
*D. M. Jones c and b Symcox	38	– c sub (D. J. Cullinan) b Donald 34
B. J. Hodge c Stewart b Rundle	80	– not out 8
W. G. Ayres c McMillan b Rundle	9	– lbw b Matthews 0
R. J. Herman lbw b McMillan	1	– not out 4
A. I. C. Dodemaide lbw b Donald	2	
†D. S. Berry c Stewart b McMillan	0	
D. W. Fleming not out	54	
C. Howard not out	41	
B 7, l-b 17, n-b 3	27	B 10, l-b 5, w 1, n-b 3 19
1/9 2/79 3/185 4/218 5/219 6/219 7/219 8/229	(8 wkts dec.) 330	1/28 2/88 3/95 4/96 (4 wkts) 110

S. H. Cook did not bat.

Bowling: *First Innings*—Donald 23.5–6–59–1; Snell 24–4–65–1; Matthews 17–1–42–0; McMillan 12.1–2–26–3; Rundle 17–1–58–2; Symcox 20–4–56–1. *Second Innings*—Donald 11–4–22–2; Snell 6–0–21–0; Matthews 9.1–1–33–2; Cronje 4–1–12–0; Callaghan 3–1–7–0.

Umpires: D. W. Holt, L. J. King and W. P. Sheahan.

South Africa's matches v Australia and New Zealand in the Benson and Hedges World Series (December 9–December 18) may be found in that section.

QUEENSLAND v SOUTH AFRICANS

At Brisbane, December 20, 21, 22, 23. Drawn. Toss: South Africans.

The tourists warmed up for the First Test by having the better of this match, in which three of their batsmen made centuries. Cronje, who hit 19 fours and two sixes, and Cullinan put on 242 after they had slumped to 38 for three against Kasprowicz, who finished with five for 92. Only Law and Healy passed 20 as Queensland struggled to 183, conceding a lead of 152, but Wessels chose not to enforce the follow-on. A patient five-hour century from Hudson enabled Wessels to set his old state an unlikely target of 377. A sound opening stand of 116 between Foley and Barsby stopped thoughts of a South African victory: Barsby was eventually out for 99, trapped lbw by de Villiers, whose impressive display assured him of a first Test cap. Maher, in his second first-class match, reached his maiden half-century before stumps were drawn.

Close of play: First day, South Africans 297-4 (D. J. Cullinan 109*, D. J. Callaghan 4*); Second day, South Africans 1-0 (A. C. Hudson 0*, G. Kirsten 0*); Third day, Queensland 12-0 (G. I. Foley 7*, T. J. Barsby 4*).

South Africans

A. C. Hudson c Healy b Kasprowicz	11	– c Foley b McDermott 105
G. Kirsten c Healy b Rowell	9	– b Jackson 24
*K. C. Wessels c Foley b Kasprowicz	8	– c Love b Kasprowicz 24
W. J. Cronje c Maher b Jackson	145	– (6) st Healy b Border 15
D. J. Cullinan c Rowell b Kasprowicz	113	– lbw b Kasprowicz 0
D. J. Callaghan not out	24	– (4) lbw b Law 0
†D. J. Richardson lbw b Kasprowicz	7	– c Border b Foley 26
D. B. Rundle c Law b Kasprowicz	5	– c Rowell b Jackson 4
C. R. Matthews (did not bat)		– not out 13
P. S. de Villiers (did not bat)		– not out 2
L-b 1, n-b 12	13	L-b 4, n-b 7 11
1/24 2/29 3/38 4/280 5/306 6/324 7/335	(7 wkts dec.) 335	1/63 2/116 3/121 4/122 5/151 6/200 7/201 8/209 (8 wkts dec.) 224

A. A. Donald did not bat.

Bowling: *First Innings*—McDermott 24–4–58–0; Rowell 24–2–81–1; Kasprowicz 26–6–92–5; Jackson 22–3–72–1; Law 6–3–17–0; Maher 3–0–10–0; Foley 1–0–4–0. *Second Innings*—McDermott 9–2–26–1; Rowell 15–4–30–0; Kasprowicz 10–1–42–2; Jackson 26–8–67–2; Border 17–6–23–1; Law 7–0–22–1; Foley 4–1–10–1.

Queensland

T. J. Barsby c Callaghan b de Villiers	15	– (2) lbw b de Villiers	99
G. I. Foley st Richardson b Rundle	18	– (1) c Richardson b Donald	39
M. L. Love lbw b de Villiers	5	– c Richardson b Matthews	6
S. G. Law c Cronje b de Villiers	56	– c and b Callaghan	33
A. R. Border c Wessels b Rundle	6		
J. P. Maher c and b Rundle	1	– (5) not out	50
G. J. Rowell c Wessels b Kirsten	17	– (6) b de Villiers	16
*†I. A. Healy c Callaghan b Matthews	41	– (7) not out	5
M. S. Kasprowicz c Richardson b Matthews	2		
C. J. McDermott st Richardson b Kirsten	16		
P. W. Jackson not out	1		
L-b 2, n-b 3	5	B 4, l-b 9, n-b 7	20
1/17 2/25 3/56 4/85 5/90 6/111 7/158 8/160 9/177	183	1/116 2/139 3/171 4/210 5/262	(5 wkts) 268

Bowling: *First Innings*—Donald 11–0–43–0; de Villiers 15–3–34–3; Matthews 14.5–5–34–2; Rundle 23–9–51–3; Kirsten 5–0–19–2. *Second Innings*—Donald 20–3–55–1; de Villiers 22.1–4–53–2; Rundle 26–3–71–0; Matthews 13–5–27–1; Kirsten 4–0–18–0; Cronje 6–1–18–0; Callaghan 4–0–13–1.

Umpires: M. R. Jay, P. D. Parker and C. D. Timmins.

AUSTRALIA v SOUTH AFRICA

First Test Match

At Melbourne, December 26, 27, 28, 29, 30. Drawn. Toss: Australia. Test debuts: P. S. de Villiers, G. Kirsten.

The long-awaited first Test between these two teams since South Africa took the 1969-70 series 4-0 was ruined by bad weather. There was little more than two hours' play on each of the first and third days, and no play at all on the second, when some four inches of rain fell in Melbourne. With a draw certain, the later stages were of interest mainly to the statisticians, who were kept busy by Taylor. Playing in his 50th Test, he compiled 170 – his 12th Test century – in 495 minutes. He became the second batsman, after Martin Crowe of New Zealand, to score Test centuries against seven different countries, and also the first to score a hundred on debut against four (he had already achieved the feat against England, Sri Lanka and Pakistan). He also passed 1,000 Test runs in 1993.

Taylor's dismissal signalled the declaration and South Africa batted out the remaining time. Cronje scored 71 before becoming the last of leg-spinner Warne's 72 Test wickets in the calendar year 1993 – 13 short of Dennis Lillee's record of 85 in 1981. He put on 103 with Hudson before the latter retired hurt, shortly after being hit on the forearm by a shy at the stumps from Warne. Wessels, the first cricketer to play for and against Australia in Tests since W. E. Midwinter in 1881-82, and Rhodes completed another century stand – though Wessels was handicapped by a painful knee and Rhodes by a fractured finger.

Man of the Match: M. A. Taylor. *Attendance:* 48,565.

Close of play: First day, Australia 71-2 (M. A. Taylor 30*, D. C. Boon 4*); Second day, No play; Third day, Australia 140-3 (M. A. Taylor 63*, M. E. Waugh 11*); Fourth day, South Africa 59-1 (A. C. Hudson 35*, W. J. Cronje 3*).

Australia

M. A. Taylor b Symcox	170	†I. A. Healy not out	7
M. J. Slater c Kirsten b Donald	32	B 2, l-b 7, n-b 5	14
S. K. Warne lbw b de Villiers	0		—
D. C. Boon b Matthews	25	1/57 (2) 2/58 (3) (7 wkts dec.)	342
M. E. Waugh lbw b Matthews	84	3/127 (4) 4/296 (5)	
*A. R. Border c Richardson b Matthews	2	5/300 (6) 6/327 (7)	
D. R. Martyn b Symcox	8	7/342 (1)	

P. R. Reiffel, T. B. A. May and C. J. McDermott did not bat.

Bowling: Donald 30–4–108–1; de Villiers 32–6–83–1; Matthews 24–5–68–3; Cronje 13–4–25–0; Symcox 16.5–3–49–2.

South Africa

A. C. Hudson retired hurt	64	*K. C. Wessels not out	63
G. Kirsten c Taylor b Waugh	16	L-b 2, w 7	9
W. J. Cronje c Boon b Warne	71		—
D. J. Cullinan c Border b McDermott	0	1/49 (2) 2/157 (4) (3 wkts)	258
J. N. Rhodes not out	35	3/157 (3)	

†D. J. Richardson, P. L. Symcox, C. R. Matthews, P. S. de Villiers and A. A. Donald did not bat.

A. C. Hudson retired hurt at 152.

Bowling: McDermott 23–5–60–1; Reiffel 21–4–55–0; Waugh 12–3–20–1; May 28–7–58–0; Warne 31–8–63–1.

Umpires: D. B. Hair and T. A. Prue. Referee: J. L. Hendriks (West Indies).

AUSTRALIA v SOUTH AFRICA

Second Test Match

At Sydney, January 2, 3, 4, 5, 6. South Africa won by five runs. Toss: South Africa.

An Australian collapse reminiscent of Botham's Test at Headingley in 1981 – the eventual total of 111 was exactly the same – allowed South Africa to take an unexpected lead in the series after the home side had made most of the running. South Africa's unlikely hero was de Villiers, in only his second Test: he took ten wickets, and his second-innings six for 43 included the first four as Australia slumped to 56 for four before the end of the fourth day. By then they might well have been celebrating victory but for some late-order South African resistance organised by Rhodes, who came in at 107 for four and saw 132 added.

The last part of South Africa's stunning success was presided over by Cronje after Wessels broke a finger attempting a slip catch. The young deputy marshalled his troops well on the tense final morning, and his turn, throw and direct hit to run out Warne from wide mid-off was a devastating blow for Australia. The Australians, who brought in McGrath for Reiffel, had seemed to be in control from the first day, when only a second-wicket stand of 90 between Kirsten and Cronje stood in the way of another dazzling display of leg-spin variations from Warne. Two years to the day after his undistinguished Test debut, when he took one for 150 against India in Sydney, Warne swept away the middle order, finishing with seven for 56. The flipper accounted for Cullinan, Rhodes and Kirsten; Richardson and Matthews fell to classic leg-breaks which found the edge and curled to slip; Symcox was fooled by the massive behind-the-legs turner – and Wessels fell for the sucker punch, driving a full toss back to the bowler.

Slater made light of an untrustworthy pitch to score 92 and led Australia to 292, a lead of 123. Border, who passed Greg Chappell's record of 1,150 runs in Sydney Tests – and needed stitches after top-edging Symcox into his face – lasted four hours for 49, and Martyn contributed 59. There were four wickets apiece for Donald and de Villiers, while the burly off-spinner Symcox bowled 46 overs – 33 in one spell – without looking unduly threatening.

Wessels, despite his broken finger and a still-painful knee, came in at No. 4 to steady the tourists, but soon became the first of another five victims for Warne – the first time he had taken ten wickets in any match. South Africa lost five wickets before clearing the first-innings deficit, but Rhodes organised the tail to good effect, sharing stands of 72 with Richardson and 36 for the last wicket with Donald. His unbeaten 76 in 195 minutes included six fours and a hooked six off McDermott.

Needing only 117 to win, Australia looked to have shrugged off the early loss of Slater, reaching 51 before de Villiers rocked them with three wickets in five balls. South Africa felt victory depended on the quick removal of Border. They got their wish in the first over of the final day, when he played no shot at one from Donald which cut back and clipped his off bail. Waugh – leg-before to Donald's Waqar-like yorker – and Healy soon followed, as did Warne, needlessly run out. In came McDermott, a veteran of a similarly pulsating situation at Adelaide the previous season. He spanked four quick fours on his way to 29, the top score of the innings, but his partner Martyn's nerve failed after 106 minutes and six singles. He holed out to cover, and McGrath (whose first-innings nine represented the sum total of his first-class runs on his home ground) soon followed, sparking off emotional scenes in the South African dressing-room. UCBSA managing director Ali Bacher – who led his country to the 4-0 thrashing of Australia when the two last met in 1969-70 – called it "our finest achievement ever". It was their 12th victory in 55 Tests against Australia (who had won 29), but their ninth in the last 13, a sequence dating back to South Africa's last tour of Australia in 1963-64.

Man of the Match: P. S. de Villiers. *Attendance:* 107,587.

Close of play: First day, Australia 20-1 (M. J. Slater 5*, D. C. Boon 7*); Second day, Australia 200-5 (D. R. Martyn 15*, I. A. Healy 6*); Third day, South Africa 94-2 (W. J. Cronje 37*, K. C. Wessels 7*); Fourth day, Australia 63-4 (M. E. Waugh 4*, A. R. Border 7*).

South Africa

First innings		Second innings	
A. C. Hudson lbw b McGrath	0	– c Healy b McDermott	1
G. Kirsten st Healy b Warne	67	– b McDermott	41
W. J. Cronje c Waugh b McDermott	41	– b McDermott	38
D. J. Cullinan b Warne	9	– (5) lbw b Warne	2
J. N. Rhodes lbw b Warne	4	– (6) not out	76
*K. C. Wessels c and b Warne	3	– (4) b Warne	18
†D. J. Richardson c Taylor b Warne	4	– lbw b McGrath	24
P. L. Symcox b Warne	7	– c Healy b McDermott	4
C. R. Matthews c Taylor b Warne	0	– c Waugh b Warne	4
P. S. de Villiers c Waugh b McDermott	18	– lbw b Warne	2
A. A. Donald not out	0	– c Healy b Warne	10
B 1, l-b 4, n-b 11	16	B 13, l-b 1, n-b 5	19
1/1 (1) 2/91 (3) 3/110 (4) 4/133 (5) 5/134 (2) 6/141 (7) 7/142 (6) 8/142 (9) 9/152 (8) 10/169 (10)	169	1/2 (1) 2/75 (2) 3/101 (3) 4/107 (4) 5/110 (5) 6/182 (7) 7/188 (8) 8/197 (9) 9/203 (10) 10/239 (11)	239

Bowling: *First Innings*—McDermott 18.1–2–42–2; McGrath 19–5–32–1; Warne 27–8–56–7; May 10–1–34–0. *Second Innings*—McDermott 28–9–62–4; McGrath 14–3–30–1; May 22–4–53–0; Warne 42–17–72–5; Border 3–1–8–0.

Australia

First innings		Second innings	
M. J. Slater b Donald	92	– (2) b de Villiers	1
M. A. Taylor c Richardson b Donald	7	– (1) c Richardson b de Villiers	27
D. C. Boon b de Villiers	19	– c Kirsten b de Villiers	24
M. E. Waugh lbw b Symcox	7	– (5) lbw b Donald	11
*A. R. Border c Richardson b de Villiers	49	– (6) b Donald	7
D. R. Martyn c Richardson b de Villiers	59	– (7) c Hudson b Donald	6
†I. A. Healy c Richardson b Donald	19	– (8) b de Villiers	1
S. K. Warne c Rhodes b Symcox	11	– (9) run out	1
C. J. McDermott c Cronje b de Villiers	6	– (10) not out	29
T. B. A. May not out	8	– (4) lbw b de Villiers	0
G. D. McGrath b Donald	9	– c and b de Villiers	1
B 1, l-b 2, n-b 3	6	L-b 3	3
1/10 (2) 2/58 (3) 3/75 (4) 4/179 (5) 5/179 (1) 6/229 (7) 7/250 (8) 8/266 (9) 9/281 (6) 10/292 (11)	292	1/4 (2) 2/51 (3) 3/51 (4) 4/56 (1) 5/63 (6) 6/72 (5) 7/73 (8) 8/75 (9) 9/110 (7) 10/111 (11)	111

Bowling: *First Innings*—Donald 31.2–8–83–4; de Villiers 36–12–80–4; Matthews 28–11–44–0; Symcox 46–11–82–2. *Second Innings*—Donald 17–5–34–3; de Villiers 23.3–8–43–6; Matthews 6–5–9–0; Symcox 10–3–22–0.

Umpires: S. G. Randell and W. P. Sheahan. Referee: J. L. Hendriks (West Indies).

South Africa's matches v Australia and New Zealand in the Benson and Hedges World Series (January 8–January 25) may be found in that section.

AUSTRALIA v SOUTH AFRICA

Third Test Match

At Adelaide, January 28, 29, 30, 31, February 1. Australia won by 191 runs. Toss: Australia.

Australia squared the three-match series with a convincing win. The chief architect was Steve Waugh, playing his first match of the series after a hamstring injury kept him out of the first two. Waugh's 164, his seventh Test century, was the mainstay of Australia's impressive first-innings 469, which occupied most of the first two days. He hit 19 fours and shared a 208-run partnership for the fifth wicket with Border, who became the first man to score 11,000 Test runs during his five-and-a-half-hour 84, which included only three boundaries.

After Hudson and Gary Kirsten put on 100, South Africa's only resistance came from Peter Kirsten, whose 79 occupied 310 minutes. Peter Kirsten, drafted in since Wessels's departure, had an animated conversation with umpire Darrell Hair after three of his team-mates were given out lbw, and was fined 25 per cent of his match fee for his pains. Another outburst when he was leg-before himself in the second innings cost Kirsten a further 40 per cent of his match fee, as he became the first player to be found guilty of breaching the ICC Code of Conduct twice in the same match. A Johannesburg radio station launched an appeal to cover his fine. Meanwhile, Waugh followed his earlier century with four for 26, accounting for the middle order. Cronje, who became South Africa's second-youngest Test captain, aged 24 (Murray Bisset was 22 when he first took the job in 1898-99), had earlier fallen to Reiffel for a duck.

After South Africa narrowly avoided the follow-on, Australia embarked on an unimpressive search for quick runs, losing six wickets in scoring 124 from 40 overs. Border, in what was apparently his last innings in a home Test, was run out by the predatory Rhodes for four. South Africa's notional target of 321 in seven and a half hours soon became academic: during the 22 overs remaining on the fourth day, they slumped to 18 for three. But Australia's march to victory was held up by a heroic innings from de Villiers, as the night-watchman. He was on pain-killers after McDermott broke his thumb early on, but survived for three and a quarter hours before he drove distractedly to mid-off. "He couldn't take any more tablets because he would have begun to feel drowsy," said coach Mike Procter. With Peter Kirsten batting four and a half hours for 42, South Africa had hopes of forcing a draw, but the later batsmen collapsed, the last seven wickets going down for 29. Warne took his 100th wicket in his 23rd Test, despite tendinitis in his shoulder, while off-spinner May took his first of the series, in his 108th over. Wicket-keeper Healy made his 200th Test dismissal when a ball from McDermott flicked the upraised bat of the ducking Cullinan.

Man of the Match: S. R. Waugh. *Man of the Series:* S. R. Waugh. *Attendance:* 79,637.

Close of play: First day, Australia 240-4 (A. R. Border 28*, S. R. Waugh 32*); Second day, South Africa 39-0 (A. C. Hudson 17*, G. Kirsten 16*); Third day, South Africa 235-7 (P. N. Kirsten 52*, R. P. Snell 7*); Fourth day, South Africa 18-3 (P. N. Kirsten 1*, P. S. de Villiers 0*).

Australia

M. A. Taylor b G. Kirsten	62 – (2) b Snell	38
M. J. Slater c Rhodes b Donald	53 – (1) lbw b Donald	7
D. C. Boon c de Villiers b Donald	50 – c Hudson b McMillan	38
M. E. Waugh c Snell b McMillan	2 – c Richardson b Donald	12
*A. R. Border c Richardson b McMillan	84 – run out	4
S. R. Waugh c Richardson b Donald	164 – c Richardson b Snell	1
†I. A. Healy c Rhodes b McMillan	0 – not out	14
P. R. Reiffel not out	32 – not out	2
S. K. Warne not out	4	
L-b 9, n-b 9	18	L-b 7, n-b 1 8
1/83 (2) 2/152 (1) 3/159 (4) 4/183 (3) 5/391 (5) 6/391 (7) 7/464 (6) (7 wkts dec.)	469	1/23 (1) 2/79 (2) 3/91 (3) 4/99 (5) 5/103 (6) 6/109 (4) (6 wkts dec.) 124

C. J. McDermott and T. B. A. May did not bat.

Bowling: *First Innings*—Donald 38–7–122–3; de Villiers 41–11–105–0; Snell 19–6–44–0; McMillan 30–3–89–3; Cronje 9–3–21–0; G. Kirsten 23–8–62–1; P. N. Kirsten 4–0–17–0. *Second Innings*—Donald 11–2–26–2; McMillan 11–0–33–1; Cronje 6–1–20–0; Snell 12–3–38–2.

South Africa

A. C. Hudson lbw b S. R. Waugh	90 – c S. R. Waugh b McDermott	2
G. Kirsten c May b McDermott	43 – b Warne	7
*W. J. Cronje c Healy b Reiffel	0 – lbw b Warne	3
P. N. Kirsten c M. E. Waugh b Warne	79 – lbw b McDermott	42
J. N. Rhodes b S. R. Waugh	5 – (6) lbw b May	4
D. J. Cullinan b S. R. Waugh	10 – (7) c Healy b McDermott	5
B. M. McMillan lbw b S. R. Waugh	2 – (8) lbw b Warne	4
†D. J. Richardson lbw b McDermott	6 – (9) c Taylor b May	10
R. P. Snell c Healy b McDermott	10 – (10) c and b Warne	1
P. S. de Villiers run out	4 – (5) c Reiffel b McDermott	30
A. A. Donald not out	1 – not out	0
B 3, l-b 10, w 1, n-b 9	23	B 9, l-b 7, w 2, n-b 3 21
1/100 (2) 2/103 (3) 3/173 (1) 4/179 (5) 5/195 (6) 6/203 (7) 7/222 (8) 8/243 (9) 9/270 (4) 10/273 (10)	273	1/12 (1) 2/17 (3) 3/18 (2) 4/100 (5) 5/105 (6) 6/113 (4) 7/116 (7) 8/128 (9) 9/128 (8) 10/129 (10) 129

Bowling: *First Innings*—McDermott 27–9–49–3; Reiffel 15–4–36–1; May 25–9–57–0; Warne 44.2–15–85–1; M. E. Waugh 3–1–7–0; S. R. Waugh 18–7–26–4. *Second Innings*—McDermott 19–8–33–4; Reiffel 11–4–15–0; Warne 30.5–15–31–4; May 32–20–26–2; S. R. Waugh 6–3–4–0; Border 4–3–1–0; M. E. Waugh 3–2–3–0.

Umpires: D. B. Hair and T. A. Prue. Referee: J. L. Hendriks (West Indies).

THE SRI LANKANS IN INDIA, 1993-94

By R. MOHAN

For the second time the Sri Lankans came to the rescue when Pakistan cancelled their visit to India amid fears about security. The fact that they were soundly beaten in all three Tests, each time by an innings and inside four days, was somehow insignificant compared to the need to keep up these exchange tours in the Asian subcontinent.

The only real controversy, as in India's visit to Sri Lanka a few months earlier, was provoked by the umpiring. Sri Lankan manager Bandula Warnapura claimed the batting failures of the first two Tests owed as much to his players' nerves, waiting for the next bad decision, as to bad shots. But after the Third Test, in which the umpires avoided giving anyone lbw unless he was playing right back, captain Arjuna Ranatunga agreed that Sri Lanka had been beaten fair and square. The Sri Lankans were not the first side to disparage home umpiring, and probably not the last, even though these were the last Tests played with two local umpires rather than one local and one overseas umpire from the ICC's panel.

The series was played on the turning pitches – some might say doctored – on which India had built up an amazing record. Not even an Asian side, accustomed to such conditions, could resist the Indian Juggernaut, running on the wheels of wristy batsmanship and spiteful spin bowling. An eighth straight home win since the defeat of Sri Lanka in 1990-91, a second successive whitewash after beating England 3-0 in 1992-93, and only the second series in history in which a team won all three Tests by an innings (following England v West Indies in 1928), all pointed to India's apparent invincibility at home under Mohammad Azharuddin. Contrary to old theories that Indian Tests mean dull draws, this series meant that the last 12 matches, from Madras in 1987-88, had produced a win – 11 of them for India. Azharuddin joined Mansur Ali Khan (the Nawab of Pataudi, junior) and Sunil Gavaskar as India's most successful captains, with nine wins each. He was also the leading batsman in the series, with two centuries: his 152 in Ahmedabad was scored on a pitch so bad-tempered that only two other players reached 50.

The series attracted a fair audience – at least when India were batting. The one-day internationals, which India won 2-1, were unremarkable, but pulled huge crowds, defying the official capacity of the stadiums which staged them. The Indians were rewarded for such popularity, too; thanks to team sponsorship, their pay multiplied several-fold and was buttressed by performance bonuses.

Further cause for celebration came from the indefatigable all-rounder, Kapil Dev. He became Test cricket's highest wicket-taker on passing Sir Richard Hadlee's mark of 431, which had stood for three and a half years. Although he took 130 Tests, 44 more than Hadlee, Kapil played 65 of them at home, where he often had to grind it out on pitches far from helpful to seam bowling. With Anil Kumble, despite injuries to his bowling arm and fingers, ripping the Sri Lankan batting apart in the opening Test, there was little work for Kapil. It was on the firmer pitch in Bangalore that he picked up five wickets to close the gap, and the record – No. 432 – came in Ahmedabad, when Hashan Tillekeratne was caught at forward short leg. By then the tourists almost automatically displayed surprise at any decision. But umpire Narasimhan was delighted; thanks to Tillekeratne's refusal to walk, he had a chance to make history in his maiden Test.

The umpiring may have been unkind to the visitors in the First Test, where debutant umpire Sharma gave three of the top order out to questionable decisions. But that hastened defeat rather than causing it. The Sri Lankans were never able to control the flow of runs, allowing India to build up winning totals with plenty of time to bowl the opposition out. Ranatunga's only gambit was to ask slow left-armer Don Anurasiri to bowl to a negative line far beyond leg stump, with seven men on the on side. The Indian batsmen were wristily dismissive of such tactics and their spinners, Kumble, Venkatapathy Raju and Rajesh Chauhan, bowled far more positively in beguiling the Sri Lankans, while Manoj Prabhakar and Kapil used the new ball craftily.

Ironically, the Sri Lankans, who used to complain of their lack of international cricket, were jaded by a crowded programme. From August 1992, when Test cricket resumed on the island after five years, to December 1993, they played 13 Tests and 29 one-day internationals. On the third afternoon of the First Test they were 120 without loss, a strong position. They betrayed themselves with two ill-advised sweep shots, the first by Roshan Mahanama, their outstanding batsman of the tour. The woeful form of two other senior players, Ranatunga and his deputy Aravinda de Silva, was hardly likely to inspire confidence in the younger players. Of the main bowlers, only off-spinner Muttiah Muralitharan, who took 12 wickets, averaged less than 70. Asked when he expected his team to win a Test abroad, Ranatunga flippantly replied "when neutral umpires stand". But it was arguable which was more debilitating, Indian umpiring or Sri Lanka's suicidal batting.

SRI LANKAN TOURING PARTY

A. Ranatunga (Sinhalese SC) (*captain*), P. A. de Silva (Nondescripts CC) (*vice-captain*), S. D. Anurasiri (Panadura SC), M. S. Atapattu (Sinhalese SC), P. B. Dassanayake (Board Under-23 XI), U. N. K. Fernando (Sinhalese SC), A. A. W. Gunawardene (Sinhalese SC), S. T. Jayasuriya (Colombo CC), R. S. Kalpage (Nondescripts CC), D. K. Liyanage (Colts CC), R. S. Mahanama (Colombo CC), M. Muralitharan (Tamil Union), K. R. Pushpakumara (Singha SC), D. P. Samaraweera (Colts CC), H. P. Tillekeratne (Nondescripts CC), G. P. Wickremasinghe (Sinhalese SC).

W. P. U. J. C. Vaas (Colts) replaced the injured Liyanage.

Manager: B. Warnapura. *Coach:* A. Polonowitta.

SRI LANKAN TOUR RESULTS

Test matches – Played 3: Lost 3.
First-class matches – Played 5: Lost 3, Drawn 2.
Losses – India (3).
Draws – Indian Board President's XI, Punjab.
One-day internationals – Played 3: Won 1, Lost 2.

TEST MATCH AVERAGES

INDIA – BATTING

	T	I	NO	R	HS	100s	Avge	Ct/St
M. Azharuddin	3	3	0	307	152	2	102.33	10
N. S. Sidhu	3	3	0	266	124	1	88.66	3
S. R. Tendulkar	3	3	0	244	142	1	81.33	2
Kapil Dev	3	3	1	99	53*	0	49.50	0
V. G. Kambli	3	3	0	144	82	0	48.00	1
S. V. Manjrekar	3	3	0	116	61	0	38.66	1
N. R. Mongia	3	3	1	76	44	0	38.00	7/2
M. Prabhakar	3	3	0	49	21	0	16.33	5

Played in three Tests: R. K. Chauhan 3, 9 (3 ct); A. Kumble 4, 15 (2 ct); S. L. V. Raju 5*, 1* (1 ct).

* *Signifies not out.*

BOWLING

	O	M	R	W	BB	5W/i	Avge
S. L. V. Raju	106.2	33	228	16	6-87	2	14.25
A. Kumble	136.3	36	317	18	7-59	1	17.61
R. K. Chauhan	93	34	181	10	3-8	0	18.10
M. Prabhakar	65.4	16	198	8	4-82	0	24.75
Kapil Dev	56.4	14	176	7	3-73	0	25.14

Also bowled: S. R. Tendulkar 4–1–7–0.

SRI LANKA – BATTING

	T	I	NO	R	HS	100s	Avge	Ct
R. S. Mahanama	3	6	0	282	73	0	47.00	1
H. P. Tillekeratne	3	6	0	179	80	0	29.83	2
M. Muralitharan	3	6	4	46	20*	0	23.00	1
P. B. Dassanayake	3	6	1	98	36	0	19.60	1
A. Ranatunga	3	6	0	107	29	0	17.83	2
R. S. Kalpage	3	6	0	96	63	0	16.00	3
D. P. Samaraweera	3	6	0	94	42	0	15.66	2
P. A. de Silva	3	6	0	70	17	0	11.66	0
G. P. Wickremasinghe	3	6	1	37	22	0	7.40	2
S. D. Anurasiri	3	6	0	27	7	0	4.50	0

Played in one Test: M. S. Atapattu 0, 0; S. T. Jayasuriya 22, 1; D. K. Liyanage 12, 23.

* *Signifies not out.*

BOWLING

	O	M	R	W	BB	5W/i	Avge
P. A. de Silva	23	5	50	3	3-50	0	16.66
M. Muralitharan	143.2	20	420	12	5-162	1	35.00
G. P. Wickremasinghe	76	12	290	4	2-108	0	72.50
S. D. Anurasiri	131	18	380	5	2-75	0	76.00

Also bowled: S. T. Jayasuriya 8–2–26–0; R. S. Kalpage 48–5–122–0; D. K. Liyanage 17–6–55–1; A. Ranatunga 15–3–30–0.

Note: Matches in this section which were not first-class are signified by a dagger.

INDIAN BOARD PRESIDENT'S XI v SRI LANKANS

At New Delhi, January 13, 14, 15. Drawn. Toss: Sri Lankans.

With no play on the first two days, the warm-up fixture became a five-hour farce, in which the touring batsmen fared poorly. In fact they had almost lost the match on the second day; the umpires threatened to award it to the home team when Sri Lankan captain Ranatunga and his deputy de Silva left the ground without informing them. They had to rush back to apologise. Sri Lankan wickets fell frequently after an opening stand of 60. With nine down, they declared, and managed to take one themselves.

Close of play: First day, No play; Second day, No play.

Sri Lankans

R. S. Mahanama lbw b P. S. Vaidya	39
D. P. Samaraweera c A. Vaidya b P. S. Vaidya	25
H. P. Tillekeratne lbw b Bhupinder Singh, sen.	28
P. A. de Silva c Puri b Hirwani	7
S. T. Jayasuriya c Puri b Hirwani	2
M. S. Atapattu b Hirwani	19
R. S. Kalpage c Kapoor b Bhupinder Singh, sen.	0
*A. Ranatunga c P. S. Vaidya b Chatterjee	24
†P. B. Dassanayake not out	4
G. P. Wickremasinghe b Hirwani	5
B 1, l-b 1, n-b 2	4
1/60 2/71 3/78 4/83 5/105 6/105 7/131 8/151 9/157 (9 wkts dec.)	157

K. R. Pushpakumara did not bat.

Bowling: Bhupinder Singh, sen. 11–4–28–2; Prasad 12–4–25–0; Hirwani 14–2–49–4; P. S. Vaidya 10–2–32–2; Kapoor 1–0–13–0; Chatterjee 3–1–8–1.

Indian Board President's XI

A. R. Kapoor c Jayasuriya b Wickremasinghe	17
Vikram Rathore not out	11
R. Puri not out	4
W 1, n-b 1	2
1/30 (1 wkt)	34

Saurav C. Ganguly, *R. S. Dravid, †A. Vaidya, U. Chatterjee, Bhupinder Singh, sen., B. K. V. Prasad, P. S. Vaidya and N. D. Hirwani did not bat.

Bowling: Wickremasinghe 3.3–0–17–1; Pushpakumara 3–1–17–0.

Umpires: K. Parthasarathy and R. C. Sharma.

INDIA v SRI LANKA

First Test Match

At K. D. Singh "Babu" Stadium, Lucknow, January 18, 19, 20, 22. India won by an innings and 119 runs. Toss: India. Test debut: N. R. Mongia.

The tourists were hardly prepared for the perils of Test cricket in India – pitches tailored for spin bowling and batsmen adept at piling runs up on them. The home team's start, however, was uninspiring. The openers struggled to find their rhythm against Wickremasinghe, who bowled his heart out on a desperately slow pitch at the world's 72nd Test ground. Not until mid-afternoon, when the assured Tendulkar helped place conditions in perspective, did India resemble the side so used to dominating visiting teams. Sidhu, flowering during a 121-run stand with Tendulkar, was particularly severe on off-spinner Muralitharan, striking him for six of his eight sixes – two hits short of Walter Hammond's

Test record of ten sixes against New Zealand in 1932-33. Despite this rough treatment, the bowler never lost heart and was rewarded when Sidhu holed out, failing to clear the fence at long-on. Another century stand, between Tendulkar and Azharuddin, sent India soaring towards 511, the kind of total to prompt early thoughts of an innings victory. Yet Sri Lanka seemed to be ruling out such a possibility as Mahanama, elegantly, and Samaraweera kept the Indians at bay, taking their stand to 120. Kumble looked desperate as he tried to tempt Mahanama into sweeping, but the batsman fell for it, providing the breakthrough for India and a first catch for their new wicket-keeper, Nayan Mongia. In the very next over Samaraweera swept in front of the stumps and missed.

Suddenly the floodgates were open, and the rest of the Test became a procession of batsmen. Given the Sri Lankans' propensity to commit themselves to shots even when plagued by doubt, it did not take the spinners long to finish the job. Though three of the top order suspected they were victims of a trigger-happy debutant umpire – Sharma – the visitors were incapable of recovering from such blows. Their second innings subsided so quickly that the fifth day was not required. Kumble, only modestly successful by his own standards with four first-innings wickets, was irresistible in the second. He returned Test-best figures of seven for 59 and his first haul of ten or more in a Test with 11 for 128. This feat he achieved even though his spinning finger had been battered out of shape, through an injury sustained while batting in an earlier game, and though the webbing of his bowling hand had been damaged in the field.

Man of the Match: A. Kumble.

Close of play: First day, India 269-3 (S. R. Tendulkar 88*, M. Azharuddin 20*); Second day, India 511; Third day, Sri Lanka 197-7 (D. K. Liyanage 6*, S. D. Anurasiri 2*).

India

Batsman	Runs
M. Prabhakar lbw b Liyanage	21
N. S. Sidhu c Kalpage b Muralitharan	124
V. G. Kambli run out	5
S. R. Tendulkar c Samaraweera b Anurasiri	142
*M. Azharuddin c Tillekeratne b Anurasiri	47
S. V. Manjrekar c and b Muralitharan	61
Kapil Dev c Wickremasinghe b Muralitharan	42
†N. R. Mongia c Samaraweera b Muralitharan	44
A. Kumble b Wickremasinghe	4
R. K. Chauhan c Tillekeratne b Muralitharan	3
S. L. V. Raju not out	5
L-b 3, w 2, n-b 8	13
1/63 (1) 2/84 (3) 3/205 (2) 4/347 (4) 5/370 (5) 6/446 (6) 7/459 (7) 8/482 (9) 9/501 (10) 10/511 (8)	511

Bowling: Wickremasinghe 20–3–84–1; Liyanage 17–6–55–1; Ranatunga 3–2–1–0; Anurasiri 58–13–147–2; Kalpage 22–2–59–0; Muralitharan 41.5–3–162–5.

Sri Lanka

First innings	Runs	Second innings	Runs
R. S. Mahanama c Mongia b Kumble	73	c Azharuddin b Kumble	45
D. P. Samaraweera lbw b Chauhan	42	lbw b Kumble	12
H. P. Tillekeratne c Mongia b Kumble	7	c Prabhakar b Kumble	47
P. A. de Silva c Azharuddin b Kumble	13	b Kumble	11
*A. Ranatunga c Chauhan b Raju	9	c Mongia b Kumble	0
R. S. Kalpage c Azharuddin b Kumble	2	c Kumble b Raju	2
†P. B. Dassanayake st Mongia b Raju	36	b Prabhakar	15
D. K. Liyanage lbw b Prabhakar	12	c Mongia b Chauhan	23
S. D. Anurasiri b Prabhakar	2	lbw b Kumble	4
G. P. Wickremasinghe lbw b Kapil Dev	6	not out	0
M. Muralitharan not out	9	b Kumble	0
L-b 7	7	B 5, l-b 6, w 4	15
1/120 (1) 2/120 (2) 3/132 (3) 4/149 (5) 5/149 (4) 6/158 (6) 7/191 (7) 8/197 (9) 9/208 (10) 10/218 (8)	218	1/29 (2) 2/100 (1) 3/109 (3) 4/109 (5) 5/122 (6) 6/122 (4) 7/162 (7) 8/174 (8) 9/174 (9) 10/174 (11)	174

Bowling: *First Innings*—Prabhakar 16.4–7–36–2; Kapil Dev 10–3–27–1; Raju 20–10–25–2; Kumble 37–10–69–4; Chauhan 23–7–54–1. *Second Innings*—Prabhakar 16–3–38–1; Kapil Dev 3–0–8–0; Raju 14–5–28–1; Kumble 27.3–9–59–7; Chauhan 13–2–30–1.

Umpires: R. C. Sharma and S. Venkataraghavan. Referee: E. D. Weekes (West Indies).

INDIA v SRI LANKA

Second Test Match

At Bangalore, January 26, 27, 29, 30. India won by an innings and 95 runs. Toss: India.

India assumed control of the Test soon after Azharuddin came back from the toss with a smile on his face. He was still smiling four days later when he handed over his own Man-of-the-Match award to Kapil Dev, who had equalled Sir Richard Hadlee's record of 341 Test wickets. The pitch was certain to deteriorate once it lost its firm-looking surface, but for the first two days it allowed the ball to come on to the bat, ideal conditions for the Indian batsmen. It was a matter of surprise, then, that three top-order Indian batsmen failed to pass the century mark after looking in command. Only Azharuddin held his nerve, though Sidhu came close enough before succumbing to the Nervous Nineties in bizarre fashion, given out leg-before, while running what he believed was the vital single to give him his second hundred in the series. Sidhu had already been dismissed on 97 and 98 in Tests. Tendulkar, who had cornered the honours on the first day, cracking the bowling at will to get to 90, was strangely subdued on the second morning; he added only six before he aimed an inventive off-glide, missed and was bowled. Azharuddin finally unravelled the mystery, giving himself plenty of time to get to his 13th Test century. A brisk fifty from Kapil Dev, off 68 balls, speeded up the declaration.

Sri Lanka, up against another total well past 500, began on a poor note, losing Samaraweera and, worse, de Silva, a victim of the hook trap set especially for him, on the second evening. The back of the Sri Lankan resistance was broken quickly next day after another classy effort by Mahanama, who batted for just over 100 minutes, a feat seemingly beyond the rest. Most of the wickets were taken by the Indian seamers, Prabhakar and Kapil Dev, which demonstrated how firm this pitch was compared to Lucknow, where Kapil bowled very little.

By the time they followed on, the Sri Lankans seemed to want to get the match over as soon as possible, like a patient undergoing painful surgery. Support spinners Raju and Chauhan undid the top order, while Kumble picked the rest off; Sri Lanka ended the third day still 131 behind with only three wickets left. Given the state of the match on the fourth morning, Azharuddin could instruct Kumble to bowl wide of the stumps, in order to leave Kapil enough batsmen to get near Hadlee's record. Kapil drew level when he had Anurasiri caught at slip; he broke down as the emotions of the moment overwhelmed him and months of tension were washed away. The wicket also completed India's victory in the Test and the series.

Man of the Match: M. Azharuddin.

Close of play: First day, India 339-3 (S. R. Tendulkar 90*, M. Azharuddin 32*); Second day, Sri Lanka 59-2 (R. S. Mahanama 25*, A. Ranatunga 11*); Third day, Sri Lanka 179-7 (R. S. Kalpage 10*).

India

M. Prabhakar c Dassanayake b Wickremasinghe	14
N. S. Sidhu lbw b Muralitharan	99
V. G. Kambli c Wickremasinghe b Muralitharan	82
S. R. Tendulkar b Anurasiri	96
*M. Azharuddin lbw b Muralitharan	108
S. V. Manjrekar c Mahanama b Muralitharan	39
Kapil Dev not out	53
†N. R. Mongia not out	18
B 6, l-b 6, n-b 20	32
1/34 (1) 2/182 (3) 3/248 (2) 4/372 (4) 5/459 (6) 6/468 (5) (6 wkts dec.)	541

A. Kumble, R. K. Chauhan and S. L. V. Raju did not bat.

Bowling: Wickremasinghe 20–0–98–1; Jayasuriya 8–2–26–0; Muralitharan 65–11–179–4; Ranatunga 4–0–14–0; Anurasiri 45–2–158–1; Kalpage 19–1–54–0.

Sri Lanka

R. S. Mahanama c and b Kumble .... 47 – c Azharuddin b Raju 36
D. P. Samaraweera c Prabhakar b Kapil Dev .. 0 – c Tendulkar b Prabhakar 4
P. A. de Silva c Chauhan b Prabhakar .... 17 – (4) lbw b Raju 8
*A. Ranatunga lbw b Kapil Dev .... 26 – (5) c Sidhu b Kumble 28
S. T. Jayasuriya c Prabhakar b Kumble .... 22 – (6) c sub (A. D. Jadeja) b Chauhan . 1
R. S. Kalpage lbw b Kapil Dev .... 63 – (7) lbw b Kumble............. 18
H. P. Tillekeratne c Raju b Kumble .... 0 – (3) c and b Chauhan 80
†P. B. Dassanayake lbw b Prabhakar .... 16 – lbw b Kumble 0
S. D. Anurasiri c Tendulkar b Prabhakar ...... 4 – c Azharuddin b Kapil Dev 7
G. P. Wickremasinghe c Mongia b Prabhakar .. 8 – c Sidhu b Kapil Dev 1
M. Muralitharan not out .... 8 – not out...................... 20
L-b 12, n-b 8 .... 20 B 9, l-b 3 12

1/7 (2) 2/36 (3) 3/94 (1) 4/116 (4) 5/132 (5) 6/132 (7) 7/189 (8) 8/196 (9) 9/208 (10) 10/231 (6) — 231
1/5 (2) 2/69 (1) 3/97 (4) 4/164 (3) 5/168 (5) 6/176 (6) 7/179 (8) 8/188 (7) 9/189 (10) 10/215 (9) — 215

Bowling: *First Innings*—Prabhakar 20–4–82–4; Kapil Dev 21.1–5–73–3; Kumble 13–2–50–3; Raju 4–0–14–0. *Second Innings*—Prabhakar 3–0–18–1; Kapil Dev 8.3–1–41–2; Kumble 16–3–64–3; Raju 12–2–36–2; Chauhan 16–3–44–2.

Umpires: S. K. Bansal and K. Parathasarathy. Referee: E. D. Weekes (West Indies).

PUNJAB v SRI LANKANS

At Mohali, February 3, 4, 5. Drawn. Toss: Sri Lankans.

Away from the tensions of the Test arena, the Sri Lankan batsmen prospered as never before on this tour against the Ranji Trophy champions, Punjab. Tillekeratne, the left-hander who had scored a stroke-filled 80 in the Second Test, batted more than seven hours for a stodgy 176 not out and shared a stand of 207 with Samaraweera for the second wicket. Punjab's equally firm reply centred on an unbeaten 143 scored off 171 balls by opener Vikram Rathore. The home team declared 107 behind but the Sri Lankans were in no mood to take up the challenge, preferring to extend their batting practice.

Close of play: First day, Sri Lankans 280-2 (H. P. Tillekeratne 142*, P. A. de Silva 34*); Second day, Punjab 234-3 (Vikram Rathore 143*, Bhupinder Singh, jun. 52*).

Sri Lankans

D. P. Samaraweera c and b Vij 89
A. A. W. Gunawardene c Kalsi b Obaid Kamal 1 – (1) c Arun Sharma b Vij 61
H. P. Tillekeratne not out ....176 – (7) not out.................. 5
*P. A. de Silva c Gursharan Singh b Bhupinder Singh, sen.. 36 – (6) not out.................. 25
S. T. Jayasuriya c Amit Sharma b Bhupinder Singh, sen.. 0 – (3) c Ajay Mehra b Bhupinder Singh, sen.. 59
M. S. Atapattu c Arun Sharma b Bhupinder Singh, sen.. 15 – (4) c and b Vij 0
R. S. Kalpage c Arun Sharma b Bhupinder Singh, sen.. 0 – (5) b Kapoor................. 6
†P. B. Dassanayake c Gursharan Singh b Kapoor 6 – (2) lbw b Vij................. 25
B 1, l-b 11, w 2, n-b 4 .... 18 B 1, l-b 4, n-b 1 6

1/2 2/209 3/284 4/284 5/325 6/330 7/341 (7 wkts dec.) 341
1/51 2/132 3/133 4/142 5/166 (5 wkts dec.) 187

K. R. Pushpakumara, W. P. U. J. C. Vaas and S. D. Anurasiri did not bat.

Bowling: *First Innings*—Bhupinder Singh, sen. 35–10–83–4; Obaid Kamal 27–8–59–1; Kapoor 21–3–79–1; Vij 30–3–105–1; Ajay Mehra 3–1–3–0. *Second Innings*—Bhupinder Singh, sen. 12–3–34–1; Obaid Kamal 7–1–21–0; Kapoor 12–0–64–1; Vij 19–2–62–3; Ajay Mehra 1–1–0–0; Kalsi 1–0–1–0; Gursharan Singh 0.2–0–0–0.

Punjab

Vikram Rathore not out	143	– c sub (M. Muralitharan) b Anurasiri	42
Ajay Mehra c Gunawardene b Pushpakumara	18	– not out	28
R. Kalsi lbw b Pushpakumara	7	– run out	16
*Gursharan Singh b Vaas	7		
Bhupinder Singh, jun. not out	52		
Amit Sharma (did not bat)		– (4) not out	0
B 4, l-b 2, n-b 1	7		
1/32 2/48 3/90	(3 wkts dec.) 234	1/60 2/85	(2 wkts) 86

A. R. Kapoor, †Arun Sharma, Bhupinder Singh, sen., B. Vij and Obaid Kamal did not bat.

Bowling: *First Innings*—Pushpakumara 17–2–77–2; Vaas 18–3–44–1; de Silva 4–0–21–0; Kalpage 18–3–70–0; Jayasuriya 4–0–16–0. *Second Innings*—Pushpakumara 6–2–22–0; Vaas 7–0–27–0; Kalpage 7–2–21–0; Anurasiri 6–3–11–1; Atapattu 2–1–4–0; Tillekeratne 1–0–1–0.

Umpires: S. Porel and H. S. Sekhon.

INDIA v SRI LANKA

Third Test Match

At Ahmedabad, February 8, 9, 10, 12. India won by an innings and 17 runs. Toss: Sri Lanka.

A third successive innings victory for a clean sweep in a series had been achieved only once in history, when England beat Test debutants West Indies in 1928. India could hardly have predicted such a result when Sri Lanka won the toss, for the first time in the series, and opted to bat on a doubtful-looking pitch, certain to be the worst behaved of the series. But losing the toss proved a blessing in disguise for India; moisture under the surface meant it was at its most difficult on the first day. Raju, an accomplished bowler on bad pitches, ran through the visitors; his persistent line and low-arm action allowed the ball to skid through and keep very low, a deadly cocktail. He got his chance late in the day. The morning had been reserved for the wicket Kapil Dev needed to pass Sir Richard Hadlee as the leading wicket-taker in Tests. He took it just after the first break for drinks: Tillekeratne was caught at forward short leg in Kapil's eighth over, sparking off a long round of celebrations in the middle and, later, in the dressing-room – it was also Azharuddin's birthday.

When Sidhu and Kambli were rattling up the runs in a second-wicket stand of 83, there was little indication of how bad the pitch really was. But the Sri Lankans did not quite know how to exploit it. Considering the conditions, Azharuddin's 152 was near-miraculous. He batted for a minute over six hours – the next longest innings was Sidhu, at three hours – with virtually no durable support. He looked as if he was on a plumb pitch, despatching the bad balls for four while keeping out the good ones with polished defence.

The eventual lead was 239 and, even if the pitch seemed to be getting slightly better, Azharuddin's three diving catches at silly point and silly mid-off hastened the demise of Sri Lanka's second innings. But India's sixth consecutive home win by an innings in 12 months since England were downed in Madras was sealed by Raju. His destructive second-innings spell of six for 87 gave him his best Test figures of 11 for 125. Kumble went wicketless for the first time in 20 Test innings.

Man of the Match: M. Azharuddin.

Close of play: First day, India 90-1 (N. S. Sidhu 29*, V. G. Kambli 45*); Second day, India 329-8 (M. Azharuddin 134*, R. K. Chauhan 0*); Third day, Sri Lanka 154-5 (A. Ranatunga 5*, R. S. Kalpage 0*).

Sri Lanka

R. S. Mahanama lbw b Kumble	18	– lbw b Raju	63
D. P. Samaraweera b Chauhan	16	– run out	20
H. P. Tillekeratne c Manjrekar b Kapil Dev	5	– c Azharuddin b Raju	40
P. A. de Silva lbw b Raju	7	– c Azharuddin b Chauhan	14
*A. Ranatunga c Azharuddin b Raju	15	– c Sidhu b Raju	29
M. S. Atapattu b Chauhan	0	– c Mongia b Chauhan	0
R. S. Kalpage c Azharuddin b Chauhan	2	– c Azharuddin b Chauhan	9
†P. B. Dassanayake c Kambli b Raju	10	– not out	21
S. D. Anurasiri b Raju	4	– c Prabhakar b Raju	6
G. P. Wickremasinghe st Mongia b Raju	22	– c Prabhakar b Raju	0
M. Muralitharan not out	5	– c Mongia b Raju	4
B 8, l-b 7	15	B 4, l-b 11, n-b 1	16
1/34 (1) 2/39 (3) 3/47 (4) 4/59 (2) 5/59 (6) 6/71 (5) 7/79 (7) 8/89 (8) 9/108 (9) 10/119 (10)	119	1/67 (2) 2/98 (1) 3/149 (3) 4/149 (4) 5/153 (6) 6/167 (7) 7/193 (5) 8/214 (9) 9/214 (10) 10/222 (11)	222

Bowling: *First Innings*—Prabhakar 5–0–13–0; Kapil Dev 9–4–15–1; Kumble 15–3–30–1; Raju 23.5–7–38–5; Chauhan 11–8–8–3. *Second Innings*—Prabhakar 5–2–11–0; Kapil Dev 5–1–12–0; Raju 32.3–9–87–6; Kumble 28–9–45–0; Chauhan 30–14–45–3; Tendulkar 4–1–7–0.

India

M. Prabhakar b Anurasiri	14
N. S. Sidhu c Kalpage b Muralitharan	43
V. G. Kambli c Ranatunga b Wickremasinghe	57
S. R. Tendulkar b Wickremasinghe	6
*M. Azharuddin b Muralitharan	152
S. V. Manjrekar c Ranatunga b de Silva	16
Kapil Dev lbw b de Silva	4
†N. R. Mongia lbw b Anurasiri	14
A. Kumble c Kalpage b de Silva	15
R. K. Chauhan b Muralitharan	9
S. L. V. Raju not out	1
B 17, l-b 5, n-b 5	27
1/27 (1) 2/110 (3) 3/123 (4) 4/123 (2) 5/169 (6) 6/203 (7) 7/249 (8) 8/288 (9) 9/355 (5) 10/358 (10)	358

Bowling: Wickremasinghe 36 9 108 2; Ranatunga 8–1–15–0; Anurasiri 28–3–75–2; Muralitharan 36.3–6–79–3; Kalpage 7–2–9–0; de Silva 23–5–50–3.

Umpires: A. L. Narasimhan and V. K. Ramaswamy. Referee: E. D. Weekes (West Indies).

†INDIA v SRI LANKA

First One-Day International

At Rajkot, February 15. India won by eight runs. Toss: Sri Lanka. International debuts: U. N. K. Fernando, W. P. U. J. C. Vaas.

Sidhu's sparkling form extended into the one-day series: his 108 off 132 balls, without a six, carried the Indian innings. After his opening stand of 122 with Prabhakar was ended by the first of three run-outs, India struggled to make the most of the closing overs. Sri Lanka were always in with a chance of scoring 247, especially when Jayasuriya and de Silva added 63 for the fifth wicket. But once de Silva fell at 218, the later batsmen could not quite cope with the climbing asking-rate; they scored only seven of the 16 needed from Srinath's final over.

Man of the Match: N. S. Sidhu.

India

M. Prabhakar run out 67	Kapil Dev not out 4
N. S. Sidhu c Mahanama b Vaas 108	
V. G. Kambli run out 25	B 1, l-b 1, w 8, n-b 1 11
*M. Azharuddin run out 14	—
S. R. Tendulkar c Ranatunga b Kalpage 1	1/122 2/181 3/211 (5 wkts, 50 overs) 246
P. K. Amre not out 16	4/214 5/236

A. Kumble, †N. R. Mongia, J. Srinath and R. K. Chauhan did not bat.

Bowling: Vaas 8–2–40–1; Wickremasinghe 10–2–41–0; Ranatunga 2–0–18–0; Anurasiri 7–0–43–0; Kalpage 10–0–37–1; Jayasuriya 10–0–47–0; de Silva 3–0–18–0.

Sri Lanka

R. S. Mahanama c and b Tendulkar . . . 35	†U. N. K. Fernando not out. 2
D. P. Samaraweera st Mongia b Tendulkar . 14	G. P. Wickremasinghe b Srinath 1
H. P. Tillekeratne c Mongia b Kumble . 35	S. D. Anurasiri not out 0
P. A. de Silva b Kumble. 67	L-b 6, w 5, n-b 9. 20
*A. Ranatunga c Mongia b Tendulkar . 8	—
S. T. Jayasuriya c Kambli b Kumble. . . 31	1/56 2/66 3/119 (8 wkts, 50 overs) 238
R. S. Kalpage b Srinath 25	4/137 5/200 6/218 7/235 8/238

W. P. U. J. C. Vaas did not bat.

Bowling: Prabhakar 10–0–53–0; Srinath 7–0–37–2; Kapil Dev 6–0–25–0; Tendulkar 8–0–43–3; Kumble 10–0–41–3; Chauhan 9–0–33–0.

Umpires: J. Kurishankel and P. D. Reporter.

†INDIA v SRI LANKA

Second One-Day International

At Hyderabad, February 18. India won by seven wickets. Toss: India. International debuts: A. A. W. Gunawardene, K. R. Pushpakumara.

A fine innings of 98 from Ranatunga, his highest in limited-overs internationals, and an aggressive fifty from Kalpage revived Sri Lanka from 65 for five. They had suffered from having to bat first on a pitch which was liveliest at the start. Prabhakar was the chief beneficiary, with his first haul of five wickets in a one-day international, though he was considerably helped by the pace and lift obtained by Srinath. India were left with a target of 227, which they chased in orderly fashion; the openers put on 98 and Kambli added pep with an unbeaten 56 off 64 balls.

Man of the Match: M. Prabhakar.

Sri Lanka

R. S. Mahanama c Tendulkar b Prabhakar . 15	R. S. Kalpage c and b Srinath 51
A. A. W. Gunawardene c Mongia b Prabhakar . 2	†U. N. K. Fernando not out. 20
H. P. Tillekeratne c Mongia b Prabhakar . 0	K. R. Pushpakumara not out 4
P. A. de Silva c Chauhan b Prabhakar . 0	B 3, l-b 9, w 9, n-b 6 27
*A. Ranatunga c Mongia b Prabhakar . 98	—
S. T. Jayasuriya c Mongia b Tendulkar . 9	1/7 2/11 3/17 (7 wkts, 50 overs) 226
	4/31 5/65 6/197 7/217

M. Muralitharan and W. P. U. J. C. Vaas did not bat.

Bowling: Prabhakar 10–0–35–5; Srinath 10–1–44–1; Kapil Dev 6–1–19–0; Tendulkar 8–0–36–1; Chauhan 9–0–40–0; Kumble 7–0–40–0.

India

M. Prabhakar c Jayasuriya b Muralitharan	39	S. R. Tendulkar not out	11
N. S. Sidhu run out	79		
V. G. Kambli not out	56	B 10, l-b 7, w 6, n-b 3	26
*M. Azharuddin c Pushpakumara b Jayasuriya	16	1/98 2/161 3/197 (3 wkts, 48.2 overs)	227

P. K. Amre, Kapil Dev, A. Kumble, †N. R. Mongia, J. Srinath and R. K. Chauhan did not bat.

Bowling: Pushpakumara 7.2–0–30–0; Vaas 7–1–22–0; de Silva 6–0–34–0; Muralitharan 10–0–39–1; Jayasuriya 8–0–38–1; Kalpage 10–0–47–0.

Umpires: S. Chowdhury and H. K. Sharma.

†INDIA v SRI LANKA

Third One-Day International

At Jalandhar, February 20. Sri Lanka won by four wickets, their target having been revised to 141 from 33 overs. Toss: Sri Lanka.

Wintry Jalandhar witnessed a most exciting finish. But few realised that Sri Lanka's gallant chase had ended in victory when they took 15 off the last over. After a third interruption for rain, the umpires had not informed the scorers or the public of the last adjustment in the target. The 30,000 spectators still assumed Sri Lanka needed 145 in 34 overs, rather than 141 in 33. Bowling the 33rd over, Srinath was spanked for nine off the first three balls. Striving for more pace, he gave away two wides, then de Silva struck his penultimate ball over point for four. De Silva's 32 at the death swung the game after his team had been 99 for six, and was consolation for Sri Lanka on an otherwise disastrous tour. The Indian innings was marked by a fifty from Tendulkar, who marshalled the second half of the batting after Sidhu made a quick 46 on his home ground.

Man of the Match: P. A. de Silva. *Man of the Series:* N. S. Sidhu.

India

A. D. Jadeja b Kalpage	37	J. Srinath c Samaraweera b de Silva	7
N. S. Sidhu b Muralitharan	46	R. K. Chauhan not out	26
V. G. Kambli c Tillekeratne b Muralitharan	12	S. A. Ankola b Vaas	0
P. K. Amre b Jayasuriya	3	S. L. V. Raju not out	1
S. R. Tendulkar run out	52	B 2, l-b 1, w 8, n-b 4	15
*M. Azharuddin c Samaraweera b de Silva	11	1/83 2/102 3/112 4/112 5/136 6/142 7/161 8/209 9/209 (9 wkts, 50 overs)	213
†N. R. Mongia run out	3		

Bowling: Vaas 10–2–43–1; Wickremasinghe 9–0–34–0; Kalpage 10–0–36–1; Muralitharan 10–2–40–2; Jayasuriya 4–0–27–1; de Silva 7–0–30–2.

Sri Lanka

R. S. Mahanama lbw b Srinath	6	R. S. Kalpage st Mongia b Tendulkar	4
D. P. Samaraweera run out	49	†P. B. Dassanayake not out	20
H. P. Tillekeratne lbw b Raju	23	B 2, l-b 3, w 2	7
P. A. de Silva not out	32		
S. T. Jayasuriya b Raju	0	1/8 2/72 3/88 4/88 5/88 6/99 (6 wkts, 32.5 overs)	141
*A. Ranatunga c Mongia b Raju	0		

M. Muralitharan, G. P. Wickremasinghe and W. P. U. J. C. Vaas did not bat.

Bowling: Srinath 7.5–0–53–1; Ankola 5–0–23–0; Raju 8–0–19–3; Chauhan 8–2–18–0; Tendulkar 4–0–23–1.

Umpires: K. S. Giridharan and M. R. Singh.

THE PAKISTANIS IN NEW ZEALAND, 1993-94

By TERRY POWER

Amply demonstrating the old truth that great fast bowlers win Test matches – and one-day series – Wasim Akram and Waqar Younis rampaged through New Zealand in February and March of 1994, compensating for the inadequacies of their support troops and the all-round failings of Pakistan's fieldsmen. But the series raised fresh hope for New Zealand, too. At Christchurch, Pakistan looked like making a clean sweep of the Test series, having left a target of 324, more than New Zealand had ever made to win a Test. But Bryan Young and Shane Thomson rose to the challenge. Both scored maiden Test hundreds as they pulled off a most unexpected victory. The one-day games followed a similar course: Pakistan won the first three but the fourth was tied and New Zealand revived morale by taking the fifth.

Young had decided, after much soul-searching, to give up wicket-keeping a year earlier; having gone to Australia as the extra batsman, he was called on to open because of Greatbatch's disastrous loss of form. His patient century in the Third Test was a revelation to his warmest admirers and triumphant justification of his change of direction. Thomson, his Northern Districts colleague, is a natural cricketer, a fluent and adventurous strokemaker. He had played four Tests for an average of 40.33 but never a complete series before this, an indictment of recent New Zealand selection panels.

But New Zealand's top order remained an acute worry. They had lost John Wright before the season opened and Martin Crowe, invalided home from Perth for knee surgery in November, was not mending as soon as he had hoped. Andrew Jones, their steadiest batsman during this series, announced his retirement at its conclusion (later rescinded). All-rounder Chris Cairns appeared only once against the tourists, doubting his own fitness after injury. The inability to get a start was the biggest failure; ten times in 20 Test innings, from Australia in November to England in July, New Zealand's first wicket fell before the score passed three, and four times there were no runs on the board.

The selection of the touring party had launched a major row in Pakistan, initially in protest at Javed Miandad's omission but soon turning to objections to the "domineering" captaincy of Wasim. After a mutiny led by Waqar, his vice-captain, both were replaced, with Salim Malik leading the team and Asif Mujtaba deputising, though there was no change to the original selection of players. Despite this tumult before their arrival, the tour was unexpectedly harmonious, and the relief from leadership duties did Wasim no harm; he took 25 wickets and Waqar 18. The other bowlers managed ten between them. Though the batting was all too often unreliable, Basit Ali, who scored a maiden Test hundred at Christchurch, looked the natural successor to Miandad. There were also centuries for Saeed Anwar – resuming his Test career after a long run as a one-day player – Malik and Inzamam-ul-Haq during Pakistan's Second Test total of 548, one of the few occasions when batsmen on either side got on top of the bowling.

Apart from Wasim and Waqar, Pakistan enjoyed a clear superiority in the wicket-keeping of Rashid Latif, short and unobtrusive but reliable. He took 13 catches in the Test series, nine of them at Auckland. His New Zealand counterpart, Tony Blain, batted well but his keeping began to show the strain of playing 24 successive matches (eight Tests and 16 one-days) for New Zealand since March 1993. By the end of the one-day series, the selectors had recalled Adam Parore, whose injury in the Wellington nets 13 months earlier had given Blain his chance.

The Auckland Test was the first to feature a third-country umpire from the International Cricket Council's panel – Dickie Bird of England, in his 56th Test. (Previous schemes were arranged by the boards concerned.) But there was little controversy to trouble him; the players' attitude seemed good, which owed much to the management of Majid Khan; it also helped that the team coaches, Intikhab Alam and Geoff Howarth, had once been team-mates at Surrey. Outside the Tests, New Zealand Cricket again deprived all provinces of what were traditionally treasured encounters with the tourists. Instead they fielded conglomerations of players who interested the national selectors in some capacity or other. But such matches lack competitive interest and the public stayed away in droves.

PAKISTANI TOURING PARTY

Salim Malik (Lahore/Habib Bank) (*captain*), Asif Mujtaba (Karachi/PIA) (*vice-captain*), Aamir Nazir (Income Tax), Aamir Sohail (Sargodha/Habib Bank), Ashfaq Ahmed (PIA), Ata-ur-Rehman (Lahore/PACO), Atif Rauf (Islamabad/ADBP), Basit Ali (Karachi/United Bank), Inzamam-ul-Haq (Multan/United Bank), Mushtaq Ahmed (Multan/United Bank), Rashid Latif (Karachi/United Bank), Saeed Anwar (ADBP), Shakeel Ahmed (Islamabad/Habib Bank), Shoaib Mohammad (Karachi/PIA), Waqar Younis (Multan/United Bank), Wasim Akram (Lahore/PIA).

Akram Raza (Habib Bank/Sargodha) joined the tour after Mushtaq Ahmed returned home with a back injury.

Tour manager: Intikhab Alam. *Team manager:* Majid Khan.

PAKISTANI TOUR RESULTS

Test matches – Played 3: Won 2, Lost 1.
First-class matches – Played 5: Won 2, Lost 1, Drawn 2.
Wins – New Zealand (2).
Loss – New Zealand.
Draws – New Zealand XI, New Zealand Emerging Players.
One-day internationals – Played 5: Won 3, Lost 1, Tied 1.
Other non first-class match – Won v Sir Ron Brierley's XI.

TEST MATCH AVERAGES

NEW ZEALAND – BATTING

	T	*I*	*NO*	*R*	*HS*	*100s*	*Avge*	*Ct/St*
A. H. Jones	3	6	0	298	81	0	49.66	1
S. A. Thomson	3	6	1	206	120*	1	41.20	0
B. A. Young	3	6	0	191	120	1	31.83	9
D. K. Morrison	2	3	1	53	42	0	26.50	0
T. E. Blain	3	6	1	127	78	0	25.40	7/1
K. R. Rutherford	3	6	0	122	63	0	20.33	0
M. J. Greatbatch	3	6	0	105	48	0	17.50	3

	T	*I*	*NO*	*R*	*HS*	*100s*	*Avge*	*Ct*
S. B. Doull	3	5	0	78	29	0	15.60	3
M. N. Hart	2	3	1	25	12*	0	12.50	2
B. A. Pocock	2	4	0	26	16	0	6.50	0
R. P. de Groen	2	4	2	7	4	0	3.50	0

Played in one Test: C. L. Cairns 6, 31 (1 ct); B. R. Hartland 3, 10 (3 ct); M. B. Owens 2*, 0; C. Pringle 0 (1 ct).

* *Signifies not out.*

BOWLING

	O	*M*	*R*	*W*	*BB*	*5W/i*	*Avge*
S. B. Doull	88	11	332	12	5-66	1	27.66
D. K. Morrison	76.3	12	310	10	4-66	0	31.00
M. N. Hart	58.2	16	186	5	3-47	0	37.20
R. P. de Groen	61.4	16	192	5	3-40	0	38.40

Also bowled: C. L. Cairns 24–3–90–2; M. B. Owens 9–1–38–0; C. Pringle 50–9–124–1; S. A. Thomson 31–4–129–3.

PAKISTAN – BATTING

	T	*I*	*NO*	*R*	*HS*	*100s*	*Avge*	*Ct*
Inzamam-ul-Haq	3	5	2	223	135*	1	74.33	4
Basit Ali	3	5	0	287	103	1	57.40	3
Saeed Anwar	3	5	0	261	169	1	52.20	1
Salim Malik	3	5	0	210	140	1	42.00	4
Aamir Sohail	3	5	0	159	78	0	31.80	0
Akram Raza	2	3	1	55	29*	0	27.50	2
Rashid Latif	3	4	1	73	30	0	24.33	13
Wasim Akram	3	3	0	57	35	0	19.00	0
Waqar Younis	3	3	0	23	11	0	7.66	1

Played in two Tests: Asif Mujtaba 8, 0 (2 ct); Ata-ur-Rehman 2* (1 ct). Played in one Test: Aamir Nazir 0, 0*; Atif Rauf 16, 9; Mushtaq Ahmed 0 (2 ct).

* *Signifies not out.*

BOWLING

	O	*M*	*R*	*W*	*BB*	*5W/i*	*Avge*
Wasim Akram	159.4	41	431	25	7-119	2	17.24
Waqar Younis	118.2	21	405	18	6-78	1	22.50
Ata-ur-Rehman	53	9	214	6	3-50	0	35.66

Also bowled: Aamir Nazir 21–2–113–1; Aamir Sohail 3–1–6–0; Akram Raza 37–13–81–0; Mushtaq Ahmed 17–1–79–3; Saeed Anwar 1–0–4–0; Salim Malik 6–1–26–0.

Note: Matches in this section which were not first-class are signified by a dagger.

†At Hamilton, January 30. Pakistanis won by four runs. Toss: Pakistanis. Pakistanis 211 for six (50 overs) (Inzamam-ul-Haq 105, Shoaib Mohammad 51 not out); Sir Ron Brierley's XI 207 for seven (50 overs) (G. E. Bradburn 83 not out, A. C. Parore 30; Salim Malik three for 29).

NEW ZEALAND XI v PAKISTANIS

At Hamilton, January 31, February 1, 2. Drawn. Toss: New Zealand XI.

Gavin Smith, New Zealand's groundsman of the year, was told to prepare a pitch for batting practice and followed his instructions to the letter: 14 wickets fell in three full days and a result never looked likely. Without Waqar Younis and Wasim Akram, the Pakistani bowlers were harmless and Hartland and Pocock batted with more assurance than at full international level. Greatbatch rushed to 65 in 48 balls and Germon, the Canterbury wicket-keeper who was noisily aggrieved when the Test selectors preferred Blain to him a year before, registered an unbeaten second-innings century to bolster his claims. But the biggest score came from Saeed Anwar, who played himself into the fine form he retained throughout the tour and hit 100 in boundaries. Though the home team was officially New Zealand's second eleven, North Island and South Island were given first choice of players for their one-day match at Dunedin, which clashed.

Close of play: First day, New Zealand XI 318-5 (M. J. Greatbatch 65*, L. K. Germon 0*); Second day, New Zealand XI 24-1 (B. R. Hartland 20*, L. G. Howell 0*).

New Zealand XI

First innings		Second innings	
B. R. Hartland c Shakeel Ahmed b Ashfaq Ahmed	49	– c sub (Atif Rauf) b Shoaib Mohammad	50
B. A. Pocock c Shakeel Ahmed b Ashfaq Ahmed	95		
G. P. Burnett c Shakeel Ahmed b Ashfaq Ahmed	59	– (2) c Shakeel Ahmed b Aamir Nazir	2
L. G. Howell lbw b Ata-ur-Rehman	1	– (3) c Aamir Sohail b Asif Mujtaba	59
*M. J. Greatbatch not out	65	– retired hurt	50
M. N. Hart c Ashfaq Ahmed b Shoaib Mohammad	26	– (7) not out	18
†L. K. Germon not out	0	– (4) not out	100
D. N. Patel (did not bat)		– (6) c Shakeel Ahmed b Aamir Sohail	4
L-b 7, n-b 16	23	L-b 2, n-b 5	7
1/90 2/211 3/220 4/225 5/312 (5 wkts dec.)	318	1/9 2/79 3/155 4/261 (4 wkts dec.)	290

S. B. Doull, R. P. de Groen and M. B. Owens did not bat.

In the second innings M. J. Greatbatch retired hurt at 249-3.

Bowling: *First Innings*—Ata-ur-Rehman 22–4–83–1; Aamir Nazir 18–2–85–0; Ashfaq Ahmed 20–2–71–3; Asif Mujtaba 19–9–29–0; Salim Malik 6–0–21–0; Shoaib Mohammad 8–2–11–1; Basit Ali 4–1–11–0. *Second Innings*—Ata-ur-Rehman 7–2–24–0; Aamir Nazir 12–0–48–1; Asif Mujtaba 10.1–3–38–1; Ashfaq Ahmed 7–1–29–0; Shoaib Mohammad 16–2–67–1; Basit Ali 13–0–54–0; Aamir Sohail 4–0–28–1.

Pakistanis

First innings		Second innings	
Aamir Sohail c and b Doull	23	– c Burnett b de Groen	55
Saeed Anwar retired hurt	131		
Asif Mujtaba c Germon b de Groen	33	– (4) not out	7
Basit Ali lbw b Doull	49		
*Salim Malik not out	53		
Inzamam-ul-Haq not out	50		
†Shakeel Ahmed (did not bat)		– (2) c Howell b Patel	68
Shoaib Mohammad (did not bat)		– (3) not out	23
L-b 3, w 1, n-b 1	5	L-b 1, n-b 1	2
1/49 2/143 3/236 (3 wkts dec.)	344	1/93 2/147 (2 wkts)	155

Ata-ur-Rehman, Aamir Nazir and Ashfaq Ahmed did not bat.

In the first innings Saeed Anwar retired hurt at 249-3.

Bowling: *First Innings*—Owens 16–5–54–0; de Groen 18–3–59–1; Doull 17–3–59–2; Patel 13–2–78–0; Hart 18–2–91–0. *Second Innings*—Owens 4–0–29–0; Doull 5–0–19–0; de Groen 9–0–38–1; Hart 12–0–52–0; Patel 4–2–16–1.

Umpires: B. F. Bowden and D. M. Quested.

NEW ZEALAND EMERGING PLAYERS v PAKISTANIS

At Napier, February 4, 5, 6, 7. Drawn. Toss: Pakistanis.

After the first scheduled day was washed out, the next two were so one-sided as to recall Archie MacLaren's scornful remark after his New Zealand tour in 1922-23, that numerous opponents did not seem to know one end of a bat from the other. The Emerging Players were submerged for 93 by the tourists' pace: Wasim Akram took three wickets and conceded only 16 runs in 18 overs. Then their bowlers could do nothing to stop the Pakistanis adding 405 in a day, with Saeed Anwar retiring after another century and Basit Ali for his first of the tour. But the final day restored some local dignity. Fleming took another decisive step towards a Test career, making an undefeated 109 against Pakistan's Test attack.

Close of play: First day, No play; Second day, Pakistanis 80-1 (Saeed Anwar 50*, Asif Mujtaba 23*); Third day, Pakistanis 485-8 (Waqar Younis 25*, Ashfaq Ahmed 0*).

New Zealand Emerging Players

First innings		Second innings	
B. A. Young c Saeed Anwar b Aamir Nazir	19	b Waqar Younis	49
D. J. Murray c Inzamam-ul-Haq b Wasim Akram	7	c Waqar Younis b Aamir Sohail	8
S. W. J. Wilson c Saeed Anwar b Waqar Younis	11	b Wasim Akram	12
S. P. Fleming c Rashid Latif b Aamir Nazir	11	not out	109
S. A. Thomson lbw b Ashfaq Ahmed	0	st Rashid Latif b Salim Malik	77
*G. R. Larsen c Rashid Latif b Wasim Akram	2	not out	18
†A. C. Parore lbw b Wasim Akram	0		
D. J. Nash c Rashid Latif b Aamir Nazir	21		
M. C. Goodson lbw b Waqar Younis	0		
C. D. Lee not out	0		
H. T. Davis lbw b Ashfaq Ahmed	0		
B 1, l-b 12, n-b 9	22	B 4, l-b 4, w 1, n-b 8	17
1/23 2/39 3/54 4/54 5/65 6/65 7/66 8/81 9/92	93	1/42 2/66 3/83 4/221 (4 wkts)	290

In the first innings G. R. Larsen, when 0, retired hurt at 65-4 and resumed at 66.

Bowling: *First Innings*—Wasim Akram 18–9–16–3; Waqar Younis 13–7–22–2; Aamir Nazir 9–2–20–3; Ashfaq Ahmed 12.3–4–22–2. *Second Innings*—Waqar Younis 19–4–63–1; Wasim Akram 19–5–39–1; Aamir Nazir 14–3–59–0; Ashfaq Ahmed 11–2–38–0; Aamir Sohail 6–2–9–1; Salim Malik 19–3–71–1; Basit Ali 3–2–3–0; Inzamam-ul-Haq 1–1–0–0.

Pakistanis

Aamir Sohail c Nash b Davis	5
Saeed Anwar retired out	114
Asif Mujtaba c Larsen b Thomson	76
*Salim Malik c Parore b Lee	59
Basit Ali retired out	100
Inzamam-ul-Haq retired out	65
†Rashid Latif c Larsen b Goodson	9
Wasim Akram c Goodson b Thomson	15
Waqar Younis not out	25
Ashfaq Ahmed not out	0
B 1, l-b 9, w 2, n-b 5	17
1/16 2/177 3/237 4/292 5/427 6/436 7/454 8/460 (8 wkts dec.)	485

Aamir Nazir did not bat.

Bowling: Davis 25–2–91–1; Nash 23–3–79–0; Lee 24–1–89–1; Larsen 20–6–42–0; Goodson 20–2–86–1; Thomson 21–1–88–2.

Umpires: D. B. Cowie and R. S. Dunne.

NEW ZEALAND v PAKISTAN

First Test Match

At Auckland, February 10, 11, 12. Pakistan won by five wickets. Toss: Pakistan.

The match set the pattern for the series: classy pace bowling was made to look even better by undisciplined batting on a poor pitch, of erratic and spasmodically excessive bounce. Wasim Akram took nine for 93 and Waqar Younis six for 81 – passing 200 and 150 Test wickets respectively – and Doull, who achieved pronounced swing without their pace, seven for 114, easily his best figures in four Tests.

Salim Malik, in his first Test as captain, inserted New Zealand. Though Wasim despatched Pocock immediately, there was little hint that 14 wickets would fall that day when New Zealand took lunch at 67 for one. On resuming, Young was caught behind, the second of Rashid Latif's nine victims, a Pakistan Test record. But Jones played the biggest and most mature innings of the match for New Zealand, looking orthodox and confident. Briefly, he had the support of Greatbatch, who made 48 from 34 deliveries, punishing Mushtaq Ahmed heavily before misreading his googly: instead of reaching New Zealand's fastest Test 50, he offered a high outside edge to Malik, running back at cover. That was the fourth wicket, at 170, and Jones followed five runs later, caught behind off the same bowler. It was Mushtaq's last significant contribution to the series before returning home with back trouble. The middle and lower order then subsided.

Pakistan looked no more secure, however, losing their first four for 50 on the first evening. That became 93 for six before some effective aggression from Inzamam-ul-Haq, whose dynamic innings beat New Zealand on this ground in the World Cup semi-final two years before. They were well served, too, by their tail. De Groen used his height well in extracting help from the pitch and shared the honours with Doull. Still, Pakistan's deficit was only 27.

New Zealand's second innings looked like a one-day effort, and the overs were indeed limited – just 32.1. Wasim bowled throughout for his best analysis in Tests. New Zealand were 44 for six before Cairns and Doull thrashed around to take them into three figures. Thirty wickets had fallen during the first two days.

As Pakistan set out to score 138, Saeed Anwar and Asif Mujtaba went cheaply. But the decisive innings of a low-scoring match was played by Aamir Sohail, who showed good judgment of when to play attacking stokes as he hit ten fours and a six. New Zealand lost their last realistic chance of bowling out Pakistan when Blain dropped an under edge just before lunch. Greatbatch had also dropped Sohail, in the slips, not the best position for his fielding talents. It was Young, a former wicket-keeper better suited to close fielding, who finally held the ball, stomach-high, when Sohail forced it hard at short leg; it was Young's sixth catch in the match, a New Zealand Test record. By then it was far too late: Latif completed Pakistan's five-wicket win with a six to mid-wicket not long after lunch. Just over half the available playing time remained.

Man of the Match: Wasim Akram.

Close of play: First day, Pakistan 61-4 (Salim Malik 5*, Basit Ali 8*); Second day, Pakistan 3-0 (Saeed Anwar 1*, Aamir Sohail 1*).

New Zealand

First innings		Second innings	
B. A. Pocock c Rashid Latif b Wasim Akram	0	(2) c Asif Mujtaba b Wasim Akram	10
B. A. Young c Rashid Latif b Waqar Younis	29	(1) c Rashid Latif b Wasim Akram	0
A. H. Jones c Rashid Latif b Mushtaq Ahmed	66	c Rashid Latif b Wasim Akram	6
*K. R. Rutherford b Waqar Younis	14	b Waqar Younis	18
M. J. Greatbatch c Salim Malik b Mushtaq Ahmed	48	c Inzamam-ul-Haq b Wasim Akram	0
S. A. Thomson c Rashid Latif b Waqar Younis	29	c Rashid Latif b Waqar Younis	0
C. L. Cairns c Salim Malik b Mushtaq Ahmed	6	c Asif Mujtaba b Ata-ur-Rehman	31
†T. E. Blain c Mushtaq Ahmed b Wasim Akram	26	c Rashid Latif b Ata-ur-Rehman	4
S. B. Doull c and b Waqar Younis	0	c Salim Malik b Wasim Akram	29
R. P. de Groen c Mushtaq Ahmed b Wasim Akram	2	not out	0
M. B. Owens not out	2	c Rashid Latif b Wasim Akram	0
B 4, l-b 8, w 1, n-b 7	20	B 4, l-b 5, n-b 3	12
1/3 (1) 2/67 (2) 3/95 (4) 4/170 (5) 5/175 (3) 6/185 (7) 7/228 (6) 8/228 (9) 9/233 (10) 10/242 (8)	242	1/0 (1) 2/8 (3) 3/31 (2) 4/35 (5) 5/40 (6) 6/44 (4) 7/67 (8) 8/103 (9) 9/110 (7) 10/110 (11)	110

Bowling: *First Innings*—Wasim Akram 22.3–9–50–3; Waqar Younis 15–2–46–4; Ata-ur-Rehman 14–3–55–0; Mushtaq Ahmed 17–1–79–3. *Second Innings*—Wasim Akram 16.1–4–43–6; Waqar Younis 10–3–35–2; Ata-ur-Rehman 6–1–23–2.

Pakistan

Saeed Anwar c Blain b Cairns	16	– c Young b de Groen	7
Aamir Sohail c Jones b de Groen	16	– c Young b Thomson	78
Asif Mujtaba c Blain b Doull	8	– c and b Doull	0
Mushtaq Ahmed c Young b Doull	0		
*Salim Malik c Young b Doull	18	– (4) c Young b de Groen	11
Basit Ali c Blain b Cairns	25	– (5) c and b Doull	7
Inzamam-ul-Haq c Young b de Groen	43	– (6) not out	20
†Rashid Latif lbw b Doull	30	– (7) not out	13
Wasim Akram c Blain b de Groen	35		
Waqar Younis c Cairns b Doull	11		
Ata-ur-Rehman not out	2		
L-b 6, n-b 5	11	L-b 3, n-b 2	5
1/17 (1) 2/36 (3) 3/48 (2) 4/50 (4) 5/87 (6) 6/93 (5) 7/141 (8) 8/176 (7) 9/207 (10) 10/215 (9)	215	1/21 (1) 2/25 (3) 3/56 (4) 4/73 (5) 5/119 (2)	(5 wkts) 141

Bowling: *First Innings*—Cairns 18–2–75–2; Owens 7–1–28–0; Doull 15–2–66–5; de Groen 17.4–5–40–3. *Second Innings*—Cairns 6–1–15–0; de Groen 13–3–48–2; Doull 16–0–48–2; Owens 2–0–10–0; Thomson 4–1–17–1.

Umpires: H. D. Bird (England) and R. S. Dunne. Referee: R. Subba Row (England).

NEW ZEALAND v PAKISTAN

Second Test Match

At Wellington, February 17, 18, 19, 20. Pakistan won by an innings and 12 runs. Toss: New Zealand. Test debut: M. N. Hart.

Pakistan produced the only authoritative team batting display of the series to take a decisive 2-0 lead, while New Zealand went down to their fourth successive Test defeat and their third by an innings. Compared with Auckland, this was a truer, harder pitch, prepared by the retiring groundsman Wes Armstrong. In 22 years working on the Basin Reserve, he had never seen the home country lose a Test there; now he did, and they made a real job of it.

Rutherford chose to bat on a hot morning, while the Pakistani pace bowlers could use the initial life in the pitch. He did nothing to justify the decision himself – falling cheaply when he failed to move his feet towards the ball outside off stump – and neither did most of his fellow-batsmen. After Wasim Akram removed Young in the first over, the rest of the early damage was done by the third seamer, Ata-ur-Rehman. Jones reached an earnest 43 in 168 minutes, Greatbatch a fortunate 45 from 56 balls and nobody else made 20.

Pakistan lost Aamir Sohail that evening, but then took full advantage of the conditions. On the second morning, the left-hander Saeed Anwar had what appeared to be an inside edge off Doull caught by Blain before adding to his overnight 30, but Dickie Bird spared him and he proceeded to 169 – his maiden Test century in his third Test, after a pair on debut. Saeed played some sumptuous off-side drives in an elegant five-hour innings. He offered only one more real chance, to Blain, who also missed stumping Basit Ali in Hart's second over. That was another costly escape: Basit made a brutal 85, in a style taken up by Inzamam-ul-Haq in the last session. During the second day, Pakistan added 363 for three wickets, including the night-watchman for a duck. On Saturday, Inzamam and Salim Malik also completed centuries and carried their fifth-wicket stand to 258. Hart, the 21-year-old slow left-armer, was the most economical bowler, conceding 3.25 an over, and took his first Test wicket when he caught and bowled Salim Malik, who immediately declared on 548, 373 ahead.

In a typically shaky start for New Zealand, both openers were dismissed by the fast bowlers as the second-innings total reached six. They recovered, but it was already too late to change the result. Jones developed his consistent form in a 114-run stand with Rutherford, who played numerous thrilling shots without ever looking likely to remain. New Zealand's top score of the match came from Blain, whose batting was holding up better than his wicket-keeping and brought him 78, his highest innings in Tests. But what was needed and the batsmen failed to provide was a pair of big centuries, ground out if necessary.

In conditions far from favourable for him, Wasim Akram improved on his best Test figures for the second game running, with seven for 119. This time he was not terrifying or suddenly devastating, but persevering and continually testing; he collected his 20th wicket of the series and his second match award.

Man of the Match: Wasim Akram.

Close of play: First day, Pakistan 35-1 (Saeed Anwar 30*, Akram Raza 0*); Second day, Pakistan 398-4 (Salim Malik 62*, Inzamam-ul-Haq 63*); Third day, New Zealand 189-4 (A. H. Jones 66*, S. A. Thomson 37*).

New Zealand

First innings		Second innings	
B. A. Young lbw b Wasim Akram	0	(2) b Wasim Akram	4
B. A. Pocock b Ata-ur-Rehman	16	(1) b Waqar Younis	0
A. H. Jones lbw b Ata-ur-Rehman	43	b Wasim Akram	76
*K. R. Rutherford c Akram Raza b Ata-ur-Rehman	7	c Akram Raza b Ata-ur-Rehman	63
M. J. Greatbatch c Rashid Latif b Waqar Younis	45	c Rashid Latif b Wasim Akram	10
S. A. Thomson b Wasim Akram	7	c Ata-ur-Rehman b Wasim Akram	47
†T. E. Blain c Saeed Anwar b Waqar Younis	8	c Basit Ali b Wasim Akram	78
M. N. Hart not out	12	b Wasim Akram	7
D. K. Morrison c Rashid Latif b Wasim Akram	5	(10) lbw b Waqar Younis	42
S. B. Doull c Basit Ali b Waqar Younis	17	(9) c Salim Malik b Wasim Akram	15
R. P. de Groen b Wasim Akram	4	not out	1
L-b 7, n-b 4	11	B 1, l-b 5, n-b 12	18
1/0 (1) 2/40 (2) 3/49 (4) 4/100 (3) 5/126 (5) 6/128 (6) 7/140 (7) 8/149 (9) 9/170 (10) 10/175 (11)	175	1/3 (1) 2/6 (2) 3/120 (4) 4/143 (5) 5/209 (3) 6/216 (6) 7/244 (8) 8/276 (9) 9/350 (7) 10/361 (10)	361

Bowling: *First Innings*—Wasim Akram 24–10–60–4; Waqar Younis 22–5–51–3; Ata-ur-Rehman 15–4–50–3; Akram Raza 6–4–7–0. *Second Innings*—Wasim Akram 37–7–119–7; Waqar Younis 25.2–4–111–2; Ata-ur-Rehman 18–1–86–1; Akram Raza 12–4–25–0; Aamir Sohail 1–0–1–0; Salim Malik 2–0–13–0.

Pakistan

Saeed Anwar run out	169
Aamir Sohail lbw b Morrison	2
Akram Raza c Blain b Morrison	0
Basit Ali b Thomson	85
*Salim Malik c and b Hart	140
Inzamam-ul-Haq not out	135
B 5, l-b 6, n-b 6	17
1/34 (2) 2/36 (3) 3/233 (4) 4/290 (1) 5/548 (5) (5 wkts dec.)	548

Asif Mujtaba, †Rashid Latif, Wasim Akram, Waqar Younis and Ata-ur-Rehman did not bat.

Bowling: Morrison 31–4–139–2; de Groen 31–8–104–0; Doull 27–6–112–0; Hart 31.2–9–102–1; Thomson 17–3–80–1.

Umpires: H. D. Bird (England) and B. L. Aldridge. Referee: R. Subba Row (England)

NEW ZEALAND v PAKISTAN

Third Test Match

At Christchurch, February 24, 25, 26, 27, 28. New Zealand won by five wickets. Toss: New Zealand. Test debut: Atif Rauf.

New Zealand – in fact Thomson and Young, with minimal support – achieved their highest-ever fourth-innings total to win a Test after Pakistan looked to be on their way to a clean sweep of the series.

New Zealand had never scored more than 278 for a Test victory. Now they needed 324. Although they had more than two days to get them, at 133 for four, with Jones gone, it did not look likely. But the stand between Young and Thomson, two naturally aggressive players, transformed the match. Young, who batted throughout the fourth day, pushed his 100th run to mid-wicket before stumps and kissed the silver fern on his helmet as he completed it. Thomson's century – like Young's, his first in Test cricket – came fortuitously next morning, with a shot over the keeper's head instead of over slips as intended. He immediately redeemed himself with much better-looking boundaries to long-on and behind point. Though Young became Wasim Akram's 25th and last wicket of the series, Thomson remained to supervise one of New Zealand's best victories. Blain, who had been at the crease last time his country won, against Australia nearly a year before, hit the winning four over mid-off.

Rutherford, who decided to play on the first morning despite a bruised left hand, had asked Pakistan to bat. Saeed Anwar pulled Morrison's first ball to Rutherford's injured hand at mid-on; he dropped it. In Morrison's next over, Blain grassed an outside edge from Saeed. Pakistan went on to raise the only century opening stand of the series, after which Basit Ali reached a confident 98, which he converted into a maiden Test century on the second morning.

That afternoon, Waqar Younis sliced through New Zealand's first innings in familiar fashion, taking five for 19. Within three deliveries, Thomson had to play at a late out-swinger, which took the edge, and Blain was lbw to a magnificent in-swinger. Jones, in what he said would be his last Test, deserved three figures, but ran himself out for 81, attempting a single to mid-on; he was to fall the same way in the next innings. The other batting failed and Pakistan led by 144. But they lost both their openers cheaply on the second evening and only Basit Ali looked the part next day, adding 67 to his first-innings hundred. Morrison, who claimed four wickets in each innings, and Hart both deserved their successes in dismissing Pakistan for 179. Even then, the visitors seemed the most likely winners.

While Waqar was creating havoc on the second afternoon there was some discussion between umpire Francis and the two captains about the state of the ball. This was interpreted by some commentators to mean a ball-tampering controversy. But Intikhab Alam, the Pakistan manager, said his players had been worried that the ball was getting wet when it was hit into the concrete gutters beyond the boundary.

Men of the Match: S. A. Thomson and B. A. Young.

Man of the Series: Wasim Akram.

Close of play: First day, Pakistan 334-7 (Basit Ali 98*, Akram Raza 27*); Second day, Pakistan 8-2 (Atif Rauf 3*, Akram Raza 2*); Third day, New Zealand 9-0 (B. A. Young 3*, B. R. Hartland 3*); Fourth day, New Zealand 277-4 (B. A. Young 115*, S. A. Thomson 93*).

Pakistan

First innings		Second innings	
Saeed Anwar c Young b Doull	69	c Blain b Morrison	0
Aamir Sohail c Hartland b Doull	60	c Young b Doull	3
Atif Rauf c Greatbatch b Morrison	16	c Young b Doull	9
*Salim Malik b Hart	18	(5) c Pringle b Morrison	23
Basit Ali c Hartland b Pringle	103	(6) run out	67
Inzamam-ul-Haq c Greatbatch b Doull	5	(7) c sub (M. A. Hastings) b Morrison	20
†Rashid Latif c Hartland b Thomson	27	(8) c and b Hart	3
Wasim Akram c Greatbatch b Morrison	5	(9) b Hart	17
Akram Raza not out	29	(4) st Blain b Hart	26
Waqar Younis c Doull b Morrison	2	c Blain b Morrison	10
Aamir Nazir b Morrison	0	not out	0
L-b 6, w 1, n-b 3	10	N-b 1	1
1/125 (1) 2/147 (2) 3/159 (3) 4/195 (4) 5/206 (6) 6/254 (7) 7/261 (8) 8/339 (5) 9/344 (10) 10/344 (11)	344	1/0 (1) 2/4 (2) 3/26 (3) 4/53 (4) 5/77 (5) 6/133 (7) 7/152 (6) 8/154 (8) 9/171 (9) 10/179 (10)	179

Bowling: *First Innings*—Morrison 24–3–105–4; Doull 25–3–93–3; Pringle 33–6–83–1; Hart 9–2–37–1; Thomson 6–0–20–1. *Second Innings*—Morrison 21.3–5–66–4; Pringle 17–3–41–0; Doull 5–0–13–2; Hart 18–5–47–3; Thomson 4–0–12–0.

New Zealand

First innings		Second innings	
B. R. Hartland c Basit Ali b Waqar Younis	3	(2) c Inzamam-ul-Haq b Wasim Akram	10
B. A. Young lbw b Aamir Nazir	38	(1) b Wasim Akram	120
A. H. Jones run out	81	run out	26
*K. R. Rutherford c Inzamam-ul-Haq b Waqar Younis	7	lbw b Wasim Akram	13
M. J. Greatbatch lbw b Wasim Akram	1	c Inzamam-ul-Haq b Waqar Younis	1
S. A. Thomson c Rashid Latif b Waqar Younis	3	not out	120
†T. E. Blain lbw b Waqar Younis	0	not out	11
M. N. Hart b Wasim Akram	6		
S. B. Doull lbw b Waqar Younis	17		
D. K. Morrison not out	6		
C. Pringle b Waqar Younis	0		
B 5, l-b 9, n-b 24	38	L-b 5, n-b 18	23
1/12 (1) 2/109 (2) 3/134 (4) 4/139 (5) 5/147 (6) 6/147 (7) 7/171 (8) 8/186 (3) 9/198 (9) 10/200 (11)	200	1/22 (2) 2/76 (3) 3/119 (4) 4/133 (5) 5/287 (1)	(5 wkts) 324

Bowling: *First Innings*—Wasim Akram 22–5–54–2; Waqar Younis 19–1–78–6; Aamir Nazir 15–2–54–1. *Second Innings*—Wasim Akram 38–6–105–3; Waqar Younis 27–6–84–1; Aamir Nazir 16–0–59–0; Akram Raza 19–5–49–0; Aamir Sohail 2–1–5–0; Salim Malik 4–1–13–0; Saeed Anwar 1–0–4–0.

Umpires: K. T. Francis (Sri Lanka) and R. S. Dunne. Referee: R. Subba Row (England).

†NEW ZEALAND v PAKISTAN

First One-Day International

At Dunedin, March 3. Pakistan won by five wickets. Toss: New Zealand.

Rutherford misjudged his home city's weather when he chose to bat, believing it would not rain. After New Zealand had reached a useful 32 for one in 9.2 overs, a long interruption meant the match was reduced to 30 overs. Under pressure to score quick runs, numerous batsmen then committed suicide; the innings staggered to 122 for nine without anyone passing 20. Though the seamers gave their side some chance by breaking through early – Pakistan were 35 for four – they could not remove Saeed Anwar, who was far and away the best batsman on the day. Rashid Latif joined in with three sixes near the end.

Man of the Match: Saeed Anwar.

New Zealand

M. J. Greatbatch run out 14
B. A. Young c Salim Malik b Akram Raza . 20
A. H. Jones c Wasim Akram b Akram Raza . 15
C. L. Cairns c Asif Mujtaba b Akram Raza . 13
*K. R. Rutherford st Rashid Latif b Aamir Sohail . 3
S. A. Thomson st Rashid Latif b Aamir Sohail . 8
C. Z. Harris c and b Salim Malik 19
†T. E. Blain c Asif Mujtaba b Salim Malik . 5
G. R. Larsen not out 9
D. K. Morrison c Asif Mujtaba b Salim Malik . 1
C. Pringle not out 6
L-b 5, w 1, n-b 3 9

1/18 2/54 3/58 4/72 5/74 6/99 7/105 8/109 9/114 (9 wkts, 30 overs) 122

Bowling: Wasim Akram 6–2–18–0; Waqar Younis 4–1–14–0; Ata-ur-Rehman 4–0–17–0; Akram Raza 6–1–18–3; Aamir Sohail 6–0–33–2; Salim Malik 4–0–17–3.

Pakistan

Saeed Anwar not out 60
Aamir Sohail c Blain b Pringle 5
Inzamam-ul-Haq c Jones b Pringle 1
*Salim Malik lbw b Cairns 2
Basit Ali lbw b Cairns 4
Asif Mujtaba c Cairns b Morrison 14
†Rashid Latif not out 32
L-b 2, w 3 5

1/17 2/24 3/27 4/35 5/74 (5 wkts, 26.1 overs) 123

Wasim Akram, Akram Raza, Waqar Younis and Ata-ur-Rehman did not bat.

Bowling: Pringle 5–0–20–2; Thomson 4–1–21–0; Larsen 5–1–15–0; Cairns 6–1–33–2; Harris 3–0–17–0; Morrison 3.1–0–15–1.

Umpires: R. S. Dunne and C. E. King.

†NEW ZEALAND v PAKISTAN

Second One-Day International

At Auckland, March 6. Pakistan won by 36 runs. Toss: New Zealand.

Feeble batting by New Zealand was accompanied by an even more discreditable performance from some parts of the crowd. For the first time in New Zealand, the players had to come off because of fears for their safety, when Ata-ur-Rehman, fielding near the fine-leg boundary, was hit on the head, apparently by a bottle. He was led to the dressing-rooms with an icebag over the wound; his team-mates followed. The crowd was told, several hours after they had started bombarding the playing area with beer cans: "From now on, anyone seen throwing anything will be arrested." The match resumed after 11 minutes. Some of the 25,000 spectators might have claimed cause for grievance. "For $25 We Want Crowe" proclaimed one banner, referring to the rise in admission price. New Zealand's bowlers did well enough on a slow, unsatisfactory pitch, but Pakistan were saved from rout, after being reduced to 65 for six, by their patient opener, Aamir Sohail, and the more aggressive Wasim Akram. Once brilliant catches had despatched Jones and Greatbatch, however, New Zealand's dismal effort revolved around the out-of-touch Rutherford and fell far behind an asking-rate of under three an over.

Man of the Match: Wasim Akram.

Pakistan

Saeed Anwar c Blain b Morrison	9	Akram Raza run out	3
Aamir Sohail c Rutherford b Thomson	48	Waqar Younis b Thomson	7
Inzamam-ul-Haq lbw b Pringle	14	Ata-ur-Rehman not out	0
*Salim Malik c Blain b Larsen	5	B 1, l-b 4, w 8, n-b 2	15
Basit Ali c Blain b Larsen	8		—
Asif Mujtaba lbw b Morrison	1	1/10 2/33 3/41 (43.3 overs)	146
†Rashid Latif c Greatbatch b Harris	3	4/60 5/61 6/65	
Wasim Akram c Greatbatch b Thomson	33	7/127 8/139 9/139	

Bowling: Morrison 8–2–16–2; Pringle 8–0–31–1; Cairns 7–1–24–0; Larsen 10–0–27–2; Harris 7–0–29–1; Thomson 3.3–1–14–3.

New Zealand

M. J. Greatbatch c Akram Raza b Ata-ur-Rehman	23	†T. E. Blain st Rashid Latif b Akram Raza	2
B. A. Young lbw b Wasim Akram	0	G. R. Larsen b Wasim Akram	5
A. H. Jones c Aamir Sohail b Wasim Akram	1	D. K. Morrison c Rashid Latif b Wasim Akram	0
*K. R. Rutherford run out	37	C. Pringle not out	4
S. A. Thomson c Salim Malik b Akram Raza	6	L-b 2, w 8, n-b 1	11
			—
C. L. Cairns b Aamir Sohail	3	1/3 2/8 3/45 (44.3 overs)	110
C. Z. Harris c Rashid Latif b Waqar Younis	18	4/62 5/71 6/86	
		7/90 8/104 9/105	

Bowling: Wasim Akram 7.3–0–23–4; Waqar Younis 8–0–18–1; Ata-ur-Rehman 9–2–25–1; Salim Malik 2–0–4–0; Akram Raza 10–1–21–2; Aamir Sohail 8–0–17–1.

Umpires: D. B. Cowie and D. M. Quested.

†NEW ZEALAND v PAKISTAN

Third One-Day International

At Wellington, March 9. Pakistan won by 11 runs. Toss: New Zealand.

The first decent total of the one-day series set up a victory for Pakistan rather more comfortable than the 11-run margin suggested. Their score of 213 revolved around strong hitting in a second-wicket stand of 142 between Aamir Sohail and Inzamam-ul-Haq. New Zealand had short-lived hopes when, at 168 for three with Rutherford and Thomson together, they needed 46 from the last six overs. But they could not cope with the return of Waqar Younis and Wasim Akram. The run-flow was greatly reduced and the next four wickets fell for 13. A third successive win assured Pakistan of the Bank of New Zealand Cup.

Man of the Match: Inzamam-ul-Haq.

Pakistan

Saeed Anwar b Cairns	16	†Rashid Latif b Larsen	3
Aamir Sohail c Young b Morrison	76	Asif Mujtaba not out	1
Inzamam-ul-Haq c Cairns b Pringle	88	B 4, l-b 9, w 3, n-b 2	18
Basit Ali b Morrison	1		—
Wasim Akram b Morrison	0	1/29 2/171 3/174 (6 wkts, 48 overs)	213
*Salim Malik not out	10	4/174 5/206 6/209	

Akram Raza, Waqar Younis and Ata-ur-Rehman did not bat.

Bowling: Pringle 9–0–52–1; Morrison 10–1–32–3; Larsen 10–1–42–1; Cairns 10–0–26–1; Thomson 2–0–14–0; Harris 7–0–34–0.

New Zealand

B. A. Young run out 37
M. J. Greatbatch c Aamir Sohail b Ata-ur-Rehman . 9
A. H. Jones run out 38
*K. R. Rutherford c Salim Malik b Waqar Younis . 46
S. A. Thomson b Wasim Akram 38
C. L. Cairns b Wasim Akram 2
C. Z. Harris not out 8
†T. E. Blain run out 3
G. R. Larsen b Waqar Younis 6
D. K. Morrison not out 4
B 3, l-b 5, w 3 11

1/32 2/76 3/106 4/168 5/176 6/177 7/181 8/193 (8 wkts, 48 overs) 202

C. Pringle did not bat.

Bowling: Wasim Akram 10–1–41–2; Waqar Younis 10–0–43–2; Ata-ur-Rehman 6–0–15–1; Aamir Sohail 6–0–29–0; Salim Malik 10–0–37–0; Akram Raza 6–0–29–0.

Umpires: B. L. Aldridge and D. M. Quested.

†NEW ZEALAND v PAKISTAN

Fourth One-Day International

At Auckland, March 13. Tied. Toss: Pakistan.

Superbly hostile bowling by Waqar Younis, added to unnecessary risk-taking by the middle order, salvaged a tie for Pakistan, the first ever involving New Zealand. The swinging yorker with which Waqar bowled Young in his opening burst and the fast break-back which skittled Hart were especially memorable. When de Groen was given out lbw, after setting out for what he hoped would be the winning leg-bye, Waqar had six for 30 and New Zealand's last six had gone for 19. Earlier, no Pakistani batsman had managed a major innings. Larsen's four wickets confirmed the effectiveness of his variable medium-slow pace when the ball is not coming on to the bat.

Man of the Match: Waqar Younis.

Pakistan

Saeed Anwar c Blain b Larsen 25
Aamir Sohail c Blain b Larsen 24
Inzamam-ul-Haq c Young b Larsen 7
*Salim Malik b Thomson 7
Basit Ali run out 34
Asif Mujtaba c Rutherford b Hart 5
†Rashid Latif b Thomson 5
Wasim Akram b Larsen 15
Akram Raza not out 11
Waqar Younis c Hartland b Pringle . . . 2
Ata-ur-Rehman not out 11
B 2, l-b 8, w 5 15

1/38 2/59 3/60 4/80 5/85 6/101 7/126 8/139 9/146 (9 wkts, 50 overs) 161

Bowling: Pringle 10–0–29–1; de Groen 6–2–26–0; Cairns 7–1–21–0; Larsen 10–0–24–4; Hart 10–1–29–1; Thomson 7–1–22–2.

New Zealand

B. A. Young b Waqar Younis 5
B. R. Hartland b Waqar Younis 3
A. H. Jones c Basit Ali b Akram Raza . 21
*K. R. Rutherford c Waqar Younis b Salim Malik . 47
C. L. Cairns run out 39
S. A. Thomson c Rashid Latif b Waqar Younis . 24
†T. E. Blain c Rashid Latif b Wasim Akram . 0
G. R. Larsen lbw b Waqar Younis 1
M. N. Hart b Waqar Younis 6
C. Pringle not out 1
R. P. de Groen lbw b Waqar Younis . . 2
L-b 5, w 7 12

1/8 2/9 3/65 4/85 5/142 6/144 7/152 8/152 9/159 (49.4 overs) 161

Bowling: Wasim Akram 10–1–24–1; Waqar Younis 9.4–1–30–6; Ata-ur-Rehman 4–0–22–0; Akram Raza 10–1–21–1; Aamir Sohail 9–0–29–0; Salim Malik 7–0–30–1.

Umpires: D. B. Cowie and R. S. Dunne.

†NEW ZEALAND v PAKISTAN

Fifth One-Day International

At Christchurch, March 16. New Zealand won by seven wickets. Toss: New Zealand.

New Zealand returned to the scene of their triumph in the Third Test for another consolatory win – with nearly 16 overs to spare. Again they owed their success to a partnership between Thomson and an opener – this time Hartland. Pakistan were put in to bat while the pitch had a green tinge, and New Zealand's pace bowlers removed the top four for 19. A total of 145 depended almost entirely on Basit Ali, who hit Cairns over his head for six. By their 14th over, New Zealand had three batsmen out for a combined score of five. But Hartland, encouraged by an 11,000 crowd on his home ground, anchored the innings, while Thomson played some admirable off-side attacking shots. Wasim Akram's triumphant tour ended on a low note, when he retired mid-over with a bad shoulder.

Man of the Match: B. R. Hartland.

Pakistan

Saeed Anwar c Hart b Pringle	2
Aamir Sohail c Rutherford b Morrison	1
Inzamam-ul-Haq c Young b Pringle	4
Asif Mujtaba b Cairns	3
*Salim Malik c Young b Cairns	15
Basit Ali c Young b Pringle	57
†Rashid Latif c Parore b Morrison	9
Wasim Akram c Parore b Larsen	7
Akram Raza not out	23
Waqar Younis c Cairns b Morrison	4
Ata-ur-Rehman not out	3
L-b 6, w 8, n-b 3	17
1/3 2/8 3/17 4/19 5/45 6/65 7/86 8/121 9/136 (9 wkts, 50 overs)	145

Bowling: Morrison 10–2–20–3; Pringle 10–1–21–3; Cairns 10–0–36–2; Larsen 10–1–21–1; Hart 4–0–17–0; Thomson 6–0–24–0.

New Zealand

B. A. Young c Rashid Latif b Waqar Younis	3
B. R. Hartland not out	68
A. H. Jones c Rashid Latif b Waqar Younis	1
*K. R. Rutherford c Akram Raza b Ata-ur-Rehman	1
S. A. Thomson not out	48
L-b 8, w 14, n-b 3	25
1/26 2/34 3/45 (3 wkts, 34.1 overs)	146

C. L. Cairns, M. N. Hart, †A. C. Parore, G. R. Larsen, D. K. Morrison and C. Pringle did not bat.

Bowling: Wasim Akram 6.3–0–17–0; Waqar Younis 8.1–1–33–2; Ata-ur-Rehman 9–0–44–1; Aamir Sohail 4–0–18–0; Akram Raza 3.3–0–14–0; Salim Malik 3–0–12–0.

Umpires: B. L. Aldridge and C. E. King.

THE AUSTRALIANS IN SOUTH AFRICA, 1993-94

By JACK BANNISTER

Australia's tour of South Africa in early 1994 was a big success on and off the field, and honour was mutually satisfied when they split the three-Test series 1-1 and the one-day international series 4-4. The results of the Tests matched those in the series played just beforehand in Australia, though they were an utter contrast to Australia's previous visit 24 years earlier when South Africa won 4-0. In this case, the greater pride was with the South Africans since the same Australian players had slaughtered England a few months before.

Except for two spectacular lapses, the spirit displayed by both teams was good, but doubts must remain about the wisdom of two countries playing each other in back-to-back series in more than four months of non-stop travel. The imbalance of five-day and one-day cricket is a problem which the United Cricket Board of South Africa must redress as soon as financial constraints imposed by their vast development programme for disadvantaged young cricketers are eased. The problems are best illustrated by the personal landmarks achieved by opening batsmen Michael Slater and Andrew Hudson. Both young men reached 1,000 Test runs, each in his 14th Test, and in their 23rd and 25th innings respectively. But Slater's milestone came only 291 days after his debut at Old Trafford, while Hudson's came 23 months after his first Test in Barbados. Since that match South Africa had played 39 one-day internationals. The South Africans do have a problem: the three five-day Tests drew 170,000 spectators, at grounds in Johannesburg, Cape Town and Durban which have a daily capacity of 30,000, 20,000 and 19,000 respectively; the eight limited-overs games were all sell-outs, and were watched by 157,000.

The first two Tests produced one-sided results after fluctuating matches containing the best elements of five-day cricket. After South Africa had been 126 for six on the first day in Johannesburg, only a supremely resilient innings from Jonty Rhodes kept his side in the match and enabled Hansie Cronje to score a century and set up the victory. At Newlands, the match seemed a certain draw until, in the final half-hour on the fourth day, South Africa lost four wickets for three runs, beginning with a hairline run-out of Kepler Wessels, settled by the third umpire.

The much-anticipated decider at Kingsmead never caught fire. The Australians lost their way in the first innings, and the sudden loss of three wickets by South Africa on the second day removed all the batsmen's sense of urgency. Allan Border's final Test before he announced his retirement was thus an anticlimax, although his unbeaten 42 ensured a draw. The most durable cricketer of his time walked out with a proud record of 32 wins in his 93 consecutive Tests as captain. His aggregate of 11,174 runs in 156 Tests may be beaten, but perhaps no one will ever make quite such a contribution to his country's cricket.

The one-day series was also halved: Australia retrieved a 3-1 deficit and won the eighth game in Bloemfontein by one run. Steve Waugh achieved the rare distinction of being named Man of the Series in both Tests and limited-overs internationals, to add to the same award in the three-Test series in Australia: he played the best cricket of his life, excelling in the field as well as with bat and ball. Slater confirmed his reputation as an unusually positive young player, but the remainder of the batting was patchy. Shane Warne carried the bowling with 15 wickets, giving him 33 against South Africa in six Tests. Disappointments included the recurrence of Craig McDermott's knee injury, Merv Hughes's lack of form and fitness, Tim May's failure to make an impact and the poor tour of Dean Jones, who announced his retirement from international cricket at its conclusion. He did not play in a Test and was omitted from the final one-day match.

For South Africa, Hudson's 293 runs in five innings were unusually polished and attractive for an opener. Cronje had a golden stretch of 742 runs in all cricket against the Australians from seven completed innings in 15 days, but followed it with only 123 from his next seven innings. Rhodes was electrifying, turning the First Test with a fighting 69 and then a brilliant run-out of Border. As captain, Wessels's policy was always safety-first, but he could be satisfied with his part in South Africa's successful international come-back.

The behavioural lapses were both on the Australian side in the Johannesburg Test. Hughes was reported to the referee, Donald Carr, for several cases of verbal abuse of batsmen, making this the third time since November 1992 he had been reported. In 15 Tests since then, his match fees totalled A$60,000, but Carr fined him just ten per cent of his match fee, bringing his total fines for the three offences to A$800. Carr was the referee who, after the second offence in Perth 13 months earlier, had reprimanded Hughes and warned him about his future conduct.

The incident involving Warne was much worse, if less characteristic. Border had kept him out of the attack for the first 44 overs of the second innings. When he did come on, he bowled Hudson in his first over, and immediately raced down the pitch shouting volleys of abuse. Wicket-keeper Ian Healy, spotting that Warne was then heading for thc dcparting batsman in the square leg area, had to restrain his colleague.

A worse example of misbehaviour it would be difficult to imagine, but Carr again deducted just ten per cent off the match fee. The Australian Board then moved in and withheld both players' entire fee for the Test. Carr compounded his errors by fining Rhodes the same ten per cent for transgressing the regulation about advertising logos on the straps of his pads.

The TV umpire, an idea which South Africa introduced to the world in 1992, had his duties widened to deal with all line decisions, including boundary-rope infringements by fielders. But lack of direct communication between the umpires on and off the field resulted in at least four such boundaries not being given. Even more important was the flaw exposed in the use of television to judge run-outs, when a fielder obstructed the camera at the crucial moment. The broadcasting authorities refused to meet the considerable cost of installing two extra cameras, on either side of the pitch. A further problem arose in the Third Test, when Hudson could not be given run out because he finished well wide of the crease. The line was subsequently extended six metres either side of the pitch, but even that might not be enough for incidents involving a runner standing by the square-leg umpire.

AUSTRALIAN TOURING PARTY

A. R. Border (Queensland) (*captain*), M. A. Taylor (New South Wales) (*vice-captain*), D. C. Boon (Tasmania), M. L. Hayden (Queensland), I. A. Healy (Queensland), M. G. Hughes (Victoria), D. M. Jones (Victoria), C. J. McDermott (Queensland), G. D. McGrath (New South Wales), T. B. A. May (South Australia), P. R. Reiffel (Victoria), M. J. Slater (New South Wales), S. K. Warne (Victoria), M. E. Waugh (New South Wales), S. R. Waugh (New South Wales).

D. W. Fleming (Victoria) joined the party when McDermott returned home with a knee injury.

Manager: Dr C. Battersby. *Coach:* R. B. Simpson.

AUSTRALIAN TOUR RESULTS

Test matches – Played 3: Won 1, Lost 1, Drawn 1.
First-class matches – Played 6: Won 3, Lost 1, Drawn 2.
Wins – South Africa, Northern Transvaal, Orange Free State.
Loss – South Africa.
Draws – South Africa, Boland.
One-day internationals – Played 8: Won 4, Lost 4.
Other non first-class matches – Played 2: Drawn 1, No result 1. *Draw* – N. F. Oppenheimer's XI. *No result* – UCBSA President's XI.

TEST MATCH AVERAGES

SOUTH AFRICA – BATTING

	T	*I*	*NO*	*R*	*HS*	*100s*	*Avge*	*Ct*
A. C. Hudson	3	5	0	293	102	1	58.60	1
J. N. Rhodes	3	5	0	193	78	0	38.60	2
W. J. Cronje	3	5	0	190	122	1	38.00	0
P. N. Kirsten	3	5	0	187	70	0	37.40	4
B. M. McMillan	3	5	0	185	84	0	37.00	2
D. J. Richardson	3	5	0	175	59	0	35.00	7
G. Kirsten	3	5	0	162	47	0	32.40	4
C. R. Matthews	3	5	3	45	31*	0	22.50	0
K. C. Wessels	3	5	0	89	50	0	17.80	2
A. A. Donald	3	5	3	22	15*	0	11.00	2
P. S. de Villiers	3	5	0	27	16	0	5.40	2

* *Signifies not out.*

BOWLING

	O	*M*	*R*	*W*	*BB*	*5W/i*	*Avge*
C. R. Matthews	134	44	297	13	5-80	1	22.84
A. A. Donald	128	21	425	12	3-66	0	35.41
P. S. de Villiers	147.3	33	405	11	4-117	0	36.81
B. M. McMillan	108	25	321	6	3-61	0	53.50

Also bowled: W. J. Cronje 36.3–10–61–1; G. Kirsten 18.1–2–50–0; J. N. Rhodes 1–1–0–0.

AUSTRALIA – BATTING

	T	*I*	*NO*	*R*	*HS*	*100s*	*Avge*	*Ct*
S. R. Waugh	3	4	1	195	86	0	65.00	3
M. E. Waugh	3	5	1	233	113*	1	58.25	2
D. C. Boon	3	6	1	277	96	0	55.40	3
M. J. Slater	3	6	1	251	95	0	50.20	1
I. A. Healy	3	4	0	157	61	0	39.25	5
A. R. Border	3	5	1	152	45	0	38.00	4
M. A. Taylor	2	4	0	97	70	0	24.25	2
M. G. Hughes	2	3	1	33	26*	0	16.50	1
C. J. McDermott	3	4	0	48	31	0	12.00	0
S. K. Warne	3	5	0	41	15	0	8.20	0

Played in two Tests: G. D. McGrath 1*, 0*. Played in one Test: M. L. Hayden 15, 5 (1 ct); T. B. A. May 2, 11; P. R. Reiffel 13 (1 ct).

* *Signifies not out.*

BOWLING

	O	*M*	*R*	*W*	*BB*	*5W/i*	*Avge*
S. R. Waugh	77.5	29	130	10	5-28	1	13.00
S. K. Warne	190.5	69	336	15	4-86	0	22.40
G. D. McGrath	83.1	21	169	4	3-65	0	42.25
T. B. A. May	61	16	169	4	2-62	0	42.25
C. J. McDermott	128.2	26	370	7	3-63	0	52.85
M. G. Hughes	70	13	237	4	3-59	0	59.25

Also bowled: A. R. Border 9–3–17–0; P. R. Reiffel 30–7–77–2; M. E. Waugh 30–9–86–0.

AUSTRALIAN AVERAGES – FIRST-CLASS MATCHES

BATTING

	M	*I*	*NO*	*R*	*HS*	*100s*	*Avge*	*Ct/St*
M. E. Waugh	6	10	2	573	154	3	71.62	3
S. R. Waugh	5	7	1	400	102	1	66.66	6
M. J. Slater	6	12	1	548	105	1	49.81	1
I. A. Healy	6	10	3	277	61	0	39.57	21/2
D. C. Boon	6	11	1	392	96	0	39.20	7
A. R. Border	3	5	1	152	45	0	38.00	4
M. A. Taylor	5	10	0	373	75	0	37.30	3
M. L. Hayden	3	6	1	151	50	0	30.20	3
M. G. Hughes	5	5	1	71	30	0	17.75	1
P. R. Reiffel	4	5	1	53	22	0	13.25	5
S. K. Warne	5	8	1	84	34	0	12.00	1
C. J. McDermott	3	4	0	48	31	0	12.00	0

Played in four matches: G. D. McGrath 4, 1*, 0*. Played in three matches: T. B. A. May 1*, 2, 11. Played in two matches: D. M. Jones 85, 63, 20.

* *Signifies not out.*

BOWLING

	O	*M*	*R*	*W*	*BB*	*5W/i*	*Avge*
S. R. Waugh	89.5	31	157	11	5-28	1	14.27
P. R. Reiffel	116.1	24	320	14	4-27	0	22.85
S. K. Warne	278	96	552	24	4-86	0	23.00
G. D. McGrath	145.1	34	348	14	4-38	0	24.85
M. G. Hughes	161	27	563	17	4-127	0	33.11
T. B. A. May	143.1	33	437	12	5-98	1	36.41
C. J. McDermott	128.2	26	370	7	3-63	0	52.85

Also bowled: A. R. Border 9–3–17–0; D. M. Jones 2–0–6–1; M. E. Waugh 39–9–119–0.

Note: Matches in this section which were not first-class are signified by a dagger.

†At Randjesfontein, February 10. Drawn. Australians batted first by mutual agreement. Australians 223 (M. L. Hayden 40, D. M. Jones 60; E. A. E. Baptiste four for 56, J. Malao three for 59); N. F. Oppenheimer's XI 121-4 (H. H. Gibbs 32 not out, A. P. Kuiper 56).

NORTHERN TRANSVAAL v AUSTRALIANS

At Verwoerdburg, February 12, 13, 14. Australians won by 249 runs. Toss: Northern Transvaal.

The Australians' opening first-class match was a successful loosener against one of the Castle Cup's weaker sides, and several of their batsmen hit form in the first innings. In the second, Mark Waugh, with a three-hour hundred, and Taylor added 165 at more than a run a minute, to set Northern Transvaal a target of 436, with which they never came to terms. Reiffel had match figures of eight for 84 and the tourists won with more than a day to spare. Australian wicket-keeper Healy had 11 dismissals in the match, which was a record for a game in South Africa, a figure beaten only three times in history and equalled six times.

Close of play: First day, Australians 274-5 (D. M. Jones 72*, I. A. Healy 1*); Second day, Australians 10-0 (M. A. Taylor 4*, M. J. Slater 5*).

Australians

M. J. Slater b van Noordwyk	51	– (2) b Smith	8
*M. A. Taylor b van Noordwyk	28	– (1) c Smith b van Zyl	75
D. C. Boon run out	48	– (5) lbw b van Zyl	1
M. E. Waugh c Rule b Elworthy	8	– (3) st Rule b Sommerville	134
M. L. Hayden c Rule b Smith	50	– (6) not out	14
D. M. Jones c Rule b Elworthy	85		
†I. A. Healy c Vorster b Smith	12	– (4) not out	38
P. R. Reiffel c Rule b Elworthy	22		
M. G. Hughes c and b Elworthy	30		
T. B. A. May not out	1		
G. D. McGrath b Bosch	4		
L-b 7, w 1, n-b 16	24	B 4, w 2, n-b 5	11
1/62 2/99 3/141 4/147 5/273 6/298 7/309 8/350 9/358	363	1/19 2/184 3/244 4/245 (4 wkts dec.)	281

Bowling: *First Innings*—Elworthy 25–5–85–4; Smith 20–1–97–2; Bosch 18.2–4–48–1; van Noordwyk 19–4–70–2; Pienaar 7–1–39–0; van Zyl 5–0–17–0. *Second Innings*—Elworthy 11–0–54–0; Smith 6–0–38–1; Bosch 4–0–23–0; van Zyl 21–4–83–2; Sommerville 12–0–37–1; van Noordwyk 8–1–42–0.

Northern Transvaal

B. J. Sommerville c Healy b Reiffel	10	– lbw b Reiffel	21
V. F. du Preez c Boon b McGrath	25	– c Healy b Hughes	0
R. F. Pienaar c Healy b Reiffel	0	– b Hughes	42
*J. J. Strydom c Waugh b Reiffel	22	– c Taylor b Reiffel	0
†K. J. Rule b McGrath	1	– c Healy b Reiffel	13
L. P. Vorster c Healy b McGrath	25	– c Healy b McGrath	12
D. J. van Zyl not out	63	– st Healy b May	8
S. Elworthy c Healy b Hughes	29	– c Healy b May	31
T. Bosch lbw b Hughes	0	– c Healy b Reiffel	4
C. van Noordwyk c Healy b Hughes	0	– not out	18
G. Smith c Hayden b Reiffel	4	– b Jones	21
L-b 6, w 6, n-b 18	30	B 2, l-b 6, w 3, n-b 5	16
1/35 2/35 3/47 4/49 5/94 6/113 7/187 8/187 9/187	209	1/0 2/31 3/31 4/82 5/82 6/96 7/114 8/142 9/146	186

Bowling: *First Innings*—McGrath 20–3–50–3; Hughes 20–1–72–3; Reiffel 12.1–4–27–4; Waugh 4–0–19–0; May 11–2–35–0. *Second Innings*—McGrath 11–2–61–1; Hughes 8–1–30–2; Reiffel 11–0–57–4; May 10–2–24–2; Jones 2–0–6–1.

Umpires: S. B. Lambson and K. E. Liebenberg.

†At Potchefstroom, February 17. No result. Toss: President's XI. Australians 142 for five (35 overs) (D. C. Boon 42, M. E. Waugh 55) v UCBSA President's XI.

†SOUTH AFRICA v AUSTRALIA

First One-Day International

At Johannesburg, February 19. South Africa won by five runs. Toss: South Africa. International debut: E. O. Simons.

A capacity crowd of 30,000 watched de Villiers bowl one of the best-ever penultimate overs in a one-day international. It contained six successive yorkers which yielded one run and the wicket of Border. A home total of 232 for three was based on 112 from 120 balls from Cronje, his maiden century in limited-overs internationals. He had good support from Peter Kirsten and Rhodes, with whom he added 106 in just 14 overs. McGrath was Australia's best bowler, but their more experienced players disappointed, both with ball and bat. The top six all reached double figures, but none went on to play a major innings and de Villiers's over upset all Australia's calculations: they finished five runs behind, even though they had five wickets in hand. Simons marked his debut with two for 29 in ten overs after conceding 12 in his first two; Donald's erratic form was worrying for South Africa.

Man of the Match: W. J. Cronje.

South Africa

P. N. Kirsten c Reiffel b McGrath	47	A. P. Kuiper not out	2
G. Kirsten c Healy b Reiffel	12	L-b 5, w 2, n-b 5	12
W. J. Cronje c Reiffel b McDermott	112		
J. N. Rhodes not out	47	1/39 2/123 3/229 (3 wkts, 50 overs)	232

*K. C. Wessels, †D. J. Richardson, E. O. Simons, R. P. Snell, P. S. de Villiers and A. A. Donald did not bat.

Bowling: McDermott 10–0–52–1; Reiffel 10–1–36–1; McGrath 10–1–29–1; S. R. Waugh 10–0–54–0; Warne 10–0–56–0.

Australia

M. A. Taylor b Snell	30	†I. A. Healy not out	4
D. C. Boon c Rhodes b Kuiper	58		
D. M. Jones c Cronje b Simons	42	L-b 4, w 3, n-b 1	8
M. E. Waugh c Richardson b Simons	14		—
S. R. Waugh not out	46	1/61 2/108 3/143 (5 wkts, 50 overs)	227
*A. R. Border b de Villiers	25	4/155 5/209	

P. R. Reiffel, S. K. Warne, C. J. McDermott and G. D. McGrath did not bat.

Bowling: Donald 9–1–46–0; de Villiers 10–0–43–1; Snell 10–0–55–1; Simons 10–0–29–2; Kuiper 7–0–30–1; Cronje 4–0–20–0.

Umpires: S. B. Lambson and C. J. Mitchley.

†SOUTH AFRICA v AUSTRALIA

Second One-Day International

At Verwoerdburg, February 20. South Africa won by 56 runs. Toss: South Africa.

Cronje continued his domination of Warne, with three more sixes to follow two in three balls the previous day. His 97 from 102 balls ensured a good total before Kuiper played an innings which was violent even by his standards. He hit an unbeaten 47 off 22 balls, including three successive sixes off the last three balls of the innings, bowled by McDermott. The over cost 26 in all. Australia were then well beaten, thanks to a fine three-wicket burst from Matthews, although Steve Waugh and Border put on 107 for the fifth wicket, with Border's savage 41 rivalling the earlier onslaught of Kuiper. Donald was dropped for the match, underlining the strength in depth of South Africa's pace bowling.

Man of the Match: W. J. Cronje.

South Africa

P. N. Kirsten b M. E. Waugh	22	E. O. Simons not out	2
G. Kirsten c S. R. Waugh b McGrath	18		
W. J. Cronje run out	97	L-b 6, w 3, n-b 4	13
J. N. Rhodes lbw b Warne	44		—
*K. C. Wessels c Healy b McGrath	22	1/45 2/58 3/152 (5 wkts, 50 overs)	265
A. P. Kuiper not out	47	4/203 5/229	

†D. J. Richardson, R. P. Snell, P. S. de Villiers and C. R. Matthews did not bat.

Bowling: McDermott 10–3–46–0; Reiffel 8–0–50–0; M. E. Waugh 9–1–52–1; McGrath 10–1–42–2; S. R. Waugh 5–0–28–0; Warne 8–1–41–1.

Australia

D. C. Boon c Cronje b Matthews	2	S. K. Warne c Wessels b Cronje	9
M. A. Taylor run out	21	C. J. McDermott run out	16
D. M. Jones b Matthews	5	G. D. McGrath not out	0
M. E. Waugh lbw b Matthews	0	L-b 12, w 3	15
S. R. Waugh b Simons	86		—
*A. R. Border run out	41	1/11 2/19 3/19 (42.4 overs)	209
†I. A. Healy c G. Kirsten b Kuiper	4	4/34 5/141 6/145	
P. R. Reiffel c Simons b de Villiers	10	7/174 8/189 9/209	

Bowling: de Villiers 8–2–20–1; Matthews 8–2–26–3; Simons 7.4–0–39–1; Snell 8–0–38–0; Kuiper 6–0–38–1; Cronje 5–0–36–1.

Umpires: W. Diedricks and K. E. Liebenberg.

†SOUTH AFRICA v AUSTRALIA

Third One-Day International

At Port Elizabeth, February 22. Australia won by 88 runs. Toss: Australia.

Border's first successful toss of the series brought Australia's first win – the ninth successive limited-overs game between the two teams to be won by the side batting first. Despite taking 20 balls to get off the mark, Jones eventually passed 6,000 runs in one-day internationals, and his busy partnership of 123 for the second wicket with Boon stole the initiative. Only Matthews conceded fewer than five runs per over. Mark Waugh rammed home the advantage with a fluent 60 and Border himself smashed an unbeaten 40 off 17 balls. Once Cronje went for 45 and Kuiper for 33 from 16 balls, Warne and McDermott were too much for the home batsmen. Warne, who was hit for 97 from 18 overs in the first two matches, returned four for 36.

Man of the Match: M. E. Waugh.

Australia

M. A. Taylor c Richardson b de Villiers	2
D. C. Boon b de Villiers	76
D. M. Jones run out	67
M. E. Waugh c Rhodes b Matthews	60
C. J. McDermott run out	15
S. R. Waugh c Matthews b Donald	18
*A. R. Border not out	40
†I. A. Healy not out	1
L-b 1, w 1	2
1/12 2/135 3/180 4/198 5/233 6/276 (6 wkts, 50 overs)	281

P. R. Reiffel, S. K. Warne and G. D. McGrath did not bat.

Bowling: de Villiers 10–1–55–2; Matthews 10–1–46–1; Donald 10–0–60–1; Cronje 10–1–62–0; Symcox 4–0–25–0; Kuiper 6–0–32–0.

South Africa

P. N. Kirsten c McGrath b Warne	27
G. Kirsten b McDermott	6
W. J. Cronje c McDermott b S. R. Waugh	45
J. N. Rhodes c Healy b M. E. Waugh	36
*K. C. Wessels run out	5
A. P. Kuiper b McDermott	33
†D. J. Richardson not out	23
P. L. Symcox c Boon b Warne	4
C. R. Matthews b Warne	0
P. S. de Villiers b Warne	4
A. A. Donald b McDermott	0
L-b 6, n-b 4	10
1/8 2/49 3/115 4/125 5/127 6/165 7/178 8/181 9/188 (43 overs)	193

Bowling: McDermott 10–1–35–3; McGrath 7–2–17–0; Reiffel 8–0–40–0; Warne 10–0–36–4; S. R. Waugh 4–0–33–1; M. E. Waugh 4–0–26–1.

Umpires: R. E. Koertzen and C. J. Mitchley.

†SOUTH AFRICA v AUSTRALIA

Fourth One-Day International

At Durban, February 24. South Africa won by seven wickets. Toss: Australia.

More superb seam bowling by Matthews and Simons had Australia in such trouble that only three batsmen reached double figures. A well-grassed pitch meant that a total of around 200 would have been useful, but without Border's unbeaten 69 the visitors would not have managed half that. South Africa galloped home with five overs to spare: Cronje capped a magnificent four games with 50 not out, to take his aggregate to 304 in three completed innings. He was accompanied by Wessels, whose unbeaten 40 settled home nerves following three early setbacks. The easy win gave South Africa a 3-1 lead after the first four one-day games, with the remaining four to be played under lights after the Test series.

Man of the Match: C. R. Matthews.

Australia

D. C. Boon c de Villiers b Simons	34	S. K. Warne b Matthews	23
M. J. Slater c Richardson b de Villiers	1	C. J. McDermott b Matthews	0
D. M. Jones lbw b Matthews	8	G. D. McGrath c Richardson b Cronje	0
M. E. Waugh c Hudson b Matthews	3	L-b 7, w 4, n-b 3	14
S. R. Waugh lbw b Simons	2		—
*A. R. Border not out	69	1/3 2/12 3/18 (43.2 overs)	154
†I. A. Healy c Richardson b Kuiper	0	4/23 5/91 6/93	
P. R. Reiffel c Wessels b Kuiper	0	7/100 8/138 9/138	

Bowling: de Villiers 8–0–30–1; Matthews 8–5–10–4; Simons 10–4–22–2; Snell 9–1–42–0; Cronje 3.2–0–19–1; Kuiper 5–0–24–2.

South Africa

A. C. Hudson lbw b Reiffel	37	*K. C. Wessels not out	40
P. N. Kirsten c Healy b Reiffel	15	L-b 1, w 8, n-b 3	12
W. J. Cronje not out	50		—
J. N. Rhodes c M. E. Waugh b Warne	3	1/51 2/55 3/69 (3 wkts, 45 overs)	157

A. P. Kuiper, E. O. Simons, †D. J. Richardson, R. P. Snell, C. R. Matthews and P. S. de Villiers did not bat.

Bowling: McDermott 10–0–35–0; McGrath 10–4–20–0; S. R. Waugh 4–0–24–0; Reiffel 10–1–31–2; Warne 8–2–32–1; M. E. Waugh 3–0–14–0.

Umpires: W. Diedricks and K. E. Liebenberg.

ORANGE FREE STATE v AUSTRALIANS

At Bloemfontein, February 26, 27, 28, March 1. Australians won by 60 runs. Toss: Australians.

Although Slater and the Waugh twins scored hundreds and the Australians won by 60 runs, everything was overshadowed by the performance in defeat of Cronje, who scored 251, his maiden double-century, 63 per cent of the second-innings total of 396. The next-highest score was Liebenberg's 39. The majestic innings brought Cronje's aggregate against the Australians to 599 in 11 days. He batted for 409 minutes and faced 306 deliveries, hitting 28 fours and four sixes – three off consecutive balls from May. He was also severe on Hughes, who hardly looked back to full fitness and form. In the Australian first innings the Waughs had put on 232 for the fourth wicket, and Slater hit six sixes in the second innings, with his second 50 coming off 30 balls, to set Orange Free State a target of 457. While Cronje was batting, they always had a chance of scoring it.

Close of play: First day, Australians 416-5 (M. L. Hayden 25*, I. A. Healy 16*); Second day, Orange Free State 264; Third day, Orange Free State 102-1 (G. F. J. Liebenberg 35*, W. J. Cronje 51*).

Australians

M. J. Slater c Liebenberg b Player	65	– (2) c Arthur b Boje	105
*M. A. Taylor c Radley b van Zyl	35	– (1) c sub (C. F. Craven) b Venter	54
D. C. Boon c Radley b Player	9	– b Venter	5
M. E. Waugh c Arthur b Player	154		
S. R. Waugh c Player b Bakkes	102		
M. L. Hayden c Cronje b van Zyl	31	– (4) c Arthur b Venter	36
†I. A. Healy c Radley b Player	38	– (6) not out	23
P. R. Reiffel c Arthur b van Zyl	2		
S. K. Warne not out	0	– (5) c Steyn b Venter	34
M. G. Hughes (did not bat)		– (7) c Liebenberg b Venter	8
B 1, l-b 6, w 1, n-b 6	14	L-b 4, n-b 1	5
	—		—
1/66 2/86 3/135 4/367 5/382 (8 wkts dec.)	450	1/81 2/107 3/203 (6 wkts dec.)	270
6/443 7/449 8/450		4/204 5/261 6/270	

T. B. A. May did not bat.

Bowling: *First Innings*—Bakkes 18–3–73–1; Player 28.3–2–107–4; van Zyl 27–4–76–3; Boje 22–4–90–0; Venter 12–0–68–0; Cronje 10–2–29–0. *Second Innings*—van Zyl 13–1–34–0; Player 7–1–20–0; Bakkes 8–1–24–0; Cronje 4–1–19–0; Venter 26–4–101–5; Boje 17–1–68–1.

Orange Free State

J. M. Arthur b Warne	51	– lbw b Hughes	10
G. F. J. Liebenberg c Healy b Hughes	28	– lbw b Hughes	39
*W. J. Cronje c Hayden b May	44	– c Reiffel b May	251
L. J. Wilkinson c Reiffel b May	53	– b Reiffel	5
P. J. R. Steyn c S. R. Waugh b Hughes	5	– c Healy b S. R. Waugh	22
J. F. Venter c Boon b May	13	– run out	16
C. J. P. G. van Zyl c S. R. Waugh b May	22	– c Healy b Hughes	2
B. T. Player lbw b Warne	10	– c Healy b Hughes	17
N. Boje st Healy b Warne	7	– b Warne	6
†P. J. L. Radley not out	16	– lbw b Warne	4
H. C. Bakkes c Boon b May	2	– not out	12
B 5, l-b 5, w 1, n-b 2	13	B 5, l-b 2, w 2, n-b 3	12
1/52 2/127 3/133 4/142 5/174 6/206 7/219 8/231 9/247	264	1/19 2/127 3/150 4/225 5/271 6/286 7/314 8/374 9/384	396

Bowling: *First Innings*—Hughes 18–5–47–2; Reiffel 10–1–36–0; May 35.1–9–98–5; Warne 23–5–73–3. *Second Innings*—Hughes 25–2–127–4; Reiffel 23–3–60–1; Warne 28.2–6–70–2; May 26–4–111–1; S. R. Waugh 6–0–21–1.

Umpires: R. A. Noble and D. L. Orchard.

SOUTH AFRICA v AUSTRALIA

First Test Match

At Johannesburg, March 4, 5, 6, 7, 8. South Africa won by 197 runs. Toss: South Africa. Test debut: M. L. Hayden.

South Africa's win by 197 runs signalled their return to the upper bracket of Test-playing countries. In Australia, they had hung on for a drawn series, following a wonderful but slightly freakish win in Sydney with a defeat in Adelaide. At the magnificently refurbished Wanderers ground, they achieved the best of their four Test wins since their return, not only outplaying Australia, but outfighting them.

Resilience, courage and the refusal to lie down are well-known Australian traits, but the home side were superior in all aspects of the game, including discipline. It was a pity that such an enthralling contest should have been sullied by Warne and Hughes, both found guilty of verbally abusing the batsmen, while Hughes also reacted over-aggressively to a spectator.

On the opening day South Africa recovered from 126 for six to a respectable 251, thanks to a fighting 69 from Rhodes, whose runs came in two crucial partnerships of 68 and 46 with Richardson and de Villiers. The pitch was cracked, but proved home forecasts right and those from the Australian camp wrong, by lasting the five days and not offering inordinate turn to the spinners. None the less it seemed curious that Border did not bowl Warne until the 49th over of the first innings and the 44th of the second, which is thought to have put him in the temper that led to his disgraceful – and almost unprecedented – outburst when he finally came on and dismissed Hudson. Rarely on a cricket field has physical violence seemed so close.

The all-pace attack of South Africa, in contrast, showed commendable discipline and application in bowling Australia out twice, although they were helped by the run-outs of Mark Waugh and Border on the second day. After two almost equal first innings, the failure of anyone but Rhodes to achieve a half-century was put into context in South Africa's second innings. Hudson batted beautifully for 60, and fifties from Peter Kirsten and Wessels provided ideal support for Cronje, whose second Test hundred contained a six and 16 fours. His 122 took four hours and enabled Wessels to set a target of 454 – never achieved to win in Test history – in a minimum of 133 overs. At 136 for two, with Boon in residence, Australia were making a fight of it after the unfortunate Hayden's debut ended with a broken thumb. But poor middle-order batting enabled South Africa to clinch victory with a session to spare, though the Australian last-wicket pair survived for an hour. With storm clouds gathering, May was dismissed by Cronje.

Man of the Match: W. J. Cronje.

Close of play: First day, Australia 34-0 (M. J. Slater 26*, M. L. Hayden 6*); Second day, South Africa 42-0 (A. C. Hudson 22*, G. Kirsten 17*); Third day, South Africa 335-5 (P. N. Kirsten 32*, P. S. de Villiers 4*); Fourth day, Australia 123-2 (D. C. Boon 56*, M. E. Waugh 16*).

South Africa

A. C. Hudson c Healy b McDermott	17	– b Warne	60
G. Kirsten b Hughes	47	– c Hughes b May	35
W. J. Cronje c Border b S. R. Waugh	21	– c S. R. Waugh b Hughes	122
*K. C. Wessels c Hayden b Hughes	18	– c Border b Warne	50
P. N. Kirsten b May	12	– c Boon b May	53
J. N. Rhodes c M. E. Waugh b McDermott	69	– c Healy b S. R. Waugh	14
B. M. McMillan c Boon b May	0	– (8) b Warne	24
†D. J. Richardson lbw b Warne	31	– (9) c Border b Warne	20
C. R. Matthews c Boon b Hughes	6	– (10) not out	31
P. S. de Villiers b McDermott	16	– (7) b McDermott	4
A. A. Donald not out	0	– not out	15
B 1, l-b 10, n-b 3	14	B 13, l-b 4, n-b 5	22
1/21 (1) 2/70 (3) 3/103 (2) 4/116 (4) 5/126 (5) 6/126 (7) 7/194 (8) 8/203 (9) 9/249 (6) 10/251 (10)	251	1/76 (2) 2/123 (1) 3/258 (4) 4/289 (3) 5/324 (6) 6/343 (7) 7/366 (5) 8/403 (9) 9/406 (8)	(9 wkts dec.) 450

Bowling: *First Innings*—McDermott 15.2–3–63–3; Hughes 20–6–59–3; May 22–5–62–2; S. R. Waugh 9–2–14–1; Warne 14–4–42–1. *Second Innings*—McDermott 35–3–112–1; Hughes 25–5–86–1; May 39–11–107–2; S. R. Waugh 10–3–28–1; M. E. Waugh 6–2–14–0; Warne 44.5–14–86–4.

Australia

M. J. Slater c Hudson b de Villiers	26	– (2) b de Villiers	41
M. L. Hayden c Richardson b Donald	15	– (1) b de Villiers	5
D. C. Boon c de Villiers b Donald	17	– b Matthews	83
M. E. Waugh run out	42	– c Richardson b Donald	28
*A. R. Border run out	34	– c G. Kirsten b McMillan	14
S. R. Waugh not out	45	– c Richardson b Matthews	0
†I. A. Healy b Matthews	11	– c and b Donald	30
M. G. Hughes c G. Kirsten b McMillan	7	– not out	26
S. K. Warne lbw b Matthews	15	– lbw b McMillan	1
C. J. McDermott lbw b Donald	31	– b McMillan	10
T. B. A. May lbw b de Villiers	2	– c G. Kirsten b Cronje	11
B 1, l-b 1, n-b 1	3	L-b 5, n-b 2	7
1/35 (1) 2/56 (2) 3/70 (3) 4/136 (4) 5/142 (5) 6/169 (7) 7/176 (8) 8/201 (9) 9/245 (10) 10/248 (11)	248	1/18 (1) 2/95 (2) 3/136 (4) 4/164 (5) 5/164 (6) 6/191 (3) 7/219 (7) 8/225 (9) 9/235 (10) 10/256 (11)	256

Bowling: *First Innings*—Donald 19–0–86–3; de Villiers 19.3–1–74–2; McMillan 14–3–46–1; Matthews 15–4–40–2. *Second Innings*—Donald 23–3–71–2; de Villiers 30–11–70–2; McMillan 19–2–61–3; Matthews 20–6–42–2; G. Kirsten 4–0–7–0; Cronje 0.3–0–0–1.

Umpires: D. R. Shepherd (England) and S. B. Lambson. Referee: D. B. Carr (England).

BOLAND v AUSTRALIANS

At Stellenbosch, March 12, 13, 14. Drawn. Toss: Boland.

The tourists were looking for batting practice and hoped to restore Hughes to full fitness and form. He managed only two for 50 but raised some laughs by ostentatiously applauding the arrival of the Australian officials who had just fined him. McGrath, however, pushed his claims for a Test place by taking six for 68 in the match. The Australians declared twice, with Taylor, who missed the First Test because of illness, scoring 74 in the second innings, and they left Boland 328 to win; the match was called off, in intense heat, with an hour remaining. Dalrymple, originally 12th man, was allowed to play for Boland, after Wayne Truter was injured on the first day.

Close of play: First day, Australians 254-7 dec.; Second day, Australians 154-2 (S. R. Waugh 49*, D. M. Jones 0*).

Australians

M. J. Slater c Henderson b Erasmus	40	– (2) c Germishuys b Erasmus	28
*M. A. Taylor c Erasmus b Smith	10	– (1) st Germishuys b Drew	74
D. C. Boon lbw b Drew	52		
M. E. Waugh st Germishuys b Henderson	43	– (8) not out	1
D. M. Jones b Drew	63	– (4) c Jackson b Henderson	20
S. R. Waugh run out	32	– (3) lbw b Henderson	71
†I. A. Healy c Roos b Drew	1	– not out	8
P. R. Reiffel not out	8	– (6) lbw b Erasmus	8
S. K. Warne (did not bat)		– (5) st Germishuys b Henderson	9
L-b 1, w 1, n-b 3	5	B 7, l-b 2	9
1/15 2/88 3/138 4/156 5/221 6/229 7/254 (7 wkts dec.)	254	1/68 2/140 3/199 4/206 5/215 6/219 (6 wkts dec.)	228

M. G. Hughes and G. D. McGrath did not bat.

Bowling: *First Innings*—Smith 12–2–32–1; Roos 13–3–40–0; Henderson 15–2–49–1; Erasmus 21–4–64–1; Drew 16–2–68–3. *Second Innings*—Smith 10–1–29–0; Erasmus 21–5–37–2; Roos 3–1–8–0; Henderson 20–1–73–3; Drew 15–4–72–1.

Boland

L. Ferreira c Reiffel b Hughes	3	– (3) lbw b McGrath	41
K. C. Jackson b Warne	27	– c Healy b Reiffel	4
*T. N. Lazard c Boon b Hughes	4	– (1) b Reiffel	44
J. B. Commins lbw b Reiffel	4	– b McGrath	0
R. I. Dalrymple c Healy b McGrath	33	– not out	17
J. S. Roos lbw b McGrath	40	– c Reiffel b Warne	9
†L-M. Germishuys c Warne b McGrath	2	– not out	4
M. Erasmus lbw b McGrath	0		
C. W. Henderson not out	19		
B. J. Drew c S. R. Waugh b Warne	4		
D. Smith lbw b Warne	3		
B 1, l-b 3, n-b 12	16	B 1, l-b 8, w 2, n-b 2	13
1/5 2/18 3/30 4/48 5/123 6/126 7/126 8/129 9/141	155	1/11 2/96 3/96 4/96 5/120 (5 wkts)	132

Bowling: *First Innings*—Hughes 9–2–21–2; Reiffel 18–6–40–1; McGrath 18–6–38–4; Warne 20.5–9–49–3; S. R. Waugh 4–1–3–0. *Second Innings*—Hughes 11–3–29–0; Reiffel 12–3–23–2; Warne 15–7–24–1; McGrath 13–2–30–2; M. E. Waugh 5–0–14–0; S. R. Waugh 2–1–3–0.

Umpires: W. Diedricks and S. F. Marais.

SOUTH AFRICA v AUSTRALIA

Second Test Match

At Cape Town, March 17, 18, 19, 20, 21. Australia won by nine wickets. Toss: South Africa.

A memorable all-round performance by Steve Waugh brought Australia a nine-wicket win with more than a session to spare. For most of the first four days, the match seemed to be drifting to a draw on a slow, low pitch. But Australia gradually gained the advantage as Waugh shared a sixth-wicket partnership of 108 with Healy, steering his side towards 435 and a lead of 74. Then, when South Africa were 69 for one that evening, he changed the course of the match. First he took a return catch off Cronje; next, after Border ran out Wessels, he trapped Hudson lbw. There were two wickets for Warne before the close and Waugh returned to dismiss McMillan next morning on the way to Test-best figures of 22.3–9–28–5. The collapse of six wickets for 34 runs proved near-terminal.

Had Australia not fallen foul of the rule for recalculating the daily quota of overs, they might have created further damage on that fourth evening. But South Africa's slow over-rate in the first half of the day robbed the tourists – and the public – of five overs. The argument that a side bowling second in a split day should not have to make up overs lost by the other team is not valid. Particularly on the penultimate day, a fielding side should not be encouraged to slow their over-rate to improve their chance of saving the match.

On the first day, Wessels elected to bat and South Africa raced away, with Hudson and Gary Kirsten scoring 71 in the first 14 overs against a pace attack in which only McGrath was impressive. Kirsten was run out by a diving Slater, but Hudson completed a lovely hundred – his second in Test cricket – on his birthday, before he, too, was brilliantly run out by Steve Waugh. With Cronje and Wessels dismissed cheaply, the innings was in the balance at 198 for five, but 70 from Peter Kirsten and 74 from McMillan ensured a respectable 361.

That total occupied nine and a half hours and Australia were no more able to score quickly, taking eleven and a half hours over 435. Taylor made a successful return with 70 and Boon scored an obdurate 96. Despite the herculean efforts of de Villiers and Matthews, South Africa's all-seam attack could only settle for disciplined containment on the first Newlands Test pitch prepared by former Essex and Warwickshire groundsman Andy Atkinson. Its lack of pace and bounce made the pitch equally unsuitable for wrist spin, but Warne still returned magnificent match figures of 77–31–116–6. It was a fine effort all round from Australia after the defeat at Johannesburg.

Man of the Match: S. R. Waugh.

Close of play: First day, South Africa 237-5 (P. N. Kirsten 62*, B. M. McMillan 16*); Second day, Australia 112-1 (M. A. Taylor 57*, D. C. Boon 26*); Third day, Australia 336-5 (S. R. Waugh 50*, I. A. Healy 15*); Fourth day, South Africa 100-6 (J. N. Rhodes 1*, B. M. McMillan 1*).

South Africa

A. C. Hudson run out	102	– lbw b S. R. Waugh	49
G. Kirsten run out	29	– lbw b Warne	10
W. J. Cronje b McGrath	2	– c and b S. R. Waugh	19
*K. C. Wessels c M. E. Waugh b McDermott	11	– run out	9
P. N. Kirsten lbw b Warne	70	– c Taylor b Warne	3
J. N. Rhodes lbw b McGrath	5	– c Border b S. R. Waugh	27
B. M. McMillan b Warne	74	– (8) lbw b S. R. Waugh	3
†D. J. Richardson lbw b McDermott	34	– (9) c Healy b McGrath	31
C. R. Matthews not out	7	– (10) not out	0
P. S. de Villiers c Taylor b Warne	7	– (7) lbw b Warne	0
A. A. Donald c Healy b McGrath	7	– b S. R. Waugh	0
L-b 6, n-b 7	13	B 4, l-b 6, n-b 3	13
1/71 (2) 2/78 (3) 3/100 (4) 4/189 (1) 5/198 (6) 6/260 (5) 7/335 (8) 8/339 (7) 9/348 (10) 10/361 (11)	361	1/33 (2) 2/69 (3) 3/94 (4) 4/97 (1) 5/97 (5) 6/97 (7) 7/103 (8) 8/164 (9) 9/164 (6) 10/164 (11)	164

Bowling: *First Innings*—McDermott 27-6-80-2; Hughes 20-1-80-0; McGrath 26.1-4-65-3; S. R. Waugh 9-3-20-0; Warne 47-18-78-3; M. E. Waugh 10-3-23-0; Border 5-2-9-0. *Second Innings*—McDermott 13-3-39-0; Hughes 5-1-12-0; Warne 30-13-38-3; McGrath 16-6-26-1; S. R. Waugh 22.3-9-28-5; Border 1-1-0-0; M. E. Waugh 3-1-11-0.

Australia

M. J. Slater c P. N. Kirsten b de Villiers	26	– (2) not out	43
M. A. Taylor c Richardson b de Villiers	70	– (1) b Donald	14
D. C. Boon c Richardson b de Villiers	96	– not out	32
M. E. Waugh c P. N. Kirsten b McMillan	7		
*A. R. Border c Richardson b Matthews	45		
S. R. Waugh b Matthews	86		
†I. A. Healy c de Villiers b Matthews	61		
M. G. Hughes lbw b Matthews	0		
S. K. Warne c McMillan b de Villiers	11		
C. J. McDermott c P. N. Kirsten b Matthews	1		
G. D. McGrath not out	1		
B 6, l-b 17, w 1, n-b 7	31	B 1, n-b 2	3
1/40 (1) 2/145 (2) 3/153 (4) 4/244 (3) 5/310 (5) 6/418 (7) 7/418 (8) 8/430 (6) 9/434 (10) 10/435 (9)	435	1/30 (1)	(1 wkt) 92

Bowling: *First Innings*—Donald 35-10-111-0; de Villiers 44.4-11-117-4; Matthews 36-12-80-5; McMillan 29-9-82-1; G. Kirsten 4-0-13-0; Cronje 11-4-9-0. *Second Innings*—Matthews 6-1-14-0; de Villiers 6-0-20-0; Donald 5-0-20-1; McMillan 5-0-23-0; Cronje 2-0-4-0; G. Kirsten 1.1-0-10-0.

Umpires: D. R. Shepherd (England) and K. E. Liebenberg. Referee: D. B. Carr (England).

SOUTH AFRICA v AUSTRALIA

Third Test Match

At Durban, March 25, 26, 27, 28, 29. Drawn. Toss: South Africa.

What could have been a thrilling climax to four months of hard-fought and fluctuating cricket between two aggressive, competitive sides ended tamely, with South Africa ignoring their chance to push for victory. By choosing to bowl first on a hard, grassy pitch, Wessels seemed determined to carry the attack to Australia. But once he had bowled them out for 269 and then seen his openers rattle up 100 for the first wicket – all before the end of the second day – his tactics over the next day and a half became baffling.

The loss of three quick wickets on the second evening was a set-back, but not one that should have dictated an overall run-rate of 2.05 an over, in a total of 422 which took nearly 14 hours to compile. It made no sense for the last 100 runs of the innings to use up 50 overs. Even when McMillan and Richardson were out, after adding 143, the tail-end batsmen came in to push and prod, putting on five insignificant runs as the last four wickets fell. The futility of such an approach considerably eased Australia's task of saving the match. Border diplomatically confined himself to an expression of disappointment about the dull nature of the game.

Hudson and Rhodes were the most positive in a batting order which chose to put safety first and then pursued it for at least two sessions more than necessary. Warne again proved his worth with four for 92 from 55 overs, and Steve Waugh's three for 40 from 27.2 overs made up for the absence of Hughes and the restricted mobility of McDermott, who returned home with a knee injury soon afterwards.

Waugh and Healy had rescued Australia from a desperate first-day situation of 123 for five with a fighting partnership of 92, but the tourists badly needed a major innings in the last four sessions if they were to save the game and the series. In fact they got two, of contrasting methods. Slater hit 95 from 202 balls, and Mark Waugh followed his first-day 43 with his sixth Test hundred. Once Slater was, perhaps unluckily, lbw for 95 – his third dismissal in the 90s in nine Tests – Waugh took over. His polished 113 not out was studded with his favourite drives and flicks between straight and square leg. Fittingly, it was Border, dropping anchor for over three hours in what was presumed to be his final Test appearance, who helped him to clinch the draw. Donald and Matthews were the pick of the home bowlers, but the match had already proved to be one contest too many.

Man of the Match: M. E. Waugh. *Man of the Series:* S. R. Waugh.

Close of play: First day, Australia 241-6 (S. R. Waugh 50*, P. R. Reiffel 8*); Second day, South Africa 143-3 (W. J. Cronje 16*, P. N. Kirsten 14*); Third day, South Africa 322-6 (B. M. McMillan 35*, D. J. Richardson 16*); Fourth day, Australia 89-2 (M. J. Slater 56*, S. K. Warne 4*).

Australia

First innings		Second innings	
M. J. Slater c Rhodes b Matthews	20	(2) lbw b Donald	95
M. A. Taylor lbw b Donald	1	(1) lbw b de Villiers	12
D. C. Boon c G. Kirsten b Donald	37	c P. N. Kirsten b Donald	12
M. E. Waugh c Richardson b Donald	43	(5) not out	113
*A. R. Border c Rhodes b McMillan	17	(6) not out	42
S. R. Waugh c Wessels b Matthews	64		
†I. A. Healy b Matthews	55		
P. R. Reiffel lbw b de Villiers	13		
S. K. Warne c Wessels b Matthews	2	(4) c McMillan b Donald	12
C. J. McDermott c Donald b de Villiers	6		
G. D. McGrath not out	0		
L-b 1, w 1, n-b 9	11	L-b 6, w 1, n-b 4	11
1/7 (2) 2/45 (1) 3/81 (3) 4/123 (5) 5/123 (4) 6/215 (7) 7/250 (8) 8/256 (9) 9/269 (6) 10/269 (10)	269	1/55 (1) 2/81 (3) 3/109 (4) 4/157 (2)	(4 wkts) 297

Bowling: *First Innings*—Donald 18–1–71–3; de Villiers 24.2–5–55–2; Matthews 29–9–65–4; McMillan 19–5–56–1; Cronje 5–1–8–0; G. Kirsten 6–1–13–0. *Second Innings*—Donald 28–7–66–3; de Villiers 24–5–69–1; McMillan 22–6–53–0; Matthews 28–12–56–0; Cronje 18–5–40–0; G. Kirsten 3–1–7–0; Rhodes 1–1–0–0.

South Africa

A. C. Hudson lbw b Reiffel	65
G. Kirsten c Healy b Reiffel	41
W. J. Cronje c S. R. Waugh b Warne	26
*K. C. Wessels lbw b McDermott	1
P. N. Kirsten lbw b S. R. Waugh	49
J. N. Rhodes lbw b Warne	78
B. M. McMillan c Slater b S. R. Waugh	84
†D. J. Richardson c Reiffel b Warne	59
C. R. Matthews lbw b Warne	1
P. S. de Villiers lbw b S. R. Waugh	0
A. A. Donald not out	0
B 3, l-b 10, n-b 5	18
1/100 (1) 2/117 (2) 3/118 (4) 4/155 (3) 5/256 (5) 6/274 (6) 7/417 (8) 8/422 (7) 9/422 (9) 10/422 (10)	422

Bowling: McDermott 38–11–76–1; Reiffel 30–7–77–2; McGrath 41–11–78–0; Warne 55–20–92–4; S. R. Waugh 27.2–12–40–3; M. E. Waugh 11–3–38–0; Border 3–0–8–0.

Umpires: Mahboob Shah (Pakistan) and C. J. Mitchley. Referee: D. B. Carr (England).

†SOUTH AFRICA v AUSTRALIA

Fifth One-Day International

At East London, April 2 (day/night). Australia won by seven wickets. Toss: South Africa.

Poor selection cost South Africa the match. On a slow, turning pitch, they stuck to their all-pace attack, while Australia not only chose both their specialist spinners but used Border's own left-arm spin with great success. Only Peter Kirsten offered resistance, with a patient 53. Once he was out, South Africa collapsed for 158. Even then, the loss of three wickets in quick succession posed problems. But Steve Waugh completed a splendid game with a scintillating unbeaten 67 at more than a run a ball, to secure victory with ten overs to spare. Donald missed this game and the rest of the one-day series, pleading exhaustion.

Man of the Match: A. R. Border.

South Africa

A. C. Hudson c Warne b Reiffel	14	†D. J. Richardson not out	7
P. N. Kirsten c M. E. Waugh b Warne	53	C. R. Matthews c Healy b Border	0
W. J. Cronje c Warne b May	10	P. S. de Villiers st Healy b Border	0
J. N. Rhodes st Healy b May	16	L-b 4, w 1, n-b 3	8
A. P. Kuiper run out	12		—
*K. C. Wessels run out	15	1/35 2/62 3/87 (49.5 overs)	158
E. O. Simons st Healy b Border	6	4/109 5/118 6/129	
B. M. McMillan b S. R. Waugh	17	7/139 8/155 9/158	

Bowling: McGrath 6–1–20–0; Reiffel 7–1–13–1; S. R. Waugh 9–1–25–1; May 10–0–35–2; Warne 10–0–34–1; Border 7.5–0–27–3.

Australia

M. J. Slater c P. N. Kirsten b Simons	31	S. R. Waugh not out	67
D. C. Boon run out	30	L-b 2	2
D. M. Jones lbw b Simons	8		—
M. E. Waugh not out	21	1/57 2/66 3/71 (3 wkts, 40 overs)	159

*A. R. Border, †I. A. Healy, P. R. Reiffel, S. K. Warne, T. B. A. May and G. D. McGrath did not bat.

Bowling: de Villiers 8–0–31–0; Matthews 8–0–34–0; Simons 10–2–32–2; McMillan 6–0–21–0; Cronje 7–0–32–0; Kuiper 1–0–7–0.

Umpires: R. E. Koertzen and K. E. Liebenberg.

†SOUTH AFRICA v AUSTRALIA

Sixth One-Day International

At Port Elizabeth, April 4 (day/night). South Africa won by 26 runs. Toss: South Africa.

A floodlight failure delayed Australia's innings and they eventually had to bat with two banks of lights on diminished power. South Africa's 227 for six included fine half-centuries from Hudson and Rhodes, who put on 105 in 20 overs, and the victory looked secure when the top seven Australian batsmen scored only 67 between them. But Warne joined Reiffel at 77 for seven to share a one-day international record of 119 for the eighth wicket, taking Australia unexpectedly close to victory. Both batsmen hit selectively for their fifties, and only a narrow run-out ended the partnership and clinched the match for the relieved South Africans.

Man of the Match: J. N. Rhodes.

South Africa

A. C. Hudson c Warne b May	63	B. M. McMillan not out	2
P. N. Kirsten b Reiffel	10	†D. J. Richardson not out	2
W. J. Cronje c Healy b M. E. Waugh	11	B 1, l-b 15, w 5, n-b 2	23
J. N. Rhodes c Jones b S. R. Waugh	66		—
*K. C. Wessels b Reiffel	27	1/18 2/48 3/153 (6 wkts, 50 overs)	227
E. O. Simons run out	23	4/175 5/216 6/223	

T. G. Shaw, C. R. Matthews and P. S. de Villiers did not bat.

Bowling: McGrath 10–1–41–0; Reiffel 10–1–33–2; M. E. Waugh 7–0–26–1; S. R. Waugh 10–1–48–1; May 10–0–45–1; Warne 3–0–18–0.

Australia

D. C. Boon c Wessels b de Villiers	4	S. K. Warne run out	55
M. J. Slater c Richardson b Matthews	16	T. B. A. May c and b de Villiers	4
D. M. Jones b Simons	13	G. D. McGrath not out	0
M. E. Waugh b Simons	17	L-b 13, w 4	17
S. R. Waugh lbw b McMillan	7		
*A. R. Border lbw b Shaw	5	1/4 2/35 3/50 (49.1 overs)	201
†I. A. Healy c Wessels b Shaw	5	4/59 5/65 6/68	
P. R. Reiffel c Simons b Matthews	58	7/77 8/196 9/201	

Bowling: de Villiers 9–1–42–2; Matthews 9.1–1–35–2; McMillan 8–0–38–1; Simons 10–3–24–2; Shaw 8–2–19–2; Cronje 5–1–30–0.

Umpires: W. Diedricks and S. B. Lambson.

†SOUTH AFRICA v AUSTRALIA

Seventh One-Day International

At Cape Town, April 6 (day/night). Australia won by 36 runs. Toss: Australia.

Australia reduced South Africa's lead to 4-3 with one to play. They made a dreadful start, losing Hayden and Jones for ten runs. But Taylor and Mark Waugh added 123 for the third wicket, and a rapid unbeaten 40 from Border took them to 242 for six. Hudson's 62 gave the crowd some hope of a win, provided that local hero Kuiper could cut loose. By the time he came in, the required run-rate was too high; an unbeaten 38 off as many balls showed what he might have achieved higher in the order. Warne bowled beautifully after just three expensive overs in the previous game.

Man of the Match: M. E. Waugh.

Australia

M. A. Taylor run out	63	†I. A. Healy c Wessels b Matthews	26
M. L. Hayden lbw b Matthews	0		
D. M. Jones c Richardson b Matthews	8	L-b 8, w 1, n-b 2	11
M. E. Waugh b Matthews	71		
S. R. Waugh b Simons	23	1/0 2/10 3/133 (6 wkts, 50 overs)	242
*A. R. Border not out	40	4/163 5/180 6/242	

P. R. Reiffel, S. K. Warne, T. B. A. May and G. D. McGrath did not bat.

Bowling: de Villiers 10–1–52–0; Matthews 10–0–47–4; McMillan 10–0–46–0; Simons 10–0–31–1; Cronje 5–0–40–0; Kuiper 5–0–18–0.

South Africa

A. C. Hudson lbw b Warne	62	E. O. Simons not out	9
G. Kirsten c M. E. Waugh b Reiffel	3		
W. J. Cronje c Taylor b Warne	37	B 1, l-b 8, n-b 1	10
J. N. Rhodes st Healy b Warne	35		
A. P. Kuiper not out	38	1/22 2/101 3/114 (5 wkts, 50 overs)	206
*K. C. Wessels c Border b M. E. Waugh	12	4/163 5/186	

B. M. McMillan, †D. J. Richardson, C. R. Matthews and P. S. de Villiers did not bat.

Bowling: McGrath 10–1–38–0; Reiffel 7–2–18–1; May 10–0–38–0; S. R. Waugh 4–0–22–0; Warne 10–0–31–3; M. E. Waugh 9–0–50–1.

Umpires: R. E. Koertzen and C. J. Mitchley.

†SOUTH AFRICA v AUSTRALIA

Eighth One-Day International

At Bloemfontein, April 8 (day/night). Australia won by one run. Toss: Australia.

Australia claimed an improbable victory to square the series after South Africa seemingly had the match won at 158 for three, needing 46 from the last nine overs. The final over was bowled by Fleming – in his first match of the tour – with six runs needed, and he held his nerve; Richardson was run out off the last ball trying to level the scores for a tie. Hudson made the only half-century of the match, and his 84 deserved to win it. But once he was caught by Border off Reiffel, the rot set in. Border, in his farewell international, astutely saved three Warne overs for the impatient Kuiper, who was first tied down and then caught, by Mark Waugh. Healy's unbeaten 41 off 31 balls for Australia had given them a total that proved just enough.

Man of the Match: A. C. Hudson. *Man of the Series:* S. R. Waugh.

Australia

M. J. Slater st Richardson b Shaw	34
M. A. Taylor c Wessels b Matthews	1
M. E. Waugh c Wessels b Simons	13
D. C. Boon c Wessels b Matthews	45
S. R. Waugh c McMillan b de Villiers	42
*A. R. Border c McMillan b Matthews	11
†I. A. Healy not out	41
P. R. Reiffel not out	8
L-b 6, w 1, n-b 1	8
1/7 2/31 3/69 4/140 5/143 6/184 (6 wkts, 50 overs)	203

S. K. Warne, D. W. Fleming and G. D. McGrath did not bat.

Bowling: de Villiers 10–1–44–1; Matthews 10–0–40–3; Simons 10–2–36–1; Shaw 10–0–30–1; McMillan 7–0–34–0; Kuiper 3–0–13–0.

South Africa

A. C. Hudson c Border b Reiffel	84
*K. C. Wessels b S. R. Waugh	28
W. J. Cronje b McGrath	18
J. N. Rhodes c S. R. Waugh b Reiffel	13
A. P. Kuiper c M. E. Waugh b Warne	6
B. M. McMillan run out	4
†D. J. Richardson run out	18
E. O. Simons b S. R. Waugh	18
T. G. Shaw not out	2
L-b 6, w 4, n-b 1	11
1/82 2/111 3/143 4/158 5/162 6/164 7/196 8/202 (8 wkts, 50 overs)	202

C. R. Matthews and P. S. de Villiers did not bat.

Bowling: McGrath 10–0–44–1; Fleming 10–2–33–0; Reiffel 10–0–34–2; Warne 10–0–37–1; S. R. Waugh 10–0–48–2.

Umpires: S. B. Lambson and K. E. Liebenberg.

MINOR COUNTIES IN SOUTH AFRICA, 1993-94

The Minor Counties Cricket Association undertook their first overseas tour for eight years when they visited South Africa in January and February 1994. A party of 15 players won five games and lost five, with one rained off.

The tour party consisted of: I. Cockbain (Cheshire) (*captain*), K. A. Arnold (Oxfordshire), C. K. Bullen (Bedfordshire), S. Burrow (Buckinghamshire), S. J. Dean (Staffordshire), K. Donohue (Devon), R. A. Evans (Oxfordshire), R. J. Evans (Lincolnshire), M. R. Gouldstone (Hertfordshire), T. M. Heap (Staffordshire), M. I. Humphries (Staffordshire), S. G. Plumb (Norfolk), B. Roberts (Cambridgeshire), M. J. Roberts (Buckinghamshire) and L. K. Smith (Wiltshire).

Manager: D. C. Wing. *Coach:* P. R. Oliver.

THE INDIANS IN NEW ZEALAND, 1993-94

By QAMAR AHMED

Encouraged by their convincing five-wicket victory over Pakistan in the third and final Test, and another consolation win in the ensuing one-day series, New Zealand were more at ease against the Indians. A docile Indian seam attack – Manoj Prabhakar had flown home with an ankle injury – doubtless came as a relief after facing the fire of Wasim Akram and Waqar Younis. They looked less certain against the Indian spinners – Anil Kumble, Rajesh Chauhan and Venkatapathy Raju – but, given that their star batsman, Martin Crowe, was still recovering from his knee operation, and all-rounder Chris Cairns and medium-pacer Simon Doull were also injured, New Zealand did well to draw the one-off Test. That Test – hindered by rain and bad light – was added to the programme at the tourists' insistence: originally the New Zealand authorities had planned only limited-overs matches. The four one-day internationals were shared 2-2.

Interest was heightened by the fact that Indian all-rounder Kapil Dev had recently passed local hero Sir Richard Hadlee's Test record of 431 wickets. Though past his best, Kapil deserved his rousing reception at the Hamilton Test. But the pitch offered little to seamers and he finished with match figures of two for 72. The highlight of the visit for India was the batting of Sachin Tendulkar, which became ever more scintillating as time went on. He reached 2,000 Test runs a month before his 21st birthday and scored a total of 200 in the four one-day games, delighting the crowds. Navjot Sidhu also batted well, though he fell just short of a century in the Test – not an unfamiliar misfortune for him. Nayan Mongia, who had to take over as Sidhu's opening partner at Hamilton after Prabhakar's injury, lived up to the responsibility and also took some brilliant catches.

For New Zealand, Ken Rutherford made two fifties in the Test – the first, in a total of 187, was especially valuable – and Bryan Young followed up his century against Pakistan with 85. But the man who attracted most attention was Stephen Fleming, a 20-year-old left-hander from Canterbury. He missed a hundred on Test debut by only eight runs and followed that with 90 in his first one-day international. His confidence, elegance and wide array of strokes impressed everyone. Danny Morrison, who completed the first hat-trick for his country in limited-overs matches, was the best of the bowlers. He had strong support, however, from Dion Nash and Chris Pringle, and spinners Matthew Hart and Shane Thomson, as the players seized their last chance to impress the selectors before the trip to England.

INDIAN TOURING PARTY

M. Azharuddin (Hyderabad) (*captain*), S. R. Tendulkar (Bombay) (*vice-captain*), P. K. Amre (Rajasthan), S. A. Ankola (Bombay), R. K. Chauhan (Madhya Pradesh), A. D. Jadeja (Haryana), V. G. Kambli (Bombay), Kapil Dev (Haryana), A. Kumble (Karnataka), S. V. Manjrekar (Bombay), N. R. Mongia (Baroda), M. Prabhakar (Delhi), S. L. V. Raju (Hyderabad), N. S. Sidhu (Punjab), J. Srinath (Karnataka).

B. K. V. Prasad (Karnataka) replaced Prabhakar, who was injured after one match.

Tour manager: M. Ranga Reddy. *Cricket manager:* A. L. Wadekar.

INDIAN TOUR RESULTS

Test match – Played 1: Drawn 1.
First-class matches – Played 3: Drawn 3.
Draws – New Zealand, New Zealand Emerging Players, New Zealand Academy XI.
One-day internationals – Played 4: Won 2, Lost 2.

INDIAN AVERAGES – FIRST-CLASS MATCHES

BATTING

	M	*I*	*NO*	*R*	*HS*	*100s*	*Avge*	*Ct*
S. V. Manjrekar	3	3	1	171	134	1	85.50	2
N. S. Sidhu	3	4	0	149	98	0	37.25	0
N. R. Mongia	3	3	0	83	45	0	27.66	6
V. G. Kambli	3	3	0	48	20	0	16.00	1

Played in three matches: A. Kumble 0, 7 (2 ct); S. L. V. Raju 0, 2; J. Srinath 4, 1. Played in two matches: S. A. Ankola 10*, 2* (1 ct); M. Azharuddin 7, 63 (2 ct); R. K. Chauhan 12* (2 ct); Kapil Dev 9, 18 (1 ct); S. R. Tendulkar 43, 11*. Played in one match: A. D. Jadeja 55*; M. Prabhakar 147 (2 ct).

* *Signifies not out.*

BOWLING

	O	*M*	*R*	*W*	*BB*	*5W/i*	*Avge*
R. K. Chauhan	64	12	175	7	3-97	0	25.00
J. Srinath	135	31	321	8	4-60	0	40.12
A. Kumble	128	38	229	4	2-37	0	57.25
S. L. V. Raju	117.2	32	233	4	2-14	0	58.25

Also bowled: S. A. Ankola 47–11–129–3; A. D. Jadeja 3–1–11–0; V. G. Kambli 1–0–6–0; Kapil Dev 30-5-82-2; N. R. Mongia 1–0–4–0; M. Prabhakar 12–2–22–0; N. S. Sidhu 5–0–10–0.

Note: Matches in this section which were not first-class are signified by a dagger.

NEW ZEALAND EMERGING PLAYERS v INDIANS

At Dunedin, March 10, 11, 12. Drawn. Toss: New Zealand Emerging Players.

The final day was little more than batting practice for the home side. Only two wickets fell and Hartland, one of three players who made 50, retired and caught a plane to Auckland for the next day's international against Pakistan. (Officially, he was diagnosed as having cramp in one hand.) Hartland also dominated the first day, when he made 98, and shared a brisk opening stand of 167 with Lawson before both fell to Ankola. The Emerging Players declared at their overnight 233 for four and bowled the Indians out by the close – though the tourists led by 119, having scored at a much faster rate. The bulk of their 352 came from Prabhakar and Manjrekar, who both made centuries and put on 193 for the fourth wicket.

Close of play: First day, New Zealand Emerging Players 233-4 (S. W. J. Wilson 42*, G. E. Bradburn 12*); Second day, India 352.

New Zealand Emerging Players

B. R. Hartland c Prabhakar b Ankola	98	– (2) retired hurt	54
R. A. Lawson c and b Ankola	62	– (1) c Prabhakar b Raju	24
S. W. J. Wilson not out	42	– c Mongia b Ankola	24
M. W. Douglas c Azharuddin b Srinath	6	– not out	64
M. D. Bailey c Mongia b Srinath	1	– not out	52
G. E. Bradburn not out	12		
B 2, l-b 6, n-b 4	12	B 10, l-b 8	18
1/167 2/170 3/180 4/186 (4 wkts dec.)	233	1/56 2/111 (2 wkts)	236

*†L. K. Germon, N. J. Astle, M. F. Sharpe, P. J. Wiseman and M. B. Owens did not bat.

In the second innings B. R. Hartland retired hurt at 91.

Bowling: *First Innings*—Prabhakar 6–1–12–0; Srinath 23–6–42–2; Ankola 15–3–44–2; Raju 31–10–69–0; Kumble 33–11–52–0; Kambli 1–0–6–0. *Second Innings*—Prabhakar 6–1–10–0; Kapil Dev 5–1–10–0; Ankola 12–2–42–1; Srinath 18–5–33–0; Raju 32–3–71–1; Kumble 18–6–38–0; Sidhu 5–0–10–0; Mongia 1–0–4–0.

Indians

M. Prabhakar c Wiseman b Owens	147
N. S. Sidhu c Germon b Owens	11
V. G. Kambli st Germon b Bradburn	20
*M. Azharuddin c Wiseman b Bradburn	7
S. V. Manjrekar c Lawson b Astle	134
Kapil Dev c Bailey b Sharpe	9
†N. R. Mongia lbw b Sharpe	0
A. Kumble c Hartland b Sharpe	0
J. Srinath c and b Bradburn	4
S. L. V. Raju c Hartland b Bradburn	0
S. A. Ankola not out	10
B 3, l-b 3, n-b 4	10
1/23 2/61 3/81 4/274 5/304 6/310 7/310 8/330 9/330	352

Bowling: Owens 21–5–43–2; Sharpe 23–4–59–3; Astle 19.3–4–68–1; Bradburn 26–3–99–4; Wiseman 19–0–77–0.

Umpires: R. J. Ebert and C. E. King.

NEW ZEALAND ACADEMY XI v INDIANS

At New Plymouth, March 14, 15, 16. Drawn. Toss: Indians.

Weather ruled out play on the final day, a disappointment for the tourists as they prepared for the Test. Only the Indian openers had had any chance of practice: Jadeja and Sidhu put on 93 in 27 overs. The first day was notable for Pocock's unbeaten century, made out of 171 for four. Asked to bat, the Academy had reached lunch at 46 without loss and, despite losing a couple of partners during the afternoon, Pocock grew in confidence to reach 100 just before the close. He hit nine fours in nearly five hours and advanced to 139 before Murray declared.

Close of play: First day, New Zealand Academy XI 171-4 (B. A. Pocock 100*, L. K. Germon 1*); Second day, Indians 96-1 (A. D. Jadeja 55*, S. A. Ankola 2*).

New Zealand Academy XI

B. A. Pocock not out	139
*D. J. Murray c Mongia b Srinath	25
G. P. Burnett b Kumble	7
S. P. Fleming c Kumble b Chauhan	20
R. A. Jones b Chauhan	6
†L. K. Germon b Kumble	26
D. J. Nash not out	10
B 7, l-b 9, n-b 4	20
1/64 2/97 3/147 4/161 5/204 (5 wkts dec.)	253

M. C. Goodson, H. T. Davis, M. J. Haslam and R. L. Hayes did not bat.

Bowling: Srinath 30–8–83–1; Ankola 20–6–43–0; Jadeja 3–1–11–0; Kumble 27–10–37–2; Raju 17–6–26–0; Chauhan 14–1–37–2.

Indians

A. D. Jadeja not out	55
N. S. Sidhu c Burnett b Goodson	30
S. A. Ankola not out	2
B 4, l-b 3, w 2	9
1/93 (1 wkt)	96

V. G. Kambli, *S. R. Tendulkar, S. V. Manjrekar, †N. R. Mongia, A. Kumble, R. K. Chauhan, J. Srinath and S. L. V. Raju did not bat.

Bowling: Davis 8–2–10–0; Hayes 7–1–42–0; Nash 7–2–12–0; Goodson 4–0–20–1; Haslam 1.3–0–5–0.

Umpires: B. F. Bowden and E. A. Watkin.

NEW ZEALAND v INDIA

Test Match

At Hamilton, March 19, 20, 21, 22, 23. Drawn. Toss: New Zealand. Test debut: S. P. Fleming.

Rain and bad light ensured a dismal draw, most memorable for the debut of Fleming. Nine days before his 21st birthday, Fleming took New Zealand to safety with a brilliant 92. He hit 12 fours in three hours and his strokeplay, on a pitch of uneven bounce and pace, delighted the crowd. He enabled Rutherford to declare at 368 for seven and set India a rather improbable target of 310 in 66 overs. Sidhu and the emergency opener, Mongia, started off with 102 and India were still interested when Kambli came in first wicket down. But when Pringle bowled him they batted out time. Sidhu made 98, with eight fours and three sixes, before he was caught behind off Hart's left-arm spin.

Play on the first day was delayed until 3.15 p.m. and restricted to 38.5 overs by rain. Rutherford chose to bat, though he must have had doubts with the pitch so moist at the start. Hartland went for a duck, caught at third slip off Kapil Dev, and Srinath, bowling with sustained accuracy, dismissed Young and the out-of-form Greatbatch. Fleming was dropped by Azharuddin just after he came in but survived to put on 51 with his captain, the only batsman to pass 20. New Zealand were all out for 187 before tea on the second day; Srinath claimed four for 60, though it was the spinners who had put most pressure on the batsmen.

India then reached 104 for three in the final session, with Tendulkar playing a dazzling cameo. He hit 43 from 47 balls, with seven fours, out of a third-wicket stand of 51 with Mongia. During his innings he passed 2,000 runs in his 32nd Test; for comparison, Rutherford, who reached 2,000 in the second innings, took 13 more Tests and was Tendulkar's senior by seven and a half years; even Fleming was three weeks older. Azharuddin's record stood comparison, as he clocked up his 4,000th run in 62 Tests, though his batting on the third day was painfully slow. He took nearly three hours over his 63 and after he was bowled, sweeping at Thomson, India's last five went for 30. Morrison was rewarded with four for 52.

New Zealand reduced the deficit from 59 to 20 by the close and prospered next day. None of the batsmen failed completely: Young struck 11 fours in his 85 and Rutherford five fours and two sixes in his second fifty of the match. But the game belonged to Fleming, who had an unbeaten 67 overnight and so nearly a century on debut in the morning.

Man of the Match: S. P. Fleming.

Close of play: First day, New Zealand 81-3 (K. R. Rutherford 43*, S. P. Fleming 10*); Second day, India 104-3 (N. R. Mongia 33*, M. Azharuddin 8*); Third day, New Zealand 39-0 (B. A. Young 19*, B. R. Hartland 18*); Fourth day, New Zealand 306-5 (S. P. Fleming 67*, A. C. Parore 10*).

New Zealand

	First innings		Second innings	
B. R. Hartland c Chauhan b Kapil Dev	0	– (2) c Mongia b Srinath	25
B. A. Young c Kumble b Srinath	13	– (1) c Mongia b Chauhan	85
*K. R. Rutherford b Kumble	63	– b Chauhan	59
M. J. Greatbatch c Azharuddin b Srinath	12	– c Manjrekar b Kumble	27
S. P. Fleming c Kambli b Srinath	16	– c Kapil Dev b Chauhan	92
S. A. Thomson c Manjrekar b Raju	12	– b Raju	26
†A. C. Parore c and b Chauhan	9	– c Mongia b Kapil Dev	17
M. N. Hart b Chauhan	17	– not out	20
D. J. Nash not out	10	– not out	9
D. K. Morrison lbw b Srinath	3		
C. Pringle b Raju	18		
L-b 9, n-b 5	14	B 2, l-b 1, n-b 5	8
1/1 (1) 2/21 (2) 3/49 (4) 4/100 (5) 5/122 (3) 6/124 (6) 7/154 (7) 8/155 (8) 9/158 (10) 10/187 (11)	187	1/56 (2) 2/172 (3) 3/176 (1) 4/220 (4) 5/265 (6) 6/317 (7) 7/355 (5) (7 wkts dec.)	368

Bowling: *First Innings*—Srinath 31–8–60–4; Kapil Dev 9–2–29–1; Kumble 23–8–34–1; Raju 13.2–5–14–2; Chauhan 21–6–41–2. *Second Innings*—Srinath 33–4–104–1; Kapil Dev 16–2–43–1; Raju 24–6–53–1; Kumble 27–6–68–1; Chauhan 29–5–97–3.

India

	First innings		Second innings	
†N. R. Mongia run out	45	– b Hart	38
N. S. Sidhu b Morrison	10	– c Parore b Hart	98
V. G. Kambli c Young b Pringle	9	– b Pringle	19
S. R. Tendulkar c Nash b Thomson	43	– not out	11
*M. Azharuddin b Thomson	63		
S. V. Manjrekar c Young b Morrison	29	– (5) not out	8
Kapil Dev c Fleming b Nash	18		
A. Kumble c Fleming b Morrison	7		
R. K. Chauhan not out	12		
S. L. V. Raju c Young b Morrison	2		
J. Srinath c Parore b Pringle	1		
L-b 6, w 1	7	L-b 3	3
1/25 (2) 2/38 (3) 3/89 (4) 4/138 (1) 5/183 (5) 6/216 (7) 7/226 (6) 8/227 (8) 9/237 (10) 10/246 (11)	246	1/102 (1) 2/140 (3) 3/167 (2) (3 wkts)	177

Bowling: *First Innings*—Morrison 30–9–52–4; Nash 20–5–57–1; Pringle 22.3–8–52–2; Hart 19–5–33–0; Thomson 11–1–46–2. *Second Innings*—Morrison 8–1–15–0; Nash 13–6–25–0; Thomson 11–1–39–0; Pringle 12–2–29–1; Hart 15–2–66–2.

Umpires: Khizar Hayat (Pakistan) and B. L. Aldridge. Referee: R. Subba Row (England).

†NEW ZEALAND v INDIA

First One-Day International

At Napier, March 25. New Zealand won by 28 runs. Toss: India.

Spirited batting and accurate bowling saw New Zealand home. The Indian innings started well, reaching 123 for one, but gave way under pressure. Morrison devastated the tail with a hat-trick – bowling Kapil Dev and Ankola with the last two balls of his eighth over and Mongia with the first of his ninth. It was the first hat-trick for New Zealand in limited-overs internationals. India, less able to exploit the conditions, failed to contain New Zealand, despite reducing them to 60 for three – all caught by Mongia – in 18 overs. Two young batsmen combined to add 144 runs: Fleming, who followed his 92 on Test debut with 90 in his first one-day international, hit eight fours and Thomson seven fours and a six in an equally impressive 83.

Man of the Match: S. A. Thomson.

New Zealand

B. R. Hartland c Mongia b Srinath 8
B. A. Young c Mongia b Srinath 11
*K. R. Rutherford c Mongia b Ankola . 23
S. P. Fleming run out 90
S. A. Thomson c Jadeja b Kumble 83
C. Z. Harris not out 18
D. J. Nash not out 1
L-b 2, w 3, n-b 1 6

1/17 2/26 3/60 4/204 5/230 (5 wkts, 50 overs) 240

G. R. Larsen, †A. C. Parore, C. Pringle and D. K. Morrison did not bat.

Bowling: Kapil Dev 10–0–36–0; Srinath 10–1–59–2; Ankola 7–0–24–1; Jadeja 8–1–41–0; Kumble 10–0–41–1; Tendulkar 5–0–37–0.

India

A. D. Jadeja c Pringle b Harris 55
N. S. Sidhu c Parore b Larsen 34
V. G. Kambli st Parore b Thomson.... 37
*M. Azharuddin b Harris 9
S. R. Tendulkar c Rutherford b Nash .. 15
S. V. Manjrekar not out 22
Kapil Dev b Morrison 17
S. A. Ankola b Morrison 0
J. Srinath c Hartland b Pringle 4
†N. R. Mongia b Morrison 0
A. Kumble not out 1
B 2, l-b 10, w 5, n-b 1 18

1/65 2/123 3/150 4/152 5/176 6/206 7/206 8/211 9/211 (9 wkts, 50 overs) 212

Bowling: Pringle 10–1–33–1; Morrison 9–1–35–3; Nash 9–0–34–1; Larsen 9–1–40–1; Harris 8–0–32–2; Thomson 5–0–26–1.

Umpires: R. S. Dunne and D. M. Quested.

†NEW ZEALAND v INDIA

Second One-Day International

At Auckland, March 27. India won by seven wickets. Toss: New Zealand.

Tendulkar played a blazing innings of 82 from 49 balls, with 15 fours and two sixes, and India achieved a thumping victory in less than half their allocated 50 overs. Opening because of Sidhu's neck strain, Tendulkar put on 61 with Jadeja in nine overs, and 56 in six with Kambli. He smashed three fours and a six off Larsen's first over and Kambli was just as hard on Morrison. Rutherford had chosen to bat but, on the same pitch on which Pakistan had won the First Test inside three days, half the side went for 34. Parore and Harris staged a minor recovery, with 52 for the sixth wicket, but off-spinner Chauhan destroyed the tail. As New Zealand limped to 142, Harris reached an unbeaten 50.

Man of the Match: S. R. Tendulkar.

New Zealand

B. A. Young c Mongia b Ankola 16
B. R. Hartland c Azharuddin b Kapil Dev . 0
*K. R. Rutherford c Azharuddin b Srinath . 6
S. P. Fleming c Mongia b Kapil Dev .. 6
S. A. Thomson c Mongia b Ankola 1
C. Z. Harris not out 50
†A. C. Parore run out 23
M. N. Hart b Chauhan 10
G. R. Larsen st Mongia b Chauhan ... 5
D. K. Morrison st Mongia b Chauhan . 2
C. Pringle b Srinath 17
L-b 2, w 3, n-b 1 6

1/1 2/11 3/31 4/33 5/34 6/86 7/105 8/111 9/115 (49.4 overs) 142

Bowling: Kapil Dev 10–1–18–2; Srinath 7.4–2–17–2; Ankola 8–0–27–2; Jadeja 4–0–6–0; Kumble 10–2–29–0; Chauhan 10–1–43–3.

India

A. D. Jadeja c Rutherford b Pringle ... 18
S. R. Tendulkar c and b Hart......... 82
V. G. Kambli c Hart b Harris........ 21
*M. Azharuddin not out............. 12
S. V. Manjrekar not out............. 7
W 2, n-b 1.................. 3

1/61 2/117 3/126 (3 wkts, 23.2 overs) 143

†N. R. Mongia, Kapil Dev, S. A. Ankola, R. K. Chauhan, J. Srinath and A. Kumble did not bat.

Bowling: Morrison 6–0–46–0; Pringle 6–1–41–1; Larsen 2–0–24–0; Hart 5.2–0–19–1; Harris 4–1–13–1.

Umpires: B. L. Aldridge and C. E. King.

†NEW ZEALAND v INDIA

Third One-Day International

At Wellington, March 30. India won by 12 runs. Toss: New Zealand.

A target of 256 for New Zealand briefly looked attainable as Thomson and Parore put on 85 for the sixth wicket. Thomson reached 50 in 51 balls but Kumble had him stumped and bowled Parore, and 28 off the last two overs was too much for the tail. Earlier, Kumble removed both Harris – promoted to open after his fifty in Auckland – and Hartland, after they had put on 60 for the second wicket, and finished with five for 33. India's first wicket put on 105 at five an over, and the other batsmen kept up that rate. Tendulkar scored 63 from 75 balls, with nine fours, and Sidhu an unbeaten 71 from 78.

Man of the Match: A. Kumble.

India

A. D. Jadeja b Morrison............. 56
S. R. Tendulkar lbw b Larsen........ 63
N. S. Sidhu not out................. 71
V. G. Kambli c Pringle b Nash....... 23
*M. Azharuddin b Morrison.......... 24
Kapil Dev c Thomson b Pringle....... 4
†N. R. Mongia not out.............. 3
B 1, l-b 4, w 6.............. 11

1/105 2/154 3/199 4/237 5/248 (5 wkts, 50 overs) 255

J. Srinath, R. K. Chauhan, A. Kumble and S. A. Ankola did not bat.

Bowling: Pringle 7–0–36–1; Morrison 10–0–57–2; Nash 9–0–55–1; Larsen 10–1–33–1; Harris 5–0–30–0; Thomson 9–0–39–0.

New Zealand

C. Z. Harris c Jadeja b Kumble....... 44
B. A. Young b Srinath.............. 2
B. R. Hartland st Mongia b Kumble... 21
*K. R. Rutherford c Kapil Dev b Srinath. 35
S. P. Fleming run out............... 2
S. A. Thomson st Mongia b Kumble... 60
†A. C. Parore b Kumble............. 47
G. R. Larsen b Srinath.............. 2
D. J. Nash c Kapil Dev b Kumble.... 6
C. Pringle not out.................. 8
D. K. Morrison not out.............. 4
B 1, l-b 6, w 4, n-b 1........ 12

1/5 2/65 3/70 4/76 5/131 6/216 7/221 8/231 9/232 (9 wkts, 50 overs) 243

Bowling: Kapil Dev 8–0–40–0; Srinath 10–3–31–3; Ankola 10–0–55–0; Kumble 10–0–33–5; Chauhan 5–0–30–0; Jadeja 5–0–35–0; Tendulkar 2–0–12–0.

Umpires: R. S. Dunne and C. E. King.

†NEW ZEALAND v INDIA

Fourth One-Day International

At Christchurch, April 2. New Zealand won by six wickets. Toss: India. International debut: B. K. V. Prasad.

New Zealand levelled the series with a ball to spare, thanks to another stand between Thomson and Parore. This time they added 88 for the fifth wicket. At 135 for four from 35 overs, New Zealand were well behind the asking-rate until Thomson scored 40 in 43 balls and Parore 47 in 46. In contrast, India started by raising 50 in eight overs and Jadeja went on to reach 68, but the middle order failed to force the pace. It was left to Mongia and Kumble to take the total past 200. The match was marred by the only trouble to disrupt the Indian tour. Several spectators, evidently drunk, invaded the pitch and uprooted the stumps during New Zealand's innings. Police made 39 arrests for disorderly behaviour.

Man of the Match: A. C. Parore.

India

A. D. Jadeja c Rutherford b Pringle	68
S. R. Tendulkar b Larsen	40
N. S. Sidhu c Nash b Harris	9
V. G. Kambli run out	19
*M. Azharuddin c Larsen b Hart	1
Kapil Dev b Morrison	15
†N. R. Mongia not out	40
A. Kumble not out	18
L-b 7, w 5	12
	—
1/61 2/80 3/114 4/118 5/150 6/183 (6 wkts, 50 overs)	222

S. A. Ankola, J. Srinath and B. K. V. Prasad did not bat.

Bowling: Morrison 10–1–47–1; Pringle 6–0–43–1; Nash 5–0–33–0; Larsen 9–1–37–1; Harris 10–1–25–1; Hart 10–1–30–1.

New Zealand

B. A. Young b Kumble	43
C. Z. Harris lbw b Kapil Dev	0
*K. R. Rutherford c and b Kumble	61
S. P. Fleming c Prasad b Kumble	25
S. A. Thomson not out	40
†A. C. Parore not out	47
L-b 2, w 4, n-b 1	7
	—
1/7 2/89 3/135 4/135 (4 wkts, 49.5 overs)	223

D. J. Nash, G. R. Larsen, M. N. Hart, D. K. Morrison and C. Pringle did not bat.

Bowling: Kapil Dev 8–3–20–1; Srinath 9.5–0–46–0; Prasad 9–0–49–0; Ankola 8–0–37–0; Kumble 10–0–47–3; Tendulkar 5–0–22–0.

Umpires: B. C. Aldridge and D. B. Cowie.

PEPSI CHAMPIONS TROPHY, 1993-94

West Indies' triumph prevented Pakistan claiming their seventh successive trophy in Sharjah since 1989. They entered the final on equal terms, having beaten Sri Lanka twice apiece and each other once. But a series of injuries left Pakistan weakened, and even a spectacular century from Basit Ali could not set up a total big enough to daunt the West Indians, for whom Lara struck magnificent form.

In what proved to be a batsman's tournament, the qualifying rounds were dominated by a remarkable run of innings from Saeed Anwar, a limited-overs specialist still with only one Test to his name. In the previous final at Sharjah, nine months earlier, he had scored 110; now he piled on 107, 131 and 111 in successive matches, a triple feat previously achieved in one-day internationals only by Zaheer Abbas, also for Pakistan, against India in 1982-83. Even so, it was the consistency of Phil Simmons, who averaged 82.50 in his five matches for West Indies, which earned the award for the player of the series. With the Indians still absenting themselves because of grievances concerning their last appearance at Sharjah, Sri Lanka made up the numbers. They showed only once, in their second match against Pakistan, how they could have stretched their opponents had more than one batsman fired in each innings.

The Cricketers' Benefit Fund presented $US35,000 each to Desmond Haynes of West Indies and Pakistanis Mohammad Nazir and Shoaib Mohammad. West Indies won $US37,500, Pakistan $US22,500 and Sri Lanka $US10,000.

Note: Matches in this section were not first-class.

SRI LANKA v WEST INDIES

At Sharjah, October 28. West Indies won by eight wickets. Toss: West Indies.

Except for Ranatunga, who struck six fours and three sixes in an unbeaten 83 from 92 balls, Sri Lanka could make little headway against Benjamin and Cummins. Simmons and Richardson added 137 in 34 overs for West Indies' second wicket; Simmons was bowled only two short of their target.

Man of the Match: P. V. Simmons.

Sri Lanka

R. S. Mahanama c Lara b Cummins . . . 27
U. C. Hathurusinghe run out 2
A. P. Gurusinha b Cummins 8
P. A. de Silva c Lara b Benjamin 1
H. P. Tillekeratne c Murray b Benjamin 1
*A. Ranatunga not out 83
S. T. Jayasuriya c Ambrose b Benjamin 23
†R. S. Kaluwitharana c Simmons b Hooper . 0
R. S. Kalpage c Murray b Cummins . . . 7
C. P. H. Ramanayake c Richardson b Ambrose . 9
G. P. Wickremasinghe c and b Ambrose 0
B 1, l-b 6, w 3, n-b 1 11

1/6 2/24 3/27 4/29 5/71 6/117 7/119 8/138 9/171 (48.5 overs) 172

Bowling: Ambrose 7.5–1–20–2; Walsh 7–4–10–0; Benjamin 9–1–34–3; Cummins 10–1–32–3; Simmons 5–0–17–0; Hooper 10–1–52–1.

West Indies

P. V. Simmons b Jayasuriya	92
B. C. Lara c Ranatunga b Gurusinha	5
*R. B. Richardson not out	69
K. L. T. Arthurton not out	1
W 4, n-b 2	6
1/34 2/171 (2 wkts, 46 overs)	173

C. L. Hooper, J. C. Adams, †J. R. Murray, A. C. Cummins, C. E. L. Ambrose, C. A. Walsh and K. C. G. Benjamin did not bat.

Bowling: Wickremasinghe 7–1–27–0; Ramanayake 8–2–22–0; Gurusinha 3–0–14–1; Kalpage 10–0–25–0; Jayasuriya 9–0–41–1; de Silva 6–0–34–0; Hathurusinghe 2–0–10–0; Tillekeratne 1–1–0–0.

Umpires: H. D. Bird and D. R. Shepherd.

PAKISTAN v WEST INDIES

At Sharjah, October 29. West Indies won by 39 runs. Toss: Pakistan.

West Indies recorded their second victory in two days, thanks to Arthurton and Adams, who joined forces at an uneasy 82 for four to share a stand of 119 in 22 overs. Pakistan also lost their first four wickets in 20 overs, but the efforts of Basit Ali and Asif Mujtaba to rally the innings foundered when Basit was run out. Waqar Younis suffered a calf injury while bowling, which kept him out of the next three matches.

Man of the Match: J. C. Adams.

West Indies

P. V. Simmons c Rashid Latif b Waqar Younis	25
B. C. Lara c Rashid Latif b Wasim Akram	14
*R. B. Richardson c Saeed Anwar b Aqib Javed	2
K. L. T. Arthurton c Aamir Sohail b Mushtaq Ahmed	84
C. L. Hooper c Rashid Latif b Mushtaq Ahmed	6
J. C. Adams not out	81
†J. R. Murray lbw b Wasim Akram	6
A. C. Cummins b Wasim Akram	18
W. K. M. Benjamin not out	2
B 1, l-b 19, w 7, n-b 2	29
1/32 2/35 3/57 4/82 5/201 6/225 7/263 (7 wkts, 50 overs)	267

C. E. L. Ambrose and K. C. G. Benjamin did not bat.

Bowling: Wasim Akram 10–0–36–3; Aqib Javed 10–0–38–1; Waqar Younis 7.1–0–57–1; Mushtaq Ahmed 10–1–44–2; Aamir Sohail 4.5–0–31–0; Asif Mujtaba 8–0–41–0.

Pakistan

Aamir Sohail lbw b K. C. G. Benjamin	3
Saeed Anwar c Lara b Cummins	22
Inzamam-ul-Haq c K. C. G. Benjamin b Hooper	25
Javed Miandad b K. C. G. Benjamin	0
Basit Ali run out	46
Asif Mujtaba not out	60
*Wasim Akram c Adams b Ambrose	28
†Rashid Latif c Lara b Ambrose	0
Mushtaq Ahmed c Murray b Hooper	2
Waqar Younis c Lara b Hooper	15
Aqib Javed not out	6
L-b 6, w 14, n-b 1	21
1/4 2/47 3/48 4/59 5/147 6/185 7/190 8/194 9/213 (9 wkts, 50 overs)	228

Bowling: Ambrose 9–1–29–2; K. C. G. Benjamin 9–1–37–2; W. K. M. Benjamin 6–0–40–0; Cummins 10–1–44–1; Hooper 10–0–33–3; Simmons 6–0–39–0.

Umpires: J. W. Holder and D. R. Shepherd.

PAKISTAN v SRI LANKA

At Sharjah, October 30. Pakistan won by 114 runs. Toss: Sri Lanka.

Left-handers Saeed Anwar and Asif Mujtaba, promoted to open, started with 171 in 31 overs, which some hard hitting from the middle order came close to doubling. Saeed contributed a dashing 107 in 109 balls, while Mujtaba advanced to an unbeaten century, his first in limited-overs internationals. In contrast, Sri Lanka had lost both their openers by the seventh over, and Jayasuriya's best efforts could not lift his team-mates anywhere near a daunting run-rate of 6.26.

Man of the Match: Asif Mujtaba.

Pakistan

Saeed Anwar c Muralitharan b Ranatunga . 107
Asif Mujtaba not out . 113
Inzamam-ul-Haq b Ramanayake . 37
*Wasim Akram b Ramanayake . 15
Basit Ali not out . 29
L-b 4, w 4, n-b 4 . 12

1/171 2/247 3/270 (3 wkts, 50 overs) 313

Javed Miandad, Salim Malik, †Rashid Latif, Mushtaq Ahmed, Aqib Javed and Ata-ur-Rehman did not bat.

Bowling: Wickremasinghe 10–2–59–0; Ramanayake 10–1–54–2; Gurusinha 4–1–22–0; Kalpage 10–0–63–0; Jayasuriya 3–0–31–0; Muralitharan 6–0–42–0; Ranatunga 7–0–38–1.

Sri Lanka

R. S. Mahanama lbw b Wasim Akram . 1
A. P. Gurusinha lbw b Wasim Akram . 6
S. T. Jayasuriya c Inzamam-ul-Haq b Mushtaq Ahmed . 58
P. A. de Silva run out . 14
H. P. Tillekeratne c Saeed Anwar b Salim Malik . 20
*A. Ranatunga c Rashid Latif b Mushtaq Ahmed . 24
†R. S. Kaluwitharana c Wasim Akram b Asif Mujtaba . 31
R. S. Kalpage not out . 16
C. P. H. Ramanayake not out . 14
B 2, l-b 5, w 7, n-b 1 . 15

1/4 2/26 3/53 4/103 5/114 6/145 7/173 (7 wkts, 50 overs) 199

G. P. Wickremasinghe and M. Muralitharan did not bat.

Bowling: Wasim Akram 8–1–21–2; Aqib Javed 3–0–15–0; Ata-ur-Rehman 8–1–35–0; Salim Malik 10–0–44–1; Mushtaq Ahmed 10–1–45–2; Asif Mujtaba 9–0–28–1; Basit Ali 2–0–4–0.

Umpires: H. D. Bird and J. W. Holder.

PAKISTAN v WEST INDIES

At Sharjah, November 1. Pakistan won by five wickets. Toss: West Indies.

Saeed Anwar's second consecutive century was the highest score for Pakistan in limited-overs internationals. He hit 12 fours and three sixes and did not fall until the target was down to ten runs from 15 balls. Haynes returned for West Indies after a throat infection, but managed only six; the innings leant heavily on Simmons and Arthurton, who put on 132 in 23.2 overs. West Indies had dropped Murray, their specialist wicket-keeper, and relied on Adams; Abdul Qadir made his first appearance for Pakistan since December 1990.

Man of the Match: Saeed Anwar.

West Indies

B. C. Lara c Rashid Latif b Mushtaq Ahmed . 14
D. L. Haynes c Mushtaq Ahmed b Wasim Akram . 6
P. V. Simmons b Ata-ur-Rehman 81
K. L. T. Arthurton c Saeed Anwar b Mushtaq Ahmed . 63
*R. B. Richardson c Salim Malik b Mushtaq Ahmed . 7
C. L. Hooper c Asif Mujtaba b Wasim Akram . 18
†J. C. Adams not out 18
R. A. Harper b Wasim Akram 2
A. C. Cummins st Rashid Latif b Abdul Qadir . 10
K. C. G. Benjamin b Wasim Akram . . . 4
C. A. Walsh not out 2
B 3, l-b 10, w 20, n-b 2 35

1/26 2/57 3/189 4/201 5/204 6/222 7/234 8/251 9/256 (9 wkts, 50 overs) 260

Bowling: Wasim Akram 10–1–40–4; Ata-ur-Rehman 10–1–59–1; Mushtaq Ahmed 10–1–46–3; Abdul Qadir 10–0–43–1; Salim Malik 7–0–35–0; Asif Mujtaba 3–0–24–0.

Pakistan

Saeed Anwar c Lara b Hooper 131
Asif Mujtaba c Arthurton b Cummins . . 15
Inzamam-ul-Haq run out 20
Javed Miandad c Adams b Benjamin . . 20
Basit Ali run out 16
Salim Malik not out 34
*Wasim Akram not out 5
B 1, l-b 9, w 9, n-b 1 20

1/42 2/86 3/143 4/186 5/251 (5 wkts, 49 overs) 261

†Rashid Latif, Abdul Qadir, Mushtaq Ahmed and Ata-ur-Rehman did not bat.

Bowling: Walsh 10–1–39–0; Benjamin 10–1–54–1; Cummins 10–0–69–1; Simmons 2–0–10–0; Harper 8–0–36–0; Hooper 9–0–43–1.

Umpires: J. W. Holder and D. R. Shepherd.

PAKISTAN v SRI LANKA

At Sharjah, November 2. Pakistan won by two wickets. Toss: Sri Lanka. International debut: Aamer Hanif.

Saeed Anwar scored his third hundred in a row, hitting 11 fours and two sixes off 104 balls, but Pakistan won with only two balls to spare. After Saeed and Asif Mujtaba opened at a frenetic six an over, the middle order lost steam. Saeed departed in the 40th over, and another five wickets fell – three to run-outs – before Aamer Hanif, flown in to reinforce the injury-ridden squad, saw them home. Mahanama and Jayasuriya had compiled Sri Lanka's first century partnership of the week, Jayasuriya hitting 65 from 56 balls. The result confirmed that Pakistan would play West Indies in the final, but without their captain: Wasim Akram fractured his hand while batting. Abdul Qadir's comeback was halted when he twisted his ankle.

Man of the Match: Saeed Anwar.

Sri Lanka

R. S. Mahanama st Rashid Latif b Mushtaq Ahmed . 59
A. P. Gurusinha lbw b Aamer Hanif . . . 7
S. T. Jayasuriya c Mushtaq Ahmed b Salim Malik . 65
*A. Ranatunga st Rashid Latif b Salim Malik . 35
P. A. de Silva run out 62
†R. S. Kaluwitharana c Inzamam-ul-Haq b Ata-ur-Rehman . 23
R. S. Kalpage not out 1
L-b 5, w 10, n-b 3 18

1/26 2/131 3/153 4/197 5/263 6/270 (6 wkts, 50 overs) 270

H. P. Tillekeratne, C. P. H. Ramanayake, G. P. Wickremasinghe and D. K. Liyanage did not bat.

Bowling: Wasim Akram 10–1–42–0; Ata-ur-Rehman 10–1–53–1; Aamer Hanif 3.4–0–27–1; Mushtaq Ahmed 10–1–56–1; Abdul Qadir 7.2–0–35–0; Salim Malik 9–0–52–2.

Pakistan

Saeed Anwar c Mahanama b Liyanage . 111
Asif Mujtaba c Kaluwitharana b Liyanage . 34
Inzamam-ul-Haq c Wickremasinghe b Liyanage . 53
Basit Ali run out 13
Salim Malik c and b Ramanayake 14
Aamer Hanif not out 17
*Wasim Akram run out 5
†Rashid Latif c Mahanama b Wickremasinghe . 2
Mushtaq Ahmed run out 6
Abdul Qadir not out 7
L-b 1, w 1, n-b 7 9

1/86 2/195 3/209 4/225 5/233 6/244 7/254 8/260 (8 wkts, 49.4 overs) 271

Ata-ur-Rehman did not bat.

Bowling: Wickremasinghe 9.4–0–35–1; Ramanayake 8–0–62–1; Liyanage 10–0–49–3; Kalpage 10–0–37–0; Jayasuriya 5–0–37–0; Ranatunga 2–0–17–0; de Silva 5–1–33–0.

Umpires: H. D. Bird and J. W. Holder.

SRI LANKA v WEST INDIES

At Sharjah, November 3. West Indies won by eight wickets. Toss: Sri Lanka. International debuts: D. P. Samaraweera; R. I. C. Holder.

The result being academic, Richardson rested and Haynes captained West Indies. He gave his spinners a full 20 overs, in which Harper picked up three Sri Lankan wickets. Though Haynes himself was bowled in the first over, Simmons led the team to victory with 11.2 overs to spare.

Man of the Match: P. V. Simmons.

Sri Lanka

R. S. Mahanama c Murray b Simmons . 23
D. P. Samaraweera c Hooper b Walsh . 3
S. T. Jayasuriya c Murray b W. K. M. Benjamin . 27
P. A. de Silva c and b Harper 14
H. P. Tillekeratne c Walsh b Hooper . . 26
*A. Ranatunga c Haynes b Harper 17
†R. S. Kaluwitharana c Holder b Harper 0
R. S. Kalpage c W. K. M. Benjamin b K. C. G. Benjamin . 30
D. K. Liyanage c Harper b K. C. G. Benjamin . 14
C. P. H. Ramanayake not out 9
G. P. Wickremasinghe not out 6
L-b 9, w 2, n-b 2 13

1/16 2/50 3/62 4/74 5/110 6/110 7/132 8/167 9/167 (9 wkts, 50 overs) 182

Bowling: Walsh 10–2–34–1; K. C. G. Benjamin 8–0–30–2; Simmons 4–0–19–1; W. K. M. Benjamin 8–0–32–1; Harper 10–1–31–3; Hooper 10–0–27–1.

West Indies

B. C. Lara c Kaluwitharana b Kalpage . 42
*D. L. Haynes b Wickremasinghe 0
P. V. Simmons not out 90
C. L. Hooper not out 47
N-b 4 4

1/1 2/87 (2 wkts, 38.4 overs) 183

R. I. C. Holder, J. C. Adams, R. A. Harper, †J. R. Murray, W. K. M. Benjamin, K. C. G. Benjamin and C. A. Walsh did not bat.

Bowling: Wickremasinghe 8–1–37–1; Ramanayake 7–0–33–0; Liyanage 5–0–30–0; Kalpage 7.4–1–32–1; Jayasuriya 10–0–48–0; Tillekeratne 1–0–3–0.

Umpires: J. W. Holder and D. R. Shepherd.

QUALIFYING TABLE

	Played	*Won*	*Lost*	*Points*
Pakistan	4	3	1	6
West Indies......	4	3	1	6
Sri Lanka	4	0	4	0

FINAL

PAKISTAN v WEST INDIES

At Sharjah, November 5. West Indies won by six wickets. Toss: West Indies.

Two brilliant centuries dominated the game. Basit Ali transformed Pakistan's innings, in dire straits at 87 for three in the 28th over, with an unbeaten 127 – his maiden international hundred – from only 79 balls, with 12 fours and five sixes. He reached three figures in 67 balls, just short of Mohammad Azharuddin's record of 62 balls against New Zealand in 1988-89. Salim Malik helped him add 172 in 21 overs. But Pakistan's bowling, with Waqar Younis just back from injury and without Wasim Akram, Abdul Qadir or Aqib Javed, struggled to contain the West Indian reply. Lara rose to the occasion with 153, his highest limited-overs score, from 144 balls, including 21 fours. He shared a second-wicket stand of 111 in 15 overs with Simmons. Only his dismissal, caught behind off Mushtaq Ahmed, stemmed the flow a little; Richardson and Hooper took four overs to complete the 12 runs needed for victory – but even then they had 27 balls to spare.

Man of the Match: B. C. Lara. *Man of the Series:* P. V. Simmons.

Pakistan

Saeed Anwar b Cummins 16
Aamir Sohail c Lara b Benjamin 10
Inzamam-ul-Haq c Haynes b Walsh.... 30
Salim Malik c Walsh b Ambrose 84
Basit Ali not out 127
†Rashid Latif not out 2
B 1, l-b 5, w 4, n-b 5 15

1/28 2/30 3/87 4/259 (4 wkts, 50 overs) 284

Asif Mujtaba, Mushtaq Ahmed, *Waqar Younis, Ata-ur-Rehman and Aamir Nazir did not bat.

Bowling: Ambrose 10–2–64–1; Walsh 10–4–33–1; Cummins 9–0–57–1; Benjamin 8–0–37–1; Hooper 10–1–65–0; Simmons 3–0–22–0.

West Indies

B. C. Lara c Rashid Latif b Mushtaq Ahmed .153
D. L. Haynes c Rashid Latif b Ata-ur-Rehman . 3
P. V. Simmons c and b Salim Malik ... 42
K. L. T. Arthurton c sub (Aamer Hanif) b Ata-ur-Rehman . 44
*R. B. Richardson not out 15
C. L. Hooper not out................ 5
L-b 10, w 8, n-b 5........... 23

1/29 2/140 3/213 4/273 (4 wkts, 45.3 overs) 285

†J. C. Adams, K. C. G. Benjamin, C. E. L. Ambrose, A. C. Cummins and C. A. Walsh did not bat.

Bowling: Waqar Younis 8–0–65–0; Ata-ur-Rehman 8–0–43–2; Aamir Nazir 8.3–0–54–0; Mushtaq Ahmed 10–1–46–1; Aamir Sohail 2–0–20–0; Salim Malik 9–1–47–1.

Umpires: H. D. Bird and D. R. Shepherd.

HERO CUP, 1993-94

The Hero Cup, staged to commemorate the diamond jubilee of the Cricket Association of Bengal, produced a repeat of the 1983 World Cup final. Once again, India unexpectedly defeated the favourites, West Indies, who had headed the table after the preliminary rounds with three wins in four matches. India's route to the final was less smooth: they lost heavily in their previous game with West Indies and could only tie with Zimbabwe. But a two-run win over much-fancied South Africa in their semi-final prepared the way for a home success. The fifth team to take part was Sri Lanka, whose captain, Arjuna Ranatunga, complained that his players were treated "shabbily" by Indian officials. Pakistan had withdrawn yet again from a visit to India for fear of Hindu militants.

With India, Pakistan and Sri Lanka due to host the World Cup in early 1996, these were not the only embarrassments for the organisers. Both India's matches with West Indies were disrupted by crowd trouble: at Ahmedabad, play was halted for 40 minutes ("the worst crowd I have ever seen", according to Indian captain Mohammad Azharuddin) and at Calcutta a firecracker exploded in Keith Arthurton's face. The Indian board was even more alarmed when the government, claiming that state television network Doordashan had a monopoly on events in India, prevented Trans-World International, who had bought the international TV rights, from broadcasting the opening rounds. The dispute was settled as the board anxiously assured visiting ICC officials that there would be no repetition in 1996.

Note: Matches in this section were not first-class.

INDIA v SRI LANKA

At Kanpur, November 7. India won by seven wickets. Toss: India.

The host country began their campaign by defeating Sri Lanka with 5.2 overs to spare. Srinath took five wickets in a one-day international for the first time and only Mahanama, who batted for two and a half hours, made a significant score for Sri Lanka. Though Raman was lbw to his first ball, a 100-run stand between Kambli and Azharuddin ensured that India had few problems.

Man of the Match: J. Srinath.

Sri Lanka

R. S. Mahanama lbw b Chauhan...... 73
A. P. Gurusinha c Yadav b Srinath.... 11
S. T. Jayasuriya c Sharma b Srinath ... 7
P. A. de Silva run out 33
*A. Ranatunga c and b Tendulkar..... 1
H. P. Tillekeratne c Srinath b Prabhakar 35
†R. S. Kaluwitharana c Sharma b Chauhan . 20
D. K. Liyanage c Kapil Dev b Srinath . 4
R. S. Kalpage c Kumble b Srinath 3
C. P. H. Ramanayake not out 3
G. P. Wickremasinghe c Kapil Dev b Srinath . 0
L-b 5, w 8 13

1/43 2/53 3/116 4/117 5/147 6/175 7/188 8/200 9/202 (49.4 overs) 203

Bowling: Prabhakar 7–2–27–1; Kapil Dev 7–0–30–0; Srinath 6.4–1–24–5; Kumble 10–0–46–0; Tendulkar 10–2–27–1; Chauhan 6–0–28–2; Sharma 3–0–16–0.

India

M. Prabhakar c Kalpage b Wickremasinghe . 20	*M. Azharuddin not out 75
W. V. Raman lbw b Wickremasinghe . . 0	S. R. Tendulkar not out 26
V. G. Kambli c Ramanayake b Liyanage . 78	L-b 4, w 2 6
	1/1 2/46 3/146 (3 wkts, 44.4 overs) 205

Ajay Sharma, Kapil Dev, †V. S. Yadav, A. Kumble, R. K. Chauhan and J. Srinath did not bat.

Bowling: Wickremasinghe 6–1–13–2; Ramanayake 5.4–0–31–0; Liyanage 7–0–40–1; Ranatunga 3–0–19–0; Tillekeratne 9–0–39–0; Jayasuriya 6–0–32–0; Kalpage 8–0–27–0.

Umpires: S. A. Bucknor and I. D. Robinson.

SRI LANKA v WEST INDIES

At Wankhede Stadium, Bombay, November 9. West Indies won by 46 runs. Toss: Sri Lanka.

With West Indies' captain, Richardson, and leading bowler Ambrose resting, Winston Benjamin made the most of his chance, taking five wickets. His first spell – three for four in six overs – reduced Sri Lanka to 21 for three. Though Tillekeratne scored 104, which was to be the only century of the tournament, no one could help him chase a target of 269. After a sound start from Lara, followed by a run-a-ball 55 from Adams, West Indies had plundered 50 runs from their last five overs, 41 of them through Cummins, who faced only 19 balls.

Men of the Match: W. K. M. Benjamin and H. P. Tillekeratne.

West Indies

B. C. Lara c Muralitharan b Ranatunga 67	†J. R. Murray not out 11
*D. L. Haynes c Mahanama b Wickremasinghe . 0	A. C. Cummins c sub (C. P. H. Ramanayake) b Kalpage . 41
P. V. Simmons c Mahanama b Liyanage 3	W. K. M. Benjamin not out 0
C. L. Hooper b Ranatunga 38	
K. L. T. Arthurton st Kaluwitharana b Muralitharan . 6	B 1, l-b 18, w 8 27
J. C. Adams st Kaluwitharana b Kalpage . 55	1/10 2/26 3/104 (8 wkts, 50 overs) 268
R. A. Harper lbw b Kalpage 20	4/111 5/172 6/211 7/220 8/268

C. A. Walsh did not bat.

Bowling: Wickremasinghe 10–2–54–1; Liyanage 8–0–24–1; Hathurusinghe 2–0–22–0; Ranatunga 10–1–44–2; Kalpage 10–0–64–3; Muralitharan 10–1–41–1.

Sri Lanka

R. S. Mahanama lbw b Benjamin 11	R. S. Kalpage not out 29
U. C. Hathurusinghe b Benjamin 1	D. K. Liyanage b Benjamin 3
S. T. Jayasuriya c Haynes b Benjamin . . 2	M. Muralitharan not out 4
H. P. Tillekeratne b Benjamin 104	B 1, l-b 14, w 2, n-b 2 19
D. P. Samaraweera c and b Harper 25	
*A. Ranatunga st Murray b Hooper . . . 14	1/10 2/16 3/21 (8 wkts, 50 overs) 222
†R. S. Kaluwitharana c Arthurton b Hooper . 10	4/72 5/118 6/143 7/204 8/214

G. P. Wickremasinghe did not bat.

Bowling: Walsh 8–2–25–0; Benjamin 10–3–22–5; Cummins 8–2–37–0; Harper 5–0–36–1; Simmons 10–0–38–0; Hooper 9–0–49–2.

Umpires: S. K. Bansal and R. T. Ramchandran.

SOUTH AFRICA v ZIMBABWE

At Bangalore, November 10. No result. Toss: Zimbabwe. International debuts: J. A. Rennie, H. H. Streak.

Rain, which had delayed the start and reduced the match to 37 overs a side, returned to end the game just after South Africa lost their first wicket.

South Africa

*K. C. Wessels not out	10
A. C. Hudson lbw b Brain	5
W. J. Cronje not out	4
W 3	3
1/18 (1 wkt, 9 overs)	22

D. J. Cullinan, J. N. Rhodes, D. J. Callaghan, B. M. McMillan, †D. J. Richardson, P. S. de Villiers, A. A. Donald and C. R. Matthews did not bat.

Bowling: Brain 5–0–12–1; Streak 4–0–10–0.

Zimbabwe

*†A. Flower, G. W. Flower, A. D. R. Campbell, D. L. Houghton, A. C. Waller, S. G. Peall, H. H. Streak, D. H. Brain, M. H. Dekker, J. A. Rennie and I. P. Butchart.

Umpires: P. D. Reporter and S. K. Sharma.

SOUTH AFRICA v WEST INDIES

At Brabourne Stadium, Bombay, November 14. South Africa won by 41 runs. Toss: West Indies.

Heavy overnight rain leaked on to the pitch at the Brabourne Stadium – the Test ground superseded by the Wankhede almost 20 years before – and reduced the match to 40 overs a side. Cullinan and Rhodes responded well after South Africa had been put in and lost both openers for 11 runs. They added 65 in 11 overs for the fourth wicket, though Cullinan was eventually forced to retire through heat exhaustion. Rhodes starred in the West Indian innings too: his athleticism secured five catches, a record for a fielder in one-day internationals, and a straightforward victory for South Africa.

Man of the Match: J. N. Rhodes.

South Africa

A. C. Hudson c Simmons b K. C. G. Benjamin	5
*K. C. Wessels c Lara b Ambrose	3
W. J. Cronje lbw b Hooper	12
D. J. Cullinan retired ill	70
J. N. Rhodes b W. K. M. Benjamin	40
B. M. McMillan b W. K. M. Benjamin	24
†D. J. Richardson not out	17
P. L. Symcox not out	3
L-b 2, w 3, n-b 1	6
1/9 2/11 3/52 4/117 5/176 (5 wkts, 40 overs)	180

R. P. Snell, P. S. de Villiers and A. A. Donald did not bat.

D. J. Cullinan retired ill at 136.

Bowling: Ambrose 8–1–23–1; K. C. G. Benjamin 8–0–41–1; W. K. M. Benjamin 8–0–40–2; Cummins 8–1–43–0; Hooper 8–0–31–1.

West Indies

B. C. Lara c Rhodes b Snell	7	W. K. M. Benjamin c Cronje b McMillan	0
D. L. Haynes c Rhodes b Snell	28	C. E. L. Ambrose c Snell b McMillan	0
P. V. Simmons c Rhodes b Symcox	29	K. C. G. Benjamin not out	7
K. L. T. Arthurton st Richardson b Symcox	16	B 4, l-b 7, w 2	13
C. L. Hooper lbw b Cronje	17		
*R. B. Richardson c and b Cronje	1	1/14 2/50 3/73	(37 overs) 139
†J. C. Adams c Rhodes b Symcox	4	4/78 5/87 6/95	
A. C. Cummins c Rhodes b Donald	17	7/120 8/124 9/131	

D. L. Haynes, when 7, retired hurt at 15 and resumed at 87.

Bowling: Donald 5–0–15–1; de Villiers 5–2–5–0; Snell 6–0–30–2; McMillan 5–0–25–2; Symcox 8–1–20–3; Cronje 8–1–33–2.

Umpires: R. C. Sharma and V. K. Ramaswamy.

SRI LANKA v ZIMBABWE

At Patna, November 15. Sri Lanka won by 55 runs. Toss: Zimbabwe. International debut: G. J. Whittal.

The tournament's two underdogs came to Patna, the 28th city in India to stage a limited-overs international, and Sri Lanka emerged on top. Their total of 263 was underpinned by 96 in 18 overs from de Silva and Ranatunga, while Ratnayake, called up after Gurusinha was injured, smashed 32 from 15 balls. For Zimbabwe, Waller hit a 46-ball fifty, but only Campbell and the newcomer Guy Whittal offered much support. Both fell to Jayasuriya, whose left-arm spin earned four wickets in four overs.

Man of the Match: A. Ranatunga.

Sri Lanka

R. S. Mahanama c Dekker b Brain	16	R. J. Ratnayake not out	32
S. T. Jayasuriya c Waller b Brain	23	†R. S. Kaluwitharana not out	4
H. P. Tillekeratne lbw b Shah	24	B 8, l-b 5, w 15, n-b 1	29
P. A. de Silva c and b Shah	68		
*A. Ranatunga c Rennie b Dekker	59	1/38 2/49 3/114	(6 wkts, 50 overs) 263
D. K. Liyanage b Rennie	8	4/210 5/221 6/225	

R. S. Kalpage, M. Muralitharan and G. P. Wickremasinghe did not bat.

Bowling: Brain 10–1–45–2; Streak 8–0–67–0; Rennie 9–0–37–1; Peall 10–0–35–0; Shah 10–0–50–2; Dekker 3–0–16–1.

Zimbabwe

*†A. Flower run out	11	S. G. Peall c Tillekeratne b Kalpage	12
D. H. Brain lbw b Ratnayake	2	H. H. Streak st Kaluwitharana b Jayasuriya	5
A. D. R. Campbell c Ratnayake b Jayasuriya	37	J. A. Rennie not out	3
D. L. Houghton b Liyanage	12	B 5, l-b 4, w 9, n-b 2	20
A. C. Waller c Tillekeratne b Ranatunga	55		
M. H. Dekker lbw b Ranatunga	1	1/6 2/22 3/53	(49 overs) 208
G. J. Whittall b Jayasuriya	36	4/130 5/132 6/133	
A. H. Shah b Jayasuriya	14	7/188 8/189 9/202	

Bowling: Wickremasinghe 6–1–13–0; Ratnayake 7–0–12–1; Liyanage 10–1–36–1; Muralitharan 10–0–43–0; Kalpage 6–0–46–1; Jayasuriya 4–0–19–4; Ranatunga 5–0–24–2; Tillekeratne 1–0–6–0.

Umpires: S. Chowdhury and K. Parthasarathy.

INDIA v WEST INDIES

At Ahmedabad, November 16. West Indies won by 69 runs, India's target having been revised to 170 from 38 overs. Toss: West Indies.

A crowd of 50,000 packed the Gujarat Stadium, and some lost patience after India had tumbled to 55 for six, answering West Indies' 202. Hurling stones, firecrackers and empty plastic bottles, they forced the fielders into the middle of the pitch. After 22 minutes the game resumed, but it halted again two balls later; the West Indians felt unsafe chasing the ball to the boundary. More than 40 minutes – 12 overs – were lost in all, but India's eventual total of 100 was way under even their revised target. Hooper's spin finished what Winston Benjamin's pace began and West Indies went through to the semi-finals with nearly ten overs to spare.

Man of the Match: W. K. M. Benjamin.

West Indies

B. C. Lara b Kumble	23	R. A. Harper run out	2
P. V. Simmons run out	9	W. K. M. Benjamin not out	14
*R. B. Richardson c Kambli b Kumble	41	B 1, l-b 21, w 6	28
K. L. T. Arthurton b Kumble	41		—
C. L. Hooper c Yadav b Srinath	8	1/34 2/36 3/114 (7 wkts, 50 overs)	202
†J. C. Adams not out	26	4/128 5/157	
R. I. C. Holder c Chauhan b Srinath	10	6/177 7/186	

C. E. L. Ambrose and C. A. Walsh did not bat.

Bowling: Prabhakar 10–1–50–0; Srinath 10–1–33–2; Kumble 10–1–24–3; Kapil Dev 8–0–21–0; Chauhan 10–2–41–0; Tendulkar 2–0–11–0.

India

M. Prabhakar c Adams b Walsh	11	A. Kumble c Benjamin b Hooper	14
Kapil Dev lbw b Ambrose	1	R. K. Chauhan not out	3
V. G. Kambli c Lara b Benjamin	10	J. Srinath c Harper b Hooper	2
*M. Azharuddin c Ambrose b Simmons	23	L-b 2, w 8	10
S. R. Tendulkar lbw b Walsh	2		—
W. V. Raman c Lara b Benjamin	4	1/12 2/18 3/37 (28.3 overs)	100
Ajay Sharma b Benjamin	0	4/40 5/55 6/55	
†V. S. Yadav st Adams b Hooper	20	7/77 8/85 9/96	

Bowling: Ambrose 6–0–18–1; Walsh 7–2–25–2; Benjamin 6–0–27–3; Simmons 5–0–19–1; Hooper 4.3–1–9–3.

Umpires: K. E. Liebenberg and I. D. Robinson.

INDIA v ZIMBABWE

At Indore, November 18. Tied. Toss: Zimbabwe.

Zimbabwe's best effort of the tournament found them ten short of victory with one wicket standing when Prabhakar began the final over. Streak and Rennie took eight off the first five balls and than a leg-bye, but Streak was run out attempting a second. Under competition rules the points were shared, although India had lost only five wickets. Earlier, Prabhakar fell just short of his century, after putting on 122 with Kambli. Azharuddin scored a rapid 54, and the other captain, Andy Flower, also scored fifty before the middle order's momentum almost won the match for Zimbabwe.

Man of the Match: M. Prabhakar.

India

M. Prabhakar st A. Flower b Peall 91
W. V. Raman c Houghton b Brain 0
V. G. Kambli c Rennie b Peall 55
†V. S. Yadav c G. W. Flower b Peall .. 0
*M. Azharuddin not out 54
S. R. Tendulkar c and b Streak 24
P. K. Amre not out 1
B 4, l-b 8, w 8, n-b 3 23

1/6 2/128 3/128 4/197 5/239 (5 wkts, 50 overs) 248

Kapil Dev, A. Kumble, J. Srinath and R. K. Chauhan did not bat.

Bowling: Brain 10–0–37–1; Streak 10–2–44–1; Rennie 9–0–36–0; Shah 5–0–31–0; Peall 10–0–54–3; G. W. Flower 6–0–34–0.

Zimbabwe

*†A. Flower st Yadav b Chauhan 56
G. W. Flower b Prabhakar........... 2
A. D. R. Campbell b Srinath 7
D. L. Houghton lbw b Kapil Dev 22
A. C. Waller c Azharuddin b Tendulkar 32
G. J. Whittall run out 33
A. H. Shah c Chauhan b Srinath...... 37
S. G. Peall c Yadav b Srinath 17
D. H. Brain c Azharuddin b Prabhakar 1
H. H. Streak run out 11
J. A. Rennie not out 9
L-b 10, w 11 21

1/10 2/23 3/67 4/131 5/143 6/207 7/208 8/212 9/237 (50 overs) 248

Bowling: Prabhakar 10–0–41–2; Srinath 10–0–44–3; Tendulkar 8–0–48–1; Kapil Dev 6–0–31–1; Kumble 8–0–42–0; Chauhan 8–0–32–1.

Umpires: S. A. Bucknor and K. E. Liebenberg.

SOUTH AFRICA v SRI LANKA

At Gauhati, November 19. South Africa won by 78 runs. Toss: Sri Lanka.

Snell hustled out Sri Lanka with almost ten overs left. Coming on first change, he took three wickets for eight runs in his first six-over spell, reducing the opposition from 48 for one to 59 for four. South Africa had not been able to set an enormous target, despite solid contributions from Wessels, Cullinan and McMillan.

Man of the Match: R. P. Snell.

South Africa

*K. C. Wessels st Kaluwitharana b Muralitharan . 53
A. C. Hudson c Kaluwitharana b Ratnayake . 5
W. J. Cronje b Muralitharan 28
D. J. Cullinan b Jayasuriya 41
J. N. Rhodes c Mahanama b Jayasuriya 16
B. M. McMillan not out 31
P. L. Symcox b Jayasuriya 4
R. P. Snell b Ratnayake 20
†D. J. Richardson not out............ 1
L-b 7, w 6, n-b 2............ 15

1/18 2/81 3/101 4/132 5/163 6/171 7/212 (7 wkts, 50 overs) 214

P. S. de Villiers and A. A. Donald did not bat.

Bowling: Wickremasinghe 6–0–29–0; Ratnayake 8–2–24–2; Liyanage 5–1–27–0; Muralitharan 10–1–36–2; Kalpage 10–1–40–0; Jayasuriya 7–0–30–3; de Silva 4–0–21–0.

Sri Lanka

R. S. Mahanama c Richardson b Donald 10
S. T. Jayasuriya c Richardson b Snell .. 27
H. P. Tillekeratne lbw b Snell 4
P. A. de Silva lbw b Snell............ 2
*A. Ranatunga lbw b Symcox 6
†R. S. Kaluwitharana c Rhodes b Cronje 17
R. S. Kalpage c de Villiers b Cronje ... 1
R. J. Ratnayake run out 21
D. K. Liyanage c Cronje b de Villiers.. 16
G. P. Wickremasinghe b Snell 17
M. Muralitharan not out............. 0
L-b 5, w 4, n-b 6............ 15

1/25 2/48 3/50 4/59 5/78 6/80 7/81 8/109 9/135 (40.1 overs) 136

Bowling: Donald 8–0–33–1; de Villiers 9–1–29–1; Snell 7.1–2–12–4; McMillan 5–0–16–0; Cronje 6–1–21–2; Symcox 5–0–20–1.

Umpires: S. Chowdhury and V. K. Ramaswamy.

WEST INDIES v ZIMBABWE

At Hyderabad, November 21 (day/night). West Indies won by 134 runs. Toss: West Indies.

Zimbabwe – one man short after an injury to Brandes – were dismissed in double figures for the first time in an international match. West Indies' second string wrapped up the match with 13.3 overs in hand, only Andy Flower and Houghton passing ten. Earlier, Haynes had hit 11 fours in 75 and Holder had reached his maiden international fifty.

Man of the Match: D. L. Haynes.

West Indies

B. C. Lara c Streak b Brain 4
D. L. Haynes run out 75
P. V. Simmons lbw b Streak 0
*R. B. Richardson c A. Flower b Streak 5
R. I. C. Holder c Brandes b Peall 50
K. L. T. Arthurton run out 16
R. A. Harper b Rennie 26
A. C. Cummins c Brain b Rennie 26
W. K. M. Benjamin run out 8
K. C. G. Benjamin not out 1
B 2, l-b 9, w 9, n-b 2 22

1/10 2/24 3/38 4/130 5/156 6/169 7/212 8/231 9/233 (9 wkts, 50 overs) 233

†J. R. Murray did not bat.

Bowling: Brain 6–1–24–1; Streak 10–2–44–2; Rennie 9–0–42–2; Brandes 9.3–0–56–0; Peall 10–0–34–1; Campbell 5–0–16–0; Whittall 0.3–0–6–0.

Zimbabwe

*†A. Flower c Haynes b K. C. G. Benjamin . 22
G. W. Flower c Simmons b W. K. M. Benjamin . 7
A. D. R. Campbell lbw b W. K. M. Benjamin . 0
D. L. Houghton c Murray b Simmons . . 22
A. C. Waller b Simmons 9
G. J. Whittall c Cummins b Harper . . . 9
S. G. Peall b Cummins 10
D. H. Brain c Harper b Simmons 1
H. H. Streak not out 0
J. A. Rennie lbw b Cummins 0
E. A. Brandes absent injured
L-b 9, w 5, n-b 5 19

1/23 2/23 3/43 4/67 5/80 6/88 7/91 8/98 9/99 (36.3 overs) 99

Bowling: K. C. G. Benjamin 7–1–19–1; W. K. M. Benjamin 6–2–13–2; Cummins 5.3–0–19–2; Simmons 10–0–23–3; Harper 8–2–16–1.

Umpires: S. K. Bansal and R. C. Sharma.

INDIA v SOUTH AFRICA

At Mohali, November 22. India won by 43 runs. Toss: South Africa.

India won with surprising ease after South Africa had reached 112 for three from 30 overs. The later batsmen failed to rise to the requirement of 5.5 from the remaining 20, only Richardson reaching double figures. Jadeja and Kambli set up India's total of 221 with a stand of 88 in 18 overs; Kambli went on to score 86. This was the inaugural match at the Punjab CA's ground at Mohali, a few miles from Chandigarh.

Man of the Match: V. G. Kambli.

India

M. Prabhakar lbw b de Villiers 1
A. D. Jadeja run out 39
V. G. Kambli b Cronje 86
S. R. Tendulkar c Richardson b Cronje. 3
*M. Azharuddin run out 31
P. K. Amre c Donald b Cronje 2
Kapil Dev c Wessels b de Villiers 22
†V. S. Yadav b Snell 2
A. Kumble run out 2
J. Srinath c Hudson b Snell 1
S. A. Ankola not out 2
B 1, l-b 10, w 16, n-b 3 30

1/6 2/94 3/129 4/180 5/188 6/192 7/196 8/199 9/211 (49.2 overs) 221

Bowling: Donald 8–0–39–0; de Villiers 8.2–0–27–2; Snell 10–0–54–2; McMillan 10–0–45–0; Cronje 10–0–29–3; Symcox 3–0–16–0.

South Africa

A. C. Hudson lbw b Kapil Dev	27	R. P. Snell c Kumble b Ankola	2
*K. C. Wessels c Yadav b Srinath	1	P. S. de Villiers c Yadav b Ankola	1
W. J. Cronje b Jadeja	39	A. A. Donald not out	5
J. N. Rhodes lbw b Ankola	56	L-b 4, w 7, n-b 3	14
D. J. Callaghan c Kapil Dev b Jadeja	6		
B. M. McMillan lbw b Kumble	2	1/7 2/40 3/108 (9 wkts, 50 overs)	178
†D. J. Richardson not out	23	4/124 5/127 6/144	
P. L. Symcox b Prabhakar	2	7/147 8/150 9/157	

Bowling: Prabhakar 10–0–36–1; Srinath 7–1–22–1; Ankola 10–1–33–3; Kapil Dev 8–1–32–1; Kumble 10–0–35–1; Jadeja 5–1–16–2.

Umpires: S. A. Bucknor and I. D. Robinson.

QUALIFYING TABLE

	Played	Won	Lost	Tied	No result	Points	Net run-rate
West Indies	4	3	1	0	0	6	1.05
South Africa	4	2	1	0	1	5	0.54
India	4	2	1	1	0	5	0.08
Sri Lanka	4	1	3	0	0	2	−0.47
Zimbabwe	4	0	2	1	1	2	−1.26

South Africa took second place on net run-rate; Sri Lanka were placed fourth, having won one match to Zimbabwe's none.

SEMI-FINALS

INDIA v SOUTH AFRICA

At Calcutta, November 24 (day/night). India won by two runs. Toss: India.

India's second successive win over South Africa was a much tighter affair. The match was the first played under lights at Eden Gardens – smoke bombs were deployed to deter vast swarms of insects, though a local mongoose remained and fielded enthusiastically in this and the next two games. It was also the first match in India to feature a video replay umpire: S. K. Bansal made his mark early on when he sent back Kambli and Prabhakar, both run out by Cullinan. Azharuddin pulled his team round with Amre's help, but India failed to reach 200. South Africa came to the last five overs needing 45, which was down to seven when they lost Richardson. They entered the final over – Tendulkar's first – looking for six, but they managed only three, and de Villiers became the seventh run-out of the game.

Man of the Match: M. Azharuddin.

India

M. Prabhakar run out	3	A. Kumble c McMillan b Snell	0
A. D. Jadeja lbw b de Villiers	6	J. Srinath b de Villiers	4
V. G. Kambli run out	4	S. A. Ankola not out	2
*M. Azharuddin c Richardson b Snell	90	L-b 5, w 5, n-b 3	13
S. R. Tendulkar c Richardson b Snell	15		
P. K. Amre run out	48	1/12 2/18 3/18 (50 overs)	195
Kapil Dev run out	7	4/53 5/148 6/173	
†V. S. Yadav c Rhodes b de Villiers	3	7/184 8/189 9/192	

Bowling: Donald 8–0–44–0; de Villiers 10–1–19–3; Snell 8–0–33–3; McMillan 9–0–41–0; Cronje 9–0–25–0; Symcox 6–0–28–0.

South Africa

*K. C. Wessels lbw b Srinath	5	†D. J. Richardson run out	15
A. C. Hudson b Kumble	62	P. S. de Villiers run out	0
W. J. Cronje run out	13	A. A. Donald not out	1
D. J. Cullinan lbw b Kapil Dev	10	L-b 9, w 4, n-b 3	16
J. N. Rhodes c Azharuddin b Jadeja	16		—
B. M. McMillan not out	48	1/10 2/45 3/65 (9 wkts, 50 overs)	193
P. L. Symcox c Amre b Jadeja	6	4/106 5/130 6/141	
R. P. Snell st Yadav b Kumble	1	7/145 8/189 9/191	

Bowling: Prabhakar 8–1–30–0; Srinath 8–0–39–1; Kapil Dev 8–0–31–1; Ankola 6–0–21–0; Kumble 10–0–29–2; Jadeja 9–0–31–2; Tendulkar 1–0–3–0.

Umpires: S. A. Bucknor and I. D. Robinson.

SRI LANKA v WEST INDIES

At Calcutta, November 25 (day/night). West Indies won by seven wickets. Toss: West Indies.

West Indies reached the final in style, with 8.1 overs to spare. They had restricted Sri Lanka to a disappointing 188, a total which owed almost everything to de Silva and Kalpage. Joining forces at 77 for five, they added 109 in 19 overs; de Silva hit 38 from his last 18 balls. Though West Indies lost Haynes and Simmons for ducks, the left-handers Lara and Arthurton then combined in a stand of 163 to put the result beyond doubt.

Man of the Match: B. C. Lara.

Sri Lanka

R. S. Mahanama lbw b Cummins	31	R. S. Kalpage not out	41
S. T. Jayasuriya c Simmons b Benjamin	18	R. J. Ratnayake not out	2
H. P. Tillekeratne lbw b Cummins	11	B 11, w 3	14
P. A. de Silva run out	68		—
*A. Ranatunga c Lara b Hooper	2	1/33 2/65 3/68 (6 wkts, 50 overs)	188
†R. S. Kaluwitharana b Hooper	1	4/73 5/77 6/186	

G. P. Wickremasinghe, C. P. H. Ramanayake and M. Muralitharan did not bat.

Bowling: Ambrose 10–0–59–0; Walsh 10–3–33–0; Benjamin 10–2–29–1; Cummins 10–0–38–2; Hooper 10–3–18–2.

West Indies

B. C. Lara b Muralitharan	82	*R. B. Richardson not out	15
D. L. Haynes lbw b Wickremasinghe	0		
P. V. Simmons c Mahanama b Wickremasinghe	0	L-b 2, w 12, n-b 7	21
			—
K. L. T. Arthurton not out	72	1/1 2/3 3/166 (3 wkts, 41.5 overs)	190

C. L. Hooper, †J. C. Adams, A. C. Cummins, W. K. M. Benjamin, C. E. L. Ambrose and C. A. Walsh did not bat.

Bowling: Wickremasinghe 6–0–27–2; Ramanayake 3–0–18–0; Ratnayake 4–0–11–0; Kalpage 9.5–0–47–0; Muralitharan 10–0–37–1; Jayasuriya 2–0–14–0; de Silva 3–0–16–0; Ranatunga 4–0–18–0.

Umpires: S. K. Bansal and S. Chowdhury.

FINAL

INDIA v WEST INDIES

At Calcutta, November 27 (day/night). India won by 102 runs. Toss: West Indies.

A crowd widely estimated as close to 100,000 watched with delight as West Indies' batting collapsed. From 57 for one they lost nine wickets for 66, and were all out with nearly ten overs remaining; Kumble took the last six for four runs in 26 balls. His full figures of six for 12 were the best for India in one-day internationals. One of his victims, Holder, notched up the dubious first of being given out bowled by a TV umpire. In theory, Sekhar Chowdhury's judgments were limited to line decisions, but umpires Robinson and Liebenberg called for advice because they were uncertain whether the ball had been deflected off the wicket-keeper. This was not West Indies' only misfortune: during India's innings, cordite from a firecracker entered Arthurton's eye, forcing him to leave the field. But Richardson had chosen to bat second on a wearing pitch, already used in both semi-finals. India began well enough, with Kambli and Azharuddin adding 80 in 14 overs, before three wickets fell at 161 – including Kambli, run out when Ambrose kicked the ball on to his wicket. They scored only eight between the 37th and 43rd overs. But when West Indies went so cheaply it hardly mattered.

Man of the Match: A. Kumble. *Man of the Series:* M. Azharuddin.

India

M. Prabhakar c Adams b Ambrose 11
A. D. Jadeja c Richardson b W. K. M. Benjamin . 30
V. G. Kambli run out 68
*M. Azharuddin c Adams b Cummins . 38
S. R. Tendulkar not out 28
P. K. Amre lbw b Cummins.......... 0
Kapil Dev c Hooper b Cummins 24
†V. S. Yadav b Ambrose 3
A. Kumble not out.................. 5
B 2, l-b 12, w 2, n-b 2 18

1/25 2/81 3/161 4/161 5/161 6/207 7/218 (7 wkts, 50 overs) 225

J. Srinath and S. L. V. Raju did not bat.

Bowling: Ambrose 10–1–35–2; K. C. G. Benjamin 10–1–35–0; W. K. M. Benjamin 10–1–47–1; Cummins 10–1–38–3; Hooper 8–0–42–0; Simmons 2–0–14–0.

West Indies

B. C. Lara b Tendulkar.............. 33
P. V. Simmons b Prabhakar 0
*R. B. Richardson c and b Kapil Dev.. 18
K. L. T. Arthurton lbw b Kapil Dev... 5
C. L. Hooper lbw b Kumble.......... 23
R. I. C. Holder b Kumble............ 15
†J. C. Adams c Azharuddin b Kumble . 4
A. C. Cummins b Kumble 1
W. K. M. Benjamin b Kumble........ 3
C. E. L. Ambrose b Kumble 0
K. C. G. Benjamin not out........... 0
L-b 12, w 8, n-b 1........... 21

1/1 2/57 3/57 4/63 5/101 6/113 7/118 8/122 9/122 (40.1 overs) 123

Bowling: Prabhakar 6–0–21–1; Srinath 6–0–12–0; Jadeja 1–0–18–0; Kapil Dev 10–3–18–2; Tendulkar 7–1–24–1; Kumble 6.1–2–12–6; Raju 4–0–6–0.

Umpires: K. E. Liebenberg and I. D. Robinson.

BENSON AND HEDGES WORLD SERIES, 1993-94

By STEVEN LYNCH

Note: Matches in this section were not first-class.

AUSTRALIA v SOUTH AFRICA

At Melbourne, December 9 (day/night). South Africa won by seven wickets. Toss: Australia.

South Africa began the tournament with an easy win. Though Australia made a good start, reaching 100 without loss in the 20th over, they struggled thereafter and were bowled out with 4.1 overs remaining. Slater, in his first one-day international, made 73 from 69 balls, with eight fours and a six, but the others could muster only two boundaries between them – the outfield had suffered from recent pop concerts. Three batsmen were run out, with direct hits from Rhodes accounting for Boon (via a remarkable throw from point while falling) and Steve Waugh. Wessels and Cronje ensured victory with a stand of 140. McGrath, dismissed by his first ball on his Test debut, against New Zealand a month earlier, completed an unwanted double when he succumbed first ball on his one-day debut.

Man of the Match: W. J. Cronje. *Attendance:* 58,030.

Australia

M. A. Taylor b Cronje	30
M. J. Slater c and b Symcox	73
D. C. Boon run out	1
M. E. Waugh c Symcox b Cronje	8
S. R. Waugh run out	33
*A. R. Border b Snell	11
†I. A. Healy not out	21
S. K. Warne run out	3
P. R. Reiffel lbw b de Villiers	0
C. J. McDermott c Richardson b de Villiers	5
G. D. McGrath b de Villiers	0
L-b 2, w 2	4
1/105 2/106 3/106 4/119 5/151 6/166 7/180 8/181 9/189 (45.5 overs)	189

Bowling: Donald 10–1–32–0; de Villiers 7.5–0–30–3; Snell 8–0–43–1; Cronje 10–0–42–2; Symcox 10–0–40–1.

South Africa

A. C. Hudson c Taylor b McDermott	4
*K. C. Wessels b McDermott	70
W. J. Cronje not out	91
D. J. Cullinan b Warne	0
J. N. Rhodes not out	20
L-b 2, w 1, n-b 2	5
1/4 2/144 3/149 (3 wkts, 48.4 overs)	190

D. J. Callaghan, †D. J. Richardson, P. L. Symcox, R. P. Snell, P. S. de Villiers and A. A. Donald did not bat.

Bowling: McDermott 10–1–31–2; McGrath 8.4–1–28–0; Reiffel 4–0–19–0; S. R. Waugh 10–0–37–0; Border 3–0–15–0; Warne 10–0–43–1; M. E. Waugh 3–0–15–0.

Umpires: T. A. Prue and W. P. Sheahan.

NEW ZEALAND v SOUTH AFRICA

At Adelaide, December 11. Abandoned.

Rain prevented any play in this match, which was officially abandoned at 3.15 p.m. South Africa won an impromptu game of touch-football played on the wet outfield.

AUSTRALIA v NEW ZEALAND

At Adelaide, December 12. Australia won by eight wickets. Toss: New Zealand.

Warne and McGrath took four wickets each as New Zealand were bowled out for 135 inside 49 overs. Only Greatbatch and Cairns passed 20, and the last seven wickets went down for only 31. Australia strolled to victory with 11.1 overs remaining, as Hayden – returning to international cricket after a prolific run with the bat for Queensland – and Boon made unhurried and unbeaten half-centuries.

Man of the Match: S. K. Warne. *Attendance*: 16,865.

New Zealand

B. A. Young b Reiffel	18
R. T. Latham c M. E. Waugh b McGrath	1
*K. R. Rutherford c Reiffel b McGrath	15
M. J. Greatbatch lbw b Warne	28
C. L. Cairns c Border b Warne	31
C. Z. Harris c and b Warne	4
†T. E. Blain not out	9
D. N. Patel c Healy b McDermott	1
G. R. Larsen c Reiffel b Warne	8
C. Pringle c Border b McGrath	4
D. K. Morrison c Healy b McGrath	3
L-b 8, w 3, n-b 2	13
1/6 2/33 3/45 4/104 5/109 6/112 7/113 8/124 9/132 (48.2 overs)	135

Bowling: McDermott 10–2–15–1; McGrath 8.2–2–32–4; Reiffel 8–2–20–1; S. R. Waugh 7–0–16–0; M. E. Waugh 5–0–19–0; Warne 10–1–25–4.

Australia

M. J. Slater lbw b Pringle	8
M. L. Hayden not out	50
M. E. Waugh run out	21
D. C. Boon not out	51
L-b 4, w 1, n-b 1	6
1/16 2/42 (2 wkts, 38.5 overs)	136

S. R. Waugh, *A. R. Border, †I. A. Healy, P. R. Reiffel, S. K. Warne, C. J. McDermott and G. D. McGrath did not bat.

Bowling: Morrison 8–2–31–0; Pringle 8–3–18–1; Cairns 9.5–0–27–0; Larsen 9–0–37–0; Patel 4–0–19–0.

Umpires: A. J. McQuillan and W. P. Sheahan.

AUSTRALIA v SOUTH AFRICA

At Sydney, December 14 (day/night). Australia won by 103 runs. Toss: South Africa. International debut: G. Kirsten.

Australia's first limited-overs victory over South Africa was clouded by misgivings about the pitch – described by Border as "very ordinary" – which allowed generous bounce and movement to the seamers. Replying to Australia's 172 for nine, in which Healy's 38 was the highest score, South Africa were shot out for 69 – less than half their previous lowest one-day total, 152 against West Indies in 1991-92 – in just 28 overs. Only Wessels and Cronje (who looked unlucky to be given out caught behind) reached double figures, while Rhodes, who had broken his left hand in the field, came in at No. 9. The match award went to Reiffel, who scored 29 not out, took four wickets for 13, made two catches and ran out de Villiers with a direct hit.

Man of the Match: P. R. Reiffel. *Attendance*: 39,634.

Australia

M. A. Taylor run out 11
M. J. Slater c Rhodes b de Villiers 10
M. E. Waugh c Kirsten b Matthews . . . 36
D. C. Boon c Richardson b Matthews . . 4
S. R. Waugh c Richardson b Cronje . . . 13
*A. R. Border c de Villiers b Matthews. 8
†I. A. Healy c Cronje b Donald 38
P. R. Reiffel not out 29
S. K. Warne c Cullinan b de Villiers . . . 0
C. J. McDermott c Cronje b de Villiers. 3

B 1, l-b 4, w 7, n-b 8 20

1/28 2/30 3/44 4/76 5/95 6/96 7/164 8/164 9/172 (9 wkts, 50 overs) 172

G. D. McGrath did not bat.

Bowling: Donald 10–1–49–1; de Villiers 10–0–37–3; Matthews 10–0–23–3; Snell 10–0–44–0; Cronje 10–4–14–1.

South Africa

A. C. Hudson c Reiffel b McDermott . . 0
G. Kirsten c Healy b McGrath 4
*K. C. Wessels lbw b Reiffel 19
W. J. Cronje c Healy b Reiffel 20
D. J. Cullinan c S. R. Waugh b McGrath . 1
†D. J. Richardson c Healy b Reiffel . . . 1
R. P. Snell b Reiffel 0
C. R. Matthews c Reiffel b S. R. Waugh 7
J. N. Rhodes not out 4
P. S. de Villiers run out 0
A. A. Donald b S. R. Waugh 0

L-b 3, w 8, n-b 2 13

1/0 2/23 3/34 4/38 5/47 6/48 7/59 8/65 9/69 (28 overs) 69

Bowling: McDermott 6–2–8–1; McGrath 8–0–25–2; Reiffel 8–4–13–4; S. R. Waugh 6–0–20–2.

Umpires: D. B. Hair and P. D. Parker.

AUSTRALIA v NEW ZEALAND

At Melbourne, December 16 (day/night). Australia won by three runs. Toss: Australia.

New Zealand almost upset Australia, doing well to restrict them to 202. Taylor's 81 occupied 130 balls, and the home batsmen hit only five fours – and 100 singles. Steve Waugh, who struck three of those boundaries, retired on 25 after tearing a hamstring, and subsequently missed the first two Tests against South Africa. Warne, with four for 19 from his ten overs, hindered New Zealand's reply. They needed 11 from the last over, bowled by McDermott. Morrison survived being given run out by umpire Len King – he convinced the official that the wicket had been broken prematurely – but still had to hit six off the last ball, which was beyond him.

Man of the Match: S. K. Warne. *Attendance:* 25,893.

Australia

M. L. Hayden c Cairns b Pringle 5
M. A. Taylor c Blain b Cairns 81
M. E. Waugh c Rutherford b de Groen. 53
D. C. Boon c Morrison b de Groen 14
S. R. Waugh retired hurt 25
*A. R. Border run out 9
†I. A. Healy not out 5

L-b 7, w 3 10

1/8 2/97 3/131 4/183 5/202 (5 wkts, 50 overs) 202

P. R. Reiffel, S. K. Warne, T. B. A. May and C. J. McDermott did not bat.

S. R. Waugh retired hurt at 188.

Bowling: Pringle 9–1–26–1; Morrison 7–2–17–0; Cairns 7–0–33–1; Larsen 10–0–57–0; de Groen 10–0–40–2; Thomson 7–0–22–0.

New Zealand

B. A. Young lbw b McDermott	0	C. Pringle run out	4
R. T. Latham st Healy b Warne	39	D. K. Morrison not out	2
*K. R. Rutherford b M. E. Waugh	39	R. P. de Groen not out	2
M. J. Greatbatch lbw b Warne	41	B 1, l-b 5, w 1	7
C. L. Cairns c Healy b Warne	5		—
S. A. Thomson c Border b McDermott	42	1/0 2/66 3/99 (9 wkts, 50 overs)	199
†T. E. Blain c Border b Warne	1	4/109 5/146 6/154	
G. R. Larsen b M. E. Waugh	17	7/187 8/193 9/194	

Bowling: McDermott 9–1–40–2; Reiffel 10–1–44–0; M. E. Waugh 9–0–42–2; May 10–0–35–0; Warne 10–1–19–4; Border 2–0–13–0.

Umpires: L. J. King and A. J. McQuillan.

NEW ZEALAND v SOUTH AFRICA

At Hobart, December 18. New Zealand won by four wickets. Toss: South Africa.

New Zealand recorded their first win of the competition, overhauling South Africa's modest total of 147 with 5.5 overs to spare. Opener Young made 74, with seven fours, but only Cairns of his colleagues reached double figures as Matthews, with four for 38, made inroads. Earlier, South Africa had found batting equally difficult: they were 112 for six after 45 overs, and hit only five boundaries throughout. Medium-pacer Larsen conceded just 12 runs from his ten overs.

Man of the Match: G. R. Larsen. *Attendance:* 3,957.

South Africa

A. C. Hudson c Blain b Pringle	8	P. L. Symcox c Blain b Cairns	8
G. Kirsten c Young b Pringle	7	R. P. Snell not out	13
*K. C. Wessels c Blain b Larsen	15	L-b 4, w 3	7
W. J. Cronje c Morrison b Larsen	18		—
D. J. Cullinan c Blain b Thomson	8	1/15 2/22 3/50 (7 wkts, 50 overs)	147
D. J. Callaghan b Pringle	25	4/53 5/66	
†D. J. Richardson not out	38	6/101 7/119	

C. R. Matthews and P. S. de Villiers did not bat.

Bowling: Pringle 10–1–28–3; Morrison 8–1–32–0; Larsen 10–5–12–2; Cairns 7–0–27–1; Patel 10–2–25–0; Thomson 5–0–19–1.

New Zealand

B. A. Young lbw b Matthews	74	†T. E. Blain c Richardson b Matthews	5
R. T. Latham c Wessels b Matthews	7	G. R. Larsen not out	4
*K. R. Rutherford run out	9	W 1, n-b 1	2
M. J. Greatbatch run out	8		—
C. L. Cairns not out	30	1/22 2/54 3/66 (6 wkts, 44.1 overs)	148
S. A. Thomson b Matthews	9	4/112 5/132 6/142	

D. N. Patel, C. Pringle and D. K. Morrison did not bat.

Bowling: de Villiers 9.1–1–23–0; Matthews 10–1–38–4; Snell 10–2–29–0; Cronje 5–0–33–0; Symcox 10–0–25–0.

Umpires: S. J. Davis and S. G. Randell.

NEW ZEALAND v SOUTH AFRICA

At Brisbane, January 8. New Zealand won by nine runs, South Africa's target having been revised to 229 from 39 overs. Toss: South Africa.

New Zealand recovered from 86 for five to total 256, mainly thanks to a stand of 111 from 16 overs between Thomson and Cairns, both making their maiden one-day international fifties. Cairns smashed 70 from 54 balls, hitting successive deliveries from Matthews for six, four and six. A thunderstorm after five overs of South Africa's reply clipped an hour off the available playing time, and the revised target of 229 proved beyond them. Peter Kirsten kept them in the fight, in his first match since arriving to replace the injured Wessels: despite straining a thigh muscle, he hit six fours and a six in his 97 – and drove his runner, Errol Stewart, to the point of exhaustion, provoking some to ask whether a runner could himself retire.

Man of the Match: P. N. Kirsten. *Attendance:* 7,477.

New Zealand

B. A. Young c Cullinan b McMillan	28	†T. E. Blain not out	36
R. T. Latham c McMillan b Donald	11	G. R. Larsen not out	6
A. H. Jones c Kirsten b Matthews	9	L-b 2, w 2, n-b 2	6
*K. R. Rutherford b McMillan	1		—
M. J. Greatbatch c Rhodes b Donald	21	1/33 2/47 3/52 (7 wkts, 50 overs)	256
S. A. Thomson c Donald b Cronje	68	4/55 5/86	
C. L. Cairns run out	70	6/197 7/221	

C. Pringle and R. P. de Groen did not bat.

Bowling: Donald 8–0–38–2; de Villiers 10–2–40–0; Matthews 10–2–52–1; McMillan 10–0–59–2; Symcox 7–1–26–0; Cronje 5–0–39–1.

South Africa

A. C. Hudson c Thomson b Pringle	14	C. R. Matthews c Latham b Pringle	1
P. N. Kirsten c Jones b Cairns	97	P. S. de Villiers not out	0
†E. L. R. Stewart c and b Thomson	19		
*W. J. Cronje c Greatbatch b Thomson	19	L-b 4, w 2, n-b 1	7
D. J. Cullinan c Greatbatch b de Groen	37		—
J. N. Rhodes c Blain b Cairns	21	1/24 2/62 3/96 (8 wkts, 39 overs)	219
B. M. McMillan b Pringle	0	4/181 5/207 6/213	
P. L. Symcox not out	4	7/215 8/217	

A. A. Donald did not bat.

Bowling: Pringle 8–1–38–3; Cairns 8–1–44–2; Larsen 8–0–42–0; de Groen 7–0–41–1; Thomson 6–0–38–2; Latham 2–0–12–0.

Umpires: I. S. Thomas and C. D. Timmins.

AUSTRALIA v SOUTH AFRICA

At Brisbane, January 9. Australia won by 48 runs. Toss: South Africa. International debut: D. B. Rundle.

South Africa completed a miserable weekend in Brisbane with another defeat. Despite four wickets (including three in five balls) from off-spinner Dave Rundle, Australia made 230, with Jones, accorded a hero's welcome on his return to the side, scoring 98 in typically forthright style. South Africa passed 100 for the loss of only two wickets, but an over-cautious approach left the later batsmen too much to do, and the last eight went down for 64 in 15 overs, with McGrath taking four and Border – who ran out Callaghan – two. Border had words with Rhodes when he refused to walk after seemingly being caught and bowled. Earlier, the first of Healy's three catches took him past Rod Marsh's Australian record of 124 dismissals in one-day internationals.

Man of the Match: D. M. Jones. *Attendance:* 17,223.

Australia

D. C. Boon c Rundle b McMillan	45	C. J. McDermott run out	2
M. A. Taylor b de Villiers	12	T. B. A. May not out	5
D. M. Jones b Rundle	98		
M. E. Waugh c Cullinan b Symcox	10	L-b 4, w 6, n-b 1	11
D. R. Martyn c Cronje b Rundle	23		—
*A. R. Border c Kirsten b Rundle	15	1/20 2/108 3/127 (9 wkts, 50 overs)	230
†I. A. Healy c and b Rundle	0	4/180 5/205 6/208	
P. R. Reiffel run out	9	7/211 8/214 9/230	

G. D. McGrath did not bat.

Bowling: de Villiers 10–0–28–1; Snell 8–0–36–0; McMillan 10–2–42–1; Cronje 5–0–31–0; Symcox 8–0–47–1; Rundle 9–0–42–4.

South Africa

*W. J. Cronje c Healy b Reiffel	17	R. P. Snell c Martyn b McGrath	9
G. Kirsten c Healy b Waugh	51	D. B. Rundle c Border b McGrath	0
D. J. Cullinan c Reiffel b Border	27	P. S. de Villiers not out	1
J. N. Rhodes c Healy b May	46	L-b 6, w 2, n-b 1	9
D. J. Callaghan run out	1		—
B. M. McMillan c and b Border	6	1/33 2/88 3/118 (46.5 overs)	182
†D. J. Richardson lbw b McGrath	15	4/119 5/138 6/168	
P. L. Symcox lbw b McGrath	0	7/168 8/175 9/181	

Bowling: McDermott 5–1–14–0; McGrath 8.5–0–24–4; Reiffel 7–0–24–1; May 9–0–45–1; Waugh 7–0–29–1; Border 10–0–40–2.

Umpires: D. B. Hair and A. J. McQuillan.

AUSTRALIA v NEW ZEALAND

At Sydney, January 11 (day/night). New Zealand won by 13 runs. Toss: New Zealand.

New Zealand looked to have assured themselves of a place in the finals with their only victory over Australia in 1993-94; they led South Africa by four points with two matches to play and a vastly superior net run-rate. Greatbatch, who survived an apparent caught and bowled by Warne (with Border's displeasure again evident), and Rutherford were the main contributors to New Zealand's 198, which looked more imposing as Australia slumped to 87 for five. Boon, who was culpable in the run-outs of Taylor and Martyn, batted for three hours. Healy made 48 with a runner, after injuring his ankle, and survived a spectacular one-handed catch by Greatbatch in the covers when the square-leg umpire called no-ball, ruling that the ball bounced above shoulder-height. Three late wickets from Pringle settled the issue with nine balls to spare.

Man of the Match: C. Pringle. *Attendance*: 37,248.

New Zealand

B. A. Young b Waugh	19	G. R. Larsen not out	29
R. T. Latham c Taylor b Reiffel	0	C. Pringle b McGrath	1
A. H. Jones lbw b McGrath	6	R. P. de Groen not out	7
*K. R. Rutherford c Healy b Border	65	B 3, l-b 1	4
M. J. Greatbatch lbw b Warne	50		—
S. A. Thomson st Healy b Warne	1	1/4 2/13 3/40 (9 wkts, 50 overs)	198
C. L. Cairns c Healy b McGrath	16	4/129 5/131 6/152	
†T. E. Blain c and b Border	0	7/152 8/164 9/168	

Bowling: McGrath 10–3–29–3; Reiffel 9–0–33–1; Waugh 7–0–38–1; May 10–1–43–0; Warne 10–1–27–2; Border 4–0–24–2.

Australia

M. A. Taylor run out 1
D. C. Boon b Pringle 67
D. M. Jones c Pringle b de Groen 21
M. E. Waugh b Pringle 15
D. R. Martyn run out 7
*A. R. Border b Thomson 1
†I. A. Healy c Blain b de Groen 48
P. R. Reiffel lbw b Pringle 3
S. K. Warne b Cairns 9
T. B. A. May not out 4
G. D. McGrath b Pringle 4
W 4, n-b 1 5

1/1 2/38 3/76 4/86 5/87 6/164 7/166 8/171 9/180 (48.3 overs) 185

Bowling: de Groen 10–0–34–2; Pringle 9.3–0–40–4; Cairns 9–2–18–1; Larsen 9–0–43–0; Thomson 9–0–40–1; Latham 2–0–10–0.

Umpires: S. J. Davis and S. G. Randell.

NEW ZEALAND v SOUTH AFRICA

At Perth, January 14 (day/night). South Africa won by five wickets. Toss: New Zealand.

After three defeats and a wash-out, South Africa recorded their first win in limited-overs internationals against New Zealand, put their recent poor one-day form behind them and significantly reduced the gap in net run-rate between the teams. Donald, back to his best after being rested in some of the earlier matches, and McMillan both took three wickets, as New Zealand were bowled out for 150, a total which South Africa surpassed with almost 20 overs to spare. The Kirstens launched their reply with a stand of 80 in 19 overs, then Cronje added 40 off 35 balls. Both sides suffered injuries: Gary Kirsten needed stitches in his mouth, after a delivery from Pringle hit his visor, while New Zealand lost Greatbatch, who twisted knee ligaments in the field.

Man of the Match: A. A. Donald. *Attendance:* 14,778.

New Zealand

B. A. Young c Richardson b de Villiers. 2
A. H. Jones lbw b Donald 0
*K. R. Rutherford b McMillan 25
M. J. Greatbatch c Richardson b Matthews . 16
S. A. Thomson c Richardson b McMillan . 0
C. L. Cairns c Richardson b Callaghan . 29
C. Z. Harris not out 29
†T. E. Blain run out 32
G. R. Larsen c Matthews b McMillan . . 2
C. Pringle b Donald 1
R. P. de Groen c Cullinan b Donald . . . 0
L-b 7, w 6, n-b 1 14

1/1 2/3 3/45 4/46 5/58 6/84 7/133 8/145 9/148 (44.2 overs) 150

Bowling: Donald 8.2–3–15–3; de Villiers 8–0–15–1; Matthews 10–1–46–1; McMillan 10–2–39–3; Callaghan 5–1–15–1; Cronje 3–0–13–0.

South Africa

P. N. Kirsten run out 50
G. Kirsten c Blain b Pringle 31
*W. J. Cronje c sub (R. T. Latham) b Thomson . 40
J. N. Rhodes c de Groen b Pringle 3
D. J. Cullinan not out 5
D. J. Callaghan c Rutherford b Pringle . 2
B. M. McMillan not out 1
L-b 10, w 8, n-b 1 19

1/80 2/117 3/139 4/141 5/148 (5 wkts, 30.3 overs) 151

†D. J. Richardson, C. R. Matthews, P. S. de Villiers and A. A. Donald did not bat.

Bowling: Pringle 8.3–0–24–3; de Groen 5–0–30–0; Cairns 7–0–32–0; Larsen 8–0–36–0; Thomson 2–0–19–1.

Umpires: R. J. Evans and D. J. Harper.

AUSTRALIA v SOUTH AFRICA

At Perth, January 16. South Africa won by 82 runs. Toss: Australia. International debut: D. W. Fleming.

South Africa continued their last-gasp push to the finals, this time at Australia's expense, bowling them out for 126 to take their net run-rate past that of New Zealand. The day had not started well for South Africa, with Peter Kirsten suffering a broken cheekbone after the grille of his helmet was hit by a McGrath bouncer. But his brother's 55 and solid contributions down the order lifted the total to 208. To the delight of a record Perth crowd, local man Zoehrer, deputising for the injured Healy, kept wicket well in his first international for nearly seven years; he caught Gary Kirsten and brought off a smart stumping. Only Taylor, captain for the day (Border was 12th man), and Steve Waugh reached 20, and substitute McMillan took three catches.

Man of the Match: D. J. Callaghan. *Attendance:* 28,223.

South Africa

P. N. Kirsten retired hurt 5
G. Kirsten c Zoehrer b M. E. Waugh . . 55
*W. J. Cronje c Warne b Reiffel 11
J. N. Rhodes run out 14
D. J. Cullinan c Warne b M. E. Waugh 34
D. J. Callaghan lbw b Warne 26
†D. J. Richardson run out 25
R. P. Snell not out 20
C. R. Matthews st Zoehrer b Warne . . . 0
P. S. de Villiers not out 0
B 1, l-b 8, w 9 18

1/27 2/69 3/133 4/133 5/176 6/196 7/196 (7 wkts, 50 overs) 208

A. A. Donald did not bat.

P. N. Kirsten retired hurt at 6.

Bowling: McGrath 10–1–38–0; Reiffel 10–2–25–1; Fleming 7–0–42–0; S. R. Waugh 6–0–32–0; Warne 10–0–36–2; M. E. Waugh 7–0–26–2.

Australia

D. C. Boon c sub (B. M. McMillan) b Snell . 11
*M. A. Taylor c Richardson b Snell . . . 29
D. M. Jones c sub (B. M. McMillan) b Matthews . 10
M. E. Waugh c sub (B. M. McMillan) b Callaghan . 14
S. R. Waugh c Richardson b Callaghan 25
D. R. Martyn c Richardson b Cronje . . 0
†T. J. Zoehrer lbw b de Villiers 9
P. R. Reiffel not out 10
S. K. Warne run out 1
D. W. Fleming lbw b Matthews 2
G. D. McGrath b Snell 4
L-b 9, w 1, n-b 1 11

1/22 2/49 3/57 4/92 5/93 6/93 7/109 8/110 9/121 (41 overs) 126

Bowling: Donald 8–0–20–0; de Villiers 8–2–19–1; Snell 7–0–26–3; Matthews 7–1–20–2; Cronje 6–1–17–1; Callaghan 5–1–15–2.

Umpires: T. A. Prue and W. P. Sheahan.

AUSTRALIA v NEW ZEALAND

At Melbourne, January 19 (day/night). Australia won by 51 runs. Toss: Australia.

Needing to win to secure a place in the finals, New Zealand were never in the hunt. Their frailty against Warne's leg-spin was exposed again as they were bowled out for 166 in reply to Australia's 217 for three. It was a good day for the locals: Jones, who hit only three fours, scored 82 from 120 balls, and his fellow-Victorians – Reiffel, Fleming and Warne – took eight wickets between them, on a pitch that slowed down as the match went on.

Man of the Match: D. M. Jones. *Attendance:* 61,788.

Australia

M. L. Hayden c Blain b Watson	13	S. R. Waugh not out	0
D. C. Boon c Rutherford b Cairns	65	L-b 12	12
D. M. Jones c Cairns b Pringle	82		—
M. E. Waugh not out	45	1/15 2/136 3/214 (3 wkts, 50 overs)	217

*A. R. Border, †I. A. Healy, P. R. Reiffel, S. K. Warne, D. W. Fleming and G. D. McGrath did not bat.

Bowling: Pringle 10–0–45–1; Watson 10–2–33–1; Cairns 10–0–53–1; Larsen 10–1–23–0; Thomson 4–0–27–0; Latham 6–0–24–0.

New Zealand

B. A. Young b Warne	43	G. R. Larsen not out	17
R. T. Latham c Warne b Reiffel	10	C. Pringle b Reiffel	6
A. H. Jones lbw b Fleming	9	W. Watson c Healy b Reiffel	0
*K. R. Rutherford run out	0	L-b 4, w 8, n-b 1	13
M. J. Greatbatch c Reiffel b Warne	13		—
S. A. Thomson lbw b McGrath	12	1/37 2/60 3/64 (47.5 overs)	166
C. L. Cairns lbw b Fleming	39	4/80 5/82 6/107	
†T. E. Blain c Hayden b Warne	4	7/124 8/147 9/166	

Bowling: McGrath 9–1–48–1; Reiffel 9.5–2–35–3; Fleming 9–2–15–2; S. R. Waugh 10–0–36–0; Warne 10–1–28–3.

Umpires: P. D. Parker and S. G. Randell.

QUALIFYING TABLE

	Played	*Won*	*Lost*	*No result*	*Points*	*Net run-rate*
Australia	8	5	3	0	10	0.36
South Africa	8	3	4	1	7	−0.06
New Zealand	8	3	4	1	7	−0.40

AUSTRALIA v SOUTH AFRICA

First Final Match

At Melbourne, January 21 (day/night). South Africa won by 28 runs. Toss: South Africa.

South Africa took the lead in the best-of-three finals. Peter Kirsten, returning only five days after his serious facial injury, shared an opening stand of 53 with his half-brother Gary, who went on to his maiden international century and the first of this tournament, cutting fiercely and driving well. Warne was subdued for once, perhaps unsettled when his first ball was called a wide after pitching in line with the stumps and turning extravagantly away from the batsman. In reply, Hayden soon played on, while the wickets of Boon (run out by the ubiquitous Rhodes) and Jones – well caught one-handed by a leaping Cronje in the covers – set back Australia's chances. Two good catches in four balls by Peter Kirsten inside the 30-metre circle left Border a tough task and Snell, using the yorker to good effect, returned to complete his first five-wicket haul in one-day internationals.

Attendance: 69,384.

South Africa

P. N. Kirsten c Healy b S. R. Waugh	28	D. J. Callaghan not out	3
G. Kirsten not out	112		
*W. J. Cronje c Jones b Warne	40	L-b 2, w 3, n-b 1	6
J. N. Rhodes c Healy b McGrath	31		—
D. J. Cullinan c Hayden b McDermott	7	1/53 2/143 3/196 (5 wkts, 50 overs)	230
R. P. Snell c Jones b McGrath	3	4/217 5/223	

B. M. McMillan, †D. J. Richardson, P. S. de Villiers and A. A. Donald did not bat.

Bowling: McDermott 10–1–40–1; McGrath 9–0–52–2; Reiffel 7–2–23–0; S. R. Waugh 7–0–27–1; Warne 10–1–45–1; Border 4–0–26–0; M. E. Waugh 3–0–15–0.

Australia

D. C. Boon run out	45	S. K. Warne c McMillan b de Villiers	1
M. L. Hayden b Snell	20	C. J. McDermott b Snell	1
D. M. Jones c Cronje b McMillan	3	G. D. McGrath not out	5
M. E. Waugh c Richardson b Donald	36		
S. R. Waugh c P. N. Kirsten b Snell	27	L-b 1, w 3	4
*A. R. Border b Snell	42		—
†I. A. Healy c P. N. Kirsten b de Villiers	0	1/41 2/53 3/84 4/128 5/150 6/150 7/192 8/195 9/197	(48.5 overs) 202
P. R. Reiffel b Snell	18		

Bowling: Donald 10–0–48–1; de Villiers 9–1–26–2; Snell 9.5–0–40–5; McMillan 10–2–38–1; Callaghan 5–0–27–0; Cronje 5–0–22–0.

Umpires: T. A. Prue and W. P. Sheahan.

AUSTRALIA v SOUTH AFRICA

Second Final Match

At Sydney, January 23 (day/night). Australia won by 69 runs. Toss: Australia.

Australia squared the finals with a convincing victory. The match was all but settled by a rapid third-wicket stand of 175 between Jones and Mark Waugh, who stroked an elegant century, hitting eight fours in 111 balls. Donald took four wickets, including both openers, but Snell – the bowling hero of the previous match – conceded 59 from his ten overs. When South Africa batted, a run-out ended another half-century opening stand between the Kirstens and later resistance was patchy. Rhodes top-scored with 52 from 59 balls, sweeping Warne for a defiant six. But Warne claimed Cullinan, Cronje – a stumping for Healy in his 100th one-day international – and McMillan, who, not for the first time, made a hash of the flipper. Three wickets in eight balls from McDermott, who also helped to run out Symcox, saw South Africa bowled out with 4.1 overs remaining.

Attendance: 39,808.

Australia

M. L. Hayden c Snell b Donald	16	†I. A. Healy not out	10
D. C. Boon c Rhodes b Donald	14	P. R. Reiffel not out	5
D. M. Jones c Cronje b Donald	79		
M. E. Waugh c G. Kirsten b de Villiers	107	L-b 5, w 3, n-b 1	9
			—
S. R. Waugh b Donald	1	1/33 2/35 3/210 4/221 5/227 6/241	(6 wkts, 50 overs) 247
*A. R. Border c Richardson b de Villiers	6		

S. K. Warne, T. B. A. May and C. J. McDermott did not bat.

Bowling: Donald 10–0–40–4; de Villiers 10–2–39–2; Snell 10–0–59–0; McMillan 7–0–40–0; Symcox 6–0–26–0; Cronje 7–0–38–0.

South Africa

P. N. Kirsten run out	11	P. L. Symcox run out	12
G. Kirsten c Boon b May	42	P. S. de Villiers not out	0
*W. J. Cronje st Healy b Warne	28	A. A. Donald c and b McDermott	0
J. N. Rhodes b McDermott	52	L-b 7, n-b 1	8
D. J. Cullinan c S. R. Waugh b Warne	3		—
B. M. McMillan lbw b Warne	0	1/50 2/74 3/102 4/106 5/107 6/156 7/160 8/174 9/178	(45.5 overs) 178
†D. J. Richardson b Border	16		
R. P. Snell b McDermott	6		

Bowling: McDermott 8.5–0–39–3; Reiffel 8–0–23–0; S. R. Waugh 5–0–11–0; May 10–1–35–1; Warne 10–0–42–3; Border 4–0–21–1.

Umpires: D. B. Hair and S. G. Randell.

AUSTRALIA v SOUTH AFRICA

Third Final Match

At Sydney, January 25 (day/night). Australia won by 35 runs. Toss: Australia.

Australia wrapped up the finals 2-1, the first time they had come from behind to win this competition since 1980-81, the year of the Chappell "under-arm" incident. Their triumph came on the pitch used two days earlier, despite South African objections that this would assist the Australian spinners. Once again, Boon was the mainstay of Australia's total, while Mark Waugh contributed a flowing 60 from 53 balls. When South Africa batted, Peter Kirsten was given out by the third umpire in the closest of run-out decisions, and they lost Cronje even more cruelly the same way when McDermott touched a Gary Kirsten straight-drive into the stumps. South Africa never looked likely to recover from 26 for three: Rhodes top-scored again before becoming Warne's 22rd wicket of the tournament. Border, captaining Australia for the 100th time in World Series matches, bowled the last over and was then chaired from the field after what turned out to be his last home one-day international before his retirement.

Player of the Finals: M. E. Waugh. *Attendance:* 37,722.

Australia

D. C. Boon c Rhodes b de Villiers	64	P. R. Reiffel run out	2
M. L. Hayden st Richardson b Rundle	20	S. K. Warne not out	1
D. M. Jones c Rundle b Donald	25	L-b 3, w 1	4
M. E. Waugh run out	60		—
S. R. Waugh b Cronje	17	1/62 2/112 3/114 (8 wkts, 50 overs)	223
*A. R. Border b de Villiers	30	4/150 5/218 6/220	
†I. A. Healy run out	0	7/221 8/223	

T. B. A. May and C. J. McDermott did not bat.

Bowling: Donald 10–1–40–1; de Villiers 10–2–41–2; Snell 10–1–34–0; Cronje 10–0–35–1; Rundle 7–0–53–1; Callaghan 3–0–17–0.

South Africa

P. N. Kirsten run out	14	D. B. Rundle lbw b May	6
G. Kirsten c M. E. Waugh b Reiffel	10	P. S. de Villiers b S. R. Waugh	15
*W. J. Cronje run out	0	A. A. Donald not out	7
J. N. Rhodes c Healy b Warne	43	B 1, l-b 2, w 3	6
E. L. R. Stewart b Warne	13		—
D. J. Callaghan c Healy b McDermott	30	1/21 2/23 3/26 (9 wkts, 50 overs)	188
†D. J. Richardson not out	38	4/51 5/110 6/117	
R. P. Snell run out	6	7/124 8/136 9/166	

Bowling: McDermott 10–1–41–1; Reiffel 9–0–32–1; S. R. Waugh 10–2–39–1; Warne 10–0–36–2; May 10–0–31–1; Border 1–0–6–0.

Umpires: D. B. Hair and S. G. Randell.

PEPSI AUSTRAL-ASIA CUP, 1993-94

By QAMAR AHMED

Pakistan won the Austral-Asia Cup for the third time out of three since its inauguration in 1985-86. But the most important event of the tournament was the return of India, who had avoided Sharjah for two and a half years, claiming that they were the victims of bias. They reached the final, just as they had on their previous visit. Their participation, however, was interpreted as a reconciliatory move in the preparations for the 1995-96 World Cup to be held in India, Pakistan and Sri Lanka. Before both Pakistan–India matches, which were staged under strict security, the cricketers walked hand in hand to demonstrate that politics, not personal animosity, had kept them apart over the past two years.

The other teams taking part were Australia, New Zealand, Sri Lanka and the hosts, the United Arab Emirates. The Emirates, recent winners of the ICC Trophy, were playing their first full international matches; they replaced Bangladesh, who had appeared in the Cup four years before. Sri Lanka were weakened by a dispute before their arrival; star batsman Aravinda de Silva was dropped for failing a fitness test and captain Arjuna Ranatunga and several others pulled out in protest. New Zealand were also without some of their senior players, giving Gavin Larsen his first chance to lead the side. The Australians were on their way back from South Africa, although some, including Allan Border, Craig McDermott and Ian Healy, had gone straight home; despite reinforcements, there was no regular wicket-keeper. Nevertheless, they were one of the stronger sides and their defeat by India in the semi-final was a surprise. New Zealand were more predictably beaten by Pakistan.

Note: Matches in this section were not first-class.

GROUP A

UNITED ARAB EMIRATES v INDIA

At Sharjah, April 13. India won by 71 runs. Toss: United Arab Emirates. International debuts: United Arab Emirates (all); A. C. Bedade, Bhupinder Singh, sen.

The public drama of the Emirates' first senior international and India's first game in Sharjah since October 1991 was overshadowed by a personal crisis. Ajit Wadekar, the Indian manager, suffered a mild heart attack before the start, news which Azharuddin kept from his players as long as possible. His worries did not show in his innings of 81. Kambli scored a spectacular unbeaten 82, striking three sixes and four fours in 65 balls. The Emirates' reply of 202 was more than respectable and lasted the full 50 overs. Former Maharashtra opener Poonawala raced to 22 from 14 balls, but the biggest contribution was Hussain's 70.

Man of the Match: V. G. Kambli.

India

A. D. Jadeja c Arshad Laiq b Sohail Butt . 25
S. R. Tendulkar c Imtiaz Abbasi b Zarawani . 63
N. S. Sidhu b Sohail Butt 0
*M. Azharuddin c Samarasekera b Saleem Raza . 81
V. G. Kambli not out 82
A. C. Bedade c Imtiaz Abbasi b Samarasekera . 7
†N. R. Mongia not out 4
B 1, l-b 2, w 6, n-b 2 11

1/49 2/55 3/130 4/230 5/254 (5 wkts, 50 overs) 273

A. Kumble, S. L. V. Raju, J. Srinath and Bhupinder Singh, sen. did not bat.

Bowling: Samarasekera 10–0–48–1; Sohail Butt 10–0–52–2; Arshad Laiq 10–0–56–0; Azhar Saeed 10–1–38–0; Zarawani 3–0–22–1; Saleem Raza 7–0–54–1.

United Arab Emirates

R. Poonawala c Mongia b Bhupinder Singh . 22
Azhar Saeed c Mongia b Srinath 3
Mazhar Hussain c Jadeja b Bhupinder Singh . 70
V. Mehra c Mongia b Bhupinder Singh 43
Mohammad Ishaq c Jadeja b Srinath . . 23
Saleem Raza c Mongia b Srinath 6
J. A. Samarasekera c Tendulkar b Raju 3
Arshad Laiq b Kumble 4
Sultan M. Zarawani b Kumble 4
†Imtiaz Abbasi not out 6
Sohail Butt not out 6
L-b 4, w 5, n-b 3 12

1/26 2/26 3/120 4/161 5/169 6/182 7/183 8/188 9/191 (9 wkts, 50 overs) 202

Bowling: Srinath 10–1–48–3; Bhupinder Singh 10–1–34–3; Jadeja 5–0–32–0; Tendulkar 5–0–22–0; Raju 10–0–32–1; Kumble 10–0–30–2.

Umpires: K. Kanjee and S. B. Lambson.

INDIA v PAKISTAN

At Sharjah, April 15. Pakistan won by six wickets. Toss: Pakistan.

The teams had not met since the World Cup, more than two years earlier, and Pakistan comfortably reversed India's win then. Opener Saeed Anwar, who had hit three successive hundreds in Sharjah a few months earlier, scored 72 from 69 balls, while Basit Ali, with a run-a-ball 75, completed the victory with five and a half overs to spare. India had thrown away an equally impressive start, given them by Tendulkar, who scored 73 from 64 balls. But India collapsed from 156 for two to 219 all out.

Man of the Match: Saeed Anwar.

India

A. D. Jadeja c Rashid Latif b Aqib Javed . 19
S. R. Tendulkar c Basit Ali b Akram Raza . 73
N. S. Sidhu c Rashid Latif b Ata-ur-Rehman . 47
*M. Azharuddin c Inzamam-ul-Haq b Salim Malik . 29
A. C. Bedade st Rashid Latif b Salim Malik . 1
V. G. Kambli c Akram Raza b Ata-ur-Rehman . 4
†N. R. Mongia run out 5
A. Kumble b Wasim Akram 6
Bhupinder Singh, sen. run out 6
R. K. Chauhan c Saeed Anwar b Aqib Javed . 13
J. Srinath not out 1
L-b 2, w 10, n-b 3 15

1/62 2/111 3/156 4/164 5/179 6/187 7/187 8/197 9/218 (46.3 overs) 219

Bowling: Wasim Akram 8.3–1–36–1; Aqib Javed 9–1–41–2; Ata-ur-Rehman 9–0–50–2; Salim Malik 10–0–49–2; Akram Raza 10–0–41–1.

Pakistan

Saeed Anwar lbw b Chauhan 72
Aamir Sohail b Chauhan. 20
Inzamam-ul-Haq c Mongia b Chauhan . 1
*Salim Malik c Azharuddin b Srinath . . 25
Basit Ali not out 75
Asif Mujtaba not out 16
L-b 4, w 7, n-b 3. 14

1/77 2/89 3/106 4/171 (4 wkts, 44.3 overs) 223

Wasim Akram, †Rashid Latif, Akram Raza, Aqib Javed and Ata-ur-Rehman did not bat.

Bowling: Srinath 9.3–0–58–1; Bhupinder Singh 7–1–44–0; Kumble 9–0–27–0; Chauhan 10–0–47–3; Tendulkar 8–0–34–0; Jadeja 1–0–9–0.

Umpires: S. B. Lambson and K. E. Liebenberg.

UNITED ARAB EMIRATES v PAKISTAN

At Sharjah, April 17. Pakistan won by nine wickets. Toss: United Arab Emirates.

Pakistan's crushing victory ensured that they and India would be in the last four. It was a disappointing performance by the Emirates after their promising debut four days earlier. They were 68 for six at the mid-point of their innings, though a stand of 57 between Johanne Samarasekera, brother of Sri Lankan opener Athula, and Arshad Laiq took them well into three figures. Pakistan needed less than half their 50 overs to knock off 146 runs. Saeed Anwar and Aamir Sohail set off with a breakneck 76 in ten overs, and Inzamam-ul-Haq scored a 47-ball fifty.

Man of the Match: Ata-ur-Rehman.

United Arab Emirates

R. Poonawala c Rashid Latif b Ata-ur-Rehman . 22
Azhar Saeed c Akram Raza b Wasim Akram . 0
Mazhar Hussain c Rashid Latif b Ata-ur-Rehman . 10
V. Mehra c Aamir Sohail b Salim Malik 5
Mohammad Ishaq c Rashid Latif b Salim Malik . 4
Saleem Raza c Akram Raza b Wasim Akram . 16
J. A. Samarasekera not out 31
Arshad Laiq c Wasim Akram b Salim Malik . 31
*Sultan M. Zarawani run out 6
†Imtiaz Abbasi b Wasim Akram 2
Sohail Butt b Ata-ur-Rehman 2
L-b 2, w 10, n-b 4. 16

1/7 2/40 3/45 4/45 5/65 6/68 7/125 8/138 9/141 (49.5 overs) 145

Bowling: Wasim Akram 10–1–19–3; Aqib Javed 10–2–29–0; Ata-ur-Rehman 9.5–0–32–3; Salim Malik 10–1–42–3; Akram Raza 10–3–21–0.

Pakistan

Saeed Anwar c Poonawala b Saleem Raza . 39
Aamir Sohail not out 51
Inzamam-ul-Haq not out 50
L-b 2, w 4 6

1/76 (1 wkt, 23.1 overs) 146

*Salim Malik, Basit Ali, Asif Mujtaba, Wasim Akram, †Rashid Latif, Akram Raza, Ata-ur-Rehman and Aqib Javed did not bat.

Bowling: Samarasekera 5–0–31–0; Sohail Butt 3–0–27–0; Arshad Laiq 4–0–25–0; Saleem Raza 3–1–17–1; Azhar Saeed 4.1–0–18–0; Zarawani 4–0–26–0.

Umpires: K. Kanjee and K. E. Liebenberg.

GROUP A FINAL TABLE

	Played	*Won*	*Lost*	*Points*
Pakistan	2	2	0	4
India	2	1	1	2
United Arab Emirates	2	0	2	0

GROUP B

AUSTRALIA v SRI LANKA

At Sharjah, April 14. Australia won by nine wickets. Toss: Sri Lanka. International debuts: M. G. Bevan; U. U. Chandana, M. Munasinghe.

Though both teams were short of several senior players, Australia's strength in depth ensured a convincing victory, with nine wickets and 13 overs to spare. Taylor and Mark Waugh shared an unbroken second-wicket stand of 133 in 27 overs, and only Ramanayake could put any brake on the scoring. Sri Lanka's new captain, Mahanama, had decided to bat but was first out as his team struggled to 91 for five – including two run-outs – in 31 overs. Tillekeratne made 64, but no one else reached 30. Warne satisfied an eager crowd with three for 29.

Man of the Match: M. E. Waugh.

Sri Lanka

*R. S. Mahanama lbw b Reiffel	10
M. A. R. Samarasekera c Langer b S. R. Waugh	24
A. P. Gurusinha run out	1
S. T. Jayasuriya run out	8
H. P. Tillekeratne c Taylor b S. R. Waugh	64
R. S. Kalpage c Bevan b Warne	4
U. U. Chandana c Bevan b Reiffel	18
†P. B. Dassanayake lbw b Warne	7
C. P. H. Ramanayake lbw b Warne	2
M. Munasinghe b Fleming	2
W. P. U. J. C. Vaas not out	0
L-b 10, w 1, n-b 3	14
1/30 2/38 3/40 4/61 5/91 6/124 7/136 8/142 9/153 (49.3 overs)	154

Bowling: Reiffel 10–1–28–2; Fleming 9.3–1–27–1; S. R. Waugh 6–0–17–2; May 10–0–25–0; Warne 10–1–29–3; M. E. Waugh 4–0–18–0.

Australia

*M. A. Taylor not out	68
M. J. Slater b Vaas	15
M. E. Waugh not out	64
B 1, l-b 7, w 3	11
1/25 (1 wkt, 36.5 overs)	158

S. R. Waugh, M. L. Hayden, †J. L. Langer, M. G. Bevan, P. R. Reiffel, S. K. Warne, T. B. A. May and D. W. Fleming did not bat.

Bowling: Ramanayake 8–1–15–0; Vaas 10–1–35–1; Munasinghe 6.5–0–28–0; Jayasuriya 4–0–22–0; Kalpage 5–0–29–0; Chandana 3–0–21–0.

Umpires: K. Kanjee and K. E. Liebenberg.

AUSTRALIA v NEW ZEALAND

At Sharjah, April 16. Australia won by seven wickets. Toss: New Zealand. International debut: M. W. Douglas.

Australia's second win made them the first team to reach the semi-finals. They achieved it comfortably after Warne wrecked New Zealand's batting and Hayden and Boon put on 123 for the second wicket. Warne took four wickets for 34, three lbw and one caught and bowled, while Fleming almost matched his figures with four for 39. It was a disappointing start for Larsen, who led New Zealand for the first time in his 52nd limited-overs international, though he still awaited his Test debut.

Man of the Match: S. K. Warne.

New Zealand

B. A. Young c and b Fleming 63
B. R. Hartland lbw b Warne 23
M. W. Douglas lbw b Warne 0
S. P. Fleming c Taylor b Fleming 35
S. A. Thomson c Taylor b Fleming 32
†A. C. Parore c and b Warne......... 12
C. Z. Harris lbw b Warne 14
*G. R. Larsen not out 9
M. N. Hart c Hayden b Fleming 2
D. K. Morrison b McGrath 2
C. Pringle not out 2
B 1, l-b 6, w 2, n-b 4 13

1/75 2/75 3/126 4/135 5/170 6/184 7/192 8/202 9/204 (9 wkts, 50 overs) 207

Bowling: Reiffel 10–0–35–0; McGrath 10–0–44–1; S. R. Waugh 10–1–48–0; Warne 10–0–34–4; Fleming 10–0–39–4.

Australia

M. J. Slater b Morrison.............. 0
M. L. Hayden c Harris b Pringle...... 67
D. C. Boon c sub (D. J. Nash) b Thomson . 68
M. G. Bevan not out 39
†J. L. Langer not out................ 20
L-b 11, w 3 14

1/0 2/123 3/166 (3 wkts, 47.5 overs) 208

*M. A. Taylor, S. R. Waugh, D. W. Fleming, G. D. McGrath, S. K. Warne and P. R. Reiffel did not bat.

Bowling: Morrison 6–2–22–1; Pringle 9.5–1–43–1; Larsen 9–0–42–0; Harris 6–0–25–0; Hart 7–0–26–0; Thomson 10–2–39–1.

Umpires: K. Kanjee and S. B. Lambson.

NEW ZEALAND v SRI LANKA

At Sharjah, April 18. New Zealand won by two runs. Toss: Sri Lanka. International debuts: H. T. Davis; A. P. Weerakkody.

New Zealand scraped through in the contest to meet Pakistan in the semi-finals. Sri Lanka needed ten from Nash's last two deliveries. Gurusinha, who had made a heroic century, hit the first for six but then could make only a single instead of the four he wanted. He had revived the innings from a seemingly hopeless 41 for four, with Chandana his principal support in a stand of 88. New Zealand started rather slowly, until Thomson arrived and reached his fifty in 41 balls. Sri Lanka deserved credit for completing their 50 overs on time despite a ten-minute interruption for rain.

Man of the Match: A. P. Gurusinha.

New Zealand

B. R. Hartland run out 5
B. A. Young c Jayasuriya b Gurusinha . 34
†A. C. Parore c Dassanayake b Jayasuriya . 37
M. W. Douglas run out 30
S. P. Fleming c Tillekeratne b Kalpage. 14
S. A. Thomson c Chandana b Vaas.... 50
C. Z. Harris c Chandana b Ramanayake 22
D. J. Nash run out 2
*G. R. Larsen not out............... 14
C. Pringle not out 0
B 1, l-b 5, w 3............. 9

1/12 2/68 3/94 4/121 5/135 6/194 7/198 8/206 (8 wkts, 50 overs) 217

H. T. Davis did not bat.

Bowling: Ramanayake 10–1–41–1; Vaas 10–1–31–1; Weerakkody 6–0–41–0; Gurusinha 10–1–30–1; Jayasuriya 7–0–37–1; Kalpage 7–0–31–1.

Sri Lanka

*R. S. Mahanama lbw b Pringle 18
M. A. R. Samarasekera c Fleming b Nash . 4
A. P. Gurusinha not out 117
S. T. Jayasuriya c Davis b Nash 5
H. P. Tillekeratne run out 0
U. U. Chandana c Young b Nash 26
R. S. Kalpage c Harris b Thomson 6
†P. B. Dassanayake c Parore b Larsen . 5
C. P. H. Ramanayake b Pringle 21
A. P. Weerakkody c Nash b Pringle . . . 2
W. P. U. J. C. Vaas not out 1
B 1, l-b 6, w 3 10

1/24 2/24 3/30 4/41 5/129 6/147 7/152 8/189 9/202 (9 wkts, 50 overs) 215

Bowling: Pringle 10–1–46–3; Davis 2–0–14–0; Nash 10–1–43–3; Larsen 10–1–34–1; Harris 9–0–33–0; Thomson 9–0–38–1.

Umpires: S. B. Lambson and K. E. Liebenberg.

GROUP B FINAL TABLE

	Played	*Won*	*Lost*	*Points*
Australia	2	2	0	4
New Zealand	2	1	1	2
Sri Lanka	2	0	2	0

SEMI-FINALS

AUSTRALIA v INDIA

At Sharjah, April 19. India won by seven wickets. Toss: Australia.

India staged a minor upset by beating Australia, in their first match under the management of Sunil Gavaskar, who replaced Ajit Wadekar after his heart attack. They rose to the challenge of 245, thanks to Jadeja and Sidhu, who added 130 after Tendulkar went quickly. In the closing stages Kambli hit two fours and two sixes in one over from Warne. Australia had started slowly, reaching 66 in 20 overs. But the pace really quickened when Langer joined Hayden. They put on 64 in six overs: Langer's share was 36 in 22 balls and he hit Kumble for three sixes. Mongia was fined $US750 by the tournament referee, A. M. Ebrahim of Zimbabwe, for excessive appealing.

Man of the Match: A. D. Jadeja.

Australia

*M. A. Taylor b Srinath 11
D. C. Boon b Kumble 21
M. E. Waugh run out 16
S. R. Waugh c Mongia b Srinath 53
M. G. Bevan c Jadeja b Kumble 25
M. L. Hayden c Jadeja b Kumble 48
†J. L. Langer run out 36
P. R. Reiffel c Tendulkar b Srinath 7
S. K. Warne run out 4
D. W. Fleming not out 2
G. D. McGrath not out 0
L-b 14, w 6, n-b 1 21

1/29 2/53 3/62 4/115 5/158 6/222 7/227 8/241 9/244 (9 wkts, 50 overs) 244

Bowling: Srinath 9–1–32–3; Prasad 8–1–39–0; Kumble 10–1–50–3; Chauhan 10–2–37–0; Tendulkar 8–0–39–0; Jadeja 5–0–33–0.

India

A. D. Jadeja c Boon b Warne 87
S. R. Tendulkar c Taylor b McGrath . . 6
N. S. Sidhu st Langer b Warne 80
*M. Azharuddin not out 36
V. G. Kambli not out 28
L-b 4, w 2, n-b 2 8

1/11 2/141 3/210 (3 wkts, 45.4 overs) 245

A. C. Bedade, †N. R. Mongia, A. Kumble, B. K. V. Prasad, R. K. Chauhan and J. Srinath did not bat.

Bowling: McGrath 8–0–35–1; Reiffel 8–0–32–0; S. R. Waugh 8–0–52–0; Fleming 9.4–0–59–0; Warne 9–0–40–2; M. E. Waugh 3–0–23–0.

Umpires: K. Kanjee and S. B. Lambson.

NEW ZEALAND v PAKISTAN

At Sharjah, April 20. Pakistan won by 62 runs. Toss: New Zealand.

A phenomenal partnership between Aamir Sohail and Inzamam-ul-Haq put Pakistan in the final. Joining forces at 57 for one, they put on 263, the highest stand for any wicket in one-day internationals, in 42 overs. The previous record was an unbroken 224 for Australia's third wicket, by Dean Jones and Allan Border, against Sri Lanka in 1984-85. Sohail scored 134 from 146 balls, with 12 fours, and Inzamam's 137 not out – a record for Pakistan in one-day internationals – came from 129 balls, with 15 fours. But it was their sharp running between wickets which made the record possible. New Zealand gallantly attempted to pursue an asking-rate of six and a half an over – Young opened with a run-a-ball 36 and Parore and Thomson added 133 – until they lost five wickets for 19. Nash was fined $US350 for swearing at Saeed Anwar, who had punished him heavily during his 23-ball 37.

Man of the Match: Inzamam-ul-Haq.

Pakistan

Saeed Anwar c Parore b Nash	37
Aamir Sohail c Douglas b Pringle	134
Inzamam-ul-Haq not out	137
Wasim Akram not out	7
B 1, l-b 2, w 8, n-b 2	13
1/57 2/320 (2 wkts, 50 overs)	328

*Salim Malik, Basit Ali, Asif Mujtaba, †Rashid Latif, Akram Raza, Ata-ur-Rehman and Aqib Javed did not bat.

Bowling: Pringle 10–0–57–1; Davis 4–0–37–0; Nash 9–0–60–1; Larsen 10–0–71–0; Thomson 7–0–44–0; Harris 10–0–56–0.

New Zealand

B. A. Young c Saeed Anwar b Ata-ur-Rehman	36
B. R. Hartland c Rashid Latif b Wasim Akram	11
†A. C. Parore c sub (Ijaz Ahmed) b Salim Malik	82
S. A. Thomson run out	62
S. P. Fleming b Aamir Sohail	1
M. W. Douglas b Salim Malik	3
C. Z. Harris not out	34
D. J. Nash b Wasim Akram	2
*G. R. Larsen not out	18
L-b 6, w 7, n-b 4	17
1/19 2/66 3/199 4/202 5/204 6/207 7/218 (7 wkts, 50 overs)	266

C. Pringle and H. T. Davis did not bat.

Bowling: Wasim Akram 10–0–50–2; Aqib Javed 10–0–56–0; Ata-ur-Rehman 5–0–35–1; Akram Raza 10–0–42–0; Salim Malik 10–0–55–2; Aamir Sohail 5–0–22–1.

Umpires: K. Kanjee and K. E. Liebenberg.

FINAL

INDIA v PAKISTAN

At Sharjah, April 22. Pakistan won by 39 runs. Toss: India.

Pakistan beat India for the second time in a week to retain the Austral-Asia Cup. They scored only 250, despite an entertaining opening stand of 96 between Saeed Anwar and Aamir Sohail. Off-spinner Chauhan ended this and dismissed both Inzamam-ul-Haq and Salim Malik in one over, before Basit Ali made 57 from 58 balls. India started badly, when

Jadeja was out in Wasim Akram's first over and, despite 59 in 11 overs from Tendulkar and Sidhu, slumped to 83 for four. Kambli found an ally in Bedade, who overcame a nervous start to score 44 from 45 balls, with four sixes, in his fourth international match. He was caught attempting another six and the last five wickets could add only 48. Sohail claimed the match award for his 69, two wickets and two catches, one of them in the covers, cutting off Tendulkar in full flight.

Man of the Match: Aamir Sohail. *Man of the Series:* Aamir Sohail.

Pakistan

Saeed Anwar c Prasad b Chauhan 47
Aamir Sohail b Srinath 69
Inzamam-ul-Haq st Mongia b Chauhan . 12
*Salim Malik c Azharuddin b Chauhan . 1
Basit Ali b Srinath 57
Asif Mujtaba not out 34
Wasim Akram c Azharuddin b Srinath . 2
†Rashid Latif not out 17
L-b 3, w 3, n-b 5 11

1/96 2/125 3/127 (6 wkts, 50 overs) 250
4/149 5/215 6/219

Akram Raza, Ata-ur-Rehman and Aqib Javed did not bat.

Bowling: Srinath 10–0–56–3; Prasad 9–1–44–0; Kumble 10–0–56–0; Chauhan 9–0–29–3; Tendulkar 8–0–45–0; Jadeja 4–0–17–0.

India

A. D. Jadeja c Basit Ali b Wasim Akram . 0
S. R. Tendulkar c Aamir Sohail b Ata-ur-Rehman . 24
N. S. Sidhu c and b Akram Raza 36
*M. Azharuddin c Rashid Latif b Aqib Javed . 3
V. G. Kambli c Akram Raza b Salim Malik . 56
A. C. Bedade c Asif Mujtaba b Aamir Sohail . 44
†N. R. Mongia c and b Aamir Sohail . . 3
A. Kumble c Rashid Latif b Salim Malik . 12
R. K. Chauhan run out 5
J. Srinath not out 6
B. K. V. Prasad lbw b Wasim Akram . . 0
L-b 4, w 10, n-b 8 22

1/1 2/60 3/63 (47.4 overs) 211
4/83 5/163 6/180
7/182 8/203 9/209

Bowling: Wasim Akram 8.4–0–39–2; Aqib Javed 7–1–27–1; Ata-ur-Rehman 8–0–27–1; Akram Raza 10–0–47–1; Salim Malik 9–0–45–2; Aamir Sohail 5–0–22–2.

Umpires: S. B. Lambson and K. E. Liebenberg.

THE ABN-AMRO ICC TROPHY, 1993-94

By DAVID TOWNSEND

The 1994 ICC Trophy was dominated both on and off the field by a United Arab Emirates team that won the tournament – and an invitation to the 1996 World Cup finals – on its first appearance, with only one indigenous player in a 16-man squad. The hosts, Kenya, and favourites Holland, finished second and third to claim the other two World Cup places on offer to the 20 competing Associate Members of the International Cricket Council.

There was no doubting the superiority of the Emirates' cricket as they beat eight different opponents before easing past Kenya to win the Trophy final with considerably more to spare than a two-wicket victory would suggest. However, the sight of seven Pakistanis, two Indians and a Sri Lankan doing a lap of honour at the Ruaraka ground after the final suggested the UAE flag they were flying was very much one of convenience, and a widespread suspicion lingered among opponents and officials that the Emirates' real triumph had been over the tournament's four-year residential qualification rule.

From the moment their players arrived in Nairobi there were rumours about Mercedes-per-man win bonuses and dark mutterings from other teams that the oil-rich Gulf state had imported a team with the sole purpose of winning a World Cup place. Members of the organising committee subjected the Emirates' hierarchy to a four-hour grilling on the residential status of each player, but manager Vikram Kaul maintained throughout that his side were only abiding by rules that they had no part in framing and the 15 members of his squad who were born on the Indian sub-continent (all except the captain, Sultan Zarawani) were all now full-time employees in the Gulf and played cricket in their spare time. This was never disproved, but the bitterness spilled over into the celebration dinner. The UAE party walked out in protest against criticism levelled at them. As they left, the Kenyan Cricket Association chairman Basheer Mauladad told the gathering: "We too can import slaves to win a tournament." The dispute was certain to lead to a review of the residential rule, with Bermuda pushing for new restrictions on the number of non-indigenes eligible for future tournaments.

Such a rule may prove easier to advocate than to draft, though, because the Emirates are not alone in having a predominance of expatriate players. Not one of the USA team was born there, Canada's squad was also mostly West Indian and Asian by origin, and Hong Kong leaned heavily on Australian and English migrants. As Kaul observed, "The world is changing, people no longer stay in one place. You only have to look at the England team to see how many have been born elsewhere."

Feelings that the UAE were in breach of the spirit – if not the rules – of the Trophy detracted from an otherwise happy three-week festival. The group structure of the qualifying round ensured each team played four games in the main competition and provided inevitable mismatches, with several of the smaller outposts fielding teams not much better than village green standard. Two poor sides can, of course, produce a keen contest and one of the tightest finishes was Israel's two-wicket win in the penultimate over against Singapore.

Hong Kong managed to finish with the scores level in two matches, beating Denmark (having lost fewer wickets) and losing to Bermuda, with whom they progressed to the last eight. The Danes were the only surprise casualties of the first round, finishing third in Group D despite some vintage grunting and pouting from Derbyshire seamer Ole Mortensen. Holland qualified as expected from Group A, along with Ireland, who owed their place in the quarter-finals to the mopping up efforts of their 40-odd supporters and a lax interpretation of the playing conditions that enabled them to score a rain-affected win over Papua New Guinea. Bangladesh recovered from 36 for five to beat a talented but ill-disciplined USA team, and qualified with the Emirates from Group B. In Group C, Namibia's dreams of a World Cup ticket were ended in 16.3 overs as they were dismissed for 51 by Canada on a wet wicket at the Nairobi Club. Bhowan Singh's seven for 21 were the Trophy's best bowling figures. Kenya needed only 15 overs at the crease to better a score of 99 by Israel and 9.2 to pass Singapore's 76 and coasted into the last eight with Canada.

Some scoffed at the poor quality of the early cricket but, as Argentinia's coach John Carr stressed: "The only way to improve is to play against better sides." His team beat East and Central Africa and celebrated only their second ICC win in 21 attempts by leaping *en masse* and fully clothed into the hotel swimming pool. A Plate competition gave those beaten in the first round a chance to regain some pride, although the teams who should have contested the final – the USA and Papua New Guinea – flew home early, leaving Namibia to beat Denmark.

The weather improved for the quarter-final group matches and, as pitches hardened, scores rocketed. Although no target ever proved beyond them, the Emirates were not overpowering and beat both Canada and Bermuda by only one wicket. The shortcomings of both Ireland and Hong Kong were shown up by competent opposition – they lost all their quarter-final games. But Bangladesh's failure to qualify for the World Cup was disappointing, because there is a bigger following for cricket in that country than in the Emirates, Kenya and The Netherlands combined.

Maurice Odumbe's majestic 158 not out saw Kenya through the first semi-final against Bermuda and then Holland batted poorly to lose to the Emirates. With both finalists already assured of entry to the World Cup, there was actually more at stake in the third-place play-off. Nolan Clarke settled Dutch nerves with his third century of the tournament and Bermuda faded gracefully. On this evidence, both the UAE and Kenya need to find bowlers to be a threat in 1996, and Holland must be concerned that their first three batsmen are all over 40: Flavian Aponso, Steve Lubbers and Nolan Clarke. It has been suggested that a composite side of the best players from the ICC associates might prove better opposition to the Test-playing nations and, certainly, a team containing wicket-keeper Dean Minors of Bermuda, Hong Kong all-rounder Stewart Brew and USA pace bowler Hopeton Barrett would not be overawed. Mohammad Ishaq and Saleem Raza, the Emirates' two big-hitters, and their opener Riaz Poonawala, who was once 12th man for India, are unlikely to disgrace themselves in the World Cup. Nor will Kenya's three Tikolo brothers, especially the classy strokemaker Steve, or Maurice Odumbe. But both teams' attacks may well be horribly exposed by the major countries.

It was a bold move to stage the tournament in Kenya but, with ten grounds within 15 minutes of the city centre, Nairobi was a perfect venue. Delightfully, the first ICC Trophy to be held outside Europe had a distinctly African flavour: the joy and enthusiasm of the Kenyan people, pipers serenading play, birds of prey circling, sun-baked batting pitches and outfields as bumpy as a local taxi ride.

But if the location was exotic, the organisation was often chaotic and, with the exception of an efficient transport system, seemed more appropriate to a bank holiday six-a-side than a World Cup qualifying competition. Although most of the wrinkles had been ironed out by the final week, the Kenyan Cricket Association's reluctance to accept outside advice did not help. It seems strange that such an important tournament should be run by inexperienced volunteers. Official scoreboards with incorrect totals and team lists giving players alphabetically, with no guide to their batting order, were a minor nuisance. The organisers did manage to provide a white glove for every scorer so they could acknowledge umpiring signals, but they failed to come up with something far more crucial for a one-day tournament: a mechanism in the playing conditions to revise the target and overs in rain-affected matches. The only concession to the weather was that a result could be awarded on run-rate if the team batting second had faced a minimum of 30 overs.

This omission, apparently the result of dissatisfaction with established formulae, almost guaranteed storms, and a six-week drought broke on the eve of the tournament. There was a rule cutting off play at 5.40 on the second day. But the problems were compounded by the Irish umpire Paddy O'Hara, who decreed that if play did not start on the first day, then the second day must be the first day. O'Hara's ruling in the game between Singapore and Canada (the only match not to produce a winner) allowed play to continue on that day if the umpires deemed a finish obtainable. This well-intentioned nonsense was far too hastily backed by the organisers, without thought to the potential consequences.

Inevitably, a couple of days later, it led to farce, with Papua New Guinea being asked to bat on as the equatorial night fell fast, with no idea of the final number of overs they would face – except that, due to darkness, it could not be the full 50. This injustice was the subject of a protest but was dismissed, seemingly on the grounds that Papua New Guinea, who were 88 for seven when their innings was cut short, had been outplayed by Ireland and did not deserve to escape with an abandonment.

Six thousand people watched the final, mainly Asians, who traditionally have been the backbone of Kenyan cricket. However, there were signs that the tournament added to the game's appeal among the local African population, if only because of the potential rewards. The Kenyan players are believed to have received about £2,500 each for finishing runners-up, perhaps three years' salary for a Nairobi clerk.

GROUP A

At Jaffrey's, February 12, 13. Papua New Guinea won by 135 runs. Toss: Gibraltar. Papua New Guinea 248 for five (50 overs) (C. Amini 63, L. Leka 45, V. Pala 66 not out); Gibraltar 113 (38.2 overs) (V. Kenny 34; T. Raka three for 16, F. Arua five for 31).

At Nairobi Club, February 12. Holland won by nine wickets. Toss: Holland. Malaysia 118 for nine (50 overs); Holland 119 for one (28.4 overs) (N. E. Clarke 64 not out, S. W. Lubbers 42 not out).

At Premier, February 14. Holland won by ten wickets. Toss: Holland. Gibraltar 80 (44.4 overs); Holland 85 for no wkt (10 overs) (N. E. Clarke 49 not out, G. J. A. F. Aponso 31 not out).

At Ngara, February 14, 15. Ireland won on scoring-rate. Toss: Papua New Guinea. Ireland 230 for eight (50 overs) (J. D. R. Benson 46, D. A. Lewis 50, A. R. Dunlop 30); Papua New Guinea 88 for seven (32 overs) (C. J. Hoey five for 29).

At Sir Ali, February 16, 17. Ireland won by six wickets. Toss: Ireland. Gibraltar 136 for nine (50 overs) (R. Buzaglo 42; C. McCrum four for 16); Ireland 138 for four (37.3 overs) (D. A. Lewis 44).

At Gymkhana, February 16, 17. Papua New Guinea won by 44 runs. Toss: Malaysia. Papua New Guinea 165 (47.5 overs) (G. Rarua 50, A. Noka 33, Tau Ao 39; V. Muniandy four for 28, D. Ramadass three for 24); Malaysia 121 (46.4 overs) (K. Ila three for 23).

At Ngara, February 18. Malaysia won by 134 runs. Toss: Gibraltar. Malaysia 253 for four (50 overs) (E. Seah 62, D. Talalla 112 not out, Tan Kim Heng 32 not out); Gibraltar 119 for nine (50 overs) (T. Buzaglo 49; Tan Kim Heng three for 15).

At Ruaraka, February 18. Holland won by 70 runs. Toss: Holland. Holland 235 for eight (50 overs) (N. E. Clarke 119; E. R. Moore three for 39, C. McCrum three for 58); Ireland 165 (48 overs) (J. D. R. Benson 39, A. R. Dunlop 31; J. Leemhuis three for 34).

At Simba Union, February 20. Ireland won by nine wickets. Toss: Malaysia. Malaysia 110 (48.2 overs) (C. J. Hoey four for 18); Ireland 111 for one (24.3 overs) (J. D. R. Benson 74 not out).

At Aga Khan, February 20. Holland won by 99 runs. Toss: Holland. Holland 212 for five (50 overs) (R. P. Lefebvre 34, R. H. Scholte 90 not out); Papua New Guinea 113 (41 overs) (H. F. Visee four for 22).

	Played	*Won*	*Lost*	*No result*	*Points*
Holland	4	4	0	0	16
Ireland	4	3	1	0	12
Papua New Guinea	4	2	2	0	8
Malaysia	4	1	3	0	4
Gibraltar	4	0	4	0	0

GROUP B

At Simba Union, February 13, 14. Bangladesh won by seven wickets. Toss: Bangladesh. Argentina 120 (43.2 overs) (D. Forrester 39; Enam-ul-Haque three for 23, G. M. Nawsher three for 25); Bangladesh 123 for three (35.2 overs) (Ather Ali Khan 41, J. Jahangir 37).

At Sir Ali, February 13, 14. United Arab Emirates won by seven wickets. Toss: United Arab Emirates. East and Central Africa 92 (37.3 overs) (K. Sabzali 36; J. A. Samarasekera four for 14, Arshad Laiq three for 18); United Arab Emirates 93 for three (26.5 overs) (Azhar Saeed 44 not out; S. Kapere three for 20).

At Impala, February 15, 16. Bangladesh won by seven wickets. Toss: Bangladesh. East and Central Africa 98 (36.2 overs) (Minhaz-ul-Abedin three for 20, G. M. Nawsher four for 36); Bangladesh 99 for three (22.5 overs).

At Aga Khan, February 15, 16. United Arab Emirates won by four wickets. Toss: United Arab Emirates. USA 206 (47.5 overs) (K. Williams 36, R. Denny 61; J. A. Samarasekera three for 32, Azhar Saeed four for 24); United Arab Emirates 209 for six (47.1 overs) (Azhar Saeed 32, Mazhar Hussain 34, V. Mehra 34, Saleem Raza 32; H. Barrett three for 29).

At Jaffrey's, February 17. United Arab Emirates won by eight wickets. Toss: United Arab Emirates. Argentina 128 (49.2 overs) (G. Ferguson 34; Sohail Butt three for 30); United Arab Emirates 130 for two (24.3 overs) (R. Poonawala 35, Saleem Raza 46 not out).

At Nairobi Club, February 17. USA won by nine wickets. Toss: USA. East and Central Africa 105 (35.1 overs) (D. Kallicharran three for 18); USA 106 for one (14.4 overs) (E. Lewis 68 not out).

At Premier, February 19. Argentina won by 47 runs. Toss: East and Central Africa. Argentina 190 (48 overs) (D. Forrester 43, G. Kirschbaum 33); East and Central Africa 143 (38.1 overs) (I. Brohi 48; L. Jooris three for 35, C. Tunon five for 37).

At Jaffrey's, February 19. Bangladesh won by three wickets. Toss: Bangladesh. USA 145 (45.4 overs) (P. Singh 69); Bangladesh 147 for seven (46 overs) (Akram Khan 64 not out; A. Howard three for 21).

At Sir Ali, February 21. USA won by 111 runs. Toss: USA. USA 337 for six (50 overs) (E. Lewis 45, S. Skeete 67, R. Latchman 75 not out, D. Kallicharran 58; H. Pereyra three for 46); Argentina 226 for six (50 overs) (G. Kirschbaum 57, D. Forrester 33, M. Morris 31).

At Ngara, February 21. United Arab Emirates won by six wickets. Toss: United Arab Emirates. Bangladesh 233 for seven (50 overs) (J. Alam Talukdar 117 not out, S. Shahed 56); United Arab Emirates 236 for four (46.3 overs) (R. Poonawala 54, V. Mehra 50, Mohammad Ishaq 49 not out, Saleem Raza 61 not out).

	Played	*Won*	*Lost*	*No result*	*Points*
United Arab Emirates	4	4	0	0	16
Bangladesh	4	3	1	0	12
USA	4	2	2	0	8
Argentina	4	1	3	0	4
East and Central Africa	4	0	4	0	0

GROUP C

At Impala, February 12, 13. No result. Toss: Singapore. Canada 159 for eight (30 overs) (I. Liburd 45, P. Prashad 41; J. Stevenson three for 23); Singapore 50 for eight (20.1 overs) (T. Gardner five for 12).

At Premier, February 12, 13. Kenya won by nine wickets. Toss: Kenya. Israel 99 (41.4 overs) (R. Ali four for 26, D. Tikolo four for 30); Kenya 100 for one (15 overs) (D. Chudasama 44, Tariq Iqbal 32 not out).

At Nairobi Club, February 14. Canada won by ten wickets. Toss: Canada. Namibia 51 (16.3 overs) (Bhowan Singh seven for 21); Canada 52 for no wkt (11.5 overs) (I. Liburd 31 not out).

At Ruaraka, February 14. Kenya won by nine wickets. Toss: Kenya. Singapore 76 (34.5 overs) (A. V. Karim five for 20, R. Ali four for 9); Kenya 77 for one (9.2 overs) (K. Otieno 35 not out).

At Ruaraka, February 16, 17. Canada won by eight wickets. Toss: Canada. Israel 89 (29.1 overs) (D. Joseph five for 19, T. Gardner three for 17); Canada 90 for two (21.4 overs) (N. Isaac 34 not out).

At Ngara, February 16. Namibia won by five wickets. Toss: Namibia. Singapore 116 (38 overs) (W. Ackerman three for 20); Namibia 117 for five (32.3 overs) (D. Karg 50).

At Gymkhana, February 18. Israel won by two wickets. Toss: Israel. Singapore 120 (49.3 overs) (C. Kilbee 33; S. Perlman three for 32); Israel 121 for eight (48.2 overs).

At Simba Union, February 18. Kenya won by 29 runs. Toss: Namibia. Kenya 198 (48.3 overs) (D. Chudasama 37, S. Tikolo 47, T. Tikolo 41; L. Louw three for 27); Namibia 169 for nine (49.4 overs) (D. Karg 51, M. Martins 35; R. Ali three for 38, A. V. Karim three for 34).

At Gymkhana, February 20. Kenya won by three wickets. Toss: Kenya. Canada 210 for nine (50 overs) (P. Prashad 84, D. Maxwell 38); Kenya 213 for seven (47 overs) (D. Chudasama 62, D. Tikolo 40 not out).

At Impala, February 20. Namibia won by 59 runs. Toss: Namibia. Namibia 257 for nine (50 overs) (G. Murgatroyd 93, M. Martins 56; R. Aston three for 41, R. Shimshon three for 36); Israel 198 (47.3 overs) (N. Wald 92; M. Martins three for 19, G. Murgatroyd three for 26).

	Played	*Won*	*Lost*	*No result*	*Points*
Kenya	4	4	0	0	16
Canada	4	2	1	1	10
Namibia	4	2	2	0	8
Israel	4	1	3	0	4
Singapore	4	0	3	1	2

GROUP D

At Aga Khan, February 13, 14. Bermuda won by eight wickets. Toss: West Africa. West Africa 93 (46.3 overs) (Kwesi Sague 41); Bermuda 94 for two (21.4 overs) (D. Smith 54 not out).

At Gymkhana, February 13, 14. Hong Kong won by virtue of losing fewer wickets. Toss: Hong Kong. Denmark 192 (46.5 overs) (A. Butt 38, Aftab Ahmed 61; S. J. Brew four for 43, including a hat-trick, D. Cross three for 19); Hong Kong 192 for eight (50 overs) (S. J. Brew 42, J. O. D. Orders 63 not out, J. Garden 32; O. H. Mortensen four for 21).

At Jaffrey's, February 15, 16. Bermuda won by virtue of losing fewer wickets. Toss: Bermuda. Hong Kong 154 (47.2 overs) (J. Fordham 79; A. Edwards five for 27); Bermuda 154 for eight (50 overs) (D. Smith 44, D. Minors 46 not out; Y. Vachha three for nine).

At Simba Union, February 15, 16. Denmark won by 93 runs. Toss: Fiji. Denmark 219 (49.3 overs) (J. Gregerson 50, A. From Hansen 50; L. Sorovakatini three for 37, T. Batina three for 55); Fiji 126 (35.3 overs) (A. Sorovakatini 31 not out; O. H. Mortensen three for 21, S. Henriksen five for 56).

At Premier, February 17. Denmark won by four wickets. Toss: Denmark. West Africa 146 (47.4 overs) (U. Ntiwu 46; S. Henriksen four for ten); Denmark 148 for six (37.2 overs) (D. Orgle four for 39).

At Aga Khan, February 17. Hong Kong won by seven wickets. Toss: Fiji. Fiji 126 (35 overs) (A. Tawatatau 31 not out; S. J. Brew four for 16); Hong Kong 127 for three (17 overs) (J. Fordham 50 not out, M. Farcy 48).

At Nairobi Club, February 19. Bermuda won by nine wickets. Toss: Fiji. Fiji 84 (29.4 overs) (L. Sorovakatini 41; C. P. Wade four for 28); Bermuda 85 for one (16 overs) (D. Smith 56 not out).

At Sir Ali, February 19. Hong Kong won by 245 runs. Toss: West Africa. Hong Kong 355 for eight (50 overs) (S. J. Brew 124, S. Atkinson 68, J. Fordham 58, M. Farcy 47; S. Kpundeh four for 65); West Africa 110 (30.5 overs).

At Ruaraka, February 21. Bermuda won by six wickets. Toss: Denmark. Denmark 183 for seven (50 overs) (A. Butt 70, J. Gregerson 53); Bermuda 185 for four (43.5 overs) (D. Smith 31, C. Smith 51, C. M. Marshall 48 not out, A. E. Manders 38 not out; M. Seider three for 42).

At Jaffrey's, February 21. Fiji won by 144 runs. Toss: Fiji. Fiji 232 for nine (50 overs) (L. Sorovakatini 84, T. Cakacaka 46; T. Ayama three for 17); West Africa 88 (39.1 overs) (S. Campbell four for 17).

	Played	*Won*	*Lost*	*No result*	*Points*
Bermuda	4	4	0	0	16
Hong Kong	4	3	1	0	12
Denmark	4	2	2	0	8
Fiji	4	1	3	0	4
West Africa	4	0	4	0	0

QUARTER-FINAL GROUP MATCHES

GROUP E

At Premier, February 23. Holland won by 47 runs. Toss: Bangladesh. Holland 205 (48.3 overs) (R. van Oosterom 64, S. W. Lubbers 34; Minhaz-ul-Abedin three for 33); Bangladesh 158 (48 overs) (J. Alam Talukdar 48; H. F. Visee four for 32).

At Gymkhana, February 23. Kenya won by eight wickets. Toss: Hong Kong. Hong Kong 86 (33.1 overs) (M. Suji three for 17, A. Njuguna five for 24); Kenya 90 for two (16 overs) (K. Otieno 52 not out).

At Simba Union, February 25. Kenya won by 13 runs. Toss: Bangladesh. Kenya 295 for six (50 overs) (D. Chudasama 75, M. Odumbe 119); Bangladesh 282 for eight (50 overs) (J. Alam Talukdar 57, Amin-ul-Islam 74, Minhaz-ul-Abedin 68, Akram Khan 30; A. V. Karim three for 55).

At Nairobi Club, February 25. Holland won by 134 runs. Toss: Hong Kong. Holland 288 for eight (50 overs) (N. E. Clarke 113, S. W. Lubbers 63, B. Kuijlman 34 not out; S. J. Brew three for 43); Hong Kong 154 (41.1 overs) (S. J. Brew 61; G. J. A. F. Aponso three for 43).

At Aga Khan, February 27. Bangladesh won by 57 runs. Toss: Hong Kong. Bangladesh 238 for eight (50 overs) (Faruq Ahmed 43, Minhaz-ul-Abedin 66, S. Shahed 42 not out; S. J. Brew three for 58); Hong Kong 181 (48.5 overs) (J. O. D. Orders 58, J. Fordham 39; Minhaz-ul-Abedin four for 40, Enam-ul-Haque three for 27).

At Ruaraka, February 27. Kenya won by two wickets. Toss: Kenya. Holland 250 for eight (50 overs) (S. W. Lubbers 67, T. B. M. de Leede 51, R. P. Lefebvre 36, R. H. Scholte 32; E. Tito three for 39); Kenya 251 for eight (49.5 overs) (S. Tikolo 95, S. Kasamali 49).

	Played	*Won*	*Lost*	*Points*
Kenya	3	3	0	12
Holland	3	2	1	8
Bangladesh	3	1	2	4
Hong Kong	3	0	3	0

GROUP F

At Simba Union, February 23. Bermuda won by eight wickets. Toss: Bermuda. Canada 149 (43.2 overs) (I. Liburd 42, S. Jayasekera 39; N. A. Gibbons four for 31); Bermuda 151 for two (34.5 overs) (D. Smith 44, A. Steede 48).

At Ruaraka, February 23. United Arab Emirates won by 59 runs. Toss: Ireland. United Arab Emirates 295 for four (50 overs) (Azhar Saeed 58, Mazhar Hussain 122, Mohammad Ishaq 41, Saleem Raza 36 not out); Ireland 236 for nine (50 overs) (M. P. Rea 36, D. A. Lewis 32, A. R. Dunlop 44; Arshad Laiq four for 37).

At Gymkhana, February 25. Bermuda won by seven wickets. Toss: Bermuda. Ireland 202 (48.4 overs) (G. D. Harrison 36, C. McCrum 54; N. A. Gibbons three for 33); Bermuda 206 for three (45.5 overs) (C. Smith 89, C. M. Marshall 62 not out).

At Aga Khan, February 25. United Arab Emirates won by one wicket. Toss: United Arab Emirates. Canada 278 for seven (50 overs) (I. Liburd 87, T. Gardner 76; Arshad Laiq three for 51); United Arab Emirates 279 for nine (49.2 overs) (Azhar Saeed 126 not out).

At Nairobi Club, February 27. United Arab Emirates won by one wicket. Toss: United Arab Emirates. Bermuda 329 for nine (50 overs) (D. Smith 110, A. Steede 76, C. Smith 71); United Arab Emirates 330 for nine (48.4 overs) (R. Poonawala 53, Saleem Raza 78, Arshad Laiq 47 not out; N. A. Gibbons three for 75).

At Premier, February 27. Canada won by five wickets. Toss: Ireland. Ireland 212 for seven (50 overs) (M. F. Cohen 74); Canada 213 for five (46 overs) (D. Singh 47, D. Maxwell 40, S. Dutchin 38 not out).

	Played	*Won*	*Lost*	*Points*
United Arab Emirates....	3	3	0	12
Bermuda	3	2	1	8
Canada	3	1	2	4
Ireland	3	0	3	0

SEMI-FINALS

At Aga Khan, March 1. Kenya won by 64 runs. Toss: Kenya. Kenya 318 for five (50 overs) (D. Chudasama 40, M. Odumbe 158 not out, S. Tikolo 67); Bermuda 254 for nine (50 overs) (A. Steede 31, C. Smith 108, N. A. Gibbons 47; M. Odumbe three for 49, S. Tikolo three for 49).

At Nairobi Club, March 3. United Arab Emirates won by six wickets. Toss: United Arab Emirates. Holland 194 (47.3 overs) (T. B. M. de Leede 52, R. P. Lefebvre 45; Sohail Butt three for 20); United Arab Emirates 195 for four (44.4 overs) (Mohammad Ishaq 72 not out, Saleem Raza 65 not out).

THIRD-PLACE PLAY-OFF

BERMUDA v HOLLAND

At Simba Union, March 5. Holland won by 103 runs. Toss: Bermuda.

Clarke's third century of the tournament set up a straightforward win to assure Holland of the last place in the next World Cup in early 1996. He shared an opening stand of 114 with Aponso and then 138 with his captain, Lubbers, who hit 81 off 55 balls. Bermuda's bowlers had conceded a total of over 300 for the third match running, and none of their batsmen could reach 40; they were bowled out with 7.4 overs to spare.

Man of the Match: S. W. Lubbers.

Holland

N. E. Clarke not out 121
G. J. A. F. Aponso run out 53
*S. W. Lubbers c Steede b Edwards . . . 81
T. B. M. de Leede not out 32
B 1, l-b 13, w 5 19

1/114 2/252 (2 wkts, 50 overs) 306

R. P. Lefebvre, †R. H. Scholte, R. van Oosterom, E. de Man, B. Kuijlman, H. F. Visee and F. Jansen did not bat.

Bowling: Burgess 7–2–25–0; Edwards 10–0–67–1; Gibbons 5–0–25–0; Wade 8–0–67–0; Perinchief 10–0–61–0; C. Smith 10–0–47–0.

Bermuda

D. Smith run out 39
*A. Steede run out 4
C. Smith c Lubbers b Jansen 32
C. M. Marshall c de Leede b Visee 30
A. E. Manders c Kuijlman b Aponso . . 1
N. A. Gibbons c Scholte b Lefebvre . . . 28
C. P. Wade c sub (J. Leemhuis) b Lubbers . 13
†D. Minors c Lubbers b Jansen 28
A. Edwards run out 17
T. W. A. Burgess c Clarke b Jansen . . . 0
B. Perinchief not out 0
L-b 7, w 3, n-b 1 11

1/11 2/64 3/103 4/111 5/115 6/139 7/172 8/192 9/199 (42.2 overs) 203

Bowling: Lefebvre 8–1–36–1; Lubbers 10–1–40–1; Aponso 10–3–29–1; Jansen 8–0–61–3; Visee 6.2–0–30–1.

Umpires: P. L. O'Hara (Ireland) and L. van Reenan (Namibia).

FINAL

KENYA v UNITED ARAB EMIRATES

At Ruaraka, March 6. United Arab Emirates won by two wickets. Toss: United Arab Emirates.

A crowd of 6,000 was delighted to see another fine batting performance from Odumbe – 87 to follow his 119 against Bangladesh and 158 not out in the semi-final against Bermuda. But despite strong support from Otieno and the Tikolo brothers, a total of 281 was not enough to deter the Emirates. Their opening pair, Poonawala and Azhar Saeed, had halved the target before they were parted, after 28 overs, and Man of the Match Mohammad Ishaq followed up with a 36-ball fifty. It was a surprise that the victory was delayed until the final over with only two wickets to spare.

Man of the Match: Mohammad Ishaq.

Kenya

D. Chudasama c Saleem Raza b Sohail Butt . 0
†K. Otieno c and b Azhar Saeed 49
M. Odumbe b Samarasekera 87
S. Tikolo b Saleem Raza 54
S. Kasamali c Imtiaz Abbasi b Saleem Raza . 0
*T. Tikolo not out 42
E. Tito run out 25
M. Orewa not out 1
B 1, l-b 16, w 6 23

1/1 2/99 3/201 4/202 5/211 6/268 (6 wkts, 50 overs) 281

A. V. Karim, M. Suji and R. Ali did not bat.

Bowling: Samarasekera 9–1–38–1; Sohail Butt 10–0–59–1; Arshad Laiq 9–0–50–0; Azhar Saeed 9–0–46–1; Saleem Raza 10–0–48–2; Zarawani 3–0–23–0.

United Arab Emirates

R. Poonawala lbw b Tito 71
Azhar Saeed c Odumbe b Tito 59
Mazhar Hussain b Suji 9
Mohammad Ishaq c Chudasama b Suji . 51
V. Mehra run out 34
Saleem Raza c T. Tikolo b Suji 6
J. A. Samarasekera run out 4
Arshad Laiq c T. Tikolo b Suji 20
†Imtiaz Abbasi not out 1
Sohail Butt not out 0
B 1, l-b 13, w 12, n-b 1 27

1/141 2/148 3/177 4/233 5/242 6/254 7/276 8/281 (8 wkts, 49.1 overs) 282

*Sultan M. Zarawani did not bat.

Bowling: Suji 10–0–61–4; Ali 6–0–27–0; Orewa 2–0–14–0; Odumbe 10–0–44–0; Karim 9–0–56–0; S. Tikolo 3–0–14–0; Tito 9.1–0–52–2.

Umpires: W. Molenaar (The Netherlands) and P. L. O'Hara (Ireland).

PREVIOUS ICC TROPHY FINALS

1979 SRI LANKA beat Canada by 60 runs at Worcester.
1982 ZIMBABWE beat Bermuda by five wickets at Leicester.
1986 ZIMBABWE beat Holland by 25 runs at Lord's.
1990 ZIMBABWE beat Holland by six wickets at The Hague.

FIFTY YEARS AGO

From WISDEN CRICKETERS' ALMANACK 1945

FLYING-BOMB STOPS CRICKET: "During the Army innings against the Royal Air Force at Lord's on July 29 a flying-bomb, apparently heading for the ground, caused players and spectators to take 'evasive action' . . . Danger having passed, the game went on and Robertson celebrated the escape by promptly hitting a 6."

NOTES BY THE EDITOR: "The urgent need for strict adherence to the laws of the game on all occasions cannot be emphasised too strongly. Under the MCC every nicety is observed, but carelessness does creep in . . . handling the ball by a batsman should be avoided in all circumstances, no matter if asked by a fieldsman or on his own initiative. A flagrant case at Weston-super-Mare, where a batsman played the ball dead at his feet, picked it up and threw it to the bowler, made me gasp."

MISCELLANEA: "James Cannon, frequently referred to by Sir Pelham Warner as 'The King of Lord's', retired on pension after 65 years' continuous service with MCC. From ball-boy for the six lawn-tennis courts at the age of 12, he rose to be chief clerk. He recalled that his earlier duties included holding the mounts of members who arrived on horseback at the ground."

ENGLISH COUNTIES OVERSEAS, 1993-94

Scorecards of matches granted first-class status, played by English counties on pre-season tours to other countries.

ZIMBABWE B v WORCESTERSHIRE

At Harare Sports Club, Harare, April 6, 7, 8. Worcestershire won by 109 runs. Toss: Worcestershire.

Close of play: First day, Zimbabwe B 12-0 (K. J. Arnott 3*, D. N. Erasmus 7*); Second day, Worcestershire 66-0 (W. P. C. Weston 30*, C. M. Tolley 32*).

Worcestershire

*T. S. Curtis c Ranchod b Hira	68		
W. P. C. Weston c and b Strang	37	– (1) c Erasmus b Jarvis	37
G. R. Haynes b Strang	41	– (4) not out	26
D. A. Leatherdale b Jarvis	38	– (5) c James b Matambanadzo	54
D. B. D'Oliveira c Erasmus b Martin	43		
†S. J. Rhodes c and b Martin	3		
P. J. Newport not out	14		
S. R. Lampitt not out	17	– (3) c James b Jarvis	12
C. M. Tolley (did not bat)		– (2) b Matambanadzo	32
B 7, l-b 1, w 2, n-b 8	18	L-b 3, w 3, n-b 2	8
1/77 2/160 3/162 4/235 5/244 6/249 (6 wkts dec.)	279	1/75 2/87 3/87 4/169 (4 wkts dec.)	169

R. K. Illingworth and N. V. Radford did not bat.

Bowling: *First Innings*—Jarvis 27–9–68–1; Matambanadzo 12–4–33–0; Martin 24–7–52–2; Hira 15.5–2–40–1; Strang 21–5–55–2; Ranchod 7–3–23–0. *Second Innings*—Jarvis 22–11–30–2; Matambanadzo 14–3–38–2; Martin 13–2–28–0; Strang 3–0–16–0; Hira 6–1–27–0; Ranchod 7–0–27–0.

Zimbabwe B

K. J. Arnott c Rhodes b Newport	9	– c Rhodes b Illingworth	21
D. N. Erasmus c D'Oliveira b Tolley	9	– run out	2
G. C. Martin c and b Newport	4	– c Rhodes b Newport	6
C. B. Wishart c and b Illingworth	32	– c Lampitt b Illingworth	0
G. K. Bruk-Jackson c Weston b Illingworth	0	– st Rhodes b Illingworth	8
*†W. R. James c Lampitt b Newport	59	– lbw b D'Oliveira	47
P. A. Strang c Rhodes b Illingworth	2	– b Illingworth	21
H. J. Hira c Weston b Illingworth	9	– (11) not out	0
U. Ranchod c Tolley b Illingworth	23	– (8) st Rhodes b Haynes	24
M. P. Jarvis st Rhodes b Illingworth	25	– (9) c D'Oliveira b Illingworth	15
E. Matambanadzo not out	1	– (10) c Lampitt b Newport	0
L-b 3, w 1, n-b 10	14	L-b 2, n-b 6	8
1/14 2/23 3/24 4/28 5/118 6/126 7/135 8/138 9/181	187	1/18 2/23 3/25 4/31 5/74 6/92 7/128 8/146 9/152	152

Bowling: *First Innings*—Radford 17–7–35–0; Newport 18–8–25–3; Tolley 13–6–27–1; Illingworth 22.5–7–56–6; Lampitt 6–1–20–0; D'Oliveira 1–1–0–0; Haynes 5–0–16–0; Weston 3–0–5–0. *Second Innings*—Radford 5.3–2–3–0; Tolley 7–3–11–0; Newport 11.3–2–32–2; Illingworth 24.3–6–38–5; Lampitt 3–0–22–0; D'Oliveira 9–1–40–1; Haynes 3–1–4–1.

Umpires: N. Fleming and K. Kanjee.

MASHONALAND XI v WARWICKSHIRE

At Old Hararians Sports Club, Harare, April 12, 13, 14. Drawn. Toss: Warwickshire.

Close of play: First day, Warwickshire 322-1 (R. G. Twose 101*, Asif Din 204*); Second day, Mashonaland XI 233-6 (A. Flower 84*, D. J. R. Campbell 23*).

Warwickshire

First innings		Second innings	
J. D. Ratcliffe c A. D. R. Campbell b Matambanadzo	5	(2) c and b Brain	17
R. G. Twose retired hurt	101	(10) not out	1
Asif Din b Brain	217		
T. L. Penney c Rennie b Matambanadzo	13	(3) run out	0
†K. J. Piper c Bruk-Jackson b G. W. Flower	39	c A. Flower b Peall	35
R. P. Davis run out	2	(8) c A. Flower b A. D. R. Campbell	2
M. A. V. Bell not out	4	(9) c and b Peall	1
*D. A. Reeve (did not bat)	–	(1) c Rennie b Matambanadzo	2
N. M. K. Smith (did not bat)	–	(4) st D. J. R. Campbell b Peall	45
G. C. Small (did not bat)	–	(6) b Peall	11
T. A. Munton (did not bat)	–	(7) st D. J. R. Campbell b Rennie	47
B 3, l-b 7, w 4, n-b 1	15	B 3, l-b 1	4
1/5 2/350 3/356 4/366 5/396 (5 wkts dec.)	396	1/5 2/5 3/29 4/76 5/96 6/133 7/160 8/161 9/165 (9 wkts dec.)	165

In the first innings, R. G. Twose retired hurt at 322.

Bowling: *First Innings*—Brain 28–6–86–1; Matambanadzo 22–4–60–2; Martin 13–2–59–0; Peall 33–7–113–0; G. W. Flower 8.4–1–28–1; A. D. R. Campbell 11–0–35–0; A. Flower 1–0–5–0. *Second Innings*—Brain 8–2–36–1; Matambanadzo 6–0–30–1; G. W. Flower 11–2–30–0; Peall 16–1–39–4; A. D. R. Campbell 6–0–22–1; Rennie 1–0–4–1.

Mashonaland XI

First innings		Second innings	
G. W. Flower c Smith b Bell	48	c Bell b Reeve	19
G. J. Rennie c Munton b Small	2	(3) lbw b Reeve	0
A. D. R. Campbell c Reeve b Small	4	(5) not out	4
G. K. Bruk-Jackson lbw b Bell	11	(2) run out	67
D. N. Erasmus b Bell	21	(4) c Bell b Ratcliffe	46
*A. Flower c Asif Din b Penney	113		
G. C. Martin c Piper b Small	33		
†D. J. R. Campbell b Davis	27		
D. H. Brain st Piper b Davis	15		
S. G. Peall not out	13		
B 4, l-b 3, n-b 2	9	B 1, w 1	2
1/5 2/21 3/34 4/81 5/98 6/181 7/256 8/276 9/296 (9 wkts dec.)	296	1/47 2/49 3/119 4/138 (4 wkts)	138

D. Matambanadzo did not bat.

Bowling: *First Innings*—Small 13–3–23–3; Munton 12–3–38–0; Reeve 5–0–16–0; Bell 15–4–37–3; Smith 14–0–67–0; Davis 15.3–4–50–2; Asif Din 5–0–18–0; Penney 6–0–40–1. *Second Innings*—Small 1–0–6–0; Munton 6–2–14–0; Bell 5–0–27–0; Reeve 4–2–11–2; Twose 4–0–22–0; Penney 3–0–15–0; Davis 4–0–16–0; Smith 3–0–22–0; Ratcliffe 0.4–0–4–1.

Umpires: G. Batte and I. D. Robinson.

MATABELELAND INVITATION XI v WORCESTERSHIRE

At Bulawayo Athletic Club, April 13, 14, 15. Drawn. Toss: Matabeleland Invitation XI. First-class debut: J. E. Brinkley.

Close of play: First day, Worcestershire 45-2 (R. K. Illingworth 8*, G. R. Haynes 0*); Second day, Matabeleland Invitation XI 37-3 (L. P. Vorster 14*, G. J. Whittall 0*).

Matabeleland Invitation XI

First innings		Second innings	
M. H. Dekker c Lampitt b Brinkley	36	– c D'Oliveira b Newport	6
J. R. Craig c Lampitt b Tolley	9	– run out	3
N. R. van Rensburg c Rhodes b Brinkley	24	– c Newport b Lampitt	9
L. P. Vorster c Curtis b Newport	4	– c Lampitt b Tolley	83
G. J. Whittall c Haynes b Newport	5	– c Weston b Brinkley	10
M. J. Hammett lbw b Brinkley	7	– c Rhodes b Tolley	32
M. D. Abrams c Illingworth b Newport	11	– (8) c Rhodes b Illingworth	8
B. A. Clark lbw b Haynes	17	– (10) c Rhodes b Brinkley	0
H. H. Streak c Curtis b Weston	62	– b Newport	18
*†W. R. James c Rhodes b Lampitt	32	– (7) c sub (D. A. Leatherdale) b Brinkley	96
J. A. Rennie not out	0	– not out	6
L-b 8, w 1, n-b 8	17	L-b 6, w 9, n-b 5	20
1/14 2/68 3/69 4/75 5/82 6/98 7/104 8/146 9/220	224	1/6 2/21 3/29 4/69 5/141 6/152 7/187 8/271 9/272	291

Bowling: *First Innings*—Newport 16–4–44–3; Tolley 12–0–38–1; Lampitt 19–1–61–1; Brinkley 14–6–23–3; Illingworth 20–4–45–0; Haynes 3–1–4–1; Weston 1.3–0–1–1. *Second Innings*—Newport 20–3–46–2; Tolley 13–2–43–2; Lampitt 10–1–33–1; Brinkley 18.1–6–56–3; Illingworth 18–7–42–1; D'Oliveira 13–3–28–0; Weston 7–1–37–0.

Worcestershire

First innings		Second innings	
*T. S. Curtis lbw b Rennie	11	– not out	7
W. P. C. Weston c Dekker b Whittall	14	– not out	17
R. K. Illingworth b Streak	8		
G. R. Haynes b Rennie	83		
A. C. H. Seymour c James b Rennie	30		
D. B. D'Oliveira b Whittall	66		
†S. J. Rhodes c van Rensburg b Dekker	9		
P. J. Newport not out	36		
S. R. Lampitt c Streak b Craig	5		
C. M. Tolley c James b Whittall	18		
J. E. Brinkley not out	10		
B 4, l-b 11, w 2, n-b 15	32	N-b 3	3
1/29 2/32 3/51 4/119 5/204 6/236 7/251 8/259 9/300 (9 wkts dec.)	322	(no wkt)	27

Bowling: *First Innings*—Streak 20–2–67–1; Rennie 35–5–110–3; Whittall 27–7–81–3; Dekker 18–5–39–1; Craig 6–3–10–1. *Second Innings*—Rennie 3–0–9–0; Streak 2–2–0–0; Craig 3–0–8–0; Dekker 3–1–10–0.

Umpires: P. Brown and J. Fenwick.

CRICKET IN AUSTRALIA, 1993-94

By JOHN MACKINNON

For the second year running, New South Wales scooped the pool of domestic cricket, winning both the Sheffield Shield and the Mercantile Mutual Cup. Their back-to-back successes were even more impressive because so many key players were away on international duty or unavailable. By the Sheffield Shield final, only three men survived from the previous year's fixture: the stand-in captain, Phil Emery, Michael Bevan and Brad McNamara.

In December, such an outcome appeared most unlikely. After an embarrassing two-day defeat by Western Australia, which followed the news that Greg Matthews's future had been put in doubt when he suffered head injuries outside a nightclub, many were ready to write them off. Much credit was due to the positive attitudes of Bob Radford, the NSWCA chief executive, coach Steve Rixon, Emery and his team who won five of their last seven matches outright, including a completely one-sided final after they headed the table by 14 points. The question of who would challenge them for their Shield remained open until the last round, when all five of the other states were still in with a chance. Tasmania's batting strength carried them through to their first ever Shield final – the climax of a remarkable ten weeks in which they had fought their way up from bottom place, with just two points, to finish with 24. They had been the last team to defeat New South Wales, but completely failed to repeat that victory.

The ability of New South Wales to bowl sides out was critical. Losing the services of Mike Whitney – injured in the first match of the season, against the New Zealanders – and Matthews meant, in essence, that at least 80 wickets had to be taken by other players. Neil Maxwell and Gavin Robertson, medium-pace and off-spin respectively, performed heroically to obtain 61 between them; Robertson, to his own great surprise, earned a place on the tour of Pakistan and Sri Lanka. Fast left-armer Phil Alley, of great potential and, at 6ft 8in, even greater stature, did well enough at times to look like a serious strike bowler but Wayne Holdsworth's value was spasmodic and eventually he lost his place. Spin resources, Robertson apart, were conspicuously slender. Adrian Tucker made a fleeting return but gave way to David Freedman, whose left-arm chinamen too often landed in the wrong half. New South Wales needed high-quality catching and fielding and they got it: as usual Emery missed very little behind the stumps and McNamara caught superbly.

Batting is traditionally the state's forte, but finding replacements for the Test players at Nos. 1 to 4 – Mark Taylor, Michael Slater and the Waugh twins – was a big challenge. The left-handed Bevan thrived on the added responsibility and went through his last 11 first-class innings without being dismissed for under 50; he fell in single figures only three times, all to Shane Warne. His casual manner has led some to doubt his concentration, but this year he looked a much tighter player. The Waughs and Slater all made hundreds during their few state appearances while their youthful understudies, especially Rodney Davison and Richard Chee Quee, played their part admirably.

Tasmania reached their first final without ever enjoying the services of their official captain, David Boon. All three of their outright wins were achieved courtesy of third-innings declarations by their opponents, but their gusto in chasing targets without their star player owed much to an array of talented batsmen. They boasted two accomplished openers in Dene Hills and Jamie Cox, two exciting youngsters in Ricky Ponting and Michael Di Venuto and a sturdy middle order. But the omission of 29-year-old Danny Buckingham from the final devastated the player and deprived the Tasmanians of a much-needed older head. The bowling, a modest proposition at best, was hampered by the moribund Hobart pitch; Colin Miller and Shaun Young were always competitive, Chris Matthews less so, due to nagging injury.

Western Australia's record of three wins, all on the fast Perth wicket, represented a poor return for a side containing so much talent and experience. Certainly both Jo Angel and Justin Langer enhanced their reputations, earning selection for the Pakistan tour. But three heavy defeats exposed a disconcerting inability to grit it out when the going was tough. Langer had a terrific year, averaging 70, and overtook Damien Martyn as a Test candidate. Martyn's season lost impetus after his nervous surrender to South Africa in the Sydney Test. Tom Moody often looked more at home with the ball rather than the bat and Geoff Marsh had a moderate season. The bowling was mostly Angel, with support from Brendon Julian. The English-born Duncan Spencer, despite getting rave reviews from Kent, lacked the discipline to capitalise on his talents. Again Tim Zoehrer and Mike Veletta shared the keeping so that Zoehrer could bowl leg-spin, but to the benefit of neither.

South Australia welcomed back Darren Lehmann and Paul Nobes from Victoria. As a result, their batting was just about the strongest in the competition – their first innings exceeded 400 in all but two Shield matches – but their bowling, with Tim May available only three times, was pretty friendly. Lehmann enjoyed his return to Adelaide, batting imperiously, Greg Blewett hit a rich vein late in the season with two double-centuries, and Jamie Siddons played some delightful innings. Darren Webber, too, looked to be a batsman of considerable promise. Shane George was the pick of the pace bowlers.

Victoria beat Western Australia and New South Wales early in the season as they responded to Dean Jones's hyperactive captaincy and the fine batting of newcomer Brad Hodge. Subsequently, Jones found his very best form, averaging 76.50. Warne was a huge, though occasional, asset; he took 27 wickets in the four games he played. In his absence, fast bowler Damien Fleming and Simon Cook responded splendidly. Merv Hughes was restricted to two games, Paul Reiffel to four. Yet Victoria could have made the final rather than finishing next to bottom, given a bit of luck in their last match.

Queensland's season was a triumph for Matthew Hayden. Seven hundreds in six matches demonstrated his total command of Shield bowling. He toured South Africa, after which a career of 86 innings had brought him 15 centuries and not a single nought. Yet he had played only one Test, in Johannesburg, and the selectors overlooked him for the Pakistan tour. Without the batting of Hayden and Allan Border, Queensland struggled. Defeats in their final two matches consigned them to last place and Jeff Thomson lost his job as coach. Nevertheless, Trevor Barsby, Stuart Law and Martin Love all played innings of substance, while

Carl Rackemann carried the pace bowling and Paul Jackson the spin. Craig McDermott could appear in only three Shield games and the reserve resources were not quite adequate to sustain a realistic challenge.

The season marked the end of some distinguished careers, with the retirement of Border and, at least temporarily, Jones from international cricket, though not from the Sheffield Shield. New South Wales lost Whitney, whose knees finally gave up, and Matthews might have tested the patience of his state selectors just once too often. Simon O'Donnell found the lure of a television career and racing horses more attractive than playing for Victoria. In mid-season, Dirk Wellham and Peter Anderson retired, depriving Queensland of two senior players.

In 1994-95 the Shield competition was to be more ravaged than ever by international demands. Once the national team returned from Pakistan in November, they faced not only a five-Test series against England but the World Series Cup, including for the first time a second native side, Australia A, and then tours to New Zealand and the West Indies running from February to May. This represents a great opportunity for blooding young hopefuls but it also indicates the developmental role consigned to the competition by the Cricket Board.

While Australia's batting resources look healthy enough, it has to be said that the season's welter of runs came off some fairly plain bowling on some very plain pitches. Hayden's difficulty in converting Shield opulence into international success underlined the current imbalance.

To their credit, the Board implemented a 100-over daily minimum, which meant that even Western Australia had to play a spinner. However, other special rules continued to apply, including the use of three umpires in rotation, disliked by the umpires and not apparently making much impact on standards at the top. The umpires voted Hayden their Player of the Year; the Lord's Taverners award, decided by the players, went, predictably enough, to the irrepressible Warne.

FIRST-CLASS AVERAGES, 1993-94

BATTING

(Qualification: 500 runs)

	M	*I*	*NO*	*R*	*HS*	*100s*	*Avge*
M. L. Hayden (*Qld*)	6	12	3	1,136	173*	7	126.22
S. R. Waugh (*NSW*)	9	15	4	976	190*	4	88.72
M. G. Bevan (*NSW*)	12	22	5	1,312	203*	5	77.17
D. M. Jones (*Vic.*)	7	14	2	918	158*	4	76.50
J. L. Langer (*WA*)	11	19	2	1,198	233	3	70.47
M. N. Atkinson (*Tas.*)	12	20	12	534	69	0	66.75
G. S. Blewett (*SA*)	11	19	1	1,036	268	2	57.55
D. S. Lehmann (*SA*)	11	19	0	1,087	200	4	57.21
B. J. Hodge (*Vic.*)	11	21	2	991	106	1	52.15
M. A. Taylor (*NSW*)	10	16	1	763	170	2	50.86
D. R. Martyn (*WA*)	12	19	2	855	197	2	50.29
S. Young (*Tas.*)	12	21	4	842	124*	1	49.52
D. F. Hills (*Tas.*)	12	23	1	1,068	158*	3	48.54
J. Cox (*Tas.*)	8	15	2	630	129	2	48.46
A. R. Border (*Qld*)	10	14	1	629	125*	2	48.38

	M	*I*	*NO*	*R*	*HS*	*100s*	*Avge*
R. T. Ponting (*Tas.*)	12	22	2	965	161	3	48.25
M. E. Waugh (*NSW*)	10	16	0	765	119	2	47.81
M. T. G. Elliott (*Vic.*)......	7	14	1	621	175*	2	47.76
D. J. Buckingham (*Tas.*)....	9	16	2	627	100*	1	44.78
T. M. Moody (*WA*)........	11	17	0	741	115	2	43.58
M. J. Slater (*NSW*)........	11	19	0	802	168	2	42.21
P. C. Nobes (*SA*)..........	11	20	1	796	141	3	41.89
T. J. Barsby (*Qld*).........	11	22	0	900	129	2	40.90
J. A. Brayshaw (*SA*)	11	20	1	766	146	2	40.31
J. D. Siddons (*SA*).........	10	17	1	640	161	2	40.00
M. J. Di Venuto (*Tas.*)	10	18	0	678	125	2	37.66
J. P. Maher (*Qld*)	8	16	1	557	122	1	37.13
D. S. Webber (*SA*)	10	17	1	581	176	2	36.31
G. R. Marsh (*WA*)	11	19	2	615	128	1	36.17
M. L. Love (*Qld*)..........	9	17	1	571	138	2	35.68
S. G. Law (*Qld*)	11	21	0	747	118	3	35.57
W. N. Phillips (*Vic.*).......	10	20	1	674	156*	2	35.47
R. J. Tucker (*Tas.*)	12	20	4	558	107	1	34.87
D. J. Ramshaw (*Vic.*)	10	19	0	614	85	0	32.31

* *Signifies not out.*

BOWLING

(Qualification: 20 wickets)

	O	*M*	*R*	*W*	*BB*	*5W/i*	*Avge*
S. K. Warne (*Vic.*)........	574.2	176	1,255	63	7-56	5	19.92
N. D. Maxwell (*NSW*)	221.2	52	641	31	4-31	0	20.67
J. Angel (*WA*)	347.5	90	1,024	47	5-32	4	21.78
D. W. Fleming (*Vic.*)......	298.4	69	903	38	6-86	3	23.76
C. J. McDermott (*Qld*)	424.1	121	1.060	41	5-62	1	25.85
T. M. Moody (*WA*)	222.2	68	570	20	4-43	0	28.50
C. R. Miller (*Tas.*)........	375.4	88	1,143	40	7-83	2	28.57
C. G. Rackemann (*Qld*) ...	379.2	90	1,097	38	6-93	2	28.86
S. H. Cook (*Vic.*)	254.5	45	885	30	5-114	1	29.50
G. D. McGrath (*NSW*)....	301.2	88	690	23	4-60	0	30.00
P. J. S. Alley (*NSW*)......	278.2	56	944	30	5-24	2	31.46
G. R. Robertson (*NSW*) ...	379.3	93	998	30	6-54	3	33.26
B. P. Julian (*WA*).........	324	72	1,021	30	5-34	1	34.03
S. P. George (*SA*).........	384.3	84	1,221	34	5-102	1	35.91
D. J. Spencer (*WA*)	183.1	20	750	20	4-85	0	37.50
T. B. A. May (*SA*)........	437	131	1,015	25	5-65	2	40.60
M. S. Kasprowicz (*Qld*) ...	262.4	55	844	20	5-92	1	42.20
S. Herzberg (*Tas.*)	317.5	57	942	22	4-66	0	42.81
P. W. Jackson (*Qld*)	474	126	1,220	28	4-86	0	43.57
S. Young (*Tas.*)...........	431	108	1,258	28	4-85	0	44.92
W. J. Holdsworth (*NSW*) ..	260.2	51	901	20	3-73	0	45.05
C. Howard (*Vic.*)	312.1	71	1,046	22	5-42	2	47.54
P. E. McIntyre (*SA*).......	510	91	1,572	29	5-61	1	54.20

SHEFFIELD SHIELD, 1993-94

	Played	*Won*	*Lost*	*Drawn*	*1st-inns Points*	*Points*
New South Wales	10	6	3	1	2	38
Tasmania	10	3	1	6	6	24
Western Australia	10	3	3*	4	5.8†	23.8
South Australia	10	2	5§	3	10	22
Victoria	10	3	3*	4	3‡	21
Queensland	10	2	4*	4	6	18

Final: New South Wales beat Tasmania by an innings and 61 runs.

* *One outright loss after leading on first innings.*
§ *Three outright losses after leading on first innings.*
† *0.2 points deducted for slow over-rates.* ‡ *1 point deducted for slow over-rates.*

Outright win = 6 pts; lead on first innings in a drawn or lost game = 2 pts.

Under Australian Cricket Board playing conditions for Sheffield Shield matches, two extras are scored for every no-ball bowled whether scored off or not. Any runs scored off the bat are credited to the batsman, while byes and leg-byes are counted as no-balls, in accordance with Law 24.9, in addition to the initial penalty.

*In the following scores, * by the name of a team indicates that they won the toss.*

At Brisbane, October 21, 22, 23, 24. Drawn. South Australia* 522 (D. S. Lehmann 128, D. S. Webber 176, J. C. Scuderi 54, S. P. George 50; C. J. McDermott four for 111, P. W. Jackson four for 90); Queensland 352 (M. L. Hayden 125, D. M. Wellham 34, I. A. Healy 46; B. N. Wigney three for 95, T. B. A. May four for 112) and 416 for four (T. J. Barsby 116, S. G. Law 100, A. R. Border 125 not out, M. L. Love 56 not out). *South Australia 2 pts.*

At Adelaide, October 27, 28, 29, 30. South Australia won by nine wickets. Victoria* 357 for nine dec. (W. N. Phillips 60, M. T. G. Elliott 54, D. M. Jones 33, D. J. Ramshaw 58, A. I. C. Dodemaide 52, D. S. Berry 33; S. P. George three for 73, P. E. McIntyre four for 101) and 198 (M. T. G. Elliott 99; T. B. A. May five for 80, P. E. McIntyre five for 61); South Australia 430 (G. S. Blewett 34, P. C. Nobes 141, J. A. Brayshaw 134, D. S. Webber 47; S. H. Cook five for 114, S. K. Warne four for 119) and 127 for one (P. C. Nobes 63 not out, J. A. Brayshaw 54 not out). *South Australia 6 pts.*

At Perth, October 29, 30, 31, November 1. Queensland won by nine wickets. Western Australia 211 (J. L. Langer 65, D. R. Martyn 59; C. J. McDermott five for 62, C. G. Rackemann three for 57) and 373 (J. L. Langer 96, D. R. Martyn 56, T. J. Zoehrer 57, Extras 55; C. G. Rackemann six for 93); Queensland* 430 (T. J. Barsby 82, S. G. Law 33, A. R. Border 65, I. A. Healy 79, C. J. McDermott 61, Extras 43) and 158 for one (T. J. Barsby 34, M. L. Hayden 96 not out). *Queensland 6 pts.*

This was Queensland's first outright win in Perth for 18 years.

At Brisbane, November 4, 5, 6, 7. New South Wales won by eight wickets. Queensland 257 (T. J. Barsby 46, A. R. Border 85; P. J. S. Alley four for 45) and 281 (M. L. Hayden 173 not out, carrying his bat); New South Wales* 382 (S. R. Waugh 43, M. E. Waugh 61, B. E. McNamara 40, P. A. Emery 30, G. R. Robertson 85, W. J. Holdsworth 34; P. W. Jackson four for 86) and 157 for two (M. E. Waugh 85). *New South Wales 6 pts.*

Having scored 30 in the first innings, Border became the second Australian, after Bradman, to reach 25,000 first-class runs.

At Melbourne, November 4, 5, 6, 7. Victoria won by six wickets. Western Australia* 322 (M. P. Lavender 31, J. L. Langer 144, T. M. Moody 33; A. I. C. Dodemaide five for 85, S. K. Warne three for 92) and 185 (D. R. Martyn 89 not out, T. M. Moody 37; S. H. Cook three for 38, S. K. Warne six for 42); Victoria 230 (D. M. Jones 47, B. J. Hodge 95, D. S. Berry 38 not out; J. Angel three for 38, D. J. Spencer three for 66) and 278 for four (M. T. G. Elliott 175 not out, D. J. Ramshaw 43). *Victoria 6 pts, Western Australia 2 pts.*

Victoria's first Sheffield Shield win since December 1991.

At Hobart, November 11, 12, 13, 14. Drawn. Western Australia 473 for five dec. (G. R. Marsh 43, J. L. Langer 135, D. R. Martyn 100, T. M. Moody 65, M. R. J. Veletta 65 not out, T. J. Zoehrer 44 not out) and 56 for two; Tasmania* 514 (D. F. Hills 43, N. C. P. Courtney 41, M. J. Di Venuto 125, R. T. Ponting 105, S. Young 63, Extras 41; J. Angel three for 118). *Tasmania 2 pts.*

At Melbourne, November 19, 20, 21, 22. Victoria won by one wicket. New South Wales* 227 (M. J. Slater 77, M. E. Waugh 58; S. K. Warne four for 72) and 268 for seven dec. (M. A. Taylor 50, S. R. Waugh 122, G. R. J. Matthews 30 not out; P. R. Reiffel five for 73); Victoria 233 (D. J. Ramshaw 85, B. J. Hodge 54; B. E. McNamara six for 43) and 263 for nine (D. M. Jones 72, B. J. Hodge 92). *Victoria 6 pts.*

Victoria won when Holdsworth struck last man Cook on the pads, and umpire Walpole signalled a no-ball rather than a dismissal.

At Sydney, November 25, 26, 27, 28. New South Wales won by 69 runs. New South Wales 353 for five dec. (R. Chee Quee 69, M. G. Bevan 141, G. R. J. Matthews 55 not out, Extras 36) and 274 for nine dec. (R. J. Davison 133 not out, on first-class debut, G. R. J. Matthews 40; S. Herzberg four for 82, S. Young three for 68); Tasmania* 343 (D. F. Hills 88, N. C. P. Courtney 55, M. J. Di Venuto 53, S. Young 52 not out; G. R. J. Matthews seven for 99) and 215 (R. T. Ponting 35, S. Young 42, M. N. Atkinson 49; G. R. J. Matthews four for 82, A. E. Tucker four for 64). *New South Wales 6 pts.*

At Adelaide, November 25, 26, 27, 28. South Australia won by five wickets. Queensland* 330 (T. J. Barsby 79, M. L. Hayden 165, Extras 30; B. N. Wigney three for 78, D. A. Reeves three for 52) and 351 for four dec. (T. J. Barsby 129, M. L. Hayden 116, G. I. Foley 43 not out, S. G. Law 38); South Australia 420 (P. C. Nobes 140, J. D. Siddons 46, D. S. Lehmann 38, D. S. Webber 100, Extras 40) and 262 for five (P. C. Nobes 106, D. S. Lehmann 50; S. G. Law three for 42). *South Australia 6 pts.*

At Hobart, December 10, 11, 12, 13. Drawn. Tasmania* 328 (D. F. Hills 71, R. J. Tucker 107, M. N. Atkinson 47; S. H. Cook four for 84, D. W. Fleming three for 77) and 308 for six dec. (D. F. Hills 59, R. T. Ponting 66, S. Young 49, R. J. Tucker 32 not out; C. Howard five for 112); Victoria 329 for three dec. (D. M. Jones 158 not out, B. J. Hodge 106) and 267 for eight (D. J. Ramshaw 53, D. M. Jones 60, B. J. Hodge 38, A. I. C. Dodemaide 32). *Victoria 2 pts.*

At Perth, December 10, 11. Western Australia won by an innings and 253 runs. Western Australia 503 for eight dec. (G. R. Marsh 128, D. R. Martyn 197, T. M. Moody 68, Extras 53; P. J. S. Alley five for 101): New South Wales* 73 (J. Angel three for 25, B. P. Julian five for 34) and 177 (M. G. Bevan 50, R. J. Green 32, P. A. Emery 33 not out; J. Angel five for 57, B. P. Julian three for 45). *Western Australia 6 pts.*

The first two-day Shield match since March 1976. NSW were bowled out twice in a day for the first time since 1882-83.

At Sydney, December 18, 19, 20, 21. Drawn. Victoria* 264 (W. N. Phillips 57, B. J. Hodge 57, D. J. Ramshaw 40, I. J. Harvey 37; W. J. Holdsworth three for 73, G. D. McGrath four for 60) and 324 for six dec. (D. M. Jones 155, B. J. Hodge 33, D. J. Ramshaw 80); New South Wales 283 (P. A. Emery 31, M. E. Waugh 119, B. E. McNamara 44; D. W. Fleming three for 63, S. K. Warne five for 77) and 275 for nine (M. G. Bevan 81, R. Chee Quee 76; P. R. Reiffel four for 68, S. K. Warne three for 90). *New South Wales 2 pts.*

At Perth, December 18, 19, 20. Western Australia won by nine wickets. South Australia* 179 (D. S. Webber 58; J. Angel three for 30, T. M. Moody four for 43) and 283 (J. A. Brayshaw 39, J. D. Siddons 129, T. J. Nielsen 33; J. Angel five for 59, D. R. Martyn three for 29); Western Australia 304 (M. R. J. Veletta 40, J. L. Langer 34, T. M. Moody 65, T. J. Zoehrer 30, Extras 35; S. P. George three for 54, T. B. A. May three for 96) and 160 for one (G. R. Marsh 62 not out, J. L. Langer 90 not out). *Western Australia 6 pts.*

At Brisbane, December 31, January 1, 2, 3. Drawn. Queensland 245 (S. G. Law 43, M. S. Kasprowicz 35, Extras 33; C. R. Miller three for 41, S. Young three for 38) and 339 for six dec. (G. I. Foley 45, M. L. Love 138, M. L. Hayden 121 not out); Tasmania* 190 (S. Young 55, R. J. Tucker 41; M. S. Kasprowicz four for 56) and 329 for seven (R. T. Ponting 64, S. Young 31, D. J. Buckingham 77, R. J. Tucker 44 not out, M. N. Atkinson 40 not out; C. G. Rackemann three for 81). *Queensland 2 pts.*

At Adelaide, December 31, January 1, 2, 3. New South Wales won by 109 runs. New South Wales* 395 for nine dec. (R. J. Davison 56, S. R. Waugh 73, M. G. Bevan 103, N. D. Maxwell 61, P. A. Emery 35; S. P. George five for 102) and 337 (R. Chee Quee 47, S. R. Waugh 46, M. G. Bevan 89, B. E. McNamara 47, N. D. Maxwell 42, A. E. Tucker 36; S. P. George three for 31, P. E. McIntyre three for 128); South Australia 465 for eight dec. (G. S. Blewett 93, P. C. Nobes 78, J. A. Brayshaw 36, J. D. Siddons 64, D. S. Lehmann 85, T. J. Nielsen 34 not out, Extras 42; G. R. Robertson three for 83) and 158 (J. D. Siddons 31, D. S. Webber 30; G. R. Robertson five for 43, N. D. Maxwell three for 27). *New South Wales 6 pts, South Australia 2 pts.*

At Adelaide, January 7, 8, 9, 10. Drawn. Western Australia 446 for seven dec. (M. R. J. Veletta 75, G. R. Marsh 98, J. L. Langer 96, T. M. Moody 58, D. A. Fitzgerald 35, T. J. Zoehrer 37 not out; S. P. George three for 120, D. J. Marsh three for 65) and 174 for three (G. R. Marsh 32, J. L. Langer 56 not out, T. M. Moody 38); South Australia* 437 (J. A. Brayshaw 146, D. S. Lehmann 200; B. P. Julian four for 108, D. J. Spencer four for 85). *Western Australia 1.8 pts.*

Lehmann's 200 lasted 277 minutes and 212 balls and included 30 fours and one six.

At Hobart, January 7, 8, 9, 10. Tasmania won by four wickets. New South Wales* 398 (S. R. Waugh 190 not out, M. G. Bevan 71, N. D. Maxwell 35, G. R. Robertson 42; C. R. Miller seven for 83) and 296 for four dec. (M. J. Slater 107, M. G. Bevan 117 not out, N. D. Maxwell 30 not out); Tasmania 401 for six dec. (D. F. Hills 158 not out, M. J. Di Venuto 42, D. J. Buckingham 52, R. J. Tucker 42, M. N. Atkinson 44 not out, Extras 41; P. J. S. Alley three for 84) and 294 for six (D. F. Hills 68, N. C. P. Courtney 31, D. J. Buckingham 88 not out, M. N. Atkinson 40 not out). *Tasmania 6 pts.*

At Brisbane, January 13, 14, 15, 16. Queensland won by 194 runs. Queensland 347 (T. J. Barsby 44, M. L. Hayden 126, M. L. Love 50, J. P. Maher 70; M. G. Hughes five for 70, A. I. C. Dodemaide three for 74) and 331 for six dec. (T. J. Barsby 58, M. L. Hayden 155, S. G. Law 76); Victoria* 272 (W. N. Phillips 47, G. J. Allardice 86, D. J. Ramshaw 41, A. I. C. Dodemaide 34; M. S. Kasprowicz four for 76, A. J. Bichel four for 69) and 212 (B. J. Hodge 64, A. I. C. Dodemaide 35; C. G. Rackemann five for 32). *Queensland 6 pts.*

Hayden scored two centuries in a match for the second time in a season and took his sequence to six centuries in seven innings.

At Hobart, January 18, 19, 20, 21. Tasmania won by four wickets. South Australia* 519 (G. S. Blewett 51, J. A. Brayshaw 47, J. D. Siddons 161, D. S. Lehmann 137, D. J. Marsh 48 not out, S. P. George 30; C. R. Miller four for 108, S. Herzberg three for 133) and 209 for three dec. (J. A. Brayshaw 37, J. D. Siddons 89 not out, D. S. Webber 44 not out); Tasmania 401 for eight dec. (D. F. Hills 63, S. Young 124 not out, D. J. Buckingham 57, M. N. Atkinson 45; S. P. George three for 96) and 329 for six (M. J. Di Venuto 112, R. T. Ponting 40, S. Young 48, D. J. Buckingham 37, R. J. Tucker 33 not out; D. J. Marsh three for 74). *Tasmania 6 pts, South Australia 2 pts.*

At Brisbane, January 19, 20, 21, 22. Drawn. Queensland 244 (T. J. Barsby 46, S. G. Law 118; J. Angel four for 64, B. P. Julian three for 52) and 375 for eight (J. M. Thomas 30, M. L. Love 119, J. P. Maher 122, A. J. Bichel 37, M. S. Kasprowicz 33); Western Australia* 413 (M. R. J. Veletta 80 retired hurt, J. L. Langer 89, D. R. Martyn 30, T. J. Zoehrer 69, J. Angel 52, D. J. Spencer 38; P. W. Jackson three for 118, G. I. Foley three for 64). *Western Australia 2 pts.*

At Melbourne, January 28, 29, 30, 31. Drawn. Victoria* 377 for nine dec. (M. T. G. Elliott 72, D. M. Jones 145, B. J. Hodge 49, G. J. Allardice 41, A. I. C. Dodemaide 33; S. P. George three for 38) and 337 for one dec. (W. N. Phillips 156 not out, D. M. Jones 152 not out); South Australia 499 (G. S. Blewett 268, P. C. Nobes 43, J. D. Siddons 46, D. S. Lehmann 86; D. W. Fleming four for 130, C. Howard four for 144) and 177 for eight (D. S. Lehmann 67, D. S. Webber 35; D. W. Fleming four for 65). *South Australia 2 pts.*

Blewett's 268 lasted 496 minutes and 389 balls and included 38 fours.

At Sydney, February 2, 3, 4, 5. New South Wales won by nine wickets. Western Australia* 379 (M. R. J. Veletta 71, T. M. Moody 115, J. Angel 84 not out; N. D. Maxwell three for 47) and 135 (T. M. Moody 33, B. P. Julian 36; N. D. Maxwell three for 21, G. R. Robertson five for 71); New South Wales 409 (R. Chee Quee 32, R. J. Davison 56, M. G. Bevan 203 not out, P. A. Emery 50; J. Angel three for 87, W. K. Wishart four for 90) and 106 for one (R. J. Davison 49 not out, R. Chee Quee 50). *New South Wales 6 pts.*

Bevan's 203 lasted 490 minutes and 409 balls and included 17 fours.*

At Hobart, February 10, 11, 12, 13. Drawn. Queensland 339 (J. M. Thomas 38, J. P. Maher 43, G. I. Foley 52, W. A. Seccombe 37, A. J. Bichel 61 not out, C. G. Rackemann 33, Extras 31; S. Young three for 66) and 208 for nine dec. (J. P. Maher 89, G. I. Foley 31; C. R. Miller four for 56); Tasmania* 248 (R. T. Ponting 49, S. Young 68, Extras 32; A. J. Bichel three for 31, D. Tazelaar five for 49) and 293 for six (D. F. Hills 91, J. Cox 81, M. J. Di Venuto 34; C. G. Rackemann four for 72). *Queensland 2 pts.*

At Sydney, February 16, 17, 18. New South Wales won by an innings and 70 runs. New South Wales* 391 (R. Chee Quee 58, M. G. Bevan 67, M. T. Haywood 39, B. E. McNamara 59, N. D. Maxwell 75; S. P. George four for 88, P. E. McIntyre three for 123); South Australia 123 (P. J. S. Alley three for 45, N. D. Maxwell four for 31) and 198 (G. S. Blewett 90, J. A. Brayshaw 37; G. R. Robertson six for 54). *New South Wales 6 pts.*

At Melbourne, February 17, 18, 19, 20. Drawn. Tasmania* 444 for nine dec. (J. Cox 32, M. J. Di Venuto 89, R. T. Ponting 42, D. J. Buckingham 71, R. J. Tucker 57, M. N. Atkinson 43 not out, C. D. Matthews 75; S. H. Cook four for 114) and 213 for two dec. (D. F. Hills 52, J. Cox 103 not out); Victoria 331 (W. N. Phillips 130, G. J. Allardice 42, B. J. Hodge 62; S. Young four for 85, R. J. Tucker four for 56) and 236 for nine (G. J. Allardice 65, B. J. Hodge 72; C. R. Miller three for 44, S. Herzberg four for 66). *Tasmania 2 pts.*

At Melbourne, February 24, 25, 26, 27. Victoria won by three runs. Victoria 242 (M. T. G. Elliott 30, W. N. Phillips 41, D. J. Ramshaw 33, I. A. Wrigglesworth 58; C. G. Rackemann three for 57, P. W. Jackson three for 75) and 250 (M. T. G. Elliott 113, B. J. Hodge 32; D. Tazelaar three for 54, C. G. Rackemann four for 38); Queensland* 275 (J. M. Thomas 34, G. I. Foley 89, W. A. Seccombe 95; D. W. Fleming five for 61, I. A. Wrigglesworth three for 72) and 214 (S. G. Law 58, J. P. Maher 90; S. M. McCooke six for 35). *Victoria 5.6 pts, Queensland 2 pts.*

At Perth, February 24, 25, 26, 27. Drawn. Western Australia 454 (M. R. J. Veletta 66, J. L. Langer 233, D. R. Martyn 41, G. B. Hogg 44, Extras 30; C. R. Miller three for 87, M. W. Ridgway four for 127) and 286 for six dec. (G. R. Marsh 81, D. R. Martyn 58, T. M. Moody 39, G. B. Hogg 33 not out); Tasmania* 487 for four dec. (J. Cox 129, M. J. Di Venuto 31, R. T. Ponting 101, S. Young 73 not out, D. J. Buckingham 100 not out) and 53 for one (J. Cox 35 not out). *Tasmania 2 pts.*

Langer's 233 lasted 408 minutes and 314 balls and included 27 fours and one six.

At Sydney, March 17, 18, 19, 20. New South Wales won by 51 runs. New South Wales 412 for six dec. (R. J. Davison 81, M. G. Bevan 50, S. Lee 104 not out, B. E. McNamara 51, D. A. Freedman 50; A. J. Bichel three for 89) and 207 for four dec. (R. J. Davison 42, R. Chee Quee 40, M. G. Bevan 69 not out); Queensland* 200 (W. A. Seccombe 37, A. J. Bichel 47; N. D. Maxwell four for 45) and 368 (T. J. Barsby 36, G. I. Foley 68, S. G. Law 108, J. P. Maher 44; N. D. Maxwell three for 54, G. R. Robertson three for 111). *New South Wales 6 pts.*

At Adelaide, March 17, 18, 19, 20. Tasmania won by four wickets. South Australia* 489 (G. S. Blewett 214, P. C. Nobes 54, D. S. Lehmann 157; C. R. Miller five for 82, M. G. Farrell three for 93) and 246 for six dec. (G. S. Blewett 80, M. P. Faull 66, P. C. Nobes 35, D. S. Lehmann 37; B. A. Robinson three for 75); Tasmania 370 for five dec. (D. F. Hills 114, J. Cox 98, R. T. Ponting 84 not out; P. E. McIntyre three for 75) and 366 for six (D. F. Hills 126, R. T. Ponting 161; P. E. McIntyre four for 97). *Tasmania 6 pts, South Australia 2 pts.*

At Perth, March 17, 18, 19. Western Australia won by three wickets. Victoria 118 (B. J. Hodge 43 not out; B. A. Reid three for 34, T. M. Moody three for 32) and 155 (G. J. Allardice 53; B. A. Reid five for 34, J. Angel three for 47); Western Australia* 112 (G. R. Marsh 42; D. W. Fleming five for 34, S. H. Cook four for 41) and 162 for seven (J. L. Langer 34; S. H. Cook four for 43). *Western Australia 6 pts, Victoria 1.4 pts.*

Blewett's 214 lasted 412 minutes and 363 balls and included 20 fours and a six.

FINAL

NEW SOUTH WALES v TASMANIA

At Sydney, March 25, 26, 27, 28, 29. New South Wales won by an innings and 61 runs. Toss: Tasmania.

What faint hopes Tasmania might have had of winning their first Sheffield Shield disappeared on the first morning when they lost their four best batsmen in 27 minutes while moving from 47 to 52. Thanks to a fine partnership between Young and Tucker, they recovered to 230 for six by the close but the last four men were soon out next morning. They had wasted their chance; Maxwell and McNamara bowled well enough, but the pitch was flat and the other New South Wales bowlers quite prodigal. The rest of the second day belonged to Bevan, who stroked his way to an enchanting hundred. It was his fifth of the season and Haywood responded with an important innings of 73. When Bevan was out, McNamara took control. The third day produced 177 runs off 97 overs as McNamara set out to score his maiden hundred, in his fifth season. It took him seven hours and cost him a painful crack on the head – he wore no helmet – when he missed a hook off Miller. However his batting – following his four wickets, one catch and a run-out – knocked the fight out of the Tasmanians, whose second innings showed it. Alley got the best figures, with his usual mixture of good and bad deliveries, but Maxwell was on the mark again and McNamara capped his performance with two splendid slip catches.

Close of play: First day, Tasmania 230-6 (M. N. Atkinson 38*, M. G. Farrell 14*); Second day, New South Wales 204-2 (M. G. Bevan 102*, M. T. Haywood 39*); Third day, New South Wales 381-8 (B. E. McNamara 91*, D. A. Freedman 3*); Fourth day, Tasmania 92-5 (S. Young 4*, R. J. Tucker 0*).

Tasmania

D. F. Hills c Emery b McNamara	20	– c Chee Quee b Robertson	17
J. Cox c McNamara b Maxwell	23	– lbw b Maxwell	11
M. J. Di Venuto c Emery b Maxwell	4	– b Alley	27
R. T. Ponting b McNamara	1	– c Davison b Alley	28
S. Young b Alley	62	– b Maxwell	9
*R. J. Tucker run out	49	– (7) c Emery b Alley	2
†M. N. Atkinson run out	44	– (8) not out	3
M. G. Farrell c Maxwell b McNamara	18	– (9) c McNamara b Maxwell	1
C. D. Matthews c Emery b Maxwell	0	– (10) b Alley	5
B. A. Robinson not out	1	– (6) c Emery b Maxwell	0
C. R. Miller c Bevan b McNamara	4	– c McNamara b Alley	10
B 4, l-b 5, w 8, n-b 12	29	B 2, l-b 1, w 8, n-b 2	13
1/47 2/51 3/52 4/52 5/152 6/201 7/243 8/246 9/249	255	1/17 2/43 3/80 4/89 5/92 6/103 7/105 8/107 9/116	126

Bowling: *First Innings*—Alley 19–3–51–1; Lee 10–1–49–0; Maxwell 32–12–61–3; McNamara 24.2–13–24–4; Robertson 20–6–42–0; Freedman 6–0–19–0. *Second Innings*—Maxwell 21–3–50–4; Robertson 16–5–34–1; McNamara 8–4–15–0; Alley 12.2–4–24–5.

New South Wales

R. Chee Quee c Ponting b Tucker 43	G. R. Robertson b Robinson 5
R. J. Davison c Atkinson b Matthews.. 5	D. A. Freedman run out 5
M. G. Bevan b Young...............113	P. J. S. Alley not out................ 17
M. T. Haywood c Cox b Matthews 73	
S. Lee c Di Venuto b Young 0	B 4, l-b 15, w 1, n-b 16 36
B. E. McNamara lbw b Robinson 128	
N. D. Maxwell c Ponting b Young 15	1/30 2/77 3/229 4/233 5/269 442
*†P. A. Emery c Atkinson b Tucker ... 2	6/311 7/337 8/360 9/383

Bowling: Miller 36–10–99–0; Matthews 40–12–99–2; Young 36–14–65–3; Tucker 28–13–47–2; Robinson 44.3–19–84–2; Farrell 12–3–26–0; Ponting 1–0–3–0.

Umpires: D. B. Hair, T. A. Prue and S. G. Randell.

SHEFFIELD SHIELD WINNERS

1892-93	Victoria	1947-48	Western Australia
1893-94	South Australia	1948-49	New South Wales
1894-95	Victoria	1949-50	New South Wales
1895-96	New South Wales	1950-51	Victoria
1896-97	New South Wales	1951-52	New South Wales
1897-98	Victoria	1952-53	South Australia
1898-99	Victoria	1953-54	New South Wales
1899-1900	New South Wales	1954-55	New South Wales
1900-01	Victoria	1955-56	New South Wales
1901-02	New South Wales	1956-57	New South Wales
1902-03	New South Wales	1957-58	New South Wales
1903-04	New South Wales	1958-59	New South Wales
1904-05	New South Wales	1959-60	New South Wales
1905-06	New South Wales	1960-61	New South Wales
1906-07	New South Wales	1961-62	New South Wales
1907-08	Victoria	1962-63	Victoria
1908-09	New South Wales	1963-64	South Australia
1909-10	South Australia	1964-65	New South Wales
1910-11	New South Wales	1965-66	New South Wales
1911-12	New South Wales	1966-67	Victoria
1912-13	South Australia	1967-68	Western Australia
1913-14	New South Wales	1968-69	South Australia
1914-15	Victoria	1969-70	Victoria
1915-19	No competition	1970-71	South Australia
1919-20	New South Wales	1971-72	Western Australia
1920-21	New South Wales	1972-73	Western Australia
1921-22	Victoria	1973-74	Victoria
1922-23	New South Wales	1974-75	Western Australia
1923-24	Victoria	1975-76	South Australia
1924-25	Victoria	1976-77	Western Australia
1925-26	New South Wales	1977-78	Western Australia
1926-27	South Australia	1978-79	Victoria
1927-28	Victoria	1979-80	Victoria
1928-29	New South Wales	1980-81	Western Australia
1929-30	Victoria	1981-82	South Australia
1930-31	Victoria	1982-83	New South Wales
1931-32	New South Wales	1983-84	Western Australia
1932-33	New South Wales	1984-85	New South Wales
1933-34	Victoria	1985-86	New South Wales
1934-35	Victoria	1986-87	Western Australia
1935-36	South Australia	1987-88	Western Australia
1936-37	Victoria	1988-89	Western Australia
1937-38	New South Wales	1989-90	New South Wales
1938-39	South Australia	1990-91	Victoria
1939-40	New South Wales	1991-92	Western Australia
1940-46	No competition	1992-93	New South Wales
1946-47	Victoria	1993-94	New South Wales

New South Wales have won the Shield 42 times, Victoria 25, Western Australia 13, South Australia 12, Queensland 0, Tasmania 0.

MERCANTILE MUTUAL INSURANCE CUP

Note: Matches in this section were not first-class.

At Perth, October 9. Western Australia won by 21 runs. Western Australia 281 for four (50 overs) (M. W. McPhee 97, G. R. Marsh 55, D. R. Martyn 54, T. M. Moody 31, J. L. Langer 34 not out); South Australia* 260 for nine (50 overs) (G. S. Blewett 40, P. C. Nobes 60, J. A. Brayshaw 35, J. D. Siddons 40; J. Angel three for 47).

At Brisbane, October 10. New South Wales won by 127 runs. New South Wales 278 for four (50 overs) (M. A. Taylor 55, M. J. Slater 96, S. R. Waugh 59, M. E. Waugh 33); Queensland* 151 (36.4 overs) (M. L. Hayden 31, D. M. Wellham 49, M. L. Love 31 not out; G. D. McGrath four for 17).

At Perth, October 15 (day/night). Western Australia won by two wickets. Tasmania 208 for six (50 overs) (D. F. Hills 68, D. C. Boon 45); Western Australia* 209 for eight (50 overs) (G. R. Marsh 56, T. M. Moody 41, J. L. Langer 42).

At Melbourne, October 17. Queensland won by seven wickets. Victoria* 224 for four (50 overs) (D. M. Jones 68, D. J. Ramshaw 82); Queensland 225 for three (46.3 overs) (D. M. Wellham 70, S. G. Law 107 not out).

At North Sydney, October 24. New South Wales won by 59 runs. New South Wales 307 for seven (50 overs) (S. R. Waugh 35, M. E. Waugh 68, R. Chee Quee 56, W. J. Holdsworth 49 not out); Tasmania* 248 for eight (50 overs) (D. F. Hills 59, D. C. Boon 52, M. J. Di Venuto 34 not out; G. R. J. Matthews three for 44).

At Adelaide, October 31. Victoria won by seven wickets. South Australia 226 for four (50 overs) (G. S. Blewett 48, J. D. Siddons 90 not out, D. S. Webber 43 not out); Victoria* 227 for three (46.4 overs) (D. S. Berry 34, D. M. Jones 95 not out, D. J. Ramshaw 36, B. J. Hodge 43 not out).

At Brisbane, November 21. Queensland won by 92 runs. Queensland 320 for four (50 overs) (M. L. Hayden 110, S. G. Law 159); Tasmania* 228 for seven (50 overs) (D. C. Boon 56, R. T. Ponting 36, D. J. Buckingham 61; P. W. Jackson three for 51).

At Hobart, January 22. South Australia won by four wickets. Tasmania* 240 for six (50 overs) (D. F. Hills 64, D. J. Buckingham 42, S. Young 42; B. N. Wigney three for 47); South Australia 243 for six (47.4 overs) (D. S. Lehmann 34, P. C. Nobes 64, J. D. Siddons 32, G. S. Blewett 38 not out, T. J. Nielsen 36).

At Brisbane, January 23. Queensland won by 29 runs. Queensland* 283 for six (50 overs) (J. M. Thomas 71, S. G. Law 114, J. P. Maher 38 not out); Western Australia 254 (48.2 overs) (G. R. Marsh 95, D. R. Martyn 53, T. J. Zoehrer 30, R. S. Russell 34; S. G. Law four for 33).

At Hobart, February 5. Tasmania won by seven wickets. Victoria* 162 (47.5 overs) (D. J. Ramshaw 32; C. D. Matthews four for 31); Tasmania 164 for three (38.5 overs) (D. F. Hills 46, R. J. Tucker 31, M. J. Di Venuto 44, R. T. Ponting 31 not out).

At Sydney, February 6. New South Wales won by six wickets. Western Australia* 162 (49.1 overs) (B. P. Julian 39); New South Wales 163 for four (45.5 overs) (R. Chee Quee 66, M. G. Bevan 64 not out; J. Stewart three for 42).

At Adelaide, February 6. South Australia won by ten wickets. Queensland 119 (40.3 overs) (T. J. Barsby 37); South Australia* 120 for no wkt (28 overs) (D. S. Lehmann 76 not out, P. C. Nobes 37 not out).

At Melbourne, February 11 (day/night). Western Australia won by 50 runs. Western Australia 173 for seven (40 overs) (D. R. Martyn 36, T. J. Zoehrer 48 not out; I. J. Harvey three for 36); Victoria* 123 (37.5 overs) (D. J. Ramshaw 52; J. Stewart three for 32).

At Melbourne, February 13. New South Wales won by four wickets. Victoria* 183 (48.2 overs) (W. N. Phillips 46, I. J. Harvey 35, D. A. Harris 33; B. E. McNamara three for 25); New South Wales 184 for six (49.1 overs) (R. J. Davison 51).

At Sydney, February 20. South Australia won by three wickets, their target having been revised to 216 from 45 overs. New South Wales* 225 for eight (50 overs) (R. Chee Quee 55, M. G. Bevan 38, S. Lee 44); South Australia 218 for seven (44.2 overs) (D. S. Lehmann 40, G. S. Blewett 80 not out, J. D. Siddons 37).

Qualifying Final

At Adelaide, March 5. Western Australia won by 51 runs. Western Australia 248 for seven (50 overs) (T. M. Moody 69, G. R. Marsh 43, D. R. Martyn 50 not out, M. R. J. Veletta 32); South Australia* 197 (45.3 overs) (J. D. Siddons 39, J. A. Brayshaw 41, D. S. Webber 30; J. Stewart three for 51).

FINAL

NEW SOUTH WALES v WESTERN AUSTRALIA

At Sydney, March 12. New South Wales won by 43 runs, Western Australia's target having been revised to 262 from 49 overs. Toss: New South Wales.

Man of the Match: R. Chee Quee.

New South Wales

R. Chee Quee b Martyn	131
M. T. Haywood run out	4
M. G. Bevan c Martyn b Angel	77
T. H. Bayliss not out	36
S. Lee b Martyn	4
N. D. Maxwell not out	7
L-b 5	5
1/13 2/212 3/226 4/242 (4 wkts, 50 overs)	264

B. E. McNamara, *†P. A. Emery, G. R. Robertson, W. J. Holdsworth and P. J. S. Alley did not bat.

Bowling: Angel 10–0–40–1; Atkinson 10–0–47–0; Julian 10–0–42–0; Moody 6–0–46–0; Stewart 10–0–53–0; Martyn 4–0–31–2.

Western Australia

T. M. Moody c Alley b Maxwell	12
*G. R. Marsh lbw b Holdsworth	11
J. L. Langer c Maxwell b Lee	65
D. R. Martyn c McNamara b Alley	0
M. R. J. Veletta lbw b McNamara	1
G. B. Hogg run out	5
B. P. Julian c Lee b Robertson	19
†T. J. Zoehrer b McNamara	61
M. P. Atkinson c Maxwell b Robertson	10
J. Angel not out	19
J. Stewart not out	1
L-b 9, w 1, n-b 4	14
1/16 2/39 3/43 4/52 5/73 6/109 7/126 8/172 9/209 (9 wkts, 49 overs)	218

Bowling: Holdsworth 10–0–39–1; Maxwell 6–0–23–1; McNamara 10–0–39–2; Alley 10–0–34–1; Robertson 10–0–56–2; Lee 3–0–18–1.

Umpires: D. B. Hair and S. G. Randell.

SHEFFIELD SHIELD PLAYER OF THE YEAR

The Sheffield Shield Player of the Year Award for 1993-94 was won by Matthew Hayden of Queensland. The award, instituted in 1975-76, is adjudicated by the umpires over the course of the season. Each of the three umpires standing in each of the 30 Sheffield Shield matches during 1993-94 (excluding the final) allocated marks of 3, 2 and 1 to the three players who most impressed them during the game. Hayden earned 30 votes in his six matches, one ahead of Michael Bevan of New South Wales.

CRICKET IN SOUTH AFRICA, 1993-94

By COLIN BRYDEN and FRANK HEYDENRYCH

The summer of 1993-94 featured tall scores, uneven performances and a remarkable triumph by Orange Free State.

The domestic programme was more cohesive than in the previous season, when the local game was relegated to a distant second place behind international fixtures. Whereas India, West Indies and Pakistan had visited South Africa in their first home season after readmission to the Test arena, this time there was only one Test side, Australia, and that was towards the end of the summer. But as that tour followed straight on from the national team's three-month absence in India and Australia, the provinces saw even less of their leading players than in 1992-93.

For those left behind, there was an expanded Castle Cup competition, with Boland being promoted, and a tour by England A, who played first-class matches against all the senior provinces except Boland. Limited-overs cricket was rationalised, with the demise of the daytime knockout competition, launched in 1969-70. It had literally paled in the eyes of the public compared to the bright colours and floodlights of the Benson and Hedges Series, initiated in 1981-82.

The season began with a record and a controversy, fully two weeks before the time-honoured official start of the summer game. In mid-September, at the seldom-used first-class venue of Worcester in the Western Cape winelands, Boland played hosts to their neighbours, Western Province, in a friendly match. On a perfect batting pitch, Terence Lazard, recently of Western Province but now the Boland captain, scored a monumental 307 not out. This bettered the South African record held by Eric Rowan since 1939-40, when he made 306 not out for Transvaal against Natal at the old Wanderers. Questions were immediately asked about the status of the match. Apart from Eric Simons, Western Province's front-line bowlers were elsewhere – on Test duty in Sri Lanka, at a training camp or injured. The United Cricket Board of South Africa nevertheless ruled the match first-class, as a three-day fixture between the best available players of the two provinces, and Lazard was confirmed as the new record-holder.

His triumph lasted only five weeks, however, until Daryll Cullinan of Transvaal played a remarkable innings in a Castle Cup match at the Wanderers. Replying to a Northern Transvaal total of 517 for eight declared, in which the Guyanese left-hander, Clayton Lambert, made 214 on his provincial debut, Transvaal were in trouble at 23 for three. Cullinan and Jimmy Cook then joined forces. They put on 283 before Cook was dismissed and Cullinan batted on relentlessly against a high-quality pace attack, spearheaded by international bowlers Fanie de Villiers and Tertius Bosch. Cullinan could not afford to lose concentration, as seven men were out with Transvaal still 49 behind; only when first-innings points were secured could he enjoy the luxury of record-hunting. He passed Allan Lamb's Cup record of 294, for Orange Free State in 1987-88, and then surged to 337 not out, without having offered a chance. This time there could be no doubting the record's validity. Sadly, Cullinan was unable to take this form to Australia when he toured with the national team.

In addition to these two triple-centuries, there were four double-hundreds, including Lambert's; John Crawley made 286 for England A against Eastern Province, while Peter Kirsten piled up a career-best 271 for Border, on the eve of his call-up to replace the injured Kepler Wessels in Australia. And when the Australians arrived for the return trip, Hansie Cronje went on the rampage for Orange Free State against the tourists, hitting 251 in a total of 396 all out.

Such astounding individual performances were a rarity, however. And when the national selectors sat down to pick a South Africa A team to oppose the English tourists, they were hard put to find top-order batsmen with solid current form. Indeed, the most consistent batsman was the 40-year-old Jimmy Cook, who hit four centuries in six Castle Cup matches, amassing 669 runs at an average of 83.62. Having failed in Sri Lanka to rekindle his brief international career, Cook gained some recognition for his efforts when he was named captain of South Africa A. Although his team performed adequately against England A, administrators expressed serious concern about the depth of talent at first-class level. This was hardly surprising with the leading players out of the country and the remaining talent dispersed across eight senior provincial teams. Before 1985-86, the top competition was contested by only five teams, which made the rivalry, especially in the years of isolation, very fierce.

For the time being, the United Board is committed to a broad base, at first-class level, not least to provide more openings for black players. To strengthen the pool, however, it decided to introduce an academy system similar to that in Australia. From 1995 a group of young players will live on the Rand Afrikaans University campus in Johannesburg and spend between six and nine months polishing their cricket skills.

Orange Free State retained the Castle Cup, which they had won for the first time in 1992-93. As in the previous season, they won their last match and then saw their nearest rivals – Western Province, this time – falter at the last hurdle, though they had an agonising two-week wait. It was a noble effort by a team with one of the smallest player bases in the country, especially as their captain, Cronje, and strike bowler Allan Donald were rarely available. Corrie van Zyl again proved an able deputy for Cronje, while Jack Birkenshaw, in his first season as coach, fitted comfortably into the tight-knit family that is Free State cricket. Rudolf Steyn and Gerhardus Liebenberg shone with the bat, but the star was the Barbadian all-rounder Franklyn Stephenson, who scored 420 runs and took 29 wickets in seven matches to be named Castle Cup Player of the Season. Free State also owed much to two young spin bowlers, left-armer Nicky Boje and off-spinner Kosie Venter, the former a serious international prospect and the latter an audacious batsman as well.

Western Province were trailing by four points when Free State finished their season and needed an outright win over Border to take the trophy. But they were firm favourites, fielding seven internationals (all available, as the Australians were playing Free State). After a poor first innings, Western Province batted much better the second time and set Border a target of 307. Nevertheless, Border pulled off a remarkable victory with their last two batsmen at the crease; it completed a glorious day for Cronje, who had just made his 251. For Western Province, it was a disappointing end to a season that had started with immense promise: Gary Kirsten was in outstanding form, which earned him a late call-up to the national team in Australia when Brian McMillan was injured. But he was the mainstay of an otherwise inconsistent batting line-up and although Meyrick Pringle, discarded by the selectors, topped the Castle Cup bowling averages and left-arm fast bowler Aubrey Martyn showed promise, Western Province could not overcome the loss of three bowlers to the national team. Eric Simons – the province's third captain of the season in the absence of Craig Matthews and Kirsten – had another outstanding season as a determined lower-order batsman and steady seam bowler and was deservedly picked for the one-day internationals against Australia.

Transvaal played below standard again. Their bowling lacked penetration, although left-arm spinner Clive Eksteen was the leading wicket-taker in the Castle Cup, with 32. Steven Jack failed to fulfil expectations until the last match of the season, when he ripped through Natal's second innings, taking six for 30. After Cullinan's departure, too much of the batting revolved around Cook. Eastern Province were ahead on first innings in their first five matches but gained only one outright win, in their final match, against Boland. Without Wessels and Dave Callaghan for most of the season, their batting was not as solid as in previous years. Eldine Baptiste, Tim Shaw and Ross Veenstra all enjoyed good days but seldom fired in unison.

Border could be proud of their effort in finishing fifth in the table. Peter Kirsten was prolific, scoring 685 runs for the province at 76.11, and the left-handed opener Andrew Lawson performed steadily in a more stable batting order. The bowling was inconsistent, although the 35-year-old left-arm slow bowler Ian Howell had one of his best seasons. Natal won only one match outright and suffered from inconsistent batting. The stand-in captain, Malcolm Marshall, was their most successful batsman, but the former West Indies Test star was less effective as a bowler. However, Neil Johnson, an all-rounder, and batsman Dale Benkenstein emerged as good prospects.

Newcomers Boland proved tougher opponents than most would have expected. The triple-centurion Lazard and John Commins provided the backbone of a surprisingly resilient batting order, while their two English imports, all-rounder Phillip DeFreitas and coach Bob Woolmer, both played important roles. Northern Transvaal again finished last and Roy Pienaar and Mike Rindel, expected to be heavy scorers, were both dropped towards the end of the season, while Lambert, who began with 214 and 137 in his first two matches, fell away markedly. Their wicket-keeper, Kevin Rule, had a golden spell early in the season, when he notched up successive scores of 122, 101 not out and 92 with thrilling strokeplay. But the chief let-down was the fast bowling, supposedly their strength. Once de Villiers joined the national team, only Steve Elworthy lived up to his reputation.

Orange Free State completed the double by winning the Benson and Hedges Series, beating Natal by seven wickets in a one-sided final at Kingsmead in Durban, with Donald and Bradley Player exploiting a seamers' pitch. It was the fourth time in five seasons that Natal had been beaten in the final, and the third time on their home ground.

After a one-season experiment when an Under-24 competition superseded the participation of the B teams of senior provinces in the Bowl, the B teams returned in force and with their first-class status renewed. Whether what is essentially a second-team competition should be deemed first-class continued to be a matter for debate. The eight B teams joined Griqualand

West, Eastern Transvaal, Western Transvaal and a Zimbabwe Board XI, and the competition was split into two sections of six. Within their groups, teams played each other once over three days and again in a limited-overs game. Western Province B and Transvaal B won their respective sections and met in the final at the Wanderers; although Transvaal achieved a 211-run lead on the first innings, Western Province B batted out the last day to earn a share of the honours. Western Province B also reached the one-day final but were convincingly beaten at Newlands by Orange Free State B, whose senior team had been in the Bowl themselves nine seasons earlier. – C.B.

FIRST-CLASS AVERAGES, 1993-94

BATTING

(Qualification: 8 innings, average 40.00)

	M	*I*	*NO*	*R*	*HS*	*100s*	*Avge*
C. J. van Heerden (*OFS*)	6	8	3	364	126*	1	72.80
W. J. Cronje (*OFS*)	7	13	0	870	251	4	66.92
T. N. Lazard (*Boland*)	9	16	3	853	307*	2	65.61
P. N. Kirsten (*Border*)	9	14	0	872	271	2	62.28
S. J. Cook (*Transvaal*)	8	14	2	745	136	4	62.08
M. D. Marshall (*Natal*)	8	11	4	420	120*	1	60.00
L. M. Germishuys (*Boland*)	8	13	4	493	108*	1	54.77
C. R. Norris (*E. Transvaal*)	5	9	1	434	78	0	54.25
G. Kirsten (*W. Province*)	7	12	0	650	192	2	54.16
M. P. Stonier (*Border*)	8	13	1	596	121	2	49.66
L. P. Vorster (*N. Transvaal*)	6	9	1	394	188	2	49.25
T. J. Mitchell (*W. Province B*)	5	8	2	289	90	0	48.16
A. C. Hudson (*Natal*)	7	13	0	622	102	1	47.84
R. A. Koster (*W. Province*)	6	9	2	332	95	0	47.42
J. F. Venter (*OFS*)	9	13	0	604	193	1	46.46
B. M. McMillan (*W. Province*)	6	9	0	414	116	1	46.00
P. J. R. Steyn (*OFS*)	9	18	3	688	90	0	45.86
H. H. Gibbs (*W. Province*)	6	12	2	456	152*	1	45.60
M. W. Rushmere (*Transvaal*)	9	14	2	546	188	1	45.50
J. B. Commins (*Boland*)	9	16	0	726	165	2	45.37
C. R. B. Armstrong (*Natal*)	7	9	1	361	97	0	45.12
P. A. J. DeFreitas (*Boland*)	7	11	1	451	103*	1	45.10
P. C. Strydom (*Border*)	6	8	1	313	117	1	44.71
D. J. Watson (*Natal*)	7	11	0	486	87	0	44.18
A. G. Lawson (*Border*)	8	13	1	522	110	1	43.50
G. Morgan (*E. Province*)	6	10	5	216	60*	0	43.20
P. M. Boa (*Transvaal*)	7	11	2	380	69	0	42.22
L. J. Wilkinson (*OFS*)	7	12	1	460	105	1	41.81
G. F. J. Liebenberg (*OFS*)	9	18	1	705	142	1	41.47
P. G. Amm (*E. Province*)	9	15	0	615	77	0	41.00
J. N. Rhodes (*Natal*)	6	11	0	450	114	1	40.90
K. J. Rule (*N. Transvaal*)	9	18	4	563	122	2	40.21

* *Signifies not out.*

BOWLING

(Qualification: 20 wickets)

	O	*M*	*R*	*W*	*BB*	*5W/i*	*Avge*
M. J. Vandrau (*Transvaal*)	217.1	67	476	26	5-42	2	18.30
M. P. Jarvis (*Zimbabwe Board XI*)	161.3	45	399	20	6-74	2	19.95
L. Klusener (*Natal*)	201.4	37	567	27	4-38	0	21.00
M. W. Pringle (*W Province*)	254.4	68	601	28	4-43	0	21.46
C. R. Matthews (*W. Province*)	214.3	64	456	21	5-80	1	21.71
B. C. Fourie (*Border*)	274.4	65	660	30	6-74	1	22.00
F. D. Stephenson (*OFS*)	306	79	715	32	4-57	0	22.34
A. G. Elgar (*Boland*)	195.1	73	475	21	4-83	0	22.61
M. Erasmus (*Boland*)	240.1	63	554	24	5-54	1	23.08
A. Badenhorst (*Border*)	233	46	650	27	5-52	1	24.07
A. Martyn (*W. Province*)	378.2	93	961	39	6-60	1	24.64
E. A. E. Baptiste (*E. Province*)	316.3	106	629	25	5-41	1	25.16
S. D. Jack (*Transvaal*)	304.2	57	864	33	6-30	1	26.18
T. G. Shaw (*E. Province*)	441.5	166	867	33	4-23	0	26.27
P. A. J. DeFreitas (*Boland*)	200.3	44	530	20	5-80	1	26.50
R. E. Veenstra (*E. Province*)	289	82	667	25	4-32	0	26.68
D. MacHelm (*W. Province*)	320.4	84	832	29	7-85	2	28.68
T. Bosch (*N. Transvaal*)	236.3	56	685	23	4-32	0	29.78
C. E. Eksteen (*Transvaal*)	462.4	150	1,014	34	7-29	2	29.82
M. R. Hobson (*Transvaal*)	216.5	27	780	26	7-61	1	30.00
I. L. Howell (*Border*)	411.4	145	830	27	5-72	1	30.74
N. Boje (*OFS*)	477.3	152	1,115	35	6-101	1	31.85
J. F. Venter (*OFS*)	181.4	34	661	20	5-14	2	33.05
C. van Noordwyk (*N. Transvaal*)	193.4	25	704	20	5-51	1	35.20
A. A. Donald (*OFS*)	246.1	42	780	22	4-32	0	35.45
A. G. Huckle (*E. Province*)	396.4	78	1,212	34	6-99	1	35.64
C. W. Henderson (*Boland*)	347.2	105	885	24	4-25	0	36.87
D. N. Crookes (*Natal*)	367.5	97	892	23	5-84	1	38.78
S. Elworthy (*N. Transvaal*)	300.5	60	971	25	4-55	0	38.84

CASTLE CUP, 1993-94

	Played	*Won*	*Lost*	*Drawn*	*1st-inns Points*	*Points*
Orange Free State	7	4	0	3	0	24
Western Province	7	3	2	2	2	20
Transvaal	7	2	1	4	4	16
Eastern Province	7	1	1	5	10	16
Border	7	2	2	3	2	14
Natal	7	1	2	4	6	12
Boland	7	1	3	3	4	10
Northern Transvaal	7	1	4	2	2	8

Outright win = 6 pts; lead on first innings in a drawn or lost game = 2 pts.

*In the following scores, * by the name of a team indicates that they won the toss.*

At Coetzenburg Oval, Stellenbosch, October 22, 23, 24, 25. Western Province won by ten wickets. Western Province* 366 (G. Kirsten 58, A. P. Kuiper 47, B. M. McMillan 116, D. B. Rundle 81; P. A. J. DeFreitas five for 80, M. Erasmus three for 59) and 73 for no wkt (F. B. Touzel 33 not out, D. Jordaan 39 not out); Boland 139 (T. N. Lazard 44; B. M. McMillan three for 32, D. B. Rundle three for 36) and 296 (W. N. van As 44, C. S. N. Marais 38, O. Henry 39, P. A. J. DeFreitas 54; D. MacHelm four for 74, A. Martyn three for 78). *Western Province 6 pts.*

At Kingsmead, Durban, October 22, 23, 24, 25. Drawn. Natal 359 (A. C. Hudson 37, N. E. Wright 72, J. N. Rhodes 43, E. L. R. Stewart 79; R. E. Veenstra three for 61, E. A. E. Baptiste three for 83) and 170 for five (A. C. Hudson 90, J. N. Rhodes 43; R. E. Veenstra three for 47); Eastern Province* 422 (M. C. Venter 31, P. G. Amm 59, K. C. Wessels 58, D. J. Callaghan 113, D. J. Richardson 67; P. L. Symcox three for 124). *Eastern Province 2 pts.*

At Springbok Park, Bloemfontein, October 22, 23, 24, 25. Orange Free State won by five wickets. Border* 323 (A. G. Lawson 110, P. N. Kirsten 36, B. M. Osborne 55, P. J. Botha 38; A. A. Donald four for 78, F. D. Stephenson three for 60) and 212 (P. N. Kirsten 46, G. C. Victor 74; A. A. Donald four for 32, N. Boje three for 46); Orange Free State 277 (J. M. Arthur 91, W. J. Cronje 74; O. D. Gibson four for 50) and 261 for five (G. F. J. Liebenberg 63, W. J. Cronje 38, L. J. Wilkinson 62, P. J. R. Steyn 63). *Orange Free State 6 pts, Border 2 pts.*

At Wanderers Stadium, Johannesburg, October 22, 23, 24, 25. Drawn. Northern Transvaal* 517 for eight dec. (C. B. Lambert 214, J. J. Strydom 109, R. F. Pienaar 73, Extras 53; C. E. Eksteen four for 144) and 159 for four (P. H. Barnard 89); Transvaal 602 for nine dec. (D. J. Cullinan 337 not out, S. J. Cook 102, N. Pothas 45, S. D. Jack 36; P. S. de Villiers four for 106). *Transvaal 2 pts.*

At Coetzenberg Oval, Stellenbosch, October 29, 30, 31, November 1. Drawn. Boland* 454 (T. N. Lazard 110, J. B. Commins 137, O. Henry 49, P. A. J. DeFreitas 63; S. D. Jack four for 119) and 328 for six dec. (C. P. Dettmer 93, W. S. Truter 110 not out, J. B. Commins 37, M. Erasmus 37 not out); Transvaal 351 (M. Yachad 30, S. Jacobs 37, S. J. Cook 119 not out, D. R. Laing 52, S. D. Jack 42; A. N. Newman five for 96). *Boland 2 pts.*

At St George's Park, Port Elizabeth, October 29, 30, 31, November 1. Drawn. Border* 322 (A. G. Lawson 86, B. M. Osborne 32, P. J. Botha 124; T. G. Shaw three for 85) and 342 for seven (P. N. Kirsten 181, M. P. Stonier 75; T. G. Shaw three for 93); Eastern Province 457 for nine dec. (P. G. Amm 34, K. C. Wessels 41, D. J. Callaghan 71, D. J. Richardson 128, E. A. E. Baptiste 97; O. D. Gibson three for 105). *Eastern Province 2 pts.*

At Centurion Park, Verwoerdburg, October 29, 30, 31, November 1. Western Province won by seven wickets. Western Province* 510 for seven dec. (G. Kirsten 192, C. A. Best 71, A. P. Kuiper 90, B. M. McMillan 34) and 67 for three (F. B. Touzel 36 not out); Northern Transvaal 210 (P. S. de Villiers 39; A. Martyn three for 36) and 366 (C. B. Lambert 137, R. F. Pienaar 42, K. J. Rule 122; G. Kirsten six for 68, M. W. Pringle four for 43). *Western Province 6 pts.*

At Springbok Park, Bloemfontein, October 29, 30, 31, November 1. Orange Free State won by 151 runs. Orange Free State 450 for eight dec. (J. M. Arthur 99, W. J. Cronje 150, L. J. Wilkinson 34, F. D. Stephenson 49) and 317 for four dec. (G. F. J. Liebenberg 142, W. J. Cronje 107, L. J. Wilkinson 38; P. W. E. Rawson three for 109); Natal* 435 (N. E. Wright 39, J. N. Rhodes 114, N. C. Johnson 95, M. D. Marshall 59 not out; F. D. Stephenson three for 73, N. Boje three for 83) and 181 (A. C. Hudson 36, E. L. R. Stewart 38, P. L. Symcox 34 not out). *Orange Free State 6 pts.*

At Buffalo Park, East London, November 25, 26, 27, 28. Drawn. Border* 392 (P. N. Kirsten 73, A. G. Lawson 60, F. J. C. Cronje 36, S. J. Palframan 132; N. C. Johnson five for 114, D. N. Crookes three for 132) and 152 for one (A. G. Lawson 68 not out, B. M. Osborne 58 not out); Natal 443 (C. R. B. Armstrong 37, N. E. Wright 32, C. E. B. Rice 59, N. C. Johnson 136, S. M. Pollock 56, Extras 40; I. L. Howell four for 123). *Natal 2 pts.*

At St George's Park, Port Elizabeth, November 25, 26, 27, 28. Western Province won by 65 runs. Western Province 188 (E. O. Simons 31; R. E. Veenstra four for 32) and 294 (G. Kirsten 116, A. P. Kuiper 53, E. O. Simons 40, Extras 44; E. A. E. Baptiste four for 43, T. G. Shaw three for 51); Eastern Province* 231 (P. G. Amm 64, M. Michau 32, E. A. E. Baptiste 58; A. Martyn four for 60) and 186 (P. G. Amm 36, M. Michau 32; A. C. Dawson three for 20, M. W. Pringle three for 37). *Western Province 6 pts, Eastern Province 2 pts.*

At Centurion Park, Verwoerdburg, November 25, 26, 27, 28. Northern Transvaal won by 111 runs. Northern Transvaal 274 (C. B. Lambert 37, V. F. du Preez 36, R. F. Pienaar 33, K. J. Rule 101 not out; M. Erasmus five for 54) and 258 (V. F. du Preez 35, R. F. Pienaar 42, K. J. Rule 92; C. W. Henderson three for 39, M. Erasmus three for 76); Boland* 149 (J. B. Commins 45, M. Erasmus 30; R. E. Bryson three for 35) and 272 (W. S. Truter 62, J. B. Commins 67, C. S. N. Marais 45; T. Bosch four for 32, S. Elworthy three for 68). *Northern Transvaal 6 pts.*

At Kingsmead, Durban, December 10, 11, 12, 13. Drawn. Western Province 300 (C. A. Best 63, E. O. Simons 96, A. C. Dawson 56; P. W. E. Rawson four for 29, M. D. Marshall three for 62) and 173 for six (C. A. Best 44, A. P. Kuiper 49); Natal* 429 (C. R. B. Armstrong 39, N. E. Wright 89, D. M. Benkenstein 50, M. D. Marshall 120 not out, D. N. Crookes 46, Extras 36; A. Martyn three for 91). *Natal 2 pts.*

At Springbok Park, Bloemfontein, December 10, 11, 12, 13. Drawn. Orange Free State 323 (P. J. R. Steyn 90, L. J. Wilkinson 72, F. D. Stephenson 42; P. A. J. DeFreitas four for 59) and 302 for six dec. (P. J. R. Steyn 40, F. D. Stephenson 95, J. F. Venter 76, C. J. P. G. van Zyl 41); Boland* 365 (K. C. Jackson 90, W. S. Truter 78, J. B. Commins 50, P. A. J. DeFreitas 52; N. Boje six for 101) and 139 for three (W. S. Truter 35, T. N. Lazard 32). *Boland 2 pts.*

At Buffalo Park, East London, December 26, 27, 28, 29. Drawn. Boland* 238 for four (T. N. Lazard 89 not out, P. A. J. DeFreitas 103 not out; A. Badenhorst three for 59) v Border.

At Kingsmead, Durban, December 26, 27, 28, 29. Natal won by 136 runs. Natal 346 (D. J. Watson 57, N. E. Wright 82, M. L. Bruyns 40, P. W. E. Rawson 46 not out; R. E. Bryson three for 64) and 91 for two dec. (C. R. B. Armstrong 48 not out, M. L. Bruyns 40 not out); Northern Transvaal* 103 for four dec. (M. D. Marshall three for 35) and 198 (R. F. Pienaar 30, M. J. R. Rindel 75; D. N. Crookes five for 84, N. C. Johnson three for 17). *Natal 6 pts.*

At Wanderers Stadium, Johannesburg, December 26, 27, 28, 29. Drawn. Eastern Province 160 (M. Michau 36; S. D. Jack four for 44, D. R. Laing three for 18) and 217 (P. G. Amm 37, M. Michau 52, E. A. E. Baptiste 60; M. R. Hobson seven for 61); Transvaal* 126 (E. A. E. Baptiste five for 41, S. C. Pope three for 12) and 218 for eight (B. M. White 59, M. D. Haysman 46; E. A. E. Baptiste three for 29, A. G. Huckle three for 71). *Eastern Province 2 pts.*

At Buffalo Park, East London, January 1, 2, 3, 4. Border won by an innings and 99 runs. Northern Transvaal* 146 (B. J. Sommerville 33, R. F. Pienaar 37; A. Badenhorst four for 26, B. C. Fourie three for 33, I. L. Howell three for 54) and 230 (B. J. Sommerville 40, R. F. Pienaar 32, K. J. Rule 69; I. L. Howell five for 72, P. C. Strydom three for 77); Border 475 for four dec. (P. N. Kirsten 271, A. G. Lawson 83, F. J. C. Cronje 42, P. C. Strydom 60 not out). *Border 6 pts.*

At St George's Park, Port Elizabeth, January 1, 2, 3, 4. Drawn. Orange Free State* 309 (F. D. Stephenson 53, J. F. Venter 55, C. J. P. G. van Zyl 51, B. T. Player 33, N. Boje 36; T. G. Shaw three for 79) and 251 for two dec. (J. M. Arthur 105 not out, G. F. J. Liebenberg 45, P. J. R. Steyn 88 not out); Eastern Province 310 for eight dec. (P. G. Amm 44, M. Michau 56, S. C. Pope 67 not out, G. Morgan 42) and 226 for nine (P. G. Amm 50, E. A. E. Baptiste 39, M. Michau 44, R. E. Veenstra 31; F. D. Stephenson four for 57). *Eastern Province 2 pts.*

At Newlands, Cape Town, January 1, 2, 3, 4. Transvaal won by 180 runs. Transvaal* 255 (B. M. White 108, M. D. Haysman 42; E. O. Simons four for 41, M. W. Pringle three for 34) and 282 for seven dec. (M. Yachad 51, M. D. Haysman 37, M. W. Rushmere 37, S. J. Cook 85, N. Pothas 32; M. W. Pringle three for 47); Western Province 131 (C. A. Best 33; C. E. Eksteen seven for 29) and 226 (A. P. Kuiper 76, R. J. Ryall 58; C. E. Eksteen five for 66). *Transvaal 6 pts.*

At Centurion Park, Verwoerdburg, January 21, 22, 23, 24. Drawn. Northern Transvaal 215 (B. J. Sommerville 33, A. J. Seymore 32, K. J. Rule 63; T. G. Shaw three for 34, R. E. Veenstra three for 55) and 201 for nine dec. (B. J. Sommerville 46, S. Elworthy 30, D. J. van Zyl 49 not out; T. G. Shaw three for 20, A. G. Huckle three for 47); Eastern Province* 67 (G. M. Smith five for 24). *Northern Transvaal 2 pts.*

At Newlands, Cape Town, January 21, 22, 23, 24. Drawn. Western Province* 318 (S. G. Koenig 64, H. H. Gibbs 31, L. F. Bleekers 87; N. Boje four for 96, C. J. P. G. van Zyl three for 21) and 220 for nine dec. (S. G. Koenig 52, C. A. Best 33, E. O. Simons 54 not out, M. W. Pringle 33; B. T. Player three for 35, F. D. Stephenson three for 43); Orange Free State 273 (P. J. R. Steyn 46, L. J. Wilkinson 105; M. W. Pringle four for 55, A. Martyn four for 65) and 49 for one. *Western Province 2 pts.*

At Springbok Park, Bloemfontein, January 28, 29, 30. Orange Free State won by ten wickets. Orange Free State* 339 (M. I. Gidley 36, J. F. Venter 83, F. D. Stephenson 35, C. J. van Heerden 40 not out, B. T. Player 47; S. Elworthy three for 73) and 14 for no wkt; Northern Transvaal 159 (C. B. Lambert 39, J. J. Strydom 37, D. J. van Zyl 38; N. Boje four for 39) and 193 (B. J. Sommerville 72, C. B. Lambert 33, J. J. Strydom 30; M. I. Gidley five for 48). *Orange Free State 6 pts.*

At Wanderers Stadium, Johannesburg, January 28, 29, 30, 31. Transvaal won by three wickets. Border* 251 (M. P. Stonier 42, P. C. Strydom 117; M. J. Vandrau four for 72) and 214 (M. P. Stonier 51, P. C. Strydom 35; M. J. Vandrau five for 42); Transvaal 271 (M. Yachad 77, M. W. Rushmere 69; B. C. Fourie six for 74) and 197 for seven (M. Yachad 100 not out, M. D. Haysman 32). *Transvaal 6 pts.*

At Coetzenburg Oval, Stellenbosch, February 11, 12, 13, 14. Boland won by 134 runs. Boland* 351 (J. B. Commins 55, P. A. J. DeFreitas 68, L. M. Germishuys 47, M. Erasmus 73, C. W. Henderson 53 not out; N. C. Johnson five for 79) and 276 for eight dec. (K. C. Jackson 61, T. N. Lazard 44, P. A. J. DeFreitas 36, Extras 38); Natal 306 (A. C. Hudson 92, M. D. Marshall 73, D. N. Crookes 48; H. Williams three for 69, P. A. J. DeFreitas three for 85) and 187 (N. E. Wright 32, D. N. Crookes 52, P. L. Symcox 34; C. W. Henderson four for 25). *Boland 6 pts.*

At Wanderers Stadium, Johannesburg, February 11, 12, 13, 14. Orange Free State won by four wickets. Transvaal* 418 for seven dec. (M. Yachad 31, B. M. White 43, D. J. Cullinan 66, S. J. Cook 110, M. W. Rushmere 82 not out, R. P. Snell 33; F. D. Stephenson three for 79) and 118 (M. D. Haysman 39; J. F. Venter five for 14, F. D. Stephenson three for 29); Orange Free State 327 for nine dec. (P. J. R. Steyn 64, J. F. Venter 63, F. D. Stephenson 78, B. T. Player 36; M. R. Hobson three for 65, R. P. Snell three for 83) and 210 for six (G. F. J. Liebenberg 62, J. F. Venter 31, F. D. Stephenson 33). *Orange Free State 6 pts, Transvaal 2 pts.*

At St George's Park, Port Elizabeth, February 26, 27, 28, March 1. Eastern Province won by eight wickets. Boland* 307 (T. N. Lazard 77, J. B. Commins 92, L. M. Germishuys 58; A. G. Huckle six for 99) and 176 (M. Erasmus 66; T. G. Shaw four for 23, R. E. Veenstra three for 35); Eastern Province 308 for seven dec. (P. G. Amm 41, K. C. Wessels 62, D. J. Callaghan 63, T. G. Shaw 36 not out; B. J. Drew three for 57) and 177 for two (P. G. Amm 46, M. C. Venter 32, K. C. Wessels 53 not out, D. J. Callaghan 43 not out). *Eastern Province 6 pts.*

At Kingsmead, Durban, February 26, 27, 28, March 1. Drawn. Natal* 464 (A. C. Hudson 47, N. E. Wright 102, J. N. Rhodes 46, N. C. Johnson 55, D. M. Benkenstein 71, D. N. Crookes 59; S. D. Jack three for 75) and 144 (D. M. Benkenstein 39 not out, M. D. Marshall 47; S. D. Jack six for 30, C. E. Eksteen four for 53); Transvaal 296 (M. Yachad 31, S. J. Cook 136, M. W. Rushmere 45; P. L. Symcox four for 64, M. D. Marshall three for 61) and 123 for three (D. J. Cullinan 47 not out). *Natal 2 pts.*

At Newlands, Cape Town, February 26, 27, 28, March 1. Border won by one wicket. Western Province 210 (B. M. McMillan 61, C. R. Matthews 34; A. Badenhorst four for 37, P. J. Botha four for 45) and 327 for seven dec. (S. G. Koenig 121 not out, G. Kirsten 78, E. O. Simons 47; B. C. Fourie three for 85, I. L. Howell three for 86); Border* 231 (M. P. Stonier 32, B. M. Osborne 39, P. J. Botha 35, I. L. Howell 52 not out) and 309 for nine (M. P. Stonier 59, A. G. Lawson 38, P. N. Kirsten 51, P. C. Strydom 31, I. L. Howell 30 not out, S. J. Base 32; B. M. McMillan three for 48). *Border 6 pts.*

CURRIE CUP AND CASTLE CUP WINNERS

The Currie Cup was replaced by the Castle Cup after the 1990-91 season.

1889-90	Transvaal
1890-91	Kimberley
1892-93	Western Province
1893-94	Western Province
1894-95	Transvaal
1896-97	Western Province
1897-98	Western Province
1902-03	Transvaal
1903-04	Transvaal
1904-05	Transvaal
1906-07	Transvaal
1908-09	Western Province
1910-11	Natal
1912-13	Natal
1920-21	Western Province
1921-22	Transvaal/Natal/W. Prov. (Tied)
1923-24	Transvaal
1925-26	Transvaal
1926-27	Transvaal
1929-30	Transvaal
1931-32	Western Province
1933-34	Natal
1934-35	Transvaal
1936-37	Natal
1937-38	Natal/Transvaal (Tied)
1946-47	Natal
1947-48	Natal
1950-51	Transvaal
1951-52	Natal
1952-53	Western Province
1954-55	Natal
1955-56	Western Province
1958-59	Transvaal
1959-60	Natal
1960-61	Natal
1962-63	Natal
1963-64	Natal
1965-66	Natal/Transvaal (Tied)
1966-67	Natal
1967-68	Natal
1968-69	Transvaal
1969-70	Transvaal/W. Province (Tied)
1970-71	Transvaal
1971-72	Transvaal
1972-73	Transvaal
1973-74	Natal
1974-75	Western Province
1975-76	Natal
1976-77	Natal
1977-78	Western Province
1978-79	Transvaal
1979-80	Transvaal
1980-81	Natal
1981-82	Western Province
1982-83	Transvaal
1983-84	Transvaal
1984-85	Transvaal
1985-86	Western Province
1986-87	Transvaal
1987-88	Transvaal
1988-89	Eastern Province
1989-90	E. Province/W. Province (Shared)
1990-91	Western Province
1991-92	Eastern Province
1992-93	Orange Free State
1993-94	Orange Free State

UCB BOWL, 1993-94

Section 1

	Played	*Won*	*Lost*	*Drawn*	*1st-inns Points*	*Points*
Transvaal B	5	2	1	2	2	14
Northern Transvaal B	5	1	2	2	4	10
Border B	5	1	1	3	2	8
Zimbabwe Board XI	5	1	0	4	0	6
Natal B	5	0	1	4	6	6
Orange Free State B	5	0	0	5	2	2

Section 2

	Played	*Won*	*Lost*	*Drawn*	*1st-inns Points*	*Points*
Western Province B	5	2	0	3	4	16
Boland B	5	2	1	2	0	12
Griqualand West	5	1	2	2	6	12
Eastern Province B	5	1	0	4	4	10
Eastern Transvaal	5	0	2	3	4	4
Western Transvaal	5	0	1	4	2	2

Final: Transvaal B and Western Province B drew to share the UCB Bowl.

Outright win = 6 pts; lead on first innings in a drawn or lost game = 2 pts.

*In the following scores, * by the name of a team indicates that they won the toss.*

Section 1

At Buffalo Park, East London, October 29, 30, November 1. Drawn. Natal B* 291 (D. J. Watson 50, C. B. Rhodes 31, B. A. Nash 49, M. Badat 54, S. J. S. Kimber 35; A. W. Schoeman four for 64) and 221 (M. L. Bruyns 82; Q. R. Still five for 53); Border B 277 (F. J. C. Cronje 85, K. G. Bauermeister 47, B. Ndzundzu 32 not out, Extras 32; M. W. Handman three for 45, L. Klusener three for 54, S. McKenzie three for 75) and 89 for four (L. Klusener three for 17). *Natal B 2 pts.*

At Wanderers Stadium, Johannesburg, October 29, 30, 31. Transvaal B won by 54 runs. Transvaal B* 317 for eight dec. (B. M. White 93, W. V. Rippon 51, G. A. Pollock 64, C. Grainger 42, P. M. Boa 35 not out) and 223 for seven dec. (B. M. White 109, P. M. Boa 44); Northern Transvaal B 245 (B. J. Sommerville 53, G. Dros 42, L. P. Vorster 38; P. A. Smith four for 60, M. J. Vandrau three for 58) and 241 (B. J. Sommerville 77, G. Dros 30, D. J. van Zyl 42; M. J. Vandrau five for 85). *Transvaal B 6 pts.*

At Harare Sports Club, Harare, October 29, 30, November 1. Drawn. Zimbabwe Board XI* 275 for nine dec. (G. K. Bruk-Jackson 58, I. P. Butchart 60, U. Ranchod 48, Extras 31; N. W. Pretorius three for 56, C. A. van Ee four for 19) and 331 for nine dec. (G. K. Bruk-Jackson 130, I. P. Butchart 39, P. A. Strang 31; N. W. Pretorius three for 93, S. Cronje three for 63); Orange Free State B 343 (M. I. Gidley 47, C. F. Craven 152, C. J. van Heerden 69; M. P. Jarvis four for 86, P. A. Strang four for 93) and 102 for one (M. I. Gidley 34 not out, C. Light 62 not out). *Orange Free State B 2 pts.*

At Springbok Park, Bloemfontein, November 24, 25, 26. Drawn. Northern Transvaal B* 409 (G. Dros 80, L. P. Vorster 188, Extras 33; H. C. Bakkes three for 71) and 121 for one (P. H. Barnard 63 not out, J. Groenewald 50 not out); Orange Free State B 387 (J. F. Venter 193, C. J. van Heerden 43, H. C. Bakkes 33, Extras 35; G. M. Smith five for 59). *Northern Transvaal B 2 pts.*

At Kingsmead, Durban, November 25, 26, 27. Transvaal B won by seven wickets. Transvaal B* 339 (B. M. White 34, P. M. Boa 57, M. O. Johnston 108, G. D. Stevenson 35) and 73 for three; Natal B 167 (D. J. Watson 57; M. J. Vandrau four for 29, A. G. Pollock three for 39) and 243 (D. J. Watson 38, G. W. Bashford 46, L. Klusener 36, Extras 30; A. G. Pollock four for 57). *Transvaal B 6 pts.*

At Bulawayo Athletic Club, Bulawayo, November 25, 26, 27. Drawn. Zimbabwe Board XI 294 (R. P. Gifford 30, G. C. Martin 40, P. A. Strang 35, D. N. Erasmus 41 not out, G. A. Paterson 37, C. B. Wishart 77; P. A. N. Emslie five for 103); Border B* 21 for no wkt.

At The Feathers, East London, December 10, 11, 12. Border B won by an innings and 24 runs. Transvaal B* 135 (C. Grainger 45; A. Badenhorst five for 52, B. C. Fourie three for 22) and 196 (M. J. Vandrau 36, P. M. Boa 57, G. D. Stevenson 40 not out; B. C. Fourie four for 37, Q. R. Still three for 59); Border B 355 (M. P. Stonier 101, B. W. Lones 104, G. W. Thompson 36; G. P. Cooke four for 68, M. J. Vandrau three for 127). *Border B 6 pts.*

At Centurion Park, Verwoerdburg, December 10, 11, 12. Zimbabwe Board XI won by four wickets. Northern Transvaal B 279 (D. J. van Zyl 77, G. J. Dros 49, J. Groenewald 44; M. P. Jarvis six for 74) and 220 (W. M. Dry 75, D. Smith 88 not out; M. P. Jarvis five for 51); Zimbabwe Board XI* 190 (D. J. R. Campbell 41, N. R. van Rensburg 31, G. A. Paterson 49; C. van Noordwyk five for 51, A. Serfontein four for 63) and 311 for six (G. J. Rennie 37, S. V. Carlisle 70, G. C. Martin 54, N. R. van Rensburg 32 not out, I. P. Butchart 60 not out). *Zimbabwe Board XI 6 pts, Northern Transvaal B 2 pts.*

At U OFS Oval, Bloemfontein, December 17, 18, 20. Drawn. Orange Free State B* 260 (M. I. Gidley 60, C. Light 85; L. Klusener four for 38, S. J. S. Kimber three for 49) and 262 for six dec. (M. I. Gidley 82, S. Nicolson 76, R. A. Brown 55 not out, N. W. Pretorius 33); Natal B 268 for eight dec. (D. J. Watson 71, B. Sugden 38, J. Payn 44, B. A. Nash 50 not out) and 207 for six (D. J. Watson 70, M. Badat 40 not out, J. Payn 41; S. Cronje three for 64). *Natal B 2 pts.*

At Sandringham Ground, Queenstown, January 14, 15, 16. Drawn. Orange Free State B 230 (S. Nicolson 51, A. Moreby 66; D. Taljard four for 47) and 319 for seven (S. Nicolson 30, C. Light 32, C. J. van Heerden 126 not out, S. Cronje 50 not out; P. A. N. Emslie three for 71); Border B* 411 for eight dec. (M. P. Stonier 121, Q. R. Still 129 not out, G. W. Thompson 35; P. Wille three for 60). *Border B 2 pts.*

At Jan Smuts Stadium, Pietermaritzburg, January 21, 22, 23. Drawn. Natal B 379 for eight dec. (C. R. B. Armstrong 30, D. J. Watson 36, W. Bond 75, G. W. Bashford 100; A. Serfontein three for 81); Northern Transvaal B* 68 for two (R. F. Pienaar 42).

At Wanderers Stadium, Johannesburg, January 21, 22, 23. Drawn. Zimbabwe Board XI 167 (G. K. Bruk-Jackson 33, P. A. Strang 45; G. D. Stevenson three for 44, G. P. Cooke three for 47) and 163 for eight (G. A. Paterson 73); Transvaal B* 387 for five dec. (N. R. Rhodes 67, M. W. Rushmere 188, P. M. Boa 69, C. Grainger 30; I. P. Butchart three for 52). *Transvaal B 2 pts.*

At Kingsmead, Durban, January 27, 28, 29. Drawn. Zimbabwe Board XI* 329 (S. V. Carlisle 45, D. J. R. Campbell 37, G. C. Martin 73, G. K. Bruk-Jackson 58, P. A. Strang 45; M. W. Handman four for 94) and 236 for three (S. V. Carlisle 111 not out, G. C. Martin 68); Natal B 360 (C. R. B. Armstrong 54, W. Bond 61, J. Payn 42, G. W. Bashford 115, D. J. Pryke 48; P. A. Strang three for 144, U. Ranchod three for 64). *Natal B 2 pts.*

At Berea Park, Pretoria, January 28, 29, 30. Northern Transvaal B won by one wicket. Border B 297 (B. W. Lones 75, G. C. Victor 65, A. C. Dewar 51, J. A. Ehrke 32; A. Serfontein five for 50) and 221 for five dec. (B. W. Lones 36, G. W. Thompson 106, A. C. Dewar 42); Northern Transvaal B* 303 for eight dec. (C. Bloemink 36, L. P. Vorster 107 not out, W. M. Dry 67, N. Martin 49; J. A. Ehrke four for 51) and 216 for nine (M. J. Davis 33, R. F. Pienaar 56, N. Martin 41; Q. R. Still five for 56). *Northern Transvaal B 6 pts.*

At Springbok Park, Bloemfontein, February 11, 12, 13. Drawn. Orange Free State B 292 for nine dec. (S. Nicolson 114 not out, C. J. van Heerden 60; G. P. Cooke three for 50); Transvaal B* 90 for eight (C. F. Craven three for 22).

Section 2

At PAM Brink Stadium, Springs, October 7, 8, 9. Drawn. Western Province B 244 for six dec. (S. G. Koenig 57, H. D. Ackerman 30, L. F. Bleekers 33, T. J. Mitchell 53 not out, C. V. English 35 not out, Extras 31; L. C. R. Jordaan four for 59) and 224 for five dec. (S. G. Koenig 33, H. D. Ackerman 57, P. A. W. Upton 37 not out, T. J. Mitchell 32 not out); Eastern Transvaal* 207 (W. R. Radford 68, C. R. Norris 73 not out; A. Martyn six for 60) and 174 for nine (C. R. Norris 68; F. Benjamin four for 40). *Western Province B 2 pts.*

At Witrand Cricket Field, Potchefstroom, October 7, 8, 9. Drawn. Griqualand West 194 (P. Kirsten 40, F. C. Brooker 72; A. H. Gray three for 21, L. Botes three for 66) and 84 for four (N. E. Alexander 31, F. C. Brooker 31); Western Transvaal* 175 (J. D. Nel 39, L. Botes 40 not out, Extras 30; B. E. van der Vyver four for 32, J. E. Johnson three for 29). *Griqualand West 2 pts.*

At Witrand Cricket Field, Potchefstroom, October 28, 29, 30. Drawn. Western Transvaal 240 (H. Coetzee 40, A. Cilliers 56, H. M. de Vos 50 not out) and 340 (H. G. Prinsloo 31, A. J. van Deventer 55, A. Cilliers 56, H. M. de Vos 95, Extras 49; S. M. Skeete six for 88); Eastern Transvaal* 336 (C. R. Norris 78, T. Jamaal 114, T. A. Marsh 50, Extras 30; F. Baird five for 72, A. H. Gray four for 83) and 175 for seven (C. R. Norris 35, T. Jamaal 41, T. A. Marsh 50 not out; A. H. Gray three for 45). *Eastern Transvaal 2 pts.*

At Kimberley Country Club, Kimberley, October 29, 30, November 1. Boland B won by one wicket. Griqualand West 120 (S. T. Jefferies four for 20, J. S. Roos three for 24) and 415 (W. E. Schonegevel 82, F. C. Brooker 42, P. Kirsten 46, M. N. Angel 51, J. E. Johnson 79; D. Smith five for 80, B. A. S. Chedburn three for 81); Boland B* 321 (B. H. Richards 43, K. C. Jackson 51, J. Wahl 43, A. G. Elgar 44, L. M. Germishuys 80 not out; M. N. Angel four for 50, I. M. Kidson three for 86) and 219 for nine (J. S. Roos 30, A. G. Elgar 41; I. M. Kidson three for 59). *Boland B 6 pts.*

At Goodwood Stadium, Goodwood, October 29, 30, 31. Drawn. Eastern Province B* 403 for nine dec. (M. G. Beamish 62, S. C. Pope 65, M. Michau 35, C. Wait 103 on first-class debut, P. A. Tullis 76, P. A. Rayment 32; T. J. Mitchell three for 61, A. Meyer three for 65); Western Province B 244 (H. H. Gibbs 43, R. A. Koster 43, T. J. Mitchell 39, A. Meyer 34 not out; G. Roe four for 42, A. V. Birrell three for 45) and 322 for three (H. H. Gibbs 152 not out, L. F. Bleekers 55, R. A. Koster 68 not out). *Eastern Province B 2 pts.*

At Brackenfell Sports Fields, Brackenfell, November 25, 26, 27. Drawn. Boland B* 186 (M. J. Cann 45, A. T. Holdstock 32; A. V. Birrell three for 29, G. Roe three for 41) and 293 (W. N. van As 35, R. I. Dalrymple 85, J. S. Roos 32; A. V. Birrell four for 95, P. A. Rayment three for 90); Eastern Province B 215 (A. Botha 30, A. V. Birrell 50, P. A. Rayment 43; A. G. Elgar three for 63) and 212 for seven (A. Botha 62, C. Wait 30, A. V. Birrell 33; A. T. Holdstock three for 25, A. G. Elgar three for 78). *Eastern Province B 2 pts.*

At St George's Park, Port Elizabeth, December 10, 11, 12. Eastern Province B won by five wickets. Eastern Transvaal 279 (C. R. Norris 37, T. Jamaal 53, B. Randall 59, L. D. Botha 32, Extras 30; A. G. Huckle four for 98) and 152 (B. N. Schultz seven for 70); Eastern Province B* 277 (A. Botha 31, G. K. Miller 57, P. A. Rayment 66, L. Masikazana 48, Extras 31; S. M. Skeete four for 74, L. C. R. Jordaan three for 52) and 158 for five (A. Botha 47, L. J. Koen 54). *Eastern Province B 6 pts, Eastern Transvaal 2 pts.*

At Field Crescent, Athlone, December 10, 11, 13. Western Province B won by 169 runs. Western Province B 299 for eight dec. (F. B. Touzel 35, H. D. Ackerman 42, M. C. de Villiers 50 not out, T. J. Mitchell 68, A. Meyer 42; S. T. Jefferies four for 93) and 185 for five dec. (F. B. Touzel 36, H. D. Ackerman 54, R. A. Koster 32; A. G. Elgar three for 34); Boland B* 207 (W. N. van As 62, L. M. Germishuys 68; A. Meyer seven for 67) and 108 (W. N. van As 33; F. Benjamin four for 41, T. J. Mitchell three for seven). *Western Province B 6 pts.*

At Brackenfell Sports Fields, Brackenfell, December 17, 18, 19. Boland B won by 115 runs. Boland B* 215 (L. M. Germishuys 108 not out; D. J. van Schalkwyk three for 52) and 231 for four dec. (C. P. Dettmer 58, A. Wylie 46, F. Davids 51, S. Nackerdien 46 not out); Western Transvaal 146 (H. M. de Vos 36, A. Cilliers 31; M. J. Cann three for 19, A. G. Elgar three for 38) and 185 (A. J. van Deventer 34, A. Cilliers 30, A. H. Gray 36, L. Botes 49; M. J. Cann five for 68, A. G. Elgar four for 83). *Boland B 6 pts.*

At PAM Brink Stadium, Springs, December 18, 19, 20. Griqualand West won by 46 runs. Griqualand West* 438 for nine dec. (J. E. Morris 65, W. E. Schonegevel 32, F. C. Brooker 89, B. E. van der Vyver 44, P. Kirsten 89, F. J. J. Viljoen 75 not out, Extras 33; L. D. Botha three for 37, T. A. Marsh three for 80) and 213 for two dec. (J. E. Morris 109, W. E. Schonegevel 79); Eastern Transvaal 381 (W. R. Radford 157, T. A. Marsh 106, L. D. Botha 32; B. K. Williams three for 44, J. E. Johnson three for 74) and 224 (A. Norris 39, C. R. Norris 76, T. A. Marsh 33; M. N. Angel four for 50). *Griqualand West 6 pts.*

At PAM Brink Stadium, Springs, January 21, 22, 23. Drawn. Eastern Transvaal* 223 (W. R. Radford 101, C. R. Norris 35; R. Hoffman five for 26); Boland B 34 for no wkt.

At Kimberley Country Club, Kimberley, January 21, 22, 24. Drawn. Griqualand West 142 (J. E. Johnson 31; C. Wait four for 18) and 232 for eight dec. (J. E. Morris 44, B. E. van der Vyver 40, F. J. J. Viljoen 61, P. Kirsten 30; S. Abrahams three for 60); Eastern Province B* 101 (C. Bradfield 30; J. E. Johnson five for 28) and 250 for seven (M. G. Beamish 111, J. P. Heath 48; M. N. Angel four for 62). *Griqualand West 2 pts.*

At Witrand Cricket Field, Potchefstroom, January 21, 22, 23. Drawn. Western Province B* 384 for eight dec. (F. B. Touzel 47, J. H. Kallis 30, T. J. Mitchell 90, R. J. Ryall 61, A. Meyer 89; A. H. Gray three for 45); Western Transvaal 169 (A. J. van Deventer 61 not out; D. MacHelm six for 31) and 116 for three (H. M. Smith 37 not out, H. G. Prinsloo 30 not out). *Western Province B 2 pts.*

At Kimberley Country Club, February 10, 11, 12. Western Province B won by 43 runs. Western Province B* 284 for four dec. (H. D. Ackerman 154, J. H. Kallis 54 not out) and 259 for one dec. (D. Jordaan 105 not out, F. B. Touzel 128 not out); Griqualand West 285 (W. E. Schonegevel 59, B. E. van der Vyver 127; D. MacHelm seven for 85) and 215 (J. E. Morris 41, K. C. Dugmore 66; D. MacHelm four for 82, D. Jordaan three for 73). *Western Province B 6 pts, Griqualand West 2 pts.*

At St George's Park, Port Elizabeth, February 11, 12, 13. Drawn. Western Transvaal* 246 (A. J. van Deventer 48, A. Cilliers 31, L. Botes 43 not out; A. G. Huckle three for 88) and 135 for three dec. (H. P. Roesch 32); Eastern Province B 112 (C. Bradfield 32, G. Morgan 34) and 255 for nine (J. P. Heath 120 not out, S. C. Pope 44, G. K. Miller 34; A. Cilliers three for 57). *Western Transvaal 2 pts.*

Final

At Wanderers Stadium, Johannesburg, March 12, 13, 14. Drawn. Transvaal B and Western Province B share title. Western Province B* 171 (H. H. Gibbs 35, R. A. Koster 54, A. C. Dawson 37; A. G. Pollock three for 20) and 313 for six (D. Jordaan 58, J. H. Kallis 69, H. H. Gibbs 57 not out, R. A. Koster 95); Transvaal B 382 for six dec. (N. R. Rhodes 37, W. V. Rippon 92, P. M. Boa 63, C. Grainger 70, S. Jacobs 41 not out, J. P. van der Westhuizen 33 not out, Extras 33).

OTHER FIRST-CLASS MATCHES

At Prospect Field, Grahamstown, September 14, 15, 16. Drawn. Eastern Province* 298 for six dec. (P. G. Amm 77, D. J. Callaghan 104, S. C. Pope 43; R. M. Ford three for 35, M. F. Sharpe three for 53) and 242 for six dec. (M. C. Venter 54, P. G. Amm 71, L. J. Koen 56; C. Z. Harris three for 60); Canterbury 270 for six dec. (L. G. Howell 94, C. Z. Harris 118 not out; T. G. Shaw three for 40) and 167 for four (B. Z. Harris 35, L. G. Howell 33, C. Z. Harris 40 not out).

At Boland Park, Worcester, September 16, 17, 18. Drawn. Western Province* 345 for five dec. (F. B. Touzel 44, D. Jordaan 63, A. P. Kuiper 129 not out, E. O. Simons 32, R. A. Koster 31 not out) and 152 for four (D. Jordaan 76 not out, A. P. Kuiper 34); Boland 575 for five dec. (T. N. Lazard 307 not out, J. B. Commins 165).

At Centurion Park, Verwoerdburg, September 24, 25, 26. Barbados won by six wickets. Northern Transvaal* 339 for six dec. (M. J. R. Rindel 137, K. J. Rule 38, J. J. Strydom 31 not out, S. Elworthy 45 not out) and 207 for six dec. (A. J. Seymore 59, J. J. Strydom 50, S. Elworthy 46); Barbados 246 (V. C. Drakes 100, F. L. Reifer 39; T. Bosch three for 44, R. E. Bryson three for 60) and 303 for four (P. A. Wallace 76, S. L. Campbell 53, C. A. Best 37, R. I. C. Holder 32, H. R. Waldron 47 not out, F. L. Reifer 51 not out; C. van Noordwyk three for 52).

BENSON AND HEDGES SERIES

(*Day/night matches of 50 overs a side, not first-class.*)

At St George's Park, Port Elizabeth, October 15. Eastern Province won by three wickets. Northern Transvaal* 161 (K. J. Rule 44, S. Elworthy 38; B. N. Schultz three for 34); Eastern Province 162 for seven (K. C. Wessels 47, L. J. Koen 43, D. J. Callaghan 32).

At PAM Brink Stadium, Springs, October 15. Natal won by 47 runs. Natal 212 for eight (C. E. B. Rice 32, D. M. Benkenstein 42, P. L. Symcox 38; M. N. Angel three for 35); Impalas* 165 for seven (W. E. Schonegevel 30; D. N. Crookes four for 37).

At Wanderers Stadium, Johannesburg, October 20. Transvaal won by 78 runs after rain had revised Impalas' target to 260 from 43 overs. Transvaal* 275 for six (M. W. Rushmere 54, D. J. Cullinan 111 not out, D. R. Laing 42; J. E. Johnson three for 33); Impalas 181 for five (W. E. Schonegevel 55, W. R. Radford 39).

At Springbok Park, Bloemfontein, November 5. Orange Free State won by 68 runs. Orange Free State 227 for seven (P. J. R. Steyn 31, G. F. J. Liebenberg 46, B. T. Player 36 not out; D. J. Callaghan three for 40); Eastern Province* 159 for nine (P. G. Amm 41; N. Boje four for 18).

At Wanderers Stadium, Johannesburg, November 5. No result. Transvaal 166 for five (M. Yachad 56, S. J. Cook 52, D. R. Laing 38 not out; D. B. Rundle three for 63) v Western Province*.

At PAM Brink Stadium, Springs, November 6. Northern Transvaal won by 45 runs in a match reduced by rain to 23 overs a side. Northern Transvaal 142 for seven (V. F. du Preez 42; T. A. Marsh three for 24); Impalas* 97 for eight (T. A. Marsh 37 not out; R. E. Bryson three for 18).

At Centurion Park, Verwoerdburg, November 10. Border won by five wickets. Northern Transvaal* 239 for six (M. J. R. Rindel 73, K. J. Rule 35, J. J. Strydom 51; O. D. Gibson four for 62); Border 243 for five (P. N. Kirsten 134 not out, P. J. Botha 43).

At Springbok Park, Bloemfontein, November 10. Orange Free State won by eight wickets after rain had revised their target to 55 from 20 overs. Impalas* 108 for eight (B. T. Player four for seven); Orange Free State 56 for two.

At Buffalo Park, East London, November 12. Western Province won by 21 runs. Western Province 252 for four (D. Jordaan 91, G. Kirsten 68, A. P. Kuiper 56 not out); Border* 231 (P. J. Botha 73, O. D. Gibson 36, I. L. Howell 50; A. Martyn four for 52).

At Kingsmead, Durban, November 12. Natal won by 17 runs after rain had revised Boland's target to 117 from 23 overs. Natal 154 for seven in 39 overs (N. E. Wright 35; O. Henry three for 37); Boland* 99 for one (T. N. Lazard 45 not out).

At St George's Park, Port Elizabeth, November 17. Eastern Province won by six wickets. Transvaal* 193 for seven (B. M. White 39, S. D. Jack 30; R. E. Veenstra three for 25); Eastern Province 197 for four (P. G. Amm 31, M. Michau 104 not out, E. A. E. Baptiste 30).

At PAM Brink Stadium, Springs, November 19. Border won by seven wickets. Impalas 205 for six (W. E. Schonegevel 51, J. E. Morris 65, P. Kirsten 35); Border* 206 for three (P. N. Kirsten 71, A. G. Lawson 81; J. E. Johnson three for 26).

At Springbok Park, Bloemfontein, November 19. Orange Free State won by 61 runs. Orange Free State* 271 for eight (J. M. Arthur 38, J. F. Venter 55, C. J. P. G. van Zyl 59 not out; A. C. Dawson three for 45); Western Province 210 (G. Kirsten 31, A. P. Kuiper 66, A. C. Dawson 31; F. D. Stephenson three for 19).

At Centurion Park, Verwoerdburg, December 8. Northern Transvaal won by 62 runs. Northern Transvaal 247 for six (C. B. Lambert 40, R. F. Pienaar 87, K. J. Rule 30, J. J. Strydom 38, B. J. Sommerville 31 not out); Natal* 185 (C. E. B. Rice 43; S. Elworthy three for 26).

At Springbok Park, Bloemfontein, December 8. Orange Free State won by 20 runs. Orange Free State 189 for nine (P. J. R. Steyn 55, C. J. P. G. van Zyl 32); Transvaal* 169 (M. Yachad 49; J. F. Venter five for 21).

At Centurion Park, Verwoerdburg, December 15. Orange Free State won by four wickets. Northern Transvaal* 131 (J. J. Strydom 47 not out; H. C. Bakkes three for 38); Orange Free State 133 for six (J. F. Venter 42 not out; T. Bosch three for 32).

At Buffalo Park, East London, December 15. Border won by five wickets. Eastern Province* 186 for nine (M. Michau 30; P. J. Botha three for 31); Border 187 for five (P. N. Kirsten 36, B. M. Osborne 30, P. J. Botha 46 not out; T. G. Shaw three for 26).

At Newlands, Cape Town, December 15. Western Province won by 30 runs. Western Province* 257 for five (D. Jordaan 116, A. P. Kuiper 75, Extras 34); Impalas 227 for eight (J. E. Morris 68, W. E. Schonegevel 46, A. J. van Deventer 47; A. C. Dawson four for 45).

At Wanderers Stadium, Johannesburg, December 17. Natal won by 97 runs. Natal* 222 for four (C. E. B. Rice 103, N. C. Johnson 41, D. M. Benkenstein 39 not out); Transvaal 125 (H. A. Page 36).

At Newlands, Cape Town, December 17. Western Province won by 95 runs. Western Province* 217 for eight (A. P. Kuiper 52, E. O. Simons 67; P. A. J. DeFreitas three for 22); Boland 122 (E. O. Simons four for 14).

At Danie Craven Stadium, Coetzenburg, December 18. Border won by two wickets. Boland 237 for nine (T. N. Lazard 67, W. S. Truter 35, J. B. Commins 32; B. C. Fourie three for 37, F. J. C. Cronje three for 54); Border* 238 for eight (P. N. Kirsten 38, M. P. Stonier 34, F. J. C. Cronje 55 not out, I. L. Howell 41 not out; A. T. Holdstock three for 54).

At Kingsmead, Durban, December 20. Natal won by 26 runs. Natal* 210 for eight (N. E. Wright 80, M. D. Marshall 32, M. L. Bruyns 55; C. J. P. G. van Zyl three for 54); Orange Free State 184 (F. D. Stephenson 45, J. F. Venter 36; C. E. B. Rice three for 39).

At Buffalo Park, East London, December 21. Border won by seven wickets. Transvaal 235 for eight (M. Yachad 86, M. D. Haysman 31, H. A. Page 36; B. C. Fourie four for 44); Border* 238 for three (P. N. Kirsten 86, B. M. Osborne 85 not out).

At Newlands, Cape Town, December 22. Western Province won by five wickets. Northern Transvaal* 161 (M. J. R. Rindel 82; M. W. Pringle four for 36, E. O. Simons three for 20, A. C. Dawson three for 33); Western Province 162 for five (D. Jordaan 40, H. H. Gibbs 53 not out).

At Danie Craven Stadium, Coetzenburg, December 23. Orange Free State won by 93 runs. Orange Free State* 205 for nine (P. J. R. Steyn 35, L. J. Wilkinson 33, C. J. P. G. van Zyl 48); Boland 112 (F. D. Stephenson four for 11).

At St George's Park, Port Elizabeth, December 23. Natal won by 59 runs. Natal* 192 (N. E. Wright 35, N. C. Johnson 61); Eastern Province 133 (E. A. E. Baptiste 32; N. C. Johnson four for 32, S. M. Pollock three for 25).

At Buffalo Park, East London, January 7. No result. Border 89 for six in 35.4 overs; Orange Free State* seven for no wkt.

At PAM Brink Stadium, Springs, January 7. Impalas won by 62 runs. Impalas* 262 for four (W. E. Schonegevel 103, W. R. Radford 101); Boland 200 (J. B. Commins 52, A. G. Elgar 35; J. E. Johnson three for 22, T. A. Marsh three for 32, L. D. Botha three for 55).

At Newlands, Cape Town, January 7. Western Province won by 11 runs. Western Province* 206 for seven (C. A. Best 57, A. P. Kuiper 30, A. C. Dawson 44 not out; T. G. Shaw three for 22); Eastern Province 195 for seven (T. G. Shaw 56 not out, P. A. Rayment 45 not out; A. P. Kuiper three for 26, A. C. Dawson three for 39).

At Kingsmead, Durban, January 12. Natal won by 102 runs. Natal* 249 for seven (N. E. Wright 40, M. L. Bruyns 38, D. M. Benkenstein 33, M. D. Marshall 63, D. N. Crookes 37 not out); Western Province 147 (E. O. Simons 31; L. Klusener three for 24).

At Wanderers Stadium, Johannesburg, January 12. Transvaal won by three wickets. Boland* 230 for seven (K. C. Jackson 31, J. B. Commins 52, A. T. Holdstock 66); Transvaal 232 for seven (B. M. White 84, D. R. Laing 85).

At Danie Craven Stadium, Coetzenburg, January 14. Eastern Province won by 84 runs. Eastern Province* 185 (M. Michau 59, P. A. Rayment 57; M. Erasmus three for 25); Boland 101 (T. G. Shaw three for 19).

At Centurion Park, Verwoerdburg, January 14. Northern Transvaal won by five wickets after rain had revised their target to 102 from 20 overs. Transvaal* 208 for nine (M. Yachad 113, M. D. Haysman 37; G. M. Smith three for 43); Northern Transvaal 102 for five.

At Danie Craven Stadium, Coetzenburg, January 19. Boland won by two wickets. Northern Transvaal* 138 (J. J. Strydom 47); Boland 143 for eight (J. B. Commins 35, P. A. J. DeFreitas 30; T. Bosch three for 34).

At St George's Park, Port Elizabeth, January 19. Eastern Province won by 91 runs. Eastern Province* 220 for eight (P. G. Amm 65, E. A. E. Baptiste 56; A. Cilliers three for 31); Impalas 129 (A. J. van Deventer 48 not out; T. G. Shaw three for 28).

At Kingsmead, Durban, January 19. Natal won by 15 runs. Natal* 234 for nine (M. L. Bruyns 40, N. C. Johnson 62, M. D. Marshall 37; F. J. C. Cronje three for 32); Border 219 for eight (P. J. Botha 73, P. C. Strydom 67; D. N. Crookes four for 53).

Natal 28 pts, Orange Free State 26 pts, Western Province 22 pts, Border 22 pts, Eastern Province 16 pts, Northern Transvaal 12 pts, Transvaal 10 pts, Impalas 4 pts, Boland 4 pts.

Semi-finals

At Buffalo Park, East London, February 2. Border won by three wickets. Natal* 134 (D. M. Benkenstein 57; S. J. Base three for 22, K. G. Bauermeister three for 35); Border 139 for seven (A. G. Lawson 40; L. Klusener three for 18).

At Kingsmead, Durban, February 4. Natal won by four wickets. Border 183 for nine (P. J. Botha 33, P. C. Strydom 72; M. D. Marshall three for 25, D. N. Crookes three for 47); Natal* 185 for six (M. L. Bruyns 85 not out, D. M. Benkenstein 36).

At Kingsmead, Durban, February 6. Natal won by 53 runs. Natal* 244 for six (A. C. Hudson 88, M. D. Marshall 64 not out; K. G. Bauermeister three for 60); Border 191 (B. M. Osborne 45, G. C. Victor 41; D. N. Crookes four for 32).

Natal won 2-1

At Newlands, Cape Town, February 2. Western Province won by 74 runs. Western Province* 192 for nine (M. W. Pringle 31, E. O. Simons 55 not out; B. T. Player four for 41); Orange Free State 118 (E. O. Simons four for 19, A. Meyer four for 26).

At Springbok Park, Bloemfontein, February 4. Orange Free State won by 63 runs. Orange Free State* 237 for seven (J. M. Arthur 44, W. J. Cronje 120); Western Province 174 (A. P. Kuiper 52; N. Boje three for 38).

At Springbok Park, Bloemfontein, February 6. Orange Free State won by five runs. Orange Free State* 145 (F. D. Stephenson 44, N. Boje 34 not out; D. B. Rundle three for 33); Western Province 140 (D. B. Rundle 44, C. R. Matthews 31 not out; F. D. Stephenson three for 12).

Orange Free State won 2-1

Final

At Kingsmead, Durban, March 11. Orange Free State won by seven wickets. Natal* 103 (A. C. Hudson 47; B. T. Player five for 27, A. A. Donald four for 21); Orange Free State 107 for three (J. F. Venter 37 not out).

CRICKET IN THE WEST INDIES, 1993-94

By TONY COZIER

For once fulfilling their status as favourites, the Leeward Islands became the first team since Guyana in 1982-83 to win both the first-class and the limited-overs championships outright.

With no conflicting overseas tour as in the previous two seasons, most of the main players were available, though Carlisle Best of Barbados and Clayton Lambert of Guyana, two of the most durable batsmen in regional cricket, chose to stay on in South Africa on professional contracts. The Leewards benefited most. They boasted five current Test players – captain Richie Richardson, Keith Arthurton, Curtly Ambrose and the two unrelated Benjamins, Kenneth and Winston – and were clearly the strongest, best-balanced team. They had been that before but, in the 13 years since they and the Windward Islands became separate entities, only once had they won the first-class title, claiming the Red Stripe Cup in 1989-90. Their only outright success in the one-day tournament had been in 1981-82. Even without Richardson, exhausted by West Indies' tours of Sharjah, India and Sri Lanka, for the first three of the five Red Stripe Cup matches, the Leewards were sufficiently well-equipped to defeat Trinidad & Tobago and the Windwards by emphatic margins after starting with first-innings points in a draw against Barbados. They won a third victory, over Jamaica, when Richardson scored a painstaking 151 over seven and a half hours, though their celebrations were somewhat muted when reigning champions Guyana beat them in their last match. But a month later, they confirmed their pre-eminence with an away win over Barbados in a high-scoring final of the limited-overs Geddes Grant Shield – despite some shaky performances in the preliminary rounds.

If the Leewards' successes were predictable, the revival of Trinidad & Tobago was not. Over the previous two seasons, they had not won a single Cup match; in 1992-93 they finished bottom. Now victories over the Windwards, Jamaica and Guyana carried them to second position, just five points behind the champions. Had it not been for rain, which prevented them from beating Barbados in their final match, the Cup might well have gone to Port-of-Spain – a week later, the Leewards were faltering against Guyana. The transformation was due almost solely to the inspiration of the captain, Brian Lara, indisputably the player of the year. His record-breaking season, culminating in his 375 against England in April, began with him surpassing Desmond Haynes's tournament aggregate of 654, set in 1990-91, with 715 in five matches at an average of 79.44. While his three centuries – 180 against Jamaica, 169 against Guyana and 206 against Barbados – were all of high quality, that against Jamaica was exceptional. It represented 70.03 per cent of the total of 257. Only E. F. Wright with 123, which was 73.21 per cent of Demerara's 168 against Trinidad, in Georgetown in 1882-83, has scored a higher proportion in a first-class match in the West Indies. Lara's runs were actually made out of 219 while he was at the wicket, of which 18 were extras. On the second day, he accumulated 131 while his four partners contributed 12. Lara's role was decisive. Trinidad & Tobago's other Test player, Phil Simmons, missed two matches with a broken thumb, while another experienced batsman, Ken

Williams, played only one before he tried to hook Winston Benjamin in a one-day match, was struck on the head and lost the sight of his left eye. Williams, 30, and a first-class cricketer for ten years, announced his retirement at once.

Barbados, meanwhile, were left to reflect on an unwanted piece of history. The island that boasts more championships and more Test players than any other failed to win a match for the first time since the annual first-class tournament was inaugurated as the Shell Shield in 1965-66. That they did not lose one either was of small consolation, for they finished above only the Windwards. As West Indies entered the final Test against England without a Barbadian for the first time in 305 Tests spread over 67 years, the island's strong cricketing pride was badly dented.

Guyana's defence of the Cup was hindered by the weather that allowed them only two days' play against Barbados and almost certainly cost them a victory over the Windwards. Their triumph over the new champions Leewards was consolation, especially as it was the last match for the 36-year-old off-spinner Clyde Butts, who announced his retirement after becoming the leading wicket-taker ever in regional cricket. In 14 seasons of Shell Shield and Red Stripe Cup, he dismissed 270 batsmen, passing the 256 of another off-spinner, Ranjie Nanan of Trinidad & Tobago.

Jamaica, three times winners since the Red Stripe Cup was inaugurated in 1987-88, relied too heavily on their Test players, captain Courtney Walsh and Jimmy Adams, and could not make the most of three home matches. Their sole victory was over last-placed Windwards, whose batting remained lamentably weak. For the second successive season, not one of their batsmen managed a century; 273 was the highest of their eight completed totals.

Lara's dominance was so emphatic that he was 279 runs ahead of the second-best aggregates in the Red Stripe Cup, 436 by Adams and Stuart Williams. The left-handed Adams started with centuries for Jamaica against Guyana and Barbados before strengthening his position in the Test team against England. Williams, the Leewards opener from Nevis, finally turned his potential into consistent form for a Cup average of 54.50. Compact in method, attacking in nature and attractive in execution, he took 157 off Barbados and 107 off the Windwards; his subsequent unbeaten 102 for the Board XI against the England tourists ensured his first West Indies cap in Antigua when Richardson and Haynes were injured. As Haynes's lengthy career neared its end, Williams, at 24, seemed a ready replacement. Haynes himself was steady but never reached three figures. In his previous seven Cup matches, in 1990-91 and 1991-92, he had accumulated six centuries.

Lara, Adams and Arthurton – who also averaged 50 in the Cup – were all aged under 30 and there were others, similarly young, who suggested that West Indian batting would be in capable hands for some time. Besides Williams, Sherwin Campbell, Shivnarine Chanderpaul and Keith Semple pushed themselves to the fore. Campbell's off-side strokeplay brought him three centuries and flattering comparisons to his fellow-Barbadian, Everton Weekes, whose short, powerful physique he also shares. He had taken some time to find his feet at first-class level, but Chanderpaul's temperament was evident from the time he scored 90 on debut for Guyana in 1991-92. His development into the Cup's leading all-rounder, with 389 solid runs and 12 wickets from his quick, flat leg-spin, was impressive enough for the selectors to choose him as West Indies' ninth teenage Test cricketer. With

Lambert in South Africa and Carl Hooper enduring a modest season, Guyana depended for their runs mainly on him and Semple, who had 142 against Jamaica and four fifties, including 76 for the Board President's XI against England, in 11 innings in his second full season. The loss of form of Roland Holder, the 26-year-old Barbados captain, after his prolific 1992-93 season and his selection for the West Indies touring team, was untimely and disappointing. But a dogged, unbeaten 116 against Trinidad & Tobago in his team's last match and scores of 85, 43 and 116 against England would have restored his confidence – and that of the selectors.

The leading Cup bowlers included some familiar names. Ambrose's 19 Cup wickets cost 11.68 each and he and the Benjamins ensured that the Leewards conceded only one total over 300. Walsh claimed 26 wickets, more than any other fast bowler, and Barrington Browne, the lively if under-estimated Guyanese, passed 20 for the second successive season. More relevant to the future was the form of Cameron Cuffy, a fast bowler from St Vincent with Ambrose's attributes of height and accuracy, who earned 24 wickets for the Windwards at 14.87, and the successes of several leg-spinners. Rajindra Dhanraj, a first-class cricketer since he was 18, enjoyed by far the best season of an inconsistent career, with 30 wickets at 15.70 for Trinidad & Tobago, including eight for 51 against Barbados, while Robert Haynes, the tall Jamaican, had 21 at 23.76. At 25, Dhanraj seemed overdue for inclusion in the West Indies team (he finally made his debut in November 1994); at 29, Haynes might not add to his eight one-day internationals. But with young fast bowlers of quality scarce, two teenage leg-spinners, Rawl Lewis of the Windwards and Dinanath Ramnarine of Trinidad & Tobago, looked distinct prospects. Both had toured England with West Indies Under-19 the previous summer: Lewis's promise was confirmed with nine wickets for the Board XI against England in his native Grenada, Ramnarine's by the support he gave to Dhanraj.

Keen to prepare younger players for international cricket, the West Indies Cricket Board of Control arranged an A tour of Canada in July, following one to Bermuda a year earlier, and a return Under-19 series against England in January 1995. Barbados players gained further experience on their first ever trip to South Africa, as guests of the Orange Free State Cricket Association's centenary celebrations. They played one first-class match, against Northern Transvaal, and nine limited-overs games.

In November 1993, the WICBC appointed a special committee to advise on cricket, as distinct from administration, including Sir Garfield Sobers and other former Test players. Peter Short, president of the Barbados Cricket Association for 21 years, was elected president of the Board in succession to Sir Clyde Walcott, who had become chairman of the International Cricket Council in October.

FIRST-CLASS AVERAGES, 1993-94

BATTING

(Qualification: 200 runs)

	M	*I*	*NO*	*R*	*HS*	*100s*	*Avge*
B. C. Lara (*T & T*)	10	17	0	1,513	375	5	89.00
S. C. Williams (*Leeward I.*)	7	13	3	592	157	3	59.20
J. C. Adams (*Jamaica*)	10	16	2	810	137	3	57.85

	M	*I*	*NO*	*R*	*HS*	*100s*	*Avge*
S. L. Campbell (*Barbados*)	7	12	2	547	141	3	54.70
K. F. Semple (*Guyana*)	6	11	2	489	142	1	54.33
R. I. C. Holder (*Barbados*)	7	11	2	440	116*	2	48.88
K. L. T. Arthurton (*Leeward I.*)	10	15	1	662	126	2	47.28
N. O. Perry (*Jamaica*)	6	9	1	357	160	1	44.62
S. Chanderpaul (*Guyana*)	10	17	3	608	101	1	43.42
R. A. Harper (*Guyana*)	5	7	0	287	79	0	41.00
R. B. Richardson (*Leeward I.*)	6	11	2	348	151	1	38.66
D. L. Haynes (*Barbados*)	9	15	2	489	84	0	37.61
C. W. Walwyn (*Leeward I.*)	4	7	0	255	80	0	36.42
D. A. Joseph (*Windward I.*)	6	12	1	395	88	0	35.90
P. A. Wallace (*Barbados*)	6	10	0	347	72	0	34.70
K. Mason (*T & T*)	6	10	1	297	63	0	33.00
R. D. Jacobs (*Leeward I.*)	7	11	2	276	71*	0	30.66
J. R. Murray (*Windward I.*)	10	16	1	446	95	0	29.73
C. O. Browne (*Barbados*)	7	10	1	259	55	0	28.77
P. V. Simmons (*T & T*)	6	11	1	271	69	0	27.10
R. G. Samuels (*Jamaica*)	6	11	0	272	68	0	24.72
L. A. Harrigan (*Leeward I.*)	6	11	0	267	61	0	24.27
R. W. Staple (*Jamaica*)	5	9	0	211	42	0	23.44
R. C. Haynes (*Jamaica*)	5	9	0	205	50	0	22.77
W. K. M. Benjamin (*Leeward I.*)	10	13	0	279	71	0	21.46

* *Signifies not out.*

BOWLING

(Qualification: 15 wickets)

	O	*M*	*R*	*W*	*BB*	*5W/i*	*Avge*
C. E. L. Ambrose (*Leeward I.*)	336	96	741	45	6-24	2	16.46
C. E. Cuffy (*Windward I.*)	172	45	431	24	6-81	2	17.95
R. Dhanraj (*T & T*)	202.3	33	609	31	8-51	1	19.64
W. D. Phillip (*Leeward I.*)	149.2	39	359	16	4-55	0	22.43
B. St A. Browne (*Guyana*)	130	13	555	24	5-27	1	23.12
C. A. Walsh (*Jamaica*)	403.4	87	1,048	45	6-109	3	23.28
R. C. Haynes (*Jamaica*)	205.5	39	499	21	6-82	1	23.76
O. D. Gibson (*Barbados*)	145.1	34	405	17	5-87	1	23.82
K. C. G. Benjamin (*Leeward I.*)	337.4	70	1,056	42	6-66	2	25.14
D. Ramnarine (*T & T*)	125.4	23	379	15	5-48	1	25.26
C. G. Butts (*Guyana*)	194.3	44	481	18	4-38	0	26.72
A. C. Cummins (*Barbados*)	142.5	21	483	17	4-92	0	28.41
R. N. Lewis (*Windward I.*)	189	30	625	21	5-95	2	29.76
N. O. Perry (*Jamaica*)	187.2	42	460	15	3-39	0	30.66
F. A. Rose (*Jamaica*)	122.1	16	470	15	4-74	0	31.33
V. C. Drakes (*Barbados*)	155.5	18	568	17	4-63	0	33.41
W. K. M. Benjamin (*Leeward I.*)	324.4	80	909	27	4-44	0	33.66

RED STRIPE CUP, 1993-94

	Played	*Won*	*Lost*	*Drawn*	*1st-inns Points*	*Points*
Leeward Islands	5	3	1	1	9	61
Trinidad & Tobago	5	3	1	1	4	56
Guyana	5	1	1	3	13	41
Jamaica	5	1	2	2	4	28
Barbados	5	0	0	5	4	24
Windward Islands	5	0	3	2	0	8

Win = 16 pts; draw = 4 pts; 1st-innings lead in drawn match = 4 pts; 1st-innings lead in lost match = 5 pts.

*In the following scores, * by the name of a team indicates that they won the toss.*

At Kensington Oval, Bridgetown, January 7, 8, 9, 10. Drawn. Leeward Islands 384 (S. C. Williams 157, L. A. Harrigan 40, C. W. Walwyn 47, K. L. T. Arthurton 58; A. C. Cummins three for 89, V. C. Drakes four for 63) and 282 (L. A. Harrigan 33, R. D. Jacobs 68, S. C. Williams 60, K. C. G. Benjamin 30; S. M. Skeete three for 50, W. E. Reid four for 56); Barbados* 343 (D. L. Haynes 61, S. L. Campbell 141, H. R. Waldron 39, Extras 33; C. E. L. Ambrose three for 64) and 80 for two (D. L. Haynes 44 not out). *Barbados 4 pts, Leeward Islands 8 pts.*

At Sabina Park, Kingston, January 7, 8, 9, 10. Drawn. Guyana 316 (N. A. McKenzie 39, K. F. Semple 142, C. L. Hooper 32, S. Chanderpaul 41; C. A. Walsh four for 65) and 216 (N. A. McKenzie 32, C. L. Hooper 49, S. Chanderpaul 34, R. A. Harper 45; C. A. Walsh three for 43, R. C. Haynes four for 67); Jamaica* 314 (J. C. Adams 112, R. C. Haynes 50, F. R. Redwood 34, F. A. Rose 47 not out; B. St A. Browne four for 84, C. G. Butts four for 63) and 124 for four (D. S. Morgan 30, J. C. Adams 58 not out; B. St A. Browne three for 60). *Guyana 8 pts, Jamaica 4 pts.*

At Mindoo Phillip Park, Castries (St Lucia), January 7, 8, 9, 10. Trinidad & Tobago won by one wicket. Windward Islands* 143 (M. I. Black three for 69) and 253 (D. A. Joseph 57, J. R. Murray 79, G. Cupid 30; P. V. Simmons three for 52, R. Dhanraj four for 37); Trinidad & Tobago 241 (A. Balliram 76, P. V. Simmons 69, K. Mason 46; R. N. Lewis three for 65) and 158 for nine (D. Williams 46; C. E. Cuffy four for 24). *Trinidad & Tobago 16 pts.*

At Kensington Oval, Bridgetown, January 14, 15, 16, 17. Drawn. Jamaica 406 (R. G. Samuels 68, J. C. Adams 133, R. W. Staple 42, F. R. Redwood 62 not out, Extras 35) and 118 (D. S. Morgan 30, R. G. Samuels 35; D. R. Maynard three for 12, S. M. Skeete three for 13); Barbados* 232 (D. L. Haynes 84; R. C. Haynes four for 82) and 250 for eight (P. A. Wallace 44, V. C. Drakes 91 not out; C. A. Walsh six for 109). *Barbados 4 pts, Jamaica 8 pts.*

At Sturge Park, Plymouth (Montserrat), January 14, 15, 16. Leeward Islands won by an innings and 110 runs. Trinidad & Tobago* 99 (C. E. L. Ambrose four for 12, K. C. G. Benjamin five for 19) and 183 (B. C. Lara 84; W. D. Phillip four for 55); Leeward Islands 392 (L. A. Harrigan 51, C. W. Walwyn 80, K. L. T. Arthurton 93, L. L. Lawrence 56; R. Dhanraj three for 122, D. Ramnarine three for 49). *Leeward Islands 16 pts.*

At Queen's Park, St George's (Grenada), January 14, 15, 16, 17. Drawn. Guyana 286 (K. F. Semple 58, S. Chanderpaul 57, Sunil Dhaniram 44, L. A. Joseph 52; C. E. Cuffy five for 50) and 109 for three dec. (C. L. Hooper 54 not out); Windward Islands* 183 (J. R. Murray 83, C. A. Davis 33; C. G. Butts three for 57) and 63 for six (D. A. Joseph 34 not out; S. Chanderpaul three for 26). *Windward Islands 4 pts, Guyana 8 pts.*

At Bourda, Georgetown, January 21, 22, 23, 24. Drawn. Barbados* 292 (P. A. Wallace 40, A. F. G. Griffith 38, S. L. Campbell 103; C. L. Hooper five for 77, S. Chanderpaul three for 32); Guyana 174 for four (P. D. Persaud 52, K. F. Semple 51 not out; W. E. Reid three for 47). *Guyana 4 pts, Barbados 4 pts.*

At Warner Park, Basseterre (St Kitts), January 21, 22, 23, 24. Leeward Islands won by seven wickets. Windward Islands* 267 (D. A. Joseph 47, R. A. Marshall 40, J. R. Murray 95; K. C. G. Benjamin four for 96, V. A. Walsh three for 36) and 162 (G. Cupid 34, C. A. Davis 43 not out; V. A. Walsh three for 22); Leeward Islands 323 (S. C. Williams 107, K. L. T. Arthurton 32, R. D. Jacobs 71 not out; C. E. Cuffy four for 49) and 110 for three (K. L. T. Arthurton 43 not out). *Leeward Islands 16 pts.*

At Queen's Park Oval, Port-of-Spain, January 21, 22, 23, 24. Trinidad & Tobago won by three wickets. Jamaica 206 (R. W. Staple 30, T. O. Powell 49; D. Ramnarine five for 48) and 217 (R. W. Staple 32, F. R. Redwood 57, R. C. Haynes 43, N. O. Perry 34; R. Dhanraj four for 40); Trinidad & Tobago* 257 (B. C. Lara 180; F. A. Rose four for 74, R. C. Haynes six for 82) and 167 for seven (K. Mason 52 not out; C. A. Walsh three for 40). *Trinidad & Tobago 16 pts.*

At Kensington Oval, Bridgetown, January 28, 29, 30, 31. Drawn. Windward Islands 273 (D. A. Joseph 49, K. K. Sylvester 44, G. Cupid 49, D. Thomas 45 not out; S. M. Skeete three for 58) and 194 for eight (D. A. Joseph 88; O. D. Gibson four for 40); Barbados* 321 for seven dec. (D. L. Haynes 36, P. A. Wallace 72, S. L. Campbell 100 not out, C. O. Browne 55; R. N. Lewis five for 103). *Barbados 8 pts, Windward Islands 4 pts.*

At Guaracara Park, Pointe-à-Pierre (Trinidad), January 28, 29, 30, 31. Trinidad & Tobago won by 78 runs. Trinidad & Tobago 178 (D. Williams 41, K. Mason 42; B. St A. Browne five for 27) and 382 (S. Ragoonath 74, B. C. Lara 169, P. V. Simmons 31, Extras 40; B. St A. Browne three for 113, C. G. Butts four for 115); Guyana* 282 (S. Chanderpaul 101, R. A. Harper 39; R. Dhanraj three for 64) and 200 (S. Chanderpaul 64, R. A. Harper 47; E. C. Antoine four for 36, R. Dhanraj three for 46). *Trinidad & Tobago 16 pts, Guyana 5 pts.*

At Sabina Park, Kingston, January 29, 30, 31, February 1. Leeward Islands won by nine wickets. Leeward Islands* 439 (R. B. Richardson 151, K. L. T. Arthurton 118, W. D. Phillip 41 not out; F. A. Rose three for 118) and 26 for one; Jamaica 249 (F. R. Redwood 59, N. O. Perry 60; C. E. L. Ambrose four for 40, W. K. M Benjamin four for 44) and 215 (R. G. Samuels 44, J. C. Adams 37, R. C. Haynes 32, N. O. Perry 40 not out; C. E. L. Ambrose four for 40, W. K. M. Benjamin three for 39, W. D. Phillip three for 32). *Leeward Islands 16 pts.*

At Queen's Park Oval, Port-of-Spain, February 4, 5, 6, 7. Drawn. Trinidad & Tobago 435 (A. Balliram 33, P. V. Simmons 62, B. C. Lara 206, K. Mason 63; A. C. Cummins four for 92; V. C. Drakes three for 104); Barbados* 198 (P. A. Wallace 47, A. F. G. Griffith 50; R. Dhanraj eight for 51) and 240 for five (R. I. C. Holder 116 not out, L. K. Puckerin 55, C. O. Browne 34). *Trinidad & Tobago 8 pts, Barbados 4 pts.*

At Sabina Park, Kingston, February 5, 6, 7, 8. Jamaica won by an innings and 136 runs. Windward Islands* 122 (C. A. Walsh five for 21) and 159 (E. J. Warrican 30; C. A. Walsh three for 18, N. O. Perry three for 39); Jamaica 417 (J. C. Adams 81, O. G. Pennant 38, N. O. Perry 160, R. C. Haynes 40; C. E. Cuffy six for 81, E. J. Warrican three for 77). *Jamaica 16 pts.*

At Blairmont, Berbice (Guyana), February 10, 11, 12, 13. Guyana won by 40 runs. Guyana* 241 (R. A. Harper 79, Sunil Dhaniram 57; K. C. G. Benjamin four for 50) and 222 (S. Chanderpaul 73, K. F. Semple 67; L. C. Weekes four for 54, W. D. Phillip four for 67); Leeward Islands 289 (L. A. Harrigan 61, L. C. Weekes 46, R. D. Jacobs 34, W. K. M. Benjamin 71, Extras 38; B. St A. Browne three for 72, R. A. Harper five for 61) and 134 (R. B. Richardson 31; R. A. Harper five for 38, C. G. Butts four for 38). *Guyana 16 pts, Leeward Islands 5 pts.*

SHELL SHIELD AND RED STRIPE CUP WINNERS

The Shell Shield was replaced by the Red Stripe Cup after the 1986-87 season.

1965-66	Barbados	1980-81	Combined Islands
1966-67	Barbados	1981-82	Barbados
1968-69	Jamaica	1982-83	Guyana
1969-70	Trinidad	1983-84	Barbados
1970-71	Trinidad	1984-85	Trinidad & Tobago
1971-72	Barbados	1985-86	Barbados
1972-73	Guyana	1986-87	Guyana
1973-74	Barbados	1987-88	Jamaica
1974-75	Guyana	1988-89	Jamaica
1975-76	Trinidad Barbados	1989-90	Leeward Islands
		1990-91	Barbados
1976-77	Barbados	1991-92	Jamaica
1977-78	Barbados	1992-93	Guyana
1978-79	Barbados	1993-94	Leeward Islands
1979-80	Barbados		

GEDDES GRANT SHIELD, 1993-94

Note: Matches in this section were not first-class.

At Kensington Oval, Bridgetown, January 5. Barbados won by eight wickets. Leeward Islands 138 (39.5 overs) (S. C. Williams 33, K. L. T. Arthurton 35; A. C. Cummins five for 16); Barbados* 139 for two (37.5 overs) (A. F. G. Griffith 41, S. L. Campbell 31).

At Sabina Park, Kingston, January 5. Jamaica won by 28 runs. Jamaica 229 for three (50 overs) (D. S. Morgan 53, R. G. Samuels 103, J. C. Adams 40); Guyana* 201 for six (50 overs) (Sudesh Dhaniram 48, C. L. Hooper 32, S. Chanderpaul 35).

At Mindoo Phillip Park, Castries (St Lucia), January 5. Windward Islands won by four wickets. Trinidad & Tobago 114 (40.4 overs) (K. Mason 37; I. B. A. Allen three for 16); Windward Islands* 115 for six (28 overs) (D. A. Joseph 31; R. Dhanraj four for 41).

At Kensington Oval, Bridgetown, January 12. Barbados won by nine wickets, their target having been revised by rain to 174 from 43 overs. Jamaica 194 for nine (48 overs) (S. M. Skeete three for 41); Barbados* 178 for one (31.3 overs) (S. L. Campbell 80 not out, R. I. C. Holder 48 not out).

At Antigua Recreation Ground, St John's, January 12. Leeward Islands won by one run. Leeward Islands* 194 (49.2 overs) (S. C. Williams 55; R. Dhanraj four for 41); Trinidad & Tobago 193 for seven (50 overs) (B. C. Lara 84, K. A. Williams 61 retired hurt; C. E. L. Ambrose three for 45).

At Queen's Park, St George's (Grenada), January 12. Guyana won by six wickets. Windward Islands 104 (38.4 overs) (L. A. Joseph four for 27); Guyana* 105 for four (33.3 overs) (Sudesh Dhaniram 40, C. L. Hooper 37 not out).

At Hampton Court, Essequibo (Guyana), January 19. Guyana won by four wickets. Barbados 140 (47.3 overs); Guyana* 143 for six (41.2 overs) (C. L. Hooper 49).

At Grove Park, Charlestown (Nevis), January 19. Leeward Islands won by 59 runs. Leeward Islands 220 (46.5 overs) (R. D. Jacobs 80, H. W. Williams 31 not out; C. A. Davis four for 22, C. E. Cuffy four for 57); Windward Islands* 161 (43.5 overs) (D. Thomas 54).

At Queen's Park Oval, Port-of-Spain, January 19. Jamaica won by 111 runs. Jamaica 266 for five (50 overs) (J. C. Adams 75, R. W. Staple 57, T. O. Powell 54 not out); Trinidad & Tobago* 155 (42.5 overs) (B. C. Lara 34, D. Williams 53; R. C. Haynes three for 32).

At Kensington Oval, Bridgetown, January 26. Barbados won by five wickets. Windward Islands* 161 (45.1 overs) (R. A. Marshall 49, Extras 30; S. M. Skeete three for 29); Barbados 164 for five (44.3 overs) (S. L. Campbell 45, C. O. Browne 51 not out, V. C. Drakes 46 not out).

At Guaracara Park, Pointe-à-Pierre (Trinidad), January 26. Trinidad & Tobago won by three wickets. Guyana 206 for nine (50 overs) (P. D. Persaud 36, S. Chanderpaul 51 not out, L. A. Joseph 34; R. Dhanraj five for 26); Trinidad & Tobago* 210 for seven (44.1 overs) (S. Ragoonath 35, B. C. Lara 86 not out).

At Sabina Park, Kingston, January 27. Leeward Islands won by six runs. Leeward Islands* 201 (49.3 overs) (K. L. T. Arthurton 33, C. W. Walwyn 32, W. K. M. Benjamin 30; F. R. Redwood four for 30); Jamaica 195 (49.2 overs) (D. S. Morgan 43, J. C. Adams 69; C. E. L. Ambrose three for 29, W. K. M. Benjamin three for 25).

At Queen's Park Oval, Port-of-Spain, February 2. Barbados won by nine wickets. Trinidad & Tobago 131 (41.3 overs) (K. Mason 68; O. D. Gibson five for 25); Barbados* 133 for one (33.3 overs) (P. A. Wallace 70 not out, S. L. Campbell 37 not out).

At Sabina Park, Kingston, February 3. Jamaica won by seven wickets. Windward Islands* 200 for six (50 overs) (J. Eugene 31, R. A. Marshall 77 not out; R. C. Haynes four for 27); Jamaica 201 for three (45.3 overs) (R. G. Samuels 99 not out, F. R. Redwood 52 not out).

At Blairmont, Berbice (Guyana), February 8. Leeward Islands won on scoring-rate, Guyana's target having been revised by rain to 139 from 27 overs. Leeward Islands 159 for seven (31 overs) (S. C. Williams 50); Guyana* 129 for five (27 overs) (A. F. Sattaur 38 not out).

Barbados 8 pts, Leeward Islands 8 pts, Jamaica 6 pts, Guyana 4 pts, Windward Islands 2 pts, Trinidad & Tobago 2 pts.

Final

At Kensington Oval, Bridgetown, March 12. Leeward Islands won by 34 runs. Leeward Islands 289 for six (50 overs) (S. C. Williams 85, L. A. Harrigan 68, R. B. Richardson 43); Barbados* 255 (46.1 overs) (D. L. Haynes 35, P. A. Wallace 38, S. L. Campbell 61, L. K. Puckerin 43; K. L. T. Arthurton four for 35).

BRIAN LARA'S FIRST-CLASS RECORD IN 1994

Jan. 7, 8, 9, 10	Castries	Trinidad & Tobago v Windward Islands	5 & 28
Jan. 14, 15, 16	Plymouth	Trinidad & Tobago v Leeward Islands	2 & 84
Jan. 21, 22, 23, 24	Port-of-Spain	Trinidad & Tobago v Jamaica	180 & 23
Jan. 28, 29, 30, 31	Pointe-à-Pierre	Trinidad & Tobago v Guyana	18 & 169
Feb. 4, 5, 6, 7	Port-of-Spain	Trinidad & Tobago v Barbados	206
Feb. 19, 20, 21, 23, 24	Kingston	West Indies v England	83 & 28
March 17, 18, 19, 20, 22	Georgetown	West Indies v England	167
March 25, 26, 27, 29, 30	Port-of-Spain	West Indies v England	43 & 12
April 8, 9, 10, 12, 13	Bridgetown	West Indies v England	26 & 64
April 16, 17, 18, 20, 21	St John's	West Indies v England	375
April 28, 29, 30, May 1	Birmingham	Warwickshire v Glamorgan	147
May 5, 6, 7, 9	Birmingham	Warwickshire v Leicestershire	106 & 120*
May 19, 20, 21, 23	Taunton	Warwickshire v Somerset	136
May 26, 27, 28, 30	Lord's	Warwickshire v Middlesex	26 & 140
June 2, 3, 4, 6	Birmingham	Warwickshire v Durham	501*
June 16, 17, 18, 20	Birmingham	Warwickshire v Kent	19 & 31
June 23, 24, 25, 27	Northampton	Warwickshire v Northamptonshire	197 & 2
July 14, 15, 16, 18	Guildford	Warwickshire v Surrey	2 & 44
July 21, 22, 23	Birmingham	Warwickshire v Essex	70 & 9
July 28, 29, 30	Chesterfield	Warwickshire v Derbyshire	142 & 51
Aug. 4, 5, 6, 8	Worcester	Warwickshire v Worcestershire	5 & 57
Aug. 11, 12, 13, 15	Birmingham	Warwickshire v Nottinghamshire	15 & 0
Aug. 18, 19, 20, 22	Scarborough	Warwickshire v Yorkshire	21 & 17
Aug. 25, 26, 27	Hove	Warwickshire v Sussex	17
Aug. 30, 31, Sept. 1, 2	Birmingham	Warwickshire v Hampshire	191
Nov. 13, 14, 15	Bangalore	West Indians v Rest of India	22
Nov. 18, 19, 20, 21, 22	Bombay	West Indies v India	14 & 0
Nov. 25, 26, 27	Kozikhode	West Indians v Bombay	29
Dec. 1, 2, 3, 4, 5	Nagpur	West Indies v India	50 & 3
Dec. 10, 11, 12, 13, 14	Mohali	West Indies v India	40 & 91

Brian Lara played in 30 first-class matches in 1994. In 50 innings, he scored 3,828 runs and was not out twice for an overall average of 79.75.

CRICKET IN NEW ZEALAND, 1993-94

By TERRY POWER

New Zealand's shift towards one-day cricket continued: there were 34 50-overs Shell Cup matches and only 18 in the first-class Shell Trophy. The Cup was extended to two full rounds, with a revised play-off system. Meanwhile, the championship was played entirely over four days for the first time since 1949-50. A mixture of three and four-day matches had been tried in 1992-93, after a generation of the three-day format. Now the six provinces played each other once, with the top four advancing to a knockout. But although there were fewer first-class fixtures, the semi-finals and final clashed directly with the Second and Third Tests against Pakistan. Apart from removing star players when they were most wanted, this drove Canterbury out of their Lancaster Park headquarters for the final. Refused a postponement, they decamped to Rangiora, where they defeated Auckland within an hour of New Zealand's famous Test victory. Peter McDermott, chairman of New Zealand Cricket, made a clear-cut acknowledgment of error and promised there would be no repeat.

Canterbury, who had finished bottom the previous season, acquired a new coach, former Central Districts pace bowler Denis Aberhart, and swapped places with title-holders Northern Districts. They also kept the Shell Cup for a third successive year; that final, too, was displaced from Lancaster Park, because of damage suffered during pop concerts. Their outstanding all-round performer was Mark Priest, who spent the early summer establishing himself as a self-employed electrician, but emerged from the wiring in January. He started with match figures of eight for 86 off 59 overs against Northern Districts and finished with the decisive innings of the final against Auckland. Arriving when Canterbury were six wickets down, needing another 131 to win, he reached 88 before being caught with the scores level. He had also featured in Canterbury's remarkable semi-final against Central Districts, when the first five wickets put on only 159 and the second five 400, with Nos. 7, 8 and 9 – captain Lee Germon, leg-spinner Gary Stead and Priest – all making centuries. Despite missing two rounds, Priest took 28 wickets at 16.35, with slow left-armers that genuinely turned, and scored 279 runs at 55.80. He still failed to earn an international recall. But there was recognition for his fellow left-hander Stephen Fleming, who developed from promising colt to successful Test batsman against India. Tall, dark and a handsome strokemaker, Fleming was vulnerable when despatching deliveries from on or outside off stump to leg but looked the most promising batsman to arrive in the 1990s. He scored 633 runs, six fewer than Darrin Murray, whose aggregate in his first two full seasons rose to 1,187 at 43.96. Chris Harris topped the batting averages with 60.20, after a disappointing visit to Australia, only to be omitted from the England tour. Canterbury also took the first three places in the bowling averages, through left-armer Chris Flanagan (who returned after four seasons off with 11 for 67 against Auckland), Michael Sharpe and Priest.

Auckland, under Justin Vaughan, their eighth captain in as many years, lost six successive one-day matches, but their first-class form carried them to the Trophy final. On paper, and periodically in practice, their greatest strength lay in three Test pace bowlers, Willie Watson, Chris Pringle and Murphy Su'a. It was Pringle who lifted Auckland to second place, taking 14 for 119 to beat Otago in a rain-affected match. Newcomer Chris Brown had a magnificent ten-wicket debut against Canterbury and Aaron Barnes became the first Aucklander to take a wicket with his first delivery in first-class cricket. Auckland's outstanding player, however, was Adam Parore. Though occasionally careless when on top, cometh the hour he was the most determined of fighters. Having lost his Test place through injury, he kept wicket efficiently, but gave the gloves to Jason Mills when he was needed to bolster the early batting. He made 133, 84 and 91 in his last three Trophy matches, followed by 134 and 67 for the Academy XI, and had the season's highest aggregate, 742.

Central Districts lost Mark Greatbatch and Tony Blain to international duty, while Mark Douglas, an aggressive batsman and top fielder, moved to Wellington and last year's best bowler, Dean Askew, pulled out with back trouble. They did well to reach the one-day final and the last four of the Trophy. The most successful bowler was slow left-armer Stu Duff, with a modest 18 wickets at 32.38. Roger Twose of Warwickshire, who was thinking of qualifying for New Zealand, became captain and plugged away to claim second place in the batting averages, with 56.42, though his highest score was 99.

Wellington launched their season amid a PR campaign which dubbed them "The Force". Only in their first match did they live up to it, reaching 506 for four to beat Central Districts by an innings; Michael Austen scored 202, the season's only double-century, and Ron Hart 120 after an opening stand of 316. But they were also-rans in the Cup and were shot out for 108 in the Trophy semi-final. The highlight was the blossoming of leg-spinner Matthew Goodson. He took 24 wickets at 22.45, including match figures of nine for 108 in that victory over Central Districts at Wanganui, one of the best batting pitches in New Zealand. The marketing men probably envisaged a Force more like Heath Davis, the fastest bowler in the country. He took 31 wickets – more than anyone else – and was lethal when straight, but left trails of no-balls and wides in his wake and became only the second bowler to be taken off in New Zealand for running on the danger area.

When Lindsay Breen reached 100 against the Academy XI in Otago's last match, it was the province's first first-class century since February 1992. With Ken Rutherford leading New Zealand, the batting was short of substance, but the pace bowling, coached by Lance Cairns, was strong, even after Otago decided they could no longer afford Neil Mallender. Dion Nash led the way with 26 wickets and Aaron Gale had 22, both at a little over 20 apiece. A worthwhile import was the 36-year-old slow left-armer Dick Wixon. A compact man, Wixon almost appears to be squatting when he releases the ball. He was the hardest worked and most economical bowler, sending down 273.3 overs at 1.72 each.

Northern Districts' decline from the top to the bottom of the table owed much to New Zealand's heavy international programme. The previous season none of their winning team played in New Zealand's home matches; in 1993-94, six appeared in the Second Test against Pakistan. Earlier, captain David White was sent to Australia as a reinforcement despite a suspect knee; further trouble put him out for the summer. Grant Bradburn took over the captaincy and had his best all-round season. But Northern Districts' treatment of up-and-coming pace bowlers came home to roost –

Su'a, Nash, Askew and left-armer David Blake had all established careers elsewhere.

In March, an Academy XI – promoting the national cricket academy in Christchurch – played the provinces who had not reached the Shell Trophy semi-finals, beating both, and then met the Indians at New Plymouth. McDermott argued that youngsters would gain more experience playing against older first-class players. "Action cricket" – the 20-overs thrash – was thrown out after one season. Two more worthwhile one-day ventures were North v South Island, officially reinstated after the idea was revived for Rod Latham's benefit in 1992-93, and the encounter of the Australian and New Zealand champions, New South Wales and Canterbury.

FIRST-CLASS AVERAGES, 1993-94

BATTING

(Qualification: 5 completed innings, average 35.00)

	M	*I*	*NO*	*R*	*HS*	*100s*	*Avge*
C. Z. Harris (*Canterbury*)	4	6	1	301	140*	1	60.20
R. G. Twose (*C. Districts*)	6	9	2	395	99	0	56.42
M. W. Priest (*Canterbury*)	5	6	1	279	102	1	55.80
M. H. Austen (*Wellington*)	6	10	0	484	202	1	48.40
G. E. Bradburn (*N. Districts*)	6	11	3	362	73*	0	45.25
A. C. Parore (*Auckland*)	10	18	1	742	134	2	43.64
M. W. Douglas (*Wellington*)	7	12	1	472	106	1	42.90
D. J. Murray (*Canterbury*)	10	16	1	639	112*	1	42.60
L. K. Germon (*Canterbury*)	9	12	2	412	114	2	41.20
D. J. Boyle (*Canterbury*)	5	8	1	282	117	1	40.28
L. J. Doull (*Wellington*)	5	7	1	240	79	0	40.00
S. P. Fleming (*Canterbury*)	11	17	1	633	109*	2	39.56
S. W. J. Wilson (*C. Districts*)	7	13	3	369	105	1	36.90
E. B. McSweeney (*Wellington*)	5	8	1	253	111	1	36.14
B. A. Young (*N. Districts*)	5	10	0	357	120	1	35.70
S. A. Thomson (*N. Districts*)	5	10	1	321	120*	1	35.66

* *Signifies not out.*

BOWLING

(Qualification: 15 wickets)

	O	*M*	*R*	*W*	*BB*	*5W/i*	*Avge*
C. W. Flanagan (*Canterbury*)	162.3	63	335	23	6-30	2	14.56
M. F. Sharpe (*Canterbury*)	122	31	299	19	4-59	0	15.73
M. W. Priest (*Canterbury*)	261.2	102	458	28	6-72	1	16.35
C. M. Brown (*Auckland*)	145.1	51	330	20	6-50	1	16.50
C. Pringle (*Auckland*)	176.3	50	397	22	7-56	2	18.04
W. Watson (*Auckland*)	134.4	40	296	16	4-30	0	18.50
A. J. Gale (*Otago*)	197.5	60	446	22	6-75	2	20.27
D. J. Nash (*Otago*)	230.1	63	537	26	6-30	3	20.65
M. B. Owens (*Canterbury*)	143	42	342	16	3-31	0	21.37
R. L. Hayes (*N. Districts*)	168.3	47	415	19	4-41	0	21.84
M. C. Goodson (*Wellington*)	260.3	76	539	24	6-48	2	22.45

	O	*M*	*R*	*W*	*BB*	*5W/i*	*Avge*
G. R. Jonas (*Wellington*)	144.4	43	340	15	4-48	0	22.66
S. J. Roberts (*Canterbury*)	170	38	454	19	5-70	1	23.89
M. L. Su'a (*Auckland*)	134.3	33	444	18	6-56	2	24.66
G. E. Bradburn (*N. Districts*)	193	51	489	18	4-99	0	27.16
E. J. Marshall (*Otago*)	170.2	39	469	17	5-27	1	27.58
H. T. Davis (*Wellington*)	287.1	68	861	31	5-37	1	27.77
R. P. Wixon (*Otago*)	273.3	98	471	16	5-83	2	29.43
S. W. Duff (*C. Districts*)	270.2	70	583	18	4-111	0	32.38
M. N. Hart (*N. Districts*)	253.2	59	738	22	5-66	1	33.54

SHELL TROPHY, 1993-94

	Played	*Won*	*Lost*	*Drawn*	*1st-inns Points*	*Points*
Canterbury	5	3	0	2	16	52
Auckland	5	3	2	0	8	44
Wellington	5	2	2	1	12	36
Central Districts	5	1	1	3	12	24
Otago	5	1	3	1	8	20
Northern Districts	5	1	3	1	4	16

Semi-finals: Auckland drew with Wellington but proceeded to the final by virtue of their higher placing in the table; Canterbury beat Central Districts by an innings and 123 runs.

Final: Canterbury beat Auckland by three wickets.

Win = 12 pts; lead on first innings = 4 pts.

*In the following scores, * by the name of a team indicates that they won the toss.*

At Dudley Park, Rangiora, December 11, 12, 13. Canterbury won by 48 runs. Canterbury* 128 (D. J. Murray 36, L. G. Howell 30; C. M. Brown six for 50, J. T. C. Vaughan four for 27) and 146 (D. J. Boyle 30, S. P. Fleming 57; C. D. Lee three for 45, C. M. Brown four for 40); Auckland 121 (A. T. Reinholds 38; C. W. Flanagan six for 30) and 105 (A. T. Reinholds 30; M. B. Owens three for 31, C. W. Flanagan five for 37). *Canterbury 16 pts.*

At Victoria Park, Wanganui, December 11, 12, 13, 14. Wellington won by an innings and 12 runs. Central Districts* 308 (C. D. Ingham 72, S. W. J. Wilson 105, C. D. Garner 37; H. T. Davis four for 61, M. C. Goodson three for 60) and 186 (S. W. J. Wilson 42, R. G. Twose 81; M. C. Goodson six for 48); Wellington 506 for four dec. (M. H. Austen 202, R. T. Hart 120, M. W. Douglas 95, E. B. McSweeney 34 not out). *Wellington 16 pts.*

At Trust Bank Park, Hamilton, December 11, 12, 13. Otago won by seven wickets. Otago 233 (J. M. Allan 56, I. S. Billcliff 38, R. P. Wixon 34 not out; R. L. Hayes three for 49, G. E. Bradburn three for 32) and 104 for three (R. A. Lawson 54 not out); Northern Districts* 82 (G. E. Bradburn 32; D. J. Nash five for 18) and 254 (G. E. Bradburn 61, M. D. Bailey 45, A. Somani 40; A. J. Gale five for 72). *Otago 16 pts.*

At Eden Park Outer Oval, Auckland, December 16, 17, 18, 19. Auckland won by 41 runs. Auckland 291 (A. T. Reinholds 71, J. T. C. Vaughan 69, M. J. Horne 33, A. C. Parore 87 not out; R. L. Hayes three for 74) and 215 for nine dec. (A, T. Reinholds 38, J. T. C. Vaughan 79 not out; M. N. Hart five for 66); Northern Districts* 221 (G. P. Burnett 71, G. E. Bradburn 39, M. D. Bailey 43; C. D. Lee three for 34, C. M. Brown three for 68) and 244 (C. P. Burnett 34, M. D. Bailey 57, B. G. Cooper 87; S. W. Brown five for 56). *Auckland 16 pts.*

At Carisbrook, Dunedin, December 16, 17, 18, 19. Drawn. Central Districts 95 for one dec. (S. W. J. Wilson 40 not out) and 116 for three dec. (C. D. Ingham 54, R. G. Twose 33 not out); Otago* first innings forfeited and 182 for seven (P. W. Dobbs 82, D. J. Nash 51). *Central Districts 4 pts.*

At Basin Reserve, Wellington, December 16, 17, 18, 19. Drawn. Wellington* 287 (D. S. McHardy 60, E. B. McSweeney 111, L. J. Doull 40 not out; C. W. Flanagan three for 82) and 281 for seven (M. W. Douglas 57, E. B. McSweeney 99, S. R. Mather 39 not out; C. W. Flanagan four for 50); Canterbury 257 (B. R. Hartland 65, L. G. Howell 60, Extras 41; J. D. Wells six for 59). *Wellington 4 pts.*

At Fitzherbert Park, Palmerston North, January 18, 19, 20, 21. Central Districts won by ten wickets. Central Districts* 449 (C. D. Ingham 73, R. G. Twose 99, S. W. Duff 32, R. K. Brown 90, M. E. L. Lane 84, Extras 36; M. L. Su'a three for 120) and 33 for no wkt; Auckland 151 (M. L. Su'a 38, Extras 33; D. J. Leonard three for 18) and 330 (J. T. C. Vaughan 37, D. N. Patel 59, J. I. Pamment 98, A. C. Parore 40, M. L. Su'a 31; S. W. Duff four for 111). *Central Districts 16 pts.*

At Trust Bank Park, Hamilton, January 18, 19, 20. Canterbury won by an innings and 15 runs. Canterbury* 407 (B. R. Hartland 32, D. J. Murray 95, S. P. Fleming 105, L. K. Germon 89; M. J. Stephens five for 101, R. G. Morgan three for 97); Northern Districts 138 (G. P. Burnett 31, B. G. Cooper 32; M. W. Priest four for 32) and 254 (K. A. Wealleans 32, G. E. Bradburn 63, R. G. Hart 36; S. J. Roberts three for 55, M. W. Priest four for 54). *Canterbury 16 pts.*

At Basin Reserve, Wellington, January 18, 19, 20, 21. Wellington won by 99 runs. Wellington 330 (M. H. Austen 89, J. M. Aiken 37, L. J. Doull 79, M. C. Goodson 38; R. P. Wixon five for 95) and 165 (M. H. Austen 48, M. W. Douglas 35; E. J. Marshall five for 27, R. P. Wixon three for 70); Otago* 272 (I. S. Billcliff 39, L. C. Breen 73, R. P. Wixon 32 not out; G. R. Jonas three for 65, M. C. Goodson four for 65) and 124 (M. C. Goodson five for 40). *Wellington 16 pts.*

At Eden Park Outer Oval, Auckland, February 3, 4, 5. Auckland won by ten wickets. Wellington 116 (M. L. Su'a six for 56) and 152 (M. H. Austen 58; D. N. Patel six for 43); Auckland* 266 (D. N. Patel 37, J. M. Mills 46, M. L. Su'a 45, C. Pringle 45 not out; G. R. Jonas four for 85, R. Rotch three for 67, R. G. Petrie three for 43) and three for no wkt. *Auckland 16 pts.*

At Dudley Park, Rangiora, February 3, 4, 5. Canterbury won by nine wickets. Otago* 179 (P. W. Dobbs 63, G. R. Baker 53; M. B. Owens three for 34) and 145 (P. W. Dobbs 31, K. R. Rutherford 41; M. W. Priest six for 72); Canterbury 303 (D. J. Boyle 117, N. J. Astle 69; A. J. Gale six for 75) and 22 for one. *Canterbury 16 pts.*

At Trafalgar Park, Nelson, February 3, 4, 5, 6. Drawn. Central Districts* 272 (G. P. McRae 62, R. K. Brown 31, S. W. Duff 59, D. J. Hartshorn 35, J. B. M. Furlong 51 not out; R. P. de Groen five for 89) and 247 for six dec. (C. D. Ingham 41, G. P. McRae 45, R. G. Twose 44 not out, R. K. Brown 32, T. E. Blain 50; M. N. Hart three for 77); Northern Districts 217 (M. E. Parlane 75, M. D. Bailey 84; S. W. Duff three for 65, D. J. Hartshorn three for 51) and 300 for nine (K. A. Wealleans 51, M. E. Parlane 89, G. E. Bradburn 73 not out, S. B. Doull 32; D. J. Hartshorn four for 124, S. W. Duff three for 92). *Central Districts 4 pts.*

At Lancaster Park, Christchurch, February 10, 11, 12, 13. Drawn. Canterbury 341 (D. J. Murray 70, C. Z. Harris 48, L. K. Germon 40, M. W. Priest 73 not out, M. F. Sharpe 33; D. J. Leonard three for 52) and 400 for four (B. R. Hartland 55, D. J. Murray 85, C. Z. Harris 140 not out, S. P. Fleming 46, N. J. Astle 52 not out); Central Districts* 261 (S. W. J. Wilson 49, R. G. Twose 39, R. K. Brown 43, S. W. Duff 40, D. J. Hartshorn 32 not out; S. J. Roberts five for 70, M. F. Sharpe three for 53.) *Canterbury 4 pts.*

At Trust Bank Park, Hamilton, February 10, 11, 12, 13. Northern Districts won by six wickets. Wellington* 218 (J. D. Wells 43, M. W. Douglas 66, L. J. Doull 47; R. L. Hayes four for 41, G. E. Bradburn three for 82) and 255 (M. W. Douglas 106; R. L. Hayes three for 61, G. E. Bradburn three for 91); Northern Districts 312 (G. P. Burnett 131, B. G. Cooper 48, M. J. Stephens 49 not out; H. T. Davis four for 95, J. D. Wells three for 59) and 164 for four (G. P. Burnett 45, G. E. Bradburn 47 not out, B. G. Cooper 30 not out). *Northern Districts 16 pts.*

At Carisbrook, Dunedin, February 10, 11, 12, 13. Auckland won by 74 runs. Auckland 141 (J. M. Mills 33; J. W. Wilson four for 29, E. J. Marshall three for 44) and 269 (A. T. Reinholds 61, A. C. Parore 133; R. P. Wixon five for 83); Otago* 163 (P. W. Dobbs 44, J. W. Wilson 48; C. Pringle seven for 63) and 173 (P. W. Dobbs 36, J. M. Allan 38, I. S. Billcliff 31 not out; C. Pringle seven for 56, W. Watson three for 63). *Auckland 12 pts, Otago 4 pts.*

Semi-finals

At Eden Park, Auckland, February 17, 18, 19, 20. Drawn. Auckland reached the final by virtue of their higher placing in the table. Auckland 170 (A. T. Reinholds 52; H. T. Davis four for 48, G. R. Jonas four for 48) and 322 for four (A. C. Parore 84, D. N. Patel 84, J. T. C. Vaughan 35 not out; G. R. Jonas three for 68); Wellington* 108 (M. H. Austen 30; M. L. Su'a five for 44, W. Watson four for 30).

At Lancaster Park, Christchurch, February 17, 18, 19, 20. Canterbury won by an innings and 123 runs. Central Districts* 195 (S. W. Duff 85, D. J. Leonard 34; S. J. Roberts three for 73, M. F. Sharpe three for 41, M. W. Priest three for 43) and 241 (R. G. Twose 70, D. M. Cooper 37; S. J. Roberts three for 67, M. F. Sharpe three for 45, M. W. Priest four for 76); Canterbury 559 (C. Z. Harris 70, L. K. Germon 114, M. W. Priest 102, G. R. Stead 113 not out; W. A. Wisneski five for 115).

Final

At Dudley Park, Rangiora, February 25, 26, 27, 28. Canterbury won by three wickets. Auckland* 179 (A. T. Reinholds 32, J. T. C. Vaughan 48 not out; M. F. Sharpe three for 42) and 204 (A. C. Parore 91; M. F. Sharpe four for 59, M. W. Priest three for 45); Canterbury 94 (L. K. Germon 37; W. Watson four for 31) and 290 for seven (D. J. Boyle 92 not out, M. W. Priest 88).

PLUNKET SHIELD AND SHELL TROPHY WINNERS

The Plunket Shield was replaced by the Shell Trophy after the 1974-75 season.

1921-22	Auckland	1929-30	Wellington
1922-23	Canterbury	1930-31	Canterbury
1923-24	Wellington	1931-32	Wellington
1924-25	Otago	1932-33	Otago
1925-26	Wellington	1933-34	Auckland
1926-27	Auckland	1934-35	Canterbury
1927-28	Wellington	1935-36	Wellington
1928-29	Auckland	1936-37	Auckland

1937-38	Auckland	1968-69	Auckland
1938-39	Auckland	1969-70	Otago
1939-40	Auckland	1970-71	Central Districts
1940-45	No competition	1971-72	Otago
1945-46	Canterbury	1972-73	Wellington
1946-47	Auckland	1973-74	Wellington
1947-48	Otago	1974-75	Otago
1948-49	Canterbury	1975-76	Canterbury
1949-50	Wellington	1976-77	Otago
1950-51	Otago	1977-78	Auckland
1951-52	Canterbury	1978-79	Otago
1952-53	Otago	1979-80	Northern Districts
1953-54	Central Districts	1980-81	Auckland
1954-55	Wellington	1981-82	Wellington
1955-56	Canterbury	1982-83	Wellington
1956-57	Wellington	1983-84	Canterbury
1957-58	Otago	1984-85	Wellington
1958-59	Auckland	1985-86	Otago
1959-60	Canterbury	1986-87	Central Districts
1960-61	Wellington	1987-88	Otago
1961-62	Wellington	1988-89	Auckland
1962-63	Northern Districts	1989-90	Wellington
1963-64	Auckland	1990-91	Auckland
1964-65	Canterbury	1991-92	Central Districts Northern Districts
1965-66	Wellington		
1966-67	Central Districts	1992-93	Northern Districts
1967-68	Central Districts	1993-94	Canterbury

OTHER FIRST-CLASS MATCHES

At Molyneux Park, Alexandra, March 4, 5, 6, 7. New Zealand Academy XI won by 93 runs. New Zealand Academy XI 312 (D. J. Murray 44, A. C. Parore 134; A. J. Gale four for 68, J. M. Paul three for 34) and 191 for one dec. (D. J. Murray 112 not out, B. A. Pocock 33); Otago* 173 (P. W. Dobbs 50; D. J. Nash five for 34, C. M. Brown four for 19) and 237 (J. M. Allan 42, L. C. Breen 100; H. T. Davis five for 37).

At Smallbone Park, Rotorua, March 9, 10, 11. New Zealand Academy XI won by 261 runs. New Zealand Academy XI 269 (G. P. Burnett 63, S. P. Fleming 77, A. C. Parore 67; K. P. Smith five for 39, R. G. Morgan three for 74) and 203 for eight dec. (D. J. Murray 84, H. T. Davis 30 not out; M. J. Stephens four for 64); Northern Districts* 120 (D. J. Nash six for 30) and 91 (H. T. Davis four for 18, R. L. Hayes three for 21).

SHELL CUP, 1993-94

Note: Matches in this section were not first-class.

At Trust Bank Park, Hamilton, December 27. Northern Districts won by seven runs. Northern Districts 223 for seven (50 overs) (B. A. Young 64, B. A. Pocock 30, G. E. Bradburn 42 not out, M. D. Bailey 35; R. G. Twose three for 34); Central Districts* 216 (49.4 overs) (M. J. Greatbatch 30, S. W. J. Wilson 91; S. B. Doull three for 41, A. R. Tait three for 44).

At Molyneux Park, Alexandra, December 27. Canterbury won by 114 runs. Canterbury* 288 for five (50 overs) (R. T. Latham 53, C. Z. Harris 94 not out, C. L. Cairns 63); Otago 174 (48.5 overs) (I. S. Billcliff 56; P. D. Unwin three for 32, C. L. Cairns three for 15. C. Z. Harris three for 20).

At Basin Reserve, Wellington, December 27. Auckland won by nine wickets. Wellington* 186 (49.5 overs) (D. S. McHardy 48, A. H. Jones 40, M. W. Douglas 33; C. Pringle three for 40); Auckland 187 for one (39.4 overs) (A. T. Reinholds 37, J. I. Pamment 105 not out, J. T. C. Vaughan 33 not out).

At Eden Park Outer Oval, Auckland, December 29. Canterbury won by eight wickets. Auckland* 164 (48 overs) (A. C. Barnes 31; M. F. Sharpe four for 30); Canterbury 165 for two (40 overs) (B. R. Hartland 54, R. T. Latham 51).

At Molyneux Park, Alexandra, December 29. Northern Districts won by 114 runs. Northern Districts* 233 (49.1 overs) (G. P. Burnett 37, S. A. Thomson 64, G. E. Bradburn 48); Otago 119 (39 overs) (P. W. Dobbs 51; G. E. Bradburn three for 28).

At Basin Reserve, Wellington, December 29. Central Districts won by 72 runs. Central Districts 238 (49.2 overs) (C. D. Ingham 67, R. K. Brown 50); Wellington* 166 (43.4 overs) (R. G. Twose four for 25).

At Hagley Oval, Christchurch, December 31. Canterbury won by 85 runs. Canterbury* 244 for eight (50 overs) (B. R. Hartland 32, C. L. Cairns 84; L. J. Doull three for 44); Wellington 159 for eight (50 overs) (A. H. Jones 33, R. J. Kerr 32).

At Pukekura Park, New Plymouth, December 31. Central Districts won by five wickets. Otago* 165 for seven (50 overs) (I. S. Billcliff 52, D. J. Nash 33 not out, C. J. W. Finch 51 not out; D. C. Blake three for 55, M. J. Pawson three for 18); Central Districts 168 for five (41.1 overs) (C. D. Ingham 46, R. G. Twose 43).

At Blake Park, Mount Maunganui, December 31. Northern Districts won by three runs. Northern Districts* 193 for seven (50 overs) (B. A. Young 32, S. A. Thomson 57); Auckland 190 for nine (50 overs) (J. I. Pamment 48; S. A. Thomson three for 18).

At Eden Park Outer Oval, Auckland, January 2. Otago won by 57 runs. Otago* 184 (48.2 overs) (K. R. Rutherford 40, D. J. Nash 32, E. J. Marshall 51); Auckland 127 (46 overs) (J. I. Pamment 43; E. J. Marshall three for 21, J. M. Paul three for 26).

At Pukekura Park, New Plymouth, January 2. Central Districts won by five wickets. Canterbury* 200 for seven (50 overs) (N. J. Astle 42, D. J. Murray 30, R. T. Latham 44; R. G. Twose three for 32); Central Districts 201 for five (44.5 overs) (G. P. McRae 38, M. J. Greatbatch 69, T. E. Blain 36 not out).

At Basin Reserve, Wellington, January 2. Wellington won by nine wickets. Northern Districts* 187 (49.4 overs) (B. A. Young 38, M. N. Hart 33; M. J. Sears three for 22); Wellington 189 for one (47.3 overs) (M. H. Austen 95 not out, A. H. Jones 45, M. W. Douglas 43 not out).

At Eden Park Outer Oval, Auckland, January 4. Central Districts won by 105 runs. Central Districts* 217 for four (50 overs) (C. D. Ingham 33, G. P. McRae 48, M. J. Greatbatch 56); Auckland 112 (40.4 overs) (S. W. Brown 36; D. W. Lamason three for 23, S. W. Duff three for 22).

At Aorangi Park, Timaru, January 4. Canterbury won by 105 runs. Canterbury* 313 for seven (50 overs) (B. R. Hartland 161, L. G. Howell 59, C. Z. Harris 34; B. G. Cooper three for 44); Northern Districts 208 for seven (50 overs) (S. A. Thomson 61, M. D. Bailey 33, B. G. Cooper 32 not out; R. T. Latham three for 40).

At Molyneux Park, Alexandra, January 4. Otago won by 49 runs. Otago* 254 for nine (50 overs) (K. R. Rutherford 102, P. W. Dobbs 81, I. S. Billcliff 30; M. J. Sears three for 40, M. H. Austen three for 62); Wellington 205 (48.2 overs) (L. J. Doull 68 not out, B. R. Williams 33).

At Hagley Oval, Christchurch, January 6. Canterbury won by eight wickets. Auckland* 175 for six (50 overs) (A. T. Reinholds 34, A. C. Parore 37 not out, A. C. Barnes 31 not out); Canterbury 176 for two (41.2 overs) (L. G. Howell 38 not out, S. P. Fleming 74 not out).

At Queen Elizabeth Park, Masterton, January 6. Central Districts won by one wicket. Wellington* 225 (49.2 overs) (J. M. Aiken 42, S. R. Mather 33, R. J. Kerr 35); Central Districts 228 for nine (49.4 overs) (R. K. Brown 47, C. D. Garner 87; L. J. Doull three for 49).

At Blake Park, Mount Maunganui, January 6. Northern Districts won by four wickets. Otago* 200 for eight (50 overs) (I. S. Billcliff 50, D. J. Nash 43; B. G. Cooper three for 27); Northern Districts 201 for six (48.3 overs) (B. G. Cooper 61, G. E. Bradburn 49).

At Eden Park Outer Oval, Auckland, January 9. Northern Districts won by 31 runs. Northern Districts* 227 (49.5 overs) (B. G. Cooper 61, G. E. Bradburn 49, A. R. Tait 37; M. L. Su'a five for 42, J. T. C. Vaughan three for 46); Auckland 196 (46.4 overs) (A. T. Reinholds 41, C. M. Spearman 32, A. C. Barnes 33).

At Basin Reserve, Wellington, January 9. Wellington won by 40 runs. Wellington* 197 for nine (50 overs) (E. B. McSweeney 69; M. B. Owens three for 46); Canterbury 157 (47.1 overs) (D. J. Murray 40, L. G. Howell 37; G. R. Jonas three for 23, M. H. Austen three for 31).

At Centennial Park, Oamaru, January 10. Otago won by 55 runs. Otago 188 for six (37 overs) (I. S. Billcliff 45, D. J. Nash 37, L. C. Breen 31 not out); Central Districts* 133 (36.5 overs) (C. D. Garner 59).

At Waikanae Park, Kapiti, January 11. Auckland won by five wickets. Central Districts* 123 (48.5 overs) (S. W. Brown three for 21, J. T. C. Vaughan three for eight); Auckland 124 for five (40.4 overs) (J. I. Pamment 51 not out).

At Smallbone Park, Rotorua, January 11. Canterbury won by four runs. Canterbury* 138 for eight (50 overs) (N. J. Astle 60 not out; A. R. Tait three for 13); Northern Districts 134 (48.2 overs) (G. P. Burnett 40; R. M. Ford three for 22).

At Basin Reserve, Wellington, January 11. Wellington won by 110 runs. Wellington* 217 for nine (50 overs) (M. H. Austen 41, R. J. Kerr 61, S. R. Mather 31; D. J. Nash four for 25); Otago 107 (37.3 overs) (B. R. Williams four for 22).

At Eden Park, Auckland, January 13. Auckland won by 24 runs. Auckland* 155 (47.1 overs) (A. T. Reinholds 34, C. M. Spearman 66; M. H. Austen three for 15); Wellington 131 (47 overs) (E. B. McSweeney 32; J. T. C. Vaughan three for 25).

At Hagley Oval, Christchurch, January 13. Otago won by four wickets. Canterbury 137 for nine (50 overs) (M. A. Hastings 31); Otago* 140 for six (49.5 overs) (P. W. Dobbs 39).

At Horton Park, Blenheim, January 13. Central Districts won by four wickets. Northern Districts* 163 (49.3 overs) (M. E. Parlane 33, K. A. Wealleans 40; A. J. Alcock three for 23); Central Districts 165 for six (49.3 overs) (R. G. Twose 36, R. K. Brown 39 not out).

At Hagley Oval, Christchurch, January 16. Canterbury won by seven wickets. Central Districts* 121 for eight (50 overs) (R. G. Twose 51, D. W. Lamason 30); Canterbury 122 for three (40 overs) (B. R. Hartland 33, D. J. Murray 45 not out, S. P. Fleming 32).

At Harry Barker Reserve, Gisborne, January 16. Wellington won by seven wickets. Northern Districts* 132 (48.3 overs) (K. A. Wealleans 31, B. G. Cooper 34; J. D. Wells four for 26); Wellington 133 for three (39 overs) (M. D. Crowe 49).

At Carisbrook, Dunedin, January 17. Otago won by 109 runs. Otago* 214 for nine (50 overs) (I. S. Billcliff 35, D. J. Nash 84; M. L. Su'a four for 47); Auckland 105 (15.1 overs) (E. J. Marshall seven for 49).

Canterbury 14 pts, Central Districts 12 pts, Northern Districts 10 pts, Otago 10 pts, Wellington 8 pts, Auckland 6 pts.

Play-offs

The first two teams played each other for immediate entry to the final; the loser played the winner of the third-place play-off for the right to join them.

At Hagley Oval, Christchurch, January 23. No result. Canterbury reached the final by virtue of their placing in the qualifying rounds. Canterbury 151 (45.2 overs) (C. Z. Harris 51, D. J. Murray 36; A. J. Alcock five for 31); Central Districts* 33 for one (12 overs).

At Trust Bank Park, Hamilton, January 23. Northern Districts won by 72 runs. Northern Districts* 240 for five (50 overs) (B. A. Young 51, B. G. Cooper 37, G. P. Burnett 38 not out, M. D. Bailey 45 not out); Otago 168 (44.1 overs) (I. S. Billcliff 60, L. C. Breen 43; B. G. Cooper three for 40).

At McLean Park, Napier, January 27. Central Districts won by three wickets. Northern Districts* 179 for seven (47 overs) (G. P. Burnett 76 not out, S. A. Thomson 31; S. W. Duff three for 37); Central Districts 181 for seven (46.1 overs) (G. P. McRae 35, M. J. Greatbatch 35, T. E. Blain 33; S. B. Doull three for 21).

Final

At McLean Park, Napier, January 29. Canterbury won by 25 runs. Canterbury* 240 for seven (50 overs) (C. L. Cairns 99, S. P. Fleming 58; A. J. Alcock three for 39); Central Districts 215 (49 overs) (C. D. Ingham 34, M. J. Greatbatch 44, R. G. Twose 38, T. E. Blain 31; C. L. Cairns four for 44, C. Z. Harris three for 32).

OTHER MATCHES

At Carisbrook, Dunedin, February 1. South Island won by five wickets. North Island* 166 for nine (50 overs) (M. H. Austen 42, S. A. Thomson 40; R. T. Latham three for 28); South Island 167 for five (47.3 overs) (S. P. Fleming 52, C. Z. Harris 64 not out).

At Lancaster Park, Christchurch, April 2. New South Wales won by 86 runs. New South Wales* 260 for eight (50 overs) (R. J. Davison 34, M. G. Bevan 90, T. H. Bayliss 52); Canterbury 174 (37 overs) (B. R. Hartland 59, R. T. Latham 57; G. R. Robertson five for 34, S. Thompson five for 11).

CRICKET IN INDIA, 1993-94

By R. MOHAN and SUDHIR VAIDYA

The most important development of another long and crowded season was the long-awaited reform of the Duleep Trophy, which prepared the way for it to become India's premier first-class competition. It was declared an unqualified success by the players, who were able to play meaningful cricket at the highest possible standard on the domestic circuit. Instead of four knockout matches – a preliminary qualifier followed by the semi-finals and final – the five zonal teams played ten games in all, in a round-robin league. The international stars available for the first half of the tournament also lent it lustre in this vital year of change, before they went off to boost Indian cricket's morale further by conquering West Indies in the final of the limited-overs Hero Cup in Bengal and steam-rollering Sri Lanka in a three-Test series.

North Zone, always a powerful side in the Duleep Trophy thanks to their bowling prowess, proved their supremacy again on a wide range of pitches in host West Zone's territory, from those assisting the bowlers outright to more traditional featherbeds. Despite losing several key players, including their inspirational captain, Kapil Dev, to the Hero Cup, they took first-innings points in the vital match against East Zone to earn a two-point lead over West, East and South, who could only be separated on run quotient.

The other significant highlight of 1993-94 was the return of the Ranji Trophy, in its 60th season, to Bombay after nearly a decade. The team once called India's New South Wales, for their many titles (30 before this, including 15 in succession from 1958-59 to 1972-73), or its Yorkshire – the well-being of their game indicating the health of the national side – had fallen upon hard days. Their bowling standards dropped as they underwent transition and they had not regained their championship since 1984-85. During the intervening eight seasons, none of the six sides who claimed the crown could quite emulate their supremacy, though Delhi had a good attempt, with three titles. But Sachin Tendulkar led Bombay to victory in all four of their zonal matches, and then the resourceful all-rounder Ravi Shastri took over to marshal the bowling during the tougher knockout section and claim the Trophy by beating Bengal in the final.

With the expansion of the Ranji Trophy the previous season, so that three teams instead of two from each zone advanced to the knockout rounds of five-day matches, and the one-day Deodhar Trophy – retained by East Zone – the quantity of cricket certainly increased. This was important for the players, all of whom are employed by private and public companies on the strength of their cricketing talent, but many of whom have suffered from the lack of match-practice at first-class level.

The changes in the Ranji Trophy created more intense competition at the end of the season, but at the expense of the earlier games, where the fancied sides have a relatively simple passage to the knockout. The changes also included a simpler points system, replacing batting and bowling bonuses with rewards for first-innings lead, and the abolition of penalty runs for slow over-rates; fines are now levied instead. But the Duleep reforms, providing top-class competitive cricket for the better players, may ease the Ranji Trophy into second place.

Bombay boasted the most prolific batsman of the season in Sanjay Manjrekar, who scored 1,100 first-class runs in all. He collected 497 in four matches for West Zone in the Duleep Trophy and added 438 in four games for Bombay before his recall to the Test team against Sri Lanka. Only Vikram Rathore of Punjab joined him in passing 1,000, though Ajay Sharma of Delhi might have beaten them had he not been summoned to the Indian squad for the Hero Cup halfway through the Duleep tournament; he finished with 504 runs from just five first-class innings. Bombay's acting-captain, Shastri, scored 963, the most by any batsman in the two domestic competitions. His enthusiasm for opening the batting remained undimmed, though he dropped down the order when he assumed the captaincy in Tendulkar's absence. Shastri also took 17 wickets for Bombay at 15.41 with his left-arm spin. Three Bengal bowlers featured among the leading wicket-takers: Chetan Sharma, who moved from Haryana through a new free transfer system allowing up to three players to be registered as professionals, and Prasant Vaidya both passed 50 and Utpal Chatterjee fell only just short. But the aggregates were topped by another Test discard, Madhya Pradesh leg-spinner Narendra Hirwani, who took 58, including two innings hauls of eight. Such performances were worth their while, with private sponsors stepping in to present cash prizes to the leading batsman and bowler from each of the five zones, supplementing the substantial prizes for trophy-winning teams from the Board.

One young batsman who made his mark in sensational fashion was 19-year-old Amol Muzumdar of Bombay. Another protégé of Ramakant Achrekar, who coached Tendulkar, Vinod Kambli and Pravin Amre, he ran up 260 on his first-class debut in the pre-quarter-final against Haryana at Faridabad. He batted for 639 minutes and struck 31 boundaries from 516 balls. The previous world record for a debutant was 240 by W. F. E. Marx, for Transvaal against Griqualand West, at Johannesburg in 1920-21. Meanwhile, Atul Bedade of Baroda developed into an extraordinary hitter: he scored regularly at more than a run a ball, and his 657 runs included 35 sixes. There was less cheer on the bowling front, with little evidence of new bowlers emerging or of the slightly more experienced making progress. Hirwani played his last Test in November 1990 and the other successes also tended to be among the older players. Venkatesh Prasad, a 24-year-old graduate of the Dennis Lillee school of pace bowling in Madras, took 18 wickets in the Duleep Trophy, to Hirwani's 21, and 50 in all; he was drafted in to replace the injured Manoj Prabhakar on the tour of New Zealand. A few more young pace bowlers showed some promise at Ranji level.

Apart from Muzumdar's double-century debut, a host of records were rewritten when Hyderabad played Andhra in their South Zone match in January. Hyderabad scored 944 for six declared, the highest total ever made in India and the fourth highest anywhere. On the third day they added 467 runs in 95 overs for the loss of one wicket. Maturi Sridhar contributed 366, the third highest score by an Indian, and put on 344 with Vivek Jaisimha and 326 with Noel David, who both made double-hundreds, the first time that three batsmen had passed 200 in the same innings. It was David's second first-class match. – R.M.

FIRST-CLASS AVERAGES, 1993-94

BATTING

(Qualification: 500 runs, average 50.00)

	M	*I*	*NO*	*R*	*HS*	*100s*	*Avge*
Ajay Sharma (*Delhi*)	5	5	1	504	235*	3	126.00
S. S. Sugwekar (*Maharashtra*)	5	8	2	728	225	4	121.33
M. Azharuddin (*Hyderabad*)	8	9	1	677	155	4	84.62
Rizwan Shamshad (*Uttar Pradesh*)	8	12	1	867	169	4	78.81
M. V. Sridhar (*Hyderabad*)	7	11	1	757	366	2	75.70
S. V. Manjrekar (*Bombay*)	12	18	3	1,100	156	5	73.33
P. K. Amre (*Rajasthan*)	5	10	2	564	218	2	70.50
S. Chopra (*Services*)	5	8	0	555	186	2	69.37
Bhupinder Singh, jun. (*Punjab*)	7	11	3	511	132	2	63.87
J. Arun Kumar (*Karnataka*)	6	9	0	566	141	2	62.88
G. K. Pandey (*Uttar Pradesh*)	7	11	2	559	106*	2	62.11
Vikram Rathore (*Punjab*)	11	19	2	1,047	250	3	61.58
A. C. Bedade (*Baroda*)	7	11	0	657	159	3	59.72
S. R. Tendulkar (*Bombay*)	9	11	1	594	142	2	59.40
Abhay Sharma (*Railways*)	7	12	3	525	143	2	58.33
R. J. Shastri (*Bombay*)	12	18	1	963	151	4	56.64
Arun Lal (*Bengal*)	8	14	1	729	177	2	56.07
N. S. Sidhu (*Punjab*)	8	10	0	558	124	1	55.80
R. S. Dravid (*Karnataka*)	13	20	4	846	151*	2	52.87
N. R. Mongia (*Baroda*)	9	14	4	525	100*	1	52.50
S. V. Jedhe (*Maharashtra*)	11	16	2	734	150*	2	52.42
H. A. Kinikar (*Maharashtra*)	8	12	0	628	184	1	52.33
S. S. Karim (*Bihar*)	7	12	2	510	138	1	51.00
S. S. Bhave (*Maharashtra*)	11	17	1	805	180	4	50.31
Saurav C. Ganguly (*Bengal*)	14	19	2	854	200*	3	50.23
C. S. Pandit (*Assam*)	7	11	1	500	125	2	50.00

* *Signifies not out.*

BOWLING

(Qualification: 20 wickets, average 25.00)

	O	*M*	*R*	*W*	*BB*	*5W/i*	*Avge*
Kanwaljit Singh (*Hyderabad*)	189.3	64	366	24	4-22	0	15.25
K. N. A. Padmanabhan (*Kerala*)	258.4	80	511	33	8-57	3	15.48
S. L. V. Raju (*Hyderabad*)	335.5	109	678	42	6-87	5	16.14
U. Chatterjee (*Bengal*)	362	111	811	49	7-71	3	16.55
P. Jain (*Haryana*)	328.4	99	814	46	8-67	6	17.69
B. Vij (*Punjab*)	279.1	63	786	44	7-58	5	17.86
Javed Zaman (*Assam*)	147.3	30	439	24	6-65	3	18.29
B. K. V. Prasad (*Karnataka*)	411.2	124	930	50	7-37	3	18.60
Arshad Ayub (*Hyderabad*)	196.3	49	437	23	5-28	2	19.00
Chetan Sharma (*Bengal*)	344.5	62	1,059	54	6-30	2	19.61
M. Venkataramana (*Tamil Nadu*)	245.2	67	594	30	5-29	1	19.80
S. Subramaniam (*Tamil Nadu*)	298.3	110	562	28	5-14	2	20.07
Bhupinder Singh, sen. (*Punjab*)	431.4	127	1,068	53	7-46	2	20.15
P. S. Vaidya (*Bengal*)	372.1	77	1,081	53	5-68	1	20.39
M. V. Rao (*Services*)	157.1	29	466	22	7-77	2	21.18
R. B. Biswal (*Orissa*)	257	55	658	31	7-45	3	21.22

	O	M	R	W	BB	5W/i	Avge
A. S. Wassan (*Delhi*)	160.4	33	491	23	4-13	0	21.34
A. Kumble (*Karnataka*)	255.2	74	654	30	7-59	1	21.80
D. Vasu (*Tamil Nadu*)	238.4	76	512	23	5-87	1	22.26
R. J. Shastri (*Bombay*)	185.1	35	589	26	6-73	2	22.65
S. Sensharma (*Bengal*)	167.5	26	534	23	4-31	0	23.21
N. D. Hirwani (*Madhya Pradesh*)	462.1	91	1,349	58	8-52	4	23.25
J. Srinath (*Karnataka*)	173.1	30	560	24	5-62	1	23.33
P. Mhambre (*Bombay*)	256.4	62	712	30	6-47	2	23.73
S. V. Bahutule (*Bombay*)	319.2	56	958	39	4-42	0	24.56
Maninder Singh (*Delhi*)	290.1	79	690	28	6-51	3	24.64

*In the following scores, * by the name of a team indicates that they won the toss.*

IRANI CUP, 1993-94

Ranji Trophy Champions (Punjab) v Rest of India

At Punjab Agricultural University Ground, Ludhiana. October 1, 2, 3, 4, 5. Rest of India won by 181 runs. Rest of India* 347 (A. D. Jadeja 64, S. V. Manjrekar 49, R. S. Dravid 93, S. V. Jedhe 76; Bhupinder Singh, sen. six for 103, A. S. Bedi three for 76) and 253 (S. V. Jedhe 43, N. R. Mongia 100 not out; Bhupinder Singh, sen. four for 81, Obaid Kamal three for 72); Punjab 234 (Vikram Rathore 74, Gursharan Singh 64; P. S. Vaidya four for 69) and 185 (N. S. Sidhu 88, Gursharan Singh 51; R. K. Chauhan five for 29).

DULEEP TROPHY, 1993-94

	Played	Won	Lost	Drawn	1st-inns Points	Points	Quotient
North Zone	4	2	1	1	2	14	3.33
West Zone	4	2	2	0	0	12	3.00
East Zone	4	2	1	1	0	12	2.98
South Zone	4	2	2	0	0	12	2.81
Central Zone	4	1	3	0	2	8	3.14

Outright win = 6 pts; lead on first innings in a drawn or lost game = 2 pts.
Quotient = runs scored per over.

At Motibaug Palace Ground, Baroda, October 10, 11, 12, 13. North Zone won by an innings and 97 runs. Central Zone* 250 (P. K. Amre 71, R. K. Chauhan 36 not out; Bhupinder Singh, sen. three for 43, A. R. Kapoor four for 60) and 361 (Yusuf Ali Khan 62, A. R. Khurasia 103, P. K. Amre 114 not out; A. R. Kapoor three for 118, Maninder Singh four for 70); North Zone 708 for nine dec. (N. S. Sidhu 57, A. D. Jadeja 264, Ajay Sharma 151, V. S. Yadav 45, A. R. Kapoor 103 not out; R. K. Chauhan five for 195). *North Zone 6 pts.*

At Corporation Stadium, Rajkot, October 10, 11, 12, 13. West Zone won by an innings and 55 runs. West Zone* 551 for eight dec. (R. J. Shastri 77, V. G. Kambli 151, S. R. Tendulkar 52, S. V. Manjrekar 144 not out, K. S. More 58, Extras 41; B. K. V. Prasad three for 63); South Zone 289 (W. V. Raman 33, M. Azharuddin 39, S. Sharath 30, A. Vaidya 55, J. Srinath 35; A. Kuruvilla four for 85) and 207 (M. Azharuddin 43, A. Vaidya 46; S. A. Ankola three for 30, R. J. Shastri five for 55). *West Zone 6 pts.*

At Corporation Stadium, Rajkot, October 19, 20, 21, 22. South Zone won by an innings and 47 runs. East Zone* 206 (Saurav C. Ganguly 51, S. S. Karim 34, C. S. Pandit 67; J. Srinath four for 41) and 80 (B. K. V. Prasad three for 31, J. Srinath three for 28, A. Kumble three for seven); South Zone 333 (V. B. Chandrasekhar 67, Robin Singh 109, J. Srinath 55; P. S. Vaidya three for 84, U. Chatterjee four for 57). *South Zone 6 pts.*

At Motibaug Palace Ground, Baroda, October 19, 20, 21, 22. North Zone won by an innings and 47 runs. West Zone* 187 (S. S. Bhave 55, S. V. Manjrekar 63; M. Prabhakar three for 37, Bhupinder Singh, sen. three for 51, A. R. Kapoor three for 52) and 169 (S. S. Bhave 32, S. V. Jedhe 51, S. V. Manjrekar 32 not out; Bhupinder Singh, sen. three for 37, Obaid Kamal three for 30); North Zone 403 (Ajay Sharma 110, Gursharan Singh 39, V. S. Yadav 40, A. R. Kapoor 48, Bhupinder Singh, sen. 50, Obaid Kamal 34 not out; A. Kuruvilla three for 131). *North Zone 6 pts.*

At Wankhede Stadium, Bombay, October 28, 29, 30, 31. East Zone won by an innings and 23 runs. East Zone* 462 (S. J. Kalyani 114, S. S. Karim 60, C. S. Pandit 125, S. T. Banerjee 81; A. W. Zaidi three for 62, N. D. Hirwani four for 133); Central Zone 197 (P. K. Dwevedi 50, G. K. Pandey 38; P. S. Vaidya four for 41, Avinash Kumar three for 47) and 242 (G. K. Pandey 106 not out; P. S. Vaidya three for 40, Chetan Sharma three for 64, U. Chatterjee four for 80). *East Zone 6 pts.*

At Sardar Patel Stadium, Valsad, October 28, 29, 30. South Zone won by seven wickets. North Zone 170 (A. D. Jadeja 30, R. Puri 30, Bhupinder Singh, sen. 32, Extras 42; B. K. V. Prasad seven for 38) and 99 (A. D. Jadeja 40, Gursharan Singh 34; Robin Singh four for 30, S. Subramaniam five for 14); South Zone* 200 (Robin Singh 60, S. Sharath 61; Bhupinder Singh, sen. three for 41, A. S. Bedi three for 35, Obaid Kamal four for 25) and 73 for three (V. B. Chandrasekhar 30). *South Zone 6 pts.*

At Poona Club, Pune, November 6, 7, 8, 9, 10. Central Zone won by 285 runs. Central Zone* 252 (M. Mudgal 65, G. K. Pandey 64; Robin Singh four for 50) and 387 (Yusuf Ali Khan 48, Rizwan Shamshad 141, P. V. Gandhe 80, R. Rathore 34; D. Vasu three for 55, M. Venkataramana four for 77); South Zone 200 (A. Pathak 35, D. Vasu 77; R. Rathore three for 58, N. D. Hirwani four for 72, P. V. Gandhe three for 42) and 154 (A. Pathak 30, V. B. Chandrasekhar 37, D. Vasu 30; N. D. Hirwani five for 48). *Central Zone 6 pts.*

At Lalbhai Contractor Stadium, Vesu, Surat, November 6, 7, 8. East Zone won by an innings and 101 runs. West Zone 235 (S. V. Manjrekar 113; S. T. Banerjee three for 51, U. Chatterjee three for 33) and 103 (S. T. Banerjee six for 48, P. S. Vaidya three for 24); East Zone* 439 (L. S. Rajput 73, Tarun Kumar 30, S. J. Kalyani 41, Saurav C. Ganguly 37, S. S. Karim 79, C. S. Pandit 48, Chetan Sharma 48, Avinash Kumar 30, Extras 30; Iqbal Siddiqui four for 97, T. B. Arothe three for 83). *East Zone 6 pts.*

At Wankhede Stadium, Bombay, November 15, 16, 17, 18, 19. West Zone won by 79 runs. West Zone 407 (R. J. Shastri 87, H. A. Kinikar 56, N. R. Mongia 81, T. B. Arothe 63, M. S. Narula 38 not out; R. Rathore three for 56, N. D. Hirwani three for 123) and 328 for six dec. (R. J. Shastri 126, S. V. Manjrekar 116; N. D. Hirwani four for 109); Central Zone* 424 (Yusuf Ali Khan 63, Rizwan Shamshad 133, G. K. Pandey 104, P. K. Dwevedi 31, Abhay Sharma 47 not out; A. Kuruvilla four for 71) and 232 (G. K. Pandey 72; Iqbal Siddiqui five for 55, M. S. Narula three for 18). *West Zone 6 pts, Central Zone 2 pts.*

At Poona Club, Pune, November 15, 16, 17, 18, 19. Drawn. North Zone 415 (Vikram Rathore 43, R. Puri 151, Bhupinder Singh, sen. 73, Maninder Singh 35, Extras 31; S. T. Banerjee three for 89, S. Sensharma three for 52, Chetan Sharma three for 137) and 274 for eight dec. (A. R. Kapoor 42, Bantoo Singh 63, A. D. Jadeja 62, Obaid Kamal 40); East Zone* 329 (L. S. Rajput 64, S. J. Kalyani 36, S. S. Karim 78, C. S. Pandit 60, Chetan Sharma 45) and 208 for six (L. S. Rajput 41, Chetan Sharma 60, S. S. Karim 52 not out; A. D. Jadeja four for 99). *North Zone 2 pts.*

DULEEP TROPHY WINNERS

1961-62	West Zone	1973-74	North Zone	1985-86	West Zone
1962-63	West Zone	1974-75	South Zone	1986-87	South Zone
1963-64	West Zone	1975-76	South Zone	1987-88	North Zone
1964-65	West Zone	1976-77	West Zone	1988-89	North Zone / West Zone
1965-66	South Zone	1977-78	West Zone		
1966-67	South Zone	1978-79	North Zone	1989-90	South Zone
1967-68	South Zone	1979-80	North Zone	1990-91	North Zone
1968-69	West Zone	1980-81	West Zone	1991-92	North Zone
1969-70	West Zone	1981-82	West Zone	1992-93	North Zone
1970-71	South Zone	1982-83	North Zone	1993-94	North Zone
1971-72	Central Zone	1983-84	North Zone		
1972-73	West Zone	1984-85	South Zone		

RANJI TROPHY, 1993-94

Central Zone

At M. B. College Ground, Udaipur, November 29, 30, December 1, 2. Rajasthan won by four wickets. Madhya Pradesh 187 (A. V. Vijayvargiya 68, R. K. Chauhan 52 not out; S. V. Mudkavi three for 29) and 393 (P. K. Dwevedi 99, D. K. Nilosey 123 not out, S. S. Lahore 38; R. Rathore four for 102, R. Sanghi three for 18); Rajasthan* 420 (R. Sanghi 108, on first-class debut, P. K. Amre 218; D. K. Nilosey four for 74, N. D. Hirwani four for 79) and 161 for six (G. Gautam 78 not out; H. S. Sodhi three for 33). *Rajasthan 6 pts.*

At OEF Stadium, Kanpur, November 29, 30, December 1, 2. Drawn. Vidarbha* 335 (K. S. M. Iyer 40, P. B. Hingnikar 68, Y. T. Ghare 36, U. I. Ghani 48, P. V. Gandhe 78; A. W. Zaidi four for 93, Gopal Sharma four for 71) and 367 for five dec. (M. G. Gogte 51, K. S. M. Iyer 89, Y. T. Ghare 107 not out, U. I. Ghani 87); Uttar Pradesh 583 for eight dec. (M. Mudgal 45, R. Pal 40, S. S. Khandkar 121, Rizwan Shamshad 160, R. V. Sapru 139 not out; V. S. Baddallu three for 117, P. B. Hingnikar three for 112). *Uttar Pradesh 2 pts.*

At Karnail Singh Stadium, Delhi, December 7, 8, 9, 10. Drawn. Railways 535 for four dec. (Yusuf Ali Khan 215, P. Shepherd 36, K. B. Kala 112, Manvinder Singh 56, Abhay Sharma 65 not out, P. S. Rawat 43 not out); Uttar Pradesh* 472 (M. Mudgal 129, S. S. Khandkar 43, Rizwan Shamshad 169, A. Gautam 48; Iqbal Thakur five for 144, K. Bharathan three for 101). *Railways 2 pts.*

At Indira Gandhi Stadium, Alwar, December 7, 8, 9, 10. Vidarbha won by four wickets. Rajasthan* 264 (G. Khoda 39, R. Sanghi 68, P. K. Amre 34; M. S. Doshi four for 44) and 208 (V. Yadav 80 not out, carrying his bat, G. Khoda 35; P. V. Gandhe eight for 61, including a hat-trick); Vidarbha 261 (K. S. M. Iyer 50, U. S. Phate 63, S. G. Gujar 31, U. I. Ghani 30; R. Rathore four for 50) and 212 for six (U. S. Phate 53, K. S. M. Iyer 32; S. V. Mudkavi three for 54). *Vidarbha 6 pts, Rajasthan 2 pts.*

At Bhilai Steel Plant Ground, Bhilai, December 15, 16, 17, 18. Drawn. Madhya Pradesh* 330 (M. S. Sahni 67, S. S. Lahore 78, N. D. Hirwani 59; Jasbir Singh four for 58) and 291 (A. Prabhakar 30, K. K. Patel 47, M. S. Sahni 71, D. K. Nilosey 31, R. K. Chauhan 35; Jasbir Singh eight for 125); Uttar Pradesh 303 (M. Mudgal 47, Rizwan Shamshad 84, R. V. Sapru 61, G. K. Pandey 37, S. Shukla 30; N. D. Hirwani five for 82) and 26 for one. *Madhya Pradesh 2 pts.*

At VCA Ground, Nagpur, December 15, 16, 17. Vidarbha won by six wickets. Railways* 179 (K. B. Kala 49, S. B. Bangar 45; P. V. Gandhe three for 45, M. S. Doshi three for 18) and 221 (P. Shepherd 30, P. S. Rawat 63, Abhay Sharma 62; P. V. Gandhe six for 76); Vidarbha 324 (P. B. Hingnikar 130, S. G. Gujar 51, Y. T. Ghare 49 not out; M. Majithia three for 97, Javed Alam seven for 99) and 80 for four (S. P. Thakre 40 not out). *Vidarbha 6 pts.*

At Karnail Singh Stadium, Delhi, December 23, 24, 25. Railways won by an innings and 31 runs. Railways 308 (K. B. Kala 62, Abhay Sharma 143, Manvinder Singh 34; Mohammad Aslam four for 75); Rajasthan* 156 (G. Khoda 37; K. Bharathan five for 39, Javed Alam four for 57) and 121 (Iqbal Thakur five for 36, Javed Alam three for 21). *Railways 6 pts.*

At VCA Ground, Nagpur, December 23, 24, 25, 26. Madhya Pradesh won by eight wickets. Madhya Pradesh 385 (A. V. Vijayvargiya 53, K. K. Patel 50, A. R. Khurasia 142, D. K. Nilosey 54; V. S. Baddallu three for 80, M. S. Doshi three for 78) and 47 for two (S. S. Lahore 36); Vidarbha* 165 (K. S. M. Iyer 43; N. D. Hirwani eight for 52) and 266 (M. G. Gogte 36, K. S. M. Iyer 41, U. I. Ghani 93; R. K. Chauhan three for 92, S. S. Lahore five for 66). *Madhya Pradesh 6 pts.*

At Roop Singh Stadium, Gwalior, January 1, 2, 3, 4. Madhya Pradesh won by three wickets. Railways* 339 (Yusuf Ali Khan 61, K. B. Kala 41, A. S. Negi 34, Abhay Sharma 103, K. Bharathan 45 retired hurt; R. K. Chauhan five for 130) and 279 (Yusuf Ali Khan 55, P. Shepherd 54, K. B. Kala 71, A. S. Negi 33, Abhay Sharma 30 not out; N. D. Hirwani eight for 66); Madhya Pradesh 324 (K. K. Patel 55, M. S. Sahni 59, A. R. Khurasia 104; M. Majithia four for 97, S. V. Bhosle three for 71) and 296 for seven (K. K. Patel 32, P. K. Dwevedi 93, D. K. Nilosey 80; Iqbal Thakur three for 87, K. Bharathan three for 60). *Madhya Pradesh 6 pts, Railways 2 pts.*

At Chowk Stadium, Lucknow, January 1, 2, 3, 4. Rajasthan won by two wickets. Uttar Pradesh* 448 (M. Mudgal 54, S. S. Khandkar 121, Rizwan Shamshad 83, G. K. Pandey 74, S. Shukla 40 not out; P. Krishnakumar six for 162, Mohammad Aslam four for 115) and 188 for two dec. (M. Mudgal 58, R. Pal 54, G. K. Pandey 34 not out, Rizwan Shamshad 30 not out); Rajasthan 403 (V. Yadav 157, G. Khoda 93, P. K. Amre 41, V. Joshi 31; Gopal Sharma six for 122) and 235 for eight (V. Yadav 30, G. Khoda 50; Jasbir Singh three for 39). *Rajasthan 6 pts, Uttar Pradesh 2 pts.*

Rajasthan 14 pts, Madhya Pradesh 14 pts, Vidarbha 12 pts, Railways 10 pts, Uttar Pradesh 4 pts. Rajasthan, Madhya Pradesh and Vidarbha qualified for the knockout stage.

East Zone

At Eden Gardens, Calcutta, November 30, December 1, 2, 3. Bengal won by an innings and 83 runs. Bengal 529 for three dec. (Arun Lal 43, S. J. Kalyani 208, Saurav C. Ganguly 200 not out, including a hundred before lunch); Tripura* 175 (R. Deb-Burman 67; P. S. Vaidya five for 68, Chetan Sharma three for 62) and 271 (Arup Deb-Burman 63, S. Paul 56, S. Dasgupta 76 not out, R. Vals 40; P. S. Vaidya three for 64, Chetan Sharma four for 72). *Bengal 6 pts.*

At Moinul Haq Stadium, Patna, November 30, December 1, 2, 3. Drawn. Assam* 398 (Deepak Das 76, Rajinder Singh 42, C. S. Pandit 111, Z. Zuffri 38, Extras 36; D. K. Singh five for 100) and 240 for five dec. (Deepak Das 51, Z. Zuffri 52, L. S. Rajput 54 not out, C. S. Pandit 39 not out); Bihar 254 (Adil Hussain 60, S. R. Sinha 36; Javed Zaman four for 80) and 179 for five (Sanjeev Kumar 54; R. C. Thakkar three for 50). *Assam 2 pts.*

At Eden Gardens, Calcutta, December 9, 10, 11, 12. Bengal won by 348 runs. Bengal 274 (Saurav C. Ganguly 148, Chetan Sharma 65; Javed Zaman five for 68) and 441 for three dec. (I. B. Roy 130, P. S. Vaidya 51, Chetan Sharma 114 not out, Saurav C. Ganguly 100 not out); Assam* 192 (D. Chakraborty 34, Rajinder Singh 36, R. C. Thakkar 45; U. Chatterjee six for 29) and 175 (L. S. Rajput 33, G. Dutta 32; Chetan Sharma three for 25, U. Chatterjee five for 44). *Bengal 6 pts.*

At Sports Stadium, Berhampur, December 10, 11, 12. Orissa won by nine wickets. Tripura* 172 (G. Banik 38; R. B. Biswal four for 61) and 163 (R. Deb-Burman 53; R. B. Biswal five for 46); Orissa 284 (M. Roy 31, Ameya Roy 72, B. D. Mohanty 76; S. Roy three for 38) and 53 for one. *Orissa 6 pts.*

At Government High School Ground, Karimganj, December 18, 19, 20. Assam won by an innings and 59 runs. Assam* 396 (L. S. Rajput 74, D. Chakraborty 33, K. K. Barua 50, Rajinder Singh 96 not out, G. Dutta 43, Extras 49; A. Saha three for 67); Tripura 188 (P. Debnath 38, R. Deb-Burman 33; Javed Zaman six for 65, R. Bora three for 18) and 149 (S. Paul 42, S. Dasgupta 32; Javed Zaman five for 51). *Assam 6 pts.*

At Ispat Stadium, Rourkela, December 19, 20, 21, 22. Drawn. Bihar* 426 (Indranil Bose 38, Sanjeev Kumar 51, S. S. Karim 138, S. T. Banerjee 77; P. Sushil Kumar three for 137) and 151 for six (Indranil Bose 33, Deepak Kumar 38; M. Roy three for 63); Orissa 293 (Suresh Kumar 35, K. Dube 63, Ameya Roy 65, R. B. Biswal 37, A. Khatua 30; Avinash Kumar four for 79, K. V. P. Rao four for 56). *Bihar 2 pts.*

At Mecon, Ranchi, December 26, 27, 28. Bengal won by an innings and 172 runs. Bihar* 150 (Indranil Bose 57; U. Chatterjee three for 25, Chetan Sharma six for 30) and 131 (P. S. Vaidya four for 72); Bengal 453 (Arun Lal 142, S. J. Kalyani 132, Ashok Malhotra 33, Chetan Sharma 38 not out; D. K. Singh five for 102, Avinash Kumar four for 119). *Bengal 6 pts.*

At Sports Stadium, Berhampur, December 27, 28, 29. Orissa won by an innings and 79 runs. Assam* 160 (R. Bora 51; R. B. Biswal seven for 45) and 157 (G. Dutta 52, Izaz Hussain 38 not out; P. Sushil Kumar five for 60, R. B. Biswal three for 30); Orissa 396 (P. Mohapatra 50, Ameya Roy 88, R. B. Biswal 48, A. Khatua 48, B. D. Mohanty 30, Extras 54; R. Bora three for 112). *Orissa 6 pts.*

At Permit Ground, Balasore, January 4, 5, 6, 7. Bengal won by eight wickets. Orissa* 204 (P. Mohapatra 47, K. Dube 41, A. Khatua 32; Chetan Sharma five for 52, U. Chatterjee three for 62) and 158 (P. Mohapatra 37, A. Khatua 40, Extras 31; Chetan Sharma four for 34); Bengal 313 (Arun Lal 40, S. J. Kalyani 30, Saurav C. Ganguly 34, Ashok Malhotra 39, Snehashish C. Ganguly 64, A. Sheikh 43 not out; V. Arvind three for 51, Sushil Kumar three for 100, R. B. Biswal three for 78) and 51 for two (Arun Lal 30 not out). *Bengal 6 pts.*

At Polytechnic Ground, Agartala, January 4, 5, 6. Bihar won by an innings and 121 runs. Bihar 227 (Indranil Bose 50, Sunil Kumar 39, Extras 30; S. Roy three for 38, R. Vals three for 49); Tripura* 62 (K. V. P. Rao six for 12) and 44 (Avinash Kumar three for two, K. V. P. Rao five for 22). *Bihar 6 pts.*

Bengal 24 pts, Orissa 12 pts, Assam 8 pts, Bihar 8 pts, Tripura 0 pts. Bengal, Orissa and Assam (on better quotient) qualified for the knockout stage.

North Zone

At Feroz Shah Kotla Ground, Delhi, November 26, 27, 28, 29. Drawn. Delhi* 114 (Bantoo Singh 47; V. Jain five for 48, Dhanraj Singh four for 19) and 365 (Hitesh Sharma 32, M. Nayyar 50, Bantoo Singh 81, G. Vadhera 32, A. S. Wassan 104 not out, F. Ghayas 42; P. Jain six for 86); Haryana 475 (Jitender Singh 31, N. R. Goel 166, Avtar Singh 53, A. S. Kaypee 74, Dhanraj Singh 36, Extras 38; Maninder Singh five for 120). *Haryana 2 pts.*

At PCA Stadium, Mohali, Chandigarh, December 2, 3, 4, 5. Punjab won by 203 runs. Punjab* 169 (Vikram Rathore 54, Bhupinder Singh, sen. 62; M. V. Rao seven for 77) and 385 for eight dec. (Vikram Rathore 45, Ajay Mehra 136, R. Kalsi 45, Bhupinder Singh, jun. 100 not out, Extras 31; M. V. Rao five for 85); Services 181 (S. Chopra 35, V. Purushottam 32; B. Vij six for 67) and 170 (S. Chopra 52, Chinmoy Sharma 37; Bhupinder Singh, sen. four for 37). *Punjab 6 pts, Services 2 pts.*

At Indira Gandhi Stadium, Una, December 8, 9, 10. Services won by an innings and 94 runs. Himachal Pradesh* 150 (R. Bittu 45; M. Subramaniam six for 32) and 137 (R. Bittu 83; P. Maitreya four for 30, S. Shirsat five for 38); Services 381 (H. Bhaskar 30, S. Chopra 129, R. Vinayak 77, Rashid Mohsin 99 not out; Jaswant Rai five for 125). *Services 6 pts.*

At PCA Stadium, Mohali, Chandigarh, December 8, 9, 10. Punjab won by an innings and 151 runs. Punjab* 525 for three dec. (Vikram Rathore 250, Ajay Mehra 88, Amit Sharma 97, Gursharan Singh 50 not out); Jammu and Kashmir 243 (Kanwaljit Singh 32, A. Gupta 87, Ranjit Bali 38; B. Vij seven for 58) and 131 (Vishal Sharma 32; A. R. Kapoor five for 57, B. Vij four for 32). *Punjab 6 pts.*

At Nahar Singh Stadium, Faridabad, December 14, 15, 16, 17. Haryana won by an innings and 94 runs. Services* 314 (R. Vinayak 55, S. Chopra 61, Chinmoy Sharma 74; A. D. Jadeja three for 65, P. Jain five for 112) and 120 (R. Vinayak 46; V. Jain seven for 45); Haryana 528 for seven dec. (Jitender Singh 71, R. Puri 143, A. S. Kaypee 88, A. D. Jadeja 54, V. S. Yadav 67, Extras 40; M. Subramaniam four for 98). *Haryana 6 pts.*

At Indira Gandhi Stadium, Una, December 14, 15, 16, 17. Drawn. Himachal Pradesh* 223 (R. Bittu 103; Sanjay Sharma six for 66) and 454 for seven dec. (R. Bittu 150, R. Nayyar 97, N. Gour 45, Shambhu Sharma 74, Extras 31; Abdul Qayyum three for 117); Jammu and Kashmir 345 (Raju Sharma 39, V. Bhaskar 30, Ranjit Bali 37, Sanjay Sharma 75, Arun Sharma 50 not out, Extras 32; S. Thakur five for 116) and 211 for six (Vishal Sharma 49, Ranjit Bali 68, V. Bhaskar 52). *Jammu and Kashmir 2 pts.*

At Punjab Agricultural University Ground, Ludhiana, December 14, 15, 16. Delhi won by four wickets. Punjab 109 (A. S. Wassan four for 13, F. Ghayas three for 16) and 201 (Vikram Rathore 34, Amit Sharma 35, A. R. Kapoor 49, Bhupinder Singh, sen. 43; A. S. Wassan four for 43); Delhi* 97 (Bhupinder Singh, sen. three for 33, A. S. Bedi three for 30, Obaid Kamal four for 29) and 214 for six (M. Prabhakar 107 not out). *Delhi 6 pts, Punjab 2 pts.*

At Vishkarma School Ground, Rohtak, December 20, 21, 22. Haryana won by an innings and 132 runs. Haryana* 470 (A. D. Jadeja 40, Jitender Singh 120, A. S. Kaypee 129, V. S. Yadav 37, Dhanraj Singh 47; A. Gupta four for 98, Sanjay Sharma four for 128); Jammu and Kashmir 114 (P. Jain six for 32) and 224 (A. Bhatia 69, Sanjay Sharma 41 not out; P. Jain five for 85, P. Thakur five for 69). *Haryana 6 pts.*

At PCA Stadium, Mohali, Chandigarh, December 20, 21, 22. Punjab won by an innings and 225 runs. Punjab* 496 for four dec. (Vikram Rathore 155, N. S. Sidhu 59, Bhupinder Singh, jun. 132, K. Mohan 57, Gursharan Singh 77 not out); Himachal Pradesh 135 (N. Gour 50; B. Vij six for 44) and 136 (R. Nayyar 30; B. Vij six for 32). *Punjab 6 pts.*

At Air Force Complex, Palam, Delhi, December 20, 21, 22, 23. Drawn. Services* 514 (S. Chopra 186, S. Narula 102, Chinmoy Sharma 41, P. Maitreya 44, M. Subramaniam 33, Extras 35; Maninder Singh three for 135) and 68 for three (Chinmoy Sharma 31 not out); Delhi 389 (V. Dahiya 64, M. Prabhakar 31, Akash Malhotra 40, S. Dogra 152 not out, Maninder Singh 39; P. Maitreya four for 89, S. Shirsat three for 108). *Services 2 pts.*

At Nehru Stadium, Gurgaon, December 26, 27, 28, 29. Punjab won by 277 runs. Punjab* 303 (Vikram Rathore 33, N. S. Sidhu 50, Bhupinder Singh, jun. 47, B. Vij 42; P. Jain three for 88) and 229 for seven dec. (Gursharan Singh 69, Bhupinder Singh, jun. 42, Amit Sharma 39 not out; P. Thakur five for 78); Haryana 126 (R. Puri 35; Bhupinder Singh, sen. seven for 46) and 129 (R. Puri 39; B. Vij five for 19). *Punjab 6 pts.*

At Indira Gandhi Stadium, Una, December 26, 27, 28. Delhi won by an innings and 120 runs. Himachal Pradesh 156 (Shambhu Sharma 33; Shakti Singh four for 46, Maninder Singh five for 39) and 156 (R. Bittu 31, N. Gour 32, R. Nayyar 43 not out; Maninder Singh six for 51); Delhi* 432 for three dec. (Bantoo Singh 130, Ajay Sharma 235 not out). *Delhi 6 pts.*

At Air Force Complex, Palam, Delhi, December 26, 27, 28, 29. Services won by ten wickets. Services* 467 (S. Chopra 51, S. Narula 64, R. Vinayak 97, P. Maitreya 45, M. Subramaniam 85, S. Shirsat 47; Vishal Sharma three for 75, A. Gupta three for 106) and four for no wkt; Jammu and Kashmir 274 (A. Bhatia 64, A. Gupta 59, Abdul Qayyum 46; M. V. Rao four for 68) and 194 (Vishal Sharma 43, Sarabjit Singh 63; S. Shirsat five for 65). *Services 6 pts.*

At Feroz Shah Kotla Ground, Delhi, January 1, 2, 3. Delhi won by an innings and 30 runs, Jammu and Kashmir 109 (Kanwaljit Singh 51; A. S. Wassan four for 34, Akash Malhotra three for seven) and 203 (Raju Sharma 60; Shakti Singh three for 58); Delhi* 342 (V. Dahiya 66, M. Prabhakar 165; Abdul Qayyum six for 130). *Delhi 6 pts.*

At T. I. T. School Ground, Bhiwani, January 1, 2, 3. Haryana won by an innings and 185 runs. Haryana* 476 for six dec. (Jitender Singh 82, N. R. Goel 112, A. S. Kaypee 78, R. Puri 101 not out, Avtar Singh 50 not out); Himachal Pradesh 145 (Rajnish Kumar 32, Brijinder Sharma 38; P. Jain seven for 73) and 146 (R Nayyar 64; P. Jain eight for 67). *Haryana 6 pts.*

Punjab 26 pts, Haryana 20 pts, Delhi 18 pts, Services 16 pts, Jammu and Kashmir 2 pts, Himachal Pradesh 0 pts. Punjab, Haryana and Delhi qualified for the knockout stage.

South Zone

At Indira Gandhi Stadium, Vijayawada, December 3, 4, 5, 6. Drawn. Karnataka* 311 for six (P. V. Shashikanth 89, J. Arun Kumar 84, R. S. Dravid 54, K. A. Jeshwant 37) v Andhra. *Andhra 1 pt, Karnataka 1 pt.*

At Panji Gymkhana, Panjim, December 3, 4, 5, 6. Drawn. Goa* 204 (A. Dabholkar 37, A. Shetty 71 not out; Suresh Kumar four for 64) and 11 for no wkt; Kerala 353 for nine dec. (V. Narayan Kutty 63, P. T. Subramaniam 53, S. Oasis 35, B. Ramaprakash 45, F. V. Rashid 91, K. N. A. Padmanabhan 43; A. Shetty four for 95). *Kerala 2 pts.*

At M. A. Chidambaram Stadium, Madras, December 3, 4, 5, 6. Drawn. Hyderabad 78 for three (R. A. Swarup 44) v Tamil Nadu*. *Tamil Nadu 1 pt, Hyderabad 1 pt.*

At DNR College Ground, Bhimavaram, December 11, 12, 13. Tamil Nadu won by 122 runs. Tamil Nadu 208 (Tanveer Jabbar 51, M. Senthilnathan 54, Extras 31; V. Vijayasarathy three for 52, G. V. V. Gopalraju five for 35) and 135 (Tanveer Jabbar 46; H. Ramkishen four for 28); Andhra* 109 (M. F. Rehman 42; D. Vasu three for 11, M. Venkataramana four for 20) and 112 (S. Subramaniam three for 29, M. Venkataramana three for 12). *Tamil Nadu 6 pts.*

At M. Chinnaswamy Stadium, Bangalore, December 11, 12, 13. Karnataka won by an innings and 85 runs. Karnataka 392 (J. Arun Kumar 141, P. V. Shashikanth 58, A. Vaidya 68, S. Joshi 64 not out; A. Shetty four for 113); Goa* 139 (A. Gaikwad 48; J. Srinath three for 61, B. K. V. Prasad five for 41) and 168 (P. A. Amonkar 42, N. A. Vernekar 32; J. Srinath four for 55, R. Ananth four for 56). *Karnataka 6 pts.*

At Nehru Stadium, Kottayam, December 11, 12, 13. Hyderabad won by 169 runs. Hyderabad* 176 (V. Jaisimha 57, V. Pratap 31; K. N. A. Padmanabhan five for 35, B. Ramaprakash three for 49) and 268 for nine dec. (R. A. Swarup 38, M. V. Sridhar 124, Yuvraj Singh 43; K. N. A. Padmanabhan four for 98, B. Ramaprakash four for 77); Kerala 65 (S. L. V. Raju five for 18, Arshad Ayub five for 28, including a hat-trick) and 210 (S. Oasis 38, F. V. Rashid 43, K. N. A. Padmanabhan 42 not out; S. L. V. Raju five for 77). *Hyderabad 6 pts.*

At Port Trust Golden Jubilee Stadium, Vishakhapatnam, December 19, 20, 21, 22. Drawn. Andhra* 301 (O. Vinod Kumar 36, K. V. S. D. Kamaraju 31, V. Vijayasarathy 66, V. Vinay Kumar 74; N. Kambli three for 60) and 180 (A. Pathak 52, M. F. Rehman 51; S. Mahadevan six for 60, A. Shetty three for 56); Goa 251 (A. Gaikwad 48, S. Dhuri 43, N. A. Vernekar 39; H. Ramkishen five for 77) and 148 for nine (Y. Barde 30, A. Gaikwad 30, M. Sawkar 37; V. Vijayasarathy four for 52). *Andhra 2 pts.*

At M. A. Chidambaram Stadium, Madras, December 19, 20, 21, 22. Drawn. Tamil Nadu* 267 (V. B. Chandrasekhar 62, Robin Singh 112, M. Senthilnathan 36; B. Ramaprakash five for 90, K. N. A. Padmanabhan three for 87); Kerala nought for no wkt. *Tamil Nadu 1 pt, Kerala 1 pt.*

At Gymkhana Ground, Secunderabad, December 20, 21, 22, 23. Hyderabad won by eight wickets. Karnataka* 252 (R. S. Dravid 60, A. Vaidya 30, J. Srinath 46; S. L. V. Raju four for 49, Arshad Ayub five for 78) and 227 (P. V. Shashikanth 46, K. Srinath 44, K. A. Jeshwant 68; S. L. V. Raju three for 53, Arshad Ayub three for 95, Kanwaljit Singh three for 44); Hyderabad 322 (M. Azharuddin 120, V. Jaisimha 30, V. Pratap 36, Kanwaljit Singh 50; B. K. V. Prasad three for 59) and 158 for two (Abdul Azeem 33, R. A. Swarup 45, M. V. Sridhar 46 not out). *Hyderabad 6 pts.*

At Dr Rajendra Prasad Stadium, Futardo, Margao, December 27, 28, 29. Hyderabad won by an innings and 125 runs. Hyderabad 362 (M. Azharuddin 155, V. Jaisimha 95; R. D. Kambli four for 119, A. Shetty three for 62); Goa* 88 (P. A. Amonkar 39; S. L. V. Raju five for 23, Arshad Ayub four for 26) and 149 (A. Gaikwad 50, M. Sawkar 50; N. P. Singh four for 29, Kanwaljit Singh three for 28). *Hyderabad 6 pts.*

At Nehru Stadium, Kottayam, December 27, 28, 29. Kerala won by ten wickets. Andhra* 169 (A. Pathak 53, V. Vijayasarathy 51 not out; K. N. A. Padmanabhan eight for 57) and 86 (Suresh Kumar four for 19, K. N. A. Padmanabhan six for 37); Kerala 232 (V. Narayan Kutty 47, P. G. Sunder 103, F. V. Rashid 32; G. V. V. Gopalraju six for 54) and 27 for no wkt. *Kerala 6 pts.*

At M. Chinnaswamy Stadium, Bangalore, December 31, January 1, 2, 3. Karnataka won by 131 runs. Karnataka* 148 (R. S. Dravid 37, K. A. Jeshwant 36; D. Vasu three for 49, M. Venkataramana five for 29) and 376 for seven dec. (J. Arun Kumar 68, R. S. Dravid 151 not out, A. Kumble 34; D. Vasu three for 81, S. Subramaniam three for 120); Tamil Nadu 222 (W. V. Raman 31, M. Senthilnathan 43, S. Subramaniam 43, J. Gokulkrishnan 34; J. Srinath five for 62, A. Kumble three for 56) and 171 (V. B. Chandrasekhar 30, Arjan Kripal Singh 64 not out; B. K. V. Prasad four for 31, A. Kumble three for 57). *Karnataka 6 pts, Tamil Nadu 2 pts.*

HYDERABAD v ANDHRA

At Gymkhana Ground, Secunderabad, January 8, 9, 10, 11. Drawn. Hyderabad 2 pts. Toss: Andhra.

Close of play: First day, Andhra 224-6 (V. Vinay Kumar 10*, Pawan Kumar 10*); Second day, Hyderabad 296-3 (M. V. Sridhar 127*, V. Jaisimha 44*); Third day, Hyderabad 763-4 (M. V. Sridhar 290*, N. David 126*).

Andhra

First innings		Second innings	
G. N. Srinivas c Yuvraj Singh b N. P. Singh	99	– (2) c Yuvraj Singh b N. P. Singh	21
A. Pathak c M. V. Sridhar b Pratap	4	– (1) b R. Sridhar	64
*M. F. Rehman c Kanwaljit Singh b Pratap	73	– b Kanwaljit Singh	9
K. V. S. D. Kamaraju lbw b Kanwaljit Singh	18	– b Kanwaljit Singh	27
†K. Veerbrahman c M. V. Sridhar b N. P. Singh	0	– (7) not out	15
V. Vijayasarathy c and b N. P. Singh	0	– (5) lbw b Kanwaljit Singh	23
V. Vinay Kumar c Yuvraj Singh b Pratap	19	– (6) c Yuvraj Singh b N. P. Singh	17
Pawan Kumar c Yuvraj Singh b N. P. Singh	24	– b Kanwaljit Singh	0
P. Prakash c Pratap b Kanwaljit Singh	0	– not out	1
G. V. V. Gopalraju c Yuvraj Singh b N. P. Singh	10		
H. Ramkishen not out	0		
B 8, l-b 4, w 4	16	L-b 2, w 1	3
1/15 2/168 3/190 4/192 5/192 6/213 7/245 8/249 9/263	263	1/37 2/64 3/118 4/130 5/147 6/163 7/164 (7 wkts)	180

Bowling: *First Innings*—N. P. Singh 30–7–84–5; Pratap 17–3–55–3; Arshad Ayub 16–4–25–0; Kanwaljit Singh 19.1–6–38–2; R. Sridhar 17–4–46–0; Swarup 4–2–2–0; David 2–1–1–0. *Second Innings*—N. P. Singh 14–2–57–2; Pratap 6–0–32–0; Kanwaljit Singh 21–8–53–4; R. Sridhar 14–4–36–1.

Hyderabad

Abdul Azeem c Srinivas b Prakash	85
R. A. Swarup c Gopalraju b Ramkishen	13
M. V. Sridhar c Vinay Kumar b Rehman	366
V. Pratap run out	17
V. Jaisimha c Pawan Kumar b Prakash	211
N. David not out	207
†Yuvraj Singh c Rehman b Gopalraju	15
N. P. Singh not out	3
B 11, l-b 8, w 1, n-b 7	27
1/30 2/174 3/210 4/554 5/880 6/941 (6 wkts dec.)	944

*Arshad Ayub, R. Sridhar and Kanwaljit Singh did not bat.

Bowling: Ramkishen 37–5–154–1; Pawan Kumar 13–0–55–0; Vijayasarathy 27–1–132–0; Gopalraju 54–4–225–1; Prakash 53–3–241–2; Pathak 1–0–8–0; Rehman 16–1–59–1; Vinay Kumar 7–2–33–0; Srinivas 3–0–18–0.

Umpires: A. R. Bhat and V. N. Kulkarni.

At M. Chinnaswamy Stadium, Bangalore, January 8, 9, 10, 11. Karnataka won by eight wickets. Karnataka* 265 (S. Bhat 31, R. S. Dravid 105 not out, A. Vaidya 35; Suresh Kumar three for 66, K. N. A. Padmanabhan four for 89) and 136 for two (S. Bhat 64 not out, R. S. Dravid 56 not out); Kerala 89 (B. K. V. Prasad seven for 37) and 310 (S. Oasis 110, B. Ramaprakash 67, F. V. Rashid 39; B. K. V. Prasad three for 21, R. Ananth three for 123). *Karnataka 6 pts.*

At M. A. Chidambaram Stadium, Madras, January 8, 9, 10. Tamil Nadu won by ten wickets. Goa 184 (P. A. Amonkar 58; S. Mahesh three for 40, M. Venkataramana three for 44) and 160 (P. A. Amonkar 38, Y. Barde 36; S. Subramaniam five for 49, M. Venkataramana four for 45); Tamil Nadu* 295 (D. Vasu 55, Tanveer Jabbar 30, M. Senthilnathan 47, Arjan Kripal Singh 85, M. Sanjay 34; U. Naik six for 74) and 53 for no wkt (D. Vasu 34 not out). *Tamil Nadu 6 pts.*

Hyderabad 21 pts, Karnataka 19 pts, Tamil Nadu 16 pts, Kerala 9 pts, Andhra 3 pts, Goa 0 pts. Hyderabad, Karnataka and Tamil Nadu qualified for the knockout stage.

West Zone

At GSFC Ground, Baroda, December 1, 2, 3, 4. Bombay won by an innings and 118 runs. Bombay 523 (J. V. Paranjpe 40, V. G. Kambli 75, S. R. Tendulkar 50, S. V. Manjrekar 156, S. S. Dighe 102, S. V. Bahutule 39 not out; T. B. Arothe five for 178); Baroda* 279 (K. S. Chavan 33, A. C. Bedade 133; R. J. Shastri six for 73) and 126 (N. R. Mongia 51; S. V. Bahutule four for 42). *Bombay 6 pts.*

At Shastri Ground, Vallabh Vidyanagar, December 1, 2, 3, 4. Maharashtra won by an innings and 44 runs. Gujarat 157 (Maqbul Malam 71; Iqbal Siddiqui three for 65) and 259 (M. H. Parmar 69, Parashar Patel 31, N. A. Patel 69; Iqbal Siddiqui five for 70, P. J. Kanade three for 52); Maharashtra* 460 for six dec. (H. A. Kinikar 90, S. S. Sugwekar 96, J. Narse 139 not out, S. J. Jadhav 50). *Maharashtra 6 pts.*

At Dadoji Konddeo Stadium, Thane, December 8, 9, 10. Bombay won by nine wickets. Maharashtra 285 (H. A. Kinikar 34, S. V. Jedhe 67, R. Manohar 76, P. Rai 32 not out; A. Kuruvilla three for 68, R. J. Shastri three for 36) and 75 (P. Mhambre five for 35); Bombay* 344 (Z. Bharucha 93, S. V. Manjrekar 41, S. R. Tendulkar 138, Extras 31; P. J. Kanade four for 77) and 17 for one. *Bombay 6 pts.*

At Corporation Stadium, Rajkot, December 8, 9, 10, 11. Baroda won by an innings and 28 runs. Baroda 459 (R. B. Parikh 77, K. S. Chavan 118, T. B. Arothe 31, A. C. Bedade 81, K. S. More 56); Saurashtra* 217 (S. S. Tanna 67, M. P. Rana 42; T. B. Arothe six for 76) and 214 (N. R. Odedra 61, S. Kotak 82; R. G. M. Patel five for 33). *Baroda 6 pts.*

At Poona Club, Pune, December 16, 17, 18, 19. Drawn. Baroda 462 (N. R. Mongia 30, T. B. Arothe 48, A. C. Bedade 122, J. J. Martin 134, K. S. More 51, M. S. Narula 31 not out; Iqbal Siddiqui seven for 139) and 68 for one; Maharashtra* 451 (H. A. Kinikar 65, S. S. Bhave 111, A. V. Kale 132, on first-class debut, J. Narse 72; M. S. Narula six for 101). *Baroda 2 pts.*

At Corporation Stadium, Rajkot, December 16, 17, 18, 19. Drawn. Gujarat* 378 (M. H. Parmar 138, Umesh Patel 41, N. Modi 36, K. Patadiwala 66 not out; R. R. Garsondia four for 82, N. P. Rana three for 79) and 154 for nine dec. (N. Modi 47; B. M. Radia four for 48); Saurashtra 321 (S. S. Tanna 71, N. R. Odedra 52, S. Kotak 81; B. H. Mistry four for 73) and 163 for seven (B. Dutta 63, N. R. Odedra 75; D. T. Patel four for 55). *Gujarat 2 pts.*

At Sardar Patel Stadium, Ahmedabad, December 24, 25, 26, 27. Bombay won by ten wickets. Bombay* 414 (R. J. Shastri 100, S. V. Manjrekar 146, S. V. Bahutule 40; D. T. Patel three for 74) and seven for no wkt; Gujarat 125 (M. H. Parmar 45; S. S. Patil four for 35) and 295 (K. Patadiwala 152, B. Mehta 32; S. V. Bahutule four for 77). *Bombay 6 pts.*

At Nehru Stadium, Pune, December 24, 25, 26, 27. Drawn. Maharashtra* 589 for three dec. (H. A. Kinikar 184, S. S. Bhave 180, S. V. Jedhe 138 not out, A. V. Kale 58); Saurashtra 372 (N. R. Odedra 137, B. Dutta 39, S. Kotak 87; P. J. Kanade four for 57) and 193 for two (S. S. Tanna 57 not out, B. M. Jadeja 75). *Maharashtra 2 pts.*

At IPCL Sports Complex Ground, Baroda, December 31, January 1, 2, 3. Drawn. Baroda 558 for eight dec. (R. B. Parikh 54, N. R. Mongia 87, T. B. Arothe 31, A. C. Bedade 57, J. J. Martin 152 not out, K. S. More 115, Extras 33; Mukesh Patel three for 111) and 124 for six dec. (R. B. Parikh 40; Mukesh Patel three for 51); Gujarat* 216 (N. Modi 50, N. A. Patel 55; R. G. M. Patel three for 53, V. Buch three for 53, T. B. Arothe three for 27) and 163 for six (N. Bakriwala 56, N. A. Patel 59; T. B. Arothe three for 37). *Baroda 2 pts.*

At Wankhede Stadium, Bombay, December 31, January 1, 2, 3. Bombay won by eight wickets. Saurashtra 335 (S. S. Tanna 35, N. R. Odedra 31, B. M. Jadeja 40, B. Dutta 69, S. Kotak 71, M. Parmar 33; A. Kuruvilla three for 39, P. Mhambre three for 94, S. V. Bahutule three for 65) and 190 (S. S. Tanna 38, S. Kotak 40; S. A. Ankola four for 67, P. Mhambre six for 47); Bombay* 320 (Z. Bharucha 36, S. V. Manjrekar 68, S. S. Dighe 51, S. V. Bahutule 47, S. S. Patil 35; M. P. Rana five for 98) and 206 for two (R. J. Shastri 93 not out, S. R. Tendulkar 80 not out). *Bombay 6 pts, Saurashtra 2 pts.*

Bombay 24 pts, Baroda 10 pts, Maharashtra 8 pts, Gujarat 2 pts, Saurashtra 2 pts. Bombay, Baroda and Maharashtra qualified for the knockout stage.

Pre-quarter-finals

At IPCL Sports Complex Ground, Baroda, February 12, 13, 14, 15, 16. Drawn. Baroda were declared winners by virtue of their first-innings lead. Baroda 366 (R. B. Parikh 99, K. S. Chavan 42, T. B. Arothe 70, J. J. Martin 54, Extras 40; D. Vasu five for 87) and 368 (P. Dave 80, R. G. M. Patel 38, K. S. Chavan 67, A. C. Bedade 46, K. S. More 40, M. S. Narula 38 not out; S. Mahesh three for 60, S. Subramaniam four for 83); Tamil Nadu* 268 (Robin Singh 87; M. S. Narula three for 39, V. Buch three for 103, T. B. Arothe four for 35) and 97 for four (D. Vasu 51; V. Buch three for 17).

At Eden Gardens, Calcutta, February 12, 13, 14, 15, 16. Drawn. Bengal were declared winners by virtue of their first-innings lead. Bengal* 213 (Arun Lal 43, Snehashish C. Ganguly 68 not out) and 445 for eight (Arun Lal 177, I. B. Roy 49, S. J. Kalyani 51, Saurav C. Ganguly 38, Ashok Malhotra 64 not out; Akash Malhotra three for 42); Delhi 178 (Akash Malhotra 34, Shakti Singh 31; P. S. Vaidya three for 61, S. Sensharma four for 45, including a hat-trick, Chetan Sharma three for 48).

At Nahar Singh Stadium, Faridabad, February 12, 13, 14, 15. Bombay won by an innings and 202 runs. Bombay* 718 (J. V. Paranjpe 117, A. A. Muzumdar 260, on first-class debut, R. J. Shastri 118, S. S. Dighe 111, S. V. Bahutule 44, Extras 32; P. Thakur seven for 254); Haryana 291 (Avtar Singh 37, V. S. Yadav 131, Ashok Singh 42; Manish Patel five for 80, S. V. Bahutule three for 66) and 225 (N. R. Goel 49, Parender Sharma 43, Avtar Singh 44, V. S. Yadav 50; S. V. Bahutule four for 81, Iqbal Khan five for 37).

At M. Chinnaswamy Stadium, Bangalore, February 12, 13, 14. Karnataka won by an innings and 186 runs. Karnataka 468 (J. Arun Kumar 75, P. V. Shashikanth 95, R. S. Dravid 38, K. A. Jeshwant 123, S. M. H. Kirmani 30, R. Ananth 30, Extras 30; S. Chakraborty five for 128); Assam* 107 (D. Johnson eight for 55) and 175 (Rajinder Singh 44; B. K. V. Prasad three for 49, R. Ananth three for 40).

At Nehru Stadium, Indore, February 12, 13, 14, 15, 16. Drawn. Orissa were declared winners by virtue of their first-innings lead. Orissa* 437 (P. Mohapatra 140, R. B. Biswal 138, B. D. Mohanty 35, P. Sushil Kumar 42; S. S. Lahore three for 96, N. D. Hirwani three for 133, D. Parmar three for 72) and 244 (P. Sushil Kumar 65, S. S. Das 98; D. Parmar six for 105); Madhya Pradesh 370 (A. R. Khurasia 91, P. K. Dwevedi 64, A. Prabhakar 37, S. S. Lahore 43, Extras 32; P. Sushil Kumar three for 113, R. B. Biswal three for 117) and 230 for nine (M. S. Sahni 37, D. K. Nilosey 111 not out; V. Arvind four for 102).

At Mansarovar Stadium, Jaipur, February 12, 13, 14, 15, 16. Hyderabad won by 167 runs. Hyderabad* 272 (M. V. Sridhar 89, V. Pratap 67, Yuvraj Singh 33 not out; P. Krishnakumar five for 78) and 233 (R. A. Swarup 48, N. David 47; R. Rathore three for 58, P. Krishnakumar three for 54); Rajasthan 202 (S. V. Mudkavi 56, D. Jain 45; N. P. Singh three for 39, Kanwaljit Singh three for ten) and 136 (V. Yadav 33; S. Meeraj three for 24, Kanwaljit Singh four for 22).

At VCA Ground, Nagpur, February 12, 13, 14, 15, 16. Drawn. Maharashtra were declared winners by virtue of their first-innings lead. Maharashtra* 535 (S. S. Bhave 129, S. V. Jedhe 47, S. S. Sugwekar 106, A. V. Kale 61, J. Narse 67, S. M. Kondhalkar 35, Iqbal Siddiqui 33; M. S. Doshi five for 157) and 350 for two dec. (H. A. Kinikar 50, S. S. Bhave 34, S. V. Jedhe 150 not out, S. S. Sugwekar 106 not out); Vidarbha 356 (M. Samdurkar 33, P. B. Hingnikar 37, Y. T. Ghare 103, U. I. Ghani 43, P. Hedaoo 47; S. J. Jadhav three for 61, P. Chitale three for 72) and 131 for five (U. I. Ghani 37 not out, U. Gandhe 37 not out; Iqbal Siddiqui three for 31).

Quarter-finals

At IPCL Sports Complex Ground, Baroda, February 26, 27, 28, March 1, 2. Drawn. Baroda were declared winners by virtue of their first-innings lead. Baroda* 592 (K. S. Chavan 190, T. B. Arothe 39, A. C. Bedade 159, M. S. Narula 131; Obaid Kamal four for 130, A. R. Kapoor four for 106); Punjab 349 (Vikram Rathore 50, Ajay Mehra 152 not out, carrying his bat, Gursharan Singh 60; T. B. Arothe three for 103, S. S. Hazare five for 66) and 287 for eight (Vikram Rathore 54, Ajay Mehra 37, Gursharan Singh 35, Bhupinder Singh, jun. 70, Bhupinder Singh, sen. 37; S. S. Hazare three for 69).

At Eden Gardens, Calcutta, February 26, 27, 28, March 1. Bengal won by nine wickets. Hyderabad 261 (V. Jaisimha 38, N. David 43, S. Meeraj 42 not out; P. S. Vaidya three for 51, Chetan Sharma three for 84, U. Chatterjee three for 43) and 209 (M. V. Sridhar 43, Arshad Ayub 32, S. Meeraj 39 not out; Chetan Sharma four for 47, U. Chatterjee three for 48); Bengal* 392 (Snehashish C. Ganguly 149, Chetan Sharma 62; S. Meeraj three for 119, Kanwaljit Singh four for 79) and 79 for one (I. B. Roy 34 not out).

At M. Chinnaswamy Stadium, Bangalore, February 26, 27, 28, March 1, 2. Drawn. Bombay were declared winners by virtue of their first-innings lead. Karnataka* 406 (J. Arun Kumar 65, R. S. Dravid 47, S. M. H. Kirmani 139, S. Joshi 118; P. Mhambre four for 86, S. V. Bahutule four for 103) and 305 for five dec. (J. Arun Kumar 105, P. V. Shashikanth 51, R. S. Dravid 69, K. A. Jeshwant 47); Bombay 460 (S. More 66, S. K. Kulkarni 55, R. J. Shastri 151, S. V. Bahutule 134 not out; R. Ananth three for 179, K. A. Jeshwant three for 19) and 89 for five (Z. Bharucha 44 not out; S. Joshi five for 29).

At Poona Club, Pune, February 26, 27, 28, March 1, 2. Drawn. Maharashtra were declared winners by virtue of their first-innings lead. Maharashtra* 645 for nine dec. (A. V. Kale 58, S. V. Jedhe 50, S. S. Sugwekar 225, S. S. Bhave 104, S. J. Jadhav 62, Iqbal Siddiqui 76, Extras 36; R. B. Biswal five for 172) and 175 for seven dec. (H. A. Kinikar 47, S. S. Bhave 60; P. Sushil Kumar three for 45, S. Raul three for 13); Orissa 398 (Ameya Roy 116, K. Dube 30, S. Raul 70, A. Khatua 40, B. D. Mohanty 49, Extras 31; Iqbal Siddiqui three for 64, P. J. Kanade three for 103, P. Chitale three for 98) and 33 for three.

Semi-finals

At Eden Gardens, Calcutta, March 12, 13, 14, 15. Bengal won by eight wickets. Baroda 249 (P. Dave 31, K. S. Chavan 75, M. S. Narula 36 not out; P. S. Vaidya four for 49, Chetan Sharma three for 69) and 123 (K. S. More 37; S. Sensharma four for 31, A. Verma three for ten); Bengal* 278 (Arun Lal 89, Snehashish C. Ganguly 36, P. S. Vaidya 35; R. G. M. Patel three for 79, S. S. Hazare four for 68) and 98 for two (S. J. Kalyani 35 not out).

At Nehru Stadium, Pune, March 12, 13, 14, 15, 16. Drawn. Bombay were declared winners by virtue of their first-innings lead. Bombay* 509 (S. More 170, A. A. Muzumdar 55, R. J. Shastri 65, S. K. Kulkarni 139; S. J. Jadhav three for 74) and 316 for seven (Z. Bharucha 51, S. S. Dighe 39, J. V. Paranjpe 42, S. More 34, A. A. Muzumdar 101 not out; S. V. Jedhe four for 75); Maharashtra 338 (H. A. Kinikar 59, S. S. Sugwekar 142, S. M. Kondhalkar 30 not out, Extras 31; P. Mhambre four for 100, S. V. Bahutule four for 68).

Final

At Wankhede Stadium, Bombay, March 27, 28, 29, 30. Bombay won by eight wickets. Bengal* 193 (Arun Lal 62, Saurav C. Ganguly 40; Manish Patel four for 59, S. V. Bahutule four for 49) and 257 (Snehashish C. Ganguly 30, Ashok Malhotra 62, Saurav C. Ganguly 88, Chetan Sharma 35; Manish Patel three for 35, S. V. Bahutule three for 108, R. J. Shastri three for 47); Bombay 256 (A. A. Muzumdar 78, S. K. Kulkarni 35; U. Chatterjee seven for 71) and 195 for two (S. More 83 not out, S. V. Bahutule 40, J. V. Paranjpe 44 not out).

RANJI TROPHY WINNERS

1934-35	Bombay	1954-55	Madras	1974-75	Bombay
1935-36	Bombay	1955-56	Bombay	1975-76	Bombay
1936-37	Nawanagar	1956-57	Bombay	1976-77	Bombay
1937-38	Hyderabad	1957-58	Baroda	1977-78	Karnataka
1938-39	Bengal	1958-59	Bombay	1978-79	Delhi
1939-40	Maharashtra	1959-60	Bombay	1979-80	Delhi
1940-41	Maharashtra	1960-61	Bombay	1980-81	Bombay
1941-42	Bombay	1961-62	Bombay	1981-82	Delhi
1942-43	Baroda	1962-63	Bombay	1982-83	Karnataka
1943-44	Western India	1963-64	Bombay	1983-84	Bombay
1944-45	Bombay	1964-65	Bombay	1984-85	Bombay
1945-46	Holkar	1965-66	Bombay	1985-86	Delhi
1946-47	Baroda	1966-67	Bombay	1986-87	Hyderabad
1947-48	Holkar	1967-68	Bombay	1987-88	Tamil Nadu
1948-49	Bombay	1968-69	Bombay	1988-89	Delhi
1949-50	Baroda	1969-70	Bombay	1989-90	Bengal
1950-51	Holkar	1970-71	Bombay	1990-91	Haryana
1951-52	Bombay	1971-72	Bombay	1991-92	Delhi
1952-53	Holkar	1972-73	Bombay	1992-93	Punjab
1953-54	Bombay	1973-74	Karnataka	1993-94	Bombay

AUSTRALIA UNDER-19 IN INDIA, 1993-94

Australia Under-19 toured India in February and March 1994, playing 11 games. They won four, lost four and drew three. The three-match "Test" series with India Under-19 was drawn 1-1; after a draw at Madras, India took the second match at Thiruvananthapuram by 226 runs but Australia drew level with a six-wicket win in Bombay. India Under-19 won the one-day series 2-1. Australia also played three three-day games against Indian teams, winning one with two drawn, and two one-day games, of which the first was lost and the second won.

The party of 13 was as follows: R. Baker (*captain*), B. Birrell, C. J. Burton, J. Cantrill, J. Cassell, J. Gillespie, M. Hussey, J. Jurgensen, B. Lee, M. Nicholson, C. Richards, P. J. Roach, A. Symonds. *Manager:* D. Guy. *Cricket manager:* R. Done.

First Under-19 "Test": At Madras, February 25, 26, 27, 28. Drawn. Toss: India Under-19. India Under-19 346 (Tarun Kumar 45, Jitender Singh 66, Amit Sharma 43, V. V. S. Laxman 88 not out, Javed Alam 35; M. Nicholson three for 37) and 275 for five (Tarun Kumar 99, Amit Sharma 64, H. Kanitkar 38 not out, Extras 30); Australia Under-19 438 for eight dec. (M. Hussey 50, C. J. Burton 30, C. Richards 133, M. Nicholson 75, P. J. Roach 59 not out; Javed Alam three for 135).

Second Under-19 "Test": At Thiruvananthapuram, March 3, 4, 5, 6. India Under-19 won by 226 runs. Toss: India Under-19. India Under-19 383 (P. Dharmani 36, Amit Sharma 84, V. V. S. Laxman 151 not out, M. Mewada 50; M. Nicholson three for 39, B. Birrell three for 60) and 328 for seven dec. (M. Mewada 126, Jitender Singh 55, V. V. S. Laxman 77; M. Hussey three for 32); Australia Under-19 286 (M. Hussey 50, C. Richards 33, A. Symonds 163; R. Sanghvi four for 88, H. Kanitkar six for 83) and 199 (C. J. Burton 38, M. Nicholson 35, P. J. Roach 42; R. Sanghvi four for 72, H. Kanitkar five for 56).

Third Under-19 "Test": At Bombay, March 14, 15, 16, 17. Australia Under-19 won by six wickets. Toss: India Under-19. India Under-19 313 (V. V. S. Laxman 36, H. Kanitkar 60, S. Sriram 77; B. Lee four for 61, J. Cassell four for 48) and 267 (Jitender Singh 58, V. V. S. Laxman 84, M. Mewada 50 not out; B. Lee four for 70); Australia Under-19 270 (M. Hussey 38, C. Richards 44, A. Symonds 93, C. J. Burton 40; S. Sriram three for 89) and 311 for four (J. Cassell 44, M. Hussey 46, C. Richards 63, R. Baker 95 not out, A. Symonds 58).

CRICKET IN PAKISTAN, 1993-94

By ABID ALI KAZI

Pakistan's success on the field, with series wins over Zimbabwe and New Zealand and victory in the Austral-Asia Cup, was accompanied by controversy off it, as national politicians took a direct hand in affairs. Before the tour of New Zealand, Farooq Ahmed Khan Leghari, the state president and patron of the Board of Control for Cricket in Pakistan, dissolved the board and appointed an ad hoc committee. A few days later, when the party was announced – retaining the selection made by the Board before its dissolution – Javed Miandad had been dropped for the first tour since his debut in 1976-77, along with Aqib Javed and Ramiz Raja. This was followed by the rebellion of nine players, led by vice-captain Waqar Younis, who demanded the removal of their "domineering" captain, Wasim Akram – to be replaced by Waqar.

After prolonged consultations, both Wasim and Waqar lost their jobs, with Salim Malik, who had not played against Zimbabwe, appointed captain and Asif Mujtaba his deputy. None of the ousted players was reinstated. When Miandad was also omitted from the Austral-Asia Cup, he tearfully announced his retirement. Subsequent public protests, demonstrations and threats of hunger strikes ended only when the prime minister, Benazir Bhutto, summoned Miandad and asked him to change his mind. Acceding to her request, he joined trials for the Sri Lankan tour in June, scored a century and earned selection – only to miss the trip through injury.

On the domestic front, the Quaid-e-Azam Trophy returned to Lahore after 25 years when Lahore City beat Karachi Whites, champions for the past three seasons, in an argumentative final. Karachi Whites (who had headed the league by 38 points to Lahore City's 20) conceded a first-innings lead of 83 and, resuming, reached 156 for six before Rashid Latif, the Test wicket-keeper, was given out caught behind. Disagreeing with the decision, he called the other batsman, Asim Rizvi, to accompany him to the pavilion. Karachi Whites at first refused to continue. Under protest, they declared, at 176, having been awarded 20 penalty runs, owing to Lahore City's slow over-rate, leaving a target of 94. To devalue the game further, Latif opened the bowling. He was later fined. Karachi Whites took revenge two days later when they defeated Lahore City in the 40-overs final.

In the earlier league match between the two, Karachi Whites set a ninth-wicket record for any Pakistani team in first-class cricket. Mahmood Hamid, with 202 not out, and Athar Laeeq, with 80, added 207, beating the 190 scored by Asif Iqbal and Intikhab Alam for Pakistan against England at The Oval in 1967.

Bahawalpur were scratched from the tournament and relegated when they conceded their final game to Karachi Blues by failing to turn up. All points for and against them were cancelled. Earlier, Bahawalpur batsman Mazhar Qayyum earned a lifetime ban from all Board tournaments for attacking umpire Abid Naqvi in an argument after the match with Islamabad. Peshawar were promoted, despite losing the Grade II final to Rawalpindi B, because the Board had ruled that only Karachi and Lahore should field two first-class teams.

In the first half of the season, ADBP ended Habib Bank's hopes of a hat-trick in the Patron's Trophy, winning their final on first-innings lead; the previous year's experiment with bonus points for batting and bowling had been abandoned. Nine teams contested the Trophy instead of eight: National Bank had successfully protested against their relegation, on the grounds that they had lost their leading players either to the Test side or to a series of matches arranged to raise money for flood victims. This meant two teams were to be relegated, and Pakistan Railways faced an abrupt return to Grade II with HBFC. But they were saved when the Pakistan Automobile Corporation (PACO) announced that they were disbanding their team. Allied Bank were promoted.

Pakistan's leading one-day tournament, the 50-overs Wills Cup, included a record 17 teams. The four groups formed by the Patron's and Quaid-e-Azam teams were won by ADBP, Habib Bank, PIA and Rawalpindi: Habib Bank beat Rawalpindi in the final to regain the title they lost to National Bank the previous season. But Rawalpindi's Under-19 team won their national championship, now known as the Pepsi Junior Cup, when they defeated Karachi Blues.

Atif Rauf of Islamabad and ADBP headed the first-class batting averages with 66.71. His 934 runs in 12 matches included four centuries. But the highest aggregate was achieved by Zahid Fazal, of Lahore City and PIA, who scored 1,205 at 57.38 in 17 matches. His team-mate Aamer Malik, Mahmood Hamid (Karachi Whites and United Bank) and Ghulam Ali (Karachi Whites and PACO) also passed 1,000. The highest individual score of the season was 267, scored by Shahid Nawaz for Faisalabad against Lahore City. The bowling averages were headed by Habib Bank's Naved Anjum, who took 42 wickets at 15.80 in just seven matches, including nine for 56 in an innings against United Bank, the best figures of the season. Mohammad Ali of Lahore City and Railways was the leading wicket-taker, with 56 wickets at 28.57, though he needed 16 games; other bowlers who reached 50 wickets were Sajjad Akbar (Sargodha and PNSC) and Athar Laeeq (Karachi Whites and National Bank). Sajjad also scored 775 runs and made six catches. The leading wicket-keeper was again Tahir Rashid of Karachi Whites and Habib Bank, with 38 dismissals. Sajid Ali, of Karachi Whites and National Bank, Ijaz Ahmed, of Faisalabad and Railways, and Zahid Fazal held 12 catches each. Mohtashim Rasheed of HBFC became the sixth of the Rasheed brothers – after Haroon, Farooq, Ahmed, Mahmood and Umar – to play first-class cricket.

FIRST-CLASS AVERAGES, 1993-94

BATTING

(Qualification: 500 runs)

	M	*I*	*NO*	*R*	*HS*	*100s*	*Avge*
Atif Rauf (*Islamabad/ADBP*)	12	15	1	934	120	4	66.71
Idrees Baig (*Sargodha/Habib Bank*)	10	13	2	719	158	3	65.36
Aamer Malik (*Lahore City/PIA*)	17	21	2	1,159	200*	5	61.00
Mansoor Rana (*Lahore City/ADBP*)	14	18	5	767	115	3	59.00
Zahid Fazal (*Lahore City/PIA*)	17	23	2	1,205	199	3	57.38

	M	I	NO	R	HS	100s	Avge
Akram Raza (*Sargodha/Habib Bank*)	13	15	3	657	145*	1	54.75
Shakeel Ahmed (*Islamabad/Habib Bank*)	11	12	0	628	200	2	52.33
Sajjad Akbar (*Sargodha/PNSC*)	13	17	2	775	143	3	51.66
Shahid Saeed (*Lahore City/PACO*)	14	21	2	939	229	3	49.42
Shahid Nawaz (*Faisalabad/PACO*)	15	21	2	891	267	2	46.89
Asif Mohammad (*Rawalpindi/PIA*)	11	15	1	637	183	2	45.50
Mahmood Hamid (*Karachi Whites/United Bank*)	17	28	4	1,088	202*	4	45.33
Sohail Miandad (*Karachi Blues/PIA*)	10	17	1	695	142	2	43.43
Ghaffar Kazmi (*Rawalpindi/ADBP*)	13	17	1	694	133	2	43.37
Ijaz Ahmed (*Faisalabad/Railways*)	13	20	3	725	159	3	42.64
Nadeem Younis (*Rawalpindi/Railways*)	14	21	0	894	105	2	42.57
Sajid Ali (*Karachi Whites/National Bank*)	12	22	0	895	154	3	40.68
Shahid Javed (*Rawalpindi/Habib Bank*)	17	23	2	800	131	1	38.09
Ghulam Ali (*Karachi Whites/PACO*)	18	30	2	1,048	138	3	37.42
Mohammad Ramzan (*Faisalabad/Railways*)	14	22	2	747	161*	3	37.35
Mohammad Javed (*Karachi Whites/National Bank*)	12	17	2	542	116*	1	36.13
Mazhar Qayyum (*Bahawalpur/Railways*)	11	18	0	634	74	0	35.22
Shahid Anwar (*Lahore City/National Bank*)	15	23	2	683	84	0	32.52
Moin Khan (*Karachi Whites/PIA*)	15	20	2	569	97	0	31.61
Kamran Khan (*Lahore City/PACO*)	12	20	0	582	150	2	29.10
Aamer Hanif (*Karachi Whites/PACO*)	14	20	1	523	47	0	27.52

* *Signifies not out.*

BOWLING

(Qualification: 25 wickets)

	O	M	R	W	BB	5W/i	Avge
Naved Anjum (*Habib Bank*)	216	45	664	42	9-56	4	15.80
Waqar Younis (*United Bank*)	224.3	46	674	42	7-91	6	16.04
Haaris Khan (*Karachi Whites*)	408.3	114	919	45	5-71	2	20.42
Naeem Ashraf (*Lahore City/National Bank*)	340.3	49	1,064	48	6-45	2	22.16
Raja Afaq (*Rawalpindi/ADBP*)	376.5	71	985	44	6-53	4	22.38
Ashfaq Ahmed (*PIA*)	219.2	40	697	31	7-127	4	22.48
Manzoor Elahi (*ADBP*)	251	62	720	32	6-113	2	22.50
Masood Anwar (*United Bank*)	278.5	59	752	33	7-95	3	22.78
Sajjad Akbar (*Sargodha/PNSC*)	436	79	1,234	54	6-68	3	22.85
Zahid Ahmed (*Faisalabad/PIA*)	313	98	719	31	6-15	1	23.19
Nadeem Ghauri (*Lahore City/National Bank*)	322.3	77	895	34	8-51	3	26.32
Athar Laeeq (*Karachi Whites/National Bank*)	427.4	89	1,324	50	5-38	2	26.48
Asadullah Butt (*Rawalpindi/Habib Bank*)	258.3	57	851	32	4-34	0	26.59
Mohammad Zahid (*Bahawalpur/PACO*)	361.4	76	931	35	8-114	3	26.60
Imran Adil (*Bahawalpur/Railways*)	266.1	41	922	34	6-85	2	27.11
Mohsin Kamal (*Lahore City/PNSC*)	291.1	33	1,147	42	5-66	3	27.30
Arshad Khan (*Railways*)	274.4	49	765	28	6-109	1	27.32
Mohammad Ali (*Lahore City/Railways*)	433.3	59	1,600	56	6-37	4	28.57
Nadeem Khan (*Karachi Whites/National Bank*)	493.5	127	1,231	41	6-72	4	30.02
Nadeem Afzal (*Faisalabad/PIA*)	262.5	46	825	27	5-57	1	30.55
Akram Raza (*Sargodha/Habib Bank*)	431.3	97	1,188	37	5-56	1	32.10
Javed Hayat (*Lahore City/ADBP*)	356	69	964	30	5-118	1	32.13
Murtaza Hussain (*Bahawalpur/PACO*)	406.2	92	1,013	31	5-118	1	32.67
Naved Nazir (*Faisalabad/PNSC*)	300.4	64	885	25	5-38	1	35.40
Mohammad Asif (*Lahore City/ADBP*)	526.2	105	1,312	31	5-71	1	42.32

QUAID-E-AZAM TROPHY, 1993-94

	Played	*Won*	*Lost*	*Drawn*	*1st-inns Points*	*Points*
Karachi Whites......	7	3	0	4	8	38
Lahore City.........	7	0	0	7	20	20
Karachi Blues.......	7	2	1	4	8	18
Rawalpindi	6	1	2	3	4	14
Faisalabad..........	6	0	0	6	8	8
Sargodha	7	0	0	7	8	8
Islamabad	7	0	2	5	0	0
Bahawalpur.........	5	0	1	4	0	0

Note: Bahawalpur were disqualified after failing to turn up for their match against Karachi Blues; points earned by them and against them were cancelled.

Semi-finals: Lahore City beat Rawalpindi by virtue of their first-innings lead; Karachi Whites beat Karachi Blues by virtue of their first-innings lead.

Final: Lahore City beat Karachi Whites by nine wickets.

Outright win = 10 pts; lead on first innings in a drawn game = 4 pts.

*In the following scores, * by the name of a team indicates that they won the toss.*

At Marghzar Cricket Ground, Islamabad, January 8, 9, 10, 11. Drawn. Sargodha 291 for eight (Mohammad Nawaz 57, Mohammad Hasnain 34, Akram Raza 67, Asad Malik 41, Sajjad Akbar 37; Ayaz Jilani four for 92); Islamabad* 279 (Mujahid Jamshed 31, Rehan Farooqi 33, Zahid Umar 57, Sajjad Ali 50, Tariq Rashid 34; Naeem Khan three for 50, Sajjad Akbar six for 82). *Sargodha 4 pts (first innings restricted to 85 overs after first two days washed out.)*

At National Stadium, Karachi, January 8, 9, 10, 11. Drawn. Karachi Whites* 141 (Sajid Ali 35, Tahir Rashid 30 not out; Zahid Ahmed six for 15) and 201 for seven (Tahir Rashid 33; Zahid Ahmed four for 65); Faisalabad 274 (Sami-ul-Haq 48, Zahid Ahmed 58, Saadat Gul 58, Extras 38; Athar Laeeq four for 44, Wasim-ur-Rehman three for 86). *Faisalabad 4 pts.*

At LCCA Ground, Lahore, January 8, 9, 10, 11. Drawn. Lahore City* 430 (Shahid Saeed 92, Shahid Anwar 47, Aamer Malik 54, Mansoor Rana 115, Extras 47; Imran Adil three for 125, Murtaza Hussain five for 118); Bahawalpur 262 (Tariq Mahmood 31, Saifullah 50, Mazhar Qayyum 64; Mohammad Ali five for 87, Javed Hayat three for 41) and seven for two. *Points cancelled.*

At KRL Cricket Ground, Rawalpindi, January 8, 9, 10, 11. Karachi Blues won by ten wickets. Rawalpindi 150 (Shahid Javed 35; Ali Gohar five for 63, Shakeel Sajjad four for 34) and 256 (Sher Ali 52, Mohammad Riaz 59 not out, Shahid Mahboob 45; Ali Gohar five for 90, Mohammad Javed three for 56); Karachi Blues* 406 for eight dec. (Sohail Miandad 37, Ata-ur-Rehman 103, Iqbal Saleem 32, Mohammad Javed 76, Iqbal Imam 58, Shakeel Sajjad 35 not out; Mohammad Akram four for 112) and four for no wkt. *Karachi Blues 10 pts.*

At Iqbal Stadium, Faisalabad, January 15, 16, 17, 18. Faisalabad v Bahawalpur. Abandoned.

At KRL Cricket Ground, Rawalpindi, January 15, 16, 17, 18. Drawn. Islamabad 255 for nine (Rizwan Umar 33, Tanvir Razzaq 86, Tariq Rashid 48; Ali Gohar three for 102, Iqbal Imam three for 66); Karachi Blues* 256 for three (Sohail Miandad 142, Sohail Jaffer 63 not out). *Karachi Blues 4 pts (first innings restricted to 65 overs after first two days washed out).*

At National Stadium, Karachi, January 15, 16, 17. 18. Drawn. Lahore City* 260 (Shahid Anwar 58, Babar Zaman 72, Aamer Malik 32; Athar Laeeq three for 49, Haaris Khan four for 72) and 225 for two (Zahid Fazal 67 not out, Shahid Saeed 80, Kamran Khan 36); Karachi Whites 501 for nine dec. (Ghulam Ali 59, Aamer Hanif 38, Mahmood Hamid 202 not out, Athar Laeeq 80, Extras 35; Shahid Ali Khan four for 140). *Karachi Whites 4 pts.*

At Rawalpindi Cricket Stadium, Rawalpindi, January 15, 16, 17, 18. Drawn. Sargodha 239 for six (Asad Malik 100 not out, Akram Raza 58; Shahid Mahboob three for 48) v Rawalpindi*.

At National Stadium, Karachi, January 22, 23, 24, 25. Drawn. Bahawalpur* 319 (Tariq Mahmood 79, Saifullah 32, Mohammad Khalid 93 not out, Extras 33; Haaris Khan three for 91) and 228 (Aamir Sohail 42, Mazhar Qayyum 74, Mohammad Zahid 30; Athar Laeeq three for 47, Haaris Khan four for 82); Karachi Whites 384 (Saeed Azad 39, Aamer Hanif 40, Mahmood Hamid 102, Moin Khan 97, Extras 36; Mohammad Zahid five for 126, Murtaza Hussain four for 134) and 65 for five. *Points cancelled.*

At Rawalpindi Cricket Stadium, Rawalpindi, January 22, 23, 24. Rawalpindi won by an innings and 18 runs. Islamabad 92 (Raja Afaq five for 37, Mohammad Riaz four for 30) and 171 (Ramiz Raja 48, Gulrez Shahid 34, Ayaz Jilani 33; Raja Afaq six for 84, Mohammad Riaz three for 55); Rawalpindi* 281 (Nadeem Younis 95, Shahid Naqi 72, Ghaffar Kazmi 66; Ayaz Jilani eight for 104). *Rawalpindi 10 pts.*

At Sargodha Stadium, Sargodha, January 22, 23, 24, 25. Drawn. Karachi Blues* 198 (Sohail Jaffer 37, Sohail Mehdi 60; Sajjad Akbar four for 64) and 415 for five (Ameer-ud-Din 64, Sohail Miandad 69, Manzoor Akhtar 115 not out, Mohammad Javed 116 not out; Sajjad Akbar three for 83); Sargodha 301 (Mohammad Hasnain 78, Tanvir Hussain 45, Akram Raza 97, Talat Imtiaz 36; Ali Gohar three for 69). *Sargodha 4 pts.*

At LCCA Ground, Lahore, January 23, 24, 25, 26. Drawn. Faisalabad* 460 (Shahid Nawaz 267, Ijaz Ahmed 105; Mohammad Ali five for 142, Shahid Anwar three for six); Lahore City 485 for four (Shahid Saeed 229, Tariq Bashir 30, Shahid Anwar 35, Zahid Fazal 152). *Lahore City 4 pts.*

At Bahawal Stadium, Bahawalpur, January 29, 30, 31, February 1. Bahawalpur v Rawalpindi. Abandoned, owing to non-availability of ground.

At Boranwalla Ground, Faisalabad, January 29, 30, 31, February 1. Drawn. Faisalabad* 321 (Shahid Nawaz 54, Wasim Haider 44, Tanvir Afzal 37 not out, Nadeem Afzal 38, Naved Nazir 30; Amanullah four for 86) and 194 (Mohammad Ramzan 54, Sami-ul-Haq 31, Nadeem Arshad 59; Mohammad Nawaz three for 81, Mohammad Hasnain four for eight); Sargodha 262 (Mohammad Nawaz 140 not out, carrying his bat, Abid Rafiq 40; Zahid Ahmed three for 56, Tanvir Afzal four for 85). *Faisalabad 4 pts.*

At National Stadium, Karachi, January 29, 30, 31, February 1. Karachi Whites won by four wickets. Karachi Whites 344 (Sajid Ali 35, Mahmood Hamid 157, Moin Khan 45, Nadeem Khan 33; Azhar Mahmood three for 97, Ayaz Jilani four for 72) and 196 for six (Sajid Ali 50, Aamer Hanif 47); Islamabad* 155 (Aamer Ishaq 56, Asif Ali 39; Humayun Hussain four for 63, Haaris Khan four for 21) and 382 (Mujahid Jamshed 71, Aamer Ishaq 93, Azhar Mahmood 35, Shakeel Khan 39; Humayun Hussain three for 117, Nadeem Khan three for 96, Haaris Khan three for 85). *Karachi Whites 10 pts.*

At LCCA Ground, Lahore, January 29, 30, 31, February 1. Drawn. Lahore City* 499 for nine dec. (Shahid Anwar 65, Shahid Saeed 49, Zahid Fazal 199, Aamer Malik 63, Mansoor Rana 34, Extras 38; Manzoor Akhtar four for 147, Sohail Mehdi four for 120); Karachi Blues 329 (Sohail Miandad 31, Sohail Jaffer 39, Manzoor Akhtar 124 not out, Iqbal Imam 45, Zahid Ali 38; Mohammad Ali three for 58, Mohammad Asif four for 110, Javed Hayat three for 50) and 387 for five (Ameer-ud-Din 82, Ata-ur-Rehman 42, Iqbal Saleem 101 not out, Mohammad Javed 93). *Lahore City 4 pts.*

At Iqbal Stadium, Faisalabad, February 6, 7, 8, 9. Drawn. Karachi Blues* 212 (Sohail Jaffer 67; Naved Nazir five for 38) and 291 for five (Sohail Miandad 50, Manzoor Akhtar 100 not out, Sohail Mehdi 102 not out; Tanvir Afzal three for 86); Faisalabad 154 (Sami-ul-Haq 31, Shahid Nawaz 66; Ali Gohar four for 64, Manzoor Akhtar three for 14). *Karachi Blues 4 pts.*

At National Stadium, Karachi, February 6, 7, 8, 9. Karachi Whites won by three wickets. Rawalpindi* 190 (Nadeem Younis 74, Shahid Javed 52; Nadeem Khan four for 66, Haaris Khan four for 68) and 206 (Shahid Naqi 46, Shahid Javed 31; Nadeem Khan five for 84, Haaris Khan five for 93); Karachi Whites 206 (Ghulam Ali 64, Azam Khan 32, Aamer Hanif 30; Shahid Mahboob three for 42, Shakeel Ahmed seven for 69) and 194 for seven (Aaley Haider 93 not out; Shakeel Ahmed four for 65). *Karachi Whites 10 pts.*

At LCCA Ground, Lahore, February 6, 7, 8, 9. Drawn. Bahawalpur 154 (Mohammad Khalid 32; Azhar Mahmood six for 68) and 156 for five (Mazhar Qayyum 66, Saifullah 35); Islamabad* 244 (Tanvir Razzaq 34, Aamer Ishaq 49, Ayaz Jilani 51, Extras 31; Imran Adil five for 104). *Points cancelled.*

At Sargodha Stadium, Sargodha, February 6, 7, 8, 9. Drawn. Sargodha* 361 (Mohammad Nawaz 75, Mohammad Hasnain 31, Sajjad Akbar 143, Ashraf Bashir 68; Mohammad Ali three for 74, Tahir Shah four for 69); Lahore City 465 for three (Shahid Saeed 32, Shahid Anwar 32, Zahid Fazal 80, Aamer Malik 200 not out, Mansoor Rana 100 not out). *Lahore City 4 pts.*

At Iqbal Stadium, Faisalabad, March 19, 20, 21, 22. Drawn. Rawalpindi 385 (Nadeem Younis 71, Mujahid Hameed 110, Tasawwar Hussain 30, Asadullah Butt 47; Naved Nazir three for 86); Faisalabad* 140 (Shahid Nawaz 54; Asadullah Butt three for 29, Raja Afaq four for 32) and 126 for four (Ijaz Ahmed 73 not out; Asadullah Butt three for 25). *Rawalpindi 4 pts.*

At National Stadium, Karachi, March 19, 20, 21, 22. Karachi Whites won by ten wickets. Karachi Blues* 130 (Zahid Ali 37; Nadeem Khan three for 39, Haaris Khan four for 41) and 241 (Iqbal Saleem 36, Zahid Ali 31, Munir-ul-Haq 61, Mohammad Hasnain 34; Nadeem Khan three for 82, Haaris Khan five for 71); Karachi Whites 304 (Irfanullah 42, Mahmood Hamid 70, Athar Laeeq 30, Nadeem Khan 62 not out; Mohammad Hasnain four for 48, Iqbal Imam three for 50) and 71 for no wkt (Ghulam Ali 53 not out). *Karachi Whites 10 pts.*

At Sargodha Stadium, Sargodha, March 19, 20, 21, 22. Drawn. Sargodha 277 (Mohammad Nawaz 38, Idrees Baig 128 not out, Mohammad Sarfraz 36; Mohammad Altaf five for 91, Murtaza Hussain three for 86); Bahawalpur* 215 (Tariq Mahmood 87; Mohammad Sarfraz four for 59, Sajjad Akbar three for 62). *Points cancelled.*

At Karachi Development Authority Ground, Karachi, March 26, 27, 28, 29. Karachi Blues v Bahawalpur. Karachi Blues awarded match after the Bahawalpur side failed to turn up. *Points cancelled.*

At National Stadium, Karachi, March 26, 27, 28, 29. Drawn. Sargodha* 265 (Tanvir Hussain 45, Sajjad Akbar 138; Nadeem Khan three for 88, Haaris Khan three for 67); Karachi Whites 444 for seven (Sohail Taqi 47, Aamer Hanif 31, Asim Rizvi 110 not out, Moin Khan 94, Zafar Iqbal 115). *Karachi Whites 4 pts.*

At Rawalpindi Cricket Stadium, Rawalpindi, March 26, 27, 28, 29. Drawn. Lahore City 458 (Babar Zaman 80, Shahid Anwar 55, Zahid Fazal 133, Tariq Aziz 34, Naeem Ashraf 41, Aslam Raza 57 not out; Naeem Akhtar five for 115) and 28 for three (Naeem Akhtar three for 15); Rawalpindi* 280 (Maqsood Ahmed 68, Mujahid Hameed 36, Nadeem Abbasi 53, Naeem Akhtar 35; Naeem Ashraf four for 95, Mohammad Ali four for 115) and 301 (Nadeem Younis 103, Shahid Javed 30, Pervez Iqbal 52; Naeem Ashraf five for 79). *Lahore City 4 pts.*

At Marghzar Cricket Ground, Islamabad, April 2, 3, 4, 5. Drawn. Faisalabad* 309 for four (Mohammad Ramzan 103, Shahid Nawaz 78 retired hurt, Nadeem Afzal 52 not out) v Islamabad.

At LCCA Ground, Lahore, April 7, 8, 9, 10. Drawn. Lahore City 405 (Aamer Manzoor 63, Zahid Fazal 94, Mohammad Asif 53, Ali Kamran 54 not out, Extras 30; Aamir Nazir four for 136) and 295 for nine (Aamer Malik 107, Ali Kamran 50, Mohammad Asif 50; Aqib Javed four for 92, Tariq Rasheed three for 42); Islamabad* 297 (Ramiz Raja 80, Tanvir Razzaq 30, Atif Rauf 100; Mohammad Ali three for 95, Afzaal Haider four for 77). *Lahore City 4 pts.*

Semi-finals

At Gaddafi Stadium, Lahore, April 14, 15, 16, 17. Drawn. Lahore City were declared winners by virtue of their first-innings lead. Rawalpindi 244 (Mujahid Hameed 45, Asadullah Butt 38, Naeem Akhtar 36; Mohsin Kamal three for 74, Mohammad Ali three for 86) and 253 for eight (Nadeem Younis 74, Ehsan Butt 53 not out; Mohammad Ali three for 64); Lahore City* 294 (Shahid Anwar 60, Pervez Shah 30, Tahir Shah 39, Naeem Ashraf 68, Mohsin Kamal 42; Naeem Akhtar six for 98).

At National Stadium, Karachi, April 15, 16, 17, 18. Drawn. Karachi Whites were declared winners by virtue of their first-innings lead. Karachi Whites* 560 (Ghulam Ali 138, Asim Rizvi 32, Mahmood Hamid 34, Irfanullah 128, Zafar Iqbal 128, Extras 47; Mohammad Hasnain five for 62) and 175 for five (Asim Rizvi 77 not out; Mohammad Hasnain three for 35); Karachi Blues 242 (Kamran Hussain 31, Ameer-ud-Din 38, Iqbal Saleem 47, Manzoor Akhtar 30, Zafar Ali 39; Haaris Khan four for 85, Nadeem Khan six for 72).

Final

At Gaddafi Stadium, Lahore, April 25, 26, 27. Lahore City won by nine wickets. Karachi Whites 172 (Basit Ali 68; Mohsin Kamal three for 84, Naeem Ashraf six for 45) and 176 for seven dec. (Mahmood Hamid 33, Rashid Latif 36; Mohsin Kamal five for 84); Lahore City* 255 (Babar Zaman 68, Aamer Manzoor 33, Mohammad Ali 33 not out; Zafar Iqbal seven for 65) and 94 for one (Aamer Manzoor 45 not out).

QUAID-E-AZAM TROPHY WINNERS

1953-54	Bahawalpur	1969-70	PIA	1982-83	United Bank
1954-55	Karachi	1970-71	Karachi Blues	1983-84	National Bank
1956-57	Punjab	1972-73	Railways	1984-85	United Bank
1957-58	Bahawalpur	1973-74	Railways	1985-86	Karachi
1958-59	Karachi	1974-75	Punjab A	1986-87	National Bank
1959-60	Karachi	1975-76	National Bank	1987-88	PIA
1961-62	Karachi Blues	1976-77	United Bank	1988-89	ADBP
1962-63	Karachi A	1977-78	Habib Bank	1989-90	PIA
1963-64	Karachi Blues	1978-79	National Bank	1990-91	Karachi Whites
1964-65	Karachi Blues	1979-80	PIA	1991-92	Karachi Whites
1966-67	Karachi	1980-81	United Bank	1992-93	Karachi Whites
1968-69	Lahore	1981-82	National Bank	1993-94	Lahore City

BCCP PATRON'S TROPHY, 1993-94

	Played	*Won*	*Lost*	*Drawn*	*1st-inns Points*	*Points*
Habib Bank	8	3	0	5	12	42
PIA	8	2	1	5	20	40
ADBP	8	2	0	6	16	36
PACO	8	1	1	6	20	30
PNSC	8	2	1	5	4	20†
National Bank	8	1	0	7	8	16‡
United Bank	8	1	1	6	8	14†
Pakistan Railways	8	1	3	4	4	14
HBFC	8	0	6	2	0	0

Semi-finals: Habib Bank beat PACO by eight wickets; ADBP beat PIA by virtue of their higher score after 40 overs.

Final: ADBP beat Habib Bank by virtue of their first-innings lead.

† 4 points deducted for slow over-rates. ‡ 2 points deducted for slow over-rates.

Outright win = 10 pts; lead on first innings in a drawn game = 4 pts.

*In the following scores, * by the name of a team indicates that they won the toss.*

At Iqbal Stadium, Faisalabad, October 23, 24, 25, 26. Drawn. ADBP 456 (Zahoor Elahi 84, Atif Rauf 80, Ghaffar Kazmi 56, Javed Hayat 49, Mujahid Hameed 77 not out, Extras 56; Athar Laeeq four for 86, Hafeez-ur-Rehman three for 98); National Bank* 268 (Sajid Ali 107, Tahir Shah 30, Athar Laeeq 39 not out; Mohammad Asif four for 82, Raja Afaq six for 91) and 323 for four (Sajid Ali 84, Saeed Azad 61, Ameer Akbar 100 not out). *ADBP 4 pts.*

At Bagh-e-Jinnah Ground, Lahore, October 24, 25, 26, 27. Habib Bank won by an innings and 72 runs. HBFC 186 (Faisal Qureshi 50, Tariq Alam 34; Asadullah Butt three for 33, Akram Raza five for 56) and 226 (Nusrat Mahboob 77; Nadeem Ghauri five for 70, Akram Raza four for 75); Habib Bank* 484 for seven dec. (Mohammad Hasnain 45, Ijaz Ahmed 92, Shahid Javed 92, Shaukat Mirza 43, Akram Raza 38, Tahir Rashid 64 not out, Asadullah Butt 51 not out; Kabir Khan three for 65, Ijaz Elahi four for 147). *Habib Bank 10 pts.*

At Niaz Stadium, Hyderabad, October 24, 25, 26, 27. PNSC won by 14 runs. PNSC* 75 (Shahid Hussain four for 20, Murtaza Hussain four for 12) and 211 (Azam Khan 74, Sher Ali 53, Extras 41; Shahid Hussain five for 57, Yahya Toor four for 26); PACO 168 (Umar Rasheed 55, Yahya Toor 42 not out; Sajjad Ali three for 61) and 104 (Aamer Hanif 41; Mohsin Kamal three for 43, Naved Nazir four for 12). *PNSC 10 pts.*

At UBL Sports Complex, Karachi, October 24, 25, 26, 27. Drawn. United Bank 368 (Javed Sami 51, Mansoor Akhtar 118, Mahmood Hamid 79, Aamer Bashir 41, Extras 41; Ashfaq Ahmed five for 123, Wasim Haider three for 74) and 111 for four (Mahmood Hamid 33 not out); PIA* 493 (Rizwan-uz-Zaman 134, Zahid Fazal 73, Aamer Malik 60, Asif Mohammad 89 not out, Zahid Ahmed 55, Moin Khan 41; Tauseef Ahmed five for 146). *PIA 4 pts.*

At Gaddafi Stadium, Lahore, October 30, 31, November 1. National Bank won by an innings and 75 runs. National Bank 373 (Sajid Ali 52, Ameer Akbar 30, Tahir Shah 117 not out, Naeem Ashraf 48, Athar Laeeq 31; Ijaz Elahi six for 132); HBFC* 145 (Munir-ul-Haq 50. Tariq Alam 33; Naeem Ashraf three for 30, Athar Laeeq three for 31) and 153 (Tariq Alam 38; Naeem Ashraf three for 52, Athar Laeeq five for 38). *National Bank 10 pts.*

At National Stadium, Karachi, October 30, 31, November 1, 2. Drawn. PIA* 412 for seven dec. (Rizwan-uz-Zaman 57, Aamer Malik 164, Asif Mohammad 104, Zahid Ahmed 41 not out, Extras 35; Murtaza Hussain three for 133); PACO 353 (Ghulam Ali 120, Kamran Khan 37, Umar Rasheed 72, Extras 43; Tanvir Ali five for 89). *PIA 4 pts.*

At UBL Sports Complex, Karachi, October 30, 31, November 1, 2. Drawn. PNSC* 242 (Sohail Jaffer 57, Sher Ali 93, Sajjad Akbar 63 not out; Tauseef Ahmed six for 90) and 185 (Sher Ali 39, Azam Khan 77; Masood Anwar five for 73, Tauseef Ahmed five for 61); United Bank 271 (Raees Ahmed 57, Mahmood Hamid 66, Mansoor Akhtar 33, Pervez Shah 30, Iqbal Imam 48 not out; Mohsin Kamal four for 71, Sajjad Ali four for 54) and 112 for seven (Iqbal Imam 32). *United Bank 4 pts.*

At Bagh-e-Jinnah Ground, Lahore, October 31, November 1, 2, 3. Drawn. Pakistan Railways* 401 (Nadeem Younis 71, Ijaz Ahmed 126, Mazhar Qayyum 43, Naseer Ahmed 37, Tariq Rana 47 not out; Naved Anjum three for 73, Nadeem Ghauri three for 82, Akram Raza four for 127) and 42 for two; Habib Bank 414 (Shakeel Ahmed 83, Ijaz Ahmed 74, Shahid Javed 131, Shaukat Mirza 69; Arshad Khan six for 109). *Habib Bank 4 pts.*

At Sargodha Stadium, Sargodha, November 6, 7, 8, 9. Drawn. Habib Bank 412 (Shakeel Ahmed 156, Shaukat Mirza 45, Akram Raza 66, Tahir Rashid 52 not out, Asadullah Butt 31; Manzoor Elahi six for 113); ADBP* 416 for six (Atif Rauf 100, Ghaffar Kazmi 129, Javed Hayat 74; Naved Anjum three for 83). *ADBP 4 pts.*

At Shahi Bagh Cricket Stadium, Peshawar, November 6, 7, 8, 9. Drawn. HBFC 179 (Faisal Qureshi 30, Tariq Alam 33; Tauseef Ahmed three for 53, Masood Anwar seven for 95); United Bank* 181 for two (Mansoor Akhtar 88, Aamer Bashir 69 not out). *United Bank 4 pts.*

At Municipal Stadium, Gujranwala, November 6, 7, 8, 9. Drawn. PACO 420 (Ghulam Ali 97, Kamran Khan 150; Shahid Sadiq three for 70, Aamer Wasim four for 84) and 242 for five (Shahid Saeed 115 not out, Zulqarnain 36, Umar Rasheed 32; Ijaz Ahmed three for 66); Pakistan Railways* 299 (Mohammad Ramzan 110, Mazhar Qayyum 33, Extras 40; Mohammad Aslam four for 123, Umar Rasheed three for 32). *PACO 4 pts.*

At National Stadium, Karachi, November 6, 7,8, 9. Drawn. PIA 269 (Babar Zaman 56, Rizwan-uz-Zaman 96, Extras 31; Sajjad Akbar four for 84, Sohail Farooqi four for 38) and 270 for four (Rizwan-uz-Zaman 117 not out, Zahid Fazal 49, Asif Mohammad 72, Extras 30); PNSC* 221 (Farrukh Bari 33, Nasir Wasti 42, Tahir Mahmood 33, Mutahir Shah 46; Nadeem Afzal five for 57). *PIA 4 pts.*

At Sargodha Stadium, Sargodha, November 13, 14, 15, 16. ADBP won by an innings and five runs. Pakistan Railways* 241 (Mohammad Ramzan 161 not out; Mohammad Asif five for 71) and 225 (Ijaz Ahmed 64, Mazhar Qayyum 53; Raja Afaq four for 80); ADBP 471 for seven dec. (Saeed Anwar 43, Zahoor Elahi 73, Atif Rauf 120, Ghaffar Kazmi 45, Mujahid Hameed 68 not out, Manzoor Elahi 67 not out; Arshad Khan four for 165). *ADBP 10 pts.*

At Rawalpindi Cricket Stadium, Rawalpindi, November 13, 14, 15. Habib Bank won by an innings and 127 runs. Habib Bank 398 (Tahir Rashid 97, Ijaz Ahmed 32, Shahid Javed 81, Salim Malik 103, Waqar Younis five for 134); United Bank* 121 (Basit Ali 56; Naved Anjum nine for 56) and 150 (Inzamam-ul-Haq 42; Naved Anjum five for 47). *Habib Bank 10 pts.*

At Iqbal Stadium, Faisalabad, November 13, 14, 15, 16. PIA won by nine wickets. HBFC 163 (Wasim Yousufi 34, Tariq Alam 39; Nadeem Afzal three for 45, Ashfaq Ahmed five for 54) and 140 (Faisal Qureshi 64; Ashfaq Ahmed six for 52); PIA* 97 (Moin Khan 33; Shahzad Ilyas four for 33, Kabir Khan five for 42) and 210 for one (Shoaib Mohammad 65, Aamer Malik 104 not out). *PIA 10 pts.*

At Gaddafi Stadium, Lahore, November 13, 14, 15, 16. Drawn. National Bank 182 (Sajid Ali 35, Saeed Azad 35, Extras 39; Umar Rasheed four for 38) and 196 (Sajid Ali 50, Ameer Akbar 34; Umar Rasheed six for 39, Aamer Hanif three for 67); PACO* 186 (Ghulam Ali 39, Mujahid Jamshed 34; Barkatullah four for 46, Naeem Ashraf four for 30) and 71 for four. *PACO 4 pts.*

At LCCA Ground, Lahore, November 20, 21, 22, 23. Drawn. PACO 440 (Ghulam Ali 46, Shahid Saeed 101, Aamer Hanif 40, Shahid Nawaz 143, Extras 40; Mohammad Asif four for 121, Javed Hayat four for 112); ADBP* 290 (Zahoor Elahi 39, Tariq Mohammad 43, Atif Rauf 64, Manzoor Elahi 75; Mohammad Zahid four for 99, Murtaza Hussain four for 92) and 242 for three (Mansoor Rana 110 not out, Atif Rauf 71). *PACO 4 pts.*

At Rawalpindi Cricket Stadium, Rawalpindi, November 20, 21, 22, 23. Habib Bank won by 169 runs. Habib Bank* 229 (Shahid Javed 41, Idrees Baig 48, Asadullah Butt 36; Nadeem Afzal four for 70) and 287 (Mohammad Hasnain 33, Tahir Rashid 30, Naved Anjum 49, Sohail Fazal 61, Asadullah Butt 58 not out; Ashfaq Ahmed seven for 127); PIA 109 (Aamer Malik 36, Moin Khan 40; Naved Anjum four for 35, Asadullah Butt four for 34) and 238 (Zahid Fazal 61, Moin Khan 67; Naved Anjum three for 54, Asadullah Butt three for 72). *Habib Bank 10 pts.*

At Gaddafi Stadium, Lahore, November 20, 21, 22, 23. Drawn. National Bank 304 (Sajid Ali 122, Ameer Akbar 35, Tahir Shah 33, Wasim Arif 46; Waqar Younis four for 83) and 194 (Ameer Akbar 30, Naeem Ashraf 31; Waqar Younis six for 84, Saleem Jaffer four for 51); United Bank* 258 (Aamer Bashir 46, Mahmood Hamid 101; Athar Laeeq four for 79, Naeem Ashraf four for 71) and 87 for three (Mansoor Akhtar 30). *National Bank 4 pts.*

At Municipal Stadium, Gujranwala, November 20, 21, 22, 23. Drawn. PNSC 235 (Sher Ali 60, Nasir Wasti 45, Mutahir Shah 32; Mohammad Ali five for 68, Arshad Khan three for 26) and 229 (Farrukh Bari 80, Sajjad Akbar 69; Mohammad Ali three for 44, Iqbal Zahoor five for 52); Pakistan Railways* 181 (Mohammad Ramzan 50, Naseer Ahmed 32; Sajjad Akbar four for 48) and 131 for six (Mazhar Qayyum 43; Alauddin four for 53). *PNSC 4 pts.*

At Municipal Stadium, Gujranwala, November 27, 28, 29, 30. Drawn. United Bank 101 (Manzoor Elahi five for 57, Sabih Azhar three for 23) and 276 for five (Saifullah 80, Pervez Shah 80, Mahmood Hamid 64, Iqbal Imam 32 not out); ADBP* 255 (Tariq Mohammad 30, Mansoor Rana 38, Ghaffar Kazmi 69; Masood Anwar four for 69). *ADBP 4 pts.*

At LCCA Ground, Lahore, November 27, 28, 29, 30. Drawn. PACO 319 (Ghulam Ali 53, Kamran Khan 69, Aamer Hanif 33, Yahya Toor 47 not out; Asadullah Butt three for 52, Nadeem Ghauri three for 68, Nadeem Nazar three for 62) and 83 for three (Shahid Saeed 31 not out, Murtaza Hussain 33 not out); Habib Bank* 287 (Mohammad Hasnain 61, Azhar Khan 41, Shaukat Mirza 80 not out; Mohammad Zahid eight for 114). *PACO 4 pts.*

At Model Town Cricket Club Ground, Lahore, November 27, 28, 29, 30. PNSC won by eight wickets. HBFC 196 (Nusrat Mahboob 34, Wasim Ali 58; Sajjad Akbar six for 68, Tahir Mahmood three for 32) and 203 (Faisal Qureshi 57, Wasim Yousufi 41; Mohsin Kamal three for 56, Sajjad Akbar five for 49); PNSC* 310 (Sohail Jaffer 59, Sher Ali 52, Sajjad Akbar 53, Mutahir Shah 68 not out; Kazim Mehdi four for 101, Nusrat Mahboob three for 46) and 93 for two (Sohail Jaffer 63 not out). *PNSC 10 pts.*

At Iqbal Stadium, Faisalabad, November 27, 28, 29, 30. Drawn. Pakistan Railways* 151 (Athar Laeeq five for 58, Hafeez-ur-Rehman three for 44) and 338 (Mohammad Ramzan 60, Majid Saeed 43, Mazhar Qayyum 50, Babar Javed 65, Iqbal Zahoor 47, Extras 38; Hafeez-ur-Rehman five for 75); National Bank 111 (Ameer Akbar 40; Imran Adil four for 46, Mohammad Ali six for 37) and 139 for six (Mohammad Javed 34, Naeem Ashraf 33; Mohammad Ali three for 42). *Pakistan Railways 4 pts.*

At UBL Sports Complex, Karachi, December 4, 5, 6, 7. Drawn. PIA 231 (Asif Mohammad 89; Manzoor Elahi three for 67, Ghayyur Qureshi five for 71) and 343 for nine dec. (Sohail Miandad 30, Zahid Fazal 64, Aamer Malik 36, Wasim Haider 100 not out, Rashid Khan 45; Javed Hayat five for 118); ADBP* 205 (Mansoor Rana 67, Ghaffar Kazmi 37, Manzoor Elahi 31; Nadeem Afzal three for 44, Zahid Ahmed three for 35) and 88 for two (Tariq Mohammad 35 not out, Atif Rauf 43). *PIA 4 pts.*

At Multan Cricket Club Stadium, Multan, December 4, 5, 6, 7. Pakistan Railways won by an innings and 54 runs. Pakistan Railways* 502 for six dec. (Majid Saeed 45, Nadeem Younis 105, Ijaz Ahmed 159, Naseer Ahmed 102 not out, Extras 30; Muhtashim Rasheed four for 133); HBFC 199 (Wasim Ali 30, Wasim Yousufi 101; Iqbal Zahoor three for 57) and 249 (Wasim Ali 102, Tariq Alam 49; Imran Adil three for 50, Iqbal Zahoor four for 78). *Pakistan Railways 10 pts.*

At Iqbal Stadium, Faisalabad, December 4, 5, 6, 7. Drawn. National Bank 480 (Sajid Ali 66, Wasim Arif 73, Ameer Akbar 100, Tahir Shah 41, Shahid Tanvir 109; Alauddin three for 93, Naved Nazir four for 111) and 205 for five (Shahid Anwar 84, Saeed Azad 67); PNSC* 352 (Azam Khan 61, Sajjad Akbar 132 not out, Sajjad Ali 50, Mohsin Kamal 36, Extras 30; Athar Laeeq three for 65, Naeem Ashraf four for 112, Hafeez-ur-Rehman three for 59). *National Bank 4 pts.*

At Bagh-e-Jinnah Ground, Lahore, December 5, 6, 7, 8. Drawn. PACO 369 (Kamran Khan 58, Ghulam Ali 85, Murtaza Hussain 53, Extras 39) and 213 for three (Ghulam Ali 115 not out, Mujahid Jamshed 62); United Bank* 236 (Javed Sami 63, Aamer Bashir 61, Extras 44; Shahid Hussain four for 30). *PACO 4 pts.*

At Iqbal Stadium, Faisalabad, December 11, 12, 13, 14. ADBP won by five wickets. PNSC 243 (R. I. Alikhan 45, Aamer Ishaq 46, Mutahir Shah 37; Manzoor Elahi four for 71, Javed Hayat three for 27) and 128 (Azam Khan 35; Manzoor Elahi three for 66, Ghaffar Kazmi five for 40); ADBP* 235 (Zahoor Elahi 46, Mansoor Rana 34, Ghaffar Kazmi 68, Mujahid Hameed 30 retired hurt; Mohsin Kamal five for 66, Alauddin three for 47) and 138 for five (Mansoor Rana 43 not out, Manzoor Elahi 40 not out). *ADBP 10 pts.*

At Municipal Stadium, Gujranwala, December 11, 12, 13, 14. Drawn. National Bank 137 (Shahid Anwar 35, Tahir Shah 37 not out; Nadeem Ghauri eight for 51) and 385 for seven dec. (Sajid Ali 154, Saeed Azad 61, Ameer Akbar 32; Akram Raza four for 90); Habib Bank* 190 (Shahid Javed 61, Extras 30; Maqsood Rana three for 58, Athar Laeeq three for 45) and 323 for nine (Shakeel Ahmed 44, Idrees Baig 83, Shahid Javed 36, Shaukat Mirza 41, Tahir Rashid 42, Akram Raza 38 not out; Nadeem Khan five for 80). *Habib Bank 4 pts.*

At LCCA Ground, Lahore, December 11, 12, 13, 14. PACO won by an innings and 11 runs. PACO* 326 (Mujahid Jamshed 59, Kamran Khan 135, Shahid Saeed 63; Shahid Ali Khan eight for 123, including a hat-trick); HBFC 173 (Faisal Qureshi 51, Raffat Alam 40; Mohammad Zahid three for 42) and 142 (Shahid Ali Khan 34 not out; Aamer Hanif seven for 71). *PACO 10 pts.*

At UBL Sports Complex, Karachi, December 11, 12, 13, 14. PIA won by eight wickets. Pakistan Railways* 328 (Majid Saeed 30, Nadeem Younis 68, Mazhar Qayyum 64, Naseer Ahmed 30; Rashid Khan four for 93) and 121 (Mazhar Qayyum 56; Zahid Ahmed four for 11, Wasim Haider four for 40); PIA 295 (Sohail Miandad 64, Zahid Fazal 74, Aamer Malik 42; Imran Adil six for 85) and 157 for two (Nasir Khan 61, Sohail Miandad 72). *PIA 10 pts.*

At Iqbal Stadium, Faisalabad, December 18, 19, 20, 21. Drawn. HBFC 179 (Tariq Alam 46, Raffat Alam 43; Javed Hayat three for 77, Raja Afaq six for 53) and 75 for no wkt (Jehangir Khan 61 not out); ADBP* 303 (Mansoor Rana 64, Ghaffar Kazmi 133; Shahid Ali Khan five for 101). *ADBP 4 pts.*

At LCCA Ground, Lahore, December 18, 19, 20, 21. Drawn. PNSC 297 (R. I. Alikhan 54, Aamer Ishaq 63, Nasir Wasti 65, Sajjad Akbar 40, Extras 30; Naved Anjum five for 61, Sohail Fazal three for 46); Habib Bank* 744 for seven (Shakeel Ahmed 200, Idrees Baig 158, Shaukat Mirza 160 not out, Akram Raza 145 not out; Mohsin Kamal five for 168). *Habib Bank 4 pts.*

At Niaz Stadium, Hyderabad, December 18, 19, 20, 21. Drawn. PIA* 540 (Sohail Miandad 142, Aamer Malik 125, Zahid Fazal 53, Asif Mohammad 62, Sagheer Abbas 51, Zahid Ahmed 37; Nadeem Khan five for 164, Hafeez-ur-Rehman three for 156); National Bank 265 (Mohammad Javed 73, Naeem Ashraf 104; Zahid Ahmed three for 98, Ayaz Jilani three for 66) and 51 for one (Shahid Anwar 32 not out). *PIA 4 pts.*

At UBL Sports Complex, Karachi, December 18, 19, 20. United Bank won by three wickets. Pakistan Railways* 178 (Nadeem Younis 45, Ijaz Ahmed 61; Masood Anwar five for 65, Iqbal Imam three for 21) and 141 (Masood Anwar three for 52, Iqbal Imam five for 26); United Bank 136 (Mansoor Akhtar 39; Iqbal Zahoor five for 57, Arshad Khan three for 35) and 187 for seven (Raees Ahmed 35, Aamer Bashir 48 not out; Iqbal Zahoor three for 77, Arshad Khan three for 76). *United Bank 10 pts.*

Semi-finals

At LCCA Ground, Lahore, December 25, 26, 27, 28. Drawn. ADBP reached the final by virtue of scoring 101 in their first 40 overs to PIA's 76. PIA 455 (Asif Mohammad 183, Zahid Ahmed 61, Moin Khan 41, Wasim Haider 30, Ayaz Jilani 78; Manzoor Elahi three for 79); ADBP* 215 for two (Atif Rauf 88 not out, Mansoor Rana 83 not out).

At UBL Sports Complex, Karachi, December 25, 26, 27, 28. Habib Bank won by eight wickets. PACO 180 (Mujahid Jamshed 40, Umar Rasheed 40 not out; Nadeem Ghauri six for 55) and 255 (Zulqarnain 45, Shahid Saeed 35, Shahid Nawaz 76; Nadeem Ghauri four for 72, Akram Raza three for 75); Habib Bank* 285 (Idrees Baig 42, Sohail Fazal 82, Shaukat Mirza 30, Akram Raza 37; Aamer Hanif three for 55, Mohammad Zahid five for 68) and 151 for two (Mohammad Hasnain 41, Idrees Baig 65 not out).

Final

At Gaddafi Stadium, Lahore, January 1, 2, 3, 4, 5. Drawn. ADBP were declared winners by virtue of their first-innings lead. ADBP 475 (Saeed Anwar 52, Zahoor Elahi 122, Atif Rauf 118, Javed Hayat 48, Extras 47; Naved Anjum three for 146, Asadullah Butt four for 91) and 159 for six (Atif Rauf 85; Naved Anjum five for 44); Habib Bank* 383 (Idrees Baig 141, Salim Malik 39, Akram Raza 76 not out, Extras 42; Manzoor Elahi three for 98, Ghayyur Qureshi four for 105, Qasim Shera three for 91).

AYUB TROPHY AND BCCP PATRON'S TROPHY WINNERS

The Ayub Trophy was replaced by the BCCP Trophy after the 1969-70 season and by the BCCP Patron's Trophy after the 1971-72 season.

1960-61	Railways-Quetta	1974-75	National Bank	1985-86	Karachi Whites
1961-62	Karachi	1975-76	National Bank	1986-87	National Bank
1962-63	Karachi	1976-77	Habib Bank	1987-88	Habib Bank
1964-65	Karachi	1977-78	Habib Bank	1988-89	Karachi
1965-66	Karachi Blues	1978-79	National Bank	1989-90	Karachi Whites
1967-68	Karachi Blues	†1979-80	IDBP	1990-91	ADBP
1969-70	PIA	†1980-81	Rawalpindi	1991-92	Habib Bank
1970-71	PIA	†1981-82	Allied Bank	1992-93	Habib Bank
1971-72	PIA	†1982-83	PACO	1993-94	ADBP
1972-73	Karachi Blues	1983-84	Karachi Blues		
1973-74	Railways	1984-85	Karachi Whites		

† *The competition was not first-class between 1979-80 and 1982-83, when it served as a qualifying competition for the Quaid-e-Azam Trophy.*

Note: Matches in the following section were not first-class.

PEPSI JUNIOR CUP UNDER-19 CHAMPIONSHIP

Final

At Rawalpindi Cricket Stadium, Rawalpindi, December 28, 29, 30, 31. Rawalpindi won by 178 runs. Rawalpindi 243 (Tasawwar Hussain 47, Mohammad Nadeem 37, Alamgir Khan 41; Imranullah six for 95, Kazim Rizvi three for 70) and 252 (Tasawwar Hussain 74, Naved Ashraf 33, Mohammad Nadeem 61; Imranullah five for 71, Kazim Rizvi three for 100); Karachi Blues* 181 (Ghayas-ud-Din 51, Zeeshan Pervez 40; Shoaib Akhtar five for 45, Alamgir Khan three for 38) and 136 (Ghayas-ud-Din 34; Pervez Iqbal three for 47, Shoaib Akhtar five for 57).

WILLS CUP

Semi-finals

At National Stadium, Karachi, October 15. Habib Bank won by 12 runs. Habib Bank 199 for nine (50 overs) (Ijaz Ahmed 64, Akram Raza 51 not out); ADBP* 187 (48.4 overs) (Atif Rauf 66, Javed Hayat 53; Naved Anjum three for 14, Asadullah Butt four for 32).

At Arbab Niaz Cricket Stadium, Peshawar, October 15. Rawalpindi won by virtue of losing fewer wickets. PIA 164 (48 overs) (Zahid Fazal 55; Naeem Akhtar three for 27, Mohammad Akram three for 35); Rawalpindi* 164 for seven (50 overs) (Azmat Jalil 31, Tariq Mahboob 32, Maqsood Ahmed 34).

Final

At Gaddafi Stadium, Lahore, October 22. Habib Bank won by 46 runs. Habib Bank 249 for five (50 overs) (Shakeel Ahmed 83, Ijaz Ahmed 71); Rawalpindi* 203 for eight (50 overs) (Nadeem Abbasi 32, Mohammad Riaz 39; Akram Raza three for 33).

BCCP PATRON'S TROPHY ONE-DAY LEAGUE

Final

At Gaddafi Stadium, Lahore, December 30. National Bank won by six wickets. ADBP 177 for seven (40 overs) (Atif Rauf 38, Mansoor Rana 74 not out; Athar Laeeq three for 36, Shahid Tanvir three for 20); National Bank* 178 for four (31.2 overs) (Sajid Ali 79, Ameer Akbar 48).

QUAID-E-AZAM TROPHY ONE-DAY LEAGUE

Final

At Gaddafi Stadium, Lahore, April 29. Karachi Whites won by 86 runs. Karachi Whites 300 for four (40 overs) (Ghulam Ali 156 not out, Aaley Haider 52, Rashid Latif 51 not out); Lahore City* 214 for eight (40 overs) (Sohail Fazal 33, Ashraf Ali 61 not out; Athar Laeeq four for 46).

CRICKET IN SRI LANKA, 1993-94

By GERRY VAIDYASEKERA

Another busy international season began with India's tour in July and continued with the historic first visit of the South Africans in August and the first Test series with the West Indians in December. The national team also toured India and played in three one-day tournaments – the last of them, the Austral-Asia Cup, without their usual captain, Arjuna Ranatunga, his deputy, Aravinda de Silva, and several others, after a dispute with the board over fitness tests and their unauthorised participation in some benefit matches in India.

Domestic first-class cricket was less plentiful in 1993-94, though it also had its share of controversy. The Super Tournament introduced the previous year was dropped and the final rounds of the P. Saravanamuttu Trophy – Division I of the inter-club tournament – were contested by eight teams, down from 14, though still divided into two groups. The Trophy matches were played immediately after the Singer inter-provincial tournament, with both finals staged in April, as the season again stretched across most of the year.

Title-holders Western Province (North) met Western Province (City) in the Singer final. North had won three of their five round-robin games, and City only one, though they took first-innings lead in the other four. City were not confirmed as finalists until after an enquiry into the bizarre conclusion of their match with Southern Province, which ended on the third day when no suitable balls could be found for the start of the second innings. Southern Province were bystanders in another dramatic curtailment, with North-Western Province. North-Western batsman Priyankara Liyanage, the non-striker, was so incensed when his team-mate, Nishantha Munasinghe, was given lbw that he attacked the umpire with his bat. This led to a crowd riot. All points were subsequently cancelled and Liyanage was given a ten-year ban.

Eventually, Western Province (City) were allowed to enter the final, which was held three weeks late. They took the title by 341 runs, thanks largely to Kumara Dharmasena, who took ten for 88 in the match and prevented North from reaching 200 in either innings. City had taken first use of the pitch and scored 276, but their batsmen really came into their own in the second innings, when Chandika Hathurusinghe and Naveed Nawaz helped them to 344. Hathurusinghe had been a key player for City, scoring 435 at 48.33, including 143 out of 503 for six against Western Province (South), and picking up 19 cheap wickets. North fielded four Ranatunga brothers – Arjuna, Dhammika, Nishantha and Sanjeeva – who dominated their batting. They also had the bowler of the tournament, Manjula Munasinghe, who took 34 at 13.58, including nine for 38 in an innings against Central Province, earning his international debut. Munasinghe was closely followed by Ajith Ekanayake, with 33 at 15.20 for North-Western Province, playing an important role in their two victories.

Two Colombo clubs battled out the P. Saravanamuttu final. Invited to bat, Colombo Cricket Club ran up 368 on the first day, with four half-centuries, one from Lalith Sagara, who scored 74 at No. 8; Wendell Labrooy took seven for 147. Nondescripts conceded a 25-run advantage. But Colombo collapsed to 143 for nine on the third day, Labrooy adding another four wickets and Hashan Tillekeratne three. Colombo owed their eventual 216 to a partnership between last man Kenneth Quinn, their Antiguan pace bowler, who scored 48, and Mario Villavarayan. Chasing 242, Nondescripts lost five wickets for 111. But Tillekeratne and Amal Silva made the most of missed chances, adding 65, and Silva and Gamini Wickremasinghe settled the issue with an unbroken stand of 67 in 14 overs.

Nondescripts had qualified ahead of their chief rivals, Sinhalese Sports Club; both had beaten the other two teams in Group B, so their match with each other turned out to have been crucial. Nondescripts took first-innings lead through a massive 538, with de Silva scoring 222, the only double-century of the season. Sinhalese made up for this hammering by dismissing Kurunegala Youth for 31, the lowest total in Sri Lankan first-class cricket; two batsmen were absent. In Group A, Colombo, Colts and Tamil Union had one win and one first-innings lead each; Colombo went through, thanks in part to Quinn, who took seven for 65 against Colts, and Athula Samarasekera, who scored the fastest hundred of the season off 97 balls against Moratuwa. Colts and Tamil Union were involved in yet another controversy. Their match was called off when Tamil opener Ruwan Peiris finally arrived to bat with eight wickets down, having absented himself, apparently, for another game. Tailender Chaminda Hathurusinghe attempted to retire in his favour, but the Colts fielders objected and the match never resumed.

Nondescripts also won the limited-overs R. Premadasa Trophy, in the floodlit final at Khettarama. Sinhalese, their opponents, collapsed from 93 for one to 177 all out. De Silva and Sanjeeva Ranatunga added an unbroken 103 to see Nondescripts to a comfortable eight-wicket victory, after rain reduced their target to 149 from 42 overs. The Sri Lankan board revived the GTE Yellow Pages Under-23 Tournament, which was won by Panadura, an outstation club. They beat Colts through their acting-captain, Surendra Kumara, who played an heroic innings of 90.

In Division II of the inter-club competition, Sinhalese Sports Club and Bloomfield shared the title after drawing the two-day final. Gamini Perera hit a stylish 126 for Sinhalese and Indika Batuwitarachchi an unbeaten 108 for Bloomfield. Earlier, Perera's team-mate, Naresh Adhikaram, hit 201 not out for Sinhalese against Police. Chilaw Marians piled up 402 for six in 45 overs, a Sri Lankan one-day record, in a Division III game against Chettarama, and won by 263 runs. Vesuvius, who entered Division III in 1986, finally secured their first win, defeating Old Rajans by five wickets. Puttalam-Chilaw became the Minor Districts Champions, beating Monaragala, who had reached their second final in their second year in the competition.

In schools cricket, Nalanda Vidyalaya won the limited-overs Coca Cola Bottlers' Trophy, snatching a 17-run victory over St Joseph's College, six of whose batsmen were run out. St Sylvester's College from Kandy became the first outstation club to win the A Division league tournament. The highest score by a schoolboy was an unbeaten 211 by left-hander Sanjeeva Warusumaine, for D. S. Senanayake Vidyalaya against Kalutara Maha Vidyalaya. Malintha Perera of De Mazenod scored 1,000 runs for the second successive season; Nuwan Shiroman of St Aloysius's, who hit twin centuries against President's College, and Sampath Perera of D. S. Senanayake also reached four figures. Sean Mackay of Raddoluwa scored a remarkable sequence of 111 not out, 105 not out, 113 not out, 63 and 117 not out – 509 in five innings for one dismissal – in the Astra Margarine Under-17 competition.

Six regimental units took part in a six-a-side tournament organised by the Sri Lanka Army Medical Services, at the request of soldiers wounded in the war in the north; Light Infantry beat Special Force in the final.

*In the following scores, * by the name of a team indicates that they won the toss.*

SINGER INTER-PROVINCIAL TOURNAMENT, 1993-94

At Welagedera Stadium, Kurunegala, February 5, 6, 7, 8. Drawn. North-Western Province 324 (R. J. Jaymon 82, M. P. Liyanage 57, J. Kulatunga 54, Extras 63; M. J. H. Rushdie seven for 148); Central Province* 123 (T. P. Kodikara 37; A. W. Ekanayake six for 20) and 29 for no wkt.

At Uyanwatta Stadium, Matara, February 5, 6, 7, 8. Western Province (North) won by 46 runs. Western Province (North) 214 (V. S. Sittamige 68, N. Ranatunga 40, G. F. Labrooy 36 not out; R. Priyadarshana three for 50) and 136 (N. Ranatunga 56; S. M. Faumi four for 37); Southern Province* 69 (G. F. Labrooy four for 30, M. Munasinghe four for 34) and 235 (H. S. S. Fonseka 47, M. A. R. Samarasekera 33, S. Jayantha 53, H. Premasiri 30; M. Munasinghe five for 67, V. D. Surendra four for 54).

At Maitland Place, Colombo (SSC), February 5, 6, 7, 8. Drawn. Western Province (South) 293 (N. S. Bopage 30, S. Jayawardene 43, R. S. Kaluwitharana 85, R. de Soysa 32; C. M. Hathurusinghe three for 73, U. C. Hathurusinghe three for 62); Western Province (City)* 503 for six (U. C. Hathurusinghe 143, R. Peiris 30, R. P. A. H. Wickremaratne 133, M. V. Perera 60, M. N. Nawaz 48, Extras 32).

At Welagedera Stadium, Kurunegala, February 10, 11, 12, 13. Drawn. Western Province (City)* 174 (R. P. A. H. Wickremaratne 47, P. W. Gunaratne 30; R. K. B. Amunugama three for 34, T. Herath three for 45) and 70 for two dec.; North-Western Province 64 (U. C. Hathurusinghe five for 15) and 101 for six (T. Herath 43).

At Braybrook Place, Colombo (Moors), February 10, 11, 12, 13. Western Province (North) won by an innings and 138 runs. Central Province 118 (M. Munasinghe five for 41, N. Ranatunga three for 14) and 98 (M. Munasinghe nine for 38); Western Province (North)* 354 for six dec. (E. F. M. U. Fernando 40, S. Ranatunga 121, N. Ranatunga 52, C. I. Dunasinghe 50 not out, Extras 31; T. P. Kodikara three for 85).

At P. Saravanamuttu Stadium, Colombo, February 10, 11, 12, 13. Drawn. Southern Province 292 (U. U. Chandana 105, K. G. Priyantha 52 not out; N. A. C. P. Rodrigo six for 50) and 351 for three dec. (H. S. S. Fonseka 93, W. M. J. Kumudu 37, M. A. R. Samarasekera 191); Western Province (South)* 168 (R. S. Kaluwitharana 56, C. Mahesh 39; K. P. J. Warnaweera six for 43) and 240 for eight (R. S. Kaluwitharana 94, M. Jayasena 51; C. P. H. Ramanayake three for 59, S. M. Faumi three for 65).

At Braybrook Place, Colombo (Moors), February 17, 18, 19, 20. Southern Province won by an innings and 52 runs. Southern Province 274 (H. Premasiri 110, U. U. Chandana 39; P. K. Wijetunge four for 47); Central Province* 110 (S. I. Fernando 57; C. P. H. Ramanayake four for 47, K. P. J. Warnaweera four for 11) and 112 (C. P. H. Ramanayake seven for 41).

At Welagedera Stadium, Kurunegala, February 17, 18, 19, 20. North-Western Province won by 105 runs. North-Western Province* 189 (M. P. Liyanage 48, J. Kulatunga 46; Sanjeeva Silva five for 40) and 154 (M. P. Liyanage 41 not out; Sanjeeva Silva three for 56, N. Dabare five for 33); Western Province (South) 56 (A. W. Ekanayake six for 17, A. W. R. Madurasinghe three for seven) and 182 (S. Jayawardene 52, R. S. Kaluwitharana 56; T. Herath three for 48, A. W. Ekanayake three for 49, A. W. R. Madurasinghe three for 44).

At P. Saravanamuttu Stadium, Colombo, February 17, 18, 19, 20. Drawn. Western Province (North) 196 (S. Ranatunga 63, N. Ranatunga 39; P. W. Gunaratne four for 46, H. D. P. K. Dharmasena three for 31) and 202 (S. Ranatunga 48, E. A. R. de Silva 50 not out; U. C. Hathurusinghe four for 51, A. P. Gurusinha three for 28); Western Province (City)* 279 (R. David 83, R. P. A. H. Wickremaratne 52; N. Ranatunga three for 76, E. A. R. de Silva four for 47) and seven for one.

At Maitland Crescent, Colombo (CCC), February 24, 25, 26, 27. Western Province (South) won by ten wickets. Central Province* 167 (S. I. Fernando 47; Sanjeeva Silva seven for 73) and 108 (D. N. Nadarajah 41, U. H. Kodituwakku 32; Sanjeeva Silva six for 40, N. A. C. P. Rodrigo three for 52); Western Province (South) 255 (C. Mendis 75, C. de Silva 43 not out, Extras 46; P. K. Wijetunge five for 83) and 23 for no wkt.

At Galle Stadium, Galle, February 24, 25, 26, 27. Drawn. Southern Province* 310 (D. D. Wickremasinghe 34, M. A. R. Samarasekera 37, S. Jayantha 58, U. U. Chandana 86, C. P. H. Ramanayake 36; A. P. Gurusinha three for 69); Western Province (City) 377 (U. C. Hathurusinghe 53, A. P. Gurusinha 126, H. D. P. K. Dharmasena 34, Y. N. Tillekeratne 47 not out, A. G. D. Wickremasinghe 32, Extras 59; C. P. H. Ramanayake four for 89, C. Bandara six for 98).

At P. Saravanamuttu Stadium, Colombo, February 24, 25, 26, 27. North-Western Province won by three wickets. Western Province (North)* 324 (V. S. Sittamige 140; A. W. Ekanayake five for 103) and 260 for eight dec. (D. Ranatunga 81, E. F. M. U. Fernando 54, S. Alexander 33; A. W. Ekanayake four for 90, A. W. R. Madurasinghe three for 91); North-Western Province 206 (J. Kulatunga 45, T. Herath 37; W. P. U. J. C. Vaas three for 58, M. Munasinghe three for 40) and 379 for seven (J. A. Jaymon 64, R. J. Jaymon 32, N. Munasinghe 31, J. Kulatunga 65, M. P. Liyanage 85 not out, Extras 36).

At Welagedera Stadium, Kurunegala, March 3, 4, 5, 6. Drawn. Southern Province* 106 (R. K. B. Amunugama three for 38, A. W. Ekanayake five for 17) and 410 (M. A. R. Samarasekera 81, M. S. Atapattu 104, S. Jayantha 45, H. Premasiri 41, C. P. H. Ramanayake 43; A. W. R. Madurasinghe five for 91); North-Western Province 212 (J. A. Jaymon 44, C. T. Ratnayake 43, Extras 31; S. T. Jayasuriya four for 44) and 97 for four (R. J. Jaymon 31).

At Maitland Crescent, Colombo, March 3, 4, 5, 6. Western Province (City) won by ten wickets. Central Province* 209 (M. Rifan 32, T. P. Kodikara 34, D. N. Nadarajah 36; H. D. P. K. Dharmasena four for 53) and 186 (S. I. Fernando 41, U. H. Kodituwakku 67; P. W. Gunaratne four for 52); Western Province (City) 377 (U. C. Hathurusinghe 66, R. P. A. H. Wickremaratne 54, M. V. Perera 102 not out, Y. N. Tillekeratne 66, Extras 34; M. J. H. Rushdie four for 86) and 22 for no wkt.

At Braybrook Place, Colombo (Moors), March 3, 4, 5, 6. Western Province (North) won by an innings and 92 runs. Western Province (South) 82 (W. P. U. J. C. Vaas five for 33, M. Munasinghe four for 39) and 147 (N. S. Bopage 32, G. R. M. A. Perera 34; W. P. U. J. C. Vaas four for 44, E. A. R. de Silva three for 27); Western Province (North)* 321 (D. Ranatunga 44, S. Ranatunga 72, N. Ranatunga 54, M. Munasinghe 37 not out; K. R. Pushpakumara four for 109, G. Perera three for 44).

Final

At Uyanwatta Stadium, Matara, April 21, 22, 23, 24. Western Province (City) won by 341 runs. Western Province (City)* 276 (V. S. K. Waragoda 47, M. V. Perera 49, M. N. Nawaz 31, C. Ranasinghe 46; E. A. R. de Silva six for 120) and 344 (U. C. Hathurusinghe 80, M. V. Perera 47, M. N. Nawaz 91 not out, Extras 52; G. F. Labrooy three for 92, D. P. Samaraweera three for 46); Western Province (North) 153 (A. Ranatunga 38; H. D. P. K. Dharmasena four for 52) and 126 (D. P. Samaraweera 40; H. D. P. K. Dharmasena six for 36).

P. SARAVANAMUTTU TROPHY, 1993-94

Group A

At Havelock Park, Colombo (Colts), March 11, 12, 13. Drawn. Colts CC 218 (S. I. Fernando 35, N. Ranatunga 35, S. Wijesekera 38; M. Muralitharan four for 46); Tamil Union C and AC* 204 for eight (D. N. Nadarajah 40, I. de Saram 36, N. Bandaratilleke 32 not out, M. Perera 36; J. C. Gamage three for 60).

At Maitland Crescent, Colombo (CCC), March 12, 13, 14. Colombo CC won by seven wickets. Moratuwa SC 135 (I. Anthony 39; J. Jayaratne five for 28) and 211 (P. Perera 36, A. Perera 95; K. Quinn three for 43, H. M. L. Sagara four for 30); Colombo CC* 283 (M. A. R. Samarasekera 129, V. S. K. Waragoda 44, P. Jayawardene 36 not out; M. P. A. Cooray three for 58, P. Perera five for 33) and 67 for three (G. W. J. Bandara 38).

At Havelock Park, Colombo (Colts), March 18, 19, 20. Colts CC won by an innings and 146 runs. Moratuwa SC 112 (A. Perera 43 not out; W. P. U. J. C. Vaas three for 42, J. C. Gamage four for 54) and 102 (I. Anthony 34 retired hurt; W. P. U. J. C. Vaas three for 42, J. C. Gamage three for 17); Colts CC* 360 for nine dec. (C. Mendis 62, D. P. Samaraweera 51, N. Ranatunga 61, W. P. U. J. C. Vaas 58 not out, J. C. Gamage 40 not out; P. Perera five for 103).

At Maitland Crescent, Colombo (CCC), March 19, 20, 21. Drawn. Tamil Union C and AC 261 (U. C. Hathurusinghe 33, W. T. de Silva 35, D. N. Nadarajah 43; K. Quinn four for 86, H. M. L. Sagara three for 23) and 342 (U. C. Hathurusinghe 35, U. U. Chandana 163, M. Muralitharan 36; K. Quinn three for 90); Colombo CC* 174 (V. S. K. Waragoda 50, H. M. L. Sagara 37 not out; C. P. H. Ramanayake six for 28) and 137 for six (C. P. Senanayake 43, M. A. R. Samarasekera 32 not out; M. Perera five for 38).

At Maitland Crescent, Colombo (CCC), March 25, 26, 27. Drawn. Colombo CC* 295 (C. P. Senanayake 92, D. D. Madurapperuma 55, C. R. Thenuwara 45; W. P. U. J. C. Vaas three for 89, S. I. Fernando three for 77, N. Ranatunga three for 58) and 248 (A. C. Seneviratne 32, M. A. R. Samarasekera 56; W. P. U. J. C. Vaas three for 85, N. Ranatunga three for 32); Colts CC 216 (D. P. Samaraweera 50, M. V. Perera 52, N. Ranatunga 39, Extras 40; K. Quinn seven for 65) and 208 for seven (D. P. Samaraweera 84, S. I. Fernando 70; H. M. L. Sagara four for 73).

At P. Saravanamuttu Stadium, Colombo, April 1, 2, 3. Tamil Union C and AC won by 186 runs. Tamil Union C and AC* 260 for nine dec. (U. C. Hathurusinghe 43, W. T. de Silva 76, M. Perera 38; P. Perera four for 55, R. Fernando three for 93) and 215 for five dec. (U. C. Hathurusinghe 100, I. de Saram 57); Moratuwa SC 186 (S. Perera 34, C. Fernando 45; C. P. H. Ramanayake three for 78, M. Muralitharan three for 30) and 103 (C. Fernando 53; M. Muralitharan three for 25, N. Bandaratilleke five for 24).

Group B

At Havelock Park, Colombo (BRC), March 11, 12, 13. Kurunegala Youth CC won by ten runs. Kurunegala Youth CC* 269 (N. Munasinghe 106, A. W. Ekanayake 36; D. Dias four for 42, M. H. A. Jabbar three for 64) and 93 (A. Jabbar four for 25, G. R. M. A. Perera five for 25); Sebastianites C and AC 222 (C. Mahesh 47, R. S. Kaluwitharana 53 retired hurt, R. Wickremaratne 40, A. W. Ekanayake five for 69, A. W. R. Madurasinghe three for 71) and 130 (R. Wickremaratne 57; S. Guruge three for 35, A. W. Ekanayake three for 55).

At Maitland Place, Colombo (NCC), March 12, 13, 14. Drawn. Nondescripts CC* 538 (S. Weerasinghe 42, P. A. de Silva 222, R. P. Arnold 42, S. A. R. Silva 43, A. G. D. Wickremasinghe 66, Extras 45; M. Munasinghe three for 106, S. Dodanwela three for 77) and 129 for one (R. David 50 not out, S. Ranatunga 55 not out); Sinhalese SC 333 (D. Ranatunga 76, U. N. K. Fernando 45, M. Munasinghe 53, R. S. Jayawardene 39, P. K. Wijetunge 34, Extras 30; P. A. de Silva four for 106, C. D. U. S. Weerasinghe four for 75).

At Royal College Ground, Colombo, March 18, 19, 20. Sinhalese SC won by an innings and 89 runs. Sebastianites C and AC 108 (A. P. Gurusinha four for 17, C. N. Fernando three for 19) and 154 (Sanjeeva Silva 53, K. N. Waduge 53; C. Ranasinghe three for four); Sinhalese SC* 351 for five dec. (D. Ranatunga 40, A. A. W. Gunawardene 31, A. P. Gurusinha 87, M. S. Atapattu 118 not out, C. N. Fernando 39).

At Welagedera Stadium, Kurunegala, March 19, 20, 21. Nondescripts CC won by nine wickets. Kurunegala Youth CC* 149 (R. Kariyawasam 38; A. P. Weerakkody five for 39) and 118 (A. P. Weerakkody six for 55, C. D. U. S. Weerasinghe three for 34); Nondescripts CC 214 (C. P. Handunettige 50, A. G. D. Wickremasinghe 86; A. W. Ekanayake three for 64, A. W. R. Madurasinghe seven for 85) and 57 for one (S. Weerasinghe 37 retired hurt).

At Maitland Place, Colombo (NCC), March 25, 26, 27. Nondescripts CC won by 214 runs. Nondescripts CC 228 (S. Ranatunga 39, C. P. Handunettige 30, Shantha Silva 40; S. Chanaka three for 74, M. H. A. Jabbar four for 48) and 227 for six dec. (S. Weerasinghe 55, R. David 51, P. A. de Silva 38, S. Ranatunga 68; Surajith Silva three for 80); Sebastianites C and AC* 137 (Anusha Perera 46, K. N. Waduge 34; A. P. Weerakkody five for 59, P. A. de Silva four for 19) and 104 (P. A. de Silva five for 39).

At Maitland Place, Colombo (SSC), March 25, 26, 27. Sinhalese SC won by an innings and 119 runs. Kurunegala Youth CC 31 (M. Munasinghe three for ten) and 203 (W. Kumara 30, A. W. R. Madurasinghe 48 not out; M. Munasinghe three for 42); Sinhalese SC* 353 for three dec. (A. A. W. Gunawardene 118, A. P. Gurusinha 65, M. S. Atapattu 77 not out, R. P. A. H. Wickremaratne 63 not out).

Final

At P. Saravanamuttu Stadium, Colombo, April 27, 28, 29, 30. Nondescripts CC won by four wickets. Colombo CC 368 (C. P. Senanayake 57, G. W. J. Bandara 36, V. S. K. Waragoda 50, M. A. R. Samarasekera 52, H. M. L. Sagara 74, M. Villavarayan 39 not out, Extras 31; W. Labrooy seven for 147) and 216 (G. W. J. Bandara 34, M. A. R. Samarasekera 46, K. Quinn 48; W. Labrooy four for 70, H. P. Tillekeratne three for 87); Nondescripts CC* 343 (S. Weerasinghe 79, R. P. Arnold 86, H. P. Tillekeratne 32, Extras 58; J. Jayaratne three for 34) and 243 for six (H. P. Tillekeratne 78, S. A. R. Silva 56 not out).

P. SARAVANAMUTTU TROPHY, 1992-93

The following scores of Colts CC's matches before they were disqualified from the 1992-93 tournament were not available when Wisden *1994 went to press.*

At Havelock Park, Colombo (Colts), January 15, 16, 17, 1993. Colts CC won by an innings and 125 runs. Kurunegala SC 101 (A. H. Bandaranayake 32; N. Ranatunga three for 18, W. P. U. J. C. Vaas three for 38, E. A. Upashantha three for 37) and 154 (M. P. Liyanage 32, D. K. Bandara 30; N. Ranatunga four for 40, E. A. Upashantha three for 33, R. Wijesuriya three for 36); Colts CC 380 for one dec. (C. Mendis 53, D. P. Samaraweera 200 not out, M. V. Perera 113 not out).

At Havelock Park, Colombo (Colts), January 21, 22, 23, 1993. Colts CC won by an innings and 34 runs. Singha SC 77 (W. P. U. J. C. Vaas five for 29, E. A. Upashantha four for 11) and 165 (H. W. Kumara 50; R. Wijesuriya three for 46, N. Kalpage six for 37); Colts CC* 276 (C. Mendis 46, D. P. Samaraweera 38, M. V. Perera 39, E. A. Upashantha 45; H. M. N. C. Dhanasinghe three for 43, L. Ranasinghe four for 63).

CRICKET IN ZIMBABWE, 1993-94

By TERRY YATES-ROUND and JOHN WARD

While their international cricketers upheld their honour abroad – almost achieving a first Test win in Pakistan – Zimbabwe continued to develop the domestic roots their new status demanded. For the first time, the Zimbabwe Cricket Union staged its own first-class competition, the Logan Cup; they entered a team in the South African UCBSA Bowl; they hosted further visits from overseas teams; and, most important for the future, they kept up the expansion in coaching facilities. It was pleasing to note that the black community was taking to the game with greater enthusiasm, with great strides made in the townships.

The Logan Cup featured four teams, three from Mashonaland and one from Matabeleland, who played each other once over three days. Mashonaland Under-24 and Matabeleland topped the league table and went forward to the final, which ended in a draw. Put in on a greenish pitch, the Under-24 team managed 286, built around Gavin Rennie's 76. But they soon dismissed Matabeleland for 140; the captain, Wayne James, made 52 not out, and no one else reached 20. First-innings lead ensured that Mashonaland Under-24 took the Cup.

James also made the only double-century of the season, 215 against Mashonaland Country Districts at Bulawayo. But though he and Matabeleland team-mate Guy Whittall headed the batting and bowling averages, the continuing dominance of Mashonaland, which includes Harare, was reflected in the composition of the teams. In Mashonaland, cricket facilities and equipment are more readily available and the population, more closely knit, have easier access to them.

Zimbabwe's own first-class tournament brought some younger players, who might have gone unnoticed, to the attention of the selectors. But the return to first-class competition in South Africa, for the first time since Zimbabwe gained independence, provided important experience. The lessons learned were invaluable, though the weaknesses of Zimbabwe's top cricketers were apparent. The Zimbabwe Board XI were unbeaten, but won only one match, against Northern Transvaal B in Verwoerdburg, and never claimed first-innings lead. Their bowlers struggled to take wickets, apart from Malcolm Jarvis, whose left-arm swing earned 20 at 19.95 and put him second in South Africa's domestic bowling averages. The rest took 23 between them at an average of just over 53. Spinners Ujesh Ranchod and Paul Strang, highly rated in Zimbabwe, returned averages of 40, though it is true that pitches in modern South African cricket hardly encourage slow bowling.

There were also visits from Western Province in October and English counties Warwickshire and Worcestershire, on pre-season tours, in April, giving local cricketers some more first-class opposition – and spectators some entertainment. Zimbabwean teams did win a few of the one-day games, though they had less success over three days. The selectors made a point of picking some of the younger hopefuls, such as the Matambanadzo brothers – Everton, who could be the genuine pace bowler Zimbabwe are looking for, and Darling, whose batting technique suggests an international future. At club level, Harare Sports Club claimed the Rothmans National

League and Mashonaland's Vigne Cup, taking over as the most successful team from Old Georgians, who won both in 1992-93.

But the ZCU has always realised that, if cricket is to grow in Zimbabwe, it has to be from grassroots level. The long-awaited Cricket Academy now offers professional coaching on a regular basis. It is funded by the Wakeford Trust and 24 other sponsors, and managed by Mike Wiley and director of coaching Dave Levy. The ZCU have also engaged 11 full-time and ten part-time black coaches. In the Mufakose township, eight teachers have passed the elementary coaching course with distinction and are putting it into practice. Country Districts employ two full-time coaches, who work in the Bindura and Shamva districts; at the Shamva mine, a football pitch has been converted for cricketing purposes, with a concrete wicket being laid, in addition to three nets with concrete strips. Each week, the ZCU buses in 12 black youngsters from the Chitungwiza and High Glen townships to the Academy, where they are able to play on grass pitches. Thanks to this coaching programme, all five provinces have junior leagues.

In the senior schools league, run by Clive Barnes, headmaster of Prince Edward School in Harare, 20 schools from the five provinces take part. The progress resulting from all this activity is indicated by the growing enthusiasm among young black Zimbabweans for the Primary Schools Annual Cricket Festival. All provinces were expected to send teams, with four more coming from the Country Districts, to the festival in December 1994, organised again by Barnes.

The ZCU also established a professional secretariat, with offices at the Harare Sports Club, and Don Arnott as chief executive. His long experience of cricket, as player and organiser in Mashonaland Country Districts, and of business, was expected to be an invaluable asset in the development of cricket in Zimbabwe. – T. Y.-R.

FIRST-CLASS AVERAGES, 1993-94

BATTING

(Qualification: 200 runs)

	M	*I*	*NO*	*R*	*HS*	*100s*	*Avge*
W. R. James (*Matabeleland*)	6	10	1	620	215	1	68.88
A. Flower (*Mashonaland*)	5	8	1	392	113	1	56.00
G. W. Flower (*Mashonaland Under-24*)	6	12	1	534	96	0	48.54
G. K. Bruk-Jackson (*Mashonaland Country Districts*)	6	12	1	496	130	1	45.09
S. V. Carlisle (*Mashonaland Under-24*)	6	11	1	385	111*	1	38.50
I. P. Butchart (*Zimbabwe Board XI*)	4	7	1	209	60*	0	34.83
A. C. Waller (*Mashonaland Country Districts*)	3	6	0	206	62	0	34.33
G. A. Paterson (*Mashonaland Country Districts*)	5	8	0	250	73	0	31.25
A. D. R. Campbell (*Mashonaland Country Districts*)	5	10	1	279	73	0	31.00
U. Ranchod (*Mashonaland*)	7	11	4	201	48	0	28.71
G. J. Rennie (*Mashonaland Under-24*)	6	12	1	309	76	0	28.09
D. N. Erasmus (*Mashonaland Under-24*)	10	18	1	441	76	0	25.94
G. C. Martin (*Mashonaland*)	9	14	0	342	73	0	24.42
D. J. R. Campbell (*Mashonaland Country Districts*)	9	15	0	274	41	0	18.26
P. A. Strang (*Mashonaland Country Districts*)	8	12	0	219	45	0	18.25
C. B. Wishart (*Mashonaland Under-24*)	10	18	0	323	77	0	17.94

* *Signifies not out.*

BOWLING

(Qualification: 10 wickets)

	O	*M*	*R*	*W*	*BB*	*5W/i*	*Avge*
G. J. Whittall (*Matabeleland*)	135	33	323	16	6-34	1	20.18
D. Matambanadzo (*Mashonaland Under-24*)	92.5	15	286	13	3-43	0	22.00
M. P. Jarvis (*Mashonaland*)	357.3	119	753	33	6-74	2	22.81
E. Matambanadzo (*Mashonaland Under-24*)	78	17	241	10	3-20	0	24.10
J. A. Rennie (*Matabeleland*)	222.5	54	651	23	6-34	2	28.30
H. J. Hira (*Mashonaland Under-24*)	121.1	36	322	11	3-43	0	29.27
S. G. Peall (*Mashonaland Country Districts*)	165	36	453	14	4-39	0	32.35
G. J. Crocker (*Mashonaland Country Districts*)	127.2	33	337	10	6-84	1	33.70
P. A. Strang (*Mashonaland Country Districts*)	250	55	775	21	4-45	0	36.90
G. C. Martin (*Mashonaland*)	231	67	522	10	3-44	0	52.20

Note: These averages include performances for the Zimbabwe Board XI in the UCB Bowl.

LOGAN CUP, 1993-94

					1st-inns	*Bonus points*		
	Played	*Won*	*Lost*	*Drawn*	*Points*	*Batting*	*Bowling*	*Points*
Mashonaland Under-24	3	1	0	2	5	12	29	56
Matabeleland	3	1	0	2	5	12	22.5	49.5
Mashonaland Country Districts	3	0	1	2	5	15	20	40
Mashonaland	3	0	1	2	5	10	22.5	37.5

Final: Mashonaland Under-24 drew with Matabeleland, but took the Logan Cup by virtue of their first-innings lead.

Outright win = 10 pts; lead on first innings in a drawn game = 5 pts.
Bonus points: One point is awarded for the first 100 runs in each innings and for every subsequent 60 (restricted to the first 85 overs in the first innings). Half a point is awarded for every wicket taken throughout both innings.

*In the following scores, * by the name of a team indicates that they won the toss.*

At Harare South Country Club, January 14, 15, 16. Drawn. Mashonaland Country Districts* 210 (A. D. R. Campbell 33, G. K. Bruk-Jackson 49, G. A. Paterson 44; G. C. Martin three for 44) and 203 for six (G. K. Bruk-Jackson 59, A. C. Waller 62; M. P. Jarvis three for 72); Mashonaland 140 (J. M. A. Inglis 36, A. Flower 35; P. A. Strang four for 45). *Mashonaland Country Districts 14 pts, Mashonaland 9 pts.*

At Queens Sports Club, Bulawayo, January 14, 15, 16. Drawn. Matabeleland 296 (W. R. James 66, B. A. Clark 55, H. H. Streak 42 not out, Extras 35; D. J. Rowett four for 65) and 200 (G. J. Whittall 73; S. G. Davies three for 14); Mashonaland Under-24* 251 (G. W. Flower 66, G. J. Rennie 34, S. G. Davies 34, H. J. Hira 46; J. A. Rennie five for 47) and 137 for five (D. N. Erasmus 46, R. P. Gifford 44; J. A. Rennie three for 35). *Matabeleland 17.5 pts, Mashonaland Under-24 14 pts.*

At Harare Sports Club, Harare, February 11, 12, 13. Mashonaland Under-24 won by ten wickets. Mashonaland Under-24 284 (G. W. Flower 55, G. J. Rennie 41, D. N. Erasmus 47, S. G. Davies 50, Extras 39; T. L. Penney three for 18) and 45 for no wkt; Mashonaland* 75 (E. Matambanadzo three for 20) and 253 (A. Flower 59, T. L. Penney 36, G. C. Martin 43, M. G. Burmester 52; C. A. Joseph three for 24). *Mashonaland Under-24 21 pts, Mashonaland 8 pts.*

At Bulawayo Athletic Club, Bulawayo, February 11, 12, 13. Matabeleland won by an innings and 34 runs. Matabeleland* 433 (M. H. Dekker 31, N. R. van Rensburg 40, W. R. James 215, B. A. Clark 56; G. J. Crocker six for 84); Mashonaland Country Districts 220 for seven dec. (K. J. Arnott 30, A. D. R. Campbell 33, G. J. Crocker 31 not out, Extras 34) and 179 (A. C. Waller 51, C. M. Robertson 43; J. A. Rennie six for 34). *Matabeleland 20.5 pts, Mashonaland Country Districts 10 pts.*

At Harare Sports Club, Harare, March 4, 5, 6. Drawn. Mashonaland* 358 (M. G. Burmester 32, A. Flower 85, D. L. Houghton 48, A. H. Shah 31, U. Ranchod 36, Extras 46; H. R. Olonga three for 48) and 160 for three dec. (A. Flower 40 not out, D. L. Houghton 80); Matabeleland 214 (M. H. Dekker 48, M. D. Abrams 64; D. H. Brain five for 56) and 253 for nine (W. R. James 39, M. D. Abrams 33, M. Ranchod 41, J. A. Rennie 32 not out; M. P. Jarvis four for 41). *Mashonaland 20.5 pts, Matabeleland 11.5 pts.*

At Alexandra Sports Club, Harare, March 4, 5, 6. Drawn. Mashonaland Under-24* 283 (G. W. Flower 96, C. B. Wishart 66, E. Matambanadzo 32 not out; P. A. Strang three for 80, T. D. Coughlan three for 40) and 292 (G. W. Flower 96, G. J. Rennie 57, D. N. Erasmus 76; P. A. Strang four for 97); Mashonaland Country Districts 249 (K. J. Arnott 51, A. D. R. Campbell 39, A. C. Waller 40; H. J. Hira three for 43, D. Matambanadzo three for 43) and 296 for eight (A. D. R. Campbell 73, A. C. Waller 30, C. M. Robertson 36, T. G. Bartlett 45, S. G. Peall 44; D. Matambanadzo three for 67). *Mashonaland Under-24 21 pts, Mashonaland Country Districts 16 pts.*

Final

At Harare Sports Club, March 18, 19, 20. Drawn. Mashonaland Under-24 286 (G. J. Rennie 76, C. B. Wishart 48, S. V. Carlisle 44, S. G. Davies 30, H. J. Hira 30 not out; J. A. Rennie three for 78) and 245 (D. N. Erasmus 41, G. W. Flower 37, C. B. Wishart 30, S. V. Carlisle 54; G. J. Whittall six for 34); Matabeleland* 140 (W. R. James 52 not out; S. G. Davies three for 33, D. D. Stannard four for 23). Logan Cup awarded to Mashonaland Under-24 by virtue of their first-innings lead.

Zimbabwe Board XI's matches in the UCB Bowl (October 29-January 29) may be found in Cricket in South Africa, 1993-94.

OTHER FIRST-CLASS MATCHES

At Harare Sports Club, Harare, October 12, 13, 14. Western Province won by 91 runs. Western Province* 310 for six dec. (F. B. Touzel 57, G. Kirsten 75, D. B. Rundle 59 not out, C. R. Matthews 36 not out) and 143 for four dec. (F. B. Touzel 40, D. Jordaan 39, A. P. Kuiper 36 not out; S. G. Peall three for 26); Mashonaland XI 116 (A. Flower 43; D. B. Rundle four for 14) and 246 (G. W. Flower 71, A. D. R. Campbell 64; A. C. Dawson four for 49, G. Kirsten three for 26).

Zimbabwe B v Worcestershire (April 6, 7, 8), Mashonaland XI v Warwickshire (April 12, 13, 14) and Matabeleland Invitation XI v Worcestershire (April 13, 14, 15) may be found in English Counties Overseas, 1993-94.

CRICKET IN DENMARK, 1994

By PETER S. HARGREAVES

Following two abysmal seasons, the Danish cricket *landshold* – or national side – hardly surprised the better-informed pundits in Nairobi in February when finishing with their poorest performance in the ICC Trophy to date.

At the end of July, however, a series of successes in The Netherlands emphasised that a number of changes, not least in the leadership of the side, rendered the team once more a force to be reckoned with. In a quadrangular tournament, Denmark swept aside by decisive margins Holland A, Scotland – for the first time ever – and Holland B. The Dutch were without their captain, Steven Lubbers, but went down heavily in a manner not particularly encouraging for a country preparing for participation in the World Cup. The Danish victories were above all team efforts, especially in the field where nothing was given away.

At the end of August, history was created when Derbyshire became the first county ever to visit Denmark – as part of Ole Mortensen's benefit programme just before the Dane bowed out after 12 seasons with the club. In the first 50-overs match the home team made a healthy 206 for five and then routed the visitors for 105. The tall, young left-handed opener, Mogens Christiansen, scored 54, and the captain, Søren Henriksen, an unbeaten 51. The dismissal of Derbyshire was more of an all-round effort, however, backed up by good fielding. Admittedly, Derbyshire were short of full strength, but the Danish victory was impressive. In a 40-overs match the next day, Gordon Greenidge was brought in to bolster the visitors' batting, which saw them reach 176, with Chris Adams scoring 58. Held down by Mortensen and Base, the home side could reply with only 142 for nine, but the public revelled in seeing Mortensen in action again.

The domestic season saw the champions, Svanholm, beaten early in the knockout competition by the all-Pakistani team, Nørrebro, mainly through the efforts of Aftab Ahmed. The final against Herning then produced a thriller, with Nørrebro passing the home team's score of 226 for eight with five wickets and an over to spare.

In the league, Svanholm went through completely unscathed, to be followed at a distance by Herning, with Esbjerg third. At the foot of the table, Skanderborg and the newly promoted Husum were relegated, despite achieving nine victories between them in a none too stable season.

Two records were created on May 7, when Svanholm scored 413 for four against Skanderborg, with Allan From Hansen making 248 not out. Christiansen had the highest league aggregate, with 846, just heading From Hansen, with 838. In all cricket, Christiansen's grand total of 1,354 runs was a new record for a Danish batsman. The bowling suffered somewhat compared with previous years, with Morten Hedegaard, of Nykøbing Mors, securing the most wickets with 36, followed by Sagib Tasneem of KB with 30.

During the season the young Svanholm all-rounder, Søren Vestergaard, was permitted to play as an amateur during his school holidays for Warwickshire, and was expected to continue with this arrangement in 1995. Mortensen, at the other end of a county career, is expected to become national coach with the Dansk Cricket-Forbund, where a new era will begin with the team playing with renewed confidence.

CRICKET IN THE NETHERLANDS, 1994

By DAVID HARDY

March 5, 1994 was a day to remember in Dutch cricket. Hundreds of Dutch supporters were in Nairobi, Kenya, to witness Holland at last secure a place alongside the Test countries in the 1996 World Cup, albeit through the back door, winning the third-place play-off of the ICC Trophy against Bermuda.

In any other year, the comprehensive victory against South Africa in The Hague on September 4 would have been the main story. Perhaps Holland are getting used to beating Test countries (two wins against England XIs and one against West Indies in recent years). For whatever reason, South Africa turned in a lacklustre performance, losing by nine wickets. Against a below-strength attack, Nolan Clarke helped himself to 78 and, along with Peter Cantrell, guided the Dutch almost past South Africa without losing a wicket. Dutch fast-medium bowler Floris Jansen took three for eight in eight overs, and in so doing went past 100 wickets for his country.

Other internationals were played against Scotland (won) and Denmark (lost, for the first time in some while) during a round-robin tournament at Vught in July and against a very weak MCC, who also ought to bring more bowlers next time, as a curtain-raiser to the South African match. Clarke added another record to his illustrious list, becoming the first Dutch player to pass 1,000 runs in internationals in a calendar year.

On the domestic scene, VOC Rotterdam took the Hoofdklasse (Premier League) championship for the first time since 1987 in a play-off against Excelsior Schiedam. The young VOC team, led by Davy Bakker, whose father Anton also led a VOC team to the championship, was superbly served by young New Zealand professional Nathan Astle, whose run-aggregate (1,257) set a new league record. He also took 44 wickets. Two others passed the 1,000 runs mark: another New Zealander, Darrin Murray of VRA Amsterdam, with 1,234, and one Dutchman, Voorburg CC's Tim de Leede, with 1,071. Four bowlers captured 50 wickets, three of them overseas professionals (Sean Cary of Excelsior, 63, Aaron Barnes of Sparta, 62, Dean Askew of KUD Deventer, 56), and one, Marc Nota of Voorburg CC, a Dutchman. He took exactly 50.

There was no relegation from the Hoofdklasse in 1994 – a relief to KUD Deventer, who achieved only three wins – because of a bizarre set of circumstances on August 6, another date which will be forever etched in Dutch cricket history, but for all the wrong reasons. In the Second Division (Eerste Klasse), HCC The Hague and Gandhi CC of Amsterdam were, with a few matches remaining, both striving for promotion to the Hoofdklasse. Gandhi were well ahead on "wicket average" (runs per wicket scored divided by runs per wicket conceded), which was to decide the championship in the event of a tie on points. Unless something extraordinary was to happen, Gandhi would be promoted for the first time. Something extraordinary did happen.

HCC happened to be fulfilling a fixture against their own Second Eleven and won the 55-overs match by 702 runs; HCC scored 703 for one (Jackson 329 not out, van Alkemade 277); HCC Seconds scored one all out. Six of the wickets fell to stumpings. On the same day Gandhi rattled up 813 for one (Gomes 429 not out, Bhoelan 277 not out) against a team inaptly called Success CC which, like Gandhi, comprised almost exclusively non-Dutch players. They replied with a spirited 16 all out.

The following day the Royal Dutch Cricket Association declared the results void, fined all four teams, deducted points as well, suspended all four captains to the end of the season and declared that there would be no promotion to the Hoofdklasse. Gandhi and Success maintained that their match was not fixed – Success did turn up with only ten men – but HCC made no attempt to deny the allegation. Had there been provision for a play-off for the championship in this league, as there was in the Hoofdklasse, all this would have been avoided.

A more valid achievement came when Steven Lubbers finally passed Wally van Weelde's all-time record of runs for the Hoofdklasse and the Dutch team combined, going over the 14,000 mark in the process.

The Test and County Cricket Board decided that Holland would, in 1995, become the first team from outside the British Isles to compete in an English competition, the NatWest Trophy, starting at Northampton. All Holland's matches will be away for the time being, until grass wickets are ready. The go-ahead for two of them was given in 1994, in Amstelveen and Deventer. They will be ready, at the earliest, in 1996, the year of the World Cup. That could be a really historic year.

HOLLAND v SOUTH AFRICANS

At The Hague CC, September 4 (not first-class). Holland won by nine wickets. Toss: Holland. South Africans 134 for eight (40 overs) (D. J. Richardson 35 not out; F. Jansen three for eight); Holland 138 for one (30.5 overs) (N. E. Clarke 78, P. E. Cantrell 43 not out).

ONE HUNDRED YEARS AGO

From JOHN WISDEN'S CRICKETERS' ALMANACK FOR 1895

CRICKETERS – PAST AND PRESENT By an old Cambridge captain: "In weighing the difference between past and present players much is said about the improved state of the grounds. While this is quite true, still such grounds as Fenner's at Cambridge, the Canterbury ground, the Oval etc., etc., were both true and good. They had not, indeed, the advantage of the mowing machine, but they were well kept and sheep-eaten, and the ball travelled truly. What the over-hand balls would have done on those wickets I cannot say. On Lord's they would probably have broken our heads!"

FIVE YOUNG BATSMEN OF THE SEASON: MR. CHARLES B. FRY: "Since the days of C. J. Ottaway and the Hon. Alfred Lyttelton there has been no such Admirable Crichton in the way of outdoor sports at either University as Mr. Fry, and if we had to deal with him as a long jumper, sprint runner, and football player, the demands upon our space would be extreme."

GLOUCESTERSHIRE: "A review of Gloucestershire cricket in 1894 cannot be otherwise than unpleasant reading. From whatever point of view regarded the condition of affairs is most unsatisfactory. The recent past affords no room for congratulation, and in the immediate future little prospect of improvement can be discerned. We do not desire to take a pessimistic view of the situation, but the fact cannot be denied that Gloucestershire cricket is in a very bad way."

CRICKET ROUND THE WORLD, 1994

ARGENTINA

The annual North v South match, played over three days and the highlight of the Argentine calendar for over a century, fizzled out into a draw. Hurlingham won the 1993-94 First Division championship.

AUSTRIA

Concordia CC, champions in both indoor and outdoor competitions in 1993, again swept the board in 1994. The most exciting domestic match was the final of the Austrian Championship, in which each team must field at least nine Austrian passport-holders. In failing late-September light at Concordia's home ground in Bad Vöslau, Franz Welt swept the ball to the boundary to give the home team a one-wicket win over Vienna CC "A". The youth development programme flourished; about 80 youngsters were playing cricket in clubs and schools in Vienna and Velden. Highlight of the year was the visit of Clive Radley and Kevin Lyons to hold a train-the-trainer programme. Unfortunately, the development of the game is under threat: although there is land available for new grounds, the cost is too much for the slim pockets of a self-financing cricket community. The indoor game, however, has grown in importance an effective way of introducing the game to Austrian schoolchildren. – Andrew Simpson-Parker.

BANGLADESH

Abahani KC and Bangladesh Biman were joint champions of the Navana Premier Division, the major cricket league in Bangladesh, in 1993-94. Both won ten games and lost one. All the matches were 45-over one-day games. Usually, the teams play each other twice, but the competition was reduced because of Bangladesh's participation in the ICC Trophy and the non-availability of Dhaka Stadium in December due to the South Asian Games. All the top players in the country play in Dhaka and the game's popularity is reflected in crowds exceeding 40,000 for some club matches. More and more young players are taking up the game and five of the Under-19 boys represented the national side. One of the most far-reaching steps taken by the Bangladesh Cricket Control Board has been organising the Nirman School Tournament for Under-16 boys. The tournament began in Dhaka in 1982 with 45 schools. Today the trophy boasts 252 schools in 21 cities and has spread cricket to places where the game was not played at all. Narayangang High School were the 1993-94 champions. – Tanjeeb Ahsan Saad.

BERMUDA

Bermuda's narrow failure to qualify for the 1996 World Cup was obviously the disappointment of the year: they were impressive throughout the ICC Trophy but lost both the semi-final and the third-place match. At home, the

Premier Division went up to 17 clubs and reverted to regular cricket instead of a limited-overs format. As in 1993, St George's were the only undefeated team, but they won one match fewer than Bailey's Bay, who became champions for the first time in 16 years. Bailey's Bay also won the knockout cup, the Camel Cup and the Eastern Counties Trophy and were deservedly named as Team of the Year. Bermuda's unique two-day cricketing festival – Cup Match – reached an exciting conclusion when St George's scored 80 runs in six overs to beat Somerset with just nine balls remaining; all four innings were over 230 runs and the match was regarded as one of the best in recent memory. Clay Smith of St George's was chosen as the Most Valuable Player. He had a productive season in the Northumberland County League with Benwell, commuting between the UK and Bermuda for important games. – Maurice F. Hankey.

BRUNEI

Cricket is almost totally an expatriate game in Brunei; it is a matter of some regret that only one Bruneian plays cricket on a regular basis. The season roughly follows the northern hemisphere summer. In 1994, six teams competed: Manggis and Cavaliers were joint league champions, and Cavaliers won the knockout cup. The annual fixture against Sabah was played in Kota Kinabalu in September – Sabah won by eight wickets. – Derek Thursby.

CANADA

Canada were well-pleased with their performances at international level, both in the ICC Trophy and at home where Canadian sides won one game out of five against a strong West Indian A team, led by Roland Holder. Canada's captain, the all-rounder Danny Singh, led Cavaliers to the Toronto & District Championship, Canada's top league. British Columbia beat Quebec to win the national championship. – Gerald Howat.

CHINA

The first games in Shanghai since 1948 were reported to have been played over the weekend of November 12 and 13 between the Craigengower Cricket Club of Hong Kong and a Shanghai team, captained by Richard Graham. The teams played on a matting wicket on a football pitch borrowed from the Shanghai Sports Institute.

EAST AND CENTRAL AFRICA

Malawi won the 27th annual Quadrangular Tournament, beating their traditional rivals, Tanzania, Uganda and Zambia, in a competition staged in Uganda, at the Logogo Stadium in Kampala and the Entebbe Oval, which has Lake Victoria as its backdrop. Tanzania, scheduled to stage the 28th tournament, has been effecting a change from matting to turf wickets.

FIJI

Fiji's results in the ICC Trophy in Kenya were disappointing, especially after the relative success in The Netherlands in 1990. Two leading players were unavailable – one of them, Neil Maxwell, gained a place in the New South Wales team. There has also been a lack of good competition since 1990; Fiji is so isolated it is very expensive to travel anywhere. The annual Crompton Cup competition, played over Easter, was won in its 43rd year by the New South Wales Police team, which beat Suva in a close-fought final. Suva won the Colonial Mutual Inter-District competition, beating Moce, an island team, in the final. This year marked the retirement of Philip Snow as Fiji's ICC representative after 30 years' service and consecutive attendance. He has done a wonderful job for Fiji and will be sadly missed, but has been ably replaced by his son-in-law Peter Wain. Umpiring continues to be a problem, but we have managed to eradicate the misconception that the first ball of an innings is "a trial ball" and our coaching programme has led to a better understanding of the Laws. Our plans for 1995-96 are to continue with our development programme, with emphasis on coaching schools and grassroots, and to send the national and Under-21 teams to New Zealand or Australia. To do this, we have to rely on Fiji's share of the World Cup proceeds. Without this, the future of cricket in Fiji would not be very bright. – Peter Knight.

FRANCE

The inaugural Ligue Française for club sides containing at least seven French nationals (of whom five must be native-born) was won by Château de Thoiry, who beat Chauny by five wickets in the final. Thoiry also defeated Northern by 11 runs to win the French Cup, and had three batsmen who passed 1,000 runs for the season, including 14-year-old Delhi-born Rishi Seth, who hit 105 on his club's visit to Fenner's in July. In the "Open" championship (no nationality restrictions) the Pakistani-based Paris Université Club finished ahead of Sri Lankan CC. An exclusively native-born French side was created in July and celebrated with a six-wicket win over its German counterpart. The full national side (containing seven passport-holders) drew at home to Germany and away to Belgium in the annual three-day game. Heavy rain marred Nottinghamshire's visit to Saumur, with Chris Lewis ripping through both the batting and the grass top as France collapsed to 48 all out. But the second game saw France earn a shock four-wicket victory. There were new clubs in 1994 in Marseilles, Montpellier and Villy-en-Auxois, near Dijon, while four clubs from New Caledonia, a *territoire d'outre-mer*, joined the French federation. In June 1995, an MCC team is due to visit France on a tour combining cricket and fact-finding that will be of crucial importance to the game in France. The TCCB have agreed to back France's bid for ICC associate status in July if MCC report favourably. – Simon Hewitt.

GERMANY

Germany had mixed fortunes in international cricket in 1994. The nationals-only team lost to both Italy – for the first time – and France. However, the day after the French defeat, the countries met again under ICC nationality-rules, and a German side packed with batting dominated the game, scoring 268 for five, leaving the French to play out time. The season ended on a winning note when the Deutscher Cricket Bund XI won a tournament in Osnabrück. This grew out of the twin-town connection between Derby, Osnabrück and the Dutch town of Haarlem. Four Derbyshire League teams took part, along with Rood en Wit Haarlem and a British Army team. The DCB bowled the Army out for 79 in the final. Hassloch Cosmopolitans won the German Championship for the second year in succession and also impressively took the European Cricket Federation club championship in Corfu. Northern Germany was the growth area in the game. After some hiccups at the beginning of the season, the new Northern League took off and produced some good, competitive cricket. – Brian Fell.

GIBRALTAR

Although they failed to win any matches in the ICC Trophy, the Gibraltar squad gave of its best, and some of the contests were close ones. It was encouraging to see several teenagers make the trip to Nairobi; this augurs well. At home, the Combined Services again swept all before them in the senior competitions, but with the rapid rundown of the defence presence on the Rock, they are unlikely to be as strong in the future. – T. J. Finlayson.

HONG KONG

Hong Kong's domestic season followed its established pattern of separate leagues and cups on Saturdays and Sundays. Templars from the Kowloon Cricket Club again won the Sunday League and the Hong Kong Cricket Club's Nomads won on Saturdays. Vagabonds took the Sunday Cup, having needed six for victory off the last ball; Kai Tak won the Saturday Cup. A dozen non-league teams are affiliated to the Association but are unable to enter the leagues because of a shortage of grounds. An experiment with orange balls was not wholly successful; it is planned to try again with yellow balls of a better quality.

IRAN

Over the past two years, cricket has begun thriving among migrant workers from the subcontinent and there are 12 local teams. A cricket ground has been built at the Azadi Stadium in Teheran with a capacity of 5,000. Teams from Sharjah and Baluchistan have visited. A national coach, Hossain Ali Salimian from Karachi University, has been appointed, and the Baseball Federation of the Islamic Republic of Iran, which also covers cricket, is keen to affiliate to ICC. The British are not playing a role in this: the small diplomatic staff in Teheran did not contain any cricketers in 1994, and the city's British community now comprises one resident businessman.

ISRAEL

In a marked attempt to run the game in a more professional manner, a new, young and more aggressive board of directors was elected in May to replace the previous board. A coaching scheme has been set up for children between ten and 16, along with the introduction of a youth league, the selection of an Under-25 team and a drive to improve umpiring standards. These decisions bore fruit immediately in a successful 1994 season. We have acquired double practice nets for four centres and cricket will now be played throughout the winter. The league was won, for the first time, by Neve Yonathan of Ashdod, who beat the holders Ashdod A in a close finish. Neve Yonathan, needing four to win with four balls to go, made the winning hit with a six over mid-wicket which the fielder caught as he fell over the boundary. Israeli international Neil Ward scored 83 for the winners, while Hillel Awaskar shone for Ashdod with 44 not out and six for 32. – Stanley Perlman.

ITALY

Despite the partial setback of being deferred in request for ICC Associate status, Italian cricket enjoyed another season of growth in 1994. Pianoro wrested the National Championship from Cesena. Under the brilliant chairmanship of Professor Arcido Parisi, this club has risen from the Second Division to the pennant, thanks to a youth policy that is probably unequalled in Europe; the average age of the team's nine Italians was 22. Cesena were runners-up in both the championship and the Italian Cup, which was won by Capanelle for the sixth time out of seven. The national team had a very positive season, beating Germany in the two-day passport-holders' game – helped by an outstanding all-round performance from Edmondo Ciappina – and holding its own on a tough tour of The Netherlands. The outstanding performer of the season was Pianoro's new recruit from Cesena, Akhlaq Qureshi, the first man to score 1,000 runs in an Italian season. – Simone Gambino.

JAPAN

Though expatriates still account for the bulk of cricket played in Japan, the game is now being played all over the country and locals are gaining in numbers and enthusiasm. We are seeing at least one new university team a year and all but two of the positions in the Japan Cricket Association are now held by Japanese. Japan's only cricket magazine, *The Straight Bat*, sponsored a competition of two-day matches, with five teams entered. The winning team, Tokyo Bay CC, was founded only two years ago by one of the new pioneers of Japanese cricket, Mr Fumito Miyakawa. Having previously experienced only 35-over cricket, it took some time for the locals to become accustomed to the longer game, but Mr Miyakawa, who had been to New Zealand to study cricket, led his team to a well-deserved victory over Senshu University. *The Straight Bat* also sponsored the second annual Challenge Cup for beginners, with 65 players vying for honours. The cup was won by Ms Miki Koyama for her dedication, enthusiasm and all-round cricket skills. The Yokohama Country and Athletic Club's fourth annual six-a-side competition had to be held over two days to accommodate all those who wanted to play, and even then some missed out; victory went for the second year running to the Edogawa Falcons. The season ended with a bang when Jeff Thomson came to Tokyo and conducted three days of coaching on behalf of the JCA. – Trevor Bayley.

KENYA

With Kenya hosting a most successful 20-nation ICC Trophy in February/March 1994 and its team qualifying for the 1996 World Cup by finishing runners-up, the game suddenly took on a new sense of purpose. The league, comprising the top ten teams, was played in a very competitive manner, even though there were fewer overseas professionals. Swamibapa, dominated by the three Tikolo brothers, retained the championship in 1993-94. David Tikolo captained the team but the star was his younger brother Steve, who broke his own record by scoring 1,959 runs in 18 innings, including three double-centuries. His highest score was 224 off 108 balls with 12 sixes and 24 fours. The return of South Africa to international cricket has been a big help to Kenya. In September and October 1994 there were visits from three leading South African teams – Transvaal and Border, who both included several Test players, and the Students XI. Kenya won only one match, against Border, but the players acquitted themselves well and Steve Tikolo scored three more centuries. He and Martin Awiti were invited to play club cricket in Transvaal. The game is healthy in Kenya: the indigenous Kenyans have taken to cricket extremely well and form two-thirds of the national team, after many years when it was dominated by Asians and Europeans; and all top-level club cricket is now played on grass wickets. – Jasmer Singh.

MALAYSIA

New clubs and new competitions are starting all the time in Malaysia, with commercial sponsorship now taking a front seat. The Government is committed to ensure that we produce a team of some strength to compete in the cricket competition at the 1998 Commonwealth Games in Kuala Lumpur. We have to date laid seven artificial strips to prepare for the Games and have plans to lay 20 more by 1997. The Carlsberg National League was split into two divisions. Kuala Lumpur were champions again but Singapore, the runners-up, had revenge in the MCA Carlsberg Cup for the top four teams. For the first time, an international youth tournament was held: Bangladesh beat Sri Lanka by 20 runs in a final witnessed by a good crowd, including both the King of Malaysia and Kapil Dev. In a friendly match against Kajang Ceylonese, the Royal Selangor Club, chasing 164 and including some very senior First Division players, were bowled out for two. One was a bye and the other was scored by the groundsman, who had been hastily recruited to make up the numbers. – Charlie Chelliah.

MAURITIUS

There are currently four teams in Mauritius: Maurindia, Young Muslim, Star Knitwear, and United Cricket Clubs. They all play against each other regularly at Vacoas Gymkhana ground and entertain teams from overseas – in 1994 there were touring sides from India, Singapore and The Seychelles – and visiting shops. The MRF Peace Foundation from India, including the former Test player T. A. Sekar, beat the Maurindia Cricket Club (MCC) in two matches in November, on both occasions by 79 runs. Although Mauritius is part of the Commonwealth, cricket is not played in schools and the locals are more interested in football and horse racing. However, we have been trying to form a Cricket Federation of Mauritius, and it is expected that 1995 will be a lively year. – Bidhan Kumar.

NAMIBIA

Namibia was proud of its national team, which won two out of four matches in the ICC Trophy and won the Philip Snow Plate. A new cricket board has been established, which was expected to take radical action to prevent clubs entering teams in the various leagues and then being unable to fulfil their commitments. "Cricket must be encouraged and not be put in jeopardy by a happy-go-lucky attitude," the chairman Laurie Pieters said. Wanderers won both the Super League and the Senior League but came second to Mariental in the Second League. A pleasing feature was that teams from the *platteland*, the country areas, were becoming more prominent.

NEPAL

There is no problem of interest in cricket in Nepal. What is lacking is infrastructure and finance. To overcome this, the Cricket Association of Nepal has signed an agreement for live TV transmission of international matches in Kathmandu in 1995. In 1994 a tournament was held in Birgunj, involving teams from India, Pakistan and Bangladesh. The winners were Muslim Commercial Bank of Karachi. The third Rameshwore Memorial Tournament was held in Kathmandu involving 22 teams: Tirupati Cricket Club of Lumbini Zone beat Baneshwore of Kathmandu by six runs in an exciting final. The Arjun Bahadur Memorial tournament for schools was won by Brihaspati Vidya Sadan; 17 schools wanted to participate but owing to lack of playing fields the organisers accepted only six. – Jai Kumar Shah.

ST HELENA

The cricket season on St Helena (population 5,500) runs from January to July. Eight teams play one-day matches of two innings a side on a matting pitch at Francis Plain, where in 1886 a fielder is alleged to have died chasing a ball over the cliff; a repetition is still theoretically possible. After many years of ascendancy by Jamestown B, Western B won the 1994 championship ahead of Levelwood A, who won the knockout. Jamestown

B, however, provided two individual highlights: left-arm spinner Eric George, the chairman of the Cricket Association who is in his 60s, took eight for 39 before announcing his retirement at the end of the season; his son Gavin averaged 71 with the bat. Play traditionally continues in the rain, but two matches had to be postponed in 1994 because the Royal Mail ship, the only link with the outside world, was in port for its bimonthly visit. – Fraser M. Simm.

SOUTH KOREA

Cricket revived in Korea in the late 1980s through the expatriate Indian community. It is played by six teams of nine a side (representing Australia, India, New Zealand, British Embassy, International All Stars and the Rest of the World) over 15 overs on a small, irregular-shaped soccer field controlled by the US Military in the UN Compound. We bowl only from one end, on a wicket that consists of bare ground, covered by one layer of rubberised matting overlaid by felt carpet; despite the small ground, bowlers tend to have the upper hand – shooters and fliers are par for the course. The scoring rules are modified but complex, taking into account the back wall (four if hit on the full), the willow tree (six) and the embankment with the blackberries. The regular competition is played twice a year, spring and autumn. India were the winners in spring 1994. In the autumn, the New Zealanders arranged for the former Test player, Rod Latham, to turn up as a casual late inclusion. The game was washed out, even though the Kiwis were still keen to play in half an inch of mud. Anyone wandering through Korea is welcome to view this grand spectacle on Sunday afternoons. – John A. Kaminsky.

UNITED STATES

The United States remains the dozing giant of world cricket, but it is not sleeping comfortably. There are now more than ten thousand players; leagues are growing rapidly, especially in New York/New Jersey and Florida, where there has been large-scale immigration from the Caribbean and South Asia. Cricket is beginning to acquire the kind of ambition that marks the American approach to everything else and, after the soccer World Cup was held in the US in 1994, there was talk of cricket doing the same. One organisation, the Center to Advance Cricket, wants to raise $10 million by 2000 with the goal of "an American Test team". But ninety per cent of players in the US are migrants who learned the game in another country, and there has been little attempt to change this. A coaching scheme for schools in New Jersey, sponsored by Haverford College, a traditional home of cricket, served to emphasise how little was being done anywhere else. Following the American team's failure in the ICC Trophy, there has been growing criticism of the USA Cricket Association, the official ICC-affiliated body. The magazine *Cricket USA* (the North American edition of *The Cricketer*) attacked the USACA as "seriously out of touch with the realities", while the *US Cricketer* claimed the Association was "not interested". There have been allegations of financial mismanagement, ethnic polarisation and even vote-rigging. It is very clear that the potential dynamism of the game is not being adequately directed. A scheduled match in Central Park, New York, in August between the US and a West Indies A team was cancelled without explanation – "just one more mystery from the Byzantine world of cricket as played in the Big Apple," said *Cricket USA*. The 150th-anniversary match between the US and Canada did go ahead in Marine Park, Brooklyn over Labour Day weekend in September, but what might have been a great occasion was close to a fiasco, with negligible media coverage and only 300 spectators. There was, at least, a thrilling finish; Canada won by four runs.

VIETNAM

The Sri Lankan Nalliah Sellathurai was reported to have become the first batsman to score a century in the Vietnamese capital, Hanoi, scoring 106 for an Indian subcontinent team against an Australian-English side on a matting pitch.

ERRATA

WISDEN, 1977

Page 385 In Essex's second innings against Hampshire at Chelmsford in 1976, B. R. Hardie scored 21 not out and G. A. Gooch was c Lewis b Richards for 27. Their overall batting aggregates and averages remain unchanged.

WISDEN, 1984

Page 422 R. M. Ellison's bowling average in County Championship matches was 29.69.

WISDEN, 1987

Page 442 M. R. Benson played 35 innings in County Championship matches for Kent and was not out twice. He scored 1,242 runs at 37.63.

WISDEN, 1988

Page 266 D. L. Houghton scored 142, not 141, for Zimbabwe against New Zealand in the World Cup (see Errata in *Wisden*, 1993, page 996); in addition, extras for Zimbabwe included seven leg-byes, not eight, and J. G. Bracewell conceded 48 runs, not 47.

WISDEN, 1994

Page 363 Mike Atherton was the sixth Lancashire player to captain England in Tests.

Page 472 R. M. Ellison's bowling analysis in County Championship matches was 31–13–72–2.

Page 790 457 hundreds had been scored in the Sunday League by the end of 1993.

Picture vi Ockley is in Surrey.

PART FIVE: ADMINISTRATION AND LAWS

INTERNATIONAL CRICKET COUNCIL

On June 15, 1909, representatives of cricket in England, Australia and South Africa met at Lord's and founded the Imperial Cricket Conference. Membership was confined to the governing bodies of cricket in countries within the British Commonwealth where Test cricket was played. India, New Zealand and West Indies were elected as members on May 31, 1926, Pakistan on July 28, 1952, Sri Lanka on July 21, 1981, and Zimbabwe on July 8, 1992. South Africa ceased to be a member of ICC on leaving the British Commonwealth in May, 1961, but was elected as a Full Member on July 10, 1991.

On July 15, 1965, the Conference was renamed the International Cricket Conference and new rules were adopted to permit the election of countries from outside the British Commonwealth. This led to the growth of the Conference, with the admission of Associate Members, who were each entitled to one vote, while the Foundation and Full Members were each entitled to two votes, on ICC resolutions. On July 12, 13, 1989, the Conference was renamed the International Cricket Council and revised rules were adopted.

On July 7, 1993, ICC ceased to be administered by MCC and became an independent organisation with its own chief executive, the headquarters remaining at Lord's. The category of Foundation Member, with its special rights, was abolished. On October 1, 1993, Sir Clyde Walcott became the first non-British chairman of ICC.

Officers

Chairman: Sir Clyde Walcott. *Chief Executive:* D. L. Richards. *Administration officer:* C. D. Hitchcock.

Constitution

Chairman: Elected for a three-year term from the date of the Council's annual conference. Normally, a new chairman will be chosen at the conference a year before the previous Chairman's term expires. Sir Clyde Walcott's term ends in 1997.

Chief Executive: Appointed by the Council. D. L. Richards has been given a contract until 1998.

Membership

Full Members: Australia, England, India, New Zealand, Pakistan, South Africa, Sri Lanka, West Indies and Zimbabwe.

Associate Members*: Argentina (1974), Bangladesh (1977), Bermuda (1966), Canada (1968), Denmark (1966), East and Central Africa (1966), Fiji (1965), Gibraltar (1969), Hong Kong (1969), Ireland (1993), Israel (1974), Kenya (1981), Malaysia (1967), Namibia (1992), Netherlands (1966), Papua New Guinea (1973), Scotland (1994), Singapore (1974), United Arab Emirates (1990), USA (1965) and West Africa (1976).

Affiliate Members*: Austria (1992), Bahamas (1987), Belgium (1991), Brunei (1992), France (1987), Germany (1991), Italy (1984), Japan (1989), Nepal (1988), Spain (1992) and Switzerland (1985).

* *Year of election shown in parentheses.*

The following governing bodies for cricket shall be eligible for election.

Full Members: The governing body for cricket recognised by ICC of a country, or countries associated for cricket purposes, or a geographical area, from which representative teams are qualified to play official Test matches.

Associate Members: The governing body for cricket recognised by ICC of a country, or countries associated for cricket purposes, or a geographical area, which does not qualify as a Full Member but where cricket is firmly established and organised.

Affiliate Members: The governing body for cricket recognised by ICC of a country, or countries associated for cricket purposes, or a geographical area (which is not part of one of those already constituted as a Full or Associate Member) where ICC recognises that cricket is played in accordance with the Laws of Cricket. Affiliate Members have no right to vote or to propose or second resolutions at ICC meetings.

THE CRICKET COUNCIL

The Cricket Council, which was set up in 1968 and reconstituted in 1974 and 1983, acts as the governing body for cricket in England and Wales. It comprises the following.

Chairman: W. R. F. Chamberlain.
Vice-Chairman: J. D. Robson.
8 Representatives of the Test and County Cricket Board: J. R. T. Barclay, Sir Lawrence Byford, W. R. F. Chamberlain, D. J. Insole, M. P. Murray, H. J. Pocock, D. Rich, D. R. W. Silk.
5 Representatives of the National Cricket Association: F. H. Elliott, E. K. Ingman, J. G. Overy, J. D. Robson, M. J. K. Smith.
3 Representatives of the Marylebone Cricket Club: Field Marshal The Rt Hon. The Lord Bramall, M. E. L. Melluish, D. R. W. Silk.
1 Representative (non-voting) of the Minor Counties Cricket Association: J. E. O. Smith.

Secretary: A. C. Smith.

THE TEST AND COUNTY CRICKET BOARD

The TCCB was set up in 1968 to be responsible for Test matches, official tours, and first-class and minor county competitions. It is composed of representatives of the 18 first-class counties, Marylebone Cricket Club and Minor Counties Cricket Association (voting members); as well as Oxford University Cricket Club, Cambridge University Cricket Club, the Irish Cricket Union and the Scottish Cricket Union (non-voting members).

Officers

Chairman: D. R. W. Silk.

Chairmen of Committees: D. R. W. Silk (Executive); D. L. Acfield (Cricket); P. R. Bromage (Discipline); D. B. Carr (Pitches); B. G. K. Downing (Marketing); R. Illingworth (England); D. J. Insole (International); M. P. Murray (Finance); D. H. Newton (Test match advisory); A. C. Smith (Appointment of Umpires); M. J. K. Smith (Development); Rev. M. D. Vockins (Second Eleven Competitions); A. Wheelhouse (Registration).

Chief Executive: A. C. Smith. *Cricket Secretary:* T. M. Lamb. *Administration Secretary:* A. S. Brown. *Accountant:* C. A. Barker. *Marketing Manager:* T. D. M. Blake. *Public Relations Manager:* R. E. Little. *England Team Manager:* K. W. R. Fletcher.

THE NATIONAL CRICKET ASSOCIATION

With the setting up of the Cricket Council in 1968 it was thought necessary to form a separate organisation to represent the interests of all cricket below the first-class game: the NCA comprises representatives from 51 county cricket associations and 19 national cricketing organisations.

Officers

President: M. J. K. Smith.
Chairman: J. D. Robson.
Vice-Chairman: F. H. Elliott.
Director of Finance: C. A. Barker.
Director of Coaching: M. J. Stewart.
Director of Administration and Development: T. N. Bates.
Marketing Executive: D. A. Clarke.
Hon. Treasurer: D. W. Carter.

The position of the above three bodies was being reviewed in 1995 with a view to possible merger. K. V. Andrew, who retired as chief executive of the NCA on April 30, 1994, has not been replaced pending the creation of the new organisation.

THE MARYLEBONE CRICKET CLUB

The Marylebone Cricket Club evolved out of the White Conduit Club in 1787, when Thomas Lord laid out his first ground in Dorset Square. Its members revised the Laws in 1788 and gradually took responsibility for cricket throughout the world. However, it relinquished control of the game in the UK in 1968 and the International Cricket Council finally established its own secretariat in 1993. MCC still owns Lord's and remains the guardian of the Laws. It calls itself "a private club with a public function" and aims to support cricket everywhere, especially at grassroots level and in countries where the game is least developed.

Patron: HER MAJESTY THE QUEEN

Officers

President: 1994-96 – The Hon. Sir Oliver Popplewell.

Treasurer: M. E. L. Melluish. *Chairman of Finance:* D. L. Hudd.

Trustees: The Rt Hon. The Lord Griffiths, J. J. Warr, Field Marshal The Rt Hon. The Lord Bramall.

Hon. Life Vice-Presidents: Sir Donald Bradman, D. G. Clark, G. H. G. Doggart, D. J. Insole, F. G. Mann, C. H. Palmer, C. G. A. Paris, E. W. Swanton, R. E. S. Wyatt.

Secretary: R. D. V. Knight.

Assistant Secretaries: M. R. Blow (Finance), J. A. Jameson (Cricket), J. R. Smith (Administration). *Personal Assistant to Secretary:* Miss S. A. Lawrence. *Curator:* S. E. A. Green. *Ground Administrator:* A. W. P. Fleming.

MCC Committee, elected members 1994-95: C. A. Fry, S. P. Henderson, C. B. Howland, Sir Ian MacLaurin, D. R. Male, N. E. J. Pocock, T. M. B. Sissons, M. O. C. Sturt, G. J. Toogood, J. A. F. Vallance, J. C. Woodcock. P. B. H. May was elected, but died on December 27, 1994.

Chairmen of main sub-committees: Sir Colin Cowdrey (Cricket); B. M. Thornton (Estates); R. V. C. Robins (General Purposes). *Chairmen of specialist sub-committees:* J. R. T. Barclay (Indoor School Management); R. P. Hodson (Players and Fixtures); A. J. B. Mason (Tennis and Squash); H. M. Wyndham (Arts and Libraries).

EUROPEAN CRICKET FEDERATION

The ECF was founded in Munich in 1989 by the national cricket associations of Austria, Germany, Italy and Switzerland to help promote and develop cricket in Europe. Portugal became the 11th member country in 1994, joining the original four plus Belgium, France, Greece, Luxembourg, Malta and Sweden.

Chairman: R. D. V. Knight. *Secretary:* G. Lees.

ADDRESSES

INTERNATIONAL CRICKET COUNCIL

D. L. Richards, The Clock Tower, Lord's Cricket Ground, London NW8 8QN (0171-266 1818; fax 0171-266 1777).

Full Members

AUSTRALIA: Australian Cricket Board, G. W. Halbish, 90 Jolimont Street, Jolimont, Victoria 3002.
ENGLAND: Cricket Council, A. C. Smith, Lord's Ground, London NW8 8QZ.
INDIA: Board of Control for Cricket in India, J. Dalmiya, Dr B. C. Roy Club House, Eden Gardens, Calcutta 700 021.
NEW ZEALAND: New Zealand Cricket Inc., G. T. Dowling, OBE, ACA, PO Box 958, 109 Cambridge Terrace, Christchurch.
PAKISTAN: Board of Control for Cricket in Pakistan, Ghulam Mustafa Khan, Gaddafi Stadium, Lahore 54600.
SOUTH AFRICA: United Cricket Board of South Africa, Dr A. Bacher, PO Box 55009, Northlands 2116, Transvaal.
SRI LANKA: Board of Control for Cricket in Sri Lanka, A. P. B. Tennekoon, 35 Maitland Place, Colombo 7.
WEST INDIES: West Indies Cricket Board of Control, G. S. Camacho, Letchworth Complex, The Garrison, St Michael, Barbados.
ZIMBABWE: Zimbabwe Cricket Union, P. Chingoka, PO Box 2739, Harare.

Associate and Affiliate Members

ARGENTINA: Argentine Cricket Association, C. M. Gibson, c/o The English Club, 25 de Mayo 586, 1002 Buenos Aires.
AUSTRIA: Austrian Cricket Association, A. Simpson-Parker, Brunner Strasse 34-38/17/16, A-1210 Vienna.
BAHAMAS: Bahamas Cricket Association, S. Deveaux, PO Box N-10101, Nassau.
BANGLADESH: Bangladesh Cricket Control Board, M. Aminul Huq Moni, National Stadium, Dhaka 1000.
BELGIUM: Belgian Cricket Federation, C. Wolfe, Rue de l'Eglise St Martin 12, B-1390 BIEZ.
BERMUDA: Bermuda Cricket Board of Control, W. Smith, PO Box HM992, Hamilton HM DX.
BRUNEI: Brunei Darussalam National Cricket Association, c/o Panaga Club, Seria 7082, Brunei Darussalam via Singapore.
CANADA: Canadian Cricket Association, Capt. J. Siew, 1650 Abbey Road, Ottawa, Ontario, K1G 0H3.
DENMARK: Danish Cricket Association, J. Holmen, Idraettens Hus, Brøndby, DK 2605.
EAST AND CENTRAL AFRICA: East and Central African Cricket Conference, T. B. McCarthy, PO Box 34321, Lusaka 1010, Zambia.
FIJI: Fiji Cricket Association, P. I. Knight, PO Box 300, Suva.
FRANCE: Fédération Française du Cricket, O. Dubaut, 73 Rue Curial, 75019 Paris.
GERMANY: Deutscher Cricket Bund, R. Schwiete, Teichweg 4a, 63452 Hanau.
GIBRALTAR: Gibraltar Cricket Association, T. J. Finlayson, 21 Sandpits House, Withams Road.
HONG KONG: Hong Kong Cricket Association, J. A. Cribbin, University of Hong Kong, School of Professional and Continuing Education, Pokfulam Road.
IRELAND: Irish Cricket Union, D. Scott, 45 Foxrock Park, Foxrock, Dublin 18.
ISRAEL: Israel Cricket Association, S. Perlman, PO Box 65085, Tel-Aviv 61650.
ITALY: Associazione Italiana Cricket, S. Gambino, Via S. Ignazio 9, 00186 Roma.
JAPAN: Japan Cricket Association, R. G. Martineau, Shizuoka City, Chiyoda 736, Yamadai Corp. 305, Japan 420.
KENYA: Kenya Cricket Association, J. Rayani, PO Box 48363, Nairobi.

MALAYSIA: Malaysian Cricket Association, C. Chelliah, 1st Floor, Wisma OCM, Jalan Hang Jebat, 50150 Kuala Lumpur.

NAMIBIA: Namibia Cricket Board, L. Pieters, PO Box 457, Windhoek 9000.

NEPAL: Cricket Association of Nepal, Jaikumar N. Shah, Dasharath Stadium, PO Box 1432, Kathmandu.

NETHERLANDS: Royal Netherlands Cricket Board, A. de la Mar, Neuiwe Kalfjeslaan 21-B, 1182 AA Amstelveen.

PAPUA NEW GUINEA: Papua New Guinea Cricket Board of Control, W. Satchell, PO Box 83, Konedobu.

SCOTLAND: Scottish Cricket Union, R. W. Barclay, Caledonia House, South Gyle, Edinburgh EH12 9DQ.

SINGAPORE: Singapore Cricket Association, J. Grimberg, c/o The Ceylon Sports Club, 101 Balestier Road, Singapore 1232.

SPAIN: Asociacion Española de Cricket, C. E. Woodbridge, Villa Valor A14 Hacienda Guadalupe, 29692 Sabinillas, Manilva (Malaga).

SWITZERLAND: Swiss Cricket Association, P. Barnes, Spitzackerstrasse 32, 4103 Bottmingen.

UNITED ARAB EMIRATES: Emirates Cricket Board, Abdul Rahman Bukhatir, Sharjah Cricket Stadium, PO Box 88, Sharjah.

USA: United States of America Cricket Association, Naseeruddin Khan, 2361 Hickory Road, Plymouth Meeting, Pennsylvania 19462.

WEST AFRICA: West Africa Cricket Conference, Mrs Tayo Oreweme, Tafawa Balewa Square, Surulere, Lagos, Nigeria.

UK ADDRESSES

TEST AND COUNTY CRICKET BOARD: A. C. Smith, Lord's Ground, London NW8 8QZ (0171-286 4405; fax 0171-289 5619).

MARYLEBONE CRICKET CLUB: R. D. V. Knight, Lord's Ground, London NW8 8QN (0171-289 1611; fax 0171-289 9100. Club office 0171-289 8979; fax 0171-266 3459).

First-Class Counties

DERBYSHIRE: County Ground, Nottingham Road, Derby DE21 6DA (01332-383211; fax 01332-290251).

DURHAM: County Ground, Riverside, Chester-le-Street, County Durham DH3 3QR (0191-387 1717; fax 0191-387 1616).

ESSEX: County Ground, New Writtle Street, Chelmsford CM2 0PG (01245-252420; fax 01245-491607).

GLAMORGAN: Sophia Gardens, Cardiff CF1 9XR (01222-343478; fax 01222-377044).

GLOUCESTERSHIRE: Phoenix County Ground, Nevil Road, Bristol BS7 9EJ (0117-924 5216; fax 0117-924 1193).

HAMPSHIRE: Northlands Road, Southampton SO9 2TY (01703-333788; fax 01703-330121).

KENT: St Lawrence Ground, Old Dover Road, Canterbury CT1 3NZ (01227-456886; fax 01227-762168).

LANCASHIRE: County Cricket Ground, Old Trafford, Manchester M16 0PX (0161-848 7021; fax 0161-848 9021).

LEICESTERSHIRE: County Cricket Ground, Grace Road, Leicester LE2 8AD (0116-283 1880/2128; fax 0116-244 0363).

MIDDLESEX: Lord's Cricket Ground, London NW8 8QN (0171-289 1300; fax 0171-289 5831).

NORTHAMPTONSHIRE: County Ground, Wantage Road, Northampton NN1 4TJ (01604-32917; fax 01604-232855).

NOTTINGHAMSHIRE: County Cricket Ground, Trent Bridge, Nottingham NG2 6AG (0115-982 1525; fax 0115-945 5730).

SOMERSET: County Ground, St James's Street, Taunton TA1 1JT (01823-272946; fax 01823-332395).

SURREY: The Oval, London SE11 5SS (0171-582 6660; fax 0171-735 7769).

SUSSEX: County Ground, Eaton Road, Hove BN3 3AN (01273-732161; fax 01273-771549).

WARWICKSHIRE: County Ground, Edgbaston, Birmingham B5 7QU (0121-446 4422; fax 0121-446 4544).

WORCESTERSHIRE: County Ground, New Road, Worcester WR2 4QQ (01905-748474; fax 01905-748005).

YORKSHIRE: Headingley Cricket Ground, Leeds LS6 3BU (0113-278 7394; fax 0113-278 4099).

Minor Counties

MINOR COUNTIES CRICKET ASSOCIATION: D. J. M. Armstrong, Thorpe Cottage, Mill Common, Ridlington, North Walsham NR28 9TY. (01692-650563).

BEDFORDSHIRE: D. J. F. Hoare, 5 Brecon Way, Bedford MK41 8DF (01234-266648).

BERKSHIRE: C. M. S. Crombie, Orchard Cottage, Waltham St Lawrence, Reading, Berkshire RG10 0JH (01734-343387 home, 01491-578555 business).

BUCKINGHAMSHIRE: S. J. Tomlin, Orchardleigh Cottage, Bigfrith Lane, Cookham Dean, Berkshire SL6 9PH (01628-482202 home, 016285-24922 business).

CAMBRIDGESHIRE: P. W. Gooden, The Redlands, Oakington Road, Cottenham, Cambridge CB4 4TW (01954-250429).

CHESHIRE: J. B. Pickup, 2 Castle Street, Northwich, Cheshire CW8 1AB (01606-74970 home, 01606-74301 business; fax 01606-871034).

CORNWALL: The Rev. Canon Kenneth Rogers, The Rectory, Priory Road, Bodmin, Cornwall PL31 2AB (01208-73867).

CUMBERLAND: D. Lamb, 42 Croft Road, Carlisle, Cumbria CA3 9AG (01228-23017).

DEVON: G. R. Evans, Blueberry Haven, 20 Boucher Road, Budleigh Salterton, Devon EX9 6JF (01395-445216 home, 01392-58406 business; fax 01392-411697).

DORSET: K. H. House, The Barn, Higher Farm, Bagber Common, Sturminster Newton, Dorset DT10 2HB (01258-473394).

HEREFORDSHIRE: P. Sykes, 5 Dale Drive, Holmer Grange, Hereford HR4 9RF (01432-264703 home, 01432-382684 business).

HERTFORDSHIRE: D. S. Dredge, "Trevellis", 38 Santers Lane, Potters Bar, Hertfordshire EN6 2BX (01707-658377).

LINCOLNSHIRE: C. J. White, "Lyndonholme", Castle Terrace Road, Sleaford, Lincolnshire NG34 7QF (01529-302341 home, 01529-302181 business).

NORFOLK: S. J. Skinner, 27 Colkett Drive, Old Catton, Norwich NR6 7ND (01603-485940 home – weekend, 01354-59026 – midweek, 01733-412152 business).

NORTHUMBERLAND: A. B. Stephenson, Northumberland County Cricket Club, Osborne Avenue, Jesmond, Newcastle-upon-Tyne NE2 1JS (0191-281 2738).

OXFORDSHIRE: A. W. Moss, 14 Croft Avenue, Kidlington, Oxford OX5 2HU (01865-372399 home, 01865-226733/742277 business; fax 01865-226886).

SHROPSHIRE: N. H. Birch, 8 Port Hill Close, Shrewsbury, Shropshire SY3 8RR (01743-233650).

STAFFORDSHIRE: W. S. Bourne, 10 The Pavement, Brewood, Staffordshire ST19 9BZ (01902-850325 home, 01902-23038 business).

SUFFOLK: Toby Pound, 94 Henley Road, Ipswich IP1 4NJ (01473-213288 home, 01473-232121 business).

WALES MINOR COUNTIES: Bill Edwards, 59a King Edward Road, Swansea SA1 4LN (01792-462233).

WILTSHIRE: C. R. Sheppard, 45 Ipswich Street, Swindon SN2 1DB (01793-511811 home, 01793-530784 business, 0831-565866 mobile).

Other Bodies

ASSOCIATION OF CRICKET UMPIRES AND SCORERS: G. J. Bullock, PO Box 399, Camberley, Surrey GU16 5ZJ (01276 27962).

BRITISH UNIVERSITIES SPORTS ASSOCIATION: 8 Union Street, London SE1 1SZ (0171-357 8555).

CLUB CRICKET CONFERENCE: A. E. F. Stevens, 361 West Barnes Lane, New Malden, Surrey KT3 6JF.

COMBINED SERVICES: Lt-Col. K. Hitchcock, c/o Army Sport Control Board, Clayton Barracks, Aldershot, Hampshire GU11 2BG.

ENGLISH SCHOOLS' CRICKET ASSOCIATION: K. S. Lake, 38 Mill House, Woods Lane, Cottingham, Hull HU16 4HQ.

EUROPEAN CRICKET FEDERATION: G. Lees, 56 Ashfield Road, Altrincham, Cheshire WA15 9QN (0161-929 5897).

LEAGUE CRICKET CONFERENCE: N. Edwards, 1 Longfield, Freshfield, Formby, Merseyside.

MIDLAND CLUB CRICKET CONFERENCE: D. R. Thomas, 4 Silverdale Gardens, Wordsley, Stourbridge, W. Midlands DY8 5NU.

NATIONAL CRICKET ASSOCIATION: Lord's Ground, London NW8 8QZ.

SCARBOROUGH CRICKET FESTIVAL: Colin T. Adamson, Cricket Ground, North Marine Road, Scarborough, North Yorkshire YO12 7TJ.

WOMEN'S CRICKET ASSOCIATION: Warwickshire County Cricket Ground, Edgbaston Road, Birmingham B5 7QX (0121-440 0520; fax 0121-446 6344).

CRICKET ASSOCIATIONS AND SOCIETIES

AUSTRALIAN CRICKET SOCIETY: D. Manning, Ravenstone, 240-246 Oban Road, North Ringwood, Victoria 3134, Australia.

BLACKLEY CRICKET SOCIETY: D. N. Butterfield, 7 Bayswater Terrace, Halifax, West Yorkshire HX3 0NB.

CAMBRIDGE UNIVERSITY CRICKET SOCIETY: R. J. Singh, Trinity Hall, Cambridge CB2 1TJ.

CHELTENHAM CRICKET SOCIETY: P. Murphy, 1 Colesbourne Road, Benhall, Cheltenham, Gloucestershire GL51 6DJ.

CHESTERFIELD CRICKET SOCIETY: J. S. Cook, 44 Morris Avenue, Newbold, Chesterfield, Derbyshire S41 7BA.

COUNCIL OF CRICKET SOCIETIES, THE: B. Rickson, 31 Grange Avenue, Cheadle Hulme, Cheshire SK8 5EN.

COUNTY CRICKET SUPPORTERS ASSOCIATION: W. Horsley, 10 Delamere Road, Northampton NN4 9QG.

CRICKET MEMORABILIA SOCIETY: A. Sheldon, 29 Highclere Road, Crumpsall, Manchester M8 6WS.

CRICKET SOCIETY, THE: D. Lodge, 2 Highfield Close, Amersham, Buckinghamshire HP6 6HG.

CRICKET STATISTICIANS AND HISTORIANS, ASSOCIATION OF: P. Wynne-Thomas, 3 Radcliffe Road, West Bridgford, Nottingham NG2 5FF.

CRICKET STATISTICIANS AND SCORERS OF INDIA, ASSOCIATION OF: T. Braganza, 63a Gokhale Road (North), Dadar, Bombay 400 028, India.

DERBYSHIRE CRICKET SOCIETY: O. Kinselle, 27 Wilsthorpe Road, Breaston, Derbyshire DE72 3EA.

DUKINFIELD CRICKET LOVERS' SOCIETY: F. Stafford, 17 Clarence Road, Wallasey, Wirral L44 9ES.

EAST RIDING CRICKET SOCIETY: S. J. Clarke, 12 Meadow Lane, Newport, North Humberside HU15 2QN.

ESSEX CRICKET SOCIETY: M. K. Smith, 321 Westbourne Grove, Westcliff-on-Sea, Essex SS0 0PU.

GLOUCESTERSHIRE CRICKET LOVERS' SOCIETY: M. Simpson, 318 Canford Lane, Westbury-on-Trym, Bristol BS9 3PL.

GOOD EGG CRICKET SOCIETY: R. Whitaker, c/o 15 Sunnyfield Avenue, Cliviger, Burnley, Lancashire BB10 4TE.

HAMPSHIRE CRICKET SOCIETY: J. Moore, 85 Kingsway, Chandlers Ford, Eastleigh, Hampshire SO53 1FD.

HIGH PEAK CRICKET SOCIETY: G. K. Watson, Stubbins Lea, Stubbins Lane, Chinley, Stockport SK12 6ED.

INDIA, THE CRICKET SOCIETY OF: Sander Nakai, 1047 Pocket-B, Sector-A, Vasant Kunj, New Delhi 1120 030, India.

LANCASHIRE AND CHESHIRE CRICKET SOCIETY: H. W. Pardoe, "Crantock", 117a Barlow Moor Road, Didsbury, Manchester M20 2TS.

LINCOLNSHIRE CRICKET LOVERS' SOCIETY: C. Kennedy, 26 Eastwood Avenue, Great Grimsby, South Humberside DN34 5BE.

MERSEYSIDE CRICKET SOCIETY: W. T. Robins, 11 Yew Tree Road, Hunts Cross, Liverpool L25 9QN.

MIDLAND CRICKET SOCIETY: Dr A. A. Walker, "Sarnia", Hernes Nest, Bewdley, Worcester, Worcestershire DY12 2ET.

NEEDWOOD CRICKET LOVERS' SOCIETY: A. D. Campion, 45 Fallowfield Drive, Barton-under-Needwood, Staffordshire DE13 8DH.

NEW ZEALAND, CRICKET SOCIETY OF: J. H. Palmer, Eden Park, PO Box 2860, Auckland 1, New Zealand.

NORFOLK CRICKET SOCIETY: A. V. Burgess, 41 Ashby Street, Norwich, Norfolk NR1 3PT.

NORTHERN CRICKET SOCIETY: K. Harvey, 5 St Margaret's Drive, Gledhow Lane, Roundhay, Leeds, Yorkshire LS8 1RU.

NOTTINGHAM CRICKET LOVERS' SOCIETY: G. Blagdurn, 2 Inham Circus, Chilwell, Beeston, Nottingham NG9 4FN.

PAKISTAN ASSOCIATION OF CRICKET STATISTICIANS: Abid Ali Kazi, 5-A, II/I Sunset Lane, Phase II, Defence Housing Authority, Karachi 75500, Pakistan.

ROTHERHAM CRICKET SOCIETY: J. A. R. Atkin, 15 Gallow Tree Road, Rotherham, South Yorkshire S65 3FE.

SCOTLAND, CRICKET SOCIETY OF: A. J. Robertson, 5 Riverside Road, Eaglesham, Glasgow G76 0DQ.

SOMERSET WYVERNS: G. Evison, 61 Welbeck Avenue, Bedgrove, Aylesbury, Buckinghamshire HP21 7BJ.

SOUTH AFRICA, CRICKET SOCIETY OF: Mrs J. Gleason, PO Box 78040, Sandton, Transvaal 2146, South Africa.

STOURBRIDGE AND DISTRICT CRICKET SOCIETY: R. Barber, 6 Carlton Avenue, Pedmore, Stourbridge, West Midlands DY9 9ED.

SUSSEX CRICKET SOCIETY: Mrs P. Brabyn, 4 Wolstonbury Walk, Shoreham-by-Sea, West Sussex BN43 5GU.

SWISS CRICKET ASSOCIATION: Dr B. Pattison, 9 Ch. du Bois Contens, 1291 Commugny, Switzerland.

WEST LANCASHIRE CRICKET SOCIETY: G. D. Anderson, 32 Dunster Road, Southport PR8 2EN.

WOMBWELL CRICKET LOVERS' SOCIETY: M. Pope, 107 Piccadilly Road, Swinton, Mexborough, South Yorkshire S64 8JT.

YORKSHIRE CCC SOUTHERN GROUP: D. M. Wood, 15 Rothschild Road, Linslade, Leighton Buzzard, Bedfordshire LU7 7SY.

ZIMBABWE, CRICKET SOCIETY OF: J. B. Stockwell, 6 Howard Close, Mount Pleasant, Harare, Zimbabwe.

THE LAWS OF CRICKET

(1980 CODE)

INDEX TO THE LAWS

LAW 1. THE PLAYERS

1. Number of Players and Captain

A match is played between two sides each of 11 players, one of whom shall be captain. In the event of the captain not being available at any time, a deputy shall act for him.

2. Nomination of Players

Before the toss for innings, the captain shall nominate his players, who may not thereafter be changed without the consent of the opposing captain.

Note

(a) More or Less than 11 Players a Side
A match may be played by agreement between sides of more or less than 11 players, but not more than 11 players may field.

LAW 2. SUBSTITUTES AND RUNNERS: BATSMAN OR FIELDSMAN LEAVING THE FIELD: BATSMAN RETIRING: BATSMAN COMMENCING INNINGS

1. Substitutes

In normal circumstances, a substitute shall be allowed to field only for a player who satisfies the umpires that he has become injured or become ill during the match. However, in very exceptional circumstances, the umpires may use their discretion to allow a substitute for a player who has to leave the field for other wholly acceptable reasons, subject to consent being given by the opposing captain. If a player wishes to change his shirt, boots, etc., he may leave the field to do so (no changing on the field), but no substitute will be allowed.

2. Objection to Substitutes

The opposing captain shall have no right of objection to any player acting as substitute in the field, nor as to where he shall field; however, no substitute shall act as wicket-keeper.

3. Substitute not to Bat or Bowl

A substitute shall not be allowed to bat or bowl.

4. A Player for whom a Substitute has Acted

A player may bat, bowl or field even though a substitute has acted for him.

5. Runner

A runner shall be allowed for a batsman who, during the match, is incapacitated by illness or injury. The person acting as runner shall be a member of the batting side and shall, if possible, have already batted in that innings.

6. Runner's Equipment

The player acting as runner for an injured batsman shall wear the same external protective equipment as the injured batsman.

7. Transgression of the Laws by an Injured Batsman or Runner

An injured batsman may be out should his runner break any one of Laws 33 (Handled the Ball), 37 (Obstructing the Field) or 38 (Run Out). As striker he remains himself subject to the Laws. Furthermore, should he be out of his ground for any purpose and the wicket at the wicket-keeper's end be put down he shall be out under Law 38 (Run Out) or Law 39 (Stumped), irrespective of the position of the other batsman or the runner, and no runs shall be scored.

When not the striker, the injured batsman is out of the game and shall stand where he does not interfere with the play. Should he bring himself into the game in any way, then he shall suffer the penalties that any transgression of the Laws demands.

8. Fieldsman Leaving the Field

No fieldsman shall leave the field or return during a session of play without the consent of the umpire at the bowler's end. The umpire's consent is also necessary if a substitute is required for a fieldsman, when his side returns to the field after an interval. If a member of the fielding side leaves the field or fails to return after an interval and is absent from the field for longer than 15 minutes, he shall not be permitted to bowl after his return until he has been on the field for at least that length of playing time for which he was absent. This restriction shall not apply at the start of a new day's play.

9. Batsman Leaving the Field or Retiring

A batsman may leave the field or retire at any time owing to illness, injury or other unavoidable cause, having previously notified the umpire at the bowler's end. He may resume his innings at the fall of a wicket, which for the purposes of this Law shall include the retirement of another batsman.

If he leaves the field or retires for any other reason he may resume his innings only with the consent of the opposing captain.

When a batsman has left the field or retired and is unable to return owing to illness, injury or other unavoidable cause, his innings is to be recorded as "retired, not out". Otherwise it is to be recorded as "retired, out".

10. Commencement of a Batsman's Innings

A batsman shall be considered to have commenced his innings once he has stepped on to the field of play.

Note

(a) Substitutes and Runners
For the purpose of these Laws, allowable illnesses or injuries are those which occur at any time after the nomination by the captains of their teams.

LAW 3. THE UMPIRES

1. Appointment

Before the toss for innings, two umpires shall be appointed, one for each end, to control the game with absolute impartiality as required by the Laws.

2. Change of Umpires

No umpire shall be changed during a match without the consent of both captains.

3. Special Conditions

Before the toss for innings, the umpires shall agree with both captains on any special conditions affecting the conduct of the match.

4. The Wickets

The umpires shall satisfy themselves before the start of the match that the wickets are properly pitched.

5. Clock or Watch

The umpires shall agree between themselves and inform both captains before the start of the match on the watch or clock to be followed during the match.

6. Conduct and Implements

Before and during a match the umpires shall ensure that the conduct of the game and the implements used are strictly in accordance with the Laws.

7. Fair and Unfair Play

The umpires shall be the sole judges of fair and unfair play.

8. Fitness of Ground, Weather and Light

(a) The umpires shall be the sole judges of the fitness of the ground, weather and light for play.

(i) However, before deciding to suspend play, or not to start play, or not to resume play after an interval or stoppage, the umpires shall establish whether both captains (the batsmen at the wicket may deputise for their captain) wish to commence or to continue in the prevailing conditions; if so, their wishes shall be met.

(ii) In addition, if during play the umpires decide that the light is unfit, only the batting side shall have the option of continuing play. After agreeing to continue to play in unfit light conditions, the captain of the batting side (or a batsman at the wicket) may appeal against the light to the umpires, who shall uphold the appeal only if, in their opinion, the light has deteriorated since the agreement to continue was made.

(b) After any suspension of play, the umpires, unaccompanied by any of the players or officials, shall, on their own initiative, carry out an inspection immediately the conditions improve and shall continue to inspect at intervals. Immediately the umpires decide that play is possible they shall call upon the players to resume the game.

9. Exceptional Circumstances

In exceptional circumstances, other than those of weather, ground or light, the umpires may decide to suspend or abandon play. Before making such a decision the umpires shall establish, if the circumstances allow, whether both captains (the batsmen at the wicket may deputise for their captain) wish to continue in the prevailing conditions; if so, their wishes shall be met.

10. Position of Umpires

The umpires shall stand where they can best see any act upon which their decision may be required.

Subject to this over-riding consideration, the umpire at the bowler's end shall stand where he does not interfere with either the bowler's run-up or the striker's view.

The umpire at the striker's end may elect to stand on the off instead of the leg side of the pitch, provided he informs the captain of the fielding side and the striker of his intention to do so.

11. Umpires Changing Ends

The umpires shall change ends after each side has had one innings.

12. Disputes

All disputes shall be determined by the umpires, and if they disagree the actual state of things shall continue.

13. Signals

The following code of signals shall be used by umpires who will wait until a signal has been answered by a scorer before allowing the game to proceed.

Boundary	– by waving the arm from side to side.
Boundary 6	– by raising both arms above the head.
Bye	– by raising an open hand above the head.
Dead Ball	– by crossing and re-crossing the wrists below the waist.
Leg-bye	– by touching a raised knee with the hand.
No-ball	– by extending one arm horizontally.
Out	– by raising the index finger above the head. If not out, the umpire shall call "not out".
Short Run	– by bending the arm upwards and by touching the nearer shoulder with the tips of the fingers.
Wide	– by extending both arms horizontally.

14. Correctness of Scores

The umpires shall be responsible for satisfying themselves on the correctness of the scores throughout and at the conclusion of the match. See Law 21.6 (Correctness of Result).

Notes

(a) Attendance of Umpires
The umpires should be present on the ground and report to the ground executive or the equivalent at least 30 minutes before the start of a day's play.

(b) Consultation between Umpires and Scorers
Consultation between umpires and scorers over doubtful points is essential.

(c) Fitness of Ground
The umpires shall consider the ground as unfit for play when it is so wet or slippery as to deprive the bowlers of a reasonable foothold, the fieldsmen, other than the deep-fielders, of the power of free movement, or the batsmen of the ability to play their strokes or to run between the wickets. Play should not be suspended merely because the grass and the ball are wet and slippery.

(d) Fitness of Weather and Light
The umpires should suspend play only when they consider that the conditions are so bad that it is unreasonable or dangerous to continue.

LAW 4. THE SCORERS

1. Recording Runs

All runs scored shall be recorded by scorers appointed for the purpose. Where there are two scorers they shall frequently check to ensure that the score-sheets agree.

2. Acknowledging Signals

The scorers shall accept and immediately acknowledge all instructions and signals given to them by the umpires.

LAW 5. THE BALL

1. Weight and Size

The ball, when new, shall weigh not less than $5\frac{1}{2}$ ounces/155.9g, nor more than $5\frac{3}{4}$ ounces/163g; and shall measure not less than $8\frac{13}{16}$ inches/22.4cm, nor more than 9 inches/22.9cm in circumference.

2. Approval of Balls

All balls used in matches shall be approved by the umpires and captains before the start of the match.

3. New Ball

Subject to agreement to the contrary, having been made before the toss, either captain may demand a new ball at the start of each innings.

4. New Ball in Match of Three or More Days' Duration

In a match of three or more days' duration, the captain of the fielding side may demand a new ball after the prescribed number of overs has been bowled with the old one. The governing body for cricket in the country concerned shall decide the number of overs applicable in that country, which shall be not less than 75 six-ball overs (55 eight-ball overs).

5. Ball Lost or Becoming Unfit for Play

In the event of a ball during play being lost or, in the opinion of the umpires, becoming unfit for play, the umpires shall allow it to be replaced by one that in their opinion has had a similar amount of wear. If a ball is to be replaced, the umpires shall inform the batsman.

Note

(a) Specifications
The specifications, as described in 1 above, shall apply to top-grade balls only. The following degrees of tolerance will be acceptable for other grades of ball.

(i) *Men's Grades 2–4*
Weight: $5\frac{5}{16}$ ounces/150g to $5\frac{13}{16}$ ounces/165g.
Size: $8\frac{11}{16}$ inches/22.0cm to $9\frac{1}{16}$ inches/23.0cm.

(ii) *Women's*
Weight: $4\frac{15}{16}$ ounces/140g to $5\frac{5}{16}$ ounces/150g.
Size: $8\frac{1}{4}$ inches/21.0cm to $8\frac{7}{8}$ inches/22.5cm.

(iii) *Junior*
Weight: $4\frac{11}{16}$ ounces/133g to $5\frac{1}{16}$ ounces/143g.
Size: $8\frac{1}{16}$ inches/20.5cm to $8\frac{11}{16}$ inches/22.0cm.

LAW 6. THE BAT

1. Width and Length

The bat overall shall not be more than 38 inches/96.5cm in length; the blade of the bat shall be made of wood and shall not exceed $4\frac{1}{4}$ inches/10.8cm at the widest part.

Note

(a) The blade of the bat may be covered with material for protection, strengthening or repair. Such material shall not exceed $\frac{1}{16}$ inch/1.56mm in thickness.

LAW 7. THE PITCH

1. Area of Pitch

The pitch is the area between the bowling creases – see Law 9 (The Bowling and Popping Creases). It shall measure 5 feet/1.52m in width on either side of a line joining the centre of the middle stumps of the wickets – see Law 8 (The Wickets).

2. Selection and Preparation

Before the toss for innings, the executive of the ground shall be responsible for the selection and preparation of the pitch; thereafter the umpires shall control its use and maintenance.

3. Changing Pitch

The pitch shall not be changed during a match unless it becomes unfit for play, and then only with the consent of both captains.

4. Non-Turf Pitches

In the event of a non-turf pitch being used, the following shall apply:

(a) Length: That of the playing surface to a minimum of 58 feet/17.68m.

(b) Width: That of the playing surface to a minimum of 6 feet/1.83m.

See Law 10 (Rolling, Sweeping, Mowing, Watering the Pitch and Re-marking of Creases) Note (a).

LAW 8. THE WICKETS

1. Width and Pitching

Two sets of wickets, each 9 inches/22.86cm wide, and consisting of three wooden stumps with two wooden bails upon the top, shall be pitched opposite and parallel to each other at a distance of 22 yards/20.12m between the centres of the two middle stumps.

2. Size of Stumps

The stumps shall be of equal and sufficient size to prevent the ball from passing between them. Their tops shall be 28 inches/71.1cm above the ground, and shall be dome-shaped except for the bail grooves.

3. Size of Bails

The bails shall be each $4\frac{3}{8}$ inches/11.1cm in length and when in position on the top of the stumps shall not project more than $\frac{1}{2}$ inch/1.3cm above them.

Notes

(a) Dispensing with Bails
In a high wind the umpires may decide to dispense with the use of bails.

(b) Junior Cricket
For junior cricket, as defined by the local governing body, the following measurements for the wickets shall apply:

Width – 8 inches/20.32cm.
Pitched – 21 yards/19.20m.
Height – 27 inches/68.58cm.
Bails – each $3\frac{7}{8}$ inches/9.84cm in length and should not project more than $\frac{1}{2}$ inch/1.3cm above the stumps.

LAW 9. THE BOWLING, POPPING AND RETURN CREASES

1. The Bowling Crease

The bowling crease shall be marked in line with the stumps at each end and shall be 8 feet 8 inches/2.64m in length, with the stumps in the centre.

2. The Popping Crease

The popping crease, which is the back edge of the crease marking, shall be in front of and parallel with the bowling crease. It shall have the back edge of the crease marking 4 feet/1.22m from the centre of the stumps and shall extend to a minimum of 6 feet/1.83m on either side of the line of the wicket.

The popping crease shall be considered to be unlimited in length.

3. The Return Crease

The return crease marking, of which the inside edge is the crease, shall be at each end of the bowling crease and at right angles to it. The return crease shall be marked to a minimum of 4 feet/1.22m behind the wicket and shall be considered to be unlimited in length. A forward extension shall be marked to the popping crease.

LAW 10. ROLLING, SWEEPING, MOWING, WATERING THE PITCH AND RE-MARKING OF CREASES

1. Rolling

During the match the pitch may be rolled at the request of the captain of the batting side, for a period of not more than seven minutes before the start of each innings, other than the first innings of the match, and before the start of each day's play. In addition, if, after the toss and before the first innings of the match, the start is delayed, the captain of the batting side may request to have the pitch rolled for not more than seven minutes. However, if in the opinion of the umpires the delay has had no significant effect upon the state of the pitch, they shall refuse any request for the rolling of the pitch.

The pitch shall not otherwise be rolled during the match.

The seven minutes' rolling permitted before the start of a day's play shall take place not earlier than half an hour before the start of play and the captain of the batting side may delay such rolling until ten minutes before the start of play should he so desire.

If a captain declares an innings closed less than 15 minutes before the resumption of play, and the other captain is thereby prevented from exercising his option of seven minutes' rolling or if he is so prevented for any other reason, the time for rolling shall be taken out of the normal playing time.

2. Sweeping

Such sweeping of the pitch as is necessary during the match shall be done so that the seven minutes allowed for rolling the pitch, provided for in 1 above, is not affected.

3. Mowing

(a) Responsibilities of Ground Authority and of Umpires
All mowings which are carried out before the toss for innings shall be the responsibility of the ground authority; thereafter they shall be carried out under the supervision of the umpires. See Law 7.2 (Selection and Preparation).

(b) Initial Mowing
The pitch shall be mown before play begins on the day the match is scheduled to start, or in the case of a delayed start on the day the match is expected to start. See 3(a) above (Responsibilities of Ground Authority and of Umpires).

(c) Subsequent Mowings in a Match of Two or More Days' Duration
In a match of two or more days' duration, the pitch shall be mown daily before play begins. Should this mowing not take place because of weather conditions, rest days or other reasons, the pitch shall be mown on the first day on which the match is resumed.

(d) Mowing of the Outfield in a Match of Two or More Days' Duration
In order to ensure that conditions are as similar as possible for both sides, the outfield shall normally be mown before the commencement of play on each day of the match, if ground and weather conditions allow. See Note (b) to this Law.

4. Watering

The pitch shall not be watered during a match.

5. Re-marking Creases

Whenever possible the creases shall be re-marked.

6. Maintenance of Foot-holes

In wet weather, the umpires shall ensure that the holes made by the bowlers and batsmen are cleaned out and dried whenever necessary to facilitate play. In matches of two or more days' duration, the umpires shall allow, if necessary, the re-turfing of foot-holes made by the bowler in his delivery stride, or the use of quick-setting fillings for the same purpose, before the start of each day's play.

7. Securing of Footholds and Maintenance of Pitch

During play, the umpires shall allow either batsman to beat the pitch with his bat and players to secure their footholds by the use of sawdust, provided that no damage to the pitch is so caused, and Law 42 (Unfair Play) is not contravened.

Notes

(a) Non-turf Pitches
The above Law 10 applies to turf pitches.

The game is played on non-turf pitches in many countries at various levels. Whilst the conduct of the game on these surfaces should always be in accordance with the Laws of Cricket, it is recognised that it may sometimes be necessary for governing bodies to lay down special playing conditions to suit the type of non-turf pitch used in their country.

In matches played against touring teams, any special playing conditions should be agreed in advance by both parties.

(b) Mowing of the Outfield in a Match of Two or More Days' Duration
If, for reasons other than ground and weather conditions, daily and complete mowing is not possible, the ground authority shall notify the captains and umpires, before the toss for innings, of the procedure to be adopted for such mowing during the match.

(c) Choice of Roller
If there is more than one roller available, the captain of the batting side shall have a choice.

LAW 11. COVERING THE PITCH

1. Before the Start of a Match

Before the start of a match, complete covering of the pitch shall be allowed.

2. During a Match

The pitch shall not be completely covered during a match unless prior arrangement or regulations so provide.

3. Covering Bowlers' Run-up

Whenever possible, the bowlers' run-up shall be covered, but the covers so used shall not extend further than 4 feet/1.22m in front of the popping crease.

Note

(a) Removal of Covers
The covers should be removed as promptly as possible whenever the weather permits.

LAW 12. INNINGS

1. Number of Innings

A match shall be of one or two innings of each side according to agreement reached before the start of play.

2. Alternate Innings

In a two-innings match each side shall take their innings alternately except in the case provided for in Law 13 (The Follow-on).

3. The Toss

The captains shall toss for the choice of innings on the field of play not later than 15 minutes before the time scheduled for the match to start, or before the time agreed upon for play to start.

4. Choice of Innings

The winner of the toss shall notify his decision to bat or to field to the opposing captain not later than ten minutes before the time scheduled for the match to start, or before the time agreed upon for play to start. The decision shall not thereafter be altered.

5. Continuation after One Innings of Each Side

Despite the terms of 1 above, in a one-innings match, when a result has been reached on the first innings, the captains may agree to the continuation of play if, in their opinion, there is a prospect of carrying the game to a further issue in the time left. See Law 21 (Result).

Notes

(a) Limited Innings – One-innings Match
In a one-innings match, each innings may, by agreement, be limited by a number of overs or by a period of time.

(b) Limited Innings – Two-innings Match
In a two-innings match, the first innings of each side may, by agreement, be limited to a number of overs or by a period of time.

LAW 13. THE FOLLOW-ON

1. Lead on First Innings

In a two-innings match the side which bats first and leads by 200 runs in a match of five days or more, by 150 runs in a three-day or four-day match, by 100 runs in a two-day match, or by 75 runs in a one-day match, shall have the option of requiring the other side to follow their innings.

2. Day's Play Lost

If no play takes place on the first day of a match of two or more days' duration, 1 above shall apply in accordance with the number of days' play remaining from the actual start of the match.

LAW 14. DECLARATIONS

1. Time of Declaration

The captain of the batting side may declare an innings closed at any time during a match, irrespective of its duration.

2. Forfeiture of Second Innings

A captain may forfeit his second innings, provided his decision to do so is notified to the opposing captain and umpires in sufficient time to allow seven minutes' rolling of the pitch. See Law 10 (Rolling, Sweeping, Mowing, Watering the Pitch and Re-marking of Creases). The normal ten-minute interval between innings shall be applied.

LAW 15. START OF PLAY

1. Call of Play

At the start of each innings and of each day's play, and on the resumption of play after any interval or interruption, the umpire at the bowler's end shall call "play".

2. Practice on the Field

At no time on any day of the match shall there be any bowling or batting practice on the pitch.

No practice may take place on the field if, in the opinion of the umpires, it could result in a waste of time.

3. Trial Run-up

No bowler shall have a trial run-up after "play" has been called in any session of play, except at the fall of a wicket when an umpire may allow such a trial run-up if he is satisfied that it will not cause any waste of time.

LAW 16. INTERVALS

1. Length

The umpire shall allow such intervals as have been agreed upon for meals, and ten minutes between each innings.

2. Luncheon Interval – Innings Ending or Stoppage within Ten Minutes of Interval

If an innings ends or there is a stoppage caused by weather or bad light within ten minutes of the agreed time for the luncheon interval, the interval shall be taken immediately.

The time remaining in the session of play shall be added to the agreed length of the interval but no extra allowance shall be made for the ten-minute interval between innings.

3. Tea Interval – Innings Ending or Stoppage within 30 Minutes of Interval

If an innings ends or there is a stoppage caused by weather or bad light within 30 minutes of the agreed time for the tea interval, the interval shall be taken immediately.

The interval shall be of the agreed length and, if applicable, shall include the ten-minute interval between innings.

4. Tea Interval – Continuation of Play

If, at the agreed time for the tea interval, nine wickets are down, play shall continue for a period not exceeding 30 minutes or until the innings is concluded.

5. Tea Interval – Agreement to Forgo

At any time during the match, the captains may agree to forgo a tea interval.

6. Intervals for Drinks

If both captains agree before the start of a match that intervals for drinks may be taken, the option to take such intervals shall be available to either side. These intervals shall be restricted to one per session, shall be kept as short as possible, shall not be taken in the last hour of the match, and in any case shall not exceed five minutes.

The agreed times for these intervals shall be strictly adhered to, except that if a wicket falls within five minutes of the agreed time then drinks shall be taken out immediately.

If an innings ends or there is a stoppage caused by weather or bad light within 30 minutes of the agreed time for a drinks interval, there will be no interval for drinks in that session.

At any time during the match the captains may agree to forgo any such drinks interval.

Notes

(a) Tea Interval – One-day Match
In a one-day match, a specific time for the tea interval need not necessarily be arranged, and it may be agreed to take this interval between the innings of a one-innings match.

(b) Changing the Agreed Time of Intervals
In the event of the ground, weather or light conditions causing a suspension of play, the umpires, after consultation with the captains, may decide in the interests of time-saving to bring forward the time of the luncheon or tea interval.

LAW 17. CESSATION OF PLAY

1. Call of Time

The umpire at the bowler's end shall call "time" on the cessation of play before any interval or interruption of play, at the end of each day's play, and at the conclusion of the match. See Law 27 (Appeals).

2. Removal of Bails

After the call of "time", the umpires shall remove the bails from both wickets.

3. Starting a Last Over

The last over before an interval or the close of play shall be started provided the umpire, after walking at his normal pace, has arrived at his position behind the stumps at the bowler's end before time has been reached.

4. Completion of the Last Over of a Session

The last over before an interval or the close of play shall be completed unless a batsman is out or retires during that over within two minutes of the interval or the close of play or unless the players have occasion to leave the field.

5. Completion of the Last Over of a Match

An over in progress at the close of play on the final day of a match shall be completed at the request of either captain, even if a wicket falls after time has been reached.

If, during the last over, the players have occasion to leave the field, the umpires shall call "time" and there shall be no resumption of play and the match shall be at an end.

6. Last Hour of Match – Number of Overs

The umpires shall indicate when one hour of playing time of the match remains according to the agreed hours of play. The next over after that moment shall be the first of a minimum of 20 six-ball overs (15 eight-ball overs), provided a result is not reached earlier or there is no interval or interruption of play.

7. Last Hour of Match – Intervals between Innings and Interruptions of Play

If, at the commencement of the last hour of the match, an interval or interruption of play is in progress or if, during the last hour, there is an interval between innings or an interruption of play, the minimum number of overs to be bowled on the resumption of play shall be reduced in proportion to the duration, within the last hour of the match, of any such interval or interruption.

The minimum number of overs to be bowled after the resumption of play shall be calculated as follows:

(a) In the case of an interval or interruption of play being in progress at the commencement of the last hour of the match, or in the case of a first interval or interruption, a deduction shall be made from the minimum of 20 six-ball overs (or 15 eight-ball overs).

(b) If there is a later interval or interruption, a further deduction shall be made from the minimum number of overs which should have been bowled following the last resumption of play.

(c) These deductions shall be based on the following factors:

(i) The number of overs already bowled in the last hour of the match or, in the case of a later interval or interruption, in the last session of play.

(ii) The number of overs lost as a result of the interval or interruption allowing one six-ball over for every full three minutes (or one eight-ball over for every full four minutes) of interval or interruption.

(iii) Any over left uncompleted at the end of an innings to be excluded from these calculations.

(iv) Any over of the minimum number to be played which is left uncompleted at the start of an interruption of play to be completed when play is resumed and to count as one over bowled.

(v) An interval to start with the end of an innings and to end ten minutes later; an interruption to start on the call of "time" and to end on the call of "play".

(d) In the event of an innings being completed and a new innings commencing during the last hour of the match, the number of overs to be bowled in the new innings shall be calculated on the basis of one six-ball over for every three minutes or part thereof remaining for play (or one eight-ball over for every four minutes or part thereof remaining for play); or alternatively on the basis that sufficient overs be bowled to enable the full minimum quota of overs to be completed under circumstances governed by (a), (b) and (c) above. In all such cases the alternative which allows the greater number of overs shall be employed.

8. Bowler Unable to Complete an Over during Last Hour of the Match

If, for any reason, a bowler is unable to complete an over during the period of play referred to in 6 above, Law 22.7 (Bowler Incapacitated or Suspended during an Over) shall apply.

LAW 18. SCORING

1. A Run

The score shall be reckoned by runs. A run is scored:

(a) So often as the batsmen, after a hit or at any time while the ball is in play, shall have crossed and made good their ground from end to end.

(b) When a boundary is scored. See Law 19 (Boundaries).

(c) When penalty runs are awarded. See 6 below.

2. Short Runs

(a) If either batsman runs a short run, the umpire shall call and signal "one short" as soon as the ball becomes dead and that run shall not be scored. A run is short if a batsman fails to make good his ground on turning for a further run.

(b) Although a short run shortens the succeeding one, the latter, if completed, shall count.

(c) If either or both batsmen deliberately run short the umpire shall, as soon as he sees that the fielding side have no chance of dismissing either batsman, call and signal "dead ball" and disallow any runs attempted or previously scored. The batsmen shall return to their original ends.

(d) If both batsmen run short in one and the same run, only one run shall be deducted.

(e) Only if three or more runs are attempted can more than one be short and then, subject to (c) and (d) above, all runs so called shall be disallowed. If there has been more than one short run the umpires shall instruct the scorers as to the number of runs disallowed.

3. Striker Caught

If the striker is caught, no run shall be scored.

4. Batsman Run Out

If a batsman is run out, only that run which was being attempted shall not be scored. If, however, an injured striker himself is run out, no runs shall be scored. See Law 2.7 (Transgression of the Laws by an Injured Batsman or Runner).

5. Batsman Obstructing the Field

If a batsman is out Obstructing the Field, any runs completed before the obstruction occurs shall be scored unless such obstruction prevents a catch being made, in which case no runs shall be scored.

6. Runs Scored for Penalties

Runs shall be scored for penalties under Laws 20 (Lost Ball), 24 (No-ball), 25 (Wide-ball), 41.1 (Fielding the Ball) and for boundary allowances under Law 19 (Boundaries).

7. Batsman Returning to Wicket he has Left

If, while the ball is in play, the batsmen have crossed in running, neither shall return to the wicket he has left, even though a short run has been called or no run has been scored as in the case of a catch. Batsmen, however, shall return to the wickets they originally left in the cases of a boundary and of any disallowance of runs and of an injured batsman being, himself, run out. See Law 2.7 (Transgression by an Injured Batsman or Runner).

Note

(a) Short Run
A striker taking stance in front of his popping crease may run from that point without penalty.

LAW 19. BOUNDARIES

1. The Boundary of the Playing Area

Before the toss for innings, the umpires shall agree with both captains on the boundary of the playing area. The boundary shall, if possible, be marked by a white line, a rope laid on the ground, or a fence. If flags or posts only are used to mark a boundary, the imaginary line joining such points shall be regarded as the boundary. An obstacle, or person, within the playing area shall not be regarded as a boundary unless so decided by the umpires before the toss for innings. Sightscreens within, or partially within, the playing area shall be regarded as the boundary and when the ball strikes or passes within or under or directly over any part of the screen, a boundary shall be scored.

2. Runs Scored for Boundaries

Before the toss for innings, the umpires shall agree with both captains the runs to be allowed for boundaries, and in deciding the allowance for them, the umpires and captains shall be guided by the prevailing custom of the ground. The allowance for a boundary shall normally be four runs, and six runs for all hits pitching over and clear of the boundary line or fence, even though the ball has been previously touched by a fieldsman. Six runs shall also be scored if a fieldsman, after catching a ball, carries it over the boundary. See Law 32 (Caught) Note (a). Six runs shall not be scored when a ball struck by the striker hits a sightscreen full pitch if the screen is within, or partially within, the playing area, but if the ball is struck directly over a sightscreen so situated, six runs shall be scored.

3. A Boundary

A boundary shall be scored and signalled by the umpire at the bowler's end whenever, in his opinion:

(a) A ball in play touches or crosses the boundary, however marked.

(b) A fieldsman with ball in hand touches or grounds any part of his person on or over a boundary line.

(c) A fieldsman with ball in hand grounds any part of his person over a boundary fence or board. This allows the fieldsman to touch or lean on or over a boundary fence or board in preventing a boundary.

4. Runs Exceeding Boundary Allowance

The runs completed at the instant the ball reaches the boundary shall count if they exceed the boundary allowance.

5. Overthrows or Wilful Act of a Fieldsman

If the boundary results from an overthrow or from the wilful act of a fieldsman, any runs already completed and the allowance shall be added to the score. The run in progress shall count provided that the batsmen have crossed at the instant of the throw or act.

Note

(a) Position of Sightscreens
Sightscreens should, if possible, be positioned wholly outside the playing area, as near as possible to the boundary line.

LAW 20. LOST BALL

1. Runs Scored

If a ball in play cannot be found or recovered, any fieldsman may call "lost ball" when six runs shall be added to the score; but if more than six have been run before "lost ball" is called, as many runs as have been completed shall be scored. The run in progress shall count provided that the batsmen have crossed at the instant of the call of "lost ball".

2. How Scored

The runs shall be added to the score of the striker if the ball has been struck, but otherwise to the score of byes, leg-byes, no-balls or wides as the case may be.

LAW 21. THE RESULT

1. A Win – Two-innings Matches

The side which has scored a total of runs in excess of that scored by the opposing side in its two completed innings shall be the winner.

2. A Win – One-innings Matches

(a) One-innings matches, unless played out as in 1 above, shall be decided on the first innings, but see Law 12.5 (Continuation after One Innings of Each Side).

(b) If the captains agree to continue play after the completion of one innings of each side in accordance with Law 12.5 (Continuation after One Innings of Each Side) and a result is not achieved on the second innings, the first innings result shall stand.

3. Umpires Awarding a Match

(a) A match shall be lost by a side which, during the match, (i) refuses to play, or (ii) concedes defeat, and the umpires shall award the match to the other side.

(b) Should both batsmen at the wickets or the fielding side leave the field at any time without the agreement of the umpires, this shall constitute a refusal to play and, on appeal, the umpires shall award the match to the other side in accordance with (a) above.

4. A Tie

The result of a match shall be a tie when the scores are equal at the conclusion of play, but only if the side batting last has completed its innings.

If the scores of the completed first innings of a one-day match are equal, it shall be a tie but only if the match has not been played out to a further conclusion.

5. A Draw

A match not determined in any of the ways as in 1, 2, 3 and 4 above shall count as a draw.

6. Correctness of Result

Any decision as to the correctness of the scores shall be the responsibility of the umpires. See Law 3.14 (Correctness of Scores).

If, after the umpires and players have left the field in the belief that the match has been concluded, the umpires decide that a mistake in scoring has occurred, which affects the result, and provided time has not been reached, they shall order play to resume and to continue until the agreed finishing time unless a result is reached earlier.

If the umpires decide that a mistake has occurred and time has been reached, the umpires shall immediately inform both captains of the necessary corrections to the scores and, if applicable, to the result.

7. Acceptance of Result

In accepting the scores as notified by the scorers and agreed by the umpires, the captains of both sides thereby accept the result.

Notes

(a) Statement of Results
The result of a finished match is stated as a win by runs, except in the case of a win by the side batting last when it is by the number of wickets still then to fall.

(b) Winning Hit or Extras
As soon as the side has won, see 1 and 2 above, the umpire shall call "time", the match is finished, and nothing that happens thereafter other than as a result of a mistake in scoring (see 6 above) shall be regarded as part of the match.

However, if a boundary constitutes the winning hit – or extras – and the boundary allowance exceeds the number of runs required to win the match, such runs scored shall be credited to the side's total and, in the case of a hit, to the striker's score.

LAW 22. THE OVER

1. Number of Balls

The ball shall be bowled from each wicket alternately in overs of either six or eight balls according to agreement before the match.

2. Call of "Over"

When the agreed number of balls has been bowled, and as the ball becomes dead or when it becomes clear to the umpire at the bowler's end that both the fielding side and the batsmen at the wicket have ceased to regard the ball as in play, the umpire shall call "over" before leaving the wicket.

3. No-ball or Wide-ball

Neither a no-ball nor a wide-ball shall be reckoned as one of the over.

4. Umpire Miscounting

If an umpire miscounts the number of balls, the over as counted by the umpire shall stand.

5. Bowler Changing Ends

A bowler shall be allowed to change ends as often as desired, provided only that he does not bowl two overs consecutively in an innings.

6. The Bowler Finishing an Over

A bowler shall finish an over in progress unless he be incapacitated or be suspended under Law 42.8 (The Bowling of Fast Short-pitched Balls), 9 (The Bowling of Fast High Full Pitches), 10 (Time Wasting) and 11 (Players Damaging the Pitch). If an over is left incomplete for any reason at the start of an interval or interruption of play, it shall be finished on the resumption of play.

7. Bowler Incapacitated or Suspended during an Over

If, for any reason, a bowler is incapacitated while running up to bowl the first ball of an over, or is incapacitated or suspended during an over, the umpire shall call and signal "dead ball" and another bowler shall be allowed to bowl or complete the over from the same end, provided only that he shall not bowl two overs, or part thereof, consecutively in one innings.

8. Position of Non-striker

The batsman at the bowler's end shall normally stand on the opposite side of the wicket to that from which the ball is being delivered, unless a request to do otherwise is granted by the umpire.

LAW 23. DEAD BALL

1. The Ball Becomes Dead

When:

(a) It is finally settled in the hands of the wicket-keeper or the bowler.

(b) It reaches or pitches over the boundary.

(c) A batsman is out.

(d) Whether played or not, it lodges in the clothing or equipment of a batsman or the clothing of an umpire.

(e) A ball lodges in a protective helmet worn by a member of the fielding side.

(f) A penalty is awarded under Law 20 (Lost Ball) or Law 41.1 (Fielding the Ball).

(g) The umpire calls "over" or "time".

2. Either Umpire Shall Call and Signal "Dead Ball"

When:

(a) He intervenes in a case of unfair play.

(b) A serious injury to a player or umpire occurs.

(c) He is satisfied that, for an adequate reason, the striker is not ready to receive the ball and makes no attempt to play it.

(d) The bowler drops the ball accidentally before delivery, or the ball does not leave his hand for any reason other than in an attempt to run out the non-striker (See Law 24.5 – Bowler Attempting to Run Out Non-striker before Delivery).

(e) One or both bails fall from the striker's wicket before he receives delivery.

(f) He leaves his normal position for consultation.

(g) He is required to do so under Law 26.3 (Disallowance of Leg-byes), etc.

3. The Ball Ceases to be Dead

When:

(a) The bowler starts his run-up or bowling action.

4. The Ball is Not Dead

When:

(a) It strikes an umpire (unless it lodges in his dress).

(b) The wicket is broken or struck down (unless a batsman is out thereby).

(c) An unsuccessful appeal is made.

(d) The wicket is broken accidentally either by the bowler during his delivery or by a batsman in running.

(e) The umpire has called "no-ball" or "wide".

Notes

(a) Ball Finally Settled
Whether the ball is finally settled or not – see 1(a) above – must be a question for the umpires alone to decide.

(b) Action on Call of "Dead Ball"

(i) If "dead ball" is called prior to the striker receiving a delivery, the bowler shall be allowed an additional ball.

(ii) If "dead ball" is called after the striker receives a delivery, the bowler shall not be allowed an additional ball, unless a "no-ball" or "wide" has been called.

LAW 24. NO-BALL

1. Mode of Delivery

The umpire shall indicate to the striker whether the bowler intends to bowl over or round the wicket, overarm or underarm, right or left-handed. Failure on the part of the bowler to indicate in advance a change in his mode of delivery is unfair and the umpire shall call and signal "no-ball".

2. Fair Delivery – The Arm

For a delivery to be fair the ball must be bowled, not thrown – see Note (a) below. If either umpire is not entirely satisfied with the absolute fairness of a delivery in this respect he shall call and signal "no-ball" instantly upon delivery.

3. Fair Delivery – The Feet

The umpire at the bowler's wicket shall call and signal "no-ball" if he is not satisfied that in the delivery stride:

(a) The bowler's back foot has landed within and not touching the return crease or its forward extension; or

(b) Some part of the front foot whether grounded or raised was behind the popping crease.

4. Bowler Throwing at Striker's Wicket before Delivery

If the bowler, before delivering the ball, throws it at the striker's wicket in an attempt to run him out, the umpire shall call and signal "no-ball". See Law 42.12 (Batsman Unfairly Stealing a Run) and Law 38 (Run Out).

5. Bowler Attempting to Run Out Non-striker before Delivery

If the bowler, before delivering the ball, attempts to run out the non-striker, any runs which result shall be allowed and shall be scored as no-balls. Such an attempt shall not count as a ball in the over. The umpire shall not call "no-ball". See Law 42.12 (Batsman Unfairly Stealing a Run).

6. Infringement of Laws by a Wicket-keeper or a Fieldsman

The umpire shall call and signal "no-ball" in the event of the wicket-keeper infringing Law 40.1 (Position of Wicket-keeper) or a fieldsman infringing Law 41.2 (Limitation of On-side Fieldsmen) or Law 41.3 (Position of Fieldsmen).

7. Revoking a Call

An umpire shall revoke the call "no-ball" if the ball does not leave the bowler's hand for any reason. See Law 23.2 (Either Umpire Shall Call and Signal "Dead Ball").

8. Penalty

A penalty of one run for a no-ball shall be scored if no runs are made otherwise.

9. Runs from a No-ball

The striker may hit a no-ball and whatever runs result shall be added to his score. Runs made otherwise from a no-ball shall be scored no-balls.

10. Out from a No-ball

The striker shall be out from a no-ball if he breaks Law 34 (Hit the Ball Twice) and either batsman may be run out or shall be given out if either breaks Law 33 (Handled the Ball) or Law 37 (Obstructing the Field).

11. Batsman Given Out off a No-ball

Should a batsman be given out off a no-ball the penalty for bowling it shall stand unless runs are otherwise scored.

Notes

(a) Definition of a Throw
A ball shall be deemed to have been thrown if, in the opinion of either umpire, the process of straightening the bowling arm, whether it be partial or complete, takes place during that part of the delivery swing which directly precedes the ball leaving the hand. This definition shall not debar a bowler from the use of the wrist in the delivery swing.

(b) No-ball Not Counting in Over
A no-ball shall not be reckoned as one of the over. See Law 22.3 (No-ball or Wide-ball).

LAW 25. WIDE-BALL

1. Judging a Wide

If the bowler bowls the ball so high over or so wide of the wicket that, in the opinion of the umpire, it passes out of reach of the striker, standing in a normal guard position, the umpire shall call and signal "wide-ball" as soon as it has passed the line of the striker's wicket.

The umpire shall not adjudge a ball as being wide if:

(a) The striker, by moving from his guard position, causes the ball to pass out of his reach.

(b) The striker moves and thus brings the ball within his reach.

2. Penalty

A penalty of one run for a wide shall be scored if no runs are made otherwise.

3. Ball Coming to Rest in Front of the Striker

If a ball which the umpire considers to have been delivered comes to rest in front of the line of the striker's wicket, "wide" shall not be called. The striker has a right, without interference from the fielding side, to make one attempt to hit the ball. If the fielding side interfere, the umpire shall replace the ball where it came to rest and shall order the fieldsmen to resume the places they occupied in the field before the ball was delivered.

The umpire shall call and signal "dead ball" as soon as it is clear that the striker does not intend to hit the ball, or after the striker has made an unsuccessful attempt to hit the ball.

4. Revoking a Call

The umpire shall revoke the call if the striker hits a ball which has been called "wide".

5. Ball Not Dead

The ball does not become dead on the call of "wide-ball" – see Law 23.4 (The Ball is Not Dead).

6. Runs Resulting from a Wide

All runs which are run or result from a wide-ball which is not a no-ball shall be scored wide-balls, or if no runs are made one shall be scored.

7. Out from a Wide

The striker shall be out from a wide-ball if he breaks Law 35 (Hit Wicket), or Law 39 (Stumped). Either batsman may be run out and shall be out if he breaks Law 33 (Handled the Ball), or Law 37 (Obstructing the Field).

8. Batsman Given Out off a Wide

Should a batsman be given out off a wide, the penalty for bowling it shall stand unless runs are otherwise made.

Note

(a) Wide-ball Not Counting in Over
A wide-ball shall not be reckoned as one of the over – see Law 22.3 (No-ball or Wide-ball).

LAW 26. BYE AND LEG-BYE

1. Byes

If the ball, not having been called "wide" or "no-ball", passes the striker without touching his bat or person, and any runs are obtained, the umpire shall signal "bye" and the run or runs shall be credited as such to the batting side.

2. Leg-byes

If the ball, not having been called "wide" or "no-ball", is unintentionally deflected by the striker's dress or person, except a hand holding the bat, and any runs are obtained the umpire shall signal "leg-bye" and the run or runs so scored shall be credited as such to the batting side.

Such leg-byes shall be scored only if, in the opinion of the umpire, the striker has:

(a) Attempted to play the ball with his bat; or

(b) Tried to avoid being hit by the ball.

3. Disallowance of Leg-byes

In the case of a deflection by the striker's person, other than in 2(a) and (b) above, the umpire shall call and signal "dead ball" as soon as one run has been completed or when it is clear that a run is not being attempted, or the ball has reached the boundary.

On the call and signal of "dead ball" the batsmen shall return to their original ends and no runs shall be allowed.

LAW 27. APPEALS

1. Time of Appeals

The umpires shall not give a batsman out unless appealed to by the other side which shall be done prior to the bowler beginning his run-up or bowling action to deliver the next ball. Under Law 23.1 (g) (The Ball Becomes Dead), the ball is dead on "over" being called; this does not, however, invalidate an appeal made prior to the first ball of the following over provided "time" has not been called – see Law 17.1 (Call of Time).

2. An Appeal "How's That?"

An appeal "How's That?" shall cover all ways of being out.

3. Answering Appeals

The umpire at the bowler's wicket shall answer appeals before the other umpire in all cases except those arising out of Law 35 (Hit Wicket) or Law 39 (Stumped) or Law 38 (Run Out) when this occurs at the striker's wicket.

When either umpire has given a batsman not out, the other umpire shall, within his jurisdiction, answer the appeal or a further appeal, provided it is made in time in accordance with 1 above (Time of Appeals).

4. Consultation by Umpires

An umpire may consult with the other umpire on a point of fact which the latter may have been in a better position to see and shall then give his decision. If, after consultation, there is still doubt remaining the decision shall be in favour of the batsman.

5. Batsman Leaving his Wicket under a Misapprehension

The umpires shall intervene if satisfied that a batsman, not having been given out, has left his wicket under a misapprehension that he has been dismissed.

6. Umpire's Decision

The umpire's decision is final. He may alter his decision, provided that such alteration is made promptly.

7. Withdrawal of an Appeal

In exceptional circumstances the captain of the fielding side may seek permission of the umpire to withdraw an appeal provided the outgoing batsman has not left the playing area. If this is allowed, the umpire shall cancel his decision.

LAW 28. THE WICKET IS DOWN

1. Wicket Down

The wicket is down if:

(a) Either the ball or the striker's bat or person completely removes either bail from the top of the stumps. A disturbance of a bail, whether temporary or not, shall not constitute a complete removal, but the wicket is down if a bail in falling lodges between two of the stumps.

(b) Any player completely removes with his hand or arm a bail from the top of the stumps, provided that the ball is held in that hand or in the hand of the arm so used.

(c) When both bails are off, a stump is struck out of the ground by the ball, or a player strikes or pulls a stump out of the ground, providing that the ball is held in the hand(s) or in the hand of the arm so used.

2. One Bail Off

If one bail is off, it shall be sufficient for the purpose of putting the wicket down to remove the remaining bail, or to strike or pull any of the three stumps out of the ground in any of the ways stated in 1 above.

3. All the Stumps Out of the Ground

If all the stumps are out of the ground, the fielding side shall be allowed to put back one or more stumps in order to have an opportunity of putting the wicket down.

4. Dispensing with Bails

If, owing to the strength of the wind, it has been agreed to dispense with the bails in accordance with Law 8, Note (a) (Dispensing with Bails), the decision as to when the wicket is down is one for the umpires to decide on the facts before them. In such circumstances and if the umpires so decide, the wicket shall be held to be down even though a stump has not been struck out of the ground.

Note

(a) Remaking the Wicket
If the wicket is broken while the ball is in play, it is not the umpire's duty to remake the wicket until the ball has become dead – see Law 23 (Dead Ball). A member of the fielding side, however, may remake the wicket in such circumstances.

LAW 29. BATSMAN OUT OF HIS GROUND

1. When out of his Ground

A batsman shall be considered to be out of his ground unless some part of his bat in his hand or of his person is grounded behind the line of the popping crease.

LAW 30. BOWLED

1. Out Bowled

The striker shall be out *Bowled* if:

(a) His wicket is bowled down, even if the ball first touches his bat or person.

(b) He breaks his wicket by hitting or kicking the ball on to it before the completion of a stroke, or as a result of attempting to guard his wicket. See Law 34.1 (Out Hit the Ball Twice).

Note

(a) Out Bowled – Not lbw
The striker is out bowled if the ball is deflected on to his wicket even though a decision against him would be justified under Law 36 (lbw).

LAW 31. TIMED OUT

1. Out Timed Out

An incoming batsman shall be out *Timed Out* if he wilfully takes more than two minutes to come in – the two minutes being timed from the moment a wicket falls until the new batsman steps on to the field of play.

If this is not complied with and if the umpire is satisfied that the delay was wilful and if an appeal is made, the new batsman shall be given out by the umpire at the bowler's end.

2. Time to be Added

The time taken by the umpires to investigate the cause of the delay shall be added at the normal close of play.

Notes

(a) Entry in Scorebook
The correct entry in the scorebook when a batsman is given out under this Law is "timed out", and the bowler does not get credit for the wicket.

(b) Batsmen Crossing on the Field of Play
It is an essential duty of the captains to ensure that the in-going batsman passes the out-going one before the latter leaves the field of play.

LAW 32. CAUGHT

1. Out Caught

The striker shall be out *Caught* if the ball touches his bat or if it touches below the wrist his hand or glove, holding the bat, and is subsequently held by a fieldsman before it touches the ground.

2. A Fair Catch

A catch shall be considered to have been fairly made if:

(a) The fieldsman is within the field of play throughout the act of making the catch.

(i) The act of making the catch shall start from the time when the fieldsman first handles the ball and shall end when he both retains complete control over the further disposal of the ball and remains within the field of play.

(ii) In order to be within the field of play, the fieldsman may not touch or ground any part of his person on or over a boundary line. When the boundary is marked by a fence or board the fieldsman may not ground any part of his person over the boundary fence or board, but may touch or lean over the boundary fence or board in completing the catch.

(b) The ball is hugged to the body of the catcher or accidentally lodges in his dress or, in the case of the wicket-keeper, in his pads. However, a striker may not be caught if a ball lodges in a protective helmet worn by a fieldsman, in which case the umpire shall call and signal "dead ball". See Law 23 (Dead Ball).

(c) The ball does not touch the ground even though a hand holding it does so in effecting the catch.

(d) A fieldsman catches the ball, after it has been lawfully played a second time by the striker, but only if the ball has not touched the ground since being first struck.

(e) A fieldsman catches the ball after it has touched an umpire, another fieldsman or the other batsman. However, a striker may not be caught if a ball has touched a protective helmet worn by a fieldsman.

(f) The ball is caught off an obstruction within the boundary provided it has not previously been agreed to regard the obstruction as a boundary.

3. Scoring of Runs

If a striker is caught, no run shall be scored.

Notes

(a) Scoring from an Attempted Catch
When a fieldsman carrying the ball touches or grounds any part of his person on or over a boundary marked by a line, six runs shall be scored.

(b) Ball Still in Play
If a fieldsman releases the ball before he crosses the boundary, the ball will be considered to be still in play and it may be caught by another fieldsman. However, if the original fieldsman returns to the field of play and handles the ball, a catch may not be made.

LAW 33. HANDLED THE BALL

1. Out Handled the Ball

Either batsman on appeal shall be out *Handled the Ball* if he wilfully touches the ball while in play with the hand not holding the bat unless he does so with the consent of the opposite side.

Note

(a) Entry in Scorebook
The correct entry in the scorebook when a batsman is given out under this Law is "handled the ball', and the bowler does not get credit for the wicket.

LAW 34. HIT THE BALL TWICE

1. Out Hit the Ball Twice

The striker, on appeal, shall be out *Hit the Ball Twice* if, after the ball is struck or is stopped by any part of his person, he wilfully strikes it again with his bat or person except for the sole purpose of guarding his wicket: this he may do with his bat or any part of his person other than his hands, but see Law 37.2 (Obstructing a Ball From Being Caught).

For the purpose of this Law, a hand holding the bat shall be regarded as part of the bat.

2. Returning the Ball to a Fieldsman

The striker, on appeal, shall be out under this Law if, without the consent of the opposite side, he uses his bat or person to return the ball to any of the fielding side.

3. Runs from Ball Lawfully Struck Twice

No runs except those which result from an overthrow or penalty – see Law 41 (The Fieldsman) – shall be scored from a ball lawfully struck twice.

Notes

(a) Entry in Scorebook
The correct entry in the scorebook when the striker is given out under this Law is "hit the ball twice", and the bowler does not get credit for the wicket.

(b) Runs Credited to the Batsman
Any runs awarded under 3 above as a result of an overthrow or penalty shall be credited to the striker, provided the ball in the first instance has touched the bat, or, if otherwise, as extras.

LAW 35. HIT WICKET

1. Out Hit Wicket

The striker shall be out *Hit Wicket* if, while the ball is in play:

(a) His wicket is broken with any part of his person, dress, or equipment as a result of any action taken by him in preparing to receive or in receiving a delivery, or in setting off for his first run, immediately after playing, or playing at, the ball.

(b) He hits down his wicket whilst lawfully making a second stroke for the purpose of guarding his wicket within the provisions of Law 34.1 (Out Hit the Ball Twice).

Notes

(a) Not Out Hit Wicket
A batsman is not out under this Law should his wicket be broken in any of the ways referred to in 1(a) above if:

(i) It occurs while he is in the act of running, other than in setting off for his first run immediately after playing at the ball, or while he is avoiding being run out or stumped.

(ii) The bowler after starting his run-up or bowling action does not deliver the ball; in which case the umpire shall immediately call and signal "dead ball".

(iii) It occurs whilst he is avoiding a throw-in at any time.

LAW 36. LEG BEFORE WICKET

1. Out lbw

The striker shall be out *lbw* in the circumstances set out below:

(a) Striker Attempting to Play the Ball
The striker shall be out lbw if he first intercepts with any part of his person, dress or equipment a fair ball which would have hit the wicket and which has not previously touched his bat or a hand holding the bat, provided that:

(i) The ball pitched in a straight line between wicket and wicket or on the off side of the striker's wicket, or was intercepted full pitch; and

(ii) The point of impact is in a straight line between wicket and wicket, even if above the level of the bails.

(b) Striker Making No Attempt to Play the Ball
The striker shall be out lbw even if the ball is intercepted outside the line of the off stump if, in the opinion of the umpire, he has made no genuine attempt to play the ball with his bat, but has intercepted the ball with some part of his person and if the other circumstances set out in (a) above apply.

LAW 37. OBSTRUCTING THE FIELD

1. Wilful Obstruction

Either batsman, on appeal, shall be out *Obstructing the Field* if he wilfully obstructs the opposite side by word or action.

2. Obstructing a Ball From Being Caught

The striker, on appeal, shall be out should wilful obstruction by either batsman prevent a catch being made.

This shall apply even though the striker causes the obstruction in lawfully guarding his wicket under the provisions of Law 34. See Law 34.1 (Out Hit the Ball Twice).

Notes

(a) Accidental Obstruction
The umpires must decide whether the obstruction was wilful or not. The accidental interception of a throw-in by a batsman while running does not break this Law.

(b) Entry in Scorebook
The correct entry in the scorebook when a batsman is given out under this Law is "obstructing the field", and the bowler does not get credit for the wicket.

LAW 38. RUN OUT

1. Out Run Out

Either batsman shall be out *Run Out* if in running or at any time while the ball is in play – except in the circumstances described in Law 39 (Stumped) – he is out of his ground and his wicket is put down by the opposite side. If, however, a batsman in running makes good his ground he shall not be out run out if he subsequently leaves his ground, in order to avoid injury, and the wicket is put down.

2. "No-ball" Called

If a no-ball has been called, the striker shall not be given run out unless he attempts to run.

3. Which Batsman Is Out

If the batsmen have crossed in running, he who runs for the wicket which is put down shall be out; if they have not crossed, he who has left the wicket which is put down shall be out. If a batsman remains in his ground or returns to his ground and the other batsman joins him there, the latter shall be out if his wicket is put down.

4. Scoring of Runs

If a batsman is run out, only that run which is being attempted shall not be scored. If, however, an injured striker himself is run out, no runs shall be scored. See Law 2.7 (Transgression of the Laws by an Injured Batsman or Runner).

Notes

(a) Ball Played on to Opposite Wicket
If the ball is played on to the opposite wicket, neither batsman is liable to be run out unless the ball has been touched by a fieldsman before the wicket is broken.

(b) Entry in Scorebook
The correct entry in the scorebook when a batsman is given out under this Law is "run out", and the bowler does not get credit for the wicket.

(c) Run Out off a Fieldsman's Helmet
If, having been played by a batsman, or having come off his person, the ball rebounds directly from a fieldsman's helmet on to the stumps, with either batsman out of his ground, the batsman shall be "not out".

LAW 39. STUMPED

1. Out Stumped

The striker shall be out *Stumped* if, in receiving the ball, not being a no-ball, he is out of his ground otherwise than in attempting a run and the wicket is put down by the wicket-keeper without the intervention of another fieldsman.

2. Action by the Wicket-keeper

The wicket-keeper may take the ball in front of the wicket in an attempt to stump the striker only if the ball has touched the bat or person of the striker.

Note

(a) Ball Rebounding from Wicket-keeper's Person
The striker may be out stumped if, in the circumstances stated in 1 above, the wicket is broken by a ball rebounding from the wicket-keeper's person or equipment other than a protective helmet or is kicked or thrown by the wicket-keeper on to the wicket.

LAW 40. THE WICKET-KEEPER

1. Position of Wicket-keeper

The wicket-keeper shall remain wholly behind the wicket until a ball delivered by the bowler touches the bat or person of the striker, or passes the wicket, or until the striker attempts a run.

In the event of the wicket-keeper contravening this Law, the umpire at the striker's end shall call and signal "no-ball" at the instant of delivery or as soon as possible thereafter.

2. Restriction on Actions of the Wicket-keeper

If the wicket-keeper interferes with the striker's right to play the ball and to guard his wicket, the striker shall not be out except under Laws 33 (Handled the Ball), 34 (Hit the Ball Twice), 37 (Obstructing the Field) and 38 (Run Out).

3. Interference with the Wicket-keeper by the Striker

If, in the legitimate defence of his wicket, the striker interferes with the wicket-keeper, he shall not be out, except as provided for in Law 37.2 (Obstructing a Ball From Being Caught).

LAW 41. THE FIELDSMAN

1. Fielding the Ball

The fieldsman may stop the ball with any part of his person, but if he wilfully stops it otherwise, five runs shall be added to the run or runs already scored; if no run has been scored five penalty runs shall be awarded. The run in progress shall count provided that the batsmen have crossed at the instant of the act. If the ball has been struck, the penalty shall be added to the score of the striker, but otherwise to the score of byes, leg-byes, no-balls or wides as the case may be.

2. Limitation of On-side Fieldsmen

The number of on-side fieldsmen behind the popping crease at the instant of the bowler's delivery shall not exceed two. In the event of infringement by the fielding side the umpire at the striker's end shall call and signal "no-ball" at the instant of delivery or as soon as possible thereafter.

3. Position of Fieldsmen

Whilst the ball is in play and until the ball has made contact with the bat or the striker's person or has passed his bat, no fieldsman, other than the bowler, may stand on or have any part of his person extended over the pitch (measuring 22 yards/20.12m × 10 feet/3.05m). In the event of a fieldsman contravening this Law, the umpire at the bowler's end shall call and signal "no-ball" at the instant of delivery or as soon as possible thereafter. See Law 40.1 (Position of Wicket-keeper).

4. Fieldsmen's Protective Helmets

Protective helmets, when not in use by members of the fielding side, shall be placed, if above the surface, only on the ground behind the wicket-keeper. In the event of the ball, when in play, striking a helmet whilst in this position, five penalty runs shall be awarded as laid down in Law 41.1 and Note (a).

Note

(a) Batsmen Changing Ends
The five runs referred to in 1 and 4 above are a penalty and the batsmen do not change ends solely by reason of this penalty.

LAW 42. UNFAIR PLAY

1. Responsibility of Captains

The captains are responsible at all times for ensuring that play is conducted within the spirit of the game as well as within the Laws.

2. Responsibility of Umpires

The umpires are the sole judges of fair and unfair play.

3. Intervention by the Umpire

The umpires shall intervene without appeal by calling and signalling "dead ball" in the case of unfair play, but should not otherwise interfere with the progress of the game except as required to do so by the Laws.

4. Lifting the Seam

A player shall not lift the seam of the ball for any reason. Should this be done, the umpires shall change the ball for one of similar condition to that in use prior to the contravention. See Note (a).

5. Changing the Condition of the Ball

Any member of the fielding side may polish the ball provided that such polishing wastes no time and that no artificial substance is used. No-one shall rub the ball on the ground or use any artificial substance or take any other action to alter the condition of the ball.

In the event of a contravention of this Law, the umpires, after consultation, shall change the ball for one of similar condition to that in use prior to the contravention.

This Law does not prevent a member of the fielding side from drying a wet ball, or removing mud from the ball. See Note (b).

6. Incommoding the Striker

An umpire is justified in intervening under this Law and shall call and signal "dead ball" if, in his opinion, any player of the fielding side incommodes the striker by any noise or action while he is receiving a ball.

7. Obstruction of a Batsman in Running

It shall be considered unfair if any fieldsman wilfully obstructs a batsman in running. In these circumstances the umpire shall call and signal "dead ball" and allow any completed runs and the run in progress, or alternatively any boundary scored.

8. The Bowling of Fast Short-pitched Balls

The bowling of fast short-pitched balls is unfair if, in the opinion of the umpire at the bowler's end, it constitutes an attempt to intimidate the striker. See Note (d).

Umpires shall consider intimidation to be the deliberate bowling of fast short-pitched balls which by their length, height and direction are intended or likely to inflict physical injury on the striker. The relative skill of the striker shall also be taken into consideration.

In the event of such unfair bowling, the umpire at the bowler's end shall adopt the following procedure:

(a) In the first instance the umpire shall call and signal "no-ball", caution the bowler and inform the other umpire, the captain of the fielding side and the batsmen of what has occurred.

(b) If this caution is ineffective, he shall repeat the above procedure and indicate to the bowler that this is a final warning.

(c) Both the above caution and final warning shall continue to apply even though the bowler may later change ends.

(d) Should the above warnings prove ineffective the umpire at the bowler's end shall:

- (i) At the first repetition call and signal "no-ball" and when the ball is dead direct the captain to take the bowler off forthwith and to complete the over with another bowler, provided that the bowler does not bowl two overs or part thereof consecutively. See Law 22.7 (Bowler Incapacitated or Suspended during an Over).
- (ii) Not allow the bowler, thus taken off, to bowl again in the same innings.
- (iii) Report the occurrence to the captain of the batting side as soon as the players leave the field for an interval.
- (iv) Report the occurrence to the executive of the fielding side and to any governing body responsible for the match, who shall take any further action which is considered to be appropriate against the bowler concerned.

9. The Bowling of Fast High Full Pitches

The bowling of fast high full pitches is unfair.

A fast high full-pitched ball is defined as a ball that passes, or would have passed, on the full above waist height of a batsman standing upright at the crease. Should a bowler bowl a fast high full-pitched ball, either umpire shall call and signal "no-ball" and adopt the procedure of caution, final warning, action against the bowler and reporting as set out in Law 42.8.

10. Time Wasting

Any form of time wasting is unfair.

(a) In the event of the captain of the fielding side wasting time or allowing any member of his side to waste time, the umpire at the bowler's end shall adopt the following procedure:

- (i) In the first instance he shall caution the captain of the fielding side and inform the other umpire of what has occurred.
- (ii) If this caution is ineffective he shall repeat the above procedure and indicate to the captain that this is a final warning.
- (iii) The umpire shall report the occurrence to the captain of the batting side as soon as the players leave the field for an interval.
- (iv) Should the above procedure prove ineffective the umpire shall report the occurrence to the executive of the fielding side and to any governing body responsible for that match, who shall take appropriate action against the captain and the players concerned.

(b) In the event of a bowler taking unnecessarily long to bowl an over the umpire at the bowler's end shall adopt the procedures, other than the calling of "no-ball", of caution, final warning, action against the bowler and reporting as set out in 8 above.

(c) In the event of a batsman wasting time (See Note (e)) other than in the manner described in Law 31 (Timed Out), the umpire at the bowler's end shall adopt the following procedure:

(i) In the first instance he shall caution the batsman and inform the other umpire at once, and the captain of the batting side, as soon as the players leave the field for an interval, of what has occurred.

(ii) If this proves ineffective, he shall repeat the caution, indicate to the batsman that this is a final warning and inform the other umpire.

(iii) The umpire shall report the occurrence to both captains as soon as the players leave the field for an interval.

(iv) Should the above procedure prove ineffective, the umpire shall report the occurrence to the executive of the batting side and to any governing body responsible for that match, who shall take appropriate action against the player concerned.

11. Players Damaging the Pitch

The umpires shall intervene and prevent players from causing damage to the pitch which may assist the bowlers of either side. See Note (c).

(a) In the event of any member of the fielding side damaging the pitch, the umpire shall follow the procedure of caution, final warning and reporting as set out in 10(a) above.

(b) In the event of a bowler contravening this Law by running down the pitch after delivering the ball, the umpire at the bowler's end shall first caution the bowler. If this caution is ineffective the umpire shall adopt the procedures, other than the calling of "no-ball", as set out in 8 above.

(c) In the event of a batsman damaging the pitch the umpire at the bowler's end shall follow the procedures of caution, final warning and reporting as set out in 10(c) above.

12. Batsman Unfairly Stealing a Run

Any attempt by the batsman to steal a run during the bowler's run-up is unfair. Unless the bowler attempts to run out either batsman – see Law 24.4 (Bowler Throwing at Striker's Wicket before Delivery) and Law 24.5 (Bowler Attempting to Run Out Non-striker before Delivery) – the umpire shall call and signal "dead ball" as soon as the batsmen cross in any such attempt to run. The batsmen shall then return to their original wickets.

13. Player's Conduct

In the event of a player failing to comply with the instructions of an umpire, criticising his decisions by word or action, or showing dissent, or generally behaving in a manner which might bring the game into disrepute, the umpire concerned shall, in the first place, report the matter to the other umpire and to the player's captain, requesting the latter to take action. If this proves ineffective, the umpire shall report the incident as soon as possible to the executive of the player's team and to any governing body responsible for the match, who shall take any further action which is considered appropriate against the player or players concerned.

Notes

(a) The Condition of the Ball
Umpires shall make frequent and irregular inspections of the condition of the ball.

(b) Drying of a Wet Ball
A wet ball may be dried on a towel or with sawdust.

(c) Danger Area
The danger area on the pitch, which must be protected from damage by a bowler, shall be regarded by the umpires as the area contained by an imaginary line 4 feet/1.22m from the popping crease, and parallel to it, and within two imaginary and parallel lines drawn down the pitch from points on that line 1 foot/30.48cm on either side of the middle stump.

(d) Fast Short-pitched Balls
As a guide, a fast short-pitched ball is one which pitches short and passes, or would have passed, above the shoulder height of the striker standing in a normal batting stance at the crease.

(e) Time Wasting by Batsmen
Other than in exceptional circumstances, the batsman should always be ready to take strike when the bowler is ready to start his run-up.

REGULATIONS OF THE INTERNATIONAL CRICKET COUNCIL

Extracts

1. Playing Conditions

The official Laws of Cricket shall be followed on all tours unless an agreement to meet special cases is arrived at between the Members concerned before the visiting team commences the first match of any tour.

2. Classification of First-Class Matches

1. Definitions

A match of three or more days' duration between two sides of 11 players officially adjudged first-class shall be regarded as a first-class fixture.

2. Rules

(a) Full Members of ICC shall decide the status of matches of three or more days' duration played in their countries.

(b) In matches of three or more days' duration played in countries which are not Full Members of ICC:

(i) If the visiting team comes from a country which is a Full Member of ICC, that country shall decide the status of matches.

(ii) If the visiting team does not come from a country which is a Full Member of ICC, or is a Commonwealth team composed of players from different countries, ICC shall decide the status of matches.

Notes

(a) Governing bodies agree that the interest of first-class cricket will be served by ensuring that first-class status is *not* accorded to any match in which one or other of the teams taking part cannot on a strict interpretation of the definition be adjudged first-class.

(b) In case of any disputes arising from these Rules, the Chief Executive of ICC shall refer the matter for decision to the Council, failing unanimous agreement by postal communication being reached.

3. First-Class Status

The following matches shall be regarded as first-class, subject to the provisions of 2.1 (Definitions) being completely complied with:

(a) **In the British Isles and Eire:** (i) County Championship matches. (ii) Official representative tourist matches from Full Member countries unless specifically excluded. (iii) MCC v any first-class county. (iv) Oxford v Cambridge and either University against first-class counties. (v) Scotland v Ireland.

(b) **In Australia:** (i) Sheffield Shield matches. (ii) Matches played by teams representing states of the Commonwealth of Australia between each other or against opponents adjudged first-class.

(c) **In India:** (i) Ranji Trophy matches. (ii) Duleep Trophy matches. (iii) Irani Trophy matches. (iv) Matches played by teams representing state or regional associations affiliated to the Board of Control between each other or against opponents adjudged first-class. (v) All three-day matches played against representative visiting sides.

(d) **In New Zealand:** (i) Shell Trophy matches. (ii) Matches played by teams representing major associations of the North and South Islands, between each other or against opponents adjudged first-class.

(e) **In Pakistan:** (i) Matches played by teams representing divisional associations affiliated to the Board of Control, between each other or against teams adjudged first-class. (ii) Quaid-e-Azam Trophy matches. (iii) BCCP Patron's Trophy matches.

(f) **In South Africa:** (i) Castle Cup competition four-day matches between Transvaal, Northern Transvaal, OFS, Western Province, Eastern Province, Border, Natal and Boland. (ii) The United Cricket Board Bowl competition three-day matches between Eastern Transvaal, Western Transvaal, Griqualand West, the Zimbabwe Board XI and the B teams of the Castle Cup provinces.

(g) **In Sri Lanka:** (i) Matches of three days or more against touring sides adjudged first-class. (ii) Singer Inter-Provincial Cricket tournament matches played over four days for the President's Trophy. (iii) Inter-Club Division I tournament matches played over three days for the P. Saravanamuttu Trophy.

(h) **In West Indies:** Matches played by teams representing Barbados, Guyana, Jamaica, Trinidad & Tobago, the Windward Islands and the Leeward Islands, either for the Red Stripe Cup or against other opponents adjudged first-class.

(i) **In Zimbabwe:** Logan Cup competition three-day matches between Mashonaland, Mashonaland Country Districts, Mashonaland Under-24 and Matabeleland.

(j) **In all Full Member countries represented on the Council:** (i) Test matches and matches against teams adjudged first-class played by official touring teams. (ii) Official Test Trial matches. (iii) Special matches between teams adjudged first-class by the governing body or bodies concerned.

3. Classification of One-Day International Matches

The following should be classified as limited-overs internationals:

(a) All matches played between the Full Member countries of ICC as part of an official tour itinerary.

(b) All matches played as part of an official tournament by Full Member countries. These need not necessarily be held in a Full Member country.

(c) All matches played in the official World Cup competition, including matches involving Associate Member countries.

(d) All matches played in the Asia Cup competition.

Note: Matches involving the United Arab Emirates in the 1993-94 Austral-Asia Cup were accorded full international status. ICC ruled that matches involving Australia A in the 1994-95 World Series should not be regarded as official internationals.

4. Qualification Rules for Test Matches and One-Day International Matches

Qualification by Birth

A cricketer is qualified to play cricket for the country of his birth provided he has not played cricket for any other Member country during the two immediately preceding years.

Qualification by Residence

A cricketer is qualified to play cricket for any Full or Associate Member country in which he has resided for at least 183 days in each of the four immediately preceding years provided that in each such case he has not played cricket for any other Member country during that period of four years.

Notes: A player who has represented his country at Under-19 level or above shall not be eligible, from October 1, 1994, to play international cricket for any other country, except through qualification by birth or residence as above.

The governing body for cricket of any Member country may impose more stringent qualification rules for that country.

REGULATIONS OF ICC FULL MEMBERS

Extracts

Duration of Test Matches

Within a maximum of 30 hours' playing time, the duration of Test matches shall be a matter for negotiation and agreement between the two countries in any particular series of Test matches.

When agreeing the Playing Conditions prior to the commencement of a Test series, the participating countries may:

(a) Extend the playing hours of the last Test beyond the limit of 30 hours, in a series in which, at the conclusion of the penultimate match, one side does not hold a lead of more than one match.

(b) In the event of play being suspended for any reason other than normal intervals, extend the playing time on that day by the amount of time lost up to a maximum of one hour, except in the last hour of the match.

(c) Play on the rest day, conditions and circumstances permitting, should a full day's play be lost on either the second or third scheduled days of play.

(d) Make up time lost in excess of five minutes in each day's play owing to circumstances outside the game, other than acts of God.

Note: The umpires shall determine when such time shall be made up. This could, if conditions and circumstances permit, include the following day.

Minimum Overs in the Day in Test Matches

Regulation for Test matches only.

(a) Play shall continue on each day until the completion of a minimum number of overs or until the scheduled cessation time, whichever is the later. The minimum number of overs to be completed, unless an innings ends or an interruption occurs, shall be:

(i) on days other than the last day – a minimum of 90 overs.

(ii) on the last day – a minimum of 75 overs (or 15 overs per hour) for playing time other than the last hour when a minimum of 15 six-ball overs shall be bowled. All calculations with regard to suspensions of play or the start of a new innings shall be based on one over for each full four minutes. If, however, at any time after 30 minutes of the last hour have elapsed both captains (the batsmen at the wicket may act for their captain) accept that there is no prospect of a result to the match, they may agree to cease play at that time.

Penalties for Slow Over-rates

(i) **Test Matches**

Over-rates shall be assessed on 15 overs per hour, i.e. a minimum of 90 overs in a six-hour day, subject to the following deductions:

Two minutes per wicket taken;
Actual time where treatment by authorised medical personnel is required on the ground, and also for a player leaving the field owing to serious injury;
Four minutes for one drinks break per session, except in the West Indies, where it is accepted that an additional drinks break should be permitted.

Overs will be calculated at the end of the match. For each over short of the target number, five per cent of each player's match fee in the fielding side (including the twelfth man) is to be deducted.

(ii) **One-Day International Matches**

The target over-rate is to be 15 overs per hour. In the event of the target over-rate not being reached, for each over short of the number required to be bowled in the scheduled time, the fielding side (including the twelfth man) will be fined an amount equal to five per cent of each player's match fee.

A penalty may be reviewed by the referee if, after consultation with the umpires, he is of the opinion that events beyond the control of the fielding side, including time-wasting by the batting side, prevented that team from bowling the required number of overs. The batting side may be fined at the same rate as the fielding side if, in the opinion of the referee, the batting side is guilty of slowing down the over-rate.

THE BOWLING OF FAST, SHORT-PITCHED BALLS: LAW 42.8

Experimental Regulation for Test matches only for three years with effect from October 1, 1994

1. A bowler shall be limited to two fast, short-pitched deliveries per over.
2. A fast, short-pitched ball is defined as a ball which passes or would have passed above the shoulder height of the batsman standing upright at the crease.
3. In the event of a bowler bowling more than two fast, short-pitched deliveries in an over, either umpire shall call and signal "no-ball" on each occasion.
4. The penalty for a fast, short-pitched no-ball shall be two runs, plus any runs scored from the delivery.
5. The umpire shall call and signal "no-ball" and then raise the other arm across the chest.

Where a bowler delivers a third fast, short-pitched ball in one over which is also a no-ball under Law 24, e.g. a front-foot no-ball, the penalty will be two runs plus any runs scored from that delivery, i.e. the greater penalty will apply.

The above Regulation is not a substitute for Law 42.8 (as amended below), which umpires are able to apply at any time:

The bowling of fast, short-pitched balls is unfair if the umpire at the bowler's end considers that, by their repetition and taking into account their length, height and direction, they are likely to inflict physical injury on the striker, irrespective of the protective clothing and equipment he may be wearing. The relative skill of the striker shall also be taken into consideration.

The umpire at the bowler's end shall adopt the procedures of caution, final warning, action against the bowler and reporting as set out in Law 42.8.

BALL LOST OR BECOMING UNFIT FOR PLAY: LAW 5.5

Experimental Law

In the event of a ball during play being lost or, in the opinion of the umpires, being unfit for play through normal use, the umpires shall allow it to be replaced by one that in their opinion has had a similar amount of wear. If the ball is to be replaced, the umpires shall inform the batsmen.

PRACTICE ON THE FIELD: LAW 15.2

Experimental Law

At no time on any day of the match shall there be any bowling or batting practice on the pitch. In addition there shall be no bowling or batting practice on any part of the square or the area immediately adjacent to the match pitch after the commencement of play on any day. Any fielder contravening this Law may not bowl the next over.

No practice may take place on the field if, in the opinion of the umpires, it could result in a waste of time.

FIELDSMAN LEAVING THE FIELD: LAW 2.8

No fieldsman shall leave the field or return during a session of play without the consent of the umpire at the bowler's end. The umpire's consent is also necessary if a substitute is required for a fieldsman at the start of play or when his side returns to the field after an interval.

If a member of the fielding side does not take the field at the start of play, leaves the field, or fails to return after an interval and is absent from the field longer than 15 minutes, he shall not be permitted to bowl in that innings after his return until he has been on the field for at least the length of playing time for which he was absent; nor shall he be permitted to bat unless or until, in the aggregate, he has returned to the field and/or his side's innings has been in progress for at least the length of playing time for which he was absent or, if earlier, when his side has lost five wickets. The restrictions shall not apply if he has suffered an external blow (as opposed to an internal injury such as a pulled muscle) while batting earlier in the match and consequently been forced to retire hurt, nor if he has been absent for exceptional and acceptable reasons (other than injury or illness) and consent for a substitute has been granted by the opposing captain.

ICC CODE OF CONDUCT

1. The captains are responsible at all times for ensuring that play is conducted within the spirit of the game as well as within the Laws.

2. Players and team officials shall not at any time engage in conduct unbecoming to an international player or team official which could bring them or the game into disrepute.

3. Players and team officials must at all times accept the umpire's decision. Players must not show dissent at the umpire's decision.

4. Players and team officials shall not intimidate, assault or attempt to intimidate or assault an umpire, another player or a spectator.

5. Players and team officials shall not use crude or abusive language (known as "sledging") nor make offensive gestures.

6. Players and team officials shall not use or in any way be concerned in the use or distribution of illegal drugs.

7. Players and team officials shall not disclose or comment upon any alleged breach of the Code or upon any hearing, report or decision arising from such breach.

8. Players and team officials shall not make any public pronouncement or media comment which is detrimental either to the game in general; or to a particular tour in which they are involved; or about any tour between other countries which is taking place; or to relations between the Boards of the competing teams.

Application, Interpretation and Enforcement of the Code

1. The Code shall apply:

   (a) To players and, where applicable, to team officials of both teams for all Test matches and one-day international matches;

   (b) To players and, where applicable, to team officials of official touring teams for all matches, other than Test matches and one-day internationals ("other matches") with such modifications as ICC shall consider necessary in the absence of a referee for other matches.

2. The Code shall also apply to Associate and Affiliate members of ICC although its application, interpretation and enforcement shall be determined in the way deemed most suitable by those concerned with the running of the game at these levels.

3. Breaches of the Code shall be deemed also to include a breach of any ICC Regulation in force from time to time, including (without limitation) those relating to advertising on cricket clothing and equipment, and, in Test matches, those relating to minimum over-rates.

4. The Code, breach of which may render a player or team official liable to disciplinary action, shall be enforced:

(a) In the case of Test matches and one-day internationals in accordance with procedures and guidelines laid down for the referee; and

(b) In the case of other matches, in such manner as ICC shall consider appropriate at the time when the incident occurs. This shall, so far as is practicable, follow the procedures and guidelines laid down for the referee.

Note: A breach of Clause 8 of the Code of Conduct (public pronouncements) should be dealt with by referees during a tour (except where related to a non-international match) and the home board of the player or official concerned in other circumstances.

ICC MATCH REFEREE

Extracts

1. Objective

To act on behalf of ICC:

(a) to see that the full implications of Law 42.1 are properly understood and upheld; and

(b) to ensure that the spirit of the game is observed and the conduct of the game maintained during Test matches and one-day internationals by players, umpires and team officials, either on or off the field, his responsibility being confined to the precincts of the ground.

2. Terms of Reference

(a) To be the independent representative of ICC (appointed by the Chairman or the Chief Executive, after consultation with the Boards concerned), at all Test matches and one-day internationals, the latter being part of a Test match tour, respecting the authority of the host country which is promoting a series, or the ground authority which is administering a match or series of matches.

(b) To liaise with the appointed umpires, but not in any way to interfere with their traditional role.

(c) To carry out the following duties:

(i) Observe and adjudicate upon breaches of the Code of Conduct.

(ii) Impose penalties for failure to maintain the minimum over-rate as set by ICC (presently 15 overs per hour).

(iii) Impose penalties for deliberate acts of unfair play, e.g. the deliberate slowing-down of over-rates and the deliberate speeding-up of overs to make up for any shortfall during a day's play.

(iv) Impose penalties for infringements of the ICC Regulation relating to advertising on cricket clothing and equipment.

(v) Impose penalties incurred under any other ICC Regulation which may be passed from time to time and which falls within the Terms of Reference.

(vi) Ensure the conduct of the game is upheld by the umpires in accordance with the Laws of Cricket and the Playing Conditions as agreed by the two Boards concerned in a series, and to give support to the umpires in this regard if required.

3. Method of Operation

The referee must be present on all days of the match or matches assigned to him from the time the players arrive within the precincts of the ground until a reasonable time after close of play, bearing in mind that reports can be submitted up to one hour after the end of the day's play. He must ensure, in conjunction with the ground authority, that he has a good view of the match and has access to a television monitor and video equipment.

The referee must lay down the standards expected from the players, making it clear that the captains are responsible for their teams and for the good conduct of the game. The referee must make it clear that *no* public criticism of the umpires will be tolerated.

The referee must not interfere with the traditional role of umpires but should urge umpires to be decisive in upholding the Law.

4. Disciplinary Procedures

Should an umpire decide to report a player for an alleged breach of the Code of Conduct or other offence, he must inform the player's captain or manager and the match referee of his intention at the earliest opportunity and complete a report and hand it to the match referee not later than one hour after the close of the day's play . . . the match referee's decision is final.

5. Penalties

The referee may in his absolute discretion impose any penalty by way of reprimand and/or fine and/or suspension including a suspended fine or suspended suspension.

(a) Maximum fine to be imposed for breaches of the Code of Conduct and other ICC Regulations (excluding over-rates) – 75 per cent of a player's match fee.

When on tour, the fine shall be calculated on the last match fee paid to that player in his previous domestic season. If a player did not participate in an international match during his previous domestic season, that player shall be fined on the basis which would have applied had he played in an international match in his previous domestic season.

(b) Maximum suspension to be imposed for breaches of the Code of Conduct and other ICC Regulations – three Test matches.

If any matches of international standard take place between Test matches, the ban will also include these. This ban may well carry over into another future series. In a series of one-day internationals, the maximum suspension will be three internationals but may not be carried over. A player's participation in his own domestic cricket during the period of any ban imposed by the ICC referee will be up to his own Board to determine.

6. Payment of Fines

Fines must be paid within one calendar month by the player(s) to his (their) Board who will, in turn, forward such fine(s) to the Chief Executive of ICC. Any player(s) failing to meet this requirement will be rendered unavailable for selection in any fixture under the control of his (their) own Board.

INTERNATIONAL UMPIRES' PANEL

On December 21, 1993, the International Cricket Council announced the formation of an international umpires' panel, backed by £1.1 million sponsorship over three years from National Grid. Each Full Member of ICC was to nominate two officials – apart from England, who named four, because of their large number of professional umpires and the fact that most Tests take place during the English winter. A third-country member of the panel was to stand with a "home" umpire, not necessarily from the panel, in every Test staged from February 1994. Teams would have no right of objection to appointments.

The following umpires were appointed to serve on the panel from October 1994:
B. L. Aldridge (New Zealand), L. H. Barker (West Indies), H. D. Bird (England), S. A. Bucknor (West Indies), B. C. Cooray (Sri Lanka), R. S. Dunne (New Zealand), K. T. Francis (Sri Lanka), D. B. Hair (Australia), K. Kanjee (Zimbabwe), Khizar Hayat (Pakistan), M. J. Kitchen (England), K. E. Liebenberg (South Africa), Mahboob Shah (Pakistan), C. J. Mitchley (South Africa), N. T. Plews (England), V. K. Ramaswamy (India), S. G. Randell (Australia), I. D. Robinson (Zimbabwe), D. R. Shepherd (England), S. Venkataraghavan (India).

Note: Compared with the 1993-94 list, M. J. Kitchen has replaced K. E. Palmer and C. J. Mitchley has replaced S. B. Lambson.

REGULATIONS FOR FIRST-CLASS MATCHES IN BRITAIN, 1994

Hours of Play

1st, 2nd, 3rd days.... 11.00 a.m. to 6.30 p.m. or after 110 overs, whichever is the later.
4th day .... 11.00 a.m. to 6.00 p.m. or after 102 overs, whichever is the later.

Non-Championship matches:

1st, 2nd days........ 11.30 a.m. to 6.30 p.m. (11.00 a.m. to 6.30 p.m. or after 104 overs, whichever is the later, in tourist matches)
3rd day .... 11.00 a.m. to 6.00 p.m. (or after 96 overs in tourist matches)

Note: The hours of play, including intervals, are brought forward by half an hour for matches scheduled to start in September.

(*a*) If play is suspended (including any interval between innings) the minimum number of overs to be bowled in a day to be reduced by one over for each 3½ minutes or part thereof of such suspension or suspensions in aggregate (including the last hour).

(*b*) If at 5.00 p.m. on the final day, 19 overs or less remain to be bowled, the umpires shall indicate that play shall continue until a minimum of a further 20 overs has been bowled, or until 6.00 p.m., whichever is the later (a minimum of 16 overs must be bowled in tourist matches). Play may cease on the final day at any time between 5.30 p.m. and 6.00 p.m. by mutual agreement of the captains. Should an innings end between 4.50 p.m. and 5.00 p.m., the time at the end of the ten-minute interval to replace 5.00 p.m. (all timings brought forward by half an hour for matches in September).

(*c*) The captains may agree or, in the event of disagreement, the umpires may decide to play 30 minutes (a minimum ten overs, or eight in tourist matches) extra time at the end of the first and/or second day's play (and/or the third day of four) if, in their opinion, it would bring about a definite result on that day. In the event of the possibility of a finish disappearing before the full period has expired, the whole period must be played out. Any time so claimed does not affect the timing for cessation of play on the final day.

(*d*) The minimum number of overs remaining to be bowled in the day shall be shown on the scoreboard.

(*e*) If an innings ends during the course of an over, that part shall count as a full over so far as the minimum number of overs per day is concerned.

(*f*) Notwithstanding any other provision, there shall be no further play on any day, other than the last day, if a wicket falls during the last minimum over within two minutes of the scheduled cessation time or thereafter.

(*g*) If play is suspended for the day in the middle of an over, that over must be completed next day in addition to the minimum overs required that day.

Intervals

Lunch: 1.15 p.m. to 1.55 p.m. (1st, 2nd [3rd] days) in Championship and tourist matches, 1.30 p.m. to 2.10 p.m. in others
1.00 p.m. to 1.40 p.m. (final day)
In the event of lunch being taken early because of a stoppage caused by weather or bad light (Law 16.2), the interval shall be limited to 40 minutes.

Tea: (Championship matches) A tea interval of 20 minutes shall normally be taken at 4.10 p.m. (3.40 p.m. on final day), or when 40 overs or less remain to be bowled. The over in progress shall be completed unless a batsman is out or retires during that over within two minutes of the interval or the players have occasion to leave the field.

(Other matches) 4.10 p.m. to 4.30 p.m. (1st, 2nd [3rd] days), 3.40 p.m. to 4.00 p.m. (final day).

If an innings ends or there is a stoppage caused by weather within 30 minutes of the scheduled time, the tea interval shall be taken immediately. There will be no tea interval if the scheduled timing for the cessation of play is earlier than 5.30 p.m.

Substitutes

(Domestic matches only) Law 2.1 will apply, but in addition:

No substitute may take the field until the player for whom he is to substitute has been absent from the field for five consecutive complete overs, with the exception that if a fieldsman sustains an obvious, serious injury or is taken ill, a substitute shall be allowed immediately. In the event of any disagreement between the two sides as to the seriousness of an injury or illness, the umpires shall adjudicate. If a player leaves the field during an over, the remainder of that over shall not count in the calculation of the five complete overs.

A substitute shall be allowed by right immediately in the event of a cricketer currently playing in a Championship match being required to join the England team for a Test match (or one-day international). Such a substitute may be permitted to bat or bowl in that match, subject to the approval of the TCCB. The player who is substituted may not take further part in the match, even though he might not be required by England. If batting at the time, the player substituted shall be retired "not out" and his substitute may be permitted to bat later in that innings subject to the approval of the TCCB.

Fieldsmen Leaving the Field

ICC regulations apply.

New Ball

The captain of the fielding side shall have the choice of taking the new ball after 100 overs (85 in tourist matches) have been bowled with the old one.

Covering of Pitches and Bowler's Run-up

The whole pitch shall be covered:

(*a*) The night before a match and, if necessary, until the first ball is bowled; and whenever necessary and possible at any time prior to that during the preparation of the pitch.

(*b*) On each night of a match and, if necessary, throughout any rest days.

(*c*) In the event of play being suspended because of bad light or rain, during the hours of play.

The bowler's run-up shall be covered to a distance of at least ten yards, with a width of four yards.

Declarations

Law 14 will apply, but, in addition, a captain may also forfeit his first innings, subject to the provisions set out in Law 14.2. If, owing to weather conditions, a County Championship match has not started when fewer than eight hours of playing time remain, the first innings of each side shall automatically be forfeited and a one-innings match played.

MEETINGS IN 1994

TCCB SPRING MEETING

At its spring meeting on March 8 and 9, the Test and County Cricket Board announced that Ray Illingworth was to be the new chairman of selectors, having defeated another former England captain, M. J. K. Smith, in a postal ballot. No voting figures were given. At a press conference after the announcement, Illingworth said: "The players work hard enough running round the ground but not hard enough at the basics of cricket." Dennis Silk, the president of MCC, was elected as the next chairman of the TCCB to succeed Frank Chamberlain from October 1, the day after his MCC term expired. The Board decided to form a new committee to consider ways of maximising income from the Test grounds. It was decided to make the role of Harry Brind, the Board's part-time pitches consultant, full-time on his retirement from his job at Surrey after the 1994 season. The Board was unable to agree on a scheme to revamp the Benson and Hedges Cup; a plan that would have involved the inclusion of Holland was shelved.

MCC ANNUAL GENERAL MEETING

At the 207th annual general meeting of the Marylebone Cricket Club, held on May 4, the President, Dennis Silk, announced that his successor for two years from October 1 would be Sir Oliver Popplewell. The annual report was adopted, mentioning MCC's support of the Minor Counties and the European Cricket Federation and its role in funding Conrad Hunte as MCC coaching representative for all Africa as well as national development coach for South Africa. A resolution to increase subscriptions in 1995 was approved. At a special general meeting after the AGM approval was given for the redevelopment of the indoor cricket school. Membership of the club on December 31, 1993, was 19,549, made up of 16,935 full members, 1,996 associate members, 535 honorary members and 83 senior members. There were 9,835 candidates awaiting election. In 1993, 484 vacancies arose.

ICC ANNUAL CONFERENCE

The International Cricket Council's full members' meeting at Lord's on July 5 abandoned the regulation permitting only one bouncer per batsman per over in Test matches. An Australian proposal allowing two bouncers per over regardless of which batsman was facing was accepted instead, to run for three years from October 1, 1994. A new definition was devised to be used in an experimental law which supersedes Law 42.8 in Test cricket, emphasising that the bowling of bouncers is unfair – whether or not there have been two in an over – if it is likely that the batsman will be hurt. The no-ball that would result from a third bouncer would be worth two runs, plus any runs scored. It was decided that the number of referees used to control matches would be reduced and they would be expected to be sterner on indiscipline. "We are aiming for more consistency," Sir Clyde Walcott, the ICC chairman, said. "We are opposed to indiscipline in any form and we expect the referees to be tougher, issuing especially stiff penalties for the second offence." The meeting also decided to ban tournaments involving more than four full member countries in order to protect the World Cup. It adopted the English regulation barring players who have not fielded from batting for the length of time they have been off the field. It ruled that, where "traffic lights" are used to display the decision of the third umpire, red must mean out, and green not out – reversing the colour scheme of the original South African prototype. The above decisions, affecting only Test-playing countries, were reported to the full ICC annual conference the following day. The conference, where associate members can also vote, decided that a player representing one country at under-19 level or above will be allowed to play for another country only after four years, or two years if he was born in the country he wishes to play for. Dates for the next World Cup in India, Pakistan and Sri Lanka were formally agreed: February 14 to March 17, 1996. The following World Cup, in England, was put back until 1999 and future tournaments will be held at four-yearly intervals rather than three, meaning that South Africa's first Cup will be in early 2003. Sir Clyde Walcott was re-elected as ICC chairman for a further three years.

TCCB SUMMER MEETING

At its summer meeting on August 16, the Test and County Cricket Board approved the four-year deal negotiated with the BBC and BSkyB Television whereby the Board would receive £58.5 million for Tests and one-day competitions between 1995 and 1998, an increase of about 50 per cent. Under the deal, the BBC would continue to show live coverage of Tests and the NatWest Trophy, while BSkyB would show the Texaco Trophy and the Benson and Hedges Cup. The BBC would present highlights of these two competitions in prime time i.e. between eight and ten p.m., and agreed to start three-quarters of its other nightly highlight programmes before 11.15 p.m. After a discussion initiated by Lancashire, counties agreed to a moratorium on signing overseas players beyond 1996 until the December meeting pending a possible ban. It was agreed to start a new Under-17 county competition, organised regionally, from 1995.

TCCB WINTER MEETING

At its winter meeting on December 7 and 8, the Test and County Cricket Board unanimously approved the idea of an English Cricket Board to take over its functions and those of the Cricket Council and National Cricket Association. The provisional mission statement of the new Board read: "To promote and develop the well-being and enjoyment of the game of cricket by encouraging participation and interest in the national summer game from the playground to the Test arena, and to strive for the highest standards of excellence throughout the country, and to attain success at all levels of international competition, and to maintain and build upon the long-established traditions and spirit of the game." The Board decided to maintain the status quo on overseas players, with a moratorium on contracts extending beyond 1998 to allow for the possibility of a complete ban in 1999 when the World Cup is in England. After a lengthy discussion on pitches, it was agreed that they should be designed to encourage spin bowling, but there was disagreement about how this might be done; there was some support for the idea of allowing pitches to be barer at the ends than in the middle. The Pitches Committee were asked to reconsider this problem and the 25-point penalty.

PRESIDENTS OF MCC SINCE 1970-71

1970-71	Sir Cyril Hawker	1982-83	Sir Anthony Tuke
1971-72	F. R. Brown	1983-84	A. H. A. Dibbs
1972-73	A. M. Crawley	1984-85	F. G. Mann
1973-74	Lord Caccia	1985-86	J. G. W. Davies
1974-75	HRH The Duke of Edinburgh	1986-87	M. C. Cowdrey
1975-76	C. G. A. Paris	1987-88	J. J. Warr
1976-77	W. H. Webster	1988-89	Field Marshal The Lord Bramhall
1977-78	D. G. Clark	1989-90	The Hon. Sir Denys Roberts
1978-79	C. H. Palmer	1990-91	The Rt Hon. The Lord Griffiths
1979-80	S. C. Griffith	1991-92	M. E. L. Melluish
1980-81	P. B. H. May	1992-94	D. R. W. Silk
1981-82	G. H. G. Doggart	1994-	The Hon. Sir Oliver Popplewell

Since 1951, Presidents of MCC have taken office on October 1. Since 1992, Presidents have been eligible for two consecutive years of office.

PART SIX: MISCELLANEOUS

CHRONICLE OF 1994

JANUARY

11 Hyderabad reach 944 for six, the fourth-highest total in history, in Ranji Trophy match against Andhra, three batsmen passing 200, an unprecedented feat. **12** Pakistan Board sacked by the state president and replaced by a three-man ad hoc committee. **16** Wasim Akram sacked as Pakistan captain after players' rebellion over selection. Salim Malik appointed. **30** In Bangalore, Kapil Dev equals Sir Richard Hadlee's 431 Test wickets.

FEBRUARY

1 Peter Kirsten of South Africa fined a second time for dissent in the Adelaide Test. Australia square the three-Test series 1-1. **8** In Ahmedabad, Kapil Dev has Hashan Tillekeratne caught at forward short leg, his 432nd Test wicket, passing Hadlee. **14** Amol Muzumdar, 19, makes 260 for Bombay v Haryana, the highest score on first-class debut, beating W. F. E. Marx's 240; Ian Healy makes 11 dismissals for Australians v Northern Transvaal.

MARCH

1 CPP "1", a consortium of cable operators unknown to the public, announces it has won the UK TV rights to the 1996 World Cup. **6** Crowd trouble halts a one-day international between New Zealand and Pakistan in Auckland. **9** Ray Illingworth named as new chairman of England selectors, having beaten M. J. K. Smith in TCCB ballot. **30** England bowled out for 46, their lowest score this century, as West Indies win the Port-of-Spain Test, and the Wisden Trophy for the 11th consecutive time.

APRIL

7 Sri Lankan captain Arjuna Ranatunga and five of the seven selectors resign after the whole international squad fails a mandatory fitness test; Brian Lara signs for Warwickshire. **12** Alec Stewart becomes first England player to score two centuries in a match against West Indies. **13** England become first team in 59 years to beat West Indies in a Barbados Test. **15** Fred Titmus and Brian Bolus elected to the new England selection panel under Ray Illingworth. **18** In the Antigua Test against England, Brian Lara scores 375, the highest individual score in Test cricket; Sir Garfield Sobers, who had held the record for 36 years, goes on to the field to shake his hand. **27** England bowler Phil Tufnell spends the night in a police cell after being arrested for allegedly beating up his ex-lover. **28** Phil Simmons of Leicestershire becomes the first player to score a double-century on debut in the County Championship.

MAY

11 Allan Border, Australia's captain since 1984, angrily announces his retirement from international cricket, in the mistaken belief that officials were pushing him. **15** Imran Khan resigns from ICC's cricket committee after admitting in his biography that he had once illegally roughened a ball in a county match in 1981. **19** Mark Taylor named as Border's successor as Australian captain. **23** Brian Lara becomes fifth man in history to score five successive first-class centuries.

JUNE

3 At Edgbaston, Brian Lara becomes first batsman to score seven centuries in eight innings. **6** Lara takes his score for Warwickshire against Durham to 501 not out, the highest in the history of first-class cricket.

JULY

2 Richard Johnson of Middlesex becomes the first player for 30 years to take ten wickets in an innings in a first-class match in England: ten for 45 at Derby. **9** Warwickshire win Benson and Hedges Cup. **23** TV pictures appear to show England captain Mike Atherton rubbing something on to the ball during the Lord's Test against South Africa. Alamgir Sheriyar of Leicestershire becomes the first player since 1906 to take a hat-trick on Championship debut. **24** South Africa win the Lord's Test, their first against England in 29 years, by 356 runs; Atherton denies cheating but admits having dirt in his pocket and not confessing this to the referee when asked – Ray Illingworth, chairman of selectors, fines him £2,000. West Indies captain Richie Richardson leaves Yorkshire because of exhaustion and plans a long break. **29** Jamie Hall of Sussex scores the slowest 50 in County Championship history, taking 302 minutes.

AUGUST

4 Courtney Walsh named to replace Richardson as West Indies captain for the tour of India. **10** David Acfield defeats Brian Close to become chairman of TCCB cricket committee in succession to Ossie Wheatley. **14** West Indies Board announce plan to put leading players on winter contracts. **16** TCCB announce new £58.5 million TV contract for next four years, giving one-day internationals to satellite channel, BSkyB. **19** Second Test between Sri Lanka and Pakistan cancelled because of political tension. Mike Atherton fined half of his match fee at the Oval Test by referee Peter Burge for dissent. **20** Devon Malcolm takes nine for 57 for England against South Africa at The Oval, the sixth-best bowling figures in Test history. **21** England win the Oval Test by eight wickets to tie the series 1-1. **30** Geoff Marsh announces retirement from first-class cricket. **31** Graham Gooch becomes the 15th player to score 40,000 runs.

SEPTEMBER

2 Warwickshire win County Championship. **4** Warwickshire's hopes of an unprecedented grand slam disappear when they lose the NatWest final to Worcestershire. **8** Ravi Shastri announces his retirement from first-class cricket. **18** Warwickshire win Sunday League to complete unprecedented treble of domestic competitions. Mike Procter sacked as South African coach. **22** Harold Larwood, 89, collapses after being presented with his MBE in Sydney. **24** Bob Woolmer, the Warwickshire coach, named as Procter's successor.

OCTOBER

9 In Rawalpindi, Damien Fleming of Australia becomes the third man in history to take a hat-trick on Test debut. **14** Victoria begin wearing shorts to play their one-day Mercantile Mutual Cup fixtures. **21** In Bulawayo, Dave Houghton becomes the first player to score a Test double-century for Zimbabwe, 266 against Sri Lanka. **24** Assassination of Sri Lankan Board president and state presidential candidate Gamini Dissanayake. **26** In Gujranwala, at least 60 people reported injured in a crowd stampede at one-day international between Pakistan and Australia. **27** England lose an experimental "quartered" one-day match to Western Australia in which the innings were split. In Goa, Brian Lara becomes the second player (following Aqib Javed in 1992-93) to be suspended from international cricket for a match, for dissent in a one-day game against New Zealand.

NOVEMBER

2 Kapil Dev, leading wicket-taker in Test cricket, announces his retirement. **3** Kepler Wessels resigns as South African captain "to concentrate on batting". **13** The *Sunday Mirror* alleges that Essex and Lancashire conspired to rig two matches in 1991, "categorically denied" by the players involved. **24** Sheffield Shield game between Western Australia and Queensland played in Perth believed to be the first ever first-class match under floodlights.

DECEMBER

14 West Indies beat India in the Third Test at Mohali to level the series 1-1 and stretch their 14-year-old unbeaten record in Test series to 28 rubbers (including one-off Tests). **18** Brian Lara dismissed at Sydney Cricket Ground by a woman: for 23, by Australian Test player Zoe Goss in a charity match. **20** Kepler Wessels retires from international cricket. **27** Former England captain Peter May dies, aged 64. **29** Shane Warne takes a hat-trick against England in Melbourne Test as Australia take 2-0 lead in Ashes series.

The following were also among the cricketing items reported in the press during 1994:

Denise Annetts, who has won 13 Test caps, claimed she had been omitted from the Australian national women's team because she was not a lesbian. Her complaint was rejected by the selectors, who said she had lost form, and by Australia's Anti-Discrimination Board, which said it was illegal to discriminate against homosexuals but not heterosexuals. (*The Times*, January 18)

Corey Hojnacki, 19, scored 426 out of a total of 710 for Heinz Southern Districts against Silverton in the Dandenong and District Association C grade, adding 338 on Saturday to the 88 he scored a week earlier. He hit 31 sixes and 36 fours. Hojnacki's own bat had been stolen and he used his father's old "Austral" bat. "It's as thick as a tree trunk," Hojnacki said. "I only had to block and the ball went for four." (*Herald-Sun*, Melbourne, February 28)

The match between Methodists and Sandown Park in the Dandenong and District Cricket Association, Victoria, was declared a draw ten days after it finished, following four hearings, when local officials finally sought advice from MCC. Methodists lost their ninth wicket to the last available ball and Sandown claimed victory because they knew the last man was missing. (*Sunday Age*, Melbourne, March 13)

Durham County Cricket Club were cleared of racial discrimination by an industrial tribunal in Newcastle upon Tyne after a student, Joher Yaqub, sent two letters asking for a trial. He was rejected but his alter ego "Tom Jacobs" was asked for more details. The chairman dismissed the application, saying the letters were clearly different. (*Daily Telegraph*, March 17)

The father of the fourth bride in the successful film *Four Weddings and a Funeral* was played by Rupert Webb, the Sussex wicket-keeper from 1948 to 1960. (*Daily Telegraph*, May 2)

Two three-inch wartime mortar bombs, one of them live, were discovered by a contractor excavating for a new concrete practice wicket at the Abbey Lawns, Bourne, Lincolnshire. Bomb disposal experts staged a controlled explosion which showered the nearby square with soil. (*Bourne Local*, May 12)

Sharon Scott of Kington, Herefordshire, was taken to hospital for observation after being hit on the head by a six struck by her husband, Clive (who played in the 1993 village final at Lord's), while she was wheeling their baby round the boundary. "She probably cost me a century," Clive said. "I went into my shell for a while after that." (*Hereford Times*, May 12)

Thomas Seward, 11, and Nicholas Brothers, ten, shared an unbroken opening stand of 235 for Oakley Hall Prep School, Cirencester, against Beaudesert School, Stroud. (*Daily Express*, May 14)

The match between Codicote and Luton College in the North Hertfordshire League was abandoned after a Luton bowler kicked an umpire for rejecting a run-out appeal. The Codicote players walked off in protest. (*Daily Telegraph*, May 21)

Thieves failed in an attempt to steal the artificial wicket at Coaver Cricket Club, Exeter, when they discovered it was too heavy to carry. (*Independent on Sunday*, June 5)

The match between Marsden and South Hetton in the Durham Coast League was left drawn after Marsden batted throughout the allotted five hours, scored 136 for six, and then left. One batsman, Tony Shields, scored four not out in 187 minutes. South Hetton captain Bobby Steel had insisted on Marsden batting first because he said their captain Colin Marshall had not spun the coin within the required time. (*Newcastle Journal*, June 6)

Burton Latimer beat Weldon in the Corby & District Under-15 League without scoring a run off the bat. Weldon were all out for three in 5.4 overs, with Jeremy Nicholls and Carl Davidson taking five wickets each, then conceded four wides in the first over they bowled. (*Northamptonshire Evening Telegraph*, June 18)

A judge who asked to borrow a television to watch the Lord's Test against New Zealand while the jury was out at Maidstone Crown Court was refused by security guards: they were watching Royal Ascot. (*Daily Telegraph*, June 18)

Mark Hubbard, who plays for Seaton in the Devon League, received seven stitches in his testicles after they were caught by a hook on a sightscreen he was repairing. (*Sidmouth Midweek Herald*, June 22)

Alex Kelly, a 17-year-old schoolboy, took ten wickets for no runs – all bowled – in 27 deliveries, bowling medium-pace for Bishop Auckland against Newton Aycliffe in the Durham County Junior League. Kelly took two wickets with his first three balls, three in his second over, two in both his third and fourth, and one in the fifth. He came on to bowl when Newton Aycliffe were 36 for nought; they were all out for 47. "I have never played so well before," he said, "and the only thing I can think of was that I was angry because I'd been dropped to number four in the batting order." John Wisden is the only player to have bowled all ten in first-class cricket. (*Newcastle Journal/Daily Telegraph*, June 25)

The England bowler Phil DeFreitas was praised for saving the life of an elderly neighbour at Bretby, Derbyshire, whose kitchen caught fire. DeFreitas climbed through a window and, when he found 85-year-old Ted Graham asleep in the smoke-filled room, carried him to safety. (*Daily Express*, June 28)

Play in the Barbados League match between St John the Baptist and Police was halted when Fidel Castro, the President of Cuba and a former baseball player, stopped as he was being driven past the ground and asked if he could try the game. Castro, in his military uniform, faced three balls from a Police bowler and missed them all before thanking his hosts and leaving. (*Caribbean Cricket Quarterly*, July)

The match between Dominica and Grenada in the Windward Islands tournament at Windsor Park, Dominica, was abandoned midway through the final day when a mob protesting against an increase in motor licence fees invaded the field and uprooted the stumps. Protesters said their views were being ignored: the island's radio station was broadcasting the cricket. (*Caribbean Cricket Quarterly*, July)

The former England captain Brian Close, playing in a charity match for Norma Major's XI against the EMP Bunburys, was caught one-handed in the gully by the former Rolling Stone Bill Wyman, who had a cigarette in his other hand. (*Daily Express*, July 22)

Wayne Killian of Offchurch scored 408 in a Coventry League Division Four match, out of a team total of 555 for four declared off 44 overs against the Hinckley club, Ashby Road. Killian, who was batting with one knee strapped because of injury, hit 18 sixes and 62 fours. Ashby Road, bowled out for 117, lost by 438 runs. It was Offchurch's first season in the League. "I think they put us in the wrong division," said one of their players, Mike Kiernan. (*Warwick Courier*, July 22)

An armed umpire officiated in a match played by Lady Gass's XI against the village team at Holford, Somerset. He was the bodyguard of the former Northern Ireland secretary Tom King. Among those he gave out was King himself, run out for nought. (*The Times*, August 3)

The League fixture between Manor House and Barnsley in Yorkshire was abandoned after the Barnsley fielders refused to retrieve a ball that had gone for six. The umpires awarded the match to Manor House under Law 21. One umpire, Brian Exley, said the incident was the culmination of a "shambolic, disgusting display". Only three Barnsley players were present for the scheduled start; several played in non-cricket gear and one, who had batted in whites, changed into a red T-shirt and shorts to field. (*Barnsley Chronicle*, August 12)

Wally Lloyd, a spectator at a match between Kington and a Herefordshire Select XI, caught an escaped pet kestrel on the outfield by tempting it with a piece of ham. (*Western Daily Press*, August 17)

A ball bowled by Chris Thomas at Trimdon, Co. Durham, hit and killed a swallow and was deflected on to batsman Joe Hall's stumps. After a long conference, the umpires ruled that the delivery was missing the stumps, declared the ball dead as well as the swallow, and said Hall was not out. (*The Sun*, August 27)

Ivor McIvor of Fochabers, Morayshire, who at 73 claims to be Britain's oldest village league cricketer, received a letter of congratulations from the Prime Minister after concluding his 48th season. "I don't know if he's the oldest but he's certainly the most stupid. He's had nine operations for varicose veins and he still insists on playing," said his wife Rita. (*The Times*, September 9)

Lash Dem Lara, a three-year-old roan colt named after Brian Lara, won the Trinidad Derby in record time. The horse was bred, owned and trained by members of the Hadeed family who, like Lara, were educated at Fatima College. (*Caribbean Cricket Quarterly*, October)

The match between the South African Under-19 team and the Northern Transvaal Colts at the Correctional Services ground in Pretoria was reduced from 55 overs a side to 50 after the start was delayed because the stumps had been stolen. (*SA Cricket Action*, October)

A vicar who swore and bowled roast potatoes at fellow-guests while speaking at the Minehead club dinner was pardoned by his bishop after apologising for having "one drink too many". Rev. Richard Allen, vicar of

Williton, Somerset, was finally led from the room after spilling coffee into the club president's lap. "I may be a vicar," he said, "but I am an ordinary man." (*Daily Telegraph*, October 7)

Mohammed Isaq was banned for three years by the Quaid-e-Azam league in Yorkshire after sending in a fictitious score showing that his team Horton Print had beaten Bradford Shalima and thus won promotion; the game had actually been cancelled because they could not find a pitch. (*News of the World*, November 20)

The former West Indian captain Viv Richards apologised to Prince Charles after forgetting to collect his OBE at Buckingham Palace. (*Daily Express*, December 2)

New Earswick Cricket Club in Yorkshire paid £105 for a £10,000 carpet with the letters NCC woven into it. The carpet became a symbol of bureaucratic waste when a government agency threw it out after only three years because the Funding Agency for Schools had taken over from the National Curriculum Council. "The lettering is near enough," said club trustee Geoff Clarkson, "and it also happens to match our colour scheme." (*The Guardian*, December 8)

Further to the report in *Wisden* 1994, researchers at the University of Durham have now concluded that left-handed bowlers are not necessarily likely to die younger than right-handers. However, left-handed bowlers have proved more likely to die in warfare; this may be because equipment and training are designed for right-handers. (*British Medical Journal*, December 24)

Four per cent of county cricketers have red-green colour-blindness, according to researchers at the Royal Free Hospital, London. This compares to eight per cent in the general male population. The batting averages of the 12 players involved were not significantly lower than normal, and the white ball seemed to make no difference to them, suggesting that they somehow found a way of seeing a red ball on a green pitch. (*British Medical Journal*, December 24)

A London insurance broker paid £6,000 at a benefit auction for a short-sleeved shirt said to have been worn by Brian Lara during his innings of 375. Tipped off by a friend, he later watched the video and discovered that Lara wore a long-sleeved shirt throughout. (*Daily Telegraph*, December 29)

Contributions from readers for this feature are very welcome, particularly from local or non-UK newspapers. Please send them to the editor, with the title and date of the publication clearly marked.

CRICKET BOOKS, 1994

By CHRISTOPHER BOOKER

It is an odd experience reading through a year's ration of cricket books. It brings home vividly how one of the deepest reasons we love cricket – and why it has produced more good literature than all other sports put together – is the unique way in which it appeals to our love of story-telling.

Far more subtly and intricately than other games, any cricket match unfolds through all its various stages like a story. And what we value above all when we read about the game is a well-told tale – an account of some particular match or Test series perhaps, preferably with dramatic reversals of fortune, or an essay on some outstanding player. Always, of course, this must be underpinned by the foundation of scores and statistics which are so essential to our appreciation of the tale, coupled with the historical references and analysis which help us better to understand the "plot", where the game has come from and how it stands now. But all this becomes woven together into that incredibly rich mythology we all share, peopled by a host of players dead and alive, each adding the colour of his individual personality to the game, and extended with the fresh dramas of each new year that passes. And it is precisely because we find all these ingredients together in *Wisden* that it will always remain the backbone of cricket literature.

Against this, how does the past year's crop of cricket books measure up? The list includes the biographies of two players whose names will be forever linked. And, if I have a personal reason for kicking off with Edrich and Compton, it is because they were where I myself began. I remember, as a small boy, buying my first *Wisden* on holiday down in Devon in that sunlit September of 1947, when all England was agog to see whether Compton could beat Hobbs's record of 16 centuries in a season and Hayward's record, of 3,518 runs. In one innings at the Hastings Festival he passed them both. This was followed by that unbelievable climax at The Oval, where, against The Rest, the Middlesex twins crowned their incredible summer, Compton with 246 and Edrich with 180, which also edged him ahead of Hayward.

Alan Hill's **Bill Edrich: A Biography**, with a foreword by Compton, opens 15 years before those glory days of 1947, with the picture of a 16-year-old schoolboy facing one of the fastest bowlers of the time, Mohammad Nissar of All-India. Norfolk were 21 for five. By the time they were all out for 49, Nissar six for 14, the young farmer's son had stayed in for 40 minutes, scoring 20. It is an appropriately dramatic opening to a most engaging account of Bill Edrich's battling career. Time is spent on such highlights as his 1,000 in May in 1938 (to be pedantic, 989 in May and 21 in April), his marathon 219 in the Durban timeless Test, his heroic war – including the day Squadron Leader Edrich destroyed an enemy vessel before 9 a.m., fought a desperate air battle over the Channel before 11, scored 80 in under half an hour before tea, then had a rendezvous with a handsome village girl in the evening. And then, of course, the three wonderful years after the war, when he was such a mainstay of England's batting and attack. In 1954, having been put in hospital by a Frank Tyson bumper which fractured his cheekbone, he insisted on resuming next morning, to be greeted by Tyson with another ferocious bouncer. With head bandaged, he made 20, and facing Tyson again a week later, at Northampton, hit 102. What makes this book particularly delightful is partly the happy account of Edrich's later years – when he almost led Norfolk to the Minor Counties title, and at the age of 54 was still capable of hitting 93 not out in 24 overs – but even more the picture it conjures up of an irrepressible personality, lovable if not always easy to live with, particularly for his succession of long-suffering wives.

One turns in eager anticipation to its companion volume, somewhat portentously titled **Denis: The Authorized Biography of the Incomparable Compton** by Tim Heald. The book opens with a rambling account of the author meeting the great man to discuss his book at Lord's during the 1993 Test against Australia, dropping rather too many names of minor celebrities who happened to be on hand. When the story proper begins, it is clear that the author has been industrious enough, but the stage machinery becomes intrusive. Here he quotes from *Wisden* or a *Times* cutting, there from an anecdote by Ian Peebles, who we are informed was "a fine spinner of the ball", until one has the sense that we are looking back at Compton's career only through the wrong end of a very long telescope. It is strange to see the drama of such a magical progress across the cricket grounds of the world reduced to such pedestrian prose. There is a throwaway reference to the extraordinary wartime game in which Sergeant-Instructor Compton scored 249 not out in the final innings of what was then the highest-scoring match of all time, Holkar v Bombay. Even the account of the golden summer of 1947 is curiously flat, with no sense of that mounting excitement we all felt as the season came to its fairy-tale climax. Compton's 300 in 181 minutes at Benoni is even described by way of playwright Ronald Harwood's memory of a film he once saw of the innings, Arsenal's Cup Final victory in 1950 on the basis of an old newsreel. And by the time Compton limps off the stage into his long years of perfunctorily described retirement, one has never once felt that electricity which used to charge the air as a packed house at Lord's watched one of the most charismatic figures in cricket history cheekily cutting and sweeping his way to another hundred.

Another figure who remarkably quickly became identified with English cricket in those early post-war years was John Arlott, although his charisma lay in his gravelly Hampshire burr over the airwaves. In **John Arlott: A Memoir**, his son Tim Arlott has written a very moving account of the policeman-poet who rose from obscurity to become the best-known of all commentators, all the more effective for the simple, direct fashion in which he conveys not only his father's charm and virtues but also his failings.

The story opens on a note of horror – the New Year's night of 1965 when Arlott's eldest son Jim, the author's brother, drove off into the darkness, and an hour or two later a policeman stumbled into the house to say that he had been found dead in a car crash. And one cannot do better than the author's own words to sum up the story he then sets out to tell, of "the best story-teller and most diverting company you could ever meet; a talker, listener, enthusiast, funny, lovable, shrewd and wise beyond credit; who got divorced, lost his eldest son, young wife and a baby in successive and terrible blows and became – partly because of these blows and two strokes – a selfish, demanding, limited and impossible old man." The son deserves all credit for the deft and humorous way in which he has reconstructed his father's early life, obviously drawing on many a well-polished paternal anecdote.

He gives us an outline of the public career, including journalism and politics. But the book is above all a picture of the private Arlott, as he enlarged his confidence and horizons, developing his interests in wine and

book collecting, and casually abandoning his first wife for his second, blissfully happy, marriage to his secretary Valerie. This golden period of the sixties, when his commentating and cricket writing were at their expansive best, was first punctuated by the death of his son Jim, then ten years later abruptly ended by that of Valerie herself. After he had been battered by these shocks, although he married once more, Arlott's cricket commentating lost much of its old joyous, bubbling energy. His voice thickened, he began to find it all a chore and, by his own choice, during the 1980 Centenary Test at Lord's, he signed off. He simply handed over to Trevor Bailey at the end of an over, without a word to listeners that they had heard him for the last time – although he was deeply moved when the whole ground rose in a standing ovation. As his son says, with loving honesty, his last years on Alderney were increasingly sad, although he was visited by a continual stream of cricket-loving friends like Ian Botham, and he kept up contributing this yearly book review to *Wisden* to the end of his life, which came just before Christmas in 1991.

One thing which can never really be recaptured about John Arlott is the sheer spontaneous magic of him talking about cricket, his plucking from the air of the *mot juste* to describe a player or a pigeon running over the ground, the way he could invest any match with romance, his throwaway humour. During one Test when Australia reached 400, I recall him soliloquising that this was "quite a score . . . in fact, when you think about it, it's a score of scores". It is hard for David Rayvern Allen in his **Arlott: The Authorised Biography** to compete with the son's version, and not seem as though he is just reconstructing the story at second hand. But he does it competently enough, and he at least includes one thing Tim omits, by giving transcripts of some authentic Arlott commentary – although, as I say, without the voice and the occasion, that magic is really impossible to recreate.

The other more recent loss from the *Test Match Special* team is, of course, the ebullient figure commemorated by many of his friends in **Summers Will Never Be The Same: A Tribute to Brian Johnston**, edited by Christopher Martin-Jenkins and Pat Gibson. Contributors range from politicians like John Major, who supplied the title, and Lord Whitelaw to Richie Benaud, Trevor Bailey, Colin Cowdrey and Godfrey Evans, who recalls how, when he was working for Ladbrokes, Johnston would hail him with a cry of, "Ah, here comes Godders with the odders from Ladders." Much of this book is in similar after-dinner anecdotal vein. But even those who found the Johnston style not entirely their cup of tea, or plate of cake, would find it hard to skim through without feeling more warmly about a man who made cricket sound fun even to those who knew nothing of the game.

The careers of Arlott and "Johnners" bridge that far-off post-war era with the cricket of the recent past, and three books marking the departure of "superstars" of our own time. One day someone may write a proper account of the meteoric career of the Somerset boy who exploded through the late 1970s and 1980s as one of the most dazzling, exasperating all-rounders ever to dominate a cricket field. But, as one might expect, **Botham: My Autobiography** is a maundering, self-justifying, two-dimensional ramble, not particularly aimed at a cricket-loving audience. **Beyond Ten Thousand: My Life Story** by Allan Border is an even more perfunctory hack job, which whisks us through the career of the batsman who compiled more Test runs than anyone else in the hyped-up fashion of a commentator on Kerry Packer's Channel Nine.

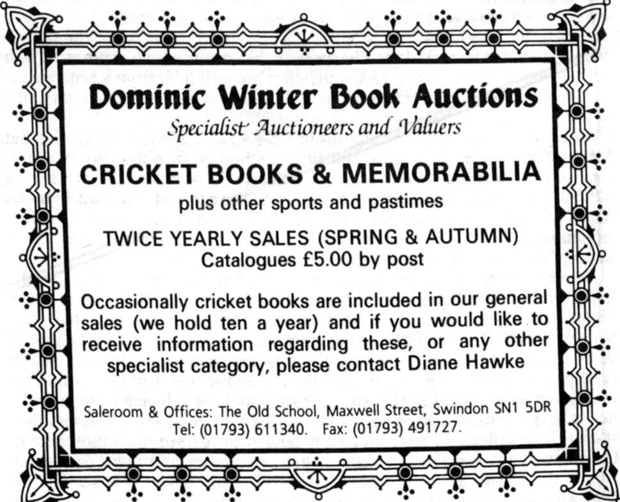

Dominic Winter Book Auctions
Specialist Auctioneers and Valuers
CRICKET BOOKS & MEMORABILIA
plus other sports and pastimes
TWICE YEARLY SALES (SPRING & AUTUMN)
Catalogues £5.00 by post
Occasionally cricket books are included in our general sales (we hold ten a year) and if you would like to receive information regarding these, or any other specialist category, please contact Diane Hawke
Saleroom & Offices: The Old School, Maxwell Street, Swindon SN1 5DR
Tel: (01793) 611340. Fax: (01793) 491727.

A biography of a cricketer which includes full-page pictures of his girlfriends – rather than his wives, like some of this year's subjects – means that it must be Imran Khan, one of the supreme examples of the way our tabloid and television age has turned cricketers into "celebrities". This is reflected in Ivo Tennant's life story, **Imran Khan**, which begins in a modest middle-class suburb of Lahore and on the small family farm in the Indus valley, takes us through Oxford and the night-club round of London in the 1980s, to culminate in Pakistan's triumph in the 1992 World Cup. This Imran was determined to inspire his team to win, not least because it would boost his fund-raising for the cancer hospital to commemorate his mother. Yet the irony is that Imran was not only one of the most dynamic fast bowlers and all-rounders the game has known, but is a highly perceptive writer, capable himself of producing a much more illuminating book on the cricket of his time than this.

In fact, the pick of the biographies of contemporary players is of one who has not yet fully retired. **Kepler: The Biography** by Edward Griffiths tells the story of the rather dour, determined little cricket-mad boy from Orange Free State who grew up to have his career shaped by two of the great cricketing dramas of our time – the isolation of South Africa from the international scene, and the Packer circus which did so much to create the media and money-dominated modern game. At the age of 18, young Kepler Wessels found himself playing for Sussex under his fellow South African Tony Greig. This led to his recruitment to the breakaway World Series squad, to his playing for Australia during those roller-coaster days under Kim Hughes and Allan Border of the mid-1980s, and finally, as the fairy-tale happy ending, South Africa's return to world cricket, with Wessels eventually taking over as captain. The difference between this and the preceding books is that cricket is firmly centre-stage, although the touching picture of Wessels's marriage (to an Australian) shows what a strength this has been in his battle through the tempests of modern cricket. The tales of his many heroic innings in tight corners and of a succession of key matches are well told, from a school game to his Tests. Forget mere "personality" – this is the inspiring story of a cricketer with real character.

After those three stunning months in 1994 when a 25-year-old Trinidadian hit the highest-ever Test score and then the highest first-class innings of all time, it was inevitable that at least one book would be rushed out to mark the 375/501 double. Jack Bannister's **Brian Lara: The Story of a Record-Breaking Year**, packed with pictures and all the relevant statistics, concisely summarises Lara's short career and is a perfect commemoration of an earthquake which made all batting records seem suddenly unreal.

It might seem odd to get too pessimistic about the overall condition of a game which can still produce a Lara or a Shane Warne. Indulgence in gloom about "the state of cricket" has been with us as long as mutterings about "the state of the novel", and with considerably less justification. But in the past 15 years concern has centred on a cluster of issues, many of which at a deeper level become linked. There has been the rise in the power of money and the marketing men, linked to the way television and the tabloids have turned a newly harsh, intrusive glare on cricket, seeing it more as show business than sport. These influences have inevitably tended to coarsen the atmosphere of the game at the top level, making it harder, brasher and more egotistical. And if this has built up the sense of aggression in cricket, it has coincided with an era particularly associated with relentless barrages of fast, often

intimidatory bowling. Such is the theme of one of the best books of the year, **Letting Rip: The Fast-Bowling Threat From Lillee to Waqar** by Simon Wilde.

The book opens with the gripping device of putting the reader in to open the innings with Geoffrey Boycott against West Indies at Lord's in the early 1980s. For eighty minutes one is standing there, trying to survive against the successive onslaught of Michael Holding, Malcolm Marshall, Colin Croft and Joel Garner, probably the most terrifying quartet of fast bowlers ever to play in a side together. Just reading about it leaves one limp. It is a brilliant introduction to a superb analysis of the domination of Test cricket by fast bowling in the past twenty years. The real skill of the book is to see it all the way from the batsman's point of view. How have the leading players of the past two decades managed to cope with this terrifying physical and mental ordeal which, as a table at the end reminds us, has led to more than a hundred broken bones and other serious injuries?

Some outstanding batsmen, such as Glenn Turner and Zaheer Abbas, cracked. Some of the most heroic resistance has come from players below the top rank, like David Steele against Lillee and Thomson in 1975. Many brave and skilful players succeeded for a while, like Lamb in 1984. No one ever wholly mastered what at one time became so brutal and oppressive a force in cricket – those 200 bouncers in a day at Sabina Park – that it threatened to upset the whole equilibrium of the game. But nothing in cricket stands still. Proportion and balance returned, not least with the emergence of a spinner, Warne, as the most feared bowler in the world. And Wilde ends with a tribute to Waqar Younis and Wasim Akram as the new fast-bowling kings, who have developed skills which he suggests even Curtly Ambrose would use, if only he knew how. Perhaps the only slight imbalance in his splendid book is its paucity of historical reference to similar episodes in the past, as when Lindwall knocked Compton about in 1948, or Larwood put Ponsford out of the 1928-29 series as a portent of the shadow that was to descend on cricket four years later.

A favourite sub-plot to the perennial introspection over "what's wrong with cricket?" is the local version, "why is English cricket so awful?", with such variants as "why is England now in the second division?", "why doesn't England produce fast bowlers any more?" or "why did they drop David Gower?" The answers given to such questions usually take the form of some complex discussion of the class-system, the "north-south divide" and how the English game should be re-organised, or just a suggestion that the selectors should be shot. An intelligent and civilised version of this discussion was contained in Graeme Wright's **Betrayal: The Struggle for Cricket's Soul**, now reissued in paperback, and which was most unfairly attacked in these pages last year by Geoffrey Moorhouse for containing too many quotations from such cricketing authorities as Montaigne, Goethe and Wittgenstein. If my predecessor thought Wright was "solemn", at least he was spared the full Marxist analysis of the problem given by Mike Marqusee in **Anyone But England: Cricket and the National Malaise**.

This American observer, taking his title from the answer given by Labour MP Dennis Skinner to the question "Who do you support in Test matches?", may well be right that "English cricket neatly mirrors the decline of Britain as an economic and political power". But I am not sure that the low drone of two hundred pages of Dave Spart prose on "feudal elites" leaves us very much further forward in understanding why England can't produce fast

bowlers, particularly from an author who sees English society in such cartoon strip terms that he imagines that Lord Lansdowne and Lord Bessborough must have sat in Harold Macmillan's Cabinet because they were both members of MCC. I am sure these long-forgotten junior ministers would have appreciated the honour. The only time this book becomes human is in Marqusee's description of taking a group of cocky, Asian-despising, London/West Indian layabouts to the final of the 1983 World Cup, and how their jeers at nearby Indian supporters faded in horror as Madan Lal and Amarnath skittled out Richards and Co. 44 runs short of victory.

Another perennial theme in the "what's wrong with English cricket?" argument has been debate over the part played in the English game by overseas stars. In **The Enemy Within: The Impact of Overseas Players on English Cricket**, Alastair McLellan gives an extremely industrious, county-by-county picture of all the outsiders who have adorned our first-class scene since the modern system began in 1968. Although there is much of interest here, at times he seems almost submerged in statistics, and he comes up with an equivocal answer to whether on balance English cricket has gained or lost. The best moment is when he forgets his learned study and simply regales us with the fascinating story of the match in 1904 involving the black West Indian C. A. Ollivierre. Essex hit 597, declaring at mid-morning on the second day with Perrin 343 not out. Derbyshire's reply, with Ollivierre hitting 229 in little over three hours, was to reach 548. Everyone had something to celebrate. On the third day Essex were all out for 97, and Ollivierre, nursing a raging hangover, hit 92 not out in 80 minutes to win the match.

At least we have said goodbye to one vexatious topic which has bedevilled cricket with clouds of humbug and righteous argument for the past quarter of a century. Several books mark the return of South Africa to the fold after she disappeared from view in the wake of the D'Oliveira affair, leaving the best Test team in the world without an opponent. One of that galaxy, Mike Procter ("with", as they say, Patrick Murphy) has produced **South Africa: The Years of Isolation and the Return to International Cricket**. This is a fairly humdrum account of the rebel tours of the 1980s, Ali Bacher's township programme to show young black Africans "how much enjoyment there could be in hitting a ball with a piece of wood" (as Procter/Murphy puts it) and of course the happy ending. In **Omar Henry: The Man in the Middle**, D'Oliveira's protégé, Omar Henry, gives an account of what it was like to be the first Cape Coloured to be admitted to first-class cricket in South Africa, in 1977-78. Mihir Bose's politically correct **Sporting Colours: Sport and Politics in South Africa** manages not to mention a single game of cricket, except for the ritual reference to D'Oliveira's 158 against Australia at The Oval in 1968 which set the whole crisis off. Although this legendary innings should win some prize for being mentioned in nearly a dozen of this year's books, none mentions its really compelling feature for those of us who saw it. D'Oliveira came in at five past six and was so determined to succeed that he was already 24 not out when stumps were drawn 25 minutes later. In fact, none of these books says as much about South Africa's years of isolation as the one on Wessels reviewed above.

A good anthology should take many years to mature. The problem with so many modern versions is that they are hastily scrambled together to fill some publisher's bill. This may explain why Christopher Martin-Jenkins's **The Spirit of Cricket: A Personal Anthology** is so patchy and could happily have been cut to half its length. As usual, the best items are stories of

individual matches, such as Mike Brearley on the Headingley Test of 1981; or A. E. J. Collins's astounding feat in 1899, when he not only outscored Lara by 127 but took 11 for 67 into the bargain. There is a series of delightful individual studies – Trevor Bailey on Godfrey Evans, Arlott on Alan Knott, Frank Keating on Tom Graveney, C. L. R. James on George Headley, George Cox on himself. I would even agree that those on Shane Warne, Derek Randall, Richie Benaud and Majid Khan merit reprinting, although I am not sure that the laws of anthologising should allow quite so many entries penned by the anthologist himself.

From its newspaper-cutting layout, **The Daily Telegraph Chronicle of Cricket**, edited by Norman Barrett, might seem to be providing a year-by-year account of almost every major cricketing highlight of the past century, as it was reported at the time. Only with some sense of letdown does one realise that many reports have in fact been rewritten for this book. Nevertheless, there is much of fascination here, such as the fact that, when W. H. Ponsford hit his world record 429 against Tasmania, it was not initially accepted as a first-class match.

I would not normally have included Ashley Mallett's **Clarrie Grimmett: The Bradman of Spin** among the tailenders except that it is a paperback. He justifies his perhaps surprising sub-title by pointing out that, if you equate a haul of five wickets with a century, Grimmett's record of 127 such hauls in 248 matches is startingly close to Bradman's unique batting record of 117 centuries in 234 matches. This is a solid account of the old fox's career, which began in his native New Zealand, by his pupil and successor as a top Australian spinner. Walter Hadlee's **The Innings of a Lifetime** is a worthy autobiography by a man who captained a fine New Zealand team in 1949, but is today better known as Richard's father.

A delightful curiosity is **101 Not Out: Prof. D. B. Deodhar** by Dr Vasant Naik, a little tribute to the man who was the world's oldest surviving first-class cricketer, before he died in 1993. Deodhar made his debut in 1911, played with Wilfred Rhodes and C. B. Fry, once put on 112 with Hobbs, hit 246 when he was 48 and became the oldest man to score a century in each innings of a first-class match when he was 52. Yet another re-issue of C. L. R. James's classic **Beyond a Boundary** is worth re-reading, if only for the essay explaining just why W. G. Grace, the first man to play off both the front and the back foot, should still be looked on as one of the greatest all-round players of all time. There have been many specialist books on statistics in the past year, but Andrew Hignell's **Glamorgan County Cricket Club: First-Class Records 1921-1993** (part of the Limlow series) is a model of its kind, reminding us that Malcolm Nash was not only the man hit for 36 in an over by Sobers and for 34 by Lancashire's Frank Hayes, but also once hit nine sixes himself in an innings of 89 against Gloucestershire.

Finally, to remind us where it all began, and to some extent still is, there are two histories of teams who won the National Village Championship: **Village Champions: Cricket at St Fagans 1862-1993** by David Allen and **150 Not Out**, a charming little memoir of the Kington Cricket Club, Herefordshire, who came to Lord's to win the final in 1993, an even greater thrill than the day the great S. F. Barnes played for them in the 1930s, aged 62, and took eight for 37. As old Pearl Lara wisely said, when her boy knocked up 501, "To God be the glory".

Christopher Booker is a columnist in the Sunday Telegraph *and was the first editor of* Private Eye.

BOOKS RECEIVED IN 1994

GENERAL

Allen, Peter and Kemsley, James, ed. **Images of Bradman: Rare and Famous Photographs of a Cricket Legend** (Bradman Museum, $A49.95; deluxe limited edition, $A650; collector's edition $A80)

Arlott, Timothy **John Arlott: A Memoir** (Andre Deutsch, £14.99)

Armstrong, Geoff and Gately, Mark **The People's Game: Australia in International One-day Cricket** (Ironbark, Sydney; obtainable from Sportspages, 94-96 Charing Cross Road, London WC2H 0JG and Barton Square, St Ann's Square, Manchester M2 7HA, £16.50)

Bannister, Jack **Brian Lara: The Story of a Record-Breaking Year** (Stanley Paul, £7.99)

Barrett, Norman ed. **The Daily Telegraph Chronicle of Cricket** (Guinness Publishing, £17.95)

Bell, Pat **Long Shies and Slow Twisters: 150 Years of Cricket in Kildare** (Templemills Bridge, Celbridge, Co. Kildare, Ireland, £5)

Border, Allan **Beyond Ten Thousand: My Life Story** Foreword by Richie Benaud (Souvenir Press, £18.99)

Bose, Mihir **Sporting Colours: Sport and Politics in South Africa** (Robson Books, £17.95)

Botham, Ian with Peter Hayter **Botham: My Autobiography – Don't Tell Kath** (HarperCollins, £15.99)

Coward, Mike (photographs by Michael Rayner) **Australia vs The New South Africa: Cricket Contact Renewed** (Simon & Schuster Australia, 20 Barcoo Street, East Roseville, NSW 2069, Australia, $A29.95)

Craven, Nico **A Summer Ball of a Game** Foreword by Graeme Wright (from the author, The Coach House, Ponsonby, Seascale, Cumberland CA20 1BX, £5.55)

Dawson, Marc **Cricket Extras** Foreword by David Gower (Blandford Press, £10.99)

Derriman, Philip **80 Not Out: A Celebration of Test Cricket at the Sydney Cricket Ground** (Sydney Cricket Ground Classic/Playbill, no price given)

De Vitre, Fredun **Willow Tales: The Lighter Side of Indian Cricket** (Marine Sports, 63A Gokhale Road (North), Dadar, Bombay 400 028, Rs 25; available from Martin Wood, 2 St John's Road, Sevenoaks, Kent TN13 3LW, £4.50 inc. p&p)

English, David and Brychta, Jan **The Bumper Bunbury Album** (HarperCollins, £6.99)

Frith, David **Stoddy's Mission: The First Great Test Series 1894-1895** (Queen Anne Press, £12.99)

The Googly **The Googly Annual: Highlights from Cricket's Dangerously Funny Magazine** (Robson Books, £6.99)

Griffiths, Edward **Kepler: The Biography** (Pelham Books, £16.99)

Hadlee, Walter with Joseph Romanos **The Innings of a Lifetime** (David Bateman, Auckland; obtainable from Sportspages, addresses as above, £19.95)

Haigh, Gideon **The Border Years** (Text Publishing, Melbourne; obtainable from Sportspages, addresses as above, £19.95)

Harris, Norman **From Stinchcombe to Lord's: The 1994 Village Cup as featured in The Independent** (BH Communications, PO Box 4589, London SW13 0XJ, £3.50 inc. p&p)

Heald, Tim **Denis: The Authorized Biography of the Incomparable Compton** (Pavilion Books, £16.99)

Henry, Omar with Keith Graham **Omar Henry: The Man in the Middle** (Lennard/Queen Anne Press, £16.99)

Hill, Alan **Bill Edrich: A Biography** (Andre Deutsch, £14.99)

Holmes, Bob and Marks, Vic eds. **Fifty Cricket Stars Describe My Greatest Game** (Mainstream, £12.99)

McCann, Mike **Cricket's Ultimate Ashes Test** Foreword by Dennis Lillee (Australian Broadcasting Corporation, PO Box 9994, Sydney, NSW 2001, no price given)

McLellan, Alastair **The Enemy Within: The Impact of Overseas Players on English Cricket** (Blandford Press, £14.99)

Mallett, Ashley **Clarrie Grimmett: The Bradman of Spin** (University of Queensland Press; obtainable from Sportspages, addresses as above, £11.95)

Marqusee, Mike **Anyone But England: Cricket and the National Malaise** (Verso, £16.95)

Martin-Jenkins, Christopher and Gibson, Pat, eds. **Summers Will Never Be The Same: A Tribute to Brian Johnston** (Partridge Press, £12.99)

Maxwell, Jim comp. **The ABC Cricket Book: The First 60 Years** (Australian Broadcasting Corporation, address as above, no price given)

Meher-Homji, Kersi **The Nervous Nineties** Foreword by Michael Slater (Kangaroo Press, 3 Whitehall Road, Kenthurst, NSW 2156, no price given)

Midwinter, Eric **First Knock: Cricket's Opening Pairs** (Cricket Lore, 22 Grazebrook Road, London N16 0HS, £13.95 inc. p&p, £11.95 to Cricket Lore subscribers)

Naik, Dr Vasant **101 Not Out: Prof. D. B. Deodhar** (Marine Sports, Bombay, obtainable from Martin Wood, address as above, £21 inc. p&p)

Nicholson, Chris **Ambidexterity in Cricket** (Harmony Publications, 15 Mount Argus Road, Umgeni Heights 4051, Natal, South Africa; obtainable from Sportspages, addresses as above, £3.50)

Over to You Richie: Classics from the Captains of Commentary (Swan Publishing, Perth; obtainable from Sportspages, addresses as above, £16.50).

Powell, William A. **Cricket Grounds Then and Now** (Dial Press, £14.99)

Powell, William comp. **The South Africans in England 1894-1965** (Limlow Books, St Peter's Hill, Litlington, Royston, Herts. SG8 0QF, £9.95 + 75p p&p)

Procter, Mike with Patrick Murphy **South Africa: The Years of Isolation and the Return to International Cricket** (Lennard/Queen Anne Press, £16.99)

Qamar Ahmed **Showdown: The Story of Pakistan's Tour of the West Indies – 1993** (Cricketprint, A-10 Bridge Apartments, Clifton Road, Karachi, Pakistan, Rs 100)

Rayvern Allen, David **Arlott: The Authorised Biography** (HarperCollins, £20)

Smith, Rick **ABC Guide to Australian Test Cricketers** (Queen Anne Press, £9.99)

Tennant, Ivo **Imran Khan** (H. F. & G. Witherby, £16.99)

Waugh, Steve **Steve Waugh's South African Tour Diary** (Ironbark, Sydney; obtainable from Sportspages, addresses as above, £16.50)

Whitney, Mike **Quick Whit: The Mike Whitney Story** Foreword by Alan Davidson (Ironbark, Sydney; obtainable from Sportspages, addresses as above, £13.50)

Wilde, Simon **Letting Rip: The Fast-Bowling Threat from Lillee to Waqar** (H. F. & G. Witherby, £15.99)

Woodward, Ian **Cricket, Not War: The Australian Services XI and The "Victory Tests" of 1945** Limited edition of 1,000 (SMK Enterprises, 7 Canberra Grove, Brighton East, Victoria 3187, Australia, $A18 + $A2 p&p)

ANTHOLOGIES

Martin-Jenkins, Christopher **The Spirit of Cricket: A Personal Anthology** (Faber and Faber, £17.50)

West, William T. comp. **An Anthology of the Writings of E. H. D. Sewell** (available from William West, 3 Roundhay Road, Bridlington, YO15 3JZ, £3.99)

FICTION

George, Elizabeth **Playing for the Ashes** (Bantam Press, £15.99)

Heller, Richard **A Tale of Ten Wickets** (Oval Publishing, 30 Crewdson Road, London SW9 0LJ, £5.99 or £6.50 inc. p&p)

PAMPHLETS

Derriman, Philip **Our Don Bradman: The Don at the SCG** (Sydney Cricket Ground Classic/Playbill; obtainable from Sportspages, 94-96 Charing Cross Road, London WC2H 0JG and Barton Square, St Ann's Square, Manchester M2 7HA, £4.95)

Pollard, Jack **The Gregorys' Great SCG Tradition** (Sydney Cricket Ground Classic/Playbill; obtainable from Sportspages, addresses as above)

Pollard, Jack **"Mary Anne" Noble at the SCG** (Sydney Cricket Ground Classic/Playbill; obtainable from Sportspages, addresses as above)

Whimpress, Bernard **W. G. Grace at Kadina: Champion Cricketer or Scoundrel** (from the author, Adelaide – limited edition of 300 copies; obtainable from Sportspages, addresses as above, £3.50)

REPRINTS AND UPDATES

Boycott, Geoff **Learn Cricket with Geoff Boycott** Revised edition of Geoff Boycott's Book for Young Cricketers (1976) (Stanley Paul, £9.99)

Gooch, Graham with Patrick Murphy **Captaincy** Paperback edition, updated to events of 1993 (Stanley Paul, £9.99)

James, C. L. R. **Beyond a Boundary** New paperback edition containing Robert Lipsyte's introduction to the US edition (Serpent's Tail, £13.99)

Smith, Tom **Cricket Umpiring and Scoring** Second edition (paperback), reprinted and revised (Weidenfeld & Nicolson, £4.99)

Ward, Andrew **Cricket's Strangest Matches** Paperback edition (Robson Books, £8.99)

John Wisden's Cricketers' Almanack for 1896 (reprint from Willows Publishing, 17 The Willows, Stone, Staffs. ST15 0DE, £42 inc. p&p UK, £44 inc. p&p overseas; £5 extra for version with facsimile of original hard cloth cover).

John Wisden's Cricketers' Almanack for 1897 (reprint from Willows Publishing, address as above, £42 inc. p&p UK, £44 inc. p&p overseas; £5 extra for version with facsimile of original hard cloth cover).

Wright, Graeme **Betrayal: The Struggle for Cricket's Soul** Paperback edition (H. F. & G. Witherby, £6.99)

TECHNICAL

Lewis, Tony **MCC Masterclass: The New MCC Coaching Book** Foreword by Dennis Silk (Weidenfeld & Nicolson, £16.99)

Malcolm Marshall's Bowling & Fielding Skills: A Complete Step-by-Step Guide (Hamlyn, £7.99)

Robin Smith's Batting Skills: A Complete Step-by-Step Guide (Hamlyn, £7.99)

STATISTICAL

Association of Cricket Statisticians **Cricket Matches 1839-1844** (ACS, 3 Radcliffe Road, West Bridgford, Nottingham NG2 5FF, £8.50)
Association of Cricket Statisticians **Cricket Matches 1845-1849** (ACS, address as above, £8.50)
Association of Cricket Statisticians **First Class Cricket Matches 1900** (ACS, address as above, £11.50)
Bailey, Philip J. comp. **Sri Lanka First Class Matches Season 1988-89** (ACS, address as above, £3.50)
Bailey, Philip J. comp. **Sri Lanka First Class Matches Season 1989-90** (ACS, address as above, £3.50)
Bartlett, C. J. **Brian Close: His Record Innings-by-Innings** (Famous Cricketers Series – no. 21) (ACS, address as above, £6)
Brooke, Robert **Warwickshire County Cricket Club: First-Class Records 1894-1993** (Limlow Books, St Peter's Hill, Litlington, Royston, Herts. SG8 0QF, £8 + 50p p&p)
Harte, Wesley **Bert Sutcliffe: His Record Innings-by-Innings** (Famous Cricketers Series – no. 23) (ACS, address as above, £6)
Hartshorn, Peter **A. R. Morris: His Record Innings-by-Innings** (Famous Cricketers Series – no. 22) (ACS, address as above, £2.50)
Heald, Brian ed. **Statistical Survey 1869** (ACS, address as above, £3.50)
Hignell, Andrew **Glamorgan County Cricket Club: First-Class Records 1921-1993** (Limlow Books, address as above, £8 + 50p p&p)
Ledbetter, Jim ed. **First-Class Cricket: A Complete Record 1936** (Limlow Books, address as above, £14.95 + £1.50 p&p)
Milton, Howard **Kent Cricket Records 1815-1993** (Limlow Books, address as above, £8.50 + 50p p&p)
Sheen, Steven **F. R. Spofforth: His Record Innings-by-Innings** (Famous Cricketers Series – no. 24) (ACS, address as above, £4.50)
Torrens, Warwick **Ray Lindwall: His Record Innings-by-Innings** (Famous Cricketers Series – no. 19) (ACS, address as above, £5.50)
Wynne-Thomas, Peter **George Parr: His Record Innings-by-Innings** (Famous Cricketers Series – no. 20) (ACS, address as above, £3.50)
Wynne-Thomas, Peter **Sir Julien Cahn's Team 1923 to 1941** (ACS, address as above, £1.75)

FIRST-CLASS COUNTY YEARBOOKS

The 18 first-class counties all now publish annual handbooks, mostly of a high standard, though the quality can vary as wildly as the price and without regard to it. The Yorkshire yearbook, up to its 96th edition in 1994, maintains an air of aloof leadership the county's cricket has lost in almost every other respect, with a hard cover, small format, clear but discreet typography and an air of permanence; the influence of another annual cricketing publication is obvious and flattering. The other counties all go in for glossy paperbacks. Of these, Lancashire produced the chunkiest (384 pages) in 1994, Essex the most confusing, Northamptonshire – who spray-painted every page with maroon – the most alarming, Gloucestershire the skimpiest and Sussex, whose publication had the virtues of both good looks and clarity, perhaps the best. – M.E.

Derbyshire (£4.50), Durham (£6), Essex (£6), Glamorgan (£5), Gloucestershire (£3), Hampshire (£5.50), Kent (£5), Lancashire (£6), Leicestershire (£4), Middlesex (£7), Northamptonshire (£7), Nottinghamshire (£4), Somerset (£5.50), Surrey (£5), Sussex (£5.50), Warwickshire (£4), Worcestershire (£3.50), Yorkshire (£7.50).
1995 prices may change; some counties may add charges for p&p.

OTHER HANDBOOKS AND ANNUALS

Armstrong, David ed. **Minor Counties Cricket Annual and Official Handbook** (ACS, 3 Radcliffe Road, West Bridgford, Nottingham NG2 5FF, £4)
Bailey, Philip comp. **ACS International Cricket Year Book 1994** (ACS, address as above, £8)
Club Cricket Conference Official Handbook (78th edition, 1994) (361 West Barnes Lane, New Malden, Surrey KT3 6JF; £5 to affiliates)
Derriman, Philip ed. **The ABC Australian Cricket Almanac, 1994** (Australian Broadcasting Corporation, PO Box 9994, Sydney, NSW 2001, no price given)
The Forty Club Handbook and Directory (The Forty Club, 133 Palace View, Bromley, Kent BR1 3EP, no price given)
Frindall, Bill ed. **Playfair Cricket Annual 1994** (Headline, paperback, £3.99; hardback, £7.99)
Hatton, Les comp. **ACS First Class Counties Second Eleven Annual** (ACS, address as above, £4)
Herefordshire Cricket Yearbook 1994 (Herefordshire CCC, £2)
Il Cricket Italiano, 1994 (Associazione Italiana Cricket, Via S. Ignazio 9, 00186 Roma, no price given)
Leitch, Neil ed. **The 1994 Miller Guide to Scottish Cricket** (Scottish Cricket Union, Caledonia House, South Gyle, Edinburgh EH12 9DQ, £3 + 70p p&p)
Lemmon, David ed. **Benson and Hedges Cricket Year** Thirteenth Edition. Foreword by Mike Atherton (Headline, £19.99)
Maxwell, Jim, ed. **ABC Cricket 1994-95** (Australian Broadcasting Corporation/Gore & Osment, $A4.95)
Menon, Mohandas ed. **Cricontrol Statistical Annual 1993-94** (Board of Control for Cricket in India)
Miller, Allan ed. **Allan's Australian Cricket Annual 1993-94** (from Allan Miller, PO Box 974, Busselton, WA 6280, $A30 inc. p&p; available in UK from Sport in Print, 3 Radcliffe Road, West Bridgford, Nottingham NG2 5FF, £14 inc. p&p)
The Cricketers' Who's Who, 1994 Statistics by Richard Lockwood. Introduction by Matthew Fleming (Lennard/Queen Anne Press, £11.99)

PERSONAL ORGANISERS

The Complete Cricket Companion (Gaymer's Guides, 46 Sefton Street, London SW15 1LZ, vinyl £14.99 + £2 p&p, leather £29.99 + £2 p&p – first three updates included)

PERIODICALS

The Cricketer International (monthly) editorial director Richard Hutton (Beech Hanger, Ashurst, Tunbridge Wells, Kent TN3 9ST, £2.30)
The Cricketer Quarterly: Facts and Figures ed. Richard Lockwood (The Cricketer International, address as above, annual subscription £11.70, Europe airmail £12, overseas surface £11.80, airmail £15.70)
Cricket Lore (ten per volume, frequency variable) ed. Richard Hill (Cricket Lore, 22 Grazebrook Road, London N16 0HS, £35 per volume)
The Cricket Statistician (quarterly) ed. Philip J. Bailey (ACS, 3 Radcliffe Road, West Bridgford, Nottingham NG2 5FF, £1.50, free to ACS members)
Cricket World (monthly) editorial director Michael Blumberg (The Club Cricketer, 2a Chelverton Road, London SW15 1RH, £1.95)
The Googly (fanzine, monthly) (Googly Subscriptions, 29b Meteor Street, London SW11 5NZ, £1)
The Indian Cricket Quarterly: Facts and Figures ed. Mohandas Menon (Valsa Publications, 2 Prem Jivan, Caesar Road, Amboli, Andheri (W), Bombay 400 058, India, Rs 70, annual subscription Rs 200; available in UK from Brian Croudy, 4 Burdett Road, West Croydon, Surrey CR0 2HH, annual airmail subscription £12)

JM 96* – Johnny Miller 96 Not Out (fanzine, monthly) (Two Heads Publishing, 12A Franklyn Suite, The Priory, Haywards Heath, West Sussex RH16 3LB, £1.50, annual subscription £18)

The Journal of the Cricket Society (twice yearly) ed. Clive W. Porter (from Mr P. Ellis, 63 Groveland Road, Beckenham, Kent BR3 3PX, £3)

The Minor Counties Newsletter (eight in 1994, scheduled to be weekly during 1995 season) (Mike Berry, Idsworth, Fair Close, Frankton, Rugby CV23 9PL, apply for subscription details)

Primestats ed. Sudhir Vaidya (published quarterly, available from India Book House, annual subscription Rs 100; in UK from Martin Wood, 2 St John's Road, Sevenoaks, Kent TN13 3LW, annual subscription £15)

Red Stripe Caribbean Quarterly ed. Tony Cozier (Cozier Publishing, PO Box 40W, Worthing, Christ Church, Barbados, annual subscription £12 Europe, BDS$22 Barbados, BDS$28/US$14 rest of the West Indies, US$18 US, Can$24 Canada, US$24 elsewhere)

South African Cricket Action (ten issues a year) (Cricket Action Subscriptions, PO Box 32797 Braamfontein 2017, South Africa, R6.95, annual subscription R55)

Third Man (quarterly) (Third Man Publications, 23 Yarnfield Square, Consort Road, London SE15 5JD, £1.50, annual subscription £6)

The White Rose Magazine (quarterly) (Yorkshire CCC, 80p, free to members)

Wisden Cricket Monthly ed. David Frith (25 Down Road, Merrow, Guildford, Surrey GU1 2PY, £2.20)

SOUVENIRS

Australian Cricket Tour of Sri Lanka August/September 1992 (Available from the Board of Control for Cricket in Sri Lanka, 35 Maitland Place, Colombo 7, Sri Lanka)

Lara 375: A Souvenir Tribute to a World Record (Cozier Publishing, PO Box 40W, Worthing, Christ Church, Barbados)

Pakistan Cricket Tour of Sri Lanka July-August 1994 (Available from the Board of Control for Cricket in Sri Lanka)

West Indies Cricket Tour of Sri Lanka December 1993 (Available from the Board of Control for Cricket in Sri Lanka)

CLUB HISTORIES

Allen, David **Village Champions: Cricket at St Fagans 1862-1993** Foreword by Wilfred Wooller (from the author, 35 Egremont Road, Penylan, Cardiff CF2 5LP, £10 + 75p p&p)

Bailey, John and Dockrell, Morgan ed. **St Columba's Cricket: Not Out 150** (from Morgan Dockrell, St Columba's College, Whitchurch, Dublin 16, Ireland, £2).

Kington Cricket Club: 150 Not Out (from David Hill, The Coopers, Prospect Lane, Kington, Herefords. HR5 3AY, £2.50 + 25p p&p)

Magee, Colm ed. **First Class Service: A History of Civil Service Cricket Club [Ireland] from 1863** (from A. Morrissey, 17 Hazelwood Lane, Clondalkin, Dublin 22, Ireland)

THE CRICKET SOCIETY LITERARY AWARD

The Cricket Society Literary Award has been presented since 1970 to the author of the cricket book judged as best of the year. The 1994 award went to David Rayvern Allen for **Arlott: The Authorised Biography**.

CRICKET VIDEOS, 1994

By STEVEN LYNCH

Video technology is playing an ever-increasing role in life, so it should come as no surprise that the cricket-video industry is a healthy one. Many enthusiasts will have created their own self-service library after tracking down the times of the notoriously nomadic TV highlights programmes, but pre-recorded cassettes remain very popular.

There was a definite wedding feel about the cricket videos issued in 1994: something old, something new, something borrowed (usually from the BBC) . . . and even something faintly blue, in the shape of **Freddie Trueman Bowls You Over**, Fred's stage show. The old was represented by Sir Donald Bradman, whose **How to Play Cricket** coaching session was filmed in England (Alexandra Park CC in North London, to be precise) during the 1934 Australian tour. Sixty years on, much good sense is contained in the grainy, monochrome frames of cricket's greatest batsman.

The double cassette **MCC Masterclass** is also invaluable for those anxious to improve. After watching David Gower bat while miked-up, absorbing bowling tutorials from Illy 'n' Lillee, or simply listening to Brearley on captaincy or Jonty Rhodes – grass-stained trousers and all – expound on the joys of fielding, it would be almost impossible not to be better informed about the game. Those who watch motor-racing for the accidents will be satisfied by **Bats, Balls and Bouncers**, where the main attraction is big fast bowlers bouncing the ball at helmeted batsmen, who occasionally avoid injury for long enough to bludgeon the ball to the boundary.

Inevitably, a certain West Indian left-hander features prominently. **Lara's Innings** replays the Test-record 375 in Antigua, while he is well represented too on **Caribbean Crusade**, the tour highlights package. Lara's Other Innings, his 501 not out, has not inspired its own video, since the media attention switched to Edgbaston only towards the end. However, brief snippets can be seen in Issue 3 of **Cover Point**, the well-produced video magazine. Issue 2 contained a thought-provoking look at ball-tampering, "as shown to the High Court" (in the truncated Sarfraz Nawaz v Allan Lamb libel case). Each issue, lasting about an hour, has a mix of recent action (including some footage from overseas Tests), news and views: a quibble might be that the sound quality is sometimes patchy. Five issues of the magazine, which deserves to be an ongoing success, had been received by the time this review was written, the fifth being a 90-minute end-of-season review.

VIDEOS RECEIVED IN 1994

Mike Atherton and the England Team's Caribbean Crusade (BMG, £10.99)
Lara's Innings (BMG, £10.99)
MCC Masterclass presented by Tony Lewis (Telstar, £12.99 for each of two tapes – **Batting, Bowling & Captaincy** and **Bowling, Fielding & Wicketkeeping**)
Bats, Balls and Bouncers presented by Geoff Boycott (Telstar, £10.99)
How to Play Cricket by Sir Donald Bradman (Quadrant, £10.99)
Cover Point Video Magazine (Cover Point Cricket Ltd, 113 Upper Tulse Hill, London SW2 2RD; Issues 1–4 and 6 £8.99 Issue 5 (season review) £12.99; subscription rates available). Issue 5 also available as **The Story of the 1994 Cricket Season** (£12.99), only from W. H. Smith
Freddie Trueman Bowls You Over (Big Life, £12.99)
The Year of the Bear: The Greatest Ever Cricket Season (Warwickshire CCC, £14.99 + £1.50 p&p)

Prices shown are Recommended Retail Prices

CRICKET AND THE MEDIA IN 1994

By TIM DE LISLE

This was going to be the story of how one player changed the face of cricket reporting, and persuaded some deeply cynical newspapers that mere excellence could be as interesting as rows, storms and ball-tampering. Brian Lara was so successful in 1994, he was sensational. The tabloids, sometimes too bored by county cricket to publish scorecards, covered every Warwickshire game. When the *Daily Mail* launched a cartoon strip, "Learn with Lara", we were back in the age of innocence. Even the England captain was being portrayed sympathetically – as boyish, able, an exemplary batsman and promising leader.

All this changed on a sweaty Saturday afternoon in July, when a BBC cameraman captured Mike Atherton doing something to the ball. The first reaction, from the commentator Tony Lewis, was no comment. His gut feeling was uncertainty: "Was the captain cheating . . . or sending up the media?" So he watched the film again, arranged for viewers to do the same, and prepared a legally watertight remark. Before the replay could be shown, Atherton did it again, in full view of the Grandstand audience. "Looks like Michael's trying the Aladdin's Lamp treatment," Lewis said. The third umpire alerted the referee. The rest is journalism.

At the close, the Test and County Cricket Board said a statement would be made in half an hour. When it wasn't, reporters were offered a glass of wine. The *vino* had come out, but the *veritas* took longer. The statements that followed are recorded elsewhere in *Wisden*. All Atherton said was: "I've got nothing further to say, and I won't be saying anything tomorrow either."

Next morning, the story led the Sunday papers' sports sections. Several muttered about unanswered questions and showed blurred stills from the TV footage; none demanded resignation. All the same, Atherton was taken aback: "It was only when I saw the newspapers that I realised how serious it was." The fact that he had misled the referee emerged that night. At a "hot, crowded and unfriendly" press conference (Atherton again), Ray Illingworth, chairman of the selectors, pronounced a sentence which sounded harsh but turned out to be a neck-saver. Atherton took it like a boy, mixing contrition and defiance. "That," said Illingworth, "closes the matter."

"Here was a story created entirely by television," Alan Lee wrote in *The Times* on Monday. Yes, but nurtured by the press and radio. That same issue of his paper had it leading not just the sports pages but page one as well. It was the same in the *Daily Telegraph*. Unfamiliar action, unfamiliar reaction. *The Times* also ran a leader, and thundered: "Not since Bodyline . . . has an England captain stood accused of conduct unbecoming." It was hard to think of a recent one who hadn't done so. Even tosh will do as tinder, but the days have gone when *Times* leaders set the nation's agenda: the role has passed to Radio Four's "Today". To prove it, the programme had Jonathan Agnew, BBC cricket correspondent, urging Atherton to resign. This was the start of a sub-saga, of which more later. It also thickened the main plot. Monday's tabloid headlines had been plays on dirt – "The soiled skipper" etc. Tuesday's were not so subtle: GO! (*Daily*

Mirror), QUIT NOW (*The Sun*), Why Atherton has got to go! (*Daily Express*). The *Express* piece was by Agnew; the others quoted him prominently. Overnight, the mood had changed. Puzzled disapproval turned to bloodlust.

The giveaway was the phrase used in the *Telegraph*, *Sun* and *Daily Mail* – "mounting pressure". This is a cliché, but a potent one, because self-fulfulling: several of John Major's ministers had lately been driven from office by a din consisting largely of this phrase. Geoffrey Boycott ("a trusted advisor" – Atherton) advised packing it in to concentrate on batting. No other big names sang along, but in the phone-in era any name will do: the *Mirror* held a poll (i.e. printed a fax number for people to call) and declared that 100 per cent of its readers were for resignation. "Good grief," Matthew Engel retorted in *The Guardian*. "Even the Kremlin used to get 0.1 per cent voting the other way."

The papers evidently expected Atherton to "do the decent thing", if they just carried on doing the indecent thing. Instead, the snowball began to melt. Agnew became a distraction: *The Guardian* (Wednesday) and *The Independent* (Thursday) both suggested he might resign, arguing that, as in politics, the BBC should be impartial. Agnew ended the week as the subject of the Michael Parkinson interview in the *Telegraph*: "Accuser who stands accused . . . has not slept for three nights."

Meanwhile, Illingworth was unwavering: "This now completely closes the matter" (Monday); "It is finished" (Tuesday). Atherton, "on the run" in the Lake District because his home was under siege, wavered, consulted friends and his father, and didn't read the papers. The South Africans, sportingly, called the affair "a relatively minor matter" (Allan Donald, Wednesday). Nor were the papers themselves unanimous. While sports editors bayed for blood, columnists hollered for tolerance. James Lawton (*Express*) argued that Atherton was young and the game "has not exactly bludgeoned him with the moral verities". Ian Wooldridge (*Mail*) roasted the leaders of the "witch-hunt" (among them, unmentioned, his sports editor, Vic Robbie): in 38 years he could not recall "any sportsperson so vilified on such lack of evidence." The *Telegraph* was solidly behind Atherton, and published a letter from Rev. Andrew Wingfield Digby, who rose above the fact that Illingworth had just fired him as England's chaplain, and drew a biblical parallel: "The media hacks of today" were as bad as "the scribes and Pharisees of Jesus's time." A second *Times* leader in two days came out for dismissal; but the rest of the broadsheets (including the *Times* sportswriters) offered broad support.

The story grew tentacles. *Sports Illustrated*, of the USA, helpfully identified Atherton as "captain of England's woebegone cricket team and its best bowler". The *Sportstar*, of Madras, said that "the soil of the hallowed Lord's ground has been defiled by the enormity of the blow to the sport that prides itself as being courted only by gentlemen". By Friday, *The Sun* was the only British paper making much noise, and that took the form of pictures of Atherton leaving his "hideaway" with his "stunning" girlfriend. It was this, not the calls for his head, that Atherton said led him to make a much-criticised reference the following week to "the gutter press".

All this was presumably intended to sell newspapers. The only evidence that it did came from Pakistan, where some papers were said to have doubled their circulation. The *schadenfreude* was understandable. Less so was the point, widely made, that a Pakistani in Atherton's shoes would not have got off so lightly. One reason why the 1992 ball-tampering allegations rumbled on was the fact that nobody was punished at all.

In the end, an apparently irresistible force met two immovable objects, Atherton and Illingworth. "Raymond saved my job," Atherton told *The Times* in September; though he still considered resigning, and only didn't because "it would be for the wrong reasons . . . the press furore". The heavy artillery turned out to have been using boomerangs. Both sides were left to ponder unanswered questions. If Atherton was innocent, why did he defend himself with a lie and, later, with evasions and self-contradictions? If he was guilty, why did he risk so much for so little – if you're going to cheat, why choose a transparently ineffectual method? Whichever view you took, the picture remained blurred. Maybe this is what really inflamed the tabloids. Their world view leaves no room for doubt. That's why they like sport: it supplies winners and losers, but especially, if you're British, losers. The Atherton Affair, rather than offering an escape from life, held a mirror to it. And, as T. S. Eliot almost said, newsmankind cannot bear very much reality.

Tim de Lisle is arts editor of the Independent on Sunday. *He was formerly the paper's cricket correspondent.*

CRICKET AND THE LAW IN 1994

The following cricket-related court cases were reported during 1994:

Cricket returned to the Buckinghamshire village of Jordans on August 29, with a special six-and-out rule on the east side of the ground to protect Linden Cottage. The owner, David Lacey, had taken the club to court, saying the game should not be played on the village green unless a 25ft net was erected in front of his house, forcing a year-long break in cricket there. However, on May 12 he lost his claim in Slough County Court, before Judge Nigel Hague (who had played for his Cambridge college), who ruled that the risk of serious injury or damage was minimal. Cricket had been played on the green for 60 years and, Judge Hague said, the plaintiff should have realised when he bought the house that balls would occasionally be hit into the garden. Mr Lacey was ordered to pay costs, estimated at £20,000. "Thank God for the winter arriving soon," said Mrs Lacey.

Lincoln Crown Court ordered Fraser Hinchcliffe, 27, of Wragby, Lincolnshire, to pay £50 compensation and do 100 hours community service for head-butting an opponent, Stephen Blythe, as he celebrated scoring his fifty in a match between Legbourne and Hainton in May, 1993. Police were called and the game was abandoned after the attack. Hinchcliffe thought Blythe should have been given out caught on 46. He admitted assault, and was also banned by the club for five years.

John Wright of Blackpool Cricket Club was fined £100 with £40 costs after admitting punching a St Annes fielder, Stuart McGill, on the nose.

Carl Fraser, a 57-year-old former bus conductor, was awarded £113,094 damages in the High Court after a fire engine on an emergency call ran over his foot, causing him to have all his toes amputated and forcing him to give up playing cricket. The judge found Mr Fraser ten per cent to blame for the accident. Mr Fraser, who played for the North Middlesex club, was reported as saying: "I have lost the passion of my life. No amount of money can ever replace cricket."

Three helicopter pilots who buzzed their clubhouse after winning a match against a team of fixed-wing pilots at White Waltham, Berkshire, were told by Maidenhead magistrates that they behaved with extreme folly. They were fined a total of £2,800 on charges of reckless, dangerous and negligent flying.

Michael McEvoy, father of the England bowler Phil Tufnell's former girlfriend, Jayne, was fined £2,500 by Enfield magistrates in June and ordered to pay Tufnell £500 for hitting him over the head with a brick and causing a wound that required eight stitches. In the same court the previous week, Tufnell had himself been fined £800 and ordered to pay £250 compensation after admitting hitting Miss McEvoy twice during a row over their baby daughter. McEvoy then went round to Tufnell's house, tried to force his way in and struck Tufnell with the brick. "If I had the opportunity to do what I did I would do it again," McEvoy said as he left the court.

CRICKETANA IN 1994

By DAVID FRITH

Wisden's good name was patently evident over 90 years ago when Australia's wicket-keeper, Yorkshire-born Hanson "Sammy" Carter, presented John Wisden & Company's proprietor Harry Luff with an exquisite ink-stand as a mark of esteem. That unique item of cricketana fetched £1,788 (including premium and VAT) at Christie's sale in London last July.

Midst the welter of cricket books, which are offered in increasingly weighty bundles, sometimes as many as 100 in a lot, selling for derisory sums, there seem to arise, with comforting regularity, special pieces which excite both widespread curiosity and high prices. During that same Christie's auction, a souvenir album compiled by E. G. Wynyard after his sole Test appearance against Australia, at The Oval in 1896, caused frenzied bidding that climaxed at £9,500, three times the estimate. Idealists' joy at this proud assertion of proper value was short-lived as word spread that the successful dealer aimed to capitalise by dismembering the photographic and ephemeral components of his prize to sell them individually.

No such surgical profit-seeking indignity could befall an original watercolour, and some gems in this category were sold at this sale. Works by the celebrated John Corbet Anderson made from £726 up to £3,352, for a portrait of William Hillyer. Also intact was a precious G. F. Watts charcoal, *Forward*, which made £2,682. Class always tells.

It told also in the response to Jack Hobbs's bat which brought him his 100th century for Surrey. Newspaper reports were misleading. Prior to the auction, at Sotheby's Ayr sale-room, it was erroneously stated that the bat was used in his 100th *first-class* hundred, which would have made it slightly

more tempting. Together with a presentation walking-stick, it still fetched £3,528 (including 15 per cent premium and VAT) against a net estimate of £600-£900, presumably to become an expensive object of fantasy for its new owner, who could flourish it and imitate Hobbs's deferential doffing of the cap as yet again he reached three figures – always being careful not to smash the glass frontage of the display cabinet.

Sir Jack's daughter-in-law also let go the silver tea-set presented to him by admirers in Melbourne during England's 1924-25 tour. This changed hands for £1,000 gross, while a gold cigarette-case inscribed by Ranjitsinhji to Hobbs made £1,882, further demonstrating that association with the great names is practically a guarantee of lasting value.

It was not surprising, therefore, that a large cache of intimate letters written by Wally Hammond attracted much interest when offered early in the year. Firstly, Christie's listed more than thirty written by the awesome but enigmatic cricketer to his first wife. Chronicles of deep moodiness, and ultimately of marital deception, they expose a sense of insecurity and a recurringly turbulent state of mind. This new insight into the Hammond persona was deemed important by some, an unwarranted intrusion by others, who seemed less disturbed by a second batch of letters offered shortly afterwards by Vennett-Smith of Nottingham. These were written to a girlfriend when Hammond was a bachelor in his early twenties, and might have been written by any young chap struggling to control his impulses. These 40 *billets-doux* sold for between £100 and £200 each, with some failing to meet high protective reserves. The first collection had gone for just £2,700 in one lot.

Wisdens also seem to occupy prominent space at every sale. During 1994, first issues (1864) were sold at Phillips (£2,011: this was once owned by *Wisden* editor Sydney H. Pardon), Dominic Winter of Swindon (£2,570 for a leather re-bound copy), and Bonhams Knightsbridge (£5,140 for 1864 to 1867 bound in pairs), with an 1865 making £1,900 and an 1875 £2,180. The existence of facsimiles thus seems to have had no deleterious effect upon the value of originals.

Autograph albums, it seems, cannot be bought cheaply, unless they are modern. A sheet bearing 15 signatures of the 1896 Australian touring team made £1,250 at Acorn's of Manchester, with the 1896 England team making £1,400. Postcards also command a high price. Less common are matchbox labels, and an example from the firm of Octavius Hill, bearing an illustration of W. G. Grace, drove bidding up to £90 at a Cricket Memorabilia Society sale in which the 1950s England batsman, Willie Watson, sold his blazers and sweaters. The collector who paid £160 (premium-free) for the 1953 England sweater was well satisfied.

The trading base continues to broaden: cricketers stage auctions in aid of their benefits (David Smith raised £12,000 at Hove last September), the London sale-rooms compete fiercely, and provincial sale-rooms know that a few dozen cricket lots will bring positive results. The dealer or collector who wishes to take in all that is on offer will be spending a small fortune on travel, accommodation and catalogues alone. Meanwhile, the 1994 award for the most grievously underestimated lot must go to Phillips' Solihull sale-room, where six albums containing 3,000 postcards and photographs, mostly signed, were estimated at £20-£30, only to be hammered for £3,117. It's all a matter of perception.

CRICKET EQUIPMENT IN 1993

By NORMAN HARRIS

Bat-makers have always striven for the extra edge, as you might say, but they are now struggling to go beyond it. At the same time they have reached the end of the line in word-play. *Ultimate* was the name chosen by Gray-Nicolls for their top bat in 1994, but how can you improve on the ultimate? The makers' answer is to call their top 1995 model the *Optimum*. We must leave it to lexicographers to debate which word has the greater value.

Evidently making little progress on the bat front, the cricket equipment trade has been exploring other parts of the market; and 1994 was quite definitely the Year of the Boot. Sponsorship from Quaser saw Leicestershire players wearing a boot with a huge tongue piece that stuck out at an eye-catching angle. But the Quaser boots were about much more than style. The inspiration was the world of athletics, especially javelin-throwing – where the stresses are argued to be comparable to those in fast bowling. David Millns and other players provided input. But, interestingly, the model that had the most support and looked most like a javelin boot (it was called the "Waqar") was not popular with Millns and company because it was rather heavy. All fast bowlers, it seems, want a boot that is both as light and as strong as possible.

Meanwhile, Pony were bringing to the cricket market the technology developed in their running shoes. The standard material which cushions foot-strike is EVA, a rubber-plastic compound with a cellular structure (from the many tiny air pockets formed as it is injected). Though light, it tends in time to break down and compress. Pony's answer was to use their own "Actilite" midsole: a polyurethane which they claim suffers much less from compression and is also lightweight. Leading players wearing Pony boots included Andy Caddick, Darren Gough and Graeme Hick.

Meanwhile, a number of professionals who were prepared to pay – and pay substantially – for their boots rather than be paid were again using the services of Ian Mason, a Sutton Coldfield part-timer for whom bootmaking has become an "out-of-control hobby". It was his boots that were worn by Devon Malcolm when he took his historic nine wickets at The Oval. Mason's clients tend to be bowlers who have had particular problems. For example, Neal Radford's front-foot action involves a fierce twisting movement and the likelihood of twisting the back out of the boot. Mason says he puts in "every conceivable protection" but he, too, is aware that players do not want heavy boots. He claims to be continually searching out the latest materials – including mid-soles from Italy – and to have reduced the weight of his boots by about 20 per cent in recent years.

In every trade, it seems, greater efficiency in production and materials stimulates a cottage-industry sector. So it is, too, with clothing. Modern synthetic materials provide a trouser more conducive to running and sliding, and more easily washed and dried. And it is the professional player, who is unlikely to have bought his own kit, who effectively dictates what is offered to cricketers at large. But a significant part of that larger market – especially players of mature years – regret the passing of genuine flannels and dislike being forced into tight-fitting polyester. The mainstream trade, of course, insists there is "no demand" for traditional flannels.

The response of Philip Allen, a village cricketer in Worcestershire, was to start a company called "A Load of Old Flannel". Allen is a carer for the mentally and physically disabled, another partner is a surveyor, while the third, "Wizzy", works with costumes at Covent Garden. What they have in common is a hatred of what Allen calls "elasticated pyjamas".

ALOOF (a rather suitable acronym that emerged quite by accident) has been pottering along in Malvern for several years. Their splendidly original marketing literature, spiced with references to Bristol Beaufighter sports cars and a pub called The Boat, is just as impressive as their traditional barathea wool flannels – which, with pleats, waist adjusters and fly buttons, come with an £85 price tag. One customer even returned his flannels with the complaint that they were "too good to play cricket in".

They were worn by the Worcestershire captain, Tim Curtis, before he made the mistake of giving them a hot wash instead of dry-cleaning them. Curtis did find that they made fielding rather hot work. But at least he was prepared to try them. It is good to know that some cricketers – including those who buy their own boots – will make their own decisions in these matters, rather than be dressed according to the dictates of a contract.

UMPIRING IN 1994

By JACK BAILEY

England's representatives on the international umpires' panel for the period ending October 1995 are David Shepherd, Dickie Bird, Nigel Plews and Mervyn Kitchen. They will all be delighted to have been chosen to travel and adjudicate in various parts of the world. There is the extra money for one thing; the avoidance, all expenses paid, of the worst aspects of the English winter for another; and most importantly, a continuation of the camaraderie, still present in the game at all levels, which makes each new series something to anticipate with relish.

Yes, relish. There is always the chance of a fair amount of anguish in these days of endless TV scrutiny of every close decision, and extravagant reactions by players who feel they have received rough justice and seize the opportunity to let everyone know – in close-up. The 1994 season in England again produced examples which must have stretched the old camaraderie to somewhere near breaking point at times, not least during a couple of incidents in the match between England and South Africa at The Oval, following as they did the controversy surrounding Mike Atherton at Lord's.

These incidents underlined the way in which Test match umpires have been consistently taking second place to Test match referees in the public consciousness. Both now yield pride of place to the television camera, even though Law 42 still quaintly asserts: "The umpires are the sole judges of fair and unfair play."

When South Africa played England at Lord's, though, Atherton's actions involving the ball, dirt (in and out of the pocket), and the hand which had been in contact with the dirt, put that notion severely to the test. As far as the umpires were concerned, the ball had not been interfered with and they said so when questioned by the referee. This, one assumes, is why Peter Burge's initial pronouncement on the subject was, in effect, an acceptance of the umpires' view.

If the Test match referee has a function it is to uphold the authority of the umpires. Burge has been the subject of much criticism for his refereeing of the England–South Africa series. (Too strict, too heavy-handed, too vindictive, even.) But Burge ranks high in the esteem of those umpires who stood in Test matches in which he was involved.

He took stick for the weight of punishment meted out to Atherton and Fanie de Villiers during the Oval Test. However, it is immaterial whether the England captain nicked the ball before being given out lbw. England captains, above all, cannot display public dissent towards an umpire's decision. Television pictures may have magnified the glancing at the bat and the shaking of the head which denoted to millions that Atherton had been given out by an umpire who didn't know his job but, if TV is there, England captains and everyone else must rein themselves in.

In the same way, de Villiers sought to put pressure on the umpire when he failed to look towards him after an appeal for a catch behind the wicket, preferring to run down the pitch to offer and receive congratulations, then to express disbelief some long moments later when it became apparent that his pressurising tactics had failed. He, too, was duly fined and Burge at least struck a blow for umpires in the long term. Whether other referees will do their job in the same fearless spirit remains open to question, although Brian Lara's punishment for dissent in India leaves room for hope.

During 1994, decisions by the third umpire played an increasingly large part in the umpiring of televised matches in England. Once introduced, they were bound to. Meanwhile, any attempt to widen the powers of the third eye will, one hopes, be kept in check.

The unsatisfactory over-rate in the English domestic game continues to highlight the problems of a system in which the umpires are subject to the judgment of the same county captains over whom they adjudicate. There are all kinds of ways in which the over-rate could be accelerated to an acceptable level. Among these would be a reasonable enforcement of Law 15.2: "No practice may take place on the field if, in the opinion of the umpires, it could result in a waste of time."

Each time a bowler is handed the ball for a new spell he has, as a matter of habit, two or three trial balls to a colleague standing some ten to fifteen yards distant. Often, the batsman is waiting while this meaningless performance takes place. Time is lost, the game is slowed and nobody gains. Yet the umpires fail to act. This is understandable – but regrettable.

CRICKET GROUNDS IN 1994

The first ground in Britain to be specifically designed with Test cricket in mind was opened in 1994 when Durham Second Eleven played the first two matches at the new Riverside Ground in Chester-le-Street. Riverside is due to stage seven of Durham's ten first-class fixtures in 1995, starting with the match against champions Warwickshire on May 18, and the club have serious hopes – encouraged by the TCCB – of hosting a Test match in 2000.

The stadium is being built in "modules" (which will eventually acquire prettier names). The first is a large pavilion, including dressing-rooms, a boardroom, offices, ten hospitality suites (all sold) and members' facilities. Module Two should be completed in 1996. Initially, the ground will have about 7,000 seats (maybe 10,000 with temporary stands). When all five modules plus a South Stand are finished, the ground should hold 20,000.

At the opening, there was much praise for the work of both groundsman Tom Flintoft and local architect Bill Ainsworth, who designed a cricket stadium for his thesis at Durham University in 1960. The club are keen to emphasise both the beauty of the site, with the River Wear snaking through and Lumley Castle rising above it, and its practicality – it is less than two minutes off the A1(M) with at least 3,000 parking places. It is part of the Riverside development, which also includes a playground, soccer pitches, parkland and a nature reserve.

Durham's nomadic existence will henceforth be curtailed. Durham University, Gateshead Fell and the old Ropery Lane ground at Chester-le-Street have all disappeared from the first-class fixture list. The last will clearly not reappear; Gateshead Fell, where there are access difficulties, has probably also been discarded; but the county still feel an emotional tug to the University ground, where their Championship career began in 1992, and they may play there again, even though it is only five miles from the new stadium. For the time being, Darlington, Hartlepool and Stockton retain their fixtures. Officials are anxious to make these more like festival games to keep them viable; in 1995 Sussex are playing at Hartlepool over August Bank Holiday weekend and the fixture is to be the centre of a festival advertising the town's under-rated seaside charms.

A new and happier era is also beginning at Northampton. In October – just before the Channel Tunnel opened, and after a similar gestation period – Northampton Town Football Club finally vacated the County Ground. They moved to a new stadium on the edge of town, Sixfields, where the facilities seemed likely to outshine the team. The dilapidated County Ground terracing was to be demolished and the floodlights sold to Ghana. This will at last allow the cricket club to expand and improve their facilities. The Cockerill Trust, which controls the ground, is obliged, under the terms of the trust, to use the extra space for sporting purposes; a decision on exactly what these might be was due to be taken in early 1995; a new indoor school was considered a certainty. In the meantime, Northamptonshire now have unrestricted access to the ground and will at last play a September fixture there in 1995.

Elsewhere, Derbyshire have withdrawn from their annual fixture at Ilkeston, after the end of a local sponsorship deal; and the Lincolnshire seaside town of Cleethorpes will stage one of Nottinghamshire's Sunday League matches in 1995 for the first time since 1983.

CHARITIES IN 1994

THE LORD'S TAVERNERS raised a record £1.7 million in 1994. The overall aim is "to give youngsters, especially the disadvantaged and disabled, a sporting chance". At least half the money distributed goes back into grassroots cricket, principally through the National Cricket Association and the English Schools Cricket Association. The other half is directed towards sporting opportunities for disabled youngsters, such as the New Horizons minibus programme.

There were two particularly successful fund-raising events in 1994: the President's Ball, sponsored by Guinness, and the dinner for the South Africans, sponsored by Tesco, on the eve of the Lord's Test. There are plans for a Lord's Taverners South Africa in 1995; there is already an Australian branch. The Lady Taverners, formed in 1987, passed the £1 million fund-raising mark during 1994. Sir Colin Cowdrey succeeded Prince Edward as president of the Taverners at the start of 1995; he is the first cricketer to hold the position since Alf Gover in 1974.

The Director: Patrick Shervington, The Lord's Taverners, 22 Queen Anne's Gate, London SW1H 9AA. Telephone: 0171-222 0707.

THE FOUNDATION FOR SPORT AND THE ARTS is funded by the Pools Promoters' Association, with the help of a tax concession from the Government. It gave away over £60 million in 1994, of which two-thirds went to sport. Cricket is the largest recipient (soccer being covered by a different organisation) and several hundred clubs benefited in 1994. Grants range from £50 to the current upper limit of £150,000. Preference is given to projects that benefit the community. The chairman of the Foundation is Sir Tim Rice.

Administrator: Jean Beynon, PO Box 20, Liverpool L9 6EA. Telephone: 0151-524 0235.

THE JOHN ARLOTT MEMORIAL TRUST was launched in June 1993 to help provide affordable housing and improve recreational facilities in rural areas, by raising funds for the Rural Housing Trust and the National Playing Fields Association. It organised three celebrity cricket matches in 1994 and is anxious to make contact with people who would like to organise their own fund-raising matches or other events. A small range of merchandise is available, including ties at £8.99 post free.

Janet Hart, John Arlott Memorial Trust, Hobart House, 40 Grosvenor Place, London SW1X 7AN. Telephone: 0171-235 6318.

THE PRIMARY CLUB, one of the favourite charities of the late Brian Johnston, started at Beckenham Cricket Club in 1955. In 1994 it raised about £70,000 for cricket and other sports for the visually handicapped. Most of the money goes to Dorton House School, Sevenoaks, which is now building a swimming pool for kindergarten children, but equipment has been provided for schools for the blind throughout the country. Membership is nominally restricted to players who have been dismissed first ball in any form of cricket.

Mike Thomas, 6 Denbigh Close, Chislehurst, Kent BR7 5EB. Telephone: 0181-467 5665.

THE HORNSBY PROFESSIONAL CRICKETERS FUND was established in 1928, from the estate of J. H. J. Hornsby, who played for Middlesex, MCC and the Gentlemen. It provides money to assist "former professional cricketers [not necessarily first-class] or their wives, widows until remarriage, children and other dependents, provided the persons concerned shall be in necessitous circumstances". Assistance is given by monthly allowances, special grants or, in certain cases, loans. Donations, requests for help or information about potential recipients are all welcome.

Clerk to the Trustees: A. K. James, "Dunroamin", 65 Keyhaven Road, Milford-on-Sea, Lymington, Hampshire SO41 0QX. Telephone: 01590-644720.

THE CRICKETERS ASSOCIATION CHARITY was founded in 1983 to relieve financial hardship amongst present or former members of the Association, anyone who has played cricket for a first-class county or their "wives, widows, children, parents and dependents". It is becoming the custom for cricketers in their benefit year to donate half of one per cent of their proceeds to the fund. Donations are welcome; also requests for help and information about cricketers who may be in need.

Chairman of the Trustees: Harold Goldblatt, 60 Doughty Street, London WC1N 2LS. Telephone: 0171-405 9855.

CRICKET AND RELIGION IN 1994

Cricket and Christianity had an improbable collision at the Trent Bridge Test in June when it was reported that Ray Illingworth, the chairman of the England selectors, had sacked the Oxford Blue, Rev. Andrew Wingfield Digby, as the team's chaplain, saying that if England players needed a shoulder to cry on, they should not be in the team. This brought forth the memorable headline: "Illy Bans God."

The story was only slightly spoiled later when it became clearer that Wingfield Digby did not hold a formal chaplaincy from which he could be sacked. He had been invited by Illingworth's predecessor, Ted Dexter, to act informally as the team's spiritual adviser. The TCCB later apologised and Illingworth said the vicar would still be welcome in the dressing-room.

On the eve of the Oval Test, Wingfield Digby switched sides to take the Bible class which is a regular feature of touring life for several of the South African players. Six of them attended; they were not rewarded with worldly success in the game that followed.

In the winter, Wingfield Digby joined the England A team in India and, as director of the organisation Christians in Sport, took part in a tour to Zimbabwe, captained by the Northamptonshire batsman Alan Fordham. Christians in Sport had previously run tours to India, and plan to repeat the Zimbabwe visit in 1995-96.

Six of the 18 first-class counties did have official chaplains at the end of 1994, not counting Worcestershire, whose secretary Mike Vockins is an ordained minister. "People are recognising that having professionals on all different levels is a good thing to do in sport," said Wingfield Digby. "Having people to look after the staff spiritually, if and when required, is part of running a good professional set-up."

CRICKET BETTING IN 1994

One of the most extraordinary sideshows of the 1994 season was the story of how 19 men of Warwickshire shared a £100,000 payout, and saw even more money – £126,512.50 – slip through their fingers.

The affair began when the bookmakers Surrey Racing wrote to all the counties offering them the opportunity to place a bet on their team, thinking they might want to insure against their club having to pay their players win bonuses. This is standard practice in other sports. However, Warwickshire had other plans. A syndicate of 19 committee men and friends, including the chief executive Dennis Amiss, decided to place a private £5 yankee (doubles, trebles and one accumulator on all four possibilities) on their team to win the County Championship at 16 to 1 and the Sunday League at 18 to 1 and to reach the two one-day finals, at 17 to 2 and 10 to 1.

Many cricketing punters back their teams to win everything. Normally, these are regarded by bookmakers as sentimental mug-bets which are certain to lose. However, in mid-season, when the idea of Warwickshire winning all four competitions began to seem possible, what one bookmaker described as "panic" spread through the industry as it considered millions of pounds of liabilities.

The Warwickshire committee bet was the best-publicised of these. But Surrey Racing said that, because the bet was not to win every competition but, in the case of the knockouts, only to reach the finals, it was a "speciality bet", which the firm could not hedge, and was thus subject to a special limit of £100,000. Warwickshire disputed this and went to the *Sporting Life*, the industry's traditional arbitrators, which censured the bookmakers for not sending out a copy of their rules when it solicited the bet and making the terms clear from the start – but supported their interpretation. So the committee members were paid £100,000 (£5,263.15 each) rather than the £226,512.50 that would otherwise have been their due. "We were disappointed," said Amiss, "but it was still enough for a very decent holiday."

In theory, a £5 yankee on Warwickshire to win the grand slam could have netted £647,635 (almost as much as Brian Lara's reputed 1994 earnings) had it happened. In practice, bookmakers have limits for winnings of a quarter or half a million pounds, and many would have paid even less on the grounds of "related contingencies", the theory that, because a team wins one competition, it is more likely to win another, and therefore reduced odds apply. The rules about similar bets will definitely be spelled out more clearly when they are struck in 1995.

Generally, cricket betting continued to grow in 1994, and now has a more central place in the game than it has had since Napoleonic times. Betting shops are commonplace on English Test and county grounds and one industry estimate is that about £10 million was gambled on cricket in the year.

DIRECTORY OF BOOK DEALERS

AARDVARK BOOKS, "Copperfield", High Street, Harmston, Lincoln LN5 9SN. Tel: 01522 722671. Peter Taylor specialises in Wisdens. Send SAE for list. Wisden cleaning and repair service available. Wisdens purchased, *any* condition.

NEIL BARNARD, 99 Lime Avenue, Leamington Spa, Warwickshire CV32 7DG. Tel: 01926 424895. Catalogue available; please send large SAE. Books bought. Booksearch service; please send "wants" list; no search fee.

TIM BEDDOW CRICKET BOOKS, 62a Stanmore Road, Edgbaston, Birmingham B16 9TB. Tel: 0121-420 3466 (24-hour answerphone). Require antiquarian, modern and remainders. Highest price paid. Catalogues also available. (Send 1st/2nd class stamp.)

BOUNDARY BOOKS, Southlands, Sandy Lane, Goostrey, Cheshire CW4 8NT. Tel: 01477 533106. Second-hand and antiquarian cricket books, autographs and memorabilia bought and sold. Deluxe limited editions published. Catalogues issued.

PETER BRIGHT, 11 Ravens Court, Ely, Cambs. CB6 3ED. Tel: 01353 661727. Send stamp for sample catalogue of Wisdens, general cricket books and printed ephemera. Books bought and "wants" serviced.

CRICKET LIBRARIES, Gracelands, Lakeside, Littleborough, Lancashire OL15 0DD. Tel: 01706 374379. Illustrated catalogues published regularly include books, prints, ceramics, photographs, postcards, autographed material and a wide range of interesting ephemera.

IAN DYER, 29 High Street, Gilling West, Richmond, North Yorkshire DL10 5JG. Tel/fax: 01748 822786. Ian Dyer specialises in antiquarian and second-hand cricket books, Wisdens and annuals. Collections purchased and collected. Send stamp for catalogue.

C. P. W. JONKERS BOOKS, 4 Ewin Court, Cherwell Drive, Oxford OX3 0NY. Tel: 01865 247086 & 0850 774828. Specialist in rare cricket books, especially Wisdens. Books bought and sold, catalogues issued; please send SAE.

E. O. KIRWAN, 3 Pine Tree Garden, Oadby, Leics. LE2 5UT. Tel: 0116-271 4267 (evenings and weekends only). Second-hand and antiquarian cricket books, Wisdens, autograph material and cricket ephemera of all kinds.

J. W. McKENZIE, 12 Stoneleigh Park Road, Ewell, Epsom, Surrey KT19 0QT. Tel: 0181-393 7700; fax: 0181-393 1694. Specialists in antiquarian, second-hand cricket books, particularly Wisdens. Books and collections bought. Catalogues sent on request.

ROGER PAGE, 10 Ekari Court, Yallambie, Victoria 3085, Australia. Tel: (03) 435 6332; fax: (03) 432 2050. Dealer in new and second-hand cricket books. Distributor of overseas cricket annuals and magazines. Agent for Cricket Statisticians and Cricket Memorabilia Society.

RED ROSE BOOKS (BOLTON), 196 Belmont Road, Astley Bridge, Bolton BL1 7AR. Tel: 01204 598080. Antiquarian and second-hand cricket books. Please send stamp for latest catalogue.

GILL & DAVID ROBERTSON, "Hedges", St Georges Lees, Sandwich, CT13 9JS. Tel: 01304 612876. Seek Wisdens, books and ephemera for current clients and future catalogues. Anything relating to Kent Cricket urgently required.

CHRISTOPHER SAUNDERS, Orchard Books, Kingston House, High Street, Newnham-on-Severn, Gloucestershire GL14 1BB. Tel: 01594 516030; fax: 01594 517273. Visitors by appointment only. See advertisement on page 1338.

DONALD SCOTT, 3 Windridge Close, St Albans, Herts. AL3 4JP. Tel: 01727 868186. Cricket books purchased and collected. Catalogues issued. Currently running second-hand book stall with related ephemera at Essex and Gloucestershire home matches.

SPORTSPAGES, Caxton Walk, 94–96 Charing Cross Road, London WC2H 0JG. Tel: 0171-240 9604. Barton Square, St Ann's Square, Manchester M2 7HA. Tel: 0161-832 8530. New cricket books, audio and videotapes, including imports, especially from Australasia; retail and mail order service.

DOMINIC WINTER, The Old School, Maxwell Street, Swindon SN1 5DR. Tel: 01793 611340; fax: 01793 491727. Book auctions, specialist auctioneers and valuers. Saleroom and offices at the above address. Specialist sales twice yearly. Valuations undertaken.

WISTERIA BOOKS, Wisteria Cottage, Birt Street, Birtsmorton, Malvern WR13 6AW. Tel: 01684 833578. Visit our family-run stall at county grounds for new, second-hand, antiquarian cricket books and ephemera, or contact Grenville Simons at the address above. Send SAE for catalogue.

MARTIN WOOD, 2 St John's Road, Sevenoaks, Kent TN13 3LW. Tel: 01732 457205. Martin Wood has been dealing in cricket books since 1970 and has now posted 20,000 parcels. For a copy of his 1995 catalogue listing 2,750 items, send 25p stamp to the address above.

DIRECTORY OF CRICKET SUPPLIERS

CRICKET EQUIPMENT

CLASSIC BAT CO., 53 High Street, Keynsham, Bristol BS18 1DS. Tel: 0117-986 2714; fax: 0117-986 1753. Hand-made bats, balls, pads, gloves, helmets, coffins and clothing. Free colour catalogue available. League and Young Player Sponsorships considered.

GRAY-NICOLLS, Robertsbridge, East Sussex TN32 5DH. Tel: 01580-880357; fax: 01580-881156. The definitive range of products to cater for cricketers at all levels, from village green to Test arena.

GUNN & MOORE LTD, 119-121 Stanstead Road, Forest Hill, London SE23 1HJ. Tel: 0181-291 3344; fax: 0181-699 4008. Gunn & Moore, established in 1885, are the world's most comprehensive provider of cricket bats, equipment, footwear and clothing.

HUNTS COUNTY BATS, Royal Oak Passage, Huntingdon, Cambs. PE18 9DN. Tel: 01480-451234. Probably the best range of cricket bats, hand-made by craftsmen to your specification, plus full range of equipment, clothing, holdalls and coffins.

MIKE INGHAM BATS AND CRICKET EQUIPMENT, 69 Helmshore Road, Haslingden BB4 4BW. All your cricketing needs at discount prices. Write for a brochure, or ring 01706-213121.

NOMAD BOX CO. LTD. Tel: 01858-464878. The original "coffin" available in red, black, blue, grey, green, yellow, maroon, brown or white, as used by Test and county players alike.

ALFRED READER, Invicta Works, Teston, Maidstone, Kent ME18 5AW. Tel: 01622-812230. Contact: Graham Brown. England's largest manufacturer of cricket balls. Distributors of Albion head protection and Sovereign cricket clothing and equipment.

BOWLING MACHINES

JUGS, 53 High Street, Keynsham, Bristol BS18 1DS. Tel: 0117-986 9519; fax: 0117-986 1753. The *original* bowling machine company. New machines from £895 + VAT. Used by Lancashire, Hampshire, Gloucestershire. Free colour catalogue and video available.

STUART & WILLIAMS, 6 Brookfield Road, Cotham, Bristol BS6 5PQ. Tel: 0117-924 3569; fax 0117-944 6194. Manufacturers of cricket bowling machines and ball-throwing machines for other sports. Machines for domestic and commercial applications. Exporters to all cricket-playing nations.

CLOTHING

CLASSIC CLUBWEAR, 53 High Street, Keynsham, Bristol BS18 1DS. Tel: 0117-986 9519; fax: 0117-986 1753. Fast, efficient embroidery and screenprinting service on cricket shirts, wool or acrylic sweaters, caps, sweatshirts, leisurewear. Free colour catalogue available.

CLUB COLOURS, Hercies Road, Hillingdon, Middlesex. Tel: 01895-232525. Suppliers of traditional cricket sweaters, shirts, ties, caps, blazers and club casual wear direct to clubs and to the trade.

CRUSADER SPORTS, Main Road, Hallow, Worcester WR2 6LL. Tel: 01905-641841; fax: 01905-641485. Suppliers of top-quality cricket clothing and protective wear. Available from stock at competitive prices and normally despatched in 48 hours.

DIRECT SPORTS SUPPLIES LTD, 2B Addington Street, Ramsgate CT11 9JL. Tel: 01843-590159. Trade and retail suppliers of high-quality cricket shirts and trousers, printing service for badges, etc. available.

LUKE EYRES, Freepost, Denny Industrial Estate, Pembroke Avenue, Waterbeach, Cambridge CB5 8BR. Tel: 01223-440501. 100% wool, cotton or acrylic sweaters as supplied to major county club, international cricket teams and schools.

ROCHFORD SPORTS KNITWEAR, 1 Lower Backway, Bruton, Somerset BA10 0EA. Tel: 01749-813240. Traditional hand-made cable pattern cricket sweaters, individually made from 100% pure new wool in your own club colours.

GROUND EQUIPMENT

JETMARINE LTD. Tel: 0161-487 1648. Glass fibre cricket pitch covers. Stronger and more durable than canvas types. Heavy steel understructure with wide caster wheels. Resists weather and vandalism. Telephone for information.

RADFORD EZY-NET, Charford House, Machine Farm, Bishampton, Worcestershire WR10 2NE. Tel. and fax: 01386-861029. A revolutionary new demountable/portable net system. Providing simplicity, security, longevity, safety and flexibility. A boon to groundsmen.

S.L.R. CRICKET COMPANY, 21 Middlefield Road, Cossington, Leicester LE7 8UT. Tel: 01509-816169; fax: 01509-816661. Suppliers of scoreboards and boxes mechanical and electrical, sightscreens, county turf wickets and all other ground equipment.

RALPH SPRING. Tel: 0181-428 5919. First-class tandem cricket rollers completely rebuilt to better than new – widely used by clubs, schools and local authorities. Ballasting available. Also all other grass machinery.

STUART CANVAS PRODUCTS (Props. Kenyon Textiles Ltd), Warren Works, Hardwick Grange, Warrington, Cheshire WA1 4RF. Tel: 01925-814525; fax: 01925-831709. Designers, manufacturers and suppliers of sports ground covering equipment.

TILDENET LTD, Longbrook House, Ashton Vale Road, Bristol BS3 2HA. Tel: 0117-966 9684; fax 0117-923 1251. Suppliers of germination sheets as used at Lord's. Cricket nets including mobiles, sightscreens, covers, perimeter nets.

MAIL ORDER/RETAIL CRICKET SPECIALISTS

FORDHAM SPORTS CRICKET EQUIPMENT SPECIALIST, 81 Robin Hood Way, Kingston Vale, London SW15. Tel: 0181-974 5654. 168-172 East Hill Wandsworth, London SW18. Tel: 0181-871 2500. Largest range of branded stock in south of England at discount prices.

MORRANT GROUP LTD, The Factory, 1 Walpole Road, South Woodford, London E18 2LN. Tel: 0181-504 7701; fax: 0181-559 0948. Leading cricket mail order specialists. Widest choice of branded equipment at the lowest prices – guaranteed.

ROMIDA SPORTS, 18 Shaw Road, New Hey, Rochdale OL16 4LT. Tel: 01706-882444; fax: 01706-882160. Possibly the largest supplier of personal cricket equipment in the world. Ring for free colour catalogue.

VEE-KAY SPORTS, 31 Bond Street, Ealing W5 5AS. Tel: 0181-579 3389; fax: 0181-567 2786. Cricket Specialists. Largest selection, lowest prices. Phone for free colour catalogue.

NON-TURF PITCHES

CLUB SURFACES LIMITED, The Barn, Bisham Grange, Marlow, Bucks. SL7 1RS. Tel: 01628-485969; fax: 01628-471944. Contact Derek Underwood for full information on **ClubTurf** pitches – world leaders since 1978.

NOTTS. SPORT, Launde House, Harborough Road, Oadby, Leicester LE2 4LE. Tel: 0116-272 0222; fax: 0116-272 0617. Non-turf cricket pitches supplied. Write or telephone for free site survey at your club without obligation.

TROPHIES AND AWARDS

COLBORNE TROPHIES LTD. Tel: 01225-764101. Manufacturers and suppliers of quality awards at factory prices. Huge choice and full engraving service. Mail order specialists. Telephone for free catalogue.

CRICKET TOURS (OVERSEAS)

MIKE BURTON SPORTS TRAVEL, Bastion House, Brunswick Road, Gloucester GL1 1JJ. Tel: 01452-419666; fax: 01452-527500. Specialists in the arrangement of inbound and outbound sports tours, for supporters, clubs and schools.

EDWIN DORAN SPORTS TRAVEL, 9 York Street, Twickenham, Middlesex TW1 3JZ. Tel: 0181-744 1212; fax: 0181-744 1169. Experienced and highly professional organisers of cricket tours around the world for both players and spectators alike.

GULLIVERS SPORTS TRAVEL, Fiddington Manor, Tewkesbury, Glos. GL20 7BJ. Tel: 01684-293175; fax: 01684-297926. The No. 1 cricket tour company for top quality and good value worldwide tours for supporters and teams.

KESTOURS, Travel House, Elmers End, Beckenham, Kent BR3 3QY. Tel: 0181-658 7313. Specialist tour operators arranging international cricket tours for players and supporters. ABTA and ATOL bonded.

FRED RUMSEY TRAVEL, 19 Main Street, Barton-under-Needwood, Staffs. DE13 8AA. Tel: 01283-716677. 20 years experience in worldwide cricket tours. Annual Pro-Am Cricket Festival in Barbados. South Africa Xmas 95/96. Club tours. Ring now.

SARtravel. Tel: 0171-287 1133. Offers a wide range of travel facilities. Tailor-made tours, package tours, special interest tours, sports teams and clubs, fly-drive, flights only, car hire, to South and Southern Africa.

SPORT ABROAD LTD, Wix Hill House, West Horsley KT24 6DZ. Tel: 01483-225000. (ABTA, ATOL). Advance register South Africa 1995 now. European Pro-Am Spain October 1995. Club/school tours tailor-made.

SUN LIVING, 10 Milton Court, Ravenshead, Nottingham NG15 9BD. Tel: 01623-795365; fax 01623-797421. Since 1974 Sun Living have specialised in tours for cricketers at all levels, including our ever popular supporters' tours.

SUNSPORT TOURS. Tel: Barry Dudleston 01604-31626. Specialists in cricket tours to South Africa, Zimbabwe, Kenya and beyond. Playing itineraries for clubs, schools, colleges. Leading operator of county pre-season tours. Supporter holidays a speciality. ATOL 2883.

TEAM EVENTS TRAVEL, 47 Palmerston Street, Bollington, Macclesfield, Cheshire SK10 5PX. Tel: 01625-576260; fax: 01625-575705. Offering a highly professional tailor-made service to major worldwide events for groups and individuals.

WORLDS END TRAVEL. Tel: 01582-481636. Club and supporters' cricket tours arranged throughout the world. Phone for quotations.

CRICKET TOURS (UK)

THE FORESTER'S ARMS, Williton, Somerset TA4 4QY. Tel: 01984-632508. 17th century coaching inn close to Brendon and Quantock Hills. Hosts to touring sides for many years. Good food, real ales, fixtures arranged.

SOUTH WALES FIXTURE BUREAU (Est. 1983). Mike Ashton, 42 Colcot Road, Barry, South Glamorgan CF62 8HN. Tel: 01446-740646. Tours arranged across ten counties – all fixtures and accommodation provided.

OBITUARY

ABBOTT, ROY, who died in September 1993, aged 77, was head groundsman at Perth's WACA ground for 36 years from the late 1940s. His skill at pitch preparation was vital in winning Perth Test status in 1970 and in sustaining the ground's reputation for having one of the fastest and truest pitches in the world.

ABEYSEKERA, CLARENCE, who died on December 16, 1993, aged 77, won an unofficial cap for Ceylon against Pakistan in 1949.

AITCHISON, Rev. JAMES, who died in Glasgow on February 13, 1994, aged 73, was regarded as Scotland's finest post-war batsman. He may even have been the finest Scottish batsman too, but no comparison is possible since, unlike Mike Denness, he never played county cricket. He was an orthodox but attractive player who appeared in 50 first-class matches for Scotland and was a regular in the team from 1946 to 1963, scoring 2,786 runs at 32.77. He scored seven centuries for Scotland, a record until 1992. Five of them were first-class, including 190 not out against Ireland in Dublin in 1959. In two-day matches he made 106 not out, carrying his bat, against the South Africans at Paisley in 1947 and 100 against the Australians at the end of their 1956 tour; Ray Lindwall and Keith Miller later called it the best innings they had seen all summer. Aitchison made 56 centuries in Scottish club cricket. He was a minister in the Church of Scotland, in Edinburgh for 11 years and in Glasgow for 23, until his retirement in 1986. After Aitchison played a long, chancy innings against Worcestershire, Roly Jenkins said that with his luck he should be an Archbishop.

ALSTON, ARTHUR REX, died on September 8, 1994, aged 93. Rex Alston was, along with John Arlott and E. W. Swanton, one of the triumvirate who dominated radio cricket commentary in the years after the war while Brian Johnston was still concentrating on television. He was an all-round sports broadcaster and in the 1940s and 1950s his precise, light baritone was a familiar sound on rugby, tennis and athletics as well as cricket. He looked rather like a vicar – his father was a Suffragan Bishop – and sounded like a schoolmaster: he taught at Bedford School until the war, when some BBC men were billeted on him and one suggested his voice might be just right. He was a considerable sportsman: on the wing for Bedford and Rosslyn Park, running second in the 1923 University athletics match to Harold Abrahams – later his partner in the commentary box – and playing cricket for the Crusaders at Cambridge and for Bedfordshire, whom he captained in 1932. Alston commentated on about a hundred Tests, but did hardly any after 1964, three years after he had officially retired from the BBC. Thereafter he wrote a column in *Playfair Cricket Monthly*, notable for its fierce opposition to the break with South Africa, and continued reporting county matches for the *Daily Telegraph* until 1987. He made a broadcasting comeback that year on the Saturday of the MCC bicentenary game when, despite some understandable difficulties ("It's little Abdul what-not. He's a good bowler, my word he is"), he delighted everyone so much he was given a 20-minute encore. His broadcasting style was described as "pleasant and courteous" in an obituary in *The Times* in 1985. This was accurate; however, Alston was not dead. A mix-up in the office had led to his obituary being published instead of merely updated for the files. By a horrid coincidence, Alston had collapsed the previous evening at a dinner and so had the doubly disconcerting experience of being shown his obituary by a nurse at the Westminster Hospital. Reports that he found it all very humorous were as exaggerated as his death. The following year he proved his fitness by remarrying and became perhaps the first man to have his death and marriage reported in *The Times* in that order. He ascribed his continuing vigour to daily cold baths.

BALASKAS, XENOPHON CONSTANTINE, died at his home in Johannesburg on May 12, 1994, aged 83. "Bally" Balaskas was the leg-spinner who bowled South Africa to their first victory in England, at Lord's in 1935. It was his only Test of the tour and the only one that produced a result. The pitch, ravaged by leather-jackets, turned from an early stage; Bruce Mitchell and Jock Cameron batted far better than anyone on the England team and Balaskas, bowling tirelessly and with great accuracy from the Pavilion End, had figures of 32–8–49–5 in England's first innings and 27–8–54–4 in the second. Balaskas was not merely one of the most improbably-named of all Test players, he had one of the most improbable backgrounds. His parents were Greek migrants who owned the first restaurant in the diamond town of Kimberley. Pre-war South African cricketers usually came from a narrow, English social background but De Beers, the diamond company that controlled Kimberley, always ensured the two local high schools had big-name coaches and Charlie Hallows taught Balaskas. He played first-class cricket for Griqualand West when he was 15, and in 1929-30 was both leading run-scorer and wicket-taker in the Currie Cup, with 644 – including 206 against Rhodesia – and 39.

Balaskas made his Test debut at 20 the following year: he made little impact with bat or ball in two Tests at home to England and never made the Test team when South Africa travelled to Australia in 1931-32, though he scored 122 not out against New Zealand in the Second Test at Wellington. When he came to England in 1935, he was not chosen for the First Test. Years later he told the story of how he established his superiority over Leyland the week before the Lord's Test, bowling him with a huge leg-break and drawing the response: "Why don't you turn the effing ball, Bally?" Leyland was his first victim at Lord's – with a straight one. Balaskas missed the rest of the series through injury and his subsequent Test career was anticlimactic. He played for five different provincial teams, moving round partly for cricketing reasons, partly because of his work as a pharmacist. He took more than 40 wickets for Transvaal in 1945-46 and, but for a knee injury, might have been picked for the 1947 England tour. Instead, he finally retired. Apart from his century, his batting was never a success in Test cricket: he scored 174 runs at 14.50 and took 22 wickets at 36.63; his first-class figures were 2,696 runs at 28.68 and 276 wickets at 24.11. He settled in Johannesburg, bought a lovely house very cheaply and laid out a concrete pitch with a net in his garden; many players would go there for advice and he would always try to get them to play his way: vigorous body-action when bowling, and forward defence *à la* Hallows, planting the foot forward first and keeping the bat close to the pad. "He was always discovering some new theory about his bowling," said Bruce Mitchell. He was a cheerful, twinkling man in old age and he still loved cricketing theory.

BARKER, HUGHLEY WOODBINE, who died in April 1994, aged 68, was a tall and powerfully built Barbadian fast bowler, a prototype of the great generation that followed him. A terror while playing for the Empire club, he made four first-class appearances for Barbados between 1952 and 1956, but took only 12 wickets, averaging 30.66.

BENAUD, LOUIS RICHARD, who died at Sydney on January 9, 1994, was father of the Test players Richie and John. Lou Benaud was a schoolteacher who never became a first-class cricketer, but he played bush and grade games until he was past 50, and once took 20 wickets in a match, a feat his sons could not emulate. He was the author of *The Young Cricketer*, published in 1964.

BLAKELY, DOUGLAS JAMES, died on July 22, 1994, aged 72. Jim Blakely was a middle-order batsman who played five matches for Otago between 1940-41 and 1950-51.

BODKIN, Dr PETER ERNEST, who died on September 18, 1994, aged 70, won wartime Blues at Cambridge and went on to captain the University in the first post-war contest at Lord's in 1946. He was a promising schoolboy left-arm medium-pace bowler at Bradfield, but his batting had taken over by the time he was at university. He played nine first-class matches, all for Cambridge in 1946.

BOURNE, GORDON ALISTER, who died on September 13, 1993, aged 80, was the one of the youngest players ever to appear for Queensland: 17 years, 241 days against Victoria at Melbourne in 1930-31, a summer of dissension among the Queensland players. He scored four and six not out and never played again.

BOTEK, FRANZ IVOR, who died on March 23, 1994, aged 52, after a long illness, was formerly treasurer of the West Indies Cricket Board of Control and chairman of its Marketing Committee. He played a major role in setting up the Board's sponsorship deals. He was an opening batsman at club level and captained the University of the West Indies team in the Jamaica Senior Cup.

BURROUGH, HERBERT DICKINSON, died on April 9, 1994, aged 85. "Dickie" Burrough was a notably enthusiastic amateur batsman who played 171 matches for Somerset from 1927 to 1947. He was a front-foot hitter, who made 5,316 runs at 20.92, including four centuries, and chased round outfields with great zest through the 1930s, whenever he could break away from his law firm. His 135 at Kettering in 1932 lasted only three hours. His father also played for Somerset and an uncle and a cousin played first-class cricket as well. He failed to win a Blue at Cambridge for either cricket or hockey but played three times for England at hockey.

BYERLEY, FREDERICK WILLIAM ALFRED, who died on August 19, 1994, aged 84, made one first-class appearance, for Auckland against the South Africans in 1931-32, but distinguished himself by scoring 77 in a tail-end partnership of 117 with Mal Matheson, rescuing his team from 123 for six.

CALDWELL, TIMOTHY CHARLES JOHN, OBE, died on June 17, 1994, aged 80. Tim Caldwell succeeded Sir Donald Bradman as Chairman of the Australian Cricket Board in 1972, and held the job for three years. He played Sydney grade cricket for 21 years, having converted from leg-spin to off-spin, and three matches for New South Wales in the mid-1930s. During the Packer controversy, he joined Bradman and the then-chairman, Bob Parish, on the three-man ACB Emergency Committee which first fought Packer's organisation and then negotiated. He was a successful banker and is remembered as an astute administrator.

CARR, JAMES LLOYD, who died on February 26, 1994, aged 81, was an author and publisher who ran a one-man business from his home in Kettering. Two of J. L. Carr's eight novels were short-listed for the Booker Prize; another, *A Season in Sinji*, is arguably the best of all novels with a cricketing backdrop. He also published, in 1977, *Carr's Dictionary of Extraordinary English Cricketers*, with an enlarged edition in 1983. Factually not for the purist, the book remains a humorous gem. Carr was originally a schoolmaster and enthusiastic club cricketer, whose literary ability surfaced when he was editing the Northamptonshire County League handbook in the 1950s and contributing his own idiosyncratic notes. He was the *Wisden* book reviewer in 1993.

CARTER, HORATIO STRATTON, died on October 9, 1994, aged 80. "Raich" Carter was a lower-order batsman and medium-pace bowler who played three away matches for Derbyshire in June 1946. He had appeared for Durham in 1933 and 1934. He managed only eight runs and two wickets in first-class cricket, but achieved considerably more fame as a footballer. He scored 216 goals in 451 league games with Sunderland, Derby County and Hull City, won one League Championship, two FA Cups and 13 England caps (in a career interrupted by the war) and was described by *The Times* on his death as one of the half-dozen geniuses of the game in England. He was one of five England footballers to play first-class cricket for Derbyshire – the others being Billy Foulke, the 21-stone goalkeeper, John Goodall, Ernest Needham and Harry Storer (jun.). He was, though, almost certainly the only man in history to be out for a duck in a county match at Stourbridge six weeks after receiving an FA Cup winner's medal.

CHATTERJEE, CHANDRANATH, died in hospital in Calcutta on March 4, 1994, aged 40, after collapsing from a heart attack while batting in a local league match at Eden Gardens. Chandu Chatterjee made one appearance for Bengal in the Ranji Trophy, in 1986-87.

CHOUDHARY, YOGENDRA MOHAN, who died on July 11, 1994, aged 59, was a successful right-hand batsman for Delhi and Railways in the Ranji Trophy between 1953-54 and 1966-67, scoring 2,600 runs at 40.62. He scored 211 for Delhi against Patiala in 1955-56, but considered his 113 against a much stronger Bombay attack six weeks later to be his best-ever innings. In November 1956 Choudhary was a member of a strong Indian team, led by Polly Umrigar, which toured Ceylon.

COHEN, HARRY ALFRED, died on June 23, 1994, aged 90. Hal Cohen had been interested in cricketana since the 1920s and built one of the world's foremost collections, which made £257,010 net at auction in January 1995. He was Birmingham's chief dental officer for many years.

CORKE, MARTIN DEWE, who died on June 8, 1994, his 71st birthday, played in five first-class matches for the Free Foresters between 1953 and 1958. He was a forceful, somewhat unorthodox, batsman who played for Suffolk from 1946 to 1964, for the last 11 seasons as captain.

CORNISH, DOUGLAS JOHN, died on March 22, 1994, aged 74. "Kicker" Cornish was a good medium-pace bowler and made himself into a capable fielder, even though his left arm was a stump from birth and almost entirely useless. He played in a first-class friendly for Rhodesia against Transvaal at Salisbury in March 1947, and had first-innings figures of 7–2–9–1.

CORRALL, PERCY, who died in February 1994, aged 87, was the oldest surviving Leicestershire player. "Paddy" Corrall kept wicket for the county in 285 matches from 1930 to 1951. He was barely 5ft 2in tall and in 1933 suffered one of the most frightening injuries ever seen in county cricket. Cyril Washbrook chased a ball from Ewart Astill on the leg side and hit Corrall on the head with his bat, fracturing his skull. He was on the danger list for several weeks, but not only did he pull through, he returned next season better than ever and played in every Championship match. He lost his place to George Dawkes for the two seasons before the war, but Dawkes was in the RAF in 1946 and Corrall regained his place, forcing Dawkes – famously – to join Derbyshire. Past his 40th birthday, Corrall successfully kept wicket to the Australian wrist-spinner Jack Walsh. Almost a third, 187 out of 568, of his first-class dismissals were stumpings. He was on the umpires' list from 1952 to 1958 and for many years cheerfully kept a pub, even though he was a teetotaller.

COWIE, JOHN, OBE, died in Lower Hutt on June 3, 1994, aged 82. Jack Cowie played in only nine Tests, owing to the Second World War and New Zealand's limited international programme. But a couple of generations later his career might have been very different. He is widely regarded as New Zealand's best-ever bowler apart from Sir Richard Hadlee, with similar command of line and length for long spells, and the same ability to move the ball sharply at high speed. He also had something of Hadlee's aggression. Cowie was a very strong man known to his team-mates as "Bull" and his trademark was a hand-raised appeal-cum-roar of "Aaaaaat?", though his next remark to the umpire could be: "You know, I reckon it's getting a bit chilly. D'you think I could have my sweater?"

Cowie began as a batsman who could bowl a bit and when he played as a 14-year-old for the Auckland Under-21 side he began with a 14-ball over – he was no-balled six times for his drag. He was said to have bowled only two more no-balls in his career. Cowie concentrated on bowling because the Auckland team was then packed with batting, and rapidly established himself. In 1937 he toured England and was praised lavishly by both *Wisden* – "Had he been an Australian he might have been termed a wonder of the age" – and Len Hutton, who recalled later: "Terrific pace off the pitch, a forked-lightning off-break, and lift and swing away from the right-hand batsman." He spoke with feeling: when they both made their Test debut at Lord's that year, Cowie dismissed Hutton for nought and one. At Old Trafford, he took ten wickets in the match and had England 75 for seven in the second innings, but was plagued by dropped catches. Cowie took 19 of the 41 England wickets (at 20.78) that fell in the three Tests in 1937, but it was almost nine years before he could play another Test: the one-off match at Wellington in March 1946, where he took six of the eight Australian wickets to fall. He played in only four other matches against Australian opposition: against South Australia, on the way home from England, he had Bradman caught behind for 11 off the first ball he faced in the morning, while the crowds were still queuing outside. Cowie struggled against injury on the 1949 tour of England, but still took 14 wickets in the four Tests and *Wisden* said his figures did him "far less than justice". After the tour, he announced his retirement and became an umpire, standing in three Tests. His highest score was 54 against Otago, part of a last-wicket partnership of 119, an Auckland record that still stands; his overall batting average was 10.16. His bowling figures in his 86 first-class matches were 359 wickets at 22.28 and in Tests 45 wickets at 21.53. Cowie was also Auckland's goalkeeper and had 14 years on the New Zealand FA council, seven of them as chairman. He was a stickler for the national soccer team retaining their black-with-silver-fern colours; after he retired, they became the All Whites. He was appointed OBE in 1972.

CRANMER, PETER, who died on May 29, 1994, aged 79, was a golden boy of English sport in the 1930s. He was a brilliant rugger player and played in all 16 of England's internationals between 1933-34 and 1937-38. It was Cranmer, playing centre, who sent away Alex Obolensky to score one of the most famous tries in history against the 1936 All Blacks. His cricket was less spectacular but had something of the same exuberance. Born in Birmingham, son of the well-known bass soloist Arthur Cranmer, he played no first-class cricket at Oxford but made his debut for Warwickshire in 1934 and hit a six off Reg Sinfield the fifth ball he received. In 1938 he was controversially offered the Warwickshire captaincy in place of R. E. S. Wyatt. No reason was given but it was believed the committee wanted a more adventurous approach. Cranmer certainly provided it. He led the team with all of his rugby athleticism and adventure plus enormous unselfishness: at Hove he declared after hitting 98 in 80 minutes. He continued as captain for two years after the war. Warwickshire were never very successful under his leadership but it could be argued that the seeds were sown that blossomed into the 1951 Championship team and, anyway, everyone had a great deal of fun, including the spectators – he scored one of his four first-class centuries in 90 minutes against the 1947 South Africans. He was generally less successful when he had to defend. He played occasionally for Warwickshire after 1947; his last first-class match was for MCC in 1959 and he captained Warwickshire Second Eleven when he was past 50. He scored 5,853 runs in all, averaging 21.59. For some years he worked as a journalist and broadcaster and briefly joined the Test match commentary team. Brian Johnston later wrote that Cranmer was "completely natural – almost conversational" but added that he was not so good at more tedious disciplines like timekeeping. He was exceptionally kind to tyro colleagues. In 1976 he had a stroke and the last two decades of his life were very cruel. Before he died, he had both legs amputated but even then he could cheerfully tell friends he was "legless again". He was a magnificent sportsman and a delightful man.

CRISP, ROBERT JAMES, DSO, MC, who died in Essex on March 3, 1994, aged 82, was one of the most extraordinary men ever to play Test cricket. His cricket, which is only a fraction of the story, was explosive enough: he is the only bowler to have taken four wickets in four balls twice. Born in Calcutta, he was educated in Rhodesia and, after taking nine for 64 for Western Province against Natal in 1933-34, which included his second set of four in four, was chosen for the South Africans' 1935 tour of England. He took 107 wickets on the tour at a brisk fast-medium, including five for 99 in the Old Trafford Test. Crisp played four further Tests against Australia in 1935-36 and appeared eight times for Worcestershire in 1938 without ever achieving a huge amount.

But it is astonishing that he ever found a moment for such a time-consuming game as cricket. He was essentially an adventurer – he had just climbed Kilimanjaro when he got news that he was wanted for the 1935 tour – with something of an attention span problem. Like other such characters, his defining moment came in the Second World War when he was an outstanding but turbulent tank commander, fighting his own personal war against better-armoured Germans in Greece and North Africa. He had six tanks blasted from under him in a month but carried on fighting and was awarded the DSO "for outstanding ability and great gallantry". However, he annoyed authority so much that General Montgomery intervened personally and prevented him being given a Bar a year later; his second honour was downgraded to an MC. Crisp was mentioned in despatches four times before being invalided out in Normandy. The King asked if his bowling would be affected. "No, sire," he is alleged to have replied. "I was hit in the head."

Crisp never did play again and found that the tedium of peacetime presented him with a problem far harder than anything offered by the Germans. He was briefly a journalist for a succession of newspapers, and went back to South Africa where he founded the now firmly-established paper for blacks, *Drum*. But he wanted a magazine about tribal matters rather than something appealing to urban blacks and rapidly fell out with his proprietor. He returned to England, tried mink farming and, for an unusually long time by Crisp standards, worked as a leader-writer on the *East Anglian Daily Times*. While there he wrote two accounts of his war exploits, *Brazen Chariots* (1957) and *The Gods Were Neutral* (1960). Then he suddenly left and lived in a Greek hut for a year. Told he had incurable cancer, he spent a year walking round Crete, selling accounts to the *Sunday Express*. He died with a copy of the *Sporting Life* on his lap, reportedly having just lost a £20 bet, a risk-taker to the last. Crisp's 276 career wickets came at an average of only 19.88, but statistics are absurd for such a man.

DAWSON, HAROLD, who died on May 13, 1994, aged 79, played ten matches for Hampshire in 1947 and 1948 without establishing himself in the side. He was a prolific batsman for Todmorden and scored a fifty on every ground in the Lancashire League.

DISSANAYAKE, GAMINI, was assassinated by a suicide bomber in Colombo on October 24, 1994, aged 52, in an explosion that killed fifty other people. He was leader of Sri Lanka's political opposition and a candidate for the presidency. Four months earlier, he had started his second term as president of Sri Lanka's cricketing Board of Control, having previously served from 1981 to 1989. He successfully campaigned for Sri Lanka's elevation to Test status in 1981, promising an improvement in the country's cricketing infrastructure: among his achievements was the transformation of the ground at his old school, Trinity College, Kandy, into the Asgiriya Stadium.

FORD, CECIL WILLIAM, DSC, who died on July 11, 1994, aged 81, topped the Hertfordshire batting averages when they won the Minor County Championship for the first time in 1936 and made one first-class appearance that year, for the Minor Counties against the Indians at Lord's. He won the DSC in Normandy.

FORTUNE, CHARLES ARTHUR FREDERICK, who died on November 22, 1994, aged 89, was South Africa's best-known cricket commentator. Fortune was born in Wiltshire and taught at Rutlish, John Major's old school, in London before emigrating to take up a science teaching post in Grahamstown in 1935. He began broadcasting just before the war and built up a reputation for gentle, discursive commentaries in the English manner which made him exceptionally popular among South African cricket followers. Sometimes they found him too discursive: once he received a telegram saying simply "What's the score?" He retired from Radio South Africa in 1972, and then for 12 years was secretary of the South African Cricket Association (later Union), a post which at that stage was more secretarial than executive. He continued broadcasting until a stroke in 1989. Fortune was a conservative, and appeared to take South Africa's exclusion from world cricket as something of a personal affront. His death came hours before the new media centre at the Wanderers ground in Johannesburg was due to be named after him.

FOSTER, PETER GEOFFREY, who died on December 7, 1994, aged 78, was a son of G. N. Foster, one of the seven brothers who played for Worcestershire. He won Blues for Oxford at golf and rackets, but not cricket, although he played five games for the University between 1936 and 1938 and 25 for Kent in the seasons immediately before and after the war. He scored 107 at Leicester in 1939 for a side captained by his brother-in-law, F. G. H. Chalk.

FREEMAN, DOUGLAS LINFORD, who died in Sydney on May 31, 1994, aged 79, was the youngest man ever to play a Test for New Zealand. When he was still a schoolboy at Nelson College, he appeared in two Tests against Douglas Jardine's England team in 1932-33, the first starting when he was 18 years 197 days. Freeman had made his first-class debut only two months earlier and taken five for 102 for Wellington against Auckland with his leg-spin. There was evidently a feeling that a promising youngster should be encouraged, rather than the 35-year-old D. R. Garrard. Freeman, 6ft 3in, had a sharp leg-break and a hard-to-pick googly but, against England, New Zealand were out of their depth; they were saved by the weather from defeat but not from two massive innings by Hammond: 227 at Christchurch and a world Test record 336 not out at Auckland. Freeman took one wicket in the two games (Sutcliffe) for 169. He played only one further match, for Wellington against Auckland the following year, making a first-class career that lasted just 16 cricketing days. In 1935 he took a job with the Colonial Sugar Refining Co.; he was employed by them for the next 40 years, the first 20 in Fiji, the next 20 in Sydney. He was active in Fijian cricket and managed the side that toured New Zealand in 1953-54; he would have been captain but for injury. In Sydney he concentrated on golf. Before he died, Freeman recalled having the temerity to say to England's acting-captain: "Excuse me, Mr Wyatt, but are you leaving your crease before I have bowled?" "He apologised," said Freeman, "but continued his illegal and disconcerting backing-up. I shudder to think of the outcry if I had taken off the bails and run him out." He also recalled seeing George Duckworth take a handful of autograph books and make a perfect replica of every MCC player's signature.

GARDINER, JOHN RICHARD, who died on April 23, 1994, aged 81, was a tireless cricketing enthusiast, as a player for MCC and innumerable other clubs, and a member of 11 counties. He was match secretary of the XL Club and represented the United States on ICC; he donated the ICC Trophy, contested by the associate members in Kenya in 1994.

GITTENS, STANTON O'CONNOR, who died on April 20, 1994, aged 82, played in 11 first-class matches for Barbados between 1934-35 and 1945-46. He was a solid batsman – making 105 against Trinidad in 1936-37 – and an efficient wicket-keeper. Gittens had great influence on Barbados cricket as a teacher at two of the island's leading boys' schools – he became principal of Combermere – as a leading light of the Empire club, and as a member of the Barbados Cricket Association board, to which he was first elected in 1942. He served until 1973, for six years as vice-president. He also kept goal for the island soccer team.

GRIFFITHS, GORDON CRAVEN, who died on September 10, 1994, aged 89, was an amateur wicket-keeper who played for Worcestershire five times between 1932 and 1935.

GROBLER, GERBRAND, who died on November 7, 1994, aged 32, after a car crash the previous day, was one of the most talented all-round sportsmen in South Africa. He made 58 appearances for Orange Free State and Northern Transvaal between 1981-82 and 1992-93 as a left-arm swing bowler. He took seven for 69 for Northern Transvaal against Eastern Province in 1989-90, and scored a first-class century for the province's B team in 1991-92. Grobler played full back for the South African A rugby team and was an official reserve for the 1994 tour of Britain. He scored a try for Transvaal in the 1994 Currie Cup final.

HAINES, MURRAY CHESTON, who died on October 26, 1994, aged 90, was the last survivor of the heyday of Philadelphian cricket. He was a useful medium-pace bowler who toured Canada and England in the 1920s. From 1969 until his death he was secretary of the C. C. Morris Library at Haverford College, the most important cricket library in the United States, and was himself a fount of knowledge of the game in America.

HARDY, Col. EVAN MICHAEL PEARCE, who died on January 13, 1994, aged 66, played in one first-class match: for the Combined Services against Warwickshire in 1959, a game best remembered for Jack Bannister's ten for 41. He was capped for England at rugby three times in 1950-51 and had a distinguished military career.

HAYTER, REGINALD JAMES, died on March 13, 1994, aged 80. Reg Hayter was a Fleet Street legend who began his own sports reporting agency, Hayters, in 1955, which has functioned ever since as a finishing school for young sports journalists. They were worked hard at not over-generous rates and either sank, or swam into the leading jobs in Fleet Street: four current national cricket correspondents are graduates, including Reg's son Peter. Hayter started as a junior with Pardon's, the agency that then produced *Wisden*, in 1933; the editor's notes on the Bodyline tour were dictated to him for transcription. He was associated with the Almanack for many years, covering a number of tours, and also edited *The Cricketer* between 1978 and 1981. He is thought to be responsible for the idea of the cricketer's agent, having persuaded Denis Compton to let Bagenal Harvey take charge of his affairs. Hayter himself acted as agent to players like Basil D'Oliveira and Ian Botham, and as an informal adviser to many others. Dozens of cricketers, particularly the more sociable sort, were among his friends and there was a huge turnout at his 80th birthday party. He was a capable and fanatical club cricketer. During the war, he turned out for the British Empire XI; he played for Stanmore until he was past 60 and spoke at the club's annual dinner two days before he died.

HEATH, DAVID MICHAEL WILLIAM, who died after a long illness, on June 13, 1994, aged 62, played 16 matches as an amateur for Warwickshire between 1949 and 1953 and scored a first-class century for the Combined Services against Worcestershire in 1952. He captained Moseley to seven Birmingham League titles, and was president of the League and then chairman of Warwickshire's cricket committee before becoming, amid much complicated internal politics, successor to A. C. Smith as club secretary in 1986, later acquiring the title chief executive. His illness forced him to step down a few months before he died. He laid much of the groundwork for Warwickshire's triumphant summer of 1994 but did not live to see it come to fruition.

HOARE, ERNEST STANLEY, died on February 24, 1994, aged 90. "Monkey" Hoare was given a trial as a Freshman at Cambridge in 1923 but made no further progress. In 1929 he made three appearances for Gloucestershire as a middle-order batsman. He won a Blue at hockey and went on to captain England.

HODGE, ROBERT STEVENSON, who died on September 15, 1994, aged 79, was a fast-medium bowler from Scotland who made a startling entrance at Lord's in 1945. Playing for Under-33 against a strong Over-33 team, he twice dismissed two batsmen in an over and finished with five for 82. He made nine other first-class appearances, all for Scotland.

HOLT, ARTHUR GEORGE, who died on July 28, 1994, aged 83, played for Hampshire between 1935 and 1948 as a batsman, but is best remembered for his years as chief coach, between 1949 and 1965. Holt was a shrewd and never over-hasty judge of a cricketer. He was a particularly fine coach of youngsters, whom he charmed with his attention to detail and his humour: "No one was ever bored in the nets," said Colin Ingleby-Mackenzie. "He had a lovely, light touch." He ran a Southampton sports shop, Holt and Haskell, and insisted on giving all his friends enormous discounts; since most people in the city were his friends this did not help the profits. He ran the county's youth team ("Holt's Colts") for years out of his own pocket. He scored two first-class centuries in his 79 matches, but his career was much curtailed by the war. Holt was also a skilful inside-left who made 202 appearances for Southampton, often alongside his friend Ted Drake.

HUNT, RAYMOND THOMAS, died on August 15, 1994, aged 72, following a heart attack during the Golden Oldies tournament in Birmingham. Ray Hunt was a modest first-class batsman in New Zealand, who played 14 matches for Otago and four for Canterbury, but an original cricket thinker. Among his innovations as Otago coach was the "Hunt shuffle", whereby no bowler could send down more than two overs in a spell to bamboozle the opposition batsmen. It was tried against Canterbury and Otago won. He built a batting machine in his basement, the bat permanently playing the forward defensive. He also forced his players to stand with their backs to him at fielding practice and not to turn round until they heard bat on ball; his first shot hit the leg-spinner, Carl Dickel, straight between the shoulder blades.

JONES, WATKIN EDWARD, died on August 23, 1994, aged 77. "Wat" Jones, which is what he was called even in *Wisden* scorecards to distinguish him from Glamorgan's other W. E. Jones, was a pace bowler who slowed down to bowl off-cutters and made five first-class appearances for Glamorgan in 1946 and 1947 as an amateur. Glamorgan wanted him to sign as a professional after the war, but he chose to join the police instead, agreeing to help out when he could. Glamorgan would have appreciated him more often: he took seven for 92 against Kent at Newport in 1947.

JOSHI, A. R., died on March 2, 1994, aged 81. "Bapu" Joshi umpired in 12 Tests in India between 1948-49 and 1964-65. He was joint honorary secretary of the Maharashtra Cricket Association for more than 20 years.

KARMARKAR, NARAYAN DAMODAR, who died on August 30, 1992, aged 83, managed the Indian team which toured Ceylon in 1965-66 and was assistant secretary to the Indian Board of Control for 31 years from 1949. In 1974, he was made an Honorary Life Member of MCC.

KEMP, JOHN GREGORY, who died on December 28, 1993, aged 53, was a left-handed batsman who made 1,076 runs for Auckland in the 1960s. The first of his three first-class centuries, 106 against Northern Districts, was made in only 162 minutes after he had come in at 45 for four. Kemp also won 23 soccer caps for New Zealand between 1960 and 1964. He died in a Sydney hospital a week after a second liver transplant.

KIPPAX, HORACE GRANVILLE, who died on February 23, 1993, aged 83, shared his debut for Yorkshire Colts with Leonard Hutton at Halifax in 1933. Hutton got a duck, while Kippax made 57. Thereafter, their careers diverged, but Kippax played a great deal of league cricket, and his son Peter did appear for Yorkshire.

KORE, JANARDAN JAGANATH, who died on February 1, 1994, aged 71, was a leg-spinning all-rounder who played in seven Ranji Trophy matches for Bombay in the 1940s. He helped develop India's best leg-spinner of the next decade, Subhash Gupte.

LAMASON, INA MABEL, MBE, who died on April 30, 1994, two days before her 83rd birthday, was a former captain of the New Zealand women's team. She was chosen for her batting against England at Christchurch in 1935 but was injured and had to wait 13 years for her Test debut. By the time she did play, she was captain, against Australia in 1947-48 and England a year later. She toured England under Rona McKenzie in 1954 and topped the batting averages in Tests at 44. She managed the New Zealand team at the 1973 World Cup, and also played international hockey. Born Ina Pickering, she was married to Jack Lamason, the Wellington captain, who toured England in 1937.

LANGLEY, BRIAN, who died on January 31, 1994, aged 65, worked at Lord's for more than 40 years, first for MCC and then for the TCCB. As the Board's assistant secretary (administration) until his retirement in 1988, he was responsible for much of the detailed organisation of the county game.

LEE, MARSHALL GILMOUR, who died suddenly on October 7, 1994, aged 57, was a journalist and gifted club cricketer in South Africa, and an unusually far-sighted one. In the early 1970s, along with two other white friends, he began playing for a coloured team at Vrededorp in Natal. This move was considered revolutionary at the time – "They left themselves open to charges of being communists and God knows what," Ali Bacher said later. In 1977, Lee moved to England and briefly presented a sports segment on BBC *Newsnight*. His last campaign, to have run-outs credited to the fielders on scorecards, was also conducted against the odds, but with the same vigour and passion that marked his stand against apartheid.

LUYT, Sir RICHARD EDMONDS, GCMG, KCVO, DCM, who died in Cape Town, his birthplace, on February 12, 1994, aged 78, was a Rhodes Scholar and played three matches for Oxford University in 1938 as a wicket-keeper without getting a Blue. He was involved in the end of colonial rule as Governor of British Guiana – where he found himself in the middle of something close to civil war – and Chief Secretary of Northern Rhodesia. He later became vice-chancellor and principal of the University of Cape Town, and was often in conflict with the apartheid regime.

McKAY, DOUGLAS GORDON, who died on April 9, 1994, aged 89, was the oldest surviving South Australian Shield player. He played ten times between 1925-26 and 1928-29, averaging 34.64 down the order with a highest score of 87 against Queensland in 1928-29. He only took ten first-class wickets, but he was regarded as a partnership-breaker, and those victims included Bradman, whom he caught and bowled for two, Hobbs, Macartney, Jackson and Kippax – twice. He later became a distinguished paediatric surgeon.

McRAE, DONALD ALEXANDER NOEL, died on August 10, 1986, aged 73, but his death did not become known to cricket writers until 1994. McRae was a left-arm medium-pace bowler for Canterbury who was successful in wartime cricket in New Zealand, and was chosen to share the new ball in the Test against Australia at Wellington in 1945-46. He took nought for 44 and played no more first-class cricket.

MATHIAS, WALLIS, who died on September 1, 1994, after a brain haemorrhage, aged 59, was the first non-Muslim to play for Pakistan. He made his debut in November 1955 as a 20-year-old and played in 21 Tests over the next seven years. His greatest merit was his fielding; he was the safe pair of hands in the slips that Pakistan's strong medium-pace attack of that era desperately wanted. He had exceptional reflexes and, though he took some spectacular catches, his great skill was to make hard chances look simple. He was also a middle-order batsman whose figures did not do justice to the usefulness of his runs: he scored 783 runs in Tests at 23.72, but regularly played critical little innings. The 64 and 45 he scored in Pakistan's win over West Indies at Dacca in 1958-59 made him easily the most successful batsman in a low-scoring game; a year earlier he had scored 73 and 77 in successive Tests in the Caribbean. He played three Tests in England in 1962, but the following year he suffered a finger injury in the nets which left him with a slight deformity that restricted his brilliant catching. He continued in domestic cricket and scored 278 not out for Karachi Blues against Railway Greens in 1965-66. In 1969-70 he became National Bank's first captain and played on until 1975-76 before becoming coach, selector and manager. In 146 first-class matches he made 7,520 runs, average 44.49, including 16 centuries. He held 130 catches, 22 in Tests. He was a popular captain and a much respected man.

MAY, PETER BARKER HOWARD, CBE, died at his home in Hampshire on December 27, 1994, four days short of his 65th birthday. In the 1950s P. B. H. May – the initials were part of the style of the man – came to represent the *beau ideal* of English batsmanship and sportsmanship. He was tall and handsome with a batting style that was close to classical, and he was the hero of a generation of schoolboys. To his contemporaries at Charterhouse he was a heroic figure much earlier: from a very young age it was clear that he was going to play for England and he glided towards greatness in an effortless-looking manner.

Peter May was born at Reading on December 31, 1929. He was an instinctive cricketer, though there was no background of the game in his family. When he was 13, the headmaster of Charterhouse barred him from the First XI for his own good, but as a 14-year-old in 1944 he made 108 against Harrow, an innings that had an extraordinary impact on the school. In four years in the school First XI he made 1,794 runs, averaging 54.36. He was advised, but not all that much, by the former England player George Geary. By 1947, his last year at school, he was clearly the best schoolboy batsman in the country, scoring an unbeaten 183 against Eton and 148 and 146 in the representative matches at Lord's.

He then had to do two years' national service as Writer May of the Royal Navy – the scorecard abbreviation Wtr puzzling at least one MCC member who thought he must be the mess waiter. By his second year, his clerical duties were being heavily interspersed with cricket and in 1949 he played enough to come third in the national averages behind Hardstaff and Hutton. That autumn he went up to Cambridge: in 1950 their batting side was as strong as any in the country and he was not immediately dominant, but he scored an unbeaten 227 against Hampshire, stepped into the Surrey team and quickly won his county cap.

By 1951 he had made enough runs in every type of cricket – including a century for the Gentlemen – to be picked for the Fourth Test against South Africa at Headingley. He scored 138, an innings that seemed like a revelation. He played in all four Tests against India in 1952 and, though he was dropped for the three middle Ashes Tests of 1953, he returned to score 39 and 37, important in context, at The Oval and was picked for the West Indies tour, where he made his second Test century, a far more dogged 135 on a matting pitch at Port-of-Spain to earn a draw.

This secured May's place once and for all, and he became a crucial member of two of the most successful teams English cricket has ever seen: Surrey, who won the Championship every year between 1952 and 1958, and an England team that never lost a series in the same period. May adapted his method and his mental approach to Test cricket and moved from being a promising batsman to a great one. Once Gubby Allen saw him get out at Fenner's and muttered: "That was the most unconscious stroke I have ever seen." After his Headingley century Allen sent him a telegram: "Charge of unconsciousness unconditionally withdrawn."

In Australia in 1954-55, May was Hutton's vice-captain, and the following year, when Hutton became ill, inherited the leadership. He captained England in 41 Tests, still a record despite the later growth of Test cricket, and was an unchallenged figure of authority. England won 20 of those Tests and lost only ten. May's stature as a batsman increased each year, even on the indifferent pitches of 1956. In the First Test at Edgbaston against West Indies in 1957, he scored 285 not out, sharing a stand of 411, England's highest ever, with Colin Cowdrey, saving the match and blunting Sonny Ramadhin's mastery of English batsmen once and for all. England went on to win the series 3-0. In 1958, in the wettest, most bowler-friendly summer of the century, he averaged almost 64, 17 more than any other batsman. In both these years, he followed on where Stuart Surridge had left off in 1956 and captained Surrey to the Championship.

That was May's apogee. England went to Australia in 1958-59 as hot favourites, but were met by bowlers widely suspected of throwing, and slumped to a 4-0 defeat. May was greatly upset by newspaper criticism of the presence on tour of his fiancée, Virginia Gilligan, especially when one report said they had been secretly married. They actually married that April, and from then on his enthusiasm for the game semed to wane. He missed much of the 1959 season with an abscess, which also forced him home from the West Indies tour that winter. It was 1961 before he returned to cricket and, when he was bowled round his legs by Richie Benaud at Old Trafford, his dismissal sealed the fate of the Ashes. Three weeks later he played his last Test and in 1962 effectively retired from first-class cricket, though there was always the hope, in other minds, that he might return, and *Wisden* delayed its retirement tribute until 1971.

May became an insurance broker and underwriter at Lloyd's and concentrated on his growing family: four girls, all of them sharing their mother's love of horses, which their father, though no horseman, happily took on. For many years his cricketing involvement was low-profile, though he served as a Test selector from 1965 to 1968, and was president of MCC in 1980-81. However, in 1982 he agreed to return to the limelight by becoming chairman of selectors with a specific brief to get a grip on the players' behaviour. He never gained a rapport with a new generation of cricketers and did not seem to have much disposition to choose between them. Had he stuck to the original plan and retired after the 1985 Ashes series, his reputation would have been largely undamaged, but he stayed on until 1988, working through four captains in the last summer alone. By the end, players were being picked and dropped with bewildering rapidity.

England were less strong relative to other countries in the 1980s than in the 1950s. Both as a batsman and as a captain, May had the advantage that the best bowlers were nearly always on his side. His failure against Heine and Adcock in South Africa in 1956-57 has led some to wonder whether he could have coped with the sustained battering that modern batsmen receive. But, 18 months earlier in England, he dealt with the same bowlers so effectively that he was close to a century in every match. Richie Benaud, perhaps his most formidable opponent, called him not merely the greatest English batsman to emerge since the war – which is the conventional judgment – but the only great one. As a captain, May was a hard but unfailingly courteous competitor. He was not an imaginative tactician but his resources meant this was not a serious disadvantage. He was helped too by the presence of a great chairman of selectors in Gubby Allen.

Peter May will be remembered best as a batsman, upright in everything he did, especially the on-drive which, famously, he perfected as a schoolboy. In 66 Tests he scored 4,537 runs at 46.77; in first-class cricket he scored 27,592 runs at 51.00 with 282 catches. He scored 85 centuries, his early retirement preventing him becoming the first amateur since W. G. Grace to score a hundred hundreds. His gifts were sublime, indeed mysterious, and he bore them with honour, modesty

[*Patrick Eagar*

Peter May, pictured in 1981.

and distinction. The fear that we will never see his like again meant his early death was felt all the more keenly.

An appreciation by Doug Insole begins on page 25. Peter May's full career figures can be found in the 1971 Wisden *on pages 105-113.*

MERRALL, JOHN EDWIN, who died on October 5, 1993, aged 84, was a Yorkshire-born fast-medium bowler, who played twice for Surrey, in 1932 and 1933, and took six wickets. In 1934 he represented Minor Counties against Oxford University.

MULCOCK, EDWARD, died on July 15, 1994, aged 85. Ted (or E.T.) Mulcock was a medium-pace in-swing bowler who had one miraculous hour at first-class level, when he took eight wickets for 32 in 63 balls for Canterbury against Otago in 1937-38, including a hat-trick; he had already toiled through 19 eight-ball overs and taken nought for 39. A few days earlier, he had had figures of six for 53 against Wellington. He took 55 wickets in a dozen first-class matches, but many more in New Zealand club cricket, which he played past his 65th birthday.

NICHOLLS, RONALD BERNARD, who died after a short illness on July 21, 1994, aged 60, was a Gloucestershire man and a county stalwart for a quarter of a century. Without ever attracting much notice, he scored 23,607 runs, more than anyone for Gloucestershire except Hammond, Milton and Dipper. He was an orthodox, straight and willowy player with an excellent on-drive and one flamboyant touch: a flourishing and uncharacteristically risky square-drive which he curbed as time went by. He finally established himself in the first team in 1957 after Jack Crapp's retirement and thereafter hit 1,000 runs every year until 1971, passing 2,000 in 1962. Nicholls was, above all, an unselfish cricketer; he preferred to open but readily dropped down in the mid-1960s to bolster a shaky middle order. His career average of 26.17 does him little justice. He was a superb athlete all his life, fielding well in the outfield and making 161 League appearances as a goalkeeper for Bristol Rovers, Cardiff City, Fulham and Bristol City. Nicholls was still playing cricket, for Cheltenham, a couple of days before he was taken ill; he died in the hospital by the College ground. He was a quiet, pleasant man, given to occasional wry comments after much thought.

OSBORN, GEORGE HENRY, MBE, who died in Sao Paulo on July 1, 1994, aged 78, was the president of the Brazilian Cricket Association and its driving force for many years.

OUTSCHOORN, LADISLAUS, died in London on January 9, 1994, aged 75. "Laddie" Outschoorn was one of the first Ceylonese players to succeed in English cricket. He went to Malaya to work and was captured by the Japanese, suffering greatly. He came to England after the war for rehabilitation and was spotted by Worcestershire playing for Kidderminster. He was already 27 and established himself at once as a stylish batsman, quick on his feet, and a superb close fielder, especially in his early days: in 1949, when Worcestershire came third, he took 55 catches at slip and gully, making him the leading fielder in the country. His best batting season was 1951, when he made 1,761 runs. In all, he played 346 matches and made 15,496 runs at 28.59, including 25 centuries. In 1966 he became Ceylon's national coach.

PARKIN, REGINALD HENRY, who died on April 16, 1994, aged 84, was the son of the England bowler Cecil Parkin, and played for Lancashire 20 times himself between 1931 and 1939 as a batsman and off-spinner.

PEARCE, THOMAS NEILL, OBE, TD, who died at Worthing on April 10, 1994, aged 88, was at the heart of Essex cricket all his adult life. Tom Pearce made his debut in 1929; he was captain, either alone or jointly, from 1933 to 1950 (except in 1939), chairman from 1952 to 1972 and president from 1970 until the month before he died. When he first became captain, the club was about to leave its headquarters at Leyton and its survival was uncertain; when he died Essex had spent 15 years as the most successful team in the country. Before the war, he shared the captaincy with Denys Wilcox: Pearce was in the wine trade and could not spare the whole season and Wilcox was a schoolmaster who could do only the second half. The arrangement worked far better in practice than in theory and Essex rose steadily up the table. Pearce was an imperturbable character both in his batting, which was strong in defence and on the leg side and at its best in a crisis, and in his captaincy, which relied on unflappability and charm rather than tactical niceties. Trevor Bailey recalled him issuing the dressing-room instruction, "Play your shots, but don't get out." He also remembered him scoring 211 not out against Leicestershire in 1948, without ever picking Jack Walsh, and smiling every time he played and missed. Pearce hit 21 other hundreds in his 250 first-class matches, scoring 12,061 runs at 34.26. He was chosen for the Gentlemen twice, served as a Test selector in 1949 and 1950, and managed MCC's tour of the subcontinent in 1961-62. From 1951 to 1976 he was the match-manager at the Scarborough Festival, prominently assisted by his wife Stella, and T. N. Pearce's XI featured on the fixture list for more than a quarter of a century. From 1956 to 1987, he was also honorary secretary of the British Sportsmen's Club, which traditionally welcomed visiting cricket and rugby teams to England, usually with a meal at the Savoy. He was a good rugby player – as a wing forward for Middlesex and London Counties – but an even better referee. He took charge of ten internationals and it was said that the calmness that served him so well at Essex was even more useful in a packed Stade Colombes. He was appointed OBE for services to sport in 1979. E. W. Swanton called him "the quintessential amateur sportsman of his times, a tough, generous, cheerful competitor, who never made an enemy".

PERERA, FREDERICK, who died on November 26, 1993, aged 76, was one of Ceylon's greatest all-round sportsmen. The war prevented him representing the country at cricket, as he did at soccer and hockey. His 352 not out for Port Commission v Excise in 1957 (not first-class) is regarded as the highest score in any match on the island.

PETTIGREW, ALAN CHARLES, who died on December 16, 1993, aged 58, became the youngest delegate to the Australian Cricket Board when he was 39. He served the Queensland Cricket Association in various capacities and was chairman from 1988 to 1993.

PHAYRE, Brig. ROBERT ARTHUR, DSO, who died on December 31, 1993, aged 92, played in two first-class matches in 1928-29 when on service in India, for the Europeans and the Punjab Governor's XI against the Muslims. In 1921 he captained RMA Woolwich. He won the DSO during the Normandy landings.

PORTER, ARTHUR, who died on February 20, 1994, aged 79, made 38 first-class appearances for Glamorgan between 1936 and 1949, as a middle-order batsman and occasional off-spinner. He played as an amateur, taking time off from his job as a police sergeant in Newport. He scored two centuries, both in 1946, including 105 off a strong Surrey attack at The Oval.

POTTER, WILFRED, who died on March 4, 1994, aged 83, was a Yorkshire-born leg-spinner and cousin of Maurice Leyland, who made one first-class appearance, for Warwickshire against Derbyshire in 1932. He was also an assistant groundsman at Edgbaston.

QURESHI, GHULAM DASTAGIR, who died on January 11, 1994, aged 75, played in 14 matches for Hyderabad, making his debut in 1936-37. His highest Ranji Trophy score was 66 against Madhya Pradesh at Nagpur in 1950-51. He was captain in three of his games and later president of the Hyderabad Cricket Association.

RAMSAMOOJ, DONALD, died on May 24, 1994, after a heart attack in Toronto, aged 61. He played for his native Trinidad and then for Northamptonshire, who signed him in 1957 in the hope that he was going to develop into a great attacking batsman. Unfortunately, by the time he had qualified, he was 28 and the edge had gone off his game. He made a thrilling Championship debut in 1960, with an innings of 123 in only 147 minutes against Derbyshire that seemed like a breath of fresh air. But thereafter he blew more cold than hot, failed to pass 50 in 15 further innings that season, and averaged only 16 in 1961. The club remained patient until 1964, when he left with a first-class average of only 20.55, but a lot of friends. Frank Tyson described him as "brilliantly disappointing".

RICHARDSON, COLIN GEORGE, died on December 22, 1993, aged 73. Col Richardson was a left-arm swing bowler who played eight matches for Tasmania after the Second World War. He was one of five brothers to play first-class cricket for Tasmania; a sixth was a first-class umpire and his father and uncle also represented the island.

ROBINSON, MAURICE, who died on August 8, 1994, aged 73, was an amateur batsman and occasional fast-medium bowler from Ulster who played first-class cricket for several teams: the Europeans, Hyderabad and Madras in India during the war and then Glamorgan and Warwickshire. In 83 first-class matches, he scored 2,719 runs at 22.10. On his day, he was an entertaining batsman: one of his two centuries was a magnificent 190 for Glamorgan at Bournemouth in 1949 and the 264 he put on there with Stan Montgomery for the fifth wicket is still a county record. He was more generally entertaining for those closer at hand, since his cricket was punctuated by Irish drollery and irreverence.

RUSSELL, SIDNEY EDWARD JAMES, died in Quebec on June 18, 1994, aged 56, after suffering a heart attack while on holiday. Sid Russell had a curious career, split between two counties: Middlesex, from 1960 to 1964, and Gloucestershire, the team on the receiving end of his two centuries for Middlesex, from 1965 to 1968. He was a solid batsman, despite a rather ungainly style, and made 1,000 runs in his debut season for both counties, but not otherwise. He was a good footballer and made 61 League appearances for Brentford.

SMITH, CYRIL, who died on January 12, 1994, aged 92, scored for Northamptonshire's first and second teams from 1962 and was the club statistician.

STEPTOE, DOUGLAS GEORGE, BEM, died on June 11, 1994, aged 71, in Copenhagen, where he was born. He was secretary of the Danish Cricket Association for many years and translated the Laws into Danish several times. For about 30 years he worked on a detailed history of the game in Denmark, and completed it days before he died. He was awarded the BEM while in the Royal Navy in 1943, for his part in the Sicily landings.

STEVENS, JAMES NORMAN, who died on December 23, 1993, aged 83, was an amateur fast-medium bowler and tail-end batsman, who was brought into the struggling Northamptonshire side in August 1937. Given the new ball in five Championship games, he took nine wickets at 48.88.

STEVENSON, MICHAEL HAMILTON, died on September 19, 1994, aged 67. Mike Stevenson was up at Cambridge from 1949 to 1952 and won his Blue in all four years, in a line-up that included, at various times, six batsmen who were to play for England: Dewes, Doggart, Insole, May, Sheppard and Subba Row. In his freshman year, Stevenson made 70 and 37 and played an important part in an unexpected Cambridge victory. Thereafter, his batting, though often pugnacious, was unreliable and he lost his bowling action. His subsequent cricketing career was not as glamorous as that of most of his team-mates: he played three matches for Derbyshire and a few for Ireland and MCC. But he remained associated with the game all his life: he was a successful cricket master at both Queen Elizabeth Grammar School, Blackburn and Pocklington School. Later, he wrote about cricket as a freelance, mainly for the *Daily Telegraph*, and published books about Yorkshire cricket and Ray Illingworth. He was steeped in cricket, and his tireless zest for the game shone through both his coaching and his reporting.

STIMPSON, ALLAN PETER, who drowned in Manakua Harbour, Auckland, in 1994, aged 43, was a fast bowler who played in 24 first-class matches for Northern Districts during the 1970s. He took 61 wickets, including six for 46 against Wellington in 1975-76. He represented a New Zealand Invitation XI against the Australians in a one-day match at Eden Park the following season.

SUNDARESAN, P. N., died on March 3, 1994. A lawyer by profession, he was a respected cricket writer who edited *Indian Cricket* from 1966 to 1974 and was *Wisden's* Indian correspondent from 1967 to 1990.

TAYFIELD, HUGH JOSEPH, who died in hospital at Durban on February 25, 1994, aged 65, was the most successful bowler yet produced by South Africa and one of the greatest off-spinners the game has seen. Between 1949-50 and 1960 he took 170 wickets in Tests at a cost of 25.91 in 37 matches. Tayfield took more wickets per Test match (4.59) than either Jim Laker or Lance Gibbs (4.19 and 3.91), and though he was not in Laker's class as a spinner of the ball, he was exceptionally accurate and could bowl all day without wavering. He preferred to bowl over the wicket, extremely close to the stumps, which gave him the perfect angle for the ball to drift away and break back. Though his variations were subtle, his field settings were often flamboyantly unorthodox, with a large, tempting, gap around extra cover but two straightish silly mid-ons waiting for the mistimed shot. Tayfield was, with Trevor Goddard, at the centre of South Africa's containing cricket of the 1950s; he bowled 137 consecutive balls without conceding a run against England at Durban in 1956-57. But, with South Africa's superb fielding to back him up, he ran through teams as well: he took 37 wickets that series at 17.18, including nine for 113 in the second innings of the Fourth Test at Johannesburg, when he bowled unchanged on the last day and sent down 35 eight-ball overs; the longer he bowled the more inhibited England's batsmen became. Tayfield was chaired off the field.

The Tayfields were a cricketing family: Hugh's uncle S. H. Martin played for Worcestershire and his brothers Arthur and Cyril both played for Transvaal, as did two cousins. It was Arthur, as substitute, who took the final catch to seal the Johannesburg triumph. Hugh first appeared for Natal as a 17-year-old in 1945-46. At 18, he took a hat-trick against Transvaal and in 1949-50 was drafted into the Test team against Australia when Athol Rowan was injured. He played in all five Tests and, on a sticky wicket at Durban, took seven for 23 when Australia crashed

[*Popperfoto*

Hugh Tayfield in 1956.

from 31 for no wicket to 75 all out (South Africa did not enforce the follow-on and Neil Harvey won the match for Australia). He was summoned late to England in 1951 as standby for Rowan, but did not enhance his reputation. It was in Australia, in 1952-53, as the attacking linchpin of Jack Cheetham's young side that stunned Australia by halving the series, that he moved into the front rank. Tayfield took 30 wickets, 13 of them at Melbourne to secure South Africa's first win over Australia in 42 years. In England in 1955, Tayfield took 143 wickets on the tour and 26 in the series. He took nine wickets in South Africa's victory at Headingley. At The Oval, when South Africa lost the deciding Test, he returned figures of 53.4–29–60–5. *The Times* said the batsmen treated him as respectfully as if he were a bishop on a diocesan visit. After his triumphs in 1956-57 his good days became less frequent. In England in 1960 he took 123 wickets on the tour but failed in the Tests; in 1961-62 he lost his place.

Tall and good-looking, he was an imposing figure in the 1950s, and something of a playboy. His later years were spent largely in shadow. He married and divorced five times. He was reported to have had a difficult time in business and was ill for some years before his death. Tayfield played 37 Tests and his 170 wickets came at 25.91 each; in first-class cricket his total was 864 at 21.86. He scored 862 Test runs at 16.90, and took 26 catches – he was one of South Africa's best fielders himself. He was known as "Toey" because before every delivery he stubbed his toes into the ground, a mannerism that became essential to his rhythm. Before each over, he would also kiss the badge on his cap before handing it to the umpire.

THOMAS, WESLEY LEON, died from cancer of the liver in Grenada on February 1, 1994, aged 29. Wes Thomas played in 21 first-class matches for the Windward Islands, in which he made 418 runs and took 46 wickets. For seven seasons he was a successful and popular all-rounder for Blaydon in the Tyneside Senior League.

THOY, REGINALD ERNEST, who died in 1994, aged 72, played in two first-class matches, both at Eastbourne, for D. R. Jardine's XI against Oxford University in 1955 and 1957. In 1955 he opened the batting with R. E. S. Wyatt, then 54.

TINDALL, MARK, MBE, who died on July 10, 1994, aged 80, was elegant both as a cricketer and as a man. He was regarded as a tremendous teenage prospect and scored 1,000 runs over his last two years at Harrow, including an unbeaten 202 against MCC. Making his debut for Middlesex as a 19-year-old only weeks after leaving school, he hit 85 against a Nottinghamshire attack led by Bill Voce. He made a century in his Freshmen's Match at Cambridge, won a Blue in his first year, passed 1,000 runs in all first-class cricket in 1936 and was captain in 1937. However, little went right for Cambridge that year and his own form declined. He played no first-class cricket after 1938 but became master-in-charge of cricket at Harrow from 1946 to 1959. He was a good enough player to lead the Harrow Wanderers in the Cricketer Cup when he was 55. But he affected a languid indifference in all circumstances. During a game for the St Edward's Martyrs at Oxford – he had taught at the school before the war – he was seen to produce a newly pressed silk handkerchief to sit on at the fall of a wicket. He was fielding at cover and his immaculate creams, just right for a Victorian picnic, had to be protected at all costs. He was once heard to ask with his usual world-weary air: "Do I have to do all the bloody batting, all the bloody bowling and all the bloody pouching in this team?" The weariness disguised the fact that he actually cared. He was awarded the MBE for war services in Italy.

TOVEY, GORDON CHARLES, who died on April 16, 1994, aged 81, made one first-class appearance, for Cambridge University against Northamptonshire, in 1933 but played for Dorset from 1929 until 1953. In 1947 he founded Tockington Manor, a prep school near Bristol.

TOWNSEND, ARNOLD FREDERICK, who died on February 25, 1994, aged 81, was the younger brother of the England all-rounder Leslie, who died in 1993. He played as a professional for Derbyshire from 1934 until 1950, when his career was ended by the after-effects of an eye injury sustained while fielding at short leg the previous year: his ability to focus properly was seriously impaired. He had hit form properly only after the war: he passed 1,000 runs in both 1946 and 1947. Overall, his record – 4,327 runs at 23.13 with five centuries – was not impressive, but he was batting at a time when Derbyshire habitually played on greentops and he was the epitome of their patient, watchful batting.

TREANOR, JOHN CASSIMAR, who died on November 7, 1993, aged 71, took a hat-trick on his first-class debut, for New South Wales against Queensland at Brisbane in 1954-55. Jack Treanor bowled leg-breaks and was enormously successful in grade cricket; he played 16 matches for the state over three seasons.

TUKE-HASTINGS, MICHAEL, who died on January 26, 1993, aged 73, was the producer in charge of cricket on BBC radio from the mid-1950s until 1972 and was responsible for the start of *Test Match Special* in 1957. He initially joined the BBC as a sound effects man; his work included *The Goon Show*. He retired to Alderney in 1979 and became a member of the legislature, The States. Although John Arlott was a neighbour, they were not close friends.

VANCE, ROBERT ALAN, CBE, who died on November 7, 1994, aged 69, was one of New Zealand cricket's most important administrators. He was a gruff, plain-spoken man with a forceful personality who helped ensure that New

Zealand moved into a front seat in world cricket. He was chairman of the New Zealand Cricket Council from 1978 to 1987. He managed the tour to England in 1986, and used his influence to ensure that his country was joint-host with Australia for the 1992 World Cup. As a player, he was a dashing but inconsistent batsman who played 40 matches for Wellington over 15 seasons, starting in 1949. His son, also Robert, played four Tests for New Zealand in the late 1980s.

WALLACE, BOON, who died on June 25, 1994, aged 84, was president of the South African Cricket Association (later Union) four times between 1963 and 1980. Wallace – christened Bryan – was one of the game's most important administrators there in the hopeless period as South Africa was frozen out of world cricket, before a new, more activist generation of leaders began the rebel tours. His personal relations with Lord's remained warm; as the world was refusing recognition of his country, MCC made him, in 1974, an honorary life member. He played 14 Currie Cup matches for Western Province in the 1930s. In the 1960s, as their president, he combined with Eddie Barlow as captain to pull the team round. He was said to be the only man Barlow was scared of.

WARN, EDWIN JAMES, died on June 13, 1994, aged 82. Ted Warn was Surrey's head groundsman from 1965 to 1975, having served his apprenticeship under "Bosser" Martin and Bert Lock. His moment of glory came at the 1968 Test against Australia when The Oval was flooded at lunchtime on the final day and Australian journalists filed the news that the series was won. When the sun came out at 2.15, Warn asked for volunteers from the crowd and Ted's Army, armed with brooms and blankets, cleared the pitch in time for Derek Underwood to bowl England to an astonishing victory and square the series.

WARNE, FRANK BELMONT, who died in South Africa on May 29, 1994, aged 87, was a cricketing nomad who played first-class domestic cricket on four continents. His father, T. S. Warne, played 40 games for Victoria at the turn of the century. Frank played only two, in 1926-27 and 1928-29, before qualifying for Worcestershire. He played 78 times for the county between 1934 and 1938 as a useful but unspectacular left-hand bat (he hit exactly 1,000 runs in 1935) and sometimes very effective leg-spinner. He spent three winters during this time playing for the Europeans in India, and helped the semi-official Australian team on its Indian tour in 1935-36. He went to South Africa during the war, playing once for Transvaal; his final first-class match was in Johannesburg for the Rest of South Africa against an Air Force XI in 1942-43 – he scored 108, the last of his three centuries.

WATSON, THOMAS MEAD, who died on August 7, 1994, aged 81, was a left-hand bat who played in three matches for Oxford University in 1933-34. He subsequently taught French at his old school, Monkton Combe, and was commissioned by MCC to write a guide to cricket in French, *Le Jeu de Cricket*.

YOUNG, JAMES OSWALD, who died on March 7, 1994, aged 80, was an all-rounder, who bowled both pace and spin in his career, and made one of the fastest centuries in South African cricket. Playing for Eastern Province against Orange Free State in 1947-48, he reached 100 in 62 minutes.

YOUNGMAN, DAVID THOMAS EVELYN, who died on December 28, 1993, aged 62, was honorary treasurer of Sussex CCC from 1989 to 1993, and for two years a member of the TCCB's finance committee.

MEMORIAL SERVICE

More than 2,000 people gathered in Westminster Abbey on May 16, 1994, to celebrate the life of the commentator Brian Johnston, who had died on January 5. His obituary appeared in the 1994 *Wisden.*

Sir Colin Cowdrey spoke of the cry "Good luck, Cowders" that sent him out to bat in his first Test and quoted the broadcaster Wynford Vaughan Thomas on Johnston: "That gallant Guards officer who could talk the turret off one of his own tanks." He was followed by the prime minister, John Major, who spoke of Johnston's essential Englishness and his ability to make everyone feel better for meeting him. He quoted the citation for Johnston's Military Cross: "His dynamic personality, his determination and cheerfulness under fire proved an inspiration to all those around him."

Among the other speakers were a blind listener, Melvin Collins – "He was a friend to those who never knew him. Eyes to those who cannot see. Warmth to those who were alone and depressed" – and the entertainer Richard Stilgoe, who wrote these verses for the occasion:

Eternal paradise, at first glance, looks very nice –
This is heaven. Every moment is sublime.
For the first few weeks it's great, then it starts to irritate –
Eternity's a hell of a long time.

But heaven's dull perfection's had a recent shock injection –
A muffled titter's running through the pews.
The cause of all this change'll be the maverick new angel
With ears like wings, and co-respondent shoes.

The cherubim and seraphim are starting to despair of him
They've never known a shade so entertaining.
He chats to total strangers, calls the angel Gabriel "Ainjers"
And talks for even longer if it's raining.

He has told them all his stories – the countless broadcast glories –
They listen as the narrative's unfolding.
Motorcycling through a wall, the Crazy Gang, but best of all
They like the line that starts "The bowler's Holding . . ."

He'd have liked to play the halls, or be Ralph Lynn or Tom Walls,
But actors almost always end in hell.
So he wrote himself a role, and with all his heart and soul,
Cast himself as him, and played him awfully well.

He made twenty million friends, for the broadcast voice extends
Far beyond those you encounter face to face
And those he never met have a chance to meet him yet
For all of us end up in the same place.

And when St Peter's done the honours he will pass you on to Johnners,
Who will cry "Good morning – welcome to the wake.
You're batting number seven for the Heaven fourth eleven.
While you're waiting, have some Angel cake!"

So if you think that Heaven's like a wet weekend in Devon
When you get there, he'll be sure to change your views.
Up there the big-nosed cherub'll be telling really terrible
Old jokes while wearing co-respondent shoes.

INDEX TO TEST MATCHES

SOUTH AFRICA v AUSTRALIA, 1993-94

NEW ZEALAND v INDIA, 1993-94

WEST INDIES v ENGLAND, 1993-94

ENGLAND v NEW ZEALAND, 1994

ENGLAND v SOUTH AFRICA, 1994

TEST MATCHES, 1994-95

Full details of these Tests, and others too late for inclusion, will appear in the 1996 edition of *Wisden*.

SRI LANKA v PAKISTAN

First Test: At P. Saravanamuttu Stadium, Colombo, August 9, 10, 11, 13. Pakistan won by 301 runs. Toss: Pakistan. Pakistan 390 (Saeed Anwar 94, Aamir Sohail 41, Asif Mujtaba 44, Inzamam-ul-Haq 81, Wasim Akram 37, Extras 33; H. D. P. K. Dharmasena six for 99, K. P. J. Warnaweera three for 63) and 318 for four dec. (Saeed Anwar 136, Aamir Sohail 65, Asif Mujtaba 31, Salim Malik 50 not out); Sri Lanka 226 (P. A. de Silva 127, H. P. Tillekeratne 34; Wasim Akram three for 30, Mushtaq Ahmed three for 57, Akram Raza three for 46) and 181 (R. S. Mahanama 37, A. Ranatunga 41, H. D. P. K. Dharmasena 30; Wasim Akram five for 43, Akram Raza three for 83).

Ranatunga became the first Sri Lankan to play in 50 Tests. De Silva reached 100 with a six, for the third time in Tests.

Second Test: At Sinhalese Sports Club, Colombo, August 19, 20, 21, 23, 24.

Cancelled without a ball bowled because of civil unrest following the general election.

Third Test: At Kandy, August 26, 27, 28. Pakistan won by an innings and 52 runs. Toss: Pakistan. Sri Lanka 71 (Wasim Akram four for 32, Waqar Younis six for 34) and 234 (A. Ranatunga 34, H. P. Tillekeratne 83 not out, R. S. Kalpage 62; Waqar Younis five for 85, Mushtaq Ahmed three for 34); Pakistan 357 for nine dec. (Saeed Anwar 31, Aamir Sohail 74, Basit Ali 53, Inzamam-ul-Haq 100 not out; K. R. Pushpakumara four for 145, H. D. P. K. Dharmasena four for 75).

Sri Lanka were dismissed for their lowest Test total, in 28.2 overs from Wasim Akram and Waqar Younis, bowling unchanged. Only P. B. Dassanayake (19 not out) reached double figures.

PAKISTAN v AUSTRALIA

First Test: At National Stadium, Karachi, September 28, 29, 30, October 1, 2. Pakistan won by one wicket. Toss: Australia. Australia 337 (M. J. Slater 36, M. G. Bevan 82, S. R. Waugh 73, I. A. Healy 57; Wasim Akram three for 75, Waqar Younis three for 75, Mushtaq Ahmed three for 97) and 232 (D. C. Boon 114 not out, M. E. Waugh 61; Wasim Akram five for 63, Waqar Younis four for 69); Pakistan 256 (Saeed Anwar 85, Aamir Sohail 36, Wasim Akram 39; J. Angel three for 54, S. K. Warne three for 61) and 315 for nine (Saeed Anwar 77, Aamir Sohail 34, Salim Malik 43, Inzamam-ul-Haq 58 not out, Rashid Latif 35; S. K. Warne five for 89).

H. D. Bird became the first umpire to stand in 60 Tests. M. A. Taylor was out for nought twice in his first Test as Australian captain. Pakistan won after Inzamam-ul-Haq and Mushtaq Ahmed added 57 for the last wicket, the winning runs coming when Healy missed a stumping and the ball went for four leg-byes.

Second Test: At Rawalpindi, October 5, 6, 7, 8, 9. Drawn. Toss: Pakistan. Australia 521 for nine dec. (M. A. Taylor 69, M. J. Slater 110, M. E. Waugh 68, M. G. Bevan 70, S. R. Waugh 98, I. A. Healy 58; Mohsin Kamal three for 109) and 14 for one; Pakistan 260 (Aamir Sohail 80, Salim Malik 33, Wasim Akram 45 not out; C. J. McDermott four for 74, D. W. Fleming four for 75) and 537 (Saeed Anwar 75, Aamir Sohail 72, Salim Malik 237, Aamir Malik 65, Rashid Latif 38, Extras 34; D. W. Fleming three for 86).

Pakistan followed on 261 behind, but Salim Malik hit a maiden double-hundred in Tests, batting 460 minutes and hitting 37 fours before he became the third victim in a hat-trick by Test debutant Fleming.

Third Test: At Lahore, November 1, 2, 3, 4, 5. Drawn. Toss: Pakistan. Pakistan 373 (Saeed Anwar 30, Inzamam-ul-Haq 66, Salim Malik 75, Ijaz Ahmed 48, Moin Khan 115 not out; S. K. Warne six for 136, T. B. A. May three for 69) and 404 (Saeed Anwar 32, Salim Malik

143, Aamir Sohail 105, Akram Raza 32, Extras 36; G. D. McGrath four for 92, S. K. Warne three for 104); Australia 455 (M. J. Slater 74, M. A. Taylor 32, M. E. Waugh 71, M. G. Bevan 91, J. L. Langer 69, S. K. Warne 33, Extras 30; Mohsin Kamal four for 116, Mushtaq Ahmed four for 121).

Wasim Akram and Waqar Younis pulled out unfit before the start. Moin Khan, in his first Test since April 1993, scored a maiden Test century. Warne took 18 wickets in the series, which Pakistan won 1-0.

ZIMBABWE v SRI LANKA

First Test: At Harare, October 11, 12, 13, 15, 16. Drawn. Toss: Sri Lanka. Sri Lanka 383 (A. P. Gurusinha 128, S. Ranatunga 118, A. Ranatunga 62; H. H. Streak four for 79, G. J. Whittall four for 70); Zimbabwe 319 for eight (G. W. Flower 41, M. H. Dekker 40, A. D. R. Campbell 44, D. L. Houghton 58, Extras 65; W. P. U. J. C. Vaas four for 74).

Rain prevented any play after the fourth afternoon. Gurusinha reached his 100 in 535 minutes, the third slowest Test century. Whittall was fined 25 per cent of his match fee by referee P. L. van der Merwe for dissent when caught behind.

Second Test: At Queens Club, Bulawayo, October 20, 21, 22, 23, 24. Drawn. Toss: Zimbabwe. Zimbabwe 462 for nine dec. (D. L. Houghton 266, A. Flower 50, W. R. James 33, S. G. Peall 30, Extras 33; W. P. U. J. C. Vaas four for 85); Sri Lanka 218 (A. P. Gurusinha 63, A. Ranatunga 34, H. D. P. K. Dharmasena 54; H. H. Streak three for 68, M. P. Jarvis three for 30) and 193 for four (S. Ranatunga 100 not out).

Queens Club became Test cricket's 73rd ground and Bulawayo's second. Houghton scored Zimbabwe's first Test double-hundred and they enforced the follow-on for the first time. S. Ranatunga scored a century in his second successive Test.

Third Test: At Harare, October 26, 27, 28, 30, 31. Drawn. Toss: Sri Lanka. Sri Lanka 402 (A. P. Gurusinha 54, S. Ranatunga 43, H. P. Tillekeratne 116, A. Ranatunga 39, Extras 32; H. H. Streak four for 97, P. A. Strang three for 65) and 89 for three (P. A. de Silva 41 not out); Zimbabwe 375 (A. D. R. Campbell 99, D. L. Houghton 142, G. J. Whittall 61 not out; K. R. Pushpakumara seven for 116).

Houghton scored his second Test century in successive innings. Pushpakumara returned the second-best figures for Sri Lanka in Tests (behind J. R. Ratnayeke's eight for 83 against Pakistan in 1985-86). The series was drawn.

INDIA v WEST INDIES

First Test: At Bombay, November 18, 19, 20, 21, 22. India won by 96 runs. Toss: India. India 272 (V. G. Kambli 40, S. R. Tendulkar 34, S. V. Manjrekar 51, N. R. Mongia 80; C. A. Walsh six for 79, K. C. G. Benjamin three for 48) and 333 (S. R. Tendulkar 85, S. V. Manjrekar 66, A. Kumble 42, J. Srinath 60, Extras 37; K. C. G. Benjamin four for 82); West Indies 243 (S. C. Williams 49, K. L. T. Arthurton 42, J. C. Adams 39; A. Kumble three for 48, S. L. V. Raju five for 60) and 266 (J. C. Adams 81, J. R. Murray 85; J. Srinath four for 48, S. L. V. Raju three for 85).

India's tenth successive home victory in Tests since December 1988 and M. Azharuddin's tenth victory as Test captain, an Indian record.

Second Test: At Nagpur, December 1, 2, 3, 4, 5. Drawn. Toss: India. India 546 for nine dec. (N. S. Sidhu 107, S. R. Tendulkar 179, M. Azharuddin 97, N. R. Mongia 44, A. Kumble 52 not out, Extras 39; C. L. Hooper five for 116) and 208 for seven dec. (N. S. Sidhu 76, S. R. Tendulkar 54, M. Azharuddin 32 not out); West Indies 428 (P. V. Simmons 50, B. C. Lara 50, J. C. Adams 125 not out, C. L. Hooper 81, J. R. Murray 54; S. L. V. Raju five for 127, A. Kumble three for 131) and 132 for five (C. L. Hooper 67; A. Kumble three for 45).

West Indian captain C. A. Walsh led his players off the field twice on the first day when the crowd threw stones at them.

Third Test: At Mohali, December 10, 11, 12, 13, 14. West Indies won by 243 runs. Toss: West Indies. West Indies 443 (S. C. Williams 34, B. C. Lara 40, J. C. Adams 174 not out, C. L. Hooper 43, J. R. Murray 31, A. C. Cummins 50, Extras 38; S. L. V. Raju three for 73, A. Kumble four for 90) and 301 for three dec. (B. C. Lara 91, J. C. Adams 78 not out, K. L. T. Arthurton 70 not out); India 387 (M. Prabhakar 120, S. V. Manjrekar 40, S. R. Tendulkar 40, N. R. Mongia 34, J. Srinath 52 not out; K. C. G. Benjamin three for 106, C. E. Cuffy three for 80) and 114 (C. A. Walsh three for 34, K. C. G. Benjamin five for 65).

Mohali, near Chandigarh, became Test cricket's 74th ground. India's first home defeat since November 1988 levelled the series, preserving West Indies' record of not losing a Test series since March 1980. Adams finished with 520 runs in the series for an average of 173.33. Prabhakar scored his maiden Test century in his 36th match.

SOUTH AFRICA v NEW ZEALAND

First Test: At Johannesburg, November 25, 26, 27, 28, 29. New Zealand won by 137 runs. Toss: New Zealand. New Zealand 411 (S. P. Fleming 48, M. D. Crowe 83, K. R. Rutherford 68, S. A. Thomson 84, S. B. Doull 31 not out; R. P. Snell three for 112, C. R. Matthews three for 98) and 194 (A. C. Parore 49, M. N. Hart 34; P. S. de Villiers four for 52, C. R. Matthews five for 42); South Africa 279 (D. J. Cullinan 58, J. N. Rhodes 37, D. J. Richardson 93; D. J. Nash three for 81, M. N. Hart three for 57) and 189 (G. Kirsten 33, B. M. McMillan 42, W. J. Cronje 62; S. B. Doull four for 33, M. N. Hart five for 77).

South Africa began the last day on 128 for two, needing another 199, but were all out before lunch.

Second Test: At Durban, December 26, 27, 28, 29, 30. South Africa won by eight wickets. Toss: New Zealand. New Zealand 185 (D. J. Murray 38, S. A. Thomson 82; P. S. de Villiers five for 64, B. M. McMillan three for 40) and 192 (B. A. Young 51, S. P. Fleming 31, S. A. Thomson 35; P. S. de Villiers three for 56, B. M. McMillan three for 53); South Africa 226 (J. B. Commins 30, D. J. Cullinan 34, D. J. Richardson 39 not out; D. K. Morrison four for 70, S. B. Doull five for 73) and 153 for two (G. Kirsten 66 not out, J. B. Commins 45).

M. D. Crowe passed J. G. Wright (5,334) as New Zealand's leading run-scorer in Tests. Young made the third slowest fifty recorded in Tests – 333 minutes.

Third Test: At Cape Town, January 2, 3, 4, 5, 6. South Africa won by seven wickets. Toss: New Zealand. New Zealand 288 (B. A. Young 45, K. R. Rutherford 56, S. P. Fleming 79, C. Pringle 30; S. D. Jack four for 69, B. M. McMillan four for 65) and 239 (B. A. Young 51, A. C. Parore 34, S. P. Fleming 53; P. S. de Villiers five for 61, B. M. McMillan three for 52); South Africa 440 (G. Kirsten 64, P. J. R. Steyn 38, W. J. Cronje 112, D. J. Richardson 109; M. N. Hart three for 141, S. A. Thomson three for 65) and 89 for three.

South Africa took the series 2-1; the only other team to win a three-Test series after going one down was England v Australia, in 1888. Richardson scored his maiden Test hundred. Rutherford was fined 75 per cent of his match fee and given a two-Test suspended ban by referee P. J. P. Burge after abusive dissent when given lbw in the second innings. Umpire S. B. Lambson gave Fleming out caught when nine but changed his mind and recalled him just before he reached the pavilion.

SOUTH AFRICA v PAKISTAN

Only Test: At Johannesburg, January 19, 20, 21, 22, 23. South Africa won by 324 runs. Toss: South Africa. South Africa 460 (G. Kirsten 62, W. J. Cronje 41, J. N. Rhodes 72, B. M. McMillan 113, P. S. de Villiers 66 not out, Extras 64; Aqib Javed three for 102) and 259 for seven dec. (G. Kirsten 42, W. J. Cronje 48, D. J. Cullinan 69 not out, B. M. McMillan 33); Pakistan 230 (Salim Malik 99, Wasim Akram 41; P. S. de Villiers six for 81) and 165 (Inzamam-ul-Haq 95; P. S. de Villiers four for 27).

South Africa recorded their biggest ever win by runs in their inaugural Test with Pakistan. Aamir Nazir, flown in from Pakistan as emergency cover, entered the match 95 minutes after landing in South Africa; he took two wickets on the first day despite breaking down with cramp twice. McMillan scored his maiden Test century. D. J. Richardson was out first ball in both innings, after scoring a hundred in his previous Test. De Villiers was the first South African to score a fifty and take ten wickets in a Test.

AUSTRALIA v ENGLAND

First Test Match

At Brisbane, November 25, 26, 27, 28, 29. Australia won by 184 runs. Toss: Australia.

Australia

M. J. Slater c Gatting b Gooch	176	– (2) lbw b Gough 45
*M. A. Taylor run out	59	– (1) c Stewart b Tufnell 58
D. C. Boon b Gough	3	– b Tufnell 28
M. E. Waugh c Stewart b Gough	140	– b Tufnell 15
M. G. Bevan c Hick b Gough	7	– c Rhodes b DeFreitas 21
S. K. Warne c Rhodes b Gough	2	– (8) c sub (C. White) b DeFreitas 0
S. R. Waugh c Hick b DeFreitas	19	– (6) c sub (C. White) b Tufnell 7
†I. A. Healy c Hick b DeFreitas	7	– (7) not out 45
C. J. McDermott c Gough b McCague	2	– c Rhodes b Gough 6
T. B. A. May not out	3	– not out 9
G. D. McGrath c Gough b McCague	0	
B 5, l-b 2, n-b 1	8	B 2, l-b 9, w 2, n-b 1 14
1/99 2/126 3/308 4/326 5/352 6/379 7/407 8/419 9/425	426	1/109 2/117 3/139 4/174 5/183 6/190 7/191 8/201 (8 wkts dec.) 248

Bowling: *First Innings*—DeFreitas 31–8–102–2; McCague 19.2–4–96–2; Gough 32–7–107–4; Tufnell 25–3–72–0; Hick 4–0–22–0; Gooch 9–2–20–1. *Second Innings*—DeFreitas 22–1–74–2; Gough 23–3–78–2; Tufnell 38–10–79–4; Gooch 3–2–5–0; Hick 2–1–1–0.

England

*M. A. Atherton c Healy b McDermott	54	– lbw b Warne 23
A. J. Stewart c Healy b McDermott	16	– b Warne 33
G. A. Hick c Healy b McDermott	3	– c Healy b Warne 80
G. P. Thorpe c and b Warne	28	– b Warne 67
G. A. Gooch c Healy b May	20	– c Healy b Warne 56
M. W. Gatting lbw b McDermott	10	– c Healy b McDermott 13
M. J. McCague b McDermott	1	– (10) b Warne 0
†S. J. Rhodes lbw b McDermott	4	– (7) c Healy b McDermott 2
P. A. J. DeFreitas c Healy b Warne	7	– (8) b Warne 11
D. Gough not out	17	– (9) c M. E. Waugh b Warne 10
P. C. R. Tufnell c Taylor b Warne	0	– not out 2
L-b 1, n-b 6	7	B 9, l-b 5, n-b 12 26
1/22 2/35 3/82 4/105 5/131 6/133 7/140 8/147 9/151	167	1/50 2/59 3/219 4/220 5/250 6/280 7/309 8/310 9/310 323

Bowling: *First Innings*—McDermott 19–3–53–6; McGrath 10–2–40–0; May 17–3–34–1; Warne 21.2–7–39–3. *Second Innings*—McDermott 23–4–90–2; McGrath 19–4–61–0; Warne 50.2–22–71–8; May 35–16–59–0; M. E. Waugh 7–1–17–0; Bevan 3–0–11–0.

Umpires: C. J. Mitchley (South Africa) and S. G. Randell.
Referee: J. R. Reid (New Zealand).

England were bowled out 259 behind but Taylor did not enforce the follow-on. McCague did not bowl in the second innings because of stomach cramps. Hick and Thorpe batted four and a half hours adding 160 in the second innings before Warne returned career-best figures. Healy's nine dismissals in the match equalled the Australian Test record.

AUSTRALIA v ENGLAND

Second Test Match

At Melbourne, December 24, 26, 27, 28, 29. Australia won by 295 runs. Toss: England.

Australia

First innings		Second innings	
M. J. Slater run out	3	(2) st Rhodes b Tufnell	44
*M. A. Taylor lbw b DeFreitas	9	(1) lbw b Gough	19
D. C. Boon c Hick b Tufnell	41	lbw b DeFreitas	131
M. E. Waugh c Thorpe b DeFreitas	71	c and b Gough	29
M. G. Bevan c Atherton b Gough	3	c sub (J. P. Crawley) b Tufnell	35
S. R. Waugh not out	94	not out	26
†I. A. Healy c Rhodes b Tufnell	17	c Thorpe b Tufnell	17
S. K. Warne c Hick b Gough	6	c DeFreitas b Gough	0
T. B. A. May lbw b Gough	9		
C. J. McDermott b Gough	0	(9) not out	2
D. W. Fleming c Hick b Malcolm	16		
L-b 7, n-b 3	10	B 1, l-b 9, w 1, n-b 6	17
1/10 2/39 3/91 4/100 5/171 6/208 7/220 8/242 9/242	279	1/61 2/81 3/157 4/269 5/275 6/316 7/317 (7 wkts dec.)	320

Bowling: *First Innings*—Malcolm 28.3–4–78–1; DeFreitas 23–4–66–2; Gough 26–9–60–4; Tufnell 28–7–59–2; Hick 2–0–9–0. *Second Innings*—Malcolm 22–3–86–0; DeFreitas 26–2–70–1; Tufnell 48–8–90–3; Gough 25–6–59–3; Hick 3–2–5–0.

England

First innings		Second innings	
*M. A. Atherton lbw b Warne	44	(2) c Healy b McDermott	25
A. J. Stewart c and b Warne	16	(7) not out	8
G. A. Hick c Healy b McDermott	23	b Fleming	2
G. P. Thorpe c M. E. Waugh b Warne	51	c Healy b McDermott	9
G. A. Gooch c and b McDermott	15	(1) c Healy b Fleming	2
M. W. Gatting c S. R. Waugh b Warne	9	(5) c Taylor b McDermott	25
D. Gough c Healy b McDermott	20	(9) c Healy b Warne	0
†S. J. Rhodes c M. E. Waugh b Warne	0	(6) c M. E. Waugh b McDermott	16
P. A. J. DeFreitas st Healy b Warne	14	(8) lbw b Warne	0
D. E. Malcolm not out	11	c Boon b Warne	0
P. C. R. Tufnell run out	0	c Healy b McDermott	0
L-b 7, n-b 2	9	L-b 2, n-b 3	5
1/40 2/119 3/124 4/140 5/148 6/151 7/185 8/189 9/207	212	1/3 2/10 3/23 4/43 5/81 6/88 7/91 8/91 9/91	92

In the first innings A. J. Stewart, when 1, retired hurt at 10 and resumed at 151.

Bowling: *First Innings*—McDermott 24–6–72–3; Fleming 11–5–30–0; M. E. Waugh 3–1–11–0; Warne 27.4–8–64–6; May 18–5–28–0. *Second Innings*—McDermott 16.5–5–42–5; Fleming 9–1–24–2; Warne 13–6–16–3; May 4–1–8–0.

Umpires: S. A. Bucknor (West Indies) and S. G. Randell.
Referee: J. R. Reid (New Zealand).

Stewart's right index finger – recently mended after earlier injury – was broken again by a McDermott delivery on the second day. Warne passed 150 wickets in his 31st Test. In the second innings, Atherton completed 1,136 runs in 13 Tests in 1994, McDermott reached 250 wickets in his 62nd Test, Healy moved into fourth place in the Test wicket-keepers' list, with 230 dismissals, and Warne took the first hat-trick in Ashes Tests since H. Trumble in 1903-04. England were all out in 42.5 overs; they entered the last day 79 for four but the last six wickets fell for 13 runs inside an hour.

AUSTRALIA v ENGLAND

Third Test Match

At Sydney, January 1, 2, 3, 4, 5. Drawn. Toss: England.

England

G. A. Gooch c Healy b Fleming	1	– lbw b Fleming	29
*M. A. Atherton b McDermott	88	– c Taylor b Fleming	67
G. A. Hick b McDermott	2	– not out	98
G. P. Thorpe lbw b McDermott	10	– not out	47
J. P. Crawley c M. E. Waugh b Fleming	72		
M. W. Gatting c Healy b McDermott	0		
A. R. C. Fraser c Healy b Fleming	27		
†S. J. Rhodes run out	1		
D. Gough c Fleming b McDermott	51		
D. E. Malcolm b Warne	29		
P. C. R. Tufnell not out	4		
B 8, l-b 7, n-b 9	24	L-b 6, w 1, n-b 7	14
1/1 2/10 3/20 4/194 5/194 6/196 7/197 8/255 9/295	309	1/54 2/158 (2 wkts dec.)	255

Bowling: *First Innings*—McDermott 30–7–101–5; Fleming 26.2–12–52–3; Warne 36–10–88–1; May 17–4–35–0; M. E. Waugh 6–1–10–0; Bevan 4–1–8–0. *Second Innings*—McDermott 24–2–76–0; Fleming 20–3–66–2; M. E. Waugh 2–1–4–0; Warne 16–2–48–0; May 10–1–55–0.

Australia

M. J. Slater b Malcolm	11	– (2) c Tufnell b Fraser	103
*M. A. Taylor c and b Gough	49	– (1) b Malcolm	113
D. C. Boon b Gough	3	– c Hick b Gough	17
M. E. Waugh c Rhodes b Malcolm	3	– lbw b Fraser	25
M. G. Bevan c Thorpe b Fraser	8	– c Rhodes b Fraser	7
S. R. Waugh b Gough	1	– c Rhodes b Fraser	0
†I. A. Healy c Hick b Gough	10	– c Rhodes b Fraser	5
S. K. Warne c Gatting b Fraser	0	– not out	36
T. B. A. May c Hick b Gough	0	– not out	10
C. J. McDermott not out	21		
D. W. Fleming b Gough	0		
B 6, l-b 1, n-b 3	10	B 12, l-b 3, w 1, n-b 12	28
1/12 2/15 3/18 4/38 5/39 6/57 7/62 8/65 9/116	116	1/208 2/239 3/265 4/282 5/286 6/289 7/292 (7 wkts)	344

Bowling: *First Innings*—Malcolm 13–4–34–2; Gough 18.5–4–49–6; Fraser 11–1–26–2. *Second Innings*—Malcolm 21–4–75–1; Gough 28–4–72–1; Fraser 25–3–73–5; Tufnell 35.4–9–61–0; Hick 5–0–21–0; Gooch 7–1–27–0.

Umpires: S. A. Bucknor (West Indies) and D. B. Hair. Referee: J. R. Reid (New Zealand).

McDermott took four wickets on the first day despite stomach cramps. Australia, set 449 to win, were 206 without loss at lunch on the final day, before collapsing to Fraser. Play continued until 7.26 p.m. because of a break for rain; the umpires were rebuked by the referee for failing to notice that England had completed the minimum 15 overs inside the final hour, so that the players had to be called back for one more over. Australia retained the Ashes.

AUSTRALIA v ENGLAND

Fourth Test Match

At Adelaide, January 26, 27, 28, 29, 30. England won by 106 runs. Toss: England.

England

G. A. Gooch c M. E. Waugh b Fleming	47	– c Healy b McDermott	34
*M. A. Atherton c Boon b Fleming	80	– lbw b M. E. Waugh	14
M. W. Gatting c S. R. Waugh b McIntyre	117	– b M. E. Waugh	0
G. P. Thorpe c Taylor b Warne	26	– c Warne b McDermott	83
J. P. Crawley b Warne	28	– c and b M. E. Waugh	71
†S. J. Rhodes c Taylor b McDermott	6	– c Fleming b Warne	2
C. C. Lewis c Blewett b McDermott	10	– b Fleming	7
P. A. J. DeFreitas c Blewett b McIntyre	21	– c Healy b M. E. Waugh	88
A. R. C. Fraser run out	7	– c McDermott b M. E. Waugh	5
D. E. Malcolm b McDermott	0	– not out	10
P. C. R. Tufnell not out	0	– lbw b Warne	0
B 2, l-b 5, w 2, n-b 2	11	B 6, l-b 8	14
1/93 2/175 3/211 4/286 5/293 6/307 7/334 8/353 9/353	353	1/26 2/30 3/83 4/154 5/169 6/181 7/270 8/317 9/317	328

Bowling: *First Innings*—McDermott 41–15–66–3; Fleming 25–6–65–2; Blewett 16–4–59–0; Warne 31–9–72–2; McIntyre 19.3–3–51–2; M. E. Waugh 9–1–33–0. *Second Innings*—McDermott 27–5–96–2; Fleming 11–3–37–1; Warne 30.5–9–82–2; M. E. Waugh 14–4–40–5; McIntyre 8–0–36–0; Blewett 4–0–23–0.

Australia

M. J. Slater c Atherton b DeFreitas	67	– (2) c Tufnell b Malcolm	5
*M. A. Taylor lbw b Lewis	90	– (1) c Thorpe b Malcolm	13
D. C. Boon c Rhodes b DeFreitas	0	– c Rhodes b Fraser	4
M. E. Waugh c Rhodes b Fraser	39	– c Gatting b Tufnell	24
S. R. Waugh c Atherton b Lewis	19	– b Malcolm	0
G. S. Blewett not out	102	– c Rhodes b Lewis	12
†I. A. Healy c Rhodes b Malcolm	74	– not out	51
S. K. Warne c Thorpe b Fraser	7	– lbw b Lewis	2
D. W. Fleming c Rhodes b Malcolm	0	– (10) lbw b Lewis	24
P. E. McIntyre b Malcolm	0	– (11) lbw b Malcolm	0
C. J. McDermott c Crawley b Fraser	5	– (9) c Rhodes b Lewis	0
B 2, l-b 7, n-b 7	16	B 3, l-b 5, n-b 13	21
1/128 2/130 3/202 4/207 5/232 6/396 7/405 8/406 9/414	419	1/17 2/22 3/22 4/23 5/64 6/75 7/83 8/83 9/152	156

Bowling: *First Innings*—Malcolm 26–5–78–3; Fraser 28.5–6–95–3; Tufnell 24–5–64–0; DeFreitas 20–3–70–2; Lewis 18–1–81–2; Gooch 5–0–22–0. *Second Innings*—Malcolm 16.1–3–39–4; Fraser 12–1–37–1; DeFreitas 11–3–31–0; Lewis 13–4–24–4; Tufnell 9–3–17–1.

Umpires: S. Venkataraghavan (India) and P. D. Parker.
Referee: J. R. Reid (New Zealand).

Gatting made his tenth Test century but his first in 20 Tests since August 1987. Blewett reached his hundred on Test debut on his home ground. Gooch announced he would retire from international cricket after Perth; he later overtook Javed Miandad (8,832) as the third highest run-scorer in Tests. DeFreitas scored his Test-best 88 in 95 balls, hitting McDermott for 22 in one over with the new ball. England secured their first Test victory in Australia since December 1986. Referee J. R. Reid fined Lewis 30 per cent of his match fee for pointing McDermott to the dressing-room on dismissing him, and reprimanded Atherton for not ensuring the game was played in the right spirit; the whole England team were fined 15 per cent of their match fee for their slow over-rate.

AUSTRALIA v ENGLAND

Fifth Test Match

At Perth, February 3, 4, 5, 6, 7. Australia won by 329 runs. Toss: Australia.

Australia

First innings		Second innings	
M. J. Slater c Lewis b DeFreitas	124	(2) c Atherton b Fraser	45
*M. A. Taylor c Rhodes b Lewis	9	(1) b Fraser	52
D. C. Boon c Ramprakash b Lewis	1	(4) c Rhodes b Malcolm	18
M. E. Waugh c DeFreitas b Lewis	88	(5) c Rhodes b DeFreitas	1
S. R. Waugh not out	99	(6) c Ramprakash b Lewis	80
G. S. Blewett c Rhodes b Fraser	20	(7) c Malcolm b Lewis	115
†I. A. Healy c Lewis b DeFreitas	12	(8) not out	11
S. K. Warne c Rhodes b DeFreitas	1	(9) c Lewis b Malcolm	6
J. Angel run out	11	(3) run out	0
G. D. McGrath run out	0		
C. J. McDermott run out	6		
B 14, l-b 4, w 4, n-b 9	31	B 1, l-b 9, n-b 7	17
1/47 2/55 3/238 4/247 5/287 6/320 7/328 8/386 9/388	402	1/75 2/79 3/102 4/115 5/123 6/326 7/333 8/345 (8 wkts dec.)	345

Bowling: *First Innings*—Malcolm 31–6–93–0; DeFreitas 29–8–91–3; Fraser 32–11–84–1; Lewis 31.5–8–73–3; Gooch 1–1–0–0; Ramprakash 11–0–43–0. *Second Innings*—Malcolm 23.3–3–105–2; Fraser 21–3–74–2; Lewis 16–1–71–2; DeFreitas 22–10–54–1; Ramprakash 8–1–31–0.

England

First innings		Second innings	
G. A. Gooch lbw b M. E. Waugh	37	c and b McDermott	4
*M. A. Atherton c Healy b McGrath	4	c Healy b McGrath	8
M. W. Gatting b McGrath	0	b McDermott	8
G. P. Thorpe st Healy b Warne	123	(5) c Taylor b McGrath	0
J. P. Crawley c Warne b M. E. Waugh	0	(6) c M. E. Waugh b McDermott	0
M. R. Ramprakash b Warne	72	(7) c S. R. Waugh b M. E. Waugh	42
†S. J. Rhodes b Angel	2	(8) not out	39
C. C. Lewis c Blewett b McGrath	40	(9) lbw b McDermott	11
P. A. J. DeFreitas b Angel	0	(10) c Taylor b McDermott	0
A. R. C. Fraser c Warne b Angel	9	(4) lbw b McGrath	5
D. E. Malcolm not out	0	b McDermott	0
B 4, l-b 1, n-b 3	8	L-b 1, w 1, n-b 4	6
1/5 2/5 3/77 4/77 5/235 6/246 7/246 8/247 9/293	295	1/4 2/17 3/26 4/26 5/27 6/27 7/95 8/121 9/123	123

Bowling: *First Innings*—Angel 22.3–7–65–3; McGrath 25–6–88–3; Blewett 4–1–9–0; M. E. Waugh 9–2–29–2; Warne 23–8–58–2; McDermott 13–5–41–0. *Second Innings*—McDermott 15–4–38–6; McGrath 13–4–40–3; Angel 3–0–20–0; Warne 7–3–11–0; M. E. Waugh 3–0–13–1.

Umpires: K. E. Liebenberg (South Africa) and S. G. Randell.
Referee: J. R. Reid (New Zealand).

Gooch played his 118th Test, passing D. I. Gower's England record, and ending his international career with 8,900 runs at 42.58. Gatting also announced his international retirement after a first-ball duck in the first innings, finishing with 4,409 at 35.55 in 79 Tests. McDermott injured his back before the match; he batted with a runner (M. E. Waugh, who became the last of three run-outs in the innings, leaving his twin stranded on 99) but still ended with 32 wickets in the series. Slater broke his right thumb in the second innings. Blewett became the fifth player in history to score centuries in each of his first two Tests. Australia took the series 3-1 and England were fined another 15 per cent of their match fee for their slow over-rate. Three England players (Fraser, Lewis and Ramprakash) were not in the original tour 16. Three of those in the 16 (J. E. Benjamin, S. D. Udal and C. White) did not play in the series. Three others (N. H. Fairbrother, M. C. Ilott and R. C. Russell) were also called in as replacements.

FIXTURES, 1995

** Indicates Sunday play.* *† Not first-class.*

All County Championship matches are of four days' duration. Other first-class matches are of three days' duration unless stated.

Thursday, April 13

Cambridge	Cambridge U. v Yorks.
Oxford	Oxford U. v Durham

Tuesday, April 18

Birmingham	Warwicks. v England A (4 days)
Cambridge	Cambridge U. v Lancs.
Oxford	Oxford U. v Glam.
Taunton	†Somerset 2nd XI v England Under-19 (4 days)

Friday, April 21

Cambridge	†Combined Univs. v Northants (1 day)

Sunday, April 23

†Benson and Hedges Cup (1 day)

Derby	Derbys. v Northants
Stockton-on-Tees	Durham v Leics.
Chelmsford	Essex v Glam.
Bristol	Glos. v Combined Univs.
Lord's	Middx v Hants
Leek	Minor Counties v Lancs.
Nottingham	Notts. v Warwicks.
Taunton	Somerset v Sussex
The Oval	Surrey v Ireland
Worcester	Worcs. v Scotland

Tuesday, April 25

†Benson and Hedges Cup (1 day)

Chelmsford	Essex v Middx
Cardiff	Glam. v Combined Univs.
Southampton	Hants v Glos.
Canterbury	Kent v Surrey
Manchester	Lancs. v Leics.
Leek	Minor Counties v Notts.
Glasgow (Titwood)	Scotland v Derbys.
Hove	Sussex v Ireland
Birmingham	Warwicks. v Durham
Leeds	Yorks. v Worcs.

Thursday, April 28

Derby*	Derbys. v Sussex
Stockton-on-Tees*	Durham v Hants
Chelmsford*	Essex v Leics.
Canterbury*	Kent v Northants
Taunton*	Somerset v Glam.
The Oval*	Surrey v Glos.
Birmingham*	Warwicks. v Middx
Leeds	Yorks. v Lancs. ("friendly" match, 4 days)
Cambridge	Cambridge U. v Notts.
Oxford	Oxford U. v Worcs.

Sunday, April 30

Leeds	†Yorks. v Lancs. (1 day)

Tuesday, May 2

†Benson and Hedges Cup (1 day)

Cambridge	Combined Univs. v Essex
Stockton-on-Tees	Durham v Notts.
Bristol	Glos. v Middx
Southampton	Hants v Glam.
Canterbury	Kent v Somerset
Leicester	Leics. v Minor Counties
Northampton	Northants v Worcs.
Glasgow (Hamilton Crescent)	Scotland v Yorks.
The Oval	Surrey v Sussex
Birmingham	Warwicks. v Lancs.

Wednesday, May 3

Lord's	†MCC v MCC Young Cricketers (1 day)

Thursday, May 4

Chelmsford Essex v Worcs.
Cardiff Glam. v Northants
Manchester Lancs. v Durham
Leicester Leics. v Yorks.
Lord's Middx v Hants
Nottingham Notts. v Derbys.
Taunton Somerset v Glos.
Hove Sussex v Kent
Birmingham Warwicks. v Surrey

Tuesday, May 9

†**Benson and Hedges Cup** (1 day)

Oxford Combined Univs. v Hants
Chelmsford Essex v Glos.
Cardiff Glam. v Middx
Comber (North Down CC) Ireland v Kent
Manchester Lancs. v Notts.
Leicester Leics. v Warwicks.
Jesmond Minor Counties v Durham
Taunton Somerset v Surrey
Worcester Worcs. v Derbys.
Leeds Yorks. v Northants

Thursday, May 11

Chesterfield Derbys. v Yorks.
Swansea Glam. v Sussex
Bristol Glos. v Notts.
Canterbury Kent v Leics.
Manchester Lancs. v Warwicks.
Northampton Northants v Somerset
The Oval Surrey v Durham
Worcester Worcs. v Middx
Cambridge Cambridge U. v Essex
Oxford Oxford U. v Hants

Saturday, May 13

Arundel †Lavinia, Duchess of Norfolk's XI v West Indians (1 day)

Sunday, May 14

Southampton †Hants v West Indians (1 day)
Cambridge †Cambridge U. v Oxford U. (1 day)

Tuesday, May 16

†**Benson and Hedges Cup** (1 day)

Chesterfield Derbys. v Yorks.
Swansea Glam. v Glos.
Southampton Hants v Essex
Eglinton Ireland v Somerset
Manchester Lancs. v Durham
Lord's Middx v Combined Univs.
Northampton Northants v Scotland
Nottingham Notts. v Leics.
Hove Sussex v Kent
Birmingham Warwicks. v Minor Counties

Worcester Worcs. v West Indians

Thursday, May 18

Chester-le-Street Durham v Warwicks.
Southampton Hants v Kent
Leicester Leics. v Derbys.
Lord's Middx v Lancs.
Northampton Northants v Surrey
Hove Sussex v Essex
Bradford Yorks. v Glam.
Oxford Oxford U. v Notts.

Friday, May 19

Taunton* Somerset v West Indians

Wednesday, May 24

Nottingham †ENGLAND v WEST INDIES (1st 1-day Texaco Trophy)
Tunbridge Wells Kent v Glam.

Thursday, May 25

Chelmsford Essex v Middx
Gloucester Glos. v Worcs.
Portsmouth Hants v Sussex
Liverpool Lancs. v Notts.
Leicester Leics. v Durham
Birmingham Warwicks. v Somerset
Sheffield Yorks. v Northants
Oxford Oxford U. v Derbys.

Friday, May 26

The Oval †ENGLAND v WEST INDIES (2nd 1-day Texaco Trophy)

Sunday, May 28

Lord's †ENGLAND v WEST INDIES (3rd 1-day Texaco Trophy)

Tuesday, May 30

†Benson and Hedges Cup – Quarter-finals
(1 day)

Leicester or Manchester	Leics. or Lancs. v West Indians

Or Warwicks. if both Leics. and Lancs. in B&H Cup quarter-finals.

Thursday, June 1

Chester-le-Street	Durham v Kent
Cardiff	Glam. v Hants
Lord's	Middx v Derbys.
Nottingham	Notts. v Essex
Taunton	Somerset v Yorks.
Hove	Sussex v Glos.
Worcester	Worcs. v Surrey

Friday, June 2

Oxford	Oxford U. v Leics.

Saturday, June 3

Northampton*	Northants v West Indians

Wednesday, June 7

Basingstoke	Hants v Leics.
Lord's	†MCC v Ireland (2 days)

Thursday, June 8

Leeds*	ENGLAND v WEST INDIES (1st Cornhill Test, 5 days)
Derby	Derbys. v Northants
Chelmsford	Essex v Durham
Canterbury	Kent v Glos.
Manchester	Lancs. v Glam.
Nottingham	Notts. v Worcs.
The Oval	Surrey v Somerset
Birmingham	Warwicks. v Sussex

Friday, June 9

Cambridge*	Cambridge U. v Middx

Tuesday, June 13

†Benson and Hedges Cup – Semi-finals
(1 day)

Thursday, June 15

Derby	Derbys. v Somerset
Colwyn Bay	Glam. v Middx
Bristol	Glos. v Hants
Leicester	Leics. v Notts.
Luton	Northants v Essex
Horsham	Sussex v Surrey
Worcester	Worcs. v Lancs.
Leeds	Yorks. v Kent
Edinburgh	†Scotland v West Indians (1 day)

Friday, June 16

Cambridge*	Cambridge U. v Warwicks.

Saturday, June 17

Chester-le-Street*	Durham v West Indians

Tuesday, June 20

Oxford	Oxford U. v Middx

Thursday, June 22

Lord's*	ENGLAND v WEST INDIES (2nd Cornhill Test, 5 days)
Chester-le-Street	Durham v Derbys.
Southampton	Hants v Worcs.
Manchester	Lancs. v Essex
Northampton	Northants v Leics.
Nottingham	Notts. v Kent
Bath	Somerset v Sussex
The Oval	Surrey v Glam.
Birmingham	Warwicks. v Yorks.

Friday, June 23

Bristol*	Glos. v Oxford U.

Tuesday, June 27

†NatWest Bank Trophy – First Round
(1 day)

March	Cambs. v Derbys.
Chester (Boughton Hall)	Cheshire v Essex
St Austell	Cornwall v Middx
Chester-le-Street	Durham v Herefords.
Cardiff	Glam. v Dorset
Bristol	Glos. v Suffolk
Manchester	Lancs. v Norfolk
Leicester	Leics. v Hants
Northampton	Northants v Holland
Nottingham	Notts. v Scotland

Stone — Staffs. v Kent
The Oval — Surrey v Berks.
Hove — Sussex v Devon
Birmingham — Warwicks. v Somerset
Worcester — Worcs. v Cumb.
Leeds — Yorks. v Ireland

Lord's — †Eton v Harrow (1 day)

Wednesday, June 28

Oxford — Combined Univs. v West Indians

Thursday, June 29

Derby — Derbys. v Hants
Ilford — Essex v Warwicks.
Swansea — Glam. v Durham
Lord's — Middx v Surrey
Nottingham — Notts. v Somerset
Worcester — Worcs. v Leics.
Middlesbrough — Yorks. v Glos.

Saturday, July 1

Hove* — Sussex v West Indians
Folkestone* — Kent v Cambridge U.
Canterbury — †England Under-19 v South Africa Under-19 (1st 1-day)

Monday, July 3

Trowbridge — †NCA England v Australia A (1 day)

Tuesday, July 4

Chelmsford — †England Under-19 v South Africa Under-19 (2nd 1-day)

Wednesday, July 5

Maidstone — Kent v Derbys.
Taunton — Somerset v Australia A
Lord's — Oxford U. v Cambridge U.

Thursday, July 6

Birmingham — ENGLAND v WEST INDIES (3rd Cornhill Test, 5 days)
Darlington — Durham v Worcs.
Bristol — Glos. v Middx
Southampton — Hants v Yorks.
Manchester — Lancs. v Northants
Leicester — Leics. v Warwicks.
The Oval — Surrey v Essex
Arundel — Sussex v Notts.

Saturday, July 8

Neath* — Glam. v Australia A

Wednesday, July 12

†NatWest Bank Trophy – Second Round (1 day)

Chester (Boughton Hall) or Chelmsford — Cheshire or Essex v Yorks. or Ireland
Chester-le-Street or Brockhampton — Durham or Herefords. v Glos. or Suffolk
Manchester or Lakenham — Lancs. or Norfolk v Worcs. or Cumb.
Leicester or Southampton — Leics. or Hants v Glam. or Dorset
Nottingham or Forfar (Strathmore CC) — Notts. or Scotland v Northants or Holland
The Oval or Finchampstead — Surrey or Berks. v Cornwall or Middx
Hove or Torquay — Sussex or Devon v Cambs. or Derbys.
Birmingham or Taunton — Warwicks. or Somerset v Staffs. or Kent

Reading — †Minor Counties v Australia A (1 day)

Thursday, July 13

Reading — †Minor Counties v West Indians (1 day)

Saturday, July 15

Lord's — †BENSON AND HEDGES CUP FINAL (1 day)
Dublin (Castle Avenue) — †Ireland v West Indians (1 day)

Monday, July 17

Harrogate — †Costcutter Cup (3 days)

Tuesday, July 18

Leeds — †Yorks. v Australia A (1 day)
Lord's — †MCC v MCC Schools (1 day)

Wednesday, July 19

Canterbury	Kent v West Indians
Chesterfield	Derbys. v Australia A
Lord's	†MCC Schools v NAYC (1 day)
Ireland	†Triple Crown Tournament (3 days)

Thursday, July 20

Southend	Essex v Somerset
Cardiff	Glam. v Warwicks.
Cheltenham	Glos. v Lancs.
Northampton	Northants v Hants
Guildford	Surrey v Notts.
Hove	Sussex v Leics.
Harrogate	Yorks. v Durham
Taunton	†England Under-19 v South Africa Under-19 (1st "Test", 4 days)
Lord's	†NCA Young Cricketers v Combined Services (1 day)

Saturday, July 22

Lord's*	Middx v West Indians
Worcester*	Worcs. v Australia A

Wednesday, July 26

Cheltenham	†Glos. v Australia A (1 day)

Thursday, July 27

Manchester*	ENGLAND v WEST INDIES (4th Cornhill Test, 5 days)
Derby	Derbys. v Glam.
Cheltenham	Glos. v Essex
Leicester	Leics. v Surrey
Lord's	Middx v Sussex
Nottingham	Notts. v Yorks.
Taunton	Somerset v Lancs.
Birmingham	Warwicks. v Northants
Worcester	Worcs. v Kent

Friday, July 28

Southampton*	Hants v Australia A (4 days)

Tuesday, August 1

†NatWest Bank Trophy – Quarter-finals (1 day)

Wednesday, August 2

Derby or Birmingham	Derbys. or Warwicks. v West Indians

Or Somerset if both Derbys. and Warwicks. in NWT Cup quarter-finals.

Thursday, August 3

Colchester	Essex v Hants
Canterbury	Kent v Surrey
Lytham	Lancs. v Sussex
Lord's	Middx v Notts.
Northampton	Northants v Durham
Scarborough	Yorks. v Worcs.
Leicester*	Leics. v Australia A (4 days)
Worcester	†England Under-19 v South Africa Under-19 (2nd "Test", 4 days)

Saturday, August 5

Bristol*	Glos. v West Indians

Monday, August 7

Cambridge and Oxford	†NAYC Under-19 County Festivals (6 days)

Tuesday, August 8

The Oval	†Surrey v Australia A (1 day)

Wednesday, August 9

Lord's	†MCC v Wales (2 days)

Thursday, August 10

Nottingham*	ENGLAND v WEST INDIES (5th Cornhill Test, 5 days)
Chester-le-Street	Durham v Middx
Swansea	Glam. v Essex
Southampton	Hants v Warwicks.
Leicester	Leics. v Lancs.
Northampton	Northants v Glos.
Taunton	Somerset v Kent
The Oval	Surrey v Yorks.
Kidderminster	Worcs. v Derbys.
Leeds*	†England Under-19 v South Africa Under-19 (3rd "Test", 4 days)

Friday, August 11

Hove* Sussex v Australia A (4 days)

Saturday, August 12

Dublin (Rathmines)* Ireland v Scotland

Tuesday, August 15

†**NatWest Bank Trophy – Semi-finals** (1 day)

Wednesday, August 16

Pontypridd or Southampton Glam. or Hants v West Indians

Or Leics. if both Glam. and Hants in NWT semi-finals.

Thursday, August 17

Chester-le-Street Durham v Somerset
Bristol Glos. v Derbys.
Manchester Lancs. v Yorks.
Lord's Middx v Kent
Nottingham Notts. v Warwicks.
Eastbourne Sussex v Worcs.
Birmingham* TCCB XI v Australia A (4 days)

†Bain Hogg Trophy Semi-finals (1 day)

Friday, August 18

†Bain Hogg Trophy Semi-finals (1 day) (if not played on August 17)

Saturday, August 19

Chelmsford* Essex v West Indians

Wednesday, August 23

Abergavenny Glam. v Glos.
Lord's †Minor Counties Knockout Final (1 day)

Thursday, August 24

The Oval* ENGLAND v WEST INDIES (6th Cornhill Test, 5 days)
Derby Derbys. v Surrey
Hartlepool Durham v Sussex
Portsmouth Hants v Lancs.
Canterbury Kent v Essex
Northampton Northants v Notts.
Weston-super-Mare Somerset v Leics.
Birmingham Warwicks. v Worcs.
Leeds Yorks. v Middx

Friday, August 25

Lord's †National Club Championship Final (1 day)

Sunday, August 27

Lord's †National Village Championship Final (1 day)

Tuesday, August 29

Chelmsford Essex v Derbys.
Leicester Leics. v Glam.
Uxbridge Middx v Northants
Nottingham Notts. v Hants
The Oval Surrey v Lancs.
Birmingham Warwicks. v Glos.
Worcester Worcs. v Somerset

Wednesday, August 30

Scarborough Yorks. v West Indians

Saturday, September 2

Lord's †NATWEST BANK TROPHY FINAL (1 day)
Scarborough †Yorks. v Durham (Northern Electric Trophy, 1 day)

Sunday, September 3

Scarborough †President's XI v West Indians (1 day)

Monday, September 4

†Bain Hogg Trophy Final (1 day).

Scarborough †Tetley Bitter Festival Trophy (3 days)

Tuesday, September 5

Lord's †MCC v Minor Counties CA (1 day)

Wednesday, September 6

The Oval — Surrey v New South Wales

Thursday, September 7

Cardiff — Glam. v Notts.
Bristol — Glos. v Durham
Southampton — Hants v Somerset
Manchester — Lancs. v Kent
Uxbridge — Middx v Leics.
Northampton — Northants v Worcs.
Birmingham — Warwicks. v Derbys.
Scarborough — Yorks. v Sussex

Sunday, September 10

The Oval — †Surrey v New South Wales (1 day)

Thursday, September 14

Derby — Derbys. v Lancs.
Chester-le-Street — Durham v Notts.
Chelmsford — Essex v Yorks.
Canterbury — Kent v Warwicks.
Leicester — Leics. v Glos.
Taunton — Somerset v Middx
The Oval — Surrey v Hants
Hove — Sussex v Northants
Worcester — Worcs. v Glam.

WEST INDIAN TOUR, 1995

MAY

13 Arundel — †v Lavinia, Duchess of Norfolk's XI (1 day)
14 Southampton — †v Hants (1 day)
16 Worcester — v Worcs.
19 Taunton* — v Somerset
24 Nottingham — †v ENGLAND (1st 1-day Texaco Trophy)
26 The Oval — †v ENGLAND (2nd 1-day Texaco Trophy)
28 Lord's — †v ENGLAND (3rd 1-day Texaco Trophy)
30 Leicester or Manchester — v Leics. or Lancs.

Or Warwicks. if both Leics. and Lancs. in B&H Cup quarter-finals.

JUNE

3 Northampton* — v Northants
8 Leeds* — v ENGLAND (1st Cornhill Test, 5 days)
15 Edinburgh — †v Scotland (1 day)
17 Chester-le-Street* — v Durham
22 Lord's* — v ENGLAND (2nd Cornhill Test, 5 days)
28 Oxford — v Combined Univs

JULY

1 Hove* — v Sussex
6 Birmingham — v ENGLAND (3rd Cornhill Test, 5 days)
13 Reading — †v Minor Counties (1 day)
15 Dublin (Castle Avenue) — †v Ireland (1 day)
19 Canterbury — v Kent
22 Lord's* — v Middx
27 Manchester* — v ENGLAND (4th Cornhill Test, 5 days)

AUGUST

2 Derby or Birmingham — v Derbys. or Warwicks.

Or Somerset if both Derbys. and Warwicks. in NWT quarter-finals.

5 Bristol* — v Glos.
10 Nottingham* — v ENGLAND (5th Cornhill Test, 5 days)
16 Pontypridd or Southampton — v Glam. or Hants

Or Leics. if both Glam. and Hants in NWT semi-finals.

19 Chelmsford* — v Essex
24 The Oval* — v ENGLAND (6th Cornhill Test, 5 days)
30 Scarborough — v Yorks.

SEPTEMBER

3 Scarborough — †v President's XI (1 day)

AUSTRALIA A TOUR, 1995

JULY

3	Trowbridge	†v NCA England (1 day)
5	Taunton	v Somerset
8	Neath*	v Glam.
12	Reading	†v Minor Counties (1 day)
18	Leeds	†v Yorks. (1 day)
19	Chesterfield	v Derbys.
22	Worcester*	v Worcs.
26	Cheltenham	†v Glos. (1 day)
28	Southampton*	v Hants (4 days)

AUGUST

3	Leicester*	v Leics. (4 days)
8	The Oval	†v Surrey (1 day)
11	Hove*	v Sussex (4 days)
17	Birmingham*	v TCCB XI (4 days)

†AXA EQUITY & LAW LEAGUE, 1995

All matches are of one day's duration.

MAY

7–Essex v Worcs. (Chelmsford); Glam. v Northants (Cardiff); Lancs. v Durham (Manchester); Leics. v Yorks. (Leicester); Middx v Hants (Lord's); Notts. v Derbys. (Nottingham); Somerset v Glos. (Taunton); Sussex v Kent (Hove); Warwicks. v Surrey (Birmingham).

14–Derbys. v Yorks. (Chesterfield); Glam. v Sussex (Swansea); Glos. v Notts. (Bristol); Kent v Leics. (Canterbury); Lancs. v Warwicks. (Manchester); Northants v Somerset (Northampton); Surrey v Durham (The Oval); Worcs. v Middx (Worcester).

21–Durham v Warwicks. (Chester-le-Street); Hants v Kent (Southampton); Leics. v Derbys. (Leicester); Middx v Lancs. (Lord's); Northants v Surrey (Northampton); Sussex v Essex (Hove); Yorks. v Glam. (Leeds).

28–Essex v Middx (Chelmsford); Glos. v Worcs. (Gloucester); Hants v Sussex (Portsmouth); Kent v Glam. (Tunbridge Wells); Lancs. v Notts. (Manchester); Leics. v Durham (Leicester); Warwicks. v Somerset (Birmingham); Yorks. v Northants (Sheffield).

JUNE

4–Durham v Kent (Chester-le-Street); Glam. v Hants (Cardiff); Middx v Derbys. (Lord's); Notts. v Essex (Nottingham); Somerset v Yorks. (Taunton); Sussex v Glos. (Hove); Worcs. v Surrey (Worcester).

11–Derbys. v Northants (Derby); Essex v Durham (Chelmsford); Hants v Leics. (Basingstoke); Kent v Glos. (Canterbury); Lancs. v Glam. (Manchester); Notts. v Worcs. (Nottingham); Surrey v Somerset (The Oval); Warwicks. v Sussex (Birmingham).

18–Derbys. v Somerset (Derby); Glam. v Middx (Colwyn Bay); Glos. v Hants (Bristol); Leics. v Notts. (Leicester); Northants v Essex (Luton); Sussex v Surrey (Horsham); Worcs. v Lancs. (Worcester); Yorks. v Kent (Leeds).

25–Durham v Derbys. (Chester-le-Street); Hants v Worcs. (Southampton); Lancs. v Essex (Manchester); Northants v Leics. (Northampton); Notts. v Kent (Nottingham); Somerset v Sussex (Bath); Surrey v Glam. (The Oval); Warwicks. v Yorks. (Birmingham).

JULY

2–Derbys. v Hants (Derby); Essex v Warwicks. (Ilford); Glam. v Durham (Swansea); Middx v Surrey (Lord's); Notts. v Somerset (Nottingham); Worcs. v Leics. (Worcester); Yorks. v Glos. (Middlesbrough).

9–Durham v Worcs. (Darlington); Glos. v Middx (Bristol); Hants v Yorks. (Southampton); Kent v Derbys. (Maidstone); Lancs. v Northants (Manchester); Leics. v Warwicks. (Leicester); Surrey v Essex (The Oval); Sussex v Notts. (Arundel).

16–Derbys. v Sussex (Derby); Durham v Hants (Chester-le-Street); Essex v Leics. (Chelmsford); Kent v Northants (Canterbury); Somerset v Glam. (Taunton); Surrey v Glos. (The Oval); Warwicks. v Middx (Birmingham). *Note: Matches involving B&H Cup finalists to be played on July 18.*

23–Essex v Somerset (Southend); Glam. v Warwicks. (Cardiff); Glos. v Lancs. (Cheltenham); Northants v Hants (Northampton); Surrey v Notts. (Guildford); Sussex v Leics. (Hove); Yorks. v Durham (Leeds).

30–Derbys. v Glam. (Derby); Glos. v Essex (Cheltenham); Leics. v Surrey (Leicester); Middx v Sussex (Lord's); Notts. v Yorks. (Cleethorpes); Somerset v Lancs. (Taunton); Warwicks. v Northants (Birmingham); Worcs. v Kent (Worcester).

AUGUST

6–Essex v Hants (Colchester); Kent v Surrey (Canterbury); Lancs. v Sussex (Manchester); Middx v Notts. (Lord's); Northants v Durham (Northampton); Yorks. v Worcs. (Scarborough).

13–Durham v Middx (Chester-le-Street); Glam. v Essex (Pontypridd); Hants v Warwicks. (Southampton); Leics. v Lancs. (Leicester); Northants v Glos. (Northampton); Somerset v Kent (Taunton); Surrey v Yorks. (The Oval); Worcs. v Derbys. (Worcester).

20–Durham v Somerset (Chester-le-Street); Glos. v Derbys. (Bristol); Lancs. v Yorks. (Manchester); Middx v Kent (Lord's); Notts. v Warwicks. (Nottingham); Sussex v Worcs. (Eastbourne).

27–Derbys. v Surrey (Derby); Durham v Sussex (Hartlepool); Glam. v Glos. (Ebbw Vale); Hants v Lancs. (Portsmouth); Kent v Essex (Canterbury); Northants v Notts. (Northampton); Somerset v Leics. (Weston-super-Mare); Worcs. v Warwicks. (Worcester); Yorks. v Middx (Leeds).

SEPTEMBER

3–Essex v Derbys. (Chelmsford); Leics. v Glam. (Leicester); Middx v Northants (Uxbridge); Notts. v Hants (Nottingham); Surrey v Lancs. (The Oval); Warwicks. v Glos. (Birmingham); Worcs. v Somerset (Worcester). *Note: Matches involving NWT finalists to be played on September 5.*

10–Glam. v Notts. (Cardiff); Glos. v Durham (Bristol); Hants v Somerset (Southampton); Lancs. v Kent (Manchester); Middx v Leics. (Uxbridge); Northants v Worcs. (Northampton); Warwicks. v Derbys. (Birmingham); Yorks. v Sussex (Scarborough).

17–Derbys. v Lancs. (Derby); Durham v Notts. (Chester-le-Street); Essex v Yorks. (Chelmsford); Kent v Warwicks. (Canterbury); Leics. v Glos. (Leicester); Somerset v Middx (Taunton); Surrey v Hants (The Oval); Sussex v Northants (Hove); Worcs. v Glam. (Worcester).

†MINOR COUNTIES CHAMPIONSHIP, 1995

All matches are of two days' duration.

MAY

28–Berks. v Salop (Kidmore End); Lincs. v Herts. (Sleaford); Wales v Herefords. (Colwyn Bay); Wilts. v Devon (Swindon).

30–Oxon. v Salop (Thame CC); Suffolk v Herts. (Mildenhall).

JUNE

4–Devon v Cornwall (Exmouth); Herts. v Norfolk (Hitchin); Northumb. v Lincs. (Jesmond); Oxon. v Wilts. (Challow & Childrey); Wales v Cheshire (Pontarddulais).

6–Bucks. v Staffs. (High Wycombe); Cambs. v Norfolk (Wisbech); Herefords. v Cheshire (Dales, Leominster).

12–Salop v Cornwall (Shifnal).

14–Cheshire v Cornwall (Toft); Staffs. v Cambs. (Leek).

18–Beds. v Suffolk (Bedford Town); Cumb. v Lincs. (Millom); Herefords. v Berks. (Colwall CC); Herts. v Northumb. (Radlett); Oxon. v Dorset (Pressed Steel); Wales v Wilts. (Marchwiel).

20–Bucks. v Northumb. (Beaconsfield).

21–Suffolk v Cambs. (Ransome's, Ipswich).

25–Lincs. v Bucks. (Cleethorpes).

JULY

4–Staffs. v Northumb. (Wolverhampton).

5–Bucks. v Cambs. (Marlow); Dorset v Herefords. (Weymouth).

9–Berks. v Dorset (Falkland CC); Bucks. v Cumb. (Slough); Lincs. v Norfolk (Bourne); Salop v Devon (Wellington); Wales v Oxon. (Pontypridd); Wilts. v Herefords. (Marlborough CC).

11–Cheshire v Devon (Bowdon); Herts. v Cumb. (St Albans).

16–Cumb. v Cambs. (Netherfield); Dorset v Wales (Dean Park, Bournemouth); Herefords. v Oxon. (Brockhampton); Northumb. v Beds. (Jesmond); Salop v Cheshire (Shrewsbury).

17–Herts. v Staffs. (Shenley Park).

18–Cumb. v Beds. (Barrow); Northumb. v Cambs. (Jesmond).

24–Cornwall v Berks. (Truro). *Note: To be rearranged if either Cornwall or Berks. in MCC Trophy semi-finals.*

25–Norfolk v Cumb. (Lakenham); Staffs. v Lincs. (Longton).

26–Devon v Berks. (Sidmouth).

27–Norfolk v Beds. (Lakenham); Suffolk v Cumb. (Ipswich School).

30–Cornwall v Wales (Camborne); Dorset v Devon (Sherborne School); Oxon. v Cheshire (Christ Church); Wilts. v Salop (Trowbridge).

31–Norfolk v Bucks. (Lakenham); Suffolk v Staffs. (Copdock CC).

AUGUST

1–Berks. v Cheshire (Finchampstead); Herefords. v Salop (Hereford City).

2–Cambs. v Lincs. (March); Norfolk v Staffs. (Lakenham); Suffolk v Bucks. (Bury St Edmunds).

6–Beds. v Bucks. (Dunstable); Wales v Berks. (Usk); Wilts. v Cornwall (Westbury).

8–Beds. v Staffs. (Wardown Park); Dorset v Cornwall (Dorchester).

10–Cambs. v Herts. (March).

13–Berks. v Wilts. (Reading); Cheshire v Dorset (Oxton); Cornwall v Oxon. (St Austell); Herts. v Beds. (Hertford); Lincs. v Suffolk (Lincoln Lindum); Northumb. v Norfolk (Jesmond).

14–Staffs. v Cumb. (Brewood).

15–Devon v Oxon. (Plymouth); Northumb. v Suffolk (Jesmond); Salop v Dorset (Bridgnorth).

20–Beds. v Lincs. (Southill Park); Cheshire v Wilts. (New Brighton); Cumb. v Northumb. (Carlisle); Devon v Herefords. (Torquay); Salop v Wales (Oswestry).

22–Cornwall v Herefords. (Falmouth). *Note: To be rearranged if either Cornwall or Herefords. in MCC Trophy final.*

27–Bucks. v Herts. (Amersham); Devon v Wales (Bovey Tracey); Dorset v Wilts. (Dean Park, Bournemouth); Norfolk v Suffolk (North Runcton); Oxon. v Berks. (Banbury CC).

30–Cambs. v Beds. (Saffron Walden).

SEPTEMBER

10–Final at Worcester.

†MCC TROPHY KNOCKOUT COMPETITION, 1995

All matches are of one day's duration.

Preliminary Round

May 21 Bucks. v Beds. (Aylesbury); Cheshire v Staffs. (Warrington); Cornwall v Devon (Falmouth); Salop v Dorset (Shrewsbury).

First Round

June 11 Cheshire or Staffs. v Bucks. or Beds. (Warrington or Walsall); Salop or Dorset v Cornwall or Devon (Wrekin College or Sherborne School); Herefords. v Norfolk (Brockhampton); Herts. v Lincs. (Shenley Park); Oxon. v Berks. (Thame CC); Suffolk v Northumb. (Framlingham College); Wales v Cumb. (Northop Hall); Wilts. v Cambs. (Trowbridge).

Quarter-finals to be played on July 2.

Semi-finals to be played on July 23.

Final to be played on August 23 at Lord's.

†SECOND ELEVEN CHAMPIONSHIP, 1995

All matches are of three days' duration.

APRIL

17–Leics. v Glos. (Leicester).

18–Derbys. v Lancs. (Derby); Middx v Glam. (Uxbridge).

23–Somerset v Sussex (King's College, Taunton).

24–Lancs. v Northants (Ramsbottom); Leics. v Kent (Leicester); Worcs. v Warwicks. (Kidderminster).

MAY

1–Durham v Glam. (Chester-le-Street CC); Essex v Derbys. (Chelmsford); Leics. v Yorks. (Oakham); Somerset v Glos. (North Perrott); Surrey v Middx (Cheam); Sussex v Lancs. (Hove); Warwicks. v Northants (Knowle & Dorridge).

8–Derbys. v Durham (Derby); Glam. v Kent (Ammanford); Glos. v Northants (Bristol); Middx v Lancs. (Uxbridge); Surrey v Essex (The Oval); Yorks. v Warwicks. (Bingley).

10–Notts. v Somerset (Nottingham).

15–Essex v Sussex (Chelmsford); Glos. v Surrey (Dowty Arle Court, Cheltenham); Hants v Notts. (Finchampstead); Middx v Leics. (Uxbridge); Somerset v Glam. (Taunton); Warwicks. v Durham (Coventry & N. Warwicks.); Yorks. v Derbys. (Harrogate).

22–Durham v Surrey (Felling); Glam. v Yorks. (Swansea); Glos. v Essex (Bristol); Kent v Sussex (Canterbury); Middx v Northants (Harrow); Somerset v Lancs. (Taunton); Warwicks. v Hants (Solihull CC); Worcs. v Leics. (Worcester).

29–Derbys. v Sussex (Derby); Durham v Glos. (Shildon CC); Glam. v Worcs. (Pontarddulais); Kent v Somerset (Maidstone); Leics. v Notts. (Barwell); Northants v Yorks. (Oundle School).

30–Hants v Essex (Bournemouth Sports Club).

JUNE

5–Essex v Middx (Southend); Glos. v Notts. (Bristol); Hants v Kent (Southampton); Lancs. v Durham (Manchester); Northants v Somerset (Old Northamptonians); Sussex v Warwicks. (Middleton); Worcs. v Derbys. (Old Hill).

12–Derbys. v Middx (Abbotsholme School, Rocester); Durham v Hants (Darlington); Leics. v Glam. (Melton Mowbray); Northants v Worcs. (Oundle School); Notts. v Kent (Collingham); Surrey v Warwicks. (Oxted); Yorks. v Lancs. (York).

19–Essex v Durham (Chelmsford); Glam. v Glos. (Swansea); Kent v Warwicks. (Gore Court, Sittingbourne); Leics. v Northants (Hinckley); Notts. v Lancs. (Worksop); Surrey v Yorks. (Cheam); Sussex v Hants (Hove); Worcs. v Somerset (Kidderminster).

26–Derbys. v Leics. (Abbotsholme School, Rocester); Durham v Notts. (South Shields CC); Essex v Warwicks. (Ilford); Kent v Worcs. (Ashford); Lancs. v Glam. (Preston); Middx v Sussex (Southgate); Surrey v Somerset (Cheam).

28–Hants v Glos. (Southampton).

JULY

3–Durham v Kent (Riverside, Chester-le-Street); Glam. v Notts. (Pontymister); Glos. v Yorks. (Bristol); Hants v Worcs. (Portsmouth); Lancs. v Leics. (Rossall School); Northants v Essex (Northampton); Warwicks. v Middx (Studley).

4–Derbys. v Somerset (Derby); Sussex v Surrey (Hove).

10–Glam. v Hants (Usk); Kent v Essex (Canterbury); Leics. v Surrey (Kibworth); Middx v Glos. (Harrow); Northants v Notts. (Northampton); Sussex v Durham (Horsham); Worcs. v Lancs. (Worcester).

11–Yorks. v Somerset (Elland).

17–Lancs. v Hants (Manchester); Northants v Kent (Wellingborough School); Notts. v Yorks. (Nottingham); Somerset v Leics. (Taunton); Surrey v Derbys. (The Oval); Warwicks. v Glam. (Griff & Coton, Nuneaton); Worcs. v Middx (Worcester).

24–Essex v Lancs. (Chelmsford); Middx v Hants (Southgate); Northants v Derbys. (Bedford School); Notts. v Sussex (Southwell CC); Surrey v Kent (The Oval); Warwicks. v Leics. (Moseley CC); Yorks. v Durham (Marske-by-Sea).

31–Kent v Derbys. (Maidstone); Lancs. v Glos. (Northern, Crosby); Middx v Durham (Lensbury CC); Notts. v Essex (Nottingham High School); Somerset v Hants (Clevedon); Yorks. v Worcs. (Park Avenue, Bradford).

AUGUST

7–Derbys. v Glam. (Derby); Hants v Northants (Bournemouth Sports Club); Lancs. v Kent (Manchester); Notts. v Surrey (Worksop College); Somerset v Warwicks. (Taunton); Sussex v Glos. (Hove); Worcs. v Essex (Worcester).

14–Derbys. v Hants (Chesterfield); Durham v Northants (Seaton Carew); Essex v Glam. (Colchester); Glos. v Kent (King's School, Gloucester); Surrey v Worcs. (Oxted); Sussex v Leics. (Middleton); Warwicks. v Notts. (Walmley); Yorks. v Middx (Sheffield).

21–Glam. v Northants (Cardiff); Glos. v Derbys. (Tuffley Park, Gloucester); Hants v Surrey (Southampton); Middx v Notts. (RAF Vine Lane, Uxbridge); Somerset v Durham (Taunton); Warwicks. v Lancs. (Solihull CC); Worcs. v Sussex (Worcester); Yorks. v Essex (Todmorden).

28–Durham v Leics. (Riverside, Chester-le-Street); Glos. v Worcs. (Bristol); Kent v Middx (Folkestone).

29–Derbys. v Warwicks. (Derby); Essex v Somerset (Coggeshall); Hants v Yorks. (Southampton); Northants v Surrey (Northampton); Sussex v Glam. (Hove).

SEPTEMBER

6–Essex v Leics. (Chelmsford); Glam. v Surrey (Pontypridd); Kent v Yorks. (British Gas, Eltham); Notts. v Derbys. (Nottingham); Sussex v Northants (Hove); Warwicks. v Glos. (Stratford-upon-Avon); Worcs. v Durham (Worcester).

11–Leics. v Hants (Hinckley); Notts. v Worcs. (Nottingham); Somerset v Middx (Taunton); Yorks. v Sussex (Leeds).

12–Lancs. v Surrey (Manchester).

†BAIN HOGG TROPHY, 1995

All matches are of one day's duration.

APRIL

21–Derbys. v Lancs. (Derby).

MAY

4–Surrey v Essex (The Oval).

5–Hants v Somerset (Southampton); Kent v MCC Young Cricketers (Canterbury); Worcs. v Glos. (Worcester).

11–Derbys. v Durham (Derby); Leics. v Middx (Leicester).

12–Sussex v Kent (Hove).

18–Essex v Sussex (Chelmsford); Middx v Leics. (Uxbridge); Yorks. v Derbys. (Leeds).

19–Kent v Surrey (Canterbury); Lancs. v Derbys. (Manchester); Warwicks. v Northants (Birmingham).

25–Kent v Sussex (Canterbury); Minor Counties v Leics. (Walsall); Somerset v Hants (Taunton).

26–Durham v Lancs. (Durham City CC); Minor Counties v Warwicks. (Walsall); Worcs. v Hants (Worcester); Yorks. v Notts. (Castleford).

JUNE

1–Derbys. v Yorks. (Chesterfield).

2–Essex v Kent (Chelmsford); Glos. v Glam. (Bristol); Lancs. v Yorks. (Manchester); MCC Young Cricketers v Sussex (Slough); Middx v Northants (Uxbridge).

8–Lancs. v Durham (Lancaster); MCC Young Cricketers v Surrey (Southgate); Somerset v Worcs. (Taunton).

9–Glam. v Worcs. (Panteg); MCC Young Cricketers v Essex (Slough); Middx v Minor Counties (Southgate); Northants v Warwicks. (Northampton); Notts. v Durham (Worksop College).

15–Durham v Derbys. (Bishop Auckland); Sussex v MCC Young Cricketers (Haywards Heath); Yorks. v Lancs. (Park Avenue, Bradford).

16–Essex v Surrey (Wickford); Lancs. v Notts. (Manchester).

22–Leics. v Northants (Leicester); Notts. v Lancs. (Farnsfield); Sussex v Essex (Hove).

23–Warwicks. v Minor Counties (Stratford-upon-Avon); Worcs. v Glam. (Bromsgrove School).

27–Hants v Glos. (Southampton).

29–Durham v Notts. (Philadelphia CC); Minor Counties v Middx (Marlow).

30–Leics. v Warwicks. (Leicester); MCC Young Cricketers v Kent (Slough); Northants v Minor Counties (Old Northamptonians); Somerset v Glam. (Glastonbury).

JULY

6–Hants v Worcs. (Bournemouth Sports Club); Warwicks. v Middx (Aston University).

7–Essex v MCC Young Cricketers (Chelmsford); Northants v Middx (Tring); Notts. v Derbys. (Caythorpe CC); Sussex v Surrey (Hove).

13–Glam. v Hants (Swansea); Kent v Essex (Canterbury); Northants v Leics. (Northampton).

14–Glos. v Somerset (Bristol); Middx v Warwicks. (Harrow).

20–Glos. v Hants (Bristol); Leics. v Minor Counties (Barwell); Notts. v Yorks. (Welbeck CC); Worcs. v Somerset (Halesowen).

21–Derbys. v Notts. (Belper Meadows CC); Hants v Glam. (Southampton); Minor Counties v Northants (Sleaford); Somerset v Glos. (Weston-super-Mare); Surrey v Sussex (The Oval).

26–Glam. v Glos. (Bridgend).

27–Glos. v Worcs. (Bristol); Surrey v Kent (The Oval); Warwicks. v Leics. (Old Edwardians); Yorks. v Durham (Marske-by-Sea).

28–Durham v Yorks. (Boldon CC); Glam. v Somerset (Swansea); Surrey v MCC Young Cricketers (The Oval).

Semi-finals to be played on August 17 or 18.

Final to be played on September 4 (reserve day September 5).

Second Eleven fixtures were subject to confirmation when Wisden *went to press.*

†OTHER SECOND ELEVEN MATCHES, 1995

APRIL

18–Somerset v England Under-19 (4 days) (Taunton).

MAY

8–Sussex v England Under-19 (3 days) (Horsham).

JUNE

26–Yorks. v England Under-19 (3 days) (Park Avenue, Bradford).

AUGUST

24–TCCB Second Eleven Regional Challenge semi-finals (4 days): Central v North (Leicester); South-East v South-West (Chelmsford).

SEPTEMBER

14–TCCB Second Eleven Regional Challenge final at Birmingham (4 days).

†WOMEN'S CRICKET, 1995

JUNE

4–England v Lord's Taverners (Windsor).

JULY

2–Under-17 Eight-a-Side Championship (To be arranged).

7–England Under-20 v Irish XI (Campbell Park, Milton Keynes).

17–European Cup (7 days) (Dublin).

29–Area Championships (5 days) (Cambridge).

AUGUST

5–England Under-20 v WCA Chairman's XI (Malvern – provisional).

25–England Representative Match (4 days).

26–Under-17 Territorial Tournament (3 days) (Denstone College, Staffs.).

SEPTEMBER

2–National Club Knockout/Plate finals.

3–Under-20 Championship finals.

9–England Under-20 v England XI (To be arranged).

10–Premier League final.

ENGLAND IN SOUTH AFRICA, 1995-96

All fixtures subject to confirmation.

OCTOBER

24	Randjesfontein	†v N. F. Oppenheimer's XI (1 day)
25	Springs	†v Eastern Transvaal (1 day, d/n)
27	Soweto	v South Africa Invitation XI (4 days)

NOVEMBER

2	East London	v Border (4 days)
9	Kimberley	v South Africa A (4 days)
16	Verwoerdburg	v SOUTH AFRICA (1st Test, 5 days)
23	Bloemfontein	v Orange Free State (4 days)
30	Johannesburg	v SOUTH AFRICA (2nd Test, 5 days)

DECEMBER

7	Paarl	v Boland (4 days)
14	Durban	v SOUTH AFRICA (3rd Test, 5 days)
20	Chatsworth, Durban	v Combined SA Universities (3 days)
26	Port Elizabeth	v SOUTH AFRICA (4th Test, 5 days)

JANUARY

2	Cape Town	v SOUTH AFRICA (5th Test, 5 days)
9	Cape Town	†v SOUTH AFRICA (1st 1-day international, d/n)
11	Bloemfontein	†v SOUTH AFRICA (2nd 1-day international, d/n)
13	Johannesburg	†v SOUTH AFRICA (3rd 1-day international)
14	Verwoerdburg	†v SOUTH AFRICA (4th 1-day international)
17	Durban	†v SOUTH AFRICA (5th 1-day international, d/n)
19	East London	†v SOUTH AFRICA (6th 1-day international, d/n)
21	Port Elizabeth	†v SOUTH AFRICA (7th 1-day international)

†WORLD CUP, 1996

All fixtures subject to confirmation.

Group A

FEBRUARY

16 India	West Indies v Zimbabwe
17 Sri Lanka	Sri Lanka v Australia
18 India	India v Kenya
21 India	India v West Indies
21 Sri Lanka	Sri Lanka v Zimbabwe
23 India	Australia v Kenya
25 Sri Lanka	Sri Lanka v West Indies
26 India	Kenya v Zimbabwe
27 India	India v Australia
29 India	Kenya v West Indies

MARCH

1 India	Australia v Zimbabwe
2 India	India v Sri Lanka
4 India	Australia v West Indies
6 India	India v Zimbabwe
6 Sri Lanka	Sri Lanka v Kenya

Group B

FEBRUARY

14 India	England v New Zealand
15 Pakistan	South Africa v UAE
17 India	Holland v New Zealand
18 Pakistan	England v UAE
20 Pakistan	New Zealand v South Africa
22 Pakistan	England v Holland
24 Pakistan	Pakistan v UAE
25 Pakistan	England v South Africa
26 Pakistan	Pakistan v Holland
27 Pakistan	New Zealand v UAE
29 Pakistan	Pakistan v South Africa

MARCH

1 Pakistan	Holland v UAE
3 Pakistan	Pakistan v England
5 Pakistan	Holland v South Africa
6 Pakistan	Pakistan v New Zealand

QUARTER-FINALS

Saturday, March 9

Pakistan	Group A winners v Group B 4th
India	Group A 3rd v Group B 2nd

Monday, March 11

Pakistan	Group B winners v Group A 4th
India	Group B 3rd v Group A 2nd

SEMI-FINALS

Wednesday, March 13

India	Winners of March 9 quarter-finals

Thursday, March 14

India	Winners of March 11 quarter-finals

The World Cup final will be played on Sunday, March 17, 1996 in Lahore.

DICTIONARY
DICTIONNAIRE
Anglais-Français

Michael Janes

PARRAGON

French Consultant
Fabrice Antoine

English Consultants
Hazel Curties
Stuart Fortey

First published in Great Britain 1988
by Harrap Books Ltd
Chelsea House, 26 Market Square
Bromley, Kent BR1 1NA

This edition published in 1993
by Parragon Book Service, Bristol

Printed and bound in Great Britain by BPCC Paperbacks Ltd

Contents/Table des matières

Preface

This dictionary is an entirely new publication designed to provide an up-to-date, practical and concise work of reference giving translations of the most useful French and English vocabulary.

The aim has been to achieve a work of great clarity of equal value to French and to English speakers, whether students, tourists, businessmen or -women or general readers, and to produce a text offering the maximum amount of guidance in pinpointing and understanding translations. Equal importance has been given to the presentation of French and English. Different translations of the same word or phrase are clearly labelled by means of bracketed context indicators and/or style and field labels. A single translation of a word is also often labelled as an additional aid to the user (e.g. **hedgehog** *n* (*animal*) hérisson *m*; **ungainly** *a* (*clumsy*) gauche; **béotien, -ienne** *nmf* (*inculte*) philistine). The user is helped by having indicators and labels in French in the French section and in English in the English section of the dictionary.

Style and field labels follow bracketed indicators (e.g. **grid** *n* . . . (*system*) *El* réseau *m*; **bidule** *nm* (*chose*) *Fam* thingummy). In the event of more than one translation within a grammatical category being qualified by the same style or field label, the label may then precede (see **café, liquidizer, trucker**).

The user will find in the text important abbreviations, useful geographical information such as names of countries, and a wide coverage of American words and usage. The vocabulary treated includes French and English colloquialisms and slang, and important technical jargon. Comparatives and superlatives of English adjectives are also indicated.

In order to save space, derived words are usually included within the entry of a headword. All such words are highlighted by means of a lozenge. Derivatives may be written in full or abbreviated, as is usually the case for important derived forms (such as English **-ly** or French **-ment**).

An oblique stroke in bold is used to mark the stem of a headword at which point the derived ending is added. A bold dash stands for a headword or the portion of a headword to the left of the oblique stroke (e.g. **awkward** *a* . . . **◆—ly** *adv* . . . **◆—ness** *n* . . . ; **boulevers/er** *vt* . . . **◆—ant** *a* . . . **◆—ement** *nm*).

An oblique stroke within an entry is another space-saving device. It is used to separate non equivalent alternative parts of a phrase or expression matched exactly in French and English (e.g. **les basses/hautes classes** the lower/upper classes is to be understood as: **les basses classes** the lower classes and **les hautes classes** the upper classes; **to give s.o./sth a push** pousser qn/qch as: **to give s.o. a push** pousser qn and **to give sth a push** pousser qch).

A further typographical device, a filled square, may be used to introduce a string of English phrasal verbs (see **come, take**).

In common with other Harrap dictionaries, when a headword appears in an example in the same form, it is represented by its initial letter. This applies whether the headword starts a new line (e.g. **advance** *n* **in a. of s.o.** avant qn) or appears within an entry, either in full form (e.g. **◆arterial** *a* **a. road** route *f* principale), or in abbreviated form (e.g. (where **◆—ed** stands for **advanced**) **◆—ed** *a* **a. in years** âgé).

The pronunciation of both English and French is shown using the latest symbols of the International Phonetic Alphabet. Pronunciation is given for headwords at the start of an entry, and, as an additional help to the user, for a word within an entry where the correct pronunciation may be difficult to derive from the form of the word (e.g. **◆aristocratie** [-asi]; **◆aoûtien, -ienne** [ausjɛ̃, -jɛn]; **◆rabid** ['ræbɪd]; **◆prayer** [preər]).

Stress in English is indicated for headwords and for derived words in which stress differs from that of a headword (e.g. **civilize** ['sɪvɪlaɪz] and **◆civili'zation**). American English pronunciation is listed wherever it is considered to differ substantially from that of British English (e.g. **aristocrat** ['ærɪstəkræt, *Am* ə'rɪstəkræt], **quinine** ['kwɪniːn, *Am* 'kwaɪnaɪn]). American spelling is also given if considered sufficiently different (e.g. **tire** and **tyre, plow** and **plough**).

An original feature of this dictionary is its semantic approach to the order and arrangement of entries. An approach whereby the meaning of words is allowed to influence the structure of entries is felt to be of particular benefit to the user in his or her understanding of language.

Important semantic categories have been indicated by bold Arabic numerals within an entry (see **bolt**, **tail**, **général**) or have been entered as separate headwords (see **bug**[1] and **bug**[2], **draw**[1] and **draw**[2], **start**[1] and **start**[2]). Note that grammatical categories, apart from the first, have been marked by a dash.

Words are entered under the headword from which they are considered to derive (e.g. **approfondi**, abbreviated as **◆—i** follows **approfond/ir**; **◆astronomer** and **◆astro'nomical** follow **astronomy**). Present and past participles (used adjectivally) are felt to be closely associated in meaning and form with the infinitive from which they derive. They are entered, usually in abbreviated form, within an entry immediately after the infinitive, any other derivatives there may be following in alphabetical order (e.g. **exalt/er** *vt* ... **◆—ant** *a* ... **◆—é** *a* ... **◆exaltation** *nf*: **accommodat/e** *vt* ... **◆—ing** *a* ... **◆accommo'dation** *n*: **expir/e** *vi* . . . **◆—ed** *a* . . . **◆expi'ration** *n* . . . **◆expiry** *n*).

Derived words and compounds are felt to be semantically distinct and are, wherever possible, grouped together alphabetically and listed separately from each other (e.g. **base** *n* . . . **◆—less** *a* . . . **◆—ness** *n* . . . **◆baseball** *n* . . . **◆baseboard** *n*: **bouton** *nm* . . . **◆b.-d'or** *nm* . . . **◆b.-pression** *nm* . . . **◆boutonner** *vt* . . . **◆boutonneux, -euse** *a* . . . **◆boutonnière** *nf*). Compounds may be listed in the place within an entry where they are felt best to belong by virtue of meaning.

The author wishes to express his gratitude to Monsieur F. Antoine, Mrs H. Curties and Mr S. Fortey for their advice and help, to Mrs R. Hillmore for her assistance with proofreading, and to Mr J.-L. Barbanneau for his support and encouragement.

M. Janes
London, 1988

Préface

Ce dictionnaire entièrement nouveau a pour ambition d'être un ouvrage de référence moderne, pratique et compact, offrant les traductions des termes les plus courants du français comme de l'anglais.

Il veut être un ouvrage qui, par sa grande clarté, soit utile autant au francophone qu'à l'anglophone, pour les études, le tourisme, les affaires aussi bien que pour l'usage courant: il tente de fournir le plus d'indications possible pour aider l'utilisateur à cerner et à comprendre les traductions proposées. On a accordé la même importance à la présentation du français qu'à celle de l'anglais. Les différentes traductions d'un même mot ou d'une même expression sont clairement définies à l'aide d'indications de contexte entre parenthèses et/ou de symboles indiquant le niveau de langue et le domaine d'utilisation. Lorsqu'un mot est accompagné d'une seule traduction, celle-ci est également souvent précédée d'une indication destinée à fournir à l'utilisateur une aide supplémentaire (par exemple **hedgehog** *n* (*animal*) hérisson *m*; **ungainly** *a* (*clumsy*) gauche; **béotien, -ienne** *nmf* (*inculte*) philistine). L'accès à cet ouvrage est facilité par l'utilisation d'indications en français dans la partie français-anglais et en anglais dans la partie anglais-français.

Les indications de niveau de langue et de domaine d'utilisation viennent à la suite de celles entre parenthèses (par example **grid** *n* . . . (*system*) *El* réseau *m*; **bidule** *nm* (*chose*) *Fam* thingummy). Lorsque plusieurs traductions dans la même catégorie grammaticale sont définies par la même indication, celle-ci peut alors venir en tête (voir **café**, **liquidizer**, **trucker**).

L'utilisateur trouvera dans cet ouvrage des abréviations importantes, de précieux éléments de géographie tels que des noms de pays, ainsi qu'une large sélection d'américanismes. Le lexique retenu comprend des mots et des expressions familiers et argotiques, tant en français qu'en anglais, et des termes techniques courants. De plus, les comparatifs et superlatifs des adjectifs anglais sont donnés.

Par souci de concision, les mots dérivés sont généralement donnés dans le corps des articles. Tous ces mots sont repérés par un losange. Les dérivés sont donnés soit sous leur forme complète, soit en abrégé, ce qui est généralement le cas pour les formes dérivées courantes (telles que celles en **-ly** en anglais ou en **-ment** en français).

On utilise une barre oblique pour indiquer le radical d'une entrée à la suite duquel la terminaison d'un dérivé sera ajoutée. Un tiret en gras remplace le mot d'entrée ou la partie de ce mot qui précède la barre oblique (par exemple **awkward** *a* . . . **◆—ly** *adv* . . . **◆—ness** *n* . . . ; **boulevers/er** *vt* . . . **◆—ant** *a* . . . **◆—ement** *nm*).

Toujours par souci de concision, une barre oblique est utilisée dans un article pour éviter la répétition d'un même élément de phrase (par exemple **les basses/hautes classes** the lower/upper classes se lira: **les basses classes** the lower classes et **les hautes classes** the upper classes; **to give s.o./sth a push** pousser qn/qch se lira: **to give s.o. a push** pousser qn et **to give sth a push** pousser qch).

Enfin, un carré plein peut être utilisé pour introduire une série de verbes à particule en anglais (voir **come**, **take**).

Comme il est d'usage dans les autres dictionnaires Harrap, lorsqu'un mot d'entrée est repris sous la même forme dans un exemple, il est remplacé par sa première lettre. Cela est le cas aussi bien lorsque le mot est au début d'un article (par exemple **advance** *n* **in a. of s.o.** avant qn) ou apparaît dans un article, sous sa forme complète (par exemple **◆arterial** *a* **a. road** route *f* principale) ou en abrégé (par exemple (**◆—ed** remplaçant **advanced**) **◆—ed** *a* **a. in years** âgé).

La prononciation de l'anglais comme du français est fournie; elle utilise la notation la plus moderne de l'Alphabet Phonétique International. La phonétique est donnée pour les mots d'entrée au début de l'article et, pour aider l'utilisateur, pour tout mot dans un article dont il pourrait être difficile de déduire la prononciation à partir de l'orthographe (par exemple **◆aristocratie** [-asi]; **◆soûtien**, **-ienne** [ausjɛ̃, -jɛn]; **◆rabid** ['ræbɪd]; **◆prayer** [preər]).

En anglais, l'accent tonique est indiqué pour les mots d'entrée et pour les dérivés chaque fois que l'accentuation diffère de celle de l'entrée (par exemple **civilize** et **◆civili'zation**). Les prononciations américaines sont indiquées chaque fois qu'elles diffèrent de façon substantielle de celles de l'anglais britannique (par exemple **aristocrat** ['ærɪstəkræt, *Am* ə'rɪstəkræt], **quinine** ['kwɪniːn, *Am* 'kwaɪnaɪn]). On indique également l'orthographe américaine lorsqu'elle est suffisamment différente de celle de l'anglais britannique (par exemple **tire** et **tyre**, **plow** et **plough**).

Une des caractérisques originales de ce dictionnaire est son approche sémantique du classement et de l'organisation des articles. On a considéré que cette approche, où le sens des mots détermine pour une part l'organisation des articles, serait d'un grand secours à l'utilisateur en ce qui concerne sa compréhension de la langue.

Les catégories sémantiques importantes sont indiquées dans un article par des chiffres arabes en gras (voir **bolt**, **tail**, **général**) ou sont présentées comme des mots distincts (voir **bug**[1] et **bug**[2], **draw**[1] et **draw**[2], **start**[1] et **start**[2]). Les catégories grammaticales autres que la première traitée sont indiquées par un tiret.

Les mots apparaissent sous les mots d'entrée dont ils sont dérivés (par exemple **approfondi**, abrégé en **◆—i** suit **approfond/ir**; **◆astronomer** et **◆astro'nomical** suivent **astronomy**). Les participes présents et passés (utilisés comme adjectifs) sont considérés comme étant étroitement associés par le sens et par la forme à l'infinitif dont ils sont dérivés. Ils sont placés dans l'article, généralement en abrégé, immédiatement après l'infinitif; tous les autres dérivés éventuels apparaissent ensuite par ordre alphabétique (par exemple **exalt/er** *vt* . . . **◆—ant** *a* . . . **◆—é** *a* . . . **◆exaltation** *nf*; **accommodat/e** *vt* . . . **◆—ing** *a* . . . **◆accommo'dation** *n*; **expir/e** *vi* . . . **◆—ed** *a* . . . **◆expi'ration** *n* . . . **◆expiry** *n*).

Les mots dérivés et les mots composés sont considérés comme étant distincts, du point de vue du sens, et sont, chaque fois que possible, regroupés séparément (par exemple **base** *n* . . . **◆—less** *a* . . . **◆—ness** *n* . . . **◆baseball** *n* . . . **◆baseboard** *n*; **bouton** *nm* . . . **◆b.-d'or** *nm* . . . **◆b.-pression** *nm* . . . **◆boutonner** *vt* . . . **◆boutonneux**, **-euse** *a* . . . **◆boutonnière** *nf*). Les composés se trouvent placés dans les articles là où leur sens a semblé devoir les appeler.

L'auteur tient à exprimer sa gratitude à Monsieur F. Antoine, à Mrs H. Curties et à Mr S. Fortey pour leurs conseils et leur collaboration, à Mrs R. Hillmore qui a bien voulu nous aider à relire les épreuves, et à Monsieur J.-L. Barbanneau pour son soutien et ses encouragements.

M. Janes
Londres, 1988

Grammar notes

In French, the feminine of an adjective is formed as a rule by adding **e** to the masculine form (e.g. grand, grande; carré, carrée; chevalin, chevaline). If the masculine already ends in **e**, the feminine is the same as the masculine (e.g. utile). Irregular feminine forms of adjectives (e.g. généreux, généreuse; léger, légère; doux; douce) are given in the French-English side of the dictionary. In the English-French side, French adjectives are shown in the masculine form only. Irregular feminines of adjectives are listed in the following way: généreux, -euse; léger, -ère; doux, douce.

To form the plural of a French noun or adjective **s** is usually added to the singular (e.g. arbre, arbres; taxi, taxis; petit, petits). The plural form of a noun ending in **s**, **x** or **z** (e.g. pois, croix, nez) is the same as that of the singular. Plurals of nouns and adjectives which do not follow these general rules are listed in the French section, including the plurals of French compounds where the formation of the plural involves a change other than the addition of final s (e.g. arc-en-ciel, arcs-en-ciel). Those nouns and adjectives where **x** or **aux** is added in the plural are shown in the following way: cerveau, -x; général, -aux.

In English also, **s** is added to form the plural of a noun (e.g. cat, cats; taxi, taxis) but a noun ending in **ch**, **s**, **sh**, **x** or **z** forms its plural by the addition of **es** (e.g. glass, glasses; match, matches). (Note that when **ch** is pronounced [k], the plural is in **s**, e.g. monarch, monarchs.) When a noun ends in **y** preceded by a consonant, **y** is changed to **ies** to form the plural (e.g. army, armies). Irregular English plurals are given in the English-French side, including the plurals of English compounds where the formation of the plural involves a change other than the addition of final s (e.g. brother-in-law, brothers-in-law).

English nouns may be used as adjectives. When a French adjective is translated in this way, this use is made clear by the addition of a hyphen following the noun translation (e.g. farm- as a translation of **agricole**).

Most French verbs have regular conjugations though some display spelling anomalies (see French verb conjugations on p (i)). In the French section an asterisk is used to mark an irregular verb, and refers the user to the table of irregular verbs on p (ii).

Most English verbs form their past tense and past participle by adding **ed** to the infinitive (e.g. look, looked) or **d** to an infinitive already ending in **e** (e.g. love, loved). When a verb ends in **y** preceded by a consonant **y** becomes **ied** (e.g. satisfy, satisfied). To form the third person singular of a verb in the present tense **s** is added to the infinitive (e.g. know, knows) but an infinitive in **ch**, **s**, **sh**, **x** or **z** forms its third person singular by the addition of **es** (e.g. dash, dashes). When an infinitive ends in **y** preceded by a consonant, **y** is changed to **ies** to form the third person singular (e.g. satisfy, satisfies).

The English present participle is formed by the addition of **ing** to the infinitive (e.g. look, looking) but final **e** is omitted when an infinitive ends in **e** (e.g. love, loving). When the infinitive ends in a single consonant preceded by a vowel (e.g. tug), the final consonant is usually doubled in the past tense, past and present participles (e.g. tug, tugged, tugging).

Irregular English verb conjugations are given in the English headword list, and a summary of the most important irregular verbs may also be found on p (vii). The doubling of consonants in English verbs is indicated in the text. The latter is shown in the following way: **tug** . . . *vt* (**-gg-**).

Notes sur la grammaire

En français, le féminin d'un adjectif se forme en général en ajoutant **e** au masculin (par exemple grand, grande; carré, carrée; chevalin, chevaline). Lorsque le masculin se termine déjà par **e**, le féminin est identique (par exemple utile). Les féminins d'adjectifs qui ne se conforment pas à ces règles (par exemple généreux, généreuse; léger, légère; doux, douce) sont donnés dans la partie français-anglais où ils sont notés comme suit: généreux, -euse; léger, -ère; doux, douce. Dans la partie anglais-français, on ne donne que la forme masculine des adjectifs.

On forme en général le pluriel d'un nom ou d'un adjectif français en ajoutant **s** au singulier (par exemple arbre, arbres; taxi, taxis; petit, petits). Le pluriel d'un nom se terminant par **s**, **x** ou **z** (par exemple pois, croix, nez) est identique au singulier. Les pluriels des noms et adjectifs qui font exception à ces règles générales sont signalés dans la partie français-anglais, de même que les pluriels des mots composés français dont le passage au pluriel appelle une modification autre que le simple ajout d'un **s** final (par exemple arc-en-ciel, arcs-en-ciel). Les noms et adjectifs dont le pluriel se forme à l'aide d'un **x** ou de **aux** sont notés comme suit: cerveau, -x; général, -aux.

De la même façon, en anglais, on forme le pluriel des noms en ajoutant **s** (par exemple cat, cats; taxi, taxis) mais on ajoutera **es** aux noms qui se terminent par **ch**, **s**, **sh**, **x** ou **z** (par exemple glass, glasses; match, matches). (Noter cependant que lorsque **ch** se prononce [k], le pluriel est en **s**, comme dans monarch, monarchs.) Lorsqu'un nom se termine par un **y** précédé d'une consonne, ce **y** devient **ies** au pluriel (par exemple army, armies). Les pluriels irréguliers de l'anglais sont signalés dans la partie anglais-français, de même que les pluriels des mots composés anglais dont le passage au pluriel entraîne une modification autre que le simple ajout d'un **s** final (par exemple brother-in-law, brothers-in-law).

Les noms anglais peuvent s'utiliser comme adjectifs. Lorsqu'un adjectif français est traduit par un nom, cela est signalé par l'ajout d'un trait d'union à la suite de ce nom (par exemple farm- comme traduction de **agricole**).

La plupart des verbes français ont des conjugaisons régulières; cependant, certains subissent des variations orthographiques (voir: Conjugaisons des verbes français à la page (i)) Dans la partie français-anglais, un astérisque signale un verbe irrégulier et renvoie à la table des verbes irréguliers donnée en page (ii).

En anglais, le passé et le participe passé des verbes se forment dans la plupart des cas en ajoutant **ed** à l'infinitif (par exemple look, looked) ou seulement **d** lorsque l'infinitif se termine par un **e** (par exemple love, loved). Lorsqu'un verbe se termine par un **y** précédé d'une consonne, ce **y** devient **ied** (par exemple satisfy, satisfied). La troisième personne du singulier d'un verbe au présent se forme en ajoutant **s** à l'infinitif (par exemple know, knows), mais on ajoutera **es** aux infinitifs qui se terminent par **ch**, **s**, **sh**, **x** ou **z** (par exemple dash, dashes). Enfin, lorsqu'un verbe se termine par un **y** précédé d'une consonne, ce **y** devient **ies** à la troisième personne du singulier (par exemple satisfy, satisfies).

Le participe présent en anglais se forme en ajoutant la désinence **ing** à l'infinitif (par exemple look, looking); lorsqu'un infinitif comporte un **e** final, celui-ci disparaît (par exemple love, loving). Lorsque l'infinitif se termine par une seule consonne précédée d'une voyelle (par exemple tug), la consonne finale est le plus souvent doublée au passé et aux participes passé et présent (par exemple tug, tugged, tugging).

Les formes des verbes irréguliers anglais sont données dans la partie anglais-français et une liste récapitulative des verbes irréguliers usuels figure en page (vii). Le doublement des consonnes dans les verbes anglais est signalé dans le corps de l'ouvrage; il est noté comme suit: **tug** . . . *vt* (**-gg-**).

Abbreviations		Abréviations
adjective	*a*	adjectif
abbreviation	*abbr, abrév*	abréviation
adverb	*adv*	adverbe
agriculture	*Agr*	agriculture
American	*Am*	américain
anatomy	*Anat*	anatomie
architecture	*Archit*	architecture
slang	*Arg*	argot
article	*art*	article
cars, motoring	*Aut*	automobile
auxiliary	*aux*	auxiliaire
aviation, aircraft	*Av*	aviation
biology	*Biol*	biologie
botany	*Bot*	botanique
British	*Br*	britannique
Canadian	*Can*	canadien
carpentry	*Carp*	menuiserie
chemistry	*Ch*	chimie
cinema	*Cin*	cinéma
commerce	*Com*	commerce
conjunction	*conj*	conjonction
cookery	*Culin*	cuisine
definite	*def, déf*	défini
demonstrative	*dem, dém*	démonstratif
economics	*Econ, Écon*	économie
electricity	*El, Él*	électricité
et cetera	*etc*	et cetera
feminine	*f*	féminin
familiar	*Fam*	familier
football	*Fb*	football
figurative	*Fig*	figuré
finance	*Fin*	finance
feminine plural	*fpl*	féminin pluriel
French	*Fr*	français
geography	*Geog, Géog*	géographie
geology	*Geol, Géol*	géologie
geometry	*Geom, Géom*	géométrie
grammar	*Gram*	grammaire
history	*Hist*	histoire
humorous	*Hum*	humoristique
indefinite	*indef, indéf*	indéfini
indicative	*indic*	indicatif
infinitive	*inf*	infinitif
interjection	*int*	interjection
invariable	*inv*	invariable
ironic	*Iron*	ironique
journalism	*Journ*	journalisme
legal, law	*Jur*	juridique
linguistics	*Ling*	linguistique
literary	*Lit, Litt*	littéraire
literature	*Liter, Littér*	littérature

masculine	*m*	masculin
mathematics	*Math*	mathématique
medicine	*Med, Méd*	médecine
carpentry	*Menuis*	menuiserie
meteorology	*Met, Mét*	météorologie
military	*Mil*	militaire
masculine plural	*mpl*	masculin pluriel
music	*Mus*	musique
noun	*n*	nom
nautical	*Nau*	nautique
noun feminine	*nf*	nom féminin
noun masculine	*nm*	nom masculin
noun masculine and feminine	*nmf*	nom masculin et féminin
pejorative	*Pej, Péj*	péjoratif
philosophy	*Phil*	philosophie
photography	*Phot*	photographie
physics	*Phys*	physique
plural	*pl*	pluriel
politics	*Pol*	politique
possessive	*poss*	possessif
past participle	*pp*	participe passé
prefix	*pref, préf*	préfixe
preposition	*prep, prép*	préposition
present participle	*pres p*	participe présent
present tense	*pres t*	temps présent
pronoun	*pron*	pronom
psychology	*Psy*	psychologie
past tense	*pt*	prétérit
	qch	quelque chose
	qn	quelqu'un
registered trademark	®	marque déposée
radio	*Rad*	radio
railway, *Am* railroad	*Rail*	chemin de fer
relative	*rel*	relatif
religion	*Rel*	religion
school	*Sch, Scol*	école
singular	*sing*	singulier
slang	*Sl*	argot
someone	*s.o.*	
sport	*Sp*	sport
something	*sth*	
subjunctive	*sub*	subjonctif
technical	*Tech*	technique
telephone	*Tel, Tél*	téléphone
textiles	*Tex*	industrie textile
theatre	*Th*	théâtre
television	*TV*	télévision
typography, printing	*Typ*	typographie
university	*Univ*	université
United States	*US*	États-Unis
auxiliary verb	*v aux*	verbe auxiliaire
intransitive verb	*vi*	verbe intransitif
impersonal verb	*v imp*	verbe impersonnel
pronominal verb	*vpr*	verbe pronominal
transitive verb	*vt*	verbe transitif
transitive and intransitive verb	*vti*	verbe transitif et intransitif

Pronunciation of French

TABLE OF PHONETIC SYMBOLS

Vowels

[i]	vite, cygne	[y]	cru, sûr
[e]	été, donner	[ø]	feu, meule
[ɛ]	elle, mais	[œ]	œuf, jeune
[a]	chat, fameux	[ə]	le, refaire
[ɑ]	pas, âgé	[ɛ̃]	vin, plein, faim
[ɔ]	donne, fort	[ɑ̃]	enfant, temps
[o]	dos, chaud, peau	[ɔ̃]	mon, nombre
[u]	tout, cour	[œ̃]	lundi, humble

Consonants

[p]	pain, absolu	[z]	cousin, zéro
[b]	beau, abbé	[ʃ]	chose, schéma
[t]	table, nette	[ʒ]	gilet, jeter
[d]	donner, sud	[l]	lait, facile
[k]	camp, képi	[r]	rare, rhume
[g]	garde, second	[m]	mon, flamme
[f]	feu, phrase	[n]	né, canne
[v]	voir, wagon	[ɲ]	campagne
[s]	sou, cire	[ŋ]	jogging
		[']	hanche (*i.e. no liaison or elision*)

Semi-consonants

[j]	piano, voyage
[w]	ouest, noir
[ɥ]	muet, lui

Prononciation de l'anglais

TABLEAU DES SIGNES PHONÉTIQUES

Voyelles et diphtongues

[iː]	bee, police
[ɪə]	beer, real
[ɪ]	bit, added
[e]	bet, said
[eɪ]	date, nail
[eə]	bear, air
[æ]	bat, plan
[aɪ]	fly, life
[ɑː]	art, ask
[aʊ]	fowl, house
[ɒ]	lot, what
[ɔː]	all, saw
[ɔɪ]	boil, toy
[əʊ]	low, soap
[ʊ]	put, wool
[uː]	shoe, too
[ʊə]	poor, sure
[ʌ]	cut, some
[ɜː]	burn, learn
[ə]	china, annoy
[(ə)]	relation

Consonnes

[p]	pat, top
[b]	but, tab
[t]	tap, patter
[d]	dab, sadder
[k]	cat, kite
[g]	go, rogue
[f]	fat, phrase
[v]	veal, rave
[s]	sat, ace
[z]	zero, houses
[ʃ]	dish, pressure
[ʒ]	pleasure
[tʃ]	charm, rich
[dʒ]	judge, rage
[θ]	thatch, breath
[ð]	that, breathe
[h]	hat, rehearse
[l]	lad, all
[r]	red, barring
[ʳ]	better, here (*représente un r final qui se prononce en liaison devant une voyelle, par exemple* 'here is' [hɪəʳɪz])
[m]	mat, hammer
[n]	no, banner
[ŋ]	singing, link
[j]	yet, onion
[w]	wall, quite
[ˈ]	*marque l'accent tonique; précède la syllabe accentuée*

A

A, a [ɑ] *nm* A, a.
a [a] *voir* **avoir.**
à [a] *prép* (**à + le = au** [o], **à + les = aux** [o]) **1** (*direction*: *lieu*) to; (*temps*) till, to; **aller à Paris** to go to Paris; **de 3 à 4 h** from 3 till *ou* to 4 (o'clock). **2** (*position*: *lieu*) at, in; (*surface*) on; (*temps*) at; **être au bureau/à la ferme/au jardin/à Paris** to be at *ou* in the office/on *ou* at the farm/in the garden/in Paris; **à la maison** at home; **à l'horizon** on the horizon; **à 8 h** at 8 (o'clock); **à mon arrivée** on (my) arrival; **à lundi!** see you (on) Monday! **3** (*description*) **l'homme à la barbe** the man with the beard; **verre à liqueur** liqueur glass. **4** (*attribution*) **donner qch à qn** to give sth to s.o., give s.o. sth. **5** (*devant inf*) **apprendre à lire** to learn to read; **travail à faire** work to do; **maison à vendre** house for sale; **prêt à partir** ready to leave. **6** (*appartenance*) **c'est (son livre) à lui** it's his (book); **c'est à vous de** (*décider, protester etc*) it's up to you to; (*lire, jouer etc*) it's your turn to. **7** (*prix*) for; **pain à 2F** loaf for 2F. **8** (*poids*) by; **vendre au kilo** to sell by the kilo. **9** (*moyen, manière*) **à bicyclette** by bicycle; **à la main** by hand; **à pied** on foot; **au crayon** with a pencil, in pencil; **au galop** at a gallop; **à la française** in the French style *ou* way; **deux à deux** two by two. **10** (*appel*) **au voleur!** (stop) thief!
abaiss/er [abese] *vt* to lower; **a. qn** to humiliate s.o.; **— s'a.** *vpr* (*barrière*) to lower; (*température*) to drop; **s'a. à faire** to stoop to doing. **◆—ement** [-ɛsmɑ̃] *nm* (*chute*) drop.
abandon [abɑ̃dɔ̃] *nm* abandonment; surrender; desertion; *Sp* withdrawal; (*naturel*) abandon; (*confiance*) lack of restraint; **à l'a.** in a neglected state. **◆abandonner** *vt* (*renoncer à*) to give up, abandon; (*droit*) to surrender; (*quitter*) to desert, abandon; **—** *vi* to give up; *Sp* to withdraw; **— s'a.** *vpr* (*se détendre*) to let oneself go; (*se confier*) to open up; **s'a. à** to give oneself up to, abandon oneself to.
abasourdir [abazurdir] *vt* to stun, astound.
abat-jour [abaʒur] *nm inv* lampshade.
abats [aba] *nmpl* offal; (*de volaille*) giblets.
abattant [abatɑ̃] *nm* leaf, flap.
abattis [abati] *nmpl* giblets.
abatt/re* [abatr] *vt* (*mur*) to knock down; (*arbre*) to cut down, fell; (*animal etc*) to slaughter; (*avion*) to shoot down; (*déprimer*) to demoralize; (*épuiser*) to exhaust; **— s'a.** *vpr* (*tomber*) to collapse; (*oiseau*) to swoop down; (*pluie*) to pour down. **◆—u** *a* (*triste*) dejected, demoralized; (*faible*) at a low ebb. **◆—age** *nm* felling; slaughter(ing). **◆—ement** *nm* (*faiblesse*) exhaustion; (*désespoir*) dejection. **◆abattoir** *nm* slaughterhouse.
abbaye [abei] *nf* abbey.
abbé [abe] *nm* (*chef d'abbaye*) abbot; (*prêtre*) priest. **◆abbesse** *nf* abbess.
abcès [apsɛ] *nm* abscess.
abdiquer [abdike] *vti* to abdicate. **◆abdication** *nf* abdication.
abdomen [abdɔmɛn] *nm* abdomen. **◆abdominal, -aux** *a* abdominal.
abeille [abɛj] *nf* bee.
aberrant [aberɑ̃] *a* (*idée etc*) ludicrous, absurd. **◆aberration** *nf* (*égarement*) aberration; (*idée*) ludicrous idea; **dire des aberrations** to talk sheer nonsense.
abhorrer [abɔre] *vt* to abhor, loathe.
abîme [abim] *nm* abyss, chasm, gulf.
abîmer [abime] *vt* to spoil, damage; **— s'a.** *vpr* to get spoilt; **s'a. dans ses pensées** *Litt* to lose oneself in one's thoughts.
abject [abʒɛkt] *a* abject, despicable.
abjurer [abʒyre] *vti* to abjure.
ablation [ablɑsjɔ̃] *nf* (*d'organe*) removal.
ablutions [ablysjɔ̃] *nfpl* ablutions.
abnégation [abnegɑsjɔ̃] *nf* self-sacrifice, abnegation.
abois (aux) [ozabwa] *adv* at bay.
abolir [abɔlir] *vt* to abolish. **◆abolition** *nf* abolition.
abominable [abɔminabl] *a* abominable, obnoxious. **◆abomination** *nf* abomination.
abondant [abɔ̃dɑ̃] *a* abundant, plentiful. **◆abondamment** *adv* abundantly. **◆abondance** *nf* abundance (**de** of); **en a.** in abundance; **années d'a.** years of plenty. **◆abonder** *vi* to abound (**en** in).
abonné, -ée [abɔne] *nmf* (*à un journal, au téléphone*) subscriber; *Rail Sp Th* season ticket holder; (*du gaz etc*) consumer.

◆**abonnement** *nm* subscription; (**carte d'**)**a.** season ticket. ◆**s'abonner** *vpr* to subscribe (**à** to); to buy a season ticket.

abord [abɔr] **1** *nm* (*accès*) **d'un a. facile** easy to approach. **2** *nm* (*vue*) **au premier a.** at first sight. **3** *nmpl* (*environs*) surroundings; **aux abords de** around, nearby. ◆**abordable** *a* (*personne*) approachable; (*prix, marchandises*) affordable.

abord (d') [dabɔr] *adv* (*avant tout*) first; (*au début*) at first.

aborder [abɔrde] *vi* to land; – *vt* (*personne*) to approach, accost; (*lieu*) to approach, reach; (*problème*) to tackle, approach; (*attaquer*) *Nau* to board; (*heurter*) *Nau* to run foul of. ◆**abordage** *nm* (*assaut*) *Nau* boarding; (*accident*) *Nau* collision.

aborigène [abɔriʒɛn] *a* & *nm* aboriginal.

about/ir [abutir] *vi* to succeed; **a. à** to end at, lead to, end up in; **n'a. à rien** to come to nothing. ◆**—issants** *nmpl voir* **tenants.** ◆**—issement** *nm* (*résultat*) outcome; (*succès*) success.

aboyer [abwaje] *vi* to bark. ◆**aboiement** *nm* bark; *pl* barking.

abrasif, -ive [abrazif, -iv] *a* & *nm* abrasive.

abrég/er [abreʒe] *vt* (*récit*) to shorten, abridge; (*mot*) to abbreviate. ◆**—é** *nm* summary; **en a.** (*phrase*) in shortened form; (*mot*) in abbreviated form.

abreuver [abrœve] *vt* (*cheval*) to water; – **s'a.** *vpr* to drink. ◆**abreuvoir** *nm* (*récipient*) drinking trough; (*lieu*) watering place.

abréviation [abrevjasjɔ̃] *nf* abbreviation.

abri [abri] *nm* shelter; **à l'a. de** (*vent*) sheltered from; (*besoin*) safe from; **sans a.** homeless. ◆**abriter** *vt* (*protéger*) to shelter; (*loger*) to house; – **s'a.** *vpr* to (take) shelter.

abricot [abriko] *nm* apricot. ◆**abricotier** *nm* apricot tree.

abroger [abrɔʒe] *vt* to abrogate.

abrupt [abrypt] *a* (*versant*) sheer; (*sentier*) steep, abrupt; (*personne*) abrupt.

abrut/ir [abrytir] *vt* (*alcool*) to stupefy (*s.o.*); (*propagande*) to brutalize (*s.o.*); (*travail*) to leave (*s.o.*) dazed, wear (*s.o.*) out. ◆**—i, -ie** *nmf* idiot; – *a* idiotic.

absence [apsɑ̃s] *nf* absence. ◆**absent, -e** *a* (*personne*) absent, away; (*chose*) missing; **air a.** faraway look; – *nmf* absentee. ◆**absentéisme** *nm* absenteeism. ◆**s'absenter** *vpr* to go away.

abside [apsid] *nf* (*d'une église*) apse.

absolu [apsɔly] *a* & *nm* absolute. ◆**—ment** *adv* absolutely.

absolution [absɔlysjɔ̃] *nf* absolution.

absorb/er [apsɔrbe] *vt* to absorb. ◆**—ant** *a* absorbent; **travail a.** absorbing job. ◆**absorption** *nf* absorption.

absoudre* [apsudr] *vt* to absolve.

abstenir* (s') [sapstənir] *vpr* to abstain; **s'a. de** to refrain *ou* abstain from. ◆**abstention** *nf* abstention.

abstinence [apstinɑ̃s] *nf* abstinence.

abstraire* [apstrɛr] *vt* to abstract. ◆**abstrait** *a* & *nm* abstract. ◆**abstraction** *nf* abstraction; **faire a. de** to disregard, leave aside.

absurde [apsyrd] *a* & *nm* absurd. ◆**absurdité** *nf* absurdity; **dire des absurdités** to talk nonsense.

abus [aby] *nm* abuse, misuse; over-indulgence; (*injustice*) abuse. ◆**abuser 1** *vi* to go too far; **a. de** (*situation, personne*) to take unfair advantage of; (*autorité*) to abuse, misuse; (*friandises*) to over-indulge in. **2 s'a.** *vpr* to be mistaken.

abusi/f, -ive [abyzif, -iv] *a* excessive; **emploi a.** *Ling* improper use, misuse. ◆**—vement** *adv Ling* improperly.

acabit [akabi] *nm* **de cet a.** *Péj* of that ilk *ou* sort.

acacia [akasja] *nm* (*arbre*) acacia.

académie [akademi] *nf* academy; *Univ* = (regional) education authority. ◆**académicien, -ienne** *nmf* academician. ◆**académique** *a* academic.

acajou [akaʒu] *nm* mahogany; **cheveux a.** auburn hair.

acariâtre [akarjɑtr] *a* cantankerous.

accabl/er [akɑble] *vt* to overwhelm, overcome; **a. d'injures** to heap insults upon; **accablé de dettes** (over)burdened with debt. ◆**—ement** *nm* dejection.

accalmie [akalmi] *nf* lull.

accaparer [akapare] *vt* to monopolize; (*personne*) *Fam* to take up all the time of.

accéder [aksede] *vi* **a. à** (*lieu*) to have access to, reach; (*pouvoir, trône, demande*) to accede to.

accélérer [akselere] *vi Aut* to accelerate; – *vt* (*travaux etc*) to speed up; (*allure, pas*) to quicken, speed up; – **s'a.** *vpr* to speed up. ◆**accélérateur** *nm Aut* accelerator. ◆**accélération** *nf* acceleration; speeding up.

accent [aksɑ̃] *nm* accent; (*sur une syllabe*) stress; **mettre l'a. sur** to stress. ◆**accentuation** *nf* accentuation. ◆**accentuer** *vt* to emphasize, accentuate, stress; – **s'a.** *vpr* to become more pronounced.

accepter [aksɛpte] *vt* to accept; **a. de faire**

to agree to do. ◆**acceptable** *a* acceptable. ◆**acceptation** *nf* acceptance.

acception [aksɛpsjɔ̃] *nf* sense, meaning.

accès [aksɛ] *nm* access (**à** to); (*de folie, colère, toux*) fit; (*de fièvre*) attack, bout; *pl* (*routes*) approaches. ◆**accessible** *a* accessible; (*personne*) approachable. ◆**accession** *nf* accession (**à** to); (*à un traité*) adherence; **a. à la propriété** home ownership.

accessoire [akseswar] *a* secondary; – *nmpl Th* props; (*de voiture etc*) accessories; **accessoires de toilette** toilet requisites.

accident [aksidɑ̃] *nm* accident; **a. d'avion/de train** plane/train crash; **par a.** by accident, by chance. ◆**accidenté, -ée** *a* (*terrain*) uneven; (*région*) hilly; (*voiture*) damaged (in an accident); – *nmf* accident victim, casualty. ◆**accidentel, -elle** *a* accidental. ◆**accidentellement** *adv* accidentally, unintentionally.

acclamer [aklame] *vt* to cheer, acclaim. ◆**acclamations** *nfpl* cheers, acclamations.

acclimater [aklimate] *vt*, — **s'a.** *vpr* to acclimatize, *Am* acclimate. ◆**acclimatation** *nf* acclimatization, *Am* acclimation.

accointances [akwɛ̃tɑ̃s] *nfpl Péj* contacts.

accolade [akɔlad] *nf* (*embrassade*) embrace; *Typ* brace, bracket.

accoler [akɔle] *vt* to place (side by side) (**à** against).

accommod/er [akɔmɔde] *vt* to adapt; *Culin* to prepare; **s'a. à** to adapt (oneself) to; **s'a. de** to make the best of. ◆**—ant** *a* accommodating, easy to please. ◆**—ement** *nm* arrangement, compromise.

accompagner [akɔ̃paɲe] *vt* (*personne*) to accompany, go *ou* come with, escort; (*chose*) & *Mus* to accompany; **s'a. de** to be accompanied by, go with. ◆**accompagnateur, -trice** *nmf Mus* accompanist; (*d'un groupe*) guide. ◆**accompagnement** *nm Mus* accompaniment.

accompl/ir [akɔ̃plir] *vt* to carry out, fulfil, accomplish. ◆**—i** *a* accomplished. ◆**—issement** *nm* fulfilment.

accord [akɔr] *nm* agreement; (*harmonie*) harmony; *Mus* chord; **être d'a.** to agree, be in agreement (**avec** with); **d'a.!** all right! ◆**accorder** *vt* (*donner*) to grant; *Mus* to tune; *Gram* to make agree; — **s'a.** *vpr* to agree; (*s'entendre*) to get along.

accordéon [akɔrdeɔ̃] *nm* accordion; **en a.** (*chaussette etc*) wrinkled.

accoster [akɔste] *vt* to accost; *Nau* to come alongside; – *vi Nau* to berth.

accotement [akɔtmɑ̃] *nm* roadside, verge.

accouch/er [akuʃe] *vi* to give birth (**de** to); – *vt* (*enfant*) to deliver. ◆**—ement** *nm* delivery. ◆**—eur** *nm* (**médecin**) **a.** obstetrician.

accouder (s') [sakude] *vpr* **s'a. à** *ou* **sur** to lean on (*with one's elbows*). ◆**accoudoir** *nm* armrest.

accoupl/er [akuple] *vt* to couple; — **s'a.** *vpr* (*animaux*) to mate (**à** with). ◆**—ement** *nm* coupling, mating.

accourir* [akurir] *vi* to come running, run over.

accoutrement [akutrəmɑ̃] *nm Péj* garb, dress.

accoutumer [akutyme] *vt* to accustom; — **s'a.** *vpr* to get accustomed (**à** to); **comme à l'accoutumée** as usual. ◆**accoutumance** *nf* familiarization (**à** with); *Méd* addiction.

accréditer [akredite] *vt* (*ambassadeur*) to accredit; (*rumeur*) to lend credence to.

accroc [akro] *nm* (*déchirure*) tear; (*difficulté*) hitch, snag.

accroch/er [akrɔʃe] *vt* (*déchirer*) to catch; (*fixer*) to hook; (*suspendre*) to hang up (*on a hook*); (*heurter*) to hit, knock; – *vi* (*affiche etc*) to grab one's attention; — **s'a.** *vpr* (*ne pas céder*) to persevere; (*se disputer*) *Fam* to clash; **s'a. à** (*se cramponner etc*) to cling to; (*s'écorcher*) to catch oneself on. ◆**—age** *nm Aut* knock, slight hit; (*friction*) *Fam* clash. ◆**—eur, -euse** *a* (*personne*) tenacious; (*affiche etc*) eyecatching, catchy.

accroître* [akrwatr] *vt* to increase; — **s'a.** *vpr* to increase, grow. ◆**accroissement** *nm* increase; growth.

accroup/ir (s') [sakrupir] *vpr* to squat *ou* crouch (down). ◆**—i** *a* squatting, crouching.

accueil [akœj] *nm* reception, welcome. ◆**accueill/ir*** *vt* to receive, welcome, greet. ◆**—ant** *a* welcoming.

acculer [akyle] *vt* **a. qn à qch** to drive s.o. to *ou* against sth.

accumuler [akymyle] *vt*, — **s'a.** *vpr* to pile up, accumulate. ◆**accumulateur** *nm* accumulator, battery. ◆**accumulation** *nf* accumulation.

accus/er [akyze] *vt* (*dénoncer*) to accuse; (*rendre responsable*) to blame (**de** for); (*révéler*) to show; (*faire ressortir*) to bring out; **a. réception** to acknowledge receipt (**de** of); **a. le coup** to stagger under the blow. ◆**—é, -ée 1** *nmf* accused; (*cour d'assises*) defendant. **2** *a* prominent. ◆**accusateur, -trice** *a* (*regard*) accusing;

(*document*) incriminating; – *nmf* accuser. ◆**accusation** *nf* accusation; *Jur* charge.
acerbe [aserb] *a* bitter, caustic.
acéré [asere] *a* sharp.
acétate [asetat] *nm* acetate. ◆**acétique** *a* acetic.
achalandé [aʃalɑ̃de] *a* **bien a.** (*magasin*) well-stocked.
acharn/er (s') [saʃarne] *vpr* **s'a. sur** (*attaquer*) to set upon, lay into; **s'a. contre** (*poursuivre*) to pursue (relentlessly); **s'a. à faire** to struggle to do, try desperately to do. ◆**—é, -ée** *a* relentless; – *nmf* (*du jeu etc*) fanatic. ◆**—ement** *nm* relentlessness.
achat [aʃa] *nm* purchase; *pl* shopping.
acheminer [aʃmine] *vt* to dispatch; **— s'a.** *vpr* to proceed (vers towards).
achet/er [aʃte] *vti* to buy, purchase; **a. à qn** (*vendeur*) to buy from s.o.; (*pour qn*) to buy for s.o. ◆**—eur, -euse** *nmf* buyer, purchaser; (*dans un magasin*) shopper.
achever [aʃve] *vt* to finish (off); **a. de faire qch** (*personne*) to finish doing sth; **a. qn** (*tuer*) to finish s.o. off; **— s'a.** *vpr* to end, finish. ◆**achèvement** *nm* completion.
achoppement [aʃɔpmɑ̃] *nm* **pierre d'a.** stumbling block.
acide [asid] *a* acid, sour; – *nm* acid. ◆**acidité** *nf* acidity.
acier [asje] *nm* steel. ◆**aciérie** *nf* steelworks.
acné [akne] *nf* acne.
acolyte [akɔlit] *nm Péj* confederate, associate.
acompte [akɔ̃t] *nm* part payment, deposit.
à-côté [akote] *nm* (*d'une question*) side issue; *pl* (*gains*) little extras.
à-coup [aku] *nm* jerk, jolt; **sans à-coups** smoothly; **par à-coups** in fits and starts.
acoustique [akustik] *a* acoustic; – *nf* acoustics.
acquérir* [akerir] *vt* to acquire, gain; (*par achat*) to purchase; **s'a. une réputation/***etc* to win a reputation/*etc*; **être acquis à** (*idée, parti*) to be a supporter of. ◆**acquéreur** *nm* purchaser. ◆**acquis** *nm* experience. ◆**acquisition** *nf* acquisition; purchase.
acquiesc/er [akjese] *vi* to acquiesce (**à** to). ◆**—ement** *nm* acquiescence.
acquit [aki] *nm* receipt; **'pour a.'** 'paid'; **par a. de conscience** for conscience sake. ◆**acquitt/er** *vt* (*dette*) to clear, pay; (*accusé*) to acquit; **s'a. de** (*devoir, promesse*) to discharge; **s'a. envers qn** to repay s.o. ◆**—ement** *nm* payment; acquittal; discharge.
âcre [ɑkr] *a* bitter, acrid, pungent.
acrobate [akrɔbat] *nmf* acrobat. ◆**acrobatie(s)** *nf(pl)* acrobatics. ◆**acrobatique** *a* acrobatic.
acrylique [akrilik] *a & nm* acrylic.
acte [akt] *nm* act, deed; *Th* act; **un a. de** an act of; **a. de naissance** birth certificate; **prendre a. de** to take note of.
acteur, -trice [aktœr, -tris] *nmf* actor, actress.
actif, -ive [aktif, -iv] *a* active; – *nm Fin* assets; **à son a.** to one's credit; (*vols, meurtres*) *Hum* to one's name.
action [aksjɔ̃] *nf* action; *Fin* share. ◆**actionnaire** *nmf* shareholder. ◆**actionner** *vt* to set in motion, activate, actuate.
activer [aktive] *vt* to speed up; (*feu*) to boost; **— s'a.** *vpr* to bustle about; (*se dépêcher*) *Fam* to get a move on.
activiste [aktivist] *nmf* activist.
activité [aktivite] *nf* activity; **en a.** (*personne*) fully active; (*volcan*) active.
actuaire [aktɥɛr] *nmf* actuary.
actualité [aktɥalite] *nf* (*d'un problème*) topicality; (*événements*) current events; *pl TV Cin* news; **d'a.** topical.
actuel, -elle [aktɥɛl] *a* (*présent*) present; (*contemporain*) topical. ◆**actuellement** *adv* at present, at the present time.
acuité [akɥite] *nf* (*de douleur*) acuteness; (*de vision*) keenness.
acupuncture [akypɔ̃ktyr] *nf* acupuncture. ◆**acupuncteur, -trice** *nmf* acupuncturist.
adage [adaʒ] *nm* (*maxime*) adage.
adapter [adapte] *vt* to adapt; (*ajuster*) to fit (**à** to); **s'a. à** (*s'habituer*) to adapt to; (*tuyau etc*) to fit. ◆**adaptable** *a* adaptable. ◆**adaptateur, -trice** *nmf* adapter. ◆**adaptation** *nf* adaptation.
additif [aditif] *nm* additive.
addition [adisjɔ̃] *nf* addition; (*au restaurant*) bill, *Am* check. ◆**additionnel, -elle** *a* additional. ◆**additionner** *vt* to add (**à** to); (*nombres*) to add up.
adepte [adɛpt] *nmf* follower.
adéquat [adekwa] *a* appropriate.
adhérer [adere] *vi* **a. à** (*coller*) to adhere *ou* stick to; (*s'inscrire*) to join; (*pneu*) to grip. ◆**adhérence** *nf* (*de pneu*) grip. ◆**adhérent, -ente** *nmf* member.
adhésif, -ive [adezif, -iv] *a & nm* adhesive. ◆**adhésion** *nf* membership; (*accord*) support.
adieu, -x [adjø] *int & nm* farewell, goodbye.
adipeux, -euse [adipø, -øz] *a* (*tissu*) fatty; (*visage*) fat.

adjacent [adʒasɑ̃] *a* (*contigu*) & *Géom* adjacent.

adjectif [adʒɛktif] *nm* adjective.

adjoindre* [adʒwɛ̃dr] *vt* (*associer*) to appoint (*s.o.*) as an assistant (à to); (*ajouter*) to add; **s'a. qn** to appoint s.o. ◆**adjoint, -ointe** *nmf* & *a* assistant; **a. au maire** deputy mayor.

adjudant [adʒydɑ̃] *nm* warrant officer.

adjuger [adʒyʒe] *vt* (*accorder*) to award; **s'a. qch** *Fam* to grab sth for oneself.

adjurer [adʒyre] *vt* to beseech, entreat.

admettre* [admɛtr] *vt* (*laisser entrer, accueillir, reconnaître*) to admit; (*autoriser, tolérer*) to allow; (*supposer*) to admit, grant; (*candidat*) to pass; **être admis à** (*examen*) to have passed.

administrer [administre] *vt* (*gérer, donner*) to administer. ◆**administrateur, -trice** *nmf* administrator. ◆**administratif, -ive** *a* administrative. ◆**administration** *nf* administration; **l'A.** (*service public*) government service, the Civil Service.

admirer [admire] *vt* to admire. ◆**admirable** *a* admirable. ◆**admirateur, -trice** *nmf* admirer. ◆**admiratif, -ive** *a* admiring. ◆**admiration** *nf* admiration.

admissible [admisibl] *a* acceptable, admissible; (*après un concours*) eligible (à for). ◆**admission** *nf* admission.

adolescent, -ente [adɔlesɑ̃, -ɑ̃t] *nmf* adolescent, teenager; — *a* teenage. ◆**adolescence** *nf* adolescence.

adonner (s') [sadɔne] *vpr* **s'a. à** (*boisson*) to take to; (*étude*) to devote oneself to.

adopter [adɔpte] *vt* to adopt. ◆**adoptif, -ive** *a* (*fils, patrie*) adopted. ◆**adoption** *nf* adoption; **suisse d'a.** Swiss by adoption.

adorer [adɔre] *vt* (*personne*) & *Rel* to worship, adore; (*chose*) *Fam* to adore, love; **a. faire** to adore *ou* love doing. ◆**adorable** *a* adorable. ◆**adoration** *nf* adoration, worship.

adosser [adose] *vt* **a. qch à** to lean sth back against; **s'a. à** to lean back against.

adouc/ir [adusir] *vt* (*voix, traits etc*) to soften; (*boisson*) to sweeten; (*chagrin*) to mitigate, ease; — **s'a.** *vpr* (*temps*) to turn milder; (*caractère*) to mellow. ◆**—issement** *nm* **a. de la température** milder weather.

adrénaline [adrenalin] *nf* adrenalin(e).

adresse [adrɛs] *nf* **1** (*domicile*) address. **2** (*habileté*) skill. ◆**adresser** *vt* (*lettre*) to send; (*compliment, remarque etc*) to address; (*coup*) to direct, aim; (*personne*) to direct (à to); **a. la parole à** to speak to; **s'a. à** to speak to; (*aller trouver*) to go and see; (*bureau*) to enquire at; (*être destiné à*) to be aimed at.

Adriatique [adriatik] *nf* **l'A.** the Adriatic.

adroit [adrwa] *a* skilful, clever.

adulation [adylɑsjɔ̃] *nf* adulation.

adulte [adylt] *a* & *nmf* adult, grown-up.

adultère [adyltɛr] *a* adulterous; — *nm* adultery.

advenir [advənir] *v imp* to occur; **a. de** (*devenir*) to become of; **advienne que pourra** come what may.

adverbe [advɛrb] *nm* adverb. ◆**adverbial, -aux** *a* adverbial.

adversaire [advɛrsɛr] *nmf* opponent, adversary. ◆**adverse** *a* opposing.

adversité [advɛrsite] *nf* adversity.

aérer [aere] *vt* (*chambre*) to air (out), ventilate; (*lit*) to air (out); — **s'a.** *vpr Fam* to get some air. ◆**aéré** *a* airy. ◆**aération** *nf* ventilation. ◆**aérien, -ienne** *a* (*ligne, attaque etc*) air-; (*photo*) aerial; (*câble*) overhead; (*léger*) airy.

aérobic [aerɔbik] *nf* aerobics.

aéro-club [aerɔklœb] *nm* flying club. ◆**aérodrome** *nm* aerodrome. ◆**aérodynamique** *a* streamlined, aerodynamic. ◆**aérogare** *nf* air terminal. ◆**aéroglisseur** *nm* hovercraft. ◆**aérogramme** *nm* air letter. ◆**aéromodélisme** *nm* model aircraft building and flying. ◆**aéronautique** *nf* aeronautics. ◆**aéronavale** *nf* = *Br* Fleet Air Arm, = *Am* Naval Air Force. ◆**aéroport** *nm* airport. ◆**aéroporté** *a* airborne. ◆**aérosol** *nm* aerosol.

affable [afabl] *a* affable.

affaiblir [afeblir] *vt*, — **s'a.** *vpr* to weaken.

affaire [afɛr] *nf* (*question*) matter, affair; (*marché*) deal; (*firme*) concern, business; (*scandale*) affair; (*procès*) *Jur* case; *pl Com* business; (*d'intérêt public, personnel*) affairs; (*effets*) belongings, things; **avoir a. à** to have to deal with; **c'est mon a.** that's my business *ou* affair *ou* concern; **faire une bonne a.** to get a good deal, get a bargain; **ça fera l'a.** that will do nicely; **toute une a.** (*histoire*) quite a business.

affair/er (s') [safere] *vpr* to busy oneself, run *ou* bustle about. ◆**—é** *a* busy. ◆**affairiste** *nm* (political) racketeer.

affaiss/er (s') [safese] *vpr* (*personne*) to collapse; (*plancher*) to cave in, give way; (*sol*) to subside, sink. ◆**—ement** [afɛsmɑ̃] *nm* (*du sol*) subsidence.

affaler (s') [safale] *vpr* to flop down, collapse.

affamé [afame] *a* starving; **a. de** *Fig* hungry for.

affect/er [afɛkte] *vt* (*destiner*) to earmark, assign; (*nommer à un poste*) to post; (*feindre, émouvoir*) to affect. ◆**—é** *a* (*manières, personne*) affected. ◆**affectation** *nf* assignment; posting; (*simulation*) affectation.

affectif, -ive [afɛktif, -iv] *a* emotional.

affection [afɛksjɔ̃] *nf* (*attachement*) affection; (*maladie*) ailment. ◆**affectionn/er** *vt* to be fond of. ◆**—é** *a* loving. ◆**affectueux, -euse** *a* affectionate.

affermir [afermir] *vt* (*autorité*) to strengthen; (*muscles*) to tone up; (*voix*) to steady.

affiche [afiʃ] *nf* poster; *Th* bill. ◆**affich/er** *vt* (*affiche etc*) to post *ou* stick up; *Th* to bill; (*sentiment*) *Péj* to display; **a. qn** *Péj* to parade s.o., flaunt s.o. ◆**—age** *nm* (bill-)posting; **panneau d'a.** hoarding, *Am* billboard.

affilée (d') [dafile] *adv* (*à la suite*) in a row, at a stretch.

affiler [afile] *vt* to sharpen.

affilier (s') [safilje] *vpr* **s'a. à** to join, become affiliated to. ◆**affiliation** *nf* affiliation.

affiner [afine] *vt* to refine.

affinité [afinite] *nf* affinity.

affirmatif, -ive [afirmatif, -iv] *a* (*ton*) assertive, positive; (*proposition*) affirmative; **il a été a.** he was quite positive; – *nf* **répondre par l'affirmative** to reply in the affirmative.

affirmer [afirme] *vt* to assert; (*proclamer solennellement*) to affirm. ◆**affirmation** *nf* assertion.

affleurer [aflœre] *vi* to appear on the surface.

affliger [afliʒe] *vt* to distress; **affligé de** stricken *ou* afflicted with.

affluence [aflyɑ̃s] *nf* crowd; **heures d'a.** rush hours.

affluent [aflyɑ̃] *nm* tributary.

affluer [aflye] *vi* (*sang*) to flow, rush; (*gens*) to flock. ◆**afflux** *nm* flow; (*arrivée*) influx.

affol/er [afɔle] *vt* to drive out of one's mind; (*effrayer*) to terrify; — **s'a.** *vpr* to panic. ◆**—ement** *nm* panic.

affranch/ir [afrɑ̃ʃir] *vt* (*timbrer*) to stamp; (*émanciper*) to free. ◆**—issement** *nm* **tarifs d'a.** postage.

affréter [afrete] *vt* (*avion*) to charter; (*navire*) to freight.

affreux, -euse [afrø, -øz] *a* hideous, dreadful, ghastly. ◆**affreusement** *adv* dreadfully.

affriolant [afriɔlɑ̃] *a* enticing.

affront [afrɔ̃] *nm* insult, affront; **faire un a. à** to insult.

affront/er [afrɔ̃te] *vt* to confront, face; (*mauvais temps, difficultés etc*) to brave. ◆**—ement** *nm* confrontation.

affubler [afyble] *vt* *Péj* to dress, rig out (**de** in).

affût [afy] *nm* **à l'a. de** *Fig* on the look-out for.

affûter [afyte] *vt* (*outil*) to sharpen, grind.

Afghanistan [afganistɑ̃] *nm* Afghanistan.

afin [afɛ̃] *prép* **a. de** (+ *inf*) in order to; – *conj* **a. que** (+ *sub*) so that.

Afrique [afrik] *nf* Africa. ◆**africain, -aine** *a & nmf* African.

agac/er [agase] *vt* (*personne*) to irritate, annoy. ◆**—ement** *nm* irritation.

âge [ɑʒ] *nm* age; **quel â. as-tu?** how old are you?; **avant l'â.** before one's time; **d'un certain â.** middle-aged; **l'â. adulte** adulthood; **la force de l'â.** the prime of life; **le moyen â.** the Middle Ages. ◆**âgé** *a* elderly; **â. de six ans** six years old; **un enfant â. de six ans** a six-year-old child.

agence [aʒɑ̃s] *nf* agency; (*succursale*) branch office; **a. immobilière** estate agent's office, *Am* real estate office.

agenc/er [aʒɑ̃se] *vt* to arrange; **bien agencé** (*maison etc*) well laid-out; (*phrase*) well put-together. ◆**—ement** *nm* (*de maison etc*) lay-out.

agenda [aʒɛ̃da] *nm* diary, *Am* datebook.

agenouiller (s') [saʒnuje] *vpr* to kneel (down); **être agenouillé** to be kneeling (down).

agent [aʒɑ̃] *nm* agent; **a. (de police)** policeman; **a. de change** stockbroker; **a. immobilier** estate agent, *Am* real estate agent.

aggloméré [aglɔmere] *nm & a* (*bois*) chipboard, fibreboard.

agglomérer (s') [saglɔmere] *vpr* (*s'entasser*) to conglomerate. ◆**agglomération** *nf* conglomeration; (*habitations*) built-up area; (*ville*) town.

aggraver [agrave] *vt* to worsen, aggravate; — **s'a.** *vpr* to worsen. ◆**aggravation** *nf* worsening.

agile [aʒil] *a* agile, nimble. ◆**agilité** *nf* agility, nimbleness.

agir [aʒir] **1** *vi* to act; **a. auprès de** to intercede with. **2 s'agir** *v imp* **il s'agit d'argent**/*etc* it's a question *ou* matter of money/*etc*, it concerns money/*etc*; **de quoi s'agit-il?** what is it?, what's it about?; **il s'agit de se dépêcher**/*etc* we have to

hurry/*etc*. ◆**agissant** *a* active, effective. ◆**agissements** *nmpl Péj* dealings.
agit/er [aʒite] *vt* (*remuer*) to stir; (*secouer*) to shake; (*brandir*) to wave; (*troubler*) to agitate; (*discuter*) to debate; — **s'a.** *vpr* (*enfant*) to fidget; (*peuple*) to stir. ◆**—é** *a* (*mer*) rough; (*malade*) restless, agitated; (*enfant*) fidgety, restless. ◆**agitateur, -trice** *nmf* (political) agitator. ◆**agitation** *nf* (*de la mer*) roughness; (*d'un malade etc*) restlessness; (*nervosité*) agitation; (*de la rue*) bustle; *Pol* unrest.
agneau, -x [aɲo] *nm* lamb.
agonie [agɔni] *nf* death throes; **être à l'a.** to be suffering the pangs of death. ◆**agoniser** *vi* to be dying.
agrafe [agraf] *nf* hook; (*pour papiers*) staple. ◆**agrafer** *vt* to fasten, hook, do up; (*papiers*) to staple. ◆**agrafeuse** *nf* stapler.
agrand/ir [agrɑ̃dir] *vt* to enlarge; (*grossir*) to magnify; — **s'a.** *vpr* to expand, grow. ◆**—issement** *nm* (*de ville*) expansion; (*de maison*) extension; (*de photo*) enlargement.
agréable [agreabl] *a* pleasant, agreeable, nice. ◆**—ment** [-əmɑ̃] *adv* pleasantly.
agré/er [agree] *vt* to accept; **veuillez a. mes salutations distinguées** (*dans une lettre*) yours faithfully. ◆**—é** *a* (*fournisseur, centre*) approved.
agrégation [agregasjɔ̃] *nf competitive examination for recruitment of lycée teachers.* ◆**agrégé, -ée** *nmf teacher who has passed the agrégation.*
agrément [agremɑ̃] *nm* (*attrait*) charm; (*accord*) assent; **voyage d'a.** pleasure trip. ◆**agrémenter** *vt* to embellish; **a. un récit d'anecdotes** to pepper a story with anecdotes.
agrès [agrɛ] *nmpl Nau* tackle, rigging; (*de gymnastique*) apparatus.
agresser [agrese] *vt* to attack. ◆**agresseur** *nm* attacker; (*dans la rue*) mugger; (*dans un conflit*) aggressor. ◆**agressif, -ive** *a* aggressive. ◆**agression** *nf* (*d'un État*) aggression; (*d'un individu*) attack. ◆**agressivité** *nf* aggressiveness.
agricole [agrikɔl] *a* (*peuple*) agricultural, farming; (*ouvrier, machine*) farm-.
agriculteur [agrikyltœr] *nm* farmer. ◆**agriculture** *nf* agriculture, farming.
agripper [agripe] *vt* to clutch, grip; **s'a. à** to cling to, clutch, grip.
agronomie [agrɔnɔmi] *nf* agronomics.
agrumes [agrym] *nmpl* citrus fruit(s).
aguerri [ageri] *a* seasoned, hardened.
aguets (aux) [ozagɛ] *adv* on the look-out.
aguich/er [agiʃe] *vt* to tease, excite. ◆**—ant** *a* enticing.
ah! [a] *int* ah!, oh!
ahur/ir [ayrir] *vt* to astound, bewilder. ◆**—i, -ie** *nmf* idiot.
ai [e] *voir* **avoir.**
aide [ɛd] *nf* help, assistance, aid; — *nmf* (*personne*) assistant; **à l'a. de** with the help *ou* aid of. ◆**a.-électricien** *nm* electrician's mate. ◆**a.-familiale** *nf* home help. ◆**a.-mémoire** *nm inv Scol* handbook (*of facts etc*).
aider [ede] *vt* to help, assist, aid (**à faire** to do); **s'a. de** to make use of.
aïe! [aj] *int* ouch!, ow!
aïeul, -e [ajœl] *nmf* grandfather, grandmother.
aïeux [ajø] *nmpl* forefathers, forebears.
aigle [ɛgl] *nmf* eagle. ◆**aiglon** *nm* eaglet.
aiglefin [egləfɛ̃] *nm* haddock.
aigre [ɛgr] *a* (*acide*) sour; (*voix, vent, parole*) sharp, cutting. ◆**a.-doux, -douce** *a* bitter-sweet. ◆**aigreur** *nf* sourness; (*de ton*) sharpness; *pl* heartburn.
aigrette [ɛgrɛt] *nf* (*de plumes*) tuft.
aigr/ir (s') [segrir] *vpr* (*vin*) to turn sour; (*caractère*) to sour. ◆**—i** [egri] *a* (*personne*) embittered, bitter.
aigu, -uë [egy] *a* (*crise etc*) acute; (*dents*) sharp, pointed; (*voix*) shrill.
aiguille [egɥij] *nf* (*à coudre, de pin*) needle; (*de montre*) hand; (*de balance*) pointer; **a. (rocheuse)** peak.
aiguill/er [egɥije] *vt* (*train*) to shunt, *Am* switch; *Fig* to steer, direct. ◆**—age** *nm* (*appareil*) *Rail* points, *Am* switches. ◆**—eur** *nm Rail* pointsman, *Am* switchman; **a. du ciel** air traffic controller.
aiguillon [egɥijɔ̃] *nm* (*dard*) sting; (*stimulant*) spur. ◆**aiguillonner** *vt* to spur (on), goad.
aiguiser [eg(ɥ)ize] *vt* (*affiler*) to sharpen; (*appétit*) to whet.
ail [aj] *nm* garlic.
aile [ɛl] *nf* wing; (*de moulin à vent*) sail; *Aut* wing, *Am* fender; **battre de l'a.** to be in a bad way; **d'un coup d'a.** (*avion*) in continuous flight. ◆**ailé** [ele] *a* winged. ◆**aileron** *nm* (*de requin*) fin; (*d'avion*) aileron; (*d'oiseau*) pinion. ◆**ailier** [elje] *nm Fb* wing(er).
ailleurs [ajœr] *adv* somewhere else, elsewhere; **partout a.** everywhere else; **d'a.** (*du reste*) besides, anyway; **par a.** (*en outre*) moreover; (*autrement*) otherwise.
ailloli [ajɔli] *nm* garlic mayonnaise.
aimable [ɛmabl] *a* (*complaisant*) kind;

(*sympathique*) likeable, amiable; (*agréable*) pleasant. ◆**—ment** [-əmɑ̃] *adv* kindly.
aimant [ɛmɑ̃] **1** *nm* magnet. **2** *a* loving. ◆**aimanter** *vt* to magnetize.
aimer [eme] *vt* (*chérir*) to love; **a. (bien)** (*apprécier*) to like, be fond of; **a. faire** to like doing *ou* to do; **a. mieux** to prefer; **ils s'aiment** they're in love.
aine [ɛn] *nf* groin.
aîné, -e [ene] *a* (*de deux frères etc*) elder, older; (*de plus de deux*) eldest, oldest; – *nmf* (*enfant*) elder *ou* older (child); eldest *ou* oldest (child); **c'est mon a.** he's my senior.
ainsi [ɛ̃si] *adv* (*comme ça*) (in) this *ou* that way, thus; (*alors*) so; **a. que** as well as; **et a. de suite** and so on; **pour a. dire** so to speak.
air [ɛr] *nm* **1** air; **en plein a.** in the open (air), outdoors; **ficher** *ou* **flanquer en l'a.** *Fam* (*jeter*) to chuck away; (*gâcher*) to mess up, upset; **en l'a.** (*jeter*) (up) in the air; (*paroles, menaces*) empty; (*projets*) uncertain, (up) in the air; **dans l'a.** (*grippe, idées*) about, around. **2** (*expression*) look, appearance; **avoir l'a.** to look, seem; **avoir l'a. de** to look like; **a. de famille** family likeness. **3** (*mélodie*) tune; **a. d'opéra** aria.
aire [ɛr] *nf* (*de stationnement etc*) & *Math* area; (*d'oiseau*) eyrie; **a. de lancement** launching site.
airelle [ɛrɛl] *nf* bilberry, *Am* blueberry.
aisance [ɛzɑ̃s] *nf* (*facilité*) ease; (*prospérité*) easy circumstances, affluence.
aise [ɛz] *nf* **à l'a.** (*dans un vêtement etc*) comfortable; (*dans une situation*) at ease; (*fortuné*) comfortably off; **aimer ses aises** to like one's comforts; **mal à l'a.** uncomfortable, ill at ease. ◆**aisé** [eze] *a* (*fortuné*) comfortably off; (*naturel*) free and easy; (*facile*) easy. ◆**aisément** *adv* easily.
aisselle [ɛsɛl] *nf* armpit.
ait [ɛ] *voir* **avoir.**
ajonc(s) [aʒɔ̃] *nm(pl)* gorse, furze.
ajouré [aʒure] *a* (*dentelle etc*) openwork.
ajourn/er [aʒurne] *vt* to postpone, adjourn. ◆**—ement** *nm* postponement, adjournment.
ajout [aʒu] *nm* addition. ◆**ajouter** *vti* to add (**à** to); **s'a. à** to add to.
ajust/er [aʒyste] *vt* (*pièce, salaires*) to adjust; (*coiffure*) to arrange; (*coup*) to aim; **a. à** (*adapter*) to fit to. ◆**—é** *a* (*serré*) close-fitting. ◆**—ement** *nm* adjustment. ◆**—eur** *nm* (*ouvrier*) fitter.
alaise [alɛz] *nf* (waterproof) undersheet.
alambic [alɑ̃bik] *nm* still.
alambiqué [alɑ̃bike] *a* convoluted, over-subtle.
alanguir [alɑ̃gir] *vt* to make languid.
alarme [alarm] *nf* (*signal, inquiétude*) alarm; **jeter l'a.** to cause alarm. ◆**alarmer** *vt* to alarm; **s'a. de** to become alarmed at.
Albanie [albani] *nf* Albania. ◆**albanais, -aise** *a* & *nmf* Albanian.
albâtre [albɑtr] *nm* alabaster.
albatros [albatros] *nm* albatross.
albinos [albinos] *nmf* & *a inv* albino.
album [albɔm] *nm* (*de timbres etc*) album; (*de dessins*) sketchbook.
alcali [alkali] *nm* alkali. ◆**alcalin** *a* alkaline.
alchimie [alʃimi] *nf* alchemy.
alcool [alkɔl] *nm* alcohol; (*spiritueux*) spirits; **a. à brûler** methylated spirit(s); **lampe à a.** spirit lamp. ◆**alcoolique** *a* & *nmf* alcoholic. ◆**alcoolisé** *a* (*boisson*) alcoholic. ◆**alcoolisme** *nm* alcoholism. ◆**alcootest®** *nm* breath test; (*appareil*) breathalyzer.
alcôve [alkov] *nf* alcove.
aléas [alea] *nmpl* hazards, risks. ◆**aléatoire** *a* chancy, uncertain; (*sélection*) random.
alentour [alɑ̃tur] *adv* round about, around; **d'a.** surrounding; – *nmpl* surroundings, vicinity; **aux alentours de** in the vicinity of.
alerte [alɛrt] **1** *a* (*leste*) agile, spry; (*éveillé*) alert. **2** *nf* alarm; **en état d'a.** on the alert; **a. aérienne** air-raid warning. ◆**alerter** *vt* to warn, alert.
alezan, -ane [alzɑ̃ -an] *a* & *nmf* (*cheval*) chestnut.
algarade [algarad] *nf* (*dispute*) altercation.
algèbre [alʒɛbr] *nf* algebra. ◆**algébrique** *a* algebraic.
Alger [alʒe] *nm ou f* Algiers.
Algérie [alʒeri] *nf* Algeria. ◆**algérien, -ienne** *a* & *nmf* Algerian.
algue(s) [alg] *nf(pl)* seaweed.
alias [aljɑs] *adv* alias.
alibi [alibi] *nm* alibi.
alién/er [aljene] *vt* to alienate; **s'a. qn** to alienate s.o. ◆**—é, -ée** *nmf* insane person; *Péj* lunatic. ◆**aliénation** *nf* alienation; *Méd* derangement.
align/er [aliɲe] *vt* to align, line up; **les a.** *Arg* to fork out, pay up; **— s'a.** *vpr* (*personnes*) to fall into line, line up; *Pol* to align oneself (**sur** with). ◆**—ement** *nm* alignment.
aliment [alimɑ̃] *nm* food. ◆**alimentaire** *a* (*industrie, produit etc*) food-. ◆**alimentation** *nf* feeding; supply(ing); (*régime*) diet,

nutrition; (*nourriture*) food; **magasin d'a.** grocer's, grocery store. ◆**alimenter** *vt* (*nourrir*) to feed; (*fournir*) to supply (**en** with); (*débat, feu*) to fuel.
alinéa [alinea] *nm* paragraph.
alité [alite] *a* bedridden.
allaiter [alete] *vti* to (breast)feed.
allant [alɑ̃] *nm* drive, energy, zest.
allécher [aleʃe] *vt* to tempt, entice.
allée [ale] *nf* path, walk, lane; (*de cinéma*) aisle; **allées et venues** comings and goings, running about.
allégation [alegɑsjɔ̃] *nf* allegation.
alléger [aleʒe] *vt* to alleviate, lighten.
allégorie [alegɔri] *nf* allegory.
allègre [alɛgr] *a* gay, lively, cheerful. ◆**allégresse** *nf* gladness, rejoicing.
alléguer [alege] *vt* (*excuse etc*) to put forward.
alléluia [aleluja] *nm* hallelujah.
Allemagne [almaɲ] *nf* Germany. ◆**allemand, -ande** *a* & *nmf* German; – *nm* (*langue*) German.
aller* [ale] **1** *vi* (*aux* **être**) to go; (*montre etc*) to work, go; **a. à** (*convenir à*) to suit; **a. avec** (*vêtement*) to go with, match; **a. bien/mieux** (*personne*) to be well/better; **il va savoir/venir/***etc* he'll know/come/*etc*, he's going to know/come/*etc*; **il va partir** he's about to leave, he's going to leave; **va voir!** go and see!; **comment vas-tu?, (comment) ça va?** how are you?; **ça va!** all right!, fine!; **ça va (comme ça)!** that's enough!; **allez-y** go on, go ahead; **j'y vais** I'm coming; **allons (donc)!** come on!, come off it!; **allez! au lit!** come on *ou* go on to bed!; **ça va de soi** that's obvious; **— s'en aller** *vpr* to go away; (*tache*) to come out. **2** *nm* outward journey; **a. (simple)** single (ticket), *Am* one-way (ticket); **a. (et) retour** return (ticket), *Am* round-trip (ticket).
allergie [alɛrʒi] *nf* allergy. ◆**allergique** *a* allergic (**à** to).
alliage [aljaʒ] *nm* alloy.
alliance [aljɑ̃s] *nf* (*anneau*) wedding ring; *Pol* alliance; *Rel* covenant; (*mariage*) marriage.
alli/er [alje] *vt* (*associer*) to combine (**à** with); (*pays*) to ally (**à** with); **— s'a.** *vpr* (*couleurs*) to combine; (*pays*) to become allied (**à** with, to); **s'a. à** (*famille*) to ally oneself with. ◆**—é, -ée** *nmf* ally.
alligator [aligatɔr] *nm* alligator.
allô! [alo] *int Tél* hullo!, hallo!, hello!
allocation [alɔkɑsjɔ̃] *nf* (*somme*) allowance; **a. (de) chômage** unemployment benefit. ◆**allocataire** *nmf* claimant.
allocution [alɔkysjɔ̃] *nf* (short) speech, address.
allong/er [alɔ̃ʒe] *vt* (*bras*) to stretch out; (*jupe*) to lengthen; (*sauce*) to thin; – *vi* (*jours*) to get longer; **— s'a.** *vpr* to stretch out. ◆**—é** *a* (*oblong*) elongated.
allouer [alwe] *vt* to allocate.
allum/er [alyme] *vt* (*feu, pipe etc*) to light; (*électricité*) to turn *ou* switch on; (*désir, colère*) *Fig* to kindle; **— s'a.** *vpr* to light up; (*feu, guerre*) to flare up. ◆**—age** *nm* lighting; *Aut* ignition. ◆**allume-gaz** *nm inv* gas lighter. ◆**allumeuse** *nf* (*femme*) teaser.
allumette [alymɛt] *nf* match.
allure [alyr] *nf* (*vitesse*) pace; (*de véhicule*) speed; (*démarche*) gait, walk; (*maintien*) bearing; (*air*) look; *pl* (*conduite*) ways.
allusion [alyzjɔ̃] *nf* allusion; (*voilée*) hint; **faire a. à** to refer *ou* allude to; to hint at.
almanach [almana] *nm* almanac.
aloi [alwa] *nm* **de bon a.** genuine, worthy.
alors [alɔr] *adv* (*en ce temps-là*) then; (*en ce cas-là*) so, then; **a. que** (*lorsque*) when; (*tandis que*) whereas.
alouette [alwɛt] *nf* (sky)lark.
alourd/ir [alurdir] *vt* to weigh down; **— s'a.** *vpr* to become heavy *ou* heavier. ◆**—i** *a* heavy.
aloyau [alwajo] *nm* sirloin.
alpaga [alpaga] *nm* (*tissu*) alpaca.
alpage [alpaʒ] *nm* mountain pasture. ◆**Alpes** *nfpl* **les A.** the Alps. ◆**alpestre** *a*, ◆**alpin** *a* alpine. ◆**alpinisme** *nm* mountaineering. ◆**alpiniste** *nmf* mountaineer.
alphabet [alfabɛ] *nm* alphabet. ◆**alphabétique** *a* alphabetic(al). ◆**alphabétiser** *vt* to teach to read and write.
altercation [altɛrkɑsjɔ̃] *nf* altercation.
altérer [altere] *vt* (*denrée, santé*) to impair, spoil; (*voix, vérité*) to distort; (*monnaie, texte*) to falsify; (*donner soif à*) to make thirsty; **— s'a.** *vpr* (*santé, relations*) to deteriorate. ◆**altération** *nf* deterioration, change (**de** in); (*de visage*) distortion.
alternatif, -ive [altɛrnatif, -iv] *a* alternating. ◆**alternative** *nf* alternative; *pl* alternate periods. ◆**alternativement** *adv* alternately.
altern/er [altɛrne] *vti* to alternate. ◆**—é** *a* alternate. ◆**alternance** *nf* alternation.
altesse [altɛs] *nf* (*titre*) Highness.
altier, -ière [altje, -jɛr] *a* haughty.
altitude [altityd] *nf* altitude, height.
alto [alto] *nm* (*instrument*) viola.
aluminium [alyminjɔm] *nm* aluminium, *Am*

aluminum; **papier a.**, *Fam* **papier alu** tin foil.
alunir [alynir] *vi* to land on the moon.
alvéole [alveɔl] *nf* (*de ruche*) cell; (*dentaire*) socket. ◆**alvéolé** *a* honeycombed.
amabilité [amabilite] *nf* kindness; **faire des amabilités à** to show kindness to.
amadouer [amadwe] *vt* to coax, persuade.
amaigr/ir [amegrir] *vt* to make thin(ner). ◆**—i** *a* thin(ner). ◆**—issant** *a* (*régime*) slimming.
amalgame [amalgam] *nm* amalgam, mixture. ◆**amalgamer** *vt*, **— s'a.** *vpr* to blend, mix, amalgamate.
amande [amɑ̃d] *nf* almond.
amant [amɑ̃] *nm* lover.
amarre [amar] *nf* (mooring) rope, hawser; *pl* moorings. ◆**amarrer** *vt* to moor; *Fig* to tie down, make fast.
amas [amɑ] *nm* heap, pile. ◆**amasser** *vt* to pile up; (*richesse, preuves*) to amass, gather; **— s'a.** *vpr* to pile up; (*gens*) to gather.
amateur [amatœr] *nm* (*d'art etc*) lover; *Sp* amateur; (*acheteur*) *Fam* taker; **d'a.** (*talent*) amateur; (*travail*) *Péj* amateurish; **une équipe a.** an amateur team. ◆**amateurisme** *nm Sp* amateurism; *Péj* amateurishness.
amazone [amazɔn] *nf* horsewoman; **monter en a.** to ride sidesaddle.
ambages (sans) [sɑ̃zɑ̃baʒ] *adv* to the point, in plain language.
ambassade [ɑ̃basad] *nf* embassy. ◆**ambassadeur, -drice** *nmf* ambassador.
ambiance [ɑ̃bjɑ̃s] *nf* atmosphere. ◆**ambiant** *a* surrounding.
ambigu, -guë [ɑ̃bigy] *a* ambiguous. ◆**ambiguïté** [-gɥite] *nf* ambiguity.
ambitieux, -euse [ɑ̃bisjø, -øz] *a* ambitious. ◆**ambition** *nf* ambition. ◆**ambitionner** *vt* to aspire to; **il ambitionne de** his ambition is to.
ambre [ɑ̃br] *nm* (*jaune*) amber; (*gris*) ambergris.
ambulance [ɑ̃bylɑ̃s] *nf* ambulance. ◆**ambulancier, -ière** *nmf* ambulance driver.
ambulant [ɑ̃bylɑ̃] *a* itinerant, travelling.
âme [ɑm] *nf* soul; **â. qui vive** a living soul; **état d'â.** state of mind; **â. sœur** soul mate; **â. damnée** evil genius, henchman; **avoir charge d'âmes** to be responsible for human life.
améliorer [ameljɔre] *vt*, **— s'a.** *vpr* to improve. ◆**amélioration** *nf* improvement.
amen [amen] *adv* amen.
aménag/er [amenaʒe] *vt* (*arranger, installer*) to fit up, fit out (**en** as); (*bateau*) to fit out; (*transformer*) to convert (**en** into); (*construire*) to set up; (*ajuster*) to adjust. ◆**—ement** *nm* fitting up; fitting out; conversion; setting up; adjustment.
amende [amɑ̃d] *nf* fine; **frapper d'une a.** to impose a fine on; **faire a. honorable** to make an apology.
amender [amɑ̃de] *vt Pol* to amend; (*terre*) to improve; **— s'a.** *vpr* to mend *ou* improve one's ways.
amener [amne] *vt* to bring; (*causer*) to bring about; **— s'a.** *vpr Fam* to come along, turn up.
amenuiser (s') [samənɥize] *vpr* to grow smaller, dwindle.
amer, -ère [amer] *a* bitter. ◆**amèrement** *adv* bitterly.
Amérique [amerik] *nf* America; **A. du Nord/du Sud** North/South America. ◆**américain, -aine** *a* & *nmf* American.
amerrir [amerir] *vi* to make a sea landing; (*cabine spatiale*) to splash down.
amertume [amertym] *nf* bitterness.
améthyste [ametist] *nf* amethyst.
ameublement [amœbləmɑ̃] *nm* furniture.
ameuter [amøte] *vt* (*soulever*) to stir up; (*attrouper*) to gather, muster; (*voisins*) to bring out; **— s'a.** *vpr* to gather, muster.
ami, -e [ami] *nmf* friend; (*des livres, de la nature etc*) lover (**de** of); **petit a.** boyfriend; **petite amie** girlfriend; – *a* friendly.
amiable (à l') [alamjabl] *a* amicable; – *adv* amicably.
amiante [amjɑ̃t] *nm* asbestos.
amical, -aux [amikal, -o] *a* friendly. ◆**—ement** *adv* in a friendly manner.
amicale [amikal] *nf* association.
amidon [amidɔ̃] *nm* starch. ◆**amidonner** *vt* to starch.
amincir [amɛ̃sir] *vt* to make thin(ner); – *vi* (*personne*) to slim; **— s'a.** *vpr* to become thinner.
amiral, -aux [amiral, -o] *nm* admiral. ◆**amirauté** *nf* admiralty.
amitié [amitje] *nf* friendship; (*amabilité*) kindness; *pl* kind regrds; **prendre en a.** to take a liking to.
ammoniac [amɔnjak] *nm* (*gaz*) ammonia. ◆**ammoniaque** *nf* (*liquide*) ammonia.
amnésie [amnezi] *nf* amnesia.
amnistie [amnisti] *nf* amnesty.
amocher [amɔʃe] *vt Arg* to mess up, bash.

amoindrir [amwɛ̃drir] *vt*, **— s'a.** *vpr* to decrease, diminish.
amoll/ir [amɔlir] *vt* to soften; (*affaiblir*) to weaken. **◆—issant** *a* enervating.
amonceler [amɔ̃sle] *vt*, **— s'a.** *vpr* to pile up. **◆amoncellement** *nm* heap, pile.
amont (en) [ɑ̃namɔ̃] *adv* upstream.
amoral, -aux [amɔral, -o] *a* amoral.
amorce [amɔrs] *nf* (*début*) start; *Pêche* bait; (*détonateur*) fuse, detonator; (*de pistolet d'enfant*) cap. **◆amorcer** *vt* to start; (*hameçon*) to bait; (*pompe*) to prime; **— s'a.** *vpr* to start.
amorphe [amɔrf] *a* listless, apathetic.
amort/ir [amɔrtir] *vt* (*coup*) to cushion, absorb; (*bruit*) to deaden; (*dette*) to pay off; **il a vite amorti sa voiture** his car has been made to pay for itself quickly. **◆—issement** *nm Fin* redemption. **◆—isseur** *nm* shock absorber.
amour [amur] *nm* love; (*liaison*) romance, love; (*Cupidon*) Cupid; **pour l'a. de** for the sake of; **mon a.** my darling, my love. **◆a.-propre** *nm* self-respect, self-esteem. **◆s'amouracher** *vpr Péj* to become infatuated (**de** with). **◆amoureux, -euse** *nmf* lover; – *a* amorous, loving; **a. de** (*personne*) in love with; (*gloire*) *Fig* enamoured of.
amovible [amɔvibl] *a* removable, detachable.
ampère [ɑ̃pɛr] *nm Él* amp(ere).
amphi [ɑ̃fi] *nm Univ Fam* lecture hall.
amphibie [ɑ̃fibi] *a* amphibious; – *nm* amphibian.
amphithéâtre [ɑ̃fiteɑtr] *nm Hist* amphitheatre; *Univ* lecture hall.
ample [ɑ̃pl] *a* (*vêtement*) ample, roomy; (*provision*) full; (*vues*) broad. **◆amplement** *adv* amply, fully; **a. suffisant** ample. **◆ampleur** *nf* (*de robe*) fullness; (*importance, étendue*) scale, extent; **prendre de l'a.** to grow.
amplifier [ɑ̃plifje] *vt* (*accroître*) to develop; (*exagérer*) to magnify; (*son, courant*) to amplify; **— s'a.** *vpr* to increase. **◆amplificateur** *nm* amplifier. **◆amplification** *nf* (*extension*) increase.
amplitude [ɑ̃plityd] *nf Fig* magnitude.
ampoule [ɑ̃pul] *nf* (*électrique*) (light) bulb; (*aux pieds etc*) blister; (*de médicament*) phial.
ampoulé [ɑ̃pule] *a* turgid.
amputer [ɑ̃pyte] *vt* **1** (*membre*) to amputate; **a. qn de la jambe** to amputate s.o.'s leg. **2** (*texte*) to curtail, cut (**de** by). **◆amputation** *nf* amputation; curtailment.
amuse-gueule [amyzgœl] *nm inv* cocktail snack, appetizer.
amus/er [amyze] *vt* (*divertir*) to amuse, entertain; (*occuper*) to divert the attention of; **— s'a.** *vpr* to enjoy oneself, have fun; (*en chemin*) to dawdle, loiter; **s'a. avec** to play with; **s'a. à faire** to amuse oneself doing. **◆—ant** *a* amusing. **◆—ement** *nm* amusement; (*jeu*) game. **◆amusette** *nf* frivolous pursuit.
amygdale [amidal] *nf* tonsil.
an [ɑ̃] *nm* year; **il a dix ans** he's ten (years old); **par a.** per annum, per year; **bon a., mal a.** putting the good years and the bad together; **Nouvel A.** New Year.
anachronisme [anakrɔnism] *nm* anachronism.
anagramme [anagram] *nf* anagram.
analogie [analɔʒi] *nf* analogy. **◆analogue** *a* similar; – *nm* analogue.
analphabète [analfabɛt] *a & nmf* illiterate. **◆analphabétisme** *nm* illiteracy.
analyse [analiz] *nf* analysis; **a. grammaticale** parsing. **◆analyser** *vt* to analyse; (*phrase*) to parse. **◆analytique** *a* analytic(al).
ananas [anana(s)] *nm* pineapple.
anarchie [anarʃi] *nf* anarchy. **◆anarchique** *a* anarchic. **◆anarchiste** *nmf* anarchist; – *a* anarchistic.
anathème [anatɛm] *nm Rel* anathema.
anatomie [anatɔmi] *nf* anatomy. **◆anatomique** *a* anatomical.
ancestral, -aux [ɑ̃sɛstral, -o] *a* ancestral.
ancêtre [ɑ̃sɛtr] *nm* ancestor.
anche [ɑ̃ʃ] *nf Mus* reed.
anchois [ɑ̃ʃwa] *nm* anchovy.
ancien, -ienne [ɑ̃sjɛ̃, -jɛn] *a* (*vieux*) old; (*meuble*) antique; (*qui n'est plus*) former, ex-, old; (*antique*) ancient; (*dans une fonction*) senior; **a. élève** old boy, *Am* alumnus; **a. combattant** ex-serviceman, *Am* veteran; – *nmf* (*par l'âge*) elder; (*dans une fonction*) senior; **les anciens** (*auteurs, peuples*) the ancients. **◆anciennement** *adv* formerly **◆ancienneté** *nf* age; (*dans une fonction*) seniority.
ancre [ɑ̃kr] *nf* anchor; **jeter l'a.** to (cast) anchor; **lever l'a.** to weigh anchor. **◆ancrer** *vt Nau* to anchor; (*idée*) *Fig* to root, fix; **ancré dans** rooted in.
andouille [ɑ̃duj] *nf* sausage (*made from chitterlings*); **espèce d'a.!** *Fam* (you) nitwit!
âne [ɑn] *nm* (*animal*) donkey, ass; (*personne*) *Péj* ass; **bonnet d'â.** dunce's

cap; **dos d'â.** (*d'une route*) hump; **pont en dos d'â.** humpback bridge.

anéant/ir [aneɑ̃tir] *vt* to annihilate, wipe out, destroy; **— s'a.** *vpr* to vanish. **◆—i** *a* (*épuisé*) exhausted; (*stupéfait*) dismayed; (*accablé*) overwhelmed. **◆—issement** *nm* annihilation; (*abattement*) dejection.

anecdote [anɛkdɔt] *nf* anecdote. **◆anecdotique** *a* anecdotal.

anémie [anemi] *nf* an(a)emia. **◆anémique** *a* an(a)emic. **◆s'anémier** *vpr* to become an(a)emic.

anémone [anemɔn] *nf* anemone.

ânerie [ɑnri] *nf* stupidity; (*action etc*) stupid thing. **◆ânesse** *nf* she-ass.

anesthésie [anɛstezi] *nf* an(a)esthesia; **a. générale/locale** general/local an(a)esthetic. **◆anesthésier** *vt* to an(a)esthetize. **◆anesthésique** *nm* an(a)esthetic.

anfractuosité [ɑ̃fraktɥɔzite] *nf* crevice, cleft.

ange [ɑ̃ʒ] *nm* angel; **aux anges** in seventh heaven. **◆angélique** *a* angelic.

angélus [ɑ̃ʒelys] *nm Rel* angelus.

angine [ɑ̃ʒin] *nf* sore throat; **a. de poitrine** angina (pectoris).

anglais, -aise [ɑ̃glɛ, -ɛz] *a* English; – *nmf* Englishman, Englishwoman; – *nm* (*langue*) English; **filer à l'anglaise** to take French leave.

angle [ɑ̃gl] *nm* (*point de vue*) & *Géom* angle; (*coin*) corner.

Angleterre [ɑ̃glətɛr] *nf* England.

anglican, -ane [ɑ̃glikɑ̃, -an] *a* & *nmf* Anglican.

anglicisme [ɑ̃glisism] *nm* Anglicism. **◆angliciste** *nmf* English specialist.

anglo- [ɑ̃glɔ] *préf* Anglo-. **◆anglo-normand** *a* Anglo-Norman; **îles a.-normandes** Channel Islands. **◆anglophile** *a* & *nmf* anglophile. **◆anglophone** *a* English-speaking; – *nmf* English speaker. **◆anglo-saxon, -onne** *a* & *nmf* Anglo-Saxon.

angoisse [ɑ̃gwas] *nf* anguish. **◆angoissant** *a* distressing. **◆angoissé** *a* (*personne*) in anguish; (*geste, cri*) anguished.

angora [ɑ̃gɔra] *nm* (*laine*) angora.

anguille [ɑ̃gij] *nf* eel.

angulaire [ɑ̃gylɛr] *a* **pierre a.** cornerstone. **◆anguleux, -euse** *a* (*visage*) angular.

anicroche [anikrɔʃ] *nf* hitch, snag.

animal, -aux [animal, -o] *nm* animal; (*personne*) *Péj* brute, animal; – *a* animal.

animer [anime] *vt* (*inspirer*) to animate; (*encourager*) to spur on; (*débat, groupe*) to lead; (*soirée*) to enliven; (*regard*) to light up, brighten up; (*mécanisme*) to actuate, drive; **a. la course** *Sp* to set the pace; **animé de** (*sentiment*) prompted by; **— s'a.** *vpr* (*rue etc*) to come to life; (*yeux*) to light up, brighten up. **◆animé** *a* (*rue*) lively; (*conversation*) animated, lively; (*doué de vie*) animate. **◆animateur, -trice** *nmf TV* compere, *Am* master of ceremonies, emcee; (*de club*) leader, organizer; (*d'entreprise*) driving force, spirit. **◆animation** *nf* (*des rues*) activity; (*de réunion*) liveliness; (*de visage*) brightness; *Cin* animation.

animosité [animɔzite] *nf* animosity.

anis [ani(s)] *nm* (*boisson, parfum*) aniseed. **◆anisette** *nf* (*liqueur*) anisette.

ankylose [ɑ̃kiloz] *nf* stiffening. **◆s'ankylos/er** *vpr* to stiffen up. **◆—é** *a* stiff.

annales [anal] *nfpl* annals.

anneau, -x [ano] *nm* ring; (*de chaîne*) link.

année [ane] *nf* year; **bonne a.!** Happy New Year!

annexe [anɛks] *nf* (*bâtiment*) annex(e); – *a* (*pièces*) appended; **bâtiment a.** annex(e). **◆annexer** *vt* (*pays*) to annex; (*document*) to append. **◆annexion** *nf* annexation.

annihiler [aniile] *vt* to destroy, annihilate.

anniversaire [anivɛrsɛr] *nm* (*d'événement*) anniversary; (*de naissance*) birthday; – *a* anniversary.

annonce [anɔ̃s] *nf* (*avis*) announcement; (*publicitaire*) advertisement; (*indice*) sign; **petites annonces** classified advertisements, small ads. **◆annoncer** *vt* (*signaler*) to announce, report; (*être l'indice de*) to indicate; (*vente*) to advertise; **a. le printemps** to herald spring; **s'a. pluvieux/difficile/***etc* to look like being rainy/difficult/*etc*. **◆annonceur** *nm* advertiser; *Rad TV* announcer.

annonciation [anɔ̃sjasjɔ̃] *nf* Annunciation.

annoter [anɔte] *vt* to annotate. **◆annotation** *nf* annotation.

annuaire [anɥɛr] *nm* yearbook; (*téléphonique*) directory, phone book.

annuel, -elle [anɥɛl] *a* annual, yearly. **◆annuellement** *adv* annually. **◆annuité** *nf* annual instalment.

annulaire [anylɛr] *nm* ring *ou* third finger.

annuler [anyle] *vt* (*visite etc*) to cancel; (*mariage*) to annul; (*jugement*) to quash; **— s'a.** *vpr* to cancel each other out. **◆annulation** *nf* cancellation; annulment; quashing.

anoblir [anɔblir] *vt* to ennoble.

anodin [anɔdɛ̃] *a* harmless; (*remède*) ineffectual.
anomalie [anɔmali] *nf* (*irrégularité*) anomaly; (*difformité*) abnormality.
ânonner [ɑnɔne] *vt* (*en hésitant*) to stumble through; (*d'une voix monotone*) to drone out.
anonymat [anɔnima] *nm* anonymity; **garder l'a.** to remain anonymous. ◆**anonyme** *a* & *nmf* anonymous (person).
anorak [anɔrak] *nm* anorak.
anorexie [anɔrɛksi] *nf* anorexia.
anormal, -aux [anɔrmal, -o] *a* abnormal; (*enfant*) educationally subnormal.
anse [ɑ̃s] *nf* (*de tasse etc*) handle; (*baie*) cove.
antagonisme [ɑ̃tagɔnism] *nm* antagonism. ◆**antagoniste** *a* antagonistic; – *nmf* antagonist.
antan (d') [dɑ̃tɑ̃] *a Litt* of yesteryear.
antarctique [ɑ̃tarktik] *a* antarctic; – *nm* **l'A.** the Antarctic, Antarctica.
antécédent [ɑ̃tesedɑ̃] *nm Gram* antecedent; *pl* past history, antecedents.
antenne [ɑ̃tɛn] *nf TV Rad* aerial, *Am* antenna; (*station*) station; (*d'insecte*) antenna, feeler; **a. chirurgicale** surgical outpost; *Aut* emergency unit; **sur** *ou* **à l'a.** on the air.
antérieur [ɑ̃terjœr] *a* (*précédent*) former, previous, earlier; (*placé devant*) front; **membre a.** forelimb; **a. à** prior to. ◆**antérieurement** *adv* previously. ◆**antériorité** *nf* precedence.
anthologie [ɑ̃tɔlɔʒi] *nf* anthology.
anthropologie [ɑ̃trɔpɔlɔʒi] *nf* anthropology.
anthropophage [ɑ̃trɔpɔfaʒ] *nm* cannibal. ◆**anthropophagie** *nf* cannibalism.
antiaérien, -ienne [ɑ̃tiaerjɛ̃, -jɛn] *a* (*canon*) antiaircraft; (*abri*) air-raid.
antiatomique [ɑ̃tiatɔmik] *a* **abri a.** fallout shelter.
antibiotique [ɑ̃tibjɔtik] *a* & *nm* antibiotic.
antibrouillard [ɑ̃tibrujar] *a* & *nm* **(phare) a.** fog lamp.
anticancéreux, -euse [ɑ̃tikɑ̃serø, -øz] *a* **centre a.** cancer hospital.
antichambre [ɑ̃tiʃɑ̃br] *nf* antechamber, anteroom.
antichoc [ɑ̃tiʃɔk] *a inv* shockproof.
anticip/er [ɑ̃tisipe] *vti* **a. (sur)** to anticipate. ◆**—é** *a* (*retraite etc*) early; (*paiement*) advance; **avec mes remerciements anticipés** thanking you in advance. ◆**anticipation** *nf* anticipation; **par a.** in advance; **d'a.** (*roman etc*) science-fiction.
anticlérical, -aux [ɑ̃tiklerikal, -o] *a* anticlerical.
anticonformiste [ɑ̃tikɔ̃fɔrmist] *a* & *nmf* nonconformist.
anticonstitutionnel, -elle [ɑ̃tikɔ̃stitysjɔnɛl] *a* unconstitutional.
anticorps [ɑ̃tikɔr] *nm* antibody.
anticyclone [ɑ̃tisiklon] *nm* anticyclone.
antidater [ɑ̃tidate] *vt* to backdate, antedate.
antidémocratique [ɑ̃tidemɔkratik] *a* undemocratic.
antidérapant [ɑ̃tiderapɑ̃] *a* non-skid.
antidote [ɑ̃tidɔt] *nm* antidote.
antigel [ɑ̃tiʒɛl] *nm* antifreeze.
Antilles [ɑ̃tij] *nfpl* **les A.** the West Indies. ◆**antillais, -aise** *a* & *nmf* West Indian.
antilope [ɑ̃tilɔp] *nf* antelope.
antimite [ɑ̃timit] *a* mothproof; – *nm* mothproofing agent.
antiparasite [ɑ̃tiparazit] *a* **dispositif a.** *Rad* suppressor.
antipathie [ɑ̃tipati] *nf* antipathy. ◆**antipathique** *a* disagreeable.
antipodes [ɑ̃tipɔd] *nmpl* **aux a.** (*partir*) to the antipodes; **aux a. de** at the opposite end of the world from; *Fig* poles apart from.
antique [ɑ̃tik] *a* ancient. ◆**antiquaire** *nmf* antique dealer. ◆**antiquité** *nf* (*temps, ancienneté*) antiquity; (*objet ancien*) antique; *pl* (*monuments etc*) antiquities.
antirabique [ɑ̃tirabik] *a* (anti-)rabies.
antisémite [ɑ̃tisemit] *a* anti-Semitic. ◆**antisémitisme** *nm* anti-Semitism.
antiseptique [ɑ̃tisɛptik] *a* & *nm* antiseptic.
antisudoral, -aux [ɑ̃tisydɔral, -o] *nm* antiperspirant.
antithèse [ɑ̃titɛz] *nf* antithesis.
antivol [ɑ̃tivɔl] *nm* anti-theft lock *ou* device.
antonyme [ɑ̃tɔnim] *nm* antonym.
antre [ɑ̃tr] *nm* (*de lion etc*) den.
anus [anys] *nm* anus.
Anvers [ɑ̃vɛr(s)] *nm ou f* Antwerp.
anxiété [ɑ̃ksjete] *nf* anxiety. ◆**anxieux, -euse** *a* anxious; – *nmf* worrier.
août [u(t)] *nm* August. ◆**aoûtien, -ienne** [ausjɛ̃, -jɛn] *nmf* August holidaymaker *ou Am* vacationer.
apais/er [apeze] *vt* (*personne*) to appease, calm; (*scrupules, faim*) to appease; (*douleur*) to allay; **— s'a.** *vpr* (*personne*) to calm down. ◆**—ant** *a* soothing. ◆**—ements** *nmpl* reassurances.
apanage [apanaʒ] *nm* privilege, monopoly (de of).
aparté [aparte] *nm Th* aside; (*dans une réunion*) private exchange; **en a.** in private.
apartheid [apartɛd] *nm* apartheid.

apathie [apati] *nf* apathy. ◆**apathique** *a* apathetic, listless.

apatride [apatrid] *nmf* stateless person.

apercevoir* [apɛrsəvwar] *vt* to see, perceive; (*brièvement*) to catch a glimpse of; **s'a. de** to notice, realize. ◆**aperçu** *nm* overall view, general outline; (*intuition*) insight.

apéritif [aperitif] *nm* aperitif. ◆**apéro** *nm* *Fam* aperitif.

apesanteur [apəzɑ̃tœr] *nf* weightlessness.

à-peu-près [apøprɛ] *nm inv* vague approximation.

apeuré [apœre] *a* frightened, scared.

aphone [afɔn] *a* voiceless.

aphorisme [afɔrism] *nm* aphorism.

aphrodisiaque [afrɔdizjak] *a & nm* aphrodisiac.

aphte [aft] *nm* mouth ulcer. ◆**aphteuse** *af* **fièvre a.** foot-and-mouth disease.

apiculture [apikyltyr] *nf* beekeeping.

apit/oyer [apitwaje] *vt* to move (to pity); **s'a. sur** to pity. ◆**—oiement** *nm* pity, commiseration.

aplanir [aplanir] *vt* (*terrain*) to level; (*difficulté*) to iron out, smooth out.

aplat/ir [aplatir] *vt* to flatten (out); **— s'a.** *vpr* (*s'étendre*) to lie flat; (*s'humilier*) to grovel; (*tomber*) *Fam* to fall flat on one's face; **s'a. contre** to flatten oneself against. ◆**—i** *a* flat. ◆**—issement** *nm* (*état*) flatness.

aplomb [aplɔ̃] *nm* self-possession, self-assurance; *Péj* impudence; **d'a.** (*équilibré*) well-balanced; (*sur ses jambes*) steady; (*bien portant*) in good shape; **tomber d'a.** (*soleil*) to beat down.

apocalypse [apɔkalips] *nf* apocalypse; **d'a.** (*vision etc*) apocalyptic. ◆**apocalyptique** *a* apocalyptic.

apogée [apɔʒe] *nm* apogee; *Fig* peak, apogee.

apolitique [apɔlitik] *a* apolitical.

Apollon [apɔlɔ̃] *nm* Apollo.

apologie [apɔlɔʒi] *nf* defence, vindication. ◆**apologiste** *nmf* apologist.

apoplexie [apɔplɛksi] *nf* apoplexy. ◆**apoplectique** *a* apoplectic.

apostolat [apɔstɔla] *nm* (*prosélytisme*) proselytism; (*mission*) *Fig* calling. ◆**apostolique** *a* apostolic.

apostrophe [apɔstrɔf] *nf* **1** (*signe*) apostrophe. **2** (*interpellation*) sharp *ou* rude remark. ◆**apostropher** *vt* to shout at.

apothéose [apɔteoz] *nf* final triumph, apotheosis.

apôtre [apotr] *nm* apostle.

apparaître* [aparɛtr] *vi* (*se montrer, sembler*) to appear.

apparat [apara] *nm* pomp; **d'a.** (*tenue etc*) ceremonial, formal.

appareil [aparɛj] *nm* (*instrument etc*) apparatus; (*électrique*) appliance; *Anat* system; *Tél* telephone; (*avion*) aircraft; (*législatif etc*) *Fig* machinery; **a. (photo)** camera; **a. (auditif)** hearing aid; **a. (dentier)** brace; **qui est à l'a.?** *Tél* who's speaking?

appareiller [apareje] **1** *vi Nau* to get under way. **2** *vt* (*assortir*) to match (up).

apparence [aparɑ̃s] *nf* appearance; (*vestige*) semblance; **en a.** outwardly; **sous l'a. de** under the guise of; **sauver les apparences** to keep up appearances. ◆**apparemment** [-amɑ̃] *adv* apparently. ◆**apparent** *a* apparent; (*ostensible*) conspicuous.

apparent/er (s') [saparɑ̃te] *vpr* (*ressembler*) to be similar *ou* akin (**à** to). ◆**—é** *a* (*allié*) related; (*semblable*) similar.

appariteur [aparitœr] *nm Univ* porter.

apparition [aparisjɔ̃] *nf* appearance; (*spectre*) apparition.

appartement [apartəmɑ̃] *nm* flat, *Am* apartment.

appartenir* [apartənir] **1** *vi* to belong (**à** to); **il vous appartient de** it's your responsibility to. **2 s'a.** *vpr* to be one's own master. ◆**appartenance** *nf* membership (**à** of).

appât [apɑ] *nm* (*amorce*) bait; (*attrait*) lure. ◆**appâter** *vt* (*attirer*) to lure.

appauvrir [apovrir] *vt* to impoverish; **— s'a.** *vpr* to become impoverished *ou* poorer.

appel [apɛl] *nm* (*cri, attrait etc*) call; (*demande pressante*) & *Jur* appeal; *Mil* call-up; **faire l'a.** *Scol* to take the register; *Mil* to have a roll call; **faire a. à** to appeal to, call upon; (*requérir*) to call for.

appel/er [aple] *vt* (*personne, nom etc*) to call; (*en criant*) to call out to; *Mil* to call up; (*nécessiter*) to call for; **a. à l'aide** to call for help; **en a. à** to appeal to; **il est appelé à** (*de hautes fonctions*) he is marked out for; (*témoigner etc*) he is called upon to; **— s'a.** *vpr* to be called; **il s'appelle Paul** his name is Paul. ◆**—é** *nm Mil* conscript. ◆**appellation** *nf* (*nom*) term; **a. contrôlée** *trade name guaranteeing quality of wine.*

appendice [apɛ̃dis] *nm* appendix; (*d'animal*) appendage. ◆**appendicite** *nf* appendicitis.

appentis [apɑ̃ti] *nm* (*bâtiment*) lean-to.

appesantir (s') [sapəzɑ̃tir] *vpr* to become heavier; **s'a. sur** (*sujet*) to dwell upon.

appétit [apeti] *nm* appetite (**de** for); **mettre**

qn en a. to whet s.o.'s appetite; **bon a.!** enjoy your meal! ◆**appétissant** *a* appetizing.

applaud/ir [aplodir] *vti* to applaud, clap; **a. à** (*approuver*) to applaud. ◆**—issements** *nmpl* applause.

applique [aplik] *nf* wall lamp.

appliqu/er [aplike] *vt* to apply (**à** to); (*surnom, baiser, gifle*) to give; (*loi, décision*) to put into effect; **s'a. à** (*un travail*) to apply oneself to; (*concerner*) to apply to; **s'a. à faire** to take pains to do. ◆**—é** *a* (*travailleur*) painstaking; (*sciences*) applied. ◆**applicable** *a* applicable. ◆**application** *nf* application.

appoint [apwɛ̃] *nm* contribution; **faire l'a.** to give the correct money *ou* change.

appointements [apwɛ̃tmɑ̃] *nmpl* salary.

appontement [apɔ̃tmɑ̃] *nm* landing stage.

apport [apɔr] *nm* contribution.

apporter [apɔrte] *vt* to bring.

apposer [apoze] *vt Jur* to affix. ◆**apposition** *nf Gram* apposition.

apprécier [apresje] *vt* (*évaluer*) to appraise; (*aimer, percevoir*) to appreciate. ◆**appréciable** *a* appreciable. ◆**appréciation** *nf* appraisal; appreciation.

appréhender [apreɑ̃de] *vt* (*craindre*) to fear; (*arrêter*) to apprehend. ◆**appréhension** *nf* apprehension.

apprendre* [aprɑ̃dr] *vti* (*étudier*) to learn; (*événement, fait*) to hear of, learn of; (*nouvelle*) to hear; **a. à faire** to learn to do; **a. qch à qn** (*enseigner*) to teach s.o. sth; (*informer*) to tell s.o. sth; **a. à qn à faire** to teach s.o. to do; **a. que** to learn that; (*être informé*) to hear that.

apprenti, -ie [aprɑ̃ti] *nmf* apprentice; (*débutant*) novice. ◆**apprentissage** *nm* apprenticeship; **faire l'a. de** *Fig* to learn the experience of.

apprêt/er [aprete] *vt*, **— s'a.** *vpr* to prepare. ◆**—é** *a Fig* affected.

apprivois/er [aprivwaze] *vt* to tame; **— s'a.** *vpr* to become tame. ◆**—é** *a* tame.

approbation [aprɔbasjɔ̃] *nf* approval. ◆**approbateur, -trice** *a* approving.

approche [aprɔʃ] *nf* approach. ◆**approch/er** *vt* (*chaise etc*) to bring up, draw up (**de** to, close to); (*personne*) to approach, come close to; *— vi* to approach, draw near(er); **a. de, s'a. de** to approach, come close(r) *ou* near(er) to. ◆**—ant** *a* similar. ◆**—é** *a* approximate. ◆**—able** *a* approachable.

approfond/ir [aprɔfɔ̃dir] *vt* (*trou etc*) to deepen; (*question*) to go into thoroughly; (*mystère*) to plumb the depths of. ◆**—i** *a* thorough. ◆**—issement** *nm* deepening; (*examen*) thorough examination.

approprié [aprɔprije] *a* appropriate.

approprier (s') [saprɔprije] *vpr* **s'a. qch** to appropriate sth.

approuver [apruve] *vt* (*autoriser*) to approve; (*apprécier*) to approve of.

approvisionn/er [aprɔvizjɔne] *vt* (*ville etc*) to supply (with provisions); (*magasin*) to stock; **— s'a.** *vpr* to stock up (**de** with), get one's supplies (**de** of). ◆**—ements** *nmpl* stocks, supplies.

approximat/if, -ive [aprɔksimatif, -iv] *a* approximate. ◆**—ivement** *adv* approximately. ◆**approximation** *nf* approximation.

appui [apɥi] *nm* support; (*pour coude etc*) rest; (*de fenêtre*) sill; **à hauteur d'a.** breast-high. ◆**appuie-tête** *nm inv* headrest. ◆**appuyer** *vt* (*soutenir*) to support; (*accentuer*) to stress; **a. qch sur** (*poser*) to lean *ou* rest sth on; (*presser*) to press sth on; *— vi* **a. sur** to rest on; (*bouton etc*) to press (on); (*mot, élément etc*) to stress; **s'a. sur** to lean on, rest on; (*compter*) to rely on; (*se baser*) to base oneself on.

âpre [ɑpr] *a* harsh, rough; **a. au gain** grasping.

après [aprɛ] *prép* (*temps*) after; (*espace*) beyond; **a. un an** after a year; **a. le pont** beyond the bridge; **a. coup** after the event; **a. avoir mangé** after eating; **a. qu'il t'a vu** after he saw you; **d'a.** (*selon*) according to, from; *— adv* after(wards); **l'année d'a.** the following year; **et a.?** and then what?

après-demain [aprɛdmɛ̃] *adv* the day after tomorrow. ◆**a.-guerre** *nm* post-war period; **d'a.-guerre** post-war. ◆**a.-midi** *nm ou f inv* afternoon. ◆**a.-shampooing** *nm* (hair) conditioner. ◆**a.-ski** *nm* ankle boot, snow boot.

a priori [aprijɔri] *adv* at the very outset, without going into the matter; *— nm inv* premiss.

à-propos [aprɔpo] *nm* timeliness, aptness.

apte [apt] *a* suited (**à** to), capable (**à** of). ◆**aptitude** *nf* aptitude, capacity (**à, pour** for).

aquarelle [akwarɛl] *nf* watercolour, aquarelle.

aquarium [akwarjɔm] *nm* aquarium.

aquatique [akwatik] *a* aquatic.

aqueduc [akdyk] *nm* aqueduct.

aquilin [akilɛ̃] *a* aquiline.

arabe [arab] *a & nmf* Arab; *— a & nm* (*langue*) Arabic; **chiffres arabes** Arabic

numerals; **désert a.** Arabian desert. ◆**Arabie** *nf* Arabia; **A. Séoudite** Saudi Arabia.
arabesque [arabɛsk] *nf* arabesque.
arable [arabl] *a* arable.
arachide [araʃid] *nf* peanut, groundnut.
araignée [areɲe] *nf* spider.
arbalète [arbalɛt] *nf* crossbow.
arbitraire [arbitrɛr] *a* arbitrary.
arbitre [arbitr] *nm Jur* arbitrator; (*maître absolu*) arbiter; *Fb* referee; *Tennis* umpire; **libre a.** free will. ◆**arbitr/er** *vt* to arbitrate; to referee; to umpire. ◆**—age** *nm* arbitration; refereeing; umpiring.
arborer [arbɔre] *vt* (*insigne, vêtement*) to sport, display.
arbre [arbr] *nm* tree; *Aut* shaft, axle. ◆**arbrisseau, -x** *nm* shrub. ◆**arbuste** *nm* (small) shrub, bush.
arc [ark] *nm* (*arme*) bow; (*voûte*) arch; *Math* arc; **tir à l'a.** archery. ◆**arcade** *nf* arch(way); *pl* arcade.
arc-boutant [arkbutɑ̃] *nm* (*pl* **arcs-boutants**) flying buttress. ◆**s'arc-bouter** *vpr* **s'a. à** *ou* **contre** to brace oneself against.
arceau, -x [arso] *nm* (*de voûte*) arch.
arc-en-ciel [arkɑ̃sjɛl] *nm* (*pl* **arcs-en-ciel**) rainbow.
archaïque [arkaik] *a* archaic.
archange [arkɑ̃ʒ] *nm* archangel.
arche [arʃ] *nf* (*voûte*) arch; **l'a. de Noé** Noah's ark.
archéologie [arkeɔlɔʒi] *nf* arch(a)eology. ◆**archéologue** *nmf* arch(a)eologist.
archer [arʃe] *nm* archer, bowman.
archet [arʃɛ] *nm Mus* bow.
archétype [arketip] *nm* archetype.
archevêque [arʃəvɛk] *nm* archbishop.
archicomble [arʃikɔ̃bl] *a* jam-packed.
archipel [arʃipɛl] *nm* archipelago.
archiplein [arʃiplɛ̃] *a* chock-full, chock-a-block.
architecte [arʃitɛkt] *nm* architect. ◆**architecture** *nf* architecture.
archives [arʃiv] *nfpl* archives, records. ◆**archiviste** *nmf* archivist.
arctique [arktik] *a* arctic; – *nm* **l'A.** the Arctic.
ardent [ardɑ̃] *a* (*chaud*) burning, scorching; (*actif, passionné*) ardent, fervent; (*empressé*) eager. ◆**ardemment** [-amɑ̃] *adv* eagerly, fervently. ◆**ardeur** *nf* heat; (*énergie*) ardour, fervour.
ardoise [ardwaz] *nf* slate.
ardu [ardy] *a* arduous, difficult.
are [ar] *nm* (*mesure*) 100 square metres.
arène [arɛn] *nf Hist* arena; (*pour taureaux*) bullring; *pl Hist* amphitheatre; bullring.
arête [arɛt] *nf* (*de poisson*) bone; (*de cube etc*) & *Géog* ridge.
argent [arʒɑ̃] *nm* (*métal*) silver; (*monnaie*) money; **a. comptant** cash. ◆**argenté** *a* (*plaqué*) silver-plated; (*couleur*) silvery. ◆**argenterie** *nf* silverware.
Argentine [arʒɑ̃tin] *nf* Argentina. ◆**argentin, -ine** *a* & *nmf* Argentinian.
argile [arʒil] *nf* clay. ◆**argileux, -euse** *a* clayey.
argot [argo] *nm* slang. ◆**argotique** *a* (*terme*) slang.
arguer [argɥe] *vi* **a. de qch** to put forward sth as an argument; **a. que** (*protester*) to protest that. ◆**argumentation** *nf* argumentation, arguments. ◆**argumenter** *vi* to argue.
argument [argymɑ̃] *nm* argument.
argus [argys] *nm* guide to secondhand cars.
argutie [argysi] *nf* specious argument, quibble.
aride [arid] *a* arid, barren.
aristocrate [aristɔkrat] *nmf* aristocrat. ◆**aristocratie** [-asi] *nf* aristocracy. ◆**aristocratique** *a* aristocratic.
arithmétique [aritmetik] *nf* arithmetic; – *a* arithmetical.
arlequin [arləkɛ̃] *nm* harlequin.
armateur [armatœr] *nm* shipowner.
armature [armatyr] *nf* (*charpente*) framework; (*de lunettes, tente*) frame.
arme [arm] *nf* arm, weapon; **a. à feu** firearm; **carrière des armes** military career. ◆**arm/er** *vt* (*personne etc*) to arm (**de** with); (*fusil*) to cock; (*appareil photo*) to wind on; (*navire*) to equip; (*béton*) to reinforce; **— s'a.** *vpr* to arm oneself (**de** with). ◆**—ement(s)** *nm(pl)* arms.
armée [arme] *nf* army; **a. active/de métier** regular/professional army; **a. de l'air** air force.
armistice [armistis] *nm* armistice.
armoire [armwar] *nf* cupboard, *Am* closet; (*penderie*) wardrobe, *Am* closet; **a. à pharmacie** medicine cabinet.
armoiries [armwari] *nfpl* (coat of) arms.
armure [armyr] *nf* armour.
armurier [armyrje] *nm* gunsmith.
arôme [arom] *nm* aroma. ◆**aromate** *nm* spice. ◆**aromatique** *a* aromatic.
arpent/er [arpɑ̃te] *vt* (*terrain*) to survey; (*trottoir etc*) to pace up and down. ◆**—eur** *nm* (land) surveyor.
arqué [arke] *a* arched, curved; (*jambes*) bandy.

arrache-pied (d') [daraʃpje] *adv* unceasingly, relentlessly.

arrach/er [araʃe] *vt* (*clou, dent etc*) to pull out; (*cheveux, page*) to tear out, pull out; (*plante*) to pull up; (*masque*) to tear off, pull off; **a. qch à qn** to snatch sth from s.o.; (*aveu, argent*) to force sth out of s.o.; **a. un bras à qn** (*obus etc*) to blow s.o.'s arm off; **a. qn de son lit** to drag s.o. out of bed. ◆**—age** *nm* (*de plante*) pulling up.

arraisonner [arezɔne] *vt* (*navire*) to board and examine.

arrang/er [arɑ̃ʒe] *vt* (*chambre, visite etc*) to arrange, fix up; (*voiture, texte*) to put right; (*différend*) to settle; **a. qn** (*maltraiter*) *Fam* to fix s.o.; **ça m'arrange** that suits me (fine); **— s'a.** *vpr* (*se réparer*) to be put right; (*se mettre d'accord*) to come to an agreement *ou* arrangement; (*finir bien*) to turn out fine; **s'a. pour faire** to arrange to do, manage to do. ◆**—eant** *a* accommodating. ◆**—ement** *nm* arrangement.

arrestation [arɛstɑsjɔ̃] *nf* arrest.

arrêt [arɛ] *nm* (*halte, endroit*) stop; (*action*) stopping; *Méd* arrest; *Jur* decree; **temps d'a.** pause; **à l'a.** stationary; **a. de travail** (*grève*) stoppage; (*congé*) sick leave; **sans a.** constantly, non-stop.

arrêté [arete] *nm* order, decision.

arrêt/er [arete] *vt* to stop; (*appréhender*) to arrest; (*regard, jour*) to fix; (*plan*) to draw up; – *vi* to stop; **il n'arrête pas de critiquer/***etc* he doesn't stop criticizing/*etc*, he's always criticizing/*etc*; **— s'a.** *vpr* to stop; **s'a. de faire** to stop doing. ◆**—é** *a* (*projet*) fixed; (*volonté*) firm.

arrhes [ar] *nfpl Fin* deposit.

arrière [arjɛr] *adv* **en a.** (*marcher*) backwards; (*rester*) behind; (*regarder*) back; **en a. de qn/qch** behind s.o./sth; – *nm & a inv* rear, back; – *nm Fb* (full) back; **faire marche a.** to reverse, back.

arrière-boutique [arjɛrbutik] *nm* back room (*of a shop*). ◆**a.-garde** *nf* rearguard. ◆**a.-goût** *nm* aftertaste. ◆**a.-grand-mère** *nf* great-grand-mother. ◆**a.-grand-père** *nm* (*pl* **arrière-grands-pères**) great-grand-father. ◆**a.-pays** *nm* hinterland. ◆**a.-pensée** *nf* ulterior motive. ◆**a.-plan** *nm* background. ◆**a.-saison** *nf* end of season, (late) autumn. ◆**a.-train** *nm* hindquarters.

arriéré [arjere] **1** *a* (*enfant*) (mentally) retarded; (*idée*) backward. **2** *nm* (*dette*) arrears.

arrimer [arime] *vt* (*fixer*) to rope down, secure.

arriv/er [arive] *vi* (*aux* **être**) (*venir*) to arrive, come; (*réussir*) to succeed; (*survenir*) to happen; **a. à** (*atteindre*) to reach; **a. à faire** to manage to do, succeed in doing; **a. à qn** to happen to s.o.; **il m'arrive d'oublier/***etc* I happen (sometimes) to forget/*etc*, I (sometimes) forget/*etc*; **en a. à faire** to get to the point of doing. ◆**—ant, -ante** *nmf* new arrival. ◆**—ée** *nf* arrival; *Sp* (winning) post. ◆**—age** *nm* consignment. ◆**arriviste** *nmf Péj* social climber, self-seeker.

arrogant [arɔgɑ̃] *a* arrogant. ◆**arrogance** *nf* arrogance.

arroger (s') [sarɔʒe] *vpr* (*droit etc*) to assume (falsely).

arrond/ir [arɔ̃dir] *vt* to make round; (*somme, chiffre*) to round off. ◆**—i** *a* rounded.

arrondissement [arɔ̃dismɑ̃] *nm* (*d'une ville*) district.

arros/er [aroze] *vt* (*terre*) to water; (*repas*) to wash down; (*succès*) to drink to. ◆**—age** *nm* watering; *Fam* booze-up, celebration. ◆**arrosoir** *nm* watering can.

arsenal, -aux [arsənal, -o] *nm Nau* dockyard; *Mil* arsenal.

arsenic [arsənik] *nm* arsenic.

art [ar] *nm* art; **film/critique d'a.** art film/critic; **arts ménagers** domestic science.

artère [artɛr] *nf Anat* artery; *Aut* main road. ◆**artériel, -elle** *a* arterial.

artichaut [artiʃo] *nm* artichoke.

article [artikl] *nm* (*de presse, de commerce*) & *Gram* article; (*dans un contrat, catalogue*) item; **a. de fond** feature (article); **articles de toilette/de voyage** toilet/travel requisites; **à l'a. de la mort** at death's door.

articuler [artikyle] *vt* (*mot etc*) to articulate; **— s'a.** *vpr Anat* to articulate; *Fig* to connect. ◆**articulation** *nf Ling* articulation; *Anat* joint; **a. du doigt** knuckle.

artifice [artifis] *nm* trick, contrivance; **feu d'a.** (*spectacle*) fireworks, firework display.

artificiel, -elle [artifisjɛl] *a* artificial. ◆**artificiellement** *adv* artificially.

artillerie [artijri] *nf* artillery. ◆**artilleur** *nm* gunner.

artisan [artizɑ̃] *nm* craftsman, artisan. ◆**artisanal, -aux** *a* (*métier*) craftsman's. ◆**artisanat** *nm* (*métier*) craftsman's trade; (*classe*) artisan class.

artiste [artist] *nmf* artist; *Th Mus Cin* performer, artist. ◆**artistique** *a* artistic.

as [ɑs] *nm* (*carte, champion*) ace; **a. du volant** crack driver.

ascendant [asɑ̃dɑ̃] *a* ascending, upward; – *nm* ascendancy, power; *pl* ancestors. ◆**ascendance** *nf* ancestry.
ascenseur [asɑ̃sœr] *nm* lift, *Am* elevator.
ascension [asɑ̃sjɔ̃] *nf* ascent; **l'A.** Ascension Day.
ascète [asɛt] *nmf* ascetic. ◆**ascétique** *a* ascetic. ◆**ascétisme** *nm* asceticism.
Asie [azi] *nf* Asia. ◆**Asiate** *nmf* Asian. ◆**asiatique** *a* & *nmf* Asian, Asiatic.
asile [azil] *nm* (*abri*) refuge, shelter; (*pour vieillards*) home; *Pol* asylum; **a. (d'aliénés)** *Péj* (lunatic) asylum; **a. de paix** haven of peace.
aspect [aspɛ] *nm* (*vue*) sight; (*air*) appearance; (*perspective*) & *Gram* aspect.
asperge [aspɛrʒ] *nf* asparagus.
asperger [aspɛrʒe] *vt* to spray, sprinkle (**de** with).
aspérité [asperite] *nf* rugged edge, bump.
asphalte [asfalt] *nm* asphalt.
asphyxie [asfiksi] *nf* suffocation. ◆**asphyxier** *vt* to suffocate, asphyxiate.
aspic [aspik] *nm* (*vipère*) asp.
aspirant [aspirɑ̃] *nm* (*candidat*) candidate.
aspirateur [aspiratœr] *nm* vacuum cleaner, hoover®; **passer (à) l'a.** to vacuum, hoover.
aspir/er [aspire] *vt* (*respirer*) to breathe in, inhale; (*liquide*) to suck up; **a. à** to aspire to. ◆**—é** *a Ling* aspirate(d). ◆**aspiration** *nf* inhaling; suction; (*ambition*) aspiration.
aspirine [aspirin] *nf* aspirin.
assagir (s') [sasaʒir] *vpr* to sober (down), settle down.
assaill/ir [asajir] *vt* to assault, attack; **a. de** (*questions etc*) to assail with. ◆**—ant** *nm* assailant, attacker.
assainir [asenir] *vt* (*purifier*) to clean up; *Fin* to stabilize.
assaisonn/er [asezɔne] *vt* to season. ◆**—ement** *nm* seasoning.
assassin [asasɛ̃] *nm* murderer; assassin. ◆**assassinat** *nm* murder; assassination. ◆**assassiner** *vt* to murder; (*homme politique etc*) to assassinate.
assaut [aso] *nm* assault, onslaught; **prendre d'a.** to (take by) storm.
assécher [aseʃe] *vt* to drain.
assemblée [asɑ̃ble] *nf* (*personnes réunies*) gathering; (*réunion*) meeting; *Pol Jur* assembly; (*de fidèles*) *Rel* congregation.
assembl/er [asɑ̃ble] *vt* to assemble, put together; **— s'a.** *vpr* to assemble, gather. ◆**—age** *nm* (*montage*) assembly; (*réunion d'objets*) collection.
asséner [asene] *vt* (*coup*) to deal, strike.
assentiment [asɑ̃timɑ̃] *nm* assent, consent.
asseoir* [aswar] *vt* (*personne*) to sit (down), seat (**sur** on); (*fondations*) to lay; (*autorité, réputation*) to establish; **a. sur** (*théorie etc*) to base on; **— s'a.** *vpr* to sit (down).
assermenté [asɛrmɑ̃te] *a* sworn.
assertion [asɛrsjɔ̃] *nf* assertion.
asserv/ir [asɛrvir] *vt* to enslave. ◆**—issement** *nm* enslavement.
assez [ase] *adv* enough; **a. de pain/de gens** enough bread/people; **j'en ai a.** I've had enough; **a. grand/intelligent/***etc* (*suffisamment*) big/clever/*etc* enough (**pour** to); **a. fatigué/***etc* (*plutôt*) fairly *ou* rather *ou* quite tired/*etc*.
assidu [asidy] *a* (*appliqué*) assiduous, diligent; **a. auprès de** attentive to. ◆**assiduité** *nf* assiduousness, diligence; *pl* (*empressement*) attentiveness. ◆**assidûment** *adv* assiduously.
assiég/er [asjeʒe] *vt* (*ville*) to besiege; (*guichet*) to mob, crowd round; (*importuner*) to pester, harry; **assiégé de** (*demandes*) besieged with; (*maux*) beset by. ◆**—eant, -eante** *nmf* besieger.
assiette [asjɛt] *nf* **1** (*récipient*) plate; **a. anglaise** *Culin* (assorted) cold meats, *Am* cold cuts. **2** (*à cheval*) seat; **il n'est pas dans son a.** he's feeling out of sorts.
assigner [asiɲe] *vt* (*attribuer*) to assign; *Jur* to summon, subpoena. ◆**assignation** *nf Jur* subpoena, summons.
assimiler [asimile] *vt* to assimilate; **— s'a.** *vpr* (*immigrants*) to assimilate, become assimilated (**à** with). ◆**assimilation** *nf* assimilation.
assis [asi] *a* sitting (down), seated; (*caractère*) settled; (*situation*) stable, secure.
assise [asiz] *nf* (*base*) *Fig* foundation; *pl Jur* assizes; *Pol* congress; **cour d'assises** court of assizes.
assistance [asistɑ̃s] *nf* **1** (*assemblée*) audience; (*nombre de personnes présentes*) attendance, turn-out. **2** (*aide*) assistance; **l'A. (publique)** the child care service; **enfant de l'A.** child in care. ◆**assist/er 1** *vt* (*aider*) to assist, help. **2** *vi* **a. à** (*réunion, cours etc*) to attend, be present at; (*accident*) to witness. ◆**—ant, -ante** *nmf* assistant; – *nmpl* (*spectateurs*) members of the audience; (*témoins*) those present; **assistante sociale** social worker; **assistante maternelle** mother's help.
associ/er [asɔsje] *vt* to associate (**à** with); **a. qn à** (*ses travaux, profits*) to involve s.o. in; **s'a. à** (*collaborer*) to associate with, become associated with; (*aux vues ou au chagrin de qn*) to share; (*s'harmoniser*) to combine

with. ◆**—é, -ée** *nmf* partner, associate; – *a* associate. ◆**association** *nf* association; (*amitié, alliance*) partnership, association.

assoiffé [aswafe] *a* thirsty (**de** for).

assombrir [asɔ̃brir] *vt* (*obscurcir*) to darken; (*attrister*) to cast a cloud over, fill with gloom; **— s'a.** *vpr* to darken; to cloud over.

assomm/er [asɔme] *vt* (*animal*) to stun, brain; (*personne*) to knock unconscious; (*ennuyer*) to bore stiff. ◆**—ant** *a* tiresome, boring.

assomption [asɔ̃psjɔ̃] *nf Rel* Assumption.

assort/ir [asɔrtir] *vt*, **— s'a.** *vpr* to match. ◆**—i** *a* **bien a.** (*magasin*) well-stocked; – *apl* (*objets semblables*) matching; (*fromages etc variés*) assorted; **époux bien assortis** well-matched couple. ◆**—iment** *nm* assortment.

assoup/ir [asupir] *vt* (*personne*) to make drowsy; (*douleur, sentiment etc*) *Fig* to dull; **— s'a.** *vpr* to doze off; *Fig* to subside. ◆**—i** *a* (*personne*) drowsy. ◆**—issement** *nm* drowsiness.

assoupl/ir [asuplir] *vt* (*étoffe, muscles*) to make supple; (*corps*) to limber up; (*caractère*) to soften; (*règles*) to ease, relax. ◆**—issement** *nm* **exercices d'a.** limbering up exercises.

assourd/ir [asurdir] *vt* (*personne*) to deafen; (*son*) to muffle. ◆**—issant** *a* deafening.

assouvir [asuvir] *vt* to appease, satisfy.

assujett/ir [asyʒetir] *vt* (*soumettre*) to subject (**à** to); (*peuple*) to subjugate; (*fixer*) to secure; **s'a. à** to subject oneself to, submit to. ◆**—issant** *a* (*travail*) constraining. ◆**—issement** *nm* subjection; (*contrainte*) constraint.

assumer [asyme] *vt* (*tâche, rôle*) to assume, take on; (*emploi*) to take up, assume; (*remplir*) to fill, hold.

assurance [asyrɑ̃s] *nf* (*aplomb*) (self-)assurance; (*promesse*) assurance; (*contrat*) insurance; **a. au tiers/tous risques** third-party/comprehensive insurance; **assurances sociales** = national insurance, *Am* = social security.

assur/er [asyre] *vt* (*rendre sûr*) to ensure, *Am* insure; (*par un contrat*) to insure; (*travail etc*) to carry out; (*fixer*) to secure; **a. à qn que** to assure s.o. that; **a. qn de qch, a. qch à qn** to assure s.o. of sth; **— s'a.** *vpr* (*se procurer*) to ensure, secure; (*par un contrat*) to insure oneself, get insured (**contre** against); **s'a. que/de** to make sure that/of. ◆**—é, -ée** *a* (*succès*) assured, certain; (*pas*) firm, secure; (*air*) (self-)assured, (self-)confident; – *nmf* policyholder, insured person. ◆**—ément** *adv* certainly, assuredly. ◆**assureur** *nm* insurer.

astérisque [asterisk] *nm* asterisk.

asthme [asm] *nm* asthma. ◆**asthmatique** *a & nmf* asthmatic.

asticot [astiko] *nm* maggot, worm.

astiquer [astike] *vt* to polish.

astre [astr] *nm* star.

astreindre* [astrɛ̃dr] *vt* **a. à** (*discipline*) to compel to accept; **a. à faire** to compel to do. ◆**astreignant** *a* exacting ◆**astreinte** *nf* constraint.

astrologie [astrɔlɔʒi] *nf* astrology. ◆**astrologue** *nm* astrologer.

astronaute [astrɔnot] *nmf* astronaut. ◆**astronautique** *nf* space travel.

astronomie [astrɔnɔmi] *nf* astronomy. ◆**astronome** *nm* astronomer. ◆**astronomique** *a* astronomical.

astuce [astys] *nf* (*pour faire qch*) knack, trick; (*invention*) gadget; (*plaisanterie*) clever joke, wisecrack; (*finesse*) astuteness; **les astuces du métier** the tricks of the trade. ◆**astucieux, -euse** *a* clever, astute.

atelier [atəlje] *nm* (*d'ouvrier*) workshop; (*de peintre*) studio.

atermoyer [atermwaje] *vi* to procrastinate.

athée [ate] *a* atheistic; – *nmf* atheist. ◆**athéisme** *nm* atheism.

Athènes [aten] *nm ou f* Athens.

athlète [atlet] *nmf* athlete. ◆**athlétique** *a* athletic. ◆**athlétisme** *nm* athletics.

atlantique [atlɑ̃tik] *a* Atlantic; – *nm* **l'A.** the Atlantic.

atlas [atlɑs] *nm* atlas.

atmosphère [atmɔsfer] *nf* atmosphere. ◆**atmosphérique** *a* atmospheric.

atome [atom] *nm* atom. ◆**atomique** [atɔmik] *a* atomic; **bombe a.** atom *ou* atomic bomb.

atomis/er [atɔmize] *vt* (*liquide*) to spray; (*région*) to destroy (*by atomic weapons*). ◆**—eur** *nm* spray.

atone [atɔn] *a* (*personne*) lifeless; (*regard*) vacant.

atours [atur] *nmpl Hum* finery.

atout [atu] *nm* trump (card); (*avantage*) *Fig* trump card, asset; **l'a. est cœur** hearts are trumps.

âtre [ɑtr] *nm* (*foyer*) hearth.

atroce [atrɔs] *a* atrocious; (*crime*) heinous, atrocious. ◆**atrocité** *nf* atrociousness; *pl* (*actes*) atrocities.

atrophie [atrɔfi] *nf* atrophy. ◆**atrophié** *a* atrophied.

attabl/er (s') [satable] *vpr* to sit down at the table. ◆**—é** *a* (seated) at the table.

attache [ataʃ] *nf* (*objet*) attachment, fastening; *pl* (*liens*) links.

attach/er [ataʃe] *vt* (*lier*) to tie (up), attach (**à** to); (*boucler, fixer*) to fasten; **a. du prix/un sens à qch** to attach great value/a meaning to sth; **cette obligation m'attache à lui** this obligation binds me to him; **s'a. à** (*adhérer*) to stick to; (*se lier*) to become attached to; (*se consacrer*) to apply oneself to. ◆**—ant** *a* (*enfant etc*) engaging, appealing. ◆**—é, -ée** *nmf* (*personne*) *Pol Mil* attaché. ◆**—ement** *nm* attachment, affection.

attaque [atak] *nf* attack; **a. aérienne** air raid; **d'a.** in tip-top shape, on top form. ◆**attaqu/er** *vt*, **s'a. à** to attack; (*difficulté, sujet*) to tackle; – *vi* to attack. ◆**—ant, -ante** *nmf* attacker.

attard/er (s') [satarde] *vpr* (*chez qn*) to linger (on), stay on; (*en chemin*) to loiter, dawdle; **s'a. sur** *ou* **à** (*détails etc*) to linger over; **s'a. derrière qn** to lag behind s.o. ◆**—é** *a* (*enfant etc*) backward; (*passant*) late.

atteindre* [atɛ̃dr] *vt* (*parvenir à*) to reach; (*idéal*) to attain; (*blesser*) to hit, wound; (*toucher*) to affect; (*offenser*) to hurt, wound; **être atteint de** (*maladie*) to be suffering from.

atteinte [atɛ̃t] *nf* attack; **porter a. à** to attack, undermine; **a. à** (*honneur*) slur on; **hors d'a.** (*objet, personne*) out of reach; (*réputation*) unassailable.

attel/er [atle] *vt* (*bêtes*) to harness, hitch up; (*remorque*) to couple; **s'a. à** (*travail etc*) to apply oneself to. ◆**—age** *nm* harnessing; coupling; (*bêtes*) team.

attenant [atnɑ̃] *a* **a. (à)** adjoining.

attend/re [atɑ̃dr] *vt* to wait for, await; (*escompter*) to expect (**de** of, from); **elle attend un bébé** she's expecting a baby; – *vi* to wait; **s'a. à** to expect; **a. d'être informé** to wait to be informed; **a. que qn vienne** to wait for s.o. to come, wait until s.o. comes; **faire a. qn** to keep s.o. waiting; **se faire a.** (*réponse, personne etc*) to be a long time coming; **attends voir** *Fam* let me see; **en attendant** meanwhile; **en attendant que** (+ *sub*) until. ◆**—u** *a* (*avec joie*) eagerly-awaited; (*prévu*) expected; – *prép* considering; **a. que** considering that.

attendr/ir [atɑ̃drir] *vt* (*émouvoir*) to move (to compassion); (*viande*) to tenderize; — **s'a.** *vpr* to be moved (**sur** by). ◆**—i** *a* compassionate. ◆**—issant** *a* moving. ◆**—issement** *nm* compassion.

attentat [atɑ̃ta] *nm* attempt (*on s.o.'s life*), murder attempt; *Fig* crime, outrage (**à** against); **a. (à la bombe)** (bomb) attack. ◆**attenter** *vi* **a. à** (*la vie de qn*) to make an attempt on; *Fig* to attack.

attente [atɑ̃t] *nf* (*temps*) wait(ing); (*espérance*) expectation(s); **une a. prolongée** a long wait; **être dans l'a. de** to be waiting for; **salle d'a.** waiting room.

attentif, -ive [atɑ̃tif, -iv] *a* (*personne*) attentive; (*travail, examen*) careful; **a. à** (*plaire etc*) anxious to; (*ses devoirs etc*) mindful of. ◆**attentivement** *adv* attentively.

attention [atɑ̃sjɔ̃] *nf* attention; *pl* (*égards*) consideration; **faire** *ou* **prêter a. à** (*écouter, remarquer*) to pay attention to; **faire a. à/que** (*prendre garde*) to be careful of/that; **a.!** look out!, be careful!; **a. à la voiture!** mind *ou* watch the car! ◆**attentionné** *a* considerate.

atténu/er [atenɥe] *vt* to attenuate, mitigate; — **s'a.** *vpr* to subside. ◆**—antes** *afpl* **circonstances a.** extenuating circumstances.

atterrer [atere] *vt* to dismay.

atterr/ir [aterir] *vi Av* to land. ◆**—issage** *nm Av* landing; **a. forcé** crash *ou* emergency landing.

attester [ateste] *vt* to testify to; **a. que** to testify that. ◆**attestation** *nf* (*document*) declaration, certificate.

attifer [atife] *vt Fam Péj* to dress up, rig out.

attirail [atiraj] *nm* (*équipement*) *Fam* gear.

attir/er [atire] *vt* (*faire venir*) to attract, draw; (*plaire à*) to attract; (*attention*) to draw (**sur** on); **a. qch à qn** (*causer*) to bring s.o. sth; (*gloire etc*) to win *ou* earn s.o. sth; **a. dans** (*coin, guet-apens*) to draw into; — **s'a.** *vpr* (*ennuis etc*) to bring upon oneself; (*sympathie de qn*) to win; **a. sur soi** (*colère de qn*) to bring down upon oneself. ◆**—ant** *a* attractive. ◆**attirance** *nf* attraction.

attiser [atize] *vt* (*feu*) to poke; (*sentiment*) *Fig* to rouse.

attitré [atitre] *a* (*représentant*) appointed; (*marchand*) regular.

attitude [atityd] *nf* attitude; (*maintien*) bearing.

attraction [atraksjɔ̃] *nf* attraction.

attrait [atrɛ] *nm* attraction.

attrape [atrap] *nf* trick. ◆**a.-nigaud** *nm* con, trick.

attraper [atrape] *vt* (*ballon, maladie, voleur, train etc*) to catch; (*accent, contravention etc*) to pick up; **se laisser a.** (*duper*) to get taken in *ou* tricked; **se faire a.** (*gronder*) *Fam* to get a telling off. ◆**attrapade** *nf* (*gronderie*) *Fam* telling off.

attrayant [atrɛjɑ̃] *a* attractive.

attribuer [atribɥe] *vt* (*donner*) to assign, allot (**à** to); (*imputer, reconnaître*) to attribute, ascribe (**à** to); (*décerner*) to grant, award (**à** to). ◆**attribuable** *a* attributable. ◆**attribution** *nf* assignment; attribution; (*de prix*) awarding; *pl* (*compétence*) powers.

attribut [atriby] *nm* attribute.

attrister [atriste] *vt* to sadden.

attroup/er [atrupe] *vt*, **— s'a.** *vpr* to gather. ◆**—ement** *nm* gathering, (disorderly) crowd.

au [o] *voir* **à**.

aubaine [obɛn] *nf* **(bonne) a.** stroke of good luck, godsend.

aube [ob] *nf* dawn; **dès l'a.** at the crack of dawn.

aubépine [obepin] *nf* hawthorn.

auberge [obɛrʒ] *nf* inn; **a. de jeunesse** youth hostel. ◆**aubergiste** *nmf* innkeeper.

aubergine [obɛrʒin] *nf* aubergine, eggplant.

aucun, -une [okœ̃, -yn] *a* no, not any; **il n'a a. talent** he has no talent, he doesn't have any talent; **a. professeur n'est venu** no teacher has come; *– pron* none, not any; **il n'en a a.** he has none (at all), he doesn't have any (at all); **plus qu'a.** more than any(one); **d'aucuns** some (people). ◆**aucunement** *adv* not at all.

audace [odas] *nf* (*courage*) daring, boldness; (*impudence*) audacity; *pl* daring innovations. ◆**audacieux, -euse** *a* daring, bold.

au-dedans, au-dehors, au-delà *voir* **dedans** *etc*.

au-dessous [odsu] *adv* (*en bas*) (down) below, underneath; (*moins*) below, under; (*à l'étage inférieur*) downstairs; *– prép* **au-d. de** (*arbre etc*) below, under, beneath; (*âge, prix*) under; (*température*) below; **au-d. de sa tâche** not up to *ou* unequal to one's task.

au-dessus [odsy] *adv* above; over; on top; (*à l'étage supérieur*) upstairs; *– prép* **au-d. de** above; (*âge, température, prix*) over; (*posé sur*) on top of.

au-devant de [odvɑ̃də] *prép* **aller au-d. de** (*personne*) to go to meet; (*danger*) to court; (*désirs de qn*) to anticipate.

audible [odibl] *a* audible.

audience [odjɑ̃s] *nf Jur* hearing; (*entretien*) audience.

audio [odjo] *a inv* (*cassette etc*) audio. ◆**audiophone** *nm* hearing aid. ◆**audio-visuel, -elle** *a* audio-visual.

auditeur, -trice [oditœr, -tris] *nmf Rad* listener; **les auditeurs** the audience; **a. libre** *Univ* auditor, *student allowed to attend classes but not to sit examinations.* ◆**auditif, -ive** *a* (*nerf*) auditory. ◆**audition** *nf* (*ouïe*) hearing; (*séance d'essai*) *Th* audition; (*séance musicale*) recital. ◆**auditionner** *vti* to audition. ◆**auditoire** *nm* audience. ◆**auditorium** *nm Rad* recording studio (*for recitals*).

auge [oʒ] *nf* (feeding) trough.

augmenter [ɔgmɑ̃te] *vt* to increase (**de** by); (*salaire, prix, impôt*) to raise, increase; **a. qn** to give s.o. a rise *ou Am* raise; *– vi* to increase (**de** by); (*prix, population*) to rise, go up. ◆**augmentation** *nf* increase (**de** in, of); **a. de salaire** (pay) rise, *Am* raise; **a. de prix** price rise *ou* increase.

augure [ɔgyr] *nm* (*présage*) omen; (*devin*) oracle; **être de bon/mauvais a.** to be a good/bad omen. ◆**augurer** *vt* to augur, predict.

auguste [ogyst] *a* august.

aujourd'hui [oʒurdɥi] *adv* today; (*actuellement*) nowadays, today; **a. en quinze** two weeks today.

aumône [omon] *nf* alms.

aumônier [omonje] *nm* chaplain.

auparavant [oparavɑ̃] *adv* (*avant*) before(hand); (*d'abord*) first.

auprès de [oprɛdə] *prép* (*assis, situé etc*) by, close to, next to; (*en comparaison de*) compared to; **agir a. de** (*ministre etc*) to use one's influence with; **accès a. de qn** access to s.o.

auquel [okɛl] *voir* **lequel**.

aura, aurait [ora, orɛ] *voir* **avoir**.

auréole [ɔreɔl] *nf* (*de saint etc*) halo; (*trace*) ring.

auriculaire [ɔrikylɛr] *nm* **l'a.** the little finger.

aurore [ɔrɔr] *nf* dawn, daybreak.

ausculter [ɔskylte] *vt* (*malade*) to examine (*with a stethoscope*); (*cœur*) to listen to. ◆**auscultation** *nf Méd* auscultation.

auspices [ospis] *nmpl* **sous les a. de** under the auspices of.

aussi [osi] *adv* **1** (*comparaison*) as; **a. sage que** as wise as. **2** (*également*) too, also, as well; **moi a.** so do, can, am *etc* I; **a. bien que** as well as. **3** (*tellement*) so; **un repas a. délicieux** so delicious a meal, such a delicious meal. **4** *conj* (*donc*) therefore.

aussitôt [osito] *adv* immediately, at once; **a. que** as soon as; **a. levé, il partit** as soon as he was up, he left; **a. dit, a. fait** no sooner said than done.

austère [ɔster] *a* austere. ◆**austérité** *nf* austerity.

austral, *mpl* **-als** [ostral] *a* southern.

Australie [ostrali] *nf* Australia. ◆**australien, -ienne** *a* & *nmf* Australian.

autant [otɑ̃] *adv* **1 a. de . . . que** (*quantité*) as much . . . as; (*nombre*) as many . . . as; **il a a. d'argent/de pommes que vous** he has as much money/as many apples as you. **2 a. de** (*tant de*) so much; (*nombre*) so many; **je n'ai jamais vu a. d'argent/de pommes** I've never seen so much money/so many apples; **pourquoi manges-tu a.?** why are you eating so much? **3 a. que** (*souffrir, lire etc*) as much as; **il lit a. que vous/que possible** he reads as much as you/as possible; **il n'a jamais souffert a.** he's never suffered as *ou* so much; **a. que je sache** as far as I know; **d'a. (plus) que** all the more (so) since; **d'a. moins que** even less since; **a. avouer**/*etc* we, you *etc* might as well confess/*etc*; **en faire/dire a.** to do/say the same; **j'aimerais a. aller au cinéma** I'd just as soon go to the cinema.

autel [otɛl] *nm* altar.

auteur [otœr] *nm* (*de livre*) author, writer; (*de chanson*) composer; (*de procédé*) originator; (*de crime*) perpetrator; (*d'accident*) cause; **droit d'a.** copyright; **droits d'a.** royalties.

authenticité [otɑ̃tisite] *nf* authenticity. ◆**authentifier** *vt* to authenticate. ◆**authentique** *a* genuine, authentic.

autiste [otist] *a,* **autistique** *a* autistic.

auto [oto] *nf* car; **autos tamponneuses** bumper cars, dodgems.

auto- [oto] *préf* self-.

autobiographie [otobjɔgrafi] *nf* autobiography.

autobus [otobys] *nm* bus.

autocar [otokar] *nm* coach, bus.

autochtone [ɔtɔktɔn] *a* & *nmf* native.

autocollant [otokɔlɑ̃] *nm* sticker.

autocrate [otokrat] *nm* autocrat. ◆**autocratique** *a* autocratic.

autocuiseur [otokɥizœr] *nm* pressure cooker.

autodéfense [otodefɑ̃s] *nf* self-defence.

autodestruction [otodɛstryksjɔ̃] *nf* self-destruction.

autodidacte [otodidakt] *a* & *nmf* self-taught (person).

autodrome [otodrom] *nm* motor-racing track.

auto-école [otoekɔl] *nf* driving school, school of motoring.

autographe [otograf] *nm* autograph.

automate [ɔtɔmat] *nm* automaton. ◆**automation** *nf* automation. ◆**automatisation** *nf* automation. ◆**automatiser** *vt* to automate.

automatique [ɔtɔmatik] *a* automatic; – *nm* **l'a.** *Tél* direct dialling. ◆**—ment** *adv* automatically.

automne [otɔn] *nm* autumn, *Am* fall. ◆**automnal, -aux** *a* autumnal.

automobile [otɔmɔbil] *nf* & *a* (motor)car, *Am* automobile; **l'a.** *Sp* motoring; **Salon de l'a.** Motor Show; **canot a.** motor boat. ◆**automobiliste** *nmf* motorist.

autonome [otonɔm] *a* (*région etc*) autonomous, self-governing; (*personne*) *Fig* independent. ◆**autonomie** *nf* autonomy.

autopsie [ɔtɔpsi] *nf* autopsy, post-mortem.

autoradio [otoradjo] *nm* car radio.

autorail [ɔtɔrɑj] *nm* railcar.

autoris/er [ɔtɔrize] *vt* (*habiliter*) to authorize (**à faire** to do); (*permettre*) to permit (**à faire** to do). ◆**—é** *a* (*qualifié*) authoritative. ◆**autorisation** *nf* authorization; permission.

autorité [ɔtɔrite] *nf* authority. ◆**autoritaire** *a* authoritarian; (*homme, ton*) authoritative.

autoroute [otorut] *nf* motorway, *Am* highway, freeway.

auto-stop [otostɔp] *nm* hitchhiking; **faire de l'a.** to hitchhike. ◆**autostoppeur, -euse** *nmf* hitchhiker.

autour [otur] *adv* around; – *prép* **a. de** around.

autre [otr] *a* & *pron* other; **un a. livre** another book; **un a.** another (one); **d'autres** others; **as-tu d'autres questions?** have you any other *ou* further questions?; **qn/personne/rien d'a.** s.o./no one/nothing else; **a. chose/part** sth/somewhere else; **qui/quoi d'a.?** who/what else?; **l'un l'a., les uns les autres** each other; **l'un et l'a.** both (of them); **l'un ou l'a.** either (of them); **ni l'un ni l'a.** neither (of them); **les uns . . . les autres** some . . . others; **nous/vous autres Anglais** we/you English; **d'un moment à l'a.** any moment (now); **. . . et autres . . .** and so on. ◆**autrement** *adv* (*différemment*) differently; (*sinon*) otherwise; (*plus*) far more (**que** than); **pas a. satisfait**/*etc* not particularly satisfied/*etc*.

autrefois [otrəfwa] *adv* in the past, in days gone by.

Autriche [otriʃ] *nf* Austria. ◆**autrichien, -ienne** *a & nmf* Austrian.
autruche [otryʃ] *nf* ostrich.
autrui [otrɥi] *pron* others, other people.
auvent [ovɑ̃] *nm* awning, canopy.
aux [o] *voir* **à**.
auxiliaire [ɔksiljɛr] *a* auxiliary; – *nm Gram* auxiliary; – *nmf (aide)* helper, auxiliary.
auxquels, -elles [okɛl] *voir* **lequel**.
avachir (s') [savaʃir] *vpr (soulier, personne)* to become flabby *ou* limp.
avait [avɛ] *voir* **avoir**.
aval (en) [ɑ̃naval] *adv* downstream (**de** from).
avalanche [avalɑ̃ʃ] *nf* avalanche; *Fig* flood, avalanche.
avaler [avale] *vt* to swallow; *(livre)* to devour; *(mots)* to mumble; – *vi* to swallow.
avance [avɑ̃s] *nf (marche, acompte)* advance; *(de coureur, chercheur etc)* lead; *pl (galantes)* advances; **à l'a., d'a., par a.** in advance; **en a.** *(arriver, partir)* early; *(avant l'horaire prévu)* ahead (of time); *(dans son développement)* ahead, in advance; *(montre etc)* fast; **en a. sur** *(qn, son époque etc)* ahead of, in advance of; **avoir une heure d'a.** *(train etc)* to be an hour early.
avanc/er [avɑ̃se] *vt (thèse, argent)* to advance; *(date)* to bring forward; *(main, chaise)* to move forward; *(travail)* to speed up; – *vi* to advance, move forward; *(montre)* to be fast; *(faire saillie)* to jut out (**sur** over); **a. en âge** to be getting on (in years); – **s'a.** *vpr* to advance, move forward; *(faire saillie)* to jut out. ◆**—é** *a* advanced; *(saison)* well advanced. ◆**—ée** *nf* projection, overhang. ◆**—ement** *nm* advancement.
avanie [avani] *nf* affront, insult.
avant [avɑ̃] *prép* before; **a. de voir** before seeing; **a. qu'il (ne) parte** before he leaves; **a. huit jours** within a week; **a. tout** above all; **a. toute chose** first and foremost; **a. peu** before long; – *adv* before; **en a.** *(mouvement)* forward; *(en tête)* ahead; **en a. de** in front of; **bien a. dans** *(creuser etc)* very deep(ly) into; **la nuit d'a.** the night before; – *nm & a inv* front; – *nm (joueur) Sp* forward.
avantage [avɑ̃taʒ] *nm* advantage; *(bénéfice) Fin* benefit; **tu as a. à le faire** it's worth your while to do it; **tirer a. de** to benefit from. ◆**avantager** *vt (favoriser)* to favour; *(faire valoir)* to show off to advantage. ◆**avantageux, -euse** *a* worthwhile, attractive; *(flatteur)* flattering; *Péj* conceited; **a. pour qn** advantageous to s.o.
avant-bras [avɑ̃bra] *nm inv* forearm. ◆**a.-centre** *nm Sp* centre-forward. ◆**a.-coureur** *am* **a.-coureur de** *(signe)* heralding. ◆**a.-dernier, -ière** *a & nmf* last but one. ◆**a.-garde** *nf Mil* advance guard; **d'a.-garde** *(idée, film etc)* avant-garde. ◆**a.-goût** *nm* foretaste. ◆**a.-guerre** *nm ou f* pre-war period; **d'a.-guerre** pre-war. ◆**a.-hier** [avɑ̃tjɛr] *adv* the day before yesterday. ◆**a.-poste** *nm* outpost. ◆**a.-première** *nf* preview. ◆**a.-propos** *nm inv* foreword. ◆**a.-veille** *nf* **l'a.-veille (de)** two days before.
avare [avar] *a* miserly; **a. de** *(compliments etc)* sparing of; – *nmf* miser. ◆**avarice** *nf* avarice.
avarie(s) [avari] *nf(pl)* damage. ◆**avarié** *a (aliment)* spoiled, rotting.
avatar [avatar] *nm Péj Fam* misadventure.
avec [avɛk] *prép* with; *(envers)* to(wards); **et a. ça?** *(dans un magasin) Fam* anything else?; – *adv* **il est venu a.** *(son chapeau etc) Fam* he came with it.
avenant [avnɑ̃] *a* pleasing, attractive; **à l'a.** in keeping (**de** with).
avènement [avɛnmɑ̃] *nm* **l'a. de** the coming *ou* advent of; *(roi)* the accession of.
avenir [avnir] *nm* future; **d'a.** *(personne, métier)* with future prospects; **à l'a.** *(désormais)* in future.
aventure [avɑ̃tyr] *nf* adventure; *(en amour)* affair; **à l'a.** *(marcher etc)* aimlessly; **dire la bonne a. à qn** to tell s.o.'s fortune. ◆**aventur/er** *vt* to risk; *(remarque)* to venture; *(réputation)* to risk; – **s'a.** *vpr* to venture (**sur** on to, **à faire** to do). ◆**—é** *a* risky. ◆**aventureux, -euse** *a (personne, vie)* adventurous; *(risqué)* risky. ◆**aventurier, -ière** *nmf Péj* adventurer.
avenue [avny] *nf* avenue.
avér/er (s') [savere] *vpr (juste etc)* to prove (to be); **il s'avère que** it turns out that. ◆**—é** *a* established.
averse [avɛrs] *nf* shower, downpour.
aversion [avɛrsjɔ̃] *nf* aversion (**pour** to).
avert/ir [avɛrtir] *vt (mettre en garde, menacer)* to warn; *(informer)* to notify, inform. ◆**—i** *a* informed. ◆**—issement** *nm* warning; notification; *(dans un livre)* foreword. ◆**—isseur** *nm Aut* horn; **a. d'incendie** fire alarm.
aveu, -x [avø] *nm* confession; **de l'a. de** by the admission of.
aveugle [avœgl] *a* blind; – *nmf* blind man, blind woman; **les aveugles** the blind. ◆**aveuglément** [-emɑ̃] *adv* blindly.

◆aveugl/er *vt* to blind. **◆—ement** [-əmɑ̃] *nm* (*égarement*) blindness.
aveuglette (à l') [alavœglet] *adv* blindly; **chercher qch à l'a.** to grope for sth.
aviateur, -trice [avjatœr, -tris] *nmf* airman, airwoman. **◆aviation** *nf* (*industrie, science*) aviation; (*armée de l'air*) air force; (*avions*) aircraft; **l'a.** *Sp* flying; **d'a.** (*terrain, base*) air-.
avide [avid] *a* (*rapace*) greedy (**de** for); **a. d'apprendre/***etc* (*désireux*) eager to learn/*etc*. **◆—ment** *adv* greedily. **◆avidité** *nf* greed.
avilir [avilir] *vt* to degrade, debase.
avion [avjɔ̃] *nm* aircraft, (aero)plane, *Am* airplane; **a. à réaction** jet; **a. de ligne** airliner; **par a.** (*lettre*) airmail; **en a., par a.** (*voyager*) by plane, by air; **aller en a.** to fly.
aviron [avirɔ̃] *nm* oar; **faire de l'a.** to row, practise rowing.
avis [avi] *nm* opinion; *Pol Jur* judgement; (*communiqué*) notice; (*conseil*) & *Fin* advice; **à mon a.** in my opinion, to my mind; **changer d'a.** to change one's mind.
avis/er [avize] *vt* to advise, inform; (*voir*) to notice; **s'a. de qch** to realize sth suddenly; **s'a. de faire** to venture to do. **◆—é** *a* prudent, wise; **bien/mal a.** well-/ill-advised.
aviver [avive] *vt* (*couleur*) to bring out; (*douleur*) to sharpen.
avocat, -ate [avɔka, -at] **1** *nmf* barrister, counsel, *Am* attorney, counselor; (*d'une cause*) *Fig* advocate. **2** *nm* (*fruit*) avocado (pear).
avoine [avwan] *nf* oats; **farine d'a.** oatmeal.
avoir* [avwar] **1** *v aux* to have; **je l'ai vu** I've seen him. **2** *vt* (*posséder*) to have; (*obtenir*) to get; (*tromper*) *Fam* to take for a ride; **il a** he has, he's got; **qu'est-ce que tu as?** what's the matter with you?, what's wrong with you?; **j'ai à lui parler** I have to speak to her; **il n'a qu'à essayer** he only has to try; **a. faim/chaud/***etc* to be *ou* feel hungry/hot/*etc*; **a. cinq ans/***etc* to be five (years old)/*etc*; **en a. pour longtemps** to be busy for quite a while; **j'en ai pour dix minutes** this will take me ten minutes; (*ne bougez pas*) I'll be with you in ten minutes; **en a. pour son argent** to get *ou* have one's money's worth; **en a. après** *ou* **contre** to have a grudge against. **3** *v imp* **il y a** there is, *pl* there are; **il y a six ans** six years ago; **il n'y a pas de quoi!** don't mention it!; **qu'est-ce qu'il y a?** what's the matter?, what's wrong? **4** *nm* assets, property; (*d'un compte*) *Fin* credit.
avoisin/er [avwazine] *vt* to border on. **◆—ant** *a* neighbouring, nearby.
avort/er [avɔrte] *vi* (*projet etc*) *Fig* to miscarry, fail; **(se faire) a.** (*femme*) to have *ou* get an abortion. **◆—ement** *nm* abortion; *Fig* failure. **◆avorton** *nm Péj* runt, puny shrimp.
avou/er [avwe] *vt* to confess, admit (**que** that); **s'a. vaincu** to admit defeat; – *vi* (*coupable*) to confess. **◆—é** *a* (*ennemi, but*) avowed; – *nm* solicitor, *Am* attorney.
avril [avril] *nm* April; **un poisson d'a.** (*farce*) an April fool joke.
axe [aks] *nm Math* axis; (*essieu*) axle; (*d'une politique*) broad direction; **grands axes** (*routes*) main roads. **◆axer** *vt* to centre; **il est axé sur** his mind is drawn towards.
axiome [aksjom] *nm* axiom.
ayant [ɛjɑ̃] *voir* **avoir**.
azalée [azale] *nf* (*plante*) azalea.
azimuts [azimyt] *nmpl* **dans tous les a.** *Fam* all over the place, here there and everywhere; **tous a.** (*guerre, publicité etc*) all-out.
azote [azot] *nm* nitrogen.
azur [azyr] *nm* azure, (sky) blue; **la Côte d'A.** the (French) Riviera.
azyme [azim] *a* (*pain*) unleavened.

B

B, b [be] *nm* B, b.
babeurre [babœr] *nm* buttermilk.
babill/er [babije] *vi* to prattle, babble. **◆—age** *nm* prattle, babble.
babines [babin] *nfpl* (*lèvres*) chops, chaps.
babiole [babjɔl] *nf* (*objet*) knick-knack; (*futilité*) trifle.
bâbord [bɑbɔr] *nm Nau Av* port (side).
babouin [babwɛ̃] *nm* baboon.
baby-foot [babifut] *nm inv* table *ou* miniature football.
bac [bak] *nm* **1** (*bateau*) ferry(boat). **2** (*cuve*) tank; **b. à glace** ice tray; **b. à laver** washtub. **3** *abrév* = **baccalauréat**.
baccalauréat [bakalɔrea] *nm* school leaving certificate.

bâche [bɑʃ] *nf* (*toile*) tarpaulin. ◆**bâcher** *vt* to cover over (*with a tarpaulin*).
bachelier, -ière [baʃəlje, -jɛr] *nmf* holder of the *baccalauréat*.
bachot [baʃo] *nm abrév* = **baccalauréat.** ◆**bachoter** *vi* to cram (*for an exam*).
bacille [basil] *nm* bacillus, germ.
bâcler [bɑkle] *vt* (*travail*) to dash off carelessly, botch (up).
bactéries [bakteri] *nfpl* bacteria. ◆**bactériologique** *a* bacteriological; **la guerre b.** germ warfare.
badaud, -aude [bado, -od] *nmf* (inquisitive) onlooker, bystander.
baderne [badɛrn] *nf* **vieille b.** *Péj* old fogey, old fuddy-duddy.
badigeon [badiʒɔ̃] *nm* whitewash. ◆**badigeonner** *vt* (*mur*) to whitewash, distemper; (*écorchure*) *Méd* to paint, coat.
badin [badɛ̃] *a* (*peu sérieux*) light-hearted, playful. ◆**badin/er** *vi* to jest, joke; **b. avec** (*prendre à la légère*) to trifle with. ◆**—age** *nm* banter, jesting.
badine [badin] *nf* cane, switch.
bafouer [bafwe] *vt* to mock *ou* scoff at.
bafouiller [bafuje] *vti* to stammer, splutter.
bâfrer [bɑfre] *vi Fam* to stuff oneself (with food).
bagage [bagaʒ] *nm* (*valise etc*) piece of luggage *ou* baggage; (*connaissances*) *Fig* (fund of) knowledge; *pl* (*ensemble des valises*) luggage, baggage. ◆**bagagiste** *nm* baggage handler.
bagarre [bagar] *nf* brawl. ◆**bagarrer** *vi Fam* to fight, struggle; **— se b.** *vpr* to fight, brawl; (*se disputer*) to fight, quarrel.
bagatelle [bagatɛl] *nf* trifle, mere bagatelle; **la b. de** *Iron* the trifling sum of.
bagne [baɲ] *nm* convict prison; **c'est le b. ici** *Fig* this place is a real hell hole *ou* workhouse. ◆**bagnard** *nm* convict.
bagnole [baɲɔl] *nf Fam* car; **vieille b.** *Fam* old banger.
bagou(t) [bagu] *nm Fam* glibness; **avoir du b.** to have the gift of the gab.
bague [bag] *nf* (*anneau*) ring; (*de cigare*) band. ◆**bagué** *a* (*doigt*) ringed.
baguenauder [bagnode] *vi*, **— se b.** *vpr* to loaf around, saunter.
baguette [bagɛt] *nf* (*canne*) stick; (*de chef d'orchestre*) baton; (*pain*) (long thin) loaf, stick of bread; *pl* (*de tambour*) drumsticks; (*pour manger*) chopsticks; **b. (magique)** (magic) wand; **mener à la b.** to rule with an iron hand.
bah! [bɑ] *int* really!, bah!
bahut [bay] *nm* (*meuble*) chest, cabinet; (*lycée*) *Fam* school.
baie [bɛ] *nf* **1** *Géog* bay. **2** *Bot* berry. **3** (*fenêtre*) picture window.
baignade [bɛɲad] *nf* (*bain*) bathe, bathing; (*endroit*) bathing place. ◆**baign/er** *vt* (*immerger*) to bathe; (*enfant*) to bath, *Am* bathe; **b. les rivages** (*mer*) to wash the shores; **baigné de** (*sueur, lumière*) bathed in; (*sang*) soaked in; **—** *vi* **b. dans** (*tremper*) to soak in; (*être imprégné de*) to be steeped in; **— se b.** *vpr* to go swimming *ou* bathing; (*dans une baignoire*) to have *ou* take a bath. ◆**—eur, -euse 1** *nmf* bather. **2** *nm* (*poupée*) baby doll. ◆**baignoire** *nf* bath (tub).
bail, *pl* baux [baj, bo] *nm* lease. ◆**bailleur** *nm Jur* lessor; **b. de fonds** financial backer.
bâill/er [bɑje] *vi* to yawn; (*chemise etc*) to gape; (*porte*) to stand ajar. ◆**—ement** *nm* yawn; gaping.
bâillon [bɑjɔ̃] *nm* gag. ◆**bâillonner** *vt* (*victime, presse etc*) to gag.
bain [bɛ̃] *nm* bath; (*de mer*) swim, bathe; **salle de bain(s)** bathroom; **être dans le b.** (*au courant*) *Fam* to have got into the swing of things; **petit/grand b.** (*piscine*) shallow/deep end; **b. de bouche** mouthwash. ◆**b.-marie** *nm* (*pl* **bains-marie**) *Culin* double boiler.
baïonnette [bajɔnɛt] *nf* bayonet.
baiser [beze] **1** *vt* **b. au front/sur la joue** to kiss on the forehead/cheek; **—** *nm* kiss; **bons baisers** (*dans une lettre*) (with) love. **2** *vt* (*duper*) *Fam* to con.
baisse [bɛs] *nf* fall, drop (**de** in); **en b.** (*température*) falling.
baisser [bese] *vt* (*voix, prix etc*) to lower, drop; (*tête*) to bend; (*radio, chauffage*) to turn down; **—** *vi* (*prix, niveau etc*) to drop, go down; (*soleil*) to go down, sink; (*marée*) to go out, ebb; (*santé, popularité*) to decline; **— se b.** *vpr* to bend down, stoop.
bajoues [baʒu] *nfpl* (*d'animal, de personne*) chops.
bal, *pl* bals [bal] *nm* (*réunion de grand apparat*) ball; (*populaire*) dance; (*lieu*) dance hall.
balade [balad] *nf Fam* walk; (*en auto*) drive; (*excursion*) tour. ◆**balader** *vt* (*enfant etc*) to take for a walk *ou* drive; (*objet*) to trail around; **— se b.** *vpr* (*à pied*) to (go for a) walk; (*excursionner*) to tour (around); **se b. (en voiture)** to go for a drive. ◆**baladeur** *nm* Walkman®. ◆**baladeuse** *nf* inspection lamp.
balafre [balafr] *nf* (*blessure*) gash, slash;

(*cicatrice*) scar. ◆**balafrer** *vt* to gash, slash; to scar.

balai [balɛ] *nm* broom; **b. mécanique** carpet sweeper; **manche à b.** broomstick; *Av* joystick. ◆**b.-brosse** *nm* (*pl* **balais-brosses**) garden brush *ou* broom (*for scrubbing paving stones*).

balance [balɑ̃s] *nf* (*instrument*) (pair of) scales; (*équilibre*) *Pol Fin* balance; **la B.** (*signe*) Libra; **mettre en b.** to balance, weigh up.

balanc/er [balɑ̃se] *vt* (*bras*) to swing; (*hanches, tête, branches*) to sway; (*lancer*) *Fam* to chuck; (*se débarrasser de*) *Fam* to chuck out; **b. un compte** *Fin* to balance an account; **— se b.** *vpr* (*personne*) to swing (from side to side); (*arbre, bateau etc*) to sway; **je m'en balance!** I couldn't care less! ◆**—é** *a* **bien b.** (*phrase*) well-balanced; (*personne*) *Fam* well-built. ◆**—ement** *nm* swinging; swaying. ◆**balancier** *nm* (*d'horloge*) pendulum; (*de montre*) balance wheel. ◆**balançoire** *nf* (*escarpolette*) swing; (*bascule*) seesaw.

balayer [baleje] *vt* (*chambre, rue*) to sweep (out *ou* up); (*enlever, chasser*) to sweep away; **le vent balayait la plaine** the wind swept the plain. ◆**balayette** [balejɛt] *nf* (hand) brush; (*balai*) short-handled broom. ◆**balayeur, -euse** [balejœr, -øz] *nmf* roadsweeper.

balbutier [balbysje] *vti* to stammer.

balcon [balkɔ̃] *nm* balcony; *Th Cin* dress circle.

baldaquin [baldakɛ̃] *nm* (*de lit etc*) canopy.

baleine [balɛn] *nf* (*animal*) whale; (*fanon*) whalebone; (*de parapluie*) rib. ◆**baleinier** *nm* (*navire*) whaler. ◆**baleinière** *nf* whaleboat.

balise [baliz] *nf Nau* beacon; *Av* (ground) light; *Aut* road sign. ◆**balis/er** *vt* to mark with beacons *ou* lights; (*route*) to signpost. ◆**—age** *nm Nau* beacons; *Av* lighting; *Aut* signposting.

balistique [balistik] *a* ballistic.

balivernes [balivɛrn] *nfpl* balderdash, nonsense.

ballade [balad] *nf* (*légende*) ballad; (*poème court*) & *Mus* ballade.

ballant [balɑ̃] *a* (*bras, jambes*) dangling.

ballast [balast] *nm* ballast.

balle [bal] *nf* (*de tennis, golf etc*) ball; (*projectile*) bullet; (*paquet*) bale; *pl* (*francs*) *Fam* francs; **se renvoyer la b.** to pass the buck (to each other).

ballet [balɛ] *nm* ballet. ◆**ballerine** *nf* ballerina.

ballon [balɔ̃] *nm* (*jouet d'enfant*) & *Av* balloon; (*sport*) ball; **b. de football** football; **lancer un b. d'essai** *Fig* to put out a feeler. ◆**ballonné** *a* (*ventre*) bloated, swollen. ◆**ballot** *nm* (*paquet*) bundle; (*imbécile*) *Fam* idiot.

ballottage [balɔtaʒ] *nm* (*scrutin*) second ballot (*no candidate having achieved the required number of votes*).

ballotter [balɔte] *vti* to shake (about); **ballotté entre** (*sentiments contraires*) torn between.

balnéaire [balneɛr] *a* **station b.** seaside resort.

balourd, -ourde [balur, -urd] *nmf* (clumsy) oaf. ◆**balourdise** *nf* clumsiness, oafishness; (*gaffe*) blunder.

Baltique [baltik] *nf* **la B.** the Baltic.

balustrade [balystrad] *nf* (hand)rail, railing(s).

bambin [bɑ̃bɛ̃] *nm* tiny tot, toddler.

bambou [bɑ̃bu] *nm* bamboo.

ban [bɑ̃] *nm* (*de tambour*) roll; (*applaudissements*) round of applause; *pl* (*de mariage*) banns; **mettre qn au b. de** to cast s.o. out from, outlaw s.o. from; **un b. pour . . .** three cheers for . . . .

banal, *mpl* **-als** [banal] *a* (*fait, accident etc*) commonplace, banal; (*idée, propos*) banal, trite. ◆**banalisé** *a* (*voiture de police*) unmarked. ◆**banalité** *nf* banality; *pl* (*propos*) banalities.

banane [banan] *nf* banana.

banc [bɑ̃] *nm* (*siège, établi*) bench; (*de poissons*) shoal; **b. d'église** pew; **b. d'essai** *Fig* testing ground; **b. de sable** sandbank; **b. des accusés** *Jur* dock.

bancaire [bɑ̃kɛr] *a* (*opération*) banking-; (*chèque*) bank-.

bancal, *mpl* **-als** [bɑ̃kal] *a* (*personne*) bandy, bow-legged; (*meuble*) wobbly; (*idée*) shaky.

bande [bɑ̃d] *nf* **1** (*de terrain, papier etc*) strip; (*de film*) reel; (*de journal*) wrapper; (*rayure*) stripe; (*de fréquences*) *Rad* band; (*pansement*) bandage; (*sur la chaussée*) line; **b. (magnétique)** tape; **b. vidéo** videotape; **b. sonore** sound track; **b. dessinée** comic strip, strip cartoon; **par la b.** indirectly. **2** (*groupe*) gang, troop, band; (*de chiens*) pack; (*d'oiseaux*) flock; **on a fait b. à part** we split into our own group; **b. d'idiots!** you load of idiots! ◆**bandeau, -x** *nm* (*sur les yeux*) blindfold; (*pour la tête*) headband; (*pansement*) head bandage. ◆**band/er** *vt* (*blessure etc*) to bandage; (*yeux*) to blindfold; (*arc*) to bend; (*muscle*) to tense. ◆**—age** *nm* (*pansement*) bandage.

banderole [bɑ̃drɔl] *nf* (*sur mât*) pennant, streamer; (*sur montants*) banner.

bandit [bɑ̃di] *nm* robber, bandit; (*enfant*) *Fam* rascal. ◆**banditisme** *nm* crime.

bandoulière [bɑ̃duljɛr] *nf* shoulder strap; **en b.** slung across the shoulder.

banjo [bɑ̃(d)ʒo] *nm Mus* banjo.

banlieue [bɑ̃ljø] *nf* suburbs, outskirts; **la grande b.** the outer suburbs; **de b.** (*magasin etc*) suburban; (*train*) commuter-. ◆**banlieusard, -arde** *nmf* (*habitant*) suburbanite; (*voyageur*) commuter.

banne [ban] *nf* (*de magasin*) awning.

bannière [banjɛr] *nf* banner.

bann/ir [banir] *vt* (*exiler*) to banish; (*supprimer*) to ban, outlaw. ◆**—issement** *nm* banishment.

banque [bɑ̃k] *nf* bank; (*activité*) banking.

banqueroute [bɑ̃krut] *nf* (fraudulent) bankruptcy.

banquet [bɑ̃kɛ] *nm* banquet.

banquette [bɑ̃kɛt] *nf* (bench) seat.

banquier [bɑ̃kje] *nm* banker.

banquise [bɑ̃kiz] *nf* ice floe *ou* field.

baptême [batɛm] *nm* christening, baptism; **b. du feu** baptism of fire; **b. de l'air** first flight. ◆**baptiser** *vt* (*enfant*) to christen, baptize; (*appeler*) *Fig* to christen.

baquet [bakɛ] *nm* tub, basin.

bar [bar] *nm* **1** (*lieu, comptoir, meuble*) bar. **2** (*poisson marin*) bass.

baragouin [baragwɛ̃] *nm* gibberish, gabble. ◆**baragouiner** *vt* (*langue*) to gabble (a few words of); – *vi* to gabble away.

baraque [barak] *nf* hut, shack; (*maison*) *Fam* house, place; *Péj* hovel; (*de forain*) stall. ◆**—ment** *nm* (makeshift) huts.

baratin [baratɛ̃] *nm Fam* sweet talk; *Com* patter. ◆**baratiner** *vt* to chat up; *Am* sweet-talk.

barbare [barbar] *a* (*manières, crime*) barbaric; (*peuple, invasions*) barbarian; – *nmf* barbarian. ◆**barbarie** *nf* (*cruauté*) barbarity. ◆**barbarisme** *nm Gram* barbarism.

barbe [barb] *nf* beard; **une b. de trois jours** three days' growth of beard; **se faire la b.** to shave; **à la b. de** under the nose(s) of; **rire dans sa b.** to laugh up one's sleeve; **la b.!** enough!; **quelle b.!** what a drag!; **b. à papa** candyfloss, *Am* cotton candy.

barbecue [barbəkju] *nm* barbecue.

barbelé [barbəle] *a* barbed; – *nmpl* barbed wire.

barb/er [barbe] *vt Fam* to bore (stiff); **— se b.** *vpr* to be *ou* get bored (stiff). ◆**—ant** *a Fam* boring.

barbiche [barbiʃ] *nf* goatee (beard).

barbiturique [barbityrik] *nm* barbiturate.

barbot/er [barbɔte] **1** *vi* (*s'agiter*) to splash about, paddle. **2** *vt* (*voler*) *Fam* to filch. ◆**—euse** *nf* (*de bébé*) rompers.

barbouill/er [barbuje] *vt* (*salir*) to smear; (*peindre*) to daub; (*gribouiller*) to scribble; **avoir l'estomac barbouillé** *Fam* to feel queasy. ◆**—age** *nm* smear; daub; scribble.

barbu [barby] *a* bearded.

barda [barda] *nm Fam* gear; (*de soldat*) kit.

bardé [barde] *a* **b. de** (*décorations etc*) covered with.

barder [barde] *v imp* **ça va b.!** *Fam* there'll be fireworks!

barème [barɛm] *nm* (*des tarifs*) table; (*des salaires*) scale; (*livre de comptes*) ready reckoner.

baril [bari(l)] *nm* barrel; **b. de poudre** powder keg.

bariolé [barjɔle] *a* brightly-coloured.

barman, *pl* **-men** *ou* **-mans** [barman, -mɛn] *nm* barman, *Am* bartender.

baromètre [barɔmɛtr] *nm* barometer.

baron, -onne [barɔ̃, -ɔn] *nm* baron; – *nf* baroness.

baroque [barɔk] **1** *a* (*idée etc*) bizarre, weird. **2** *a & nm Archit Mus etc* baroque.

baroud [barud] *nm* **b. d'honneur** *Arg* gallant last fight.

barque [bark] *nf* (small) boat.

barre [bar] *nf* bar; (*trait*) line, stroke; *Nau* helm; **b. de soustraction** minus sign; **b. fixe** *Sp* horizontal bar. ◆**barreau, -x** *nm* (*de fenêtre etc*) & *Jur* bar; (*d'échelle*) rung.

barr/er [bare] **1** *vt* (*route etc*) to block (off), close (off); (*porte*) to bar; (*chèque*) to cross; (*phrase*) to cross out; *Nau* to steer; **b. la route à qn, b. qn** to bar s.o.'s way; **'rue barrée'** 'road closed'. **2 se b.** *vpr Arg* to hop it, make off. ◆**—age** *nm* (*sur une route*) roadblock; (*barrière*) barrier; (*ouvrage hydraulique*) dam; (*de petite rivière*) weir; **le b. d'une rue** the closure of a street; **tir de b.** barrage fire; **b. d'agents** cordon of police. ◆**—eur** *nm Sp Nau* cox.

barrette [barɛt] *nf* (*pince*) (hair)slide, *Am* barrette.

barricade [barikad] *nf* barricade. ◆**barricader** *vt* to barricade; **— se b.** *vpr* to barricade oneself.

barrière [barjɛr] *nf* (*porte*) gate; (*clôture*) fence; (*obstacle, mur*) barrier.

barrique [barik] *nf* (large) barrel.

baryton [baritɔ̃] *nm* baritone.

bas[1], **basse** [bɑ, bɑs] *a* (*table, prix etc*) low; (*âme, action*) base, mean; (*partie de ville etc*) lower; (*origine*) lowly; **au b. mot** at the very least; **enfant en b. âge** young child; **avoir la vue basse** to be short-sighted; **le b. peuple** *Péj* the lower orders; **coup b.** *Boxe* blow below the belt; – *adv* low; (*parler*) in a whisper, softly; **mettre b.** (*animal*) to give birth; **mettre b. les armes** to lay down one's arms; **jeter b.** to overthrow; **plus b.** further *ou* lower down; **en b.** down (below); (*par l'escalier*) downstairs, down below; **en** *ou* **au b. de** at the foot *ou* bottom of; **de haut en b.** from top to bottom; **sauter à b. du lit** to jump out of bed; **à b. les dictateurs/***etc***!** down with dictators/*etc*!; – *nm* (*de côte, page etc*) bottom, foot; **du b.** (*tiroir, étagère*) bottom.

bas[2] [bɑ] *nm* (*chaussette*) stocking; **b. de laine** *Fig* nest egg.

basané [bazane] *a* (*visage etc*) tanned.

bas-bleu [bɑblø] *nm Péj* bluestocking.

bas-côté [bɑkote] *nm* (*de route*) roadside, shoulder.

bascule [baskyl] *nf* **(jeu de) b.** (game of) seesaw; **(balance à) b.** weighing machine; **cheval/fauteuil à b.** rocking horse/chair. ◆**basculer** *vti* (*personne*) to topple over; (*benne*) to tip up.

base [bɑz] *nf* base; (*principe fondamental*) basis, foundation; **de b.** (*salaire etc*) basic; **produit à b. de lait** milk-based product; **militant de b.** rank-and-file militant. ◆**baser** *vt* to base; **se b. sur** to base oneself on.

bas-fond [bɑfɔ̃] *nm* (*eau*) shallows; (*terrain*) low ground; *pl* (*population*) *Péj* dregs.

basilic [bazilik] *nm Bot Culin* basil.

basilique [bazilik] *nf* basilica.

basket(-ball) [basket(bol)] *nm* basketball.

basque [bask] **1** *a & nmf* Basque. **2** *nfpl* (*pans de veste*) skirts.

basse [bɑs] **1** *voir* **bas**[1]. **2** *nf Mus* bass.

basse-cour [bɑskur] *nf* (*pl* **basses-cours**) farmyard.

bassement [bɑsmɑ̃] *adv* basely, meanly. ◆**bassesse** *nf* baseness, meanness; (*action*) base *ou* mean act.

bassin [basɛ̃] *nm* (*pièce d'eau*) pond; (*piscine*) pool; (*cuvette*) bowl, basin; (*rade*) dock; *Anat* pelvis; *Géog* basin; **b. houiller** coalfield. ◆**bassine** *nf* bowl.

basson [bɑsɔ̃] *nm* (*instrument*) bassoon; (*musicien*) bassoonist.

bastingage [bastɛ̃gaʒ] *nm Nau* bulwarks, rail.

bastion [bastjɔ̃] *nm* bastion.

bastringue [bastrɛ̃g] *nm* (*bal*) *Fam* popular dance hall; (*tapage*) *Arg* shindig, din; (*attirail*) *Arg* paraphernalia.

bas-ventre [bɑvɑ̃tr] *nm* lower abdomen.

bat [ba] *voir* **battre.**

bât [bɑ] *nm* packsaddle.

bataclan [bataklɑ̃] *nm Fam* paraphernalia; **et tout le b.** *Fam* and the whole caboodle.

bataille [batɑj] *nf* battle; *Cartes* beggar-my-neighbour. ◆**bataill/er** *vi* to fight, battle. ◆**—eur, -euse** *nmf* fighter; – *a* belligerent. ◆**bataillon** *nm* batallion.

bâtard, -arde [bɑtar, -ard] *a & nmf* bastard; **chien b.** mongrel; **œuvre bâtarde** hybrid work.

bateau, -x [bato] *nm* boat; (*grand*) ship. ◆**b.-citerne** *nm* (*pl* **bateaux-citernes**) tanker. ◆**b.-mouche** *nm* (*pl* **bateaux-mouches**) (*sur la Seine*) pleasure boat.

batifoler [batifɔle] *vi Hum* to fool *ou* lark about.

bâtiment [bɑtimɑ̃] *nm* (*édifice*) building; (*navire*) vessel; **le b., l'industrie du b.** the building trade; **ouvrier du b.** building worker. ◆**bât/ir** *vt* (*construire*) to build; (*coudre*) to baste, tack; **terrain à b.** building site. ◆**—i** *a* **bien b.** well-built; – *nm Menuis* frame, support. ◆**bâtisse** *nf Péj* building. ◆**bâtisseur, -euse** *nmf* builder (**de** of).

bâton [bɑtɔ̃] *nm* (*canne*) stick; (*de maréchal, d'agent*) baton; **b. de rouge** lipstick; **donner des coups de b. à qn** to beat s.o. (with a stick); **parler à bâtons rompus** to ramble from one subject to another; **mettre des bâtons dans les roues à qn** to put obstacles in s.o.'s way.

batterie [batri] *nf Mil Aut* battery; **la b.** *Mus* the drums; **b. de cuisine** set of kitchen utensils.

batt/re* [batr] **1** *vt* (*frapper, vaincre*) to beat; (*blé*) to thresh; (*cartes*) to shuffle; (*pays, chemins*) to scour; (*à coups redoublés*) to batter, pound; **b. la mesure** to beat time; **b. à mort** to batter *ou* beat to death; **b. pavillon** to fly a flag; – *vi* to beat; (*porte*) to bang; **b. des mains** to clap (one's hands); **b. des paupières** to blink; **b. des ailes** (*oiseau*) to flap its wings; **le vent fait b. la porte** the wind bangs the door. **2 se b.** *vpr* to fight. ◆**—ant 1** *a* (*pluie*) driving; (*porte*) swing-. **2** *nm* (*de cloche*) tongue; (*vantail de porte etc*) flap; **porte à deux battants** double door. **3** *nm* (*personne*) fighter. ◆**—u** *a* **chemin** *ou* **sentier b.** beaten track. ◆**—age** *nm* (*du blé*) threshing; (*publicité*) *Fam* publicity, hype, ballyhoo. ◆**—ement** *nm* (*de cœur, de tambour*) beat; (*délai*) interval; **battements de cœur** palpitations. ◆**—eur** *nm* (*musicien*) percussionist; **b. à œufs** egg beater.

baudet [bodɛ] *nm* donkey.

baume [bom] *nm* (*résine*) & *Fig* balm.

baux [bo] *voir* **bail.**

bavard, -arde [bavar, -ard] *a* (*loquace*) talkative; (*cancanier*) gossipy; – *nmf* chatterbox; gossip. ◆**bavard/er** *vi* to chat, chatter; (*papoter*) to gossip; (*divulguer*) to blab. ◆**—age** *nm* chatting, chatter(ing); gossip(ing).

bave [bav] *nf* dribble, slobber; foam; (*de limace*) slime. ◆**baver** *vi* to dribble, slobber; (*chien enragé*) to foam; (*encre*) to smudge; **en b.** *Fam* to have a rough time of it. ◆**bavette** *nf* bib. ◆**baveux, -euse** *a* (*bouche*) slobbery; (*omelette*) runny. ◆**bavoir** *nm* bib. ◆**bavure** *nf* smudge; (*erreur*) blunder; **sans b.** perfect(ly), flawless(ly).

bazar [bazar] *nm* (*magasin, marché*) bazaar; (*désordre*) mess, clutter; (*attirail*) *Fam* stuff, gear. ◆**bazarder** *vt Fam* to sell off, get rid of.

bazooka [bazuka] *nm* bazooka.

béant [beɑ̃] *a* (*plaie*) gaping; (*gouffre*) yawning.

béat [bea] *a Péj* smug; (*heureux*) *Hum* blissful. ◆**béatitude** *nf Hum* bliss.

beau (*or* **bel** *before vowel or mute h*), **belle,** *pl* **beaux, belles** [bo, bɛl] *a* (*femme, fleur etc*) beautiful, attractive; (*homme*) handsome, good-looking; (*voyage, temps etc*) fine, lovely; **au b. milieu** right in the middle; **j'ai b. crier/essayer/***etc* it's no use (my) shouting/trying/*etc*; **un b. morceau** a good *or* sizeable bit; **de plus belle** (*recommencer etc*) worse than ever; **bel et bien** really; – *nm* **le b.** the beautiful; **faire le b.** (*chien*) to sit up and beg; **le plus b. de l'histoire** the best part of the story; – *nf* (*femme*) beauty; *Sp* deciding game.

beaucoup [boku] *adv* (*lire etc*) a lot, a great deal; **aimer b.** to like very much; **s'intéresser b. à** to be very interested in; **b. de** (*livres etc*) many, a lot *ou* a great deal of; (*courage etc*) a lot *ou* a great deal of, much; **pas b. d'argent/***etc* not much money/*etc*; **j'en ai b.** (*quantité*) I have a lot; (*nombre*) I have many; **b. plus/moins** much more/less; many more/fewer; **b. trop** much too much; much too many; **de b.** by far; **b. sont . . .** many are . . . .

beau-fils [bofis] *nm* (*pl* **beaux-fils**) (*d'un précédent mariage*) stepson; (*gendre*) son-in-law. ◆**b.-frère** *nm* (*pl* **beaux-frères**) brother-in-law. ◆**b.-père** *nm* (*pl* **beaux-pères**) father-in-law; (*parâtre*) stepfather.

beauté [bote] *nf* beauty; **institut** *ou* **salon de b.** beauty parlour; **en b.** (*gagner etc*) magnificently; **être en b.** to look one's very best; **de toute b.** beautiful.

beaux-arts [bozar] *nmpl* fine arts. ◆**b.-parents** *nmpl* parents-in-law.

bébé [bebe] *nm* baby; **b.-lion/***etc* (*pl* **bébés-lions/***etc*) baby lion/*etc.*

bébête [bebɛt] *a Fam* silly.

bec [bɛk] *nm* (*d'oiseau*) beak, bill; (*de cruche*) lip, spout; (*de plume*) nib; (*bouche*) *Fam* mouth; *Mus* mouthpiece; **coup de b.** peck; **b. de gaz** gas lamp; **clouer le b. à qn** *Fam* to shut s.o. up; **tomber sur un b.** *Fam* to come up against a serious snag. ◆**b.-de-cane** *nm* (*pl* **becs-de-cane**) door handle.

bécane [bekan] *nf Fam* bike.

bécarre [bekar] *nm Mus* natural.

bécasse [bekas] *nf* (*oiseau*) woodcock; (*personne*) *Fam* simpleton.

bêche [bɛʃ] *nf* spade. ◆**bêcher** *vt* **1** (*cultiver*) to dig. **2** *Fig* to criticize; (*snober*) to snub. ◆**bêcheur, -euse** *nmf* snob.

bécot [beko] *nm Fam* kiss. ◆**bécoter** *vt*, – **se b.** *vpr Fam* to kiss.

becquée [beke] *nf* beakful; **donner la b. à** (*oiseau, enfant*) to feed. ◆**becqueter** *vt* (*picorer*) to peck (at); (*manger*) *Fam* to eat.

bedaine [bədɛn] *nf Fam* paunch, potbelly.

bedeau, -x [bədo] *nm* beadle, verger.

bedon [bədɔ̃] *nm Fam* paunch. ◆**bedonnant** *a* paunchy, potbellied.

bée [be] *a* **bouche b.** open-mouthed.

beffroi [befrwa] *nm* belfry.

bégayer [begeje] *vi* to stutter, stammer. ◆**bègue** [bɛg] *nmf* stutterer, stammerer; – *a* **être b.** to stutter, stammer.

bégueule [begœl] *a* prudish; – *nf* prude.

béguin [begɛ̃] *nm* **avoir le b. pour qn** *Fam* to have taken a fancy to s.o.

beige [bɛʒ] *a* & *nm* beige.

beignet [bɛɲɛ] *nm Culin* fritter.

bel [bɛl] *voir* **beau.**

bêler [bele] *vi* to bleat.

belette [bəlɛt] *nf* weasel.

Belgique [bɛlʒik] *nf* Belgium. ◆**belge** *a* & *nmf* Belgian.

bélier [belje] *nm* (*animal, machine*) ram; **le B.** (*signe*) Aries.

belle [bɛl] *voir* **beau.**

belle-fille [bɛlfij] *nf* (*pl* **belles-filles**) (*d'un *précédent mariage*) stepdaughter; (*bru*) daughter-in-law. ◆**b.-mère** *nf* (*pl* **belles-mères**) mother-in-law; (*marâtre*) stepmother. ◆**b.-sœur** *nf* (*pl* **belles-sœurs**) sister-in-law.

belligérant [beliʒerɑ̃] *a & nm* belligerent.

belliqueux, -euse [belikø, -øz] *a* warlike; *Fig* aggressive.

belvédère [belvedɛr] *nm* (*sur une route*) viewpoint.

bémol [bemɔl] *nm Mus* flat.

bénédiction [benediksjɔ̃] *nf* blessing, benediction.

bénéfice [benefis] *nm* (*gain*) profit; (*avantage*) benefit; **b.** (*ecclésiastique*) living, benefice. ◆**bénéficiaire** *nmf* beneficiary; – *a* (*marge, solde*) profit-. ◆**bénéficier** *vi* **b. de** to benefit from, have the benefit of. ◆**bénéfique** *a* beneficial.

Bénélux [benelyks] *nm* Benelux.

benêt [bənɛ] *nm* simpleton; – *am* simple-minded.

bénévole [benevɔl] *a* voluntary, unpaid.

bénin, -igne [benɛ̃, -iɲ] *a* (*tumeur, critique*) benign; (*accident*) minor.

bénir [benir] *vt* to bless; (*exalter, remercier*) to give thanks to. ◆**bénit** *a* (*pain*) consecrated; **eau bénite** holy water. ◆**bénitier** [-itje] *nm* (holy-water) stoup.

benjamin, -ine [bɛ̃ʒamɛ̃, -in] *nmf* youngest child; *Sp* young junior.

benne [bɛn] *nf* (*de grue*) scoop; (*à charbon*) tub, skip; (*de téléphérique*) cable car; **camion à b. basculante** dump truck; **b. à ordures** skip.

béotien, -ienne [beɔsjɛ̃, -jɛn] *nmf* (*inculte*) philistine.

béquille [bekij] *nf* (*canne*) crutch; (*de moto*) stand.

bercail [bɛrkaj] *nm* (*famille etc*) *Hum* fold.

berceau, -x [bɛrso] *nm* cradle.

berc/er [bɛrse] *vt* (*balancer*) to rock; (*apaiser*) to lull; (*leurrer*) to delude (**de** with); **se b. d'illusions** to delude oneself. ◆**–euse** *nf* lullaby.

béret [berɛ] *nm* beret.

berge [bɛrʒ] *nm* (*rivage*) (raised) bank.

berger, -ère [bɛrʒe, -ɛr] **1** *nm* shepherd; **chien (de) b.** sheepdog; – *nf* shepherdess. **2** *nm* **b. allemand** Alsatian (dog), *Am* German shepherd. ◆**bergerie** *nf* sheepfold.

berline [bɛrlin] *nf Aut* (four-door) saloon, *Am* sedan.

berlingot [bɛrlɛ̃go] *nm* (*bonbon aux fruits*) boiled sweet; (*à la menthe*) mint; (*emballage*) (milk) carton.

berlue [bɛrly] *nf* **avoir la b.** to be seeing things.

berne (en) [ɑ̃bɛrn] *adv* at half-mast.

berner [bɛrne] *vt* to fool, hoodwink.

besogne [bəzɔɲ] *nf* work, job, task. ◆**besogneux, -euse** *a* needy.

besoin [bəzwɛ̃] *nm* need; **avoir b. de** to need; **au b.** if necessary, if need(s) be; **dans le b.** in need, needy.

bestial, -aux [bɛstjal, -o] *a* bestial, brutish. ◆**bestiaux** *nmpl* livestock; (*bovins*) cattle. ◆**bestiole** *nf* (*insecte*) creepy-crawly, bug.

bétail [betaj] *nm* livestock; (*bovins*) cattle.

bête[1] [bɛt] *nf* animal; (*bestiole*) bug, creature; **b. de somme** beast of burden; **b. à bon dieu** ladybird, *Am* ladybug; **b. noire** pet hate, pet peeve; **chercher la petite b.** (*critiquer*) to pick holes.

bête[2] [bɛt] *a* silly, stupid. ◆**bêtement** *adv* stupidly; **tout b.** quite simply. ◆**bêtise** [betiz] *nf* silliness, stupidity; (*action, parole*) silly *ou* stupid thing; (*bagatelle*) mere trifle.

béton [betɔ̃] *nm* concrete; **en b.** concrete-; **b. armé** reinforced concrete. ◆**bétonnière** *nf*, ◆**bétonneuse** *nf* cement *ou* concrete mixer.

betterave [bɛtrav] *nf Culin* beetroot, *Am* beet; **b. sucrière** *ou* **à sucre** sugar beet.

beugler [bøgle] *vi* (*taureau*) to bellow; (*vache*) to moo; (*radio*) to blare (out).

beurre [bœr] *nm* butter; **b. d'anchois** anchovy paste. ◆**beurrer** *vt* to butter. ◆**beurrier** *nm* butter dish.

beuverie [bøvri] *nf* drinking session, booze-up.

bévue [bevy] *nf* blunder, mistake.

biais [bjɛ] *nm* (*moyen détourné*) device, expedient; (*aspect*) angle; **regarder de b.** to look at sidelong; **traverser en b.** to cross at an angle. ◆**biaiser** [bjeze] *vi* to prevaricate, hedge.

bibelot [biblo] *nm* curio, trinket.

biberon [bibrɔ̃] *nm* (feeding) bottle.

bible [bibl] *nf* bible; **la B.** the Bible. ◆**biblique** *a* biblical.

bibliobus [biblijɔbys] *nm* mobile library.

bibliographie [biblijɔgrafi] *nf* bibliography.

bibliothèque [biblijɔtɛk] *nf* library; (*meuble*) bookcase; (*à la gare*) bookstall. ◆**bibliothécaire** *nmf* librarian.

bic® [bik] *nm* ballpoint, biro®.

bicarbonate [bikarbɔnat] *nm* bicarbonate.

bicentenaire [bisɑ̃tnɛr] *nm* bicentenary, bicentennial.

biceps [bisɛps] *nm Anat* biceps.

biche [biʃ] *nf* doe, hind; **ma b.** *Fig* my pet.

bichonner [biʃɔne] *vt* to doll up.
bicoque [bikɔk] *nf Péj* shack, hovel.
bicyclette [bisiklɛt] *nf* bicycle, cycle; **la b.** *Sp* cycling: **aller à b.** to cycle.
bide [bid] *nm* (*ventre*) *Fam* belly; **faire un b.** *Arg* to flop.
bidet [bidɛ] *nm* (*cuvette*) bidet.
bidon [bidɔ̃] **1** *nm* (*d'essence*) can; (*pour boissons*) canteen; (*ventre*) *Fam* belly. **2** *nm* **du b.** *Fam* rubbish, bluff; – *a inv* (*simulé*) *Fam* fake, phoney. ◆**se bidonner** *vpr Fam* to have a good laugh.
bidonville [bidɔ̃vil] *nf* shantytown.
bidule [bidyl] *nm* (*chose*) *Fam* thingummy, whatsit.
bielle [bjɛl] *nf Aut* connecting rod.
bien [bjɛ̃] *adv* well; **il joue b.** he plays well; **je vais b.** I'm fine *ou* well; **b. fatigué/souvent/***etc* (*très*) very tired/often/*etc*; **merci b.!** thanks very much!; **b.!** fine!, right!; **b. du courage/***etc* a lot of courage/*etc*; **b. des fois/des gens/***etc* lots of *ou* many times/people/*etc*; **je l'ai b. dit** (*intensif*) I *did* say so; **c'est b. compris?** is that quite understood?; **c'est b. toi?** is it really you?; **tu as b. fait** you did right; **c'est b. fait (pour lui)** it serves him right; – *a inv* (*convenable*) all right, fine; (*agréable*) nice, fine; (*compétent, bon*) good, fine; (*à l'aise*) comfortable, fine; (*beau*) attractive; (*en forme*) well; (*moralement*) nice; **une fille b.** a nice *ou* respectable girl; – *nm* (*avantage*) good; (*capital*) possession; **ça te fera du b.** it will do you good; **le b. et le mal** good and evil; **biens de consommation** consumer goods. ◆**b.-aimé, -ée** *a & nmf* beloved. ◆**b.-être** *nm* wellbeing. ◆**b.-fondé** *nm* validity, soundness.
bienfaisance [bjɛ̃fəzɑ̃s] *nf* benevolence, charity; **de b.** (*société etc*) benevolent, charitable. ◆**bienfaisant** *a* beneficial.
bienfait [bjɛ̃fɛ] *nm* (*générosité*) favour; *pl* benefits, blessings. ◆**bienfaiteur, -trice** *nmf* benefactor, benefactress.
bienheureux, -euse [bjɛ̃nœrø, -øz] *a* blessed, blissful.
biennal, -aux [bjenal, -o] *a* biennial.
bien que [bjɛ̃k(ə)] *conj* although.
bienséant [bjɛ̃seɑ̃] *a* proper. ◆**bienséance** *nf* propriety.
bientôt [bjɛ̃to] *adv* soon; **à b.!** see you soon!; **il est b. dix heures/***etc* it's nearly ten o'clock/*etc*.
bienveillant [bjɛ̃vɛjɑ̃] *a* kindly. ◆**bienveillance** *nf* kindliness.
bienvenu, -ue [bjɛ̃vny] *a* welcome; – *nmf* **soyez le b.!** welcome!; – *nf* welcome; **souhaiter la bienvenue à** to welcome.
bière [bjɛr] *nf* **1** (*boisson*) beer; **b. pression** draught beer. **2** (*cercueil*) coffin.
biffer [bife] *vt* to cross *ou* strike out.
bifteck [biftɛk] *nm* steak; **gagner son b.** *Fam* to earn one's (daily) bread.
bifurquer [bifyrke] *vi* to branch off, fork. ◆**bifurcation** *nf* fork, junction.
bigame [bigam] *a* bigamous; – *nmf* bigamist. ◆**bigamie** *nf* bigamy.
bigarré [bigare] *a* (*bariolé*) mottled; (*hétéroclite*) motley, mixed.
bigler [bigle] *vi* (*loucher*) *Fam* to squint; – *vti* **b. (sur)** (*lorgner*) *Fam* to leer at. ◆**bigleux, -euse** *a Fam* cock-eyed.
bigorneau, -x [bigɔrno] *nm* (*coquillage*) winkle.
bigot, -ote [bigo, -ɔt] *nmf Péj* religious bigot; – *a* over-devout, fanatical.
bigoudi [bigudi] *nm* (hair)curler *ou* roller.
bigrement [bigrəmɑ̃] *adv Fam* awfully.
bijou, -x [biʒu] *nm* jewel; (*ouvrage élégant*) *Fig* gem. ◆**bijouterie** *nf* (*commerce*) jeweller's shop; (*bijoux*) jewellery. ◆**bijoutier, -ière** *nmf* jeweller.
bikini [bikini] *nm* bikini.
bilan [bilɑ̃] *nm Fin* balance sheet; (*résultat*) outcome; (*d'un accident*) (casualty) toll; **b. de santé** checkup; **faire le b.** to make an assessment **(de** of).
bilboquet [bilbɔkɛ] *nm* cup-and-ball (game).
bile [bil] *nf* bile; **se faire de la b.** *Fam* to worry, fret. ◆**bilieux, -euse** *a* bilious.
bilingue [bilɛ̃g] *a* bilingual.
billard [bijar] *nm* (*jeu*) billiards; (*table*) billiard table; *Méd Fam* operating table; **c'est du b.** *Fam* it's a cinch.
bille [bij] *nf* (*d'un enfant*) marble; (*de billard*) billiard ball; **stylo à b.** ballpoint pen, biro®.
billet [bijɛ] *nm* ticket; **b. (de banque)** (bank)note, *Am* bill; **b. aller, b. simple** single ticket, *Am* one-way ticket; **b. (d')aller et retour** return ticket, *Am* round trip ticket; **b. doux** love letter.
billion [biljɔ̃] *nm* billion, *Am* trillion.
billot [bijo] *nm* (*de bois*) block.
bimensuel, -elle [bimɑ̃sɥɛl] *a* bimonthly, fortnightly.
bimoteur [bimɔtœr] *a* twin-engined.
binaire [binɛr] *a* binary.
biner [bine] *vt* to hoe. ◆**binette** *nf* hoe; (*visage*) *Arg* mug, face.
biochimie [bjɔʃimi] *nf* biochemistry.

biodégradable [bjɔdegradabl] *a* biodegradable.
biographie [bjɔgrafi] *nf* biography. ◆**biographe** *nmf* biographer.
biologie [bjɔlɔʒi] *nf* biology. ◆**biologique** *a* biological.
bip-bip [bipbip] *nm* bleeper.
bipède [bipɛd] *nm* biped.
bique [bik] *nf Fam* nanny-goat.
Birmanie [birmani] *nf* Burma. ◆**birman, -ane** *a & nmf* Burmese.
bis[1] [bis] *adv* (*cri*) *Th* encore; *Mus* repeat; **4 bis** (*numéro*) 4A; – *nm Th* encore.
bis[2], **bise** [bi, biz] *a* greyish-brown.
bisbille [bisbij] *nf* squabble; **en b. avec** *Fam* at loggerheads with.
biscornu [biskɔrny] *a* (*objet*) distorted, misshapen; (*idée*) cranky.
biscotte [biskɔt] *nf* (*pain*) Melba toast; (*biscuit*) rusk, *Am* zwieback.
biscuit [biskɥi] *nm* (*salé*) biscuit, *Am* cracker; (*sucré*) biscuit, *Am* cookie; **b. de** Savoie sponge (cake). ◆**biscuiterie** *nf* biscuit factory.
bise [biz] *nf* **1** (*vent*) north wind. **2** (*baiser*) *Fam* kiss.
biseau, -x [bizo] *nm* bevel.
bison [bizɔ̃] *nm* bison, (American) buffalo.
bisou [bizu] *nm Fam* kiss.
bisser [bise] *vt* (*musicien, acteur*) to encore.
bissextile [bisɛkstil] *af* **année b.** leap year.
bistouri [bisturi] *nm* scalpel, lancet.
bistre [bistr] *a inv* bistre, dark-brown.
bistro(t) [bistro] *nm* bar, café.
bitume [bitym] *nm* (*revêtement*) asphalt.
bivouac [bivwak] *nm Mil* bivouac.
bizarre [bizar] *a* peculiar, odd, bizarre. ◆**—ment** *adv* oddly. ◆**bizarrerie** *nf* peculiarity.
blabla(bla) [blabla(bla)] *nm* claptrap, bunkum.
blafard [blafar] *a* pale, pallid.
blague [blag] *nf* **1** (*à tabac*) pouch. **2** (*plaisanterie, farce*) *Fam* joke; *pl* (*absurdités*) *Fam* nonsense; **sans b.!** you're joking! ◆**blagu/er** *vi* to be joking; – *vt* to tease. ◆**—eur, -euse** *nmf* joker.
blair [blɛr] *nm* (*nez*) *Arg* snout, conk. ◆**blairer** *vt Arg* to stomach.
blaireau, -x [blɛro] *nm* **1** (*animal*) badger. **2** (*brosse*) (shaving) brush.
blâme [blɑm] *nm* (*réprimande*) rebuke; (*reproche*) blame. ◆**blâmable** *a* blameworthy. ◆**blâmer** *vt* to rebuke; to blame.
blanc, blanche [blɑ̃, blɑ̃ʃ] **1** *a* white; (*page etc*) blank; **nuit blanche** sleepless night; **voix blanche** expressionless voice; – *nmf* (*personne*) white (man *ou* woman); – *nm* (*couleur*) white; (*de poulet*) white meat, breast; (*espace, interligne*) blank; **b. (d'œuf)** (egg) white; **le b.** (*linge*) whites; **magasin de b.** linen shop; **laisser en b.** to leave blank; **chèque en b.** blank cheque; **cartouche à b.** blank (cartridge); **saigner à b.** to bleed white. **2** *nf Mus* minim, *Am* half-note. ◆**blanchâtre** *a* whitish. ◆**blancheur** *nf* whiteness.
blanchir [blɑ̃ʃir] *vt* to whiten; (*draps*) to launder; (*mur*) to whitewash; *Culin* to blanch; (*argent*) *Fig* to launder; **b. qn** (*disculper*) to clear s.o.; – *vi* to turn white, whiten. ◆**blanchissage** *nm* laundering. ◆**blanchisserie** *nf* (*lieu*) laundry. ◆**blanchisseur, -euse** *nmf* laundryman, laundrywoman.
blanquette [blɑ̃kɛt] *nf* **b. de veau** veal stew in white sauce.
blasé [blɑze] *a* blasé.
blason [blazɔ̃] *nm* (*écu*) coat of arms; (*science*) heraldry.
blasphème [blasfɛm] *nf* blasphemy. ◆**blasphématoire** *a* (*propos*) blasphemous. ◆**blasphémer** *vti* to blaspheme.
blatte [blat] *nf* cockroach.
blazer [blazœr] *nm* blazer.
blé [ble] *nm* wheat; (*argent*) *Arg* bread.
bled [blɛd] *nm Péj Fam* (dump of a) village.
blême [blɛm] *a* sickly pale, wan; **b. de colère** livid with anger.
bless/er [blese] *vt* to injure, hurt; (*avec un couteau, une balle etc*) to wound; (*offenser*) to hurt, offend, wound; **se b. le** *ou* **au bras/***etc* to hurt one's arm/*etc*. ◆**—ant** [blɛsɑ̃] *a* (*parole, personne*) hurtful. ◆**—é, -ée** *nmf* casualty, injured *ou* wounded person. ◆**blessure** *nf* injury; wound.
blet, blette [blɛ, blɛt] *a* (*fruit*) overripe.
bleu [blø] *a* blue; **b. de colère** blue in the face; **steak b.** *Culin* very rare steak; – *nm* (*couleur*) blue; (*contusion*) bruise; (*vêtement*) overalls; (*conscrit*) raw recruit; **bleus de travail** overalls. ◆**bleuir** *vti* to turn blue.
bleuet [bløɛ] *nm* cornflower.
blind/er [blɛ̃de] *vt Mil* to armour(-plate). ◆**—é** *a* (*train etc*) *Mil* armoured; **porte blindée** reinforced steel door; – *nm Mil* armoured vehicle.
bloc [blɔk] *nm* block; (*de pierre*) lump, block; (*de papier*) pad; (*masse compacte*) unit; *Pol* bloc; **en b.** all together; **à b.** (*serrer etc*) tight, hard; **travailler à b.** *Fam* to work flat out. ◆**b.-notes** *nm* (*pl* **blocs-notes**) writing pad.

blocage [blɔkaʒ] *nm* (*des roues*) locking; *Psy* mental block; **b. des prix** price freeze.
blocus [blɔkys] *nm* blockade.
blond, -onde [blɔ̃, -ɔ̃d] *a* fair(-haired), blond; – *nm* fair-haired man; (*couleur*) blond; – *nf* fair-haired woman, blonde; (**bière**) **blonde** lager, pale *ou* light ale. ◆**blondeur** *nf* fairness, blondness.
bloquer [blɔke] *vt* (*obstruer*) to block; (*coincer*) to jam; (*grouper*) to group together; (*ville*) to blockade; (*freins*) to slam *ou* jam on; (*roue*) to lock; (*salaires, prix*) to freeze; **bloqué par la neige/la glace** snowbound/icebound; – **se b.** *vpr* to stick, jam; (*roue*) to lock.
blottir (se) [səblɔtir] *vpr* (*dans un coin etc*) to crouch; (*dans son lit*) to snuggle down; **se b. contre** to huddle *ou* snuggle up to.
blouse [bluz] *nf* (*tablier*) overall, smock; (*corsage*) blouse. ◆**blouson** *nm* (waist-length) jacket.
blue-jean [bludʒin] *nm* jeans, denims.
bluff [blœf] *nm* bluff. ◆**bluffer** *vti* to bluff.
boa [bɔa] *nm* (*serpent, tour de cou*) boa.
bobard [bɔbar] *nm Fam* fib, yarn, tall story.
bobine [bɔbin] *nf* (*de fil, film etc*) reel, spool; (*pour machine à coudre*) bobbin, spool.
bobo [bobo] *nm* (*langage enfantin*) pain; **j'ai b., ça fait b.** it hurts.
bocage [bɔkaʒ] *nm* copse.
bocal, -aux [bɔkal, -o] *nm* glass jar; (*à poissons*) bowl.
bock [bɔk] *nm* (*récipient*) beer glass; (*contenu*) glass of beer.
bœuf, *pl* **-fs** [bœf, bø] *nm* (*animal*) ox (*pl* oxen), bullock; (*viande*) beef.
bohème [bɔɛm] *a* & *nmf* bohemian. ◆**bohémien, -ienne** *a* & *nmf* gipsy.
boire* [bwar] *vt* to drink; (*absorber*) to soak up; (*paroles*) *Fig* to take *ou* drink in; **b. un coup** to have a drink; **offrir à b. à qn** to offer s.o. a drink; **b. à petits coups** to sip; – *vi* to drink.
bois[1] [bwa] *voir* **boire.**
bois[2] [bwa] *nm* (*matière, forêt*) wood; (*de construction*) timber; (*gravure*) woodcut; *pl* (*de cerf*) antlers; *Mus* woodwind instruments; **en** *ou* **de b.** wooden; **b. de chauffage** firewood; **b. de lit** bedstead. ◆**boisé** *a* wooded. ◆**boiserie(s)** *nf(pl)* panelling.
boisson [bwasɔ̃] *nf* drink, beverage.
boit [bwa] *voir* **boire.**
boîte [bwat] *nf* box; (*de conserve*) tin, *Am* can; (*lieu de travail*) *Fam* firm; **b. aux** *ou* **à lettres** letterbox; **b. de nuit** nightclub; **mettre qn en b.** *Fam* to pull s.o.'s leg. ◆**boîtier** *nm* (*de montre etc*) case.
boiter [bwate] *vi* (*personne*) to limp. ◆**boiteux, -euse** *a* lame; (*meuble*) wobbly; (*projet etc*) *Fig* shaky.
bol [bɔl] *nm* (*récipient*) bowl; **prendre un b. d'air** to get a breath of fresh air; **avoir du b.** *Fam* to be lucky.
bolide [bɔlid] *nm* (*véhicule*) racing car.
Bolivie [bɔlivi] *nf* Bolivia. ◆**bolivien, -ienne** *a* & *nmf* Bolivian.
bombard/er [bɔ̃barde] *vt* (*ville etc*) to bomb; (*avec des obus*) to shell; **b. qn** *Fam* (*nommer*) to pitchfork s.o. (**à un poste** into a job); **b. de** (*questions*) to bombard with; (*objets*) to pelt with. ◆**—ement** *nm* bombing; shelling. ◆**bombardier** *nm* (*avion*) bomber.
bombe [bɔ̃b] *nf* (*projectile*) bomb; (*atomiseur*) spray; **tomber comme une b.** *Fig* to be a bombshell, be quite unexpected; **faire la b.** *Fam* to have a binge.
bomb/er [bɔ̃be] **1** *vi* (*gonfler*) to bulge; – *vt* **b. la poitrine** to throw out one's chest. **2** *vi* (*véhicule etc*) *Fam* to bomb *ou* belt along. ◆**—é** *a* (*verre etc*) rounded; (*route*) cambered.
bon[1]**, bonne**[1] [bɔ̃, bɔn] *a* **1** (*satisfaisant etc*) good. **2** (*charitable*) kind, good. **3** (*agréable*) nice, good; **il fait b. se reposer** it's nice *ou* good to rest; **b. anniversaire!** happy birthday! **4** (*qui convient*) right; **c'est le b. clou** it's the right nail. **5** (*approprié, apte*) fit; **b. à manger** fit to eat; **b. pour le service** fit for service; **ce n'est b. à rien** it's useless; **comme b. te semble** as you think fit *ou* best; **c'est b. à savoir** it's worth knowing. **6** (*prudent*) wise, good; **croire b. de** to think it wise *ou* good to. **7** (*compétent*) good; **b. en français** good at French. **8** (*valable*) good; **ce billet est encore b.** this ticket's still good. **9** (*intensif*) **un b. moment** a good while. **10 à quoi b.?** what's the use *ou* point *ou* good?; **pour de b.** in earnest; **tenir b.** to stand firm; **ah b.?** is that so? **11** *nm* **du b.** some good; **les bons** the good.
bon[2] [bɔ̃] *nm* (*billet*) coupon, voucher; (*titre*) *Fin* bond; (*formulaire*) slip.
bonasse [bɔnas] *a* feeble, soft.
bonbon [bɔ̃bɔ̃] *nm* sweet, *Am* candy. ◆**bonbonnière** *nf* sweet box, *Am* candy box.
bonbonne [bɔ̃bɔn] *nf* (*récipient*) demijohn.
bond [bɔ̃] *nm* leap, bound; (*de balle*) bounce; **faire faux b. à qn** to stand s.o. up, let s.o. down (*by not turning up*). ◆**bondir** *vi* to leap, bound.
bonde [bɔ̃d] *nf* (*bouchon*) plug; (*trou*) plughole.

bondé [bɔ̃de] *a* packed, crammed.
bonheur [bɔnœr] *nm* (*chance*) good luck, good fortune; (*félicité*) happiness; **par b.** luckily; **au petit b.** haphazardly.
bonhomie [bɔnɔmi] *nf* good-heartedness.
bonhomme, *pl* **bonshommes** [bɔnɔm, bɔ̃zɔm] **1** *nm* fellow, guy; **b. de neige** snowman; **aller son petit b. de chemin** to go on in one's own sweet way. **2** *a inv* good-hearted.
boniment(s) [bɔnimɑ̃] *nm(pl)* (*bobard*) claptrap; (*baratin*) patter.
bonjour [bɔ̃ʒur] *nm & int* good morning; (*après-midi*) good afternoon; **donner le b. à, dire b. à** to say hello to.
bonne² [bɔn] *nf* (*domestique*) maid; **b. d'enfants** nanny.
bonnement [bɔnmɑ̃] *adv* **tout b.** simply.
bonnet [bɔnɛ] *nm* cap; (*de femme, d'enfant*) bonnet; (*de soutien-gorge*) cup; **gros b.** *Fam* bigshot, bigwig. ◆**bonneterie** *nf* hosiery.
bonsoir [bɔ̃swar] *nm & int* (*en rencontrant qn*) good evening; (*en quittant qn*) goodbye; (*au coucher*) good night.
bonté [bɔ̃te] *nf* kindness, goodness.
bonus [bɔnys] *nm* no claims bonus.
bonze [bɔ̃z] *nm Péj Fam* bigwig.
boom [bum] *nm Écon* boom.
bord [bɔr] *nm* (*rebord*) edge; (*rive*) bank; (*de vêtement*) border; (*de chapeau*) brim; (*de verre*) rim, brim, edge; **au b. de la mer/route** at *ou* by the seaside/roadside; **b. du trottoir** kerb, *Am* curb; **au b. de** (*précipice*) on the brink of; **au b. des larmes** on the verge of tears; **à bord (de)** *Nau Av* on board; **jeter par-dessus b.** to throw overboard. ◆**border** *vt* (*vêtement*) to border, edge; (*lit, personne*) to tuck in; **b. la rue/***etc* (*maisons, arbres etc*) to line the street/*etc.* ◆**bordure** *nf* border; **en b. de** bordering on.
bordeaux [bɔrdo] *a inv* maroon.
bordée [bɔrde] *nf* (*salve*) *Nau* broadside; (*d'injures*) *Fig* torrent, volley.
bordel [bɔrdɛl] *nm* **1** *Fam* brothel. **2** (*désordre*) *Fam* mess.
bordereau, -x [bɔrdəro] *nm* (*relevé*) docket, statement; (*formulaire*) note.
borgne [bɔrɲ] *a* (*personne*) one-eyed, blind in one eye; (*hôtel etc*) *Fig* shady.
borne [bɔrn] *nf* (*pierre*) boundary mark; *Él* terminal; *pl* (*limites*) *Fig* bounds; **b. kilométrique** = milestone; **dépasser** *ou* **franchir les bornes** to go too far. ◆**born/er** *vt* (*limiter*) to confine; **se b. à** to confine oneself to. ◆**—é** *a* (*personne*) narrow-minded; (*intelligence*) narrow, limited.
bosquet [bɔskɛ] *nm* grove, thicket, copse.
bosse [bɔs] *nf* (*grosseur dorsale*) hump; (*enflure*) bump, lump; (*de terrain*) bump; **avoir la b. de** *Fam* to have a flair for; **rouler sa b.** *Fam* to knock about the world. ◆**bossu, -ue** *a* hunchbacked; **dos b.** hunchback; – *nmf* (*personne*) hunchback.
bosseler [bɔsle] *vt* (*orfèvrerie*) to emboss; (*déformer*) to dent.
bosser [bɔse] *vi Fam* to work (hard).
bot [bo] *am* **pied b.** club foot.
botanique [bɔtanik] *a* botanical; – *nf* botany.
botte [bɔt] *nf* (*chaussure*) boot; (*faisceau*) bunch, bundle. ◆**botter** *vt* (*ballon etc*) *Fam* to boot. ◆**bottier** *nm* bootmaker. ◆**bottillon** *nm,* ◆**bottine** *nf* (ankle) boot.
Bottin® [bɔtɛ̃] *nm* telephone book.
bouc [buk] *nm* billy goat; (*barbe*) goatee; **b. émissaire** scapegoat.
boucan [bukɑ̃] *nm Fam* din, row, racket.
bouche [buʃ] *nf* mouth; **faire la petite** *ou* **fine b.** *Péj* to turn up one's nose; **une fine b.** a gourmet; **b. de métro** métro entrance; **b. d'égout** drain opening, manhole; **b. d'incendie** fire hydrant; **le b.-à-b.** the kiss of life. ◆**bouchée** *nf* mouthful.
bouch/er¹ [buʃe] **1** *vt* (*évier, nez etc*) to block (up), stop up; (*bouteille*) to close, cork; (*vue, rue etc*) to block; **se b. le nez** to hold one's nose. ◆**—é** *a* (*vin*) bottled; (*temps*) overcast; (*personne*) *Fig* stupid, dense. ◆**bouche-trou** *nm* stopgap. ◆**bouchon** *nm* stopper, top; (*de liège*) cork; (*de tube, bidon*) cap, top; *Pêche* float; (*embouteillage*) *Fig* traffic jam.
boucher² [buʃe] *nm* butcher. ◆**boucherie** *nf* butcher's (shop); (*carnage*) butchery.
boucle [bukl] *nf* **1** (*de ceinture*) buckle; (*de fleuve etc*) & *Av* loop; (*de ruban*) bow; **b. d'oreille** earring. **2 b. (de cheveux)** curl. ◆**boucl/er 1** *vt* to fasten, buckle; (*travail etc*) to finish off; (*enfermer, fermer*) *Fam* to lock up; (*budget*) to balance; (*circuit*) to lap; (*encercler*) to surround, cordon off; **b. la boucle** *Av* to loop the loop; **la b.** *Fam* to shut up. **2** *vt* (*cheveux*) to curl; – *vi* to be curly. ◆**—é** *a* (*cheveux*) curly.
bouclier [buklije] *nm* shield.
bouddhiste [budist] *a & nmf* Buddhist.
bouder [bude] *vi* to sulk; – *vt* (*personne, plaisirs etc*) to steer clear of. ◆**bouderie** *nf* sulkiness. ◆**boudeur, -euse** *a* sulky, moody.
boudin [budɛ̃] *nm* black pudding, *Am* blood pudding.
boue [bu] *nf* mud. ◆**boueux, -euse 1** *a*

muddy. **2** *nm* dustman, *Am* garbage collector.

bouée [bwe] *nf* buoy; **b. de sauvetage** lifebuoy.

bouffe [buf] *nf Fam* food, grub, nosh.

bouffée [bufe] *nf* (*de fumée*) puff; (*de parfum*) whiff; (*d'orgueil*) fit; **b. de chaleur** *Méd* hot flush. ◆**bouff/er 1** *vi* to puff out. **2** *vti* (*manger*) *Fam* to eat. ◆**—ant** *a* (*manche*) puff(ed). ◆**bouffi** *a* puffy, bloated.

bouffon, -onne [bufɔ̃, -ɔn] *a* farcical; – *nm* buffoon. ◆**bouffonneries** *nfpl* antics, buffoonery.

bouge [buʒ] *nm* (*bar*) dive; (*taudis*) hovel.

bougeotte [buʒɔt] *nf* **avoir la b.** *Fam* to have the fidgets.

bouger [buʒe] *vi* to move; (*agir*) to stir; (*rétrécir*) to shrink; – *vt* to move; **— se b.** *vpr Fam* to move.

bougie [buʒi] *nf* candle; *Aut* spark(ing) plug. ◆**bougeoir** *nm* candlestick.

bougon, -onne [bugɔ̃, -ɔn] *a Fam* grumpy; – *nmf* grumbler, grouch. ◆**bougonner** *vi Fam* to grumble, grouch.

bougre [bugr] *nm* fellow, bloke; (*enfant*) *Péj* (little) devil. ◆**bougrement** *adv Arg* damned.

bouillabaisse [bujabɛs] *nf* fish soup.

bouillie [buji] *nf* porridge; **en b.** in a mush, mushy.

bouill/ir* [bujir] *vi* to boil; **b. à gros bouillons** to bubble, boil hard; **faire b. qch** to boil sth. ◆**—ant** *a* boiling; **b. de colère/***etc* seething with anger/*etc*. ◆**bouilloire** *nf* kettle. ◆**bouillon** *nm* (*eau*) broth, stock; (*bulle*) bubble. ◆**bouillonner** *vi* to bubble. ◆**bouillotte** *nf* hot water bottle.

boulanger, -ère [bulɑ̃ʒe, -ɛr] *nmf* baker. ◆**boulangerie** *nf* baker's (shop).

boule [bul] *nf* (*sphère*) ball; *pl* (*jeu*) bowls; **b. de neige** snowball; **faire b. de neige** to snowball; **perdre la b.** *Fam* to go out of one's mind; **se mettre en b.** (*chat etc*) to curl up into a ball; **boules Quiès®** earplugs. ◆**boulet** *nm* (*de forçat*) ball and chain; **b. de canon** cannonball. ◆**boulette** *nf* (*de papier*) pellet; (*de viande*) meatball; (*gaffe*) *Fam* blunder.

bouleau, -x [bulo] *nm* (silver) birch.

bouledogue [buldɔg] *nm* bulldog.

boulevard [bulvar] *nm* boulevard.

boulevers/er [bulvɛrse] *vt* (*déranger*) to turn upside down; (*émouvoir*) to upset deeply, distress; (*vie de qn, pays*) to disrupt. ◆**—ant** *a* upsetting, distressing. ◆**—ement** *nm* upheaval.

boulon [bulɔ̃] *nm* bolt.

boulot, -otte [bulo, -ɔt] **1** *a* dumpy. **2** *nm* (*travail*) *Fam* work.

boum [bum] **1** *int & nm* bang. **2** *nf* (*surprise-partie*) *Fam* party.

bouquet [bukɛ] *nm* (*de fleurs*) bunch, bouquet; (*d'arbres*) clump; (*de vin*) bouquet; (*crevette*) prawn; **c'est le b.!** that's the last straw!

bouquin [bukɛ̃] *nm Fam* book. ◆**bouquiner** *vti Fam* to read. ◆**bouquiniste** *nmf* second-hand bookseller.

bourbeux, -euse [burbø, -øz] *a* muddy. ◆**bourbier** *nm* (*lieu, situation*) quagmire, morass.

bourde [burd] *nf* blunder, bloomer.

bourdon [burdɔ̃] *nm* (*insecte*) bumblebee. ◆**bourdonn/er** *vi* to buzz, hum. ◆**—ement** *nm* buzzing, humming.

bourg [bur] *nm* (small) market town. ◆**bourgade** *nf* (large) village.

bourgeois, -oise [burʒwa, -waz] *a & nmf* middle-class (person); *Péj* bourgeois. ◆**bourgeoisie** *nf* middle class, bourgeoisie.

bourgeon [burʒɔ̃] *nm* bud. ◆**bourgeonner** *vi* to bud; (*nez*) *Fam* to be pimply.

bourgmestre [burgmɛstr] *nm* (*en Belgique, Suisse*) burgomaster.

bourgogne [burgɔɲ] *nm* (*vin*) Burgundy.

bourlinguer [burlɛ̃ge] *vi* (*voyager*) *Fam* to knock about.

bourrade [burad] *nf* (*du coude*) poke.

bourrasque [burask] *nf* squall.

bourratif, -ive [buratif, -iv] *a* (*aliment*) *Fam* filling, stodgy.

bourreau, -x [buro] *nm* executioner; **b. d'enfants** child batterer; **b. de travail** workaholic.

bourrelet [burlɛ] *nm* weather strip; **b. de graisse** roll of fat, spare tyre.

bourr/er [bure] **1** *vt* to stuff, cram (full) (**de** with); (*pipe, coussin*) to fill; **b. de coups** to thrash; **b. le crâne à qn** to brainwash s.o. **2** **se b.** *vpr* (*s'enivrer*) *Fam* to get plastered. ◆**—age** *nm* **b. de crâne** brainwashing.

bourrique [burik] *nf* ass.

bourru [bury] *a* surly, rough.

bourse [burs] *nf* (*sac*) purse; *Scol Univ* grant, scholarship; **la B.** the Stock Exchange; **sans b. délier** without spending a penny. ◆**boursier, -ière 1** *a* Stock Exchange-. **2** *nmf Scol Univ* grant holder, scholar.

boursouflé [bursufle] *a* (*visage etc*) puffy; (*style*) *Fig* inflated.

bousculer [buskyle] *vt* (*heurter, pousser*) to

jostle; (*presser*) to rush, push; **b. qch** (*renverser*) to knock sth over; **b. les habitudes/***etc* to turn one's habits/*etc* upside down. ◆**bousculade** *nf* rush, jostling.

bouse [buz] *nf* **b. de vache** cow dung.

bousiller [buzije] *vt Fam* to mess up, wreck.

boussole [busɔl] *nf* compass.

bout [bu] *nm* end; (*de langue, canne, doigt*) tip; (*de papier, pain, ficelle*) bit; **un b. de temps/chemin** a little while/way; **au b. d'un moment** after a moment; **à b.** exhausted; **à b. de souffle** out of breath; **à b. de bras** at arm's length; **venir à b. de** (*travail*) to get through; (*adversaire*) to get the better of; **à tout b. de champ** at every turn, every minute; **à b. portant** point-blank.

boutade [butad] *nf* (*plaisanterie*) quip, witticism.

boute-en-train [butɑ̃trɛ̃] *nm inv* (*personne*) live wire.

bouteille [butɛj] *nf* bottle; (*de gaz*) cylinder.

bouteur [butœr] *nm* bulldozer.

boutique [butik] *nf* shop; (*d'un grand couturier*) boutique. ◆**boutiquier, -ière** *nmf Péj* shopkeeper.

boutoir [butwar] *nm* **coup de b.** staggering blow.

bouton [butɔ̃] *nm* (*bourgeon*) bud; (*pustule*) pimple, spot; (*de vêtement*) button; (*poussoir*) (push-)button; (*de porte, de télévision*) knob; **b. de manchette** cuff link. ◆**b.-d'or** *nm* (*pl* **boutons-d'or**) buttercup. ◆**b.-pression** *nm* (*pl* **boutons-pression**) press-stud, *Am* snap. ◆**boutonner** *vt*, **— se b.** *vpr* to button (up). ◆**boutonneux, -euse** *a* pimply, spotty. ◆**boutonnière** *nf* buttonhole.

bouture [butyr] *nf* (*plante*) cutting.

bouvreuil [buvrœj] *nm* (*oiseau*) bullfinch.

bovin [bɔvɛ̃] *a* bovine; **–** *nmpl* cattle.

bowling [boliŋ] *nm* (tenpin) bowling; (*lieu*) bowling alley.

box, *pl* **boxes** [bɔks] *nm* (*d'écurie*) (loose) box; (*de dortoir*) cubicle; *Jur* dock; *Aut* lockup *ou* individual garage.

boxe [bɔks] *nf* boxing. ◆**boxer** *vi Sp* to box; **–** *vt Fam* to whack, punch. ◆**boxeur** *nm* boxer.

boyau, -x [bwajo] *nm Anat* gut; (*corde*) catgut; (*de bicyclette*) (racing) tyre *ou Am* tire.

boycott/er [bɔjkɔte] *vt* to boycott. ◆**—age** *nm* boycott.

BP [bepe] *abrév* (*boîte postale*) PO Box.

bracelet [braslɛ] *nm* bracelet, bangle; (*de montre*) strap.

braconner [brakɔne] *vi* to poach. ◆**braconnier** *nm* poacher.

brader [brade] *vt* to sell off cheaply. ◆**braderie** *nf* open-air (clearance) sale.

braguette [bragɛt] *nf* (*de pantalon*) fly, flies.

braille [brɑj] *nm* Braille.

brailler [brɑje] *vti* to bawl. ◆**braillard** *a* bawling.

braire* [brɛr] *vi* (*âne*) to bray.

braise(s) [brɛz] *nf(pl)* embers, live coals. ◆**braiser** [breze] *vt Culin* to braise.

brancard [brɑ̃kar] *nm* (*civière*) stretcher; (*de charrette*) shaft. ◆**brancardier** *nm* stretcher-bearer.

branche [brɑ̃ʃ] *nf* (*d'un arbre, d'une science etc*) branch; (*de compas*) leg; (*de lunettes*) side piece. ◆**branchages** *nmpl* (cut *ou* fallen) branches.

branch/er [brɑ̃ʃe] *vt Él* to plug in; (*installer*) to connect. ◆**—é** *a* (*informé*) *Fam* with it. ◆**—ement** *nm Él* connection.

brandir [brɑ̃dir] *vt* to brandish, flourish.

brandon [brɑ̃dɔ̃] *nm* (*paille, bois*) firebrand.

branle [brɑ̃l] *nm* impetus; **mettre en b.** to set in motion. ◆**b.-bas** *nm inv* turmoil. ◆**branl/er** *vi* to be shaky, shake. ◆**—ant** *a* shaky.

braqu/er [brake] **1** *vt* (*arme etc*) to point, aim; (*yeux*) to fix; **b. qn contre qn** to set *ou* turn s.o. against s.o. **2** *vti Aut* to steer, turn. ◆**—age** *nm Aut* steering; **rayon de b.** turning circle.

bras [bra] *nm* arm; **en b. de chemise** in one's shirtsleeves; **b. dessus b. dessous** arm in arm; **sur les b.** *Fig* on one's hands; **son b. droit** *Fig* his right-hand man; **à b. ouverts** with open arms; **à tour de b.** with all one's might; **faire le b. d'honneur** *Fam* to make an obscene gesture; **à b.-le-corps** round the waist. ◆**brassard** *nm* armband. ◆**brassée** *nf* armful. ◆**brassière** *nf* (*de bébé*) vest, *Am* undershirt.

brasier [brazje] *nm* inferno, blaze.

brasse [bras] *nf* (*nage*) breaststroke; (*mesure*) fathom; **b. papillon** butterfly stroke.

brasser [brase] *vt* to mix; (*bière*) to brew. ◆**brassage** *nm* mixture; brewing. ◆**brasserie** *nf* (*usine*) brewery; (*café*) brasserie. ◆**brasseur** *nm* **b. d'affaires** *Péj* big businessman.

bravache [bravaʃ] *nm* braggart.

bravade [bravad] *nf* **par b.** out of bravado.

brave [brav] *a & nm* (*hardi*) brave (man); (*honnête*) good (man). ◆**bravement** *adv* bravely. ◆**braver** *vt* to defy; (*danger*) to brave. ◆**bravoure** *nf* bravery.

bravo [bravo] *int* well done, bravo, good show; – *nm* cheer.
break [brɛk] *nm* estate car, *Am* station wagon.
brebis [brəbi] *nf* ewe; **b. galeuse** black sheep.
brèche [brɛʃ] *nf* breach, gap; **battre en b.** (*attaquer*) to attack (mercilessly).
bredouille [brəduj] *a* **rentrer b.** to come back empty-handed.
bredouiller [brəduje] *vti* to mumble.
bref, brève [brɛf, brɛv] *a* brief, short; – *adv* (**enfin**) **b.** in a word.
breloque [brəlɔk] *nf* charm, trinket.
Brésil [brezil] *nm* Brazil. ◆**brésilien, -ienne** *a & nmf* Brazilian.
Bretagne [brətaɲ] *nf* Brittany. ◆**breton, -onne** *a & nmf* Breton.
bretelle [brətɛl] *nf* strap; (*voie de raccordement*) *Aut* access road; *pl* (*pour pantalon*) braces, *Am* suspenders.
breuvage [brœvaʒ] *nm* drink, brew.
brève [brɛv] *voir* **bref.**
brevet [brəvɛ] *nm* diploma; **b. (d'invention)** patent. ◆**brevet/er** *vt* to patent. ◆**—é** *a* (*technicien*) qualified.
bréviaire [brevjɛr] *nm* breviary.
bribes [brib] *nfpl* scraps, bits.
bric-à-brac [brikabrak] *nm inv* bric-à-brac, jumble, junk.
brick [brik] *nm* (*de lait, jus d'orange etc*) carton.
bricole [brikɔl] *nf* (*objet, futilité*) trifle. ◆**bricol/er** *vi* to do odd jobs; – *vt* (*réparer*) to patch up; (*fabriquer*) to put together. ◆**—age** *nm* (*petits travaux*) odd jobs; (*passe-temps*) do-it-yourself; **salon/rayon du b.** do-it-yourself exhibition/department. ◆**—eur, -euse** *nmf* handyman, handywoman.
bride [brid] *nf* (*de cheval*) bridle; **à b. abattue** at full gallop. ◆**brider** *vt* (*cheval*) to bridle; (*personne, désir*) to curb; *Culin* to truss; **avoir les yeux bridés** to have slit eyes.
bridge [bridʒ] *nm* (*jeu*) bridge.
brièvement [briɛvmɑ̃] *adv* briefly. ◆**brièveté** *nf* brevity.
brigade [brigad] *nf* (*de gendarmerie*) squad; *Mil* brigade; **b. des mœurs** vice squad. ◆**brigadier** *nm* police sergeant; *Mil* corporal.
brigand [brigɑ̃] *nm* robber; (*enfant*) rascal.
briguer [brige] *vt* to covet; (*faveurs, suffrages*) to court.
brillant [brijɑ̃] *a* (*luisant*) shining; (*astiqué*) shiny; (*couleur*) bright; (*magnifique*) *Fig* brilliant; – *nm* shine; brightness; *Fig* brilliance; (*diamant*) diamond. ◆**brillamment** *adv* brilliantly.
briller [brije] *vi* to shine; **faire b.** (*meuble*) to polish (up).
brimer [brime] *vt* to bully. ◆**brimade** *nm Scol* bullying, ragging, *Am* hazing; *Fig* vexation.
brin [brɛ̃] *nm* (*d'herbe*) blade; (*de corde, fil*) strand; (*de muguet*) spray; **un b. de** *Fig* a bit of.
brindille [brɛ̃dij] *nf* twig.
bringue [brɛ̃g] *nf* **faire la b.** *Fam* to have a binge.
bringuebaler [brɛ̃gbale] *vi* to wobble about.
brio [brijo] *nm* (*virtuosité*) brilliance.
brioche [brijɔʃ] *nf* **1** brioche (*light sweet bun*). **2** (*ventre*) *Fam* paunch.
brique [brik] *nf* brick. ◆**briquette** *nf* (*aggloméré*) breezeblock.
briquer [brike] *vt* to polish (up).
briquet [brikɛ] *nm* (cigarette) lighter.
brise [briz] *nf* breeze.
bris/er [brize] *vt* to break; (*en morceaux*) to smash, break; (*espoir, carrière*) to shatter; (*fatiguer*) to exhaust; **— se b.** *vpr* to break. ◆**—ants** *nmpl* reefs. ◆**brise-lames** *nm inv* breakwater.
britannique [britanik] *a* British; – *nmf* Briton; **les Britanniques** the British.
broc [bro] *nm* pitcher, jug.
brocanteur, -euse [brɔkɑ̃tœr, -øz] *nmf* secondhand dealer (*in furniture etc*).
broche [brɔʃ] *nf Culin* spit; (*bijou*) brooch, *Méd* pin. ◆**brochette** *nf* (*tige*) skewer; (*plat*) kebab.
broché [brɔʃe] *a* **livre b.** paperback.
brochet [brɔʃɛ] *nm* (*poisson*) pike.
brochure [brɔʃyr] *nf* brochure, booklet, pamphlet.
broder [brɔde] *vt* to embroider (**de** with). ◆**broderie** *nf* embroidery.
broncher [brɔ̃ʃe] *vi* (*bouger*) to budge; (*reculer*) to flinch; (*regimber*) to balk.
bronches [brɔ̃ʃ] *nfpl* bronchial tubes. ◆**bronchite** *nf* bronchitis.
bronze [brɔ̃z] *nm* bronze.
bronz/er [brɔ̃ze] *vt* to tan; – *vi*, **— se b.** *vpr* to get (sun)tanned; **se (faire) b.** to sunbathe. ◆**—age** *nm* (sun)tan, sunburn.
brosse [brɔs] *nf* brush; **b. à dents** toothbrush; **cheveux en b.** crew cut. ◆**brosser** *vt* to brush; **b. un tableau de** to give an outline of; **se b. les dents/les cheveux** to brush one's teeth/one's hair.
brouette [bruɛt] *nf* wheelbarrow.
brouhaha [bruaa] *nm* hubbub.

brouillard [brujar] *nm* fog; **il fait du b.** it's foggy.
brouille [bruj] *nf* disagreement, quarrel. ◆**brouiller 1** *vt* (*papiers, idées etc*) to mix up; (*vue*) to blur; (*œufs*) to scramble; *Rad* to jam; — **se b.** *vpr* (*idées*) to be *ou* get confused; (*temps*) to cloud over; (*vue*) to blur. **2** *vt* (*amis*) to cause a split between; — **se b.** *vpr* to fall out (**avec** with). ◆**brouillon, -onne 1** *a* confused. **2** *nm* rough draft.
broussailles [brusɑj] *nfpl* brushwood.
brousse [brus] *nf* **la b.** the bush.
brouter [brute] *vti* to graze.
broyer [brwaje] *vt* to grind; (*doigt, bras*) to crush; **b. du noir** to be (down) in the dumps.
bru [bry] *nf* daughter-in-law.
brugnon [bryɲɔ̃] *nm* (*fruit*) nectarine.
bruine [brɥin] *nf* drizzle. ◆**bruiner** *v imp* to drizzle.
bruissement [brɥismɑ̃] *nm* (*de feuilles*) rustle, rustling.
bruit [brɥi] *nm* noise, sound; (*nouvelle*) rumour; **faire du b.** to be noisy, make a noise. ◆**bruitage** *nm Cin* sound effects.
brûle-pourpoint (à) [abrylpurpwɛ̃] *adv* point-blank.
brûl/er [bryle] *vt* to burn; (*consommer*) to use up, burn; (*signal, station*) to go through (without stopping); **b. un feu (rouge)** to jump *ou* go through the lights; **ce désir le brûlait** this desire consumed him; – *vi* to burn; **b. (d'envie) de faire** to be burning to do; **ça brûle** (*temps*) it's baking *ou* scorching; — **se b.** *vpr* to burn oneself. ◆**—ant** *a* (*objet, soleil*) burning (hot); (*sujet*) *Fig* red-hot. ◆**—é 1** *nm* **odeur de b.** smell of burning. **2** *a* **cerveau b., tête brûlée** hothead. ◆**brûlure** *nf* burn; **brûlures d'estomac** heartburn.
brume [brym] *nf* mist, haze. ◆**brumeux, -euse** *a* misty, hazy; (*obscur*) *Fig* hazy.
brun, brune [brœ̃, bryn] *a* brown; (*cheveux*) dark, brown; (*personne*) dark-haired; – *nm* (*couleur*) brown; – *nmf* dark-haired person. ◆**brunette** *nf* brunette. ◆**brunir** *vt* (*peau*) to tan; – *vi* to turn brown; (*cheveux*) to go darker.
brushing [brœʃiŋ] *nm* blow-dry.
brusque [brysk] *a* (*manière etc*) abrupt, blunt; (*subit*) sudden, abrupt. ◆**brusquement** *adv* suddenly, abruptly. ◆**brusquer** *vt* to rush. ◆**brusquerie** *nf* abruptness, bluntness.
brut [bryt] *a* (*pétrole*) crude; (*diamant*) rough; (*sucre*) unrefined; (*soie*) raw; (*poids*) & *Fin* gross.
brutal, -aux [brytal, -o] *a* (*violent*) savage, brutal; (*franchise, réponse*) crude, blunt; (*fait*) stark. ◆**brutaliser** *vt* to ill-treat. ◆**brutalité** *nf* (*violence, acte*) brutality. ◆**brute** *nf* brute.
Bruxelles [brysɛl] *nm ou f* Brussels.
bruyant [brɥijɑ̃] *a* noisy. ◆**bruyamment** *adv* noisily.
bruyère [bryjɛr] *nf* (*plante*) heather; (*terrain*) heath.
bu [by] *voir* **boire.**
buanderie [bɥɑ̃dri] *nf* (*lieu*) laundry.
bûche [byʃ] *nf* log; **ramasser une b.** *Fam* to come a cropper, *Am* take a spill. ◆**bûcher 1** *nm* (*local*) woodshed; (*supplice*) stake. **2** *vt* (*étudier*) *Fam* to slog away at. ◆**bûcheron** *nm* woodcutter, lumberjack.
budget [bydʒɛ] *nm* budget. ◆**budgétaire** *a* budgetary; (*année*) financial.
buée [bɥe] *nf* condensation, mist.
buffet [byfɛ] *nm* (*armoire*) sideboard; (*table, restaurant, repas*) buffet.
buffle [byfl] *nm* buffalo.
buis [bɥi] *nm* (*arbre*) box; (*bois*) boxwood.
buisson [bɥisɔ̃] *nm* bush.
buissonnière [bɥisɔnjɛr] *af* **faire l'école b.** to play truant *ou Am* hookey.
bulbe [bylb] *nm* bulb. ◆**bulbeux, -euse** *a* bulbous.
Bulgarie [bylgari] *nf* Bulgaria. ◆**bulgare** *a* & *nmf* Bulgarian.
bulldozer [byldozœr] *nm* bulldozer.
bulle [byl] *nf* **1** bubble; (*de bande dessinée*) balloon. **2** (*décret du pape*) bull.
bulletin [byltɛ̃] *nm* (*communiqué, revue*) bulletin; (*de la météo*) & *Scol* report; (*de bagages*) ticket, *Am* check; **b. de paie** pay slip; **b. de vote** ballot paper.
buraliste [byralist] *nmf* (*à la poste*) clerk; (*au tabac*) tobacconist.
bureau, -x [byro] *nm* **1** (*table*) desk. **2** (*lieu*) office; (*comité*) board; **b. de change** bureau de change; **b. de location** *Th Cin* box office; **b. de tabac** tobacconist's (shop). ◆**bureaucrate** *nmf* bureaucrat. ◆**bureaucratie** [-asi] *nf* bureaucracy ◆**bureautique** *nf* office automation.
burette [byrɛt] *nf* oilcan; *Culin* cruet.
burlesque [byrlɛsk] *a* (*idée etc*) ludicrous; (*genre*) burlesque.
bus[1] [bys] *nm Fam* bus.
bus[2] [by] *voir* **boire.**
busqué [byske] *a* (*nez*) hooked.
buste [byst] *nm* (*torse, sculpture*) bust. ◆**bustier** *nm* long-line bra(ssiere).
but[1] [by(t)] *nm* (*dessein, objectif*) aim, goal;

(*cible*) target; *Fb* goal; **de b. en blanc** point-blank; **aller droit au b.** to go straight to the point; **j'ai pour b. de . . .** my aim is to . . . .
but² [by] *voir* **boire.**
butane [bytan] *nm* (*gaz*) butane.
but/er [byte] **1** *vi* **b. contre** to stumble over; (*difficulté*) *Fig* to come up against. **2 se b.** *vpr* (*s'entêter*) to get obstinate. ◆**—é** *a* obstinate.
butin [bytɛ̃] *nm* loot, booty.
butiner [bytine] *vi* (*abeille*) to gather nectar.
butoir [bytwar] *nm Rail* buffer; (*de porte*) stop(per).
butor [bytɔr] *nm Péj* lout, oaf, boor.
butte [byt] *nf* hillock, mound; **en b. à** (*calomnie etc*) exposed to.
buvable [byvabl] *a* drinkable. ◆**buveur, -euse** *nmf* drinker.
buvard [byvar] *a* & *nm* **(papier) b.** blotting paper.
buvette [byvɛt] *nf* refreshment bar.

C

C, c [se] *nm* C, c
c *abrév* centime.
c' [s] *voir* **ce¹.**
ça [sa] *pron dém* (*abrév de* **cela**) (*pour désigner*) that; (*plus près*) this; (*sujet indéfini*) it, that; **ça m'amuse que . . .** it amuses me that . . . ; **où/quand/comment/***etc* **ça?** where?/when?/how?/*etc*; **ça va (bien)?** how's it going?; **ça va!** fine!, OK!; **ça alors!** (*surprise, indignation*) well I never!, how about that!; **c'est ça** that's right; **et avec ça?** (*dans un magasin*) anything else?
çà [sa] *adv* **çà et là** here and there.
caban [kabɑ̃] *nm* (*veste*) reefer.
cabane [kaban] *nf* hut, cabin; (*à outils*) shed; (*à lapins*) hutch.
cabaret [kabarɛ] *nm* night club, cabaret.
cabas [kabɑ] *nm* shopping bag.
cabillaud [kabijo] *nm* (fresh) cod.
cabine [kabin] *nf Nau Av* cabin; *Tél* phone booth, phone box; (*de camion*) cab; (*d'ascenseur*) car, cage; **c. (de bain)** beach hut; (*à la piscine*) cubicle; **c. (de pilotage)** cockpit; (*d'un grand avion*) flight deck; **c. d'essayage** fitting room; **c. d'aiguillage** signal box.
cabinet [kabinɛ] *nm* (*local*) *Méd* surgery, *Am* office; (*d'avocat*) office, chambers; (*clientèle de médecin ou d'avocat*) practice; *Pol* cabinet; *pl* (*toilettes*) toilet; **c. de toilette** bathroom, toilet; **c. de travail** study.
câble [kɑbl] *nm* cable; (*cordage*) rope; **la télévision par c.** cable television; **le c.** *TV* cable. ◆**câbler** *vt* (*message*) to cable; **être câblé** *TV* to have cable.
caboche [kabɔʃ] *nf* (*tête*) *Fam* nut, noddle.
cabosser [kabɔse] *vt* to dent.
caboteur [kabɔtœr] *nm* (*bateau*) coaster.
cabotin, -ine [kabɔtɛ̃, -in] *nmf Th* ham actor, ham actress; *Fig* play-actor. ◆**cabotinage** *nm* histrionics, play-acting.
cabrer (se) [sәkabre] *vpr* (*cheval*) to rear (up); (*personne*) to rebel.
cabri [kabri] *nm* (*chevreau*) kid.
cabrioles [kabriɔl] *nfpl* **faire des c.** (*sauts*) to cavort, caper.
cabriolet [kabriɔlɛ] *nm Aut* convertible.
cacah(o)uète [kakawɛt] *nf* peanut.
cacao [kakao] *nm* (*boisson*) cocoa.
cacatoès [kakatoɛs] *nm* cockatoo.
cachalot [kaʃalo] *nm* sperm whale.
cache-cache [kaʃkaʃ] *nm inv* hide-and-seek. ◆**c.-col** *nm inv*, ◆**c.-nez** *nm inv* scarf, muffler. ◆**c.-sexe** *nm inv* G-string.
cachemire [kaʃmir] *nm* (*tissu*) cashmere.
cacher [kaʃe] *vt* to hide, conceal (**à** from); **je ne cache pas que . . .** I don't hide the fact that . . . ; **c. la lumière à qn** to stand in s.o.'s light; **— se c.** *vpr* to hide. ◆**cachette** *nf* hiding place; **en c.** in secret; **en c. de qn** without s.o. knowing.
cachet [kaʃɛ] *nm* (*sceau*) seal; (*de la poste*) postmark; (*comprimé*) tablet; (*d'acteur etc*) fee; *Fig* distinctive character. ◆**cacheter** *vt* to seal.
cachot [kaʃo] *nm* dungeon.
cachotteries [kaʃɔtri] *nfpl* secretiveness; (*petits secrets*) little mysteries. ◆**cachottier, -ière** *a* & *nmf* secretive (person).
cacophonie [kakɔfɔni] *nf* cacophony.
cactus [kaktys] *nm* cactus.
cadastre [kadastr] *nm* (*registre*) land register.
cadavre [kadɑvr] *nm* corpse. ◆**cadavéri-**

que *a* (*teint etc*) cadaverous; **rigidité c.** rigor mortis.

caddie® [kadi] *nm* supermarket trolly *ou Am* cart.

cadeau, -x [kado] *nm* present, gift.

cadenas [kadnɑ] *nm* padlock. ◆**cadenasser** *vt* to padlock.

cadence [kadɑ̃s] *nf* rhythm; *Mus* cadence; (*taux, vitesse*) rate; **en c.** in time. ◆**cadencé** *a* rhythmical.

cadet, -ette [kadɛ, -ɛt] *a* (*de deux frères etc*) younger; (*de plus de deux*) youngest; – *nmf* (*enfant*) younger (child); youngest (child); *Sp* junior; **c'est mon c.** he's my junior.

cadran [kadrɑ̃] *nm* (*de téléphone etc*) dial; (*de montre*) face; **c. solaire** sundial; **faire le tour du c.** to sleep round the clock.

cadre [kɑdr] *nm* **1** (*de photo, vélo etc*) frame; (*décor*) setting; (*sur un imprimé*) box; **dans le c. de** (*limites, contexte*) within the framework *ou* scope of, as part of. **2** (*chef*) *Com* executive, manager; *pl* (*personnel*) *Mil* officers; *Com* management, managers.

cadr/er [kɑdre] *vi* to tally (**avec** with); – *vt* (*image*) *Cin Phot* to centre. ◆**—eur** *nm* cameraman.

caduc, -uque [kadyk] *a* (*usage*) obsolete; *Bot* deciduous; *Jur* null and void.

cafard, -arde [kafar, -ard] **1** *nmf* (*espion*) sneak. **2** *nm* (*insecte*) cockroach; **avoir le c.** to be in the dumps; **ça me donne le c.** it depresses me. ◆**cafardeux, -euse** *a* (*personne*) in the dumps; (*qui donne le cafard*) depressing.

café [kafe] *nm* coffee; (*bar*) café; **c. au lait, c. crème** white coffee, coffee with milk; **c. noir, c. nature** black coffee; **tasse de c.** cup of black coffee. ◆**caféine** *nf* caffeine. ◆**cafétéria** *nf* cafeteria. ◆**cafetier** *nm* café owner. ◆**cafetière** *nf* percolator, coffeepot.

cafouiller [kafuje] *vi Fam* to make a mess (of things). ◆**cafouillage** *nm Fam* mess, muddle, snafu.

cage [kaʒ] *nf* cage; (*d'escalier*) well; (*d'ascenseur*) shaft; **c. des buts** *Fb* goal (area).

cageot [kaʒo] *nm* crate.

cagibi [kaʒibi] *nm* (storage) room, cubbyhole.

cagneux, -euse [kaɲø, -øz] *a* knock-kneed.

cagnotte [kaɲɔt] *nf* (*tirelire*) kitty.

cagoule [kagul] *nf* (*de bandit, pénitent*) hood.

cahier [kaje] *nm* (*carnet*) (note)book; *Scol* exercise book.

cahin-caha [kaɛ̃kaa] *adv* **aller c.-caha** to jog along (with ups and downs).

cahot [kao] *nm* jolt, bump. ◆**cahot/er** *vt* to jolt, bump; – *vi* (*véhicule*) to jolt along. ◆**—ant** *a*, ◆**cahoteux, -euse** *a* bumpy.

caïd [kaid] *nm Fam* big shot, leader.

caille [kɑj] *nf* (*oiseau*) quail.

cailler [kɑje] *vti*, — **se c.** *vpr* (*sang*) to clot, congeal; (*lait*) to curdle; **faire c.** (*lait*) to curdle; **ça caille** *Fam* it's freezing cold. ◆**caillot** *nm* (blood) clot.

caillou, -x [kaju] *nm* stone; (*galet*) pebble. ◆**caillouté** *a* gravelled. ◆**caillouteux, -euse** *a* stony.

caisse [kɛs] *nf* (*boîte*) case, box; (*cageot*) crate; (*guichet*) cash desk, pay desk; (*de supermarché*) checkout; (*fonds*) fund; (*bureau*) (paying-in) office; *Mus* drum; *Aut* body; **c. (enregistreuse)** cash register, till; **c. d'épargne** savings bank; **de c.** (*livre, recettes*) cash-. ◆**caissier, -ière** *nmf* cashier; (*de supermarché*) checkout assistant.

caisson [kɛsɔ̃] *nm* (*de plongeur*) & *Mil* caisson.

cajoler [kaʒɔle] *vt* (*câliner*) to pamper, pet, cosset. ◆**cajolerie(s)** *nf(pl)* pampering.

cajou [kaʒu] *nm* (*noix*) cashew.

cake [kɛk] *nm* fruit cake.

calamité [kalamite] *nf* calamity.

calandre [kalɑ̃dr] *nf Aut* radiator grille.

calcaire [kalkɛr] *a* (*terrain*) chalky; (*eau*) hard; – *nm Géol* limestone.

calciné [kalsine] *a* charred, burnt to a cinder.

calcium [kalsjɔm] *nm* calcium.

calcul [kalkyl] *nm* **1** calculation; (*estimation*) calculation, reckoning; (*discipline*) arithmetic; (*différentiel*) calculus. **2** *Méd* stone. ◆**calcul/er** *vt* (*compter*) to calculate, reckon; (*évaluer, combiner*) to calculate. ◆**—é** *a* (*risque etc*) calculated. ◆**calculateur** *nm* calculator, computer ◆**calculatrice** *nf* (*ordinateur*) calculator.

cale [kal] *nf* **1** (*pour maintenir*) wedge. **2** *Nau* hold; **c. sèche** dry dock.

calé [kale] *a Fam* (*instruit*) clever (**en qch** at sth); (*difficile*) tough.

caleçon [kalsɔ̃] *nm* underpants; **c. de bain** bathing trunks.

calembour [kalɑ̃bur] *nm* pun.

calendrier [kalɑ̃drije] *nm* (*mois et jours*) calendar; (*programme*) timetable.

cale-pied [kalpje] *nm* (*de bicyclette*) toe-clip.

calepin [kalpɛ̃] *nm* (pocket) notebook.

caler [kale] **1** *vt* (*meuble etc*) to wedge (up); (*appuyer*) to prop (up). **2** *vi* (*moteur*) to stall; – *vi* to stall; (*abandonner*) *Fam* give up.

calfeutrer [kalføtre] *vt* (*avec du bourrelet*) to draughtproof; **se c. (chez soi)** to shut oneself away, hole up.

calibre [kalibr] *nm* (*diamètre*) calibre; (*d'œuf*) grade; **de ce c.** (*bêtise etc*) of this degree. ◆**calibrer** *vt* (*œufs*) to grade.

calice [kalis] *nm* (*vase*) *Rel* chalice.

calicot [kaliko] *nm* (*tissu*) calico.

califourchon (à) [akalifurʃɔ̃] *adv* astride; **se mettre à c. sur** to straddle.

câlin [kɑlɛ̃] *a* endearing, cuddly. ◆**câliner** *vt* (*cajoler*) to make a fuss of; (*caresser*) to cuddle. ◆**câlineries** *nfpl* endearing ways.

calleux, -euse [kalø, -øz] *a* callous, horny.

calligraphie [kaligrafi] *nf* calligraphy.

calme [kalm] *a* calm; (*flegmatique*) calm, cool; (*journée etc*) quiet, calm; – *nm* calm(ness); **du c.!** keep quiet!; (*pas de panique*) keep calm!; **dans le c.** (*travailler, étudier*) in peace and quiet. ◆**calm/er** *vt* (*douleur*) to soothe; (*inquiétude*) to calm; (*ardeur*) to damp(en); **c. qn** to calm s.o. (down); – **se c.** *vpr* to calm down. ◆**—ant** *nm* sedative; **sous calmants** under sedation.

calomnie [kalɔmni] *nf* slander; (*par écrit*) libel. ◆**calomnier** *vt* to slander; to libel. ◆**calomnieux, -euse** *a* slanderous; libellous.

calorie [kalɔri] *nf* calorie.

calorifère [kalɔrifɛr] *nm* stove.

calorifuge [kalɔrifyʒ] *a* (heat-)insulating. ◆**calorifuger** *vt* to lag.

calot [kalo] *nm Mil* forage cap.

calotte [kalɔt] *nf Rel* skull cap; (*gifle*) *Fam* slap; **c. glaciaire** icecap.

calque [kalk] *nm* (*dessin*) tracing; (*imitation*) (exact *ou* carbon) copy; **(papier-)c.** tracing paper. ◆**calquer** *vt* to trace; to copy; **c. sur** to model on.

calumet [kalymɛ] *nm* **c. de la paix** peace pipe.

calvaire [kalvɛr] *nm Rel* calvary; *Fig* agony.

calvitie [kalvisi] *nf* baldness.

camarade [kamarad] *nmf* friend, chum; *Pol* comrade; **c. de jeu** playmate; **c. d'atelier** workmate. ◆**camaraderie** *nf* friendship, companionship.

cambouis [kɑ̃bwi] *nm* grease, (engine) oil.

cambrer [kɑ̃bre] *vt* to arch; **c. les reins** *ou* **le buste** to throw out one's chest; – **se c.** *vpr* to throw back one's shoulders. ◆**cambrure** *nf* curve; (*de pied*) arch, instep.

cambriol/er [kɑ̃brijɔle] *vt* to burgle, *Am* burglarize. ◆**—age** *nm* burglary. ◆**—eur, -euse** *nmf* burglar.

came [kam] *nf Tech* cam; **arbre à cames** camshaft.

camée [kame] *nm* (*pierre*) cameo.

caméléon [kameleɔ̃] *nm* (*reptile*) chameleon.

camélia [kamelja] *nm Bot* camellia.

camelot [kamlo] *nm* street hawker. ◆**camelote** *nf* cheap goods, junk.

camembert [kamɑ̃bɛr] *nm* Camembert (cheese).

camer (se) [sәkame] *vpr Fam* to get high (on drugs).

caméra [kamera] *nf* (TV *ou* film) camera. ◆**caméraman** *nm* (*pl* **-mans** *ou* **-men**) cameraman.

camion [kamjɔ̃] *nm* lorry, *Am* truck. ◆**c.-benne** *nm* (*pl* **camions-bennes**) dustcart, *Am* garbage truck. ◆**c.-citerne** *nm* (*pl* **camions-citernes**) tanker, *Am* tank truck. ◆**camionnage** *nm* (road) haulage, *Am* trucking. ◆**camionnette** *nf* van. ◆**camionneur** *nm* (*entrepreneur*) haulage contractor, *Am* trucker; (*conducteur*) lorry *ou Am* truck driver.

camisole [kamizɔl] *nf* **c. de force** straitjacket.

camomille [kamɔmij] *nf Bot* camomile; (*tisane*) camomile tea.

camoufl/er [kamufle] *vt* to camouflage. ◆**—age** *nm* camouflage.

camp [kɑ̃] *nm* camp; **feu de c.** campfire; **lit de c.** camp bed; **c. de concentration** concentration camp; **dans mon c.** (*jeu*) on my side; **ficher** *ou* **foutre le c.** *Arg* to clear off. ◆**camp/er** *vi* to camp; – *vt* (*personnage*) to portray (boldly); (*chapeau etc*) to plant boldly; – **se c.** *vpr* to plant oneself (boldly) (**devant** in front of). ◆**—ement** *nm* encampment, camp. ◆**—eur, -euse** *nmf* camper. ◆**camping** *nm* camping; (*terrain*) camp(ing) site. ◆**camping-car** *nm* camper.

campagne [kɑ̃paɲ] *nf* **1** country(side); **à la c.** in the country. **2** (*électorale, militaire etc*) campaign. ◆**campagnard, -arde** *a* country-; – *nm* countryman; – *nf* countrywoman.

campanile [kɑ̃panil] *nm* belltower.

camphre [kɑ̃fr] *nm* camphor.

campus [kɑ̃pys] *nm Univ* campus.

camus [kamy] *a* (*personne*) snub-nosed; **nez c.** snub nose.

Canada [kanada] *nm* Canada. ◆**canadien, -ienne** *a* & *nmf* Canadian; – *nf* fur-lined jacket.

canaille [kanɑj] *nf* rogue, scoundrel; – *a* vulgar, cheap.

canal, -aux [kanal, -o] *nm* (*artificiel*) canal; (*bras de mer*) & *TV* channel; (*conduite*) & *Anat* duct; **par le c. de** via, through. ◆**canalisation** *nf* (*de gaz etc*) mains. ◆**canaliser** *vt* (*rivière etc*) to canalize; (*diriger*) *Fig* to channel.

canapé [kanape] *nm* **1** (*siège*) sofa, couch, settee. **2** (*tranche de pain*) canapé.

canard [kanar] *nm* **1** duck; (*mâle*) drake. **2** *Mus* false note. **3** (*journal*) *Péj* rag. ◆**canarder** *vt* (*faire feu sur*) to fire at *ou* on.

canari [kanari] *nm* canary.

cancans [kɑ̃kɑ̃] *nmpl* (malicious) gossip. ◆**cancaner** *vi* to gossip. ◆**cancanier, -ière** *a* gossipy.

cancer [kɑ̃sɛr] *nm* cancer; **le C.** (*signe*) Cancer. ◆**cancéreux, -euse** *a* cancerous; – *nmf* cancer patient. ◆**cancérigène** *a* carcinogenic. ◆**cancérologue** *nmf* cancer specialist.

cancre [kɑ̃kr] *nm Scol Péj* dunce.

cancrelat [kɑ̃krəla] *nm* cockroach.

candélabre [kɑ̃delɑbr] *nm* candelabra.

candeur [kɑ̃dœr] *nf* innocence, artlessness. ◆**candide** *a* artless, innocent.

candidat, -ate [kɑ̃dida, -at] *nmf* candidate; (*à un poste*) applicant, candidate; **être** *ou* **se porter c. à** to apply for. ◆**candidature** *nf* application; *Pol* candidacy; **poser sa c.** to apply (**à** for).

cane [kan] *nf* (female) duck. ◆**caneton** *nm* duckling.

canette [kanɛt] *nf* **1** (*de bière*) (small) bottle. **2** (*bobine*) spool.

canevas [kanva] *nm* (*toile*) canvas; (*ébauche*) framework, outline.

caniche [kaniʃ] *nm* poodle.

canicule [kanikyl] *nf* scorching heat; (*période*) dog days.

canif [kanif] *nm* penknife.

canine [kanin] **1** *af* (*espèce, race*) canine; **exposition c.** dog show. **2** *nf* (*dent*) canine.

caniveau, -x [kanivo] *nm* gutter (*in street*).

canne [kan] *nf* (walking) stick; (*à sucre, de bambou*) cane; (*de roseau*) reed; **c. à pêche** fishing rod.

cannelle [kanɛl] *nf Bot Culin* cinnamon.

cannelure [kanlyr] *nf* groove; *Archit* flute.

cannette [kanɛt] *nf* = **canette.**

cannibale [kanibal] *nmf* & *a* cannibal. ◆**cannibalisme** *nm* cannibalism.

canoë [kanɔe] *nm* canoe; *Sp* canoeing. ◆**canoéiste** *nmf* canoeist.

canon [kanɔ̃] *nm* **1** (big) gun; *Hist* cannon; (*de fusil etc*) barrel; **c. lisse** smooth bore; **chair à c.** cannon fodder. **2** (*règle*) canon. ◆**canoniser** *vt* to canonize. ◆**canonnade** *nf* gunfire. ◆**canonnier** *nm* gunner.

cañon [kaɲɔ̃] *nm* canyon.

canot [kano] *nm* boat; **c. de sauvetage** lifeboat; **c. pneumatique** rubber dinghy. ◆**canot/er** *vi* to boat, go boating. ◆**—age** *nm* boating.

cantaloup [kɑ̃talu] *nm* (*melon*) cantaloup(e).

cantate [kɑ̃tat] *nf Mus* cantata.

cantatrice [kɑ̃tatris] *nf* opera singer.

cantine [kɑ̃tin] *nf* **1** (*réfectoire*) canteen; **manger à la c.** *Scol* to have school dinners. **2** (*coffre*) tin trunk.

cantique [kɑ̃tik] *nm* hymn.

canton [kɑ̃tɔ̃] *nm* (*en France*) district (*division of arrondissement*); (*en Suisse*) canton. ◆**cantonal, -aux** *a* divisional; cantonal.

cantonade (à la) [alakɑ̃tɔnad] *adv* (*parler etc*) to all and sundry, to everyone in general.

cantonn/er [kɑ̃tɔne] *vt Mil* to billet; (*confiner*) to confine; – *vi Mil* to be billeted; — **se c.** *vpr* to confine oneself (**dans** to). ◆**—ement** *nm* (*lieu*) billet, quarters.

cantonnier [kɑ̃tɔnje] *nm* road mender.

canular [kanylar] *nm* practical joke, hoax.

canyon [kaɲɔ̃] *nm* canyon.

caoutchouc [kautʃu] *nm* rubber; (*élastique*) rubber band; *pl* (*chaussures*) galoshes; **en c.** (*balle etc*) rubber-; **c. mousse** foam. ◆**caoutchouter** *vt* to rubberize. ◆**caoutchouteux, -euse** *a* rubbery.

CAP [seape] *nm abrév* (*certificat d'aptitude professionnelle*) technical and vocational diploma.

cap [kap] *nm Géog* cape, headland; *Nau* course; **mettre le c. sur** to steer a course for; **franchir** *ou* **doubler le c. de** (*difficulté*) to get over the worst of; **franchir** *ou* **doubler le c. de la trentaine/***etc* to turn thirty/*etc*.

capable [kapabl] *a* capable, able; **c. de faire** able to do, capable of doing. ◆**capacité** *nf* ability, capacity; (*contenance*) capacity.

cape [kap] *nf* cape; (*grande*) cloak.

CAPES [kapɛs] *nm abrév* (*certificat d'aptitude professionnelle à l'enseignement secondaire*) teaching diploma.

capillaire [kapilɛr] *a* (*huile, lotion*) hair-.

capitaine [kapitɛn] *nm* captain.

capital, -ale, -aux [kapital, -o] **1** *a* major, fundamental, capital; (*peine*) capital; (*péché*) deadly. **2** *a* (*lettre*) capital; – *nf* (*lettre, ville*) capital. **3** *nm* & *nmpl Fin* capital. ◆**capitaliser** *vt* (*accumuler*) to build up; – *vi* to save up. ◆**capitalisme** *nm*

capitalism. ◆**capitaliste** *a* & *nmf* capitalist.
capiteux, -euse [kapitø, -øz] *a* (*vin, parfum*) heady.
capitonn/er [kapitɔne] *vt* to pad, upholster. ◆**—age** *nm* (*garniture*) padding, upholstery.
capituler [kapityle] *vi* to surrender, capitulate. ◆**capitulation** *nf* surrender, capitulation.
caporal, -aux [kapɔral, -o] *nm* corporal.
capot [kapo] *nm Aut* bonnet, *Am* hood.
capote [kapɔt] *nf Aut* hood, *Am* (convertible) top; *Mil* greatcoat; **c. (anglaise)** (*préservatif*) *Fam* condom. ◆**capoter** *vi Aut Av* to overturn.
câpre [kɑpr] *nf Bot Culin* caper.
caprice [kapris] *nm* (passing) whim, caprice. ◆**capricieux, -euse** *a* capricious.
Capricorne [kaprikɔrn] *nm* **le C.** (*signe*) Capricorn.
capsule [kapsyl] *nf* (*spatiale*) & *Méd etc* capsule; (*de bouteille, pistolet d'enfant*) cap.
capter [kapte] *vt* (*faveur etc*) to win; (*attention*) to capture, win; (*eau*) to draw off; *Rad* to pick up.
captif, -ive [kaptif, -iv] *a* & *nmf* captive. ◆**captiver** *vt* to captivate, fascinate. ◆**captivité** *nf* captivity.
capture [kaptyr] *nf* capture; catch. ◆**capturer** *vt* (*criminel, navire*) to capture; (*animal*) to catch, capture.
capuche [kapyʃ] *nf* hood. ◆**capuchon** *nm* hood; (*de moine*) cowl; (*pèlerine*) hooded (rain)coat; (*de stylo*) cap, top.
capucine [kapysin] *nf* (*plante*) nasturtium.
caquet [kakɛ] *nm* (*bavardage*) cackle. ◆**caquet/er** *vi* (*poule, personne*) to cackle. ◆**—age** *nm* cackle.
car [kar] **1** *conj* because, for. **2** *nm* coach, bus, *Am* bus; **c. de police** police van.
carabine [karabin] *nf* rifle, carbine; **c. à air comprimé** airgun.
carabiné [karabine] *a Fam* violent; (*punition, amende*) very stiff.
caracoler [karakɔle] *vi* to prance, caper.
caractère [karaktɛr] *nm* **1** (*lettre*) *Typ* character; **en petits caractères** in small print; **caractères d'imprimerie** block capitals *ou* letters; **caractères gras** bold type *ou* characters. **2** (*tempérament, nature*) character, nature; (*attribut*) characteristic; **aucun c. de gravité** no serious element; **son c. inégal** his *ou* her uneven temper; **avoir bon c.** to be good-natured. ◆**caractériel, -ielle** *a* (*trait, troubles*) character-; – *a* & *nmf* disturbed (child). ◆**caractériser** *vt* to characterize; **se c. par** to be characterized by. ◆**caractéristique** *a* & *nf* characteristic.
carafe [karaf] *nf* decanter, carafe.
carambol/er [karɑ̃bɔle] *vt Aut* to smash into. ◆**—age** *nm* pileup, multiple smash-up.
caramel [karamɛl] *nm* caramel; (*bonbon dur*) toffee.
carapace [karapas] *nf* (*de tortue etc*) & *Fig* shell.
carat [kara] *nm* carat.
caravane [karavan] *nf* (*dans le désert*) caravan; *Aut* caravan, *Am* trailer; **c. publicitaire** publicity convoy. ◆**caravaning** *n*, ◆**caravanage** *n* caravanning.
carbone [karbɔn] *nm* carbon; **(papier) c.** carbon (paper). ◆**carboniser** *vt* to burn (to ashes), char; (*substance*) *Ch* to carbonize; **être mort carbonisé** to be burned to death.
carburant [karbyrɑ̃] *nm Aut* fuel. ◆**carburateur** *nm* carburettor, *Am* carburetor.
carcan [karkɑ̃] *nm Hist* iron collar; (*contrainte*) *Fig* yoke.
carcasse [karkas] *nf Anat* carcass; (*d'immeuble etc*) frame, shell.
cardiaque [kardjak] *a* (*trouble etc*) heart-; **crise c.** heart attack; **arrêt c.** cardiac arrest; – *nmf* heart patient.
cardinal, -aux [kardinal, -o] **1** *a* (*nombre, point*) cardinal. **2** *nm Rel* cardinal.
Carême [karɛm] *nm* Lent.
carence [karɑ̃s] *nf* inadequacy, incompetence; *Méd* deficiency.
carène [karɛn] *nf Nau* hull. ◆**caréné** *a Aut Av* streamlined.
caresse [karɛs] *nf* caress. ◆**caress/er** [karese] *vt* (*animal, enfant etc*) to stroke, pat, fondle; (*femme, homme*) to caress; (*espoir*) to cherish. ◆**—ant** *a* endearing, loving.
cargaison [kargɛzɔ̃] *nf* cargo, freight. ◆**cargo** *nm* freighter, cargo boat.
caricature [karikatyr] *nf* caricature. ◆**caricatural, -aux** *a* ludicrous; **portrait c.** portrait in caricature. ◆**caricaturer** *vt* to caricature.
carie [kari] *nf* **la c. (dentaire)** tooth decay; **une c.** a cavity. ◆**carié** *a* (*dent*) decayed, bad.
carillon [karijɔ̃] *nm* (*cloches*) chimes, peal; (*horloge*) chiming clock. ◆**carillonner** *vi* to chime, peal.
carlingue [karlɛ̃g] *nf* (*fuselage*) *Av* cabin.

carnage [karnaʒ] *nm* carnage.
carnassier, -ière [karnasje, -jɛr] *a* carnivorous; — *nm* carnivore.
carnaval, *pl* **-als** [karnaval] *nm* carnival.
carné [karne] *a* (*régime*) meat-.
carnet [karnɛ] *nm* notebook; (*de timbres, chèques, adresses etc*) book; **c. de notes** school report; **c. de route** logbook; **c. de vol** *Av* logbook.
carnivore [karnivɔr] *a* carnivorous; — *nm* carnivore.
carotte [karɔt] *nf* carrot.
carotter [karɔte] *vt Arg* to wangle, cadge (**à qn** from s.o.).
carpe [karp] *nf* carp.
carpette [karpɛt] *nf* rug.
carquois [karkwa] *nm* (*étui*) quiver.
carré [kare] *a* square; (*en affaires*) *Fig* plain-dealing; — *nm* square; (*de jardin*) patch; *Nau* messroom; **c. de soie** (square) silk scarf.
carreau, -x [karo] *nm* (*vitre*) (window) pane; (*pavé*) tile; (*sol*) tiled floor; *Cartes* diamonds; **à carreaux** (*nappe etc*) check(ed); **se tenir à c.** to watch one's step; **rester sur le c.** to be left for dead; (*candidat*) *Fig* to be left out in the cold. ◆**carrel/er** *vt* to tile. ◆**—age** *nm* (*sol*) tiled floor; (*action*) tiling.
carrefour [karfur] *nm* crossroads.
carrelet [karlɛ] *nm* (*poisson*) plaice, *Am* flounder.
carrément [karemɑ̃] *adv* (*dire etc*) straight out, bluntly; (*complètement*) downright, well and truly.
carrer (se) [səkare] *vpr* to settle down firmly.
carrière [karjɛr] *nf* **1** (*terrain*) quarry. **2** (*métier*) career.
carrosse [karɔs] *nm Hist* (horse-drawn) carriage. ◆**carrossable** *a* suitable for vehicles. ◆**carrosserie** *nf Aut* body(work).
carrousel [karuzɛl] *nm* (*tourbillon*) *Fig* whirl, merry-go-round.
carrure [karyr] *nf* breadth of shoulders, build; *Fig* calibre.
cartable [kartabl] *nm Scol* satchel.
carte [kart] *nf* card; (*de lecteur*) ticket; *Géog* map; *Nau Mét* chart; *Culin* menu; *pl* (*jeu*) cards; **c. (postale)** (post)card; **c. à jouer** playing card; **c. de crédit** credit card; **c. des vins** wine list; **c. grise** *Aut* vehicle registration; **c. blanche** *Fig* free hand.
cartel [kartɛl] *nm Écon Pol* cartel.
carter [kartɛr] *nm* (*de moteur*) *Aut* crankcase; (*de bicyclette*) chain guard.
cartilage [kartilaʒ] *nm* cartilage.
carton [kartɔ̃] *nm* cardboard; (*boîte*) cardboard box, carton; **c. à dessin** portfolio; **en c.-pâte** (*faux*) *Péj* pasteboard; **faire un c. sur** *Fam* to take a potshot at. ◆**cartonn/er** *vt* (*livre*) to case; **livre cartonné** hardback. ◆**—age** *nm* (*emballage*) cardboard package.
cartouche [kartuʃ] *nf* cartridge; (*de cigarettes*) carton; *Phot* cassette. ◆**cartouchière** *nf* (*ceinture*) cartridge belt.
cas [kɑ] *nm* case; **en tout c.** in any case *ou* event; **en aucun c.** on no account; **en c. de besoin** if need(s) be; **en c. d'accident** in the event of an accident; **en c. d'urgence** in (case of) an emergency; **faire c. de/peu de c. de** to set great/little store by; **au c. où elle tomberait** if she should fall; **pour le c. où il pleuvrait** in case it rains.
casanier, -ière [kazanje, -jɛr] *a & nmf* home-loving (person); (*pantouflard*) *Péj* stay-at-home (person).
casaque [kazak] *nf* (*de jockey*) shirt, blouse.
cascade [kaskad] *nf* **1** waterfall; (*série*) *Fig* spate; **en c.** in succession. **2** *Cin* stunt. ◆**cascadeur, -euse** *nmf Cin* stunt man, stunt woman.
case [kɑz] *nf* **1** pigeonhole; (*de tiroir*) compartment; (*d'échiquier etc*) square; (*de formulaire*) box. **2** (*hutte*) hut, cabin.
caser [kaze] *vt Fam* (*ranger*) to park, place; **c. qn** (*dans un logement ou un travail*) to find a place for s.o.; (*marier*) to marry s.o. off; — **se c.** *vpr* to settle down.
caserne [kazɛrn] *nf Mil* barracks; **c. de pompiers** fire station.
casier [kɑzje] *nm* pigeonhole, compartment; (*meuble à tiroirs*) filing cabinet; (*fermant à clef, à consigne automatique*) locker; **c. à bouteilles/à disques** bottle/record rack; **c. judiciaire** criminal record.
casino [kazino] *nm* casino.
casque [kask] *nm* helmet; (*pour cheveux*) (hair) dryer; **c. (à écouteurs)** headphones; **les Casques bleus** the UN peace-keeping force. ◆**casqué** *a* helmeted, wearing a helmet.
casquer [kaske] *vi Fam* to pay up, cough up.
casquette [kaskɛt] *nf* (*coiffure*) cap.
cassation [kasɑsjɔ̃] *nf* **Cour de c.** supreme court of appeal.
casse [1] [kɑs] *nf* **1** (*action*) breakage; (*objets*) breakages; (*grabuge*) *Fam* trouble; **mettre à la c.** to scrap; **vendre à la c.** to sell for

scrap. **2** *Typ* case; **bas/haut de c.** lower/upper case.
casse² [kɑs] *nm* (*cambriolage*) *Arg* break-in.
casse-cou [kɑsku] *nmf inv* (*personne*) *Fam* daredevil. **◆c.-croûte** *nm inv* snack. **◆c.-gueule** *nm inv Fam* death trap; – *a inv* perilous. **◆c.-noisettes** *nm inv*, **◆c.-noix** *nm inv* nut-cracker(s). **◆c.-pieds** *nmf inv* (*personne*) *Fam* pain in the neck. **◆c.-tête** *nm inv* **1** (*massue*) club. **2** (*problème*) headache; (*jeu*) puzzle, brain teaser.
cass/er [kɑse] *vt* to break; (*noix*) to crack; (*annuler*) *Jur* to annul; (*dégrader*) *Mil* to cashier; – *vi*, — **se c.** *vpr* to break; **il me casse la tête** *Fam* he's giving me a headache; **elle me casse les pieds** *Fam* she's getting on my nerves; **se c. la tête** *Fam* to rack one's brains; **c. la figure à qn** *Fam* to smash s.o.'s face in; **se c. la figure** (*tomber*) *Fam* to come a cropper, *Am* take a spill; **ça ne casse rien** *Fam* it's nothing special; **ça vaut 50F à tout c.** *Fam* it's worth 50F at the very most; **il ne s'est pas cassé** *Iron Fam* he didn't bother himself *ou* exhaust himself. **◆—ant** *a* (*fragile*) brittle; (*brusque*) curt, imperious; (*fatigant*) *Fam* exhausting. **◆—eur** *nm Aut* breaker, scrap merchant; (*manifestant*) demonstrator who damages property.
casserole [kasrɔl] *nf* (sauce)pan.
cassette [kasɛt] *nf* (*pour magnétophone ou magnétoscope*) cassette; **sur c.** (*film*) on video; **faire une c. de** (*film*) to make a video of.
cassis 1 [kasis] *nm Bot* blackcurrant; (*boisson*) blackcurrant liqueur. **2** [kasi] *nm Aut* dip (*across road*).
cassoulet [kasulɛ] *nm* stew (*of meat and beans*).
cassure [kɑsyr] *nf* (*fissure, rupture*) break; *Géol* fault.
castagnettes [kastaɲɛt] *nfpl* castanets.
caste [kast] *nf* caste; **esprit de c.** class consciousness.
castor [kastɔr] *nm* beaver.
castrer [kastre] *vt* to castrate. **◆castration** *nf* castration.
cataclysme [kataklism] *nm* cataclysm.
catacombes [katakɔ̃b] *nfpl* catacombs.
catalogue [katalɔg] *nm* catalogue. **◆cataloguer** *vt* (*livres etc*) to catalogue; **c. qn** *Péj* to categorize s.o.
catalyseur [katalizœr] *nm Ch & Fig* catalyst.
cataphote® [katafɔt] *nm Aut* reflector.
cataplasme [kataplasm] *nm Méd* poultice.
catapulte [katapylt] *nf Hist Av* catapult. **◆catapulter** *vt* to catapult.
cataracte [katarakt] *nf* **1** *Méd* cataract. **2** (*cascade*) falls, cataract.
catastrophe [katastrɔf] *nf* disaster, catastrophe; **atterrir en c.** to make an emergency landing. **◆catastrophique** *a* disastrous, catastrophic.
catch [katʃ] *nm* (all-in) wrestling. **◆catcheur, -euse** *nmf* wrestler.
catéchisme [kateʃism] *nm Rel* catechism.
catégorie [kategɔri] *nf* category. **◆catégorique** *a* categorical.
cathédrale [katedral] *nf* cathedral.
catholicisme [katɔlisism] *nm* Catholicism. **◆catholique** *a & nmf* Catholic; **pas (très) c.** (*affaire, personne*) *Fig* shady, doubtful.
catimini (en) [ɑ̃katimini] *adv* on the sly.
cauchemar [koʃmar] *nm* nightmare.
cause [koz] *nf* cause; *Jur* case; **à c. de** because of, on account of; **et pour c.!** for a very good reason!; **pour c. de** on account of; **en connaissance de c.** in full knowledge of the facts; **mettre en c.** (*la bonne foi de qn etc*) to (call into) question; (*personne*) to implicate; **en c.** involved, in question.
caus/er [koze] **1** *vt* (*provoquer*) to cause. **2** *vi* (*bavarder*) to chat (**de** about); (*discourir*) to talk; (*jaser*) to blab. **◆—ant** *a Fam* chatty, talkative. **◆causerie** *nf* talk. **◆causette** *nf* **faire la c.** *Fam* to have a little chat.
caustique [kostik] *a* (*substance, esprit*) caustic.
cauteleux, -euse [kotlø, -øz] *a* wily, sly.
cautériser [koterize] *vt Méd* to cauterize.
caution [kosjɔ̃] *nf* surety; (*pour libérer qn*) *Jur* bail; **sous c.** on bail; **sujet à c.** (*nouvelle etc*) very doubtful. **◆cautionn/er** *vt* (*approuver*) to sanction. **◆—ement** *nm* (*garantie*) surety.
cavalcade [kavalkad] *nf Fam* stampede; (*défilé*) cavalcade. **◆cavale** *nf* **en c.** *Arg* on the run. **◆cavaler** *vi Fam* to run, rush.
cavalerie [kavalri] *nf Mil* cavalry; (*de cirque*) horses. **◆cavalier, -ière 1** *nmf* rider; – *nm Mil* trooper, cavalryman; *Échecs* knight; – *af* **allée cavalière** bridle path. **2** *nmf* (*pour danser*) partner, escort. **3** *a* (*insolent*) offhand.
cave [kav] **1** *nf* cellar, vault. **2** *a* sunken, hollow. **◆caveau, -x** *nm* (*sépulture*) (burial) vault.
caverne [kavɛrn] *nf* cave, cavern; **homme**

des cavernes caveman. ◆**caverneux, -euse** *a* (*voix, rire*) hollow, deep-sounding.
caviar [kavjar] *nm* caviar(e).
cavité [kavite] *nf* cavity.
CCP [sesepe] *nm abrév* (*Compte chèque postal*) PO Giro account, *Am* Post Office checking account.
ce[1] [s(ə)] (**c'** *before e and é*) *pron dém* **1** it, that; **c'est toi/bon/demain/***etc* it's *ou* that's you/good/tomorrow/*etc*; **c'est mon médecin** he's my doctor; **ce sont eux qui . . .** they are the ones who . . . ; **c'est à elle de jouer** it's her turn to play; **est-ce que tu viens?** are you coming?; **sur ce** at this point, thereupon. **2 ce que, ce qui** what; **je sais ce qui est bon/ce que tu veux** I know what is good/what you want; **ce que c'est beau!** how beautiful it is!
ce[2]**, cette,** *pl* **ces** [s(ə), sɛt, se] (**ce** *becomes* **cet** *before a vowel or mute h*) *a dém* this, that, *pl* these, those; (**+** *-ci*) this, *pl* these; (**+** *-là*) that, *pl* those; **cet homme** this *ou* that man; **cet homme-ci** this man; **cet homme-là** that man.
ceci [səsi] *pron dém* this; **écoutez bien c.** listen to this.
cécité [sesite] *nf* blindness.
céder [sede] *vt* to give up (**à** to); *Jur* to transfer; **c. le pas à** to give way *ou* precedence to; – *vi* (*personne*) to give way, give in, yield (**à** to); (*branche, chaise etc*) to give way.
cédille [sedij] *nf Gram* cedilla.
cèdre [sɛdr] *nm* (*arbre, bois*) cedar.
CEE [seøø] *nf abrév* (*Communauté économique européenne*) EEC.
ceindre [sɛ̃dr] *vt* (*épée*) *Lit* to gird on.
ceinture [sɛ̃tyr] *nf* belt; (*de robe de chambre*) cord; (*taille*) *Anat* waist; (*de remparts*) *Hist* girdle; **petite/grande c.** *Rail* inner/outer circle; **c. de sécurité** *Aut Av* seatbelt; **c. de sauvetage** lifebelt. ◆**ceinturer** *vt* to seize round the waist; *Rugby* to tackle; (*ville*) to girdle, surround.
cela [s(ə)la] *pron dém* (*pour désigner*) that; (*sujet indéfini*) it, that; **c. m'attriste que . . .** it saddens me that . . . ; **quand/comment/***etc* **c.?** when?/how?/*etc*; **c'est c.** that is so.
célèbre [selɛbr] *a* famous. ◆**célébrité** *nf* fame; (*personne*) celebrity.
célébrer [selebre] *vt* to celebrate. ◆**célébration** *nf* celebration (**de** of).
céleri [sɛlri] *nm* (*en branches*) celery.
céleste [selɛst] *a* celestial, heavenly.
célibat [seliba] *nm* celibacy. ◆**célibataire** *a* (*non marié*) single, unmarried; (*chaste*) celibate; – *nm* bachelor; – *nf* unmarried woman, spinster.
celle *voir* **celui.**
cellier [selje] *nm* storeroom (*for wine etc*).
cellophane® [selɔfan] *nf* cellophane®.
cellule [selyl] *nf* cell. ◆**cellulaire** *a* (*tissu etc*) *Biol* cell-; **voiture c.** prison van.
celluloïd [selylɔid] *nm* celluloid.
cellulose [selyloz] *nf* cellulose.
celtique *ou* **celte** [sɛltik, sɛlt] *a* Celtic.
celui, celle, *pl* **ceux, celles** [səlɥi, sɛl, sø, sɛl] *pron dém* **1** the one, *pl* those, the ones; **c. de Jean** John's (one); **ceux de Jean** John's (ones), those of John. **2** (**+** *-ci*) this one, *pl* these (ones); (*dont on vient de parler*) the latter; (**+** *-là*) that one, *pl* those (ones); the former; **ceux-ci sont gros** these (ones) are big.
cendre [sɑ̃dr] *nf* ash. ◆**cendré** *a* ash(-coloured), ashen. ◆**cendrée** *nf Sp* cinder track.
Cendrillon [sɑ̃drijɔ̃] *nm* Cinderella.
censé [sɑ̃se] *a* supposed; **il n'est pas c. le savoir** he's not supposed to know.
censeur [sɑ̃sœr] *nm* censor; *Scol* assistant headmaster, vice-principal. ◆**censure** *nf* **la c.** (*examen*) censorship; (*comité, service*) the censor; **motion de c.** *Pol* censure motion. ◆**censurer** *vt* (*film etc*) to censor; (*critiquer*) & *Pol* to censure.
cent [sɑ̃] ([sɑ̃t] *pl* [sɑ̃z] *before vowel and mute h except* **un** *and* **onze**) *a* & *nm* hundred; **c. pages** a *ou* one hundred pages; **deux cents pages** two hundred pages; **deux c. trois pages** two hundred and three pages; **cinq pour c.** five per cent. ◆**centaine** *nf* **une c.** a hundred (or so); **des centaines de** hundreds of. ◆**centenaire** *a* & *nmf* centenarian; – *nm* (*anniversaire*) centenary. ◆**centième** *a* & *nmf* hundredth; **un c.** a hundredth. ◆**centigrade** *a* centigrade. ◆**centime** *nm* centime. ◆**centimètre** *nm* centimetre; (*ruban*) tape measure.
central, -aux [sɑ̃tral, -o] **1** *a* central; **pouvoir c.** (power of) central government. **2** *nm* **c. (téléphonique)** (telephone) exchange. ◆**centrale** *nf* (*usine*) power station. ◆**centraliser** *vt* to centralize. ◆**centre** *nm* centre; **c. commercial** shopping centre. ◆**c.-ville** *nm inv* city *ou* town centre. ◆**centrer** *vt* to centre. ◆**centrifuge** *a* centrifugal. ◆**centrifugeuse** *nf* liquidizer, juice extractor.
centuple [sɑ̃typl] *nm* hundredfold; **au c.** a hundredfold. ◆**centupler** *vti* to increase a hundredfold.

cep [sɛp] *nm* vine stock. ◆**cépage** *nm* vine (plant).
cependant [səpɑ̃dɑ̃] *conj* however, yet.
céramique [seramik] *nf* (*art*) ceramics; (*matière*) ceramic; **de** *ou* **en c.** ceramic.
cerceau, -x [sɛrso] *nm* hoop.
cercle [sɛrkl] *nm* (*forme, groupe, étendue*) circle; **c. vicieux** vicious circle.
cercueil [sɛrkœj] *nm* coffin.
céréale [sereal] *nf* cereal.
cérébral, -aux [serebral, -o] *a* cerebral.
cérémonie [seremɔni] *nf* ceremony; **de c.** (*tenue etc*) ceremonial; **sans c.** (*inviter, manger*) informally; **faire des cérémonies** *Fam* to make a lot of fuss. ◆**cérémonial,** *pl* **-als** *nm* ceremonial. ◆**cérémonieux, -euse** *a* ceremonious.
cerf [sɛr] *nm* deer; (*mâle*) stag. ◆**cerf-volant** *nm* (*pl* **cerfs-volants**) (*jouet*) kite.
cerise [s(ə)riz] *nf* cherry. ◆**cerisier** *nm* cherry tree.
cerne [sɛrn] *nm* (*cercle, marque*) ring. ◆**cerner** *vt* to surround; (*problème*) to define; **les yeux cernés** with rings under one's eyes.
certain [sɛrtɛ̃] **1** *a* (*sûr*) certain, sure; **il est** *ou* **c'est c. que tu réussiras** you're certain *ou* sure to succeed; **je suis c. de réussir** I'm certain *ou* sure I'll succeed; **être c. de qch** to be certain *ou* sure of sth. **2** *a* (*imprécis, difficile à fixer*) certain; *pl* certain, some; **un c. temps** a certain (amount of) time; – *pron pl* some (people), certain people; (*choses*) some. ◆**certainement** *adv* certainly. ◆**certes** *adv* indeed.
certificat [sɛrtifika] *nm* certificate. ◆**certifi/er** *vt* to certify; **je vous certifie que** I assure you that. ◆**—é** *a* (*professeur*) qualified.
certitude [sɛrtityd] *nf* certainty; **avoir la c. que** to be certain that.
cerveau, -x [sɛrvo] *nm* (*organe*) brain; (*intelligence*) mind, brain(s); **rhume de c.** head cold; **fuite des cerveaux** brain drain.
cervelas [sɛrvəla] *nm* saveloy.
cervelle [sɛrvɛl] *nf* (*substance*) brain; *Culin* brains; **tête sans c.** scatterbrain.
ces *voir* **ce**[2].
CES [seəɛs] *nm abrév* (*collège d'enseignement secondaire*) comprehensive school, *Am* high school.
césarienne [sezarjɛn] *nf Méd* Caesarean (section).
cessation [sɛsɑsjɔ̃] *nf* (*arrêt, fin*) suspension.
cesse [sɛs] *nf* **sans c.** incessantly; **elle n'a (pas) eu de c. que je fasse . . .** she had no rest until I did . . . .
cesser [sese] *vti* to stop; **faire c.** to put a stop *ou* halt to; **il ne cesse (pas) de parler** he doesn't stop talking. ◆**cessez-le-feu** *nm inv* ceasefire.
cession [sɛsjɔ̃] *nf Jur* transfer.
c'est-à-dire [setadir] *conj* that is (to say), in other words.
cet, cette *voir* **ce**[2].
ceux *voir* **celui.**
chacal, *pl* **-als** [ʃakal] *nm* jackal.
chacun, -une [ʃakœ̃, -yn] *pron* each (one), every one; (*tout le monde*) everyone.
chagrin [ʃagrɛ̃] **1** *nm* sorrow, grief; **avoir du c.** to be very upset. **2** *a Lit* doleful. ◆**chagriner** *vt* to upset, distress.
chahut [ʃay] *nm* racket, noisy disturbance. ◆**chahut/er** *vi* to create a racket *ou* a noisy disturbance; – *vt* (*professeur*) to be rowdy with, play up. ◆**—eur, -euse** *nmf* rowdy.
chai [ʃɛ] *nm* wine and spirits storehouse.
chaîne [ʃɛn] *nf* chain; *TV* channel, network; *Géog* chain, range; *Nau* cable; *Tex* warp; *pl* (*liens*) *Fig* shackles, chains; **c. de montage** assembly line; **travail à la c.** production-line work; **c. haute fidélité, c. hi-fi** hi-fi system; **c. de magasins** chain of shops *ou Am* stores; **collision en c.** *Aut* multiple collision; **réaction en c.** chain reaction. ◆**chaînette** *nf* (small) chain. ◆**chaînon** *nm* (*anneau, lien*) link.
chair [ʃɛr] *nf* flesh; **(couleur) c.** flesh-coloured; **en c. et en os** in the flesh; **la c. de poule** goose pimples, gooseflesh; **bien en c.** plump; **c. à saucisses** sausage meat.
chaire [ʃɛr] *nf Univ* chair; *Rel* pulpit.
chaise [ʃɛz] *nf* chair, seat; **c. longue** (*siège pliant*) deckchair; **c. d'enfant, c. haute** high-chair.
chaland [ʃalɑ̃] *nm* barge, lighter.
châle [ʃɑl] *nm* shawl.
chalet [ʃalɛ] *nm* chalet.
chaleur [ʃalœr] *nf* heat; (*douce*) warmth; (*d'un accueil, d'une voix etc*) warmth; (*des convictions*) ardour; (*d'une discussion*) heat. ◆**chaleureux, -euse** *a* warm.
challenge [ʃalɑ̃ʒ] *nm Sp* contest.
chaloupe [ʃalup] *nf* launch, long boat.
chalumeau, -x [ʃalymo] *nm* blowlamp, *Am* blowtorch; *Mus* pipe.
chalut [ʃaly] *nm* trawl net, drag net. ◆**chalutier** *nm* (*bateau*) trawler.
chamailler (se) [səʃamɑje] *vpr* to squabble, bicker. ◆**chamailleries** *nfpl* squabbling, bickering.

chamarré [ʃamare] *a* (*robe etc*) richly coloured; **c. de** (*décorations etc*) *Péj* bedecked with.
chambard [ʃɑ̃bar] *nm Fam* (*tapage*) rumpus, row. ◆**chambarder** *vt Fam* to turn upside down; **il a tout chambardé dans** he's turned everything upside down in.
chambouler [ʃɑ̃bule] *vt Fam* to make topsy-turvy, turn upside down.
chambre [ʃɑ̃br] *nf* (bed)room; *Pol Jur Tech Anat* chamber; **c. à coucher** bedroom; (*mobilier*) bedroom suite; **c. à air** (*de pneu*) inner tube; **C. des Communes** *Pol* House of Commons; **c. d'ami** guest *ou* spare room; **c. forte** strongroom; **c. noire** *Phot* darkroom; **garder la c.** to stay indoors. ◆**chambrée** *nf Mil* barrack room. ◆**chambrer** *vt* (*vin*) to bring to room temperature.
chameau, -x [ʃamo] *nm* camel.
chamois [ʃamwa] **1** *nm* (*animal*) chamois; **peau de c.** chamois (leather), shammy. **2** *a inv* buff(-coloured).
champ [ʃɑ̃] *nm* field; (*domaine*) *Fig* scope, range; **c. de bataille** battlefield; **c. de courses** racecourse, racetrack; **c. de foire** fairground; **c. de tir** (*terrain*) rifle range; **laisser le c. libre à qn** to leave the field open for s.o. ◆**champêtre** *a* rustic, rural.
champagne [ʃɑ̃paɲ] *nm* champagne; **c. brut** extra-dry champagne.
champignon [ʃɑ̃piɲɔ̃] *nm* **1** *Bot* mushroom; **c. vénéneux** toadstool, poisonous mushroom; **c. atomique** mushroom cloud. **2** *Aut Fam* accelerator pedal.
champion [ʃɑ̃pjɔ̃] *nm* champion. ◆**championnat** *nm* championship.
chance [ʃɑ̃s] *nf* luck; (*probabilité de réussir, occasion*) chance; **avoir de la c.** to be lucky; **tenter** *ou* **courir sa c.** to try one's luck; **c'est une c. que ...** it's a stroke of luck that ...; **mes chances de succès** my chances of success. ◆**chanceux, -euse** *a* lucky.
chancel/er [ʃɑ̃sle] *vi* to stagger, totter; (*courage*) *Fig* to falter. ◆**—ant** *a* (*pas, santé*) faltering, shaky.
chancelier [ʃɑ̃səlje] *nm* chancellor. ◆**chancellerie** *nf* chancellery.
chancre [ʃɑ̃kr] *nm Méd & Fig* canker.
chandail [ʃɑ̃daj] *nm* (thick) sweater, jersey.
chandelier [ʃɑ̃dəlje] *nm* candlestick.
chandelle [ʃɑ̃dɛl] *nf* candle; **voir trente-six chandelles** *Fig* to see stars; **en c.** *Av Sp* straight into the air.
change [ʃɑ̃ʒ] *nm Fin* exchange; **le contrôle des changes** exchange control; **donner le c. à qn** to deceive s.o. ◆**chang/er** *vt* (*modifier, remplacer, échanger*) to change; **c. qn en** to change s.o. into; **ça la changera de ne pas travailler** it'll be a change for her not to be working; – *vi* to change; **c. de voiture/d'adresse/***etc* to change one's car/address/*etc*; **c. de train/de place** to change trains/places; **c. de vitesse/de cap** to change gear/course; **c. de sujet** to change the subject; **— se c.** *vpr* to change (one's clothes). ◆**—eant** *a* (*temps*) changeable; (*humeur*) fickle; (*couleurs*) changing. ◆**—ement** *nm* change; **aimer le c.** to like change. ◆**—eur** *nm* moneychanger; **c. de monnaie** change machine.
chanoine [ʃanwan] *nm* (*personne*) *Rel* canon.
chanson [ʃɑ̃sɔ̃] *nf* song. ◆**chant** *nm* singing; (*chanson*) song; (*hymne*) chant; **c. de Noël** Christmas carol. ◆**chant/er** *vi* to sing; (*psalmodier*) to chant; (*coq*) to crow; **si ça te chante** *Fam* if you feel like it; **faire c. qn** to blackmail s.o.; – *vt* to sing; (*glorifier*) to sing of; (*dire*) *Fam* to say. ◆**—ant** *a* (*air, voix*) melodious. ◆**—age** *nm* blackmail. ◆**—eur, -euse** *nm* singer.
chantier [ʃɑ̃tje] *nm* (building) site; (*entrepôt*) builder's yard; **c. naval** shipyard; **mettre un travail en c.** to get a task under way.
chantonner [ʃɑ̃tɔne] *vti* to hum.
chantre [ʃɑ̃tr] *nm Rel* cantor.
chanvre [ʃɑ̃vr] *nm* hemp; **c. indien** (*plante*) cannabis.
chaos [kao] *nm* chaos. ◆**chaotique** *a* chaotic.
chaparder [ʃaparde] *vt Fam* to filch, pinch (**à** from).
chapeau, -x [ʃapo] *nm* hat; (*de champignon, roue*) cap; **c.!** well done!; **donner un coup de c.** (*pour saluer etc*) to raise one's hat; **c. mou** trilby, *Am* fedora. ◆**chapelier** *nm* hatter.
chapelet [ʃaplɛ] *nm* rosary; **dire son c.** to tell one's beads; **un c. de** (*saucisses, injures etc*) a string of.
chapelle [ʃapɛl] *nf* chapel; **c. ardente** chapel of rest.
chaperon [ʃaprɔ̃] *nm* chaperon(e). ◆**chaperonner** *vt* to chaperon(e).
chapiteau, -x [ʃapito] *nm* (*de cirque*) big top; (*pour expositions etc*) marquee, tent; (*de colonne*) *Archit* capital.
chapitre [ʃapitr] *nm* chapter; **sur le c. de** on the subject of. ◆**chapitrer** *vt* to scold, lecture.
chaque [ʃak] *a* each, every.
char [ʃar] *nm Hist* chariot; (*de carnaval*)

float: *Can Fam* car; **c. à bœufs** oxcart; **c. (d'assaut)** *Mil* tank.

charabia [ʃarabja] *nm Fam* gibberish.

charade [ʃarad] *nf (énigme)* riddle; *(mimée)* charade.

charbon [ʃarbɔ̃] *nm* coal; *(fusain)* charcoal; **c. de bois** charcoal; **sur des charbons ardents** like a cat on hot bricks. ◆**charbonnages** *nmpl* coalmines, collieries. ◆**charbonnier, -ière** *a* coal-; – *nm* coal merchant.

charcuter [ʃarkyte] *vt (opérer) Fam Péj* to cut up (badly).

charcuterie [ʃarkytri] *nf* pork butcher's shop; *(aliment)* cooked (pork) meats. ◆**charcutier, -ière** *nmf* pork butcher.

chardon [ʃardɔ̃] *nm Bot* thistle.

chardonneret [ʃardɔnrɛ] *nm (oiseau)* goldfinch.

charge [ʃarʒ] *nf (poids)* load; *(fardeau)* burden; *Jur Él Mil* charge; *(fonction)* office; *pl Fin* financial obligations; *(dépenses)* expenses; *(de locataire)* (maintenance) charges; **charges sociales** national insurance contributions, *Am* Social Security contributions; **à c.** *(enfant, parent)* dependent; **être à c. à qn** to be a burden to s.o.; **à la c. de qn** *(personne)* dependent on s.o.; *(frais)* payable by s.o.; **prendre en c.** to take charge of, take responsibility for.

charg/er [ʃarʒe] *vt* to load; *Él Mil* to charge; *(passager) Fam* to pick up; **se c. de** *(enfant, tâche etc)* to take charge of; **c. qn de** *(impôts etc)* to burden s.o. with; *(paquets etc)* to load s.o. with; *(tâche etc)* to entrust s.o. with; **c. qn de faire** to instruct s.o. to do. ◆**—é, -ée** *a (personne, véhicule, arme etc)* loaded; *(journée etc)* heavy, busy; *(langue)* coated; **c. de** *(arbre, navire etc)* laden with; – *nmf* **c. de cours** *Univ* (temporary) lecturer. ◆**—ement** *nm (action)* loading; *(objet)* load. ◆**—eur** *nm (de piles)* charger.

chariot [ʃarjo] *nm (à bagages etc)* trolley, *Am* cart; *(de ferme)* waggon; *(de machine à écrire)* carriage.

charité [ʃarite] *nf (vertu, secours)* charity; *(acte)* act of charity; **faire la c.** to give to charity; **faire la c. à** *(mendiant)* to give to. ◆**charitable** *a* charitable.

charivari [ʃarivari] *nm Fam* hubbub, hullabaloo.

charlatan [ʃarlatɑ̃] *nm* charlatan, quack.

charme [ʃarm] *nm* **1** charm; *(magie)* spell. **2** *(arbre)* hornbeam. ◆**charm/er** *vt* to charm; **je suis charmé de vous voir** I'm delighted to see you. ◆**—ant** *a* charming. ◆**—eur, -euse** *nmf* charmer; – *a* engaging.

charnel, -elle [ʃarnɛl] *a* carnal.

charnier [ʃarnje] *nm* mass grave.

charnière [ʃarnjɛr] *nf* hinge; *Fig* meeting point (**de** between).

charnu [ʃarny] *a* fleshy.

charogne [ʃarɔɲ] *nf* carrion.

charpente [ʃarpɑ̃t] *nf* frame(work); *(de personne)* build. ◆**charpenté** *a* **bien c.** solidly built. ◆**charpenterie** *nf* carpentry. ◆**charpentier** *nm* carpenter.

charpie [ʃarpi] *nf* **mettre en c.** *(déchirer) & Fig* to tear to shreds.

charrette [ʃarɛt] *nf* cart. ◆**charretier** *nm* carter. ◆**charrier 1** *vt (transporter)* to cart; *(rivière)* to carry along, wash down *(sand etc)*. **2** *vti (taquiner) Fam* to tease.

charrue [ʃary] *nf* plough, *Am* plow.

charte [ʃart] *nf Pol* charter.

charter [ʃartɛr] *nm Av* charter (flight).

chas [ʃa] *nm* eye *(of a needle)*.

chasse [ʃas] *nf* **1** hunting, hunt; *(poursuite)* chase; *Av* fighter forces; **de c.** *(pilote, avion)* fighter-; **c. sous-marine** underwater (harpoon) fishing; **c. à courre** hunting; **tableau de c.** *(animaux abattus)* bag; **faire la c. à** to hunt down, hunt for; **donner la c. à** to give chase to; **c. à l'homme** manhunt. **2** **c. d'eau** toilet flush; **tirer la c.** to flush the toilet.

châsse [ʃɑs] *nf* shrine.

chassé-croisé [ʃasekrwaze] *nm (pl* **chassés-croisés**) *Fig* confused coming(s) and going(s).

chass/er [ʃase] *vt (animal)* to hunt; *(papillon)* to chase; *(faire partir)* to drive out *ou* off; *(employé)* to dismiss; *(mouche)* to brush away; *(odeur)* to get rid of; – *vi* to hunt; *Aut* to skid. ◆**—eur, -euse** *nmf* hunter; – *nm (domestique)* pageboy, bellboy; *Av* fighter; **c. à pied** infantryman. ◆**chasse-neige** *nm inv* snowplough, *Am* snowplow.

châssis [ʃɑsi] *nm* frame; *Aut* chassis.

chaste [ʃast] *a* chaste, pure. ◆**chasteté** *nf* chastity.

chat, chatte [ʃa, ʃat] *nmf* cat; **un c. dans la gorge** a frog in one's throat; **d'autres chats à fouetter** other fish to fry; **pas un c.** not a soul; **ma (petite) chatte** *Fam* my darling; **c. perché** *(jeu)* tag.

châtaigne [ʃatɛɲ] *nf* chestnut. ◆**châtaignier** *nm* chestnut tree. ◆**châtain** *a inv* (chestnut) brown.

château, -x [ʃɑto] *nm (forteresse)* castle; *(palais)* palace, stately home; **c. fort** fortified castle; **châteaux en Espagne** *Fig* castles in the air; **c. d'eau** water tower; **c. de cartes** house of cards. ◆**châtelain, -aine** *nmf* lord of the manor, lady of the manor.

châtier [ʃɑtje] *vt Litt* to chastise, castigate; (*style*) to refine.

châtiment [ʃɑtimɑ̃] *nm* punishment.

chaton [ʃatɔ̃] *nm* **1** (*chat*) kitten. **2** (*de bague*) setting, mounting. **3** *Bot* catkin.

chatouill/er [ʃatuje] *vt* (*pour faire rire*) to tickle; (*exciter, plaire à*) *Fig* to titillate. ◆**—ement** *nm* tickle; (*action*) tickling. ◆**chatouilleux, -euse** *a* ticklish; (*irritable*) touchy.

chatoyer [ʃatwaje] *vi* to glitter, sparkle.

châtrer [ʃɑtre] *vt* to castrate.

chatte [ʃat] *voir* **chat.**

chatteries [ʃatri] *nfpl* cuddles; (*friandises*) delicacies.

chatterton [ʃatɛrtɔn] *nm* adhesive insulating tape.

chaud [ʃo] *a* hot; (*doux*) warm; (*fervent*) *Fig* warm; **pleurer à chaudes larmes** to cry bitterly; – *nm* heat; warmth; **avoir c.** to be hot; to be warm; **il fait c.** it's hot; it's warm; **être au c.** to be in the warm(th); **ça ne me fait ni c. ni froid** it leaves me indifferent. ◆**chaudement** *adv* warmly; (*avec passion*) hotly.

chaudière [ʃodjɛr] *nf* boiler.

chaudron [ʃodrɔ̃] *nm* cauldron.

chauffard [ʃofar] *nm* road hog, reckless driver.

chauff/er [ʃofe] *vt* to heat up, warm up; (*métal etc*) *Tech* to heat; – *vi* to heat up, warm up; *Aut* to overheat; **ça va c.** *Fam* things are going to hot up; **— se c.** *vpr* to warm oneself up. ◆**—ant** *a* (*couverture*) electric; (*plaque*) hot-; (*surface*) heating. ◆**—age** *nm* heating. ◆**—eur** *nm* **1** (*de chaudière*) stoker. **2** *Aut* driver; (*employé, domestique*) chauffeur. ◆**chauffe-bain** *nm*, ◆**chauffe-eau** *nm inv* water heater. ◆**chauffe-plats** *nm inv* hotplate.

chaume [ʃom] *nm* (*tiges coupées*) stubble, straw; (*pour toiture*) thatch; **toit de c.** thatched roof. ◆**chaumière** *nf* thatched cottage.

chaussée [ʃose] *nf* road(way).

chausser [ʃose] *vt* (*chaussures*) to put on; (*fournir*) to supply in footwear; **c. qn** to put shoes on (to) s.o.; **c. du 40** to take a size 40 shoe; **ce soulier te chausse bien** this shoe fits (you) well; **— se c.** *vpr* to put on one's shoes. ◆**chausse-pied** *nm* shoehorn. ◆**chausson** *nm* slipper; (*de danse*) shoe; **c. (aux pommes)** apple turnover. ◆**chaussure** *nf* shoe; *pl* shoes, footwear; **chaussures à semelles compensées** platform shoes.

chaussette [ʃosɛt] *nf* sock.

chauve [ʃov] *a & nmf* bald (person).

chauve-souris [ʃovsuri] *nf* (*pl* **chauves-souris**) (*animal*) bat.

chauvin, -ine [ʃovɛ̃, -in] *a & nmf* chauvinist.

chaux [ʃo] *nf* lime; **blanc de c.** whitewash.

chavirer [ʃavire] *vti Nau* to capsize.

chef [ʃɛf] *nm* **1 de son propre c.** on one's own authority. **2** leader, head; (*de tribu*) chief; *Culin* chef; **en c.** (*commandant, rédacteur*) in chief; **c'est un c.!** (*personne remarquable*) he's an ace!; **c. d'atelier** (shop) foreman; **c. de bande** ringleader, gang leader; **c. d'entreprise** company head; **c. d'équipe** foreman; **c. d'État** head of state; **c. d'état-major** chief of staff; **c. de famille** head of the family; **c. de file** leader; **c. de gare** stationmaster; **c. d'orchestre** conductor. ◆**chef-lieu** *nm* (*pl* **chefs-lieux**) chief town (*of a département*).

chef-d'œuvre [ʃɛdœvr] *nm* (*pl* **chefs-d'œuvre**) masterpiece.

chemin [ʃ(ə)mɛ̃] *nm* **1** road, path; (*trajet, direction*) way; **beaucoup de c. à faire** a long way to go; **dix minutes de c.** ten minutes' walk; **se mettre en c.** to start out, set out; **faire du c.** to come a long way; (*idée*) to make considerable headway; **c. faisant** on the way; **à mi-c.** half-way. **2 c. de fer** railway, *Am* railroad. ◆**chemin/er** *vi* to proceed; (*péniblement*) to trudge (along) on foot; (*évoluer*) *Fig* to progress. ◆**—ement** *nm Fig* progress. ◆**cheminot** *nm* railway *ou Am* railroad employee.

cheminée [ʃ(ə)mine] *nf* (*sur le toit*) chimney; (*de navire*) funnel; (*âtre*) fireplace; (*encadrement*) mantelpiece.

chemise [ʃ(ə)miz] *nf* shirt; (*couverture cartonnée*) folder; **c. de nuit** nightdress. ◆**chemiserie** *nf* men's shirt (and underwear) shop. ◆**chemisette** *nf* short-sleeved shirt. ◆**chemisier** *nm* (*vêtement*) blouse.

chenal, -aux [ʃənal, -o] *nm* channel.

chenapan [ʃ(ə)napɑ̃] *nm Hum* rogue, scoundrel.

chêne [ʃɛn] *nm* (*arbre, bois*) oak.

chenet [ʃ(ə)nɛ] *nm* firedog, andiron.

chenil [ʃ(ə)ni(l)] *nm* kennels.

chenille [ʃ(ə)nij] *nf* caterpillar; (*de char*) *Mil* caterpillar track.

cheptel [ʃɛptɛl] *nm* livestock.

chèque [ʃɛk] *nm* cheque, *Am* check; **c. de voyage** traveller's cheque, *Am* traveler's check. ◆**c.-repas** *nm* (*pl* **chèques-repas**) luncheon voucher. ◆**chéquier** *nm* cheque book, *Am* checkbook.

cher, chère [ʃɛr] **1** *a* (*aimé*) dear (**à** to); – *nmf* **mon c.** my dear fellow; **ma chère** my dear (woman). **2** *a* (*coûteux*) dear, expensive; (*quartier, hôtel etc*) expensive; **la vie chère** the high cost of living; **payer c.** (*objet*) to pay a lot for; (*erreur etc*) *Fig* to pay dearly for. ◆**chèrement** *adv* dearly.

cherch/er [ʃɛrʃe] *vt* to look for, search for; (*du secours, la paix etc*) to seek; (*dans un dictionnaire*) to look up; **c. ses mots** to fumble for one's words; **aller c.** to (go and) fetch *ou* get; **c. à faire** to attempt to do; **tu l'as bien cherché!** it's your own fault!, you asked for it! ◆**—eur, -euse** *nmf* research worker; **c. d'or** gold-digger.

chér/ir [ʃerir] *vt* to cherish. ◆**—i, -ie** *a* dearly loved, beloved; – *nmf* darling.

chérot [ʃero] *am Fam* pricey.

cherté [ʃɛrte] *nf* high cost, expensiveness.

chétif, -ive [ʃetif, -iv] *a* puny; (*dérisoire*) wretched.

cheval, -aux [ʃ(ə)val, -o] *nm* horse; **c. (vapeur)** *Aut* horsepower; **à c.** on horseback; **faire du c.** to go horse riding; **à c. sur** straddling; **à c. sur les principes** a stickler for principle; **monter sur ses grands chevaux** to get excited; **c. à bascule** rocking horse; **c. d'arçons** *Sp* vaulting horse; **c. de bataille** (*dada*) hobbyhorse; **chevaux de bois** (*manège*) merry-go-round. ◆**chevaleresque** *a* chivalrous. ◆**chevalier** *nm* knight. ◆**chevalin** *a* equine; (*boucherie*) horse-.

chevalet [ʃ(ə)vale] *nm* easel; *Menuis* trestle.

chevalière [ʃ(ə)valjɛr] *nf* signet ring.

chevauchée [ʃ(ə)voʃe] *nf* (horse) ride.

chevaucher [ʃ(ə)voʃe] *vt* to straddle; – *vi*, – **se c.** *vpr* to overlap.

chevet [ʃ(ə)vɛ] *nm* bedhead; **table/livre de c.** bedside table/book; **au c. de** at the bedside of.

cheveu, -x [ʃ(ə)vø] *nm* **un c.** a hair; **les cheveux** hair; **couper les cheveux en quatre** *Fig* to split hairs; **tiré par les cheveux** (*argument*) far-fetched. ◆**chevelu** *a* hairy. ◆**chevelure** *nf* (head of) hair.

cheville [ʃ(ə)vij] *nf Anat* ankle; *Menuis* peg, pin; (*pour vis*) (wall)plug; **c. ouvrière** *Aut & Fig* linchpin; **en c. avec** *Fam* in cahoots with. ◆**cheviller** *vt Menuis* to pin, peg.

chèvre [ʃɛvr] *nf* goat; (*femelle*) nanny-goat. ◆**chevreau, -x** *nm* kid.

chèvrefeuille [ʃɛvrəfœj] *nm* honeysuckle.

chevreuil [ʃəvrœj] *nm* roe deer; *Culin* venison.

chevron [ʃəvrɔ̃] *nm* (*poutre*) rafter; *Mil* stripe, chevron; **à chevrons** (*tissu, veste etc*) herringbone.

chevronné [ʃəvrɔne] *a* seasoned, experienced.

chevroter [ʃəvrɔte] *vi* to quaver, tremble.

chez [ʃe] *prép* **c. qn** at s.o.'s house, flat *etc*; **il est c. Jean/c. l'épicier** he's at John's (place)/at the grocer's; **il va c. Jean/c. l'épicier** he's going to John's (place)/to the grocer's; **c. moi, c. nous** at home; **je vais c. moi** I'm going home; **c. les Suisses/les jeunes** among the Swiss/the young; **c. Camus** in Camus; **c. l'homme** in man; **une habitude c. elle** a habit with her; **c. Mme Dupont** (*adresse*) care of *ou* c/o Mme Dupont. ◆**c.-soi** *nm inv* **un c.-soi** a home (of one's own).

chialer [ʃjale] *vi* (*pleurer*) *Fam* to cry.

chic [ʃik] **1** *a inv* stylish, smart; (*gentil*) *Fam* decent, nice; – *int* **c. (alors)!** great!; – *nm* style, elegance. **2** *nm* **avoir le c. pour faire** to have the knack of doing.

chicane [ʃikan] **1** *nf* (*querelle*) quibble. **2** *nfpl* (*obstacles*) zigzag barriers. ◆**chicaner** *vt* to quibble with (*s.o.*); – *vi* to quibble.

chiche [ʃiʃ] **1** *a* mean, niggardly; **c. de** sparing of. **2** *int* (*défi*) *Fam* I bet you I do, can *etc*; **c. que je parte sans lui** I bet I leave without him.

chichis [ʃiʃi] *nmpl* **faire des c.** to make a lot of fuss.

chicorée [ʃikɔre] *nf* (*à café*) chicory; (*pour salade*) endive.

chien [ʃjɛ̃] *nm* dog; **c. d'arrêt** pointer, retriever; **un mal de c.** a hell of a job; **temps de c.** filthy weather; **vie de c.** *Fig* dog's life; **entre c. et loup** at dusk, in the gloaming. ◆**c.-loup** *nm* (*pl* **chiens-loups**) wolfhound. ◆**chienne** *nf* dog, bitch.

chiendent [ʃjɛ̃dɑ̃] *nm Bot* couch grass.

chiffon [ʃifɔ̃] *nm* rag; **c. (à poussière)** duster. ◆**chiffonner** *vt* to crumple; (*ennuyer*) *Fig* to bother, distress. ◆**chiffonnier** *nm* ragman.

chiffre [ʃifr] *nm* figure, number; (*romain, arabe*) numeral; (*code*) cipher; **c. d'affaires** *Fin* turnover. ◆**chiffrer** *vt* (*montant*) to assess, work out; (*message*) to cipher, code; – *vi* to mount up; **se c. à** to amount to, work out at.

chignon [ʃiɲɔ̃] *nm* bun, chignon.

Chili [ʃili] *nm* Chile. ◆**chilien, -ienne** *a & nmf* Chilean.

chimère [ʃimɛr] *nf* fantasy, (wild) dream. ◆**chimérique** *a* fanciful.

chimie [ʃimi] *nf* chemistry. ◆**chimique** *a* chemical. ◆**chimiste** *nmf* (research) chemist.

chimpanzé [ʃɛ̃pɑ̃ze] *nm* chimpanzee.

Chine [ʃin] *nf* China. ◆**chinois, -oise** *a* & *nmf* Chinese; – *nm* (*langue*) Chinese. ◆**chinoiser** *vi* to quibble. ◆**chinoiserie** *nf* (*objet*) Chinese curio; *pl* (*bizarreries*) *Fig* weird complications.

chiner [ʃine] *vi* (*brocanteur etc*) to hunt for bargains.

chiot [ʃjo] *nm* pup(py).

chiper [ʃipe] *vt Fam* to swipe, pinch (à from).

chipie [ʃipi] *nf* **vieille c.** (*femme*) *Péj* old crab.

chipoter [ʃipɔte] *vi* **1** (*manger*) to nibble. **2** (*chicaner*) to quibble.

chips [ʃips] *nmpl* (potato) crisps, *Am* chips.

chiquenaude [ʃiknod] *nf* flick (of the finger).

chiromancie [kirɔmɑ̃si] *nf* palmistry.

chirurgie [ʃiryrʒi] *nf* surgery. ◆**chirurgical, -aux** *a* surgical. ◆**chirurgien** *nm* surgeon.

chlore [klɔr] *nm* chlorine. ◆**chloroforme** *nm* chloroform. ◆**chlorure** *nm* chloride.

choc [ʃɔk] *nm* (*heurt*) impact, shock; (*émotion*) & *Méd* shock; (*collision*) crash; (*des opinions, entre manifestants etc*) clash.

chocolat [ʃɔkɔla] *nm* chocolate; **c. à croquer** plain *ou Am* bittersweet chocolate; **c. au lait** milk chocolate; **c. glacé** choc-ice; – *a inv* chocolate(-coloured). ◆**chocolaté** *a* chocolate-flavoured.

chœur [kœr] *nm* (*chanteurs, nef*) *Rel* choir; (*composition musicale*) & *Fig* chorus; **en c.** (all) together, in chorus.

choir [ʃwar] *vi* **laisser c. qn** *Fam* to turn one's back on s.o.

chois/ir [ʃwazir] *vt* to choose, pick, select. ◆**—i** *a* (*œuvres*) selected; (*terme, langage*) well-chosen; (*public*) select. ◆**choix** *nm* choice; (*assortiment*) selection; **morceau de c.** choice piece; **au c. du client** according to choice.

choléra [kɔlera] *nm* cholera.

cholestérol [kɔlesterɔl] *nm* cholesterol.

chôm/er [ʃome] *vi* (*ouvrier etc*) to be unemployed; **jour chômé** (public) holiday. ◆**—age** *nm* unemployment; **en** *ou* **au c.** unemployed; **mettre en c. technique** to lay off, dismiss.

chope [ʃɔp] *nf* beer mug, tankard; (*contenu*) pint.

choqu/er [ʃɔke] *vt* to offend, shock; (*verres*) to clink; (*commotionner*) to shake up. ◆**—ant** *a* shocking, offensive.

choral, *mpl* **-als** [kɔral] *a* choral. ◆**chorale** *nf* choral society. ◆**choriste** *nmf* chorister.

chorégraphe [kɔregraf] *nmf* choreographer. ◆**chorégraphie** *nf* choreography.

chose [ʃoz] *nf* thing; **état de choses** state of affairs; **par la force des choses** through force of circumstance; **dis-lui bien des choses de ma part** remember me to him *ou* her; **ce monsieur C.** that Mr What's-his-name; **se sentir tout c.** *Fam* (*décontenancé*) to feel all funny; (*malade*) to feel out of sorts.

chou, -x [ʃu] *nm* cabbage; **choux de Bruxelles** Brussels sprouts; **mon c.!** my pet!; **c. à la crème** cream puff. ◆**c.-fleur** *nm* (*pl* **choux-fleurs**) cauliflower.

choucas [ʃuka] *nm* jackdaw.

chouchou, -oute [ʃuʃu, -ut] *nmf* (*favori*) *Fam* pet, darling. ◆**chouchouter** *vt* to pamper.

choucroute [ʃukrut] *nf* sauerkraut.

chouette [ʃwɛt] **1** *nf* (*oiseau*) owl. **2** *a* (*chic*) *Fam* super, great.

choyer [ʃwaye] *vt* to pet, pamper.

chrétien, -ienne [kretjɛ̃, -jɛn] *a* & *nmf* Christian. ◆**chrétienté** *nf* Christendom. ◆**Christ** [krist] *nm* Christ. ◆**christianisme** *nm* Christianity.

chrome [krom] *nm* chromium, chrome. ◆**chromé** *a* chromium-plated.

chromosome [krɔmozom] *nm* chromosome.

chronique [krɔnik] **1** *a* (*malade, chômage etc*) chronic. **2** *nf* (*annales*) chronicle; *Journ* report, news; (*rubrique*) column. ◆**chroniqueur** *nm* chronicler; *Journ* reporter, columnist.

chronologie [krɔnɔlɔʒi] *nf* chronology. ◆**chronologique** *a* chronological.

chronomètre [krɔnɔmɛtr] *nm* stopwatch. ◆**chronométr/er** *vt Sp* to time. ◆**—eur** *nm Sp* timekeeper.

chrysanthème [krizɑ̃tɛm] *nm* chrysanthemum.

chuchot/er [ʃyʃɔte] *vti* to whisper. ◆**—ement** *nm* whisper(ing). ◆**chuchoteries** *nfpl Fam* whispering.

chuinter [ʃwɛ̃te] *vi* (*vapeur*) to hiss.

chut! [ʃyt] *int* sh!, hush!

chute [ʃyt] *nf* fall; (*défaite*) (down)fall; **c. d'eau** waterfall; **c. de neige** snowfall; **c. de pluie** rainfall; **c. des cheveux** hair loss. ◆**chuter** *vi Fam* to fall.

Chypre [ʃipr] *nf* Cyprus. ◆**chypriote** *a* & *nmf* Cypriot.
ci [si] **1** *adv* **par-ci par-là** here and there. **2** *pron dém* **comme ci comme ça** so so. **3** *voir* **ce**[2], **celui.**
ci-après [siaprɛ] *adv* below, hereafter. ◆**ci-contre** *adv* opposite. ◆**ci-dessous** *adv* below. ◆**ci-dessus** *adv* above. ◆**ci-gît** *adv* here lies (*on gravestones*). ◆**ci-inclus** *a*, ◆**ci-joint** *a* (*inv before n*) (*dans une lettre*) enclosed (herewith).
cible [sibl] *nf* target.
ciboulette [sibulɛt] *nf Culin* chives.
cicatrice [sikatris] *nf* scar. ◆**cicatriser** *vt*, — **se c.** *vpr* to heal up (*leaving a scar*).
cidre [sidr] *nm* cider.
Cie *abrév* (*compagnie*) Co.
ciel [sjɛl] *nm* **1** (*pl* **ciels**) sky; **à c. ouvert** (*piscine etc*) open-air; **c. de lit** canopy. **2** (*pl* **cieux** [sjø]) *Rel* heaven; **juste c.!** good heavens!; **sous d'autres cieux** *Hum* in other climes.
cierge [sjɛrʒ] *nm Rel* candle.
cigale [sigal] *nf* (*insecte*) cicada.
cigare [sigar] *nm* cigar. ◆**cigarette** *nf* cigarette.
cigogne [sigɔɲ] *nf* stork.
cil [sil] *nm* (**eye**)**lash.**
cime [sim] *nf* (*d'un arbre*) top; (*d'une montagne*) & *Fig* peak.
ciment [simɑ̃] *nm* cement. ◆**cimenter** *vt* to cement.
cimetière [simtjɛr] *nm* cemetery, graveyard; **c. de voitures** scrapyard, breaker's yard, *Am* auto graveyard.
ciné [sine] *nm Fam* cinema. ◆**c.-club** *nm* film society. ◆**cinéaste** *nm* film maker. ◆**cinéphile** *nmf* film buff.
cinéma [sinema] *nm* cinema; **faire du c.** to make films. ◆**cinémascope** *nm* cinemascope. ◆**cinémathèque** *nf* film library; (*salle*) film theatre. ◆**cinématographique** *a* cinema-.
cinglé [sɛ̃gle] *a Fam* crazy.
cingl/er [sɛ̃gle] *vt* to lash. ◆—**ant** *a* (*vent, remarque*) cutting, biting.
cinoche [sinɔʃ] *nm Fam* cinema.
cinq [sɛ̃k] *nm* five; – *a* ([sɛ̃] *before consonant*) five. ◆**cinquième** *a* & *nmf* fifth; **un c.** a fifth.
cinquante [sɛ̃kɑ̃t] *a* & *nm* fifty. ◆**cinquantaine** *nf* about fifty. ◆**cinquantenaire** *a* & *nmf* fifty-year-old (person); – *nm* fiftieth anniversary. ◆**cinquantième** *a* & *nmf* fiftieth.
cintre [sɛ̃tr] *nm* coathanger; *Archit* arch. ◆**cintré** *a* arched; (*veste etc*) tailored, slim-fitting.
cirage [siraʒ] *nm* (shoe) polish.
circoncis [sirkɔ̃si] *a* circumcised. ◆**circoncision** *nf* circumcision.
circonférence [sirkɔ̃ferɑ̃s] *nf* circumference.
circonflexe [sirkɔ̃flɛks] *a Gram* circumflex.
circonlocution [sirkɔ̃lɔkysjɔ̃] *nf* circumlocution.
circonscrire [sirkɔ̃skrir] *vt* to circumscribe. ◆**circonscription** *nf* division; **c. (électorale)** constituency.
circonspect, -ecte [sirkɔ̃spɛ(kt), -ɛkt] *a* cautious, circumspect. ◆**circonspection** *nf* caution.
circonstance [sirkɔ̃stɑ̃s] *nf* circumstance; **pour/en la c.** for/on this occasion; **de c.** (*habit, parole etc*) appropriate. ◆**circonstancié** *a* detailed. ◆**circonstanciel, -ielle** *a Gram* adverbial.
circonvenir [sirkɔ̃vnir] *vt* to circumvent.
circuit [sirkɥi] *nm Sp Él Fin* circuit; (*périple*) tour, trip; (*détour*) roundabout way; *pl Él* circuitry, circuits.
circulaire [sirkylɛr] *a* circular; – *nf* (*lettre*) circular. ◆**circulation** *nf* circulation; *Aut* traffic. ◆**circuler** *vi* to circulate; (*véhicule, train*) to move, travel; (*passant*) to walk about; (*rumeur*) to go round, circulate; **faire c.** to circulate; (*piétons etc*) to move on; **circulez!** keep moving!
cire [sir] *nf* wax; (*pour meubles*) polish, wax. ◆**cir/er** *vt* to polish, wax. ◆—**é** *nm* (*vêtement*) oilskin(s). ◆—**eur** *nm* bootblack. ◆—**euse** *nf* (*appareil*) floor polisher. ◆**cireux, -euse** *a* waxy.
cirque [sirk] *nm Th Hist* circus.
cirrhose [siroz] *nf Méd* cirrhosis.
cisaille(s) [sizaj] *nf(pl)* shears. ◆**ciseau, -x** *nm* chisel; *pl* scissors. ◆**ciseler** *vt* to chisel.
citadelle [sitadɛl] *nf* citadel.
cité [site] *nf* city; **c. (ouvrière)** housing estate (*for workers*), *Am* housing project *ou* development; **c. universitaire** (students') halls of residence. ◆**citadin, -ine** *nmf* city dweller; – *a* city-, urban.
citer [site] *vt* to quote; *Jur* to summon; *Mil* to mention, cite. ◆**citation** *nf* quotation; *Jur* summons; *Mil* mention, citation.
citerne [sitɛrn] *nf* (*réservoir*) tank.
cithare [sitar] *nf* zither.
citoyen, -enne [sitwajɛ̃, -ɛn] *nmf* citizen. ◆**citoyenneté** *nf* citizenship.
citron [sitrɔ̃] *nm* lemon; **c. pressé** (fresh)

lemon juice. ◆**citronnade** *nf* lemon drink, (still) lemonade.
citrouille [sitruj] *nf* pumpkin.
civet [sivɛ] *nm* stew; **c. de lièvre** jugged hare.
civière [sivjɛr] *nf* stretcher.
civil [sivil] **1** *a* (*droits, guerre, mariage etc*) civil; (*non militaire*) civilian; (*courtois*) civil; **année civile** calendar year. **2** *nm* civilian; **dans le c.** in civilian life; **en c.** (*policier*) in plain clothes; (*soldat*) in civilian clothes. ◆**civilité** *nf* civility.
civilis/er [sivilize] *vt* to civilize; — **se c.** *vpr* to become civilized. ◆**civilisation** *nf* civilization.
civique [sivik] *a* civic; **instruction c.** *Scol* civics. ◆**civisme** *nm* civic sense.
clair [klɛr] *a* (*distinct, limpide, évident*) clear; (*éclairé*) light; (*pâle*) light(-coloured); (*sauce, chevelure*) thin; **bleu/vert c.** light blue/green; **il fait c.** it's light *ou* bright; — *adv* (*voir*) clearly; — *nm* **c. de lune** moonlight; **le plus c. de** the major *ou* greater part of; **tirer au c.** (*question etc*) to clear up. ◆**—ement** *adv* clearly. ◆**claire-voie** *nf* **à c.-voie** (*barrière*) lattice-; (*caisse*) openwork; (*porte*) louvre(d).
clairière [klɛrjɛr] *nf* clearing, glade.
clairon [klɛrɔ̃] *nm* bugle; (*soldat*) bugler. ◆**claironner** *vt* (*annoncer*) to trumpet forth.
clairsemé [klɛrsəme] *a* sparse.
clairvoyant [klɛrvwajɑ̃] *a* (*perspicace*) clear-sighted. ◆**clairvoyance** *nf* clear-sightedness.
clam/er [klame] *vt* to cry out. ◆**—eur** *nf* clamour, outcry.
clan [klɑ̃] *nm* clan, clique, set.
clandestin [klɑ̃dɛstɛ̃] *a* secret, clandestine; (*journal, mouvement*) underground; **passager c.** stowaway.
clapet [klapɛ] *nm Tech* valve; (*bouche*) *Arg* trap.
clapier [klapje] *nm* (rabbit) hutch.
clapot/er [klapɔte] *vi* (*vagues*) to lap. ◆**—ement** *nm*, ◆**clapotis** *nm* lap(ping).
claque [klak] *nf* smack, slap. ◆**claquer** *vt* (*porte*) to slam, bang; (*gifler*) to smack, slap; (*fouet*) to crack; (*fatiguer*) *Fam* to tire out; (*dépenser*) *Arg* to blow; **se c. un muscle** to tear a muscle; **faire c.** (*doigts*) to snap; (*langue*) to click; (*fouet*) to crack; — *vi* (*porte*) to slam, bang; (*drapeau*) to flap; (*coup de revolver*) to ring out; (*mourir*) *Fam* to die; (*tomber en panne*) *Fam* to break down; **c. des mains** to clap one's hands; **elle claque des dents** her teeth are chattering.
claquemurer (se) [səklakmyre] *vpr* to shut oneself up, hole up.
claquettes [klakɛt] *nfpl* tap dancing.
clarifier [klarifje] *vt* to clarify. ◆**clarification** *nf* clarification.
clarinette [klarinɛt] *nf* clarinet.
clarté [klarte] *nf* light, brightness; (*précision*) clarity, clearness.
classe [klɑs] *nf* class; **aller en c.** to go to school; **c. ouvrière/moyenne** working/middle class; **avoir de la c.** to have class.
class/er [klɑse] *vt* to classify, class; (*papiers*) to file; (*candidats*) to grade; (*affaire*) to close; **se c. parmi** to rank *ou* be classed among; **se c. premier** to come first. ◆**—ement** *nm* classification; filing; grading; (*rang*) place; *Sp* placing. ◆**—eur** *nm* (*meuble*) filing cabinet; (*portefeuille*) (loose leaf) file. ◆**classification** *nf* classification. ◆**classifier** *vt* to classify.
classique [klasik] *a* classical; (*typique*) classic; — *nm* (*œuvre, auteur*) classic. ◆**classicisme** *nm* classicism.
clause [kloz] *nf* clause.
claustrophobie [klostrɔfɔbi] *nf* claustrophobia. ◆**claustrophobe** *a* claustrophobic.
clavecin [klavsɛ̃] *nm Mus* harpsichord.
clavicule [klavikyl] *nf* collarbone.
clavier [klavje] *nm* keyboard.
clé, clef [kle] *nf* key; (*outil*) spanner, wrench; *Mus* clef; **fermer à c.** to lock; **sous c.** under lock and key; **c. de contact** ignition key; **c. de voûte** keystone; **poste/industrie c.** key post/industry; **clés en main** (*acheter une maison etc*) ready to move in; **prix clés en main** (*voiture*) on the road price.
clément [klemɑ̃] *a* (*temps*) mild, clement; (*juge*) lenient, clement. ◆**clémence** *nf* mildness; leniency; clemency.
clémentine [klemɑ̃tin] *nf* clementine.
clerc [klɛr] *nm Rel* cleric; (*de notaire*) clerk. ◆**clergé** *nm* clergy. ◆**clérical, -aux** *a Rel* clerical.
cliché [kliʃe] *nm Phot* negative; *Typ* plate; (*idée*) cliché.
client, -ente [klijɑ̃, -ɑ̃t] *nmf* (*de magasin etc*) customer; (*d'un avocat etc*) client; (*d'un médecin*) patient; (*d'hôtel*) guest. ◆**clientèle** *nf* customers, clientele; (*d'un avocat*) practice, clientele; (*d'un médecin*) practice, patients; **accorder sa c. à** to give one's custom to.
cligner [kliɲe] *vi* **c. des yeux** (*ouvrir et fermer*) to blink; (*fermer à demi*) to screw up one's eyes; **c. de l'œil** to wink.

◆**clignot/er** *vi* to blink; (*lumière*) to flicker; *Aut* to flash; (*étoile*) to twinkle. ◆**–ant** *nm Aut* indicator, *Am* directional signal.
climat [klima] *nm Mét & Fig* climate. ◆**climatique** *a* climatic. ◆**climatisation** *nf* air-conditioning. ◆**climatiser** *vt* to air-condition.
clin d'œil [klɛ̃dœj] *nm* wink; **en un c. d'œil** in the twinkling of an eye.
clinique [klinik] *a* clinical; – *nf* (*hôpital*) (private) clinic.
clinquant [klɛ̃kɑ̃] *a* tawdry.
clique [klik] *nf Péj* clique; *Mus Mil* (drum and bugle) band.
cliqueter [klikte] *vi* to clink. ◆**cliquetis** *nm* clink(ing).
clivage [klivaʒ] *nm* split, division (**de** in).
cloaque [klɔak] *nm* cesspool.
clochard, -arde [klɔʃar, -ard] *nmf* tramp, vagrant.
cloche [klɔʃ] *nf* **1** bell; **c. à fromage** cheese cover. **2** (*personne*) *Fam* idiot, oaf. ◆**clocher 1** *nm* bell tower; (*en pointe*) steeple; **de c.** *Fig* parochial; **esprit de c.** parochialism. **2** *vi* to be wrong *ou* amiss. ◆**clochette** *nf* (small) bell.
cloche-pied (à) [aklɔʃpje] *adv* **sauter à c.-pied** to hop on one foot.
cloison [klwazɔ̃] *nf* partition; *Fig* barrier. ◆**cloisonner** *vt* to partition; (*activités etc*) *Fig* to compartmentalize.
cloître [klwɑtr] *nm* cloister. ◆**se cloîtrer** *vpr* to shut oneself away, cloister oneself.
clopin-clopant [klɔpɛ̃klɔpɑ̃] *adv* **aller c.-clopant** to hobble.
cloque [klɔk] *nf* blister.
clore [klɔr] *vt* (*débat, lettre*) to close. ◆**clos** *a* (*incident etc*) closed; (*espace*) enclosed; – *nm* (enclosed) field.
clôture [klotyr] *nf* (*barrière*) enclosure, fence; (*fermeture*) closing. ◆**clôturer** *vt* to enclose; (*compte, séance etc*) to close.
clou [klu] *nm* nail; (*furoncle*) boil; **le c. (du spectacle)** *Fam* the star attraction; **les clous** (*passage*) pedestrian crossing; **des clous!** *Fam* nothing at all! ◆**clouer** *vt* to nail; **cloué au lit** confined to (one's) bed; **cloué sur place** nailed to the spot; **c. le bec à qn** *Fam* to shut s.o. up. ◆**clouté** *a* (*chaussures*) hobnailed; (*ceinture, pneus*) studded; **passage c.** pedestrian crossing, *Am* crosswalk.
clown [klun] *nm* clown.
club [klœb] *nm* (*association*) club.
cm *abrév* (*centimètre*) cm.
co- [kɔ] *préf* co-.
coaguler [kɔagyle] *vti*, — **se c.** *vpr* to coagulate.
coaliser (se) [səkɔalize] *vpr* to form a coalition, join forces. ◆**coalition** *nf* coalition.
coasser [kɔase] *vi* (*grenouille*) to croak.
cobaye [kɔbaj] *nm* (*animal*) & *Fig* guinea pig.
cobra [kɔbra] *nm* (*serpent*) cobra.
coca [kɔka] *nm* (*Coca-Cola®*) coke.
cocagne [kɔkaɲ] *nf* **pays de c.** dreamland, land of plenty.
cocaïne [kɔkain] *nf* cocain.
cocarde [kɔkard] *nf* rosette, cockade; *Av* roundel. ◆**cocardier, -ière** *a Péj* flag-waving.
cocasse [kɔkas] *a* droll, comical. ◆**cocasserie** *nf* drollery.
coccinelle [kɔksinɛl] *nf* ladybird, *Am* lady-bug.
cocher[1] [kɔʃe] *vt* to tick (off), *Am* to check (off).
cocher[2] [kɔʃe] *nm* coachman. ◆**cochère** *af* **porte c.** main gateway.
cochon, -onne [kɔʃɔ̃, -ɔn] **1** *nm* pig; (*mâle*) hog; **c. d'Inde** guinea pig. **2** *nmf* (*personne sale*) (dirty) pig; (*salaud*) swine; – *a* (*histoire, film*) dirty, filthy. ◆**cochonnerie(s)** *nf(pl)* (*obscénité(s)*) filth; (*pacotille*) *Fam* rubbish.
cocktail [kɔktɛl] *nm* (*boisson*) cocktail; (*réunion*) cocktail party.
coco [kɔko] *nm* **noix de c.** coconut. ◆**cocotier** *nm* coconut palm.
cocon [kɔkɔ̃] *nm* cocoon.
cocorico [kɔkɔriko] *int & nm* cock-a-doodle-doo; **faire c.** (*crier victoire*) *Fam* to give three cheers for France, wave the flag.
cocotte [kɔkɔt] *nf* (*marmite*) casserole; **c. minute®** pressure cooker.
cocu [kɔky] *nm Fam* cuckold.
code [kɔd] *nm* code; **codes, phares c.** *Aut* dipped headlights, *Am* low beams; **C. de la route** Highway Code. ◆**coder** *vt* to code. ◆**codifier** *vt* to codify.
coefficient [kɔefisjɑ̃] *nm Math* coefficient, (*d'erreur, de sécurité*) *Fig* margin.
coéquipier, -ière [kɔekipje, -jɛr] *nmf* team mate.
cœur [kœr] *nm* heart; *Cartes* hearts; **au c. de** (*ville, hiver etc*) in the heart of; **par c.** by heart; **ça me (sou)lève le c.** that turns my stomach; **à c. ouvert** (*opération*) open-heart; (*parler*) freely; **avoir mal au c.** to feel sick; **avoir le c. gros** *ou* **serré** to have a heavy heart; **ça me tient à c.** that's close to my heart; **avoir bon c.** to be

kind-hearted; **de bon c.** (*offrir*) with a good heart, willingly; (*rire*) heartily; **si le c. vous en dit** if you so desire.

coexister [kɔegziste] *vi* to coexist. ◆**coexistence** *nf* coexistence.

coffre [kɔfr] *nm* chest; (*de banque*) safe; (*de voiture*) boot, *Am* trunk; (*d'autocar*) luggage *ou Am* baggage compartment. ◆**c.-fort** *nm* (*pl* **coffres-forts**) safe. ◆**coffret** *nm* casket, box.

cogiter [kɔʒite] *vi Iron* to cogitate.

cognac [kɔɲak] *nm* cognac.

cogner [kɔɲe] *vti* to knock; **c. qn** *Arg* (*frapper*) to thump s.o.; (*tabasser*) to beat s.o. up; **se c. la tête/***etc* to knock one's head/*etc*.

cohabiter [kɔabite] *vi* to live together. ◆**cohabitation** *nf* living together; *Pol Fam* power sharing.

cohérent [kɔerɑ̃] *a* coherent. ◆**cohérence** *nf* coherence. ◆**cohésion** *nf* cohesion, cohesiveness.

cohorte [kɔɔrt] *nf* (*groupe*) troop, band, cohort.

cohue [kɔy] *nf* crowd, mob.

coiffe [kwaf] *nf* headdress.

coiff/er [kwafe] *vt* (*chapeau*) to put on, wear; (*surmonter*) *Fig* to cap; (*être à la tête de*) to head; **c. qn** to do s.o.'s hair; **c. qn d'un chapeau** to put a hat on s.o.; **— se c.** *vpr* to do one's hair; **se c. d'un chapeau** to put on a hat. ◆**—eur, -euse**[1] *nmf* (*pour hommes*) barber, hairdresser; (*pour dames*) hairdresser. ◆**—euse**[2] *nf* dressing table. ◆**coiffure** *nf* headgear, hat; (*arrangement*) hairstyle; (*métier*) hairdressing.

coin [kwɛ̃] *nm* (*angle*) corner; (*endroit*) spot; (*de terre, de ciel*) patch; (*cale*) wedge; **du c.** (*magasin etc*) local; **dans le c.** in the (local) area; **au c. du feu** by the fireside; **petit c.** *Fam* loo, *Am* john.

coinc/er [kwɛ̃se] *vt* (*mécanisme, tiroir*) to jam; (*caler*) to wedge; **c. qn** *Fam* to catch s.o., corner s.o.; **— se c.** *vpr* (*mécanisme etc*) to get jammed *ou* stuck. ◆**—é** *a* (*tiroir etc*) stuck, jammed; (*personne*) *Fam* stuck.

coïncider [kɔɛ̃side] *vi* to coincide. ◆**coïncidence** *nf* coincidence.

coin-coin [kwɛ̃kwɛ̃] *nm inv* (*de canard*) quack.

coing [kwɛ̃] *nm* (*fruit*) quince.

coke [kɔk] *nm* (*combustible*) coke.

col [kɔl] *nm* (*de chemise*) collar; (*de bouteille*) & *Anat* neck; *Géog* pass; **c. roulé** polo neck, *Am* turtleneck.

colère [kɔlɛr] *nf* anger; **une c.** (*accès*) a fit of anger; **en c.** angry (**contre** with); **se mettre en c.** to lose one's temper. ◆**coléreux, -euse** *a*, ◆**colérique** *a* quick-tempered.

colibri [kɔlibri] *nm* hummingbird.

colifichet [kɔlifiʃɛ] *nm* trinket.

colimaçon (en) [ɑ̃kɔlimasɔ̃] *adv* **escalier en c.** spiral staircase.

colin [kɔlɛ̃] *nm* (*poisson*) hake.

colique [kɔlik] *nf* diarrh(o)ea; (*douleur*) stomach pain, colic.

colis [kɔli] *nm* parcel, package.

collaborer [kɔlabɔre] *vi* collaborate (**avec** with, **à on**); **c. à** (*journal*) to contribute to. ◆**collaborateur, -trice** *nmf* collaborator; contributor. ◆**collaboration** *nf* collaboration; contribution.

collage [kɔlaʒ] *nm* (*œuvre*) collage.

collant [kɔlɑ̃] **1** *a* (*papier*) sticky; (*vêtement*) skin-tight; **être c.** (*importun*) *Fam* to be a pest. **2** *nm* (pair of) tights; (*de danse*) leotard.

collation [kɔlasjɔ̃] *nf* (*repas*) light meal.

colle [kɔl] *nf* (*transparente*) glue; (*blanche*) paste; (*question*) *Fam* poser, teaser; (*interrogation*) *Scol Arg* oral; (*retenue*) *Scol Arg* detention.

collecte [kɔlɛkt] *nf* (*quête*) collection. ◆**collect/er** *vt* to collect. ◆**—eur** *nm* collector; **(égout) c.** main sewer.

collectif, -ive [kɔlɛktif, -iv] *a* collective; (*hystérie, démission*) mass-; **billet c.** group ticket. ◆**collectivement** *adv* collectively. ◆**collectivisme** *nm* collectivism. ◆**collectivité** *nf* community, collectivity.

collection [kɔlɛksjɔ̃] *nf* collection. ◆**collectionn/er** *vt* (*timbres etc*) to collect. ◆**—eur, -euse** *nmf* collector.

collège [kɔlɛʒ] *nm* (secondary) school, *Am* (high) school; (*électoral, sacré*) college. ◆**collégien** *nm* schoolboy. ◆**collégienne** *nf* schoolgirl.

collègue [kɔlɛg] *nmf* colleague.

coller [kɔle] *vt* (*timbre etc*) to stick; (*à la colle transparente*) to glue; (*à la colle blanche*) to paste; (*affiche*) to stick up; (*papier peint*) to hang; (*mettre*) *Fam* to stick, shove; **c. contre** (*nez, oreille etc*) to press against; **c. qn** (*embarrasser*) *Fam* to stump s.o., catch s.o. out; (*consigner*) *Scol* to keep s.o. in; **être collé à** (*examen*) *Fam* to fail, flunk; **se c. contre** to cling (close) to; **se c. qn/qch** *Fam* to get stuck with s.o./sth; – *vi* to stick, cling; **c. à** (*s'adapter*) to fit, correspond to; **ça colle!** *Fam* everything's just fine! ◆**colleur, -euse** *nmf* **c. d'affiches** billsticker.

collet [kɔlɛ] *nm* (*lacet*) snare; **prendre qn au c.** to grab s.o. by the scruff of the neck; **elle**

est/ils sont c. monté she is/they are prim and proper *ou* straight-laced.

collier [kɔlje] *nm* (*bijou*) necklace; (*de chien, cheval*) & *Tech* collar.

colline [kɔlin] *nf* hill.

collision [kɔlizjɔ̃] *nf* (*de véhicules*) collision; (*bagarre, conflit*) clash; **entrer en c. avec** to collide with.

colloque [kɔlɔk] *nm* symposium.

collusion [kɔlyzjɔ̃] *nf* collusion.

colmater [kɔlmate] *vt* (*fuite, fente*) to seal; (*trou*) to fill in; (*brèche*) *Mil* to close, seal.

colombe [kɔlɔ̃b] *nf* dove.

colon [kɔlɔ̃] *nm* settler, colonist; (*enfant*) *child taking part in a holiday camp*. **◆colonial, -aux** *a* colonial. **◆colonie** *nf* colony; **c. de vacances** (children's) holiday camp *ou Am* vacation camp.

coloniser [kɔlɔnize] *vt Pol* to colonize; (*peupler*) to settle. **◆colonisateur, -trice** *a* colonizing; – *nmf* colonizer. **◆colonisation** *nf* colonization.

côlon [kolɔ̃] *nm Anat* colon.

colonel [kɔlɔnɛl] *nm* colonel.

colonne [kɔlɔn] *nf* column; **c. vertébrale** spine. **◆colonnade** *nf* colonnade.

color/er [kɔlɔre] *vt* to colour. **◆–ant** *a* & *nm* colouring. **◆–é** *a* (*verre etc*) coloured; (*teint*) ruddy; (*style, foule*) colourful. **◆coloration** *nf* colouring, colour. **◆coloriage** *nm* colouring; (*dessin*) coloured drawing. **◆colorier** *vt* (*dessin etc*) to colour (in). **◆coloris** *nm* (*effet*) colouring; (*nuance*) shade.

colosse [kɔlɔs] *nm* giant, colossus. **◆colossal, -aux** *a* colossal, gigantic.

colporter [kɔlpɔrte] *vt* to peddle, hawk.

coltiner [kɔltine] *vt* (*objet lourd*) *Fam* to lug, haul; — **se c.** *vpr* (*tâche pénible*) *Fam* to take on, tackle.

coma [kɔma] *nm* coma; **dans le c.** in a coma.

combat [kɔ̃ba] *nm* fight; *Mil* combat. **◆combatif, -ive** *a* (*personne*) eager to fight; (*instinct, esprit*) fighting. **◆combatt/re*** *vt* to fight; (*maladie, inflation etc*) to combat, fight; – *vi* to fight. **◆–ant** *nm Mil* combattant; (*bagarreur*) *Fam* brawler; – *a* (*unité*) fighting.

combien [kɔ̃bjɛ̃] **1** *adv* (*quantité*) how much; (*nombre*) how many; **c. de** (*temps, argent etc*) how much; (*gens, livres etc*) how many. **2** *adv* (*à quel point*) how; **tu verras c. il est bête** you'll see how silly he is. **3** *adv* (*distance*) **c. y a-t-il d'ici à . . . ?** how far is it to . . . ? **4** *nm inv* **le c. sommes-nous?** (*date*) *Fam* what date is it?; **tous les c.?** (*fréquence*) *Fam* how often?

combine [kɔ̃bin] *nf* (*truc, astuce*) *Fam* trick.

combin/er [kɔ̃bine] *vt* (*disposer*) to combine; (*calculer*) to devise, plan (out). **◆–é** *nm* (*de téléphone*) receiver. **◆combinaison** *nf* **1** combination; (*manœuvre*) scheme. **2** (*vêtement de femme*) slip; (*de mécanicien*) boiler suit, *Am* overalls; (*de pilote*) flying suit; **c. de ski** ski suit.

comble [kɔ̃bl] **1** *nm* **le c. de** (*la joie etc*) the height of; **pour c. (de malheur)** to crown *ou* cap it all; **c'est un** *ou* **le c.!** that's the limit! **2** *nmpl* (*mansarde*) attic, loft; **sous les combles** beneath the roof, in the loft *ou* attic. **3** *a* (*bondé*) packed, full.

combler [kɔ̃ble] *vt* (*trou, lacune etc*) to fill; (*retard, perte*) to make good; (*vœu*) to fulfil; **c. qn de** (*cadeaux etc*) to lavish on s.o.; (*joie*) to fill s.o. with; **je suis comblé** I'm completely satisfied; **vous me comblez!** you're too good to me!

combustible [kɔ̃bystibl] *nm* fuel; – *a* combustible. **◆combustion** *nf* combustion.

comédie [kɔmedi] *nf* comedy; (*complication*) *Fam* fuss, palaver; **c. musicale** musical; **jouer la c.** *Fig* to put on an act, play-act; **c'est de la c.** (*c'est faux*) it's a sham. **◆comédien** *nm Th & Fig* actor **◆comédienne** *nf Th & Fig* actress.

comestible [kɔmɛstibl] *a* edible; – *nmpl* foods.

comète [kɔmɛt] *nf* comet.

comique [kɔmik] *a* (*style etc*) *Th* comic; (*amusant*) *Fig* comical, funny; **(auteur) c.** comedy writer; – *nm* comedy; (*acteur*) comic (actor); **le c.** (*genre*) comedy; *Fig* the comical side (**de** of).

comité [kɔmite] *nm* committee; **c. de gestion** board (of management); **en petit c.** in a small group.

commande [kɔmɑ̃d] **1** *nf* (*achat*) order; **sur c.** to order. **2** *nfpl* **les commandes** *Av Tech* the controls; **tenir les commandes** (*diriger*) *Fig* to have control.

command/er [kɔmɑ̃de] **1** *vt* (*diriger, exiger, dominer*) to command; (*faire fonctionner*) to control; – *vi* **c. à** (*ses passions etc*) to have control over; **c. à qn de faire** to command s.o. to do. **2** *vt* (*acheter*) to order. **◆–ant** *nm Nau* captain; (*grade*) *Mil* major; (*grade*) *Av* squadron leader; **c. de bord** *Av* captain. **◆–ement** *nm* (*autorité*) command; *Rel* commandment. **◆commando** *nm* commando.

commanditaire [kɔmɑ̃ditɛr] *nm Com* sleeping *ou* limited partner, *Am* silent partner.

comme [kɔm] **1** *adv & conj* as, like; **un peu**

c. a bit like; **c. moi** like me; **c. cela** like that; **blanc c. neige** (as) white as snow; **c. si** as if; **c. pour faire** as if to do; **c. par hasard** as if by chance; **joli c. tout** *Fam* ever so pretty; **c. ami** as a friend; **c. quoi** (*disant que*) to the effect that; (*ce qui prouve que*) so, which goes to show that; **qu'as-tu c. diplômes?** what do you have in the way of certificates? **2** *adv* (*exclamatif*) **regarde c. il pleut!** look how it's raining!; **c. c'est petit!** isn't it small! **3** *conj* (*temps*) as; (*cause*) as, since; **c. je pars** as I'm leaving; **c. elle entrait** (just) as she was coming in.

commémorer [kɔmemɔre] *vt* to commemorate. ◆**commémoratif, -ive** *a* commemorative. ◆**commémoration** *nf* commemoration.

commenc/er [kɔmɑ̃se] *vti* to begin, start (**à faire** to do, doing; **par** with; **par faire** by doing); **pour c.** to begin with. ◆**—ement** *nm* beginning, start.

comment [kɔmɑ̃] *adv* how; **c. le sais-tu?** how do you know?; **et c.!** and how!; **c.?** (*répétition, surprise*) what?; **c.!** (*indignation*) what!; **c. est-il?** what is he like?; **c. faire?** what's to be done?; **c. t'appelles-tu?** what's your name?; **c. allez-vous?** how are you?

commentaire [kɔmɑ̃tɛr] *nm* (*explications*) commentary; (*remarque*) comment. ◆**commentateur, -trice** *nmf* commentator. ◆**commenter** *vt* to comment (up)on.

commérage(s) [kɔmeraʒ] *nm(pl)* gossip.

commerce [kɔmɛrs] *nm* trade, commerce; (*magasin*) shop, business; **de c.** (*voyageur, maison, tribunal*) commercial; (*navire*) trading; **chambre de c.** chamber of commerce; **faire du c.** to trade; **dans le c.** (*objet*) (on sale) in the shops. ◆**commercer** *vi* to trade. ◆**commerçant, -ante** *nmf* shopkeeper; **c. en gros** wholesale dealer; – *a* (*nation*) trading, mercantile; (*rue, quartier*) shopping-; (*personne*) business-minded. ◆**commercial, -aux** *a* commercial, business-. ◆**commercialiser** *vt* to market.

commère [kɔmɛr] *nf* (*femme*) gossip.

commettre* [kɔmɛtr] *vt* (*délit etc*) to commit; (*erreur*) to make.

commis [kɔmi] *nm* (*de magasin*) assistant, *Am* clerk; (*de bureau*) clerk, *Am* clerical worker.

commissaire [kɔmisɛr] *nm Sp* steward; **c. (de police)** police superintendent *ou Am* chief; **c. aux comptes** auditor; **c. du bord** *Nau* purser. ◆**c.-priseur** *nm* (*pl* **commissaires-priseurs**) auctioneer. ◆**commissariat** *nm* **c. (de police)** (central) police station.

commission [kɔmisjɔ̃] *nf* (*course*) errand; (*message*) message; (*réunion*) commission, committee; (*pourcentage*) *Com* commission (**sur** on); **faire les commissions** to do the shopping. ◆**commissionnaire** *nm* messenger; (*d'hôtel*) commissionaire; *Com* agent.

commod/e [kɔmɔd] **1** *a* (*pratique*) handy; (*simple*) easy; **il n'est pas c.** (*pas aimable*) he's unpleasant; (*difficile*) he's a tough one. **2** *nf* chest of drawers, *Am* dresser. ◆**—ément** *adv* comfortably. ◆**commodité** *nf* convenience.

commotion [kɔmosjɔ̃] *nf* shock; **c. (cérébrale)** concussion. ◆**commotionner** *vt* to shake up.

commuer [kɔmɥe] *vt* (*peine*) *Jur* to commute (**en** to).

commun [kɔmœ̃] **1** *a* (*collectif, comparable, habituel*) common; (*frais, cuisine etc*) shared; (*action, démarche etc*) joint; **ami c.** mutual friend; **peu c.** uncommon; **en c.** in common; **transports en c.** public transport; **avoir** *ou* **mettre en c.** to share; **vivre en c.** to live together; **il n'a rien de c. avec** he has nothing in common with. **2** *nm* **le c. des mortels** ordinary mortals. ◆**—ément** [kɔmynemɑ̃] *adv* commonly.

communauté [kɔmynote] *nf* community. ◆**communautaire** *a* community-.

commune [kɔmyn] *nf* (*municipalité française*) commune; **les Communes** *Br Pol* the Commons. ◆**communal, -aux** *a* communal, local, municipal.

communi/er [kɔmynje] *vi* to receive Holy Communion, communicate. ◆**—ant, -ante** *nmf Rel* communicant. ◆**communion** *nf* communion; *Rel* (Holy) Communion.

communiqu/er [kɔmynike] *vt* to communicate, pass on; (*mouvement*) to impart, communicate; **se c. à** (*feu, rire*) to spread to; – *vi* (*personne, pièces etc*) to communicate. ◆**—é** *nm* (*avis*) *Pol* communiqué; (*publicitaire*) message; **c. de presse** press release. ◆**communicatif, -ive** *a* communicative; (*contagieux*) infectious. ◆**communication** *nf* communication; **c. (téléphonique)** (telephone) call; **mauvaise c.** *Tél* bad line.

communisme [kɔmynism] *nm* communism. ◆**communiste** *a* & *nmf* communist.

communs [kɔmœ̃] *nmpl* (*bâtiments*) outbuildings.

commutateur [kɔmytatœr] *nm* (*bouton*) *Él* switch.

compact [kɔ̃pakt] *a* dense; (*mécanisme, disque, véhicule*) compact.

compagne [kɔ̃paɲ] *nf* (*camarade*) friend; (*épouse, maîtresse*) companion. ◆**compagnie** *nf* (*présence, société*) & *Com Mil* company; **tenir c. à qn** to keep s.o. company. ◆**compagnon** *nm* companion; (*ouvrier*) workman; **c. de route** travelling companion, fellow traveller; **c. de jeu/de travail** playmate/workmate.

comparaître* [kɔ̃parɛtr] *vi Jur* to appear (in court) (**devant** before).

compar/er [kɔ̃pare] *vt* to compare; **— se c.** *vpr* to be compared (**à** to). ◆**—é** *a* (*science etc*) comparative. ◆**—able** *a* comparable. ◆**comparaison** *nf* comparison; *Littér* simile. ◆**comparatif, -ive** *a* (*méthode etc*) comparative; – *nm Gram* comparative.

comparse [kɔ̃pars] *nmf Jur* minor accomplice, stooge.

compartiment [kɔ̃partimɑ̃] *nm* compartment. ◆**compartimenter** *vt* to compartmentalize, divide up.

comparution [kɔ̃parysjɔ̃] *nf Jur* appearance (in court).

compas [kɔ̃pa] *nm* **1** (*pour mesurer etc*) (pair of) compasses, *Am* compass. **2** (*boussole*) *Nau* compass.

compassé [kɔ̃pɑse] *a* (*affecté*) starchy, stiff.

compassion [kɔ̃pɑsjɔ̃] *nf* compassion.

compatible [kɔ̃patibl] *a* compatible. ◆**compatibilité** *nf* compatibility.

compat/ir [kɔ̃patir] *vi* to sympathize; **c. à** (*la douleur etc de qn*) to share in. ◆**—issant** *a* sympathetic.

compatriote [kɔ̃patrijɔt] *nmf* compatriot.

compenser [kɔ̃pɑ̃se] *vt* to make up for, compensate for; – *vi* to compensate. ◆**compensation** *nf* compensation; **en c. de** in compensation for.

compère [kɔ̃pɛr] *nm* accomplice.

compétent [kɔ̃petɑ̃] *a* competent. ◆**compétence** *nf* competence.

compétition [kɔ̃petisjɔ̃] *nf* competition; (*épreuve*) *Sp* event; **de c.** (*esprit, sport*) competitive. ◆**compétitif, -ive** *a* competitive. ◆**compétitivité** *nf* competitiveness.

compiler [kɔ̃pile] *vt* (*documents*) to compile.

complainte [kɔ̃plɛ̃t] *nf* (*chanson*) lament.

complaire (se) [səkɔ̃plɛr] *vpr* **se c. dans qch/à faire** to delight in sth/in doing.

complaisant [kɔ̃plezɑ̃] *a* kind, obliging; (*indulgent*) self-indulgent, complacent. ◆**complaisance** *nf* kindness, obligingness; self-indulgence, complacency.

complément [kɔ̃plemɑ̃] *nm* complement; **le c.** (*le reste*) the rest; **un c. d'information** additional information. ◆**complémentaire** *a* complementary; (*détails*) additional.

complet, -ète [kɔ̃plɛ, -ɛt] **1** *a* complete; (*train, hôtel, examen etc*) full; (*aliment*) whole; **au (grand) c.** in full strength. **2** *nm* (*costume*) suit. ◆**complètement** *adv* completely. ◆**compléter** *vt* to complete; (*ajouter à*) to complement; (*somme*) to make up; **— se c.** *vpr* (*caractères*) to complement each other.

complexe [kɔ̃plɛks] **1** *a* complex. **2** *nm* (*sentiment, construction*) complex. ◆**complexé** *a Fam* hung up, inhibited. ◆**complexité** *nf* complexity.

complication [kɔ̃plikɑsjɔ̃] *nf* complication; (*complexité*) complexity.

complice [kɔ̃plis] *nm* accomplice; – *a* (*regard*) knowing; (*silence, attitude*) conniving; **c. de** *Jur* a party to. ◆**complicité** *nf* complicity.

compliment [kɔ̃plimɑ̃] *nm* compliment; *pl* (*éloges*) compliments; (*félicitations*) congratulations. ◆**complimenter** *vt* to compliment (**sur, pour** on).

compliqu/er [kɔ̃plike] *vt* to complicate; **— se c.** *vpr* (*situation*) to get complicated. ◆**—é** *a* complicated; (*mécanisme etc*) intricate; complicated; (*histoire, problème etc*) involved, complicated.

complot [kɔ̃plo] *nm* plot, conspiracy. ◆**comploter** [kɔ̃plɔte] *vti* to plot (**de faire** to do).

comport/er [kɔ̃pɔrte] **1** *vt* (*impliquer*) to involve, contain; (*comprendre en soi, présenter*) to contain, comprise, have. **2 se c.** *vpr* to behave; (*joueur, voiture*) to perform. ◆**—ement** *nm* behaviour; (*de joueur etc*) performance.

compos/er [kɔ̃poze] *vt* (*former, constituer*) to compose, make up; (*musique, visage*) to compose; (*numéro*) *Tél* to dial; (*texte*) *Typ* to set (up); **se c. de, être composé de** to be composed of; – *vi Scol* to take an examination; **c. avec** to come to terms with. ◆**—ant** *nm* (*chimique, électronique*) component. ◆**—ante** *nf* (*d'une idée etc*) component. ◆**—é** *a* & *nm* compound. ◆**compositeur, -trice** *nmf Mus* composer; *Typ* typesetter. ◆**composition** *nf* (*action*) composing, making up; *Typ* typesetting; *Mus Littér Ch* composition; *Scol* test, class exam; **c. française** *Scol* French essay *ou* composition.

composter [kɔ̃pɔste] *vt* (*billet*) to cancel, punch.

compote [kɔ̃pɔt] *nf* stewed fruit; **c. de pommes** stewed apples, apple sauce. ◆**compotier** *nm* fruit dish.

compréhensible [kɔ̃preɑ̃sibl] *a* understandable, comprehensible. ◆**compréhensif, -ive** *a* (*personne*) understanding. ◆**compréhension** *nf* understanding, comprehension.

comprendre* [kɔ̃prɑ̃dr] *vt* to understand, comprehend; (*comporter*) to include, comprise; **je n'y comprends rien** I don't understand anything about it; **ça se comprend** that's understandable. ◆**compris** *a* (*inclus*) included (**dans** in); **frais c.** including expenses; **tout c.** (all) inclusive; **y c.** including; **c. entre** (situated) between; **(c'est) c.!** it's agreed!

compresse [kɔ̃prɛs] *nf Méd* compress.

compresseur [kɔ̃presœr] *a* **rouleau c.** steam roller.

comprim/er [kɔ̃prime] *vt* to compress; (*colère etc*) to repress; (*dépenses*) to reduce. ◆**—é** *nm Méd* tablet. ◆**compression** *nf* compression; (*du personnel etc*) reduction.

compromettre* [kɔ̃prɔmɛtr] *vt* to compromise. ◆**compromis** *nm* compromise. ◆**compromission** *nf* compromising action, compromise.

comptable [kɔ̃tabl] *a* (*règles etc*) bookkeeping-; – *nmf* bookkeeper; (*expert*) accountant. ◆**comptabilité** *nf* (*comptes*) accounts; (*science*) bookkeeping, accountancy; (*service*) accounts department.

comptant [kɔ̃tɑ̃] *a* **argent c.** (hard) cash; – *adv* **payer c.** to pay (in) cash; **(au) c.** (*acheter, vendre*) for cash.

compte [kɔ̃t] *nm* (*comptabilité*) account; (*calcul*) count; (*nombre*) (right) number; **avoir un c. en banque** to have a bank(ing) account; **c. chèque** cheque account, *Am* checking account; **tenir c. de** to take into account; **c. tenu de** considering; **entrer en ligne de c.** to be taken into account; **se rendre c. de** to realize; **rendre c. de** (*exposer*) to report on; (*justifier*) to account for; **c. rendu** report; (*de livre, film*) review; **demander des comptes à** to call to account; **faire le c. de** to count; **à son c.** (*travailler*) for oneself; (*s'installer*) on one's own; **pour le c. de** on behalf of; **pour mon c.** for my part; **sur le c. de qn** about s.o.; **en fin de c.** all things considered; **à bon c.** (*acheter*) cheap(ly); **s'en tirer à bon c.** to get off lightly; **avoir un c. à régler avec qn** to have a score to settle with s.o.; **c. à rebours** countdown. ◆**c.-gouttes** *nm inv Méd* dropper; **au c.-gouttes** very sparingly. ◆**c.-tours** *nm inv Aut* rev counter.

compt/er [kɔ̃te] *vt* (*calculer*) to count; (*prévoir*) to reckon, allow; (*considérer*) to consider; (*payer*) to pay; **c. faire** to expect to do; (*avoir l'intention de*) to intend to do; **c. qch à qn** (*facturer*) to charge s.o. for sth; **il compte deux ans de service** he has two years' service; **ses jours sont comptés** his *ou* her days are numbered; – *vi* (*calculer, avoir de l'importance*) to count; **c. sur** to rely on; **c. avec** to reckon with; **c. parmi** to be (numbered) among. ◆**—eur** *nm Él* meter; **c. (de vitesse)** *Aut* speedometer; **c. (kilométrique)** milometer, clock; **c. Geiger** Geiger counter.

comptoir [kɔ̃twar] *nm* **1** (*de magasin*) counter; (*de café*) bar; (*de bureau*) (reception) desk. **2** *Com* branch, agency.

compulser [kɔ̃pylse] *vt* to examine.

comte [kɔ̃t] *nm* (*noble*) count; *Br* earl. ◆**comté** *nm* county. ◆**comtesse** *nf* countess.

con, conne [kɔ̃, kɔn] *a* (*idiot*) *Fam* stupid; – *nmf Fam* stupid fool.

concave [kɔ̃kav] *a* concave.

concéder [kɔ̃sede] *vt* to concede, grant (**à** to, **que** that).

concentr/er [kɔ̃sɑ̃tre] *vt* to concentrate; (*attention etc*) to focus, concentrate; – **se c.** *vpr* (*réfléchir*) to concentrate. ◆**—é** *a* (*solution*) concentrated; (*lait*) condensed; (*attentif*) in a state of concentration; – *nm Ch* concentrate; **c. de tomates** tomato purée. ◆**concentration** *nf* concentration.

concentrique [kɔ̃sɑ̃trik] *a* concentric.

concept [kɔ̃sɛpt] *nm* concept. ◆**conception** *nf* (*idée*) & *Méd* conception.

concern/er [kɔ̃sɛrne] *vt* to concern; **en ce qui me concerne** as far as I'm concerned. ◆**—ant** *prép* concerning.

concert [kɔ̃sɛr] *nm Mus* concert; (*de louanges*) chorus; **de c.** (*agir*) together, in concert.

concert/er [kɔ̃sɛrte] *vt* to arrange, devise (*in agreement*); – **se c.** *vpr* to consult together. ◆**—é** *a* (*plan*) concerted. ◆**concertation** *nf* (*dialogue*) dialogue.

concession [kɔ̃sesjɔ̃] *nf* concession (**à** to); (*terrain*) plot (of land). ◆**concessionnaire** *nmf Com* (authorized) dealer, agent.

concev/oir* [kɔ̃səvwar] **1** *vt* (*imaginer, éprouver, engendrer*) to conceive; (*comprendre*) to understand; **ainsi conçu** (*dépêche etc*) worded as follows. **2** *vi* (*femme*) to conceive. ◆**—able** *a* conceivable.

concierge [kɔ̃sjɛrʒ] *nmf* caretaker, *Am* janitor.
concile [kɔ̃sil] *nm Rel* council.
concili/er [kɔ̃silje] *vt* (*choses*) to reconcile; **se c. l'amitié/***etc* **de qn** to win (over) s.o.'s friendship/*etc*. ◆**—ant** *a* conciliatory. ◆**conciliateur, -trice** *nmf* conciliator. ◆**conciliation** *nf* conciliation.
concis [kɔ̃si] *a* concise, terse. ◆**concision** *nf* concision.
concitoyen, -enne [kɔ̃sitwajɛ̃, -ɛn] *nmf* fellow citizen.
conclu/re* [kɔ̃klyr] *vt* (*terminer, régler*) to conclude; **c. que** (*déduire*) to conclude that; – *vi* (*orateur etc*) to conclude; **c. à** to conclude in favour of. ◆**—ant** *a* conclusive. ◆**conclusion** *nf* conclusion.
concombre [kɔ̃kɔ̃br] *nm* cucumber.
concorde [kɔ̃kɔrd] *nf* concord, harmony. ◆**concord/er** *vi* (*faits etc*) to agree; (*caractères*) to match; **c. avec** to match. ◆**—ant** *a* in agreement. ◆**concordance** *nf* agreement; (*de situations, résultats*) similarity; **c. des temps** *Gram* sequence of tenses.
concourir* [kɔ̃kurir] *vi* (*candidat*) to compete (**pour** for); (*directions*) to converge; **c. à** (*un but*) to contribute to. ◆**concours** *nm Scol Univ* competitive examination; (*jeu*) competition; (*aide*) assistance; (*de circonstances*) combination; **c. hippique** horse show.
concret, -ète [kɔ̃krɛ, -ɛt] *a* concrete. ◆**concrétiser** *vt* to give concrete form to; — **se c.** *vpr* to materialize.
conçu [kɔ̃sy] *voir* **concevoir**; – *a* **c. pour faire** designed to do; **bien c.** (*maison etc*) well-designed.
concubine [kɔ̃kybin] *nf* (*maîtresse*) concubine. ◆**concubinage** *nm* cohabitation; **en c.** as husband and wife.
concurrent, -ente [kɔ̃kyrɑ̃, -ɑ̃t] *nmf* competitor; *Scol Univ* candidate. ◆**concurrence** *nf* competition; **faire c. à** to compete with; **jusqu'à c. de** up to the amount of. ◆**concurrencer** *vt* to compete with. ◆**concurrentiel, -ielle** *a* (*prix etc*) competitive.
condamn/er [kɔ̃dane] *vt* to condemn; *Jur* to sentence (à to); (*porte*) to block up, bar; (*pièce*) to keep locked; **c. à une amende** to fine. ◆**—é, -ée** *nmf Jur* condemned man, condemned woman; **être c.** (*malade*) to be doomed, be a hopeless case. ◆**condamnation** *nf Jur* sentence; (*censure*) condemnation.
condenser [kɔ̃dɑ̃se] *vt*, — **se c.** *vpr* to condense. ◆**condensateur** *nm Él* condenser. ◆**condensation** *nf* condensation.
condescendre [kɔ̃desɑ̃dr] *vi* to condescend (à to). ◆**condescendance** *nf* condescension.
condiment [kɔ̃dimɑ̃] *nm* condiment.
condisciple [kɔ̃disipl] *nm Scol* classmate, schoolfellow; *Univ* fellow student.
condition [kɔ̃disjɔ̃] *nf* (*état, stipulation, rang*) condition; *pl* (*clauses, tarifs*) *Com* terms; **à c. de faire, à c. que l'on fasse** providing *ou* provided (that) one does; **mettre en c.** (*endoctriner*) to condition; **sans c.** (*se rendre*) unconditionally. ◆**conditionnel, -elle** *a* conditional. ◆**conditionn/er** *vt* **1** (*influencer*) to condition. **2** (*article*) *Com* to package. ◆**—é** *a* (*réflexe*) conditioned; **à air c.** (*pièce etc*) air-conditioned. ◆**—ement** *nm* conditioning; packaging.
condoléances [kɔ̃dɔleɑ̃s] *nfpl* condolences.
conducteur, -trice [kɔ̃dyktœr, -tris] **1** *nmf Aut Rail* driver. **2** *a & nm* (**corps**) **c.** *Él* conductor; (**fil**) **c.** *Él* lead (wire).
conduire* [kɔ̃dɥir] **1** *vt* to lead; *Aut* to drive; (*affaire etc*) & *Él* to conduct; (*eau*) to carry; **c. qn à** (*accompagner*) to take s.o. to. **2 se c.** *vpr* to behave. ◆**conduit** *nm* duct. ◆**conduite** *nf* conduct, behaviour; *Aut* driving (**de** of); (*d'entreprise etc*) conduct; (*d'eau, de gaz*) main; **c. à gauche** (*volant*) left-hand drive; **faire un bout de c. à qn** to go with s.o. part of the way; **sous la c. de** under the guidance of.
cône [kon] *nm* cone.
confection [kɔ̃fɛksjɔ̃] *nf* making (**de** of); **vêtements de c.** ready-made clothes; **magasin de c.** ready-made clothing shop. ◆**confectionner** *vt* (*gâteau, robe*) to make.
confédération [kɔ̃federasjɔ̃] *nf* confederation. ◆**confédéré** *a* confederate.
conférence [kɔ̃ferɑ̃s] *nf* conference; (*exposé*) lecture. ◆**conférencier, -ière** *nmf* lecturer. ◆**conférer** *vt* (*attribuer, donner*) to confer (à on).
confess/er [kɔ̃fese] *vt* to confess; — **se c.** *vpr Rel* to confess (à to). ◆**—eur** *nm* (*prêtre*) confessor. ◆**confession** *nf* confession. ◆**confessionnal, -aux** *nm Rel* confessional. ◆**confessionnel, -elle** *a* (*école*) *Rel* denominational.
confettis [kɔ̃feti] *nmpl* confetti.
confiance [kɔ̃fjɑ̃s] *nf* trust, confidence; **faire c. à qn, avoir c. en qn** to trust s.o.; **c. en soi** (self-)confidence; **poste/abus de c.** posi-

tion/breach of trust; **homme de c.** reliable man; **en toute c.** (*acheter*) quite confidently; **poser la question de c.** *Pol* to ask for a vote of confidence. ◆**confiant** *a* trusting; (*sûr de soi*) confident; **être c. en** *ou* **dans** to have confidence in.

confidence [kɔ̃fidɑ̃s] *nf* (*secret*) confidence; **en c.** in confidence; **il m'a fait une c.** he confided in me. ◆**confident** *nm* confidant. ◆**confidente** *nf* confidante. ◆**confidentiel, -ielle** *a* confidential.

confier [kɔ̃fje] *vt* **c. à qn** (*enfant, objet*) to give s.o. to look after, entrust s.o. with; **c. un secret/etc à qn** to confide a secret/*etc* to s.o.; **— se c.** *vpr* to confide (**à qn** in s.o.).

configuration [kɔ̃figyrɑsjɔ̃] *nf* configuration.

confin/er [kɔ̃fine] *vt* to confine; – *vi* **c. à** to border on; **— se c.** *vpr* to confine oneself (**dans** to). ◆**—é** *a* (*atmosphère*) stuffy.

confins [kɔ̃fɛ̃] *nmpl* confines.

confire [kɔ̃fir] *vt* (*cornichon*) to pickle; (*fruit*) to preserve.

confirmer [kɔ̃firme] *vt* to confirm (**que** that); **c. qn dans sa résolution** to confirm s.o.'s resolve. ◆**confirmation** *nf* confirmation.

confiserie [kɔ̃fizri] *nf* (*magasin*) sweet shop, *Am* candy store; *pl* (*produits*) confectionery, sweets, *Am* candy. ◆**confiseur, -euse** *nmf* confectioner.

confisquer [kɔ̃fiske] *vt* to confiscate (**à qn** from s.o.). ◆**confiscation** *nf* confiscation.

confit [kɔ̃fi] *a* **fruits confits** crystallized *ou* candied fruit. ◆**confiture** *nf* jam, preserves.

conflit [kɔ̃fli] *nm* conflict. ◆**conflictuel, -elle** *a Psy* conflict-provoking.

confluent [kɔ̃flyɑ̃] *nm* (*jonction*) confluence.

confondre [kɔ̃fɔ̃dr] *vt* (*choses, personnes*) to confuse, mix up; (*consterner, étonner*) to confound; (*amalgamer*) to fuse; **c. avec** to mistake for; **— se c.** *vpr* (*s'unir*) to merge; **se c. en excuses** to be very apologetic.

conforme [kɔ̃fɔrm] *a* **c. à** in accordance with; **c. (à l'original)** (*copie*) true (to the original). ◆**conform/er** *vt* to model, adapt; **— se c.** *vpr* to conform (**à** to). ◆**—ément** *adv* **c. à** in accordance with. ◆**conformisme** *nm* conformity, conformism. ◆**conformiste** *a* & *nmf* conformist. ◆**conformité** *nf* conformity.

confort [kɔ̃fɔr] *nm* comfort. ◆**confortable** *a* comfortable.

confrère [kɔ̃frɛr] *nm* colleague. ◆**confrérie** *nf Rel* brotherhood.

confronter [kɔ̃frɔ̃te] *vt Jur etc* to confront (**avec** with); (*textes*) to collate; **confronté à** confronted with. ◆**confrontation** *nf* confrontation; collation.

confus [kɔ̃fy] *a* (*esprit, situation, bruit*) confused; (*idée, style*) confused, jumbled, hazy; (*gêné*) embarrassed; **je suis c.!** (*désolé*) I'm terribly sorry!; (*comblé de bienfaits*) I'm overwhelmed! ◆**confusément** *adv* indistinctly, vaguely. ◆**confusion** *nf* confusion; (*gêne, honte*) embarrassment.

congé [kɔ̃ʒe] *nm* leave (of absence); (*avis pour locataire*) notice (to quit); (*pour salarié*) notice (of dismissal); (*vacances*) holiday, *Am* vacation; **c. de maladie** sick leave; **congés payés** holidays with pay, paid holidays; **donner son c. à** (*employé, locataire*) to give notice to; **prendre c. de** to take leave of. ◆**congédier** *vt* (*domestique etc*) to dismiss.

congeler [kɔ̃ʒle] *vt* to freeze. ◆**congélateur** *nm* freezer, deep-freeze. ◆**congélation** *nf* freezing.

congénère [kɔ̃ʒenɛr] *nmf* fellow creature. ◆**congénital, -aux** *a* congenital.

congère [kɔ̃ʒɛr] *nf* snowdrift.

congestion [kɔ̃ʒɛstjɔ̃] *nf* congestion; **c. cérébrale** *Méd* stroke. ◆**congestionn/er** *vt* to congest. ◆**—é** *a* (*visage*) flushed.

Congo [kɔ̃go] *nm* Congo. ◆**congolais, -aise** *a* & *nmf* Congolese.

congratuler [kɔ̃gratyle] *vt Iron* to congratulate.

congrégation [kɔ̃gregɑsjɔ̃] *nf* (*de prêtres etc*) congregation.

congrès [kɔ̃grɛ] *nm* congress. ◆**congressiste** *nmf* delegate (*to a congress*).

conifère [kɔnifɛr] *nm* conifer.

conique [kɔnik] *a* conic(al), cone-shaped.

conjecture [kɔ̃ʒɛktyr] *nf* conjecture. ◆**conjectural, -aux** *a* conjectural. ◆**conjecturer** *vt* to conjecture, surmise.

conjoint [kɔ̃ʒwɛ̃] **1** *a* (*problèmes, action etc*) joint. **2** *nm* spouse; *pl* husband and wife. ◆**conjointement** *adv* jointly.

conjonction [kɔ̃ʒɔ̃ksjɔ̃] *nf Gram* conjunction.

conjoncture [kɔ̃ʒɔ̃ktyr] *nf* circumstances; *Écon* economic situation. ◆**conjoncturel, -elle** *a* (*prévisions etc*) economic.

conjugal, -aux [kɔ̃ʒygal, -o] *a* conjugal.

conjuguer [kɔ̃ʒyge] *vt* (*verbe*) to conjugate; (*efforts*) to combine; **— se c.** *vpr* (*verbe*) to be conjugated. ◆**conjugaison** *nf Gram* conjugation.

conjur/er [kɔ̃ʒyre] *vt* (*danger*) to avert; (*mauvais sort*) to ward off; **c. qn** (*implorer*) to entreat s.o. (**de faire** to do). ◆**—é, -ée** *nmf* conspirator. ◆**conjuration** *nf* (*complot*) conspiracy.

connaissance [kɔnɛsɑ̃s] *nf* knowledge; (*personne*) acquaintance; *pl* (*science*) knowledge (**en** of); **faire la c. de qn, faire c. avec qn** to make s.o.'s acquaintance, meet s.o.; (*ami, époux etc*) to get to know s.o.; **à ma c.** as far as I know; **avoir c. de** to be aware of; **perdre c.** to lose consciousness, faint; **sans c.** unconscious. ◆**connaisseur** *nm* connoisseur.

connaître* [kɔnɛtr] *vt* to know; (*rencontrer*) to meet; (*un succès etc*) to have; (*un malheur etc*) to experience; **faire c.** to make known; **— se c.** *vpr* (*amis etc*) to get to know each other; **nous nous connaissons déjà** we've met before; **s'y c. à** *ou* **en qch** to know (all) about sth; **il ne se connaît plus** he's losing his cool.

connecter [kɔnɛkte] *vt Él* to connect. ◆**connexe** *a* (*matières*) allied. ◆**connexion** *nf Él* connection.

connerie [kɔnri] *nf Fam* (*bêtise*) stupidity; (*action*) stupid thing; *pl* (*paroles*) stupid nonsense.

connivence [kɔnivɑ̃s] *nf* connivance.

connotation [kɔnɔtɑsjɔ̃] *nf* connotation.

connu *voir* **connaître;** — *a* (*célèbre*) well-known.

conquér/ir* [kɔ̃kerir] *vt* (*pays, marché etc*) to conquer. ◆**—ant, -ante** *nmf* conqueror. ◆**conquête** *nf* conquest; **faire la c. de** (*pays, marché etc*) to conquer.

consacrer [kɔ̃sakre] *vt* (*temps, vie etc*) to devote (**à** to); (*église etc*) *Rel* to consecrate; (*coutume etc*) to establish, sanction, consecrate; **se c. à** to devote oneself to.

conscience [kɔ̃sjɑ̃s] *nf* **1** (*psychologique*) consciousness; **la c. de qch** the awareness *ou* consciousness of sth; **c. de soi** self-awareness; **avoir/prendre c. de** to be/become aware *ou* conscious of; **perdre c.** to lose consciousness. **2** (*morale*) conscience; **avoir mauvaise c.** to have a guilty conscience; **c. professionnelle** conscientiousness. ◆**consciemment** [kɔ̃sjamɑ̃] *adv* consciously. ◆**consciencieux, -euse** *a* conscientious. ◆**conscient** *a* conscious; **c. de** aware *ou* conscious of.

conscrit [kɔ̃skri] *nm Mil* conscript. ◆**conscription** *nf* conscription.

consécration [kɔ̃sekrɑsjɔ̃] *nf Rel* consecration; (*confirmation*) sanction, consecration.

consécuti/f, -ive [kɔ̃sekytif, -iv] *a* consecutive; **c. à** following upon. ◆**—vement** *adv* consecutively.

conseil [kɔ̃sɛj] *nm* **1 un c.** a piece of advice, some advice; **des conseils** advice; **(expert-)c.** consultant. **2** (*assemblée*) council, committee; **c. d'administration** board of directors; **C. des ministres** *Pol* Cabinet; (*réunion*) Cabinet meeting. ◆**conseiller**[1] *vt* (*guider, recommander*) to advise; **c. qch à qn** to recommend sth to s.o.; **c. à qn de faire** to advise s.o. to do. ◆**conseiller**[2], **-ère** *nmf* (*expert*) consultant; (*d'un conseil*) councillor.

consent/ir* [kɔ̃sɑ̃tir] *vi* **c. à** to consent to; — *vt* to grant (**à** to). ◆**—ement** *nm* consent.

conséquence [kɔ̃sekɑ̃s] *nf* consequence; (*conclusion*) conclusion; **en c.** accordingly; **sans c.** (*importance*) of no importance. ◆**conséquent** *a* logical; (*important*) *Fam* important; **par c.** consequently.

conservatoire [kɔ̃sɛrvatwar] *nm* academy, school (*of music, drama*).

conserve [kɔ̃sɛrv] *nf* **conserves** tinned *ou* canned food; **de** *ou* **en c.** tinned, canned; **mettre en c.** to tin, can.

conserv/er [kɔ̃sɛrve] *vt* (*ne pas perdre*) to retain, keep; (*fruits, vie, tradition etc*) to preserve; **— se c.** *vpr* (*aliment*) to keep. ◆**—é** *a* **bien c.** (*vieillard*) well-preserved. ◆**conservateur, -trice 1** *a* & *nmf Pol* Conservative. **2** *nm* (*de musée*) curator; (*de bibliothèque*) (chief) librarian. **3** *nm* (*produit*) *Culin* preservative. ◆**conservation** *nf* preservation; **instinct de c.** survival instinct. ◆**conservatisme** *nm* conservatism.

considér/er [kɔ̃sidere] *vt* to consider (**que** that); **c. qn** (*faire cas de*) to respect s.o.; **c. comme** to consider to be, regard as; **tout bien considéré** all things considered. ◆**—able** *a* considerable. ◆**considération** *nf* (*motif, examen*) consideration; (*respect*) regard, esteem; *pl* (*remarques*) observations; **prendre en c.** to take into consideration.

consigne [kɔ̃siɲ] *nf* (*instruction*) orders; *Rail* left-luggage office, *Am* baggage checkroom; *Scol* detention; *Mil* confinement to barracks; (*somme*) deposit; **c. automatique** *Rail* luggage lockers, *Am* baggage lockers. ◆**consignation** *nf* (*somme*) deposit. ◆**consigner** *vt* (*écrire*) to record; (*bouteille etc*) to charge a deposit on; (*bagages*) to deposit in the left-luggage office, *Am* to check; (*élève*) *Scol* to keep in;

(*soldat*) *Mil* to confine (to barracks); (*salle*) to seal off, close.
consistant [kɔ̃sistɑ̃] *a* (*sauce, bouillie*) thick; (*argument, repas*) solid. ◆**consistance** *nf* (*de liquide*) consistency; **sans c.** (*rumeur*) unfounded; (*esprit*) irresolute.
consister [kɔ̃siste] *vi* **c. en/dans** to consist of/in; **c. à faire** to consist in doing.
consistoire [kɔ̃sistwar] *nm Rel* council.
console [kɔ̃sɔl] *nf Tech Él* console.
consoler [kɔ̃sɔle] *vt* to console, comfort (**de** for); **se c. de** (*la mort de qn etc*) to get over. ◆**consolation** *nf* consolation, comfort.
consolider [kɔ̃sɔlide] *vt* to strengthen, consolidate. ◆**consolidation** *nf* strengthening, consolidation.
consomm/er [kɔ̃sɔme] *vt* (*aliment, carburant etc*) to consume; (*crime, œuvre*) *Litt* to accomplish; – *vi* (*au café*) to drink; **c. beaucoup/peu** (*véhicule*) to be heavy/light on petrol *ou Am* gas. ◆**—é 1** *a* (*achevé*) consummate. **2** *nm* clear meat soup, consommé. ◆**consommateur, -trice** *nmf Com* consumer; (*au café*) customer. ◆**consommation** *nf* consumption; drink; **biens/société de c.** consumer goods/society.
consonance [kɔ̃sɔnɑ̃s] *nf Mus* consonance; *pl* (*sons*) sounds.
consonne [kɔ̃sɔn] *nf* consonant.
consortium [kɔ̃sɔrsjɔm] *nm Com* consortium.
consorts [kɔ̃sɔr] *nmpl* **et c.** *Péj* and people of that ilk.
conspirer [kɔ̃spire] *vi* **1** to conspire, plot (**contre** against). **2 c. à faire** (*concourir*) to conspire to do. ◆**conspirateur, -trice** *nmf* conspirator. ◆**conspiration** *nf* conspiracy.
conspuer [kɔ̃spɥe] *vt* (*orateur etc*) to boo.
constant, -ante [kɔ̃stɑ̃, -ɑ̃t] *a* constant; – *nf Math* constant. ◆**constamment** *adv* constantly. ◆**constance** *nf* constancy.
constat [kɔ̃sta] *nm* (official) report; **dresser un c. d'échec** to acknowledge one's failure.
constater [kɔ̃state] *vt* to note, observe (**que** that); (*vérifier*) to establish; (*enregistrer*) to record; **je ne fais que c.** I'm merely stating a fact. ◆**constatation** *nf* (*remarque*) observation.
constellation [kɔ̃stelɑsjɔ̃] *nf* constellation. ◆**constellé** *a* **c. de** (*étoiles, joyaux*) studded with.
consterner [kɔ̃stɛrne] *vt* to distress, dismay. ◆**consternation** *nf* distress, (profound) dismay.
constip/er [kɔ̃stipe] *vt* to constipate. ◆**—é** *a* constipated; (*gêné*) *Fam* embarrassed, stiff. ◆**constipation** *nf* constipation.
constitu/er [kɔ̃stitɥe] *vt* (*composer*) to make up, constitute; (*être, représenter*) to constitute; (*organiser*) to form; (*instituer*) *Jur* to appoint; **constitué de** made up of; **se c. prisonnier** to give oneself up. ◆**—ant** *a* (*éléments*) component, constituent; (*assemblée*) *Pol* constituent. ◆**constitutif, -ive** *a* constituent. ◆**constitution** *nf* (*santé*) & *Pol* constitution; (*fondation*) formation (**de** of); (*composition*) composition. ◆**constitutionnel, -elle** *a* constitutional.
constructeur [kɔ̃stryktœr] *nm* builder; (*fabricant*) maker (**de** of). ◆**constructif, -ive** *a* constructive. ◆**construction** *nf* (*de pont etc*) building, construction (**de** of); (*édifice*) building, structure; (*de théorie etc*) & *Gram* construction; **de c.** (*matériaux, jeu*) building-.
construire* [kɔ̃strɥir] *vt* (*maison, route etc*) to build, construct; (*phrase, théorie etc*) to construct.
consul [kɔ̃syl] *nm* consul. ◆**consulaire** *a* consular. ◆**consulat** *nm* consulate.
consulter [kɔ̃sylte] **1** *vt* to consult; – **se c.** *vpr* to consult (each other), confer. **2** *vi* (*médecin*) to hold surgery, *Am* hold office hours. ◆**consultatif, -ive** *a* consultative, advisory. ◆**consultation** *nf* consultation; **cabinet de c.** *Méd* surgery, *Am* office; **heures de c.** *Méd* surgery hours, *Am* office hours.
consumer [kɔ̃syme] *vt* (*détruire, miner*) to consume.
contact [kɔ̃takt] *nm* contact; (*toucher*) touch; *Aut* ignition; **être en c. avec** to be in touch *ou* contact with; **prendre c.** to get in touch (**avec** with); **entrer en c. avec** to come into contact with; **prise de c.** first meeting; **mettre/couper le c.** *Aut* to switch on/off the ignition. ◆**contacter** *vt* to contact.
contagieux, -euse [kɔ̃taʒjø, -øz] *a* (*maladie, rire*) contagious, infectious; **c'est c.** it's catching *ou* contagious. ◆**contagion** *nf Méd* contagion, infection; (*de rire etc*) contagiousness.
contaminer [kɔ̃tamine] *vt* to contaminate. ◆**contamination** *nf* contamination.
conte [kɔ̃t] *nm* tale; **c. de fée** fairy tale.
contempler [kɔ̃tɑ̃ple] *vt* to contemplate, gaze at. ◆**contemplatif, -ive** *a* contemplative. ◆**contemplation** *nf* contemplation.
contemporain, -aine [kɔ̃tɑ̃pɔrɛ̃, -ɛn] *a* & *nmf* contemporary.

contenance [kɔ̃tnɑ̃s] *nf* **1** (*contenu*) capacity. **2** (*allure*) bearing; **perdre c.** to lose one's composure.

conten/ir* [kɔ̃tnir] *vt* (*renfermer*) to contain; (*avoir comme capacité*) to hold; (*contrôler*) to hold back, contain; **— se c.** *vpr* to contain oneself. ◆**—ant** *nm* container. ◆**—eur** *nm* (freight) container.

content [kɔ̃tɑ̃] **1** *a* pleased, happy, glad (**de faire** to do); **c. de qn/qch** pleased *ou* happy with s.o./sth; **c. de soi** self-satisfied; **non c. d'avoir fait** not content with having done. **2** *nm* **avoir son c.** to have had one's fill (**de** of). ◆**content/er** *vt* to satisfy, please; **se c. de** to be content with, content oneself with. ◆**—ement** *nm* contentment, satisfaction.

contentieux [kɔ̃tɑ̃sjø] *nm* (*affaires*) matters in dispute; (*service*) legal *ou* claims department.

contenu [kɔ̃tny] *nm* (*de récipient*) contents; (*de texte, film etc*) content.

cont/er [kɔ̃te] *vt* (*histoire etc*) to tell, relate. ◆**—eur, -euse** *nmf* storyteller.

conteste (sans) [sɑ̃kɔ̃tɛst] *adv* indisputably.

contest/er [kɔ̃tɛste] **1** *vt* (*fait etc*) to dispute, contest. **2** *vi* (*étudiants etc*) to protest; **–** *vt* to protest against. ◆**—é** *a* (*théorie etc*) controversial. ◆**—able** *a* debatable. ◆**contestataire** *a* **étudiant/ouvrier c.** student/worker protester; **–** *nmf* protester. ◆**contestation** *nf* (*discussion*) dispute; **faire de la c.** to protest (against the establishment).

contexte [kɔ̃tɛkst] *nm* context.

contigu, -uë [kɔ̃tigy] *a* **c. (à)** (*maisons etc*) adjoining. ◆**contiguïté** *nf* close proximity.

continent [kɔ̃tinɑ̃] *nm* continent; (*opposé à une île*) mainland. ◆**continental, -aux** *a* continental.

contingent [kɔ̃tɛ̃ʒɑ̃] **1** *a* (*accidentel*) contingent. **2** *nm Mil* contingent; (*part, quota*) quota. ◆**contingences** *nfpl* contingencies.

continu [kɔ̃tiny] *a* continuous. ◆**continuel, -elle** *a* continual, unceasing. ◆**continuellement** *adv* continually.

continuer [kɔ̃tinɥe] *vt* to continue, carry on (**à** *ou* **de faire** doing); (*prolonger*) to continue; **–** *vi* to continue, go on. ◆**continuation** *nf* continuation; **bonne c.!** *Fam* I hope the rest of it goes well, keep up the good work! ◆**continuité** *nf* continuity.

contondant [kɔ̃tɔ̃dɑ̃] *a* **instrument c.** *Jur* blunt instrument.

contorsion [kɔ̃tɔrsjɔ̃] *nf* contortion. ◆**se contorsionner** *vpr* to contort oneself. ◆**contorsionniste** *nmf* contortionist.

contour [kɔ̃tur] *nm* outline, contour; *pl* (*de route, rivière*) twists, bends. ◆**contourn/er** *vt* (*colline etc*) to go round, skirt; (*difficulté, loi*) to get round. ◆**—é** *a* (*style*) convoluted, tortuous.

contraception [kɔ̃trasɛpsjɔ̃] *nf* contraception. ◆**contraceptif, -ive** *a* & *nm* contraceptive.

contract/er [kɔ̃trakte] *vt* (*muscle, habitude, dette etc*) to contract; **— se c.** *vpr* (*cœur etc*) to contract. ◆**—é** *a* (*inquiet*) tense. ◆**contraction** *nf* contraction.

contractuel, -elle [kɔ̃traktɥɛl] **1** *nmf* traffic warden; **–** *nf Am* meter maid. **2** *a* contractual.

contradicteur [kɔ̃tradiktœr] *nm* contradictor. ◆**contradiction** *nf* contradiction. ◆**contradictoire** *a* (*propos etc*) contradictory; (*rapports, théories*) conflicting; **débat c.** debate.

contraindre* [kɔ̃trɛ̃dr] *vt* to compel, force (**à faire** to do); **— se c.** *vpr* to compel *ou* force oneself; (*se gêner*) to restrain oneself. ◆**contraignant** *a* constraining, restricting. ◆**contraint** *a* (*air etc*) forced, constrained. ◆**contrainte** *nf* compulsion, constraint; (*gêne*) constraint, restraint.

contraire [kɔ̃trɛr] *a* opposite; (*défavorable*) contrary; **c. à** contrary to; **–** *nm* opposite; **(bien) au c.** on the contrary. ◆**—ment** *adv* **c. à** contrary to.

contrari/er [kɔ̃trarje] *vt* (*projet, action*) to thwart; (*personne*) to annoy. ◆**—ant** *a* (*action etc*) annoying; (*personne*) difficult, perverse. ◆**contrariété** *nf* annoyance.

contraste [kɔ̃trast] *nm* contrast. ◆**contraster** *vi* to contrast (**avec** with); **faire c.** (*mettre en contraste*) to contrast.

contrat [kɔ̃tra] *nm* contract.

contravention [kɔ̃travɑ̃sjɔ̃] *nf* (*amende*) *Aut* fine; (*pour stationnement interdit*) (parking) ticket; **en c.** contravening the law; **en c. à** in contravention of.

contre [kɔ̃tr] **1** *prép* & *adv* against; (*en échange de*) (in exchange) for; **échanger c.** to exchange for; **fâché c.** angry with; **s'abriter c.** to shelter from; **il va s'appuyer c.** he's going to lean against it; **six voix c. deux** six votes to two; **Nîmes c. Arras** *Sp* Nîmes versus Arras; **un médicament c.** (*toux, grippe etc*) a medicine for; **par c.** on the other hand; **tout c.** close to *ou* by. **2** *nm* (*riposte*) *Sp* counter.

contre- [kɔ̃tr] *préf* counter-.

contre-attaque [kɔ̃tratak] *nf* counterattack. ◆**contre-attaquer** *vt* to counterattack.
contrebalancer [kɔ̃trəbalɑ̃se] *vt* to counterbalance.
contrebande [kɔ̃trəbɑ̃d] *nf* (*fraude*) smuggling, contraband; (*marchandise*) contraband; **de c.** (*tabac etc*) contraband, smuggled; **faire de la c.** to smuggle; **passer qch en c.** to smuggle sth. ◆**contrebandier, -ière** *nmf* smuggler.
contrebas (en) [ɑ̃kɔ̃trəba] *adv & prép* **en c. (de)** down below.
contrebasse [kɔ̃trəbɑs] *nf Mus* double-bass.
contrecarrer [kɔ̃trəkare] *vt* to thwart, frustrate.
contrecœur (à) [akɔ̃trəkœr] *adv* reluctantly.
contrecoup [kɔ̃trəku] *nm* (indirect) effect *ou* consequence; **par c.** as an indirect consequence.
contre-courant (à) [akɔ̃trəkurɑ̃] *adv* against the current.
contredanse [kɔ̃trədɑ̃s] *nf* (*amende*) *Aut Fam* ticket.
contredire* [kɔ̃trədir] *vt* to contradict; — **se c.** *vpr* to contradict oneself.
contrée [kɔ̃tre] *nf* region, land.
contre-espionnage [kɔ̃trɛspjɔnaʒ] *nm* counterespionage.
contrefaçon [kɔ̃trəfasɔ̃] *nf* counterfeiting, forgery; (*objet imité*) counterfeit, forgery. ◆**contrefaire** *vt* (*parodier*) to mimic; (*déguiser*) to disguise; (*monnaie etc*) to counterfeit, forge.
contreforts [kɔ̃trəfɔr] *nmpl Géog* foothills.
contre-indiqué [kɔ̃trɛ̃dike] *a* (*médicament*) dangerous, not recommended.
contre-jour (à) [akɔ̃trəʒur] *adv* against the (sun)light.
contremaître [kɔ̃trəmɛtr] *nm* foreman.
contre-offensive [kɔ̃trɔfɑ̃siv] *nf* counteroffensive.
contrepartie [kɔ̃trəparti] *nf* compensation; **en c.** in exchange.
contre-performance [kɔ̃trəpɛrfɔrmɑ̃s] *nf Sp* bad performance.
contre-pied [kɔ̃trəpje] *nm* **le c.-pied d'une opinion/attitude** the (exact) opposite view/attitude; **à c.-pied** *Sp* on the wrong foot.
contre-plaqué [kɔ̃trəplake] *nm* plywood.
contrepoids [kɔ̃trəpwa] *nm Tech & Fig* counterbalance; **faire c. (à)** to counterbalance.
contrepoint [kɔ̃trəpwɛ̃] *nm Mus* counterpoint.
contrer [kɔ̃tre] *vt* (*personne, attaque*) to counter.
contre-révolution [kɔ̃trərevɔlysjɔ̃] *nf* counter-revolution.
contresens [kɔ̃trəsɑ̃s] *nm* misinterpretation; (*en traduisant*) mistranslation; (*non-sens*) absurdity; **à c.** the wrong way.
contresigner [kɔ̃trəsiɲe] *vt* to countersign.
contretemps [kɔ̃trətɑ̃] *nm* hitch, mishap; **à c.** (*arriver etc*) at the wrong moment.
contre-torpilleur [kɔ̃trətɔrpijœr] *nm* (*navire*) destroyer, torpedo boat.
contrevenir [kɔ̃trəvnir] *vi* **c. à** (*loi etc*) to contravene.
contre-vérité [kɔ̃trəverite] *nf* untruth.
contribu/er [kɔ̃tribɥe] *vi* to contribute (à to). ◆**—able** *nmf* taxpayer. ◆**contribution** *nf* contribution; (*impôt*) tax; *pl* (*administration*) tax office; **mettre qn à c.** to use s.o.'s services.
contrit [kɔ̃tri] *a* (*air etc*) contrite. ◆**contrition** *nf* contrition.
contrôle [kɔ̃trol] *nm* (*vérification*) inspection, check(ing) (**de** of); (*des prix, de la qualité*) control; (*maîtrise*) control; (*sur bijou*) hallmark; **un c.** (*examen*) a check (**sur on**); **le c. de soi(-même)** self-control; **le c. des naissances** birth control; **un c. d'identité** an identity check. ◆**contrôl/er** *vt* (*examiner*) to inspect, check; (*maîtriser, surveiller*) to control; — **se c.** *vpr* (*se maîtriser*) to control oneself. ◆**—eur, -euse** *nmf* (*de train*) (ticket) inspector; (*au quai*) ticket collector; (*de bus*) conductor, conductress.
contrordre [kɔ̃trɔrdr] *nm* change of orders.
controverse [kɔ̃trɔvɛrs] *nf* controversy. ◆**controversé** *a* controversial.
contumace (par) [parkɔ̃tymas] *adv Jur* in one's absence, in absentia.
contusion [kɔ̃tyzjɔ̃] *nf* bruise. ◆**contusionner** *vt* to bruise.
convainc/re* [kɔ̃vɛ̃kr] *vt* to convince (**de** of); (*accusé*) to prove guilty (**de** of); **c. qn de faire** to persuade s.o. to do. ◆**—ant** *a* convincing. ◆**—u** *a* (*certain*) convinced (**de** of).
convalescent, -ente [kɔ̃valesɑ̃, -ɑ̃t] *nmf* convalescent; – *a* **être c.** to convalesce. ◆**convalescence** *nf* convalescence; **être en c.** to convalesce; **maison de c.** convalescent home.
conven/ir [kɔ̃vnir] *vi* **c. à** (*être approprié à*) to be suitable for; (*plaire à, aller à*) to suit; **ça convient** (*date etc*) that's suitable; **c. de** (*lieu etc*) to agree upon; (*erreur*) to admit; **c. que** to admit that; **il convient de** it's

advisable to; (*selon les usages*) it is proper *ou* fitting to. ◆**—u** *a* (*prix etc*) agreed. ◆**—able** *a* (*approprié, acceptable*) suitable; (*correct*) decent, proper. ◆**—ablement** *adv* suitably; decently. ◆**convenance** *nf* **convenances** (*usages*) convention(s), proprieties; **à sa c.** to one's satisfaction *ou* taste.

convention [kɔ̃vɑ̃sjɔ̃] *nf* (*accord*) agreement, convention; (*règle*) & *Am Pol* convention; **c. collective** collective bargaining; **de c.** (*sentiment etc*) conventional. ◆**conventionné** *a* (*prix, tarif*) regulated (by voluntary agreement); **médecin c.** = National Health Service doctor (*bound by agreement with the State*). ◆**conventionnel, -elle** *a* conventional.

convergent [kɔ̃vɛrʒɑ̃] *a* converging, convergent. ◆**convergence** *nf* convergence. ◆**converger** *vi* to converge.

converser [kɔ̃vɛrse] *vi* to converse. ◆**conversation** *nf* conversation.

conversion [kɔ̃vɛrsjɔ̃] *nf* conversion. ◆**convert/ir** *vt* to convert (**à** to, **en** into); **— se c.** *vpr* to be converted, convert. ◆**—i, -ie** *nmf* convert. ◆**convertible** *a* convertible; **–** *nm* **(canapé) c.** bed settee.

convexe [kɔ̃vɛks] *a* convex.

conviction [kɔ̃viksjɔ̃] *nf* (*certitude, croyance*) conviction; **pièce à c.** *Jur* exhibit.

convier [kɔ̃vje] *vt* to invite (**à une soirée**/*etc* to a party/*etc*, **à faire** to do).

convive [kɔ̃viv] *nmf* guest (*at table*).

convoi [kɔ̃vwa] *nm* (*véhicules, personnes etc*) convoy; *Rail* train; **c. (funèbre)** funeral procession. ◆**convoy/er** *vt* to escort. ◆**—eur** *nm Nau* escort ship; **c. de fonds** security guard.

convoiter [kɔ̃vwate] *vt* to desire, envy, covet. ◆**convoitise** *nf* desire, envy.

convoquer [kɔ̃vɔke] *vt* (*candidats, membres etc*) to summon *ou* invite (to attend); (*assemblée*) to convene, summon; **c. à** to summon *ou* invite to. ◆**convocation** *nf* (*action*) summoning; convening; (*ordre*) summons (to attend); (*lettre*) (written) notice (to attend).

convulser [kɔ̃vylse] *vt* to convulse. ◆**convulsif, -ive** *a* convulsive. ◆**convulsion** *nf* convulsion.

coopérer [kɔɔpere] *vi* to co-operate (**à** in, **avec** with). ◆**coopératif, -ive** *a* co-operative; **–** *nf* co-operative (society). ◆**coopération** *nf* co-operation.

coopter [kɔɔpte] *vt* to co-opt.

coordonn/er [kɔɔrdɔne] *vt* to co-ordinate. ◆**—ées** *nfpl Math* co-ordinates; (*adresse, téléphone*) *Fam* particulars, details. ◆**coordination** *nf* co-ordination.

copain [kɔpɛ̃] *nm Fam* (*camarade*) pal; (*petit ami*) boyfriend; **être c. avec** to be pals with.

copeau, -x [kɔpo] *nm* (*de bois*) shaving.

copie [kɔpi] *nf* copy; (*devoir, examen*) *Scol* paper. ◆**copier** *vti* to copy; *Scol* to copy, crib (**sur** from). ◆**copieur, -euse** *nmf* (*élève etc*) copycat, copier.

copieux, -euse [kɔpjø, -øz] *a* copious, plentiful.

copilote [kɔpilɔt] *nm* co-pilot.

copine [kɔpin] *nf Fam* (*camarade*) pal; (*petite amie*) girlfriend; **être c. avec** to be pals with.

copropriété [kɔprɔprijete] *nf* joint ownership; **(immeuble en) c.** block of flats in joint ownership, *Am* condominium.

copulation [kɔpylɑsjɔ̃] *nf* copulation.

coq [kɔk] *nm* cock, rooster; **c. au vin** coq au vin (*chicken cooked in wine*); **passer du c. à l'âne** to jump from one subject to another.

coque [kɔk] *nf* **1** (*de noix*) shell; (*mollusque*) cockle; **œuf à la c.** boiled egg. **2** *Nau* hull.

coquelicot [kɔkliko] *nm* poppy

coqueluche [kɔklyʃ] *nf Méd* whooping-cough; **la c. de** *Fig* the darling of.

coquet, -ette [kɔkɛ, -ɛt] *a* (*chic*) smart; (*joli*) pretty; (*provocant*) coquettish, flirtatious; (*somme*) *Fam* tidy; **–** *nf* coquette, flirt. ◆**coquetterie** *nf* (*élégance*) smartness; (*goût de la toilette*) dress sense; (*galanterie*) coquetry.

coquetier [kɔktje] *nm* egg cup.

coquille [kɔkij] *nf* shell; *Typ* misprint; **c. Saint-Jacques** scallop. ◆**coquillage** *nm* (*mollusque*) shellfish; (*coquille*) shell.

coquin, -ine [kɔkɛ̃, -in] *nmf* rascal; **–** *a* mischievous, rascally; (*histoire etc*) naughty.

cor [kɔr] *nm Mus* horn; **c. (au pied)** corn; **réclamer** *ou* **demander à c. et à cri** to clamour for.

corail, -aux [kɔraj, -o] *nm* coral.

Coran [kɔrɑ̃] *nm* **le C.** the Koran.

corbeau, -x [kɔrbo] *nm* crow; **(grand) c.** raven.

corbeille [kɔrbɛj] *nf* basket; **c. à papier** waste paper basket.

corbillard [kɔrbijar] *nm* hearse.

corde [kɔrd] *nf* rope; (*plus mince*) (fine) cord; (*de raquette, violon etc*) string; **c. (raide)** (*d'acrobate*) tightrope; **instrument à cordes** *Mus* string(ed) instrument; **c. à linge** (washing *ou* clothes) line; **c. à sauter** skipping rope, *Am* jump rope; **usé jusqu'à**

la c. threadbare; **cordes vocales** vocal cords; **prendre un virage à la c.** *Aut* to hug a bend; **pas dans mes cordes** *Fam* not my line. ◆**cordage** *nm Nau* rope. ◆**cordée** *nf* roped (climbing) party. ◆**cordelette** *nf* (fine) cord. ◆**corder** *vt* (*raquette*) to string. ◆**cordon** *nm* (*de tablier, sac etc*) string; (*de soulier*) lace; (*de rideau*) cord, rope; (*d'agents de police*) cordon; (*décoration*) ribbon, sash; (*ombilical*) *Anat* cord. ◆**c.-bleu** *nm* (*pl* **cordons-bleus**) cordon bleu (cook), first-class cook.

cordial, -aux [kɔrdjal, -o] *a* cordial, warm; – *nm Méd* cordial. ◆**cordialité** *nf* cordiality.

cordonnier [kɔrdɔnje] *nm* shoe repairer, cobbler. ◆**cordonnerie** *nf* shoe repairer's shop.

Corée [kɔre] *nf* Korea. ◆**coréen, -enne** *a* & *nmf* Korean.

coriace [kɔrjas] *a* (*aliment, personne*) tough.

corne [kɔrn] *nf* (*de chèvre etc*) horn; (*de cerf*) antler; (*matière, instrument*) horn; (*angle, pli*) corner.

cornée [kɔrne] *nf Anat* cornea.

corneille [kɔrnɛj] *nf* crow.

cornemuse [kɔrnəmyz] *nf* bagpipes.

corner [kɔrne] **1** *vt* (*page*) to turn down the corner of, dog-ear. **2** *vi* (*véhicule*) to sound its horn. **3** [kɔrnɛr] *nm Fb* corner.

cornet [kɔrnɛ] *nm* **1 c. (à pistons)** *Mus* cornet. **2** (*de glace*) cornet, cone; **c. (de papier)** (paper) cone.

corniaud [kɔrnjo] *nm* (*chien*) mongrel; (*imbécile*) *Fam* drip, twit.

corniche [kɔrniʃ] *nf Archit* cornice; (*route*) cliff road.

cornichon [kɔrniʃɔ̃] *nm* (*concombre*) gherkin; (*niais*) *Fam* clot, twit.

cornu [kɔrny] *a* (*diable etc*) horned.

corollaire [kɔrɔlɛr] *nm* corollary.

corporation [kɔrpɔrɑsjɔ̃] *nf* trade association, professional body.

corps [kɔr] *nm Anat Ch Fig etc* body; *Mil Pol* corps; **c. électoral** electorate; **c. enseignant** teaching profession; **c. d'armée** army corps; **garde du c.** bodyguard; **un c. de bâtiment** a main building; **c. et âme** body and soul; **lutter c. à c.** to fight hand-to-hand; **à son c. défendant** under protest; **prendre c.** (*projet*) to take shape; **donner c. à** (*rumeur, idée*) to give substance to; **faire c. avec** to form a part of, belong with; **perdu c. et biens** *Nau* lost with all hands; **esprit de c.** corporate spirit. ◆**corporel, -elle** *a* bodily; (*châtiment*) corporal.

corpulent [kɔrpylɑ̃] *a* stout, corpulent. ◆**corpulence** *nf* stoutness, corpulence.

corpus [kɔrpys] *nm Ling* corpus.

correct [kɔrɛkt] *a* (*exact*) correct; (*bienséant, honnête*) proper, correct; (*passable*) adequate. ◆**—ement** *adv* correctly; properly; adequately. ◆**correcteur, -trice 1** *a* (*verres*) corrective. **2** *nmf Scol* examiner; *Typ* proofreader. ◆**correctif, -ive** *a* & *nm* corrective.

correction [kɔrɛksjɔ̃] *nf* (*rectification etc*) correction; (*punition*) thrashing; (*exactitude, bienséance*) correctness; **la c. de** (*devoirs, examen*) the marking of; **c. d'épreuves** *Typ* proofreading. ◆**correctionnel, -elle** *a* **tribunal c.**, – *nf* magistrates' court, *Am* police court.

corrélation [kɔrelɑsjɔ̃] *nf* correlation.

correspond/re [kɔrɛspɔ̃dr] **1** *vi* (*s'accorder*) to correspond (**à** to, with); (*chambres etc*) to communicate; **c. avec** *Rail* to connect with; **— se c.** *vpr* (*idées etc*) to correspond; (*chambres etc*) to communicate. **2** *vi* (*écrire*) to correspond (**avec** with). ◆**—ant, -ante** *a* corresponding; – *nmf* correspondent; (*d'un élève, d'un adolescent*) pen friend; *Tél* caller. ◆**correspondance** *nf* correspondence; (*de train, d'autocar*) connection, *Am* transfer.

corrida [kɔrida] *nf* bullfight.

corridor [kɔridɔr] *nm* corridor.

corrig/er [kɔriʒe] *vt* (*texte, injustice etc*) to correct; (*épreuve*) *Typ* to read; (*devoir*) *Scol* to mark, correct; (*châtier*) to beat, punish; **c. qn de** (*défaut*) to cure s.o. of; **se c. de** to cure oneself of. ◆**—é** *nm Scol* model (answer), correct version, key.

corroborer [kɔrɔbɔre] *vt* to corroborate.

corroder [kɔrɔde] *vt* to corrode. ◆**corrosif, -ive** *a* corrosive. ◆**corrosion** *nf* corrosion.

corromp/re* [kɔrɔ̃pr] *vt* to corrupt; (*soudoyer*) to bribe; (*aliment, eau*) to taint. ◆**—u** *a* corrupt; (*altéré*) tainted. ◆**corruption** *nf* (*dépravation*) corruption; (*de juge etc*) bribery.

corsage [kɔrsaʒ] *nm* (*chemisier*) blouse; (*de robe*) bodice.

corsaire [kɔrsɛr] *nm* (*marin*) *Hist* privateer.

Corse [kɔrs] *nf* Corsica. ◆**corse** *a* & *nmf* Corsican.

cors/er [kɔrse] *vt* (*récit, action*) to heighten; **l'affaire se corse** things are hotting up. ◆**—é** *a* (*vin*) full-bodied; (*café*) strong; (*sauce, histoire*) spicy; (*problème*) tough; (*addition de restaurant*) steep.

corset [kɔrsɛ] *nm* corset.

cortège [kɔrtɛʒ] *nm* (*défilé*) procession; (*suite*) retinue; **c. officiel** (*automobiles*) motorcade.

corvée [kɔrve] *nf* chore, drudgery; *Mil* fatigue (duty).

cosaque [kɔzak] *nm* Cossack.

cosmopolite [kɔsmɔpɔlit] *a* cosmopolitan.

cosmos [kɔsmɔs] *nm* (*univers*) cosmos; (*espace*) outer space. ◆**cosmique** *a* cosmic. ◆**cosmonaute** *nmf* cosmonaut.

cosse [kɔs] *nf* (*de pois etc*) pod.

cossu [kɔsy] *a* (*personne*) well-to-do; (*maison etc*) opulent.

costaud [kɔsto] *a Fam* brawny, beefy; – *nm Fam* strong man.

costume [kɔstym] *nm* (*pièces d'habillement*) costume, dress; (*complet*) suit. ◆**costum/er** *vt* **c. qn** to dress s.o. up (**en** as). ◆**–é** *a* **bal c.** fancy-dress ball.

cote [kɔt] *nf* (*marque de classement*) mark, letter, number; (*tableau des valeurs*) (official) listing; (*des valeurs boursières*) quotation; (*évaluation, popularité*) rating; (*de cheval*) odds (**de** on); **c. d'alerte** danger level.

côte [kot] *nf* **1** *Anat* rib; (*de mouton*) chop; (*de veau*) cutlet; **à côtes** (*étoffe*) ribbed; **c. à c.** side by side; **se tenir les côtes** to split one's sides (laughing). **2** (*montée*) hill; (*versant*) hillside. **3** (*littoral*) coast.

côté [kote] *nm* side; (*direction*) way; **de l'autre c.** on the other side (**de** of); (*direction*) the other way; **de ce c.** (*passer*) this way; **du c. de** (*vers, près de*) towards; **de c.** (*se jeter, mettre de l'argent etc*) to one side; (*regarder*) sideways, to one side; **à c.** close by, nearby; (*pièce*) in the other room; (*maison*) next door; **la maison (d')à c.** the house next door; **à c. de** next to, beside; (*comparaison*) compared to; **passer à c.** (*balle*) to fall wide (**de** of); **venir de tous côtés** to come from all directions; **d'un c.** on the one hand; **de mon c.** for my part; **à mes côtés** by my side; **laisser de c.** (*travail*) to neglect; **(du) c. argent/***etc Fam* as regards money/*etc*, moneywise/*etc*; **le bon c.** (*d'une affaire*) the bright side (**de** of).

coteau, -x [kɔto] *nm* (small) hill; (*versant*) hillside.

côtelé [kotle] *a* (*étoffe*) ribbed; **velours c.** cord(uroy).

côtelette [kotlɛt] *nf* (*d'agneau, de porc*) chop; (*de veau*) cutlet.

cot/er [kɔte] *vt* (*valeur boursière*) to quote. ◆**–é** *a* **bien c.** highly rated.

coterie [kɔtri] *nf Péj* set, clique.

côtier, -ière [kotje, -jɛr] *a* coastal; (*pêche*) inshore.

cotiser [kɔtize] *vi* to contribute (**à** to, **pour** towards); **c. (à)** (*club*) to subscribe (to); – **se c.** *vpr* to club together (**pour acheter** to buy). ◆**cotisation** *nf* (*de club*) dues, subscription; (*de pension etc*) contribution(s).

coton [kɔtɔ̃] *nm* cotton; **c. (hydrophile)** cottonwool, *Am* (absorbent) cotton. ◆**cotonnade** *nf* cotton (fabric). ◆**cotonnier, -ière** *a* (*industrie*) cotton-.

côtoyer [kotwaje] *vt* (*route, rivière*) to run along, skirt; (*la misère, la folie etc*) *Fig* to be *ou* come close to; **c. qn** (*fréquenter*) to rub shoulders with s.o.

cotte [kɔt] *nf* (*de travail*) overalls.

cou [ku] *nm* neck; **sauter au c. de qn** to throw one's arms around s.o.; **jusqu'au c.** *Fig* up to one's eyes *ou* ears.

couche [kuʃ] *nf* **1** (*épaisseur*) layer; (*de peinture*) coat; *Géol* stratum; **couches sociales** social strata. **2** (*linge de bébé*) nappy, *Am* diaper. **3 faire une fausse c.** *Méd* to have a miscarriage; **les couches** *Méd* confinement.

couch/er [kuʃe] *vt* to put to bed; (*héberger*) to put up; (*allonger*) to lay (down *ou* out); (*blé*) to flatten; **c. (par écrit)** to put down (in writing); **c. qn en joue** to aim at s.o.; – *vi* to sleep (**avec** with); – **se c.** *vpr* to go to bed; (*s'allonger*) to lie flat *ou* down; (*soleil*) to set, go down; – *nm* (*moment*) bedtime; **c. de soleil** sunset. ◆**–ant** *a* (*soleil*) setting; – *nm* (*aspect*) sunset; **le c.** (*ouest*) west. ◆**–é** *a* **être c.** to be in bed; (*étendu*) to be lying (down). ◆**–age** *nm* sleeping (situation); (*matériel*) bedding; **sac de c.** sleeping bag. ◆**couchette** *nf Rail* sleeping berth, couchette; *Nau* bunk.

couci-couça [kusikusa] *adv Fam* so-so.

coucou [kuku] *nm* (*oiseau*) cuckoo; (*pendule*) cuckoo clock; *Bot* cowslip.

coude [kud] *nm* elbow; (*de chemin, rivière*) bend; **se serrer** *ou* **se tenir les coudes** to help one another, stick together; **c. à c.** side by side; **coup de c.** poke *ou* dig (with one's elbow), nudge; **pousser du c.** to nudge. ◆**coudoyer** *vt* to rub shoulders with.

cou-de-pied [kudpje] *nm* (*pl* **cous-de-pied**) instep.

coudre* [kudr] *vti* to sew.

couenne [kwan] *nf* (pork) crackling.

couette [kwɛt] *nf* (*édredon*) duvet, continental quilt.

couffin [kufɛ̃] *nm* (*de bébé*) Moses basket, *Am* bassinet.

couic! [kwik] *int* eek!, squeak! ◆**couiner** *vi* *Fam* to squeal; (*pleurer*) to whine.

couillon [kujɔ̃] *nm* (*idiot*) *Arg* drip, cretin.

coul/er¹ [kule] *vi* (*eau etc*) to flow; (*robinet, nez, sueur*) to run; (*fuir*) to leak; **c. de source** *Fig* to follow naturally; **faire c. le sang** to cause bloodshed; – *vt* (*métal, statue*) to cast; (*vie*) *Fig* to pass, lead; (*glisser*) to slip; **se c. dans** (*passer*) to slip into; **se la c. douce** to have things easy. ◆**—ant** *a* (*style*) flowing; (*caractère*) easygoing. ◆**—ée** *nf* (*de métal*) casting; **c. de lave** lava flow. ◆**—age** *nm* (*de métal, statue*) casting; (*gaspillage*) *Fam* wastage.

couler² [kule] *vi* (*bateau, nageur*) to sink; **c. à pic** to sink to the bottom; – *vt* to sink; (*discréditer*) *Fig* to discredit.

couleur [kulœr] *nf* colour; (*colorant*) paint; *Cartes* suit; *pl* (*teint, carnation*) colour; **c. chair** flesh-coloured; **de c.** (*homme, habit etc*) coloured; **en couleurs** (*photo, télévision*) colour-; **téléviseur c.** colour TV set; **haut en c.** colourful; **sous c. de faire** while pretending to do.

couleuvre [kulœvr] *nf* (grass) snake.

coulisse [kulis] *nf* **1** (*de porte*) runner; **à c.** (*porte etc*) sliding. **2 dans les coulisses** *Th* in the wings, backstage; **dans la c.** (*caché*) *Fig* behind the scenes. ◆**coulissant** *a* (*porte etc*) sliding.

couloir [kulwar] *nm* corridor; (*de circulation*) & *Sp* lane; (*dans un bus*) gangway.

coup [ku] *nm* blow, knock; (*léger*) tap, touch; (*choc moral*) blow; (*de fusil etc*) shot; (*de crayon, d'horloge*) & *Sp* stroke; (*aux échecs etc*) move; (*fois*) *Fam* time; **donner des coups à** to hit; **c. de brosse** brush(-up); **c. de chiffon** wipe (with a rag); **c. de sonnette** ring (on a bell); **c. de dents** bite; **c. de chance** stroke of luck; **c. d'État** coup; **c. dur** *Fam* nasty blow; **sale c.** dirty trick; **mauvais c.** piece of mischief; **c. franc** *Fb* free kick; **tenter le c.** *Fam* to have a go *ou* try; **réussir son c.** to bring it off; **faire les quatre cents coups** to get into all kinds of mischief; **tenir le c.** to hold out; **avoir/attraper le c.** to have/get the knack; **sous le c. de** (*émotion etc*) under the influence of; **il est dans le c.** *Fam* he's in the know; **après c.** after the event, afterwards; **sur le c. de midi** on the stroke of twelve; **sur le c.** (*alors*) at the time; **tué sur le c.** killed outright; **à c. sûr** for sure; **c. sur c.** (*à la suite*) one after the other, in quick succession; **tout à c., tout d'un c.** suddenly; **à tout c.** at every go; **d'un seul c.** in one go; **du premier c.** *Fam* (at the) first go; **du c.** suddenly; (*de ce fait*) as a result; **pour le c.** this time. ◆**c.-de-poing** *nm* (*pl* **coups-de-poing**) **c.-de-poing (américain)** knuckle-duster.

coupable [kupabl] *a* guilty (**de** of); (*plaisir, désir*) sinful; **déclarer c.** *Jur* to convict; – *nmf* guilty person, culprit.

coupe [kup] *nf* **1** *Sp* cup; (*à fruits*) dish; (*à boire*) goblet, glass. **2** (*de vêtement etc*) cut; *Géom* section; **c. de cheveux** haircut. ◆**coup/er** *vt* to cut; (*arbre*) to cut down; (*vivres etc*) & *Tél* to cut off; (*courant etc*) to switch off; (*voyage*) to break (off); (*faim, souffle etc*) to take away; (*vin*) to water down; (*morceler*) to cut up; (*croiser*) to cut across; **c. la parole à** to cut short; – *vi* to cut; **c. à** (*corvée*) *Fam* to get out of; **ne coupez pas!** *Tél* hold the line!; – **se c.** *vpr* (*routes*) to intersect; (*se trahir*) to give oneself away; **se c. au doigt** to cut one's finger. ◆**—ant** *a* sharp; – *nm* (cutting) edge. ◆**—é** *nm Aut* coupé.

coupe-circuit [kupsirkɥi] *nm inv Él* cutout, circuit breaker. ◆**c.-file** *nm inv* (*carte*) official pass. ◆**c.-gorge** *nm inv* cut-throat alley. ◆**c.-ongles** *nm inv* (finger nail) clippers. ◆**c.-papier** *nm inv* paper knife.

couperet [kuprɛ] *nm* (meat) chopper; (*de guillotine*) blade.

couperosé [kuproze] *a* (*visage*) blotchy.

couple [kupl] *nm* pair, couple. ◆**coupler** *vt* to couple, connect.

couplet [kuplɛ] *nm* verse.

coupole [kupɔl] *nf* dome.

coupon [kupɔ̃] *nm* (*tissu*) remnant, oddment; (*pour la confection d'un vêtement*) length; (*ticket, titre*) coupon; **c. réponse** reply coupon.

coupure [kupyr] *nf* cut; (*de journal*) cutting, *Am* clipping; (*billet*) banknote.

cour [kur] *nf* **1** court(yard); (*de gare*) forecourt; **c. (de récréation)** *Scol* playground. **2** (*de roi*) & *Jur* court. **3** (*de femme, d'homme*) courtship; **faire la c. à qn** to court s.o., woo s.o.

courage [kuraʒ] *nm* courage; (*zèle*) spirit; **perdre c.** to lose heart *ou* courage; **s'armer de c.** to pluck up courage; **bon c.!** keep your chin up! ◆**courageux, -euse** *a* courageous; (*énergique*) spirited.

couramment [kuramɑ̃] *adv* (*parler*) fluently; (*souvent*) frequently.

courant [kurɑ̃] **1** *a* (*fréquent*) common; (*compte, année, langage*) current; (*eau*) running; (*modèle, taille*) standard; (*affaires*) routine; **le dix/etc c.** *Com* the tenth/*etc* inst(ant). **2** *nm* (*de l'eau, élec-*

trique) current; **c. d'air** draught; **coupure de c.** *Él* power cut; **dans le c. de** (*mois etc*) during the course of; **être/mettre au c.** to know/tell (**de** about); **au c.** (*à jour*) up to date.

courbature [kurbatyr] *nf* (muscular) ache. ◆**courbaturé** *a* aching (all over).

courbe [kurb] *a* curved; – *nf* curve. ◆**courber** *vti* to bend; – **se c.** *vpr* to bend (over).

courge [kurʒ] *nf* marrow, *Am* squash. ◆**courgette** *nf* courgette, *Am* zucchini.

cour/ir* [kurir] *vi* to run; (*se hâter*) to rush; (*à bicyclette, en auto*) to race; **en courant** (*vite*) in a rush; **le bruit court que...** there's a rumour going around that...; **faire c.** (*nouvelle*) to spread; **il court encore** (*voleur*) he's still at large; – *vt* (*risque*) to run; (*épreuve sportive*) to run (in); (*danger*) to face, court; (*rues, monde*) to roam; (*magasins, cafés*) to go round; (*filles*) to run after. ◆**—eur** *nm Sp etc* runner; (*cycliste*) cyclist; *Aut* racing driver; (*galant*) *Péj* womanizer.

couronne [kurɔn] *nf* (*de roi, dent*) crown, (*funéraire*) wreath. ◆**couronn/er** *vt* to crown; (*auteur, ouvrage*) to award a prize to. ◆**—é** *a* (*tête*) crowned; (*ouvrage*) prize-. ◆**—ement** *nm* (*sacre*) coronation; *Fig* crowning achievement.

courrier [kurje] *nm* post, mail; (*transport*) postal *ou* mail service; (*article*) *Journ* column; **par retour du c.** by return of post, *Am* by return mail.

courroie [kurwa] *nf* (*attache*) strap; (*de transmission*) *Tech* belt.

courroux [kuru] *nm Litt* wrath.

cours [kur] *nm* **1** (*de maladie, rivière, astre, pensées etc*) course; (*cote*) rate, price; **c. d'eau** river, stream; **suivre son c.** (*déroulement*) to follow its course; **avoir c.** (*monnaie*) to be legal tender; (*théorie*) to be current; **en c.** (*travail*) in progress; (*année*) current; (*affaires*) outstanding; **en c. de route** on the way; **au c. de** during; **donner libre c. à** to give free rein to. **2** (*leçon*) class; (*série de leçons*) course; (*conférence*) lecture; (*établissement*) school; (*manuel*) textbook; **c. magistral** lecture. **3** (*allée*) avenue.

course [kurs] *nf* **1** (*action*) run(ning); (*épreuve de vitesse*) & *Fig* race; (*trajet*) journey, run; (*excursion*) hike; (*de projectile etc*) path, flight; *pl* (*de chevaux*) races; **il n'est plus dans la c.** *Fig* he's out of touch; **cheval de c.** racehorse; **voiture de c.** racing car. **2** (*commission*) errand; *pl* (*achats*) shopping; **faire une c.** to run an errand; **faire les courses** to do the shopping.

coursier, -ière [kursje, -jɛr] *nmf* messenger.

court [kur] **1** *a* short; **c'est un peu c.** *Fam* that's not very much; – *adv* short; **couper c. à** (*entretien*) to cut short; **tout c.** quite simply; **à c. de** (*argent etc*) short of; **pris de c.** caught unawares. **2** *nm Tennis* court. ◆**c.-bouillon** *nm* (*pl* **courts-bouillons**) court-bouillon (*spiced water for cooking fish*). ◆**c.-circuit** *nm* (*pl* **courts-circuits**) *Él* short circuit. ◆**c.-circuiter** *vt* to short-circuit.

courtier, -ière [kurtje, -jɛr] *nmf* broker. ◆**courtage** *nm* brokerage.

courtisan [kurtizɑ̃] *nm Hist* courtier. ◆**courtisane** *nf Hist* courtesan. ◆**courtiser** *vt* to court.

courtois [kurtwa] *a* courteous. ◆**courtoisie** *nf* courtesy.

couru [kury] *a* (*spectacle, lieu*) popular; **c'est c. (d'avance)** *Fam* it's a sure thing.

couscous [kuskus] *nm Culin* couscous.

cousin, -ine [kuzɛ̃, -in] **1** *nmf* cousin. **2** *nm* (*insecte*) gnat, midge.

coussin [kusɛ̃] *nm* cushion.

cousu [kuzy] *a* sewn; **c. main** handsewn.

coût [ku] *nm* cost. ◆**coût/er** *vti* to cost; **ça coûte combien?** how much is it?, how much does it cost?; **ça lui en coûte de faire** it pains him *ou* her to do; **coûte que coûte** at all costs; **c. les yeux de la tête** to cost the earth. ◆**—ant** *a* **prix c.** cost price. ◆**coûteux, -euse** *a* costly, expensive.

couteau, -x [kuto] *nm* knife; **coup de c.** stab; **à couteaux tirés** at daggers drawn (**avec** with); **visage en lame de c.** hatchet face; **retourner le c. dans la plaie** *Fig* to rub it in.

coutume [kutym] *nf* custom; **avoir c. de faire** to be accustomed to doing; **comme de c.** as usual; **plus que de c.** more than is customary. ◆**coutumier, -ière** *a* customary.

couture [kutyr] *nf* sewing, needlework; (*métier*) dressmaking; (*raccord*) seam; **maison de c.** fashion house. ◆**couturier** *nm* fashion designer. ◆**couturière** *nf* dressmaker.

couvent [kuvɑ̃] *nm* (*pour religieuses*) convent; (*pour moines*) monastery; (*pensionnat*) convent school.

couv/er [kuve] *vt* (*œufs*) to sit on, hatch; (*projet*) *Fig* to hatch; (*rhume etc*) to be getting; **c. qn** to pamper s.o.; **c. des yeux** (*convoiter*) to look at enviously; – *vi* (*poule*) to brood; (*mal*) to be brewing;

(*feu*) to smoulder. ◆**—ée** *nf* (*petits*) brood; (*œufs*) clutch. ◆**couveuse** *nf* (*pour nouveaux-nés, œufs*) incubator.

couvercle [kuvɛrkl] *nm* lid, cover.

couvert [kuvɛr] **1** *nm* (*cuiller, fourchette, couteau*) (set of) cutlery; (*au restaurant*) cover charge; **mettre le c.** to lay the table; **table de cinq couverts** table set for five. **2** *nm* **sous (le) c. de** (*apparence*) under cover of; **se mettre à c.** to take cover. **3** *a* covered (**de** with, in); (*ciel*) overcast. ◆**couverture** *nf* (*de lit*) blanket, cover; (*de livre etc*) & *Fin Mil* cover; (*de toit*) roofing; **c. chauffante** electric blanket; **c. de voyage** travelling rug.

couvre-chef [kuvrəʃɛf] *nm Hum* headgear. ◆**c.-feu** *nm* (*pl* -x) curfew. ◆**c.-lit** *nm* bedspread. ◆**c.-pied** *nm* quilt.

couvr/ir* [kuvrir] *vt* to cover (**de** with); (*voix*) to drown; **— se c.** *vpr* (*se vêtir*) to cover up, wrap up; (*se coiffer*) to cover one's head; (*ciel*) to cloud over. ◆**—eur** *nm* roofer.

cow-boy [kɔbɔj] *nm* cowboy.

crabe [krab] *nm* crab.

crac! [krak] *int* (*rupture*) snap!; (*choc*) bang!, smash!

crach/er [kraʃe] *vi* to spit; (*stylo*) to splutter; (*radio*) to crackle; – *vt* to spit (out); **c. sur qch** (*dédaigner*) *Fam* to turn one's nose up at sth. ◆**—é** *a* **c'est son portrait tout c.** *Fam* that's the spitting image of him *ou* her. ◆**crachat** *nm* spit, spittle.

crachin [kraʃɛ̃] *nm* (fine) drizzle.

crack [krak] *nm Fam* ace, wizard, real champ.

craie [krɛ] *nf* chalk.

craindre* [krɛ̃dr] *vt* (*personne, mort, douleur etc*) to be afraid of, fear, dread; (*chaleur etc*) to be sensitive to; **c. de faire** to be afraid of doing, dread doing; **je crains qu'elle ne vienne** I'm afraid *ou* I fear *ou* I dread (that) she might come; **c. pour qch** to fear for sth; **ne craignez rien** have no fear. ◆**crainte** *nf* fear, dread; **de c. de faire** for fear of doing; **de c. que** (+ *sub*) for fear that. ◆**craintif, -ive** *a* timid.

cramoisi [kramwazi] *a* crimson.

crampe [krɑ̃p] *nf Méd* cramp.

crampon [krɑ̃pɔ̃] **1** *nm* (*personne*) *Fam* leech, hanger-on. **2** *nmpl* (*de chaussures*) studs.

cramponner (se) [səkrɑ̃pɔne] *vpr* **se c. à** to hold on to, cling to.

cran [krɑ̃] *nm* **1** (*entaille*) notch; (*de ceinture*) hole; **c. d'arrêt** catch; **couteau à c. d'arrêt** flick-knife, *Am* switchblade; **c. de sûreté** safety catch. **2** (*de cheveux*) wave. **3** (*audace*) *Fam* pluck, guts. **4 à c.** (*excédé*) *Fam* on edge.

crâne [krɑn] *nm* skull; (*tête*) *Fam* head. ◆**crânienne** *af* **boîte c.** cranium, brain pan.

crâner [krɑne] *vi Péj* to show off, swagger.

crapaud [krapo] *nm* toad.

crapule [krapyl] *nf* villain, (filthy) scoundrel. ◆**crapuleux, -euse** *a* vile, sordid.

craqueler [krakle] *vt*, **— se c.** *vpr* to crack.

craqu/er [krake] *vi* (*branche*) to snap; (*chaussure*) to creak; (*bois sec*) to crack; (*sous la dent*) to crunch; (*se déchirer*) to split, rip; (*projet, entreprise etc*) to come apart at the seams, crumble; (*personne*) to break down, reach breaking point; – *vt* (**faire**) **c.** (*allumette*) to strike. ◆**—ement** *nm* snapping *ou* creaking *ou* cracking (sound).

crasse [kras] **1** *a* (*ignorance*) crass. **2** *nf* filth. ◆**crasseux, -euse** *a* filthy.

cratère [kratɛr] *nm* crater.

cravache [kravaʃ] *nf* horsewhip, riding crop.

cravate [kravat] *nf* (*autour du cou*) tie. ◆**cravaté** *a* wearing a tie.

crawl [krol] *nm* (*nage*) crawl. ◆**crawlé** *a* **dos c.** backstroke.

crayeux, -euse [krɛjø, -øz] *a* chalky.

crayon [krɛjɔ̃] *nm* (*en bois*) pencil; (*de couleur*) crayon; **c. à bille** ballpoint (pen). ◆**crayonner** *vt* to pencil.

créance [kreɑ̃s] *nf* **1** *Fin Jur* claim (*for money*). **2 lettres de c.** *Pol* credentials. ◆**créancier, -ière** *nmf* creditor.

créateur, -trice [kreatœr, -tris] *nmf* creator; – *a* creative; **esprit c.** creativeness. ◆**créatif, -ive** *a* creative. ◆**création** *nf* creation. ◆**créativité** *nf* creativity. ◆**créature** *nf* (*être*) creature.

crécelle [kresɛl] *nf* (*de supporter*) rattle.

crèche [krɛʃ] *nf* (*de Noël*) *Rel* crib, manger; *Scol* day nursery, crèche. ◆**crécher** *vi* (*loger*) *Arg* to bed down, hang out.

crédible [kredibl] *a* credible. ◆**crédibilité** *nf* credibility.

crédit [kredi] *nm* (*influence*) & *Fin* credit; *pl* (*sommes*) funds; **à c.** (*acheter*) on credit, on hire purchase; **faire c.** *Fin* to give credit (**à** to). ◆**créditer** *vt Fin* to credit (**de** with). ◆**créditeur, -euse** *a* (*solde, compte*) credit-; **son compte est c.** his account is in credit, he is in credit.

credo [kredo] *nm* creed.

crédule [kredyl] *a* credulous. ◆**crédulité** *nf* credulity.

créer [kree] *vt* to create.

crémaillère [kremajɛr] *nf* **pendre la c.** to have a house-warming (party).

crématoire [krematwar] *a* **four c.** crematorium. ◆**crémation** *nf* cremation.

crème [krɛm] *nf* cream; (*dessert*) cream dessert; **café c.** white coffee, coffee with cream *ou* milk; **c. Chantilly** whipped cream; **c. glacée** ice cream; **c. à raser** shaving cream; **c. anglaise** custard; – *a inv* cream(-coloured); – *nm* (*café*) white coffee. ◆**crémerie** *nf* (*magasin*) dairy (shop). ◆**crémeux, -euse** *a* creamy. ◆**crémier, -ière** *nmf* dairyman, dairywoman.

créneau, -x [kreno] *nm Hist* crenellation; (*trou*) *Fig* slot, gap; *Écon* market opportunity, niche; **faire un c.** *Aut* to park between two vehicles.

créole [kreɔl] *nmf* Creole; – *nm Ling* Creole.

crêpe [krɛp] **1** *nf Culin* pancake. **2** *nm* (*tissu*) crepe; (*caoutchouc*) crepe (rubber). ◆**crêperie** *nf* pancake bar.

crépi [krepi] *a & nm* roughcast.

crépit/er [krepite] *vi* to crackle. ◆**—ement** *nm* crackling (sound).

crépu [krepy] *a* (*cheveux, personne*) frizzy.

crépuscule [krepyskyl] *nm* twilight, dusk. ◆**crépusculaire** *a* (*lueur etc*) twilight-, dusk-.

crescendo [kreʃendo] *adv & nm inv* crescendo.

cresson [kresɔ̃] *nm* (water) cress.

crête [krɛt] *nf* (*d'oiseau, de vague, de montagne*) crest; **c. de coq** cockscomb.

Crète [krɛt] *nf* Crete.

crétin, -ine [kretɛ̃, -in] *nmf* cretin; – *a* cretinous.

creus/er [krøze] **1** *vt* (*terre, sol*) to dig (a hole *ou* holes in); (*trou, puits*) to dig; (*évider*) to hollow (out); (*idée*) *Fig* to go deeply into; **c. l'estomac** to whet the appetite. **2 se c.** *vpr* (*joues etc*) to become hollow; (*abîme*) *Fig* to form; **se c. la tête** *ou* **la cervelle** to rack one's brains. ◆**—é** *a* **c. de rides** (*visage*) furrowed with wrinkles.

creuset [krøzɛ] *nm* (*récipient*) crucible; (*lieu*) *Fig* melting pot.

creux, -euse [krø, -øz] *a* (*tube, joues, paroles etc*) hollow; (*estomac*) empty; (*sans activité*) slack; **assiette creuse** soup plate; – *nm* hollow; (*de l'estomac*) pit; (*moment*) slack period; **c. des reins** small of the back.

crevaison [krəvɛzɔ̃] *nf* puncture.

crevasse [krəvas] *nf* crevice, crack; (*de glacier*) crevasse; *pl* (*aux mains*) chaps. ◆**crevasser** *vt*, — **se c.** *vpr* to crack; (*peau*) to chap.

crève [krɛv] *nf* (*rhume*) *Fam* bad cold.

crev/er [krəve] *vi* (*bulle etc*) to burst; (*pneu*) to puncture, burst; (*mourir*) *Fam* to die, drop dead; **c. d'orgueil** to be bursting with pride; **c. de rire** *Fam* to split one's sides; **c. d'ennui/de froid** *Fam* to be bored/to freeze to death; **c. de faim** *Fam* to be starving; – *vt* to burst; (*œil*) to put *ou* knock out; **c. qn** *Fam* to wear *ou* knock s.o. out; **ça (vous) crève les yeux** *Fam* it's staring you in the face; **c. le cœur** to be heartbreaking. ◆**—ant** *a* (*fatigant*) *Fam* exhausting; (*drôle*) *Arg* hilarious, killing. ◆**—é** *a* (*fatigué*) *Fam* worn *ou* knocked out; (*mort*) *Fam* dead. ◆**crève-cœur** *nm inv* heartbreak.

crevette [krəvɛt] *nf* (*grise*) shrimp; (*rose*) prawn.

cri [kri] *nm* (*de joie, surprise*) cry, shout; (*de peur*) scream; (*de douleur, d'alarme*) cry; (*appel*) call, cry; **c. de guerre** war cry; **un chapeau/*etc* dernier c.** the latest hat/*etc*. ◆**criard** *a* (*enfant*) bawling; (*son*) screeching; (*couleur*) gaudy, showy.

criant [krijɑ̃] *a* (*injustice etc*) glaring.

crible [kribl] *nm* sieve, riddle. ◆**cribler** *vt* to sift; **criblé de** (*balles, dettes etc*) riddled with.

cric [krik] *nm* (*instrument*) *Aut* jack.

cricket [krikɛt] *nm Sp* cricket.

crier [krije] *vi* to shout (out), cry (out); (*de peur*) to scream; (*oiseau*) to chirp; (*grincer*) to creak, squeak; **c. au scandale/*etc*** to proclaim sth to be a scandal/*etc*; **c. après qn** *Fam* to shout at s.o.; – *vt* (*injure, ordre*) to shout (out); (*son innocence etc*) to proclaim; **c. vengeance** to cry out for vengeance. ◆**crieur, -euse** *nmf* **c. de journaux** newspaper seller.

crime [krim] *nm* crime; (*assassinat*) murder. ◆**criminalité** *nf* crime (in general), criminal practice. ◆**criminel, -elle** *a* criminal; – *nmf* criminal; (*assassin*) murderer.

crin [krɛ̃] *nm* horsehair; **c. végétal** vegetable fibre; **à tous crins** (*pacifiste etc*) out-and-out. ◆**crinière** *nf* mane.

crique [krik] *nf* creek, cove.

criquet [krikɛ] *nm* locust.

crise [kriz] *nf* crisis; (*accès*) attack; (*de colère etc*) fit; (*pénurie*) shortage; **c. de conscience** (moral) dilemma.

crisp/er [krispe] *vt* (*muscle*) to tense; (*visage*) to make tense; (*poing*) to clench; **c. qn** *Fam* to aggravate s.o.; **se c. sur** (*main*) to grip tightly. ◆**—ant** *a* aggravating. ◆**—é**

a (*personne*) tense. ◆**crispation** *nf* (*agacement*) aggravation.

crisser [krise] *vi* (*pneu, roue*) to screech; (*neige*) to crunch.

cristal, -aux [kristal, -o] *nm* crystal; *pl* (*objets*) crystal(ware); (*pour nettoyer*) washing soda. ◆**cristallin** *a* (*eau, son*) crystal-clear. ◆**cristalliser** *vti*, **— se c.** *vpr* to crystallize.

critère [kriter] *nm* criterion.

critérium [kriterjɔm] *nm* (*épreuve*) *Sp* eliminating heat.

critique [kritik] *a* critical; – *nf* (*reproche*) criticism; (*analyse de film, livre etc*) review; (*de texte*) critique; **faire la c. de** (*film etc*) to review; **affronter la c.** to confront the critics; – *nm* critic. ◆**critiqu/er** *vt* to criticize. ◆**—able** *a* open to criticism.

croasser [krɔase] *vi* (*corbeau*) to caw.

croc [kro] *nm* (*crochet*) hook; (*dent*) fang. ◆**c.-en-jambe** *nm* (*pl* **crocs-en-jambe**) = **croche-pied.**

croche [krɔʃ] *nf Mus* quaver, *Am* eighth (note).

croche-pied [krɔʃpje] *nm* **faire un c.-pied à qn** to trip s.o. up.

crochet [krɔʃɛ] *nm* (*pour accrocher*) & *Boxe* hook; (*aiguille*) crochet hook; (*travail*) crochet; (*clef*) picklock; *Typ* (square) bracket; **faire qch au c.** to crochet sth; **faire un c.** (*route*) to make a sudden turn; (*personne*) to make a detour *ou* side trip; (*pour éviter*) to swerve; **vivre aux crochets de qn** *Fam* to sponge off *ou* on s.o. ◆**crocheter** *vt* (*serrure*) to pick. ◆**crochu** *a* (*nez*) hooked.

crocodile [krɔkɔdil] *nm* crocodile.

crocus [krɔkys] *nm Bot* crocus.

croire* [krwar] *vt* to believe; (*estimer*) to think, believe (**que** that); **j'ai cru la voir** I thought I saw her; **je crois que oui** I think *ou* believe so; **je n'en crois pas mes yeux** I can't believe my eyes; **à l'en c.** according to him; **il se croit malin/quelque chose** he thinks he's smart/quite something; – *vi* to believe (**à, en** in).

croisé[1] [krwaze] *nm Hist* crusader. ◆**croisade** *nf* crusade.

crois/er [krwaze] *vt* to cross; (*bras*) to fold, cross; **c. qn** to pass *ou* meet s.o.; – *vi* (*veston*) to fold over; *Nau* to cruise; **— se c.** *vpr* (*voitures etc*) to pass *ou* meet (each other); (*routes*) to cross, intersect; (*lettres*) to cross in the post. ◆**—é**[2], **-ée** *a* (*bras*) folded, crossed; (*veston*) double-breasted; **mots croisés** crossword; **tirs croisés** crossfire; **race croisée** crossbreed; – *nf* (*fenêtre*) casement; **croisée des chemins** crossroads. ◆**—ement** *nm* (*action*) crossing; (*de routes*) crossroads, intersection; (*de véhicules*) passing. ◆**—eur** *nm* (*navire de guerre*) cruiser. ◆**croisière** *nf* cruise; **vitesse de c.** *Nau Av* & *Fig* cruising speed.

croître* [krwatr] *vi* (*plante etc*) to grow; (*augmenter*) to grow, increase; (*lune*) to wax. ◆**croissant 1** *a* (*nombre etc*) growing. **2** *nm* crescent; (*pâtisserie*) croissant. ◆**croissance** *nf* growth.

croix [krwa] *nf* cross.

croque-mitaine [krɔkmitɛn] *nm* bogeyman. ◆**c.-monsieur** *nm inv* toasted cheese and ham sandwich. ◆**c.-mort** *nm Fam* undertaker's assistant.

croqu/er [krɔke] **1** *vt* (*manger*) to crunch; – *vi* (*fruit etc*) to be crunchy, crunch. **2** *vt* (*peindre*) to sketch; **joli à c.** pretty as a picture. ◆**—ant** *a* (*biscuit etc*) crunchy. ◆**croquette** *nf Culin* croquette.

croquet [krɔkɛ] *nm Sp* croquet.

croquis [krɔki] *nm* sketch.

crosse [krɔs] *nf* (*d'évêque*) crook; (*de fusil*) butt; (*de hockey*) stick.

crotte [krɔt] *nf* (*de lapin etc*) mess, droppings. ◆**crottin** *nm* (horse) dung.

crotté [krɔte] *a* (*bottes etc*) muddy.

croul/er [krule] *vi* (*édifice, projet etc*) to crumble, collapse; **c. sous une charge** (*porteur etc*) to totter beneath a burden; **faire c.** (*immeuble etc*) to bring down. ◆**—ant** *a* (*mur etc*) tottering; – *nm* (*vieux*) *Fam* old-timer.

croupe [krup] *nf* (*de cheval*) rump; **monter en c.** (*à cheval*) to ride pillion. ◆**croupion** *nm* (*de poulet*) parson's nose.

croupier [krupje] *nm* (*au casino*) croupier.

croupir [krupir] *vi* (*eau*) to stagnate, become foul; **c. dans** (*le vice etc*) to wallow in; **eau croupie** stagnant water.

croustill/er [krustije] *vi* to be crusty; to be crunchy. ◆**—ant** *a* (*pain*) crusty; (*biscuit*) crunchy; (*histoire*) *Fig* spicy, juicy.

croûte [krut] *nf* (*de pain etc*) crust; (*de fromage*) rind; (*de plaie*) scab; **casser la c.** *Fam* to have a snack; **gagner sa c.** *Fam* to earn one's bread and butter. ◆**croûton** *nm* crust (*at end of loaf*); *pl* (*avec soupe*) croûtons.

croyable [krwajabl] *a* credible, believable. ◆**croyance** *nf* belief (**à, en** in). ◆**croyant, -ante** *a* **être c.** to be a believer; – *nmf* believer.

CRS [seɛrɛs] *nmpl abrév* (*Compagnies républicaines de sécurité*) French state security police, riot police.

cru[1] [kry] *voir* **croire.**
cru[2] [kry] **1** *a* (*aliment etc*) raw; (*lumière*) glaring; (*propos*) crude; **monter à c.** to ride bareback. **2** *nm* (*vignoble*) vineyard; **un grand c.** (*vin*) a vintage wine; **vin du c.** local wine.
cruauté [kryote] *nf* cruelty (**envers** to).
cruche [kryʃ] *nf* pitcher, jug.
crucial, -aux [krysjal, -o] *a* crucial.
crucifier [krysifje] *vt* to crucify. ◆**crucifix** [krysifi] *nm* crucifix. ◆**crucifixion** *nf* crucifixion.
crudité [krydite] *nf* (*grossièreté*) crudeness; *pl Culin* assorted raw vegetables.
crue [kry] *nf* (*de cours d'eau*) swelling, flood; **en c.** in spate.
cruel, -elle [kryɛl] *a* cruel (**envers, avec** to).
crûment [krymɑ̃] *adv* crudely.
crustacés [krystase] *nmpl* shellfish, crustaceans.
crypte [kript] *nf* crypt.
Cuba [kyba] *nm* Cuba. ◆**cubain, -aine** *a* & *nmf* Cuban.
cube [kyb] *nm* cube; *pl* (*jeu*) building blocks; – *a* (*mètre etc*) cubic. ◆**cubique** *a* cubic.
cueillir* [kœjir] *vt* to gather, pick; (*baiser*) to snatch; (*voleur*) *Fam* to pick up, run in. ◆**cueillette** *nf* gathering, picking; (*fruits cueillis*) harvest.
cuiller, cuillère [kɥijɛr] *nf* spoon; **petite c., c. à café** teaspoon; **c. à soupe** table spoon. ◆**cuillerée** *nf* spoonful.
cuir [kɥir] *nm* leather; (*peau épaisse d'un animal vivant*) hide; **c. chevelu** scalp.
cuirasse [kɥiras] *nf Hist* breastplate. ◆**se cuirass/er** *vpr* to steel oneself (**contre** against). ◆**–é** *nm* battleship.
cuire* [kɥir] *vt* to cook; (*à l'eau*) to boil; (*porcelaine*) to bake, fire; **c. (au four)** to bake; (*viande*) to roast; – *vi* to cook; to boil; to bake; to roast; (*soleil*) to bake, boil; **faire c.** to cook. ◆**cuisant** *a* (*affront, blessure etc*) stinging. ◆**cuisson** *nm* cooking; (*de porcelaine*) baking, firing.
cuisine [kɥizin] *nf* (*pièce*) kitchen; (*art*) cooking, cuisine, cookery; (*aliments*) cooking; (*intrigues*) *Péj* scheming; **faire la c.** to cook, do the cooking; **livre de c.** cook(ery) book; **haute c.** high-class cooking. ◆**cuisiner** *vti* to cook; **c. qn** (*interroger*) *Fam* to grill s.o. ◆**cuisinier, -ière** *nmf* cook; – *nf* (*appareil*) cooker, stove, *Am* range.
cuisse [kɥis] *nf* thigh; (*de poulet, mouton*) leg.
cuit [kɥi] **1** *voir* **cuire;** – *a* cooked; **bien c.** well done *ou* cooked. **2** *a* (*pris*) *Fam* done for.
cuite [kɥit] *nf* **prendre une c.** *Fam* to get plastered *ou* drunk.
cuivre [kɥivr] *nm* (*rouge*) copper; (*jaune*) brass; *pl* (*ustensiles*) & *Mus* brass. ◆**cuivré** *a* copper-coloured, coppery.
cul [ky] *nm* (*derrière*) *Fam* backside; (*de bouteille etc*) bottom. ◆**c.-de-jatte** *nm* (*pl* **culs-de-jatte**) legless cripple. ◆**c.-de-sac** *nm* (*pl* **culs-de-sac**) dead end, cul-de-sac.
culasse [kylas] *nf Aut* cylinder head; (*d'une arme à feu*) breech.
culbute [kylbyt] *nf* (*cabriole*) sommersault; (*chute*) (backward) tumble; **faire une c.** to sommersault; to tumble. ◆**culbuter** *vi* to tumble over (backwards); – *vt* (*personne, chaise*) to knock over.
culinaire [kylinɛr] *a* (*art*) culinary; (*recette*) cooking.
culmin/er [kylmine] *vi* (*montagne*) to reach its highest point, peak (**à** at); (*colère*) *Fig* to reach a peak. ◆**–ant** *a* **point c.** (*de réussite, montagne etc*) peak.
culot [kylo] *nm* **1** (*aplomb*) *Fam* nerve, cheek. **2** (*d'ampoule, de lampe etc*) base. ◆**culotté** *a* **être c.** *Fam* to have plenty of nerve *ou* cheek.
culotte [kylɔt] *nf Sp* (pair of) shorts; (*de femme*) (pair of) knickers *ou Am* panties; **culottes (courtes)** (*de jeune garçon*) short trousers *ou Am* pants; **c. de cheval** riding breeches.
culpabilité [kylpabilite] *nf* guilt.
culte [kylt] *nm* (*hommage*) *Rel* worship, cult; (*pratique*) *Rel* religion; (*service protestant*) service; (*admiration*) *Fig* cult.
cultiv/er [kyltive] *vt* (*terre*) to farm, cultivate; (*plantes*) to grow, cultivate; (*goût, relations etc*) to cultivate; **– se c.** *vpr* to cultivate one's mind. ◆**–é** *a* (*esprit, personne*) cultured, cultivated. ◆**cultivateur, -trice** *nmf* farmer. ◆**culture** *nf* (*action*) farming, cultivation; (*agriculture*) farming; (*horticulture*) growing, cultivation; (*éducation, civilisation*) culture; *pl* (*terres*) fields (under cultivation); (*plantes*) crops; **c. générale** general knowledge. ◆**culturel, -elle** *a* cultural.
cumin [kymɛ̃] *nm Bot Culin* caraway.
cumul [kymyl] *nm* **c. de fonctions** plurality of offices. ◆**cumulatif, -ive** *a* cumulative. ◆**cumuler** *vt* **c. deux fonctions** to hold two offices (at the same time).
cupide [kypid] *a* avaricious. ◆**cupidité** *nf* avarice, cupidity.
Cupidon [kypidɔ̃] *nm* Cupid.

cure [kyr] *nf* **1** (course of) treatment, cure. **2** (*fonction*) office (of a parish priest); (*résidence*) presbytery. ◆**curable** *a* curable. ◆**curatif, -ive** *a* curative. ◆**curé** *nm* (parish) priest.

curer [kyre] *vt* to clean out; **se c. le nez/les dents** to pick one's nose/teeth. ◆**cure-dent** *nm* toothpick. ◆**cure-ongles** *nm inv* nail cleaner. ◆**cure-pipe** *nm* pipe cleaner.

curieux, -euse [kyrjø, -øz] *a* (*bizarre*) curious; (*indiscret*) inquisitive, curious (**de** about); **c. de savoir** curious to know; – *nmf* inquisitive *ou* curious person; (*badaud*) onlooker. ◆**curieusement** *adv* curiously. ◆**curiosité** *nf* (*de personne, forme etc*) curiosity; (*chose*) curiosity; (*spectacle*) unusual sight.

curriculum (vitæ) [kyrikylɔm(vite)] *nm inv* curriculum (vitae), *Am* résumé.

curseur [kyrsœr] *nm* (*d'un ordinateur*) cursor.

cutané [kytane] *a* (*affection etc*) skin-. ◆**cuti(-réaction)** *nf* skin test.

cuve [kyv] *nf* vat; (*réservoir*) & *Phot* tank. ◆**cuvée** *nf* (*récolte de vin*) vintage. ◆**cuver** *vt* **c. son vin** *Fam* to sleep it off. ◆**cuvette** *nf* (*récipient*) & *Géog* basin, bowl; (*des cabinets*) pan, bowl.

cyanure [sjanyr] *nm* cyanide.

cybernétique [sibernetik] *nf* cybernetics.

cycle [sikl] *nm* **1** (*série, révolution*) cycle. **2** (*bicyclette*) cycle. ◆**cyclable** *a* (*piste*) cycle-. ◆**cyclique** *a* cyclic(al). ◆**cyclisme** *nm Sp* cycling. ◆**cycliste** *nmf* cyclist; – *a* (*course*) cycle-; (*champion*) cycling; **coureur c.** racing cyclist. ◆**cyclomoteur** *nm* moped.

cyclone [siklon] *nm* cyclone.

cygne [siɲ] *nm* swan; **chant du c.** *Fig* swan song.

cylindre [silɛ̃dr] *nm* cylinder; (*de rouleau compresseur*) roller. ◆**cylindrée** *nf Aut* (engine) capacity. ◆**cylindrique** *a* cylindrical.

cymbale [sɛ̃bal] *nf* cymbal.

cynique [sinik] *a* cynical; – *nmf* cynic. ◆**cynisme** *nm* cynicism.

cyprès [siprɛ] *nm* (*arbre*) cypress.

cypriote [siprijɔt] *a* & *nmf* Cypriot.

cytise [sitiz] *nf Bot* laburnum.

D

D, d [de] *nm* D, d.

d' [d] *voir* **de**[1,2].

d'abord [dabɔr] *adv* (*en premier lieu*) first; (*au début*) at first.

dactylo [daktilo] *nf* (*personne*) typist; (*action*) typing. ◆**dactylographie** *nf* typing. ◆**dactylographier** *vt* to type.

dada [dada] *nm* (*manie*) hobby horse, pet subject.

dadais [dadɛ] *nm* **(grand) d.** big oaf.

dahlia [dalja] *nm* dahlia.

daigner [deɲe] *vt* **d. faire** to condescend *ou* deign to do.

daim [dɛ̃] *nm* fallow deer; (*mâle*) buck; (*cuir*) suede.

dais [dɛ] *nm* (*de lit, feuillage etc*) canopy.

dalle [dal] *nf* paving stone; (*funèbre*) (flat) gravestone. ◆**dallage** *nm* (*action, surface*) paving. ◆**dallé** *a* (*pièce, cour etc*) paved.

daltonien, -ienne [daltɔnjɛ̃, -jɛn] *a* & *n* colour-blind (person). ◆**daltonisme** *nm* colour blindness.

dame [dam] *nf* **1** lady; (*mariée*) married lady. **2** *Échecs Cartes* queen; (*au jeu de dames*) king; **(jeu de) dames** draughts, *Am* checkers. ◆**damer** *vt* (*au jeu de dames*) to crown; **d. le pion à qn** to outsmart s.o. ◆**damier** *nm* draughtboard, *Am* checkerboard.

damner [dane] *vt* to damn; **faire d.** *Fam* to torment, drive mad; **– se d.** *vpr* to be damned. ◆**damnation** *nf* damnation.

dancing [dɑ̃siŋ] *nm* dance hall.

dandiner (se) [sədɑ̃dine] *vpr* to waddle.

dandy [dɑ̃di] *nm* dandy.

Danemark [danmark] *nm* Denmark. ◆**danois, -oise** *a* Danish; – *nmf* Dane; – *nm* (*langue*) Danish.

danger [dɑ̃ʒe] *nm* danger; **en d.** in danger *ou* jeopardy; **mettre en d.** to endanger, jeopardize; **en cas de d.** in an emergency; **en d. de mort** in peril of death; **'d. de mort'** (*panneau*) 'danger'; **sans d.** (*se promener etc*) safely; **être sans d.** to be safe; **pas de d.!** *Fam* no way!, no fear! ◆**dangereux, -euse** *a* dangerous (**pour** to). ◆**dangereusement** *adv* dangerously.

dans [dɑ̃] *prép* in; (*changement de lieu*) into; (*à l'intérieur de*) inside, within; **entrer d.** to go in(to); **d. Paris** in Paris, within Paris;

d. un rayon de within (a radius of); **boire/prendre/***etc* **d.** to drink/take/*etc* from *ou* out of; **marcher d. les rues** (*à travers*) to walk through *ou* about the streets; **d. ces circonstances** under *ou* in these circumstances; **d. deux jours/***etc* (*temps futur*) in two days/*etc*, in two days'/*etc* time; **d. les dix francs/***etc* (*quantité*) about ten francs/*etc*.

danse [dɑ̃s] *nf* dance; (*art*) dancing. ◆**dans/er** *vti* to dance; **faire d. l'anse du panier** (*domestique*) to fiddle on the shopping money. ◆**—eur, -euse** *nmf* dancer; **en danseuse** (*cycliste*) standing on the pedals.

dard [dar] *nm* (*d'abeille etc*) sting; (*de serpent*) tongue. ◆**darder** *vt Litt* (*flèche*) to shoot; (*regard*) to flash, dart; **le soleil dardait ses rayons** the sun cast down its burning rays.

dare-dare [dardar] *adv Fam* at *ou* on the double.

date [dat] *nf* date; **de vieille d.** (*amitié etc*) (of) long-standing; **faire d.** (*événement*) to mark an important date, be epoch-making; **en d. du ...** dated the ... ; **d. limite** deadline. ◆**datation** *nf* dating. ◆**dater** *vt* (*lettre etc*) to date; – *vi* (*être dépassé*) to date, be dated; **d. de** to date back to, date from; **à d. de** as from. ◆**dateur** *nm* (*de montre*) date indicator; – *a & nm* **(tampon) d.** date stamp.

datte [dat] *nf* (*fruit*) date. ◆**dattier** *nm* date palm.

daube [dob] *nf* **bœuf en d.** braised beef stew.

dauphin [dofɛ̃] *nm* (*mammifère marin*) dolphin.

davantage [davɑ̃taʒ] *adv* (*quantité*) more; (*temps*) longer; **d. de temps/***etc* more time/*etc*; **d. que** more than; longer than.

de[1] [d(ə)] (**d'** *before a vowel or mute h*; **de + le = du, de + les = des**) *prép* **1** (*complément d'un nom*) of; **les rayons du soleil** the rays of the sun, the sun's rays; **la ville de Paris** the town of Paris; **le livre de Paul** Paul's book; **un pont de fer** an iron bridge; **le train de Londres** the London train; **une augmentation/diminution de** an increase/decrease in. **2** (*complément d'un adjectif*) **digne de** worthy of; **heureux de partir** happy to leave; **content de qch** pleased with sth. **3** (*complément d'un verbe*) **parler de** to speak of *ou* about; **se souvenir de** to remember; **décider de faire** to decide to do; **traiter de lâche** to call a coward. **4** (*provenance*: *lieu & temps*) from; **venir/dater de** to come/date from; **mes amis du village** my friends from the village, my village friends; **le train de Londres** the train from London. **5** (*agent*) **accompagné de** accompanied by. **6** (*moyen*) **armé de** armed with; **se nourrir de** to live on. **7** (*manière*) **d'une voix douce** in *ou* with a gentle voice. **8** (*cause*) **puni de** punished for; **mourir de faim** to die of hunger. **9** (*temps*) **travailler de nuit** to work by night; **six heures du matin** six o'clock in the morning. **10** (*mesure*) **avoir six mètres de haut, être haut de six mètres** to be six metres high; **retarder de deux heures** to delay by two hours; **homme de trente ans** thirty-year-old man; **gagner cent francs de l'heure** to earn one hundred francs an hour.

de[2] [d(ə)] *art partitif* some; **elle boit du vin** she drinks (some) wine; **il ne boit pas de vin** (*négation*) he doesn't drink (any) wine; **des fleurs** (some) flowers; **de jolies fleurs** (some) pretty flowers; **d'agréables soirées** (some) pleasant evenings; **il y en a six de tués** (*avec un nombre*) there are six killed.

dé [de] *nm* (*à jouer*) dice; (*à coudre*) thimble; **les dés** the dice; (*jeu*) dice; **les dés sont jetés** *Fig* the die is cast; **couper en dés** *Culin* to dice.

déambuler [deɑ̃byle] *vi* to stroll, saunter.

débâcle [debɑkl] *nf Mil* rout; (*ruine*) *Fig* downfall; (*des glaces*) *Géog* breaking up.

déball/er [debale] *vt* to unpack; (*étaler*) to display. ◆**—age** *nm* unpacking; display.

débandade [debɑ̃dad] *nf* (mad) rush, stampede; *Mil* rout; **à la d.** in confusion; **tout va à la d.** everything's going to rack and ruin.

débaptiser [debatize] *vt* (*rue*) to rename.

débarbouiller [debarbuje] *vt* **d. qn** to wash s.o.'s face; **se d.** to wash one's face.

débarcadère [debarkadɛr] *nm* landing stage, quay.

débardeur [debardœr] *nm* **1** (*docker*) stevedore. **2** (*vêtement*) slipover, *Am* (sweater) vest.

débarqu/er [debarke] *vt* (*passagers*) to land; (*marchandises*) to unload; **d. qn** (*congédier*) *Fam* to sack s.o.; – *vi* (*passagers*) to disembark, land; (*être naïf*) *Fam* not to be quite with it; **d. chez qn** *Fam* to turn up suddenly at s.o.'s place. ◆**—ement** *nm* landing; unloading; *Mil* landing.

débarras [debara] *nm* lumber room, *Am* storeroom; **bon d.!** *Fam* good riddance! ◆**débarrasser** *vt* (*voie, table etc*) to clear (**de** of); **d. qn de** (*ennemi, soucis etc*) to rid s.o. of; (*manteau etc*) to relieve s.o. of; **se d. de** to get rid of, rid oneself of.

débat [deba] *nm* discussion, debate; *pl Pol Jur* proceedings. ◆**débattre*** *vt* to discuss, debate; **— se d.** *vpr* to struggle *ou* fight (to get free), put up a fight.

débauche [deboʃ] *nf* debauchery; **une d. de** *Fig* a wealth *ou* profusion of. ◆**débauch/er** *vt* **d. qn** (*détourner*) *Fam* to entice s.o. away from his work; (*licencier*) to dismiss s.o., lay s.o. off. ◆**—é, -ée** *a* (*libertin*) debauched, profligate; – *nmf* debauchee, profligate.

débile [debil] *a* (*esprit, enfant etc*) weak, feeble; *Péj Fam* idiotic; – *nmf Péj Fam* idiot, moron. ◆**débilité** *nf* debility, weakness; *pl* (*niaiseries*) *Fam* sheer nonsense. ◆**débiliter** *vt* to debilitate, weaken.

débiner [debine] **1** *vt* (*décrier*) *Fam* to run down. **2 se d.** *vpr* (*s'enfuir*) *Arg* to hop it, bolt.

débit [debi] *nm* **1** (*vente*) turnover, sales; (*de fleuve*) (rate of) flow; (*d'un orateur*) delivery; **d. de tabac** tobacconist's shop, *Am* tobacco store; **d. de boissons** bar, café. **2** (*compte*) *Fin* debit. ◆**débiter** *vt* **1** (*découper*) to cut up, slice up (**en** into); (*vendre*) to sell; (*fournir*) to yield; (*dire*) *Péj* to utter, spout. **2** *Fin* to debit. ◆**débiteur, -trice** *nmf* debtor; – *a* (*solde, compte*) debit-; **son compte est d.** his account is in debit, he is in debit.

déblais [deble] *nmpl* (*terre*) earth; (*décombres*) rubble. ◆**déblayer** *vt* (*terrain, décombres*) to clear.

débloquer [debloke] **1** *vt* (*machine*) to unjam; (*crédits, freins, compte*) to release; (*prix*) to decontrol. **2** *vi* (*divaguer*) *Fam* to talk through one's hat, talk nonsense.

déboires [debwar] *nmpl* disappointments, setbacks.

déboît/er [debwate] **1** *vt* (*tuyau*) to disconnect; (*os*) *Méd* to dislocate. **2** *vi Aut* to pull out, change lanes. ◆**—ement** *nm Méd* dislocation.

débonnaire [debɔnɛr] *a* good-natured, easy-going.

débord/er [debɔrde] *vi* (*fleuve, liquide*) to overflow; (*en bouillant*) to boil over; **d. de** (*vie, joie etc*) *Fig* to be overflowing *ou* bubbling over with; **l'eau déborde du vase** the water is running over the top of the vase *ou* is overflowing the vase; – *vt* (*dépasser*) to go *ou* extend beyond; (*faire saillie*) to stick out from; *Mil Sp* to outflank; **débordé de travail/de visites** snowed under with work/visits. ◆**—ement** *nm* overflowing; (*de joie, activité*) outburst.

débouch/er [debuʃe] **1** *vt* (*bouteille*) to open, uncork; (*lavabo, tuyau*) to clear, unblock. **2** *vi* (*surgir*) to emerge, come out (**de** from); **d. sur** (*rue*) to lead out onto, lead into; *Fig* to lead up to. ◆**—é** *nm* (*carrière*) & *Géog* opening; (*de rue*) exit; (*marché*) *Com* outlet.

débouler [debule] *vi* (*arriver*) *Fam* to burst in, turn up.

déboulonner [debulɔne] *vt* to unbolt; **d. qn** *Fam* (*renvoyer*) to sack *ou* fire s.o.; (*discréditer*) to bring s.o. down.

débours [debur] *nmpl* expenses. ◆**débourser** *vt* to pay out.

debout [d(ə)bu] *adv* standing (up); **mettre d.** (*planche etc*) to stand up, put upright; **se mettre d.** to stand *ou* get up; **se tenir *ou* rester d.** (*personne*) to stand (up), remain standing (up); **rester d.** (*édifice etc*) to remain standing; **être d.** (*levé*) to be up (and about); **d.!** get up!; **ça ne tient pas d.** (*théorie etc*) that doesn't hold water *ou* make sense.

déboutonner [debutɔne] *vt* to unbutton, undo; **— se d.** *vpr* (*personne*) to undo one's buttons.

débraillé [debraje] *a* (*tenue etc*) slovenly, sloppy; – *nm* slovenliness, sloppiness.

débrancher [debrɑ̃ʃe] *vt Él* to unplug, disconnect.

débrayer [debreje] *vi* **1** *Aut* to declutch, release the clutch. **2** (*se mettre en grève*) to stop work. ◆**débrayage** (*grève*) strike, walk-out.

débridé [debride] *a* (*effréné*) unbridled.

débris [debri] *nmpl* fragments, scraps; (*restes*) remains; (*détritus*) rubbish, debris.

débrouiller [debruje] **1** *vt* (*écheveau etc*) to unravel, disentangle; (*affaire*) to sort out. **2 se d.** *vpr* to manage, get by, make out; **se d. pour faire** to manage (somehow) to do. ◆**débrouillard** *a* smart, resourceful. ◆**débrouillardise** *nf* smartness, resourcefulness.

débroussailler [debrusaje] *vt* (*chemin*) to clear (of brushwood); (*problème*) *Fig* to clarify.

débusquer [debyske] *vt* (*gibier, personne*) to drive out, dislodge.

début [deby] *nm* start, beginning; **au d.** at the beginning; **faire ses débuts** (*sur la scène etc*) to make one's debut. ◆**début/er** *vi* to start, begin; (*dans une carrière*) to start out in life; (*sur la scène etc*) to make one's debut. ◆**—ant, -ante** *nmf* beginner; – *a* novice.

déca [deka] *nm Fam* decaffeinated coffee.

deçà (en) [ɑ̃d(ə)sa] *adv* (on) this side; – *prép* **en d. de** (on) this side of; (*succès, prix etc*) *Fig* short of.

décacheter [dekaʃte] *vt* (*lettre etc*) to open, unseal.

décade [dekad] *nf* (*dix jours*) period of ten days; (*décennie*) decade.

décadent [dekadɑ̃] *a* decadent. ◆**décadence** *nf* decay, decadence.

décaféiné [dekafeine] *a* decaffeinated.

décalaminer [dekalamine] *vt* (*moteur*) *Aut* to decoke, decarbonize.

décalcomanie [dekalkɔmani] *nf* (*image*) transfer, *Am* decal.

décal/er [dekale] *vt* **1** (*avancer*) to shift; (*départ, repas*) to shift (the time of). **2** (*ôter les cales de*) to unwedge. ◆**—age** *nm* (*écart*) gap, discrepancy; **d. horaire** time difference.

décalque [dekalk] *nm* tracing. ◆**décalquer** *vt* (*dessin*) to trace.

décamper [dekɑ̃pe] *vi* to make off, clear off.

décanter [dekɑ̃te] *vt* (*liquide*) to settle, clarify; **d. ses idées** to clarify one's ideas; **— se d.** *vpr* (*idées, situation*) to become clearer, settle.

décap/er [dekape] *vt* (*métal*) to clean, scrape down; (*surface peinte*) to strip. ◆**—ant** *nm* cleaning agent; (*pour enlever la peinture*) paint stripper. ◆**—eur** *nm* **d. thermique** hot-air paint stripper.

décapiter [dekapite] *vt* to decapitate, behead.

décapotable [dekapɔtabl] *a* (*voiture*) convertible.

décapsul/er [dekapsyle] *vt* **d. une bouteille** to take the cap *ou* top off a bottle. ◆**—eur** *nm* bottle-opener.

décarcasser (se) [sədekarkase] *vpr Fam* to flog oneself to death (**pour faire** doing).

décathlon [dekatlɔ̃] *nm Sp* decathlon.

décati [dekati] *a* worn out, decrepit.

décavé [dekave] *a Fam* ruined.

décéd/er [desede] *vi* to die. ◆**—é** *a* deceased.

déceler [desle] *vt* (*trouver*) to detect, uncover; (*révéler*) to reveal.

décembre [desɑ̃br] *nm* December.

décennie [deseni] *nf* decade.

décent [desɑ̃] *a* (*bienséant, acceptable*) decent. ◆**décemment** [-amɑ̃] *adv* decently. ◆**décence** *nf* decency.

décentraliser [desɑ̃tralize] *vt* to decentralize. ◆**décentralisation** *nf* decentralization.

déception [desɛpsjɔ̃] *nf* disappointment. ◆**décevoir*** *vt* to disappoint. ◆**décevant** *a* disappointing.

décerner [desɛrne] *vt* (*prix etc*) to award; (*mandat d'arrêt etc*) *Jur* to issue.

décès [desɛ] *nm* death.

déchaîn/er [deʃene] *vt* (*colère, violence*) to unleash, let loose; **d. l'enthousiasme/les rires** to set off wild enthusiasm/a storm of laughter; **— se d.** *vpr* (*tempête, rires*) to break out; (*foule*) to run amok *ou* riot; (*colère, personne*) to explode. ◆**—é** *a* (*foule, flots*) wild, raging. ◆**—ement** [-ɛnmɑ̃] *nm* (*de rires, de haine etc*) outburst; (*de violence*) outbreak, eruption; **le d. de la tempête** the raging of the storm.

déchanter [deʃɑ̃te] *vi Fam* to become disillusioned; (*changer de ton*) to change one's tune.

décharge [deʃarʒ] *nf Jur* discharge; **d. (publique)** (rubbish) dump *ou* tip, *Am* (garbage) dump; **d. (électrique)** (electrical) discharge, shock; **recevoir une d. (électrique)** to get a shock; **à la d. de qn** in s.o.'s defence. ◆**décharg/er** *vt* to unload; (*batterie*) *Él* to discharge; (*accusé*) *Jur* to discharge, exonerate; **d. qn de** (*travail etc*) to relieve s.o. of; **d. sur qn** (*son arme*) to fire at s.o.; (*sa colère*) to vent on s.o.; **— se d.** *vpr* (*batterie*) to go flat; **se d. sur qn du soin de faire qch** to unload onto s.o. the job of doing sth. ◆**—ement** *nm* unloading.

décharné [deʃarne] *a* skinny, bony.

déchausser [deʃose] *vt* **d. qn** to take s.o.'s shoes off; **se d.** to take one's shoes off; (*dent*) to get loose.

dèche [dɛʃ] *nf* **être dans la d.** *Arg* to be flat broke.

déchéance [deʃeɑ̃s] *nf* (*déclin*) decline, decay, degradation.

déchet [deʃɛ] *nm* **déchets** (*résidus*) scraps, waste; **il y a du d.** there's some waste *ou* wastage.

déchiffrer [deʃifre] *vt* (*message*) to decipher; (*mauvaise écriture*) to make out, decipher.

déchiquet/er [deʃikte] *vt* to tear to shreds, cut to bits. ◆**—é** *a* (*drapeau etc*) (all) in shreds; (*côte*) jagged.

déchir/er [deʃire] *vt* to tear (up), rip (up); (*vêtement*) to tear, rip; (*ouvrir*) to tear *ou* rip open; (*pays, groupe*) to tear apart; **d. l'air** (*bruit*) to rend the air; **ce bruit me déchire les oreilles** this noise is ear-splitting; **— se d.** *vpr* (*robe etc*) to tear.

rip. ◆**—ant** *a* (*navrant*) heart-breaking; (*aigu*) ear-splitting. ◆**—ement** *nm* (*souffrance*) heartbreak; *pl* (*divisions*) *Pol* deep rifts. ◆**déchirure** *nf* tear, rip; **d. musculaire** torn muscle.

déchoir [deʃwar] *vi* to lose prestige. ◆**déchu** *a* (*ange*) fallen; **être d. de** (*ses droits etc*) to have forfeited.

décibel [desibel] *nm* decibel.

décid/er [deside] *vt* (*envoi, opération*) to decide on; **d. que** to decide that; **d. qn à faire** to persuade s.o. to do; – *vi* **d. de** (*destin de qn*) to decide; (*voyage etc*) to decide on; **d. de faire** to decide to do; **— se d.** *vpr* (*question*) to be decided; **se d. à faire** to make up one's mind to do; **se d. pour qch** to decide on sth *ou* in favour of sth. ◆**—é** *a* (*air, ton*) determined, decided; (*net, pas douteux*) decided; **c'est d.** it's settled; **être d. à faire** to be decided about doing *ou* determined to do. ◆**—ément** *adv* undoubtedly.

décilitre [desilitr] *nm* decilitre.

décimal, -aux [desimal, -o] *a* decimal. ◆**décimale** *nf* decimal.

décimer [desime] *vt* to decimate.

décimètre [desimɛtr] *nm* decimetre; **double d.** ruler.

décisif, -ive [desizif, -iv] *a* decisive; (*moment*) crucial. ◆**décision** *nf* decision; (*fermeté*) determination.

déclamer [deklame] *vt* to declaim; *Péj* to spout. ◆**déclamatoire** *a Péj* bombastic.

déclarer [deklare] *vt* to declare (**que** that); (*décès, vol etc*) to notify; **d. coupable** to convict, find guilty; **d. la guerre** to declare war (à on); **— se d.** *vpr* (*s'expliquer*) to declare one's views; (*incendie, maladie*) to break out; **se d. contre** to come out against. ◆**déclaration** *nf* declaration; (*de décès etc*) notification; (*commentaire*) statement, comment; **d. de revenus** tax return.

déclasser [deklɑse] *vt* (*livres etc*) to put out of order; (*hôtel etc*) to downgrade; **d. qn** *Sp* to relegate s.o. (in the placing).

déclench/er [deklɑ̃ʃe] *vt* (*mécanisme*) to set *ou* trigger off, release; (*attaque*) to launch; (*provoquer*) to trigger off, spark off; **d. le travail** *Méd* to induce labour; **— se d.** *vpr* (*sonnerie*) to go off; (*attaque, grève*) to start. ◆**—ement** *nm* (*d'un appareil*) release.

déclic [deklik] *nm* (*mécanisme*) catch, trigger; (*bruit*) click.

déclin [deklɛ̃] *nm* decline; (*du jour*) close; (*de la lune*) wane. ◆**décliner 1** *vt* (*refuser*) to decline. **2** *vt* (*réciter*) to state. **3** *vi* (*forces etc*) to decline, wane; (*jour*) to draw to a close.

déclivité [deklivite] *nf* slope.

décocher [dekɔʃe] *vt* (*flèche*) to shoot, fire; (*coup*) to let fly, aim; (*regard*) to flash.

décoder [dekɔde] *vt* (*message*) to decode.

décoiffer [dekwafe] *vt* **d. qn** to mess up s.o.'s hair.

décoincer [dekwɛ̃se] *vt* (*engrenage*) to unjam.

décoll/er [dekɔle] **1** *vi* (*avion etc*) to take off; **elle ne décolle pas d'ici** *Fam* she won't leave *ou* budge. **2** *vt* (*timbre etc*) to unstick; **— se d.** *vpr* to come unstuck. ◆**—age** *nm Av* takeoff.

décolleté [dekɔlte] *a* (*robe*) low-cut; – *nm* (*de robe*) low neckline; (*de femme*) bare neck and shoulders.

décoloniser [dekɔlɔnize] *vt* to decolonize. ◆**décolonisation** *nf* decolonization.

décolor/er [dekɔlɔre] *vt* to discolour, fade; (*cheveux*) to bleach. ◆**—ant** *nm* bleach. ◆**décoloration** *nf* discolo(u)ration; bleaching.

décombres [dekɔ̃br] *nmpl* ruins, rubble, debris.

décommander [dekɔmɑ̃de] *vt* (*marchandises, invitation*) to cancel; (*invités*) to put off; **— se d.** *vpr* to cancel (one's appointment).

décomposer [dekɔ̃poze] *vt* to decompose; (*visage*) to distort; **— se d.** *vpr* (*pourrir*) to decompose; (*visage*) to become distorted. ◆**décomposition** *nf* decomposition.

décompresser [dekɔ̃prese] *vi Psy Fam* to unwind.

décompression [dekɔ̃prɛsjɔ̃] *nf* decompression.

décompte [dekɔ̃t] *nm* deduction; (*détail*) breakdown. ◆**décompter** *vt* to deduct.

déconcerter [dekɔ̃sɛrte] *vt* to disconcert.

déconfit [dekɔ̃fi] *a* downcast. ◆**déconfiture** *nf* (state of) collapse *ou* defeat; (*faillite*) *Fam* financial ruin.

décongeler [dekɔ̃ʒle] *vt* (*aliment*) to thaw, defrost.

décongestionner [dekɔ̃ʒɛstjɔne] *vt* (*rue*) & *Méd* to relieve congestion in.

déconnecter [dekɔnɛkte] *vt Él & Fig* to disconnect.

déconner [dekɔne] *vi* (*divaguer*) *Fam* to talk nonsense.

déconseiller [dekɔ̃seje] *vt* **d. qch à qn** to advise s.o. against sth; **d. à qn de faire** to advise s.o. against doing; **c'est déconseillé** it is inadvisable.

déconsidérer [dekɔ̃sidere] *vt* to discredit.

décontaminer [dekɔ̃tamine] *vt* to decontaminate.
décontenancer [dekɔ̃tnɑ̃se] *vt* to disconcert; **— se d.** *vpr* to lose one's composure, become flustered.
décontracter [dekɔ̃trakte] *vt*, **— se d.** *vpr* to relax. **◆décontraction** *nf* relaxation.
déconvenue [dekɔ̃vny] *nf* disappointment.
décor [dekɔr] *nm Th* scenery, decor; *Cin* set; (*paysage*) scenery; (*d'intérieur*) decoration; (*cadre, ambiance*) setting; **entrer dans le d.** (*véhicule*) *Fam* to run off the road.
décorer [dekɔre] *vt* (*maison, soldat etc*) to decorate (**de** with). **◆décorateur, -trice** *nmf* (interior) decorator; *Th* stage designer; *Cin* set designer. **◆décoratif, -ive** *a* decorative. **◆décoration** *nf* decoration.
décortiquer [dekɔrtike] *vt* (*graine*) to husk; (*homard etc*) to shell; (*texte*) *Fam* to take to pieces, dissect.
découcher [dekuʃe] *vi* to stay out all night.
découdre [dekudr] *vt* to unstitch; – *vi* **en d.** *Fam* to fight it out; **— se d.** *vpr* to come unstitched.
découler [dekule] *vi* **d. de** to follow from.
découp/er [dekupe] *vt* (*poulet etc*) to carve; (*article etc*) *Journ* to cut out; **se d. sur** to stand out against. **◆—é** *a* (*côte*) jagged. **◆—age** *nm* carving; cutting out; (*image*) cut-out. **◆découpure** *nf* (*contour*) jagged outline; (*morceau*) piece cut out, cut-out.
découplé [dekuple] *a* **bien d.** (*personne*) well-built, strapping.
décourag/er [dekuraʒe] *vt* (*dissuader*) to discourage (**de** from); (*démoraliser*) to dishearten, discourage; **— se d.** *vpr* to get discouraged *ou* disheartened. **◆—ement** *nm* discouragement.
décousu [dekuzy] *a* (*propos, idées*) disconnected.
découvrir* [dekuvrir] *vt* (*trésor, terre etc*) to discover; (*secret, vérité etc*) to find out, discover; (*casserole etc*) to take the lid off; (*dévoiler*) to disclose (**à** to); (*dénuder*) to uncover, expose; (*voir*) to perceive; **d. que** to discover *ou* find out that; **— se d.** *vpr* (*se dénuder*) to uncover oneself; (*enlever son chapeau*) to take one's hat off; (*ciel*) to clear (up). **◆découvert 1** *a* (*terrain*) open; (*tête etc*) bare; **à d.** exposed, unprotected; **agir à d.** to act openly. **2** *nm* (*d'un compte*) *Fin* overdraft. **◆découverte** *nf* discovery; **partir** *ou* **aller à la d. de** to go in search of.
décrasser [dekrase] *vt* (*éduquer*) to take the rough edges off.
décrépit [dekrepi] *a* (*vieillard*) decrepit.
◆décrépitude *nf* (*des institutions etc*) decay.
décret [dekrɛ] *nm* decree. **◆décréter** *vt* to order, decree.
décrier [dekrije] *vt* to run down, disparage.
décrire* [dekrir] *vt* to describe.
décroch/er [dekrɔʃe] **1** *vt* (*détacher*) to unhook; (*tableau*) to take down; (*obtenir*) *Fam* to get, land; **d. (le téléphone)** to pick up the phone. **2** *vi Fam* (*abandonner*) to give up; (*perdre le fil*) to be unable to follow, lose track. **◆—é** *a* (*téléphone*) off the hook.
décroître* [dekrwatr] *vi* (*mortalité etc*) to decrease, decline; (*eaux*) to subside; (*jours*) to draw in. **◆décroissance** *nf* decrease, decline (**de** in, of).
décrotter [dekrɔte] *vt* (*chaussures*) to clean *ou* scrape (the mud off). **◆décrottoir** *nm* shoe scraper.
décrypter [dekripte] *vt* (*message*) to decipher, decode.
déçu [desy] *voir* **décevoir**; – *a* disappointed.
déculotter (se) [sədekylɔte] *vpr* to take off one's trousers *ou Am* pants. **◆déculottée** *nf Fam* thrashing.
décupler [dekyple] *vti* to increase tenfold.
dédaigner [dedeɲe] *vt* (*personne, richesse etc*) to scorn, despise; (*repas*) to turn up one's nose at; (*offre*) to spurn; (*ne pas tenir compte de*) to disregard. **◆dédaigneux, -euse** *a* scornful, disdainful (**de** of). **◆dédain** *nm* scorn, disdain (**pour, de** for).
dédale [dedal] *nm* maze, labyrinth.
dedans [d(ə)dɑ̃] *adv* inside; **de d.** from (the) inside, from within; **en d.** on the inside; **au-d. (de), au d. (de)** inside; **au-d.** *ou* **au d. de lui-même** inwardly; **tomber d.** (*trou*) to fall in (it); **donner d.** (*être dupé*) *Fam* to fall in; **mettre d.** *Fam* (*en prison*) to put inside; (*tromper*) to take in; **je me suis fait rentrer d.** (*accident de voiture*) *Fam* someone went *ou* crashed into me; – *nm* **le d.** the inside.
dédicace [dedikas] *nf* dedication, inscription. **◆dédicacer** *vt* (*livre etc*) to dedicate, inscribe (**à** to).
dédier [dedje] *vt* to dedicate.
dédire (se) [sədedir] *vpr* to go back on one's word; **se d. de** (*promesse etc*) to go back on. **◆dédit** *nm* (*somme*) *Com* forfeit, penalty.
dédommag/er [dedɔmaʒe] *vt* to compensate (**de** for). **◆—ement** *nm* compensation.
dédouaner [dedwane] *vt* (*marchandises*) to clear through customs; **d. qn** to restore s.o.'s prestige.

dédoubl/er [deduble] *vt* (*classe etc*) to split into two; **d. un train** to run an extra train; **— se d.** *vpr* to be in two places at once. **◆—ement** *nm* **d. de la personnalité** *Psy* split personality.

déduire* [dedɥir] *vt* (*retirer*) to deduct (**de** from); (*conclure*) to deduce (**de** from). **◆déductible** *a* (*frais*) deductible, allowable. **◆déduction** *nf* (*raisonnement*) & *Com* deduction.

déesse [dees] *nf* goddess.

défaill/ir* [defajir] *vi* (*s'évanouir*) to faint; (*forces*) to fail, flag; **sans d.** without flinching. **◆—ant** *a* (*personne*) faint; (*témoin*) *Jur* defaulting. **◆défaillance** *nf* (*évanouissement*) fainting fit; (*faiblesse*) weakness; (*panne*) fault; **une d. de mémoire** a lapse of memory.

défaire* [defɛr] *vt* (*nœud etc*) to undo, untie; (*bagages*) to unpack; (*installation*) to take down; (*coiffure*) to mess up; **d. qn de** to rid s.o. of; **— se d.** *vpr* (*nœud etc*) to come undone *ou* untied; **se d. de** to get rid of. **◆défait** *a* (*lit*) unmade; (*visage*) drawn; (*armée*) defeated. **◆défaite** *nf* defeat. **◆défaitisme** *nm* defeatism.

défalquer [defalke] *vt* (*frais etc*) to deduct (**de** from).

défaut [defo] *nm* (*faiblesse*) fault, shortcoming, failing, defect; (*de diamant etc*) flaw; (*désavantage*) drawback; (*contumace*) *Jur* default; **le d. de la cuirasse** the chink in the armour; **faire d.** to be lacking; **le temps me fait d.** I lack time; **à d. de** for want of; **en d.** at fault; **prendre qn en d.** to catch s.o. out; **ou, à d.** . . . . or, failing that . . . .

défaveur [defavœr] *nf* disfavour. **◆défavorable** *a* unfavourable (**à** to). **◆défavoriser** *vt* to put at a disadvantage, be unfair to.

défection [defɛksjɔ̃] *nf* defection, desertion; **faire d.** to desert; (*ne pas venir*) to fail to turn up.

défectueux, -euse [defɛktɥø, -øz] *a* faulty, defective. **◆défectuosité** *nf* defectiveness; (*défaut*) defect (**de** in).

défendre [defɑ̃dr] **1** *vt* (*protéger*) to defend; **— se d.** *vpr* to defend oneself; **se d. de** (*pluie etc*) to protect oneself from; **se d. de faire** (*s'empêcher de*) to refrain from doing; **je me défends (bien)** *Fam* I can hold my own. **2** *vt* **d. à qn de faire** (*interdire*) to forbid s.o. to do, not allow s.o. to do; **d. qch à qn** to forbid s.o. sth. **◆défendable** *a* defensible.

défense [defɑ̃s] *nf* **1** (*protection*) defence, *Am* defense; **sans d.** defenceless. **2** (*interdiction*) **'d. de fumer'** 'no smoking'; **'d. d'entrer'** 'no entry', 'no admittance'. **3** (*d'éléphant*) tusk. **◆défenseur** *nm* defender; (*des faibles*) protector, defender. **◆défensif, -ive** *a* defensive; **–** *nf* **sur la défensive** on the defensive.

déférent [deferɑ̃] *a* deferential. **◆déférence** *nf* deference.

déférer [defere] **1** *vt* (*coupable*) *Jur* to refer (**à** to). **2** *vi* **d. à l'avis de qn** to defer to s.o.'s opinion.

déferler [defɛrle] *vi* (*vagues*) to break; (*haine etc*) to erupt; **d. dans** *ou* **sur** (*foule*) to surge *ou* sweep into.

défi [defi] *nm* challenge; **lancer un d. à qn** to challenge s.o.; **mettre qn au d. de faire** to defy *ou* dare *ou* challenge s.o. to do.

déficient [defisjɑ̃] *a* *Méd* deficient. **◆déficience** *nf* *Méd* deficiency.

déficit [defisit] *nm* deficit. **◆déficitaire** *a* (*budget etc*) in deficit; (*récolte etc*) *Fig* short, insufficient.

défier[1] [defje] *vt* (*provoquer*) to challenge (**à** to); (*braver*) to defy; **d. qn de faire** to defy *ou* challenge s.o. to do.

défier[2] (se) [sədefje] *vpr* **se d. de** *Litt* to distrust. **◆défiance** *nf* distrust (**de** of). **◆défiant** *a* distrustful (**à l'égard de** of).

défigur/er [defigyre] *vt* (*visage*) to disfigure; (*vérité etc*) to distort. **◆—ement** *nm* disfigurement; distortion.

défil/er [defile] *vi* (*manifestants*) to march (**devant** past); *Mil* to march *ou* file past; (*paysage, jours*) to pass by; (*visiteurs*) to keep coming and going, stream in and out; (*images*) *Cin* to flash by (on the screen); **— se d.** *vpr* *Fam* (*s'éloigner*) to sneak off; (*éviter d'agir*) to cop out. **◆—é** *nm* **1** (*cortège*) procession; (*de manifestants*) march; *Mil* parade, march past; (*de visiteurs*) stream, succession. **2** *Géog* gorge, pass.

défin/ir [definir] *vt* to define. **◆—i** *a* (*article*) *Gram* definite. **◆définition** *nf* definition; (*de mots croisés*) clue.

définitif, -ive [definitif, -iv] *a* final, definitive; **–** *nf* **en définitive** in the final analysis, finally. **◆définitivement** *adv* (*partir*) permanently, for good; (*exclure*) definitively.

déflagration [deflagrɑsjɔ̃] *nf* explosion.

déflation [deflɑsjɔ̃] *nf* *Écon* deflation.

déflorer [deflɔre] *vt* (*idée, sujet*) to spoil the freshness of.

défonc/er [defɔ̃se] **1** *vt* (*porte, mur etc*) to smash in *ou* down; (*trottoir, route etc*) to dig up, break up. **2 se d.** *vpr* (*drogué*) *Fam* to get high (à on). ◆**—é** *a* **1** (*route*) full of potholes, bumpy. **2** (*drogué*) *Fam* high.

déform/er [defɔrme] *vt* (*objet*) to put *ou* knock out of shape; (*doigt, main*) to deform; (*faits, image etc*) to distort; (*goût*) to corrupt; **— se d.** *vpr* to lose its shape. ◆**—é** *a* (*objet*) misshapen; (*corps etc*) deformed, misshapen; **chaussée déformée** uneven road surface. ◆**déformation** *nf* distortion; corruption; (*de membre*) deformity; **c'est de la d. professionnelle** it's an occupational hazard, it's a case of being conditioned by one's job.

défouler (se) [sədefule] *vpr Fam* to let off steam.

défraîchir (se) [sədefreʃir] *vpr* (*étoffe etc*) to lose its freshness, become faded.

défrayer [defreje] *vt* **d. qn** to pay *ou* defray s.o.'s expenses; **d. la chronique** to be the talk of the town.

défricher [defriʃe] *vt* (*terrain*) to clear (for cultivation); (*sujet etc*) *Fig* to open up.

défriser [defrize] *vt* (*cheveux*) to straighten; **d. qn** (*contrarier*) *Fam* to ruffle *ou* annoy s.o.

défroisser [defrwase] *vt* (*papier*) to smooth out.

défroqué [defrɔke] *a* (*prêtre*) defrocked.

défunt, -unte [defœ̃, -œ̃t] *a* (*mort*) departed; **son d. mari** her late husband; *– nmf* **le d., la défunte** the deceased, the departed.

dégag/er [degaʒe] *vt* (*lieu, table*) to clear (**de** of); (*objet en gage*) to redeem; (*odeur*) to give off; (*chaleur*) to give out; (*responsabilité*) to disclaim; (*idée, conclusion*) to bring out; **d. qn de** (*promesse*) to release s.o. from; (*décombres*) to free s.o. from, pull s.o. out of; **cette robe dégage la taille** this dress leaves the waist free and easy; *– vi Fb* to clear the ball (down the pitch); **d.!** clear the way!; **— se d.** *vpr* (*rue, ciel*) to clear; **se d. de** (*personne*) to release oneself from (*promise*); to get free from, free oneself from (*rubble*); **se d. de** (*odeur*) to issue *ou* emanate from; (*vérité, impression*) to emerge from. ◆**—é** *a* (*ciel*) clear; (*ton, allure*) easy-going, casual; (*vue*) open. ◆**—ement** *nm* **1** (*action*) clearing; redemption; (*d'odeur*) emanation; (*de chaleur*) emission; release; freeing; *Fb* clearance, kick; **itinéraire de d.** *Aut* relief road. **2** (*espace libre*) clearing; (*de maison*) passage.

dégainer [degene] *vti* (*arme*) to draw.

dégarn/ir [degarnir] *vt* to clear, empty; (*arbre, compte*) to strip; **— se d.** *vpr* (*crâne*) to go bald; (*salle*) to clear, empty ◆**—i** *a* (*salle*) empty, bare; (*tête*) balding; **front d.** receding hairline.

dégâts [dega] *nmpl* damage; **limiter les d.** *Fig* to prevent matters getting worse.

dégel [deʒɛl] *nm* thaw. ◆**dégeler** *vt* to thaw (out); (*crédits*) to unfreeze; *– vi* to thaw (out); *– v imp* to thaw; **— se d.** *vpr* (*personne, situation*) to thaw (out).

dégénér/er [deʒenere] *vi* to degenerate (**en** into). ◆**—é, -ée** *a* & *nmf* degenerate. ◆**dégénérescence** *nf* degeneration.

dégingandé [deʒɛ̃gɑ̃de] *a* gangling, lanky.

dégivrer [deʒivre] *vt Aut Av* to de-ice; (*réfrigérateur*) to defrost.

déglingu/er (se) [sədeglɛ̃ge] *vpr Fam* to fall to bits. ◆**—é** *a* falling to bits, in bits.

dégobiller [degɔbije] *vt Fam* to spew up.

dégonfl/er [degɔ̃fle] *vt* (*pneu etc*) to deflate, let down; **— se d.** *vpr* (*flancher*) *Fam* to chicken out, get cold feet. ◆**—é, -ée** *a* (*pneu*) flat; (*lâche*) *Fam* chicken, yellow; *– nmf Fam* yellow belly.

dégorger [degɔrʒe] *vi* (*se déverser*) to discharge (**dans** into); **faire d.** (*escargots*) *Culin* to cover with salt.

dégot(t)er [degɔte] *vt Fam* to find, turn up.

dégouliner [deguline] *vi* to trickle, drip, run.

dégourd/ir [degurdir] *vt* (*doigts etc*) to take the numbness out of; **d. qn** *Fig* to smarten *ou* wise s.o. up, sharpen s.o.'s wits; **— se d.** *vpr* to smarten up, wise up; **se d. les jambes** to stretch one's legs. ◆**—i** *a* (*malin*) smart, sharp.

dégoût [degu] *nm* disgust; **le d. de** (*la vie, les gens etc*) disgust for; **avoir un** *ou* **du d. pour qch** to have a (strong) dislike *ou* distaste for sth. ◆**dégoût/er** *vt* to disgust; **d. qn de qch** to put s.o. off sth; **se d. de** to take a (strong) dislike to, become disgusted with. ◆**—ant** *a* disgusting. ◆**—é** *a* disgusted; **être d. de** to be sick of *ou* disgusted with *ou* by *ou* at; **elle est partie dégoûtée** she left in disgust; **il n'est pas d.** (*difficile*) he's not too fussy; **faire le d.** to be fussy.

dégrad/er [degrade] **1** *vt* (*avilir*) to degrade; (*mur etc*) to deface, damage; **— se d.** *vpr* (*s'avilir*) to degrade oneself; (*édifice, situation*) to deteriorate. **2** *vt* (*couleur*) to shade off. ◆**—ant** *a* degrading. ◆**—é** *nm* (*de couleur*) shading off, gradation. ◆**dégradation** *nf* (*de drogué etc*) & *Ch* degradation; (*de situation etc*) deterioration; *pl* (*dégâts*) damage.

dégrafer [degrafe] *vt* (*vêtement*) to unfasten, unhook.

dégraisser [degrese] *vt* **1** (*bœuf*) to take the

fat off; (*bouillon*) to skim. **2** (*entreprise*) *Fam* to slim down, trim down the size of (*by laying off workers*).

degré [dəgre] *nm* **1** degree; **enseignement du premier/second d.** primary/secondary education; **au plus haut d.** (*avare etc*) extremely. **2** (*gradin*) *Litt* step.

dégrever [degrəve] *vt* (*contribuable*) to reduce the tax burden on.

dégriffé [degrife] *a* **vêtement d.** unlabelled designer garment.

dégringoler [degrɛ̃gɔle] *vi* to tumble (down); **faire d. qch** to topple sth over; – *vt* (*escalier*) to rush down. ◆**dégringolade** *nf* tumble.

dégriser [degrize] *vt* **d. qn** to sober s.o. (up).

dégrossir [degrosir] *vt* (*travail*) to rough out; **d. qn** to refine s.o.

déguerpir [degɛrpir] *vi* to clear off *ou* out.

dégueulasse [degœlas] *a Fam* lousy, disgusting.

dégueuler [degœle] *vi* (*vomir*) *Arg* to puke.

déguis/er [degize] *vt* (*pour tromper*) to disguise; **d. qn en** (*costumer*) to dress s.o. up as, disguise s.o. as; – **se d.** *vpr* to dress oneself up, disguise oneself (**en** as). ◆**—ement** *nm* disguise; (*de bal costumé etc*) fancy dress.

déguster [degyste] **1** *vt* (*goûter*) to taste, sample; (*apprécier*) to relish. **2** *vi* (*subir des coups*) *Fam* to cop it, get a good hiding. ◆**dégustation** *nf* tasting, sampling.

déhancher (se) [sədeɑ̃ʃe] *vpr* (*femme etc*) to sway *ou* wiggle one's hips; (*boiteux*) to walk lop-sided.

dehors [dəɔr] *adv* out(side); (*à l'air*) outdoors, outside; **en d.** on the outside; **en d. de** outside; (*excepté*) apart from; **en d. de la ville/fenêtre** out of town/the window; **au-d. (de), au d. (de)** outside; **déjeuner/jeter/***etc* **d.** to lunch/throw/*etc* out; – *nm* (*extérieur*) outside; *pl* (*aspect*) outward appearance.

déjà [deʒa] *adv* already; **est-il d. parti?** has he left yet *ou* already?; **elle l'a d. vu** she's seen it before, she's already seen it; **c'est d. pas mal** that's not bad at all; **quand partez-vous, d.?** when are you leaving, again?

déjeuner [deʒœne] *vi* (*à midi*) to (have) lunch; (*le matin*) to (have) breakfast; – *nm* lunch; **petit d.** breakfast.

déjouer [deʒwe] *vt* (*intrigue etc*) to thwart, foil.

déjuger (se) [sədeʒyʒe] *vpr* to go back on one's opinion *ou* decision.

delà [d(ə)la] *adv* **au-d. (de), au d. (de), par-d., par d.** beyond; **au-d. du pont/***etc* beyond *ou* past the bridge/*etc*; – *nm* **l'au-d.** the (world) beyond.

délabr/er (se) [sədelabre] *vpr* (*édifice*) to become dilapidated, fall into disrepair; (*santé*) to become impaired. ◆**—ement** *nm* dilapidation, disrepair; impaired state.

délacer [delase] *vt* (*chaussures*) to undo.

délai [delɛ] *nm* time limit; (*répit, sursis*) extra time, extension; **dans un d. de dix jours** within ten days; **sans d.** without delay; **à bref d.** at short notice; **dans les plus brefs délais** as soon as possible; **dernier d.** final date.

délaisser [delese] *vt* to forsake, desert, abandon; (*négliger*) to neglect.

délass/er [delɑse] *vt*, – **se d.** *vpr* to relax. ◆**—ement** *nm* relaxation, diversion.

délateur, -trice [delatœr, -tris] *nmf* informer.

délavé [delave] *a* (*tissu, jean*) faded; (*ciel*) watery; (*terre*) waterlogged.

délayer [deleje] *vt* (*mélanger*) to mix (with liquid); (*discours, texte*) *Fig* to pad out, drag out.

delco [dɛlko] *nm Aut* distributor.

délect/er (se) [sədelɛkte] *vpr* **se d. de qch/à faire** to (take) delight in sth/in doing. ◆**—able** *a* delectable. ◆**délectation** *nf* delight.

délégu/er [delege] *vt* to delegate (**à** to). ◆**—é, -ée** *nmf* delegate. ◆**délégation** *nf* delegation.

délest/er [delɛste] *vt Él* to cut the power from; **d. qn de** (*voler à qn*) *Fam* to relieve s.o. of. ◆**—age** *nm Aut* relief; **itinéraire de d.** alternative route (*to relieve congestion*).

délibér/er [delibere] *vi* (*réfléchir*) to deliberate (**sur** upon); (*se consulter*) to confer, deliberate (**de** about). ◆**—é** *a* (*résolu*) determined; (*intentionnel*) deliberate; **de propos d.** deliberately. ◆**—ément** *adv* (*à dessein*) deliberately. ◆**délibération** *nf* deliberation.

délicat [delika] *a* (*santé, travail etc*) delicate; (*question*) tricky, delicate; (*geste*) tactful; (*conscience*) scrupulous; (*exigeant*) particular. ◆**délicatement** *adv* delicately; tactfully. ◆**délicatesse** *nf* delicacy; tact(fulness); scrupulousness.

délice [delis] *nm* delight; – *nfpl* delights. ◆**délicieux, -euse** *a* (*mets, fruit etc*) delicious; (*endroit, parfum etc*) delightful.

délié [delje] **1** *a* (*esprit*) sharp; (*doigts*) nimble; (*mince*) slender. **2** *nm* (*d'une lettre*) (thin) upstroke.

délier [delje] *vt* to untie, undo; (*langue*) *Fig*

to loosen; **d. qn de** to release s.o. from; — **se d.** *vpr* (*paquet etc*) to come undone *ou* untied.

délimiter [delimite] *vt* to mark off, delimit; (*définir*) to define. ◆**délimitation** *nf* demarcation, delimitation; definition.

délinquant, -ante [delɛ̃kɑ̃, -ɑ̃t] *a* & *nmf* delinquent. ◆**délinquance** *nf* delinquency.

délire [delir] *nm Méd* delirium; (*exaltation*) *Fig* frenzy. ◆**délir/er** *vi Méd* to be delirious; (*dire n'importe quoi*) *Fig* to rave; **d. de** (*joie etc*) to be wild with. ◆**—ant** *a* (*malade*) delirious; (*joie*) frenzied, wild; (*déraisonnable*) utterly absurd.

délit [deli] *nm* offence, misdemeanour.

délivrer [delivre] *vt* **1** (*prisonnier*) to release, deliver; (*ville*) to deliver; **d. qn de** (*souci etc*) to rid s.o. of. **2** (*billet, diplôme etc*) to issue. ◆**délivrance** *nf* release; deliverance; issue; (*soulagement*) relief.

déloger [delɔʒe] *vi* to move out; — *vt* to force *ou* drive out; *Mil* to dislodge.

déloyal, -aux [delwajal, -o] *a* disloyal; (*concurrence*) unfair. ◆**déloyauté** *nf* disloyalty; unfairness; (*action*) disloyal act.

delta [delta] *nm* (*de fleuve*) delta.

deltaplane® [dɛltaplan] *nm* (*engin*) hang-glider; **faire du d.** to practise hang-gliding.

déluge [delyʒ] *nm* flood; (*de pluie*) downpour; (*de compliments, coups*) shower.

déluré [delyre] *a* (*malin*) smart, sharp; (*fille*) *Péj* brazen.

démagogie [demagɔʒi] *nf* demagogy. ◆**démagogue** *nmf* demagogue.

demain [d(ə)mɛ̃] *adv* tomorrow; **à d.!** see you tomorrow!; **ce n'est pas d. la veille** *Fam* that won't happen for a while yet.

demande [d(ə)mɑ̃d] *nf* request; (*d'emploi*) application; (*de renseignements*) inquiry; *Écon* demand; (*question*) question; **d. (en mariage)** proposal (of marriage); **demandes d'emploi** *Journ* situations wanted. ◆**demander** *vt* to ask for; (*emploi*) to apply for; (*autorisation*) to request, ask for; (*charité*) to beg for; (*prix*) to charge; (*nécessiter, exiger*) to require; **d. un nom/le chemin/l'heure** to ask a name/the way/the time; **d. qch à qn** to ask s.o. for sth; **d. à qn de faire** to ask s.o. to do; **d. si/où** to ask *ou* inquire whether/where; **on te demande!** you're wanted!; **ça demande du temps/une heure** it takes time/an hour; **d. en mariage** to propose (marriage) to; — **se d.** *vpr* to wonder, ask oneself (**pourquoi** why, **si** if).

démanger [demɑ̃ʒe] *vti* to itch; **son bras le** *ou* **lui démange** his arm itches; **ça me démange de...** *Fig* I'm itching to.... ◆**démangeaison** *nf* itch; **avoir des démangeaisons** to be itching; **j'ai une d. au bras** my arm's itching.

démanteler [demɑ̃tle] *vt* (*bâtiment*) to demolish; (*organisation etc*) to break up.

démantibuler [demɑ̃tibyle] *vt* (*meuble etc*) *Fam* to pull to pieces.

démaquill/er (se) [sədemakije] *vpr* to take off one's make-up. ◆**—ant** *nm* make-up remover.

démarcation [demarkɑsjɔ̃] *nf* demarcation.

démarche [demarʃ] *nf* walk, step, gait; (*de pensée*) process; **faire des démarches** to take the necessary steps (**pour faire** to do).

démarcheur, -euse [demarʃœr, -øz] *nmf Pol* canvasser; *Com* door-to-door salesman *ou* saleswoman.

démarquer [demarke] *vt* (*prix*) to mark down; **se d. de** *Fig* to dissociate oneself from.

démarr/er [demare] *vi* (*moteur*) *Aut* to start (up); (*partir*) *Aut* to move *ou* drive off; (*entreprise etc*) *Fig* to get off the ground; — *vt* (*commencer*) *Fam* to start. ◆**—age** *nm Aut* start; **d. en côte** hill start. ◆**—eur** *nm Aut* starter.

démasquer [demaske] *vt* to unmask.

démêl/er [demele] *vt* to disentangle; (*discerner*) to fathom. ◆**—é** *nm* (*dispute*) squabble; *pl* (*ennuis*) trouble (**avec** with).

démembrer [demɑ̃bre] *vt* (*pays etc*) to dismember.

déménag/er [demenaʒe] *vi* to move (out), move house; — *vt* (*meubles*) to (re)move. ◆**—ement** *nm* move, moving (house); (*de meubles*) removal, moving (**de** of); **voiture de d.** removal van, *Am* moving van. ◆**—eur** *nm* removal man, *Am* (furniture) mover.

démener (se) [sədemne] *vpr* to fling oneself about; **se d. pour faire** to spare no effort to do.

dément, -ente [demɑ̃, -ɑ̃t] *a* insane; (*génial*) *Iron* fantastic; — *nmf* lunatic. ◆**démence** *nf* insanity. ◆**démentiel, -ielle** *a* insane.

dément/ir [demɑ̃tir] *vt* (*infirmer*) to belie; (*nouvelle, faits etc*) to deny; **d. qn** to give the lie to s.o. ◆**—i** *nm* denial.

démerder (se) [sədemerde] *vpr* (*se débrouiller*) *Arg* to manage (by oneself).

démesure [deməzyr] *nf* excess. ◆**démesuré** *a* excessive, inordinate.

démettre [demetr] *vt* **1** (*os*) to dislocate; **se d. le pied** to dislocate one's foot. **2 d. qn de**

to dismiss s.o. from; **se d. de ses fonctions** to resign one's office.

demeurant (au) [odəmœrɑ̃] *adv* for all that, after all.

demeure [dəmœr] *nf* **1** dwelling (place), residence. **2 mettre qn en d. de faire** to summon *ou* instruct s.o. to do. ◆**demeur/er** *vi* **1** (*aux* **être**) (*rester*) to remain; **en d. là** (*affaire etc*) to rest there. **2** (*aux* **avoir**) (*habiter*) to live, reside. ◆**—é** *a Fam* (mentally) retarded.

demi, -ie [d(ə)mi] *a* half; **d.-journée** half-day; **une heure et demie** an hour and a half; (*horloge*) half past one; – *adv* (**à**) **d. plein** half-full; **à d. nu** half-naked; **ouvrir à d.** to open halfway; **faire les choses à d.** to do things by halves; – *nmf* (*moitié*) half; – *nm* (*verre*) (half-pint) glass of beer; *Fb* half-back; – *nf* (*à l'horloge*) half-hour.

demi-cercle [d(ə)miscrkl] *nm* semicircle. ◆**d.-douzaine** *nf* **une d.-douzaine (de)** a half-dozen, half a dozen. ◆**d.-finale** *nf Sp* semifinal. ◆**d.-frère** *nm* stepbrother. ◆**d.-heure** *nf* **une d.-heure** a half-hour, half an hour. ◆**d.-mesure** *nf* half-measure. ◆**d.-mot** *nm* **tu comprendras à d.-mot** you'll understand without my having to spell it out. ◆**d.-pension** *nf* half-board. ◆**d.-pensionnaire** *nmf* day boarder, *Am* day student. ◆**d.-saison** *nf* **de d.-saison** (*vêtement*) between seasons. ◆**d.-sel** *a inv* (*beurre*) slightly salted; (**fromage**) **d.-sel** cream cheese. ◆**d.-sœur** *nf* stepsister. ◆**d.-tarif** *nm & a inv* (*billet*) (**à**) **d.-tarif** half-price. ◆**d.-tour** *nm* about turn, *Am* about face; *Aut* U-turn; **faire d.-tour** to turn back.

démission [demisjɔ̃] *nf* resignation. ◆**démissionnaire** *a* (*ministre etc*) outgoing. ◆**démissionner** *vi* to resign.

démobiliser [demɔbilize] *vt* to demobilize. ◆**démobilisation** *nf* demobilization.

démocrate [demɔkrat] *nmf* democrat; – *a* democratic. ◆**démocratie** [-asi] *nf* democracy. ◆**démocratique** *a* democratic.

démod/er (se) [sədemɔde] *vpr* to go out of fashion. ◆**—é** *a* old-fashioned.

démographie [demɔgrafi] *nf* demography.

demoiselle [d(ə)mwazɛl] *nf* (*célibataire*) spinster, single woman; (*jeune fille*) young lady; **d. d'honneur** (*à un mariage*) bridesmaid; (*de reine*) maid of honour.

démolir [demɔlir] *vt* (*maison, jouet etc*) to demolish; (*projet etc*) to shatter; **d. qn** (*battre, discréditer*) *Fam* to tear s.o. to pieces. ◆**démolition** *nf* demolition; **en d.** being demolished.

démon [demɔ̃] *nm* demon; **petit d.** (*enfant*) little devil. ◆**démoniaque** *a* devilish, fiendish.

démonstrateur, -trice [demɔ̃stratœr, -tris] *nmf* (*dans un magasin etc*) demonstrator. ◆**démonstratif, -ive** *a* demonstrative. ◆**démonstration** *nf* demonstration; **d. de force** show of force.

démonter [demɔ̃te] *vt* (*assemblage*) to dismantle, take apart; (*installation*) to take down; **d. qn** (*troubler*) *Fig* to disconcert s.o.; **une mer démontée** a stormy sea; **— se d.** *vpr* to come apart; (*installation*) to come down; (*personne*) to be put out *ou* disconcerted.

démontrer [demɔ̃tre] *vt* to demonstrate, show.

démoraliser [demɔralize] *vt* to demoralize; **— se d.** *vpr* to become demoralized. ◆**démoralisation** *nf* demoralization.

démordre [demɔrdr] *vi* **il ne démordra pas de** (*son opinion etc*) he won't budge from.

démouler [demule] *vt* (*gâteau*) to turn out (*from its mould*).

démunir [demynir] *vt* **d. qn de** to deprive s.o. of; **se d. de** to part with.

démystifier [demistifje] *vt* (*public etc*) to disabuse; (*idée etc*) to debunk.

dénationaliser [denasjɔnalize] *vt* to denationalize.

dénatur/er [denatyre] *vt* (*propos, faits etc*) to misrepresent, distort. ◆**—é** (*goût, père etc*) unnatural.

dénégation [denegɑsjɔ̃] *nf* denial.

déneiger [deneʒe] *vt* to clear of snow.

dénicher [deniʃe] *vt* (*trouver*) to dig up, turn up; (*ennemi, fugitif*) to hunt out, flush out.

dénier [denje] *vt* to deny; (*responsabilité*) to disclaim, deny; **d. qch à qn** to deny s.o. sth.

dénigr/er [denigre] *vt* to denigrate, disparage. ◆**—ement** *nm* denigration, disparagement.

dénivellation [denivelɑsjɔ̃] *nf* unevenness; (*pente*) gradient; *pl* (*accidents*) bumps.

dénombrer [denɔ̃bre] *vt* to count, number.

dénomm/er [denɔme] *vt* to name. ◆**—é, -ée** *nmf* **un d. Dupont** a man named Dupont. ◆**dénomination** *nf* designation, name.

dénonc/er [denɔ̃se] *vt* (*injustice etc*) to denounce (**à** to); **d. qn** to inform on s.o., denounce s.o. (**à** to); *Scol* to tell on s.o. (**à** to); **— se d.** *vpr* to give oneself up (**à** to). ◆**dénonciateur, -trice** *nmf* informer. ◆**dénonciation** *nf* denunciation.

dénoter [denɔte] *vt* to denote.
dénouer [denwe] *vt* (*nœud, corde*) to undo, untie; (*cheveux*) to undo; (*situation, intrigue*) to unravel; (*problème, crise*) to clear up; — **se d.** *vpr* (*nœud*) to come undone *ou* untied; (*cheveux*) to come undone. ◆**dénouement** *nm* outcome, ending; *Th* dénouement.
dénoyauter [denwajote] *vt* (*prune etc*) to stone, *Am* to pit.
denrée [dɑ̃re] *nf* food(stuff); **denrées alimentaires** foodstuffs.
dense [dɑ̃s] *a* dense. ◆**densité** *nf* density.
dent [dɑ̃] *nf* tooth; (*de roue*) cog; (*de fourche*) prong; (*de timbre-poste*) perforation; **d. de sagesse** wisdom tooth; **rien à se mettre sous la d.** nothing to eat; **manger à belles dents/du bout des dents** to eat whole-heartedly/half-heartedly; **faire ses dents** (*enfant*) to be teething; **coup de d.** bite; **sur les dents** (*surmené*) exhausted; (*énervé*) on edge; **avoir une d. contre qn** to have it in for s.o. ◆**dentaire** *a* dental. ◆**dentée** *af* **roue d.** cogwheel. ◆**dentier** *nm* denture(s), (set of) false teeth. ◆**dentifrice** *nm* toothpaste. ◆**dentiste** *nmf* dentist; **chirurgien d.** dental surgeon. ◆**dentition** *nf* (*dents*) (set of) teeth.
dentelé [dɑ̃tle] *a* (*côte*) jagged; (*feuille*) serrated. ◆**dentelure** *nf* jagged outline *ou* edge.
dentelle [dɑ̃tɛl] *nf* lace.
dénud/er [denyde] *vt* to (lay) bare. ◆**—é** *a* bare.
dénué [denɥe] *a* **d. de** devoid of, without.
dénuement [denymɑ̃] *nm* destitution; **dans le d.** poverty-stricken.
déodorant [deɔdɔrɑ̃] *nm* deodorant.
dépann/er [depane] *vt* (*mécanisme*) to get going (again), repair; **d. qn** *Fam* to help s.o. out. ◆**—age** *nm* (emergency) repair; **voiture/service de d.** breakdown vehicle/service. ◆**—eur** *nm* repairman; *Aut* breakdown mechanic. ◆**—euse** *nf* (*voiture*) *Aut* breakdown lorry, *Am* wrecker, tow truck.
dépareillé [depareje] *a* (*chaussure etc*) odd, not matching; (*collection*) incomplete.
déparer [depare] *vt* to mar, spoil.
départ [depar] *nm* departure; (*début*) start, beginning; *Sp* start; **point/ligne de d.** starting point/post; **au d.** at the outset, at the start; **au d. de Paris/***etc* (*excursion etc*) departing from Paris/*etc*.
départager [departaʒe] *vt* (*concurrents*) to decide between; **d. les votes** to give the casting vote.
département [departəmɑ̃] *nm* department. ◆**départemental, -aux** *a* departmental; **route départementale** secondary road.
départir (se) [sədepartir] *vpr* **se d. de** (*attitude*) to depart from, abandon.
dépass/er [depase] *vt* (*durée, attente etc*) to go beyond, exceed; (*endroit*) to go past, go beyond; (*véhicule, bicyclette etc*) to overtake, pass; (*pouvoir*) to go beyond, overstep; **d. qn** (*en hauteur*) to be taller than s.o.; (*surclasser*) to be ahead of s.o.; **ça me dépasse** *Fig* that's (quite) beyond me; – *vi* (*jupon, clou etc*) to stick out, show. ◆**—é** *a* (*démodé*) outdated; (*incapable*) unable to cope. ◆**—ement** *nm Aut* overtaking, passing.
dépays/er [depeize] *vt* to disorientate, *Am* disorient. ◆**—ement** *nm* disorientation; (*changement*) change of scenery.
dépecer [depəse] *vt* (*animal*) to cut up, carve up.
dépêche [depɛʃ] *nf* telegram; (*diplomatique*) dispatch. ◆**dépêcher** *vt* to dispatch; — **se d.** *vpr* to hurry (up).
dépeign/er [depeɲe] *vt* **d. qn** to make s.o.'s hair untidy. ◆**—é** *a* **être d.** to have untidy hair; **sortir d.** to go out with untidy hair.
dépeindre* [depɛ̃dr] *vt* to depict, describe.
dépenaillé [depənaje] *a* in tatters *ou* rags.
dépend/re [depɑ̃dr] **1** *vi* to depend (**de** on); **d. de** (*appartenir à*) to belong to; (*être soumis à*) to be dependent on; **ça dépend de toi** that depends on you, that's up to you. **2** *vt* (*décrocher*) to take down. ◆**—ant** *a* dependent (**de** on). ◆**dépendance 1** *nf* dependence; **sous la d. de qn** under s.o.'s domination. **2** *nfpl* (*bâtiments*) outbuildings.
dépens [depɑ̃] *nmpl Jur* costs; **aux d. de** at the expense of; **apprendre à ses d.** to learn to one's cost.
dépense [depɑ̃s] *nf* (*action*) spending; (*frais*) expense, expenditure; (*d'électricité etc*) consumption; (*physique*) exertion. ◆**dépenser** *vt* (*argent*) to spend; (*électricité etc*) to use; (*forces*) to exert; (*énergie*) to expend; — **se d.** *vpr* to exert oneself. ◆**dépensier, -ière** *a* wasteful, extravagant.
déperdition [deperdisjɔ̃] *nf* (*de chaleur etc*) loss.
dépér/ir [deperir] *vi* (*personne*) to waste away; (*plante*) to wither; (*santé etc*) to decline. ◆**—issement** *nm* (*baisse*) decline.
dépêtrer [depɛtre] *vt* to extricate; — **se d.** *vpr* to extricate oneself (**de** from).
dépeupl/er [depœple] *vt* to depopulate. ◆**—ement** *nm* depopulation.

dépilatoire [depilatwar] *nm* hair-remover.
dépist/er [depiste] *vt* (*criminel etc*) to track down; (*maladie, fraude*) to detect. ◆**—age** *nm Méd* detection.
dépit [depi] *nm* resentment, chagrin; **en d. de** in spite of. ◆**dépiter** *vt* to vex, chagrin; **— se d.** *vpr* to feel resentment *ou* chagrin.
déplac/er [deplase] *vt* to shift, move; (*fonctionnaire*) to transfer; **— se d.** *vpr* to move (about); (*voyager*) to get about, travel (about). ◆**—é** *a* (*mal à propos*) out of place; **personne déplacée** (*réfugié*) displaced person. ◆**—ement** *nm* (*voyage*) (business *ou* professional) trip; (*d'ouragan, de troupes*) movement; **les déplacements** (*voyages*) travel(ling); **frais de d.** travelling expenses.
déplaire* [depler] *vi* **d. à qn** to displease s.o.; **cet aliment lui déplaît** he *ou* she dislikes this food; **n'en déplaise à** *Iron* with all due respect to; – *v imp* **il me déplaît de faire** I dislike doing, it displeases me to do; **— se d.** *vpr* to dislike it. ◆**déplaisant** *a* unpleasant, displeasing. ◆**déplaisir** *nm* displeasure.
dépli/er [deplije] *vt* to open out, unfold. ◆**—ant** *nm* (*prospectus*) leaflet.
déplor/er [deplore] *vt* (*regretter*) to deplore; (*la mort de qn*) to mourn (over), lament (over); **d. qn** to mourn (for) s.o.; **d. que** (+ *sub*) to deplore the fact that, regret that. ◆**—able** *a* deplorable, lamentable.
déployer [deplwaje] *vt* (*ailes*) to spread; (*journal, carte etc*) to unfold, spread (out); (*objets, courage etc*) to display; (*troupes*) to deploy; **— se d.** *vpr* (*drapeau*) to unfurl. ◆**déploiement** *nm* (*démonstration*) display; *Mil* deployment.
dépoli [depoli] *a* **verre d.** frosted glass.
déport/er [deporte] *vt* **1** (*exiler*) *Hist* to deport (to a penal colony); (*dans un camp de concentration*) *Hist* to send to a concentration camp, deport. **2** (*dévier*) to veer *ou* carry (off course). ◆**—é, -ée** *nmf* deportee; (concentration camp) inmate. ◆**déportation** *nf* deportation; internment (in a concentration camp).
dépos/er [depoze] *vt* (*poser*) to put down; (*laisser*) to leave; (*argent, lie*) to deposit; (*plainte*) to lodge; (*armes*) to lay down; (*gerbe*) to lay; (*ordures*) to dump; (*marque de fabrique*) to register; (*projet de loi*) to introduce; (*souverain*) to depose; **d. qn** *Aut* to drop s.o. (off), put s.o. off; **d. son bilan** *Fin* to go into liquidation, file for bankruptcy; – *vi Jur* to testify; (*liquide*) to leave a deposit; **— se d.** *vpr* (*poussière, lie*) to settle. ◆**dépositaire** *nmf Fin* agent; (*de secret*) custodian. ◆**déposition** *nf Jur* statement; (*de souverain*) deposing.
déposséder [deposede] *vt* to deprive, dispossess (**de** of).
dépôt [depo] *nm* (*d'ordures etc*) dumping, (*lieu*) dump; (*de gerbe*) laying; (*d'autobus, de trains*) depot; (*entrepôt*) warehouse; (*argent*) deposit; (*de vin*) deposit, sediment; **d. (calcaire)** (*de chaudière etc*) deposit; **laisser qch à qn en d.** to give s.o. sth for safekeeping *ou* in trust.
dépotoir [depɔtwar] *nm* rubbish dump, *Am* garbage dump.
dépouille [depuj] *nf* hide, skin; (*de serpent*) slough; *pl* (*butin*) spoils; **d. (mortelle)** mortal remains. ◆**dépouill/er** *vt* (*animal*) to skin, flay; (*analyser*) to go through, analyse; **d. de** (*dégarnir*) to strip of; (*déposséder*) to deprive of; **se d. de** to rid *ou* divest oneself of, cast off; **d. un scrutin** to count votes. ◆**—é** *a* (*arbre*) bare; (*style*) austere, spare; **d. de** bereft of. ◆**—ement** *nm* (*de document etc*) analysis; (*privation*) deprivation; (*sobriété*) austerity; **d. du scrutin** counting of the votes.
dépourvu [depurvy] *a* **d. de** devoid of; **prendre qn au d.** to catch s.o. unawares *ou* off his guard.
dépraver [deprave] *vt* to deprave. ◆**dépravation** *nf* depravity.
dépréci/er [depresje] *vt* (*dénigrer*) to disparage; (*monnaie, immeuble etc*) to depreciate; **— se d.** *vpr* (*baisser*) to depreciate, lose (its) value. ◆**dépréciation** *nf* depreciation.
déprédations [depredɑsjɔ̃] *nfpl* damage, ravages.
dépression [depresjɔ̃] *nf* depression; **zone de d.** trough of low pressure; **d. nerveuse** nervous breakdown; **d. économique** slump. ◆**dépressif, -ive** *a* depressive. ◆**déprime** *nf* **la d.** (*dépression*) *Fam* the blues. ◆**déprim/er** *vt* to depress. ◆**—é** *a* depressed.
depuis [dəpɥi] *prép* since; **d. lundi** since Monday; **d. qu'elle est partie** since she left; **j'habite ici d. un mois** I've been living here for a month; **d. quand êtes-vous là?** how long have you been here?; **d. peu/longtemps** for a short/long time; **d. Paris jusqu'à Londres** from Paris to London; – *adv* since (then), ever since.
députation [depytɑsjɔ̃] *nf* (*groupe*) deputation, delegation; **candidat à la d.** parliamentary candidate. ◆**député** *nm* dele-

gate, deputy; (*au parlement*) deputy, = *Br* MP, = *Am* congressman, congresswoman.

déracin/er [derasine] *vt* (*personne, arbre etc*) to uproot; (*préjugés etc*) to eradicate, root out. **◆—ement** *nm* uprooting; eradication.

déraill/er [derαje] *vi* **1** (*train*) to jump the rails, be derailed; **faire d.** to derail. **2** (*divaguer*) *Fam* to drivel, talk through one's hat. **◆—ement** *nm* (*de train*) derailment. **◆—eur** *nm* (*de bicyclette*) derailleur (gear change).

déraisonnable [derezɔnabl] *a* unreasonable. **◆déraisonner** *vi* to talk nonsense.

dérang/er [derɑ̃ʒe] *vt* (*affaires*) to disturb, upset; (*estomac*) to upset; (*projets*) to mess up, upset; (*vêtements*) to mess up; (*cerveau, esprit*) to derange; **d. qn** to disturb *ou* bother *ou* trouble s.o.; **je viendrai si ça ne te dérange pas** I'll come if that doesn't put you out *ou* if that's not imposing; **ça vous dérange si je fume?** do you mind if I smoke?; **— se d.** *vpr* to put oneself to a lot of trouble (**pour faire** to do), (*se déplacer*) to move; **ne te dérange pas!** don't trouble yourself!, don't bother! **◆—ement** *nm* (*gêne*) bother, inconvenience; (*désordre*) disorder; **en d.** (*téléphone etc*) out of order.

dérap/er [derape] *vi* to skid. **◆—age** *nm* skid; (*des prix, de l'inflation*) *Fig* loss of control (**de** over).

dératé [derate] *nm* **courir comme un d.** to run like mad.

dérégl/er [deregle] *vt* (*mécanisme*) to put out of order; (*estomac, habitudes*) to upset; (*esprit*) to unsettle; **— se d.** *vpr* (*montre, appareil*) to go wrong. **◆—é** *a* out of order; (*vie, mœurs*) dissolute, wild; (*imagination*) wild. **◆dérèglement** *nm* (*de mécanisme*) breakdown; (*d'esprit*) disorder; (*d'estomac*) upset.

dérider [deride] *vt*, **— se d.** *vpr* to cheer up.

dérision [derizjɔ̃] *nf* derision, mockery; **tourner en d.** to mock, deride; **par d.** derisively; **de d.** derisive. **◆dérisoire** *a* ridiculous, derisory, derisive.

dérive [deriv] *nf Nau* drift; **partir à la d.** (*navire*) to drift out to sea; **aller à la d.** (*navire*) to go adrift; (*entreprise etc*) *Fig* to drift (towards ruin). **◆dériv/er** *vi Nau Av* to drift; **d. de** (*venir*) to derive from, be derived from; – *vt* (*cours d'eau*) to divert; *Ling* to derive (**de** from). **◆—é** *nm Ling Ch* derivative; (*produit*) by-product. **◆dérivatif** *nm* distraction (**à** from). **◆dérivation** *nf* (*de cours d'eau*) diversion; *Ling* derivation; (*déviation routière*) bypass.

dermatologie [dɛrmatɔlɔʒi] *nf* dermatology.

dernier -ière [dɛrnje, -jɛr] *a* last; (*nouvelles, mode*) latest; (*étage*) top; (*degré*) highest; (*qualité*) lowest; **le d. rang** the back *ou* last row; **ces derniers mois** these past few months, these last *ou* final months; **de la dernière importance** of (the) utmost importance; **en d.** last; – *nmf* last (person *ou* one); **ce d.** (*de deux*) the latter; (*de plusieurs*) the last-mentioned; **être le d. de la classe** to be (at the) bottom of the class; **le d. des derniers** the lowest of the low; **le d. de mes soucis** the least of my worries. **◆d.-né, ◆dernière-née** *nmf* youngest (child). **◆dernièrement** *adv* recently.

dérob/er [derɔbe] *vt* (*voler*) to steal (**à** from); (*cacher*) to hide (**à** from); **— se d.** *vpr* to get out of one's obligations; (*s'éloigner*) to slip away; (*éviter de répondre*) to dodge the issue; **se d. à** (*obligations*) to shirk, get out of; (*regards*) to hide from; **ses jambes se sont dérobées sous lui** his legs gave way beneath him. **◆—é** *a* (*porte etc*) hidden, secret; **à la dérobée** *adv* on the sly, stealthily. **◆dérobade** *nf* dodge, evasion.

déroger [derɔʒe] *vi* **d. à une règle**/*etc* to depart from a rule/*etc.* **◆dérogation** *nf* exemption, (special) dispensation.

dérouiller [deruje] *vt* **d. qn** (*battre*) *Arg* to thrash *ou* thump s.o.; **se d. les jambes** *Fam* to stretch one's legs.

déroul/er [derule] *vt* (*carte etc*) to unroll; (*film*) to unwind; **— se d.** *vpr* (*événement*) to take place, pass off; (*paysage, souvenirs*) to unfold; (*récit*) to develop. **◆—ement** *nm* (*d'une action*) unfolding, development; (*cours*) course;

dérouter [derute] *vt* (*avion, navire*) to divert, reroute; (*candidat etc*) to baffle; (*poursuivant*) to throw off the scent.

derrick [derik] *nm* derrick.

derrière [dɛrjɛr] *prép & adv* behind; **d. moi** behind me, *Am* in back of me; **assis d.** (*dans une voiture*) sitting in the back; **de d.** (*roue*) back, rear; (*pattes*) hind; **par d.** (*attaquer*) from behind, from the rear; – *nm* (*de maison etc*) back, rear; (*fesses*) behind, bottom.

des [de] *voir* **de**[1,2], **le.**

dès [dɛ] *prép* from; **d. cette époque** (as) from that time, from that time on; **d. le début** (right) from the start; **d. son enfance** since *ou* from (his *ou* her) childhood; **d. le**

sixième siècle as early as *ou* as far back as the sixth century; **d. l'aube** at (the crack of) dawn; **d. qu'elle viendra** as soon as she comes.

désabusé [dezabyze] *a* disenchanted, disillusioned.

désaccord [dezakɔr] *nm* disagreement. ◆**désaccordé** *a Mus* out of tune.

désaccoutumer (se) [sədezakutyme] *vpr* se **d. de** to lose the habit of.

désaffecté [dezafɛkte] *a* (*école etc*) disused.

désaffection [dezafɛksjɔ̃] *nf* loss of affection, disaffection (**pour** for).

désagréable [dezagreabl] *a* unpleasant, disagreeable. ◆**—ment** [-əmɑ̃] *adv* unpleasantly.

désagréger [dezagreʒe] *vt*, **— se d.** *vpr* to disintegrate, break up. ◆**désagrégation** *nf* disintegration.

désagrément [dezagremɑ̃] *nm* annoyance, trouble.

désaltér/er [dezaltere] *vt* **d. qn** to quench s.o.'s thirst; **se d.** to quench one's thirst. ◆**—ant** *a* thirst-quenching.

désamorcer [dezamɔrse] *vt* (*obus, situation*) to defuse.

désappointer [dezapwɛ̃te] *vt* to disappoint.

désapprouver [dezapruve] *vt* to disapprove of; – *vi* to disapprove. ◆**désapprobateur, -trice** *a* disapproving. ◆**désapprobation** *nf* disapproval.

désarçonner [dezarsɔne] *vt* (*jockey*) to throw, unseat; (*déconcerter*) *Fig* to nonpluss, throw.

désarm/er [dezarme] *vt* (*émouvoir*) & *Mil* to disarm; – *vi Mil* to disarm; (*céder*) to let up. ◆**—ant** *a* (*charme etc*) disarming. ◆**—é** *a* (*sans défense*) unarmed; *Fig* helpless. ◆**—ement** *nm* (*de nation*) disarmament.

désarroi [dezarwa] *nm* (*angoisse*) distress.

désarticuler [dezartikyle] *vt* (*membre*) to dislocate.

désastre [dezastr] *nm* disaster. ◆**désastreux, -euse** *a* disastrous.

désavantage [dezavɑ̃taʒ] *nm* disadvantage, handicap; (*inconvénient*) drawback, disadvantage. ◆**désavantager** *vt* to put at a disadvantage, handicap. ◆**désavantageux, -euse** *a* disadvantageous.

désaveu, -x [dezavø] *nm* repudiation. ◆**désavouer** *vt* (*livre, personne etc*) to disown, repudiate.

désaxé, -ée [dezakse] *a* & *nmf* unbalanced (person).

desceller [desele] *vt* (*pierre etc*) to loosen; **— se d.** *vpr* to come loose.

descend/re [desɑ̃dr] *vi* (*aux* **être**) to come *ou* go down, descend (**de** from); (*d'un train etc*) to get off *ou* out, alight (**de** from); (*d'un arbre*) to climb down (**de** from); (*nuit, thermomètre*) to fall; (*marée*) to go out; **d. à** (*une bassesse*) to stoop to; **d. à l'hôtel** to put up at a hotel; **d. de** (*être issu de*) to be descended from; **d. de cheval** to dismount; **d. en courant/flânant/***etc* to run/stroll/*etc* down; – *vt* (*aux* **avoir**) (*escalier*) to come *ou* go down, descend; (*objets*) to bring *ou* take down; (*avion*) to bring *ou* shoot down; **d. qn** (*tuer*) *Fam* to bump s.o. off. ◆**—ant, -ante 1** *a* descending; (*marée*) outgoing. **2** *nmf* (*personne*) descendant. ◆**descendance** *nf* (*enfants*) descendants; (*origine*) descent.

descente [desɑ̃t] *nf* (*action*) descent; (*irruption*) raid (**dans** upon); (*en parachute*) drop; (*pente*) slope; **la d. des bagages** bringing *ou* taking down the luggage; **il fut accueilli à sa d. d'avion** he was met as he got off the plane; **d. à skis** downhill run; **d. de lit** (*tapis*) bedside rug.

descriptif, -ive [dɛskriptif, -iv] *a* descriptive. ◆**description** *nf* description.

déségrégation [desegregasjɔ̃] *nf* desegregation.

désemparé [dezɑ̃pare] *a* distraught, at a loss; (*navire*) crippled.

désemplir [dezɑ̃plir] *vi* **ce magasin/***etc* **ne désemplit pas** this shop/*etc* is always crowded.

désenchant/er [dezɑ̃ʃɑ̃te] *vt* to disenchant. ◆**—ement** *nm* disenchantment.

désencombrer [dezɑ̃kɔ̃bre] *vt* (*passage etc*) to clear.

désenfler [dezɑ̃fle] *vi* to go down, become less swollen.

déséquilibre [dezekilibr] *nm* (*inégalité*) imbalance; (*mental*) unbalance; **en d.** (*meuble etc*) unsteady. ◆**déséquilibrer** *vt* to throw off balance; (*esprit, personne*) *Fig* to unbalance.

désert [dezɛr] *a* deserted; **île déserte** desert island; – *nm* desert, wilderness. ◆**désertique** *a* (*région etc*) desert-.

déserter [dezɛrte] *vti* to desert. ◆**déserteur** *nm Mil* deserter. ◆**désertion** *nf* desertion.

désespér/er [dezɛspere] *vi* to despair (**de** of); – *vt* to drive to despair; **— se d.** *vpr* to (be in) despair. ◆**—ant** *a* (*enfant etc*) that drives one to despair, hopeless. ◆**—é, -ée** *a* (*personne*) in despair, despairing; (*cas, situation*) desperate, hopeless; (*efforts, cris*) desperate; – *nmf* (*suicidé*) person driven to despair *ou* desperation. ◆**–ément** *adv* desperately. ◆**désespoir** *nm* despair; **au d.** in despair; **en d. de cause** in desperation, as a (desperate) last resort.

déshabiller [dezabije] *vt* to undress, strip; **— se d.** *vpr* to get undressed, undress.

déshabituer [dezabitɥe] *vt* **d. qn de** to break s.o. of the habit of.

désherb/er [dezɛrbe] *vti* to weed. ◆**–ant** *nm* weed killer.

déshérit/er [dezerite] *vt* to disinherit. ◆**–é** *a* (*pauvre*) underprivileged; (*laid*) ill-favoured.

déshonneur [dezɔnœr] *nm* dishonour, disgrace. ◆**déshonor/er** *vt* to disgrace, dishonour. ◆**–ant** *a* dishonourable.

déshydrater [dezidrate] *vt* to dehydrate; **— se d.** *vpr* to become dehydrated.

désigner [deziɲe] *vt* (*montrer*) to point to, point out; (*élire*) to appoint, designate; (*signifier*) to indicate, designate; **ses qualités le désignent pour** his qualities mark him out for. ◆**désignation** *nf* designation.

désillusion [dezilyzjɔ̃] *nf* disillusion(ment). ◆**désillusionner** *vt* to disillusion.

désincarné [dezɛ̃karne] *a* (*esprit*) disembodied.

désinence [dezinɑ̃s] *nf Gram* ending.

désinfect/er [dezɛ̃fɛkte] *vt* to disinfect. ◆**–ant** *nm* & *a* disinfectant. ◆**désinfection** *nf* disinfection.

désinformation [dezɛ̃fɔrmasjɔ̃] *nf Pol* misinformation.

désintégrer (se) [sədezɛ̃tegre] *vpr* to disintegrate. ◆**désintégration** *nf* disintegration.

désintéress/er (se) [sədezɛ̃terese] *vpr* **se d. de** to lose interest in, take no further interest in. ◆**–é** *a* (*altruiste*) disinterested. ◆**–ement** [-ɛsmɑ̃] *nm* (*altruisme*) disinterestedness. ◆**désintérêt** *nm* lack of interest.

désintoxiquer [dezɛ̃tɔksike] *vt* (*alcoolique, drogué*) to cure.

désinvolte [dezɛ̃vɔlt] *a* (*dégagé*) easy-going, casual; (*insolent*) offhand, casual. ◆**désinvolture** *nf* casualness; offhandedness.

désir [dezir] *nm* desire, wish. ◆**désirable** *a* desirable. ◆**désirer** *vt* to want, desire; (*convoiter*) to desire; **je désire venir** I would like to come, I wish *ou* want to come; **je désire que tu viennes** I want you to come; **ça laisse à d.** it leaves something *ou* a lot to be desired. ◆**désireux, -euse** *a* **d. de faire** anxious *ou* eager to do, desirous of doing.

désist/er (se) [sədeziste] *vpr* (*candidat etc*) to withdraw. ◆**–ement** *nm* withdrawal.

désobé/ir [dezɔbeir] *vi* to disobey; **d. à qn** to disobey s.o. ◆**–issant** *a* disobedient. ◆**désobéissance** *nf* disobedience (**à** to).

désobligeant [dezɔbliʒɑ̃] *a* disagreeable, unkind.

désodorisant [dezɔdɔrizɑ̃] *nm* air freshener.

désœuvré [dezœvre] *a* idle, unoccupied. ◆**désœuvrement** *nm* idleness.

désol/er [dezɔle] *vt* to distress, upset (very much); **— se d.** *vpr* to be distressed *ou* upset (**de** at). ◆**–ant** *a* distressing, upsetting. ◆**–é** *a* (*région*) desolate; (*affligé*) distressed; **être d.** (*navré*) to be sorry (**que** (+ *sub*) that, **de faire** to do). ◆**désolation** *nf* (*peine*) distress, grief.

désolidariser (se) [sədesɔlidarize] *vpr* to dissociate oneself (**de** from).

désopilant [dezɔpilɑ̃] *a* hilarious, screamingly funny.

désordre [dezɔrdr] *nm* (*de papiers, affaires, idées*) mess, muddle, disorder; (*de cheveux, pièce*) untidiness; *Méd* disorder; *pl* (*émeutes*) disorder, unrest; **en d.** untidy, messy. ◆**désordonné** *a* (*personne, chambre*) untidy, messy.

désorganiser [dezɔrganize] *vt* to disorganize. ◆**désorganisation** *nf* disorganization.

désorienter [dezɔrjɑ̃te] *vt* **d. qn** to disorientate *ou Am* disorient s.o., make s.o. lose his bearings; (*déconcerter*) to bewilder s.o. ◆**désorientation** *nf* disorientation.

désormais [dezɔrmɛ] *adv* from now on, in future, henceforth.

désosser [dezɔse] *vt* (*viande*) to bone.

despote [dɛspɔt] *nm* despot. ◆**despotique** *a* despotic. ◆**despotisme** *nm* despotism.

desquels, desquelles [dekɛl] *voir* **lequel.**

dessaisir (se) [sədesezir] *vpr* **se d. de qch** to part with sth, relinquish sth.

dessaler [desale] *vt* (*poisson etc*) to remove the salt from (*by smoking*).

dessécher [deseʃe] *vt* (*végétation*) to dry up, wither; (*gorge, bouche*) to dry, parch; (*fruits*) to desiccate, dry; (*cœur*) to harden; **— se d.** *vpr* (*plante*) to wither, dry up; (*peau*) to dry (up), get dry; (*maigrir*) to waste away.

dessein [desɛ̃] *nm* aim, design; **dans le d. de faire** with the aim of doing; **à d.** intentionally.

desserrer [desere] *vt* (*ceinture etc*) to loosen, slacken; (*poing*) to open, unclench;

(*frein*) to release; **il n'a pas desserré les dents** he didn't open his mouth; **— se d.** *vpr* to come loose.

dessert [desɛr] *nm* dessert, sweet.

desserte [desɛrt] *nf* **assurer la d. de** (*village etc*) to provide a (bus *ou* train) service to. **◆desservir** *vt* **1** (*table*) to clear (away). **2** **d. qn** to harm s.o., do s.o. a disservice. **3** **l'autobus/*etc* dessert ce village** the bus/*etc* provides a service to *ou* stops at this village; **ce quartier est bien desservi** this district is well served by public transport.

dessin [desɛ̃] *nm* drawing; (*rapide*) sketch; (*motif*) design, pattern; (*contour*) outline; **d. animé** *Cin* cartoon; **d. humoristique** *Journ* cartoon; **école de d.** art school; **planche à d.** drawing board. **◆dessinateur, -trice** *nmf* drawer; sketcher; **d. humoristique** cartoonist; **d. de modes** dress designer; **d. industriel** draughtsman, *Am* draftsman. **◆dessiner** *vt* to draw; (*rapidement*) to sketch; (*meuble, robe etc*) to design; (*indiquer*) to outline, trace; **d. (bien) la taille** (*vêtement*) to show off the figure; **— se d.** *vpr* (*colline etc*) to stand out, be outlined; (*projet*) to take shape.

dessoûler [desule] *vti Fam* to sober up.

dessous [d(ə)su] *adv* under(neath), beneath, below; **en d.** (*sous*) under(neath); (*agir*) *Fig* in an underhand way; **vêtement de d.** undergarment; **drap de d.** bottom sheet; – *nm* underneath; *pl* (*vêtements*) underclothes; **d. de table** backhander, bribe; **les gens du d.** the people downstairs *ou* below; **avoir le d.** to be defeated, get the worst of it. **◆d.-de-plat** *nm inv* table mat.

dessus [d(ə)sy] *adv* (*marcher, écrire*) on it; (*monter*) on top (of it), on it; (*lancer, passer*) over it; **de d. la table** off *ou* from the table; **vêtement de d.** outer garment; **drap de d.** top sheet; **par-d.** (*sauter etc*) over (it); **par-d. tout** above all; – *nm* top; (*de chaussure*) upper; **avoir le d.** to have the upper hand, get the best of it; **les gens du d.** the people upstairs *ou* above. **◆d.-de-lit** *nm inv* bedspread.

déstabiliser [destabilize] *vt* to destabilize.

destin [dɛstɛ̃] *nm* fate, destiny. **◆destinée** *nf* fate, destiny (*of an individual*).

destin/er [dɛstine] *vt* **d. qch à qn** to intend *ou* mean sth for s.o.; **d. qn à** (*carrière, fonction*) to intend *ou* destine s.o. for; **se d. à** (*carrière etc*) to intend *ou* mean to take up; **destiné à mourir/*etc*** (*condamné*) destined *ou* fated to die/*etc*. **◆destinataire** *nmf* addressee. **◆destination** *nf* (*usage*) purpose; (*lieu*) destination; **à d. de** (*train etc*) (going) to, (bound) for.

destituer [dɛstitɥe] *vt* (*fonctionnaire etc*) to dismiss (from office). **◆destitution** *nf* dismissal.

destructeur, -trice [dɛstryktœr, -tris] *a* destructive; – *nmf* (*personne*) destroyer. **◆destructif, -ive** *a* destructive. **◆destruction** *nf* destruction.

désuet, -ète [desɥɛ, -ɛt] *a* antiquated, obsolete.

désunir [dezynir] *vt* (*famille etc*) to divide, disunite. **◆désunion** *nf* disunity, dissension.

détach/er¹ [detaʃe] *vt* (*ceinture, vêtement*) to undo; (*nœud*) to untie, undo; (*personne, mains*) to untie; (*ôter*) to take off, detach; (*mots*) to pronounce clearly; **d. qn** (*libérer*) to let s.o. loose; (*affecter*) to transfer s.o. (on assignment) (**à** to); **d. les yeux de qn/qch** to take one's eyes off s.o./sth; **— se d.** *vpr* (*chien, prisonnier*) to break loose; (*se dénouer*) to come undone; **se d. (de qch)** (*fragment*) to come off (sth); **se d. de** (*amis*) to break away from, grow apart from; **se d. (sur)** (*ressortir*) to stand out (against). **◆—é** *a* **1** (*nœud*) loose, undone. **2** (*air, ton etc*) detached. **◆—ement** *nm* **1** (*indifférence*) detachment. **2** (*de fonctionnaire*) (temporary) transfer; *Mil* detachment.

détach/er² [detaʃe] *vt* (*linge etc*) to remove the spots *ou* stains from. **◆—ant** *nm* stain remover.

détail [detaj] *nm* **1** detail; **en d.** in detail; **le d. de** (*dépenses etc*) a detailing *ou* breakdown of. **2** **de d.** (*magasin, prix*) retail; **vendre au d.** to sell retail; (*par petites quantités*) to sell separately; **faire le d.** to retail to the public. **◆détaill/er** *vt* **1** (*vendre*) to sell in small quantities *ou* separately; (*au détail*) to (sell) retail. **2** (*énumérer*) to detail. **◆—ant, -ante** *nmf* retailer. **◆—é** *a* (*récit etc*) detailed.

détaler [detale] *vi Fam* to run off, make tracks.

détartrer [detartre] *vt* (*chaudière, dents etc*) to scale.

détaxer [detakse] *vt* (*denrée etc*) to reduce the tax on; (*supprimer*) to take the tax off; **produit détaxé** duty-free article.

détecter [detɛkte] *vt* to detect. **◆détecteur** *nm* (*appareil*) detector. **◆détection** *nf* detection.

détective [detɛktiv] *nm* **d. (privé)** (private) detective.

déteindre* [detɛ̃dr] *vi* (*couleur ou étoffe au lavage*) to run; (*au soleil*) to fade; **ton**

tablier bleu a déteint sur ma chemise the blue of your apron has come off on(to) my shirt; **d. sur qn** (*influencer*) to leave one's mark on s.o.

dételer [detle] *vt* (*chevaux*) to unhitch, unharness.

détend/re [detɑ̃dr] *vt* (*arc etc*) to slacken, relax; (*situation, atmosphère*) to ease; **d. qn** to relax s.o.; — **se d.** *vpr* to slacken, get slack; to ease; (*se reposer*) to relax; (*rapports*) to become less strained. ◆**—u** *a* (*visage, atmosphère*) relaxed; (*ressort, câble*) slack. ◆**détente** *nf* **1** (*d'arc*) slackening; (*de relations*) easing of tension, *Pol* détente; (*repos*) relaxation; (*saut*) leap, spring. **2** (*gâchette*) trigger.

déten/ir* [detnir] *vt* to hold; (*secret, objet volé*) to be in possession of; (*prisonnier*) to hold, detain. ◆**—u, -ue** *nmf* prisoner. ◆**détenteur, -trice** *nmf* (*de record etc*) holder. ◆**détention** *nf* (*d'armes*) possession; (*captivité*) detention; **d. préventive** *Jur* custody.

détergent [deterʒɑ̃] *nm* detergent.

détériorer [deterjɔre] *vt* (*abîmer*) to damage; — **se d.** *vpr* (*empirer*) to deteriorate. ◆**détérioration** *nf* damage (**de** to); (*d'une situation etc*) deterioration (**de** in).

détermin/er [determine] *vt* (*préciser*) to determine; (*causer*) to bring about; **d. qn à faire** to induce s.o. to do, make s.o. do; **se d. à faire** to resolve *ou* determine to do. ◆**—ant** *a* (*motif*) determining, deciding; (*rôle*) decisive. ◆**—é** *a* (*précis*) specific; (*résolu*) determined. ◆**détermination** *nf* (*fermeté*) determination; (*résolution*) resolve.

déterrer [detere] *vt* to dig up, unearth.

détest/er [deteste] *vt* to hate, detest; **d. faire** to hate doing *ou* to do, detest doing. ◆**—able** *a* awful, foul.

détonateur [detɔnatœr] *nm* detonator. ◆**détonation** *nf* explosion, blast.

détonner [detɔne] *vi* (*contraster*) to jar, be out of place.

détour [detur] *nm* (*de route etc*) bend, curve; (*crochet*) detour; **sans d.** (*parler*) without beating about the bush; **faire des détours** (*route*) to wind.

détourn/er [deturne] *vt* (*fleuve, convoi etc*) to divert; (*tête*) to turn (away); (*coups*) to ward off; (*conversation, sens*) to change; (*fonds*) to embezzle, misappropriate; (*avion*) to hijack; **d. qn de** (*son devoir, ses amis*) to take *ou* turn s.o. away from; (*sa route*) to lead s.o. away from; (*projet*) to talk s.o. out of; **d. les yeux** to look away, avert one's eyes; — **se d.** *vpr* to turn aside *ou* away; **se d. de** (*chemin*) to wander *ou* stray from. ◆**—é** *a* (*chemin, moyen*) roundabout, indirect. ◆**—ement** *nm* (*de cours d'eau*) diversion; **d.** (**d'avion**) hijack(ing); **d.** (**de fonds**) embezzlement.

détraqu/er [detrake] *vt* (*mécanisme*) to break, put out of order; — **se d.** *vpr* (*machine*) to go wrong; **se d. l'estomac** to upset one's stomach; **se d. la santé** to ruin one's health. ◆**—é, -ée** *a* out of order; (*cerveau*) deranged; — *nmf* crazy *ou* deranged person.

détremper [detrɑ̃pe] *vt* to soak, saturate.

détresse [detrɛs] *nf* distress; **en d.** (*navire, âme*) in distress; **dans la d.** (*misère*) in (great) distress.

détriment de (au) [odetrimɑ̃də] *prép* to the detriment of.

détritus [detritys] *nmpl* refuse, rubbish.

détroit [detrwa] *nm Géog* strait(s), sound.

détromper [detrɔ̃pe] *vt* **d. qn** to undeceive s.o., put s.o. right; **détrompez-vous!** don't you believe it!

détrôner [detrone] *vt* (*souverain*) to dethrone; (*supplanter*) to supersede, oust.

détrousser [detruse] *vt* (*voyageur etc*) to rob.

détruire* [detrɥir] *vt* (*ravager, tuer*) to destroy; (*projet, santé*) to ruin, wreck, destroy.

dette [dɛt] *nf* debt; **faire des dettes** to run *ou* get into debt; **avoir des dettes** to be in debt.

deuil [dœj] *nm* (*affliction, vêtements*) mourning; (*mort de qn*) bereavement; **porter le d., être en d.** to be in mourning.

deux [dø] *a* & *nm* two; **d. fois** twice, two times; **tous (les) d.** both; **en moins de d.** *Fam* in no time. ◆**d.-pièces** *nm inv* (*vêtement*) two-piece; (*appartement*) two-roomed flat *ou Am* apartment. ◆**d.-points** *nm inv Gram* colon. ◆**d.-roues** *nm inv* two-wheeled vehicle. ◆**d.-temps** *nm inv* two-stroke (engine).

deuxième [døzjɛm] *a* & *nmf* second. ◆**—ment** *adv* secondly.

dévaler [devale] *vt* (*escalier etc*) to hurtle *ou* race *ou* rush down; – *vi* (*tomber*) to tumble down, come tumbling down.

dévaliser [devalize] *vt* (*détrousser*) to clean out, strip, rob (of everything).

dévaloriser [devalɔrize] **1** *vt*, — **se d.** *vpr* (*monnaie*) to depreciate. **2** *vt* (*humilier etc*) to devalue, disparage. ◆**dévalorisation** *nf* (*de monnaie*) depreciation.

dévaluer [devalɥe] *vt* (*monnaie*) & *Fig* to devalue. ◆**dévaluation** *nf* devaluation.

devancer [d(ə)vɑ̃se] *vt* to get *ou* be ahead of; (*question etc*) to anticipate, forestall; (*surpasser*) to outstrip; **tu m'as devancé** (*action*) you did it before me; (*lieu*) you got there before me. ◆**devancier, -ière** *nmf* predecessor.

devant [d(ə)vɑ̃] *prép & adv* in front (of); **d. (l'hôtel/***etc***)** in front (of the hotel/*etc*); **marcher d. (qn)** to walk in front (of s.o.) *ou* ahead (of s.o.); **passer d. (l'église/***etc***)** to go past (the church/*etc*); **assis d.** (*dans une voiture*) sitting in the front; **l'avenir est d. toi** the future is ahead of you; **loin d.** a long way ahead *ou* in front; **d. le danger** (*confronté à*) in the face of danger; **d. mes yeux/la loi** before my eyes/the law; – *nm* front; **de d.** (*roue, porte*) front; **patte de d.** foreleg; **par d.** from *ou* at the front; **prendre les devants** (*action*) to take the initiative. ◆**devanture** *nf* (*vitrine*) shop window; (*façade*) shop front.

dévaster [devaste] *vt* (*ruiner*) to devastate. ◆**dévastation** *nf* devastation.

déveine [devɛn] *nf Fam* tough *ou* bad luck.

développ/er [devlɔpe] *vt* to develop; *Phot* to develop, process; — **se d.** *vpr* to develop. ◆**—ement** *nm* development; *Phot* developing, processing; **les pays en voie de d.** the developing countries.

devenir* [dəvnir] *vi* (*aux* **être**) to become; (*vieux, difficile etc*) to get, grow, become; (*rouge, bleu etc*) to turn, go, become; **d. un papillon/un homme/***etc* to grow into a butterfly/a man/*etc*; **qu'est-il devenu?** what's become of him *ou* it?, where's he *ou* it got to?; **qu'est-ce que tu deviens?** *Fam* how are you doing?

dévergond/er (se) [sədevɛrgɔ̃de] *vpr* to fall into dissolute ways. ◆**—é** *a* dissolute, licentious.

déverser [devɛrse] *vt* (*liquide, rancune*) to pour out; (*bombes, ordures*) to dump; — **se d.** *vpr* (*liquide*) to empty, pour out (**dans** into).

dévêtir [devetir] *vt*, — **se d.** *vpr Litt* to undress.

dévier [devje] *vt* (*circulation, conversation*) to divert; (*coup, rayons*) to deflect; – *vi* (*de ses principes etc*) to deviate (**de** from); (*de sa route*) to veer (off course). ◆**déviation** *nf* deflection; deviation; (*chemin*) bypass; (*itinéraire provisoire*) diversion.

deviner [d(ə)vine] *vt* to guess (**que** that); (*avenir*) to predict; **d. (le jeu de) qn** to see through s.o. ◆**devinette** *nf* riddle.

devis [d(ə)vi] *nm* estimate (*of cost of work to be done*).

dévisager [devizaʒe] *vt* **d. qn** to stare at s.o.

devise [d(ə)viz] *nf* (*légende*) motto; *pl* (*monnaie*) (foreign) currency.

dévisser [devise] *vt* to unscrew, undo; — **se d.** *vpr* (*bouchon etc*) to come undone.

dévoiler [devwale] *vt* (*révéler*) to disclose; (*statue*) to unveil; — **se d.** *vpr* (*mystère*) to come to light.

devoir* [1] [d(ə)vwar] *v aux* **1** (*nécessité*) **je dois refuser** I must refuse, I have (got) to refuse; **j'ai dû refuser** I had to refuse. **2** (*forte probabilité*) **il doit être tard** it must be late; **elle a dû oublier** she must have forgotten; **il ne doit pas être bête** he can't be stupid. **3** (*obligation*) **tu dois l'aider** you should help her, you ought to help her; **il aurait dû venir** he should have come, he ought to have come; **vous devriez rester** you should stay, you ought to stay. **4** (*supposition*) **elle doit venir** she should be coming, she's supposed to be coming, she's due to come; **le train devait arriver à midi** the train was due (to arrive) at noon; **je devais le voir** I was (due) to see him.

devoir* [2] [d(ə)vwar] **1** *vt* to owe; **d. qch à qn** to owe s.o. sth, owe sth to s.o.; **l'argent qui m'est dû** the money due to *ou* owing to me, the money owed (to) me; **se d. à** to have to devote oneself to; **comme il se doit** as is proper. **2** *nm* duty; *Scol* exercise; **devoir(s)** (*travail à faire à la maison*) *Scol* homework; **présenter ses devoirs à qn** to pay one's respects to s.o.

dévolu [devɔly] **1** *a* **d. à qn** (*pouvoirs, tâche*) vested in s.o., allotted to s.o. **2** *nm* **jeter son d. sur** to set one's heart on.

dévor/er [devɔre] *vt* (*manger*) to gobble up, devour; (*incendie*) to engulf, devour; (*tourmenter, lire*) to devour. ◆**—ant** *a* (*faim*) ravenous; (*passion*) devouring.

dévot, -ote [devo, -ɔt] *a & nmf* devout *ou* pious (person). ◆**dévotion** *nf* devotion.

dévou/er (se) [sədevwe] *vpr* (*à une tâche*) to dedicate oneself, devote oneself (**à** to); **se d. (pour qn)** (*se sacrifier*) to sacrifice oneself (for s.o.). ◆**—é** *a* (*ami, femme etc*) devoted (**à qn** to s.o.); (*domestique, soldat etc*) dedicated. ◆**—ement** [-umɑ̃] *nm* devotion, dedication; (*de héros*) devotion to duty.

dévoyé, -ée [devwaje] *a & nmf* delinquent.

dextérité [dɛksterite] *nf* dexterity, skill.

diabète [djabɛt] *nm Méd* diabetes. ◆**diabétique** *a & nmf* diabetic.

diable [djɑbl] *nm* devil; **d.!** heavens!; **où/pourquoi/que d.?** where/why/what the devil?; **un bruit/vent/***etc* **du d.** the devil of

a noise/wind/*etc*; **à la d.** anyhow; **habiter au d.** to live miles from anywhere. ◆**diablerie** *nf* devilment, mischief. ◆**diablesse** *nf* **c'est une d.** *Fam* she's a devil. ◆**diablotin** *nm* (*enfant*) little devil. ◆**diabolique** *a* diabolical, devilish.
diabolo [djabɔlo] *nm* (*boisson*) lemonade *ou Am* lemon soda flavoured with syrup.
diacre [djakr] *nm Rel* deacon.
diadème [djadɛm] *nm* diadem.
diagnostic [djagnɔstik] *nm* diagnosis. ◆**diagnostiquer** *vt* to diagnose.
diagonal, -aux [djagɔnal, -o] *a* diagonal. ◆**diagonale** *nf* diagonal (line); **en d.** diagonally.
diagramme [djagram] *nm* (*schéma*) diagram; (*courbe*) graph.
dialecte [djalɛkt] *nm* dialect.
dialogue [djalɔg] *nm* conversation; *Pol Cin Th Littér* dialogue. ◆**dialoguer** *vi* to have a conversation *ou* dialogue.
dialyse [djaliz] *nf Méd* dialysis.
diamant [djamɑ̃] *nm* diamond.
diamètre [djamɛtr] *nm* diameter. ◆**diamétralement** *adv* **d. opposés** (*avis etc*) diametrically opposed, poles apart.
diapason [djapazɔ̃] *nm Mus* tuning fork; **être/se mettre au d. de** *Fig* to be/get in tune with.
diaphragme [djafragm] *nm* diaphragm.
diapositive, *Fam* **diapo** [djapozitiv, djapo] *nf* (colour) slide, transparency.
diarrhée [djare] *nf* diarrh(o)ea.
diatribe [djatrib] *nf* diatribe.
dictateur [diktatœr] *nm* dictator. ◆**dictatorial, -aux** *a* dictatorial. ◆**dictature** *nf* dictatorship.
dict/er [dikte] *vt* to dictate (**à** to). ◆**—ée** *nf* dictation. ◆**dictaphone®** *nm* dictaphone®.
diction [diksjɔ̃] *nf* diction, elocution.
dictionnaire [diksjɔnɛr] *nm* dictionary.
dicton [diktɔ̃] *nm* saying, adage, dictum.
didactique [didaktik] *a* didactic.
dièse [djɛz] *a & nm Mus* sharp.
diesel [djezɛl] *a & nm* **(moteur) d.** diesel (engine).
diète [djɛt] *nf* (*jeûne*) starvation diet; **à la d.** on a starvation diet. ◆**diététicien, -ienne** *nmf* dietician. ◆**diététique** *nf* dietetics; – *a* (*magasin etc*) health-; **aliment *ou* produit d.** health food.
dieu, -x [djø] *nm* god; **D.** God; **D. merci!** thank God!, thank goodness!
diffamer [difame] *vt* (*en paroles*) to slander; (*par écrit*) to libel. ◆**diffamation** *nf* defamation; (*en paroles*) slander; (*par écrit*) libel; **campagne de d.** smear campaign. ◆**diffamatoire** *a* slanderous; libellous.
différent [diferɑ̃] *a* different; *pl* (*divers*) different, various; **d. de** different from *ou* to, unlike. ◆**différemment** [-amɑ̃] *adv* differently (**de** from, to). ◆**différence** *nf* difference (**de** in); **à la d. de** unlike; **faire la d. entre** to make a distinction between.
différencier [diferɑ̃sje] *vt* to differentiate (**de** from); **— se d.** *vpr* to differ (**de** from).
différend [diferɑ̃] *nm* difference (of opinion).
différentiel, -ielle [diferɑ̃sjɛl] *a* differential.
différ/er [difere] **1** *vi* to differ (**de** from). **2** *vt* (*remettre*) to postpone, defer. ◆**—é** *nm* **en d.** (*émission*) (pre)recorded.
difficile [difisil] *a* difficult; (*exigeant*) fussy, particular, hard *ou* difficult to please; **c'est d. à faire** it's hard *ou* difficult to do; **il (nous) est d. de faire ça** it's hard *ou* difficult (for us) to do that. ◆**—ment** *adv* with difficulty; **d. lisible** not easily read. ◆**difficulté** *nf* difficulty (**à faire** in doing); **en d.** in a difficult situation.
difforme [difɔrm] *a* deformed, misshapen. ◆**difformité** *nf* deformity.
diffus [dify] *a* (*lumière, style*) diffuse.
diffuser [difyze] *vt* (*émission, nouvelle etc*) to broadcast; (*lumière, chaleur*) *Phys* to diffuse; (*livre*) to distribute. ◆**diffusion** *nf* broadcasting; (*de connaissances*) & *Phys* diffusion; (*de livre*) distribution.
digérer [diʒere] *vt* to digest; (*endurer*) *Fam* to stomach; – *vi* to digest. ◆**digeste** *a*, ◆**digestible** *a* digestible. ◆**digestif, -ive** *a* digestive; – *nm* after-dinner liqueur. ◆**digestion** *nf* digestion.
digitale [diʒital] *af* **empreinte d.** fingerprint.
digne [diɲ] *a* (*fier*) dignified; (*honnête*) worthy; **d. de qn** worthy of s.o.; **d. d'admiration/***etc* worthy of *ou* deserving of admiration/*etc*; **d. de foi** reliable. ◆**dignement** *adv* with dignity. ◆**dignitaire** *nm* dignitary. ◆**dignité** *nf* dignity.
digression [digresjɔ̃] *nf* digression.
digue [dig] *nf* dyke, dike.
dilapider [dilapide] *vt* to squander, waste.
dilater [dilate] *vt*, **— se d.** *vpr* to dilate, expand. ◆**dilatation** *nf* dilation, expansion.
dilatoire [dilatwar] *a* **manœuvre *ou* moyen d.** delaying tactic.
dilemme [dilɛm] *nm* dilemma.
dilettante [dilɛtɑ̃t] *nmf Péj* dabbler, amateur.
diligent [diliʒɑ̃] *a* (*prompt*) speedy and effi-

cient; (*soin*) diligent. ◆**diligence** *nf* 1 (*célérité*) speedy efficiency; **faire d.** to make haste. 2 (*véhicule*) *Hist* stagecoach.

diluer [dilɥe] *vt* to dilute. ◆**dilution** *nf* dilution.

diluvienne [dilyvjɛn] *af* **pluie d.** torrential rain.

dimanche [dimɑ̃ʃ] *nm* Sunday.

dimension [dimɑ̃sjɔ̃] *nf* dimension; **à deux dimensions** two-dimensional.

diminuer [diminɥe] *vt* to reduce, decrease; (*frais*) to cut down (on), reduce; (*mérite, forces*) to diminish, lessen, reduce; **d. qn** (*rabaisser*) to diminish s.o., lessen s.o.; – *vi* (*réserves, nombre*) to decrease, diminish; (*jours*) to get shorter, draw in; (*prix*) to drop, decrease. ◆**diminutif, -ive** *a* & *nm Gram* diminutive; – *nm* (*prénom*) nickname. ◆**diminution** *nf* reduction, decrease (**de** in).

dinde [dɛ̃d] *nf* turkey (hen), *Culin* turkey. ◆**dindon** *nm* turkey (cock).

dîner [dine] *vi* to have dinner, dine; (*au Canada, en Belgique etc*) to (have) lunch; – *nm* dinner; lunch; (*soirée*) dinner party. ◆**dînette** *nf* (*jouet*) doll's dinner service; (*jeu*) doll's dinner party. ◆**dîneur, -euse** *nmf* diner.

dingue [dɛ̃g] *a Fam* nuts, screwy, crazy; – *nmf Fam* nutcase.

dinosaure [dinozɔr] *nm* dinosaur.

diocèse [djɔsɛz] *nm Rel* diocese.

diphtérie [difteri] *nf* diphtheria.

diphtongue [diftɔ̃g] *nf Ling* diphthong.

diplomate [diplɔmat] *nm Pol* diplomat; – *nmf* (*négociateur*) diplomatist; – *a* (*habile, plein de tact*) diplomatic. ◆**diplomatie** [-asi] *nf* (*tact*) & *Pol* diplomacy; (*carrière*) diplomatic service. ◆**diplomatique** *a Pol* diplomatic.

diplôme [diplom] *nm* certificate, diploma; *Univ* degree. ◆**diplômé, -ée** *a* & *nmf* qualified (person); **être d. (de)** *Univ* to be a graduate (of).

dire* [dir] *vt* (*mot, avis etc*) to say; (*vérité, secret, heure etc*) to tell; (*penser*) to think (**de** of, about); **d. des bêtises** to talk nonsense; **elle dit que tu mens** she says (that) you're lying; **d. qch à qn** to tell s.o. sth, say sth to s.o.; **d. à qn que** to tell s.o. that, say to s.o. that; **d. à qn de faire** to tell s.o. to do; **dit-il** he said; **dit-on** they say; **d. que oui/non** to say yes/no; **d. du mal/du bien de** to speak ill/well of; **on dirait un château** it looks like a castle; **on dirait du Mozart** it sounds like Mozart; **on dirait du cabillaud** it tastes like cod; **on dirait que** it would seem that; **ça ne me dit rien** (*envie*) I don't feel like *ou* fancy that; (*souvenir*) it doesn't ring a bell; **ça vous dit de rester?** do you feel like staying?; **dites donc!** I say!; **ça va sans d.** that goes without saying; **autrement dit** in other words; **c'est beaucoup d.** that's going too far; **à l'heure dite** at the agreed time; **à vrai d.** to tell the truth; **il se dit malade/etc** he says he's ill/*etc*; **ça ne se dit pas** that's not said; – *nm* **au d. de** according to; **les dires de** (*déclarations*) the statements of.

direct [dirɛkt] *a* direct; (*chemin*) straight, direct; (*manière*) straightforward, direct; **train d.** through train, non-stop train; – *nm* **en d.** (*émission*) live; **un d. du gauche** *Boxe* a straight left. ◆**—ement** *adv* directly; (*immédiatement*) straight (away), directly.

directeur, -trice [dirɛktœr, -tris] *nmf* director; (*d'entreprise*) manager(ess), director; (*de journal*) editor; *Scol* headmaster, headmistress; – *a* (*principe*) guiding; **idées** *ou* **lignes directrices** guidelines.

direction [dirɛksjɔ̃] *nf* 1 (*de société*) running, management; (*de club*) leadership, running; (*d'études*) supervision; (*mécanisme*) *Aut* steering; **avoir la d. de** to be in charge of; **sous la d. de** (*orchestre*) conducted by; **la d.** (*équipe dirigeante*) the management; **une d.** (*fonction*) *Com* a directorship; *Scol* a headmastership; *Journ* an editorship. 2 (*sens*) direction; **en d. de** (*train*) (going) to, for.

directive [dirɛktiv] *nf* directive, instruction.

dirig/er [diriʒe] *vt* (*société*) to run, manage, direct; (*débat, cheval*) to lead; (*véhicule*) to steer; (*orchestre*) to conduct; (*études*) to supervise, direct; (*conscience*) to guide; (*orienter*) to turn (**vers** towards); (*arme, lumière*) to point, direct (**vers** towards); **se d. vers** (*lieu, objet*) to make one's way towards, head *ou* make for; (*dans une carrière*) to turn towards. ◆**—eant** *a* (*classe*) ruling; – *nm* (*de pays, club*) leader; (*d'entreprise*) manager. ◆**—é** *a* (*économie*) planned. ◆**—eable** *a* & *nm* **(ballon) d.** airship. ◆**dirigisme** *nm Écon* state control.

dis [di] *voir* **dire**.

discern/er [discrne] *vt* (*voir*) to make out, discern; (*différencier*) to distinguish. ◆**—ement** *nm* discernment, discrimination.

disciple [disipl] *nm* disciple, follower.

discipline [disiplin] *nf* (*règle, matière*) discipline. ◆**disciplinaire** *a* disciplinary. ◆**disciplin/er** *vt* (*contrôler, éduquer*) to

discipline; — **se d.** *vpr* to discipline oneself. ◆**—é** *a* well-disciplined.
disco [disko] *nf Fam* disco; **aller en d.** to go to a disco.
discontinu [diskɔ̃tiny] *a* (*ligne*) discontinuous; (*bruit etc*) intermittent. ◆**discontinuer** *vi* **sans d.** without stopping.
disconvenir [diskɔ̃vnir] *vi* **je n'en disconviens pas** I don't deny it.
discorde [diskɔrd] *nf* discord. ◆**discordance** *nf* (*de caractères*) clash, conflict; (*de son*) discord. ◆**discordant** *a* (*son*) discordant; (*témoignages*) conflicting; (*couleurs*) clashing.
discothèque [diskɔtɛk] *nf* record library; (*club*) discotheque.
discours [diskur] *nm* speech; (*écrit littéraire*) discourse. ◆**discourir** *vi Péj* to speechify, ramble on.
discourtois [diskurtwa] *a* discourteous.
discrédit [diskredi] *nm* disrepute, discredit. ◆**discréditer** *vt* to discredit, bring into disrepute; — **se d.** *vpr* (*personne*) to become discredited.
discret, -ète [diskrɛ, -ɛt] *a* (*personne, manière etc*) discreet; (*vêtement*) simple. ◆**discrètement** *adv* discreetly; (*s'habiller*) simply. ◆**discrétion** *nf* discretion; **vin/***etc* **à d.** as much wine/*etc* as one wants. ◆**discrétionnaire** *a* discretionary.
discrimination [diskriminɑsjɔ̃] *nf* (*ségrégation*) discrimination. ◆**discriminatoire** *a* discriminatory.
disculper [diskylpe] *vt* to exonerate (**de** from).
discussion [diskysjɔ̃] *nf* discussion; (*conversation*) talk; (*querelle*) argument; **pas de d.!** no argument! ◆**discut/er** *vt* to discuss; (*familièrement*) to talk over; (*contester*) to question; **ça peut se d., ça se discute** that's arguable; — *vi* (*parler*) to talk (**de** about, **avec** with); (*répliquer*) to argue; **d. de** *ou* **sur qch** to discuss sth. ◆**—é** *a* (*auteur*) much discussed *ou* debated; (*théorie, question*) disputed, controversial. ◆**—able** *a* arguable, debatable.
disette [dizɛt] *nf* food shortage.
diseuse [dizœz] *nf* **d. de bonne aventure** fortune-teller.
disgrâce [disgrɑs] *nf* disgrace, disfavour. ◆**disgracier** *vt* to disgrace.
disgracieux, -euse [disgrasjø, -øz] *a* ungainly.
disjoindre [disʒwɛ̃dr] *vt* (*questions*) to treat separately. ◆**disjoint** *a* (*questions*) unconnected, separate. ◆**disjoncteur** *nm Él* circuit breaker.
disloquer [dislɔke] *vt* (*membre*) to dislocate; (*meuble, machine*) to break; — **se d.** *vpr* (*cortège*) to break up; (*meuble etc*) to fall apart; **se d. le bras** to dislocate one's arm. ◆**dislocation** *nf* (*de membre*) dislocation.
dispar/aître* [disparɛtr] *vi* to disappear; (*être porté manquant*) to be missing; (*mourir*) to die; **d. en mer** to be lost at sea; **faire d.** to remove, get rid of. ◆**—u, -ue** *a* (*soldat etc*) missing, lost; — *nmf* (*absent*) missing person; (*mort*) departed; **être porté d.** to be reported missing. ◆**disparition** *nf* disappearance; (*mort*) death.
disparate [disparat] *a* ill-assorted.
disparité [disparite] *nf* disparity (**entre, de** between).
dispendieux, -euse [dispɑ̃djø, -øz] *a* expensive, costly.
dispensaire [dispɑ̃sɛr] *nm* community health centre.
dispense [dispɑ̃s] *nf* exemption; **d. d'âge** waiving of the age limit. ◆**dispenser** *vt* (*soins, bienfaits etc*) to dispense; **d. qn de** (*obligation*) to exempt *ou* excuse s.o. from; **je vous dispense de** (*vos réflexions etc*) I can dispense with; **se d. de faire** to spare oneself the bother of doing.
disperser [disperse] *vt* to disperse, scatter; (*efforts*) to dissipate; — **se d.** *vpr* (*foule*) to disperse; **elle se disperse trop** she tries to do too many things at once. ◆**dispersion** *nf* (*d'une armée etc*) dispersal, dispersion.
disponible [disponibl] *a* available; (*place*) spare, available; (*esprit*) alert. ◆**disponibilité** *nf* availability; *pl Fin* available funds.
dispos [dispo] *a* fit, in fine fettle; **frais et d.** refreshed.
dispos/er [dispoze] *vt* to arrange; (*troupes*) *Mil* to dispose; **d. qn à** (*la bonne humeur etc*) to dispose *ou* incline s.o. towards; **se d. à faire** to prepare to do; — *vi* **d. de qch** to have sth at one's disposal; (*utiliser*) to make use of sth; **d. de qn** *Péj* to take advantage of s.o., abuse s.o. ◆**—é** *a* **bien/mal d.** in a good/bad mood; **bien d. envers** well-disposed towards; **d. à faire** prepared *ou* disposed to do. ◆**disposition** *nf* arrangement; (*de troupes*) disposition; (*de maison, page*) layout; (*humeur*) frame of mind; (*tendance*) tendency, (pre)disposition (**à** to); (*clause*) *Jur* provision; *pl* (*aptitudes*) ability, aptitude (**pour** for): **à la d. de qn** at s.o.'s disposal; **prendre ses** *ou* **des dispositions** (*préparatifs*) to make arrangements, prepare; (*pour l'avenir*) to

make provision; **dans de bonnes dispositions à l'égard de** well-disposed towards.

dispositif [dispozitif] *nm* (*mécanisme*) device; **d. de défense** *Mil* defence system; **d. antiparasite** *Él* suppressor.

disproportion [disprɔpɔrsjɔ̃] *nf* disproportion. ◆**disproportionné** *a* disproportionate.

dispute [dispyt] *nf* quarrel. ◆**disputer** *vt* (*match*) to play; (*terrain, droit etc*) to contest, dispute; (*rallye*) to compete in; **d. qch à qn** (*prix, première place etc*) to fight with s.o. for *ou* over sth, contend with s.o. for sth; **d. qn** (*gronder*) *Fam* to tell s.o. off; — **se d.** *vpr* to quarrel (**avec** with); (*match*) to take place; **se d. qch** to fight over sth.

disqualifier [diskalifje] *vt Sp* to disqualify; — **se d.** *vpr Fig* to become discredited. ◆**disqualification** *nf Sp* disqualification.

disque [disk] *nm Mus* record; *Sp* discus; (*cercle*) disc, *Am* disk; (*pour ordinateur*) disk. ◆**disquaire** *nmf* record dealer. ◆**disquette** *nf* (*pour ordinateur*) floppy disk.

dissection [disɛksjɔ̃] *nf* dissection.

dissemblable [disɑ̃blabl] *a* dissimilar (**à** to).

disséminer [disemine] *vt* (*graines, mines etc*) to scatter; (*idées*) *Fig* to disseminate. ◆**dissémination** *nf* scattering; (*d'idées*) *Fig* dissemination.

dissension [disɑ̃sjɔ̃] *nf* dissension.

disséquer [diseke] *vt* to dissect.

disserter [disɛrte] *vi* **d. sur** to comment upon, discuss. ◆**dissertation** *nf Scol* essay.

dissident, -ente [disidɑ̃, -ɑ̃t] *a & nmf* dissident. ◆**dissidence** *nf* dissidence.

dissimul/er [disimyle] *vt* (*cacher*) to conceal, hide (**à** from); — *vi* (*feindre*) to pretend; — **se d.** *vpr* to hide, conceal oneself. ◆**—é** *a* (*enfant*) *Péj* secretive. ◆**dissimulation** *nf* concealment; (*duplicité*) deceit.

dissip/er [disipe] *vt* (*brouillard, craintes*) to dispel; (*fortune*) to squander, dissipate; **d. qn** to lead s.o. astray, distract s.o.; — **se d.** *vpr* (*brume*) to clear, lift; (*craintes*) to disappear; (*élève*) to misbehave. ◆**—é** *a* (*élève*) unruly; (*vie*) dissipated. ◆**dissipation** *nf* (*de brouillard*) clearing; (*indiscipline*) misbehaviour; (*débauche*) *Litt* dissipation.

dissocier [disɔsje] *vt* to dissociate (**de** from).

dissolu [disɔly] *a* (*vie etc*) dissolute.

dissoudre* [disudr] *vt*, — **se d.** *vpr* to dissolve. ◆**dissolution** *nf* dissolution. ◆**dissolvant** *a & nm* solvent; (*pour vernis à ongles*) nail polish remover.

dissuader [disɥade] *vt* to dissuade, deter (**de qch** from sth, **de faire** from doing). ◆**dissuasif, -ive** *a* (*effet*) deterrent; **être d.** *Fig* to be a deterrent. ◆**dissuasion** *nf* dissuasion; **force de d.** *Mil* deterrent.

distant [distɑ̃] *a* distant; (*personne*) aloof, distant; **d. de dix kilomètres** (*éloigné*) ten kilometres away; (*à intervalles*) ten kilometres apart. ◆**distance** *nf* distance; **à deux mètres de d.** two metres apart; **à d.** at *ou* from a distance; **garder ses distances** to keep one's distance. ◆**distancer** *vt* to leave behind, outstrip.

distendre [distɑ̃dr] *vt*, — **se d.** *vpr* to distend.

distiller [distile] *vt* to distil. ◆**distillation** *nf* distillation. ◆**distillerie** *nf* (*lieu*) distillery.

distinct, -incte [distɛ̃, -ɛ̃kt] *a* (*différent*) distinct, separate (**de** from); (*net*) clear, distinct. ◆**distinctement** *adv* distinctly, clearly. ◆**distinctif, -ive** *a* distinctive. ◆**distinction** *nf* (*différence, raffinement*) distinction.

distingu/er [distɛ̃ge] *vt* (*différencier*) to distinguish; (*voir*) to make out; (*choisir*) to single out; **d. le blé de l'orge** to tell wheat from barley, distinguish between wheat and barley; — **se d.** *vpr* (*s'illustrer*) to distinguish oneself; **se d. de** (*différer*) to be distinguishable from; **se d. par** (*sa gaieté, beauté etc*) to be conspicuous for. ◆**—é** *a* (*bien élevé, éminent*) distinguished; **sentiments distingués** (*formule épistolaire*) *Com* yours faithfully.

distorsion [distɔrsjɔ̃] *nf* (*du corps, d'une image etc*) distortion.

distraction [distraksjɔ̃] *nf* amusement, distraction; (*étourderie*) (fit of) absent-mindedness. ◆**distraire*** *vt* (*divertir*) to entertain, amuse; **d. qn (de)** (*détourner*) to distract s.o. (from); — **se d.** *vpr* to amuse oneself, enjoy oneself. ◆**distrait** *a* absent-minded. ◆**distraitement** *adv* absent-mindedly. ◆**distrayant** *a* entertaining.

distribuer [distribɥe] *vt* (*répartir*) to distribute; (*donner*) to give *ou* hand out, distribute; (*courrier*) to deliver; (*eau*) to supply; (*cartes*) to deal; **bien distribué** (*appartement*) well-arranged. ◆**distributeur** *nm Aut Cin* distributor; **d. (automatique)** vending machine; **d. de billets** *Rail* ticket machine; (*de billets de banque*) cash dispenser *ou* machine. ◆**distribution** *nf* distribution; (*du courrier*) delivery; (*de l'eau*) supply; (*acteurs*) *Th Cin* cast; **d. des prix** prize giving.

district [distrikt] *nm* district.

dit [di] *voir* **dire**; – *a* (*convenu*) agreed; (*surnommé*) called.

dites [dit] *voir* **dire.**

divaguer [divage] *vi* (*dérailler*) to rave, talk drivel. ◆**divagations** *nfpl* ravings.

divan [divɑ̃] *nm* divan, couch.

divergent [divɛrʒɑ̃] *a* diverging, divergent. ◆**divergence** *nf* divergence. ◆**diverger** *vi* to diverge (**de** from).

divers, -erses [divɛr, -ɛrs] *apl* (*distincts*) varied, diverse; **d. groupes** (*plusieurs*) various *ou* sundry groups. ◆**diversement** *adv* in various ways. ◆**diversifier** *vt* to diversify; — **se d.** *vpr Écon* to diversify. ◆**diversité** *nf* diversity.

diversion [divɛrsjɔ̃] *nf* diversion.

divert/ir [divɛrtir] *vt* to amuse, entertain; — **se d.** *vpr* to enjoy oneself, amuse oneself. ◆**—issement** *nm* amusement, entertainment.

dividende [dividɑ̃d] *nm Math Fin* dividend.

divin [divɛ̃] *a* divine. ◆**divinité** *nf* divinity.

diviser [divize] *vt*, — **se d.** *vpr* to divide (**en** into). ◆**divisible** *a* divisible. ◆**division** *nf* division.

divorce [divɔrs] *nm* divorce. ◆**divorc/er** *vi* to get *ou* be divorced, divorce; **d. d'avec qn** to divorce s.o. ◆**—é, -ée** *a* divorced (**d'avec** from); – *nmf* divorcee.

divulguer [divylge] *vt* to divulge. ◆**divulgation** *nf* divulgence.

dix [dis] ([di] *before consonant*, [diz] *before vowel*) *a* & *nm* ten. ◆**dixième** [dizjɛm] *a* & *nmf* tenth; **un d.** a tenth. ◆**dix-huit** [dizɥit] *a* & *nm* eighteeen. ◆**dix-huitième** *a* & *nmf* eighteenth. ◆**dix-neuf** [diznœf] *a* & *nm* nineteen. ◆**dix-neuvième** *a* & *nmf* nineteenth. ◆**dix-sept** [dissɛt] *a* & *nm* seventeen. ◆**dix-septième** *a* & *nmf* seventeenth.

dizaine [dizɛn] *nf* about ten.

docile [dɔsil] *a* submissive, docile. ◆**docilité** *nf* submissiveness, docility.

dock [dɔk] *nm Nau* dock. ◆**docker** [dɔkɛr] *nm* docker.

docteur [dɔktœr] *nm Méd Univ* doctor (**ès**, **en** of). ◆**doctorat** *nm* doctorate, = PhD (**ès**, **en** in).

doctrine [dɔktrin] *nf* doctrine. ◆**doctrinaire** *a* & *nmf Péj* doctrinaire.

document [dɔkymɑ̃] *nm* document. ◆**documentaire** *a* documentary; – *nm* (*film*) documentary. ◆**documentaliste** *nmf* information officer.

document/er [dɔkymɑ̃te] *vt* (*informer*) to document; — **se d.** *vpr* to collect material *ou* information. ◆**—é** *a* (**bien** *ou* **très**) **d.** (*personne*) well-informed. ◆**documentation** *nf* (*documents*) documentation, *Com* literature; (*renseignements*) information.

dodeliner [dɔdline] *vi* **d. de la tête** to nod (one's head).

dodo [dodo] *nm* (*langage enfantin*) **faire d.** to sleep; **aller au d.** to go to bye-byes.

dodu [dɔdy] *a* chubby, plump.

dogme [dɔgm] *nm* dogma. ◆**dogmatique** *a* dogmatic. ◆**dogmatisme** *nm* dogmatism.

dogue [dɔg] *nm* (*chien*) mastiff.

doigt [dwa] *nm* finger; **d. de pied** toe; **à deux doigts de** within an ace of; **montrer du d.** to point (to); **savoir sur le bout du d.** to have at one's finger tips. ◆**doigté** *nm Mus* fingering, touch; (*savoir-faire*) tact, expertise. ◆**doigtier** *nm* fingerstall.

dois, doit [dwa] *voir* **devoir**[1,2].

doléances [dɔleɑ̃s] *nfpl* (*plaintes*) grievances.

dollar [dɔlar] *nm* dollar.

domaine [dɔmɛn] *nm* (*terres*) estate, domain; (*sphère*) province, domain.

dôme [dom] *nm* dome.

domestique [dɔmɛstik] *a* (*animal*) domestic(ated); (*de la famille*) family-, domestic; (*ménager*) domestic, household; – *nmf* servant. ◆**domestiquer** *vt* to domesticate.

domicile [dɔmisil] *nm* home; *Jur* abode; **travailler à d.** to work at home; **livrer à d.** (*pain etc*) to deliver (to the house). ◆**domicilié** *a* resident (**à, chez** at).

domin/er [dɔmine] *vt* to dominate; (*situation, sentiment*) to master, dominate; (*être supérieur à*) to surpass, outclass; (*tour, rocher*) to tower above, dominate (*valley, building etc*); – *vi* (*être le plus fort*) to be dominant, dominate; (*être le plus important*) to predominate; — **se d.** *vpr* to control oneself. ◆**—ant** *a* dominant. ◆**—ante** *nf* dominant feature; *Mus* dominant. ◆**dominateur, -trice** *a* domineering. ◆**domination** *nf* domination.

dominicain, -aine [dɔminikɛ̃, -ɛn] *a* & *nmf Rel* Dominican.

dominical, -aux [dɔminikal, -o] *a* (*repos*) Sunday-.

domino [dɔmino] *nm* domino; *pl* (*jeu*) dominoes.

dommage [dɔmaʒ] *nm* **1** (**c'est**) **d.!** it's a

pity *ou* a shame! (que that); **quel d.!** what a pity *ou* a shame! **2** (*tort*) prejudice, harm; *pl* (*dégâts*) damage; **dommages-intérêts** *Jur* damages.

dompt/er [dɔ̃te] *vt* (*animal*) to tame; (*passions, rebelles*) to subdue. **◆—eur, -euse** *nmf* (*de lions*) lion tamer.

don [dɔ̃] *nm* (*cadeau, aptitude*) gift; (*aumône*) donation; **le d. du sang/***etc* (the) giving of blood/*etc*; **faire d. de** to give; **avoir le d. de** (*le chic pour*) to have the knack of. **◆donateur, -trice** *nmf Jur* donor. **◆donation** *nf Jur* donation.

donc [dɔ̃(k)] *conj* so, then; (*par conséquent*) so, therefore; **asseyez-vous d.!** (*intensif*) will you sit down!, sit down then!; **qui/quoi d.?** who?/what?; **allons d.!** come on!

donjon [dɔ̃ʒɔ̃] *nm* (*de château*) keep.

donne [dɔn] *nf Cartes* deal.

donner [dɔne] *vt* to give; (*récolte, résultat*) to produce; (*sa place*) to give up; (*pièce, film*) to put on; (*cartes*) to deal; **d. un coup à** to hit, give a blow to; **d. le bonjour à qn** to say hello to s.o.; **d. à réparer** to take (in) to be repaired; **d. raison à qn** to say s.o. is right; **ça donne soif/faim** it makes you thirsty/hungry; **je lui donne trente ans** I'd say *ou* guess he *ou* she was thirty; **ça n'a rien donné** (*efforts*) it hasn't got us anywhere; **c'est donné** *Fam* it's dirt cheap; **étant donné** (*la situation etc*) considering, in view of; **étant donné que** seeing (that), considering (that); **à un moment donné** at some stage; – *vi* **d. sur** (*fenêtre*) to look out onto, overlook; (*porte*) to open onto; **d. dans** (*piège*) to fall into; **d. de la tête contre** to hit one's head against; **— se d.** *vpr* (*se consacrer*) to devote oneself (à to); **se d. du mal** to go to a lot of trouble (**pour faire** to do); **s'en d. à cœur joie** to have a whale of a time, enjoy oneself to the full. **◆données** *nfpl* (*information*) data; (*de problème*) (known) facts; (*d'un roman*) basic elements. **◆donneur, -euse** *nmf* giver; (*de sang, d'organe*) donor; *Cartes* dealer.

dont [dɔ̃] *pron rel* (= **de qui, duquel, de quoi** *etc*) (*personne*) of whom; (*chose*) of which; (*appartenance: personne*) whose, of whom; (*appartenance: chose*) of which, whose; **une mère d. le fils est malade** a mother whose son is ill; **la fille d. il est fier** the daughter he is proud of *ou* of whom he is proud; **les outils d. j'ai besoin** the tools I need; **la façon d. elle joue** the way (in which) she plays; **voici ce d. il s'agit** here's what it's about.

doper [dɔpe] *vt* (*cheval, sportif*) to dope; **— se d.** *vpr* to dope oneself. **◆doping** *nm* (*action*) doping; (*substance*) dope.

dorénavant [dɔrenavɑ̃] *adv* henceforth.

dor/er [dɔre] *vt* (*objet*) to gild; **d. la pilule** *Fig* to sugar the pill; **se (faire) d. au soleil** to bask in the sun; – *vi Culin* to brown. **◆—é** *a* (*objet*) gilt; (*couleur*) golden; – *nm* (*couche*) gilt. **◆dorure** *nf* gilding.

dorloter [dɔrlɔte] *vt* to pamper, coddle.

dormir* [dɔrmir] *vi* to sleep; (*être endormi*) to be asleep; (*argent*) to lie idle; **histoire à d. debout** tall story, cock-and-bull story; **eau dormante** stagnant water. **◆dortoir** *nm* dormitory.

dos [do] *nm* back; (*de nez*) bridge; (*de livre*) spine; **voir qn de d.** to have a back view of s.o.; **à d. de chameau** (riding) on a camel; **'voir au d.'** (*verso*) 'see over'; **j'en ai plein le d.** *Fam* I'm sick of it; **mettre qch sur le d. de qn** (*accusation*) to pin sth on s.o. **◆dossard** *nm Sp* number (*fixed on back*). **◆dossier** *nm* **1** (*de siège*) back. **2** (*papiers, compte rendu*) file, dossier; (*classeur*) folder, file.

dose [doz] *nf* dose; (*quantité administrée*) dosage. **◆dos/er** *vt* (*remède*) to measure out the dose of; (*équilibrer*) to strike the correct balance between. **◆—age** *nm* measuring out (*of dose*); (*équilibre*) balance; **faire le d. de** = **doser**. **◆—eur** *nm* **bouchon d.** measuring cap.

dot [dɔt] *nf* dowry.

doter [dɔte] *vt* (*hôpital etc*) to endow; **d. de** (*matériel*) to equip with; (*qualité*) *Fig* to endow with. **◆dotation** *nf* endowment; equipping.

douane [dwan] *nf* customs. **◆douanier, -ière** *nm* customs officer; – *a* (*union etc*) customs-.

double [dubl] *a* double; (*rôle, avantage etc*) twofold, double; – *adv* double; – *nm* (*de personne*) double; (*copie*) copy, duplicate; (*de timbre*) swap, duplicate; **le d. (de)** (*quantité*) twice as much (as). **◆doublage** *nm* (*de film*) dubbing. **◆doublement** *adv* doubly; – *nm* doubling. **◆doubler 1** *vt* (*augmenter*) to double; (*vêtement*) to line; (*film*) to dub; (*acteur*) to stand in for; (*classe*) *Scol* to repeat; (*cap*) *Nau* to round; **se d. de** to be coupled with; – *vi* (*augmenter*) to double. **2** *vti Aut* to overtake, pass. **◆doublure** *nf* (*étoffe*) lining; *Th* understudy; *Cin* stand-in, double.

douce [dus] *voir* **doux**. **◆doucement** *adv* (*délicatement*) gently; (*à voix basse*) softly; (*sans bruit*) quietly; (*lentement*) slowly; (*sans à-coups*) smoothly; (*assez bien*) *Fam* so-so. ◆**douceur** *nf* (*de miel etc*) sweetness; (*de personne, pente etc*) gentleness; (*de peau etc*) softness; (*de temps*) mildness; *pl* (*sucreries*) sweets, *Am* candies; **en d.** (*démarrer etc*) smoothly.

douche [duʃ] *nf* shower. ◆**doucher** *vt* **d. qn** to give s.o. a shower; **— se d.** *vpr* to take *ou* have a shower.

doué [dwe] *a* gifted, talented (**en** at); (*intelligent*) clever; **d. de** gifted with; **il est d. pour** he has a gift *ou* talent for.

douille [duj] *nf* (*d'ampoule*) *Él* socket; (*de cartouche*) case.

douillet, -ette [dujɛ, -ɛt] *a* (*lit etc*) soft, cosy, snug; **il est d.** (*délicat*) *Péj* he's soft.

douleur [dulœr] *nf* (*mal*) pain; (*chagrin*) sorrow, grief. ◆**douloureux, -euse** *a* (*maladie, membre, décision, perte etc*) painful.

doute [dut] *nm* doubt; *pl* (*méfiance*) doubts, misgivings; **sans d.** no doubt, probably; **sans aucun d.** without (any *ou* a) doubt; **mettre en d.** to cast doubt on; **dans le d.** uncertain, doubtful; **ça ne fait pas de d.** there is no doubt about it. ◆**douter** *vi* to doubt; **d. de qch/qn** to doubt sth/s.o.; **d. que** (+ *sub*) to doubt whether *ou* that; **se d. de qch** to suspect sth; **je m'en doute** I suspect so, I would think so. ◆**douteux, -euse** *a* doubtful; (*louche, médiocre*) dubious; **il est d. que** (+ *sub*) it's doubtful whether *ou* that.

douve(s) [duv] *nf(pl)* (*de château*) moat.

Douvres [duvr] *nm ou f* Dover.

doux, douce [du, dus] *a* (*miel, son etc*) sweet; (*personne, pente etc*) gentle; (*peau, lumière, drogue etc*) soft; (*émotion, souvenir etc*) pleasant; (*temps, climat*) mild; **en douce** on the quiet.

douze [duz] *a & nm* twelve. ◆**douzaine** *nf* (*douze*) dozen; (*environ*) about twelve; **une d. d'œufs/***etc* a dozen eggs/*etc*. ◆**douzième** *a & nmf* twelfth; **un d.** a twelfth.

doyen, -enne [dwajɛ̃, -ɛn] *nmf Rel Univ* dean; **d. (d'âge)** oldest person.

draconien, -ienne [drakɔnjɛ̃, -jɛn] *a* (*mesures*) drastic.

dragée [draʒe] *nf* sugared almond; **tenir la d. haute à qn** (*tenir tête à qn*) to stand up to s.o.

dragon [dragɔ̃] *nm* (*animal*) dragon; *Mil Hist* dragoon.

drague [drag] *nf* (*appareil*) dredge; (*filet*) drag net. ◆**draguer** *vt* **1** (*rivière etc*) to dredge. **2** *Arg* (*racoler*) to try and pick up; (*faire du baratin à*) to chat up, *Am* smooth-talk.

drainer [drene] *vt* to drain.

drame [dram] *nm* drama; (*catastrophe*) tragedy. ◆**dramatique** *a* dramatic; **critique d.** drama critic; **auteur d.** playwright, dramatist; **film d.** drama. ◆**dramatiser** *vt* (*exagérer*) to dramatize. ◆**dramaturge** *nmf* dramatist.

drap [dra] *nm* (*de lit*) sheet; (*tissu*) cloth; **dans de beaux draps** *Fig* in a fine mess.

drapeau, -x [drapo] *nm* flag; **être sous les drapeaux** *Mil* to be in the services.

draper [drape] *vt* to drape (**de** with). ◆**draperie** *nf* (*étoffe*) drapery.

dresser [drese] **1** *vt* (*échelle, statue*) to put up, erect; (*piège*) to lay, set; (*oreille*) to prick up; (*liste*) to draw up, make out; **— se d.** *vpr* (*personne*) to stand up; (*statue, montagne*) to rise up, stand; **se d. contre** (*abus*) to stand up against. **2** *vt* (*animal*) to train; (*personne*) *Péj* to drill, teach. ◆**dressage** *nm* training. ◆**dresseur, -euse** *nmf* trainer.

dribbler [drible] *vti Fb* to dribble.

drogue [drɔg] *nf* (*médicament*) *Péj* drug; **une d.** (*stupéfiant*) a drug; **la d.** drugs, dope. ◆**drogu/er** *vt* (*victime*) to drug; (*malade*) to dose up; **— se d.** *vpr* to take drugs, be on drugs; (*malade*) to dose oneself up. ◆**—é, -ée** *nmf* drug addict.

droguerie [drɔgri] *nf* hardware shop *ou Am* store. ◆**droguiste** *nmf* owner of a *droguerie*.

droit[1] [drwa] *nm* (*privilège*) right; (*d'inscription etc*) fee(s), dues; *pl* (*de douane*) duty; **le d.** (*science juridique*) law; **avoir d. à** to be entitled to; **avoir le d. de faire** to be entitled to do, have the right to do; **à bon d.** rightly; **d. d'entrée** entrance fee.

droit[2] [drwa] *a* (*ligne, route etc*) straight; (*personne, mur etc*) upright, straight; (*angle*) right; (*veston*) single-breasted; (*honnête*) *Fig* upright; *— adv* straight; **tout d.** straight *ou* right ahead. ◆**droite**[1] *nf* (*ligne*) straight line.

droit[3] [drwa] *a* (*côté, bras etc*) right; *— nm* (*coup*) *Boxe* right. ◆**droite**[2] *nf* **la d.** (*côté*) the right (side); *Pol* the right (wing); **à d.** (*tourner*) (to the) right; (*rouler, se tenir*) on the right(-hand) side; **de d.** (*fenêtre etc*) right-hand; (*politique, candidat*) right-wing; **à d. de** on *ou* to the right of; **à d. et à gauche** (*voyager etc*) here, there and everywhere. ◆**droitier, -ière** *a & nmf* right-handed (person). ◆**droiture** *nf* uprightness.

drôle [drol] *a* funny; **d. d'air/de type** funny look/fellow. ◆**—ment** *adv* funnily; (*extrêmement*) *Fam* dreadfully.
dromadaire [drɔmadɛr] *nm* dromedary.
dru [dry] *a* (*herbe etc*) thick, dense; – *adv* **tomber d.** (*pluie*) to pour down heavily; **pousser d.** to grow thick(ly).
du [dy] = **de** + **le**.
dû, due [dy] *a* **d. à** (*accident etc*) due to; – *nm* due; (*argent*) dues.
dualité [dɥalite] *nf* duality.
dubitatif, -ive [dybitatif, -iv] *a* (*regard etc*) dubious.
duc [dyk] *nm* duke. ◆**duché** *nm* duchy. ◆**duchesse** *nf* duchess.
duel [dɥɛl] *nm* duel.
dûment [dymɑ̃] *adv* duly.
dune [dyn] *nf* (sand) dune.
duo [dɥo] *nm Mus* duet; (*couple*) *Hum* duo.
dupe [dyp] *nf* dupe, fool; – *a* **d. de** duped by, fooled by. ◆**duper** *vt* to fool, dupe.
duplex [dyplɛks] *nm* split-level flat, *Am* duplex; **(émission en) d.** *Tél* link-up.
duplicata [dyplikata] *nm inv* duplicate.
duplicateur [dyplikatœr] *nm* (*machine*) duplicator.
duplicité [dyplisite] *nf* duplicity, deceit.
dur [dyr] *a* (*substance*) hard; (*difficile*) hard, tough; (*viande*) tough; (*hiver, leçon, ton*) harsh; (*personne*) hard, harsh; (*brosse, carton*) stiff; (*œuf*) hard-boiled; **d. d'oreille** hard of hearing; **d. à cuire** *Fam* hard-bitten, tough; – *adv* (*travailler*) hard; – *nm Fam* tough guy. ◆**durement** *adv* harshly. ◆**dureté** *nf* hardness; harshness; toughness.
durant [dyrɑ̃] *prép* during.
durc/ir [dyrsir] *vti*, — **se d.** *vpr* to harden. ◆**—issement** *nm* hardening.
durée [dyre] *nf* (*de film, événement etc*) length; (*période*) duration; (*de pile*) *Él* life; **de longue d.** (*disque*) long-playing. ◆**dur/er** *vi* to last; **ça dure depuis . . .** it's been going on for . . . . ◆**—able** *a* durable, lasting.
durillon [dyrijɔ̃] *nm* callus.
duvet [dyvɛ] *nm* **1** (*d'oiseau, de visage*) down. **2** (*sac*) sleeping bag. ◆**duveté** *a*, ◆**duveteux, -euse** *a* downy.
dynamique [dinamik] *a* dynamic; – *nf* (*force*) *Fig* dynamic force, thrust. ◆**dynamisme** *nm* dynamism.
dynamite [dinamit] *nf* dynamite. ◆**dynamiter** *vt* to dynamite.
dynamo [dinamo] *nf* dynamo.
dynastie [dinasti] *nf* dynasty.
dysenterie [disɑ̃tri] *nf Méd* dysentery.
dyslexique [dislɛksik] *a* & *nmf* dyslexic.

E

E, e [ə, ø] *nm* E, e.
eau, -x [o] *nf* water; **il est tombé beaucoup d'e.** a lot of rain fell; **e. douce** (*non salée*) fresh water; (*du robinet*) soft water; **e. salée** salt water; **e. de Cologne** eau de Cologne; **e. de toilette** toilet water; **grandes eaux** (*d'un parc*) ornamental fountains; **tomber à l'e.** (*projet*) to fall through; **ça lui fait venir l'e. à la bouche** it makes his *ou* her mouth water; **tout en e.** sweating; **prendre l'e.** (*chaussure*) to take water, leak. ◆**e.-de-vie** *nf* (*pl* **eaux-de-vie**) brandy. ◆**e.-forte** *nf* (*pl* **eaux-fortes**) (*gravure*) etching.
ébah/ir [ebair] *vt* to astound, dumbfound, amaze. ◆**—issement** *nm* amazement.
ébattre (s') [sebatr] *vpr* to frolic, frisk about. ◆**ébats** *nmpl* frolics.
ébauche [eboʃ] *nf* (*esquisse*) (rough) outline, (rough) sketch; (*début*) beginnings. ◆**ébaucher** *vt* (*projet, tableau, œuvre*) to sketch out, outline; **e. un sourire** to give a faint smile; — **s'é.** *vpr* to take shape.
ébène [ebɛn] *nf* (*bois*) ebony.
ébéniste [ebenist] *nm* cabinet-maker. ◆**ébénisterie** *nf* cabinet-making.
éberlué [ebɛrlɥe] *a Fam* dumbfounded.
éblou/ir [ebluir] *vt* to dazzle. ◆**—issement** *nm* (*aveuglement*) dazzling, dazzle; (*émerveillement*) feeling of wonder; (*malaise*) fit of dizziness.
éboueur [ebwœr] *nm* dustman, *Am* garbage collector.
ébouillanter [ebujɑ̃te] *vt* to scald; — **s'é.** *vpr* to scald oneself.
éboul/er (s') [sebule] *vpr* (*falaise etc*) to crumble; (*terre, roches*) to fall. ◆**—ement** *nm* landslide. ◆**éboulis** *nm* (mass of) fallen debris.
ébouriffant [eburifɑ̃] *a Fam* astounding.
ébouriffer [eburife] *vt* (*cheveux*) to dishevel, ruffle, tousle.

ébranl/er [ebrɑ̃le] *vt* (*mur, confiance etc*) to shake; (*santé*) to weaken, affect; (*personne*) to shake, shatter; **— s'é.** *vpr* (*train, cortège etc*) to move off. ◆**—ement** *nm* (*secousse*) shaking, shock; (*nerveux*) shock.

ébrécher [ebreʃe] *vt* (*assiette*) to chip; (*lame*) to nick. ◆**ébréchure** *nf* chip; nick.

ébriété [ebrijete] *nf* drunkenness.

ébrouer (s') [sebrue] *vpr* (*cheval*) to snort; (*personne*) to shake oneself (about).

ébruiter [ebrɥite] *vt* (*nouvelle etc*) to make known, divulge.

ébullition [ebylisjɔ̃] *nf* boiling; **être en é.** (*eau*) to be boiling; (*ville*) *Fig* to be in turmoil.

écaille [ekɑj] *nf* **1** (*de poisson*) scale; (*de tortue, d'huître*) shell; (*résine synthétique*) tortoise-shell. **2** (*de peinture*) flake. ◆**écailler 1** *vt* (*poisson*) to scale; (*huître*) to shell. **2 s'é.** *vpr* (*peinture*) to flake (off), peel.

écarlate [ekarlat] *a & nf* scarlet.

écarquiller [ekarkije] *vt* **é. les yeux** to open one's eyes wide.

écart [ekar] *nm* (*intervalle*) gap, distance; (*mouvement, embardée*) swerve; (*différence*) difference (**de** in, **entre** between); **écarts de** (*conduite, langage etc*) lapses in; **le grand é.** (*de gymnaste*) the splits; **à l'é.** out of the way; **tenir qn à l'é.** *Fig* to keep s.o. out of things; **à l'é. de** away from, clear of. ◆**écart/er** *vt* (*objets*) to move away from each other, move apart; (*jambes*) to spread, open; (*rideaux*) to draw (aside), open; (*crainte, idée*) to brush aside, dismiss; (*carte*) to discard; **é. qch de qch** to move sth away from sth; **é. qn de** (*éloigner*) to keep *ou* take s.o. away from; (*exclure*) to keep s.o. out of; **— s'é.** *vpr* (*s'éloigner*) to move away (**de** from); (*se séparer*) to move aside (**de** from); **s'é. de** (*sujet, bonne route*) to stray *ou* deviate from. ◆**—é** *a* (*endroit*) remote; **les jambes écartées** with legs (wide) apart. ◆**—ement** *nm* (*espace*) gap, distance (**de** between).

écartelé [ekartəle] *a* **é. entre** (*tiraillé*) torn between.

ecchymose [ekimoz] *nf* bruise.

ecclésiastique [eklezjastik] *a* ecclesiastical; – *nm* ecclesiastic, clergyman.

écervelé, -ée [eservəle] *a* scatterbrained; – *nmf* scatterbrain.

échafaud [eʃafo] *nm* (*pour exécution*) scaffold.

échafaudage [eʃafodaʒ] *nm* (*construction*) scaffold(ing); (*tas*) heap; (*système*) *Fig* fabric. ◆**échafauder** *vi* to put up scaffolding *ou* a scaffold; – *vt* (*projet etc*) to put together, think up.

échalas [eʃala] *nm* **grand é.** tall skinny person.

échalote [eʃalɔt] *nf Bot Culin* shallot, scallion.

échancré [eʃɑ̃kre] *a* (*encolure*) V-shaped, scooped. ◆**échancrure** *nf* (*de robe*) opening.

échange [eʃɑ̃ʒ] *nm* exchange; **en é.** in exchange (**de** for). ◆**échanger** *vt* to exchange (**contre** for). ◆**échangeur** *nm* (*intersection*) *Aut* interchange.

échantillon [eʃɑ̃tijɔ̃] *nm* sample. ◆**échantillonnage** *nm* (*collection*) range (of samples).

échappatoire [eʃapatwar] *nf* evasion, way out.

échapp/er [eʃape] *vi* **é. à qn** to escape from s.o.; **é. à la mort/un danger/***etc* to escape death/a danger/*etc*; **ce nom m'échappe** that name escapes me; **ça lui a échappé (des mains)** it slipped out of his *ou* her hands; **laisser é.** (*cri*) to let out; (*objet, occasion*) to let slip; **l'é. belle** to have a close shave; **ça m'a échappé** (*je n'ai pas compris*) I didn't catch it; **— s'é.** *vpr* (*s'enfuir*) to escape (**de** from); (*s'éclipser*) to slip away; *Sp* to break away; (*gaz, eau*) to escape, come out. ◆**—é, -ée** *nmf* runaway. ◆**—ée** *nf Sp* breakaway; (*vue*) vista. ◆**—ement** *nm* **tuyau d'é.** *Aut* exhaust pipe; **pot d'é.** *Aut* silencer, *Am* muffler.

écharde [eʃard] *nf* (*de bois*) splinter.

écharpe [eʃarp] *nf* scarf; (*de maire*) sash; **en é.** (*bras*) in a sling; **prendre en é.** *Aut* to hit sideways.

écharper [eʃarpe] *vt* **é. qn** to cut s.o. to bits.

échasse [eʃas] *nf* (*bâton*) stilt. ◆**échassier** *nm* wading bird.

échauder [eʃode] *vt* **être échaudé, se faire é.** (*déçu*) *Fam* to be taught a lesson.

échauffer [eʃofe] *vt* (*moteur*) to overheat; (*esprit*) to excite; **— s'é.** *vpr* (*discussion*) & *Sp* to warm up.

échauffourée [eʃofure] *nf* (*bagarre*) clash, brawl, skirmish.

échéance [eʃeɑ̃s] *nf Com* date (due), expiry *ou Am* expiration date; (*paiement*) payment (due); (*obligation*) commitment; **à brève/longue é.** (*projet, emprunt*) short-/long-term.

échéant (le cas) [ləkɑzeʃeɑ̃] *adv* if the occasion should arise, possibly.

échec [eʃɛk] *nm* **1** (*insuccès*) failure; **faire é. à** (*inflation etc*) to hold in check. **2 les**

échecs (*jeu*) chess; **en é.** in check; **é.!** check!; **é. et mat!** checkmate!

échelle [eʃɛl] *nf* **1** (*marches*) ladder; **faire la courte é. à qn** to give s.o. a leg up. **2** (*mesure, dimension*) scale; **à l'é. nationale** on a national scale. ◆**échelon** *nm* (*d'échelle*) rung; (*de fonctionnaire*) grade; (*dans une organisation*) echelon; **à l'é. régional/national** on a regional/national level. ◆**échelonner** *vt* (*paiements*) to spread out, space out; — **s'é.** *vpr* to be spread out.

écheveau, -x [eʃvo] *nm* (*de laine*) skein; *Fig* muddle, tangle.

échevelé [eʃəvle] *a* (*ébouriffé*) dishevelled; (*course, danse etc*) *Fig* wild.

échine [eʃin] *nf Anat* backbone, spine.

échiner (s') [seʃine] *vpr* (*s'évertuer*) *Fam* to knock oneself out (**à faire** doing).

échiquier [eʃikje] *nm* (*tableau*) chessboard.

écho [eko] *nm* (*d'un son*) echo; (*réponse*) response; *pl Journ* gossip (items), local news; **avoir des échos de** to hear some news about; **se faire l'é. de** (*opinions etc*) to echo. ◆**échotier, -ière** *nmf Journ* gossip columnist.

échographie [ekografi] *nf* (ultrasound) scan; **passer une é.** (*femme enceinte*) to have a scan.

échoir* [eʃwar] *vi* (*terme*) to expire; **é. à qn** (*part*) to fall to s.o.

échouer [eʃwe] **1** *vi* to fail; **é. à** (*examen*) to fail. **2** *vi*, — **s'é.** *vpr* (*navire*) to run aground.

éclabousser [eklabuse] *vt* to splash, spatter (**de** with); (*salir*) *Fig* to tarnish the image of. ◆**éclaboussure** *nf* splash, spatter.

éclair [eklɛr] **1** *nm* (*lumière*) flash; **un é.** *Mét* a flash of lightning. **2** *nm* (*gâteau*) éclair. **3** *a inv* (*visite, raid*) lightning.

éclairc/ir [eklɛrsir] *vt* (*couleur etc*) to lighten, make lighter; (*sauce*) to thin out; (*question, mystère*) to clear up, clarify; — **s'é.** *vpr* (*ciel*) to clear (up); (*idées*) to become clear(er); (*devenir moins dense*) to thin out; **s'é. la voix** to clear one's throat. ◆**—ie** *nf* (*dans le ciel*) clear patch; (*durée*) sunny spell. ◆**—issement** *nm* (*explication*) clarification.

éclair/er [eklere] *vt* (*pièce etc*) to light (up); (*situation*) *Fig* to throw light on; **é. qn** (*avec une lampe etc*) to give s.o. some light; (*informer*) *Fig* to enlighten s.o.; — *vi* (*lampe*) to give light; — **s'é.** *vpr* (*visage*) to light up, brighten up; (*question, situation*) *Fig* to become clear(er); **s'é. à la bougie** to use candlelight. ◆**—é** *a* (*averti*) enlightened; **bien/mal é.** (*illuminé*) well/badly lit. ◆**—age** *nm* (*de pièce etc*) light(ing); (*point de vue*) *Fig* light.

éclaireur, -euse [eklerœr, -øz] *nm Mil* scout; — *nmf* (boy) scout, (girl) guide.

éclat [ekla] *nm* **1** (*de la lumière*) brightness; (*de phare*) *Aut* glare; (*du feu*) blaze; (*splendeur*) brilliance, radiance; (*de la jeunesse*) bloom; (*de diamant*) glitter, sparkle. **2** (*fragment de verre ou de bois*) splinter; (*de rire, colère*) (out)burst; **é. d'obus** shrapnel; **éclats de voix** noisy outbursts, shouts. ◆**éclat/er** *vi* (*pneu, obus etc*) to burst; (*pétard, bombe*) to go off, explode; (*verre*) to shatter, break into pieces; (*guerre, incendie*) to break out; (*orage, scandale*) to break; (*parti*) to break up; **é. de rire** to burst out laughing; **é. en sanglots** to burst into tears. ◆**—ant** *a* (*lumière, couleur, succès*) brilliant; (*bruit*) thunderous; (*vérité*) blinding; (*beauté*) radiant. ◆**—ement** *nm* (*de pneu etc*) bursting; (*de bombe etc*) explosion; (*de parti*) break-up.

éclectique [eklektik] *a* eclectic.

éclipse [eklips] *nf* (*du soleil*) & *Fig* eclipse. ◆**éclipser** *vt* to eclipse; — **s'é.** *vpr* (*soleil*) to be eclipsed; (*partir*) *Fam* to slip away.

éclopé, -ée [eklɔpe] *a & nmf* limping *ou* lame (person).

éclore [eklɔr] *vi* (*œuf*) to hatch; (*fleur*) to open (out), blossom. ◆**éclosion** *nf* hatching; opening, blossoming.

écluse [eklyz] *nf Nau* lock.

écœur/er [ekœre] *vt* (*aliment etc*) to make (*s.o.*) feel sick; (*au moral*) to sicken, nauseate. ◆**—ement** *nm* (*répugnance*) nausea, disgust.

école [ekɔl] *nf* school; (*militaire*) academy; **aller à l'é.** to go to school; **é. de danse/dessin** dancing/art school; **faire é.** to gain a following; **les grandes écoles** *university establishments giving high-level professional training*; **é. normale** teachers' training college. ◆**écolier, -ière** *nmf* schoolboy, schoolgirl.

écologie [ekɔlɔʒi] *nf* ecology. ◆**écologique** *a* ecological. ◆**écologiste** *nmf Pol* environmentalist.

éconduire [ekɔ̃dɥir] *vt* (*repousser*) to reject.

économe [ekɔnɔm] **1** *a* thrifty, economical. **2** *nmf* (*de collège etc*) bursar, steward. ◆**économie** *nf* (*activité économique, vertu*) economy; *pl* (*pécule*) savings; **une é. de** (*gain*) a saving of; **faire une é. de temps** to save time; **faire des économies** to save (up); **é. politique** economics. ◆**économique** *a* **1** (*doctrine etc*) economic; **science é.** economics. **2** (*bon marché, *avantageux*) economical. ◆**économiquement** *adv* economically. ◆**économiser** *vt* (*forces, argent, énergie etc*) to save; – *vi* to economize (**sur** on). ◆**économiste** *nmf* economist.

écoper [ekɔpe] **1** *vt* (*bateau*) to bail out, bale out. **2** *vi Fam* to cop it; **é. (de)** (*punition*) to cop, get.

écorce [ekɔrs] *nf* (*d'arbre*) bark; (*de fruit*) peel, skin; **l'é. terrestre** the earth's crust.

écorcher [ekɔrʃe] *vt* (*animal*) to skin, flay; (*érafler*) to graze; (*client*) *Fam* to fleece; (*langue étrangère*) *Fam* to murder; **é. les oreilles** to grate on one's ears; **— s'é.** *vpr* to graze oneself. ◆**écorchure** *nf* graze.

Écosse [ekɔs] *nf* Scotland. ◆**écossais, -aise** *a* Scottish; (*tissu*) tartan; (*whisky*) Scotch; – *nmf* Scot.

écosser [ekɔse] *vt* (*pois*) to shell.

écot [eko] *nm* (*quote-part*) share.

écoul/er [ekule] **1** *vt* (*se débarrasser de*) to dispose of; (*produits*) *Com* to sell (off), clear. **2 s'é.** *vpr* (*eau*) to flow out, run out; (*temps*) to pass, elapse; (*foule*) to disperse. ◆**—é** *a* (*années etc*) past. ◆**—ement** *nm* **1** (*de liquide, véhicules*) flow; (*de temps*) passage. **2** (*débit*) *Com* sale, selling.

écourter [ekurte] *vt* (*séjour, discours etc*) to cut short; (*texte, tige etc*) to shorten.

écoute [ekut] *nf* listening; **à l'é.** *Rad* tuned in, listening in (**de** to); **être aux écoutes** (*attentif*) to keep one's ears open (**de** for). ◆**écout/er** *vt* to listen to; (*radio*) to listen (in) to; – *vi* to listen; (*aux portes etc*) to eavesdrop, listen; **si je m'écoutais** if I did what I wanted. ◆**—eur** *nm* (*de téléphone*) earpiece; *pl* (*casque*) headphones, earphones.

écrabouiller [ekrabuje] *vt Fam* to crush to a pulp.

écran [ekrɑ̃] *nm* screen; **le petit é.** television.

écras/er [ekraze] *vt* (*broyer*) to crush; (*fruit, insecte*) to squash, crush; (*cigarette*) to put out; (*tuer*) *Aut* to run over; (*vaincre*) to beat (hollow), crush; (*dominer*) to outstrip; **écrasé de** (*travail, douleur*) overwhelmed with; **se faire é.** *Aut* to get run over; **— s'é.** *vpr* (*avion, voiture*) to crash (**contre** into); **s'é. dans** (*foule*) to crush *ou* squash into. ◆**—ant** *a* (*victoire, nombre, chaleur*) overwhelming. ◆**—é** *a* (*nez*) snub. ◆**—ement** *nm* crushing.

écrémer [ekreme] *vt* (*lait*) to skim, cream; (*collection etc*) *Fig* to cream off the best from.

écrevisse [ekrəvis] *nf* (*crustacé*) crayfish.

écrier (s') [sekrije] *vpr* to cry out, exclaim (**que** that).

écrin [ekrɛ̃] *nm* (jewel) case.

écrire* [ekrir] *vt* to write; (*noter*) to write (down); (*orthographier*) to spell; **é. à la machine** to type; – *vi* to write; **— s'é.** *vpr* (*mot*) to be spelt. ◆**écrit** *nm* written document, paper; (*examen*) *Scol* written paper; *pl* (*œuvres*) writings; **par é.** in writing. ◆**écriteau, -x** *nm* notice, sign. ◆**écriture** *nf* (*système*) writing; (*personnelle*) (hand)writing; *pl Com* accounts; **l'É.** *Rel* the Scripture(s). ◆**écrivain** *nm* author, writer.

écrou [ekru] *nm Tech* nut.

écrouer [ekrue] *vt* to imprison.

écroul/er (s') [sekrule] *vpr* (*édifice, projet etc*) to collapse; (*blessé etc*) to slump down, collapse. ◆**—ement** *nm* collapse.

écrue [ekry] *af* **toile é.** unbleached linen; **soie é.** raw silk.

écueil [ekœj] *nm* (*rocher*) reef; (*obstacle*) *Fig* pitfall.

écuelle [ekɥɛl] *nf* (*bol*) bowl.

éculé [ekyle] *a* (*chaussure*) worn out at the heel; *Fig* hackneyed.

écume [ekym] *nf* (*de mer, bave d'animal etc*) foam; *Culin* scum. ◆**écumer** *vt Culin* to skim; (*piller*) to plunder; – *vi* to foam (**de rage** with anger). ◆**écumoire** *nf Culin* skimmer.

écureuil [ekyrœj] *nm* squirrel.

écurie [ekyri] *nf* stable.

écusson [ekysɔ̃] *nm* (*emblème d'étoffe*) badge.

écuyer, -ère [ekɥije, -ɛr] *nmf* (*cavalier*) (horse) rider, equestrian.

eczéma [ɛgzema] *nm Méd* eczema.

édenté [edɑ̃te] *a* toothless.

édicter [edikte] *vt* to enact, decree.

édifice [edifis] *nm* building, edifice; (*ensemble organisé*) *Fig* edifice. ◆**édification** *nf* construction; edification; enlightenment. ◆**édifier** *vt* (*bâtiment*) to construct, erect; (*théorie*) to construct; **é. qn** (*moralement*) to edify s.o.; (*détromper*) *Iron* to enlighten s.o.

Édimbourg [edɛ̃bur] *nm ou f* Edinburgh.

édit [edi] *nm Hist* edict.

éditer [edite] *vt* (*publier*) to publish; (*annoter*) to edit. ◆**éditeur, -trice** *nmf* publisher; editor. ◆**édition** *nf* (*livre, journal*) edition; (*diffusion, métier*) publishing. ◆**éditorial, -aux** *nm* (*article*) editorial.

édredon [edrədɔ̃] *nm* eiderdown.

éducation [edykɑsjɔ̃] *nf* (*enseignement*) education; (*façon d'élever*) upbringing, education; **avoir de l'é.** to have good manners, be well-bred. **◆éducateur, -trice** *nmf* educator. **◆éducatif, -ive** *a* educational. **◆éduquer** *vt* (*à l'école*) to educate (*s.o.*); (*à la maison*) to bring (*s.o.*) up, educate (*s.o.*) (**à faire** to do); (*esprit*) to educate, train.

effac/er [efase] *vt* (*gommer*) to rub out, erase; (*en lavant*) to wash out; (*avec un chiffon*) to wipe away; (*souvenir*) *Fig* to blot out, erase; **— s'e.** *vpr* (*souvenir, couleur etc*) to fade; (*se placer en retrait*) to step *ou* draw aside. **◆—é** *a* (*modeste*) self-effacing. **◆—ement** *nm* (*modestie*) self-effacement.

effar/er [efare] *vt* to scare, alarm. **◆—ement** *nm* alarm.

effaroucher [efaruʃe] *vt* to scare away, frighten away.

effectif, -ive [efɛktif, -iv] **1** *a* (*réel*) effective, real. **2** *nm* (*nombre*) (total) strength; (*de classe*) *Scol* size, total number; *pl* (*employés*) & *Mil* manpower. **◆effectivement** *adv* (*en effet*) actually, effectively, indeed.

effectuer [efɛktɥe] *vt* (*expérience etc*) to carry out; (*paiement, trajet etc*) to make.

efféminé [efemine] *a* effeminate.

effervescent [efɛrvesɑ̃] *a* (*mélange, jeunesse*) effervescent. **◆effervescence** *nf* (*exaltation*) excitement, effervescence; (*de liquide*) effervescence.

effet [efɛ] *nm* **1** (*résultat*) effect; (*impression*) impression, effect (**sur** on); **faire de l'e.** (*remède etc*) to be effective; **rester sans e.** to have no effect; **à cet e.** to this end, for this purpose; **en e.** indeed, in fact; **il me fait l'e. d'être fatigué** he seems to me to be tired; **sous l'e. de la colère** (*agir*) in anger, out of anger. **2 e. de commerce** bill, draft.

effets [efɛ] *nmpl* (*vêtements*) clothes, things.

efficace [efikas] *a* (*mesure etc*) effective; (*personne*) efficient. **◆efficacité** *nf* effectiveness; efficiency.

effigie [efiʒi] *nf* effigy.

effilé [efile] *a* tapering, slender.

effilocher (s') [sefilɔʃe] *vpr* to fray.

efflanqué [eflɑ̃ke] *a* emaciated.

effleurer [eflœre] *vt* (*frôler*) to skim, touch lightly; (*égratigner*) to graze; (*question*) *Fig* to touch on; **e. qn** (*pensée etc*) to cross s.o.'s mind.

effondr/er (s') [sefɔ̃dre] *vpr* (*projet, édifice, personne*) to collapse; (*toit*) to cave in, collapse. **◆—ement** *nm* collapse; *Com* slump; (*abattement*) dejection.

efforcer (s') [sefɔrse] *vpr* **s'e. de faire** to try (hard) *ou* endeavour *ou* strive to do.

effort [efɔr] *nm* effort; **sans e.** (*réussir etc*) effortlessly; (*réussite etc*) effortless.

effraction [efraksjɔ̃] *nf* **pénétrer par e.** (*cambrioleur*) to break in; **vol avec e.** housebreaking.

effranger (s') [sefrɑ̃ʒe] *vpr* to fray.

effray/er [efreje] *vt* to frighten, scare; **— s'e.** *vpr* to be frightened *ou* scared. **◆—ant** *a* frightening, scary.

effréné [efrene] *a* unrestrained, wild.

effriter [efrite] *vt*, **— s'e.** *vpr* to crumble (away).

effroi [efrwa] *nm* (*frayeur*) dread. **◆effroyable** *a* dreadful, appalling. **◆effroyablement** *adv* dreadfully.

effronté [efrɔ̃te] *a* (*enfant etc*) cheeky, brazen; (*mensonge*) shameless. **◆effronterie** *nf* effrontery.

effusion [efyzjɔ̃] *nf* **1 e. de sang** bloodshed. **2** (*manifestation*) effusion; **avec e.** effusively.

égailler (s') [segaje] *vpr* to disperse.

égal, -ale, -aux [egal, -o] *a* equal (**à** to); (*uniforme, régulier*) even; **ça m'est é.** I don't care, it's all the same to me; **—** *nmf* (*personne*) equal; **traiter qn d'é. à é.** *ou* **en é.** to treat s.o. as an equal; **sans é.** without match. **◆—ement** *adv* (*au même degré*) equally; (*aussi*) also, as well. **◆égaler** *vt* to equal, match (**en** in); (*en quantité*) *Math* to equal. **◆égalisation** *nf Sp* equalization; levelling. **◆égaliser** *vt* to equalize; (*terrain*) to level; **—** *vi Sp* to equalize. **◆égalitaire** *a* egalitarian. **◆égalité** *nf* equality; (*regularité*) evenness; **à é. (de score)** *Sp* equal (on points); **signe d'é.** *Math* equals sign.

égard [egar] *nm* **à l'é. de** (*concernant*) with respect *ou* regard to; (*envers*) towards; **avoir des égards pour** to have respect *ou* consideration for; **à cet é.** in this respect; **à certains égards** in some respects.

égarer [egare] *vt* (*objet*) to mislay; **é. qn** (*dérouter*) to mislead s.o.; (*aveugler, troubler*) to lead s.o. astray, misguide s.o.; **— s'é.** *vpr* to lose one's way, get lost; (*objet*) to get mislaid, go astray; (*esprit*) to wander.

égayer [egeje] *vt* (*pièce*) to brighten up; **é. qn** (*réconforter, amuser*) to cheer s.o. up; **— s'é.** *vpr* (*par la moquerie*) to be amused.

égide [eʒid] *nf* **sous l'é. de** under the aegis of.

églantier [eglɑ̃tje] *nm* (*arbre*) wild rose. **◆églantine** *nf* (*fleur*) wild rose.

église [egliz] *nf* church.
égocentrique [egɔsɑ̃trik] *a* egocentric.
égoïne [egɔin] *nf* **(scie) é.** hand saw.
égoïsme [egɔism] *nm* selfishness, egoism. ◆**égoïste** *a* selfish, egoistic(al); – *nmf* egoist.
égorger [egɔrʒe] *vt* to cut *ou* slit the throat of.
égosiller (s') [segozije] *vpr* to scream one's head off, bawl out.
égotisme [egɔtism] *nm* egotism.
égout [egu] *nm* sewer; **eaux d'é.** sewage.
égoutter [egute] *vt* (*vaisselle*) to drain; (*légumes*) to strain, drain; – *vi*, – **s'é.** *vpr* to drain; to strain; (*linge*) to drip. ◆**égouttoir** *nm* (*panier*) (dish) drainer.
égratigner [egratiɲe] *vt* to scratch. ◆**égratignure** *nf* scratch.
égrener [egrəne] *vt* (*raisins*) to pick off; (*épis*) to shell; **é. son chapelet** *Rel* to count one's beads.
Égypte [eʒipt] *nf* Egypt. ◆**égyptien, -ienne** [-sjɛ̃, -sjɛn] *a* & *nmf* Egyptian.
eh! [e] *int* hey!; **eh bien!** well!
éhonté [eɔ̃te] *a* shameless; **mensonge é.** barefaced lie.
éjecter [eʒɛkte] *vt* to eject. ◆**éjectable** *a* **siège é.** *Av* ejector seat. ◆**éjection** *nf* ejection.
élaborer [elabɔre] *vt* (*système etc*) to elaborate. ◆**élaboration** *nf* elaboration.
élaguer [elage] *vt* (*arbre, texte etc*) to prune.
élan [elɑ̃] *nm* **1** (*vitesse*) momentum, impetus; (*impulsion*) impulse; (*fougue*) fervour, spirit; **prendre son é.** *Sp* to take a run (up); **d'un seul é.** in one bound. **2** (*animal*) elk.
élanc/er [elɑ̃se] **1** *vi* (*dent etc*) to give shooting pains. **2 s'é.** *vpr* (*bondir*) to leap *ou* rush (forward); **s'é. vers le ciel** (*tour*) to soar up (high) into the sky. ◆**–é** *a* (*personne, taille etc*) slender. ◆**–ement** *nm* shooting pain.
élargir [elarʒir] **1** *vt* (*chemin*) to widen; (*esprit, débat*) to broaden; – **s'é.** *vpr* (*sentier etc*) to widen out. **2** *vt* (*prisonnier*) to free.
élastique [elastik] *a* (*objet, caractère*) elastic; (*règlement, notion*) flexible, supple; – *nm* (*tissu*) elastic; (*lien*) elastic *ou* rubber band. ◆**élasticité** *nf* elasticity.
élection [elɛksjɔ̃] *nf* election; **é. partielle** by-election. ◆**électeur, -trice** *nmf* voter, elector. ◆**électoral, -aux** *a* (*campagne, réunion*) election-; **collège é.** electoral college. ◆**électorat** *nm* (*électeurs*) electorate, voters.
électricien [elɛktrisjɛ̃] *nm* electrician. ◆**électricité** *nf* electricity; **coupure d'é.** power cut. ◆**électrifier** *vt Rail* to electrify. ◆**électrique** *a* (*pendule, décharge*) electric; (*courant, fil*) electric(al); (*phénomène, effet*) *Fig* electric. ◆**électriser** *vt* (*animer*) *Fig* to electrify. ◆**électrocuter** *vt* to electrocute.
électrode [elɛktrɔd] *nf Él* electrode.
électrogène [elɛktrɔʒɛn] *a* **groupe é.** *Él* generator.
électroménager [elɛktrɔmenaʒe] *am* **appareil é.** household electrical appliance.
électron [elɛktrɔ̃] *nm* electron. ◆**électronicien, -ienne** *nmf* electronics engineer. ◆**électronique** *a* electronic; (*microscope*) electron-; – *nf* electronics.
électrophone [elɛktrɔfɔn] *nm* record player.
élégant [elegɑ̃] *a* (*style, mobilier, solution etc*) elegant; (*bien habillé*) smart, elegant. ◆**élégamment** *adv* elegantly; smartly. ◆**élégance** *nf* elegance.
élégie [eleʒi] *nf* elegy.
élément [elemɑ̃] *nm* (*composante, personne*) & *Ch* element; (*de meuble*) unit; (*d'ensemble*) *Math* member; *pl* (*notions*) rudiments, elements; **dans son é.** (*milieu*) in one's element. ◆**élémentaire** *a* elementary.
éléphant [elefɑ̃] *nm* elephant. ◆**éléphantesque** *a* (*énorme*) *Fam* elephantine.
élévateur [elevatœr] *am* **chariot é.** forklift truck.
élévation [elevɑsjɔ̃] *nf* raising; *Géom* elevation; **é. de** (*hausse*) rise in.
élève [elɛv] *nmf Scol* pupil.
élev/er [elve] *vt* (*prix, objection, voix etc*) to raise; (*enfant*) to bring up, raise; (*animal*) to breed, rear; (*âme*) to uplift, raise; – **s'é.** *vpr* (*prix, montagne, ton, avion etc*) to rise; **s'é. à** (*prix etc*) to amount to; **s'é. contre** to rise up against. ◆**–é** *a* (*haut*) high; (*noble*) noble; **bien/mal é.** well-/bad-mannered. ◆**–age** *nm* (*de bovins*) cattle rearing; **l'é. de** the breeding *ou* rearing of. ◆**–eur, -euse** *nmf* breeder.
élider [elide] *vt Ling* to elide.
éligible [eliʒibl] *a Pol* eligible (**à** for).
élimé [elime] *a* (*tissu*) threadbare, worn thin.
éliminer [elimine] *vt* to eliminate. ◆**élimination** *nf* elimination. ◆**éliminatoire** *a* & *nf* **(épreuve) é.** *Sp* heat, qualifying round.
élire* [elir] *vt Pol* to elect (**à** to).
élision [elizjɔ̃] *nf Ling* elision.
élite [elit] *nf* elite (**de** of); **d'é.** (*chef, sujet etc*) top-notch.
elle [ɛl] *pron* **1** (*sujet*) she; (*chose, animal*) it;

pl they; **e. est** she is; it is; **elles sont** they are. **2** (*complément*) her; (*chose, animal*) it; *pl* them; **pour e.** for her; **pour elles** for them; **plus grande qu'e./qu'elles** taller than her/them. ◆**e.-même** *pron* herself; (*chose, animal*) itself; *pl* themselves.

ellipse [elips] *nf Géom* ellipse. ◆**elliptique** *a* elliptical.

élocution [elɔkysjɔ̃] *nf* diction; **défaut d'é.** speech defect.

éloge [elɔʒ] *nm* praise; (*panégyrique*) eulogy; **faire l'é. de** to praise. ◆**élogieux, -euse** *a* laudatory.

éloign/er [elwaɲe] *vt* (*chose, personne*) to move *ou* take away (**de** from); (*clients*) to keep away; (*crainte, idée*) to get rid of, banish; (*date*) to put off; **é. qn de** (*sujet, but*) to take *ou* get s.o. away from; **— s'é.** *vpr* (*partir*) to move *ou* go away (**de** from); (*dans le passé*) to become (more) remote; **s'é. de** (*sujet, but*) to get away from. ◆**—é** *a* far-off, remote, distant; (*parent*) distant; **é. de** (*village, maison etc*) far (away) from; (*très différent*) far removed from. ◆**—ement** *nm* remoteness, distance; (*absence*) separation (**de** from); **avec l'é.** (*avec le recul*) with time.

élongation [elɔ̃gasjɔ̃] *nf Méd* pulled muscle.

éloquent [elɔkɑ̃] *a* eloquent. ◆**éloquence** *nf* eloquence.

élu, -ue [ely] *voir* **élire;** – *nmf Pol* elected member *ou* representative; **les élus** *Rel* the chosen, the elect.

élucider [elyside] *vt* to elucidate. ◆**élucidation** *nf* elucidation.

éluder [elyde] *vt* to elude, evade.

émacié [emasje] *a* emaciated.

émail, -aux [emaj, -o] *nm* enamel; **en é.** enamel-. ◆**émailler** *vt* to enamel.

émaillé [emaje] *a* **é. de fautes/***etc* (*texte*) peppered with errors/*etc*.

émanciper [emɑ̃sipe] *vt* (*femmes*) to emancipate; **— s'é.** *vpr* to become emancipated. ◆**émancipation** *nf* emancipation.

émaner [emane] *vi* to emanate. ◆**émanation** *nf* emanation; **une é. de** *Fig* a product of.

emball/er [ɑ̃bale] **1** *vt* (*dans une caisse etc*) to pack; (*dans du papier*) to wrap (up). **2** *vt* (*moteur*) to race; **e. qn** (*passionner*) *Fam* to enthuse s.o., thrill s.o.; **— s'e.** *vpr* (*personne*) *Fam* to get carried away; (*cheval*) to bolt; (*moteur*) to race. ◆**—é** *a Fam* enthusiastic. ◆**—age** *nm* (*action*) packing; wrapping; (*caisse*) packaging; (*papier*) wrapping (paper). ◆**—ement** *nm Fam* (sudden) enthusiasm.

embarcadère [ɑ̃barkadɛr] *nm* landing place, quay.

embarcation [ɑ̃barkasjɔ̃] *nf* (small) boat.

embardée [ɑ̃barde] *nf Aut* (sudden) swerve; **faire une e.** to swerve.

embargo [ɑ̃bargo] *nm* embargo.

embarqu/er [ɑ̃barke] *vt* (*passagers*) to embark, take on board; (*marchandises*) to load (up); (*voler*) *Fam* to walk off with; (*prisonnier*) *Fam* to cart off; **e. qn dans** (*affaire*) *Fam* to involve s.o. in, launch s.o. into; – *vi.* **— s'e.** *vpr* to embark, (go on) board; **s'e. dans** (*aventure etc*) *Fam* to embark on. ◆**—ement** *nm* (*de passagers*) boarding.

embarras [ɑ̃bara] *nm* (*malaise, gêne*) embarrassment; (*difficulté*) difficulty, trouble; (*obstacle*) obstacle; **dans l'e.** in difficulty; **faire des e.** (*chichis*) to make a fuss. ◆**embarrass/er** *vt* (*obstruer*) to clutter, encumber; **e. qn** to be in s.o.'s way; (*déconcerter*) to embarrass s.o., bother s.o.; **s'e. de** to burden oneself with; (*se soucier*) to bother oneself about. ◆**—ant** *a* (*paquet*) cumbersome; (*question*) embarrassing.

embauche [ɑ̃boʃ] *nf* (*action*) hiring; (*travail*) work. ◆**embaucher** *vt* (*ouvrier*) to hire, take on.

embaumer [ɑ̃bome] **1** *vt* (*cadavre*) to embalm. **2** *vt* (*parfumer*) to give a sweet smell to; – *vi* to smell sweet.

embell/ir [ɑ̃belir] *vt* (*texte, vérité*) to embellish; **e. qn** to make s.o. attractive. ◆**—issement** *nm* (*de ville etc*) improvement, embellishment.

embêt/er [ɑ̃bete] *vt Fam* (*contrarier, taquiner*) to annoy, bother; (*raser*) to bore; **— s'e.** *vpr Fam* to get bored. ◆**—ant** *a Fam* annoying; boring. ◆**—ement** [-ɛtmɑ̃] *nm Fam* **un e.** (some) trouble *ou* bother; **des embêtements** trouble(s), bother.

emblée (d') [dɑ̃ble] *adv* right away.

emblème [ɑ̃blɛm] *nm* emblem.

embobiner [ɑ̃bɔbine] *vt* (*tromper*) *Fam* to hoodwink.

emboîter [ɑ̃bwate] *vt*, **— s'e.** *vpr* (*pièces*) to fit into each other, fit together; **e. le pas à qn** to follow on s.o.'s heels; (*imiter*) *Fig* to follow in s.o.'s footsteps.

embonpoint [ɑ̃bɔ̃pwɛ̃] *nm* plumpness.

embouchure [ɑ̃buʃyr] *nf* (*de cours d'eau*) mouth; *Mus* mouthpiece.

embourber (s') [sɑ̃burbe] *vpr* (*véhicule*) & *Fig* to get bogged down.

embourgeoiser (s') [sɑ̃burʒwaze] *vpr* to become middle-class.

embout [ɑ̃bu] *nm* (*de canne*) tip, end piece; (*de seringue*) nozzle.

embouteill/er [ɑ̃buteje] *vt Aut* to jam, congest. ◆**—age** *nm* traffic jam.

emboutir [ɑ̃butir] *vt* (*voiture*) to bash *ou* crash into; (*métal*) to stamp, emboss.

embranch/er (s') [sɑ̃brɑ̃ʃe] *vpr* (*voie*) to branch off. ◆**—ement** *nm* (*de voie*) junction, fork; (*de règne animal*) branch.

embras/er [ɑ̃brɑze] *vt* to set ablaze; **— s'e.** *vpr* (*prendre feu*) to flare up. ◆**—ement** *nm* (*troubles*) flare-up.

embrasser [ɑ̃brase] *vt* (*adopter, contenir*) to embrace; **e. qn** to kiss s.o.; (*serrer*) to embrace *ou* hug s.o.; **— s'e.** *vpr* to kiss (each other). ◆**embrassade** *nf* embrace, hug.

embrasure [ɑ̃brazyr] *nf* (*de fenêtre, porte*) opening.

embray/er [ɑ̃breje] *vi* to let in *ou* engage the clutch. ◆**—age** *nm* (*mécanisme, pédale*) *Aut* clutch.

embrigader [ɑ̃brigade] *vt* to recruit.

embrocher [ɑ̃brɔʃe] *vt Culin & Fig* to skewer.

embrouiller [ɑ̃bruje] *vt* (*fils*) to tangle (up); (*papiers etc*) to muddle (up), mix up; **e. qn** to confuse s.o., get s.o. muddled; **— s'e.** *vpr* to get confused *ou* muddled (**dans** in, with). ◆**embrouillamini** *nm Fam* muddle, mix-up. ◆**embrouillement** *nm* confusion, muddle.

embroussaillé [ɑ̃brusaje] *a* (*barbe, chemin*) bushy.

embruns [ɑ̃brœ̃] *nmpl* (sea) spray.

embryon [ɑ̃brijɔ̃] *nm* embryo. ◆**embryonnaire** *a Méd & Fig* embryonic.

embûches [ɑ̃byʃ] *nfpl* (*difficultés*) traps, pitfalls.

embuer [ɑ̃bɥe] *vt* (*vitre, yeux*) to mist up.

embusquer (s') [sɑ̃byske] *vpr* to lie in ambush. ◆**embuscade** *nf* ambush.

éméché [emeʃe] *a* (*ivre*) *Fam* tipsy.

émeraude [ɛmrod] *nf* emerald.

émerger [emɛrʒe] *vi* to emerge (**de** from).

émeri [ɛmri] *nm* **toile (d')é.** emery cloth.

émerveill/er [emɛrveje] *vt* to amaze; **— s'é.** *vpr* to marvel, be filled with wonder (**de** at). ◆**—ement** *nm* wonder, amazement.

émett/re* [emɛtr] *vt* (*lumière, son etc*) to give out, emit; *Rad* to transmit, broadcast; (*cri*) to utter; (*opinion, vœu*) to express; (*timbre-poste, monnaie*) to issue; (*chèque*) to draw; (*emprunt*) *Com* to float. ◆**—eur** *nm* (**poste**) **é.** *Rad* transmitter.

émeute [emøt] *nf* riot. ◆**émeutier, -ière** *nmf* rioter.

émietter [emjete] *vt*, **— s'é.** *vpr* (*pain etc*) to crumble.

émigr/er [emigre] *vi* (*personne*) to emigrate. ◆**—ant, -ante** *nmf* emigrant. ◆**—é, -ée** *nmf* exile, émigré. ◆**émigration** *nf* emigration.

éminent [eminɑ̃] *a* eminent. ◆**éminemment** [-amɑ̃] *adv* eminently. ◆**éminence** *nf* **1** (*colline*) hillock. **2 son É.** *Rel* his Eminence.

émissaire [emisɛr] *nm* emissary.

émission [emisjɔ̃] *nf* (*programme*) *TV Rad* broadcast; (*action*) emission (**de** of); (*de programme*) *TV Rad* transmission; (*de timbre-poste, monnaie*) issue.

emmagasiner [ɑ̃magazine] *vt* to store (up).

emmanchure [ɑ̃mɑ̃ʃyr] *nf* (*de vêtement*) arm hole.

emmêler [ɑ̃mele] *vt* to tangle (up).

emménag/er [ɑ̃menaʒe] *vi* (*dans un logement*) to move in; **e. dans** to move into. ◆**—ement** *nm* moving in.

emmener [ɑ̃mne] *vt* to take (**à** to); (*prisonnier*) to take away; **e. qn faire une promenade** to take s.o. for a walk.

emmerd/er [ɑ̃mɛrde] *vt Arg* to annoy, bug; (*raser*) to bore stiff; **— s'e.** *vpr Arg* to get bored stiff. ◆**—ement** *nm Arg* bother, trouble. ◆**—eur, -euse** *nmf* (*personne*) *Arg* pain in the neck.

emmitoufler (s') [sɑ̃mitufle] *vpr* to wrap (oneself) up.

emmurer [ɑ̃myre] *vt* (*personne*) to wall in.

émoi [emwa] *nm* excitement; **en é.** agog, excited.

émoluments [emɔlymɑ̃] *nmpl* remuneration.

émotion [emosjɔ̃] *nf* (*trouble*) excitement; (*sentiment*) emotion; **une é.** (*peur*) a scare. ◆**émotif, -ive** *a* emotional. ◆**émotionné** *a Fam* upset.

émouss/er [emuse] *vt* (*pointe*) to blunt; (*sentiment*) to dull. ◆**—é** *a* (*pointe*) blunt; (*sentiment*) dulled.

émouv/oir* [emuvwar] *vt* (*affecter*) to move, touch; **— s'é.** *vpr* to be moved *ou* touched. ◆**—ant** *a* moving, touching.

empailler [ɑ̃paje] *vt* (*animal*) to stuff.

empaler (s') [sɑ̃pale] *vpr* to impale oneself.

empaqueter [ɑ̃pakte] *vt* to pack(age).

emparer (s') [sɑ̃pare] *vpr* **s'e. de** to seize, take hold of.

empât/er (s') [sɑ̃pɑte] *vpr* to fill out, get fat(ter). ◆**—é** *a* fleshy, fat.

empêch/er [ɑ̃peʃe] *vt* to prevent, stop; **e. qn de faire** to prevent *ou* stop s.o. (from) doing; **n'empêche qu'elle a raison** *Fam* all the same she's right; **n'empêche!** *Fam* all the same!; **elle ne peut pas s'e. de rire** she can't help laughing. **◆—ement** [-ɛʃmɑ̃] *nm* difficulty, hitch; **avoir un e.** to be unavoidably detained.

empereur [ɑ̃prœr] *nm* emperor.

empeser [ɑ̃pəze] *vt* to starch.

empester [ɑ̃pɛste] *vt* (*pièce*) to make stink, stink out; (*tabac etc*) to stink of; **e. qn** to stink s.o. out; – *vi* to stink.

empêtrer (s') [sɑ̃petre] *vpr* to get entangled (**dans** in).

emphase [ɑ̃faz] *nf* pomposity. **◆emphatique** *a* pompous.

empiéter [ɑ̃pjete] *vi* **e. sur** to encroach upon. **◆empiétement** *nm* encroachment.

empiffrer (s') [sɑ̃pifre] *vpr Fam* to gorge *ou* stuff oneself (**de** with).

empil/er [ɑ̃pile] *vt*, **— s'e.** *vpr* to pile up (**sur** on); **s'e. dans** (*personnes*) to pile into (*building, car etc*). **◆—ement** *nm* (*tas*) pile.

empire [ɑ̃pir] *nm* (*territoires*) empire; (*autorité*) hold, influence; **sous l'e. de** (*peur etc*) in the grip of.

empirer [ɑ̃pire] *vi* to worsen, get worse.

empirique [ɑ̃pirik] *a* empirical. **◆empirisme** *nm* empiricism.

emplacement [ɑ̃plasmɑ̃] *nm* site, location; (*de stationnement*) place.

emplâtre [ɑ̃plɑtr] *nm* (*onguent*) *Méd* plaster.

emplette [ɑ̃plɛt] *nf* purchase; *pl* shopping.

emplir [ɑ̃plir] *vt*, **— s'e.** *vpr* to fill (**de** with).

emploi [ɑ̃plwa] *nm* **1** (*usage*) use; **e. du temps** timetable; **mode d'e.** directions (for use). **2** (*travail*) job, position, employment; **l'e.** (*travail*) *Écon Pol* employment; **sans e.** unemployed. **◆employ/er** *vt* (*utiliser*) to use; **e. qn** (*occuper*) to employ s.o.; **— s'e.** *vpr* (*expression etc*) to be used; **s'e. à faire** to devote oneself to doing. **◆—é, -ée** *nmf* employee; (*de bureau, banque*) clerk, employee; **e. des postes/***etc* postal/*etc* worker; **e. de magasin** shop assistant, *Am* sales clerk. **◆employeur, -euse** *nmf* employer.

empocher [ɑ̃pɔʃe] *vt* (*argent*) to pocket.

empoigner [ɑ̃pwaɲe] *vt* (*saisir*) to grab, grasp; **— s'e.** *vpr* to come to blows, fight. **◆empoignade** *nf* (*querelle*) fight.

empoisonn/er [ɑ̃pwazɔne] *vt* (*personne, aliment, atmosphère*) to poison; (*empester*) to stink out; (*gâter, altérer*) to trouble, bedevil; **e. qn** (*embêter*) *Fam* to get on s.o.'s nerves; **— s'e.** *vpr* (*par accident*) to be poisoned; (*volontairement*) to poison oneself. **◆—ant** *a* (*embêtant*) *Fam* irritating. **◆—ement** *nm* poisoning; (*ennui*) *Fam* problem, trouble.

emport/er [ɑ̃pɔrte] *vt* (*prendre*) to take (away) (**avec soi** with one); (*enlever*) to take away; (*prix, trophée*) to carry off; (*décision*) to carry; (*entraîner*) to carry along *ou* away; (*par le vent*) to blow off *ou* away; (*par les vagues*) to sweep away; (*par la maladie*) to carry off; **l'e. sur qn** to get the upper hand over s.o.; **se laisser e.** *Fig* to get carried away (**par** by); **— s'e.** *vpr* to lose one's temper (**contre** with). **◆—é** *a* (*caractère*) hot-tempered. **◆—ement** *nm* anger; *pl* fits of anger.

empoté [ɑ̃pɔte] *a Fam* clumsy.

empourprer (s') [sɑ̃purpre] *vpr* to turn crimson.

empreint [ɑ̃prɛ̃] *a* **e. de** stamped with, heavy with.

empreinte [ɑ̃prɛ̃t] *nf* (*marque*) & *Fig* mark, stamp; **e. digitale** fingerprint; **e. des pas** footprint.

empress/er (s') [sɑ̃prese] *vpr* **s'e. de faire** to hasten to do; **s'e. auprès de qn** to busy oneself with s.o., be attentive to s.o.; **s'e. autour de qn** to rush around s.o. **◆—é** *a* eager, attentive; **e. à faire** eager to do. **◆—ement** [-ɛsmɑ̃] *nm* (*hâte*) eagerness; (*auprès de qn*) attentiveness.

emprise [ɑ̃priz] *nf* ascendancy, hold (**sur** over).

emprisonn/er [ɑ̃prizɔne] *vt Jur* to imprison; (*enfermer*) *Fig* to confine. **◆—ement** *nm* imprisonment.

emprunt [ɑ̃prœ̃] *nm* (*argent*) *Com* loan; (*mot*) *Ling* borrowed word; **un e. à** *Ling* a borrowing from; **l'e. de qch** the borrowing of sth; **d'e.** borrowed; **nom d'e.** assumed name. **◆emprunt/er** *vt* (*obtenir*) to borrow (**à qn** from s.o.); (*route etc*) to use; (*nom*) to assume; **e. à** (*tirer de*) to derive *ou* borrow from. **◆—é** *a* (*gêné*) ill-at-ease.

empuantir [ɑ̃pɥɑ̃tir] *vt* to make stink, stink out.

ému [emy] *voir* **émouvoir;** – *a* (*attendri*) moved; (*apeuré*) nervous; (*attristé*) upset; **une voix émue** a voice charged with emotion.

émulation [emylɑsjɔ̃] *nf* emulation.

émule [emyl] *nmf* imitator, follower.

en[1] [ɑ̃] *prép* **1** (*lieu*) in; (*direction*) to; **être en ville/en France** to be in town/in France; **aller en ville/en France** to go (in)to town/to France. **2** (*temps*) in; **en été** in summer; **en février** in February; **d'heure en heure** from hour to hour. **3** (*moyen, état etc*) by; in; at; on; **en avion** by plane; **en groupe**

in a group; **en mer** at sea; **en guerre** at war; **en fleur** in flower; **en congé** on leave; **en vain** in vain. **4** (*matière*) in; **en bois** wooden, in wood; **chemise en nylon** nylon shirt; **c'est en or** it's (made of) gold. **5** (*comme*) **en cadeau** as a present; **en ami** as a friend. **6** (+ *participe présent*) **en mangeant/chantant/***etc* while eating/singing/*etc*; **en apprenant que . . .** on hearing that . . . ; **en souriant** smiling, with a smile; **en ne disant rien** by saying nothing; **sortir en courant** to run out. **7** (*transformation*) into; **traduire en** to translate into.

en² [ɑ̃] *pron & adv* **1** (= *de là*) from there; **j'en viens** I've just come from there. **2** (= *de ça, lui, eux etc*) **il en est content** he's pleased with it *ou* him *ou* them; **en parler** to talk about it; **en mourir** to die of *ou* from it; **elle m'en frappa** she struck me with it. **3** (*partitif*) some; **j'en ai** I have some; **en veux-tu?** do you want some *ou* any?; **je t'en supplie** I beg you (to).

encadr/er [ɑ̃kadre] *vt* (*tableau*) to frame; (*entourer d'un trait*) to box in; (*troupes, étudiants*) to supervise, train; (*prisonnier, accusé*) to flank. **◆—ement** *nm* (*action*) framing; supervision; (*de porte, photo*) frame; (*décor*) setting; (*personnel*) training and supervisory staff.

encaissé [ɑ̃kese] *a* (*vallée*) deep.

encaisser [ɑ̃kese] *vt* (*argent, loyer etc*) to collect; (*effet, chèque*) *Com* to cash; (*coup*) *Fam* to take; **je ne peux pas l'e.** *Fam* I can't stand him *ou* her. **◆encaissement** *nm* (*de loyer etc*) collection; (*de chèque*) cashing.

encapuchonné [ɑ̃kapyʃɔne] *a* hooded.

encart [ɑ̃kar] *nm* (*feuille*) insert. **◆encarter** *vt* to insert.

en-cas [ɑ̃kɑ] *nm inv* (*repas*) snack.

encastrer [ɑ̃kastre] *vt* to build in (**dans** to), embed (**dans** into).

encaustique [ɑ̃kostik] *nf* (wax) polish. **◆encaustiquer** *vt* to wax, polish.

enceinte [ɑ̃sɛ̃t] **1** *af* (*femme*) pregnant; **e. de six mois/***etc* six months/*etc* pregnant. **2** *nf* (*muraille*) (surrounding) wall; (*espace*) enclosure; **e. acoustique** (loud)speakers.

encens [ɑ̃sɑ̃] *nm* incense. **◆encensoir** *nm Rel* censer.

encercler [ɑ̃sɛrkle] *vt* to surround, encircle.

enchaîner [ɑ̃ʃene] *vt* (*animal*) to chain (up); (*prisonnier*) to put in chains, chain (up); (*assembler*) to link (up), connect; — *vi* (*continuer à parler*) to continue; — **s'e.** *vpr* (*idées etc*) to be linked (up). **◆enchaînement** *nm* (*succession*) chain, series; (*liaison*) link(ing) (**de** between, of).

enchant/er [ɑ̃ʃɑ̃te] *vt* (*ravir*) to delight, enchant; (*ensorceler*) to bewitch, enchant. **◆—é** *a* (*ravi*) delighted (**de** with, **que** (+ *sub*) that); **e. de faire votre connaissance!** pleased to meet you! **◆—ement** *nm* delight; enchantment; **comme par e.** as if by magic. **◆—eur** *a* delightful, enchanting; — *nm* (*sorcier*) magician.

enchâsser [ɑ̃ʃɑse] *vt* (*diamant*) to set, embed.

enchère [ɑ̃ʃɛr] *nf* (*offre*) bid; **vente aux enchères** auction; **mettre aux enchères** to (put up for) auction. **◆enchér/ir** *vi* **e. sur qn** to outbid s.o. **◆—isseur** *nm* bidder.

enchevêtrer [ɑ̃ʃvetre] *vt* to (en)tangle; — **s'e.** *vpr* to get entangled (**dans** in). **◆enchevêtrement** *nm* tangle, entanglement.

enclave [ɑ̃klav] *nf* enclave. **◆enclaver** *vt* to enclose (completely).

enclencher [ɑ̃klɑ̃ʃe] *vt Tech* to engage.

enclin [ɑ̃klɛ̃] *am* **e. à** inclined *ou* prone to.

enclore [ɑ̃klɔr] *vt* (*terrain*) to enclose. **◆enclos** *nm* (*terrain, clôture*) enclosure.

enclume [ɑ̃klym] *nf* anvil.

encoche [ɑ̃kɔʃ] *nf* notch, nick (**à** in).

encoignure [ɑ̃kwaɲyr] *nf* corner.

encoller [ɑ̃kɔle] *vt* to paste.

encolure [ɑ̃kɔlyr] *nf* (*de cheval, vêtement*) neck; (*tour du cou*) collar (size).

encombre (sans) [sɑ̃zɑ̃kɔ̃br] *adv* without a hitch.

encombr/er [ɑ̃kɔ̃bre] *vt* (*couloir, pièce etc*) to clutter up (**de** with); (*rue*) to congest, clog (**de** with); **e. qn** to hamper s.o.; **s'e. de** to burden *ou* saddle oneself with. **◆—ant** *a* (*paquet*) bulky, cumbersome; (*présence*) awkward. **◆—é** *a* (*profession, marché*) overcrowded, saturated. **◆—ement** *nm* (*embarras*) clutter; *Aut* traffic jam; (*volume*) bulk(iness).

encontre de (à l') [alɑ̃kɔ̃trədə] *adv* against; (*contrairement à*) contrary to.

encore [ɑ̃kɔr] *adv* **1** (*toujours*) still; **tu es e. là?** are you still here? **2** (*avec négation*) yet; **pas e.** not yet; **ne pars pas e.** don't go yet; **je ne suis pas e. prêt** I'm not ready yet, I'm still not ready. **3** (*de nouveau*) again; **essaie e.** try again. **4** (*de plus*) **e. un café** another coffee, one more coffee; **e. une fois** (once) again, once more; **e. un** another (one), one more; **e. du pain** (some) more bread; **que veut-il e.?** what else *ou* more does he want?; **e. quelque chose** something else; **qui/quoi e.?** who/what else?; **chante e.** sing some more. **5** (*avec comparatif*) even, still; **e. mieux** even better, better still. **6** (*aussi*) also. **7 si e.** (*si seulement*) if only; **et e.!** (*à peine*) if that!, only just! **8 e. que** (+ *sub*) although.

encourag/er [ɑ̃kuraʒe] *vt* to encourage (à faire to do). ◆**—eant** *a* encouraging. ◆**—ement** *nm* encouragement.

encourir* [ɑ̃kurir] *vt* (*amende etc*) to incur.

encrasser [ɑ̃krase] *vt* to clog up (with dirt).

encre [ɑ̃kr] *nf* ink; **e. de Chine** Indian ink; **e. sympathique** invisible ink. ◆**encrier** *nm* inkwell, inkpot.

encroûter (s') [sɑ̃krute] *vpr Péj* to get set in one's ways; **s'e. dans** (*habitude*) to get stuck in.

encyclique [ɑ̃siklik] *nf Rel* encyclical.

encyclopédie [ɑ̃siklɔpedi] *nf* encyclop(a)edia. ◆**encyclopédique** *a* encyclop(a)edic.

endémique [ɑ̃demik] *a* endemic.

endetter [ɑ̃dete] *vt* **e. qn** to get s.o. into debt; **— s'e.** *vpr* to get into debt. ◆**endettement** *nm* (*dettes*) debts.

endeuiller [ɑ̃dœje] *vt* to plunge into mourning.

endiablé [ɑ̃djɑble] *a* (*rythme etc*) frantic, wild.

endiguer [ɑ̃dige] *vt* (*fleuve*) to dam (up); (*réprimer*) *Fig* to stem.

endimanché [ɑ̃dimɑ̃ʃe] *a* in one's Sunday best.

endive [ɑ̃div] *nf* chicory, endive.

endoctrin/er [ɑ̃dɔktrine] *vt* to indoctrinate. ◆**—ement** *nm* indoctrination.

endolori [ɑ̃dɔlɔri] *a* painful, aching.

endommager [ɑ̃dɔmaʒe] *vt* to damage.

endorm/ir* [ɑ̃dɔrmir] *vt* (*enfant, patient*) to put to sleep; (*ennuyer*) to send to sleep; (*soupçons etc*) to lull; (*douleur*) to deaden; **— s'e.** *vpr* to fall asleep, go to sleep. ◆**—i** *a* asleep, sleeping; (*indolent*) *Fam* sluggish.

endosser [ɑ̃dose] *vt* (*vêtement*) to put on, don; (*responsabilité*) to assume; (*chèque*) to endorse.

endroit [ɑ̃drwa] *nm* **1** place, spot; (*de film, livre*) part, place. **2** (*de tissu*) right side; **à l'e.** (*vêtement*) right side out, the right way round.

enduire* [ɑ̃dɥir] *vt* to smear, coat (**de** with). ◆**enduit** *nm* coating; (*de mur*) plaster.

endurant [ɑ̃dyrɑ̃] *a* hardy, tough. ◆**endurance** *nf* endurance.

endurc/ir [ɑ̃dyrsir] *vt* to harden; **s'e. à** (*personne*) to become hardened to (*pain etc*). ◆**—i** *a* hardened; (*célibataire*) confirmed. ◆**—issement** *nm* hardening.

endurer [ɑ̃dyre] *vt* to endure, bear.

énergie [enɛrʒi] *nf* energy; **avec é.** (*protester etc*) forcefully. ◆**énergétique** *a* (*ressources etc*) energy-. ◆**énergique** *a* (*dynamique*) energetic; (*remède*) powerful; (*mesure, ton*) forceful. ◆**énergiquement** *adv* (*protester etc*) energetically.

énergumène [enɛrgymɛn] *nmf Péj* rowdy character.

énerv/er [enɛrve] *vt* **é. qn** (*irriter*) to get on s.o.'s nerves; (*rendre énervé*) to make s.o. nervous; **— s'é.** *vpr* to get worked up. ◆**—é** *a* on edge, irritated. ◆**—ement** *nm* irritation, nervousness.

enfant [ɑ̃fɑ̃] *nmf* child (*pl* children); **e. en bas âge** infant; **un e. de** (*originaire*) a native of; **attendre un e.** to expect a baby *ou* a child; **e. trouvé** foundling; **e. de chœur** *Rel* altar boy; **e. prodige** child prodigy; **e. prodigue** prodigal son; **bon e.** (*caractère*) good natured. ◆**enfance** *nf* childhood; **première e.** infancy, early childhood; **dans son e.** (*science etc*) in its infancy. ◆**enfanter** *vt* to give birth to; **–** *vi* to give birth. ◆**enfantillage** *nm* childishness. ◆**enfantin** *a* (*voix, joie*) childlike; (*langage, jeu*) children's; (*puéril*) childish; (*simple*) easy.

enfer [ɑ̃fɛr] *nm* hell; **d'e.** (*vision, bruit*) infernal; **feu d'e.** roaring fire; **à un train d'e.** at breakneck speed.

enfermer [ɑ̃fɛrme] *vt* (*personne etc*) to shut up, lock up; (*objet précieux*) to lock up, shut away; (*jardin*) to enclose; **s'e. dans** (*chambre etc*) to shut *ou* lock oneself (up) in; (*attitude etc*) *Fig* to maintain stubbornly.

enferrer (s') [sɑ̃fere] *vpr* **s'e. dans** to get caught up in.

enfiévré [ɑ̃fjevre] *a* (*surexcité*) feverish.

enfiler [ɑ̃file] *vt* (*aiguille*) to thread; (*perles etc*) to string; (*vêtement*) *Fam* to slip on, pull on; (*rue, couloir*) to take; **s'e. dans** (*rue etc*) to take. ◆**enfilade** *nf* (*série*) row, string.

enfin [ɑ̃fɛ̃] *adv* (*à la fin*) finally, at last; (*en dernier lieu*) lastly; (*en somme*) in a word; (*conclusion résignée*) well; **e. bref** (*en somme*) *Fam* in a word; **il est grand, e. pas trop petit** he's tall – well, not too short anyhow; **mais e.** but; **(mais) e.!** for heaven's sake!

enflamm/er [ɑ̃flame] *vt* to set fire to, ignite; (*allumette*) to light; (*irriter*) *Méd* to inflame; (*imagination, colère*) to excite, inflame; **— s'e.** *vpr* to catch fire, ignite; **s'e. de colère** to flare up. ◆**—é** *a* (*discours*) fiery.

enfler [ɑ̃fle] *vt* to swell; (*voix*) to raise; – *vi Méd* to swell (up). ◆**enflure** *nf* swelling.

enfonc/er [ɑ̃fɔ̃se] *vt* (*clou etc*) to knock in, drive in; (*chapeau*) to push *ou* force down; (*porte, voiture*) to smash in; **e. dans** (*couteau, mains etc*) to plunge into; – *vi*, — **s'e.** *vpr* (*s'enliser*) to sink (**dans** into); **s'e. dans** (*pénétrer*) to plunge into, disappear (deep) into. ◆**—é** *a* (*yeux*) sunken.

enfouir [ɑ̃fwir] *vt* to bury.

enfourcher [ɑ̃furʃe] *vt* (*cheval etc*) to mount, bestride.

enfourner [ɑ̃furne] *vt* to put in the oven.

enfreindre* [ɑ̃frɛ̃dr] *vt* to infringe.

enfuir* (s') [sɑ̃fɥir] *vpr* to run away *ou* off, flee (**de** from).

enfumer [ɑ̃fyme] *vt* (*pièce*) to fill with smoke; (*personne*) to smoke out.

engag/er [ɑ̃gaʒe] *vt* (*bijou etc*) to pawn; (*parole*) to pledge; (*discussion, combat*) to start; (*clef etc*) to insert (**dans** into); (*capitaux*) to tie up, invest; **e. la bataille avec** to join battle with; **e. qn** (*lier*) to bind s.o., commit s.o.; (*embaucher*) to hire s.o., engage s.o.; **e. qn dans** (*affaire etc*) to involve s.o. in; **e. qn à faire** (*exhorter*) to urge s.o. to do; — **s'e.** *vpr* (*s'inscrire*) *Mil* to enlist; *Sp* to enter; (*au service d'une cause*) to commit oneself; (*action*) to start; **s'e. à faire** to commit oneself to doing, undertake to do; **s'e. dans** (*voie*) to enter; (*affaire etc*) to get involved in. ◆**—eant** *a* engaging, inviting. ◆**—é** *a* (*écrivain etc*) committed. ◆**—ement** *nm* (*promesse*) commitment; (*commencement*) start; (*de recrues*) *Mil* enlistment; (*inscription*) *Sp* entry; (*combat*) *Mil* engagement; **prendre l'e. de** to undertake to.

engelure [ɑ̃ʒlyr] *nf* chilblain.

engendrer [ɑ̃ʒɑ̃dre] *vt* (*procréer*) to beget; (*causer*) to generate, engender.

engin [ɑ̃ʒɛ̃] *nm* machine, device; (*projectile*) missile; **e. explosif** explosive device.

englober [ɑ̃glɔbe] *vt* to include, embrace.

engloutir [ɑ̃glutir] *vt* (*avaler*) to wolf (down), gobble (up); (*faire sombrer ou disparaître*) to engulf.

engorger [ɑ̃gɔrʒe] *vt* to block up, clog.

engouement [ɑ̃gumɑ̃] *nm* craze.

engouffrer [ɑ̃gufre] *vt* (*avaler*) to wolf (down); (*fortune*) to consume; **s'e. dans** to sweep *ou* rush into.

engourd/ir [ɑ̃gurdir] *vt* (*membre*) to numb; (*esprit*) to dull; — **s'e.** *vpr* to go numb; to become dull. ◆**—issement** *nm* numbness; dullness.

engrais [ɑ̃grɛ] *nm* (*naturel*) manure; (*chimique*) fertilizer.

engraisser [ɑ̃grese] *vt* (*animal*) to fatten (up); – *vi*, — **s'e.** *vpr* to get fat, put on weight.

engrenage [ɑ̃grənaʒ] *nm Tech* gears; *Fig* mesh, chain, web.

engueuler [ɑ̃gœle] *vt* **e. qn** *Fam* to swear at s.o., give s.o. hell. ◆**engueulade** *nf Fam* (*réprimande*) dressing-down, severe talking-to; (*dispute*) slanging match, row.

enhardir [ɑ̃ardir] *vt* to make bolder; **s'e. à faire** to make bold to do.

énième [ɛnjɛm] *a Fam* umpteenth, nth.

énigme [enigm] *nf* enigma, riddle. ◆**énigmatique** *a* enigmatic.

enivrer [ɑ̃nivre] *vt* (*soûler, troubler*) to intoxicate; — **s'e.** *vpr* to get drunk (**de** on).

enjamber [ɑ̃ʒɑ̃be] *vt* to step over; (*pont etc*) to span (*river etc*). ◆**enjambée** *nf* stride.

enjeu, -x [ɑ̃ʒø] *nm* (*mise*) stake(s).

enjoindre [ɑ̃ʒwɛ̃dr] *vt* **e. à qn de faire** *Litt* to order s.o. to do.

enjôler [ɑ̃ʒole] *vt* to wheedle, coax.

enjoliv/er [ɑ̃ʒɔlive] *vt* to embellish. ◆**—eur** *nm Aut* hubcap.

enjoué [ɑ̃ʒwe] *a* playful. ◆**enjouement** *nm* playfulness.

enlacer [ɑ̃lase] *vt* to entwine; (*serrer dans ses bras*) to clasp.

enlaidir [ɑ̃ledir] *vt* to make ugly; – *vi* to grow ugly.

enlev/er [ɑ̃lve] *vt* to take away *ou* off, remove (**à qn** from s.o.); (*ordures*) to collect; (*vêtement*) to take off, remove; (*tache*) to take out, lift, remove; (*enfant etc*) to kidnap, abduct; — **s'e.** *vpr* (*tache*) to come out; (*vernis*) to come off. ◆**—é** *a* (*scène, danse etc*) well-rendered. ◆**enlèvement** *nm* kidnapping, abduction; (*d'un objet*) removal; (*des ordures*) collection.

enliser (s') [sɑ̃lize] *vpr* (*véhicule*) & *Fig* to get bogged down (**dans** in).

enneigé [ɑ̃neʒe] *a* snow-covered. ◆**enneigement** *nm* snow coverage; **bulletin d'e.** snow report.

ennemi, -ie [ɛnmi] *nmf* enemy; – *a* (*personne*) hostile (**de** to); (*pays etc*) enemy-.

ennui [ɑ̃nɥi] *nm* boredom; (*mélancolie*) weariness; **un e.** (*tracas*) (some) trouble *ou* bother; **des ennuis** trouble(s), bother; **l'e., c'est que . . .** the annoying thing is that . . . .

ennuy/er [ɑ̃nɥije] *vt* (*agacer*) to annoy, bother; (*préoccuper*) to bother; (*fatiguer*) to bore; — **s'e.** *vpr* to get bored. ◆**—é**

a (*air*) bored; **je suis e.** that annoys *ou* bothers me. ◆**ennuyeux, -euse** *a* (*fastidieux*) boring; (*contrariant*) annoying.

énonc/er [enɔ̃se] *vt* to state, express. ◆**—é** *nm* (*de texte*) wording, terms; (*phrase*) *Ling* utterance.

enorgueillir [ɑ̃nɔrgœjir] *vt* to make proud; **s'e. de** to pride oneself on.

énorme [enɔrm] *a* enormous, huge, tremendous. ◆**énormément** *adv* enormously, tremendously; **e. de** an enormous *ou* tremendous amount of. ◆**énormité** *nf* (*dimension*) enormity; (*faute*) (enormous) blunder.

enquérir (s') [sɑ̃kerir] *vpr* **s'e. de** to inquire about.

enquête [ɑ̃kɛt] *nf* (*de police etc*) investigation; (*judiciaire, administrative*) inquiry; (*sondage*) survey. ◆**enquêter** *vi* (*police etc*) to investigate; **e. sur** (*crime*) to investigate. ◆**enquêteur, -euse** *nmf* investigator.

enquiquiner [ɑ̃kikine] *vt* *Fam* to annoy, bug.

enraciner (s') [sɑ̃rasine] *vpr* to take root; **enraciné dans** (*personne, souvenir*) rooted in; **bien enraciné** (*préjugé etc*) deep-rooted.

enrag/er [ɑ̃raʒe] *vi* **e. de faire** to be furious about doing; **faire e. qn** to get on s.o.'s nerves. ◆**—eant** *a* infuriating. ◆**—é** *a* (*chien*) rabid, mad; (*joueur etc*) *Fam* fanatical (**de** about); **rendre/devenir e.** (*furieux*) to make/become furious.

enrayer [ɑ̃reje] *vt* (*maladie etc*) to check; — **s'e.** *vpr* (*fusil*) to jam.

enregistr/er [ɑ̃rʒistre] *vt* **1** (*inscrire*) to record; (*sur registre*) to register; (*constater*) to note, register; **(faire) e.** (*bagages*) to register, *Am* check. **2** (*musique, émission etc*) to record. ◆**—ement** *nm* (*des bagages*) registration, *Am* checking; (*d'un acte*) registration; (*sur bande etc*) recording. ◆**—eur, -euse** *a* (*appareil*) recording-; **caisse enregistreuse** cash register.

enrhumer [ɑ̃ryme] *vt* **e. qn** to give s.o. a cold; **être enrhumé** to have a cold; — **s'e.** *vpr* to catch a cold.

enrich/ir [ɑ̃riʃir] *vt* to enrich (**de** with); — **s'e.** *vpr* (*personne*) to get rich. ◆**—issement** *nm* enrichment.

enrober [ɑ̃rɔbe] *vt* to coat (**de** in); **enrobé de chocolat** chocolate-coated.

enrôl/er [ɑ̃role] *vt*, — **s'e.** *vpr* to enlist. ◆**—ement** *nm* enlistment.

enrou/er (s') [sɑ̃rwe] *vpr* to get hoarse. ◆**—é** *a* hoarse. ◆**—ement** [ɑ̃rumɑ̃] *nm* hoarseness.

enrouler [ɑ̃rule] *vt* (*fil etc*) to wind; (*tapis, cordage*) to roll up; **s'e. dans** (*couvertures*) to roll *ou* wrap oneself up in; **s'e. sur** *ou* **autour de qch** to wind round sth.

ensabler [ɑ̃sable] *vt*, — **s'e.** *vpr* (*port*) to silt up.

ensanglanté [ɑ̃sɑ̃glɑ̃te] *a* bloodstained.

enseigne [ɑ̃sɛɲ] **1** *nf* (*de magasin etc*) sign; **e. lumineuse** neon sign; **logés à la même e.** *Fig* in the same boat. **2** *nm* **e. de vaisseau** lieutenant, *Am* ensign.

enseign/er [ɑ̃seɲe] *vt* to teach; **e. qch à qn** to teach s.o. sth; — *vi* to teach. ◆**—ant, -ante** [-ɛɲɑ̃, -ɑ̃t] *a* (*corps*) teaching-; — *nmf* teacher. ◆**—ement** [-ɛɲmɑ̃] *nm* education; (*action, métier*) teaching.

ensemble [ɑ̃sɑ̃bl] **1** *adv* together. **2** *nm* (*d'objets*) group, set; *Math* set; *Mus* ensemble; (*mobilier*) suite; (*vêtement féminin*) outfit; (*harmonie*) unity; **l'e. du personnel** (*totalité*) the whole (of the) staff; **l'e. des enseignants** all (of) the teachers; **dans l'e.** on the whole; **d'e.** (*vue etc*) general; **grand e.** (*quartier*) housing complex *ou* *Am* development; (*ville*) = new town, = *Am* planned community. ◆**ensemblier** *nm* (interior) decorator.

ensemencer [ɑ̃smɑ̃se] *vt* (*terre*) to sow.

ensevelir [ɑ̃səvlir] *vt* to bury.

ensoleillé [ɑ̃sɔleje] *a* (*endroit, journée*) sunny.

ensommeillé [ɑ̃sɔmeje] *a* sleepy.

ensorceler [ɑ̃sɔrsəle] *vt* (*envoûter, séduire*) to bewitch. ◆**ensorcellement** *nm* (*séduction*) spell.

ensuite [ɑ̃sɥit] *adv* (*puis*) next, then; (*plus tard*) afterwards.

ensuivre* (s') [sɑ̃sɥivr] *vpr* to follow, ensue; — *v imp* **il s'ensuit que** it follows that.

entacher [ɑ̃taʃe] *vt* (*honneur etc*) to sully, taint.

entaille [ɑ̃taj] *nf* (*fente*) notch; (*blessure*) gash, slash. ◆**entailler** *vt* to notch; to gash, slash.

entame [ɑ̃tam] *nf* first slice.

entamer [ɑ̃tame] *vt* (*pain, peau etc*) to cut (into); (*bouteille, boîte etc*) to start (on); (*négociations etc*) to enter into, start; (*sujet*) to broach; (*capital*) to break *ou* eat into; (*métal, plastique*) to damage; (*résolution, réputation*) to shake.

entass/er [ɑ̃tɑse] *vt*, — **s'e.** *vpr* (*objets*) to pile up, heap up; **(s')e. dans** (*passagers etc*) to crowd *ou* pack *ou* pile into; **ils s'entassaient sur la plage** they were crowded *ou* packed (together) on the beach.

◆—**ement** *nm* (*tas*) pile, heap; (*de gens*) crowding.
entend/re [ɑ̃tɑ̃dr] *vt* to hear; (*comprendre*) to understand; (*vouloir*) to intend, mean; **e. parler de** to hear of; **e. dire que** to hear (it said) that; **e. raison** to listen to reason; **laisser e. à qn que** to give s.o. to understand that; **— s'e.** *vpr* (*être entendu*) to be heard; (*être compris*) to be understood; **s'e. (sur)** (*être d'accord*) to agree (on); **s'e. (avec qn)** (*s'accorder*) to get on (with s.o.); **on ne s'entend plus!** (*à cause du bruit etc*) we can't hear ourselves speak!; **il s'y entend** (*est expert*) he knows all about that. ◆—**u** *a* (*convenu*) agreed; (*compris*) understood; (*sourire, air*) knowing; **e.!** all right!; **bien e.** of course. ◆—**ement** *nm* (*faculté*) understanding. ◆**entente** *nf* (*accord*) agreement, understanding; **(bonne) e.** (*amitié*) good relationship, harmony.
entériner [ɑ̃terine] *vt* to ratify.
enterrer [ɑ̃tere] *vt* (*mettre en ou sous terre*) to bury; (*projet*) *Fig* to scrap. ◆**enterrement** *nm* burial; (*funérailles*) funeral.
entêtant [ɑ̃tɛtɑ̃] *a* (*enivrant*) heady.
en-tête [ɑ̃tɛt] *nm* (*de papier*) heading; **papier à en-tête** headed paper.
entêt/er (s') [sɑ̃tete] *vpr* to persist (**à faire** in doing). ◆—**é** *a* (*têtu*) stubborn; (*persévérant*) persistent. ◆—**ement** [ɑ̃tɛtmɑ̃] *nm* stubbornness; (*à faire qch*) persistence.
enthousiasme [ɑ̃tuzjasm] *nm* enthusiasm. ◆**enthousiasmer** *vt* to fill with enthusiasm, enthuse; **s'e. pour** to be *ou* get enthusiastic over, enthuse over. ◆**enthousiaste** *a* enthusiastic.
enticher (s') [sɑ̃tiʃe] *vpr* **s'e. de** to become infatuated with.
entier, -ière [ɑ̃tje, -jɛr] **1** *a* (*total*) whole, entire; (*absolu*) absolute, complete, entire; (*intact*) intact; **payer place entière** to pay full price; **le pays tout e.** the whole *ou* entire country; **—** *nm* (*unité*) whole; **en e., dans son e.** in its entirety, completely. **2** *a* (*caractère, personne*) unyielding. ◆**entièrement** *adv* entirely.
entité [ɑ̃tite] *nf* entity.
entonner [ɑ̃tɔne] *vt* (*air*) to start singing.
entonnoir [ɑ̃tɔnwar] *nm* (*ustensile*) funnel.
entorse [ɑ̃tɔrs] *nf Méd* sprain; **e. à** (*règlement*) infringement of.
entortill/er [ɑ̃tɔrtije] *vt* **e. qch autour de qch** (*papier etc*) to wrap sth around sth; **e. qn** *Fam* to dupe s.o., get round s.o.; **— s'e.** *vpr* (*lierre etc*) to wind, twist. ◆—**é** *a* (*phrase etc*) convoluted.
entour/er [ɑ̃ture] *vt* to surround (**de** with); (*envelopper*) to wrap (**de** in); **e. qn de ses bras** to put one's arms round s.o.; **s'e. de** to surround oneself with. ◆—**age** *nm* (*proches*) circle of family and friends.
entourloupette [ɑ̃turlupɛt] *nf Fam* nasty trick.
entracte [ɑ̃trakt] *nm Th* interval, *Am* intermission.
entraide [ɑ̃trɛd] *nf* mutual aid. ◆**s'entraider** [sɑ̃trede] *vpr* to help each other.
entrailles [ɑ̃traj] *nfpl* entrails.
entrain [ɑ̃trɛ̃] *nm* spirit, liveliness; **plein d'e.** lively.
entraîn/er [ɑ̃trene] **1** *vt* (*charrier*) to sweep *ou* carry away; (*roue*) *Tech* to drive; (*causer*) to bring about; (*impliquer*) to entail, involve; **e. qn** (*emmener*) to lead *ou* draw s.o. (away); (*de force*) to drag s.o. (away); (*attirer*) *Péj* to lure s.o.; (*charmer*) to carry s.o. away; **e. qn à faire** (*amener*) to lead s.o. to do. **2** *vt* (*athlète, cheval etc*) to train (**à** for); **— s'e.** *vpr* to train oneself; *Sp* to train. ◆—**ant** [-ɛnɑ̃] *a* (*musique*) captivating. ◆—**ement** [-ɛnmɑ̃] *nm* **1** *Sp* training. **2** *Tech* drive; (*élan*) impulse. ◆—**eur** [-ɛnœr] *nm* (*instructeur*) *Sp* trainer, coach; (*de cheval*) trainer.
entrave [ɑ̃trav] *nf* (*obstacle*) *Fig* hindrance (**à** to). ◆**entraver** *vt* to hinder, hamper.
entre [ɑ̃tr(ə)] *prép* between; (*parmi*) among(st); **l'un d'e. vous** one of you; **(soit dit) e. nous** between you and me; **se dévorer e. eux** (*réciprocité*) to devour each other; **e. deux âges** middle-aged; **e. autres** among other things; **e. les mains de** in the hands of.
entrebâill/er [ɑ̃trəbaje] *vt* (*porte*) to open slightly. ◆—**é** *a* ajar, slightly open. ◆—**eur** *nm* **e. (de porte)** door chain.
entrechoquer (s') [sɑ̃trəʃɔke] *vpr* (*bouteilles etc*) to knock against each other, chink.
entrecôte [ɑ̃trəkot] *nf* (boned) rib steak.
entrecouper [ɑ̃trəkupe] *vt* (*entremêler*) to punctuate (**de** with), intersperse (**de** with).
entrecroiser [ɑ̃trəkrwaze] *vt*, **— s'e.** *vpr* (*fils*) to interlace; (*routes*) to intersect.
entre-deux-guerres [ɑ̃trədøgɛr] *nm inv* inter-war period.
entrée [ɑ̃tre] *nf* (*action*) entry, entrance; (*porte*) entrance; (*accès*) entry, admission (**de** to); (*vestibule*) entrance hall, entry; (*billet*) ticket (of admission); *Culin* first course, entrée; (*mot dans un dictionnaire etc*) entry; (*processus informatique*) input; **à son e.** as he *ou* she came in; **'e. interdite'** 'no entry', 'no admittance'; **'e. libre'** 'ad-

mission free'; **e. en matière** (*d'un discours*) opening.

entrefaites (sur ces) [syrsezɑ̃trəfɛt] *adv* at that moment.

entrefilet [ɑ̃trəfilɛ] *nm Journ* (news) item.

entrejambes [ɑ̃trəʒɑ̃b] *nm inv* (*de pantalon*) crutch, crotch.

entrelacer [ɑ̃trəlase] *vt*, — **s'e.** *vpr* to intertwine.

entremêler [ɑ̃trəmele] *vt*, — **s'e.** *vpr* to intermingle.

entremets [ɑ̃trəmɛ] *nm* (*plat*) sweet, dessert.

entremetteur, -euse [ɑ̃trəmɛtœr, -øz] *nmf Péj* go-between.

entremise [ɑ̃trəmiz] *nf* intervention; **par l'e. de qn** through s.o.

entreposer [ɑ̃trəpoze] *vt* to store; *Jur* to bond. ◆**entrepôt** *nm* warehouse; (*de la douane*) *Jur* bonded warehouse.

entreprendre* [ɑ̃trəprɑ̃dr] *vt* (*travail, voyage etc*) to start on, undertake; **e. de faire** to undertake to do. ◆**entreprenant** *a* enterprising; (*galant*) brash, forward. ◆**entrepreneur** *nm* (*en bâtiment*) (building) contractor. ◆**entreprise** *nf* **1** (*opération*) undertaking. **2** (*firme*) company, firm.

entrer [ɑ̃tre] *vi* (*aux* **être**) (*aller*) to go in, enter; (*venir*) to come in, enter; **e. dans** to go into; (*carrière*) to enter, go into; (*club*) to join, enter; (*détail, question*) to go *ou* enter into; (*pièce*) to come *ou* go into, enter; (*arbre etc*) *Aut* to crash into; **e. en action** to go *ou* get into action; **e. en ébullition** to start boiling; **entrez!** come in!; **faire/laisser e. qn** to show/let s.o. in.

entresol [ɑ̃trəsɔl] *nm* mezzanine (floor).

entre-temps [ɑ̃trətɑ̃] *adv* meanwhile.

entreten/ir* [ɑ̃trətnir] *vt* **1** (*voiture, maison etc*) to maintain; (*relations, souvenir*) to keep up; (*famille*) to keep, maintain; (*sentiment*) to entertain; **e. sa forme/sa santé** to keep fit/healthy. **2 e. qn de** to talk to s.o. about; **s'e. de** to talk about (**avec** with). ◆**—u** *a* (*femme*) kept. ◆**entretien** *nm* **1** (*de route, maison etc*) maintenance, upkeep; (*subsistance*) keep. **2** (*dialogue*) conversation; (*entrevue*) interview.

entre-tuer (s') [sɑ̃trətɥe] *vpr* to kill each other.

entrevoir* [ɑ̃trəvwar] *vt* (*rapidement*) to catch a glimpse of; (*pressentir*) to (fore)see.

entrevue [ɑ̃trəvy] *nf* interview.

entrouvrir* [ɑ̃truvrir] *vt*, — **s'e.** *vpr* to half-open. ◆**entrouvert** *a* (*porte, fenêtre*) ajar, half-open.

énumérer [enymere] *vt* to enumerate, list. ◆**énumération** *nf* enumeration.

envah/ir [ɑ̃vair] *vt* to invade; (*herbe etc*) to overrun; **e. qn** (*doute, peur etc*) to overcome s.o. ◆**—issant** *a* (*voisin etc*) intrusive. ◆**—issement** *nm* invasion. ◆**—isseur** *nm* invader.

enveloppe [ɑ̃vlɔp] *nf* (*pli*) envelope; (*de colis*) wrapping; (*de pneu*) casing; (*d'oreiller*) cover; (*apparence*) *Fig* exterior; **mettre sous e.** to put into an envelope. ◆**envelopp/er** *vt* to wrap (up); **e. la ville** (*brouillard etc*) to envelop the town; **enveloppé de mystère** shrouded *ou* enveloped in mystery; — **s'e.** *vpr* to wrap oneself (up) (**dans** in). ◆**—ant** *a* (*séduisant*) captivating.

envenimer [ɑ̃vnime] *vt* (*plaie*) to make septic; (*querelle*) *Fig* to envenom; — **s'e.** *vpr* to turn septic; *Fig* to become envenomed.

envergure [ɑ̃vɛrgyr] *nf* **1** (*d'avion, d'oiseau*) wingspan. **2** (*de personne*) calibre; (*ampleur*) scope, importance; **de grande e.** wide-ranging, far-reaching.

envers [ɑ̃vɛr] **1** *prép* towards, *Am* toward(s). **2** *nm* (*de tissu*) wrong side; (*de médaille*) reverse side; **à l'e.** (*chaussette*) inside out; (*pantalon*) back to front; (*à contresens, de travers*) the wrong way; (*en désordre*) upside down.

envie [ɑ̃vi] *nf* **1** (*jalousie*) envy; (*désir*) longing, desire; **avoir e. de qch** to want sth; **j'ai e. de faire** I feel like doing, I would like to do; **elle meurt d'e. de faire** she's dying *ou* longing to do. **2** (*peau autour des ongles*) hangnail. ◆**envier** *vt* to envy (**qch à qn** s.o. sth). ◆**envieux, -euse** *a* & *nmf* envious (person); **faire des envieux** to cause envy.

environ [ɑ̃virɔ̃] *adv* (*à peu près*) about; — *nmpl* outskirts, surroundings; **aux environs de** (*Paris, Noël, dix francs etc*) around, in the vicinity of. ◆**environn/er** *vt* to surround. ◆**—ant** *a* surrounding. ◆**—ement** *nm* environment.

envisag/er [ɑ̃vizaʒe] *vt* to consider; (*imaginer comme possible*) to envisage, *Am* envision, consider; **e. de faire** to consider *ou* contemplate doing. ◆**—eable** *a* thinkable.

envoi [ɑ̃vwa] *nm* (*action*) dispatch, sending; (*paquet*) consignment; **coup d'e.** *Fb* kick-off.

envol [ɑ̃vɔl] *nm* (*d'oiseau*) taking flight; (*d'avion*) take-off; **piste d'e.** *Av* runway. ◆**s'envol/er** *vpr* (*oiseau*) to fly away; (*avion*) to take off; (*emporté par le vent*) to blow away; (*espoir*) *Fig* to vanish. ◆**—ée** *nf* (*élan*) *Fig* flight.

envoût/er [ɑ̃vute] *vt* to bewitch. ◆**—ement** *nm* bewitchment.

envoy/er* [ɑ̃vwaje] *vt* to send; (*pierre*) to throw; (*gifle*) to give; **e. chercher qn** to send for s.o.; **— s'e.** *vpr Fam* (*travail etc*) to take on, do; (*repas etc*) to put *ou* stash away. ◆**—é, -ée** *nmf* envoy; *Journ* correspondent. ◆**—eur** *nm* sender.

épagneul, -eule [epaɲœl] *nmf* spaniel.

épais, -aisse [epɛ, -ɛs] *a* thick; (*personne*) thick-set; (*esprit*) dull. ◆**épaisseur** *nf* thickness; (*dimension*) depth. ◆**épaissir** *vt* to thicken; *– vi*, **— s'é.** *vpr* to thicken; (*grossir*) to fill out; **le mystère s'épaissit** the mystery is deepening.

épanch/er [epɑ̃ʃe] *vt* (*cœur*) *Fig* to pour out; **— s'é.** *vpr* (*parler*) to pour out one's heart, unbosom oneself. ◆**—ement** *nm* (*aveu*) outpouring; *Méd* effusion.

épanou/ir (s') [sepanwir] *vpr* (*fleur*) to open out; (*personne*) *Fig* to fulfil oneself, blossom (out); (*visage*) to beam. ◆**—i** *a* (*fleur, personne*) in full bloom; (*visage*) beaming. ◆**—issement** *nm* (*éclat*) full bloom; (*de la personnalité*) fulfilment.

épargne [eparɲ] *nf* saving (**de** of); (*qualité, vertu*) thrift; (*sommes d'argent*) savings. ◆**épargn/er** *vt* (*ennemi etc*) to spare; (*denrée rare etc*) to be sparing with; (*argent, temps*) to save; **e. qch à qn** (*ennuis, chagrin etc*) to spare s.o. sth. ◆**—ant, -ante** *nmf* saver.

éparpiller [eparpije] *vt*, **— s'é.** *vpr* to scatter; (*efforts*) to dissipate. ◆**épars** *a* scattered.

épaté [epate] *a* (*nez*) flat. ◆**épatement** *nm* flatness.

épat/er [epate] *vt Fam* to stun, astound. ◆**—ant** *a Fam* stunning, marvellous.

épaule [epol] *nf* shoulder. ◆**épauler** *vt* (*fusil*) to raise (to one's shoulder); **é. qn** (*aider*) to back s.o. up.

épave [epav] *nf* (*bateau, personne*) wreck; *pl* (*débris*) *Nau* (pieces of) wreckage.

épée [epe] *nf* sword; **un coup d'é.** a sword thrust.

épeler [ɛple] *vt* (*mot*) to spell.

éperdu [epɛrdy] *a* frantic, wild (**de** with); (*regard*) distraught. ◆**—ment** *adv* (*aimer*) madly; **elle s'en moque e.** she couldn't care less.

éperon [eprɔ̃] *nm* (*de cavalier, coq*) spur. ◆**éperonner** (*cheval, personne*) to spur (on).

épervier [epɛrvje] *nm* sparrowhawk.

éphémère [efemɛr] *a* short-lived, ephemeral, transient.

épi [epi] *nm* (*de blé etc*) ear; (*mèche de cheveux*) tuft of hair.

épice [epis] *nf Culin* spice. ◆**épic/er** *vt* to spice. ◆**—é** *a* (*plat, récit etc*) spicy.

épicier, -ière [episje, -jɛr] *nmf* grocer. ◆**épicerie** *nf* (*magasin*) grocer's (shop); (*produits*) groceries.

épidémie [epidemi] *nf* epidemic. ◆**épidémique** *a* epidemic.

épiderme [epidɛrm] *nm Anat* skin.

épier [epje] *vt* (*observer*) to watch closely; (*occasion*) to watch out for; **é. qn** to spy on s.o.

épilepsie [epilɛpsi] *nf* epilepsy. ◆**épileptique** *a* & *nmf* epileptic.

épiler [epile] *vt* (*jambe*) to remove unwanted hair from; (*sourcil*) to pluck.

épilogue [epilɔg] *nm* epilogue.

épinard [epinar] *nm* (*plante*) spinach; *pl* (*feuilles*) *Culin* spinach.

épine [epin] *nf* **1** (*de buisson*) thorn; (*d'animal*) spine, prickle. **2 é. dorsale** *Anat* spine. ◆**épineux, -euse** *a* (*tige, question*) thorny.

épingle [epɛ̃gl] *nf* pin; **é. de nourrice, é. de sûreté** safety pin; **é. à linge** clothes peg, *Am* clothes pin; **virage en é. à cheveux** hairpin bend; **tiré à quatre épingles** very spruce. ◆**épingler** *vt* to pin; **é. qn** (*arrêter*) *Fam* to nab s.o.

épique [epik] *a* epic.

épiscopal, -aux [episkɔpal, -o] *a* episcopal.

épisode [epizɔd] *nm* episode; **film à épisodes** serial. ◆**épisodique** *a* occasional, episodic; (*accessoire*) minor.

épitaphe [epitaf] *nf* epitaph.

épithète [epitɛt] *nf* epithet; *Gram* attribute.

épître [epitr] *nf* epistle.

éploré [eplɔre] *a* (*personne, air*) tearful.

éplucher [eplyʃe] *vt* (*pommes de terre*) to peel; (*salade*) to clean, pare; (*texte*) *Fig* to dissect. ◆**épluchure** *nf* peeling.

éponge [epɔ̃ʒ] *nf* sponge. ◆**éponger** *vt* (*liquide*) to sponge up, mop up; (*carrelage*) to sponge (down), mop; (*dette etc*) *Fin* to absorb; **s'é. le front** to mop one's brow.

épopée [epɔpe] *nf* epic.

époque [epɔk] *nf* (*date*) time, period; (*historique*) age; **meubles d'é.** period furniture; **à l'é.** at the *ou* that time.

épouse [epuz] *nf* wife, *Jur* spouse.

épouser [epuze] *vt* **1 é. qn** to marry s.o. **2** (*opinion etc*) to espouse; (*forme*) to assume, adopt.

épousseter [epuste] *vt* to dust.

époustoufler [epustufle] *vt Fam* to astound.
épouvantail [epuvɑ̃taj] *nm* (*à oiseaux*) scarecrow.
épouvante [epuvɑ̃t] *nf* (*peur*) terror; (*appréhension*) dread; **d'é.** (*film etc*) horror-. **◆épouvant/er** *vt* to terrify. **◆—able** *a* terrifying; (*très mauvais*) appalling.
époux [epu] *nm* husband, *Jur* spouse; *pl* husband and wife.
éprendre* (s') [seprɑ̃dr] *vpr* **s'é. de qn** to fall in love with s.o. **◆épris** *a* in love (**de** with).
épreuve [eprøv] *nf* (*essai, examen*) test; *Sp* event, heat; *Phot* print; *Typ* proof; (*malheur*) ordeal, trial; **mettre à l'é.** to put to the test. **◆éprouv/er** [epruve] *vt* to test, try; (*sentiment etc*) to experience, feel; **é. qn** (*mettre à l'épreuve*) to put s.o. to the test; (*faire souffrir*) to distress s.o. **◆—ant** *a* (*pénible*) trying. **◆—é** *a* (*sûr*) well-tried.
éprouvette [epruvɛt] *nf* test tube; **bébé é.** test tube baby.
épuis/er [epɥize] *vt* (*personne, provisions, sujet*) to exhaust; — **s'é.** *vpr* (*réserves, patience*) to run out; **s'é. à faire** to exhaust oneself doing. **◆—ant** *a* exhausting. **◆—é** *a* exhausted; (*édition*) out of print; (*marchandise*) out of stock. **◆—ement** *nm* exhaustion.
épuisette [epɥizɛt] *nf* fishing net (*on pole*).
épurer [epyre] *vt* to purify; (*personnel etc*) to purge; (*goût*) to refine. **◆épuration** *nf* purification; purging; refining.
équateur [ekwatœr] *nm* equator; **sous l'é.** at *ou* on the equator. **◆équatorial, -aux** *a* equatorial.
équation [ekwasjɔ̃] *nf Math* equation.
équerre [ekɛr] *nf* **é. (à dessiner)** setsquare, *Am* triangle; **d'é.** straight, square.
équestre [ekɛstr] *a* (*figure etc*) equestrian; (*exercices etc*) horseriding-.
équilibre [ekilibr] *nm* balance; **tenir** *ou* **mettre en é.** to balance (**sur** on); **se tenir en é.** to (keep one's) balance; **perdre l'é.** to lose one's balance. **◆équilibrer** *vt* (*charge, budget etc*) to balance; — **s'é.** *vpr* (*équipes etc*) to (counter)balance each other; (*comptes*) to balance.
équinoxe [ekinɔks] *nm* equinox.
équipage [ekipaʒ] *nm Nau Av* crew.
équipe [ekip] *nf* team; (*d'ouvriers*) gang; **é. de nuit** night shift; **é. de secours** search party; **faire é. avec** to team up with. **◆équipier, -ière** *nmf* team member.
équipée [ekipe] *nf* escapade.
équip/er [ekipe] *vt* to equip (**de** with); — **s'é.** *vpr* to equip oneself. **◆—ement** *nm* equipment; (*de camping, ski etc*) gear, equipment.
équitation [ekitasjɔ̃] *nf* (horse) riding.
équité [ekite] *nf* fairness. **◆équitable** *a* fair, equitable. **◆équitablement** *adv* fairly.
équivalent [ekivalɑ̃] *a* & *nm* equivalent. **◆équivalence** *nf* equivalence. **◆équivaloir** *vi* **é. à** to be equivalent to.
équivoque [ekivɔk] *a* (*ambigu*) equivocal; (*douteux*) dubious; — *nf* ambiguity.
érable [erabl] *nm* (*arbre, bois*) maple.
érafler [erafle] *vt* to graze, scratch. **◆éraflure** *nf* graze, scratch.
éraillée [eraje] *af* (*voix*) rasping.
ère [ɛr] *nf* era.
érection [erɛksjɔ̃] *nf* (*de monument etc*) erection.
éreinter [erɛ̃te] *vt* (*fatiguer*) to exhaust; (*critiquer*) to tear to pieces, slate, slam.
ergot [ɛrgo] *nm* (*de coq*) spur.
ergoter [ɛrgɔte] *vi* to quibble, cavil.
ériger [eriʒe] *vt* to erect; **s'é. en** to set oneself up as.
ermite [ɛrmit] *nm* hermit.
érosion [erozjɔ̃] *nf* erosion. **◆éroder** *vt* to erode.
érotique [erɔtik] *a* erotic. **◆érotisme** *nm* eroticism.
err/er [ɛre] *vi* to wander, roam. **◆—ant** *a* wandering, roving; (*animal*) stray.
erreur [ɛrœr] *nf* (*faute*) error, mistake; (*action blâmable, opinion fausse*) error; **par e.** by mistake, in error; **dans l'e.** mistaken. **◆erroné** *a* erroneous.
ersatz [ɛrzats] *nm* substitute.
éructer [erykte] *vi Litt* to belch.
érudit, -ite [erydi, -it] *a* scholarly, erudite; — *nmf* scholar. **◆érudition** *nf* scholarship, erudition.
éruption [erypsjɔ̃] *nf* (*de volcan, colère*) eruption (**de** of); *Méd* rash.
es *voir* **être**.
ès [ɛs] *prép* of; **licencié/docteur ès lettres** = BA/PhD.
escabeau, -x [ɛskabo] *nm* stepladder, (pair of) steps; (*tabouret*) stool.
escadre [ɛskadr] *nf Nau Av* fleet, squadron. **◆escadrille** *nf* (*unité*) *Av* flight. **◆escadron** *nm* squadron.
escalade [ɛskalad] *nf* climbing; (*de prix*) & *Mil* escalation. **◆escalader** *vt* to climb, scale.
escale [ɛskal] *nf Av* stop(over); *Nau* port of call; **faire e. à** *Av* to stop (over) at; *Nau* to put in at; **vol sans e.** non-stop flight.
escalier [ɛskalje] *nm* staircase, stairs; **e. mé-**

canique *ou* **roulant** escalator; **e. de secours** fire escape.

escalope [ɛskalɔp] *nf Culin* escalope.

escamot/er [ɛskamɔte] *vt* (*faire disparaître*) to make vanish; (*esquiver*) to dodge. ◆**—able** *a Av Tech* retractable.

escapade [ɛskapad] *nf* (*excursion*) jaunt; **faire une e.** to run off.

escargot [ɛskargo] *nm* snail.

escarmouche [ɛskarmuʃ] *nf* skirmish.

escarpé [ɛskarpe] *a* steep. ◆**escarpement** *nm* (*côte*) steep slope.

escarpin [ɛskarpɛ̃] *nm* (*soulier*) pump, court shoe.

escient [ɛsjɑ̃] *nm* **à bon e.** discerningly, wisely.

esclaffer (s') [sɛsklafe] *vpr* to roar with laughter.

esclandre [ɛsklɑ̃dr] *nm* (noisy) scene.

esclave [ɛsklav] *nmf* slave; **être l'e. de** to be a slave to. ◆**esclavage** *nm* slavery.

escompte [ɛskɔ̃t] *nm* discount; **taux d'e.** bank rate. ◆**escompter** *vt* **1** (*espérer*) to anticipate (**faire** doing), expect (**faire** to do). **2** *Com* to discount.

escorte [ɛskɔrt] *nf Mil Nau etc* escort. ◆**escorter** *vt* to escort.

escouade [ɛskwad] *nf* (*petite troupe*) squad.

escrime [ɛskrim] *nf Sp* fencing. ◆**escrimeur, -euse** *nmf* fencer.

escrimer (s') [sɛskrime] *vpr* to slave away (**à faire** at doing).

escroc [ɛskro] *nm* swindler, crook. ◆**escroquer** *vt* **e. qn** to swindle s.o.; **e. qch à qn** to swindle s.o. out of sth. ◆**escroquerie** *nf* swindling; **une e.** a swindle.

espace [ɛspas] *nm* space; **e. vert** garden, park. ◆**espacer** *vt* to space out; **espacés d'un mètre** (spaced out) one metre apart; — **s'e.** (*maisons, visites etc*) to become less frequent.

espadon [ɛspadɔ̃] *nm* swordfish.

espadrille [ɛspadrij] *nf* rope-soled sandal.

Espagne [ɛspaɲ] *nf* Spain. ◆**espagnol, -ole** *a* Spanish; — *nmf* Spaniard; — *nm* (*langue*) Spanish.

espèce [ɛspɛs] **1** *nf* (*race*) species; (*genre*) kind, sort; **c'est une e. d'idiot** he's a silly fool; **e. d'idiot!/de maladroit!/***etc* (you) silly fool!/oaf!/*etc*. **2** *nfpl* (*argent*) **en espèces** in cash.

espérance [ɛsperɑ̃s] *nf* hope; **avoir des espérances** to have expectations; **e. de vie** life expectancy. ◆**espérer** *vt* to hope for; **e. que** to hope that; **e. faire** to hope to do; — *vi* to hope; **e. en qn/qch** to trust in s.o./sth.

espiègle [ɛspjɛgl] *a* mischievous. ◆**espièglerie** *nf* mischievousness; (*farce*) mischievous trick.

espion, -onne [ɛspjɔ̃, -ɔn] *nmf* spy. ◆**espionnage** *nm* espionage, spying. ◆**espionner** *vt* to spy on; — *vi* to spy.

esplanade [ɛsplanad] *nf* esplanade.

espoir [ɛspwar] *nm* hope; **avoir de l'e.** to have hope(s); **sans e.** (*cas etc*) hopeless.

esprit [ɛspri] *nm* (*attitude, fantôme*) spirit; (*intellect*) mind; (*humour*) wit; (*être humain*) person; **avoir de l'e.** to be witty; **cette idée m'est venue à l'e.** this idea crossed my mind.

esquimau, -aude, -aux [ɛskimo, -od, -o] **1** *a* & *nmf* Eskimo. **2** *nm* (*glace*) choc-ice (*on a stick*).

esquinter [ɛskɛ̃te] *vt Fam* (*voiture etc*) to damage, bash; (*critiquer*) to slam, pan (*author, film etc*); **s'e. la santé** to damage one's health; **s'e. à faire** (*se fatiguer*) to wear oneself out doing.

esquisse [ɛskis] *nf* (*croquis, plan*) sketch. ◆**esquisser** *vt* to sketch; **e. un geste** to make a (slight) gesture.

esquive [ɛskiv] *nf Boxe* dodge; **e. de** (*question*) dodging of, evasion of. ◆**esquiver** *vt* (*coup, problème*) to dodge; — **s'e.** *vpr* to slip away.

essai [esɛ] *nm* (*épreuve*) test, trial; (*tentative*) try, attempt; *Rugby* try; *Littér* essay; **à l'e.** (*objet*) *Com* on trial, on approval; **pilote d'e.** test pilot; **période d'e.** trial period.

essaim [esɛ̃] *nm* swarm (*of bees etc*).

essayer [eseje] *vt* to try (**de faire** to do); (*vêtement*) to try on; (*méthode*) to try (out); **s'e. à qch/à faire** to try one's hand at sth/at doing. ◆**essayage** *nm* (*de costume*) fitting.

essence [esɑ̃s] *nf* **1** (*extrait*) *Ch Culin* essence; *Aut* petrol, *Am* gas; **poste d'e.** filling station. **2** *Phil* essence. **3** (*d'arbres*) species. ◆**essentiel, -ielle** *a* essential (**à, pour** for); — *nm* **l'e.** the main thing *ou* point; (*quantité*) the main part (**de** of). ◆**essentiellement** *adv* essentially.

essieu, -x [esjø] *nm* axle.

essor [esɔr] *nm* (*de pays, d'entreprise etc*) development, rise, expansion; **en plein e.** (*industrie etc*) booming.

essor/er [esɔre] *vt* (*linge*) to wring; (*dans une essoreuse*) to spin-dry; (*dans une machine à laver*) to spin. ◆**—euse** *nf* (*à main*) wringer; (*électrique*) spin dryer.

essouffler [esufle] *vt* to make (*s.o.*) out of breath; — **s'e.** *vpr* to get out of breath.

essuyer [esɥije] **1** *vt* to wipe; — **s'e.** *vpr* to wipe oneself. **2** *vt* (*subir*) to suffer. ◆**es-**

suie-glace *nm inv* windscreen wiper, *Am* windshield wiper. ◆**essuie-mains** *nm inv* (hand) towel.
est[1] [ɛ] *voir* être.
est[2] [ɛst] *nm* east; – *a inv* (*côte*) east(ern); **d'e.** (*vent*) east(erly); **de l'e.** eastern; **Allemagne de l'E.** East Germany. ◆**e.-allemand, -ande** *a* & *nmf* East German.
estafilade [ɛstafilad] *nf* gash, slash.
estampe [ɛstɑ̃p] *nf* (*gravure*) print.
estamper [ɛstɑ̃pe] *vt* (*rouler*) *Fam* to swindle.
estampille [ɛstɑ̃pij] *nf* mark, stamp.
esthète [ɛstɛt] *nmf* aesthete, *Am* esthete. ◆**esthétique** *a* aesthetic, *Am* esthetic.
esthéticienne [ɛstetisjɛn] *nf* beautician.
estime [ɛstim] *nf* esteem, regard. ◆**estim/er** *vt* (*objet*) to value; (*juger*) to consider (**que** that); (*calculer*) to estimate; (*apprécier*) to appreciate; **e. qn** to have high regard for s.o., esteem s.o.; **s'e. heureux/***etc* to consider oneself happy/*etc.* ◆**—able** *a* respectable. ◆**estimation** *nf* (*de mobilier etc*) valuation; (*calcul*) estimation.
estival, -aux [ɛstival, -o] *a* (*période etc*) summer-. ◆**estivant, -ante** *nmf* holidaymaker, *Am* vacationer.
estomac [ɛstɔma] *nm* stomach.
estomaquer [ɛstɔmake] *vt Fam* to flabbergast.
estomper [ɛstɔ̃pe] *vt* (*rendre flou*) to blur; – **s'e.** *vpr* to become blurred.
estrade [ɛstrad] *nf* (*tribune*) platform.
estropi/er [ɛstrɔpje] *vt* to cripple, maim. ◆**—é, -ée** *nmf* cripple.
estuaire [ɛstɥɛr] *nm* estuary.
esturgeon [ɛstyrʒɔ̃] *nm* (*poisson*) sturgeon.
et [e] *conj* and; **vingt et un/***etc* twenty-one/*etc.*
étable [etabl] *nf* cowshed.
établi [etabli] *nm Menuis* (work)bench.
établ/ir [etablir] *vt* to establish; (*installer*) to set up; (*plan, chèque, liste*) to draw up; – **s'é.** *vpr* (*habiter*) to settle; (*épicier etc*) to set up shop as, set (oneself) up as. ◆**—issement** *nm* (*action, bâtiment, institution*) establishment; *Com* firm, establishment; **é. scolaire** school.
étage [etaʒ] *nm* (*d'immeuble*) floor, storey, *Am* story; (*de fusée etc*) stage; **à l'é.** upstairs; **au premier é.** on the first *ou Am* second floor. ◆**étager** *vt*, – **s'é.** *vpr* (*rochers, maisons etc*) to range above one another.
étagère [etaʒɛr] *nf* shelf; (*meuble*) shelving unit.
étai [etɛ] *nm Tech* prop, stay.
étain [etɛ̃] *nm* (*métal*) tin; (*de gobelet etc*) pewter.
était [etɛ] *voir* être.
étal, *pl* **étals** [etal] *nm* (*au marché*) stall.
étalage [etalaʒ] *nm* display; (*vitrine*) display window; **faire é. de** to make a show *ou* display of. ◆**étalagiste** *nmf* window dresser.
étaler [etale] *vt* (*disposer*) to lay out; (*luxe etc*) & *Com* to display; (*crème, beurre etc*) to spread; (*vacances*) to stagger; — **s'é.** *vpr* (*s'affaler*) to sprawl; (*tomber*) *Fam* to fall flat; **s'é. sur** (*congés, paiements etc*) to be spread over.
étalon [etalɔ̃] *nm* **1** (*cheval*) stallion. **2** (*modèle*) standard.
étanche [etɑ̃ʃ] *a* watertight; (*montre*) waterproof.
étancher [etɑ̃ʃe] *vt* (*sang*) to stop the flow of; (*soif*) to quench, slake.
étang [etɑ̃] *nm* pond.
étant [etɑ̃] *voir* être.
étape [etap] *nf* (*de voyage etc*) stage; (*lieu*) stop(over); **faire é. à** to stop off *ou* over at.
état [eta] *nm* **1** (*condition, manière d'être*) state; (*registre, liste*) statement, list; **en bon é.** in good condition; **en é. de faire** in a position to do; **é. d'esprit** state *ou* frame of mind; **é. d'âme** mood; **é. civil** civil status (*birth, marriage, death etc*); **é. de choses** situation, state of affairs; **à l'é. brut** in a raw state; **de son é.** (*métier*) by trade; **faire é. de** (*mention*) to mention, put forward. **2 É.** (*nation*) State; **homme d'É.** statesman. ◆**étatisé** *a* state-controlled, state-owned.
état-major [etamaʒɔr] *nm* (*pl* **états-majors**) (*d'un parti etc*) senior staff.
États-Unis [etazyni] *nmpl* **É.-Unis (d'Amérique)** United States (of America).
étau, -x [eto] *nm Tech* vice, *Am* vise.
étayer [eteje] *vt* to prop up, support.
été[1] [ete] *nm* summer.
été[2] [ete] *voir* être.
éteindre* [etɛ̃dr] *vt* (*feu, cigarette etc*) to put out, extinguish; (*lampe etc*) to turn *ou* switch off; (*dette, espoir*) to extinguish; – *vi* to switch off; — **s'é.** *vpr* (*feu*) to go out; (*personne*) to pass away; (*race*) to die out. ◆**éteint** *a* (*feu*) out; (*volcan, race, amour*) extinct; (*voix*) faint.
étendard [etɑ̃dar] *nm* (*drapeau*) standard.
étend/re [etɑ̃dr] *vt* (*nappe*) to spread (out); (*beurre*) to spread; (*linge*) to hang out; (*agrandir*) to extend; **é. le bras/***etc* to stretch out one's arm/*etc*; **é. qn** to stretch s.o. out; — **s'é.** *vpr* (*personne*) to stretch

(oneself) out; (*plaine etc*) to stretch; (*feu*) to spread; (*pouvoir*) to extend; **s'é. sur** (*sujet*) to dwell on. ◆**—u** *a* (*forêt, vocabulaire etc*) extensive; (*personne*) stretched out. ◆**—ue** *nf* (*importance*) extent; (*surface*) area; (*d'eau*) expanse, stretch.

éternel, -elle [eternel] *a* eternal. ◆**éternellement** *adv* eternally, for ever. ◆**éterniser** *vt* to perpetuate; — **s'é.** *vpr* (*débat etc*) to drag on endlessly; (*visiteur etc*) to stay for ever. ◆**éternité** *nf* eternity.

éternu/er [eternɥe] *vi* to sneeze. ◆**—ement** [-ymɑ̃] *nm* sneeze.

êtes [ɛt] *voir* **être**.

éther [eter] *nm* ether.

Éthiopie [etjɔpi] *nf* Ethiopia. ◆**éthiopien, -ienne** *a* & *nmf* Ethiopian.

éthique [etik] *a* ethical; – *nf Phil* ethics; **l'é. puritaine/***etc* the Puritan/*etc* ethic.

ethnie [ɛtni] *nf* ethnic group. ◆**ethnique** *a* ethnic.

étinceler [etɛ̃sle] *vi* to sparkle. ◆**étincelle** *nf* spark. ◆**étincellement** *nm* sparkle.

étioler (s') [setjɔle] *vpr* to wilt, wither.

étiqueter [etikte] *vt* to label. ◆**étiquette** *nf* **1** (*marque*) label. **2** (*protocole*) (diplomatic *ou* court) etiquette.

étirer [etire] *vt* to stretch; — **s'é.** *vpr* to stretch (oneself).

étoffe [etɔf] *nf* material, cloth, fabric; (*de héros etc*) *Fig* stuff (of).

étoffer [etɔfe] *vt*, — **s'é.** *vpr* to fill out.

étoile [etwal] *nf* **1** star; **à la belle é.** in the open. **2 é. de mer** starfish. ◆**étoilé** *a* (*ciel, nuit*) starry; (*vitre*) cracked (*star-shaped*); **é. de** (*rubis etc*) studded with; **la bannière étoilée** *Am* the Star-Spangled Banner.

étonn/er [etɔne] *vt* to surprise, astonish; — **s'é.** *vpr* to be surprised *ou* astonished (**de qch** at sth, **que** (+ *sub*) that). ◆**—ant** *a* (*ahurissant*) surprising; (*remarquable*) amazing. ◆**—ement** *nm* surprise, astonishment.

étouff/er [etufe] *vt* (*tuer*) to suffocate, smother; (*bruit*) to muffle; (*feu*) to smother; (*révolte, sentiment*) to stifle; (*scandale*) to hush up; **é. qn** (*chaleur*) to stifle s.o.; (*aliment, colère*) to choke s.o.; – *vi* to suffocate; **on étouffe!** it's stifling!; **é. de colère** to choke with anger. — **s'é.** *vpr* (*en mangeant*) to choke, gag (**sur, avec** on); (*mourir*) to suffocate. ◆**—ant** *a* (*air*) stifling. ◆**—ement** *nm Méd* suffocation.

étourdi, -ie [eturdi] *a* thoughtless; – *nmf* scatterbrain. ◆**étourderie** *nf* thoughtlessness; **une é.** (*faute*) a thoughtless blunder.

étourd/ir [eturdir] *vt* to stun, daze; (*vertige, vin*) to make dizzy; (*abrutir*) to deafen. ◆**—issant** *a* (*bruit*) deafening; (*remarquable*) stunning. ◆**—issement** *nm* dizziness; (*syncope*) dizzy spell.

étourneau, -x [eturno] *nm* starling.

étrange [etrɑ̃ʒ] *a* strange, odd. ◆**—ment** *adv* strangely, oddly. ◆**étrangeté** *nf* strangeness, oddness.

étranger, -ère [etrɑ̃ʒe, -ɛr] *a* (*d'un autre pays*) foreign; (*non familier*) strange (**à** to); **il m'est é.** he's unknown to me; – *nmf* foreigner; (*inconnu*) stranger; **à l'é.** abroad; **de l'é.** from abroad.

étrangl/er [etrɑ̃gle] *vt* **é. qn** (*tuer*) to strangle s.o.; (*col, aliment*) to choke s.o.; — **s'é.** *vpr* (*de colère, en mangeant etc*) to choke. ◆**—é** *a* (*voix*) choking; (*passage*) constricted. ◆**—ement** *nm* (*d'une victime*) strangulation. ◆**—eur, -euse** *nmf* strangler.

être* [ɛtr] **1** *vi* to be; **il est tailleur** he's a tailor; **est-ce qu'elle vient?** is she coming?; **il vient, n'est-ce pas?** he's coming, isn't he?; **est-ce qu'il aime le thé?** does he like tea?; **nous sommes dix** there are ten of us; **nous sommes le dix** today is the tenth (of the month); **où en es-tu?** how far have you got?; **il a été à Paris** (*est allé*) he's been to Paris; **elle est de Paris** she's from Paris; **elle est de la famille** she's one of the family; **c'est à faire tout de suite** it must be done straight away; **c'est à lui** it's his; **cela étant** that being so. **2** *v aux* (*avec venir, partir etc*) to have; **elle est déjà arrivée** she has already arrived. **3** *nm* (*personne*) being; **ê. humain** human being; **les êtres chers** the loved ones.

étreindre [etrɛ̃dr] *vt* to grip; (*ami*) to embrace. ◆**étreinte** *nf* grip; (*amoureuse etc*) embrace.

étrenner [etrene] *vt* to use *ou* wear for the first time.

étrennes [etrɛn] *nfpl* New Year gift; (*gratification*) = Christmas box *ou* tip.

étrier [etrije] *nm* stirrup.

étriper (s') [setripe] *vpr Fam* to fight (each other) to the kill.

étriqué [etrike] *a* (*vêtement*) tight, skimpy; (*esprit, vie*) narrow.

étroit [etrwa] *a* narrow; (*vêtement*) tight; (*parenté, collaboration etc*) close; (*discipline*) strict; **être à l'é.** to be cramped. ◆**étroitement** *adv* (*surveiller etc*) closely. ◆**étroitesse** *nf* narrowness; closeness; **é. d'esprit** narrow-mindedness.

étude [etyd] *nf* **1** (*action, ouvrage*) study; (*salle*) *Scol* study room; **à l'é.** (*projet*) under consideration; **faire des études de** (*médecine etc*) to study. **2** (*de notaire etc*) office. **◆étudiant, -ante** *nmf* & *a* student. **◆étudier** *vti* to study.

étui [etɥi] *nm* (*à lunettes, à cigarettes etc*) case; (*de revolver*) holster.

étymologie [etimɔlɔʒi] *nf* etymology.

eu, eue [y] *voir* **avoir**.

eucalyptus [økaliptys] *nm* (*arbre*) eucalyptus.

Eucharistie [økaristi] *nf Rel* Eucharist.

euh! [ø] *int* hem!, er!, well!

euphémisme [øfemism] *nm* euphemism.

euphorie [øfɔri] *nf* euphoria.

eurent [yr] *voir* **avoir**.

euro- [øro] *préf* Euro-.

Europe [ørɔp] *nf* Europe. **◆européen, -enne** *a* & *nmf* European.

eut [y] *voir* **avoir**.

euthanasie [øtanazi] *nf* euthanasia.

eux [ø] *pron* (*sujet*) they; (*complément*) them; (*réfléchi, emphase*) themselves. **◆eux-mêmes** *pron* themselves.

évacuer [evakɥe] *vt* to evacuate; (*liquide*) to drain off. **◆évacuation** *nf* evacuation.

évad/er (s') [sevade] *vpr* to escape (**de** from). **◆—é, -ée** *nmf* escaped prisoner.

évaluer [evalɥe] *vt* (*chiffre, foule etc*) to estimate; (*meuble etc*) to value. **◆évaluation** *nf* estimation; valuation.

évangile [evɑ̃ʒil] *nm* gospel; **É.** Gospel. **◆évangélique** *a* evangelical.

évanou/ir (s') [sevanwir] *vpr Méd* to black out, faint; (*espoir, crainte etc*) to vanish. **◆—i** *a Méd* unconscious. **◆—issement** *nm* (*syncope*) blackout, fainting fit; (*disparition*) vanishing.

évaporer (s') [sevapɔre] *vpr Ch* to evaporate; (*disparaître*) *Fam* to vanish into thin air. **◆évaporation** *nf* evaporation.

évasif, -ive [evazif, -iv] *a* evasive.

évasion [evazjɔ̃] *nf* escape (**d'un lieu** from a place, **devant un danger**/*etc* from a danger/*etc*); (*hors de la réalité*) escapism; **é. fiscale** tax evasion.

évêché [eveʃe] *nm* (*territoire*) bishopric, see.

éveil [evɛj] *nm* awakening; **en é.** on the alert; **donner l'é. à** to alert.

éveill/er [eveje] *vt* (*susciter*) to arouse; **é. qn** to awake(n) s.o.; **— s'é.** *vpr* to awake(n) (**à** to); (*sentiment, idée*) to be aroused. **◆—é** *a* awake; (*vif*) lively, alert.

événement [evɛnmɑ̃] *nm* event.

éventail [evɑ̃taj] *nm* **1** (*instrument portatif*) fan; **en é.** (*orteils*) spread out. **2** (*choix*) range.

évent/er [evɑ̃te] *vt* **1** (*secret*) to discover. **2** **é. qn** to fan s.o. **3 s'é.** *vpr* (*bière, vin etc*) to turn stale. **◆—é** *a* (*bière, vin etc*) stale.

éventrer [evɑ̃tre] *vt* (*animal etc*) to disembowel; (*sac*) to rip open.

éventuel, -elle [evɑ̃tɥɛl] *a* possible. **◆éventuellement** *adv* possibly. **◆éventualité** *nf* possibility; **dans l'é. de** in the event of.

évêque [evɛk] *nm* bishop.

évertuer (s') [sevɛrtɥe] *vpr* **s'é. à faire** to do one's utmost to do, struggle to do.

éviction [eviksjɔ̃] *nf* (*de concurrent etc*) & *Pol* ousting.

évident [evidɑ̃] *a* obvious, evident (**que** that). **◆évidemment** [-amɑ̃] *adv* certainly, obviously. **◆évidence** *nf* obviousness; **une é.** an obvious fact; **nier l'é.** to deny the obvious; **être en é.** to be conspicuous *ou* in evidence; **mettre en é.** (*fait*) to underline.

évider [evide] *vt* to hollow out.

évier [evje] *nm* (kitchen) sink.

évincer [evɛ̃se] *vt* (*concurrent etc*) & *Pol* to oust.

éviter [evite] *vt* to avoid (**de faire** doing); **é. qch à qn** to spare *ou* save s.o. sth.

évolu/er [evɔlɥe] *vi* **1** (*changer*) to develop, change; (*société, idée, situation*) to evolve. **2** (*se déplacer*) to move; *Mil* to manœuvre, *Am* maneuver. **◆—é** *a* (*pays*) advanced; (*personne*) enlightened. **◆évolution** *nf* **1** (*changement*) development; evolution. **2** (*d'un danseur etc*) & *Mil* movement.

évoquer [evɔke] *vt* to evoke, call to mind. **◆évocateur, -trice** *a* evocative. **◆évocation** *nf* evocation, recalling.

ex [ɛks] *nmf* (*mari, femme*) *Fam* ex.

ex- [ɛks] *préf* ex-; **ex-mari** ex-husband.

exacerber [ɛgzasɛrbe] *vt* (*douleur etc*) to exacerbate.

exact [ɛgzakt] *a* (*précis*) exact, accurate; (*juste, vrai*) correct, exact, right; (*ponctuel*) punctual. **◆exactement** *adv* exactly. **◆exactitude** *nf* exactness; accuracy; correctness; punctuality.

exaction [ɛgzaksjɔ̃] *nf* exaction.

ex aequo [ɛgzeko] *adv* **être classés ex ae.** *Sp* to tie, be equally placed.

exagér/er [ɛgzaʒere] *vt* to exaggerate; **–** *vi* (*parler*) to exaggerate; (*agir*) to overdo it, go too far. **◆—é** *a* excessive. **◆—ément** *adv* excessively. **◆exagération** *nf* exaggeration; (*excès*) excessiveness.

exalt/er [ɛgzalte] *vt* (*glorifier*) to exalt; (*animer*) to fire, stir. **◆—ant** *a* stirring. **◆—é, -ée** *a* (*sentiment*) impassioned, wild; – *nmf Pėj* fanatic. ◆**exaltation** *nf* (*délire*) elation, excitement.

examen [ɛgzamɛ̃] *nm* examination; *Scol* exam(ination); **e. blanc** *Scol* mock exam(ination). ◆**examinateur, -trice** *nmf Scol* examiner. ◆**examiner** *vt* (*considérer, regarder*) to examine.

exaspérer [ɛgzaspere] *vt* (*énerver*) to aggravate, exasperate. ◆**exaspération** *nf* exasperation, aggravation.

exaucer [ɛgzose] *vt* (*désir*) to grant; **e. qn** to grant s.o.'s wish(es).

excavation [ɛkskavɑsjɔ̃] *nf* (*trou*) hollow.

excéder [ɛksede] *vt* **1** (*dépasser*) to exceed. **2 é. qn** (*fatiguer, énerver*) to exasperate s.o. ◆**excédent** *nm* surplus, excess; **e. de bagages** excess luggage *ou Am* baggage. ◆**excédentaire** *a* (*poids etc*) excess-.

excellent [ɛkselɑ̃] *a* excellent. ◆**excellence** *nf* **1** excellence; **par e.** above all else *ou* all others. **2 E.** (*titre*) Excellency. ◆**exceller** *vi* to excel (**en qch** in sth, **à faire** in doing).

excentrique [ɛksɑ̃trik] **1** *a & nmf* (*original*) eccentric. **2** *a* (*quartier*) remote. ◆**excentricité** *nf* (*bizarrerie*) eccentricity.

excepté [ɛksɛpte] *prép* except. ◆**excepter** *vt* to except. ◆**exception** *nf* exception; **à l'e. de** except (for), with the exception of; **faire e.** to be an exception. ◆**exceptionnel, -elle** *a* exceptional. ◆**exceptionnellement** *adv* exceptionally.

excès [ɛksɛ] *nm* excess; (*de table*) over-eating; **e. de vitesse** *Aut* speeding. ◆**excessif, -ive** *a* excessive. ◆**excessivement** *adv* excessively.

excit/er [ɛksite] *vt* (*faire naître*) to excite, rouse, stir; **e. qn** (*mettre en colère*) to provoke s.o.; (*agacer*) to annoy s.o.; (*enthousiasmer*) to thrill s.o., excite s.o.; **e. qn à faire** to incite s.o. to do; — **s'e.** *vpr* (*nerveux, enthousiaste*) to get excited. ◆**—ant** *a* exciting; – *nm* stimulant. ◆**—é** *a* excited. ◆**—able** *a* excitable. ◆**excitation** *nf* (*agitation*) excitement; **e. à** (*haine etc*) incitement to.

exclamer (s') [sɛksklame] *vpr* to exclaim. ◆**exclamatif, -ive** *a* exclamatory. ◆**exclamation** *nf* exclamation.

excl/ure* [ɛksklyr] *vt* (*écarter*) to exclude (**de** from); (*chasser*) to expel (**de** from); **e. qch** (*rendre impossible*) to preclude sth. ◆**—u** *a* (*solution etc*) out of the question; (*avec une date*) exclusive. ◆**exclusif, -ive** *a* (*droit, modèle, préoccupation*) exclusive. ◆**exclusion** *nf* exclusion. ◆**exclusivement** *adv* exclusively. ◆**exclusivité** *nf Com* exclusive rights; **en e.** (*film*) having an exclusive showing (**à** at).

excommunier [ɛkskɔmynje] *vt* to excommunicate. ◆**excommunication** *nf* excommunication.

excrément(s) [ɛkskremɑ̃] *nm(pl)* excrement.

excroissance [ɛkskrwasɑ̃s] *nf* (out)growth.

excursion [ɛkskyrsjɔ̃] *nf* outing, excursion, tour; (*à pied*) hike.

excuse [ɛkskyz] *nf* (*prétexte*) excuse; *pl* (*regrets*) apology; **des excuses** an apology; **faire des excuses** to apologize (**à** to); **toutes mes excuses** (my) sincere apologies. ◆**excuser** *vt* (*justifier, pardonner*) to excuse (**qn d'avoir fait, qn de faire** s.o. for doing); — **s'e.** *vpr* to apologize (**de** for, **auprès de** to); **excusez-moi!, je m'excuse!** excuse me!

exécrer [ɛgzekre] *vt* to loathe. ◆**exécrable** *a* atrocious.

exécut/er [ɛgzekyte] *vt* **1** (*projet, tâche etc*) to carry out, execute; (*statue, broderie etc*) to produce; (*jouer*) *Mus* to perform. **2 e. qn** (*tuer*) to execute s.o. **3 s'e.** *vpr* to comply. ◆**—ant, -ante** *nmf Mus* performer. ◆**—able** *a* practicable. ◆**exécutif** *am* (*pouvoir*) executive; – *nm* **l'e.** *Pol* the executive. ◆**exécution** *nf* **1** carrying out, execution; production; performance. **2** (*mise à mort*) execution.

exemple [ɛgzɑ̃pl] *nm* example; **par e.** for example, for instance; **(ça) par e.!** *Fam* good heavens!; **donner l'e.** to set an example (**à** to). ◆**exemplaire 1** *a* exemplary. **2** *nm* (*livre etc*) copy.

exempt [ɛgzɑ̃] *a* **e. de** (*dispensé de*) exempt from; (*sans*) free from. ◆**exempter** *vt* to exempt (**de** from). ◆**exemption** *nf* exemption.

exercer [ɛgzɛrse] *vt* (*muscles, droits*) to exercise; (*autorité, influence*) to exert (**sur** over); (*métier*) to carry on, work at; (*profession*) to practise; **e. qn à** (*couture etc*) to train s.o. in; **e. qn à faire** to train s.o. to do; – *vi* (*médecin*) to practise; — **s'e.** *vpr* (*influence etc*) to be exerted; **s'e. (à qch)** (*sportif etc*) to practise (sth); **s'e. à faire** to practise doing. ◆**exercice** *nm* (*physique etc*) & *Scol* exercise; *Mil* drill, exercise; (*de métier*) practice; **l'e. de** (*pouvoir etc*) the exercise of; **en e.** (*fonctionnaire*) in office; (*médecin*) in practice; **faire de l'e., prendre de l'e.** to (take) exercise.

exhaler [ɛgzale] *vt* (*odeur etc*) to give off.

exhaustif, -ive [ɛgzostif, -iv] *a* exhaustive.

exhiber [ɛgzibe] *vt* to exhibit, show.

◆**exhibition** *nf* exhibition. ◆**exhibitionniste** *nmf* exhibitionist.

exhorter [ɛgzɔrte] *vt* to urge, exhort (**à faire** to do).

exhumer [ɛgzyme] *vt* (*cadavre*) to exhume: (*vestiges*) to dig up.

exiger [ɛgziʒe] *vt* to demand, require (**de** from, **que** (+ *sub*) that). ◆**exigeant** *a* demanding, exacting. ◆**exigence** *nf* demand, requirement; **d'une grande e.** very demanding.

exigu, -uë [ɛgzigy] *a* (*appartement etc*) cramped, tiny. ◆**exiguïté** *nf* crampedness.

exil [ɛgzil] *nm* (*expulsion*) exile. ◆**exil/er** *vt* to exile; — **s'e.** *vpr* to go into exile. ◆**—é, -ée** *nmf* (*personne*) exile.

existence [ɛgzistɑ̃s] *nf* existence. ◆**existentialisme** *nm* existentialism. ◆**exist/er** *vi* to exist; — *v imp* **il existe . . .** (*sing*) there is . . . ; (*pl*) there are . . . . ◆**—ant** *a* existing.

exode [ɛgzɔd] *nm* exodus.

exonérer [ɛgzɔnere] *vt* to exempt (**de** from). ◆**exonération** *nf* exemption.

exorbitant [ɛgzɔrbitɑ̃] *a* exorbitant.

exorciser [ɛgzɔrsize] *vt* to exorcize. ◆**exorcisme** *nm* exorcism.

exotique [ɛgzɔtik] *a* exotic. ◆**exotisme** *nm* exoticism.

expansif, -ive [ɛkspɑ̃sif, -iv] *a* expansive, effusive.

expansion [ɛkspɑ̃sjɔ̃] *nf Com Phys Pol* expansion; **en (pleine) e.** (fast *ou* rapidly) expanding.

expatri/er (s') [sɛkspatrije] *vpr* to leave one's country. ◆**—é, -ée** *a & nmf* expatriate.

expectative [ɛkspɛktativ] *nf* **être dans l'e.** to be waiting to see what happens.

expédient [ɛkspedjɑ̃] *nm* (*moyen*) expedient.

expédier [ɛkspedje] *vt* **1** (*envoyer*) to send off. **2** (*affaires, client*) to dispose of quickly, dispatch. ◆**expéditeur, -trice** *nmf* sender. ◆**expéditif, -ive** *a* expeditious, quick. ◆**expédition** *nf* **1** (*envoi*) dispatch. **2** (*voyage*) expedition.

expérience [ɛksperjɑ̃s] *nf* (*pratique, connaissance*) experience; (*scientifique*) experiment; **faire l'e. de qch** to experience sth. ◆**expérimental, -aux** *a* experimental. ◆**expérimentation** *nf* experimentation. ◆**expériment/er** *vt Phys Ch* to try out, experiment with; — *vi* to experiment. ◆**—é** *a* experienced.

expert [ɛkspɛr] *a* expert, skilled (**en** in); — *nm* expert; (*d'assurances*) valuer. ◆**e.-comptable** *nm* (*pl* **experts-comptables**) = chartered accountant, = *Am* certified public accountant. ◆**expertise** *nf* (*évaluation*) (expert) appraisal; (*compétence*) expertise.

expier [ɛkspje] *vt* (*péchés, crime*) to expiate, atone for. ◆**expiation** *nf* expiation (**de** of).

expir/er [ɛkspire] **1** *vti* to breathe out. **2** *vi* (*mourir*) to pass away; (*finir, cesser*) to expire. ◆**—ant** *a* dying. ◆**expiration** *nf* (*échéance*) expiry, *Am* expiration.

explicite [ɛksplisit] *a* explicit. ◆**—ment** *adv* explicitly.

expliquer [ɛksplike] *vt* to explain (**à** to); — **s'e.** *vpr* to explain oneself; (*discuter*) to talk things over, have it out (**avec** with); **s'e. qch** (*comprendre*) to understand sth; **ça s'explique** that is understandable. ◆**explicable** *a* understandable. ◆**explicatif, -ive** *a* explanatory. ◆**explication** *nf* explanation; (*mise au point*) discussion.

exploit [ɛksplwa] *nm* exploit, feat.

exploit/er [ɛksplwate] *vt* **1** (*champs*) to farm; (*ferme, entreprise*) to run; (*mine*) to work; (*situation*) *Fig* to exploit. **2** (*abuser de*) *Péj* to exploit (*s.o.*). ◆**—ant, -ante** *nmf* farmer. ◆**exploitation** *nf* **1** *Péj* exploitation. **2** farming; running; working; (*entreprise*) concern; (*agricole*) farm.

explorer [ɛksplɔre] *vt* to explore. ◆**explorateur, -trice** *nmf* explorer. ◆**exploration** *nf* exploration.

exploser [ɛksploze] *vi* (*gaz etc*) to explode; (*bombe*) to blow up, explode; **e. (de colère)** *Fam* to explode, blow up; **faire e.** (*bombe*) to explode. ◆**explosif, -ive** *a & nm* explosive. ◆**explosion** *nf* explosion; (*de colère, joie*) outburst.

exporter [ɛkspɔrte] *vt* to export (**vers** to, **de** from). ◆**exportateur, -trice** *nmf* exporter; — *a* exporting. ◆**exportation** *nf* (*produit*) export; (*action*) export(ation), exporting.

expos/er [ɛkspoze] *vt* (*présenter, soumettre*) & *Phot* to expose (**à** to); (*marchandises*) to display; (*tableau etc*) to exhibit; (*idée, théorie*) to set out; (*vie, réputation*) to risk, endanger; **s'e. à** to expose oneself to. ◆**—ant, -ante** *nmf* exhibitor. ◆**—é 1** *a* **bien e.** (*édifice*) having a good exposure; **e. au sud** facing south. **2** *nm* (*compte rendu*) account (**de** of); (*discours*) talk; *Scol* paper. ◆**exposition** *nf* (*de marchandises etc*) display; (*salon*) exhibition; (*au danger etc*) &

Phot exposure (à to); (*de maison etc*) aspect.

exprès[1] [ɛksprɛ] *adv* on purpose, intentionally; (*spécialement*) specially.

exprès[2], **-esse** [ɛksprɛs] **1** *a* (*ordre, condition*) express. **2** *a inv* **lettre/colis e.** express letter/parcel. ◆**expressément** *adv* expressly.

express [ɛksprɛs] *a & nm inv* (*train*) express; (*café*) espresso.

expressif, -ive [ɛkspresif, -iv] *a* expressive. ◆**expression** *nf* (*phrase, mine etc*) expression. ◆**exprimer** *vt* to express; **— s'e.** *vpr* to express oneself.

exproprier [ɛksprɔprije] *vt* to seize the property of by compulsory purchase.

expulser [ɛkspylse] *vt* to expel (**de** from); (*joueur*) *Sp* to send off; (*locataire*) to evict. ◆**expulsion** *nf* expulsion; eviction; sending off.

expurger [ɛkspyrʒe] *vt* to expurgate.

exquis [ɛkski] *a* exquisite.

extase [ɛkstɑz] *nf* ecstasy, rapture. ◆**s'extasi/er** *vpr* to be in raptures (**sur** over, about). ◆**—é** *a* ecstatic.

extensible [ɛkstɑ̃sibl] *a* expandable. ◆**extension** *nf* extension; (*essor*) expansion.

exténuer [ɛkstenɥe] *vt* (*fatiguer*) to exhaust. ◆**exténuation** *nf* exhaustion.

extérieur [ɛksterjœr] *a* (*monde etc*) outside; (*surface*) outer; (*signe*) outward, external; (*politique*) foreign; **e. à** external to; **—** *nm* outside, exterior; **à l'e. (de)** outside; **à l'e.** (*match*) away; **en e.** *Cin* on location. ◆**—ement** *adv* externally; (*en apparence*) outwardly. ◆**extérioriser** *vt* to express.

exterminer [ɛkstɛrmine] *vt* to exterminate, wipe out. ◆**extermination** *nf* extermination.

externe [ɛkstɛrn] **1** *a* external. **2** *nmf Scol* day pupil; *Méd* non-resident hospital doctor, *Am* extern.

extincteur [ɛkstɛ̃ktœr] *nm* fire extinguisher. ◆**extinction** *nf* (*de feu*) extinguishing; (*de voix*) loss; (*de race*) extinction.

extirper [ɛkstirpe] *vt* to eradicate.

extorquer [ɛkstɔrke] *vt* to extort (**à** from). ◆**extorsion** *nf* extortion.

extra [ɛkstra] **1** *a inv* (*très bon*) *Fam* top-quality. **2** *nm inv Culin* (extra-special) treat; (*serviteur*) extra hand *ou* help.

extra- [ɛkstra] *préf* extra-. ◆**e.-fin** *a* extra-fine. ◆**e.-fort** *a* extra-strong.

extradition [ɛkstradisjɔ̃] *nf* extradition. ◆**extrader** *vt* to extradite.

extraire* [ɛkstrɛr] *vt* to extract (**de** from); (*charbon*) to mine. ◆**extraction** *nf* extraction. ◆**extrait** *nm* extract; **un e. de naissance** a (copy of one's) birth certificate.

extraordinaire [ɛkstraɔrdinɛr] *a* extraordinary. ◆**—ment** *adv* exceptionally; (*très, bizarrement*) extraordinarily.

extravagant [ɛkstravagɑ̃] *a* extravagant. ◆**extravagance** *nf* extravagance.

extrême [ɛkstrɛm] *a* extreme; **—** *nm* extreme; **pousser à l'e.** to take *ou* carry to extremes. ◆**—ment** *adv* extremely. ◆**extrémiste** *a & nmf* extremist. ◆**extrémité** *nf* (*bout*) extremity, end; *pl* (*excès*) extremes.

exubérant [ɛgzyberɑ̃] *a* exuberant. ◆**exubérance** *nf* exuberance.

exulter [ɛgzylte] *vi* to exult, rejoice. ◆**exultation** *nf* exultation.

F

F, f [ɛf] *nm* F, f.

F *abrév* **franc(s).**

fable [fɑbl] *nf* fable.

fabrique [fabrik] *nf* factory; **marque de f.** trade mark.

fabriquer [fabrike] *vt* (*objet*) to make; (*industriellement*) to manufacture; (*récit*) *Péj* to fabricate, make up; **qu'est-ce qu'il fabrique?** *Fam* what's he up to? ◆**fabricant, -ante** *nmf* manufacturer. ◆**fabrication** *nf* manufacture; (*artisanale*) making; **de f. française** of French make.

fabuleux, -euse [fabylø, -øz] *a* (*légendaire, incroyable*) fabulous.

fac [fak] *nf Univ Fam* = **faculté 2.**

façade [fasad] *nf* (*de bâtiment*) front, façade; (*apparence*) *Fig* pretence, façade; **de f.** (*luxe etc*) sham.

face [fas] *nf* face; (*de cube etc*) side; (*de monnaie*) head; **de f.** (*photo*) full-face; (*vue*) front; **faire f. à** (*situation etc*) to face, face up to; **en f.** opposite; **en f. de** opposite, facing; (*en présence de*) in front of; **en f. d'un problème, f. à un problème** in the face of a problem, faced with a problem; **f. à** (*vis-à-vis de*) facing; **regarder qn en f.** to look s.o. in the face; **f. à f.** face to face; **un f. à f.** *TV* a face to face encounter; **sauver/perdre la f.** to save/lose face.

facétie [fasesi] *nf* joke, jest. ◆**facétieux, -euse** [-esjø, -øz] *a* (*personne*) facetious.

facette [faset] *nf* (*de diamant, problème etc*) facet.

fâch/er [faʃe] *vt* to anger; **— se f.** *vpr* to get angry *ou* annoyed (**contre** with); **se f. avec qn** (*se brouiller*) to fall out with s.o. ◆**—é** *a* (*air*) angry; (*amis*) on bad terms; **f. avec** *ou* **contre qn** angry *ou* annoyed with s.o.; **f. de qch** sorry about sth. ◆**fâcherie** *nf* quarrel. ◆**fâcheux, -euse** *a* (*nouvelle etc*) unfortunate.

facho [faʃo] *a & nmf Fam* fascist.

facile [fasil] *a* easy; (*caractère, humeur*) easygoing; (*banal*) *Péj* facile; **c'est f. à faire** it's easy to do; **il est f. de faire ça** it's easy to do that; **f. à vivre** easy to get along with, easygoing. ◆**—ment** *adv* easily. ◆**facilité** *nf* (*simplicité*) easiness; (*aisance*) ease; **facilités de paiement** *Com* easy terms; **avoir de la f.** to be gifted; **avoir toutes facilités pour** to have every facility *ou* opportunity to. ◆**faciliter** *vt* to facilitate, make easier.

façon [fasɔ̃] *nf* **1** way; **la f. dont elle parle** the way (in which) she talks; **f. (d'agir)** behaviour; **je n'aime pas ses façons** I don't like his *ou* her manners *ou* ways; **une f. de parler** a manner of speaking; **à la f. de** in the fashion of; **de toute f.** anyway, anyhow; **de f. à** so as to; **de f. générale** generally speaking; **à ma f.** my way, (in) my own way; **faire des façons** to make a fuss; **table f. chêne** imitation oak table. **2** (*coupe de vêtement*) cut, style. ◆**façonner** *vt* (*travailler, former*) to fashion, shape; (*fabriquer*) to manufacture.

facteur [faktœr] *nm* **1** postman, *Am* mailman. **2** (*élément*) factor. ◆**factrice** *nf Fam* postwoman.

factice [faktis] *a* false, artificial; (*diamant*) imitation-.

faction [faksjɔ̃] *nf* **1** (*groupe*) *Pol* faction. **2 de f.** *Mil* on guard (duty), on sentry duty.

facture [faktyr] *nf Com* invoice, bill. ◆**facturer** *vt* to invoice, bill.

facultatif, -ive [fakyltatif, -iv] *a* optional; **arrêt f.** request stop.

faculté [fakylte] *nf* **1** (*aptitude*) faculty; (*possibilité*) freedom (**de faire** to do); **une f. de travail** a capacity for work. **2** *Univ* faculty; **à la f.** *Fam* at university, *Am* at school.

fadaises [fadez] *nfpl* twaddle, nonsense.

fade [fad] *a* insipid. ◆**fadasse** *a Fam* wishy-washy.

fagot [fago] *nm* bundle (of firewood).

fagoter [fagɔte] *vt Péj* to dress, rig out.

faible [fɛbl] *a* weak, feeble; (*bruit, voix*) faint; (*vent, quantité, chances*) slight; (*revenus*) small; **f. en anglais/***etc* poor at English/*etc*; – *nm* (*personne*) weakling; **les faibles** the weak; **avoir un f. pour** to have a weakness *ou* a soft spot for. ◆**faiblement** *adv* weakly; (*légèrement*) slightly; (*éclairer, parler*) faintly. ◆**faiblesse** *nf* weakness, feebleness; faintness; slightness; smallness; (*défaut, syncope*) weakness. ◆**faiblir** *vi* (*forces*) to weaken; (*courage, vue*) to fail; (*vent*) to slacken.

faïence [fajɑ̃s] *nf* (*matière*) earthenware; *pl* (*objets*) crockery, earthenware.

faille [faj] *nf Géol* fault; *Fig* flaw.

faillible [fajibl] *a* fallible.

faillir* [fajir] *vi* **1 il a failli tomber** he almost *ou* nearly fell. **2 f. à** (*devoir*) to fail in.

faillite [fajit] *nf Com* bankruptcy; *Fig* failure; **faire f.** to go bankrupt.

faim [fɛ̃] *nf* hunger; **avoir f.** to be hungry; **donner f. à qn** to make s.o. hungry; **manger à sa f.** to eat one's fill; **mourir de f.** to die of starvation; (*avoir très faim*) *Fig* to be starving.

fainéant, -ante [feneɑ̃, -ɑ̃t] *a* idle; – *nmf* idler. ◆**fainéanter** *vi* to idle. ◆**fainéantise** *nf* idleness.

faire* [fɛr] **1** *vt* (*bruit, pain, faute etc*) to make; (*devoir, dégâts, ménage etc*) to do; (*rêve, chute*) to have; (*sourire, grognement*) to give; (*promenade, sieste*) to have, take; (*guerre*) to wage, make; **ça fait dix mètres de large** (*mesure*) it's ten metres wide; **2 et 2 font 4** 2 and 2 are 4; **ça fait dix francs** that is *ou* comes to ten francs; **qu'a-t-il fait (de)?** what's he done (with)?; **que f.?** what's to be done?; **f. du tennis/du piano/***etc* to play tennis/the piano/*etc*; **f. l'idiot** to act *ou* play the fool; **ça ne fait rien** that doesn't matter; **comment as-tu fait pour . . . ?** how did you manage to . . . ?; **il ne fait que travailler** he does nothing but work, he keeps on working; **je ne fais que d'arriver** I've just arrived; **oui, fit-elle** yes, she said. **2** *vi* (*agir*) to do; (*paraître*) to look; **il fait vieux** he looks old; **il fera un bon médecin** he'll be *ou* make a good doctor; **elle ferait bien de partir** she'd do well to leave. **3** *v imp* **il fait beau/froid/***etc* it's fine/cold/*etc*; **quel temps fait-il?** what's the weather like?; **ça fait deux ans que je ne l'ai pas vu** I haven't seen him for two years, it's (been) two years since I saw him. **4** *v aux* (+ *inf*): **f. construire une maison** to have *ou* get a house built (**à qn, par qn** by s.o.); **f. crier/souffrir/***etc* **qn** to make s.o. shout/suffer/*etc*; **se f. couper les cheveux** to have one's hair cut; **se f. craindre/obéir/***etc* to make oneself feared/obeyed/*etc*; **se f. tuer/renverser/***etc* to get *ou* be killed/knocked down/*etc*. **5 se f.** *vpr* (*fabrication*) to be made; (*activité*) to be done; **se f. des illusions** to have illusions; **se f. des amis** to make friends; **se f. vieux/***etc* (*devenir*) to get old/*etc*; **il se fait tard** it's getting late; **comment se fait-il que?** how is it that?; **se f. à** to get used to, adjust to; **ne t'en fais pas!** don't worry!

faire-part [fɛrpar] *nm inv* (*de mariage etc*) announcement.

faisable [fəzabl] *a* feasible.

faisan [fəzɑ̃] *nm* (*oiseau*) pheasant.

faisandé [fəzɑ̃de] *a* (*gibier*) high.

faisceau, -x [fɛso] *nm* (*lumineux*) beam; (*de tiges etc*) bundle.

fait [fɛ] **1** *voir* **faire**; – *a* (*fromage*) ripe; (*homme*) grown; (*yeux*) made up; (*ongles*) polished; **tout f.** ready made; **bien f.** (*jambes, corps etc*) shapely; **c'est bien f.!** it serves you right! **2** *nm* event, occurrence; (*donnée, réalité*) fact; **prendre sur le f.** *Jur* to catch in the act; **du f. de** on account of; **f. divers** *Journ* (miscellaneous) news item; **au f.** (*à propos*) by the way; **aller au f.** to get to the point; **faits et gestes** actions; **en f.** in fact; **en f. de** in the matter of.

faîte [fɛt] *nm* (*haut*) top; (*apogée*) *Fig* height.

faites [fɛt] *voir* **faire**.

faitout [fɛtu] *nm* stewing pot, casserole.

falaise [falɛz] *nf* cliff.

falloir* [falwar] **1** *v imp* **il faut qch/qn** I, you, we *etc* need sth/s.o.; **il lui faut un stylo** he *ou* she needs a pen; **il faut partir/***etc* I, you, we *etc* have to go/*etc*; **il faut que je parte** I have to go; **il faudrait qu'elle reste** she ought to stay; **il faut un jour** it takes a day (**pour faire** to do); **comme il faut** proper(ly); **s'il le faut** if need be. **2 s'en f.** *v imp* **peu s'en est fallu qu'il ne pleure** he almost cried; **tant s'en faut** far from it.

falsifier [falsifje] *vt* (*texte etc*) to falsify. ◆**falsification** *nf* falsification.

famé (mal) [malfame] *a* of ill repute.

famélique [famelik] *a* ill-fed, starving.

fameux, -euse [famø, -øz] *a* famous; (*excellent*) *Fam* first-class; **pas f.** *Fam* not much good.

familial, -aux [familjal, -o] *a* family-.

familier, -ière [familje, -jɛr] *a* (*bien connu*) familiar (**à** to); (*amical*) friendly, informal; (*locution*) colloquial, familiar; **f. avec qn** (over)familiar with s.o.; – *nm* (*de club etc*) regular visitor. ◆**familiariser** *vt* to familiarize (**avec** with); — **se f.** *vpr* to familiarize oneself (**avec** with). ◆**familiarité** *nf* familiarity; *pl Péj* liberties. ◆**familièrement** *adv* familiarly; (*parler*) informally.

famille [famij] *nf* family; **en f.** (*dîner etc*) with one's family; **un père de f.** a family man.

famine [famin] *nf* famine.

fan [fɑ̃] *nm* (*admirateur*) *Fam* fan.

fana [fana] *nmf Fam* fan; **être f. de** to be crazy about.

fanal, -aux [fanal, -o] *nm* lantern, light.

fanatique [fanatik] *a* fanatical; – *nmf* fanatic. ◆**fanatisme** *nm* fanaticism.

fan/er (se) [səfane] *vpr* (*fleur, beauté*) to fade. ◆**—é** *a* faded.

fanfare [fɑ̃far] *nf* (*orchestre*) brass band; (*air, musique*) fanfare.

fanfaron, -onne [fɑ̃farɔ̃, -ɔn] *a* boastful; – *nmf* braggart.

fange [fɑ̃ʒ] *nf Litt* mud, mire.

fanion [fanjɔ̃] *nm* (*drapeau*) pennant.

fantaisie [fɑ̃tezi] *nf* (*caprice*) fancy, whim; (*imagination*) imagination, fantasy; **(de) f.** (*bouton etc*) fancy. ◆**fantaisiste** *a* (*pas sérieux*) fanciful; (*irrégulier*) unorthodox.

fantasme [fɑ̃tasm] *nm Psy* fantasy. ◆**fantasmer** *vi* to fantasize (**sur** about).

fantasque [fɑ̃task] *a* whimsical.

fantassin [fɑ̃tasɛ̃] *nm Mil* infantryman.

fantastique [fɑ̃tastik] *a* (*imaginaire, excellent*) fantastic.

fantoche [fɑ̃tɔʃ] *nm & a* puppet.

fantôme [fɑ̃tom] *nm* ghost, phantom; – *a* (*ville, train*) ghost-; (*firme*) bogus.

faon [fɑ̃] *nm* (*animal*) fawn.

faramineux, -euse [faraminø, -øz] *a Fam* fantastic.

farce¹ [fars] *nf* practical joke, prank; *Th* farce; **magasin de farces et attrapes** joke shop. ◆**farceur, -euse** *nmf* (*blagueur*) wag, joker.

farce² [fars] *nf Culin* stuffing. ◆**farcir** *vt* **1** *Culin* to stuff. **2 se f. qn/qch** *Fam* to put up with s.o./sth.

fard [far] *nm* make-up. ◆**farder** *vt* (*vérité*) to camouflage; — **se f.** *vpr* (*se maquiller*) to make up.

fardeau, -x [fardo] *nm* burden, load.

farfelu, -ue [farfəly] *a Fam* crazy, bizarre; – *nmf Fam* weirdo.

farine [farin] *nf* (*de blé*) flour; **f. d'avoine**

oatmeal. ◆**farineux, -euse** *a Péj* floury, powdery.

farouche [faruʃ] *a* **1** (*timide*) shy, unsociable; (*animal*) easily scared. **2** (*violent, acharné*) fierce. ◆**—ment** *adv* fiercely.

fart [far(t)] *nm* (ski) wax. ◆**farter** *vt* (*skis*) to wax.

fascicule [fasikyl] *nm* volume.

fasciner [fasine] *vt* to fascinate. ◆**fascination** *nf* fascination.

fascisme [faʃism] *nm* fascism. ◆**fasciste** *a & nmf* fascist.

fasse(nt) [fas] *voir* **faire.**

faste [fast] *nm* ostentation, display.

fastidieux, -euse [fastidjø, -øz] *a* tedious, dull.

fatal, *mpl* **-als** [fatal] *a* (*mortel*) fatal; (*inévitable*) inevitable; (*moment, ton*) fateful; **c'était f.!** it was bound to happen! ◆**—ement** *adv* inevitably. ◆**fataliste** *a* fatalistic; – *nmf* fatalist. ◆**fatalité** *nf* (*destin*) fate. ◆**fatidique** *a* (*jour, date*) fateful.

fatigue [fatig] *nf* tiredness, fatigue, weariness. ◆**fatigant** *a* (*épuisant*) tiring; (*ennuyeux*) tiresome. ◆**fatigu/er** *vt* to tire, fatigue; (*yeux*) to strain; (*importuner*) to annoy; (*raser*) to bore; – *vi* (*moteur*) to strain; **— se f.** *vpr* (*se lasser*) to get tired, tire (**de** of); (*travailler*) to tire oneself out (**à faire** doing). ◆**—é** *a* tired, weary (**de** of).

fatras [fatra] *nm* jumble, muddle.

faubourg [fobur] *nm* suburb. ◆**faubourien, -ienne** *a* (*accent etc*) suburban, common.

fauché [foʃe] *a* (*sans argent*) *Fam* broke.

fauch/er [foʃe] *vt* **1** (*herbe*) to mow; (*blé*) to reap; (*abattre, renverser*) *Fig* to mow down. **2** (*voler*) *Fam* to snatch, pinch. ◆**—euse** *nf* (*machine*) reaper.

faucille [fosij] *nf* (*instrument*) sickle.

faucon [fokɔ̃] *nm* (*oiseau*) falcon, hawk; (*personne*) *Fig* hawk.

faudra, faudrait [fodra, fodrɛ] *voir* **falloir.**

faufiler (se) [səfofile] *vpr* to edge *ou* inch one's way (**dans** through, into; **entre** between).

faune [fon] *nf* wildlife, fauna; (*gens*) *Péj* set.

faussaire [fosɛr] *nm* (*faux-monnayeur*) forger.

fausse [fos] *voir* **faux** [1]. ◆**faussement** *adv* falsely.

fausser [fose] *vt* (*sens, réalité etc*) to distort; (*clé etc*) to buckle; **f. compagnie à qn** to give s.o. the slip.

fausseté [foste] *nf* (*d'un raisonnement etc*) falseness; (*hypocrisie*) duplicity.

faut [fo] *voir* **falloir.**

faute [fot] *nf* (*erreur*) mistake; (*responsabilité*) fault; (*délit*) offence; (*péché*) sin; *Fb* foul; **c'est ta f.** it's your fault, you're to blame; **f. de temps/***etc* for lack of time/*etc*; **f. de mieux** for want of anything better; **en f.** at fault; **sans f.** without fail. ◆**fautif, -ive** *a* (*personne*) at fault; (*erroné*) faulty.

fauteuil [fotœj] *nm* armchair; (*de président*) chair; **f. d'orchestre** *Th* seat in the stalls; **f. roulant** wheelchair; **f. pivotant** swivel chair.

fauteur [fotœr] *nm* **f. de troubles** troublemaker.

fauve [fov] **1** *a & nm* (*couleur*) fawn. **2** *nm* wild beast; **chasse aux fauves** big game hunting.

faux [1]**, fausse** [fo, fos] *a* (*inauthentique*) false; (*pas vrai*) untrue, false; (*pas exact*) wrong; (*monnaie*) counterfeit, forged; (*bijou, marbre*) imitation-, fake; (*voix*) out of tune; (*col*) detachable; – *adv* (*chanter*) out of tune; – *nm* (*contrefaçon*) forgery; **le f.** the false, the untrue. ◆**f.-filet** *nm Culin* sirloin. ◆**f.-fuyant** *nm* subterfuge. ◆**f.-monnayeur** *nm* counterfeiter.

faux [2] [fo] *nf* (*instrument*) scythe.

faveur [favœr] *nf* favour; **en f. de** (*au profit de*) in favour of; **de f.** (*billet*) complimentary; (*traitement, régime*) preferential. ◆**favorable** *a* favourable (**à** to). ◆**favori, -ite** *a & nmf* favourite. ◆**favoriser** *vt* to favour. ◆**favoritisme** *nm* favouritism.

favoris [favɔri] *nmpl* sideburns, side whiskers.

fébrile [febril] *a* feverish. ◆**fébrilité** *nf* feverishness.

fécond [fekɔ̃] *a* (*femme, idée etc*) fertile. ◆**féconder** *vt* to fertilize. ◆**fécondité** *nf* fertility.

fécule [fekyl] *nf* starch. ◆**féculents** *nmpl* (*aliments*) carbohydrates.

fédéral, -aux [federal, -o] *a* federal. ◆**fédération** *nf* federation. ◆**fédérer** *vt* to federate.

fée [fe] *nf* fairy. ◆**féerie** *nf Th* fantasy extravaganza; *Fig* fairy-like spectacle. ◆**féerique** *a* fairy(-like), magical.

feindre* [fɛ̃dr] *vt* to feign, sham; **f. de faire** to pretend to do. ◆**feint** *a* feigned, sham. ◆**feinte** *nf* sham, pretence; *Boxe Mil* feint.

fêler [fele] *vt*, **— se f.** *vpr* (*tasse*) to crack. ◆**fêlure** *nf* crack.

félicité [felisite] *nf* bliss, felicity.

féliciter [felisite] *vt* to congratulate (**qn de** *ou* **sur** s.o. on); **se f. de** to congratulate oneself on. ◆**félicitations** *nfpl* congratulations (pour on).

félin [felɛ̃] *a* & *nm* feline.

femelle [fəmɛl] *a* & *nf* (*animal*) female.

féminin [feminɛ̃] *a* (*prénom, hormone etc*) female; (*trait, intuition etc*) & *Gram* feminine; (*mode, revue, équipe etc*) women's. ◆**féministe** *a* & *nmf* feminist. ◆**féminité** *nf* femininity.

femme [fam] *nf* woman; (*épouse*) wife; **f. médecin** woman doctor; **f. de chambre** (chamber)maid; **f. de ménage** cleaning lady, maid; **bonne f.** *Fam* woman.

fémur [femyr] *nm* thighbone, femur.

fendiller (se) [səfɑ̃dije] *vpr* to crack.

fendre [fɑ̃dr] *vt* (*bois etc*) to split; (*foule*) to force one's way through; (*onde, air*) to cleave; (*cœur*) *Fig* to break, rend; **— se f.** *vpr* (*se fissurer*) to crack.

fenêtre [f(ə)nɛtr] *nf* window.

fenouil [fənuj] *nm Bot Culin* fennel.

fente [fɑ̃t] *nf* (*de tirelire, palissade, jupe etc*) slit; (*de rocher*) split, crack.

féodal, -aux [feɔdal, -o] *a* feudal.

fer [fɛr] *nm* iron; (*partie métallique de qch*) metal (part); **de f., en f.** (*outil etc*) iron-; **fil de f.** wire; **f. à cheval** horseshoe; **f. (à repasser)** iron; **f. à friser** curling tongs; **f. de lance** *Fig* spearhead; **de f.** (*santé*) *Fig* cast-iron; (*main, volonté*) *Fig* iron-. ◆**fer-blanc** *nm* (*pl* **fers-blancs**) tin(-plate).

fera, ferait [fəra, fərɛ] *voir* **faire**.

férié [ferje] *a* **jour f.** (public) holiday.

ferme¹ [fɛrm] *nf* farm; (*maison*) farm(house).

ferme² [fɛrm] *a* (*beurre, décision etc*) firm; (*autoritaire*) firm (**avec** with); (*pas, voix*) steady; (*pâte*) stiff; – *adv* (*travailler, boire*) hard; (*discuter*) keenly; **tenir f.** to stand firm *ou* fast. ◆**—ment** [-əmɑ̃] *adv* firmly.

ferment [fɛrmɑ̃] *nm* ferment. ◆**fermentation** *nf* fermentation. ◆**fermenter** *vi* to ferment.

ferm/er [fɛrme] *vt* to close, shut; (*gaz, radio etc*) to turn *ou* switch off; (*passage*) to block; (*vêtement*) to do up; **f. (à clef)** to lock; **f. la marche** to bring up the rear; – *vi*, **— se f.** *vpr* to close, shut. ◆**—é** *a* (*porte, magasin etc*) closed, shut; (*route, circuit etc*) closed; (*gaz etc*) off. ◆**fermeture** *nf* closing, closure; (*heure*) closing time; (*mécanisme*) catch; **f. éclair®** zip (fastener), *Am* zipper. ◆**fermoir** *nm* clasp, (snap) fastener.

fermeté [fɛrməte] *nf* firmness; (*de geste, voix*) steadiness.

fermier, -ière [fɛrmje, -jɛr] *nmf* farmer; – *a* (*poulet, produit*) farm-.

féroce [ferɔs] *a* fierce, ferocious. ◆**férocité** *nf* ferocity, fierceness.

ferraille [fɛrɑj] *nf* scrap-iron; **mettre à la f.** to scrap. ◆**ferrailleur** *nm* scrap-iron merchant.

ferré [fɛre] *a* **1** (*canne*) metal-tipped; **voie ferrée** railway, *Am* railroad; (*rails*) track. **2** (*calé*) *Fam* well up (**en** in, **sur** on).

ferrer [fɛre] *vt* (*cheval*) to shoe.

ferronnerie [fɛrɔnri] *nf* ironwork.

ferroviaire [fɛrɔvjɛr] *a* (*compagnie etc*) railway-, *Am* railroad-.

ferry-boat [fɛribot] *nm* ferry.

fertile [fɛrtil] *a* (*terre, imagination*) fertile; **f. en incidents** eventful. ◆**fertiliser** *vt* to fertilize. ◆**fertilité** *nf* fertility.

fervent, -ente [fɛrvɑ̃, -ɑ̃t] *a* fervent; – *nmf* devotee (**de** of). ◆**ferveur** *nf* fervour.

fesse [fɛs] *nf* buttock; **les fesses** one's behind. ◆**fessée** *nf* spanking.

festin [fɛstɛ̃] *nm* (*banquet*) feast.

festival, *pl* **-als** [fɛstival] *nm Mus Cin* festival.

festivités [fɛstivite] *nfpl* festivities.

festoyer [fɛstwaje] *vi* to feast, carouse.

fête [fɛt] *nf* (*civile*) holiday; *Rel* festival, feast; (*entre amis*) party; **f. du village** village fair *ou* fête; **f. de famille** family celebration; **c'est sa f.** it's his *ou* her saint's day; **f. des Mères** Mother's Day; **jour de f.** (public) holiday; **faire la f.** to make merry, revel; **air de f.** festive air. ◆**fêter** *vt* (*événement*) to celebrate.

fétiche [fetiʃ] *nm* (*objet de culte*) fetish; (*mascotte*) *Fig* mascot.

fétide [fetid] *a* fetid, stinking.

feu¹, -x [fø] *nm* fire; (*lumière*) *Aut Nau Av* light; (*de réchaud*) burner; (*de dispute*) *Fig* heat; *pl* (*de signalisation*) traffic lights; **feux de position** *Aut* parking lights; **feux de croisement** *Aut* dipped headlights, *Am* low beams; **f. rouge** *Aut* (*lumière*) red light; (*objet*) traffic lights; **tous feux éteints** *Aut* without lights; **mettre le f. à** to set fire to; **en f.** on fire, ablaze; **avez-vous du f.?** have you got a light?; **donner le f. vert** to give the go-ahead (**à** to); **ne pas faire long f.** not to last very long; **à f. doux** *Culin* on a low light; **au f.!** (there's a) fire!; **f.!** *Mil* fire!; **coup de f.** (*bruit*) gunshot; **feux croisés** *Mil* crossfire.

feu² [fø] *a inv* late; **f. ma tante** my late aunt.

feuille [fœj] *nf* leaf; (*de papier etc*) sheet; (*de température*) chart; *Journ* newssheet; **f. d'impôt** tax form *ou* return; **f. de paye** pay slip. ◆**feuillage** *nm* foliage. ◆**feuillet** *nm* (*de livre*) leaf. ◆**feuilleter** *vt* (*livre*) to flip *ou* leaf through; **pâte feuilletée** puff *ou* flaky pastry. ◆**feuilleton** *nm* (*roman, film etc*) serial. ◆**feuillu** *a* leafy.

feutre [føtr] *nm* felt; (*chapeau*) felt hat; **crayon f.** felt-tip(ped) pen. ◆**feutré** *a* (*bruit*) muffled; **à pas feutrés** silently.

fève [fɛv] *nf* bean.

février [fevrije] *nm* February.

fiable [fjabl] *a* reliable. ◆**fiabilité** *nf* reliability.

fiacre [fjakr] *nm Hist* hackney carriage.

fianc/er (se) [səfjɑ̃se] *vpr* to become engaged (avec to). ◆**—é** *nm* fiancé; *pl* engaged couple. ◆**—ée** *nf* fiancée. ◆**fiançailles** *nfpl* engagement.

fiasco [fjasko] *nm* fiasco; **faire f.** to be a fiasco.

fibre [fibr] *nf* fibre; **f. (alimentaire)** roughage, (dietary) fibre; **f. de verre** fibreglass.

ficelle [fisɛl] *nf* **1** string; **connaître les ficelles** (*d'un métier etc*) to known the ropes. **2** (*pain*) long thin loaf. ◆**ficeler** *vt* to tie up.

fiche [fiʃ] *nf* **1** (*carte*) index *ou* record card; (*papier*) slip, form; **f. technique** data record. **2** *Él* (*broche*) pin; (*prise*) plug. ◆**fichier** *nm* card index, file.

fiche(r) [fiʃ(e)] *vt* (*pp* **fichu**) *Fam* (*faire*) to do; (*donner*) to give; (*jeter*) to throw; (*mettre*) to put; **f. le camp** to shove off; **fiche-moi la paix!** leave me alone!; **se f. de qn** to make fun of s.o.; **je m'en fiche!** I don't give a damn!

ficher [fiʃe] *vt* **1** (*enfoncer*) to drive in. **2** (*renseignement, personne*) to put on file.

fichu [fiʃy] **1** *a Fam* (*mauvais*) lousy, rotten; (*capable*) able (**de faire** to do); **il est f.** he's had it, he's done for; **mal f.** (*malade*) not well. **2** *nm* (head) scarf.

fictif, -ive [fiktif, -iv] *a* fictitious. ◆**fiction** *nf* fiction.

fidèle [fidɛl] *a* faithful (**à** to); – *nmf* faithful supporter; (*client*) regular (customer); **les fidèles** (*croyants*) the faithful; (*à l'église*) the congregation. ◆**—ment** *adv* faithfully. ◆**fidélité** *nf* fidelity, faithfulness.

fief [fjɛf] *nm* (*spécialité, chasse gardée*) domain.

fiel [fjɛl] *nm* gall.

fier (se) [səfje] *vpr* **se f. à** to trust.

fier, fière [fjɛr] *a* proud (**de** of); **un f. culot** *Péj* a rare cheek. ◆**fièrement** *adv* proudly. ◆**fierté** *nf* pride.

fièvre [fjɛvr] *nf* (*maladie*) fever; (*agitation*) frenzy; **avoir de la f.** to have a temperature *ou* a fever. ◆**fiévreux, -euse** *a* feverish.

fig/er [fiʒe] *vt* (*sang, sauce etc*) to congeal; **f. qn** (*paralyser*) *Fig* to freeze s.o.; – *vi* (*liquide*) to congeal; **— se f.** *vpr* (*liquide*) to congeal; (*sourire, personne*) *Fig* to freeze. ◆**—é** *a* (*locution*) set, fixed; (*regard*) frozen; (*société*) petrified.

fignol/er [fiɲɔle] *vt Fam* to round off meticulously, refine. ◆**—é** *a Fam* meticulous.

figue [fig] *nf* fig; **mi-f., mi-raisin** (*accueil etc*) neither good nor bad, mixed. ◆**figuier** *nm* fig tree.

figurant, -ante [figyrɑ̃, -ɑ̃t] *nmf Cin Th* extra.

figure [figyr] *nf* **1** (*visage*) face. **2** (*personnage*) & *Géom* figure; (*de livre*) figure, illustration; **faire f. de riche/d'imbécile/***etc* to look rich/a fool/*etc.* ◆**figurine** *nf* statuette.

figur/er [figyre] *vt* to represent; – *vi* to appear, figure; **— se f.** *vpr* to imagine; **figurez-vous que . . . ?** would you believe that . . . ? ◆**—é** *a* (*sens*) figurative; – *nm* **au f.** figuratively.

fil [fil] *nm* **1** (*de coton, pensée etc*) thread; (*lin*) linen; **f. dentaire** dental floss; **de f. en aiguille** bit by bit. **2** (*métallique*) wire; **f. de fer** wire; **f. à plomb** plumbline; **au bout du f.** *Tél* on the line; **passer un coup de f. à qn** *Tél* to give s.o. a ring *ou* a call. **3** (*de couteau*) edge. **4 au f. de l'eau/des jours** with the current/the passing of time.

filament [filamɑ̃] *nm Él* filament.

filandreux, -euse [filɑ̃drø, -øz] *a* (*phrase*) long-winded.

filante [filɑ̃t] *af* **étoile f.** shooting star.

file [fil] *nf* line; (*couloir*) *Aut* lane; **f. d'attente** queue, *Am* line; **en f. (indienne)** in single file; **chef de f.** leader; **(se) mettre en f.** to line up.

filer [file] **1** *vt* (*coton etc*) to spin. **2** *vt* **f. qn** (*suivre*) to shadow s.o., tail s.o. **3** *vt Fam* **f. qch à qn** (*objet*) to slip s.o. sth; **f. un coup de pied/***etc* **à qn** to give s.o. a kick/*etc.* **4** *vi* (*partir*) to shoot off, bolt; (*aller vite*) to speed along; (*temps*) to fly; (*bas, collant*) to ladder, run; (*liquide*) to trickle, run; **filez!** hop it!; **f. entre les doigts de qn** to slip through s.o.'s fingers; **f. doux** to be obedient. ◆**filature** *nf* **1** (*usine*) textile mill. **2** (*de policiers etc*) shadowing; **prendre en f.** to shadow.

filet [filɛ] *nm* **1** (*de pêche*) & *Sp* net; (*à bagages*) *Rail* (luggage) rack; **f. (à provisions)** string *ou* net bag (*for shopping*). **2** (*d'eau*) trickle. **3** (*de poisson, viande*) fillet.

filial, -aux [filjal, -o] *a* filial.

filiale [filjal] *nf* subsidiary (company).

filiation [filjasjɔ̃] *nf* relationship.
filière [filjɛr] *nf* (*de drogue*) network; **suivre la f.** (*pour obtenir qch*) to go through the official channels; (*employé*) to work one's way up.
filigrane [filigran] *nm* (*de papier*) watermark.
filin [filɛ̃] *nm Nau* rope.
fille [fij] *nf* **1** girl; **petite f.** (little *ou* young) girl; **jeune f.** girl, young lady; **vieille f.** *Péj* old maid; **f. (publique)** *Péj* prostitute. **2** (*parenté*) daughter, girl. ◆**f.-mère** *nf* (*pl* filles-mères) *Péj* unmarried mother. ◆**fillette** *nf* little girl.
filleul [fijœl] *nm* godson. ◆**filleule** *nf* goddaughter.
film [film] *nm* film, movie; (*pellicule*) film; **f. muet/parlant** silent/talking film *ou* movie; **le f. des événements** the sequence of events. ◆**filmer** *vt* (*personne, scène*) to film.
filon [filɔ̃] *nm Géol* seam; **trouver le (bon) f.** to strike it lucky.
filou [filu] *nm* rogue, crook.
fils [fis] *nm* son; **Dupont f.** Dupont junior.
filtre [filtr] *nm* filter; **(à bout) f.** (*cigarette*) (filter-)tipped; **(bout) f.** filter tip. ◆**filtrer** *vt* to filter; (*personne, nouvelles*) to scrutinize; – *vi* to filter (through).
fin [fɛ̃] **1** *nf* end; (*but*) end, aim; **mettre f. à** to put an end *ou* a stop to; **prendre f.** to come to an end; **tirer à sa f.** to draw to an end *ou* a close; **sans f.** endless; **à la f.** in the end; **arrêtez, à la f.!** stop, for heaven's sake!; **f. de semaine** weekend; **f. mai** at the end of May; **à cette f.** to this end. **2** *a* (*pointe, travail, tissu etc*) fine; (*taille, tranche*) thin; (*plat*) delicate, choice; (*esprit, oreille*) sharp; (*observation*) sharp, fine; (*gourmet*) discerning; (*rusé*) shrewd; (*intelligent*) clever; **au f. fond de** in the depths of; – *adv* (*couper, moudre*) finely; (*écrire*) small.
final, -aux *ou* **-als** [final, -o] *a* final; – *nm Mus* finale. ◆**finale** *nf Sp* final; *Gram* final syllable; – *nm Mus* finale. ◆**finalement** *adv* finally; (*en somme*) after all. ◆**finaliste** *nmf Sp* finalist.
finance [finɑ̃s] *nf* finance. ◆**financ/er** *vt* to finance. ◆**—ement** *nm* financing. ◆**financier, -ière** *a* financial; – *nm* financier. ◆**financièrement** *adv* financially.
fine [fin] *nf* liqueur brandy.
finement [finmɑ̃] *adv* (*broder, couper etc*) finely; (*agir*) cleverly.
finesse [finɛs] *nf* (*de pointe etc*) fineness; (*de taille etc*) thinness; (*de plat*) delicacy; (*d'esprit, de goût*) finesse; *pl* (*de langue*) niceties.
fin/ir [finir] *vt* to finish; (*discours, vie*) to end, finish; – *vi* to finish, end; **f. de faire** to finish doing; (*cesser*) to stop doing; **f. par faire** to end up *ou* finish up doing; **f. par qch** to finish (up) *ou* end (up) with sth; **en f. avec** to put an end to, finish with; **elle n'en finit pas** there's no end to it, she goes on and on. ◆**—i** *a* (*produit*) finished; (*univers etc*) & *Math* finite; **c'est f.** it's over *ou* finished; **il est f.** (*fichu*) he's done for *ou* finished; – *nm* (*poli*) finish. ◆**—issant** *a* (*siècle*) declining. ◆**finish** *nm Sp* finish. ◆**finition** *nf* (*action*) *Tech* finishing; (*résultat*) finish.
Finlande [fɛ̃lɑ̃d] *nf* Finland. ◆**finlandais, -aise** *a* Finnish; – *nmf* Finn. ◆**finnois, -oise** *a* Finnish; – *nmf* Finn; – *nm* (*langue*) Finnish.
fiole [fjɔl] *nf* phial, flask.
firme [firm] *nf* (*entreprise*) *Com* firm.
fisc [fisk] *nm* tax authorities, = Inland Revenue, = *Am* Internal Revenue. ◆**fiscal, -aux** *a* fiscal, tax-. ◆**fiscalité** *nf* tax system; (*charges*) taxation.
fission [fisjɔ̃] *nf Phys* fission.
fissure [fisyr] *nf* split, crack, fissure. ◆**se fissurer** *vpr* to split, crack.
fiston [fistɔ̃] *nm Fam* son, sonny.
fixe [fiks] *a* fixed; (*prix, heure*) set, fixed; **idée f.** obsession; **regard f.** stare; **être au beau f.** *Mét* to be set fair; – *nm* (*paie*) fixed salary. ◆**—ment** [-əmɑ̃] *adv* **regarder f.** to stare at. ◆**fixer** *vt* (*attacher*) to fix (**à** to); (*choix*) to settle; (*règle, date etc*) to decide, fix; **f. (du regard)** to stare at; **f. qn sur** to inform s.o. clearly about; **être fixé** (*décidé*) to be decided; **comme ça on est fixé!** (*renseigné*) we've got the picture!; **— se f.** *vpr* (*regard*) to become fixed; (*s'établir*) to settle. ◆**fixateur** *nm Phot* fixer; (*pour cheveux*) setting lotion. ◆**fixation** *nf* (*action*) fixing; (*dispositif*) fastening, binding; *Psy* fixation.
flacon [flakɔ̃] *nm* bottle, flask.
flageoler [flaʒɔle] *vi* to shake, tremble.
flageolet [flaʒɔlɛ] *nm Bot Culin* (dwarf) kidney bean.
flagrant [flagrɑ̃] *a* (*injustice etc*) flagrant, glaring; **pris en f. délit** caught in the act *ou* red-handed.
flair [flɛr] *nm* **1** (*d'un chien etc*) (sense of) smell, scent. **2** (*clairvoyance*) intuition, flair. ◆**flairer** *vt* to sniff at, smell; (*discerner*) *Fig* to smell, sense.
flamand, -ande [flamɑ̃, -ɑ̃d] *a* Flemish; – *nmf* Fleming; – *nm* (*langue*) Flemish.
flamant [flamɑ̃] *nm* (*oiseau*) flamingo.

flambant [flɑ̃bɑ̃] *adv* **f. neuf** brand new.
flambeau, -x [flɑ̃bo] *nm* torch.
flamb/er [flɑ̃be] **1** *vi* to burn, blaze; – *vt* (*aiguille*) *Méd* to sterilize; (*poulet*) to singe. **2** *vi* (*jouer*) *Fam* to gamble for big money. ◆**—é** *a* (*ruiné*) *Fam* done for. ◆**—ée** *nf* blaze; (*de colère, des prix etc*) *Fig* surge; (*de violence*) flare-up, eruption. ◆**—eur** *nm Fam* big gambler. ◆**flamboyer** *vi* to blaze, flame.
flamme [flam] *nf* flame; (*ardeur*) *Fig* fire; **en flammes** on fire. ◆**flammèche** *nf* spark.
flan [flɑ̃] *nm* **1** *Culin* custard tart *ou* pie. **2 au f.** *Fam* on the off chance, on the spur of the moment.
flanc [flɑ̃] *nm* side; (*d'une armée, d'un animal*) flank; **tirer au f.** *Arg* to shirk, idle.
flancher [flɑ̃ʃe] *vi Fam* to give in, weaken.
Flandre(s) [flɑ̃dr] *nf*(*pl*) Flanders.
flanelle [flanɛl] *nf* (*tissu*) flannel.
flâner [flɑne] *vi* to stroll, dawdle. ◆**flânerie** *nf* (*action*) strolling; (*promenade*) stroll.
flanquer [flɑ̃ke] *vt* **1** to flank (**de** with). **2** *Fam* (*jeter*) to chuck; (*donner*) to give; **f. qn à la porte** to throw s.o. out.
flaque [flak] *nf* puddle, pool.
flash, *pl* **flashes** [flaʃ] *nm* **1** *Phot* (*éclair*) flashlight; (*dispositif*) flash(gun). **2** *TV Rad* (news)flash.
flasque [flask] *a* flabby, floppy.
flatt/er [flate] *vt* to flatter; **se f. d'être malin/de réussir** to flatter oneself on being smart/on being able to succeed. ◆**—é** *a* flattered (**de qch** by sth, **de faire** to do, **que** that). ◆**flatterie** *nf* flattery. ◆**flatteur, -euse** *nmf* flatterer; – *a* flattering.
fléau, -x [fleo] *nm* **1** (*calamité*) scourge; (*personne, chose*) bane, plague. **2** *Agr* flail.
flèche [flɛʃ] *nf* arrow; (*d'église*) spire; **monter en f.** (*prix*) to (sky)rocket, shoot ahead. ◆**flécher** [fleʃe] *vt* to signpost (with arrows). ◆**fléchette** *nf* dart; *pl* (*jeu*) darts.
fléchir [fleʃir] *vt* (*membre*) to flex, bend; **f. qn** *Fig* to move s.o., persuade s.o.; – *vi* (*membre*) to bend; (*poutre*) to sag; (*faiblir*) to give way; (*baisser*) to fall off.
flegme [flɛgm] *nm* composure. ◆**flegmatique** *a* phlegmatic, stolid.
flemme [flɛm] *nf Fam* laziness; **il a la f.** he can't be bothered, he's just too lazy. ◆**flemmard, -arde** *a Fam* lazy; – *nmf Fam* lazybones.
flétrir [fletrir] **1** *vt*, **— se f.** *vpr* to wither. **2** *vt* (*blâmer*) to stigmatize, brand.
fleur [flœr] *nf* flower; (*d'arbre, d'arbuste*) blossom; **en f.** in flower, in bloom; **in blossom; à** *ou* **dans la f. de l'âge** in the prime of life; **à f. d'eau** just above the water; **à fleurs** (*tissu*) floral. ◆**fleur/ir** *vi* to flower, bloom; (*arbre etc*) to blossom; (*art, commerce etc*) *Fig* to flourish; – *vt* (*table etc*) to decorate with flowers. ◆**—i** *a* (*fleur, jardin*) in bloom; (*tissu*) flowered, floral; (*teint*) florid; (*style*) flowery, florid. ◆**fleuriste** *nmf* florist.
fleuve [flœv] *nm* river.
flexible [flɛksibl] *a* flexible, pliable. ◆**flexibilité** *nf* flexibility.
flexion [flɛksjɔ̃] *nf* **1** *Anat* flexion, flexing. **2** *Gram* inflexion.
flic [flik] *nm Fam* cop, policeman.
flinguer [flɛ̃ge] *vt* **f. qn** *Arg* to shoot s.o.
flipper [flipœr] *nm* (*jeu*) pinball.
flirt [flœrt] *nm* (*rapports*) flirtation; (*personne*) flirt. ◆**flirter** *vi* to flirt (**avec** with). ◆**flirteur, -euse** *a* flirtatious; – *nmf* flirt.
flocon [flɔkɔ̃] *nm* (*de neige*) flake; (*de laine*) flock; **flocons d'avoine** *Culin* porridge oats. ◆**floconneux, -euse** *a* fluffy.
floraison [flɔrɛzɔ̃] *nf* flowering; **en pleine f.** in full bloom. ◆**floral, -aux** *a* floral. ◆**floralies** *nfpl* flower show.
flore [flɔr] *nf* flora.
florissant [flɔrisɑ̃] *a* flourishing.
flot [flo] *nm* (*de souvenirs, larmes*) flood, stream; (*marée*) floodtide; *pl* (*de mer*) waves; (*de lac*) waters; **à flots** in abundance; **à f.** (*bateau, personne*) afloat; **mettre à f.** (*bateau, firme*) to launch; **remettre qn à f.** to restore s.o.'s fortunes.
flotte [flɔt] *nf* **1** *Nau Av* fleet. **2** *Fam* (*pluie*) rain; (*eau*) water. ◆**flottille** *nf Nau* flotilla.
flott/er [flɔte] *vi* to float; (*drapeau*) to fly; (*cheveux*) to flow; (*pensées*) to drift; (*pleuvoir*) *Fam* to rain. ◆**—ant** *a* **1** (*bois, dette etc*) floating; (*vêtement*) flowing, loose. **2** (*esprit*) indecisive. ◆**—ement** *nm* (*hésitation*) indecision. ◆**—eur** *nm Pêche etc* float.
flou [flu] *a* (*photo*) fuzzy, blurred; (*idée*) hazy, fuzzy; – *nm* fuzziness.
fluctuant [flyktɥɑ̃] *a* (*prix, opinions*) fluctuating. ◆**fluctuations** *nfpl* fluctuation(s) (**de** in).
fluet, -ette [flyɛ, -ɛt] *a* thin, slender.
fluide [flyid] *a* (*liquide*) & *Fig* fluid; – *nm* (*liquide*) fluid. ◆**fluidité** *nf* fluidity.
fluorescent [flyɔresɑ̃] *a* fluorescent.
flûte [flyt] **1** *nf Mus* flute. **2** *nf* (*verre*) champagne glass. **3** *int* heck!, darn!, dash it! ◆**flûté** *a* (*voix*) piping. ◆**flûtiste** *nmf* flautist, *Am* flutist.
fluvial, -aux [flyvjal, -o] *a* river-, fluvial.

flux [fly] *nm* (*abondance*) flow; **f. et reflux** ebb and flow.

focal, -aux [fɔkal, -o] *a* focal. **◆focaliser** *vt* (*intérêt etc*) to focus.

fœtus [fetys] *nm* foetus, *Am* fetus.

foi [fwa] *nf* faith; **sur la f. de** on the strength of; **agir de bonne/mauvaise f.** to act in good/bad faith; **ma f., oui!** yes, indeed!

foie [fwa] *nm* liver.

foin [fwɛ̃] *nm* hay; **faire du f.** (*scandale*) *Fam* to make a stink.

foire [fwar] *nf* fair; **faire la f.** *Fam* to go on a binge, have a ball.

fois [fwa] *nf* time; **une f.** once; **deux f.** twice, two times; **chaque f. que** each time (that), whenever; **une f. qu'il sera arrivé** (*dès que*) once he has arrived; **à la f.** at the same time, at once; **à la f. riche et heureux** both rich and happy; **une autre f.** (*elle fera attention etc*) next time; **des f.** *Fam* sometimes; **non mais des f.!** *Fam* you must be joking!; **une f. pour toutes, une bonne f.** once and for all.

foison [fwazɔ̃] *nf* **à f.** in plenty. **◆foisonn/er** *vi* to abound (**de, en** in). **◆—ement** *nm* abundance.

fol [fɔl] *voir* **fou.**

folâtre [fɔlatr] *a* playful. **◆folâtrer** *vi* to romp, frolic.

folichon, -onne [fɔliʃɔ̃, -ɔn] *a* **pas f.** not very funny, not much fun.

folie [fɔlie] *nf* madness, insanity; **faire une f.** to do a foolish thing; (*dépense*) to be wildly extravagant; **aimer qn à la f.** to be madly in love with s.o..

folklore [fɔlklɔr] *nm* folklore. **◆folklorique** *a* (*danse etc*) folk-; (*pas sérieux*) *Fam* lightweight, trivial, silly.

folle [fɔl] *voir* **fou. ◆follement** *adv* madly.

fomenter [fɔmɑ̃te] *vt* (*révolte etc*) to foment.

foncé [fɔ̃se] *a* (*couleur*) dark.

foncer [fɔ̃se] **1** *vi* (*aller vite*) to tear *ou* charge along; **f. sur qn** to charge into *ou* at s.o. **2** *vti* (*couleur*) to darken.

foncier, -ière [fɔ̃sje, -jɛr] *a* **1** fundamental, basic. **2** (*propriété*) landed. **◆foncièrement** *adv* fundamentally.

fonction [fɔ̃ksjɔ̃] *nf* (*rôle*) & *Math* function; (*emploi*) office, function, duty; **f. publique** civil service; **faire f. de** (*personne*) to act as; (*objet*) to serve *ou* act as; **en f. de** according to. **◆fonctionnaire** *nmf* civil servant. **◆fonctionnel, -elle** *a* functional. **◆fonctionn/er** *vi* (*machine etc*) to work, operate, function; (*organisation*) to function; **faire f.** to operate, work. **◆—ement** *nm* working.

fond [fɔ̃] *nm* (*de boîte, jardin, vallée etc*) bottom; (*de salle, armoire etc*) back; (*de culotte*) seat; (*de problème, débat etc*) essence; (*arrière-plan*) background; (*contenu*) content; (*du désespoir*) *Fig* depths; **au f. de** at the bottom of; at the back of; **fonds de verre** dregs; **f. de teint** foundation cream; **f. sonore** background music; **un f. de bon sens** a stock of good sense; **au f.** basically, in essence; **à f.** (*connaître etc*) thoroughly; **de f. en comble** from top to bottom; **de f.** (*course*) long-distance; (*bruit*) background-.

fondamental, -aux [fɔ̃damɑ̃tal, -o] *a* fundamental, basic.

fond/er [fɔ̃de] *vt* (*ville etc*) to found; (*commerce*) to set up; (*famille*) to start; **(se) f. sur** to base (oneself) on; **être fondé à croire/***etc* to be justified in thinking/*etc*; **bien fondé** well-founded. **◆—ement** *nm* foundation. **◆fondateur, -trice** *nmf* founder; – *a* (*membre*) founding, founder-. **◆fondation** *nf* (*création, œuvre*) foundation (**de** of).

fond/re [fɔ̃dr] *vt* to melt; (*métal*) to smelt; (*cloche*) to cast; (*amalgamer*) *Fig* to fuse (**avec** with); **faire f.** (*dissoudre*) to dissolve; – *vi* to melt; (*se dissoudre*) to dissolve; **f. en larmes** to burst into tears; **f. sur** to swoop on; **— se f.** *vpr* to merge, fuse. **◆—ant** *a* (*fruit*) which melts in the mouth. **◆—u** *nm* **f. enchaîné** *Cin* dissolve. **◆—ue** *nf Culin* fondue. **◆fonderie** *nf* (*usine*) smelting works, foundry.

fonds [fɔ̃] **1** *nm* **un f. (de commerce)** a business. **2** *nmpl* (*argent*) funds. **3** *nm* (*culturel etc*) *Fig* fund.

font [fɔ̃] *voir* **faire.**

fontaine [fɔ̃tɛn] *nf* (*construction*) fountain; (*source*) spring.

fonte [fɔ̃t] *nf* **1** (*des neiges*) melting; (*d'acier*) smelting. **2** (*fer*) cast iron; **en f.** (*poêle etc*) cast-iron.

fonts [fɔ̃] *nmpl* **f. baptismaux** *Rel* font.

football [futbol] *nm* football, soccer. **◆footballeur, -euse** *nmf* footballer.

footing [futiŋ] *nm Sp* jogging, jog-trotting.

forage [fɔraʒ] *nm* drilling, boring.

forain [fɔrɛ̃] *a* (*marchand*) itinerant; **fête foraine** (fun)fair.

forçat [fɔrsa] *nm* (*prisonnier*) convict.

force [fɔrs] *nf* force; (*physique, morale*) strength; (*atomique etc*) power; **de toutes ses forces** with all one's strength; **les forces armées** the armed forces; **de f.** by force, forcibly; **en f.** (*attaquer, venir*) in force; **cas de f. majeure** circumstances beyond one's control; **dans la f. de l'âge** in the prime of life; **à f. de** through sheer force of, by dint of. ◆**forc/er** *vt* (*porte, fruits etc*) to force; (*attention*) to force, compel; (*voix*) to strain; (*sens*) to stretch; **f. qn à faire** to force *ou* compel s.o. to do; – *vi* (*y aller trop fort*) to overdo it; – **se f.** *vpr* to force oneself (**à faire** to do). ◆**—é** *a* forced (**de faire** to do); **un sourire f.** a forced smile; **c'est f.** *Fam* it's inevitable *ou* obvious. ◆**—ément** *adv* inevitably, obviously; **pas f.** not necessarily.

forcené, -ée [fɔrsəne] *a* frantic, frenzied; – *nmf* madman, madwoman.

forceps [fɔrsɛps] *nm* forceps.

forcir [fɔrsir] *vi* (*grossir*) to fill out.

forer [fɔre] *vt* to drill, bore. ◆**foret** *nm* drill.

forêt [fɔrɛ] *nf* forest. ◆**forestier, -ière** *a* forest-; – *nm* **(garde) f.** forester, *Am* (forest) ranger.

forfait [fɔrfɛ] *nm* **1** (*prix*) all-inclusive price; **travailler à f.** to work for a lump sum. **2** **déclarer f.** *Sp* to withdraw from the game. **3** (*crime*) *Litt* heinous crime. ◆**forfaitaire** *a* **prix f.** all-inclusive price.

forge [fɔrʒ] *nf* forge. ◆**forg/er** *vt* (*métal, liens etc*) to forge; (*inventer*) to make up. ◆**—é** *a* **fer f.** wrought iron. ◆**forgeron** *nm* (black)smith.

formaliser (se) [səfɔrmalize] *vpr* to take offence (**de** at).

formalité [fɔrmalite] *nf* formality.

format [fɔrma] *nm* format, size.

forme [fɔrm] *nf* (*contour*) shape, form; (*manière, genre*) form; *pl* (*de femme, d'homme*) figure; **en f. de** in the form of; **en f. d'aiguille/de poire/***etc* needle-/pear-/*etc* shaped; **dans les formes** in due form; **en (pleine) f.** in good shape *ou* form, on form; **prendre f.** to take shape. ◆**formateur, -trice** *a* formative. ◆**formation** *nf* formation; (*éducation*) education, training. ◆**formel, -elle** *a* (*structure, logique etc*) formal; (*démenti*) categorical, formal; (*preuve*) positive, formal. ◆**formellement** *adv* (*interdire*) strictly. ◆**form/er** *vt* (*groupe, caractère etc*) to form; (*apprenti etc*) to train; – **se f.** *vpr* (*apparaître*) to form; (*institution*) to be formed. ◆**—é** *a* (*personne*) fully-formed.

formidable [fɔrmidabl] *a* tremendous.

formule [fɔrmyl] *nf* **1** formula; (*phrase*) (set) expression; (*méthode*) method; **f. de politesse** polite expression. **2** (*feuille*) form. ◆**formulaire** *nm* (*feuille*) form. ◆**formulation** *nf* formulation. ◆**formuler** *vt* to formulate.

fort[1] [fɔr] *a* strong; (*pluie, mer*) heavy; (*voix*) loud; (*fièvre*) high; (*femme, homme*) large; (*élève*) bright; (*pente*) steep; (*ville*) fortified; (*chances*) good; **f. en** (*maths etc*) good at; **c'est plus f. qu'elle** she can't help it; **c'est un peu f.** *Fam* that's a bit much; **à plus forte raison** all the more reason; – *adv* **1** (*frapper*) hard; (*pleuvoir*) hard, heavily; (*parler*) loud; (*serrer*) tight; **sentir f.** to have a strong smell. **2** (*très*) *Vieilli* very; (*beaucoup*) *Litt* very much; – *nm* **son f.** one's strong point; **les forts** the strong; **au plus f. de** in the thick of. ◆**fortement** *adv* greatly; (*frapper*) hard.

fort[2] [fɔr] *nm Hist Mil* fort. ◆**forteresse** *nf* fortress.

fortifi/er [fɔrtifje] *vt* to strengthen, fortify; – **se f.** *vpr* (*malade*) to fortify oneself. ◆**—ant** *nm Méd* tonic. ◆**—é** *a* (*ville, camp*) fortified. ◆**fortification** *nf* fortification.

fortuit [fɔrtɥi] *a* (*rencontre etc*) chance-, fortuitous. ◆**fortuitement** *adv* by chance.

fortune [fɔrtyn] *nf* (*argent, hasard*) fortune; **avoir de la f.** to have (private) means; **faire f.** to make one's fortune; **de f.** (*moyens etc*) makeshift; **dîner à la f. du pot** to take pot luck. ◆**fortuné** *a* (*riche*) well-to-do.

forum [fɔrɔm] *nm* forum.

fosse [fos] *nf* (*trou*) pit; (*tombe*) grave; **f. d'aisances** cesspool.

fossé [fose] *nm* ditch; (*douve*) moat; (*dissentiment*) *Fig* gulf, gap.

fossette [fosɛt] *nf* dimple.

fossile [fɔsil] *nm* & *a* fossil.

fossoyeur [fɔswajœr] *nm* gravedigger.

fou (*or* **fol** *before vowel or mute h*), **folle** [fu, fɔl] *a* (*personne, projet etc*) mad, insane, crazy; (*envie*) wild, mad; (*espoir*) foolish; (*rire*) uncontrollable; (*cheval, camion*) runaway; (*succès, temps*) tremendous; **f. à lier** raving mad; **f. de** (*musique, personne etc*) mad *ou* wild *ou* crazy about; **f. de joie** wild with joy; – *nmf* madman, madwoman; – *nm* (*bouffon*) jester; *Échecs* bishop; **faire le f.** to play the fool.

foudre [fudr] *nf* **la f.** lightning; **coup de f.** *Fig* love at first sight. ◆**foudroy/er** *vt* to strike by lightning; *Él* to electrocute; (*malheur etc*) *Fig* to strike (*s.o.*) down. ◆**—ant** *a* (*succès, vitesse etc*) staggering. ◆**—é** *a* (*stupéfait*) thunderstruck.

fouet [fwɛ] *nm* whip; *Culin* (egg) whisk. ◆**fouetter** *vt* to whip; (*œufs*) to whisk; (*pluie etc*) to lash (*face, windows etc*); **crème fouettée** whipped cream.

fougère [fuʒɛr] *nf* fern.

fougue [fug] *nf* fire, ardour. ◆**fougueux, -euse** *a* fiery, ardent.
fouille [fuj] *nf* **1** (*archéologique*) excavation, dig. **2** (*de personne, bagages etc*) search. ◆**fouiller 1** *vti* (*creuser*) to dig. **2** *vt* (*personne, maison etc*) to search; – *vi* **f. dans** (*tiroir etc*) to rummage *ou* search through.
fouillis [fuji] *nm* jumble.
fouine [fwin] *nf* (*animal*) stone marten.
fouin/er [fwine] *vi Fam* to nose about. ◆**—eur, -euse** *a Fam* nosy; – *nmf Fam* nosy parker.
foulard [fular] *nm* (head) scarf.
foule [ful] *nf* crowd; **en f.** in mass; **une f. de** (*objets etc*) a mass of; **un bain de f.** a walkabout.
foulée [fule] *nf Sp* stride; **dans la f.** *Fam* at one and the same time.
fouler [fule] *vt* to press; (*sol*) to tread; **f. aux pieds** to trample on; **se f. la cheville/***etc* to sprain one's ankle/*etc*; **il ne se foule pas (la rate)** *Fam* he doesn't exactly exert himself. ◆**foulure** *nf* sprain.
four [fur] *nm* **1** oven; (*de potier etc*) kiln. **2 petit f.** (*gâteau*) (small) fancy cake. **3** *Th Cin* flop; **faire un f.** to flop.
fourbe [furb] *a* deceitful; – *nmf* cheat. ◆**fourberie** *nf* deceit.
fourbi [furbi] *nm* (*choses*) *Fam* stuff, gear, rubbish.
fourbu [furby] *a* (*fatigué*) dead beat.
fourche [furʃ] *nf* fork; **f. à foin** pitchfork. ◆**fourchette** *nf* **1** *Culin* fork. **2** (*de salaires etc*) *Écon* bracket. ◆**fourchu** *a* forked.
fourgon [furgɔ̃] *nm* (*camion*) van; (*mortuaire*) hearse; *Rail* luggage van, *Am* baggage car. ◆**fourgonnette** *nf* (small) van.
fourmi [furmi] *nf* **1** (*insecte*) ant. **2 avoir des fourmis** *Méd* to have pins and needles (**dans** in). ◆**fourmilière** *nf* anthill. ◆**fourmiller** *vi* **1** to teem, swarm (**de** with). **2** *Méd* to tingle.
fournaise [furnɛz] *nf* (*chambre etc*) *Fig* furnace.
fourneau, -x [furno] *nm* (*poêle*) stove; (*four*) furnace; **haut f.** blast furnace.
fournée [furne] *nf* (*de pain, gens*) batch.
fourn/ir [furnir] *vt* to supply, provide; (*effort*) to make; **f. qch à qn** to supply s.o. with sth; – *vi* **f. à** (*besoin etc*) to provide for; – **se f.** *vpr* to get one's supplies (**chez** from), shop (**chez** at). ◆**—i** *a* (*barbe*) bushy; **bien f.** (*boutique*) well-stocked. ◆**fournisseur** *nm* (*commerçant*) supplier. ◆**fourniture** *nf* (*action*) supply(ing) (**de** of); *pl* (*objets*) supplies.
fourrage [furaʒ] *nm* fodder.
fourrager [furaʒe] *vi Fam* to rummage (**dans** in, through).
fourreau, -x [furo] *nm* (*gaine*) sheath.
fourr/er [fure] **1** *vt Culin* to fill, stuff; (*vêtement*) to fur-line. **2** *vt Fam* (*mettre*) to stick; (*flanquer*) to chuck; **f. qch dans la tête de qn** to knock sth into s.o.'s head; **f. son nez dans** to poke one's nose into; – **se f.** *vpr* to put *ou* stick oneself (**dans** in). ◆**—é 1** *a* (*gant etc*) fur-lined; (*gâteau*) jam- *ou* cream-filled; **coup f.** (*traîtrise*) stab in the back. **2** *nm Bot* thicket. ◆**—eur** *nm* furrier. ◆**fourrure** *nf* (*pour vêtement etc, de chat etc*) fur.
fourre-tout [furtu] *nm inv* (*pièce*) junk room; (*sac*) holdall, *Am* carryall.
fourrière [furjɛr] *nf* (*lieu*) pound.
fourvoyer (se) [səfurvwaje] *vpr* to go astray.
foutre* [futr] *vt Arg* = **fiche(r)**. ◆**foutu** *a Arg* = **fichu 1.** ◆**foutaise** *nf Arg* rubbish, rot.
foyer [fwaje] *nm* (*domicile*) home; (*d'étudiants etc*) hostel; (*âtre*) hearth; (*lieu de réunion*) club; *Th* foyer; *Géom Phys* focus; **f. de** (*maladie etc*) seat of; (*énergie, lumière*) source of; **fonder un f.** to start a family.
fracas [fraka] *nm* din; (*d'un objet qui tombe*) crash. ◆**fracass/er** *vt*, – **se f.** *vpr* to smash. ◆**—ant** *a* (*nouvelle, film etc*) sensational.
fraction [fraksjɔ̃] *nf* fraction. ◆**fractionner** *vt*, – **se f.** *vpr* to split (up).
fracture [fraktyr] *nf* fracture; **se faire une f. au bras/***etc* to fracture one's arm/*etc*. ◆**fracturer** *vt* (*porte etc*) to break (open); **se f. la jambe/***etc* to fracture one's leg/*etc*.
fragile [fraʒil] *a* (*verre, santé etc*) fragile; (*enfant etc*) frail; (*équilibre*) shaky. ◆**fragilité** *nf* fragility; (*d'un enfant etc*) frailty.
fragment [fragmɑ̃] *nm* fragment. ◆**fragmentaire** *a* fragmentary, fragmented. ◆**fragmentation** *nf* fragmentation. ◆**fragmenter** *vt* to fragment, divide.
frais[1], fraîche [frɛ, frɛʃ] *a* (*poisson, souvenir etc*) fresh; (*temps*) cool, fresh, (*plutôt désagréable*) chilly; (*œufs*) new-laid, fresh; (*boisson*) cold, cool; (*peinture*) wet; (*date*) recent; **boire f.** to drink something cold *ou* cool; **servir f.** (*vin etc*) to serve chilled; – *nm* **prendre le f.** to get some fresh air; **il fait f.** it's cool; (*froid*) it's chilly; **mettre au f.** to put in a cool place. ◆**fraîchement** *adv* **1** (*récemment*) freshly. **2** (*accueillir etc*) coolly. ◆**fraîcheur** *nf* freshness; coolness;

chilliness. ◆**fraîchir** *vi* (*temps*) to get cooler *ou* chillier, freshen.

frais[2] [frɛ] *nmpl* expenses; (*droits*) fees; **à mes f.** at my expense; **faire des f.** to go to some expense; **faire les f.** to bear the cost (**de** of); **j'en ai été pour mes f.** I wasted my time and effort; **faux f.** incidental expenses; **f. généraux** running expenses, overheads.

fraise [frɛz] *nf* **1** (*fruit*) strawberry. **2** (*de dentiste*) drill. ◆**fraisier** *nm* (*plante*) strawberry plant.

framboise [frɑ̃bwaz] *nf* raspberry. ◆**framboisier** *nm* raspberry cane.

franc[1], **franche** [frɑ̃, frɑ̃ʃ] *a* **1** (*personne, réponse etc*) frank; (*visage, gaieté*) open; (*net*) clear; (*cassure, coupe*) clean; (*vrai*) *Péj* downright. **2** (*zone*) free; **coup f.** *Fb* free kick; **f. de port** carriage paid. ◆**franchement** *adv* (*honnêtement*) frankly; (*sans ambiguïté*) clearly; (*vraiment*) really. ◆**franchise** *nf* **1** frankness; openness; **en toute f.** quite frankly. **2** (*exemption*) *Com* exemption; **en f.** (*produit*) duty-free; **'f. postale'** 'official paid'. **3** (*permis de vendre*) *Com* franchise.

franc[2] [frɑ̃] *nm* (*monnaie*) franc.

France [frɑ̃s] *nf* France. ◆**français, -aise** *a* French; – *nmf* Frenchman, Frenchwoman; **les F.** the French; – *nm* (*langue*) French.

franch/ir [frɑ̃ʃir] *vt* (*fossé*) to jump (over), clear; (*frontière, seuil etc*) to cross; (*porte*) to go through; (*distance*) to cover; (*limites*) to exceed; (*mur du son*) to break (through), go through. ◆**—issable** *a* (*rivière, col*) passable.

franc-maçon [frɑ̃masɔ̃] *nm* (*pl* **francs-maçons**) Freemason. ◆**franc-maçonnerie** *nf* Freemasonry.

franco [frɑ̃ko] *adv* carriage paid.

franco- [frɑ̃ko] *préf* Franco-.

francophile [frɑ̃kɔfil] *a & nmf* francophile. ◆**francophone** *a* French-speaking; – *nmf* French speaker. ◆**francophonie** *nf* **la f.** the French-speaking community.

frange [frɑ̃ʒ] *nf* (*de vêtement etc*) fringe; (*de cheveux*) fringe, *Am* bangs.

frangin [frɑ̃ʒɛ̃] *nm Fam* brother. ◆**frangine** *nf Fam* sister.

franquette (à la bonne) [alabɔnfrɑ̃kɛt] *adv* without ceremony.

frappe [frap] *nf* **1** (*dactylographie*) typing; (*de dactylo etc*) touch; **faute de f.** typing error. **2 force de f.** *Mil* strike force. ◆**frapp/er** *vt* (*battre*) to strike, hit; (*monnaie*) to mint; **f. qn** (*surprendre, affecter*) to strike s.o.; (*impôt, mesure etc*) to hit s.o.; **frappé de** (*horreur etc*) stricken with; **frappé de panique** panic-stricken; – *vi* (*à la porte etc*) to knock, bang (**à** at); **f. du pied** to stamp (one's foot); — **se f.** *vpr* (*se tracasser*) to worry. ◆**—ant** *a* striking. ◆**—é** *a* (*vin*) chilled.

frasque [frask] *nf* prank, escapade.

fraternel, -elle [fratɛrnɛl] *a* fraternal, brotherly. ◆**fraterniser** *vi* to fraternize (**avec** with). ◆**fraternité** *nf* fraternity, brotherhood.

fraude [frod] *nf Jur* fraud; (*à un examen*) cheating; **passer qch en f.** to smuggle sth; **prendre qn en f.** to catch s.o. cheating. ◆**fraud/er** *vt* to defraud; – *vi Jur* to commit fraud; (*à un examen*) to cheat (**à** in); **f. sur** (*poids etc*) to cheat on *ou* over. ◆**—eur, -euse** *nmf Jur* defrauder. ◆**frauduleux, -euse** *a* fraudulent.

frayer [freje] *vt* (*voie etc*) to clear; **se f. un passage** to clear a way, force one's way (**à travers, dans** through).

frayeur [frɛjœr] *nf* fear, fright.

fredaine [frədɛn] *nf* prank, escapade.

fredonner [frədɔne] *vt* to hum.

freezer [frizœr] *nm* (*de réfrigérateur*) freezer.

frégate [fregat] *nf* (*navire*) frigate.

frein [frɛ̃] *nm* brake; **donner un coup de f.** to brake; **mettre un f. à** *Fig* to put a curb on. ◆**frein/er** *vi Aut* to brake; – *vt* (*gêner*) *Fig* to check, curb. ◆**—age** *nm Aut* braking.

frelaté [frəlate] *a* (*vin etc*) & *Fig* adulterated.

frêle [frɛl] *a* frail, fragile.

frelon [frəlɔ̃] *nm* (*guêpe*) hornet.

frémir [fremir] *vi* to shake, shudder (**de** with); (*feuille*) to quiver; (*eau chaude*) to simmer.

frêne [frɛn] *nm* (*arbre, bois*) ash.

frénésie [frenezi] *nf* frenzy. ◆**frénétique** *a* frenzied, frantic.

fréquent [frekɑ̃] *a* frequent. ◆**fréquemment** [-amɑ̃] *adv* frequently. ◆**fréquence** *nf* frequency.

fréquent/er [frekɑ̃te] *vt* (*lieu*) to visit, frequent; (*école, église*) to attend; **f. qn** to see *ou* visit s.o.; — **se f.** *vpr* (*fille et garçon*) to see each other, go out together; (*voisins*) to see each other socially. ◆**—é** *a* **très f.** (*lieu*) very busy. ◆**fréquentable** *a* **peu f.** (*personne, endroit*) not very commendable. ◆**fréquentation** *nf* visiting; *pl* (*personnes*) company.

frère [frɛr] *nm* brother.

fresque [frɛsk] *nf* (*œuvre peinte*) fresco.

fret [frɛ] *nm* freight.

frétiller [fretije] *vi* (*poisson*) to wriggle; **f. de** (*impatience*) to quiver with; **f. de joie** to tingle with excitement.

fretin [frətɛ̃] *nm* **menu f.** small fry.

friable [frijabl] *a* crumbly.

friand [frijɑ̃] *a* **f. de** fond of, partial to. ◆**friandises** *nfpl* sweet stuff, sweets, *Am* candies.

fric [frik] *nm* (*argent*) *Fam* cash, dough.

fric-frac [frikfrak] *nm* (*cambriolage*) *Fam* break-in.

friche (en) [ɑ̃friʃ] *adv* fallow.

friction [friksjɔ̃] *nf* **1** massage, rub(-down); (*de cheveux*) friction. **2** (*désaccord*) friction. ◆**frictionner** *vt* to rub (down).

frigidaire® [friʒidɛr] *nm* fridge. ◆**frigo** *nm Fam* fridge. ◆**frigorifié** *a* (*personne*) *Fam* very cold. ◆**frigorifique** *a* (*vitrine*) refrigerated; (*wagon*) refrigerator-.

frigide [friʒid] *a* frigid. ◆**frigidité** *nf* frigidity.

frileux, -euse [frilø, -øz] *a* sensitive to cold, chilly.

frime [frim] *nf Fam* sham, show.

frimousse [frimus] *nf Fam* little face.

fringale [frɛ̃gal] *nf Fam* raging appetite.

fringant [frɛ̃gɑ̃] *a* (*allure etc*) dashing.

fringues [frɛ̃g] *nfpl* (*vêtements*) *Fam* togs, clothes.

frip/er [fripe] *vt* to crumple; **— se f.** *vpr* to get crumpled. ◆**—é** *a* (*visage*) crumpled, wrinkled.

fripier, -ière [fripje, -jɛr] *nmf* secondhand clothes dealer.

fripon, -onne [fripɔ̃, -ɔn] *nmf* rascal; – *a* rascally.

fripouille [fripuj] *nf* rogue, scoundrel.

frire* [frir] *vti* to fry; **faire f.** to fry.

frise [friz] *nf Archit* frieze.

fris/er [frize] **1** *vti* (*cheveux*) to curl, wave; **f. qn** to curl *ou* wave s.o.'s hair. **2** *vt* (*effleurer*) to skim; (*accident etc*) to be within an ace of; **f. la trentaine** to be close on thirty. ◆**—é** *a* curly. ◆**frisette** *nf* ringlet, little curl.

frisquet [friskɛ] *am* chilly, coldish.

frisson [frisɔ̃] *nm* shiver; shudder; **donner le f. à qn** to give s.o. the creeps *ou* shivers. ◆**frissonner** *vi* (*de froid*) to shiver; (*de peur etc*) to shudder (**de** with).

frit [fri] *voir* **frire**; – *a* (*poisson etc*) fried. ◆**frites** *nfpl* chips, *Am* French fries. ◆**friteuse** *nf* (deep) fryer. ◆**friture** *nf* (*matière*) (frying) oil *ou* fat; (*aliment*) fried fish; (*bruit*) *Rad Tél* crackling.

frivole [frivɔl] *a* frivolous. ◆**frivolité** *nf* frivolity.

froid [frwa] *a* cold; **garder la tête froide** to keep a cool head; – *nm* cold; **avoir/prendre f.** to be/catch cold; **il fait f.** it's cold; **coup de f.** *Méd* chill; **jeter un f.** to cast a chill (**dans** over); **démarrer à f.** *Aut* to start (from) cold; **être en f.** to be on bad terms (**avec** with). ◆**froidement** *adv* coldly. ◆**froideur** *nf* (*de sentiment, personne etc*) coldness.

froisser [frwase] **1** *vt*, **— se f.** *vpr* (*tissu etc*) to crumple, rumple; **se f. un muscle** to strain a muscle. **2** *vt* **f. qn** to offend s.o.; **se f.** to take offence (**de** at).

frôler [frole] *vt* (*toucher*) to brush against, touch lightly; (*raser*) to skim; (*la mort etc*) to come within an ace of.

fromage [frɔmaʒ] *nm* cheese; **f. blanc** soft white cheese. ◆**fromager, -ère** *a* (*industrie*) cheese-; – *nm* (*fabricant*) cheesemaker. ◆**fromagerie** *nf* cheese dairy.

froment [frɔmɑ̃] *nm* wheat.

fronce [frɔ̃s] *nf* (*pli dans un tissu*) gather, fold. ◆**fronc/er** *vt* **1** (*étoffe*) to gather. **2 f. les sourcils** to frown. ◆**—ement** *nm* **f. de sourcils** frown.

fronde [frɔ̃d] *nf* **1** (*arme*) sling. **2** (*sédition*) revolt.

front [frɔ̃] *nm* forehead, brow; *Mil Pol* front; **de f.** (*heurter*) head-on; (*côte à côte*) abreast; (*à la fois*) (all) at once; **faire f. à** to face.

frontière [frɔ̃tjɛr] *nf* border, frontier; – *a inv* **ville/***etc* **f.** border town/*etc.* ◆**frontalier, -ière** *a* border-, frontier-.

fronton [frɔ̃tɔ̃] *nm Archit* pediment.

frott/er [frɔte] *vt* to rub; (*astiquer*) to rub (up), shine; (*plancher*) to scrub; (*allumette*) to strike; **se f. à qn** (*défier*) to meddle with s.o., provoke s.o.; – *vi* to rub; (*nettoyer, laver*) to scrub. ◆**—ement** *nm* rubbing; *Tech* friction.

froufrou(s) [frufru] *nm(pl)* (*bruit*) rustling.

frousse [frus] *nf Fam* funk, fear; **avoir la f.** to be scared. ◆**froussard, -arde** *nmf Fam* coward.

fructifier [fryktifje] *vi* (*arbre, capital*) to bear fruit. ◆**fructueux, -euse** *a* (*profitable*) fruitful.

frugal, -aux [frygal, -o] *a* frugal. ◆**frugalité** *nf* frugality.

fruit [frɥi] *nm* fruit; **des fruits, les fruits** fruit; **porter f.** to bear fruit; **fruits de mer** seafood; **avec f.** fruitfully. ◆**fruité** *a* fruity. ◆**fruitier, -ière** *a* (*arbre*) fruit-; – *nmf* fruiterer.

frusques [frysk] *nfpl* (*vêtements*) *Fam* togs, clothes.

fruste [fryst] *a* (*personne*) rough.

frustr/er [frystre] *vt* **f. qn** to frustrate s.o.; **f. qn de** to deprive s.o. of. ◆**—é** *a* frustrated. ◆**frustration** *nf* frustration.

fuel [fjul] *nm* (fuel) oil.

fugace [fygas] *a* fleeting.

fugitif, -ive [fyʒitif, -iv] **1** *nmf* runaway, fugitive. **2** *a* (*passager*) fleeting.

fugue [fyg] *nf* **1** *Mus* fugue. **2** (*absence*) flight; **faire une f.** to run away.

fuir* [fɥir] *vi* to flee, run away; (*temps*) to fly; (*gaz, robinet, stylo etc*) to leak; – *vt* (*éviter*) to shun, avoid. ◆**fuite** *nf* (*évasion*) flight (**de** from); (*de gaz etc*) leak(age); (*de documents*) leak; **en f.** on the run; **prendre la f.** to take flight; **f. des cerveaux** brain drain; **délit de f.** *Aut* hit-and-run offence.

fulgurant [fylgyrɑ̃] *a* (*regard*) flashing; (*vitesse*) lightning-; (*idée*) spectacular, striking.

fulminer [fylmine] *vi* (*personne*) to thunder forth (**contre** against).

fumée [fyme] *nf* smoke; (*vapeur*) steam, fumes; *pl* (*de vin*) fumes. ◆**fum/er** *vi* to smoke; (*liquide brûlant*) to steam; (*rager*) *Fam* to fume; – *vt* to smoke. ◆**—é** *a* (*poisson, verre etc*) smoked. ◆**—eur, -euse** *nmf* smoker; **compartiment fumeurs** *Rail* smoking compartment. ◆**fume-cigarette** *nm inv* cigarette holder.

fumet [fymɛ] *nm* aroma, smell.

fumeux, -euse [fymø, -øz] *a* (*idée etc*) hazy, woolly.

fumier [fymje] *nm* manure, dung; (*tas*) dunghill.

fumigation [fymigɑsjɔ̃] *nf* fumigation.

fumigène [fymiʒɛn] *a* (*bombe, grenade etc*) smoke-.

fumiste [fymist] *nmf* (*étudiant etc*) time-waster, good-for-nothing. ◆**fumisterie** *nf Fam* farce, con.

funambule [fynɑ̃byl] *nmf* tightrope walker.

funèbre [fynɛbr] *a* (*service, marche etc*) funeral-; (*lugubre*) gloomy. ◆**funérailles** *nfpl* funeral. ◆**funéraire** *a* (*frais, salon etc*) funeral-.

funeste [fynɛst] *a* (*désastreux*) catastrophic.

funiculaire [fynikylɛr] *nm* funicular.

fur et à mesure (au) [ofyreamzyr] *adv* as one goes along, progressively; **au f. et à m. que** as.

furent [fyr] *voir* **être**.

furet [fyrɛ] *nm* (*animal*) ferret. ◆**furet/er** *vi* to pry *ou* ferret about. ◆**—eur, -euse** *a* inquisitive, prying; – *nmf* inquisitive person.

fureur [fyrœr] *nf* (*violence*) fury; (*colère*) rage, fury; (*passion*) passion (**de** for); **en f.** furious; **faire f.** (*mode etc*) to be all the rage. ◆**furibond** *a* furious. ◆**furie** *nf* (*colère, mégère*) fury. ◆**furieux, -euse** *a* (*violent, en colère*) furious (**contre** with, at); (*vent*) raging; (*coup*) *Fig* tremendous.

furoncle [fyrɔ̃kl] *nm Méd* boil.

furtif, -ive [fyrtif, -iv] *a* furtive, stealthy.

fusain [fyzɛ̃] *nm* **1** (*crayon, dessin*) charcoal. **2** *Bot* spindle tree.

fuseau, -x [fyzo] *nm* **1** *Tex* spindle; **en f.** (*jambes*) spindly. **2 f. horaire** time zone. **3** (*pantalon*) ski pants. ◆**fuselé** *a* slender.

fusée [fyze] *nf* rocket; (*d'obus*) fuse; **f. éclairante** flare.

fuselage [fyzlaʒ] *nm Av* fuselage.

fuser [fyze] *vi* (*rires etc*) to burst forth.

fusible [fyzibl] *nm Él* fuse.

fusil [fyzi] *nm* rifle, gun; (*de chasse*) shotgun; **coup de f.** gunshot, report; **un bon f.** (*personne*) a good shot. ◆**fusillade** *nf* (*tirs*) gunfire; (*exécution*) shooting. ◆**fusiller** *vt* (*exécuter*) to shoot; **f. qn du regard** to glare at s.o.

fusion [fyzjɔ̃] *nf* **1** melting; *Phys Biol* fusion; **point de f.** melting point; **en f.** (*métal*) molten. **2** (*union*) fusion; *Com* merger. ◆**fusionner** *vti Com* to merge.

fut [fy] *voir* **être**.

fût [fy] *nm* **1** (*tonneau*) barrel, cask. **2** (*d'arbre*) trunk. ◆**futaie** *nf* timber forest.

futé [fyte] *a* cunning, smart.

futile [fytil] *a* (*propos, prétexte etc*) frivolous, futile; (*personne*) frivolous; (*tentative, action*) futile. ◆**futilité** *nf* futility; *pl* (*bagatelles*) trifles.

futur, -ure [fytyr] *a* future; **future mère** mother-to-be; – *nmf* **f. (mari)** husband-to-be; **future (épouse)** wife-to-be; – *nm* future.

fuyant [fɥijɑ̃] *voir* **fuir**; – *a* (*front, ligne*) receding; (*personne*) evasive. ◆**fuyard** *nm* (*soldat*) runaway, deserter.

G

G, g [ʒe] *nm* G, g.
gabardine [gabardin] *nf* (*tissu, imperméable*) gabardine.
gabarit [gabari] *nm* (*de véhicule etc*) size, dimension.
gâcher [gɑʃe] *vt* **1** (*gâter*) to spoil; (*occasion, argent*) to waste; (*vie, travail*) to mess up. **2** (*plâtre*) to mix. ◆**gâchis** *nm* (*désordre*) mess; (*gaspillage*) waste.
gâchette [gɑʃɛt] *nf* (*d'arme à feu*) trigger; **une fine g.** (*personne*) *Fig* a marksman.
gadget [gadʒɛt] *nm* gadget.
gadoue [gadu] *nf* (*boue*) dirt, sludge; (*neige*) slush.
gaffe [gaf] *nf* (*bévue*) *Fam* blunder, gaffe. ◆**gaff/er** *vi* to blunder. ◆**—eur, -euse** *nmf* blunderer.
gag [gag] *nm* (*effet comique*) *Cin Th* (sight) gag.
gaga [gaga] *a Fam* senile, gaga.
gage [gaʒ] **1** *nm* (*promesse*) pledge; (*témoignage*) proof; (*caution*) security; **mettre en g.** to pawn. **2** *nmpl* (*salaire*) pay; **tueur à gages** hired killer, hitman.
gager [gaʒe] *vt* **g. que** *Litt* to wager that. ◆**gageure** [gaʒyr] *nf Litt* (impossible) wager.
gagn/er [gɑɲe] **1** *vt* (*par le travail*) to earn; (*mériter*) *Fig* to earn. **2** *vt* (*par le jeu*) to win; (*réputation, estime etc*) *Fig* to win, gain; **g. qn** to win s.o. over (**à** to); **g. une heure**/*etc* (*économiser*) to save an hour/*etc*; **g. du temps** (*temporiser*) to gain time; **g. du terrain/du poids** to gain ground/weight; – *vi* (*être vainqueur*) to win; **g. à être connu** to be well worth getting to know. **3** *vt* (*atteindre*) to reach; **g. qn** (*sommeil, faim etc*) to overcome s.o.; – *vi* (*incendie etc*) to spread, gain. ◆**—ant, -ante** *a* (*billet, cheval*) winning; – *nmf* winner. ◆**gagne-pain** *nm inv* (*emploi*) job, livelihood.
gai [ge] *a* (*personne, air etc*) cheerful, gay, jolly; (*ivre*) merry, tipsy; (*couleur, pièce*) bright, cheerful. ◆**gaiement** *adv* cheerfully, gaily. ◆**gaieté** *nf* (*de personne etc*) gaiety, cheerfulness, jollity.
gaillard [gajar] *a* vigorous; (*grivois*) coarse; – *nm* (*robuste*) strapping fellow; (*type*) *Fam* fellow. ◆**gaillarde** *nf Péj* brazen wench.
gain [gɛ̃] *nm* (*profit*) gain, profit; (*avantage*) *Fig* advantage; *pl* (*salaire*) earnings; (*au jeu*) winnings; **un g. de temps** a saving of time.
gaine [gɛn] *nf* **1** (*sous-vêtement*) girdle. **2** (*étui*) sheath.
gala [gala] *nm* official reception, gala.
galant [galɑ̃] *a* (*homme*) gallant; (*ton, propos*) *Hum* amorous; – *nm* suitor. ◆**galanterie** *nf* (*courtoisie*) gallantry.
galaxie [galaksi] *nf* galaxy.
galbe [galb] *nm* curve, contour. ◆**galbé** *a* (*jambes*) shapely.
gale [gal] *nf* **la g.** *Méd* the itch, scabies; (*d'un chien*) mange; **une (mauvaise) g.** (*personne*) *Fam* a pest.
galère [galɛr] *nf* (*navire*) *Hist* galley. ◆**galérien** *nm Hist* & *Fig* galley slave.
galerie [galri] *nf* **1** (*passage, magasin etc*) gallery; *Th* balcony. **2** *Aut* roof rack.
galet [galɛ] *nm* pebble, stone; *pl* shingle, pebbles.
galette [galɛt] *nf* **1** round, flat, flaky cake; (*crêpe*) pancake. **2** (*argent*) *Fam* dough, money.
galeux, -euse [galø, -øz] *a* (*chien*) mangy.
galimatias [galimatja] *nm* gibberish.
Galles [gal] *nfpl* **pays de G.** Wales. ◆**gallois, -oise** *a* Welsh; – *nm* (*langue*) Welsh; – *nmf* Welshman, Welshwoman.
gallicisme [galisism] *nm* (*mot etc*) gallicism.
galon [galɔ̃] *nm* (*ruban*) braid; (*signe*) *Mil* stripe; **prendre du g.** *Mil* & *Fig* to get promoted.
galop [galo] *nm* gallop; **aller au g.** to gallop; **g. d'essai** *Fig* trial run. ◆**galopade** *nf* (*ruée*) stampede. ◆**galop/er** *vi* (*cheval*) to gallop; (*personne*) to rush. ◆**—ant** *a* (*inflation etc*) *Fig* galloping.
galopin [galɔpɛ̃] *nm* urchin, rascal.
galvaniser [galvanize] *vt* (*métal*) & *Fig* to galvanize.
galvauder [galvode] *vt* (*talent, avantage etc*) to debase, misuse.
gambade [gɑ̃bad] *nf* leap, caper. ◆**gambader** *vi* to leap *ou* frisk about.
gambas [gɑ̃bas] *nfpl* scampi.
gamelle [gamɛl] *nf* (*de soldat*) mess tin; (*de campeur*) billy(can).
gamin, -ine [gamɛ̃, -in] *nmf* (*enfant*) *Fam*

kid; – *a* playful, naughty. ◆**gaminerie** *nf* playfulness; (*acte*) naughty prank.
gamme [gam] *nf Mus* scale; (*série*) range.
gammée [game] *af* croix g. swastika.
gang [gɑ̃g] *nm* (*de malfaiteurs*) gang. ◆**gangster** *nm* gangster.
gangrène [gɑ̃grɛn] *nf* gangrene. ◆**se gangrener** [səgɑ̃grəne] *vpr Méd* to become gangrenous.
gangue [gɑ̃g] *nf* (*enveloppe*) *Fig Péj* outer crust.
gant [gɑ̃] *nm* glove; **g. de toilette** face cloth, cloth glove (*for washing*); **jeter/relever le g.** *Fig* to throw down/take up the gauntlet; **boîte à gants** glove compartment. ◆**ganté** *a* (*main*) gloved; (*personne*) wearing gloves.
garage [garaʒ] *nm Aut* garage; **voie de g.** *Rail* siding; *Fig* dead end. ◆**garagiste** *nmf* garage owner.
garant, -ante [garɑ̃, -ɑ̃t] *nmf* (*personne*) *Jur* guarantor; **se porter g. de** to guarantee, vouch for; – *nm* (*garantie*) guarantee. ◆**garantie** *nf* guarantee; (*caution*) security; (*protection*) *Fig* safeguard; **garantie(s)** (*de police d'assurance*) cover. ◆**garantir** *vt* to guarantee (**contre** against); **g. (à qn) que** to guarantee (s.o.) that; **g. de** (*protéger*) to protect from.
garce [gars] *nf Péj Fam* bitch.
garçon [garsɔ̃] *nm* boy, lad; (*jeune homme*) young man; (*célibataire*) bachelor; **g. (de café)** waiter; g. **d'honneur** (*d'un mariage*) best man; **g. manqué** tomboy; **de g.** (*comportement*) boyish. ◆**garçonnet** *nm* little boy. ◆**garçonnière** *nf* bachelor flat *ou Am* apartment.
garde [gard] **1** *nm* (*gardien*) guard; *Mil* guardsman; **g. champêtre** rural policeman; **g. du corps** bodyguard; **G. des Sceaux** Justice Minister. **2** *nf* (*d'enfants, de bagages etc*) care, custody (**de** of); **avoir la g. de** to be in charge of; **faire bonne g.** to keep a close watch; **prendre g.** to pay attention (**à qch** to sth), be careful (**à qch** of sth); **prendre g. de ne pas faire** to be careful not to do; **mettre en g.** to warn (**contre** against); **mise en g.** warning; **de g.** on duty; (*soldat*) on guard duty; **monter la g.** to stand *ou* mount guard; **sur ses gardes** on one's guard; **g. à vue** (police) custody; **chien de g.** watchdog. **3** *nf* (*escorte, soldats*) guard.
garde-à-vous [gardavu] *nm inv Mil* (position of) attention. ◆**g.-boue** *nm inv* mudguard, *Am* fender. ◆**g.-chasse** *nm* (*pl* **gardes-chasses**) gamekeeper. ◆**g.-côte** *nm* (*personne*) coastguard. ◆**g.-fou** *nm* railing(s), parapet. ◆**g.-malade** *nmf* (*pl* **gardes-malades**) nurse. ◆**g.-manger** *nm inv* (*armoire*) food safe; (*pièce*) larder. ◆**g.-robe** *nf* (*habits, armoire*) wardrobe.
garder [garde] *vt* (*maintenir, conserver, mettre de côté*) to keep; (*vêtement*) to keep on; (*surveiller*) to watch (over); (*défendre*) to guard; (*enfant*) to look after, watch; (*habitude*) to keep up; **g. qn** (*retenir*) to keep s.o.; **g. la chambre** to keep to one's room; **g. le lit** to stay in bed; — **se g.** *vpr* (*aliment*) to keep; **se g. de qch** (*éviter*) to beware of sth; **se g. de faire** to take care not to do. ◆**garderie** *nf* day nursery. ◆**gardeuse** *nf* **g. d'enfants** babysitter.
gardien, -ienne [gardjɛ̃, -jɛn] *nmf* (*d'immeuble, d'hôtel*) caretaker; (*de prison*) (prison) guard, warder; (*de zoo, parc*) keeper; (*de musée*) attendant; **g. de but** *Fb* goalkeeper; **gardienne d'enfants** child minder; **g. de nuit** night watchman; **g. de la paix** policeman; **g. de** (*libertés etc*) *Fig* guardian of; – *am* **ange g.** guardian angel.
gare [gar] **1** *nf Rail* station; **g. routière** bus *ou* coach station. **2** *int* **g. à** watch *ou* look out for; **g. à toi!** watch *ou* look out!; **sans crier g.** without warning.
garer [gare] *vt* (*voiture etc*) to park; (*au garage*) to garage; — **se g.** *vpr* (*se protéger*) to get out of the way (**de** of); *Aut* to park.
gargariser (se) [səgargarize] *vpr* to gargle. ◆**gargarisme** *nm* gargle.
gargote [gargɔt] *nf* cheap eating house.
gargouille [garguj] *nf Archit* gargoyle.
gargouiller [garguje] *vi* (*fontaine, eau*) to gurgle; (*ventre*) to rumble. ◆**gargouillis** *nm* gurgling; rumbling.
garnement [garnəmɑ̃] *nm* rascal, urchin.
garn/ir [garnir] *vt* (*équiper*) to furnish, fit out (**de** with); (*magasin*) to stock; (*tissu*) to line; (*orner*) to adorn (**de** with); (*enjoliver*) to trim (**de** with); (*couvrir*) to cover; *Culin* to garnish; — **se g.** *vpr* (*lieu*) to fill (up) (**de** with). ◆**—i** *a* (*plat*) served with vegetables; **bien g.** (*portefeuille*) *Fig* well-lined. ◆**garniture** *nf Culin* garnish, trimmings; *pl Aut* fittings, upholstery; **g. de lit** bed linen.
garnison [garnizɔ̃] *nf Mil* garrison.
gars [gɑ] *nm Fam* fellow, guy.
gas-oil [gɑzwal] *nm* diesel (oil).
gaspill/er [gaspije] *vt* to waste. ◆**—age** *nm* waste.
gastrique [gastrik] *a* gastric. ◆**gastronome** *nmf* gourmet. ◆**gastronomie** *nf* gastronomy.
gâteau, -x [gɑto] *nm* cake; **g. de riz** rice pudding; **g. sec** (sweet) biscuit, *Am* cookie;

c'était du g. (*facile*) *Fam* it was a piece of cake.

gât/er [gate] *vt* to spoil; (*plaisir, vue*) to mar, spoil; **— se g.** *vpr* (*aliment, dent*) to go bad; (*temps, situation*) to get worse; (*relations*) to turn sour. **◆—é** *a* (*dent, fruit etc*) bad. **◆gâteries** *nfpl* (*cadeaux*) treats.

gâteux, -euse [gatø, -øz] *a* senile, soft in the head.

gauche¹ [goʃ] *a* (*côté, main etc*) left; – *nf* **la g.** (*côté*) the left (side); *Pol* the left (wing); **à g.** (*tourner etc*) (to the) left; (*marcher, se tenir*) on the left(-hand) side; **de g.** (*fenêtre etc*) left-hand; (*parti, politique etc*) left-wing; **à g. de** on *ou* to the left of. **◆gaucher, -ère** *a* & *nmf* left-handed (person). **◆gauchisant** *a Pol* leftish. **◆gauchiste** *a* & *nmf Pol* (extreme) leftist.

gauche² [goʃ] *a* (*maladroit*) awkward. **◆—ment** *adv* awkwardly. **◆gaucherie** *nf* awkwardness; (*acte*) blunder.

gauchir [goʃir] *vti* to warp.

gaufre [gofr] *nf Culin* waffle. **◆gaufrette** *nf* wafer (biscuit).

gaule [gol] *nf* long pole; *Pêche* fishing rod.

Gaule [gol] *nf* (*pays*) *Hist* Gaul. **◆gaulois** *a* Gallic; (*propos etc*) *Fig* broad, earthy; – *nmpl* **les G.** *Hist* the Gauls. **◆gauloiserie** *nf* broad joke.

gausser (se) [səgose] *vpr Litt* to poke fun (de at).

gaver [gave] *vt* (*animal*) to force-feed; (*personne*) *Fig* to cram (**de** with); **— se g.** *vpr* to gorge *ou* stuff oneself (**de** with).

gaz [gaz] *nm inv* gas; **usine à g.** gasworks; **chambre/réchaud à g.** gas chamber/stove; **avoir des g.** to have wind *ou* flatulence.

gaze [gaz] *nf* (*tissu*) gauze.

gazelle [gazɛl] *nf* (*animal*) gazelle.

gazer [gaze] **1** *vi Aut Fam* to whizz along; **ça gaze!** everything's just fine! **2** *vt Mil* to gas.

gazette [gazɛt] *nf Journ* newspaper.

gazeux, -euse [gazø, -øz] *a* (*état*) gaseous; (*boisson, eau*) fizzy. **◆gazomètre** *nm* gasometer.

gazinière [gazinjɛr] *nf* gas cooker *ou Am* stove.

gazole [gazɔl] *nm* diesel (oil).

gazon [gazɔ̃] *nm* grass, lawn.

gazouiller [gazuje] *vi* (*oiseau*) to chirp; (*bébé, ruisseau*) to babble. **◆gazouillis** *nm* chirping; babbling.

geai [ʒɛ] *nm* (*oiseau*) jay.

géant, -ante [ʒeɑ̃, -ɑ̃t] *a* & *nmf* giant.

Geiger [ʒeʒɛr] *nm* **compteur G.** Geiger counter.

geindre [ʒɛ̃dr] *vi* to whine, whimper.

gel [ʒɛl] *nm* **1** (*temps, glace*) frost; (*de crédits*) *Écon* freezing. **2** (*substance*) gel. **◆gel/er** *vti* to freeze; **on gèle ici** it's freezing here; – *v imp* **il gèle** it's freezing. **◆—é** *a* frozen; (*doigts*) *Méd* frostbitten. **◆—ée** *nf* frost; *Culin* jelly, *Am* jello; **g. blanche** ground frost.

gélatine [ʒelatin] *nf* gelatin(e).

gélule [ʒelyl] *nf* (*médicament*) capsule.

Gémeaux [ʒemo] *nmpl* **les G.** (*signe*) Gemini.

gém/ir [ʒemir] *vi* to groan, moan. **◆—issement** *nm* groan, moan.

gencive [ʒɑ̃siv] *nf Anat* gum.

gendarme [ʒɑ̃darm] *nm* gendarme, policeman (*soldier performing police duties*). **◆gendarmerie** *nf* police force; (*local*) police headquarters.

gendre [ʒɑ̃dr] *nm* son-in-law.

gène [ʒɛn] *nm Biol* gene.

gêne [ʒɛn] *nf* (*trouble physique*) discomfort; (*confusion*) embarrassment; (*dérangement*) bother, trouble; **dans la g.** *Fin* in financial difficulties. **◆gên/er** *vt* (*déranger, irriter*) to bother, annoy; (*troubler*) to embarrass; (*mouvement, action*) to hamper, hinder; (*circulation*) *Aut* to hold up, block; **g. qn** (*vêtement*) to be uncomfortable on s.o.; (*par sa présence*) to be in s.o.'s way; **ça ne me gêne pas** I don't mind (**si** if); **— se g.** *vpr* (*se déranger*) to put oneself out; **ne te gêne pas pour moi!** don't mind me! **◆—ant** *a* (*objet*) cumbersome; (*présence, situation*) awkward; (*personne*) annoying. **◆—é** *a* (*intimidé*) embarrassed; (*mal à l'aise*) uneasy, awkward; (*silence, sourire*) awkward; (*sans argent*) short of money.

généalogie [ʒenealɔʒi] *nf* genealogy. **◆généalogique** *a* genealogical; **arbre g.** family tree.

général, -aux [ʒeneral, -o] **1** *a* (*global, commun*) general; **en g.** in general. **2** *nm* (*officier*) *Mil* general. **◆générale** *nf Th* dress rehearsal. **◆généralement** *adv* generally; **g. parlant** broadly *ou* generally speaking. **◆généralisation** *nf* generalization. **◆généraliser** *vti* to generalize; **— se g.** *vpr* to become general *ou* widespread. **◆généraliste** *nmf Méd* general practitioner, GP. **◆généralité** *nf* generality; **la g. de** the majority of.

générateur [ʒeneratœr] *nm*, **◆génératrice** *nf Él* generator.

génération [ʒenerasjɔ̃] *nf* generation.

généreux, -euse [ʒenerø, -øz] *a* generous (**de** with). **◆généreusement** *adv* generously. **◆générosité** *nf* generosity.

générique [ʒenerik] *nm Cin* credits.

genèse [ʒənɛz] *nf* genesis.

genêt [ʒənɛ] *nm (arbrisseau)* broom.

génétique [ʒenetik] *nf* genetics; – *a* genetic.

Genève [ʒənɛv] *nm ou f* Geneva.

génie [ʒeni] *nm* **1** *(aptitude, personne)* genius; **avoir le g. pour faire/de qch** to have a genius for doing/for sth. **2** *(lutin)* genie, spirit. **3 g. civil** civil engineering; **g. militaire** engineering corps. ◆**génial, -aux** *a (personne, invention)* brilliant; *(formidable) Fam* fantastic.

génisse [ʒenis] *nf (vache)* heifer.

génital, -aux [ʒenital, -o] *a* genital; **organes génitaux** genitals.

génocide [ʒenɔsid] *nm* genocide.

genou, -x [ʒ(ə)nu] *nm* knee; **être à genoux** to be kneeling (down); **se mettre à genoux** to kneel (down); **prendre qn sur ses genoux** to take s.o. on one's lap *ou* knee. ◆**genouillère** *nf Fb etc* knee pad.

genre [ʒɑ̃r] *nm* **1** *(espèce)* kind, sort; *(attitude)* manner, way; **g. humain** mankind; **g. de vie** way of life. **2** *Littér Cin* genre; *Gram* gender; *Biol* genus.

gens [ʒɑ̃] *nmpl ou nfpl* people; **jeunes g.** young people; *(hommes)* young men.

gentil, -ille [ʒɑ̃ti, -ij] *a (agréable)* nice, pleasant; *(aimable)* kind, nice; *(mignon)* pretty; **g. avec qn** nice *ou* kind to s.o.; **sois g.** *(sage)* be good. ◆**gentillesse** *nf* kindness; **avoir la g. de faire** to be kind enough to do. ◆**gentiment** *adv (aimablement)* kindly; *(sagement)* nicely.

gentilhomme, *pl* **gentilshommes** [ʒɑ̃tijɔm, ʒɑ̃tizɔm] *nm (noble) Hist* gentleman.

géographie [ʒeɔgrafi] *nf* geography. ◆**géographique** *a* geographical.

geôlier, -ière [ʒolje, -jɛr] *nmf* jailer, gaoler.

géologie [ʒeɔlɔʒi] *nf* geology. ◆**géologique** *a* geological. ◆**géologue** *nmf* geologist.

géomètre [ʒeɔmɛtr] *nm (arpenteur)* surveyor.

géométrie [ʒeɔmetri] *nf* geometry. ◆**géométrique** *a* geometric(al).

géranium [ʒeranjɔm] *nm Bot* geranium.

gérant, -ante [ʒerɑ̃, -ɑ̃t] *nmf* manager, manageress; **g. d'immeubles** landlord's agent. ◆**gérance** *nf (gestion)* management.

gerbe [ʒɛrb] *nf (de blé)* sheaf; *(de fleurs)* bunch; *(d'eau)* spray; *(d'étincelles)* shower.

gercer [ʒɛrse] *vti,* — **se g.** *vpr (peau, lèvres)* to chap, crack. ◆**gerçure** *nf* chap, crack.

gérer [ʒere] *vt (fonds, commerce etc)* to manage.

germain [ʒɛrmɛ̃] *a* **cousin g.** first cousin.

germanique [ʒɛrmanik] *a* Germanic.

germe [ʒɛrm] *nm Méd Biol* germ; *Bot* shoot; *(d'une idée) Fig* seed, germ. ◆**germer** *vi Bot & Fig* to germinate.

gésir [ʒezir] *vi (être étendu) Litt* to be lying; **il gît/gisait** he is/was lying; **ci-gît** here lies.

gestation [ʒɛstasjɔ̃] *nf* gestation.

geste [ʒɛst] *nm* gesture; **ne pas faire un g.** *(ne pas bouger)* not to make a move. ◆**gesticuler** *vi* to gesticulate.

gestion [ʒɛstjɔ̃] *nf (action)* management, administration. ◆**gestionnaire** *nmf* administrator.

geyser [ʒɛzɛr] *nm Géol* geyser.

ghetto [gɛto] *nm* ghetto.

gibecière [ʒibsjɛr] *nf* shoulder bag.

gibier [ʒibje] *nm (animaux, oiseaux)* game.

giboulée [ʒibule] *nf* shower, downpour.

gicl/er [ʒikle] *vi (liquide)* to spurt, squirt; *(boue)* to splash; **faire g.** to spurt, squirt. ◆**—ée** *nf* jet, spurt. ◆**—eur** *nm (de carburateur) Aut* jet.

gifle [ʒifl] *nf* slap (in the face). ◆**gifler** *vt* **g. qn** to slap s.o., slap s.o.'s face.

gigantesque [ʒigɑ̃tɛsk] *a* gigantic.

gigogne [ʒigɔɲ] *a* **table g.** nest of tables.

gigot [ʒigo] *nm* leg of mutton *ou* lamb.

gigoter [ʒigɔte] *vi Fam* to kick, wriggle.

gilet [ʒilɛ] *nm* waistcoat, *Am* vest; *(cardigan)* cardigan; **g. (de corps)** vest, *Am* undershirt; **g. pare-balles** bulletproof jacket *ou Am* vest; **g. de sauvetage** life jacket.

gin [dʒin] *nm (eau-de-vie)* gin.

gingembre [ʒɛ̃ʒɑ̃br] *nm Bot Culin* ginger.

girafe [ʒiraf] *nf* giraffe.

giratoire [ʒiratwar] *a* **sens g.** *Aut* roundabout, *Am* traffic circle.

girl [gœrl] *nf (danseuse)* chorus girl.

girofle [ʒirɔfl] *nm* **clou de g.** *Bot* clove.

giroflée [ʒirɔfle] *nf Bot* wall flower.

girouette [ʒirwɛt] *nf* weathercock, weather vane.

gisement [ʒizmɑ̃] *nm (de minerai, pétrole) Géol* deposit.

gitan, -ane [ʒitɑ̃, -an] *nmf* (Spanish) gipsy.

gîte [ʒit] *nm (abri)* resting place.

gîter [ʒite] *vi (navire)* to list.

givre [ʒivr] *nm* (hoar)frost. ◆**se givrer** *vpr (pare-brise etc)* to ice up, frost up. ◆**givré** *a* frost-covered.

glabre [glabr] *a (visage)* smooth.

glace [glas] *nf* **1** *(eau gelée)* ice; *(crème glacée)* ice cream. **2** *(vitre)* window; *(miroir)* mirror; *(verre)* plate glass.

glacer [glase] **1** *vt* (*sang*) *Fig* to chill; **g. qn** (*transir, paralyser*) to chill s.o.; **— se g.** *vpr* (*eau*) to freeze. **2** *vt* (*gâteau*) to ice, (*au jus*) to glaze; (*papier*) to glaze. ◆**glaçant** *a* (*attitude etc*) chilling, icy. ◆**glacé** *a* **1** (*eau, main, pièce*) ice-cold, icy; (*vent*) freezing, icy; (*accueil*) *Fig* icy, chilly. **2** (*thé*) iced; (*fruit, marron*) candied; (*papier*) glazed. ◆**glaçage** *nm* (*de gâteau etc*) icing. ◆**glacial, -aux** *a* icy. ◆**glacier** *nm* **1** *Géol* glacier. **2** (*vendeur*) ice-cream man. ◆**glacière** *nf* (*boîte, endroit*) icebox. ◆**glaçon** *nm Culin* ice cube; *Géol* block of ice; (*sur le toit*) icicle.

glaïeul [glajœl] *nm Bot* gladiolus.

glaires [glɛr] *nfpl Méd* phlegm.

glaise [glɛz] *nf* clay.

gland [glɑ̃] *nm* **1** *Bot* acorn. **2** (*pompon*) *Tex* tassel.

glande [glɑ̃d] *nf* gland.

glander [glɑ̃de] *vi Arg* to fritter away one's time.

glaner [glane] *vt* (*blé, renseignement etc*) to glean.

glapir [glapir] *vi* to yelp, yap.

glas [glɑ] *nm* (*de cloche*) knell.

glauque [glok] *a* sea-green.

gliss/er [glise] *vi* (*involontairement*) to slip; (*patiner, coulisser*) to slide; (*sur l'eau*) to glide; **g. sur** (*sujet*) to slide *ou* gloss over; **ça glisse** it's slippery; – *vt* (*introduire*) to slip (**dans** into); (*murmurer*) to whisper; **se g. dans/sous** to slip into/under. ◆**—ant** *a* slippery. ◆**glissade** *nf* (*involontaire*) slip; (*volontaire*) slide. ◆**glissement** *nm* (*de sens*) *Ling* shift; **g. à gauche** *Pol* swing *ou* shift to the left; **g. de terrain** *Géol* landslide. ◆**glissière** *nf* groove; **porte à g.** sliding door; **fermeture à g.** zip (fastener), *Am* zipper.

global, -aux [glɔbal, -o] *a* total, global; **somme globale** lump sum. ◆**—ement** *adv* collectively, as a whole.

globe [glɔb] *nm* globe; **g. de l'œil** eyeball.

globule [glɔbyl] *nm* (*du sang*) corpuscle.

gloire [glwar] *nf* (*renommée, louange, mérite*) glory; (*personne célèbre*) celebrity; **se faire g. de** to glory in; **à la g. de** in praise of. ◆**glorieux, -euse** *a* (*plein de gloire*) glorious. ◆**glorifier** *vt* to glorify; **se g. de** to glory in.

glossaire [glɔsɛr] *nm* glossary.

glouglou [gluglu] *nm* (*de liquide*) gurgle. ◆**glouglouter** *vi* to gurgle.

glouss/er [gluse] *vi* (*poule*) to cluck; (*personne*) to chuckle. ◆**—ement** *nm* cluck; chuckle.

glouton, -onne [glutɔ̃, -ɔn] *a* greedy, gluttonous; – *nmf* glutton. ◆**gloutonnerie** *nf* gluttony.

gluant [glyɑ̃] *a* sticky.

glucose [glykoz] *nm* glucose.

glycérine [gliserin] *nf* glycerin(e).

glycine [glisin] *nf Bot* wisteria.

gnome [gnom] *nm* (*nain*) gnome.

gnon [ɲɔ̃] *nm Arg* blow, punch.

goal [gol] *nm Fb* goalkeeper.

gobelet [gɔblɛ] *nm* tumbler; (*de plastique, papier*) cup.

gober [gɔbe] *vt* (*œuf, mouche etc*) to swallow (whole); (*propos*) *Fig* to swallow.

godasse [gɔdas] *nf Fam* shoe.

godet [gɔdɛ] *nm* (*récipient*) pot; (*verre*) *Arg* drink.

goéland [gɔelɑ̃] *nm* (sea)gull.

gogo [gogo] *nm* (*homme naïf*) *Fam* sucker.

gogo (à) [agogo] *adv Fam* galore.

goguenard [gɔgnar] *a* mocking.

goguette (en) [ɑ̃gɔgɛt] *adv Fam* on the spree.

goinfre [gwɛ̃fr] *nm* (*glouton*) *Fam* pig, guzzler. ◆**se goinfrer** *vpr Fam* to stuff oneself (**de** with).

golf [gɔlf] *nm* golf; (*terrain*) golf course. ◆**golfeur, -euse** *nmf* golfer.

golfe [gɔlf] *nm* gulf, bay.

gomme [gɔm] *nf* **1** (*substance*) gum. **2** (*à effacer*) rubber, *Am* eraser. ◆**gommé** *a* (*papier*) gummed. ◆**gommer** *vt* (*effacer*) to rub out, erase.

gomme (à la) [alagɔm] *adv Fam* useless.

gond [gɔ̃] *nm* (*de porte etc*) hinge.

gondole [gɔ̃dɔl] *nf* (*bateau*) gondola. ◆**gondolier** *nm* gondolier.

gondoler [gɔ̃dɔle] **1** *vi*, **— se g.** *vpr* (*planche*) to warp. **2 se g.** *vpr* (*rire*) *Fam* to split one's sides.

gonfl/er [gɔ̃fle] *vt* to swell; (*pneu*) to inflate, pump up; (*en soufflant*) to blow up; (*poitrine*) to swell out; (*grossir*) *Fig* to inflate; – *vi*, **— se g.** *vpr* to swell; **se g. de** (*orgueil, émotion*) to swell with. ◆**—é** *a* swollen; **être g.** *Fam* (*courageux*) to have plenty of pluck; (*insolent*) to have plenty of nerve. ◆**—able** *a* inflatable. ◆**—ement** *nm* swelling. ◆**—eur** *nm* (air) pump.

gong [gɔ̃g] *nm* gong.

gorge [gɔrʒ] *nf* **1** throat; (*seins*) *Litt* bust. **2** *Géog* gorge. ◆**gorg/er** *vt* (*remplir*) to stuff (**de** with); **se g. de** to stuff *ou* gorge oneself with. ◆**—é** *a* **g. de** (*saturé*) gorged with. ◆**—ée** *nf* mouthful; **petite g.** sip; **d'une seule g.** in *ou* at one gulp.

gorille [gɔrij] *nm* **1** (*animal*) gorilla. **2** (*garde du corps*) *Fam* bodyguard.
gosier [gozje] *nm* throat, windpipe.
gosse [gɔs] *nmf* (*enfant*) *Fam* kid, youngster.
gothique [gɔtik] *a* & *nm* Gothic.
gouache [gwaʃ] *nf* (*peinture*) gouache.
goudron [gudrɔ̃] *nm* tar. ◆**goudronner** *vt* to tar.
gouffre [gufr] *nm* gulf, chasm.
goujat [guʒa] *nm* churl, lout.
goulasch [gulaʃ] *nf Culin* goulash.
goulot [gulo] *nm* (*de bouteille*) neck; **boire au g.** to drink from the bottle.
goulu, -ue [guly] *a* greedy; – *nmf* glutton. ◆**goulûment** *adv* greedily.
goupille [gupij] *nf* (*cheville*) pin.
goupiller [gupije] *vt* (*arranger*) *Fam* to work out, arrange.
gourde [gurd] *nf* **1** (*à eau*) water bottle, flask. **2** (*personne*) *Péj Fam* chump, oaf.
gourdin [gurdɛ̃] *nm* club, cudgel.
gourer (se) [səgure] *vpr Fam* to make a mistake.
gourmand, -ande [gurmɑ̃, -ɑ̃d] *a* fond of eating, *Péj* greedy; **g. de** fond of; **être g. (de sucreries)** to have a sweet tooth; – *nmf* hearty eater, *Péj* glutton. ◆**gourmandise** *nf* good eating, *Péj* gluttony; *pl* (*mets*) delicacies.
gourmet [gurmɛ] *nm* gourmet, epicure.
gourmette [gurmɛt] *nf* chain *ou* identity bracelet.
gousse [gus] *nf* **g. d'ail** clove of garlic.
goût [gu] *nm* taste; **de bon g.** in good taste; **prendre g. à qch** to take a liking to sth; **par g.** from *ou* by choice; **sans g.** tasteless. ◆**goûter** *vt* (*aliment*) to taste; (*apprécier*) to relish, enjoy; **g. à qch** to taste (a little of) sth; **g. de** (*pour la première fois*) to try out, taste; – *vi* to have a snack, have tea; – *nm* snack, tea.
goutte [gut] *nf* **1** drop. **couler g. à g.** to drip. **2** (*maladie*) gout. ◆**g.-à-goutte** *nm inv Méd* drip. ◆**gouttelette** *nf* droplet. ◆**goutter** *vi* (*eau, robinet, nez*) to drip (**de** from).
gouttière [gutjɛr] *nf* (*d'un toit*) gutter.
gouvernail [guvɛrnaj] *nm* (*pale*) rudder; (*barre*) helm.
gouvernante [guvɛrnɑ̃t] *nf* governess.
gouvernement [guvɛrnəmɑ̃] *nm* government. ◆**gouvernemental, -aux** *a* (*parti, politique etc*) government-.
gouvern/er [guvɛrne] *vti Pol* & *Fig* to govern, rule. ◆**—ants** *nmpl* rulers. ◆**—eur** *nm* governor.
grabuge [grabyʒ] *nm* **du g.** (*querelle*) *Fam* a rumpus.
grâce [grɑs] **1** *nf* (*charme*) & *Rel* grace; (*avantage*) favour; (*miséricorde*) mercy; **crier g.** to cry for mercy; **de bonne/mauvaise g.** with good/bad grace; **donner le coup de g. à** to finish off; **faire g. de qch à qn** to spare s.o. sth. **2** *prép* **g. à** thanks to. ◆**gracier** *vt* (*condamné*) to pardon.
gracieux, -euse [grasjø, -øz] *a* **1** (*élégant*) graceful; (*aimable*) gracious. **2** (*gratuit*) gratuitous; **à titre g.** free (of charge). ◆**gracieusement** *adv* gracefully; graciously; free (of charge).
gracile [grasil] *a Litt* slender.
gradation [gradɑsjɔ̃] *nf* gradation.
grade [grad] *nm Mil* rank; **monter en g.** to be promoted. ◆**gradé** *nm Mil* non-commissioned officer.
gradin [gradɛ̃] *nm Th etc* row of seats, tier.
graduel, -elle [gradɥɛl] *a* gradual.
graduer [gradɥe] *vt* (*règle*) to graduate; (*exercices*) to grade, make gradually more difficult.
graffiti [grafiti] *nmpl* graffiti.
grain [grɛ̃] *nm* **1** (*de blé etc*) & *Fig* grain; (*de café*) bean; (*de chapelet*) bead; (*de poussière*) speck; *pl* (*céréales*) grain; **le g.** (*de cuir, papier*) the grain; **g. de beauté** mole; (*sur le visage*) beauty spot; **g. de raisin** grape. **2** *Mét* shower
graine [grɛn] *nf* seed; **mauvaise g.** (*enfant*) *Péj* bad lot, rotten egg.
graisse [grɛs] *nf* fat; (*lubrifiant*) grease. ◆**graissage** *nm Aut* lubrication. ◆**graisser** *vt* to grease. ◆**graisseux, -euse** *a* (*vêtement etc*) greasy, oily; (*bourrelets, tissu*) fatty.
grammaire [gramɛr] *nf* grammar. ◆**grammatical, -aux** *a* grammatical.
gramme [gram] *nm* gram(me).
grand, grande [grɑ̃, grɑ̃d] *a* big, large; (*en hauteur*) tall; (*mérite, âge, chaleur, ami etc*) great; (*bruit*) loud, great; (*différence*) wide, great, big; (*adulte, mûr, plus âgé*) grown up, big; (*officier, maître*) grand; (*âme*) noble; **g. frère/**etc (*plus âgé*) big brother/*etc*; **le g. air** the open air; **il est g. temps** it's high time (**que** that); – *adv* **g. ouvert** (*yeux, fenêtre*) wide-open; **ouvrir g.** to open wide; **en g.** on a grand *ou* large scale; – *nmf Scol* senior; (*adulte*) grown-up; **les quatre Grands** *Pol* the Big Four. ◆**grandement** *adv* (*beaucoup*) greatly; (*généreusement*) grandly; **avoir g. de quoi vivre** to have plenty to live on. ◆**grandeur** *nf* (*importance, gloire*) greatness; (*dimension*) size, magni-

tude; (*majesté, splendeur*) grandeur; **g. nature** life-size; **g. d'âme** generosity.

grand-chose [grɑ̃ʃoz] *pron* **pas g.-chose** not much. ◆**g.-mère** *nf* (*pl* **grands-mères**) grandmother. ◆**grands-parents** *nmpl* grandparents. ◆**g.-père** *nm* (*pl* **grands-pères**) grandfather.

Grande-Bretagne [grɑ̃dbrətaɲ] *nf* Great Britain.

grandiose [grɑ̃djoz] *a* grandiose, grand.

grandir [grɑ̃dir] *vi* to grow; (*bruit*) to grow louder; – *vt* (*grossir*) to magnify; **g. qn** (*faire paraître plus grand*) to make s.o. seem taller.

grange [grɑ̃ʒ] *nf* barn.

granit(e) [granit] *nm* granite.

graphique [grafik] *a* (*signe, art*) graphic; – *nm* graph.

grappe [grap] *nf* (*de fruits etc*) cluster; **g. de raisin** bunch of grapes.

grappin [grapɛ̃] *nm* **mettre le g. sur** *Fam* to grab hold of.

gras, grasse [grɑ, grɑs] *a* (*personne, ventre etc*) fat; (*aliment*) fatty; (*graisseux*) greasy, oily; (*caractère*) *Typ* bold, heavy; (*plante, contour*) thick; (*rire*) throaty, deep; (*toux*) loose, phlegmy; (*récompense*) rich; **matières grasses** fat; **foie g.** *Culin* foie gras, fatted goose liver; – *nm* (*de viande*) fat. ◆**grassement** *adv* (*abondamment*) handsomely. ◆**grassouillet, -ette** *a* plump.

gratifier [gratifje] *vt* **g. qn de** to present *ou* favour s.o. with. ◆**gratification** *nf* (*prime*) bonus.

gratin [gratɛ̃] *nm* **1 au g.** *Culin* baked with breadcrumbs and grated cheese. **2** (*élite*) *Fam* upper crust.

gratis [gratis] *adv Fam* free (of charge), gratis.

gratitude [gratityd] *nf* gratitude.

gratte-ciel [gratsjɛl] *nm inv* skyscraper.

gratte-papier [gratpapje] *nm* (*employé*) *Péj* pen-pusher.

gratter [grate] *vt* (*avec un outil etc*) to scrape; (*avec les ongles, les griffes etc*) to scratch; (*boue*) to scrape off; (*effacer*) to scratch out; **ça me gratte** *Fam* it itches, I have an itch; – *vi* (*à la porte etc*) to scratch; (*tissu*) to be scratchy; **– se g.** *vpr* to scratch oneself. ◆**grattoir** *nm* scraper.

gratuit [gratɥi] *a* (*billet etc*) free; (*hypothèse, acte*) gratuitous. ◆**gratuité** *nf* **la g. de l'enseignement/***etc* free education/*etc*. ◆**gratuitement** *adv* free (of charge); gratuitously.

gravats [gravɑ] *nmpl* rubble, debris.

grave [grav] *a* serious; (*juge, visage*) grave, solemn; (*voix*) deep, low; (*accent*) *Gram* grave; **ce n'est pas g.!** it's not important! ◆**—ment** *adv* (*malade, menacé*) seriously; (*dignement*) gravely.

grav/er [grave] *vt* (*sur métal etc*) to engrave; (*sur bois*) to carve; (*disque*) to cut; (*dans sa mémoire*) to imprint, engrave. ◆**—eur** *nm* engraver.

gravier [gravje] *nm* gravel. ◆**gravillon** *nm* gravel; *pl* gravel, (loose) chippings.

gravir [gravir] *vt* to climb (*with effort*).

gravité [gravite] *nf* **1** (*de situation etc*) seriousness; (*solennité*) gravity. **2** *Phys* gravity.

graviter [gravite] *vi* to revolve (**autour de** around). ◆**gravitation** *nf* gravitation.

gravure [gravyr] *nf* (*action, art*) engraving; (*à l'eau forte*) etching; (*estampe*) print; (*de disque*) recording; **g. sur bois** (*objet*) woodcut.

gré [gre] *nm* **à son g.** (*goût*) to his *ou* her taste; (*désir*) as he *ou* she pleases; **de bon g.** willingly; **contre le g. de** against the will of; **bon g. mal g.** willy-nilly; **au g. de** (*vent etc*) at the mercy of.

Grèce [grɛs] *nf* Greece. ◆**grec, grecque** *a* & *nmf* Greek; – *nm* (*langue*) Greek.

greffe [grɛf] **1** *nf* (*de peau*) & *Bot* graft; (*d'organe*) transplant. **2** *nm Jur* record office. ◆**greffer** *vt* (*peau etc*) & *Bot* to graft (**à** on to); (*organe*) to transplant. ◆**greffier** *nm* clerk (of the court). ◆**greffon** *nm* (*de peau*) & *Bot* graft.

grégaire [gregɛr] *a* (*instinct*) gregarious.

grêle [grɛl] **1** *nf Mét* & *Fig* hail. **2** *a* (*fin*) spindly, (very) slender *ou* thin. ◆**grêler** *v imp* to hail. ◆**grêlon** *nm* hailstone.

grêlé [grele] *a* (*visage*) pockmarked.

grelot [grəlo] *nm* (small round) bell.

grelotter [grəlɔte] *vi* to shiver (**de** with).

grenade [grənad] *nf* **1** *Bot* pomegranate. **2** (*projectile*) *Mil* grenade. ◆**grenadine** *nf* pomegranate syrup, grenadine.

grenat [grəna] *a inv* (*couleur*) dark red.

grenier [grənje] *nm* attic; *Agr* granary.

grenouille [grənuj] *nf* frog.

grès [grɛ] *nm* (*roche*) sandstone; (*poterie*) stoneware.

grésiller [grezije] *vi Culin* to sizzle; *Rad* to crackle.

grève [grɛv] *nf* **1** strike; **g. de la faim** hunger strike; **g. du zèle** work-to-rule, *Am* rule-book slow-down; **g. perlée** go-slow, *Am* slow-down (strike); **g. sauvage/sur le tas** wildcat/sit-down strike; **g. tournante** strike by rota. **2** (*de mer*) shore; (*de rivière*) bank. ◆**gréviste** *nmf* striker.

gribouiller [gribuje] *vti* to scribble. ◆**gribouillis** *nm* scribble.

grief [grijɛf] *nm* (*plainte*) grievance.

grièvement [grijɛvmɑ̃] *adv* **g. blessé** seriously *ou* badly injured.

griffe [grif] *nf* **1** (*ongle*) claw; **sous la g. de qn** (*pouvoir*) in s.o.'s clutches. **2** (*de couturier*) (designer) label; (*tampon*) printed signature; (*d'auteur*) *Fig* mark, stamp. ◆**griffé** *a* (*vêtement*) designer-. ◆**griffer** *vt* to scratch, claw.

griffonn/er [grifɔne] *vt* to scrawl, scribble. ◆**—age** *nm* scrawl, scribble.

grignoter [griɲɔte] *vti* to nibble.

gril [gril] *nm Culin* grill, grid(iron). ◆**grillade** [grijad] *nf* (*viande*) grill. ◆**grille-pain** *nm inv* toaster. ◆**griller** *vt* (*viande*) to grill, broil; (*pain*) to toast; (*café*) to roast; (*ampoule*) *El* to blow; (*brûler*) to scorch; (*cigarette*) *Fam* to smoke; **g. un feu rouge** *Aut Fam* to drive through *ou* jump a red light; – *vi* **mettre à g.** to put on the grill; **on grille ici** *Fam* it's scorching; **g. de faire** to be itching to do.

grille [grij] *nf* (*clôture*) railings; (*porte*) (iron) gate; (*de fourneau, foyer*) grate; (*de radiateur*) *Aut* grid, grille; (*des salaires*) *Fig* scale; *pl* (*de fenêtre*) bars, grating; **g.** (**des horaires**) schedule. ◆**grillage** *nm* wire netting.

grillon [grijɔ̃] *nm* (*insecte*) cricket.

grimace [grimas] *nf* (*pour faire rire*) (funny) face, grimace; (*de dégoût, douleur*) grimace. ◆**grimacer** *vi* to grimace (**de** with).

grimer [grime] *vt*, **— se g.** *vpr* (*acteur*) to make up.

grimp/er [grɛ̃pe] *vi* to climb (**à qch** up sth); (*prix*) *Fam* to rocket; – *vt* to climb. ◆**—ant** *a* (*plante*) climbing.

grinc/er [grɛ̃se] *vi* to grate, creak; **g. des dents** to grind *ou* gnash one's teeth. ◆**—ement** *nm* grating; grinding.

grincheux, -euse [grɛ̃ʃø, -øz] *a* grumpy, peevish.

gringalet [grɛ̃galɛ] *nm* (*homme*) *Péj* puny runt, weakling.

grippe [grip] *nf* **1** (*maladie*) flu, influenza. **2** **prendre qch/qn en g.** to take a strong dislike to sth/s.o. ◆**grippé** *a* **être g.** to have (the) flu.

gripper [gripe] *vi*, **— se g.** *vpr* (*moteur*) to seize up.

grippe-sou [gripsu] *nm* skinflint, miser.

gris [gri] *a* grey, *Am* gray; (*temps*) dull, grey; (*ivre*) tipsy; – *nm* grey. ◆**grisaille** *nf* (*de vie*) dullness, greyness, *Am* grayness. ◆**grisâtre** *a* greyish, *Am* grayish. ◆**griser** *vt* (*vin etc*) to make (*s.o.*) tipsy, intoxicate (*s.o.*); (*air vif, succès*) to exhilarate (*s.o.*). ◆**griserie** *nf* intoxication; exhilaration. ◆**grisonn/er** *vi* (*cheveux, personne*) to go grey. ◆**—ant** *a* greying.

grisou [grizu] *nm* (*gaz*) firedamp.

grive [griv] *nf* (*oiseau*) thrush.

grivois [grivwa] *a* bawdy. ◆**grivoiserie** *nf* (*propos*) bawdy talk.

Groenland [grɔenlɑ̃d] *nm* Greenland.

grog [grɔg] *nm* (*boisson*) grog, toddy.

grogn/er [grɔɲe] *vi* to growl, grumble (**contre** at); (*cochon*) to grunt. ◆**—ement** *nm* growl, grumble; grunt. ◆**grognon, -onne** *a* grumpy, peevish.

grommeler [grɔmle] *vti* to grumble, mutter.

gronder [grɔ̃de] *vi* (*chien*) to growl; (*tonnerre*) to rumble; – *vt* (*réprimander*) to scold. ◆**grondement** *nm* growl; rumble. ◆**gronderie** *nf* scolding.

gros, grosse [gro, gros] *a* big; (*gras*) fat; (*épais*) thick; (*effort, progrès*) great; (*fortune, somme*) large; (*bruit*) loud; (*averse, mer, rhume*) heavy; (*faute*) serious, gross; (*traits, laine, fil*) coarse; **g. mot** swear word; – *adv* **gagner g.** to earn big money; **risquer g.** to take a big risk; **en g.** (*globalement*) roughly; (*écrire*) in big letters; (*vendre*) in bulk, wholesale; – *nmf* (*personne*) fat man, fat woman; – *nm* **le g. de** the bulk of; **de g.** (*maison, prix*) wholesale.

groseille [grozɛj] *nf* (white *ou* red) currant; **g. à maquereau** gooseberry.

grossesse [grosɛs] *nf* pregnancy.

grosseur [grosœr] *nf* **1** (*volume*) size; (*obésité*) weight. **2** (*tumeur*) *Méd* lump.

grossier, -ière [grosje, -jɛr] *a* (*matière, tissu, traits*) coarse, rough; (*idée, solution*) rough, crude; (*instrument*) crude; (*erreur*) gross; (*personne, manières*) coarse, uncouth, rude; **être g. envers** (*insolent*) to be rude to. ◆**grossièrement** *adv* (*calculer*) roughly; (*se tromper*) grossly; (*répondre*) coarsely, rudely. ◆**grossièreté** *nf* coarseness; roughness; (*insolence*) rudeness; (*mot*) rude word.

gross/ir [grosir] *vi* (*personne*) to put on weight; (*fleuve*) to swell; (*nombre, bosse, foule*) to swell, get bigger; (*bruit*) to get louder; – *vt* to swell; (*exagérer*) *Fig* to magnify; – *vti* (*verre, loupe etc*) to magnify; **verre grossissant** magnifying glass. ◆**—issement** *nm* increase in weight; swelling, increase in size; (*de microscope etc*) magnification.

grossiste [grosist] *nmf Com* wholesaler.

grosso modo [grosomɔdo] *adv* (*en gros*) roughly.
grotesque [grɔtɛsk] *a* (*risible*) ludicrous, grotesque.
grotte [grɔt] *nf* grotto.
grouill/er [gruje] **1** *vi* (*rue, fourmis, foule etc*) to be swarming (**de** with). **2 se g.** *vpr* (*se hâter*) *Arg* to step on it. **◆—ant** *a* swarming (**de** with).
groupe [grup] *nm* group; **g. scolaire** (*bâtiments*) school block. **◆groupement** *nm* (*action*) grouping; (*groupe*) group. **◆grouper** *vt* to group (together); **— se g.** *vpr* to band together, group (together).
grue [gry] *nf* (*machine, oiseau*) crane.
grumeau, -x [grymo] *nm* (*dans une sauce etc*) lump. **◆grumeleux, -euse** *a* lumpy.
gruyère [gryjɛr] *nm* gruyère (cheese).
gué [ge] *nm* ford; **passer à g.** to ford.
guenilles [gənij] *nfpl* rags (and tatters).
guenon [gənɔ̃] *nf* female monkey.
guépard [gepar] *nm* cheetah.
guêpe [gɛp] *nf* wasp. **◆guêpier** *nm* (*nid*) wasp's nest; (*piège*) *Fig* trap.
guère [gɛr] *adv* (**ne**) . . . **g.** hardly, scarcely; **il ne sort g.** he hardly *ou* scarcely goes out.
guéridon [geridɔ̃] *nm* pedestal table.
guérilla [gerija] *nf* guerrilla warfare. **◆guérillero** *nm* guerrilla.
guér/ir [gerir] *vt* (*personne, maladie*) to cure (**de** of); (*blessure*) to heal; **–** *vi* to recover; (*blessure*) to heal; (*rhume*) to get better; **g. de** (*fièvre etc*) to get over, recover from. **◆—i** *a* cured, better, well. **◆guérison** *nf* (*de personne*) recovery; (*de maladie*) cure; (*de blessure*) healing. **◆guérisseur, -euse** *nmf* faith healer.
guérite [gerit] *nf Mil* sentry box.
guerre [gɛr] *nf* war; (*chimique etc*) warfare; **en g.** at war (**avec** with); **faire la g.** to wage *ou* make war (**à** on, against); **g. d'usure** war of attrition; **conseil de g.** court-martial. **◆guerrier, -ière** *a* (*chant, danse*) war-; (*nation*) war-like; **–** *nmf* warrior. **◆guerroyer** *vi Litt* to war.
guet [gɛ] *nm* **faire le g.** to be on the look-out. **◆guett/er** *vt* to be on the look-out for, watch (out) for; (*gibier*) to lie in wait for. **◆—eur** *nm* (*soldat*) look-out.
guet-apens [gɛtapɑ̃] *nm inv* ambush.
guêtre [gɛtr] *nf* gaiter.
gueule [gœl] *nf* (*d'animal, de canon*) mouth; (*de personne*) *Fam* mouth; (*figure*) *Fam* face; **avoir la g. de bois** *Fam* to have a hangover; **faire la g.** *Fam* to sulk. **◆gueuler** *vti* to bawl (out). **◆gueuleton** *nm* (*repas*) *Fam* blow-out, feast.
gui [gi] *nm Bot* mistletoe.
guichet [giʃɛ] *nm* (*de gare, cinéma etc*) ticket office; (*de banque etc*) window; *Th* box office, ticket office; **à guichets fermés** *Th Sp* with all tickets sold in advance. **◆guichetier, -ière** *nmf* (*à la poste etc*) counter clerk; (*à la gare*) ticket office clerk.
guide [gid] **1** *nm* (*personne, livre etc*) guide. **2** *nf* (*éclaireuse*) (girl) guide. **3** *nfpl* (*rênes*) reins. **◆guider** *vt* to guide; **se g. sur** to guide oneself by.
guidon [gidɔ̃] *nm* (*de bicyclette etc*) handlebar(s).
guigne [giɲ] *nf* (*malchance*) *Fam* bad luck.
guignol [giɲɔl] *nm* (*spectacle*) = Punch and Judy show.
guillemets [gijmɛ] *nmpl Typ* inverted commas, quotation marks.
guilleret, -ette [gijrɛ, -ɛt] *a* lively, perky.
guillotine [gijɔtin] *nf* guillotine.
guimauve [gimov] *nf Bot Culin* marshmallow.
guimbarde [gɛ̃bard] *nf* (*voiture*) *Fam* old banger, *Am* (old) wreck.
guindé [gɛ̃de] *a* (*affecté*) stiff, stilted, stuck-up.
guingois (de) [dəgɛ̃gwa] *adv* askew.
guirlande [girlɑ̃d] *nf* garland, wreath.
guise [giz] *nf* **n'en faire qu'à sa g.** to do as one pleases; **en g. de** by way of.
guitare [gitar] *nf* guitar. **◆guitariste** *nmf* guitarist.
guttural, -aux [gytyral, -o] *a* guttural.
gymnase [ʒimnɑz] *nm* gymnasium. **◆gymnaste** *nmf* gymnast. **◆gymnastique** *nf* gymnastics.
gynécologie [ʒinekɔlɔʒi] *nf* gynaecology, *Am* gynecology. **◆gynécologue** *nmf* gynaecologist, *Am* gynecologist.

H

H, h [aʃ] *nm* H, h; **l'heure H** zero hour; **bombe H** H-bomb.

ha! ['ɑ] *int* ah!, oh!; **ha, ha!** (*rire*) ha-ha!

habile [abil] *a* clever, skilful (**à qch** at sth, **à faire** at doing). **◆habilement** *adv* cleverly, skilfully. **◆habileté** *nf* skill, ability.

habill/er [abije] *vt* to dress (**de** in); (*fournir en vêtements*) to clothe; (*couvrir*) to cover (**de** with); **h. qn en soldat/***etc* (*déguiser*) to dress s.o. up as a soldier/*etc*; **– s'h.** *vpr* to dress (oneself), get dressed; (*avec élégance, se déguiser*) to dress up. **◆–é** *a* dressed (**de** in); (*costume, robe*) smart, dressy. **◆–ement** *nm* (*vêtements*) clothing, clothes.

habit [abi] *nm* costume, outfit; (*tenue de soirée*) evening dress, tails; *pl* (*vêtements*) clothes.

habit/er [abite] *vi* to live (**à, en, dans** in); – *vt* (*maison, région*) to live in; (*planète*) to inhabit. **◆–ant, -ante** *nmf* (*de pays etc*) inhabitant; (*de maison*) resident, occupant. **◆–é** *a* (*région*) inhabited; (*maison*) occupied. **◆–able** *a* (in)habitable. **◆habitat** *nm* (*d'animal, de plante*) habitat; (*conditions*) housing, living conditions. **◆habitation** *nf* house, dwelling; (*action de résider*) living.

habitude [abityd] *nf* habit; **avoir l'h. de qch** to be used to sth; **avoir l'h. de faire** to be used to doing, be in the habit of doing; **prendre l'h. de faire** to get into the habit of doing; **d'h.** usually; **comme d'h.** as usual. **◆habituel, -elle** *a* usual, customary. **◆habituellement** *adv* usually. **◆habitu/er** *vt* **h. qn à** to accustom s.o. to; **être habitué à** to be used *ou* accustomed to; **– s'h.** *vpr* to get accustomed (**à** to). **◆–é, -ée** *nmf* regular (customer *ou* visitor).

hache ['aʃ] *nf* axe, *Am* ax. **◆hachette** *nf* hatchet.

hach/er ['aʃe] *vt* (*au couteau*) to chop (up); (*avec un appareil*) to mince, *Am* grind; (*déchiqueter*) to cut to pieces. **◆–é** *a* **1** (*viande*) minced, *Am* ground; chopped. **2** (*style*) staccato, broken. **◆hachis** *nm* (*viande*) mince, minced *ou Am* ground meat. **◆hachoir** *nm* (*couteau*) chopper; (*appareil*) mincer, *Am* grinder.

hagard ['agar] *a* wild-looking, frantic.

haie ['ɛ] *nf* (*clôture*) *Bot* hedge; (*rangée*) row; (*de coureur*) *Sp* hurdle; (*de chevaux*) *Sp* fence, hurdle; **course de haies** (*coureurs*) hurdle race; (*chevaux*) steeplechase.

haillons ['ɑjɔ̃] *nmpl* rags (and tatters).

haine ['ɛn] *nf* hatred, hate. **◆haineux, -euse** *a* full of hatred.

haïr* ['air] *vt* to hate. **◆haïssable** *a* hateful, detestable.

hâle ['ɑl] *nm* suntan. **◆hâlé** *a* (*par le soleil*) suntanned; (*par l'air*) weather-beaten.

haleine [alɛn] *nf* breath; **hors d'h.** out of breath; **perdre h.** to get out of breath; **reprendre h.** to get one's breath back, catch one's breath; **de longue h.** (*travail*) long-term; **tenir en h.** to hold in suspense.

hal/er ['ale] *vt Nau* to tow. **◆–age** *nm* towing; **chemin de h.** towpath.

halet/er ['alte] *vi* to pant, gasp. **◆–ant** *a* panting, gasping.

hall ['ol] *nm* (*de gare*) main hall, concourse; (*d'hôtel*) lobby, hall; (*de maison*) hall(way).

halle ['al] *nf* (covered) market; **les halles** the central food market.

hallucination [alysinɑsjɔ̃] *nf* hallucination. **◆hallucinant** *a* extraordinary.

halo ['alo] *nm* (*auréole*) halo.

halte ['alt] *nf* (*arrêt*) stop, *Mil* halt; (*lieu*) stopping place, *Mil* halting place; **faire h.** to stop; – *int* stop!, *Mil* halt!

haltère [altɛr] *nm* (*poids*) *Sp* dumbbell. **◆haltérophilie** *nf* weight lifting.

hamac ['amak] *nm* hammock.

hameau, -x ['amo] *nm* hamlet.

hameçon [amsɔ̃] *nm* (fish) hook; **mordre à l'h.** *Pêche & Fig* to rise to *ou* swallow the bait.

hamster ['amstɛr] *nm* hamster.

hanche ['ɑ̃ʃ] *nf Anat* hip.

hand(-)ball ['ɑdbal] *nm Sp* handball.

handicap ['ɑdikap] *nm* (*désavantage*) & *Sp* handicap. **◆handicap/er** *vt* to handicap. **◆–é, -ée** *a* & *nmf* handicapped (person); **h. moteur** spastic.

hangar ['ɑ̃gar] *nm* (*entrepôt*) shed; (*pour avions*) hangar.

hanneton ['antɔ̃] *nm* (*insecte*) cockchafer.

hanter ['ɑ̃te] *vt* to haunt.

hantise ['ɑ̃tiz] *nf* **la h. de** an obsession with.

happer ['ape] *vt* (*saisir*) to catch, snatch; (*par la gueule*) to snap up.
haras ['arɑ] *nm* stud farm.
harasser ['arase] *vt* to exhaust.
harceler ['arsəle] *vt* to harass, torment (**de** with). ◆**harcèlement** *nm* harassment.
hardi ['ardi] *a* bold, daring. ◆**—ment** *adv* boldly. ◆**hardiesse** *nf* boldness, daring; **une h.** (*action*) *Litt* an audacity.
harem ['arɛm] *nm* harem.
hareng ['arɑ̃] *nm* herring.
hargne ['arɲ] *nf* aggressive bad temper. ◆**hargneux, -euse** *a* bad-tempered, aggressive.
haricot ['ariko] *nm* (*blanc*) (haricot) bean; (*vert*) French bean, green bean.
harmonica [armɔnika] *nm* harmonica, mouthorgan.
harmonie [armɔni] *nf* harmony. ◆**harmonieux, -euse** *a* harmonious. ◆**harmonique** *a* & *nm Mus* harmonic. ◆**harmoniser** *vt*, **— s'h.** *vpr* to harmonize. ◆**harmonium** *nm Mus* harmonium.
harnacher ['arnaʃe] *vt* (*cheval etc*) to harness. ◆**harnais** *nm* (*de cheval, bébé*) harness.
harpe ['arp] *nf* harp. ◆**harpiste** *nmf* harpist.
harpon ['arpɔ̃] *nm* harpoon. ◆**harponner** *vt* (*baleine*) to harpoon; **h. qn** (*arrêter*) *Fam* to waylay s.o.
hasard ['azar] *nm* **le h.** chance; **un h.** (*coïncidence*) a coincidence; **un heureux h.** a stroke of luck; **un malheureux h.** a rotten piece of luck; **par h.** by chance; **si par h.** if by any chance; **au h.** at random, haphazardly; **à tout h.** just in case; **les hasards de** (*risques*) the hazards of. ◆**hasard/er** *vt* (*remarque, démarche*) to venture, hazard; (*vie, réputation*) to risk; **se h. dans** to venture into; **se h. à faire** to risk doing, venture to do. ◆**—é** *a*, ◆**hasardeux, -euse** *a* risky, hazardous.
haschisch ['aʃiʃ] *nm* hashish.
hâte ['ɑt] *nf* haste, speed; (*impatience*) eagerness; **en h., à la h.** hurriedly, in a hurry, in haste; **avoir h. de faire** (*désireux*) to be eager to do, be in a hurry to do. ◆**hâter** *vt* (*pas, départ etc*) to hasten; **— se h.** *vpr* to hurry, make haste (**de faire** to do). ◆**hâtif, -ive** *a* hasty, hurried; (*développement*) precocious; (*fruit*) early.
hausse ['os] *nf* rise (**de** in); **en h.** rising. ◆**hausser** *vt* (*prix, voix etc*) to raise; (*épaules*) to shrug; **se h. sur la pointe des pieds** to stand on tip-toe.
haut ['o] *a* high; (*de taille*) tall; (*classes*) upper, higher; (*fonctionnaire etc*) high-ranking; **le h. Rhin** the upper Rhine; **la haute couture** high fashion; **à haute voix** aloud, in a loud voice; **h. de 5 mètres** 5 metres high *ou* tall; – *adv* (*voler, viser etc*) high (up); (*estimer*) highly; (*parler*) loud, loudly; **tout h.** (*lire, penser*) aloud, out loud; **h. placé** (*personne*) in a high position; **plus h.** (*dans un texte*) above, further back; – *nm* (*partie haute*) top; **en h. de** at the top of; **en h.** (*loger*) upstairs; (*regarder*) up; (*mettre*) on (the) top; **d'en h.** (*de la partie haute, du ciel etc*) from high up, from up above; **avoir 5 mètres de h.** to be 5 metres high *ou* tall; **des hauts et des bas** *Fig* ups and downs.
hautain ['otɛ̃] *a* haughty.
hautbois ['obwa] *nm Mus* oboe.
haut-de-forme ['odfɔrm] *nm* (*pl* **hauts-de-forme**) top hat.
hautement ['otmɑ̃] *adv* (*tout à fait, très*) highly. ◆**hauteur** *nf* height; *Géog* hill; (*orgueil*) *Péj* haughtiness; *Mus* pitch; **à la h. de** (*objet*) level with; (*rue*) opposite; (*situation*) *Fig* equal to; **il n'est pas à la h.** he isn't up to it; **saut en h.** *Sp* high jump.
haut-le-cœur ['olkœr] *nm inv* **avoir des h.-le-cœur** to retch, gag.
haut-le-corps ['olkɔr] *nm inv* (*sursaut*) sudden start, jump.
haut-parleur ['oparlœr] *nm* loudspeaker.
hâve ['ɑv] *a* gaunt, emaciated.
havre ['ɑvr] *nm* (*refuge*) *Litt* haven.
Haye (La) [la'ɛ] *nf* The Hague.
hayon ['ɛjɔ̃] *nm* (*porte*) *Aut* tailgate, hatchback.
hé! [e] *int* **hé (là)** (*appel*) hey!; **hé! hé!** well, well!
hebdomadaire [ɛbdɔmadɛr] *a* weekly; – *nm* (*publication*) weekly.
héberg/er [eberʒe] *vt* to put up, accommodate. ◆**—ement** *nm* accommodation; **centre d'h.** shelter.
hébété [ebete] *a* dazed, stupefied.
hébreu, -x [ebrø] *am* Hebrew; – *nm* (*langue*) Hebrew. ◆**hébraïque** *a* Hebrew.
hécatombe [ekatɔ̃b] *nf* (great) slaughter.
hectare [ɛktar] *nm* hectare (= *2.47 acres*).
hégémonie [eʒemɔni] *nf* hegemony, supremacy.
hein! [ɛ̃] *int* (*surprise, interrogation etc*) eh!
hélas! ['elɑs] *int* alas!, unfortunately.
héler ['ele] *vt* (*taxi etc*) to hail.
hélice [elis] *nf Av Nau* propeller.
hélicoptère [elikɔptɛr] *nm* helicopter. ◆**héliport** *nm* heliport.
hellénique [elenik] *a* Hellenic, Greek.

helvétique [ɛlvetik] *a* Swiss.

hem! ['ɛm] *int* (a)hem!, hm!

hémicycle [emisikl] *nm* semicircle; *Pol Fig* French National Assembly.

hémisphère [emisfɛr] *nm* hemisphere.

hémorragie [emɔraʒi] *nf Méd* h(a)emorrhage; (*de capitaux*) *Com* outflow, drain.

hémorroïdes [emɔrɔid] *nfpl* piles, h(a)emorrhoids.

henn/ir ['enir] *vi* (*cheval*) to neigh. ◆**—issement** *nm* neigh.

hep! ['ɛp] *int* hey!, hey there!

hépatite [epatit] *nf* hepatitis.

herbe [ɛrb] *nf* grass; (*médicinale etc*) herb; **mauvaise h.** weed; **fines herbes** *Culin* herbs; **en h.** (*blés*) green; (*poète etc*) *Fig* budding. ◆**herbage** *nm* grassland. ◆**herbeux, -euse** *a* grassy. ◆**herbicide** *nm* weed killer. ◆**herbivore** *a* grass-eating, herbivorous. ◆**herbu** *a* grassy.

hercule [ɛrkyl] *nm* Hercules, strong man. ◆**herculéen, -enne** *a* herculean.

hérédité [eredite] *nf* heredity. ◆**héréditaire** *a* hereditary.

hérésie [erezi] *nf* heresy. ◆**hérétique** *a* heretical; – *nmf* heretic.

hériss/er ['erise] *vt* (*poils*) to bristle (up); **h. qn** (*irriter*) to ruffle s.o., ruffle s.o.'s feathers; **— se h.** *vpr* to bristle (up); to get ruffled. ◆**—é** *a* (*cheveux*) bristly; (*cactus*) prickly; **h. de** bristling with.

hérisson ['erisɔ̃] *nm* (*animal*) hedgehog.

hérit/er [erite] *vti* to inherit (**qch de qn** sth from s.o.); **h. de qch** to inherit sth. ◆**—age** *nm* (*biens*) inheritance; (*culturel, politique etc*) *Fig* heritage. ◆**héritier** *nm* heir. ◆**héritière** *nf* heiress.

hermétique [ɛrmetik] *a* hermetically sealed, airtight; (*obscur*) *Fig* impenetrable. ◆**—ment** *adv* hermetically.

hermine [ɛrmin] *nf* (*animal, fourrure*) ermine.

hernie ['ɛrni] *nf Méd* hernia, rupture; (*de pneu*) swelling.

héron ['erɔ̃] *nm* (*oiseau*) heron.

héros ['ero] *nm* hero. ◆**héroïne** [erɔin] *nf* **1** (*femme*) heroine. **2** (*stupéfiant*) heroin. ◆**héroïque** [erɔik] *a* heroic. ◆**héroïsme** [erɔism] *nm* heroism.

hésit/er [ezite] *vi* to hesitate (**sur** over, about; **à faire** to do); (*en parlant*) to falter, hesitate. ◆**—ant** *a* (*personne*) hesitant; (*pas, voix*) faltering, unsteady, wavering. ◆**hésitation** *nf* hesitation; **avec h.** hesitantly.

hétéroclite [eterɔklit] *a* (*disparate*) motley.

hétérogène [eterɔʒɛn] *a* heterogeneous.

hêtre ['ɛtr] *nm* (*arbre, bois*) beech.

heu! ['ø] *int* (*hésitation*) er!

heure [œr] *nf* (*mesure*) hour; (*moment*) time; **quelle h. est-il?** what time is it?; **il est six heures** it's six (o'clock); **six heures moins cinq** five to six; **six heures cinq** five past *ou Am* after six; **à l'h.** (*arriver*) on time; (*être payé*) by the hour; **dix kilomètres à l'h.** ten kilometres an hour; **à l'h. qu'il est** (by) now; **de dernière h.** (*nouvelle*) last minute; **de bonne h.** early; **à une h. avancée** at a late hour, late at night; **tout à l'h.** (*futur*) in a few moments, later; (*passé*) a moment ago; **à toute h.** (*continuellement*) at all hours; **faire des heures supplémentaires** to work *ou* do overtime; **heures creuses** off-peak *ou* slack periods; **l'h. d'affluence, l'h. de pointe** (*circulation etc*) rush hour; (*dans les magasins*) peak period; **l'h. de pointe** (*électricité etc*) peak period.

heureux, -euse [œrø, -øz] *a* happy; (*chanceux*) lucky, fortunate; (*issue, changement*) successful; (*expression, choix*) apt; **h. de qch/de voir qn** (*satisfait*) happy *ou* pleased *ou* glad about sth/to see s.o.; – *adv* (*vivre, mourir*) happily. ◆**heureusement** *adv* (*par chance*) fortunately, luckily, happily (**pour** for); (*avec succès*) successfully; (*exprimer*) aptly.

heurt ['œr] *nm* bump, knock; (*d'opinions etc*) *Fig* clash; **sans heurts** smoothly. ◆**heurt/er** *vt* (*cogner*) to knock, bump, hit (**contre** against); (*mur, piéton*) to bump into, hit; **h. qn** (*choquer*) to offend s.o., upset s.o.; **se h. à** to bump into, hit; (*difficultés*) *Fig* to come up against. ◆**—é** *a* (*couleurs, tons*) clashing; (*style, rythme*) jerky. ◆**heurtoir** *nm* (door) knocker.

hexagone [ɛgzagɔn] *nm* hexagon; **l'H.** *Fig* France. ◆**hexagonal, -aux** *a* hexagonal; *Fig Fam* French.

hiatus [jatys] *nm Fig* hiatus, gap.

hiberner [iberne] *vi* to hibernate. ◆**hibernation** *nf* hibernation.

hibou, -x ['ibu] *nm* owl.

hic ['ik] *nm* **voilà le h.** *Fam* that's the snag.

hideux, -euse ['idø, -øz] *a* hideous.

hier [(i)jɛr] *adv & nm* yesterday; **h. soir** last *ou* yesterday night, yesterday evening; **elle n'est pas née d'h.** *Fig* she wasn't born yesterday.

hiérarchie ['jerarʃi] *nf* hierarchy. ◆**hiérarchique** *a* (*ordre*) hierarchical; **par la voie h.** through (the) official channels. ◆**hiérarchiser** *vt* (*emploi, valeurs*) to grade.

hi-fi ['ifi] *a inv & nf inv Fam* hi-fi.

hilare [ilar] *a* merry. ◆**hilarant** *a* (*drôle*) hilarious. ◆**hilarité** *nf* (sudden) laughter.
hindou, -oue [ɛ̃du] *a* & *nmf* Hindu.
hippie ['ipi] *nmf* hippie.
hippique [ipik] *a* **un concours h.** a horse show, a show-jumping event. ◆**hippodrome** *nm* racecourse, racetrack (*for horses*).
hippopotame [ipɔpɔtam] *nm* hippopotamus.
hirondelle [irɔ̃dɛl] *nf* (*oiseau*) swallow.
hirsute [irsyt] *a* (*personne, barbe*) unkempt, shaggy.
hispanique [ispanik] *a* Spanish, Hispanic.
hisser ['ise] *vt* (*voile, fardeau etc*) to hoist, raise; — **se h.** *vpr* to raise oneself (up).
histoire [istwar] *nf* (*science, événements*) history; (*récit, mensonge*) story; (*affaire*) *Fam* business, matter; *pl* (*ennuis*) trouble; (*façons, chichis*) fuss; **toute une h.** (*problème*) quite a lot of trouble; (*chichis*) quite a lot of fuss; **h. de voir/***etc* (so as) to see/*etc*; **h. de rire** for (the sake of) a laugh; **sans histoires** (*voyage etc*) uneventful. ◆**historien, -ienne** *nmf* historian. ◆**historique** *a* historical; (*lieu, événement*) historic; – *nm* **faire l'h. de** to give an historical account of.
hiver [ivɛr] *nm* winter. ◆**hivernal, -aux** *a* (*froid etc*) winter-.
HLM ['aʃɛlɛm] *nm ou f abrév* (*habitation à loyer modéré*) = council flats, *Am* = low-rent apartment building (*sponsored by government*).
hoch/er ['ɔʃe] *vt* **h. la tête** (*pour dire oui*) to nod one's head; (*pour dire non*) to shake one's head. ◆**—ement** *nm* **h. de tête** nod; shake of the head.
hochet ['ɔʃɛ] *nm* (*jouet*) rattle.
hockey ['ɔkɛ] *nm* hockey; **h. sur glace** ice hockey.
holà! ['ɔla] *int* (*arrêtez*) hold on!, stop!, (*pour appeler*) hallo!; – *nm inv* **mettre le h. à** to put a stop to.
hold-up ['ɔldœp] *nm inv* (*attaque*) holdup, stick-up.
Hollande ['ɔlɑ̃d] *nf* Holland. ◆**hollandais, -aise** *a* Dutch; – *nmf* Dutchman, Dutchwoman; – *nm* (*langue*) Dutch.
holocauste [ɔlɔkost] *nm* (*massacre*) holocaust.
homard ['ɔmar] *nm* lobster.
homélie [ɔmeli] *nf* homily.
homéopathie [ɔmeɔpati] *nf* hom(o)eopathy.
homicide [ɔmisid] *nm* murder, homicide; **h. involontaire** manslaughter.
hommage [ɔmaʒ] *nm* tribute, homage (**à** to); *pl* (*civilités*) respects; **rendre h. à** to pay (a) tribute to, pay homage to.
homme [ɔm] *nm* man; **l'h.** (*espèce*) man(kind); **des vêtements d'h.** men's clothes; **d'h. à h.** man to man; **l'h. de la rue** *Fig* the man in the street; **h. d'affaires** businessman. ◆**h.-grenouille** *nm* (*pl* **hommes-grenouilles**) frogman.
homogène [ɔmɔʒɛn] *a* homogeneous. ◆**homogénéité** *nf* homogeneity.
homologue [ɔmɔlɔg] *a* equivalent (**de** to); – *nmf* counterpart, opposite number.
homologuer [ɔmɔlɔge] *vt* to approve *ou* recognize officially, validate.
homonyme [ɔmɔnim] *nm* (*personne, lieu*) namesake.
homosexuel, -elle [ɔmɔsɛksɥɛl] *a* & *nmf* homosexual. ◆**homosexualité** *nf* homosexuality.
Hongrie ['ɔ̃gri] *nf* Hungary. ◆**hongrois, -oise** *a* & *nmf* Hungarian; – *nm* (*langue*) Hungarian.
honnête [ɔnɛt] *a* (*intègre*) honest; (*satisfaisant, passable*) decent, fair. ◆**honnêtement** *adv* honestly; decently. ◆**honnêteté** *nf* honesty.
honneur [ɔnœr] *nm* (*dignité, faveur*) honour; (*mérite*) credit; **en l'h. de** in honour of; **faire h. à** (*sa famille etc*) to be a credit to; (*par sa présence*) to do honour to; (*promesse etc*) to honour; (*repas*) to do justice to; **en h.** (*roman etc*) in vogue; **invité d'h.** guest of honour; **membre d'h.** honorary member; **avoir la place d'h.** to have pride of place *ou* the place of honour. ◆**honorabilité** *nf* respectability. ◆**honorable** *a* honourable; (*résultat, salaire etc*) *Fig* respectable. ◆**honoraire 1** *a* (*membre*) honorary. **2** *nmpl* (*d'avocat etc*) fees. ◆**honorer** *vt* to honour (**de** with); **h. qn** (*conduite etc*) to do credit to s.o.; **s'h. d'être** to pride oneself *ou* itself on being. ◆**honorifique** *a* (*titre*) honorary.
honte ['ɔ̃t] *nf* shame; **avoir h.** to be *ou* feel ashamed (**de qch/de faire** of sth/to do, of doing); **faire h. à** to put to shame; **fausse h.** self-consciousness. ◆**honteux, -euse** *a* (*déshonorant*) shameful; (*penaud*) ashamed, shamefaced; **être h. de** to be ashamed of. ◆**honteusement** *adv* shamefully.
hop! ['ɔp] *int* **allez, h.!** jump!, move!
hôpital, -aux [ɔpital, -o] *nm* hospital; **à l'h.** in hospital, *Am* in the hospital.
hoquet ['ɔkɛ] *nm* hiccup; **le h.** (the) hiccups. ◆**hoqueter** *vi* to hiccup.

horaire [ɔrɛr] *a* (*salaire etc*) hourly; (*vitesse*) per hour; – *nm* timetable, schedule.
horde ['ɔrd] *nf* (*troupe*) *Péj* horde.
horizon [ɔrizɔ̃] *nm* horizon; (*vue, paysage*) view; **à l'h.** on the horizon.
horizontal, -aux [ɔrizɔ̃tal, -o] *a* horizontal. ◆**—ement** *adv* horizontally.
horloge [ɔrlɔʒ] *nf* clock. ◆**horloger, -ère** *nmf* watchmaker. ◆**horlogerie** *nf* (*magasin*) watchmaker's (shop); (*industrie*) watchmaking.
hormis ['ɔrmi] *prép Litt* save, except (for).
hormone [ɔrmɔn] *nf* hormone. ◆**hormonal, -aux** *a* (*traitement etc*) hormone-.
horoscope [ɔrɔskɔp] *nm* horoscope.
horreur [ɔrœr] *nf* horror; *pl* (*propos*) horrible things; **faire h. à** to disgust; **avoir h. de** to hate, loathe. ◆**horrible** *a* horrible, awful. ◆**horriblement** *adv* horribly. ◆**horrifiant** *a* horrifying, horrific. ◆**horrifié** *a* horrified.
horripiler [ɔripile] *vt* to exasperate.
hors ['ɔr] *prép* **h. de** (*maison, boîte etc*) outside, out of; (*danger, haleine etc*) *Fig* out of; **h. de doute** beyond doubt; **h. de soi** (*furieux*) beside oneself; **être h. jeu** *Fb* to be offside. ◆**h.-bord** *nm inv* speedboat; **moteur h.-bord** outboard motor. ◆**h.-concours** *a inv* non-competing. ◆**h.-d'œuvre** *nm inv Culin* starter, hors-d'œuvre. ◆**h.-jeu** *nm inv Fb* offside. ◆**h.-la-loi** *nm inv* outlaw. ◆**h.-taxe** *a inv* (*magasin, objet*) duty-free.
hortensia [ɔrtɑ̃sja] *nm* (*arbrisseau*) hydrangea.
horticole [ɔrtikɔl] *a* horticultural. ◆**horticulteur, -trice** *nmf* horticulturalist. ◆**horticulture** *nf* horticulture.
hospice [ɔspis] *nm* (*pour vieillards*) geriatric hospital.
hospitalier, -ière [ɔspitalje, -jɛr] *a* **1** (*accueillant*) hospitable. **2** (*personnel etc*) *Méd* hospital-. ◆**hospitaliser** *vt* to hospitalize. ◆**hospitalité** *nf* hospitality.
hostie [ɔsti] *nf* (*pain*) *Rel* host.
hostile [ɔstil] *a* hostile (**à** to, towards). ◆**hostilité** *nf* hostility (**envers** to, towards); *pl Mil* hostilities.
hôte [ot] **1** *nm* (*maître*) host. **2** *nmf* (*invité*) guest. ◆**hôtesse** *nf* hostess; **h. (de l'air)** (air) hostess.
hôtel [otɛl] *nm* hotel; **h. particulier** mansion, town house; **h. de ville** town hall; **h. des ventes** auction rooms. ◆**hôtelier, -ière** *nmf* hotel-keeper, hotelier; – *a* (*industrie etc*) hotel-. ◆**hôtellerie** *nf* **1** (*auberge*) inn, hostelry. **2** (*métier*) hotel trade.
hotte ['ɔt] *nf* **1** (*panier*) basket (*carried on back*). **2** (*de cheminée etc*) hood.
houblon ['ublɔ̃] *nm* **le h.** *Bot* hops.
houille ['uj] *nf* coal; **h. blanche** hydroelectric power. ◆**houiller, -ère** *a* (*bassin, industrie*) coal-; – *nf* coalmine, colliery.
houle ['ul] *nf* (*de mer*) swell, surge. ◆**houleux, -euse** *a* (*mer*) rough; (*réunion etc*) *Fig* stormy.
houppette ['upɛt] *nf* powder puff.
hourra ['ura] *nm* & *int* hurray, hurrah.
houspiller ['uspije] *vt* to scold, upbraid.
housse ['us] *nf* (protective) cover.
houx ['u] *nm* holly.
hublot ['yblo] *nm Nau Av* porthole.
huche ['yʃ] *nf* **h. à pain** bread box *ou* chest.
hue! ['y] *int* gee up! (*to horse*).
huer ['ɥe] *vt* to boo. ◆**huées** *nfpl* boos.
huile [ɥil] *nf* **1** oil; **peinture à l'h.** oil painting. **2** (*personnage*) *Fam* big shot. ◆**huiler** *vt* to oil. ◆**huileux, -euse** *a* oily.
huis [ɥi] *nm* **à h. clos** *Jur* in camera.
huissier [ɥisje] *nm* (*introducteur*) usher; (*officier*) *Jur* bailiff.
huit ['ɥit] *a* (['ɥi] *before consonant*) eight; **h. jours** a week; – *nm* eight. ◆**huitaine** *nf* (about) eight; (*semaine*) week. ◆**huitième** *a* & *nmf* eighth; **un h.** an eighth.
huître [ɥitr] *nf* oyster.
hululer ['ylyle] *vi* (*hibou*) to hoot.
humain [ymɛ̃] *a* human; (*compatissant*) humane; – *nmpl* humans. ◆**humainement** *adv* (*possible etc*) humanly; (*avec humanité*) humanely. ◆**humaniser** *vt* (*prison, ville etc*) to humanize, make more humane. ◆**humanitaire** *a* humanitarian. ◆**humanité** *nf* (*genre humain, sentiment*) humanity.
humble [œbl] *a* humble. ◆**humblement** *adv* humbly.
humecter [ymɛkte] *vt* to moisten, damp(en).
humer ['yme] *vt* (*respirer*) to breathe in; (*sentir*) to smell.
humeur [ymœr] *nf* (*caprice*) mood, humour; (*caractère*) temperament; (*irritation*) bad temper; **bonne h.** (*gaieté*) good humour; **de bonne/mauvaise h.** in a good/bad mood *ou* humour; **égalité d'h.** evenness of temper.
humide [ymid] *a* damp, wet; (*saison, route*) wet; (*main, yeux*) moist; **climat/temps h.** (*chaud*) humid climate/weather; (*froid, pluvieux*) damp *ou* wet climate/weather. ◆**humidifier** *vt* to humidify. ◆**humidité** *nf* humidity; (*plutôt froide*) damp(ness); (*vapeur*) moisture.
humili/er [ymilje] *vt* to humiliate, humble.

◆—ant *a* humiliating. **◆humiliation** *nf* humiliation. **◆humilité** *nf* humility.
humour [ymur] *nm* humour; **avoir de l'h.** *ou* **beaucoup d'h.** *ou* **le sens de l'h.** to have a sense of humour. **◆humoriste** *nmf* humorist. **◆humoristique** *a* (*livre, ton etc*) humorous.
huppé ['ype] *a* (*riche*) *Fam* high-class, posh.
hurl/er ['yrle] *vi* (*loup, vent*) to howl; (*personne*) to scream, yell; – *vt* (*slogans, injures etc*) to scream. **◆—ement** *nm* howl; scream, yell.
hurluberlu [yrlyberly] *nm* (*personne*) scatterbrain.
hutte ['yt] *nf* hut.
hybride [ibrid] *a* & *nm* hybrid.
hydrater [idrate] *vt* (*peau*) to moisturize; **crème hydratante** moisturizing cream.
hydraulique [idrolik] *a* hydraulic.
hydravion [idravjɔ̃] *nm* seaplane.
hydro-électrique [idrɔelɛktrik] *a* hydroelectric.
hydrogène [idrɔʒɛn] *nm Ch* hydrogen.
hydrophile [idrɔfil] *a* **coton h.** cotton wool, *Am* (absorbent) cotton.
hyène [jɛn] *nf* (*animal*) hyena.
hygiaphone [iʒjafɔn] *nm* (hygienic) grill.
hygiène [iʒjɛn] *nf* hygiene. **◆hygiénique** *a* hygienic; (*promenade*) healthy; (*serviette, conditions*) sanitary; **papier h.** toilet paper.
hymne [imn] *nm Rel Littér* hymn; **h. national** national anthem.
hyper- [ipɛr] *préf* hyper-.
hypermarché [ipɛrmarʃe] *nm* hypermarket.
hypertension [ipɛrtɑ̃sjɔ̃] *nf* high blood pressure.
hypnose [ipnoz] *nf* hypnosis. **◆hypnotique** *a* hypnotic. **◆hypnotiser** *vt* to hypnotize. **◆hypnotiseur** *nm* hypnotist. **◆hypnotisme** *nm* hypnotism.
hypocrisie [ipɔkrizi] *nf* hypocrisy. **◆hypocrite** *a* hypocritical; – *nmf* hypocrite.
hypodermique [ipɔdɛrmik] *a* hypodermic.
hypothèque [ipɔtɛk] *nf* mortgage. **◆hypothéquer** (*maison, avenir*) to mortgage.
hypothèse [ipɔtɛz] *nf* assumption; (*en sciences*) hypothesis; **dans l'h. où . . .** supposing (that) . . . . **◆hypothétique** *a* hypothetical.
hystérie [isteri] *nf* hysteria. **◆hystérique** *a* hysterical.

I

I, i [i] *nm* I, i.
iceberg [isbɛrg] *nm* iceberg.
ici [isi] *adv* here; **par i.** (*passer*) this way; (*habiter*) around here, hereabouts; **jusqu'i.** (*temps*) up to now; (*lieu*) as far as this *ou* here; **d'i. à mardi** by Tuesday, between now and Tuesday; **d'i. à une semaine** within a week; **d'i. peu** before long; **i. Dupont** *Tél* this is Dupont, Dupont here; **je ne suis pas d'i.** I'm a stranger around here; **les gens d'i.** the people (from) around here, the locals. **◆i.-bas** *adv* on earth.
icône [ikon] *nf Rel* icon.
idéal, -aux [ideal, -o] *a* & *nm* ideal; **l'i.** (*valeurs spirituelles*) ideals; **c'est l'i.** *Fam* that's the ideal thing. **◆idéalement** *adv* ideally. **◆idéaliser** *vt* to idealize. **◆idéalisme** *nm* idealism. **◆idéaliste** *a* idealistic; – *nmf* idealist.
idée [ide] *nf* idea (**de** of, **que** that); **changer d'i.** to change one's mind; **il m'est venu à l'i. que** it occurred to me that; **se faire une i. de** (*rêve*) to imagine; (*concept*) to get *ou* have an idea of; **avoir dans l'i. de faire** to have it in mind to do; **i. fixe** obsession.
idem [idɛm] *adv* ditto.
identifier [idɑ̃tifje] *vt* to identify (**à, avec** with). **◆identification** *nf* identification. **◆identique** *a* identical (**à** to, with). **◆identité** *nf* identity; **carte d'i** identity card.
idéologie [ideɔlɔʒi] *nf* ideology. **◆idéologique** *a* ideological.
idiome [idjom] *nm* (*langue*) idiom. **◆idiomatique** *a* idiomatic.
idiot, -ote [idjo, -ɔt] *a* idiotic, silly; – *nmf* idiot. **◆idiotement** *adv* idiotically. **◆idiotie** [-ɔsi] *nf* (*état*) idiocy; **une i.** an idiotic *ou* silly thing.
idole [idɔl] *nm* idol. **◆idolâtrer** *vt* to idolize.
idylle [idil] *nf* (*amourette*) romance.
idyllique [idilik] *a* (*merveilleux*) idyllic.
if [if] *nm* yew (tree).
igloo [iglu] *nm* igloo.
ignare [iɲar] *a Péj* ignorant; – *nmf* ignoramus.

ignifugé [iɲifyʒe] *a* fireproof(ed).
ignoble [iɲɔbl] *a* vile, revolting.
ignorant [iɲɔrɑ̃] *a* ignorant (**de** of). ◆**ignorance** *nf* ignorance. ◆**ignor/er** *vt* not to know, be ignorant of; **j'ignore si** I don't know if; **i. qn** (*être indifférent à*) to ignore s.o., cold-shoulder s.o. ◆**—é** *a* (*inconnu*) unknown.
il [il] *pron* (*personne*) he; (*chose, animal*) it; **il est** he is; it is; **il pleut** it's raining; **il est vrai que** it's true that; **il y a** there is; *pl* there are; **il y a six ans** (*temps écoulé*) six years ago; **il y a une heure qu'il travaille** (*durée*) he's been working for an hour; **qu'est-ce qu'il y a?** what's the matter?, what's wrong?; **il n'y a pas de quoi!** don't mention it!; **il doit/peut y avoir** there must/may be.
île [il] *nf* island; **les îles Britanniques** the British Isles.
illégal, -aux [ilegal, -o] *a* illegal. ◆**illégalité** *nf* illegality.
illégitime [ileʒitim] *a* (*enfant, revendication*) illegitimate; (*non fondé*) unfounded.
illettré, -ée [iletre] *a* & *nmf* illiterate.
illicite [ilisit] *a* unlawful, illicit.
illico [iliko] *adv* **i. (presto)** *Fam* straightaway.
illimité [ilimite] *a* unlimited.
illisible [ilizibl] *a* (*écriture*) illegible; (*livre*) unreadable.
illogique [ilɔʒik] *a* illogical.
illumin/er [ilymine] *vt* to light up, illuminate; **— s'i.** *vpr* (*visage, personne, ciel*) to light up. ◆**—é** *a* (*monument*) floodlit, lit up. ◆**illumination** *nf* (*action, lumière*) illumination.
illusion [ilyzjɔ̃] *nf* illusion (**sur** about); **se faire des illusions** to delude oneself. ◆**s'illusionner** *vpr* to delude oneself (**sur** about). ◆**illusionniste** *nmf* conjurer. ◆**illusoire** *a* illusory, illusive.
illustre [ilystr] *a* famous, illustrious.
illustr/er [ilystre] *vt* (*d'images, par des exemples*) to illustrate (**de** with); **— s'i.** *vpr* to become famous. ◆**—é** *a* (*livre, magazine*) illustrated; – *nm* (*périodique*) comic. ◆**illustration** *nf* illustration.
îlot [ilo] *nm* **1** (*île*) small island. **2** (*maisons*) block.
ils [il] *pron* they; **ils sont** they are.
image [imaʒ] *nf* picture; (*ressemblance, symbole*) image; (*dans une glace*) reflection; **i. de marque** (*de firme etc*) (public) image. ◆**imagé** *a* (*style*) colourful, full of imagery.
imagination [imaʒinɑsjɔ̃] *nf* imagination; *pl* (*chimères*) imaginings.
imaginer [imaʒine] *vt* (*envisager, supposer*) to imagine; (*inventer*) to devise; **— s'i.** *vpr* (*se figurer*) to imagine (**que** that); (*se voir*) to imagine oneself. ◆**imaginable** *a* imaginable. ◆**imaginaire** *a* imaginary. ◆**imaginatif, -ive** *a* imaginative.
imbattable [ɛ̃batabl] *a* unbeatable.
imbécile [ɛ̃besil] *a* idiotic; – *nmf* imbecile, idiot. ◆**imbécillité** *nf* (*état*) imbecility; **une i.** (*action, parole*) an idiotic thing.
imbiber [ɛ̃bibe] *vt* to soak (**de** with, in); **— s'i.** *vpr* to become soaked.
imbriquer (s') [sɛ̃brike] *vpr* (*questions etc*) to overlap, be bound up with each other.
imbroglio [ɛ̃brɔljo] *nm* muddle, foul-up.
imbu [ɛ̃by] *a* **i. de** imbued with.
imbuvable [ɛ̃byvabl] *a* undrinkable; (*personne*) *Fig* insufferable.
imiter [imite] *vt* to imitate; (*contrefaire*) to forge; **i. qn** (*pour rire*) to mimic s.o., take s.o. off; (*faire comme*) to do the same as s.o., follow suit. ◆**imitateur, -trice** *nmf* imitator; (*artiste*) *Th* impersonator, mimic. ◆**imitatif, -ive** *a* imitative. ◆**imitation** *nf* imitation.
immaculé [imakyle] *a* (*sans tache, sans péché*) immaculate.
immangeable [ɛ̃mɑ̃ʒabl] *a* inedible.
immanquable [ɛ̃mɑ̃kabl] *a* inevitable.
immatriculer [imatrikyle] *vt* to register; **se faire i.** to register. ◆**immatriculation** *nf* registration.
immédiat [imedja] *a* immediate; – *nm* **dans l'i.** for the time being. ◆**immédiatement** *adv* immediately.
immense [imɑ̃s] *a* immense, vast. ◆**immensément** *adv* immensely. ◆**immensité** *nf* immensity, vastness.
immerger [imɛrʒe] *vt* to immerse, put under water; **— s'i.** *vpr* (*sous-marin*) to submerge. ◆**immersion** *nf* immersion; submersion.
immettable [ɛ̃metabl] *a* (*vêtement*) unfit to be worn.
immeuble [imœbl] *nm* building; (*d'habitation*) block of flats, *Am* apartment building; (*de bureaux*) office block.
immigr/er [imigre] *vi* to immigrate. ◆**—ant, -ante** *nmf* immigrant. ◆**—é, -ée** *a* & *nmf* immigrant. ◆**immigration** *nf* immigration.
imminent [iminɑ̃] *a* imminent. ◆**imminence** *nf* imminence.
immiscer (s') [simise] *vpr* to interfere (**dans** in).
immobile [imɔbil] *a* still, motionless. ◆**immobiliser** *vt* to immobilize; (*arrêter*) to

stop; — **s'i.** *vpr* to stop, come to a standstill. ◆**immobilité** *nf* stillness; (*inactivité*) immobility.

immobilier, -ière [imɔbilje, -jɛr] *a* (*vente*) property-; (*société*) construction-; **agent i.** estate agent, *Am* real estate agent.

immodéré [imɔdere] *a* immoderate.

immonde [imɔ̃d] *a* filthy. ◆**immondices** *nfpl* refuse, rubbish.

immoral, -aux [imɔral, -o] *a* immoral. ◆**immoralité** *nf* immorality.

immortel, -elle [imɔrtɛl] *a* immortal. ◆**immortaliser** *vt* to immortalize. ◆**immortalité** *nf* immortality.

immuable [imɥabl] *a* immutable, unchanging.

immuniser [imynize] *vt* to immunize (**contre** against); **immunisé contre** (*à l'abri de*) *Méd & Fig* immune to *ou* from. ◆**immunitaire** *a* (*déficience etc*) *Méd* immune. ◆**immunité** *nf* immunity.

impact [ɛ̃pakt] *nm* impact (**sur** on).

impair [ɛ̃pɛr] **1** *a* (*nombre*) odd, uneven. **2** *nm* (*gaffe*) blunder.

imparable [ɛ̃parabl] *a* (*coup etc*) unavoidable.

impardonnable [ɛ̃pardɔnabl] *a* unforgivable.

imparfait [ɛ̃parfɛ] **1** *a* (*connaissance etc*) imperfect. **2** *nm* (*temps*) *Gram* imperfect.

impartial, -aux [ɛ̃parsjal, -o] *a* impartial, unbiased. ◆**impartialité** *nf* impartiality.

impartir [ɛ̃partir] *vt* to grant (**à** to).

impasse [ɛ̃pɑs] *nf* (*rue*) dead end, blind alley; (*situation*) *Fig* impasse; **dans l'i.** (*négociations*) in deadlock.

impassible [ɛ̃pasibl] *a* impassive, unmoved. ◆**impassibilité** *nf* impassiveness.

impatient [ɛ̃pasjɑ̃] *a* impatient; **i. de faire** eager *ou* impatient to do. ◆**impatiemment** [-amɑ̃] *adv* impatiently. ◆**impatience** *nf* impatience. ◆**impatienter** *vt* to annoy, make impatient; — **s'i.** *vpr* to get impatient.

impayable [ɛ̃pɛjabl] *a* (*comique*) *Fam* hilarious, priceless.

impayé [ɛ̃peje] *a* unpaid.

impeccable [ɛ̃pekabl] *a* impeccable, immaculate. ◆**—ment** [-əmɑ̃] *adv* impeccably, immaculately.

impénétrable [ɛ̃penetrabl] *a* (*forêt, mystère etc*) impenetrable.

impénitent [ɛ̃penitɑ̃] *a* unrepentant.

impensable [ɛ̃pɑ̃sabl] *a* unthinkable.

imper [ɛ̃pɛr] *nm Fam* raincoat, mac.

impératif, -ive [ɛ̃peratif, -iv] *a* (*consigne, ton*) imperative; — *nm* (*mode*) *Gram* imperative.

impératrice [ɛ̃peratris] *nf* empress.

imperceptible [ɛ̃pɛrsɛptibl] *a* imperceptible (**à** to).

imperfection [ɛ̃pɛrfɛksjɔ̃] *nf* imperfection.

impérial, -aux [ɛ̃perjal, -o] *a* imperial. ◆**impérialisme** *nm* imperialism.

impériale [ɛ̃perjal] *nf* (*d'autobus*) top deck.

impérieux, -euse [ɛ̃perjø, -øz] *a* (*autoritaire*) imperious; (*besoin*) pressing, imperative.

imperméable [ɛ̃pɛrmeabl] **1** *a* impervious (**à** to); (*manteau, tissu*) waterproof. **2** *nm* raincoat, mackintosh. ◆**imperméabilisé** *a* waterproof.

impersonnel, -elle [ɛ̃pɛrsɔnɛl] *a* impersonal.

impertinent [ɛ̃pɛrtinɑ̃] *a* impertinent (**envers** to). ◆**impertinence** *nf* impertinence.

imperturbable [ɛ̃pɛrtyrbabl] *a* unruffled, imperturbable.

impétueux, -euse [ɛ̃petɥø, -øz] *a* impetuous. ◆**impétuosité** *nf* impetuosity.

impitoyable [ɛ̃pitwajabl] *a* ruthless, pitiless, merciless.

implacable [ɛ̃plakabl] *a* implacable, relentless.

implanter [ɛ̃plɑ̃te] *vt* (*industrie, mode etc*) to establish; — **s'i.** *vpr* to become established. ◆**implantation** *nf* establishment.

implicite [ɛ̃plisit] *a* implicit. ◆**—ment** *adv* implicitly.

impliquer [ɛ̃plike] *vt* (*entraîner*) to imply; **i. que** (*supposer*) to imply that; **i. qn** (*engager*) to implicate s.o. (**dans** in). ◆**implication** *nf* (*conséquence, participation*) implication.

implorer [ɛ̃plɔre] *vt* to implore (**qn de faire** s.o. to do).

impoli [ɛ̃pɔli] *a* impolite, rude. ◆**impolitesse** *nf* impoliteness, rudeness; **une i.** an act of rudeness.

impopulaire [ɛ̃pɔpylɛr] *a* unpopular.

important [ɛ̃pɔrtɑ̃] *a* (*personnage, événement etc*) important; (*quantité, somme etc*) considerable, big, great; — *nm* **l'i., c'est de ...** the important thing is to.... ◆**importance** *nf* importance, significance; (*taille*) size; (*de dégâts*) extent; **ça n'a pas d'i.** it doesn't matter.

importer [ɛ̃pɔrte] **1** *v imp* to matter, be important (**à** to); **il importe de faire** it's important to do; **peu importe, n'importe** it doesn't matter; **n'importe qui/quoi/où/quand/comment** anyone/anything/anywhere/any time/anyhow. **2** *vt* (*marchandises etc*) to import (**de** from). ◆**im-**

portateur, -trice *nmf* importer; – *a* importing. ◆**importation** *nf* (*objet*) import; (*action*) import(ing), importation; **d'i.** (*article*) imported.

importun, -une [ɛ̃pɔrtœ̃, -yn] *a* troublesome, intrusive; – *nmf* nuisance, intruder. ◆**importuner** *vt* to inconvenience, trouble.

impos/er [ɛ̃poze] **1** *vt* to impose, enforce (**à** on); (*exiger*) to demand; (*respect*) to command; – *vi* **en i. à qn** to impress s.o., command respect from s.o.; – **s'i.** *vpr* (*chez qn*) *Péj* to impose; (*s'affirmer*) to assert oneself, compel recognition; (*aller de soi*) to stand out; (*être nécessaire*) to be essential. **2** *vt* *Fin* to tax. ◆**—ant** *a* imposing. ◆**—able** *a* *Fin* taxable. ◆**imposition** *nf Fin* taxation.

impossible [ɛ̃pɔsibl] *a* impossible (**à faire** to do); **il (nous) est i. de faire** it is impossible (for us) to do; **il est i. que** (+ *sub*) it is impossible that; **ça m'est i.** I cannot possibly; – *nm* **faire l'i.** to do the impossible. ◆**impossibilité** *nf* impossibility.

imposteur [ɛ̃pɔstœr] *nm* impostor. ◆**imposture** *nf* deception.

impôt [ɛ̃po] *nm* tax; *pl* (*contributions*) (income) tax, taxes; **i. sur le revenu** income tax.

impotent, -ente [ɛ̃pɔtɑ̃, -ɑ̃t] *a* crippled, disabled; – *nmf* cripple, invalid.

impraticable [ɛ̃pratikabl] *a* (*projet etc*) impracticable; (*chemin etc*) impassable.

imprécis [ɛ̃presi] *a* imprecise. ◆**imprécision** *nf* lack of precision.

imprégner [ɛ̃preɲe] *vt* to saturate, impregnate (**de** with); – **s'i.** *vpr* to become saturated *ou* impregnated (**de** with); **imprégné de** (*idées*) imbued *ou* infused with. ◆**imprégnation** *nf* saturation.

imprenable [ɛ̃prənabl] *a Mil* impregnable.

impresario [ɛ̃presarjo] *nm* (business) manager, impresario.

impression [ɛ̃presjɔ̃] *nf* **1** impression; **avoir l'i. que** to have the feeling *ou* impression that, be under the impression that; **faire une bonne i. à qn** to make a good impression on s.o. **2** *Typ* printing.

impressionn/er [ɛ̃presjɔne] *vt* (*influencer*) to impress; (*émouvoir, troubler*) to make a strong impression on. ◆**—ant** *a* impressive. ◆**—able** *a* impressionable.

imprévisible [ɛ̃previzibl] *a* unforeseeable. ◆**imprévoyance** *nf* lack of foresight. ◆**imprévoyant** *a* shortsighted. ◆**imprévu** *a* unexpected, unforeseen; – *nm* **en cas d'i.** in case of anything unexpected.

imprim/er [ɛ̃prime] *vt* **1** (*livre etc*) to print; (*trace*) to impress (**dans** in); (*cachet*) to stamp. **2** (*communiquer*) *Tech* to impart (**à** to). ◆**—ante** *nf* (*d'ordinateur*) printer. ◆**—é** *nm* (*formulaire*) printed form; – *nm(pl)* (*par la poste*) printed matter. ◆**imprimerie** *nf* (*technique*) printing; (*lieu*) printing works. ◆**imprimeur** *nm* printer.

improbable [ɛ̃prɔbabl] *a* improbable, unlikely. ◆**improbabilité** *nf* improbability, unlikelihood.

impromptu [ɛ̃prɔ̃pty] *a* & *adv* impromptu.

impropre [ɛ̃prɔpr] *a* inappropriate; **i. à qch** unfit for sth. ◆**impropriété** *nf* (*incorrection*) *Ling* impropriety.

improviser [ɛ̃prɔvise] *vti* to improvise. ◆**improvisation** *nf* improvisation.

improviste (à l') [alɛ̃prɔvist] *adv* unexpectedly; **une visite à l'i.** an unexpected visit; **prendre qn à l'i.** to catch s.o. unawares.

imprudent [ɛ̃prydɑ̃] *a* (*personne, action*) careless, rash; **il est i. de** it is unwise to. ◆**imprudemment** [-amɑ̃] *adv* carelessly. ◆**imprudence** *nf* carelessness; **une i.** an act of carelessness.

impudent [ɛ̃pydɑ̃] *a* impudent ◆**impudence** *nf* impudence.

impudique [ɛ̃pydik] *a* lewd.

impuissant [ɛ̃pɥisɑ̃] *a* helpless; *Méd* impotent; **i. à faire** powerless to do. ◆**impuissance** *nf* helplessness; *Méd* impotence.

impulsif, -ive [ɛ̃pylsif, -iv] *a* impulsive. ◆**impulsion** *nf* impulse; **donner une i. à** (*élan*) *Fig* to give an impetus *ou* impulse to.

impunément [ɛ̃pynemɑ̃] *adv* with impunity. ◆**impuni** *a* unpunished.

impur [ɛ̃pyr] *a* impure. ◆**impureté** *nf* impurity.

imputer [ɛ̃pyte] *vt* to attribute, impute (**à** to); (*affecter*) *Fin* to charge (**à** to). ◆**imputable** *a* attributable (**à** to). ◆**imputation** *nf Jur* accusation.

inabordable [inabɔrdabl] *a* (*lieu*) inaccessible; (*personne*) unapproachable; (*prix*) prohibitive.

inacceptable [inakseptabl] *a* unacceptable.

inaccessible [inaksesibl] *a* inaccessible.

inaccoutumé [inakutyme] *a* unusual, unaccustomed.

inachevé [inaʃve] *a* unfinished.

inactif, -ive [inaktif, -iv] *a* inactive. ◆**inaction** *nf* inactivity, inaction. ◆**inactivité** *nf* inactivity.

inadapté, -ée [inadapte] *a* & *nmf* maladjusted (person). ◆**inadaptation** *nf* maladjustment.

inadmissible [inadmisibl] *a* unacceptable, inadmissible.
inadvertance (par) [parinadvertɑ̃s] *adv* inadvertently.
inaltérable [inalterabl] *a* (*couleur*) fast; (*sentiment*) unchanging.
inamical, -aux [inamikal, -o] *a* unfriendly.
inanimé [inanime] *a* (*mort*) lifeless; (*évanoui*) unconscious; (*matière*) inanimate.
inanité [inanite] *nf* (*vanité*) futility.
inanition [inanisjɔ̃] *nf* **mourir d'i.** to die of starvation.
inaperçu [inapersy] *a* **passer i.** to go unnoticed.
inapplicable [inaplikabl] *a* inapplicable (**à** to).
inappliqué [inaplike] *a* (*élève etc*) inattentive.
inappréciable [inapresjabl] *a* invaluable.
inapte [inapt] *a* unsuited (**à qch** to sth), inept (**à qch** at sth); *Mil* unfit ◆**inaptitude** *nf* ineptitude, incapacity.
inarticulé [inartikyle] *a* (*son*) inarticulate.
inattaquable [inatakabl] *a* unassailable.
inattendu [inatɑ̃dy] *a* unexpected.
inattentif, -ive [inatɑ̃tif, -iv] *a* inattentive, careless; **i. à** (*soucis, danger etc*) heedless of. ◆**inattention** *nf* lack of attention; **dans un moment d'i.** in a moment of distraction.
inaudible [inodibl] *a* inaudible.
inaugurer [inogyre] *vt* (*politique, édifice*) to inaugurate; (*école, congrès*) to open, inaugurate; (*statue*) to unveil. ◆**inaugural, -aux** *a* inaugural. ◆**inauguration** *nf* inauguration; opening; unveiling.
inauthentique [inotɑ̃tik] *a* not authentic.
inavouable [inavwabl] *a* shameful.
incalculable [ɛ̃kalkylabl] *a* incalculable.
incandescent [ɛ̃kɑ̃desɑ̃] *a* incandescent.
incapable [ɛ̃kapabl] *a* incapable; **i. de faire** unable to do, incapable of doing; – *nmf* (*personne*) incompetent. ◆**incapacité** *nf* incapacity, inability (**de faire** to do); *Méd* disability, incapacity.
incarcérer [ɛ̃karsere] *vt* to incarcerate. ◆**incarcération** *nf* incarceration.
incarné [ɛ̃karne] *a* (*ongle*) ingrown.
incarner [ɛ̃karne] *vt* to embody, incarnate. ◆**incarnation** *nf* embodiment, incarnation.
incartade [ɛ̃kartad] *nf* indiscretion, prank.
incassable [ɛ̃kɑsabl] *a* unbreakable.
incendie [ɛ̃sɑ̃di] *nm* fire; (*guerre*) *Fig* conflagration. ◆**incendiaire** *nmf* arsonist; – *a* (*bombe*) incendiary; (*discours*) inflammatory. ◆**incendier** *vt* to set fire to, set on fire.
incertain [ɛ̃sertɛ̃] *a* uncertain; (*temps*) unsettled; (*entreprise*) chancy; (*contour*) indistinct. ◆**incertitude** *nf* uncertainty.
incessamment [ɛ̃sesamɑ̃] *adv* without delay, shortly.
incessant [ɛ̃sesɑ̃] *a* incessant.
inceste [ɛ̃sest] *nm* incest. ◆**incestueux, -euse** *a* incestuous.
inchangé [ɛ̃ʃɑ̃ʒe] *a* unchanged.
incidence [ɛ̃sidɑ̃s] *nf* (*influence*) effect.
incident [ɛ̃sidɑ̃] *nm* incident; (*accroc*) hitch.
incinérer [ɛ̃sinere] *vt* (*ordures*) to incinerate; (*cadavre*) to cremate. ◆**incinération** *nf* incineration; cremation.
inciser [ɛ̃size] *vt* to make an incision in. ◆**incision** *nf* (*entaille*) incision.
incisif, -ive[1] [ɛ̃sizif, -iv] *a* incisive, sharp.
incisive[2] [ɛ̃siziv] *nf* (*dent*) incisor.
inciter [ɛ̃site] *vt* to urge, incite (**à faire** to do). ◆**incitation** *nf* incitement (**à** to).
incliner [ɛ̃kline] *vt* (*courber*) to bend; (*pencher*) to tilt, incline; **i. la tête** (*approuver*) to nod one's head; (*révérence*) to bow (one's head); **i. qn à faire** to make s.o. inclined to do, incline s.o. to do; – *vi* **i. à** to be inclined towards; **– s'i.** *vpr* (*se courber*) to bow (down); (*s'avouer vaincu*) to admit defeat; (*chemin*) to slope down. ◆**inclinaison** *nf* incline, slope. ◆**inclination** *nf* (*goût*) inclination; (*de tête*) nod, (*révérence*) bow.
incl/ure* [ɛ̃klyr] *vt* to include; (*enfermer*) to enclose. ◆**—us** *a* inclusive; **du quatre jusqu'au dix mai i.** from the fourth to the tenth of May inclusive; **jusqu'à lundi i.** up to and including (next) Monday. ◆**inclusion** *nf* inclusion. ◆**inclusivement** *adv* inclusively.
incognito [ɛ̃kɔɲito] *adv* incognito.
incohérent [ɛ̃kɔerɑ̃] *a* incoherent. ◆**incohérence** *nf* incoherence.
incollable [ɛ̃kɔlabl] *a Fam* infallible, unable to be caught out.
incolore [ɛ̃kɔlɔr] *a* colourless; (*verre, vernis*) clear.
incomber [ɛ̃kɔ̃be] *vi* **i. à qn** (*devoir*) to fall to s.o.; **il lui incombe de faire** it's his *ou* her duty *ou* responsiblity to do.
incommode [ɛ̃kɔmɔd] *a* awkward. ◆**incommodité** *nf* awkwardness.
incommod/er [ɛ̃kɔmɔde] *vt* to bother, annoy. ◆**—ant** *a* annoying.
incomparable [ɛ̃kɔ̃parabl] *a* incomparable.
incompatible [ɛ̃kɔ̃patibl] *a* incompatible, inconsistent (**avec** with). ◆**incompatibilité** *nf* incompatibility, inconsistency.

incompétent [ɛ̃kɔ̃petɑ̃] *a* incompetent. ◆**incompétence** *nf* incompetence.
incomplet, -ète [ɛ̃kɔ̃plɛ, -ɛt] *a* incomplete; (*fragmentaire*) scrappy, sketchy.
incompréhensible [ɛ̃kɔ̃preɑ̃sibl] *a* incomprehensible. ◆**incompréhensif, -ive** *a* uncomprehending, lacking understanding. ◆**incompréhension** *nf* lack of understanding. ◆**incompris** *a* misunderstood.
inconcevable [ɛ̃kɔ̃svabl] *a* inconceivable.
inconciliable [ɛ̃kɔ̃siljabl] *a* irreconcilable.
inconditionnel, -elle [ɛ̃kɔ̃disjɔnɛl] *a* unconditional.
inconfort [ɛ̃kɔ̃fɔr] *nm* lack of comfort. ◆**inconfortable** *a* uncomfortable.
incongru [ɛ̃kɔ̃gry] *a* unseemly, incongruous.
inconnu, -ue [ɛ̃kɔny] *a* unknown (**à** to); – *nmf* (*étranger*) stranger; (*auteur*) unknown; – *nm* **l'i.** the unknown; – *nf Math* unknown (quantity).
inconscient [ɛ̃kɔ̃sjɑ̃] *a* unconscious (**de** of); (*irréfléchi*) thoughtless, senseless; – *nm* **l'i.** *Psy* the unconscious. ◆**inconsciemment** [-amɑ̃] *adv* unconsciously. ◆**inconscience** *nf* (*physique*) unconsciousness; (*irréflexion*) utter thoughtlessness.
inconséquence [ɛ̃kɔ̃sekɑ̃s] *nf* inconsistency.
inconsidéré [ɛ̃kɔ̃sidere] *a* thoughtless.
inconsolable [ɛ̃kɔ̃sɔlabl] *a* inconsolable.
inconstant [ɛ̃kɔ̃stɑ̃] *a* fickle. ◆**inconstance** *nf* fickleness.
incontestable [ɛ̃kɔ̃tɛstabl] *a* undeniable, indisputable. ◆**incontesté** *a* undisputed.
incontinent [ɛ̃kɔ̃tinɑ̃] *a* incontinent.
incontrôlé [ɛ̃kɔ̃trole] *a* unchecked. ◆**incontrôlable** *a* unverifiable.
inconvenant [ɛ̃kɔ̃vnɑ̃] *a* improper. ◆**inconvenance** *nf* impropriety.
inconvénient [ɛ̃kɔ̃venjɑ̃] *nm* (*désavantage*) drawback; (*risque*) risk; (*objection*) objection.
incorporer [ɛ̃kɔrpɔre] *vt* (*introduire, admettre*) to incorporate (**dans** into); (*ingrédient*) to blend (**à** with); *Mil* to enrol. ◆**incorporation** *nf* incorporation (**de** of); *Mil* enrolment.
incorrect [ɛ̃kɔrɛkt] *a* (*inexact*) incorrect; (*inconvenant*) improper; (*grossier*) impolite. ◆**incorrection** *nf* (*faute*) impropriety, error; (*inconvenance*) impropriety; **une i.** (*grossièreté*) an impolite word *ou* act.
incorrigible [ɛ̃kɔriʒibl] *a* incorrigible.
incorruptible [ɛ̃kɔryptibl] *a* incorruptible.
incrédule [ɛ̃kredyl] *a* incredulous. ◆**incrédulité** *nf* disbelief, incredulity.
increvable [ɛ̃krəvabl] *a* (*robuste*) *Fam* tireless.
incriminer [ɛ̃krimine] *vt* to incriminate.
incroyable [ɛ̃krwajabl] *a* incredible, unbelievable. ◆**incroyablement** *adv* incredibly. ◆**incroyant, -ante** *a* unbelieving; – *nmf* unbeliever.
incrusté [ɛ̃kryste] *a* (*de tartre*) encrusted; **i. de** (*orné*) inlaid with. ◆**incrustation** *nf* (*ornement*) inlay; (*action*) inlaying.
incruster (s') [sɛ̃kryste] *vpr* (*chez qn*) *Fig* to dig oneself in, be difficult to get rid of.
incubation [ɛ̃kybɑsjɔ̃] *nf* incubation.
inculp/er [ɛ̃kylpe] *vt Jur* to charge (**de** with), indict (**de** for). ◆**–é, -ée** *nmf* **l'i.** the accused. ◆**inculpation** *nf* charge, indictment.
inculquer [ɛ̃kylke] *vt* to instil (**à** into).
inculte [ɛ̃kylt] *a* (*terre*) uncultivated; (*personne*) uneducated.
incurable [ɛ̃kyrabl] *a* incurable.
incursion [ɛ̃kyrsjɔ̃] *nf* incursion, inroad (**dans** into).
incurver [ɛ̃kyrve] *vt* to curve.
Inde [ɛ̃d] *nf* India.
indécent [ɛ̃desɑ̃] *a* indecent. ◆**indécemment** [-amɑ̃] *adv* indecently. ◆**indécence** *nf* indecency.
indéchiffrable [ɛ̃deʃifrabl] *a* undecipherable.
indécis [ɛ̃desi] *a* (*victoire, résultat*) undecided; (*indistinct*) vague; **être i.** (*hésiter*) to be undecided; (*de tempérament*) to be indecisive *ou* irresolute. ◆**indécision** *nf* indecisiveness, indecision.
indéfectible [ɛ̃defɛktibl] *a* unfailing.
indéfendable [ɛ̃defɑ̃dabl] *a* indefensible.
indéfini [ɛ̃defini] *a* (*indéterminé*) indefinite; (*imprécis*) undefined. ◆**indéfiniment** *adv* indefinitely. ◆**indéfinissable** *a* indefinable.
indéformable [ɛ̃defɔrmabl] *a* (*vêtement*) which keeps its shape.
indélébile [ɛ̃delebil] *a* (*encre, souvenir*) indelible.
indélicat [ɛ̃delika] *a* (*grossier*) indelicate; (*malhonnête*) unscrupulous.
indemne [ɛ̃dɛmn] *a* unhurt, unscathed.
indemniser [ɛ̃dɛmnize] *vt* to indemnify, compensate (**de** for). ◆**indemnisation** *nf* compensation. ◆**indemnité** *nf* (*dédommagement*) indemnity; (*allocation*) allowance.
indémontable [ɛ̃demɔ̃tabl] *a* that cannot be taken apart.
indéniable [ɛ̃denjabl] *a* undeniable.
indépendant [ɛ̃depɑ̃dɑ̃] *a* independent (**de**

of); (*chambre*) self-contained; (*journaliste*) freelance. ◆**indépendamment** *adv* independently (**de** of); **i. de** (*sans aucun égard à*) apart from. ◆**indépendance** *nf* independence.

indescriptible [ɛ̃deskriptibl] *a* indescribable.

indésirable [ɛ̃dezirabl] *a* & *nmf* undesirable.

indestructible [ɛ̃destryktibl] *a* indestructible.

indéterminé [ɛ̃determine] *a* indeterminate. ◆**indétermination** *nf* (*doute*) indecision.

index [ɛ̃dɛks] *nm* (*liste*) index; *Anat* forefinger, index finger.

indexer [ɛ̃dɛkse] *vt* *Écon* to index-link, tie (**sur** to).

indicateur, -trice [ɛ̃dikatœr, -tris] **1** *nmf* (*espion*) (police) informer. **2** *nm Rail* guide, timetable; *Tech* indicator, gauge. **3** *a* **poteau i.** signpost. ◆**indicatif, -ive 1** *a* indicative (**de** of); – *nm Mus* signature tune; *Tél* dialling code, *Am* area code. **2** *nm* (*mode*) *Gram* indicative. ◆**indication** *nf* indication (**de** of); (*renseignement*) (piece of) information; (*directive*) instruction.

indice [ɛ̃dis] *nm* (*indication*) sign; (*dans une enquête*) *Jur* clue; (*des prix*) index; (*de salaire*) grade; **i. d'écoute** *TV Rad* rating.

indien, -ienne [ɛ̃djɛ̃, -jɛn] *a* & *nmf* Indian.

indifférent [ɛ̃diferɑ̃] *a* indifferent (**à** to); **ça m'est i.** that's all the same to me. ◆**indifféremment** [-amɑ̃] *adv* indifferently. ◆**indifférence** *nf* indifference (**à** to).

indigène [ɛ̃diʒɛn] *a* & *nmf* native.

indigent [ɛ̃diʒɑ̃] *a* (very) poor. ◆**indigence** *nf* poverty.

indigeste [ɛ̃diʒɛst] *a* indigestible. ◆**indigestion** *nf* (attack of) indigestion.

indigne [ɛ̃diɲ] *a* (*personne*) unworthy; (*chose*) shameful; **i. de qn/qch** unworthy of s.o./sth. ◆**indignité** *nf* unworthiness; **une i.** (*honte*) an indignity.

indigner [ɛ̃diɲe] *vt* **i. qn** to make s.o. indignant; – **s'i.** *vpr* to be *ou* become indignant (**de** at). ◆**indignation** *nf* indignation.

indigo [ɛ̃digo] *nm* & *a inv* (*couleur*) indigo.

indiqu/er [ɛ̃dike] *vt* (*montrer*) to show, indicate; (*dire*) to point out, tell; (*recommander*) to recommend; **i. du doigt** to point to *ou* at. ◆**–é** *a* (*heure*) appointed; (*conseillé*) recommended; (*adéquat*) appropriate.

indirect [ɛ̃dirɛkt] *a* indirect. ◆**–ement** *adv* indirectly.

indiscipline [ɛ̃disiplin] *nf* lack of discipline. ◆**indiscipliné** *a* unruly.

indiscret, -ète [ɛ̃diskrɛ, -ɛt] *a* (*indélicat*) indiscreet, tactless; (*curieux*) *Péj* inquisitive, prying. ◆**indiscrétion** *nf* indiscretion.

indiscutable [ɛ̃diskytabl] *a* indisputable.

indispensable [ɛ̃dispɑ̃sabl] *a* indispensable, essential.

indispos/er [ɛ̃dispoze] *vt* (*incommoder*) to make unwell, upset; **i. qn (contre soi)** (*mécontenter*) to antagonize s.o. ◆**–é** *a* (*malade*) indisposed, unwell. ◆**indisposition** *nf* indisposition.

indissoluble [ɛ̃disɔlybl] *a* (*liens etc*) solid, indissoluble.

indistinct, -incte [ɛ̃distɛ̃(kt), -ɛ̃kt] *a* indistinct. ◆**–ement** [-ɛ̃ktəmɑ̃] *adv* indistinctly; (*également*) without distinction.

individu [ɛ̃dividy] *nm* individual. ◆**individualiser** *vt* to individualize. ◆**individualiste** *a* individualistic; – *nmf* individualist. ◆**individualité** *nf* (*originalité*) individuality. ◆**individuel, -elle** *a* individual. ◆**individuellement** *adv* individually.

indivisible [ɛ̃divizibl] *a* indivisible.

Indochine [ɛ̃dɔʃin] *nf* Indo-China.

indolent [ɛ̃dɔlɑ̃] *a* indolent. ◆**indolence** *nf* indolence.

indolore [ɛ̃dɔlɔr] *a* painless.

indomptable [ɛ̃dɔ̃tabl] *a* (*énergie, volonté*) indomitable. ◆**indompté** *a* (*animal*) untamed.

Indonésie [ɛ̃dɔnezi] *nf* Indonesia.

indubitable [ɛ̃dybitabl] *a* beyond doubt.

indue [ɛ̃dy] *af* **à une heure i.** at an ungodly hour.

induire* [ɛ̃dɥir] *vt* **i. qn en erreur** to lead s.o. astray.

indulgent [ɛ̃dylʒɑ̃] *a* indulgent (**envers** to, **avec** with). ◆**indulgence** *nf* indulgence.

industrie [ɛ̃dystri] *nf* industry. ◆**industrialisé** *a* industrialized. ◆**industriel, -elle** *a* industrial; – *nmf* industrialist.

inébranlable [inebrɑ̃labl] *a* (*certitude, personne*) unshakeable, unwavering.

inédit [inedi] *a* (*texte*) unpublished; (*nouveau*) *Fig* original.

ineffable [inefabl] *a Litt* inexpressible, ineffable.

inefficace [inefikas] *a* (*mesure, effort etc*) ineffective, ineffectual; (*personne*) inefficient. ◆**inefficacité** *nf* ineffectiveness; inefficiency.

inégal, -aux [inegal, -o] *a* unequal; (*sol, humeur*) uneven. ◆**inégalable** *a* incomparable. ◆**inégalé** *a* unequalled. ◆**inégalité** *nf* (*morale*) inequality; (*physique*)

difference; (*irrégularité*) unevenness; *pl* (*bosses*) bumps.
inélégant [inelegɑ̃] *a* coarse, inelegant.
inéligible [inelizibl] *a* (*candidat*) ineligible.
inéluctable [inelyktabl] *a* inescapable.
inepte [inɛpt] *a* absurd, inept. ◆**ineptie** [-si] *nf* absurdity, ineptitude.
inépuisable [inepɥizabl] *a* inexhaustible.
inerte [inɛrt] *a* inert; (*corps*) lifeless. ◆**inertie** [-si] *nf* inertia.
inespéré [inɛspere] *a* unhoped-for.
inestimable [inɛstimabl] *a* priceless.
inévitable [inevitabl] *a* inevitable, unavoidable.
inexact [inɛgzakt] *a* (*erroné*) inaccurate, inexact; **c'est i.!** it's incorrect! ◆**inexactitude** *nf* inaccuracy, inexactitude; (*manque de ponctualité*) lack of punctuality.
inexcusable [inɛkskyzabl] *a* inexcusable.
inexistant [inɛgzistɑ̃] *a* non-existent.
inexorable [inɛgzɔrabl] *a* inexorable.
inexpérience [inɛksperjɑ̃s] *nf* inexperience. ◆**inexpérimenté** *a* (*personne*) inexperienced; (*machine, arme*) untested.
inexplicable [inɛksplikabl] *a* inexplicable. ◆**inexpliqué** *a* unexplained.
inexploré [inɛksplɔre] *a* unexplored.
inexpressif, -ive [inɛkspresif, -iv] *a* expressionless.
inexprimable [inɛksprimabl] *a* inexpressible.
inextricable [inɛkstrikabl] *a* inextricable.
infaillible [ɛ̃fajibl] *a* infallible. ◆**infaillibilité** *nf* infallibility.
infaisable [ɛ̃fəzabl] *a* (*travail etc*) that cannot be done.
infamant [ɛ̃famɑ̃] *a* ignominious.
infâme [ɛ̃fɑm] *a* (*odieux*) vile, infamous; (*taudis*) squalid. ◆**infamie** *nf* infamy.
infanterie [ɛ̃fɑ̃tri] *nf* infantry.
infantile [ɛ̃fɑ̃til] *a* (*maladie, réaction*) infantile.
infarctus [ɛ̃farktys] *nm* **un i.** *Méd* a coronary.
infatigable [ɛ̃fatigabl] *a* tireless, indefatigable.
infect [ɛ̃fɛkt] *a* (*puant*) foul; (*mauvais*) lousy, vile.
infecter [ɛ̃fɛkte] **1** *vt* (*air*) to contaminate, foul. **2** *vt Méd* to infect; — **s'i.** *vpr* to get infected. ◆**infectieux, -euse** *a* infectious. ◆**infection** *nf* **1** *Méd* infection. **2** (*odeur*) stench.
inférer [ɛ̃fere] *vt* (*conclure*) to infer (**de** from, **que** that).
inférieur, -eure [ɛ̃ferjœr] *a* (*partie*) lower; (*qualité, personne*) inferior; **à l'étage i.** on the floor below; **i. à** inferior to; (*plus petit que*) smaller than; — *nmf* (*personne*) *Péj* inferior. ◆**infériorité** *nf* inferiority.
infernal, -aux [ɛ̃fɛrnal, -o] *a* infernal.
infest/er [ɛ̃fɛste] *vt* to infest, overrun (**de** with). ◆**—é** *a* **i. de requins/de fourmis/***etc* shark-/ant-/*etc* infested.
infidèle [ɛ̃fidɛl] *a* unfaithful (**à** to). ◆**infidélité** *nf* unfaithfulness; **une i.** (*acte*) an infidelity.
infiltrer (s') [sɛ̃filtre] *vpr* (*liquide*) to seep *ou* percolate (through) (**dans** into); (*lumière*) to filter (through) (**dans** into); **s'i. dans** (*groupe, esprit*) *Fig* to infiltrate. ◆**infiltration** *nf* (*de personne, idée, liquide*) infiltration.
infime [ɛ̃fim] *a* (*très petit*) tiny; (*personne*) *Péj* lowly.
infini [ɛ̃fini] *a* infinite; — *nm Math Phot* infinity; *Phil* infinite; **à l'i.** (*beaucoup*) ad infinitum, endlessly; *Math* to infinity. ◆**infiniment** *adv* infinitely; (*regretter, remercier*) very much. ◆**infinité** *nf* **une i. de** an infinite amount of.
infinitif [ɛ̃finitif] *nm Gram* infinitive.
infirme [ɛ̃firm] *a* disabled, crippled; — *nmf* disabled person. ◆**infirmité** *nf* disability.
infirmer [ɛ̃firme] *vt* to invalidate.
infirmerie [ɛ̃firməri] *nf* infirmary, sickbay. ◆**infirmier** *nm* male nurse. ◆**infirmière** *nf* nurse.
inflammable [ɛ̃flamabl] *a* (in)flammable.
inflammation [ɛ̃flamɑsjɔ̃] *nf Méd* inflammation.
inflation [ɛ̃flɑsjɔ̃] *nf Écon* inflation. ◆**inflationniste** *a Écon* inflationary.
infléchir [ɛ̃fleʃir] *vt* (*courber*) to inflect, bend; (*modifier*) to shift. ◆**inflexion** *nf* bend; (*de voix*) tone, inflexion; **une i. de la tête** a nod.
inflexible [ɛ̃flɛksibl] *a* inflexible.
infliger [ɛ̃fliʒe] *vt* to inflict (**à** on); (*amende*) to impose (**à** on).
influence [ɛ̃flyɑ̃s] *nf* influence. ◆**influencer** *vt* to influence. ◆**influençable** *a* easily influenced. ◆**influent** *a* influential. ◆**influer** *vi* **i. sur** to influence.
information [ɛ̃fɔrmɑsjɔ̃] *nf* information; (*nouvelle*) piece of news; (*enquête*) *Jur* inquiry; *pl* information; *Journ Rad TV* news.
informatique [ɛ̃fɔrmatik] *nf* (*science*) computer science; (*technique*) data processing. ◆**informaticien, -ienne** *nmf* computer scientist. ◆**informatiser** *vt* to computerize.
informe [ɛ̃fɔrm] *a* shapeless.
informer [ɛ̃fɔrme] *vt* to inform (**de** of, about;

que that); **— s'i.** *vpr* to inquire (**de** about; **si** if, whether). ◆**informateur, -trice** *nmf* informant.

infortune [ɛ̃fɔrtyn] *nf* misfortune. ◆**infortuné** *a* ill-fated, hapless.

infraction [ɛ̃fraksjɔ̃] *nf* (*délit*) offence; **i. à** breach of, infringement of.

infranchissable [ɛ̃frɑ̃ʃisabl] *a* (*mur, fleuve*) impassable; (*difficulté*) *Fig* insuperable.

infrarouge [ɛ̃fraruʒ] *a* infrared.

infroissable [ɛ̃frwasabl] *a* crease-resistant.

infructueux, -euse [ɛ̃fryktɥø, -øz] *a* fruitless.

infuser [ɛ̃fyze] *vt* (**faire**) **i.** (*thé*) to infuse. ◆**infusion** *nf* (*tisane*) (herb *ou* herbal) tea, infusion.

ingénier (s') [sɛ̃ʒenje] *vpr* to exercise one's wits (**à faire** in order to do).

ingénieur [ɛ̃ʒenjœr] *nm* engineer. ◆**ingénierie** [-iri] *nf* engineering.

ingénieux, -euse [ɛ̃ʒenjø, -øz] *a* ingenious. ◆**ingéniosité** *nf* ingenuity.

ingénu [ɛ̃ʒeny] *a* artless, naïve.

ingérer (s') [sɛ̃ʒere] *vpr* to interfere (**dans** in). ◆**ingérence** *nf* interference.

ingrat [ɛ̃gra] *a* (*personne*) ungrateful (**envers** to); (*sol*) barren; (*tâche*) thankless; (*visage, physique*) unattractive; (*âge*) awkward. ◆**ingratitude** *nf* ingratitude.

ingrédient [ɛ̃gredjɑ̃] *nm* ingredient.

inguérissable [ɛ̃gerisabl] *a* incurable.

ingurgiter [ɛ̃gyrʒite] *vt* to gulp down.

inhabitable [inabitabl] *a* uninhabitable. ◆**inhabité** *a* uninhabited.

inhabituel, -elle [inabitɥɛl] *a* unusual.

inhalateur [inalatœr] *nm Méd* inhaler. ◆**inhalation** *nf* inhalation; **faire des inhalations** to inhale.

inhérent [inerɑ̃] *a* inherent (**à** in).

inhibé [inibe] *a* inhibited. ◆**inhibition** *nf* inhibition.

inhospitalier, -ière [inɔspitalje, -jɛr] *a* inhospitable.

inhumain [inymɛ̃] *a* (*cruel, terrible*) inhuman.

inhumer [inyme] *vt* to bury, inter. ◆**inhumation** *nf* burial.

inimaginable [inimaʒinabl] *a* unimaginable.

inimitable [inimitabl] *a* inimitable.

inimitié [inimitje] *nf* enmity.

ininflammable [inɛ̃flamabl] *a* (*tissu etc*) non-flammable.

inintelligent [inɛ̃teliʒɑ̃] *a* unintelligent.

inintelligible [inɛ̃teliʒibl] *a* unintelligible.

inintéressant [inɛ̃teresɑ̃] *a* uninteresting.

ininterrompu [inɛ̃terɔ̃py] *a* uninterrupted, continuous.

inique [inik] *a* iniquitous. ◆**iniquité** *nf* iniquity.

initial, -aux [inisjal, -o] *a* initial. ◆**initiale** *nf* (*lettre*) initial. ◆**initialement** *adv* initially.

initiative [inisjativ] *nf* **1** initiative. **2 syndicat d'i.** tourist office.

initi/er [inisje] *vt* to initiate (**à** into); **s'i. à** (*art, science*) to become acquainted with *ou* initiated into. ◆**—é, -ée** *nmf* initiate; **les initiés** the initiated. ◆**initiateur, -trice** *nmf* initiator. ◆**initiation** *nf* initiation.

injecter [ɛ̃ʒɛkte] *vt* to inject; **injecté de sang** bloodshot. ◆**injection** *nf* injection.

injonction [ɛ̃ʒɔ̃ksjɔ̃] *nf* order, injunction.

injure [ɛ̃ʒyr] *nf* insult; *pl* abuse, insults. ◆**injurier** *vt* to abuse, insult, swear at. ◆**injurieux, -euse** *a* abusive, insulting (**pour** to).

injuste [ɛ̃ʒyst] *a* (*contraire à la justice*) unjust; (*partial*) unfair. ◆**injustice** *nf* injustice.

injustifiable [ɛ̃ʒystifjabl] *a* unjustifiable. ◆**injustifié** *a* unjustified.

inlassable [ɛ̃lɑsabl] *a* untiring.

inné [ine] *a* innate, inborn.

innocent, -ente [inɔsɑ̃, -ɑ̃t] *a* innocent (**de** of); **—** *nmf Jur* innocent person; (*idiot*) simpleton. ◆**innocemment** [-amɑ̃] *adv* innocently. ◆**innocence** *nf* innocence. ◆**innocenter** *vt* **i. qn** to clear s.o. (**de** of).

innombrable [inɔ̃brabl] *a* innumerable.

innommable [inɔmabl] *a* (*dégoûtant*) unspeakable, foul.

innover [inɔve] *vi* to innovate. ◆**innovateur, -trice** *nmf* innovator. ◆**innovation** *nf* innovation.

inoccupé [inɔkype] *a* unoccupied.

inoculer [inɔkyle] *vt* **i. qch à qn** to infect *ou* inoculate s.o. with sth. ◆**inoculation** *nf* (*vaccination*) inoculation.

inodore [inɔdɔr] *a* odourless.

inoffensif, -ive [inɔfɑ̃sif, -iv] *a* harmless, inoffensive.

inonder [inɔ̃de] *vt* to flood, inundate; (*mouiller*) to soak; **inondé de** (*envahi*) inundated with; **inondé de soleil** bathed in sunlight. ◆**inondable** *a* (*chaussée etc*) liable to flooding. ◆**inondation** *nf* flood; (*action*) flooding (**de** of).

inopérant [inɔperɑ̃] *a* inoperative.

inopiné [inɔpine] *a* unexpected.

inopportun [inɔpɔrtœ̃] *a* inopportune.

inoubliable [inublijabl] *a* unforgettable.

inouï [inwi] *a* incredible, extraordinary.

inox [inɔks] *nm* stainless steel; **en i.** (*couteau etc*) stainless-steel. ◆**inoxydable** *a* (*couteau etc*) stainless-steel; **acier i.** stainless steel.

inqualifiable [ɛ̃kalifjabl] *a* (*indigne*) unspeakable.

inquiet, -iète [ɛ̃kjɛ, -jɛt] *a* anxious, worried (de about). ◆**inquiét/er** *vt* (*préoccuper*) to worry; (*police*) to bother, harass (*suspect etc*); — **s'i.** *vpr* to worry (**de** about). ◆**—ant** *a* worrying. ◆**inquiétude** *nf* anxiety, concern, worry.

inquisiteur, -trice [ɛ̃kizitœr, -tris] *a* (*regard*) *Péj* inquisitive. ◆**inquisition** *nf* inquisition.

insaisissable [ɛ̃sezisabl] *a* elusive.

insalubre [ɛ̃salybr] *a* unhealthy, insalubrious.

insanités [ɛ̃sanite] *nfpl* (*idioties*) absurdities.

insatiable [ɛ̃sasjabl] *a* insatiable.

insatisfait [ɛ̃satisfɛ] *a* unsatisfied, dissatisfied.

inscrire* [ɛ̃skrir] *vt* to write *ou* put down; (*sur un registre*) to register; (*graver*) to inscribe; **i. qn** to enrol s.o.; — **s'i.** *vpr* to enrol (**à** at); **s'i. à** (*parti, club*) to join, enrol in; (*examen*) to enter *ou* enrol *ou* register for; **s'i. dans (le cadre de)** to be part of; **s'i. en faux contre** to deny absolutely. ◆**inscription** *nf* writing down; enrolment; registration; (*de médaille, sur écriteau etc*) inscription; **frais d'i.** *Univ* tuition fees.

insecte [ɛ̃sɛkt] *nm* insect. ◆**insecticide** *nm* insecticide.

insécurité [ɛ̃sekyrite] *nf* insecurity.

insémination [ɛ̃seminɑsjɔ̃] *nf Méd* insemination.

insensé [ɛ̃sɑ̃se] *a* senseless, absurd.

insensible [ɛ̃sɑ̃sibl] *a* (*indifférent*) insensitive (**à** to); (*graduel*) imperceptible, very slight. ◆**insensiblement** *adv* imperceptibly. ◆**insensibilité** *nf* insensitivity.

inséparable [ɛ̃separabl] *a* inseparable (**de** from).

insérer [ɛ̃sere] *vt* to insert (**dans** into, in); **s'i. dans** (*programme etc*) to be part of. ◆**insertion** *nf* insertion.

insidieux, -euse [ɛ̃sidjø, -øz] *a* insidious.

insigne [ɛ̃siɲ] *nm* badge, emblem; *pl* (*de maire etc*) insignia.

insignifiant [ɛ̃siɲifjɑ̃] *a* insignificant, unimportant. ◆**insignifiance** *nf* insignificance.

insinuer [ɛ̃sinɥe] *vt Péj* to insinuate (**que** that); — **s'i.** *vpr* to insinuate oneself (**dans** into). ◆**insinuation** *nf* insinuation.

insipide [ɛ̃sipid] *a* insipid.

insist/er [ɛ̃siste] *vi* to insist (**pour faire** on doing); (*continuer*) *Fam* to persevere; **i. sur** (*détail, syllabe etc*) to stress; **i. pour que** (+ *sub*) to insist that. ◆**—ant** *a* insistent, persistent. ◆**insistance** *nf* insistence, persistence.

insolation [ɛ̃sɔlɑsjɔ̃] *nf Méd* sunstroke.

insolent [ɛ̃sɔlɑ̃] *a* (*impoli*) insolent; (*luxe*) indecent. ◆**insolence** *nf* insolence.

insolite [ɛ̃sɔlit] *a* unusual, strange.

insoluble [ɛ̃sɔlybl] *a* insoluble.

insolvable [ɛ̃sɔlvabl] *a Fin* insolvent.

insomnie [ɛ̃sɔmni] *nf* insomnia; *pl* (periods of) insomnia; **nuit d'i.** sleepless night. ◆**insomniaque** *nmf* insomniac.

insondable [ɛ̃sɔ̃dabl] *a* unfathomable.

insonoriser [ɛ̃sɔnɔrize] *vt* to soundproof, insulate. ◆**insonorisation** *nf* soundproofing, insulation.

insouciant [ɛ̃susjɑ̃] *a* carefree; **i. de** unconcerned about. ◆**insouciance** *nf* carefree attitude, lack of concern.

insoumis [ɛ̃sumi] *a* rebellious. ◆**insoumission** *nf* rebelliousness.

insoupçonnable [ɛ̃supsɔnabl] *a* beyond suspicion. ◆**insoupçonné** *a* unsuspected.

insoutenable [ɛ̃sutnabl] *a* unbearable; (*théorie*) untenable.

inspecter [ɛ̃spɛkte] *vt* to inspect. ◆**inspecteur, -trice** *nmf* inspector. ◆**inspection** *nf* inspection.

inspir/er [ɛ̃spire] **1** *vt* to inspire; **i. qch à qn** to inspire s.o. with sth; **s'i. de** to take one's inspiration from. **2** *vi Méd* to breathe in. ◆**—é** *a* inspired; **être bien i. de faire** to have the good idea to do. ◆**inspiration** *nf* **1** inspiration. **2** *Méd* breathing in.

instable [ɛ̃stabl] *a* (*meuble*) unsteady, shaky; (*temps*) unsettled; (*caractère, situation*) unstable. ◆**instabilité** *nf* unsteadiness; instability.

install/er [ɛ̃stale] *vt* (*équiper*) to fit out, fix up; (*appareil, meuble etc*) to install, put in; (*étagère*) to put up; **i. qn** (*dans une fonction, un logement*) to install s.o. (**dans** in); — **s'i.** *vpr* (*s'asseoir, s'établir*) to settle (down); (*médecin etc*) to set oneself up; **s'i. dans** (*maison, hôtel*) to move into. ◆**installateur** *nm* fitter. ◆**installation** *nf* fitting out; installation; putting in; moving in; *pl* (*appareils*) fittings; (*bâtiments*) facilities.

instance [ɛ̃stɑ̃s] **1** *nf* (*juridiction, autorité*) authority; **tribunal de première i.** = magistrates' court; **en i. de** (*divorce, départ*) in the process of. **2** *nfpl* (*prières*) insistence, entreaties.

instant [ɛ̃stɑ̃] *nm* moment, instant; **à l'i.** a moment ago; **pour l'i.** for the moment. ◆**instantané** *a* instantaneous; **café i.** instant coffee; – *nm Phot* snapshot.

instaurer [ɛ̃stɔre] *vt* to found, set up.

instigateur, -trice [ɛ̃stigatœr, -tris] *nmf* instigator. ◆**instigation** *nf* instigation.

instinct [ɛ̃stɛ̃] *nm* instinct; **d'i.** instinctively, by instinct. ◆**instinctif, -ive** *a* instinctive.

instituer [ɛ̃stitɥe] *vt* (*règle, régime*) to establish, institute.

institut [ɛ̃stity] *nm* institute; **i. de beauté** beauty salon *ou* parlour; **i. universitaire de technologie** polytechnic, technical college.

instituteur, -trice [ɛ̃stitytœr, -tris] *nmf* primary school teacher.

institution [ɛ̃stitysjɔ̃] *nf* (*règle, organisation, structure etc*) institution; *Scol* private school. ◆**institutionnel, -elle** *a* institutional.

instructif, -ive [ɛ̃stryktif, -iv] *a* instructive.

instruction [ɛ̃stryksjɔ̃] *nf* education, schooling; *Mil* training; *Jur* investigation; (*document*) directive; *pl* (*ordres*) instructions. ◆**instructeur** *nm* (*moniteur*) & *Mil* instructor.

instruire* [ɛ̃strɥir] *vt* to teach, educate; *Mil* to train; *Jur* to investigate; **i. qn de** to inform *ou* instruct s.o. of; **– s'i.** *vpr* to educate oneself; **s'i. de** to inquire about. ◆**instruit** *a* educated.

instrument [ɛ̃strymɑ̃] *nm* instrument; (*outil*) implement, tool. ◆**instrumental, -aux** *a Mus* instrumental. ◆**instrumentiste** *nmf Mus* instrumentalist.

insu de (à l') [alɛ̃syd(ə)] *prép* without the knowledge of.

insuccès [ɛ̃syksɛ] *nm* failure.

insuffisant [ɛ̃syfizɑ̃] *a* (*en qualité*) inadequate; (*en quantité*) insufficient, inadequate. ◆**insuffisance** *nf* inadequacy.

insulaire [ɛ̃sylɛr] *a* insular; – *nmf* islander.

insuline [ɛ̃sylin] *nf Méd* insulin.

insulte [ɛ̃sylt] *nf* insult (**à** to). ◆**insulter** *vt* to insult.

insupportable [ɛ̃sypɔrtabl] *a* unbearable.

insurg/er (s') [sɛ̃syrʒe] *vpr* to rise (up), rebel (**contre** against). ◆**–é, -ée** *nmf* & *a* insurgent, rebel. ◆**insurrection** *nf* insurrection, uprising.

insurmontable [ɛ̃syrmɔ̃tabl] *a* insurmountable, insuperable.

intact [ɛ̃takt] *a* intact.

intangible [ɛ̃tɑ̃ʒibl] *a* intangible.

intarissable [ɛ̃tarisabl] *a* inexhaustible.

intégral, -aux [ɛ̃tegral, -o] *a* full, complete; (*édition*) unabridged. ◆**intégralement** *adv* in full, fully. ◆**intégralité** *nf* whole (**de** of); **dans son i.** in full.

intègre [ɛ̃tɛgr] *a* upright, honest. ◆**intégrité** *nf* integrity.

intégr/er [ɛ̃tegre] *vt* to integrate (**dans** in); **– s'i.** *vpr* to become integrated, adapt. ◆**–ante** *af* **faire partie i. de** to be part and parcel of. ◆**intégration** *nf* integration.

intellectuel, -elle [ɛ̃telɛktɥɛl] *a* & *nmf* intellectual.

intelligent [ɛ̃teliʒɑ̃] *a* intelligent, clever. ◆**intelligemment** [-amɑ̃] *adv* intelligently. ◆**intelligence** *nf* (*faculté*) intelligence; *pl Mil Pol* secret relations; **avoir l'i. de qch** (*compréhension*) to have an understanding of sth; **d'i. avec qn** in complicity with s.o. ◆**intelligentsia** [-dʒɛntsja] *nf* intelligentsia.

intelligible [ɛ̃teliʒibl] *a* intelligible. ◆**intelligibilité** *nf* intelligibility.

intempérance [ɛ̃tɑ̃perɑ̃s] *nf* intemperance.

intempéries [ɛ̃tɑ̃peri] *nfpl* **les i.** the elements, bad weather.

intempestif, -ive [ɛ̃tɑ̃pɛstif, -iv] *a* untimely.

intenable [ɛ̃tnabl] *a* (*position*) untenable; (*enfant*) unruly, uncontrollable.

intendant, -ante [ɛ̃tɑ̃dɑ̃, -ɑ̃t] *nmf Scol* bursar. ◆**intendance** *nf Scol* bursar's office.

intense [ɛ̃tɑ̃s] *a* intense; (*circulation, trafic*) heavy. ◆**intensément** *adv* intensely. ◆**intensif, -ive** *a* intensive. ◆**intensifier** *vt*, **– s'i.** *vpr* to intensify. ◆**intensité** *nf* intensity.

intenter [ɛ̃tɑ̃te] *vt* **i. un procès à** *Jur* to institute proceedings against.

intention [ɛ̃tɑ̃sjɔ̃] *nf* intention; *Jur* intent; **avoir l'i. de faire** to intend to do; **à l'i. de qn** for s.o.; **à votre i.** for you. ◆**intentionné** *a* **bien i.** well-intentioned. ◆**intentionnel, -elle** *a* intentional, wilful. ◆**intentionnellement** *adv* intentionally.

inter- [ɛ̃tɛr] *préf* inter-.

interaction [ɛ̃tɛraksjɔ̃] *nf* interaction.

intercaler [ɛ̃tɛrkale] *vt* to insert.

intercéder [ɛ̃tɛrsede] *vt* to intercede (**auprès de** with).

intercepter [ɛ̃tɛrsɛpte] *vt* to intercept. ◆**interception** *nf* interception.

interchangeable [ɛ̃tɛrʃɑ̃ʒabl] *a* interchangeable.

interclasse [ɛ̃tɛrklas] *nm Scol* break (between classes).

intercontinental, -aux [ɛ̃tɛrkɔ̃tinɑ̃tal, -o] *a* intercontinental.

interdépendant [ɛ̃tɛrdepɑ̃dɑ̃] *a* interdependent.

interd/ire* [ɛ̃tɛrdir] *vt* to forbid, not to allow (**qch à qn** s.o. sth); (*meeting, film etc*) to ban; **i. à qn de faire** (*médecin, père etc*) not to allow s.o. to do, forbid s.o. to do; (*attitude, santé etc*) to prevent s.o. from doing, not allow s.o. to do. ◆**—it** *a* **1** forbidden, not allowed; **il est i. de** it is forbidden to; **'stationnement i.'** 'no parking'. **2** (*étonné*) nonplussed. ◆**interdiction** *nf* ban (**de** on); **'i. de fumer'** 'no smoking'.

intéress/er [ɛ̃terese] *vt* to interest; (*concerner*) to concern; **s'i. à** to take an interest in, be interested in. ◆**—ant** *a* (*captivant*) interesting; (*affaire, prix etc*) attractive, worthwhile. ◆**—é, -ée** *a* (*avide*) self-interested; (*motif*) selfish; (*concerné*) concerned; – *nmf* **l'i.** the interested party.

intérêt [ɛ̃terɛ] *nm* interest; *Péj* self-interest; *pl Fin* interest; **tu as i. à faire** it would pay you to do, you'd do well to do; **des intérêts dans** *Com* an interest *ou* stake in.

interface [ɛ̃tɛrfas] *nf Tech* interface.

intérieur [ɛ̃terjœr] *a* (*cour, paroi*) inner, interior; (*poche*) inside; (*vie, sentiment*) inner, inward; (*mer*) inland; (*politique, vol*) internal, domestic; – *nm* (*de boîte etc*) inside (**de** of); (*de maison*) interior, inside; (*de pays*) interior; **à l'i. (de)** inside; **d'i.** (*vêtement, jeux*) indoor; **femme d'i.** home-loving woman; **ministère de l'I.** Home Office, *Am* Department of the Interior. ◆**—ement** *adv* (*dans le cœur*) inwardly.

intérim [ɛ̃terim] *nm* **pendant l'i.** in the interim; **assurer l'i.** to deputize (**de** for); **ministre/***etc* **par i.** acting minister/*etc.* ◆**intérimaire** *a* temporary, interim; – *nmf* (*fonctionnaire*) deputy; (*secrétaire*) temporary.

interligne [ɛ̃tɛrliɲ] *nm Typ* space (between the lines).

interlocuteur, -trice [ɛ̃tɛrlɔkytœr, -tris] *nmf Pol* negotiator; **mon i.** the person I am, was *etc* speaking to.

interloqué [ɛ̃tɛrlɔke] *a* dumbfounded.

interlude [ɛ̃tɛrlyd] *nm Mus TV* interlude.

intermède [ɛ̃tɛrmɛd] *nm* (*interruption*) & *Th* interlude.

intermédiaire [ɛ̃tɛrmedjɛr] *a* intermediate; – *nmf* intermediary; **par l'i. de** through (the medium of).

interminable [ɛ̃tɛrminabl] *a* endless, interminable.

intermittent [ɛ̃tɛrmitɑ̃] *a* intermittent. ◆**intermittence** *nf* **par i.** intermittently.

international, -aux [ɛ̃tɛrnasjɔnal, -o] *a* international; – *nm* (*joueur*) *Sp* international.

interne [ɛ̃tɛrn] **1** *a* (*douleur etc*) internal; (*oreille*) inner. **2** *nmf Scol* boarder; **i. (des hôpitaux)** houseman, *Am* intern. ◆**internat** *nm* (*école*) boarding school.

intern/er [ɛ̃tɛrne] *vt* (*réfugié*) to intern; (*aliéné*) to confine. ◆**—ement** *nm* internment; confinement.

interpeller [ɛ̃tɛrpele] *vt* to shout at, address sharply; (*dans une réunion*) to question, (*interrompre*) to heckle; (*arrêter*) *Jur* to take in for questioning. ◆**interpellation** *nf* sharp address; questioning; heckling; (*de police*) arrest.

interphone [ɛ̃tɛrfɔn] *nm* intercom.

interplanétaire [ɛ̃tɛrplanetɛr] *a* interplanetary.

interpoler [ɛ̃tɛrpɔle] *vt* to interpolate.

interposer (s') [sɛ̃tɛrpoze] *vpr* (*dans une dispute etc*) to intervene (**dans** in); **s'i. entre** to come between.

interprète [ɛ̃tɛrprɛt] *nmf Ling* interpreter; (*chanteur*) singer; *Th Mus* performer; (*porte-parole*) spokesman, spokeswoman; **faire l'i.** *Ling* to interpret. ◆**interprétariat** *nm* (*métier*) *Ling* interpreting. ◆**interprétation** *nf* interpretation; *Th Mus* performance. ◆**interpréter** *vt* (*expliquer*) to interpret; (*chanter*) to sing; (*jouer*) *Th* to play, perform; (*exécuter*) *Mus* to perform.

interroger [ɛ̃terɔʒe] *vt* to question; *Jur* to interrogate; (*faits*) to examine. ◆**interrogateur, -trice** *a* (*air*) questioning; – *nmf Scol* examiner. ◆**interrogatif, -ive** *a & nm Gram* interrogative. ◆**interrogation** *nf* question; (*action*) questioning; (*épreuve*) *Scol* test. ◆**interrogatoire** *nm Jur* interrogation.

interrompre* [ɛ̃terɔ̃pr] *vt* to interrupt, break off; **i. qn** to interrupt s.o.; – **s'i.** *vpr* (*personne*) to break off, stop. ◆**interrupteur** *nm* (*bouton*) *Él* switch. ◆**interruption** *nf* interruption; (*des hostilités, du courant*) break (**de** in).

intersection [ɛ̃tɛrsɛksjɔ̃] *nf* intersection.

interstice [ɛ̃tɛrstis] *nm* crack, chink.

interurbain [ɛ̃tɛryrbɛ̃] *a & nm* **(téléphone) i.** long-distance telephone service.

intervalle [ɛ̃tɛrval] *nm* (*écart*) space, gap; (*temps*) interval; **dans l'i.** (*entretemps*) in the meantime.

intervenir* [ɛ̃tɛrvənir] *vi* (*s'interposer, agir*) to intervene; (*survenir*) to occur; (*opérer*) *Méd* to operate; **être intervenu** (*accord*) to be reached. ◆**intervention** *nf* intervention; **i. (chirurgicale)** operation.

intervertir [ɛ̃tɛrvɛrtir] *vt* to invert. ◆**interversion** *nf* inversion.

interview [ɛ̃tɛrvju] *nf Journ TV* interview. ◆**interviewer** [-vjuve] *vt* to interview.

intestin [ɛ̃tɛstɛ̃] *nm* intestine, bowel. ◆**intestinal, -aux** *a* intestinal, bowel-.

intime [ɛ̃tim] *a* intimate; (*ami*) close, intimate; (*vie, fête, journal*) private; (*pièce, coin*) cosy; (*cérémonie*) quiet; – *nmf* close *ou* intimate friend. ◆**—ment** *adv* intimately. ◆**intimité** *nf* intimacy; privacy; cosiness; **dans l'i.** (*mariage etc*) in private.

intimider [ɛ̃timide] *vt* to intimidate, frighten. ◆**intimidation** *nf* intimidation.

intituler [ɛ̃tityle] *vt* to entitle; **— s'i.** *vpr* to be entitled.

intolérable [ɛ̃tɔlerabl] *a* intolerable (**que** that). ◆**intolérance** *nf* intolerance. ◆**intolérant** *a* intolerant (**de** of).

intonation [ɛ̃tɔnɑsjɔ̃] *nf Ling* intonation; (*ton*) tone.

intoxiqu/er [ɛ̃tɔksike] *vt* (*empoisonner*) to poison; *Psy Pol* to brainwash; **— s'i.** *vpr* to be *ou* become poisoned. ◆**—é, -ée** *nmf* addict. ◆**intoxication** *nf* poisoning; *Psy Pol* brainwashing.

intra- [ɛ̃tra] *préf* intra-.

intraduisible [ɛ̃tradɥizibl] *a* untranslatable.

intraitable [ɛ̃trɛtabl] *a* uncompromising.

intransigeant [ɛ̃trɑ̃ziʒɑ̃] *a* intransigent. ◆**intransigeance** *nf* intransigence.

intransitif, -ive [ɛ̃trɑ̃zitif, -iv] *a & nm Gram* intransitive.

intraveineux, -euse [ɛ̃travɛnø, -øz] *a Méd* intravenous.

intrépide [ɛ̃trepid] *a* (*courageux*) fearless, intrepid; (*obstiné*) headstrong. ◆**intrépidité** *nf* fearlessness.

intrigue [ɛ̃trig] *nf* intrigue; *Th Cin Littér* plot. ◆**intrigant, -ante** *nmf* schemer. ◆**intriguer 1** *vi* to scheme, intrigue. **2** *vt* **i.** qn (*intéresser*) to intrigue s.o., puzzle s.o.

intrinsèque [ɛ̃trɛ̃sɛk] *a* intrinsic. ◆**—ment** *adv* intrinsically.

introduire* [ɛ̃trɔdɥir] *vt* (*présenter*) to introduce, bring in; (*insérer*) to insert (**dans** into), put in (**dans** to); (*faire entrer*) to show (*s.o.*) in; **s'i. dans** to get into. ◆**introduction** *nf* (*texte, action*) introduction.

introspectif, -ive [ɛ̃trɔspɛktif, -iv] *a* introspective. ◆**introspection** *nf* introspection.

introuvable [ɛ̃truvabl] *a* that cannot be found anywhere.

introverti, -ie [ɛ̃trɔvɛrti] *nmf* introvert.

intrus, -use [ɛ̃try, -yz] *nmf* intruder. ◆**intrusion** *nf* intrusion (**dans** into).

intuition [ɛ̃tɥisjɔ̃] *nf* intuition. ◆**intuitif, -ive** *a* intuitive.

inusable [inyzabl] *a Fam* hard-wearing.

inusité [inyzite] *a Gram* unused.

inutile [inytil] *a* unnecessary, useless; **c'est i. de crier** it's pointless *ou* useless to shout. ◆**inutilement** *adv* (*vainement*) needlessly. ◆**inutilité** *nf* uselessness.

inutilisable [inytilizabl] *a* unusable. ◆**inutilisé** *a* unused.

invalider [ɛ̃valide] *vt* to invalidate.

invariable [ɛ̃varjabl] *a* invariable. ◆**—ment** [-əmɑ̃] *adv* invariably.

invasion [ɛ̃vɑsjɔ̃] *nf* invasion.

invective [ɛ̃vɛktiv] *nf* invective. ◆**invectiver** *vt* to abuse; – *vi* **i. contre** to inveigh against.

invendable [ɛ̃vɑ̃dabl] *a* unsaleable. ◆**invendu** *a* unsold.

inventaire [ɛ̃vɑ̃tɛr] *nm* (*liste*) *Com* inventory; (*étude*) *Fig* survey; **faire l'i.** *Com* to do the stocktaking (**de** of).

inventer [ɛ̃vɑ̃te] *vt* (*découvrir*) to invent; (*imaginer*) to make up. ◆**inventeur, -trice** *nmf* inventor. ◆**inventif, -ive** *a* inventive. ◆**invention** *nf* invention.

inverse [ɛ̃vɛrs] *a* (*sens*) opposite; (*ordre*) reverse; *Math* inverse; – *nm* **l'i.** the reverse, the opposite. ◆**inversement** *adv* conversely. ◆**inverser** *vt* (*ordre*) to reverse. ◆**inversion** *nf Gram Anat etc* inversion.

investigation [ɛ̃vɛstigɑsjɔ̃] *nf* investigation.

invest/ir [ɛ̃vɛstir] **1** *vti Com* to invest (**dans** in). **2** *vt* **i. qn de** (*fonction etc*) to invest s.o. with. ◆**—issement** *nm Com* investment. ◆**investiture** *nf Pol* nomination.

invétéré [ɛ̃vetere] *a* inveterate.

invincible [ɛ̃vɛ̃sibl] *a* invincible.

invisible [ɛ̃vizibl] *a* invisible.

invit/er [ɛ̃vite] *vt* to invite; **i. qn à faire** to invite *ou* ask s.o. to do; (*inciter*) to tempt s.o. to do. ◆**—é, -ée** *nmf* guest. ◆**invitation** *nf* invitation.

invivable [ɛ̃vivabl] *a* unbearable.

involontaire [ɛ̃vɔlɔ̃tɛr] *a* involuntary. ◆**—ment** *adv* accidentally, involuntarily.

invoquer [ɛ̃vɔke] *vt* (*argument etc*) to put forward; (*appeler*) to invoke, call upon. ◆**invocation** *nf* invocation (**à** to).

invraisemblable [ɛ̃vrɛsɑ̃blabl] *a* incredible; (*improbable*) improbable. ◆**invraisemblance** *nf* improbability.

invulnérable [ɛ̃vylnerabl] *a* invulnerable.

iode [jɔd] *nm* **teinture d'i.** *Méd* iodine.

ira, irait [ira, irɛ] *voir* **aller 1**.

Irak [irak] *nm* Iraq. ◆**irakien, -ienne** *a & nmf* Iraqi.

Iran [irɑ̃] *nm* Iran. ◆**iranien, -ienne** *a* & *nmf* Iranian.
irascible [irasibl] *a* irascible.
iris [iris] *nm Anat Bot* iris.
Irlande [irlɑ̃d] *nf* Ireland. ◆**irlandais, -aise** *a* Irish; – *nmf* Irishman, Irishwoman; – *nm (langue)* Irish.
ironie [irɔni] *nf* irony. ◆**ironique** *a* ironic(al).
irradier [iradje] *vt* to irradiate.
irraisonné [irɛzɔne] *a* irrational.
irréconciliable [irekɔ̃siljabl] *a* irreconcilable.
irrécusable [irekyzabl] *a* irrefutable.
irréel, -elle [ireɛl] *a* unreal.
irréfléchi [irefleʃi] *a* thoughtless, unthinking.
irréfutable [irefytabl] *a* irrefutable.
irrégulier, -ière [iregylje, -jɛr] *a* irregular. ◆**irrégularité** *nf* irregularity.
irrémédiable [iremedjabl] *a* irreparable.
irremplaçable [irɑ̃plasabl] *a* irreplaceable.
irréparable [ireparabl] *a (véhicule etc)* beyond repair; *(tort, perte)* irreparable.
irrépressible [irepresibl] *a (rires etc)* irrepressible.
irréprochable [ireprɔʃabl] *a* beyond reproach, irreproachable.
irrésistible [irezistibl] *a (personne, charme etc)* irresistible.
irrésolu [irezɔly] *a* irresolute.
irrespirable [irespirabl] *a* unbreathable; *Fig* stifling.
irresponsable [irespɔ̃sabl] *a (personne)* irresponsible.
irrévérencieux, -euse [ireverɑ̃sjø, -øz] *a* irreverent.
irréversible [ireversibl] *a* irreversible.
irrévocable [irevɔkabl] *a* irrevocable.
irriguer [irige] *vt* to irrigate. ◆**irrigation** *nf* irrigation.
irrit/er [irite] *vt* to irritate; – **s'i.** *vpr* to get angry (**de, contre** at). ◆**—ant** *a* irritating; – *nm* irritant. ◆**irritable** *a* irritable. ◆**irritation** *nf (colère)* & *Méd* irritation.
irruption [irypsjɔ̃] *nf* **faire i. dans** to burst into.
islam [islam] *nm* Islam. ◆**islamique** *a* Islamic.
Islande [islɑ̃d] *nf* Iceland. ◆**islandais, -aise** *a* Icelandic.
isol/er [izɔle] *vt* to isolate (**de** from); *(contre le froid etc)* & *Él* to insulate; – **s'i.** *vpr* to cut oneself off, isolate oneself. ◆**—ant** *a* insulating; – *nm* insulating material. ◆**—é** *a* isolated; *(écarté)* remote, isolated; **i. de** cut off *ou* isolated from. ◆**isolation** *nf* insulation. ◆**isolement** *nm* isolation. ◆**isolément** *adv* in isolation, singly. ◆**isoloir** *nm* polling booth.
isorel® [izɔrɛl] *nm* hardboard.
Israël [israɛl] *nm* Israel. ◆**israélien, -ienne** *a* & *nmf* Israeli. ◆**israélite** *a* Jewish; – *nm* Jew; – *nf* Jewess.
issu [isy] *a* **être i. de** to come from.
issue [isy] *nf (sortie)* exit, way out; *(solution) Fig* way out; *(résultat)* outcome; **à l'i. de** at the close of; **rue** *etc* **sans i.** dead end; **situation** *etc* **sans i.** *Fig* dead end.
isthme [ism] *nm Géog* isthmus.
Italie [itali] *nf* Italy. ◆**italien, -ienne** *a* & *nmf* Italian; – *nm (langue)* Italian.
italique [italik] *a Typ* italic; – *nm* italics.
itinéraire [itinerɛr] *nm* itinerary, route.
itinérant [itinerɑ̃] *a* itinerant.
IVG [iveʒe] *nf abrév (interruption volontaire de grossesse)* (voluntary) abortion.
ivoire [ivwar] *nm* ivory.
ivre [ivr] *a* drunk (**de** with). ◆**ivresse** *nf* drunkenness; **en état d'i.** under the influence of drink. ◆**ivrogne** *nmf* drunk(ard).

J

J, j [ʒi] *nm* J, j; **le jour J.** D-day.
j' [ʒ] *voir* **je.**
jacasser [ʒakase] *vi (personne, pie)* to chatter.
jachère (en) [ɑ̃ʒaʃɛr] *adv (champ etc)* fallow.
jacinthe [ʒasɛ̃t] *nf* hyacinth.
jacousi [ʒakuzi] *nm (baignoire, piscine)* jacuzzi.
jade [ʒad] *nm (pierre)* jade.
jadis [ʒadis] *adv* at one time, once.
jaguar [ʒagwar] *nm (animal)* jaguar.
jaill/ir [ʒajir] *vi (liquide)* to spurt (out), gush (out); *(lumière)* to flash, stream; *(cri)* to burst out; *(vérité)* to burst forth; *(étincelle)* to fly out. ◆**—issement** *nm (de liquide)* gush.
jais [ʒɛ] *nm* **(noir) de j.** jet-black.

jalon [ʒalɔ̃] *nm* (*piquet*) marker; **poser les jalons** *Fig* to prepare the way (**de** for). ◆**jalonner** *vt* to mark (out); (*border*) to line.

jaloux, -ouse [ʒalu, -uz] *a* jealous (**de** of). ◆**jalouser** *vt* to envy. ◆**jalousie** *nf* **1** jealousy. **2** (*persienne*) venetian blind.

Jamaïque [ʒamaik] *nf* Jamaica.

jamais [ʒamɛ] *adv* **1** (*négatif*) never; **sans j. sortir** without ever going out; **elle ne sort j.** she never goes out. **2** (*positif*) ever; **à (tout) j.** for ever; **si j.** if ever.

jambe [ʒɑ̃b] *nf* leg; **à toutes jambes** as fast as one can; **prendre ses jambes à son cou** to take to one's heels.

jambon [ʒɑ̃bɔ̃] *nm Culin* ham. ◆**jambonneau, -x** *nm* knuckle of ham.

jante [ʒɑ̃t] *nf* (*de roue*) rim.

janvier [ʒɑ̃vje] *nm* January.

Japon [ʒapɔ̃] *nm* Japan. ◆**japonais, -aise** *a* & *nmf* Japanese; – *nm* (*langue*) Japanese.

japp/er [ʒape] *vi* (*chien etc*) to yap, yelp. ◆**—ement** *nm* yap, yelp.

jaquette [ʒakɛt] *nf* (*d'homme*) tailcoat, morning coat; (*de femme, livre*) jacket.

jardin [ʒardɛ̃] *nm* garden; **j. d'enfants** kindergarten, playschool; **j. public** park; (*plus petit*) gardens. ◆**jardinage** *nm* gardening. ◆**jardiner** *vi* to do the garden, be gardening. ◆**jardinerie** *nf* garden centre. ◆**jardinier** *nm* gardener. ◆**jardinière** *nf* (*personne*) gardener; (*caisse à fleurs*) window box; **j. (de légumes)** *Culin* mixed vegetable dish; **j. d'enfants** kindergarten teacher.

jargon [ʒargɔ̃] *nm* jargon.

jarret [ʒarɛ] *nm Anat* back of the knee.

jarretelle [ʒartɛl] *nf* (*de gaine*) suspender, *Am* garter. ◆**jarretière** *nf* (*autour de la jambe*) garter.

jaser [ʒaze] *vi* (*bavarder*) to jabber.

jasmin [ʒasmɛ̃] *nm Bot* jasmine.

jatte [ʒat] *nf* (*bol*) bowl.

jauge [ʒoʒ] *nf* **1** (*instrument*) gauge. **2** (*capacité*) capacity; *Nau* tonnage. ◆**jauger** *vt* (*personne*) *Litt* to size up.

jaune [ʒon] **1** *a* yellow; – *nm* (*couleur*) yellow; **j. d'œuf** (egg) yolk. **2** *nm* (*ouvrier*) *Péj* blackleg, scab. ◆**jaunâtre** *a* yellowish. ◆**jaunir** *vti* to (turn) yellow. ◆**jaunisse** *nf Méd* jaundice.

Javel (eau de) [odʒavɛl] *nf* bleach. ◆**javelliser** *vt* to chlorinate.

javelot [ʒavlo] *nm* javelin.

jazz [dʒaz] *nm* jazz.

je [ʒ(ə)] *pron* (**j'** *before vowel or mute h*) I; **je suis** I am.

jean [dʒin] *nm* (pair of) jeans.

jeep [dʒip] *nf* jeep.

je-m'en-fichisme [ʒmɑ̃fiʃism] *nm inv Fam* couldn't-care-less attitude.

jérémiades [ʒeremjad] *nfpl Fam* lamentations.

jerrycan [(d)ʒerikan] *nm* jerry can.

jersey [ʒɛrzɛ] *nm* (*tissu*) jersey.

Jersey [ʒɛrzɛ] *nf* Jersey.

jésuite [ʒezɥit] *nm* Jesuit.

Jésus [ʒezy] *nm* Jesus; **J.-Christ** Jesus Christ.

jet [ʒɛ] *nm* throw; (*de vapeur*) burst, gush; (*de lumière*) flash; **j. d'eau** fountain; **premier j.** (*ébauche*) first draft; **d'un seul j.** in one go.

jetée [ʒ(ə)te] *nf* pier, jetty.

jeter [ʒ(ə)te] *vt* to throw (**à** to, **dans** into); (*mettre à la poubelle*) to throw away; (*ancre, regard, sort*) to cast; (*bases*) to lay; (*cri, son*) to let out, utter; (*éclat, lueur*) to throw out, give out; (*noter*) to jot down; **j. un coup d'œil sur** *ou* **à** to have *ou* take a look at; (*rapidement*) to glance at; **— se j.** *vpr* to throw oneself; **se j. sur** to fall on, pounce on; **se j. contre** (*véhicule*) to crash into; **se j. dans** (*fleuve*) to flow into. ◆**jetable** *a* (*rasoir etc*) disposable.

jeton [ʒ(ə)tɔ̃] *nm* (*pièce*) token; (*pour compter*) counter; (*à la roulette*) chip.

jeu, -x [ʒø] *nm* **1** game; (*amusement*) play; (*d'argent*) gambling; *Th* acting; *Mus* playing; **j. de mots** play on words, pun; **jeux de société** parlour *ou* party games; **j. télévisé** television quiz; **maison de jeux** gambling club; **en j.** (*en cause*) at stake; (*forces etc*) at work; **entrer en j.** to come into play. **2** (*série complète*) set; (*de cartes*) pack, deck, *Am* deck; (*cartes en main*) hand; **j. d'échecs** (*boîte, pièces*) chess set. **3** (*de ressort, verrou*) *Tech* play.

jeudi [ʒødi] *nm* Thursday.

jeun (à) [aʒœ̃] *adv* on an empty stomach; **être à j.** to have eaten no food.

jeune [ʒœn] *a* young; (*inexpérimenté*) inexperienced; **Dupont j.** Dupont junior; **d'allure j.** young-looking; **jeunes gens** young people; – *nmf* young person; **les jeunes** young people. ◆**jeunesse** *nf* youth; (*apparence*) youthfulness; **la j.** (*jeunes*) the young, youth.

jeûne [ʒøn] *nm* fast; (*action*) fasting. ◆**jeûner** *vi* to fast.

joaillier, -ière [ʒɔaje, -jɛr] *nmf* jeweller.

◆**joaillerie** *nf* jewellery; (*magasin*) jewellery shop.
jockey [ʒɔkɛ] *nm* jockey.
jogging [dʒɔgiŋ] *nm Sp* jogging; (*chaussure*) running *ou* jogging shoe; **faire du j.** to jog.
joie [ʒwa] *nf* joy, delight; **feu de j.** bonfire.
joindre* [ʒwɛ̃dr] *vt* (*mettre ensemble, relier*) to join; (*efforts*) to combine; (*insérer dans une enveloppe*) to enclose (**à** with); (*ajouter*) to add (**à** to); **j. qn** (*contacter*) to get in touch with s.o.; **j. les deux bouts** *Fig* to make ends meet; **se j. à** (*se mettre avec, participer à*) to join. ◆**joint** *a* (*efforts*) joint, combined; **à pieds joints** with feet together; – *nm Tech* joint; (*de robinet*) washer. ◆**jointure** *nf Anat* joint.
joker [ʒɔkɛr] *nm Cartes* joker.
joli [ʒɔli] *a* nice, lovely; (*femme, enfant*) pretty. ◆**—ment** *adv* nicely; (*très, beaucoup*) awfully.
jonc [ʒɔ̃] *nm Bot* (bul)rush.
joncher [ʒɔ̃ʃe] *vt* to litter (**de** with); **jonché de** strewn *ou* littered with.
jonction [ʒɔ̃ksjɔ̃] *nf* (*de tubes, routes etc*) junction.
jongl/er [ʒɔ̃gle] *vi* to juggle. ◆**—eur, -euse** *nmf* juggler.
jonquille [ʒɔ̃kij] *nf* daffodil.
Jordanie [ʒɔrdani] *nf* Jordan.
joue [ʒu] *nf Anat* cheek; **coucher qn en j.** to aim (a gun) at s.o.
jouer [ʒwe] *vi* to play; *Th* to act; (*au tiercé etc*) to gamble, bet; (*à la Bourse*) to gamble; (*entrer en jeu*) to come into play; (*être important*) to count; (*fonctionner*) to work; **j. au tennis/aux cartes/***etc* to play tennis/cards/*etc*; **j. du piano/du violon/***etc* to play the piano/violin/*etc*; **j. des coudes** to use one's elbows; – *vt* (*musique, tour, jeu*) to play; (*risquer*) to gamble, bet (**sur** on); (*cheval*) to bet on; (*personnage, rôle*) *Th* to play; (*pièce*) *Th* to perform, put on; (*film*) to show, put on; **j. gros jeu** to play for high stakes; **se j. de** to scoff at; (*difficultés*) to make light of. ◆**jouet** *nm* toy; **le j. de qn** *Fig* s.o.'s plaything. ◆**joueur, -euse** *nmf* player; (*au tiercé etc*) gambler; **beau j., bon j.,** good loser.
joufflu [ʒufly] *a* (*visage*) chubby; (*enfant*) chubby-cheeked.
joug [ʒu] *nm Agr* & *Fig* yoke.
jouir [ʒwir] *vi* **1 j. de** (*savourer, avoir*) to enjoy. **2** (*éprouver le plaisir sexuel*) to come. ◆**jouissance** *nf* enjoyment; (*usage*) *Jur* use.
joujou, -x [ʒuʒu] *nm Fam* toy.
jour [ʒur] *nm* day; (*lumière*) (day)light; (*ouverture*) gap, opening; (*aspect*) *Fig* light; **il fait j.** it's (day)light; **grand j., plein j.** broad daylight; **de nos jours** nowadays, these days; **au j. le j.** from day to day; **du j. au lendemain** overnight; **mettre à j.** to bring up to date; **mettre au j.** to bring into the open; **se faire j.** to come to light; **donner le j. à** to give birth to; **le j. de l'An** New Year's day. ◆**journalier, -ière** *a* daily. ◆**journée** *nf* day; **pendant la j.** during the day(time); **toute la j.** all day (long). ◆**journellement** *adv* daily.
journal, -aux [ʒurnal, -o] *nm* (news)paper; (*spécialisé*) journal; (*intime*) diary; **j. (parlé)** *Rad* news bulletin; **j. de bord** *Nau* logbook. ◆**journalisme** *nm* journalism. ◆**journaliste** *nmf* journalist. ◆**journalistique** *a* (*style etc*) journalistic.
jovial, -aux [ʒɔvjal, -o] *a* jovial, jolly. ◆**jovialité** *nf* jollity.
joyau, -aux [ʒwajo] *nm* jewel.
joyeux, -euse [ʒwajø, -øz] *a* merry, happy, joyful; **j. anniversaire!** happy birthday!; **j. Noël!** merry *ou* happy Christmas!
jubilé [ʒybile] *nm* (golden) jubilee.
jubiler [ʒybile] *vi* to be jubilant. ◆**jubilation** *nf* jubilation.
jucher [ʒyʃe] *vt*, – **se j.** *vpr* to perch (**sur** on).
judaïque [ʒydaik] *a* Jewish. ◆**judaïsme** *nm* Judaism.
judas [ʒyda] *nm* (*de porte*) peephole, spy hole.
judiciaire [ʒydisjɛr] *a* judicial, legal.
judicieux, -euse [ʒydisjø, -øz] *a* sensible, judicious.
judo [ʒydo] *nm* judo. ◆**judoka** *nmf* judo expert.
juge [ʒyʒ] *nm* judge; *Sp* referee, umpire; **j. d'instruction** examining magistrate; **j. de paix** Justice of the Peace; **j. de touche** *Fb* linesman. ◆**juger** *vt* (*personne, question etc*) to judge; (*affaire*) *Jur* to try; (*estimer*) to consider (**que** that); **j. qn** *Jur* to try s.o.; – *vi* **j. de** to judge; **jugez de ma surprise/***etc* imagine my surprise/*etc*. ◆**jugement** *nm* judg(e)ment; (*verdict*) *Jur* sentence; **passer en j.** *Jur* to stand trial. ◆**jugeote** *nf Fam* commonsense.
jugé (au) [oʒyʒe] *adv* by guesswork.
juguler [ʒygyle] *vt* to check, suppress.
juif, juive [ʒɥif, ʒɥiv] *a* Jewish; – *nm* Jew; – *nf* Jew(ess).
juillet [ʒɥijɛ] *nm* July.
juin [ʒɥɛ̃] *nm* June.
jumeau, -elle, *pl* **-eaux, -elles** [ʒymo, -ɛl] **1** *a* (*frères, lits etc*) twin; – *nmf* twin. **2** *nfpl*

(*longue-vue*) binoculars; **jumelles de théâtre** opera glasses. ◆**jumel/er** *vt*.(*villes*) to twin. ◆**—age** *nm* twinning.
jument [ʒymɑ̃] *nf* (*cheval*) mare.
jungle [ʒœ̃gl] *nf* jungle.
junior [ʒynjɔr] *nm* & *a* (*inv au sing*) *Sp* junior.
junte [ʒœ̃t] *nf Pol* junta.
jupe [ʒyp] *nf* skirt. ◆**jupon** *nm* petticoat.
jurer [ʒyre] **1** *vi* (*blasphémer*) to swear. **2** *vt* (*promettre*) to swear (**que** that, **de faire** to do); – *vi* **j. de qch** to swear to sth. **3** *vi* (*contraster*) to clash (**avec** with). ◆**juré** *a* (*ennemi*) sworn; – *nm Jur* juror. ◆**juron** *nm* swearword, oath.
juridiction [ʒyridiksjɔ̃] *nf* jurisdiction.
juridique [ʒyridik] *a* legal. ◆**juriste** *nmf* legal expert, jurist.
jury [ʒyri] *nm Jur* jury; (*de concours*) panel (of judges), jury.
jus [ʒy] *nm* (*des fruits etc*) juice; (*de viande*) gravy; (*café*) *Fam* coffee; (*électricité*) *Fam* power.
jusque [ʒysk] *prép* **jusqu'à** (*espace*) as far as, (right) up to; (*temps*) until, (up) till, to; (*même*) even; **jusqu'à dix francs/***etc* (*limite*) up to ten francs/*etc*; **jusqu'en mai/***etc* until May/*etc*; **jusqu'où?** how far?; **j. dans/sous/***etc* right into/under/*etc*; **j. chez moi** as far as my place; **jusqu'ici** as far as this; (*temps*) up till now; **en avoir j.-là** *Fam* to be fed up; – *conj* **jusqu'à ce qu'il vienne** until he comes.
juste [ʒyst] *a* (*équitable*) fair, just; (*légitime*) just; (*calcul, heure, réponse*) correct, right, accurate; (*remarque*) sound; (*oreille*) good; (*voix*) *Mus* true; (*vêtement*) tight; **un peu j.** (*quantité, repas etc*) barely enough; **très j.!** quite so *ou* right!; **à 3 heures j.** on the stroke of 3; – *adv* (*deviner, compter*) correctly, right, accurately; (*chanter*) in tune; (*exactement, seulement*) just; **au j.** exactly; **tout j.** (*à peine, seulement*) only just; **c'était j.!** (*il était temps*) it was a near thing!; **un peu j.** (*mesurer, compter*) a bit on the short side; – *nm* (*homme*) just man. ◆**justement** *adv* precisely, exactly, just; (*avec justesse ou justice*) justly. ◆**justesse** *nf* (*exactitude*) accuracy; **de j.** (*éviter, gagner etc*) just.
justice [ʒystis] *nf* justice; (*organisation, autorités*) law; **en toute j.** in all fairness; **rendre j. à** to do justice to. ◆**justicier, -ière** *nmf* dispenser of justice.
justifier [ʒystifje] *vt* to justify; – *vi* **j. de** to prove; – **se j.** *vpr Jur* to clear oneself (**de** of); (*attitude etc*) to be justified. ◆**justifiable** *a* justifiable. ◆**justificatif, -ive** *a* **document j.** supporting document, proof. ◆**justification** *nf* justification; (*preuve*) proof.
jute [ʒyt] *nm* (*fibre*) jute.
juteux, -euse [ʒytø, -øz] *a* juicy.
juvénile [ʒyvenil] *a* youthful.
juxtaposer [ʒykstapoze] *vt* to juxtapose. ◆**juxtaposition** *nf* juxtaposition.

K

K, k [kɑ] *nm* K, k.
kaki [kaki] *a inv* & *nm* khaki.
kaléidoscope [kaleidɔskɔp] *nm* kaleidoscope.
kangourou [kɑ̃guru] *nm* **1** (*animal*) kangaroo. **2**® (*porte-bébé*) baby sling.
karaté [karate] *nm Sp* karate.
kart [kart] *nm Sp* (go-)kart, go-cart. ◆**karting** [-iŋ] *nm Sp* (go-)karting.
kascher [kaʃɛr] *a inv Rel* kosher.
kayac [kajak] *nm* (*bateau*) *Sp* canoe.
képi [kepi] *nm* (*coiffure*) *Mil* kepi.
kermesse [kɛrmɛs] *nf* charity fête; (*en Belgique etc*) village fair.
kérosène [kerozɛn] *nm* kerosene, aviation fuel.
kibboutz [kibuts] *nm* kibbutz.
kidnapp/er [kidnape] *vt* to kidnap. ◆**—eur, -euse** *nmf* kidnapper.
kilo(gramme) [kilo, kilɔgram] *nm* kilo(gramme).
kilomètre [kilɔmɛtr] *nm* kilometre. ◆**kilométrage** *nm Aut* = mileage. ◆**kilométrique** *a* **borne k.** = milestone.
kilowatt [kilɔwat] *nm* kilowatt.
kimono [kimɔno] *nm* (*tunique*) kimono.
kinésithérapie [kineziterapi] *nf* physiotherapy. ◆**kinésithérapeute** *nmf* physiotherapist.
kiosque [kjɔsk] *nm* (*à journaux*) kiosk, stall; **k. à musique** bandstand.
kit [kit] *nm* (*meuble etc prêt à monter*) kit; **en k.** in kit form, ready to assemble.

klaxon® [klaksɔn] *nm Aut* horn. ◆**klaxonner** *vi* to hoot, *Am* honk.
km *abrév* (*kilomètre*) km.
k.-o. [kao] *a inv* **mettre k.-o.** *Boxe* to knock out.
kyrielle [kirjɛl] *nf* **une k. de** a long string of.
kyste [kist] *nm Méd* cyst.

L

L, l [ɛl] *nm* L, l.
l', la [l, la] *voir* **le**.
là [la] **1** *adv* there; (*chez soi*) in, home; **je reste là** I'll stay here; **c'est là que** *ou* **où** that's where; **c'est là ton erreur** that's *ou* there's your mistake; **là où il est** where he is; **à cinq mètres de là** five metres away; **de là son échec** (*cause*) hence his *ou* her failure; **jusque-là** (*lieu*) as far as that; **passe par là** go that way. **2** *adv* (*temps*) then; **jusque-là** up till then. **3** *int* **là, là!** (*pour rassurer*) there, there!; **alors là!** well!; **oh là là!** oh dear! **4** *voir* **ce**[2], **celui**.
là-bas [labɑ] *adv* over there.
label [label] *nm Com* label, mark (*of quality, origin etc*).
labeur [labœr] *nm Litt* toil.
labo [labo] *nm Fam* lab. ◆**laboratoire** *nm* laboratory; **l. de langues** language laboratory.
laborieux, -euse [labɔrjø, -øz] *a* (*pénible*) laborious; (*personne*) industrious; **les classes laborieuses** the working classes.
labour [labur] *nm* ploughing, *Am* plowing; digging over. ◆**labour/er** *vt* (*avec charrue*) to plough, *Am* plow; (*avec bêche*) to dig over; (*visage etc*) *Fig* to furrow. ◆**—eur** *nm* ploughman, *Am* plowman.
labyrinthe [labirɛ̃t] *nm* maze, labyrinth.
lac [lak] *nm* lake.
lacer [lase] *vt* to lace (up). ◆**lacet** *nm* **1** (shoe- *ou* boot-)lace. **2** (*de route*) twist, zigzag; **route en l.** winding *ou* zigzag road.
lacérer [lasere] *vt* (*papier etc*) to tear; (*visage etc*) to lacerate.
lâche [lɑʃ] **1** *a* cowardly; – *nmf* coward. **2** *a* (*détendu*) loose, slack. ◆**lâchement** *adv* in a cowardly manner. ◆**lâcheté** *nf* cowardice; **une l.** (*action*) a cowardly act.
lâch/er [lɑʃe] *vt* (*main, objet etc*) to let go of; (*bombe, pigeon*) to release; (*place, études*) to give up; (*juron*) to utter, let slip; (*secret*) to let out; **l. qn** (*laisser tranquille*) to leave s.o. (alone); (*abandonner*) *Fam* to drop s.o.; **l. prise** to let go; – *vi* (*corde*) to give way; – *nm* release. ◆**—eur, -euse** *nmf Fam* deserter.
laconique [lakɔnik] *a* laconic.
lacrymogène [lakrimɔʒɛn] *a* **gaz l.** tear gas.
lacté [lakte] *a* (*régime*) milk-; **la Voie lactée** the Milky Way.
lacune [lakyn] *nf* gap, deficiency.
lad [lad] *nm* stable boy, groom.
là-dedans [lad(ə)dɑ̃] *adv* (*lieu*) in there, inside. ◆**là-dessous** *adv* underneath. ◆**là-dessus** *adv* on it, on that; (*monter*) on top; (*alors*) thereupon. ◆**là-haut** *adv* up there; (*à l'étage*) upstairs.
lagon [lagɔ̃] *nm* (small) lagoon. ◆**lagune** *nf* lagoon.
laid [lɛ] *a* ugly; (*ignoble*) wretched. ◆**laideur** *nf* ugliness.
laine [lɛn] *nf* wool; **de l., en l.** woollen. ◆**lainage** *nm* (*vêtement*) woollen garment, woolly; (*étoffe*) woollen material; *pl* (*vêtements, objets fabriqués*) woollens. ◆**laineux, -euse** *a* woolly.
laïque [laik] *a* (*vie*) secular; (*habit, tribunal*) lay; – *nmf* (*non-prêtre*) layman, laywoman.
laisse [lɛs] *nf* lead, leash; **en l.** on a lead *ou* leash.
laisser [lese] *vt* to leave; **l. qn partir/entrer/etc** (*permettre*) to let s.o. go/come in/*etc*; **l. qch à qn** (*confier, donner*) to let s.o. have sth, leave sth with s.o.; (*vendre*) to let s.o. have sth; **laissez-moi le temps de le faire** give me *ou* leave me time to do it; **se l. aller/faire** to let oneself go/be pushed around. ◆**laissé(e)-pour-compte** *nmf* (*personne*) misfit, reject. ◆**laisser-aller** *nm inv* carelessness, slovenliness; ◆**laissez-passer** *nm inv* (*sauf-conduit*) pass.
lait [lɛ] *nm* milk; **frère/sœur de l.** foster-brother/-sister; **dent de l.** milk tooth. ◆**laitage** *nm* milk product *ou* food. ◆**laiterie** *nf* dairy. ◆**laiteux, -euse** *a* milky. ◆**laitier, -ière** *a* (*produits*) dairy-; – *nm* (*livreur*) milkman; (*vendeur*) dairyman; – *nf* dairywoman.
laiton [lɛtɔ̃] *nm* brass.

laitue [lety] *nf* lettuce.
laïus [lajys] *nm Fam* speech.
lama [lama] *nm* (*animal*) llama.
lambeau, -x [lɑ̃bo] *nm* shred, bit; **mettre en lambeaux** to tear to shreds; **tomber en lambeaux** to fall to bits.
lambin, -ine [lɑ̃bɛ̃, -in] *nmf* dawdler. ◆**lambiner** *vi* to dawdle.
lambris [lɑ̃bri] *nm* panelling. ◆**lambrisser** *vt* to panel.
lame [lam] *nf* **1** (*de couteau, rasoir etc*) blade; (*de métal*) strip, plate; **l. de parquet** floorboard. **2** (*vague*) wave; **l. de fond** ground swell.
lamelle [lamɛl] *nf* thin strip; **l. de verre** (*pour microscope*) slide.
lamenter (se) [səlamɑ̃te] *vpr* to moan, lament; **se l. sur** to lament (over). ◆**lamentable** *a* (*mauvais*) deplorable; (*voix, cri*) mournful. ◆**lamentation** *nf* lament(ation).
laminé [lamine] *a* (*métal*) laminated.
lampadaire [lɑ̃padɛr] *nm* standard lamp; (*de rue*) street lamp.
lampe [lɑ̃p] *nf* lamp; (*au néon*) light; (*de vieille radio*) valve, *Am* (vacuum) tube; **l. de poche** torch, *Am* flashlight.
lampée [lɑ̃pe] *nf Fam* gulp.
lampion [lɑ̃pjɔ̃] *nm* Chinese lantern.
lance [lɑ̃s] *nf* spear; (*de tournoi*) *Hist* lance; (*extrémité de tuyau*) nozzle; **l. d'incendie** fire hose.
lance-flammes [lɑ̃sflam] *nm inv* flame thrower. ◆**l.-pierres** *nm inv* catapult. ◆**l.-roquettes** *nm inv* rocket launcher.
lanc/er [lɑ̃se] *vt* (*jeter*) to throw (**à** to); (*avec force*) to hurl; (*navire, mode, acteur, idée*) to launch; (*regard*) to cast (**à** at); (*moteur*) to start; (*ultimatum*) to issue; (*bombe*) to drop; (*gifle*) to give; (*cri*) to utter; — **se l.** *vpr* (*se précipiter*) to rush; **se l. dans** (*aventure, discussion*) to launch into; – *nm* **un l.** a throw; **le l. de** the throwing of. ◆**—ée** *nf* momentum. ◆**—ement** *nm Sp* throwing; (*de fusée, navire etc*) launch(ing).
lancinant [lɑ̃sinɑ̃] *a* (*douleur*) shooting; (*obsédant*) haunting.
landau [lɑ̃do] *nm* (*pl* **-s**) pram, *Am* baby carriage.
lande [lɑ̃d] *nf* moor, heath.
langage [lɑ̃gaʒ] *nm* (*système, faculté d'expression*) language; **l. machine** computer language.
lange [lɑ̃ʒ] *nm* (baby) blanket. ◆**langer** *vt* (*bébé*) to change.
langouste [lɑ̃gust] *nf* (spiny) lobster. ◆**langoustine** *nf* (Dublin) prawn, Norway lobster.
langue [lɑ̃g] *nf Anat* tongue; *Ling* language; **de l. anglaise/française** English-/French-speaking; **l. maternelle** mother tongue; **mauvaise l.** (*personne*) gossip. ◆**languette** *nf* (*patte*) tongue.
langueur [lɑ̃gœr] *nf* languor. ◆**langu/ir** *vi* to languish (**après** for, after); (*conversation*) to flag. ◆**—issant** *a* languid; (*conversation*) flagging.
lanière [lanjɛr] *nf* strap; (*d'étoffe*) strip.
lanterne [lɑ̃tɛrn] *nf* lantern; (*électrique*) lamp; *pl Aut* sidelights.
lanterner [lɑ̃tɛrne] *vi* to loiter.
lapalissade [lapalisad] *nf* statement of the obvious, truism.
laper [lape] *vt* (*boire*) to lap up; – *vi* to lap.
lapider [lapide] *vt* to stone.
lapin [lapɛ̃] *nm* rabbit; **mon (petit) l.!** my dear!; **poser un l. à qn** *Fam* to stand s.o. up.
laps [laps] *nm* **un l. de temps** a lapse of time.
lapsus [lapsys] *nm* slip (of the tongue).
laquais [lakɛ] *nm Hist & Fig* lackey.
laque [lak] *nf* lacquer; **l. à cheveux** hair spray, (hair) lacquer. ◆**laquer** *vt* to lacquer.
laquelle [lakɛl] *voir* **lequel**.
larbin [larbɛ̃] *nm Fam* flunkey.
lard [lar] *nm* (*fumé*) bacon; (*gras*) (pig's) fat. ◆**lardon** *nm Culin* strip of bacon *ou* fat.
large [larʒ] *a* wide, broad; (*vêtement*) loose; (*idées, esprit*) broad; (*grand*) large; (*généreux*) liberal; **l. d'esprit** broad-minded; **l. de six mètres** six metres wide; – *adv* (*calculer*) liberally, broadly; – *nm* breadth, width; **avoir six mètres de l.** to be six metres wide; **le l.** (*mer*) the open sea; **au l. de Cherbourg** *Nau* off Cherbourg; **être au l.** to have lots of room. ◆**—ment** *adv* widely; (*ouvrir*) wide; (*servir, payer*) liberally; (*au moins*) easily; **avoir l. le temps** to have plenty of time, have ample time. ◆**largesse** *nf* liberality. ◆**largeur** *nf* width, breadth; (*d'esprit*) breadth.
larguer [large] *vt* (*bombe, parachutiste*) to drop; **l. qn** (*se débarrasser de*) to drop s.o.; **l. les amarres** *Nau* to cast off.
larme [larm] *nf* tear; (*goutte*) *Fam* drop; **en larmes** in tears; **rire aux larmes** to laugh till one cries. ◆**larmoyer** *vi* (*yeux*) to water.
larve [larv] *nf* (*d'insecte*) larva, grub.
larvé [larve] *a* latent, underlying.
larynx [larɛ̃ks] *nm Anat* larynx ◆**laryngite** *nf Méd* laryngitis.
las, lasse [lɑ, lɑs] *a* tired, weary (**de** of).

◆**lasser** *vt* to tire, weary; **se l. de** to tire of. ◆**lassitude** *nf* tiredness, weariness.
lascar [laskar] *nm Fam* (clever) fellow.
lascif, -ive [lasif, -iv] *a* lascivious.
laser [lazɛr] *nm* laser.
lasso [laso] *nm* lasso.
latent [latɑ̃] *a* latent.
latéral, -aux [lateral, -o] *a* lateral, side-.
latin, -ine [latɛ̃, -in] *a & nmf* Latin; – *nm* (*langue*) Latin.
latitude [latityd] *nf Géog & Fig* latitude.
latrines [latrin] *nfpl* latrines.
latte [lat] *nf* slat, lath; (*de plancher*) board.
lauréat, -ate [lɔrea, -at] *nmf* (prize)winner; – *a* prize-winning.
laurier [lɔrje] *nm Bot* laurel, bay; **du l.** *Culin* bay leaves.
lavabo [lavabo] *nm* washbasin, sink; *pl* (*cabinet*) toilet(s), *Am* washroom.
lavande [lavɑ̃d] *nf* lavender.
lave [lav] *nf Géol* lava.
lave-auto [lavoto] *nm* car wash. ◆**l.-glace** *nm* windscreen *ou Am* windshield washer. ◆**l.-linge** *nm* washing machine. ◆**l.-vaisselle** *nm* dishwasher.
laver [lave] *vt* to wash; **l. qn de** (*soupçon etc*) to clear s.o. of; – **se l.** *vpr* to wash (oneself), *Am* wash up; **se l. les mains** to wash one's hands (*Fig* **de** of). ◆**lavable** *a* washable. ◆**lavage** *nm* washing; **l. de cerveau** *Psy* brainwashing. ◆**laverie** *nf* (*automatique*) launderette, *Am* laundromat. ◆**lavette** *nf* dish cloth; (*homme*) *Péj* drip. ◆**laveur** *nm* **l. de carreaux** window cleaner *ou Am* washer. ◆**lavoir** *nm* (*bâtiment*) washhouse.
laxatif, -ive [laksatif, -iv] *nm & a Méd* laxative.
laxisme [laksism] *nm* permissiveness, laxity. ◆**laxiste** *a* permissive, lax.
layette [lɛjɛt] *nf* baby clothes, layette.
le, la, *pl* **les** [l(ə), la, le] (**le** & **la** *become* **l'** *before a vowel or mute h*) **1** *art déf* (**à + le = au, à + les = aux; de + le = du, de + les = des**) the; **le garçon** the boy; **la fille** the girl; **venez, les enfants!** come children!; **les petits/rouges/***etc* the little ones/red ones/*etc*; **mon ami le plus intime** my closest friend. **2** (*généralisation, abstraction*) **la beauté** beauty; **la France** France; **les Français** the French; **les hommes** men; **aimer le café** to like coffee. **3** (*possession*) **il ouvrit la bouche** he opened his mouth; **se blesser au pied** to hurt one's foot; **avoir les cheveux blonds** to have blond hair. **4** (*mesure*) **dix francs le kilo** ten francs a kilo. **5** (*temps*) **elle vient le lundi** she comes on Monday(s); **elle passe le soir** she comes over in the evening(s); **l'an prochain** next year; **une fois l'an** once a year. **6** *pron* (*homme*) him; (*femme*) her; (*chose, animal*) it; *pl* them; **je la vois** I see her; I see it; **je le vois** I see him; I see it; **je les vois** I see them; **es-tu fatigué?** – **je le suis** are you tired? – I am; **je le crois** I think so.
leader [lidœr] *nm Pol* leader.
lécher [leʃe] *vt* to lick; **se l. les doigts** to lick one's fingers. ◆**lèche-vitrines** *nm* **faire du l.-vitrines** to go window-shopping.
leçon [ləsɔ̃] *nf* lesson; **faire la l. à qn** to lecture s.o.
lecteur, -trice [lɛktœr, -tris] *nmf* reader; *Univ* (foreign language) assistant; **l. de cassettes** cassette player. ◆**lecture** *nf* reading; *pl* (*livres*) books; **faire de la l. à qn** to read to s.o.; **de la l.** some reading matter.
légal, -aux [legal, -o] *a* legal; (*médecine*) forensic. ◆**légalement** *adv* legally. ◆**légaliser** *vt* to legalize. ◆**légalité** *nf* legality (**de** of); **respecter la l.** to respect the law.
légation [legasjɔ̃] *nf Pol* legation.
légende [leʒɑ̃d] *nf* **1** (*histoire, fable*) legend. **2** (*de plan, carte*) key, legend; (*de photo*) caption. ◆**légendaire** *a* legendary.
léger, -ère [leʒe, -ɛr] *a* light; (*bruit, faute, fièvre etc*) slight; (*café, thé, argument*) weak; (*bière, tabac*) mild; (*frivole*) frivolous; (*irréfléchi*) careless; **à la légère** (*agir*) rashly. ◆**légèrement** *adv* lightly; (*un peu*) slightly; (*à la légère*) rashly. ◆**légèreté** *nf* lightness; frivolity.
légiférer [leʒifere] *vi* to legislate.
légion [leʒjɔ̃] *nf Mil & Fig* legion. ◆**légionnaire** *nm* (*de la Légion étrangère*) legionnaire.
législatif, -ive [leʒislatif, -iv] *a* legislative; (*élections*) parliamentary. ◆**législation** *nf* legislation. ◆**législature** *nf* (*période*) *Pol* term of office.
légitime [leʒitim] *a* (*action, enfant etc*) legitimate; **en état de l. défense** acting in self-defence. ◆**légitimité** *nf* legitimacy.
legs [lɛg] *nm Jur* legacy, bequest; (*héritage*) *Fig* legacy. ◆**léguer** *vt* to bequeath (**à** to).
légume [legym] **1** *nm* vegetable. **2** *nf* **grosse l.** (*personne*) *Fam* bigwig.
lendemain [lɑ̃dmɛ̃] *nm* **le l.** the next day; (*avenir*) *Fig* the future; **le l. de** the day after; **le l. matin** the next morning.
lent [lɑ̃] *a* slow. ◆**lentement** *adv* slowly. ◆**lenteur** *nf* slowness.
lentille [lɑ̃tij] *nf* **1** *Bot Culin* lentil. **2** (*verre*) lens.
léopard [leɔpar] *nm* leopard.

lèpre [lɛpr] *nf* leprosy. ◆**lépreux, -euse** *a* leprous; – *nmf* leper.
lequel, laquelle, *pl* **lesquels, lesquelles** [ləkɛl, lakɛl, lekɛl] (+ **à** = **auquel, à laquelle, auxquel(le)s;** + **de** = **duquel, de laquelle, desquel(le)s**) *pron* (*chose, animal*) which; (*personne*) who, (*indirect*) whom; (*interrogatif*) which (one); **dans l.** in which; **parmi lesquels** (*choses, animaux*) among which; (*personnes*) among whom; **l. préférez-vous?** which (one) do you prefer?
les [le] *voir* **le.**
lesbienne [lɛsbjɛn] *nf* & *af* lesbian.
léser [leze] *vt* (*personne*) *Jur* to wrong.
lésiner [lezine] *vi* to be stingy (**sur** with).
lésion [lezjɔ̃] *nf Méd* lesion.
lessive [lesiv] *nf* (*produit*) washing powder; (*linge*) washing; **faire la l.** to do the wash(ing). ◆**lessiv/er** *vt* to scrub, wash. ◆**—é** *a Fam* (*fatigué*) washed-out; (*ruiné*) washed-up. ◆**—euse** *nf* (laundry) boiler.
lest [lɛst] *nm* ballast. ◆**lester** *vt* to ballast, weight down; (*remplir*) *Fam* to overload.
leste [lɛst] *a* (*agile*) nimble; (*grivois*) coarse.
léthargie [letarʒi] *nf* lethargy. ◆**léthargique** *a* lethargic.
lettre [lɛtr] *nf* (*missive, caractère*) letter; **en toutes lettres** (*mot*) in full; (*nombre*) in words; **les lettres** (*discipline*) *Univ* arts; **homme de lettres** man of letters. ◆**lettré, -ée** *a* well-read; – *nmf* scholar.
leucémie [løsemi] *nf* leuk(a)emia.
leur [lœr] **1** *a poss* their; **l. chat** their cat; **leurs voitures** their cars; – *pron poss* **le l., la l., les leurs** theirs. **2** *pron inv* (*indirect*) (to) them; **il l. est facile de . . .** it's easy for them to . . . .
leurre [lœr] *nm* illusion; (*tromperie*) trickery. ◆**leurrer** *vt* to delude.
lev/er [l(ə)ve] *vt* to lift (up), raise; (*blocus, interdiction*) to lift; (*séance*) to close; (*camp*) to strike; (*plan*) to draw up; (*impôts, armée*) to levy; **l. les yeux** to look up; – *vi* (*pâte*) to rise; (*blé*) to come up; – **se l.** *vpr* to get up; (*soleil, rideau*) to rise; (*jour*) to break; (*brume*) to clear, lift; – *nm* **le l. du soleil** sunrise; **le l. du rideau** *Th* the curtain. ◆**—ant** *a* (*soleil*) rising; – *nm* **le l.** the east. ◆**—é** *a* **être l.** (*debout*) to be up. ◆**—ée** *nf* (*d'interdiction*) lifting; (*d'impôts*) levying; (*du courrier*) collection; **l. de boucliers** public outcry.
levier [ləvje] *nm* lever; (*pour soulever*) crowbar.
lèvre [lɛvr] *nf* lip; **du bout des lèvres** half-heartedly, grudgingly.
lévrier [levrije] *nm* greyhound.
levure [ləvyr] *nf* yeast.
lexique [lɛksik] *nm* vocabulary, glossary.
lézard [lezar] *nm* lizard.
lézarde [lezard] *nf* crack, split. ◆**lézarder** **1** *vi Fam* to bask in the sun. **2 se l.** *vpr* to crack, split.
liaison [ljɛzɔ̃] *nf* (*rapport*) connection; (*routière etc*) link; *Gram Mil* liaison; **l. (amoureuse)** love affair; **en l. avec qn** in contact with s.o.
liane [ljan] *nf Bot* jungle vine.
liant [ljɑ̃] *a* sociable.
liasse [ljas] *nf* bundle.
Liban [libɑ̃] *nm* Lebanon. ◆**libanais, -aise** *a* & *nmf* Lebanese.
libell/er [libele] *vt* (*contrat etc*) to word, draw up; (*chèque*) to make out. ◆**—é** *nm* wording.
libellule [libelyl] *nf* dragonfly.
libéral, -ale, -aux [liberal, -o] *a* & *nmf* liberal. ◆**libéraliser** *vt* to liberalize. ◆**libéralisme** *nm* liberalism. ◆**libéralité** *nf* liberality; (*don*) liberal gift.
libérer [libere] *vt* (*prisonnier etc*) to (set) free, release; (*pays, esprit*) to liberate (**de** from); **l. qn de** to free s.o. of *ou* from; – **se l.** *vpr* to get free, free oneself (**de** of, from). ◆**libérateur, -trice** *a* (*sentiment etc*) liberating; – *nmf* liberator. ◆**libération** *nf* freeing, release; liberation; **l. conditionnelle** *Jur* parole. ◆**liberté** *nf* freedom, liberty; **en l. provisoire** *Jur* on bail; **mettre en l.** to free, release; **mise en l.** release.
libraire [librɛr] *nmf* bookseller. ◆**librairie** *nf* (*magasin*) bookshop.
libre [libr] *a* free (**de qch** from sth, **de faire** to do); (*voie, route*) clear; (*place*) vacant, free; (*école*) private (and religious); **l. penseur** freethinker. ◆**l.-échange** *nm Écon* free trade. ◆**l.-service** *nm* (*pl* **libres-services**) (*système, magasin etc*) self-service. ◆**librement** *adv* freely.
Libye [libi] *nf* Libya. ◆**libyen, -enne** *a* & *nmf* Libyan.
licence [lisɑ̃s] *nf Sp Com Littér* licence; *Univ* (bachelor's) degree; **l. ès lettres/sciences** arts/science degree, = BA/BSc, = *Am* BA/BS. ◆**licencié, -ée** *a* & *nmf* graduate; **l. ès lettres/sciences** bachelor of arts/science, = BA/BSc, = *Am* BA/BS.
licencier [lisɑ̃sje] *vt* (*ouvrier*) to lay off, dismiss. ◆**licenciement** *nm* dismissal.
licite [lisit] *a* licit, lawful.
licorne [likɔrn] *nf* unicorn.
lie [li] *nf* dregs.
liège [ljɛʒ] *nm* (*matériau*) cork.
lien [ljɛ̃] *nm* (*rapport*) link, connection; (*de*

parenté) tie, bond; (*attache, ficelle*) tie. ◆**lier** *vt* (*attacher*) to tie (up), bind; (*relier*) to link (up), connect; (*conversation, amitié*) to strike up; **l. qn** (*unir, engager*) to bind s.o.; **— se l.** *vpr* (*idées etc*) to connect, link together; **se l. avec qn** to make friends with s.o.; **amis très liés** very close friends.
lierre [ljɛr] *nm* ivy.
lieu, -x [ljø] *nm* place; (*d'un accident*) scene; **les lieux** (*locaux*) the premises; **sur les lieux** on the spot; **avoir l.** to take place, be held; **au l. de** instead of; **avoir l. de faire** (*des raisons*) to have good reason to do; **en premier l.** in the first place, firstly; **en dernier l.** lastly; **l. commun** commonplace. ◆**l.-dit** *nm* (*pl* **lieux-dits**) *Géog* locality.
lieue [ljø] *nf* (*mesure*) *Hist* league.
lieutenant [ljøtnɑ̃] *nm* lieutenant.
lièvre [ljɛvr] *nm* hare.
ligament [ligamɑ̃] *nm* ligament.
ligne [liɲ] *nf* (*trait, règle, contour, transport*) line; (*belle silhouette de femme etc*) figure; (*rangée*) row, line; **(se) mettre en l.** to line up; **en l.** *Tél* connected, through; **entrer en l. de compte** to be of consequence, count; **faire entrer en l. de compte** to take into account; **grande l.** *Rail* main line; **les grandes lignes** *Fig* the broad outline; **pilote de l.** airline pilot; **à la l.** *Gram* new paragraph.
lignée [liɲe] *nf* line, ancestry.
ligoter [ligɔte] *vt* to tie up.
ligue [lig] *nf* (*alliance*) league. ◆**se liguer** *vpr* to join together, gang up (**contre** against).
lilas [lilɑ] *nm* lilac; – *a inv* (*couleur*) lilac.
limace [limas] *nf* (*mollusque*) slug.
limaille [limɑj] *nf* filings.
limande [limɑ̃d] *nf* (*poisson*) dab.
lime [lim] *nf* (*outil*) file. ◆**limer** *vt* to file.
limier [limje] *nm* (*chien*) bloodhound.
limite [limit] *nf* limit; (*de propriété, jardin etc*) boundary; *pl Fb* boundary lines; **dépasser la l.** to go beyond the bounds; – *a* (*cas*) extreme; (*vitesse, prix, âge etc*) maximum; **date l.** latest date, deadline; **date l. de vente** *Com* sell-by date. ◆**limitatif, -ive** *a* restrictive. ◆**limitation** *nf* limitation; (*de vitesse*) limit. ◆**limiter** *vt* to limit, restrict; (*délimiter*) to border; **se l. à faire** to limit *ou* restrict oneself to doing.
limoger [limɔʒe] *vt* (*destituer*) to dismiss.
limonade [limɔnad] *nf* (fizzy) lemonade.
limpide [lɛ̃pid] *a* (*eau, explication*) (crystal) clear. ◆**limpidité** *nf* clearness.
lin [lɛ̃] *nm Bot* flax; (*tissu*) linen; **huile de l.** linseed oil.
linceul [lɛ̃sœl] *nm* shroud.
linéaire [lineɛr] *a* linear.
linge [lɛ̃ʒ] *nm* (*pièces de tissu*) linen; (*à laver*) washing, linen; (*torchon*) cloth; **l. (de corps)** underwear. ◆**lingerie** *nf* (*de femmes*) underwear; (*local*) linen room.
lingot [lɛ̃go] *nm* ingot.
linguiste [lɛ̃gɥist] *nmf* linguist. ◆**linguistique** *a* linguistic; – *nf* linguistics.
lino [lino] *nm* lino. ◆**linoléum** *nm* linoleum.
linotte [linɔt] *nf* (*oiseau*) linnet; **tête de l.** *Fig* scatterbrain.
lion [ljɔ̃] *nm* lion. ◆**lionceau, -x** *nm* lion cub. ◆**lionne** *nf* lioness.
liquéfier [likefje] *vt*, **— se l.** *vpr* to liquefy.
liqueur [likœr] *nf* liqueur.
liquide [likid] *a* liquid; **argent l.** ready cash; – *nm* liquid; **du l.** (*argent*) ready cash.
liquider [likide] *vt* (*dette, stock etc*) to liquidate; (*affaire, travail*) to wind up, finish off; **l. qn** (*tuer*) *Fam* to liquidate s.o. ◆**liquidation** *nf* liquidation; winding up; (*vente*) (clearance) sale.
lire[1*] [lir] *vti* to read.
lire[2] [lir] *nf* (*monnaie*) lira.
lis[1] [lis] *nm* (*plante, fleur*) lily.
lis[2], **lisent** [li, liz] *voir* **lire**[1].
liseron [lizrɔ̃] *nm Bot* convolvulus.
lisible [lizibl] *a* (*écriture*) legible; (*livre*) readable. ◆**lisiblement** *adv* legibly.
lisière [lizjɛr] *nf* edge, border.
lisse [lis] *a* smooth. ◆**lisser** *vt* to smooth; (*plumes*) to preen.
liste [list] *nf* list; **l. électorale** register of electors, electoral roll; **sur la l. rouge** *Tél* ex-directory, *Am* unlisted.
lit[1] [li] *nm* bed; **l. d'enfant** cot, *Am* crib; **lits superposés** bunk beds; **garder le l.** to stay in bed. ◆**literie** *nf* bedding, bed clothes.
lit[2] [li] *voir* **lire**[1].
litanie [litani] **1** *nf* (*énumération*) long list (de of). **2** *nfpl* (*prière*) *Rel* litany.
litière [litjɛr] *nf* (*couche de paille*) litter.
litige [litiʒ] *nm* dispute; *Jur* litigation. ◆**litigieux, -euse** *a* contentious.
litre [litr] *nm* litre.
littéraire [literɛr] *a* literary. ◆**littérature** *nf* literature.
littéral, -aux [literal, -o] *a* literal. ◆**—ement** *adv* literally.
littoral, -aux [litɔral, -o] *a* coastal; – *nm* coast(line).
liturgie [lityrʒi] *nf* liturgy. ◆**liturgique** *a* liturgical.
livide [livid] *a* (*bleuâtre*) livid; (*pâle*) (ghastly) pale, pallid.
livre [livr] **1** *nm* book; **l. de bord** *Nau* log-

book; **l. de poche** paperback (book); **le l., l'industrie du l.** the book industry. **2** *nf* (*monnaie, poids*) pound. ◆**livresque** *a* (*savoir*) *Péj* bookish. ◆**livret** *nm* (*registre*) book; *Mus* libretto; **l. scolaire** school report book; **l. de famille** family registration book; **l. de caisse d'épargne** bankbook, passbook.

livrée [livre] *nf* (*uniforme*) livery.

livrer [livre] *vt* (*marchandises*) to deliver (**à** to); (*secret*) to give away; **l. qn à** (*la police etc*) to give s.o. up *ou* over to; **l. bataille** to do *ou* join battle; **— se l.** *vpr* (*se rendre*) to give oneself up (**à** to); (*se confier*) to confide (**à** in); **se l. à** (*habitude, excès etc*) to indulge in; (*tâche*) to devote oneself to; (*désespoir, destin*) to abandon oneself to. ◆**livraison** *nf* delivery. ◆**livreur, -euse** *nmf* delivery man, delivery woman.

lobe [lɔb] *nm Anat* lobe.

local, -aux [lɔkal, -o] **1** *a* local. **2** *nm & nmpl* (*pièce, bâtiment*) premises. ◆**localement** *adv* locally. ◆**localiser** *vt* (*déterminer*) to locate; (*limiter*) to localize. ◆**localité** *nf* locality.

locataire [lɔkatɛr] *nmf* tenant; (*hôte payant*) lodger.

location [lɔkasjɔ̃] *nf* (*de maison etc*) renting; (*à bail*) leasing; (*de voiture*) hiring; (*réservation*) booking; (*par propriétaire*) renting (out), letting; leasing (out); hiring (out); (*loyer*) rental; (*bail*) lease; **bureau de l.** booking office; **en l.** on hire.

lock-out [lɔkawt] *nm inv* (*industriel*) lock-out.

locomotion [lɔkɔmosjɔ̃] *nf* locomotion. ◆**locomotive** *nf* locomotive, engine.

locuteur [lɔkytœr] *nm Ling* speaker. ◆**locution** *nf* phrase, idiom; *Gram* phrase.

logarithme [lɔgaritm] *nm* logarithm.

loge [lɔʒ] *nf* (*de concierge*) lodge; (*d'acteur*) dressing-room; (*de spectateur*) *Th* box.

log/er [lɔʒe] *vt* (*recevoir, mettre*) to accommodate, house; (*héberger*) to put up; **être logé et nourri** to have board and lodging; – *vi* (*à l'hôtel etc*) to put up, lodge; (*habiter*) to live; **(trouver à) se l.** to find somewhere to live; (*temporairement*) to find somewhere to stay; **se l. dans** (*balle*) to lodge (itself) in. ◆**—eable** *a* habitable. ◆**—ement** *nm* accommodation, lodging; (*habitat*) housing; (*appartement*) lodgings, flat, *Am* apartment; (*maison*) dwelling. ◆**—eur, -euse** *nmf* landlord, landlady.

logiciel [lɔʒisjɛl] *nm* (*d'un ordinateur*) software *inv*.

logique [lɔʒik] *a* logical; – *nf* logic. ◆**—ment** *adv* logically.

logistique [lɔʒistik] *nf* logistics.

logo [lɔgo] *nm* logo.

loi [lwa] *nf* law; *Pol* act; **projet de l.** *Pol* bill; **faire la l.** to lay down the law (**à** to).

loin [lwɛ̃] *adv* far (away *ou* off); **Boston est l. (de Paris)** Boston is a long way away (from Paris); **plus l.** further, farther; (*ci-après*) further on; **l. de là** *Fig* far from it; **au l.** in the distance, far away; **de l.** from a distance; (*de beaucoup*) by far; **de l. en l.** every so often. ◆**lointain** *a* distant, far-off; – *nm* **dans le l.** in the distance.

loir [lwar] *nm* (*animal*) dormouse.

loisir [lwazir] *nm* **le l. de faire** the time to do; **moment de l.** moment of leisure; **loisirs** (*temps libre*) spare time, leisure (time); (*distractions*) spare-time *ou* leisure activities.

Londres [lɔ̃dr] *nm ou f* London. ◆**londonien, -ienne** *a* London-; – *nmf* Londoner.

long, longue [lɔ̃, lɔ̃g] *a* long; **être l. (à faire)** to be a long time *ou* slow (in doing); **l. de deux mètres** two metres long; – *nm* **avoir deux mètres de l.** to be two metres long; **tomber de tout son l.** to fall flat; **(tout) le l. de** (*espace*) (all) along; **tout le l. de** (*temps*) throughout; **de l. en large** (*marcher etc*) up and down; **en l. et en large** thoroughly; **en l.** lengthwise; **à la longue** in the long run. ◆**l.-courrier** *nm Av* long-distance airliner. ◆**longue-vue** *nf* (*pl* **longues-vues**) telescope.

longer [lɔ̃ʒe] *vt* to pass *ou* go along; (*forêt, mer*) to skirt; (*mur*) to hug.

longévité [lɔ̃ʒevite] *nf* longevity.

longitude [lɔ̃ʒityd] *nf* longitude.

longtemps [lɔ̃tɑ̃] *adv* (for) a long time; **trop/avant l.** too/before long; **aussi l. que** as long as.

longue [lɔ̃g] *voir* **long.** ◆**longuement** *adv* at length. ◆**longuet, -ette** *a Fam* (fairly) lengthy. ◆**longueur** *nf* length; *pl* (*de texte, film*) over-long passages; **saut en l.** *Sp* long jump; **à l. de journée** all day long; **l. d'onde** *Rad & Fig* wavelength.

lopin [lɔpɛ̃] *nm* **l. de terre** plot *ou* patch of land.

loquace [lɔkas] *a* loquacious.

loque [lɔk] **1** *nfpl* rags. **2** *nf* **l. (humaine)** (*personne*) human wreck.

loquet [lɔkɛ] *nm* latch.

lorgner [lɔrɲe] *vt* (*regarder, convoiter*) to eye.

lors [lɔr] *adv* **l. de** at the time of; **depuis l.,**

dès l. from then on; **dès l. que** (*puisque*) since.

losange [lɔzɑ̃ʒ] *nm Géom* diamond, lozenge.

lot [lo] *nm* **1** (*de loterie*) prize; **gros l.** top prize, jackpot. **2** (*portion, destin*) lot. ◆**loterie** *nf* lottery, raffle. ◆**lotir** *vt* (*terrain*) to divide into lots; **bien loti** *Fig* favoured by fortune. ◆**lotissement** *nm* (*terrain*) building plot; (*habitations*) housing estate *ou* development.

lotion [losjɔ̃] *nf* lotion.

loto [lɔto] *nm* (*jeu*) lotto.

louche [luʃ] **1** *a* (*suspect*) shady, fishy. **2** *nf Culin* ladle.

loucher [luʃe] *vi* to squint; **l. sur** *Fam* to eye.

louer [lwe] *vt* **1** (*prendre en location*) to rent (*house, flat etc*); (*à bail*) to lease; (*voiture*) to hire, rent; (*réserver*) to book; (*donner en location*) to rent (out), let; to lease (out); to hire (out); **maison/chambre à l.** house/room to let. **2** (*exalter*) to praise (**de** for); **se l. de** to be highly satisfied with. ◆**louable** *a* praiseworthy, laudable. ◆**louange** *nf* praise; **à la l. de** in praise of.

loufoque [lufɔk] *a* (*fou*) *Fam* nutty, crazy.

loukoum [lukum] *nm* Turkish delight.

loup [lu] *nm* wolf; **avoir une faim de l.** to be ravenous. ◆**l.-garou** *nm* (*pl* **loups-garous**) werewolf.

loupe [lup] *nf* magnifying glass.

louper [lupe] *vt Fam* (*train etc*) to miss; (*examen*) to fail; (*travail*) to mess up.

lourd [lur] *a* heavy (*Fig* **de** with); (*temps, chaleur*) close, sultry; (*faute*) gross; (*tâche*) arduous; (*esprit*) dull; – *adv* **peser l.** (*malle etc*) to be heavy. ◆**lourdaud, -aude** *a* loutish, oafish; – *nmf* lout, oaf. ◆**lourdement** *adv* heavily. ◆**lourdeur** *nf* heaviness; (*de temps*) closeness; (*d'esprit*) dullness.

loutre [lutr] *nf* otter.

louve [luv] *nf* she-wolf. ◆**louveteau, -x** *nm* (*scout*) cub (scout).

louvoyer [luvwaje] *vi* (*tergiverser*) to hedge, be evasive.

loyal, -aux [lwajal, -o] *a* (*fidèle*) loyal (**envers** to); (*honnête*) honest, fair (**envers** to). ◆**loyalement** *adv* loyally; fairly. ◆**loyauté** *nf* loyalty; honesty, fairness.

loyer [lwaje] *nm* rent.

lu [ly] *voir* **lire**[1].

lubie [lybi] *nf* whim.

lubrifi/er [lybrifje] *vt* to lubricate. ◆**–ant** *nm* lubricant.

lubrique [lybrik] *a* lewd, lustful.

lucarne [lykarn] *nf* (*ouverture*) skylight; (*fenêtre*) dormer window.

lucide [lysid] *a* lucid. ◆**lucidité** *nf* lucidity.

lucratif, -ive [lykratif, -iv] *a* lucrative.

lueur [lɥœr] *nf* (*lumière*) & *Fig* glimmer.

luge [lyʒ] *nf* toboggan, sledge.

lugubre [lygybr] *a* gloomy, lugubrious.

lui [lɥi] **1** *pron mf* (*complément indirect*) (to) him; (*femme*) (to) her; (*chose, animal*) (to) it; **je le lui ai montré** I showed it to him *ou* to her, I showed him it *ou* her it; **il lui est facile de . . .** it's easy for him *ou* her to . . . . **2** *pron m* (*complément direct*) him; (*chose, animal*) it; (*sujet emphatique*) he; **pour lui** for him; **plus grand que lui** taller than him; **il ne pense qu'à lui** he only thinks of himself. ◆**lui-même** *pron* himself; (*chose, animal*) itself.

luire* [lɥir] *vi* to shine, gleam. ◆**luisant** *a* (*métal etc*) shiny.

lumbago [lɔ̃bago] *nm* lumbago.

lumière [lymjer] *nf* light; **à la l. de** by the light of; (*grâce à*) *Fig* in the light of; **faire toute la l. sur** *Fig* to clear up; **mettre en l.** to bring to light. ◆**luminaire** *nm* (*appareil*) lighting appliance. ◆**lumineux, -euse** *a* (*idée, ciel etc*) bright, brilliant; (*ondes, source etc*) light-; (*cadran, corps etc*) *Tech* luminous.

lunaire [lyner] *a* lunar; **clarté l.** light *ou* brightness of of the moon.

lunatique [lynatik] *a* temperamental.

lunch [lœʃ, lœntʃ] *nm* buffet lunch, snack.

lundi [lœ̃di] *nm* Monday.

lune [lyn] *nf* moon; **l. de miel** honeymoon.

lunette [lynet] *nf* **1 lunettes** glasses, spectacles; (*de protection, de plongée*) goggles; **lunettes de soleil** sunglasses. **2** (*astronomique*) telescope; **l. arrière** *Aut* rear window.

lurette [lyret] *nf* **il y a belle l.** a long time ago.

luron [lyrɔ̃] *nm* **gai l.** gay fellow.

lustre [lystr] *nm* (*éclairage*) chandelier; (*éclat*) lustre. ◆**lustré** *a* (*par l'usure*) shiny.

luth [lyt] *nm Mus* lute.

lutin [lytɛ̃] *nm* elf, imp, goblin.

lutte [lyt] *nf* fight, struggle; *Sp* wrestling; **l. des classes** class warfare *ou* struggle. ◆**lutter** *vi* to fight, struggle; *Sp* to wrestle. ◆**lutteur, -euse** *nmf* fighter; *Sp* wrestler.

luxe [lyks] *nm* luxury; **un l. de** a wealth of; **de l.** (*article*) luxury-; (*modèle*) de luxe. ◆**luxueux, -euse** *a* luxurious.

Luxembourg [lyksɑ̃bur] *nm* Luxembourg.

luxure [lyksyr] *nf* lewdness, lust.

luxuriant [lyksyrjɑ̃] *a* luxuriant.

luzerne [lyzɛrn] *nf Bot* lucerne, *Am* alfalfa.
lycée [lise] *nm* (secondary) school, *Am* high school. ◆**lycéen, -enne** *nmf* pupil (*at lycée*).
lymphathique [lɛ̃fatik] *a* (*apathique*) sluggish.
lynch/er [lɛ̃ʃe] *vt* to lynch. ◆**—age** *nm* lynching.
lynx [lɛ̃ks] *nm* (*animal*) lynx.
lyre [lir] *nf Mus Hist* lyre.
lyrique [lirik] *a* (*poème etc*) lyric; (*passionné*) *Fig* lyrical. ◆**lyrisme** *nm* lyricism.
lys [lis] *nm* (*plante, fleur*) lily.

M

M, m [ɛm] *nm* M, m.
m *abrév* (*mètre*) metre.
M [məsjø] *abrév* = **Monsieur.**
m' [m] *voir* **me.**
ma [ma] *voir* **mon.**
macabre [makɑbr] *a* macabre, gruesome.
macadam [makadam] *nm* (*goudron*) tarmac.
macaron [makarɔ̃] *nm* (*gâteau*) macaroon; (*insigne*) (round) badge.
macaroni(s) [makarɔni] *nm(pl)* macaroni.
macédoine [masedwan] *nf* **m. (de légumes)** mixed vegetables; **m. (de fruits)** fruit salad.
macérer [masere] *vti Culin* to soak. ◆**macération** *nf* soaking.
mâcher [mɑʃe] *vt* to chew; **il ne mâche pas ses mots** he doesn't mince matters *ou* his words.
machiavélique [makjavelik] *a* Machiavellian.
machin [maʃɛ̃] *nm Fam* (*chose*) thing, what's-it; (*personne*) what's-his-name.
machinal, -aux [maʃinal, -o] *a* (*involontaire*) unconscious, mechanical. ◆**—ement** *adv* unconsciously, mechanically.
machination [maʃinɑsjɔ̃] *nf* machination.
machine [maʃin] *nf* (*appareil, avion, système etc*) machine; (*locomotive, moteur*) engine; *pl Tech* machines, (heavy) machinery; **m. à coudre** sewing machine; **m. à écrire** typewriter; **m. à laver** washing machine. ◆**machinerie** *nf Nau* engine room. ◆**machiniste** *nm Th* stage-hand.
macho [matʃo] *nm* macho *m*; – *a* (*f inv*) (*attitude etc*) macho.
mâchoire [mɑʃwar] *nf* jaw.
mâchonner [mɑʃɔne] *vt* to chew, munch.
maçon [masɔ̃] *nm* builder; bricklayer; mason. ◆**maçonnerie** *nf* (*travaux*) building work; (*ouvrage de briques*) brickwork; (*de pierres*) masonry, stonework.
maculer [makyle] *vt* to stain (**de** with).
Madagascar [madagaskar] *nf* Madagascar.
madame, *pl* **mesdames** [madam, medam] *nf* madam; **oui m.** yes (madam); **bonjour mesdames** good morning (ladies); **Madame** *ou* **Mme Legras** Mrs Legras; **Madame** (*sur une lettre*) *Com* Dear Madam.
madeleine [madlɛn] *nf* (small) sponge cake.
mademoiselle, *pl* **mesdemoiselles** [madmwazɛl, medmwazɛl] *nf* miss; **oui m.** yes (miss); **bonjour mesdemoiselles** good morning (ladies); **Mademoiselle** *ou* **Mlle Legras** Miss Legras; **Mademoiselle** (*sur une lettre*) *Com* Dear Madam.
madère [madɛr] *nm* (*vin*) Madeira.
madone [madɔn] *nf Rel* madonna.
madrier [madrije] *nm* (*poutre*) beam.
maestro [maɛstro] *nm Mus* maestro.
maf(f)ia [mafja] *nf* Mafia.
magasin [magazɛ̃] *nm* shop, *Am* store; (*entrepôt*) warehouse; (*d'arme*) & *Phot* magazine; **grand m.** department store. ◆**magasinier** *nm* warehouseman.
magazine [magazin] *nm* (*revue*) magazine.
magie [maʒi] *nf* magic. ◆**magicien, -ienne** *nmf* magician. ◆**magique** *a* (*baguette, mot*) magic; (*mystérieux, enchanteur*) magical.
magistral, -aux [maʒistral, -o] *a* masterly, magnificent. ◆**—ement** *adv* magnificently.
magistrat [maʒistra] *nm* magistrate. ◆**magistrature** *nf* judiciary, magistracy.
magnanime [maɲanim] *a* magnanimous.
magnat [magna] *nm* tycoon, magnate.
magner (se) [səmaɲe] *vpr Fam* to hurry up.
magnésium [maɲezjɔm] *nm* magnesium.
magnétique [maɲetik] *a* magnetic. ◆**magnétiser** *vt* to magnetize. ◆**magnétisme** *nm* magnetism.
magnétophone [maɲetɔfɔn] *nm* (*Fam* **magnéto**) tape recorder; **m. à cassettes** cassette recorder. ◆**magnétoscope** *nm* video (cassette) recorder.

magnifique [maɲifik] *a* magnificent. ◆**magnificence** *nf* magnificence. ◆**magnifiquement** *adv* magnificently.

magnolia [maɲɔlja] *nm* (*arbre*) magnolia.

magot [mago] *nm* (*économies*) nest egg, hoard.

magouille(s) [maguj] *nf(pl)* *Pol Fam* fiddling, graft.

mai [mɛ] *nm* May.

maigre [mɛgr] *a* thin, lean; (*viande*) lean; (*fromage, yaourt*) low-fat; (*repas, salaire, espoir*) meagre; **faire m.** to abstain from meat ◆**maigrement** *adv* (*chichement*) meagrely. ◆**maigreur** *nf* thinness; (*de viande*) leanness; (*médiocrité*) *Fig* meagreness. ◆**maigrichon, -onne** *a & nmf* skinny (person). ◆**maigrir** *vi* to get thin(ner); – *vt* to make thin(ner).

maille [mɑj] *nf* (*de tricot*) stitch; (*de filet*) mesh; **m. filée** (*de bas*) run, ladder. ◆**maillon** *nm* (*de chaîne*) link.

maillet [majɛ] *nm* (*outil*) mallet.

maillot [majo] *nm* (*de sportif*) jersey; (*de danseur*) leotard, tights; **m. (de corps)** vest, *Am* undershirt; **m. (de bain)** (*de femme*) swimsuit; (*d'homme*) (swimming) trunks.

main [mɛ̃] *nf* hand; **tenir à la m.** to hold in one's hand; **à la m.** (*livrer, faire etc*) by hand; **la m. dans la m.** hand in hand; **haut les mains!** hands up!; **donner un coup de m. à qn** to lend s.o. a (helping) hand; **coup de m.** (*habileté*) knack; **sous la m.** at hand, handy; **en venir aux mains** to come to blows; **avoir la m. heureuse** to be lucky, have a lucky streak; **mettre la dernière m. à** to put the finishing touches to; **en m. propre** (*remettre qch*) in person; **attaque/vol à m. armée** armed attack/robbery; **homme de m.** henchman, hired man; **m. courante** handrail; **prêter m.-forte à** to lend assistance to. ◆**m.-d'œuvre** *nf* (*pl* **mains-d'œuvre**) (*travail*) manpower, labour; (*salariés*) labour *ou* work force.

maint [mɛ̃] *a Litt* many a; **maintes fois, à maintes reprises** many a time.

maintenant [mɛ̃tnɑ̃] *adv* now; (*de nos jours*) nowadays; **m. que** now that; **dès m.** from now on.

maintenir* [mɛ̃tnir] *vt* (*conserver*) to keep, maintain; (*retenir*) to hold, keep; (*affirmer*) to maintain (**que** that); **— se m.** *vpr* (*durer*) to be maintained; (*rester*) to keep; (*malade, vieillard*) to hold one's own. ◆**maintien** *nm* (*action*) maintenance (**de** of); (*allure*) bearing.

maire [mɛr] *nm* mayor. ◆**mairie** *nf* town hall; (*administration*) town council.

mais [mɛ] *conj* but; **m. oui, m. si** yes of course; **m. non** definitely not.

maïs [mais] *nm* (*céréale*) maize, *Am* corn; **farine de m.** cornflour, *Am* cornstarch.

maison [mɛzɔ̃] *nf* (*bâtiment*) house; (*immeuble*) building; (*chez-soi, asile*) home; *Com* firm; (*famille*) household; **à la m.** (*être*) at home; (*rentrer, aller*) home; – *a inv* (*pâté, tartes etc*) homemade; **m. de la culture** arts *ou* cultural centre; **m. d'étudiants** student hostel; **m. des jeunes** youth club; **m. de repos** rest home; **m. de retraite** old people's home. ◆**maisonnée** *nf* household. ◆**maisonnette** *nf* small house.

maître [mɛtr] *nm* master; **se rendre m. de** (*incendie*) to master, control; (*pays*) to conquer; **être m. de** (*situation etc*) to be in control of, be master of; **m. de soi** in control of oneself; **m. d'école** teacher; **m. d'hôtel** (*restaurant*) head waiter; **m. de maison** host; **m. chanteur** blackmailer; **m. nageur (sauveteur)** swimming instructor (and lifeguard). ◆**maîtresse** *nf* mistress; **m. d'école** teacher; **m. de maison** hostess; (*ménagère*) housewife; **être m. de** (*situation etc*) to be in control of; – *af* (*idée, poutre*) main; (*carte*) master.

maîtrise [metriz] *nf* (*habileté, contrôle*) mastery (**de** of); (*grade*) *Univ* master's degree (**de** in); **m. (de soi)** self-control. ◆**maîtriser** *vt* (*émotion*) to master, control; (*sujet*) to master; (*incendie*) to (bring under) control; **m. qn** to subdue s.o.; **— se m.** *vpr* to control oneself.

majesté [maʒeste] *nf* majesty; **Votre M.** (*titre*) Your Majesty. ◆**majestueux, -euse** *a* majestic, stately.

majeur [maʒœr] **1** *a* (*primordial*) & *Mus* major; **être m.** *Jur* to be of age; **la majeure partie de** most of; **en majeure partie** for the most part. **2** *nm* (*doigt*) middle finger.

majorer [maʒɔre] *vt* to raise, increase. ◆**majoration** *nf* (*hausse*) increase (**de** in).

majorette [maʒɔrɛt] *nf* (drum) majorette.

majorité [maʒɔrite] *nf* majority (**de** of); (*âge*) *Jur* coming of age, majority; (*gouvernement*) party in office, government; **en m.** in the *ou* a majority; (*pour la plupart*) in the main. ◆**majoritaire** *a* (*vote etc*) majority-; **être m.** to be in the *ou* a majority; **être m. aux élections** to win the elections.

Majorque [maʒɔrk] *nf* Majorca.

majuscule [maʒyskyl] *a* capital; – *nf* capital letter.

mal, maux [mal, mo] **1** *nm* *Phil Rel* evil;

(*dommage*) harm; (*douleur*) pain; (*maladie*) illness; (*malheur*) misfortune; **dire du m. de** to speak ill of; **m. de dents** toothache; **m. de gorge** sore throat; **m. de tête** headache; **m. de ventre** stomachache; **m. de mer** seasickness; **m. du pays** homesickness; **avoir le m. du pays/*etc*** to be homesick/*etc*; **avoir m. à la tête/à la gorge/*etc*** to have a headache/sore throat/*etc*; **ça (me) fait m., j'ai m.** it hurts (me); **faire du m. à** to harm, hurt; **avoir du m. à faire** to have trouble (in) doing; **se donner du m. pour faire** to go to a lot of trouble to do. **2** *adv* (*travailler etc*) badly; (*entendre, comprendre*) not too well; **aller m.** (*projet etc*) to be going badly; (*personne*) *Méd* to be bad *or* ill; **m. (à l'aise)** uncomfortable; **se trouver m.** to (feel) faint; **(ce n'est) pas m.** (*mauvais*) (that's) not bad; **pas m.** (*beaucoup*) *Fam* quite a lot (**de** of); **c'est m. de jurer/*etc*** (*moralement*) it's wrong to swear/*etc*; **de m. en pis** from bad to worse; **m. renseigner/interpréter/*etc*** to misinform/misinterpret/*etc*.

malade [malad] *a* ill, sick; (*arbre, dent*) diseased; (*estomac, jambe*) bad; **être m. du foie/cœur** to have a bad liver/heart; – *nmf* sick person; (*à l'hôpital, d'un médecin*) patient; **les malades** the sick. **◆maladie** *nf* illness, sickness, disease. **◆maladif, -ive** *a* (*personne*) sickly; (*morbide*) morbid.

maladroit [maladrwa] *a* (*malhabile*) clumsy, awkward; (*indélicat*) tactless. **◆maladresse** *nf* clumsiness, awkwardness; tactlessness; (*bévue*) blunder.

malaise [malɛz] *nm* (*angoisse*) uneasiness, malaise; (*indisposition*) faintness, dizziness; **avoir un m.** to feel faint *ou* dizzy.

malaisé [maleze] *a* difficult.

Malaisie [malɛzi] *nf* Malaysia.

malaria [malarja] *nf* malaria.

malavisé [malavize] *a* ill-advised (**de faire** to do).

malax/er [malakse] *vt* (*pétrir*) to knead; (*mélanger*) to mix. **◆—eur** *nm Tech* mixer.

malchance [malʃɑ̃s] *nf* bad luck; **une m.** (*mésaventure*) a mishap. **◆malchanceux, -euse** *a* unlucky.

malcommode [malkɔmɔd] *a* awkward.

mâle [mal] *a* male; (*viril*) manly; – *nm* male.

malédiction [malediksjɔ̃] *nf* curse.

maléfice [malefis] *nm* evil spell. **◆maléfique** *a* baleful, evil.

malencontreux, -euse [malɑ̃kɔ̃trø, -øz] *a* unfortunate.

malentendant, -ante [malɑ̃tɑ̃dɑ̃, -ɑ̃t] *nmf* person who is hard of hearing.

malentendu [malɑ̃tɑ̃dy] *nm* misunderstanding.

malfaçon [malfasɔ̃] *nf* defect.

malfaisant [malfəzɑ̃] *a* evil, harmful.

malfaiteur [malfɛtœr] *nm* criminal.

malformation [malfɔrmasjɔ̃] *nf* malformation.

malgré [malgre] *prép* in spite of; **m. tout** for all that, after all; **m. soi** (*à contrecœur*) reluctantly.

malhabile [malabil] *a* clumsy.

malheur [malœr] *nm* (*événement*) misfortune; (*accident*) mishap; (*malchance*) bad luck, misfortune; **par m.** unfortunately. **◆malheureusement** *adv* unfortunately. **◆malheureux, -euse** *a* (*misérable, insignifiant*) wretched, miserable; (*fâcheux*) unfortunate; (*malchanceux*) unlucky, unfortunate; – *nmf* (*infortuné*) (poor) wretch; (*indigent*) needy person.

malhonnête [malɔnɛt] *a* dishonest. **◆malhonnêteté** *nf* dishonesty; **une m.** (*action*) a dishonest act.

malice [malis] *nf* mischievousness. **◆malicieux, -euse** *a* mischievous.

malin, -igne [malɛ̃, -iɲ] *a* (*astucieux*) smart, clever; (*plaisir*) malicious; (*tumeur*) *Méd* malignant. **◆malignité** *nf* (*méchanceté*) malignity; *Méd* malignancy.

malingre [malɛ̃gr] *a* puny, sickly.

malintentionné [malɛ̃tɑ̃sjɔne] *a* ill-intentioned (**à l'égard de** towards).

malle [mal] *nf* (*coffre*) trunk; (*de véhicule*) boot, *Am* trunk. **◆mallette** *nf* small suitcase; (*pour documents*) attaché case.

malléable [maleabl] *a* malleable.

malmener [malməne] *vt* to manhandle, treat badly.

malodorant [malɔdɔrɑ̃] *a* smelly.

malotru, -ue [malɔtry] *nmf* boor, lout.

malpoli [malpɔli] *a* impolite.

malpropre [malprɔpr] *a* (*sale*) dirty. **◆malpropreté** *nf* dirtiness.

malsain [malsɛ̃] *a* unhealthy, unwholesome.

malséant [malseɑ̃] *a* unseemly.

malt [malt] *nm* malt.

Malte [malt] *nf* Malta. **◆maltais, -aise** *a* *nmf* Maltese.

maltraiter [maltrete] *vt* to ill-treat.

malveillant [malvɛjɑ̃] *a* malevolent. **◆malveillance** *nf* malevolence, ill will.

malvenu [malvəny] *a* (*déplacé*) uncalled-for.

maman [mamɑ̃] *nf* mum(my), *Am* mom(my).

mamelle [mamɛl] *nf* (*d'animal*) teat; (*de*

vache) udder. ◆**mamelon** *nm* **1** (*de femme*) nipple. **2** (*colline*) hillock.

mamie [mami] *nf Fam* granny, grandma.

mammifère [mamifɛr] *nm* mammal.

manche [mɑ̃ʃ] **1** *nf* (*de vêtement*) sleeve; *Sp Cartes* round; **la M.** *Géog* the Channel. **2** *nm* (*d'outil etc*) handle; **m. à balai** broomstick; (*d'avion, d'ordinateur*) joystick. ◆**manchette** *nf* **1** (*de chemise etc*) cuff. **2** *Journ* headline. ◆**manchon** *nm* (*fourrure*) muff.

manchot, -ote [mɑ̃ʃo, -ɔt] **1** *a* & *nmf* one-armed *ou* one-handed (person). **2** *nm* (*oiseau*) penguin.

mandarin [mɑ̃darɛ̃] *nm* (*lettré influent*) *Univ Péj* mandarin.

mandarine [mɑ̃darin] *nf* (*fruit*) tangerine, mandarin (orange).

mandat [mɑ̃da] *nm* **1** (*postal*) money order. **2** *Pol* mandate; *Jur* power of attorney; **m. d'arrêt** warrant (**contre qn** for s.o.'s arrest). ◆**mandataire** *nmf* (*délégué*) representative, proxy. ◆**mandater** *vt* to delegate; *Pol* to give a mandate to.

manège [manɛʒ] *nm* **1** (*à la foire*) merry-go-round, roundabout; (*lieu*) riding-school; (*piste*) ring, manège; (*exercice*) horsemanship. **2** (*intrigue*) wiles, trickery.

manette [manɛt] *nf* lever, handle.

manger [mɑ̃ʒe] *vt* to eat; (*essence, électricité*) *Fig* to guzzle; (*fortune*) to eat up; (*corroder*) to eat into; **donner à m. à** to feed; – *vi* to eat; **on mange bien ici** the food is good here; **m. à sa faim** to have enough to eat; – *nm* food. ◆**mangeable** *a* eatable. ◆**mangeaille** *nf Péj* (bad) food. ◆**mangeoire** *nf* (feeding) trough. ◆**mangeur, -euse** *nmf* eater.

mangue [mɑ̃g] *nf* (*fruit*) mango.

manie [mani] *nf* mania, craze (**de** for). ◆**maniaque** *a* finicky, fussy; – *nmf* fusspot, *Am* fussbudget; **un m. de la propreté/***etc* a maniac for cleanliness/*etc*.

manier [manje] *vt* to handle; **se m. bien** (*véhicule etc*) to handle well. ◆**maniabilité** *nf* (*de véhicule etc*) manoeuvrability. ◆**maniable** *a* easy to handle. ◆**maniement** *nm* handling; **m. d'armes** *Mil* drill.

manière [manjɛr] *nf* way, manner; *pl* (*politesse*) manners; **de toute m.** anyway, anyhow; **de m. à faire** so as to do; **à ma m.** my way, (in) my own way; **de cette m.** (in) this way; **la m. dont elle parle** the way (in which) she talks; **d'une m. générale** generally speaking; **faire des manières** (*chichis*) to make a fuss; (*être affecté*) to put on airs. ◆**maniéré** *a* affected; (*style*) mannered.

manif [manif] *nf Fam* demo.

manifeste [manifɛst] **1** *a* (*évident*) manifest, obvious. **2** *nm Pol* manifesto.

manifester [manifɛste] **1** *vt* to show, manifest; – **se m.** *vpr* (*apparaître*) to appear; (*sentiment, maladie etc*) to show *ou* manifest itself. **2** *vi Pol* to demonstrate. ◆**manifestant, -ante** *nmf* demonstrator. ◆**manifestation** *nf* **1** (*expression*) expression, manifestation; (*apparition*) appearance. **2** *Pol* demonstration; (*réunion, fête*) event.

manigance [manigɑ̃s] *nf* little scheme. ◆**manigancer** *vt* to plot.

manipuler [manipyle] *vt* (*manier*) to handle; (*faits, électeurs*) *Péj* to manipulate. ◆**manipulation** *nf* handling; *Péj* manipulation (**de** of); *pl Pol Péj* manipulation.

manivelle [manivɛl] *nf Aut* crank.

mannequin [mankɛ̃] *nm* (*femme, homme*) (fashion) model; (*statue*) dummy.

manœuvre [manœvr] **1** *nm* (*ouvrier*) labourer. **2** *nf* (*opération*) & *Mil* manoeuvre, *Am* maneuver; (*action*) manoeuvring; (*intrigue*) scheme. ◆**manœuvrer** *vt* (*véhicule, personne etc*) to manoeuvre, *Am* maneuver; (*machine*) to operate; – *vi* to manoeuvre, *Am* maneuver.

manoir [manwar] *nm* manor house.

manque [mɑ̃k] *nm* lack (**de** of); (*lacune*) gap; *pl* (*défauts*) shortcomings; **m. à gagner** loss of profit. ◆**manqu/er** *vt* (*chance, cible etc*) to miss; (*ne pas réussir*) to make a mess of, ruin; (*examen*) to fail; – *vi* (*faire défaut*) to be short *ou* lacking; (*être absent*) to be absent (**à** from); (*être en moins*) to be missing *ou* short; (*défaillir, échouer*) to fail; **m. de** (*pain, argent etc*) to be short of; (*attention, cohérence*) to lack; **ça manque de sel/***etc* it lacks salt/*etc*, there isn't any salt/*etc*; **m. à** (*son devoir*) to fail in; (*sa parole*) to break; **le temps lui manque** he's short of time, he has no time; **elle/cela lui manque** he misses her/that; **je ne manquerai pas de venir** I won't fail to come; **ne manquez pas de venir** don't forget to come; **elle a manqué (de) tomber** (*faillir*) she nearly fell; – *v imp* **il manque/il nous manque dix** tasses there are/we are ten cups short. ◆**—ant** *a* missing. ◆**—é** *a* (*médecin, pilote etc*) failed; (*livre*) unsuccessful. ◆**—ement** *nm* breach (**à** of).

mansarde [mɑ̃sard] *nf* attic.

manteau, -x [mɑ̃to] *nm* coat.

manucure [manykyr] *nmf* manicurist. ◆**manucurer** *vt Fam* to manicure.

manuel, -elle [manɥɛl] **1** *a* (*travail etc*) manual. **2** *nm* (*livre*) handbook, manual.

manufacture [manyfaktyr] *nf* factory. ◆**manufacturé** *a* (*produit*) manufactured.

manuscrit [manyskri] *nm* manuscript; (*tapé à la machine*) typescript.

manutention [manytɑ̃sjɔ̃] *nf Com* handling (*of stores*). ◆**manutentionnaire** *nmf* packer.

mappemonde [mapmɔ̃d] *nf* map of the world; (*sphère*) *Fam* globe.

maquereau, -x [makro] *nm* (*poisson*) mackerel.

maquette [makɛt] *nf* (scale) model.

maquill/er [makije] *vt* (*visage*) to make up; (*voiture etc*) *Péj* to tamper with; (*vérité etc*) *Péj* to fake; **— se m.** to make (oneself) up. ◆**—age** *nm* (*fard*) make-up.

maquis [maki] *nm Bot* scrub, bush; *Mil Hist* maquis.

maraîcher, -ère [mareʃe, -ɛʃɛr] *nmf* market gardener, *Am* truck farmer.

marais [marɛ] *nm* marsh, bog; **m. salant** saltworks, saltern.

marasme [marasm] *nm Écon* stagnation.

marathon [maratɔ̃] *nm* marathon.

maraudeur, -euse [marodœr, -øz] *nmf* petty thief.

marbre [marbr] *nm* marble. ◆**marbrier** *nm* (*funéraire*) monumental mason.

marc [mar] *nm* (*eau-de-vie*) marc, brandy; **m. (de café)** coffee grounds.

marchand, -ande [marʃɑ̃, -ɑ̃d] *nmf* trader, shopkeeper; (*de vins, charbon*) merchant; (*de cycles, meubles*) dealer; **m. de bonbons** confectioner; **m. de couleurs** hardware merchant *ou* dealer; **m. de journaux** (*dans la rue*) newsvendor; (*dans un magasin*) newsagent, *Am* news dealer; **m. de légumes** greengrocer; **m. de poissons** fishmonger; – *a* (*valeur*) market; (*prix*) trade-. ◆**marchandise(s)** *nf(pl)* goods, merchandise.

marchand/er [marʃɑ̃de] *vi* to haggle, bargain; – *vt* (*objet*) to haggle over. ◆**—age** *nm* haggling, bargaining.

marche [marʃ] *nf* **1** (*d'escalier*) step, stair. **2** (*démarche, trajet*) walk; *Mil Mus* march; (*pas*) pace; (*de train, véhicule*) movement; (*de maladie, d'événement*) progress, course; **la m.** (*action*) *Sp* walking; **faire m. arrière** *Aut* to reverse; **la bonne m. de** (*opération, machine*) the smooth running of; **un train/véhicule en m.** a moving train/vehicle; **mettre qch en m.** to start sth (up). ◆**marcher** *vi* (*à pied*) to walk; *Mil* to march; (*poser le pied*) to tread, step; (*train, véhicule etc*) to run, go, move; (*fonctionner*) to go, work, run; (*prospérer*) to go well; **faire m.** (*machine*) to work; (*entreprise*) to run; (*personne*) *Fam* to kid; **ça marche?** *Fam* how's it going?; **elle va m.** (*accepter*) *Fam* she'll go along (with it). ◆**marcheur, -euse** *nmf* walker.

marché [marʃe] *nm* (*lieu*) market; (*contrat*) deal; **faire son** *ou* **le m.** to do one's shopping (*in the market*); **être bon m.** to be cheap; **voiture(s)/***etc* **bon m.** cheap car(s)/*etc*; **vendre (à) bon m.** to sell cheap(ly); **c'est meilleur m.** it's cheaper; **par-dessus le m.** *Fig* into the bargain; **au m. noir** on the black market; **le M. commun** the Common Market.

marchepied [marʃəpje] *nm* (*de train, bus*) step(s); (*de voiture*) running board.

mardi [mardi] *nm* Tuesday; **M. gras** Shrove Tuesday.

mare [mar] *nf* (*flaque*) pool; (*étang*) pond.

marécage [marekaʒ] *nm* swamp, marsh. ◆**marécageux, -euse** *a* marshy, swampy.

maréchal, -aux [mareʃal, -o] *nm Fr Mil* marshal. ◆**m.-ferrant** *nm* (*pl* **maréchaux-ferrants**) blacksmith.

marée [mare] *nf* tide; (*poissons*) fresh (sea) fish; **m. noire** oil slick.

marelle [marɛl] *nf* (*jeu*) hopscotch.

margarine [margarin] *nf* margarine.

marge [marʒ] *nf* margin; **en m. de** (*en dehors de*) on the periphery of, on the fringe(s) of; **m. de sécurité** safety margin. ◆**marginal, -ale, -aux** *a* (*secondaire, asocial*) marginal; – *nmf* misfit, dropout; (*bizarre*) weirdo.

marguerite [margərit] *nf* (*fleur*) marguerite, daisy.

mari [mari] *nm* husband.

mariage [marjaʒ] *nm* marriage; (*cérémonie*) wedding; (*mélange*) *Fig* blend, marriage; **demande en m.** proposal (of marriage). ◆**mari/er** *vt* (*couleurs*) to blend; **m. qn** (*maire, prêtre etc*) to marry s.o.; **m. qn avec** to marry s.o. (off) to; **— se m.** *vpr* to get married, marry; **se m. avec qn** to marry s.o., get married to s.o. ◆**—é** *a* married; – *nm* (bride)groom; **les mariés** the bride and (bride)groom; **les jeunes mariés** the newly-weds. ◆**—ée** *nf* bride.

marijuana [mariʒɥana] *nf* marijuana.

marin [marɛ̃] *a* (*air, sel etc*) sea-; (*flore*) marine; (*mille*) nautical; (*costume*) sailor-; – *nm* seaman, sailor. ◆**marine** *nf* **m. (de guerre)** navy; **m. marchande** merchant navy; **(bleu) m.** (*couleur*) navy (blue).

marina [marina] *nf* marina.
mariner [marine] *vti Culin* to marinate.
marionnette [marjɔnɛt] *nf* puppet; (*à fils*) marionette.
maritalement [maritalmɑ̃] *adv* **vivre m.** to live together (as husband and wife).
maritime [maritim] *a* (*droit, province, climat etc*) maritime; (*port*) sea-; (*gare*) harbour-; (*chantier*) naval; (*agent*) shipping-.
marjolaine [marʒɔlɛn] *nf* (*aromate*) marjoram.
mark [mark] *nm* (*monnaie*) mark.
marmaille [marmɑj] *nf* (*enfants*) *Fam* kids.
marmelade [marməlad] *nf* **m. (de fruits)** stewed fruit; **en m.** *Culin Fig* in a mush.
marmite [marmit] *nf* (cooking) pot.
marmonner [marmɔne] *vti* to mutter.
marmot [marmo] *nm* (*enfant*) *Fam* kid.
marmotter [marmɔte] *vti* to mumble.
Maroc [marɔk] *nm* Morocco. ◆**marocain, -aine** *a* & *nmf* Moroccan.
maroquinerie [marɔkinri] *nf* (*magasin*) leather goods shop. ◆**maroquinier** *nm* leather dealer.
marotte [marɔt] *nf* (*dada*) *Fam* fad, craze.
marque [mark] *nf* (*trace, signe*) mark; (*de fabricant*) make, brand; (*points*) *Sp* score; **m. de fabrique** trademark; **m. déposée** registered trademark; **la m. de** (*preuve*) the stamp of; **de m.** (*hôte, visiteur*) distinguished; (*produit*) of quality. ◆**marqu/er** *vt* (*par une marque etc*) to mark; (*écrire*) to note down; (*indiquer*) to show, mark; (*point, but*) *Sp* to score; **m. qn** *Sp* to mark s.o.; **m. les points** *Sp* to keep (the) score; **m. le coup** to mark the event; – *vi* (*trace*) to leave a mark; (*date, événement*) to stand out; *Sp* to score. ◆**—ant** *a* (*remarquable*) outstanding. ◆**—é** *a* (*différence, accent etc*) marked, pronounced. ◆**—eur** *nm* (*crayon*) marker.
marquis [marki] *nm* marquis. ◆**marquise** *nf* **1** marchioness. **2** (*auvent*) glass canopy.
marraine [marɛn] *nf* godmother.
marre [mar] *nf* **en avoir m.** *Fam* to be fed up (**de** with).
marr/er (se) [səmare] *vpr Fam* to have a good laugh. ◆**—ant** *a Fam* hilarious, funny.
marron[1] [marɔ̃] **1** *nm* chestnut; (*couleur*) (chestnut) brown; **m. (d'Inde)** horse chestnut; – *a inv* (*couleur*) (chestnut) brown. **2** *nm* (*coup*) *Fam* punch, clout. ◆**marronnier** *nm* (horse) chestnut tree.
marron[2], **-onne** [marɔ̃, -ɔn] *a* (*médecin etc*) bogus.
mars [mars] *nm* March.
marsouin [marswɛ̃] *nm* porpoise.
marteau, -x [marto] *nm* hammer; (*de porte*) (door)knocker; **m. piqueur, m. pneumatique** pneumatic drill. ◆**marteler** *vt* to hammer. ◆**martèlement** *nm* hammering.
martial, -aux [marsjal, -o] *a* martial; **cour martiale** court-martial; **loi martiale** martial law.
martien, -ienne [marsjɛ̃, -jɛn] *nmf* & *a* Martian.
martinet [martinɛ] *nm* (*fouet*) (small) whip.
martin-pêcheur [martɛ̃pɛʃœr] *nm* (*pl* **martins-pêcheurs**) (*oiseau*) kingfisher.
martyr, -yre[1] [martir] *nmf* (*personne*) martyr; **enfant m.** battered child. ◆**martyre**[2] *nm* (*souffrance*) martyrdom. ◆**martyriser** *vt* to torture; (*enfant*) to batter.
marxisme [marksism] *nm* Marxism. ◆**marxiste** *a* & *nmf* Marxist.
mascara [maskara] *nm* mascara.
mascarade [maskarad] *nf* masquerade.
mascotte [maskɔt] *nf* mascot.
masculin [maskylɛ̃] *a* male; (*viril*) masculine, manly; *Gram* masculine; (*vêtement, équipe*) men's; – *nm Gram* masculine. ◆**masculinité** *nf* masculinity.
masochisme [mazɔʃism] *nm* masochism. ◆**masochiste** *nmf* masochist; – *a* masochistic.
masque [mask] *nm* mask. ◆**masquer** *vt* (*dissimuler*) to mask (**à** from); (*cacher à la vue*) to block off.
massacre [masakr] *nm* massacre, slaughter. ◆**massacr/er** *vt* to massacre, slaughter; (*abîmer*) *Fam* to ruin. ◆**—ant** *a* (*humeur*) excruciating.
massage [masaʒ] *nm* massage.
masse [mas] *nf* **1** (*volume*) mass; (*gros morceau, majorité*) bulk (**de** of); **en m.** (*venir, vendre*) in large numbers; **départ en m.** mass *ou* wholesale departure; **manifestation de m.** mass demonstration; **la m.** (*foule*) the masses; **les masses** (*peuple*) the masses; **une m. de** (*tas*) a mass of; **des masses de** *Fam* masses of. **2** (*outil*) sledgehammer. **3** *Él* earth, *Am* ground. ◆**mass/er 1** *vt*, — **se m.** *vpr* (*gens*) to mass. **2** *vt* (*frotter*) to massage. ◆**—eur** *nm* masseur. ◆**—euse** *nf* masseuse.
massif, -ive [masif, -iv] **1** *a* massive; (*départs etc*) mass-; (*or, chêne etc*) solid. **2** *nm* (*d'arbres, de fleurs*) clump; *Géog* massif. ◆**massivement** *adv* (*en masse*) in large numbers.
massue [masy] *nf* (*bâton*) club.
mastic [mastik] *nm* (*pour vitres*) putty; (*pour bois*) filler; **m. (silicone)** mastic.

◆**mastiquer** *vt* **1** (*vitre*) to putty; (*porte*) to mastic; (*bois*) to fill. **2** (*mâcher*) to chew, masticate.
mastoc [mastɔk] *a inv Péj Fam* massive.
mastodonte [mastɔdɔ̃t] *nm* (*personne*) *Péj* monster; (*véhicule*) juggernaut.
masturber (se) [səmastyrbe] *vpr* to masturbate. ◆**masturbation** *nf* masturbation.
masure [mazyr] *nf* tumbledown house.
mat [mat] **1** *a* (*papier, couleur*) mat(t); (*bruit*) dull. **2** *a inv* & *nm Échecs* (check)mate; **faire** *ou* **mettre m.** to (check)mate.
mât [mɑ] *nm* (*de navire*) mast; (*poteau*) pole.
match [matʃ] *nm Sp* match, *Am* game; **m. nul** tie, draw.
matelas [matla] *nm* mattress; **m. pneumatique** air bed. ◆**matelassé** *a* (*meuble*) padded; (*tissu*) quilted.
matelot [matlo] *nm* sailor, seaman.
mater [mate] *vt* (*enfant, passion etc*) to subdue.
matérialiser [materjalize] *vt*, — **se m.** *vpr* to materialize. ◆**matérialisation** *nf* materialization.
matérialisme [materjalism] *nm* materialism. ◆**matérialiste** *a* materialistic; – *nmf* materialist.
matériaux [materjo] *nmpl* (building) materials; (*de roman, enquête etc*) material.
matériel, -ielle [materjɛl] **1** *a* material; (*personne*) *Péj* materialistic; (*financier*) financial; (*pratique*) practical. **2** *nm* equipment, material(s); (*d'un ordinateur*) hardware *inv*. ◆**matériellement** *adv* materially; **m. impossible** physically impossible.
maternel, -elle [maternɛl] *a* motherly, maternal; (*parenté, réprimande*) maternal; – *nf* (**école**) **maternelle** nursery school. ◆**materner** *vt* to mother. ◆**maternité** *nf* (*état*) motherhood, maternity; (*hôpital*) maternity hospital *ou* unit; (*grossesse*) pregnancy; **de m.** (*congé, allocation*) maternity-.
mathématique [matematik] *a* mathematical; – *nfpl* mathematics. ◆**mathématicien, -ienne** *nmf* mathematician. ◆**maths** [mat] *nfpl Fam* maths, *Am* math.
matière [matjɛr] *nf* (*sujet*) & *Scol* subject; (*de livre*) subject matter; **une m., la m., des matières** (*substance(s)*) matter; **m. première** raw material; **en m. d'art**/*etc* as regards art/*etc*, in art/*etc*; **s'y connaître en m. de** to be experienced in.
matin [matɛ̃] *nm* morning; **de grand m., de bon m., au petit m.** very early (in the morning); **le m.** (*chaque matin*) in the morning; **à sept heures du m.** at seven in the morning; **tous les mardis m.** every Tuesday morning. ◆**matinal, -aux** *a* (*personne*) early; (*fleur, soleil etc*) morning-. ◆**matinée** *nf* morning; *Th* matinée; **faire la grasse m.** to sleep late, lie in.
matou [matu] *nm* tomcat.
matraque [matrak] *nf* (*de policier*) truncheon, *Am* billy (club); (*de malfaiteur*) cosh, club. ◆**matraqu/er** *vt* (*frapper*) to club; (*publicité etc*) to plug (away) at. ◆—**age** *nm* **m. (publicitaire)** plugging, publicity build-up.
matrice [matris] *nf* **1** *Anat* womb. **2** *Tech* matrix.
matricule [matrikyl] *nm* (registration) number; – *a* (*livret, numéro*) registration-.
matrimonial, -aux [matrimɔnjal, -o] *a* matrimonial.
mâture [mɑtyr] *nf Nau* masts.
maturité [matyrite] *nf* maturity. ◆**maturation** *nf* maturing.
maudire* [modir] *vt* to curse. ◆**maudit** *a* (*sacré*) (ac)cursed, damned.
maugréer [mogree] *vi* to growl, grumble (**contre** at).
mausolée [mozɔle] *nm* mausoleum.
maussade [mosad] *a* (*personne etc*) glum, sullen; (*temps*) gloomy.
mauvais [movɛ] *a* bad; (*méchant, malveillant*) evil, wicked; (*mal choisi*) wrong; (*mer*) rough; **plus m.** worse; **le plus m.** the worst; **il fait m.** the weather's bad; **ça sent m.** it smells bad; **être m. en** (*anglais etc*) to be bad at; **mauvaise santé** ill *ou* bad *ou* poor health; – *nm* **le bon et le m.** the good and the bad.
mauve [mov] *a* & *nm* (*couleur*) mauve.
mauviette [movjɛt] *nf personne*) *Péj* weakling.
maux [mo] *voir* **mal**.
maxime [maksim] *nf* maxim.
maximum [maksimɔm] *nm* maximum; **le m. de** (*force etc*) the maximum (amount of); **au m.** as mucn as possible; (*tout au plus*) at most; – *a* maximum; **la température m.** maximum temperature. ◆**maximal, -aux** *a* maximum.
mayonnaise [majɔnɛz] *nf* mayonnaise.
mazout [mazut] *nm* (fuel) oil.
me [m(ə)] (**m'** *before vowel or mute h*) *pron* **1** (*complément direct*) me; **il me voit** he sees me. **2** (*indirect*) (to) me; **elle me parle** she speaks to me; **tu me l'as dit** you told me. **3** (*réfléchi*) myself; **je me lave** I wash myself.
méandres [meɑ̃dr] *nmpl* meander(ing)s.

mec [mɛk] *nm* (*individu*) *Arg* guy, bloke.
mécanique [mekanik] *a* mechanical; (*jouet*) clockwork-; – *nf* (*science*) mechanics; (*mécanisme*) mechanism. ◆**mécanicien** *nm* mechanic; *Rail* train driver. ◆**mécanisme** *nm* mechanism.
mécaniser [mekanize] *vt* to mechanize. ◆**mécanisation** *nf* mechanization.
mécène [mesɛn] *nm* patron (of the arts).
méchant [meʃɑ̃] *a* (*cruel*) malicious, wicked, evil; (*désagréable*) nasty; (*enfant*) naughty; (*chien*) vicious; **ce n'est pas m.** (*grave*) *Fam* it's nothing much. ◆**méchamment** *adv* (*cruellement*) maliciously; (*très*) *Fam* terribly. ◆**méchanceté** *nf* malice, wickedness; **une m.** (*acte*) a malicious act; (*parole*) a malicious word.
mèche [mɛʃ] *nf* **1** (*de cheveux*) lock; *pl* (*reflets*) highlights. **2** (*de bougie*) wick; (*de pétard*) fuse; (*de perceuse*) drill, bit. **3 de m. avec qn** (*complicité*) *Fam* in collusion *ou* cahoots with s.o.
méconn/aître* [mekɔnɛtr] *vt* to ignore; (*méjuger*) to fail to appreciate. ◆**—u** *a* unrecognized. ◆**—aissable** *a* unrecognizable.
mécontent [mekɔ̃tɑ̃] *a* dissatisfied, discontented (**de** with). ◆**mécontent/er** *vt* to displease, dissatisfy. ◆**—ement** *nm* dissatisfaction, discontent.
médaille [medaj] *nf* (*décoration*) *Sp* medal; (*pieuse*) medallion; (*pour chien*) name tag; **être m. d'or/d'argent** *Sp* to be a gold/silver medallist. ◆**médaillé, -ée** *nmf* medal holder. ◆**médaillon** *nm* (*bijou*) locket, medallion; (*ornement*) *Archit* medallion.
médecin [medsɛ̃] *nm* doctor, physician. ◆**médecine** *nf* medicine; **étudiant en m.** medical student. ◆**médical, -aux** *a* medical. ◆**médicament** *nm* medicine. ◆**médicinal, -aux** *a* medicinal. ◆**médico-légal, -aux** *a* (*laboratoire*) forensic.
médias [medja] *nmpl* (mass) media. ◆**médiatique** *a* media-.
médiateur, -trice [medjatœr, -tris] *nmf* mediator; – *a* mediating. ◆**médiation** *nf* mediation.
médiéval, -aux [medjeval, -o] *a* medi(a)eval.
médiocre [medjɔkr] *a* mediocre, second-rate. ◆**médiocrement** *adv* (*pas très*) not very; (*pas très bien*) not very well. ◆**médiocrité** *nf* mediocrity.
médire* [medir] *vi* **m. de** to speak ill of, slander. ◆**médisance(s)** *nf(pl)* malicious gossip, slander; **une m.** a piece of malicious gossip.
méditer [medite] *vt* (*conseil etc*) to meditate on; **m. de faire** to consider doing; – *vi* to meditate (**sur** on). ◆**méditatif, -ive** *a* meditative. ◆**méditation** *nf* meditation.
Méditerranée [mediterane] *nf* **la M.** the Mediterranean. ◆**méditerranéen, -enne** *a* Mediterranean.
médium [medjɔm] *nm* (*spirite*) medium.
méduse [medyz] *nf* jellyfish.
méduser [medyze] *vt* to stun, dumbfound.
meeting [mitiŋ] *nm Pol Sp* meeting, rally.
méfait [mefɛ] *nm Jur* misdeed; *pl* (*dégâts*) ravages.
méfi/er (se) [səmefje] *vpr* **se m. de** to distrust, mistrust; (*faire attention à*) to watch out for, beware of; **méfie-toi!** watch out!, beware!; **je me méfie** I'm distrustful *ou* suspicious. ◆**—ant** *a* distrustful, suspicious. ◆**méfiance** *nf* distrust, mistrust.
mégalomane [megalɔman] *nmf* megalomaniac. ◆**mégalomanie** *nf* megalomania.
mégaphone [megafɔn] *nm* loudhailer.
mégarde (par) [parmegard] *adv* inadvertently, by mistake.
mégère [meʒɛr] *nf* (*femme*) *Péj* shrew.
mégot [mego] *nm Fam* cigarette end *ou* butt.
meilleur, -eure [mɛjœr] *a* better (**que** than); **le m. moment/résultat/***etc* the best moment/result/*etc*; – *nmf* **le m., la meilleure** the best (one).
mélancolie [melɑ̃kɔli] *nf* melancholy, gloom. ◆**mélancolique** *a* melancholy, gloomy.
mélange [melɑ̃ʒ] *nm* mixture, blend; (*opération*) mixing. ◆**mélanger** *vt* (*mêler*) to mix; (*brouiller*) to mix (up), muddle; – **se m.** *vpr* to mix; (*idées etc*) to get mixed (up) *ou* muddled.
mélasse [melas] *nf* treacle, *Am* molasses.
mêl/er [mele] *vt* to mix, mingle (**à** with); (*qualités, thèmes*) to combine; (*brouiller*) to mix (up), muddle; **m. qn à** (*impliquer*) to involve s.o. in; – **se m.** *vpr* to mix, mingle (**à** with); **se m. à** (*la foule etc*) to join; **se m. de** (*s'ingérer dans*) to meddle in; **mêle-toi de ce qui te regarde!** mind your own business! ◆**—é** *a* mixed (**de** with). ◆**—ée** *nf* (*bataille*) rough-and-tumble; *Rugby* scrum(mage).
méli-mélo [melimelo] *nm* (*pl* **mélis-mélos**) *Fam* muddle.
mélodie [melɔdi] *nf* melody. ◆**mélodieux, -euse** *a* melodious. ◆**mélodique** *a Mus* melodic. ◆**mélomane** *nmf* music lover.

mélodrame [melɔdram] *nm* melodrama. ◆**mélodramatique** *a* melodramatic.
melon [m(ə)lɔ̃] *nm* **1** (*fruit*) melon. **2** (**chapeau**) **m.** bowler (hat).
membrane [mɑ̃bran] *nf* membrane.
membre [mɑ̃br] *nm* **1** *Anat* limb. **2** (*d'un groupe*) member.
même [mɛm] **1** *a* (*identique*) same; **en m. temps** at the same time (**que** as); **ce livre/** *etc* **m.** (*exact*) this very book/*etc*; **il est la bonté m.** he is kindness itself; **lui-m./vous-m./***etc* himself/yourself/*etc*; – *pron* **le m., la m.** the same (one); **j'ai les mêmes** I have the same (ones). **2** *adv* (*y compris, aussi*) even; **m. si** even if; **tout de m., quand m.** all the same; **de m.** likewise; **de m. que** just as; **ici m.** in this very place; **à m. de** in a position to; **à m. le sol** on the ground; **à m. la bouteille** from the bottle.
mémento [memɛ̃to] *nm* (*aide-mémoire*) handbook; (*agenda*) notebook.
mémoire [memwar] **1** *nf* memory; **de m. d'homme** in living memory; **à la m. de** in memory of. **2** *nm* (*requête*) petition; *Univ* memoir; *pl Littér* memoirs. ◆**mémorable** *a* memorable. ◆**mémorandum** [memɔrɑ̃dɔm] *nm Pol Com* memorandum. ◆**mémorial, -aux** *nm* (*monument*) memorial.
menace [mənas] *nf* threat, menace. ◆**mena/cer** *vt* to threaten (**de faire** to do). ◆**—çant** *a* threatening.
ménage [menaʒ] *nm* (*entretien*) housekeeping; (*couple*) couple, household; **faire le m.** to do the housework; **faire bon m. avec** to get on happily with. ◆**ménager**[1], **-ère** *a* (*appareil*) domestic, household-; **travaux ménagers** housework; – *nf* (*femme*) housewife.
ménag/er[2] [menaʒe] *vt* (*arranger*) to prepare *ou* arrange (carefully); (*épargner*) to use sparingly, be careful with; (*fenêtre, escalier etc*) to build; **m. qn** to treat *ou* handle s.o. gently *ou* carefully. ◆**—ement** *nm* (*soin*) care.
ménagerie [menaʒri] *nf* menagerie.
mendier [mɑ̃dje] *vi* to beg; – *vt* to beg for. ◆**mendiant, -ante** *nmf* beggar. ◆**mendicité** *nf* begging.
menées [məne] *nfpl* schemings, intrigues.
men/er [məne] *vt* (*personne, vie etc*) to lead; (*lutte, enquête, tâche etc*) to carry out; (*affaires*) to run; (*bateau*) to command; **m. qn à** (*accompagner, transporter*) to take s.o. to; **m. à bien** *Fig* to carry through; – *vi Sp* to lead. ◆**—eur, -euse** *nmf* (*de révolte*) (ring)leader.
méningite [menɛ̃ʒit] *nf Méd* meningitis.
ménopause [menɔpoz] *nf* menopause.
menottes [mənɔt] *nfpl* handcuffs.
mensonge [mɑ̃sɔ̃ʒ] *nm* lie; (*action*) lying. ◆**mensonger, -ère** *a* untrue, false.
menstruation [mɑ̃stryɑsjɔ̃] *nf* menstruation.
mensuel, -elle [mɑ̃sɥɛl] *a* monthly; – *nm* (*revue*) monthly. ◆**mensualité** *nf* monthly payment. ◆**mensuellement** *adv* monthly.
mensurations [mɑ̃syrɑsjɔ̃] *nfpl* measurements.
mental, -aux [mɑ̃tal, -o] *a* mental. ◆**mentalité** *nf* mentality.
menthe [mɑ̃t] *nf* mint.
mention [mɑ̃sjɔ̃] *nf* mention, reference; (*annotation*) comment; **m. bien** *Scol Univ* distinction; **faire m. de** to mention. ◆**mentionner** *vt* to mention.
ment/ir* [mɑ̃tir] *vi* to lie, tell lies *ou* a lie (**à** to). ◆**—eur, -euse** *nmf* liar; – *a* lying.
menton [mɑ̃tɔ̃] *nm* chin.
menu [məny] **1** *a* (*petit*) tiny; (*mince*) slender, fine; (*peu important*) minor, petty; – *adv* (*hacher*) small, finely; – *nm* **par le m.** in detail. **2** *nm* (*carte*) *Culin* menu.
menuisier [mənɥizje] *nm* carpenter, joiner. ◆**menuiserie** *nf* carpentry, joinery; (*ouvrage*) woodwork.
méprendre (se) [səmeprɑ̃dr] *vpr* **se m. sur** to be mistaken about. ◆**méprise** *nf* mistake.
mépris [mepri] *nm* contempt (**de** of, for), scorn (**de** for); **au m. de** without regard to. ◆**mépris/er** *vt* to despise, scorn. ◆**—ant** *a* scornful, contemptuous. ◆**—able** *a* despicable.
mer [mɛr] *nf* sea; (*marée*) tide; **en m.** at sea; **par m.** by sea; **aller à la m.** to go to the seaside; **un homme à la m.!** man overboard!
mercantile [mɛrkɑ̃til] *a Péj* money-grabbing.
mercenaire [mɛrsənɛr] *a* & *nm* mercenary.
mercerie [mɛrsəri] *nf* (*magasin*) haberdasher's, *Am* notions store. ◆**mercier, -ière** *nmf* haberdasher, *Am* notions merchant.
merci [mɛrsi] **1** *int* & *nm* thank you, thanks (**de, pour** for); **(non) m.!** no, thank you! **2** *nf* **à la m. de** at the mercy of.
mercredi [mɛrkrədi] *nm* Wednesday.
mercure [mɛrkyr] *nm* mercury.
merde! [mɛrd] *int Fam* (bloody) hell!
mère [mɛr] *nf* mother; **m. de famille** mother (of a family); **la m. Dubois** *Fam* old Mrs Dubois; **maison m.** *Com* parent firm.
méridien [meridjɛ̃] *nm* meridian.

méridional, -ale, -aux [meridjɔnal, -o] *a* southern; – *nmf* southerner.
meringue [mərɛ̃g] *nf (gâteau)* meringue.
merisier [mərizje] *nm (bois)* cherry.
mérite [merit] *nm* merit; **homme de m.** *(valeur)* man of worth. ◆**mérit/er** *vt (être digne de)* to deserve; *(valoir)* to be worth; **m. de réussir/***etc* to deserve to succeed/*etc.* ◆**—ant** *a* deserving. ◆**méritoire** *a* commendable.
merlan [mɛrlɑ̃] *nm (poisson)* whiting.
merle [mɛrl] *nm* blackbird.
merveille [mɛrvɛj] *nf* wonder, marvel; **à m.** wonderfully (well). ◆**merveilleusement** *adv* wonderfully. ◆**merveilleux, -euse** *a* wonderful, marvellous; – *nm* **le m.** *(surnaturel)* the supernatural.
mes [me] *voir* **mon.**
mésange [mezɑ̃ʒ] *nf (oiseau)* tit.
mésaventure [mezavɑ̃tyr] *nf* misfortune, misadventure.
mesdames [medam] *voir* **madame.**
mesdemoiselles [medmwazɛl] *voir* **mademoiselle.**
mésentente [mezɑ̃tɑ̃t] *nf* misunderstanding.
mesquin [mɛskɛ̃] *a* mean, petty. ◆**mesquinerie** *nf* meanness, pettiness; **une m.** an act of meanness.
mess [mɛs] *nm inv Mil* mess.
message [mesaʒ] *nm* message. ◆**messager, -ère** *nmf* messenger.
messageries [mesaʒri] *nfpl Com* courier service.
messe [mɛs] *nf Rel* mass.
Messie [mesi] *nm* Messiah.
messieurs [mesjø] *voir* **monsieur.**
mesure [məzyr] *nf (évaluation, dimension)* measurement; *(quantité, disposition)* measure; *(retenue)* moderation; *(cadence) Mus* time, beat; **fait sur m.** made to measure; **à m. que** as, as soon *ou* as fast as; **dans la m. où** in so far as; **dans une certaine m.** to a certain extent; **en m. de** able to, in a position to; **dépasser la m.** to exceed the bounds. ◆**mesur/er** *vt* to measure; *(juger, estimer)* to calculate, assess, measure; *(argent, temps)* to ration (out); **m. 1 mètre 83** *(personne)* to be six feet tall; *(objet)* to measure six feet; **se m. à** *ou* **avec qn** *Fig* to pit oneself against s.o. ◆**—é** *a (pas, ton)* measured; *(personne)* moderate.
met [mɛ] *voir* **mettre.**
métal, -aux [metal, -o] *nm* metal. ◆**métallique** *a (objet)* metal-; *(éclat, reflet, couleur)* metallic. ◆**métallisé** *a (peinture)* metallic.
métallo [metalo] *nm Fam* steelworker. ◆**métallurgie** *nf (industrie)* steel industry; *(science)* metallurgy. ◆**métallurgique** *a* **usine m.** steelworks. ◆**métallurgiste** *a & nm* **(ouvrier) m.** steelworker.
métamorphose [metamɔrfoz] *nf* metamorphosis. ◆**métamorphoser** *vt*, **— se m.** *vpr* to transform (en into).
métaphore [metafɔr] *nf* metaphor. ◆**métaphorique** *a* metaphorical.
métaphysique [metafizik] *a* metaphysical.
météo [meteo] *nf (bulletin)* weather forecast.
météore [meteɔr] *nm* meteor. ◆**météorite** *nm* meteorite.
météorologie [meteɔrɔlɔʒi] *nf (scienee)* meteorology; *(service)* weather bureau. ◆**météorologique** *a* meteorological; *(bulletin, station, carte)* weather-.
méthode [metɔd] *nf* method; *(livre)* course. ◆**méthodique** *a* methodical.
méticuleux, -euse [metikylø, -øz] *a* meticulous.
métier [metje] *nm* **1** *(travail)* job; *(manuel)* trade; *(intellectuel)* profession; *(habileté)* professional skill; **homme de m.** specialist. **2 m. (à tisser)** loom.
métis, -isse [metis] *a & nmf* half-caste.
mètre [mɛtr] *nm (mesure)* metre; *(règle)* (metre) rule; **m. (à ruban)** tape measure. ◆**métr/er** *vt (terrain)* to survey. ◆**—age** *nm* **1** surveying. **2** *(tissu)* length; *(de film)* footage; **long m.** *(film)* full length film; **court m.** *(film)* short (film). ◆**—eur** *nm* quantity surveyor. ◆**métrique** *a* metric.
métro [metro] *nm* underground, *Am* subway.
métropole [metrɔpɔl] *nf (ville)* metropolis; *(pays)* mother country. ◆**métropolitain** *a* metropolitan.
mets [mɛ] *nm (aliment)* dish.
mett/re* [mɛtr] **1** *vt* to put; *(table)* to lay; *(vêtement, lunettes)* to put on, wear; *(chauffage, radio etc)* to put on, switch on; *(réveil)* to set (**à** for); *(dépenser)* to spend (**pour une robe/***etc* on a dress/*etc*); **m. dix heures/***etc* **à venir** *(consacrer)* to take ten hours/*etc* coming *ou* to come; **m. à l'aise** *(rassurer)* to put *ou* set at ease; *(dans un fauteuil etc)* to make comfortable; **m. en colère** to make angry; **m. en liberté** to free; **m. en bouteille(s)** to bottle; **m. du soin à faire** to take care to do; **mettons que** (+ *sub*) let's suppose that; **— se m.** *vpr (se placer)* to put oneself; *(debout)* to stand; *(assis)* to sit; *(objet)* to be put, go; **se m. en short/pyjama/***etc* to get into one's

shorts/pyjamas/*etc*; **se m. en rapport avec** to get in touch with; **se m. à** (*endroit*) to go to; (*travail*) to set oneself to, start; **se m. à faire** to start doing; **se m. à table** to sit (down) at the table; **se m. à l'aise** to make oneself comfortable; **se m. au beau/froid** (*temps*) to turn fine/cold. ◆**—able** *a* wearable. ◆**—eur** *nm* **m. en scène** *Th* producer; *Cin* director.

meuble [mœbl] *nm* piece of furniture; *pl* furniture. ◆**meubl/er** *vt* to furnish; (*remplir*) *Fig* to fill. ◆**—é** *nm* furnished flat *ou Am* apartment.

meugl/er [møgle] *vi* to moo, low. ◆**—ement(s)** *nm*(*pl*) mooing.

meule [møl] *nf* **1** (*de foin*) haystack. **2** (*pour moudre*) millstone.

meunier, -ière [mønje, -jɛr] *nmf* miller.

meurt [mœr] *voir* **mourir.**

meurtre [mœrtr] *nm* murder. ◆**meurtrier, -ière** *nmf* murderer; – *a* deadly, murderous.

meurtrir [mœrtrir] *vt* to bruise. ◆**meurtrissure** *nf* bruise.

meute [møt] *nf* (*de chiens, de creânciers etc*) pack.

Mexique [mɛksik] *nm* Mexico. ◆**mexicain, -aine** *a* & *nmf* Mexican.

mi- [mi] *préf* **la mi-mars/***etc* mid March/*etc*; **à mi-distance** mid-distance, midway.

miaou [mjau] *int* (*cri du chat*) miaow.
◆**miaul/er** [mjole] *vi* to miaow, mew. ◆**—ement(s)** *nm*(*pl*) miaowing, mewing.

mi-bas [miba] *nm inv* knee sock.

miche [miʃ] *nf* round loaf.

mi-chemin (à) [amiʃmɛ̃] *adv* halfway.

mi-clos [miklo] *a* half-closed.

micmac [mikmak] *nm* (*manigance*) *Fam* intrigue.

mi-corps (à) [amikɔr] *adv* (up) to the waist.

mi-côte (à) [amikot] *adv* halfway up *ou* down (the hill).

micro [mikro] *nm* microphone, mike. ◆**microphone** *nm* microphone.

micro- [mikro] *préf* micro-.

microbe [mikrɔb] *nm* germ, microbe.

microcosme [mikrɔkɔsm] *nm* microcosm.

microfilm [mikrɔfilm] *nm* microfilm.

micro-onde [mikrɔɔ̃d] *nf* microwave; **four à micro-ondes** microwave oven.

microscope [mikrɔskɔp] *nm* microscope. ◆**microscopique** *a* miscroscopic.

midi [midi] *nm* **1** (*heure*) midday, noon, twelve o'clock; (*heure du déjeuner*) lunchtime. **2** (*sud*) south; **le M.** the south of France.

mie [mi] *nf* soft bread, crumb.

miel [mjɛl] *nm* honey. ◆**mielleux, -euse** *a* (*parole, personne*) unctuous.

mien, mienne [mjɛ̃, mjɛn] *pron poss* **le m., la mienne** mine, my one; **les miens, les miennes** mine, my ones; **les deux miens** my two; – *nmpl* **les miens** (*amis etc*) my (own) people.

miette [mjɛt] *nf* (*de pain, de bon sens etc*) crumb; **réduire en miettes** to smash to pieces.

mieux [mjø] *adv* & *a inv* better (**que** than); (*plus à l'aise*) more comfortable; (*plus beau*) better-looking; **le m., la m., les m.** (*convenir, être etc*) the best; (*de deux*) the better; **le m. serait de . . .** the best thing would be to . . . ; **de m. en m.** better and better; **tu ferais m. de partir** you had better leave; **je ne demande pas m.** there's nothing I'd like better (**que de faire** than to do); – *nm* (*amélioration*) improvement; **faire de son m.** to do one's best.

mièvre [mjɛvr] *a* (*doucereux*) *Péj* mannered, wishy-washy.

mignon, -onne [miɲɔ̃, -ɔn] *a* (*charmant*) cute; (*agréable*) nice.

migraine [migrɛn] *nf* headache; *Méd* migraine.

migration [migrasjɔ̃] *nf* migration. ◆**migrant, -ante** *a* & *nmf* (**travailleur**) **m.** migrant worker, migrant.

mijoter [miʒɔte] *vt Culin* to cook (lovingly); (*lentement*) to simmer; (*complot*) *Fig Fam* to brew; – *vi* to simmer.

mil [mil] *nm inv* (*dans les dates*) a *ou* one thousand; **l'an deux m.** the year two thousand.

milice [milis] *nf* militia. ◆**milicien** *nm* militiaman.

milieu, -x [miljø] *nm* (*centre*) middle; (*cadre, groupe social*) environment; (*entre extrêmes*) middle course; (*espace*) *Phys* medium; *pl* (*groupes, littéraires etc*) circles; **au m. de** in the middle of; **au m. du danger** in the midst of danger; **le juste m.** the happy medium; **le m.** (*de malfaiteurs*) the underworld.

militaire [militɛr] *a* military; – *nm* serviceman; (*dans l'armeé de terre*) soldier.

milit/er [milite] *vi* (*personne*) to be a militant; (*arguments etc*) to militate (**pour** in favour of). ◆**—ant, -ante** *a* & *nmf* militant.

mille [mil] **1** *a* & *nm inv* thousand; **m. hommes/***etc* a *ou* one thousand men/*etc*; **deux m.** two thousand; **mettre dans le m.** to hit the bull's-eye. **2** *nm* (*mesure*) mile. ◆**m.-pattes** *nm inv* (*insecte*) centipede.

◆**millième** *a* & *nmf* thousandth; **un m.** a thousandth. ◆**millier** *nm* thousand; **un m. (de)** a thousand or so.

millefeuille [milfœj] *nm* (*gâteau*) cream slice.

millénaire [milenɛr] *nm* millennium.

millésime [milezim] *nm* date (*on coins, wine etc*).

millet [mijɛ] *nm Bot* millet.

milli- [mili] *préf* milli-.

milliard [miljar] *nm* thousand million, *Am* billion. ◆**milliardaire** *a* & *nmf* multimillionaire.

millimètre [milimɛtr] *nm* millimetre.

million [miljɔ̃] *nm* million; **un m. de livres/***etc* a million pounds/*etc*; **deux millions** two million. ◆**millionième** *a* & *nmf* millionth. ◆**millionnaire** *nmf* millionaire.

mime [mim] *nmf* (*acteur*) mime; **le m.** (*art*) mime. ◆**mimer** *vti* to mime. ◆**mimique** *nf* (*mine*) (funny) face; (*gestes*) signs, sign language.

mimosa [mimoza] *nm* (*arbre, fleur*) mimosa.

minable [minabl] *a* (*médiocre*) pathetic; (*lieu, personne*) shabby.

minaret [minarɛ] *nm* (*de mosquée*) minaret.

minauder [minode] *vi* to simper, make a show of affectation.

mince [mɛ̃s] **1** *a* thin; (*élancé*) slim; (*insignifiant*) slim, paltry. **2** *int* **m. (alors)!** oh heck!, blast (it)! ◆**minceur** *nf* thinness; slimness. ◆**mincir** *vi* to grow slim.

mine [min] *nf* **1** appearance; (*physionomie*) look; **avoir bonne/mauvaise m.** (*santé*) to look well/ill; **faire m. de faire** to appear to do, make as if to do. **2** (*d'or, de charbon etc*) & *Fig* mine; **m. de charbon** coalmine. **3** (*de crayon*) lead. **4** (*engin explosif*) mine. ◆**miner** *vt* **1** (*saper*) to undermine. **2** (*garnir d'explosifs*) to mine.

minerai [minrɛ] *nm* ore.

minéral, -aux [mineral, -o] *a* & *nm* mineral.

minéralogique [mineralɔʒik] *a* **numéro m.** *Aut* registration *ou Am* license number.

minet, -ette [minɛ, -ɛt] *nmf* **1** (*chat*) puss. **2** (*personne*) *Fam* fashion-conscious young man *ou* woman.

mineur, -eure [minœr] **1** *nm* (*ouvrier*) miner. **2** *a* (*jeune, secondaire*) & *Mus* minor; – *nmf Jur* minor. ◆**minier, -ière** *a* (*industrie*) mining-.

mini- [mini] *préf* mini-.

miniature [minjatyr] *nf* miniature; – *a inv* (*train etc*) miniature-.

minibus [minibys] *nm* minibus.

minime [minim] *a* trifling, minor, minimal. ◆**minimiser** *vt* to minimize.

minimum [minimɔm] *nm* minimum; **le m. de** (*force etc*) the minimum (amount of); **au (grand) m.** at the very least; **la température m.** the minimum temperature. ◆**minimal, -aux** *a* minimum, minimal.

ministre [ministr] *nm Pol Rel* minister; **m. de l'Intérieur** = Home Secretary, *Am* Secretary of the Interior. ◆**ministère** *nm* ministry; (*gouvernement*) cabinet; **m. de Intérieur** = Home Office, *Am* Department of the Interior. ◆**ministériel, -ielle** *a* ministerial; (*crise, remaniement*) cabinet-.

minorer [minɔre] *vt* to reduce.

minorité [minɔrite] *nf* minority; **en m.** in the *ou* a minority. ◆**minoritaire** *a* (*parti etc*) minority-; **être m.** to be in the *ou* a minority.

Minorque [minɔrk] *nf* Minorca.

minuit [minɥi] *nm* midnight, twelve o'clock.

minus [minys] *nm* (*individu*) *Péj Fam* moron.

minuscule [minyskyl] **1** *a* (*petit*) tiny, minute. **2** *a* & *nf* **(lettre) m.** small letter.

minute [minyt] *nf* minute; **à la m.** (*tout de suite*) this (very) minute; **d'une m. à l'autre** any minute (now); – *a inv* **aliments** *ou* **plats m.** convenience food(s). ◆**minuter** *vt* to time. ◆**minuterie** *nf* time switch.

minutie [minysi] *nf* meticulousness. ◆**minutieux, -euse** *a* meticulous.

mioche [mjɔʃ] *nmf* (*enfant*) *Fam* kid, youngster.

miracle [mirɑkl] *nm* miracle; **par m.** miraculously. ◆**miraculeux, -euse** *a* miraculous.

mirador [miradɔr] *nm Mil* watchtower.

mirage [miraʒ] *nm* mirage.

mirifique [mirifik] *a Hum* fabulous.

mirobolant [mirɔbɔlɑ̃] *a Fam* fantastic.

miroir [mirwar] *nm* mirror. ◆**miroiter** *vi* to gleam, shimmer.

mis [mi] *voir* **mettre;** – *a* **bien m.** (*vêtu*) well dressed.

misanthrope [mizɑ̃trɔp] *nmf* misanthropist; – *a* misanthropic.

mise [miz] *nf* **1** (*action de mettre*) putting; **m. en service** putting into service; **m. en marche** starting up; **m. à la retraite** pensioning off; **m. à feu** (*de fusée*) blast-off; **m. en scène** *Th* production; *Cin* direction. **2** (*argent*) stake. **3** (*tenue*) attire. ◆**miser** *vt* (*argent*) to stake (**sur** on); – *vi* **m. sur** (*cheval*) to back; (*compter sur*) to bank on.

misère [mizɛr] *nf* (grinding) poverty; (*malheur*) misery; (*bagatelle*) trifle. ◆**mi-**

sérable *a* miserable, wretched; (*indigent*) poor, destitute; (*logement, quartier*) seedy, slummy; – *nmf* (poor) wretch; (*indigent*) pauper. ◆**miséreux, -euse** *a* destitute; – *nmf* pauper.

miséricorde [mizerikɔrd] *nf* mercy. ◆**miséricordieux, -euse** *a* merciful.

misogyne [mizɔʒin] *nmf* misogynist.

missile [misil] *nm* (*fusée*) missile.

mission [misjɔ̃] *nf* mission; (*tâche*) task. ◆**missionnaire** *nm* & *a* missionary.

missive [misiv] *nf* (*lettre*) missive.

mistral [mistral] *nm inv* (*vent*) mistral.

mite [mit] *nf* (clothes) moth; (*du fromage etc*) mite. ◆**mité** *a* moth-eaten.

mi-temps [mitɑ̃] *nf* (*pause*) *Sp* half-time; (*période*) *Sp* half; **à mi-t.** (*travailler etc*) part-time.

miteux, -euse [mitø, -øz] *a* shabby.

mitigé [mitiʒe] *a* (*zèle etc*) moderate, lukewarm; (*mêlé*) *Fam* mixed.

mitraille [mitrɑj] *nf* gunfire. ◆**mitrailler** *vt* to machinegun; (*photographier*) *Fam* to click *ou* snap away at. ◆**mitraillette** *nf* submachine gun. ◆**mitrailleur** *a* **fusil m.** machinegun. ◆**mitrailleuse** *nf* machinegun.

mi-voix (à) [amivwa] *adv* in an undertone.

mixe(u)r [miksœr] *nm* (*pour mélanger*) (food) mixer.

mixte [mikst] *a* mixed; (*école*) co-educational, mixed; (*tribunal*) joint.

mixture [mikstyr] *nf* (*boisson*) *Péj* mixture.

Mlle [madmwazɛl] *abrév* = **Mademoiselle.**

MM [mesjø] *abrév* = **Messieurs.**

mm *abrév* (*millimètre*) mm.

Mme [madam] *abrév* = **Madame.**

mobile [mɔbil] **1** *a* (*pièce etc*) moving; (*personne*) mobile; (*feuillets*) detachable, loose; (*reflets*) changing; **échelle m.** sliding scale; **fête m.** mov(e)able feast; – *nm* (*œuvre d'art*) mobile. **2** *nm* (*motif*) motive (de for). ◆**mobilité** *nf* mobility.

mobilier [mɔbilje] *nm* furniture.

mobiliser [mɔbilize] *vti* to mobilize. ◆**mobilisation** *nf* mobilization.

mobylette [mɔbilɛt] *nf* moped.

mocassin [mɔkasɛ̃] *nm* (*chaussure*) moccasin.

moche [mɔʃ] *a Fam* (*laid*) ugly; (*mauvais, peu gentil*) lousy, rotten.

modalité [mɔdalite] *nf* method (**de** of).

mode [mɔd] **1** *nf* fashion; (*industrie*) fashion trade; **à la m.** in fashion, fashionable; **passé de m.** out of fashion; **à la m. de** in the manner of. **2** *nm* mode, method; **m. d'emploi** directions (for use); **m. de vie** way of life. **3** *nm Gram* mood.

modèle [mɔdɛl] *nm* (*schéma, exemple, personne*) model; **m. (réduit)** (scale) model; – *a* (*élève etc*) model-. ◆**model/er** *vt* to model (**sur** on); **se m. sur** to model oneself on. ◆**—age** *nm* (*de statue etc*) modelling. ◆**modéliste** *nmf Tex* stylist, designer.

modéré [mɔdere] *a* moderate. ◆**—ment** *adv* moderately.

modérer [mɔdere] *vt* to moderate, restrain; (*vitesse, allure*) to reduce; – **se m.** *vpr* to restrain oneself. ◆**modérateur, -trice** *a* moderating; – *nmf* moderator. ◆**modération** *nf* moderation, restraint; reduction; **avec m.** in moderation.

moderne [mɔdɛrn] *a* modern; – *nm* **le m.** (*mobilier*) modern furniture. ◆**modernisation** *nf* modernization. ◆**moderniser** *vt*, – **se m.** *vpr* to modernize. ◆**modernisme** *nm* modernism.

modeste [mɔdɛst] *a* modest. ◆**modestement** *adv* modestly. ◆**modestie** *nf* modesty.

modifier [mɔdifje] *vt* to modify, alter; – **se m.** *vpr* to alter. ◆**modification** *nf* modification, alteration.

modique [mɔdik] *a* (*salaire, prix*) modest. ◆**modicité** *nf* modesty.

module [mɔdyl] *nm* module.

moduler [mɔdyle] *vt* to modulate. ◆**modulation** *nf* modulation.

moelle [mwal] *nf Anat* marrow; **m. épinière** spinal cord.

moelleux, -euse [mwalø, -øz] *a* soft; (*voix, vin*) mellow.

mœurs [mœr(s)] *nfpl* (*morale*) morals; (*habitudes*) habits, customs.

mohair [mɔɛr] *nm* mohair.

moi [mwa] *pron* **1** (*complément direct*) me; **laissez-moi** leave me; **pour moi** for me. **2** (*indirect*) (to) me; **montrez-le-moi** show it to me, show me it. **3** (*sujet*) I; **moi, je veux** *I* want. **4** *nm inv Psy* self, ego. ◆**moi-même** *pron* myself.

moignon [mwaɲɔ̃] *nm* stump.

moindre [mwɛ̃dr] *a* **être m.** (*moins grand*) to be less; **le m. doute**/*etc* the slightest *ou* least doubt/*etc*; **le m.** (*de mes problèmes etc*) the least (**de** of); (*de deux problèmes etc*) the lesser (**de** of).

moine [mwan] *nm* monk, friar.

moineau, -x [mwano] *nm* sparrow.

moins [mwɛ̃] **1** *adv* ([mwɛ̃z] *before vowel*) less (**que** than); **m. de** (*temps, zèle etc*) less (**que** than), not so much (**que** as); (*gens, livres etc*) fewer (**que** than), not so many (**que** as); (*cent francs etc*) less than; **m. froid/grand/***etc* not as cold/big/*etc* (**que** as); **de m. en m.** less and less; **le m., la m., les m.** (*travailler etc*) the least; **le m. grand** the smallest; **au m., du m.** at least; **de m., en m.** (*qui manque*) missing; **dix ans/***etc* **de m.** ten years/*etc* less; **en m.** (*personne, objet*) less; (*personnes, objets*) fewer; **les m. de vingt ans** those under twenty, the under-twenties; **à m. que** (+ *sub*) unless. **2** *prép Math* minus; **deux heures m. cinq** five to two; **il fait m. dix (degrés)** it's minus ten (degrees).

mois [mwa] *nm* month; **au m. de juin/***etc* in (the month of) June/*etc*.

mois/ir [mwazir] *vi* to go mouldy; (*attendre*) *Fig* to hang about. ◆**—i** *a* mouldy; — *nm* mould, mildew; **sentir le m.** to smell musty. ◆**moisissure** *nf* mould, mildew.

moisson [mwasɔ̃] *nf* harvest. ◆**moissonner** *vt* to harvest. ◆**moissonneuse-batteuse** *nf* (*pl* **moissonneuses-batteuses**) combine-harvester.

moite [mwat] *a* sticky, moist. ◆**moiteur** *nf* stickiness, moistness.

moitié [mwatje] *nf* half; **la m. de la pomme/***etc* half (of) the apple/*etc*; **à m.** (*remplir etc*) halfway; **à m. fermé/cru/***etc* half closed/raw/*etc*; **à m. prix** (for *ou* at) half-price; **de m.** by half; **m.-moitié** *Fam* so-so; **partager m.-moitié** *Fam* to split fifty-fifty.

moka [mɔka] *nm* (*café*) mocha.

mol [mɔl] *voir* **mou.**

molaire [mɔlɛr] *nf* (*dent*) molar.

molécule [mɔlekyl] *nf* molecule.

moleskine [mɔleskin] *nf* imitation leather.

molester [mɔleste] *vt* to manhandle.

molette [mɔlɛt] *nf* **clé à m.** adjustable wrench *ou* spanner.

mollasse [mɔlas] *a Péj* flabby.

molle [mɔl] *voir* **mou.** ◆**mollement** *adv* feebly; (*paresseusement*) lazily. ◆**mollesse** *nf* softness; (*faiblesse*) feebleness. ◆**mollir** *vi* to go soft; (*courage*) to flag.

mollet [mɔlɛ] **1** *a* **œuf m.** soft-boiled egg. **2** *nm* (*de jambe*) calf.

mollusque [mɔlysk] *nm* mollusc.

môme [mom] *nmf* (*enfant*) *Fam* kid.

moment [mɔmɑ̃] *nm* (*instant*) moment; (*période*) time; **en ce m.** at the moment; **par moments** at times; **au m. de partir** when just about to leave; **au m. où** when, just as; **du m. que** (*puisque*) seeing that. ◆**momentané** *a* momentary. ◆**momentanément** *adv* temporarily, for the moment.

momie [mɔmi] *nf* (*cadavre*) mummy.

mon, ma, *pl* **mes** [mɔ̃, ma, me] (**ma** *becomes* **mon** [mɔ̃n] *before a vowel or mute h*) *a poss* my; **mon père** my father; **ma mère** my mother; **mon ami(e)** my friend.

Monaco [mɔnako] *nf* Monaco.

monarque [mɔnark] *nm* monarch. ◆**monarchie** *nf* monarchy. ◆**monarchique** *a* monarchic.

monastère [mɔnastɛr] *nm* monastery.

monceau, -x [mɔ̃so] *nm* heap, pile.

monde [mɔ̃d] *nm* world; (*milieu social*) set; **du m.** (*gens*) people; (*beaucoup*) a lot of people; **un m. fou** a tremendous crowd; **le (grand) m.** (high) society; **le m. entier** the whole world; **tout le m.** everybody; **mettre au m.** to give birth to; **pas le moins du m.!** not in the least *ou* slightest! ◆**mondain, -aine** *a* (*vie, réunion etc*) society-. ◆**mondanités** *nfpl* (*événements*) social events. ◆**mondial, -aux** *a* (*renommée etc*) world-; (*crise*) worldwide. ◆**mondialement** *adv* the (whole) world over.

monégasque [mɔnegask] *a* & *nmf* Monegasque.

monétaire [mɔnetɛr] *a* monetary.

mongolien, -ienne [mɔ̃gɔljɛ̃, -jɛn] *a* & *nmf Méd* mongol.

moniteur, -trice [mɔnitœr, -tris] *nmf* **1** instructor; (*de colonie de vacances*) assistant, *Am* camp counselor. **2** (*écran*) *Tech* monitor.

monnaie [mɔnɛ] *nf* (*devise*) currency, money; (*appoint, pièces*) change; **pièce de m.** coin; **(petite) m.** (small) change; **faire de la m.** to get change; **faire de la m. à qn** to give s.o. change (**sur un billet** for a note); **c'est m. courante** it's very frequent; **Hôtel de la M.** mint. ◆**monnayer** *vt* (*talent etc*) to cash in on; (*bien, titre*) *Com* to convert into cash.

mono [mɔno] *a inv* (*disque etc*) mono.

mono- [mɔno] *préf* mono-.

monocle [mɔnɔkl] *nm* monocle.

monologue [mɔnɔlɔg] *nm* monologue.

monoplace [mɔnɔplas] *a* & *nmf* (*avion, voiture*) single-seater.

monopole [mɔnɔpɔl] *nm* monopoly. ◆**monopoliser** *vt* to monopolize.

monosyllabe [mɔnɔsilab] *nm* monosyllable. ◆**monosyllabique** *a* monosyllabic.

monotone [mɔnɔtɔn] *a* monotonous. ◆**monotonie** *nf* monotony.

monseigneur [mɔ̃sɛɲœr] *nm* (*évêque*) His *ou* Your Grace; (*prince*) His *ou* Your Highness.

monsieur, *pl* **messieurs** [məsjø, mesjø] *nm* gentleman; **oui m.** yes; (*avec déférence*) yes sir; **oui messieurs** yes (gentlemen); **M. Legras** Mr Legras; **Messieurs** *ou* **MM Legras** Messrs Legras; **tu vois ce m.?** do you see that man *ou* gentleman?; **Monsieur** (*sur une lettre*) *Com* Dear Sir.

monstre [mɔ̃str] *nm* monster; – *a* (*énorme*) *Fam* colossal. ◆**monstrueux, -euse** *a* (*abominable, énorme*) monstrous. ◆**monstruosité** *nf* (*horreur*) monstrosity.

mont [mɔ̃] *nm* (*montagne*) mount.

montagne [mɔ̃taɲ] *nf* mountain; **la m.** (*zone*) the mountains; **montagnes russes** *Fig* roller coaster. ◆**montagnard, -arde** *nmf* mountain dweller; – *a* (*peuple*) mountain-. ◆**montagneux, -euse** *a* mountainous.

mont-de-piété [mɔ̃dpjete] *nm* (*pl* **monts-de-piété**) pawnshop.

monte-charge [mɔ̃tʃarʒ] *nm inv* service lift *ou Am* elevator.

mont/er [mɔ̃te] *vi* (*aux* **être**) (*personne*) to go *ou* come up; (*s'élever*) to go up; (*grimper*) to climb (up) (**sur** onto); (*prix*) to go up, rise; (*marée*) to come in; (*avion*) to climb; **m. dans un véhicule** to get in(to) a vehicle; **m. dans un train** to get on(to) a train; **m. sur** (*échelle etc*) to climb up; (*trône*) to ascend; **m. en courant/***etc* to run/*etc* up; **m. (à cheval)** *Sp* to ride (a horse); **m. en graine** (*salade etc*) to go to seed; – *vt* (*aux* **avoir**) (*côte etc*) to climb (up); (*objets*) to bring *ou* take up; (*cheval*) to ride; (*tente, affaire*) to set up; (*machine*) to assemble; (*bijou*) to set, mount; (*complot, démonstration*) to mount; (*pièce*) *Th* to stage, mount; **m. l'escalier** to go *ou* come upstairs *ou* up the stairs; **faire m.** (*visiteur etc*) to show up; **m. qn contre qn** to set s.o. against s.o.; **— se m.** *vpr* (*s'irriter*) *Fam* to get angry; **se m. à** (*frais*) to amount to. ◆**—ant 1** *a* (*chemin*) uphill; (*mouvement*) upward; (*marée*) rising; (*col*) stand-up; (*robe*) high-necked; **chaussure montante** boot. **2** *nm* (*somme*) amount. **3** *nm* (*de barrière*) post; (*d'échelle*) upright. ◆**—é** *a* (*police*) mounted. ◆**—ée** *nf* ascent, climb; (*de prix, des eaux*) rise; (*chemin*) slope. ◆**—age** *nm Tech* assembling, assembly; *Cin* editing. ◆**—eur, -euse** *nmf Tech* fitter; *Cin* editor.

montre [mɔ̃tr] *nf* **1** watch; **course contre la m.** race against time. **2 faire m. de** to show. ◆**m.-bracelet** *nf* (*pl* **montres-bracelets**) wristwatch.

Montréal [mɔ̃real] *nm ou f* Montreal.

montrer [mɔ̃tre] *vt* to show (**à** to); **m. du doigt** to point to; **m. à qn à faire qch** to show s.o. how to do sth; **— se m.** *vpr* to show oneself, appear; (*s'avérer*) to turn out to be; **se m. courageux/***etc* (*être*) to be courageous/*etc.*

monture [mɔ̃tyr] *nf* **1** (*cheval*) mount. **2** (*de lunettes*) frame; (*de bijou*) setting.

monument [mɔnymɑ̃] *nm* monument; **m. aux morts** war memorial. ◆**monumental, -aux** *a* (*imposant, énorme etc*) monumental.

moquer (se) [səmɔke] *vpr* **se m. de** (*allure etc*) to make fun of; (*personne*) to make a fool of, make fun of; **je m'en moque!** *Fam* I couldn't care less! ◆**moquerie** *nf* mockery. ◆**moqueur, -euse** *a* mocking.

moquette [mɔkɛt] *nf* fitted carpet(s), wall-to-wall carpeting.

moral, -aux [mɔral, -o] *a* moral; – *nm* **le m.** spirits, morale. ◆**morale** *nf* (*principes*) morals; (*code*) **moral code**; (*d'histoire etc*) moral; **faire la m. à qn** to lecture s.o. ◆**moralement** *adv* morally. ◆**moraliser** *vi* to moralize. ◆**moraliste** *nmf* moralist. ◆**moralité** *nf* (*mœurs*) morality; (*de fable, récit etc*) moral.

moratoire [mɔratwar] *nm* moratorium.

morbide [mɔrbid] *a* morbid.

morceau, -x [mɔrso] *nm* piece, bit; (*de sucre*) lump; (*de viande*) *Culin* cut; (*extrait*) *Littér* extract. ◆**morceler** *vt* (*terrain*) to divide up.

mordiller [mɔrdije] *vt* to nibble.

mord/re [mɔrdr] *vti* to bite; **ça mord** *Pêche* I have a bite. ◆**—ant 1** *a* (*voix, manière*) scathing; (*froid*) biting; (*personne, ironie*) caustic. **2** *nm* (*énergie*) punch. ◆**—u, -ue** *nmf* **un m. du jazz/***etc Fam* a jazz/*etc* fan.

morfondre (se) [səmɔrfɔ̃dr] *vpr* to get bored (waiting), mope (about).

morgue [mɔrg] *nf* (*lieu*) mortuary, morgue.

moribond, -onde [mɔribɔ̃, -ɔ̃d] *a* & *nmf* dying *ou* moribund (person).

morne [mɔrn] *a* dismal, gloomy, dull.

morose [mɔroz] *a* morose, sullen.

morphine [mɔrfin] *nf* morphine.

mors [mɔr] *nm* (*de harnais*) bit.

morse [mɔrs] *nm* **1** Morse (code). **2** (*animal*) walrus.

morsure [mɔrsyr] *nf* bite.

mort[1] [mɔr] *nf* death; **mettre à m.** to put to death; **silence de m.** dead silence. ◆**mortalité** *nf* death rate, mortality. ◆**mortel, -elle** *a* (*hommes, ennemi, danger etc*) mortal; (*accident*) fatal; (*chaleur*) deadly; (*pâleur*) deathly; – *nmf* mortal. ◆**mortellement** *adv* (*blessé*) fatally.

mort[2], **morte** [mɔr, mɔrt] *a* (*personne, plante, ville etc*) dead; **m. de fatigue** dead

tired; **m. de froid** numb with cold; **m. de peur** frightened to death; – *nmf* dead man, dead woman; **les morts** the dead; **de nombreux morts** (*victimes*) many deaths *ou* casualties; **le jour** *ou* **la fête des Morts** All Souls' Day. ◆**morte-saison** *nf* off season. ◆**mort-né** *a* (*enfant*) & *Fig* stillborn.
mortier [mɔrtje] *nm* mortar.
mortifier [mɔrtifje] *vt* to mortify.
mortuaire [mɔrtɥɛr] *a* (*avis, rites etc*) death-, funeral.
morue [mɔry] *nf* cod.
morve [mɔrv] *nf* (nasal) mucus. ◆**morveux, -euse** *a* (*enfant*) snotty (-nosed).
mosaïque [mɔzaik] *nf* mosaic.
Moscou [mɔsku] *nm ou f* Moscow.
mosquée [mɔske] *nf* mosque.
mot [mo] *nm* word; **envoyer un m. à** to drop a line to; **m. à** *ou* **pour m.** word for word; **bon m.** witticism; **mots croisés** crossword (puzzle); **m. d'ordre** *Pol* resolution, order; (*slogan*) watchword; **m. de passe** password.
motard [mɔtar] *nm Fam* motorcyclist.
motel [mɔtɛl] *nm* motel.
moteur[1] [mɔtœr] *nm* (*de véhicule etc*) engine, motor; *Él* motor.
moteur[2], **-trice** [mɔtœr, -tris] *a* (*force*) driving-; (*nerf, muscle*) motor.
motif [mɔtif] *nm* **1** reason, motive. **2** (*dessin*) pattern.
motion [mosjɔ̃] *nf Pol* motion; **on a voté une m. de censure** a vote of no confidence was given.
motiver [mɔtive] *vt* (*inciter, causer*) to motivate; (*justifier*) to justify. ◆**motivation** *nf* motivation.
moto [mɔto] *nf* motorcycle, motorbike. ◆**motocycliste** *nmf* motorcyclist.
motorisé [mɔtɔrize] *a* motorized.
motte [mɔt] *nf* (*de terre*) clod, lump; (*de beurre*) block.
mou (*or* **mol** *before vowel or mute h*), **molle** [mu, mɔl] *a* soft; (*faible, sans énergie*) feeble; – *nm* **avoir du m.** (*cordage*) to be slack.
mouchard, -arde [muʃar, -ard] *nmf Péj* informer. ◆**moucharder** *vt* **m. qn** *Fam* to inform on s.o.
mouche [muʃ] *nf* (*insecte*) fly; **prendre la m.** (*se fâcher*) to go into a huff; **faire m.** to hit the bull's-eye. ◆**moucheron** *nm* (*insecte*) midge.
moucher [muʃe] *vt* **m. qn** to wipe s.o.'s nose; **se m.** to blow one's nose.
moucheté [muʃte] *a* speckled, spotted.
mouchoir [muʃwar] *nm* handkerchief; (*en papier*) tissue.
moudre* [mudr] *vt* (*café, blé*) to grind.
moue [mu] *nf* long face, pout; **faire la m.** to pout, pull a (long) face.
mouette [mwɛt] *nf* (sea)gull.
moufle [mufl] *nf* (*gant*) mitt(en).
mouill/er [muje] **1** *vt* to wet, make wet; **se faire m.** to get wet; **— se m.** *vpr* to get (oneself) wet; (*se compromettre*) *Fam* to get involved (*by taking risks*). **2** *vt* **m. l'ancre** *Nau* to (drop) anchor; – *vi* to anchor. ◆**—é** *a* wet (**de** with). ◆**—age** *nm* (*action*) *Nau* anchoring; (*lieu*) anchorage.
moule[1] [mul] *nm* mould, *Am* mold; **m. à gâteaux** cake tin. ◆**moul/er** *vt* to mould, *Am* mold; (*statue*) to cast; **m. qn** (*vêtement*) to fit s.o. tightly. ◆**—ant** *a* (*vêtement*) tight-fitting. ◆**—age** *nm* moulding; casting; (*objet*) cast. ◆**moulure** *nf Archit* moulding.
moule[2] [mul] *nf* (*mollusque*) mussel.
moulin [mulɛ̃] *nm* mill; (*moteur*) *Fam* engine; **m. à vent** windmill; **m. à café** coffee-grinder.
moulinet [mulinɛ] *nm* **1** (*de canne à pêche*) reel. **2** (*de bâton*) twirl.
moulu [muly] *voir* **moudre;** – *a* (*café*) ground; (*éreinté*) *Fam* dead tired.
mour/ir* [murir] *vi* (*aux* **être**) to die (**de** of, from); **m. de froid** to die of exposure; **m. d'ennui/de fatigue** *Fig* to be dead bored/tired; **m. de peur** *Fig* to be frightened to death; **s'ennuyer à m.** to be bored to death; **— se m.** *vpr* to be dying. ◆**—ant, -ante** *a* dying; (*voix*) faint; – *nmf* dying person.
mousquetaire [muskətɛr] *nm Mil Hist* musketeeer.
mousse [mus] **1** *nf Bot* moss. **2** *nf* (*écume*) froth, foam; (*de bière*) froth; (*de savon*) lather; **m. à raser** shaving foam. **3** *nf Culin* mousse. **4** *nm Nau* ship's boy. ◆**mousser** *vi* (*bière etc*) to froth; (*savon*) to lather; (*eau savonneuse*) to foam. ◆**mousseux, -euse** *a* frothy; (*vin*) sparkling; – *nm* sparkling wine. ◆**moussu** *a* mossy.
mousseline [muslin] *nf* (*coton*) muslin.
mousson [musɔ̃] *nf* (*vent*) monsoon.
moustache [mustaʃ] *nf* moustache, *Am* mustache; *pl* (*de chat etc*) whiskers. ◆**moustachu** *a* wearing a moustache.
moustique [mustik] *nm* mosquito. ◆**moustiquaire** *nf* mosquito net; (*en métal*) screen.
moutard [mutar] *nm* (*enfant*) *Arg* kid.
moutarde [mutard] *nf* mustard.
mouton [mutɔ̃] *nm* sheep; (*viande*) mutton;

pl (*sur la mer*) white horses; (*poussière*) bits of dust; **peau de m.** sheepskin.

mouvement [muvmɑ̃] *nm* (*geste, déplacement, groupe etc*) & *Mus* movement; (*de colère*) outburst; (*impulsion*) impulse; **en m.** in motion. **◆mouvementé** *a* (*animé*) lively, exciting; (*séance, vie etc*) eventful.

mouv/oir* [muvwar] *vi*, — **se m.** *vpr* to move; **mû par** (*mécanisme*) driven by. **◆—ant** *a* (*changeant*) changing; **sables mouvants** quicksands.

moyen[1], -enne [mwajɛ̃, -ɛn] *a* average; (*format, entreprise etc*) medium(-sized); (*solution*) intermediate, middle; – *nf* average; (*dans un examen*) pass mark; (*dans un devoir*) half marks; **la moyenne d'âge** the average age; **en moyenne** on average. **◆moyennement** *adv* averagely, moderately.

moyen[2] [mwajɛ̃] *nm* (*procédé, façon*) means, way (**de faire** of doing, to do); *pl* (*capacités*) ability, powers; (*argent, ressources*) means; **au m. de** by means of; **il n'y a pas m. de faire** it's not possible to do; **je n'ai pas les moyens** (*argent*) I can't afford it; **par mes propres moyens** under my own steam.

moyennant [mwajɛnɑ̃] *prép* (*pour*) (in return) for; (*avec*) with.

moyeu, -x [mwajø] *nm* (*de roue*) hub.

mucosités [mykozite] *nfpl* mucus.

mue [my] *nf* moulting; breaking of the voice. **◆muer** [mɥe] *vi* (*animal*) to moult; (*voix*) to break; **se m. en** to become transformed into.

muet, -ette [mɥɛ, -ɛt] *a* (*infirme*) dumb; (*de surprise etc*) speechless; (*film, reproche etc*) silent; *Gram* mute; – *nmf* dumb person.

mufle [myfl] *nm* **1** (*d'animal*) nose, muzzle. **2** (*individu*) *Péj* lout.

mug/ir [myʒir] *vi* (*vache*) to moo; (*bœuf*) to bellow; (*vent*) *Fig* to roar. **◆—issement(s)** *nm*(*pl*) moo(ing); bellow(ing); roar(ing).

muguet [mygɛ] *nm* lily of the valley.

mule [myl] *nf* **1** (*pantoufle*) mule. **2** (*animal*) (she-)mule. **◆mulet[1]** *nm* (he-)mule.

mulet[2] [mylɛ] *nm* (*poisson*) mullet.

multi- [mylti] *préf* multi-.

multicolore [myltikɔlɔr] *a* multicoloured.

multinationale [myltinasjɔnal] *nf* multinational.

multiple [myltipl] *a* (*nombreux*) numerous; (*ayant des formes variées*) multiple; – *nm* *Math* multiple. **◆multiplication** *nf* multiplication; (*augmentation*) increase. **◆multiplicité** *nf* multiplicity. **◆multiplier** *vt* to multiply; — **se m.** *vpr* to increase; (*se reproduire*) to multiply.

multitude [myltityd] *nf* multitude.

municipal, -aux [mynisipal, -o] *a* municipal; **conseil m.** town council. **◆municipalité** *nf* (*corps*) town council; (*commune*) municipality.

munir [mynir] *vt* **m. de** to provide *ou* equip with; **se m. de** to provide oneself with; **muni de** (*papiers, arme etc*) in possession of.

munitions [mynisjɔ̃] *nfpl* ammunition.

muqueuse [mykøz] *nf* mucous membrane.

mur [myr] *nm* wall; **m. du son** sound barrier; **au pied du m.** *Fig* with one's back to the wall. **◆muraille** *nf* (high) wall. **◆mural, -aux** *a* (*carte etc*) wall-; **peinture murale** mural (painting). **◆murer** *vt* (*porte*) to wall up; **m. qn** to wall s.o. in.

mûr [myr] *a* (*fruit, projet etc*) ripe; (*âge, homme*) mature. **◆mûrement** *adv* (*réfléchir*) carefully. **◆mûrir** *vti* (*fruit*) to ripen; (*personne, projet*) to mature.

muret [myrɛ] *nm* low wall.

murmure [myrmyr] *nm* murmur. **◆murmurer** *vti* to murmur.

musc [mysk] *nm* (*parfum*) musk.

muscade [myskad] *nf* nutmeg.

muscle [myskl] *nm* muscle. **◆musclé** *a* (*bras*) brawny, muscular. **◆musculaire** *a* (*tissu, système etc*) muscular. **◆musculature** *nf* muscles.

museau, -x [myzo] *nm* (*de chien etc*) muzzle; (*de porc*) snout. **◆museler** *vt* (*animal, presse etc*) to muzzle. **◆muselière** *nf* (*appareil*) muzzle.

musée [myze] *nm* museum; **m. de peinture** (public) art gallery. **◆muséum** *nm* (natural history) museum.

musette [myzɛt] *nf* (*d'ouvrier*) duffel bag, kit bag.

music-hall [myzikol] *nm* variety theatre.

musique [myzik] *nf* music; (*fanfare*) *Mil* band. **◆musical, -aux** *a* musical. **◆musicien, -ienne** *nmf* musician; – *a* **être très/assez m.** to be very/quite musical.

musulman, -ane [myzylmɑ̃, -an] *a* & *nmf* Moslem, Muslim.

muter [myte] *vt* (*employé*) to transfer. **◆mutation** *nf* **1** transfer. **2** *Biol* mutation.

mutil/er [mytile] *vt* to mutilate, maim; **être mutilé** to be disabled. **◆—é, -ée** *nmf* **m. de guerre/du travail** disabled ex-serviceman/worker. **◆mutilation** *nf* mutilation.

mutin [mytɛ̃] **1** *a* (*espiègle*) saucy. **2** *nm* (*rebelle*) mutineer. **◆se mutin/er** *vpr* to mutiny. **◆—é** *a* mutinous. **◆mutinerie** *nf* mutiny.

mutisme [mytism] *nm* (stubborn) silence.

mutualité [mytɥalite] *nf* mutual insurance. **◆mutualiste** *nmf* member of a friendly *ou Am* benefit society. **◆mutuelle¹** *nf* friendly society, *Am* benefit society.

mutuel, -elle² [mytɥɛl] *a* (*réciproque*) mutual. **◆mutuellement** *adv* (*l'un l'autre*) each other (mutually).

myope [mjɔp] *a & nmf* shortsighted (person). **◆myopie** *nf* shortsightedness.

myosotis [mjozɔtis] *nm Bot* forget-me-not.

myrtille [mirtij] *nf Bot* bilberry.

mystère [mister] *nm* mystery. **◆mystérieux, -euse** *a* mysterious.

mystifier [mistifje] *vt* to fool, deceive, hoax. **◆mystification** *nf* hoax.

mystique [mistik] *a* mystic(al); – *nmf* (*personne*) mystic; – *nf* mystique (**de** of). **◆mysticisme** *nm* mysticism.

mythe [mit] *nm* myth. **◆mythique** *a* mythical. **◆mythologie** *nf* mythology. **◆mythologique** *a* mythological.

mythomane [mitɔman] *nmf* compulsive liar.

N

N, n [ɛn] *nm* N, n.

n' [n] *voir* **ne**.

nabot [nabo] *nm Péj* midget.

nacelle [nasɛl] *nf* (*de ballon*) car, gondola; (*de landau*) carriage, carrycot.

nacre [nakr] *nf* mother-of-pearl. **◆nacré** *a* pearly.

nage [naʒ] *nf* (swimming) stroke; **n. libre** freestyle; **traverser à la n.** to swim across; **en n.** *Fig* sweating. **◆nager** *vi* to swim; (*flotter*) to float; **je nage dans le bonheur** my happiness knows no bounds; **je nage complètement** (*je suis perdu*) *Fam* I'm all at sea; – *vt* (*crawl etc*) to swim. **◆nageur, -euse** *nmf* swimmer.

nageoire [naʒwar] *nf* (*de poisson*) fin; (*de phoque*) flipper.

naguère [nager] *adv Litt* not long ago.

naïf, -ïve [naif, -iv] *a* simple, naïve; – *nmf* (*jobard*) simpleton.

nain, naine [nɛ̃, nɛn] *nmf* dwarf; – *a* (*arbre, haricot*) dwarf-.

naissance [nesɑ̃s] *nf* birth; (*de bras, cou*) base; **donner n. à** *Fig* to give rise to; **de n.** from birth.

naître* [nɛtr] *vi* to be born; (*jour*) to dawn; (*sentiment, difficulté*) to arise (**de** from); **faire n.** (*soupçon, industrie etc*) to give rise to, create. **◆naissant** *a* (*amitié etc*) incipient.

naïveté [naivte] *nf* simplicity, naïveté.

nant/ir [nɑ̃tir] *vt* **n. de** to provide with. **◆–i** *a & nmpl* (*riche*) affluent.

naphtaline [naftalin] *nf* mothballs.

nappe [nap] *nf* **1** table cloth. **2** (*d'eau*) sheet; (*de gaz, pétrole*) layer; (*de brouillard*) blanket. **◆napperon** *nm* (soft) table mat; (*pour vase etc*) (soft) mat, cloth.

narcotique [narkɔtik] *a & nm* narcotic.

narguer [narge] *vt* to flout, mock.

narine [narin] *nf* nostril.

narquois [narkwa] *a* sneering.

narration [narɑsjɔ̃] *nf* (*récit, acte, art*) narration. **◆narrateur, -trice** *nmf* narrator.

nasal, -aux [nazal, -o] *a* nasal.

naseau, -x [nazo] *nm* (*de cheval*) nostril.

nasiller [nazije] *vi* (*personne*) to speak with a twang; (*micro, radio*) to crackle. **◆nasillard** *a* (*voix*) nasal; (*micro etc*) crackling.

natal, mpl -als [natal] *a* (*pays etc*) native; **sa maison natale** the house where he *ou* she was born. **◆natalité** *nf* birthrate.

natation [natɑsjɔ̃] *nf* swimming.

natif, -ive [natif, -iv] *a & nmf* native; **être n. de** to be a native of.

nation [nasjɔ̃] *nf* nation; **les Nations Unies** the United Nations. **◆national, -aux** *a* national; **◆nationale** *nf* (*route*) trunk road, *Am* highway. **◆nationaliser** *vt* to nationalize. **◆nationaliste** *a Péj* nationalistic; – *nmf* nationalist. **◆nationalité** *nf* nationality.

nativité [nativite] *nf Rel* nativity.

natte [nat] *nf* **1** (*de cheveux*) plait, *Am* braid. **2** (*tapis*) mat, (piece of) matting. **◆natt/er** *vt* to plait, *Am* braid. **◆–age** *n* (*matière*) matting.

naturaliser [natyralize] *vt* (*personne*) *Pol* to naturalize. **◆naturalisation** *nf* naturalization.

nature [natyr] *nf* (*monde naturel, caractère*) nature; **de toute n.** of every kind; **être de n. à** to be likely to; **payer en n.** *Fin* to pay in kind; **n. morte** (*tableau*) still life; **plus grand que n.** larger than life; – *a inv* (*omelette, yaourt etc*) plain; (*café*) black. **◆natura-**

liste *nmf* naturalist. ◆**naturiste** *nmf* nudist, naturist.

naturel, -elle [natyrɛl] *a* natural; **mort naturelle** death from natural causes; – *nm* (*caractère*) nature; (*simplicité*) naturalness. ◆**naturellement** *adv* naturally.

naufrage [nofraʒ] *nm* (ship)wreck; (*ruine*) *Litt Fig* ruin; **faire n.** to be (ship)wrecked. ◆**naufragé, -ée** *a & nmf* shipwrecked (person).

nausée [noze] *nf* nausea, sickness. ◆**nauséabond** *a* nauseating, sickening.

nautique [notik] *a* nautical; (*sports, ski*) water-.

naval, *mpl* **-als** [naval] *a* naval; **constructions navales** shipbuilding.

navet [navɛ] *nm* **1** *Bot Culin* turnip. **2** (*film etc*) *Péj* flop, dud.

navette [navɛt] *nf* (*transport*) shuttle (service); **faire la n.** (*véhicule, personne etc*) to shuttle back and forth (**entre** between); **n. spatiale** space shuttle.

naviguer [navige] *vi* (*bateau*) to sail; (*piloter, voler*) to navigate. ◆**navigabilité** *nf* (*de bateau*) seaworthiness; (*d'avion*) airworthiness. ◆**navigable** *a* (*fleuve*) navigable. ◆**navigant** *a* **personnel n.** *Av Nau* crew. ◆**navigateur** *nm Av* navigator. ◆**navigation** *nf* (*pilotage*) navigation; (*trafic*) *Nau* shipping.

navire [navir] *nm* ship.

navr/er [navre] *vt* to upset (greatly), grieve. ◆**—ant** *a* upsetting. ◆**—é** *a* (*air*) grieved; **je suis n.** I'm (terribly) sorry (**de faire** to do).

nazi, -ie [nazi] *a & nmf Pol Hist* Nazi.

ne [n(ə)] (**n'** *before vowel or mute h*; *used to form negative verb with* **pas, jamais, que** *etc*) *adv* **1** (+ *pas*) not; **elle ne boit pas** she does not *ou* doesn't drink; **il n'ose (pas)** he doesn't dare; **n'importe** it doesn't matter. **2** (*with* **craindre, avoir peur** *etc*) **je crains qu'il ne parte** I'm afraid he'll leave.

né [ne] *a* born; **il est né** he was born; **née Dupont** née Dupont.

néanmoins [neɑ̃mwɛ̃] *adv* nevertheless, nonetheless.

néant [neɑ̃] *nm* nothingness, void; (*sur un formulaire*) = none.

nébuleux, -euse [nebylø, -øz] *a* hazy, nebulous.

nécessaire [nesesɛr] *a* necessary; (*inéluctable*) inevitable; – *nm* **le n.** (*biens*) the necessities; **le strict n.** the bare necessities; **n. de couture** sewing box, workbox; **n. de toilette** sponge bag, dressing case; **faire le n.** to do what's necessary *ou* the necessary. ◆**nécessairement** *adv* necessarily; (*échouer etc*) inevitably. ◆**nécessité** *nf* necessity. ◆**nécessiter** *vt* to necessitate, require. ◆**nécessiteux, -euse** *a* needy.

nécrologie [nekrɔlɔʒi] *nf* obituary.

nectarine [nektarin] *nf* (*fruit*) nectarine.

néerlandais, -aise [neɛrlɑ̃dɛ, -ɛz] *a* Dutch; – *nmf* Dutchman, Dutchwoman; – *nm* (*langue*) Dutch.

nef [nɛf] *nf* (*d'église*) nave.

néfaste [nefast] *a* (*influence etc*) harmful (**à** to).

négatif, -ive [negatif, -iv] *a* negative; – *nm Phot* negative; – *nf* **répondre par la négative** to answer in the negative. ◆**négation** *nf* negation, denial (**de** of); *Gram* negation; (*mot*) negative.

négligeable [negliʒabl] *a* negligible.

négligent [negliʒɑ̃] *a* negligent, careless. ◆**négligemment** [-amɑ̃] *adv* negligently, carelessly. ◆**négligence** *nf* negligence, carelessness; (*faute*) (careless) error.

néglig/er [negliʒe] *vt* (*personne, conseil, travail etc*) to neglect; **n. de faire** to neglect to do; **— se n.** *vpr* (*négliger sa tenue ou sa santé*) to neglect oneself. ◆**—é** *a* (*tenue*) untidy, neglected; (*travail*) careless; – *nm* (*de tenue*) untidiness; (*vêtement*) negligee.

négoci/er [negɔsje] *vti Fin Pol* to negotiate. ◆**—ant, -ante** *nmf* merchant, trader. ◆**—able** *a Fin* negotiable. ◆**négociateur, -trice** *nmf* negotiator. ◆**négociation** *nf* negotiation.

nègre [nɛgr] **1** *a* (*art, sculpture etc*) Negro. **2** *nm* (*écrivain*) ghost writer.

neige [nɛʒ] *nf* snow; **n. fondue** sleet; **n. carbonique** dry ice. ◆**neiger** *v imp* to snow. ◆**neigeux, -euse** *a* snowy.

nénuphar [nenyfar] *nm* water lily.

néo [neɔ] *préf* neo-.

néon [neɔ̃] *nm* (*gaz*) neon; **au n.** (*éclairage etc*) neon-.

néophyte [neɔfit] *nmf* novice.

néo-zélandais, -aise [neɔzelɑ̃dɛ, -ɛz] *a* (*peuple etc*) New Zealand-; – *nmf* New Zealander.

nerf [nɛr] *nm Anat* nerve; **avoir du n.** (*vigueur*) *Fam* to have guts; **du n.!, un peu de n.!** buck up!; **ça me porte** *ou* **me tape sur les nerfs** it gets on my nerves; **être sur les nerfs** *Fig* to be keyed up *ou* het up. ◆**nerveux, -euse** *a* nervous; (*centre, cellule*) nerve-. ◆**nervosité** *nf* nervousness.

nervure [nɛrvyr] *nf* (*de feuille*) vein.

nescafé [nɛskafe] *nm* instant coffee.

n'est-ce pas? [nɛspɑ] *adv* isn't he?, don't

you? *etc*; **il fait beau, n'est-ce pas?** the weather's fine, isn't it?

net, nette [nɛt] **1** *a* (*conscience, idée, image, refus*) clear; (*coupure, linge*) clean; (*soigné*) neat; (*copie*) fair; – *adv* (*s'arrêter*) short, dead; (*tuer*) outright; (*parler*) plainly; (*refuser*) flat(ly); (*casser, couper*) clean. **2** *a* (*poids, prix etc*) *Com* net(t). **◆nettement** *adv* clearly, plainly; (*sensiblement*) markedly. **◆netteté** *nf* clearness; (*de travail*) neatness.

nettoyer [nɛtwaje] *vt* to clean (up); (*plaie*) to cleanse, clean (up); (*vider, ruiner*) *Fam* to clean out. **◆nettoiement** *nm* cleaning; **service du n.** refuse *ou Am* garbage collection. **◆nettoyage** *nm* cleaning; **n. à sec** dry cleaning.

neuf¹, neuve [nœf, nœv] *a* new; **quoi de n.?** what's new(s)?; – *nm* **il y a du n.** there's been something new; **remettre à n.** to make as good as new.

neuf² [nœf] *a* & *nm* ([nœv] *before* **heures** & **ans**) nine. **◆neuvième** *a* & *nmf* ninth.

neurasthénique [nørastenik] *a* depressed.

neutre [nøtr] **1** *a* (*pays, personne etc*) neutral; – *nm* *El* neutral. **2** *a* & *nm* *Gram* neuter. **◆neutraliser** *vt* to neutralize. **◆neutralité** *nf* neutrality.

neveu, -x [nəvø] *nm* nephew.

névralgie [nevralʒi] *nf* headache; *Méd* neuralgia. **◆névralgique** *a* **centre n.** *Fig* nerve centre.

névrose [nevroz] *nf* neurosis. **◆névrosé, -ée** *a* & *nmf* neurotic.

nez [ne] *nm* nose; **n. à n.** face to face (**avec** with); **au n. de qn** (*rire etc*) in s.o.'s face; **mettre le n. dehors** *Fam* to stick one's nose outside.

ni [ni] *conj* **ni . . . ni** (+ *ne*) neither . . . nor; **il n'a ni faim ni soif** he's neither hungry nor thirsty; **sans manger ni boire** without eating or drinking; **ni l'un(e) ni l'autre** neither (of them).

niais, -aise [njɛ, -ɛz] *a* silly, simple; – *nmf* simpleton. **◆niaiserie** *nf* silliness; *pl* (*paroles*) nonsense.

niche [niʃ] *nf* (*de chien*) kennel; (*cavité*) niche, recess.

nich/er [niʃe] *vi* (*oiseau*) to nest; (*loger*) *Fam* to hang out; – **se n.** *vpr* (*oiseau*) to nest; (*se cacher*) to hide oneself. **◆–ée** *nf* (*oiseaux, enfants*) brood; (*chiens*) litter.

nickel [nikɛl] *nm* (*métal*) nickel.

nicotine [nikɔtin] *nf* nicotine.

nid [ni] *nm* nest; **n. de poules** *Aut* pothole.

nièce [njɛs] *nf* niece.

nième [ɛnjɛm] *a* nth.

nier [nje] *vt* to deny (**que** that); – *vi* *Jur* to deny the charge.

nigaud, -aude [nigo, -od] *a* silly; – *nmf* silly fool.

Nigéria [niʒerja] *nm ou f* Nigeria.

n'importe [nɛ̃pɔrt] *voir* **importer 1**.

nippon, -one *ou* **-onne** [nipɔ̃, -ɔn] *a* Japanese.

niveau, -x [nivo] *nm* (*hauteur*) level; (*degré, compétence*) standard, level; **n. de vie** standard of living; **n. à bulle (d'air)** spirit level; **au n. de qn** (*élève etc*) up to s.o.'s standard. **◆niveler** *vt* (*surface*) to level; (*fortunes etc*) to even (up).

noble [nɔbl] *a* noble; – *nmf* nobleman, noblewoman. **◆noblement** *adv* nobly. **◆noblesse** *nf* (*caractère, classe*) nobility.

noce(s) [nɔs] *nf*(*pl*) wedding; **faire la noce** *Fam* to have a good time, make merry; **noces d'argent/d'or** silver/golden wedding. **◆noceur, -euse** *nmf* *Fam* fast liver, reveller.

nocif, -ive [nɔsif, -iv] *a* harmful. **◆nocivité** *nf* harmfulness.

noctambule [nɔktɑ̃byl] *nmf* (*personne*) night bird *ou* prowler. **◆nocturne** *a* nocturnal, night-; – *nm* (*de magasins etc*) late night opening; **(match en) n.** *Sp* floodlit match, *Am* night game.

Noël [nɔɛl] *nm* Christmas; **le père N.** Father Christmas, Santa Claus.

nœud [nø] *nm* **1** knot; (*ruban*) bow; **le n. du problème/***etc* the crux of the problem/*etc*; **n. coulant** noose, slipknot; **n. papillon** bow tie. **2** (*mesure*) *Nau* knot.

noir, noire [nwar] *a* black; (*nuit, lunettes etc*) dark; (*idées*) gloomy; (*âme, crime*) vile; (*misère*) dire; **roman n.** thriller; **film n.** film noir; **il fait n.** it's dark; – *nm* (*couleur*) black; (*obscurité*) dark; **N.** (*homme*) black; **vendre au n.** to sell on the black market; – *nf* *Mus* crotchet, *Am* quarter note; **Noire** (*femme*) black. **◆noirceur** *nf* blackness; (*d'une action etc*) vileness. **◆noircir** *vt* to blacken; – *vi*, – **se n.** *vpr* to turn black.

noisette [nwazɛt] *nf* hazelnut. **◆noisetier** *nm* hazel (tree).

noix [nwa] *nf* (*du noyer*) walnut; **n. de coco** coconut; **n. du Brésil** Brazil nut; **n. de beurre** knob of butter; **à la n.** *Fam* trashy, awful.

nom [nɔ̃] *nm* name; *Gram* noun; **n. de famille** surname; **n. de jeune fille** maiden name; **n. propre** *Gram* proper noun; **au n. de qn** on s.o.'s behalf; **sans n.** (*anonyme*) nameless; (*vil*) vile; **n. d'un chien!** *Fam* oh hell!

nomade [nɔmad] *a* nomadic; – *nmf* nomad.

nombre [nɔ̃br] *nm* number; **ils sont au** *ou* **du n. de** (*parmi*) they're among; **ils sont au n. de dix** there are ten of them; **elle est au n. de** she's one of; **le plus grand n. de** the majority of. ◆**nombreux, -euse** *a* (*amis, livres etc*) numerous; (*famille, collection etc*) large; **peu n.** few; **venir n.** to come in large numbers.

nombril [nɔ̃bri] *nm* navel.

nominal, -aux [nɔminal, -o] *a* nominal. ◆**nomination** *nf* appointment, nomination.

nommer [nɔme] *vt* (*appeler*) to name; **n. qn** (*désigner*) to appoint s.o. (**à un poste/***etc* to a post/*etc*); **n. qn président/lauréat** to nominate s.o. chairman/prizewinner; – **se n.** *vpr* (*s'appeler*) to be called. ◆**nommément** *adv* by name.

non [nɔ̃] *adv & nm inv* no; **n.!** no!; **tu viens ou n.?** are you coming or not?; **n. seulement** not only; **n. (pas) que (+ *sub*) . . .** not that . . . ; **c'est bien, n.?** *Fam* it's all right, isn't it?; **je crois que n.** I don't think so; **(ni) moi n. plus** neither do, am, can *etc* I; **une place n. réservée** an unreserved seat.

non- [nɔ̃] *préf* non-.

nonante [nɔnɑ̃t] *a* (*en Belgique, en Suisse*) ninety.

nonchalant [nɔ̃ʃalɑ̃] *a* nonchalant, apathetic. ◆**nonchalance** *nf* nonchalance, apathy.

non-conformiste [nɔ̃kɔ̃fɔrmist] *a & nmf* nonconformist.

non-fumeur, -euse [nɔ̃fymœr, -øz] *nmf* non-smoker.

non-sens [nɔ̃sɑ̃s] *nm inv* absurdity.

nord [nɔr] *nm* north; **au n. de** north of; **du n.** (*vent, direction*) northerly; (*ville*) northern; (*gens*) from *ou* in the north; **Amérique/Afrique du N.** North America/Africa; **l'Europe du N.** Northern Europe; – *a inv* (*côte*) north(ern). ◆**n.-africain, -aine** *a & nmf* North African. ◆**n.-américain, -aine** *a & nmf* North American. ◆**n.-est** *nm & a inv* north-east. ◆**n.-ouest** *nm & a inv* north-west.

nordique [nɔrdik] *a & nmf* Scandinavian.

normal, -aux [nɔrmal, -o] *a* normal. ◆**normale** *nf* norm, normality; **au-dessus de la n.** above normal. ◆**normalement** *adv* normally. ◆**normaliser** *vt* (*uniformiser*) to standardize; (*relations etc*) to normalize.

normand, -ande [nɔrmɑ̃, -ɑ̃d] *a & nmf* Norman. ◆**Normandie** *nf* Normandy.

norme [nɔrm] *nf* norm.

Norvège [nɔrvɛʒ] *nf* Norway. ◆**norvégien, -ienne** *a & nmf* Norwegian; – *nm* (*langue*) Norwegian.

nos [no] *voir* **notre.**

nostalgie [nɔstalʒi] *nf* nostalgia. ◆**nostalgique** *a* nostalgic.

notable [nɔtabl] *a* (*fait etc*) notable; – *nm* (*personne*) notable. ◆**—ment** [-əmɑ̃] *adv* (*sensiblement*) notably.

notaire [nɔtɛr] *nm* solicitor, notary.

notamment [nɔtamɑ̃] *adv* notably.

note [nɔt] *nf* (*remarque etc*) & *Mus* note; (*chiffrée*) *Scol* mark, *Am* grade; (*compte, facture*) bill, *Am* check; **prendre n. de** to make a note of. ◆**notation** *nf* notation; *Scol* marking. ◆**noter** *vt* (*prendre note de*) to note; (*remarquer*) to note, notice; (*écrire*) to note down; (*devoir etc*) *Scol* to mark, *Am* grade; **être bien noté** (*personne*) to be highly rated.

notice [nɔtis] *nf* (*résumé, préface*) note; (*mode d'emploi*) instructions.

notifier [nɔtifje] *vt* **n. qch à qn** to notify s.o. of sth.

notion [nosjɔ̃] *nf* notion, idea; *pl* (*éléments*) rudiments.

notoire [nɔtwar] *a* (*criminel, bêtise*) notorious; (*fait*) well-known. ◆**notoriété** *nf* (*renom*) fame; (*de fait*) general recognition.

notre, *pl* **nos** [nɔtr, no] *a poss* our. ◆**nôtre** *pron poss* **le** *ou* **la n., les nôtres** ours; – *nmpl* **les nôtres** (*parents etc*) our (own) people.

nouer [nwe] *vt* to tie, knot; (*amitié, conversation*) to strike up; **avoir la gorge nouée** to have a lump in one's throat. ◆**noueux, -euse** *a* (*bois*) knotty; (*doigts*) gnarled.

nougat [nuga] *nm* nougat.

nouille [nuj] *nf* (*idiot*) *Fam* drip.

nouilles [nuj] *nfpl* noodles.

nounours [nunurs] *nm* teddy bear.

nourrice [nuris] *nf* (*assistante maternelle*) child minder, nurse; (*qui allaite*) wet nurse; **mettre en n.** to put out to nurse.

nourr/ir [nurir] *vt* (*alimenter, faire vivre*) to feed; (*espoir etc*) *Fig* to nourish; (*esprit*) to enrich; **se n. de** to feed on; – *vi* (*aliment*) to be nourishing. ◆**—issant** *a* nourishing. ◆**nourriture** *nf* food.

nourrisson [nurisɔ̃] *nm* infant.

nous [nu] *pron* **1** (*sujet*) we; **n. sommes** we are. **2** (*complément direct*) us; **il n. connaît** he knows us. **3** (*indirect*) (to) us; **il n. l'a donné** he gave it to us, he gave us it. **4** (*réfléchi*) ourselves; **n. n. lavons** we wash ourselves. **5** (*réciproque*) each other;

n. n. **détestons** we hate each other. ◆**n.-mêmes** *pron* ourselves.

nouveau (*or* **nouvel** *before vowel or mute h*), **nouvelle**[1], *pl* **nouveaux, nouvelles** [nuvo, nuvɛl] *a* new; – *nmf Scol* new boy, new girl; – *nm* **du n.** something new; **de n., à n.** again. ◆**n.-né, -ée** *a & nmf* new-born (baby). ◆**n.-venu** *nm*, ◆**nouvelle-venue** *nf* newcomer. ◆**nouveauté** *nf* newness, novelty; *pl* (*livres*) new books; (*disques*) new releases; (*vêtements*) new fashions; **une n.** (*objet*) a novelty.

nouvelle[2] [nuvɛl] *nf* **1 nouvelle(s)** news; **une n.** a piece of news. **2** *Littér* short story.

Nouvelle-Zélande [nuvɛlzelɑ̃d] *nf* New Zealand.

novateur, -trice [nɔvatœr, -tris] *nmf* innovator.

novembre [nɔvɑ̃br] *nm* November.

novice [nɔvis] *nmf* novice; – *a* inexperienced.

noyau, -x [nwajo] *nm* (*de fruit*) stone, *Am* pit; (*d'atome, de cellule*) nucleus; (*groupe*) group; **un n. d'opposants** a hard core of opponents.

noyaut/er [nwajote] *vt Pol* to infiltrate. ◆**—age** *nm* infiltration.

noy/er[1] [nwaje] *vt* (*personne etc*) to drown; (*terres*) to flood; **— se n.** *vpr* to drown; (*se suicider*) to drown oneself; **se n. dans le détail** to get bogged down in details. ◆**—é, -ée** *nmf* (*mort*) drowned person; – *a* **être n.** (*perdu*) *Fig* to be out of one's depth. ◆**noyade** *nf* drowning.

noyer[2] [nwaje] *nm* (*arbre*) walnut tree.

nu [ny] *a* (*personne, vérité*) naked; (*mains, chambre*) bare; **tout nu** (stark) naked, (in the) nude; **voir à l'œil nu** to see with the naked eye; **mettre à nu** (*exposer*) to lay bare; **se mettre nu** to strip off; **tête nue, nu-tête** bare-headed; – *nm* (*femme, homme, œuvre*) nude.

nuage [nɥaʒ] *nm* cloud; **un n. de lait** *Fig* a dash of milk. ◆**nuageux, -euse** *a* (*ciel*) cloudy.

nuance [nɥɑ̃s] *nf* (*de sens*) nuance; (*de couleurs*) shade, nuance; (*de regret*) tinge, nuance. ◆**nuanc/er** *vt* (*teintes*) to blend, shade; (*pensée*) to qualify. ◆**—é** *a* (*jugement*) qualified.

nucléaire [nyklеɛr] *a* nuclear.

nudisme [nydism] *nm* nudism. ◆**nudiste** *nmf* nudist. ◆**nudité** *nf* nudity, nakedness; (*de mur etc*) bareness.

nuée [nɥe] *nf* **une n. de** (*foule*) a host of; (*groupe compact*) a cloud of.

nues [ny] *nfpl* **porter qn aux n.** to praise s.o. to the skies.

nuire* [nɥir] *vi* **n. à** (*personne, intérêts etc*) to harm. ◆**nuisible** *a* harmful.

nuit [nɥi] *nf* night; (*obscurité*) dark(ness); **il fait n.** it's dark; **avant la n.** before nightfall; **la n.** (*se promener etc*) at night; **cette n.** (*aujourd'hui*) tonight; (*hier*) last night. ◆**nuitée** *nf* overnight stay (*in hotel etc*).

nul, nulle [nyl] **1** *a* (*risque etc*) non-existent, nil; (*médiocre*) useless, hopeless; (*non valable*) *Jur* null (and void); **faire match n.** *Sp* to tie, draw. **2** *a* (*aucun*) no; **de nulle importance** of no importance; **sans n. doute** without any doubt; **nulle part** nowhere; – *pron m* (*aucun*) no one. ◆**nullard, -arde** *nmf Fam* useless person. ◆**nullement** *adv* not at all. ◆**nullité** *nf* (*d'un élève etc*) uselessness; (*personne*) useless person.

numéraire [nymerɛr] *nm* cash, currency.

numéral, -aux [nymeral, -o] *a & nm* numeral. ◆**numérique** *a* numerical; (*montre etc*) digital.

numéro [nymero] *nm* number; (*de journal*) issue, number; (*au cirque*) act; **un n. de danse/de chant** a dance/song number; **quel n.!** (*personne*) *Fam* what a character!; **n. vert** *Tél* = Freefone®, = *Am* tollfree number. ◆**numérot/er** *vt* (*pages, sièges*) to number. ◆**—age** *nm* numbering.

nu-pieds [nypje] *nmpl* open sandals.

nuptial, -aux [nypsjal, -o] *a* (*chambre*) bridal; (*anneau, cérémonie*) wedding-.

nuque [nyk] *nf* back *ou* nape of the neck.

nurse [nœrs] *nf* nanny, (children's) nurse.

nutritif, -ive [nytritif, -iv] *a* nutritious, nutritive. ◆**nutrition** *nf* nutrition.

nylon [nilɔ̃] *nm* (*fibre*) nylon.

nymphe [nɛ̃f] *nf* nymph. ◆**nymphomane** *nf Péj* nymphomaniac.

O

O, o [o] *nm* O, o.

oasis [ɔazis] *nf* oasis.

obédience [ɔbedjɑ̃s] *nf Pol* allegiance.

obé/ir [ɔbeir] *vi* to obey; **o. à qn/qch** to obey s.o./sth; **être obéi** to be obeyed. ◆**—issant** *a* obedient. ◆**obéissance** *nf* obedience (à to).

obélisque [ɔbelisk] *nm* (*monument*) obelisk.

obèse [ɔbɛz] *a* & *nmf* obese (person). ◆**obésité** *nf* obesity.

objecter [ɔbʒɛkte] *vt* (*prétexte*) to put forward, plead; **o. que** to object that; **on lui objecta son jeune âge** they objected that he *ou* she was too young. ◆**objecteur** *nm* **o. de conscience** conscientious objector. ◆**objection** *nf* objection.

objectif, -ive [ɔbʒɛktif, -iv] **1** *a* (*opinion etc*) objective. **2** *nm* (*but*) objective; *Phot* lens. ◆**objectivement** *adv* objectively. ◆**objectivité** *nf* objectivity.

objet [ɔbʒɛ] *nm* (*chose, sujet, but*) object; (*de toilette*) article; **faire l'o. de** (*étude, critiques etc*) to be the subject of; (*soins, surveillance*) to be given, receive; **objets trouvés** (*bureau*) lost property, *Am* lost and found.

obligation [ɔbligɑsjɔ̃] *nf* (*devoir, lieu, nécessité*) obligation; *Fin* bond. ◆**obligatoire** *a* compulsory, obligatory; (*inévitable*) *Fam* inevitable. ◆**obligatoirement** *adv* (*fatalement*) inevitably; **tu dois o. le faire** you have to do it.

oblig/er [ɔbliʒe] *vt* **1** (*contraindre*) to compel, oblige (**à faire** to do); (*engager*) to bind; **être obligé de faire** to have to do, be compelled *ou* obliged to do. **2** (*rendre service à*) to oblige; **être obligé à qn de qch** to be obliged to s.o. for sth. ◆**—eant** *a* obliging, kind. ◆**—é** *a* (*obligatoire*) necessary; (*fatal*) *Fam* inevitable. ◆**obligeamment** [-amɑ̃] *adv* obligingly. ◆**obligeance** *nf* kindness.

oblique [ɔblik] *a* oblique; **regard o.** sidelong glance; **en o.** at an (oblique) angle. ◆**obliquer** *vi* (*véhicule etc*) to turn off.

oblitérer [ɔblitere] *vt* (*timbre*) to cancel; (*billet, carte*) to stamp; **timbre oblitéré** (*non neuf*) used stamp. ◆**oblitération** *nf* cancellation; stamping.

oblong, -ongue [ɔblɔ̃, -ɔ̃g] *a* oblong.

obnubilé [ɔbnybile] *a* (*obsédé*) obsessed (par with).

obscène [ɔpsɛn] *a* obscene. ◆**obscénité** *nf* obscenity.

obscur [ɔpskyr] *a* (*noir*) dark; (*peu clair, inconnu, humble*) obscure. ◆**obscurcir** *vt* (*chambre etc*) to darken; (*rendre peu intelligible*) to obscure (*text, ideas etc*); **— s'o.** *vpr* (*ciel*) to cloud over, darken; (*vue*) to become dim. ◆**obscurément** *adv* obscurely. ◆**obscurité** *nf* dark(ness); (*de texte, d'acteur etc*) obscurity.

obséd/er [ɔpsede] *vt* to obsess, haunt. ◆**—ant** *a* haunting, obsessive. ◆**—é, -ée** *nmf* maniac (**de** for); **o. sexuel** sex maniac.

obsèques [ɔpsɛk] *nfpl* funeral.

obséquieux, -euse [ɔpsekjø, -øz] *a* obsequious.

observer [ɔpsɛrve] *vt* (*regarder*) to observe, watch; (*remarquer, respecter*) to observe; **faire o. qch à qn** (*signaler*) to point sth out to s.o. ◆**observateur, -trice** *a* observant; – *nmf* observer. ◆**observation** *nf* (*examen, remarque*) observation; (*reproche*) (critical) remark, rebuke; (*de règle etc*) observance; **en o.** (*malade*) under observation. ◆**observatoire** *nm* observatory; (*colline etc*) *Fig* & *Mil* observation post.

obsession [ɔpsesjɔ̃] *nf* obsession. ◆**obsessif, -ive** *a* (*peur etc*) obsessive. ◆**obsessionnel, -elle** *a Psy* obsessive.

obstacle [ɔpstakl] *nm* obstacle; **faire o. à** to stand in the way of.

obstétrique [ɔpstetrik] *nf Méd* obstetrics.

obstin/er (s') [sɔpstine] *vpr* to be obstinate *ou* persistent; **s'o. à faire** to persist in doing. ◆**—é** *a* stubborn, obstinate, persistent. ◆**obstination** *nf* stubbornness, obstinacy, persistence.

obstruction [ɔpstryksjɔ̃] *nf Méd Pol Sp* obstruction; **faire de l'o.** *Pol Sp* to be obstructive. ◆**obstruer** *vt* to obstruct.

obtempérer [ɔptɑ̃pere] *vi* to obey an injunction; **o. à** to obey.

obtenir° [ɔptənir] *vt* to get, obtain, secure. ◆**obtention** *nf* obtaining, getting.

obturer [ɔptyre] *vt* (*trou etc*) to stop *ou* close up. ◆**obturateur** *nm Phot* shutter; *Tech* valve.

obtus [ɔpty] *a* (*angle, esprit*) obtuse.

obus [ɔby] *nm Mil* shell.

occasion [ɔkazjɔ̃] *nf* **1** (*chance*) opportunity, chance (**de faire** to do); (*circonstance*) occasion; **à l'o.** on occasion, when the occasion arises; **à l'o. de** on the occasion of. **2** *Com* (*marché avantageux*) bargain; (*objet non neuf*) second-hand buy; **d'o.** second-hand, used. ◆**occasionner** *vt* to cause; **o. qch à qn** to cause s.o. sth.

occident [ɔksidɑ̃] *nm* **l'O.** *Pol* the West. ◆**occidental, -aux** *a Géog Pol* western; – *nmpl* **les occidentaux** *Pol* Westerners. ◆**occidentalisé** *a Pol* Westernized.

occulte [ɔkylt] *a* occult.

occup/er [ɔkype] *vt* (*maison, pays, usine etc*) to occupy; (*place, temps*) to take up, occupy; (*poste*) to hold, occupy; **o. qn** (*absorber*) to occupy s.o., keep s.o. busy; (*ouvrier etc*) to employ s.o.; **– s'o.** *vpr* to keep (oneself) busy (**à faire** doing); **s'o. de** (*affaire, problème etc*) to deal with; (*politique*) to be engaged in; **s'o. de qn** (*malade etc*) to take care of s.o.; (*client*) to see to s.o., deal with s.o.; **ne t'en occupe pas!** (*ne t'en fais pas*) don't worry!; (*ne t'en mêle pas*) mind your own business! ◆**—ant, -ante** *a* (*armée*) occupying; – *nmf* (*habitant*) occupant; – *nm Mil* forces of occupation, occupier. ◆**—é** *a* busy (**à faire** doing); (*place, maison etc*) occupied; (*ligne*) *Tél* engaged, *Am* busy; (*taxi*) hired. ◆**occupation** *nf* (*activité, travail etc*) occupation; **l'o. de** (*action*) the occupation of.

occurrence [ɔkyrɑ̃s] *nf Ling* occurrence; **en l'o.** in the circumstances, as it happens *ou* happened.

océan [ɔseɑ̃] *nm* ocean. ◆**océanique** *a* oceanic.

ocre [ɔkr] *nm & a inv* (*couleur*) ochre.

octave [ɔktav] *nf Mus* octave.

octobre [ɔktɔbr] *nm* October.

octogénaire [ɔktɔʒenɛr] *nmf* octogenarian.

octogone [ɔktɔgɔn] *nm* octagon. ◆**octogonal, -aux** *a* octagonal.

octroi [ɔktrwa] *nm Litt* granting. ◆**octroyer** *vt Litt* to grant (**à** to).

oculaire [ɔkylɛr] *a* **témoin o.** eyewitness; **globe o.** eyeball. ◆**oculiste** *nmf* eye specialist.

ode [ɔd] *nf* (*poème*) ode.

odeur [ɔdœr] *nf* smell, odour; (*de fleur*) scent. ◆**odorant** *a* sweet-smelling. ◆**odorat** *nm* sense of smell.

odieux, -euse [ɔdjø, -øz] *a* odious, obnoxious.

œcuménique [ekymenik] *a Rel* (o)ecumenical.

œil, *pl* **yeux** [œj, jø] *nm* eye; **sous mes yeux** before my very eyes; **lever/baisser les yeux** to look up/down; **fermer l'o.** (*dormir*) to shut one's eyes; **fermer les yeux sur** to turn a blind eye to; **ouvre l'o.!** keep your eyes open!; **coup d'o.** (*regard*) glance, look; **jeter un coup d'o. sur** to (have a) look *ou* glance at; **à vue d'o.** visibly; **faire les gros yeux à** to scowl at; **avoir à l'o.** (*surveiller*) to keep an eye on; **à l'o.** (*gratuitement*) *Fam* free; **faire de l'o. à** *Fam* to make eyes at; **o. au beurre noir** *Fig* black eye; **mon o.!** *Fam* (*incrédulité*) my foot!; (*refus*) no way!, no chance!

œillade [œjad] *nf* (*clin d'œil*) wink.

œillères [œjɛr] *nfpl* (*de cheval*) & *Fig* blinkers, *Am* blinders.

œillet [œjɛ] *nm* **1** *Bot* carnation. **2** (*trou de ceinture etc*) eyelet.

œuf, *pl* **œufs** [œf, ø] *nm* egg; *pl* (*de poisson*) (hard) roe; **o. sur le plat** fried egg; **étouffer qch dans l'o.** *Fig* to nip *ou* stifle sth in the bud.

œuvre [œvr] *nf* (*travail, acte, livre etc*) work; **o. (de charité)** (*organisation*) charity; **l'o. de** (*production artistique etc*) the works of; **mettre en o.** (*employer*) to make use of; **mettre tout en o.** to do everything possible (**pour faire** to do). ◆**œuvrer** *vi Litt* to work.

offense [ɔfɑ̃s] *nf* insult; *Rel* transgression. ◆**offens/er** *vt* to offend; **s'o. de** to take offence at. ◆**—ant** *a* offensive.

offensif, -ive [ɔfɑ̃sif, -iv] *a* offensive; – *nf* (*attaque*) offensive; (*du froid*) onslaught.

offert [ɔfɛr] *voir* **offrir.**

office [ɔfis] **1** *nm* (*fonction*) office; (*bureau*) office, bureau; **d'o.** (*être promu etc*) automatically; **faire o. de** to serve as; **ses bons offices** (*service*) one's good offices. **2** *nm Rel* service. **3** *nm ou f* (*pièce pour provisions*) pantry.

officiel, -ielle [ɔfisjɛl] *a* (*acte etc*) official; – *nm* (*personnage*) official. ◆**officiellement** *adv* officially. ◆**officieux, -euse** *a* unofficial.

officier [ɔfisje] **1** *vi Rel* to officiate. **2** *nm* (*dans l'armée etc*) officer.

offre [ɔfr] *nf* offer; (*aux enchères*) bid; **l'o. et la demande** *Écon* supply and demand; **offres d'emploi** *Journ* situations vacant. ◆**offrande** *nf* offering.

offr/ir* [ɔfrir] *vt* (*proposer, présenter*) to offer (**de faire** to do); (*donner en cadeau*) to give; (*démission*) to tender, offer; **je lui ai offert de le loger** I offered to put him up; **– s'o.** *vpr* (*cadeau etc*) to treat oneself to; (*se *proposer*) to offer oneself (**comme** as); **s'o. à faire** to offer *ou* volunteer to do; **s'o. (aux yeux)** (*vue etc*) to present itself. **◆—ant** *nm* **au plus o.** to the highest bidder.

offusquer [ɔfyske] *vt* to offend, shock; **s'o. de** to take offence at.

ogive [ɔʒiv] *nf* (*de fusée*) nose cone; **o. nucléaire** nuclear warhead.

ogre [ɔgr] *nm* ogre.

oh! [o] *int* oh!, o!

ohé! [ɔe] *int* hey (there)!

oie [wa] *nf* goose.

oignon [ɔɲɔ̃] *nm* (*légume*) onion; (*de tulipe, lis etc*) bulb; **occupe-toi de tes oignons!** *Fam* mind your own business!

oiseau, -x [wazo] *nm* bird; **à vol d'o.** as the crow flies; **drôle d'o.** (*individu*) *Péj* odd fish, *Am* oddball; **o. rare** (*personne étonnante*) *Iron* rare bird, perfect gem.

oiseux, -euse [wazø, -øz] *a* (*futile*) idle, vain.

oisif, -ive [wazif, -iv] *a* (*inactif*) idle; – *nmf* idler. **◆oisiveté** *nf* idleness.

oléoduc [ɔleɔdyk] *nm* oil pipeline.

olive [ɔliv] *nf* (*fruit*) olive; **huile d'o.** olive oil; – *a inv* (*couleur*) **(vert) o.** olive (green). **◆olivier** *nm* (*arbre*) olive tree.

olympique [ɔlɛ̃pik] *a* (*jeux, record etc*) Olympic.

ombilical, -aux [ɔ̃bilikal, -o] *a* (*cordon*) umbilical.

ombrage [ɔ̃braʒ] *nm* **1** (*ombre*) shade. **2 prendre o. de** (*jalousie, dépit*) to take umbrage at. **◆ombrag/er** *vt* to give shade to. **◆—é** *a* shady. **◆ombrageux, -euse** *a* (*caractère, personne*) touchy.

ombre [ɔ̃br] *nf* (*d'arbre etc*) shade; (*de personne, objet*) shadow; **l'o. d'un doute** *Fig* the shadow of a doubt; **l'o. de** (*remords, reproche etc*) the trace of; **30° à l'o.** 30° in the shade; **dans l'o.** (*comploter, travailler etc*) in secret.

ombrelle [ɔ̃brɛl] *nf* sunshade, parasol.

omelette [ɔmlɛt] *nf* omelet(te); **o. au fromage/***etc* cheese/*etc* omelet(te).

omettre* [ɔmɛtr] *vt* to omit (**de faire** to do). **◆omission** *nf* omission.

omni- [ɔmni] *préf* omni-. **◆omnipotent** *a* omnipotent.

omnibus [ɔmnibys] *a* & *nm* **(train) o.** slow train (*stopping at all stations*).

omoplate [ɔmɔplat] *nf* shoulder blade.

on [ɔ̃] (*sometimes* **l'on** [lɔ̃]) *pron* (*les gens*) they, people; (*nous*) we, one; (*vous*) you, one; **on dit** they say, people say, it is said; **on frappe** (*quelqu'un*) someone's knocking; **on me l'a donné** it was given to me, I was given it.

once [ɔ̃s] *nf* (*mesure*) & *Fig* ounce.

oncle [ɔ̃kl] *nm* uncle.

onctueux, -euse [ɔ̃ktɥø, -øz] *a* (*liquide, crème*) creamy; (*manières, paroles*) *Fig* smooth.

onde [ɔ̃d] *nf Phys Rad* wave; **grandes ondes** long wave; **ondes courtes/moyennes** short/medium wave; **sur les ondes** (*sur l'antenne*) on the radio.

ondée [ɔ̃de] *nf* (*pluie*) (sudden) shower.

on-dit [ɔ̃di] *nm inv* rumour, hearsay.

ondoyer [ɔ̃dwaje] *vi* to undulate. **◆ondulation** *nf* undulation; (*de cheveux*) wave. **◆ondul/er** *vi* to undulate; (*cheveux*) to be wavy. **◆—é** *a* wavy.

onéreux, -euse [ɔnerø, -øz] *a* costly.

ongle [ɔ̃gl] *nm* (finger) nail.

onglet [ɔ̃glɛ] *nm* (*entaille de canif etc*) (nail) groove.

ont [ɔ̃] *voir* **avoir**.

ONU [ɔny] *nf abrév* (*Organisation des nations unies*) UN.

onyx [ɔniks] *nm* (*pierre précieuse*) onyx.

onze [ɔ̃z] *a* & *nm* eleven. **◆onzième** *a* & *nmf* eleventh.

opale [ɔpal] *nf* (*pierre*) opal.

opaque [ɔpak] *a* opaque. **◆opacité** *nf* opacity.

opéra [ɔpera] *nm* (*ouvrage, art*) opera; (*édifice*) opera house. **◆opérette** *nf* operetta.

opér/er [ɔpere] **1** *vt* (*exécuter*) to carry out; (*choix*) to make; – *vi* (*agir*) to work, act; (*procéder*) to proceed; **— s'o.** *vpr* (*se produire*) to take place. **2** *vt* (*personne, organe*) *Méd* to operate on (**de** for); (*tumeur*) to remove; **cela peut s'o.** this can be removed; **se faire o.** to have an operation; – *vi* (*chirurgien*) to operate. **◆—ant** *a* (*efficace*) operative. **◆—é, -ée** *nmf Méd* patient (*operated on*). **◆opérateur, -trice** *nmf* (*de prise de vues*) *Cin* cameraman; (*sur machine*) operator. **◆opération** *nf* (*acte*) & *Méd Mil Math etc* operation; *Fin* deal. **◆opérationnel, -elle** *a* operational. **◆opératoire** *a Méd* operative; **bloc o.** operating *ou* surgical wing.

opiner [ɔpine] *vi* **o. (de la tête** *ou* **du chef)** to nod assent.

opiniâtre [ɔpinjɑtr] *a* stubborn, obstinate. **◆opiniâtreté** *nf* stubbornness, obstinacy.

opinion [ɔpinjɔ̃] *nf* opinion (**sur** about, on).

opium [ɔpjɔm] *nm* opium.

opportun [ɔpɔrtœ̃] *a* opportune, timely. **◆opportunément** *adv* opportunely.

◆**opportunisme** *nm* opportunism. ◆**opportunité** *nf* timeliness.

oppos/er [ɔpoze] *vt* (*argument, résistance*) to put up (à against); (*équipes, rivaux*) to bring together, set against each other; (*objets*) to place opposite each other; (*couleurs*) to contrast; **o. qch à qch** (*objet*) to place sth opposite sth; **o. qn à qn** to set s.o. against s.o.; **match qui oppose...** match between...; **— s'o.** *vpr* (*couleurs*) to contrast; (*équipes*) to confront each other; **s'o. à** (*mesure, personne etc*) to oppose, be opposed to; **je m'y oppose** I'm opposed to it, I oppose. ◆**—ant, -ante** *a* opposing; — *nmf* opponent. ◆**—é** *a* (*direction etc*) opposite; (*intérêts, équipe*) opposing; (*opinions*) opposite, opposing; (*couleurs*) contrasting; **être o. à** to be opposed to; — *nm* **l'o.** the opposite (**de** of); **à l'o.** (*côté*) on the opposite side (**de** from, to); **à l'o. de** (*contrairement à*) contrary to. ◆**opposition** *nf* opposition; **faire o. à** to oppose; **par o. à** as opposed to.

oppress/er [ɔprese] *vt* (*gêner*) to oppress. ◆**—ant** *a* oppressive. ◆**—eur** *nm Pol* oppressor. ◆**oppressif, -ive** *a* (*loi etc*) oppressive. ◆**oppression** *nf* oppression. ◆**opprim/er** *vt* (*tyranniser*) to oppress. ◆**—és** *nmpl* **les o.** the oppressed.

opter [ɔpte] *vi* **o. pour** to opt for.

opticien, -ienne [ɔptisjɛ̃, -jɛn] *nmf* optician.

optimisme [ɔptimism] *nm* optimism. ◆**optimiste** *a* optimistic; — *nmf* optimist.

optimum [ɔptimɔm] *nm & a* optimum; **la température o.** the optimum temperature. ◆**optimal, -aux** *a* optimal.

option [ɔpsjɔ̃] *nf* (*choix*) option; (*chose*) optional extra.

optique [ɔptik] *a* (*verre*) optical; — *nf* optics; (*aspect*) *Fig* perspective; **d'o.** (*illusion, instrument etc*) optical.

opulent [ɔpylɑ̃] *a* opulent. ◆**opulence** *nf* opulence.

or [ɔr] **1** *nm* gold; **en or** (*chaîne etc*) gold-; **d'or** (*cheveux, âge, règle*) golden; (*cœur*) of gold; **mine d'or** *Géol* goldmine; (*fortune*) *Fig* goldmine; **affaire en or** (*achat*) bargain; (*commerce*) *Fig* goldmine; **or noir** (*pétrole*) *Fig* black gold. **2** *conj* (*alors, cependant*) now, well.

oracle [ɔrakl] *nm* oracle.

orage [ɔraʒ] *nm* (thunder)storm. ◆**orageux, -euse** *a* stormy.

oraison [ɔrɛzɔ̃] *nf* prayer; **o. funèbre** funeral oration.

oral, -aux [ɔral, -o] *a* oral; — *nm* (*examen*) *Scol* oral.

orange [ɔrɑ̃ʒ] *nf* (*fruit*) orange; **o. pressée** (fresh) orange juice; — *a & nm inv* (*couleur*) orange. ◆**orangé** *a & nm* (*couleur*) orange. ◆**orangeade** *nf* orangeade. ◆**oranger** *nm* orange tree.

orang-outan(g) [ɔrɑ̃utɑ̃] *nm* (*pl* **orangs-outan(g)s**) orang-outang.

orateur [ɔratœr] *nm* speaker, orator.

orbite [ɔrbit] *nf* (*d'astre etc*) & *Fig* orbit; (*d'œil*) socket; **mettre sur o.** (*fusée etc*) to put into orbit.

orchestre [ɔrkɛstr] *nm* (*classique*) orchestra; (*moderne*) band; (*places*) *Th* stalls, *Am* orchestra. ◆**orchestrer** *vt* (*organiser*) & *Mus* to orchestrate.

orchidée [ɔrkide] *nf* orchid.

ordinaire [ɔrdinɛr] *a* (*habituel, normal*) ordinary, *Am* regular; (*médiocre*) ordinary, average; **d'o., à l'o.** usually; **comme d'o., comme à l'o.** as usual; **de l'essence o.** two-star (petrol), *Am* regular. ◆**—ment** *adv* usually.

ordinal, -aux [ɔrdinal, -o] *a* (*nombre*) ordinal.

ordinateur [ɔrdinatœr] *nm* computer.

ordination [ɔrdinɑsjɔ̃] *nf Rel* ordination.

ordonnance [ɔrdɔnɑ̃s] *nf* **1** (*de médecin*) prescription. **2** (*décret*) *Jur* order, ruling. **3** (*disposition*) arrangement. **4** (*soldat*) orderly.

ordonn/er [ɔrdɔne] *vt* **1** (*enjoindre*) to order (**que** (+ *sub*) that); **o. à qn de faire** to order s.o. to do. **2** (*agencer*) to arrange, order. **3** (*médicament etc*) to prescribe. **4** (*prêtre*) to ordain. ◆**—é** *a* (*personne, maison etc*) orderly.

ordre [ɔrdr] *nm* (*commandement, structure, association etc*) order; (*absence de désordre*) tidiness (*of room, person etc*); **en o.** (*chambre etc*) tidy; **mettre en o., mettre de l'o. dans** to tidy (up); **de premier o.** first-rate; **o. (public)** (law and) order; **par o. d'âge** in order of age; **à l'o. du jour** (*au programme*) on the agenda; (*d'actualité*) of topical interest; **les forces de l'o.** the police; **jusqu'à nouvel o.** until further notice; **de l'o. de** (*environ*) of the order of.

ordure [ɔrdyr] *nf* filth, muck; *pl* (*débris*) refuse, rubbish, *Am* garbage. ◆**ordurier, -ière** *a* (*plaisanterie etc*) lewd.

oreille [ɔrɛj] *nf* ear; **être tout oreilles** to be all ears; **faire la sourde o.** to turn a deaf ear; **casser les oreilles à qn** to deafen s.o.

oreiller [ɔreje] *nm* pillow.

oreillons [ɔrɛjɔ̃] *nmpl Méd* mumps.

ores (d') [dɔr] *adv* **d'ores et déjà** [dɔrzedeʒa] henceforth.

orfèvre [ɔrfɛvr] *nm* goldsmith, silversmith. ◆**orfèvrerie** *nf* (*magasin*) goldsmith's *ou* silversmith's shop; (*objets*) gold *ou* silver plate.

organe [ɔrgan] *nm Anat* & *Fig* organ; (*porte-parole*) mouthpiece. ◆**organique** *a* organic. ◆**organisme** *nm* **1** (*corps*) body; *Anat Biol* organism. **2** (*bureaux etc*) organization.

organisation [ɔrganizɑsjɔ̃] *nf* (*arrangement, association*) organization.

organis/er [ɔrganize] *vt* to organize; — **s'o.** *vpr* to organize oneself, get organized. ◆**—é** *a* (*esprit, groupe etc*) organized. ◆**organisateur, -trice** *nmf* organizer.

organiste [ɔrganist] *nmf Mus* organist.

orgasme [ɔrgasm] *nm* orgasm.

orge [ɔrʒ] *nf* barley.

orgie [ɔrʒi] *nf* orgy.

orgue [ɔrg] *nm Mus* organ; **o. de Barbarie** barrel organ; — *nfpl* organ; **grandes orgues** great organ.

orgueil [ɔrgœj] *nm* pride. ◆**orgueilleux, -euse** *a* proud.

orient [ɔrjɑ̃] *nm* **l'O.** the Orient, the East; **Moyen-O., Proche-O.** Middle East; **Extrême-O.** Far East. ◆**oriental, -ale, -aux** *a* eastern; (*de l'Orient*) oriental; — *nmf* oriental.

orient/er [ɔrjɑ̃te] *vt* (*lampe, antenne etc*) to position, direct; (*voyageur, élève etc*) to direct; (*maison*) to orientate, *Am* orient; — **s'o.** *vpr* to find one's bearings *ou* direction; **s'o. vers** (*carrière etc*) to move towards. ◆**—é** *a* (*ouvrage, film etc*) slanted. ◆**orientable** *a* (*lampe etc*) adjustable, flexible; (*bras de machine*) movable. ◆**orientation** *nf* direction; (*action*) positioning, directing; (*de maison*) aspect, orientation; (*tendance*) *Pol Littér etc* trend; **o. professionnelle** vocational guidance.

orifice [ɔrifis] *nm* opening, orifice.

originaire [ɔriʒinɛr] *a* **être o. de** (*natif*) to be a native of.

original, -ale, -aux [ɔriʒinal, -o] **1** *a* (*idée, artiste, version etc*) original; — *nm* (*modèle*) original. **2** *a* & *nmf* (*bizarre*) eccentric. ◆**originalité** *nf* originality; eccentricity.

origine [ɔriʒin] *nf* origin; **à l'o.** originally; **d'o.** (*pneu etc*) original; **pays d'o.** country of origin. ◆**originel, -elle** *a* (*sens, péché, habitant etc*) original.

orme [ɔrm] *nm* (*arbre, bois*) elm.

ornement [ɔrnəmɑ̃] *nm* ornament. ◆**ornemental, -aux** *a* ornamental. ◆**ornementation** *nf* ornamentation. ◆**ornementé** *a* adorned, ornamented (**de** with). ◆**orn/er** *vt* to decorate, adorn (**de** with). ◆**—é** *a* (*syle etc*) ornate.

ornière [ɔrnjɛr] *nf* (*sillon*) & *Fig* rut.

orphelin, -ine [ɔrfəlɛ̃, -in] *nmf* orphan; — *a* orphaned. ◆**orphelinat** *nm* orphanage.

orteil [ɔrtɛj] *nm* toe; **gros o.** big toe.

orthodoxe [ɔrtɔdɔks] *a* orthodox; — *nmpl* **les orthodoxes** the orthodox. ◆**orthodoxie** *nf* orthodoxy.

orthographe [ɔrtɔgraf] *nf* spelling. ◆**orthographier** *vt* (*mot*) to spell.

orthopédie [ɔrtɔpedi] *nf* orthop(a)edics.

ortie [ɔrti] *nf* nettle.

os [ɔs, *pl* o *ou* ɔs] *nm* bone; **trempé jusqu'aux os** soaked to the skin; **tomber sur un os** (*difficulté*) *Fam* to hit a snag.

OS [oɛs] *abrév* = **ouvrier spécialisé.**

oscar [ɔskar] *nm Cin* Oscar.

osciller [ɔsile] *vi Tech* to oscillate; (*se balancer*) to swing, sway; (*hésiter*) to waver; (*varier*) to fluctuate; (*flamme*) to flicker. ◆**oscillation** *nf Tech* oscillation; (*de l'opinion*) fluctuation.

oseille [ozɛj] *nf* **1** *Bot Culin* sorrel. **2** (*argent*) *Arg* dough.

os/er [oze] *vti* to dare; **o. faire** to dare (to) do. ◆**—é** *a* bold, daring.

osier [ozje] *nm* (*branches*) wicker.

ossature [ɔsatyr] *nf* (*du corps*) frame; (*de bâtiment*) & *Fig* framework. ◆**osselets** *nmpl* (*jeu*) jacks, knucklebones. ◆**ossements** *nmpl* (*de cadavres*) bones. ◆**osseux, -euse** *a* (*tissu*) bone-; (*maigre*) bony.

ostensible [ɔstɑ̃sibl] *a* conspicuous.

ostentation [ɔstɑ̃tɑsjɔ̃] *nf* ostentation.

otage [ɔtaʒ] *nm* hostage; **prendre qn en o.** to take s.o. hostage.

OTAN [ɔtɑ̃] *nf abrév* (*Organisation du traité de l'Atlantique Nord*) NATO.

otarie [ɔtari] *nf* (*animal*) sea lion.

ôter [ote] *vt* to remove, take away (**à qn** from s.o.); (*vêtement*) to take off, remove; (*déduire*) to take (away); **ôte-toi de là!** *Fam* get out of the way!

otite [ɔtit] *nf* ear infection.

oto-rhino [ɔtɔrino] *nmf Méd Fam* ear, nose and throat specialist.

ou [u] *conj* or; **ou bien** or else; **ou elle ou moi** either her or me.

où [u] *adv* & *pron* where; **le jour où** the day when, the day on which; **la table où** the table on which; **l'état où** the condition in which; **par où?** which way?; **d'où?** where from?; **d'où ma surprise/***etc* (*conséquence*) hence my surprise/*etc*; **le pays d'où** the country from which; **où qu'il soit** wherever he may be.

ouate [wat] *nf Méd* cotton wool, *Am* absorbent cotton.

oubli [ubli] *nm* (*défaut*) forgetfulness; **l'o. de qch** forgetting sth; **un o.** a lapse of memory; (*omission*) an oversight; **tomber dans l'o.** to fall into oblivion. ◆**oublier** *vt* to forget (**de faire** to do); (*faute, problème*) to overlook; **— s'o.** *vpr* (*traditions etc*) to be forgotten; (*personne*) *Fig* to forget oneself. ◆**oublieux, -euse** *a* forgetful (**de** of).

oubliettes [ublijɛt] *nfpl* (*de château*) dungeon.

ouest [wɛst] *nm* west; **à l'o. de** west of; **d'o.** (*vent*) west(erly); **de l'o.** western; **Allemagne de l'O.** West Germany; **l'Europe de l'O.** Western Europe; – *a inv* (*côte*) west(ern). ◆**o.-allemand, -ande** *a & nmf* West German.

ouf! [uf] *int* (*soulagement*) ah!, phew!

oui [wi] *adv & nm inv* yes; **o.!** yes!; **les o.** (*votes*) the ayes; **tu viens, o.?** come on, will you?; **je crois que o.** I think so; **si o.** if so.

ouï-dire [widir] *nm inv* hearsay.

ouïe[1] [wi] *nf* hearing; **être tout o.** *Fam* to be all ears.

ouïe[2]**!** [uj] *int* ouch!

ouïes [wi] *nfpl* (*de poisson*) gills.

ouille! [uj] *int* ouch!

ouragan [uragɑ̃] *nm* hurricane.

ourler [urle] *vt* to hem. ◆**ourlet** *nm* hem.

ours [urs] *nm* bear; **o. blanc/gris** polar/grizzly bear.

oursin [ursɛ̃] *nm* (*animal*) sea urchin.

ouste! [ust] *int Fam* scram!

outil [uti] *nm* tool. ◆**outill/er** *vt* to equip. ◆**—age** *nm* tools; (*d'une usine*) equipment.

outrage [utraʒ] *nm* insult (**à** to). ◆**outrag/er** *vt* to insult, offend. ◆**—eant** *a* insulting, offensive.

outrance [utrɑ̃s] *nf* (*excès*) excess; **à o.** (*travailler etc*) to excess; **guerre à o.** all-out war. ◆**outrancier, -ière** *a* excessive.

outre [utr] *prép* besides; – *adv* **en o.** besides, moreover; **o. mesure** inordinately; **passer o.** to take no notice (**à** of). ◆**o.-Manche** *adv* across the Channel. ◆**o.-mer** *adv* overseas; **d'o.-mer** (*peuple*) overseas.

outrepasser [utrəpɑse] *vt* (*limite etc*) to go beyond, exceed.

outr/er [utre] *vt* to exaggerate, overdo; **o. qn** (*indigner*) to outrage s.o. ◆**—é** *a* (*excessif*) exaggerated; (*révolté*) outraged.

outsider [awtsajdœr] *nm Sp* outsider.

ouvert [uvɛr] *voir* **ouvrir**; – *a* open; (*robinet, gaz etc*) on; **à bras ouverts** with open arms. ◆**ouvertement** *adv* openly. ◆**ouverture** *nf* opening; (*trou*) hole; (*avance*) & *Mus* overture; (*d'objectif*) *Phot* aperture; **o. d'esprit** open-mindedness.

ouvrable [uvrabl] *a* **jour o.** working day.

ouvrage [uvraʒ] *nm* (*travail, objet, livre*) work; (*couture*) (needle)work; **un o.** (*travail*) a piece of work. ◆**ouvragé** *a* (*bijou etc*) finely worked.

ouvreuse [uvrøz] *nf Cin* usherette.

ouvrier, -ière [uvrije, -jɛr] *nmf* worker; **o. agricole** farm labourer; **o. qualifié/spécialisé** skilled/unskilled worker; – *a* (*législation etc*) industrial; (*quartier, éducation*) working-class; **classe ouvrière** working class.

ouvrir* [uvrir] *vt* to open (up); (*gaz, radio etc*) to turn on, switch on; (*inaugurer*) to open; (*hostilités*) to begin; (*appétit*) to whet; (*liste, procession*) to head; – *vi* to open; (*ouvrir la porte*) to open (up); **— s'o.** *vpr* (*porte, boîte etc*) to open (up); **s'o. la jambe** to cut one's leg open; **s'o. à qn** *Fig* to open one's heart to s.o. (**de qch** about sth). ◆**ouvre-boîtes** *nm inv* tin opener, *Am* can-opener. ◆**ouvre-bouteilles** *nm inv* bottle opener.

ovaire [ɔvɛr] *nm Anat* ovary.

ovale [ɔval] *a & nm* oval.

ovation [ɔvɑsjɔ̃] *nf* (standing) ovation.

OVNI [ɔvni] *nm abrév* (*objet volant non identifié*) UFO.

oxyde [ɔksid] *nm Ch* oxide; **o. de carbone** carbon monoxide. ◆**oxyder** *vt*, **— s'o.** *vpr* to oxidize.

oxygène [ɔksiʒɛn] *nm* oxygen; **à o.** (*masque, tente*) oxygen-. ◆**oxygén/er** *vt* (*cheveux*) to bleach; **— s'o.** *vpr Fam* to breathe *ou* get some fresh air. ◆**—ée** *af* **eau o.** (hydrogen) peroxide.

P

P, p [pe] *nm* P, p.
pachyderme [paʃidɛrm] *nm* elephant.
pacifier [pasifje] *vt* to pacify. ◆**pacification** *nf* pacification. ◆**pacifique 1** *a* (*non violent, non militaire*) peaceful; (*personne, peuple*) peace-loving. **2** *a* (*côte etc*) Pacific; **Océan P.** Pacific Ocean; – *nm* **le P.** the Pacific. ◆**pacifiste** *a* & *nmf* pacifist.
pack [pak] *nm* (*de lait etc*) carton.
pacotille [pakɔtij] *nf* (*camelote*) trash.
pacte [pakt] *nm* pact. ◆**pactiser** *vi* **p. avec qn** *Péj* to be in league with s.o.
paf! [paf] **1** *int* bang!, wallop! **2** *a inv* (*ivre*) *Fam* sozzled, plastered.
pagaie [pagɛ] *nf* paddle. ◆**pagayer** *vi* (*ramer*) to paddle.
pagaïe, pagaille [pagaj] *nf* (*désordre*) *Fam* mess, shambles; **en p.** *Fam* in a mess; **avoir des livres/***etc* **en p.** *Fam* to have loads of books/*etc*.
paganisme [paganism] *nm* paganism.
page [paʒ] **1** *nf* (*de livre etc*) page; **à la p.** (*personne*) *Fig* up-to-date. **2** *nm* (*à la cour*) *Hist* page (boy).
pagne [paɲ] *nm* loincloth.
pagode [pagɔd] *nf* pagoda.
paie [pɛ] *nf* pay, wages. ◆**paiement** *nm* payment.
païen, -enne [pajɛ̃, -ɛn] *a* & *nmf* pagan, heathen.
paillasson [pajasɔ̃] *nm* (door)mat.
paille [pɑj] *nf* straw; (*pour boire*) (drinking) straw; **homme de p.** *Fig* stooge, man of straw; **tirer à la courte p.** to draw lots; **sur la p.** *Fig* penniless; **feu de p.** *Fig* flash in the pan. ◆**paillasse** *nf* **1** (*matelas*) straw mattress. **2** (*d'un évier*) draining-board.
paillette [pajɛt] *nf* (*d'habit*) sequin; *pl* (*de lessive, savon*) flakes; (*d'or*) *Géol* gold dust.
pain [pɛ̃] *nm* bread; **un p.** a loaf (of bread); **p. grillé** toast; **p. complet** wholemeal bread; **p. d'épice** gingerbread; **petit p.** roll; **p. de savon/de cire** bar of soap/wax; **avoir du p. sur la planche** (*travail*) *Fig* to have a lot on one's plate.
pair [pɛr] **1** *a* (*numéro*) even. **2** *nm* (*personne*) peer; **hors (de) p.** unrivalled, without equal; **aller de p.** to go hand in hand (**avec** with); **au p.** (*étudiante etc*) au pair; **travailler au p.** to work as an au pair.
paire [pɛr] *nf* pair (**de** of).
paisible [pezibl] *a* (*vie etc*) peaceful; (*caractère, personne*) peaceable.
paître* [pɛtr] *vi* to graze; **envoyer p.** *Fig* to send packing.
paix [pɛ] *nf* peace; (*traité*) *Pol* peace treaty; **en p.** in peace; (*avec sa conscience*) at peace (**avec** with); **avoir la p.** to have (some) peace and quiet.
Pakistan [pakistɑ̃] *nm* Pakistan. ◆**pakistanais, -aise** *a* & *nmf* Pakistani.
palabres [palabr] *nmpl* palaver.
palace [palas] *nm* luxury hotel.
palais [palɛ] *nm* **1** (*château*) palace; **P. de justice** law courts; **p. des sports** sports stadium *ou* centre. **2** *Anat* palate.
palan [palɑ̃] *nm* (*de navire etc*) hoist.
pâle [pɑl] *a* pale.
palet [palɛ] *nm* (*hockey sur glace*) puck.
paletot [palto] *nm* (knitted) cardigan.
palette [palɛt] *nf* **1** (*de peintre*) palette. **2** (*support pour marchandises*) pallet
pâleur [pɑlœr] *nf* paleness, pallor. ◆**pâlir** *vi* to go *ou* turn pale (**de** with).
palier [palje] *nm* **1** (*d'escalier*) landing; **être voisins de p.** to live on the same floor. **2** (*niveau*) level; (*phase de stabilité*) plateau; **par paliers** (*étapes*) in stages.
palissade [palisad] *nf* fence (*of stakes*).
pallier [palje] *vt* (*difficultés etc*) to alleviate. ◆**palliatif** *nm* palliative.
palmarès [palmarɛs] *nm* prize list; (*des chansons*) hit-parade.
palme [palm] *nf* **1** palm (leaf); (*symbole*) *Fig* palm. **2** (*de nageur*) flipper. ◆**palmier** *nm* palm (tree).
palmé [palme] *a* (*patte, pied*) webbed.
palombe [palɔ̃b] *nf* wood pigeon.
pâlot, -otte [pɑlo, -ɔt] *a* pale.
palourde [palurd] *nf* (*mollusque*) clam.
palp/er [palpe] *vt* to feel, finger. ◆**—able** *a* tangible.
palpit/er [palpite] *vi* (*frémir*) to quiver; (*cœur*) to palpitate, throb. ◆**—ant** *a* (*film etc*) thrilling. ◆**palpitations** *nfpl* quivering; palpitations.
pâmer (se) [sәpɑme] *vpr* **se p. de** (*joie etc*) to be paralysed *ou* ecstatic with.
pamphlet [pɑ̃flɛ] *nm* lampoon.
pamplemousse [pɑ̃plәmus] *nm* grapefruit.

pan [pɑ̃] **1** *nm* (*de chemise*) tail; (*de ciel*) patch; **p. de mur** section of wall. **2** *int* bang!

pan- [pɑ̃, pan] *préf* Pan-.

panacée [panase] *nf* panacea.

panache [panaʃ] *nm* (*plumet*) plume; **avoir du p.** (*fière allure*) to have panache; **un p. de fumée** a plume of smoke.

panaché [panaʃe] **1** *a* (*bigarré, hétéroclite*) motley. **2** *a* & *nm* **(demi) p.** shandy; **bière panachée** shandy.

pancarte [pɑ̃kart] *nf* sign, notice; (*de manifestant*) placard.

pancréas [pɑ̃kreɑs] *nm Anat* pancreas.

panda [pɑ̃da] *nm* (*animal*) panda.

pané [pane] *a Culin* breaded.

panier [panje] *nm* (*ustensile, contenu*) basket; **p. à salade** salad basket; (*voiture*) *Fam* police van, prison van. ◆**p.-repas** *nm* (*pl* **paniers-repas**) packed lunch.

panique [panik] *nf* panic; **pris de p.** panic-stricken; – *a* **peur p.** panic fear. ◆**paniqu/er** *vi* to panic. ◆**—é** *a* panic-stricken.

panne [pan] *nf* breakdown; **tomber en p.** to break down; **être en p.** to have broken down; **p. d'électricité** power cut, blackout; **avoir une p. sèche** to run out of petrol *ou Am* gas.

panneau, -x [pano] *nm* **1** (*écriteau*) sign, notice, board; **p. (de signalisation)** traffic *ou* road sign; **p. (d'affichage)** (*publicité*) hoarding, *Am* billboard. **2** (*de porte etc*) panel. ◆**panonceau, -x** *nm* (*enseigne*) sign.

panoplie [panɔpli] *nf* **1** (*jouet*) outfit. **2** (*gamme, arsenal*) (wide) range, assortment.

panorama [panɔrama] *nm* panorama. ◆**panoramique** *a* panoramic.

panse [pɑ̃s] *nf Fam* paunch, belly. ◆**pansu** *a* potbellied.

pans/er [pɑ̃se] *vt* (*plaie, main etc*) to dress, bandage; (*personne*) to dress the wound(s) of, bandage (up); (*cheval*) to groom. ◆**—ement** *nm* (*bande*) bandage, dressing; **p. adhésif** sticking plaster, *Am* Band-Aid®.

pantalon [pɑ̃talɔ̃] *nm* (pair of) trousers *ou Am* pants; **deux pantalons** two pairs of trousers *ou Am* pants; **en p.** in trousers, *Am* in pants.

pantelant [pɑ̃tlɑ̃] *a* gasping.

panthère [pɑ̃tɛr] *nf* (*animal*) panther.

pantin [pɑ̃tɛ̃] *nm* (*jouet*) jumping jack; (*personne*) *Péj* puppet.

pantois [pɑ̃twa] *a* flabbergasted.

pantoufle [pɑ̃tufl] *nf* slipper. ◆**pantouflard, -arde** *nmf Fam* stay-at-home, *Am* homebody.

paon [pɑ̃] *nm* peacock.

papa [papa] *nm* dad(dy); **de p.** (*désuet*) *Péj* outdated; **fils à p.** *Péj* rich man's son, daddy's boy.

pape [pap] *nm* pope. ◆**papauté** *nf* papacy.

paperasse(s) [papras] *nf(pl) Péj* (official) papers. ◆**paperasserie** *nf Péj* (official) papers; (*procédure*) red tape.

papeterie [papetri] *nf* (*magasin*) stationer's shop; (*articles*) stationery; (*fabrique*) paper mill. ◆**papetier, -ière** *nmf* stationer.

papi [papi] *nm Fam* grand(d)ad.

papier [papje] *nm* (*matière*) paper; **un p.** (*feuille*) a piece *ou* sheet of paper; (*formulaire*) a form; *Journ* an article; **en p.** (*sac etc*) paper-; **papiers (d'identité)** (identity) papers; **p. à lettres** writing paper; **du p. journal** (some) newspaper; **p. peint** wallpaper; **p. de verre** sandpaper.

papillon [papijɔ̃] *nm* **1** (*insecte*) butterfly; (*écrou*) butterfly nut, *Am* wing nut; **p. (de nuit)** moth. **2** (*contravention*) (parking) ticket.

papot/er [papɔte] *vi* to prattle. ◆**—age(s)** *nm(pl)* prattle.

paprika [paprika] *nm* (*poudre*) *Culin* paprika.

papy [papi] *nm Fam* grand(d)ad.

Pâque [pɑk] *nf* **la P.** *Rel* Passover.

paquebot [pakbo] *nm Nau* liner.

pâquerette [pɑkrɛt] *nf* daisy.

Pâques [pɑk] *nm* & *nfpl* Easter.

paquet [pakɛ] *nm* (*de sucre, bonbons etc*) packet; (*colis*) package; (*de cigarettes*) pack(et); (*de cartes*) pack.

par [par] *prép* **1** (*agent, manière, moyen*) by; **choisi/frappé/***etc* **p.** chosen/hit/*etc* by; **p. erreur** by mistake; **p. mer** by sea; **p. le train** by train; **p. la force/le travail/***etc* by *ou* through force/work/*etc*; **apprendre p. un voisin** to learn from *ou* through a neighbour; **commencer/s'ouvrir p. qch** (*récit etc*) to begin/open with sth; **p. malchance** unfortunately. **2** (*lieu*) through; **p. la porte/le tunnel/***etc* through *ou* by the door/tunnel/*etc*; **regarder/jeter p. la fenêtre** to look/throw out (of) the window; **p. les rues** through the streets; **p. ici/là** (*aller*) this/that way; (*habiter*) around here/there. **3** (*motif*) out of, from; **p. respect/pitié/***etc* out of *ou* from respect/pity/*etc*. **4** (*temps*) on; **p. un jour d'hiver/***etc* on a winter's day/*etc*; **p. le passé** in the past; **p. ce froid** in this cold. **5** (*distributif*) **dix fois p. an** ten times a *ou* per year; **deux p. deux** two by

two; **p. deux fois** twice. **6** (*trop*) **p. trop aimable**/*etc* far too kind/*etc*.
para [para] *nm Mil Fam* para(trooper).
para- [para] *préf* para-.
parabole [parabɔl] *nf* **1** (*récit*) parable. **2** *Math* parabola.
parachever [paraʃve] *vt* to perfect.
parachute [paraʃyt] *nf* parachute. ◆**parachuter** *vt* to parachute; (*nommer*) *Fam* to pitchfork (**à un poste** into a job). ◆**parachutisme** *nm* parachute jumping. ◆**parachutiste** *nmf* parachutist; *Mil* paratrooper.
parade [parad] *nf* **1** (*étalage*) show, parade; (*spectacle*) & *Mil* parade. **2** *Boxe Escrime* parry; (*riposte*) *Fig* reply. ◆**parader** *vi* to parade, show off.
paradis [paradi] *nm* paradise, heaven. ◆**paradisiaque** *a* (*endroit etc*) *Fig* heavenly.
paradoxe [paradɔks] *nm* paradox. ◆**paradoxalement** *adv* paradoxically.
parafe [paraf] *voir* **paraphe**. ◆**parafer** *voir* **parapher**.
paraffine [parafin] *nf* paraffin (wax).
parages [paraʒ] *nmpl* region, area (**de** of); **dans ces p.** in these parts.
paragraphe [paragraf] *nm* paragraph.
paraître* [parɛtr] **1** *vi* (*se montrer*) to appear; (*sembler*) to seem, look, appear; – *v imp* **il paraît qu'il va partir** it appears *ou* seems (that) he's leaving. **2** *vi* (*livre*) to be published, come out; **faire p.** to bring out.
parallèle [paralɛl] **1** *a* (*comparable*) & *Math* parallel (**à** with, to); (*marché*) *Com* unofficial. **2** *nm* (*comparaison*) & *Géog* parallel. ◆**—ment** *adv* **p. à** parallel to.
paralyser [paralize] *vt* to paralyse, *Am* paralyze. ◆**paralysie** *nf* paralysis. ◆**paralytique** *a* & *nmf* paralytic.
paramètre [paramɛtr] *nm* parameter.
paranoïa [paranɔja] *nf* paranoia. ◆**paranoïaque** *a* & *nmf* paranoid.
parapet [parapɛ] *nm* parapet.
paraphe [paraf] *nm* initials, signature; (*traits*) flourish. ◆**parapher** *vt* to initial, sign.
paraphrase [parafraz] *nf* paraphrase. ◆**paraphraser** *vt* to paraphrase.
parapluie [paraplɥi] *nm* umbrella.
parasite [parazit] *nm* (*personne, organisme*) parasite; *pl Rad* interference; – *a* parasitic(al).
parasol [parasɔl] *nm* parasol, sunshade.
paratonnerre [paratɔnɛr] *nm* lightning conductor *ou Am* rod.
paravent [paravɑ̃] *nm* (folding) screen.
parc [park] *nm* **1** park; (*de château*) grounds. **2** (*de bébé*) (play) pen; (*à moutons, à bétail*) pen; **p. (de stationnement)** car park, *Am* parking lot; **p. à huîtres** oyster bed.
parcelle [parsɛl] *nf* fragment, particle; (*terrain*) plot; (*de vérité*) *Fig* grain.
parce que [parsk(ə)] *conj* because.
parchemin [parʃəmɛ̃] *nm* parchment.
parcimonie [parsimɔni] *nf* **avec p.** parsimoniously. ◆**parcimonieux, -euse** *a* parsimonious.
par-ci par-là [parsiparla] *adv* here, there and everywhere.
parcmètre [parkmɛtr] *nm* parking meter.
parcourir* [parkurir] *vt* (*région*) to travel through, tour, scour; (*distance*) to cover; (*texte*) to glance through. ◆**parcours** *nm* (*itinéraire*) route; (*de fleuve*) & *Sp* course; (*voyage*) trip, journey.
par-delà [pard(ə)la] *voir* **delà**.
par-derrière [pardɛrjɛr] *voir* **derrière**.
par-dessous [pard(ə)su] *prép* & *adv* under(neath).
pardessus [pard(ə)sy] *nm* overcoat.
par-dessus [pard(ə)sy] *prép* & *adv* over (the top of); **p.-dessus tout** above all.
par-devant [pard(ə)vɑ̃] *voir* **devant**.
pardon [pardɔ̃] *nm* forgiveness, pardon; **p.?** (*pour demander*) excuse me?, *Am* pardon me?; **p.!** (*je le regrette*) sorry!; **demander p.** to apologize (**à** to). ◆**pardonn/er** *vt* to forgive; **p. qch à qn/à qn d'avoir fait qch** to forgive s.o. for sth/for doing sth. ◆**—able** *a* forgivable.
pare-balles [parbal] *a inv* **gilet p.-balles** bulletproof jacket *ou Am* vest.
pare-brise [parbriz] *nm inv Aut* windscreen, *Am* windshield.
pare-chocs [parʃɔk] *nm inv Aut* bumper.
pareil, -eille [parɛj] *a* similar; **p. à** the same as, similar to; **être pareils** to be the same, be similar *ou* alike; **un p. désordre**/*etc* such a mess/*etc*; **en p. cas** in such a case; – *nmf* (*personne*) equal; **rendre la pareille à qn** to treat s.o. the same way; **sans p.** unparalleled, unique; – *adv Fam* the same. ◆**pareillement** *adv* in the same way; (*aussi*) likewise.
parement [parmɑ̃] *nm* (*de pierre, de vêtement*) facing.
parent, -ente [parɑ̃, -ɑ̃t] *nmf* relation, relative; – *nmpl* (*père et mère*) parents; – *a* related (**de** to). ◆**parenté** *nf* (*rapport*) relationship, kinship.
parenthèse [parɑ̃tɛz] *nf* (*signe*) bracket, parenthesis; (*digression*) digression.

parer [pare] **1** *vt* (*coup*) to parry, ward off; – *vi* **p. à** to be prepared for. **2** *vt* (*orner*) to adorn (**de** with).

paresse [parɛs] *nf* laziness, idleness. ◆**paresser** *vi* to laze (about). ◆**paresseux, -euse** *a* lazy, idle; – *nmf* lazybones.

parfaire [parfɛr] *vt* to perfect. ◆**parfait** *a* perfect; **p.!** excellent!; – *nm Gram* perfect (tense). ◆**parfaitement** *adv* perfectly; (*certainement*) certainly.

parfois [parfwa] *adv* sometimes.

parfum [parfœ̃] *nm* (*odeur*) fragrance, scent; (*goût*) flavour; (*liquide*) perfume, scent. ◆**parfum/er** *vt* to perfume, scent; (*glace, crème etc*) to flavour (**à** with); — **se p.** *vpr* to put on perfume; (*habituellement*) to wear perfume. ◆**—é** *a* (*savon, mouchoir*) scented; **p. au café/***etc* coffee-/*etc* flavoured. ◆**parfumerie** *nf* (*magasin*) perfume shop.

pari [pari] *nm* bet, wager; *pl Sp* betting, bets; **p. mutuel urbain** = the tote, *Am* pari-mutuel. ◆**parier** *vti* to bet (**sur** on, **que** that). ◆**parieur, -euse** *nmf Sp* better, punter.

Paris [pari] *nm ou f* Paris. ◆**parisien, -ienne** *a* (*accent etc*) Parisian, Paris-; – *nmf* Parisian.

parité [parite] *nf* parity.

parjure [parʒyr] *nm* perjury; – *nmf* perjurer. ◆**se parjurer** *vpr* to perjure oneself.

parka [parka] *nm* parka.

parking [parkiŋ] *nm* (*lieu*) car park, *Am* parking lot.

par-là [parla] *adv voir* **par-ci.**

parlement [parləmɑ̃] *nm* parliament. ◆**parlementaire** *a* parliamentary; – *nmf* member of parliament.

parlementer [parləmɑ̃te] *vi* to parley, negotiate.

parl/er [parle] *vi* to talk, speak (**de** about, of; **à** to); **tu parles!** *Fam* you must be joking!; **sans p. de . . .** not to mention . . . ; – *vt* (*langue*) to speak; **p. affaires/***etc* to talk business/*etc*; — **se p.** *vpr* (*langue*) to be spoken; – *nm* speech; (*régional*) dialect. ◆**—ant** *a* (*film*) talking; (*regard etc*) eloquent. ◆**—é** *a* (*langue*) spoken.

parloir [parlwar] *nm* (*de couvent, prison*) visiting room.

parmi [parmi] *prép* among(st).

parodie [parɔdi] *nf* parody. ◆**parodier** *vt* to parody.

paroi [parwa] *nf* wall; (*de maison*) inside wall; (*de rocher*) (rock) face.

paroisse [parwas] *nf* parish. ◆**paroissial, -aux** *a* (*registre, activité etc*) parish-. ◆**paroissien, -ienne** *nmf* parishioner.

parole [parɔl] *nf* (*mot, promesse*) word; (*faculté, langage*) speech; **adresser la p. à** to speak to; **prendre la p.** to speak, make a speech; **demander la p.** to ask to speak; **perdre la p.** to lose one's tongue.

paroxysme [parɔksism] *nm* (*de douleur etc*) height.

parpaing [parpɛ̃] *nm* concrete block, breezeblock.

parquer [parke] *vt* (*bœufs*) to pen; (*gens*) to herd together, confine; (*véhicule*) to park; — **se p.** *vpr Aut* to park.

parquet [parkɛ] *nm* **1** (parquet) floor(ing). **2** *Jur* Public Prosecutor's office.

parrain [parɛ̃] *nm Rel* godfather; (*répondant*) sponsor. ◆**parrain/er** *vt* to sponsor. ◆**—age** *nm* sponsorship.

pars, part[1] [par] *voir* **partir.**

parsemer [parsəme] *vt* to strew, dot (**de** with).

part[2] [par] *nf* (*portion*) share, part; **prendre p. à** (*activité*) to take part in; (*la joie etc de qn*) to share; **de toutes parts** from *ou* on all sides; **de p. et d'autre** on both sides; **d'une p., . . . d'autre p.** on the one hand, . . . on the other hand; **d'autre p.** (*d'ailleurs*) moreover; **pour ma p.** as far as I'm concerned; **de la p. de** (*provenance*) from; **c'est de la p. de qui?** *Tél* who's speaking?; **faire p. de qch à qn** to inform s.o. of sth; **quelque p.** somewhere; **nulle p.** nowhere; **autre p.** somewhere else; **à p.** (*séparément*) apart; (*mettre, prendre*) aside; (*excepté*) apart from; **un cas/une place/***etc* **à p.** a separate *ou* special case/place/*etc*; **membre à p. entière** full member.

partage [partaʒ] *nm* dividing (up), division; (*participation*) sharing; (*distribution*) sharing out; (*sort*) *Fig* lot. ◆**partag/er** *vt* (*repas, frais, joie etc*) to share (**avec** with); (*diviser*) to divide (up); (*distribuer*) to share out; — **se p.** *vpr* (*bénéfices etc*) to share (between themselves *etc*); **se p. entre** to divide one's time between. ◆**—é** *a* (*avis etc*) divided; **p. entre** (*sentiments*) torn between.

partance (en) [ɑ̃partɑ̃s] *adv* (*train etc*) about to depart (**pour** for).

partant [partɑ̃] *nm* (*coureur, cheval*) *Sp* starter.

partenaire [partənɛr] *nmf* (*époux etc*) & *Sp Pol* partner.

parterre [partɛr] *nm* **1** (*de jardin etc*) flower bed. **2** *Th* stalls, *Am* orchestra.

parti [parti] *nm Pol* party; (*époux*) match; **prendre un p.** to make a decision, follow a course; **prendre p. pour** to side with; **tirer p. de** to turn to (good) account; **p. pris** (*préjugé*) prejudice; **être de p. pris** to be prejudiced (**contre** against).

partial, -aux [parsjal, -o] *a* biased. ◆**partialité** *nf* bias.

participe [partisip] *nm Gram* participle.

particip/er [partisipe] *vi* **p. à** (*activité, jeu etc*) to take part in, participate in; (*frais, joie etc*) to share (in). ◆**—ant, -ante** *nmf* participant. ◆**participation** *nf* participation; sharing; (*d'un acteur*) appearance, collaboration; **p. (aux frais)** (*contribution*) share (in the expenses).

particule [partikyl] *nf* particle.

particulier, -ière [partikylje, -jɛr] *a* (*spécial, spécifique*) particular; (*privé*) private; (*bizarre*) peculiar; **p. à** peculiar to; **en p.** (*surtout*) in particular; (*à part*) in private; – *nm* private individual *ou* citizen. ◆**particularité** *nf* peculiarity. ◆**particulièrement** *adv* particularly; **tout p.** especially.

partie [parti] *nf* part; (*de cartes, de tennis etc*) game; (*de chasse, de plaisir*) & *Jur* party; (*métier*) line, field; **en p.** partly, in part; **en grande p.** mainly; **faire p. de** to be a part of; (*adhérer à*) to belong to; (*comité*) to be on. ◆**partiel, -ielle** *a* partial; – *nm* **(examen) p.** *Univ* term exam. ◆**partiellement** *adv* partially.

part/ir* [partir] *vi* **(aux être)** (*aller, disparaître*) to go; (*s'en aller*) to leave, go (off); (*se mettre en route*) to set off; (*s'éloigner*) to go (away); (*moteur*) to start; (*fusil, coup de feu*) to go off; (*flèche*) to shoot off; (*bouton*) to come off; (*tache*) to come out; **p. de** (*commencer par*) to start (off) with; **ça part du cœur** it comes from the heart; **p. bien** to get off to a good start; **à p. de** (*date, prix*) from. ◆**—i** *a* **bien p.** off to a good start.

partisan [partizɑ̃] *nm* follower, supporter; *Mil* partisan; – *a* (*esprit*) *Péj* partisan; **être p. de qch/de faire** to be in favour of sth/of doing.

partition [partisjɔ̃] *nf Mus* score.

partout [partu] *adv* everywhere; **p. où tu vas** *ou* **iras** everywhere *ou* wherever you go; **p. sur la table**/*etc* all over the table/*etc.*

paru [pary] *voir* **paraître.** ◆**parution** *nf* (*de livre etc*) publication.

parure [paryr] *nf* (*toilette*) finery; (*bijoux*) jewellery.

parven/ir* [parvənir] *vi* (*aux* **être**) **p. à** (*lieu*) to reach; (*fortune, ses fins*) to achieve; **p. à faire** to manage to do. ◆**—u, -ue** *nmf Péj* upstart.

parvis [parvi] *nm* square (*in front of church etc*).

pas[1] [pɑ] *adv* (*négatif*) not; **(ne) . . . p.** not; **je ne sais p.** I do not *ou* don't know; **p. de pain/de café**/*etc* no bread/coffee/*etc*; **p. encore** not yet; **p. du tout** not at all.

pas[2] [pɑ] *nm* **1** step, pace; (*allure*) pace; (*bruit*) footstep; (*trace*) footprint; **à deux p. (de)** close by; **revenir sur ses p.** to go back on one's tracks; **au p.** at a walking pace; **rouler au p.** (*véhicule*) to go dead slow(ly); **au p. (cadencé)** in step; **faire les cent p.** to walk up and down; **faux p.** stumble; (*faute*) *Fig* blunder; **le p. de la porte** the doorstep. **2** (*de vis*) thread. **3** *Géog* straits; **le p. de Calais** the Straits of Dover.

pascal [paskal] *a* (*semaine, messe etc*) Easter-.

passable [pɑsabl] *a* acceptable, tolerable; **mention p.** *Scol Univ* pass. ◆**—ment** [-əmɑ̃] *adv* acceptably; (*beaucoup*) quite a lot.

passage [pɑsaʒ] *nm* (*action*) passing, passage; (*traversée*) *Nau* crossing, passage; (*extrait*) passage; (*couloir*) passage(way); (*droit*) right of way; (*venue*) arrival; (*chemin*) path; **p. clouté** *ou* **pour piétons** (pedestrian) crossing; **obstruer le p.** to block the way; **p. souterrain** subway, *Am* underpass; **p. à niveau** level crossing, *Am* grade crossing; **'p. interdit'** 'no thoroughfare'; **'cédez le p.'** *Aut* 'give way', *Am* 'yield'; **être de p.** to be passing through (**à Paris**/*etc* Paris/*etc*); **hôte de p.** passing guest. ◆**passager, -ère 1** *nmf* passenger; **p. clandestin** stowaway. **2** *a* (*de courte durée*) passing, temporary. ◆**passagèrement** *adv* temporarily.

passant, -ante [pɑsɑ̃, -ɑ̃t] **1** *a* (*rue*) busy; – *nmf* passer-by. **2** *nm* (*de ceinture etc*) loop.

passe [pɑs] *nf Sp* pass; **mot de p.** password; **en p. de faire** on the road to doing; **une mauvaise p.** *Fig* a bad patch.

passe-montagne [pɑsmɔ̃taɲ] *nm* balaclava.

passe-partout [pɑspartu] *nm inv* (*clé*) master key; – *a inv* (*compliment, phrase*) all-purpose.

passe-passe [pɑspɑs] *nm inv* **tour de p.-passe** conjuring trick.

passe-plat [pɑspla] *nm* service hatch.

passeport [pɑspɔr] *nm* passport.

passer [pɑse] *vi* (*aux* **être** *ou* **avoir**) (*aller, venir*) to pass (**à** to); (*facteur, laitier*) to come; (*temps*) to pass (by), go by; (*courant*) to flow; (*film, programme*) to be shown, be on; (*loi*) to be passed; (*douleur, mode*) to pass; (*couleur*) to fade; **p. devant** (*maison etc*) to go past *ou* by, pass (by); **p. à** *ou* **par Paris** to pass through Paris; **p. à la radio** to come *ou* go on the radio; **p. à l'ennemi/à la caisse** to go over to the enemy/the cash desk; **laisser p.** (*personne, lumière*) to let in *ou* through; (*occasion*) to let slip; **p. prendre** to pick up, fetch; **p. voir qn** to drop in on s.o.; **p. pour** (*riche etc*) to be taken for; **faire p. qn pour** to pass s.o. off as; **p. sur** (*détail etc*) to overlook, pass over; **p. capitaine/***etc* to be promoted captain/*etc*; **p. en** (*seconde etc*) *Scol* to pass up into; *Aut* to change up to; **ça passe** (*c'est passable*) that'll do; **en passant** (*dire qch*) in passing; – *vt* (*aux* **avoir**) (*frontière etc*) to pass, cross; (*maison etc*) to pass, go past; (*donner*) to pass, hand (**à** to); (*mettre*) to put; (*omettre*) to overlook; (*temps*) to spend, pass (**à faire** doing); (*disque*) to play, put on; (*film, programme*) to show, put on; (*loi, motion*) to pass; (*chemise*) to slip on; (*examen*) to take, sit (for); (*thé*) to strain; (*café*) to filter; (*commande*) to place; (*accord*) to conclude; (*colère*) to vent (**sur** on); (*limites*) to go beyond; (*visite médicale*) to go through; **p. (son tour)** to pass; **p. qch à qn** (*caprice etc*) to grant s.o. sth; (*pardonner*) to excuse s.o. sth; **je vous passe . . .** *Tél* I'm putting you through to . . . ; **p. un coup d'éponge/***etc* **à qch** to go over sth with a sponge/*etc*; **– se p.** *vpr* (*se produire*) to take place, happen; (*douleur*) to pass, go (away); **se p. de** to do *ou* go without; **se p. de commentaires** to need no comment; **ça s'est bien passé** it went off all right. ◆**passé 1** *a* (*temps etc*) past; (*couleur*) faded; **la semaine passée** last week; **dix heures passées** after *ou* gone ten (o'clock); **être passé** (*personne*) to have been (and gone); (*orage*) to be over; **avoir vingt ans passés** to be over twenty; – *nm* (*temps, vie passée*) past; *Gram* past (tense). **2** *prép* after; **p. huit heures** after eight (o'clock).

passerelle [pɑsrɛl] *nf* (*pont*) footbridge; (*voie d'accès*) *Nau Av* gangway.

passe-temps [pɑstɑ̃] *nm inv* pastime.

passeur, -euse [pɑsœr, -øz] *nmf* **1** *Nau* ferryman, ferrywoman. **2** (*contrebandier*) smuggler.

passible [pasibl] *a* **p. de** (*peine*) *Jur* liable to.

passif, -ive [pasif, -iv] **1** *a* (*rôle, personne etc*) passive; – *nm Gram* passive. **2** *nm Com* liabilities. ◆**passivité** *nf* passiveness, passivity.

passion [pasjɔ̃] *nf* passion; **avoir la p. des voitures/d'écrire/***etc* to have a passion *ou* a great love for cars/writing/*etc*. ◆**passionnel, -elle** *a* (*crime*) of passion. ◆**passionn/er** *vt* to thrill, fascinate; **se p. pour** to have a passion for. ◆**—ant** *a* thrilling. ◆**—é, -ée** *a* passionate; **p. de qch** passionately fond of sth; – *nmf* fan (**de** of). ◆**—ément** *adv* passionately.

passoire [pɑswar] *nf* (*pour liquides*) sieve; (*à thé*) strainer; (*à légumes*) colander.

pastel [pastɛl] *nm* pastel; **au p.** (*dessin*) pastel-; – *a inv* (*ton*) pastel-.

pastèque [pastɛk] *nf* watermelon.

pasteur [pastœr] *nm Rel* pastor.

pasteurisé [pastœrize] *a* (*lait, beurre etc*) pasteurized.

pastiche [pastiʃ] *nm* pastiche.

pastille [pastij] *nf* pastille, lozenge.

pastis [pastis] *nm* aniseed liqueur, pastis.

pastoral, -aux [pastɔral, -o] *a* pastoral.

patate [patat] *nf Fam* spud, potato.

patatras! [patatra] *int* crash!

pataud [pato] *a* clumsy, lumpish.

patauger [patoʒe] *vi* (*marcher*) to wade (*in the mud etc*); (*barboter*) to splash about; (*s'empêtrer*) *Fig* to flounder. ◆**pataugeoire** *nf* paddling pool.

patchwork [patʃwœrk] *nm* patchwork.

pâte [pɑt] *nf* (*substance*) paste; (*à pain, à gâteau*) dough; (*à tarte*) pastry; **pâtes (alimentaires)** pasta; **p. à modeler** plasticine®, modelling clay; **p. à frire** batter; **p. dentifrice** toothpaste.

pâté [pɑte] *nm* **1** (*charcuterie*) pâté; **p. (en croûte)** meat pie. **2 p. (de sable)** sand castle; **p. de maisons** block of houses. **3** (*tache d'encre*) (ink) blot.

pâtée [pɑte] *nf* (*pour chien, volaille etc*) mash.

patelin [patlɛ̃] *nm Fam* village.

patent [patɑ̃] *a* patent, obvious.

patère [patɛr] *nf* (coat) peg.

paternel, -elle [patɛrnɛl] *a* (*amour etc*) fatherly, paternal; (*parenté, réprimande*) paternal. ◆**paternité** *nf* (*état*) paternity, fatherhood; (*de livre*) authorship.

pâteux, -euse [pɑtø, -øz] *a* (*substance*) doughy, pasty; (*style*) woolly; **avoir la bouche** *ou* **la langue pâteuse** (*après s'être enivré*) to have a mouth full of cotton wool *ou Am* cotton.

pathétique [patetik] *a* moving; – *nm* pathos.

pathologie [patɔlɔʒi] *nf* pathology. ◆**pathologique** *a* pathological.

patient, -ente [pasjɑ̃, -ɑ̃t] **1** *a* patient. **2** *nmf Méd* patient. ◆**patiemment** [-amɑ̃] *adv* patiently. ◆**patience** *nf* patience; **prendre p.** to have patience; **perdre p.** to lose patience. ◆**patienter** *vi* to wait (patiently).

patin [patɛ̃] *nm* skate; (*pour le parquet*) cloth pad (*used for walking*); **p. à glace/à roulettes** ice/roller skate. ◆**patin/er** *vi Sp* to skate; (*véhicule, embrayage*) to slip. ◆**—age** *nm Sp* skating; **p. artistique** figure skating. ◆**—eur, -euse** *nmf Sp* skater. ◆**patinoire** *nf* (*piste*) & *Fig* skating rink, ice rink.

patine [patin] *nf* patina.

patio [patjo] *nm* patio.

pâtir [pɑtir] *vi* **p. de** to suffer from.

pâtisserie [pɑtisri] *nf* pastry, cake; (*magasin*) cake shop; (*art*) cake *ou* pastry making. ◆**pâtissier, -ière** *nmf* pastry-cook and cake shop owner.

patois [patwa] *nm Ling* patois.

patraque [patrak] *a* (*malade*) *Fam* under the weather.

patriarche [patrijarʃ] *nm* patriarch.

patrie [patri] *nf* (native) country; (*ville*) birth place. ◆**patriote** *nmf* patriot; – *a* (*personne*) patriotic. ◆**patriotique** *a* (*chant etc*) patriotic. ◆**patriotisme** *nm* patriotism.

patrimoine [patrimwan] *nm* (*biens*) & *Fig* heritage.

patron, -onne [patrɔ̃, -ɔn] **1** *nmf* (*chef*) employer, boss; (*propriétaire*) owner (**de** of); (*gérant*) manager, manageress; (*de bar*) landlord, landlady. **2** *nmf Rel* patron saint. **3** *nm* (*modèle de papier*) *Tex* pattern. ◆**patronage** *nm* **1** (*protection*) patronage. **2** (*centre*) youth club. ◆**patronal, -aux** *a* (*syndicat etc*) employers'. ◆**patronat** *nm* employers. ◆**patronner** *vt* to sponsor.

patrouille [patruj] *nf* patrol. ◆**patrouill/er** *vi* to patrol. ◆**—eur** *nm* (*navire*) patrol boat.

patte [pat] *nf* **1** (*membre*) leg; (*de chat, chien*) paw; (*main*) *Fam* hand; **à quatre pattes** on all fours. **2** (*de poche*) flap; (*languette*) tongue.

pattes [pat] *nfpl* (*favoris*) sideboards, *Am* sideburns.

pâture [pɑtyr] *nf* (*nourriture*) food; (*intellectuelle*) *Fig* fodder. ◆**pâturage** *nm* pasture.

paume [pom] *nf* (*de main*) palm.

paum/er [pome] *vt Fam* to lose; **un coin** *ou* **trou paumé** (*sans attrait*) a dump. ◆**—é, -ée** *nmf* (*malheureux*) *Fam* down-and-out, loser.

paupière [popjɛr] *nf* eyelid.

pause [poz] *nf* (*arrêt*) break; (*dans le discours etc*) pause.

pauvre [povr] *a* poor; (*terre*) impoverished, poor; **p. en** (*calories etc*) low in; (*ressources etc*) low on; – *nmf* (*indigent, malheureux*) poor man, poor woman; **les pauvres** the poor. ◆**pauvrement** *adv* poorly. ◆**pauvreté** *nf* (*besoin*) poverty; (*insuffisance*) poorness.

pavaner (se) [səpavane] *vpr* to strut (about).

pav/er [pave] *vt* to pave. ◆**—é** *nm* **un p.** a paving stone; (*rond, de vieille chaussée*) a cobblestone; **sur le p.** *Fig* on the streets. ◆**—age** *nm* (*travail, revêtement*) paving.

pavillon [pavijɔ̃] *nm* **1** (*maison*) house; (*de chasse*) lodge; (*d'hôpital*) ward; (*d'exposition*) pavilion. **2** (*drapeau*) flag.

pavoiser [pavwaze] *vt* to deck out with flags; – *vi* (*exulter*) *Fig* to rejoice.

pavot [pavo] *nm* (*cultivé*) poppy.

pay/er [peje] *vt* (*personne, somme*) to pay; (*service, objet, faute*) to pay for; (*récompenser*) to repay; **p. qch à qn** (*offrir en cadeau*) *Fam* to treat s.o. to sth; **p. qn pour faire** to pay s.o. to do *ou* for doing; – *vi* (*personne, métier, crime*) to pay; **se p. qch** (*s'acheter*) *Fam* to treat oneself to sth; **se p. la tête de qn** *Fam* to make fun of s.o. ◆**—ant** [pɛjɑ̃] *a* (*hôte, spectateur*) who pays, paying; (*place, entrée*) that one has to pay for; (*rentable*) worthwhile. ◆**payable** *a* payable. ◆**paye** *nf* pay, wages. ◆**payement** *nm* payment.

pays [pei] *nm* country; (*région*) region; (*village*) village; **p. des rêves/du soleil** land of dreams/sun; **du p.** (*vin, gens etc*) local.

paysage [peizaʒ] *nm* landscape, scenery.

paysan, -anne [peizɑ̃, -an] *nmf* (small) farmer; (*rustre*) *Péj* peasant; – *a* country-; (*monde*) farming.

Pays-Bas [peibɑ] *nmpl* **les P.-Bas** the Netherlands.

PCV [peseve] *abrév* (*paiement contre vérification*) **téléphoner en PCV** to reverse the charges, *Am* call collect.

PDG [pedeʒe] *abrév* = **président directeur général.**

péage [peaʒ] *nm* (*droit*) toll; (*lieu*) tollgate.

peau, -x [po] *nf* skin; (*de fruit*) peel, skin; (*cuir*) hide, skin; (*fourrure*) pelt; **dans la p. de qn** *Fig* in s.o.'s shoes; **faire p. neuve** *Fig* to turn over a new leaf. ◆**P.-Rouge** *nmf* (*pl* **Peaux-Rouges**) (Red) Indian.

pêche[1] [pɛʃ] *nf* (*activité*) fishing; (*poissons*) catch; **p. (à la ligne)** angling; **aller à la p.** to go fishing. ◆**pêcher**[1] *vi* to fish; – *vt* (*chercher à prendre*) to fish for; (*attraper*) to

catch; (*dénicher*) *Fam* to dig up. ◆**pêcheur** *nm* fisherman; angler.
pêche² [pɛʃ] *nf* (*fruit*) peach. ◆**pêcher²** *nm* (*arbre*) peach tree.
péché [peʃe] *nm* sin. ◆**péch/er** *vi* to sin; **p. par orgueil/***etc* to be too proud/*etc*. ◆**—eur, -eresse** *nmf* sinner.
pectoraux [pɛktɔro] *nmpl* (*muscles*) chest muscles.
pécule [pekyl] *nm* **un p.** (*économies*) (some) savings, a nest egg.
pécuniaire [pekynjɛr] *a* monetary.
pédagogie [pedagɔʒi] *nf* (*science*) education, teaching methods. ◆**pédagogique** *a* educational. ◆**pédagogue** *nmf* teacher.
pédale [pedal] *nf* **1** pedal; **p. de frein** footbrake (pedal). **2** (*homosexuel*) *Péj Fam* pansy, queer. ◆**pédaler** *vi* to pedal.
pédalo [pedalo] *nm* pedal boat, pedalo.
pédant, -ante [pedɑ̃, -ɑ̃t] *nmf* pedant; – *a* pedantic. ◆**pédantisme** *nm* pedantry.
pédé [pede] *nm* (*homosexuel*) *Péj Fam* queer.
pédiatre [pedjatr] *nmf Méd* p(a)ediatrician.
pédicure [pedikyr] *nmf* chiropodist.
pedigree [pedigre] *nm* (*de chien, cheval etc*) pedigree.
pègre [pɛgr] *nf* **la p.** the (criminal) underworld.
peigne [pɛɲ] *nm* comb; **passer au p. fin** *Fig* to go through with a fine toothcomb; **un coup de p.** (*action*) a comb. ◆**peigner** *vt* (*cheveux*) to comb; **p. qn** to comb s.o.'s hair; — **se p.** *vpr* to comb one's hair.
peignoir [pɛɲwar] *nm* dressing gown, *Am* bathrobe; **p. (de bain)** bathrobe.
peinard [pɛnar] *a Arg* quiet (and easy).
peindre* [pɛ̃dr] *vt* to paint; (*décrire*) *Fig* to depict, paint; **p. en bleu/***etc* to paint blue/*etc*; – *vi* to paint.
peine [pɛn] *nf* **1** (*châtiment*) punishment; **p. de mort** death penalty *ou* sentence; **p. de prison** prison sentence; **'défense d'entrer sous p. d'amende'** 'trespassers will be fined'. **2** (*chagrin*) sorrow, grief; **avoir de la p.** to be upset *ou* sad; **faire de la p. à** to upset, cause pain *ou* sorrow to. **3** (*effort, difficulté*) trouble; **se donner de la p.** *ou* **beaucoup de p.** to go to a lot of trouble (**pour faire** to do); **avec p.** with difficulty; **ça vaut la p. d'attendre/***etc* it's worth (while) waiting/*etc*; **ce n'est pas** *ou* **ça ne vaut pas la p.** it's not worth while *ou* worth it *ou* worth bothering. ◆**peiner 1** *vt* to upset, grieve. **2** *vi* to labour, struggle.
peine (à) [apɛn] *adv* hardly, scarcely.
peintre [pɛ̃tr] *nm* painter; **p. (en bâtiment)** (house) painter, (painter and) decorator. ◆**peinture** *nf* (*tableau, activité*) painting; (*couleur*) paint; **'p. fraîche'** 'wet paint'. ◆**peinturlurer** *vt Fam* to daub with colour; **se p. (le visage)** to paint one's face.
péjoratif, -ive [peʒɔratif, -iv] *a* pejorative, derogatory.
pékinois [pekinwa] *nm* (*chien*) pekin(g)ese.
pelage [pəlaʒ] *nm* (*d'animal*) coat, fur.
pelé [pəle] *a* bare.
pêle-mêle [pɛlmɛl] *adv* in disorder.
peler [pəle] *vt* (*fruit*) to peel; **se p. facilement** (*fruit*) to peel easily; – *vi* (*peau bronzée*) to peel.
pèlerin [pɛlrɛ̃] *nm* pilgrim. ◆**pèlerinage** *nm* pilgrimage.
pèlerine [pɛlrin] *nf* (*manteau*) cape.
pélican [pelikɑ̃] *nm* (*oiseau*) pelican.
pelisse [pəlis] *nf* fur-lined coat.
pelle [pɛl] *nf* shovel; (*d'enfant*) spade; **p. à poussière** dustpan; **ramasser** *ou* **prendre une p.** (*tomber*) *Fam* to come a cropper, *Am* take a spill; **à la p.** (*argent etc*) *Fam* galore. ◆**pelletée** *nf* shovelful. ◆**pelleteuse** *nf Tech* mechanical shovel, excavator.
pellicule [pelikyl] *nf Phot* film; (*couche*) film, layer; *pl Méd* dandruff.
pelote [plɔt] *nf* (*de laine*) ball; (*à épingles*) pincushion; **p. (basque)** *Sp* pelota.
peloter [plɔte] *vt* (*palper*) *Péj Fam* to paw.
peloton [plɔtɔ̃] *nm* **1** (*coureurs*) *Sp* pack, main body. **2** *Mil* squad; **p. d'exécution** firing squad. **3** (*de ficelle*) ball.
pelotonner (se) [səplɔtɔne] *vpr* to curl up (into a ball).
pelouse [pluz] *nf* lawn; *Sp* enclosure.
peluche [plyʃ] *nf* (*tissu*) plush; *pl* (*flocons*) fluff, lint; **une p.** (*flocon*) a bit of fluff *ou* lint; **jouet en p.** soft toy; **chien/***etc* **en p.** (*jouet*) furry dog/*etc*; **ours en p.** teddy bear. ◆**pelucher** *vi* to get fluffy *ou* linty. ◆**pelucheux, -euse** *a* fluffy, linty.
pelure [plyr] *nf* (*épluchure*) peeling; **une p.** a (piece of) peeling.
pénal, -aux [penal, -o] *a* (*droit, code etc*) penal. ◆**pénalisation** *nf Sp* penalty. ◆**pénaliser** *vt Sp Jur* to penalize (**pour** for). ◆**pénalité** *nf Jur Rugby* penalty.
penalty, *pl* **-ties** [penalti, -iz] *nm Fb* penalty.
penaud [pəno] *a* sheepish.
penchant [pɑ̃ʃɑ̃] *nm* (*goût*) liking (**pour** for); (*tendance*) inclination (**à qch** towards sth).
pench/er [pɑ̃ʃe] *vt* (*objet*) to tilt; (*tête*) to lean; – *vi* (*arbre etc*) to lean (over); **p. pour** *Fig* to be inclined towards; — **se p.** *vpr* to lean (forward); **se p. par** (*fenêtre*) to lean

out of; **se p. sur** (*problème etc*) to examine. ◆**—é** *a* leaning.

pendaison [pɑ̃dɛzɔ̃] *nf* hanging.

pendant[1] [pɑ̃dɑ̃] *prép* (*au cours de*) during; **p. la nuit** during the night; **p. deux mois** (*pour une période de*) for two months; **p. que** while, whilst.

pendentif [pɑ̃dɑ̃tif] *nm* (*collier*) pendant.

penderie [pɑ̃dri] *nf* wardrobe.

pend/re [pɑ̃dr] *vti* to hang (**à** from); **— se p.** *vpr* (*se tuer*) to hang oneself; (*se suspendre*) to hang (**à** from). ◆**—ant**[2] **1** *a* hanging; (*langue*) hanging out; (*joues*) sagging; (*question*) *Fig* pending. **2** *nm* **p. (d'oreille)** drop earring. **3** *nm* **le p. de** the companion piece to. ◆**—u, -ue** *a* (*objet*) hanging (**à** from); – *nmf* hanged man, hanged woman.

pendule [pɑ̃dyl] **1** *nf* clock. **2** *nm* (*balancier*) & *Fig* pendulum. ◆**pendulette** *nf* small clock.

pénétr/er [penetre] *vi* **p. dans** to enter; (*profondément*) to penetrate (into); – *vt* (*substance, mystère etc*) to penetrate; **se p. de** (*idée*) to become convinced of. ◆**—ant** *a* (*esprit, froid etc*) penetrating, keen. ◆**pénétration** *nf* penetration.

pénible [penibl] *a* (*difficile*) difficult; (*douloureux*) painful, distressing; (*ennuyeux*) tiresome; (*agaçant*) annoying. ◆**—ment** [-əmɑ̃] *adv* with difficulty; (*avec douleur*) painfully.

péniche [peniʃ] *nf* barge; **p. de débarquement** *Mil* landing craft.

pénicilline [penisilin] *nf* penicillin.

péninsule [penɛ̃syl] *nf* peninsula. ◆**péninsulaire** *a* peninsular.

pénis [penis] *nm* penis.

pénitence [penitɑ̃s] *nf* (*punition*) punishment; (*peine*) *Rel* penance; (*regret*) penitence. ◆**pénitent, -ente** *nmf Rel* penitent.

pénitencier [penitɑ̃sje] *nm* prison. ◆**pénitentiaire** *a* (*régime etc*) prison-.

pénombre [penɔ̃br] *nf* half-light, darkness.

pensée [pɑ̃se] *nf* **1** thought. **2** (*fleur*) pansy. ◆**pens/er** *vi* to think (**à** of, about); **p. à qch/à faire qch** (*ne pas oublier*) to remember sth/to do sth; **p. à tout** (*prévoir*) to think of everything; **penses-tu!** you must be joking!, not at all!; – *vt* to think (**que** that); (*concevoir*) to think out; (*imaginer*) to imagine (**que** that); **je pensais rester** (*intention*) I was thinking of staying, I thought I'd stay; **je pense réussir** (*espoir*) I hope to succeed; **que pensez-vous de . . . ?** what do you think of *ou* about . . . ?; **p. du bien de** to think highly of. ◆**—ant** *a* **bien p.** *Péj* orthodox. ◆**—eur** *nm* thinker. ◆**pensif, -ive** *a* thoughtful, pensive.

pension [pɑ̃sjɔ̃] *nf* **1** boarding school; (*somme, repas*) board; **être en p.** to board, be a boarder (**chez** with); **p. (de famille)** guesthouse, boarding house; **p. complète** full board. **2** (*allocation*) pension; **p. alimentaire** maintenance allowance. ◆**pensionnaire** *nmf* (*élève*) boarder; (*d'hôtel*) resident; (*de famille*) lodger. ◆**pensionnat** *nm* boarding school; (*élèves*) boarders. ◆**pensionné, -ée** *nmf* pensioner.

pentagone [pɛ̃tagɔn] *nm* **le P.** *Am Pol* the Pentagon.

pentathlon [pɛ̃tatlɔ̃] *nm Sp* pentathlon.

pente [pɑ̃t] *nf* slope; **être en p.** to slope, be sloping.

Pentecôte [pɑ̃tkot] *nf* Whitsun, *Am* Pentecost.

pénurie [penyri] *nf* scarcity, shortage (**de** of).

pépère [pepɛr] **1** *nm Fam* grand(d)ad. **2** *a* (*tranquille*) *Fam* quiet (and easy).

pépier [pepje] *vi* (*oiseau*) to cheep, chirp.

pépin [pepɛ̃] *nm* **1** (*de fruit*) pip, *Am* pit. **2** (*ennui*) *Fam* hitch, bother. **3** (*parapluie*) *Fam* brolly.

pépinière [pepinjɛr] *nf Bot* nursery.

pépite [pepit] *nf* (gold) nugget.

péquenaud, -aude [pɛkno, -od] *nmf Péj Arg* peasant, bumpkin.

perçant [pɛrsɑ̃] *a* (*cri, froid*) piercing; (*yeux*) sharp, keen.

percée [pɛrse] *nf* (*dans une forêt*) opening; (*avance technologique, attaque militaire*) breakthrough.

perce-neige [pɛrsənɛʒ] *nm ou f inv Bot* snowdrop.

perce-oreille [pɛrsɔrɛj] *nm* (*insecte*) earwig.

percepteur [pɛrsɛptœr] *nm* tax collector. ◆**perceptible** *a* perceptible (**à** to), noticeable. ◆**perception** *nf* **1** (*bureau*) tax office; (*d'impôt*) collection. **2** (*sensation*) perception.

perc/er [pɛrse] *vt* (*trouer*) to pierce; (*avec perceuse*) to drill (a hole in); (*trou, ouverture*) to make, drill; (*mystère etc*) to uncover; **p. une dent** (*bébé*) to cut a tooth; – *vi* (*soleil, ennemi, sentiment*) to break *ou* come through; (*abcès*) to burst. ◆**—euse** *nf* drill.

percevoir* [pɛrsəvwar] *vt* **1** (*sensation*) to perceive; (*son*) to hear. **2** (*impôt*) to collect.

perche [pɛrʃ] *nf* **1** (*bâton*) pole; **saut à la p.** pole-vaulting. **2** (*poisson*) perch.

perch/er [pɛrʃe] *vi* (*oiseau*) to perch; (*volailles*) to roost; (*loger*) *Fam* to hang out; –

vt (*placer*) *Fam* to perch; **— se p.** *vpr* (*oiseau, personne*) to perch. **◆—é** *a* perched. **◆perchoir** *nm* perch; (*de volailles*) roost.

percolateur [perkɔlatœr] *nm* (*de restaurant*) percolator.

percussion [perkysjɔ̃] *nf Mus* percussion.

percutant [perkytɑ̃] *a Fig* powerful.

percuter [perkyte] *vt* (*véhicule*) to crash into; *– vi* **p. contre** to crash into.

perd/re [perdr] *vt* to lose; (*gaspiller*) to waste; (*ruiner*) to ruin; (*habitude*) to get out of; **p. de vue** to lose sight of; *– vi* to lose; (*récipient, tuyau*) to leak; **j'y perds!** I lose out, I lose on the deal; **— se p.** *vpr* (*s'égarer*) to get lost; (*dans les détails*) to lose oneself; (*disparaître*) to disappear; **je m'y perds** I'm lost *ou* confused. **◆—ant, -ante** *a* (*billet*) losing; *– nmf* loser. **◆—u** *a* lost; wasted; (*malade*) finished; (*lieu*) isolated, in the middle of nowhere; **à ses moments perdus** in one's spare time; **une balle perdue** a stray bullet; **c'est du temps p.** it's a waste of time. **◆perdition (en)** *adv* (*navire*) in distress.

perdrix [perdri] *nf* partridge. **◆perdreau, -x** *nm* young partridge.

père [per] *nm* father; **Dupont p.** Dupont senior; **le p. Jean** *Fam* old John.

péremptoire [perɑ̃ptwar] *a* peremptory.

perfection [perfeksjɔ̃] *nf* perfection. **◆perfectionn/er** *vt* to improve, perfect; **se p. en anglais/***etc* to improve one's English/*etc*. **◆—é** *a* (*machine etc*) advanced. **◆—ement** *nm* improvement (**de** in, **par rapport à** on); **cours de p.** advanced *ou* refresher course. **◆perfectionniste** *nmf* perfectionist.

perfide [perfid] *a Litt* treacherous, perfidious. **◆perfidie** *nf Litt* treachery.

perforer [perfɔre] *vt* (*pneu, intestin etc*) to perforate; (*billet, carte*) to punch; **carte perforée** punch card. **◆perforateur** *nm* (*appareil*) drill. **◆perforation** *nf* perforation; (*trou*) punched hole. **◆perforatrice** *nf* (*pour cartes*) *Tech* (card) punch. **◆perforeuse** *nf* (paper) punch.

performance [perfɔrmɑ̃s] *nf* (*d'athlète, de machine etc*) performance. **◆performant** *a* (highly) efficient.

péricliter [periklite] *vi* to go to rack and ruin.

péril [peril] *nm* peril; **à tes risques et périls** at your own risk. **◆périlleux, -euse** *a* perilous; **saut p.** somersault (*in mid air*).

périm/er [perime] *vi*, **— se p.** *vpr* **laisser (se) p.** (*billet*) to allow to expire. **◆—é** *a* expired; (*désuet*) outdated.

périmètre [perimetr] *nm* perimeter.

période [perjɔd] *nf* period. **◆périodique** *a* periodic; *– nm* (*revue*) periodical.

péripétie [peripesi] *nf* (unexpected) event.

périphérie [periferi] *nf* (*limite*) periphery; (*banlieue*) outskirts. **◆périphérique** *a* (*quartier*) outlying, peripheral; *– nm* (**boulevard**) **p.** (motorway) ring road, *Am* beltway.

périphrase [perifrɑz] *nf* circumlocution.

périple [peripl] *nm* trip, tour.

pér/ir [perir] *vi* to perish, die. **◆—issable** *a* (*denrée*) perishable.

périscope [periskɔp] *nm* periscope.

perle [perl] *nf* (*bijou*) pearl; (*de bois, verre etc*) bead; (*personne*) *Fig* gem, pearl; (*erreur*) *Iron* howler, gem. **◆perler** *vi* (*sueur*) to form beads; **grève perlée** go-slow, *Am* slow-down strike.

permanent, -ente [permanɑ̃, -ɑ̃t] **1** *a* permanent; (*spectacle*) *Cin* continuous; (*comité*) standing. **2** *nf* (*coiffure*) perm. **◆permanence** *nf* permanence; (*service, bureau*) duty office; (*salle*) *Scol* study room; **être de p.** to be on duty; **en p.** permanently.

perméable [permeabl] *a* permeable.

permettre* [permetr] *vt* to allow, permit; **p. à qn de faire** (*permission, possibilité*) to allow *ou* permit s.o. to do; **permettez!** excuse me!; **vous permettez?** may I?; **se p. de faire** to allow oneself to do, take the liberty to do; **se p. qch** (*se payer*) to afford sth. **◆permis** *a* allowed, permitted; *– nm* (*autorisation*) permit, licence; **p. de conduire** (*carte*) driving licence, *Am* driver's license; **p. de travail** work permit. **◆permission** *nf* permission; (*congé*) *Mil* leave; **demander la p.** to ask (for) permission (**de faire** to do).

permuter [permyte] *vt* to change round *ou* over, permutate. **◆permutation** *nf* permutation.

pernicieux, -euse [pernisjø, -øz] *a* (*nocif*) & *Méd* pernicious.

pérorer [perɔre] *vi Péj* to speechify.

Pérou [peru] *nm* Peru.

perpendiculaire [perpɑ̃dikyler] *a* & *nf* perpendicular (**à** to).

perpétrer [perpetre] *vt* (*crime*) to perpetrate.

perpétuel, -elle [perpetɥel] *a* perpetual; (*fonction, rente*) for life. **◆perpétuellement** *adv* perpetually. **◆perpétuer** *vt* to perpetuate. ◆**perpétuité (à)** *adv* in perpetuity; (*condamné*) for life.

perplexe [perplɛks] *a* perplexed, puzzled. ◆**perplexité** *nf* perplexity.

perquisition [pɛrkizisjɔ̃] *nf* (house) search (*by police*). ◆**perquisitionner** *vti* to search.

perron [perɔ̃] *nm* (front) steps.

perroquet [perɔkɛ] *nm* parrot.

perruche [peryʃ] *nf* budgerigar, *Am* parakeet.

perruque [peryk] *nf* wig.

persan [persɑ̃] *a* (*langue, tapis, chat*) Persian; – *nm* (*langue*) Persian.

persécuter [persekyte] *vt* (*tourmenter*) to persecute; (*importuner*) to harass. ◆**persécuteur, -trice** *nmf* persecutor. ◆**persécution** *nf* persecution.

persévér/er [persevere] *vi* to persevere (**dans** in). ◆**—ant** *a* persevering. ◆**persévérance** *nf* perseverance.

persienne [persjɛn] *nf* (outside) shutter.

persil [persi] *nm* parsley.

persist/er [persiste] *vi* to persist (**à faire** in doing). ◆**—ant** *a* persistent; **à feuilles persistantes** (*arbre etc*) evergreen. ◆**persistance** *nf* persistence.

personnage [persɔnaʒ] *nm* (*célébrité*) (important) person; *Th Littér* character.

personnaliser [persɔnalize] *vt* to personalize; (*voiture*) to customize.

personnalité [persɔnalite] *nf* (*individualité, personnage*) personality.

personne [persɔn] **1** *nf* person; *pl* people; **grande p.** grown-up, adult; **jolie p.** pretty girl *ou* woman; **en p.** in person. **2** *pron* (*négatif*) nobody, no one; **ne . . . p.** nobody, no one; **je ne vois p.** I don't see anybody *ou* anyone; **mieux que p.** better than anybody *ou* anyone.

personnel, -elle [persɔnɛl] **1** *a* personal; (*joueur, jeu*) individualistic. **2** *nm* staff, personnel. ◆**personnellement** *adv* personally.

personnifier [persɔnifje] *vt* to personify. ◆**personnification** *nf* personification.

perspective [perspɛktiv] *nf* (*art*) perspective; (*point de vue*) *Fig* viewpoint, perspective; (*de paysage etc*) view; (*possibilité, espérance*) prospect; **en p.** *Fig* in view, in prospect.

perspicace [perspikas] *a* shrewd. ◆**perspicacité** *nf* shrewdness.

persuader [persɥade] *vt* to persuade (**qn de faire** s.o. to do); **se p. que** to be convinced that. ◆**persuasif, -ive** *a* persuasive. ◆**persuasion** *nf* persuasion; (*croyance*) conviction.

perte [pert] *nf* loss; (*gaspillage*) waste (**de temps/d'argent** of time/money); (*ruine*) ruin; **à p. de vue** as far as the eye can see; **vendre à p.** to sell at a loss.

pertinent [pertinɑ̃] *a* relevant, pertinent. ◆**pertinence** *nf* relevance.

perturb/er [pertyrbe] *vt* (*trafic, cérémonie etc*) to disrupt; (*ordre public, personne*) to disturb. ◆**—é** *a* (*troublé*) *Fam* perturbed. ◆**perturbateur, -trice** *a* (*élément*) disruptive; – *nmf* trouble-maker. ◆**perturbation** *nf* disruption; (*crise*) upheaval.

péruvien, -ienne [peryvjɛ̃, -jɛn] *a* & *nmf* Peruvian.

pervenche [pervɑ̃ʃ] *nf Bot* periwinkle.

pervers [perver] *a* wicked, perverse; (*dépravé*) perverted. ◆**perversion** *nf* perversion. ◆**perversité** *nf* perversity. ◆**pervert/ir** *vt* to pervert. ◆**—i, -ie** *nmf* pervert.

pesant [pəzɑ̃] *a* heavy, weighty; – *nm* **valoir son p. d'or** to be worth one's weight in gold. ◆**pesamment** *adv* heavily. ◆**pesanteur** *nf* heaviness; (*force*) *Phys* gravity.

pes/er [pəze] *vt* to weigh; – *vi* to weigh; **p. lourd** to be heavy; (*argument etc*) *Fig* to carry (a lot of) weight; **p. sur** (*appuyer*) to bear down upon; (*influer*) to bear upon; **p. sur qn** (*menace*) to hang over s.o.; **p. sur l'estomac** to lie (heavily) on the stomach. ◆**—ée** *nf* weighing; *Boxe* weigh-in; (*effort*) pressure. ◆**—age** *nm* weighing. ◆**pèse-bébé** *nm* (baby) scales. ◆**pèse-personne** *nm* (bathroom) scales.

pessimisme [pesimism] *nm* pessimism. ◆**pessimiste** *a* pessimistic; – *nmf* pessimist.

peste [pɛst] *nf Méd* plague; (*personne, enfant*) *Fig* pest.

pester [pɛste] *vi* to curse; **p. contre qch/qn** to curse sth/s.o.

pestilentiel, -ielle [pɛstilɑ̃sjɛl] *a* fetid, stinking.

pétale [petal] *nm* petal.

pétanque [petɑ̃k] *nf* (*jeu*) bowls.

pétarades [petarad] *nfpl* (*de moto etc*) backfiring. ◆**pétarader** *vi* to backfire.

pétard [petar] *nm* (*explosif*) firecracker, banger.

péter [pete] *vi Fam* (*éclater*) to go bang *ou* pop; (*se rompre*) to snap.

pétill/er [petije] *vi* (*eau, champagne*) to sparkle, fizz; (*bois, feu*) to crackle; (*yeux*) to sparkle. ◆**—ant** *a* (*eau, vin, regard*) sparkling.

petit, -ite [p(ə)ti, -it] *a* small, little; (*de taille*) short; (*bruit, espoir, coup*) slight; (*jeune*) young, small; (*mesquin, insignifiant*) petty; **tout p.** tiny; **un bon p. travail** a nice little job; **un p. Français** a (little) French boy; – *nmf* (little) boy, (little) girl; (*personne*) small person; *Scol* junior; *pl* (*d'animal*) young; (*de chien*) pups, young; (*de chat*) kittens, young; – *adv* **p. à p.** little by little. ◆**p.-bourgeois** *a Péj* middle-class. ◆**p.-suisse** *nm* soft cheese (*for dessert*). ◆**petitement** *adv* (*chichement*) shabbily, poorly. ◆**petitesse** *nf* (*de taille*) smallness; (*mesquinerie*) pettiness.

petit-fils [p(ə)tifis] *nm* (*pl* **petits-fils**) grandson, grandchild. ◆**petite-fille** *nf* (*pl* **petites-filles**) granddaughter, grandchild. ◆**petits-enfants** *nmpl* grandchildren.

pétition [petisjɔ̃] *nf* petition.

pétrifier [petrifje] *vt* (*de peur, d'émoi etc*) to petrify.

pétrin [petrɛ̃] *nm* (*situation*) *Fam* fix; **dans le p.** in a fix.

pétrir [petrir] *vt* to knead.

pétrole [petrɔl] *nm* oil, petroleum; **p. (lampant)** paraffin, *Am* kerosene; **nappe de p.** (*sur la mer*) oil slick. ◆**pétrolier, -ière** *a* (*industrie*) oil-; – *nm* (*navire*) oil tanker. ◆**pétrolifère** *a* **gisement p.** oil field.

pétulant [petylɑ̃] *a* exuberant.

pétunia [petynja] *nm Bot* petunia.

peu [pø] *adv* (*lire, manger etc*) not much, little; **elle mange p.** she doesn't eat much, she eats little; **un p.** (*lire, surpris etc*) a little, a bit; **p. de sel/de temps/***etc* not much salt/time/*etc*, little salt/time/*etc*; **un p. de fromage/***etc* a little cheese/*etc*, a bit of cheese/*etc*; **le p. de fromage que j'ai** the little cheese I have; **p. de gens/de livres/***etc* few people/books/*etc*, not many people/books/*etc*; **p. sont...** few are...; **un (tout) petit p.** a (tiny) little bit; **p. intéressant/souvent/***etc* not very interesting/often/*etc*; **p. de chose** not much; **p. à p.** gradually, little by little; **à p. près** more or less; **p. après/avant** shortly after/before.

peuplade [pœplad] *nf* tribe.

peuple [pœpl] *nm* (*nation, masse*) people; **les gens du p.** the common people. ◆**peupl/er** *vt* to populate, people. ◆**–é** *a* (*quartier etc*) populated (**de** with).

peuplier [pøplije] *nm* (*arbre, bois*) poplar.

peur [pœr] *nf* fear; **avoir p.** to be afraid *ou* frightened *ou* scared (**de** of); **faire p. à** to frighten, scare; **de p. que** (+ *sub*) for fear that; **de p. de faire** for fear of doing. ◆**peureux, -euse** *a* fearful, easily frightened.

peut, peux [pø] *voir* **pouvoir 1.**

peut-être [pøtetr] *adv* perhaps, maybe; **p.-être qu'il viendra** perhaps *ou* maybe he'll come.

phallique [falik] *a* phallic. ◆**phallocrate** *nm Péj* male chauvinist.

phare [far] *nm Nau* lighthouse; *Aut* headlight, headlamp; **rouler pleins phares** *Aut* to drive on full headlights; **faire un appel de phares** *Aut* to flash one's lights.

pharmacie [farmasi] *nf* chemist's shop, *Am* drugstore; (*science*) pharmacy; (*armoire*) medicine cabinet. ◆**pharmaceutique** *a* pharmaceutical. ◆**pharmacien, -ienne** *nmf* chemist, pharmacist, *Am* druggist.

pharynx [farɛ̃ks] *nm Anat* pharynx.

phase [fɑz] *nf* phase.

phénomène [fenɔmɛn] *nm* phenomenon; (*personne*) *Fam* eccentric. ◆**phénoménal, -aux** *a* phenomenal.

philanthrope [filɑ̃trɔp] *nmf* philanthropist. ◆**philanthropique** *a* philanthropic.

philatélie [filateli] *nf* philately, stamp collecting. ◆**philatélique** *a* philatelic. ◆**philatéliste** *nmf* philatelist, stamp collector.

philharmonique [filarmɔnik] *a* philharmonic.

Philippines [filipin] *nfpl* **les P.** the Philippines.

philosophe [filɔzɔf] *nmf* philosopher; – *a* (*sage, résigné*) philosophical. ◆**philosopher** *vi* to philosophize (**sur** about). ◆**philosophie** *nf* philosophy. ◆**philosophique** *a* philosophical.

phobie [fɔbi] *nf* phobia.

phonétique [fɔnetik] *a* phonetic; – *nf* phonetics.

phonographe [fɔnɔgraf] *nm* gramophone, *Am* phonograph.

phoque [fɔk] *nm* (*animal marin*) seal.

phosphate [fɔsfat] *nm Ch* phosphate.

phosphore [fɔsfɔr] *nm Ch* phosphorus.

photo [fɔto] *nf* photo; (*art*) photography; **prendre une p. de, prendre en p.** to take a photo of; – *a inv* **appareil p.** camera. ◆**photocopie** *nf* photocopy. ◆**photocopier** *vt* to photocopy. ◆**photocopieur** *nm*, ◆**photocopieuse** *nf* (*machine*) photocopier. ◆**photogénique** *a* photogenic. ◆**photographe** *nmf* photographer. ◆**photographie** *nf* (*art*) photography; (*image*) photograph. ◆**photographier** *vt* to photograph. ◆**photographique** *a* photographic. ◆**photomaton®** *nm* (*appareil*) photo booth.

phrase [fraz] *nf* (*mots*) sentence.

physicien, -ienne [fizisjɛ̃, -jɛn] *nmf* physicist.

physiologie [fizjɔlɔʒi] *nf* physiology. ◆**physiologique** *a* physiological.

physionomie [fizjɔnɔmi] *nf* face.

physique [fizik] **1** *a* physical; – *nm* (*corps, aspect*) physique; **au p.** physically. **2** *nf* (*science*) physics. ◆**—ment** *adv* physically.

piaffer [pjafe] *vi* (*cheval*) to stamp; **p. d'impatience** *Fig* to fidget impatiently.

piailler [pjaje] *vi* (*oiseau*) to cheep; (*enfant*) *Fam* to squeal.

piano [pjano] *nm* piano; **p. droit/à queue** upright/grand piano. ◆**pianiste** *nmf* pianist.

piaule [pjol] *nf* (*chambre*) *Arg* room, pad.

pic [pik] *nm* **1** (*cime*) peak. **2** (*outil*) pick(axe); **p. à glace** ice pick. **3** (*oiseau*) woodpecker.

pic (à) [apik] *adv* (*verticalement*) sheer; **couler à p.** to sink to the bottom; **arriver à p.** *Fig* to arrive in the nick of time.

pichet [piʃɛ] *nm* jug, pitcher.

pickpocket [pikpɔkɛt] *nm* pickpocket.

pick-up [pikœp] *nm inv* (*camionnette*) pick-up truck.

picorer [pikɔre] *vti* to peck.

picoter [pikɔte] *vt* (*yeux*) to make smart; (*jambes*) to make tingle; **les yeux me picotent** my eyes are smarting.

pie [pi] **1** *nf* (*oiseau*) magpie. **2** *a inv* (*couleur*) piebald.

pièce [pjɛs] *nf* **1** (*de maison etc*) room. **2** (*morceau, objet etc*) piece; (*de pantalon*) patch; (*écrit*) & *Jur* document; **p. (de monnaie)** coin; **p. (de théâtre)** play; **p. (d'artillerie)** gun; **p. d'identité** proof of identity, identity card; **p. d'eau** pool, pond; **pièces détachées** *ou* **de rechange** (*de véhicule etc*) spare parts; **cinq dollars/***etc* **(la) p.** five dollars/*etc* each; **travailler à la p.** to do piecework.

pied [pje] *nm* foot; (*de meuble*) leg; (*de verre, lampe*) base; *Phot* stand; **un p. de salade** a head of lettuce; **à p.** on foot; **aller à p.** to walk, go on foot; **au p. de** at the foot *ou* bottom of; **au p. de la lettre** *Fig* literally; **avoir p.** (*nageur*) to have a footing, touch the bottom; **coup de p.** kick; **donner un coup de p.** to kick (**à qn** s.o.); **sur p.** (*debout, levé*) up and about; **sur ses pieds** (*malade guéri*) up and about; **sur un p. d'égalité** on an equal footing; **comme un p.** (*mal*) *Fam* dreadfully; **faire un p. de nez** to thumb one's nose (**à** at); **mettre sur p.** (*projet*) to set up. ◆**p.-noir** *nmf* (*pl* **pieds-noirs**) Algerian Frenchman *ou* Frenchwoman.

piédestal, -aux [pjedɛstal, -o] *nm* pedestal.

piège [pjɛʒ] *nm* (*pour animal*) & *Fig* trap. ◆**piéger** *vt* (*animal*) to trap; (*voiture etc*) to booby-trap; **engin piégé** booby trap; **lettre/colis/voiture piégé(e)** letter/parcel/car bomb.

pierre [pjɛr] *nf* stone; (*précieuse*) gem, stone; **p. à briquet** flint; **geler à p. fendre** to freeze (rock) hard. ◆**pierreries** *nfpl* gems, precious stones. ◆**pierreux, -euse** *a* stony.

piété [pjete] *nf* piety.

piétiner [pjetine] *vt* (*fouler aux pieds*) to trample (on); – *vi* to stamp (one's feet); (*marcher sur place*) to mark time; (*ne pas avancer*) *Fig* to make no headway.

piéton[1] [pjetɔ̃] *nm* pedestrian. ◆**piéton**[2], **-onne** *a*, ◆**piétonnier, -ière** *a* (*rue etc*) pedestrian-.

piètre [pjɛtr] *a* wretched, poor.

pieu, -x [pjø] *nm* **1** (*piquet*) post, stake. **2** (*lit*) *Fam* bed.

pieuvre [pjœvr] *nf* octopus.

pieux, -euse [pjø, -øz] *a* pious.

pif [pif] *nm* (*nez*) *Fam* nose. ◆**pifomètre (au)** *adv* (*sans calcul*) *Fam* at a rough guess.

pigeon [piʒɔ̃] *nm* pigeon; (*personne*) *Fam* dupe; **p. voyageur** carrier pigeon. ◆**pigeonner** *vt* (*voler*) *Fam* to rip off.

piger [piʒe] *vti Fam* to understand.

pigment [pigmɑ̃] *nm* pigment.

pignon [piɲɔ̃] *nm* (*de maison etc*) gable.

pile [pil] **1** *nf Él* battery; (*atomique*) pile; **radio à piles** battery radio. **2** *nf* (*tas*) pile; **en p.** in a pile. **3** *nf* (*de pont*) pier. **4** *nf* **p. (ou face)?** heads (or tails)?; **jouer à p. ou face** to toss up. **5** *adv* **s'arrêter p.** to stop short *ou* dead; **à deux heures p.** on the dot of two.

piler [pile] **1** *vt* (*amandes*) to grind; (*ail*) to crush. **2** *vi* (*en voiture*) to stop dead. ◆**pilonner** *vt Mil* to bombard, shell.

pilier [pilje] *nm* pillar.

pilon [pilɔ̃] *nm* (*de poulet*) drumstick.

piller [pije] *vti* to loot, pillage. ◆**pillage** *nm* looting, pillage. ◆**pillard, -arde** *nmf* looter.

pilori [pilɔri] *nm* **mettre au p.** *Fig* to pillory.

pilote [pilɔt] *nm Av Nau* pilot; (*de voiture, char*) driver; (*guide*) *Fig* guide; – *a* **usine(-)/projet(-)p.** pilot factory/plan. ◆**pilot/er** *vt Av* to fly, pilot; *Nau* to pilot; **p. qn** to show s.o. around. ◆**—age** *nm* piloting; **école de p.** flying school; **poste de p.** cockpit.

pilotis [pilɔti] *nm* (*pieux*) *Archit* piles.

pilule [pilyl] *nf* pill; **prendre la p.** (*femme*) to be on the pill; **se mettre à/arrêter la p.** to go on/off the pill.

piment [pimɑ̃] *nm* pimento, pepper. ◆**pimenté** *a Culin & Fig* spicy.

pimpant [pɛ̃pɑ̃] *a* pretty, spruce.

pin [pɛ̃] *nm* (*bois, arbre*) pine; **pomme de p.** pine cone.

pinailler [pinɑje] *vi Fam* to quibble, split hairs.

pinard [pinar] *nm* (*vin*) *Fam* wine.

pince [pɛ̃s] *nf* (*outil*) pliers; *Méd* forceps; (*de cycliste*) clip; (*levier*) crowbar; *pl* (*de crabe*) pincers; **p. (à linge)** (clothes) peg *ou Am* pin; **p. (à épiler)** tweezers; **p. (à sucre)** sugar tongs; **p. à cheveux** hairgrip. ◆**pinc/er** *vt* to pinch; (*corde*) *Mus* to pluck; **p. qn** (*arrêter*) *Jur* to nab s.o., pinch s.o.; **se p. le doigt** to get one's finger caught (**dans** in). ◆**—é** *a* (*air*) stiff, constrained. ◆**—ée** *nf* (*de sel etc*) pinch (**de** of). ◆**pincettes** *nfpl* (fire) tongs; (*d'horloger*) tweezers. ◆**pinçon** *nm* pinch (mark).

pinceau, -x [pɛ̃so] *nm* (paint)brush.

pince-sans-rire [pɛ̃ssɑ̃rir] *nm inv* person of dry humour.

pinède [pinɛd] *nf* pine forest.

pingouin [pɛ̃gwɛ̃] *nm* auk, penguin.

ping-pong [piŋpɔ̃g] *nm* ping-pong.

pingre [pɛ̃gr] *a* stingy; – *nmf* skinflint.

pinson [pɛ̃sɔ̃] *nm* (*oiseau*) chaffinch.

pintade [pɛ̃tad] *nf* guinea fowl.

pin-up [pinœp] *nf inv* (*fille*) pinup.

pioche [pjɔʃ] *nf* pick(axe). ◆**piocher** *vti* (*creuser*) to dig (with a pick).

pion [pjɔ̃] *nm* **1** (*au jeu de dames*) piece; *Échecs & Fig* pawn. **2** *Scol* master (in charge of discipline).

pionnier [pjɔnje] *nm* pioneer.

pipe [pip] *nf* (*de fumeur*) pipe; **fumer la p.** to smoke a pipe.

pipeau, -x [pipo] *nm* (*flûte*) pipe.

pipe-line [piplin] *nm* pipeline.

pipi [pipi] *nm* **faire p.** *Fam* to go for a pee.

pique [pik] **1** *nm* (*couleur*) *Cartes* spades. **2** *nf* (*arme*) pike. **3** *nf* (*allusion*) cutting remark.

pique-assiette [pikasjɛt] *nmf inv* scrounger.

pique-nique [piknik] *nm* picnic. ◆**pique-niquer** *vi* to picnic.

piqu/er [pike] *vt* (*entamer, percer*) to prick; (*langue, yeux*) to sting; (*curiosité*) to rouse; (*coudre*) to (machine-)stitch; (*édredon, couvre-lit*) to quilt; (*crise de nerfs*) to have; (*maladie*) to get; **p. qn** (*abeille*) to sting s.o.; (*serpent*) to bite s.o.; *Méd* to give s.o. an injection; **p. qch dans** (*enfoncer*) to stick sth into; **p. qn** (*arrêter*) *Jur Fam* to nab s.o., pinch s.o.; **p. qch** (*voler*) *Fam* to pinch sth; **p. une colère** to fly into a rage; **p. une tête** to plunge headlong; – *vi* (*avion*) to dive; (*moutarde etc*) to be hot; **– se p.** *vpr* to prick oneself; **se p. de faire qch** to pride oneself on being able to do sth. ◆**—ant** *a* (*épine*) prickly; (*froid*) biting; (*sauce, goût*) pungent, piquant; (*mot*) cutting; (*détail*) spicy; – *nm Bot* prickle, thorn; (*d'animal*) spine, prickle. ◆**—é** *a* (*meuble*) worm-eaten; (*fou*) *Fam* crazy; – *nm Av* (nose)dive; **descente en p.** *Av* nosedive. ◆**—eur, -euse** *nmf* (*sur machine à coudre*) machinist. ◆**piqûre** *nf* (*d'épingle*) prick; (*d'abeille*) sting; (*de serpent*) bite; (*trou*) hole; *Méd* injection; (*point*) stitch.

piquet [pikɛ] *nm* **1** (*pieu*) stake, picket; (*de tente*) peg. **2 p. (de grève)** picket (line), strike picket. **3 au p.** *Scol* in the corner.

piqueté [pikte] *a* **p. de** dotted with.

pirate [pirat] *nm* pirate; **p. de l'air** hijacker; – *a* (*radio, bateau*) pirate-. ◆**piraterie** *nf* piracy; (*acte*) act of piracy; **p. (aérienne)** hijacking.

pire [pir] *a* worse (**que** than); **le p. moment/résultat/***etc* the worst moment/result/*etc*; – *nmf* **le** *ou* **la p.** the worst (one); **le p. de tout** the worst (thing) of all; **au p.** at (the very) worst; **s'attendre au p.** to expect the (very) worst.

pirogue [pirɔg] *nf* canoe, dugout.

pis [pi] **1** *nm* (*de vache*) udder. **2** *a inv & adv Litt* worse; **de mal en p.** from bad to worse; – *nm* **le p.** *Litt* the worst.

pis-aller [pizale] *nm inv* (*personne, solution*) stopgap.

piscine [pisin] *nf* swimming pool.

pissenlit [pisɑ̃li] *nm* dandelion.

pistache [pistaʃ] *nf* (*fruit, parfum*) pistachio.

piste [pist] *nf* (*trace de personne ou d'animal*) track, trail; *Sp* track, racetrack; (*de magnétophone*) track; *Av* runway; (*de cirque*) ring; (*de patinage*) rink; (*pour chevaux*) racecourse, racetrack; **p. cyclable** cycle track, *Am* bicycle path; **p. de danse** dance floor; **p. de ski** ski run; **tour de p.** *Sp* lap.

pistolet [pistɔlɛ] *nm* gun, pistol; (*de peintre*) spray gun.

piston [pistɔ̃] *nm* **1** *Aut* piston. **2 avoir du p.** (*appui*) to have connections. ◆**pistonner** *vt* (*appuyer*) to pull strings for.

pitié [pitje] *nf* pity; **j'ai p. de lui, il me fait p.** I pity him, I feel sorry for him. ◆**piteux, -euse** *a Iron* pitiful. ◆**pitoyable** *a* pitiful.

piton [pitɔ̃] *nm* **1** (*à crochet*) hook. **2** *Géog* peak.

pitre [pitr] *nm* clown. ◆**pitrerie(s)** *nf(pl)* clowning.

pittoresque [pitɔrɛsk] *a* picturesque.

pivert [pivɛr] *nm* (*oiseau*) woodpecker.

pivoine [pivwan] *nf Bot* peony.

pivot [pivo] *nm* pivot; (*personne*) *Fig* linchpin, mainspring. ◆**pivoter** *vi* (*personne*) to swing round; (*fauteuil*) to swivel; (*porte*) to revolve.

pizza [pidza] *nf* pizza. ◆**pizzeria** *nf* pizza parlour.

placage [plakaʒ] *nm* (*revêtement*) facing; (*en bois*) veneer.

placard [plakar] *nm* **1** (*armoire*) cupboard, *Am* closet. **2** (*pancarte*) poster. ◆**placarder** *vt* (*affiche*) to post (up); (*mur*) to cover with posters.

place [plas] *nf* (*endroit, rang*) & *Sp* place; (*occupée par qn ou qch*) room; (*lieu public*) square; (*siège*) seat, place; (*prix d'un trajet*) *Aut* fare; (*emploi*) job, position; **p. (forte)** *Mil* fortress; **p. (de parking)** (parking) space; **p. (financière)** (money) market; **à la p.** (*échange*) instead (**de** of); **à votre p.** in your place; **sur p.** on the spot; **en p.** (*objet*) in place; **ne pas tenir en p.** to be unable to keep still; **mettre en p.** to install, set up; **faire p. à** to give way to; **changer qch de p.** to move sth.

plac/er [plase] *vt* (*mettre*) to put, place; (*situer*) to place, position; (*invité, spectateur*) to seat; (*argent*) to invest, place (**dans** in); (*vendre*) to place, sell; **p. un mot** to get a word in edgeways *ou Am* edgewise; — **se p.** *vpr* (*personne*) to take up a position, place oneself; (*objet*) to be put *ou* placed; (*cheval, coureur*) to be placed; **se p. troisième**/*etc Sp* to come *ou* be third/*etc*. ◆**—é** *a* (*objet*) & *Sp* placed; **bien/mal p. pour faire** in a good/bad position to do; **les gens haut placés** people in high places. ◆**—ement** *nm* (*d'argent*) investment.

placide [plasid] *a* placid.

plafond [plafɔ̃] *nm* ceiling. ◆**plafonnier** *nm Aut* roof light.

plage [plaʒ] *nf* **1** beach; (*ville*) (seaside) resort. **2** (*sur disque*) track. **3 p. arrière** *Aut* parcel shelf.

plagiat [plaʒja] *nm* plagiarism. ◆**plagier** *vt* to plagiarize.

plaid [plɛd] *nm* travelling rug.

plaider [plede] *vti Jur* to plead. ◆**plaideur, -euse** *nmf* litigant. ◆**plaidoirie** *nf Jur* speech (for the defence). ◆**plaidoyer** *nm* plea.

plaie [plɛ] *nf* (*blessure*) wound; (*coupure*) cut; (*corvée, personne*) *Fig* nuisance.

plaignant, -ante [plɛɲɑ̃, -ɑ̃t] *nmf Jur* plaintiff.

plaindre* [plɛ̃dr] **1** *vt* to feel sorry for, pity. **2 se p.** *vpr* (*protester*) to complain (**de** about, **que** that); **se p. de** (*maux de tête etc*) to complain of *ou* about. ◆**plainte** *nf* complaint; (*cri*) moan, groan. ◆**plaintif, -ive** *a* sorrowful, plaintive.

plaine [plɛn] *nf Géog* plain.

plaire* [plɛr] *vi & v imp* **p. à** to please; **elle lui plaît** he likes her, she pleases him; **ça me plaît** I like it; **il me plaît de faire** I like doing; **s'il vous** *ou* **te plaît** please; — **se p.** *vpr* (*à Paris etc*) to like *ou* enjoy it; (*l'un l'autre*) to like each other.

plaisance [plɛzɑ̃s] *nf* **bateau de p.** pleasure boat; **navigation de p.** yachting.

plaisant [plɛzɑ̃] *a* (*drôle*) amusing; (*agréable*) pleasing; — *nm* **mauvais p.** *Péj* joker. ◆**plaisanter** *vi* to joke, jest; **p. avec qch** to trifle with sth; — *vt* to tease. ◆**plaisanterie** *nf* joke, jest; (*bagatelle*) trifle; **par p.** for a joke. ◆**plaisantin** *nm Péj* joker.

plaisir [plezir] *nm* pleasure; **faire p. à** to please; **faites-moi le p. de . . .** would you be good enough to . . . ; **pour le p.** for fun, for the fun of it; **au p. (de vous revoir)** see you again sometime.

plan [plɑ̃] **1** *nm* (*projet, dessin*) plan; (*de ville*) plan, map; (*niveau*) *Géom* plane; **au premier p.** in the foreground; **gros p.** *Phot Cin* close-up; **sur le p. politique**/*etc* from the political/*etc* viewpoint, politically/*etc*; **de premier p.** (*question etc*) major; **p. d'eau** stretch of water; **laisser en p.** (*abandonner*) to ditch. **2** *a* (*plat*) even, flat.

planche [plɑ̃ʃ] *nf* **1** board, plank; **p. à repasser/à dessin** ironing/drawing board; **p. (à roulettes)** skateboard; **p. (de surf)** surfboard; **p. (à voile)** sailboard; **faire de la p. (à voile)** to go windsurfing; **faire la p.** to float on one's back. **2** (*illustration*) plate. **3** (*de légumes*) bed, plot.

plancher [plɑ̃ʃe] *nm* floor.

plan/er [plane] *vi* (*oiseau*) to glide, hover; (*avion*) to glide; **p. sur qn** (*mystère, danger*) to hang over s.o.; **vol plané** glide. ◆**—eur** *nm* (*avion*) glider.

planète [planɛt] *nf* planet. ◆**planétaire** *a* planetary. ◆**planétarium** *nm* planetarium.

planifier [planifje] *vt Écon* to plan. ◆**pla-**

nification *nf* *Écon* planning. ◆**planning** *nm* (*industriel, commercial*) planning; **p familial** family planning.
planque [plɑ̃k] *nf* **1** (*travail*) *Fam* cushy job. **2** (*lieu*) *Fam* hideout. ◆**planquer** *vt*, — **se p.** *vpr Fam* to hide.
plant [plɑ̃] *nm* (*plante*) seedling; (*de légumes etc*) bed.
plante [plɑ̃t] *nf* **1** *Bot* plant; **p. d'appartement** house plant; **jardin des plantes** botanical gardens. **2 p. des pieds** sole (of the foot). ◆**plant/er** *vt* (*arbre, plante etc*) to plant; (*clou, couteau*) to drive in; (*tente, drapeau, échelle*) to put up; (*mettre*) to put (**sur** on, **contre** against); (*regard*) to fix (**sur** on); **p. là qn** to leave s.o. standing; **se p. devant** to plant oneself in front of. ◆**—é** *a* (*immobile*) standing; **bien p.** (*personne*) sturdy. ◆**plantation** *nf* (*action*) planting; (*terrain*) bed; (*de café, d'arbres etc*) plantation. ◆**planteur** *nm* plantation owner.
planton [plɑ̃tɔ̃] *nm Mil* orderly.
plantureux, -euse [plɑ̃tyrø, -øz] *a* (*repas etc*) abundant.
plaque [plak] *nf* plate; (*de verre, métal*) sheet, plate; (*de verglas*) sheet; (*de marbre*) slab; (*de chocolat*) bar; (*commémorative*) plaque; (*tache*) *Méd* blotch; **p. chauffante** *Culin* hotplate; **p. tournante** (*carrefour*) *Fig* centre; **p. minéralogique, p. d'immatriculation** *Aut* number *ou Am* license plate; **p. dentaire** (dental) plaque.
plaqu/er [plake] *vt* (*métal, bijou*) to plate; (*bois*) to veneer; (*cheveux*) to plaster (down); *Rugby* to tackle; (*aplatir*) to flatten (**contre** against); (*abandonner*) *Fam* to give (*sth*) up; **p. qn** *Fam* to ditch s.o.; **se p. contre** to flatten oneself against. ◆**—é** *a* (*bijou*) plated; **p. or** gold-plated; — *nm* **p. or** gold plate. ◆**—age** *nm Rugby* tackle.
plasma [plasma] *nm Méd* plasma.
plastic [plastik] *nm* plastic explosive. ◆**plastiquer** *vt* to blow up.
plastique [plastik] *a* (*art, substance*) plastic; **matière p.** plastic; — *nm* (*matière*) plastic; **en p.** (*bouteille etc*) plastic.
plastron [plastrɔ̃] *nm* shirtfront.
plat [pla] **1** *a* flat; (*mer*) calm, smooth; (*fade*) flat, dull; **à fond p.** flat-bottomed; **à p. ventre** flat on one's face; **à p.** (*pneu, batterie*) flat; (*déprimé, épuisé*) *Fam* low; **poser à p.** to put *ou* lay (down) flat; **tomber à p.** to fall down flat; **assiette plate** dinner plate; **calme p.** dead calm; — *nm* (*de la main*) flat. **2** *nm* (*récipient, mets*) dish; (*partie du repas*) course; **'p. du jour'** (*au restaurant*) 'today's special'.
platane [platan] *nm* plane tree.
plateau, -x [plato] *nm* (*pour servir*) tray; (*de balance*) pan; (*de tourne-disque*) turntable; (*plate-forme*) *Cin TV* set; *Th* stage; *Géog* plateau; **p. à fromages** cheeseboard.
plate-bande [platbɑ̃d] *nf* (*pl* **plates-bandes**) flower bed.
plate-forme [platfɔrm] *nf* (*pl* **plates-formes**) platform; **p.-forme pétrolière** oil rig.
platine [platin] **1** *nm* (*métal*) platinum. **2** *nf* (*d'électrophone*) deck. ◆**platiné** *a* (*cheveux*) platinum, platinum-blond(e).
platitude [platityd] *nf* platitude.
plâtre [plɑtr] *nm* (*matière*) plaster; **un p.** *Méd* a plaster cast; **dans le p.** *Méd* in plaster; **les plâtres** (*d'une maison etc*) the plasterwork; **p. à mouler** plaster of Paris. ◆**plâtr/er** *vt* (*mur*) to plaster; (*membre*) to put in plaster. ◆**—age** *nm* plastering. ◆**plâtrier** *nm* plasterer.
plausible [plozibl] *a* plausible.
plébiscite [plebisit] *nm* plebiscite.
plein [plɛ̃] *a* (*rempli, complet*) full; (*paroi*) solid; (*ivre*) *Fam* tight; **p. de** full of; **en pleine mer** on the open sea; **en p. visage**/*etc* right in the middle of the face/*etc*; **en p. jour** in broad daylight; — *prép & adv* **des billes p. les poches** pockets full of marbles; **du chocolat p. la figure** chocolate all over one's face; **p. de lettres/d'argent**/*etc* (*beaucoup de*) *Fam* lots of letters/money/*etc*; **à p.** (*travailler*) to full capacity; — *nm* **faire le p.** *Aut* to fill up (the tank); **battre son p.** (*fête*) to be in full swing. ◆**pleinement** *adv* fully.
pléonasme [pleɔnasm] *nm* (*expression*) redundancy.
pléthore [pletɔr] *nf* plethora.
pleurer [plœre] *vi* to cry, weep (**sur** over); — *vt* (*regretter*) to mourn (for). ◆**pleureur** *a* **saule p.** weeping willow. ◆**pleurnicher** *vi* to snivel, grizzle. ◆**pleurs (en)** *adv* in tears.
pleurésie [plœrezi] *nf Méd* pleurisy.
pleuvoir* [pløvwar] *v imp* to rain; **il pleut** it's raining; — *vi* (*coups etc*) to rain down (**sur** on).
pli [pli] *nm* **1** (*de papier etc*) fold; (*de jupe, robe*) pleat; (*de pantalon, de bouche*) crease; (*de bras*) bend; **(faux) p.** crease; **mise en plis** (*coiffure*) set. **2** (*enveloppe*) *Com* envelope, letter; **sous p. séparé** under separate cover. **3** *Cartes* trick. **4** (*habitude*) habit; **prendre le p. de faire** to get into the habit of doing. ◆**pli/er** *vt* to fold; (*courber*) to bend; **p. qn à** to submit s.o. to; — *vi* (*branche*) to bend; — **se p.** *vpr* (*lit, chaise*

etc) to fold (up); **se p. à** to submit to, give in to. ◆**—ant** *a* (*chaise etc*) folding; (*parapluie*) telescopic; – *nm* folding stool. ◆**—able** *a* pliable. ◆**—age** *nm* (*manière*) fold; (*action*) folding.

plinthe [plɛ̃t] *nf* skirting board, *Am* baseboard.

pliss/er [plise] *vt* (*jupe, robe*) to pleat; (*froisser*) to crease; (*lèvres*) to pucker; (*front*) to wrinkle, crease; (*yeux*) to screw up. ◆**—é** *nm* pleating, pleats.

plomb [plɔ̃] *nm* (*métal*) lead; (*fusible*) *Él* fuse; (*poids pour rideau etc*) lead weight; *pl* (*de chasse*) lead shot, buckshot; **de p.** (*tuyau etc*) lead-; (*sommeil*) *Fig* heavy; (*soleil*) blazing; (*ciel*) leaden. ◆**plomb/er** *vt* (*dent*) to fill; (*colis*) to seal (with lead). ◆**—é** *a* (*teint*) leaden. ◆**—age** *nm* (*de dent*) filling.

plombier [plɔ̃bje] *nm* plumber. ◆**plomberie** *nf* (*métier, installations*) plumbing.

plong/er [plɔ̃ʒe] *vi* (*personne, avion etc*) to dive, plunge; (*route, regard*) *Fig* to plunge; – *vt* (*mettre, enfoncer*) to plunge, thrust (**dans** into); **se p. dans** (*lecture etc*) to immerse oneself in. ◆**—eant** *a* (*décolleté*) plunging; (*vue*) bird's eye-. ◆**—é** *a* **p. dans** (*lecture etc*) immersed *ou* deep in. ◆**—ée** *nf* diving; (*de sous-marin*) submersion; **en p.** (*sous-marin*) submerged. ◆**plongeoir** *nm* diving board. ◆**plongeon** *nm* dive. ◆**plongeur, -euse** *nmf* diver; (*employé de restaurant*) dishwasher.

plouf [pluf] *nm & int* splash.

ployer [plwaje] *vti* to bend.

plu [ply] *voir* **plaire, pleuvoir.**

pluie [plɥi] *nf* rain; **une p.** (*averse*) & *Fig* a shower; **sous la p.** in the rain.

plume [plym] *nf* **1** (*d'oiseau*) feather. **2** (*pour écrire*) *Hist* quill (pen); (*pointe en acier*) (pen) nib; **stylo à p.** (fountain) pen; **vivre de sa p.** *Fig* to live by one's pen. ◆**plumage** *nm* plumage. ◆**plumeau, -x** *nm* feather duster. ◆**plumer** *vt* (*volaille*) to pluck; **p. qn** (*voler*) *Fig* to fleece s.o. ◆**plumet** *nm* plume. ◆**plumier** *nm* pencil box, pen box.

plupart (la) [laplypar] *nf* most; **la p. des cas**/*etc* most cases/*etc*; **la p. du temps** most of the time; **la p. d'entre eux** most of them; **pour la p.** mostly.

pluriel, -ielle [plyrjɛl] *a & nm Gram* plural; **au p.** (*nom*) plural, in the plural.

plus[1] [ply] ([plyz] *before vowel*, [plys] *in end position*) **1** *adv comparatif* (*travailler etc*) more (**que** than); **p. d'un kilo/de dix**/*etc* (*quantité, nombre*) more than a kilo/ten/*etc*; **p. de thé**/*etc* (*davantage*) more tea/*etc*; **p. beau/rapidement**/*etc* more beautiful/rapidly/*etc* (**que** than); **p. tard** later; **p. petit** smaller; **de p. en p.** more and more; **de p. en p. vite** quicker and quicker; **p. il crie p. il s'enroue** the more he shouts the more hoarse he gets; **p. ou moins** more or less; **en p.** in addition (**de** to); **de p.** more (**que** than); (*en outre*) moreover; **les enfants (âgés) de p. de dix ans** children over ten; **j'ai dix ans de p. qu'elle** I'm ten years older than she is; **il est p. de cinq heures** it's after five (o'clock). **2** *adv superlatif* **le p.** (*travailler etc*) (the) most; **le p. beau**/*etc* the most beautiful/*etc*; (*de deux*) the more beautiful/*etc*; **le p. grand**/*etc* the biggest/*etc*; the bigger/*etc*; **j'ai le p. de livres** I have (the) most books; **j'en ai le p.** I have (the) most; **(tout) au p.** at (the very) most.

plus[2] [ply] *adv de négation* **p. de** (*pain, argent etc*) no more; **il n'a p. de pain** he has no more bread, he doesn't have any more bread; **tu n'es p. jeune** you're no longer young, you're not young any more *ou* any longer; **elle ne le fait p.** she no longer does it, she doesn't do it any more *ou* any longer; **je ne la reverrai p.** I won't see her again.

plus[3] [plys] *prép* plus; **deux p. deux font quatre** two plus two are four; **il fait p. deux (degrés)** it's two degrees above freezing; – *nm* **le signe p.** the plus sign.

plusieurs [plyzjœr] *a & pron* several.

plus-value [plyvaly] *nf* (*bénéfice*) profit.

plutonium [plytɔnjɔm] *nm* plutonium.

plutôt [plyto] *adv* rather (**que** than).

pluvieux, -euse [plyvjø, -øz] *a* rainy, wet.

PMU [peɛmy] *abrév* = **pari mutuel urbain.**

pneu [pnø] *nm* (*pl* **-s**) **1** (*de roue*) tyre, *Am* tire. **2** (*lettre*) express letter. ◆**pneumatique 1** *a* (*matelas etc*) inflatable; **marteau p.** pneumatic drill. **2** *nm* = **pneu.**

pneumonie [pnømɔni] *nf* pneumonia.

poche [pɔʃ] *nf* pocket; (*de kangourou etc*) pouch; (*sac en papier etc*) bag; *pl* (*sous les yeux*) bags; **livre de p.** paperback; **faire des poches** (*pantalon*) to be baggy; **j'ai un franc en p.** I have one franc on me. ◆**pochette** *nf* (*sac*) bag, envelope; (*d'allumettes*) book; (*de disque*) sleeve, jacket; (*mouchoir*) pocket handkerchief; (*sac à main*) (clutch) bag.

poch/er [pɔʃe] *vt* **1 p. l'œil à qn** to give s.o. a black eye. **2** (*œufs*) to poach. ◆**—é** *a* **œil p.** black eye.

podium [pɔdjɔm] *nm Sp* rostrum, podium.

poêle [pwal] **1** *nm* stove. **2** *nf* **p. (à frire)** frying pan.

poème [pɔɛm] *nm* poem. ◆**poésie** *nf* poetry; une p. (*poème*) a piece of poetry. ◆**poète** *nm* poet; – *a* **femme p.** poetess. ◆**poétique** *a* poetic.

pognon [pɔɲɔ̃] *nm* (*argent*) *Fam* dough.

poids [pwa] *nm* weight; **au p.** by weight; **de p.** (*influent*) influential; **p. lourd** (heavy) lorry *ou Am* truck; **lancer le p.** *Sp* to put *ou* hurl the shot.

poignant [pwaɲɑ̃] *a* (*souvenir etc*) poignant.

poignard [pwaɲar] *nm* dagger; **coup de p.** stab. ◆**poignarder** *vt* to stab.

poigne [pwaɲ] *nf* (*étreinte*) grip.

poignée [pwaɲe] *nf* (*quantité*) handful (**de** of); (*de porte, casserole etc*) handle; (*d'épée*) hilt; **p. de main** handshake; **donner une p. de main à** to shake hands with.

poignet [pwaɲɛ] *nm* wrist; (*de chemise*) cuff.

poil [pwal] *nm* hair; (*pelage*) coat, fur; (*de brosse*) bristle; *pl* (*de tapis*) pile; (*d'étoffe*) nap; **à p.** (*nu*) *Arg* (stark) naked; **au p.** (*travail etc*) *Arg* top-rate; **de bon/mauvais p.** *Fam* in a good/bad mood; **de tout p.** *Fam* of all kinds. ◆**poilu** *a* hairy.

poinçon [pwɛ̃sɔ̃] *nm* (*outil*) awl, bradawl; (*marque de bijou etc*) hallmark. ◆**poinçonner** *vt* (*bijou*) to hallmark; (*billet*) to punch. ◆**poinçonneuse** *nf* (*machine*) punch.

poindre [pwɛ̃dr] *vi* (*jour*) *Litt* to dawn.

poing [pwɛ̃] *nm* fist; **coup de p.** punch.

point[1] [pwɛ̃] *nm* (*lieu, question, degré, score etc*) point; (*sur i, à l'horizon etc*) dot; (*tache*) spot; (*note*) *Scol* mark; (*de couture*) stitch; **sur le p. de faire** about to do, on the point of doing; **p. (final)** full stop, period; **p. d'exclamation** exclamation mark *ou Am* point; **p. d'interrogation** question mark; **p. de vue** point of view, viewpoint; (*endroit*) viewing point; **à p. (nommé)** (*arriver etc*) at the right moment; **à p.** (*rôti etc*) medium (cooked); (*steak*) medium rare; **mal en p.** in bad shape; **mettre au p.** *Phot* to focus; *Aut* to tune; (*technique etc*) to elaborate, perfect; (*éclaircir*) *Fig* to clarify, clear up; **mise au p.** focusing; tuning, tune-up; elaboration; *Fig* clarification; **faire le p.** *Fig* to take stock, sum up; **p. mort** *Aut* neutral; **au p. mort** *Fig* at a standstill; **p. noir** *Aut* (accident) black spot; **p. du jour** daybreak; **p. de côté** (*douleur*) stitch (in one's side). ◆**p.-virgule** *nm* (*pl* **points-virgules**) semicolon.

point[2] [pwɛ̃] *adv Litt* = **pas**[1].

pointe [pwɛ̃t] *nf* (*extrémité*) point, tip; (*pour grille*) spike; (*clou*) nail; *Géog* headland; (*maximum*) *Fig* peak; **une p. de** (*soupçon, nuance*) a touch of; **sur la p. des pieds** on tiptoe; **en p.** pointed; **de p.** (*technique etc*) latest, most advanced; **à la p. de** (*progrès etc*) *Fig* in *ou* at the forefront of.

point/er [pwɛ̃te] **1** *vt* (*cocher*) to tick (off), *Am* check (off). **2** *vt* (*braquer, diriger*) to point (**sur, vers** at). **3** *vti* (*employé*) to clock in, (*à la sortie*) to clock out; **— se p.** *vpr* (*arriver*) *Fam* to show up. **4** *vi* (*bourgeon etc*) to appear; **p. vers** to point upwards towards. ◆**—age** *nm* (*de personnel*) clocking in; clocking out.

pointillé [pwɛ̃tije] *nm* dotted line; – *a* dotted.

pointilleux, -euse [pwɛ̃tijø, -øz] *a* fussy, particular.

pointu [pwɛ̃ty] *a* (*en pointe*) pointed; (*voix*) shrill.

pointure [pwɛ̃tyr] *nf* (*de chaussure, gant*) size.

poire [pwar] *nf* **1** (*fruit*) pear. **2** (*figure*) *Fam* mug. **3** (*personne*) *Fam* sucker. ◆**poirier** *nm* pear tree.

poireau, -x [pwaro] *nm* leek.

poireauter [pwarote] *vi* (*attendre*) *Fam* to kick one's heels.

pois [pwa] *nm* (*légume*) pea; (*dessin*) (polka) dot; **petits p.** (garden) peas; **p. chiche** chickpea; **à p.** (*vêtement*) spotted, dotted.

poison [pwazɔ̃] *nm* (*substance*) poison.

poisse [pwas] *nf Fam* bad luck.

poisseux, -euse [pwasø, -øz] *a* sticky.

poisson [pwasɔ̃] *nm* fish; **p. rouge** goldfish; **les Poissons** (*signe*) Pisces. ◆**poissonnerie** *nf* fish shop. ◆**poissonnier, -ière** *nmf* fishmonger.

poitrine [pwatrin] *nf Anat* chest; (*seins*) breast, bosom; (*de veau, mouton*) *Culin* breast.

poivre [pwavr] *nm* pepper. ◆**poivr/er** *vt* to pepper. ◆**—é** *a Culin* peppery; (*plaisanterie*) *Fig* spicy. ◆**poivrier** *nm Bot* pepper plant; (*ustensile*) pepperpot. ◆**poivrière** *nf* pepperpot.

poivron [pwavrɔ̃] *nm* pepper, capsicum.

poivrot, -ote [pwavro, -ɔt] *nmf Fam* drunk(ard).

poker [pɔkɛr] *nm Cartes* poker.

polar [pɔlar] *nm* (*roman*) *Fam* whodunit.

polariser [pɔlarize] *vt* to polarize.

pôle [pol] *nm Géog* pole; **p. Nord/Sud** North/South Pole. ◆**polaire** *a* polar.

polémique [pɔlemik] *a* controversial, polemical; – *nf* controversy, polemic.

poli [pɔli] **1** *a* (*courtois*) polite (**avec** to, with). **2** *a* (*lisse, brillant*) polished; – *nm* (*aspect*) polish. ◆**—ment** *adv* politely.

police [pɔlis] *nf* **1** police; **faire *ou* assurer la**

p. to maintain order (**dans** in); **p. secours** emergency services; **p. mondaine** *ou* **des mœurs** = vice squad. **2 p. (d'assurance)** (insurance) policy. ◆**policier** *a* (*enquête, état*) police-; **roman p.** detective novel; – *nm* policeman, detective.

polichinelle [pɔliʃinɛl] *nf* **secret de p.** open secret.

polio [pɔljo] *nf* (*maladie*) polio; – *nmf* (*personne*) polio victim. ◆**poliomyélite** *nf* poliomyelitis.

polir [pɔlir] *vt* (*substance dure, style*) to polish.

polisson, -onne [pɔlisɔ̃, -ɔn] *a* naughty; – *nmf* rascal.

politesse [pɔlitɛs] *nf* politeness; **une p.** (*parole*) a polite word; (*action*) an act of politeness.

politique [pɔlitik] *a* political; **homme p.** politician; – *nf* (*science, activité*) politics; (*mesures, manières de gouverner*) *Pol* policies; **une p.** (*tactique*) a policy. ◆**politicien, -ienne** *nmf Péj* politician. ◆**politiser** *vt* to politicize.

pollen [pɔlɛn] *nm* pollen.

polluer [pɔlɥe] *vt* to pollute. ◆**polluant** *nm* pollutant. ◆**pollution** *nf* pollution.

polo [pɔlo] *nm* **1** (*chemise*) sweat shirt. **2** *Sp* polo.

polochon [pɔlɔʃɔ̃] *nm* (*traversin*) *Fam* bolster.

Pologne [pɔlɔɲ] *nf* Poland. ◆**polonais, -aise** *a* Polish; – *nmf* Pole; – *nm* (*langue*) Polish.

poltron, -onne [pɔltrɔ̃, -ɔn] *a* cowardly; – *nmf* coward.

polycopi/er [pɔlikɔpje] *vt* to mimeograph, duplicate. ◆**—é** *nm Univ* mimeographed copy (*of lecture etc*).

polyester [pɔliɛstɛr] *nm* polyester.

Polynésie [pɔlinezi] *nf* Polynesia.

polyvalent [pɔlivalɑ̃] *a* (*rôle*) multi-purpose, varied; (*professeur, ouvrier*) all-round; **école polyvalente, lycée p.** comprehensive school.

pommade [pɔmad] *nf* ointment.

pomme [pɔm] *nf* **1** apple; **p. d'Adam** *Anat* Adam's apple. **2** (*d'arrosoir*) rose. **3 p. de terre** potato; **pommes vapeur** steamed potatoes; **pommes frites** chips, *Am* French fries; **pommes chips** potato crisps *ou Am* chips. ◆**pommier** *nm* apple tree.

pommette [pɔmɛt] *nf* cheekbone.

pompe [pɔ̃p] **1** *nf* pump; **p. à essence** petrol *ou Am* gas station; **p. à incendie** fire engine; **coup de p.** *Fam* tired feeling. **2** *nf* (*chaussure*) *Fam* shoe. **3** *nf* (*en gymnastique*) press-up, *Am* push-up. **4** *nfpl* **pompes funèbres** undertaker's; **entrepreneur des pompes funèbres** undertaker. **5** *nf* **p. anti-sèche** *Scol* crib. **6** *nf* (*splendeur*) pomp. ◆**pomper** *vt* to pump; (*évacuer*) to pump out (**de** of); (*absorber*) to soak up; (*épuiser*) *Fam* to tire out; – *vi* to pump. ◆**pompeux, -euse** *a* pompous. ◆**pompier 1** *nm* fireman; **voiture des pompiers** fire engine. **2** *a* (*emphatique*) pompous. ◆**pompiste** *nmf Aut* pump attendant.

pompon [pɔ̃pɔ̃] *nm* (*ornement*) pompon.

pomponner [pɔ̃pɔne] *vt* to doll up.

ponce [pɔ̃s] *nf* **(pierre) p.** pumice (stone). ◆**poncer** *vt* to rub down, sand. ◆**ponceuse** *nf* (*machine*) sander.

ponctuation [pɔ̃ktɥasjɔ̃] *nf* punctuation. ◆**ponctuer** *vt* to punctuate (**de** with).

ponctuel, -elle [pɔ̃ktɥɛl] *a* (*à l'heure*) punctual; (*unique*) *Fig* one-off, *Am* one-of-a-kind. ◆**ponctualité** *nf* punctuality.

pondéré [pɔ̃dere] *a* level-headed. ◆**pondération** *nf* level-headedness.

pondre [pɔ̃dr] *vt* (*œuf*) to lay; (*livre, discours*) *Péj Fam* to produce; – *vi* (*poule*) to lay.

poney [pɔnɛ] *nm* pony.

pont [pɔ̃] *nm* bridge; (*de bateau*) deck; **p. (de graissage)** *Aut* ramp; **faire le p.** *Fig* to take the intervening day(s) off (*between two holidays*); **p. aérien** airlift. ◆**p.-levis** *nm* (*pl* **ponts-levis**) drawbridge.

ponte [pɔ̃t] **1** *nf* (*d'œufs*) laying. **2** *nm* (*personne*) *Fam* bigwig.

pontife [pɔ̃tif] *nm* **1** **(souverain) p.** pope. **2** (*ponte*) *Fam* bigshot. ◆**pontifical, -aux** *a* papal, pontifical.

pop [pɔp] *nm & a inv Mus* pop.

popote [pɔpɔt] *nf* (*cuisine*) *Fam* cooking.

populace [pɔpylas] *nf Péj* rabble.

populaire [pɔpylɛr] *a* (*personne, tradition, gouvernement etc*) popular; (*quartier, milieu*) lower-class; (*expression*) colloquial; (*art*) folk-. ◆**populariser** *vt* to popularize. ◆**popularité** *nf* popularity (**auprès de** with).

population [pɔpylasjɔ̃] *nf* population. ◆**populeux, -euse** *a* populous, crowded.

porc [pɔr] *nm* pig; (*viande*) pork; (*personne*) *Péj* swine.

porcelaine [pɔrsəlɛn] *nf* china, porcelain.

porc-épic [pɔrkepik] *nm* (*pl* **porcs-épics**) (*animal*) porcupine.

porche [pɔrʃ] *nm* porch.

porcherie [pɔrʃəri] *nf* pigsty.

pore [pɔr] *nm* pore. ◆**poreux, -euse** *a* porous.

pornographie [pɔrnɔgrafi] *nf* pornography. ◆**pornographique** *a* (*Fam* **porno**) pornographic.

port [pɔr] *nm* **1** port, harbour; **arriver à bon p.** to arrive safely. **2** (*d'armes*) carrying; (*de barbe*) wearing; (*prix*) **carriage**, postage; (*attitude*) bearing.

portable [pɔrtabl] *a* (*robe etc*) wearable; (*portatif*) portable.

portail [pɔrtaj] *nm* (*de cathédrale etc*) portal.

portant [pɔrtɑ̃] *a* **bien p.** in good health.

portatif, -ive [pɔrtatif, -iv] *a* portable.

porte [pɔrt] *nf* door, (*passage*) doorway; (*de jardin*) gate, (*passage*) gateway; (*de ville*) entrance, *Hist* gate. **p. (d'embarquement)** *Av* (departure) gate; **Alger, p. de . . .** Algiers, gateway **to . . .** ; **p. d'entrée** front door; **mettre à la p.** (*jeter dehors*) to throw out; (*renvoyer*) to sack. ◆**p.-fenêtre** *nf* (*pl* **portes-fenêtres**) French window.

porte-à-faux [pɔrtafo] *nm inv* **en p.-à-faux** (*en déséquilibre*) unstable.

porte-avions [pɔrtavjɔ̃] *nm inv* aircraft carrier. ◆**p.-bagages** *nm inv* luggage rack. ◆**p.-bébé** *nm* (*nacelle*) carrycot, *Am* baby basket; (*kangourou®*) baby sling. ◆**p.-bonheur** *nm inv* (*fétiche*) (lucky) charm. ◆**p.-cartes** *nm inv* card holder *ou* case. ◆**p.-clés** *nm inv* key ring. ◆**p.-documents** *nm inv* briefcase. ◆**p.-drapeau, -x** *nm Mil* standard bearer. ◆**p.-jarretelles** *nm inv* suspender *ou Am* garter belt. ◆**p.-monnaie** *nm inv* purse. ◆**p.-parapluie** *nm inv* umbrella stand. ◆**p.-plume** *nm inv* pen (*for dipping in ink*). ◆**p.-revues** *nm inv* newspaper rack. ◆**p.-savon** *nm* soapdish. ◆**p.-serviettes** *nm inv* towel rail. ◆**p.-voix** *nm inv* megaphone.

portée [pɔrte] *nf* **1** (*de fusil etc*) range; **à la p. de qn** within reach of s.o.; (*richesse, plaisir etc*) *Fig* within s.o.'s grasp; **à p. de la main** within (easy) reach; **à p. de voix** within earshot; **hors de p.** out of reach. **2** (*animaux*) litter. **3** (*importance, effet*) significance, import. **4** *Mus* stave.

portefeuille [pɔrtəfœj] *nm* wallet; *Pol Com* portfolio.

portemanteau, -x [pɔrtmɑ̃to] *nm* (*sur pied*) hatstand; (*barre*) hat *ou* coat peg.

porte-parole [pɔrtparɔl] *nm inv* (*homme*) spokesman; (*femme*) spokeswoman (**de** for, of).

port/er [pɔrte] *vt* to carry; (*vêtement, lunettes, barbe etc*) to wear; (*trace, responsabilité, fruits etc*) to bear; (*regard*) to cast; (*attaque*) to make (**contre** against); (*coup*) to strike; (*sentiment*) to have (**à** for); (*inscrire*) to enter, write down; **p. qch à** (*amener*) to bring *ou* take sth to; **p. qn à faire** (*pousser*) to lead *ou* prompt s.o. to do; **p. bonheur/malheur** to bring good/bad luck; **se faire p. malade** to report sick; – *vi* (*voix*) to carry; (*canon*) to fire; (*vue*) to extend; **p. (juste)** (*coup*) to hit the mark; (*mot, reproche*) to hit home; **p. sur** (*reposer sur*) to rest on; (*concerner*) to bear on; (*accent*) to fall on; (*heurter*) to strike; **— se p.** *vpr* (*vêtement*) to be worn; **se p. bien/mal** to be well/ill; **comment te portes-tu?** how are you?; **se p. candidat** to stand as a candidate. ◆**—ant** *a* **bien p.** in good health. ◆**—é** *a* **p. à croire**/*etc* inclined to believe/*etc*; **p. sur qch** fond of sth. ◆**—eur, -euse** *nm Rail* porter; – *nmf Méd* carrier; (*de nouvelles, chèque*) bearer; **mère porteuse** surrogate mother.

portier [pɔrtje] *nm* doorkeeper, porter. ◆**portière** *nf* (*de véhicule, train*) door. ◆**portillon** *nm* gate.

portion [pɔrsjɔ̃] *nf* (*part, partie*) portion; (*de nourriture*) helping, portion.

portique [pɔrtik] *nm* **1** *Archit* portico. **2** (*de balançoire etc*) crossbar, frame.

porto [pɔrto] *nm* (*vin*) port.

portrait [pɔrtrɛ] *nm* portrait; **être le p. de** (*son père etc*) to be the image of; **faire un p.** to paint *ou* draw a portrait (**de** of); **p. en pied** full-length portrait. ◆**p.-robot** *nm* (*pl* **portraits-robots**) identikit (picture), photofit.

portuaire [pɔrtɥɛr] *a* (*installations etc*) harbour-.

Portugal [pɔrtygal] *nm* Portugal. ◆**portugais, -aise** *a* & *nmf* Portuguese; – *nm* (*langue*) Portuguese.

pose [poz] *nf* **1** (*installation*) putting up; putting in; laying. **2** (*attitude de modèle, affectation*) pose; (*temps*) *Phot* exposure. ◆**pos/er** *vt* to put (down); (*papier peint, rideaux*) to put up; (*sonnette, chauffage*) to put in; (*mine, moquette, fondations*) to lay; (*question*) to ask (**à qn** s.o.); (*principe, conditions*) to lay down; **p. sa candidature** to apply, put in one's application (**à** for); **ça pose la question de . . .** it poses the question of . . . ; – *vi* (*modèle etc*) to pose (**pour** for); **— se p.** *vpr* (*oiseau, avion*) to land; (*problème, question*) to arise; **se p. sur** (*yeux*) to fix on; **se p. en chef**/*etc* to set oneself up as *ou* pose as a leader/*etc*; **la question se pose!** this question should be asked! ◆**—é** *a* (*calme*) calm, staid.

◆—ément *adv* calmly. **◆—eur, -euse** *nmf Péj* poseur.

positif, -ive [pozitif, -iv] *a* positive. **◆positivement** *adv* positively.

position [pozisjɔ̃] *nf* (*attitude, emplacement, opinion etc*) position; **prendre p.** *Fig* to take a stand (**contre** against); **prise de p.** stand.

posologie [pozɔlɔʒi] *nf* (*de médicament*) dosage.

posséder [pɔsede] *vt* to possess; (*maison etc*) to own, possess; (*bien connaître*) to master. **◆possesseur** *nm* possessor; owner. **◆possessif, -ive** *a* (*personne, adjectif etc*) possessive; – *nm Gram* possessive. **◆possession** *nf* possession; **en p. de** in possession of; **prendre p. de** to take possession of.

possible [pɔsibl] *a* possible (**à faire** to do); **il (nous) est p. de le faire** it is possible (for us) to do it; **il est p. que** (+ *sub*) it is possible that; **si p.** if possible; **le plus tôt**/*etc* **p.** as soon/*etc* as possible; **autant que p.** as much *ou* as many as possible; – *nm* **faire son p.** to do one's utmost (**pour faire** to do); **dans la mesure du p.** as far as possible. **◆possibilité** *nf* possibility.

post- [pɔst] *préf* post-.

postdater [pɔstdate] *vt* to postdate.

poste [pɔst] **1** *nf* (*service*) post, mail; (*local*) post office; **bureau de p.** post office; **Postes (et Télécommunications)** (*administration*) Post Office; **par la p.** by post, by mail; **p. aérienne** airmail; **mettre à la p.** to post, mail. **2** *nm* (*lieu, emploi*) post; **p. de secours** first aid post; **p. de police** police station; **p. d'essence** petrol *ou Am* gas station; **p. d'incendie** fire hydrant; **p. d'aiguillage** signal box *ou Am* tower. **3** *nm* (*appareil*) *Rad TV* set; *Tél* extension (number). **◆postal, -aux** *a* postal; **boîte postale** PO Box; **code p.** postcode, *Am* zip code. **◆poster 1** *vt* **p. qn** (*placer*) *Mil* to post s.o. **2** *vt* (*lettre*) to post, mail. **3** [pɔstɛr] *nm* poster.

postérieur [pɔsterjœr] **1** *a* (*document etc*) later; **p. à** after. **2** *nm* (*derrière*) *Fam* posterior.

postérité [pɔsterite] *nf* posterity.

posthume [pɔstym] *a* posthumous; **à titre p.** posthumously.

postiche [pɔstiʃ] *a* (*barbe etc*) false.

postier, -ière [pɔstje, -jɛr] *nmf* postal worker.

postillonner [pɔstijɔne] *vi* to sputter.

post-scriptum [pɔstskriptɔm] *nm inv* postscript.

postul/er [pɔstyle] *vt* **1** (*emploi*) to apply for. **2** (*poser*) *Math* to postulate. **◆—ant, -ante** *nmf* applicant.

posture [pɔstyr] *nf* posture.

pot [po] *nm* **1** pot; (*à confiture*) jar, pot; (*à lait*) jug; (*à bière*) mug; (*de crème, yaourt*) carton; **p. de chambre** chamber pot; **p. de fleurs** flower pot; **prendre un p.** (*verre*) *Fam* to have a drink. **2** (*chance*) *Fam* luck; **avoir du p.** to be lucky.

potable [pɔtabl] *a* drinkable; (*passable*) *Fam* tolerable; **'eau p.'** 'drinking water'.

potage [pɔtaʒ] *nm* soup.

potager, -ère [pɔtaʒe, -ɛr] *a* (*jardin*) vegetable-; **plante potagère** vegetable; – *nm* vegetable garden.

potasser [pɔtase] *vt* (*examen*) to cram for; – *vi* to cram.

pot-au-feu [pɔtofø] *nm inv* (*plat*) beef stew.

pot-de-vin [podvɛ̃] *nm* (*pl* **pots-de-vin**) bribe.

pote [pɔt] *nm* (*ami*) *Fam* pal, buddy.

poteau, -x [pɔto] *nm* post; (*télégraphique*) pole; **p. d'arrivée** *Sp* winning post.

potelé [pɔtle] *a* plump, chubby.

potence [pɔtɑ̃s] *nf* (*gibet*) gallows.

potentiel, -ielle [pɔtɑ̃sjɛl] *a* & *nm* potential.

poterie [pɔtri] *nf* (*art*) pottery; **une p.** a piece of pottery; **des poteries** (*objets*) pottery. **◆potier** *nm* potter.

potin [pɔtɛ̃] **1** *nmpl* (*cancans*) gossip. **2** *nm* (*bruit*) *Fam* row.

potion [posjɔ̃] *nf* potion.

potiron [pɔtirɔ̃] *nm* pumpkin.

pot-pourri [popuri] *nm* (*pl* **pots-pourris**) *Mus* medley.

pou, -x [pu] *nm* louse; **poux** lice.

poubelle [pubɛl] *nf* dustbin, *Am* garbage can.

pouce [pus] *nm* **1** thumb; **un coup de p.** *Fam* a helping hand. **2** (*mesure*) *Hist & Fig* inch.

poudre [pudr] *nf* powder; **p. (à canon)** (*explosif*) gunpowder; **en p.** (*lait*) powdered; (*chocolat*) drinking; **sucre en p.** castor *ou* caster sugar. **◆poudrer** *vt* to powder; – **se p.** *vpr* (*femme*) to powder one's nose. **◆poudreux, -euse** *a* powdery, dusty. **◆poudrier** *nm* (powder) compact. **◆poudrière** *nf* powder magazine; (*région*) *Fig* powder keg.

pouf [puf] **1** *int* thump! **2** *nm* (*siège*) pouf(fe).

pouffer [pufe] *vi* **p. (de rire)** to burst out laughing, guffaw.

pouilleux, -euse [pujø, -øz] *a* (*sordide*) miserable; (*mendiant*) lousy.

poulain [pulɛ̃] *nm* (*cheval*) foal; **le p. de qn** *Fig* s.o.'s protégé.

poule [pul] *nf* **1** hen. *Culin* fowl; **être p. mouillée** (*lâche*) to be chicken; **oui, ma p.!** *Fam* yes, my pet! **2** (*femme*) *Péj* tart. ◆**poulailler** *nm* **1** (hen) coop. **2 le p.** *Th Fam* the gods, the gallery. ◆**poulet** *nm* **1** (*poule, coq*) *Culin* chicken. **2** (*policier*) *Fam* cop.

pouliche [puliʃ] *nf* (*jument*) filly.

poulie [puli] *nf* pulley.

poulpe [pulp] *nm* octopus.

pouls [pu] *nm Méd* pulse.

poumon [pumɔ̃] *nm* lung; **à pleins poumons** (*respirer*) deeply; (*crier*) loudly; **p. d'acier** iron lung.

poupe [pup] *nf Nau* stern, poop.

poupée [pupe] *nf* doll.

poupin [pupɛ̃] *a* **visage p.** baby face.

poupon [pupɔ̃] *nm* (*bébé*) baby; (*poupée*) doll.

pour [pur] **1** *prép* for; **p. toi/moi/***etc* for you/me/*etc*; **faites-le p. lui** do it for him, do it for his sake; **partir p.** (*Paris etc*) to leave for; **elle va partir p. cinq ans** she's leaving for five years; **p. femme/base/***etc* as a wife/basis/*etc*; **p. moi, p. ma part** (*quant à moi*) as for me; **dix p. cent** ten per cent; **gentil p.** kind to; **elle est p.** she's in favour; **p. faire** (in order) to do, so as to do; **p. que tu saches** so (that) you may know; **p. quoi faire?** what for?; **trop petit/poli/***etc* **p. faire** too small/polite/*etc* to do; **assez grand/***etc* **p. faire** big/*etc* enough to do; **p. cela** for that reason; **jour p. jour/heure p. heure** to the day/hour; **p. intelligent/***etc* **qu'il soit** however clever/*etc* he may be; **ce n'est pas p. me plaire** it doesn't exactly please me; **acheter p. cinq francs de bonbons** to buy five francs' worth of sweets. **2** *nm* **le p. et le contre** the pros and cons.

pourboire [purbwar] *nm* (*argent*) tip.

pourcentage [pursɑ̃taʒ] *nm* percentage.

pourchasser [purʃase] *vt* to pursue.

pourparlers [purparle] *nmpl* negotiations, talks.

pourpre [purpr] *a & nm* purple.

pourquoi [purkwa] *adv & conj* why; **p. pas?** why not?; – *nm inv* reason (**de** for); **le p. et le comment** the whys and wherefores.

pourra, pourrait [pura, pure] *voir* **pouvoir 1.**

pourrir [purir] *vi*, **— se p.** *vpr* to rot; – *vt* to rot; **p. qn** to corrupt s.o. ◆**pourri** *a* (*fruit, temps, personne etc*) rotten. ◆**pourriture** *nf* rot, rottenness; (*personne*) *Péj* swine.

poursuite [pursɥit] **1** *nf* chase, pursuit; (*du bonheur, de créancier*) pursuit (**de** of); (*continuation*) continuation; **se mettre à la p. de** to go in pursuit of. **2** *nfpl Jur* legal proceedings (**contre** against). ◆**poursuiv/re* 1** *vt* (*courir après*) to chase, pursue; (*harceler, relancer*) to hound, pursue; (*obséder*) to haunt; (*but, idéal etc*) to pursue. **2** *vt* **p. qn** *Jur* (*au criminel*) to prosecute s.o.; (*au civil*) to sue s.o. **3** *vt* (*lecture, voyage etc*) to continue (with), carry on (with), pursue; – *vi*, **— se p.** *vpr* to continue, go on. ◆**—ant, -ante** *nmf* pursuer.

pourtant [purtɑ̃] *adv* yet, nevertheless.

pourtour [purtur] *nm* perimeter.

pourvoir* [purvwar] *vt* to provide (**de** with); **être pourvu de** to have, be provided with; – *vi* **p. à** (*besoins etc*) to provide for. ◆**pourvoyeur, -euse** *nmf* supplier.

pourvu que [purvyk(ə)] *conj* (*condition*) provided *ou* providing (that); **p. qu'elle soit là** (*souhait*) I only hope (that) she's there.

pousse [pus] *nf* **1** (*bourgeon*) shoot, sprout. **2** (*croissance*) growth.

pousse-café [puskafe] *nm inv* after-dinner liqueur.

pouss/er [puse] **1** *vt* to push; (*du coude*) to nudge, poke; (*véhicule, machine*) to drive hard; (*recherches*) to pursue; (*cri*) to utter; (*soupir*) to heave; **p. qn à faire** to urge s.o. to do; **p. qn à bout** to push s.o. to his limits; **p. trop loin** (*gentillesse etc*) to carry too far; **p. à la perfection** to bring to perfection; – *vi* to push; **p. jusqu'à Paris/***etc* to push on as far as Paris/*etc*; **— se p.** *vpr* (*se déplacer*) to move up *ou* over. **2** *vi* (*croître*) to grow; **faire p.** (*plante, barbe etc*) to grow. ◆**—é** *a* (*travail, études*) advanced. ◆**—ée** *nf* (*pression*) pressure; (*coup*) push; (*d'ennemi*) thrust, push; (*de fièvre etc*) outbreak; (*de l'inflation*) upsurge. ◆**poussette** *nf* pushchair, *Am* stroller; **p. canne** (baby) buggy, *Am* (collapsible) stroller; **p. de marché** shopping trolley *ou Am* cart. ◆**poussoir** *nm* (push) button.

poussière [pusjɛr] *nf* dust; **dix francs et des poussières** *Fam* a bit over ten francs. ◆**poussiéreux, -euse** *a* dusty.

poussif, -ive [pusif, -iv] *a* short-winded, puffing.

poussin [pusɛ̃] *nm* (*poulet*) chick.

poutre [putr] *nf* (*en bois*) beam; (*en acier*) girder. ◆**poutrelle** *nf* girder.

pouvoir* [puvwar] **1** *v aux* (*capacité*) to be able, can; (*permission, éventualité*) may, can; **je peux deviner** I can guess, I'm able to guess; **tu peux entrer** you may *ou* can come in; **il peut être malade** he may *ou* might be ill; **elle pourrait/pouvait venir** she might/could come; **j'ai pu l'obtenir** I managed to get it; **j'aurais pu l'obtenir** I could have got it *ou Am* gotten it; **je n'en peux plus** I'm utterly exhausted; – *v imp* **il peut neiger** it may snow; **— se p.** *vpr* **il se peut qu'elle parte** (it's possible that) she might leave. **2** *nm* (*capacité, autorité*) power; (*procuration*) power of attorney; **les pouvoirs publics** the authorities; **au p.** *Pol* in power; **en son p.** in one's power (**de faire** to do).

poux [pu] *voir* **pou.**

pragmatique [pragmatik] *a* pragmatic.

praire [prɛr] *nf* (*mollusque*) clam.

prairie [preri] *nf* meadow.

praline [pralin] *nf* sugared almond. ◆**praliné** *a* (*glace*) praline-flavoured.

praticable [pratikabl] *a* (*projet, chemin*) practicable.

praticien, -ienne [pratisjɛ̃, -jɛn] *nmf* practitioner.

pratique [pratik] **1** *a* (*connaissance, personne, instrument etc*) practical. **2** *nf* (*exercice, procédé*) practice; (*expérience*) practical experience; **la p. de la natation/du golf/***etc* swimming/golfing/*etc*; **mettre en p.** to put into practice; **en p.** (*en réalité*) in practice. ◆**pratiqu/er** *vt* (*art etc*) to practise; (*football*) to play, practise; (*trou, route*) to make; (*opération*) to carry out; **p. la natation** to go swimming; – *vi* to practise. ◆**—ant, -ante** *a Rel* practising; – *nmf* churchgoer.

pratiquement [pratikmɑ̃] *adv* (*presque*) practically; (*en réalité*) in practice.

pré [pre] *nm* meadow.

pré- [pre] *préf* pre-.

préalable [prealabl] *a* previous, preliminary; **p. à** prior to; – *nm* precondition, prerequisite; **au p.** beforehand. ◆**—ment** [-əmɑ̃] *adv* beforehand.

préambule [preɑ̃byl] *nm* (*de loi*) preamble; *Fig* prelude (**à** to).

préau, -x [preo] *nm Scol* covered playground.

préavis [preavi] *nm* (*de congé etc*) (advance) notice (**de** of).

précaire [prekɛr] *a* precarious.

précaution [prekosjɔ̃] *nf* (*mesure*) precaution; (*prudence*) caution; **par p.** as a precaution. ◆**précautionneux, -euse** *a* cautious.

précédent, -ente [presedɑ̃, -ɑ̃t] **1** *a* previous, preceding, earlier; – *nmf* previous one. **2** *nm* **un p.** (*fait, exemple*) a precedent; **sans p.** unprecedented. ◆**précédemment** [-amɑ̃] *adv* previously. ◆**précéder** *vti* to precede; **faire p. qch de qch** to precede sth by sth.

précepte [presɛpt] *nm* precept.

précepteur, -trice [presɛptœr, -tris] *nmf* (private) tutor.

prêcher [preʃe] *vti* to preach; **p. qn** *Rel & Fig* to preach to s.o.

précieux, -euse [presjø, -øz] *a* precious.

précipice [presipis] *nm* abyss, chasm.

précipit/er [presipite] *vt* (*jeter*) to throw, hurl; (*plonger*) to plunge (**dans** into); (*hâter*) to hasten; **— se p.** *vpr* (*se jeter*) to throw *ou* hurl oneself; (*foncer*) to rush (**à, sur** on to); (*s'accélérer*) to speed up. ◆**—é** *a* hasty. ◆**précipitamment** *adv* hastily. ◆**précipitation 1** *nf* haste. **2** *nfpl* (*pluie*) precipitation.

précis [presi] **1** *a* precise; (*idée, mécanisme*) accurate, precise; **à deux heures précises** at two o'clock sharp *ou* precisely. **2** *nm* (*résumé*) summary; (*manuel*) handbook. ◆**précisément** *adv* precisely. ◆**préciser** *vt* to specify (**que** that); **— se p.** *vpr* to become clear(er). ◆**précision** *nf* precision; accuracy; (*détail*) detail; (*explication*) explanation.

précoce [prekɔs] *a* (*fruit, mariage, mort etc*) early; (*personne*) precocious. ◆**précocité** *nf* precociousness; earliness.

préconçu [prekɔ̃sy] *a* preconceived.

préconiser [prekɔnize] *vt* to advocate (**que** that).

précurseur [prekyrsœr] *nm* forerunner, precursor; – *a* **un signe p. de qch** a sign heralding sth.

prédécesseur [predesesœr] *nm* predecessor.

prédestiné [predestine] *a* fated, predestined (**à faire** to do).

prédicateur [predikatœr] *nm* preacher.

prédilection [predilɛksjɔ̃] *nf* (special) liking; **de p.** favourite.

prédire* [predir] *vt* to predict (**que** that). ◆**prédiction** *nf* prediction.

prédisposer [predispoze] *vt* to predispose (**à qch** to sth, **à faire** to do). ◆**prédisposition** *nf* predisposition.

prédomin/er [predɔmine] *vi* to predominate. ◆**—ant** *a* predominant. ◆**prédominance** *nf* predominance.

préfabriqué [prefabrike] *a* prefabricated.

préface [prefas] *nf* preface. ◆**préfacer** *vt* to preface.

préfér/er [prefere] *vt* to prefer (**à** to); **p. faire** to prefer to do. ◆**—é, -ée** *a & nmf* favourite. ◆**—able** *a* preferable (**à** to). ◆**préférence** *nf* preference; **de p.** preferably; **de p. à** in preference to. ◆**préférentiel, -ielle** *a* preferential.

préfet [prefɛ] *nm* prefect, *chief administrator in a department*; **p. de police** prefect of police, *Paris chief of police*. ◆**préfecture** *nf* prefecture; **p. de police** Paris police headquarters.
préfixe [prefiks] *nm* prefix.
préhistoire [preistwar] *nf* prehistory. ◆**préhistorique** *a* prehistoric.
préjudice [preʒydis] *nm Jur* prejudice, harm; **porter p. à** to prejudice, harm. ◆**préjudiciable** *a* prejudicial (**à** to).
préjugé [preʒyʒe] *nm* (*parti pris*) prejudice; **avoir un p. ou des préjugés** to be prejudiced (**contre** against).
prélasser (se) [sәprelɑse] *vpr* to loll (about), lounge (about).
prélat [prela] *nm Rel* prelate.
prélever [prelve] *vt* (*échantillon*) to take (**sur** from); (*somme*) to deduct (**sur** from). ◆**prélèvement** *nm* taking; deduction; **p. de sang** blood sample; **p. automatique** *Fin* standing order.
préliminaire [preliminɛr] *a* preliminary; – *nmpl* preliminaries.
prélude [prelyd] *nm* prelude (**à** to).
prématuré [prematyre] *a* premature; – *nm* (*bébé*) premature baby. ◆**—ment** *adv* prematurely, too soon.
préméditer [premedite] *vt* to premeditate. ◆**préméditation** *nf Jur* premeditation.
premier, -ière [prәmje, -jɛr] *a* first; (*enfance*) early; (*page*) *Journ* front, first; (*qualité, nécessité, importance*) prime; (*état*) original; (*notion, cause*) basic; (*danseuse, rôle*) leading; (*inférieur*) bottom; (*supérieur*) top; **nombre p.** *Math* prime number; **le p. rang** the front *ou* first row; **à la première occasion** at the earliest opportunity; **P. ministre** Prime Minister, Premier; – *nmf* first (one); **arriver le p. ou en p.** to arrive first; **être le p. de la classe** to be (at the) top of the class; – *nm* (*date*) first; (*étage*) first *ou Am* second floor; **le p. de l'an** New Year's Day; – *nf Th Cin* première; *Rail* first class; *Scol* = sixth form, *Am* = twelfth grade; *Aut* first (gear); (*événement historique*) first. ◆**premier-né** *nm*, ◆**première-née** *nf* first-born (child). ◆**premièrement** *adv* firstly.
prémisse [premis] *nf* premiss.
prémonition [premɔnisjɔ̃] *nf* premonition.
prémunir [premynir] *vt* to safeguard (**contre** against).
prénatal, *mpl* **-als** [prenatal] *a* antenatal, *Am* prenatal.
prendre* [prɑ̃dr] *vt* to take (**à qn** from s.o.); (*attraper*) to catch, get; (*voyager par*) to take, travel by; (*acheter*) to get; (*douche, bain*) to take, have; (*repas*) to have; (*nouvelles*) to get; (*temps, heure*) to take (up); (*pensionnaire*) to take (in); (*ton, air*) to put on; (*engager*) to take (*s.o.*) (on); (*chercher*) to pick up, get; **p. qn pour** (*un autre*) to (mis)take s.o. for; (*considérer*) to take s.o. for; **p. qn** (*doute etc*) to seize s.o.; **p. feu** to catch fire; **p. de la place** to take up room; **p. du poids/de la vitesse** to put on weight/speed; **à tout p.** on the whole; **qu'est-ce qui te prend?** what's got *ou Am* gotten into you?; – *vi* (*feu*) to catch; (*gelée, ciment*) to set; (*greffe, vaccin*) to take; (*mode*) to catch on; **— se p.** *vpr* (*objet*) to be taken; (*s'accrocher*) to get caught; (*eau*) to freeze; **se p. pour un génie/***etc* to think one is a genius/*etc*; **s'y p.** to go *ou* set about it; **s'en p. à** (*critiquer, attaquer*) to attack; (*accuser*) to blame; **se p. à faire** to begin to do. ◆**prenant** *a* (*travail, film etc*) engrossing; (*voix*) engaging. ◆**preneur, -euse** *nmf* taker, buyer.
prénom [prenɔ̃] *nm* first name. ◆**prénommer** *vt* to name; **il se prénomme Louis** his first name is Louis.
préoccup/er [preɔkype] *vt* (*inquiéter*) to worry; (*absorber*) to preoccupy; **se p. de** to be worried about; to be preoccupied about. ◆**—ant** *a* worrying. ◆**—é** *a* worried. ◆**préoccupation** *nf* worry; (*idée, problème*) preoccupation.
préparer [prepare] *vt* to prepare; (*repas etc*) to get ready, prepare; (*examen*) to study for, prepare (for); **p. qch à qn** to prepare sth for s.o.; **p. qn à** (*examen*) to prepare *ou* coach s.o. for; **— se p.** *vpr* to get (oneself) ready, prepare oneself (**à qch** for sth); (*orage*) to brew, threaten. ◆**préparatifs** *nmpl* preparations (**de** for). ◆**préparation** *nf* preparation. ◆**préparatoire** *a* preparatory.
prépondérant [prepɔ̃derɑ̃] *a* dominant. ◆**prépondérance** *nf* dominance.
prépos/er [prepoze] *vt* **p. qn à** to put s.o. in charge of. ◆**—é, -ée** *nmf* employee; (*facteur*) postman, postwoman.
préposition [prepozisjɔ̃] *nf* preposition.
préretraite [prerәtrɛt] *nf* early retirement.
prérogative [prerɔgativ] *nf* prerogative.
près [prɛ] *adv* **p. de** (*qn, qch*) near (to), close to; **p. de deux ans/***etc* (*presque*) nearly two years/*etc*; **p. de partir/***etc* about to leave/*etc*; **tout p.** nearby (**de qn/qch** s.o./sth), close by (**de qn/qch** s.o./sth); **de p.** (*lire, examiner, suivre*) closely; **à peu de chose p.** almost; **à cela p.** except for that; **voici le**

chiffre à un franc p. here is the figure give or take a franc; calculer au franc p. to calculate to the nearest franc.

présage [prezaʒ] *nm* omen, foreboding. ◆**présager** *vt* to forebode.

presbyte [presbit] *a & nmf* long-sighted (person). ◆**presbytie** [-bisi] *nf* long-sightedness.

presbytère [presbiter] *nm Rel* presbytery.

préscolaire [preskɔler] *a* (*âge etc*) pre-school.

prescrire* [preskrir] *vt* to prescribe. ◆**prescription** *nf* (*instruction*) & *Jur* prescription.

préséance [preseɑ̃s] *nf* precedence (sur over).

présent[1] [prezɑ̃] **1** *a* (*non absent*) present; les personnes présentes those present. **2** *a* (*actuel*) present; – *nm* (*temps*) present; *Gram* present (tense); à p. now, at present; dès à p. as from now. ◆**présence** *nf* presence; (*à l'école, au bureau etc*) attendance (à at); feuille de p. attendance sheet; faire acte de p. to put in an appearance; en p. (*personnes*) face to face; en p. de in the presence of; p. d'esprit presence of mind.

présent[2] [prezɑ̃] *nm* (*cadeau*) present.

présent/er [prezɑ̃te] *vt* (*offrir, exposer, animer etc*) to present; (*montrer*) to show, present; p. qn à qn to introduce *ou* present s.o. to s.o.; – **se p.** *vpr* to introduce *ou* present oneself (à to); (*chez qn*) to show up; (*occasion etc*) to arise; se p. à (*examen*) to sit for; (*élections*) to stand in *ou* at, run in; (*emploi*) to apply for; (*autorités*) to report to; ça se présente bien it looks promising. ◆**—able** *a* presentable. ◆**présentateur, -trice** *nmf TV* announcer, presenter. ◆**présentation** *nf* presentation; introduction. ◆**présentoir** *nm* (*étagère*) (display) stand.

préserver [prezerve] *vt* to protect, preserve (de from). ◆**préservatif** *nm* sheath, condom. ◆**préservation** *nf* protection, preservation.

présidence [prezidɑ̃s] *nf* (*de nation*) presidency; (*de firme etc*) chairmanship. ◆**président, -ente** *nmf* (*de nation*) president; (*de réunion, firme*) chairman, chairwoman; p. directeur général chairman and managing director, *Am* chief executive officer. ◆**présidentiel, -ielle** *a* presidential.

présider [prezide] *vt* (*réunion*) to preside at *ou* over, chair; – *vi* to preside.

présomption [prezɔ̃psjɔ̃] *nf* (*conjecture, suffisance*) presumption.

présomptueux, -euse [prezɔ̃ptɥø, -øz] *a* presumptuous.

presque [presk(ə)] *adv* almost, nearly; p. jamais/rien hardly ever/anything.

presqu'île [preskil] *nf* peninsula.

presse [pres] *nf* (*journaux, appareil*) press; *Typ* (printing) press; de p. (*conférence, agence*) press-.

presse-citron [pressitrɔ̃] *nm inv* lemon squeezer. ◆**p.-papiers** *nm inv* paper-weight. ◆**p.-purée** *nm inv* (potato) masher.

pressentir* [presɑ̃tir] *vt* (*deviner*) to sense (que that). ◆**pressentiment** *nm* foreboding, presentiment.

press/er [prese] *vt* (*serrer*) to squeeze, press; (*bouton*) to press; (*fruit*) to squeeze; (*départ etc*) to hasten; p. qn to hurry s.o. (de faire to do); (*assaillir*) to harass s.o. (de questions with questions); p. le pas to speed up; – *vi* (*temps*) to press; (*affaire*) to be pressing *ou* urgent; rien ne presse there's no hurry; — **se p.** *vpr* (*se grouper*) to crowd, swarm; (*se serrer*) to squeeze (together); (*se hâter*) to hurry (de faire to do); presse-toi (de partir) hurry up (and go). ◆**—ant** *a* pressing, urgent. ◆**—é** *a* (*personne*) in a hurry; (*air*) hurried; (*travail*) pressing, urgent. ◆**pressing** [-iŋ] *nm* (*magasin*) dry cleaner's. ◆**pressoir** *nm* (wine) press.

pression [presjɔ̃] *nf* pressure; faire p. sur qn to put pressure on s.o., pressurize s.o.; bière (à la) p. draught beer; – *nm* (bouton-)p. press-stud, *Am* snap.

pressuriser [presyrize] *vt Av* to pressurize.

prestance [prestɑ̃s] *nf* (imposing) presence.

prestation [prestasjɔ̃] *nf* **1** (*allocation*) allowance, benefit. **2** (*performance*) performance.

prestidigitateur, -trice [prestidiʒitatœr, -tris] *nmf* conjurer. ◆**prestidigitation** *nf* conjuring.

prestige [prestiʒ] *nm* prestige. ◆**prestigieux, -euse** *a* prestigious.

presto [presto] *Fam voir* illico.

présumer [prezyme] *vt* to presume (que that).

présupposer [presypoze] *vt* to presuppose (que that).

prêt[1] [pre] *a* (*préparé, disposé*) ready (à faire to do, à qch for sth). ◆**p.-à-porter** [pretapɔrte] *nm inv* ready-to-wear clothes.

prêt[2] [pre] *nm* (*emprunt*) loan. ◆**p.-logement** *nm* (*pl* prêts-logement) mortgage.

prétend/re [pretɑ̃dr] *vt* to claim (que that); (*vouloir*) to intend (faire to do); p.

être/savoir to claim to be/to know; **elle se prétend riche** she claims to be rich; – *vi* **p. à** (*titre etc*) to lay claim to. ◆**—ant** *nm* (*amoureux*) suitor. ◆**—u** *a* so-called. ◆**—ument** *adv* supposedly.

prétentieux, -euse [pretɑ̃sjø, -øz] *a* & *nmf* pretentious (person). ◆**prétention** *nf* (*vanité*) pretension; (*revendication, ambition*) claim.

prêt/er [prete] *vt* (*argent, objet*) to lend (**à** to); (*aide, concours*) to give (**à** to); (*attribuer*) to attribute (**à** to); **p. attention** to pay attention (**à** to); **p. serment** to take an oath; – *vi* **p. à** (*phrase etc*) to lend itself to; **se p. à** (*consentir à*) to agree to; (*sujet etc*) to lend itself to. ◆**—eur, -euse** *nmf* (*d'argent*) lender; **p. sur gages** pawnbroker.

prétexte [pretɛkst] *nm* pretext, excuse; **sous p. de/que** on the pretext of/that. ◆**prétexter** *vt* to plead (**que** that).

prêtre [prɛtr] *nm* priest; **grand p.** high priest.

preuve [prœv] *nf* proof, evidence; **faire p. de** to show; **faire ses preuves** (*personne*) to prove oneself; (*méthode*) to prove itself.

prévaloir [prevalwar] *vi* to prevail (**contre** against, **sur** over).

prévenant [prevnɑ̃] *a* considerate. ◆**prévenance(s)** *nf(pl)* (*gentillesse*) consideration.

préven/ir* [prevnir] *vt* **1** (*avertir*) to warn (**que** that); (*aviser*) to tell, inform (**que** that). **2** (*désir, question*) to anticipate; (*malheur*) to avert. ◆**—u, -ue 1** *nmf Jur* defendant, accused. **2** *a* prejudiced (**contre** against). ◆**préventif, -ive** *a* preventive. ◆**prévention** *nf* **1** prevention; **p. routière** road safety. **2** (*opinion*) prejudice.

prév/oir* [prevwar] *vt* (*anticiper*) to foresee (**que** that); (*prédire*) forecast (**que** that); (*temps*) *Mét* to forecast; (*projeter, organiser*) to plan (for); (*réserver, préparer*) to allow, provide. ◆**—u** *a* (*conditions*) laid down; **un repas est p.** a meal is provided; **au moment p.** at the appointed time; **comme p.** as planned, as expected; **p. pour** (*véhicule, appareil etc*) designed for. ◆**prévisible** *a* foreseeable. ◆**prévision** *nf* (*opinion*) & *Mét* forecast; **en p. de** in expectation of.

prévoyant [prevwajɑ̃] *a* (*personne*) provident. ◆**prévoyance** *nf* foresight; **société de p.** provident society.

prier [prije] **1** *vi Rel* to pray; – *vt* **p. Dieu pour qu'il nous accorde qch** to pray (to God) for sth. **2** *vt* **p. qn de faire** to ask *ou* request s.o. to do; (*implorer*) to beg s.o. to do; **je vous en prie** (*faites donc, allez-y*) please; (*en réponse à 'merci'*) don't mention it; **je vous prie** please; **se faire p.** to wait to be asked. ◆**prière** *nf Rel* prayer; (*demande*) request; **p. de répondre/***etc* please answer/*etc*.

primaire [primɛr] *a* primary.

prime [prim] **1** *nf* (*d'employé*) bonus; (*d'État*) subsidy; (*cadeau*) *Com* free gift; **p. (d'assurance)** (insurance) premium. **2** *a* **de p. abord** at the very first glance.

primé [prime] *a* (*animal*) prize-winning.

primer [prime] *vi* to excel, prevail; – *vt* to prevail over.

primeurs [primœr] *nfpl* early fruit and vegetables.

primevère [primvɛr] *nf* (*à fleurs jaunes*) primrose.

primitif, -ive [primitif, -iv] *a* (*art, société etc*) primitive; (*état, sens*) original; – *nm* (*artiste*) primitive. ◆**primitivement** *adv* originally.

primo [primo] *adv* first(ly).

primordial, -aux [primɔrdjal, -o] *a* vital (**de faire** to do).

prince [prɛ̃s] *nm* prince. ◆**princesse** *nf* princess. ◆**princier, -ière** *a* princely. ◆**principauté** *nf* principality.

principal, -aux [prɛ̃sipal, -o] *a* main, chief, principal; – *nm* (*de collège*) *Scol* principal; **le p.** (*essentiel*) the main *ou* chief thing. ◆**—ement** *adv* mainly.

principe [prɛ̃sip] *nm* principle; **par p.** on principle; **en p.** theoretically, in principle; (*normalement*) as a rule.

printemps [prɛ̃tɑ̃] *nm* (*saison*) spring. ◆**printanier, -ière** *a* (*temps etc*) spring-, spring-like.

priorité [priɔrite] *nf* priority; **la p.** *Aut* the right of way; **la p. à droite** *Aut* right of way to traffic coming from the right; **'cédez la p.'** *Aut* 'give way', *Am* 'yield'; **en p.** as a matter of priority. ◆**prioritaire** *a* (*industrie etc*) priority-; **être p.** to have priority; *Aut* to have the right of way.

pris [pri] *voir* **prendre;** – *a* (*place*) taken; (*crème, ciment*) set; (*eau*) frozen; (*gorge*) infected; (*nez*) congested; **être (très) p.** (*occupé*) to be (very) busy; **p. de** (*peur, panique*) stricken with.

prise [priz] *voir* **prendre;** – *nf* taking; (*manière d'empoigner*) grip, hold; (*de ville*) capture, taking; (*objet saisi*) catch; (*de tabac*) pinch; **p. (de courant)** *Él* (*mâle*) plug; (*femelle*) socket; **p. multiple** *Él* adaptor; **p. d'air** air vent; **p. de conscience** awareness; **p. de contact** first meeting; **p. de position** *Fig* stand; **p. de sang** blood test; **p.**

de son (sound) recording; **p. de vue(s)** *Cin Phot* (*action*) shooting; (*résultat*) shot; **aux prises avec** at grips with.

priser [prize] **1** *vt* **tabac à p.** snuff; – *vi* to take snuff. **2** *vt* (*estimer*) to prize.

prisme [prism] *nm* prism.

prison [prizɔ̃] *nf* prison, jail, gaol; (*réclusion*) imprisonment; **mettre en p.** to imprison, put in prison. ◆**prisonnier, -ière** *nmf* prisoner; **faire qn p.** to take s.o. prisoner.

privé [prive] *a* private; **en p.** (*seul à seul*) in private; – *nm* **dans le p.** in private life; *Com Fam* in the private sector.

priver [prive] *vt* to deprive (**de** of); **se p. de** to deprive oneself of, do without. ◆**privation** *nf* deprivation (**de** of); *pl* (*sacrifices*) hardships.

privilège [privilɛʒ] *nm* privilege. ◆**privilégié, -ée** *a & nmf* privileged (person).

prix [pri] *nm* **1** (*d'un objet, du succès etc*) price; **à tout p.** at all costs; **à aucun p.** on no account; **hors (de) p.** exorbitant; **attacher du p. à** to attach importance to; **menu à p. fixe** set price menu. **2** (*récompense*) prize.

pro- [pro] *préf* pro-.

probable [prɔbabl] *a* probable, likely; **peu p.** unlikely. ◆**probabilité** *nf* probability, likelihood; **selon toute p.** in all probability. ◆**probablement** *adv* probably.

probant [prɔbɑ̃] *a* conclusive.

probité [prɔbite] *nf* (*honnêteté*) integrity.

problème [prɔblɛm] *nm* problem. ◆**problématique** *a* doubtful, problematic.

procéd/er [prɔsede] *vi* (*agir*) to proceed; (*se conduire*) to behave; **p. à** (*enquête etc*) to carry out. ◆**—é** *nm* process; (*conduite*) behaviour. ◆**procédure** *nf* procedure; *Jur* proceedings.

procès [prɔsɛ] *nm* (*criminel*) trial; (*civil*) lawsuit; **faire un p. à** to take to court.

processeur [prɔsesœr] *nm* (*d'ordinateur*) processor.

procession [prɔsesjɔ̃] *nf* procession.

processus [prɔsesys] *nm* process.

procès-verbal, -aux [prɔsɛvɛrbal, -o] *nm* (*de réunion*) minutes; (*constat*) *Jur* report; (*contravention*) fine, ticket.

prochain, -aine [prɔʃɛ̃, -ɛn] **1** *a* next; (*avenir*) near; (*parent*) close; (*mort, arrivée*) impending; (*mariage*) forthcoming; **un jour p.** one day soon; – *nf* **à la prochaine!** *Fam* see you soon!; **à la prochaine (station)** at the next stop. **2** *nm* (*semblable*) fellow (man). ◆**prochainement** *adv* shortly, soon.

proche [prɔʃ] *a* (*espace*) near, close; (*temps*) close (at hand); (*parent, ami*) close; (*avenir*) near; **p. de** near (to), close to; **une maison/etc p.** a house/*etc* nearby *ou* close by; – *nmpl* close relations.

proclamer [prɔklame] *vt* to proclaim, declare (**que** that); **p. roi** to proclaim king. ◆**proclamation** *nf* proclamation, declaration.

procréer [prɔkree] *vt* to procreate. ◆**procréation** *nf* procreation.

procuration [prɔkyrasjɔ̃] *nf* power of attorney; **par p.** (*voter*) by proxy.

procurer [prɔkyre] *vt* **p. qch à qn** (*personne*) to obtain sth for s.o.; (*occasion etc*) to afford s.o. sth; **se p. qch** to obtain sth.

procureur [prɔkyrœr] *nm* = *Br* public prosecutor, = *Am* district attorney.

prodige [prɔdiʒ] *nm* (*miracle*) wonder; (*personne*) prodigy. ◆**prodigieux, -euse** *a* prodigious, extraordinary.

prodigue [prɔdig] *a* (*dépensier*) wasteful, prodigal. ◆**prodiguer** *vt* to lavish (**à qn** on s.o.).

production [prɔdyksjɔ̃] *nf* production; (*de la terre*) yield. ◆**producteur, -trice** *nmf* *Com Cin* producer; – *a* producing; **pays p. de pétrole** oil-producing country. ◆**productif, -ive** *a* (*terre, réunion etc*) productive. ◆**productivité** *nf* productivity.

produire* [prɔdɥir] **1** *vt* (*fabriquer, présenter etc*) to produce; (*causer*) to bring about, produce. **2 se p.** *vpr* (*événement etc*) to happen, occur. ◆**produit** *nm* (*article etc*) product; (*pour la vaisselle*) liquid; (*d'une vente, d'une collecte*) proceeds; *pl* (*de la terre*) produce; **p. (chimique)** chemical; **p. de beauté** cosmetic.

proéminent [prɔeminɑ̃] *a* prominent.

prof [prɔf] *nm Fam* = **professeur.**

profane [prɔfan] **1** *nmf* lay person. **2** *a* (*art etc*) secular.

profaner [prɔfane] *vt* to profane, desecrate. ◆**profanation** *nf* profanation, desecration.

proférer [prɔfere] *vt* to utter.

professer [prɔfese] *vt* to profess (**que** that).

professeur [prɔfesœr] *nm* teacher; *Univ* lecturer, *Am* professor; (*titulaire d'une chaire*) *Univ* professor.

profession [prɔfesjɔ̃] *nf* **1** occupation, vocation; (*libérale*) profession; (*manuelle*) trade; **de p.** (*chanteur etc*) professional, by profession. **2 p. de foi** *Fig* declaration of principles. ◆**professionnel, -elle** *a* professional; (*école*) vocational, trade-; – *nmf* (*non amateur*) professional.

profil [prɔfil] *nm* (*de personne, objet*) profile;

de p. in profile. ◆**profiler** *vt* to outline, profile; – **se p.** *vpr* to be outlined *ou* profiled (sur against).

profit [prɔfi] *nm* profit; (*avantage*) advantage, profit; **vendre à p.** to sell at a profit; **tirer p. de** to benefit by, profit by; **au p. de** for the benefit of. ◆**profitable** *a* profitable (à to). ◆**profiter** *vi* **p. de** to take advantage of; **p. à qn** to profit s.o.; **p. (bien)** (*enfant*) *Fam* to thrive. ◆**profiteur, -euse** *nmf Péj* profiteer.

profond [prɔfɔ̃] *a* deep; (*esprit, joie, erreur etc*) profound, great; (*cause*) underlying; **p. de deux mètres** two metres deep; – *adv* (*pénétrer etc*) deep; – *nm* **au plus p. de** in the depths of. ◆**profondément** *adv* deeply; (*dormir*) soundly; (*triste, souhaiter*) profoundly; (*extrêmement*) thoroughly. ◆**profondeur** *nf* depth; profoundness; *pl* depths (de of); **en p.** (*étudier etc*) in depth; **à six mètres de p.** at a depth of six metres.

profusion [prɔfyzjɔ̃] *nf* profusion; **à p.** in profusion.

progéniture [prɔʒenityr] *nf Hum* offspring.

progiciel [prɔʒisjɛl] *nm* (*pour ordinateur*) (software) package.

programme [prɔgram] *nm* programme, *Am* program; (*d'une matière*) *Scol* syllabus; (*d'ordinateur*) program; **p. (d'études)** (*d'une école*) curriculum. ◆**programmation** *nf* programming. ◆**programmer** *vt Cin Rad TV* to programme, *Am* program; (*ordinateur*) to program. ◆**programmeur, -euse** *nmf* (computer) programmer.

progrès [prɔgrɛ] *nm & nmpl* progress; **faire des p.** to make (good) progress. ◆**progresser** *vi* to progress. ◆**progressif, -ive** *a* progressive. ◆**progression** *nf* progression. ◆**progressiste** *a & nmf Pol* progressive. ◆**progressivement** *adv* progressively, gradually.

prohiber [prɔibe] *vt* to prohibit, forbid. ◆**prohibitif, -ive** *a* prohibitive. ◆**prohibition** *nf* prohibition.

proie [prwa] *nf* prey; **être en p. à** to be (a) prey to, be tortured by.

projecteur [prɔʒɛktœr] *nm* (*de monument*) floodlight; (*de prison*) & *Mil* searchlight; *Th* spot(light); *Cin* projector.

projectile [prɔʒɛktil] *nm* missile.

projet [prɔʒɛ] *nm* plan; (*ébauche*) draft; (*entreprise, étude*) project.

projeter [prɔʒte] *vt* **1** (*lancer*) to hurl, project. **2** (*film, ombre*) to project; (*lumière*) to flash. **3** (*voyage, fête etc*) to plan; **p. de faire** to plan to do. ◆**projection** *nf* (*lancement*) hurling, projection; (*de film, d'ombre*) projection; (*séance*) showing.

prolétaire [prɔletɛr] *nmf* proletarian. ◆**prolétariat** *nm* proletariat. ◆**prolétarien, -ienne** *a* proletarian.

proliférer [prɔlifere] *vi* to proliferate. ◆**prolifération** *nf* proliferation.

prolifique [prɔlifik] *a* prolific.

prolixe [prɔliks] *a* verbose, wordy.

prologue [prɔlɔg] *nm* prologue (**de, à** to).

prolonger [prɔlɔ̃ʒe] *vt* to prolong, extend; – **se p.** *vpr* (*séance, rue, effet*) to continue. ◆**prolongateur** *nm* (*rallonge*) *Él* extension cord. ◆**prolongation** *nf* extension; *pl Fb* extra time. ◆**prolongement** *nm* extension.

promenade [prɔmnad] *nf* (*à pied*) walk; (*en voiture*) ride, drive; (*en vélo, à cheval*) ride; (*action*) *Sp* walking; (*lieu*) walk, promenade; **faire une p.** = **se promener.** ◆**promener** *vt* to take for a walk *ou* ride; (*visiteur*) to take *ou* show around; **p. qch sur qch** (*main, regard*) to run sth over sth; **envoyer p.** *Fam* to send packing; – **se p.** *vpr* (*à pied*) to (go for a) walk; (*en voiture*) to (go for a) ride *ou* drive. ◆**promeneur, -euse** *nmf* walker, stroller.

promesse [prɔmɛs] *nf* promise. ◆**promett/re*** *vt* to promise (**qch à qn** s.o. sth); **p. de faire** to promise to do; **c'est promis** it's a promise; – *vi* **p. (beaucoup)** *Fig* to be promising; **se p. qch** to promise oneself sth; **se p. de faire** to resolve to do. ◆**—eur, -euse** *a* promising.

promontoire [prɔmɔ̃twar] *nm Géog* headland.

promoteur [prɔmɔtœr] *nm* **p. (immobilier)** property developer.

promotion [prɔmosjɔ̃] *nf* **1** promotion; **en p.** *Com* on (special) offer. **2** (*candidats*) *Univ* year. ◆**promouvoir*** *vt* (*personne, produit etc*) to promote; **être promu** (*employé*) to be promoted (à to).

prompt [prɔ̃] *a* swift, prompt, quick. ◆**promptitude** *nf* swiftness, promptness.

promulguer [prɔmylge] *vt* to promulgate.

prôner [prone] *vt* (*vanter*) to extol; (*préconiser*) to advocate.

pronom [prɔnɔ̃] *nm Gram* pronoun. ◆**pronominal, -aux** *a* pronominal.

prononc/er [prɔnɔ̃se] *vt* (*articuler*) to pronounce; (*dire*) to utter; (*discours*) to deliver; (*jugement*) *Jur* to pronounce, pass; – *vi Jur Ling* to pronounce; – **se p.** *vpr* (*mot*) to be pronounced; (*personne*) to reach a decision (**sur** about, on); **se p. pour** to come out in favour of. ◆**—é** *a* (*visible*) pronounced, marked. ◆**prononciation** *nf* pronunciation.

pronostic [prɔnɔstik] *nm* (*prévision*) & *Sp* forecast. ◆**pronostiquer** *vt* to forecast.

propagande [prɔpagɑ̃d] *nf* propaganda. ◆**propagandiste** *nmf* propagandist.

propager [prɔpaʒe] *vt*, — **se p.** *vpr* to spread. ◆**propagation** *nf* spread(ing).

propension [prɔpɑ̃sjɔ̃] *nf* propensity (**à qch** for sth, **à faire** to do).

prophète [prɔfɛt] *nm* prophet. ◆**prophétie** [-fesi] *nf* prophecy. ◆**prophétique** *a* prophetic. ◆**prophétiser** *vti* to prophesy.

propice [prɔpis] *a* favourable (**à** to).

proportion [prɔpɔrsjɔ̃] *nf* proportion; *Math* ratio; **en p. de** in proportion to; **hors de p.** out of proportion (**avec** to). ◆**proportionnel, -elle** *a* proportional (**à** to). ◆**proportionn/er** *vt* to proportion (**à** to). ◆**—é** *a* proportionate (**à** to); **bien p.** well *ou* nicely proportioned.

propos [prɔpo] **1** *nmpl* (*paroles*) remarks, utterances. **2** *nm* (*intention*) purpose. **3** *nm* (*sujet*) subject; **à p. de** about; **à p. de rien** for no reason; **à tout p.** for no reason, at every turn. **4** *adv* **à p.** (*arriver etc*) at the right time; **à p.!** by the way!; **juger à p. de faire** to consider it fit to do.

proposer [prɔpoze] *vt* (*suggérer*) to suggest, propose (**qch à qn** sth to s.o., **que** (+ *sub*) that); (*offrir*) to offer (**qch à qn** s.o. sth, **de faire** to do); (*candidat*) to put forward, propose; **je te propose de rester** I suggest (that) you stay; **se p. pour faire** to offer to do; **se p. de faire** to propose *ou* mean to do. ◆**proposition** *nf* suggestion, proposal; (*de paix*) proposal, (*affirmation*) proposition; *Gram* clause.

propre[1] [prɔpr] *a* clean; (*soigné*) neat; (*honnête*) decent; — *nm* **mettre qch au p.** to make a fair copy of sth. ◆**proprement**[1] *adv* (*avec propreté*) cleanly; (*avec netteté*) neatly; (*comme il faut*) decently. ◆**propreté** *nf* cleanliness; (*netteté*) neatness.

propre[2] [prɔpr] **1** *a* (*à soi*) own; **mon p. argent** my own money; **ses propres mots** his very *ou* his own words. **2** *a* (*qui convient*) right, proper; **p. à** (*attribut, coutume etc*) peculiar to; (*approprié*) well-suited to; **p. à faire** likely to do; **sens p.** literal meaning; **nom p.** proper noun; — *nm* **le p. de** (*qualité*) the distinctive quality of; **au p.** (*au sens propre*) literally. ◆**proprement**[2] *adv* (*strictement*) strictly; **à p. parler** strictly speaking; **le village/*etc* p. dit** the village/*etc* proper *ou* itself.

propriété [prɔprijete] *nf* **1** (*bien*) property; (*droit*) ownership, property. **2** (*qualité*) property. **3** (*de mot*) suitability. ◆**propriétaire** *nmf* owner; (*d'hôtel*) proprietor, owner; (*qui loue*) landlord, landlady; **p. foncier** landowner.

propulser [prɔpylse] *vt* (*faire avancer, projeter*) to propel. ◆**propulsion** *nf* propulsion.

prosaïque [prozaik] *a* prosaic, pedestrian.

proscrire* [prɔskrir] *vt* to proscribe, banish. ◆**proscrit, -ite** *nmf* (*personne*) exile. ◆**proscription** *nf* banishment.

prose [proz] *nf* prose.

prospecter [prɔspɛkte] *vt* (*sol*) to prospect; (*pétrole*) to prospect for; (*région*) *Com* to canvass. ◆**prospecteur, -trice** *nmf* prospector. ◆**prospection** *nf* prospecting; *Com* canvassing.

prospectus [prɔspɛktys] *nm* leaflet, prospectus.

prospère [prɔspɛr] *a* (*florissant*) thriving, prosperous; (*riche*) prosperous. ◆**prospérer** *vi* to thrive, flourish, prosper. ◆**prospérité** *nf* prosperity.

prostate [prɔstat] *nf Anat* prostate (gland).

prostern/er (se) [səprɔstɛrne] *vpr* to prostrate oneself (**devant** before). ◆**—é** *a* prostrate. ◆**—ement** *nm* prostration.

prostituer [prɔstitɥe] *vt* to prostitute; — **se p.** *vpr* to prostitute oneself. ◆**prostituée** *nf* prostitute. ◆**prostitution** *nf* prostitution.

prostré [prɔstre] *a* (*accablé*) prostrate. ◆**prostration** *nf* prostration.

protagoniste [prɔtagɔnist] *nmf* protagonist.

protecteur, -trice [prɔtɛktœr, -tris] *nmf* protector; (*mécène*) patron; — *a* (*geste etc*) & *Écon* protective; (*ton, air*) *Péj* patronizing. ◆**protection** *nf* protection; (*mécénat*) patronage; **de p.** (*écran etc*) protective. ◆**protectionnisme** *nm Écon* protectionism.

protég/er [prɔteʒe] *vt* to protect (**de** from, **contre** against); (*appuyer*) *Fig* to patronize; — **se p.** *vpr* to protect oneself. ◆**—é** *nm* protégé. ◆**—ée** *nf* protégée. ◆**protège-cahier** *nm* exercise book cover.

protéine [prɔtein] *nf* protein.

protestant, -ante [prɔtɛstɑ̃, -ɑ̃t] *a* & *nmf* Protestant. ◆**protestantisme** *nm* Protestantism.

protester [prɔtɛste] *vi* to protest (**contre** against); **p. de** (*son innocence etc*) to protest; — *vt* to protest (**que** that). ◆**protestation** *nf* protest (**contre** against); *pl* (*d'amitié*) protestations (**de** of).

prothèse [prɔtɛz] *nf* **(appareil de) p.** (*membre*) artificial limb; (*dents*) false teeth.
protocole [prɔtɔkɔl] *nm* protocol.
prototype [prɔtɔtip] *nm* prototype.
protubérance [prɔtyberɑ̃s] *nf* protuberance. ◆**protubérant** *a* (*yeux*) bulging; (*menton*) protruding.
proue [pru] *nf Nau* prow, bow(s).
prouesse [pruɛs] *nf* feat, exploit.
prouver [pruve] *vt* to prove (**que** that).
Provence [prɔvɑ̃s] *nf* Provence. ◆**provençal, -ale, -aux** *a* & *nmf* Provençal.
provenir* [prɔvnir] *vi* **p. de** to come from. ◆**provenance** *nf* origin; **en p. de** from.
proverbe [prɔvɛrb] *nm* proverb. ◆**proverbial, -aux** *a* proverbial.
providence [prɔvidɑ̃s] *nf* providence. ◆**providentiel, -ielle** *a* providential.
province [prɔvɛ̃s] *nf* province; **la p.** the provinces; **en p.** in the provinces; **de p.** (*ville etc*) provincial. ◆**provincial, -ale, -aux** *a* & *nmf* provincial.
proviseur [prɔvizœr] *nm* (*de lycée*) headmaster.
provision [prɔvizjɔ̃] *nf* **1** (*réserve*) supply, stock; *pl* (*achats*) shopping; (*vivres*) provisions: **panier/sac à provisions** shopping basket/bag. **2** (*acompte*) advance payment; **chèque sans p.** dud cheque.
provisoire [prɔvizwar] *a* temporary, provisional. ◆**—ment** *adv* temporarily, provisionally.
provoquer [prɔvɔke] *vt* **1** (*causer*) to bring about, provoke; (*désir*) to arouse. **2** (*défier*) to provoke (*s.o.*). ◆**provocant** *a* provocative. ◆**provocateur** *nm* troublemaker. ◆**provocation** *nf* provocation.
proxénète [prɔksenɛt] *nm* pimp.
proximité [prɔksimite] *nf* closeness, proximity; **à p.** close by; **à p. de** close to.
prude [pryd] *a* prudish; – *nf* prude.
prudent [prydɑ̃] *a* (*circonspect*) cautious, careful; (*sage*) sensible. ◆**prudemment** [-amɑ̃] *adv* cautiously, carefully; (*sagement*) sensibly. ◆**prudence** *nf* caution, care, prudence; (*sagesse*) wisdom; **par p.** as a precaution.
prune [pryn] *nf* (*fruit*) plum. ◆**pruneau, -x** *nm* prune. ◆**prunelle** *nf* **1** (*fruit*) sloe. **2** (*de l'œil*) pupil. ◆**prunier** *nm* plum tree.
P.-S. [peɛs] *abrév* (*post-scriptum*) PS.
psaume [psom] *nm* psalm.
pseudo- [psødo] *préf* pseudo-.
pseudonyme [psødɔnim] *nm* pseudonym.
psychanalyse [psikanaliz] *nf* psychoanalysis. ◆**psychanalyste** *nmf* psychoanalyst.
psychiatre [psikjatr] *nmf* psychiatrist. ◆**psychiatrie** *nf* psychiatry. ◆**psychiatrique** *a* psychiatric.
psychique [psiʃik] *a* mental, psychic.
psycho [psiko] *préf* psycho-.
psychologie [psikɔlɔʒi] *nf* psychology. ◆**psychologique** *a* psychological. ◆**psychologue** *nmf* psychologist.
psychose [psikoz] *nf* psychosis.
PTT [petete] *nfpl* (*Postes, Télégraphes, Téléphones*) Post Office, = GPO.
pu [py] *voir* **pouvoir 1.**
puant [pɥɑ̃] *a* stinking. ◆**puanteur** *nf* stink, stench.
pub [pyb] *nf Fam* (*réclame*) advertising; (*annonce*) ad.
puberté [pybɛrte] *nf* puberty.
public, -ique [pyblik] *a* public; **dette publique** national debt; – *nm* public; (*de spectacle*) audience; **le grand p.** the general public; **en p.** in public. ◆**publiquement** *adv* publicly.
publication [pyblikɑsjɔ̃] *nf* (*action, livre etc*) publication. ◆**publier** *vt* to publish.
publicité [pyblisite] *nf* publicity (**pour** for); (*réclame*) advertising, publicity; (*annonce*) advertisement; *Rad TV* commercial. ◆**publicitaire** *a* (*agence, film*) publicity-, advertising-.
puce [pys] *nf* **1** flea; **le marché aux puces, les puces** the flea market. **2** (*d'un ordinateur*) chip, microchip.
puceron [pysrɔ̃] *nm* greenfly.
pudeur [pydœr] *nf* (sense of) modesty; **attentat à la p.** *Jur* indecency. ◆**pudibond** *a* prudish. ◆**pudique** *a* modest.
puer [pɥe] *vi* to stink; – *vt* to stink of.
puériculture [pɥerikyltyr] *nf* infant care, child care. ◆**puéricultrice** *nf* children's nurse.
puéril [pɥeril] *a* puerile. ◆**puérilité** *nf* puerility.
puis [pɥi] *adv* then; **et p. quoi?** and so what?
puiser [pɥize] *vt* to draw, take (**dans** from); – *vi* **p. dans** to dip into.
puisque [pɥisk(ə)] *conj* since, as.
puissant [pɥisɑ̃] *a* powerful. ◆**puissamment** *adv* powerfully. ◆**puissance** *nf* (*force, nation*) & *Math Tech* power; **en p.** (*talent, danger etc*) potential.
puits [pɥi] *nm* well; (*de mine*) shaft.
pull(-over) [pyl(ɔvɛr)] *nm* pullover, sweater.
pulluler [pylyle] *vi Péj* to swarm.
pulmonaire [pylmɔnɛr] *a* (*congestion, maladie*) of the lungs, lung-.

pulpe [pylp] *nf* (*de fruits*) pulp.
pulsation [pylsasjɔ̃] *nf* (heart)beat.
pulvériser [pylverize] *vt* (*broyer*) & *Fig* to pulverize; (*liquide*) to spray. ◆**pulvérisateur** *nm* spray, atomizer. ◆**pulvérisation** *nf* (*de liquide*) spraying.
punaise [pynez] *nf* **1** (*insecte*) bug. **2** (*clou*) drawing pin, *Am* thumbtack. ◆**punaiser** *vt* (*fixer*) to pin (up).
punch [pɔ̃ʃ] *nm* **1** (*boisson*) punch. **2** [pœnʃ] (*énergie*) punch.
punir [pynir] *vt* to punish. ◆**punissable** *a* punishable (**de** by). ◆**punition** *nf* punishment.
pupille [pypij] **1** *nf* (*de l'œil*) pupil. **2** *nmf* (*enfant sous tutelle*) ward.
pupitre [pypitr] *nm* (*d'écolier*) desk; (*d'orateur*) lectern; **p. à musique** music stand.
pur [pyr] *a* pure; (*alcool*) neat, straight. ◆**purement** *adv* purely. ◆**pureté** *nf* purity.
purée [pyre] *nf* purée; **p. (de pommes de terre)** mashed potatoes, mash.
purgatoire [pyrgatwar] *nm* purgatory.
purge [pyrʒ] *nf Pol Méd* purge.
purger [pyrʒe] *vt* **1** (*conduite*) *Tech* to drain, clear. **2** (*peine*) *Jur* to serve.
purifier [pyrifje] *vt* to purify. ◆**purification** *nf* purification.
purin [pyrɛ̃] *nm* liquid manure.
puriste [pyrist] *nmf Gram* purist.
puritain, -aine [pyritɛ̃, -ɛn] *a* & *nmf* puritan.
pur-sang [pyrsɑ̃] *nm inv* (*cheval*) thoroughbred.
pus¹ [py] *nm* (*liquide*) pus, matter.
pus², put [py] *voir* **pouvoir 1**.
putain [pytɛ̃] *nf Péj Fam* whore.
putois [pytwa] *nm* (*animal*) polecat.
putréfier [pytrefje] *vt*, — **se p.** *vpr* to putrefy. ◆**putréfaction** *nf* putrefaction.
puzzle [pœzl] *nm* (jigsaw) puzzle, jigsaw.
p.-v. [peve] *nm inv* (*procès-verbal*) (traffic) fine.
PVC [pevese] *nm* (*plastique*) PVC.
pygmée [pigme] *nm* pygmy.
pyjama [piʒama] *nm* pyjamas, *Am* pajamas; **un p.** a pair of pyjamas *ou Am* pajamas; **de p.** (*veste, pantalon*) pyjama-, *Am* pajama-.
pylône [pilon] *nm* pylon.
pyramide [piramid] *nf* pyramid.
Pyrénées [pirene] *nfpl* **les P.** the Pyrenees.
pyromane [pirɔman] *nmf* arsonist, firebug.
python [pitɔ̃] *nm* (*serpent*) python.

Q

Q, q [ky] *nm* Q, q.
QI [kyi] *nm inv abrév* (*quotient intellectuel*) IQ.
qu' [k] *voir* **que**.
quadrill/er [kadrije] *vt* (*troupes, police*) to be positioned throughout, comb, cover (*town etc*). ◆**—é** *a* (*papier*) squared. ◆**—age** *nm* (*lignes*) squares.
quadrupède [k(w)adryped] *nm* quadruped.
quadruple [k(w)adrypl] *a* **q. de** fourfold; — *nm* **le q. de** four times as much as. ◆**quadrupl/er** *vti* to quadruple. ◆**—és, -ées** *nmfpl* (*enfants*) quadruplets, quads.
quai [ke] *nm Nau* quay; (*pour marchandises*) wharf; (*de fleuve*) embankment, bank; *Rail* platform.
qualification [kalifikasjɔ̃] *nf* **1** description. **2** (*action*) *Sp* qualifying, qualification. ◆**qualificatif** *nm* (*mot*) term. ◆**qualifi/er 1** *vt* (*décrire*) to describe (**de** as); **se faire q. de menteur/*etc*** to be called a liar/*etc*. **2** *vt* (*rendre apte*) & *Sp* to qualify (**pour qch** for sth, **pour faire** to do); — **se q.** *vpr Sp* to qualify (**pour** for). **3** *vt Gram* to qualify. ◆**—é** *a* qualified (**pour faire** to do); (*ouvrier, main-d'œuvre*) skilled.
qualité [kalite] *nf* quality; (*condition sociale etc*) occupation, status; **produit/*etc* de q.** high-quality product/*etc*; **en sa q. de** in one's capacity as. ◆**qualitatif, -ive** *a* qualitative.
quand [kɑ̃] *conj* & *adv* when; **q. je viendrai** when I come; **c'est pour q.?** (*réunion, mariage*) when is it?; **q. bien même vous le feriez** even if you did it; **q. même** all the same.
quant (à) [kɑ̃ta] *prép* as for.
quantité [kɑ̃tite] *nf* quantity; **une q., des quantités** (*beaucoup*) a lot (**de** of); **en q.** (*abondamment*) in plenty. ◆**quantifier** *vt* to quantify. ◆**quantitatif, -ive** *a* quantitative.
quarante [karɑ̃t] *a* & *nm* forty. ◆**quarantaine** *nf* **1 une q. (de)** (*nombre*)

(about) forty; **avoir la q.** (*âge*) to be about forty. **2** *Méd* quarantine; **mettre en q.** *Méd* to quarantine; *Fig* to send to Coventry, *Am* give the silent treatment to. ◆**quarantième** *a & nmf* fortieth.

quart [kar] *nm* **1** quarter; **q. (de litre)** quarter litre, quarter of a litre; **q. d'heure** quarter of an hour; **un mauvais q. d'heure** *Fig* a trying time; **une heure et q.** an hour and a quarter; **il est une heure et q.** it's a quarter past *ou Am* after one; **une heure moins le q.** a quarter to one. **2** *Nau* watch; **de q.** on watch.

quartette [kwartɛt] *nm* (jazz) quartet(te).

quartier [kartje] **1** *nm* neighbourhood, district; (*chinois etc*) quarter; **de q.** (*cinéma etc*) local; **les gens du q.** the local people. **2** *nm* (*de pomme, lune*) quarter; (*d'orange*) segment. **3** *nm(pl)* **quartier(s)** *Mil* quarters; **q. général** headquarters.

quartz [kwarts] *nm* quartz; **montre/***etc* **à q.** quartz watch/*etc*.

quasi [kazi] *adv* almost. ◆**quasi-** *préf* near; **q.-obscurité** near darkness. ◆**quasiment** *adv* almost.

quatorze [katɔrz] *a & nm* fourteen. ◆**quatorzième** *a & nmf* fourteenth.

quatre [katr] *a & nm* four; **se mettre en q.** to go out of one's way (**pour faire** to do); **son q. heures** (*goûter*) one's afternoon snack; **un de ces q.** *Fam* some day soon. ◆**quatrième** *a & nmf* fourth. ◆**quatrièmement** *adv* fourthly.

quatre-vingt(s) [katrəvɛ̃] *a & nm* eighty; **q.-vingts ans** eighty years; **q.-vingt-un** eighty-one. ◆**q.-vingt-dix** *a & nm* ninety.

quatuor [kwatɥɔr] *nm Mus* quartet(te).

que [k(ə)] (**qu'** *before a vowel or mute h*) **1** *conj* that; **je pense qu'elle restera** I think (that) she'll stay; **qu'elle vienne ou non** whether she comes or not; **qu'il s'en aille!** let him leave!; **ça fait un an q. je suis là** I've been here for a year; **ça fait un an q. je suis parti** I left a year ago. **2 (ne)... q.** only; **tu n'as qu'un franc** you only have one franc. **3** (*comparaison*) than; (*avec aussi, même, tel, autant*) as; **plus/moins âgé q. lui** older/younger than him; **aussi sage/***etc* **q.** as wise/*etc* as; **le même q.** the same as. **4** *adv* **(ce) qu'il est bête!** (*comme*) how silly he is!; **q. de gens!** (*combien*) what a lot of people! **5** *pron rel* (*chose*) that, which; (*personne*) that, whom; (*temps*) when; **le livre q. j'ai** the book (that *ou* which) I have; **l'ami q. j'ai** the friend (that *ou* whom) I have; **un jour/mois/***etc* **q.** one day/month/*etc* when. **6** *pron interrogatif* what; **q. fait-il?, qu'est-ce qu'il fait?** what is he doing?; **qu'est-ce qui est dans ta poche?** what's in your pocket?; **q. préférez-vous?** which do you prefer?

Québec [kebɛk] *nm* **le Q.** Quebec.

quel, quelle [kɛl] **1** *a interrogatif* what, which; (*qui*) who; **q. livre/acteur?** what *ou* which book/actor?; **q. livre/acteur préférez-vous?** which *ou* what book/actor do you prefer?; **q. est cet homme?** who is that man?; **je sais q. est ton but** I know what your aim is; **q. qu'il soit** (*chose*) whatever it may be; (*personne*) whoever it *ou* he may be; – *pron interrogatif* which (one); **q. est le meilleur?** which (one) is the best? **2** *a exclamatif* **q. idiot!** what a fool!; **q. joli bébé!** what a pretty baby!

quelconque [kɛlkɔ̃k] *a* **1** any, some (or other); **une raison q.** any reason (whatever *ou* at all), some reason (or other). **2** (*banal*) ordinary.

quelque [kɛlk(ə)] **1** *a* some; **q. jour** some day; **quelques femmes** a few women, some women; **les quelques amies qu'elle** a the few friends she has. **2** *adv* (*environ*) about, some; **et q.** *Fam* and a bit; **q. grand qu'il soit** however tall he may be; **q. numéro qu'elle choisisse** whichever number she chooses; **q. peu** somewhat. **3** *pron* **q. chose** something; (*interrogation*) anything, something; **il a q. chose** *Fig* there's something the matter with him; **q. chose d'autre** something else; **q. chose de grand/***etc* something big/*etc*. **4** *adv* **q. part** somewhere; (*interrogation*) anywhere, somewhere.

quelquefois [kɛlkəfwa] *adv* sometimes.

quelques-uns, -unes [kɛlkəzœ̃, -yn] *pron pl* some.

quelqu'un [kɛlkœ̃] *pron* someone, somebody; (*interrogation*) anyone, anybody, someone, somebody; **q. d'intelligent/***etc* someone clever/*etc*.

quémander [kemɑ̃de] *vt* to beg for.

qu'en-dira-t-on [kɑ̃diratɔ̃] *nm inv* (*propos*) gossip.

quenelle [kənɛl] *nf Culin* quenelle, fish *ou* meat roll.

querelle [kərɛl] *nf* quarrel, dispute. ◆**se quereller** *vpr* to quarrel. ◆**querelleur, -euse** *a* quarrelsome.

question [kɛstjɔ̃] *nf* question; (*affaire, problème*) matter, issue, question; **il est q. de** it's a matter *ou* question of (**faire** doing); (*on projette de*) there's some question of (**faire** doing); **il n'en est pas q.** there's no question of it, it's out of the question; **en q.** in question; **hors de q.** out of the question;

(re)mettre en q. to (call in) question. ◆**questionner** *vt* to question (sur about).

quête [kɛt] *nf* **1** (*collecte*) collection. **2** (*recherche*) quest (**de** for); **en q. de** in quest *ou* search of. ◆**quêter** *vt* to seek, beg for; – *vi* to collect money.

queue [kø] *nf* **1** (*d'animal*) tail; (*de fleur*) stalk, stem; (*de fruit*) stalk; (*de poêle*) handle; (*de comète*) trail; (*de robe*) train; (*de cortège, train*) rear; **q. de cheval** (*coiffure*) ponytail; **faire une q. de poisson** *Aut* to cut in (**à qn** in front of s.o.); **à la q. de** (*classe*) at the bottom of; **à la q. leu leu** (*marcher*) in single file. **2** (*file*) queue, *Am* line; **faire la q.** to queue up, *Am* line up. **3** (*de billard*) cue. ◆**q.-de-pie** *nf* (*pl* **queues-de-pie**) (*habit*) tails.

qui [ki] *pron* (*personne*) who, that; (*interrogatif*) who; (*après prép*) whom; (*chose*) which, that; **l'homme q.** the man who *ou* that; **la maison q.** the house which *ou* that; **q.?** who?; **q. (est-ce q.) est là?** who's there?; **q. désirez-vous voir?, q. est-ce que vous désirez voir?** who(m) do you want to see?; **sans q.** without whom; **la femme de q. je parle** the woman I'm talking about *ou* about whom I'm talking; **l'ami sur l'aide de q. je compte** the friend on whose help I rely; **q. que vous soyez** whoever you are, whoever you may be; **q. que ce soit** anyone (at all); **à q. est ce livre?** whose book is this?

quiche [kiʃ] *nf* (*tarte*) quiche.

quiconque [kikɔ̃k] *pron* (*celui qui*) whoever; (*n'importe qui*) anyone.

quignon [kiɲɔ̃] *nm* chunk (of bread).

quille [kij] *nf* **1** (*de navire*) keel. **2** (*de jeu*) skittle; *pl* (*jeu*) skittles, ninepins. **3** (*jambe*) *Fam* leg.

quincaillier, -ière [kɛ̃kaje, -jɛr] *nmf* hardware dealer, ironmonger. ◆**quincaillerie** *nf* hardware; (*magasin*) hardware shop.

quinine [kinin] *nf Méd* quinine.

quinquennal, -aux [kɛ̃kenal, -o] *a* (*plan*) five-year.

quinte [kɛ̃t] *nf Méd* coughing fit.

quintessence [kɛ̃tesɑ̃s] *nf* quintessence.

quintette [kɛ̃tɛt] *nm Mus* quintet(te).

quintuple [kɛ̃typl] *a* **q. de** fivefold; – *nm* **le q. de** five times as much as. ◆**quintupl/er** *vti* to increase fivefold. ◆**—és, -ées** *nmfpl* (*enfants*) quintuplets, quins.

quinze [kɛ̃z] *a & nm* fifteen; **q. jours** two weeks, fortnight. ◆**quinzaine** *nf* **une q. (de)** (*nombre*) (about) fifteen; **q. (de jours)** two weeks, fortnight. ◆**quinzième** *a & nmf* fifteenth.

quiproquo [kiprɔko] *nm* misunderstanding.

quittance [kitɑ̃s] *nf* receipt.

quitte [kit] *a* quits, even (**envers** with); **q. à faire** even if it means doing; **en être q. pour une amende/***etc* to (be lucky enough to) get off with a fine/*etc*.

quitter [kite] *vt* to leave; (*ôter*) to take off; – *vi* **ne quittez pas!** *Tél* hold the line!, hold on!; **— se q.** *vpr* (*se séparer*) to part.

qui-vive (sur le) [syrləkiviv] *adv* on the alert.

quoi [kwa] *pron* what; (*après prép*) which; **à q. penses-tu?** what are you thinking about?; **après q.** after which; **ce à q. je m'attendais** what I was expecting; **de q. manger/***etc* (*assez*) enough to eat/*etc*; **de q. couper/écrire/***etc* (*instrument*) something to cut/write/*etc* with; **q. que je dise** whatever I say; **q. que ce soit** anything (at all); **q. qu'il en soit** be that as it may; **il n'y a pas de q.!** (*en réponse à 'merci'*) don't mention it!; **q.?** what?; **c'est un idiot, q.!** (*non traduit*) *Fam* he's a fool!

quoique [kwak(ə)] *conj* (+ *sub*) (al)though.

quolibet [kɔlibɛ] *nm Litt* gibe.

quorum [k(w)ɔrɔm] *nm* quorum.

quota [k(w)ɔta] *nm* quota.

quote-part [kɔtpar] *nf* (*pl* **quotes-parts**) share.

quotidien, -ienne [kɔtidjɛ̃, -jɛn] *a* (*journalier*) daily; (*banal*) everyday; – *nm* daily (paper). ◆**quotidiennement** *adv* daily.

quotient [kɔsjɑ̃] *nm* quotient.

R

R, r [ɛr] *nm* R, r.

rabâch/er [rabɑʃe] *vt* to repeat endlessly; – *vi* to repeat oneself ◆**—age** *nm* endless repetition.

rabais [rabɛ] *nm* (price) reduction, discount; **au r.** (*acheter*) cheap, at a reduction.

rabaisser [rabese] *vt* (*dénigrer*) to belittle, humble; **r. à** (*ravaler*) to reduce to.

rabat-joie [rabaʒwa] *nm inv* killjoy.

rabattre* [rabatr] *vt* (*baisser*) to put *ou* pull down; (*refermer*) to close (down); (*replier*) to fold down *ou* over; (*déduire*) to take off; **en r.** (*prétentieux*) *Fig* to climb down (from one's high horse); — **se r.** *vpr* (*se refermer*) to close; (*après avoir doublé*) *Aut* to cut in (**devant** in front of); **se r. sur** *Fig* to fall back on.

rabbin [rabɛ̃] *nm* rabbi; **grand r.** chief rabbi.

rabibocher [rabibɔʃe] *vt* (*réconcilier*) *Fam* to patch it up between; — **se r.** *vpr Fam* to patch it up.

rabiot [rabjo] *nm* (*surplus*) *Fam* extra (helping); **faire du r.** *Fam* to work extra time.

râblé [rɑble] *a* stocky, thickset.

rabot [rabo] *nm* (*outil*) plane. ◆**raboter** *vt* to plane.

raboteux, -euse [rabɔtø, -øz] *a* uneven, rough.

rabougri [rabugri] *a* (*personne, plante*) stunted.

rabrouer [rabrue] *vt* to snub, rebuff.

racaille [rakɑj] *nf* rabble, riffraff.

raccommod/er [rakɔmɔde] **1** *vt* to mend; (*chaussette*) to darn. **2** *vt* (*réconcilier*) *Fam* to reconcile; — **se r.** *vpr Fam* to make it up (**avec** with). ◆**—age** *nm* mending; darning.

raccompagner [rakɔ̃paɲe] *vt* to see *ou* take back (home); **r. à la porte** to see to the door, see out.

raccord [rakɔr] *nm* (*dispositif*) connection; (*de papier peint*) join; **r. (de peinture)** touch-up. ◆**raccord/er** *vt*, — **se r.** *vpr* to connect (up), join (up) (**à** with, to). ◆**—ement** *nm* (*action, résultat*) connection.

raccourc/ir [rakursir] *vt* to shorten; – *vi* to get shorter; (*au lavage*) to shrink. ◆**—i** *nm* **1** (*chemin*) short cut. **2 en r.** (*histoire etc*) in a nutshell.

raccroc (par) [parrakro] *adv* by (a lucky) chance.

raccrocher [rakrɔʃe] *vt* to hang back up; (*récepteur*) *Tél* to put down; (*relier*) to connect (**à** with, to); (*client*) to accost; **se r. à** to hold on to, cling to; (*se rapporter à*) to link (up) with; – *vi Tél* to hang up, ring off.

race [ras] *nf* (*groupe ethnique*) race; (*animale*) breed; (*famille*) stock; (*engeance*) *Péj* breed; **de r.** (*chien*) pedigree-; (*cheval*) thoroughbred. ◆**racé** *a* (*chien*) pedigree-; (*cheval*) thoroughbred; (*personne*) distinguished. ◆**racial, -aux** *a* racial. ◆**racisme** *nm* racism, racialism. ◆**raciste** *a* & *nmf* racist, racialist.

rachat [raʃa] *nm Com* repurchase; (*de firme*) take-over; *Rel* redemption. ◆**racheter** *vt* to buy back; (*objet d'occasion*) to buy; (*nouvel article*) to buy another; (*firme*) to take over, buy out; (*pécheur, dette*) to redeem; (*compenser*) to make up for; **r. des chaussettes/du pain/***etc* to buy (some) more socks/bread/*etc*; — **se r.** *vpr* to make amends, redeem oneself.

racine [rasin] *nf* (*de plante, personne etc*) & *Math* root; **prendre r.** (*plante*) & *Fig* to take root.

racket [rakɛt] *nm* (*association*) racket; (*activité*) racketeering.

raclée [rɑkle] *nf Fam* hiding, thrashing.

racler [rɑkle] *vt* to scrape; (*enlever*) to scrape off; **se r. la gorge** to clear one's throat. ◆**raclette** *nf* scraper; (*à vitres*) squeegee. ◆**racloir** *nm* scraper. ◆**raclures** *nfpl* (*déchets*) scrapings.

racol/er [rakɔle] *vt* (*prostituée*) to solicit (*s.o.*); (*vendeur etc*) to tout for (*s.o.*), solicit (*s.o.*). ◆**—age** *nm* soliciting; touting. ◆**—eur, -euse** *nmf* tout.

raconter [rakɔ̃te] *vt* (*histoire*) to tell, relate; (*décrire*) to describe; **r. qch à qn** (*vacances etc*) to tell s.o. about sth; **r. à qn que** to tell s.o. that, say to s.o. that. ◆**racontars** *nmpl* gossip, stories.

racornir [rakɔrnir] *vt* to harden; — **se r.** *vpr* to get hard.

radar [radar] *nm* radar; **contrôle r.** (*pour véhicules etc*) radar control. ◆**radariste** *nmf* radar operator.

rade [rad] *nf* **1** *Nau* (natural) harbour. **2 laisser en r.** to leave stranded, abandon; **rester en r.** to be left behind.

radeau, -x [rado] *nm* raft.

radiateur [radjatœr] *nm* (*à eau*) & *Aut* radiator; (*électrique, à gaz*) heater.

radiation [radjɑsjɔ̃] *nf* **1** *Phys* radiation. **2** (*suppression*) removal (**de** from).

radical, -ale, -aux [radikal, -o] *a* radical; – *nm Ling* stem; – *nmf Pol* radical.

radier [radje] *vt* to strike *ou* cross off (**de** from).

radieux, -euse [radjø, -øz] *a* (*personne, visage*) radiant, beaming; (*soleil*) brilliant; (*temps*) glorious.

radin, -ine [radɛ̃, -in] *a Fam* stingy; – *nmf Fam* skinflint.

radio [radjo] **1** *nf* radio; (*poste*) radio (set); **à la r.** on the radio. **2** *nf* (*photo*) *Méd* X-ray; **passer** *ou* **faire une r.** to be X-rayed, have an X-ray. **3** *nm* (*opérateur*) radio operator. ◆**radioactif, -ive** *a* radioactive. ◆**radioactivité** *nf* radioactivity. ◆**radiodiffuser** *vt* to broadcast (on the radio). ◆**radio-**

diffusion *nf* broadcasting. ◆**radiographie** *nf* (*photo*) X-ray; (*technique*) radiography. ◆**radiographier** *vt* to X-ray. ◆**radiologie** *nf Méd* radiology. ◆**radiologue** *nmf* (*technicien*) radiographer; (*médecin*) radiologist. ◆**radiophonique** *a* (*programme*) radio-. ◆**radiotélévisé** *a* broadcast on radio and television.

radis [radi] *nm* radish; **r. noir** horseradish.

radot/er [radɔte] *vi* to drivel (on), ramble (on). ◆**—age** *nm* (*propos*) drivel.

radouc/ir (se) [səradusir] *vpr* to calm down; (*temps*) to become milder. ◆**—issement** *nm* **r. (du temps)** milder weather.

rafale [rafal] *nf* (*vent*) gust, squall; (*de mitrailleuse*) burst; (*de balles*) hail.

raffermir [rafɛrmir] *vt* to strengthen; (*muscles etc*) to tone up; **— se r.** *vpr* to become stronger.

raffin/er [rafine] *vt* (*pétrole, sucre, manières*) to refine. ◆**—é** *a* refined. ◆**—age** *nm* (*du pétrole, sucre*) refining. ◆**—ement** *nm* (*de personne*) refinement. ◆**raffinerie** *nf* refinery.

raffoler [rafɔle] *vi* **r. de** (*aimer*) to be very fond of, be mad *ou* wild about.

raffut [rafy] *nm Fam* din, row.

rafiot [rafjo] *nm* (*bateau*) *Péj* (old) tub.

rafistoler [rafistɔle] *vt Fam* to patch up.

rafle [rɑfl] *nf* (police) raid.

rafler [rɑfle] *vt* (*enlever*) *Fam* to swipe, make off with.

rafraîch/ir [rafreʃir] *vt* to cool (down); (*remettre à neuf*) to brighten up; (*mémoire, personne*) to refresh; – *vi* **mettre à r.** *Culin* to chill; **— se r.** *vpr* (*boire*) to refresh oneself; (*se laver*) to freshen (oneself) up; (*temps*) to get cooler. ◆**—issant** *a* refreshing. ◆**—issement** *nm* **1** (*de température*) cooling. **2** (*boisson*) cold drink; *pl* (*fruits, glaces etc*) refreshments.

ragaillardir [ragajardir] *vt* to buck up.

rage [raʒ] *nf* **1** (*colère*) rage; **r. de dents** violent toothache; **faire r.** (*incendie, tempête*) to rage. **2** (*maladie*) rabies. ◆**rager** *vi* (*personne*) *Fam* to rage, fume. ◆**rageant** *a Fam* infuriating. ◆**rageur, -euse** *a* bad-tempered, furious.

ragots [rago] *nmpl Fam* gossip.

ragoût [ragu] *nm Culin* stew.

ragoûtant [ragutɑ̃] *a* **peu r.** (*mets, personne*) unsavoury.

raid [rɛd] *nm* (*incursion, attaque*) *Mil Av* raid.

raide [rɛd] *a* (*rigide, guindé*) stiff; (*côte*) steep; (*cheveux*) straight; (*corde etc*) tight; **c'est r.!** (*exagéré*) *Fam* it's a bit stiff *ou* much!; – *adv* (*grimper*) steeply; **tomber r. mort** to drop dead. ◆**raideur** *nf* stiffness; steepness. ◆**raidillon** *nm* (*pente*) short steep rise. ◆**raidir** *vt*, **— se r.** *vpr* to stiffen; (*corde*) to tighten; (*position*) to harden; **se r. contre** *Fig* to steel oneself against.

raie [rɛ] *nf* **1** (*trait*) line; (*de tissu, zèbre*) stripe; (*de cheveux*) parting, *Am* part. **2** (*poisson*) skate, ray.

rail [rɑj] *nm* (*barre*) rail; **le r.** (*transport*) rail.

railler [rɑje] *vt* to mock, make fun of. ◆**raillerie** *nf* gibe, mocking remark. ◆**railleur, -euse** *a* mocking.

rainure [renyr] *nf* groove.

raisin [rezɛ̃] *nm* **raisin(s)** grapes; **grain de r.** grape; **manger du r.** *ou* **des raisins** to eat grapes; **r. sec** raisin.

raison [rɛzɔ̃] *nf* **1** (*faculté, motif*) reason; **entendre r.** to listen to reason; **la r. pour laquelle je . . .** the reason (why *ou* that) I . . . ; **pour raisons de famille/de santé/***etc* for family/health/*etc* reasons; **en r. de** (*cause*) on account of; **à r. de** (*proportion*) at the rate of; **avoir r. de qn/de qch** to get the better of s.o./sth; **mariage de r.** marriage of convenience; **à plus forte r.** all the more so; **r. de plus** all the more reason (**pour faire** to do, for doing). **2 avoir r.** to be right (**de faire** to do, in doing); **donner r. à qn** to agree with s.o.; (*évènement etc*) to prove s.o. right; **avec r.** rightly. ◆**raisonnable** *a* reasonable. ◆**raisonnablement** *adv* reasonably.

raisonn/er [rezɔne] *vi* (*penser*) to reason; (*discuter*) to argue; – *vt* **r. qn** to reason with s.o. ◆**—é** *a* (*projet*) well-thought-out. ◆**—ement** *nm* (*faculté, activité*) reasoning; (*propositions*) argument. ◆**—eur, -euse** *a Péj* argumentative; – *nmf Péj* arguer.

rajeun/ir [raʒœnir] *vt* to make (feel *ou* look) younger; (*personnel*) to infuse new blood into; (*moderniser*) to modernize, update; (*personne âgée*) *Méd* to rejuvenate; – *vi* to get *ou* feel *ou* look younger. ◆**—issant** *a Méd* rejuvenating. ◆**—issement** *nm Méd* rejuvenation; **le r. de la population** the population getting younger.

rajout [raʒu] *nm* addition. ◆**rajouter** *vt* to add (**à** to); **en r.** *Fig* to overdo it.

rajuster [raʒyste] *vt* (*mécanisme*) to readjust; (*lunettes, vêtements*) to straighten, adjust; (*cheveux*) to rearrange; **— se r.** *vpr* to straighten *ou* tidy oneself up.

râle [rɑl] *nm* (*de blessé*) groan; (*de mourant*) death rattle. ◆**râler** *vi* (*blessé*) to groan; (*mourant*) to give the death rattle; (*protes-

er) *Fam* to grouse, moan. ◆**râleur, -euse** *nmf Fam* grouser, moaner.
ralent/ir [ralɑ̃tir] *vti*, — **se r.** *vpr* to slow down. ◆—**i** *nm Cin TV* slow motion; **au r.** (*filmer, travailler*) in slow motion; (*vivre*) at a slower pace; **tourner au r.** (*moteur, usine*) to idle, tick over, *Am* turn over.
rallier [ralje] *vt* (*rassembler*) to rally; (*rejoindre*) to rejoin; **r. qn à** (*convertir*) to win s.o. over to; — **se r.** *vpr* (*se regrouper*) to rally; **se r. à** (*point de vue*) to come over *ou* round to.
rallonge [ralɔ̃ʒ] *nf* (*de table*) extension; (*fil électrique*) extension (lead); **une r. (de)** (*supplément*) *Fam* (some) extra. ◆**rallonger** *vti* to lengthen.
rallumer [ralyme] *vt* to light again, relight; (*lampe*) to switch on again; (*conflit, haine*) to rekindle; — **se r.** *vpr* (*guerre, incendie*) to flare up again.
rallye [rali] *nm Sp Aut* rally.
ramage [ramaʒ] **1** *nm* (*d'oiseaux*) song, warbling. **2** *nmpl* (*dessin*) foliage.
ramass/er [ramɑse] **1** *vt* (*prendre par terre, réunir*) to pick up; (*ordures, copies*) to collect, pick up; (*fruits, coquillages*) to gather; (*rhume, amende*) *Fam* to pick up, get; **r. une bûche** *ou* **une pelle** *Fam* to come a cropper, *Am* take a spill. **2 se r.** *vpr* (*se pelotonner*) to curl up. ◆—**é** *a* (*trapu*) squat, stocky; (*recroquevillé*) huddled; (*concis*) compact. ◆—**age** *nm* picking up; collection; gathering; **r. scolaire** school bus service.
ramassis [ramɑsi] *nm* **r. de** (*voyous etc*) *Péj* bunch of.
rambarde [rɑ̃bard] *nf* guardrail.
rame [ram] *nf* **1** (*aviron*) oar. **2** (*de métro*) train. **3** (*de papier*) ream. ◆**ramer** *vi* to row. ◆**rameur, -euse** *nmf* rower.
rameau, -x [ramo] *nm* branch; **les Rameaux** *Rel* Palm Sunday.
ramener [ramne] *vt* to bring *ou* take back; (*paix, calme, ordre etc*) to restore, bring back; (*remettre en place*) to put back; **r. à** (*réduire à*) to reduce to; **r. à la vie** to bring back to life; — **se r.** *vpr* (*arriver*) *Fam* to turn up; **se r. à** (*problème etc*) to boil down to.
ramier [ramje] *nm* **(pigeon) r.** wood pigeon.
ramification [ramifikɑsjɔ̃] *nf* ramification.
ramoll/ir [ramɔlir] *vt*, — **se r.** *vpr* to soften. ◆—**i** *a* soft; (*personne*) soft-headed.
ramon/er [ramɔne] *vt* (*cheminée*) to sweep. ◆—**age** *nm* (chimney) sweeping. ◆—**eur** *nm* (chimney)sweep.
rampe [rɑ̃p] *nf* **1** (*pente*) ramp, slope; **r. de lancement** (*de fusées etc*) launch(ing) pad. **2** (*d'escalier*) banister(s). **3** (*projecteurs*) *Th* footlights.
ramper [rɑ̃pe] *vi* to crawl; (*plante*) to creep; **r. devant** *Fig* to cringe *ou* crawl to.
rancard [rɑ̃kar] *nm Fam* (*rendez-vous*) date; (*renseignement*) tip.
rancart [rɑ̃kar] *nm* **mettre au r.** *Fam* to throw out, scrap.
rance [rɑ̃s] *a* rancid. ◆**rancir** *vi* to turn rancid.
ranch [rɑ̃tʃ] *nm* ranch.
rancœur [rɑ̃kœr] *nf* rancour, resentment.
rançon [rɑ̃sɔ̃] *nf* ransom; **la r. de** (*inconvénient*) the price of (*success, fame etc*). ◆**rançonner** *vt* to hold to ransom.
rancune [rɑ̃kyn] *nf* grudge; **garder r. à qn** to bear s.o. a grudge; **sans r.!** no hard feelings! ◆**rancunier, -ière** *a* vindictive, resentful.
randonnée [rɑ̃dɔne] *nf* (*à pied*) walk, hike; (*en voiture*) drive, ride; (*en vélo*) ride.
rang [rɑ̃] *nm* (*rangée*) row, line; (*condition, grade, classement*) rank; **les rangs** (*hommes*) *Mil* the ranks (**de** of); **les rangs de ses ennemis** (*nombre*) *Fig* the ranks of his enemies; **se mettre en rang(s)** to line up (**par trois**/*etc* in threes/*etc*); **par r. de** in order of. ◆**rangée** *nf* row, line.
rang/er [rɑ̃ʒe] *vt* (*papiers, vaisselle etc*) to put away; (*chambre etc*) to tidy (up); (*chiffres, mots*) to arrange; (*voiture*) to park; **r. parmi** (*auteur etc*) to rank among; — **se r.** *vpr* (*élèves etc*) to line up; (*s'écarter*) to stand aside; (*voiture*) to pull over; (*s'assagir*) to settle down; **se r. à** (*avis de qn*) to fall in with. ◆—**é** *a* (*chambre etc*) tidy; (*personne*) steady; (*bataille*) pitched. ◆—**ement** *nm* putting away; (*de chambre etc*) tidying (up); (*espace*) storage space.
ranimer [ranime] *vt* (*réanimer, revigorer*) to revive; (*encourager*) to spur on; (*feu, querelle*) to rekindle.
rapace [rapas] **1** *a* (*avide*) grasping. **2** *nm* (*oiseau*) bird of prey.
rapatrier [rapatrije] *vt* to repatriate. ◆**rapatriement** *nm* repatriation.
râpe [rɑp] *nf Culin* grater; shredder; (*lime*) rasp. ◆**râp/er** *vt* (*fromage*) to grate; (*carottes etc*) to shred, (*finement*) to grate; (*bois*) to rasp. ◆—**é 1** *a* (*fromage*) grated; — *nm* grated cheese. **2** *a* (*vêtement*) threadbare.
rapetisser [raptise] *vt* to make (look) smaller; (*vêtement*) to shorten; — *vi* to get smaller; (*au lavage*) to shrink; (*jours*) to get shorter.
râpeux, -euse [rɑpø, -øz] *a* rough.

raphia [rafja] *nm* raffia.

rapide [rapid] *a* fast, quick, rapid; (*pente*) steep; – *nm* (*train*) express (train); (*de fleuve*) rapid. ◆**—ment** *adv* fast, quickly, rapidly. ◆**rapidité** *nf* speed, rapidity.

rapiécer [rapjese] *vt* to patch (up).

rappel [rapɛl] *nm* (*de diplomate etc*) recall; (*évocation, souvenir*) reminder; (*paiement*) back pay; *pl Th* curtain calls; **(vaccination de) r.** *Méd* booster; **r. à l'ordre** call to order. ◆**rappeler** *vt* (*pour faire revenir*) & *Tél* to call back; (*diplomate, souvenir*) to recall; **r. qch à qn** (*redire*) to remind s.o. of sth; – *vi Tél* to call back; – **se r.** *vpr* (*histoire, personne etc*) to remember, recall, recollect.

rappliquer [raplike] *vi* (*arriver*) *Fam* to show up.

rapport [rapɔr] *nm* **1** (*lien*) connection, link; *pl* (*entre personnes*) relations; **rapports (sexuels)** (sexual) intercourse; **par r. à** compared to *ou* with; (*envers*) towards; **se mettre en r. avec qn** to get in touch with s.o.; **en r. avec** in keeping with; **sous le r. de** from the point of view of. **2** (*revenu*) *Com* return, yield. **3** (*récit*) report. ◆**rapporter 1** *vt* (*ramener*) to bring *ou* take back; (*ajouter*) to add; – *vi* (*chien*) to retrieve. **2** *vt* (*récit*) to report; (*mot célèbre*) to repeat; – *vi* (*moucharder*) *Fam* to tell tales. **3** *vt* (*profit*) *Com* to bring in, yield; – *vi* (*investissement*) *Com* to bring in a good return. **4** *vt* **r. qch à** (*rattacher*) to relate sth to; **se r. à** to relate to, be connected with; **s'en r. à** to rely on. ◆**rapporteur, -euse 1** *nmf* (*mouchard*) telltale. **2** *nm Jur* reporter. **3** *nm Géom* protractor.

rapproch/er [raprɔʃe] *vt* to bring closer (**de** to); (*chaise*) to pull up (**de** to); (*réconcilier*) to bring together; (*réunir*) to join; (*comparer*) to compare; – **se r.** *vpr* to come *ou* get closer (**de** to); (*se réconcilier*) to come together, be reconciled; (*ressembler*) to be close (**de** to). ◆**—é** *a* close, near; (*yeux*) close-set; (*fréquent*) frequent. ◆**—ement** *nm* (*réconciliation*) reconciliation; (*rapport*) connection; (*comparaison*) comparison.

rapt [rapt] *nm* (*d'enfant*) abduction.

raquette [rakɛt] *nf* (*de tennis*) racket; (*de ping-pong*) bat.

rare [rar] *a* rare; (*argent, main-d'œuvre etc*) scarce; (*barbe, herbe*) sparse; **il est r. que** (+ *sub*) it's seldom *ou* rare that. ◆**se raréfier** *vpr* (*denrées etc*) to get scarce. ◆**rarement** *adv* rarely, seldom. ◆**rareté** *nf* rarity; scarcity; **une r.** (*objet*) a rarity.

ras [rɑ] *a* (*cheveux*) close-cropped; (*herbe, poil*) short; (*mesure*) full; **en rase campagne** in (the) open country; **à r. de** very close to; **à r. bord** (*remplir*) to the brim; **en avoir r. le bol** *Fam* to be fed up (**de** with); **pull (au) r. du cou** *ou* **à col r.** crew-neck(ed) pullover; – *adv* short.

ras/er [rɑze] **1** *vt* (*menton, personne*) to shave; (*barbe, moustache*) to shave off; – **se r.** *vpr* to (have a) shave. **2** *vt* (*démolir*) to raze, knock down. **3** *vt* (*frôler*) to skim, brush. **4** *vt* (*ennuyer*) *Fam* to bore. ◆**—ant** *a Fam* boring. ◆**—é** *a* **bien r.** clean-shaven; **mal r.** unshaven. ◆**—age** *nm* shaving. ◆**—eur, -euse** *nmf Fam* bore. ◆**rasoir 1** *nm* shaver. **2** *a inv Fam* boring.

rassasier [rasazje] *vti* to satisfy; **être rassasié** to have had enough (**de** of).

rassembler [rasɑ̃ble] *vt* to gather (together), assemble; (*courage*) to summon up, muster; – **se r.** *vpr* to gather, assemble. ◆**rassemblement** *nm* (*action, gens*) gathering.

rasseoir* (se) [səraswar] *vpr* to sit down again.

rassis, *f* rassie [rasi] *a* (*pain, brioche etc*) stale. ◆**rassir** *vti* to turn stale.

rassur/er [rasyre] *vt* to reassure; **rassure-toi** set your mind at rest, don't worry. ◆**—ant** *a* (*nouvelle*) reassuring, comforting.

rat [ra] *nm* rat; **r. de bibliothèque** *Fig* bookworm.

ratatiner (se) [səratatine] *vpr* to shrivel (up); (*vieillard*) to become wizened.

rate [rat] *nf Anat* spleen.

râteau, -x [rɑto] *nm* (*outil*) rake.

râtelier [rɑtəlje] *nm* **1** (*support pour outils, armes etc*) rack. **2** (*dentier*) *Fam* set of false teeth.

rat/er [rate] *vt* (*bus, cible, occasion etc*) to miss; (*gâcher*) to spoil, ruin; (*vie*) to waste; (*examen*) to fail; – *vi* (*projet etc*) to fail; (*pistolet*) to misfire. ◆**—é, -ée 1** *nmf* (*personne*) failure. **2** *nmpl* **avoir des ratés** *Aut* to backfire. ◆**—age** *nm* (*échec*) *Fam* failure.

ratifier [ratifje] *vt* to ratify. ◆**ratification** *nf* ratification.

ration [rɑsjɔ̃] *nf* ration; **r. de** *Fig* share of. ◆**rationn/er** *vt* (*vivres, personne*) to ration. ◆**—ement** *nm* rationing.

rationaliser [rasjɔnalize] *vt* to rationalize. ◆**rationalisation** *nf* rationalization.

rationnel, -elle [rasjɔnɛl] *a* (*pensée, méthode*) rational.

ratisser [ratise] *vt* **1** (*allée etc*) to rake; (*feuilles etc*) to rake up. **2** (*fouiller*) to comb. **3 r. qn** (*au jeu*) *Fam* to clean s.o. out.

raton [ratɔ̃] *nm* **r. laveur** rac(c)oon.

rattach/er [rataʃe] *vt* to tie up again; (*in-*

corporer, joindre) to join (à to); (*idée, question*) to link (à to); r. qn à (*son pays etc*) to bind s.o. to; se r. à to be linked to. ◆—ement *nm* (*annexion*) joining (à to).

rattrap/er [ratrape] *vt* to catch; (*prisonnier etc*) to recapture; (*erreur, temps perdu*) to make up for; r. qn (*rejoindre*) to catch up with s.o., catch s.o. up; — se r. *vpr* to catch up; (*se dédommager, prendre une compensation*) to make up for it; se r. à (*branche etc*) to catch hold of. ◆—age *nm* cours de r. *Scol* remedial classes; r. des prix/salaires adjustment of prices/wages (*to the cost of living*).

rature [ratyr] *nf* deletion. ◆**raturer** *vt* to delete, cross out.

rauque [rok] *a* (*voix*) hoarse, raucous.

ravages [ravaʒ] *nmpl* devastation; (*de la maladie, du temps*) ravages; faire des r. to wreak havoc. ◆**ravager** *vt* to devastate, ravage.

raval/er [ravale] *vt* **1** (*façade etc*) to clean (and restore). **2** (*salive, sanglots*) to swallow. **3** (*avilir*) *Litt* to lower. ◆—ement *nm* (*de façade etc*) cleaning (and restoration).

ravi [ravi] *a* delighted (de with, de faire to do).

ravier [ravje] *nm* hors-d'œuvre dish.

ravigoter [ravigɔte] *vt Fam* to buck up.

ravin [ravɛ̃] *nm* ravine, gully.

ravioli [ravjɔli] *nmpl* ravioli.

rav/ir [ravir] *vt* **1** to delight; à r. (*chanter etc*) delightfully. **2** (*emporter*) to snatch (à from). ◆—issant *a* delightful, lovely. ◆**ravisseur, -euse** *nmf* kidnapper.

raviser (se) [səravize] *vpr* to change one's mind.

ravitaill/er [ravitaje] *vt* to provide with supplies, supply; (*avion*) to refuel; — se r. *vpr* to stock up (with supplies). ◆—ement *nm* supplying; refuelling; (*denrées*) supplies; aller au r. (*faire des courses*) *Fam* to stock up, get stocks in.

raviver [ravive] *vt* (*feu, sentiment*) to revive; (*couleurs*) to brighten up.

ray/er [reje] *vt* (*érafler*) to scratch; (*mot etc*) to cross out; r. qn de (*liste*) to cross ou strike s.o. off. ◆—é *a* scratched; (*tissu*) striped; (*papier*) lined, ruled. ◆**rayure** *nf* scratch; (*bande*) stripe; à rayures striped.

rayon [rɛjɔ̃] *nm* **1** (*de lumière, soleil etc*) *Phys* ray; (*de cercle*) radius; (*de roue*) spoke; (*d'espoir*) *Fig* ray; r. X X-ray; r. d'action range; dans un r. de within a radius of. **2** (*planche*) shelf; (*de magasin*) department. **3** (*de ruche*) honeycomb. ◆**rayonnage** *nm* shelving, shelves.

rayonn/er [rɛjɔne] *vi* to radiate; (*dans une région*) to travel around (*from a central base*); r. de joie to beam with joy. ◆—ant *a* (*visage etc*) radiant, beaming (de with). ◆—ement *nm* (*éclat*) radiance; (*influence*) influence; (*radiation*) radiation.

raz-de-marée [radmare] *nm inv* tidal wave; (*bouleversement*) *Fig* upheaval; r.-de-marée électoral landslide.

razzia [ra(d)zja] *nf* faire une r. sur (*tout enlever sur*) *Fam* to raid.

re- [r(ə)] *préf* re-.

ré- [re] *préf* re-.

réabonn/er (se) [səreabɔne] *vpr* to renew one's subscription (à to). ◆—ement *nm* renewal of subscription.

réacteur [reaktœr] *nm* (*d'avion*) jet engine; (*nucléaire*) reactor.

réaction [reaksjɔ̃] *nf* reaction; r. en chaîne chain reaction; avion à r. jet (aircraft); moteur à r. jet engine. ◆**réactionnaire** *a* & *nmf* reactionary.

réadapter [readapte] *vt*, — se r. *vpr* to readjust (à to). ◆**réadaptation** *nf* readjustment.

réaffirmer [reafirme] *vt* to reaffirm.

réagir [reaʒir] *vi* to react (contre against, à to); (*se secouer*) *Fig* to shake oneself out of it.

réalis/er [realize] *vt* (*projet etc*) to carry out, realize; (*ambition, rêve*) to fulfil; (*achat, bénéfice, vente*) to make; (*film*) to direct; (*capital*) *Com* to realize; (*se rendre compte*) to realize (que that); — se r. *vpr* (*vœu*) to come true; (*projet*) to be carried out; (*personne*) to fulfil oneself. ◆—able *a* (*plan*) workable; (*rêve*) attainable. ◆**réalisateur, -trice** *nmf Cin TV* director. ◆**réalisation** *nf* realization; (*de rêve*) fulfilment; *Cin TV* direction; (*œuvre*) achievement.

réalisme [realism] *nm* realism. ◆**réaliste** *a* realistic; — *nmf* realist.

réalité [realite] *nf* reality; en r. in (actual) fact, in reality.

réanimer [reanime] *vt Méd* to resuscitate. ◆**réanimation** *nf* resuscitation; (service de) r. intensive care unit.

réapparaître [reaparɛtr] *vi* to reappear. ◆**réapparition** *nf* reappearance.

réarmer [rearme] *vt* (*fusil etc*) to reload; — *vi*, — se r. *vpr* (*pays*) to rearm. ◆**réarmement** *nm* rearmament.

rébarbatif, -ive [rebarbatif, -iv] *a* forbidding, off-putting.

rebâtir [r(ə)batir] *vt* to rebuild.

rebattu [r(ə)baty] *a* (*sujet*) hackneyed.

rebelle [rəbɛl] *a* rebellious; (*troupes*) rebel-; (*fièvre*) stubborn; (*mèche*) unruly; **r. à** resistant to; – *nmf* rebel. ◆**se rebeller** *vpr* to rebel (**contre** against). ◆**rébellion** *nf* rebellion.

rebiffer (se) [sər(ə)bife] *vpr Fam* to rebel.

rebond [r(ə)bɔ̃] *nm* bounce; (*par ricochet*) rebound. ◆**rebondir** *vi* to bounce; to rebound; (**faire**) **r.** (*affaire, discussion etc*) to get going again. ◆**rebondissement** *nm* new development (**de** in).

rebondi [r(ə)bɔ̃di] *a* chubby, rounded.

rebord [r(ə)bɔr] *nm* edge; (*de plat etc*) rim; (*de vêtement*) hem; **r. de (la) fenêtre** windowsill, window ledge.

reboucher [r(ə)buʃe] *vt* (*flacon*) to put the top back on.

rebours (à) [ar(ə)bur] *adv* the wrong way.

rebrousse-poil (à) [arbruspwal] *adv* **prendre qn à r.-poil** *Fig* to rub s.o. up the wrong way.

rebrousser [r(ə)bruse] *vt* **r. chemin** to turn back.

rebuffade [rəbyfad] *nf Litt* rebuff.

rébus [rebys] *nm inv* (*jeu*) rebus.

rebut [rəby] *nm* **mettre au r.** to throw out, scrap; **le r. de la société** *Péj* the dregs of society.

rebut/er [r(ə)byte] *vt* (*décourager*) to put off; (*choquer*) to repel. ◆**—ant** *a* off-putting; (*choquant*) repellent.

récalcitrant [rekalsitrɑ̃] *a* recalcitrant.

recaler [r(ə)kale] *vt* **r. qn** *Scol Fam* to fail s.o., flunk s.o.; **être recalé, se faire r.** *Scol Fam* to fail, flunk.

récapituler [rekapityle] *vti* to recapitulate. ◆**récapitulation** *nf* recapitulation.

recel [rəsɛl] *nm* receiving stolen goods, fencing; harbouring. ◆**receler** *vt* (*mystère, secret etc*) to contain; (*objet volé*) to receive; (*malfaiteur*) to harbour. ◆**receleur, -euse** *nmf* receiver (*of stolen goods*), fence.

recens/er [r(ə)sɑ̃se] *vt* (*population*) to take a census of; (*inventorier*) to make an inventory of. ◆**—ement** *nm* census; inventory.

récent [resɑ̃] *a* recent. ◆**récemment** [-amɑ̃] *adv* recently.

récépissé [resepise] *nm* (*reçu*) receipt.

récepteur [reseptœr] *nm Tél Rad* receiver. ◆**réceptif, -ive** *a* receptive (**à** to). ◆**réception** *nf* (*accueil, soirée*) & *Rad* reception; (*de lettre etc*) *Com* receipt; (*d'hôtel etc*) reception (desk). ◆**réceptionniste** *nmf* receptionist.

récession [resesjɔ̃] *nf Écon* recession.

recette [r(ə)sɛt] *nf* **1** *Culin* & *Fig* recipe. **2** (*argent, bénéfice*) takings; (*bureau*) tax office; **recettes** (*rentrées*) *Com* receipts; **faire r.** *Fig* to be a success.

recev/oir* [rəsvwar] *vt* to receive; (*obtenir*) to get, receive; (*accueillir*) to welcome; (*accepter*) to accept; **être reçu (à)** (*examen*) to pass; **être reçu premier** to come first; – *vi* to receive guests *ou* visitors *ou Méd* patients. ◆**—able** *a* (*excuse etc*) admissible. ◆**—eur, -euse** *nmf* (*d'autobus*) (bus) conductor, (bus) conductress; (*des impôts*) tax collector; (*des postes*) postmaster, postmistress.

rechange (de) [dər(ə)ʃɑ̃ʒ] *a* (*pièce, outil etc*) spare; (*solution etc*) alternative; **vêtements/chaussures de r.** a change of clothes/shoes.

rechapé [r(ə)ʃape] *a* **pneu r.** retread.

réchapper [reʃape] *vi* **r. de** *ou* **à** (*accident etc*) to come through.

recharge [r(ə)ʃarʒ] *nf* (*de stylo etc*) refill. ◆**recharger** *vt* (*camion, fusil*) to reload; (*briquet, stylo etc*) to refill; (*batterie*) to recharge.

réchaud [reʃo] *nm* (portable) stove.

réchauff/er [reʃofe] *vt* (*personne, aliment etc*) to warm up; **— se r.** *vpr* to warm oneself up; (*temps*) to get warmer. ◆**—é** *nm* **du r.** *Fig Péj* old hat. ◆**—ement** *nm* (*de température*) rise (**de** in).

rêche [rɛʃ] *a* rough, harsh.

recherche [r(ə)ʃɛrʃ] *nf* **1** search, quest (**de** for); **à la r. de** in search of. **2 la r., des recherches** (*scientifique etc*) research (**sur** on, into); **faire des recherches** to research; (*enquête*) to make investigations. **3** (*raffinement*) studied elegance; *Péj* affectation. ◆**recherch/er** *vt* to search *ou* hunt for; (*cause, faveur, perfection*) to seek. ◆**—é** *a* **1** (*très demandé*) in great demand; (*rare*) much sought-after; **r. pour meurtre** wanted for murder. **2** (*élégant*) elegant; *Péj* affected.

rechigner [r(ə)ʃiɲe] *vi* (*renâcler*) to jib (**à qch** at sth, **à faire** at doing).

rechute [r(ə)ʃyt] *nf Méd* relapse. ◆**rechuter** *vi Méd* to (have a) relapse.

récidive [residiv] *nf Jur* further offence; *Méd* recurrence (**de** of). ◆**récidiver** *vi Jur* to commit a further offence; (*maladie*) to recur. ◆**récidiviste** *nmf Jur* further offender.

récif [resif] *nm* reef.

récipient [resipjɑ̃] *nm* container, receptacle.

réciproque [resiprɔk] *a* mutual, reciprocal; – *nf* (*inverse*) opposite; **rendre la r. à qn** to get even with s.o. ◆**réciprocité** *nf* reci-

procity. ◆**réciproquement** *adv* (*l'un l'autre*) each other; **et r.** and vice versa.
récit [resi] *nm* (*compte rendu*) account; (*histoire*) story.
récital, *pl* **-als** [resital] *nm Mus* recital.
réciter [resite] *vt* to recite. ◆**récitation** *nf* recitation.
réclame [reklam] *nf* advertising; (*annonce*) advertisement; **en r.** *Com* on (special) offer; – *a inv* **prix r.** (special) offer price; **vente r.** (bargain) sale.
réclamer [reklame] *vt* (*demander, nécessiter*) to demand, call for; (*revendiquer*) to claim; – *vi* to complain; **se r. de qn** to invoke s.o.'s authority. ◆**réclamation** *nf* complaint; *pl* (*bureau*) complaints department.
reclasser [r(ə)klɑse] *vt* (*fiches etc*) to reclassify.
reclus, -use [rəkly, -yz] *a* (*vie*) cloistered; – *nmf* recluse.
réclusion [reklyzjɔ̃] *nf* imprisonment (with hard labour); **r. à perpétuité** life imprisonment.
recoiffer (se) [sər(ə)kwafe] *vpr* (*se peigner*) to do *ou* comb one's hair.
recoin [rəkwɛ̃] *nm* nook, recess.
recoller [r(ə)kɔle] *vt* (*objet cassé*) to stick together again; (*enveloppe*) to stick back down.
récolte [rekɔlt] *nf* (*action*) harvest; (*produits*) crop, harvest; (*collection*) *Fig* crop. ◆**récolter** *vt* to harvest, gather (in); (*recueillir*) *Fig* to collect, gather; (*coups*) *Fam* to get.
recommand/er [r(ə)kɔmɑ̃de] **1** *vt* (*appuyer, conseiller*) to recommend; **r. à qn de faire** to recommend s.o. to do. **2** *vt* (*lettre etc*) to register. **3** *vt* **r. à** (*âme*) to commend to. **4 se r.** *vpr* **se r. de qn** to invoke s.o.'s authority. ◆**—é** *nm* **en r.** (*envoyer*) by registered post. ◆**—able** *a* **peu r.** not very commendable. ◆**recommandation** *nf* **1** (*appui, conseil, louange*) recommendation. **2** (*de lettre etc*) registration.
recommenc/er [r(ə)kɔmɑ̃se] *vti* to start *ou* begin again. ◆**—ement** *nm* (*reprise*) renewal (**de** of).
récompense [rekɔ̃pɑ̃s] *nf* reward (**de** for); (*prix*) award; **en r. de** in return for. ◆**récompenser** *vt* to reward (**de, pour** for).
réconcilier [rekɔ̃silje] *vt* to reconcile; **— se r.** *vpr* to become reconciled, make it up (**avec** with). ◆**réconciliation** *nf* reconciliation.
reconduire* [r(ə)kɔ̃dɥir] *vt* **1 r. qn** to see *ou* take s.o. back; (*à la porte*) to show s.o. out. **2** (*mesures etc*) to renew. ◆**reconduction** *nf* renewal.
réconfort [rekɔ̃fɔr] *nm* comfort. ◆**réconfort/er** *vt* to comfort; (*revigorer*) to fortify. ◆**—ant** *a* comforting; (*boisson etc*) fortifying.
reconnaissant [r(ə)kɔnɛsɑ̃] *a* grateful, thankful (**à qn de qch** to s.o. for sth). ◆**reconnaissance**[1] *nf* (*gratitude*) gratitude.
reconnaître* [r(ə)kɔnɛtr] *vt* to recognize (**à qch** by sth); (*admettre*) to acknowledge, admit (**que** that); (*terrain*) *Mil* to reconnoitre; **être reconnu coupable** to be found guilty; **— se r.** *vpr* (*s'orienter*) to find one's bearings; **se r. coupable** to admit one's guilt. ◆**reconnu** *a* (*chef, fait*) acknowledged, recognized. ◆**reconnaissable** *a* recognizable (**à qch** by sth). ◆**reconnaissance**[2] *nf* recognition; (*aveu*) acknowledgement; *Mil* reconnaissance; **r. de dette** IOU.
reconsidérer [r(ə)kɔ̃sidere] *vt* to reconsider.
reconstituant [r(ə)kɔ̃stitɥɑ̃] *adj* (*aliment, régime*) restorative.
reconstituer [r(ə)kɔ̃stitɥe] *vt* (*armée, parti*) to reconstitute; (*crime, quartier*) to reconstruct; (*faits*) to piece together; (*fortune*) to build up again. ◆**reconstitution** *nf* reconstitution; reconstruction.
reconstruire* [r(ə)kɔ̃strɥir] *vt* (*ville, fortune*) to rebuild. ◆**reconstruction** *nf* rebuilding.
reconvertir [r(ə)kɔ̃vertir] **1** *vt* (*bâtiment etc*) to reconvert. **2 se r.** *vpr* to take up a new form of employment. ◆**reconversion** *nf* reconversion.
recopier [r(ə)kɔpje] *vt* to copy out.
record [r(ə)kɔr] *nm & a inv Sp* record.
recoucher (se) [sər(ə)kuʃe] *vpr* to go back to bed.
recoudre* [r(ə)kudr] *vt* (*bouton*) to sew back on.
recoup/er [r(ə)kupe] *vt* (*témoignage etc*) to tally with, confirm; **— se r.** *vpr* to tally, match *ou* tie up. ◆**—ement** *nm* cross-check(ing).
recourbé [r(ə)kurbe] *a* curved; (*nez*) hooked.
recours [r(ə)kur] *nm* recourse (**à** to); *Jur* appeal; **avoir r. à** to resort to; (*personne*) to turn to; **notre dernier r.** our last resort. ◆**recourir*** *vi* **r. à** to resort to; (*personne*) to turn to.

recouvrer [r(ə)kuvre] *vt* (*argent, santé*) to recover.
recouvrir* [r(ə)kuvrir] *vt* (*livre, meuble, sol etc*) to cover; (*de nouveau*) to recover; (*cacher*) *Fig* to conceal, mask.
récréation [rekreasjɔ̃] *nf* recreation; (*temps*) *Scol* break, playtime.
récriminer [rekrimine] *vi* to complain bitterly (**contre** about). ◆**récrimination** *nf* (bitter) complaint.
récrire [rekrir] *vt* (*lettre etc*) to rewrite.
recroqueviller (se) [sər(ə)krɔkvije] *vpr* (*papier, personne etc*) to curl up.
recrudescence [rəkrydesɑ̃s] *nf* new outbreak (**de** of).
recrue [rəkry] *nf* recruit. ◆**recrut/er** *vt* to recruit. ◆**—ement** *nm* recruitment.
rectangle [rɛktɑ̃gl] *nm* rectangle. ◆**rectangulaire** *a* rectangular.
rectifier [rɛktifje] *vt* (*erreur etc*) to correct, rectify; (*ajuster*) to adjust. ◆**rectificatif** *nm* (*document*) amendment, correction. ◆**rectification** *nf* correction, rectification.
recto [rɛkto] *nm* front (of the page).
reçu [r(ə)sy] *voir* **recevoir**; – *a* (*usages etc*) accepted; (*idée*) conventional, received; (*candidat*) successful; – *nm* (*écrit*) *Com* receipt.
recueil [r(ə)kœj] *nm* (*ouvrage*) collection (**de** of).
recueill/ir* [r(ə)kœjir] **1** *vt* to collect, gather; (*suffrages*) to win, get; (*prendre chez soi*) to take in. **2 se r.** *vpr* to meditate; (*devant un monument*) to stand in silence. ◆**—i** *a* (*air*) meditative. ◆**—ement** *nm* meditation.
recul [r(ə)kyl] *nm* (*d'armée, de négociateur, de maladie*) retreat; (*éloignement*) distance; (*déclin*) decline; (**mouvement de**) **r.** (*de véhicule*) backward movement; **avoir un mouvement de r.** (*personne*) to recoil; **phare de r.** *Aut* reversing light. ◆**reculade** *nf Péj* retreat. ◆**recul/er** *vi* to move *ou* step back; *Aut* to reverse; (*armée*) to retreat; (*épidémie, glacier*) to recede, retreat; (*renoncer*) to back down, retreat; (*diminuer*) to decline; **r. devant** *Fig* to recoil *ou* shrink from; – *vt* to move *ou* push back; (*différer*) to postpone. ◆**—é** *a* (*endroit, temps*) remote.
reculons (à) [arkylɔ̃] *adv* backwards.
récupérer [rekypere] *vt* to recover, get back; (*ferraille etc*) to salvage; (*heures*) to make up; (*mouvement, personne etc*) *Pol Péj* to take over, convert; – *vi* to recuperate, recover. ◆**récupération** *nf* recovery; salvage; recuperation.
récurer [rekyre] *vt* (*casserole etc*) to scour; **poudre à r.** scouring powder.
récuser [rekyze] *vt* to challenge; **— se r.** *vpr* to decline to give an opinion.
recycl/er [r(ə)sikle] *vt* (*reconvertir*) to retrain (*s.o.*); (*matériaux*) to recycle; **— se r.** *vpr* to retrain. ◆**—age** *nm* retraining; recycling.
rédacteur, -trice [redaktœr, -tris] *nmf* writer; (*de chronique*) *Journ* editor; (*de dictionnaire etc*) compiler; **r. en chef** *Journ* editor(-in-chief). ◆**rédaction** *nf* (*action*) writing; (*de contrat*) drawing up; (*devoir*) *Scol* essay, composition; (*rédacteurs*) *Journ* editorial staff; (*bureaux*) *Journ* editorial offices.
reddition [redisjɔ̃] *nf* surrender.
redemander [rədmɑ̃de] *vt* (*pain etc*) to ask for more; **r. qch à qn** to ask s.o. for sth back.
rédemption [redɑ̃psjɔ̃] *nf Rel* redemption.
redescendre [r(ə)desɑ̃dr] *vi* (*aux* **être**) to come *ou* go back down; – *vt* (*aux* **avoir**) (*objet*) to bring *ou* take back down.
redevable [rədvabl] *a* **être r. de qch à qn** (*argent*) to owe s.o. sth; *Fig* to be indebted to s.o. for sth.
redevance [rədvɑ̃s] *nf* (*taxe*) *TV* licence fee; *Tél* rental charge.
redevenir* [rədvənir] *vi* (*aux* **être**) to become again.
rédiger [rediʒe] *vt* to write; (*contrat*) to draw up; (*dictionnaire etc*) to compile.
redire* [r(ə)dir] **1** *vt* to repeat. **2** *vi* **avoir** *ou* **trouver à r. à qch** to find fault with sth. ◆**redite** *nf* (pointless) repetition.
redondant [r(ə)dɔ̃dɑ̃] *a* (*style*) redundant.
redonner [r(ə)dɔne] *vt* to give back; (*de nouveau*) to give more.
redoubl/er [r(ə)duble] *vti* **1** to increase; **r. de patience/***etc* to be much more patient/*etc*; **à coups redoublés** (*frapper*) harder and harder. **2 r. (une classe)** *Scol* to repeat a year *ou Am* a grade. ◆**—ant, -ante** *nmf* pupil repeating a year *ou Am* a grade. ◆**—ement** *nm* increase (**de** in); repeating a year *ou Am* a grade.
redout/er [r(ə)dute] *vt* to dread (**de faire** doing). ◆**—able** *a* formidable, fearsome.
redress/er [r(ə)drese] *vt* to straighten (out); (*économie, mât, situation, tort*) to right; **— se r.** *vpr* (*se mettre assis*) to sit up; (*debout*) to stand up; (*pays, situation etc*) to right itself. ◆**—ement** [-ɛsmɑ̃] *nm* (*essor*) recovery.

réduction [redyksjɔ̃] *nf* reduction (**de** in); **en r.** (*copie, modèle etc*) small-scale.
réduire* [redɥir] *vt* to reduce (**à** to, **de** by); **r. qn à** (*contraindre à*) to reduce s.o. to (*silence, inaction etc*); **se r. à** (*se ramener à*) to come down to, amount to; **se r. en cendres/***etc* to be reduced to ashes/*etc*; – *vi* (**faire**) **r.** (*sauce*) to reduce, boil down. ◆**réduit 1** *a* (*prix, vitesse*) reduced; (*moyens*) limited; (*à petite échelle*) small-scale. **2** *nm* (*pièce*) *Péj* cubbyhole; (*recoin*) recess.
réécrire [reekrir] *vt* (*texte*) to rewrite.
rééduquer [reedyke] *vt* (*membre*) *Méd* to re-educate; **r. qn** to rehabilitate s.o., re-educate s.o. ◆**rééducation** *nf* re-education; rehabilitation.
réel, -elle [reɛl] *a* real; **le r.** reality. ◆**réellement** *adv* really.
réélire [reelir] *vt* to re-elect.
réexpédier [reɛkspedje] *vt* (*lettre etc*) to forward; (*à l'envoyeur*) to return.
refaire* [r(ə)fɛr] *vt* to do again, redo; (*erreur, voyage*) to make again; (*réparer*) to do up, redo; (*duper*) *Fam* to take in. ◆**réfection** *nf* repair(ing).
réfectoire [refɛktwar] *nm* refectory.
référendum [referɑ̃dɔm] *nm* referendum.
référer [refere] *vi* **en r. à** to refer the matter to; **— se r.** *vpr* **se r. à** to refer to. ◆**référence** *nf* reference.
refermer [r(ə)fɛrme] *vt*, **— se r.** *vpr* to close *ou* shut (again).
refiler [r(ə)file] *vt* (*donner*) *Fam* to palm off (**à** on).
réfléch/ir [refleʃir] **1** *vt* (*image*) to reflect; **— se r.** *vpr* to be reflected. **2** *vi* (*penser*) to think (**à, sur** about); – *vt* **r. que** to realize that. ◆**—i** *a* (*personne*) thoughtful, reflective; (*action, décision*) carefully thought-out; (*verbe*) *Gram* reflexive. ◆**réflecteur** *nm* reflector. ◆**réflexion** *nf* **1** (*de lumière etc*) reflection. **2** (*méditation*) thought, reflection; (*remarque*) remark; **à la r., r. faite** on second thoughts *ou Am* thought,on reflection.
reflet [r(ə)flɛ] *nm* (*image*) & *Fig* reflection; (*lumière*) glint; (*couleur*) tint. ◆**refléter** *vt* (*image, sentiment etc*) to reflect; **— se r.** *vpr* to be reflected.
réflexe [reflɛks] *nm* & *a* reflex.
refluer [r(ə)flye] *vi* (*eaux*) to ebb, flow back; (*foule*) to surge back. ◆**reflux** *nm* ebb; backward surge.
réforme *nf* **1** (*changement*) reform. **2** (*de soldat*) discharge. ◆**réformateur, -trice** *nmf* reformer. ◆**réformer 1** *vt* to reform; **— se r.** *vpr* to mend one's ways. **2** *vt* (*soldat*) to invalid out, discharge.
refoul/er [r(ə)fule] *vt* to force *ou* drive back; (*sentiment*) to repress; (*larmes*) to hold back. ◆**—é** *a* (*personne*) *Psy* repressed. ◆**—ement** *nm Psy* repression.
réfractaire [refraktɛr] *a* **r. à** resistant to.
refrain [r(ə)frɛ̃] *nm* (*de chanson*) refrain, chorus; (*rengaine*) *Fig* tune.
refréner [r(ə)frene] *vt* to curb, check.
réfrigér/er [refriʒere] *vt* to refrigerate. ◆**—ant** *a* (*accueil, air*) *Fam* icy. ◆**réfrigérateur** *nm* refrigerator. ◆**réfrigération** *nf* refrigeration.
refroid/ir [r(ə)frwadir] *vt* to cool (down); (*décourager*) *Fig* to put off; (*ardeur*) to dampen, cool; – *vi* to get cold, cool down; **— se r.** *vpr Méd* to catch cold; (*temps*) to get cold; (*ardeur*) to cool (off). ◆**—issement** *nm* cooling; (*rhume*) chill; **r. de la température** fall in the temperature.
refuge [r(ə)fyʒ] *nm* refuge; (*pour piétons*) (traffic) island; (*de montagne*) (mountain) hut. ◆**se réfugi/er** *vpr* to take refuge. ◆**—é, -ée** *nmf* refugee.
refus [r(ə)fy] *nm* refusal; **ce n'est pas de r.** *Fam* I won't say no. ◆**refuser** *vt* to refuse (**qch à qn** s.o. sth, **de faire** to do); (*offre, invitation*) to turn down, refuse; (*client*) to turn away, refuse; (*candidat*) to fail; **— se r.** *vpr* (*plaisir etc*) to deny oneself; **se r. à** (*évidence etc*) to refuse to accept, reject; **se r. à croire/***etc* to refuse to believe/*etc*.
réfuter [refyte] *vt* to refute.
regagner [r(ə)gaɲe] *vt* (*récupérer*) to regain; (*revenir à*) to get back to. ◆**regain** *nm* **r. de** (*retour*) renewal of.
régal, *pl* **-als** [regal] *nm* treat. ◆**régaler** *vt* to treat to a delicious meal; **r. de** to treat to; **— se r.** *vpr* to have a delicious meal.
regard *nm* **1** (*coup d'œil, expression*) look; (*fixe*) stare, gaze; **chercher du r.** to look (a)round for; **attirer les regards** to attract attention; **jeter un r. sur** to glance at. **2 au r. de** in regard to; **en r. de** compared with. ◆**regard/er 1** *vt* to look at; (*fixement*) to stare at, gaze at; (*observer*) to watch; (*considérer*) to consider, regard (**comme** as); **r. qn faire** to watch s.o. do; – *vi* to look; to stare, gaze; to watch; **r. à** (*dépense, qualité etc*) to pay attention to; **r. vers** (*maison etc*) to face; **— se r.** *vpr* (*personnes*) to look at each other. **2** *vt* (*concerner*) to concern. ◆**—ant** *a* (*économe*) careful (with money).
régates [regat] *nfpl* regatta.
régence [reʒɑ̃s] *nf* regency.
régénérer [reʒenere] *vt* to regenerate.

régenter [reʒɑ̃te] *vt* to rule over.
régie [reʒi] *nf* (*entreprise*) state-owned company; *Th* stage management; *Cin TV* production department.
regimber [r(ə)ʒɛ̃be] *vi* to balk (**contre** at).
régime [reʒim] *nm* **1** system; *Pol* régime. **2** *Méd* diet; **se mettre au r.** to go on a diet; **suivre un r.** to be on a diet. **3** (*de moteur*) speed; **à ce r.** *Fig* at this rate. **4** (*de bananes, dattes*) bunch.
régiment [reʒimɑ̃] *nm Mil* regiment; **un r. de** (*quantité*) *Fig* a host of.
région [reʒjɔ̃] *nf* region, area. ◆**régional, -aux** *a* regional.
régir [reʒir] *vt* (*déterminer*) to govern.
régisseur [reʒisœr] *nm* (*de propriété*) steward; *Th* stage manager; *Cin* assistant director.
registre [rəʒistr] *nm* register.
règle [rɛgl] **1** *nf* (*principe*) rule; **en r.** (*papiers d'identité etc*) in order; **être/se mettre en r. avec qn** to be/put oneself right with s.o.; **en r. générale** as a (general) rule. **2** *nf* (*instrument*) ruler; **r. à calcul** slide rule. **3** *nfpl* (*menstruation*) period.
règlement [rɛgləmɑ̃] *nm* **1** (*arrêté*) regulation; (*règles*) regulations. **2** (*de conflit, problème etc*) settling; (*paiement*) payment; **r. de comptes** *Fig* (violent) settling of scores. ◆**réglementaire** *a* in accordance with the regulations; (*tenue*) *Mil* regulation-. ◆**réglementation** *nf* **1** (*action*) regulation. **2** (*règles*) regulations. ◆**réglementer** *vt* to regulate.
régler [regle] **1** *vt* (*conflit, problème etc*) to settle; (*mécanisme*) to regulate, adjust; (*moteur*) to tune; (*papier*) to rule; **se r. sur** to model oneself on. **2** *vti* (*payer*) to pay; **r. qn** to settle up with s.o.; **r. son compte à** *Fig* to settle old scores with. ◆**réglé** *a* (*vie*) ordered; (*papier*) ruled. ◆**réglable** *a* (*siège etc*) adjustable. ◆**réglage** *nm* adjustment; (*de moteur*) tuning.
réglisse [reglis] *nf* liquorice, *Am* licorice.
règne [rɛɲ] *nm* reign; (*animal, minéral, végétal*) kingdom. ◆**régner** *vi* to reign; (*prédominer*) to prevail; **faire r. l'ordre** to maintain (law and) order.
regorger [r(ə)gɔrʒe] *vi* **r. de** to be overflowing with.
régresser [regrese] *vi* to regress. ◆**régression** *nf* regression; **en r.** on the decline.
regret [r(ə)grɛ] *nm* regret; **à r.** with regret; **avoir le r.** *ou* **être au r. de faire** to be sorry to do. ◆**regrett/er** *vt* to regret; **r. qn** to miss s.o.; **je regrette** I'm sorry; **r. que** (+ *sub*) to be sorry that, regret that. ◆**—able** *a* regrettable.
regrouper [r(ə)grupe] *vt*, **— se r.** *vpr* to gather together.
régulariser [regylarize] *vt* (*situation*) to regularize.
régulation [regylɑsjɔ̃] *nf* (*action*) regulation.
régulier, -ière [regylje, -jɛr] *a* regular; (*progrès, vie, vitesse*) steady; (*légal*) legal; (*honnête*) honest. ◆**régularité** *nf* regularity; steadiness; legality. ◆**régulièrement** *adv* regularly; (*normalement*) normally.
réhabiliter [reabilite] *vt* (*dans l'estime publique*) to rehabilitate.
réhabituer (se) [səreabitɥe] *vpr* **se r. à qch/à faire qch** to get used to sth/to doing sth again.
rehausser [rəose] *vt* to raise; (*faire valoir*) to enhance.
réimpression [reɛ̃presjɔ̃] *nf* (*livre*) reprint.
rein [rɛ̃] *nm* kidney; *pl* (*dos*) (small of the) back; **r. artificiel** *Méd* kidney machine.
reine [rɛn] *nf* queen.
reine-claude [rɛnklod] *nf* greengage.
réintégrer [reɛ̃tegre] *vt* **1** (*fonctionnaire etc*) to reinstate. **2** (*lieu*) to return to. ◆**réintégration** *nf* reinstatement.
réitérer [reitere] *vt* to repeat.
rejaillir [r(ə)ʒajir] *vi* to spurt (up *ou* out); **r. sur** *Fig* to rebound on.
rejet [r(ə)ʒɛ] *nm* **1** (*refus*) & *Méd* rejection. **2** *Bot* shoot. ◆**rejeter** *vt* to throw back; (*épave*) to cast up; (*vomir*) to bring up; (*refuser*) & *Méd* to reject; **r. une erreur/***etc* **sur qn** to put the blame for a mistake/*etc* on s.o.
rejeton [rəʒtɔ̃] *nm* (*enfant*) *Fam* kid.
rejoindre* [r(ə)ʒwɛ̃dr] *vt* (*famille, régiment*) to rejoin, get *ou* go back to; (*lieu*) to get back to; (*route, rue*) to join; **r. qn** to join *ou* meet s.o.; (*rattraper*) to catch up with s.o.; **— se r.** *vpr* (*personnes*) to meet; (*routes, rues*) to join, meet.
réjou/ir [reʒwir] *vt* to delight; **— se r.** *vpr* to be delighted (**de** at, about; **de faire** to do). ◆**—i** *a* (*air*) joyful. ◆**—issant** *a* cheering. ◆**réjouissance** *nf* rejoicing; *pl* festivities, rejoicings.
relâche [r(ə)lɑʃ] *nf Th Cin* (temporary) closure; **faire r.** (*théâtre, cinéma*) to close; (*bateau*) to put in (**dans un port** at a port); **sans r.** without a break.
relâch/er [r(ə)lɑʃe] **1** *vt* to slacken; (*discipline, étreinte*) to relax; **r. qn** to release s.o.; **— se r.** *vpr* to slacken; (*discipline*) to get lax. **2** *vi* (*bateau*) to put in. ◆**—é** *a* lax.

◆**—ement** *nm* (*de corde etc*) slackness; (*de discipline*) slackening.

relais [r(ə)lɛ] *nm Él Rad TV* relay; **(course de) r.** *Sp* relay (race); **r. routier** transport café, *Am* truck stop (café); **prendre le r.** to take over (**de** from).

relance [r(ə)lɑ̃s] *nf* (*reprise*) revival. ◆**relancer** *vt* to throw back; (*moteur*) to restart; (*industrie etc*) to put back on its feet; **r. qn** (*solliciter*) to pester s.o.

relater [r(ə)late] *vt* to relate (**que** that).

relatif, -ive [r(ə)latif, -iv] *a* relative (**à** to). ◆**relativement** *adv* relatively; **r. à** compared to, relative to.

relation [r(ə)lasjɔ̃] *nf* (*rapport*) relation(ship); (*ami*) acquaintance; **avoir des relations** (*amis influents*) to have connections; **entrer/être en relations avec** to come into/be in contact with; **relations internationales/***etc* international/*etc* relations.

relax(e) [rəlaks] *a Fam* relaxed, informal.

relaxer (se) [sər(ə)lakse] *vpr* to relax. ◆**relaxation** *nf* relaxation.

relayer [r(ə)leje] *vt* to relieve, take over from; (*émission*) to relay; **— se r.** *vpr* to take (it in) turns (**pour faire** to do); *Sp* to take over from one another.

reléguer [r(ə)lege] *vt* to relegate (**à** to).

relent [rəlɑ̃] *nm* stench, smell.

relève [r(ə)lɛv] *nf* (*remplacement*) relief; **prendre la r.** to take over (**de** from).

relev/er [rəlve] *vt* to raise; (*ramasser*) to pick up; (*chaise etc*) to put up straight; (*personne tombée*) to help up; (*col*) to turn up; (*manches*) to roll up; (*copier*) to note down; (*traces*) to find; (*relayer*) to relieve; (*rehausser*) to enhance; (*sauce*) to season; (*faute*) to pick *ou* point out; (*compteur*) to read; (*défi*) to accept; (*économie, pays*) to put back on its feet; (*mur*) to rebuild; **r. qn de** (*fonctions*) to relieve s.o. of; *– vi* **r. de** (*dépendre de*) to come under; (*maladie*) to get over; **— se r.** *vpr* (*personne*) to get up; **se r. de** (*malheur*) to recover from; (*ruines*) to rise from. ◆**—é** *nm* list; (*de dépenses*) statement; (*de compteur*) reading; **r. de compte** (bank) statement. ◆**relèvement** *nm* (*d'économie, de pays*) recovery.

relief [rəljɛf] **1** *nm* (*forme, ouvrage*) relief; **en r.** (*cinéma*) three-D; (*livre*) pop-up; **mettre en r.** *Fig* to highlight. **2** *nmpl* (*de repas*) remains.

relier [rəlje] *vt* to link, connect (**à** to); (*ensemble*) to link (together); (*livre*) to bind.

religion [r(ə)liʒjɔ̃] *nf* religion; (*foi*) faith. ◆**religieux, -euse 1** *a* religious; **mariage r.** church wedding; *– nm* monk; *– nf* nun. **2** *nf Culin* cream bun.

reliquat [r(ə)lika] *nm* (*de dette etc*) remainder.

relique [r(ə)lik] *nf* relic.

relire* [r(ə)lir] *vt* to reread.

reliure [rəljyr] *nf* (*couverture de livre*) binding; (*art*) bookbinding.

reluire [r(ə)lɥir] *vi* to shine, gleam; **faire r.** (*polir*) to shine (up). ◆**reluisant** *a* shiny; **peu r.** *Fig* far from brilliant.

reluquer [r(ə)lyke] *vt Fig* to eye (up).

remâcher [r(ə)mɑʃe] *vt Fig* to brood over.

remanier [r(ə)manje] *vt* (*texte*) to revise; (*ministère*) to reshuffle. ◆**remaniement** *nm* revision; reshuffle.

remarier (se) [sər(ə)marje] *vpr* to remarry.

remarque [r(ə)mark] *nf* remark; (*annotation*) note; **je lui en ai fait la r.** I remarked on it to him *ou* her. ◆**remarquable** *a* remarkable (**par** for). ◆**remarquablement** *adv* remarkably. ◆**remarquer** *vt* **1** (*apercevoir*) to notice (**que** that); **faire r.** to point out (**à** to, **que** that); **se faire r.** to attract attention; **remarque!** mind (you)! **2** (*dire*) to remark (**que** that).

rembarrer [rɑ̃bare] *vt* to rebuff, snub.

remblai [rɑ̃blɛ] *nm* (*terres*) embankment. ◆**remblayer** *vt* (*route*) to bank up; (*trou*) to fill in.

rembourr/er [rɑ̃bure] *vt* (*matelas etc*) to stuff, pad; (*vêtement*) to pad. ◆**—age** *nm* (*action, matière*) stuffing; padding.

rembourser [rɑ̃burse] *vt* to pay back, repay; (*billet*) to refund. ◆**remboursement** *nm* repayment; refund; **envoi contre r.** cash on delivery.

remède [r(ə)mɛd] *nm* remedy, cure; (*médicament*) medicine. ◆**remédier** *vi* **r. à** to remedy.

remémorer (se) [sər(ə)memɔre] *vpr* (*histoire etc*) to recollect, recall.

remercier [r(ə)mɛrsje] *vt* **1** to thank (**de qch, pour qch,** for sth); **je vous remercie d'être venu** thank you for coming; **je vous remercie** (*non merci*) no thank you. **2** (*congédier*) to dismiss. ◆**remerciements** *nmpl* thanks.

remettre* [r(ə)mɛtr] *vt* to put back, replace; (*vêtement*) to put back on; (*donner*) to hand over (**à** to); (*restituer*) to give back (**à** to); (*démission, devoir*) to hand in; (*différer*) to postpone (**à** until); (*ajouter*) to add more *ou* another; (*peine*) *Jur* to remit; (*guérir*) to restore to health; (*reconnaître*) to place, remember; **r. en cause** *ou* **question** to call into question; **r. en état** to repair; **r. ça** *Fam* to start again; **se r. à** (*activité*) to go back to; **se r. à faire** to start to do again; **se r. de** (*chagrin, maladie*) to recover from, get over; **s'en r. à** to rely on. ◆**remise** *nf* **1** (*de lettre etc*) delivery; (*de peine*) *Jur* remission; (*ajournement*) postponement; **r. en cause** *ou* **question** calling into question; **r. en état** repair(ing). **2** (*rabais*) discount. **3** (*local*) shed; *Aut* garage. ◆**remiser** *vt* to put away.

réminiscences [reminisɑ̃s] *nfpl* (vague) recollections, reminiscences.

rémission [remisjɔ̃] *nf Jur Rel Méd* remission; **sans r.** (*travailler etc*) relentlessly.

remmener [rɑ̃mne] *vt* to take back.

remonte-pente [r(ə)mɔ̃tpɑ̃t] *nm* ski lift.

remont/er [r(ə)mɔ̃te] *vi* (*aux* **être**) to come *ou* go back up; (*niveau, prix*) to rise again, go back up; (*dans le temps*) to go back (**à** to); **r. dans** (*voiture*) to go *ou* get back in(to); (*bus, train*) to go *ou* get back on(to); **r. sur** (*cheval, vélo*) to remount; – *vt* (*aux* **avoir**) (*escalier, pente*) to come *ou* go back up; (*porter*) to bring *ou* take back up; (*montre*) to wind up; (*relever*) to raise; (*col*) to turn up; (*objet démonté*) to reassemble; (*garde-robe etc*) to restock; **r. qn** (*ragaillardir*) to buck s.o. up; **r. le moral à qn** to cheer s.o. up. ◆**—ant** *a* (*boisson*) fortifying; – *nm Méd* tonic. ◆**—ée** *nf* **1** (*de pente etc*) ascent; (*d'eau, de prix*) rise. **2 r. mécanique** ski lift. ◆**remontoir** *nm* (*de mécanisme, montre*) winder.

remontrance [r(ə)mɔ̃trɑ̃s] *nf* reprimand; **faire des remontrances à** to reprimand, remonstrate with.

remontrer [r(ə)mɔ̃tre] *vi* **en r. à qn** to prove one's superiority over s.o.

remords [r(ə)mɔr] *nm* & *nmpl* remorse; **avoir des r.** to feel remorse.

remorque [r(ə)mɔrk] *nf Aut* trailer; (**câble de**) **r.** towrope; **prendre en r.** to tow; **en r.** on tow. ◆**remorquer** *vt* (*voiture, bateau*) to tow. ◆**remorqueur** *nm* tug(boat).

remous [r(ə)mu] *nm* eddy; (*de foule*) bustle; (*agitation*) *Fig* turmoil.

rempart [rɑ̃par] *nm* rampart.

remplacer [rɑ̃plase] *vt* to replace (**par** with, by); (*succéder à*) to take over from; (*temporairement*) to stand in for. ◆**remplaçant, -ante** *nmf* (*personne*) replacement; (*enseignant*) supply teacher; *Sp* reserve. ◆**remplacement** *nm* (*action*) replacement; **assurer le r. de qn** to stand in for s.o.; **en r. de** in place of.

rempl/ir [rɑ̃plir] *vt* to fill (up) (**de** with); (*fiche etc*) to fill in *ou* out; (*condition, devoir, tâche*) to fulfil; (*fonctions*) to perform; **— se r.** *vpr* to fill (up). ◆**—i** *a* full (**de** of). ◆**remplissage** *nm* filling; (*verbiage*) *Péj* padding.

remporter [rɑ̃pɔrte] *vt* **1** (*objet*) to take back. **2** (*prix, victoire*) to win; (*succès*) to achieve.

remu/er [r(ə)mɥe] *vt* (*déplacer, émouvoir*) to move; (*café etc*) to stir; (*terre*) to turn over; (*salade*) to toss; – *vi* to move; (*gigoter*) to fidget; (*se rebeller*) to stir; **— se r.** *vpr* to move; (*se démener*) to exert oneself. ◆**—ant** *a* (*enfant*) restless, fidgety. ◆**remue-ménage** *nm inv* commotion.

rémunérer [remynere] *vt* (*personne*) to pay; (*travail*) to pay for. ◆**rémunérateur, -trice** *a* remunerative. ◆**rémunération** *nf* payment (**de** for).

renâcler [r(ə)nakle] *vi* **1** (*cheval*) to snort. **2 r. à** to jib at, balk at.

renaître* [r(ə)nɛtr] *vi* (*fleur*) to grow again; (*espoir, industrie*) to revive. ◆**renaissance** *nf* rebirth, renaissance.

renard [r(ə)nar] *nm* fox.

renchérir [rɑ̃ʃerir] *vi* **r. sur qn** *ou* **sur ce que qn dit**/*etc* to go further than s.o. in what one says/*etc*.

rencontre [rɑ̃kɔ̃tr] *nf* meeting; (*inattendue*) & *Mil* encounter; *Sp* match, *Am* game; (*de routes*) junction; **aller à la r. de** to go to meet. ◆**rencontrer** *vt* to meet; (*difficultés*) to come up against, encounter; (*trouver*) to come across, find; (*heurter*) to hit; (*équipe*) *Sp* to play; **— se r.** *vpr* to meet.

rendez-vous [rɑ̃devu] *nm inv* appointment; (*d'amoureux*) date; (*lieu*) meeting place; **donner r.-vous à qn, prendre r.-vous avec qn** to make an appointment with s.o.

rendormir* (se) [sərɑ̃dɔrmir] *vpr* to go back to sleep.

rend/re [rɑ̃dr] *vt* (*restituer*) to give back, return; (*hommage*) to pay; (*invitation*) to return; (*santé*) to restore; (*monnaie, son*) to give; (*justice*) to dispense; (*jugement*) to pronounce, give; (*armes*) to surrender; (*exprimer, traduire*) to render; (*vomir*) to bring up; **r. célèbre/plus grand/possible**/*etc* to make famous/bigger/possible/*etc*; – *vi* (*arbre, terre*) to yield; (*vomir*) to be sick; **— se r.** *vpr* (*capituler*) to surrender (**à** to); (*aller*) to go (**à** to); **se r. à** (*évidence, ordres*) to submit to; **se r. malade/utile**/*etc* to make oneself ill/useful/*etc*. ◆**—u** *a* (*fatigué*) exhausted; **être r.** (*arrivé*) to have arrived. ◆**rendement** *nm Agr Fin* yield; (*de personne, machine*) output.

renégat, -ate [rənega, -at] *nmf* renegade.

rênes [rɛn] *nfpl* reins.

renferm/er [rɑ̃fɛrme] *vt* to contain; **— se r.** *vpr* **se r. (en soi-même)** to withdraw into oneself. ◆**—é 1** *a* (*personne*) withdrawn. **2** *nm* **sentir le r.** (*chambre etc*) to smell stuffy.

renflé [rɑ̃fle] *a* bulging. ◆**renflement** *nm* bulge.

renflouer [rɑ̃flue] *vt* (*navire*) & *Com* to refloat.

renfoncement [rɑ̃fɔ̃smɑ̃] *nm* recess; **dans le r. d'une porte** in a doorway.

renforcer [rɑ̃fɔrse] *vt* to reinforce, strengthen. ◆**renforcement** *nm* reinforcement, strengthening. ◆**renfort** *nm* **des renforts** *Mil* reinforcements; **de r.** (*armée, personnel*) back-up; **à grand r. de** *Fig* with a great deal of.

renfrogn/er (se) [sərɑ̃frɔɲe] *vpr* to scowl. ◆**—é** *a* scowling, sullen.

rengaine [rɑ̃gɛn] *nf* **la même r.** *Fig Péj* the same old song *ou* story.

rengorger (se) [sərɑ̃gɔrʒe] *vpr* to give oneself airs.

renier [rənje] *vt* (*ami, pays etc*) to disown; (*foi, opinion*) to renounce. ◆**reniement** *nm* disowning; renunciation.

renifler [r(ə)nifle] *vti* to sniff. ◆**reniflement** *nm* sniff.

renne [rɛn] *nm* reindeer.

renom [rənɔ̃] *nm* renown; (*réputation*) reputation (**de** for). ◆**renommé** *a* famous, renowned (**pour** for). ◆**renommée** *nf* fame, renown; (*réputation*) reputation.

renoncer [r(ə)nɔ̃se] *vi* **r. à** to give up, abandon; **r. à faire** to give up (the idea of) doing. ◆**renoncement** *nm*, ◆**renonciation** *nf* renunciation (**à** of).

renouer [rənwe] **1** *vt* (*lacet etc*) to retie. **2** *vt* (*reprendre*) to renew; – *vi* **r. avec qch** (*mode, tradition etc*) to revive sth; **r. avec qn** to take up with s.o. again.

renouveau, -x [r(ə)nuvo] *nm* revival.

renouveler [r(ə)nuvle] *vt* to renew; (*action, erreur, question*) to repeat; **— se r.** *vpr* (*incident*) to recur, happen again; (*cellules, sang*) to be renewed. ◆**renouvelable** *a* renewable. ◆**renouvellement** *nm* renewal.

rénover [renɔve] *vt* (*institution, méthode*) to reform; (*édifice, meuble etc*) to renovate. ◆**rénovation** *nf* reform; renovation.

renseign/er [rɑ̃seɲe] *vt* to inform, give information to (**sur** about); **— se r.** *vpr* to inquire, make inquiries, find out (**sur** about). ◆**—ement** *nm* (piece of) information; *pl* information; *Tél* directory inquiries, *Am* information; *Mil* intelligence; **prendre** *ou* **demander des reseignements** to make inquiries.

rentable [rɑ̃tabl] *a* profitable. ◆**rentabilité** *nf* profitability.

rente [rɑ̃t] *nf* (private) income; (*pension*) pension; **avoir des rentes** to have private means. ◆**rentier, -ière** *nmf* person of private means.

rentr/er [rɑ̃tre] *vi* (*aux* **être**) to go *ou* come back, return; (*chez soi*) to go *ou* come (back) home; (*entrer*) to go *ou* come in; (*entrer de nouveau*) to go *ou* come back in; (*école*) to start again; (*argent*) to come in; **r. dans** (*entrer dans*) to go *ou* come into; (*entrer de nouveau dans*) to go *ou* come back into; (*famille, pays*) to return to; (*ses frais*) to get back; (*catégorie*) to come under; (*heurter*) to crash into; (*s'emboîter dans*) to fit into; **r. (en classe)** to start (school) again; **je lui suis rentré dedans** (*frapper*) *Fam* I laid into him *ou* her; – *vt* (*aux* **avoir**) to bring *ou* take in; (*voiture*) to put away; (*chemise*) to tuck in; (*griffes*) to draw in. ◆**—é** *a* (*colère*) suppressed; (*yeux*) sunken. ◆**—ée** *nf* **1** (*retour*) return; (*de parlement*) reassembly; (*d'acteur*) comeback; **r. (des classes)** beginning of term *ou* of the school year. **2** (*des foins etc*) bringing in; (*d'impôt*) collection; *pl* (*argent*) receipts.

renverse (à la) [alarɑ̃vɛrs] *adv* (*tomber*) backwards, on one's back.

renvers/er [rɑ̃vɛrse] *vt* (*mettre à l'envers*) to turn upside down; (*faire tomber*) to knock over *ou* down; (*piéton*) to knock down, run over; (*liquide*) to spill, knock over; (*courant, ordre*) to reverse; (*gouvernement*) to overturn, overthrow; (*projet*) to upset; (*tête*) to tip back; **— se r.** *vpr* (*en arrière*) to lean back; (*bouteille, vase etc*) to fall over. ◆**—ant** *a* (*nouvelle etc*) astounding. ◆**—ement** *nm* (*d'ordre, de situation*) reversal; (*de gouvernement*) overthrow.

renvoi [rɑ̃vwa] *nm* **1** return; dismissal; expulsion; postponement; (*dans un livre*) reference. **2** (*rot*) belch, burp. ◆**renvoyer*** *vt* to send back, return; (*importun*) to send away; (*employé*) to dismiss; (*élève*) to expel; (*balle etc*) to throw back; (*ajourner*) to postpone (**à** until); (*lumière, image etc*) to reflect; **r. qn à** (*adresser à*) to refer s.o. to.

réorganiser [reɔrganize] *vt* to reorganize.

réouverture [reuvɛrtyr] *nf* reopening.

repaire [r(ə)pɛr] *nm* den.

repaître (se) [sərəpɛtr] *vpr* **se r. de** (*sang*) *Fig* to wallow in.

répand/re [repɑ̃dr] *vt* (*liquide*) to spill;

(*idées, joie, nouvelle*) to spread; (*fumée, odeur*) to give off; (*chargement, lumière, larmes, sang*) to shed; (*gravillons etc*) to scatter; (*dons*) to lavish; **— se r.** *vpr* (*nouvelle, peur etc*) to spread; (*liquide*) to spill; **se r. dans** (*fumée, odeur*) to spread through; **se r. en louanges/***etc* to pour forth praise/*etc*. **◆—u** *a* (*opinion, usage*) widespread; (*épars*) scattered.

reparaître [r(ə)parɛtr] *vi* to reappear.

réparer [repare] *vt* to repair, mend; (*forces, santé*) to restore; (*faute*) to make amends for; (*perte*) to make good; (*erreur*) to put right. **◆réparable** *a* (*montre etc*) repairable. **◆réparateur, -trice** *nmf* repairer; – *a* (*sommeil*) refreshing. **◆réparation** *nf* repair(ing); (*compensation*) amends, compensation (**de** for); *pl Mil Hist* reparations; **en r.** under repair.

reparler [r(ə)parle] *vi* **r. de** to talk about again.

repartie [reparti] *nf* (*réponse vive*) repartee.

repartir* [r(ə)partir] *vi* (*aux* **être**) to set off again; (*s'en retourner*) to go back; (*reprendre*) to start again; **r. à** *ou* **de zéro** to go back to square one.

répartir [repartir] *vt* to distribute; (*partager*) to share (out); (*classer*) to divide (up); (*étaler dans le temps*) to spread (out) (**sur** over). **◆répartition** *nf* distribution; sharing; division.

repas [r(ə)pɑ] *nm* meal; **prendre un r.** to have *ou* eat a meal.

repass/er [r(ə)pɑse] **1** *vi* to come *ou* go back; – *vt* (*traverser*) to go back over; (*examen*) to resit; (*leçon, rôle*) to go over; (*film*) to show again; (*maladie, travail*) to pass on (**à** to). **2** *vt* (*linge*) to iron. **3** *vt* (*couteau*) to sharpen. **◆—age** *nm* ironing.

repêcher [r(ə)peʃe] *vt* to fish out; (*candidat*) *Fam* to allow to pass.

repenser [r(ə)pɑ̃se] *vt* to rethink.

repentir [r(ə)pɑ̃tir] *nm* repentance. **◆se repentir*** *vpr Rel* to repent (**de** of); **se r. de** (*regretter*) to regret, be sorry for. **◆repentant** *a*, **◆repenti** *a* repentant.

répercuter [reperkyte] *vt* (*son*) to echo; **— se r.** *vpr* to echo, reverberate; **se r. sur** *Fig* to have repercussions on. **◆répercussion** *nf* repercussion.

repère [r(ə)pɛr] *nm* (guide) mark; (*jalon*) marker; **point de r.** (*espace, temps*) landmark, point of reference. **◆repérer** *vt* to locate; (*personnne*) *Fam* to spot; **— se r.** *vpr* to get one's bearings.

répertoire [repertwar] *nm* **1** index; (*carnet*) indexed notebook; **r. d'adresses** address book. **2** *Th* repertoire. **◆répertorier** *vt* to index.

répéter [repete] *vti* to repeat; *Th* to rehearse; **— se r.** *vpr* (*radoter*) to repeat oneself; (*se reproduire*) to repeat itself. **◆répétitif, -ive** *a* repetitive. **◆répétition** *nf* repetition; *Th* rehearsal; **r. générale** *Th* (final) dress rehearsal.

repiquer [r(ə)pike] *vt* **1** (*plante*) to plant out. **2** (*disque*) to tape, record (on tape).

répit [repi] *nm* rest, respite; **sans r.** ceaselessly.

replacer [r(ə)plase] *vt* to replace, put back.

repli [r(ə)pli] *nm* fold; withdrawal; *pl* (*de l'âme*) recesses. **◆replier 1** *vt* to fold (up); (*siège*) to fold up; (*couteau, couverture*) to fold back; (*ailes, jambes*) to tuck in; **— se r.** *vpr* (*siège*) to fold up; (*couteau, couverture*) to fold back. **2** *vt*, **— se r.** *vpr Mil* to withdraw; **se r. sur soi-même** to withdraw into oneself.

réplique [replik] *nf* **1** (*réponse*) reply; (*riposte*) retort; *Th* lines; **pas de r.!** no answering back!; **sans r.** (*argument*) irrefutable. **2** (*copie*) replica. **◆répliquer** *vt* to reply (**que** that); (*riposter*) to retort (**que** that); – *vi* (*être impertinent*) to answer back.

répond/re [repɔ̃dr] *vi* to answer, reply; (*être impertinent*) to answer back; (*réagir*) to respond (**à** to); **r. à qn** to answer s.o., reply to s.o.; (*avec impertinence*) to answer s.o. back; **r. à** (*lettre, objection, question*) to answer, reply to; (*salut*) to return; (*besoin*) to meet, answer; (*correspondre à*) to correspond to; **r. de** (*garantir*) to answer for (*s.o., sth*); – *vt* (*remarque etc*) to answer *ou* reply with; **r. que** to answer *ou* reply that. **◆—ant, -ante 1** *nmf* guarantor. **2** *nm* **avoir du r.** to have money behind one. **◆—eur** *nm Tél* answering machine. **◆réponse** *nf* answer, reply; (*réaction*) response (**à** to); **en r. à** in answer *ou* reply *ou* response to.

reporter[1] [r(ə)pɔrte] *vt* to take back; (*différer*) to postpone, put off (**à** until); (*transcrire, transférer*) to transfer (**sur** to); (*somme*) *Com* to carry forward (**sur** to); **se r. à** (*texte etc*) to refer to; (*en esprit*) to go *ou* think back to. **◆report** *nm* postponement; transfer; *Com* carrying forward. **◆reportage** *nm* (news) report, article; (*en direct*) commentary; (*métier*) reporting.

reporter[2] [r(ə)pɔrtɛr] *nm* reporter.

repos [r(ə)po] *nm* rest; (*tranquillité*) peace (and quiet); (*de l'esprit*) peace of mind; **r.!** *Mil* at ease!; **jour de r.** day off; **de tout r.** (*situation etc*) safe. **◆repos/er 1** *vt* (*objet*) to put back down; (*problème, question*) to raise again. **2** *vt* (*délasser*) to rest, relax; **r. sa tête sur** (*appuyer*) to rest one's head on; – *vi* (*être enterré ou étendu*) to rest, lie; **r. sur** (*bâtiment*) to be built on; (*théorie etc*) to be based on, rest on; **laisser r.** (*vin*) to allow to settle; **— se r.** *vpr* to rest; **se r. sur qn** to rely on s.o. **◆—ant** *a* relaxing, restful. **◆—é** *a* rested, fresh.

repouss/er [r(ə)puse] **1** *vt* to push back; (*écarter*) to push away; (*attaque, ennemi*) to repulse; (*importun etc*) to turn away, repulse; (*dégoûter*) to repel; (*décliner*) to reject; (*différer*) to put off, postpone. **2** *vi* (*cheveux, feuilles*) to grow again. **◆—ant** *a* repulsive, repellent.

répréhensible [repreɑ̃sibl] *a* reprehensible, blameworthy.

reprendre* [r(ə)prɑ̃dr] *vt* (*objet*) to take back; (*évadé, ville*) to recapture; (*passer prendre*) to pick up again; (*souffle*) to get back; (*activité*) to resume, take up again; (*texte*) to go back over; (*vêtement*) to alter; (*histoire, refrain*) to take up; (*pièce*) *Th* to put on again; (*blâmer*) to admonish; (*corriger*) to correct; **r. de la viande/un œuf/***etc* to take (some) more meat/another egg/*etc*; **r. ses esprits** to come round; **r. des forces** to recover one's strength; – *vi* (*plante*) to take again; (*recommencer*) to resume, start (up) again; (*affaires*) to pick up; (*dire*) to go on, continue; **— se r.** *vpr* (*se ressaisir*) to take a hold on oneself; (*se corriger*) to correct oneself; **s'y r. à deux/plusieurs fois** to have another go/several goes (at it).

représailles [r(ə)prezaj] *nfpl* reprisals, retaliation.

représent/er [r(ə)prezɑ̃te] *vt* to represent; (*jouer*) *Th* to perform; **— se r.** *vpr* (*s'imaginer*) to imagine. **◆—ant, -ante** *nmf* representative; **r. de commerce** (travelling) salesman *ou* saleswoman, sales representative. **◆représentatif, -ive** *a* representative (**de** of). **◆représentation** *nf* representation; *Th* performance.

répression [represjɔ̃] *nf* suppression, repression; (*mesures de contrôle*) *Pol* repression. **◆répressif, -ive** *a* repressive. **◆réprimer** *vt* (*sentiment, révolte etc*) to suppress, repress.

réprimande [reprimɑ̃d] *nf* reprimand. **◆réprimander** *vt* to reprimand.

repris [r(ə)pri] *nm* **r. de justice** hardened criminal.

reprise [r(ə)priz] *nf* (*de ville*) *Mil* recapture; (*recommencement*) resumption; (*de pièce de théâtre, de coutume*) revival; *Rad TV* repeat; (*de tissu*) mend, repair; *Boxe* round; (*essor*) *Com* recovery, revival; (*d'un locataire*) money for fittings; (*de marchandise*) taking back; (*pour nouvel achat*) part exchange, trade-in; *pl Aut* acceleration; **à plusieurs reprises** on several occasions. **◆repriser** *vt* (*chaussette etc*) to mend, darn.

réprobation [reprɔbasjɔ̃] *nf* disapproval. **◆réprobateur, -trice** *a* disapproving.

reproche [r(ə)prɔʃ] *nm* reproach; **faire des reproches à qn** to reproach s.o.; **sans r.** beyond reproach. **◆reprocher** *vt* **r. qch à qn** to reproach *ou* blame s.o. for sth; **r. qch à qch** to have sth against sth; **n'avoir rien à se r.** to have nothing to reproach *ou* blame oneself for.

reproduire* [r(ə)prɔdɥir] **1** *vt* (*son, modèle etc*) to reproduce; **— se r.** *vpr Biol Bot* to reproduce. **2 se r.** *vpr* (*incident etc*) to happen again, recur. **◆reproducteur, -trice** *a* reproductive. **◆reproduction** *nf* (*de son etc*) & *Biol Bot* reproduction.

réprouver [repruve] *vt* to disapprove of, condemn.

reptile [rɛptil] *nm* reptile.

repu [rəpy] *a* (*rassasié*) satiated.

république [repyblik] *nf* republic. **◆républicain, -aine** *a* & *nmf* republican.

répudier [repydje] *vt* to repudiate.

répugnant [repyɲɑ̃] *a* repugnant, loathsome. **◆répugnance** *nf* repugnance, loathing (**pour** for); (*manque d'enthousiasme*) reluctance. **◆répugner** *vi* **r. à qn** to be repugnant to s.o.; **r. à faire** to be loath to do.

répulsion [repylsjɔ̃] *nf* repulsion.

réputation [repytɑsjɔ̃] *nf* reputation; **avoir la r. d'être franc** to have a reputation for frankness *ou* for being frank. **◆réputé** *a* (*célèbre*) renowned (**pour** for); **r. pour être** (*considéré comme*) reputed to be.

requérir [rəkerir] *vt* (*nécessiter*) to demand, require; (*peine*) *Jur* to call for. **◆requête** *nf* request; *Jur* petition. **◆requis** *a* required, requisite.

requiem [rekɥijem] *nm inv* requiem.

requin [r(ə)kɛ̃] *nm* (*poisson*) & *Fig* shark.

réquisition [rekizisjɔ̃] *nf* requisition. **◆réquisitionner** *vt* to requisition, commandeer.

réquisitoire [rekizitwar] *nm* (*critique*) indictment (**contre** of).

rescapé, -ée [rɛskape] *a* surviving; – *nmf* survivor.

rescousse (à la) [alarɛskus] *adv* to the rescue.

réseau, -x [rezo] *nm* network; **r. d'espionnage** spy ring *ou* network.

réserve [rezɛrv] *nf* **1** (*restriction, doute*) reservation; (*réticence*) reserve; **sans r.** (*admiration etc*) unqualified; **sous r. de** subject to; **sous toutes réserves** without guarantee. **2** (*provision*) reserve; (*entrepôt*) storeroom; (*de bibliothèque*) stacks; **la r.** *Mil* the reserve; **les réserves** (*soldats*) the reserves; **en r.** in reserve. **3** (*de chasse, pêche*) preserve; (*indienne*) reservation; **r. naturelle** nature reserve.

réserv/er [rezɛrve] *vt* to reserve; (*garder*) to keep, save; (*marchandises*) to put aside (**à** for); (*place, table*) to book, reserve; (*sort, surprise etc*) to hold in store (**à** for); **se r. pour** to save oneself for; **se r. de faire** to reserve the right to do. ◆**—é** *a* (*personne, place*) reserved; (*prudent*) guarded. ◆**réservation** *nf* reservation, booking. ◆**réservoir** *nm* (*lac*) reservoir; (*citerne, cuve*) tank; **r. d'essence** *Aut* petrol *ou Am* gas tank.

résidence [rezidɑ̃s] *nf* residence; **r. secondaire** second home; **r. universitaire** hall of residence. ◆**résident, -ente** *nmf* (foreign) resident. ◆**résidentiel, -ielle** *a* (*quartier*) residential. ◆**résider** *vi* to reside, be resident (**à, en, dans** in); **r. dans** (*consister dans*) to lie in.

résidu [rezidy] *nm* residue.

résigner (se) [sərezipe] *vpr* to resign oneself (**à qch** to sth, **à faire** to doing). ◆**résignation** *nf* resignation.

résilier [rezilje] *vt* (*contrat*) to terminate. ◆**résiliation** *nf* termination.

résille [rezij] *nf* (*pour cheveux*) hairnet.

résine [rezin] *nf* resin.

résistance [rezistɑ̃s] *nf* resistance (**à** to); (*conducteur*) *Él* (heating) element; **plat de r.** main dish. ◆**résist/er** *vi* **r. à** to resist; (*chaleur, fatigue, souffrance*) to withstand; (*examen*) to stand up to. ◆**—ant, -ante** *a* tough, strong; **r. à la chaleur** heat-resistant; **r. au choc** shockproof; – *nmf Mil Hist* Resistance fighter.

résolu [rezɔly] *voir* **résoudre;** – *a* resolute, determined; **r. à faire** resolved *ou* determined to do. ◆**—ment** *adv* resolutely. ◆**résolution** *nf* (*décision*) resolution; (*fermeté*) determination.

résonance [rezɔnɑ̃s] *nf* resonance.

résonner [rezɔne] *vi* to resound (**de** with); (*salle, voix*) to echo.

résorber [rezɔrbe] *vt* (*chômage*) to reduce; (*excédent*) to absorb; **— se r.** *vpr* to be reduced; to be absorbed. ◆**résorption** *nf* reduction; absorption.

résoudre* [rezudr] *vt* (*problème*) to solve; (*difficulté*) to resolve; **r. de faire** to decide *ou* resolve to do; **se r. à faire** to decide *ou* resolve to do; (*se résigner*) to bring oneself to do.

respect [rɛspɛ] *nm* respect (**pour, de** for); **mes respects à** my regards *ou* respects to; **tenir qn en r.** to hold s.o. in check. ◆**respectabilité** *nf* respectability. ◆**respectable** *a* (*honorable, important*) respectable. ◆**respecter** *vt* to respect; **qui se respecte** self-respecting. ◆**respectueux, -euse** *a* respectful (**envers** to, **de** of).

respectif, -ive [rɛspɛktif, -iv] *a* respective. ◆**respectivement** *adv* respectively.

respirer [rɛspire] *vi* to breathe; (*reprendre haleine*) to get one's breath (back); (*être soulagé*) to breathe again; – *vt* to breathe (in); (*exprimer*) *Fig* to exude. ◆**respiration** *nf* breathing; (*haleine*) breath; **r. artificielle** *Méd* artificial respiration. ◆**respiratoire** *a* breathing-, respiratory.

resplend/ir [rɛsplɑ̃dir] *vi* to shine; (*visage*) to glow (**de** with). ◆**—issant** *a* radiant.

responsable [rɛspɔ̃sabl] *a* responsible (**de qch** for sth, **devant qn** to s.o.); – *nmf* (*chef*) person in charge; (*dans une organisation*) official; (*coupable*) person responsible (**de** for). ◆**responsabilité** *nf* responsibility; (*légale*) liability.

resquiller [rɛskije] *vi* (*au cinéma, dans le métro etc*) to avoid paying; (*sans attendre*) to jump the queue, *Am* cut in (line).

ressaisir (se) [sər(ə)sezir] *vpr* to pull oneself together.

ressasser [r(ə)sase] *vt* (*ruminer*) to keep going over; (*répéter*) to keep trotting out.

ressemblance [r(ə)sɑ̃blɑ̃s] *nf* resemblance, likeness. ◆**ressembl/er** *vi* **r. à** to resemble, look *ou* be like; **cela ne lui ressemble pas** (*ce n'est pas son genre*) that's not like him *ou* her; **— se r.** *vpr* to look *ou* be alike. ◆**—ant** *a* **portrait r.** good likeness.

ressentiment [r(ə)sɑ̃timɑ̃] *nm* resentment.

ressentir* [r(ə)sɑ̃tir] *vt* to feel; **se r. de** to feel *ou* show the effects of.

resserre [r(ə)sɛr] *nf* storeroom; (*remise*) shed.

resserrer [r(ə)sere] *vt* (*nœud, boulon etc*) to tighten; (*contracter*) to close (up), contract; (*liens*) *Fig* to strengthen; **— se r.** *vpr* to tighten; (*amitié*) to become closer; (*se contracter*) to close (up), contract; (*route etc*) to narrow.

resservir [r(ə)sɛrvir] **1** *vi* (*outil etc*) to come

in useful (again). **2 se r.** *vpr* se **r. de** (*plat etc*) to have another helping of.
ressort [r(ə)sɔr] *nm* **1** *Tech* spring. **2** (*énergie*) spirit. **3 du r. de** within the competence of; **en dernier r.** (*décider etc*) in the last resort, as a last resort.
ressortir[1*] [r(ə)sɔrtir] *vi* (*aux* **être**) **1** to go *ou* come back out. **2** (*se voir*) to stand out; **faire r.** to bring out; **il ressort de** (*résulte*) it emerges from.
ressortir[2] [r(ə)sɔrtir] *vi* (*conjugated like* **finir**) **r. à** to fall within the scope of.
ressortissant, -ante [r(ə)sɔrtisɑ̃, -ɑ̃t] *nmf* (*citoyen*) national.
ressource [r(ə)surs] **1** *nfpl* (*moyens*) resources; (*argent*) means, resources. **2** *nf* (*recours*) recourse; (*possibilité*) possibility (**de faire** of doing); **dernière r.** last resort.
ressusciter [resysite] *vi* to rise from the dead; (*malade, pays*) to recover, revive; – *vt* (*mort*) to raise; (*malade, mode*) to revive.
restaurant [rɛstɔrɑ̃] *nm* restaurant.
restaurer [rɛstɔre] **1** *vt* (*réparer, rétablir*) to restore. **2 se r.** *vpr* to (have sth to) eat. ◆**restaurateur, -trice** *nmf* **1** (*de tableaux*) restorer. **2** (*hôtelier, hôtelière*) restaurant owner. ◆**restauration** *nf* **1** restoration. **2** (*hôtellerie*) catering.
reste [rɛst] *nm* rest, remainder (**de** of); *Math* remainder; *pl* remains (**de** of); (*de repas*) leftovers; **un r. de fromage/***etc* some left-over cheese/*etc*; **au r., du r.** moreover, besides.
rester [rɛste] *vi* (*aux* **être**) to stay, remain; (*calme, jeune etc*) to keep, stay, remain; (*subsister*) to remain, be left; **il reste du pain/***etc* there's some bread/*etc* left (over); **il me reste une minute/***etc* I have one minute/*etc* left; **l'argent qui lui reste** the money he *ou* she has left; **reste à savoir** it remains to be seen; **il me reste deux choses à faire** I still have two things to do; **il me reste à vous remercier** it remains for me to thank you; **en r. à** to stop at; **restons-en là** let's leave it at that. ◆**restant** *a* remaining; **poste restante** poste restante, *Am* general delivery; – *nm* **le r.** the rest, the remainder; **un r. de viande/***etc* some left-over meat/*etc*.
restituer [rɛstitɥe] *vt* **1** (*rendre*) to return, restore (**à** to). **2** (*son*) to reproduce; (*énergie*) to release. ◆**restitution** *nf* return.
restreindre* [rɛstrɛ̃dr] *vt* to restrict, limit (**à** to); **— se r.** *vpr* to decrease; (*faire des économies*) to cut back *ou* down. ◆**restreint** *a* limited, restricted (**à** to). ◆**restrictif, -ive** *a* restrictive. ◆**restriction** *nf* restriction; **sans r.** unreservedly.
résultat [rezylta] *nm* result; (*conséquence*) outcome, result; **avoir qch pour r.** to result in sth. ◆**résulter** *vi* **r. de** to result from.
résum/er [rezyme] *vt* to summarize; (*récapituler*) to sum up; **— se r.** *vpr* (*orateur etc*) to sum up; **se r. à** (*se réduire à*) to boil down to. ◆**—é** *nm* summary; **en r.** in short; (*en récapitulant*) to sum up.
résurrection [rezyrɛksjɔ̃] *nf* resurrection.
rétabl/ir [retablir] *vt* to restore; (*fait, vérité*) to re-establish; (*malade*) to restore to health; (*employé*) to reinstate; **— se r.** *vpr* to be restored; (*malade*) to recover. ◆**—issement** *nm* restoring; re-establishment; *Méd* recovery.
retaper [r(ə)tape] *vt* (*maison, voiture etc*) to do up; (*lit*) to straighten; (*malade*) *Fam* to buck up.
retard [r(ə)tar] *nm* lateness; (*sur un programme etc*) delay; (*infériorité*) backwardness; **en r.** late; (*retardé*) backward; **en r. dans qch** behind in sth; **en r. sur qn/qch** behind s.o./sth; **rattraper** *ou* **combler son r.** to catch up; **avoir du r.** to be late; (*sur un programme*) to be behind (schedule); (*montre*) to be slow; **avoir une heure de r.** to be an hour late; **prendre du r.** (*montre*) to lose (time); **sans r.** without delay. ◆**retardataire** *a* (*arrivant*) late; **enfant r.** *Méd* slow learner; – *nmf* latecomer. ◆**retardement** *nm* **à r.** delayed-action-; **bombe à r.** time bomb.
retard/er [r(ə)tarde] *vt* to delay; (*date, départ, montre*) to put back; **r. qn** (*dans une activité*) to put s.o. behind; – *vi* (*montre*) to be slow; **r. de cinq minutes** to be five minutes slow; **r. (sur son temps)** (*personne*) to be behind the times. ◆**—é, -ée** *a* (*enfant*) backward; – *nmf* backward child.
retenir* [rətnir] *vt* (*empêcher d'agir, contenir*) to hold back; (*attention, souffle*) to hold; (*réserver*) to book; (*se souvenir de*) to remember; (*fixer*) to hold (in place), secure; (*déduire*) to take off; (*candidature, proposition*) to accept; (*chiffre*) *Math* to carry; (*chaleur, odeur*) to retain; (*invité, suspect etc*) to detain, keep; **r. qn prisonnier** to keep *ou* hold s.o. prisoner; **r. qn de faire** to stop s.o. (from) doing; **— se r.** *vpr* (*se contenir*) to restrain oneself; **se r. de faire** to stop oneself (from) doing; **se r. à** to cling to. ◆**retenue** *nf* **1** (*modération*) restraint. **2** (*de salaire*) deduction, stoppage; (*chiffre*) *Math* figure carried over. **3** *Scol* detention; **en r.** in detention.

retent/ir [r(ə)tɑ̃tir] *vi* to ring (out) (**de** with). ◆**—issant** *a* resounding; (*scandale*) major. ◆**—issement** *nm* (*effet*) effect; **avoir un grand r.** (*film etc*) to create a stir.

réticent [retisɑ̃] *a* (*réservé*) reticent; (*hésitant*) reluctant. ◆**réticence** *nf* reticence; reluctance.

rétine [retin] *nf Anat* retina.

retir/er [r(ə)tire] *vt* to withdraw; (*sortir*) to take out; (*ôter*) to take off; (*éloigner*) to take away; (*reprendre*) to pick up; (*offre, plainte*) to take back, withdraw; **r. qch à qn** (*permis etc*) to take sth away from s.o.; **r. qch de** (*gagner*) to derive sth from; — **se r.** *vpr* to withdraw, retire (**de** from); (*mer*) to ebb. ◆**—é** *a* (*lieu, vie*) secluded.

retomber [r(ə)tɔ̃be] *vi* to fall; (*de nouveau*) to fall again; (*pendre*) to hang (down); (*après un saut etc*) to land; (*intérêt*) to slacken; **r. dans** (*erreur, situation*) to fall *ou* sink back into; **r. sur qn** (*frais, responsabilité*) to fall on s.o. ◆**retombées** *nfpl* (*radioactives*) fallout.

rétorquer [retɔrke] *vt* **r. que** to retort that.

retors [rətɔr] *a* wily, crafty.

rétorsion [retɔrsjɔ̃] *nf Pol* retaliation; **mesure de r.** reprisal.

retouche [r(ə)tuʃ] *nf* touching up; alteration. ◆**retoucher** *vt* (*photo, tableau*) to touch up, retouch; (*texte, vêtement*) to alter.

retour [r(ə)tur] *nm* return; (*de fortune*) reversal; **être de r.** to be back (**de** from); **en r.** (*en échange*) in return; **par r. (du courrier)** by return (of post), *Am* by return mail; **à mon retour** when I get *ou* got back (**de** from); **r. en arrière** flashback; **r. de flamme** *Fig* backlash; **match r.** return match *ou Am* game.

retourner [r(ə)turne] *vt* (*aux* **avoir**) (*tableau etc*) to turn round; (*matelas, steak etc*) to turn over; (*foin, terre etc*) to turn; (*vêtement, sac etc*) to turn inside out; (*maison*) to turn upside down; (*compliment, lettre*) to return; **r. qn** (*bouleverser*) *Fam* to upset s.o., shake s.o.; **r. contre qn** (*argument*) to turn against s.o.; (*arme*) to turn on s.o.; **de quoi il retourne** what it's about; — *vi* (*aux* **être**) to go back, return; — **se r.** *vpr* (*pour regarder*) to turn round, look back; (*sur le dos*) to turn over *ou* round; (*dans son lit*) to toss and turn; (*voiture*) to overturn; **s'en r.** to go back; **se r. contre** *Fig* to turn against.

retracer [r(ə)trase] *vt* (*histoire etc*) to retrace.

rétracter [retrakte] *vt*, — **se r.** *vpr* to retract. ◆**rétractation** *nf* (*désaveu*) retraction.

retrait [r(ə)trɛ] *nm* withdrawal; (*de bagages, billets*) collection; (*de mer*) ebb(ing); **en r.** (*maison etc*) set back.

retraite [r(ə)trɛt] *nf* **1** (*d'employé*) retirement; (*pension*) (retirement) pension; (*refuge*) retreat, refuge; **r. anticipée** early retirement; **prendre sa r.** to retire; **à la r.** retired; **mettre à la r.** to pension off. **2** *Mil* retreat; **r. aux flambeaux** torchlight tattoo. ◆**retraité, -ée** *a* retired; — *nmf* senior citizen, (old age) pensioner.

retrancher [r(ə)trɑ̃ʃe] **1** *vt* (*mot, passage etc*) to cut (**de** from); (*argent, quantité*) to deduct (**de** from). **2 se r.** *vpr* (*soldat, gangster etc*) to entrench oneself; **se r. dans/derrière** *Fig* to take refuge in/behind.

retransmettre [r(ə)trɑ̃smɛtr] *vt* to broadcast. ◆**retransmission** *nf* broadcast.

rétréc/ir [retresir] *vt* to narrow; (*vêtement*) to take in; — *vi*, — **se r.** *vpr* (*au lavage*) to shrink; (*rue etc*) to narrow. ◆**—i** *a* (*esprit, rue*) narrow.

rétribuer [retribɥe] *vt* to pay, remunerate; (*travail*) to pay for. ◆**rétribution** *nf* payment, remuneration.

rétro [retro] *a inv* (*mode etc*) which harks back to the past, retro.

rétro- [retrɔ] *préf* retro-. ◆**rétroactif, -ive** *a* retroactive.

rétrograde [retrɔgrad] *a* retrograde. ◆**rétrograder** *vi* (*reculer*) to move back; (*civilisation etc*) to go backwards; *Aut* to change down; — *vt* (*fonctionnaire, officier*) to demote.

rétrospectif, -ive [retrɔspɛktif, -iv] *a* (*sentiment etc*) retrospective; — *nf* (*de films, tableaux*) retrospective. ◆**rétrospectivement** *adv* in retrospect.

retrouss/er [r(ə)truse] *vt* (*jupe etc*) to hitch *ou* tuck up; (*manches*) to roll up ◆**—é** *a* (*nez*) snub, turned-up.

retrouver [r(ə)truve] *vt* to find (again); (*rejoindre*) to meet (again); (*forces, santé*) to regain; (*découvrir*) to rediscover; (*se rappeler*) to recall; — **se r.** *vpr* (*chose*) to be found (again); (*se trouver*) to find oneself (back); (*se rencontrer*) to meet (again); **s'y r.** (*s'orienter*) to find one's bearings *ou* way. ◆**retrouvailles** *nfpl* reunion.

rétroviseur [retrɔvizœr] *nm Aut* (rear-view) mirror.

réunion [reynjɔ̃] *nf* (*séance*) meeting; (*d'objets*) collection, gathering; (*d'éléments divers*) combination; (*jonction*) joining. ◆**réunir** *vt* to collect, gather; (*relier*) to join; (*convoquer*) to call together, assemble; (*rapprocher*) to bring together; (*qua-

lités, tendances) to combine. ◆**réunis** *apl* (*éléments*) combined.

réuss/ir [reysir] *vi* to succeed, be successful (**à faire** in doing); (*plante*) to thrive; **r. à** (*examen*) to pass; **r. à qn** to work (out) well for s.o.; (*aliment, climat*) to agree with s.o.; – *vt* to make a success of. ◆**—i** *a* successful. ◆**réussite** *nf* **1** success. **2 faire des réussites** *Cartes* to play patience.

revaloir [r(ə)valwar] *vt* **je vous le revaudrai** (*en bien ou en mal*) I'll pay you back.

revaloriser [r(ə)valɔrize] *vt* (*salaire*) to raise. ◆**revalorisation** *nf* raising.

revanche [r(ə)vɑ̃ʃ] *nf* revenge; *Sp* return game; **en r.** on the other hand.

rêve [rɛv] *nm* dream; **faire un r.** to have a dream; **maison/voiture/***etc* **de r.** dream house/car/*etc.* ◆**rêvasser** *vi* to daydream.

revêche [rəvɛʃ] *a* bad-tempered, surly.

réveil [revɛj] *nm* waking (up); *Fig* awakening; (*pendule*) alarm (clock). ◆**réveill/er** *vt* (*personne*) to wake (up); (*sentiment, souvenir*) *Fig* to revive, awaken; — **se r.** *vpr* to wake (up); *Fig* to revive, awaken. ◆**—é** *a* awake. ◆**réveille-matin** *nm inv* alarm (clock).

réveillon [revɛjɔ̃] *nm* (*repas*) midnight supper (*on Christmas Eve or New Year's Eve*). ◆**réveillonner** *vi* to take part in a *réveillon.*

révéler [revele] *vt* to reveal (**que** that); — **se r.** to be revealed; **se r. facile/***etc* to turn out to be easy/*etc.* ◆**révélateur, -trice** *a* revealing; **r. de** indicative of. ◆**révélation** *nf* revelation.

revenant [rəvnɑ̃] *nm* ghost.

revendiquer [r(ə)vɑ̃dike] *vt* to claim; (*exiger*) to demand. ◆**revendicatif, -ive** *a* (*mouvement etc*) protest-. ◆**revendication** *nf* claim; demand; (*action*) claiming; demanding.

revendre [r(ə)vɑ̃dr] *vt* to resell; **avoir (de) qch à r.** to have sth to spare. ◆**revendeur, -euse** *nmf* retailer; (*d'occasion*) second-hand dealer; **r. (de drogue)** drug pusher; **r. de billets** ticket tout. ◆**revente** *nf* resale.

revenir* [rəvnir] *vi* (*aux* **être**) to come back, return; (*date*) to come round again; (*mot*) to come *ou* crop up; (*coûter*) to cost (**à qn** s.o.); **r. à** (*activité, sujet*) to go back to, return to; (*se résumer à*) to boil down to; **r. à qn** (*forces, mémoire*) to come back to s.o., return to s.o.; (*honneur*) to fall to s.o.; **r. à soi** to come to *ou* round; **r. de** (*maladie, surprise*) to get over; **r. sur** (*décision, promesse*) to go back on; (*passé, question*) to go back over; **r. sur ses pas** to retrace one's steps; **faire r.** (*aliment*) to brown.

revenu [rəvny] *nm* income (**de** from); (*d'un État*) revenue (**de** from); **déclaration de revenus** tax return.

rêv/er [reve] *vi* to dream (**de** of, **de faire** of doing); – *vt* to dream (**que** that); (*désirer*) to dream of. ◆**—é** *a* ideal.

réverbération [reverberɑsjɔ̃] *nf* (*de lumière*) reflection; (*de son*) reverberation.

révérence [reverɑ̃s] *nf* reverence; (*salut d'homme*) bow; (*salut de femme*) curts(e)y; **faire une r.** to bow; to curts(e)y. ◆**révérer** *vt* to revere.

révérend, -ende [reverɑ̃, -ɑ̃d] *a & nm Rel* reverend.

rêverie [rɛvri] *nf* daydream; (*activité*) daydreaming.

revers [r(ə)vɛr] *nm* (*côté*) reverse; *Tennis* backhand; (*de veste*) lapel; (*de pantalon*) turn-up, *Am* cuff; (*d'étoffe*) wrong side; (*coup du sort*) setback, reverse; **r. de main** (*coup*) backhander; **le r. de la médaille** *Fig* the other side of the coin.

réversible [reversibl] *a* reversible.

revêtir* [r(ə)vetir] *vt* to cover (**de** with); (*habit*) to put on; (*caractère, forme*) to assume; (*route*) to surface; **r. qn** (*habiller*) to dress s.o. (**de** in); **r. de** (*signature*) to provide with. ◆**revêtement** *nm* (*surface*) covering; (*de route*) surface.

rêveur, -euse [rɛvœr, -øz] *a* dreamy; – *nmf* dreamer.

revient [rəvjɛ̃] *nm* **prix de r.** cost price.

revigorer [r(ə)vigɔre] *vt* (*personne*) to revive.

revirement [r(ə)virmɑ̃] *nm* (*changement*) about-turn, *Am* about-face; (*de situation, d'opinion, de politique*) reversal.

réviser [revize] *vt* (*notes, texte*) to revise; (*jugement, règlement etc*) to review; (*machine, voiture*) to overhaul, service. ◆**révision** *nf* revision; review; overhaul, service.

revivre* [r(ə)vivr] *vi* to live again; **faire r.** to revive; – *vt* (*incident etc*) to relive.

révocation [revɔkɑsjɔ̃] *nf* **1** (*de contrat etc*) revocation. **2** (*de fonctionnaire*) dismissal.

revoici [r(ə)vwasi] *prép* **me r.** here I am again.

revoilà [r(ə)vwala] *prép* **la r.** there she is again.

revoir* [r(ə)vwar] *vt* to see (again); (*texte*) to revise; **au r.** goodbye.

révolte [revɔlt] *nf* revolt. ◆**révolt/er 1** *vt* to revolt, incense. **2 se r.** *vpr* to revolt, rebel (**contre** against). ◆**—ant** *a* (*honteux*) revolting. ◆**—é, -ée** *nmf* rebel.

révolu [revɔly] *a* (*époque*) past; **avoir trente ans révolus** to be over thirty (years of age).

révolution [revɔlysjɔ̃] *nf* (*changement, rotation*) revolution. ◆**révolutionnaire** *a & nmf* revolutionary. ◆**révolutionner** *vt* to revolutionize; (*émouvoir*) *Fig* to shake up.

revolver [revɔlvɛr] *nm* revolver, gun.

révoquer [revɔke] *vt* **1** (*contrat etc*) to revoke. **2** (*fonctionnaire*) to dismiss.

revue [r(ə)vy] *nf* **1** (*examen*) & *Mil* review; **passer en r.** to review. **2** (*de music-hall*) variety show. **3** (*magazine*) magazine; (*spécialisée*) journal.

rez-de-chaussée [redʃose] *nm inv* ground floor, *Am* first floor.

rhabiller (se) [sərabije] *vpr* to get dressed again.

rhapsodie [rapsɔdi] *nf* rhapsody.

rhétorique [retɔrik] *nf* rhetoric.

Rhin [rɛ̃] *nm* **le R.** the Rhine.

rhinocéros [rinɔserɔs] *nm* rhinoceros.

rhododendron [rɔdɔdɛ̃drɔ̃] *nm* rhododendron.

rhubarbe [rybarb] *nf* rhubarb.

rhum [rɔm] *nm* rum.

rhumatisme [rymatism] *nm Méd* rheumatism; **avoir des rhumatismes** to have rheumatism. ◆**rhumatisant, -ante** *a & nmf* rheumatic. ◆**rhumatismal, -aux** *a* (*douleur*) rheumatic.

rhume [rym] *nm* cold; **r. de cerveau** head cold; **r. des foins** hay fever.

riant [rjɑ̃] *a* cheerful, smiling.

ricaner [rikane] *vi* (*sarcastiquement*) to snigger; (*bêtement*) to giggle.

riche [riʃ] *a* rich; (*personne, pays*) rich, wealthy; **r. en** (*minérai, vitamines etc*) rich in; – *nmf* rich *ou* wealthy person; **les riches** the rich. ◆**—ment** *a* (*vêtu, illustré etc*) richly. ◆**richesse** *nf* wealth; (*d'étoffe, de sol, vocabulaire*) richness; *pl* (*trésor*) riches; (*ressources*) wealth.

ricin [risɛ̃] *nm* **huile de r.** castor oil.

ricocher [rikɔʃe] *vi* to ricochet, rebound. ◆**ricochet** *nm* ricochet, rebound; **par r.** *Fig* as an indirect result.

rictus [riktys] *nm* grin, grimace.

ride [rid] *nf* wrinkle; ripple. ◆**rider** *vt* (*visage*) to wrinkle; (*eau*) to ripple; — **se r.** *vpr* to wrinkle.

rideau, -x [rido] *nm* curtain; (*métallique*) shutter; (*écran*) *Fig* screen (**de** of); **le r. de fer** *Pol* the Iron Curtain.

ridicule [ridikyl] *a* ridiculous, ludicrous; – *nm* (*moquerie*) ridicule; (*défaut*) absurdity; (*de situation etc*) ridiculousness; **tourner en r.** to ridicule. ◆**ridiculiser** *vt* to ridicule.

rien [rjɛ̃] *pron* nothing; **il ne sait r.** he knows nothing, he doesn't know anything; **r. du tout** nothing at all; **r. d'autre/de bon/***etc* nothing else/good/*etc*; **r. de tel** nothing like it; **de r.!** (*je vous en prie*) don't mention it!; **ça ne fait r.** it doesn't matter; **en moins de r.** (*vite*) in no time; **trois fois r.** (*chose insignifiante*) next to nothing; **pour r.** (*à bas prix*) for next to nothing; **il n'en est r.** (*ce n'est pas vrai*) nothing of the kind; **r. que** only, just; – *nm* trifle, (mere) nothing; **un r. de** a hint *ou* touch of; **en un r. de temps** (*vite*) in no time; **un r. trop petit/***etc* just a bit too small/*etc*.

rieur, -euse [rijœr, -øz] *a* cheerful.

riflard [riflar] *nm Fam* brolly, umbrella.

rigide [riʒid] *a* rigid; (*carton, muscle*) stiff; (*personne*) *Fig* inflexible; (*éducation*) strict. ◆**rigidité** *nf* rigidity; stiffness; inflexibility; strictness.

rigole [rigɔl] *nf* (*conduit*) channel; (*filet d'eau*) rivulet.

rigoler [rigɔle] *vi Fam* to laugh; (*s'amuser*) to have fun *ou* a laugh; (*plaisanter*) to joke (**avec** about). ◆**rigolade** *nf Fam* fun; (*chose ridicule*) joke, farce; **prendre qch à la r.** to make a joke out of sth. ◆**rigolo, -ote** *a Fam* funny; – *nmf Fam* joker.

rigueur [rigœr] *nf* rigour; harshness; strictness; (*précision*) precision; **être de r.** to be the rule; **à la r.** if absolutely necessary, at *ou Am* in a pinch; **tenir r. à qn de qch** *Fig* to hold sth against s.o. ◆**rigoureux, -euse** *a* rigorous; (*climat, punition*) harsh; (*personne, morale, sens*) strict.

rillettes [rijɛt] *nfpl* potted minced pork.

rime [rim] *nf* rhyme. ◆**rimer** *vi* to rhyme (**avec** with); **ça ne rime à rien** it makes no sense.

rincer [rɛ̃se] *vt* to rinse (out). ◆**rinçage** *nm* rinsing; (*opération*) rinse.

ring [riŋ] *nm* (boxing) ring.

ringard [rɛ̃gar] *a* (*démodé*) *Fam* unfashionable, fuddy-duddy.

ripaille [ripɑj] *nf Fam* feast.

riposte [ripɔst] *nf* (*réponse*) retort; (*attaque*) counter(attack). ◆**riposter** *vi* to retort; **r. à** (*attaque*) to counter; (*insulte*) to reply to; – *vt* **r. que** to retort that.

rire* [rir] *vi* to laugh (**de** at); (*s'amuser*) to have a good time; (*plaisanter*) to joke; **faire qch pour r.** to do sth for a laugh *ou* a joke; **se r. de qch** to laugh sth off; – *nm* laugh; *pl* laughter; **le r.** (*activité*) laughter. ◆**risée** *nf* mockery; **être la r. de** to be the laughing stock of. ◆**risible** *a* laughable.

ris [ri] *nm* **r. de veau** *Culin* (calf) sweetbread.

risque [risk] *nm* risk; **r. du métier** occupational hazard; **au r. de qch/de faire** at the risk of sth/of doing; **à vos risques et périls** at your own risk; **assurance tous risques** comprehensive insurance. ◆**risquer** *vt* to risk; (*question, regard*) to venture, hazard; **r. de faire** to stand a good chance of doing; **se r. à faire** to dare to do; **se r. dans** to venture into. ◆**risqué** *a* risky; (*plaisanterie*) daring, risqué.

ristourne [risturn] *nf* discount.

rite [rit] *nm* rite; (*habitude*) *Fig* ritual. ◆**rituel, -elle** *a* & *nm* ritual.

rivage [rivaʒ] *nm* shore.

rival, -ale, -aux [rival, -o] *a* & *nmf* rival. ◆**rivaliser** *vi* to compete (**avec** with, **de** in). ◆**rivalité** *nf* rivalry.

rive [riv] *nf* (*de fleuve*) bank; (*de lac*) shore.

rivé [rive] *a* **r. à** (*chaise etc*) *Fig* riveted to; **r. sur** *Fig* riveted on. ◆**rivet** *nm* (*tige*) rivet. ◆**riveter** *vt* to rivet (together).

riverain, -aine [rivrɛ̃, -ɛn] *a* riverside; lakeside; – *nmf* riverside resident; (*de lac*) lakeside resident; (*de rue*) resident.

rivière [rivjɛr] *nf* river.

rixe [riks] *nf* brawl, scuffle.

riz [ri] *nm* rice; **r. au lait** rice pudding. ◆**rizière** *nf* paddy (field), ricefield.

RN *abrév* = **route nationale.**

robe [rɔb] *nf* (*de femme*) dress; (*d'ecclésiastique, de juge*) robe; (*de professeur*) gown; (*pelage*) coat; **r. de soirée** *ou* **du soir** evening dress *ou* gown; **r. de grossesse/de mariée** maternity/wedding dress; **r. de chambre** dressing gown; **r. chasuble** pinafore (dress).

robinet [rɔbinɛ] *nm* tap, *Am* faucet; **eau du r.** tap water.

robot [rɔbo] *nm* robot; **r. ménager** food processor, liquidizer.

robuste [rɔbyst] *a* robust. ◆**robustesse** *nf* robustness.

roc [rɔk] *nm* rock.

rocaille [rɔkɑj] *nf* (*terrain*) rocky ground; (*de jardin*) rockery. ◆**rocailleux, -euse** *a* rocky, stony; (*voix*) harsh.

rocambolesque [rɔkɑ̃bɔlɛsk] *a* (*aventure etc*) fantastic.

roche [rɔʃ] *nf*, **rocher** [rɔʃe] *nm* (*bloc, substance*) rock. ◆**rocheux, -euse** *a* rocky.

rock [rɔk] *nm* (*musique*) rock; – *a inv* (*chanteur etc*) rock-.

rod/er [rɔde] *vt* (*moteur, voiture*) to run in, *Am* break in; **être rodé** (*personne*) *Fig* to have got *ou Am* gotten the hang of things. ◆**–age** *nm* running in, *Am* breaking in.

rôd/er [rode] *vi* to roam (about); (*suspect*) to prowl (about). ◆**–eur, -euse** *nmf* prowler.

rogne [rɔɲ] *nf Fam* anger; **en r.** in a temper.

rogner [rɔɲe] *vt* to trim, clip; (*réduire*) to cut; – *vi* **r. sur** (*réduire*) to cut down on. ◆**rognures** *nfpl* clippings, trimmings.

rognon [rɔɲɔ̃] *nm Culin* kidney.

roi [rwa] *nm* king; **fête** *ou* **jour des rois** Twelfth Night.

roitelet [rwatlɛ] *nm* (*oiseau*) wren.

rôle [rol] *nm* role, part; **à tour de r.** in turn.

romain, -aine [rɔmɛ̃, -ɛn] **1** *a* & *nmf* Roman. **2** *nf* (*laitue*) cos (lettuce), *Am* romaine.

roman [rɔmɑ̃] **1** *nm* novel; (*histoire*) *Fig* story; **r.-fleuve** saga. **2** *a* (*langue*) Romance; *Archit* Romanesque. ◆**romancé** *a* (*histoire*) fictional. ◆**romancier, -ière** *nmf* novelist.

romanesque [rɔmanɛsk] *a* romantic; (*incroyable*) fantastic.

romanichel, -elle [rɔmaniʃɛl] *nmf* gipsy.

romantique [rɔmɑ̃tik] *a* romantic. ◆**romantisme** *nm* romanticism.

romarin [rɔmarɛ̃] *nm Bot Culin* rosemary.

romp/re* [rɔ̃pr] *vt* to break; (*pourparlers, relations*) to break off; (*digue*) to burst; – *vi* to break (*Fig* **avec** with); to burst; (*fiancés*) to break it off; – **se r.** *vpr* to break; to burst. ◆**–u** *a* **1** (*fatigué*) exhausted. **2 r. à** (*expérimenté*) experienced in.

romsteck [rɔmstɛk] *nm* rump steak.

ronces [rɔ̃s] *nfpl* (*branches*) brambles.

ronchonner [rɔ̃ʃɔne] *vi Fam* to grouse, grumble.

rond [rɔ̃] *a* round; (*gras*) plump; (*honnête*) straight; (*ivre*) *Fam* tight; **dix francs tout r.** ten francs exactly; – *adv* **tourner r.** (*machine etc*) to run smoothly; – *nm* (*objet*) ring; (*cercle*) circle; (*tranche*) slice; *pl* (*argent*) *Fam* money; **r. de serviette** napkin ring; **en r.** (*s'asseoir etc*) in a ring *ou* circle; **tourner en r.** (*toupie etc*) & *Fig* to go round and round. ◆**r.-de-cuir** *nm* (*pl* **ronds-de-cuir**) *Péj* pen pusher. ◆**r.-point** *nm* (*pl* **ronds-points**) *Aut* roundabout, *Am* traffic circle. ◆**ronde** *nf* (*tour de surveillance*) round; (*de policier*) beat; (*danse*) round (dance); (*note*) *Mus* semibreve, *Am* whole note; **à la r.** around; (*boire*) in turn. ◆**rondelet, -ette** *a* chubby; (*somme*) *Fig* tidy. ◆**rondelle** *nf* (*tranche*) slice; *Tech* washer. ◆**rondement** *adv* (*efficacement*) briskly; (*franchement*) straight. ◆**rondeur** *nf* roundness; (*du corps*) plumpness. ◆**rondin** *nm* log.

ronéotyper [rɔneɔtipe] *vt* to duplicate, roneo.
ronflant [rɔ̃flɑ̃] *a* (*langage etc*) *Péj* high-flown; (*feu*) roaring.
ronfler [rɔ̃fle] *vi* to snore; (*moteur*) to hum. ◆**ronflement** *nm* snore, snoring; hum(ming).
rong/er [rɔ̃ʒe] *vt* to gnaw (at); (*ver, mer, rouille*) to eat into (*sth*); **r. qn** (*chagrin, maladie*) to consume s.o.; **se r. les ongles** to bite one's nails; **se r. les sangs** (*s'inquiéter*) to worry oneself sick. ◆**—eur** *nm* (*animal*) rodent.
ronron [rɔ̃rɔ̃] *nm*, **ronronnement** [rɔ̃rɔnmɑ̃] *nm* purr(ing). ◆**ronronner** *vi* to purr.
roquette [rɔkɛt] *nf Mil* rocket.
rosbif [rɔsbif] *nm* **du r.** (*rôti*) roast beef; (*à rôtir*) roasting beef; **un r.** a joint of roast *ou* roasting beef.
rose [roz] **1** *nf* (*fleur*) rose. **2** *a* (*couleur*) pink; (*situation, teint*) rosy; – *nm* pink. ◆**rosé** *a* pinkish; & – *a* & *nm* (*vin*) rosé. ◆**rosette** *nf* (*d'un officier*) rosette; (*nœud*) bow. ◆**rosier** *nm* rose bush.
roseau, -x [rozo] *nm* (*plante*) reed.
rosée [roze] *nf* dew.
rosse [rɔs] *a* & *nf Fam* nasty (person).
ross/er [rɔse] *vt Fam* to thrash. ◆**—ée** *nf Fam* thrashing.
rossignol [rɔsiɲɔl] *nm* **1** (*oiseau*) nightingale. **2** (*crochet*) picklock.
rot [ro] *nm Fam* burp, belch. ◆**roter** *vi Fam* to burp, belch.
rotation [rɔtɑsjɔ̃] *nf* rotation; (*de stock*) turnover. ◆**rotatif, -ive** *a* rotary; – *nf* rotary press.
rotin [rɔtɛ̃] *nm* rattan, cane.
rôt/ir [rotir] *vti*, — **se r.** *vpr* to roast; **faire r.** to roast. ◆**—i** *nm* **du r.** roasting meat; (*cuit*) roast meat; **un r.** a joint; **r. de bœuf/de porc** (joint of) roast beef/pork. ◆**rôtissoire** *nf* (roasting) spit.
rotule [rɔtyl] *nf* kneecap.
roturier, -ière [rɔtyrje, -jɛr] *nmf* commoner.
rouage [rwaʒ] *nm* (*de montre etc*) (working) part; (*d'organisation etc*) *Fig* cog.
roublard [rublar] *a* wily, foxy.
rouble [rubl] *nm* (*monnaie*) r(o)uble.
roucouler [rukule] *vi* (*oiseau, amoureux*) to coo.
roue [ru] *nf* wheel; **r. (dentée)** cog(wheel); **faire la r.** (*paon*) to spread its tail; (*se pavaner*) *Fig* to strut; **faire r. libre** *Aut* to freewheel.
roué, -ée [rwe] *a* & *nmf* sly *ou* calculating (person).
rouer [rwe] *vt* **r. qn de coups** to beat s.o. black and blue.
rouet [rwɛ] *nm* spinning wheel.
rouge [ruʒ] *a* red; (*fer*) red-hot; – *nm* (*couleur*) red; (*vin*) *Fam* red wine; **r. (à lèvres)** lipstick; **r. (à joues)** rouge; **le feu est au r.** *Aut* the (traffic) lights are red; – *nmf* (*personne*) *Pol* Red. ◆**r.-gorge** *nm* (*pl* **rouges-gorges**) robin. ◆**rougeâtre** *a* reddish. ◆**rougeaud** *a* red-faced. ◆**rougeoyer** *vi* to glow (red). ◆**rougeur** *nf* redness; (*due à la gêne ou à la honte*) blush(ing); *pl Méd* red spots *ou* blotches. ◆**rougir** *vti* to redden, turn red; – *vi* (*de gêne, de honte*) to blush (**de** with); (*de colère, de joie*) to flush (**de** with).
rougeole [ruʒɔl] *nf* measles.
rouget [ruʒɛ] *nm* (*poisson*) mullet.
rouille [ruj] *nf* rust; – *a inv* (*couleur*) rust(-coloured). ◆**rouill/er** *vi* to rust; — **se r.** *vpr* to rust; (*esprit, sportif etc*) *Fig* to get rusty. ◆**—é** *a* rusty.
roul/er [rule] *vt* to roll; (*brouette, meuble*) to wheel, push; (*crêpe, ficelle, manches etc*) to roll up; **r. qn** (*duper*) *Fam* to cheat s.o.; – *vi* to roll; (*train, voiture*) to go, travel; (*conducteur*) to drive; **r. sur** (*conversation*) to turn on; **ça roule!** *Fam* everything's fine!; — **se r.** *vpr* to roll; **se r. dans** (*couverture etc*) to roll oneself (up) in. ◆**—ant** *a* (*escalier, trottoir*) moving; (*meuble*) on wheels. ◆**—é** *nm* (*gâteau*) Swiss roll. ◆**rouleau, -x** *nm* (*outil, vague*) roller; (*de papier, pellicule etc*) roll; **r. à pâtisserie** rolling pin; **r. compresseur** steamroller. ◆**roulement** *nm* (*bruit*) rumbling, rumble; (*de tambour, de tonnerre, d'yeux*) roll; (*ordre*) rotation; **par r.** in rotation; **r. à billes** *Tech* ball bearing. ◆**roulette** *nf* (*de meuble*) castor; (*de dentiste*) drill; (*jeu*) roulette. ◆**roulis** *nm* (*de navire*) roll(ing).
roulotte [rulɔt] *nf* (*de gitan*) caravan.
Roumanie [rumani] *nf* Romania. ◆**roumain, -aine** *a* & *nmf* Romanian; – *nm* (*langue*) Romanian.
round [rawnd, rund] *nm Boxe* round.
roupiller [rupije] *vi Fam* to kip, sleep.
rouqin, -ine [rukɛ̃, -in] *a Fam* red-haired; – *nmf Fam* redhead.
rouspét/er [ruspete] *vi Fam* to grumble, complain. ◆**—eur, -euse** *nmf* grumbler.
rousse [rus] *voir* **roux.**
rousseur [rusœr] *nf* redness; **tache de r.** freckle. ◆**roussir** *vt* (*brûler*) to singe, scorch; – *vi* (*feuilles*) to turn brown; **faire r.** *Culin* to brown.
route [rut] *nf* road (**de** to); (*itinéraire*) way.

route; (*aérienne, maritime*) route; (*chemin*) *Fig* path, way; **r. nationale/départementale** main/secondary road; **grande r., grand-r.** main road; **code de la r.** Highway Code; **en r.** on the way, en route; **en r.!** let's go!; **par la r.** by road; **sur la bonne r.** *Fig* on the right track; **mettre en r.** (*voiture etc*) to start (up); **se mettre en r.** to set out (**pour** for); **une heure de r.** *Aut* an hour's drive; **bonne r.!** *Aut* have a good trip! ◆**routier, -ière** *a* (*carte etc*) road-; – *nm* (*camionneur*) (long distance) lorry *ou Am* truck driver; (*restaurant*) transport café, *Am* truck stop.

routine [rutin] *nf* routine; **de r.** (*contrôle etc*) routine-. ◆**routinier, -ière** *a* (*travail etc*) routine-; (*personne*) addicted to routine.

rouvrir* [ruvrir] *vti*, — **se r.** *vpr* to reopen.

roux, rousse [ru, rus] *a* (*cheveux*) red, ginger; (*personne*) red-haired; – *nmf* redhead.

royal, -aux [rwajal, -o] *a* royal; (*cadeau, festin etc*) fit for a king; (*salaire*) princely. ◆**royalement** *adv* (*traiter*) royally. ◆**royaliste** *a & nmf* royalist. ◆**royaume** *nm* kingdom. ◆**Royaume-Uni** *nm* United Kingdom. ◆**royauté** *nf* (*monarchie*) monarchy.

ruade [rɥad] *nf* (*d'âne etc*) kick.

ruban [rybɑ̃] *nm* ribbon; (*d'acier, de chapeau*) band; **r. adhésif** adhesive *ou* sticky tape.

rubéole [rybeɔl] *nf* German measles, rubella.

rubis [rybi] *nm* (*pierre*) ruby; (*de montre*) jewel.

rubrique [rybrik] *nf* (*article*) *Journ* column; (*catégorie, titre*) heading.

ruche [ryʃ] *nf* (bee)hive.

rude [ryd] *a* (*grossier*) crude; (*rêche*) rough; (*pénible*) tough; (*hiver, voix*) harsh; (*remarquable*) *Fam* tremendous. ◆**—ment** *adv* (*parler, traiter*) harshly; (*frapper, tomber*) hard; (*très*) *Fam* awfully. ◆**rudesse** *nf* harshness. ◆**rudoyer** *vt* to treat harshly.

rudiments [rydimɑ̃] *nmpl* rudiments. ◆**rudimentaire** *a* rudimentary.

rue [ry] *nf* street; **être à la r.** (*sans domicile*) to be on the streets. ◆**ruelle** *nf* alley(way).

ruer [rɥe] **1** *vi* (*cheval*) to kick (out). **2 se r.** *vpr* (*foncer*) to rush, fling oneself (**sur** at). ◆**ruée** *nf* rush.

rugby [rygbi] *nm* rugby. ◆**rugbyman,** *pl* **-men** [rygbiman, -mɛn] *nm* rugby player.

rug/ir [ryʒir] *vi* to roar. ◆**—issement** *nm* roar.

rugueux, -euse [rygø, -øz] *a* rough. ◆**rugosité** *nf* roughness; *pl* (*aspérités*) roughness.

ruine [rɥin] *nf* (*décombres*) & *Fig* ruin; **en r.** (*édifice*) in ruins; **tomber en r.** to fall into ruin. ◆**ruiner** *vt* to ruin; — **se r.** *vpr* (*en dépensant*) to ruin oneself. ◆**ruineux, -euse** *a* (*goûts, projet*) ruinously expensive; (*dépense*) ruinous.

ruisseau, -x [rɥiso] *nm* stream; (*caniveau*) gutter. ◆**ruisseler** *vi* to stream (**de** with).

rumeur [rymœr] *nf* (*protestation*) clamour; (*murmure*) murmur; (*nouvelle*) rumour.

ruminer [rymine] *vt* (*méditer*) to ponder on, ruminate over.

rumsteak [rɔmstɛk] *nm* rump steak.

rupture [ryptyr] *nf* break(ing); (*de fiançailles, relations*) breaking off; (*de pourparlers*) breakdown (**de** in); (*brouille*) break (up), split; (*de contrat*) breach; (*d'organe*) *Méd* rupture.

rural, -aux [ryral, -o] *a* rural, country-; – *nmpl* country people.

ruse [ryz] *nf* (*subterfuge*) trick; **la r.** (*habileté*) cunning; (*fourberie*) trickery. ◆**rusé, -ée** *a & nmf* crafty *ou* cunning (person). ◆**ruser** *vi* to resort to trickery.

Russie [rysi] *nf* Russia. ◆**russe** *a & nmf* Russian; – *nm* (*langue*) Russian.

rustique [rystik] *a* (*meuble*) rustic.

rustre [rystr] *nm* lout, churl.

rutabaga [rytabaga] *nm* (*racine*) swede, *Am* rutabaga.

rutilant [rytilɑ̃] *a* gleaming, glittering.

rythme [ritm] *nm* rhythm; (*de travail*) rate, tempo; (*de la vie*) pace; **au r. de trois par jour** at a *ou* the rate of three a day. ◆**rythmé** *a*, ◆**rythmique** *a* rhythmic(al).

S

S, s [ɛs] *nm* S, s.

s' [s] *voir* **se, si.**

sa [sa] *voir* **son**².

SA *abrév* (*société anonyme*) *Com* plc, *Am* Inc.

sabbat [saba] *nm* (Jewish) Sabbath.

◆**sabbatique** *a* (*année etc*) *Univ* sabbatical.

sable [sabl] *nm* sand; **sables mouvants** quicksand(s). ◆**sabler** *vt* (*route*) to sand. ◆**sableux, -euse** *a* (*eau*) sandy. ◆**sablier** *nm* hourglass; *Culin* egg timer. ◆**sablière** *nf* (*carrière*) sandpit. ◆**sablonneux, -euse** *a* (*terrain*) sandy.

sablé [sable] *nm* shortbread biscuit *ou Am* cookie.

saborder [saborde] *vt* (*navire*) to scuttle; (*entreprise*) *Fig* to shut down.

sabot [sabo] *nm* **1** (*de cheval etc*) hoof. **2** (*chaussure*) clog. **3** (*de frein*) *Aut* shoe; **s. (de Denver)** *Aut* (wheel) clamp.

sabot/er [sabote] *vt* to sabotage; (*bâcler*) to botch. ◆**—age** *nm* sabotage; **un s.** an act of sabotage. ◆**—eur, -euse** *nmf* saboteur.

sabre [sabr] *nm* sabre, sword.

sabrer [sabre] *vt* (*élève, candidat*) *Fam* to give a thoroughly bad mark to.

sac [sak] *nm* **1** bag; (*grand et en toile*) sack; **s. (à main)** handbag; **s. à dos** rucksack. **2** **mettre à s.** (*ville*) *Mil* to sack.

saccade [sakad] *nf* jerk, jolt; **par saccades** jerkily, in fits and starts. ◆**saccadé** *a* (*geste, style*) jerky.

saccager [sakaʒe] *vt* (*ville, région*) *Mil* to sack; (*bouleverser*) *Fig* to turn upside down.

saccharine [sakarin] *nf* saccharin.

sacerdoce [sasɛrdɔs] *nm* (*fonction*) *Rel* priesthood; *Fig* vocation.

sachet [saʃɛ] *nm* (small) bag; (*de lavande etc*) sachet; **s. de thé** teabag.

sacoche [sakɔʃ] *nf* bag; (*de vélo, moto*) saddlebag; *Scol* satchel.

sacquer [sake] *vt Fam* (*renvoyer*) to sack; (*élève*) to give a thoroughly bad mark to.

sacre [sakr] *nm* (*d'évêque*) consecration; (*de roi*) coronation. ◆**sacrer** *vt* (*évêque*) to consecrate; (*roi*) to crown.

sacré [sakre] *a* (*saint*) sacred; (*maudit*) *Fam* damned. ◆**—ment** *adv Fam* (*très*) damn(ed); (*beaucoup*) a hell of a lot.

sacrement [sakrəmɑ̃] *nm Rel* sacrament.

sacrifice [sakrifis] *nm* sacrifice. ◆**sacrifier** *vt* to sacrifice (**à** to, **pour** for); – *vi* **s. à** (*mode etc*) to pander to; — **se s.** *vpr* to sacrifice oneself (**à** to, **pour** for).

sacrilège [sakrilɛʒ] *nm* sacrilege; – *a* sacrilegious.

sacristie [sakristi] *nf* vestry.

sacro-saint [sakrɔsɛ̃] *a Iron* sacrosanct.

sadisme [sadism] *nm* sadism. ◆**sadique** *a* sadistic; – *nmf* sadist.

safari [safari] *nm* safari; **faire un s.** to be *ou* go on safari.

safran [safrɑ̃] *nm* saffron.

sagace [sagas] *a* shrewd, sagacious.

sage [saʒ] *a* wise; (*enfant*) well-behaved, good; (*modéré*) moderate; – *nm* wise man, sage. ◆**sagement** *adv* wisely; (*avec calme*) quietly. ◆**sagesse** *nf* wisdom; good behaviour; moderation.

sage-femme [saʒfam] *nf* (*pl* **sages-femmes**) midwife.

Sagittaire [saʒitɛr] *nm* **le S.** (*signe*) Sagittarius.

Sahara [saara] *nm* **le S.** the Sahara (desert).

saign/er [seɲe] *vti* to bleed. ◆**—ant** [sɛɲɑ̃] *a* (*viande*) *Culin* rare, underdone. ◆**—ée** *nf* **1** *Méd* bleeding, blood-letting; (*perte*) *Fig* heavy loss. **2 la s. du bras** *Anat* the bend of the arm. ◆**saignement** *nm* bleeding; **s. de nez** nosebleed.

saillant [sajɑ̃] *a* projecting, jutting out; (*trait etc*) *Fig* salient. ◆**saillie** *nf* projection; **en s., faisant s.** projecting.

sain [sɛ̃] *a* healthy; (*moralement*) sane; (*jugement*) sound; (*nourriture*) wholesome, healthy; **s. et sauf** safe and sound, unhurt. ◆**sainement** *adv* (*vivre*) healthily; (*raisonner*) sanely.

saindoux [sɛ̃du] *nm* lard.

saint, sainte [sɛ̃, sɛ̃t] *a* holy; (*personne*) saintly; **s. Jean** Saint John; **sainte nitouche** *Iron* little innocent; **la Sainte Vierge** the Blessed Virgin; – *nmf* saint. ◆**s.-bernard** *nm* (*chien*) St Bernard. ◆**S.-Esprit** *nm* Holy Spirit. ◆**S.-Siège** *nm* Holy See. ◆**S.-Sylvestre** *nf* New Year's Eve.

sais [sɛ] *voir* **savoir.**

saisie [sezi] *nf Jur* seizure; **s. de données** data capture *ou* entry.

sais/ir [sezir] **1** *vt* to grab (hold of), seize; (*occasion*) & *Jur* to seize; (*comprendre*) to understand, grasp; (*frapper*) *Fig* to strike; **se s. de** to grab (hold of), seize. **2** *vt* (*viande*) *Culin* to fry briskly. ◆**—i** *a* **s. de** (*joie, peur etc*) overcome by. ◆**—issant** *a* (*film etc*) gripping; (*contraste, ressemblance*) striking. ◆**—issement** *nm* (*émotion*) shock.

saison [sɛzɔ̃] *nf* season; **en/hors s.** in/out of season; **en pleine** *ou* **haute s.** in (the) high season; **en basse s.** in the low season. ◆**saisonnier, -ière** *a* seasonal.

sait [sɛ] *voir* **savoir.**

salade [salad] **1** *nf* (*laitue*) lettuce; **s. (verte)** (green) salad; **s. de fruits/de tomates/***etc* fruit/tomato/*etc* salad. **2** *nf* (*désordre*) *Fam* mess. **3** *nfpl* (*mensonges*) *Fam* stories, nonsense. ◆**saladier** *nm* salad bowl.

salaire [salɛr] *nm* wage(s), salary.
salaison [salɛzɔ̃] *nf Culin* salting; *pl* (*denrées*) salt(ed) meat *ou* fish.
salamandre [salamɑ̃dr] *nf* (*animal*) salamander.
salami [salami] *nm Culin* salami.
salarial, -aux [salarjal, -o] *a* (*accord etc*) wage-. ◆**salarié, -ée** *a* wage-earning; – *nmf* wage earner.
salaud [salo] *nm Arg Péj* bastard, swine.
sale [sal] *a* dirty; (*dégoûtant*) filthy; (*mauvais*) nasty; (*couleur*) dingy. ◆**salement** *adv* (*se conduire, manger*) disgustingly. ◆**saleté** *nf* dirtiness; filthiness; (*crasse*) dirt, filth; (*action*) dirty trick; (*camelote*) *Fam* rubbish, junk; *pl* (*détritus*) mess, dirt; (*obscénités*) filth. ◆**salir** *vt* to (make) dirty; (*réputation*) *Fig* to sully, tarnish; — **se s.** *vpr* to get dirty. ◆**salissant** *a* (*métier*) dirty, messy; (*étoffe*) easily dirtied. ◆**salissure** *nf* (*tache*) dirty mark.
sal/er [sale] *vt Culin* to salt. ◆**—é** *a* **1** (*eau*) salt-; (*saveur*) salty; (*denrées*) salted; (*grivois*) *Fig* spicy. **2** (*excessif*) *Fam* steep. ◆**salière** *nf* saltcellar.
salive [saliv] *nf* saliva. ◆**saliver** *vi* to salivate.
salle [sal] *nf* room; (*très grande, publique*) hall; *Th* auditorium; (*d'hôpital*) ward; (*public*) *Th* house, audience; **s. à manger** dining room; **s. d'eau** washroom, shower room; **s. d'exposition** *Com* showroom; **s. de jeux** (*pour enfants*) games room; (*avec machines à sous*) amusement arcade; **s. d'opération** *Méd* operating theatre.
salon [salɔ̃] *nm* sitting room, lounge; (*exposition*) show; **s. de beauté/de coiffure** beauty/hairdressing salon; **s. de thé** tearoom(s).
salope [salɔp] *nf* (*femme*) *Arg Péj* bitch, cow. ◆**saloperie** *nf Arg* (*action*) dirty trick; (*camelote*) rubbish, junk; **des saloperies** (*propos*) filth.
salopette [salɔpɛt] *nf* dungarees; (*d'ouvrier*) overalls.
salsifis [salsifi] *nf Bot Culin* salsify.
saltimbanque [saltɛ̃bɑ̃k] *nmf* (travelling) acrobat.
salubre [salybr] *a* healthy, salubrious. ◆**salubrité** *nf* healthiness; **s. publique** public health.
saluer [salɥe] *vt* to greet; (*en partant*) to take one's leave; (*de la main*) to wave to; (*de la tête*) to nod to; *Mil* to salute; **s. qn comme** *Fig* to hail s.o. as. ◆**salut 1** *nm* greeting; wave; nod; *Mil* salute; – *int Fam* hello!, hi!; (*au revoir*) bye! **2** *nm* (*de peuple etc*) salvation; (*sauvegarde*) safety. ◆**salutation** *nf* greeting.
salutaire [salytɛr] *a* salutary.
salve [salv] *nf* salvo.
samedi [samdi] *nm* Saturday.
SAMU [samy] *nm abrév* (*service d'assistance médicale d'urgence*) emergency medical service.
sanatorium [sanatɔrjɔm] *nm* sanatorium.
sanctifier [sɑ̃ktifje] *vt* to sanctify.
sanction [sɑ̃ksjɔ̃] *nf* (*approbation, peine*) sanction. ◆**sanctionner** *vt* (*confirmer, approuver*) to sanction; (*punir*) to punish.
sanctuaire [sɑ̃ktɥɛr] *nm Rel* sanctuary.
sandale [sɑ̃dal] *nf* sandal.
sandwich [sɑ̃dwitʃ] *nm* sandwich.
sang [sɑ̃] *nm* blood; **coup de s.** *Méd* stroke. ◆**sanglant** *a* bloody; (*critique, reproche*) scathing. ◆**sanguin, -ine 1** *a* (*vaisseau etc*) blood-; (*tempérament*) full-blooded. **2** *nf* (*fruit*) blood orange. ◆**sanguinaire** *a* blood-thirsty.
sang-froid [sɑ̃frwa] *nm* self-control, calm; **avec s.-froid** calmly; **de s.-froid** (*tuer*) in cold blood.
sangle [sɑ̃gl] *nf* (*de selle, parachute*) strap.
sanglier [sɑ̃glije] *nm* wild boar.
sanglot [sɑ̃glo] *nm* sob. ◆**sangloter** *vi* to sob.
sangsue [sɑ̃sy] *nf* leech.
sanitaire [sanitɛr] *a* health-; (*conditions*) sanitary; (*personnel*) medical; (*appareils etc*) bathroom-, sanitary.
sans [sɑ̃] ([sɑ̃z] *before vowel and mute h*) *prép* without; **s. faire** without doing; **ça va s. dire** that goes without saying; **s. qu'il le sache** without him *ou* his knowing; **s. cela, s. quoi** otherwise; **s. plus** (but) no more than that; **s. exception/faute** without exception/fail; **s. importance/travail** unimportant/unemployed; **s. argent/manches** penniless/sleeveless. ◆**s.-abri** *nmf inv* homeless person; **les s.-abri** the homeless. ◆**s.-gêne** *a inv* inconsiderate; – *nm inv* inconsiderateness. ◆**s.-travail** *nmf inv* unemployed person.
santé [sɑ̃te] *nf* health; **en bonne/mauvaise s.** in good/bad health, well/not well; (**à votre**) **s.!** (*en trinquant*) your health!, cheers!; **maison de s.** nursing home.
saoul [su] = **soûl**.
saper [sape] *vt* to undermine.
sapeur-pompier [sapœrpɔ̃pje] *nm* (*pl* **sapeurs-pompiers**) fireman.
saphir [safir] *nm* (*pierre*) sapphire; (*d'électrophone*) sapphire, stylus.

sapin [sapɛ̃] *nm (arbre; bois)* fir; **s. de Noël** Christmas tree.
sarbacane [sarbakan] *nf (jouet)* peashooter.
sarcasme [sarkasm] *nm* sarcasm; **un s.** a piece of sarcasm. ◆**sarcastique** *a* sarcastic.
sarcler [sarkle] *vt (jardin etc)* to weed.
Sardaigne [sardɛɲ] *nf* Sardinia.
sardine [sardin] *nf* sardine.
sardonique [sardɔnik] *a* sardonic.
SARL *abrév (société à responsabilité limitée)* Ltd, *Am* Inc.
sarment [sarmɑ̃] *nm* vine shoot.
sarrasin [sarazɛ̃] *nm* buckwheat.
sas [sɑ(s)] *nm (pièce étanche) Nau Av* airlock.
Satan [satɑ̃] *nm* Satan. ◆**satané** *a (maudit)* blasted. ◆**satanique** *a* satanic.
satellite [satelit] *nm* satellite; **pays s.** *Pol* satellite (country).
satiété [sasjete] *nf* **à s.** *(boire, manger)* one's fill; *(répéter)* ad nauseam.
satin [satɛ̃] *nm* satin. ◆**satiné** *a* satiny, silky.
satire [satir] *nf* satire (**contre** on). ◆**satirique** *a* satiric(al).
satisfaction [satisfaksjɔ̃] *nf* satisfaction. ◆**satisfaire*** *vt* to satisfy; – *vi* **s. à** *(conditions, engagement etc)* to fulfil. ◆**satisfaisant** *a (acceptable)* satisfactory. ◆**satisfait** *a* satisfied, content (**de** with).
saturateur [satyratœr] *nm (de radiateur)* humidifier.
saturer [satyre] *vt* to saturate (**de** with).
satyre [satir] *nm Fam* sex fiend.
sauce [sos] *nf* sauce; *(jus de viande)* gravy; **s. tomate** tomato sauce. ◆**saucière** *nf* sauce boat; gravy boat.
saucisse [sosis] *nf* sausage. ◆**saucisson** *nm* (cold) sausage.
sauf[1] [sof] *prép* except (**que** that); **s. avis contraire** unless you hear otherwise; **s. erreur** barring error.
sauf[2], **sauve** [sof, sov] *a (honneur)* intact, saved; **avoir la vie sauve** to be unharmed. ◆**sauf-conduit** *nm (document)* safe-conduct.
sauge [soʒ] *nf Bot Culin* sage.
saugrenu [sogrəny] *a* preposterous.
saule [sol] *nm* willow; **s. pleureur** weeping willow.
saumâtre [somɑtr] *a (eau)* briny, brackish.
saumon [somɔ̃] *nm* salmon; – *a inv (couleur)* salmon (pink).
saumure [somyr] *nf* (pickling) brine.
sauna [sona] *nm* sauna.
saupoudrer [sopudre] *vt (couvrir)* to sprinkle (**de** with).
saur [sɔr] *am* **hareng s.** smoked herring, kipper.
saut [so] *nm* jump, leap; **faire un s.** to jump, leap; **faire un s. chez qn** *(visite)* to pop round to s.o.; **au s. du lit** on getting out of bed; **s. à la corde** skipping, *Am* jumping rope. ◆**sauter** *vi* to jump, leap; *(bombe)* to go off, explode; *(poudrière etc)* to go up, blow up; *(fusible)* to blow; *(se détacher)* to come off; **faire s.** *(détruire)* to blow up; *(arracher)* to tear off; *(casser)* to break; *(renvoyer) Fam* to get rid of, fire; *(fusible)* to blow; *Culin* to sauté; **s. à la corde** to skip, *Am* jump rope; **ça saute aux yeux** it's obvious; – *vt (franchir)* to jump (over); *(mot, classe, repas)* to skip. ◆**saute-mouton** *nm (jeu)* leapfrog. ◆**sautiller** *vi* to hop. ◆**sautoir** *nm Sp* jumping area.
sauté [sote] *a & nm Culin* sauté. ◆**sauteuse** *nf* (shallow) pan.
sauterelle [sotrɛl] *nf* grasshopper.
sautes [sot] *nfpl (d'humeur, de température)* sudden changes (**de** in).
sauvage [sovaʒ] *a* wild; *(primitif, cruel)* savage; *(farouche)* unsociable, shy; *(illégal)* unauthorized; – *nmf* unsociable person; *(brute)* savage. ◆**sauvagerie** *nf* unsociability; *(cruauté)* savagery.
sauve [sov] *a voir* **sauf**[2].
sauvegarde [sovgard] *nf* safeguard (**contre** against). ◆**sauvegarder** *vt* to safeguard.
sauver [sove] **1** *vt* to save; *(d'un danger)* to rescue (**de** from); *(matériel)* to salvage; **s. la vie à qn** to save s.o.'s life. **2 se s.** *vpr (s'enfuir)* to run away *ou* off; *(partir) Fam* to get off, go. ◆**sauve-qui-peut** *nm inv* stampede. ◆**sauvetage** *nm* rescue; **canot de s.** lifeboat; **ceinture de s.** life belt; **radeau de s.** life raft. ◆**sauveteur** *nm* rescuer. ◆**sauveur** *nm* saviour.
sauvette (à la) [alasovɛt] *adv* **vendre à la s.** to hawk illicitly (on the streets).
savant [savɑ̃] *a* learned, scholarly; *(manœuvre etc)* masterly, clever; – *nm* scientist. ◆**savamment** *adv* learnedly; *(avec habileté)* cleverly, skilfully.
savate [savat] *nf* old shoe *ou* slipper.
saveur [savœr] *nf (goût)* flavour; *(piment) Fig* savour.
savoir* [savwar] *vt* to know; *(nouvelle)* to know, have heard; **j'ai su la nouvelle** I heard *ou* got to know the news; **s. lire/nager/***etc* *(pouvoir)* to know how to read/swim/*etc*; **faire s. à qn que** to inform *ou* tell s.o. that; **à s.** *(c'est-à-dire)* that is,

namely; **je ne saurais pas** I could not, I cannot; **(pas) que je sache** (not) as far as I know; **je n'en sais rien** I have no idea, I don't know; **en s. long sur** to know a lot about; **un je ne sais quoi** a something or other; – *nm* (*culture*) learning, knowledge. **◆s.-faire** *nm inv* know-how, ability. **◆s.-vivre** *nm inv* good manners.

savon [savɔ̃] *nm* **1** soap; (*morceau*) bar of soap. **2 passer un s. à qn** (*réprimander*) *Fam* to give s.o. a dressing-down *ou* a talking-to. **◆savonner** *vt* to soap. **◆savonnette** *nf* bar of soap. **◆savonneux, -euse** *a* soapy.

savourer [savure] *vt* to savour, relish. **◆savoureux, -euse** *a* tasty; (*histoire etc*) *Fig* juicy.

saxophone [saksɔfɔn] *nm* saxophone.

sbire [sbir] *nm* (*homme de main*) *Péj* henchman.

scabreux, -euse [skabrø, -øz] *a* obscene.

scalpel [skalpɛl] *nm* scalpel.

scandale [skɑ̃dal] *nm* scandal; (*tapage*) uproar; **faire s.** (*livre etc*) to scandalize people; **faire un s.** to make a scene. **◆scandaleux, -euse** *a* scandalous, outrageous. **◆scandaleusement** *adv* outrageously. **◆scandaliser** *vt* to scandalize, shock; **— se s.** *vpr* to be shocked *ou* scandalized (**de** by, **que** (+ *sub*) that).

scander [skɑ̃de] *vt* (*vers*) to scan; (*slogan*) to chant.

Scandinavie [skɑ̃dinavi] *nf* Scandinavia. **◆scandinave** *a & nmf* Scandinavian.

scanner [skanɛr] *nm* (*appareil*) *Méd* scanner.

scaphandre [skafɑ̃dr] *nm* (*de plongeur*) diving suit; (*de cosmonaute*) spacesuit; **s. autonome** aqualung. **◆scaphandrier** *nm* diver.

scarabée [skarabe] *nm* beetle.

scarlatine [skarlatin] *nf* scarlet fever.

scarole [skarɔl] *nf* endive.

sceau, -x [so] *nm* (*cachet, cire*) seal. **◆scell/er** *vt* **1** (*document etc*) to seal. **2** (*fixer*) *Tech* to cement. **◆—és** *nmpl* (*cachets de cire*) seals.

scélérat, -ate [selera, -at] *nmf* scoundrel.

scel-o-frais® [selofrɛ] *nm* clingfilm, *Am* plastic wrap.

scénario [senarjo] *nm* (*déroulement*) *Fig* scenario; (*esquisse*) *Cin* scenario; (*dialogues etc*) screenplay. **◆scénariste** *nmf Cin* scriptwriter.

scène [sɛn] *nf* **1** *Th* scene; (*estrade, art*) stage; (*action*) action; **mettre en s.** (*pièce, film*) to direct. **2** (*dispute*) scene; **faire une s.** (**à qn**) to make *ou* create a scene; **s. de ménage** domestic quarrel.

scepticisme [septisism] *nm* scepticism, *Am* skepticism. **◆sceptique** *a* sceptical, *Am* skeptical; – *nmf* sceptic, *Am* skeptic.

scheik [ʃɛk] *nm* sheikh.

schéma [ʃema] *nm* diagram; *Fig* outline. **◆schématique** *a* diagrammatic; (*succinct*) *Péj* sketchy. **◆schématiser** *vt* to represent diagrammatically; (*simplifier*) *Péj* to oversimplify.

schizophrène [skizɔfrɛn] *a & nmf* schizophrenic.

sciatique [sjatik] *nf Méd* sciatica.

scie [si] *nf* (*outil*) saw. **◆scier** *vt* to saw. **◆scierie** *nf* sawmill.

sciemment [sjamɑ̃] *adv* knowingly.

science [sjɑ̃s] *nf* science; (*savoir*) knowledge; (*habileté*) skill; **sciences humaines** social science(s); **étudier les sciences** to study science. **◆s.-fiction** *nf* science fiction. **◆scientifique** *a* scientific; – *nmf* scientist.

scinder [sɛ̃de] *vt*, **— se s.** *vpr* to divide, split.

scintill/er [sɛ̃tije] *vi* to sparkle, glitter; (*étoiles*) to twinkle. **◆—ement** *nm* sparkling; twinkling.

scission [sisjɔ̃] *nf* (*de parti etc*) split (**de** in).

sciure [sjyr] *nf* sawdust.

sclérose [skleroz] *nf Méd* sclerosis; *Fig* ossification; **s. en plaques** multiple sclerosis. **◆sclérosé** *a* (*société etc*) *Fig* ossified.

scolaire [skɔlɛr] *a* school-. **◆scolariser** *vt* (*pays*) to provide with schools; (*enfant*) to send to school, put in school. **◆scolarité** *nf* schooling.

scooter [skutɛr] *nm* (motor) scooter.

score [skɔr] *nm Sp* score.

scories [skɔri] *nfpl* (*résidu*) slag.

scorpion [skɔrpjɔ̃] *nm* scorpion; **le S.** (*signe*) Scorpio.

scotch [skɔtʃ] *nm* **1** (*boisson*) Scotch, whisky. **2®** (*ruban adhésif*) sellotape®, *Am* scotch (tape)®. **◆scotcher** *vt* to sellotape, *Am* to tape.

scout [skut] *a & nm* scout. **◆scoutisme** *nm* scout movement, scouting.

script [skript] *nm* (*écriture*) printing.

scrupule [skrypyl] *nm* scruple; **sans scrupules** unscrupulous; (*agir*) unscrupulously. **◆scrupuleux, -euse** *a* scrupulous. **◆scrupuleusement** *adv* scrupulously.

scruter [skryte] *vt* to examine, scrutinize.

scrutin [skrytɛ̃] *nm* (*vote*) ballot; (*opérations électorales*) poll(ing).

sculpter [skylte] *vt* to sculpt(ure), carve.

◆**sculpteur** *nm* sculptor. ◆**sculptural, -aux** *a* (*beauté*) statuesque. ◆**sculpture** *nf* (*art, œuvre*) sculpture; **s. sur bois** woodcarving.

se [s(ə)] (**s'** *before vowel or mute h*) *pron* **1** (*complément direct*) himself; (*sujet femelle*) herself; (*non humain*) itself; (*indéfini*) oneself; *pl* themselves; **il se lave**, he washes himself. **2** (*indirect*) to himself; to herself; to itself; to oneself; **se dire** to say to oneself; **elle se dit** she says to herself. **3** (*réciproque*) (to) each other, (to) one another; **ils s'aiment** they love each other *ou* one another; **ils** *ou* **elles se parlent** they speak to each other *ou* one another. **4** (*passif*) **ça se fait** that is done; **ça se vend bien** it sells well. **5** (*possessif*) **il se lave les mains** he washes his hands.

séance [seɑ̃s] *nf* **1** (*d'assemblée etc*) session, sitting; (*de travail etc*) session; **s. (de pose)** (*chez un peintre*) sitting. **2** *Cin Th* show, performance. **3 s. tenante** at once.

séant [seɑ̃] **1** *a* (*convenable*) seemly, proper. **2** *nm* **se mettre sur son s.** to sit up.

seau, -x [so] *nm* bucket, pail.

sec, sèche [sɛk, sɛʃ] *a* dry; (*fruits, légumes*) dried; (*ton*) curt, harsh; (*maigre*) spare; (*cœur*) *Fig* hard; **coup s.** sharp blow, tap; **bruit s.** (*rupture*) snap; – *adv* (*frapper, pleuvoir*) hard; (*boire*) neat, *Am* straight; – *nm* **à s.** dried up, dry; (*sans argent*) *Fam* broke; **au s.** in a dry place. ◆**séch/er 1** *vti* to dry; — **se s.** *vpr* to dry oneself. **2** *vt* (*cours*) *Scol Fam* to skip; – *vi* (*ignorer*) *Scol Fam* to be stumped. ◆**—age** *nm* drying. ◆**sécheresse** *nf* dryness; (*de ton*) curtness; *Mét* drought. ◆**séchoir** *nm* (*appareil*) drier; **s. à linge** clotheshorse.

sécateur [sekatœr] *nm* pruning shears, secateurs.

sécession [sesesjɔ̃] *nf* secession; **faire s.** to secede.

sèche [sɛʃ] *voir* **sec.** ◆**sèche-cheveux** *nm inv* hair drier. ◆**sèche-linge** *nm inv* tumble drier.

second, -onde[1] [sgɔ̃, -ɔ̃d] *a & nmf* second; **de seconde main** second-hand; – *nm* (*adjoint*) second in command; (*étage*) second floor, *Am* third floor; – *nf Rail* second class; *Scol* = fifth form, *Am* = eleventh grade; (*vitesse*) *Aut* second (gear). ◆**secondaire** *a* secondary.

seconde[2] [sgɔ̃d] *nf* (*instant*) second.

seconder [sgɔ̃de] *vt* to assist.

secouer [s(ə)kwe] *vt* to shake; (*paresse, poussière*) to shake off; **s. qn** (*maladie, nouvelle etc*) to shake s.o. up; **s. qch de qch** (*enlever*) to shake sth out of sth; — **se s.** *vpr* (*faire un effort*) *Fam* to shake oneself out of it.

secour/ir [skurir] *vt* to assist, help. ◆**—able** *a* (*personne*) helpful. ◆**secourisme** *nm* first aid. ◆**secouriste** *nmf* first-aid worker.

secours [s(ə)kur] *nm* assistance, help; (*aux indigents*) aid, relief; **le s., les s.** *Mil* relief; **(premiers) s.** *Méd* first aid; **au s.!** help!; **porter s. à qn** to give s.o. assistance *ou* help; **de s.** (*sortie*) emergency-; (*équipe*) rescue-; (*roue*) spare.

secousse [s(ə)kus] *nf* jolt, jerk; (*psychologique*) shock; *Géol* tremor.

secret, -ète [səkrɛ, -ɛt] *a* secret; (*cachottier*) secretive; – *nm* secret; (*discrétion*) secrecy; **en s.** in secret, secretly; **dans le s.** (*au courant*) in on the secret.

secrétaire [səkretɛr] **1** *nmf* secretary; **s. d'État** Secretary of State; **s. de mairie** town clerk; **s. de rédaction** subeditor. **2** *nm* (*meuble*) writing desk. ◆**secrétariat** *nm* (*bureau*) secretary's office; (*d'organisation internationale*) secretariat; (*métier*) secretarial work; **de s.** (*école, travail*) secretarial.

sécréter [sekrete] *vt Méd Biol* to secrete. ◆**sécrétion** *nf* secretion.

secte [sɛkt] *nf* sect. ◆**sectaire** *a & nmf Péj* sectarian.

secteur [sɛktœr] *nm Mil Com* sector; (*de ville*) district; (*domaine*) *Fig* area; (*de réseau*) *Él* supply area; (*ligne*) *Él* mains.

section [sɛksjɔ̃] *nf* section; (*de ligne d'autobus*) fare stage; *Mil* platoon. ◆**sectionner** *vt* to divide (into sections); (*artère, doigt*) to sever.

séculaire [sekylɛr] *a* (*tradition etc*) age-old.

secundo [s(ə)gɔ̃do] *adv* secondly.

sécurité [sekyrite] *nf* (*tranquillité*) security; (*matérielle*) safety; **s. routière** road safety; **s. sociale** = social services *ou* security; **de s.** (*dispositif, ceinture, marge etc*) safety-; **en s.** secure; safe. ◆**sécuriser** *vt* to reassure, make feel (emotionally) secure.

sédatif [sedatif] *nm* sedative.

sédentaire [sedɑ̃tɛr] *a* sedentary.

sédiment [sedimɑ̃] *nm* sediment.

séditieux, -euse [sedisjø, -øz] *a* seditious. ◆**sédition** *nf* sedition.

séduire* [sedɥir] *vt* to charm, attract; (*plaire à*) to appeal to; (*abuser de*) to seduce. ◆**séduisant** *a* attractive. ◆**séducteur, -trice** *a* seductive; – *nmf* seducer. ◆**séduction** *nf* attraction.

segment [sɛgmɑ̃] *nm* segment.

ségrégation [segregasjɔ̃] *nf* segregation.

seiche [sɛʃ] *nf* cuttlefish.
seigle [sɛgl] *nm* rye.
seigneur [sɛɲœr] *nm Hist* lord; **S.** *Rel* Lord.
sein [sɛ̃] *nm* (*mamelle, poitrine*) breast; *Fig* bosom; **bout de s.** nipple; **au s. de** (*parti etc*) within; (*bonheur etc*) in the midst of.
Seine [sɛn] *nf* **la S.** the Seine.
séisme [seism] *nm* earthquake.
seize [sɛz] *a & nm* sixteen. ◆**seizième** *a & nmf* sixteenth.
séjour [seʒur] *nm* stay; **(salle de) s.** living room. ◆**séjourner** *vi* to stay.
sel [sɛl] *nm* salt; (*piquant*) *Fig* spice; (*humour*) wit; *pl Méd* (smelling) salts; **sels de bain** bath salts.
sélect [selɛkt] *a Fam* select.
sélectif, -ive [selɛktif, -iv] *a* selective. ◆**sélection** *nf* selection. ◆**sélectionner** *vt* to select.
self(-service) [sɛlf(sɛrvis)] *nm* self-service restaurant *ou* shop.
selle [sɛl] **1** *nf* (*de cheval*) saddle. **2** *nfpl* **les selles** *Méd* bowel movements, stools. ◆**seller** *vt* (*cheval*) to saddle.
sellette [sɛlɛt] *nf* **sur la s.** (*personne*) under examination, in the hot seat.
selon [s(ə)lɔ̃] *prép* according to (**que** whether); **c'est s.** *Fam* it (all) depends.
Seltz (eau de) [odsɛls] *nf* soda (water).
semailles [s(ə)mɑj] *nfpl* (*travail*) sowing; (*période*) seedtime.
semaine [s(ə)mɛn] *nf* week; **en s.** (*opposé à week-end*) in the week.
sémantique [semɑ̃tik] *a* semantic; – *nf* semantics.
sémaphore [semafɔr] *nm* (*appareil*) *Rail Nau* semaphore.
semblable [sɑ̃blabl] *a* similar (**à** to); **être semblables** to be alike *ou* similar; **de semblables propos/***etc* (*tels*) such remarks/*etc*; – *nm* fellow (creature); **toi et tes semblables** you and your kind.
semblant [sɑ̃blɑ̃] *nm* **faire s.** to pretend (**de faire** to do); **un s. de** a semblance of.
sembler [sɑ̃ble] *vi* to seem (**à** to); **il (me) semble vieux** he seems *ou* looks old (to me); **s. être/faire** to seem to be/to do; – *v imp* **il semble que** (+ *sub ou indic*) it seems that, it looks as if; **il me semble que** it seems to me that, I think that.
semelle [s(ə)mɛl] *nf* (*de chaussure*) sole; (*intérieure*) insole.
semer [s(ə)me] *vt* **1** (*graines*) to sow; (*jeter*) *Fig* to strew; (*répandre*) to spread; **semé de** *Fig* strewn with, dotted with. **2** (*concurrent, poursuivant*) to shake off. ◆**semence** *nf* seed; (*clou*) tack. ◆**semeur, -euse** *nmf* sower (**de** of).
semestre [s(ə)mɛstr] *nm* half-year; *Univ* semester. ◆**semestriel, -ielle** *a* half-yearly.
semi- [səmi] *préf* semi-.
séminaire [seminɛr] *nm* **1** *Univ* seminar. **2** *Rel* seminary.
semi-remorque [səmirəmɔrk] *nm* (*camion*) articulated lorry, *Am* semi(trailer).
semis [s(ə)mi] *nm* sowing; (*terrain*) seedbed; (*plant*) seedling.
sémite [semit] *a* Semitic; – *nmf* Semite. ◆**sémitique** *a* (*langue*) Semitic.
semonce [səmɔ̃s] *nf* reprimand; **coup de s.** *Nau* warning shot.
semoule [s(ə)mul] *nf* semolina.
sempiternel, -elle [sɑ̃pitɛrnɛl] *a* endless, ceaseless.
sénat [sena] *nm Pol* senate. ◆**sénateur** *nm Pol* senator.
sénile [senil] *a* senile. ◆**sénilité** *nf* senility.
sens [sɑ̃s] *nm* **1** (*faculté, raison*) sense; (*signification*) meaning, sense; **à mon s.** to my mind; **s. commun** commonsense; **s. de l'humour** sense of humour; **ça n'a pas de s.** that doesn't make sense. **2** (*direction*) direction; **s. giratoire** *Aut* roundabout, *Am* traffic circle, rotary; **s. interdit** *ou* **unique** (*rue*) one-way street; **'s. interdit'** 'no entry'; **à s. unique** (*rue*) one-way; **s. dessus dessous** [sɑ̃dsydsu] upside down; **dans le s./le s. inverse des aiguilles d'une montre** clockwise/anticlockwise, *Am* counterclockwise.
sensation [sɑ̃sɑsjɔ̃] *nf* sensation, feeling; **faire s.** to cause *ou* create a sensation; **à s.** (*film etc*) *Péj* sensational. ◆**sensationnel, -elle** *a Fig* sensational.
sensé [sɑ̃se] *a* sensible.
sensible [sɑ̃sibl] *a* sensitive (**à** to); (*douloureux*) tender, sore; (*perceptible*) perceptible; (*progrès etc*) appreciable. ◆**sensiblement** *adv* (*notablement*) appreciably; (*à peu près*) more or less. ◆**sensibiliser** *vt* **s. qn à** (*problème etc*) to make s.o. alive to *ou* aware of. ◆**sensibilité** *nf* sensitivity.
sensoriel, -ielle [sɑ̃sɔrjɛl] *a* sensory.
sensuel, -elle [sɑ̃sɥɛl] *a* (*sexuel*) sensual; (*musique, couleur etc*) sensuous. ◆**sensualité** *nf* sensuality; sensuousness.
sentence [sɑ̃tɑ̃s] *nf* **1** *Jur* sentence. **2** (*maxime*) maxim.
senteur [sɑ̃tœr] *nf* (*odeur*) scent.
sentier [sɑ̃tje] *nm* path.
sentiment [sɑ̃timɑ̃] *nm* feeling; **avoir le s. de** (*apprécier*) to be aware of; **faire du s.** to be sentimental. ◆**sentimental, -aux** *a* senti-

mental; (*amoureux*) love-. ◆**sentimentalité** *nf* sentimentality.

sentinelle [sɑ̃tinɛl] *nf* sentry.

sentir* [sɑ̃tir] *vt* to feel; (*odeur*) to smell; (*goût*) to taste; (*racisme etc*) to smack of; (*connaître*) to sense, be conscious of; **s. le moisi/le parfum/***etc* to smell musty/of perfume/*etc*; **s. le poisson/***etc* (*avoir le goût de*) to taste of fish/*etc*; **je ne peux pas le s.** (*supporter*) *Fam* I can't bear *ou* stand him; **se faire s.** (*effet etc*) to make itself felt; **se s. fatigué/humilié/***etc* to feel tired/humiliated/*etc*; – *vi* to smell.

séparation [separɑsjɔ̃] *nf* separation; (*en deux*) division, split; (*départ*) parting. ◆**séparer** *vt* to separate (**de** from); (*diviser en deux*) to divide, split (up); (*cheveux*) to part; **— se s.** *vpr* (*se quitter*) to part; (*adversaires, époux*) to separate; (*assemblée, cortège*) to disperse, break up; (*se détacher*) to split off; **se s. de** (*objet aimé, chien etc*) to part with. ◆**séparé** *a* (*distinct*) separate; (*époux*) separated (**de** from). ◆**séparément** *adv* separately.

sept [sɛt] *a* & *nm* seven. ◆**septième** *a* & *nmf* seventh; **un s.** a seventh.

septante [sɛptɑ̃t] *a* & *nm* (*en Belgique, Suisse*) seventy.

septembre [sɛptɑ̃br] *nm* September.

septennat [sɛptena] *nm Pol* seven-year term (of office).

septentrional, -aux [sɛptɑ̃trijɔnal, -o] *a* northern.

sépulcre [sepylkr] *nm Rel* sepulchre.

sépulture [sepyltyr] *nf* burial; (*lieu*) burial place.

séquelles [sekɛl] *nfpl* (*de maladie etc*) aftereffects; (*de guerre*) aftermath.

séquence [sekɑ̃s] *nf Mus Cartes Cin* sequence.

séquestrer [sekɛstre] *vt* to confine (illegally), lock up.

sera, serait [s(ə)ra, s(ə)rɛ] *voir* **être**.

serein [sərɛ̃] *a* serene. ◆**sérénité** *nf* serenity.

sérénade [serenad] *nf* serenade.

sergent [sɛrʒɑ̃] *nm Mil* sergeant.

série [seri] *nf* series; (*ensemble*) set; **s. noire** *Fig* string *ou* series of disasters; **de s.** (*article etc*) standard; **fabrication en s.** mass production; **fins de s.** *Com* oddments; **hors s.** *Fig* outstanding.

sérieux, -euse [serjø, -øz] *a* (*personne, maladie, doute etc*) serious; (*de bonne foi*) genuine, serious; (*digne de foi, fiable*) reliable; (*bénéfices*) substantial; **de sérieuses chances de ...** a good chance of ...; – *nm* seriousness; (*fiabilité*) reliability; **prendre au s.** to take seriously; **garder son s.** to keep a straight face; **manquer de s.** (*travailleur*) to lack application. ◆**sérieusement** *adv* seriously; (*travailler*) conscientiously.

serin [s(ə)rɛ̃] *nm* canary.

seriner [s(ə)rine] *vt* **s. qch à qn** to repeat sth to s.o. over and over again.

seringue [s(ə)rɛ̃g] *nf* syringe.

serment [sɛrmɑ̃] *nm* (*affirmation solennelle*) oath; (*promesse*) pledge; **prêter s.** to take an oath; **faire le s. de faire** to swear to do; **sous s.** *Jur* on *ou* under oath.

sermon [sɛrmɔ̃] *nm Rel* sermon; (*discours*) *Péj* lecture. ◆**sermonner** *vt* (*faire la morale à*) to lecture.

serpe [sɛrp] *nf* bill(hook).

serpent [sɛrpɑ̃] *nm* snake; **s. à sonnette** rattlesnake.

serpenter [sɛrpɑ̃te] *vi* (*sentier etc*) to meander.

serpentin [sɛrpɑ̃tɛ̃] *nm* (*ruban*) streamer.

serpillière [sɛrpijɛr] *nf* floor cloth.

serre [sɛr] **1** *nf* greenhouse. **2** *nfpl* (*d'oiseau*) claws, talons.

serre-livres [sɛrlivr] *nm inv* bookend. ◆**s.-tête** *nm inv* (*bandeau*) headband.

serr/er [sere] *vt* (*saisir, tenir*) to grip, clasp; (*presser*) to squeeze, press; (*corde, nœud, vis*) to tighten; (*poing*) to clench; (*taille*) to hug; (*pieds*) to pinch; (*frein*) to apply, put on; (*rapprocher*) to close up; (*rangs*) *Mil* to close; **s. la main à** to shake hands with; **s. les dents** *Fig* to grit one's teeth; **s. qn** (*embrasser*) to hug s.o.; (*vêtement*) to be too tight for s.o.; **s. qn de près** (*talonner*) to be close behind s.o.; – *vi* **s. à droite** *Aut* to keep (to the) right; **— se s.** *vpr* (*se rapprocher*) to squeeze up *ou* together; **se s. contre** to squeeze up against. ◆**—é** *a* (*budget, nœud, vêtement*) tight; (*gens*) packed (together); (*mailles, lutte*) close; (*rangs*) serried; (*dense*) dense, thick; (*cœur*) *Fig* heavy; **avoir la gorge serrée** *Fig* to have a lump in one's throat.

serrure [seryr] *nf* lock. ◆**serrurier** *nm* locksmith.

sertir [sɛrtir] *vt* (*diamant etc*) to set.

sérum [serɔm] *nm* serum.

servante [sɛrvɑ̃t] *nf* (maid)servant.

serveur, -euse [sɛrvœr, -øz] *nmf* waiter, waitress; (*au bar*) barman, barmaid.

serviable [sɛrvjabl] *a* helpful, obliging. ◆**serviabilité** *nf* helpfulness.

service [sɛrvis] *nm* service; (*fonction, travail*) duty; (*pourboire*) service (charge); (*département*) *Com* department; *Tennis* serve, service; **un s.** (*aide*) a favour; **rendre s.** to be of service (**à qn** to s.o.), help (**à qn** s.o.); **rendre un mauvais s. à qn** to do s.o. a disservice; **ça pourrait rendre s.** *Fam* that might come in useful; **s. (non) compris** service (not) included; **s. après-vente** *Com* aftersales (service); **s. d'ordre** (*policiers*) police; **être de s.** to be on duty; **s. à café/à thé** coffee/tea service *ou* set; **à votre s.!** at your service!

serviette [sɛrvjɛt] *nf* **1** towel; **s. de bain/de toilette** bath/hand towel; **s. hygiénique** sanitary towel; **s. (de table)** serviette, napkin. **2** (*sac*) briefcase.

servile [sɛrvil] *a* servile; (*imitation*) slavish. ◆**servilité** *nf* servility; slavishness.

servir* [sɛrvir] **1** *vt* to serve (**qch à qn** s.o. with sth, sth to s.o.); (*convive*) to wait on; – *vi* to serve; – **se s.** *vpr* (*à table*) to help oneself (**de** to). **2** *vi* (*être utile*) to be useful, serve; **s. à qch/à faire** (*objet*) to be used for sth/to do *ou* for doing; **ça ne sert à rien** it's useless, it's no good *ou* use (**de faire** doing); **à quoi ça sert de protester/***etc* what's the use *ou* good of protesting/*etc*; **s. de qch** (*objet*) to be used for sth, serve as sth; **ça me sert à faire/de qch** I use it to do *ou* for doing/as sth; **s. à qn de guide/***etc* to act as a guide/*etc* to s.o. **3 se s.** *vpr* **se s. de** (*utiliser*) to use.

serviteur [sɛrvitœr] *nm* servant. ◆**servitude** *nf* (*esclavage*) servitude; (*contrainte*) *Fig* constraint.

ses [se] *voir* **son**[2].

session [sesjɔ̃] *nf* session.

set [sɛt] *nm* **1** *Tennis* set. **2 s. (de table)** (*napperon*) place mat.

seuil [sœj] *nm* doorstep; (*entrée*) doorway; (*limite*) *Fig* threshold; **au s. de** *Fig* on the threshold of.

seul, seule [sœl] **1** *a* (*sans compagnie*) alone; **tout s.** all alone, by oneself, on one's own; **se sentir s.** to feel lonely *ou* alone; – *adv* **(tout) s.** (*agir, vivre*) by oneself, alone, on one's own; (*parler*) to oneself; **s. à s.** (*parler*) in private. **2** *a* (*unique*) only; **la seule femme/***etc* the only *ou* sole woman/*etc*; **un s. chat/***etc* only one cat/*etc*; **une seule fois** only once; **pas un s. livre/***etc* not a single book/*etc*; **seuls les garçons . . . , les garçons seuls . . .** only the boys . . . ; – *nmf* **le s., la seule** the only one; **un s., une seule** only one, one only; **pas un s.** not (a single) one. ◆**seulement** *adv* only; **non s. . . . mais . . .** not only . . . but (also) . . . ; **pas s.** (*même*) not even; **sans s. faire** without even doing.

sève [sɛv] *nf Bot & Fig* sap.

sévère [sevɛr] *a* severe; (*parents, professeur*) strict. ◆**–ment** *adv* severely; (*élever*) strictly. ◆**sévérité** *nf* severity; strictness.

sévices [sevis] *nmpl* brutality.

sévir [sevir] *vi* (*fléau*) *Fig* to rage; **s. contre** to deal severely with.

sevrer [səvre] *vt* (*enfant*) to wean; **s. de** (*priver*) *Fig* to deprive of.

sexe [sɛks] *nm* (*catégorie, sexualité*) sex; (*organes*) genitals; **l'autre s.** the opposite sex. ◆**sexiste** *a & nmf* sexist. ◆**sexualité** *nf* sexuality. ◆**sexuel, -elle** *a* sexual; (*éducation, acte etc*) sex-.

sextuor [sɛkstɥɔr] *nm* sextet.

seyant [sɛjɑ̃] *a* (*vêtement*) becoming.

shampooing [ʃɑ̃pwɛ̃] *nm* shampoo; **s. colorant** rinse; **faire un s. à qn** to shampoo s.o.'s hair.

shérif [ʃerif] *nm Am* sheriff.

shooter [ʃute] *vti Fb* to shoot.

short [ʃɔrt] *nm* (pair of) shorts.

si [si] **1** (= **s'** [s] *before* **il, ils**) *conj* if; **s'il vient** if he comes; **si j'étais roi** if I were *ou* was king; **je me demande si** I wonder whether *ou* if; **si on restait?** (*suggestion*) what if we stayed?; **si je dis ça, c'est que . . .** I say this because . . . ; **si ce n'est** (*sinon*) if not; **si oui** if so. **2** *adv* (*tellement*) so; **pas si riche que toi/que tu crois** not as rich as you/as you think; **un si bon dîner** such a good dinner; **si grand qu'il soit** however big he may be; **si bien que** with the result that. **3** *adv* (*après négative*) yes; **tu ne viens pas? – si!** you're not coming? – yes (I am)!

siamois [sjamwa] *a* Siamese; **frères s., sœurs siamoises** Siamese twins.

Sicile [sisil] *nf* Sicily.

SIDA [sida] *nm Méd* AIDS. ◆**sidéen, -enne** *nmf* AIDS sufferer.

sidérer [sidere] *vt Fam* to flabbergast.

sidérurgie [sideryrʒi] *nf* iron and steel industry.

siècle [sjɛkl] *nm* century; (*époque*) age.

siège [sjɛʒ] *nm* **1** (*meuble, centre*) & *Pol* seat; (*d'autorité, de parti etc*) headquarters; **s. (social)** (*d'entreprise*) head office. **2** *Mil* siege; **mettre le s. devant** to lay siege to. ◆**siéger** *vi Pol* to sit.

sien, sienne [sjɛ̃, sjɛn] *pron poss* **le s., la sienne, les sien(ne)s** his; (*de femme*) hers; (*de chose*) its; **les deux siens** his *ou* her two; – *nmpl* **les siens** (*amis etc*) one's (own) people.

sieste [sjɛst] *nf* siesta; **faire la s.** to have *ou* take a nap.

siffler [sifle] *vi* to whistle; (*avec un sifflet*) to

blow one's whistle; (*gaz, serpent*) to hiss; (*en respirant*) to wheeze; – *vt* (*chanson*) to whistle; (*chien*) to whistle to; (*faute, fin de match*) *Sp* to blow one's whistle for; (*acteur, pièce*) to boo; (*boisson*) *Fam* to knock back. ◆**sifflement** *nm* whistling, whistle; hiss(ing). ◆**sifflet** *nm* (*instrument*) whistle; *pl Th* booing, boos; **(coup de) s.** (*son*) whistle. ◆**siffloter** *vti* to whistle.

sigle [sigl] *nm* (*initiales*) abbreviation; (*prononcé comme un mot*) acronym.

signal, -aux [siɲal, -o] *nm* signal; **s. d'alarme** *Rail* communication cord; **signaux routiers** road signs. ◆**signal/er 1** *vt* (*faire remarquer*) to point out (**à qn** to s.o., **que** that); (*annoncer, indiquer*) to indicate, signal; (*dénoncer à la police etc*) to report (**à** to). **2 se s.** *vpr* **se s. par** to distinguish oneself by. ◆**—ement** *nm* (*de personne*) description, particulars. ◆**signalisation** *nf* signalling; *Aut* signposting; **s. (routière)** (*signaux*) road signs.

signature [siɲatyr] *nf* signature; (*action*) signing. ◆**signataire** *nmf* signatory. ◆**signer 1** *vt* to sign. **2 se s.** *vpr Rel* to cross oneself.

signe [siɲ] *nm* (*indice*) sign, indication; **s. particulier/de ponctuation** distinguishing/punctuation mark; **faire s. à qn** (*geste*) to motion to *ou* beckon s.o. (**de faire** to do); (*contacter*) to get in touch with s.o.; **faire s. que oui** to nod (one's head); **faire s. que non** to shake one's head.

signet [siɲɛ] *nm* bookmark.

signification [siɲifikasjɔ̃] *nf* meaning. ◆**significatif, -ive** *a* significant, meaningful; **s. de** indicative of. ◆**signifier** *vt* to mean, signify (**que** that); **s. qch à qn** (*faire connaître*) to make sth known to s.o., signify sth to s.o.

silence [silɑ̃s] *nm* silence; *Mus* rest; **en s.** in silence; **garder le s.** to keep quiet *ou* silent (**sur** about). ◆**silencieux, -euse 1** *a* silent. **2** *nm Aut* silencer, *Am* muffler; (*d'arme*) silencer. ◆**silencieusement** *adv* silently.

silex [silɛks] *nm* (*roche*) flint.

silhouette [silwɛt] *nf* outline; (*en noir*) silhouette; (*ligne du corps*) figure.

silicium [silisjɔm] *nm* silicon. ◆**silicone** *nf* silicone.

sillage [sijaʒ] *nm* (*de bateau*) wake; **dans le s. de** *Fig* in the wake of.

sillon [sijɔ̃] *nm* furrow; (*de disque*) groove.

sillonner [sijɔne] *vt* (*traverser*) to cross; (*en tous sens*) to criss-cross.

silo [silo] *nm* silo.

simagrées [simagre] *nfpl* airs (and graces); (*cérémonies*) fuss.

similaire [similɛr] *a* similar. ◆**similitude** *nf* similarity.

similicuir [similikɥir] *nm* imitation leather.

simple [sɛ̃pl] *a* simple; (*non multiple*) single; (*employé, particulier*) ordinary; – *nmf* **s. d'esprit** simpleton; – *nm Tennis* singles. ◆**simplement** *adv* simply. ◆**simplet, -ette** *a* (*personne*) a bit simple. ◆**simplicité** *nf* simplicity. ◆**simplification** *nf* simplification. ◆**simplifier** *vt* to simplify. ◆**simpliste** *a* simplistic.

simulacre [simylakr] *nm* **un s. de** *Péj* a pretence of.

simuler [simyle] *vt* to simulate; (*feindre*) to feign. ◆**simulateur, -trice 1** *nmf* (*hypocrite*) shammer; (*tire-au-flanc*) & *Mil* malingerer. **2** *nm* (*appareil*) simulator. ◆**simulation** *nf* simulation; feigning.

simultané [simyltane] *a* simultaneous. ◆**—ment** *adv* simultaneously.

sincère [sɛ̃sɛr] *a* sincere. ◆**sincèrement** *adv* sincerely. ◆**sincérité** *nf* sincerity.

sinécure [sinekyr] *nf* sinecure.

singe [sɛ̃ʒ] *nm* monkey, ape. ◆**singer** *vt* (*imiter*) to ape, mimic. ◆**singeries** *nfpl* antics, clowning.

singulariser (se) [səsɛ̃gylarize] *vpr* to draw attention to oneself.

singulier, -ière [sɛ̃gylje, -jɛr] **1** *a* peculiar, odd. **2** *a* & *nm Gram* singular. ◆**singularité** *nf* peculiarity. ◆**singulièrement** *adv* (*notamment*) particularly; (*beaucoup*) extremely.

sinistre [sinistr] **1** *a* (*effrayant*) sinister. **2** *nm* disaster; (*incendie*) fire; (*dommage*) *Jur* damage. ◆**sinistré, -ée** *a* (*population, région*) disaster-stricken; – *nmf* disaster victim.

sinon [sinɔ̃] *conj* (*autrement*) otherwise, or else; (*sauf*) except (**que** that); (*si ce n'est*) if not.

sinueux, -euse [sinɥø, -øz] *a* winding. ◆**sinuosités** *nfpl* twists (and turns).

sinus [sinys] *nm inv Anat* sinus.

siphon [sifɔ̃] *nm* siphon; (*d'évier*) trap, U-bend.

sirène [sirɛn] *nf* **1** (*d'usine etc*) siren. **2** (*femme*) mermaid.

sirop [siro] *nm* syrup; (*à diluer, boisson*) (fruit) cordial; **s. contre la toux** cough mixture *ou* syrup.

siroter [sirɔte] *vt Fam* to sip (at).

sis [si] *a Jur* situated.

sismique [sismik] *a* seismic; **secousse s.** earth tremor.
site [sit] *nm* (*endroit*) site; (*environnement*) setting; (*pittoresque*) beauty spot; **s. (touristique)** (*monument etc*) place of interest.
sitôt [sito] *adv* **s. que** as soon as; **s. levée, elle partit** as soon as she was up, she left; **s. après** immediately after; **pas de s.** not for some time.
situation [sitɥasjɔ̃] *nf* situation, position; (*emploi*) position; **s. de famille** marital status. ◆**situ/er** *vt* to situate, locate; — **se s.** *vpr* (*se trouver*) to be situated. ◆**—é** *a* (*maison etc*) situated.
six [sis] ([si] *before consonant,* [siz] *before vowel*) *a & nm* six. ◆**sixième** *a & nmf* sixth; **un s.** a sixth.
sketch [skɛtʃ] *nm* (*pl* **sketches**) *Th* sketch.
ski [ski] *nm* (*objet*) ski; (*sport*) skiing; **faire du s.** to ski; **s. nautique** water skiing. ◆**ski/er** *vi* to ski. ◆**—eur, -euse** *nmf* skier.
slalom [slalɔm] *nm Sp* slalom.
slave [slav] *a* Slav; (*langue*) Slavonic; – *nmf* Slav.
slip [slip] *nm* (*d'homme*) briefs, (under)pants; (*de femme*) panties, pants, knickers; **s. de bain** (swimming) trunks; (*d'un bikini*) briefs.
slogan [slɔgɑ̃] *nm* slogan.
SMIC [smik] *nm abrév* (*salaire minimum interprofessionnel de croissance*) minimum wage.
smoking [smɔkiŋ] *nm* (*veston, costume*) dinner jacket, *Am* tuxedo.
snack(-bar) [snak(bar)] *nm* snack bar.
SNCF [ɛsɛnseef] *nf abrév* (*Société nationale des Chemins de fer français*) French railways.
snob [snɔb] *nmf* snob; – *a* snobbish. ◆**snober** *vt* **s. qn** to snub s.o. ◆**snobisme** *nm* snobbery.
sobre [sɔbr] *a* sober. ◆**sobriété** *nf* sobriety.
sobriquet [sɔbrikɛ] *nm* nickname.
sociable [sɔsjabl] *a* sociable. ◆**sociabilité** *nf* sociability.
social, -aux [sɔsjal, -o] *a* social. ◆**socialisme** *nm* socialism. ◆**socialiste** *a & nmf* socialist.
société [sɔsjete] *nf* society; (*compagnie*) & *Com* company; **s. anonyme** *Com* (public) limited company, *Am* incorporated company. ◆**sociétaire** *nmf* (*d'une association*) member.
sociologie [sɔsjɔlɔʒi] *nf* sociology. ◆**sociologique** *a* sociological. ◆**sociologue** *nmf* sociologist.
socle [sɔkl] *nm* (*de statue, colonne*) plinth, pedestal; (*de lampe*) base.
socquette [sɔkɛt] *nf* ankle sock.
soda [sɔda] *nm* (*à l'orange etc*) fizzy drink, *Am* soda (pop).
sœur [sœr] *nf* sister; *Rel* nun, sister.
sofa [sɔfa] *nm* sofa, settee.
soi [swa] *pron* oneself; **chacun pour s.** every man for himself; **en s.** in itself; **cela va de s.** it's self-evident (**que** that); **amour/conscience de s.** self-love/-awareness. ◆**s.-même** *pron* oneself.
soi-disant [swadizɑ̃] *a inv* so-called; – *adv* supposedly.
soie [swa] *nf* **1** silk. **2** (*de porc etc*) bristle. ◆**soierie** *nf* (*tissu*) silk.
soif [swaf] *nf* thirst (*Fig* **de** for); **avoir s.** to be thirsty; **donner s. à qn** to make s.o. thirsty.
soign/er [swaɲe] *vt* to look after, take care of; (*malade*) to tend, nurse; (*maladie*) to treat; (*détails, présentation, travail*) to take care over; **se faire s.** to have (medical) treatment; — **se s.** *vpr* to take care of oneself, look after oneself. ◆**—é** *a* (*personne*) well-groomed; (*vêtement*) neat, tidy; (*travail*) careful. ◆**soigneux, -euse** *a* careful (**de** with); (*propre*) tidy, neat. ◆**soigneusement** *adv* carefully.
soin [swɛ̃] *nm* care; (*ordre*) tidiness, neatness; *pl* care; *Méd* treatment; **avoir** *ou* **prendre s. de qch/de faire** to take care of sth/to do; **les premiers soins** first aid; **soins de beauté** beauty care *ou* treatment; **aux bons soins de** (*sur lettre*) care of, c/o; **avec s.** carefully, with care.
soir [swar] *nm* evening; **le s.** (*chaque soir*) in the evening; **à neuf heures du s.** at nine in the evening; **du s.** (*repas, robe etc*) evening-. ◆**soirée** *nf* evening; (*réunion*) party; **s. dansante** dance.
soit 1 [swa] *voir* **être. 2** [swa] *conj* (*à savoir*) that is (to say); **s. . . . s. . . .** either . . . or . . . . **3** [swat] *adv* (*oui*) very well.
soixante [swasɑ̃t] *a & nm* sixty. ◆**soixantaine** *nf* **une s. (de)** (*nombre*) (about) sixty; **avoir la s.** (*âge*) to be about sixty. ◆**soixante-dix** *a & nm* seventy. ◆**soixante-dixième** *a & nmf* seventieth. ◆**soixantième** *a & nmf* sixtieth.
soja [sɔʒa] *nm* (*plante*) soya; **graine de s.** soya bean; **germes** *ou* **pousses de s.** beansprouts.
sol [sɔl] *nm* ground; (*plancher*) floor; (*matière, territoire*) soil.

solaire [sɔlɛr] *a* solar; (*chaleur, rayons*) sun's; (*crème, filtre*) sun-; (*lotion, huile*) suntan-.

soldat [sɔlda] *nm* soldier; **simple s.** private.

solde [sɔld] **1** *nm* (*de compte, à payer*) balance. **2** *nm* **en s.** (*acheter*) at sale price, *Am* on sale; *pl* (*marchandises*) sale goods; (*vente*) (clearance) sale(s). **3** *nf Mil* pay; **à la s. de** *Fig Péj* in s.o.'s pay. ◆**sold/er 1** *vt* (*articles*) to sell off, clear. **2** *vt* (*compte*) to pay the balance of. **3 se s.** *vpr* **se s. par** (*un échec, une défaite etc*) to end in. ◆**—é** *a* (*article etc*) reduced. ◆**solderie** *nf* discount *ou* reject shop.

sole [sɔl] *nf* (*poisson*) sole.

soleil [sɔlɛj] *nm* sun; (*chaleur, lumière*) sunshine; (*fleur*) sunflower; **au s.** in the sun; **il fait (du) s.** it's sunny, the sun's shining; **prendre un bain de s.** to sunbathe; **coup de s.** *Méd* sunburn.

solennel, -elle [sɔlanɛl] *a* solemn. ◆**solennellement** *adv* solemnly. ◆**solennité** [-anite] *nf* solemnity.

solex® [sɔlɛks] *nm* moped.

solfège [sɔlfɛʒ] *nm* rudiments of music.

solidaire [sɔlidɛr] *a* **être s.** (*ouvriers etc*) to be as one, show solidarity (**de** with); (*pièce de machine*) to be interdependent (**de** with). ◆**solidairement** *adv* jointly. ◆**se solidariser** *vpr* to show solidarity (**avec** with). ◆**solidarité** *nf* solidarity; (*d'éléments*) interdependence.

solide [sɔlid] *a* (*voiture, nourriture, caractère etc*) & *Ch* solid; (*argument, qualité, raison*) sound; (*vigoureux*) robust; – *nm Ch* solid. ◆**solidement** *adv* solidly. ◆**se solidifier** *vpr* to solidify. ◆**solidité** *nf* solidity; (*d'argument etc*) soundness.

soliste [sɔlist] *nmf Mus* soloist.

solitaire [sɔlitɛr] *a* solitary; – *nmf* loner; (*ermite*) recluse, hermit; **en s.** on one's own. ◆**solitude** *nf* solitude.

solive [sɔliv] *nf* joist, beam.

solliciter [sɔlisite] *vt* (*audience, emploi etc*) to seek; (*tenter*) to tempt, entice; **s. qn** (*faire appel à*) to appeal to s.o. (**de faire** to do); **être (très) sollicité** (*personne*) to be in (great) demand. ◆**sollicitation** *nf* (*demande*) appeal; (*tentation*) temptation.

sollicitude [sɔlisityd] *nf* solicitude, concern.

solo [sɔlo] *a inv & nm Mus* solo.

solstice [sɔlstis] *nm* solstice.

soluble [sɔlybl] *a* (*substance, problème*) soluble; **café s.** instant coffee. ◆**solution** *nf* (*d'un problème etc*) & *Ch* solution (**de** to).

solvable [sɔlvabl] *a Fin* solvent. ◆**solvabilité** *nf Fin* solvency.

solvant [sɔlvɑ̃] *nm Ch* solvent.

sombre [sɔ̃br] *a* dark; (*triste*) sombre, gloomy; **il fait s.** it's dark.

sombrer [sɔ̃bre] *vi* (*bateau*) to sink, founder; **s. dans** (*folie, sommeil etc*) to sink into.

sommaire [sɔmɛr] *a* summary; (*repas, tenue*) scant; – *nm* summary, synopsis.

sommation [sɔmɑsjɔ̃] *nf Jur* summons; (*de sentinelle etc*) warning.

somme [sɔm] **1** *nf* sum; **faire la s. de** to add up; **en s., s. toute** in short. **2** *nm* (*sommeil*) nap; **faire un s.** to have *ou* take a nap.

sommeil [sɔmɛj] *nm* sleep; (*envie de dormir*) sleepiness, drowsiness; **avoir s.** to be *ou* feel sleepy *ou* drowsy. ◆**sommeiller** *vi* to doze; (*faculté, qualité*) *Fig* to slumber.

sommelier [sɔməlje] *nm* wine waiter.

sommer [sɔme] *vt* **s. qn de faire** (*enjoindre*) & *Jur* to summon s.o. to do.

sommes [sɔm] *voir* **être**.

sommet [sɔmɛ] *nm* top; (*de montagne*) summit, top; (*de la gloire etc*) *Fig* height, summit; **conférence au s.** summit (conference).

sommier [sɔmje] *nm* (*de lit*) base; **s. à ressorts** spring base.

sommité [sɔmite] *nf* leading light, top person (**de** in).

somnambule [sɔmnɑ̃byl] *nmf* sleepwalker; **être s.** to sleepwalk. ◆**somnambulisme** *nm* sleepwalking.

somnifère [sɔmnifɛr] *nm* sleeping pill.

somnolence [sɔmnɔlɑ̃s] *nf* drowsiness, sleepiness. ◆**somnolent** *a* drowsy, sleepy. ◆**somnoler** *vi* to doze, drowse.

somptueux, -euse [sɔ̃ptɥø, -øz] *a* sumptuous, magnificent. ◆**somptuosité** *nf* sumptuousness, magnificence.

son[1] [sɔ̃] *nm* **1** (*bruit*) sound. **2** (*de grains*) bran.

son[2], **sa**, *pl* **ses** [sɔ̃, sa, se] (**sa** *becomes* **son** [sɔ̃n] *before a vowel or mute h*) *a poss* his; (*de femme*) her; (*de chose*) its; (*indéfini*) one's; **son père** his *ou* her *ou* one's father; **sa durée** its duration.

sonate [sɔnat] *nf Mus* sonata.

sonde [sɔ̃d] *nf Géol* drill; *Nau* sounding line; *Méd* probe; (*pour l'alimentation*) (feeding) tube; **s. spatiale** *Av* space probe. ◆**sondage** *nm* sounding; drilling; probing; **s. (d'opinion)** opinion poll. ◆**sonder** *vt* (*rivière etc*) to sound; (*terrain*) to drill; *Av* & *Méd* to probe; (*personne, l'opinion*) *Fig* to sound out.

songe [sɔ̃ʒ] *nm* dream.

song/er [sɔ̃ʒe] *vi* **s. à qch/à faire** to think of sth/of doing; – *vt* **s. que** to consider *ou* think that. ◆**—eur, -euse** *a* thoughtful, pensive.

sonner [sɔne] *vi* to ring; (*cor, cloches etc*) to sound; **midi a sonné** it has struck twelve; – *vt* to ring; (*domestique*) to ring for; (*cor etc*) to sound; (*l'heure*) to strike; (*assommer*) to knock out. ◆**sonnantes** *afpl* **à cinq/***etc* **heures s.** on the stroke of five/*etc*. ◆**sonné** *a* **1 trois/***etc* **heures sonnées** gone *ou* past three/*etc* o'clock. **2** (*fou*) crazy. ◆**sonnerie** *nf* (*son*) ring(ing); (*de cor etc*) sound; (*appareil*) bell. ◆**sonnette** *nf* bell; **s. d'alarme** alarm (bell); **coup de s.** ring.

sonnet [sɔnɛ] *nm* (*poème*) sonnet.

sonore [sɔnɔr] *a* (*rire*) loud; (*salle, voix*) resonant; (*effet, film, ondes etc*) sound-. ◆**sonorisation** *nf* (*matériel*) sound equipment *ou* system. ◆**sonoriser** *vt* (*film*) to add sound to; (*salle*) to wire for sound. ◆**sonorité** *nf* (*de salle*) acoustics, resonance; (*de violon etc*) tone.

sont [sɔ̃] *voir* **être**.

sophistiqué [sɔfistike] *a* sophisticated.

soporifique [sɔpɔrifik] *a* (*médicament, discours etc*) soporific.

soprano [sɔprano] *nmf* (*personne*) *Mus* soprano; – *nm* (*voix*) soprano.

sorbet [sɔrbɛ] *nm Culin* water ice, sorbet.

sorcellerie [sɔrsɛlri] *nf* witchcraft, sorcery. ◆**sorcier** *nm* sorcerer. ◆**sorcière** *nf* witch; **chasse aux sorcières** *Pol* witch-hunt.

sordide [sɔrdid] *a* (*acte, affaire etc*) sordid; (*maison etc*) squalid.

sornettes [sɔrnɛt] *nfpl* (*propos*) *Péj* twaddle.

sort [sɔr] *nm* **1** (*destin, hasard*) fate; (*condition*) lot. **2** (*maléfice*) spell.

sorte [sɔrt] *nf* sort, kind (**de** of); **en quelque s.** as it were, in a way; **de (telle) s. que** so that, in such a way that; **de la s.** (*de cette façon*) in that way; **faire en s. que** (+ *sub*) to see to it that.

sortie [sɔrti] *nf* **1** departure, exit; (*de scène*) exit; (*promenade*) walk; (*porte*) exit, way out; (*de livre, modèle*) *Com* appearance; (*de disque, film*) release; (*d'ordinateur*) output; *pl* (*argent*) outgoings; **à la s. de l'école** (*moment*) when school comes out; **l'heure de la s. de qn** the time at which s.o. leaves; **première s.** (*de convalescent etc*) first time out. **2 s. de bain** (*peignoir*) bathrobe.

sortilège [sɔrtilɛʒ] *nm* (magic) spell.

sort/ir* [sɔrtir] *vi* (*aux* **être**) to go out, leave; (*venir*) to come out; (*pour s'amuser*) to go out; (*film, modèle, bourgeon etc*) to come out; (*numéro gagnant*) to come up; **s. de** (*endroit*) to leave; (*sujet*) to stray from; (*université*) to be a graduate of; (*famille, milieu*) to come from; (*légalité, limites*) to go beyond; (*compétence*) to be outside; (*gonds, rails*) to come off; **s. de l'ordinaire** to be out of the ordinary; **s. de table** to leave the table; **s. de terre** (*plante, fondations*) to come up; **s. indemne** to escape unhurt (**de** from); – *vt* (*aux* **avoir**) to take out (**de** of); (*film, modèle, livre etc*) *Com* to bring out; (*dire*) *Fam* to come out with; (*expulser*) *Fam* to throw out; **s'en s., se s. d'affaire** to pull *ou* come through, get out of trouble. ◆**—ant** *a* (*numéro*) winning; (*député etc*) *Pol* outgoing. ◆**—able** *a* (*personne*) presentable.

sosie [sozi] *nm* (*de personne*) double.

sot, sotte [so, sɔt] *a* foolish; – *nmf* fool. ◆**sottement** *adv* foolishly. ◆**sottise** *nf* foolishness; (*action, parole*) foolish thing; *pl* (*injures*) *Fam* insults; **faire des sottises** (*enfant*) to be naughty, misbehave.

sou [su] *nm* **sous** (*argent*) money; **elle n'a pas un** *ou* **le s.** she doesn't have a penny, she's penniless; **pas un s. de** (*bon sens etc*) not an ounce of; **appareil** *ou* **machine à sous** fruit machine, one-armed bandit.

soubresaut [subrəso] *nm* (*sursaut*) (sudden) start.

souche [suʃ] *nf* (*d'arbre*) stump; (*de carnet*) stub, counterfoil; (*famille, de vigne*) stock.

souci [susi] *nm* (*inquiétude*) worry, concern; (*préoccupation*) concern; **se faire du s.** to be worried, worry; **ça lui donne du s.** it worries him *ou* her. ◆**se soucier** *vpr* **se s. de** to be concerned *ou* worried about. ◆**soucieux, -euse** *a* concerned, worried (**de qch** about sth); **s. de plaire/***etc* anxious to please/*etc*.

soucoupe [sukup] *nf* saucer; **s. volante** flying saucer.

soudain [sudɛ̃] *a* sudden; – *adv* suddenly. ◆**soudainement** *adv* suddenly. ◆**soudaineté** *nf* suddenness.

Soudan [sudɑ̃] *nm* Sudan.

soude [sud] *nf Ch* soda; **cristaux de s.** washing soda.

souder [sude] *vt* to solder; (*par soudure autogène*) to weld; (*groupes etc*) *Fig* to unite (closely); **— se s.** *vpr* (*os*) to knit (together). ◆**soudure** *nf* soldering; (*métal*) solder; **s. (autogène)** welding.

soudoyer [sudwaje] *vt* to bribe.

souffle [sufl] *nm* puff, blow; (*haleine*) breath; (*respiration*) breathing; (*de bombe etc*) blast; (*inspiration*) *Fig* inspiration; **s. (d'air)** breath of air. ◆**souffler** *vi* to blow; (*haleter*) to puff; **laisser s. qn** (*reprendre haleine*) to let s.o. get his breath back; – *vt* (*bougie*) to blow out; (*fumée, poussière, verre*) to blow; (*par une explosion*) to blow down, blast; (*chuchoter*) to whisper; (*voler*) *Fam* to pinch (**à** from); (*étonner*) *Fam* to stagger; **s. son rôle à qn** *Th* to prompt s.o.; **ne pas s. mot** not to breathe a word. ◆**soufflet** *nm* **1** (*instrument*) bellows. **2** (*gifle*) *Litt* slap. ◆**souffleur, -euse** *nmf Th* prompter.

soufflé [sufle] *nm Culin* soufflé.

souffrance [sufrɑ̃s] *nf* **1** suffering. **2 en s.** (*colis etc*) unclaimed; (*affaire*) in abeyance.

souffreteux, -euse [sufrətø, -øz] *a* sickly.

souffr/ir* [sufrir] **1** *vi* to suffer; **s. de** to suffer from; (*gorge, pieds etc*) to have trouble with; **faire s. qn** (*physiquement*) to hurt s.o.; (*moralement*) to make s.o. suffer, hurt s.o. **2** *vt* (*endurer*) to suffer; **je ne peux pas le s.** I can't bear him. **3** *vt* (*exception*) to admit of. ◆**—ant** *a* unwell.

soufre [sufr] *nm* sulphur, *Am* sulfur.

souhait [swɛ] *nm* wish; **à vos souhaits!** (*après un éternuement*) bless you!; **à s.** perfectly. ◆**souhait/er** *vt* (*bonheur etc*) to wish for; **s. qch à qn** to wish s.o. sth; **s. faire** to hope to do; **s. que** (+ *sub*) to hope that. ◆**—able** *a* desirable.

souiller [suje] *vt* to soil, dirty; (*déshonorer*) *Fig* to sully.

soûl [su] **1** *a* drunk. **2** *nm* **tout son s.** (*boire etc*) to one's heart's content. ◆**soûler** *vt* to make drunk; **— se s.** *vpr* to get drunk.

soulager [sulaʒe] *vt* to relieve (**de** of). ◆**soulagement** *nm* relief.

soulever [sulve] *vt* to raise, lift (up); (*l'opinion, le peuple*) to stir up; (*poussière, question*) to raise; (*sentiment*) to arouse; **cela me soulève le cœur** it makes me feel sick, it turns my stomach; **— se s.** *vpr* (*malade etc*) to lift oneself (up); (*se révolter*) to rise (up). ◆**soulèvement** *nm* (*révolte*) (up)rising.

soulier [sulje] *nm* shoe.

souligner [suliɲe] *vt* (*d'un trait*) to underline; (*accentuer, faire remarquer*) to emphasize, underline; **s. que** to emphasize that.

soumettre* [sumetr] **1** *vt* (*pays, rebelles*) to subjugate, subdue; **s. à** (*assujettir*) to subject to; **— se s.** *vpr* to submit (**à** to). **2** *vt* (*présenter*) to submit (**à** to). ◆**soumis** *a* (*docile*) submissive; **s. à** subject to. ◆**soumission** *nf* **1** submission; (*docilité*) submissiveness. **2** (*offre*) *Com* tender.

soupape [supap] *nf* valve.

soupçon [supsɔ̃] *nm* suspicion; **un s. de** (*quantité*) *Fig* a hint *ou* touch of. ◆**soupçonner** *vt* to suspect (**de** of, **d'avoir fait** of doing, **que** that). ◆**soupçonneux, -euse** *a* suspicious.

soupe [sup] *nf* soup. ◆**soupière** *nf* (soup) tureen.

soupente [supɑ̃t] *nf* (*sous le toit*) loft.

souper [supe] *nm* supper; *– vi* to have supper.

soupeser [supəze] *vt* (*objet dans la main*) to feel the weight of; (*arguments etc*) *Fig* to weigh up.

soupir [supir] *nm* sigh. ◆**soupir/er** *vi* to sigh; **s. après** to yearn for. ◆**—ant** *nm* (*amoureux*) suitor.

soupirail, -aux [supiraj, -o] *nm* basement window.

souple [supl] *a* (*personne, esprit, règlement*) flexible; (*cuir, membre, corps*) supple. ◆**souplesse** *nf* flexibility; suppleness.

source [surs] *nf* **1** (*point d'eau*) spring; **eau de s.** spring water; **prendre sa s.** (*rivière*) to rise (**à** at, **dans** in). **2** (*origine*) source; **de s. sûre** on good authority.

sourcil [sursi] *nm* eyebrow. ◆**sourciller** *vi* **ne pas s.** *Fig* not to bat an eyelid.

sourd, sourde [sur, surd] **1** *a* deaf (*Fig* **à** to); *– nmf* deaf person. **2** *a* (*bruit, douleur*) dull; (*caché*) secret. ◆**s.-muet** (*pl* **sourds-muets**), ◆**sourde-muette** (*pl* **sourdes-muettes**) *a* deaf and dumb; *– nmf* deaf mute.

sourdine [surdin] *nf* (*dispositif*) *Mus* mute; **en s.** *Fig* quietly, secretly.

souricière [surisjɛr] *nf* mousetrap; *Fig* trap.

sourire* [surir] *vi* to smile (**à** at); **s. à qn** (*fortune*) to smile on s.o.; *– nm* smile; **faire un s. à qn** to give s.o. a smile.

souris [suri] *nf* mouse.

sournois [surnwa] *a* sly, underhand. ◆**sournoisement** *adv* slyly. ◆**sournoiserie** *nf* slyness.

sous [su] *prép* (*position*) under(neath), beneath; (*rang*) under; **s. la pluie** in the rain; **s. cet angle** from that angle *ou* point of view; **s. le nom de** under the name of; **s. Charles X** under Charles X; **s. peu** (*bientôt*) shortly.

sous- [su] *préf* (*subordination, subdivision*) sub-; (*insuffisance*) under-.

sous-alimenté [suzalimɑ̃te] *a* undernourished. ◆**sous-alimentation** *nf* undernourishment.

sous-bois [subwa] *nm* undergrowth.

sous-chef [suʃɛf] *nmf* second-in-command.

souscrire* [suskrir] *vi* **s. à** (*payer, approuver*) to subscribe to. ◆**souscription** *nf* subscription.

sous-développé [sudevlɔpe] *a* (*pays*) underdeveloped.
sous-directeur, -trice [sudirɛktœr, -tris] *nmf* assistant manager, assistant manageress.
sous-entend/re [suzɑ̃tɑ̃dr] *vt* to imply. ◆**—u** *nm* insinuation.
sous-estimer [suzɛstime] *vt* to underestimate.
sous-jacent [suʒasɑ̃] *a* underlying.
sous-louer [sulwe] *vt* (*appartement*) to sublet.
sous-main [sumɛ̃] *nm inv* desk pad.
sous-marin [sumarɛ̃] *a* underwater; **plongée sous-marine** skin diving; – *nm* submarine.
sous-officier [suzɔfisje] *nm* noncommissioned officer.
sous-payer [supeje] *vt* (*ouvrier etc*) to underpay.
sous-produit [suprɔdɥi] *nm* by-product.
soussigné, -ée [susiɲe] *a & nmf* undersigned; **je s.** I the undersigned.
sous-sol [susɔl] *nm* basement; *Géol* subsoil.
sous-titre [sutitr] *nm* subtitle. ◆**sous-titrer** *vt* (*film*) to subtitle.
soustraire* [sustrɛr] *vt* to remove; *Math* to subtract, take away (**de** from); **s. qn à** (*danger etc*) to shield *ou* protect s.o. from; **se s. à** to escape from; (*devoir, obligation*) to avoid. ◆**soustraction** *nf Math* subtraction.
sous-trait/er [sutrete] *vi Com* to subcontract. ◆**—ant** *nm* subcontractor.
sous-verre [suvɛr] *nm inv* (*encadrement*) (frameless) glass mount.
sous-vêtement [suvɛtmɑ̃] *nm* undergarment; *pl* underwear.
soutane [sutan] *nf* (*de prêtre*) cassock.
soute [sut] *nf* (*magasin*) *Nau* hold.
souten/ir* [sutnir] *vt* to support, hold up; (*droits, opinion*) to uphold, maintain; (*candidat etc*) to back, support; (*malade*) to sustain; (*effort, intérêt*) to sustain, keep up; (*thèse*) to defend; (*résister à*) to withstand; **s. que** to maintain that; **— se s.** *vpr* (*blessé etc*) to hold oneself up; (*se maintenir, durer*) to be sustained. ◆**—u** *a* (*attention, effort*) sustained; (*style*) lofty. ◆**soutien** *nm* support; (*personne*) supporter; **s. de famille** breadwinner. ◆**soutien-gorge** *nm* (*pl* **soutiens-gorge**) bra.
souterrain [sutɛrɛ̃] *a* underground; – *nm* underground passage.
soutirer [sutire] *vt* **s. qch à qn** to extract *ou* get sth from s.o.
souvenir [suvnir] *nm* memory, recollection; (*objet*) memento; (*cadeau*) keepsake; (*pour touristes*) souvenir; **en s. de** in memory of; **mon bon s. à** (give) my regards to. ◆**se souvenir*** *vpr* **se s. de** to remember, recall; **se s. que** to remember *ou* recall that.
souvent [suvɑ̃] *adv* often; **peu s.** seldom; **le plus s.** more often than not, most often.
souverain, -aine [suvrɛ̃, -ɛn] *a* sovereign; (*extrême*) *Péj* supreme; – *nmf* sovereign. ◆**souveraineté** *nf* sovereignty.
soviétique [sɔvjetik] *a* Soviet; **l'Union s.** the Soviet Union; – *nmf* Soviet citizen.
soyeux, -euse [swajø, -øz] *a* silky.
spacieux, -euse [spasjø, -øz] *a* spacious, roomy.
spaghetti(s) [spageti] *nmpl* spaghetti.
sparadrap [sparadra] *nm Méd* sticking plaster, *Am* adhesive tape.
spasme [spasm] *nm* spasm. ◆**spasmodique** *a* spasmodic.
spatial, -aux [spasjal, -o] *a* (*vol etc*) space-; **engin s.** spaceship, spacecraft.
spatule [spatyl] *nf* spatula.
speaker [spikœr] *nm*, **speakerine** [spikrin] *nf Rad TV* announcer.
spécial, -aux [spesjal, -o] *a* special; (*bizarre*) peculiar. ◆**spécialement** *adv* especially, particularly; (*exprès*) specially.
spécialiser (se) [səspesjalize] *vpr* to specialize (**dans** in). ◆**spécialisation** *nf* specialization. ◆**spécialiste** *nmf* specialist. ◆**spécialité** *nf* speciality, *Am* specialty.
spécifier [spesifje] *vt* to specify (**que** that).
spécifique [spesifik] *a Phys Ch* specific.
spécimen [spesimɛn] *nm* specimen; (*livre etc*) specimen copy.
spectacle [spɛktakl] *nm* **1** (*vue*) spectacle, sight; **se donner en s.** *Péj* to make an exhibition of oneself. **2** (*représentation*) show; **le s.** (*industrie*) show business. ◆**spectateur, -trice** *nmf Sp* spectator; (*témoin*) onlooker, witness; *pl Th Cin* audience.
spectaculaire [spɛktakylɛr] *a* spectacular.
spectre [spɛktr] *nm* **1** (*fantôme*) spectre, ghost. **2** (*solaire*) spectrum.
spéculer [spekyle] *vi Fin Phil* to speculate; **s. sur** (*tabler sur*) to bank *ou* rely on. ◆**spéculateur, -trice** *nmf* speculator. ◆**spéculatif, -ive** *a Fin Phil* speculative. ◆**spéculation** *nf Fin Phil* speculation.
spéléologie [speleɔlɔʒi] *nf* (*activité*) potholing, caving, *Am* spelunking. ◆**spéléologue** *nmf* potholer, *Am* spelunker.
sperme [spɛrm] *nm* sperm, semen.
sphère [sfɛr] *nf* (*boule, domaine*) sphere. ◆**sphérique** *a* spherical.
sphinx [sfɛ̃ks] *nm* sphinx.

spirale [spiral] *nf* spiral.

spirite [spirit] *nmf* spiritualist. ◆**spiritisme** *nm* spiritualism.

spirituel, -elle [spiritɥɛl] *a* **1** (*amusant*) witty. **2** (*pouvoir, vie etc*) spiritual.

spiritueux [spiritɥø] *nmpl* (*boissons*) spirits.

splendide [splɑ̃did] *a* (*merveilleux, riche, beau*) splendid. ◆**splendeur** *nf* splendour.

spongieux, -euse [spɔ̃ʒjø, -øz] *a* spongy.

spontané [spɔ̃tane] *a* spontaneous. ◆**spontanéité** *nf* spontaneity. ◆**spontanément** *adv* spontaneously.

sporadique [spɔradik] *a* sporadic.

sport [spɔr] *nm* sport; **faire du s.** to play sport *ou Am* sports; **(de) s.** (*chaussures, vêtements*) casual, sports; **voiture/veste de s.** sports car/jacket. ◆**sportif, -ive** *a* (*attitude, personne*) sporting; (*association, journal, résultats*) sports, sporting; (*allure*) athletic; – *nmf* sportsman, sportswoman. ◆**sportivité** *nf* (*esprit*) sportsmanship.

spot [spɔt] *nm* **1** (*lampe*) spot(light). **2 s. (publicitaire)** *Rad TV* commercial.

sprint [sprint] *nm Sp* sprint. ◆**sprint/er** *vt* to sprint; – *nm* [-œr] sprinter. ◆**—euse** *nf* sprinter.

square [skwar] *nm* public garden.

squelette [skəlɛt] *nm* skeleton. ◆**squelettique** *a* (*personne, maigreur*) skeleton-like; (*exposé*) sketchy.

stable [stabl] *a* stable. ◆**stabilisateur** *nm* stabilizer. ◆**stabiliser** *vt* to stabilize; – **se s.** *vpr* to stabilize. ◆**stabilité** *nf* stability.

stade [stad] *nm* **1** *Sp* stadium. **2** (*phase*) stage.

stage [staʒ] *nm* training period; (*cours*) (training) course. ◆**stagiaire** *a & nmf* trainee.

stagner [stagne] *vi* to stagnate. ◆**stagnant** *a* stagnant. ◆**stagnation** *nf* stagnation.

stalle [stal] *nf* (*box*) & *Rel* stall.

stand [stɑ̃d] *nm* (*d'exposition etc*) stand, stall; **s. de ravitaillement** *Sp* pit; **s. de tir** (*de foire*) shooting range; *Mil* firing range.

standard [stɑ̃dar] **1** *nm Tél* switchboard. **2** *a inv* (*modèle etc*) standard. ◆**standardiser** *vt* to standardize. ◆**standardiste** *nmf* (switchboard) operator.

standing [stɑ̃diŋ] *nm* standing, status; **de (grand) s.** (*immeuble*) luxury-.

starter [startɛr] *nm* **1** *Aut* choke. **2** *Sp* starter.

station [stasjɔ̃] *nf* (*de métro, d'observation etc*) & *Rad* station; (*de ski etc*) resort; (*d'autobus*) stop; **s. de taxis** taxi rank, *Am* taxi stand; **s. debout** standing (position); **s. (thermale)** spa. ◆**s.-service** *nf* (*pl* **stations-service**) *Aut* service station.

stationnaire [stasjɔnɛr] *vi a* stationary.

stationn/er [stasjɔne] *vi* (*se garer*) to park; (*être garé*) to be parked. ◆**—ement** *nm* parking.

statique [statik] *a* static.

statistique [statistik] *nf* (*donnée*) statistic; **la s.** (*techniques*) statistics; – *a* statistical.

statue [staty] *nf* statue. ◆**statuette** *nf* statuette.

statuer [statɥe] *vi* **s. sur** *Jur* to rule on.

statu quo [statykwo] *nm inv* status quo.

stature [statyr] *nf* stature.

statut [staty] *nm* **1** (*position*) status. **2** *pl* (*règles*) statutes. ◆**statutaire** *a* statutory.

steak [stɛk] *nm* steak.

stencil [stɛnsil] *nm* stencil.

sténo [steno] *nf* (*personne*) stenographer; (*sténographie*) shorthand, stenography; **prendre en s.** to take down in shorthand. ◆**sténodactylo** *nf* shorthand typist, *Am* stenographer. ◆**sténographie** *nf* shorthand, stenography.

stéréo [stereo] *nf* stereo; – *a inv* (*disque etc*) stereo. ◆**stéréophonique** *a* stereophonic.

stéréotype [stereɔtip] *nm* stereotype. ◆**stéréotypé** *a* stereotyped.

stérile [steril] *a* sterile; (*terre*) barren. ◆**stérilisation** *nf* sterilization. ◆**stériliser** *vt* to sterilize. ◆**stérilité** *nf* sterility; (*de terre*) barrenness.

stérilet [sterilɛ] *nm* IUD, coil.

stéthoscope [stetɔskɔp] *nm* stethoscope.

steward [stiwart] *nm Av Nau* steward.

stigmate [stigmat] *nm Fig* mark, stigma (**de** of). ◆**stigmatiser** *vt* (*dénoncer*) to stigmatize.

stimul/er [stimyle] *vt* to stimulate. ◆**—ant** *nm Fig* stimulus; *Méd* stimulant. ◆**stimulateur** *nm* **s. cardiaque** pacemaker. ◆**stimulation** *nf* stimulation.

stimulus [stimylys] *nm* (*pl* **stimuli** [-li]) (*physiologique*) stimulus.

stipuler [stipyle] *vt* to stipulate (**que** that). ◆**stipulation** *nf* stipulation.

stock [stɔk] *nm Com & Fig* stock (**de** of). ◆**stock/er** *vt* to (keep in) stock. ◆**—age** *nm* stocking.

stoïque [stɔik] *a* stoic(al). ◆**stoïcisme** *nm* stoicism.

stop [stɔp] **1** *int* stop; – *nm* (*panneau*) *Aut* stop sign; (*feu arrière*) *Aut* brake light. **2** *nm* **faire du s.** *Fam* to hitchhike. ◆**stopp/er 1** *vti* to stop. **2** *vt* (*vêtement*) to

mend (invisibly). ◆—**age** *nm* (invisible) mending.
store [stɔr] *nm* blind, *Am* (window) shade; (*de magasin*) awning.
strabisme [strabism] *nm* squint.
strapontin [strapɔ̃tɛ̃] *nm* tip-up seat.
stratagème [strataʒɛm] *nm* stratagem, ploy.
stratège [stratɛʒ] *nm* strategist. ◆**stratégie** *nf* strategy. ◆**stratégique** *a* strategic.
stress [strɛs] *nm inv Méd Psy* stress. ◆**stressant** *a* stressful. ◆**stressé** *a* under stress.
strict [strikt] *a* strict; (*langue, tenue, vérité*) plain; (*droit*) basic; **le s. minimum/nécessaire** the bare minimum/necessities. ◆**strictement** *adv* strictly; (*vêtu*) plainly.
strident [stridɑ̃] *a* strident, shrill.
strie [stri] *nf* streak; (*sillon*) groove. ◆**strier** *vt* to streak.
strip-tease [striptiz] *nm* striptease. ◆**strip-teaseuse** *nf* stripper.
strophe [strɔf] *nf* stanza, verse.
structure [stryktyr] *nf* structure. ◆**structural, -aux** *a* structural. ◆**structurer** *vt* to structure.
stuc [styk] *nm* stucco.
studieux, -euse [stydjø, -øz] *a* studious; (*vacances etc*) devoted to study.
studio [stydjo] *nm* (*de peintre*) & *Cin TV* studio; (*logement*) studio flat *ou Am* apartment.
stupéfait [stypefɛ] *a* amazed, astounded (de at, by). ◆**stupéfaction** *nf* amazement. ◆**stupéfi/er** *vt* to amaze, astound. ◆—**ant 1** *a* amazing, astounding. **2** *nm* drug, narcotic. ◆**stupeur** *nf* **1** (*étonnement*) amazement. **2** (*inertie*) stupor.
stupide [stypid] *a* stupid. ◆**stupidement** *adv* stupidly. ◆**stupidité** *nf* stupidity; (*action, parole*) stupid thing.
style [stil] *nm* style; **de s.** (*meuble*) period-. ◆**stylisé** *a* stylized. ◆**styliste** *nmf* (*de mode etc*) designer. ◆**stylistique** *a* stylistic.
stylé [stile] *a* well-trained.
stylo [stilo] *nm* pen; **s. à bille** ballpoint (pen), biro®; **s. à encre** fountain pen.
su [sy] *voir* **savoir.**
suave [sɥav] *a* (*odeur, voix*) sweet.
subalterne [sybaltɛrn] *a* & *nmf* subordinate.
subconscient [sypkɔ̃sjɑ̃] *a* & *nm* subconscious.
subdiviser [sybdivize] *vt* to subdivide (**en** into). ◆**subdivision** *nf* subdivision.
subir [sybir] *vt* to undergo; (*conséquences, défaite, perte, tortures*) to suffer; (*influence*) to be under; **s. qn** (*supporter*) *Fam* to put up with s.o.
subit [sybi] *a* sudden. ◆**subitement** *adv* suddenly.
subjectif, -ive [sybʒɛktif, -iv] *a* subjective. ◆**subjectivement** *adv* subjectively. ◆**subjectivité** *nf* subjectivity.
subjonctif [sybʒɔ̃ktif] *nm Gram* subjunctive.
subjuguer [sybʒyge] *vt* to subjugate; (*envoûter*) to captivate.
sublime [syblim] *a* & *nm* sublime.
sublimer [syblime] *vt Psy* to sublimate.
submerger [sybmɛrʒe] *vt* to submerge; (*envahir*) *Fig* to overwhelm; **submergé de** (*travail etc*) overwhelmed with; **submergé par** (*ennemi, foule*) swamped by. ◆**submersible** *nm* submarine.
subordonn/er [sybɔrdɔne] *vt* to subordinate (**à** to). ◆—**é, -ée** *a* subordinate (**à** to); **être s. à** (*dépendre de*) to depend on; – *nmf* subordinate. ◆**subordination** *nf* subordination.
subreptice [sybrɛptis] *a* surreptitious.
subside [sypsid] *nm* grant, subsidy.
subsidiaire [sybsidjɛr] *a* subsidiary; **question s.** (*de concours*) deciding question.
subsister [sybziste] *vi* (*rester*) to remain; (*vivre*) to get by, subsist; (*doutes, souvenirs etc*) to linger (on), subsist. ◆**subsistance** *nf* subsistence.
substance [sypstɑ̃s] *nf* substance; **en s.** *Fig* in essence. ◆**substantiel, -ielle** *a* substantial.
substantif [sypstɑ̃tif] *nm Gram* noun, substantive.
substituer [sypstitɥe] *vt* to substitute (**à** for); **se s. à qn** to take the place of s.o., substitute for s.o.; (*représenter*) to substitute for s.o. ◆**substitution** *nf* substitution.
subterfuge [sypterfyʒ] *nm* subterfuge.
subtil [syptil] *a* subtle. ◆**subtilité** *nf* subtlety.
subtiliser [syptilize] *vt* (*dérober*) *Fam* to make off with.
subvenir* [sybvənir] *vi* **s. à** (*besoins, frais*) to meet.
subvention [sybvɑ̃sjɔ̃] *nf* subsidy. ◆**subventionner** *vt* to subsidize.
subversif, -ive [sybvɛrsif, -iv] *a* subversive. ◆**subversion** *nf* subversion.
suc [syk] *nm* (*gastrique, de fruit*) juice; (*de plante*) sap.

succédané [syksedane] *nm* substitute (**de** for).

succéder [syksede] *vi* s. **à qn** to succeed s.o.; s. **à qch** to follow sth, come after sth; — **se s.** *vpr* to succeed one another; to follow one another. ◆**successeur** *nm* successor. ◆**successif, -ive** *a* successive. ◆**successivement** *adv* successively. ◆**succession** *nf* **1** succession (**de** of, **à** to); **prendre la s. de qn** to succeed s.o. **2** (*patrimoine*) *Jur* inheritance, estate.

succès [syksɛ] *nm* success; **s. de librairie** (*livre*) best-seller; **avoir du s.** to be successful, be a success; **à s.** (*auteur, film etc*) successful; **avec s.** successfully.

succinct [syksɛ̃] *a* succinct, brief.

succion [sy(k)sjɔ̃] *nf* suction.

succomber [sykɔ̃be] *vi* **1** (*mourir*) to die. **2** s. **à** (*céder à*) to succumb to, give in to.

succulent [sykylɑ̃] *a* succulent.

succursale [sykyrsal] *nf Com* branch; **magasin à succursales multiples** chain *ou* multiple store.

sucer [syse] *vt* to suck. ◆**sucette** *nf* lollipop; (*tétine*) dummy, comforter, *Am* pacifier.

sucre [sykr] *nm* sugar; (*morceau*) sugar lump; **s. cristallisé** granulated sugar; **s. en morceaux** lump sugar; **s. en poudre, s. semoule** caster sugar, *Am* finely ground sugar; **s. d'orge** barley sugar. ◆**sucr/er** *vt* to sugar, sweeten. ◆**—é** *a* sweet, sugary; (*artificiellement*) sweetened; (*doucereux*) *Fig* sugary, syrupy. ◆**sucrerie 1** *nf* (*usine*) sugar refinery. **2** *nfpl* (*bonbons*) sweets, *Am* candy. ◆**sucrier, -ière** *a* (*industrie*) sugar-; — *nm* (*récipient*) sugar bowl.

sud [syd] *nm* south; **au s. de** south of; **du s.** (*vent, direction*) southerly; (*ville*) southern; (*gens*) from *ou* in the south; **Amérique/Afrique du S.** South America/Africa; **l'Europe du S.** Southern Europe; — *a inv* (*côte*) south(ern). ◆**s.-africain, -aine** *a & nmf* South African. ◆**s.-américain, -aine** *a & nmf* South American. ◆**s.-est** *nm & a inv* south-east. ◆**s.-ouest** *nm & a inv* south-west.

Suède [sɥɛd] *nf* Sweden. ◆**suédois, -oise** *a* Swedish; — *nmf* Swede; — *nm* (*langue*) Swedish.

suer [sɥe] *vi* (*personne, mur etc*) to sweat; **faire s. qn** *Fam* to get on s.o.'s nerves; **se faire s.** *Fam* to be bored stiff; — *vt* (*sang etc*) to sweat. ◆**sueur** *nf* sweat; **(tout) en s.** sweating.

suffire* [syfir] *vi* to be enough *ou* sufficient, suffice (**à** for); **ça suffit!** that's enough!; **il suffit de faire** one only has to do; **il suffit d'une goutte/***etc* **pour faire** a drop/*etc* is enough to do; **il ne me suffit pas de faire** I'm not satisfied with doing; — **se s.** *vpr* se s. (**à soi-même**) to be self-sufficient. ◆**suffisant** *a* **1** sufficient, adequate. **2** (*vaniteux*) conceited. ◆**suffisamment** *adv* sufficiently; s. **de** sufficient, enough. ◆**suffisance** *nf* (*vanité*) conceit.

suffixe [syfiks] *nm Gram* suffix.

suffoquer [syfɔke] *vti* to choke, suffocate. ◆**suffocant** *a* stifling, suffocating. ◆**suffocation** *nf* suffocation; (*sensation*) feeling of suffocation.

suffrage [syfraʒ] *nm Pol* (*voix*) vote; (*droit*) suffrage.

suggérer [sygʒere] *vt* (*proposer*) to suggest (**de faire** doing, **que** (+ *sub*) that); (*évoquer*) to suggest. ◆**suggestif, -ive** *a* suggestive. ◆**suggestion** *nf* suggestion.

suicide [sɥisid] *nm* suicide. ◆**suicidaire** *a* suicidal. ◆**se suicid/er** *vpr* to commit suicide. ◆**—é, -ée** *nmf* suicide (victim).

suie [sɥi] *nf* soot.

suif [sɥif] *nm* tallow.

suinter [sɥɛ̃te] *vi* to ooze, seep. ◆**suintement** *nm* oozing, seeping.

suis [sɥi] *voir* **être, suivre.**

Suisse [sɥis] *nf* Switzerland. ◆**suisse** *a & nmf* Swiss. ◆**Suissesse** *nf* Swiss (woman *ou* girl).

suite [sɥit] *nf* (*reste*) rest; (*continuation*) continuation; (*de film, roman*) sequel; (*série*) series, sequence; (*appartement, escorte*) & *Mus* suite; (*cohérence*) order; *pl* (*résultats*) consequences; (*séquelles*) effects; **attendre la s.** to wait and see what happens next; **donner s. à** (*demande etc*) to follow up; **faire s. (à)** to follow; **prendre la s. de qn** to take over from s.o.; **par la s.** afterwards; **par s. de** as a result of; **à la s.** one after another; **à la s. de** (*derrière*) behind; (*événement, maladie etc*) as a result of; **de s.** in succession.

suiv/re* [sɥivr] *vt* to follow; (*accompagner*) to go with, accompany; (*classe*) *Scol* to attend, go to; (*malade*) to treat; **s. (des yeux** *ou* **du regard)** to watch; **s. son chemin** to go on one's way; **se s.** to follow each other; — *vi* to follow; **faire s.** (*courrier*) to forward; **'à s.'** 'to be continued'; **comme suit** as follows. ◆**—ant**[1], **-ante** *a* next, following; (*ci-après*) following; — *nmf* next (one); **au s.!** next!, the next person! ◆**—ant**[2] *prép* (*selon*) according to. ◆**—i** *a* (*régulier*) regular, steady; (*cohérent*) coherent; (*article*)

Com regularly on sale; **peu/très s.** (*cours*) poorly/well attended.

sujet[1], **-ette** [syʒɛ, -ɛt] *a* **s. à** (*maladie etc*) subject *ou* liable to; – *nmf* (*personne*) *Pol* subject.

sujet[2] [syʒɛ] *nm* **1** (*question*) & *Gram* subject; (*d'examen*) question; **au s. de** about; **à quel s.?** about what? **2** (*raison*) cause; **avoir s. de faire** to have (good) cause *ou* (good) reason to do. **3** *nm* (*individu*) subject; **un mauvais s.** (*garçon*) a rotten egg.

sulfurique [sylfyrik] *a* (*acide*) sulphuric, *Am* sulfuric.

sultan [syltɑ̃] *nm* sultan.

summum [sɔmɔm] *nm* (*comble*) *Fig* height.

super [sypɛr] **1** *a* (*bon*) *Fam* great. **2** *nm* (*supercarburant*) *Fam* four-star (petrol), *Am* premium *ou* hi-test gas.

superbe [sypɛrb] *a* superb.

supercarburant [sypɛrkarbyrɑ̃] *nm* high-octane petrol *ou Am* gasoline.

supercherie [sypɛrʃəri] *nf* deception.

superficie [sypɛrfisi] *nf* surface; (*dimensions*) area. ◆**superficiel, -ielle** *a* superficial. ◆**superficiellement** *adv* superficially.

superflu [sypɛrfly] *a* superfluous.

super-grand [sypɛrgrɑ̃] *nm Pol Fam* superpower.

supérieur, -eure [syperjœr] *a* (*étages, partie etc*) upper; (*qualité, air, ton*) superior; (*études*) higher; **à l'étage s.** on the floor above; **s. à** (*meilleur que*) superior to, better than; (*plus grand que*) above, greater than; – *nmf* superior. ◆**supériorité** *nf* superiority.

superlatif, -ive [sypɛrlatif, -iv] *a & nm Gram* superlative.

supermarché [sypɛrmarʃe] *nm* supermarket.

superposer [sypɛrpoze] *vt* (*objets*) to put on top of each other; (*images etc*) to superimpose.

superproduction [sypɛrprɔdyksjɔ̃]. *nf* (*film*) blockbuster.

superpuissance [sypɛrpɥisɑ̃s] *nf Pol* superpower.

supersonique [sypɛrsɔnik] *a* supersonic.

superstitieux, -euse [sypɛrstisjø, -øz] *a* superstitious. ◆**superstition** *nf* superstition.

superviser [sypɛrvize] *vt* to supervise.

supplanter [syplɑ̃te] *vt* to take the place of.

supplé/er [syplee] *vt* (*remplacer*) to replace; (*compenser*) to make up for; – *vi* **s. à** (*compenser*) to make up for. ◆**—ant, -ante** *a & nmf* (*personne*) substitute, replacement; (**professeur**) **s.** supply teacher.

supplément [syplemɑ̃] *nm* (*argent*) extra charge, supplement; (*de livre, revue*) supplement; **en s.** extra; **un s. de** (*information, travail etc*) extra, additional. ◆**supplémentaire** *a* extra, additional.

supplice [syplis] *nm* torture; **au s.** *Fig* on the rack. ◆**supplicier** *vt* to torture.

suppli/er [syplije] *vt* **s. qn de faire** to beg *ou* implore s.o. to do; **je vous en supplie!** I beg *ou* implore you! ◆**—ant, -ante** *a* (*regard etc*) imploring. ◆**supplication** *nf* plea, entreaty.

support [sypɔr] *nm* **1** support; (*d'instrument etc*) stand. **2** (*moyen*) *Fig* medium; **s. audio-visuel** audio-visual aid.

support/er[1] [sypɔrte] *vt* to bear, endure; (*frais*) to bear; (*affront etc*) to suffer; (*résister à*) to withstand; (*soutenir*) to support. ◆**—able** *a* bearable; (*excusable, passable*) tolerable.

supporter[2] [sypɔrtɛr] *nm Sp* supporter.

supposer [sypoze] *vt* to suppose, assume (**que** that); (*impliquer*) to imply (**que** that); **à s.** *ou* **en supposant que** (+ *sub*) supposing (that). ◆**supposition** *nf* supposition, assumption.

suppositoire [sypozitwar] *nm Méd* suppository.

supprimer [syprime] *vt* to remove, get rid of; (*institution, loi*) to abolish; (*journal etc*) to suppress; (*mot, passage*) to cut, delete; (*train etc*) to cancel; (*tuer*) to do away with; **s. qch à qn** to take sth away from s.o. ◆**suppression** *nf* removal; abolition; suppression; cutting; cancellation.

suprématie [sypremasi] *nf* supremacy. ◆**suprême** *a* supreme.

sur [syr] *prép* on, upon; (*par-dessus*) over; (*au sujet de*) on, about; **s. les trois heures** at about three o'clock; **six s. dix** six out of ten; **un jour s. deux** every other day; **coup s. coup** blow after *ou* upon blow; **six mètres s. dix** six metres by ten; **mettre/monter/***etc* **s.** to put/climb/*etc* on (to); **aller/tourner/***etc* **s.** to go/turn/*etc* towards; **s. ce** after which, and then; (*maintenant*) and now.

sur- [syr] *préf* over-.

sûr [syr] *a* sure, certain (**de** of, **que** that); (*digne de confiance*) reliable; (*avenir*) secure; (*lieu*) safe; (*main*) steady; (*goût*) unerring; (*jugement*) sound; **s. de soi** self-assured; **bien s.!** of course!

surabondant [syrabɔ̃dɑ̃] *a* over-abundant.

suranné [syrane] *a* outmoded.

surboum [syrbum] *nf Fam* party.

surcharge [syrʃarʒ] *nf* **1** overloading; (*poids*) extra load; **s. de travail** extra work; en s. (*passagers etc*) extra. **2** (*correction de texte etc*) alteration; (*de timbre-poste*) surcharge. ◆**surcharger** *vt* (*voiture, personne etc*) to overload (**de** with).
surchauffer [syrʃofe] *vt* to overheat.
surchoix [syrʃwa] *a inv Com* top-quality.
surclasser [syrklɑse] *vt* to outclass.
surcroît [syrkrwa] *nm* increase (**de** in); **de s.,** par s. in addition.
surdité [syrdite] *nf* deafness.
surdoué, -ée [syrdwe] *nmf* child who has a genius-level IQ.
surélever [syrelve] *vt* to raise (the height of).
sûrement [syrmɑ̃] *adv* certainly; (*sans danger*) safely.
surenchère [syrɑ̃ʃɛr] *nf Com* higher bid; **s. électorale** *Fig* bidding for votes. ◆**surenchérir** *vi* to bid higher (**sur** than).
surestimer [syrestime] *vt* to overestimate; (*peinture etc*) to overvalue.
sûreté [syrte] *nf* safety; (*de l'état*) security; (*garantie*) surety; (*de geste*) sureness; (*de jugement*) soundness; **être en s.** to be safe; **mettre en s.** to put in a safe place; **de s.** (*épingle, soupape etc*) safety-.
surexcité [syrɛksite] *a* overexcited.
surf [sœrf] *nm Sp* surfing; **faire du s.** to surf, go surfing.
surface [syrfas] *nf* surface; (*dimensions*) (surface) area; **faire s.** (*sous-marin etc*) to surface; **(magasin à) grande s.** hypermarket.
surfait [syrfɛ] *a* overrated.
surgelé [syrʒəle] *a* (deep-)frozen; —*. nmpl* (deep-)frozen foods.
surgir [syrʒir] *vi* to appear suddenly (**de** from); (*conflit, problème*) to arise.
surhomme [syrɔm] *nm* superman. ◆**surhumain** *a* superhuman.
sur-le-champ [syrləʃɑ̃] *adv* immediately.
surlendemain [syrlɑ̃dmɛ̃] *nm* **le s.** two days later; **le s. de** two days after.
surmen/er [syrməne] *vt*, — **se s.** *vpr* to overwork. ◆**—age** *nm* overwork.
surmonter [syrmɔ̃te] *vt* **1** (*obstacle, peur etc*) to overcome, get over. **2** (*être placé sur*) to be on top of, top.
surnager [syrnaʒe] *vi* to float.
surnaturel, -elle [syrnatyrɛl] *a & nm* supernatural.
surnom [syrnɔ̃] *nm* nickname. ◆**surnommer** *vt* to nickname.
surnombre [syrnɔ̃br] *nm* **en s.** too many; **je suis en s.** I am one too many.
surpasser [syrpɑse] *vt* to surpass (**en** in); — **se s.** *vpr* to surpass oneself.
surpeuplé [syrpœple] *a* overpopulated.
surplomb [syrplɔ̃] *nm* **en s.** overhanging. ◆**surplomber** *vti* to overhang.
surplus [syrply] *nm* surplus; *pl Com* surplus (stock).
surprendre* [syrprɑ̃dr] *vt* (*étonner, prendre sur le fait*) to surprise; (*secret*) to discover; (*conversation*) to overhear; **se s. à faire** to find oneself doing. ◆**surprenant** *a* surprising. ◆**surpris** *a* surprised (**de** at, **que** (+ *sub*) that). ◆**surprise** *nf* surprise. ◆**surprise-partie** *nf* (*pl* **surprises-parties**) party.
surréaliste [syrealist] *a* (*bizarre*) *Fam* surrealistic.
sursaut [syrso] *nm* (sudden) start *ou* jump; **en s.** with a start; **s. de** (*énergie etc*) burst of. ◆**sursauter** *vi* to start, jump.
sursis [syrsi] *nm Mil* deferment; (*répit*) *Fig* reprieve; **un an (de prison) avec s.** a one-year suspended sentence.
surtaxe [syrtaks] *nf* surcharge.
surtout [syrtu] *adv* especially; (*avant tout*) above all; **s. pas** certainly not; **s. que** especially as *ou* since.
surveill/er [syrveje] *vt* (*garder*) to watch, keep an eye on; (*épier*) to watch; (*contrôler*) to supervise; **s. son langage/sa santé** *Fig* to watch one's language/health; — **se s.** *vpr* to watch oneself. ◆**—ant, -ante** *nmf* (*de lycée*) supervisor (in charge of discipline); (*de prison*) warder; (*de chantier*) supervisor; **s. de plage** lifeguard. ◆**surveillance** *nf* watch (**sur** over); (*de travaux, d'ouvriers*) supervision; (*de la police*) surveillance, observation.
survenir* [syrvənir] *vi* to occur; (*personne*) to turn up.
survêtement [syrvɛtmɑ̃] *nm Sp* tracksuit.
survie [syrvi] *nf* survival. ◆**surviv/re*** *vi* to survive (**à qch** sth); **s. à qn** to outlive s.o., survive s.o. ◆**—ant, -ante** *nmf* survivor. ◆**survivance** *nf* (*chose*) survival, relic.
survol [syrvɔl] *nm* **le s. de** flying over; (*question*) *Fig* the overview of. ◆**survoler** *vt* (*en avion*) to fly over; (*question*) *Fig* to go over (quickly).
survolté [syrvɔlte] *a* (*surexcité*) worked up.
susceptible [sysɛptibl] *a* **1** (*ombrageux*) touchy, sensitive. **2 s. de** (*interprétations etc*) open to; **s. de faire** likely *ou* liable to do; (*capable*) able to do. ◆**susceptibilité** *nf* touchiness, sensitiveness.
susciter [sysite] *vt* (*sentiment*) to arouse; (*ennuis, obstacles etc*) to create.

suspect, -ecte [syspɛ(kt), -ɛkt] *a* suspicious, suspect; **s. de** suspected of; – *nmf* suspect. ◆**suspecter** *vt* to suspect (**de qch** of sth, **de faire** of doing); (*bonne foi etc*) to question, suspect, doubt.

suspend/re [syspɑ̃dr] *vt* **1** (*destituer, différer, interrompre*) to suspend. **2** (*fixer*) to hang (up) (**à** on); **se s. à** to hang from. ◆**—u** *a* **s. à** hanging from; **pont s.** suspension bridge. ◆**suspension** *nf* **1** (*d'hostilités, d'employé etc*) & *Aut* suspension; **points de s.** *Gram* dots, suspension points. **2** (*lustre*) hanging lamp.

suspens (en) [ɑ̃syspɑ̃] *adv* **1** (*affaire, travail*) in abeyance. **2** (*dans l'incertitude*) in suspense.

suspense [syspɛns] *nm* suspense; **film à s.** thriller, suspense film.

suspicion [syspisjɔ̃] *nf* suspicion.

susurrer [sysyre] *vti* to murmur.

suture [sytyr] *nf Méd* stitching; **point de s.** stitch. ◆**suturer** *vt* to stitch up.

svelte [svɛlt] *a* slender. ◆**sveltesse** *nf* slenderness.

SVP *abrév* (*s'il vous plaît*) please.

syllabe [silab] *nf* syllable.

symbole [sɛ̃bɔl] *nm* symbol. ◆**symbolique** *a* symbolic; (*salaire*) nominal. ◆**symboliser** *vt* to symbolize. ◆**symbolisme** *nm* symbolism.

symétrie [simetri] *nf* symmetry. ◆**symétrique** *a* symmetrical.

sympa [sɛ̃pa] *a inv Fam* = **sympathique.**

sympathie [sɛ̃pati] *nf* liking, affection; (*affinité*) affinity; (*condoléances*) sympathy; **avoir de la s. pour qn** to be fond of s.o. ◆**sympathique** *a* nice, pleasant; (*accueil, geste*) friendly. ◆**sympathis/er** *vi* to get on well (**avec** with). ◆**—ant, -ante** *nmf Pol* sympathizer.

symphonie [sɛ̃fɔni] *nf* symphony. ◆**symphonique** *a* symphonic; (*orchestre*) symphony-.

symposium [sɛ̃pozjɔm] *nm* symposium.

symptôme [sɛ̃ptom] *nm* symptom. ◆**symptomatique** *a* symptomatic (**de** of).

synagogue [sinagɔg] *nf* synagogue.

synchroniser [sɛ̃krɔnize] *vt* to synchronize.

syncope [sɛ̃kɔp] *nf Méd* blackout; **tomber en s.** to black out.

syndicat [sɛ̃dika] *nm* **1** (*d'employés, d'ouvriers*) (trade) union; (*de patrons etc*) association. **2 s. d'initiative** tourist (information) office. ◆**syndical, -aux** *a* (*réunion etc*) (trade) union-. ◆**syndicalisme** *nm* trade unionism. ◆**syndicaliste** *nmf* trade unionist; – *a* (trade) union-. ◆**syndiqu/er** *vt* to unionize; — **se s.** *vpr* (*adhérer*) to join a (trade) union. ◆**—é, -ée** *nmf* (trade) union member.

syndrome [sɛ̃drom] *nm Méd* & *Fig* syndrome.

synode [sinɔd] *nm Rel* synod.

synonyme [sinɔnim] *a* synonymous (**de** with); – *nm* synonym.

syntaxe [sɛ̃taks] *nf Gram* syntax.

synthèse [sɛ̃tɛz] *nf* synthesis. ◆**synthétique** *a* synthetic.

syphilis [sifilis] *nf* syphilis.

Syrie [siri] *nf* Syria. ◆**syrien, -ienne** *a* & *nmf* Syrian.

système [sistɛm] *nm* (*structure, réseau etc*) & *Anat* system; **le s. D** *Fam* resourcefulness. ◆**systématique** *a* systematic; (*soutien*) unconditional. ◆**systématiquement** *adv* systematically.

T

T, t [te] *nm* T, t.

t' [t] *voir* **te.**

ta [ta] *voir* **ton**[1].

tabac [taba] **1** *nm* tobacco; (*magasin*) tobacconist's (shop), *Am* tobacco store; **t. (à priser)** snuff. **2** *nm* **passer à t.** to beat up; **passage à t.** beating up. **3** *a inv* (*couleur*) buff. ◆**tabatière** *nf* (*boîte*) snuffbox.

tabasser [tabase] *vt Fam* to beat up.

table [tabl] *nf* **1** (*meuble*) table; (*nourriture*) fare; **t. de jeu/de nuit/d'opération** card/bedside/operating table; **t. basse** coffee table; **t. à repasser** ironing board; **t. roulante** (tea) trolley, *Am* (serving) cart; **mettre/débarrasser la t.** to lay *ou* set/clear the table; **être à t.** to be sitting at the table; **à t.!** (food's) ready!; **faire t. rase** *Fig* to make a clean sweep (**de** of); **mettre sur t. d'écoute** (*téléphone*) to tap. **2** (*liste*) table; **t. des matières** table of contents.

tableau, -x [tablo] *nm* **1** (*peinture*) picture, painting; (*image, description*) picture; *Th* scene; **t. de maître** (*peinture*) old master. **2** (*panneau*) board; *Rail* train-indicator;

(*liste*) list: (*graphique*) chart; **t. (noir)** (black)board; **t. d'affichage** notice board, *Am* bulletin board; **t. de bord** *Aut* dashboard; **t. de contrôle** *Tech* control panel.

tabler [table] *vi* **t. sur** to count *ou* rely on.

tablette [tablɛt] *nf* (*d'armoire, de lavabo*) shelf; (*de cheminée*) mantelpiece; (*de chocolat*) bar, slab.

tablier [tablije] *nm* **1** (*vêtement*) apron; (*d'écolier*) smock; **rendre son t.** (*démissionner*) to give notice. **2** (*de pont*) roadway.

tabou [tabu] *a* & *nm* taboo.

tabouret [taburɛ] *nm* stool.

tabulateur [tabylatœr] *nm* (*de machine à écrire etc*) tabulator.

tac [tak] *nm* **répondre du t. au t.** to give tit for tat.

tache [taʃ] *nf* spot, mark; (*salissure*) stain; **faire t.** (*détonner*) *Péj* to jar, stand out; **faire t. d'huile** *Fig* to spread. **◆tacher** *vt*, **— se t.** *vpr* (*tissu etc*) to stain; – *vi* (*vin etc*) to stain. **◆tacheté** *a* speckled, spotted.

tâche [tɑʃ] *nf* task, job; **travailler à la t.** to do piecework.

tâcher [tɑʃe] *vi* **t. de faire** to try *ou* endeavour to do.

tâcheron [tɑʃrɔ̃] *nm* drudge.

tacite [tasit] *a* tacit. **◆—ment** *adv* tacitly.

taciturne [tasityrn] *a* taciturn.

tacot [tako] *nm* (*voiture*) *Fam* (old) wreck, banger.

tact [takt] *nm* tact.

tactile [taktil] *a* tactile.

tactique [taktik] *a* tactical; – *nf* **la t.** tactics; **une t.** a tactic.

Tahiti [taiti] *nm* Tahiti. **◆tahitien, -ienne** [taisjɛ̃, -jɛn] *a* & *nmf* Tahitian.

taie [tɛ] *nf* **t. d'oreiller** pillowcase, pillowslip.

taillade [tɑjad] *nf* gash, slash. **◆taillader** *vt* to gash, slash.

taille[1] [tɑj] *nf* **1** (*stature*) height; (*dimension, mesure commerciale*) size; **de haute t.** (*personne*) tall; **de petite t.** short; **de t. moyenne** (*objet, personne*) medium-sized; **être de t. à faire** *Fig* to be capable of doing; **de t.** (*erreur, objet*) *Fam* enormous. **2** *Anat* waist; **tour de t.** waist measurement.

taille[2] [tɑj] *nf* cutting; cutting out; trimming; pruning; (*forme*) cut. **◆taill/er 1** *vt* to cut; (*vêtement*) to cut out; (*haie, barbe*) to trim; (*arbre*) to prune; (*crayon*) to sharpen. **2 se t.** *vpr* (*partir*) *Arg* to clear off. **◆—é** *a* **t. en athlète/*etc*** built like an athlete/*etc*; **t. pour faire** *Fig* cut out for doing.

taille-crayon(s) [tɑjkrɛjɔ̃] *nm inv* pencil-sharpener. **◆t.-haies** *nm inv* (garden) shears; (*électrique*) hedge trimmer.

tailleur [tɑjœr] *nm* **1** (*personne*) tailor. **2** (*costume féminin*) suit.

taillis [taji] *nm* copse, coppice.

tain [tɛ̃] *nm* (*de glace*) silvering; **glace sans t.** two-way mirror.

taire* [tɛr] *vt* to say nothing about; – *vi* **faire t. qn** to silence s.o. **— se t.** *vpr* (*rester silencieux*) to keep quiet (**sur qch** about sth); (*cesser de parler*) to fall silent, shut up; **tais-toi!** be *ou* keep quiet!, shut up!

talc [talk] *nm* talcum powder.

talent [talɑ̃] *nm* talent; **avoir du t. pour** to have a talent for. **◆talentueux, -euse** *a* talented.

taler [tale] *vt* (*fruit*) to bruise.

talion [taljɔ̃] *nm* **la loi du t.** (*vengeance*) an eye for an eye.

talisman [talismɑ̃] *nm* talisman.

talkie-walkie [talkiwalki] *nm* (*poste*) walkie-talkie.

taloche [talɔʃ] *nf* (*gifle*) *Fam* clout, smack.

talon [talɔ̃] *nm* **1** heel; (**chaussures à**) **talons hauts** high heels, high-heeled shoes. **2** (*de chèque, carnet*) stub, counterfoil; (*bout de pain*) crust; (*de jambon*) heel. **◆talonner** *vt* (*fugitif etc*) to follow on the heels of; (*ballon*) *Rugby* to heel; (*harceler*) *Fig* to hound, dog.

talus [taly] *nm* slope, embankment.

tambour [tɑ̃bur] *nm* **1** (*de machine etc*) & *Mus* drum; (*personne*) drummer. **2** (*porte*) revolving door. **◆tambourin** *nm* tambourine. **◆tambouriner** *vi* (*avec les doigts etc*) to drum (**sur** on).

tamis [tami] *nm* sieve. **◆tamiser** *vt* to sift; (*lumière*) to filter, subdue.

Tamise [tamiz] *nf* **la T.** the Thames.

tampon [tɑ̃pɔ̃] *nm* **1** (*bouchon*) plug, stopper; (*d'ouate*) wad, pad; *Méd* swab; **t. hygiénique** *ou* **périodique** tampon; **t. à récurer** scouring pad. **2** (*de train etc*) & *Fig* buffer; **état t.** buffer state. **3** (*marque, instrument*) stamp; **t. buvard** blotter; **t. encreur** ink(ing) pad. **◆tamponn/er 1** *vt* (*visage etc*) to dab; (*plaie*) to swab. **2** *vt* (*train, voiture*) to crash into; **— se t.** *vpr* to crash into each other. **3** *vt* (*lettre, document*) to stamp. **◆—euses** *afpl* **autos t.** dodgems, bumper cars.

tam-tam [tamtam] *nm* (*tambour*) tom-tom.

tandem [tɑ̃dɛm] *nm* **1** (*bicyclette*) tandem. **2** (*duo*) *Fig* duo, pair; **en t.** (*travailler etc*) in tandem.

tandis que [tɑ̃dik(ə)] *conj* (*pendant que*) while; (*contraste*) whereas, while.

tangent [tɑ̃ʒɑ̃] *a* **1** *Géom* tangential (**à** to).

2 (*juste*) *Fam* touch and go, close. ◆**tangente** *nf Géom* tangent.
tangible [tɑ̃ʒibl] *a* tangible.
tango [tɑ̃go] *nm* tango.
tang/uer [tɑ̃ge] *vi* (*bateau, avion*) to pitch. ◆**—age** *nm* pitching.
tanière [tanjɛr] *nf* den, lair.
tank [tɑ̃k] *nm Mil* tank.
tanker [tɑ̃kɛr] *nm* (*navire*) tanker.
tann/er [tane] *vt* (*cuir*) to tan. ◆**—é** *a* (*visage*) weather-beaten, tanned.
tant [tɑ̃] *adv* so much (**que** that); **t. de** (*pain, temps etc*) so much (**que** that); (*gens, choses etc*) so many (**que** that); **t. de fois** so often, so many times; **t. que** (*autant que*) as much as; (*aussi fort que*) as hard as; (*aussi longtemps que*) as long as; **en t. que** (*considéré comme*) as; **t. mieux!** good!, I'm glad!; **t. pis!** too bad!, pity!; **t. soit peu** (even) remotely *ou* slightly; **un t. soit peu** somewhat; **t. s'en faut** far from it; **t. bien que mal** more or less, so-so.
tante [tɑ̃t] *nf* aunt.
tantinet [tɑ̃tinɛ] *nm & adv* **un t.** a tiny bit (**de** of).
tantôt [tɑ̃to] *adv* **1 t. . . . t.** sometimes . . . sometimes, now . . . now. **2** (*cet après-midi*) this afternoon.
taon [tɑ̃] *nm* horsefly, gadfly.
tapage [tapaʒ] *nm* din, uproar. ◆**tapageur, -euse** *a* **1** (*bruyant*) rowdy. **2** (*criard*) flashy.
tape [tap] *nf* slap. ◆**tap/er 1** *vt* (*enfant, cuisse*) to slap; (*table*) to bang; **t. qn** (*emprunter de l'argent à qn*) *Fam* to touch s.o., tap s.o. (**de** for); – *vi* (*soleil*) to beat down; **t. sur qch** to bang on sth; **t. à la porte** to bang on the door; **t. sur qn** (*critiquer*) *Fam* to run s.o. down, knock s.o.; **t. sur les nerfs de qn** *Fam* to get on s.o.'s nerves; **t. dans** (*provisions etc*) to dig into; **t. du pied** to stamp one's foot; **t. dans l'œil à qn** *Fam* to take s.o.'s fancy; **— se t.** *vpr* (*travail*) *Fam* to do, take on; (*repas, vin*) *Fam* to put away. **2** *vti* (*écrire à la machine*) to type. ◆**—ant** *a* **à midi t.** at twelve sharp; **à huit heures tapant(es)** at eight sharp. ◆**—eur, -euse** *nmf Fam* person who borrows money.
tape-à-l'œil [tapalœj] *a inv* flashy, gaudy.
tapée [tape] *nf* **une t. de** *Fam* a load of.
tapioca [tapjɔka] *nm* tapioca.
tapir (se) [sətapir] *vpr* to crouch (down). ◆**tapi** *a* crouching, crouched.
tapis [tapi] *nm* carpet; **t. de bain** bathmat; **t. roulant** (*pour marchandises*) conveyor belt; (*pour personnes*) moving pavement *ou Am* sidewalk; **t. de sol** groundsheet; **t. de table** table cover; **envoyer qn au t.** (*abattre*) to floor s.o.; **mettre sur le t.** (*sujet*) to bring up for discussion. ◆**t.-brosse** *nm* doormat.
tapisser [tapise] *vt* (*mur*) to (wall)paper; to hang with tapestry; (*recouvrir*) *Fig* to cover. ◆**tapisserie** *nf* (*tenture*) tapestry; (*papier peint*) wallpaper. ◆**tapissier, -ière** *nmf* (*qui pose des tissus etc*) upholsterer; **t.(-décorateur)** interior decorator.
tapoter [tapɔte] *vt* to tap; (*joue*) to pat; – *vi* **t. sur** to tap (on).
taquin, -ine [takɛ̃, -in] *a* (fond of) teasing; – *nmf* tease(r). ◆**taquiner** *vt* to tease; (*inquiéter, agacer*) to bother. ◆**taquinerie(s)** *nf(pl)* teasing.
tarabiscoté [tarabiskɔte] *a* over-elaborate.
tarabuster [tarabyste] *vt* (*idée etc*) to trouble (*s.o.*).
tard [tar] *adv* late; **plus t.** later (on); **au plus t.** at the latest; **sur le t.** late in life. ◆**tarder** *vi* (*lettre, saison*) to be a long time coming; **t. à faire** to take one's time doing; (*différer*) to delay (in) doing; **ne tardez pas** (*agissez tout de suite*) don't delay; **elle ne va pas t.** she won't be long; **sans t.** without delay; **il me tarde de faire** I long to do. ◆**tardif, -ive** *a* late; (*regrets*) belated. ◆**tardivement** *adv* late.
tare [tar] *nf* **1** (*poids*) tare. **2** (*défaut*) *Fig* defect. ◆**taré** *a* (*corrompu*) corrupt; *Méd* defective; (*fou*) *Fam* mad, idiotic.
targuer (se) [sətarge] *vpr* **se t. de qch/de faire** to boast about sth/about doing.
tarif [tarif] *nm* (*prix*) rate; *Aut Rail* fare; (*tableau*) price list, tariff. ◆**tarification** *nf* (price) fixing.
tarir [tarir] *vti,* **— se t.** *vpr* (*fleuve etc*) & *Fig* to dry up; **ne pas t. d'éloges sur qn** to rave about s.o.
tartare [tartar] *a* **sauce t.** tartar sauce.
tarte [tart] **1** *nf* tart, flan, *Am* (open) pie. **2** *a inv Fam* (*sot*) silly; (*laid*) ugly. ◆**tartelette** *nf* (small) tart.
tartine [tartin] *nf* slice of bread; **t. (de beurre/de confiture)** slice of bread and butter/jam. ◆**tartiner** *vt* (*beurre*) to spread; **fromage à t.** cheese spread.
tartre [tartr] *nm* (*de bouilloire*) scale, fur; (*de dents*) tartar.
tas [tɑ] *nm* pile, heap; **un** *ou* **des t. de** (*beaucoup*) *Fam* lots of; **mettre en t.** to pile *ou* heap up; **former qn sur le t.** (*au travail*) to train s.o. on the job.
tasse [tas] *nf* cup; **t. à café** coffee cup; **t. à thé** teacup; **boire la t.** *Fam* to swallow a mouthful (*when swimming*).

tasser [tɑse] *vt* to pack, squeeze (**dans** into); (*terre*) to pack down; **un café/***etc* **bien tassé** (*fort*) a good strong coffee/*etc*; **— se t.** *vpr* (*se voûter*) to become bowed; (*se serrer*) to squeeze up; (*sol*) to sink, collapse; **ça va se t.** (*s'arranger*) *Fam* things will pan out (all right).

tâter [tɑte] *vt* to feel; (*sonder*) *Fig* to sound out; – *vi* **t. de** (*métier, prison*) to have a taste of, experience; **— se t.** *vpr* (*hésiter*) to be in *ou* of two minds. **◆tâtonn/er** *vi* to grope about, feel one's way. **◆—ement** *nm* **par t.** (*procéder*) by trial and error. **◆tâtons (à)** *adv* **avancer à t.** to feel one's way (along); **chercher à t.** to grope for.

tatillon, -onne [tatijɔ̃, -ɔn] *a* finicky.

tatou/er [tatwe] *vt* (*corps, dessin*) to tattoo. **◆—age** *nm* (*dessin*) tattoo; (*action*) tattooing.

taudis [todi] *nm* slum, hovel.

taule [tol] *nf* (*prison*) *Fam* nick, jug, *Am* can.

taupe [top] *nf* (*animal, espion*) mole. **◆taupinière** *nf* molehill.

taureau, -x [tɔro] *nm* bull; **le T.** (*signe*) Taurus. **◆tauromachie** *nf* bull-fighting.

taux [to] *nm* rate; **t. d'alcool/de cholestérol/***etc* alcohol/cholesterol/*etc* level.

taverne [tavɛrn] *nf* tavern.

taxe [taks] *nf* (*prix*) official price; (*impôt*) tax; (*douanière*) duty; **t. de séjour** tourist tax; **t. à la valeur ajoutée** value-added tax. **◆taxation** *nf* fixing of the price (**de** of); taxation (**de** of). **◆taxer** *vt* **1** (*produit*) to fix the price of; (*objet de luxe etc*) to tax. **2 t. qn de** to accuse s.o. of.

taxi [taksi] *nm* taxi.

taxiphone [taksifɔn] *nm* pay phone.

Tchécoslovaquie [tʃekɔslɔvaki] *nf* Czechoslovakia. **◆tchèque** *a & nmf* Czech; – *nm* (*langue*) Czech.

te [t(ə)] (**t'** *before vowel or mute h*) *pron* **1** (*complément direct*) you; **je te vois** I see you. **2** (*indirect*) (to) you; **il te parle** he speaks to you; **elle te l'a dit** she told you. **3** (*réfléchi*) yourself; **tu te laves** you wash yourself.

technicien, -ienne [tɛknisjɛ̃, -jɛn] *nmf* technician. **◆technique** *a* technical; – *nf* technique. **◆techniquement** *adv* technically. **◆technocrate** *nm* technocrat. **◆technologie** *nf* technology. **◆technologique** *a* technological.

teck [tɛk] *nm* (*bois*) teak.

teckel [tekɛl] *nm* (*chien*) dachshund.

tee-shirt [tiʃœrt] *nm* tee-shirt.

teindre* [tɛ̃dr] *vt* to dye; **— se t.** *vpr* to dye one's hair. **◆teinture** *nf* dyeing; (*produit*) dye. **◆teinturerie** *nf* (*boutique*) (dry) cleaner's. **◆teinturier, -ière** *nmf* dry cleaner.

teint [tɛ̃] *nm* **1** (*de visage*) complexion. **2 bon** *ou* **grand t.** (*tissu*) colourfast; **bon t.** (*catholique etc*) *Fig* staunch.

teinte [tɛ̃t] *nf* shade, tint; **une t. de** (*dose*) *Fig* a tinge of. **◆teinter** *vt* to tint; (*bois*) to stain; **se t. de** (*remarque, ciel*) *Fig* to be tinged with.

tel, telle [tɛl] *a* such; **un t. homme/livre/***etc* such a man/book/*etc*; **un t. intérêt/***etc* such interest/*etc*; **de tels mots/***etc* such words/*etc*; **t. que** such as, like; **t. que je l'ai laissé** just as I left it; **laissez-le t. quel** leave it just as it is; **en tant que t., comme t.** as such; **t. ou t.** such and such; **rien de t. que . . .** (there's) nothing like . . . ; **rien de t.** nothing like it; **Monsieur Un t.** Mr So-and-so; **t. père t. fils** like father like son.

télé [tele] *nf* (*téléviseur*) *Fam* TV, telly; **à la t.** on TV, on the telly; **regarder la t.** to watch TV *ou* the telly.

télé- [tele] *préf* tele-.

télébenne [telebɛn] *nf*, **télécabine** [telekabin] *nf* (*cabine, système*) cable car.

télécommande [telekɔmɑ̃d] *nf* remote control. **◆télécommander** *vt* to operate by remote control.

télécommunications [telekɔmynikɑsjɔ̃] *nfpl* telecommunications.

téléfilm [telefilm] *nm* TV film.

télégramme [telegram] *nm* telegram.

télégraphe [telegraf] *nm* telegraph. **◆télégraphie** *nf* telegraphy. **◆télégraphier** *vt* (*message*) to wire, cable (**que** that). **◆télégraphique** *a* (*fil, poteau*) telegraph-; (*style*) *Fig* telegraphic. **◆télégraphiste** *nm* (*messager*) telegraph boy.

téléguid/er [telegide] *vt* to radio-control. **◆—age** *nm* radio-control.

télématique [telematik] *nf* telematics, computer communications.

télépathie [telepati] *nf* telepathy.

téléphérique [teleferik] *nm* (*système*) cable car, cableway.

téléphone [telefɔn] *nm* (tele)phone; **coup de t.** (phone) call; **passer un coup de t. à qn** to give s.o. a call *ou* a ring; **au t.** on the (tele)phone; **avoir le t.** to be on the (tele)phone; **par le t. arabe** *Fig* on the grapevine. **◆téléphoner** *vt* (*nouvelle etc*) to (tele)phone (**à** to); – *vi* to (tele)phone; **t. à qn** to (tele)phone s.o., call s.o. (up). **◆téléphonique** *a* (*appel etc*) (tele)phone-. **◆téléphoniste** *nmf* operator, telephonist.

télescope [teleskɔp] *nm* telescope. ◆**télescopique** *a* telescopic.

télescop/er [teleskɔpe] *vt Aut Rail* to smash into; se t. to smash into each other. ◆**—age** *nm* smash.

téléscripteur [teleskriptœr] *nm* (*appareil*) teleprinter.

télésiège [telesjɛʒ] *nm* chair lift.

téléski [teleski] *nm* ski tow.

téléspectateur, -trice [telespɛktatœr, -tris] *nmf* (television) viewer.

téléviser [televize] *vt* to televise; **journal télévisé** television news. ◆**téléviseur** *nm* television (set). ◆**télévision** *nf* television; **à la t.** on (the) television; **regarder la t.** to watch (the) television; **de t.** (*programme etc*) television-.

télex [telɛks] *nm* (*service, message*) telex.

telle [tɛl] *voir* **tel.**

tellement [tɛlmɑ̃] *adv* (*si*) so; (*tant*) so much; **t. grand/***etc* **que** so big/*etc* that; **crier/***etc* **t. que** to shout/*etc* so much that; **t. de** (*travail etc*) so much; (*soucis etc*) so many; **personne ne peut le supporter, t. il est bavard** nobody can stand him, he's so talkative; **tu aimes ça? - pas t.** do you like it? - not much *ou* a lot.

téméraire [temerɛr] *a* rash, reckless. ◆**témérité** *nf* rashness, recklessness.

témoign/er [temwaɲe] **1** *vi Jur* to testify (**contre** against); **t. de qch** (*personne, attitude etc*) to testify to sth; — *vt* **t. que** *Jur* to testify that. **2** *vt* (*gratitude etc*) to show (**à qn** (to) s.o.). ◆**—age** *nm* **1** testimony, evidence; (*récit*) account; **faux t.** (*délit*) *Jur* perjury. **2** (*d'affection etc*) *Fig* token, sign (de of); **en t. de** as a token *ou* sign of.

témoin [temwɛ̃] **1** *nm* witness; **t. oculaire** eyewitness; **être t. de** (*accident etc*) to witness; — *a* **appartement t.** show flat *ou Am* apartment. **2** *nm Sp* baton.

tempe [tɑ̃p] *nf Anat* temple.

tempérament [tɑ̃peramɑ̃] *nm* **1** (*caractère*) temperament; (*physique*) constitution. **2 acheter à t.** to buy on hire purchase *ou Am* on the installment plan.

tempérance [tɑ̃perɑ̃s] *nf* temperance.

température [tɑ̃peratyr] *nf* temperature; **avoir** *ou* **faire de la t.** *Méd* to have a temperature.

tempér/er [tɑ̃pere] *vt Litt* to temper. ◆**—é** *a* (*climat, zone*) temperate.

tempête [tɑ̃pɛt] *nf* storm; **t. de neige** snowstorm, blizzard.

tempêter [tɑ̃pete] *vi* (*crier*) to storm, rage (**contre** against).

temple [tɑ̃pl] *nm Rel* temple; (*protestant*) church.

tempo [tempo] *nm* tempo.

temporaire [tɑ̃pɔrɛr] *a* temporary. ◆**—ment** *adv* temporarily.

temporel, -elle [tɑ̃pɔrɛl] *a* temporal.

temporiser [tɑ̃pɔrize] *vi* to procrastinate, play for time.

temps[1] [tɑ̃] *nm* (*durée, période, moment*) time; *Gram* tense; (*étape*) stage; **t. d'arrêt** pause, break; **en t. de guerre** in time of war, in wartime; **avoir/trouver le t.** to have/find (the) time (**de faire** to do); **il est t.** it is time (**de faire** to do); **il était t.!** it was about time (too)!; **pendant un t.** for a while *ou* time; **ces derniers t.** lately; **de t. en t.** [dətɑ̃zɑ̃tɑ̃], **de t. à autre** [dətɑ̃zaotr] from time to time, now and again; **en t. utile** [ɑ̃tɑ̃zytil] in good *ou* due time; **en même t.** at the same time (**que** as); **à t.** (*arriver*) in time; **à plein t.** (*travailler etc*) full-time; **à t. partiel** (*travailler etc*) part-time; **dans le t.** (*autrefois*) once, at one time; **avec le t.** (*à la longue*) in time; **tout le t.** all the time; **du t. de** in the time of; **de mon t.** in my time; **à quatre t.** (*moteur*) four-stroke.

temps[2] [tɑ̃] *nm* (*atmosphérique*) weather; **il fait beau/mauvais t.** the weather's fine/bad; **quel t. fait-il?** what's the weather like?

tenable [tənabl] *a* bearable.

tenace [tənas] *a* stubborn, tenacious. ◆**ténacité** *nf* stubbornness, tenacity.

tenailler [tənaje] *vt* (*faim, remords*) to rack, torture (*s.o.*).

tenailles [tənaj] *nfpl* (*outil*) pincers.

tenancier, -ière [tənɑ̃sje, -jɛr] *nmf* (*d'hôtel etc*) manager, manageress.

tenant, -ante [tənɑ̃, -ɑ̃t] *nmf* (*de titre*) *Sp* holder. **2** *nm* (*partisan*) supporter (**de** of).

tenants [tənɑ̃] *nmpl* **les t. et les aboutissants** (*d'une question etc*) the ins and outs (**de** of).

tendance [tɑ̃dɑ̃s] *nf* (*penchant*) tendency; (*évolution*) trend (**à** towards); **avoir t. à faire** to have a tendency to do, tend to do.

tendancieux, -euse [tɑ̃dɑ̃sjø, -øz] *a Péj* tendentious.

tendeur [tɑ̃dœr] *nm* (*pour arrimer des bagages*) elastic strap.

tendon [tɑ̃dɔ̃] *nm Anat* tendon, sinew.

tend/re[1] [tɑ̃dr] **1** *vt* to stretch; (*main*) to hold out (**à qn** to s.o.); (*bras, jambe*) to stretch out; (*cou*) to strain, crane; (*muscle*) to tense, flex; (*arc*) to bend; (*piège*) to lay, set; (*filet*) to spread; (*tapisserie*) to hang; **t. qch à qn** to hold out sth to s.o.; **t. l'oreille** *Fig* to prick up one's ears; **— se t.** *vpr* (*rap-*

ports) to become strained. **2** *vi* **t. à qch/à faire** to tend towards sth/to do. **◆—u** *a* (*corde*) tight, taut; (*personne, situation*) tense; (*rapports*) strained; (*main*) outstretched.

tendre² [tɑ̃dr] *a* **1** (*viande*) tender; (*peau*) delicate, tender; (*bois, couleur*) soft. **2** (*affectueux*) loving, tender. **◆—ment** [-əmɑ̃] *adv* lovingly, tenderly. **◆tendresse** *nf* (*affection*) affection, tenderness. **◆tendreté** *nf* (*de viande*) tenderness.

ténèbres [tenɛbr] *nfpl* darkness, gloom. **◆ténébreux, -euse** *a* dark, gloomy; (*mystérieux*) mysterious.

teneur [tənœr] *nf* (*de lettre etc*) content; **t. en alcool/***etc* alcohol/*etc* content (**de** of).

tenir* [tənir] *vt* (*à la main etc*) to hold; (*pari, promesse*) to keep; (*hôtel*) to run, keep; (*comptes*) *Com* to keep; (*propos*) to utter; (*rôle*) to play; **t. propre/chaud/***etc* to keep clean/hot/*etc*; **je le tiens!** (*je l'ai attrapé*) I've got him!; **je le tiens de** (*fait etc*) I got it from; (*caractère héréditaire*) I get it from; **t. pour** to regard as; **t. sa droite** *Aut* to keep to the right; **t. la route** (*voiture*) to hold the road; – *vi* (*nœud etc*) to hold; (*coiffure, neige*) to last, hold; (*offre*) to stand; (*résister*) to hold out; **t. à** (*personne, jouet etc*) to be attached to, be fond of; (*la vie*) to value; (*provenir*) to stem from; **t. à faire** to be anxious to do; **t. dans qch** (*être contenu*) to fit into sth; **t. de qn** to take after s.o.; **tenez!** (*prenez*) here (you are)!; **tiens!** (*surprise*) hey!, well!; – *v imp* **il ne tient qu'à vous** it's up to you (**de faire** to do); — **se t.** *vpr* (*rester*) to keep, remain; (*avoir lieu*) to be held; **se t. (debout)** to stand (up); **se t. droit** to stand up *ou* sit up straight; **se t. par la main** to hold hands; **se t. à** to hold on to; **se t. bien** to behave oneself; **tout se tient** *Fig* it all hangs together; **s'en t. à** (*se limiter à*) to stick to; **savoir à quoi s'en t.** to know what's what.

tennis [tenis] *nm* tennis; (*terrain*) (tennis) court; **t. de table** table tennis; – *nfpl* (*chaussures*) plimsolls, pumps, *Am* sneakers.

ténor [tenɔr] *nm Mus* tenor.

tension [tɑ̃sjɔ̃] *nf* tension; **t. (artérielle)** blood pressure; **t. d'esprit** concentration; **avoir de la t.** *Méd* to have high blood pressure.

tentacule [tɑ̃takyl] *nm* tentacle.

tente [tɑ̃t] *nf* tent.

tenter¹ [tɑ̃te] *vt* (*essayer*) to try; **t. de faire** to try *ou* attempt to do. **◆tentative** *nf* attempt; **t. de suicide** suicide attempt.

tent/er² [tɑ̃te] *vt* (*allécher*) to tempt; **tenté de faire** tempted to do. **◆—ant** *a* tempting. **◆tentation** *nf* temptation.

tenture [tɑ̃tyr] *nf* (wall) hanging; (*de porte*) drape, curtain.

tenu [təny] *voir* **tenir**; – *a* **t. de faire** obliged to do; **bien/mal t.** (*maison etc*) well/badly kept.

ténu [teny] *a* (*fil etc*) fine; (*soupçon, différence*) tenuous; (*voix*) thin.

tenue [təny] *nf* **1** (*vêtements*) clothes, outfit; (*aspect*) appearance; **t. de combat** *Mil* combat dress; **t. de soirée** (*smoking*) evening dress. **2** (*conduite*) (good) behaviour; (*maintien*) posture; **manquer de t.** to lack (good) manners. **3** (*de maison, hôtel*) running; (*de comptes*) *Com* keeping. **4 t. de route** *Aut* road-holding.

ter [tɛr] *a* **4 t.** (*numéro*) 4B.

térébenthine [terebɑ̃tin] *nf* turpentine.

tergal® [tɛrgal] *nm* Terylene®, *Am* Dacron®.

tergiverser [tɛrʒivɛrse] *vi* to procrastinate.

terme [tɛrm] *nm* **1** (*mot*) term. **2** (*loyer*) rent; (*jour*) rent day; (*période*) rental period. **3** (*date limite*) time (limit), date; (*fin*) end; **mettre un t. à** to put an end to; **à court/long t.** (*projet etc*) short-/long-term; **être né avant/à t.** to be born prematurely/at (full) term. **4 moyen t.** (*solution*) middle course. **5 en bons/mauvais termes** on good/bad terms (**avec qn** with s.o.).

terminer [tɛrmine] *vt* (*achever*) to finish, complete; (*lettre, phrase, débat, soirée*) to end; — **se t.** *vpr* to end (**par** with, **en** in). **◆terminaison** *nf Gram* ending. **◆terminal, -aux 1** *a* final; (*phase*) *Méd* terminal; – *a* & *nf* (**classe**) **terminale** *Scol* = sixth form, *Am* = twelfth grade. **2** *nm* (*d'ordinateur, pétrolier*) terminal.

terminologie [tɛrminɔlɔʒi] *nf* terminology.

terminus [tɛrminys] *nm* terminus.

termite [tɛrmit] *nm* (*insecte*) termite.

terne [tɛrn] *a* (*couleur, journée etc*) dull, drab; (*personne*) dull. **◆ternir** *vt* (*métal, réputation*) to tarnish; (*miroir, meuble*) to dull; — **se t.** *vpr* (*métal*) to tarnish.

terrain [tɛrɛ̃] *nm* (*sol*) & *Fig* ground; (*étendue*) land; *Mil Géol* terrain; (*à bâtir*) plot, site; **un t.** a piece of land; **t. d'aviation** airfield; **t. de camping** campsite; **t. de football/rugby** football/rugby pitch; **t. de golf** golf course; **t. de jeu** playground; **t. de sport** sports ground, playing field; **t. vague** waste ground, *Am* vacant lot; **céder/gagner/perdre du t.** *Mil* & *Fig* to give/

lose ground; **tout t., tous terrains** (*véhicule*) all-purpose.

terrasse [tɛras] *nf* **1** terrace; (*toit*) terrace (roof). **2** (*de café*) pavement *ou Am* sidewalk area; **à la t.** outside.

terrassement [tɛrasmɑ̃] *nm* (*travail*) excavation.

terrasser [tɛrase] *vt* (*adversaire*) to floor, knock down; (*accabler*) *Fig* to overcome.

terrassier [tɛrasje] *nm* labourer, navvy.

terre [tɛr] *nf* (*matière*) earth; (*sol*) ground; (*opposé à mer, étendue*) land; *pl* (*domaine*) land, estate; *Él* earth, *Am* ground; **la t.** (*le monde*) the earth; **la T.** (*planète*) Earth; **à** *ou* **par t.** (*poser, tomber*) to the ground; **par t.** (*assis, couché*) on the ground; **aller à t.** *Nau* to go ashore; **sous t.** underground; **t. cuite** (baked) clay, earthenware; **en t. cuite** (*poterie*) clay-. ◆**t.-à-terre** *a inv* down-to-earth. ◆**t.-plein** *nm* (earth) platform; (*au milieu de la route*) central reservation, *Am* median strip. ◆**terrestre** *a* (*vie, joies*) earthly; (*animaux, transport*) land-; **la surface t.** the earth's surface; **globe t.** (terrestrial) globe. ◆**terreux, -euse** *a* (*goût*) earthy; (*sale*) grubby; (*couleur*) dull; (*teint*) ashen. ◆**terrien, -ienne** *a* land-owning; **propriétaire t.** landowner; – *nmf* (*habitant de la terre*) earth dweller, earthling.

terreau [tɛro] *nm* compost.

terrer (se) [sətɛre] *vpr* (*fugitif, animal*) to hide, go to ground *ou* earth.

terreur [tɛrœr] *nf* terror; **t. de** fear of. ◆**terrible** *a* terrible; (*formidable*) *Fam* terrific. ◆**terriblement** *adv* (*extrêmement*) terribly. ◆**terrifi/er** *vt* to terrify. ◆**—ant** *a* terrifying; (*extraordinaire*) incredible.

terrier [tɛrje] *nm* **1** (*de lapin etc*) burrow. **2** (*chien*) terrier.

terrine [tɛrin] *nf* (*récipient*) *Culin* terrine; (*pâté*) pâté.

territoire [tɛritwar] *nm* territory. ◆**territorial, -aux** *a* territorial.

terroir [tɛrwar] *nm* (*sol*) soil; (*région*) region; **du t.** (*accent etc*) rural.

terroriser [tɛrɔrize] *vt* to terrorize. ◆**terrorisme** *nm* terrorism. ◆**terroriste** *a & nmf* terrorist.

tertiaire [tɛrsjɛr] *a* tertiary.

tertre [tɛrtr] *nm* hillock, mound.

tes [te] *voir* **ton**[1].

tesson [tesɔ̃] *nm* **t. de bouteille** piece of broken bottle.

test [tɛst] *nm* test. ◆**tester** *vt* (*élève, produit*) to test.

testament [tɛstamɑ̃] *nm* **1** *Jur* will; (*œuvre*) *Fig* testament. **2 Ancien/Nouveau T.** *Rel* Old/New Testament.

testicule [tɛstikyl] *nm Anat* testicle.

tétanos [tetanos] *nm Méd* tetanus.

têtard [tɛtar] *nm* tadpole.

tête [tɛt] *nf* head; (*figure*) face; (*cheveux*) (head of) hair; (*cerveau*) brain; (*cime*) top; (*de clou, cortège, lit*) head; (*de page, liste*) top, head; (*coup*) *Fb* header; **t. nucléaire** nuclear warhead; **tenir t. à** (*s'opposer à*) to stand up to; **t. nue** bare-headed; **tu n'as pas de t.!** you're a scatterbrain!; **faire la t.** (*bouder*) to sulk; **faire une t.** *Fb* to head the ball; **avoir/faire une drôle de t.** to have/give a funny look; **perdre la t.** *Fig* to lose one's head; **tomber la t. la première** to fall headlong *ou* head first; **calculer qch de t.** to work sth out in one's head; **se mettre dans la t. de faire** to get it into one's head to do; **à t. reposée** at one's leisure; **à la t. de** (*entreprise, parti*) at the head of; (*classe*) *Scol* at the top of; **de la t. aux pieds** from head *ou* top to toe; **en t.** *Sp* in the lead. ◆**t.-à-queue** *nm inv* **faire un t.-à-queue** *Aut* to spin right round. ◆**t.-à-tête** *adv* **(en) t.-à-tête** (*seul*) in private, alone together; – *nm inv* tête-à-tête. ◆**t.-bêche** *adv* head to tail.

tét/er [tete] *vt* (*lait, biberon etc*) to suck; **t. sa mère** (*bébé*) to suck, feed; – *vi* **donner à t. à** to feed, suckle. ◆**—ée** *nf* (*de bébé*) feed. ◆**tétine** *nf* **1** (*de biberon*) teat, *Am* nipple; (*sucette*) dummy, *Am* pacifier. **2** (*de vache*) udder. ◆**téton** *nm Fam* breast.

têtu [tety] *a* stubborn, obstinate.

texte [tɛkst] *nm* text; *Th* lines, text; (*de devoir*) *Scol* subject; (*morceau choisi*) *Littér* passage. ◆**textuel, -elle** *a* (*traduction*) literal.

textile [tɛkstil] *a & nm* textile.

texture [tɛkstyr] *nf* texture.

TGV [teʒeve] *abrév* = **train à grande vitesse.**

Thaïlande [tailɑ̃d] *nf* Thailand. ◆**thaïlandais, -aise** *a & nmf* Thai.

thé [te] *nm* (*boisson, réunion*) tea. ◆**théière** *nf* teapot.

théâtre [teatr] *nm* (*art, lieu*) theatre; (*œuvres*) drama; (*d'un crime*) *Fig* scene; (*des opérations*) *Mil* theatre; **faire du t.** to act. ◆**théâtral, -aux** *a* theatrical.

thème [tɛm] *nm* theme; (*traduction*) *Scol* translation, prose.

théologie [teɔlɔʒi] *nf* theology. ◆**théologien** *nm* theologian. ◆**théologique** *a* theological.

théorème [teɔrɛm] *nm* theorem.

théorie [teɔri] *nf* theory; **en t.** in theory.

◆**théoricien, -ienne** *nmf* theorist, theoretician. ◆**théorique** *a* theoretical. ◆**théoriquement** *adv* theoretically.
thérapeutique [terapøtik] *a* therapeutic; – *nf* (*traitement*) therapy. ◆**thérapie** *nf Psy* therapy.
thermal, -aux [termal, -o] *a* **station thermale** spa; **eaux thermales** hot springs.
thermique [termik] *a* (*énergie, unité*) thermal.
thermomètre [termɔmetr] *nm* thermometer.
thermonucléaire [termɔnykleer] *a* thermonuclear.
thermos® [termɔs] *nm ou f* Thermos (flask)®, vacuum flask.
thermostat [termɔsta] *nm* thermostat.
thèse [tez] *nf* (*proposition, ouvrage*) thesis.
thon [tɔ̃] *nm* tuna (fish).
thorax [tɔraks] *nm Anat* thorax.
thym [tɛ̃] *nm Bot Culin* thyme.
thyroïde [tirɔid] *a & nf Anat* thyroid.
tibia [tibja] *nm* shin bone, tibia.
tic [tik] *nm* (*contraction*) tic, twitch; (*manie*) *Fig* mannerism.
ticket [tike] *nm* ticket; **t. de quai** *Rail* platform ticket.
tic(-)tac [tiktak] *int & nm inv* tick-tock.
tiède [tjed] *a* (luke)warm, tepid; (*climat, vent*) mild; (*accueil, partisan*) half-hearted. ◆**tiédeur** *nf* (luke)warmness, tepidness; mildness; half-heartedness. ◆**tiédir** *vt* to cool (down); (*chauffer*) to warm (up); – *vi* to cool (down); to warm up.
tien, tienne [tjɛ̃, tjen] *pron poss* **le t., la tienne, les tien(ne)s** yours; **les deux tiens** your two; – *nmpl* **les tiens** (*amis etc*) your (own) people.
tiens, tient [tjɛ̃] *voir* **tenir.**
tiercé [tjerse] *nm* (*pari*) place betting (*on horses*); **gagner au t.** to win on the races.
tiers, tierce [tjer, tjers] *a* third; – *nm* (*fraction*) third; (*personne*) third party; **assurance au t.** third-party insurance. ◆**T.-Monde** *nm* Third World.
tige [tiʒ] *nf* (*de plante*) stem, stalk; (*de botte*) leg; (*barre*) rod.
tignasse [tiɲas] *nf* mop (of hair).
tigre [tigr] *nm* tiger. ◆**tigresse** *nf* tigress.
tigré [tigre] *a* (*tacheté*) spotted; (*rayé*) striped.
tilleul [tijœl] *nm* lime (tree), linden (tree); (*infusion*) lime (blossom) tea.
timbale [tɛ̃bal] *nf* **1** (*gobelet*) (metal) tumbler. **2** *Mus* kettledrum.
timbre [tɛ̃br] *nm* **1** (*marque, tampon, vignette*) stamp; (*cachet de la poste*) postmark. **2** (*sonnette*) bell. **3** (*d'instrument, de voix*) tone (quality). ◆**t.-poste** *nm* (*pl* **timbres-poste**) (postage) stamp. ◆**timbr/er** *vt* (*affranchir*) to stamp (*letter*); (*marquer*) to stamp (*document*). ◆**—é** *a* **1** (*voix*) sonorous. **2** (*fou*) *Fam* crazy.
timide [timid] *a* (*gêné*) shy, timid; (*timoré*) timid. ◆**—ment** *adv* shyly; timidly. ◆**timidité** *nf* shyness; timidity.
timonier [timɔnje] *nm Nau* helmsman.
timoré [timɔre] *a* timorous, fearful.
tintamarre [tɛ̃tamar] *nm* din, racket.
tint/er [tɛ̃te] *vi* (*cloche*) to ring, toll; (*clés, monnaie*) to jingle; (*verres*) to chink. ◆**—ement(s)** *nm(pl)* ringing; jingling; chinking.
tique [tik] *nf* (*insecte*) tick.
tiquer [tike] *vi* (*personne*) to wince.
tir [tir] *nm* (*sport*) shooting; (*action*) firing, shooting; (*feu, rafale*) fire; *Fb* shot; **t. (forain), (stand de) t.** shooting *ou* rifle range; **t. à l'arc** archery; **ligne de t.** line of fire.
tirade [tirad] *nf Th & Fig* monologue.
tiraill/er [tiraje] **1** *vt* to pull (away) at; (*harceler*) *Fig* to pester, plague; **tiraillé entre** (*possibilités etc*) torn between. **2** *vi* (*au fusil*) to shoot wildly. ◆**—ement** *nm* **1** (*conflit*) conflict (**entre** between). **2** (*crampe*) *Méd* cramp.
tire [tir] *nf* **vol à la t.** *Fam* pickpocketing.
tire-au-flanc [tiroflɑ̃] *nm inv* (*paresseux*) shirker. ◆**t.-bouchon** *nm* corkscrew. ◆**t.-d'aile (à)** *adv* swiftly.
tirelire [tirlir] *nf* moneybox, *Am* coin bank.
tir/er [tire] *vt* to pull; (*langue*) to stick out; (*trait, conclusion, rideaux*) to draw; (*chapeau*) to raise; (*balle, canon*) to fire, shoot; (*gibier*) to shoot; *Typ Phot* to print; **t. de** (*sortir*) to take *ou* pull *ou* draw out of; (*obtenir*) to get from; (*nom, origine*) to derive from; (*produit*) to extract from; **t. qn de** (*danger, lit*) to get s.o. out of; – *vi* to pull (**sur** on, at); (*faire feu*) to fire, shoot (**sur** at); *Fb* to shoot; (*cheminée*) to draw; **t. sur** (*couleur*) to verge on; **t. au sort** to draw lots; **t. à sa fin** to draw to a close; – **se t.** *vpr* (*partir*) *Fam* to beat it; **se t. de** (*problème, travail*) to cope with; (*danger, situation*) to get out of; **se t. d'affaire** to get out of trouble; **s'en t.** *Fam* (*en réchapper*) to come *ou* pull through; (*réussir*) to get along. ◆**—é** *a* (*traits, visage*) drawn; **t. par les cheveux** *Fig* far-fetched. ◆**—age** *nm* **1** (*action*) *Typ Phot* printing; (*édition*) edition; (*quantité*) (print) run; (*de journal*) circulation. **2** (*de loterie*) draw; **t. au sort**

drawing of lots. **3** (*de cheminée*) draught. ◆**—eur** *nm* gunman; **t. d'élite** marksman; **un bon/mauvais t.** a good/bad shot. ◆**—euse** *nf* **t. de cartes** fortune-teller.

tiret [tirɛ] *nm* (*trait*) dash.

tiroir [tirwar] *nm* (*de commode etc*) drawer. ◆**t.-caisse** *nm* (*pl* **tiroirs-caisses**) (cash) till.

tisane [tizan] *nf* herb(al) tea.

tison [tizɔ̃] *nm* (fire)brand, ember. ◆**tisonner** *vt* (*feu*) to poke. ◆**tisonnier** *nm* poker.

tiss/er [tise] *vt* to weave. ◆**—age** *nm* (*action*) weaving. ◆**tisserand, -ande** *nmf* weaver.

tissu [tisy] *nm* fabric, material, cloth; *Biol* tissue; **un t. de** (*mensonges etc*) a web of; **le t. social** the fabric of society, the social fabric; **du t.-éponge** (terry) towelling.

titre [titr] *nm* (*nom, qualité*) title; *Com* bond; (*diplôme*) qualification; *pl* (*droits*) claims (**à** to); **(gros) t.** *Journ* headline; **t. de propriété** title deed; **t. de transport** ticket; **à quel t.?** (*pour quelle raison*) on what grounds?; **à ce t.** (*en cette qualité*) as such; (*pour cette raison*) therefore; **à aucun t.** on no account; **au même t.** in the same way (**que** as); **à t. d'exemple/d'ami** as an example/friend; **à t. exceptionnel** exceptionally; **à t. privé** in a private capacity; **à juste t.** rightly. ◆**titr/er** *vt* (*film*) to title; *Journ* to run as a headline. ◆**—é** *a* (*personne*) titled. ◆**titulaire** *a* (*professeur*) staff-, full; **être t. de** (*permis etc*) to be the holder of; (*poste*) to hold; – *nmf* (*de permis, poste*) holder (**de** of). ◆**titulariser** *vt* (*fonctionnaire*) to give tenure to.

tituber [titybe] *vi* to reel, stagger.

toast [tost] *nm* **1** (*pain grillé*) piece *ou* slice of toast. **2** (*allocution*) toast; **porter un t. à** to drink (a toast) to.

toboggan [tɔbɔgɑ̃] *nm* **1** (*pente*) slide; (*traîneau*) toboggan. **2** *Aut* flyover, *Am* overpass.

toc [tɔk] **1** *int* **t. t.!** knock knock! **2** *nm* **du t.** (*camelote*) rubbish, trash; **en t.** (*bijou*) imitation-.

tocsin [tɔksɛ̃] *nm* alarm (bell).

tohu-bohu [tɔybɔy] *nm* (*bruit*) hubbub, commotion; (*confusion*) hurly-burly.

toi [twa] *pron* **1** (*complément*) you; **c'est t.** it's you; **avec t.** with you. **2** (*sujet*) you; **t., tu peux** *you* may. **3** (*réfléchi*) **assieds-t.** sit (yourself) down; **dépêche-t.** hurry up. ◆**t.-même** *pron* yourself.

toile [twal] *nf* **1** cloth; (*à voile*) canvas; (*à draps*) linen; **une t.** a piece of cloth *ou* canvas *ou* linen; **t. de jute** hessian; **drap de t.** linen sheet; **t. de fond** *Th & Fig* backcloth. **2** (*tableau*) canvas, painting. **3 t. d'araignée** cobweb, (spider's) web.

toilette [twalɛt] *nf* (*action*) wash(ing); (*vêtements*) outfit, clothes; **articles de t.** toiletries; **cabinet de t.** washroom; **eau/savon/trousse de t.** toilet water/soap/bag; **table de t.** dressing table; **faire sa t.** to wash (and dress); **les toilettes** (*W-C*) the toilet(s); **aller aux toilettes** to go to the toilet.

toiser [twaze] *vt* to eye scornfully.

toison [twazɔ̃] *nf* (*de mouton*) fleece.

toit [twa] *nm* roof; **t. ouvrant** *Aut* sunroof. ◆**toiture** *nf* roof(ing).

tôle [tol] *nf* **la t.** sheet metal; **une t.** a steel *ou* metal sheet; **t. ondulée** corrugated iron.

tolér/er [tɔlere] *vt* (*permettre*) to tolerate, allow; (*supporter*) to tolerate, bear; (*à la douane*) to allow. ◆**—ant** *a* tolerant (**à l'égard de** of). ◆**—able** *a* tolerable. ◆**tolérance** *nf* tolerance; (*à la douane*) allowance.

tollé [tɔle] *nm* outcry.

tomate [tɔmat] *nf* tomato; **sauce t.** tomato sauce.

tombe [tɔ̃b] *nf* grave; (*avec monument*) tomb. ◆**tombale** *af* **pierre t.** gravestone, tombstone. ◆**tombeau, -x** *nm* tomb.

tomb/er [tɔ̃be] *vi* (*aux* **être**) to fall; (*température*) to drop, fall; (*vent*) to drop (off); (*cheveux, robe*) to hang down; **t. malade** to fall ill; **t. (par terre)** to fall (down); **faire t.** (*personne*) to knock over; (*gouvernement, prix*) to bring down; **laisser t.** (*objet*) to drop; (*personne, projet etc*) *Fig* to drop, give up; **tu m'as laissé t. hier** *Fig* you let me down yesterday; **se laisser t. dans un fauteuil** to drop into an armchair; **tu tombes bien/mal** *Fig* you've come at the right/wrong time; **t. de fatigue** *ou* **de sommeil** to be ready to drop; **t. un lundi** to fall on a Monday; **t. sur** (*trouver*) to come across. ◆**—ée** *nf* **t. de la nuit** nightfall.

tombereau, -x [tɔ̃bro] *nm* (*charrette*) tip cart.

tombola [tɔ̃bɔla] *nf* raffle.

tome [tɔm] *nm* (*livre*) volume.

ton[1], **ta**, *pl* **tes** [tɔ̃, ta, te] (**ta** *becomes* **ton** [tɔ̃n] *before a vowel or mute h*) *a poss* your; **t. père** your father; **ta mère** your mother; **ton ami(e)** your friend.

ton[2] [tɔ̃] *nm* tone; (*de couleur*) shade, tone; (*gamme*) *Mus* key; (*hauteur de son*) & *Ling* pitch; **de bon t.** (*goût*) in good taste; **donner le t.** *Fig* to set the tone. ◆**tonalité** *nf* (*de* *radio etc*) tone; *Tél* dialling tone, *Am* dial tone.

tond/re [tɔ̃dr] *vt* **1** (*mouton*) to shear; (*cheveux*) to clip, crop; (*gazon*) to mow. **2 t. qn** (*escroquer*) *Fam* to fleece s.o. ◆**—euse** *nf* shears; (*à cheveux*) clippers; **t. (à gazon)** (lawn)mower.

tonifi/er [tɔnifje] *vt* (*muscles, peau*) to tone up; (*esprit, personne*) to invigorate. ◆**—ant** *a* (*activité, climat etc*) invigorating.

tonique [tɔnik] **1** *a* (*accent*) *Ling* tonic. **2** *a* (*froid, effet, vin*) tonic, invigorating; – *nm Méd* tonic.

tonitruant [tɔnitryɑ̃] *a* (*voix*) *Fam* booming.

tonnage [tɔnaʒ] *nm Nau* tonnage.

tonne [tɔn] *nf* (*poids*) metric ton, tonne; **des tonnes de** (*beaucoup*) *Fam* tons of.

tonneau, -x [tɔno] *nm* **1** (*récipient*) barrel, cask. **2** (*manœuvre*) *Av* roll; **faire un t.** *Aut* to roll over. **3** (*poids*) *Nau* ton. ◆**tonnelet** *nm* keg.

tonnelle [tɔnɛl] *nf* arbour, bower.

tonner [tɔne] *vi* (*canons*) to thunder; (*crier*) *Fig* to thunder, rage (**contre** against); – *v imp* **il tonne** it's thundering. ◆**tonnerre** *nm* thunder; **coup de t.** thunderclap; *Fig* bombshell, thunderbolt; **du t.** (*excellent*) *Fam* terrific.

tonte [tɔ̃t] *nf* (*de moutons*) shearing; (*de gazon*) mowing.

tonton [tɔ̃tɔ̃] *nm Fam* uncle.

tonus [tɔnys] *nm* (*énergie*) energy, vitality.

top [tɔp] *nm* (*signal sonore*) *Rad* stroke.

topaze [tɔpaz] *nf* (*pierre*) topaz.

topinambour [tɔpinɑ̃bur] *nm* Jerusalem artichoke.

topo [tɔpo] *nm* (*exposé*) *Fam* talk, speech.

topographie [tɔpɔgrafi] *nf* topography.

toque [tɔk] *nf* (*de fourrure*) fur hat; (*de juge, jockey*) cap; (*de cuisinier*) hat.

toqu/er (se) [sətɔke] *vpr* **se t. de qn** *Fam* to become infatuated with s.o. ◆**—é** *a* (*fou*) *Fam* crazy. ◆**toquade** *nf Fam* (*pour qch*) craze (**pour** for); (*pour qn*) infatuation (**pour** with).

torche [tɔrʃ] *nf* (*flambeau*) torch; **t. électrique** torch, *Am* flashlight.

torcher [tɔrʃe] *vt* **1** (*travail*) to skimp. **2** (*essuyer*) *Fam* to wipe.

torchon [tɔrʃɔ̃] *nm* (*à vaisselle*) tea towel, *Am* dish towel; (*de ménage*) duster, cloth.

tord/re [tɔrdr] *vt* to twist; (*linge, cou*) to wring; (*barre*) to bend; **se t. la cheville/le pied/le dos** to twist *ou* sprain one's ankle/foot/back; **— se t.** *vpr* to twist; (*barre*) to bend; **se t. de douleur** to writhe with pain; **se t. (de rire)** to split one's sides (laughing). ◆**—ant** *a* (*drôle*) *Fam* hilarious. ◆**—u** *a* twisted; (*esprit*) warped.

tornade [tɔrnad] *nf* tornado.

torpeur [tɔrpœr] *nf* lethargy, torpor.

torpille [tɔrpij] *nf* torpedo. ◆**torpill/er** *vt Mil & Fig* to torpedo. ◆**—eur** *nm* torpedo boat.

torréfier [tɔrefje] *vt* (*café*) to roast.

torrent [tɔrɑ̃] *nm* (*ruisseau*) torrent; **un t. de** (*injures, larmes*) a flood of; **il pleut à torrents** it's pouring (down). ◆**torrentiel, -ielle** *a* (*pluie*) torrential.

torride [tɔrid] *a* (*chaleur etc*) torrid, scorching.

torsade [tɔrsad] *nf* (*de cheveux*) twist, coil. ◆**torsader** *vt* to twist (together).

torse [tɔrs] *nm Anat* chest; (*statue*) torso.

torsion [tɔrsjɔ̃] *nf* twisting; *Phys Tech* torsion.

tort [tɔr] *nm* (*dommage*) wrong; (*défaut*) fault; **avoir t.** to be wrong (**de faire** to do, in doing); **tu as t. de fumer!** you shouldn't smoke!; **être dans son t.** *ou* **en t.** to be in the wrong; **donner t. à qn** (*accuser*) to blame s.o.; (*faits etc*) to prove s.o. wrong; **faire du t. à qn** to harm *ou* wrong s.o.; **à t.** wrongly; **à t. et à travers** wildly, indiscriminately; **à t. ou à raison** rightly or wrongly.

torticolis [tɔrtikɔli] *nm* stiff neck.

tortill/er [tɔrtije] *vt* to twist, twirl; (*moustache*) to twirl; (*tripoter*) to twiddle with; **— se t.** *vpr* (*ver, personne*) to wriggle; (*en dansant, des hanches*) to wiggle. ◆**—ement** *nm* wriggling, wiggling.

tortionnaire [tɔrsjɔnɛr] *nm* torturer.

tortue [tɔrty] *nf* tortoise; (*marine*) turtle; **quelle t.!** *Fig* what a slowcoach *ou Am* slowpoke!

tortueux, -euse [tɔrtɥø, -øz] *a* tortuous.

torture [tɔrtyr] *nf* torture. ◆**torturer** *vt* to torture; **se t. les méninges** to rack one's brains.

tôt [to] *adv* early; **au plus t.** at the earliest; **le plus t. possible** as soon as possible; **t. ou tard** sooner or later; **je n'étais pas plus t. sorti que . . .** no sooner had I gone out than . . . .

total, -aux [tɔtal, -o] *a & nm* total; **au t.** all in all, in total; (*somme toute*) all in all. ◆**totalement** *adv* totally, completely. ◆**totaliser** *vt* to total. ◆**totalité** *nf* entirety; **la t. de** all of; **en t.** entirely, totally.

totalitaire [tɔtalitɛr] *a Pol* totalitarian.

toubib [tubib] *nm* (*médecin*) *Fam* doctor.

touche [tuʃ] *nf* (*de peintre*) touch; *Pêche* bite; (*clavier*) key; **une t. de** (*un peu de*) a touch *ou* hint of; **(ligne de) t.** *Fb Rugby* touchline.

touche-à-tout [tuʃatu] **1** *a & nmf inv* (*qui touche*) meddlesome (person). **2** *nmf inv* (*qui se disperse*) dabbler.

touch/er [tuʃe] *vt* to touch; (*paie*) to draw; (*chèque*) to cash; (*cible*) to hit; (*émouvoir*) to touch, move; (*concerner*) to affect; **t. qn** (*contacter*) to get in touch with s.o., reach s.o.; – *vi* **t. à** to touch; (*sujet*) to touch on; (*but, fin*) to approach; **— se t.** *vpr* (*lignes etc*) to touch; – *nm* (*sens*) touch; **au t.** to the touch. ◆**—ant** *a* (*émouvant*) touching, moving.

touffe [tuf] *nf* (*de cheveux, d'herbe*) tuft; (*de plantes*) cluster. ◆**touffu** *a* (*barbe, haie*) thick, bushy; (*livre*) *Fig* heavy.

toujours [tuʒur] *adv* always; (*encore*) still; **pour t.** for ever; **essaie t.!** (*quand même*) try anyhow!; **t. est-il que ...** the fact remains that ....

toupet [tupɛ] *nm* (*audace*) *Fam* cheek, nerve.

toupie [tupi] *nf* (spinning) top.

tour¹ [tur] *nf* **1** *Archit* tower; (*immeuble*) tower block, high-rise. **2** *Échecs* rook, castle.

tour² [tur] *nm* **1** (*mouvement, ordre, tournure*) turn; (*artifice*) trick; (*excursion*) trip, outing; (*à pied*) stroll, walk; (*en voiture*) drive; **t. (de phrase)** turn of phrase; **t. (de piste)** *Sp* lap; **t. de cartes** card trick; **t. d'horizon** survey; **t. de poitrine/***etc* chest/*etc* measurement *ou* size; **de dix mètres de t.** ten metres round; **faire le t. de** to go round; (*question, situation*) to review; **faire un t.** (*à pied*) to go for a stroll *ou* walk; (*en voiture*) to go for a drive; (*voyage*) to go on a trip; **faire** *ou* **jouer un t. à qn** to play a trick on s.o.; **c'est mon t.** it's my turn; **à qui le tour?** whose turn (is it)?; **à son t.** in (one's) turn; **à t. de rôle** in turn; **t. à t.** in turn, by turns. **2** *Tech* lathe; (*de potier*) wheel.

tourbe [turb] *nf* peat. ◆**tourbière** *nf* peat bog.

tourbillon [turbijɔ̃] *nm* (*de vent*) whirlwind; (*d'eau*) whirlpool; (*de neige, sable*) eddy; (*tournoiement*) *Fig* whirl, swirl. ◆**tourbillonner** *vi* to whirl, swirl; to eddy.

tourelle [turɛl] *nf* turret.

tourisme [turism] *nm* tourism; **faire du t.** to do some sightseeing *ou* touring; **agence/office de t.** tourist agency/office. ◆**touriste** *nmf* tourist. ◆**touristique** *a* (*guide, menu etc*) tourist-; **route t., circuit t.** scenic route.

tourment [turmɑ̃] *nm* torment. ◆**tourment/er** *vt* to torment; **— se t.** *vpr* to worry (oneself). ◆**—é** *a* (*mer, vie*) turbulent, stormy; (*sol*) rough, uneven; (*expression, visage*) anguished.

tourmente [turmɑ̃t] *nf* (*troubles*) turmoil.

tourne-disque [turnədisk] *nm* record player.

tournée [turne] *nf* **1** (*de livreur etc*) round; (*théâtrale*) tour; **faire la t. de** (*magasins etc*) to make the rounds of, go round. **2** (*de boissons*) round.

tourn/er [turne] *vt* to turn; (*film*) to shoot, make; (*difficulté*) to get round; **t. en ridicule** to ridicule; – *vi* to turn; (*tête, toupie*) to spin; (*Terre*) to revolve, turn; (*moteur*) to run, go; (*usine*) to run; (*lait, viande*) to go off; *Cin* to shoot; **t. autour de** (*objet*) to go round; (*maison, personne*) to hang around; (*question*) to centre on; **t. bien/mal** (*évoluer*) to turn out well/badly; **t. au froid** (*temps*) to turn cold; **t. à l'aigre** (*ton, conversation etc*) to turn nasty *ou* sour; **t. de l'œil** *Fam* to faint; **— se t.** *vpr* to turn (**vers** to, towards). ◆**—ant 1** *a* **pont t.** swing bridge. **2** *nm* (*virage*) bend, turning; (*moment*) *Fig* turning point. ◆**—age** *nm Cin* shooting, filming. ◆**—eur** *nm* (*ouvrier*) turner. ◆**tournoyer** *vi* to spin (round), whirl. ◆**tournure** *nf* (*expression*) turn of phrase; **t. d'esprit** way of thinking; **t. des événements** turn of events; **prendre t.** (*forme*) to take shape.

tournesol [turnəsɔl] *nm* sunflower.

tournevis [turnəvis] *nm* screwdriver.

tourniquet [turnikɛ] *nm* **1** (*barrière*) turnstile. **2** (*pour arroser*) sprinkler.

tournoi [turnwa] *nm Sp & Hist* tournament.

tourte [turt] *nf* pie.

tourterelle [turtərɛl] *nf* turtledove.

Toussaint [tusɛ̃] *nf* All Saints' Day.

tousser [tuse] *vi* to cough.

tout, toute, *pl* **tous, toutes** [tu, tut, tu, tut] **1** *a* all; **tous les livres/***etc* all the books/*etc*; **t. l'argent/le village/***etc* the whole (of the) money/village/*etc*, all the money/village/*etc*; **toute la nuit** all night, the whole (of the) night; **tous (les) deux** both; **tous (les) trois** all three; **t. un problème** quite a problem. **2** *a* (*chaque*) every, each; (*n'importe quel*) any; **tous les ans/jours/***etc* every *ou* each year/day/*etc*; **tous les deux/trois mois/***etc* every second/third month/*etc*; **tous les cinq mètres** every five metres; **t. homme** [tutɔm] every *ou* any man; **à toute heure** at any time. **3** *pron pl* (**tous** = [tus]) all; **ils sont tous là, tous sont là** they're all there. **4** *pron m sing* **tout** everything;

dépenser t. to spend everything, spend it all; **t. ce que** everything that, all that; **en t.** (*au total*) in all. **5** *adv* (*tout à fait*) quite; (*très*) very; **t. petit** very small; **t. neuf** brand new; **t. simplement** quite simply; **t. seul** all alone; **t. droit** straight ahead; **t. autour** all around, right round; **t. au début** right at the beginning; **le t. premier** the very first; **t. au moins/plus** at the very least/most; **t. en chantant/***etc* while singing/*etc*; **t. rusé qu'il est** however sly he may be; **t. à coup** suddenly, all of a sudden; **t. à fait** completely, quite; **t. de même** all the same; (*indignation*) really!; **t. de suite** at once. **6** *nm* **le t.** everything, the lot; **un t.** a whole; **le t. est** (*l'important*) the main thing is (**que** that, **de faire** to do); **pas du t.** not at all; **rien du t.** nothing at all; **du t. au t.** (*changer*) entirely, completely. **♦t.-puissant, toute-puissante** *a* all-powerful.

tout-à-l'égout [tutalegu] *nm inv* mains drainage.

toutefois [tutfwa] *adv* nevertheless, however.

toutou [tutu] *nm* (*chien*) *Fam* doggie.

toux [tu] *nf* cough.

toxicomane [tɔksikɔman] *nmf* drug addict. **♦toxicomanie** *nf* drug addiction. **♦toxine** *nf* toxin. **♦toxique** *a* toxic.

trac [trak] *nm* **le t.** (*peur*) the jitters; (*de candidat*) exam nerves; *Th* stage fright.

tracas [traka] *nm* worry. **♦tracasser** *vt*, **— se t.** *vpr* to worry. **♦tracasseries** *nfpl* annoyances. **♦tracassier, -ière** *a* irksome.

trace [tras] *nf* (*quantité, tache, vestige*) trace; (*marque*) mark; (*de fugitif etc*) trail; *pl* (*de bête, de pneus*) tracks; **traces de pas** footprints; **suivre les traces de qn** *Fig* to follow in s.o.'s footsteps.

trac/er [trase] *vt* (*dessiner*) to draw; (*écrire*) to trace; **t. une route** to mark out a route; (*frayer*) to open up a route. **♦—é** *nm* (*plan*) layout; (*ligne*) line.

trachée [traʃe] *nf Anat* windpipe.

tract [trakt] *nm* leaflet.

tractations [traktɑsjɔ̃] *nfpl Péj* dealings.

tracter [trakte] *vt* (*caravane etc*) to tow. **♦tracteur** *nm* (*véhicule*) tractor.

traction [traksjɔ̃] *nf Tech* traction; *Sp* pull-up; **t. arrière/avant** *Aut* rear-/front-wheel drive.

tradition [tradisjɔ̃] *nf* tradition. **♦traditionnel, -elle** *a* traditional.

traduire* [tradɥir] *vt* **1** to translate (**de** from, **en** into); (*exprimer*) *Fig* to express. **2 t. qn en justice** to bring s.o. before the courts. **♦traducteur, -trice** *nmf* translator. **♦traduction** *nf* translation. **♦traduisible** *a* translatable.

trafic [trafik] *nm* **1** *Aut Rail etc* traffic. **2** *Com Péj* traffic, trade; **faire du t.** to traffic, trade; **faire le t. de** to traffic in, trade in. **♦trafiqu/er 1** *vi* to traffic, trade. **2** *vt* (*produit*) *Fam* to tamper with. **♦—ant, -ante** *nmf* trafficker, dealer; **t. d'armes/de drogue** arms/drug trafficker *ou* dealer.

tragédie [traʒedi] *nf Th & Fig* tragedy. **♦tragique** *a* tragic. **♦tragiquement** *adv* tragically.

trahir [trair] *vt* to betray; (*secret etc*) to betray, give away; (*forces*) to fail (*s.o.*); **— se t.** *vpr* to give oneself away, betray oneself. **♦trahison** *nf* betrayal; (*crime*) *Pol* treason.

train [trɛ̃] *nm* **1** (*locomotive, transport, jouet*) train; **t. à grande vitesse** high-speed train; **t. couchettes** sleeper; **t. auto-couchettes** (car) sleeper. **2 en t.** (*forme*) on form; **se mettre en t.** to get (oneself) into shape. **3 être en t. de faire** to be (busy) doing; **mettre qch en t.** to get sth going, start sth off. **4** (*allure*) pace; **t. de vie** life style. **5** (*de pneus*) set; (*de péniches, véhicules*) string. **6 t. d'atterrissage** *Av* undercarriage.

traîne [trɛn] *nf* **1** (*de robe*) train. **2 à la t.** (*en arrière*) lagging behind.

traîneau, -x [trɛno] *nm* sledge, sleigh, *Am* sled.

traînée [trene] *nf* **1** (*de substance*) trail, streak; (*bande*) streak; **se répandre comme une t. de poudre** (*vite*) to spread like wildfire. **2** (*prostituée*) *Arg* tart.

traîner [trene] *vt* to drag; (*mots*) to drawl; **(faire) t. en longueur** (*faire durer*) to drag out; **–** *vi* (*jouets, papiers etc*) to lie around; (*subsister*) to linger on; (*s'attarder*) to lag behind, dawdle; (*errer*) to hang around; **t. (par terre)** (*robe etc*) to trail (on the ground); **t. (en longueur)** (*durer*) to drag on; **— se t.** *vpr* (*avancer*) to drag oneself (along); (*par terre*) to crawl; (*durer*) to drag on. **♦traînant** *a* (*voix*) drawling. **♦traînailler** *vi Fam* = **traînasser. ♦traînard, -arde** *nmf* slowcoach, *Am* slowpoke. **♦traînasser** *vi Fam* to dawdle; (*errer*) to hang around.

train-train [trɛ̃trɛ̃] *nm* routine.

traire* [trɛr] *vt* (*vache*) to milk.

trait [trɛ] *nm* **1** line; (*en dessinant*) stroke; (*caractéristique*) feature, trait; *pl* (*du visage*) features; **t. d'union** hyphen; (*intermédiaire*) *Fig* link; **d'un t.** (*boire*) in one gulp, in one go; **à grands traits** in outline; **t. de** (*esprit, génie*) flash of; (*bravoure*) act of; **avoir t. à** (*se rapporter à*) to relate to. **2 cheval de t.** draught horse.

traite [trɛt] *nf* **1** (*de vache*) milking. **2** *Com* bill, draft. **3 d'une (seule) t.** (*sans interruption*) in one go. **4 t. des Noirs** slave trade; **t. des blanches** white slave trade.

traité [trete] *nm* **1** *Pol* treaty. **2** (*ouvrage*) treatise (**sur** on).

trait/er [trete] *vt* (*se comporter envers*) & *Méd* to treat; (*problème, sujet*) to deal with; (*marché*) *Com* to negotiate; (*matériau, produit*) to treat, process; **t. qn de lâche**/*etc* to call s.o. a coward/*etc*; – *vi* to negotiate, deal (**avec** with); **t. de** (*sujet*) to deal with. ◆**—ant** [-ɛtɑ̃] *a* **médecin t.** regular doctor. ◆**—ement** [-ɛtmɑ̃] *nm* **1** treatment; **mauvais traitements** rough treatment; **t. de données/de texte** data/word processing; **machine de t. de texte** word processor. **2** (*gains*) salary.

traiteur [trɛtœr] *nm* (*fournisseur*) caterer; **chez le t.** (*magasin*) at the delicatessen.

traître [trɛtr] *nm* traitor; **en t.** treacherously; – *a* (*dangereux*) treacherous; **être t. à** to be a traitor to. ◆**traîtrise** *nf* treachery.

trajectoire [traʒɛktwar] *nf* path, trajectory.

trajet [traʒɛ] *nm* journey, trip; (*distance*) distance; (*itinéraire*) route.

trame [tram] *nf* **1** (*de récit etc*) framework. **2** (*de tissu*) weft.

tramer [trame] *vt* (*évasion etc*) to plot; (*complot*) to hatch.

trampoline [trɑ̃pɔlin] *nm* trampoline.

tram(way) [tram(wɛ)] *nm* tram, *Am* streetcar.

tranche [trɑ̃ʃ] *nf* (*morceau coupé*) slice; (*bord*) edge; (*partie*) portion; (*de salaire, impôts*) bracket; **t. d'âge** age bracket.

tranchée [trɑ̃ʃe] *nf* trench.

tranch/er [trɑ̃ʃe] **1** *vt* to cut. **2** *vt* (*difficulté, question*) to settle; – *vi* (*décider*) to decide. **3** *vi* (*contraster*) to contrast (**avec, sur** with). ◆**—ant 1** *a* (*couteau*) sharp; – *nm* (cutting) edge. **2** *a* (*péremptoire*) trenchant, cutting. ◆**—é** *a* (*couleurs*) distinct; (*opinion*) clear-cut.

tranquille [trɑ̃kil] *a* quiet; (*mer*) calm, still; (*conscience*) clear; (*esprit*) easy; (*certain*) *Fam* confident; **je suis t.** (*rassuré*) my mind is at rest; **soyez t.** don't worry; **laisser t.** to leave be *ou* alone. ◆**tranquillement** *adv* calmly. ◆**tranquillis/er** *vt* to reassure; **tranquillisez-vous** set your mind at rest. ◆**—ant** *nm Méd* tranquillizer. ◆**tranquillité** *nf* (peace and) quiet; (*d'esprit*) peace of mind.

trans- [trɑ̃z, trɑ̃s] *préf* trans-.

transaction [trɑ̃zaksjɔ̃] *nf* **1** (*compromis*) compromise. **2** *Com* transaction.

transatlantique [trɑ̃zatlɑ̃tik] *a* transatlantic; – *nm* (*paquebot*) transatlantic liner; (*chaise*) deckchair.

transcend/er [trɑ̃sɑ̃de] *vt* to transcend. ◆**—ant** *a* transcendent.

transcrire* [trɑ̃skrir] *vt* to transcribe. ◆**transcription** *nf* transcription; (*document*) transcript.

transe [trɑ̃s] *nf* **en t.** (*mystique*) in a trance; (*excité*) very exited.

transférer [trɑ̃sfere] *vt* to transfer (**à** to). ◆**transfert** *nm* transfer.

transfigurer [trɑ̃sfigyre] *vt* to transform, transfigure.

transformer [trɑ̃sfɔrme] *vt* to transform, change; (*maison, matière première*) to convert; (*robe etc*) to alter; (*essai*) *Rugby* to convert; **t. en** to turn into; – **se t.** *vpr* to change, be transformed (**en** into). ◆**transformateur** *nm Él* transformer. ◆**transformation** *nf* transformation, change; conversion.

transfuge [trɑ̃sfyʒ] *nm Mil* renegade; – *nmf Pol* renegade.

transfusion [trɑ̃sfyzjɔ̃] *nf* **t. (sanguine)** (blood) transfusion.

transgresser [trɑ̃sgrese] *vt* (*loi, ordre*) to disobey.

transi [trɑ̃zi] *a* (*personne*) numb with cold; **t. de peur** paralysed by fear.

transiger [trɑ̃ziʒe] *vi* to compromise.

transistor [trɑ̃zistɔr] *nm* (*dispositif, poste*) transistor. ◆**transistorisé** *a* (*téléviseur etc*) transistorized.

transit [trɑ̃zit] *nm* transit; **en t.** in transit. ◆**transiter** *vt* **(faire) t.** to send in transit; – *vi* to be in transit.

transitif, -ive [trɑ̃zitif, -iv] *a Gram* transitive.

transition [trɑ̃zisjɔ̃] *nf* transition. ◆**transitoire** *a* (*qui passe*) transient; (*provisoire*) transitional.

transmettre* [trɑ̃smɛtr] *vt* (*héritage, message etc*) to pass on (**à** to); *Phys Tech* to transmit; *Rad TV* to broadcast, transmit. ◆**transmetteur** *nm* (*appareil*) transmitter, transmitting device. ◆**transmission** *nf* transmission; passing on.

transparaître* [trɑ̃sparɛtr] *vi* to show (through).

transparent [trɑ̃sparɑ̃] *a* transparent. ◆**transparence** *nf* transparency.

transpercer [trɑ̃sperse] *vt* to pierce, go through.
transpirer [trɑ̃spire] *vi* (*suer*) to perspire; (*information*) *Fig* to leak out. ◆**transpiration** *nf* perspiration.
transplanter [trɑ̃splɑ̃te] *vt* (*organe, plante etc*) to transplant. ◆**transplantation** *nf* transplantation; (*greffe*) *Méd* transplant.
transport [trɑ̃spɔr] *nm* **1** (*action*) transport, transportation (**de** of); *pl* (*moyens*) transport; **moyen de t.** means of transport; **transports en commun** public transport. **2** (*émotion*) *Litt* rapture. ◆**transporter 1** *vt* (*véhicule, train*) to transport, convey; (*à la main*) to carry, take; **t. d'urgence à l'hôpital** to rush to hospital; — **se t.** *vpr* (*aller*) to take oneself (**à** to). **2** *vt Litt* to enrapture. ◆**transporteur** *nm* **t. (routier)** haulier, *Am* trucker.
transposer [trɑ̃spoze] *vt* to transpose. ◆**transposition** *nf* transposition.
transvaser [trɑ̃svɑze] *vt* (*vin*) to decant.
transversal, -aux [trɑ̃sversal, -o] *a* (*barre, rue etc*) cross-, transverse.
trapèze [trapɛz] *nm* (*au cirque*) trapeze. ◆**trapéziste** *nmf* trapeze artist.
trappe [trap] *nf* (*dans le plancher*) trap door.
trappeur [trapœr] *nm* (*chasseur*) trapper.
trapu [trapy] *a* **1** (*personne*) stocky, thickset. **2** (*problème etc*) *Fam* tough.
traquenard [traknar] *nm* trap.
traquer [trake] *vt* to track *ou* hunt (down).
traumatis/er [tromatize] *vt* to traumatize. ◆**—ant** *a* traumatic. ◆**traumatisme** *nm* (*choc*) trauma.
travail, -aux [travaj, -o] *nm* (*activité, lieu*) work; (*emploi, tâche*) job; (*façonnage*) working (**de** of); (*ouvrage, étude*) work, publication; *Écon Méd* labour; *pl* work; (*dans la rue*) roadworks; (*aménagement*) alterations; **travaux forcés** hard labour; **travaux ménagers** housework; **travaux pratiques** *Scol Univ* practical work; **travaux publics** public works; **t. au noir** moonlighting; **en t.** (*femme*) *Méd* in labour.
travaill/er [travaje] **1** *vi* to work (**à qch** at *ou* on sth); – *vt* (*discipline, rôle, style*) to work on; (*façonner*) to work; (*inquiéter*) to worry; **t. la terre** to work the land. **2** *vi* (*bois*) to warp. ◆**—é** *a* (*style*) elaborate. ◆**—eur, -euse** *a* hard-working; – *nmf* worker ◆**travailliste** *a Pol* Labour-; – *nmf Pol* member of the Labour party.
travers [traver] **1** *prép* & *adv* **à t.** through; **en t. (de)** across. **2** *adv* **de t.** (*chapeau, nez etc*) crooked; (*comprendre*) badly; (*regarder*) askance; **aller de t.** *Fig* to go wrong; **j'ai avalé de t.** it went down the wrong way. **3** *nm* (*défaut*) failing.
traverse [travers] *nf* **1** *Rail* sleeper, *Am* tie. **2 chemin de t.** short cut.
travers/er [traverse] *vt* to cross, go across; (*foule, période, mur*) to go through. ◆**—ée** *nf* (*action, trajet*) crossing.
traversin [traversɛ̃] *nm* (*coussin*) bolster.
travest/ir [travestir] *vt* to disguise; (*pensée, vérité*) to misrepresent. ◆**—i** *nm Th* female impersonator; (*homosexuel*) transvestite. ◆**—issement** *nm* disguise; misrepresentation.
trébucher [trebyʃe] *vi* to stumble (**sur** over); **faire t.** to trip (up).
trèfle [trɛfl] *nm* **1** (*plante*) clover. **2** (*couleur*) *Cartes* clubs.
treille [trɛj] *nf* climbing vine.
treillis [treji] *nm* **1** lattice(work); (*en métal*) wire mesh. **2** (*tenue militaire*) combat uniform.
treize [trɛz] *a* & *nm inv* thirteen. ◆**treizième** *a* & *nmf* thirteenth.
tréma [trema] *nm Gram* di(a)eresis.
trembl/er [trɑ̃ble] *vi* to tremble, shake; (*de froid, peur*) to tremble (**de** with); (*flamme, lumière*) to flicker; (*voix*) to tremble, quaver; (*avoir peur*) to be afraid (**que** (+ *sub*) that, **de faire** to do); **t. pour qn** to fear for s.o. ◆**—ement** *nm* (*action, frisson*) trembling; **t. de terre** earthquake. ◆**trembloter** *vi* to quiver.
trémousser (se) [sətremuse] *vpr* to wriggle (about).
trempe [trɑ̃p] *nf* (*caractère*) stamp; **un homme de sa t.** a man of his stamp.
tremper [trɑ̃pe] **1** *vt* to soak, drench; (*plonger*) to dip (**dans** in); – *vi* to soak; **faire t.** to soak; — **se t.** *vpr* (*se baigner*) to take a dip. **2** *vt* (*acier*) to temper. **3** *vi* **t. dans** (*participer*) *Péj* to be mixed up in. ◆**trempette** *nf* **faire t.** (*se baigner*) to take a dip.
tremplin [trɑ̃plɛ̃] *nm Natation* & *Fig* springboard.
trente [trɑ̃t] *a* & *nm* thirty; **un t.-trois tours** (*disque*) an LP. ◆**trentaine** *nf* **une t. (de)** (*nombre*) (about) thirty; **avoir la t.** (*âge*) to be about thirty. ◆**trentième** *a* & *nmf* thirtieth.
trépidant [trepidɑ̃] *a* (*vie etc*) hectic.
trépied [trepje] *nm* tripod.
trépigner [trepiɲe] *vi* to stamp (one's feet).
très [trɛ] *adv* ([trɛz] *before vowel or mute h*) very; **t. aimé/critiqué/***etc* much liked/criticized/*etc.*
trésor [trezɔr] *nm* treasure; **le T. (public)**

(*service*) public revenue (department); (*finances*) public funds; **des trésors de** *Fig* a treasure house of. ◆**trésorerie** *nf* (*bureaux d'un club etc*) accounts department; (*capitaux*) funds; (*gestion*) accounting. ◆**trésorier, -ière** *nmf* treasurer.

tressaill/ir* [tresajir] *vi* (*sursauter*) to jump, start; (*frémir*) to shake, quiver; (*de joie, peur*) to tremble (**de** with). ◆**—ement** *nm* start; quiver; trembling.

tressauter [tresote] *vi* (*sursauter*) to start, jump.

tresse [trɛs] *nf* (*cordon*) braid; (*cheveux*) plait, *Am* braid. ◆**tresser** *vt* to braid; to plait.

tréteau, -x [treto] *nm* trestle.

treuil [trœj] *nm* winch, windlass.

trêve [trɛv] *nf Mil* truce; (*répit*) *Fig* respite.

tri [tri] *nm* sorting (out); **faire le t. de** to sort (out); **(centre de) t.** (*des postes*) sorting office. ◆**triage** *nm* sorting (out).

triangle [trijɑ̃gl] *nm* triangle. ◆**triangulaire** *a* triangular.

tribord [tribɔr] *nm Nau Av* starboard.

tribu [triby] *nf* tribe. ◆**tribal, -aux** *a* tribal.

tribulations [tribylɑsjɔ̃] *nfpl* tribulations.

tribunal, -aux [tribynal, -o] *nm Jur* court; (*militaire*) tribunal.

tribune [tribyn] *nf* **1** (*de salle publique etc*) gallery; (*de stade*) (grand)stand; (*d'orateur*) rostrum. **2 t. libre** (*dans un journal*) open forum.

tribut [triby] *nm* tribute (**à** to).

tributaire [tribytɛr] *a* **t. de** *Fig* dependent on.

tricher [triʃe] *vi* to cheat. ◆**tricherie** *nf* cheating, trickery; **une t.** a piece of trickery. ◆**tricheur, -euse** *nmf* cheat, *Am* cheater.

tricolore [trikɔlɔr] *a* **1** (*cocarde etc*) red, white and blue; **le drapeau/l'équipe t.** the French flag/team. **2 feu t.** traffic lights.

tricot [triko] *nm* (*activité, ouvrage*) knitting; (*chandail*) jumper, sweater; **un t.** (*ouvrage*) a piece of knitting; **en t.** knitted; **t. de corps** vest, *Am* undershirt. ◆**tricoter** *vti* to knit.

tricycle [trisikl] *nm* tricycle.

trier [trije] *vt* (*séparer*) to sort (out); (*choisir*) to pick *ou* sort out.

trilogie [trilɔʒi] *nf* trilogy.

trimbal(l)er [trɛ̃bale] *vt Fam* to cart about, drag around; **— se t.** *vpr Fam* to trail around.

trimer [trime] *vi Fam* to slave (away), toil.

trimestre [trimɛstr] *nm* (*période*) *Com* quarter; *Scol* term. ◆**trimestriel, -ielle** *a* (*revue*) quarterly; (*bulletin*) *Scol* end-of-term.

tringle [trɛ̃gl] *nf* rail, rod; **t. à rideaux** curtain rail *ou* rod.

Trinité [trinite] *nf* **la T.** (*fête*) Trinity; (*dogme*) the Trinity.

trinquer [trɛ̃ke] *vi* to chink glasses; **t. à** to drink to.

trio [trijo] *nm* (*groupe*) & *Mus* trio.

triomphe [trijɔ̃f] *nm* triumph (**sur** over); **porter qn en t.** to carry s.o. shoulder-high. ◆**triomphal, -aux** *a* triumphal. ◆**triomph/er** *vi* to triumph (**de** over); (*jubiler*) to be jubilant. ◆**—ant** *a* triumphant.

tripes [trip] *nfpl* (*intestins*) *Fam* guts; *Culin* tripe. ◆**tripier, -ière** *nmf* tripe butcher.

triple [tripl] *a* treble, triple; **–** *nm* **le t.** three times as much (**de** as). ◆**tripl/er** *vti* to treble, triple. ◆**—és, -ées** *nmfpl* (*enfants*) triplets.

tripot [tripo] *nm* (*café etc*) *Péj* gambling den.

tripoter [tripɔte] *vt* to fiddle about *ou* mess about with; **–** *vi* to fiddle *ou* mess about.

trique [trik] *nf* cudgel, stick.

triste [trist] *a* sad; (*couleur, temps, rue*) gloomy, dreary; (*lamentable*) unfortunate, sorry. ◆**tristement** *adv* sadly. ◆**tristesse** *nf* sadness; gloom, dreariness.

triturer [trityre] *vt* (*manipuler*) to manipulate.

trivial, -aux [trivjal, -o] *a* coarse, vulgar. ◆**trivialité** *nf* coarseness, vulgarity.

troc [trɔk] *nm* exchange, barter.

troène [trɔɛn] *nm* (*arbuste*) privet.

trognon [trɔɲɔ̃] *nm* (*de pomme, poire*) core; (*de chou*) stump.

trois [trwɑ] *a* & *nm* three. ◆**troisième** *a* & *nmf* third. ◆**troisièmement** *adv* thirdly.

trolley(bus) [trɔlɛ(bys)] *nm* trolley(bus).

trombe [trɔ̃b] *nf* **t. d'eau** (*pluie*) rainstorm, downpour; **en t.** (*entrer etc*) *Fig* like a whirlwind.

trombone [trɔ̃bɔn] *nm* **1** *Mus* trombone. **2** (*agrafe*) paper clip.

trompe [trɔ̃p] *nf* **1** (*d'éléphant*) trunk; (*d'insecte*) proboscis. **2** *Mus* horn.

tromper [trɔ̃pe] *vt* to deceive, mislead; (*escroquer*) to cheat; (*échapper à*) to elude; (*être infidèle à*) to be unfaithful to; **— se t.** *vpr* to be mistaken, make a mistake; **se t. de route/de train/***etc* to take the wrong road/train/*etc*; **se t. de date/de jour/***etc* to get the date/day/*etc* wrong. ◆**tromperie** *nf* deceit, deception. ◆**trompeur, -euse** *a* (*apparences etc*) deceptive, misleading; (*personne*) deceitful.

trompette [trɔ̃pɛt] *nf* trumpet. ◆**trompettiste** *nmf* trumpet player.

tronc [trɔ̃] *nm* **1** *Bot Anat* trunk. **2** *Rel* collection box.
tronçon [trɔ̃sɔ̃] *nm* section. ◆**tronçonn/er** *vt* to cut (into sections). ◆**—euse** *nf* chain saw.
trône [tron] *nm* throne. ◆**trôner** *vi* (*vase, personne etc*) *Fig* to occupy the place of honour.
tronquer [trɔ̃ke] *vt* to truncate; (*texte etc*) to curtail.
trop [tro] *adv* too; too much; **t. dur/loin/***etc* too hard/far/*etc*; **t. fatigué** too tired, overtired; **boire/lire/***etc* **t.** to drink/read/*etc* too much; **t. de sel/***etc* (*quantité*) too much salt/*etc*; **t. de gens/***etc* (*nombre*) too many people/*etc*; **du fromage/***etc* **de** *ou* **en t.** (*quantité*) too much cheese/*etc*; **des œufs/***etc* **de** *ou* **en t.** (*nombre*) too many eggs/*etc*; **un franc/verre/***etc* **de t.** *ou* **en t.** one franc/glass/*etc* too many; **se sentir de t.** *Fig* to feel in the way.
trophée [trɔfe] *nm* trophy.
tropique [trɔpik] *nm* tropic. ◆**tropical, -aux** *a* tropical.
trop-plein [trɔplɛ̃] *nm* (*dispositif, liquide*) overflow; (*surabondance*) *Fig* excess.
troquer [trɔke] *vt* to exchange (**contre** for).
trot [tro] *nm* trot; **aller au t.** to trot; **au t.** (*sans traîner*) *Fam* at the double. ◆**trott/er** [trɔte] *vi* (*cheval*) to trot; (*personne*) *Fig* to scurry (along).
trotteuse [trɔtøz] *nf* (*de montre*) second hand.
trottiner [trɔtine] *vi* (*personne*) to patter (along).
trottinette [trɔtinɛt] *nf* (*jouet*) scooter.
trottoir [trɔtwar] *nm* pavement, *Am* sidewalk; **t. roulant** moving walkway, travolator.
trou [tru] *nm* hole; (*d'aiguille*) eye; (*manque*) *Fig* gap (**dans** in); (*village*) *Péj* hole, dump; **t. d'homme** (*ouverture*) manhole; **t. de (la) serrure** keyhole; **t. (de mémoire)** *Fig* lapse (of memory).
trouble [trubl] **1** *a* (*liquide*) cloudy; (*image*) blurred; (*affaire*) shady; **voir t.** to see blurred. **2** *nm* (*émoi, émotion*) agitation; (*désarroi*) distress; (*désordre*) confusion; *pl Méd* trouble; (*révolte*) disturbances, troubles. ◆**troubl/er** *vt* to disturb; (*liquide*) to make cloudy; (*projet*) to upset; (*esprit*) to unsettle; (*vue*) to blur; (*inquiéter*) to trouble; **— se t.** *vpr* (*liquide*) to become cloudy; (*candidat etc*) to become flustered. ◆**—ant** *a* (*détail etc*) disquieting. ◆**trouble-fête** *nmf inv* killjoy, spoilsport.
trou/er [true] *vt* to make a hole *ou* holes in; (*silence, ténèbres*) to cut through. ◆**—ée** *nf* gap; (*brèche*) *Mil* breach.
trouille [truj] *nf* **avoir la t.** *Fam* to have the jitters, be scared. ◆**trouillard** *a* (*poltron*) *Fam* chicken.
troupe [trup] *nf Mil* troop; (*groupe*) group; *Th* company, troupe; **la t., les troupes** (*armée*) the troops.
troupeau, -x [trupo] *nm* (*de vaches*) & *Fig Péj* herd; (*de moutons, d'oies*) flock.
trousse [trus] **1** *nf* (*étui*) case, kit; (*d'écolier*) pencil case; **t. à outils** toolkit; **t. à pharmacie** first-aid kit. **2** *nfpl* **aux trousses de qn** *Fig* on s.o.'s heels.
trousseau, -x [truso] *nm* **1** (*de clés*) bunch. **2** (*de mariée*) trousseau.
trouver [truve] *vt* to find; **aller/venir t. qn** to go/come and see s.o.; **je trouve que** (*je pense que*) I think that; **comment la trouvez-vous?** what do you think of her?; **— se t.** *vpr* to be; (*être situé*) to be situated; (*se sentir*) to feel; (*dans une situation*) to find oneself; **se t. mal** (*s'évanouir*) to faint; **il se trouve que** it happens that. ◆**trouvaille** *nf* (lucky) find.
truand [tryɑ̃] *nm* crook.
truc [tryk] *nm* **1** (*astuce*) trick; (*moyen*) way; **avoir/trouver le t.** to have/get the knack (**pour faire** of doing). **2** (*chose*) *Fam* thing. ◆**—age** *nm* = **truquage.**
truchement [tryʃmɑ̃] *nm* **par le t. de qn** through (the intermediary of) s.o.
truculent [trykylɑ̃] *a* (*langage, personnage*) colourful.
truelle [tryɛl] *nf* trowel.
truffe [tryf] *nf* **1** (*champignon*) truffle. **2** (*de chien*) nose.
truff/er [tryfe] *vt* (*remplir*) to stuff (**de** with). ◆**—é** *a* (*pâté etc*) *Culin* with truffles.
truie [trɥi] *nf* (*animal*) sow.
truite [trɥit] *nf* trout.
truqu/er [tryke] *vt* (*photo etc*) to fake; (*élections, match*) to rig, fix. ◆**—é** *a* (*photo etc*) fake-; (*élections, match*) rigged, fixed; (*scène*) *Cin* trick-. ◆**—age** *nm Cin* (special) effect; (*action*) faking; rigging.
trust [trœst] *nm Com* (*cartel*) trust; (*entreprise*) corporation.
tsar [dzar] *nm* tsar, czar.
TSF [teɛsɛf] *nf abrév* (*télégraphie sans fil*) wireless, radio.
tsigane [tsigan] *a* & *nmf* (Hungarian) gipsy.
TSVP [teɛsvepe] *abrév* (*tournez s'il vous plaît*) PTO.
TTC [tetese] *abrév* (*toutes taxes comprises*) inclusive of tax.
tu[1] [ty] *pron* you (*familiar form of address*).

tu[2] [ty] *voir* taire.

tuba [tyba] *nm* **1** *Mus* tuba. **2** *Sp* snorkel.

tube [tyb] *nm* **1** tube; (*de canalisation*) pipe. **2** (*chanson, disque*) *Fam* hit. ◆**tubulaire** *a* tubular.

tuberculeux, -euse [tyberkylø, -øz] *a* tubercular; **être t.** to have tuberculosis *ou* TB. ◆**tuberculose** *nf* tuberculosis, TB.

tue-mouches [tymuʃ] *a inv* **papier t.-mouches** flypaper. ◆**t.-tête (à)** *adv* at the top of one's voice.

tu/er [tɥe] *vt* to kill; (*d'un coup de feu*) to shoot (dead), kill; (*épuiser*) *Fig* to wear out; — **se t.** *vpr* to kill oneself; to shoot oneself; (*dans un accident*) to be killed; **se t. à faire** *Fig* to wear oneself out doing. ◆**—ant** *a* (*fatigant*) exhausting. ◆**tuerie** *nf* slaughter. ◆**tueur, -euse** *nmf* killer.

tuile [tɥil] *nf* **1** tile. **2** (*malchance*) *Fam* (stroke of) bad luck.

tulipe [tylip] *nf* tulip.

tuméfié [tymefje] *a* swollen.

tumeur [tymœr] *nf* tumour, growth.

tumulte [tymylt] *nm* commotion; (*désordre*) turmoil. ◆**tumultueux, -euse** *a* turbulent.

tunique [tynik] *nf* tunic.

Tunisie [tynizi] *nf* Tunisia. ◆**tunisien, -ienne** *a* & *nmf* Tunisian.

tunnel [tynel] *nm* tunnel.

turban [tyrbɑ̃] *nm* turban.

turbine [tyrbin] *nf* turbine.

turbulences [tyrbylɑ̃s] *nfpl Phys Av* turbulence.

turbulent [tyrbylɑ̃] *a* (*enfant etc*) boisterous, turbulent.

turfiste [tyrfist] *nmf* racegoer, punter.

Turquie [tyrki] *nf* Turkey. ◆**turc, turque** *a* Turkish; — *nmf* Turk; — *nm* (*langue*) Turkish.

turquoise [tyrkwaz] *a inv* turquoise.

tuteur, -trice [tytœr, -tris] **1** *nmf Jur* guardian. **2** *nm* (*bâton*) stake, prop. ◆**tutelle** *nf Jur* guardianship; *Fig* protection.

tutoyer [tytwaje] *vt* to address familiarly (*using tu*). ◆**tutoiement** *nm* familiar address, use of *tu*.

tutu [tyty] *nm* ballet skirt, tutu.

tuyau, -x [tɥijo] *nm* **1** pipe; **t. d'arrosage** hose(pipe); **t. de cheminée** flue; **t. d'échappement** *Aut* exhaust (pipe). **2** (*renseignement*) *Fam* tip. ◆**tuyauter** *vt* **t. qn** (*conseiller*) *Fam* to give s.o. a tip. ◆**tuyauterie** *nf* (*tuyaux*) piping.

TVA [tevea] *nf abrév* (*taxe à la valeur ajoutée*) VAT.

tympan [tɛ̃pɑ̃] *nm* eardrum.

type [tip] *nm* (*modèle*) type; (*traits*) features; (*individu*) *Fam* fellow, guy, bloke; **le t. même de** *Fig* the very model of; — *a inv* (*professeur etc*) typical. ◆**typique** *a* typical (**de** of). ◆**typiquement** *adv* typically.

typhoïde [tifɔid] *nf Méd* typhoid (fever).

typhon [tifɔ̃] *nm Mét* typhoon.

typographe [tipɔgraf] *nmf* typographer. ◆**typographie** *nf* typography, printing. ◆**typographique** *a* typographical, printing-.

tyran [tirɑ̃] *nm* tyrant. ◆**tyrannie** *nf* tyranny. ◆**tyrannique** *a* tyrannical. ◆**tyranniser** *vt* to tyrannize.

tzigane [dzigan] *a* & *nmf* (Hungarian) gipsy.

U

U, u [y] *nm* U, u.

ulcère [ylser] *nm* ulcer, sore.

ulcérer [ylsere] *vt* (*blesser, irriter*) to embitter.

ultérieur [ylterjœr] *a* later. ◆**—ement** *adv* later.

ultimatum [yltimatɔm] *nm* ultimatum.

ultime [yltim] *a* final, last.

ultra- [yltra] *préf* ultra-. ◆**u.-secret, -ète** *a* (*document*) top-secret.

ultramoderne [yltramɔdern] *a* ultramodern.

ultraviolet, -ette [yltravjɔle, -ɛt] *a* ultraviolet.

un, une [œ̃, yn] **1** *art indéf* a, (*devant voyelle*) an; **une page** a page; **un ange** [œ̃nɑ̃ʒ] an angel. **2** *a* one; **la page un** page one; **un kilo** one kilo; **un type** (*un quelconque*) some *ou* a fellow. **3** *pron* & *nmf* one; **l'un** one; **les uns** some; **le numéro un** number one; **j'en ai un** I have one; **l'un d'eux** one of them; **la une** *Journ* page one.

unanime [ynanim] *a* unanimous. ◆**unanimité** *nf* unanimity; **à l'u.** unanimously.

uni [yni] *a* united; (*famille etc*) close; (*surface*) smooth; (*couleur, étoffe*) plain.
unième [ynjɛm] *a* (*après un numéral*) (-)first; **trente et u.** thirty-first; **cent u.** hundred and first.
unifier [ynifje] *vt* to unify. ◆**unification** *nf* unification.
uniforme [ynifɔrm] **1** *a* (*régulier*) uniform. **2** *nm* (*vêtement*) uniform. ◆**uniformément** *adv* uniformly. ◆**uniformiser** *vt* to standardize. ◆**uniformité** *nf* uniformity.
unijambiste [yniʒɑ̃bist] *a* & *nmf* one-legged (man *ou* woman).
unilatéral, -aux [ynilateral, -o] *a* unilateral; (*stationnement*) on one side of the road only.
union [ynjɔ̃] *nf* union; (*association*) association; (*entente*) unity. ◆**unir** *vt* to unite, join (together); **u. la force au courage/***etc* to combine strength with courage/*etc*; **— s'u.** *vpr* to unite; (*se marier*) to be joined together; (*se joindre*) to join (together).
unique [ynik] *a* **1** (*fille, fils*) only; (*espoir, souci etc*) only, sole; (*prix, salaire, voie*) single, one; **son seul et u. souci** his *ou* her one and only worry. **2** (*incomparable*) unique. ◆**uniquement** *adv* only, solely.
unisexe [ynisɛks] *a inv* (*vêtements etc*) unisex.
unisson (à l') [alynisɔ̃] *adv* in unison (**de** with).
unité [ynite] *nf* (*élément, grandeur*) & *Mil* unit; (*cohésion, harmonie*) unity. ◆**unitaire** *a* (*prix*) per unit.
univers [ynivɛr] *nm* universe.
universel, -elle [ynivɛrsɛl] *a* universal. ◆**universellement** *adv* universally. ◆**universalité** *nf* universality.
université [ynivɛrsite] *nf* university; **à l'u.** at university. ◆**universitaire** *a* university-; – *nmf* academic.
uranium [yranjɔm] *nm* uranium.
urbain [yrbɛ̃] *a* urban, town-, city-. ◆**urbaniser** *vt* to urbanize, build up. ◆**urbanisme** *nm* town planning, *Am* city planning. ◆**urbaniste** *nmf* town planner, *Am* city planner.
urgent [yrʒɑ̃] *a* urgent, pressing. ◆**urgence** *nf* (*cas*) emergency; (*de décision, tâche etc*) urgency; **d'u.** (*mesures etc*) emergency-; **état d'u.** *Pol* state of emergency; **faire qch d'u.** to do sth urgently.
urine [yrin] *nf* urine. ◆**uriner** *vi* to urinate. ◆**urinoir** *nm* (public) urinal.
urne [yrn] *nf* **1** (*électorale*) ballot box; **aller aux urnes** to go to the polls. **2** (*vase*) urn.
URSS [yrs] *nf abrév* (*Union des Républiques Socialistes Soviétiques*) USSR.
usage [yzaʒ] *nm* use; *Ling* usage; (*habitude*) custom; **faire u. de** to make use of; **faire de l'u.** (*vêtement etc*) to wear well; **d'u.** (*habituel*) customary; **à l'u. de** for (the use of); **hors d'u.** no longer usable. ◆**usagé** *a* worn; (*d'occasion*) used. ◆**usager** *nm* user. ◆**us/er** *vt* (*vêtement, personne*) to wear out; (*consommer*) to use (up); (*santé*) to ruin; – *vi* **u. de** to use; **— s'u.** *vpr* (*tissu, machine*) to wear out; (*personne*) to wear oneself out. ◆**—é** *a* (*tissu etc*) worn (out); (*sujet etc*) well-worn; (*personne*) worn out.
usine [yzin] *nf* factory; (*à gaz, de métallurgie*) works.
usiner [yzine] *vt* (*pièce*) *Tech* to machine.
usité [yzite] *a* commonly used.
ustensile [ystɑ̃sil] *nm* utensil.
usuel, -elle [yzɥɛl] *a* everyday, ordinary; – *nmpl* (*livres*) reference books.
usure [yzyr] *nf* (*détérioration*) wear (and tear); **avoir qn à l'u.** *Fig* to wear s.o. down (in the end).
usurier, -ière [yzyrje, -jɛr] *nmf* usurer.
usurper [yzyrpe] *vt* to usurp.
utérus [yterys] *nm Anat* womb, uterus.
utile [ytil] *a* useful (**à** to). ◆**utilement** *adv* usefully.
utiliser [ytilize] *vt* to use, utilize. ◆**utilisable** *a* usable. ◆**utilisateur, -trice** *nmf* user. ◆**utilisation** *nf* use. ◆**utilité** *nf* use(fulness); **d'une grande u.** very useful.
utilitaire [ytilitɛr] *a* utilitarian; (*véhicule*) utility-.
utopie [ytɔpi] *nf* (*idéal*) utopia; (*projet, idée*) utopian plan *ou* idea. ◆**utopique** *a* utopian.

V

V, v [ve] *nm* V, v.
va [va] *voir* **aller 1.**
vacances [vakɑ̃s] *nfpl* holiday(s), *Am* vacation; **en v.** on holiday, *Am* on vacation; **prendre ses v.** to take one's holiday(s) *ou* *Am* vacation; **les grandes v.** the summer

holidays *ou Am* vacation. ◆**vacancier, -ière** *nmf* holidaymaker, *Am* vacationer.
vacant [vakɑ̃] *a* vacant. ◆**vacance** *nf* (*poste*) vacancy.
vacarme [vakarm] *nm* din, uproar.
vaccin [vaksɛ̃] *nm* vaccine; **faire un v. à** to vaccinate. ◆**vaccination** *nf* vaccination. ◆**vacciner** *vt* to vaccinate.
vache [vaʃ] **1** *nf* cow; **v. laitière** dairy cow. **2** *nf* **(peau de) v.** (*personne*) *Fam* swine; – *a* (*méchant*) *Fam* nasty. ◆**vachement** *adv Fam* (*très*) damned; (*beaucoup*) a hell of a lot. ◆**vacherie** *nf Fam* (*action, parole*) nasty thing; (*caractère*) nastiness.
vacill/er [vasije] *vi* to sway, wobble; (*flamme, lumière*) to flicker; (*jugement, mémoire etc*) to falter, waver. ◆**—ant** *a* (*démarche, mémoire*) shaky; (*lumière etc*) flickering.
vadrouille [vadruj] *nf* **en v.** *Fam* roaming *ou* wandering about. ◆**vadrouiller** *vi Fam* to roam *ou* wander about.
va-et-vient [vaevjɛ̃] *nm inv* (*mouvement*) movement to and fro; (*de personnes*) comings and goings.
vagabond, -onde [vagabɔ̃, -ɔ̃d] *a* wandering; – *nmf* (*clochard*) vagrant, tramp. ◆**vagabond/er** *vi* to roam *ou* wander about; (*pensée*) to wander. ◆**—age** *nm* wandering; *Jur* vagrancy.
vagin [vaʒɛ̃] *nm* vagina.
vagir [vaʒir] *vi* (*bébé*) to cry, wail.
vague [vag] **1** *a* vague; (*regard*) vacant; (*souvenir*) dim, vague; – *nm* vagueness; **regarder dans le v.** to gaze into space, gaze vacantly; **rester dans le v.** (*être évasif*) to keep it vague. **2** *nf* (*de mer*) & *Fig* wave; **v. de chaleur** heat wave; **v. de froid** cold snap *ou* spell; **v. de fond** (*dans l'opinion*) *Fig* tidal wave. ◆**vaguement** *adv* vaguely.
vaillant [vajɑ̃] *a* brave, valiant; (*vigoureux*) healthy. ◆**vaillamment** *adv* bravely, valiantly. ◆**vaillance** *nf* bravery.
vain [vɛ̃] *a* **1** (*futile*) vain, futile; (*mots, promesse*) empty; **en v.** in vain, vainly. **2** (*vaniteux*) vain. ◆**vainement** *adv* in vain, vainly.
vainc/re* [vɛ̃kr] *vt* to defeat, beat; (*surmonter*) to overcome. ◆**—u, -ue** *nmf* defeated man *ou* woman; *Sp* loser. ◆**vainqueur** *nm* victor; *Sp* winner; – *am* victorious.
vaisseau, -x [vɛso] *nm* **1** *Anat Bot* vessel. **2** (*bateau*) ship, vessel; **v. spatial** spaceship.
vaisselle [vɛsɛl] *nf* crockery; (*à laver*) washing-up; **faire la v.** to do the washing-up, do *ou* wash the dishes.
val, *pl* **vals** *ou* **vaux** [val, vo] *nm* valley.
valable [valabl] *a* (*billet, motif etc*) valid; (*remarquable, rentable*) *Fam* worthwhile.
valet [valɛ] *nm* **1** *Cartes* jack. **2 v. (de chambre)** valet, manservant; **v. de ferme** farmhand.
valeur [valœr] *nf* value; (*mérite*) worth; (*poids*) importance, weight; *pl* (*titres*) *Com* stocks and shares; **la v. de** (*quantité*) the equivalent of; **avoir de la v.** to be valuable; **mettre en v.** (*faire ressortir*) to highlight; **de v.** (*personne*) of merit, able; **objets de v.** valuables.
valide [valid] *a* **1** (*personne*) fit, able-bodied; (*population*) able-bodied. **2** (*billet etc*) valid. ◆**valider** *vt* to validate. ◆**validité** *nf* validity.
valise [valiz] *nf* (suit)case; **v. diplomatique** diplomatic bag *ou Am* pouch; **faire ses valises** to pack (one's bags).
vallée [vale] *nf* valley. ◆**vallon** *nm* (small) valley. ◆**vallonné** *a* (*région etc*) undulating.
valoir* [valwar] *vi* to be worth; (*s'appliquer*) to apply **(pour** to); **v. mille francs/cher/***etc* to be worth a thousand francs/a lot/*etc*; **un vélo vaut bien une auto** a bicycle is as good as a car; **il vaut mieux rester** it's better to stay; **il vaut mieux que j'attende** I'd better wait; **ça ne vaut rien** it's worthless, it's no good; **ça vaut le coup** *Fam ou* **la peine** it's worthwhile **(de faire** doing); **faire v.** (*faire ressortir*) to highlight, set off; (*argument*) to put forward; (*droit*) to assert; – *vt* **v. qch à qn** to bring *ou* get s.o. sth; **— se v.** *vpr* (*objets, personnes*) to be as good as each other; **ça se vaut** *Fam* it's all the same.
valse [vals] *nf* waltz. ◆**valser** *vi* to waltz.
valve [valv] *nf* (*clapet*) valve. ◆**valvule** *nf* (*du cœur*) valve.
vampire [vɑ̃pir] *nm* vampire.
vandale [vɑ̃dal] *nmf* vandal. ◆**vandalisme** *nm* vandalism.
vanille [vanij] *nf* vanilla; **glace/***etc* **à la v.** vanilla ice cream/*etc.* ◆**vanillé** *a* vanilla-flavoured.
vanité [vanite] *nf* vanity. ◆**vaniteux, -euse** *a* vain, conceited.
vanne [van] *nf* **1** (*d'écluse*) sluice (gate), floodgate. **2** (*remarque*) *Fam* dig, jibe.
vanné [vane] *a* (*fatigué*) *Fam* dead beat.
vannerie [vanri] *nf* (*fabrication, objets*) basketwork, basketry.
vantail, -aux [vɑ̃taj, -o] *nm* (*de porte*) leaf.
vanter [vɑ̃te] *vt* to praise; **— se v.** *vpr* to boast, brag **(de** about, of). ◆**vantard, -arde** *a* boastful; – *nmf* boaster, braggart.

◆**vantardise** *nf* boastfulness; (*propos*) boast.

va-nu-pieds [vanypje] *nmf inv* tramp, beggar.

vapeur [vapœr] *nf* (*brume, émanation*) vapour; **v. (d'eau)** steam; **cuire à la v.** to steam; **bateau à v.** steamship. ◆**vaporeux, -euse** *a* hazy, misty; (*tissu*) translucent, diaphanous.

vaporiser [vaporize] *vt* to spray. ◆**vaporisateur** *nm* (*appareil*) spray.

vaquer [vake] *vi* **v. à** to attend to.

varappe [varap] *nf* rock-climbing.

varech [varɛk] *nm* wrack, seaweed.

vareuse [varøz] *nf* (*d'uniforme*) tunic.

varicelle [varisɛl] *nf* chicken pox.

varices [varis] *nfpl* varicose veins.

vari/er [varje] *vti* to vary (**de** from). ◆**—é** *a* (*diversifié*) varied; (*divers*) various. ◆**—able** *a* variable; (*humeur, temps*) changeable. ◆**variante** *nf* variant. ◆**variation** *nf* variation. ◆**variété** *nf* variety; **spectacle de variétés** *Th* variety show.

variole [varjɔl] *nf* smallpox.

vas [va] *voir* **aller 1.**

vase [vaz] **1** *nm* vase. **2** *nf* (*boue*) silt, mud.

vaseline [vazlin] *nf* Vaseline®.

vaseux, -euse [vazø, -øz] *a* **1** (*boueux*) silty, muddy. **2** (*fatigué*) off colour. **3** (*idées etc*) woolly, hazy.

vasistas [vazistas] *nm* (*dans une porte ou une fenêtre*) hinged panel.

vaste [vast] *a* vast, huge.

Vatican [vatikɑ̃] *nm* Vatican.

va-tout [vatu] *nm inv* **jouer son v.-tout** to stake one's all.

vaudeville [vodvil] *nm Th* light comedy.

vau-l'eau (à) [avolo] *adv* **aller à v.-l'eau** to go to rack and ruin.

vaurien, -ienne [vorjɛ̃, -jɛn] *nmf* good-for-nothing.

vautour [votur] *nm* vulture.

vautrer (se) [səvotre] *vpr* to sprawl; **se v. dans** (*boue, vice*) to wallow in.

va-vite (à la) [alavavit] *adv Fam* in a hurry.

veau, -x [vo] *nm* (*animal*) calf; (*viande*) veal; (*cuir*) calf(skin).

vécu [veky] *voir* **vivre;** – *a* (*histoire etc*) real(-life), true.

vedette [vədɛt] *nf* **1** *Cin Th* star; **avoir la v.** (*artiste*) to head the bill; **en v.** (*personne*) in the limelight; (*objet*) in a prominent position. **2** (*canot*) motor boat, launch.

végétal, -aux [veʒetal, -o] *a* (*huile, règne*) vegetable-; – *nm* plant. ◆**végétarien, -ienne** *a* & *nmf* vegetarian. ◆**végétation 1** *nf* vegetation. **2** *nfpl Méd* adenoids.

végéter [veʒete] *vi* (*personne*) *Péj* to vegetate.

véhément [veemɑ̃] *a* vehement. ◆**véhémence** *nf* vehemence.

véhicule [veikyl] *nm* vehicle. ◆**véhiculer** *vt* to convey.

veille [vɛj] *nf* **1 la v. (de)** (*jour précédent*) the day before; **à la v. de** (*événement*) on the eve of; **la v. de Noël** Christmas Eve. **2** (*état*) wakefulness; *pl* vigils.

veill/er [veje] *vi* to stay up *ou* awake; (*sentinelle etc*) to be on watch; **v. à qch** to attend to sth, see to sth; **v. à ce que** (+ *sub*) to make sure that; **v. sur qn** to watch over s.o.; – *vt* (*malade*) to sit with, watch over. ◆**—ée** *nf* (*soirée*) evening; (*réunion*) evening get-together; (*mortuaire*) vigil. ◆**—eur** *nm* **v. de nuit** night watchman. ◆**—euse** *nf* (*lampe*) night light; (*de voiture*) sidelight; (*de réchaud*) pilot light.

veine [vɛn] *nf* **1** *Anat Bot Géol* vein. **2** (*chance*) *Fam* luck; **avoir de la v.** to be lucky; **une v.** a piece *ou* stroke of luck. ◆**veinard, -arde** *nmf Fam* lucky devil; – *a Fam* lucky.

vêler [vele] *vi* (*vache*) to calve.

vélin [velɛ̃] *nm* (*papier, peau*) vellum.

velléité [veleite] *nf* vague desire.

vélo [velo] *nm* bike, bicycle; (*activité*) cycling; **faire du v.** to cycle, go cycling. ◆**vélodrome** *nm Sp* velodrome, cycle track. ◆**vélomoteur** *nm* (lightweight) motorcycle.

velours [v(ə)lur] *nm* velvet; **v. côtelé** corduroy, cord. ◆**velouté** *a* soft, velvety; (*au goût*) mellow, smooth; – *nm* smoothness; **v. d'asperges**/*etc* (*potage*) cream of asparagus/*etc* soup.

velu [vəly] *a* hairy.

venaison [vənɛzɔ̃] *nf* venison.

vénal, -aux [venal, -o] *a* mercenary, venal.

vendange(s) [vɑ̃dɑ̃ʒ] *nf(pl)* grape harvest, vintage. ◆**vendanger** *vi* to pick the grapes. ◆**vendangeur, -euse** *nmf* grape-picker.

vendetta [vɑ̃deta] *nf* vendetta.

vend/re [vɑ̃dr] *vt* to sell; **v. qch à qn** to sell s.o. sth, sell sth to s.o.; **v. qn** (*trahir*) to sell s.o. out; **à v.** (*maison etc*) for sale; **— se v.** *vpr* to be sold; **ça se vend bien** it sells well. ◆**—eur, -euse** *nmf* (*de magasin*) sales *ou* shop assistant, *Am* sales clerk; (*marchand*) salesman, saleswoman; *Jur* vendor, seller.

vendredi [vɑ̃drədi] *nm* Friday; **V. saint** Good Friday.

vénéneux, -euse [venenø, -øz] *a* poisonous.

vénérable [venerabl] *a* venerable. ◆**vénérer** *vt* to venerate.

vénérien, -ienne [venerjɛ̃, -jɛn] *a Méd* venereal.

venger [vɑ̃ʒe] *vt* to avenge; **— se v.** *vpr* to take (one's) revenge, avenge oneself (**de qn** on s.o., **de qch** for sth). ◆**vengeance** *nf* revenge, vengeance. ◆**vengeur, -eresse** *a* vengeful; – *nmf* avenger.

venin [vənɛ̃] *nm* (*substance*) & *Fig* venom. ◆**venimeux, -euse** *a* poisonous, venomous; (*haineux*) *Fig* venomous.

venir* [v(ə)nir] *vi* (*aux* **être**) to come (**de** from); **v. faire** to come to do; **viens me voir** come and *ou* to see me; **je viens/venais d'arriver** I've/I'd just arrived; **en v. à** (*conclusion etc*) to come to; **où veux-tu en v.?** what are you driving *ou* getting at?; **d'où vient que...?** how is it that...?; **s'il venait à faire** (*éventualité*) if he happened to do; **les jours/***etc* **qui viennent** the coming days/*etc*; **une idée m'est venue** an idea occurred to me; **faire v.** to send for, get.

vent [vɑ̃] *nm* wind; **il fait** *ou* **il y a du v.** it's windy; **coup de v.** gust of wind; **avoir v. de** (*connaissance de*) to get wind of; **dans le v.** (*à la mode*) *Fam* trendy, with it.

vente [vɑ̃t] *nf* sale; **v. (aux enchères)** auction (sale); **v. de charité** bazaar, charity sale; **en v.** (*disponible*) on sale; **point de v.** sales *ou* retail outlet; **prix de v.** selling price; **salle des ventes** auction room.

ventilateur [vɑ̃tilatœr] *nm* (*électrique*) & *Aut* fan; (*dans un mur*) ventilator. ◆**ventilation** *nf* ventilation. ◆**ventiler** *vt* to ventilate.

ventouse [vɑ̃tuz] *nf* (*pour fixer*) suction grip; **à v.** (*crochet, fléchette etc*) suction-.

ventre [vɑ̃tr] *nm* belly, stomach; (*utérus*) womb; (*de cruche etc*) bulge; **avoir/prendre du v.** to have/get a paunch; **à plat v.** flat on one's face. ◆**ventru** *a* (*personne*) pot-bellied; (*objet*) bulging.

ventriloque [vɑ̃trilɔk] *nmf* ventriloquist.

venu, -ue[1] [v(ə)ny] *voir* **venir**; – *nmf* **nouveau v., nouvelle venue** newcomer; **premier v.** anyone; – *a* **bien v.** (*à propos*) timely; **mal v.** untimely; **être bien/mal v. de faire** to have good grounds/no grounds for doing.

venue[2] [v(ə)ny] *nf* (*arrivée*) coming.

vêpres [vɛpr] *nfpl Rel* vespers.

ver [vɛr] *nm* worm; (*larve*) grub; (*de fruits, fromage etc*) maggot; **v. luisant** glow-worm; **v. à soie** silkworm; **v. solitaire** tapeworm; **v. de terre** earthworm.

véracité [verasite] *nf* truthfulness, veracity.

véranda [verɑ̃da] *nf* veranda(h).

verbe [vɛrb] *nm Gram* verb. ◆**verbal, -aux** *a* (*promesse, expression etc*) verbal.

verbeux, -euse [vɛrbø, -øz] *a* verbose. ◆**verbiage** *nm* verbiage.

verdâtre [vɛrdɑtr] *a* greenish.

verdeur [vɛrdœr] *nf* (*de fruit, vin*) tartness; (*de vieillard*) sprightliness; (*de langage*) crudeness.

verdict [vɛrdikt] *nm* verdict.

verdir [vɛrdir] *vti* to turn green. ◆**verdoyant** *a* green, verdant. ◆**verdure** *nf* (*arbres etc*) greenery.

véreux, -euse [verø, -øz] *a* (*fruit etc*) wormy, maggoty; (*malhonnête*) *Fig* dubious, shady.

verge [vɛrʒ] *nf Anat* penis.

verger [vɛrʒe] *nm* orchard.

vergetures [vɛrʒətyr] *nfpl* stretch marks.

verglas [vɛrgla] *nm* (black) ice, *Am* sleet. ◆**verglacé** *a* (*route*) icy.

vergogne (sans) [sɑ̃vɛrgɔɲ] *a* shameless; – *adv* shamelessly.

véridique [veridik] *a* truthful.

vérifier [verifje] *vt* to check, verify; (*confirmer*) to confirm; (*comptes*) to audit. ◆**vérifiable** *a* verifiable. ◆**vérification** *nf* verification; confirmation; audit(ing).

vérité [verite] *nf* truth; (*de personnage, tableau etc*) trueness to life; (*sincérité*) sincerity; **en v.** in fact. ◆**véritable** *a* true, real; (*non imité*) real, genuine; (*exactement nommé*) veritable, real. ◆**véritablement** *adv* really.

vermeil, -eille [vɛrmɛj] *a* bright red, vermilion.

vermicelle(s) [vɛrmisɛl] *nm(pl) Culin* vermicelli.

vermine [vɛrmin] *nf* (*insectes, racaille*) vermine.

vermoulu [vɛrmuly] *a* worm-eaten.

vermouth [vɛrmut] *nm* vermouth.

verni [vɛrni] *a* (*chanceux*) *Fam* lucky.

vernir [vɛrnir] *vt* to varnish; (*poterie*) to glaze. ◆**vernis** *nm* varnish; glaze; (*apparence*) *Fig* veneer; **v. à ongles** nail polish *ou* varnish. ◆**vernissage** *nm* (*d'exposition de peinture*) first day. ◆**vernisser** *vt* (*poterie*) to glaze.

verra, verrait [vɛra, vɛrɛ] *voir* **voir**.

verre [vɛr] *nm* (*substance, récipient*) glass; **boire** *ou* **prendre un v.** to have a drink; **v. à bière/à vin** beer/wine glass; **v. de contact**

contact lens. ◆**verrerie** *nf* (*objets*) glassware. ◆**verrière** *nf* (*toit*) glass roof.
verrou [veru] *nm* bolt; **fermer au v.** to bolt; **sous les verrous** behind bars. ◆**verrouiller** *vt* to bolt.
verrue [very] *nf* wart.
vers[1] [ver] *prép* (*direction*) towards, toward; (*approximation*) around, about.
vers[2] [ver] *nm* (*d'un poème*) line; *pl* (*poésie*) verse.
versant [versɑ̃] *nm* slope, side.
versatile [versatil] *a* fickle, volatile.
verse (à) [avers] *adv* in torrents; **pleuvoir à v.** to pour (down).
versé [verse] *a* **v. dans** (well-)versed in.
Verseau [verso] *nm* **le V.** (*signe*) Aquarius.
vers/er [verse] **1** *vt* to pour; (*larmes, sang*) to shed. **2** *vt* (*argent*) to pay. **3** *vti* (*basculer*) to overturn. ◆**—ement** *nm* payment. ◆**—eur** *a* **bec v.** spout.
verset [verse] *nm Rel* verse.
version [versjɔ̃] *nf* version; (*traduction*) *Scol* translation, unseen.
verso [verso] *nm* back (of the page); **'voir au v.'** 'see overleaf'.
vert [ver] *a* green; (*pas mûr*) unripe; (*vin*) young; (*vieillard*) *Fig* sprightly; – *nm* green.
vert-de-gris [verdəgri] *nm inv* verdigris.
vertèbre [vertebr] *nf* vertebra.
vertement [vertəmɑ̃] *adv* (*réprimander etc*) sharply.
vertical, -ale, -aux [vertikal, -o] *a* & *nf* vertical; **à la verticale** vertically. ◆**verticalement** *adv* vertically.
vertige [vertiʒ] *nm* (feeling of) dizziness *ou* giddiness; (*peur de tomber dans le vide*) vertigo; *pl* dizzy spells; **avoir le v.** to feel dizzy *ou* giddy. ◆**vertigineux, -euse** *a* (*hauteur*) giddy, dizzy; (*très grand*) *Fig* staggering.
vertu [verty] *nf* virtue; **en v. de** in accordance with. ◆**vertueux, -euse** *a* virtuous.
verve [verv] *nf* (*d'orateur etc*) brilliance.
verveine [verven] *nf* (*plante*) verbena.
vésicule [vezikyl] *nf* **v. biliaire** gall bladder.
vessie [vesi] *nf* bladder.
veste [vest] *nf* jacket, coat.
vestiaire [vestjer] *nm* cloakroom, *Am* locker room; (*meuble métallique*) locker.
vestibule [vestibyl] *nm* (entrance) hall.
vestiges [vestiʒ] *nmpl* (*restes, ruines*) remains; (*traces*) traces, vestiges.
vestimentaire [vestimɑ̃ter] *a* (*dépense*) clothing-; (*détail*) of dress.
veston [vestɔ̃] *nm* (suit) jacket.
vêtement [vetmɑ̃] *nm* garment, article of clothing; *pl* clothes; **du v.** (*industrie, commerce*) clothing-; **vêtements de sport** sportswear.
vétéran [veterɑ̃] *nm* veteran.
vétérinaire [veteriner] *a* veterinary; – *nmf* vet, veterinary surgeon, *Am* veterinarian.
vétille [vetij] *nf* trifle, triviality.
vêt/ir* [vetir] *vt*, — **se v.** *vpr* to dress. ◆**—u** *a* dressed (**de** in).
veto [veto] *nm inv* veto; **mettre** *ou* **opposer son v. à** to veto.
vétuste [vetyst] *a* dilapidated.
veuf, veuve [vœf, vœv] *a* widowed; – *nm* widower; – *nf* widow.
veuille [vœj] *voir* **vouloir.**
veule [vøl] *a* feeble. ◆**veulerie** *nf* feebleness.
veut, veux [vø] *voir* **vouloir.**
vex/er [vekse] *vt* to upset, hurt; — **se v.** *vpr* to be *ou* get upset (**de** at). ◆**—ant** *a* hurtful; (*contrariant*) annoying. ◆**vexation** *nf* humiliation.
viable [vjabl] *a* (*enfant, entreprise etc*) viable. ◆**viabilité** *nf* viability.
viaduc [vjadyk] *nm* viaduct.
viager, -ère [vjaʒe, -er] *a* **rente viagère** life annuity; – *nm* life annuity.
viande [vjɑ̃d] *nf* meat.
vibrer [vibre] *vi* to vibrate; (*être ému*) to thrill (**de** with); **faire v.** (*auditoire etc*) to thrill. ◆**vibrant** *a* (*émouvant*) emotional; (*voix, son*) resonant, vibrant. ◆**vibration** *nf* vibration. ◆**vibromasseur** *nm* (*appareil*) vibrator.
vicaire [viker] *nm* curate.
vice [vis] *nm* vice; (*défectuosité*) defect.
vice- [vis] *préf* vice-.
vice versa [vis(e)versa] *adv* vice versa.
vicier [visje] *vt* to taint, pollute.
vicieux, -euse [visjø, -øz] **1** *a* depraved; – *nmf* pervert. **2** *a* **cercle v.** vicious circle.
vicinal, -aux [visinal, -o] *a* **chemin v.** by-road, minor road.
vicissitudes [visisityd] *nfpl* vicissitudes.
vicomte [vikɔ̃t] *nm* viscount. ◆**vicomtesse** *nf* viscountess.
victime [viktim] *nf* victim; (*d'un accident*) casualty; **être v. de** to be the victim of.
victoire [viktwar] *nf* victory; *Sp* win. ◆**victorieux, -euse** *a* victorious; (*équipe*) winning.
victuailles [viktɥaj] *nfpl* provisions.
vidange [vidɑ̃ʒ] *nf* emptying, draining; *Aut* oil change; (*dispositif*) waste outlet. ◆**vidanger** *vt* to empty, drain.
vide [vid] *a* empty; – *nm* emptiness, void; (*absence d'air*) vacuum; (*gouffre etc*) drop;

(*trou, manque*) gap; **regarder dans le v.** to stare into space; **emballé sous v.** vacuum-packed; **à v.** empty.

vidéo [video] *a inv* video. ◆**vidéocassette** *nf* video (cassette).

vide-ordures [vidɔrdyr] *nm inv* (refuse) chute. ◆**vide-poches** *nm inv Aut* glove compartment.

vid/er [vide] *vt* to empty; (*lieu*) to vacate; (*poisson, volaille*) *Culin* to gut; (*querelle*) to settle; **v. qn** *Fam* (*chasser*) to throw s.o. out; (*épuiser*) to tire s.o. out; **— se v.** *vpr* to empty. ◆**—é** *a* (*fatigué*) *Fam* exhausted. ◆**—eur** *nm* (*de boîte de nuit*) bouncer.

vie [vi] *nf* life; (*durée*) lifetime; **coût de la v.** cost of living; **gagner sa v.** to earn one's living *ou* livelihood; **en v.** living; **à v., pour la v.** for life; **donner la v. à** to give birth to; **avoir la v. dure** (*préjugés etc*) to die hard; **jamais de la v.!** not on your life!, never!

vieill/ir [vjejir] *vi* to grow old; (*changer*) to age; (*théorie, mot*) to become old-fashioned; – *vt* **v. qn** (*vêtement etc*) to age s.o. ◆**—i** *a* (*démodé*) old-fashioned. ◆**—issant** *a* ageing. ◆**—issement** *nm* ageing.

viens, vient [vjɛ̃] *voir* **venir.**

vierge [vjɛrʒ] *nf* virgin; **la V.** (*signe*) Virgo; – *a* (*femme, neige etc*) virgin; (*feuille de papier, film*) blank; **être v.** (*femme, homme*) to be a virgin.

Viêt-nam [vjɛtnam] *nm* Vietnam. ◆**vietnamien, -ienne** *a* & *nmf* Vietnamese.

vieux (*or* **vieil** *before vowel or mute h*), **vieille,** *pl* **vieux, vieilles** [vjø, vjɛj] *a* old; **être v. jeu** (*a inv*) to be old-fashioned; **v. garçon** bachelor; **vieille fille** *Péj* old maid; – *nm* old man; *pl* old people; **mon v.** (*mon cher*) *Fam* old boy, old man; – *nf* old woman; **ma vieille** (*ma chère*) *Fam* old girl. ◆**vieillard** *nm* old man; *pl* old people. ◆**vieillerie** *nf* (*objet*) old thing; (*idée*) old idea. ◆**vieillesse** *nf* old age. ◆**vieillot** *a* antiquated.

vif, vive [vif, viv] *a* (*enfant, mouvement*) lively; (*alerte*) quick, sharp; (*intelligence, intérêt, vent*) keen; (*couleur, lumière*) bright; (*froid*) biting; (*pas*) quick, brisk; (*impression, imagination, style*) vivid; (*parole*) sharp; (*regret, satisfaction, succès etc*) great; (*coléreux*) quick-tempered; **brûler/enterrer qn v.** to burn/bury s.o. alive; – *nm* **le v. du sujet** the heart of the matter; **à v.** (*plaie*) open; **piqué au v.** (*vexé*) cut to the quick.

vigie [viʒi] *nf* (*matelot*) lookout; (*poste*) lookout post.

vigilant [viʒilɑ̃] *a* vigilant. ◆**vigilance** *nf* vigilance.

vigile [viʒil] *nm* (*gardien*) watchman; (*de nuit*) night watchman.

vigne [viɲ] *nf* (*plante*) vine; (*plantation*) vineyard. ◆**vigneron, -onne** *nmf* wine grower. ◆**vignoble** *nm* vineyard; (*région*) vineyards.

vignette [viɲɛt] *nf Aut* road tax sticker; (*de médicament*) price label (*for reimbursement by Social Security*).

vigueur [vigœr] *nf* vigour; **entrer/être en v.** (*loi*) to come into/be in force. ◆**vigoureux, -euse** *a* (*personne, style etc*) vigorous; (*bras*) sturdy.

vilain [vilɛ̃] *a* (*laid*) ugly; (*mauvais*) nasty; (*enfant*) naughty.

villa [villa] *nf* (detached) house.

village [vilaʒ] *nm* village. ◆**villageois, -oise** *a* village-; – *nmf* villager.

ville [vil] *nf* town; (*grande*) city; **aller/être en v.** to go into/be in town; **v. d'eaux** spa (town).

villégiature [vileʒjatyr] *nf* **lieu de v.** (holiday) resort.

vin [vɛ̃] *nm* wine; **v. ordinaire** *ou* **de table** table wine; **v. d'honneur** reception (*in honour of s.o.*). ◆**vinicole** *a* (*région*) wine-growing; (*industrie*) wine-.

vinaigre [vinɛgr] *nm* vinegar. ◆**vinaigré** *a* seasoned with vinegar. ◆**vinaigrette** *nf* (*sauce*) vinaigrette, French dressing, *Am* Italian dressing.

vindicatif, -ive [vɛ̃dikatif, -iv] *a* vindictive.

vingt [vɛ̃] ([vɛ̃t] *before vowel or mute h and in numbers 22–29*) *a* & *nm* twenty; **v. et un** twenty-one. ◆**vingtaine** *nf* **une v. (de)** (*nombre*) about twenty; **avoir la v.** (*âge*) to be about twenty. ◆**vingtième** *a* & *nmf* twentieth.

vinyle [vinil] *nm* vinyl.

viol [vjɔl] *nm* rape; (*de loi, lieu*) violation. ◆**violation** *nf* violation. ◆**violenter** *vt* to rape. ◆**violer** *vt* (*femme*) to rape; (*loi, lieu*) to violate. ◆**violeur** *nm* rapist.

violent [vjɔlɑ̃] *a* violent; (*remède*) drastic. ◆**violemment** [-amɑ̃] *adv* violently. ◆**violence** *nf* violence; (*acte*) act of violence.

violet, -ette [vjɔlɛ, -ɛt] **1** *a* & *nm* (*couleur*) purple, violet. **2** *nf* (*fleur*) violet. ◆**violacé** *a* purplish.

violon [vjɔlɔ̃] *nm* violin. ◆**violoncelle** *nm* cello. ◆**violoncelliste** *nmf* cellist. ◆**violoniste** *nmf* violinist.

vipère [vipɛr] *nf* viper, adder.

virage [viraʒ] *nm* (*de route*) bend; (*de véhicule*) turn; (*revirement*) *Fig* change of

course. ◆**vir/er 1** *vi* to turn, veer; (*sur soi*) to turn round; **v. au bleu/***etc* to turn blue/*etc.* **2** *vt* (*expulser*) *Fam* to throw out. **3** *vt* (*somme*) *Fin* to transfer (**à** to). ◆**—ement** *nm Fin* (bank *ou* credit) transfer.
virée [vire] *nf Fam* trip, outing.
virevolter [virvɔlte] *vi* to spin round.
virginité [virʒinite] *nf* virginity.
virgule [virgyl] *nf Gram* comma; *Math* (decimal) point; **2 v. 5** 2 point 5.
viril [viril] *a* virile, manly; (*attribut, force*) male. ◆**virilité** *nf* virility, manliness.
virtuel, -elle [virtɥɛl] *a* potential.
virtuose [virtɥoz] *nmf* virtuoso. ◆**virtuosité** *nf* virtuosity.
virulent [virylɑ̃] *a* virulent. ◆**virulence** *nf* virulence.
virus [virys] *nm* virus.
vis[1] [vi] *voir* **vivre, voir.**
vis[2] [vis] *nf* screw.
visa [viza] *nm* (*timbre*) stamp, stamped signature; (*de passeport*) visa; **v. de censure** (*d'un film*) certificate.
visage [vizaʒ] *nm* face.
vis-à-vis [vizavi] *prép* **v.-à-vis de** opposite; (*à l'égard de*) with respect to; (*envers*) towards; (*comparé à*) compared to; – *nm inv* (*personne*) person opposite; (*bois, maison etc*) opposite view.
viscères [visɛr] *nmpl* intestines. ◆**viscéral, -aux** *a* (*haine etc*) *Fig* deeply felt.
viscosité [viskozite] *nf* viscosity.
viser [vize] **1** *vi* to aim (**à** at); **v. à faire** to aim to do; – *vt* (*cible*) to aim at; (*concerner*) to be aimed at. **2** *vt* (*passeport, document*) to stamp. ◆**visées** *nfpl* (*desseins*) *Fig* aims; **avoir des visées sur** to have designs on. ◆**viseur** *nm Phot* viewfinder; (*d'arme*) sight.
visible [vizibl] *a* visible. ◆**visiblement** *adv* visibly. ◆**visibilité** *nf* visibility.
visière [vizjɛr] *nf* (*de casquette*) peak; (*en plastique etc*) eyeshade; (*de casque*) visor.
vision [vizjɔ̃] *nf* (*conception, image*) vision; (*sens*) (eye)sight, vision; **avoir des visions** *Fam* to be seeing things. ◆**visionnaire** *a* & *nmf* visionary. ◆**visionner** *vt Cin* to view. ◆**visionneuse** *nf* (*pour diapositives*) viewer.
visite [vizit] *nf* visit; (*personne*) visitor; (*examen*) inspection; **rendre v. à, faire une v. à** to visit; **v. (à domicile)** *Méd* call, visit; **v. (médicale)** medical examination; **v. guidée** guided tour; **de v.** (*carte, heures*) visiting-. ◆**visiter** *vt* to visit; (*examiner*) to inspect. ◆**visiteur, -euse** *nmf* visitor.
vison [vizɔ̃] *nm* mink.
visqueux, -euse [viskø, -øz] *a* viscous; (*surface*) sticky; (*répugnant*) *Fig* slimy.
visser [vise] *vt* to screw on.
visuel, -elle [vizɥɛl] *a* visual.
vit [vi] *voir* **vivre, voir.**
vital, -aux [vital, -o] *a* vital. ◆**vitalité** *nf* vitality.
vitamine [vitamin] *nf* vitamin. ◆**vitaminé** *a* (*biscuits etc*) vitamin-enriched.
vite [vit] *adv* quickly, fast; (*tôt*) soon; **v.!** quick(ly)! ◆**vitesse** *nf* speed; (*régime*) *Aut* gear; **boîte de vitesses** gearbox; **à toute v.** at top *ou* full speed; **v. de pointe** top speed; **en v.** quickly.
viticole [vitikɔl] *a* (*région*) wine-growing; (*industrie*) wine-. ◆**viticulteur** *nm* wine grower. ◆**viticulture** *nf* wine growing.
vitre [vitr] *nf* (window)pane; (*de véhicule*) window. ◆**vitrage** *nm* (*vitres*) windows. ◆**vitrail, -aux** *nm* stained-glass window. ◆**vitré** *a* glass-, glazed. ◆**vitreux, -euse** *a* (*regard, yeux*) *Fig* glassy. ◆**vitrier** *nm* glazier.
vitrine [vitrin] *nf* (*de magasin*) (shop) window; (*meuble*) showcase, display cabinet.
vitriol [vitrijɔl] *nm Ch* & *Fig* vitriol.
vivable [vivabl] *a* (*personne*) easy to live with; (*endroit*) fit to live in.
vivace [vivas] *a* (*plante*) perennial; (*haine*) *Fig* inveterate.
vivacité [vivasite] *nf* liveliness; (*de l'air, d'émotion*) keenness; (*agilité*) quickness; (*de couleur, d'impression, de style*) vividness; (*emportement*) petulance; **v. d'esprit** quick-wittedness.
vivant [vivɑ̃] *a* (*en vie*) alive, living; (*être, matière, preuve*) living; (*conversation, enfant, récit, rue*) lively; **langue vivante** modern language; – *nm* **de son v.** in one's lifetime; **bon v.** jovial fellow; **les vivants** the living.
vivats [viva] *nmpl* cheers.
vive[1] [viv] *voir* **vif.**
vive[2] [viv] *int* **v. le roi/***etc*! long live the king/*etc*!; **v. les vacances!** hurray for the holidays!
vivement [vivmɑ̃] *adv* quickly, briskly; (*répliquer*) sharply; (*sentir*) keenly; (*regretter*) deeply; **v. demain!** roll on tomorrow!, I can hardly wait for tomorrow!; **v. que** (+ *sub*) I'll be glad when.
vivier [vivje] *nm* fish pond.
vivifier [vivifje] *vt* to invigorate.
vivisection [vivisɛksjɔ̃] *nf* vivisection.
vivre* [vivr] **1** *vi* to live; **elle vit encore** she's still alive *ou* living; **faire v.** (*famille etc*) to

support; **v. vieux** to live to be old; **difficile/facile à v.** hard/easy to get on with; **manière de v.** way of life; **v. de** (*fruits etc*) to live on; (*travail etc*) to live by; **avoir de quoi v.** to have enough to live on; **vivent les vacances!** hurray for the holidays!; – *vt* (*vie*) to live; (*aventure, époque*) to live through; (*éprouver*) to experience. **2** *nmpl* food, supplies. ◆**vivoter** *vi* to jog along, get by.

vlan! [vlɑ̃] *int* bang!, wham!

vocable [vɔkabl] *nm* term, word.

vocabulaire [vɔkabylɛr] *nm* vocabulary.

vocal, -aux [vɔkal, -o] *a* (*cordes, musique*) vocal.

vocation [vɔkɑsjɔ̃] *nf* vocation, calling.

vociférer [vɔsifere] *vti* to shout angrily. ◆**vocifération** *nf* angry shout.

vodka [vɔdka] *nf* vodka.

vœu, -x [vø] *nm* (*souhait*) wish; (*promesse*) vow; **faire le v. de faire** to (make a) vow to do; **tous mes vœux!** (my) best wishes!

vogue [vɔg] *nf* fashion, vogue; **en v.** in fashion, in vogue.

voici [vwasi] *prép* here is, this is; *pl* here are, these are; **me v.** here I am; **me v. triste** I'm sad now; **v. dix ans/***etc* ten years/*etc* ago; **v. dix ans que** it's ten years since.

voie [vwa] *nf* (*route*) road; (*rails*) track, line; (*partie de route*) lane; (*chemin*) way; (*moyen*) means, way; (*de communication*) line; (*diplomatique*) channels; (*quai*) *Rail* platform; **en v. de** in the process of; **en v. de développement** (*pays*) developing; **v. publique** public highway; **v. navigable** waterway; **v. sans issue** cul-de-sac, dead end; **préparer la v.** *Fig* to pave the way; **sur la (bonne) v.** on the right track.

voilà [vwala] *prép* there is, that is; *pl* there are, those are; **les v.** there they are; **v., j'arrive!** all right, I'm coming!; **le v. parti** he has left now; **v. dix ans/***etc* ten years/*etc* ago; **v. dix ans que** it's ten years since.

voile[1] [vwal] *nm* (*étoffe qui cache, coiffure etc*) & *Fig* veil. ◆**voilage** *nm* net curtain. ◆**voil/er**[1] *vt* (*visage, vérité etc*) to veil; – **se v.** *vpr* (*personne*) to wear a veil; (*ciel, regard*) to cloud over. ◆**—é** *a* (*femme, allusion*) veiled; (*terne*) dull; (*photo*) hazy.

voile[2] [vwal] *nf* (*de bateau*) sail; (*activité*) sailing; **bateau à voiles** sailing boat, *Am* sailboat; **faire de la v.** to sail, go sailing. ◆**voilier** *nm* sailing ship; (*de plaisance*) sailing boat, *Am* sailboat. ◆**voilure** *nf Nau* sails.

voiler[2] [vwale] *vt*, – **se v.** *vpr* (*roue*) to buckle.

voir* [vwar] *vti* to see; **faire** *ou* **laisser v. qch** to show sth; **fais v.** let me see, show me; **v. qn faire** to see s.o. do *ou* doing; **voyons!** (*sois raisonnable*) come on!; **y v. clair** (*comprendre*) to see clearly; **je ne peux pas la v.** (*supporter*) *Fam* I can't stand (the sight of) her; **v. venir** (*attendre*) to wait and see; **on verra bien** (*attendons*) we'll see; **ça n'a rien à v. avec** that's got nothing to do with; – **se v.** *vpr* to see oneself; (*se fréquenter*) to see each other; (*objet, attitude etc*) to be seen; (*reprise, tache*) to show; **ça se voit** that's obvious.

voire [vwar] *adv* indeed.

voirie [vwari] *nf* (*enlèvement des ordures*) refuse collection; (*routes*) public highways.

voisin, -ine [vwazɛ̃, -in] *a* (*pays, village etc*) neighbouring; (*maison, pièce*) next (**de** to); (*idée, état etc*) similar (**de** to); – *nmf* neighbour. ◆**voisinage** *nm* (*quartier, voisins*) neighbourhood; (*proximité*) proximity. ◆**voisiner** *vi* **v. avec** to be side by side with.

voiture [vwatyr] *nf Aut* car; *Rail* carriage, coach, *Am* car; (*charrette*) cart; **v. (à cheval)** (horse-drawn) carriage; **v. de course/de tourisme** racing/private car; **v. d'enfant** pram, *Am* baby carriage; **en v.!** *Rail* all aboard!

voix [vwa] *nf* voice; (*suffrage*) vote; **à v. basse** in a whisper; **à portée de v.** within earshot; **avoir v. au chapitre** *Fig* to have a say.

vol [vɔl] *nm* **1** (*d'avion, d'oiseau*) flight; (*groupe d'oiseaux*) flock, flight; **v. libre** hang gliding; **v. à voile** gliding. **2** (*délit*) theft; (*hold-up*) robbery; **v. à l'étalage** shoplifting; **c'est du v.!** (*trop cher*) it's daylight robbery!

volage [vɔlaʒ] *a* flighty, fickle.

volaille [vɔlɑj] *nf* **la v.** (*oiseaux*) poultry; **une v.** (*oiseau*) a fowl. ◆**volailler** *nm* poulterer.

volatile [vɔlatil] *nm* (*oiseau domestique*) fowl.

volatiliser (se) [səvɔlatilize] *vpr* (*disparaître*) to vanish (into thin air).

vol-au-vent [vɔlovɑ̃] *nm inv Culin* vol-au-vent.

volcan [vɔlkɑ̃] *nm* volcano. ◆**volcanique** *a* volcanic.

voler [vɔle] **1** *vi* (*oiseau, avion etc*) to fly; (*courir*) *Fig* to rush. **2** *vt* (*dérober*) to steal (**à** from); **v. qn** to rob s.o.; – *vi* to steal. ◆**volant 1** *a* (*tapis etc*) flying; **feuille volante** loose sheet. **2** *nm Aut* (steering) wheel; (*objet*) *Sp* shuttlecock; (*de jupe*) flounce. ◆**volée** *nf* flight; (*groupe d'oiseaux*) flock, flight; (*de coups, flèches etc*) volley; (*suite de* *coups*) thrashing; **lancer à toute v.** to throw as hard as one can; **sonner à toute v.** to peal *ou* ring out. ◆**voleter** *vi* to flutter. ◆**voleur, -euse** *nmf* thief; **au v.!** stop thief!; – *a* thieving.

volet [vɔlɛ] *nm* **1** (*de fenêtre*) shutter. **2** (*de programme, reportage etc*) section, part.

volière [vɔljɛr] *nf* aviary.

volley(-ball) [vɔlɛ(bol)] *nm* volleyball. ◆**volleyeur, -euse** *nmf* volleyball player.

volonté [vɔlɔ̃te] *nf* (*faculté, intention*) will; (*désir*) wish; *Phil Psy* free will; **elle a de la v.** she has willpower; **bonne v.** goodwill; **mauvaise v.** ill will; **à v.** at will; (*quantité*) as much as desired. ◆**volontaire** *a* (*délibéré, qui agit librement*) voluntary; (*opiniâtre*) wilful, *Am* willful; – *nmf* volunteer. ◆**volontairement** *adv* voluntarily; (*exprès*) deliberately. ◆**volontiers** [-ɔ̃tje] *adv* willingly, gladly; (*habituellement*) readily; **v.!** (*oui*) I'd love to!

volt [vɔlt] *nm Él* volt. ◆**voltage** *nm* voltage.

volte-face [vɔltəfas] *nf inv* about turn, *Am* about face; **faire v.-face** to turn round.

voltige [vɔltiʒ] *nf* acrobatics.

voltiger [vɔltiʒe] *vi* to flutter.

volubile [vɔlybil] *a* (*bavard*) loquacious, voluble.

volume [vɔlym] *nm* (*capacité, intensité, tome*) volume. ◆**volumineux, -euse** *a* bulky, voluminous.

volupté [vɔlypte] *nf* sensual pleasure. ◆**voluptueux, -euse** *a* voluptuous.

vom/ir [vɔmir] *vt* to vomit, bring up; (*exécrer*) *Fig* to loathe; – *vi* to vomit, be sick. ◆**—i** *nm Fam* vomit. ◆**—issement** *nm* (*action*) vomiting. ◆**vomitif, -ive** *a Fam* nauseating.

vont [vɔ̃] *voir* **aller 1**.

vorace [vɔras] *a* (*appétit, lecteur etc*) voracious.

vos [vo] *voir* **votre**.

vote [vɔt] *nm* (*action*) vote, voting; (*suffrage*) vote; (*de loi*) passing; **bureau de v.** polling station. ◆**voter** *vi* to vote; – *vt* (*loi*) to pass; (*crédits*) to vote. ◆**votant, -ante** *nmf* voter.

votre, *pl* **vos** [vɔtr, vo] *a poss* your. ◆**vôtre** *pron poss* **le** *ou* **la v., les vôtres** yours; **à la v.!** (*toast*) cheers!; – *nmpl* **les vôtres** (*parents etc*) your (own) people.

vouer [vwe] *vt* (*promettre*) to vow (**à** to); (*consacrer*) to dedicate (**à** to); (*condamner*) to doom (**à** to); **se v. à** to dedicate oneself to.

vouloir* [vulwar] *vt* to want (**faire** to do); **je veux qu'il parte** I want him to go; **v. dire** to mean (**que** that); **je voudrais rester** I'd like to stay; **je voudrais un pain** I'd like a loaf of bread; **voulez-vous me suivre** will you follow me; **si tu veux** if you like *ou* wish; **en v. à qn d'avoir fait qch** to hold it against s.o. for doing sth; **l'usage veut que . . .** (+ *sub*) custom requires that . . . ; **v. du bien à qn** to wish s.o. well; **je veux bien** I don't mind (**faire** doing); **que voulez-vous!** (*résignation*) what can you expect!; **sans le v.** unintentionally; **ça ne veut pas bouger** it won't move; **ne pas v. de qch/de qn** not to want sth/s.o.; **veuillez attendre** kindly wait. ◆**voulu** *a* (*requis*) required; (*délibéré*) deliberate, intentional.

vous [vu] *pron* **1** (*sujet, complément direct*) you; **v. êtes** you are; **il v. connaît** he knows you. **2** (*complément indirect*) (to) you; **il v. l'a donné** he gave it to you, he gave you it. **3** (*réfléchi*) yourself, *pl* yourselves; **v. v. lavez** you wash yourself; you wash yourselves. **4** (*réciproque*) each other; **v. v. aimez** you love each other. ◆**v.-même** *pron* yourself. ◆**v.-mêmes** *pron pl* yourselves.

voûte [vut] *nf* (*plafond*) vault; (*porche*) arch(way). ◆**voûté** *a* (*personne*) bent, stooped.

vouvoyer [vuvwaje] *vt* to address formally (*using vous*).

voyage [vwajaʒ] *nm* trip, journey; (*par mer*) voyage; **aimer les voyages** to like travelling; **faire un v., partir en v.** to go on a trip; **être en v.** to be (away) travelling; **de v.** (*compagnon etc*) travelling-; **bon v.!** have a pleasant trip!; **v. de noces** honeymoon; **v. organisé** (package) tour. ◆**voyager** *vi* to travel. ◆**voyageur, -euse** *nmf* traveller; (*passager*) passenger; **v. de commerce** commercial traveller. ◆**voyagiste** *nm* tour operator.

voyant [vwajɑ̃] **1** *a* gaudy, loud. **2** *nm* (*signal*) (warning) light; (*d'appareil électrique*) pilot light.

voyante [vwajɑ̃t] *nf* clairvoyant.

voyelle [vwajɛl] *nf* vowel.

voyeur, -euse [vwajœr, -øz] *nmf* peeping Tom, voyeur.

voyou [vwaju] *nm* hooligan, hoodlum.

vrac (en) [ɑ̃vrak] *adv* (*en désordre*) haphazardly; (*au poids*) loose, unpackaged.

vrai [vrɛ] *a* true; (*réel*) real; (*authentique*) genuine; – *adv* **dire v.** to be right (in what one says); – *nm* (*vérité*) truth. ◆**—ment** *adv* really.

vraisemblable [vrɛsɑ̃blabl] *a* (*probable*) likely, probable; (*plausible*) plausible. ◆**vraisemblablement** *adv* probably.

◆**vraisemblance** *nf* likelihood; plausibility.

vrille [vrij] *nf* **1** (*outil*) gimlet. **2** *Av* (tail)spin.

vromb/ir [vrɔ̃bir] *vi* to hum. ◆**—issement** *nm* hum(ming).

vu [vy] **1** *voir* **voir**; – *a* **bien vu** well thought of; **mal vu** frowned upon. **2** *prép* in view of; **vu que** seeing that.

vue [vy] *nf* (*spectacle*) sight; (*sens*) (eye)sight; (*panorama, photo, idée*) view; **en v.** (*proche*) in sight; (*en évidence*) on view; (*personne*) *Fig* in the public eye; **avoir en v.** to have in mind; **à v.** (*tirer*) on sight; (*payable*) at sight; **à première v.** at first sight; **de v.** (*connaître*) by sight; **en v. de faire** with a view to doing.

vulgaire [vylgɛr] *a* (*grossier*) vulgar, coarse; (*ordinaire*) common. ◆**—ment** *adv* vulgarly, coarsely; (*appeler*) commonly. ◆**vulgariser** *vt* to popularize. ◆**vulgarité** *nf* vulgarity, coarseness.

vulnérable [vylnerabl] *a* vulnerable. ◆**vulnérabilité** *nf* vulnerability.

W

W, w [dubləve] *nm* W, w.

wagon [vagɔ̃] *nm Rail* (*de voyageurs*) carriage, coach, *Am* car; (*de marchandises*) wag(g)on, truck, *Am* freight car. ◆**w.-lit** *nm* (*pl* **wagons-lits**) sleeping car, sleeper. ◆**w.-restaurant** *nm* (*pl* **wagons-restaurants**) dining car, diner. ◆**wagonnet** *nm* (small) wagon *ou* truck.

wallon, -onne [walɔ̃, -ɔn] *a & nmf* Walloon.

waters [watɛr] *nmpl* toilet.

watt [wat] *nm Él* watt.

w-c [(dublə)vese] *nmpl* toilet.

week-end [wikɛnd] *nm* weekend.

western [wɛstɛrn] *nm Cin* western.

whisky, *pl* **-ies** [wiski] *nm* whisky, *Am* whiskey.

X

X, x [iks] *nm* X, x; **rayon X** X-ray.

xénophobe [ksenɔfɔb] *a* xenophobic; – *nmf* xenophobe. ◆**xénophobie** *nf* xenophobia.

xérès [gzerɛs] *nm* sherry.

xylophone [ksilɔfɔn] *nm* xylophone.

Y

Y, y¹ [igrɛk] *nm* Y, y.

y² [i] **1** *adv* there; (*dedans*) in it; *pl* in them; (*dessus*) on it; *pl* on them; **elle y vivra** she'll live there; **j'y entrai** I entered (it); **allons-y** let's go; **j'y suis!** (*je comprends*) now I get it!; **je n'y suis pour rien** I have nothing to do with it, that's nothing to do with me. **2** *pron* (= *à cela*) **j'y pense** I think of it; **je m'y attendais** I was expecting it; **ça y est!** that's it!

yacht [jɔt] *nm* yacht.

yaourt [jaur(t)] *nm* yog(h)urt.

yeux [jø] *voir* **œil**.

yiddish [(j)idiʃ] *nm & a* Yiddish.

yoga [jɔga] *nm* yoga.

yog(h)ourt [jɔgur(t)] *voir* **yaourt**.

Yougoslavie [jugɔslavi] *nf* Yugoslavia. ◆**yougoslave** *a & nmf* Yugoslav(ian).

yo-yo [jojo] *nm inv* yoyo.

Z

Z, z [zɛd] *nm* Z, z.
zèbre [zɛbr] *nm* zebra. ◆**zébré** *a* striped, streaked (de with).
zèle [zɛl] *nm* zeal; **faire du z.** to overdo it. ◆**zélé** *a* zealous.
zénith [zenit] *nm* zenith.
zéro [zero] *nm* (*chiffre*) nought, zero; (*dans un numéro*) 0 [əʊ]; (*température*) zero; (*rien*) nothing; (*personne*) *Fig* nobody, nonentity; **deux buts à z.** *Fb* two nil, *Am* two zero; **partir de z.** to start from scratch.
zeste [zɛst] *nm* **un z. de citron** (a piece of) lemon peel.
zézayer [zezeje] *vi* to lisp.
zibeline [ziblin] *nf* (*animal*) sable.
zigzag [zigzag] *nm* zigzag; **en z.** (*route etc*) zigzag(ging). ◆**zigzaguer** *vi* to zigzag.
zinc [zɛ̃g] *nm* (*métal*) zinc; (*comptoir*) *Fam* bar.
zizanie [zizani] *nf* discord.
zodiaque [zɔdjak] *nm* zodiac.
zona [zona] *nm Méd* shingles.
zone [zon] *nf* zone, area; (*domaine*) *Fig* sphere; (*faubourgs misérables*) shanty town; **z. bleue** restricted parking zone; **z. industrielle** trading estate, *Am* industrial park.
zoo [zo(o)] *nm* zoo. ◆**zoologie** [zɔɔlɔʒi] *nf* zoology. ◆**zoologique** *a* zoological; **jardin** *ou* **parc z.** zoo.
zoom [zum] *nm* (*objectif*) zoom lens.
zut! [zyt] *int Fam* bother!, heck!

French verb conjugations

REGULAR VERBS

	-ER Verbs	-IR Verbs	-RE Verbs
Infinitive	*donn/er*	*fin/ir*	*vend/re*
1 Present	je donne tu donnes il donne nous donnons vous donnez ils donnent	je finis tu finis il finit nous finissons vous finissez ils finissent	je vends tu vends il vend nous vendons vous vendez ils vendent
2 Imperfect	je donnais tu donnais il donnait nous donnions vous donniez ils donnaient	je finissais tu finissais il finissait nous finissions vous finissiez ils finissaient	je vendais tu vendais il vendait nous vendions vous vendiez ils vendaient
3 Past historic	je donnai tu donnas il donna nous donnâmes vous donnâtes ils donnèrent	je finis tu finis il finit nous finîmes vous finîtes ils finirent	je vendis tu vendis il vendit nous vendîmes vous vendîtes ils vendirent
4 Future	je donnerai tu donneras il donnera nous donnerons vous donnerez ils donneront	je finirai tu finiras il finira nous finirons vous finirez ils finiront	je vendrai tu vendras il vendra nous vendrons vous vendrez ils vendront
5 Subjunctive	je donne tu donnes il donne nous donnions vous donniez ils donnent	je finisse tu finisses il finisse nous finissions vous finissiez ils finissent	je vende tu vendes il vende nous vendions vous vendiez ils vendent
6 Imperative	donne donnons donnez	finis finissons finissez	vends vendons vendez
7 Present participle	donnant	finissant	vendant
8 Past participle	donné	fini	vendu

SPELLING ANOMALIES OF -ER VERBS

Verbs in **-ger** (e.g. **manger**) take an extra **e** before endings beginning with **o** or **a**: *Present* je mange, nous mangeons; *Imperfect* je mangeais, nous mangions; *Past historic* je mangeai, nous mangeâmes; *Present participle* mangeant. Verbs in **-cer** (e.g. **commencer**) change **c** to **ç** before endings beginning with **o** or **a**: *Present* je commence, nous commençons; *Imperfect* je commençais, nous commencions; *Past historic* je commençai, nous commençâmes; *Present participle* commençant. Verbs containing mute **e** in their penultimate syllable fall into two groups. In the first (e.g. **mener**, **peser**, **lever**), **e** becomes **è** before an unpronounced syllable in the present and subjunctive, and in the future and conditional tenses (e.g. je mène, ils mèneront). The second group contains most verbs ending in **-eler** and **-eter** (e.g. **appeler**, **jeter**). These verbs change **l** to **ll** and **t** to **tt** before an unpronounced syllable (e.g. j'appelle, ils appelleront; je jette, ils jetteront). However, the following verbs in **-eler** and **-eter** fall into the first group in which e changes to **è** before mute **e** (e.g. je modèle, ils modèleront; j'achète, ils achèteront): **celer**, **ciseler**, **démanteler**, **geler**, **marteler**, **modeler**, **peler**; **acheter**, **crocheter**, **fureter**, **haleter**. Derived verbs (e.g. **dégeler**, **racheter**) are conjugated in the same way. Verbs containing **e** acute in their penultimate syllable change **é** to **è** before the unpronounced endings of the present and subjunctive only (e.g. je cède but je céderai). Verbs in **-yer** (e.g. **essuyer**) change **y** to **i** before an unpronounced syllable in the present and subjunctive, and in the future and conditional tenses (e.g. j'essuie, ils essuieront). In verbs in **-ayer** (e.g. **balayer**), **y** may be retained before mute **e** (e.g. je balaie or balaye, ils balaieront or balayeront).

IRREGULAR VERBS

Listed below are those verbs considered to be the most useful. Forms and tenses not given are fully derivable. Note that the endings of the past historic fall into three categories, the 'a' and 'i' categories shown at *donner*, and at *finir* and *vendre*, and the 'u' category which has the following endings: -us, -ut, -ûmes, -ûtes, -urent. Most of the verbs listed below form their past historic with 'u'. The imperfect may usually be formed by adding -ais, -ait, -ions, -iez, -aient to the stem of the first person plural of the present tense, e.g. 'je buvais' etc may be derived from 'nous buvons' (stem 'buv-' and ending '-ons'); similarly, the present participle may generally be formed by substituting -ant for -ons (e.g. buvant). The future may usually be formed by adding -ai, -as, -a, -ons, -ez, -ont to the infinitive or to an infinitive without final 'e' where the ending is -re (e.g. conduire). The imperative usually has the same forms as the second persons singular and plural and first person plural of the present tense.

1 = Present 2 = Imperfect 3 = Past historic 4 = Future
5 = Subjunctive 6 = Imperative 7 = Present participle
8 = Past participle n = nous v = vous †verbs conjugated with **être** only.

abattre *like* **battre**

absoudre 1 j'absous, n absolvons 2 j'absolvais
3 j'absolus (*rarely used*) 5 j'absolve 7 absolvant
8 absous, absoute

†s'abstenir *like* **tenir**

abstraire 1 j'abstrais, n abstrayons 2 j'abstrayais 3 *none* 5 j'abstraie
7 abstrayant 8 abstrait

accourir *like* **courir**

accroître *like* **croître** *except* 8 accru

accueillir *like* **cueillir**

acquérir 1 j'acquiers, n acquérons 2 j'acquérais 3 j'acquis
4 j'acquerrai 5 j'acquière 7 acquérant 8 acquis

adjoindre *like* **atteindre**

admettre *like* **mettre**

†aller 1 je vais, tu vas, il va, n allons, v allez, ils vont 4 j'irai
5 j'aille, nous allions, ils aillent 6 va, allons, allez (*but note* vas-y)

apercevoir *like* **recevoir**

apparaître *like* **connaître**

appartenir *like* **tenir**

apprendre *like* **prendre**

asseoir 1 j'assieds, n asseyons, ils asseyent 2 j'asseyais 3 j'assis
4 j'assiérai 5 j'asseye 7 asseyant 8 assis

astreindre	*like* **atteindre**
atteindre	1 j'atteins, n atteignons, ils atteignent 2 j'atteignais 3 j'atteignis 4 j'atteindrai 5 j'atteigne 7 atteignant 8 atteint
avoir	1 j'ai, tu as, il a, n avons, v avez, ils ont 2 j'avais 3 j'eus 4 j'aurai 5 j'aie, il ait, n ayons, ils aient 6 aie, ayons, ayez 7 ayant 8 eu
battre	1 je bats, n battons 5 je batte
boire	1 je bois, n buvons, ils boivent 2 je buvais 3 je bus 5 je boive, n buvions 7 buvant 8 bu
bouillir	1 je bous, n bouillons, ils bouillent 2 je bouillais 3 *not used* 5 je bouille 7 bouillant
braire	(*defective*) 1 il brait, ils braient 4 il braira, ils brairont
combattre	*like* **battre**
commettre	*like* **mettre**
comparaître	*like* **connaître**
comprendre	*like* **prendre**
compromettre	*like* **mettre**
concevoir	*like* **recevoir**
conclure	1 je conclus, n concluons, ils concluent 5 je conclue
concourir	*like* **courir**
conduire	1 je condùis, n conduisons 3 je conduisis 5 je conduise 8 conduit
connaître	1 je connais, il connaît, n connaissons 3 je connus 5 je connaisse 7 connaissant 8 connu
conquérir	*like* **acquérir**
consentir	*like* **mentir**
construire	*like* **conduire**
contenir	*like* **tenir**
contraindre	*like* **atteindre**
contredire	*like* **dire** *except* 1 v contredisez
convaincre	*like* **vaincre**
convenir	*like* **tenir**
corrompre	*like* **rompre**
coudre	1 je couds, n cousons, ils cousent 3 je cousis 5 je couse 7 cousant 8 cousu
courir	1 je cours, n courons 3 je courus 4 je courrai 5 je coure 8 couru
couvrir	1 je couvre, n couvrons 2 je couvrais 5 je couvre 8 couvert
craindre	*like* **atteindre**
croire	1 je crois, n croyons, ils croient 2 je croyais 3 je crus 5 je croie, n croyions 7 croyant 8 cru
croître	1 je crois, il croît, n croissons 2 je croissais 3 je crûs 5 je croisse 7 croissant 8 crû, crue
cueillir	1 je cueille, n cueillons 2 je cueillais 4 je cueillerai 5 je cueille 7 cueillant
cuire	1 je cuis, n cuisons 2 je cuisais 3 je cuisis 5 je cuise 7 cuisant 8 cuit
débattre	*like* **battre**
décevoir	*like* **recevoir**
découvrir	*like* **couvrir**
décrire	*like* **écrire**
décroître	*like* **croître** *except* 8 décru
déduire	*like* **conduire**
défaillir	1 je défaille, n défaillons 2 je défaillais 3 je défaillis 5 je défaille 7 défaillant 8 défailli

défaire	*like* **faire**
dépeindre	*like* **atteindre**
déplaire	*like* **plaire**
déteindre	*like* **atteindre**
détenir	*like* **tenir**
détruire	*like* **conduire**
†devenir	*like* **tenir**
devoir	1 je dois, n devons, ils doivent 2 je devais 3 je dus 4 je devrai 5 je doive, n devions 6 *not used* 7 devant 8 dû, due, *pl* dus, dues
dire	1 je dis, n disons, v dites 2 je disais 3 je dis 5 je dise 7 disant 8 dit
disparaître	*like* **connaître**
dissoudre	*like* **absoudre**
distraire	*like* **abstraire**
dormir	*like* **mentir**
†échoir	(*defective*) 1 il échoit 3 il échut, ils échurent 4 il échoira 7 échéant 8 échu
écrire	1 j'écris, n écrivons 2 j'écrivais 3 j'écrivis 5 j'écrive 7 écrivant 8 écrit
élire	*like* **lire**
émettre	*like* **mettre**
émouvoir	*like* **mouvoir** *except* 8 ému
encourir	*like* **courir**
endormir	*like* **mentir**
enduire	*like* **conduire**
enfreindre	*like* **atteindre**
†s'enfuir	*like* **fuir**
†s'ensuivre	*like* **suivre** (*but third person only*)
entreprendre	*like* **prendre**
entretenir	*like* **tenir**
entrevoir	*like* **voir**
entrouvrir	*like* **couvrir**
envoyer	4 j'enverrai
†s'éprendre	*like* **prendre**
éteindre	*like* **atteindre**
être	1 je suis, tu es, il est, n sommes, v êtes, ils sont 2 j'étais 3 je fus 4 je serai 5 je sois, n soyons, ils soient 6 sois, soyons, soyez 7 étant 8 été
exclure	*like* **conclure**
extraire	*like* **abstraire**
faillir	(*defective*) 3 je faillis 4 je faillirai 8 failli
faire	1 je fais, n faisons, v faites, ils font 2 je faisais 3 je fis 4 je ferai 5 je fasse 7 faisant 8 fait
falloir	(*impersonal*) 1 il faut 2 il fallait 3 il fallut 4 il faudra 5 il faille 6 *none* 7 *none* 8 fallu
feindre	*like* **atteindre**
foutre	1 je fous, n foutons 2 je foutais 3 *none* 5 je foute 7 foutant 8 foutu
frire	(*defective*) 1 je fris, tu fris, il frit 4 je frirai (*rare*) 6 fris (*rare*) 8 frit (*for other persons and tenses use* faire frire)
fuir	1 je fuis, n fuyons, ils fuient 2 je fuyais 3 je fuis 5 je fuie 7 fuyant 8 fui
haïr	1 je hais, il hait, n haïssons
inclure	*like* **conclure**
induire	*like* **conduire**
inscrire	*like* **écrire**

instruire	*like* **conduire**
interdire	*like* **dire** *except* 1 v interdisez
interrompre	*like* **rompre**
intervenir	*like* **tenir**
introduire	*like* **conduire**
joindre	*like* **atteindre**
lire	1 je lis, n lisons 2 je lisais 3 je lus 5 je lise 7 lisant 8 lu
luire	*like* **nuire**
maintenir	*like* **tenir**
maudire	1 je maudis, n maudissons 2 je maudissais 3 je maudis 4 je maudirai 5 je maudisse 7 maudissant 8 maudit
méconnaître	*like* **connaître**
médire	*like* **dire** *except* 1 v médisez
mentir	1 je mens, n mentons 2 je mentais 5 je mente 7 mentant
mettre	1 je mets, n mettons 2 je mettais 3 je mis 5 je mette 7 mettant 8 mis
moudre	1 je mouds, n moulons 2 je moulais 3 je moulus 5 je moule 7 moulant 8 moulu
†mourir	1 je meurs, n mourons, ils meurent 2 je mourais 3 je mourus 4 je mourrai 5 je meure, n mourions 7 mourant 8 mort
mouvoir	1 je meus, n mouvons, ils meuvent 2 je mouvais 3 je mus (*rare*) 4 je mouvrai 5 je meuve, n mouvions 8 mû, mue, *pl* mus, mues
†naître	1 je nais, il naît, n naissons 2 je naissais 3 je naquis 4 je naîtrai 5 je naisse 7 naissant 8 né
nuire	1 je nuis, n nuisons 2 je nuisais 3 je nuisis 5 je nuise 7 nuisant 8 nui
obtenir	*like* **tenir**
offrir	*like* **couvrir**
omettre	*like* **mettre**
ouvrir	*like* **couvrir**
paître	(*defective*) 1 il paît 2 il paissait 3 *none* 4 il paîtra 5 il paisse 7 paissant 8 *none*
paraître	*like* **connaître**
parcourir	*like* **courir**
†partir	*like* **mentir**
†parvenir	*like* **tenir**
peindre	*like* **atteindre**
percevoir	*like* **recevoir**
permettre	*like* **mettre**
plaindre	*like* **atteindre**
plaire	1 je plais, n plaisons 2 je plaisais 3 je plus 5 je plaise 7 plaisant 8 plu
pleuvoir	(*impersonal*) 1 il pleut 2 il pleuvait 3 il plut 4 il pleuvra 5 il pleuve 6 *none* 7 pleuvant 8 plu
poursuivre	*like* **suivre**
pourvoir	*like* **voir** *except* 4 je pourvoirai
pouvoir	1 je peux *or* je puis, tu peux, il peut, n pouvons, ils peuvent 2 je pouvais 3 je pus 4 je pourrai 5 je puisse 6 *not used* 7 pouvant 8 pu
prédire	*like* **dire** *except* 1 v prédisez
prendre	1 je prends, n prenons, ils prennent 2 je prenais 3 je pris 5 je prenne 7 prenant 8 pris
prescrire	*like* **écrire**
pressentir	*like* **mentir**

prévenir *like* **tenir**
prévoir *like* **voir** *except* 4 je prévoirai
produire *like* **conduire**
promettre *like* **mettre**
promouvoir *like* **mouvoir** *except* 8 promu
proscrire *like* **écrire**
†provenir *like* **tenir**
rabattre *like* **battre**
rasseoir *like* **asseoir**
recevoir 1 je reçois, n recevons, ils reçoivent 2 je recevais 3 je reçus 4 je recevrai 5 je reçoive, n recevions, ils reçoivent 7 recevant 8 reçu
reconnaître *like* **connaître**
reconduire *like* **conduire**
reconstruire *like* **conduire**
recoudre *like* **coudre**
recourir *like* **courir**
recouvrir *like* **couvrir**
recueillir *like* **cueillir**
†redevenir *like* **tenir**
redire *like* **dire**
réduire *like* **conduire**
refaire *like* **faire**
rejoindre *like* **atteindre**
relire *like* **lire**
remettre *like* **mettre**
†renaître *like* **naître**
rendormir *like* **mentir**
renvoyer *like* **envoyer**
†repartir *like* **mentir**
repentir *like* **mentir**
reprendre *like* **prendre**
reproduire *like* **conduire**
résoudre 1 je résous, n résolvons 2 je résolvais 3 je résolus 5 je résolve 7 résolvant 8 résolu
ressentir *like* **mentir**
ressortir *like* **mentir**
restreindre *like* **atteindre**
retenir *like* **tenir**
†revenir *like* **tenir**
revêtir *like* **vêtir**
revivre *like* **vivre**
revoir *like* **voir**
rire 1 je ris, n rions 2 je riais 3 je ris 5 je rie, n riions 7 riant 8 ri
rompre *regular except* 1 il rompt
rouvrir *like* **couvrir**
satisfaire *like* **faire**
savoir 1 je sais, n savons, il savent 2 je savais 3 je sus 4 je saurai 5 je sache 6 sache, sachons, sachez 7 sachant 8 su
séduire *like* **conduire**
sentir *like* **mentir**
servir *like* **mentir**
sortir *like* **mentir**
souffrir *like* **couvrir**
soumettre *like* **mettre**
sourire *like* **rire**

souscrire	*like* **écrire**
soustraire	*like* **abstraire**
soutenir	*like* **tenir**
†se souvenir	*like* **tenir**
subvenir	*like* **tenir**
suffire	1 je suffis, n suffisons 2 je suffisais 3 je suffis 5 je suffise 7 suffisant 8 suffi
suivre	1 je suis, n suivons 2 je suivais 3 je suivis 5 je suive 7 suivant 8 suivi
surprendre	*like* **prendre**
†survenir	*like* **tenir**
survivre	*like* **vivre**
taire	1 je tais, n taisons 2 je taisais 3 je tus 5 je taise 7 taisant 8 tu
teindre	*like* **atteindre**
tenir	1 je tiens, n tenons, ils tiennent 2 je tenais 3 je tins, tu tins, il tint, n tînmes, v tîntes, ils tinrent 4 je tiendrai 5 je tienne 7 tenant 8 tenu
traduire	*like* **conduire**
traire	*like* **abstraire**
transcrire	*like* **écrire**
transmettre	*like* **mettre**
transparaître	*like* **connaître**
tressaillir	*like* **défaillir**
vaincre	1 je vaincs, il vainc, n vainquons 2 je vainquais 3 je vainquis 5 je vainque 7 vainquant 8 vaincu
valoir	1 je vaux, n valons 2 je valais 3 je valus 4 je vaudrai 5 je vaille 6 *not used* 7 valant 8 valu
†venir	*like* **tenir**
vêtir	1 je vêts, n vêtons 2 je vêtais 5 je vête 7 vêtant 8 vêtu
vivre	1 je vis, n vivons 2 je vivais 3 je vécus 5 je vive 7 vivant 8 vécu
voir	1 je vois, n voyons 2 je voyais 3 je vis 4 je verrai 5 je voie, n voyions 7 voyant 8 vu
vouloir	1 je veux, n voulons, ils veulent 2 je voulais 3 je voulus 4 je voudrai 5 je veuille 6 veuille, veuillons, veuillez 7 voulant 8 voulu.

Verbes anglais irréguliers

Infinitif	**Prétérit**	**Participe passé**
arise	arose	arisen
be	was, were	been
bear	bore	borne
beat	beat	beaten
become	became	become
begin	began	begun
bend	bent	bent
bet	bet, betted	bet, betted
bid	bade, bid	bidden, bid
bind	bound	bound
bite	bit	bitten
bleed	bled	bled
blow	blew	blown
break	broke	broken
breed	bred	bred

bring	brought	brought
broadcast	broadcast	broadcast
build	built	built
burn	burnt, burned	burnt, burned
burst	burst	burst
buy	bought	bought
cast	cast	cast
catch	caught	caught
choose	chose	chosen
cling	clung	clung
come	came	come
cost	cost	cost
creep	crept	crept
cut	cut	cut
deal	dealt	dealt
dig	dug	dug
dive	dived, *Am* dove	dived
do	did	done
draw	drew	drawn
dream	dreamed, dreamt	dreamed, dreamt
drink	drank	drunk
drive	drove	driven
dwell	dwelt	dwelt
eat	ate [et, *Am* eɪt]	eaten
fall	fell	fallen
feed	fed	fed
feel	felt	felt
fight	fought	fought
find	found	found
fling	flung	flung
fly	flew	flown
forbid	forbad(e)	forbidden
forecast	forecast	forecast
foresee	foresaw	foreseen
forget	forgot	forgotten
forgive	forgave	forgiven
forsake	forsook (*rare*)	forsaken
freeze	froze	frozen
get	got	got, *Am* gotten
give	gave	given
go	went	gone
grind	ground	ground
grow	grew	grown
hang	hung, hanged	hung, hanged
have	had	had
hear	heard	heard
hide	hid	hidden
hit	hit	hit
hold	held	held
hurt	hurt	hurt
keep	kept	kept
kneel	knelt, kneeled	knelt, kneeled
know	knew	known
lay	laid	laid
lead	led	led
lean	leant, leaned	leant, leaned
leap	leapt, leaped	leapt, leaped

learn	learnt, learned	learnt, learned
leave	left	left
lend	lent	lent
let	let	let
lie	lay	lain
light	lit, lighted	lit, lighted
lose	lost	lost
make	made	made
mean	meant	meant
meet	met	met
mislay	mislaid	mislaid
mislead	misled	misled
misunderstand	misunderstood	misunderstood
mow	mowed	mown, mowed
overcome	overcame	overcome
pay	paid	paid
put	put	put
quit	quit, quitted	quit, quitted
read	read [red]	read [red]
rid	rid	rid
ride	rode	ridden
ring	rang	rung
rise	rose	risen
run	ran	run
saw	sawed	sawn, sawed
say	said	said
see	saw	seen
seek	sought	sought
sell	sold	sold
send	sent	sent
set	set	set
sew	sewed	sewn, sewed
shake	shook	shaken
shed	shed	shed
shine	shone ([ʃɒn, *Am* ʃəun])	shone ([ʃɒn, *Am* ʃəun])
shoot	shot	shot
show	showed	shown, showed
shrink	shrank	shrunk, shrunken
shut	shut	shut
sing	sang	sung
sink	sank	sunk
sit	sat	sat
sleep	slept	slept
slide	slid	slid
sling	slung	slung
slit	slit	slit
smell	smelt, smelled	smelt, smelled
sow	sowed	sown, sowed
speak	spoke	spoken
speed	sped, speeded	sped, speeded
spell	spelt, spelled	spelt, spelled
spend	spent	spent
spill	spilt, spilled	spilt, spilled
spin	spun	spun
spit	spat, spit	spat, spit
split	split	split
spoil	spoilt, spoiled	spoilt, spoiled

spread	spread	spread
spring	sprang	sprung
stand	stood	stood
steal	stole	stolen
stick	stuck	stuck
sting	stung	stung
stink	stank, stunk	stunk
stride	strode	stridden (*rare*)
strike	struck	struck
string	strung	strung
strive	strove	striven
swear	swore	sworn
sweep	swept	swept
swell	swelled	swollen, swelled
swim	swam	swum
swing	swung	swung
take	took	taken
teach	taught	taught
tear	tore	torn
tell	told	told
think	thought	thought
throw	threw	thrown
thrust	thrust	thrust
tread	trod	trodden
undergo	underwent	undergone
understand	understood	understood
undertake	undertook	undertaken
upset	upset	upset
wake	woke	woken
wear	wore	worn
weave	wove	woven
weep	wept	wept
win	won	won
wind	wound	wound
withdraw	withdrew	withdrawn
withhold	withheld	withheld
withstand	withstood	withstood
wring	wrung	wrung
write	wrote	written

Numerals

Les nombres

Cardinal numbers

Les nombres cardinaux

nought	0	zéro
one	1	un
two	2	deux
three	3	trois
four	4	quatre
five	5	cinq
six	6	six
seven	7	sept
eight	8	huit
nine	9	neuf
ten	10	dix

eleven	11	onze
twelve	12	douze
thirteen	13	treize
fourteen	14	quatorze
fifteen	15	quinze
sixteen	16	seize
seventeen	17	dix-sept
eighteen	18	dix-huit
nineteen	19	dix-neuf
twenty	20	vingt
twenty-one	21	vingt et un
twenty-two	22	vingt-deux
thirty	30	trente
forty	40	quarante
fifty	50	cinquante
sixty	60	soixante
seventy	70	soixante-dix
seventy-five	75	soixante-quinze
eighty	80	quatre-vingts
eighty-one	81	quatre-vingt-un
ninety	90	quatre-vingt-dix
ninety-one	91	quatre-vingt-onze
a *or* one hundred	100	cent
a hundred and one	101	cent un
a hundred and two	102	cent deux
a hundred and fifty	150	cent cinquante
two hundred	200	deux cents
two hundred and one	201	deux cent un
two hundred and two	202	deux cent deux
a *or* one thousand	1,000 (1 000)	mille
a thousand and one	1,001 (1 001)	mille un
a thousand and two	1,002 (1 002)	mille deux
two thousand	2,000 (2 000)	deux mille
a *or* one million	1,000,000 (1 000 000)	un million

Ordinal numbers

Les nombres ordinaux

first	1st	1er	premier
second	2nd	2e	deuxième
third	3rd	3e	troisième
fourth	4th	4e	quatrième
fifth	5th	5e	cinquième
sixth	6th	6e	sixième
seventh	7th	7e	septième
eighth	8th	8e	huitième
ninth	9th	9e	neuvième
tenth	10th	10e	dixième
eleventh	11th	11e	onzième
twelfth	12th	12e	douzième
thirteenth	13th	13e	treizième
fourteenth	14th	14e	quatorzième
fifteenth	15th	15e	quinzième
twentieth	20th	20e	vingtième
twenty-first	21st	21e	vingt et unième
twenty-second	22nd	22e	vingt deuxième
thirtieth	30th	30e	trentième

Examples of usage	Exemples d'emplois
three (times) out of ten	*trois (fois) sur dix*
ten at a time, in *or* by tens, ten by ten	*dix par dix, dix à dix*
the ten of us/you, we ten/you ten	*nous dix/vous dix*
all ten of them *or* us *or* you	*tous les dix, toutes les dix*
there are ten of us/them	*nous sommes dix/elles sont dix*
(between) the ten of them	*à eux dix, à elles dix*
ten of them came/were living together	*ils sont venus/ils vivaient à dix*
page ten	*page dix*
Charles the Tenth	*Charles Dix*
to live at number ten	*habiter au (numéro) dix*
to be the tenth to arrive/to leave	*arriver/partir le dixième*
to come tenth, be tenth *(in a race)*	*arriver dixième, être dixième*
it's the tenth (today)	*nous sommes le dix (aujourd'hui)*
the tenth of May, May the tenth, *Am* May tenth	*le dix mai*
to arrive/be paid/*etc* on the tenth	*arriver/être payé/*etc *le dix*
to arrive/be paid/*etc* on the tenth of May *or* on May the tenth *or Am* on May tenth	*arriver/être payé/*etc *le dix mai*
by the tenth, before the tenth	*avant le dix, pour le dix*
it's ten (o'clock)	*il est dix heures*
it's half past ten	*il est dix heures et demie*
ten past ten, *Am* ten after ten	*dix heures dix*
ten to ten	*dix heures moins dix*
by ten (o'clock), before ten (o'clock)	*pour dix heures, avant dix heures*
to be ten (years old)	*avoir dix ans*
a child of ten, a ten-year-old (child)	*un enfant de dix ans*

Days and months / Les jours et les mois

Monday *lundi*; Tuesday *mardi*; Wednesday *mercredi*; Thursday *jeudi*; Friday *vendredi*; Saturday *samedi*; Sunday *dimanche*

January *janvier*; February *février*; March *mars*; April *avril*; May *mai*; June *juin*; July *juillet*; August *août*; September *septembre*; October *octobre*; November *novembre*; December *décembre*

Examples of usage	Exemples d'emplois
on Monday (*e.g.* he arrives on Monday)	*lundi* (par exemple *il arrive lundi*)
(on) Mondays	*le lundi*
see you on Monday!	*à lundi!*
by Monday, before Monday	*avant lundi, pour lundi*
Monday morning/evening	*lundi matin/soir*
a week/two weeks on Monday, *Am* a week/two weeks from Monday	*lundi en huit/en quinze*
it's Monday (today)	*nous sommes (aujourd'hui) lundi*
Monday the tenth of May, Monday May the tenth, *Am* Monday May tenth	*(le) lundi dix mai*
on Monday the tenth of May, on Monday May the tenth *or Am* May tenth	*le lundi dix mai*
tomorrow is Tuesday	*demain c'est mardi*
in May	*en mai, au mois de mai*
every May, each May	*tous les ans en mai, chaque année en mai*
by May, before May	*avant mai, pour mai*

A

A, a [eɪ] *n* A, a *m*; **5A** (*number*) 5 bis; **A1** (*dinner etc*) *Fam* super, superbe; **to go from A to B** aller du point A au point B.

a [ə, *stressed* eɪ] (*before vowel or mute h* **an** [ən, *stressed* æn]) *indef art* **1** un, une; **a man** un homme; **an apple** une pomme. **2** (= *def art in Fr*) **six pence a kilo** six pence le kilo; **50 km an hour** 50 km à l'heure; **I have a broken arm** j'ai le bras cassé. **3** (*art omitted in Fr*) **he's a doctor** il est médecin; **Caen, a town in Normandy** Caen, ville de Normandie; **what a man!** quel homme! **4** (*a certain*) **a Mr Smith** un certain M. Smith. **5** (*time*) **twice a month** deux fois par mois. **6** (*some*) **to make a noise/a fuss** faire du bruit/des histoires.

aback [ə'bæk] *adv* **taken a.** déconcerté.

abandon [ə'bændən] **1** *vt* abandonner. **2** *n* (*freedom of manner*) laisser-aller *m*, abandon *m*. ◆**—ment** *n* abandon *m*.

abase [ə'beɪs] *vt* **to a. oneself** s'humilier, s'abaisser.

abashed [ə'bæʃt] *a* confus, gêné.

abate [ə'beɪt] *vi* (*of storm, pain*) se calmer; (*of flood*) baisser; – *vt* diminuer, réduire. ◆**—ment** *n* diminution *f*, réduction *f*.

abbey ['æbɪ] *n* abbaye *f*.

abbot ['æbət] *n* abbé *m*. ◆**abbess** *n* abbesse *f*.

abbreviate [ə'briːvɪeɪt] *vt* abréger. ◆**abbrevi'ation** *n* abréviation *f*.

abdicate ['æbdɪkeɪt] *vti* abdiquer. ◆**abdi'cation** *n* abdication *f*.

abdomen ['æbdəmən] *n* abdomen *m*. ◆**ab'dominal** *a* abdominal.

abduct [æb'dʌkt] *vt Jur* enlever. ◆**abduction** *n* enlèvement *m*, rapt *m*.

aberration [æbə'reɪʃ(ə)n] *n* (*folly, lapse*) aberration *f*.

abet [ə'bet] *vt* (**-tt-**) **to aid and a. s.o.** *Jur* être le complice de qn.

abeyance [ə'beɪəns] *n* **in a.** (*matter*) en suspens.

abhor [əb'hɔːr] *vt* (**-rr-**) avoir horreur de, exécrer. ◆**abhorrent** *a* exécrable. ◆**abhorrence** *n* horreur *f*.

abide [ə'baɪd] **1** *vi* **to a. by** (*promise etc*) rester fidèle à. **2** *vt* supporter; **I can't a. him** je ne peux pas le supporter.

ability [ə'bɪlətɪ] *n* capacité *f* (**to do** pour faire), aptitude *f* (**to do** à faire); **to the best of my a.** de mon mieux.

abject ['æbdʒekt] *a* abject; **a. poverty** la misère.

ablaze [ə'bleɪz] *a* en feu; **a. with** (*light*) resplendissant de; (*anger*) enflammé de.

able ['eɪb(ə)l] *a* (**-er, -est**) capable, compétent; **to be a. to do** être capable de faire, pouvoir faire; **to be a. to swim/drive** savoir nager/conduire. ◆**a.-'bodied** *a* robuste. ◆**ably** *adv* habilement.

ablutions [ə'bluːʃ(ə)nz] *npl* ablutions *fpl*.

abnormal [æb'nɔːm(ə)l] *a* anormal. ◆**abnor'mality** *n* anomalie *f*; (*of body*) difformité *f*. ◆**abnormally** *adv Fig* exceptionnellement.

aboard [ə'bɔːd] *adv Nau* à bord; **all a.** *Rail* en voiture; – *prep* **a. the ship** à bord du navire; **a. the train** dans le train.

abode [ə'bəʊd] *n* (*house*) *Lit* demeure *f*; *Jur* domicile *m*.

abolish [ə'bɒlɪʃ] *vt* supprimer, abolir. ◆**abo'lition** *n* suppression *f*, abolition *f*.

abominable [ə'bɒmɪnəb(ə)l] *a* abominable. ◆**abomi'nation** *n* abomination *f*.

aboriginal [æbə'rɪdʒən(ə)l] *a & n* aborigène (*m*). ◆**aborigines** *npl* aborigènes *mpl*.

abort [ə'bɔːt] *vt Med* faire avorter; (*space flight, computer program*) abandonner; – *vi Med & Fig* avorter. ◆**abortion** *n* avortement *m*; **to have an a.** se faire avorter. ◆**abortive** *a* (*plan etc*) manqué, avorté.

abound [ə'baʊnd] *vi* abonder (**in, with** en).

about [ə'baʊt] *adv* **1** (*approximately*) à peu près, environ; **(at) a. two o'clock** vers deux heures. **2** (*here and there*) çà et là, ici et là; (*ideas, flu*) *Fig* dans l'air; (*rumour*) en circulation; **to look a.** regarder autour; **to follow a.** suivre partout; **to bustle a.** s'affairer; **there are lots a.** il en existe beaucoup; **(out and) a.** (*after illness*) sur pied, guéri; **(up and) a.** (*out of bed*) levé, debout; **a. turn, a. face** *Mil* demi-tour *m*; *Fig* volte-face *f inv*; – *prep* **1** (*around*) **a. the garden** autour du jardin; **a. the streets** par *or* dans les rues. **2** (*near to*) **a. here** par ici. **3** (*concerning*) au sujet de; **to talk a.** parler de; **a book a.** un livre sur; **what's it (all) a.?** de quoi s'agit-il?; **while you're a. it** pendant que vous y êtes; **what** *or* **how a. me?** et moi alors?; **what** *or* **how a. a drink?** que dirais-tu de prendre un verre? **4** (+ *inf*) **a. to do** sur le point de faire; **I was a. to say** j'étais sur le point de dire, j'allais dire.

above [ə'bʌv] *adv* au-dessus; (*in book*) ci-dessus; **from a.** d'en haut; **floor a.** étage *m* supérieur *or* du dessus; – *prep* au-dessus de; **a. all** par-dessus tout, surtout; **a. the bridge** (*on river*) en amont du pont; **he's a. me** (*in rank*) c'est mon supérieur; **a. lying** incapable de mentir; **a. asking** trop fier pour demander. ◆**a.-'mentioned** *a* susmentionné. ◆**aboveboard** *a* ouvert, honnête; – *adv* sans tricherie, cartes sur table.

abrasion [ə'breɪʒ(ə)n] *n* frottement *m*; *Med* écorchure *f*. ◆**abrasive** *a* (*substance*) abrasif; (*rough*) *Fig* rude, dur; (*irritating*) agaçant; – *n* abrasif *m*.

abreast [ə'brest] *adv* côte à côte, de front; **four a.** par rangs de quatre; **to keep a. of** *or* **with** se tenir au courant de.

abridge [ə'brɪdʒ] *vt* (*book etc*) abréger. ◆**abridg(e)ment** *n* abrégement *m* (**of** de); (*abridged version*) abrégé *m*.

abroad [ə'brɔːd] *adv* **1** (*in or to a foreign country*) à l'étranger; **from a.** de l'étranger. **2** (*over a wide area*) de tous côtés; **rumour a.** bruit *m* qui court.

abrogate ['æbrəgeɪt] *vt* abroger.

abrupt [ə'brʌpt] *a* (*sudden*) brusque; (*person*) brusque, abrupt; (*slope, style*) abrupt. ◆**—ly** *adv* (*suddenly*) brusquement; (*rudely*) avec brusquerie.

abscess ['æbses] *n* abcès *m*.

abscond [əb'skɒnd] *vi Jur* s'enfuir.

absence ['æbsəns] *n* absence *f*; **in the a. of** sth à défaut de qch, faute de qch; **a. of mind** distraction *f*.

absent ['æbsənt] *a* absent (**from** de); (*look*) distrait; – [æb'sent] *vt* **to a. oneself** s'absenter. ◆**a.-'minded** *a* distrait. ◆**a.-'mindedness** *n* distraction *f*. ◆**absen'tee** *n* absent, -ente *mf*. ◆**absen'teeism** *n* absentéisme *m*.

absolute ['æbsəluːt] *a* absolu; (*proof etc*) indiscutable; (*coward etc*) parfait, véritable. ◆**—ly** *adv* absolument; (*forbidden*) formellement.

absolve [əb'zɒlv] *vt Rel Jur* absoudre; to **a. from** (*vow*) libérer de. ◆**absolution** [æbsə'luːʃ(ə)n] *n* absolution *f*.

absorb [əb'zɔːb] *vt* absorber; (*shock*) amortir; **to become absorbed in** (*work*) s'absorber dans. ◆**—ing** *a* (*work*) absorbant; (*book, film*) prenant. ◆**absorbent** *a* & *n* absorbant (*m*); **a. cotton** *Am* coton *m* hydrophile. ◆**absorber** *n* **shock a.** *Aut* amortisseur *m*. ◆**absorption** *n* absorption *f*.

abstain [əb'steɪn] *vi* s'abstenir (**from** de). ◆**abstemious** *a* sobre, frugal. ◆**abstention** *n* abstention *f*. ◆**'abstinence** *n* abstinence *f*.

abstract ['æbstrækt] **1** *a* & *n* abstrait (*m*). **2** *n* (*summary*) résumé *m*. **3** [əb'strækt] *vt* (*remove*) retirer; (*notion*) abstraire. ◆**ab'straction** *n* (*idea*) abstraction *f*; (*absent-mindedness*) distraction *f*.

abstruse [əb'struːs] *a* obscur.

absurd [əb'sɜːd] *a* absurde, ridicule. ◆**absurdity** *n* absurdité *f*. ◆**absurdly** *adv* absurdement.

abundant [ə'bʌndənt] *a* abondant. ◆**abundance** *n* abondance *f*. ◆**abundantly** *adv* **a. clear** tout à fait clair.

abuse [ə'bjuːs] *n* (*abusing*) abus *m* (**of** de); (*curses*) injures *fpl*; – [ə'bjuːz] *vt* (*misuse*) abuser de; (*malign*) dire du mal de; (*insult*) injurier. ◆**abusive** [ə'bjuːsɪv] *a* injurieux.

abysmal [ə'bɪzm(ə)l] *a* (*bad*) *Fam* désastreux, exécrable.

abyss [ə'bɪs] *n* abîme *m*.

acacia [ə'keɪʃə] *n* (*tree*) acacia *m*.

academic [ækə'demɪk] *a* universitaire; (*scholarly*) érudit, intellectuel; (*issue etc*) *Pej* théorique; (*style, art*) académique; – *n* (*teacher*) *Univ* universitaire *mf*.

academy [ə'kædəmɪ] *n* (*society*) académie *f*; *Mil Mus* école *f*. ◆**acade'mician** *n* académicien, -ienne *mf*.

accede [ək'siːd] *vi* **to a. to** (*request, throne, position*) accéder à.

accelerate [ək'seləreɪt] *vt* accélérer; – *vi* s'accélérer; *Aut* accélérer. ◆**accele'ration** *n* accélération *f*. ◆**accelerator** *n* *Aut* accélérateur *m*.

accent ['æksənt] *n* accent *m*; – [æk'sent] *vt* accentuer. ◆**accentuate** [æk'sentʃʊeɪt] *vt* accentuer.

accept [ək'sept] *vt* accepter. ◆**—ed** *a* (*opinion etc*) reçu, admis. ◆**acceptable** *a* (*worth accepting, tolerable*) acceptable. ◆**acceptance** *n* acceptation *f*; (*approval, favour*) accueil *m* favorable.

access ['ækses] *n* accès *m* (**to sth** à qch, **to s.o.** auprès de qn). ◆**ac'cessible** *a* accessible.

accession [æk'seʃ(ə)n] *n* accession *f* (**to** à); (*increase*) augmentation *f*; (*sth added*) nouvelle acquisition *f*.

accessory [ək'sesərɪ] **1** *n* (*person*) *Jur* complice *mf.* **2** *npl* (*objects*) accessoires *mpl.*
accident ['æksɪdənt] *n* accident *m*; **by a.** (*by chance*) par accident; (*unintentionally*) accidentellement, sans le vouloir. ◆**a.-prone** *a* prédisposé aux accidents. ◆**acci'dental** *a* accidentel, fortuit. ◆**acci'dentally** *adv* accidentellement, par mégarde; (*by chance*) par accident.
acclaim [ə'kleɪm] *vt* acclamer; **to a. king** proclamer roi. ◆**accla'mation** *n* acclamation(s) *f(pl)*, louange(s) *f(pl)*.
acclimate ['æklɪmeɪt] *vti Am* = **acclimatize.** ◆**a'cclimatize** *vt* acclimater; – *vi* s'acclimater. ◆**accli'mation** *n Am*, ◆**acclimati'zation** *n* acclimatisation *f.*
accolade ['ækəleɪd] *n* (*praise*) *Fig* louange *f.*
accommodat/e [ə'kɒmədeɪt] *vt* (*of house*) loger, recevoir; (*have room for*) avoir de la place pour (mettre); (*adapt*) adapter (**to** à); (*supply*) fournir (**s.o. with sth** qch à qn); (*oblige*) rendre service à; (*reconcile*) concilier; **to a. oneself to** s'accomoder à. ◆**—ing** *a* accommodant, obligeant. ◆**accommo'dation** *n* **1** (*lodging*) logement *m*; (*rented room or rooms*) chambre(s) *f(pl)*; *pl* (*in hotel*) *Am* chambre(s) *f(pl)*. **2** (*compromise*) compromis *m*, accommodement *m.*
accompany [ə'kʌmpənɪ] *vt* accompagner. ◆**accompaniment** *n* accompagnement *m.* ◆**accompanist** *n Mus* accompagnateur, -trice *mf.*
accomplice [ə'kʌmplɪs] *n* complice *mf.*
accomplish [ə'kʌmplɪʃ] *vt* (*task, duty*) accomplir; (*aim*) réaliser. ◆**—ed** *a* accompli. ◆**—ment** *n* accomplissement *m*; (*of aim*) réalisation *f*; (*thing achieved*) réalisation *f*; *pl* (*skills*) talents *mpl.*
accord [ə'kɔːd] **1** *n* accord *m*; **of my own a.** volontairement, de mon plein gré; – *vi* concorder. **2** *vt* (*grant*) accorder. ◆**accordance** *n* **in a. with** conformément à.
according to [ə'kɔːdɪŋtuː] *prep* selon, d'après, suivant. ◆**accordingly** *adv* en conséquence.
accordion [ə'kɔːdɪən] *n* accordéon *m.*
accost [ə'kɒst] *vt* accoster, aborder.
account [ə'kaunt] **1** *n Com* compte *m*; *pl* comptabilité *f*, comptes *mpl*; **accounts department** comptabilité *f*; **to take into a.** tenir compte de; **ten pounds on a.** un acompte de dix livres; **of some a.** d'une certaine importance; **on a. of** à cause de; **on no a.** en aucun cas. **2** *n* (*report*) compte rendu *m*, récit *m*; (*explanation*) explication *f*; **by all accounts** au dire de tous; **to give a good a. of oneself** s'en tirer à son avantage; – *vi* **to a. for** (*explain*) expliquer; (*give reckoning of*) rendre compte de. **3** *vt* **to a. oneself lucky**/*etc* (*consider*) se considérer heureux/*etc.* ◆**accountable** *a* responsable (**for** de, **to** devant); (*explainable*) explicable.
accountant [ə'kauntənt] *n* comptable *mf.* ◆**accountancy** *n* comptabilité *f.*
accoutrements [ə'kuːtrəmənts] (*Am* **accouterments** [ə'kuːtəmənts]) *npl* équipement *m.*
accredit [ə'kredɪt] *vt* (*ambassador*) accréditer; **to a. s.o. with sth** attribuer qch à qn.
accrue [ə'kruː] *vi* (*of interest*) *Fin* s'accumuler; **to a. to** (*of advantage etc*) revenir à.
accumulate [ə'kjuːmjuleɪt] *vt* accumuler, amasser; – *vi* s'accumuler. ◆**accumu'lation** *n* accumulation *f*; (*mass*) amas *m.* ◆**accumulator** *n El* accumulateur *m.*
accurate ['ækjurət] *a* exact, précis. ◆**accuracy** *n* exactitude *f*, précision *f.* ◆**accurately** *adv* avec précision.
accursed [ə'kɜːsɪd] *a* maudit, exécrable.
accus/e [ə'kjuːz] *vt* accuser (**of** de). ◆**—ed** *n* **the a.** *Jur* l'inculpé, -ée *mf*, l'accusé, -ée *mf.* ◆**—ing** *a* accusateur. ◆**accu'sation** *n* accusation *f.*
accustom [ə'kʌstəm] *vt* habituer, accoutumer. ◆**—ed** *a* habitué (**to sth** à qch, **to doing** à faire); **to get a. to** s'habituer à, s'accoutumer à.
ace [eɪs] *n* (*card, person*) as *m.*
acetate ['æsɪteɪt] *n* acétate *m.*
acetic [ə'siːtɪk] *a* acétique.
ache [eɪk] *n* douleur *f*, mal *m*; **to have an a. in one's arm** avoir mal au bras; – *vi* faire mal; **my head aches** ma tête me fait mal; **it makes my heart a.** cela me serre le cœur; **to be aching to do** brûler de faire. ◆**aching** *a* douloureux.
achieve [ə'tʃiːv] *vt* accomplir, réaliser; (*success, aim*) atteindre; (*victory*) remporter. ◆**—ment** *n* accomplissement *m*, réalisation *f* (**of** de); (*feat*) réalisation *f*, exploit *m.*
acid ['æsɪd] *a* & *n* acide (*m*). ◆**a'cidity** *n* acidité *f.*
acknowledge [ək'nɒlɪdʒ] *vt* reconnaître (**as** pour); (*greeting*) répondre à; **to a. (receipt of)** accuser réception de; **to a. defeat** s'avouer vaincu. ◆**—ment** *n* reconnaissance *f*; (*of letter*) accusé *m* de réception; (*receipt*) reçu *m*, récépissé *m.*

acme ['ækmɪ] *n* sommet *m*, comble *m*.
acne ['æknɪ] *n* acné *f*.
acorn ['eɪkɔːn] *n Bot* gland *m*.
acoustic [ə'kuːstɪk] *a* acoustique; – *npl* acoustique *f*.
acquaint [ə'kweɪnt] *vt* **to a. s.o. with sth** informer qn de qch; **to be acquainted with** (*person*) connaître; (*fact*) savoir; **we are acquainted** on se connaît. ◆**acquaintance** *n* (*person, knowledge*) connaissance *f*.
acquiesce [ækwɪ'es] *vi* acquiescer (**in** à). ◆**acquiescence** *n* acquiescement *m*.
acquire [ə'kwaɪər] *vt* acquérir; (*taste*) prendre (**for** à); (*friends*) se faire; **aquired taste** goût *m* qui s'acquiert. ◆**acqui'sition** *n* acquisition *f*. ◆**acquisitive** *a* avide, cupide.
acquit [ə'kwɪt] *vt* (**-tt-**) **to a. s.o. (of a crime)** acquitter qn. ◆**acquittal** *n* acquittement *m*.
acre ['eɪkər] *n* acre *f* (= *0,4 hectare*). ◆**acreage** *n* superficie *f*.
acrid ['ækrɪd] *a* (*smell, manner etc*) âcre.
acrimonious [ækrɪ'məʊnɪəs] *a* acerbe.
acrobat ['ækrəbæt] *n* acrobate *mf*. ◆**acro'batic** *a* acrobatique; – *npl* acrobatie(s) *f*(*pl*).
acronym ['ækrənɪm] *n* sigle *m*.
across [ə'krɒs] *adv & prep* (*from side to side* (*of*)) d'un côté à l'autre (de); (*on the other side* (*of*)) de l'autre côté (de); (*crossways*) en travers (de); **to be a kilometre/***etc* **a.** (*wide*) avoir un kilomètre/*etc* de large; **to walk** *or* **go a.** (*street etc*) traverser; **to come a.** (*person*) rencontrer (par hasard), tomber sur; (*thing*) trouver (par hasard); **to get sth a. to s.o.** faire comprendre qch à qn.
acrostic [ə'krɒstɪk] *n* acrostiche *m*.
acrylic [ə'krɪlɪk] *a & n* acrylique (*m*).
act [ækt] **1** *n* (*deed*) acte *m*; **a. (of parliament)** loi *f*; **caught in the a.** pris sur le fait; **a. of walking** action *f* de marcher; **an a. of folly** une folie. **2** *n* (*of play*) *Th* acte *m*; (*turn*) *Th* numéro *m*; **in on the a.** *Fam* dans le coup; **to put on an a.** *Fam* jouer la comédie; – *vt* (*part*) *Th* jouer; **to a. the fool** faire l'idiot; – *vi Th Cin* jouer; (*pretend*) jouer la comédie. **3** *vi* (*do sth, behave*) agir; (*function*) fonctionner; **to a. as** (*secretary etc*) faire office de; (*of object*) servir de; **to a. (up)on** (*affect*) agir sur; (*advice*) suivre; **to a. on behalf of** représenter; **to a. up** (*of person, machine*) *Fam* faire des siennes. ◆**—ing 1** *a* (*manager etc*) intérimaire, provisoire. **2** *n* (*of play*) représentation *f*; (*actor's art*) jeu *m*; (*career*) théâtre *m*.
action ['ækʃ(ə)n] *n* action *f*; *Mil* combat *m*; *Jur* procès *m*, action *f*; **to take a.** prendre des mesures; **to put into a.** (*plan*) exécuter; **out of a.** hors d'usage, hors (de) service; (*person*) hors de combat; **killed in a.** mort au champ d'honneur; **to take industrial a.** se mettre en grève.
active ['æktɪv] *a* actif; (*interest*) vif; (*volcano*) en activité. ◆**activate** *vt Ch* activer; (*mechanism*) actionner. ◆**activist** *n* activiste *mf*. ◆**ac'tivity** *n* activité *f*; (*in street*) mouvement *m*.
actor ['æktər] *n* acteur *m*. ◆**actress** *n* actrice *f*.
actual ['æktʃʊəl] *a* réel, véritable; (*example*) concret; **the a. book** le livre même; **in a. fact** en réalité, effectivement. ◆**—ly** *adv* (*truly*) réellement; (*in fact*) en réalité, en fait.
actuary ['æktʃʊərɪ] *n* actuaire *mf*.
actuate ['æktʃʊeɪt] *vt* (*person*) animer; (*machine*) actionner.
acumen ['ækjʊmen, *Am* ə'kjuːmən] *n* perspicacité *f*, finesse *f*.
acupuncture ['ækjʊpʌŋktʃər] *n* acupuncture *f*.
acute [ə'kjuːt] *a* aigu; (*anxiety, emotion*) vif, profond; (*observer*) perspicace; (*shortage*) grave. ◆**—ly** *adv* (*to suffer, feel*) vivement, profondément. ◆**—ness** *n* acuité *f*; perspicacité *f*.
ad [æd] *n Fam* pub *f*; (*private, in newspaper*) annonce *f*; **small ad** petite annonce.
AD [eɪ'diː] *abbr* (*anno Domini*) après Jésus-Christ.
adage ['ædɪdʒ] *n* adage *m*.
Adam ['ædəm] *n* **A.'s apple** pomme *f* d'Adam.
adamant ['ædəmənt] *a* inflexible.
adapt [ə'dæpt] *vt* adapter (**to** à); **to a. (oneself)** s'adapter. ◆**adaptable** *a* (*person*) capable de s'adapter, adaptable. ◆**adaptor** *n* (*device*) adaptateur *m*; (*plug*) prise *f* multiple. ◆**adap'tation** *n* adaptation *f*.
add [æd] *vt* ajouter (**to** à, **that** que); **to a. (up** *or* **together)** (*total*) additionner; **to a. in** inclure; – *vi* **to a. to** (*increase*) augmenter; **to a. up to** (*total*) s'élever à; (*mean*) signifier; **it all adds up** *Fam* ça s'explique. ◆**a'ddendum,** *pl* **-da** *n* supplément *m*. ◆**adding machine** *n* machine *f* à calculer. ◆**a'ddition** *n* addition *f*; augmentation *f*; **in a.** de plus; **in a. to** en plus de. ◆**a'dditional** *a* supplémentaire. ◆**a'dditionally** *adv* de plus. ◆**additive** *n* additif *m*.
adder ['ædər] *n* vipère *f*.

addict ['ædɪkt] *n* intoxiqué, -ée *mf*; **jazz/sport a.** fanatique *mf* du jazz/du sport; **drug a.** drogué, -ée *mf*. ◆**a'ddicted** *a* **to be a. to** (*study, drink*) s'adonner à; (*music*) se passionner pour; (*to have the habit of*) avoir la manie de; **a. to cigarettes** drogué par la cigarette. ◆**a'ddiction** *n* (*habit*) manie *f*; (*dependency*) *Med* dépendance *f*; **drug a.** toxicomanie *f*. ◆**a'ddictive** *a* qui crée une dépendance.

address [ə'dres, *Am* 'ædres] *n* (*on letter etc*) adresse *f*; (*speech*) allocution *f*; **form of a.** formule *f* de politesse; – [ə'dres] *vt* (*person*) s'adresser à; (*audience*) parler devant; (*words, speech*) adresser (**to** à); (*letter*) mettre l'adresse sur; **to a. to s.o.** (*send, intend for*) adresser à qn. ◆**addressee** [ædre'siː] *n* destinataire *mf*.

adenoids ['ædɪnɔɪdz] *npl* végétations *fpl* (adénoïdes).

adept ['ædept, *Am* ə'dept] *a* expert (**in, at** à).

adequate ['ædɪkwət] *a* (*quantity*) suffisant; (*acceptable*) convenable; (*person, performance*) compétent. ◆**adequacy** *n* (*of person*) compétence *f*; **to doubt the a. of sth** douter que qch soit suffisant. ◆**adequately** *adv* suffisamment; convenablement.

adhere [əd'hɪər] *vi* **to a. to** adhérer à; (*decision*) s'en tenir à; (*rule*) respecter. ◆**adherence** *n*, ◆**adhesion** *n* (*grip*) adhérence *f*; (*support*) *Fig* adhésion *f*. ◆**adhesive** *a* & *n* adhésif (*m*).

ad infinitum [ædɪnfɪ'naɪtəm] *adv* à l'infini.

adjacent [ə'dʒeɪsənt] *a* (*house, angle etc*) adjacent (**to** à).

adjective ['ædʒɪktɪv] *n* adjectif *m*.

adjoin [ə'dʒɔɪn] *vt* avoisiner. ◆**—ing** *a* avoisinant, voisin.

adjourn [ə'dʒɜːn] *vt* (*postpone*) adjourner; (*session*) lever, suspendre; – *vi* lever la séance; **to a. to** (*go*) passer à. ◆**—ment** *n* ajournement *m*; suspension *f* (de séance), levée *f* de séance.

adjudicate [ə'dʒuːdɪkeɪt] *vti* juger. ◆**adjudi'cation** *n* jugement *m*. ◆**adjudicator** *n* juge *m*, arbitre *m*.

adjust [ə'dʒʌst] *vt* *Tech* régler, ajuster; (*prices*) (r)ajuster; (*arrange*) arranger; **to a. (oneself) to** s'adapter à. ◆**—able** *a* réglable. ◆**—ment** *n* *Tech* réglage *m*; (*of person*) adaptation *f*; (*of prices*) (r)ajustement *m*.

ad-lib [æd'lɪb] *vi* (**-bb-**) improviser; – *a* (*joke etc*) improvisé.

administer [əd'mɪnɪstər] **1** *vt* (*manage, dispense*) administrer (**to** à). **2** *vi* **to a. to** pourvoir à. ◆**admini'stration** *n* administration *f*; (*ministry*) gouvernement *m*. ◆**administrative** *a* administratif. ◆**administrator** *n* administrateur, -trice *mf*.

admiral ['ædmərəl] *n* amiral *m*.

admir/e [əd'maɪər] *vt* admirer. ◆**—ing** *a* admiratif. ◆**—er** *n* admirateur, -trice *mf*. ◆**'admirable** *a* admirable. ◆**admi'ration** *n* admiration *f*.

admit [əd'mɪt] *vt* (**-tt-**) (*let in*) laisser entrer; (*accept*) admettre; (*acknowledge*) reconnaître, avouer; – *vi* **to a. to sth** (*confess*) avouer qch; **to a. of** permettre. ◆**admittedly** *adv* c'est vrai (que). ◆**admissible** *a* admissible. ◆**admission** *n* (*entry to theatre etc*) entrée *f* (**to** à, de); (*to club, school*) admission *f*; (*acknowledgement*) aveu *m*; **a. (charge)** (prix *m* d')entrée *f*. ◆**admittance** *n* entrée *f*; **'no a.'** 'entrée interdite'.

admonish [əd'mɒnɪʃ] *vt* (*reprove*) réprimander; (*warn*) avertir.

ado [ə'duː] *n* **without further a.** sans (faire) plus de façons.

adolescent [ædə'lesənt] *n* adolescent, -ente *mf*. ◆**adolescence** *n* adolescence *f*.

adopt [ə'dɒpt] *vt* (*child, method, attitude etc*) adopter; (*candidate*) *Pol* choisir. ◆**—ed** *a* (*child*) adoptif; (*country*) d'adoption. ◆**adoption** *n* adoption *f*. ◆**adoptive** *a* (*parent*) adoptif.

adore [ə'dɔːr] *vt* adorer; **he adores being flattered** il adore qu'on le flatte. ◆**adorable** *a* adorable. ◆**ado'ration** *n* adoration *f*.

adorn [ə'dɔːn] *vt* (*room, book*) orner; (*person, dress*) parer. ◆**—ment** *n* ornement *m*; parure *f*.

adrenalin(e) [ə'drenəlɪn] *n* adrénaline *f*.

Adriatic [eɪdrɪ'ætɪk] *n* **the A.** l'Adriatique *f*.

adrift [ə'drɪft] *a* & *adv* *Nau* à la dérive; **to come a.** (*of rope, collar etc*) se détacher; **to turn s.o. a.** *Fig* abandonner qn à son sort.

adroit [ə'drɔɪt] *a* adroit, habile.

adulation [ædjʊ'leɪʃ(ə)n] *n* adulation *f*.

adult ['ædʌlt] *a* & *n* adulte (*mf*). ◆**adulthood** *n* âge *m* adulte.

adulterate [ə'dʌltəreɪt] *vt* (*food*) altérer.

adultery [ə'dʌltərɪ] *n* adultère *m*. ◆**adulterous** *a* adultère.

advanc/e [əd'vɑːns] *n* (*movement, money*) avance *f*; (*of science*) progrès *mpl*; *pl* (*of friendship, love*) avances *fpl*; **in a.** à l'avance, d'avance; (*to arrive*) en avance; **in a. of s.o.** avant qn; – *a* (*payment*) anticipé; **a. booking** réservation *f*; **a. guard** avant-garde *f*; – *vt* (*put forward, lend*) avancer; (*science, work*) faire avancer; – *vi* (*go forward, progress*) avancer; (*towards s.o.*) s'avancer, avancer. ◆**—ed** *a* avancé; (*studies*) supérieur; **a. in years** âgé. ◆**—ement** *n* (*progress, promotion*) avancement *m*.

advantage [əd'vɑːntɪdʒ] *n* avantage *m* (**over** sur); **to take a. of** profiter de; (*person*) tromper, exploiter; (*woman*) séduire; **to show (off) to a.** faire valoir. ◆**advan'tageous** *a* avantageux (**to**, pour), profitable.

advent ['ædvent] *n* arrivée *f*, avènement *m*; **A.** *Rel* l'Avent *m*.

adventure [əd'ventʃər] *n* aventure *f*; – *a* (*film etc*) d'aventures. ◆**adventurer** *n* aventurier, -ière *mf*. ◆**adventurous** *a* aventureux.

adverb ['ædvɜːb] *n* adverbe *m*.

adversary ['ædvəsərɪ] *n* adversaire *mf*.

adverse ['ædvɜːs] *a* hostile, défavorable. ◆**ad'versity** *n* adversité *f*.

advert ['ædvɜːt] *n* *Fam* pub *f*; (*private, in newspaper*) annonce *f*.

advertis/e ['ædvətaɪz] *vt* (*goods*) faire de la publicité pour; (*make known*) annoncer; – *vi* faire de la publicité; **to a. (for s.o.)** mettre une annonce (pour chercher qn). ◆**—er** *n* annonceur *m*. ◆**—ement** [əd'vɜːtɪsmənt, *Am* ædvə'taɪzmənt] *n* publicité *f*; (*private or classified in newspaper*) annonce *f*; (*poster*) affiche *f*; **classified a.** petite annonce; **the advertisements** *TV* la publicité.

advice [əd'vaɪs] *n* conseil(s) *m*(*pl*); *Com* avis *m*; **a piece of a.** un conseil.

advis/e [əd'vaɪz] *vt* (*counsel*) conseiller; (*recommend*) recommander; (*notify*) informer; **to a. s.o. to do** conseiller à qn de faire; **to a. against** déconseiller. ◆**—ed** *a* **well-a.** (*action*) prudent. ◆**—able** *a* (*wise*) prudent (**to do** de faire); (*act*) à conseiller. ◆**—edly** [-ɪdlɪ] *adv* après réflexion. ◆**—er** *n* conseiller, -ère *mf*. ◆**advisory** *a* consultatif.

advocate 1 ['ædvəkət] *n* (*of cause*) défenseur *m*, avocat, -ate *mf*; *Jur* avocat *m*. **2** ['ædvəkeɪt] *vt* préconiser, recommander.

aegis ['iːdʒɪs] *n* **under the a. of** sous l'égide de.

aeon ['iːən] *n* éternité *f*.

aerial ['eərɪəl] *n* antenne *f*; – *a* aérien.

aerobatics [eərə'bætɪks] *npl* acrobatie *f* aérienne. ◆**ae'robics** *npl* aérobic *f*. ◆**'aerodrome** *n* aérodrome *m*. ◆**aerody'namic** *a* aérodynamique. ◆**aero'nautics** *npl* aéronautique *f*. ◆**'aeroplane** *n* avion *m*. ◆**'aerosol** *n* aérosol *m*. ◆**'aerospace** *a* (*industry*) aérospatial.

aesthetic [iːs'θetɪk, *Am* es'θetɪk] *a* esthétique.

afar [ə'fɑːr] *adv* **from a.** de loin.

affable ['æfəb(ə)l] *a* affable, aimable.

affair [ə'feər] *n* (*matter, concern*) affaire *f*; (**love**) **a.** liaison *f*; **state of affairs** état *m* de choses.

affect [ə'fekt] *vt* (*move, feign*) affecter; (*concern*) toucher, affecter; (*harm*) nuire à; (*be fond of*) affectionner. ◆**—ed** *a* (*manner*) affecté; (*by disease*) atteint. ◆**affec'tation** *n* affectation *f*.

affection [ə'fekʃ(ə)n] *n* affection *f* (**for** pour). ◆**affectionate** *a* affectueux, aimant. ◆**affectionately** *adv* affectueusement.

affiliate [ə'fɪlɪeɪt] *vt* affilier; **to be affiliated** s'affilier (**to** à); **affiliated company** filiale *f*. ◆**affili'ation** *n* affiliation *f*; *pl* (*political*) attaches *fpl*.

affinity [ə'fɪnɪtɪ] *n* affinité *f*.

affirm [ə'fɜːm] *vt* affirmer. ◆**affir'mation** *n* affirmation *f*. ◆**affirmative** *a* affirmatif; – *n* affirmative *f*.

affix [ə'fɪks] *vt* apposer.

afflict [ə'flɪkt] *vt* affliger (**with** de). ◆**affliction** *n* (*misery*) affliction *f*; (*disorder*) infirmité *f*.

affluent ['æfluənt] *a* riche; **a. society** société *f* d'abondance. ◆**affluence** *n* richesse *f*.

afford [ə'fɔːd] *vt* **1** (*pay for*) avoir les moyens d'acheter, pouvoir se payer; (*time*) pouvoir trouver; **I can a. to wait** je peux me permettre d'attendre. **2** (*provide*) fournir, donner; **to a. s.o. sth** fournir qch à qn.

affray [ə'freɪ] *n* *Jur* rixe *f*, bagarre *f*.

affront [ə'frʌnt] *n* affront *m*; – *vt* faire un affront à.

Afghanistan [æf'gænɪstɑːn] *n* Afghanistan *m*. ◆**'Afghan** *a* & *n* afghan, -ane (*mf*).

afield [ə'fiːld] *adv* **further a.** plus loin; **too far a.** trop loin.

afloat [ə'fləʊt] *adv* (*ship, swimmer, business*) à flot; (*awash*) submergé; **life a.** la vie sur l'eau.

afoot [ə'fʊt] *adv* **there's sth a.** il se trame qch; **there's a plan a. to** on prépare un projet pour.

aforementioned [ə'fɔːmenʃənd] *a* susmentionné.

afraid [ə'freɪd] *a* **to be a.** avoir peur (**of, to** de; **that** que); **to make s.o. afraid** faire peur à qn; **he's a. (that) she may be ill** il a peur qu'elle (ne) soit malade; **I'm a. he's out** (*I regret to say*) je regrette, il est sorti.

afresh [əˈfreʃ] *adv* de nouveau.

Africa [ˈæfrɪkə] *n* Afrique *f*. ◆**African** *a & n* africain, -aine (*mf*).

after [ˈɑːftər] *adv* après; **the month a.** le mois suivant, le mois d'après; – *prep* après; **a. all** après tout; **a. eating** après avoir mangé; **day a. day** jour après jour; **page a. page** page sur page; **time a. time** bien des fois; **a. you!** je vous en prie!; **ten a. four** *Am* quatre heures dix; **to be a. sth/s.o.** (*seek*) chercher qch/qn; – *conj* après que; **a. he saw you** après qu'il t'a vu. ◆**aftercare** *n Med* soins *mpl* postopératoires; *Jur* surveillance *f*. ◆**aftereffects** *npl* suites *fpl*, séquelles *fpl*. ◆**afterlife** *n* vie *f* future. ◆**aftermath** [-mɑːθ] *n* suites *fpl*. ◆**after'noon** *n* après-midi *m or f inv*; **in the a.** l'après-midi; **good a.!** (*hello*) bonjour!; (*goodbye*) au revoir! ◆**after'noons** *adv Am* l'après midi. ◆**aftersales (service)** *n* service *m* après-vente. ◆**aftershave (lotion)** *n* lotion *f* après-rasage. ◆**aftertaste** *n* arrière-goût *m*. ◆**afterthought** *n* réflexion *f* après coup. ◆**afterward(s)** *adv* après, plus tard.

afters [ˈɑːftəz] *npl Fam* dessert *m*.

again [əˈgen, əˈgeɪn] *adv* de nouveau, encore une fois; (*furthermore*) en outre; **to do a.** refaire; **to go down/up a.** redescendre/remonter; **never a.** plus jamais; **half as much a.** moitié plus; **a. and a., time and (time) a.** maintes fois; **what's his name a.?** comment s'appelle-t-il déjà?

against [əˈgenst, əˈgeɪnst] *prep* contre; **to go** *or* **be a.** s'opposer à; **a law a. drinking** une loi qui interdit de boire; **his age is a. him** son âge lui est défavorable; **a. a background of** sur (un) fond de; **a. the light** à contre-jour; **a. the law** illégal; **a. the rules** interdit, contraire aux règlements.

age [eɪdʒ] *n* (*lifespan, period*) âge *m*; **(old) a.** vieillesse *f*; **the Middle Ages** le moyen âge; **what a. are you?, what's your a.?** quel âge as-tu?; **five years of a.** âgé de cinq ans; **to be of a.** être majeur; **under a.** trop jeune, mineur; **to wait (for) ages** *Fam* attendre une éternité; **a. group** tranche *f* d'âge; – *vti* (*pres p* **ag(e)ing**) vieillir. ◆**a.-old** *a* séculaire. ◆**aged** *a* [eɪdʒd] **a. ten** âgé de dix ans; [ˈeɪdʒɪd] vieux, âgé; **the a.** les personnes *fpl* âgées. ◆**ageless** *a* toujours jeune.

agenda [əˈdʒendə] *n* ordre *m* du jour.

agent [ˈeɪdʒənt] *n* agent *m*; (*dealer*) *Com* concessionnaire *mf*. ◆**agency** *n* **1** (*office*) agence *f*. **2 through the a. of s.o.** par l'intermédiaire de qn.

agglomeration [əglɒməˈreɪʃ(ə)n] *n* agglomération *f*.

aggravate [ˈægrəveɪt] *vt*. (*make worse*) aggraver; **to a. s.o.** *Fam* exaspérer qn. ◆**aggra'vation** *n* aggravation *f*; *Fam* exaspération *f*; (*bother*) *Fam* ennui(s) *m*(*pl*).

aggregate [ˈægrɪgət] *a* global; – *n* (*total*) ensemble *m*.

aggression [əˈgreʃ(ə)n] *n* agression *f*. ◆**aggressive** *a* agressif. ◆**aggressiveness** *n* agressivité *f*. ◆**agressor** *n* agresseur *m*.

aggrieved [əˈgriːvd] *a* (*offended*) blessé, froissé; (*tone*) peiné.

aghast [əˈgɑːst] *a* consterné, horrifié.

agile [ˈædʒaɪl, *Am* ˈædʒ(ə)l] *a* agile. ◆**a'gility** *n* agilité *f*.

agitate [ˈædʒɪteɪt] *vt* (*worry, shake*) agiter; – *vi* **to a. for** *Pol* faire campagne pour. ◆**agi'tation** *n* (*anxiety, unrest*) agitation *f*. ◆**agitator** *n* agitateur, -trice *mf*.

aglow [əˈgləʊ] *a* **to be a.** briller (**with** de).

agnostic [ægˈnɒstɪk] *a & n* agnostique (*mf*).

ago [əˈgəʊ] *adv* **a year a.** il y a un an; **how long a.?** il y a combien de temps (de cela)?; **as long a. as 1800** (déjà) en 1800.

agog [əˈgɒg] *a* (*excited*) en émoi; (*eager*) impatient.

agony [ˈægənɪ] *n* (*pain*) douleur *f* atroce; (*anguish*) angoisse *f*; **to be in a.** souffrir horriblement; **a. column** *Journ* courrier *m* du cœur. ◆**agonize** *vi* se faire beaucoup de souci. ◆**agonized** *a* (*look*) angoissé; (*cry*) de douleur. ◆**agonizing** *a* (*pain*) atroce; (*situation*) angoissant.

agree [əˈgriː] *vi* (*come to terms*) se mettre d'accord, s'accorder; (*be in agreement*) être d'accord, s'accorder (**with** avec); (*of facts, dates etc*) concorder; *Gram* s'accorder; **to a. upon** (*decide*) convenir de; **to a. to sth/to doing** consentir à qch/à faire; **it doesn't a. with me** (*food, climate*) ça ne me réussit pas; – *vt* (*figures*) faire concorder; (*accounts*) *Com* approuver; **to a. to do** accepter de faire; **to a. that** (*admit*) admettre que. ◆**agreed** *a* (*time, place*) convenu; **we are a.** nous sommes d'accord; **a.!** entendu! ◆**agreeable** *a* **1** (*pleasant*) agréable. **2 to be a.** (*agree*) être d'accord; **to be a. to sth** consentir à qch. ◆**agreement** *n* accord *m*; *Pol Com* convention *f*, accord *m*; **in a. with** d'accord avec.

agriculture [ˈægrɪkʌltʃər] *n* agriculture *f*. ◆**agri'cultural** *a* agricole.

aground [əˈgraʊnd] *adv* **to run a.** *Nau* (s')échouer.

ah! [ɑː] *int* ah!
ahead [ə'hed] *adv* (*in space*) en avant; (*leading*) en tête; (*in the future*) dans l'avenir; **a. (of time** *or* **of schedule)** en avance (sur l'horaire); **one hour/***etc* **a.** une heure/*etc* d'avance (**of** sur); **a. of** (*space*) devant; (*time, progress*) en avance sur; **to go a.** (*advance*) avancer; (*continue*) continuer; (*start*) commencer; **go a.!** allez-y!; **to go a. with** (*task*) poursuivre; **to get a.** prendre de l'avance; (*succeed*) réussir; **to think a.** penser à l'avenir; **straight a.** tout droit.
aid [eɪd] *n* (*help*) aide *f*; (*apparatus*) support *m*, moyen *m*; **with the a. of** (*a stick etc*) à l'aide de; **in a. of** (*charity etc*) au profit de; **what's this in a. of?** *Fam* quel est le but de tout ça?, ça sert à quoi?; – *vt* aider (**to do** à faire).
aide [eɪd] *n Pol* aide *mf*.
AIDS [eɪdz] *n Med* SIDA *m*.
ail [eɪl] *vt* **what ails you?** de quoi souffrez-vous? ◆**—ing** *a* souffrant, malade. ◆**—ment** *n* maladie *f*.
aim [eɪm] *n* but *m*; **to take a.** viser; **with the a. of** dans le but de; – *vt* (*gun*) braquer, diriger (**at** sur); (*lamp*) diriger (**at** vers); (*stone*) lancer (**at** à, vers); (*blow, remark*) décocher (**at** à); – *vi* viser; **to a. at s.o.** viser qn; **to a. to do** *or* **at doing** avoir l'intention de faire. ◆**—less** *a*, ◆**—lessly** *adv* sans but.
air [eər] **1** *n* air *m*; **in the open a.** en plein air; **by a.** (*to travel*) en *or* par avion; (*letter, freight*) par avion; **to be** *or* **go on the a.** (*person*) passer à l'antenne; (*programme*) être diffusé; **(up) in the a.** (*to throw*) en l'air; (*plan*) incertain, en l'air; **there's sth in the a.** *Fig* il se prépare qch; – *a* (*raid, base etc*) aérien; **a. force/hostess** armée *f*/hôtesse *f* de l'air; **a. terminal** aérogare *f*; – *vt* (*room*) aérer; (*views*) exposer; **airing cupboard** armoire *f* sèche-linge. **2** *n* (*appearance, tune*) air *m*; **to put on airs** se donner des airs; **with an a. of sadness/***etc* d'un air triste/*etc*.
airborne ['eəbɔːn] *a* en (cours de) vol; (*troops*) aéroporté; **to become a.** (*of aircraft*) décoller. ◆**airbridge** *n* pont *m* aérien. ◆**air-conditioned** *a* climatisé. ◆**air-conditioner** *n* climatiseur *m*. ◆**aircraft** *n inv* avion(s) *m*(*pl*); **a. carrier** porte-avions *m inv*. ◆**aircrew** *n Av* équipage *m*. ◆**airfield** *n* terrain *m* d'aviation. ◆**airgun** *n* carabine *f* à air comprimé. ◆**airletter** *n* aérogramme *m*. ◆**airlift** *n* pont *m* aérien; – *vt* transporter par avion. ◆**airline** *n* ligne *f* aérienne. ◆**airliner** *n* avion *m* de ligne. ◆**airlock** *n* (*chamber*) *Nau Av* sas *m*; (*in pipe*) bouchon *m*. ◆**airmail** *n* poste *f* aérienne; **by a.** par avion. ◆**airman** *n* (*pl* **-men**) aviateur *m*. ◆**airplane** *n Am* avion *m*. ◆**airpocket** *n* trou *m* d'air. ◆**airport** *n* aéroport *m*. ◆**airship** *n* dirigeable *m*. ◆**airsickness** *n* mal *m* de l'air. ◆**airstrip** *n* terrain *m* d'atterrissage. ◆**airtight** *a* hermétique. ◆**airway** *n* (*route*) couloir *m* aérien. ◆**airworthy** *a* en état de navigation.
airy ['eərɪ] *a* (**-ier, -iest**) (*room*) bien aéré; (*promise*) vain; (*step*) léger. ◆**a.-fairy** *a Fam* farfelu. ◆**airily** *adv* (*not seriously*) d'un ton léger.
aisle [aɪl] *n* couloir *m*; (*of church*) nef *f* latérale.
aitch [eɪtʃ] *n* (*letter*) h *m*.
ajar [ə'dʒɑːr] *a* & *adv* (*door*) entrouvert.
akin [ə'kɪn] *a* **a. (to)** apparenté (à).
alabaster ['æləbɑːstər] *n* albâtre *m*.
alacrity [ə'lækrɪtɪ] *n* empressement *m*.
à la mode [ælæ'məʊd] *a Culin Am* avec de la crème glacée.
alarm [ə'lɑːm] *n* (*warning, fear*) alarme *f*; (*apparatus*) sonnerie *f* (d'alarme); **false a.** fausse alerte *f*; **a. (clock)** réveil *m*, réveille-matin *m inv*; – *vt* (*frighten*) alarmer. ◆**alarmist** *n* alarmiste *mf*.
alas! [ə'læs] *int* hélas!
albatross ['ælbətrɒs] *n* albatros *m*.
albeit [ɔːl'biːɪt] *conj Lit* quoique.
albino [æl'biːnəʊ, *Am* æl'baɪnəʊ] *n* (*pl* **-os**) albinos *mf*.
album ['ælbəm] *n* (*book, record*) album *m*.
alchemy ['ælkəmɪ] *n* alchimie *f*. ◆**alchemist** *n* alchimiste *m*.
alcohol ['ælkəhɒl] *n* alcool *m*. ◆**alco'holic** *a* (*person*) alcoolique; (*drink*) alcoolisé; – *n* (*person*) alcoolique *mf*. ◆**alcoholism** *n* alcoolisme *m*.
alcove ['ælkəʊv] *n* alcôve *f*.
alderman ['ɔːldəmən] *n* (*pl* **-men**) conseiller, -ère *mf* municipal(e).
ale [eɪl] *n* bière *f*.
alert [ə'lɜːt] *a* (*watchful*) vigilant; (*sharp, awake*) éveillé; – *n* alerte *f*; **on the a.** sur le qui-vive; – *vt* alerter. ◆**—ness** *n* vigilance *f*.
alfalfa [æl'fælfə] *n Am* luzerne *f*.
algebra ['ældʒɪbrə] *n* algèbre *f*. ◆**algeb'raic** *a* algébrique.
Algeria [æl'dʒɪərɪə] *n* Algérie *f*. ◆**Algerian** *a* & *n* algérien, -ienne (*mf*).
alias ['eɪlɪəs] *adv* alias; – *n* nom *m* d'emprunt.
alibi ['ælɪbaɪ] *n* alibi *m*.

alien ['eɪlɪən] *a* étranger (to à); – *n* étranger, -ère *mf.* ◆**alienate** *vt* aliéner; **to a. s.o.** (*make unfriendly*) s'aliéner qn.

alight [ə'laɪt] **1** *a* (*fire*) allumé; (*building*) en feu; (*face*) éclairé; **to set a.** mettre le feu à. **2** *vi* descendre (**from** de); (*of bird*) se poser.

align [ə'laɪn] *vt* aligner. ◆**—ment** *n* alignement *m.*

alike [ə'laɪk] **1** *a* (*people, things*) semblables, pareils; **to look** *or* **be a.** se ressembler. **2** *adv* de la même manière; **summer and winter a.** été comme hiver.

alimony ['ælɪmənɪ, *Am* 'ælɪməʊnɪ] *n Jur* pension *f* alimentaire.

alive [ə'laɪv] *a* vivant, en vie; **a. to** conscient de; **a. with** grouillant de; **burnt a.** brûlé vif; **anyone a.** n'importe qui; **to keep a.** (*custom, memory*) entretenir, perpétuer; **a. and kicking** *Fam* plein de vie; **look a.!** *Fam* active-toi!

all [ɔːl] *a* tout, toute, *pl* tous, toutes; **a. day** toute la journée; **a. (the) men** tous les hommes; **with a. speed** à toute vitesse; **for a. her wealth** malgré toute sa fortune; – *pron* tous *mpl,* toutes *fpl*; (*everything*) tout; **a. will die** tous mourront; **my sisters are a. here** toutes mes sœurs sont ici; **he ate it a., he ate a. of it** il a tout mangé; **a. (that) he has** tout ce qu'il a; **a. in a.** à tout prendre; **in a., a. told** en tout; **a. but impossible/*etc*** presque impossible/*etc*; **anything at a.** quoi que ce soit; **if he comes at a.** s'il vient effectivement; **if there's any wind at a.** s'il y a le moindre vent; **not at a.** pas du tout; (*after 'thank you'*) il n'y a pas de quoi; **a. of us** nous tous; **take a. of it** prends (le) tout; – *adv* tout; **a. alone** tout seul; **a. bad** entièrement mauvais; **a. over** (*everywhere*) partout; (*finished*) fini; **a. right** (très) bien; **he's a. right** (*not harmed*) il est sain et sauf; (*healthy*) il va bien; **a. too soon** bien trop tôt; **six a.** *Fb* six buts partout; **a. there** *Fam* éveillé, intelligent; **not a. there** *Fam* simple d'esprit; **a. in** *Fam* épuisé; **a.-in price** prix global; – *n* **my a.** tout ce que j'ai. ◆**a.-'clear** *n Mil* fin *f* d'alerte. ◆**a.-night** *a* (*party*) qui dure toute la nuit; (*shop*) ouvert toute la nuit. ◆**a.-out** *a* (*effort*) violent; (*war, strike*) tous azimuts. ◆**a.-'powerful** *a* tout-puissant. ◆**a.-purpose** *a* (*tool*) universel. ◆**a.-round** *a* complet. ◆**a.-'rounder** *n* personne *f* qui fait de tout. ◆**a.-time** *a* (*record*) jamais atteint; **to reach an a.-time low/high** arriver au point le plus bas/le plus haut.

allay [ə'leɪ] *vt* calmer, apaiser.

alleg/e [ə'ledʒ] *vt* prétendre. ◆**—ed** *a* (*so-called*) prétendu; (*author, culprit*) présumé; **he is a. to be** on prétend qu'il est. ◆**—edly** [-ɪdlɪ] *adv* d'après ce qu'on dit. ◆**alle'gation** *n* allégation *f.*

allegiance [ə'liːdʒəns] *n* fidélité *f* (**to** à).

allegory ['ælɪgərɪ, *Am* 'æləgɔːrɪ] *n* allégorie *f.* ◆**alle'gorical** *a* allégorique.

allergy ['ælədʒɪ] *n* allergie *f.* ◆**a'llergic** *a* allergique (**to** à).

alleviate [ə'liːvɪeɪt] *vt* alléger.

alley ['ælɪ] *n* ruelle *f*; (*in park*) allée *f*; **blind a.** impasse *f*; **that's up my a.** *Fam* c'est mon truc. ◆**alleyway** *n* ruelle *f.*

alliance [ə'laɪəns] *n* alliance *f.*

allied ['ælaɪd] *a* (*country*) allié; (*matters*) connexe.

alligator ['ælɪgeɪtər] *n* alligator *m.*

allocate ['æləkeɪt] *vt* (*assign*) attribuer, allouer (**to** à); (*distribute*) répartir. ◆**allo'cation** *n* attribution *f.*

allot [ə'lɒt] *vt* (**-tt-**) (*assign*) attribuer; (*distribute*) répartir. ◆**—ment** *n* attribution *f*; (*share*) partage *m*; (*land*) lopin *m* de terre (*loué pour la culture*).

allow [ə'laʊ] **1** *vt* permettre; (*grant*) accorder; (*a request*) accéder à; (*deduct*) *Com* déduire; (*add*) *Com* ajouter; **to a. s.o. to do** permettre à qn de faire, autoriser qn à faire; **a. me!** permettez(-moi)!; **not allowed** interdit; **you're not allowed to go** on vous interdit de partir. **2** *vi* **to a. for** tenir compte de. ◆**—able** *a* (*acceptable*) admissible; (*expense*) déductible.

allowance [ə'laʊəns] *n* allocation *f*; (*for travel, housing, food*) indemnité *f*; (*for duty-free goods*) tolérance *f*; (*tax-free amount*) abattement *m*; **to make allowance(s) for** (*person*) être indulgent envers; (*thing*) tenir compte de.

alloy ['ælɔɪ] *n* alliage *m.*

allude [ə'luːd] *vi* **to a. to** faire allusion à. ◆**allusion** *n* allusion *f.*

allure [ə'lʊər] *vt* attirer.

ally ['ælaɪ] *n* allié, -ée *mf*; – [ə'laɪ] *vt* (*country, person*) allier.

almanac ['ɔːlmənæk] *n* almanach *m.*

almighty [ɔːl'maɪtɪ] **1** *a* tout-puissant; **the A.** le Tout-Puissant. **2** *a* (*great*) *Fam* terrible, formidable.

almond ['ɑːmənd] *n* amande *f.*

almost ['ɔːlməʊst] *adv* presque; **he a. fell/*etc*** il a failli tomber/*etc.*

alms [ɑːmz] *npl* aumône *f.*

alone [ə'ləʊn] *a & adv* seul; **an expert a. can . . .** seul un expert peut . . . ; **I did it (all) a.** je l'ai fait à moi (tout) seul, je l'ai fait (tout) seul; **to leave** *or* **let a.** (*person*) laisser tranquille *or* en paix; (*thing*) ne pas toucher à.

along [ə'lɒŋ] *prep* **(all) a.** (tout) le long de; **to go** *or* **walk a.** (*street*) passer par; **a. here** par ici; **a. with** avec; – *adv* **all a.** d'un bout à l'autre; (*time*) dès le début; **come a.!** venez!; **move a.!** avancez!

alongside [əlɒŋ'saɪd] *prep* & *adv* à côté (de); **to come a.** *Nau* accoster; **a. the kerb** le long du trottoir.

aloof [ə'luːf] *a* distant; – *adv* à distance; **to keep a.** garder ses distances **(from** par rapport à). ◆**—ness** *n* réserve *f.*

aloud [ə'laʊd] *adv* à haute voix.

alphabet ['ælfəbet] *n* alphabet *m.* ◆**alpha'betical** *a* alphabétique.

Alps [ælps] *npl* **the A.** les Alpes *fpl.* ◆**alpine** *a* (*club, range etc*) alpin; (*scenery*) alpestre.

already [ɔːl'redɪ] *adv* déjà.

alright [ɔːl'raɪt] *adv Fam* = **all right.**

Alsatian [æl'seɪʃ(ə)n] *n* (*dog*) berger *m* allemand, chien-loup *m.*

also ['ɔːlsəʊ] *adv* aussi, également. ◆**a.-ran** *n* (*person*) *Fig* perdant, -ante *mf.*

altar ['ɔːltər] *n* autel *m.*

alter ['ɔːltər] *vt* changer, modifier; (*clothing*) retoucher; – *vi* changer. ◆**alte'ration** *n* changement *m,* modification *f*; retouche *f.*

altercation [ɔːltə'keɪʃ(ə)n] *n* altercation *f.*

alternat/e [ɔːl'tɜːnət] *a* alterné; **on a. days** tous les deux jours; **a. laughter and tears** des rires et des larmes qui se succèdent; – ['ɔːltəneɪt] *vi* alterner **(with** avec); –*vt* faire alterner. ◆**—ing** *a* (*current*) *El* alternatif. ◆**—ely** *adv* alternativement. ◆**alter'nation** *n* alternance *f.*

alternative [ɔːl'tɜːnətɪv] *a* **an a. way/***etc* une autre façon/*etc*; **a. answers/***etc* d'autres réponses/*etc* (différentes); – *n* (*choice*) alternative *f.* ◆**—ly** *adv* comme alternative; **or a.** (*or else*) ou bien.

although [ɔːl'ðəʊ] *adv* bien que, quoique (+ *sub*).

altitude ['æltɪtjuːd] *n* altitude *f.*

altogether [ɔːltə'geðər] *adv* (*completely*) tout à fait; (*on the whole*) somme toute; **how much a.?** combien en tout?

aluminium [ælju'mɪnjəm] (*Am* **aluminum** [ə'luːmɪnəm]) *n* aluminium *m.*

alumnus, *pl* **-ni** [ə'lʌmnəs, -naɪ] *n Am* ancien(ne) élève *mf,* ancien(ne) étudiant, -ante *mf.*

always ['ɔːlweɪz] *adv* toujours; **he's a. criticizing** il est toujours à critiquer.

am [æm, *unstressed* əm] *see* **be.**

a.m. [eɪ'em] *adv* du matin.

amalgam [ə'mælgəm] *n* amalgame *m.* ◆**a'malgamate** *vt* amalgamer; (*society*) *Com* fusionner; – *vi* s'amalgamer; fusionner.

amass [ə'mæs] *vt* (*riches*) amasser.

amateur ['æmətər] *n* amateur *m*; – *a* (*interest, sports*) d'amateur; **a. painter/***etc* peintre/*etc* amateur. ◆**amateurish** *a* (*work*) *Pej* d'amateur; (*person*) *Pej* maladroit, malhabile. ◆**amateurism** *n* amateurisme *m.*

amaz/e [ə'meɪz] *vt* stupéfier, étonner. ◆**—ed** *a* stupéfait **(at sth** de qch), étonné **(at sth** par *or* de qch); **a. at seeing/***etc* stupéfait *or* étonné de voir/*etc.* ◆**—ing** *a* stupéfiant; *Fam* extraordinaire. ◆**—ingly** *adv* extraordinairement; (*miraculously*) par miracle. ◆**amazement** *n* stupéfaction *f.*

ambassador [æm'bæsədər] *n* ambassadeur *m*; (*woman*) ambassadrice *f.*

amber ['æmbər] *n* ambre *m*; **a. (light)** *Aut* (feu *m*) orange *m.*

ambidextrous [æmbɪ'dekstrəs] *a* ambidextre.

ambiguous [æm'bɪgjʊəs] *a* ambigu. ◆**ambi'guity** *n* ambiguïté *f.*

ambition [æm'bɪʃ(ə)n] *n* ambition *f.* ◆**ambitious** *a* ambitieux.

ambivalent [æm'bɪvələnt] *a* ambigu, équivoque.

amble ['æmb(ə)l] *vi* marcher d'un pas tranquille.

ambulance ['æmbjʊləns] *n* ambulance *f*; **a. man** ambulancier *m.*

ambush ['æmbʊʃ] *n* guet-apens *m,* embuscade *f*; – *vt* prendre en embuscade.

amen [ɑː'men, eɪ'men] *int* amen.

amenable [ə'miːnəb(ə)l] *a* docile; **a. to** (*responsive to*) sensible à; **a. to reason** raisonnable.

amend [ə'mend] *vt* (*text*) modifier; (*conduct*) corriger; *Pol* amender. ◆**—ment** *n Pol* amendement *m.*

amends [ə'mendz] *npl* **to make a. for** réparer; **to make a.** réparer son erreur.

amenities [ə'miːnɪtɪz, *Am* ə'menɪtɪz] *npl* (*pleasant things*) agréments *mpl*; (*of sports club etc*) équipement *m*; (*of town*) aménagements *mpl.*

America [ə'merɪkə] *n* Amérique *f*; **North/South A.** Amérique du Nord/du Sud. ◆**American** *a* & *n* américain, -aine (*mf*). ◆**Americanism** *n* américanisme *m.*

amethyst ['æməθɪst] *n* améthyste *f.*

amiable ['eɪmɪəb(ə)l] *a* aimable.

amicab/le ['æmɪkəb(ə)l] *a* amical. ◆**—ly** *adv* amicalement; *Jur* à l'amiable.

amid(st) [ə'mɪd(st)] *prep* au milieu de, parmi.
amiss [ə'mɪs] *adv & a* mal (à propos); **sth is a.** (*wrong*) qch ne va pas; **that wouldn't come a.** ça ne ferait pas de mal; **to take a.** prendre en mauvaise part.
ammonia [ə'məʊnjə] *n* (*gas*) ammoniac *m*; (*liquid*) ammoniaque *f*.
ammunition [æmjʊ'nɪʃ(ə)n] *n* munitions *fpl*.
amnesia [æm'niːzjə] *n* amnésie *f*.
amnesty ['æmnəstɪ] *n* amnistie *f*.
amok [ə'mɒk] *adv* **to run a.** se déchaîner, s'emballer.
among(st) [ə'mʌŋ(st)] *prep* parmi, entre; **a. themselves/friends** entre eux/amis; **a. the French**/*etc* (*group*) chez les Français/*etc*; **a. the crowd** dans *or* parmi la foule.
amoral [eɪ'mɒrəl] *a* amoral.
amorous ['æmərəs] *a* amoureux.
amount [ə'maʊnt] **1** *n* quantité *f*; (*sum of money*) somme *f*; (*total of bill etc*) montant *m*; (*scope, size*) importance *f*. **2** *vi* **to a. to** s'élever à; (*mean*) *Fig* signifier; **it amounts to the same thing** ça revient au même.
amp(ere) ['æmp(eər)] *n El* ampère *m*.
amphibian [æm'fɪbɪən] *n & a* amphibie (*m*). ◆**amphibious** *a* amphibie.
amphitheatre ['æmfɪθɪətər] *n* amphithéâtre *m*.
ample ['æmp(ə)l] *a* (*roomy*) ample; (*enough*) largement assez de; (*reasons, means*) solides; **you have a. time** tu as largement le temps. ◆**amply** *adv* largement, amplement.
amplify ['æmplɪfaɪ] *vt* amplifier. ◆**amplifier** *n El* amplificateur *m*.
amputate ['æmpjʊteɪt] *vt* amputer. ◆**ampu'tation** *n* amputation *f*.
amuck [ə'mʌk] *adv see* **amok**.
amulet ['æmjʊlət] *n* amulette *f*.
amus/e [ə'mjuːz] *vt* amuser, divertir; **to keep s.o. amused** amuser qn. ◆**—ing** *a* amusant. ◆**—ement** *n* amusement *m*, divertissement *m*; (*pastime*) distraction *f*; **a. arcade** salle *f* de jeux.
an [æn, *unstressed* ən] *see* **a**.
anachronism [ə'nækrənɪz(ə)m] *n* anachronisme *m*.
an(a)emia [ə'niːmɪə] *n* anémie *f*. ◆**an(a)emic** *a* anémique.
an(a)esthesia [ænɪs'θiːzɪə] *n* anesthésie *f*. ◆**an(a)esthetic** [ænɪs'θetɪk] *n* (*substance*) anesthésique *m*; **under the a.** sous anesthésie; **general/local a.** anesthésie *f* générale/locale. ◆**an(a)esthetize** [ə'niːsθɪtaɪz] *vt* anesthésier.
anagram ['ænəgræm] *n* anagramme *f*.
analogy [ə'næləd͡ʒɪ] *n* analogie *f*. ◆**analogous** *a* analogue (**to** à).
analyse ['ænəlaɪz] *vt* analyser. ◆**analysis**, *pl* **-yses** [ə'næləsɪs, -ɪsiːz] *n* analyse *f*. ◆**analyst** *n* analyste *mf*. ◆**ana'lytical** *a* analytique.
anarchy ['ænəkɪ] *n* anarchie *f*. ◆**a'narchic** *a* anarchique. ◆**anarchist** *n* anarchiste *mf*.
anathema [ə'næθəmə] *n Rel* anathème *m*; **it is (an) a. to me** j'ai une sainte horreur de cela.
anatomy [ə'nætəmɪ] *n* anatomie *f*. ◆**ana'tomical** *a* anatomique.
ancestor ['ænsestər] *n* ancêtre *m*. ◆**an'cestral** *a* ancestral. ◆**ancestry** *n* (*lineage*) ascendance *f*; (*ancestors*) ancêtres *mpl*.
anchor ['æŋkər] *n* ancre *f*; **to weigh a.** lever l'ancre; — *vt* (*ship*) mettre à l'ancre; — *vi* jeter l'ancre, mouiller. ◆**—ed** *a* à l'ancre. ◆**—age** *n* mouillage *m*.
anchovy ['æntʃəvɪ, *Am* æn'tʃəʊvɪ] *n* anchois *m*.
ancient ['eɪnʃənt] *a* ancien; (*pre-medieval*) antique; (*person*) *Hum* vétuste.
ancillary [æn'sɪlərɪ] *a* auxiliaire.
and [ænd, *unstressed* ən(d)] *conj* et; **a knife a. fork** un couteau et une fourchette; **two hundred a. two** deux cent deux; **better a. better** de mieux en mieux; **go a. see** va voir.
anecdote ['ænɪkdəʊt] *n* anecdote *f*.
anemone [ə'nemənɪ] *n* anémone *f*.
anew [ə'njuː] *adv Lit* de *or* à nouveau.
angel ['eɪnd͡ʒəl] *n* ange *m*. ◆**an'gelic** *a* angélique.
anger ['æŋgər] *n* colère *f*; **in a., out of a.** sous le coup de la colère; — *vt* mettre en colère, fâcher.
angl/e ['æŋg(ə)l] **1** *n* angle *m*; **at an a.** en biais. **2** *vi* (*to fish*) pêcher à la ligne; **to a. for** *Fig* quêter. ◆**—er** *n* pêcheur, -euse *mf* à la ligne. ◆**—ing** *n* pêche *f* à la ligne.
Anglican ['æŋglɪkən] *a & n* anglican, -ane (*mf*).
anglicism ['æŋglɪsɪz(ə)m] *n* anglicisme *m*.
Anglo- ['æŋgləʊ] *pref* anglo-. ◆**Anglo-'Saxon** *a & n* anglo-saxon, -onne (*mf*).
angora [æŋ'gɔːrə] *n* (*wool*) angora *m*.
angry ['æŋgrɪ] *a* (**-ier, -iest**) (*person, look*) fâché; (*letter*) indigné; **to get a.** se fâcher, se mettre en colère (**with** contre). ◆**angrily** *adv* en colère; (*to speak*) avec colère.
anguish ['æŋgwɪʃ] *n* angoisse *f*. ◆**—ed** *a* angoissé.
angular ['æŋgjʊlər] *a* (*face*) anguleux.

animal ['ænɪməl] *a* animal; – *n* animal *m*, bête *f*.
animate ['ænɪmeɪt] *vt* animer; **to become animated** s'animer; – ['ænɪmət] *a* (*alive*) animé. ◆**ani'mation** *n* animation *f*.
animosity [ænɪ'mɒsɪtɪ] *n* animosité *f*.
aniseed ['ænɪsiːd] *n* *Culin* anis *m*.
ankle ['æŋk(ə)l] *n* cheville *f*; **a. sock** socquette *f*.
annals ['æn(ə)lz] *npl* annales *fpl*.
annex [ə'neks] *vt* annexer.
annex(e) ['æneks] *n* (*building*) annexe *f*. ◆**annex'ation** *n* annexion *f*.
annihilate [ə'naɪəleɪt] *vt* anéantir, annihiler. ◆**annihi'lation** *n* anéantissement *m*.
anniversary [ænɪ'vɜːsərɪ] *n* (*of event*) anniversaire *m*, commémoration *f*.
annotate ['ænəteɪt] *vt* annoter. ◆**anno'tation** *n* annotation *f*.
announc/e [ə'naʊns] *vt* annoncer; (*birth, marriage*) faire part de. ◆**—ement** *n* annonce *f*; (*of birth, marriage*) avis *m*; (*private letter*) faire-part *m inv*. ◆**—er** *n* *TV* speaker *m*, speakerine *f*.
annoy [ə'nɔɪ] *vt* (*inconvenience*) ennuyer, gêner; (*irritate*) agacer, contrarier. ◆**—ed** *a* contrarié, fâché; **to get a.** se fâcher (**with** contre). ◆**—ing** *a* ennuyeux, contrariant. ◆**annoyance** *n* contrariété *f*, ennui *m*.
annual ['ænjʊəl] *a* annuel; – *n* (*book*) annuaire *m*. ◆**—ly** *adv* annuellement.
annuity [ə'njuːɪtɪ] *n* (*of retired person*) pension *f* viagère.
annul [ə'nʌl] *vt* (**-ll-**) annuler. ◆**—ment** *n* annulation *f*.
anoint [ə'nɔɪnt] *vt* oindre (**with** de). ◆**—ed** *a* oint.
anomalous [ə'nɒmələs] *a* anormal. ◆**anomaly** *n* anomalie *f*.
anon [ə'nɒn] *adv* *Hum* tout à l'heure.
anonymous [ə'nɒnɪməs] *a* anonyme; **to remain a.** garder l'anonymat. ◆**ano'nymity** *n* anonymat *m*.
anorak ['ænəræk] *n* anorak *m*.
anorexia [ænə'reksɪə] *n* anorexie *f*.
another [ə'nʌðər] *a* & *pron* un(e) autre; **a. man** un autre homme; **a. month** (*additional*) encore un mois, un autre mois; **a. ten** encore dix; **one a.** l'un(e) l'autre, *pl* les un(e)s les autres; **they love one a.** ils s'aiment (l'un l'autre).
answer ['ɑːnsər] *n* réponse *f*; (*to problem*) solution (**to** de); (*reason*) explication *f*; – *vt* (*person, question, phone etc*) répondre à; (*word*) répondre; (*problem*) résoudre; (*prayer, wish*) exaucer; **to a. the bell** *or* **the door** ouvrir la porte; – *vi* répondre; **to a. back** répliquer, répondre; **to a. for** (*s.o., sth*) répondre de. ◆**—able** *a* responsable (**for sth** de qch, **to s.o.** devant qn).
ant [ænt] *n* fourmi *f*. ◆**anthill** *n* fourmilière *f*.
antagonism [æn'tægənɪz(ə)m] *n* antagonisme *m*; (*hostility*) hostilité *f*. ◆**antagonist** *n* antagoniste *mf*. ◆**antago'nistic** *a* antagoniste; (*hostile*) hostile. ◆**antagonize** *vt* provoquer (l'hostilité de).
antarctic [æn'tɑːktɪk] *a* antarctique; – *n* **the A.** l'Antarctique *m*.
antecedent [æntɪ'siːd(ə)nt] *n* antécédent *m*.
antechamber ['æntɪtʃeɪmbər] *n* antichambre *f*.
antedate ['æntɪdeɪt] *vt* (*letter*) antidater.
antelope ['æntɪləʊp] *n* antilope *f*.
antenatal [æntɪ'neɪt(ə)l] *a* prénatal.
antenna[1], *pl* **-ae** [æn'tenə, -iː] *n* (*of insect etc*) antenne *f*.
antenna[2] [æn'tenə] *n* (*pl* **-as**) (*aerial*) *Am* antenne *f*.
anteroom ['æntɪrʊm] *n* antichambre *f*.
anthem ['ænθəm] *n* **national a.** hymne *m* national.
anthology [æn'θɒlədʒɪ] *n* anthologie *f*.
anthropology [ænθrə'pɒlədʒɪ] *n* anthropologie *f*.
anti- ['æntɪ, *Am* 'æntaɪ] *pref* anti-; **to be a. sth** *Fam* être contre qch. ◆**anti'aircraft** *a* antiaérien. ◆**antibi'otic** *a* & *n* antibiotique (*m*). ◆**antibody** *n* anticorps *m*. ◆**anti'climax** *n* chute *f* dans l'ordinaire; (*let-down*) déception *f*. ◆**anti'clockwise** *adv* dans le sens inverse des aiguilles d'une montre. ◆**anti'cyclone** *n* anticyclone *m*. ◆**antidote** *n* antidote *m*. ◆**antifreeze** *n* *Aut* antigel *m*. ◆**anti'histamine** *n* *Med* antihistaminique *m*. ◆**anti'perspirant** *n* antisudoral *m*. ◆**anti-Se'mitic** *a* antisémite. ◆**anti-'Semitism** *n* antisémitisme *m*. ◆**anti'septic** *a* & *n* antiseptique (*m*). ◆**anti'social** *a* (*misfit*) asocial; (*measure, principles*) antisocial; (*unsociable*) insociable.
anticipate [æn'tɪsɪpeɪt] *vt* (*foresee*) prévoir; (*forestall*) devancer; (*expect*) s'attendre à; (*the future*) anticiper sur. ◆**antici'pation** *n* prévision *f*; (*expectation*) attente *f*; **in a. of** en prévision de, dans l'attente de; **in a.** (*to thank s.o., pay etc*) d'avance.
antics ['æntɪks] *npl* bouffonneries *fpl*.
antipathy [æn'tɪpəθɪ] *n* antipathie *f*.
antipodes [æn'tɪpədiːz] *npl* antipodes *mpl*.
antiquarian [æntɪ'kweərɪən] *a* **a. bookseller**

libraire *mf* spécialisé(e) dans le livre ancien.
antiquated ['æntɪkweɪtɪd] *a* vieilli; (*person*) vieux jeu *inv*.
antique [æn'tiːk] *a* (*furniture etc*) ancien; (*of Greek etc antiquity*) antique; **a. dealer** antiquaire *mf*; **a. shop** magasin *m* d'antiquités; – *n* objet *m* ancien *or* d'époque, antiquité *f*. ◆**antiquity** *n* (*period etc*) antiquité *f*.
antithesis, *pl* **-eses** [æn'tɪθəsɪs, -ɪsiːz] *n* antithèse *f*.
antler ['æntlər] *n* (*tine*) andouiller *m*; *pl* bois *mpl*.
antonym ['æntənɪm] *n* antonyme *m*.
Antwerp ['æntwɜːp] *n* Anvers *m or f*.
anus ['eɪnəs] *n* anus *m*.
anvil ['ænvɪl] *n* enclume *f*.
anxiety [æŋ'zaɪətɪ] *n* (*worry*) inquiétude *f* (**about** au sujet de); (*fear*) anxiété *f*; (*eagerness*) impatience *f* (**for** de).
anxious ['æŋkʃəs] *a* (*worried*) inquiet (**about** de, pour); (*troubled*) anxieux; (*causing worry*) inquiétant; (*eager*) impatient (**to** do de faire); **I'm a. (that) he should go** je tiens beaucoup à ce qu'il parte. ◆**—ly** *adv* avec inquiétude; (*to wait etc*) impatiemment.
any ['enɪ] *a* **1** (*interrogative*) du, de la, des; **have you a. milk/tickets?** avez-vous du lait/des billets?; **is there a. man (at all) who . . . ?** y a-t-il un homme (quelconque) qui . . . ? **2** (*negative*) de; (*not any at all*) aucun; **he hasn't a. milk/tickets** il n'a pas de lait/de billets; **there isn't a. proof** il n'y a aucune preuve. **3** (*no matter which*) n'importe quel. **4** (*every*) tout; **at a. hour** à toute heure; **in a. case, at a. rate** de toute façon; – *pron* **1** (*no matter which one*) n'importe lequel; (*somebody*) quelqu'un; **if a. of you** si l'un d'entre vous, si quelqu'un parmi vous; **more than a.** plus qu'aucun. **2** (*quantity*) en; **have you a.?** en as-tu?; **I don't see a.** je n'en vois pas; – *adv* (*usually not translated*) **(not) a. further/happier/***etc* (pas) plus loin/plus heureux/*etc*; **I don't see her a. more** je ne la vois plus; **a. more tea?** (*a little*) encore du thé?, encore un peu de thé?; **a. better?** (un peu) mieux?
anybody ['enɪbɒdɪ] *pron* **1** (*somebody*) quelqu'un; **do you see a.?** vois-tu quelqu'un?; **more than a.** plus qu'aucun. **2** (*negative*) personne; **he doesn't know a.** il ne connaît personne. **3** (*no matter who*) n'importe qui; **a. would think that . . .** on croirait que . . . .
anyhow ['enɪhaʊ] *adv* (*at any rate*) de toute façon; (*badly*) n'importe comment; **to leave sth a.** (*in confusion*) laisser qch sens dessus dessous.
anyone ['enɪwʌn] *pron* = **anybody.**
anyplace ['enɪpleɪs] *adv Am* = **anywhere.**
anything ['enɪθɪŋ] *pron* **1** (*something*) quelque chose; **can you see a.?** voyez-vous quelque chose? **2** (*negative*) rien; **he doesn't do a.** il ne fait rien; **without a.** sans rien. **3** (*everything*) tout; **a. you like** (tout) ce que tu veux; **like a.** (*to work etc*) *Fam* comme un fou. **4** (*no matter what*) **a. (at all)** n'importe quoi.
anyway ['enɪweɪ] *adv* (*at any rate*) de toute façon.
anywhere ['enɪweər] *adv* **1** (*no matter where*) n'importe où. **2** (*everywhere*) partout; **a. you go** partout où vous allez, où que vous alliez; **a. you like** là où tu veux. **3** (*somewhere*) quelque part; **is he going a.?** va-t-il quelque part? **4** (*negative*) nulle part; **he doesn't go a.** il ne va nulle part; **without a. to put it** sans un endroit où le mettre.
apace [ə'peɪs] *adv* rapidement.
apart [ə'pɑːt] *adv* (*to or at one side*) à part; **to tear a.** (*to pieces*) mettre en pièces; **we kept them a.** (*separate*) on les tenait séparés; **with legs (wide) a.** les jambes écartées; **they are a metre a.** ils se trouvent à un mètre l'un de l'autre; **a. from** (*except for*) à part; **to take a.** démonter; **to come a.** (*of two objects*) se séparer; (*of knot etc*) se défaire; **to tell a.** distinguer entre; **worlds a.** (*very different*) diamétralement opposé.
apartheid [ə'pɑːteɪt] *n* apartheid *m*.
apartment [ə'pɑːtmənt] *n* (*flat*) *Am* appartement *m*; (*room*) chambre *f*; **a. house** *Am* immeuble *m* (*d'habitation*).
apathy ['æpəθɪ] *n* apathie *f*. ◆**apa'thetic** *a* apathique.
ape [eɪp] *n* singe; – *vt* (*imitate*) singer.
aperitif [ə'perətiːf] *n* apéritif *m*.
aperture ['æpətʃʊər] *n* ouverture *f*.
apex ['eɪpeks] *n Geom & Fig* sommet *m*.
aphorism ['æfərɪz(ə)m] *n* aphorisme *m*.
aphrodisiac [æfrə'dɪzɪæk] *a & n* aphrodisiaque (*m*).
apiece [ə'piːs] *adv* chacun; **a pound a.** une livre (la) pièce *or* chacun.
apish ['eɪpɪʃ] *a* simiesque; (*imitative*) imitateur.
apocalypse [ə'pɒkəlɪps] *n* apocalypse *f*. ◆**apoca'lyptic** *a* apocalyptique.
apocryphal [ə'pɒkrɪfəl] *a* apocryphe.
apogee ['æpədʒiː] *n* apogée *m*.
apologetic [əpɒlə'dʒetɪk] *a* (*letter*) plein d'excuses; **to be a. about** s'excuser de. ◆**apologetically** *adv* en s'excusant.

apology [ə'pɒlədʒɪ] *n* excuses *fpl*; **an a. for a dinner** *Fam Pej* un dîner minable. ♦**apologist** *n* apologiste *mf*. ♦**apologize** *vi* s'excuser (**for** de); **to a. to s.o.** faire ses excuses à qn (**for** pour).

apoplexy ['æpəpleksɪ] *n* apoplexie *f*. ♦**apo'plectic** *a* & *n* apoplectique (*mf*).

apostle [ə'pɒs(ə)l] *n* apôtre *m*.

apostrophe [ə'pɒstrəfɪ] *n* apostrophe *f*.

appal [ə'pɔːl] (*Am* **appall**) *vt* (**-ll-**) épouvanter. ♦**appalling** *a* épouvantable.

apparatus [æpə'reɪtəs, *Am* -'rætəs] *n* (*equipment, organization*) appareil *m*; (*in gym*) agrès *mpl*.

apparel [ə'pærəl] *n* habit *m*, habillement *m*.

apparent [ə'pærənt] *a* (*obvious, seeming*) apparent; **it's a. that** il est évident que. ♦**—ly** *adv* apparemment.

apparition [æpə'rɪʃ(ə)n] *n* apparition *f*.

appeal [ə'piːl] *n* (*call*) appel *m*; (*entreaty*) supplication *f*; (*charm*) attrait *m*; (*interest*) intérêt *m*; *Jur* appel *m*; – *vt* **to a. to** (*s.o., s.o.'s kindness*) faire appel à; **to a. to s.o.** (*attract*) plaire à qn, séduire qn; (*interest*) intéresser qn; **to a. to s.o. for sth** demander qch à qn; **to a. to s.o. to do** supplier qn de faire; – *vi Jur* faire appel. ♦**—ing** *a* (*begging*) suppliant; (*attractive*) séduisant.

appear [ə'pɪər] *vi* (*become visible*) apparaître; (*present oneself*) se présenter; (*seem, be published*) paraître; (*act*) *Th* jouer; *Jur* comparaître; **it appears that** (*it seems*) il semble que (+ *sub or indic*); (*it is rumoured*) il paraîtrait que (+ *indic*). ♦**appearance** *n* (*act*) apparition *f*; (*look*) apparence *f*, aspect *m*; (*of book*) parution *f*; **to put in an a.** faire acte de présence.

appease [ə'piːz] *vt* apaiser; (*curiosity*) satisfaire.

append [ə'pend] *vt* joindre, ajouter (**to** à). ♦**—age** *n Anat* appendice *m*.

appendix, *pl* **-ixes** *or* **-ices** [ə'pendɪks, -ɪksɪz, -ɪsiːz] *n* (*of book*) & *Anat* appendice *m*. ♦**appendicitis** [əpendɪ'saɪtɪs] *n* appendicite *f*.

appertain [æpə'teɪn] *vi* **to a. to** se rapporter à.

appetite ['æpɪtaɪt] *n* appétit *m*; **to take away s.o.'s a.** couper l'appétit à qn. ♦**appetizer** *n* (*drink*) apéritif *m*; (*food*) amuse-gueule *m inv*. ♦**appetizing** *a* appétissant.

applaud [ə'plɔːd] *vt* (*clap*) applaudir; (*approve of*) approuver, applaudir à; – *vi* applaudir. ♦**applause** *n* applaudissements *mpl*.

apple ['æp(ə)l] *n* pomme *f*; **stewed apples, a. sauce** compote *f* de pommes; **eating/cooking a.** pomme *f* à couteau/à cuire; **a. pie** tarte *f* aux pommes; **a. core** trognon *m* de pomme; **a. tree** pommier *m*.

appliance [ə'plaɪəns] *n* appareil *m*.

apply [ə'plaɪ] **1** *vt* (*put, carry out etc*) appliquer; (*brake*) *Aut* appuyer sur; **to a. oneself to** s'appliquer à. **2** *vi* (*be relevant*) s'appliquer (**to** à); **to a. for** (*job*) poser sa candidature à, postuler; **to a. to s.o.** (*ask*) s'adresser à qn (**for** pour). ♦**applied** *a* (*maths etc*) appliqué. ♦**applicable** *a* applicable (**to** à). ♦**'applicant** *n* candidat, -ate *mf* (**for** à). ♦**appli'cation** *n* application *f*; (*request*) demande *f*; (*for job*) candidature *f*; (*for membership*) demande *f* d'adhésion *or* d'inscription; **a. (form)** (*job*) formulaire *m* de candidature; (*club*) formulaire *m* d'inscription *or* d'adhésion.

appoint [ə'pɔɪnt] *vt* (*person*) nommer (**to sth** à qch, **to do** pour faire); (*time etc*) désigner, fixer; **at the appointed time** à l'heure dite; **well-appointed** bien équipé. ♦**—ment** *n* nomination *f*; (*meeting*) rendez-vous *m inv*; (*post*) place *f*, situation *f*.

apportion [ə'pɔːʃ(ə)n] *vt* répartir.

apposite ['æpəzɪt] *a* juste, à propos.

appraise [ə'preɪz] *vt* évaluer. ♦**appraisal** *n* évaluation *f*.

appreciate [ə'priːʃɪeɪt] **1** *vt* (*enjoy, value, assess*) apprécier; (*understand*) comprendre; (*be grateful for*) être reconnaissant de. **2** *vi* prendre de la valeur. ♦**appreciable** *a* appréciable, sensible. ♦**appreci'ation** *n* **1** (*judgement*) appréciation *f*; (*gratitude*) reconnaissance *f*. **2** (*rise in value*) plus-value *f*. ♦**appreciative** *a* (*grateful*) reconnaissant (**of** de); (*laudatory*) élogieux; **to be a. of** (*enjoy*) apprécier.

apprehend [æprɪ'hend] *vt* (*seize, arrest*) appréhender. ♦**apprehension** *n* (*fear*) appréhension *f*. ♦**apprehensive** *a* inquiet (**about** de, au sujet de); **to be a. of** redouter.

apprentice [ə'prentɪs] *n* apprenti, -ie *mf*; – *vt* mettre en apprentissage (**to** chez). ♦**apprenticeship** *n* apprentissage *m*.

approach [ə'prəʊtʃ] *vt* (*draw near to*) s'approcher de (*qn, feu, porte etc*); (*age, result, town*) approcher de; (*subject*) aborder; (*accost*) aborder (*qn*); **to a. s.o. about** parler à qn de; – *vi* (*of person, vehicle*) s'approcher; (*of date etc*) approcher; – *n* approche *f*; (*method*) façon *f* de s'y prendre; (*path*) (voie *f* d')accès *m*; **a. to** (*question*) manière *f* d'aborder; **to make approaches to** faire des avances à.

◆—**able** *a* (*place*) accessible; (*person*) abordable.

appropriate 1 [ə'prəʊprıət] *a* (*place, tools, clothes etc*) approprié, adéquat; (*remark, time*) opportun; **a. to** *or* **for** propre à, approprié à. **2** [ə'prəʊprıeıt] *vt* (*set aside*) affecter; (*steal*) s'approprier. ◆—**ly** *adv* convenablement.

approv/e [ə'pruːv] *vt* approuver; **to a. of sth** approuver qch; **I don't a. of him** il ne me plaît pas, je ne l'apprécie pas; **I a. of his going** je trouve bon qu'il y aille; **I a. of her having accepted** je l'approuve d'avoir accepté. ◆—**ing** *a* approbateur. ◆**approval** *n* approbation *f*; **on a.** (*goods*) *Com* à l'essai.

approximate [ə'prɒksımət] *a* approximatif; – [ə'prɒksımeıt] *vi* **to a. to** se rapprocher de. ◆—**ly** *adv* à peu près, approximativement. ◆**approxi'mation** *n* approximation *f*.

apricot ['eıprıkɒt] *n* abricot *m*.

April ['eıprəl] *n* avril *m*; **to make an A. fool of** faire un poisson d'avril à.

apron ['eıprən] *n* (*garment*) tablier *m*.

apse [æps] *n* (*of church*) abside *f*.

apt [æpt] *a* (*suitable*) convenable; (*remark, reply*) juste; (*word, name*) bien choisi; (*student*) doué, intelligent; **to be a. to** avoir tendance à; **a. at sth** habile à qch. ◆**aptitude** *n* aptitude *f* (**for** à, pour). ◆**aptly** *adv* convenablement; **a. named** qui porte bien son nom.

aqualung ['ækwəlʌŋ] *n* scaphandre *m* autonome.

aquarium [ə'kweərıəm] *n* aquarium *m*.

Aquarius [ə'kweərıəs] *n* (*sign*) le Verseau.

aquatic [ə'kwætık] *a* (*plant etc*) aquatique; (*sport*) nautique.

aqueduct ['ækwıdʌkt] *n* aqueduc *m*.

aquiline ['ækwılaın] *a* (*nose, profile*) aquilin.

Arab ['ærəb] *a* & *n* arabe (*mf*). ◆**Arabian** [ə'reıbıən] *a* arabe. ◆**Arabic** *a* & *n* (*language*) arabe (*m*); **A. numerals** chiffres *mpl* arabes.

arabesque [ærə'besk] *n* (*decoration*) arabesque *f*.

arable ['ærəb(ə)l] *a* (*land*) arable.

arbiter ['ɑːbıtər] *n* arbitre *m*. ◆**arbitrate** *vti* arbitrer. ◆**arbi'tration** *n* arbitrage *m*; **to go to a.** soumettre la question à l'arbitrage. ◆**arbitrator** *n* (*in dispute*) médiateur, -trice *mf*.

arbitrary ['ɑːbıtrərı] *a* arbitraire.

arbour ['ɑːbər] *n* tonnelle *f*, charmille *f*.

arc [ɑːk] *n* (*of circle*) arc *m*.

arcade [ɑː'keıd] *n* (*market*) passage *m* couvert.

arch [ɑːtʃ] *n* (*of bridge*) arche *f*; *Archit* voûte *f*, arc *m*; (*of foot*) cambrure *f*; – *vt* (*one's back etc*) arquer, courber. ◆**archway** *n* passage *m* voûté, voûte *f*.

arch- [ɑːtʃ] *pref* (*villain etc*) achevé; **a. enemy** ennemi *m* numéro un.

arch(a)eology [ɑːkı'ɒlədʒı] *n* archéologie *f*. ◆**arch(a)eologist** *n* archéologue *mf*.

archaic [ɑː'keıık] *a* archaïque.

archangel ['ɑːkeındʒəl] *n* archange *m*.

archbishop [ɑːtʃ'bıʃəp] *n* archevêque *m*.

archer ['ɑːtʃər] *n* archer *m*. ◆**archery** *n* tir *m* à l'arc.

archetype ['ɑːkıtaıp] *n* archétype *m*.

archipelago [ɑːkı'peləgəʊ] *n* (*pl* **-oes** *or* **-os**) archipel *m*.

architect ['ɑːkıtekt] *n* architecte *m*. ◆**architecture** *n* architecture *f*.

archives ['ɑːkaıvz] *npl* archives *fpl*. ◆**archivist** *n* archiviste *mf*.

arctic ['ɑːktık] *a* arctique; (*weather*) polaire, glacial; – *n* **the A.** l'Arctique *m*.

ardent ['ɑːdənt] *a* ardent. ◆—**ly** *adv* ardemment. ◆**ardour** *n* ardeur *f*.

arduous ['ɑːdjʊəs] *a* ardu.

are [ɑːr] *see* **be**.

area ['eərıə] *n Math* superficie *f*; *Geog* région *f*; (*of town*) quartier *m*; *Mil* zone *f*; (*domain*) *Fig* domaine *m*, secteur *m*, terrain *m*; **built-up a.** agglomération *f*; **parking a.** aire *f* de stationnement; **a. code** *Tel Am* indicatif *m*.

arena [ə'riːnə] *n Hist* & *Fig* arène *f*.

Argentina [ɑːdʒən'tiːnə] *n* Argentine *f*. ◆**Argentine** ['ɑːdʒəntaın] *a* & *n*, ◆**Argentinian** *a* & *n* argentin, -ine (*mf*).

argu/e ['ɑːgjuː] *vi* (*quarrel*) se disputer (**with** avec, **about** au sujet de); (*reason*) raisonner (**with** avec, **about** sur); **to a. in favour of** plaider pour; – *vt* (*matter*) discuter; **to a. that** (*maintain*) soutenir que. ◆—**able** ['ɑːgjʊəb(ə)l] *a* discutable. ◆—**ably** *adv* on pourrait soutenir que. ◆—**ment** *n* (*quarrel*) dispute *f*; (*reasoning*) argument *m*; (*debate*) discussion *f*; **to have an a.** se disputer. ◆**argu'mentative** *a* raisonneur.

aria ['ɑːrıə] *n Mus* air *m* (d'opéra).

arid ['ærıd] *a* aride.

Aries ['eəriːz] *n* (*sign*) le Bélier.

arise [ə'raız] *vi* (*pt* **arose**, *pp* **arisen**) (*of problem, opportunity etc*) se présenter; (*of cry, objection*) s'élever; (*result*) résulter (**from** de); (*get up*) *Lit* se lever.

aristocracy [ærı'stɒkrəsı] *n* aristocratie *f*. ◆**aristocrat** ['ærıstəkræt, *Am* ə'rıstəkræt] *n* aristocrate *mf*. ◆**aristo'cratic** *a* aristocratique.

arithmetic [ə'rɪθmətɪk] *n* arithmétique *f*.

ark [ɑːk] *n* **Noah's a.** l'arche *f* de Noé.

arm [ɑːm] **1** *n* bras *m*; **a. in a.** bras dessus bras dessous; **with open arms** à bras ouverts. **2** *n* (*weapon*) arme *f*; **arms race** course *f* aux armements; – *vt* armer (with de). ◆**armament** *n* armement *m*. ◆**armband** *n* brassard *m*. ◆**armchair** *n* fauteuil *m*. ◆**armful** *n* brassée *f*. ◆**armhole** *n* emmanchure *f*. ◆**armpit** *n* aisselle *f*. ◆**armrest** *n* accoudoir *m*.

armadillo [ɑːmə'dɪləʊ] *n* (*pl* **-os**) tatou *m*.

armistice ['ɑːmɪstɪs] *n* armistice *m*.

armour ['ɑːmər] *n* (*of knight etc*) armure *f*; (*of tank etc*) blindage *m*. ◆**armoured** *a*, ◆**armour-plated** *a* blindé. ◆**armoury** *n* arsenal *m*.

army ['ɑːmɪ] *n* armée *f*; – *a* (*uniform etc*) militaire; **to join the a.** s'engager; **regular a.** armée *f* active.

aroma [ə'rəʊmə] *n* arôme *m*. ◆**aro'matic** *a* aromatique.

arose [ə'rəʊz] *see* **arise**.

around [ə'raʊnd] *prep* autour de; (*approximately*) environ, autour de; **to go a. the world** faire le tour du monde; – *adv* autour; **all a.** tout autour; **to follow a.** suivre partout; **to rush a.** courir çà et là; **a. here** par ici; **he's still a.** il est encore là; **there's a lot of flu a.** il y a pas mal de grippes dans l'air; **up and a.** (*after illness*) *Am* sur pied, guéri.

arouse [ə'raʊz] *vt* éveiller, susciter; (*sexually*) exciter; **to a. from sleep** tirer du sommeil.

arrange [ə'reɪndʒ] *vt* arranger; (*time, meeting*) fixer; **it was arranged that** il était convenu que; **to a. to do** s'arranger pour faire. ◆**—ment** *n* (*layout, agreement*) arrangement *m*; *pl* (*preparations*) préparatifs *mpl*; (*plans*) projets *mpl*; **to make arrangements to** s'arranger pour.

array [ə'reɪ] *n* (*display*) étalage *m*. ◆**arrayed** *a* (*dressed*) *Lit* (re)vêtu (**in** de).

arrears [ə'rɪəz] *npl* (*payment*) arriéré *m*; **to be in a.** avoir des arriérés.

arrest [ə'rest] *vt* arrêter; – *n Jur* arrestation *f*; **under a.** en état d'arrestation; **cardiac a.** arrêt *m* du cœur. ◆**—ing** *a* (*striking*) *Fig* frappant.

arrive [ə'raɪv] *vi* arriver. ◆**arrival** *n* arrivée *f*; **new a.** nouveau venu *m*, nouvelle venue *f*; (*baby*) nouveau-né, -ée *mf*.

arrogant ['ærəgənt] *a* arrogant. ◆**arrogance** *n* arrogance *f*. ◆**arrogantly** *adv* avec arrogance.

arrow ['ærəʊ] *n* flèche *f*.

arsenal ['ɑːsən(ə)l] *n* arsenal *m*.

arsenic ['ɑːsnɪk] *n* arsenic *m*.

arson ['ɑːs(ə)n] *n* incendie *m* volontaire. ◆**arsonist** *n* incendiaire *mf*.

art [ɑːt] *n* art *m*; (*cunning*) artifice *m*; **work of a.** œuvre *f* d'art; **fine arts** beaux-arts *mpl*; **faculty of arts** *Univ* faculté *f* des lettres; **a. school** école *f* des beaux-arts.

artefact ['ɑːtɪfækt] *n* objet *m* fabriqué.

artery ['ɑːtərɪ] *n Anat Aut* artère *f*. ◆**ar'terial** *a Anat* artériel; **a. road** route *f* principale.

artful ['ɑːtfəl] *a* rusé, astucieux. ◆**—ly** *adv* astucieusement.

arthritis [ɑː'θraɪtɪs] *n* arthrite *f*.

artichoke ['ɑːtɪtʃəʊk] *n* **(globe) a.** artichaut *m*; **Jerusalem a.** topinambour *m*.

article ['ɑːtɪk(ə)l] *n* (*object, clause*) & *Journ Gram* article *m*; **a. of clothing** vêtement *m*; **articles of value** objets *mpl* de valeur; **leading a.** *Journ* éditorial *m*.

articulat/e [ɑː'tɪkjʊlət] *a* (*sound*) net, distinct; (*person*) qui s'exprime clairement; – [ɑː'tɪkjʊleɪt] *vti* (*speak*) articuler. ◆**—ed** *a* **a. lorry** semi-remorque *m*. ◆**articu'lation** *n* articulation *f*.

artifact ['ɑːtɪfækt] *n* object *m* fabriqué.

artifice ['ɑːtɪfɪs] *n* artifice *m*.

artificial [ɑːtɪ'fɪʃ(ə)l] *a* artificiel. ◆**artifici'ality** *n* caractère *m* artificiel. ◆**artificially** *adv* artificiellement.

artillery [ɑː'tɪlərɪ] *n* artillerie *f*.

artisan ['ɑːtɪzæn] *n* artisan *m*.

artist ['ɑːtɪst] *n* (*actor, painter etc*) artiste *mf*. ◆**artiste** [ɑː'tiːst] *n Th Mus* artiste *m*. ◆**ar'tistic** *a* (*sense, treasure etc*) artistique; (*person*) artiste. ◆**artistry** *n* art *m*.

artless ['ɑːtləs] *a* naturel, naïf.

arty ['ɑːtɪ] *a Pej* du genre artiste.

as [æz, *unstressed* əz] *adv & conj* **1** (*manner etc*) comme; **as you like** comme tu veux; **such as** comme, tel que; **as much** *or* **as hard as I can** (au)tant que je peux; **as it is** (*this being the case*) les choses étant ainsi; (*to leave sth*) comme ça, tel quel; **it's late as it is** il est déjà tard; **as if, as though** comme si. **2** (*comparison*) **as tall as you** aussi grand que vous; **is he as tall as you?** est-il aussi *or* si grand que vous?; **as white as a sheet** blanc comme un linge; **as much** *or* **as hard as you** autant que vous; **the same as** le même que; **twice as big as** deux fois plus grand que. **3** (*concessive*) **(as) clever as he is** si *or* aussi intelligent qu'il soit. **4** (*capacity*) **as a**

teacher comme professeur, en tant que *or* en qualité de professeur; **to act as a father** agir en père. **5** (*reason*) puisque, comme; **as it's late** puisqu'il est tard, comme il est tard. **6** (*time*) **as I left** comme je partais; **as one grows older** à mesure que l'on vieillit; **as he slept** pendant qu'il dormait; **one day as . . .** un jour que . . . ; **as from, as of** (*time*) à partir de. **7** (*concerning*) **as for that, as to that** quant à cela. **8** (+ *inf*) **so as to** de manière à; **so stupid as to** assez bête pour.

asbestos [æs'bestəs] *n* amiante *f*.

ascend [ə'send] *vi* monter; – *vt* (*throne*) monter sur; (*stairs*) monter; (*mountain*) faire l'ascension de. ◆**ascent** *n* ascension *f* (of de); (*slope*) côte *f*.

ascertain [æsə'teɪn] *vt* (*discover*) découvrir; (*check*) s'assurer de.

ascetic [ə'setɪk] *a* ascétique; – *n* ascète *mf*.

ascribe [ə'skraɪb] *vt* attribuer (to à).

ash [æʃ] *n* **1** (*of cigarette etc*) cendre *f*; **A. Wednesday** mercredi *m* des Cendres. **2** (*tree*) frêne *m*. ◆**ashen** *a* (*pale grey*) cendré; (*face*) pâle. ◆**ashcan** *n Am* poubelle *f*. ◆**ashtray** *n* cendrier *m*.

ashamed [ə'ʃeɪmd] *a* honteux; **to be a. of** avoir honte de; **to be a. (of oneself)** avoir honte.

ashore [ə'ʃɔːr] *adv* **to go a.** débarquer; **to put s.o. a.** débarquer qn.

Asia ['eɪʃə] *n* Asie *f*. ◆**Asian** *a* asiatique; – *n* Asiatique *mf*, Asiate *mf*.

aside [ə'saɪd] **1** *adv* de côté; **to draw a.** (*curtain*) écarter; **to take** *or* **draw s.o. a.** prendre qn à part; **to step a.** s'écarter; **a. from** en dehors de. **2** *n Th* aparté *m*.

asinine ['æsɪnaɪn] *a* stupide, idiot.

ask [ɑːsk] *vt* demander; (*a question*) poser; (*invite*) inviter; **to a. s.o. (for) sth** demander qch à qn; **to a. s.o. to do** demander à qn de faire; – *vi* demander; **to a. for sth/s.o.** demander qch/qn; **to a. for sth back** redemander qch; **to a. about sth** se renseigner sur qch; **to a. after** *or* **about s.o.** demander des nouvelles de qn; **to a. s.o. about** interroger qn sur; **asking price** prix *m* demandé.

askance [ə'skɑːns] *adv* **to look a. at** regarder avec méfiance.

askew [ə'skjuː] *adv* de biais, de travers.

aslant [ə'slɑːnt] *adv* de travers.

asleep [ə'sliːp] *a* endormi; (*arm, leg*) engourdi; **to be a.** dormir; **to fall a.** s'endormir.

asp [æsp] *n* (*snake*) aspic *m*.

asparagus [ə'spærəgəs] *n* (*plant*) asperge *f*; (*shoots*) *Culin* asperges *fpl*.

aspect ['æspekt] *n* aspect *m*; (*of house*) orientation *f*.

aspersions [ə'spɜːʃ(ə)nz] *npl* **to cast a. on** dénigrer.

asphalt ['æsfælt, *Am* 'æsfɔːlt] *n* asphalte *m*; – *vt* asphalter.

asphyxia [əs'fɪksɪə] *n* asphyxie *f*. ◆**asphyxiate** *vt* asphyxier. ◆**asphyxi'ation** *n* asphyxie *f*.

aspire [ə'spaɪər] *vi* **to a. to** aspirer à. ◆**aspi'ration** *n* aspiration *f*.

aspirin ['æsprɪn] *n* aspirine *f*.

ass [æs] *n* (*animal*) âne *m*; (*person*) *Fam* imbécile *mf*, âne *m*; **she-a.** ânesse *f*.

assail [ə'seɪl] *vt* assaillir (**with** de). ◆**assailant** *n* agresseur *m*.

assassin [ə'sæsɪn] *n Pol* assassin *m*. ◆**assassinate** *vt Pol* assassiner. ◆**assassi'nation** *n Pol* assassinat *m*.

assault [ə'sɔːlt] *n Mil* assaut *m*; *Jur* agression *f*; – *vt Jur* agresser; (*woman*) violenter.

assemble [ə'semb(ə)l] *vt* (*objects, ideas*) assembler; (*people*) rassembler; (*machine*) monter; – *vi* se rassembler. ◆**assembly** *n* (*meeting*) assemblée *f*; *Tech* montage *m*, assemblage *m*; *Sch* rassemblement *m*; **a. line** (*in factory*) chaîne *f* de montage.

assent [ə'sent] *n* assentiment *m*; – *vi* consentir (**to** à).

assert [ə'sɜːt] *vt* affirmer (**that** que); (*rights*) revendiquer; **to a. oneself** s'affirmer. ◆**assertion** *n* affirmation *f*; revendication *f*. ◆**assertive** *a* affirmatif; *Pej* autoritaire.

assess [ə'ses] *vt* (*estimate, evaluate*) évaluer; (*decide amount of*) fixer le montant de; (*person*) juger. ◆**—ment** *n* évaluation *f*; jugement *m*. ◆**assessor** *n* (*valuer*) expert *m*.

asset ['æset] *n* atout *m*, avantage *m*; *pl Com* biens *mpl*, avoir *m*.

assiduous [ə'sɪdjʊəs] *a* assidu.

assign [ə'saɪn] *vt* (*allocate*) assigner; (*day etc*) fixer; (*appoint*) nommer (**to** à). ◆**—ment** *n* (*task*) mission *f*; *Sch* devoirs *mpl*.

assimilate [ə'sɪmɪleɪt] *vt* assimiler; – *vi* s'assimiler. ◆**assimi'lation** *n* assimilation *f*.

assist [ə'sɪst] *vti* aider (**in doing, to do** à faire). ◆**assistance** *n* aide *f*; **to be of a. to s.o.** aider qn. ◆**assistant** *n* assistant, -ante *mf*; (*in shop*) vendeur, -euse *mf*; – *a* adjoint.

assizes [ə'saɪzɪz] *npl Jur* assises *fpl*.

associate [ə'səʊʃɪeɪt] *vt* associer (**with** à, avec); – *vi* **to a. with s.o.** fréquenter qn; **to**

a. **(oneself) with** (*in business venture*) s'associer à *or* avec; – [ə'səʊʃɪət] *n & a* associé, -ée (*mf*). ◆**associ'ation** *n* association *f*; *pl* (*memories*) souvenirs *mpl*.

assort/ed [ə'sɔːtɪd] *a* (*different*) variés; (*foods*) assortis; **well-a.** bien assorti. ◆**—ment** *n* assortiment *m*.

assuage [ə'sweɪdʒ] *vt* apaiser, adoucir.

assum/e [ə'sjuːm] *vt* **1** (*take on*) prendre; (*responsibility, role*) assumer; (*attitude, name*) adopter. **2** (*suppose*) présumer (**that** que). ◆**—ed** *a* (*feigned*) faux; **a. name** nom *m* d'emprunt. ◆**assumption** *n* (*supposition*) supposition *f*.

assur/e [ə'ʃʊər] *vt* assurer. ◆**—edly** [-ɪdlɪ] *adv* assurément. ◆**assurance** *n* assurance *f*.

asterisk ['æstərɪsk] *n* astérisque *m*.

astern [ə'stɜːn] *adv Nau* à l'arrière.

asthma ['æsmə] *n* asthme *m*. ◆**asth'matic** *a & n* asthmatique (*mf*).

astir [ə'stɜːr] *a* (*excited*) en émoi; (*out of bed*) debout.

astonish [ə'stɒnɪʃ] *vt* étonner; **to be astonished** s'étonner (**at sth** de qch). ◆**—ing** *a* étonnant. ◆**—ingly** *adv* étonnamment. ◆**—ment** *n* étonnement *m*.

astound [ə'staʊnd] *vt* stupéfier, étonner. ◆**—ing** *a* stupéfiant.

astray [ə'streɪ] *adv* **to go a.** s'égarer; **to lead a.** égarer.

astride [ə'straɪd] *adv* à califourchon; – *prep* à cheval sur.

astringent [ə'strɪndʒənt] *a* (*harsh*) sévère.

astrology [ə'strɒlədʒɪ] *n* astrologie *f*. ◆**astrologer** *n* astrologue *mf*.

astronaut ['æstrənɔːt] *n* astronaute *mf*.

astronomy [ə'strɒnəmɪ] *n* astronomie *f*. ◆**astronomer** *n* astronome *m*. ◆**astro'nomical** *a* astronomique.

astute [ə'stjuːt] *a* (*crafty*) rusé; (*clever*) astucieux.

asunder [ə'sʌndər] *adv* (*to pieces*) en pièces; (*in two*) en deux.

asylum [ə'saɪləm] *n* asile *m*; **lunatic a.** *Pej* maison *f* de fous, asile *m* d'aliénés.

at [æt, *unstressed* ət] *prep* **1** à; **at the end** à la fin; **at work** au travail; **at six (o'clock)** à six heures. **2** chez; **at the doctor's** chez le médecin; **at home** chez soi, à la maison. ◆**at-home** *n* réception *f*. **3** en; **at sea** en mer; **at war** en guerre; **good at** (*geography etc*) fort en. **4** contre; **angry at** fâché contre. **5** sur; **to shoot at** tirer sur; **at my request** sur ma demande. **6** de; **to laugh at** rire de; **surprised at** surpris de. **7** (au)près de; **at the window** (au)près de la fenêtre. **8** par; **to come in at the door** entrer par la porte; **six at a time** six par six. **9** **at night** la nuit; **to look at** regarder; **not at all** pas du tout; (*after 'thank you'*) pas de quoi!; **nothing at all** rien du tout; **to be (hard) at it** être très occupé, travailler dur; **he's always (on) at me** *Fam* il est toujours après moi.

ate [et, *Am* eɪt] *see* eat.

atheism ['eɪθɪɪz(ə)m] *n* athéisme *m*. ◆**atheist** *n* athée *mf*.

Athens ['æθɪnz] *n* Athènes *m or f*.

athlete ['æθliːt] *n* athlète *mf*; **a.'s foot** *Med* mycose *f*. ◆**ath'letic** *a* athlétique; **a. meeting** réunion *f* sportive. ◆**ath'letics** *npl* athlétisme *m*.

atishoo! [ə'tɪʃuː] (*Am* **atchoo** [ə'tʃuː]) *int* atchoum!

Atlantic [ət'læntɪk] *a* atlantique; – *n* **the A.** l'Atlantique *m*.

atlas ['ætləs] *n* atlas *m*.

atmosphere ['ætməsfɪər] *n* atmosphère *f*. ◆**atmos'pheric** *a* atmosphérique.

atom ['ætəm] *n* atome *m*; **a. bomb** bombe *f* atomique. ◆**a'tomic** *a* atomique. ◆**atomizer** *n* atomiseur *m*.

atone [ə'təʊn] *vi* **to a. for** expier. ◆**—ment** *n* expiation *f* (**for** de).

atrocious [ə'trəʊʃəs] *a* atroce. ◆**atrocity** *n* atrocité *f*.

atrophy ['ætrəfɪ] *vi* s'atrophier.

attach [ə'tætʃ] *vt* attacher (**to** à); (*document*) joindre (**to** à); **attached to** (*fond of*) attaché à. ◆**—ment** *n* (*affection*) attachement *m*; (*fastener*) attache *f*; (*tool*) accessoire *m*.

attaché [ə'tæʃeɪ] *n* **1** *Pol* attaché, -ée *mf*. **2** **a. case** attaché-case *m*.

attack [ə'tæk] *n Mil Med & Fig* attaque *f*; (*of fever*) accès *m*; (*on s.o.'s life*) attentat *m*; **heart a.** crise *f* cardiaque; – *vt* attaquer; (*problem, plan*) s'attaquer à; – *vi* attaquer. ◆**—er** *n* agresseur *m*.

attain [ə'teɪn] *vt* parvenir à, atteindre, réaliser. ◆**—able** *a* accessible. ◆**—ment** *n* (*of ambition, aim etc*) réalisation *f* (**of** de); *pl* (*skills*) talents *mpl*.

attempt [ə'tempt] *n* tentative *f*; **to make an a. to** essayer *or* tenter de; **a. on** (*record*) tentative pour battre; **a. on s.o.'s life** attentat *m* contre qn; – *vt* tenter; (*task*) entreprendre; **to a. to do** essayer *or* tenter de faire; **attempted murder** tentative de meurtre.

attend [ə'tend] *vt* (*match etc*) assister à; (*course*) suivre; (*school, church*) aller à; (*wait on, serve*) servir; (*escort*) accompagner; (*patient*) soigner; – *vi* assister; **to a. to** (*pay attention to*) prêter attention à;

(*take care of*) s'occuper de. ◆**—ed** *a* **well-a.** (*course*) très suivi; (*meeting*) où il y a du monde. ◆**attendance** *n* présence *f* (**at** à); (*people*) assistance *f*; **school a.** scolarité *f*; **in a.** de service. ◆**attendant 1** *n* employé, -ée *mf*; (*in museum*) gardien, -ienne *mf*; *pl* (*of prince, king etc*) suite *f*. **2** *a* (*fact*) concomitant.

attention [ə'tenʃ(ə)n] *n* attention *f*; **to pay a.** prêter *or* faire attention (**to** à); **a.!** *Mil* garde-à-vous!; **to stand at a.** *Mil* être au garde-à-vous; **a. to detail** minutie *f*. ◆**attentive** *a* (*heedful*) attentif (**to** à); (*thoughtful*) attentionné (**to** pour). ◆**attentively** *adv* avec attention, attentivement.

attenuate [ə'tenjʊeɪt] *vt* atténuer.

attest [ə'test] *vti* **to a. (to)** témoigner de.

attic ['ætɪk] *n* grenier *m*.

attire [ə'taɪər] *n Lit* vêtements *mpl*.

attitude ['ætɪtjuːd] *n* attitude *f*.

attorney [ə'tɜːnɪ] *n* (*lawyer*) *Am* avocat *m*; **district a.** *Am* = procureur *m* (de la République).

attract [ə'trækt] *vt* attirer. ◆**attraction** *n* attraction *f*; (*charm, appeal*) attrait *m*. ◆**attractive** *a* (*price etc*) intéressant; (*girl*) belle, jolie; (*boy*) beau; (*manners*) attrayant.

attribut/e 1 ['ætrɪbjuːt] *n* (*quality*) attribut *m*. **2** [ə'trɪbjuːt] *vt* (*ascribe*) attribuer (**to** à). ◆**—able** *a* attribuable (**to** à).

attrition [ə'trɪʃ(ə)n] *n* **war of a.** guerre *f* d'usure.

attuned [ə'tjuːnd] *a* **a. to** (*of ideas, trends etc*) en accord avec; (*used to*) habitué à.

atypical [eɪ'tɪpɪk(ə)l] *a* peu typique.

aubergine ['əʊbəʒiːn] *n* aubergine *f*.

auburn ['ɔːbən] *a* (*hair*) châtain roux.

auction ['ɔːkʃən] *n* vente *f* (aux enchères); – *vt* **to a. (off)** vendre (aux enchères). ◆**auctio'neer** *n* commissaire-priseur *m*, adjudicateur, -trice *mf*.

audacious [ɔː'deɪʃəs] *a* audacieux. ◆**audacity** *n* audace *f*.

audib/le ['ɔːdɪb(ə)l] *a* perceptible, audible. ◆**—ly** *adv* distinctement.

audience ['ɔːdɪəns] *n* assistance *f*, public *m*; (*of speaker, musician*) auditoire *m*; *Th Cin* spectateurs *mpl*; *Rad* auditeurs *mpl*; (*interview*) audience *f*.

audio ['ɔːdɪəʊ] *a* (*cassette, system etc*) audio *inv*. ◆**audiotypist** *n* dactylo *f* au magnétophone, audiotypiste *mf*. ◆**audio-'visual** *a* audio-visuel.

audit ['ɔːdɪt] *vt* (*accounts*) vérifier; – *n* vérification *f* (des comptes). ◆**auditor** *n* commissaire *m* aux comptes.

audition [ɔː'dɪʃ(ə)n] *n* audition *f*; – *vti* auditionner.

auditorium [ɔːdɪ'tɔːrɪəm] *n* salle *f* (*de spectacle, concert etc*).

augment [ɔːg'ment] *vt* augmenter (**with, by** de).

augur ['ɔːgər] *vt* présager; – *vi* **to a. well** être de bon augure.

august [ɔː'gʌst] *a* auguste.

August ['ɔːgəst] *n* août *m*.

aunt [ɑːnt] *n* tante *f*. ◆**auntie** *or* **aunty** *n Fam* tata *f*.

au pair [əʊ'peər] *adv* au pair; – *n* **au p. (girl)** jeune fille *f* au pair.

aura ['ɔːrə] *n* émanation *f*, aura *f*; (*of place*) atmosphère *f*.

auspices ['ɔːspɪsɪz] *npl* auspices *mpl*.

auspicious [ɔː'spɪʃəs] *a* favorable.

austere [ɔː'stɪər] *a* austère. ◆**austerity** *n* austérité *f*.

Australia [ɒ'streɪlɪə] *n* Australie *f*. ◆**Australian** *a* & *n* australien, -ienne (*mf*).

Austria ['ɒstrɪə] *n* Autriche *f*. ◆**Austrian** *a* & *n* autrichien, -ienne (*mf*).

authentic [ɔː'θentɪk] *a* authentique. ◆**authenticate** *vt* authentifier. ◆**authen'ticity** *n* authenticité *f*.

author ['ɔːθər] *n* auteur *m*. ◆**authoress** *n* femme *f* auteur. ◆**authorship** *n* (*of book etc*) paternité *f*.

authority [ɔː'θɒrɪtɪ] *n* autorité *f*; (*permission*) autorisation *f* (**to do** de faire); **to be in a.** (*in charge*) être responsable. ◆**authori'tarian** *a* & *n* autoritaire (*mf*). ◆**authoritative** *a* (*report*) autorisé; (*tone, person*) autoritaire.

authorize ['ɔːθəraɪz] *vt* autoriser (**to do** à faire). ◆**authori'zation** *n* autorisation *f*.

autistic [ɔː'tɪstɪk] *a* autiste, autistique.

autobiography [ɔːtəʊbaɪ'ɒgrəfɪ] *n* autobiographie *f*.

autocrat ['ɔːtəkræt] *n* autocrate *m*. ◆**auto'cratic** *a* autocratique.

autograph ['ɔːtəgrɑːf] *n* autographe *m*; – *vt* dédicacer (**for** à).

automat ['ɔːtəmæt] *n Am* cafétéria *f* à distributeurs automatiques.

automate ['ɔːtəmeɪt] *vt* automatiser. ◆**auto'mation** *n* automatisation *f*, automation *f*.

automatic [ɔːtə'mætɪk] *a* automatique. ◆**automatically** *adv* automatiquement.

automaton [ɔː'tɒmətən] *n* automate *m*.

automobile ['ɔːtəməbiːl] *n Am* auto(mobile) *f*.

autonomous [ɔː'tɒnəməs] *a* autonome. ◆**autonomy** *n* autonomie *f*.

autopsy ['ɔːtɒpsɪ] *n* autopsie *f*.

autumn ['ɔːtəm] *n* automne *m*. ◆**autumnal** [ɔː'tʌmnəl] *a* automnal.

auxiliary [ɔːg'zɪljərɪ] *a* & *n* auxiliaire (*mf*); **a.** (**verb**) (verbe *m*) auxiliaire *m*.

avail [ə'veɪl] **1** *vt* **to a. oneself of** profiter de, tirer parti de. **2** *n* **to no a.** en vain; **of no a.** inutile.

available [ə'veɪləb(ə)l] *a* (*thing, means etc*) disponible; (*person*) libre, disponible; (*valid*) valable; **a. to all** (*goal etc*) accessible à tous. ◆**availa'bility** *n* disponibilité *f*; validité *f*; accessibilité *f*.

avalanche ['ævəlɑːnʃ] *n* avalanche *f*.

avarice ['ævərɪs] *n* avarice *f*. ◆**ava'ricious** *a* avare.

avenge [ə'vendʒ] *vt* venger; **to a. oneself** se venger (**on** de).

avenue ['ævənjuː] *n* avenue *f*; (*way to a result*) *Fig* voie *f*.

average ['ævərɪdʒ] *n* moyenne *f*; **on a.** en moyenne; – *a* moyen; – *vt* (*do*) faire en moyenne; (*reach*) atteindre la moyenne de; (*figures*) faire la moyenne de.

averse [ə'vɜːs] *a* **to be a. to doing** répugner à faire. ◆**aversion** *n* (*dislike*) aversion *f*, répugnance *f*.

avert [ə'vɜːt] *vt* (*prevent*) éviter; (*turn away*) détourner (**from** de).

aviary ['eɪvɪərɪ] *n* volière *f*.

aviation [eɪvɪ'eɪʃ(ə)n] *n* aviation *f*. ◆**'aviator** *n* aviateur, -trice *mf*.

avid ['ævɪd] *a* avide (**for** de).

avocado [ævə'kɑːdəʊ] *n* (*pl* **-os**) **a. (pear)** avocat *m*.

avoid [ə'vɔɪd] *vt* éviter; **to a. doing** éviter de faire. ◆**—able** *a* évitable. ◆**avoidance** *n* **his a. of** (*danger etc*) son désir *m* d'éviter; **tax a.** évasion *f* fiscale.

avowed [ə'vaʊd] *a* (*enemy*) déclaré, avoué.

await [ə'weɪt] *vt* attendre.

awake [ə'weɪk] *vi* (*pt* **awoke**, *pp* **awoken**) s'éveiller; – *vt* (*person, hope etc*) éveiller; – *a* réveillé, éveillé; **(wide-)a.** éveillé; **to keep s.o. a.** empêcher qn de dormir, tenir qn éveillé; **he's (still) a.** il ne dort pas (encore); **a. to** (*conscious of*) conscient de. ◆**awaken 1** *vti* = **awake. 2** *vt* **to a. s.o. to sth** faire prendre conscience de qch à qn. ◆**awakening** *n* réveil *m*.

award [ə'wɔːd] *vt* (*money*) attribuer; (*prize*) décerner, attribuer; (*damages*) accorder; – *n* (*prize*) prix *m*, récompense *f*; (*scholarship*) bourse *f*.

aware [ə'weər] *a* avisé, informé; **a. of** (*conscious*) conscient de; (*informed*) au courant de; **to become a. of** prendre conscience de. ◆**—ness** *n* conscience *f*.

awash [ə'wɒʃ] *a* inondé (**with** de).

away [ə'weɪ] *adv* **1** (*distant*) loin; (**far**) **a.** au loin, très loin; **5 km a.** à 5 km (de distance). **2** (*absent*) parti, absent; **a. with you!** va-t-en!; **to drive a.** partir (en voiture); **to look a.** détourner les yeux; **to work/talk/***etc* **a.** travailler/parler/*etc* sans relâche; **to fade/melt a.** disparaître/fondre complètement. **3 to play a.** *Sp* jouer à l'extérieur.

awe [ɔː] *n* crainte *f* (*mêlée de respect*); **to be in a. of s.o.** éprouver de la crainte envers qn. ◆**a.-inspiring** *a*, ◆**awesome** *a* (*impressive*) imposant; (*frightening*) effrayant.

awful ['ɔːfəl] *a* affreux; (*terrifying*) épouvantable; (*ill*) malade; **an a. lot of** *Fam* un nombre incroyable de; **I feel a. (about it)** j'ai vraiment honte. ◆**—ly** *adv* affreusement; (*very*) *Fam* terriblement; **thanks a.** merci infiniment.

awhile [ə'waɪl] *adv* quelque temps; (*to stay, wait*) un peu.

awkward ['ɔːkwəd] *a* **1** (*clumsy*) maladroit; (*age*) ingrat. **2** (*difficult*) difficile; (*cumbersome*) gênant; (*tool*) peu commode; (*time*) inopportun; (*silence*) gêné. ◆**—ly** *adv* maladroitement; (*speak*) d'un ton gêné; (*placed*) à un endroit difficile. ◆**—ness** *n* maladresse *f*; difficulté *f*; (*discomfort*) gêne *f*.

awning ['ɔːnɪŋ] *n* auvent *m*; (*over shop*) store *m*; (*glass canopy*) marquise *f*.

awoke(n) [ə'wəʊk(ən)] *see* **awake**.

awry [ə'raɪ] *adv* **to go a.** (*of plan etc*) mal tourner.

axe [æks] (*Am* **ax**) *n* hache *f*; (*reduction*) *Fig* coupe *f* sombre; – *vt* réduire; (*eliminate*) supprimer.

axiom ['æksɪəm] *n* axiome *m*.

axis, *pl* **axes** ['æksɪs, 'æksiːz] *n* axe *m*.

axle ['æks(ə)l] *n* essieu *m*.

ay(e) [aɪ] **1** *adv* oui. **2** *n* **the ayes** (*votes*) les voix *fpl* pour.

azalea [ə'zeɪlɪə] *n* (*plant*) azalée *f*.

B

B, b [biː] *n* B, b *m*; **2B** (*number*) 2 ter.
BA *abbr* = **Bachelor of Arts.**
babble ['bæb(ə)l] *vi* (*of baby, stream*) gazouiller; (*mumble*) bredouiller; – *vt* **to b. (out)** bredouiller; – *n inv* gazouillement *m*, gazouillis *m*; (*of voices*) rumeur *f*.
babe [beɪb] *n* **1** petit(e) enfant *mf*, bébé *m*. **2** (*girl*) *Sl* pépée *f*.
baboon [bə'buːn] *n* babouin *m*.
baby ['beɪbɪ] **1** *n* bébé *m*; – *a* (*clothes etc*) de bébé; **b. boy** petit garçon *m*; **b. girl** petite fille *f*; **b. carriage** *Am* voiture *f* d'enfant; **b. sling** kangourou® *m*, porte-bébé *m*; **b. tiger/***etc* bébé-tigre/*etc m*; **b. face** visage *m* poupin. **2** *n Sl* (*girl*) pépée *f*; (*girlfriend*) copine *f*. **3** *vt Fam* dorloter. ◆**b.-batterer** *n* bourreau *m* d'enfants. ◆**b.-minder** *n* gardien, -ienne *mf* d'enfants. ◆**b.-sit** *vi* (*pt & pp* **-sat**, *pres p* **-sitting**) garder les enfants, faire du baby-sitting. ◆**b.-sitter** *n* baby-sitter *mf*. ◆**b.-snatching** *n* rapt *m* d'enfant. ◆**b.-walker** *n* trotteur *m*, youpala® *m*.
babyish ['beɪbɪɪʃ] *a Pej* de bébé; (*puerile*) enfantin.
bachelor ['bætʃələr] *n* **1** célibataire *m*; **b. flat** garçonnière *f*. **2 B. of Arts/of Science** licencié -ée *mf* ès lettres/ès sciences.
back [bæk] *n* (*of person, animal*) dos *m*; (*of chair*) dossier *m*; (*of hand*) revers *m*; (*of house*) derrière *m*, arrière *m*; (*of room*) fond *m*; (*of page*) verso *m*,(*of fabric*) envers *m*; *Fb* arrière *m*; **at the b. of** (*book*) à la fin de; (*car*) à l'arrière de; **at the b. of one's mind** derrière la tête; **b. to front** devant derrière, à l'envers; **to get s.o.'s b. up** *Fam* irriter qn; **in b. of** *Am* derrière; – *a* arrière *inv*, de derrière; (*taxes*) arriéré; **b. door** porte *f* de derrière; **b. room** pièce *f* du fond; **b. end** (*of bus*) arrière *m*; **b. street** rue *f* écartée; **b. number** vieux numéro *m*; **b. pay** rappel *m* de salaire; **b. tooth** molaire *f*; – *adv* en arrière; **far b.** loin derrière; **far b. in the past** à une époque reculée; **to stand b.** (*of house*) être en retrait (**from** par rapport à); **to go b. and forth** aller et venir; **to come b.** revenir; **he's b.** il est de retour, il est rentré *or* revenu; **a month b.** il y a un mois; **the trip there and b.** le voyage aller et retour; – *vt Com* financer; (*horse etc*) parier sur, jouer; (*car*) faire reculer; (*wall*) renforcer; **to b. s.o (up)** (*support*) appuyer qn; – *vi* (*move backwards*) reculer; **to b. down** se dégonfler; **to b. out** (*withdraw*) se retirer; *Aut* sortir en marche arrière; **to b. on to** (*of window etc*) donner par derrière sur; **to b. up** *Aut* faire marche arrière. ◆**—ing** *n* (*aid*) soutien *m*; (*material*) support *m*, renfort *m*. ◆**—er** *n* (*supporter*) partisan *m*; *Sp* parieur, -euse *mf*; *Fin* bailleur *m* de fonds.
backache ['bækeɪk] *n* mal *m* aux reins. ◆**back'bencher** *n Pol* membre *m* sans portefeuille. ◆**backbiting** *n* médisance *f*. ◆**backbreaking** *a* éreintant. ◆**backcloth** *n* toile *f* de fond. ◆**backchat** *n* impertinence *f*. ◆**back'date** *vt* (*cheque*) antidater. ◆**back'handed** *a* (*compliment*) équivoque. ◆**backhander** *n* revers *m*; (*bribe*) *Fam* pot-de-vin *m*. ◆**backrest** *n* dossier *m*. ◆**backside** *n* (*buttocks*) *Fam* derrière *m*. ◆**back'stage** *adv* dans les coulisses. ◆**backstroke** *n Sp* dos *m* crawlé. ◆**backtrack** *vi* rebrousser chemin. ◆**backup** *n* appui *m*; (*tailback*) *Am* embouteillage *m*; **b. lights** *Aut* feux *mpl* de recul. ◆**backwater** *n* (*place*) trou *m* perdu. ◆**backwoods** *npl* forêts *f* vierges. ◆**back'yard** *n* arrière-cour *f*; *Am* jardin *m* (*à l'arrière d'une maison*).
backbone ['bækbəʊn] *n* colonne *f* vertébrale; (*of fish*) grande arête *f*; (*main support*) pivot *m*.
backfire [bæk'faɪər] *vi Aut* pétarader; (*of plot etc*) *Fig* échouer.
backgammon ['bækgæmən] *n* trictrac *m*.
background ['bækgraʊnd] *n* fond *m*, arrière-plan *m*; (*events*) *Fig* antécédents *mpl*; (*education*) formation *f*; (*environment*) milieu *m*; (*conditions*) *Pol* climat *m*, contexte *m*; **to keep s.o. in the b.** tenir qn à l'écart; **b. music** musique *f* de fond.
backlash ['bæklæʃ] *n* choc *m* en retour, retour *m* de flamme.
backlog ['bæklɒg] *n* (*of work*) arriéré *m*.
backward ['bækwəd] *a* (*glance etc*) en arrière; (*retarded*) arriéré; **b. in doing** lent à faire; – *adv* = **backwards.** ◆**—ness** *n* (*of country etc*) retard *m*. ◆**backwards** *adv* en arrière; (*to walk*) à reculons; (*to fall*) à la

renverse; **to move b.** reculer; **to go b. and forwards** aller et venir.
bacon ['beɪkən] *n* lard *m*; (*in rashers*) bacon *m*; **b. and eggs** œufs *mpl* au jambon.
bacteria [bæk'tɪərɪə] *npl* bactéries *fpl*.
bad [bæd] *a* (**worse, worst**) mauvais; (*wicked*) méchant; (*sad*) triste; (*accident, wound etc*) grave; (*tooth*) carié; (*arm, leg*) malade; (*pain*) violent; (*air*) vicié; **b. language** gros mots *mpl*; **it's b. to think that . . .** ce n'est pas bien de penser que . . . ; **to feel b.** *Med* se sentir mal; **I feel b. about it** ça m'a chagriné; **things are b.** ça va mal; **she's not b.!** elle n'est pas mal!; **to go b.** se gâter; (*of milk*) tourner; **in a b. way** mal en point; (*ill*) très mal; (*in trouble*) dans le pétrin; **too b.!** tant pis! ◆**b.-'mannered** *a* mal élevé. ◆**b.-'tempered** *a* grincheux. ◆**badly** *adv* mal; (*hurt*) grièvement; **b. affected/shaken** très touché/bouleversé; **to be b. mistaken** se tromper lourdement; **b. off** dans la gêne; **to be b. off for** manquer de; **to want b.** avoir grande envie de.
badge [bædʒ] *n* insigne *m*; (*of postman etc*) plaque *f*; (*bearing slogan or joke*) badge *m*.
badger ['bædʒər] **1** *n* (*animal*) blaireau *m*. **2** *vt* importuner.
badminton ['bædmɪntən] *n* badminton *m*.
baffle ['bæf(ə)l] *vt* (*person*) déconcerter, dérouter.
bag [bæg] **1** *n* sac *m*; *pl* (*luggage*) valises *fpl*, bagages *mpl*; (*under the eyes*) poches *fpl*; **bags of** *Fam* (*lots of*) beaucoup de; **an old b.** une vieille taupe; **in the b.** *Fam* dans la poche. **2** *vt* (**-gg-**) (*take, steal*) *Fam* piquer, s'adjuger; (*animal*) *Sp* tuer.
baggage ['bægɪdʒ] *n* bagages *mpl*; *Mil* équipement *m*; **b. car** *Am* fourgon *m*; **b. room** *Am* consigne *f*.
baggy ['bægɪ] *a* (**-ier, -iest**) (*clothing*) trop ample; (*trousers*) faisant des poches.
bagpipes ['bægpaɪps] *npl* cornemuse *f*.
Bahamas [bə'hɑːməz] *npl* **the B.** les Bahamas *fpl*.
bail [beɪl] **1** *n Jur* caution *f*; **on b.** en liberté provisoire; – *vt* **to b. (out)** fournir une caution pour; **to b. out** (*ship*) écoper; (*person, company*) *Fig* tirer d'embarras. **2** *vi* **to b. out** *Am Av* sauter (en parachute).
bailiff ['beɪlɪf] *n Jur* huissier *m*; (*of landowner*) régisseur *m*.
bait [beɪt] **1** *n* amorce *f*, appât *m*; – *vt* (*fishing hook*) amorcer. **2** *vt* (*annoy*) asticoter, tourmenter.
baize [beɪz] *n* **green b.** (*on card table etc*) tapis *m* vert.
bak/e [beɪk] *vt* (faire) cuire (au four); – *vi* (*of cook*) faire de la pâtisserie *or* du pain; (*of cake etc*) cuire (au four); **we're** *or* **it's baking (hot)** *Fam* on cuit. ◆**—ed** *a* (*potatoes*) au four; **b. beans** haricots *mpl* blancs (à la tomate). ◆**—ing** *n* cuisson *f*; **b. powder** levure *f* (chimique). ◆**—er** *n* boulanger, -ère *mf*. ◆**bakery** *n* boulangerie *f*.
balaclava [bælə'klɑːvə] *n* **b. (helmet)** passe-montagne *m*.
balance ['bæləns] *n* (*scales*) & *Econ Pol Com* balance *f*; (*equilibrium*) équilibre *m*; (*of account*) *Com* solde *m*; (*remainder*) reste *m*; **to strike a b.** trouver le juste milieu; **sense of b.** sens *m* de la mesure; **in the b.** incertain; **on b.** à tout prendre; **b. sheet** bilan *m*; – *vt* tenir *or* mettre en équilibre (**on** sur); (*budget, account*) équilibrer; (*compare*) mettre en balance, peser; **to b. (out)** (*compensate for*) compenser; **to b. (oneself)** se tenir en équilibre; – *vi* (*of accounts*) être en équilibre, s'équilibrer.
balcony ['bælkənɪ] *n* balcon *m*.
bald [bɔːld] *a* (**-er, -est**) chauve; (*statement*) brutal; (*tyre*) lisse; **b. patch** *or* **spot** tonsure *f*. ◆**b.-'headed** *a* chauve. ◆**balding** *a* **to be b.** perdre ses cheveux. ◆**baldness** *n* calvitie *f*.
balderdash ['bɔːldədæʃ] *n* balivernes *fpl*.
bale [beɪl] **1** *n* (*of cotton etc*) balle *f*. **2** *vi* **to b. out** *Av* sauter (en parachute).
baleful ['beɪlfʊl] *a* sinistre, funeste.
balk [bɔːk] *vi* reculer (**at** devant), regimber (**at** contre).
ball[1] [bɔːl] *n* balle *f*; (*inflated*) *Fb Rugby etc* ballon *m*; *Billiards* bille *f*; (*of string, wool*) pelote *f*; (*sphere*) boule *f*; (*of meat or fish*) *Culin* boulette *f*; **on the b.** (*alert*) *Fam* éveillé; **he's on the b.** (*efficient, knowledgeable*) *Fam* il connaît son affaire, il est au point; **b. bearing** roulement *m* à billes; **b. game** *Am* partie *f* de baseball; **it's a whole new b. game** *or* **a different b. game** *Am Fig* c'est une tout autre affaire. ◆**ballcock** *n* robinet *m* à flotteur. ◆**ballpoint** *n* stylo *m* à bille.
ball[2] [bɔːl] *n* (*dance*) bal *m*. ◆**ballroom** *n* salle *f* de danse.
ballad ['bæləd] *n Liter* ballade *f*; *Mus* romance *f*.
ballast ['bæləst] *n* lest *m*; – *vt* lester.
ballet ['bæleɪ] *n* ballet *m*. ◆**balle'rina** *n* ballerine *f*.
ballistic [bə'lɪstɪk] *a* **b. missile** engin *m* balistique.
balloon [bə'luːn] *n* ballon *m*; *Met* ballon-sonde *m*.

ballot ['bælət] *n* (*voting*) scrutin *m*; **b.** (*paper*) bulletin *m* de vote; **b. box** urne *f*; – *vt* (*members*) consulter (par un scrutin).
ballyhoo [bælɪ'huː] *n* *Fam* battage *m* (publicitaire).
balm [bɑːm] *n* (*liquid, comfort*) baume *m*. ◆**balmy** *a* (**-ier, -iest**) **1** (*air*) *Lit* embaumé. **2** (*crazy*) *Fam* dingue, timbré.
baloney [bə'ləʊnɪ] *n* *Sl* foutaises *fpl*.
Baltic ['bɔːltɪk] *n* **the B.** la Baltique.
balustrade ['bæləstreɪd] *n* balustrade *f*.
bamboo [bæm'buː] *n* bambou *m*.
bamboozle [bæm'buːz(ə)l] *vt* (*cheat*) *Fam* embobiner.
ban [bæn] *n* interdiction *f*; – *vt* (**-nn-**) interdire; **to b. from** (*club etc*) exclure de; **to ban s.o. from doing** interdire à qn de faire.
banal [bə'nɑːl, *Am* 'beɪn(ə)l] *a* banal. ◆**ba'nality** *n* banalité *f*.
banana [bə'nɑːnə] *n* banane *f*.
band [bænd] **1** *n* (*strip*) bande *f*; (*of hat*) ruban *m*; **rubber** *or* **elastic b.** élastique *m*. **2** *n* (*group*) bande *f*; *Mus* (petit) orchestre *m*; *Mil* fanfare *f*; – *vi* **to b. together** former une bande, se grouper. ◆**bandstand** *n* kiosque *m* à musique. ◆**bandwagon** *n* **to jump on the b.** *Fig* suivre le mouvement.
bandage ['bændɪdʒ] *n* (*strip*) bande *f*; (*for wound*) pansement *m*; (*for holding in place*) bandage *m*; – *vt* **to b. (up)** (*arm, leg*) bander; (*wound*) mettre un pansement sur.
Band-Aid® ['bændeɪd] *n* pansement *m* adhésif.
bandit ['bændɪt] *n* bandit *m*. ◆**banditry** *n* banditisme *m*.
bandy ['bændɪ] **1** *a* (**-ier, -iest**) (*person*) bancal; (*legs*) arqué. ◆**b.-'legged** *a* bancal. **2** *vt* **to b. about** (*story etc*) faire circuler, propager.
bane [beɪn] *n* *Lit* fléau *m*. ◆**baneful** *a* funeste.
bang [bæŋ] **1** *n* (*hit, noise*) coup *m* (violent); (*of gun etc*) détonation *f*; (*of door*) claquement *m*; – *vt* cogner, frapper; (*door*) (faire) claquer; **to b. one's head** se cogner la tête; – *vi* cogner, frapper; (*of door*) claquer; (*of gun*) détoner; (*of firework*) éclater; **to b. down** (*lid*) rabattre (violemment); **to b. into sth** heurter qch; – *int* vlan!, pan!; **to go (off) b.** éclater. **2** *adv* (*exactly*) *Fam* exactement; **b. in the middle** en plein milieu; **b. on six** à six heures tapantes.
banger ['bæŋər] *n* **1** *Culin Fam* saucisse *f*. **2** (*firecracker*) pétard *m*. **3 old b.** (*car*) *Fam* tacot *m*, guimbarde *f*.
bangle ['bæŋg(ə)l] *n* bracelet *m* (rigide).
bangs [bæŋz] *npl* (*of hair*) *Am* frange *f*.
banish ['bænɪʃ] *vt* bannir.
banister ['bænɪstər] *n* **banister(s)** rampe *f* (d'escalier).
banjo ['bændʒəʊ] *n* (*pl* **-os** *or* **-oes**) banjo *m*.
bank [bæŋk] **1** *n* (*of river*) bord *m*, rive *f*; (*raised*) berge *f*; (*of earth*) talus *m*; (*of sand*) banc *m*; **the Left B.** (*in Paris*) la Rive gauche; – *vt* **to b. (up)** (*earth etc*) amonceler; (*fire*) couvrir. **2** *n* *Com* banque *f*; **b. account** compte *m* en banque; **b. card** carte *f* d'identité bancaire; **b. holiday** jour *m* férié; **b. note** billet *m* de banque; **b. rate** taux *m* d'escompte; – *vt* (*money*) *Com* mettre en banque; – *vi* avoir un compte en banque (**with** à). **3** *vi* *Av* virer. **4** *vi* **to b. on s.o./sth** (*rely on*) compter sur qn/qch. ◆**—ing** *a* bancaire; – *n* (*activity, profession*) la banque. ◆**—er** *n* banquier *m*.
bankrupt ['bæŋkrʌpt] *a* **to go b.** faire faillite; **b. of** (*ideas*) *Fig* dénué de; – *vt* mettre en faillite. ◆**bankruptcy** *n* faillite *f*.
banner ['bænər] *n* (*at rallies etc*) banderole *f*; (*flag*) & *Fig* bannière *f*.
banns [bænz] *npl* bans *mpl*.
banquet ['bæŋkwɪt] *n* banquet *m*.
banter ['bæntər] *vti* plaisanter; – *n* plaisanterie *f*. ◆**—ing** *a* (*tone, air*) plaisantin.
baptism ['bæptɪzəm] *n* baptême *m*. ◆**bap'tize** *vt* baptiser.
bar [bɑːr] **1** *n* barre *f*; (*of gold*) lingot *m*; (*of chocolate*) tablette *f*; (*on window*) & *Jur* barreau *m*; **b. of soap** savonnette *f*; **behind bars** *Jur* sous les verrous; **to be a b. to** *Fig* faire obstacle à. **2** *n* (*pub*) bar *m*; (*counter*) comptoir *m*. **3** *n* (*group of notes*) *Mus* mesure *f*. **4** *vt* (**-rr-**) (*way etc*) bloquer, barrer; (*window*) griller. **5** *vt* (*prohibit*) interdire (**s.o. from doing** à qn de faire); (*exclude*) exclure (**from** à). **6** *prep* sauf. ◆**barmaid** *n* serveuse *f* de bar. ◆**barman** *n*, ◆**bartender** *n* barman *m*.
Barbados [bɑː'beɪdɒs] *n* Barbade *f*.
barbarian [bɑː'beərɪən] *n* barbare *mf*. ◆**barbaric** *a* barbare. ◆**barbarity** *n* barbarie *f*.
barbecue ['bɑːbɪkjuː] *n* barbecue *m*; – *vt* griller (au barbecue).
barbed [bɑːbd] *a* **b. wire** fil *m* de fer barbelé; (*fence*) barbelés *mpl*.
barber ['bɑːbər] *n* coiffeur *m* (*pour hommes*).
barbiturate [bɑː'bɪtjʊrət] *n* barbiturique *m*.
bare [beər] *a* (**-er, -est**) nu; (*tree, hill etc*) dénudé; (*cupboard*) vide; (*mere*) simple; **the b. necessities** le strict nécessaire; **with his b. hands** à mains nues; – *vt* mettre à nu.

◆**—ness** *n* (*of person*) nudité *f*. ◆**bareback** *adv* **to ride b.** monter à cru. ◆**barefaced** *a* (*lie*) éhonté. ◆**barefoot** *adv* nu-pieds; – *a* aux pieds nus. ◆**bare'headed** *a & adv* nu-tête *inv*.

barely ['beəlɪ] *adv* (*scarcely*) à peine, tout juste.

bargain ['bɑːgɪn] *n* (*deal*) marché *m*, affaire *f*; **a (good) b.** (*cheap buy*) une occasion, une bonne affaire; **it's a b.!** (*agreed*) c'est entendu!; **into the b.** par-dessus le marché; **b. price** prix *m* exceptionnel; **b. counter** rayon *m* des soldes; – *vi* (*negotiate*) négocier; (*haggle*) marchander; **to b. for** *or* **on sth** *Fig* s'attendre à qch. ◆**—ing** *n* négociations *fpl*; marchandage *m*.

barge [bɑːdʒ] **1** *n* chaland *m*, péniche *f*. **2** *vi* **to b. in** (*enter a room*) faire irruption; (*interrupt*) interrompre; **to b. into** (*hit*) se cogner contre.

baritone ['bærɪtəʊn] *n* (*voice, singer*) baryton *m*.

bark [bɑːk] **1** *n* (*of tree*) écorce *f*. **2** *vi* (*of dog etc*) aboyer; – *n* aboiement *m*. ◆**—ing** *n* aboiements *mpl*.

barley ['bɑːlɪ] *n* orge *f*; **b. sugar** sucre *m* d'orge.

barmy [bɑːmɪ] *a* (**-ier, -iest**) *Fam* dingue, timbré.

barn [bɑːn] *n* (*for crops etc*) grange *f*; (*for horses*) écurie *f*; (*for cattle*) étable *f*. ◆**barnyard** *n* basse-cour *f*.

barometer [bə'rɒmɪtər] *n* baromètre *m*.

baron ['bærən] *n* baron *m*; (*industrialist*) *Fig* magnat *m*. ◆**baroness** *n* baronne *f*.

baroque [bə'rɒk, *Am* bə'rəʊk] *a & n Archit Mus etc* baroque (*m*).

barracks ['bærəks] *npl* caserne *f*.

barrage ['bærɑːʒ, *Am* bə'rɑːʒ] *n* (*barrier*) barrage *m*; **a b. of** (*questions etc*) un feu roulant de.

barrel ['bærəl] *n* **1** (*cask*) tonneau *m*; (*of oil*) baril *m*. **2** (*of gun*) canon *m*. **3 b. organ** orgue *m* de Barbarie.

barren ['bærən] *a* stérile; (*style*) *Fig* aride.

barrette [bə'ret] *n* (*hair slide*) *Am* barrette *f*.

barricade ['bærɪkeɪd] *n* barricade *f*; – *vt* barricader; **to b. oneself (in)** se barricader.

barrier ['bærɪər] *n* barrière *f*; *Fig* obstacle *m*, barrière *f*; **(ticket) b.** *Rail* portillon *m*; **sound b.** mur *m* du son.

barring ['bɑːrɪŋ] *prep* sauf, excepté.

barrister ['bærɪstər] *n* avocat *m*.

barrow ['bærəʊ] *n* charrette *f* *or* voiture *f* à bras; (*wheelbarrow*) brouette *f*.

barter ['bɑːtər] *vt* troquer, échanger (**for** contre); – *n* troc *m*, échange *m*.

base [beɪs] **1** *n* (*bottom, main ingredient*) base *f*; (*of tree, lamp*) pied *m*. **2** *n Mil* base *f*. **3** *vt* baser, fonder (**on** sur); **based in** *or* **on London** basé à Londres. **4** *a* (*dishonourable*) bas, ignoble; (*metal*) vil. ◆**—less** *a* sans fondement. ◆**—ness** *n* bassesse *f*. ◆**baseball** *n* base-ball *m*. ◆**baseboard** *n Am* plinthe *f*.

basement ['beɪsmənt] *n* sous-sol *m*.

bash [bæʃ] *n Fam* (*bang*) coup *m*; **to have a b.** (*try*) essayer un coup; – *vt Fam* (*hit*) cogner; **to b. (about)** (*ill-treat*) malmener; **to b. s.o. up** tabasser qn; **to b. in** *or* **down** (*door etc*) défoncer. ◆**—ing** *n* (*thrashing*) *Fam* raclée *f*.

bashful ['bæʃfəl] *a* timide.

basic ['beɪsɪk] *a* fondamental; (*pay etc*) de base; – *n* **the basics** *Fam* l'essentiel *m*. ◆**—ally** [-klɪ] *adv* au fond.

basil ['bæz(ə)l] *n Bot Culin* basilic *m*.

basilica [bə'zɪlɪkə] *n* basilique *f*.

basin ['beɪs(ə)n] *n* bassin *m*, bassine *f*; (*for soup, food*) bol *m*; (*of river*) bassin *m*; (*portable washbasin*) cuvette *f*; (*sink*) lavabo *m*.

basis, *pl* **-ses** ['beɪsɪs, -siːz] *n* base *f*; **on the b. of** d'après; **on that b.** dans ces conditions; **on a weekly/etc b.** chaque semaine/*etc*.

bask [bɑːsk] *vi* se chauffer.

basket ['bɑːskɪt] *n* panier *m*; (*for bread, laundry, litter*) corbeille *f*. ◆**basketball** *n* basket(-ball) *m*.

Basque [bæsk] *a & n* basque (*mf*).

bass[1] [beɪs] *n Mus* basse *f*; – *a* (*note, voice*) bas.

bass[2] [bæs] *n* (*sea fish*) bar *m*; (*fresh-water*) perche *f*.

bassinet [bæsɪ'net] *n* (*cradle*) *Am* couffin *m*.

bastard ['bɑːstəd] **1** *n & a* bâtard, -arde (*mf*). **2** *n Pej Sl* salaud *m*, salope *f*.

baste [beɪst] *vt* **1** (*fabric*) bâtir. **2** *Culin* arroser.

bastion ['bæstɪən] *n* bastion *m*.

bat [bæt] **1** *n* (*animal*) chauve-souris *f*. **2** *n Cricket* batte *f*; *Table Tennis* raquette *f*; **off my own b.** de ma propre initiative; – *vt* (**-tt-**) (*ball*) frapper. **3** *vt* **she didn't b. an eyelid** elle n'a pas sourcillé.

batch [bætʃ] *n* (*of people*) groupe *m*; (*of letters*) paquet *m*; (*of books*) lot *m*; (*of loaves*) fournée *f*; (*of papers*) liasse *f*.

bated ['beɪtɪd] *a* **with b. breath** en retenant son souffle.

bath [bɑːθ] *n* (*pl* **-s** [bɑːðz]) bain *m*; (*tub*) baignoire *f*; **swimming baths** piscine *f*; – *vt* baigner; – *vi* prendre un bain.

◆**bathrobe** *n* peignoir *m* (de bain); *Am* robe *f* de chambre. ◆**bathroom** *n* salle *f* de bain(s); (*toilet*) *Am* toilettes *fpl.* ◆**bathtub** *n* baignoire *f.*

bath/e [beɪð] *vt* baigner; (*wound*) laver; – *vi* se baigner; *Am* prendre un bain; – *n* bain *m* (de mer), baignade *f.* ◆**–ing** *n* baignade(s) *f(pl)*; **b. costume** *or* **suit** maillot *m* de bain.

baton ['bætən, *Am* bə'tɒn] *n Mus Mil* bâton *m*; (*truncheon*) matraque *f.*

battalion [bə'tæljən] *n* bataillon *m.*

batter ['bætər] **1** *n* pâte *f* à frire. **2** *vt* battre, frapper; (*baby*) martyriser; *Mil* pilonner; **to b. down** (*door*) défoncer. ◆**–ed** *a* (*car, hat*) cabossé; (*house*) délabré; (*face*) meurtri; (*wife*) battu. ◆**–ing** *n* **to take a b.** *Fig* souffrir beaucoup.

battery ['bætərɪ] *n Mil Aut Agr* batterie *f*; (*in radio etc*) pile *f.*

battle ['bæt(ə)l] *n* bataille *f*; (*struggle*) *Fig* lutte *f*; **that's half the b.** *Fam* c'est ça le secret de la victoire; **b. dress** tenue *f* de campagne; – *vi* se battre, lutter. ◆**battlefield** *n* champ *m* de bataille. ◆**battleship** *n* cuirassé *m.*

battlements ['bæt(ə)lmənts] *npl* (*indentations*) créneaux *mpl*; (*wall*) remparts *mpl.*

batty ['bætɪ] *a* (**-ier, -iest**) *Sl* dingue, toqué.

baulk [bɔːk] *vi* reculer (**at** devant), regimber (**at** contre).

bawdy ['bɔːdɪ] *a* (**-ier, -iest**) paillard, grossier.

bawl [bɔːl] *vti* **to b. (out)** beugler, brailler; **to b. s.o. out** *Am Sl* engueuler qn.

bay [beɪ] **1** *n Geog Archit* baie *f.* **2** *n Bot* laurier *m.* **3** *n* (*for loading etc*) aire *f.* **4** *n* (*of dog*) aboiement *m*; **at b.** aux abois; **to hold at b.** tenir à distance; – *vi* aboyer. **5** *a* (*horse*) bai.

bayonet ['beɪənɪt] *n* baïonnette *f.*

bazaar [bə'zɑːr] *n* (*market, shop*) bazar *m*; (*charity sale*) vente *f* de charité.

bazooka [bə'zuːkə] *n* bazooka *m.*

BC [biː'siː] *abbr* (*before Christ*) avant Jésus-Christ.

be [biː] *vi* (*pres t* **am, are, is**; *pt* **was, were**; *pp* **been**; *pres p* **being**) **1** être; **it is green/small** c'est vert/petit; **she's a doctor** elle est médecin; **he's an Englishman** c'est un Anglais; **it's 3 (o'clock)** il est trois heures; **it's the sixth of May** c'est *or* nous sommes le six mai. **2** avoir; **to be hot/right/lucky** avoir chaud/raison/de la chance; **my feet are cold** j'ai froid aux pieds; **he's 20** (*age*) il a 20 ans; **to be 2 metres high** avoir 2 mètres de haut; **to be 6 feet tall** mesurer 1,80 m. **3** (*health*) aller; **how are you?** comment vas-tu? **4** (*place, situation*) se trouver, être; **she's in York** elle se trouve *or* elle est à York. **5** (*exist*) être; **the best painter there is** le meilleur peintre qui soit; **leave me be** laissez-moi (tranquille); **that may be** cela se peut. **6** (*go, come*) **I've been to see her** je suis allé *or* j'ai été la voir; **he's (already) been** il est (déjà) venu. **7** (*weather*) & *Math* faire; **it's fine** il fait beau; **2 and 2 are 4** 2 et 2 font 4. **8** (*cost*) coûter, faire; **it's 20 pence** ça coûte 20 pence; **how much is it?** ça fait combien?, c'est combien? **9** (*auxiliary*) **I am/was doing** je fais/faisais; **I'm listening to the radio** (*in the process of*) je suis en train d'écouter la radio; **she's been there some time** elle est là depuis longtemps; **he was killed** il a été tué, on l'a tué; **I've been waiting (for) two hours** j'attends depuis deux heures; **it is said** on dit; **to be pitied** à plaindre; **isn't it?, aren't you?** *etc* n'est-ce pas?, non?; **I am!, he is!** *etc* oui! **10** (+ *inf*) **he is to come** (*must*) il doit venir; **he's shortly to go** (*intends to*) il va bientôt partir. **11 there is** *or* **are** il y a; (*pointing*) voilà; **here is** *or* **are** voici.

beach [biːtʃ] *n* plage *f.* ◆**beachcomber** *n* (*person*) ramasseur, -euse *mf* d'épaves.

beacon ['biːkən] *n Nau Av* balise *f*; (*lighthouse*) phare *m.*

bead [biːd] *n* (*small sphere, drop of liquid*) perle *f*; (*of rosary*) grain *m*; (*of sweat*) goutte *f*; **(string of) beads** collier *m.*

beak [biːk] *n* bec *m.*

beaker ['biːkər] *n* gobelet *m.*

beam [biːm] **1** *n* (*of wood*) poutre *f.* **2** *n* (*of light*) rayon *m*; (*of headlight, torch*) faisceau *m* (lumineux); – *vi* rayonner; (*of person*) *Fig* sourire largement. **3** *vt Rad* diffuser. ◆**–ing** *a* (*radiant*) radieux.

bean [biːn] *n* haricot *m*; (*of coffee*) grain *m*; **(broad) b.** fève *f*; **to be full of beans** *Fam* déborder d'entrain. ◆**beanshoots** *npl*, ◆**beansprouts** *npl* germes *mpl* de soja.

bear[1] [beər] *n* (*animal*) ours *m.*

bear[2] [beər] *vt* (*pt* **bore**, *pp* **borne**) (*carry, show*) porter; (*endure*) supporter; (*resemblance*) offrir; (*comparison*) soutenir; (*responsibility*) assumer; (*child*) donner naissance à; **to b. in mind** tenir compte de; **to b. out** corroborer; – *vi* **to b. left/***etc* (*turn*) tourner à gauche/*etc*; **to b. north/***etc* (*go*) aller en direction du nord/*etc*; **to b. (up)on** (*relate to*) se rapporter à; **to b. heavily on** (*of burden*) *Fig* peser sur; **to b. with** être indulgent envers, être patient avec; **to bring to b.** (*one's energies*) consacrer (**on** à);

(*pressure*) exercer (**on** sur); **to b. up** ne pas se décourager, tenir le coup; **b. up!** du courage! ◆**—ing** *n* (*posture, conduct*) maintien *m*; (*relationship, relevance*) relation *f* (**on** avec); *Nau Av* position *f*; **to get one's bearings** s'orienter. ◆**—able** *a* supportable. ◆**—er** *n* porteur, -euse *mf*.

beard [bɪəd] *n* barbe *f*. ◆**bearded** *a* barbu.

beast [biːst] *n* bête *f*, animal *m*; (*person*) *Pej* brute *f*. ◆**beastly** *a Fam* (*bad*) vilain, infect; (*spiteful*) méchant; – *adv Fam* terriblement.

beat [biːt] *n* (*of heart, drum*) battement *m*; (*of policeman*) ronde *f*; *Mus* mesure *f*, rythme *m*; – *vt* (*pt* **beat**, *pp* **beaten**) battre; (*defeat*) vaincre, battre; **to b. a drum** battre du tambour; **that beats me** *Fam* ça me dépasse; **to b. s.o. to it** devancer qn; **b. it!** *Sl* fichez le camp!; **to b. back** *or* **off** repousser; **to b. down** (*price*) faire baisser; **to b. in** *or* **down** (*door*) défoncer; **to b. out** (*rhythm*) marquer; (*tune*) jouer; **to b. s.o. up** tabasser qn; – *vi* battre; (*at door*) frapper (**at** à); **to b. about** *or* **around the bush** *Fam* tourner autour du pot; **to b. down** (*of rain*) tomber à verse; (*of sun*) taper. ◆**—ing** *n* (*blows, defeat*) raclée *f*. ◆**—er** *n* (*for eggs*) batteur *m*.

beauty ['bjuːtɪ] *n* (*quality, woman*) beauté *f*; **it's a b.!** c'est une merveille!; **the b. of it is . . .** le plus beau, c'est que . . . ; **b. parlour** institut *m* de beauté; **b. spot** (*on skin*) grain *m* de beauté; (*in countryside*) site *m* pittoresque. ◆**beau'tician** *n* esthéticienne *f*. ◆**beautiful** *a* (très) beau; (*superb*) merveilleux. ◆**beautifully** *adv* merveilleusement.

beaver ['biːvər] *n* castor *m*; – *vi* **to b. away** travailler dur (**at sth** à qch).

because [bɪ'kɒz] *conj* parce que; **b. of** à cause de.

beck [bek] *n* **at s.o.'s b. and call** aux ordres de qn.

beckon ['bekən] *vti* **to b. (to) s.o.** faire signe à qn (**to do** de faire).

becom/e [bɪ'kʌm] **1** *vi* (*pt* **became**, *pp* **become**) devenir; **to b. a painter** devenir peintre; **to b. thin** maigrir; **to b. worried** commencer à s'inquiéter; **what has b. of her?** qu'est-elle devenue? **2** *vt* **that hat becomes her** ce chapeau lui sied *or* lui va. ◆**—ing** *a* (*clothes*) seyant; (*modesty*) bienséant.

bed [bed] *n* lit *m*; *Geol* couche *f*; (*of vegetables*) carré *m*; (*of sea*) fond *m*; (*flower bed*) parterre *m*; **to go to b.** (aller) se coucher; **in b.** couché; **to get out of b.** se lever; **b. and breakfast** (*in hotel etc*) chambre *f* avec petit déjeuner; **b. settee** (canapé *m*) convertible *m*; **air b.** matelas *m* pneumatique; – *vt* (**-dd-**) **to b. (out)** (*plant*) repiquer; – *vi* **to b. down** se coucher. ◆**bedding** *n* literie *f*. ◆**bedbug** *n* punaise *f*. ◆**bedclothes** *npl* couvertures *fpl* et draps *mpl*. ◆**bedridden** *a* alité. ◆**bedroom** *n* chambre *f* à coucher. ◆**bedside** *n* chevet *m*; – *a* (*lamp, book, table*) de chevet. ◆**bed'sitter** *n*, *Fam* ◆**bedsit** *n* chambre *f* meublée. ◆**bedspread** *n* dessus-de-lit *m inv*. ◆**bedtime** *n* heure *f* du coucher.

bedeck [bɪ'dek] *vt* orner (**with** de).

bedevil [bɪ'dev(ə)l] *vt* (**-ll-**, *Am* **-l-**) (*plague*) tourmenter; (*confuse*) embrouiller; **bedevilled by** (*problems etc*) perturbé par, empoisonné par.

bedlam ['bedləm] *n* (*noise*) *Fam* chahut *m*.

bedraggled [bɪ'dræg(ə)ld] *a* (*clothes, person*) débraillé.

bee [biː] *n* abeille *f*. ◆**beehive** *n* ruche *f*. ◆**beekeeping** *n* apiculture *f*. ◆**beeline** *n* **to make a b. for** aller droit vers.

beech [biːtʃ] *n* (*tree, wood*) hêtre *m*.

beef [biːf] **1** *n* bœuf *m*. **2** *vi* (*complain*) *Sl* rouspéter. ◆**beefburger** *n* hamburger *m*. ◆**beefy** *a* (**-ier**, **-iest**) *Fam* musclé, costaud.

beer [bɪər] *n* bière *f*; **b. glass** chope *f*. ◆**beery** *a* (*room, person*) qui sent la bière.

beet [biːt] *n* betterave *f* (à sucre); *Am* = **beetroot**. ◆**beetroot** *n* betterave *f* (potagère).

beetle ['biːt(ə)l] **1** *n* cafard *m*, scarabée *m*. **2** *vi* **to b. off** *Fam* se sauver.

befall [bɪ'fɔːl] *vt* (*pt* **befell**, *pp* **befallen**) arriver à.

befit [bɪ'fɪt] *vt* (**-tt-**) convenir à.

before [bɪ'fɔːr] *adv* avant; (*already*) déjà; (*in front*) devant; **the month b.** le mois d'avant *or* précédent; **the day b.** la veille; **I've never done it b.** je ne l'ai jamais (encore) fait; – *prep* (*time*) avant; (*place*) devant; **the year b. last** il y a deux ans; – *conj* avant que (+ ne + *sub*), avant de (+ *inf*); **b. he goes** avant qu'il (ne) parte; **b. going** avant de partir. ◆**beforehand** *adv* à l'avance, avant.

befriend [bɪ'frend] *vt* offrir son amitié à, aider.

befuddled [bɪ'fʌd(ə)ld] *a* (*drunk*) ivre.

beg [beg] *vt* (**-gg-**) **to b. (for)** solliciter, demander; (*bread, money*) mendier; **to b. s.o. to do** prier *or* supplier qn de faire; **I b. to** je me permets de; **to b. the question** esquiver la question; – *vi* mendier;

(*entreat*) supplier; **to go begging** (*of food, articles*) ne pas trouver d'amateurs. ◆**beggar** *n* mendiant, -ante *mf*; (*person*) *Sl* individu *m*; **lucky b.** veinard, -arde *mf*. ◆**beggarly** *a* misérable.

beget [bɪ'get] *vt* (*pt* **begot**, *pp* **begotten**, *pres p* **begetting**) engendrer.

begin [bɪ'gɪn] *vt* (*pt* **began**, *pp* **begun**, *pres p* **beginning**) commencer; (*fashion, campaign*) lancer; (*bottle, sandwich*) entamer; (*conversation*) engager; **to b. doing** *or* **to do** commencer *or* se mettre à faire; – *vi* commencer (**with** par, **by doing** par faire); **to b. on sth** commencer qch; **beginning from** à partir de; **to b. with** (*first*) d'abord. ◆**—ning** *n* commencement *m*, début *m*. ◆**—ner** *n* débutant, -ante *mf*.

begrudge [bɪ'grʌdʒ] *vt* (*give unwillingly*) donner à contrecœur; (*envy*) envier (**s.o. sth** qch à qn); (*reproach*) reprocher (**s.o. sth** qch à qn); **to b. doing** faire à contrecœur.

behalf [bɪ'hɑːf] *n* **on b. of** pour, au nom de, de la part de; (*in the interest of*) en faveur de, pour.

behave [bɪ'heɪv] *vi* se conduire; (*of machine*) fonctionner; **to b. (oneself)** se tenir bien; (*of child*) être sage. ◆**behaviour** *n* conduite *f*, comportement *m*; **to be on one's best b.** se conduire de son mieux.

behead [bɪ'hed] *vt* décapiter.

behest [bɪ'hest] *n Lit* ordre *m*.

behind [bɪ'haɪnd] **1** *prep* derrière; (*more backward than, late according to*) en retard sur; – *adv* derrière; (*late*) en retard (**with, in** dans). **2** *n* (*buttocks*) *Fam* derrière *m*. ◆**behindhand** *adv* en retard.

beholden [bɪ'həʊldən] *a* redevable (**to** à, **for** de).

beige [beɪʒ] *a* & *n* beige (*m*).

being ['biːɪŋ] *n* (*person, life*) être *m*; **to come into b.** naître, être créé.

belated [bɪ'leɪtɪd] *a* tardif.

belch [beltʃ] **1** *vi* (*of person*) faire un renvoi, éructer; – *n* renvoi *m*. **2** *vt* **to b. (out)** (*smoke*) vomir.

beleaguered [bɪ'liːgəd] *a* (*besieged*) assiégé.

belfry ['belfrɪ] *n* beffroi *m*, clocher *m*.

Belgium ['beldʒəm] *n* Belgique *f*. ◆**Belgian** ['beldʒən] *a* & *n* belge (*mf*).

belie [bɪ'laɪ] *vt* démentir.

belief [bɪ'liːf] *n* (*believing, thing believed*) croyance *f* (**in s.o.** en qn, **in sth** à *or* en qch); (*trust*) confiance *f*, foi *f*; (*faith*) *Rel* foi *f* (**in** en).

believ/e [bɪ'liːv] *vti* croire (**in sth** à qch, **in God/s.o.** en Dieu/qn); **I b. so** je crois que oui; **I b. I'm right** je crois avoir raison; **to b. in doing** croire qu'il faut faire; **he doesn't b. in smoking** il désapprouve que l'on fume. ◆**—able** *a* croyable. ◆**—er** *n Rel* croyant, -ante *mf*; **b. in** (*supporter*) partisan, -ane *mf* de.

belittle [bɪ'lɪt(ə)l] *vt* déprécier.

bell [bel] *n* cloche *f*; (*small*) clochette *f*; (*in phone*) sonnerie *f*; (*on door, bicycle*) sonnette *f*; (*on dog*) grelot *m*. ◆**bellboy** *n*, ◆**bellhop** *n Am* groom *m*.

belle [bel] *n* (*woman*) beauté *f*, belle *f*.

belligerent [bɪ'lɪdʒərənt] *a* & *n* belligérant, -ante (*mf*).

bellow ['beləʊ] *vi* beugler, mugir.

bellows ['beləʊz] *npl* **(pair of) b.** soufflet *m*.

belly ['belɪ] *n* ventre *m*; **b. button** *Sl* nombril *m*. ◆**bellyache** *n* mal *m* au ventre; – *vi Sl* rouspéter. ◆**bellyful** *n* **to have a b.** *Sl* en avoir plein le dos.

belong [bɪ'lɒŋ] *vi* appartenir (**to** à); **to b. to** (*club*) être membre de; **the cup belongs here** la tasse se range ici. ◆**—ings** *npl* affaires *fpl*.

beloved [bɪ'lʌvɪd] *a* & *n* bien-aimé, -ée (*mf*).

below [bɪ'ləʊ] *prep* (*lower than*) au-dessous de; (*under*) sous, au-dessous de; (*unworthy of*) *Fig* indigne de; – *adv* en dessous; **see b.** (*in book etc*) voir ci-dessous.

belt [belt] **1** *n* ceinture *f*; (*area*) zone *f*, région *f*; *Tech* courroie *f*. **2** *vt* (*hit*) *Sl* rosser. **3** *vi* **to b. (along)** (*rush*) *Sl* filer à toute allure; **b. up!** (*shut up*) *Sl* boucle-la!

bemoan [bɪ'məʊn] *vt* déplorer.

bench [bentʃ] *n* (*seat*) banc *m*; (*work table*) établi *m*, banc *m*; **the B.** *Jur* la magistrature (assise); (*court*) le tribunal.

bend [bend] *n* courbe *f*; (*in river, pipe*) coude *m*; (*in road*) *Aut* virage *m*; (*of arm, knee*) pli *m*; **round the b.** (*mad*) *Sl* tordu; – *vt* (*pt* & *pp* **bent**) courber; (*leg, arm*) plier; (*direct*) diriger; **to b. the rules** faire une entorse au règlement; – *vi* (*of branch*) plier, être courbé; (*of road*) tourner; **to b. (down)** se courber; **to b. (over** *or* **forward)** se pencher; **to b. to** (*s.o.'s will*) se soumettre à.

beneath [bɪ'niːθ] *prep* au-dessous de, sous; (*unworthy of*) indigne de; – *adv* (au-)dessous.

benediction [benɪ'dɪkʃ(ə)n] *n* bénédiction *f*.

benefactor ['benɪfæktər] *n* bienfaiteur *m*. ◆**benefactress** *n* bienfaitrice *f*.

beneficial [benɪ'fɪʃəl] *a* bénéfique.

beneficiary [benɪ'fɪʃərɪ] *n* bénéficiaire *mf*.

benefit ['benɪfɪt] *n* (*advantage*) avantage *m*; (*money*) allocation *f*; *pl* (*of science, education etc*) bienfaits *mpl*; **to s.o.'s b.** dans l'intérêt de qn; **for your (own) b.** pour vous, pour votre bien; **to be of b.** faire du bien (to à); **to give s.o. the b. of the doubt** accorder à qn le bénéfice du doute; **b. concert**/*etc* concert/*etc m* de bienfaisance; – *vt* faire du bien à; (*be useful to*) profiter à; – *vi* gagner (**from doing** à faire); **you'll b. from** *or* **by the rest** le repos vous fera du bien.

Benelux ['benılʌks] *n* Bénélux *m.*

benevolent [bı'nevələnt] *a* bienveillant. ◆**benevolence** *n* bienveillance *f.*

benign [bı'naın] *a* bienveillant, bénin; (*climate*) doux; (*tumour*) bénin.

bent [bent] **1** *a* (*nail, mind*) tordu; (*dishonest*) *Sl* corrompu; **b. on doing** résolu à faire. **2** *n* (*talent*) aptitude *f* (**for** pour); (*inclination, liking*) penchant *m*, goût *m* (**for** pour).

bequeath [bı'kwiːð] *vt* léguer (**to** à). ◆**bequest** *n* legs *m.*

bereaved [bı'riːvd] *a* endeuillé; – *n* **the b.** la famille, la femme *etc* du disparu. ◆**bereavement** *n* deuil *m.*

bereft [bı'reft] *a* **b. of** dénué de.

beret ['bereı, *Am* bə'reı] *n* béret *m.*

berk [bɜːk] *n Sl* imbécile *mf.*

Bermuda [bə'mjuːdə] *n* Bermudes *fpl.*

berry ['berı] *n* baie *f.*

berserk [bə'zɜːk] *a* **to go b.** devenir fou, se déchaîner.

berth [bɜːθ] *n* (*in ship, train*) couchette *f*; (*anchorage*) mouillage *m*; – *vi* (*of ship*) mouiller.

beseech [bı'siːtʃ] *vt* (*pt & pp* **besought** *or* **beseeched**) *Lit* implorer (**to do** de faire).

beset [bı'set] *vt* (*pt & pp* **beset**, *pres p* **besetting**) assaillir (*qn*); **b. with obstacles**/*etc* semé *or* hérissé d'obstacles/*etc.*

beside [bı'saıd] *prep* à côté de; **that's b. the point** ça n'a rien à voir; **b. oneself** (*angry, excited*) hors de soi.

besides [bı'saıdz] *prep* (*in addition to*) en plus de; (*except*) excepté; **there are ten of us b. Paul** nous sommes dix sans compter Paul; – *adv* (*in addition*) de plus; (*moreover*) d'ailleurs.

besiege [bı'siːdʒ] *vt* (*of soldiers, crowd*) assiéger; (*annoy*) *Fig* assaillir (**with** de).

besotted [bı'sɒtıd] *a* (*drunk*) abruti; **b. with** (*infatuated*) entiché de.

bespatter [bı'spætər] *vt* éclabousser (**with** de).

bespectacled [bı'spektık(ə)ld] *a* à lunettes.

bespoke [bı'spəʊk] *a* (*tailor*) à façon.

best [best] *a* meilleur; **the b. page in the book** la meilleure page du livre; **the b. part of** (*most*) la plus grande partie de; **the b. thing** le mieux; **b. man** (*at wedding*) témoin *m*, garçon *m* d'honneur; – *n* **the b. (one)** le meilleur, la meilleure; **it's for the b.** c'est pour le mieux; **at b.** au mieux; **to do one's b.** faire de son mieux; **to look one's b., be at one's b.** être à son avantage; **to the b. of my knowledge** autant que je sache; **to make the b. of** (*accept*) s'accommoder de; **to get the b. of it** avoir le dessus; **in one's Sunday b.** endimanché; **all the b.!** portez-vous bien!; (*in letter*) amicalement; – *adv* **(the) b.** (*to play etc*) le mieux; **the b. loved** le plus aimé; **to think it b. to** juger prudent de. ◆**b.-'seller** *n* (*book*) best-seller *m.*

bestow [bı'stəʊ] *vt* accorder, conférer (**on** à).

bet [bet] *n* pari *m*; – *vti* (*pt & pp* **bet** *or* **betted**, *pres p* **betting**) parier (**on** sur, **that** que); **you b.!** *Fam* (*of course*) tu parles! ◆**betting** *n* pari(s) *m(pl)*; **b. shop** *or* **office** bureau *m* du pari mutuel.

betoken [bı'təʊkən] *vt Lit* annoncer.

betray [bı'treı] *vt* trahir; **to b. to s.o.** (*give away to*) livrer à qn. ◆**betrayal** *n* (*disloyalty*) trahison *f*; (*disclosure*) révélation *f.*

better ['betər] *a* meilleur (**than** que); **she's (much) b.** *Med* elle va (bien) mieux; **he's b. than** (*at games*) il joue mieux que; (*at maths etc*) il est plus fort que; **that's b.** c'est mieux; **to get b.** (*recover*) se remettre; (*improve*) s'améliorer; **it's b. to go** il vaut mieux partir; **the b. part of** (*most*) la plus grande partie de; – *adv* mieux; **I had b. go** il vaut mieux que je parte; **so much the b., all the b.** tant mieux (**for** pour); – *n* **to get the b. of s.o.** l'emporter sur qn; **change for the b.** amélioration *f*; **one's betters** ses supérieurs *mpl*; – *vt* (*improve*) améliorer; (*outdo*) dépasser; **to b. oneself** améliorer sa condition. ◆**—ment** *n* amélioration *f.*

between [bı'twiːn] *prep* entre; **we did it b. (the two of) us** nous l'avons fait à nous deux; **b. you and me** entre nous; **in b.** entre; – *adv* **in b.** (*space*) au milieu, entre les deux; (*time*) dans l'intervalle.

bevel ['bevəl] *n* (*edge*) biseau *m.*

beverage ['bevərıdʒ] *n* boisson *f.*

bevy ['bevı] *n* (*of girls*) essaim *m*, bande *f.*

beware [bı'weər] *vi* **to b. of** (*s.o., sth*) se méfier de, prendre garde à; **b.!** méfiez-vous!, prenez garde!; **b. of falling**/*etc* prenez garde de (ne .pas) tomber/*etc*; **'b. of the trains'** 'attention aux trains'.

bewilder [bı'wıldər] *vt* dérouter, rendre perplexe. ◆**—ment** *n* confusion *f.*

bewitch [bı'wıtʃ] *vt* enchanter. ◆**—ing** *a* enchanteur.

beyond [bı'jɒnd] *prep* (*further than*) au-delà

de; (*reach, doubt*) hors de; (*except*) sauf; **b. a year/etc** (*longer than*) plus d'un an/*etc*; **b. belief** incroyable; **b. his** *or* **her means** au-dessus de ses moyens; **it's b. me** ça me dépasse; – *adv* (*further*) au-delà.

bias ['baɪəs] **1** *n* penchant *m* (**towards** pour); (*prejudice*) préjugé *m*, parti pris *m*; – *vt* (**-ss-** *or* **-s-**) influencer. **2** *n* **cut on the b.** (*fabric*) coupé dans le biais. ◆**bias(s)ed** *a* partial; **to be b. against** avoir des préjugés contre.

bib [bɪb] *n* (*baby's*) bavoir *m*.

bible ['baɪb(ə)l] *n* bible *f*; **the B.** la Bible. ◆**biblical** ['bɪblɪk(ə)l] *a* biblique.

bibliography [bɪblɪ'ɒgrəfɪ] *n* bibliographie *f*.

bicarbonate [baɪ'kɑːbənət] *n* bicarbonate *m*.

bicentenary [baɪsen'tiːnərɪ] *n*, ◆**bicentennial** *n* bicentenaire *m*.

biceps ['baɪseps] *n Anat* biceps *m*.

bicker ['bɪkər] *vi* se chamailler. ◆**—ing** *n* chamailleries *fpl*.

bicycle ['baɪsɪk(ə)l] *n* bicyclette *f*; – *vi* faire de la bicyclette.

bid[1] [bɪd] *vt* (*pt & pp* **bid**, *pres p* **bidding**) offrir, faire une offre de; – *vi* faire une offre (**for** pour); **to b. for** *Fig* tenter d'obtenir; – *n* (*at auction*) offre *f*, enchère *f*; (*tender*) *Com* soumission *f*; (*attempt*) tentative *f*. ◆**—ding[1]** *n* enchères *fpl*. ◆**—der** *n* enchérisseur *m*; soumissionnaire *mf*; **to the highest b.** au plus offrant.

bid[2] [bɪd] *vt* (*pt* **bade** [bæd], *pp* **bidden** *or* **bid**, *pres p* **bidding**) (*command*) commander (**s.o. to do** à qn de faire); (*say*) dire. ◆**—ding[2]** *n* ordre(s) *m*(*pl*).

bide [baɪd] *vt* **to b. one's time** attendre le bon moment.

bier [bɪər] *n* (*for coffin*) brancards *mpl*.

bifocals [baɪ'fəʊkəlz] *npl* verres *mpl* à double foyer.

big [bɪg] *a* (**bigger, biggest**) grand, gros; (*in age, generous*) grand; (*in bulk, amount*) gros; **b. deal!** *Am Fam* (bon) et alors!; **b. mouth** *Fam* grande gueule *f*; **b. toe** gros orteil *m*; – *adv* **to do things b.** *Fam* faire grand; **to talk b.** fanfaronner. ◆**bighead** *n*, ◆**big'headed** *a Fam* prétentieux, -euse (*mf*). ◆**big-'hearted** *a* généreux. ◆**bigshot** *n*, ◆**bigwig** *n Fam* gros bonnet *m*. ◆**big-time** *a Fam* important.

bigamy ['bɪgəmɪ] *n* bigamie *f*. ◆**bigamist** *n* bigame *mf*. ◆**bigamous** *a* bigame.

bigot ['bɪgət] *n* fanatique *mf*; *Rel* bigot, -ote *mf*. ◆**bigoted** *a* fanatique; *Rel* bigot.

bike [baɪk] *n Fam* vélo *m*; – *vi Fam* aller à vélo.

bikini [bɪ'kiːnɪ] *n* bikini *m*.

bilberry ['bɪlbərɪ] *n* myrtille *f*.

bile [baɪl] *n* bile *f*. ◆**bilious** ['bɪlɪəs] *a* bilieux.

bilge [bɪldʒ] *n* (*nonsense*) *Sl* foutaises *fpl*.

bilingual [baɪ'lɪŋgwəl] *a* bilingue.

bill [bɪl] **1** *n* (*of bird*) bec *m*. **2** *n* (*invoice*) facture *f*, note *f*; (*in restaurant*) addition *f*; (*in hotel*) note *f*; (*draft*) *Com* effet *m*; (*of sale*) acte *m*; (*banknote*) *Am* billet *m*; (*law*) *Pol* projet *m* de loi; (*poster*) affiche *f*; **b. of fare** menu *m*; **b. of rights** déclaration *f* des droits; – *vt Th* mettre à l'affiche, annoncer; **to b. s.o.** *Com* envoyer la facture à qn. ◆**billboard** *n* panneau *m* d'affichage. ◆**billfold** *n Am* portefeuille *m*.

billet ['bɪlɪt] *vt Mil* cantonner; – *n* cantonnement *m*.

billiard ['bɪljəd] *a* (*table etc*) de billard. ◆**billiards** *npl* (jeu *m* de) billard *m*.

billion ['bɪljən] *n* billion *m*; *Am* milliard *m*.

billow ['bɪləʊ] *n* flot *m*; – *vi* (*of sea*) se soulever; (*of smoke*) tourbillonner.

billy-goat ['bɪlɪgəʊt] *n* bouc *m*.

bimonthly [baɪ'mʌnθlɪ] *a* (*fortnightly*) bimensuel; (*every two months*) bimestriel.

bin [bɪn] *n* boîte *f*; (*for bread*) coffre *m*, huche *f*; (*for litter*) boîte *f* à ordures, poubelle *f*.

binary ['baɪnərɪ] *a* binaire.

bind [baɪnd] **1** *vt* (*pt & pp* **bound**) lier; (*fasten*) attacher, lier; (*book*) relier; (*fabric, hem*) border; **to b. s.o. to do** *Jur* obliger *or* astreindre qn à faire. **2** *n* (*bore*) *Fam* plaie *f*. ◆**—ing 1** *a* (*contract*) irrévocable; **to be b. on s.o.** *Jur* lier qn. **2** *n* (*of book*) reliure *f*. ◆**—er** *n* (*for papers*) classeur *m*.

binge [bɪndʒ] *n* **to go on a b.** *Sl* faire la bringue.

bingo ['bɪŋgəʊ] *n* loto *m*.

binoculars [bɪ'nɒkjʊləz] *npl* jumelles *fpl*.

biochemistry [baɪəʊ'kemɪstrɪ] *n* biochimie *f*.

biodegradable [baɪəʊdɪ'greɪdəb(ə)l] *a* biodégradable.

biography [baɪ'ɒgrəfɪ] *n* biographie *f*. ◆**biographer** *n* biographe *mf*.

biology [baɪ'ɒlədʒɪ] *n* biologie *f*. ◆**bio'logical** *a* biologique.

biped ['baɪped] *n* bipède *m*.

birch [bɜːtʃ] *n* **1** (*tree*) bouleau *m*. **2** (*whip*) verge *f*; – *vt* fouetter.

bird [bɜːd] *n* oiseau *m*; (*fowl*) *Culin* volaille *f*; (*girl*) *Sl* poulette *f*, nana *f*; **b.'s-eye view**

perspective *f* à vol d'oiseau; *Fig* vue *f* d'ensemble. ◆**birdseed** *n* grains *mpl* de millet.

biro® ['baɪərəʊ] *n* (*pl* **-os**) stylo *m* à bille, bic® *m*.

birth [bɜːθ] *n* naissance *f*; **to give b. to** donner naissance à; **b. certificate** acte *m* de naissance; **b. control** limitation *f* des naissances. ◆**birthday** *n* anniversaire *m*; **happy b.!** bon anniversaire! ◆**birthplace** *n* lieu *m* de naissance; (*house*) maison *f* natale. ◆**birthrate** *n* (taux *m* de) natalité *f*. ◆**birthright** *n* droit *m* (*qu'on a dès sa naissance*), patrimoine *m*.

biscuit ['bɪskɪt] *n* biscuit *m*, gâteau *m* sec; *Am* petit pain *m* au lait.

bishop ['bɪʃəp] *n* évêque *m*; (*in chess*) fou *m*.

bison ['baɪs(ə)n] *n inv* bison *m*.

bit[1] [bɪt] *n* **1** morceau *m*; (*of string, time*) bout *m*; **a b.** (*a little*) un peu; **a tiny b.** un tout petit peu; **quite a b.** (*very*) très; (*much*) beaucoup; **not a b.** pas du tout; **a b. of luck** une chance; **b. by b.** petit à petit; **in bits (and pieces)** en morceaux; **to come to bits** se démonter. **2** (*coin*) pièce *f*. **3** (*of horse*) mors *m*. **4** (*of drill*) mèche *f*. **5** (*computer information*) bit *m*.

bit[2] [bɪt] *see* **bite**.

bitch [bɪtʃ] **1** *n* chienne *f*; (*woman*) *Pej Fam* garce *f*. **2** *vi* (*complain*) *Fam* râler. ◆**bitchy** *a* (**-ier, -iest**) *Fam* vache.

bit/e [baɪt] *n* (*wound*) morsure *f*; (*from insect*) piqûre *f*; *Fishing* touche *f*; (*mouthful*) bouchée *f*; (*of style etc*) *Fig* mordant *m*; **a b. to eat** un morceau à manger; – *vti* (*pt* **bit**, *pp* **bitten**) mordre; (*of insect*) piquer, mordre; **to b. one's nails** se ronger les ongles; **to b. on sth** mordre qch; **to b. sth off** arracher qch d'un coup de dent(s). ◆**—ing** *a* mordant; (*wind*) cinglant.

bitter ['bɪtər] **1** *a* (*person, taste, irony etc*) amer; (*cold, wind*) glacial, âpre; (*criticism*) acerbe; (*shock, fate*) cruel; (*conflict*) violent. **2** *n* bière *f* (pression). ◆**—ness** *n* amertume *f*; âpreté *f*; violence *f*. ◆**bitter'sweet** *a* aigre-doux.

bivouac ['bɪvʊæk] *n Mil* bivouac *m*; – *vi* (**-ck-**) bivouaquer.

bizarre [bɪ'zɑːr] *a* bizarre.

blab [blæb] *vi* (**-bb-**) jaser. ◆**blabber** *vi* jaser. ◆**blabbermouth** *n* jaseur, -euse *mf*.

black [blæk] *a* (**-er, -est**) noir; **b. eye** œil *m* au beurre noir; **to give s.o. a b. eye** pocher l'œil à qn; **b. and blue** (*bruised*) couvert de bleus; **b. sheep** *Fig* brebis *f* galeuse; **b. ice** verglas *m*; **b. pudding** boudin *m*; – *n* (*colour*) noir *m*; (*Negro*) Noir, -e *mf*; – *vt* noircir; (*refuse to deal with*) boycotter; – *vi* **to b. out** (*faint*) s'évanouir. ◆**blacken** *vti* noircir. ◆**blackish** *a* noirâtre. ◆**blackness** *n* noirceur *f*; (*of night*) obscurité *f*.

blackberry ['blækbərɪ] *n* mûre *f*. ◆**blackbird** *n* merle *m*. ◆**blackboard** *n* tableau *m* (noir). ◆**black'currant** *n* cassis *m*. ◆**blackleg** *n* (*strike breaker*) jaune *m*. ◆**blacklist** *n* liste *f* noire; – *vt* mettre sur la liste noire. ◆**blackmail** *n* chantage *m*; – *vt* faire chanter. ◆**blackmailer** *n* maître chanteur *m*. ◆**blackout** *n* panne *f* d'électricité; (*during war*) *Mil* black-out *m*; *Med* syncope *f*; (**news**) **b.** black-out *m*. ◆**blacksmith** *n* forgeron *m*.

blackguard ['blægɑːd, -gəd] *n* canaille *f*.

bladder ['blædər] *n* vessie *f*.

blade [bleɪd] *n* lame *f*; (*of grass*) brin *m*; (*of windscreen wiper*) caoutchouc *m*.

blame [bleɪm] *vt* accuser; (*censure*) blâmer; **to b. sth on s.o.** *or* **s.o. for sth** rejeter la responsabilité de qch sur qn; **to b. s.o. for sth** (*reproach*) reprocher qch à qn; **you're to b.** c'est ta faute; – *n* faute *f*; (*censure*) blâme *m*. ◆**—less** *a* irréprochable.

blanch [blɑːntʃ] *vt* (*vegetables*) blanchir; – *vi* (*turn pale with fear etc*) blêmir.

blancmange [blə'mɒnʒ] *n* blanc-manger *m*.

bland [blænd] *a* (**-er, -est**) doux; (*food*) fade.

blank [blæŋk] *a* (*paper, page*) blanc, vierge; (*cheque*) en blanc; (*look, mind*) vide; (*puzzled*) ébahi; (*refusal*) absolu; – *a & n* **b. (space)** blanc *m*; **b. (cartridge)** cartouche *f* à blanc; **my mind's a b.** j'ai la tête vide. ◆**blankly** *adv* sans expression.

blanket ['blæŋkɪt] **1** *n* couverture *f*; (*of snow etc*) *Fig* couche *f*; – *vt* (*cover*) *Fig* recouvrir. **2** *a* (*term etc*) général. ◆**—ing** *n* (*blankets*) couvertures *fpl*.

blare [bleər] *n* (*noise*) beuglement *m*; (*of trumpet*) sonnerie *f*; – *vi* **to b. (out)** (*of radio*) beugler; (*of music, car horn*) retentir.

blarney ['blɑːnɪ] *n Fam* boniment(s) *m(pl)*.

blasé ['blɑːzeɪ] *a* blasé.

blaspheme [blæs'fiːm] *vti* blasphémer. ◆**'blasphemous** *a* blasphématoire; (*person*) blasphémateur. ◆**'blasphemy** *n* blasphème *m*.

blast [blɑːst] **1** *n* explosion *f*; (*air from explosion*) souffle *m*; (*of wind*) rafale *f*, coup *m*; (*of trumpet*) sonnerie *f*; **(at) full b.** (*loud*) à plein volume; (*fast*) à pleine vitesse; **b. furnace** haut fourneau *m*; – *vt* (*blow up*) faire sauter; (*hopes*) *Fig* détruire; **to b. s.o.** *Fam* réprimander qn. **2** *int* zut!,

merde! ◆**—ed** *a Fam* fichu. ◆**blast-off** *n* (*of spacecraft*) mise *f* à feu.
blatant ['bleɪtənt] *a* (*obvious*) flagrant, criant; (*shameless*) éhonté.
blaz/e [bleɪz] **1** *n* (*fire*) flamme *f*, feu *m*; (*conflagration*) incendie *m*; (*splendour*) *Fig* éclat *m*; **b. of light** torrent *m* de lumière; – *vi* (*of fire*) flamber; (*of sun, colour, eyes*) flamboyer. **2** *vt* **to b. a trail** marquer la voie. ◆**—ing** *a* (*burning*) en feu; (*sun*) brûlant; (*argument*) *Fig* violent.
blazer ['bleɪzər] *n* blazer *m*.
bleach [bliːtʃ] *n* décolorant *m*; (*household detergent*) eau *f* de Javel; – *vt* (*hair*) décolorer, oxygéner; (*linen*) blanchir.
bleak [bliːk] *a* (**-er, -est**) (*appearance, future etc*) morne; (*countryside*) désolé.
bleary ['blɪərɪ] *a* (*eyes*) troubles, voilés.
bleat [bliːt] *vi* bêler.
bleed [bliːd] *vti* (*pt & pp* **bled**) saigner; **to b. to death** perdre tout son sang. ◆**—ing** *a* (*wound*) saignant; (*bloody*) *Sl* foutu.
bleep [bliːp] *n* signal *m*, bip *m*; – *vt* appeler au bip-bip. ◆**bleeper** *n* bip-bip *m*.
blemish ['blemɪʃ] *n* (*fault*) défaut *m*; (*on fruit, reputation*) tache *f*; – *vt* (*reputation*) ternir.
blend [blend] *n* mélange *m*; – *vt* mélanger; – *vi* se mélanger; (*go together*) se marier (**with** avec). ◆**—er** *n Culin* mixer *m*.
bless [bles] *vt* bénir; **to be blessed with** avoir le bonheur de posséder; **b. you!** (*sneezing*) à vos souhaits! ◆**—ed** [-ɪd] *a* saint, béni; (*happy*) *Rel* bienheureux; (*blasted*) *Fam* fichu, sacré. ◆**—ing** *n* bénédiction *f*; (*divine favour*) grâce *f*; (*benefit*) bienfait *m*; **what a b. that . . .** quelle chance que . . . .
blew [bluː] *see* **blow** [1].
blight [blaɪt] *n* (*on plants*) rouille *f*; (*scourge*) *Fig* fléau *m*; **to be** *or* **cast a b. on** avoir une influence néfaste sur; **urban b.** (*area*) quartier *m* délabré; (*condition*) délabrement *m* (de quartier). ◆**blighter** *n Pej Fam* type *m*.
blimey! ['blaɪmɪ] *int Fam* zut!, mince!
blimp [blɪmp] *n* dirigeable *m*.
blind [blaɪnd] **1** *a* aveugle; **b. person** aveugle *mf*; **b. in one eye** borgne; **he's b. to** (*fault*) il ne voit pas; **to turn a b. eye to** fermer les yeux sur; **b. alley** impasse *f*; – *n* **the b.** les aveugles *mpl*; – *vt* aveugler. **2** *n* (*on window*) store *m*; (*deception*) feinte *f*. ◆**—ly** *adv* aveuglément. ◆**—ness** *n* cécité *f*; *Fig* aveuglement *m*. ◆**blinders** *npl Am* œillères *fpl*. ◆**blindfold** *n* bandeau *m*; – *vt* bander les yeux à; – *adv* les yeux bandés.
blink [blɪŋk] *vi* cligner des yeux; (*of eyes*) cligner; (*of light*) clignoter; – *vt* **to b. one's eyes** cligner des yeux; – *n* clignement *m*; **on the b.** (*machine*) *Fam* détraqué. ◆**—ing** *a* (*bloody*) *Fam* sacré. ◆**blinkers** *npl* (*for horse*) œillères *fpl*; (*indicators*) *Aut* clignotants *mpl*.
bliss [blɪs] *n* félicité *f*. ◆**blissful** *a* (*happy*) très joyeux; (*wonderful*) merveilleux. ◆**blissfully** *adv* (*happy, unaware*) parfaitement.
blister ['blɪstər] *n* (*on skin*) ampoule *f*; – *vi* se couvrir d'ampoules.
blithe [blaɪð] *a* joyeux.
blitz [blɪts] *n* (*attack*) *Av* raid *m* éclair; (*bombing*) bombardement *m* aérien; *Fig Fam* offensive *f*; – *vt* bombarder.
blizzard ['blɪzəd] *n* tempête *f* de neige.
bloat [bləʊt] *vt* gonfler.
bloater ['bləʊtər] *n* hareng *m* saur.
blob [blɒb] *n* (*of water*) (grosse) goutte *f*; (*of ink, colour*) tache *f*.
bloc [blɒk] *n Pol* bloc *m*.
block [blɒk] **1** *n* (*of stone etc*) bloc *m*; (*of buildings*) pâté *m* (de maisons); (*in pipe*) obstruction *f*; (*mental*) blocage *m*; **b. of flats** immeuble *m*; **a b. away** *Am* une rue plus loin; **school b.** groupe *m* scolaire; **b. capitals** *or* **letters** majuscules *fpl*. **2** *vt* (*obstruct*) bloquer; (*pipe*) boucher, bloquer; (*one's view*) boucher; **to b. off** (*road*) barrer; (*light*) intercepter; **to b. up** (*pipe, hole*) bloquer. ◆**blo'ckade** *n* blocus *m*; – *vt* bloquer. ◆**blockage** *n* obstruction *f*. ◆**blockbuster** *n Cin* superproduction *f*, film *m* à grand spectacle. ◆**blockhead** *n* imbécile *mf*.
bloke [bləʊk] *n Fam* type *m*.
blond [blɒnd] *a & n* blond (*m*). ◆**blonde** *a & n* blonde (*f*).
blood [blʌd] *n* sang *m*; – *a* (*group, orange etc*) sanguin; (*donor, bath etc*) de sang; (*poisoning etc*) du sang; **b. pressure** tension *f* (artérielle); **high b. pressure** (hyper)tension *f*. ◆**bloodcurdling** *a* à vous tourner le sang. ◆**bloodhound** *n* (*dog, detective*) limier *m*. ◆**bloodletting** *n* saignée *f*. ◆**bloodshed** *n* effusion *f* de sang. ◆**bloodshot** *a* (*eye*) injecté de sang. ◆**bloodsucker** *n* (*insect, person*) sangsue *f*. ◆**bloodthirsty** *a* sanguinaire.
bloody ['blʌdɪ] **1** *a* (**-ier, -iest**) sanglant. **2** *a* (*blasted*) *Fam* sacré; – *adv Fam* vachement. ◆**b.-'minded** *a* hargneux, pas commode.
bloom [bluːm] *n* fleur *f*; **in b.** en fleur(s); – *vi* fleurir; (*of person*) *Fig* s'épanouir. ◆**—ing**

a **1** (*in bloom*) en fleur(s); (*thriving*) florissant. **2** (*blinking*) *Fam* fichu.

bloomer ['bluːmər] *n Fam* (*mistake*) gaffe *f*.

blossom ['blɒsəm] *n* fleur(s) *f(pl)*; – *vi* fleurir; **to b. (out)** (*of person*) s'épanouir; **to b. (out) into** devenir.

blot [blɒt] *n* tache *f*; – *vt* (**-tt-**) tacher; (*dry*) sécher; **to b. out** (*word*) rayer; (*memory*) effacer. ◆**blotting** *a* **b. paper** (papier *m*) buvard *m*. ◆**blotter** *n* buvard *m*.

blotch [blɒtʃ] *n* tache *f*. ◆**blotchy** *a* (**-ier, -iest**) couvert de taches; (*face*) marbré.

blouse [blaʊz, *Am* blaʊs] *n* chemisier *m*.

blow[1] [bləʊ] *vt* (*pt* **blew**, *pp* **blown**) (*of wind*) pousser (*un navire etc*), chasser (*la pluie etc*); (*smoke, glass*) souffler; (*bubbles*) faire; (*trumpet*) souffler dans; (*fuse*) faire sauter; (*kiss*) envoyer (**to** à); (*money*) *Fam* claquer; **to b. one's nose** se moucher; **to b. a whistle** siffler; **to b. away** (*of wind*) emporter; **to b. down** (*chimney etc*) faire tomber; **to b. off** (*hat etc*) emporter; (*arm*) arracher; **to b. out** (*candle*) souffler; (*cheeks*) gonfler; **to b. up** (*building etc*) faire sauter; (*tyre*) gonfler; (*photo*) agrandir; – *vi* (*of wind, person*) souffler; (*of fuse*) sauter; (*of papers etc*) s'éparpiller; **b.!** *Fam* zut!; **to b. down** (*fall*) tomber; **to b. off** *or* **away** s'envoler; **to b. out** (*of light*) s'éteindre; **to b. over** (*pass*) passer; **to b. up** (*explode*) exploser. ◆**—er** *n* (*telephone*) *Fam* bigophone *m*. ◆**blow-dry** *n* brushing *m*. ◆**blowlamp** *n* chalumeau *m*. ◆**blowout** *n* (*of tyre*) éclatement *m*; (*meal*) *Sl* gueuleton *m*. ◆**blowtorch** *n Am* chalumeau *m*. ◆**blow-up** *n Phot* agrandissement *m*.

blow[2] [bləʊ] *n* coup *m*; **to come to blows** en venir aux mains.

blowy ['bləʊɪ] *a* **it's b.** *Fam* il y a du vent.

blowzy ['blaʊzɪ] *a* **b. woman** (*slovenly*) *Fam* femme *f* débraillée.

blubber ['blʌbər] *n* graisse *f* (de baleine).

bludgeon ['blʌdʒən] *n* gourdin *m*; – *vt* matraquer.

blue [bluː] *a* (**bluer, bluest**) bleu; **to feel b.** *Fam* avoir le cafard; **b. film** *Fam* film *m* porno; – *n* bleu *m*; **the blues** (*depression*) *Fam* le cafard; *Mus* le blues. ◆**bluebell** *n* jacinthe *f* des bois. ◆**blueberry** *n* airelle *f*. ◆**bluebottle** *n* mouche *f* à viande. ◆**blueprint** *n Fig* plan *m* (de travail).

bluff [blʌf] **1** *a* (*person*) brusque, direct. **2** *vti* bluffer; – *n* bluff *m*.

blunder ['blʌndər] **1** *n* (*mistake*) bévue *f*, gaffe *f*; – *vi* faire une bévue. **2** *vi* (*move awkwardly*) avancer à tâtons. ◆**—ing** *a* maladroit; – *n* maladresse *f*.

blunt [blʌnt] *a* (**-er, -est**) (*edge*) émoussé; (*pencil*) épointé; (*person*) brusque; (*speech*) franc; – *vt* émousser; épointer. ◆**—ly** *adv* carrément. ◆**—ness** *n Fig* brusquerie *f*; (*of speech*) franchise *f*.

blur [blɜːr] *n* tache *f* floue, contour *m* imprécis; – *vt* (**-rr-**) estomper, rendre flou; (*judgment*) *Fig* troubler. ◆**blurred** *a* (*image*) flou, estompé.

blurb [blɜːb] *n Fam* résumé *m* publicitaire, laïus *m*.

blurt [blɜːt] *vt* **to b. (out)** laisser échapper, lâcher.

blush [blʌʃ] *vi* rougir (**at, with** de); – *n* rougeur *f*; **with a b.** en rougissant.

bluster ['blʌstər] *vi* (*of person*) tempêter; (*of wind*) faire rage. ◆**blustery** *a* (*weather*) de grand vent, à bourrasques.

boa ['bəʊə] *n* (*snake*) boa *m*.

boar [bɔːr] *n* (**wild**) **b.** sanglier *m*.

board[1] [bɔːd] **1** *n* (*piece of wood*) planche *f*; (*for notices, games etc*) tableau *m*; (*cardboard*) carton *m*; (*committee*) conseil *m*, commission *f*; **b. (of directors)** conseil *m* d'administration; **on b.** *Nau Av* à bord (de); **B. of Trade** *Br Pol* ministère *m* du Commerce; **across the b.** (*pay rise*) général; **to go by the b.** (*of plan*) être abandonné. **2** *vt Nau Av* monter à bord de; (*bus, train*) monter dans; **to b. up** (*door*) boucher. ◆**—ing** *n Nau Av* embarquement *m*. ◆**boardwalk** *n Am* promenade *f*.

board[2] [bɔːd] *n* (*food*) pension *f*; **b. and lodging, bed and b.** (chambre *f* avec) pension *f*; – *vi* (*lodge*) être en pension (**with** chez); **boarding house** pension *f* (de famille); **boarding school** pensionnat *m*. ◆**—er** *n* pensionnaire *mf*.

boast [bəʊst] *vi* se vanter (**about, of** de); – *vt* se glorifier de; **to b. that one can do . . .** se vanter de (pouvoir) faire . . . ; – *n* vantardise *f*. ◆**—ing** *n* vantardise *f*. ◆**boastful** *a* vantard. ◆**boastfully** *adv* en se vantant.

boat [bəʊt] *n* bateau *m*; (*small*) barque *f*, canot *m*; (*liner*) paquebot *m*; **in the same b.** *Fig* logé à la même enseigne; **b. race** course *f* d'aviron. ◆**—ing** *n* canotage *m*; **b. trip** excursion *f* en bateau.

boatswain ['bəʊs(ə)n] *n* maître *m* d'équipage.

bob [bɒb] *vi* (**-bb-**) **to b. (up and down)** (*on water*) danser sur l'eau.

bobbin ['bɒbɪn] *n* bobine *f*.

bobby ['bɒbɪ] *n* **1** (*policeman*) *Fam* flic *m*, agent *m*. **2** **b. pin** *Am* pince *f* à cheveux.

bode [bəʊd] *vi* **to b. well/ill** être de bon/mauvais augure.

bodice ['bɒdɪs] *n* corsage *m*.

body ['bɒdɪ] *n* corps *m*; (*of vehicle*) carrosserie *f*; (*quantity*) masse *f*; (*institution*) organisme *m*; **the main b. of** le gros de; **b. building** culturisme *m*. ◆**bodily** *a* physique; (*need*) matériel; – *adv* physiquement; (*as a whole*) tout entier. ◆**bodyguard** *n* garde *m* du corps, gorille *m*. ◆**bodywork** *n* carrosserie *f*.

boffin ['bɒfɪn] *n* *Fam* chercheur, -euse *mf* scientifique.

bog [bɒg] *n* marécage *m*; – *vt* **to get bogged down** s'enliser. ◆**boggy** *a* (-ier, -iest) marécageux.

bogey ['bəʊgɪ] *n* spectre *m*; **b. man** croque-mitaine *m*.

boggle ['bɒg(ə)l] *vi* **the mind boggles** cela confond l'imagination.

bogus ['bəʊgəs] *a* faux.

bohemian [bəʊ'hiːmɪən] *a* & *n* (*artist etc*) bohème (*mf*).

boil [bɔɪl] **1** *n* *Med* furoncle *m*, clou *m*. **2** *vi* bouillir; **to b. away** (*until dry*) s'évaporer; (*on and on*) bouillir sans arrêt; **to b. down to** *Fig* se ramener à; **to b. over** (*of milk, emotions etc*) déborder; – *vt* **to b. (up)** faire bouillir; – *n* **to be on the b., come to the b.** bouillir; **to bring to the b.** amener à ébullition. ◆**—ed** *a* (*beef*) bouilli; (*potato*) (cuit) à l'eau; **b. egg** œuf *m* à la coque. ◆**—ing** *n* ébullition *f*; **at b. point** à ébullition; – *a* & *adv* **b. (hot)** bouillant; **it's b. (hot)** (*weather*) il fait une chaleur infernale. ◆**—er** *n* chaudière *f*; **b. suit** bleu *m* (de travail).

boisterous ['bɔɪstərəs] *a* (*noisy*) tapageur; (*child*) turbulent; (*meeting*) houleux.

bold [bəʊld] *a* (-er, -est) hardi; **b. type** caractères *mpl* gras. ◆**—ness** *n* hardiesse *f*.

Bolivia [bə'lɪvɪə] *n* Bolivie *f*. ◆**Bolivian** *a* & *n* bolivien, -ienne (*mf*).

bollard ['bɒləd, 'bɒlɑːd] *n* *Aut* borne *f*.

boloney [bə'ləʊnɪ] *n* *Sl* foutaises *fpl*.

bolster ['bəʊlstər] **1** *n* (*pillow*) traversin *m*, polochon *m*. **2** *vt* **to b. (up)** (*support*) soutenir.

bolt [bəʊlt] **1** *n* (*on door etc*) verrou *m*; (*for nut*) boulon *m*; – *vt* (*door*) verrouiller. **2** *n* (*dash*) fuite *f*, ruée *f*; – *vi* (*dash*) se précipiter; (*flee*) détaler; (*of horse*) s'emballer. **3** *n* **b. (of lightning)** éclair *m*. **4** *vt* (*food*) engloutir. **5** *adv* **b. upright** tout droit.

bomb [bɒm] *n* bombe *f*; **letter b.** lettre *f* piégée; **b. disposal** désamorçage *m*; – *vt* bombarder. ◆**—ing** *n* bombardement *m*. ◆**—er** *n* (*aircraft*) bombardier *m*; (*terrorist*) plastiqueur *m*. ◆**bombshell** *n* **to come as a b.** tomber comme une bombe. ◆**bombsite** *n* terrain *m* vague, lieu *m* bombardé.

bombard [bɒm'bɑːd] *vt* bombarder (**with** de). ◆**—ment** *n* bombardement *m*.

bona fide [bəʊnə'faɪdɪ, *Am* -'faɪd] *a* sérieux, de bonne foi.

bonanza [bə'nænzə] *n* *Fig* mine *f* d'or.

bond [bɒnd] **1** *n* (*agreement, promise*) engagement *m*; (*link*) lien *m*; *Com* bon *m*, obligation *f*; (*adhesion*) adhérence *f*. **2** *vt* (*goods*) entreposer.

bondage ['bɒndɪdʒ] *n* esclavage *m*.

bone [bəʊn] **1** *n* os *m*; (*of fish*) arête *f*; **b. of contention** pomme *f* de discorde; **b. china** porcelaine *f* tendre; – *vt* (*meat etc*) désosser. **2** *vi* **to b. up on** (*subject*) *Am Fam* bûcher. ◆**bony** *a* (-ier, -iest) (*thin*) osseux, maigre; (*fish*) plein d'arêtes.

bone-dry [bəʊn'draɪ] *a* tout à fait sec. ◆**b.-idle** *a* paresseux comme une couleuvre.

bonfire ['bɒnfaɪər] *n* (*for celebration*) feu *m* de joie; (*for dead leaves*) feu *m* (de jardin).

bonkers ['bɒŋkəz] *a* (*crazy*) *Fam* dingue.

bonnet ['bɒnɪt] *n* (*hat*) bonnet *m*; *Aut* capot *m*.

bonus ['bəʊnəs] *n* prime *f*; **no claims b.** *Aut* bonus *m*.

boo [buː] **1** *int* bou! **2** *vti* huer; – *npl* huées *fpl*.

boob [buːb] *n* (*mistake*) gaffe *f*; – *vi* *Sl* gaffer.

booby-trap ['buːbɪtræp] *n* engin *m* piégé; – *vt* (-pp-) piéger.

book [bʊk] **1** *n* livre *m*; (*of tickets*) carnet *m*; (*record*) registre *m*; *pl* (*accounts*) comptes *mpl*; **(excercise) b.** cahier *m*. **2** *vt* **to b. (up)** (*seat etc*) réserver, retenir; **to b. s.o.** *Jur* donner un procès-verbal à qn; **to b. (down)** inscrire; **(fully) booked (up)** (*hotel, concert*) complet; (*person*) pris; – *vi* **to b. (up)** réserver des places; **to b. in** (*in hotel*) signer le registre. ◆**—ing** *n* réservation *f*; **b. clerk** guichetier, -ière *mf*; **b. office** bureau *m* de location, guichet *m*. ◆**—able** *a* (*seat*) qu'on peut réserver. ◆**bookish** *a* (*word, theory*) livresque; (*person*) studieux.

bookbinding ['bʊkbaɪndɪŋ] *n* reliure *f*. ◆**bookcase** *n* bibliothèque *f*. ◆**bookend** *n* serre-livres *m inv*. ◆**bookkeeper** *n* comptable *mf*. ◆**bookkeeping** *n* comptabilité *f*. ◆**booklet** *n* brochure *f*. ◆**book-lover** *n* bibliophile *mf*. ◆**bookmaker** *n* bookmaker *m*. ◆**bookmark** *n* marque *f.* ◆**bookseller** *n* libraire *mf.* ◆**bookshelf** *n* rayon *m.* ◆**bookshop** *n*, *Am* ◆**bookstore** *n* librairie *f.* ◆**bookstall** *n* kiosque *m* (à journaux). ◆**bookworm** *n* rat *m* de bibliothèque.

boom [buːm] **1** *vi* (*of thunder, gun etc*) gronder; – *n* grondement *m*; **sonic b.** bang *m.* **2** *n Econ* expansion *f*, essor *m*, boom *m.*

boomerang ['buːməræŋ] *n* boomerang *m.*

boon [buːn] *n* aubaine *f*, avantage *m.*

boor [bʊər] *n* rustre *m.* ◆**boorish** *a* rustre.

boost [buːst] *vt* (*push*) donner une poussée à; (*increase*) augmenter; (*product*) faire de la réclame pour; (*economy*) stimuler; (*morale*) remonter; – *n* **to give a b. to** = **to boost.** ◆**—er** *n* **b. (injection)** piqûre *f* de rappel.

boot [buːt] **1** *n* (*shoe*) botte *f*; **(ankle) b.** bottillon *m*; **(knee) b.** bottine *f*; **to get the b.** *Fam* être mis à la porte; **b. polish** cirage *m*; – *vt* (*kick*) donner un coup *or* des coups de pied à; **to b. out** mettre à la porte. **2** *n Aut* coffre *m.* **3** *n* **to b.** en plus. ◆**bootblack** *n* cireur *m.* ◆**boo'tee** *n* (*of baby*) chausson *m.*

booth [buːð, buːθ] *n Tel* cabine *f*; (*at fair*) baraque *f.*

booty ['buːtɪ] *n* (*stolen goods*) butin *m.*

booz/e [buːz] *n Fam* alcool *m*, boisson(s) *f(pl)*; (*drinking bout*) beuverie *f*; – *vi Fam* boire (beaucoup). ◆**—er** *n Fam* (*person*) buveur, -euse *mf*; (*place*) bistrot *m.*

border ['bɔːdər] *n* (*of country*) & *Fig* frontière *f*; (*edge*) bord *m*; (*of garden etc*) bordure *f*; – *a* (*town*) frontière *inv*; (*incident*) de frontière; – *vt* (*street*) border; **to b. (on)** (*country*) toucher à; **to b. (up)on** (*resemble*) être voisin de. ◆**borderland** *n* pays *m* frontière. ◆**borderline** *n* frontière *f*; **b. case** cas *m* limite.

bor/e[1] [bɔːr] **1** *vt* (*weary*) ennuyer; **to be bored** s'ennuyer; – *n* (*person*) raseur, -euse *mf*; (*thing*) ennui *m.* **2** *vt Tech* forer, creuser; (*hole*) percer; – *vi* forer. **3** *n* (*of gun*) calibre *m.* ◆**—ing** *a* ennuyeux. ◆**boredom** *n* ennui *m.*

bore[2] [bɔːr] *see* **bear**[2].

born [bɔːn] *a* né; **to be b.** naître; **he was b.** il est né.

borne [bɔːn] *see* **bear**[2].

borough ['bʌrə] *n* (*town*) municipalité *f*; (*part of town*) arrondissement *m.*

borrow ['bɒrəʊ] *vt* emprunter (**from** à). ◆**—ing** *n* emprunt *m.*

Borstal ['bɔːst(ə)l] *n* maison *f* d'éducation surveillée.

bosom ['bʊzəm] *n* (*chest*) & *Fig* sein *m*; **b. friend** ami, -ie *mf* intime.

boss [bɒs] *n Fam* patron, -onne *mf*, chef *m*; – *vt Fam* diriger; **to b. s.o. around** *or* **about** régenter qn. ◆**bossy** *a* (**-ier, -iest**) *Fam* autoritaire.

boss-eyed ['bɒsaɪd] *a* **to be b.-eyed** loucher.

bosun ['bəʊs(ə)n] *n* maître *m* d'équipage.

botany ['bɒtənɪ] *n* botanique *f.* ◆**bo'tanical** *a* botanique. ◆**botanist** *n* botaniste *mf.*

botch [bɒtʃ] *vt* **to b. (up)** (*spoil*) bâcler; (*repair*) rafistoler.

both [bəʊθ] *a* les deux, l'un(e) et l'autre; – *pron* tous *or* toutes (les) deux, l'un(e) et l'autre; **b. of us** nous deux; – *adv* (*at the same time*) à la fois; **b. you and I** vous et moi.

bother ['bɒðər] *vt* (*annoy, worry*) ennuyer; (*disturb*) déranger; (*pester*) importuner; **I can't be bothered!** je n'en ai pas envie!, ça m'embête!; – *vi* **to b. about** (*worry about*) se préoccuper de; (*deal with*) s'occuper de; **to b. doing** *or* **to do** se donner la peine de faire; – *n* (*trouble*) ennui *m*; (*effort*) peine *f*; (*inconvenience*) dérangement *m*; **(oh) b.!** zut alors!

bottle ['bɒt(ə)l] *n* bouteille *f*; (*small*) flacon *m*; (*wide-mouthed*) bocal *m*; (*for baby*) biberon *m*; **(hot-water) b.** bouillotte *f*; **b. opener** ouvre-bouteilles *m inv*; – *vt* mettre en bouteille; **to b. up** (*feeling*) contenir. ◆**b.-feed** *vt* (*pt* & *pp* **-fed**) nourrir au biberon. ◆**bottleneck** *n* (*in road*) goulot *m* d'étranglement; (*traffic holdup*) bouchon *m.*

bottom ['bɒtəm] *n* (*of sea, box, etc*) fond *m*; (*of page, hill etc*) bas *m*; (*buttocks*) *Fam* derrière *m*; (*of table*) bout *m*; **to be (at the) b. of the class** être le dernier de la classe; – *a* (*part, shelf*) inférieur, du bas; **b. floor** rez-de-chaussée *m*; **b. gear** première vitesse *f.* ◆**—less** *a* insondable.

bough [baʊ] *n Lit* rameau *m.*

bought [bɔːt] *see* **buy.**

boulder ['bəʊldər] *n* rocher *m.*

boulevard ['buːləvɑːd] *n* boulevard *m.*

bounc/e [baʊns] **1** *vi* (*of ball*) rebondir; (*of person*) faire des bonds; **to b. into** bondir dans; – *vt* faire rebondir; – *n* (re)bond *m.* **2** *vi* (*of cheque*) *Fam* être sans provision, être en bois. ◆**—ing** *a* (*baby*) robuste. ◆**—er** *n* (*at club etc*) *Fam* videur *m.*

bound[1] [baʊnd] **1** *a* **b. to do** (*obliged*) obligé de faire; (*certain*) sûr de faire; **it's b. to happen** ça arrivera sûrement; **to be b. for**

être en route pour. **2** *n* (*leap*) bond *m*; – *vi* bondir.

bound[2] [baʊnd] *see* **bind 1;** – *a* **b. up with** (*connected*) lié à.

bounds [baʊndz] *npl* limites *fpl*; **out of b.** (*place*) interdit. ◆**boundary** *n* limite *f*. ◆**bounded** *a* **b. by** limité par. ◆**boundless** *a* sans bornes.

bountiful ['baʊntɪfʊl] *a* généreux.

bounty ['baʊntɪ] *n* (*reward*) prime *f*.

bouquet [bəʊ'keɪ] *n* (*of flowers, wine*) bouquet *m*.

bourbon ['bɜːbən] *n* (*whisky*) *Am* bourbon *m*.

bout [baʊt] *n* période *f*; *Med* accès *m*, crise *f*; *Boxing* combat *m*; (*session*) séance *f*.

boutique [buː'tiːk] *n* boutique *f* (de mode).

bow[1] [bəʊ] *n* (*weapon*) arc *m*; *Mus* archet *m*; (*knot*) nœud *m*; **b. tie** nœud *m* papillon. ◆**b.-'legged** *a* aux jambes arquées.

bow[2] [baʊ] **1** *n* révérence *f*; (*nod*) salut *m*; – *vt* courber, incliner; – *vi* s'incliner (**to** devant); (*nod*) incliner la tête; **to b. down** (*submit*) s'incliner. **2** *n Nau* proue *f*.

bowels ['baʊəlz] *npl* intestins *mpl*; (*of earth*) *Fig* entrailles *fpl*.

bowl [bəʊl] **1** *n* (*for food*) bol *m*; (*basin*) & *Geog* cuvette *f*; (*for sugar*) sucrier *m*; (*for salad*) saladier *m*; (*for fruit*) corbeille *f*, coupe *f*. **2** *npl Sp* boules *fpl*. **3** *vi Cricket* lancer la balle; **to b. along** *Aut* rouler vite; – *vt* (*ball*) *Cricket* servir; **to b. s.o. over** (*knock down*) renverser qn; (*astound*) bouleverser qn. ◆**—ing** *n* (**tenpin**) **b.** bowling *m*; **b. alley** bowling *m*. ◆**—er**[1] *n Cricket* lanceur, -euse *mf*.

bowler[2] ['bəʊlər] *n* **b. (hat)** (chapeau *m*) melon *m*.

box [bɒks] **1** *n* boîte *f*; (*large*) caisse *f*; (*of cardboard*) carton *m*; *Th* loge *f*; *Jur* barre *f*, banc *m*; (*for horse*) box *m*; *TV Fam* télé *f*; **b. office** bureau *m* de location, guichet *m*; **b. room** (*lumber room*) débarras *m*; (*bedroom*) petite chambre *f* (carrée); – *vt* **to b. (up)** mettre en boîte; **to b. in** (*enclose*) enfermer. **2** *vti Boxing* boxer; **to b. s.o.'s ears** gifler qn. ◆**—ing** *n* **1** boxe *f*; **b. ring** ring *m*. **2 B. Day** le lendemain de Noël. ◆**—er** *n* boxeur *m*. ◆**boxcar** *n Rail Am* wagon *m* couvert. ◆**boxwood** *n* buis *m*.

boy [bɔɪ] *n* garçon *m*; **English b.** jeune Anglais *m*; **old b.** *Sch* ancien élève *m*; **yes, old b.!** oui, mon vieux!; **the boys** (*pals*) *Fam* les copains *mpl*; **my dear b.** mon cher ami; **oh b.!** *Am* mon Dieu! ◆**boyfriend** *n* petit ami *m*. ◆**boyhood** *n* enfance *f*. ◆**boyish** *a* de garçon; *Pej* puéril.

boycott ['bɔɪkɒt] *vt* boycotter; – *n* boycottage *m*.

bra [brɑː] *n* soutien-gorge *m*.

brac/e [breɪs] *n* (*for fastening*) attache *f*; (*dental*) appareil *m*; *pl* (*trouser straps*) bretelles *fpl*; – *vt* (*fix*) attacher; (*press*) appuyer; **to b. oneself for** (*news, shock*) se préparer à. ◆**—ing** *a* (*air etc*) fortifiant.

bracelet ['breɪslɪt] *n* bracelet *m*.

bracken ['brækən] *n* fougère *f*.

bracket ['brækɪt] *n Tech* support *m*, tasseau *m*; (*round sign*) *Typ* parenthèse *f*; (*square*) *Typ* crochet *m*; *Fig* groupe *m*, tranche *f*; – *vt* mettre entre parenthèses *or* crochets; **to b. together** *Fig* mettre dans le même groupe.

bradawl ['brædɔːl] *n* poinçon *m*.

brag [bræg] *vi* (**-gg-**) se vanter (**about, of** de). ◆**—ging** *n* vantardise *f*. ◆**braggart** *n* vantard, -arde *mf*.

braid [breɪd] *vt* (*hair*) tresser; (*trim*) galonner; – *n* tresse *f*; galon *m*.

Braille [breɪl] *n* braille *m*.

brain [breɪn] *n* cerveau *m*; (*of bird etc*) & *Pej* cervelle *f*; – *a* (*operation, death*) cérébral; – *vt Fam* assommer; **to have brains** (*sense*) avoir de l'intelligence; **b. drain** fuite *f* des cerveaux. ◆**brainchild** *n* invention *f* personnelle. ◆**brainstorm** *n Psy Fig* aberration *f*; *Am* idée *f* géniale. ◆**brainwash** *vt* faire un lavage de cerveau à. ◆**brainwave** *n* idée *f* géniale.

brainy ['breɪnɪ] *a* (**-ier, -iest**) *Fam* intelligent.

braise [breɪz] *vt Culin* braiser.

brak/e [breɪk] *vi* freiner; – *n* frein *m*; **b. light** *Aut* stop *m*. ◆**—ing** *n* freinage *m*.

bramble ['bræmb(ə)l] *n* ronce *f*.

bran [bræn] *n Bot* son *m*.

branch [brɑːntʃ] *n* branche *f*; (*of road*) embranchement *m*; (*of store etc*) succursale *f*; **b. office** succursale *f*; – *vi* **to b. off** (*of road*) bifurquer; **to b. out** (*of family, tree*) se ramifier; *Fig* étendre ses activités.

brand [brænd] *n* (*trademark, stigma & on cattle*) marque *f*; – *vt* (*mark*) marquer; (*stigmatize*) flétrir; **to be branded as** avoir la réputation de.

brandish ['brændɪʃ] *vt* brandir.

brand-new [brænd'njuː] *a* tout neuf, flambant neuf.

brandy ['brændɪ] *n* cognac *m*; (*made with pears etc*) eau-de-vie *f*.

brash [bræʃ] *a* effronté, fougueux.

brass [brɑːs] *n* cuivre *m*; (*instruments*) *Mus* cuivres *mpl*; **the top b.** (*officers, executives*) *Fam* les huiles *fpl*; **b. band** fanfare *f*.

brassiere ['bræzıər, *Am* brə'zıər] *n* soutien-gorge *m*.
brat [bræt] *n Pej* môme *mf*, gosse *mf*; (*badly behaved*) galopin *m*.
bravado [brə'vɑːdəʊ] *n* bravade *f*.
brave [breıv] *a* (**-er, -est**) courageux, brave; – *n* (*Red Indian*) guerrier *m* (indien), brave *m*; – *vt* braver. ◆**bravery** *n* courage *m*.
bravo! ['brɑːvəʊ] *int* bravo!
brawl [brɔːl] *n* (*fight*) bagarre *f*; – *vi* se bagarrer. ◆**—ing** *a* bagarreur.
brawn [brɔːn] *n* muscles *mpl*. ◆**brawny** *a* (**-ier, -iest**) musclé.
bray [breı] *vi* (*of ass*) braire.
brazen ['breız(ə)n] *a* (*shameless*) effronté; – *vt* **to b. it out** payer d'audace, faire front.
Brazil [brə'zıl] *n* Brésil *m*. ◆**Brazilian** *a* & *n* brésilien, -ienne (*mf*).
breach [briːtʃ] **1** *n* violation *f*, infraction *f*; (*of contract*) rupture *f*; (*of trust*) abus *m*; – *vt* (*law, code*) violer. **2** *n* (*gap*) brèche *f*; – *vt* (*wall etc*) ouvrir une brèche dans.
bread [bred] *n inv* pain *m*; (*money*) *Sl* blé *m*, fric *m*; **loaf of b.** pain *m*; **(slice *or* piece of) b. and butter** tartine *f*; **b. and butter** (*job*) *Fig* gagne-pain *m*. ◆**breadbin** *n*, *Am* ◆**breadbox** *n* coffre *m* à pain. ◆**breadboard** *n* planche *f* à pain. ◆**breadcrumb** *n* miette *f* (de pain); *pl Culin* chapelure *f*. ◆**breadline** *n* **on the b.** indigent. ◆**breadwinner** *n* soutien *m* de famille.
breadth [bretθ] *n* largeur *f*.
break [breık] *vt* (*pt* **broke**, *pp* **broken**) casser; (*into pieces*) briser; (*silence, vow etc*) rompre; (*strike, heart, ice etc*) briser; (*record*) *Sp* battre; (*law*) violer; (*one's word*) manquer à; (*journey*) interrompre; (*sound barrier*) franchir; (*a fall*) amortir; (*news*) révéler (**to** à); **to b. (oneself of)** (*habit*) se débarrasser de; **to b. open** (*safe*) percer; **to b. new ground** innover; – *vi* (se) casser; se briser; se rompre; (*of voice*) s'altérer; (*of boy's voice*) muer; (*of weather*) se gâter; (*of news*) éclater; (*of day*) se lever; (*of wave*) déferler; **to b. free** se libérer; **to b. loose** s'échapper; **to b. with s.o.** rompre avec qn; – *n* cassure *f*; (*in relationship, continuity etc*) rupture *f*; (*in journey*) interruption *f*; (*rest*) repos *m*; (*for tea*) pause *f*; *Sch* récréation *f*; (*change*) *Met* changement *m*; **a lucky b.** *Fam* une chance. ◆**—ing** *a* **b. point** *Tech* point *m* de rupture; **at b. point** (*patience*) à bout; (*person*) sur le point de craquer, à bout. ◆**—able** *a* cassable. ◆**—age** *n* casse *f*; *pl* (*things broken*) la casse. ◆**—er** *n* (*wave*) brisant *m*; (*dealer*) *Aut* casseur *m*. ■ **to b. away** *vi* se détacher; – *vt* détacher. ◆**breakaway** *a* (*group*) dissident; **to b. down** *vt* (*door*) enfoncer; (*resistance*) briser; (*analyse*) analyser; – *vi Aut Tech* tomber en panne; (*of negotiations etc*) échouer; (*collapse*) s'effondrer. ◆**breakdown** *n* panne *f*; analyse *f*; (*in talks*) rupture *f*; (*nervous*) dépression *f*; – *a* (*service*) *Aut* de dépannage; **b. lorry** dépanneuse *f*; **to b. in** *vi* interrompre; (*of burglar*) entrer par effraction; – *vt* (*door*) enfoncer; (*horse*) dresser; (*vehicle*) *Am* roder. ◆**break-in** *n* cambriolage *m*; **to b. into** *vt* (*safe*) forcer; (*start*) entamer; **to b. off** *vt* détacher; (*relations*) rompre; – *vi* se détacher; (*stop*) s'arrêter; **to b. off with** rompre avec; **to b. out** *vi* éclater; (*escape*) s'échapper; **to b. out in** (*pimples*) avoir une poussée de; **to b. through** *vi* (*of sun*) & *Mil* percer; – *vt* (*defences*) percer. ◆**breakthrough** *n Fig* percée *f*, découverte *f*; **to b. up** *vt* mettre en morceaux; (*marriage*) briser; (*fight*) mettre fin à; – *vi* (*end*) prendre fin; (*of group*) se disperser; (*of marriage*) se briser; *Sch* partir en vacances. ◆**breakup** *n* fin *f*; (*in friendship, marriage*) rupture *f*.
breakfast ['brekfəst] *n* petit déjeuner *m*.
breakwater ['breıkwɔːtər] *n* brise-lames *m inv*.
breast [brest] *n* sein *m*; (*chest*) poitrine *f*. ◆**b.-feed** *vt* (*pt* & *pp* **-fed**) allaiter. ◆**breaststroke** *n* (*swimming*) brasse *f*.
breath [breθ] *n* haleine *f*, souffle *m*; (*of air*) souffle *m*; **under one's b.** tout bas; **one's last b.** son dernier soupir; **out of b.** à bout de souffle; **to get a b. of air** prendre l'air; **to take a deep b.** respirer profondément. ◆**breathalyser**® *n* alcootest® *m*. ◆**breathless** *a* haletant. ◆**breathtaking** *a* sensationnel.
breath/e [briːð] *vti* respirer; **to b. in** aspirer; **to b. out** expirer; **to b. air into sth** souffler dans qch; – *vt* (*a sigh*) pousser; (*a word*) dire. ◆**—ing** *n* respiration *f*; **b. space** moment *m* de repos. ◆**—er** *n Fam* moment *m* de repos; **to go for a b.** sortir prendre l'air.
bred [bred] *see* **breed 1**; – *a* **well-b.** bien élevé.
breeches ['brıtʃız] *npl* culotte *f*.
breed [briːd] **1** *vt* (*pt* & *pp* **bred**) (*animals*) élever; (*cause*) *Fig* engendrer; – *vi* (*of animals*) se reproduire. **2** *n* race *f*, espèce *f*. ◆**—ing** *n* élevage *m*; reproduction *f*; *Fig* éducation *f*. ◆**—er** *n* éleveur, -euse *mf*.
breeze [briːz] *n* brise *f*. ◆**breezy** *a* (**-ier,**

-iest) 1 (*weather, day*) frais, venteux. 2 (*cheerful*) jovial; (*relaxed*) décontracté.

breezeblock ['bri:zblɒk] *n* parpaing *m*, briquette *f*.

brevity ['brevɪtɪ] *n* brièveté *f*.

brew [bru:] *vt* (*beer*) brasser; (*trouble, plot*) préparer; **to b. tea** préparer du thé; (*infuse*) (faire) infuser du thé; – *vi* (*of beer*) fermenter; (*of tea*) infuser; (*of storm, trouble*) se préparer; – *n* (*drink*) breuvage *m*; (*of tea*) infusion *f*. ◆**—er** *n* brasseur *m*. ◆**brewery** *n* brasserie *f*.

bribe [braɪb] *n* pot-de-vin *m*; – *vt* soudoyer, corrompre. ◆**bribery** *n* corruption *f*.

brick [brɪk] *n* brique *f*; (*child's*) cube *m*; **to drop a b.** *Fam* faire une gaffe; – *vt* **to b. up** (*gap, door*) murer. ◆**bricklayer** *n* maçon *m*. ◆**brickwork** *n* ouvrage *m* en briques; (*bricks*) briques *fpl*.

bridal ['braɪd(ə)l] *a* (*ceremony*) nuptial; **b. gown** robe *f* de mariée.

bride [braɪd] *n* mariée *f*; **the b. and groom** les mariés *mpl*. ◆**bridegroom** *n* marié *m*. ◆**bridesmaid** *n* demoiselle *f* d'honneur.

bridge [brɪdʒ] 1 *n* pont *m*; (*on ship*) passerelle *f*; (*of nose*) arête *f*; (*false tooth*) bridge *m*; – *vt* **to b. a gap** combler une lacune. 2 *n Cards* bridge *m*.

bridle ['braɪd(ə)l] *n* (*for horse*) bride *f*; – *vt* (*horse, instinct etc*) brider; **b. path** allée *f* cavalière.

brief [bri:f] 1 *a* (**-er, -est**) bref; **in b.** en résumé. 2 *n Jur* dossier *m*; (*instructions*) *Mil Pol* instructions *fpl*; *Fig* tâche *f*, fonctions *fpl*; – *vt* donner des instructions à; (*inform*) mettre au courant (**on** de). 3 *npl* (*underpants*) slip *m*. ◆**—ing** *n Mil Pol* instructions *fpl*; *Av* briefing *m*. ◆**—ly** *adv* (*quickly*) en vitesse; (*to say*) brièvement.

brigade [brɪ'geɪd] *n* brigade *f*. ◆**briga'dier** *n* général *m* de brigade.

bright [braɪt] *a* (**-er, -est**) brillant, vif; (*weather, room*) clair; (*clever*) intelligent; (*happy*) joyeux; (*future*) brillant, prometteur; (*idea*) génial; **b. interval** *Met* éclaircie *f*; – *adv* **b. and early** (*to get up*) de bonne heure. ◆**—ly** *adv* brillamment. ◆**—ness** *n* éclat *m*; (*of person*) intelligence *f*. ◆**brighten** *vt* **to b. (up)** (*person, room*) égayer; – *vi* **to b. (up)** (*of weather*) s'éclaircir; (*of face*) s'éclairer.

brilliant ['brɪljənt] *a* (*light*) éclatant; (*very clever*) brillant. ◆**brilliance** *n* éclat *m*; (*of person*) grande intelligence *f*.

brim [brɪm] *n* bord *m*; – *vi* (**-mm-**) **to b. over** déborder (**with** de).

brine [braɪn] *n Culin* saumure *f*.

bring [brɪŋ] *vt* (*pt & pp* **brought**) (*person, vehicle etc*) amener; (*thing*) apporter; (*to cause*) amener; (*action*) *Jur* intenter; **to b. along** *or* **over** *or* **round** amener; apporter; **to b. back** ramener; rapporter; (*memories*) rappeler; **to b. sth up/down** monter/descendre qch; **to b. sth in/out** rentrer/sortir qch; **to b. sth to** (*perfection, a peak etc*) porter qch à; **to b. to an end** mettre fin à; **to b. to mind** rappeler; **to b. sth on oneself** s'attirer qch; **to b. oneself to do** se résoudre à faire; **to b. about** provoquer, amener; **to b. down** (*overthrow*) faire tomber; (*reduce*) réduire; (*shoot down*) abattre; **to b. forward** (*in time or space*) avancer; (*witness*) produire; **to b. in** (*person*) faire entrer *or* venir; (*introduce*) introduire; (*income*) *Com* rapporter; **to b. off** (*task*) mener à bien; **to b. out** (*person*) faire sortir; (*meaning*) faire ressortir; (*book*) publier; (*product*) lancer; **to b. over to** (*convert to*) convertir à; **to b. round** *Med* ranimer; (*convert*) convertir (to à); **to b. s.o. to** *Med* ranimer qn; **to b. together** mettre en contact; (*reconcile*) réconcilier; **to b. up** (*child etc*) élever; (*question*) soulever; (*subject*) mentionner; (*vomit*) vomir.

brink [brɪŋk] *n* bord *m*.

brisk [brɪsk] *a* (**-er, -est**) vif; (*trade*) actif; **at a b. pace** d'un bon pas. ◆**—ly** *adv* vivement; (*to walk*) d'un bon pas. ◆**—ness** *n* vivacité *f*.

bristl/e ['brɪs(ə)l] *n* poil *m*; – *vi* se hérisser. ◆**—ing** *a* **b. with** (*difficulties*) hérissé de.

Britain ['brɪt(ə)n] *n* Grande-Bretagne *f*. ◆**British** *a* britannique; – *n* **the B.** les Britanniques *mpl*. ◆**Briton** *n* Britannique *mf*.

Brittany ['brɪtənɪ] *n* Bretagne *f*.

brittle ['brɪt(ə)l] *a* cassant, fragile.

broach [brəʊtʃ] *vt* (*topic*) entamer.

broad[1] [brɔ:d] *a* (**-er, -est**) (*wide*) large; (*outline*) grand, général; (*accent*) prononcé; **in b. daylight** au grand jour; **b. bean** fève *f*; **b. jump** *Sp Am* saut *m* en longueur. ◆**b.-'minded** *a* à l'esprit large. ◆**b.-'shouldered** *a* large d'épaules. ◆**broaden** *vt* élargir; – *vi* s'élargir. ◆**broadly** *adv* **b. (speaking)** en gros, grosso modo.

broad[2] [brɔ:d] *n* (*woman*) *Am Sl* nana *f*.

broadcast ['brɔ:dkɑ:st] *vt* (*pt & pp* **broadcast**) *Rad & Fig* diffuser; *TV* téléviser; – *vi* (*of station*) émettre; (*of person*) parler à la radio *or* à la télévision; – *a* (radio)diffusé; télévisé; – *n* émission *f*. ◆**—ing** *n* radiodiffusion *f*; télévision *f*.

broccoli ['brɒkəlɪ] *n inv* brocoli *m*.

brochure ['brəʊʃər] *n* brochure *f*, dépliant *m*.

brogue [brəʊg] *n Ling* accent *m* irlandais.

broil [brɔɪl] *vti* griller. ◆**–er** *n* poulet *m* (à rôtir); (*apparatus*) gril *m*.

broke [brəʊk] **1** *see* **break. 2** *a* (*penniless*) fauché. ◆**broken** *see* **break;** – *a* (*ground*) accidenté; (*spirit*) abattu; (*man, voice, line*) brisé; **b. English** mauvais anglais *m*; **b. home** foyer *m* brisé. ◆**broken-'down** *a* (*machine etc*) (tout) déglingué, détraqué.

brolly ['brɒlɪ] *n* (*umbrella*) *Fam* pépin *m*.

bronchitis [brɒŋ'kaɪtɪs] *n* bronchite *f*.

bronze [brɒnz] *n* bronze *m*; – *a* (*statue etc*) en bronze.

brooch [brəʊtʃ] *n* (*ornament*) broche *f*.

brood [bruːd] **1** *n* couvée *f*, nichée *f*; – *vi* (*of bird*) couver. **2** *vi* méditer tristement (**over, on** sur); **to b. over** (*a plan*) ruminer. ◆**broody** *a* (**-ier, -iest**) (*person*) maussade, rêveur; (*woman*) *Fam* qui a envie d'avoir un enfant.

brook [brʊk] **1** *n* ruisseau *m*. **2** *vt* souffrir, tolérer.

broom [bruːm] *n* **1** (*for sweeping*) balai *m*. **2** *Bot* genêt *m*. ◆**broomstick** *n* manche *m* à balai.

Bros *abbr* (*Brothers*) Frères *mpl*.

broth [brɒθ] *n* bouillon *m*.

brothel ['brɒθ(ə)l] *n* maison *f* close, bordel *m*.

brother ['brʌðər] *n* frère *m*. ◆**b.-in-law** *n* (*pl* **brothers-in-law**) beau-frère *m*. ◆**brotherhood** *n* fraternité *f*. ◆**brotherly** *a* fraternel.

brow [braʊ] *n* (*forehead*) front *m*; (*of hill*) sommet *m*.

browbeat ['braʊbiːt] *vt* (*pt* **-beat,** *pp* **-beaten**) intimider.

brown [braʊn] *a* (**-er, -est**) brun; (*reddish*) marron; (*hair*) châtain; (*tanned*) bronzé; – *n* brun *m*; marron *m*; – *vt* brunir; *Culin* faire dorer; **to be browned off** *Fam* en avoir marre. ◆**brownish** *a* brunâtre.

Brownie ['braʊnɪ] *n* **1** (*girl scout*) jeannette *f*. **2 b.** *Culin Am* petit gâteau *m* au chocolat.

browse [braʊz] *vi* (*in shop*) regarder; (*in bookshop*) feuilleter des livres; (*of animal*) brouter; **to b. through** (*book*) feuilleter.

bruis/e [bruːz] *vt* contusionner, meurtrir; (*fruit, heart*) meurtrir; – *n* bleu *m*, contusion *f*. ◆**–ed** *a* couvert de bleus.

brunch [brʌntʃ] *n* repas *m* mixte (*petit déjeuner pris comme déjeuner*).

brunette [bruː'net] *n* brunette *f*.

brunt [brʌnt] *n* **to bear the b. of** (*attack etc*) subir le plus gros de.

brush [brʌʃ] *n* brosse *f*; (*for shaving*) blaireau *m*; (*little broom*) balayette *f*; (*action*) coup *m* de brosse; (*fight*) accrochage *m*; – *vt* (*teeth, hair etc*) brosser; (*clothes*) donner un coup de brosse à; **to b. aside** écarter; **to b. away** *or* **off** enlever; **to b. up (on)** (*language*) se remettre à; – *vi* **to b. against** effleurer. ◆**b.-off** *n Fam* **to give s.o. the b.-off** envoyer promener qn. ◆**b.-up** *n* coup *m* de brosse. ◆**brushwood** *n* broussailles *fpl*.

brusque [bruːsk] *a* brusque.

Brussels ['brʌs(ə)lz] *n* Bruxelles *m or f*; **B. sprouts** choux *mpl* de Bruxelles.

brutal ['bruːt(ə)l] *a* brutal. ◆**bru'tality** *n* brutalité *f*.

brute [bruːt] *n* (*animal, person*) brute *f*; – *a* **by b. force** par la force.

BSc, *Am* **BS** *abbr* = **Bachelor of Science.**

bubble ['bʌb(ə)l] *n* (*of air, soap etc*) bulle *f*; (*in boiling liquid*) bouillon *m*; **b. and squeak** *Fam* friture *f* de purée et de viande réchauffées; **b. bath** bain *m* moussant; **b. gum** chewing-gum *m*; – *vi* bouillonner; **to b. over** déborder (**with** de). ◆**bubbly** *n Hum Fam* champagne *m*.

buck [bʌk] **1** *n Am Fam* dollar *m*. **2** *n* (*animal*) mâle *m*. **3** *vt* **to b. up** remonter le moral à; – *vi* **to b. up** prendre courage; (*hurry*) se grouiller. ◆**buckshot** *n inv* du gros plomb *m*. ◆**buck'tooth** *n* (*pl* **-teeth**) dent *f* saillante.

bucket ['bʌkɪt] *n* seau *m*.

buckle ['bʌk(ə)l] **1** *n* boucle *f*; – *vt* boucler. **2** *vti* (*warp*) voiler, gauchir. **3** *vi* **to b. down to** (*task*) s'atteler à.

bud [bʌd] *n* (*of tree*) bourgeon *m*; (*of flower*) bouton *m*; – *vi* (**-dd-**) bourgeonner; pousser des boutons. ◆**budding** *a* (*talent*) naissant; (*doctor etc*) en herbe.

Buddhist ['bʊdɪst] *a* & *n* bouddhiste (*mf*).

buddy ['bʌdɪ] *n Am Fam* copain *m*, pote *m*.

budge [bʌdʒ] *vi* bouger; – *vt* faire bouger.

budgerigar ['bʌdʒərɪgɑːr] *n* perruche *f*.

budget ['bʌdʒɪt] *n* budget *m*; – *vi* dresser un budget; **to b. for** inscrire au budget. ◆**budgetary** *a* budgétaire.

budgie ['bʌdʒɪ] *n Fam* perruche *f*.

buff [bʌf] **1** *a* **b.(-coloured)** chamois *inv*. **2** *n* **jazz/***etc* **b.** *Fam* fana(tique) *mf* du jazz/*etc*. **3** *n* **in the b.** *Fam* tout nu.

buffalo ['bʌfələʊ] *n* (*pl* **-oes** *or* **-o**) buffle *m*; **(American) b.** bison *m*.

buffer ['bʌfər] *n* (*on train*) tampon *m*; (*at end of track*) butoir *m*; **b. state** état *m* tampon.

buffet 1 ['bʌfɪt] *vt* frapper; (*of waves*) battre; (*of wind, rain*) cingler (*qn*). **2** ['bʊfeɪ] *n* (*table, meal, café*) buffet *m*; **cold b.** viandes *fpl* froides.

buffoon [bə'fuːn] *n* bouffon *m*.

bug[1] [bʌg] **1** *n* punaise *f*; (*any insect*) *Fam* bestiole *f*; *Med Fam* microbe *m*, virus *m*; **the travel b.** (*urge*) le désir de voyager. **2** *n* *Fam* (*in machine*) défaut *m*; (*in computer program*) erreur *f*. **3** *n* (*apparatus*) *Fam* micro *m*; – *vt* **(-gg-)** (*room*) *Fam* installer des micros dans.

bug[2] [bʌg] *vt* **(-gg-)** (*annoy*) *Am Fam* embêter.

bugbear ['bʌgbeər] *n* (*worry*) cauchemar *m*.

buggy ['bʌgɪ] *n* **(baby) b.** (*pushchair*) poussette *f*; (*folding*) poussette-canne *f*; (*pram*) *Am* landau *m*.

bugle ['bjuɪg(ə)l] *n* clairon *m*. ◆**bugler** *n* (*person*) clairon *m*.

build [bɪld] **1** *n* (*of person*) carrure *f*. **2** *vt* (*pt & pp* **built**) construire; (*house, town*) construire, bâtir; **to b. in** (*cupboard etc*) encastrer; – *vi* bâtir, construire. ◆**built-in** *a* (*cupboard etc*) encastré; (*element of machine etc*) incorporé; (*innate*) *Fig* inné. **3 to b. up** *vt* (*reputation*) bâtir; (*increase*) augmenter; (*accumulate*) accumuler; (*business*) monter; (*speed, one's strength*) prendre; – *vi* augmenter, monter; s'accumuler. ◆**build-up** *n* montée *f*; accumulation *f*; *Mil* concentration *f*; *Journ* publicité *f*. ◆**built-up** *a* urbanisé; **b.-up area** agglomération *f*.

builder ['bɪldər] *n* maçon *m*; (*contractor*) entrepreneur *m*; (*of cars etc*) constructeur *m*; (*labourer*) ouvrier *m*.

building ['bɪldɪŋ] *n* bâtiment *m*; (*flats, offices*) immeuble *m*; (*action*) construction *f*; **b. society** caisse *f* d'épargne-logement, = société *f* de crédit immobilier.

bulb [bʌlb] *n* *Bot* bulbe *m*, oignon *m*; *El* ampoule *f*. ◆**bulbous** *a* bulbeux.

Bulgaria [bʌl'geərɪə] *n* Bulgarie *f*. ◆**Bulgarian** *a* & *n* bulgare (*mf*).

bulg/e [bʌldʒ] *vi* **to b. (out)** se renfler, bomber; (*of eyes*) sortir de la tête; – *n* renflement *m*; (*increase*) *Fam* augmentation *f*. ◆**—ing** *a* renflé, bombé; (*eyes*) protubérant; (*bag*) gonflé (**with** de).

bulk [bʌlk] *n inv* grosseur *f*, volume *m*; **the b. of** (*most*) la majeure partie de; **in b.** (*to buy, sell*) en gros. ◆**bulky** *a* **(-ier, -iest)** gros, volumineux.

bull [bʊl] *n* **1** taureau *m*. **2** (*nonsense*) *Fam* foutaises *fpl*. ◆**bullfight** *n* corrida *f*. ◆**bullfighter** *n* matador *m*. ◆**bullring** *n* arène *f*.

bulldog ['bʊldɒg] *n* bouledogue *m*; **b. clip** pince *f* (à dessin).

bulldoz/e ['bʊldəʊz] *vt* passer au bulldozer. ◆**—er** *n* bulldozer *m*, bouteur *m*.

bullet ['bʊlɪt] *n* balle *f*. ◆**bulletproof** *a* (*jacket, Am vest*) pare-balles *inv*; (*car*) blindé.

bulletin ['bʊlətɪn] *n* bulletin *m*.

bullion ['bʊljən] *n* or *m* or argent *m* en lingots.

bullock ['bʊlək] *n* bœuf *m*.

bull's-eye ['bʊlzaɪ] *n* (*of target*) centre *m*; **to hit the b.-eye** faire mouche.

bully ['bʊlɪ] *n* (grosse) brute *f*, tyran *m*; – *vt* brutaliser; (*persecute*) tyranniser; **to b. into doing** forcer à faire.

bulwark ['bʊlwək] *n* rempart *m*.

bum [bʌm] **1** *n* (*loafer*) *Am Fam* clochard *m*; – *vi* **(-mm-) to b. (around)** se balader. **2** *vt* **(-mm-) to b. sth off s.o.** (*cadge*) *Am Fam* taper qn de qch. **3** *n* (*buttocks*) *Fam* derrière *m*.

bumblebee ['bʌmb(ə)lbiː] *n* bourdon *m*.

bumf [bʌmf] *n* *Pej Sl* paperasses *fpl*.

bump [bʌmp] *vt* (*of car etc*) heurter; **to b. one's head/knee** se cogner la tête/le genou; **to b. into** se cogner contre; (*of car*) rentrer dans; (*meet*) *Fam* tomber sur; **to b. off** (*kill*) *Sl* liquider; **to b. up** *Fam* augmenter; – *vi* **to b. along** (*on rough road*) *Aut* cahoter; – *n* (*impact*) choc *m*; (*jerk*) cahot *m*; (*on road, body*) bosse *f*. ◆**—er** *n* (*of car etc*) pare-chocs *m inv*; – *a* (*crop etc*) exceptionnel; **b. cars** autos *fpl* tamponneuses. ◆**bumpy** *a* **(-ier, -iest)** (*road, ride*) cahoteux.

bumpkin ['bʌmpkɪn] *n* rustre *m*.

bumptious ['bʌmpʃəs] *a* prétentieux.

bun [bʌn] *n* **1** *Culin* petit pain *m* au lait. **2** (*of hair*) chignon *m*.

bunch [bʌntʃ] *n* (*of flowers*) bouquet *m*; (*of keys*) trousseau *m*; (*of bananas*) régime *m*; (*of people*) bande *f*; **b. of grapes** grappe *f* de raisin; **a b. of** (*mass*) *Fam* un tas de.

bundle ['bʌnd(ə)l] **1** *n* paquet *m*; (*of papers*) liasse *f*; (*of firewood*) fagot *m*. **2** *vt* (*put*) fourrer; (*push*) pousser (**into** dans); **to b. (up)** mettre en paquet; **to b. s.o. off** expédier qn; – *vi* **to b. (oneself) up** se couvrir (bien).

bung [bʌŋ] **1** *n* (*stopper*) bonde *f*; – *vt* **to b. up** (*stop up*) boucher. **2** *vt* (*toss*) *Fam* balancer, jeter.

bungalow ['bʌŋgələʊ] *n* bungalow *m*.

bungl/e ['bʌŋg(ə)l] *vt* gâcher; – *vi* travailler

mal. ◆**—ing** *n* gâchis *m*; – *a* (*clumsy*) maladroit.

bunion ['bʌnjən] *n* (*on toe*) oignon *m*.

bunk [bʌŋk] *n* **1** *Rail Nau* couchette *f*; **b. beds** lits *mpl* superposés. **2** *Sl* = **bunkum.** ◆**bunkum** *n Sl* foutaises *fpl*.

bunker ['bʌŋkər] *n Mil Golf* bunker *m*; (*coalstore in garden*) coffre *m*.

bunny ['bʌnɪ] *n Fam* Jeannot *m* lapin.

buoy [bɔɪ] *n* bouée *f*; – *vt* **to b. up** (*support*) *Fig* soutenir.

buoyant ['bɔɪənt] *a Fig* gai, optimiste; (*market*) *Fin* ferme.

burden ['bɜːd(ə)n] *n* fardeau *m*; (*of tax*) poids *m*; – *vt* charger, accabler (**with** de).

bureau, *pl* **-eaux** ['bjʊərəʊ, -əʊz] *n* (*office*) bureau *m*; (*desk*) secrétaire *m*. ◆**bureaucracy** [bjʊə'rɒkrəsɪ] *n* bureaucratie *f*. ◆**bureaucrat** ['bjʊərəkræt] *n* bureaucrate *mf*.

burger ['bɜːgər] *n Fam* hamburger *m*.

burglar ['bɜːglər] *n* cambrioleur, -euse *mf*; **b. alarm** sonnerie *f* d'alarme. ◆**burglarize** *vt Am* cambrioler. ◆**burglary** *n* cambriolage *m*. ◆**burgle** *vt* cambrioler.

burial ['berɪəl] *n* enterrement *m*; – *a* (*service*) funèbre; **b. ground** cimetière *m*.

burlap ['bɜːlæp] *n* (*sacking*) *Am* toile *f* à sac.

burlesque [bɜː'lesk] *n* parodie *f*; *Th Am* revue *f*.

burly ['bɜːlɪ] *a* (**-ier, -iest**) costaud.

Burma ['bɜːmə] *n* Birmanie *f*. ◆**Bur'mese** *a & n* birman, -ane (*mf*).

burn [bɜːn] *n* brûlure *f*; – *vt* (*pt & pp* **burned** *or* **burnt**) brûler; **to b. down** *or* **off** *or* **up** brûler; **burnt alive** brûlé vif; – *vi* brûler; **to b. down** (*of house*) brûler (complètement), être réduit en cendres; **to b. out** (*of fire*) s'éteindre; (*of fuse*) sauter. ◆**—ing** *a* en feu; (*fire*) allumé; (*topic, fever etc*) *Fig* brûlant; – *n* **smell of b.** odeur *f* de brûlé. ◆**—er** *n* (*of stove*) brûleur *m*.

burp [bɜːp] *n Fam* rot *m*; – *vi Fam* roter.

burrow ['bʌrəʊ] *n* (*hole*) terrier *m*; – *vti* creuser.

bursar ['bɜːsər] *n* (*in school*) intendant, -ante *mf*.

bursary ['bɜːsərɪ] *n* (*grant*) bourse *f*.

burst [bɜːst] *n* éclatement *m*, explosion *f*; (*of laughter*) éclat *m*; (*of applause*) salve *f*; (*of thunder*) coup *m*; (*surge*) élan *m*; (*fit*) accès *m*; (*burst water pipe*) *Fam* tuyau *m* crevé; – *vi* (*pt & pp* **burst**) (*of bomb etc*) éclater; (*of bubble, tyre, cloud etc*) crever; **to b. into** (*room*) faire irruption dans; **to b. into tears** fondre en larmes; **to b. into flames** prendre feu, s'embraser; **to b. open** s'ouvrir avec force; **to b. out laughing** éclater de rire; – *vt* crever, faire éclater; (*rupture*) rompre; **to b. open** ouvrir avec force. ◆**—ing** *a* (*full*) plein à craquer (**with** de); **b. with** (*joy*) débordant de; **to be b. to do** mourir d'envie de faire.

bury ['berɪ] *vt* (*dead person*) enterrer; (*hide*) enfouir; (*plunge, absorb*) plonger.

bus [bʌs] *n* (auto)bus *m*; (*long-distance*) (auto)car *m*; – *a* (*driver, ticket etc*) d'autobus; d'autocar; **b. shelter** abribus *m*; **b. station** gare *f* routière; **b. stop** arrêt *m* d'autobus; – *vt* (**-ss-**) (*children*) transporter (en bus) à l'école. ◆**bussing** *n Sch* ramassage *m* scolaire.

bush [bʊʃ] *n* buisson *m*; (*of hair*) tignasse *f*; **the b.** (*land*) la brousse. ◆**bushy** *a* (**-ier, -iest**) (*hair, tail etc*) broussailleux.

bushed [bʊʃt] *a* (*tired*) *Fam* crevé.

business ['bɪznɪs] *n* affaires *fpl*, commerce *m*; (*shop*) commerce *m*; (*task, concern, matter*) affaire *f*; **the textile b.** le textile; **big b.** *Fam* les grosses entreprises *fpl* commerciales; **on b.** (*to travel*) pour affaires; **it's your b. to . . .** c'est à vous de . . . ; **you have no b. to . . .** vous n'avez pas le droit de . . . ; **that's none of your b.!** ça ne vous regarde pas!; **to mean b.** *Fam* ne pas plaisanter; – *a* commercial; (*meeting, trip*) d'affaires; **b. hours** (*office*) heures *fpl* de travail; (*shop*) heures *fpl* d'ouverture. ◆**businesslike** *a* sérieux, pratique. ◆**businessman** *n* (*pl* **-men**) homme *m* d'affaires. ◆**businesswoman** *n* (*pl* **-women**) femme *f* d'affaires.

busker ['bʌskər] *n* musicien, -ienne *mf* des rues.

bust [bʌst] **1** *n* (*sculpture*) buste *m*; (*woman's breasts*) poitrine *f*. **2** *a* (*broken*) *Fam* fichu; **to go b.** (*bankrupt*) faire faillite; – *vti* (*pt & pp* **bust** *or* **busted**) *Fam* = **to burst** & **to break.** ◆**b.-up** *n Fam* (*quarrel*) engueulade *f*; (*breakup*) rupture *f*.

bustl/e ['bʌs(ə)l] *vi* **to b. (about)** s'affairer; – *n* activité *f*, branle-bas *m*. ◆**—ing** *a* (*street*) bruyant.

bus/y ['bɪzɪ] *a* (**-ier, -iest**) occupé (**doing** à faire); (*active*) actif; (*day*) chargé; (*street*) animé; (*line*) *Tel Am* occupé; **to be b. doing** (*in the process of*) être en train de faire; – *vt* **to b. oneself** s'occuper (**with sth** à qch, **doing** à faire). ◆**—ily** *adv* activement. ◆**busybody** *n* **to be a b.** faire la mouche du coche.

but [bʌt, *unstressed* bət] **1** *conj* mais. **2** *prep* (*except*) sauf; **b. for that** sans cela; **b. for him** sans lui; **no one b. you** personne d'autre que toi. **3** *adv* (*only*) ne ... que, seulement.

butane ['bjuːteɪn] *n* (*gas*) butane *m*.

butcher ['bʊtʃər] *n* boucher *m*; **b.'s shop** boucherie *f*; – *vt* (*people*) massacrer; (*animal*) abattre. ◆**butchery** *n* massacre *m* (**of** de).

butler ['bʌtlər] *n* maître *m* d'hôtel.

butt [bʌt] **1** *n* (*of cigarette*) mégot *m*; (*of gun*) crosse *f*; (*buttocks*) *Am Fam* derrière *m*; **b. for ridicule** objet *m* de risée. **2** *vi* **to b. in** interrompre, intervenir.

butter ['bʌtər] *n* beurre *m*; **b. bean** haricot *m* blanc; **b. dish** beurrier *m*; – *vt* beurrer; **to b. s.o. up** *Fam* flatter qn. ◆**buttercup** *n* bouton-d'or *m*. ◆**buttermilk** *n* lait *m* de beurre.

butterfly ['bʌtəflaɪ] *n* papillon *m*; **to have butterflies** *Fam* avoir le trac; **b. stroke** *Swimming* brasse *f* papillon.

buttock ['bʌtək] *n* fesse *f*.

button ['bʌtən] *n* bouton *m*; – *vt* **to b. (up)** boutonner; – *vi* **to b. up** (*of garment*) se boutonner. ◆**buttonhole 1** *n* boutonnière *f*; (*flower*) fleur *f*. **2** *vt* (*person*) *Fam* accrocher.

buttress ['bʌtrɪs] *n Archit* contrefort *m*; *Fig* soutien *m*; **flying b.** arc-boutant *m*; – *vt* (*support*) *Archit & Fig* soutenir.

buxom ['bʌksəm] *a* (*woman*) bien en chair.

buy [baɪ] *vt* (*pt & pp* **bought**) acheter (**from s.o.** à qn, **for s.o.** à *or* pour qn); (*story etc*) *Am Fam* avaler, croire; **to b. back** racheter; **to b. over** (*bribe*) corrompre; **to b. up** acheter en bloc; – *n* **a good b.** une bonne affaire. ◆**—er** *n* acheteur, -euse *mf*.

buzz [bʌz] **1** *vi* bourdonner; **to b. off** *Fam* décamper; – *n* bourdonnement *m*. **2** *vt* (*building etc*) *Av* raser. **3** *vt* **to b. s.o.** *Tel* appeler qn; – *n Tel Fam* coup *m* de fil. ◆**—er** *n* interphone *m*; (*of bell, clock*) sonnerie *f*; (*hooter*) sirène *f*.

by [baɪ] *prep* **1** (*agent, manner*) par; **hit/chosen/***etc* **by** frappé/choisi/*etc* par; **surrounded/followed/***etc* **by** entouré/suivi/*etc* de; **by doing** en faisant; **by sea** par mer; **by mistake** par erreur; **by car** en voiture; **by bicycle** à bicyclette; **by moonlight** au clair de lune; **one by one** un à un; **day by day** de jour en jour; **by sight/day/far** de vue/jour/loin; **by the door** (*through*) par la porte; **(all) by oneself** tout seul. **2** (*next to*) à côté de; (*near*) près de; **by the lake/sea** au bord du lac/de la mer; **to pass by the bank** passer devant la banque. **3** (*before in time*) avant; **by Monday** avant lundi, d'ici lundi; **by now** à cette heure-ci, déjà; **by yesterday** (dès) hier. **4** (*amount, measurement*) à; **by the kilo** au kilo; **taller by a metre** plus grand d'un mètre; **paid by the hour** payé à l'heure. **5** (*according to*) d'après; – *adv* **close by** tout près; **to go by, pass by** passer; **to put by** mettre de côté; **by and by** bientôt; **by and large** en gros. ◆**by-election** *n* élection *f* partielle. ◆**by-law** *n* arrêté *m*; (*of organization*) *Am* statut *m*. ◆**by-product** *n* sous-produit *m*. ◆**by-road** *n* chemin *m* de traverse.

bye(-bye)! [baɪ('baɪ)] *int Fam* salut!, au revoir!

bygone ['baɪgɒn] *a* **in b. days** jadis.

bypass ['baɪpɑːs] *n* déviation *f* (routière), dérivation *f*; – *vt* contourner; (*ignore*) *Fig* éviter de passer par.

bystander ['baɪstændər] *n* spectateur, -trice *mf*; (*in street*) badaud, -aude *mf*.

byword ['baɪwɜːd] *n* **a b. for** *Pej* un synonyme de.

C

C, c [siː] *n* C, c *m*.

c *abbr* = **cent**.

cab [kæb] *n* taxi *m*; (*horse-drawn*) *Hist* fiacre *m*; (*of train driver etc*) cabine *f*. ◆**cabby** *n Fam* (chauffeur *m* de) taxi *m*; *Hist* cocher *m*.

cabaret ['kæbəreɪ] *n* (*show*) spectacle *m*; (*place*) cabaret *m*.

cabbage ['kæbɪdʒ] *n* chou *m*.

cabin ['kæbɪn] *n Nau Rail* cabine *f*; (*hut*) cabane *f*, case *f*; **c. boy** mousse *m*.

cabinet ['kæbɪnɪt] **1** *n* (*cupboard*) armoire *f*; (*for display*) vitrine *f*; **(filing) c.** classeur *m* (de bureau). **2** *n Pol* cabinet *m*; – *a* ministériel; **c. minister** ministre *m*. ◆**c.-maker** *n* ébéniste *m*.

cable ['keɪb(ə)l] *n* câble *m*; **c. car** (*with overhead cable*) téléphérique *m*; *Rail* funiculaire *m*; **c. television** la télévision par câble; **to have c.** *Fam* avoir le câble; – *vt* (*message etc*) câbler (**to** à).

caboose [kə'buːs] *n Rail Am* fourgon *m* (de queue).
cache [kæʃ] *n* (*place*) cachette *f*; **an arms' c.** des armes cachées, une cache d'armes.
cachet ['kæʃeɪ] *n* (*mark, character etc*) cachet *m*.
cackle ['kæk(ə)l] *vi* (*of hen*) caqueter; (*laugh*) glousser; – *n* caquet *m*; gloussement *m*.
cacophony [kə'kɒfənɪ] *n* cacophonie *f*.
cactus, *pl* **-ti** *or* **-tuses** ['kæktəs, -taɪ, -təsɪz] *n* cactus *m*.
cad [kæd] *n Old-fashioned Pej* goujat *m*.
cadaverous [kə'dævərəs] *a* cadavérique.
caddie ['kædɪ] *n Golf* caddie *m*.
caddy ['kædɪ] *n* **(tea) c.** boîte *f* à thé.
cadence ['keɪdəns] *n Mus* cadence *f*.
cadet [kə'det] *n Mil* élève *m* officier.
cadge [kædʒ] *vi* (*beg*) *Pej* quémander; – *vt* (*meal*) se faire payer (**off s.o.** par qn); **to c. money from** *or* **off s.o.** taper qn.
Caesarean [sɪ'zeərɪən] *n* **c. (section)** *Med* césarienne *f*.
café ['kæfeɪ] *n* café(-restaurant) *m*. ◆**cafeteria** [kæfɪ'tɪərɪə] *n* cafétéria *f*.
caffeine ['kæfiːn] *n* caféine *f*.
cage [keɪdʒ] *n* cage *f*; – *vt* **to c. (up)** mettre en cage.
cagey ['keɪdʒɪ] *a Fam* peu communicatif (**about** à l'égard de).
cahoots [kə'huːts] *n* **in c.** *Sl* de mèche, en cheville (**with** avec).
cajole [kə'dʒəʊl] *vt* amadouer, enjôler.
cak/e [keɪk] **1** *n* gâteau *m*; (*small*) pâtisserie *f*; **c. of soap** savonnette *f*. **2** *vi* (*harden*) durcir; – *vt* (*cover*) couvrir (**with** de). ◆**—ed** *a* (*mud*) séché.
calamine ['kæləmaɪn] *n* **c. (lotion)** lotion *f* apaisante (à la calamine).
calamity [kə'læmɪtɪ] *n* calamité *f*. ◆**calamitous** *a* désastreux.
calcium ['kælsɪəm] *n* calcium *m*.
calculat/e ['kælkjʊleɪt] *vti* calculer; **to c. that** *Fam* supposer que; **to c. on** compter sur. ◆**—ing** *a* (*shrewd*) calculateur. ◆**calcu'lation** *n* calcul *m*. ◆**calculator** *n* (*desk computer*) calculatrice *f*; **(pocket) c.** calculatrice (de poche). ◆**calculus** *n Math Med* calcul *m*.
calendar ['kælɪndər] *n* calendrier *m*; (*directory*) annuaire *m*.
calf [kɑːf] *n* (*pl* **calves**) **1** (*animal*) veau *m*. **2** *Anat* mollet *m*.
calibre ['kælɪbər] *n* calibre *m*. ◆**calibrate** *vt* calibrer.
calico ['kælɪkəʊ] *n* (*pl* **-oes** *or* **-os**) (*fabric*) calicot *m*; (*printed*) *Am* indienne *f*.
call [kɔːl] *n* appel *m*; (*shout*) cri *m*; (*vocation*) vocation *f*; (*visit*) visite *f*; **(telephone) c.** communication *f*, appel *m* téléphonique; **to make a c.** *Tel* téléphoner (**to** à); **on c.** de garde; **no c. to do** aucune raison de faire; **there's no c. for that article** *Com* cet article n'est pas très demandé; **c. box** cabine *f* (téléphonique); – *vt* appeler; (*wake up*) réveiller; (*person to meeting*) convoquer (**to** à); (*attention*) attirer (**to** sur); (*truce*) demander; (*consider*) considérer; **he's called David** il s'appelle David; **to c. a meeting** convoquer une assemblée; **to c. s.o. a liar/etc** qualifier *or* traiter qn de menteur/*etc*; **to c. into question** mettre en question; **let's c. it a day** *Fam* on va s'arrêter là, ça suffit; **to c. sth (out)** (*shout*) crier qch; – *vi* appeler; **to c. (out)** (*cry out*) crier; **to c. (in** *or* **round** *or* **by** *or* **over)** (*visit*) passer. ■ **to c. back** *vti* rappeler; **to c. for** *vt* (*require*) demander; (*summon*) appeler; (*collect*) passer prendre; **to c. in** *vt* faire venir *or* entrer; (*police*) appeler; (*recall*) rappeler, faire rentrer; – *vi* **to c. in on s.o.** passer chez qn. ◆**call-in** *a* (*programme*) *Rad* à ligne ouverte; **to c. off** *vt* (*cancel*) annuler; (*dog*) rappeler; **to c. out** *vt* (*doctor*) appeler; (*workers*) donner une consigne de grève à; – *vi* **to c. out for** demander à haute voix; **to c. up** *vt Mil Tel* appeler; (*memories*) évoquer. ◆**call-up** *n Mil* appel *m*, mobilisation *f*; **to c. (up)on** *vi* (*visit*) passer voir, passer chez; (*invoke*) invoquer; **to c. (up)on s.o. to do** inviter qn à faire; (*urge*) sommer qn de faire. ◆**calling** *n* vocation *f*; **c. card** *Am* carte *f* de visite. ◆**caller** *n* visiteur, -euse *mf*; *Tel* correspondant, -ante *mf*.
calligraphy [kə'lɪgrəfɪ] *n* calligraphie *f*.
callous ['kæləs] *a* **1** cruel, insensible. **2** (*skin*) calleux. ◆**callus** *n* durillon *m*, cal *m*.
callow ['kæləʊ] *a* inexpérimenté.
calm [kɑːm] *a* (**-er, -est**) calme, tranquille; **keep c.!** (*don't panic*) du calme!; – *n* calme *m*; – *vt* **to c. (down)** calmer; – *vi* **to c. down** se calmer. ◆**—ly** *adv* calmement. ◆**—ness** *n* calme *m*.
calorie ['kælərɪ] *n* calorie *f*.
calumny ['kæləmnɪ] *n* calomnie *f*.
calvary ['kælvərɪ] *n Rel* calvaire *m*.
calve [kɑːv] *vi* (*of cow*) vêler.
camber ['kæmbər] *n* (*in road*) bombement *m*.
came [keɪm] *see* **come**.
camel ['kæməl] *n* chameau *m*.
camellia [kə'miːlɪə] *n Bot* camélia *m*.

cameo ['kæmɪəʊ] *n* camée *m*.
camera ['kæmrə] *n* appareil(-photo) *m*; *TV Cin* caméra *f*. ◆**cameraman** *n* (*pl* -men) caméraman *m*.
camomile ['kæməmaɪl] *n Bot* camomille *f*.
camouflage ['kæməflɑːʒ] *n* camouflage *m*; – *vt* camoufler.
camp[1] [kæmp] *n* camp *m*, campement *m*; **c. bed** lit *m* de camp; – *vi* **to c. (out)** camper. ◆**—ing** *n Sp* camping *m*; **c. site** (terrain *m* de) camping *m*. ◆**—er** *n* (*person*) campeur, -euse *mf*; (*vehicle*) camping-car *m*. ◆**campfire** *n* feu *m* de camp. ◆**campsite** *n* camping *m*.
camp[2] [kæmp] *a* (*affected*) affecté, exagéré (*de façon à provoquer le rire*).
campaign [kæm'peɪn] *n Pol Mil Journ etc* campagne *f*; – *vi* faire campagne. ◆**—er** *n* militant, -ante *mf* (**for** pour).
campus ['kæmpəs] *n Univ* campus *m*.
can[1] [kæn, *unstressed* kən] *v aux* (*pres t* **can**; *pt* **could**) (*be able to*) pouvoir; (*know how to*) savoir; **if I c.** si je peux; **she c. swim** elle sait nager; **if I could swim** si je savais nager; **he could do it tomorrow** il pourrait le faire demain; **he couldn't help me** il ne pouvait pas m'aider; **he could have done it** il aurait pu le faire; **you could be wrong** (*possibility*) tu as peut-être tort; **he can't be old** (*probability*) il ne doit pas être vieux; **c. I come in?** (*permission*) puis-je entrer?; **you can't** *or* **c. not come** tu ne peux pas venir; **I c. see** je vois.
can[2] [kæn] *n* (*for water etc*) bidon *m*; (*tin for food*) boîte *f*; – *vt* (**-nn-**) mettre en boîte. ◆**canned** *a* en boîte, en conserve; **c. food** conserves *fpl*. ◆**can-opener** *n* ouvre-boîtes *m inv*.
Canada ['kænədə] *n* Canada *m*. ◆**Canadian** [kə'neɪdɪən] *a* & *n* canadien, -ienne (*mf*).
canal [kə'næl] *n* canal *m*.
canary [kə'neərɪ] *n* canari *m*, serin *m*.
cancan ['kænkæn] *n* french-cancan *m*.
cancel ['kænsəl] *vt* (**-ll-**, *Am* **-l-**) annuler; (*goods, taxi, appointment*) décommander; (*word, paragraph etc*) biffer; (*train*) supprimer; (*stamp*) oblitérer; **to c. a ticket** (*with date*) composter un billet; (*punch*) poinçonner un billet; **to c. each other out** s'annuler. ◆**cance'llation** *n* annulation *f*; suppression *f*; oblitération *f*.
cancer ['kænsər] *n* cancer *m*; **C.** (*sign*) le Cancer; **c. patient** cancéreux, -euse *mf*. ◆**cancerous** *a* cancéreux.
candelabra [kændɪ'lɑːbrə] *n* candélabre *m*.
candid ['kændɪd] *a* franc, sincère. ◆**candour** *n* franchise *f*, sincérité *f*.
candidate ['kændɪdeɪt] *n* candidat, -ate *mf*. ◆**candidacy** *n*, ◆**candidature** *n* candidature *f*.
candle ['kænd(ə)l] *n* bougie *f*; (*tallow*) chandelle *f*; *Rel* cierge *m*; **c. grease** suif *m*. ◆**candlelight** *n* **by c.** à la (lueur d'une) bougie; **to have dinner by c.** dîner aux chandelles. ◆**candlestick** *n* bougeoir *m*; (*tall*) chandelier *m*.
candy ['kændɪ] *n Am* bonbon(s) *m*(*pl*); (**sugar**) **c.** sucre *m* candi; **c. store** *Am* confiserie *f*. ◆**candied** *a* (*fruit*) confit, glacé. ◆**candyfloss** *n* barbe *f* à papa.
cane [keɪn] *n* canne *f*; (*for basket*) rotin *m*; *Sch* baguette *f*; – *vt* (*punish*) *Sch* fouetter.
canine ['keɪnaɪn] **1** *a* canin. **2** *n* (*tooth*) canine *f*.
canister ['kænɪstər] *n* boîte *f* (*en métal*).
canker ['kæŋkər] *n* (*in disease*) & *Fig* chancre *m*.
cannabis ['kænəbɪs] *n* (*plant*) chanvre *m* indien; (*drug*) haschisch *m*.
cannibal ['kænɪbəl] *n* & *a* cannibale (*mf*).
cannon ['kænən] *n* (*pl* **-s** *or inv*) canon *m*. ◆**cannonball** *n* boulet *m* (de canon).
cannot ['kænɒt] = **can not**.
canny ['kænɪ] *a* (**-ier, -iest**) rusé, malin.
canoe [kə'nuː] *n* canoë *m*, kayak *m*; – *vi* faire du canoë *or* du kayak. ◆**—ing** *n* **to go c.** *Sp* faire du canoë *or* du kayak. ◆**canoeist** *n* canoéiste *mf*.
canon ['kænən] *n* (*law*) canon *m*; (*clergyman*) chanoine *m*. ◆**canonize** *vt Rel* canoniser.
canopy ['kænəpɪ] *n* (*over bed, altar etc*) dais *m*; (*hood of pram*) capote *f*; (*awning*) auvent *m*; (*made of glass*) marquise *f*; (*of sky*) *Fig* voûte *f*.
cant [kænt] *n* (*jargon*) jargon *m*.
can't [kɑːnt] = **can not**.
cantaloup(e) ['kæntəluːp, *Am* -ləʊp] *n* (*melon*) cantaloup *m*.
cantankerous [kæn'tæŋkərəs] *a* grincheux, acariâtre.
cantata [kæn'tɑːtə] *n Mus* cantate *f*.
canteen [kæn'tiːn] *n* (*place*) cantine *f*; (*flask*) gourde *f*; **c. of cutlery** ménagère *f*.
canter ['kæntər] *n* petit galop *m*; – *vi* aller au petit galop.
cantor ['kæntər] *n Rel* chantre *m*, maître *m* de chapelle.
canvas ['kænvəs] *n* (grosse) toile *f*; (*for embroidery*) canevas *m*.
canvass ['kænvəs] *vt* (*an area*) faire du démarchage dans; (*opinions*) sonder; **to c.**

s.o. *Pol* solliciter des voix de qn; *Com* solliciter des commandes de qn. ◆**—ing** *n Com* démarchage *m*, prospection *f*; *Pol* démarchage *m* (électoral). ◆**—er** *n Pol* agent *m* électoral; *Com* démarcheur, -euse *mf*.

canyon ['kænjən] *n* cañon *m*, canyon *m*.

cap[1] [kæp] *n* **1** (*hat*) casquette *f*; (*for shower etc*) & *Nau* bonnet *m*; *Mil* képi *m*. **2** (*of bottle, tube, valve*) bouchon *m*; (*of milk or beer bottle*) capsule *f*; (*of pen*) capuchon *m*. **3** (*of child's gun*) amorce *f*, capsule *f*. **4** **(Dutch) c.** (*contraceptive*) diaphragme *m*.

cap[2] [kæp] *vt* (**-pp-**) (*outdo*) surpasser; **to c. it all** pour comble; **capped with** (*covered*) coiffé de.

capable ['keɪpəb(ə)l] *a* (*person*) capable (**of** sth de qch, **of doing** de faire), compétent; **c. of** (*thing*) susceptible de. ◆**capa'bility** *n* capacité *f*. ◆**capably** *adv* avec compétence.

capacity [kə'pæsətɪ] *n* (*of container*) capacité *f*, contenance *f*; (*ability*) aptitude *f*, capacité *f*; (*output*) rendement *m*; **in my c. as** en ma qualité de; **in an advisory/***etc* **c.** à titre consultatif/*etc*; **filled to c.** absolument plein, comble; **c. audience** salle *f* comble.

cape [keɪp] *n* **1** (*cloak*) cape *f*; (*of cyclist*) pèlerine *f*. **2** *Geog* cap *m*; **C. Town** Le Cap.

caper ['keɪpər] **1** *vi* (*jump about*) gambader. **2** *n* (*activity*) *Sl* affaire *f*; (*prank*) *Fam* farce *f*; (*trip*) *Fam* virée *f*. **3** *n Bot Culin* câpre *f*.

capital ['kæpɪtəl] **1** *a* (*punishment, letter, importance*) capital; – *n* **c. (city)** capitale *f*; **c. (letter)** majuscule *f*, capitale *f*. **2** *n* (*money*) capital *m*, capitaux *mpl*. ◆**capitalism** *n* capitalisme *m*. ◆**capitalist** *a* & *n* capitaliste (*mf*). ◆**capitalize** *vi* **to c. on** tirer parti de.

capitulate [kə'pɪtʃʊleɪt] *vi* capituler. ◆**capitu'lation** *n* capitulation *f*.

caprice [kə'priːs] *n* caprice *m*. ◆**capricious** [kə'prɪʃəs] *a* capricieux.

Capricorn ['kæprɪkɔːn] *n* (*sign*) le Capricorne.

capsize [kæp'saɪz] *vi Nau* chavirer; – *vt* (faire) chavirer.

capsule ['kæpsəl, 'kæpsjuːl] *n* (*medicine, of spaceship etc*) capsule *f*.

captain ['kæptɪn] *n* capitaine *m*; – *vt Nau* commander; *Sp* être le capitaine de.

caption ['kæpʃ(ə)n] *n Cin Journ* sous-titre *m*; (*under illustration*) légende *f*.

captivate ['kæptɪveɪt] *vt* captiver.

captive ['kæptɪv] *n* captif, -ive *mf*, prisonnier, -ière *mf*. ◆**cap'tivity** *n* captivité *f*.

capture ['kæptʃər] *n* capture *f*; – *vt* (*person, animal*) prendre, capturer; (*town*) prendre; (*attention*) capter; (*represent in words, on film etc*) rendre, reproduire.

car [kɑːr] *n* voiture *f*, auto(mobile) *f*; *Rail* wagon *m*; – *a* (*industry*) automobile; **c. ferry** ferry-boat *m*; **c. park** parking *m*; **c. radio** autoradio *m*; **c. wash** (*action*) lavage *m* automatique; (*machine*) lave-auto *m*. ◆**carfare** *n Am* frais *mpl* de voyage. ◆**carport** *n* auvent *m* (pour voiture). ◆**carsick** *a* **to be c.** être malade en voiture.

carafe [kə'ræf] *n* carafe *f*.

caramel ['kærəməl] *n* (*flavouring, toffee*) caramel *m*.

carat ['kærət] *n* carat *m*.

caravan ['kærəvæn] *n* (*in desert*) & *Aut* caravane *f*; (*horse-drawn*) roulotte *f*; **c. site** camping *m* pour caravanes.

caraway ['kærəweɪ] *n Bot Culin* cumin *m*, carvi *m*.

carbohydrates [kɑːbəʊ'haɪdreɪts] *npl* (*in diet*) féculents *mpl*.

carbon ['kɑːbən] *n* carbone *m*; **c. copy** double *m* (au carbone); *Fig* réplique *f*, double *m*; **c. paper** (papier *m*) carbone *m*.

carbuncle ['kɑːbʌŋk(ə)l] *n Med* furoncle *m*, clou *m*.

carburettor [kɑːbjʊ'retər] (*Am* **carburetor** ['kɑːbəreɪtər]) *n* carburateur *m*.

carcass ['kɑːkəs] *n* (*body, framework*) carcasse *f*.

carcinogenic [kɑːsɪnə'dʒenɪk] *a* cancérigène.

card [kɑːd] *n* carte *f*; (*cardboard*) carton *m*; **(index) c.** fiche *f*; **c. index** fichier *m*; **c. table** table *f* de jeu; **to play cards** jouer aux cartes; **on** *or Am* **in the cards** *Fam* très vraisemblable; **to get one's cards** (*be dismissed*) *Fam* être renvoyé. ◆**cardboard** *n* carton *m*. ◆**cardsharp** *n* tricheur, -euse *mf*.

cardiac ['kɑːdɪæk] *a* cardiaque.

cardigan ['kɑːdɪgən] *n* cardigan *m*, gilet *m*.

cardinal ['kɑːdɪn(ə)l] **1** *a* (*number etc*) cardinal. **2** *n* (*priest*) cardinal *m*.

care [keər] **1** *vi* **to c. about** (*feel concern about*) se soucier de, s'intéresser à; **I don't c.** ça m'est égal; **I couldn't c. less** *Fam* je m'en fiche; **who cares?** qu'est-ce que ça fait? **2** *vi* (*like*) aimer, vouloir; **would you c. to try?** voulez-vous essayer?, aimeriez-vous essayer?; **I don't c. for it** (*music etc*) je n'aime pas tellement ça; **to c. for** (*a drink, a change etc*) avoir envie de; **to c. about** *or* **for** s.o. avoir de la sympathie pour qn; **to c. for**

(*look after*) s'occuper de; (*sick person*) soigner. **3** *n* (*application, heed*) soin(s) *m*(*pl*), attention *f*; (*charge, protection*) garde *f*, soin *m*; (*anxiety*) souci *m*; **to take c. not to do** faire attention à ne pas faire; **take c. to put everything back** veillez à tout ranger; **to take c. of** s'occuper de; **to take c. of itself** (*of matter*) s'arranger; **to take c. of oneself** (*manage*) se débrouiller; (*keep healthy*) faire attention à sa santé. ◆**carefree** *a* insouciant. ◆**caretaker** *n* gardien, -ienne *mf*, concierge *mf*.

career [kə'rɪər] **1** *n* carrière *f*; – *a* (*diplomat etc*) de carrière. **2** *vi* **to c. along** aller à toute vitesse.

careful ['keəf(ə)l] *a* (*diligent*) soigneux (**about, of** de); (*cautious*) prudent; **c. (with money)** regardant; **to be c. of** *or* **with** (*heed*) faire attention à. ◆**—ly** *adv* avec soin; prudemment. ◆**careless** *a* négligent; (*thoughtless*) irréfléchi; (*inattentive*) inattentif (**of** à). ◆**carelessness** *n* négligence *f*, manque *m* de soin.

caress [kə'res] *n* caresse *f*; – *vt* (*stroke*) caresser; (*kiss*) embrasser.

cargo ['kɑːgəʊ] *n* (*pl* **-oes**, *Am* **-os**) cargaison *f*; **c. boat** cargo *m*.

Caribbean [kærɪ'biːən, *Am* kə'rɪbɪən] *a* caraïbe; – *n* **the C. (Islands)** les Antilles *fpl*.

caricature ['kærɪkətʃʊər] *n* caricature *f*; – *vt* caricaturer.

caring ['keərɪŋ] *a* (*loving*) aimant; (*understanding*) compréhensif; – *n* affection *f*.

carnage ['kɑːnɪdʒ] *n* carnage *m*.

carnal ['kɑːnəl] *a* charnel, sexuel.

carnation [kɑː'neɪʃən] *n* œillet *m*.

carnival ['kɑːnɪvəl] *n* carnaval *m*.

carnivore ['kɑːnɪvɔːr] *n* carnivore *m*. ◆**car'nivorous** *a* carnivore.

carol ['kærəl] *n* chant *m* (de Noël).

carouse [kə'raʊz] *vi* faire la fête.

carp [kɑːp] **1** *n* (*fish*) carpe *f*. **2** *vi* critiquer; **to c. at** critiquer.

carpenter ['kɑːpɪntər] *n* (*for house building*) charpentier *m*; (*light woodwork*) menuisier *m*. ◆**carpentry** *n* charpenterie *f*; menuiserie *f*.

carpet ['kɑːpɪt] *n* tapis *m*; (*fitted*) moquette *f*; **c. sweeper** balai *m* mécanique; – *vt* recouvrir d'un tapis *or* d'une moquette; (*of snow etc*) *Fig* tapisser. ◆**—ing** *n* (*carpets*) tapis *mpl*; moquette *f*.

carriage ['kærɪdʒ] *n* (*horse-drawn*) voiture *f*, équipage *m*; *Rail* voiture *f*; *Com* transport *m*; (*bearing of person*) port *m*; (*of typewriter*) chariot *m*; **c. paid** port payé. ◆**carriageway** *n* (*of road*) chaussée *f*.

carrier ['kærɪər] *n Com* entreprise *f* de transports; *Med* porteur, -euse *mf*; **c. (bag)** sac *m* (en plastique); **c. pigeon** pigeon *m* voyageur.

carrion ['kærɪən] *n* charogne *f*.

carrot ['kærət] *n* carotte *f*.

carry ['kærɪ] *vt* porter; (*goods*) transporter; (*by wind*) emporter; (*involve*) comporter; (*interest*) *Com* produire; (*extend*) faire passer; (*win*) remporter; (*authority*) avoir; (*child*) *Med* attendre; (*motion*) *Pol* faire passer, voter; (*sell*) stocker; *Math* retenir; **to c. too far** pousser trop loin; **to c. oneself** se comporter; – *vi* (*of sound*) porter. ■ **to c. away** *vt* emporter; *Fig* transporter; **to be** *or* **get carried away** (*excited*) s'emballer; **to c. back** *vt* (*thing*) rapporter; (*person*) ramener; (*in thought*) reporter; **to c. off** *vt* emporter; (*kidnap*) enlever; (*prize*) remporter; **to c. it off** réussir; **to c. on** *vt* continuer; (*conduct*) diriger, mener; (*sustain*) soutenir; – *vi* continuer (**doing** à faire); (*behave*) *Pej* se conduire (mal); (*complain*) se plaindre; **to c. on with sth** continuer qch; **to c. on about** (*talk*) causer de. ◆**carryings-'on** *npl Pej* activités *fpl*; (*behaviour*) *Pej* façons *fpl*; **to c. out** *vt* (*plan etc*) exécuter, réaliser; (*repair etc*) effectuer; (*duty*) accomplir; (*meal*) *Am* emporter; **to c. through** *vt* (*plan etc*) mener à bonne fin.

carryall ['kærɪɔːl] *n Am* fourre-tout *m inv*. ◆**carrycot** *n* (nacelle *f*) porte-bébé *m*.

cart [kɑːt] **1** *n* charrette *f*; (*handcart*) voiture *f* à bras. **2** *vt* (*goods, people*) transporter; **to c. (around)** *Fam* trimbal(l)er; **to c. away** emporter. ◆**carthorse** *n* cheval *m* de trait.

cartel [kɑː'tel] *n Econ Pol* cartel *m*.

cartilage ['kɑːtɪlɪdʒ] *n* cartilage *m*.

carton ['kɑːtən] *n* (*box*) carton *m*; (*of milk, fruit juice etc*) brick *m*, pack *m*; (*of cigarettes*) cartouche *f*; (*of cream*) pot *m*.

cartoon [kɑː'tuːn] *n Journ* dessin *m* (humoristique); *Cin* dessin *m* animé; **(strip) c.** bande *f* dessinée. ◆**cartoonist** *n Journ* dessinateur, -trice *mf* (humoristique).

cartridge ['kɑːtrɪdʒ] *n* (*of firearm, pen, camera, tape deck*) cartouche *f*; (*of record player*) cellule *f*; **c. belt** cartouchière *f*.

carv/e [kɑːv] *vt* (*cut*) tailler (**out of** dans); (*sculpt*) sculpter; (*initials etc*) graver; **to c. (up)** (*meat*) découper; **to c. up** (*country*) dépecer, morceler; **to c. out sth for oneself** (*career etc*) se tailler qch. ◆**—ing** *n* **(wood) c.** sculpture *f* (sur bois).

cascade [kæs'keɪd] *n* (*of rocks*) chute *f*; (*of*

blows) déluge *m*; (*of lace*) flot *m*; – *vi* tomber; (*hang*) pendre.

case [keɪs] *n* **1** (*instance*) & *Med* cas *m*; *Jur* affaire *f*; *Phil* arguments *mpl*; **in any c.** en tout cas; **in c. it rains** au cas où il pleuvrait; **in c. of** en cas de; **(just) in c.** à tout hasard. **2** (*bag*) valise *f*; (*crate*) caisse *f*; (*for pen, glasses, camera, violin, cigarettes*) étui *m*; (*for jewels*) coffret *m*. ◆**casing** *n* (*covering*) enveloppe *f*.

cash [kæʃ] *n* argent *m*; **to pay (in) c.** (*not by cheque*) payer en espèces *or* en liquide; **to pay c. (down)** payer comptant; **c. price** prix *m* (au) comptant; **c. box** caisse *f*; **c. desk** caisse *f*; **c. register** caisse *f* enregistreuse; – *vt* (*banknote*) changer; **to c. a cheque** (*of person*) encaisser un chèque; (*of bank*) payer un chèque; **to c. in on** *Fam* profiter de. ◆**ca'shier** **1** *n* caissier, -ière *mf*. **2** *vt* (*dismiss*) *Mil* casser.

cashew ['kæʃuː] *n* (*nut*) cajou *m*.

cashmere ['kæʃmɪər] *n* cachemire *m*.

casino [kə'siːnəʊ] *n* (*pl* **-os**) casino *m*.

cask [kɑːsk] *n* fût *m*, tonneau *m*. ◆**casket** *n* (*box*) coffret *m*; (*coffin*) cercueil *m*.

casserole ['kæsərəʊl] *n* (*covered dish*) cocotte *f*; (*stew*) ragoût *m* en cocotte.

cassette [kə'set] *n* cassette *f*; *Phot* cartouche *f*; **c. player** lecteur *m* de cassettes; **c. recorder** magnétophone *m* à cassettes.

cassock ['kæsək] *n* soutane *f*.

cast [kɑːst] **1** *n* *Th* acteurs *mpl*; (*list*) *Th* distribution *f*; (*mould*) moulage *m*; (*of dice*) coup *m*; *Med* plâtre *m*; (*squint*) léger strabisme *m*; **c. of mind** tournure *f* d'esprit. **2** *vt* (*pt & pp* **cast**) (*throw*) jeter; (*light, shadow*) projeter; (*blame*) rejeter; (*glance*) jeter; (*doubt*) exprimer; (*lose*) perdre; (*metal*) couler; (*role*) *Th* distribuer; (*actor*) donner un rôle à; **to c. one's mind back** se reporter en arrière; **to c. a vote** voter; **to c. aside** rejeter; **to c. off** (*chains etc*) se libérer de; (*shed, lose*) se dépouiller de; *Fig* abandonner. **3** *vi* **to c. off** *Nau* appareiller. **4** *n* **c. iron** fonte *f*. ◆**c.-'iron** *a* (*pan etc*) en fonte; (*will etc*) *Fig* de fer, solide.

castaway ['kɑːstəweɪ] *n* naufragé, -ée *mf*.

caste [kɑːst] *n* caste *f*.

caster ['kɑːstər] *n* (*wheel*) roulette *f*; **c. sugar** sucre *m* en poudre.

castle ['kɑːs(ə)l] *n* château *m*; (*in chess*) tour *f*.

castoffs ['kɑːstɒfs] *npl* vieux vêtements *mpl*.

castor ['kɑːstər] *n* (*wheel*) roulette *f*; **c. oil** huile *f* de ricin; **c. sugar** sucre *m* en poudre.

castrate [kæ'streɪt] *vt* châtrer. ◆**castration** *n* castration *f*.

casual ['kæʒjʊəl] *a* (*meeting*) fortuit; (*remark*) fait en passant; (*stroll*) sans but; (*offhand*) désinvolte, insouciant; (*worker*) temporaire; (*work*) irrégulier; **c. clothes** vêtements *mpl* sport; **a c. acquaintance** quelqu'un que l'on connaît un peu. ◆**—ly** *adv* par hasard; (*informally*) avec désinvolture; (*to remark*) en passant.

casualty ['kæʒjʊəltɪ] *n* (*dead*) mort *m*, morte *f*; (*wounded*) blessé, -ée *mf*; (*accident victim*) accidenté, -ée *mf*; **casualties** morts et blessés *mpl*; *Mil* pertes *fpl*; **c. department** *Med* service *m* des accidentés.

cat [kæt] *n* chat *m*, chatte *f*; **c. burglar** monte-en-l'air *m* *inv*; **c.'s eyes®** cataphotes® *mpl*, clous *mpl*. ◆**catcall** *n* sifflet *m*, huée *f*.

cataclysm ['kætəklɪzəm] *n* cataclysme *m*.

catalogue ['kætəlɒg] (*Am* **catalog**) *n* catalogue *m*; – *vt* cataloguer.

catalyst ['kætəlɪst] *n* *Ch* & *Fig* catalyseur *m*.

catapult ['kætəpʌlt] *n* lance-pierres *m* *inv*; *Hist Av* catapulte *f*; – *vt* catapulter.

cataract ['kætərækt] *n* (*waterfall*) & *Med* cataracte *f*.

catarrh [kə'tɑːr] *n* catarrhe *m*, rhume *m*.

catastrophe [kə'tæstrəfɪ] *n* catastrophe *f*. ◆**cata'strophic** *a* catastrophique.

catch [kætʃ] *vt* (*pt & pp* **caught**) (*ball, thief, illness etc*) attraper; (*grab*) prendre, saisir; (*surprise*) (sur)prendre; (*understand*) saisir; (*train etc*) attraper, (réussir à) prendre; (*attention*) attirer; (*of nail etc*) accrocher; (*finger etc*) se prendre (**in** dans); **to c. sight of** apercevoir; **to c. fire** prendre feu; **to c. s.o. (in)** *Fam* trouver qn (chez soi); **to c. one's breath** (*rest a while*) reprendre haleine; (*stop breathing*) retenir son souffle; **I didn't c. the train/***etc* j'ai manqué le train/*etc*; **to c. s.o. out** prendre qn en défaut; **to c. s.o. up** rattraper qn; – *vi* (*of fire*) prendre; **her skirt (got) caught in the door** sa jupe s'est prise *or* coincée dans la porte; **to c. on** prendre, devenir populaire; (*understand*) saisir; **to c. up** se rattraper; **to c. up with s.o.** rattraper qn; – *n* capture *f*, prise *f*; (*trick, snare*) piège *m*; (*on door*) loquet *m*. ◆**—ing** *a* contagieux. ◆**catchphrase** *n*, ◆**catchword** *n* slogan *m*.

catchy ['kætʃɪ] *a* (**-ier, -iest**) (*tune*) *Fam* facile à retenir.

catechism ['kætɪkɪzəm] *n* *Rel* catéchisme *m*.

category ['kætɪgərɪ] *n* catégorie *f*. ◆**cate-**

'gorical *a* catégorique. ◆**categorize** *vt* classer (par catégories).
cater ['keɪtər] *vi* s'occuper de la nourriture; **to c. for** *or* **to** (*need, taste*) satisfaire; (*readership*) *Journ* s'adresser à. ◆**—ing** *n* restauration *f*. ◆**—er** *n* traiteur *m*.
caterpillar ['kætəpɪlər] *n* chenille *f*.
catgut ['kætgʌt] *n* (*cord*) boyau *m*.
cathedral [kə'θiːdrəl] *n* cathédrale *f*.
catholic ['kæθlɪk] **1** *a* & *n* **C.** catholique (*mf*). **2** *a* (*taste*) universel; (*view*) libéral. ◆**Ca'tholicism** *n* catholicisme *m*.
cattle ['kæt(ə)l] *npl* bétail *m*, bestiaux *mpl*.
catty ['kætɪ] *a* (**-ier, -iest**) *Fam* rosse, méchant.
caucus ['kɔːkəs] *n* *Pol Am* comité *m* électoral.
caught [kɔːt] *see* **catch**.
cauldron ['kɔːldrən] *n* chaudron *m*.
cauliflower ['kɒlɪflaʊər] *n* chou-fleur *m*.
cause [kɔːz] *n* cause *f*; (*reason*) raison *f*; **c. for complaint** sujet *m* de plainte; – *vt* causer, occasionner; (*trouble*) créer, causer (**for** à); **to c. sth to move/***etc* faire bouger/*etc* qch.
causeway ['kɔːzweɪ] *n* chaussée *f*.
caustic ['kɔːstɪk] *a* (*remark, substance*) caustique.
cauterize ['kɔːtəraɪz] *vt* *Med* cautériser.
caution ['kɔːʃ(ə)n] *n* (*care*) prudence *f*, précaution *f*; (*warning*) avertissement *m*; – *vt* (*warn*) avertir; **to c. s.o. against sth** mettre qn en garde contre qch. ◆**cautionary** *a* (*tale*) moral. ◆**cautious** *a* prudent, circonspect. ◆**cautiously** *adv* prudemment.
cavalcade ['kævəlkeɪd] *n* (*procession*) cavalcade *f*.
cavalier [kævə'lɪər] **1** *a* (*selfish*) cavalier. **2** *n* (*horseman, knight*) *Hist* cavalier *m*.
cavalry ['kævəlrɪ] *n* cavalerie *f*.
cave [keɪv] **1** *n* caverne *f*, grotte *f*. **2** *vi* **to c. in** (*fall in*) s'effondrer. ◆**caveman** *n* (*pl* **-men**) homme *m* des cavernes. ◆**cavern** ['kævən] *n* caverne *f*.
caviar(e) ['kævɪɑːr] *n* caviar *m*.
cavity ['kævɪtɪ] *n* cavité *f*.
cavort [kə'vɔːt] *vi* *Fam* cabrioler; **to c. naked/***etc* se balader tout nu/*etc*.
cease [siːs] *vti* cesser (**doing** de faire). ◆**c.-fire** *n* cessez-le-feu *m inv*. ◆**ceaseless** *a* incessant. ◆**ceaselessly** *adv* sans cesse.
cedar ['siːdər] *n* (*tree, wood*) cèdre *m*.
cedilla [sɪ'dɪlə] *n* *Gram* cédille *f*.
ceiling ['siːlɪŋ] *n* (*of room, on wages etc*) plafond *m*.
celebrat/e ['selɪbreɪt] *vt* (*event*) fêter; (*mass, s.o.'s merits etc*) célébrer; – *vi* faire la fête; **we should c. (that)!** il faut fêter ça! ◆**—ed** *a* célèbre. ◆**cele'bration** *n* fête *f*; **the c. of** (*marriage etc*) la célébration de. ◆**ce'lebrity** *n* (*person*) célébrité *f*.
celery ['selərɪ] *n* céleri *m*.
celibate ['selɪbət] *a* (*abstaining from sex*) célibataire; (*monk etc*) abstinent. ◆**celibacy** *n* (*of young person etc*) célibat *m*; (*of monk etc*) abstinence *f*.
cell [sel] *n* cellule *f*; *El* élément *m*. ◆**cellular** *a* cellulaire; **c. blanket** couverture *f* en cellular.
cellar ['selər] *n* cave *f*.
cello ['tʃeləʊ] *n* (*pl* **-os**) violoncelle *m*. ◆**cellist** *n* violoncelliste *mf*.
cellophane® ['seləfeɪn] *n* cellophane® *f*.
celluloid ['seljʊlɔɪd] *n* celluloïd *m*.
cellulose ['seljʊləʊs] *n* cellulose *f*.
Celsius ['selsɪəs] *a* Celsius *inv*.
Celt [kelt] *n* Celte *mf*. ◆**Celtic** *a* celtique, celte.
cement [sɪ'ment] *n* ciment *m*; **c. mixer** bétonnière *f*; – *vt* cimenter.
cemetery ['semətrɪ, *Am* 'semǝterɪ] *n* cimetière *m*.
cenotaph ['senətɑːf] *n* cénotaphe *m*.
censor ['sensər] *n* censeur *m*; – *vt* (*film etc*) censurer. ◆**censorship** *n* censure *f*.
censure ['senʃər] *vt* blâmer; *Pol* censurer; – *n* blâme *m*; **c. motion, vote of c.** motion *f* de censure.
census ['sensəs] *n* recensement *m*.
cent [sent] *n* (*coin*) cent *m*; **per c.** pour cent.
centenary [sen'tiːnərɪ, *Am* sen'tenərɪ] *n* centenaire *m*.
centigrade ['sentɪgreɪd] *a* centigrade.
centimetre ['sentɪmiːtər] *n* centimètre *m*.
centipede ['sentɪpiːd] *n* mille-pattes *m inv*.
centre ['sentər] *n* centre *m*; **c. forward** *Fb* avant-centre *m*; – *vt* centrer; – *vi* **to c. on** (*of thoughts*) se concentrer sur; (*of question*) tourner autour de. ◆**central** *a* central. ◆**centralize** *vt* centraliser. ◆**centrifugal** [sen'trɪfjʊgəl] *a* centrifuge.
century ['sentʃərɪ] *n* siècle *m*; (*score*) *Sp* cent points *mpl*.
ceramic [sə'ræmɪk] *a* (*tile etc*) de *or* en céramique; – *npl* (*objects*) céramiques *fpl*; (*art*) céramique *f*.
cereal ['sɪərɪəl] *n* céréale *f*.
cerebral ['serɪbrəl, *Am* sə'riːbrəl] *a* cérébral.
ceremony ['serɪmənɪ] *n* (*event*) cérémonie *f*; **to stand on c.** faire des cérémonies *or* des façons. ◆**cere'monial** *a* de cérémonie; –

n cérémonial *m.* ◆**cere'monious** *a* cérémonieux.

certain ['sɜːtən] *a* (*particular, some*) certain; (*sure*) sûr, certain; **she's c. to come, she'll come for c.** c'est certain *or* sûr qu'elle viendra; **I'm not c. what to do** je ne sais pas très bien ce qu'il faut faire; **to be c. of sth/that** être certain de qch/que; **for c.** (*to say, know*) avec certitude; **be c. to go!** vas-y sans faute!; **to make c. of** (*fact*) s'assurer de; (*seat etc*) s'assurer. ◆**—ly** *adv* certainement; (*yes*) bien sûr; (*without fail*) sans faute; (*without any doubt*) sans aucun doute. ◆**certainty** *n* certitude *f.*

certificate [sə'tɪfɪkɪt] *n* certificat *m*; *Univ* diplôme *m.*

certify ['sɜːtɪfaɪ] *vt* certifier; **to c. (insane)** déclarer dément; – *vi* **to c. to sth** attester qch.

cervix ['sɜːvɪks] *n* col *m* de l'utérus.

cesspool ['sespuːl] *n* fosse *f* d'aisances; *Fig* cloaque *f.*

chafe [tʃeɪf] *vt* (*skin*) *Lit* frotter.

chaff [tʃæf] *vt* (*tease*) taquiner.

chaffinch ['tʃæfɪntʃ] *n* (*bird*) pinson *m.*

chagrin ['ʃægrɪn, *Am* ʃə'grɪn] *n* contrariété *f*; – *vt* contrarier.

chain [tʃeɪn] *n* (*of rings, mountains*) chaîne *f*; (*of ideas, events*) enchaînement *m*, suite *f*; (*of lavatory*) chasse *f* d'eau; **c. reaction** réaction *f* en chaîne; **to be a c.-smoker, to c.-smoke** fumer cigarette sur cigarette, fumer comme un pompier; **c. saw** tronçonneuse *f*; **c. store** magasin *m* à succursales multiples; – *vt* **to c. (down)** enchaîner; **to c. (up)** (*dog*) mettre à l'attache.

chair [tʃeər] *n* chaise *f*; (*armchair*) fauteuil *m*; *Univ* chaire *f*; **the c.** (*office*) la présidence; **c. lift** télésiège *m*; – *vt* (*meeting*) présider. ◆**chairman** *n* (*pl* **-men**) président, -ente *mf.* ◆**chairmanship** *n* présidence *f.*

chalet ['ʃæleɪ] *n* chalet *m.*

chalk [tʃɔːk] *n* craie *f*; **not by a long c.** loin de là, tant s'en faut; – *vt* marquer *or* écrire à la craie; **to c. up** (*success*) *Fig* remporter. ◆**chalky** *a* (**-ier, -iest**) crayeux.

challeng/e ['tʃælɪndʒ] *n* défi *m*; (*task*) gageure *f*; *Mil* sommation *f*; **c. for** (*bid*) tentative *f* d'obtenir; – *vt* défier (**s.o. to do** qn de faire); (*dispute*) contester; **to c. s.o. to a game** inviter qn à jouer; **to c. s.o. to a duel** provoquer qn en duel. ◆**—ing** *a* (*job*) exigeant; (*book*) stimulant. ◆**—er** *n* *Sp* challenger *m.*

chamber ['tʃeɪmbər] *n* chambre *f*; (*of judge*) cabinet *m*; – *a* (*music, orchestra*) de chambre; **c. pot** pot *m* de chambre. ◆**chambermaid** *n* femme *f* de chambre.

chameleon [kə'miːlɪən] *n* (*reptile*) caméléon *m.*

chamois ['ʃæmɪ] *n* **c. (leather)** peau *f* de chamois.

champagne [ʃæm'peɪn] *n* champagne *m.*

champion ['tʃæmpɪən] *n* champion, -onne *mf*; **c. skier** champion, -onne du ski; – *vt* (*support*) se faire le champion de. ◆**championship** *n* *Sp* championnat *m.*

chance [tʃɑːns] *n* (*luck*) hasard *m*; (*possibility*) chances *fpl*, possibilité *f*; (*opportunity*) occasion *f*; (*risk*) risque *m*; **by c.** par hasard; **by any c.** (*possibly*) par hasard; **on the off c. (that) you could help me** au cas où tu pourrais m'aider; – *a* (*remark*) fait au hasard; (*occurrence*) accidentel; – *vt* **to c. doing** prendre le risque de faire; **to c. to find/*etc*** trouver/*etc* par hasard; **to c. it** risquer le coup; – *v imp* **it chanced that** (*happened*) il s'est trouvé que.

chancel ['tʃɑːnsəl] *n* (*in church*) chœur *m.*

chancellor ['tʃɑːnsələr] *n* *Pol Jur* chancelier *m.* ◆**chancellery** *n* chancellerie *f.*

chandelier [ʃændə'lɪər] *n* lustre *m.*

chang/e [tʃeɪndʒ] *n* changement *m*; (*money*) monnaie *f*; **for a c.** pour changer; **it makes a c. from** ça change de; **to have a c. of heart** changer d'avis; **a c. of clothes** des vêtements de rechange; – *vt* (*modify*) changer; (*exchange*) échanger (**for** contre); (*money*) changer; (*transform*) transformer (**into** en); **to c. trains/one's skirt/*etc*** changer de train/de jupe/*etc*; **to c. gear** *Aut* changer de vitesse; **to c. the subject** changer de sujet; – *vi* (*alter*) changer; (*change clothes*) se changer; **to c. over** passer. ◆**—ing** *n* (*of guard*) relève *f*; **c. room** vestiaire *m.* ◆**changeable** *a* (*weather, mood etc*) changeant, variable. ◆**changeless** *a* immuable. ◆**changeover** *n* passage *m* (**from** de, **to** à).

channel ['tʃæn(ə)l] *n* (*navigable*) chenal *m*; *TV* chaîne *f*, canal *m*; (*groove*) rainure *f*; *Fig* direction *f*; **through the c. of** par le canal de; **the C.** *Geog* la Manche; **the C. Islands** les îles anglo-normandes; – *vt* (**-ll-**, *Am* **-l-**) (*energies, crowd etc*) canaliser (**into** vers).

chant [tʃɑːnt] *n* (*of demonstrators*) chant *m* scandé; *Rel* psalmodie *f*; – *vt* (*slogan*) scander; – *vi* scander des slogans.

chaos ['keɪɒs] *n* chaos *m.* ◆**cha'otic** *a* chaotique.

chap [tʃæp] **1** *n* (*fellow*) *Fam* type *m*; **old c.!**

mon vieux! **2** *n* (*on skin*) gerçure *f*; – *vi* (**-pp-**) se gercer; – *vt* gercer.

chapel ['tʃæp(ə)l] *n* chapelle *f*; (*nonconformist church*) temple *m*.

chaperon(e) ['ʃæpərəʊn] *n* chaperon *m*; – *vt* chaperonner.

chaplain ['tʃæplɪn] *n* aumônier *m*.

chapter ['tʃæptər] *n* chapitre *m*.

char [tʃɑːr] **1** *vt* (**-rr-**) (*convert to carbon*) carboniser; (*scorch*) brûler légèrement. **2** *n* *Fam* femme *f* de ménage; – *vi* **to go charring** *Fam* faire des ménages. **3** *n* (*tea*) *Sl* thé *m*.

character ['kærɪktər] *n* (*of person, place etc*) & *Typ* caractère *m*; (*in book, film*) personnage *m*; (*strange person*) numéro *m*; **c. actor** acteur *m* de genre. ◆**characte'ristic** *a* & *n* caractéristique (*f*). ◆**characte'ristically** *adv* typiquement. ◆**characterize** *vt* caractériser.

charade [ʃə'rɑːd] *n* (*game*) charade *f* (mimée); (*travesty*) parodie *f*, comédie *f*.

charcoal ['tʃɑːkəʊl] *n* charbon *m* (de bois); (*crayon*) fusain *m*, charbon *m*.

charge [tʃɑːdʒ] *n* (*in battle*) *Mil* charge *f*; *Jur* accusation *f*; (*cost*) prix *m*; (*responsibility*) responsabilité *f*, charge *f*; (*care*) garde *f*; *pl* (*expenses*) frais *mpl*; **there's a c. (for it)** c'est payant; **free of c.** gratuit; **extra c.** supplément *m*; **to take c. of** prendre en charge; **to be in c. of** (*child etc*) avoir la garde de; (*office etc*) être responsable de; **the person in c.** le *or* la responsable; **who's in c. here?** qui commande ici?; – *vt* *Mil El* charger; *Jur* accuser, inculper; **to c. s.o.** *Com* faire payer qn; **to c. (up) to** *Com* mettre sur le compte de; **how much do you c.?** combien demandez-vous?; – *vi* (*rush*) se précipiter; **c.!** *Mil* chargez! ◆**—able** *a* **c. to** aux frais de. ◆**charger** *n* (*for battery*) chargeur *m*.

chariot ['tʃærɪət] *n* *Mil* char *m*.

charisma [kə'rɪzmə] *n* magnétisme *m*.

charity ['tʃærɪtɪ] *n* (*kindness, alms*) charité *f*; (*society*) fondation *f* *or* œuvre *f* charitable; **to give to c.** faire la charité. ◆**charitable** *a* charitable.

charlady ['tʃɑːleɪdɪ] *n* femme *f* de ménage.

charlatan ['ʃɑːlətən] *n* charlatan *m*.

charm [tʃɑːm] *n* (*attractiveness, spell*) charme *m*; (*trinket*) amulette *f*; – *vt* charmer. ◆**—ing** *a* charmant. ◆**—ingly** *adv* d'une façon charmante.

chart [tʃɑːt] *n* (*map*) carte *f*; (*graph*) graphique *m*, tableau *m*; **(pop) charts** hit-parade *m*; **flow c.** organigramme *m*; – *vt* (*route*) porter sur la carte; (*figures*) faire le graphique de; (*of graph*) montrer.

charter ['tʃɑːtər] *n* (*document*) charte *f*; (*aircraft*) charter *m*; **the c. of** (*hiring*) l'affrètement *m* de; **c. flight** charter *m*; – *vt* (*aircraft etc*) affréter. ◆**—ed** *a* **c. accountant** expert-comptable *m*.

charwoman ['tʃɑːwʊmən] *n* (*pl* **-women**) femme *f* de ménage.

chary ['tʃeərɪ] *a* (**-ier, -iest**) (*cautious*) prudent.

chase [tʃeɪs] *n* poursuite *f*, chasse *f*; **to give c.** se lancer à la poursuite (**to** de); – *vt* poursuivre; **to c. away** *or* **off** chasser; **to c. sth up** *Fam* essayer d'obtenir qch, rechercher qch; – *vi* **to c. after** courir après.

chasm ['kæzəm] *n* abîme *m*, gouffre *m*.

chassis ['ʃæsɪ, *Am* 'tʃæsɪ] *n* *Aut* châssis *m*.

chaste [tʃeɪst] *a* chaste. ◆**chastity** *n* chasteté *f*.

chasten ['tʃeɪs(ə)n] *vt* (*punish*) châtier; (*cause to improve*) faire se corriger, assagir. ◆**—ing** *a* (*experience*) instructif.

chastise [tʃæ'staɪz] *vt* punir.

chat [tʃæt] *n* causette *f*; **to have a c.** bavarder; – *vi* (**-tt-**) causer, bavarder; – *vt* **to c. up** *Fam* baratiner, draguer. ◆**chatty** *a* (**-ier, -iest**) (*person*) bavard; (*style*) familier; (*text*) plein de bavardages.

chatter ['tʃætər] *vi* bavarder; (*of birds, monkeys*) jacasser; **his teeth are chattering** il claque des dents; – *n* bavardage *m*; jacassement *m*. ◆**chatterbox** *n* bavard, -arde *mf*.

chauffeur ['ʃəʊfər] *n* chauffeur *m* (de maître).

chauvinist ['ʃəʊvɪnɪst] *n* & *a* chauvin, -ine (*mf*); **male c.** *Pej* phallocrate *m*.

cheap [tʃiːp] *a* (**-er, -est**) bon marché *inv*, pas cher; (*rate etc*) réduit; (*worthless*) sans valeur; (*superficial*) facile; (*mean, petty*) mesquin; **cheaper** moins cher, meilleur marché; – *adv* (*to buy*) (à) bon marché, au rabais; (*to feel*) humilié. ◆**cheapen** *vt* *Fig* déprécier. ◆**cheaply** *adv* (à) bon marché. ◆**cheapness** *n* bas prix *m*; *Fig* mesquinerie *f*.

cheat [tʃiːt] *vt* (*deceive*) tromper; (*defraud*) frauder; **to c. s.o. out of sth** escroquer qch à qn; **to c. on** (*wife, husband*) faire une infidélité *or* des infidélités à; – *vi* tricher; (*defraud*) frauder; – *n* (*at games etc*) tricheur, -euse *mf*; (*crook*) escroc *m*. ◆**—ing** *n* (*deceit*) tromperie *f*; (*trickery*) tricherie *f*. ◆**—er** *n* *Am* = **cheat**.

check[1] [tʃek] *vt* (*examine*) vérifier; (*inspect*) contrôler; (*tick*) cocher, pointer; (*stop*) arrêter, enrayer; (*restrain*) contenir, maîtriser; (*rebuke*) réprimander; (*baggage*) *Am* mettre à la consigne; **to c. in** (*luggage*) *Av* enregistrer; **to c. sth out** confirmer qch; – *vi* vérifier; **to c. in** (*at hotel etc*) signer le registre; (*arrive at hotel*) arriver; (*at airport*) se présenter (à l'enregistrement), enregistrer ses bagages; **to c. on sth** vérifier qch; **to c. out** (*at hotel etc*) régler sa note; **to c. up** vérifier, se renseigner; – *n* vérification *f*; contrôle *m*; (*halt*) arrêt *m*; *Chess* échec *m*; (*curb*) frein *m*; (*tick*) = croix *f*; (*receipt*) *Am* reçu *m*; (*bill in restaurant etc*) *Am* addition *f*; (*cheque*) *Am* chèque *m*. ◆**c.-in** *n Av* enregistrement *m* (des bagages). ◆**checking account** *n Am* compte *m* courant. ◆**checkmate** *n Chess* échec et mat *m*. ◆**checkout** *n* (*in supermarket*) caisse *f*. ◆**checkpoint** *n* contrôle *m*. ◆**checkroom** *n Am* vestiaire *m*; (*left-luggage office*) *Am* consigne *f*. ◆**checkup** *n* bilan *m* de santé.

check[2] [tʃek] *n* (*pattern*) carreaux *mpl*; – *a* à carreaux. ◆**checked** *a* à carreaux.

checkered ['tʃekəd] *a Am* = **chequered**.

checkers ['tʃekəz] *npl Am* jeu *m* de dames.

cheddar ['tʃedər] *n* (*cheese*) cheddar *m*.

cheek [tʃiːk] *n* joue *f*; (*impudence*) *Fig* culot *m*. ◆**cheekbone** *n* pommette *f*. ◆**cheeky** *a* (**-ier, -iest**) (*person, reply etc*) effronté.

cheep [tʃiːp] *vi* (*of bird*) piauler.

cheer[1] [tʃɪər] *n* **cheers** (*shouts*) acclamations *fpl*; **cheers!** *Fam* à votre santé! – *vt* (*applaud*) acclamer; **to c. on** encourager; **to c. (up)** donner du courage à; (*amuse*) égayer; – *vi* applaudir; **to c. up** prendre courage; s'égayer; **c. up!** (du) courage! ◆**—ing** *n* (*shouts*) acclamations *fpl*; – *a* (*encouraging*) réjouissant.

cheer[2] [tʃɪər] *n* (*gaiety*) joie *f*; **good c.** (*food*) la bonne chère. ◆**cheerful** *a* gai. ◆**cheerfully** *adv* gaiement. ◆**cheerless** *a* morne.

cheerio! [tʃɪərɪ'əʊ] *int* salut!, au revoir!

cheese [tʃiːz] *n* fromage *m*. ◆**cheeseburger** *n* cheeseburger *m*. ◆**cheesecake** *n* tarte *f* au fromage blanc. ◆**cheesed** *a* **to be c. (off)** *Fam* en avoir marre (with de). ◆**cheesy** *a* (**-ier, -iest**) (*shabby, bad*) *Am Fam* miteux.

cheetah ['tʃiːtə] *n* guépard *m*.

chef [ʃef] *n Culin* chef *m*.

chemistry ['kemɪstrɪ] *n* chimie *f*. ◆**chemical** *a* chimique; – *n* produit *m* chimique. ◆**chemist** *n* (*dispensing*) pharmacien, -ienne *mf*; (*scientist*) chimiste *mf*; **chemist('s)** (*shop*) pharmacie *f*.

cheque [tʃek] *n* chèque *m*. ◆**chequebook** *n* carnet *m* de chèques.

chequered ['tʃekəd] *a* (*pattern*) à carreaux; (*career etc*) qui connaît des hauts et des bas.

cherish ['tʃerɪʃ] *vt* (*person*) chérir; (*hope*) nourrir, caresser.

cherry ['tʃerɪ] *n* cerise *f*; – *a* cerise *inv*; **c. brandy** cherry *m*.

chess [tʃes] *n* échecs *mpl*. ◆**chessboard** *n* échiquier *m*.

chest [tʃest] *n* **1** *Anat* poitrine *f*. **2** (*box*) coffre *m*; **c. of drawers** commode *f*.

chestnut ['tʃestnʌt] *n* châtaigne *f*, marron *m*; – *a* (*hair*) châtain; **c. tree** châtaignier *m*.

chew [tʃuː] *vt* **to c. (up)** mâcher; **to c. over** *Fig* ruminer; – *vi* mastiquer; **chewing gum** chewing-gum *m*.

chick [tʃɪk] *n* poussin *m*; (*girl*) *Fam* nana *f*. ◆**chicken** **1** *n* poulet *m*; *pl* (*poultry*) volaille *f*; **it's c. feed** *Fam* c'est deux fois rien, c'est une bagatelle. **2** *a Fam* froussard; – *vi* **to c. out** *Fam* se dégonfler. ◆**chickenpox** *n* varicelle *f*.

chickpea ['tʃɪkpiː] *n* pois *m* chiche.

chicory ['tʃɪkərɪ] *n* (*in coffee etc*) chicorée *f*; (*for salad*) endive *f*.

chide [tʃaɪd] *vt* gronder.

chief [tʃiːf] *n* chef *m*; (*boss*) *Fam* patron *m*, chef *m*; **in c.** (*commander, editor*) en chef; – *a* (*main, highest in rank*) principal. ◆**—ly** *adv* principalement, surtout. ◆**chieftain** *n* (*of clan etc*) chef *m*.

chilblain ['tʃɪlbleɪn] *n* engelure *f*.

child, *pl* **children** [tʃaɪld, 'tʃɪldrən] *n* enfant *mf*; **c. care** *or* **welfare** protection *f* de l'enfance; **child's play** *Fig* jeu *m* d'enfant; **c. minder** gardien, -ienne *mf* d'enfants. ◆**childbearing** *n* (*act*) accouchement *m*; (*motherhood*) maternité *f*. ◆**childbirth** *n* accouchement *m*, couches *fpl*. ◆**childhood** *n* enfance *f*. ◆**childish** *a* puéril, enfantin. ◆**childishness** *n* puérilité *f*. ◆**childlike** *a* naïf, innocent.

chill [tʃɪl] *n* froid *m*; (*coldness in feelings*) froideur *f*; *Med* refroidissement *m*; **to catch a c.** prendre froid; – *vt* (*wine, melon*) faire rafraîchir; (*meat, food*) réfrigérer; **to c. s.o.** (*with fear, cold etc*) faire frissonner qn (**with** de); **to be chilled to the bone** être transi. ◆**—ed** *a* (*wine*) frais. ◆**chilly** *a* (**-ier, -iest**) froid; (*sensitive to cold*) frileux; **it's c.** il fait (un peu) froid.

chilli ['tʃɪlɪ] *n* (*pl* **-ies**) piment *m* (de Cayenne).

chime [tʃaɪm] *vi* (*of bell*) carillonner; (*of clock*) sonner; **to c. in** (*interrupt*) interrompre; – *n* carillon *m*; sonnerie *f*.

chimney ['tʃɪmnɪ] *n* cheminée *f*. ◆**chimneypot** *n* tuyau *m* de cheminée. ◆**chimneysweep** *n* ramoneur *m*.

chimpanzee [tʃɪmpæn'ziː] *n* chimpanzé *m*.

chin [tʃɪn] *n* menton *m*.

china ['tʃaɪnə] *n inv* porcelaine *f*; – *a* en porcelaine. ◆**chinaware** *n* (*objects*) porcelaine *f*.

China ['tʃaɪnə] *n* Chine *f*. ◆**Chi'nese** *a* & *n* chinois, -oise (*mf*); – *n* (*language*) chinois *m*.

chink [tʃɪŋk] **1** *n* (*slit*) fente *f*. **2** *vi* tinter; – *vt* faire tinter; – *n* tintement *m*.

chip [tʃɪp] *vt* (**-pp-**) (*cup etc*) ébrécher; (*table etc*) écorner; (*paint*) écailler; (*cut*) tailler; – *vi* **to c. in** *Fam* contribuer; – *n* (*splinter*) éclat *m*; (*break*) ébréchure *f*; écornure *f*; (*microchip*) puce *f*; (*counter*) jeton *m*; *pl* (*French fries*) frites *fpl*; (*crisps*) *Am* chips *mpl*. ◆**chipboard** *n* (bois *m*) aggloméré *m*. ◆**chippings** *npl* **road** *or* **loose c.** gravillons *mpl*.

chiropodist [kɪ'rɒpədɪst] *n* pédicure *mf*.

chirp [tʃɜːp] *vi* (*of bird*) pépier; – *n* pépiement *m*.

chirpy ['tʃɜːpɪ] *a* (**-ier, -iest**) gai, plein d'entrain.

chisel ['tʃɪz(ə)l] *n* ciseau *m*; – *vt* (**-ll-**, *Am* **-l-**) ciseler.

chit [tʃɪt] *n* (*paper*) note *f*, billet *m*.

chitchat ['tʃɪttʃæt] *n* bavardage *m*.

chivalry ['ʃɪvəlrɪ] *n* (*practices etc*) chevalerie *f*; (*courtesy*) galanterie *f*. ◆**chivalrous** *a* (*man*) galant.

chives [tʃaɪvz] *npl* ciboulette *f*.

chloride ['klɔːraɪd] *n* chlorure *m*. ◆**chlorine** *n* chlore *m*. ◆**chloroform** *n* chloroforme *m*.

choc-ice ['tʃɒkaɪs] *n* (*ice cream*) esquimau *m*.

chock [tʃɒk] *n* (*wedge*) cale *f*; – *vt* caler.

chock-a-block [tʃɒkə'blɒk] *a*, ◆**c.-'full** *a Fam* archiplein.

chocolate ['tʃɒklɪt] *n* chocolat *m*; **milk c.** chocolat au lait; **plain** *or Am* **bittersweet c.** chocolat à croquer; – *a* (*cake*) au chocolat; (*colour*) chocolat *inv*.

choice [tʃɔɪs] *n* choix *m*; **from c., out of c.** de son propre choix; – *a* (*goods*) de choix.

choir ['kwaɪər] *n* chœur *m*. ◆**choirboy** *n* jeune choriste *m*.

chok/e [tʃəʊk] **1** *vt* (*person*) étrangler, étouffer; (*clog*) boucher, engorger; **to c. back** (*sobs etc*) étouffer; – *vi* s'étrangler, étouffer; **to c. on** (*fish bone etc*) s'étrangler avec. **2** *n Aut* starter *m*. ◆**—er** *n* (*scarf*) foulard *m*; (*necklace*) collier *m* (de chien).

cholera ['kɒlərə] *n* choléra *m*.

cholesterol [kə'lestərɒl] *n* cholestérol *m*.

choose [tʃuːz] *vt* (*pt* **chose**, *pp* **chosen**) choisir (**to do** de faire); **to c. to do** (*decide*) juger bon de faire; – *vi* choisir; **as I/you/etc c.** comme il me/vous/*etc* plaît. ◆**choos(e)y** *a* (**-sier, -siest**) difficile (**about** sur).

chop [tʃɒp] **1** *n* (*of lamb, pork*) côtelette *f*; **to lick one's chops** *Fig* s'en lécher les babines; **to get the c.** *Sl* être flanqué à la porte. **2** *vt* (**-pp-**) couper (à la hache); (*food*) hacher; **to c. down** (*tree*) abattre; **to c. off** trancher; **to c. up** hacher. **3** *vti* (**-pp-**) **to c. and change** changer constamment d'idées, de projets *etc*. ◆**chopper** *n* hachoir *m*; *Sl* hélicoptère *m*. ◆**choppy** *a* (*sea*) agité.

chopsticks ['tʃɒpstɪks] *npl Culin* baguettes *fpl*.

choral ['kɔːrəl] *a* choral; **c. society** chorale *f*. ◆**chorister** ['kɒrɪstər] *n* choriste *mf*.

chord [kɔːd] *n Mus* accord *m*.

chore [tʃɔːr] *n* travail *m* (routinier); (*unpleasant*) corvée *f*; *pl* (*domestic*) travaux *mpl* du ménage.

choreographer [kɒrɪ'ɒgrəfər] *n* chorégraphe *mf*.

chortle ['tʃɔːt(ə)l] *vi* glousser; – *n* gloussement *m*.

chorus ['kɔːrəs] *n* chœur *m*; (*dancers*) *Th* troupe *f*; (*of song*) refrain *m*; **c. girl** girl *f*.

chose, chosen [tʃəʊz, 'tʃəʊz(ə)n] *see* choose.

chowder ['tʃaʊdər] *n Am* soupe *f* aux poissons.

Christ [kraɪst] *n* Christ *m*. ◆**Christian** ['krɪstʃən] *a* & *n* chrétien, -ienne (*mf*); **C. name** prénom *m*. ◆**Christi'anity** *n* christianisme *m*.

christen ['krɪs(ə)n] *vt* (*name*) & *Rel* baptiser. ◆**—ing** *n* baptême *m*.

Christmas ['krɪsməs] *n* Noël *m*; **at C.** (**time**) à (la) Noël; **Merry C.** Joyeux Noël; **Father C.** le père Noël; – *a* (*tree, card, day, party etc*) de Noël; **C. box** étrennes *fpl*.

chrome [krəʊm] *n*, ◆**chromium** *n* chrome *m*.

chromosome ['krəʊməsəʊm] *n* chromosome *m*.

chronic ['krɒnɪk] *a* (*disease, state etc*) chronique; (*bad*) *Sl* atroce.

chronicle ['krɒnɪk(ə)l] *n* chronique *f*; – *vt* faire la chronique de.

chronology [krəˈnɒlədʒɪ] *n* chronologie *f*. ◆**chronoˈlogical** *a* chronologique.
chronometer [krəˈnɒmɪtər] *n* chronomètre *m*.
chrysanthemum [krɪˈsænθəməm] *n* chrysanthème *m*.
chubby [ˈtʃʌbɪ] *a* (**-ier, -iest**) (*body*) dodu; (*cheeks*) rebondi. ◆**c.-ˈcheeked** *a* joufflu.
chuck [tʃʌk] *vt Fam* jeter, lancer; **to c.** (**in**) *or* (**up**) (*give up*) *Fam* laisser tomber; **to c. away** *Fam* balancer; (*money*) gaspiller; **to c. out** *Fam* balancer.
chuckle [ˈtʃʌk(ə)l] *vi* glousser, rire; – *n* gloussement *m*.
chuffed [tʃʌft] *a Sl* bien content; (*displeased*) *Iron Sl* pas heureux.
chug [tʃʌg] *vi* (**-gg-**) **to c. along** (*of vehicle*) avancer lentement (*en faisant teuf-teuf*).
chum [tʃʌm] *n Fam* copain *m*. ◆**chummy** *a* (**-ier, -iest**) *Fam* amical; **c. with** copain avec.
chump [tʃʌmp] *n* (*fool*) crétin, -ine *mf*.
chunk [tʃʌŋk] *n* (gros) morceau *m*. ◆**chunky** *a* (**-ier, -iest**) (*person*) *Fam* trapu; (*coat, material etc*) de grosse laine.
church [tʃɜːtʃ] *n* église *f*; (*service*) office *m*; (*Catholic*) messe *f*; **c. hall** salle *f* paroissiale. ◆**churchgoer** *n* pratiquant, -ante *mf*. ◆**churchyard** *n* cimetière *m*.
churlish [ˈtʃɜːlɪʃ] *a* (*rude*) grossier; (*bad-tempered*) hargneux.
churn [tʃɜːn] **1** *n* (*for making butter*) baratte *f*; (*milk can*) bidon *m*. **2** *vt* **to c. out** *Pej* produire (en série).
chute [ʃuːt] *n* glissière *f*; (*in playground, pool*) toboggan *m*; (*for refuse*) vide-ordures *m inv*.
chutney [ˈtʃʌtnɪ] *n* condiment *m* épicé (*à base de fruits*).
cider [ˈsaɪdər] *n* cidre *m*.
cigar [sɪˈgɑːr] *n* cigare *m*. ◆**cigaˈrette** *n* cigarette *f*; **c. end** mégot *m*; **c. holder** fume-cigarette *m inv*; **c. lighter** briquet *m*.
cinch [sɪntʃ] *n* **it's a c.** *Fam* (*easy*) c'est facile; (*sure*) c'est (sûr et) certain.
cinder [ˈsɪndər] *n* cendre *f*; **c. track** *Sp* cendrée *f*.
Cinderella [sɪndəˈrelə] *n Liter* Cendrillon *f*; *Fig* parent *m* pauvre.
cine-camera [ˈsɪnɪkæmrə] *n* caméra *f*.
cinema [ˈsɪnəmə] *n* cinéma *m*. ◆**cinemagoer** *n* cinéphile *mf*. ◆**cinemascope** *n* cinémascope *m*.
cinnamon [ˈsɪnəmən] *n Bot Culin* cannelle *f*.
cipher [ˈsaɪfər] *n* (*code, number*) chiffre *m*; (*zero, person*) *Fig* zéro *m*.
circle [ˈsɜːk(ə)l] *n* (*shape, group, range etc*) cercle *m*; (*around eyes*) cerne *m*; *Th* balcon *m*; *pl* (*milieux*) milieux *mpl*; – *vt* (*move round*) faire le tour de; (*word etc*) entourer d'un cercle; – *vi* (*of aircraft, bird*) décrire des cercles. ◆**circular** *a* circulaire; – *n* (*letter*) circulaire *f*; (*advertisement*) prospectus *m*. ◆**circulate** *vi* circuler; – *vt* faire circuler. ◆**circuˈlation** *n* circulation *f*; *Journ* tirage *m*; **in c.** (*person*) *Fam* dans le circuit.
circuit [ˈsɜːkɪt] *n* circuit *m*; *Jur Th* tournée *f*; **c. breaker** *El* disjoncteur *m*. ◆**circuitous** [sɜːˈkjuːɪtəs] *a* (*route, means*) indirect. ◆**circuitry** *n El* circuits *mpl*.
circumcised [ˈsɜːkəmsaɪzd] *a* circoncis. ◆**circumˈcision** *n* circoncision *f*.
circumference [sɜːˈkʌmfərəns] *n* circonférence *f*.
circumflex [ˈsɜːkəmfleks] *n* circonflexe *m*.
circumscribe [ˈsɜːkəmskraɪb] *vt* circonscrire.
circumspect [ˈsɜːkəmspekt] *a* circonspect.
circumstance [ˈsɜːkəmstæns] *n* circonstance *f*; *pl Com* situation *f* financière; **in** *or* **under no circumstances** en aucun cas. ◆**circumˈstantial** *a* (*evidence*) *Jur* indirect.
circus [ˈsɜːkəs] *n Th Hist* cirque *m*.
cirrhosis [sɪˈrəʊsɪs] *n Med* cirrhose *f*.
cistern [ˈsɪstən] *n* (*in house*) réservoir *m* (d'eau).
citadel [ˈsɪtəd(ə)l] *n* citadelle *f*.
cite [saɪt] *vt* citer. ◆**citation** [saɪˈteɪʃ(ə)n] *n* citation *f*.
citizen [ˈsɪtɪz(ə)n] *n Pol Jur* citoyen, -enne *mf*; (*of town*) habitant, -ante *mf*; **Citizens' Band** *Rad* la CB. ◆**citizenship** *n* citoyenneté *f*.
citrus [ˈsɪtrəs] *a* **c. fruit(s)** agrumes *mpl*.
city [ˈsɪtɪ] *n* (grande) ville *f*, cité *f*; **c. dweller** citadin, -ine *mf*; **c. centre** centre-ville *m inv*; **c. hall** *Am* hôtel *m* de ville; **c. page** *Journ* rubrique *f* financière.
civic [ˈsɪvɪk] *a* (*duty*) civique; (*centre*) administratif; (*authorities*) municipal; – *npl* (*social science*) instruction *f* civique.
civil [ˈsɪv(ə)l] *a* **1** (*rights, war, marriage etc*) civil; **c. defence** défense *f* passive; **c. servant** fonctionnaire *mf*; **c. service** fonction *f* publique. **2** (*polite*) civil. ◆**ciˈvilian** *a & n* civil, -ile (*mf*). ◆**ciˈvility** *n* civilité *f*.
civilize [ˈsɪvɪlaɪz] *vt* civiliser. ◆**civiliˈzation** *n* civilisation *f*.
civvies [ˈsɪvɪz] *npl* **in c.** *Sl* (habillé) en civil.
clad [klæd] *a* vêtu (in de).
claim [kleɪm] *vt* (*one's due etc*) revendiquer, réclamer; (*require*) réclamer; **to c. that**

(*assert*) prétendre que; – *n* (*demand*) prétention *f*, revendication *f*; (*statement*) affirmation *f*; (*complaint*) réclamation *f*; (*right*) droit *m*; (*land*) concession *f*; **(insurance)** c. demande *f* d'indemnité; **to lay c. to** prétendre à. ◆**claimant** *n* allocataire *mf*.

clairvoyant [kleə'vɔɪənt] *n* voyant, -ante *mf*.

clam [klæm] *n* (*shellfish*) praire *f*.

clamber ['klæmbər] *vi* **to c. (up)** grimper; **to c. up** (*stairs*) grimper; (*mountain*) gravir.

clammy ['klæmɪ] *a* (*hands etc*) moite (et froid).

clamour ['klæmər] *n* clameur *f*; – *vi* vociférer (**against** contre); **to c. for** demander à grands cris.

clamp [klæmp] *n* crampon *m*; *Carp* serre-joint(s) *m*; **(wheel)** c. *Aut* sabot *m* (de Denver); – *vt* serrer; – *vi* **to c. down** *Fam* sévir (**on** contre). ◆**clampdown** *n* (*limitation*) *Fam* coup *m* d'arrêt, restriction *f*.

clan [klæn] *n* clan *m*.

clandestine [klæn'destɪn] *a* clandestin.

clang [klæŋ] *n* son *m* métallique. ◆**clanger** *n Sl* gaffe *f*; **to drop a c.** faire une gaffe.

clap [klæp] **1** *vti* **(-pp-)** (*applaud*) applaudir; **to c. (one's hands)** battre des mains; – *n* battement *m* (des mains); (*on back*) tape *f*; (*of thunder*) coup *m*. **2** *vt* **(-pp-)** (*put*) *Fam* fourrer. ◆**clapped-'out** *a* (*car, person*) *Sl* crevé. ◆**clapping** *n* applaudissements *mpl*. ◆**claptrap** *n* (*nonsense*) *Fam* boniment *m*.

claret ['klærət] *n* (*wine*) bordeaux *m* rouge.

clarify ['klærɪfaɪ] *vt* clarifier. ◆**clarifi'cation** *n* clarification *f*.

clarinet [klærɪ'net] *n* clarinette *f*.

clarity ['klærətɪ] *n* (*of water, expression etc*) clarté *f*.

clash [klæʃ] *vi* (*of plates, pans*) s'entrechoquer; (*of interests, armies*) se heurter; (*of colours*) jurer (**with** avec); (*of people*) se bagarrer; (*coincide*) tomber en même temps (**with** que); – *n* (*noise, of armies*) choc *m*, heurt *m*; (*of interests*) conflit *m*; (*of events*) coïncidence *f*.

clasp [klɑːsp] *vt* (*hold*) serrer; **to c. one's hands** joindre les mains; – *n* (*fastener*) fermoir *m*; (*of belt*) boucle *f*.

class [klɑːs] *n* classe *f*; (*lesson*) cours *m*; (*grade*) *Univ* mention *f*; **the c. of 1987** *Am* la promotion de 1987; – *vt* classer. ◆**classmate** *n* camarade *mf* de classe. ◆**classroom** *n* (salle *f* de) classe *f*.

classic ['klæsɪk] *a* classique; – *n* (*writer, work etc*) classique *m*; **to study classics** étudier les humanités *fpl*. ◆**classical** *a* classique. ◆**classicism** *n* classicisme *m*.

classif/y ['klæsɪfaɪ] *vt* classer, classifier. ◆**–ied** *a* (*information*) secret. ◆**classifi'cation** *n* classification *f*.

classy ['klɑːsɪ] *a* **(-ier, -iest)** *Fam* chic *inv*.

clatter ['klætər] *n* bruit *m*, fracas *m*.

clause [klɔːz] *n Jur* clause *f*; *Gram* proposition *f*.

claustrophobia [klɔːstrə'fəʊbɪə] *n* claustrophobie *f*. ◆**claustrophobic** *a* claustrophobe.

claw [klɔː] *n* (*of cat, sparrow etc*) griffe *f*; (*of eagle*) serre *f*; (*of lobster*) pince *f*; – *vt* (*scratch*) griffer; **to c. back** (*money etc*) *Pej Fam* repiquer, récupérer.

clay [kleɪ] *n* argile *f*.

clean [kliːn] *a* **(-er, -est)** propre; (*clear-cut*) net; (*fair*) *Sp* loyal; (*joke*) non paillard; (*record*) *Jur* vierge; **c. living** vie *f* saine; **to make a c. breast of it** tout avouer; – *adv* (*utterly*) complètement, carrément; **to break c.** se casser net; **to cut c.** couper net; – *n* **to give sth a c.** nettoyer qch; – *vt* nettoyer; (*wash*) laver; (*wipe*) essuyer; **to c. one's teeth** se brosser *or* se laver les dents; **to c. out** nettoyer; (*empty*) *Fig* vider; **to c. up** nettoyer; (*reform*) *Fig* épurer; – *vi* **to c. (up)** faire le nettoyage. ◆**–ing** *n* nettoyage *m*; (*housework*) ménage *m*; **c. woman** femme *f* de ménage. ◆**–er** *n* (*woman*) femme *f* de ménage; **(dry) c.** teinturier, -ière *mf*. ◆**–ly** *adv* (*to break, cut*) net. ◆**–ness** *n* propreté *f*. ◆**clean-'cut** *a* net. ◆**clean-'living** *a* honnête, chaste. ◆**clean-'shaven** *a* rasé (de près). ◆**clean-up** *n Fig* épuration *f*.

cleanliness ['klenlɪnɪs] *n* propreté *f*.

cleans/e [klenz] *vt* nettoyer; (*soul, person etc*) *Fig* purifier. ◆**–ing** *a* **c. cream** crème *f* démaquillante. ◆**–er** *n* (*cream, lotion*) démaquillant *m*.

clear [klɪər] *a* **(-er, -est)** (*water, sound etc*) clair; (*glass*) transparent; (*outline, photo*) net, clair; (*mind*) lucide; (*road*) libre, dégagé; (*profit*) net; (*obvious*) évident, clair; (*certain*) certain; (*complete*) entier; **to be c. of** (*free of*) être libre de; (*out of*) être hors de; **to make oneself c.** se faire comprendre; **c. conscience** conscience *f* nette *or* tranquille; – *adv* (*quite*) complètement; **c. of** (*away from*) à l'écart de; **to keep *or* steer c. of** se tenir à l'écart de; **to get c. of** (*away from*) s'éloigner de; – *vt* (*path, place, table*) débarrasser, dégager; (*land*) défricher; (*fence*) franchir (sans toucher); (*obstacle*) éviter; (*person*) *Jur* disculper;

(*cheque*) compenser; (*goods, debts*) liquider; (*through customs*) dédouaner; (*for security etc*) autoriser; **to c. s.o. of** (*suspicion*) laver qn de; **to c. one's throat** s'éclaircir la gorge; – *vi* **to c. (up)** (*of weather*) s'éclaircir; (*of fog*) se dissiper. ■ **to c. away** *vt* (*remove*) enlever; – *vi* (*of fog*) se dissiper; **to c. off** *vi* (*leave*) *Fam* filer; – *vt* (*table*) débarrasser; **to c. out** *vt* (*empty*) vider; (*clean*) nettoyer; (*remove*) enlever; **to c. up** *vt* (*mystery etc*) éclaircir; – *vti* (*tidy*) ranger. ◆**—ing** *n* (*in woods*) clairière *f*. ◆**—ly** *adv* clairement; (*to understand*) bien, clairement; (*obviously*) évidemment. ◆**—ness** *n* (*of sound*) clarté *f*, netteté *f*; (*of mind*) lucidité *f*. ◆**clearance** *n* (*sale*) soldes *mpl*; (*space*) dégagement *m*; (*permission*) autorisation *f*; (*of cheque*) compensation *f*. ◆**clear-'cut** *a* net. ◆**clear-'headed** *a* lucide.

clearway ['klɪəweɪ] *n* route *f* à stationnement interdit.

cleavage ['kliːvɪdʒ] *n* (*split*) clivage *m*; (*of woman*) *Fam* naissance *f* des seins.

cleft [kleft] *a* (*palate*) fendu; (*stick*) fourchu; – *n* fissure *f*.

clement ['klemənt] *a* clément. ◆**clemency** *n* clémence *f*.

clementine ['kleməntaɪn] *n* clémentine *f*.

clench [klentʃ] *vt* (*press*) serrer.

clergy ['klɜːdʒɪ] *n* clergé *m*. ◆**clergyman** *n* (*pl* **-men**) ecclésiastique *m*.

cleric ['klerɪk] *n Rel* clerc *m*. ◆**clerical** *a* (*job*) d'employé; (*work*) de bureau; (*error*) d'écriture; *Rel* clérical.

clerk [klɑːk, *Am* klɜːk] *n* employé, -ée *mf* (de bureau); *Jur* clerc *m*; (*in store*) *Am* vendeur, -euse *mf*; **c. of the court** *Jur* greffier *m*.

clever ['klevər] *a* (**-er, -est**) intelligent; (*smart, shrewd*) astucieux; (*skilful*) habile (**at** sth à qch, **at doing** à faire); (*ingenious*) ingénieux; (*gifted*) doué; **c. at** (*English etc*) fort en; **c. with one's hands** habile *or* adroit de ses mains. ◆**—ly** *adv* intelligemment; astucieusement; habilement. ◆**—ness** *n* intelligence *f*; astuce *f*; habileté *f*.

cliché ['kliːʃeɪ] *n* (*idea*) cliché *m*.

click [klɪk] **1** *n* déclic *m*, bruit *m* sec; – *vi* faire un déclic; (*of lovers etc*) *Fam* se plaire du premier coup; **it clicked** (*I realized*) *Fam* j'ai compris tout à coup. **2** *vt* **to c. one's heels** *Mil* claquer des talons.

client ['klaɪənt] *n* client, -ente *mf*. ◆**clientele** [kliːən'tel] *n* clientèle *f*.

cliff [klɪf] *n* falaise *f*.

climate ['klaɪmɪt] *n Met & Fig* climat *m*; **c. of opinion** opinion *f* générale. ◆**cli'matic** *a* climatique.

climax ['klaɪmæks] *n* point *m* culminant; (*sexual*) orgasme *m*; – *vi* atteindre son point culminant.

climb [klaɪm] *vt* **to c. (up)** (*steps*) monter, gravir; (*hill, mountain*) gravir, faire l'ascension de; (*tree, ladder*) monter à, grimper à; **to c. (over)** (*wall*) escalader; **to c. down (from)** descendre de; – *vi* **to c. (up)** monter; (*of plant*) grimper; **to c. down** descendre; (*back down*) *Fig* en rabattre; – *n* montée *f*. ◆**—ing** *n* montée *f*; (**mountain**) **c.** alpinisme *m*. ◆**—er** *n* grimpeur, -euse *mf*; *Sp* alpiniste *mf*; *Bot* plante *f* grimpante; **social c.** arriviste *mf*.

clinch [klɪntʃ] *vt* (*deal, bargain*) conclure; (*argument*) consolider.

cling [klɪŋ] *vi* (*pt & pp* **clung**) se cramponner, s'accrocher (to à); (*stick*) adhérer (to à). ◆**—ing** *a* (*clothes*) collant. ◆**clingfilm** *n* scel-o-frais®*m*, film *m* étirable.

clinic ['klɪnɪk] *n* (*private*) clinique *f*; (*health centre*) centre *m* médical. ◆**clinical** *a Med* clinique; *Fig* scientifique, objectif.

clink [klɪŋk] *vi* tinter; – *vt* faire tinter; – *n* tintement *m*.

clip [klɪp] **1** *vt* (**-pp-**) (*cut*) couper; (*sheep*) tondre; (*hedge*) tailler; (*ticket*) poinçonner; **to c. sth out of** (*newspaper etc*) découper qch dans. **2** *n* (*for paper*) attache *f*, trombone *m*; (*of brooch, of cyclist, for hair*) pince *f*; – *vt* (**-pp-**) **to c. (on)** attacher. **3** *n* (*of film*) extrait *m*; (*blow*) *Fam* taloche *f*. ◆**clipping** *n Journ* coupure *f*. ◆**clippers** *npl* (*for hair*) tondeuse *f*; (*for nails*) pince *f* à ongles; (*pocket-sized, for finger nails*) coupe-ongles *m inv*.

clique [kliːk] *n Pej* clique *f*. ◆**cliquey** *a Pej* exclusif.

cloak [kləʊk] *n* (grande) cape *f*; *Fig* manteau *m*; **c. and dagger** (*film etc*) d'espionnage. ◆**cloakroom** *n* vestiaire *m*; (*for luggage*) *Rail* consigne *f*; (*lavatory*) toilettes *fpl*.

clobber ['klɒbər] **1** *vt* (*hit*) *Sl* rosser. **2** *n* (*clothes*) *Sl* affaires *fpl*.

clock [klɒk] *n* (*large*) horloge *f*; (*small*) pendule *f*; *Aut* compteur *m*; **against the c.** *Fig* contre la montre; **round the c.** *Fig* vingt-quatre heures sur vingt-quatre; **c. tower** clocher *m*; – *vt Sp* chronométrer; **to c. up** (*miles*) *Aut Fam* faire; – *vi* **to c. in** *or* **out** (*of worker*) pointer. ◆**clockwise** *adv* dans le sens des aiguilles d'une montre. ◆**clockwork** *a* mécanique; *Fig* régulier;

– *n* **to go like c.** aller comme sur des roulettes.

clod [klɒd] *n* **1** (*of earth*) motte *f*. **2** (*oaf*) *Fam* balourd, -ourde *mf*.

clog [klɒg] **1** *n* (*shoe*) sabot *m*. **2** *vt* **(-gg-) to c. (up)** (*obstruct*) boucher.

cloister ['klɔɪstər] *n* cloître *m*; – *vt* cloîtrer.

close¹ [kləʊs] *a* **(-er, -est)** (*place, relative etc*) proche (**to** de); (*collaboration, resemblance, connection*) étroit; (*friend etc*) intime; (*order, contest*) serré; (*study*) rigoureux; (*atmosphere*) *Met* lourd; (*vowel*) fermé; **c. to** (*near*) près de, proche de; **c. to tears** au bord des larmes; **to have a c. shave** *or* **call** l'échapper belle; – *adv* **c. (by), c. at hand** (tout) près; **c. to** près de; **c. behind** juste derrière; **c. on** (*almost*) *Fam* pas loin de; **c. together** (*to stand*) serrés; **to follow c.** suivre de près; – *n* (*enclosed area*) enceinte *f*. ◆**c.-'cropped** *a* (*hair*) (coupé) ras. ◆**c.-'knit** *a* très uni. ◆**c.-up** *n* gros plan *m*.

close² [kləʊz] *n* fin *f*, conclusion *f*; **to bring to a c.** mettre fin à; **to draw to a c.** tirer à sa fin; – *vt* fermer; (*discussion*) terminer, clore; (*opening*) boucher; (*road*) barrer; (*gap*) réduire; (*deal*) conclure; **to c. the meeting** lever la séance; **to c. ranks** serrer les rangs; **to c. in** (*enclose*) enfermer; **to c. up** fermer; – *vi* se fermer; (*end*) (se) terminer; **to c. (up)** (*of shop*) fermer; (*of wound*) se refermer; **to c. in** (*approach*) approcher; **to c. in on s.o.** se rapprocher de qn. ■ **to c. down** *vti* (*close for good*) fermer (définitivement); – *vi TV* terminer les émissions. ◆**c.-down** *n* fermeture *f* (définitive); *TV* fin *f* (des émissions). ◆**closing** *n* fermeture *f*; (*of session*) clôture *f*; – *a* final; **c. time** heure *f* de fermeture. ◆**closure** ['kləʊʒər] *n* fermeture *f*.

closely ['kləʊslɪ] *adv* (*to link, guard*) étroitement; (*to follow*) de près; (*to listen*) attentivement; **c. contested** très disputé; **to hold s.o. c.** tenir qn contre soi. ◆**closeness** *n* proximité *f*; (*of collaboration etc*) étroitesse *f*; (*of friendship*) intimité *f*; (*of weather*) lourdeur *f*.

closet ['klɒzɪt] *n* (*cupboard*) *Am* placard *m*; (*wardrobe*) *Am* penderie *f*.

clot [klɒt] **1** *n* (*of blood*) caillot *m*; – *vt* **(-tt-)** (*blood*) coaguler; – *vi* (*of blood*) se coaguler. **2** *n* (*person*) *Fam* imbécile *mf*.

cloth [klɒθ] *n* tissu *m*, étoffe *f*; (*of linen*) toile *f*; (*of wool*) drap *m*; (*for dusting*) chiffon *m*; (*for dishes*) torchon *m*; (*tablecloth*) nappe *f*.

cloth/e [kləʊð] *vt* habiller, vêtir (**in** de). ◆**—ing** *n* habillement *m*; (*clothes*) vêtements *mpl*; **an article of c.** un vêtement.

clothes [kləʊðz] *npl* vêtements *mpl*; **to put one's c. on** s'habiller; **c. shop** magasin *m* d'habillement; **c. brush** brosse *f* à habits; **c. peg,** *Am* **c. pin** pince *f* à linge; **c. line** corde *f* à linge.

cloud [klaʊd] *n* nuage *m*; (*of arrows, insects*) *Fig* nuée *f*; – *vt* (*mind, issue*) obscurcir; (*window*) embuer; – *vi* **to c. (over)** (*of sky*) se couvrir. ◆**cloudburst** *n* averse *f*. ◆**cloudy** *a* **(-ier, -iest)** (*weather*) couvert, nuageux; (*liquid*) trouble.

clout [klaʊt] **1** *n* (*blow*) *Fam* taloche *f*; – *vt Fam* flanquer une taloche à, talocher. **2** *n Pol Fam* influence *f*, pouvoir *m*.

clove [kləʊv] *n* clou *m* de girofle; **c. of garlic** gousse *f* d'ail.

clover ['kləʊvər] *n* trèfle *m*.

clown [klaʊn] *n* clown *m*; – *vi* **to c. (around)** faire le clown.

cloying ['klɔɪɪŋ] *a* écœurant.

club [klʌb] **1** *n* (*weapon*) matraque *f*, massue *f*; **(golf) c.** (*stick*) club *m*; – *vt* **(-bb-)** matraquer. **2** *n* (*society*) club *m*, cercle *m*; – *vi* **(-bb-) to c. together** se cotiser (**to buy** pour acheter). **3** *n & npl Cards* trèfle *m*. ◆**clubhouse** *n* pavillon *m*.

clubfoot ['klʌbfʊt] *n* pied *m* bot. ◆**club-'footed** *a* pied bot *inv*.

cluck [klʌk] *vi* (*of hen*) glousser.

clue [kluː] *n* indice *m*; (*of crossword*) définition *f*; (*to mystery*) clef *f*; **I don't have a c.** *Fam* je n'en ai pas la moindre idée. ◆**clueless** *a Fam* stupide.

clump [klʌmp] *n* (*of flowers, trees*) massif *m*.

clumsy ['klʌmzɪ] *a* **(-ier, -iest)** maladroit; (*shape*) lourd; (*tool*) peu commode. ◆**clumsily** *adv* maladroitement. ◆**clumsiness** *n* maladresse *f*.

clung [klʌŋ] *see* **cling**.

cluster ['klʌstər] *n* groupe *m*; (*of flowers*) grappe *f*; (*of stars*) amas *m*; – *vi* se grouper.

clutch [klʌtʃ] **1** *vt* (*hold tight*) serrer, étreindre; (*cling to*) se cramponner à; (*grasp*) saisir; – *vi* **to c. at** essayer de saisir; – *n* étreinte *f*. **2** *n* (*apparatus*) *Aut* embrayage *m*; (*pedal*) pédale *f* d'embrayage. **3** *npl* **s.o.'s clutches** (*power*) les griffes *fpl* de qn.

clutter ['klʌtər] *n* (*objects*) fouillis *m*, désordre *m*; – *vt* **to c. (up)** encombrer (**with** de).

cm *abbr* (*centimetre*) cm.

co- [kəʊ] *prep* co-.

Co *abbr* (*company*) Cie.

coach [kəʊtʃ] **1** *n* (*horse-drawn*) carrosse *m*; *Rail* voiture *f*, wagon *m*; *Aut* autocar *m*. **2** *n* (*person*) *Sch* répétiteur, -trice *mf*; *Sp* entraîneur *m*; – *vt* (*pupil*) donner des leçons (particulières) à; (*sportsman etc*) entraîner; **to c. s.o. for** (*exam*) préparer qn à. ◆**coachman** *n* (*pl* **-men**) cocher *m*.

coagulate [kəʊ'ægjʊleɪt] *vi* (*of blood*) se coaguler; – *vt* coaguler.

coal [kəʊl] *n* charbon *m*; *Geol* houille *f*; – *a* (*basin etc*) houiller; (*merchant, fire*) de charbon; (*cellar, bucket*) à charbon. ◆**coalfield** *n* bassin *m* houiller. ◆**coalmine** *n* mine *f* de charbon.

coalition [kəʊə'lɪʃ(ə)n] *n* coalition *f*.

coarse [kɔːs] *a* (**-er, -est**) (*person, manners*) grossier, vulgaire; (*surface*) rude; (*fabric*) grossier; (*salt*) gros; (*accent*) commun, vulgaire. ◆**—ness** *n* grossièreté *f*; vulgarité *f*.

coast [kəʊst] **1** *n* côte *f*. **2** *vi* **to c. (down** *or* **along)** (*of vehicle etc*) descendre en roue libre. ◆**coastal** *a* côtier. ◆**coaster** *n* (*ship*) caboteur *m*; (*for glass etc*) dessous *m* de verre, rond *m*. ◆**coastguard** *n* (*person*) garde *m* maritime, garde-côte *m*. ◆**coastline** *n* littoral *m*.

coat [kəʊt] *n* manteau *m*; (*overcoat*) pardessus *m*; (*jacket*) veste *f*; (*of animal*) pelage *m*; (*of paint*) couche *f*; **c. of arms** blason *m*, armoiries *fpl*; **c. hanger** cintre *m*; – *vt* couvrir, enduire (**with** de); (*with chocolate*) enrober (**with** de). ◆**—ed** *a* **c. tongue** langue *f* chargée. ◆**—ing** *n* couche *f*.

coax [kəʊks] *vt* amadouer, cajoler; **to c. s.o. to do** *or* **into doing** amadouer qn pour qu'il fasse. ◆**—ing** *n* cajoleries *fpl*.

cob [kɒb] *n* **corn on the c.** épi *m* de maïs.

cobble ['kɒb(ə)l] *n* pavé *m*; – *vt* **to c. together** (*text etc*) *Fam* bricoler. ◆**cobbled** *a* pavé. ◆**cobblestone** *n* pavé *m*.

cobbler ['kɒblər] *n* cordonnier *m*.

cobra ['kəʊbrə] *n* (*snake*) cobra *m*.

cobweb ['kɒbweb] *n* toile *f* d'araignée.

cocaine [kəʊ'keɪn] *n* cocaïne *f*.

cock [kɒk] **1** *n* (*rooster*) coq *m*; (*male bird*) (oiseau *m*) mâle *m*. **2** *vt* (*gun*) armer; **to c. (up)** (*ears*) dresser. ◆**c.-a-doodle-'doo** *n* & *int* cocorico (*m*). ◆**c.-and-'bull story** *n* histoire *f* à dormir debout.

cockatoo [kɒkə'tuː] *n* (*bird*) cacatoès *m*.

cocker ['kɒkər] *n* **c. (spaniel)** cocker *m*.

cockerel ['kɒkərəl] *n* jeune coq *m*, coquelet *m*.

cock-eyed [kɒk'aɪd] *a Fam* **1** (*cross-eyed*) bigleux. **2** (*crooked*) de travers. **3** (*crazy*) absurde, stupide.

cockle ['kɒk(ə)l] *n* (*shellfish*) coque *f*.

cockney ['kɒknɪ] *a* & *n* cockney (*mf*).

cockpit ['kɒkpɪt] *n Av* poste *m* de pilotage.

cockroach ['kɒkrəʊtʃ] *n* (*beetle*) cafard *m*.

cocksure [kɒk'ʃʊər] *a Fam* trop sûr de soi.

cocktail ['kɒkteɪl] *n* (*drink*) cocktail *m*; **(fruit) c.** macédoine *f* (de fruits); **c. party** cocktail *m*; **prawn c.** crevettes *fpl* à la mayonnaise.

cocky ['kɒkɪ] *a* (**-ier, -iest**) *Fam* trop sûr de soi, arrogant.

cocoa ['kəʊkəʊ] *n* cacao *m*.

coconut ['kəʊkənʌt] *n* noix *f* de coco; **c. palm** cocotier *m*.

cocoon [kə'kuːn] *n* cocon *m*.

cod [kɒd] *n* morue *f*; (*bought fresh*) cabillaud *m*. ◆**c.-liver 'oil** *n* huile *f* de foie de morue.

COD [siːəʊ'diː] *abbr* (*cash on delivery*) livraison *f* contre remboursement.

coddle ['kɒd(ə)l] *vt* dorloter.

cod/e [kəʊd] *n* code *m*; – *vt* coder. ◆**—ing** *n* codage *m*. ◆**codify** *vt* codifier.

co-educational [kəʊedjʊ'keɪʃən(ə)l] *a* (*school, teaching*) mixte.

coefficient [kəʊɪ'fɪʃənt] *n Math* coefficient *m*.

coerce [kəʊ'ɜːs] *vt* contraindre. ◆**coercion** *n* contrainte *f*.

coexist [kəʊɪg'zɪst] *vi* coexister. ◆**coexistence** *n* coexistence *f*.

coffee ['kɒfɪ] *n* café *m*; **white c.** café *m* au lait; (*ordered in restaurant etc*) (café *m*) crème *m*; **black c.** café *m* noir, café nature; **c. bar, c. house** café *m*, cafétéria *f*; **c. break** pause-café *f*; **c. table** table *f* basse. ◆**coffeepot** *n* cafetière *f*.

coffers ['kɒfəz] *npl* (*funds*) coffres *mpl*.

coffin ['kɒfɪn] *n* cercueil *m*.

cog [kɒg] *n Tech* dent *f*; (*person*) *Fig* rouage *m*.

cogent ['kəʊdʒənt] *a* (*reason, argument*) puissant, convaincant.

cogitate ['kɒdʒɪteɪt] *vi Iron* cogiter.

cognac ['kɒnjæk] *n* cognac *m*.

cohabit [kəʊ'hæbɪt] *vi* (*of unmarried people*) vivre en concubinage.

coherent [kəʊ'hɪərənt] *a* cohérent; (*speech*) compréhensible. ◆**cohesion** *n* cohésion *f*. ◆**cohesive** *a* cohésif.

cohort ['kəʊhɔːt] *n* (*group*) cohorte *f*.

coil [kɔɪl] *n* (*of wire etc*) rouleau *m*; *El* bobine *f*; (*contraceptive*) stérilet *m*; – *vt* (*rope, hair*) enrouler; – *vi* (*of snake etc*) s'enrouler.

coin [kɔɪn] *n* pièce *f* (de monnaie); (*currency*) monnaie *f*; – *vt* (*money*) frapper; (*word*) *Fig* inventer, forger; **to c. a phrase** pour ainsi dire. ◆**c.-operated** *a* automatique. ◆**coinage** *n* (*coins*) monnaie *f*; *Fig* invention *f*.

coincide [kəʊɪn'saɪd] *vi* coïncider (**with** avec). ◆**co'incidence** *n* coïncidence *f*. ◆**coinci'dental** *a* fortuit; **it's c.** c'est une coïncidence.

coke [kəʊk] *n* **1** (*fuel*) coke *m*. **2** (*Coca-Cola®*) coca *m*.

colander ['kʌləndər] *n* (*for vegetables etc*) passoire *f*.

cold [kəʊld] *n* froid *m*; *Med* rhume *m*; **to catch c.** prendre froid; **out in the c.** *Fig* abandonné, en carafe; – *a* (**-er, -est**) froid; **to be** *or* **feel c.** (*of person*) avoir froid; **my hands are c.** j'ai les mains froides; **it's c.** (*of weather*) il fait froid; **to get c.** (*of weather*) se refroidir; (*of food*) refroidir; **to get c. feet** *Fam* se dégonfler; **in c. blood** de sang-froid; **c. cream** crème *f* de beauté; **c. meats,** *Am* **c. cuts** *Culin* assiette *f* anglaise. ◆**c.-'blooded** *a* (*person*) cruel, insensible; (*act*) de sang-froid. ◆**c.-'shoulder** *vt* snober. ◆**coldly** *adv* avec froideur. ◆**coldness** *n* froideur *f*.

coleslaw ['kəʊlslɔː] *n* salade *f* de chou cru.

colic ['kɒlɪk] *n* *Med* coliques *fpl*.

collaborate [kə'læbəreɪt] *vi* collaborer (**on** à). ◆**collabo'ration** *n* collaboration *f*. ◆**collaborator** *n* collaborateur, -trice *mf*.

collage ['kɒlɑːʒ] *n* (*picture*) collage *m*.

collapse [kə'læps] *vi* (*fall*) s'effondrer, s'écrouler; (*of government*) tomber; (*faint*) *Med* se trouver mal; – *n* effondrement *m*, écroulement *m*; (*of government*) chute *f*. ◆**collapsible** *a* (*chair etc*) pliant.

collar ['kɒlər] *n* (*on garment*) col *m*; (*of dog*) collier *m*; **to seize by the c.** saisir au collet; – *vt* *Fam* saisir (*qn*) au collet; *Fig* *Fam* retenir (*qn*); (*take, steal*) *Sl* piquer. ◆**collarbone** *n* clavicule *f*.

collate [kə'leɪt] *vt* collationner, comparer (**with** avec).

colleague ['kɒliːg] *n* collègue *mf*, confrère *m*.

collect [kə'lekt] *vt* (*pick up*) ramasser; (*gather*) rassembler, recueillir; (*taxes*) percevoir; (*rent, money*) encaisser; (*stamps etc as hobby*) collectionner; (*fetch, call for*) (passer) prendre; – *vi* (*of dust*) s'accumuler; (*of people*) se rassembler; **to c. for** (*in street, church*) quêter pour; – *adv* **to call** *or* **phone c.** *Am* téléphoner en PCV. ◆**collection** [kə'lekʃ(ə)n] *n* ramassage *m*; (*of taxes*) perception *f*; (*of objects*) collection *f*; (*of poems etc*) recueil *m*; (*of money in church etc*) quête *f*; (*of mail*) levée *f*. ◆**collective** *a* collectif. ◆**collectively** *adv* collectivement. ◆**collector** *n* (*of stamps etc*) collectionneur, -euse *mf*.

college ['kɒlɪdʒ] *n* *Pol Rel Sch* collège *m*; (*university*) université *f*; *Mus* conservatoire *m*; **teachers' training c.** école *f* normale; **art c.** école *f* des beaux-arts; **agricultural c.** institut *m* d'agronomie, lycée *m* agricole.

collide [kə'laɪd] *vi* entrer en collision (**with** avec), se heurter (**with** à). ◆**collision** *n* collision *f*; *Fig* conflit *m*, collision *f*.

colliery ['kɒlɪərɪ] *n* houillère *f*.

colloquial [kə'ləʊkwɪəl] *a* (*word etc*) familier. ◆**colloquialism** *n* expression *f* familière.

collusion [kə'luːʒ(ə)n] *n* collusion *f*.

collywobbles ['kɒlɪwɒb(ə)lz] *npl* **to have the c.** (*feel nervous*) *Fam* avoir la frousse.

cologne [kə'ləʊn] *n* eau *f* de Cologne.

colon ['kəʊlən] *n* **1** *Gram* deux-points *m inv*. **2** *Anat* côlon *m*.

colonel ['kɜːn(ə)l] *n* colonel *m*.

colony ['kɒlənɪ] *n* colonie *f*. ◆**colonial** [kə'ləʊnɪəl] *a* colonial. ◆**coloni'zation** *n* colonisation *f*. ◆**colonize** *vt* coloniser.

colossal [kə'lɒs(ə)l] *a* colossal.

colour ['kʌlər] *n* couleur *f*; – *a* (*photo, television*) en couleurs; (*television set*) couleur *inv*; (*problem*) racial; **c. supplement** *Journ* supplément *m* illustré; **off c.** (*not well*) mal fichu; (*improper*) scabreux; – *vt* colorer; **to c. (in)** (*drawing*) colorier. ◆**—ed** *a* (*person, pencil*) de couleur; (*glass, water*) coloré. ◆**—ing** *n* coloration *f*; (*with crayons*) coloriage *m*; (*hue, effect*) coloris *m*; (*matter*) colorant *m*. ◆**colour-blind** *a* daltonien. ◆**colourful** *a* (*crowd, story*) coloré; (*person*) pittoresque.

colt [kəʊlt] *n* (*horse*) poulain *m*.

column ['kɒləm] *n* colonne *f*. ◆**columnist** *n* *Journ* chroniqueur *m*; **gossip c.** échotier, -ière *mf*.

coma ['kəʊmə] *n* coma *m*; **in a c.** dans le coma.

comb [kəʊm] *n* peigne *m*; – *vt* peigner; (*search*) *Fig* ratisser; **to c. one's hair** se peigner; **to c. out** (*hair*) démêler.

combat ['kɒmbæt] *n* combat *m*; – *vti* combattre (**for** pour). ◆**'combatant** *n* combattant, -ante *mf*.

combin/e[1] [kəm'baɪn] *vt* unir, joindre (**with** à); (*elements, sounds*) combiner; (*qualities, efforts*) allier, joindre; – *vi* s'unir; **everything combined to . . .** tout s'est ligué pour . . . . ◆**—ed** *a* (*effort*) conjugué; **c. wealth/***etc* (*put together*) richesses/*etc* *fpl* réunies; **c. forces** *Mil* forces *fpl* alliées. ◆**combi'nation** *n* combinaison *f*; (*of *qualities*) réunion *f*; (*of events*) concours *m*; **in c. with** en association avec.

combine² ['kɒmbaɪn] *n Com* cartel *m*; **c. harvester** *Agr* moissonneuse-batteuse *f*.

combustion [kəm'bʌstʃ(ə)n] *n* combustion *f*.

come [kʌm] *vi* (*pt* **came**, *pp* **come**) venir (**from** de, **to** à); (*arrive*) arriver, venir; (*happen*) arriver; **c. and see me** viens me voir; **I've just c. from** j'arrive de; **to c. for** venir chercher; **to c. home** rentrer; **coming!** j'arrive!; **c. now!** voyons!; **to c. as a surprise (to)** surprendre; **to c. near** *or* **close to doing** faillir faire; **to c. on page 2** se trouver à la page 2; **nothing came of it** ça n'a abouti à rien; **to c. to** (*understand etc*) en venir à; (*a decision*) parvenir à; **to c. to an end** toucher à sa fin; **to c. true** se réaliser; **c. May/***etc* *Fam* en mai/*etc*; **the life to c.** la vie future; **how c. that . . . ?** *Fam* comment se fait-il que . . . ? ■ **to c. about** *vi* (*happen*) se faire, arriver; **to c. across** *vi* (*of speech*) faire de l'effet; (*of feelings*) se montrer; – *vt* (*thing, person*) tomber sur; **to c. along** *vi* venir (**with** avec); (*progress*) avancer; **c. along!** allons!; **to c. at** *vt* (*attack*) attaquer; **to c. away** *vi* (*leave, come off*) partir; **to c. back** *vi* revenir; (*return home*) rentrer. ◆**comeback** *n* retour *m*; *Th Pol* rentrée *f*; (*retort*) réplique *f*; **to c. by** *vt* (*obtain*) obtenir; (*find*) trouver; **to c. down** *vi* descendre; (*of rain, price*) tomber. ◆**comedown** *n Fam* humiliation *f*; **to c. forward** *vi* (*make oneself known, volunteer*) se présenter; **to c. forward with** offrir, suggérer; **to c. in** *vi* entrer; (*of tide*) monter; (*of train, athlete*) arriver; *Pol* arriver au pouvoir; (*of clothes*) devenir la mode, se faire beaucoup; (*of money*) rentrer; **to c. in for** recevoir; **to c. into** (*money*) hériter de; **to c. off** *vi* se détacher, partir; (*succeed*) réussir; (*happen*) avoir lieu; (*fare, manage*) s'en tirer; – *vt* (*fall from*) tomber de; (*get down from*) descendre de; **to c. on** *vi* (*follow*) suivre; (*progress*) avancer; (*start*) commencer; (*arrive*) arriver; (*of play*) être joué; **c. on!** allez!; **to c. out** *vi* sortir; (*of sun, book*) paraître; (*of stain*) s'enlever, partir; (*of secret*) être révélé; (*of photo*) réussir; **to c. out (on strike)** se mettre en grève; **to c. over** *vi* (*visit*) venir, passer; **to c. over funny** *or* **peculiar** se trouver mal; – *vt* (*take hold of*) saisir (*qn*), prendre (*qn*); **to c. round** *vi* (*visit*) venir, passer; (*recur*) revenir; (*regain consciousness*) revenir à soi; **to c. through** *vi* (*survive*) s'en tirer; – *vt* se tirer indemne de; **to c. to** *vi* (*regain consciousness*) revenir à soi; (*amount to*) *Com* revenir à, faire; **to c. under** *vi* être classé sous; (*s.o.'s influence*) tomber sous; **to c. up** *vi* (*rise*) monter; (*of plant*) sortir; (*of question, job*) se présenter; **to c. up against** (*wall, problem*) se heurter à; **to c. up to** (*reach*) arriver jusqu'à; (*one's hopes*) répondre à; **to c. up with** (*idea, money*) trouver; **to c. upon** *vt* (*book, reference etc*) tomber sur. ◆**coming** *a* (*future*) à venir; – *n Rel* avènement *m*; **comings and goings** allées *fpl* et venues.

comedy ['kɒmɪdɪ] *n* comédie *f*. ◆**co'median** *n* (acteur *m*) comique *m*, actrice *f* comique.

comet ['kɒmɪt] *n* comète *f*.

comeuppance [kʌm'ʌpəns] *n* **he got his c.** *Pej Fam* il n'a eu que ce qu'il mérite.

comfort ['kʌmfət] *n* confort *m*; (*consolation*) réconfort *m*, consolation *f*; (*peace of mind*) tranquillité *f* d'esprit; **to like one's comforts** aimer ses aises *fpl*; **c. station** *Am* toilettes *fpl*; – *vt* consoler; (*cheer*) réconforter. ◆**—able** *a* (*chair, house etc*) confortable; (*rich*) aisé; **he's c.** (*in chair etc*) il est à l'aise, il est bien; **make yourself c.** mets-toi à l'aise. ◆**—ably** *adv* **c. off** (*rich*) à l'aise. ◆**—er** *n* (*baby's dummy*) sucette *f*; (*quilt*) *Am* édredon *m*. ◆**comfy** *a* (**-ier, -iest**) (*chair etc*) *Fam* confortable; **I'm c.** je suis bien.

comic ['kɒmɪk] *a* comique; – *n* (*actor*) comique *m*; (*actress*) actrice *f* comique; (*magazine*) illustré *m*; **c. strip** bande *f* dessinée. ◆**comical** *a* comique, drôle.

comma ['kɒmə] *n Gram* virgule *f*.

command [kə'mɑːnd] *vt* (*order*) commander (**s.o. to do** à qn de faire); (*control, dominate*) commander (*régiment, vallée etc*); (*be able to use*) disposer de; (*respect*) imposer (**from** à); (*require*) exiger; – *vi* commander; – *n* ordre *m*; (*power*) commandement *m*; (*troops*) troupes *fpl*; (*mastery*) maîtrise *f* (**of** de); **at one's c.** (*disposal*) à sa disposition; **to be in c. (of)** (*ship, army etc*) commander; (*situation*) être maître (de). ◆**—ing** *a* (*authoritative*) imposant; (*position*) dominant; **c. officer** commandant *m*. ◆**—er** *n* chef *m*; *Mil* commandant *m*. ◆**—ment** *n Rel* commandement *m*.

commandant ['kɒməndænt] *n Mil* commandant *m* (*d'un camp etc*). ◆**comman'deer** *vt* réquisitionner.

commando [kə'mɑːndəʊ] *n* (*pl* **-os** *or* **-oes**) *Mil* commando *m*.

commemorate [kə'meməreɪt] *vt* commémorer. ◆**commemo'ration** *n* commémoration *f*. ◆**commemorative** *a* commémoratif.

commence [kə'mens] *vti* commencer (**doing** à faire). ◆**—ment** *n* commencement *m*; *Univ Am* remise *f* des diplômes.

commend [kə'mend] *vt* (*praise*) louer; (*recommend*) recommander; (*entrust*) confier (**to** à). ◆**—able** *a* louable. ◆**commen'dation** *n* éloge *m*.

commensurate [kə'menʃərət] *a* proportionné (**to, with** à).

comment ['kɒment] *n* commentaire *m*, remarque *f*; – *vi* faire des commentaires *or* des remarques (**on** sur); **to c. on** (*text, event, news item*) commenter; **to c. that** remarquer que. ◆**commentary** *n* commentaire *m*; (**live**) **c.** *TV Rad* reportage *m*. ◆**commentate** *vi TV Rad* faire un reportage (**on** sur). ◆**commentator** *n TV Rad* reporter *m*, commentateur, -trice *mf*.

commerce ['kɒmɜːs] *n* commerce *m*. ◆**co'mmercial 1** *a* commercial; (*street*) commerçant; (*traveller*) de commerce. **2** *n* (*advertisement*) *TV* publicité *f*; **the commercials** *TV* la publicité. ◆**co'mmercialize** *vt* (*event*) *Pej* transformer en une affaire de gros sous.

commiserate [kə'mɪzəreɪt] *vi* **to c. with s.o.** s'apitoyer sur (le sort de) qn. ◆**commise'ration** *n* commisération *f*.

commission [kə'mɪʃ(ə)n] *n* (*fee, group*) commission *f*; (*order for work*) commande *f*; **out of c.** hors service; **to get one's c.** *Mil* être nommé officier; – *vt* (*artist*) passer une commande à; (*book*) commander; *Mil* nommer (*qn*) officier; **to c. to do** charger de faire. ◆**commissio'naire** *n* (*in hotel etc*) commissionnaire *m*. ◆**commissioner** *n Pol* commissaire *m*; (**police**) **c.** préfet *m* (de police).

commit [kə'mɪt] *vt* (**-tt-**) (*crime*) commettre; (*entrust*) confier (**to** à); **to c. suicide** se suicider; **to c. to memory** apprendre par cœur; **to c. to prison** incarcérer; **to c. oneself** s'engager (**to** à); (*compromise oneself*) se compromettre. ◆**—ment** *n* obligation *f*; (*promise*) engagement *m*.

committee [kə'mɪtɪ] *n* comité *m*.

commodity [kə'mɒdɪtɪ] *n* produit *m*, article *m*.

common ['kɒmən] **1** *a* (**-er, -est**) (*shared, vulgar*) commun; (*frequent*) courant, fréquent, commun; **the c. man** l'homme *m* du commun; **in c.** (*shared*) en commun (**with** avec); **to have nothing in c.** n'avoir rien de commun (**with** avec); **in c. with** (*like*) comme; **c. law** droit *m* coutumier; **C. Market** Marché *m* commun; **c. room** salle *f* commune; **c. or garden** ordinaire. **2** *n* (*land*) terrain *m* communal; **House of Commons** *Pol* Chambre *f* des Communes; **the Commons** *Pol* les Communes *fpl*. ◆**—er** *n* roturier, -ière *mf*. ◆**—ly** *adv* (*generally*) communément; (*vulgarly*) d'une façon commune. ◆**—ness** *n* fréquence *f*; (*vulgarity*) vulgarité *f*. ◆**commonplace** *a* banal; – *n* banalité *f*. ◆**common'sense** *n* sens *m* commun; – *a* sensé.

Commonwealth ['kɒmənwelθ] *n* **the C.** le Commonwealth.

commotion [kə'məʊʃ(ə)n] *n* agitation *f*.

communal [kə'mjuːn(ə)l] *a* (*of the community*) communautaire; (*shared*) commun. ◆**—ly** *adv* en commun; (*to live*) en communauté.

commune 1 ['kɒmjuːn] *n* (*district*) commune *f*; (*group*) communauté *f*. **2** [kə'mjuːn] *vi Rel & Fig* communier (**with** avec). ◆**co'mmunion** *n* communion *f*; (**Holy**) **C.** communion *f*.

communicate [kə'mjuːnɪkeɪt] *vt* communiquer; (*illness*) transmettre; – *vi* (*of person, rooms etc*) communiquer. ◆**communi'cation** *n* communication *f*; **c. cord** *Rail* signal *m* d'alarme. ◆**communicative** *a* communicatif. ◆**communiqué** *n Pol* communiqué *m*.

communism ['kɒmjʊnɪz(ə)m] *n* communisme *m*. ◆**communist** *a* & *n* communiste (*mf*).

community [kə'mjuːnɪtɪ] *n* communauté *f*; – *a* (*rights, life etc*) communautaire; **the student c.** les étudiants *mpl*; **c. centre** centre *m* socio-culturel; **c. worker** animateur, -trice *mf* socio-culturel(le).

commut/e [kə'mjuːt] **1** *vt Jur* commuer (**to** en). **2** *vi* (*travel*) faire la navette (**to work** pour se rendre à son travail). ◆**—ing** *n* trajets *mpl* journaliers. ◆**—er** *n* banlieusard, -arde *mf*; **c. train** train *m* de banlieue.

compact 1 [kəm'pækt] *a* (*car, crowd, substance*) compact; (*style*) condensé; **c. disc** ['kɒmpækt] disque *m* compact. **2** ['kɒmpækt] *n* (*for face powder*) poudrier *m*.

companion [kəm'pænjən] *n* (*person*) compagnon *m*, compagne *f*; (*handbook*) manuel *m*. ◆**companionship** *n* camaraderie *f*.

company ['kʌmpənɪ] *n* (*fellowship, firm*) compagnie *f*; (*guests*) invités, -ées *mfpl*; **to keep s.o. c.** tenir compagnie à qn; **to keep good c.** avoir de bonnes fréquentations; **he's good c.** c'est un bon compagnon.

compar/e [kəm'peər] *vt* comparer; **compared to** *or* **with** en comparaison de; – *vi* être comparable, se comparer (**with** à). ◆**—able** ['kɒmpərəb(ə)l] *a* comparable. ◆**comparative** *a* comparatif; (*relative*) relatif. ◆**comparatively** *adv* relativement. ◆**comparison** *n* comparaison *f* (**between** entre; **with** à, avec).

compartment [kəm'pɑːtmənt] *n* compartiment *m*. ◆**compart'mentalize** *vt* compartimenter.

compass ['kʌmpəs] *n* **1** (*for navigation*) boussole *f*; *Nau* compas *m*; (*range*) *Fig* portée *f*. **2** (*for measuring etc*) *Am* compas *m*; (**pair of**) **compasses** compas *m*.

compassion [kəm'pæʃ(ə)n] *n* compassion *f*. ◆**compassionate** *a* compatissant; **on c. grounds** pour raisons de famille.

compatible [kəm'pætɪb(ə)l] *a* compatible. ◆**compati'bility** *n* compatibilité *f*.

compatriot [kəm'pætrɪət, kəm'peɪtrɪət] *n* compatriote *mf*.

compel [kəm'pel] *vt* (**-ll-**) contraindre (**to do** à faire); (*respect etc*) imposer (**from** à); **compelled to do** contraint de faire. ◆**compelling** *a* irrésistible.

compendium [kəm'pendɪəm] *n* abrégé *m*.

compensate ['kɒmpənseɪt] *vt* **to c. s.o.** (*with payment, recompense*) dédommager qn (**for** de); **to c. for sth** (*make up for*) compenser qch; – *vi* compenser. ◆**compen'sation** *n* (*financial*) dédommagement *m*; (*consolation*) compensation *f*, dédommagement *m*; **in c. for** en compensation de.

compère ['kɒmpeər] *n TV Rad* animateur, -trice *mf*, présentateur, -trice *mf*; – *vt* (*a show*) animer, présenter.

compete [kəm'piːt] *vi* prendre part (**in** à), concourir (**in** à); (*vie*) rivaliser (**with** avec); *Com* faire concurrence (**with** à); **to c. for** (*prize etc*) concourir pour; **to c. in a rally** courir dans un rallye.

competent ['kɒmpɪtənt] *a* (*capable*) compétent (**to do** pour faire); (*sufficient*) suffisant. ◆**—ly** *adv* avec compétence. ◆**competence** *n* compétence *f*.

competition [kɒmpə'tɪʃ(ə)n] *n* (*rivalry*) compétition *f*, concurrence *f*; **a c.** (*contest*) un concours; *Sp* une compétition. ◆**com'petitive** *a* (*price, market*) compétitif; (*selection*) par concours; (*person*) aimant la compétition; **c. exam(ination)** concours *m*. ◆**com'petitor** *n* concurrent, -ente *mf*.

compil/e [kəm'paɪl] *vt* (*dictionary*) rédiger; (*list*) dresser; (*documents*) compiler. ◆**—er** *n* rédacteur, -trice *mf*.

complacent [kəm'pleɪsənt] *a* content de soi. ◆**complacence** *n*, ◆**complacency** *n* autosatisfaction *f*, contentement *m* de soi.

complain [kəm'pleɪn] *vi* se plaindre (**of, about** de; **that** que). ◆**complaint** *n* plainte *f*; *Com* réclamation *f*; *Med* maladie *f*; (**cause for**) **c.** sujet *m* de plainte.

complement ['kɒmplɪmənt] *n* complément *m*; – ['kɒmplɪment] *vt* compléter. ◆**comple'mentary** *a* complémentaire.

complete [kəm'pliːt] *a* (*total*) complet; (*finished*) achevé; (*downright*) *Pej* parfait; – *vt* (*add sth missing*) compléter; (*finish*) achever; (*a form*) remplir. ◆**—ly** *adv* complètement. ◆**completion** *n* achèvement *m*, réalisation *f*.

complex ['kɒmpleks] **1** *a* complexe. **2** *n* (*feeling, buildings*) complexe *m*; **housing c.** grand ensemble *m*. ◆**com'plexity** *n* complexité *f*.

complexion [kəm'plekʃ(ə)n] *n* (*of the face*) teint *m*; *Fig* caractère *m*.

compliance [kəm'plaɪəns] *n* (*agreement*) conformité *f* (**with** avec).

complicat/e ['kɒmplɪkeɪt] *vt* compliquer. ◆**—ed** *a* compliqué. ◆**compli'cation** *n* complication *f*.

complicity [kəm'plɪsɪtɪ] *n* complicité *f*.

compliment ['kɒmplɪmənt] *n* compliment *m*; *pl* (*of author*) hommages *mpl*; **compliments of the season** meilleurs vœux pour Noël et la nouvelle année; – ['kɒmplɪment] *vt* complimenter. ◆**compli'mentary** *a* **1** (*flattering*) flatteur. **2** (*free*) à titre gracieux; (*ticket*) de faveur.

comply [kəm'plaɪ] *vi* obéir (**with** à); (*request*) accéder à.

component [kəm'pəʊnənt] *a* (*part*) constituant; – *n* (*chemical, electronic*) composant *m*; *Tech* pièce *f*; (*element*) *Fig* composante *f*.

compos/e [kəm'pəʊz] *vt* composer; **to c. oneself** se calmer. ◆**—ed** *a* calme. ◆**—er** *n Mus* compositeur, -trice *mf*. ◆**compo'sition** *n Mus Liter Ch* composition *f*; *Sch* rédaction *f*. ◆**composure** *n* calme *m*, sang-froid *m*.

compost ['kɒmpɒst, *Am* 'kɒmpəʊst] *n* compost *m*.

compound 1 ['kɒmpaʊnd] *n* (*substance, word*) composé *m*; (*area*) enclos *m*; – *a Ch* composé; (*sentence, number*) complexe. **2** [kəm'paʊnd] *vt Ch* composer; (*increase*) *Fig* aggraver.

comprehend [kɒmprɪ'hend] *vt* comprendre. ◆**comprehensible** *a* compréhensible. ◆**comprehension** *n* compréhension *f.* ◆**comprehensive** *a* complet; (*knowledge*) étendu; (*view, measure*) d'ensemble; (*insurance*) tous-risques *inv*; – *a* & *n* **c. (school)** = collège *m* d'enseignement secondaire.

compress [kəm'pres] *vt* comprimer; (*ideas etc*) *Fig* condenser. ◆**compression** *n* compression *f*; condensation *f*.

comprise [kəm'praɪz] *vt* comprendre, englober.

compromise ['kɒmprəmaɪz] *vt* compromettre; – *vi* accepter un compromis; – *n* compromis *m*; – *a* (*solution*) de compromis.

compulsion [kəm'pʌlʃ(ə)n] *n* contrainte *f*. ◆**compulsive** *a* (*behaviour*) *Psy* compulsif; (*smoker, gambler*) invétéré; **c. liar** mythomane *mf*.

compulsory [kəm'pʌlsərɪ] *a* obligatoire.

compunction [kəm'pʌŋkʃ(ə)n] *n* scrupule *m*.

comput/e [kəm'pjuːt] *vt* calculer. ◆**—ing** *n* informatique *f*. ◆**computer** *n* ordinateur *m*; – *a* (*system*) informatique; (*course*) d'informatique; **c. operator** opérateur, -trice *mf* sur ordinateur; **c. science** informatique *f*; **c. scientist** informaticien, -ienne *mf*. ◆**computerize** *vt* informatiser.

comrade ['kɒmreɪd] *n* camarade *mf*. ◆**comradeship** *n* camaraderie *f*.

con [kɒn] *vt* (**-nn-**) *Sl* rouler, escroquer; **to be conned** se faire avoir *or* rouler; – *n* *Sl* escroquerie *f*; **c. man** escroc *m*.

concave ['kɒnkeɪv] *a* concave.

conceal [kən'siːl] *vt* (*hide*) dissimuler (**from s.o.** à qn); (*plan etc*) tenir secret. ◆**—ment** *n* dissimulation *f*.

concede [kən'siːd] *vt* concéder (**to** à, **that** que); – *vi* céder.

conceit [kən'siːt] *n* vanité *f*. ◆**conceited** *a* vaniteux. ◆**conceitedly** *adv* avec vanité.

conceiv/e [kən'siːv] *vt* (*idea, child etc*) concevoir; – *vi* (*of woman*) concevoir; **to c. of** concevoir. ◆**—able** *a* concevable, envisageable. ◆**—ably** *adv* **yes, c.** oui, c'est concevable.

concentrate ['kɒnsəntreɪt] *vt* concentrer; – *vi* se concentrer (**on** sur); **to c. on doing** s'appliquer à faire. ◆**concen'tration** *n* concentration *f*; **c. camp** camp *m* de concentration.

concentric [kən'sentrɪk] *a* concentrique.

concept ['kɒnsept] *n* concept *m*. ◆**con'ception** *n* (*idea*) & *Med* conception *f*.

concern [kən'sɜːn] *vt* concerner; **to c. oneself with, be concerned with** s'occuper de; **to be concerned about** s'inquiéter de; – *n* (*matter*) affaire *f*; (*anxiety*) inquiétude *f*; (*share*) *Com* intérêt(s) *m(pl)* (**in** dans); **(business) c.** entreprise *f*. ◆**—ed** *a* (*anxious*) inquiet; **the department c.** le service compétent; **the main person c.** le principal intéressé. ◆**—ing** *prep* en ce qui concerne.

concert ['kɒnsət] *n* concert *m*; **in c.** (*together*) de concert (**with** avec). ◆**c.-goer** *n* habitué, -ée *mf* des concerts. ◆**con'certed** *a* (*effort*) concerté.

concertina [kɒnsə'tiːnə] *n* concertina *m*; **c. crash** *Aut* carambolage *m*.

concession [kən'seʃ(ə)n] *n* concession *f* (**to** à).

conciliate [kən'sɪlɪeɪt] *vt* **to c. s.o.** (*win over*) se concilier qn; (*soothe*) apaiser qn. ◆**concili'ation** *n* conciliation *f*; apaisement *m*. ◆**conciliatory** [kən'sɪlɪətərɪ, *Am* -tɔːrɪ] *a* conciliant.

concise [kən'saɪs] *a* concis. ◆**—ly** *adv* avec concision. ◆**—ness** *n*. ◆**concision** *n* concision *f*.

conclud/e [kən'kluːd] *vt* (*end, settle*) conclure; **to c. that** (*infer*) conclure que; – *vi* (*of event etc*) se terminer (**with** par); (*of speaker*) conclure. ◆**—ing** *a* final. ◆**conclusion** *n* conclusion *f*; **in c.** pour conclure. ◆**conclusive** *a* concluant. ◆**conclusively** *adv* de manière concluante.

concoct [kən'kɒkt] *vt* *Culin Pej* concocter, confectionner; (*scheme*) *Fig* combiner. ◆**concoction** *n* (*substance*) *Pej* mixture *f*; (*act*) confection *f*; *Fig* combinaison *f*.

concord ['kɒŋkɔːd] *n* concorde *f*.

concourse ['kɒŋkɔːs] *n* (*hall*) *Am* hall *m*; *Rail* hall *m*, salle *f* des pas perdus.

concrete ['kɒŋkriːt] **1** *a* (*real, positive*) concret. **2** *n* béton *m*; – *a* en béton; **c. mixer** bétonnière *f*, bétonneuse *f*.

concur [kən'kɜːr] *vi* (**-rr-**) **1** (*agree*) être d'accord (**with** avec). **2 to c. to** (*contribute*) concourir à.

concurrent [kən'kʌrənt] *a* simultané. ◆**—ly** *adv* simultanément.

concussion [kən'kʌʃ(ə)n] *n* *Med* commotion *f* (cérébrale).

condemn [kən'dem] *vt* condamner; (*building*) déclarer inhabitable. ◆**condem'nation** *n* condamnation *f*.

condense [kən'dens] *vt* condenser; – *vi* se condenser. ◆**conden'sation** *n* condensation *f* (**of** de); (*mist*) buée *f*.

condescend [kɒndɪ'send] *vi* condescendre (**to do** à faire). ◆**condescension** *n* condescendance *f*.

condiment ['kɒndɪmənt] *n* condiment *m*.

condition ['kəndɪʃ(ə)n] **1** *n* (*stipulation, circumstance, rank*) condition *f*; (*state*) état *m*, condition *f*; **on c. that one does** à condition de faire, à condition que l'on fasse; **in/out of c.** en bonne/mauvaise forme. **2** *vt* (*action etc*) déterminer, conditionner; **to c. s.o.** *Psy* conditionner qn (**into doing** à faire). ◆**conditional** *a* conditionnel; **to be c. upon** dépendre de. ◆**conditioner** *n* (**hair**) **c.** après-shampooing *m*.

condo ['kɒndəʊ] *n abbr* (*pl* **-os**) *Am* = **condominium.**

condolences [kən'dəʊlənsɪz] *npl* condoléances *fpl*.

condom ['kɒndəm] *n* préservatif *m*, capote *f* (anglaise).

condominium [kɒndə'mɪnɪəm] *n Am* (*building*) (immeuble *m* en) copropriété *f*; (*apartment*) appartement *m* dans une copropriété.

condone [kən'dəʊn] *vt* (*forgive*) pardonner; (*overlook*) fermer les yeux sur.

conducive [kən'djuːsɪv] *a* **c. to** favorable à.

conduct ['kɒndʌkt] *n* (*behaviour, directing*) conduite *f*; – [kən'dʌkt] *vt* (*lead*) conduire, mener; (*orchestra*) diriger; (*electricity etc*) conduire; **to c. oneself** se conduire. ◆**—ed** *a* (*visit*) guidé; **c. tour** excursion *f* accompagnée. ◆**conductor** *n Mus* chef *m* d'orchestre; (*on bus*) receveur *m*; *Rail Am* chef *m* de train; (*metal, cable etc*) conducteur *m*. ◆**conductress** *n* (*on bus*) receveuse *f*.

cone [kəʊn] *n* cône *m*; (*of ice cream*) cornet *m*; (**paper**) **c.** cornet *m* (de papier); **traffic c.** cône *m* de chantier.

confectioner [kən'fekʃənər] *n* (*of sweets*) confiseur, -euse *mf*; (*of cakes*) pâtissier, -ière *mf*. ◆**confectionery** *n* (*sweets*) confiserie *f*; (*cakes*) pâtisserie *f*.

confederate [kən'fedərət] *a* confédéré; – *n* (*accomplice*) complice *mf*, acolyte *m*. ◆**confederacy** *n*, ◆**confede'ration** *n* confédération *f*.

confer [kən'fɜːr] **1** *vt* (**-rr-**) (*grant*) conférer (**on** à); (*degree*) *Univ* remettre. **2** *vi* (**-rr-**) (*talk together*) conférer, se consulter.

conference ['kɒnfərəns] *n* conférence *f*; (*scientific etc*) congrès *m*.

confess [kən'fes] **1** *vt* avouer, confesser (**that** que, **to** à); – *vi* avouer; **to c. to** (*crime etc*) avouer, confesser. **2** *vt Rel* confesser; – *vi* se confesser. ◆**confession** *n* aveu *m*, confession *f*; *Rel* confession *f*. ◆**confessional** *n Rel* confessionnal *m*.

confetti [kən'fetɪ] *n* confettis *mpl*.

confide [kən'faɪd] *vt* confier (**to** à, **that** que); – *vi* **to c. in** (*talk to*) se confier à. ◆**'confidant, -ante** [-ænt] *n* confident, -ente *mf*. ◆**'confidence** *n* (*trust*) confiance *f*; (*secret*) confidence *f*; (**self-**)**c.** confiance *f* en soi; **in c.** en confidence; **motion of no c.** *Pol* motion *f* de censure; **c. trick** escroquerie *f*; **c. trickster** escroc *m*. ◆**'confident** *a* sûr, assuré; (**self-**)**c.** sûr de soi. ◆**confi'dential** *a* confidentiel; (*secretary*) particulier. ◆**confi'dentially** *adv* en confidence. ◆**'confidently** *adv* avec confiance.

configuration [kənfɪgjʊ'reɪʃ(ə)n] *n* configuration *f*.

confin/e [kən'faɪn] *vt* enfermer, confiner (**to, in** dans); (*limit*) limiter (**to** à); **to c. oneself to doing** se limiter à faire. ◆**—ed** *a* (*atmosphere*) confiné; (*space*) réduit; **c. to bed** obligé de garder le lit. ◆**—ement** *n Med* couches *fpl*; *Jur* emprisonnement *m*. ◆**'confines** *npl* limites *fpl*, confins *mpl*.

confirm [kən'fɜːm] *vt* confirmer (**that** que); (*strengthen*) raffermir. ◆**—ed** *a* (*bachelor*) endurci; (*smoker, habit*) invétéré. ◆**confir'mation** *n* confirmation *f*; raffermissement *m*.

confiscate ['kɒnfɪskeɪt] *vt* confisquer (**from s.o.** à qn). ◆**confis'cation** *n* confiscation *f*.

conflagration [kɒnflə'greɪʃ(ə)n] *n* (**grand**) incendie *m*, brasier *m*.

conflict ['kɒnflɪkt] *n* conflit *m*; – [kən'flɪkt] *vi* être en contradiction, être incompatible (**with** avec); (*of dates, events, TV programmes*) tomber en même temps (**with** que). ◆**—ing** *a* (*views, theories etc*) contradictoires; (*dates*) incompatibles.

confluence ['kɒnflʊəns] *n* (*of rivers*) confluent *m*.

conform [kən'fɔːm] *vi* se conformer (**to, with** à); (*of ideas etc*) être en conformité. ◆**conformist** *a* & *n* conformiste (*mf*). ◆**conformity** *n* (*likeness*) conformité *f*; *Pej* conformisme *m*.

confound [kən'faʊnd] *vt* confondre; **c. him!** que le diable l'emporte! ◆**—ed** *a* (*damned*) *Fam* sacré.

confront [kən'frʌnt] *vt* (*danger*) affronter; (*problems*) faire face à; **to c. s.o.** (*be face to face with*) se trouver en face de qn; (*oppose*) s'opposer à qn; **to c. s.o. with** (*person*) confronter qn avec; (*thing*) mettre qn en présence de. ◆**confron'tation** *n* confrontation *f*.

confus/e [kən'fjuːz] *vt* (*perplex*) confondre; (*muddle*) embrouiller; **to c. with** (*mistake for*) confondre avec. ◆**—ed** *a* (*situation,*

noises etc) confus; **to be c.** (*of person*) s'y perdre; **to get c.** s'embrouiller. ◆**—ing** *a* difficile à comprendre, déroutant. ◆**confusion** *n* confusion *f*; **in c.** en désordre.
congeal [kən'dʒiːl] *vt* figer; – *vi* (se) figer.
congenial [kən'dʒiːnɪəl] *a* sympathique.
congenital [kən'dʒenɪtəl] *a* congénital.
congested [kən'dʒestɪd] *a* (*street*) encombré; (*town*) surpeuplé; *Med* congestionné. ◆**congestion** *n* (*traffic*) encombrement(s) *m*(*pl*); (*overcrowding*) surpeuplement *m*; *Med* congestion *f*.
Congo ['kɒŋgəʊ] *n* Congo *m*.
congratulate [kən'grætʃʊleɪt] *vt* féliciter (s.o. on sth qn de qch). ◆**congratu'lations** *npl* félicitations *fpl* (**on** pour). ◆**congratu'latory** *a* (*telegram etc*) de félicitations.
congregate ['kɒŋgrɪgeɪt] *vi* se rassembler. ◆**congre'gation** *n* (*worshippers*) assemblée *f*, fidèles *mfpl*.
congress ['kɒŋgres] *n* congrès *m*; **C.** *Pol Am* le Congrès. ◆**Congressman** *n* (*pl* **-men**) *Am* membre *m* du Congrès. ◆**Con'gressional** *a Am* du Congrès.
conic(al) ['kɒnɪk(ə)l] *a* conique.
conifer ['kɒnɪfər] *n* (*tree*) conifère *m*.
conjecture [kən'dʒektʃər] *n* conjecture *f*; – *vt* conjecturer; – *vi* faire des conjectures. ◆**conjectural** *a* conjectural.
conjugal ['kɒndʒʊgəl] *a* conjugal.
conjugate ['kɒndʒʊgeɪt] *vt* (*verb*) conjuguer. ◆**conju'gation** *n Gram* conjugaison *f*.
conjunction [kən'dʒʌŋkʃ(ə)n] *n Gram* conjonction *f*; **in c. with** conjointement avec.
conjur/e ['kʌndʒər] *vt* **to c. (up)** (*by magic*) faire apparaître; **to c. up** (*memories etc*) *Fig* évoquer. ◆**—ing** *n* prestidigitation *f*. ◆**—er** *n* prestidigitateur, -trice *mf*.
conk [kɒŋk] **1** *n* (*nose*) *Sl* pif *m*. **2** *vi* **to c. out** (*break down*) *Fam* claquer, tomber en panne.
conker ['kɒŋkər] *n* (*horse-chestnut fruit*) *Fam* marron *m* (d'Inde).
connect [kə'nekt] *vt* relier (**with, to** à); (*telephone, stove etc*) brancher; **to c. with** *Tel* mettre en communication avec; (*in memory*) associer avec; – *vi* (*be connected*) être relié; **to c. with** (*of train, bus*) assurer la correspondance avec. ◆**—ed** *a* (*facts etc*) lié, connexe; (*speech*) suivi; **to be c. with** (*have dealings with*) être lié à; (*have to do with, relate to*) avoir rapport à; (*by marriage*) être allié à. ◆**connection** *n* (*link*) rapport *m*, relation *f* (**with** avec); (*train, bus etc*) correspondance *f*; (*phone call*) communication *f*; (*between pipes etc*) *Tech* raccord *m*; *pl* (*contacts*) relations *fpl*; **in c. with** à propos de.
connive [kə'naɪv] *vi* **to c. at** fermer les yeux sur; **to c. to do** se mettre de connivence pour faire (**with** avec); **to c. together** agir en complicité. ◆**connivance** *n* connivence *f*.
connoisseur [kɒnə'sɜːr] *n* connaisseur *m*.
connotation [kɒnə'teɪʃ(ə)n] *n* connotation *f*.
conquer ['kɒŋkər] *vt* (*country, freedom etc*) conquérir; (*enemy, habit*) vaincre. ◆**—ing** *a* victorieux. ◆**conqueror** *n* conquérant, -ante *mf*, vainqueur *m*. ◆**conquest** *n* conquête *f*.
cons [kɒnz] *npl* **the pros and (the) c.** le pour et le contre.
conscience ['kɒnʃəns] *n* conscience *f*. ◆**c.-stricken** *a* pris de remords.
conscientious [kɒnʃɪ'enʃəs] *a* consciencieux; **c. objector** objecteur *m* de conscience. ◆**—ness** *n* application *f*, sérieux *m*.
conscious ['kɒnʃəs] *a* conscient (**of sth** de qch); (*intentional*) délibéré; *Med* conscient; **to be c. of doing** avoir conscience de faire. ◆**—ly** *adv* (*knowingly*) consciemment. ◆**—ness** *n* conscience *f* (**of** de); *Med* connaissance *f*.
conscript ['kɒnskrɪpt] *n Mil* conscrit *m*; – [kən'skrɪpt] *vt* enrôler (par conscription). ◆**con'scription** *n* conscription *f*.
consecrate ['kɒnsɪkreɪt] *vt* (*church etc*) *Rel* consacrer. ◆**conse'cration** *n* consécration *f*.
consecutive [kən'sekjʊtɪv] *a* consécutif. ◆**—ly** *adv* consécutivement.
consensus [kən'sensəs] *n* consensus *m*, accord *m* (général).
consent [kən'sent] *vi* consentir (**to** à); – *n* consentement *m*; **by common c.** de l'aveu de tous; **by mutual c.** d'un commun accord.
consequence ['kɒnsɪkwəns] *n* (*result*) conséquence *f*; (*importance*) importance *f*, conséquence *f*. ◆**consequently** *adv* par conséquent.
conservative [kən'sɜːvətɪv] **1** *a* (*estimate*) modeste; (*view*) traditionnel. **2** *a* & *n* **C.** *Pol* conservateur, -trice (*mf*). ◆**conservatism** *n* (*in behaviour*) & *Pol Rel* conservatisme *m*.
conservatoire [kən'sɜːvətwɑːr] *n Mus* conservatoire *m*.
conservatory [kən'sɜːvətrɪ] *n* (*greenhouse*) serre *f*.
conserve [kən'sɜːv] *vt* préserver, conserver;

(*one's strength*) ménager; **to c. energy** faire des économies d'énergie. ◆**conser'vation** *n* (*energy-saving*) économies *fpl* d'énergie; (*of nature*) protection *f* de l'environnement; *Phys* conservation *f*.

consider [kən'sɪdər] *vt* considérer; (*take into account*) tenir compte de; **I'll c. it** j'y réfléchirai; **to c. doing** envisager de faire; **to c. that** estimer *or* considérer que; **he's** *or* **she's being considered (for the job)** sa candidature est à l'étude; **all things considered** en fin de compte. ◆**—ing** *prep* étant donné, vu. ◆**—able** *a* (*large*) considérable; (*much*) beaucoup de. ◆**—ably** *adv* beaucoup, considérablement. ◆**conside'ration** *n* (*thought, thoughtfulness, reason*) considération *f*; **under c.** à l'étude; **out of c. for** par égard pour; **to take into c.** prendre en considération.

considerate [kən'sɪdərət] *a* plein d'égards (**to** pour), attentionné (**to** à l'égard de).

consign [kən'saɪn] *vt* (*send*) expédier; (*give, entrust*) confier (**to** à). ◆**—ment** *n* (*act*) expédition *f*; (*goods*) arrivage *m*.

consist [kən'sɪst] *vi* consister (**of** en, **in** dans, **in doing** à faire).

consistent [kən'sɪstənt] *a* logique, conséquent; (*coherent*) cohérent; (*friend*) fidèle; **c. with** compatible avec, conforme à. ◆**—ly** *adv* (*logically*) avec logique; (*always*) constamment. ◆**consistency** *n* **1** logique *f*; cohérence *f*. **2** (*of liquid etc*) consistance *f*.

console[1] [kən'səʊl] *vt* consoler. ◆**conso'lation** *n* consolation *f*; **c. prize** prix *m* de consolation.

console[2] ['kɒnsəʊl] *n* (*control desk*) *Tech* console *f*.

consolidate [kən'sɒlɪdeɪt] *vt* consolider; – *vi* se consolider. ◆**consoli'dation** *n* consolidation *f*.

consonant ['kɒnsənənt] *n* consonne *f*.

consort 1 ['kɒnsɔːt] *n* époux *m*, épouse *f*; **prince c.** prince *m* consort. **2** [kən'sɔːt] *vi* **to c. with** *Pej* fréquenter.

consortium [kən'sɔːtɪəm] *n* *Com* consortium *m*.

conspicuous [kən'spɪkjʊəs] *a* visible, en évidence; (*striking*) remarquable, manifeste; (*showy*) voyant; **to be c. by one's absence** briller par son absence; **to make oneself c.** se faire remarquer. ◆**—ly** *adv* visiblement.

conspire [kən'spaɪər] **1** *vi* (*plot*) conspirer (**against** contre); **to c. to do** comploter de faire. **2** *vt* **to c. to do** (*of events*) conspirer à faire. ◆**conspiracy** *n* conspiration *f*.

constable ['kɒnstəb(ə)l] *n* (**police**) **c.** agent *m* (de police). ◆**con'stabulary** *n* la police.

constant ['kɒnstənt] *a* (*frequent*) incessant; (*unchanging*) constant; (*faithful*) fidèle. ◆**constancy** *n* constance *f*. ◆**constantly** *adv* constamment, sans cesse.

constellation [kɒnstə'leɪʃ(ə)n] *n* constellation *f*.

consternation [kɒnstə'neɪʃ(ə)n] *n* consternation *f*.

constipate ['kɒnstɪpeɪt] *vt* constiper. ◆**consti'pation** *n* constipation *f*.

constituent [kən'stɪtjʊənt] **1** *a* (*element etc*) constituant, constitutif. **2** *n* *Pol* électeur, -trice *mf*. ◆**constituency** *n* circonscription *f* électorale; (*voters*) électeurs *mpl*.

constitute ['kɒnstɪtjuːt] *vt* constituer. ◆**consti'tution** *n* (*of person etc*) & *Pol* constitution *f*. ◆**consti'tutional** *a* *Pol* constitutionnel.

constrain [kən'streɪn] *vt* contraindre.

constrict [kən'strɪkt] *vt* (*tighten, narrow*) resserrer; (*movement*) gêner. ◆**con'striction** *n* resserrement *m*.

construct [kən'strʌkt] *vt* construire. ◆**construction** *n* construction *f*; **under c.** en construction. ◆**constructive** *a* constructif.

construe [kən'struː] *vt* interpréter, comprendre.

consul ['kɒnsəl] *n* consul *m*. ◆**consular** *a* consulaire. ◆**consulate** *n* consulat *m*.

consult [kən'sʌlt] *vt* consulter; – *vi* **to c. with** discuter avec, conférer avec. ◆**—ing** *a* (*room*) *Med* de consultation; (*physician*) consultant. ◆**consultancy** *n* **c. (firm)** *Com* cabinet *m* d'experts-conseils; **c. fee** honoraires *mpl* de conseils. ◆**consultant** *n* conseiller, -ère *mf*; *Med* spécialiste *mf*; (*financial, legal*) conseil *m*, expert-conseil *m*; – *a* (*engineer etc*) consultant. ◆**consul'tation** *n* consultation *f*. ◆**consultative** *a* consultatif.

consum/e [kən'sjuːm] *vt* (*food, supplies etc*) consommer; (*of fire, grief, hate*) consumer. ◆**—ing** *a* (*ambition*) brûlant. ◆**—er** *n* consommateur, -trice *mf*; **c. goods/society** biens *mpl*/société *f* de consommation. ◆**con'sumption** *n* consommation *f* (**of** de).

consummate ['kɒnsəmət] *a* (*perfect*) consommé.

contact ['kɒntækt] *n* contact *m*; (*person*) relation *f*; **in c. with** en contact avec; **c. lenses** lentilles *fpl or* verres *mpl* de contact; – *vt* se mettre en contact avec, contacter.

contagious [kən'teɪdʒəs] *a* contagieux.
contain [kən'teɪn] *vt* (*enclose, hold back*) contenir; **to c. oneself** se contenir. ◆**—er** *n* récipient *m*; (*for transporting freight*) conteneur *m*, container *m*.
contaminate [kən'tæmɪneɪt] *vt* contaminer. ◆**contami'nation** *n* contamination *f*.
contemplate ['kɒntəmpleɪt] *vt* (*look at*) contempler; (*consider*) envisager (**doing** de faire). ◆**contem'plation** *n* contemplation *f*; **in c. of** en prévision de.
contemporary [kən'tempərərɪ] *a* contemporain (**with** de); – *n* (*person*) contemporain, -aine *mf*.
contempt [kən'tempt] *n* mépris *m*; **to hold in c.** mépriser. ◆**contemptible** *a* méprisable. ◆**contemptuous** *a* dédaigneux (**of** de).
contend [kən'tend] **1** *vi* **to c. with** (*problem*) faire face à; (*person*) avoir affaire à; (*compete*) rivaliser avec; (*struggle*) se battre avec. **2** *vt* **to c. that** (*claim*) soutenir que. ◆**—er** *n* concurrent, -ente *mf*. ◆**contention** *n* **1** (*argument*) dispute *f*. **2** (*claim*) affirmation *f*. ◆**contentious** *a* (*issue*) litigieux.
content[1] [kən'tent] *a* satisfait (**with** de); **he's c. to do** il ne demande pas mieux que de faire. ◆**—ed** *a* satisfait. ◆**—ment** *n* contentement *m*.
content[2] ['kɒntent] *n* (*of text, film etc*) contenu *m*; *pl* (*of container*) contenu *m*; (**table of**) **contents** (*of book*) table *f* des matières; **alcoholic/iron/***etc* **c.** teneur *f* en alcool/fer/*etc*.
contest [kən'test] *vt* (*dispute*) contester; (*fight for*) disputer; – ['kɒntest] *n* (*competition*) concours *m*; (*fight*) lutte *f*; *Boxing* combat *m*. ◆**con'testant** *n* concurrent, -ente *mf*; (*in fight*) adversaire *mf*.
context ['kɒntekst] *n* contexte *m*.
continent ['kɒntɪnənt] *n* continent *m*; **the C.** l'Europe *f* (continentale). ◆**conti'nental** *a* continental; européen; **c. breakfast** petit déjeuner *m* à la française.
contingent [kən'tɪndʒənt] **1** *a* (*accidental*) contingent; **to be c. upon** dépendre de. **2** *nm Mil* contingent *m*. ◆**contingency** *n* éventualité *f*; **c. plan** plan *m* d'urgence.
continu/e [kən'tɪnjuː] *vt* continuer (**to do** *or* **doing** à *or* de faire); (*resume*) reprendre; **to c.** (**with**) (*work, speech etc*) poursuivre, continuer; – *vi* continuer; (*resume*) reprendre; **to c. in** (*job*) garder. ◆**—ed** *a* (*interest, attention etc*) soutenu, assidu; (*presence*) continu(el); **to be c.** (*of story*) à suivre. ◆**continual** *a* continuel. ◆**continually** *adv* continuellement. ◆**continuance** *n* continuation *f*. ◆**continu'ation** *n* continuation *f*; (*resumption*) reprise *f*; (*new episode*) suite *f*. ◆**continuity** [kɒntɪ'njuːɪtɪ] *n* continuité *f*. ◆**continuous** *a* continu; **c. performance** *Cin* spectacle *m* permanent. ◆**continuously** *adv* sans interruption.
contort [kən'tɔːt] *vt* (*twist*) tordre; **to c. oneself** se contorsionner. ◆**contortion** *n* contorsion *f*. ◆**contortionist** *n* (*acrobat*) contorsionniste *mf*.
contour ['kɒntʊər] *n* contour *m*.
contraband ['kɒntrəbænd] *n* contrebande *f*.
contraception [kɒntrə'sepʃ(ə)n] *n* contraception *f*. ◆**contraceptive** *a* & *n* contraceptif (*m*).
contract 1 ['kɒntrækt] *n* contrat *m*; **c. work** travail *m* en sous-traitance; – *vi* **to c. out of** (*agreement etc*) se dégager de. **2** [kən'trækt] *vt* (*habit, debt, muscle etc*) contracter; – *vi* (*of heart etc*) se contracter. ◆**con'traction** *n* (*of muscle, word*) contraction *f*. ◆**con'tractor** *n* entrepreneur *m*.
contradict [kɒntrə'dɪkt] *vt* contredire; (*belie*) démentir. ◆**contradiction** *n* contradiction *f*. ◆**contradictory** *a* contradictoire.
contralto [kən'træltəʊ] *n* (*pl* **-os**) contralto *m*.
contraption [kən'træpʃ(ə)n] *n Fam* machin *m*, engin *m*.
contrary 1 ['kɒntrərɪ] *a* contraire (**to** à); – *adv* **c. to** contrairement à; – *n* contraire *m*; **on the c.** au contraire; **unless you, I** *etc* **hear to the c.** sauf avis contraire; **she said nothing to the c.** elle n'a rien dit contre. **2** [kən'treərɪ] *a* (*obstinate*) entêté, difficile.
contrast 1 ['kɒntrɑːst] *n* contraste *m*; **in c. to** par opposition à. **2** [kən'trɑːst] *vi* contraster (**with** avec); – *vt* faire contraster, mettre en contraste. ◆**—ing** *a* (*colours etc*) opposés.
contravene [kɒntrə'viːn] *vt* (*law*) enfreindre. ◆**contravention** *n* **in c. of** en contravention de.
contribute [kən'trɪbjuːt] *vt* donner, fournir (**to** à); (*article*) écrire (**to** pour); **to c. money to** contribuer à, verser de l'argent à; – *vi* **to c. to** contribuer à; (*publication*) collaborer à. ◆**contri'bution** *n* contribution *f*; (*to pension fund etc*) cotisation(s) *f*(*pl*); *Journ* article *m*. ◆**contributor** *n Journ* collaborateur, -trice *mf*; (*of money*) donateur, -trice *mf*. ◆**contributory** *a* **a c. factor** un facteur qui a contribué (**in** à).
contrite [kən'traɪt] *a* contrit. ◆**contrition** *n* contrition *f*.
contriv/e [kən'traɪv] *vt* inventer; **to c. to do**

trouver moyen de faire. ◆**—ed** *a* artificiel. ◆**contrivance** *n* (*device*) dispositif *m*; (*scheme*) invention *f*.

control [kən'trəʊl] *vt* (**-ll-**) (*business, organization*) diriger; (*traffic*) régler; (*prices, quality*) contrôler; (*emotion, reaction*) maîtriser, contrôler; (*disease*) enrayer; (*situation*) être maître de; **to c. oneself** se contrôler; – *n* (*authority*) autorité *f* (**over** sur); (*of traffic*) réglementation *f*; (*of prices etc*) contrôle *m*; (*of emotion etc*) maîtrise *f*; *pl* (*of train etc*) commandes *fpl*; (*knobs*) *TV Rad* boutons *mpl*; **the c. of** (*fires etc*) la lutte contre; **(self-)c.** le contrôle de soi-même; **to keep s.o. under c.** tenir qn; **everything is under c.** tout est en ordre; **in c. of** maître de; **to lose c. of** (*situation, vehicle*) perdre le contrôle de; **out of c.** (*situation, crowd*) difficilement maîtrisable; **c. tower** *Av* tour *f* de contrôle. ◆**controller** *n* **air traffic c.** aiguilleur *m* du ciel.

controversy ['kɒntrəvɜːsɪ] *n* controverse *f*. ◆**contro'versial** *a* (*book, author*) contesté, discuté; (*doubtful*) discutable.

conundrum [kə'nʌndrəm] *n* devinette *f*, énigme *f*; (*mystery*) énigme *f*.

conurbation [kɒnɜː'beɪʃ(ə)n] *n* agglomération *f*, conurbation *f*.

convalesce [kɒnvə'les] *vi* être en convalescence. ◆**convalescence** *n* convalescence *f*. ◆**convalescent** *n* convalescent, -ente *mf*; **c. home** maison *f* de convalescence.

convector [kən'vektər] *n* radiateur *m* à convection.

convene [kən'viːn] *vt* convoquer; – *vi* se réunir.

convenient [kən'viːnɪənt] *a* commode, pratique; (*well-situated*) bien situé (**for the shops/***etc* par rapport aux magasins/*etc*); (*moment*) convenable, opportun; **to be c. (for)** (*suit*) convenir (à). ◆**—ly** *adv* (*to arrive*) à propos; **c. situated** bien situé. ◆**convenience** *n* commodité *f*; (*comfort*) confort *m*; (*advantage*) avantage *m*; **to** *or* **at one's c.** à sa convenance; **c. food(s)** plats *mpl* or aliments *mpl* minute; **(public) conveniences** toilettes *fpl*.

convent ['kɒnvənt] *n* couvent *m*.

convention [kən'venʃ(ə)n] *n* (*agreement*) & *Am Pol* convention *f*; (*custom*) usage *m*, convention *f*; (*meeting*) *Pol* assemblée *f*. ◆**conventional** *a* conventionnel.

converg/e [kən'vɜːdʒ] *vi* converger. ◆**—ing** *a* convergent. ◆**convergence** *n* convergence *f*.

conversant [kən'vɜːsənt] *a* **to be c. with** (*custom etc*) connaître; (*fact*) savoir; (*cars etc*) s'y connaître en.

conversation [kɒnvə'seɪʃ(ə)n] *n* conversation *f*. ◆**conversational** *a* (*tone*) de la conversation; (*person*) loquace. ◆**conversationalist** *n* causeur, -euse *mf*.

converse 1 [kən'vɜːs] *vi* s'entretenir (**with** avec). **2** ['kɒnvɜːs] *a* & *n* inverse (*m*). ◆**con'versely** *adv* inversement.

convert [kən'vɜːt] *vt* (*change*) convertir (**into** en); (*building*) aménager (**into en**); **to c. s.o.** convertir qn (**to** à); – ['kɒnvɜːt] *n* converti, -ie *mf*. ◆**con'version** *n* conversion *f*; aménagement *m*. ◆**con'vertible** *a* convertible; – *n* (*car*) (voiture *f*) décapotable *f*.

convex ['kɒnveks] *a* convexe.

convey [kən'veɪ] *vt* (*goods, people*) transporter; (*sound, message, order*) transmettre; (*idea*) communiquer; (*evoke*) évoquer; (*water etc through pipes*) amener. ◆**conveyance** *n* transport *m*; *Aut* véhicule *m*. ◆**conveyor** *a* **c. belt** tapis *m* roulant.

convict ['kɒnvɪkt] *n* forçat *m*; – [kən'vɪkt] *vt* déclarer coupable, condamner. ◆**con'viction** *n* *Jur* condamnation *f*; (*belief*) conviction *f*; **to carry c.** (*of argument etc*) être convaincant.

convinc/e [kən'vɪns] *vt* convaincre, persuader. ◆**—ing** *a* convaincant. ◆**—ingly** *adv* de façon convaincante.

convivial [kən'vɪvɪəl] *a* joyeux, gai; (*person*) bon vivant.

convoke [kən'vəʊk] *vt* (*meeting etc*) convoquer.

convoluted [kɒnvə'luːtɪd] *a* (*argument, style*) compliqué, tarabiscoté.

convoy ['kɒnvɔɪ] *n* (*ships, cars, people*) convoi *m*.

convulse [kən'vʌls] *vt* bouleverser, ébranler; (*face*) convulser. ◆**convulsion** *n* convulsion *f*. ◆**convulsive** *a* convulsif.

coo [kuː] *vi* (*of dove*) roucouler.

cook [kʊk] *vt* (faire) cuire; (*accounts*) *Fam* truquer; **to c. up** *Fam* inventer; – *vi* (*of food*) cuire; (*of person*) faire la cuisine; **what's cooking?** *Fam* qu'est-ce qui se passe?; – *n* (*person*) cuisinier, -ière *mf*. ◆**—ing** *n* cuisine *f*; **c. apple** pomme *f* à cuire. ◆**—er** *n* (*stove*) cuisinière *f*; (*apple*) pomme *f* à cuire. ◆**cookbook** *n* livre *m* de cuisine. ◆**cookery** *n* cuisine *f*; **c. book** livre *m* de cuisine.

cookie ['kʊkɪ] *n* *Am* biscuit *m*, gâteau *m* sec.

cool [kuːl] *a* (**-er, -est**) (*weather, place etc*) frais; (*manner, person*) calme; (*reception etc*) froid; (*impertinent*) *Fam* effronté; **I feel**

c. j'ai (un peu) froid; **a c. drink** une boisson fraîche; **a c. £50** la coquette somme de 50 livres; – *n* (*of evening*) fraîcheur *f*; **to keep (in the) c.** tenir au frais; **to keep/lose one's c.** garder/perdre son sang-froid; – *vt* **to c. (down)** refroidir, rafraîchir; – *vi* **to c. (down** *or* **off)** (*of enthusiasm*) se refroidir; (*of anger, angry person*) se calmer; (*of hot liquid*) refroidir; **to c. off** (*refresh oneself by drinking, bathing etc*) se rafraîchir; **to c. off towards s.o.** se refroidir envers qn. ◆**—ing** *n* (*of air, passion etc*) refroidissement *m*. ◆**—er** *n* (*for food*) glacière *f*. ◆**—ly** *adv* calmement; (*to welcome*) froidement; (*boldly*) effrontément. ◆**—ness** *n* fraîcheur *f*; (*unfriendliness*) froideur *f*. ◆**cool-'headed** *a* calme.

coop [kuːp] **1** *n* (*for chickens*) poulailler *m*. **2** *vt* **to c. up** (*person*) enfermer.

co-op ['kəʊɒp] *n Am* appartement *m* en copropriété.

co-operate [kəʊ'ɒpəreɪt] *vi* coopérer (**in** à, **with** avec). ◆**co-ope'ration** *n* coopération *f*. ◆**co-operative** *a* coopératif; – *n* coopérative *f*.

co-opt [kəʊ'ɒpt] *vt* coopter.

co-ordinate [kəʊ'ɔːdɪneɪt] *vt* coordonner. ◆**co-ordinates** [kəʊ'ɔːdɪnəts] *npl Math* coordonnées *fpl*; (*clothes*) coordonnés *mpl*. ◆**co-ordi'nation** *n* coordination *f*.

cop [kɒp] **1** *n* (*policeman*) *Fam* flic *m*. **2** *vt* (**-pp-**) (*catch*) *Sl* piquer. **3** *vi* (**-pp-**) **to c. out** *Sl* se défiler, éviter ses responsabilités.

cope [kəʊp] *vi* **to c. with** s'occuper de; (*problem*) faire face à; **(to be able) to c.** (savoir) se débrouiller.

co-pilot ['kəʊpaɪlət] *n* copilote *m*.

copious ['kəʊpɪəs] *a* copieux.

copper ['kɒpər] *n* **1** cuivre *m*; *pl* (*coins*) petite monnaie *f*. **2** (*policeman*) *Fam* flic *m*.

coppice ['kɒpɪs] *n*, ◆**copse** [kɒps] *n* taillis *m*.

copulate ['kɒpjʊleɪt] *vi* s'accoupler. ◆**copu'lation** *n* copulation *f*.

copy ['kɒpɪ] *n* copie *f*; (*of book etc*) exemplaire *m*; *Phot* épreuve *f*; – *vti* copier; – *vt* **to c. out** *or* **down** (re)copier. ◆**copyright** *n* copyright *m*.

coral ['kɒrəl] *n* corail *m*; **c. reef** récif *m* de corail.

cord [kɔːd] **1** *n* (*of curtain, pyjamas etc*) cordon *m*; *El* cordon *m* électrique; **vocal cords** cordes *fpl* vocales. **2** *npl Fam* velours *m*, pantalon *m* en velours (côtelé).

cordial ['kɔːdɪəl] **1** *a* (*friendly*) cordial. **2** *n* **(fruit) c.** sirop *m*.

cordon ['kɔːdən] *n* cordon *m*; – *vt* **to c. off** (*place*) boucler, interdire l'accès à.

corduroy ['kɔːdərɔɪ] *n* (*fabric*) velours *m* côtelé; *pl* pantalon *m* en velours (côtelé), velours *m*.

core [kɔːr] *n* (*of fruit*) trognon *m*; (*of problem*) cœur *m*; (*group of people*) & *Geol El* noyau *m*; – *vt* (*apple*) vider. ◆**corer** *n* vide-pomme *m*.

cork [kɔːk] *n* liège *m*; (*for bottle*) bouchon *m*; – *vt* **to c. (up)** (*bottle*) boucher. ◆**corkscrew** *n* tire-bouchon *m*.

corn [kɔːn] *n* **1** (*wheat*) blé *m*; (*maize*) *Am* maïs *m*; (*seed*) grain *m*; **c. on the cob** épi *m* de maïs. **2** (*hard skin*) cor *m*. ◆**corned** *a* **c. beef** corned-beef *m*, singe *m*. ◆**cornflakes** *npl* céréales *fpl*. ◆**cornflour** *n* farine *f* de maïs, maïzena® *f*. ◆**cornflower** *n* bleuet *m*. ◆**cornstarch** *n Am* = **cornflour**.

cornea ['kɔːnɪə] *n Anat* cornée *f*.

corner ['kɔːnər] **1** *n* coin *m*; (*of street, room*) coin *m*, angle *m*; (*bend in road*) virage *m*; *Fb* corner *m*; **in a (tight) c.** dans une situation difficile. **2** *vt* (*animal, enemy etc*) acculer; (*person in corridor etc*) *Fig* coincer, accrocher; (*market*) *Com* accaparer; – *vi Aut* prendre un virage. ◆**cornerstone** *n* pierre *f* angulaire.

cornet ['kɔːnɪt] *n* (*of ice cream etc*) & *Mus* cornet *m*.

Cornwall ['kɔːnwəl] *n* Cornouailles *fpl*. ◆**Cornish** *a* de Cornouailles.

corny ['kɔːnɪ] *a* (**-ier, -iest**) (*joke etc*) rebattu.

corollary [kə'rɒlərɪ, *Am* 'kɒrəlerɪ] *n* corollaire *m*.

coronary ['kɒrənərɪ] *n Med* infarctus *m*.

coronation [kɒrə'neɪʃ(ə)n] *n* couronnement *m*, sacre *m*.

coroner ['kɒrənər] *n Jur* coroner *m*.

corporal ['kɔːpərəl] **1** *n Mil* caporal(-chef) *m*. **2** *a* **c. punishment** châtiment *m* corporel.

corporation [kɔːpə'reɪʃ(ə)n] *n* (*business*) société *f* commerciale; (*of town*) conseil *m* municipal. ◆**'corporate** *a* collectif; **c. body** corps *m* constitué.

corps [kɔːr, *pl* kɔːz] *n Mil Pol* corps *m*.

corpse [kɔːps] *n* cadavre *m*.

corpulent ['kɔːpjʊlənt] *a* corpulent. ◆**corpulence** *n* corpulence *f*.

corpus ['kɔːpəs] *n Ling* corpus *m*.

corpuscle ['kɔːpʌs(ə)l] *n Med* globule *m*.

corral [kə'ræl] *n Am* corral *m*.

correct [kə'rekt] *a* (*right, accurate*) exact, correct; (*proper*) correct; **he's c.** il a raison; – *vt* corriger. ◆**—ly** *adv* correctment.

◆—ness *n* (*accuracy, propriety*) correction *f*. **◆correction** *n* correction *f*. **◆corrective** *a* (*act, measure*) rectificatif.

correlate ['kɒrəleɪt] *vi* correspondre (**with** à); – *vt* faire correspondre. **◆corre'lation** *n* corrélation *f*.

correspond [kɒrɪ'spɒnd] *vi* **1** (*agree, be similar*) correspondre (**to** à, **with** avec). **2** (*by letter*) correspondre (**with** avec). **◆—ing** *a* (*matching*) correspondant; (*similar*) semblable. **◆correspondence** *n* correspondance *f*; **c. course** cours *m* par correspondance. **◆correspondent** *n* correspondant, -ante *mf*; *Journ* envoyé, -ée *mf*.

corridor ['kɒrɪdɔːr] *n* couloir *m*, corridor *m*.

corroborate [kə'rɒbəreɪt] *vt* corroborer.

corrode [kə'rəʊd] *vt* ronger, corroder; – *vi* se corroder. **◆corrosion** *n* corrosion *f*. **◆corrosive** *a* corrosif.

corrugated ['kɒrəgeɪtɪd] *a* (*cardboard*) ondulé; **c. iron** tôle *f* ondulée.

corrupt [kə'rʌpt] *vt* corrompre; – *a* corrompu. **◆corruption** *n* corruption *f*.

corset ['kɔːsɪt] *n* (*boned*) corset *m*; (*elasticated*) gaine *f*.

Corsica ['kɔːsɪkə] *n* Corse *f*.

cos [kɒs] *n* **c. (lettuce)** (laitue *f*) romaine *f*.

cosh [kɒʃ] *n* matraque *f*; – *vt* matraquer.

cosiness ['kəʊzɪnəs] *n* intimité *f*, confort *m*.

cosmetic [kɒz'metɪk] *n* produit *m* de beauté; – *a* esthétique; *Fig* superficiel.

cosmopolitan [kɒzmə'pɒlɪtən] *a* & *n* cosmopolite (*mf*).

cosmos ['kɒzmɒs] *n* cosmos *m*. **◆cosmic** *a* cosmique. **◆cosmonaut** *n* cosmonaute *mf*.

Cossack ['kɒsæk] *n* cosaque *m*.

cosset ['kɒsɪt] *vt* choyer.

cost [kɒst] *vti* (*pt* & *pp* **cost**) coûter; **how much does it c.?** ça coûte *or* ça vaut combien?; **to c. the earth** *Fam* coûter les yeux de la tête; – *n* coût *m*, prix *m*; **at great c.** à grands frais; **to my c.** à mes dépens; **at any c., at all costs** à tout prix; **at c. price** au prix coûtant. **◆c.-effective** *a* rentable. **◆costly** *a* (**-ier, -iest**) (*expensive*) coûteux; (*valuable*) précieux.

co-star ['kəʊstɑːr] *n* *Cin Th* partenaire *mf*.

costume ['kɒstjuːm] *n* costume *m*; (*woman's suit*) tailleur *m*; **(swimming) c.** maillot *m* (de bain); **c. jewellery** bijoux *mpl* de fantaisie.

cosy ['kəʊzɪ] **1** *a* (**-ier, -iest**) douillet, intime; **make yourself (nice and) c.** mets-toi à l'aise; **we're c.** on est bien ici. **2** *n* **(tea) c.** couvre-théière *m*.

cot [kɒt] *n* lit *m* d'enfant; (*camp bed*) *Am* lit *m* de camp.

cottage ['kɒtɪdʒ] *n* petite maison *f* de campagne; **(thatched) c.** chaumière *f*; **c. cheese** fromage *m* blanc (maigre); **c. industry** travail *m* à domicile (*activité artisanale*).

cotton ['kɒtən] **1** *n* coton *m*; (*yarn*) fil *m* (de coton); **absorbent c.** *Am*, **c. wool** coton *m* hydrophile, ouate *f*; **c. candy** *Am* barbe *f* à papa. **2** *vi* **to c. on (to)** *Sl* piger.

couch [kaʊtʃ] **1** *n* canapé *m*. **2** *vt* (*express*) formuler.

couchette [kuː'ʃet] *n* *Rail* couchette *f*.

cough [kɒf] **1** *n* toux *f*; **c. mixture** sirop *m* contre la toux; – *vi* tousser; – *vt* **to c. up** (*blood*) cracher. **2** *vt* **to c. up** (*money*) *Sl* cracher; – *vi* **to c. up** *Sl* payer, casquer.

could [kʊd, *unstressed* kəd] *see* **can** [1].

couldn't ['kʊd(ə)nt] = **could not**.

council ['kaʊns(ə)l] *n* conseil *m*; **c. flat/house** appartement *m*/maison *f* loué(e) à la municipalité, HLM *m or f*. **◆councillor** *n* conseiller, -ère *mf*; **(town) c.** conseiller *m* municipal.

counsel ['kaʊnsəl] *n* (*advice*) conseil *m*; *Jur* avocat, -ate *mf*; – *vt* (**-ll-**, *Am* **-l-**) conseiller (**s.o. to do** à qn de faire). **◆counsellor** *n* conseiller, -ère *mf*.

count[1] [kaʊnt] *vt* (*find number of, include*) compter; (*deem*) considérer; **not counting Paul** sans compter Paul; **to c. in** (*include*) inclure; **to c. out** exclure; (*money*) compter; – *vi* (*calculate, be important*) compter; **to c. against s.o.** être un désavantage pour qn, jouer contre qn; **to c. on s.o.** (*rely on*) compter sur qn; **to c. on doing** compter faire; – *n* compte *m*; *Jur* chef *m* (d'accusation); **he's lost c. of the books he has** il ne sait plus combien il a de livres. **◆countdown** *n* compte *m* à rebours.

count[2] [kaʊnt] *n* (*title*) comte *m*.

countenance ['kaʊntɪnəns] **1** *n* (*face*) mine *f*, expression *f*. **2** *vt* (*allow*) tolérer; (*approve*) approuver.

counter ['kaʊntər] **1** *n* (*in shop, bar etc*) comptoir *m*; (*in bank etc*) guichet *m*; **under the c.** *Fig* clandestinement, au marché noir; **over the c.** (*to obtain medicine*) sans ordonnance. **2** *n* (*in games*) jeton *m*. **3** *n* *Tech* compteur *m*. **4** *adv* **c. to** à l'encontre de. **5** *vt* (*plan*) contrarier; (*insult*) riposter à; (*blow*) parer; – *vi* riposter (**with** par).

counter- ['kaʊntər] *pref* contre-.

counterattack ['kaʊntərətæk] *n* contre-attaque *f*; – *vti* contre-attaquer.

counterbalance ['kaʊntəbæləns] *n* contrepoids *m*; – *vt* contrebalancer.

counterclockwise [kaʊntəˈklɒkwaɪz] *a & adv Am* dans le sens inverse des aiguilles d'une montre.
counterfeit [ˈkaʊntəfɪt] *a* faux; – *n* contrefaçon *f*, faux *m*; – *vt* contrefaire.
counterfoil [ˈkaʊntəfɔɪl] *n* souche *f*.
counterpart [ˈkaʊntəpɑːt] *n* (*thing*) équivalent *m*; (*person*) homologue *mf*.
counterpoint [ˈkaʊntəpɔɪnt] *n Mus* contrepoint *m*.
counterproductive [kaʊntəprəˈdʌktɪv] *a* (*action*) inefficace, qui produit l'effet contraire.
countersign [ˈkaʊntəsaɪn] *vt* contresigner.
countess [ˈkaʊntes] *n* comtesse *f*.
countless [ˈkaʊntləs] *a* innombrable.
countrified [ˈkʌntrɪfaɪd] *a* rustique.
country [ˈkʌntrɪ] *n* pays *m*; (*region*) région *f*, pays *m*; (*homeland*) patrie *f*; (*opposed to town*) campagne *f*; – *a* (*house etc*) de campagne; **c. dancing** la danse folklorique. ◆**countryman** *n* (*pl* **-men**) **(fellow) c.** compatriote *m*. ◆**countryside** *n* campagne *f*.
county [ˈkaʊntɪ] *n* comté *m*; **c. seat** *Am*, **c. town** chef-lieu *m*.
coup [kuː, *pl* kuːz] *n Pol* coup *m* d'État.
couple [ˈkʌp(ə)l] **1** *n* (*of people, animals*) couple *m*; **a c. of** deux ou trois; (*a few*) quelques. **2** *vt* (*connect*) accoupler. **3** *vi* (*mate*) s'accoupler.
coupon [ˈkuːpɒn] *n* (*voucher*) bon *m*; (*ticket*) coupon *m*.
courage [ˈkʌrɪdʒ] *n* courage *m*. ◆**courageous** [kəˈreɪdʒəs] *a* courageux.
courgette [kʊəˈʒet] *n* courgette *f*.
courier [ˈkʊrɪər] *n* (*for tourists*) guide *m*; (*messenger*) messager *m*; **c. service** service *m* de messagerie.
course [kɔːs] **1** *n* (*duration, movement*) cours *m*; (*of ship*) route *f*; (*of river*) cours *m*; (*way*) *Fig* route *f*, chemin *m*; (*means*) moyen *m*; **c. (of action)** ligne *f* de conduite; (*option*) parti *m*; **your best c. is to . . .** le mieux c'est de . . . ; **as a matter of c.** normalement; **in (the) c. of time** avec le temps, à la longue; **in due c.** en temps utile. **2** *n Sch Univ* cours *m*; **c. of lectures** série *f* de conférences; **c. (of treatment)** *Med* traitement *m*. **3** *n Culin* plat *m*; **first c.** entrée *f*. **4** *n* (*racecourse*) champ *m* de courses; **(golf) c.** terrain *m* (de golf). **5** *adv* **of c.!** bien sûr!, mais oui!; **of c. not!** bien sûr que non!
court [kɔːt] **1** *n* (*of monarch*) cour *f*; *Jur* cour *f*, tribunal *m*; *Tennis* court *m*; **c. of enquiry** commission *f* d'enquête; **high c.** cour *f* suprême; **to take to c.** poursuivre en justice; **c. shoe** escarpin *m*. **2** *vt* (*woman*) faire la cour à; (*danger, support*) rechercher. ◆**—ing** *a* (*couple*) d'amoureux; **they are c.** ils sortent ensemble. ◆**courthouse** *n* palais *m* de justice. ◆**courtier** *n Hist* courtisan *m*. ◆**courtroom** *n* salle *f* du tribunal. ◆**courtship** *n* (*act, period of time*) cour *f*. ◆**courtyard** *n* cour *f*.
courteous [ˈkɜːtɪəs] *a* poli, courtois. ◆**courtesy** *n* politesse *f*, courtoisie *f*.
court-martial [kɔːtˈmɑːʃəl] *n* conseil *m* de guerre; – *vt* **(-ll-)** faire passer en conseil de guerre.
cousin [ˈkʌz(ə)n] *n* cousin, -ine *mf*.
cove [kəʊv] *n* (*bay*) *Geog* anse *f*.
covenant [ˈkʌvənənt] *n Jur* convention *f*; *Rel* alliance *f*.
Coventry [ˈkɒvəntrɪ] *n* **to send s.o. to C.** *Fig* mettre qn en quarantaine.
cover [ˈkʌvər] *n* (*lid*) couvercle *m*; (*of book*) & *Fin* couverture *f*; (*for furniture, typewriter*) housse *f*; (*bedspread*) dessus-de-lit *m*; **the covers** (*blankets*) les couvertures *fpl*; **to take c.** se mettre à l'abri; **c. charge** (*in restaurant*) couvert *m*; **c. note** certificat *m* provisoire d'assurance; **under separate c.** (*letter*) sous pli séparé; – *vt* couvrir; (*protect*) protéger, couvrir; (*distance*) parcourir, couvrir; (*include*) englober, recouvrir; (*treat*) traiter; (*event*) *Journ TV Rad* couvrir, faire le reportage de; (*aim gun at*) tenir en joue; (*insure*) assurer; **to c. over** recouvrir; **to c. up** recouvrir; (*truth, tracks*) dissimuler; (*scandal*) étouffer, camoufler; – *vi* **to c. (oneself) up** se couvrir; **to c. up for s.o.** couvrir qn. ◆**c.-up** *n* tentative *f* pour étouffer *or* camoufler une affaire. ◆**covering** *n* (*wrapping*) enveloppe *f*; (*layer*) couche *f*; **c. letter** lettre *f* jointe (*à un document*).
coveralls [ˈkʌvərɔːlz] *npl Am* bleus *mpl* de travail.
covert [ˈkəʊvət, ˈkʌvət] *a* secret.
covet [ˈkʌvɪt] *vt* convoiter. ◆**covetous** *a* avide.
cow [kaʊ] **1** *n* vache *f*; (*of elephant etc*) femelle *f*; (*nasty woman*) *Fam* chameau *m*. **2** *vt* (*person*) intimider. ◆**cowboy** *n* cow-boy *m*. ◆**cowhand** *n* vacher, -ère *mf*. ◆**cowshed** *n* étable *f*.
coward [ˈkaʊəd] *n* lâche *mf*. ◆**—ly** *a* lâche. ◆**cowardice** *n* lâcheté *f*.
cower [ˈkaʊər] *vi* (*crouch*) se tapir; (*with fear*) *Fig* reculer (par peur).
cowslip [ˈkaʊslɪp] *n Bot* coucou *m*.

cox [kɒks] *vt Nau* barrer; – *n* barreur, -euse *mf*.

coy [kɔɪ] *a* (-er, -est) qui fait son *or* sa timide. ◆**coyness** *n* timidité *f* feinte.

coyote [kaɪ'əʊtɪ] *n* (*wolf*) *Am* coyote *m*.

cozy ['kəʊzɪ] *Am* = cosy.

crab [kræb] **1** *n* crabe *m*. **2** *n* **c. apple** pomme *f* sauvage. **3** *vi* (-bb-) (*complain*) *Fam* rouspéter. ◆**crabbed** *a* (*person*) grincheux.

crack[1] [kræk] *n* (*fissure*) fente *f*; (*in glass etc*) fêlure *f*; (*in skin*) crevasse *f*; (*snapping noise*) craquement *m*; (*of whip*) claquement *m*; (*blow*) coup *m*; (*joke*) *Fam* plaisanterie *f* (**at** aux dépens de); **to have a c. at doing** *Fam* essayer de faire; **at the c. of dawn** au point du jour; – *vt* (*glass, ice*) fêler; (*nut*) casser; (*ground, skin*) crevasser; (*whip*) faire claquer; (*joke*) lancer; (*problem*) résoudre; (*code*) déchiffrer; (*safe*) percer; **it's not as hard as it's cracked up to be** ce n'est pas aussi dur qu'on le dit; – *vi* se fêler; se crevasser; (*of branch, wood*) craquer; **to get cracking** (*get to work*) *Fam* s'y mettre; (*hurry*) *Fam* se grouiller; **to c. down on** sévir contre; **to c. up** (*mentally*) *Fam* craquer. ◆**c.-up** *n Fam* dépression *f* nerveuse; (*crash*) *Am Fam* accident *m*. ◆**cracked** *a* (*crazy*) *Fam* fou. ◆**cracker** *n* **1** (*cake*) biscuit *m* (salé). **2** (*firework*) pétard *m*; **Christmas c.** diablotin *m*. **3 she's a c.** *Fam* elle est sensationnelle. ◆**crackers** *a* (*mad*) *Sl* cinglé. ◆**crackpot** *a Fam* fou; – *n* fou *m*, folle *f*.

crack[2] [kræk] *a* (*first-rate*) de premier ordre, **c. shot** tireur *m* d'élite.

crackle ['kræk(ə)l] *vi* crépiter; (*of sth frying*) *Culin* grésiller; – *n* crépitement *m*; grésillement *m*.

cradle ['kreɪd(ə)l] *n* berceau *m*; – *vt* bercer.

craft [krɑːft] **1** *n* (*skill*) art *m*; (*job*) métier *m* (artisanal); – *vt* façonner. **2** *n* (*cunning*) ruse *f*. **3** *n inv* (*boat*) bateau *m*. ◆**craftsman** *n* (*pl* -men) artisan *m*. ◆**craftsmanship** *n* (*skill*) art *m*; **a piece of c.** un beau travail, une belle pièce. ◆**crafty** *a* (-ier, -iest) astucieux; *Pej* rusé.

crag [kræg] *n* rocher *m* à pic. ◆**craggy** *a* (*rock*) à pic; (*face*) rude.

cram [kræm] *vt* (-mm-) **to c. into** (*force*) fourrer dans; **to c. with** (*fill*) bourrer de; – *vi* **to c. into** (*of people*) s'entasser dans; **to c. (for an exam)** bachoter.

cramp [kræmp] *n Med* crampe *f* (**in** à). ◆**cramped** *a* (*in a room or one's clothes*) à l'étroit; **in c. conditions** à l'étroit.

cranberry ['krænbərɪ] *n Bot* canneberge *f*.

crane [kreɪn] **1** *n* (*bird*) & *Tech* grue *f*. **2** *vt* **to c. one's neck** tendre le cou.

crank [kræŋk] **1** *n* (*person*) *Fam* excentrique *mf*; (*fanatic*) fanatique *mf*. **2** *n* (*handle*) *Tech* manivelle *f*; – *vt* **to c. (up)** (*vehicle*) faire démarrer à la manivelle. ◆**cranky** *a* (-ier, -iest) excentrique; (*bad-tempered*) *Am* grincheux.

crannies ['krænɪz] *npl* **nooks and c.** coins et recoins *mpl*.

craps [kræps] *n* **to shoot c.** *Am* jouer aux dés.

crash [kræʃ] *n* accident *m*; (*of firm*) faillite *f*; (*noise*) fracas *m*; (*of thunder*) coup *m*; **c. course/diet** cours *m*/régime *m* intensif; **c. helmet** casque *m* (anti-choc); **c. landing** atterrissage *m* en catastrophe; – *int* (*of fallen object*) patatras!; – *vt* (*car*) avoir un accident avec; **to c. one's car into** faire rentrer sa voiture dans; – *vi Aut Av* s'écraser; **to c. into** rentrer dans; **the cars crashed (into each other)** les voitures se sont percutées *or* carambolées; **to c. (down)** tomber; (*break*) se casser; (*of roof*) s'effondrer. ◆**c.-land** *vi* atterrir en catastrophe.

crass [kræs] *a* grossier; (*stupidity*) crasse.

crate [kreɪt] *n* caisse *f*, cageot *m*.

crater ['kreɪtər] *n* cratère *m*; **(bomb) c.** entonnoir *m*.

cravat [krə'væt] *n* foulard *m* (*autour du cou*).

crav/e [kreɪv] *vt* **to c. (for)** éprouver un grand besoin de; (*mercy*) implorer. ◆**—ing** *n* désir *m*, grand besoin *m* (**for** de).

craven ['kreɪvən] *a Pej* lâche.

crawl [krɔːl] *vi* ramper; (*of child*) se traîner (à quatre pattes); *Aut* avancer au pas; **to be crawling with** grouiller de; – *n Swimming* crawl *m*; **to move at a c.** *Aut* avancer au pas.

crayfish ['kreɪfɪʃ] *n inv* écrevisse *f*.

crayon ['kreɪən] *n* crayon *m*, pastel *m*.

craze [kreɪz] *n* manie *f* (**for** de), engouement *m* (**for** pour). ◆**crazed** *a* affolé.

crazy ['kreɪzɪ] *a* (-ier, -iest) fou; **c. about sth** fana de qch; **c. about s.o.** fou de qn; **c. paving** dallage *m* irrégulier. ◆**craziness** *n* folie *f*.

creak [kriːk] *vi* (*of hinge*) grincer; (*of timber*) craquer. ◆**creaky** *a* grinçant; qui craque.

cream [kriːm] *n* crème *f*; (*élite*) *Fig* crème *f*, gratin *m*; – *a* (*cake*) à la crème; **c.(-coloured)** crème *inv*; **c. cheese** fromage *m* blanc; – *vt* (*milk*) écrémer; **to c. off** *Fig* écrémer. ◆**creamy** *a* (-ier, -iest) crémeux.

crease [kriːs] *vt* froisser, plisser; – *vi* se froisser; – *n* pli *m*; (*accidental*) (faux) pli *m*. ◆**c.-resistant** *a* infroissable.

create [kriː'eɪt] *vt* créer; (*impression, noise*) faire. ◆**creation** *n* création *f*. ◆**creative** *a* créateur, créatif. ◆**creativeness** *n* créativité *f*. ◆**crea'tivity** *n* créativité *f*. ◆**creator** *n* créateur, -trice *mf*.

creature ['kriːtʃər] *n* animal *m*, bête *f*; (*person*) créature *f*; **one's c. comforts** ses aises *fpl*.

crèche [kreʃ] *n* (*nursery*) crèche *f*; (*manger*) *Rel Am* crèche *f*.

credence ['kriːdəns] *n* **to give** *or* **lend c. to** ajouter foi à.

credentials [krɪ'denʃəlz] *npl* références *fpl*; (*identity*) pièces *fpl* d'identité; (*of diplomat*) lettres *fpl* de créance.

credible ['kredɪb(ə)l] *a* croyable; (*politician, information*) crédible. ◆**credi'bility** *n* crédibilité *f*.

credit ['kredɪt] *n* (*influence, belief*) & *Fin* crédit *m*; (*merit*) mérite *m*; *Univ* unité *f* de valeur; *pl Cin* générique *m*; **to give c. to** (*person*) *Fin* faire crédit à; *Fig* reconnaître le mérite de; (*statement*) ajouter foi à; **to be a c. to** faire honneur à; **on c.** à crédit; **in c.** (*account*) créditeur; **to one's c.** *Fig* à son actif; – *a* (*balance*) créditeur; **c. card** carte *f* de crédit; **c. facilities** facilités *fpl* de paiement; – *vt* (*believe*) croire; *Fin* créditer (**s.o. with sth** qn de qch); **to c. s.o. with** (*qualities*) attribuer à qn. ◆**creditable** *a* honorable. ◆**creditor** *n* créancier, -ière *mf*. ◆**creditworthy** *a* solvable.

credulous ['kredjʊləs] *a* crédule.

creed [kriːd] *n* credo *m*.

creek [kriːk] *n* (*bay*) crique *f*; (*stream*) *Am* ruisseau *m*; **up the c.** (*in trouble*) *Sl* dans le pétrin.

creep [kriːp] **1** *vi* (*pt & pp* **crept**) ramper; (*silently*) se glisser (furtivement); (*slowly*) avancer lentement; **it makes my flesh c.** ça me donne la chair de poule. **2** *n* (*person*) *Sl* salaud *m*; **it gives me the creeps** *Fam* ça me fait froid dans le dos. ◆**creepy** *a* (**-ier, -iest**) *Fam* terrifiant; (*nasty*) *Fam* vilain. ◆**creepy-'crawly** *n Fam, Am.* ◆**creepy-'crawler** *n Fam* bestiole *f*.

cremate [krɪ'meɪt] *vt* incinérer. ◆**cremation** *n* crémation *f*. ◆**crema'torium** *n* crématorium *m*. ◆**'crematory** *n Am* crématorium *m*.

Creole ['kriːəʊl] *n* créole *mf*; *Ling* créole *m*.

crêpe [kreɪp] *n* (*fabric*) crêpe *m*; **c. (rubber)** crêpe *m*; **c. paper** papier *m* crêpon.

crept [krept] *see* **creep 1.**

crescendo [krɪ'ʃendəʊ] *n* (*pl* **-os**) crescendo *m inv*.

crescent ['kres(ə)nt] *n* croissant *m*; (*street*) *Fig* rue *f* (en demi-lune).

cress [kres] *n* cresson *m*.

crest [krest] *n* (*of bird, wave, mountain*) crête *f*; (*of hill*) sommet *m*; (*on seal, letters etc*) armoiries *fpl*.

Crete [kriːt] *n* Crète *f*.

cretin ['kretɪn, *Am* 'kriːt(ə)n] *n* crétin, -ine *mf*. ◆**cretinous** *a* crétin.

crevasse [krɪ'væs] *n* (*in ice*) *Geol* crevasse *f*.

crevice ['krevɪs] *n* (*crack*) crevasse *f*, fente *f*.

crew [kruː] *n Nau Av* équipage *m*; (*gang*) équipe *f*; **c. cut** (coupe *f* en) brosse *f*. ◆**c.-neck(ed)** *a* à col ras.

crib [krɪb] **1** *n* (*cradle*) berceau *m*; (*cot*) *Am* lit *m* d'enfant; *Rel* crèche *f*. **2** *n* (*copy*) plagiat *m*; *Sch* traduction *f*; (*list of answers*) *Sch* pompe *f* anti-sèche; – *vti* (**-bb-**) copier.

crick [krɪk] *n* **c. in the neck** torticolis *m*; **c. in the back** tour *m* de reins.

cricket ['krɪkɪt] *n* **1** (*game*) cricket *m*. **2** (*insect*) grillon *m*. ◆**cricketer** *n* joueur, -euse *mf* de cricket.

crikey! ['kraɪkɪ] *int Sl* zut (alors)!

crime [kraɪm] *n* crime *m*; (*not serious*) délit *m*; (*criminal practice*) criminalité *f*. ◆**criminal** *a* & *n* criminel, -elle (*mf*).

crimson ['krɪmz(ə)n] *a* & *n* cramoisi (*m*).

cring/e [krɪndʒ] *vi* reculer (**from** devant); *Fig* s'humilier (**to, before** devant). ◆**—ing** *a Fig* servile.

crinkle ['krɪŋk(ə)l] *vt* froisser; – *vi* se froisser; – *n* fronce *f*. ◆**crinkly** *a* froissé; (*hair*) frisé.

crippl/e ['krɪpəl] *n* (*lame*) estropié, -ée *mf*; (*disabled*) infirme *mf*; – *vt* estropier; (*disable*) rendre infirme; (*nation etc*) *Fig* paralyser. ◆**—ed** *a* estropié; infirme; (*ship*) désemparé; **c. with** (*rheumatism, pains*) perclus de. ◆**—ing** *a* (*tax*) écrasant.

crisis, *pl* **-ses** ['kraɪsɪs, -siːz] *n* crise *f*.

crisp [krɪsp] **1** *a* (**-er, -est**) (*biscuit*) croustillant; (*apple etc*) croquant; (*snow*) craquant; (*air, style*) vif. **2** *npl* **(potato) crisps** (pommes *fpl*) chips *mpl*. ◆**crispbread** *n* pain *m* suédois.

criss-cross ['krɪskrɒs] *a* (*lines*) entrecroisés; (*muddled*) enchevêtrés; – *vi* s'entrecroiser; – *vt* sillonner (en tous sens).

criterion, *pl* **-ia** [kraɪ'tɪərɪən, -ɪə] *n* critère *m*.

critic ['krɪtɪk] *n* critique *m*. ◆**critical** *a* critique. ◆**critically** *adv* (*to examine etc*) en critique; (*harshly*) sévèrement; (*ill*) gravement. ◆**criticism** *n* critique *f*. ◆**criticize** *vti* critiquer. ◆**cri'tique** *n* (*essay etc*) critique *f*.

croak [krəʊk] *vi* (*of frog*) croasser; – *n* croassement *m*.
crochet ['krəʊʃeɪ] *vt* faire au crochet; – *vi* faire du crochet; – *n* (travail *m* au) crochet *m*; **c. hook** crochet *m*.
crock [krɒk] *n* **a c., an (old) c.** *Fam* (*person*) un croulant; (*car*) un tacot.
crockery ['krɒkərɪ] *n* (*cups etc*) vaisselle *f*.
crocodile ['krɒkədaɪl] *n* crocodile *m*.
crocus ['krəʊkəs] *n* crocus *m*.
crony ['krəʊnɪ] *n Pej Fam* copain *m*, copine *f*.
crook [krʊk] *n* **1** (*thief*) escroc *m*. **2** (*shepherd's stick*) houlette *f*.
crooked ['krʊkɪd] *a* courbé; (*path*) tortueux; (*hat, picture*) de travers; (*deal, person*) malhonnête; – *adv* de travers. ◆**—ly** *adv* de travers.
croon [kruːn] *vti* chanter (à voix basse).
crop [krɒp] **1** *n* (*harvest*) récolte *f*; (*produce*) culture *f*; (*of questions etc*) *Fig* série *f*; (*of people*) groupe *m*. **2** *vt* (**-pp-**) (*hair*) couper (ras); – *n* **c. of hair** chevelure *f*. **3** *vi* (**-pp-**) **to c. up** se présenter, survenir. ◆**cropper** *n* **to come a c.** *Sl* (*fall*) ramasser une pelle; (*fail*) échouer.
croquet ['krəʊkeɪ] *n* (*game*) croquet *m*.
croquette [krəʊ'ket] *n Culin* croquette *f*.
cross[1] [krɒs] **1** *n* croix *f*; **a c. between** (*animal*) un croisement entre *or* de. **2** *vt* traverser; (*threshold, barrier*) franchir; (*legs, animals*) croiser; (*thwart*) contrecarrer; (*cheque*) barrer; **to c. off** *or* **out** rayer; **it never crossed my mind that . . .** il ne m'est pas venu à l'esprit que . . . ; **crossed lines** *Tel* lignes *fpl* embrouillées; – *vi* (*of paths*) se croiser; **to c. (over)** traverser. ◆**—ing** *n Nau* traversée *f*; **(pedestrian) c.** passage *m* clouté. ◆**cross-breed** *n* métis, -isse *mf*, hybride *m*. ◆**c.-'country** *a* à travers champs; **c.-country race** cross(-country) *m*. ◆**c.-exami'nation** *n* contre-interrogatoire *m*. ◆**c.-e'xamine** *vt* interroger. ◆**c.-eyed** *a* qui louche. ◆**c.-'legged** *a* & *adv* les jambes croisées. ◆**c.-'purposes** *npl* **to be at c.-purposes** se comprendre mal. ◆**c.-'reference** *n* renvoi *m*. ◆**c.-section** *n* coupe *f* transversale; *Fig* échantillon *m*.
cross[2] [krɒs] *a* (*angry*) fâché (**with** contre). ◆**—ly** *adv* d'un air fâché.
crossbow ['krɒsbəʊ] *n* arbalète *f*.
crosscheck [krɒs'tʃek] *n* contre-épreuve *f*; – *vt* vérifier.
crossfire ['krɒsfaɪər] *n* feux *mpl* croisés.
crossroads ['krɒsrəʊdz] *n* carrefour *m*.
crosswalk ['krɒswɔːk] *n Am* passage *m* clouté.
crossword ['krɒswɜːd] *n* **c. (puzzle)** mots *mpl* croisés.
crotch [krɒtʃ] *n* (*of garment*) entre-jambes *m inv*.
crotchet ['krɒtʃɪt] *n Mus* noire *f*.
crotchety ['krɒtʃɪtɪ] *a* grincheux.
crouch [kraʊtʃ] *vi* **to c. (down)** s'accroupir, se tapir. ◆**—ing** *a* accroupi, tapi.
croupier ['kruːpɪər] *n* (*in casino*) croupier *m*.
crow [krəʊ] **1** *n* corbeau *m*, corneille *f*; **as the c. flies** à vol d'oiseau; **c.'s nest** *Nau* nid *m* de pie. **2** *vi* (*of cock*) chanter; (*boast*) *Fig* se vanter (**about** de). ◆**crowbar** *n* levier *m*.
crowd [kraʊd] *n* foule *f*; (*particular group*) bande *f*; (*of things*) *Fam* masse *f*; **quite a c.** beaucoup de monde; – *vi* **to c. into** (*of people*) s'entasser dans; **to c. round s.o.** se presser autour de qn; **to c. together** se serrer; – *vt* (*fill*) remplir; **to c. into** (*press*) entasser dans; **don't c. me!** *Fam* ne me bouscule pas! ◆**—ed** *a* plein (**with** de); (*train etc*) bondé, plein; (*city*) encombré; **it's very c.!** il y a beaucoup de monde!
crown [kraʊn] *n* (*of king, tooth*) couronne *f*; (*of head, hill*) sommet *m*; **c. court** cour *f* d'assises; **C. jewels,** joyaux *mpl* de la Couronne; – *vt* couronner. ◆**—ing** *a* (*glory etc*) suprême; **c. achievement** couronnement *m*.
crucial ['kruːʃəl] *a* crucial.
crucify ['kruːsɪfaɪ] *vt* crucifier. ◆**crucifix** ['kruːsɪfɪks] *n* crucifix *m*. ◆**cruci'fixion** *n* crucifixion *f*.
crude [kruːd] *a* (**-er, -est**) (*oil, fact*) brut; (*manners, person*) grossier; (*language, light*) cru; (*painting, work*) rudimentaire. ◆**—ly** *adv* (*to say, order etc*) crûment. ◆**—ness** *n* grossièreté *f*; crudité *f*; état *m* rudimentaire.
cruel [krʊəl] *a* (**crueller, cruellest**) cruel. ◆**cruelty** *n* cruauté *f*; **an act of c.** une cruauté.
cruet ['kruːɪt] *n* **c. (stand)** salière *f*, poivrière *f* et huilier *m*.
cruis/e [kruːz] *vi Nau* croiser; *Aut* rouler; *Av* voler; (*of taxi*) marauder; (*of tourists*) faire une croisière; – *n* croisière *f*. ◆**—ing** *a* **c. speed** *Nau Av* & *Fig* vitesse *f* de croisière. ◆**—er** *n Nau* croiseur *m*.
crumb [krʌm] *n* miette *f*; (*of comfort*) *Fig* brin *m*; **crumbs!** *Hum Fam* zut!
crumble ['krʌmb(ə)l] *vt* (*bread*) émietter; – *vi* (*collapse*) s'effondrer; **to c. (away)** (*in small pieces*) & *Fig* s'effriter. ◆**crumbly** *a* friable.
crummy ['krʌmɪ] *a* (**-ier, -iest**) *Fam* moche, minable.

crumpet ['krʌmpɪt] *n Culin* petite crêpe *f* grillée (*servie beurrée*).
crumple ['krʌmp(ə)l] *vt* froisser; – *vi* se froisser.
crunch [krʌntʃ] **1** *vt* (*food*) croquer; – *vi* (*of snow*) craquer. **2** *n* **the c.** *Fam* le moment critique. ◆**crunchy** *a* (**-ier, -iest**) (*apple etc*) croquant.
crusade [kruː'seɪd] *n Hist & Fig* croisade *f*; – *vi* faire une croisade. ◆**crusader** *n Hist* croisé *m*; *Fig* militant, -ante *mf*.
crush [krʌʃ] **1** *n* (*crowd*) cohue *f*; (*rush*) bousculade *f*; **to have a c. on s.o.** *Fam* avoir le béguin pour qn. **2** *vt* écraser; (*hope*) détruire; (*clothes*) froisser; (*cram*) entasser (**into** dans). ◆**—ing** *a* (*defeat*) écrasant.
crust [krʌst] *n* croûte *f*. ◆**crusty** *a* (**-ier, -iest**) (*bread*) croustillant.
crutch [krʌtʃ] *n* **1** *Med* béquille *f*. **2** (*crotch*) entre-jambes *m inv*.
crux [krʌks] *n* **the c. of** (*problem, matter*) le nœud de.
cry [kraɪ] *n* (*shout*) cri *m*; **to have a c.** *Fam* pleurer; – *vi* (*weep*) pleurer; **to c. (out)** pousser un cri, crier; (*exclaim*) s'écrier; **to c. (out) for** demander (à grands cris); **to be crying out for** avoir grand besoin de; **to c. off** (*withdraw*) abandonner; **to c. off (sth)** se désintéresser (de qch); **to c. over** pleurer (sur); – *vt* (*shout*) crier. ◆**—ing** *a* (*need etc*) très grand; **a c. shame** une véritable honte; – *n* cris *mpl*; (*weeping*) pleurs *mpl*.
crypt [krɪpt] *n* crypte *f*.
cryptic ['krɪptɪk] *a* secret, énigmatique.
crystal ['krɪst(ə)l] *n* cristal *m*. ◆**c.-'clear** *a* (*water, sound*) cristallin; *Fig* clair comme le jour *or* l'eau de roche. ◆**crystallize** *vt* cristalliser; – *vi* (se) cristalliser.
cub [kʌb] *n* **1** (*of animal*) petit *m*. **2** (*scout*) louveteau *m*.
Cuba ['kjuːbə] *n* Cuba *m*. ◆**Cuban** *a & n* cubain, -aine (*mf*).
cubbyhole ['kʌbɪhəʊl] *n* cagibi *m*.
cube [kjuːb] *n* cube *m*; (*of meat etc*) dé *m*. ◆**cubic** *a* (*shape*) cubique; (*metre etc*) cube; **c. capacity** volume *m*; *Aut* cylindrée *f*.
cubicle ['kjuːbɪk(ə)l] *n* (*for changing*) cabine *f*; (*in hospital*) box *m*.
cuckoo ['kʊkuː] **1** *n* (*bird*) coucou *m*; **c. clock** coucou *m*. **2** *a* (*stupid*) *Sl* cinglé.
cucumber ['kjuːkʌmbər] *n* concombre *m*.
cuddle ['kʌd(ə)l] *vt* (*hug*) serrer (dans ses bras); (*caress*) câliner; – *vi* (*of lovers*) se serrer; **to (kiss and) c.** s'embrasser; **to c. up to** (*huddle*) se serrer *or* se blottir contre; – *n* caresse *f*. ◆**cuddly** *a* (**-ier, -iest**) *a* câlin, caressant; (*toy*) doux, en peluche.
cudgel ['kʌdʒəl] *n* trique *f*, gourdin *m*.
cue [kjuː] *n* **1** *Th* réplique *f*; (*signal*) signal *m*. **2** (**billiard**) **c.** queue *f* (de billard).
cuff [kʌf] **1** *n* (*of shirt etc*) poignet *m*, manchette *f*; (*of trousers*) *Am* revers *m*; **off the c.** *Fig* impromptu; **c. link** bouton *m* de manchette. **2** *vt* (*strike*) gifler.
cul-de-sac ['kʌldəsæk] *n* impasse *f*, cul-de-sac *m*.
culinary ['kʌlɪnərɪ] *a* culinaire.
cull [kʌl] *vt* choisir; (*animals*) abattre sélectivement.
culminate ['kʌlmɪneɪt] *vi* **to c. in** finir par. ◆**culmi'nation** *n* point *m* culminant.
culprit ['kʌlprɪt] *n* coupable *mf*.
cult [kʌlt] *n* culte *m*.
cultivat/e ['kʌltɪveɪt] *vt* (*land, mind etc*) cultiver. ◆**—ed** *a* cultivé. ◆**culti'vation** *n* culture *f*; **land *or* fields under c.** cultures *fpl*.
culture ['kʌltʃər] *n* culture *f*. ◆**cultural** *a* culturel. ◆**cultured** *a* cultivé.
cumbersome ['kʌmbəsəm] *a* encombrant.
cumulative ['kjuːmjʊlətɪv] *a* cumulatif; **c. effect** (*long-term*) effet *m or* résultat *m* à long terme.
cunning ['kʌnɪŋ] *a* astucieux; *Pej* rusé; – *n* astuce *f*; ruse *f*. ◆**—ly** *adv* avec astuce; avec ruse.
cup [kʌp] *n* tasse *f*; (*goblet, prize*) coupe *f*; **that's my c. of tea** *Fam* c'est à mon goût; **c. final** *Fb* finale *f* de la coupe. ◆**c.-tie** *n Fb* match *m* éliminatoire. ◆**cupful** *n* tasse *f*.
cupboard ['kʌbəd] *n* armoire *f*; (*built-in*) placard *m*.
Cupid ['kjuːpɪd] *n* Cupidon *m*.
cupola ['kjuːpələ] *n Archit* coupole *f*.
cuppa ['kʌpə] *n Fam* tasse *f* de thé.
curate ['kjʊərɪt] *n* vicaire *m*.
curator [kjʊə'reɪtər] *n* (*of museum*) conservateur *m*.
curb [kɜːb] **1** *n* (*kerb*) *Am* bord *m* du trottoir. **2** *vt* (*feelings*) refréner, freiner; (*ambitions*) modérer; (*expenses*) limiter; – *n* frein *m*; **to put a c. on** mettre un frein à.
curdle ['kɜːd(ə)l] *vt* cailler; – *vi* se cailler; (*of blood*) *Fig* se figer.
curds [kɜːdz] *npl* lait *m* caillé. ◆**curd cheese** *n* fromage *m* blanc (maigre).
cure [kjʊər] **1** *vt* guérir (**of** de); (*poverty*) *Fig* éliminer; – *n* remède *m* (**for** contre); (*recovery*) guérison *f*; **rest c.** cure *f* de repos. **2** *vt Culin* (*smoke*) fumer; (*salt*) saler; (*dry*) sécher. ◆**curable** *a* guérissable, curable. ◆**curative** *a* curatif.
curfew ['kɜːfjuː] *n* couvre-feu *m*.

curio ['kjuərɪəʊ] *n* (*pl* **-os**) bibelot *m*, curiosité *f*.
curious ['kjuərɪəs] *a* (*odd*) curieux; (*inquisitive*) curieux (**about** de); **c. to know** curieux de savoir. ◆**—ly** *adv* (*oddly*) curieusement. ◆**curi'osity** *n* curiosité *f*.
curl [kɜːl] **1** *vti* (*hair*) boucler, friser; – *n* boucle *f*; (*of smoke*) *Fig* spirale *f*. **2** *vi* **to c. up** (*shrivel*) se racornir; **to c. oneself up** (*into a ball*) se pelotonner. ◆**—er** *n* bigoudi *m*. ◆**curly** *a* (**-ier, -iest**) bouclé, frisé.
currant ['kʌrənt] *n* (*fruit*) groseille *f*; (*dried grape*) raisin *m* de Corinthe.
currency ['kʌrənsɪ] *n* (*money*) monnaie *f*; (*acceptance*) *Fig* cours *m*; (**foreign**) **c.** devises *fpl* (étrangères).
current ['kʌrənt] **1** *a* (*fashion, trend etc*) actuel; (*opinion, use, phrase*) courant; (*year, month*) en cours, courant; **c. affairs** questions *fpl* d'actualité; **c. events** actualité *f*; **the c. issue** (*of magazine etc*) le dernier numéro. **2** *n* (*of river, air*) & *El* courant *m*. ◆**—ly** *adv* actuellement, à présent.
curriculum, *pl* **-la** [kə'rɪkjʊləm, -lə] *n* programme *m* (scolaire); **c. (vitae)** curriculum (vitae) *m inv*.
curry ['kʌrɪ] **1** *n Culin* curry *m*, cari *m*. **2** *vt* **to c. favour with** s'insinuer dans les bonnes grâces de.
curs/e [kɜːs] *n* malédiction *f*; (*swearword*) juron *m*; (*bane*) *Fig* fléau *m*; – *vt* maudire; **cursed with** (*blindness etc*) affligé de; – *vi* (*swear*) jurer. ◆**—ed** [-ɪd] *a Fam* maudit.
cursor ['kɜːsər] *n* (*on computer screen*) curseur *m*.
cursory ['kɜːsərɪ] *a* (trop) rapide, superficiel.
curt [kɜːt] *a* brusque. ◆**—ly** *adv* d'un ton brusque. ◆**—ness** *n* brusquerie *f*.
curtail [kɜː'teɪl] *vt* écourter, raccourcir; (*expenses*) réduire. ◆**—ment** *n* raccourcissement *m*; réduction *f*.
curtain ['kɜːt(ə)n] *n* rideau *m*; **c. call** *Th* rappel *m*.
curts(e)y ['kɜːtsɪ] *n* révérence *f*; – *vi* faire une révérence.
curve [kɜːv] *n* courbe *f*; (*in road*) *Am* virage *m*; *pl* (*of woman*) *Fam* rondeurs *fpl*; – *vt* courber; – *vi* se courber; (*of road*) tourner, faire une courbe.
cushion ['kʊʃən] *n* coussin *m*; – *vt* (*shock*) *Fig* amortir. ◆**cushioned** *a* (*seat*) rembourré; **c. against** *Fig* protégé contre.
cushy ['kʊʃɪ] *a* (**-ier, -iest**) (*job, life*) *Fam* pépère, facile.
custard ['kʌstəd] *n* crème *f* anglaise; (*when set*) crème *f* renversée.
custodian [kʌ'stəʊdɪən] *n* gardien, -ienne *mf*.
custody ['kʌstədɪ] *n* (*care*) garde *f*; **to take into c.** *Jur* mettre en détention préventive. ◆**cu'stodial** *a* **c. sentence** peine *f* de prison.
custom ['kʌstəm] *n* coutume *f*; (*patronage*) *Com* clientèle *f*. ◆**customary** *a* habituel, coutumier; **it is c. to** il est d'usage de. ◆**custom-built** *a*, ◆**customized** *a* (*car etc*) (fait) sur commande.
customer ['kʌstəmər] *n* client, -ente *mf*; *Pej* individu *m*.
customs ['kʌstəmz] *n* & *npl* (**the**) **c.** la douane; **c. (duties)** droits *mpl* de douane; **c. officer** douanier *m*; **c. union** union *f* douanière.
cut [kʌt] *n* coupure *f*; (*stroke*) coup *m*; (*of clothes, hair*) coupe *f*; (*in salary*) réduction *f*; (*of meat*) morceau *m*; – *vt* (*pt* & *pp* **cut**, *pres p* **cutting**) couper; (*meat*) découper; (*glass, tree*) tailler; (*record*) graver; (*hay*) faucher; (*profits, prices etc*) réduire; (*tooth*) percer; (*corner*) *Aut* prendre à la corde; **to c. open** ouvrir (*au couteau etc*); **to c. short** (*visit*) abréger; – *vi* (*of person, scissors*) couper; (*of material*) se couper; **to c. into** (*cake*) entamer. ■ **to c. away** *vt* (*remove*) enlever; **to c. back (on)** *vti* réduire. ◆**cutback** *n* réduction *f*; **to c. down** *vt* (*tree*) abattre, couper; **to c. down (on)** *vti* réduire; **to c. in** *vi* interrompre; *Aut* faire une queue de poisson (**on s.o.** à qn); **to c. off** *vt* couper; (*isolate*) isoler; **to c. out** *vi* (*of engine*) *Aut* caler; – *vt* (*article*) découper; (*garment*) tailler; (*remove*) enlever; (*leave out, get rid of*) *Fam* supprimer; **to c. out drinking** (*stop*) *Fam* s'arrêter de boire; **c. it out!** *Fam* ça suffit!; **c. out to be a doctor/***etc* fait pour être médecin/*etc*. ◆**cutout** *n* (*picture*) découpage *m*; *El* coupe-circuit *m inv*; **to c. up** *vt* couper (en morceaux); (*meat*) découper; **c. up about** démoralisé par. ◆**cutting** *n* coupe *f*; (*of diamond*) taille *f*; (*article*) *Journ* coupure *f*; (*plant*) bouture *f*; *Cin* montage *m*; – *a* (*wind, word*) cinglant; **c. edge** tranchant *m*.
cute [kjuːt] *a* (**-er, -est**) *Fam* (*pretty*) mignon; (*shrewd*) astucieux.
cuticle ['kjuːtɪk(ə)l] *n* petites peaux *fpl* (*de l'ongle*).
cutlery ['kʌtlərɪ] *n* couverts *mpl*.
cutlet ['kʌtlɪt] *n* (*of veal etc*) côtelette *f*.
cut-price [kʌt'praɪs] *a* à prix réduit.
cutthroat ['kʌtθrəʊt] *n* assassin *m*; – *a* (*competition*) impitoyable.

cv [siː'viː] *n abbr* curriculum (vitae) *m inv*.
cyanide ['saɪənaɪd] *n* cyanure *m*.
cybernetics [saɪbə'netɪks] *n* cybernétique *f*.
cycle ['saɪk(ə)l] **1** *n* bicyclette *f*, vélo *m*; – *a* (*path, track*) cyclable; (*race*) cycliste; – *vi* aller à bicyclette (**to** à); *Sp* faire de la bicyclette. **2** *n* (*series, period*) cycle *m*. ◆**cycling** *n* cyclisme *m*; – *a* (*champion*) cycliste. ◆**cyclist** *n* cycliste *mf*. ◆**cyclic(al)** ['sɪklɪk(əl)] *a* cyclique.
cyclone ['saɪkləʊn] *n* cyclone *m*.
cylinder ['sɪlɪndər] *n* cylindre *m*. ◆**cy'lindrical** *a* cylindrique.
cymbal ['sɪmbəl] *n* cymbale *f*.
cynic ['sɪnɪk] *n* cynique *mf*. ◆**cynical** *a* cynique. ◆**cynicism** *n* cynisme *m*.
cypress ['saɪprəs] *n* (*tree*) cyprès *m*.
Cyprus ['saɪprəs] *n* Chypre *f*. ◆**Cypriot** ['sɪprɪət] *a* & *n* cypriote (*mf*).
cyst [sɪst] *n Med* kyste *m*.
czar [zɑːr] *n* tsar *m*.
Czech [tʃek] *a* & *n* tchèque (*mf*). ◆**Czecho'slovak** *a* & *n* tchécoslovaque (*mf*). ◆**Czechoslo'vakia** *n* Tchécoslovaquie *f*. ◆**Czechoslo'vakian** *a* & *n* tchécoslovaque (*mf*).

D

D, d [diː] *n* D, d *m*. ◆**D.-day** *n* le jour J.
dab [dæb] *n* **a d. of** un petit peu de; – *vt* (-bb-) (*wound, brow etc*) tamponner; **to d. sth on sth** appliquer qch (à petits coups) sur qch.
dabble ['dæb(ə)l] *vi* **to d. in** s'occuper *or* se mêler un peu de.
dad [dæd] *n Fam* papa *m*. ◆**daddy** *n Fam* papa *m*; **d. longlegs** (*cranefly*) tipule *f*; (*spider*) *Am* faucheur *m*.
daffodil ['dæfədɪl] *n* jonquille *f*.
daft [dɑːft] *a* (-er, -est) *Fam* idiot, bête.
dagger ['dægər] *n* poignard *m*; **at daggers drawn** à couteaux tirés (**with** avec).
dahlia ['deɪljə, *Am* 'dæljə] *n* dahlia *m*.
daily ['deɪlɪ] *a* quotidien, journalier; (*wage*) journalier; – *adv* quotidiennement; – *n* **d. (paper)** quotidien *m*; **d. (help)** (*cleaning woman*) femme *f* de ménage.
dainty ['deɪntɪ] *a* (-ier, -iest) délicat; (*pretty*) mignon; (*tasteful*) élégant. ◆**daintily** *adv* délicatement; élégamment.
dairy ['deərɪ] *n* (*on farm*) laiterie *f*; (*shop*) crémerie *f*; – *a* (*produce, cow etc*) laitier. ◆**dairyman** *n* (*pl* **-men**) (*dealer*) laitier *m*. ◆**dairywoman** *n* (*pl* **-women**) laitière *f*.
daisy ['deɪzɪ] *n* pâquerette *f*.
dale [deɪl] *n Geog Lit* vallée *f*.
dally ['dælɪ] *vi* musarder, lanterner.
dam [dæm] *n* (*wall*) barrage *m*; – *vt* (-mm-) (*river*) barrer.
damag/e ['dæmɪdʒ] *n* dégâts *mpl*, dommages *mpl*; (*harm*) *Fig* préjudice *m*; *pl Jur* dommages-intérêts *mpl*; – *vt* (*spoil*) abîmer; (*material object*) endommager, abîmer; (*harm*) *Fig* nuire à. ◆**—ing** *a* préjudiciable (**to** à).
dame [deɪm] *n Lit* dame *f*; *Am Sl* nana *f*, fille *f*.
damn [dæm] *vt* (*condemn, doom*) condamner; *Rel* damner; (*curse*) maudire; **d. him!** *Fam* qu'il aille au diable!; – *int* **d. (it)!** *Fam* zut!, merde!; – *n* **he doesn't care a d.** *Fam* il s'en fiche pas mal; – *a Fam* fichu, sacré; – *adv Fam* sacrément; **d. all** rien du tout. ◆**—ed 1** *a* (*soul*) damné. **2** *Fam* = **damn** *a* & *adv*. ◆**—ing** *a* (*evidence etc*) accablant. ◆**dam'nation** *n* damnation *f*.
damp [dæmp] *a* (-er, -est) humide; (*skin*) moite; – *n* humidité *f*. ◆**damp(en)** *vt* humecter; **to d. (down)** (*zeal*) refroidir; (*ambition*) étouffer. ◆**damper** *n* **to put a d. on** jeter un froid sur. ◆**dampness** *n* humidité *f*.
damsel ['dæmzəl] *n Lit* & *Hum* demoiselle *f*.
damson ['dæmzən] *n* prune *f* de Damas.
danc/e [dɑːns] *n* danse *f*; (*social event*) bal *m*; **d. hall** dancing *m*; – *vi* danser; **to d. for joy** sauter de joie; – *vt* (*polka etc*) danser. ◆**—ing** *n* danse *f*; **d. partner** cavalier, -ière *mf*. ◆**—er** *n* danseur, -euse *mf*.
dandelion ['dændɪlaɪən] *n* pissenlit *m*.
dandruff ['dændrʌf] *n* pellicules *fpl*.
dandy ['dændɪ] **1** *n* dandy *m*. **2** *a* (*very good*) *Am Fam* formidable.
Dane [deɪn] *n* Danois, -oise *mf*.
danger ['deɪndʒər] *n* (*peril*) danger *m* (**to** pour); (*risk*) risque *m*; **in d.** en danger; **in d. of** (*threatened by*) menacé de; **to be in d. of falling/etc** risquer de tomber/etc; **on the d. list** *Med* dans un état critique; **d. signal** signal *m* d'alarme; **d. zone** zone *f* dangereuse. ◆**dangerous** *a* (*place, illness,*

person etc) dangereux (**to** pour). ◆**dangerously** *adv* dangereusement; (*ill*) gravement.

dangle ['dæŋg(ə)l] *vt* balancer; (*prospect*) *Fig* faire miroiter (**before s.o.** aux yeux de qn); – *vi* (*hang*) pendre; (*swing*) se balancer.

Danish ['deɪnɪʃ] *a* danois; – *n* (*language*) danois *m*.

dank [dæŋk] *a* (**-er, -est**) humide (et froid).

dapper ['dæpər] *a* pimpant, fringant.

dappled ['dæp(ə)ld] *a* pommelé, tacheté.

dar/e [deər] *vi* oser (**do** faire); **she d. not come** elle n'ose pas venir; **he doesn't d. (to) go** il n'ose pas y aller; **if you d. (to)** si tu l'oses, si tu oses le faire; **I d. say he tried** il a sans doute essayé, je suppose qu'il a essayé; **to d. s.o. to do** défier qn de faire. ◆**—ing** *a* audacieux; – *n* audace *f*. ◆**daredevil** *n* casse-cou *m inv*, risque-tout *m inv*.

dark [dɑːk] *a* (**-er, -est**) obscur, noir, sombre; (*colour*) foncé, sombre; (*skin*) brun, foncé; (*hair*) brun, noir, foncé; (*eyes*) foncé; (*gloomy*) sombre; **it's d.** il fait nuit *or* noir; **to keep sth d.** tenir qch secret; **d. glasses** lunettes *fpl* noires; – *n* noir *m*, obscurité *f*; **after d.** après la tombée de la nuit; **to keep s.o. in the d.** laisser qn dans l'ignorance (**about** de). ◆**d.-'haired** *a* aux cheveux bruns. ◆**d.-'skinned** *a* brun; (*race*) de couleur. ◆**darken** *vt* assombrir, obscurcir; (*colour*) foncer; – *vi* s'assombrir; (*of colour*) foncer. ◆**darkness** *n* obscurité *f*, noir *m*.

darkroom ['dɑːkruːm] *n Phot* chambre *f* noire.

darling ['dɑːlɪŋ] *n* (*favourite*) chouchou, -oute *mf*; **(my) d.** (mon) chéri, (ma) chérie; **he's a d.** c'est un amour; **be a d.!** sois un ange!; – *a* chéri; (*delightful*) *Fam* adorable.

darn [dɑːn] **1** *vt* (*socks*) repriser. **2** *int* **d. it!** bon sang! ◆**—ing** *n* reprise *f*; – *a* (*needle, wool*) à repriser.

dart [dɑːt] **1** *vi* se précipiter, s'élancer (**for** vers); – *n* **to make a d.** se précipiter (**for** vers). **2** *n Sp* fléchette *f*; *pl* (*game*) fléchettes *fpl*. ◆**dartboard** *n Sp* cible *f*.

dash [dæʃ] **1** *n* (*run, rush*) ruée *f*; **to make a d.** se précipiter (**for** vers); – *vi* se précipiter; (*of waves*) se briser (**against** contre); **to d. off** *or* **away** partir *or* filer en vitesse; – *vt* jeter (avec force); (*shatter*) briser; **d. (it)!** *Fam* zut!; **to d. off** (*letter*) faire en vitesse. **2** *n* **a d. of** un (petit) peu de; **a d. of milk** une goutte *or* un nuage de lait. **3** *n* (*stroke*) trait *m*; *Typ* tiret *m*. ◆**—ing** *a* (*person*) sémillant.

dashboard ['dæʃbɔːd] *n Aut* tableau *m* de bord.

data ['deɪtə] *npl* données *fpl*; **d. processing** informatique *f*.

date[1] [deɪt] *n* date *f*; (*on coin*) millésime *m*; (*meeting*) *Fam* rendez-vous *m inv*; (*person*) *Fam* copain, -ine *mf* (*avec qui on a un rendez-vous*); **up to d.** moderne; (*information*) à jour; (*well-informed*) au courant (**on** de); **out of d.** (*old-fashioned*) démodé; (*expired*) périmé; **to d.** à ce jour, jusqu'ici; **d. stamp** (*object*) (tampon *m*) dateur *m*; (*mark*) cachet *m*; – *vt* (*letter etc*) dater; (*girl, boy*) *Fam* sortir avec; – *vi* (*become out of date*) dater; **to d. back to, d. from** dater de. ◆**dated** *a* démodé.

date[2] [deɪt] *n Bot* datte *f*.

datebook ['deɪtbʊk] *n Am* agenda *m*.

daub [dɔːb] *vt* barbouiller (**with** de).

daughter ['dɔːtər] *n* fille *f*. ◆**d.-in-law** *n* (*pl* **daughters-in-law**) belle-fille *f*, bru *f*.

daunt [dɔːnt] *vt* décourager, rebuter. ◆**—less** *a* intrépide.

dawdl/e ['dɔːd(ə)l] *vi* traîner, lambiner. ◆**—er** *n* traînard, -arde *mf*.

dawn [dɔːn] *n* aube *f*, aurore *f*; – *vi* (*of day*) poindre; (*of new era, idea*) naître, voir le jour; **it dawned upon him that . . .** il lui est venu à l'esprit que . . . . ◆**—ing** *a* naissant.

day [deɪ] *n* jour *m*; (*working period, whole day long*) journée *f*; *pl* (*period*) époque *f*, temps *mpl*; **all d. (long)** toute la journée; **what d. is it?** quel jour sommes-nous?; **the following** *or* **next d.** le lendemain; **the d. before** la veille; **the d. before yesterday** avant-hier; **the d. after tomorrow** après-demain; **to the d.** jour pour jour; **d. boarder** demi-pensionnaire *mf*; **d. nursery** crèche *f*; **d. return** *Rail* aller et retour *m* (*pour une journée*); **d. tripper** excursionniste *mf*. ◆**d.-to-'d.** *a* journalier; **on a d.-to-day basis** (*every day*) journellement. ◆**daybreak** *n* point *m* du jour. ◆**daydream** *n* rêverie *f*; – *vi* rêvasser. ◆**daylight** *n* (lumière *f* du) jour *m*; (*dawn*) point *m* du jour; **it's d.** il fait jour. ◆**daytime** *n* journée *f*.

daze [deɪz] *vt* (*with drugs etc*) hébéter; (*by blow*) étourdir; – *n* **in a d.** étourdi; hébété.

dazzle ['dæz(ə)l] *vt* éblouir; – *n* éblouissement *m*.

deacon ['diːkən] *n Rel* diacre *m*.

dead [ded] *a* mort; (*numb*) engourdi; (*party etc*) qui manque de vie, mortel; (*telephone*) sans tonalité; **in (the) d. centre** au beau milieu; **to be a d. loss** (*person*) *Fam* n'être bon à rien; **it's a d. loss** *Fam* ça ne vaut rien; **d. silence** un silence de mort; **a d. stop** un arrêt complet; **d. end** (*street*) & *Fig* impasse *f*; **a d.-end job** un travail sans avenir; – *adv* (*completely*) absolument; (*very*) très; **d. beat** *Fam* éreinté; **d. drunk** *Fam* ivre mort; **to stop d.** s'arrêter net; – *n* **the d.** les morts *mpl*; **in the d. of** (*night, winter*) au cœur de. ◆**—ly** *a* (**-ier, -iest**) (*enemy, silence, paleness*) mortel; (*weapon*) meurtrier; **d. sins** péchés *mpl* capitaux; – *adv* mortellement. ◆**deadbeat** *n Am Fam* parasite *m*. ◆**deadline** *n* date *f* limite; (*hour*) heure *f* limite. ◆**deadlock** *n Fig* impasse *f*. ◆**deadpan** *a* (*face*) figé, impassible.

deaden ['ded(ə)n] *vt* (*shock*) amortir; (*pain*) calmer; (*feeling*) émousser.

deaf [def] *a* sourd (**to** à); **d. and dumb** sourd-muet; **d. in one ear** sourd d'une oreille; – *n* **the d.** les sourds *mpl*. ◆**d.-aid** *n* audiophone *m*, prothèse *f* auditive. ◆**deafen** *vt* assourdir. ◆**deafness** *n* surdité *f*.

deal[1] [diːl] **1** *n* **a good** *or* **great d.** beaucoup (**of** de). **2** *n Com* marché *m*, affaire *f*; *Cards* donne *f*; **fair d.** traitement *m or* arrangement *m* équitable; **it's a d.** d'accord; **big d.!** *Iron* la belle affaire! **3** *vt* (*pt & pp* **dealt** [delt]) (*blow*) porter; **to d. (out)** (*cards*) donner; (*money*) distribuer. **4** *vi* (*trade*) traiter (**with s.o.** avec qn); **to d. in** faire le commerce de; **to d. with** (*take care of*) s'occuper de; (*concern*) traiter de, parler de; **I can d. with him** (*handle*) je sais m'y prendre avec lui. ◆**—ings** *npl* relations *fpl* (**with** avec); *Com* transactions *fpl*. ◆**—er** *n* marchand, -ande *mf* (**in** de); (*agent*) dépositaire *mf*; (*for cars*) concessionnaire *mf*; (*in drugs*) *Sl* revendeur, -euse *mf* de drogues; *Cards* donneur, -euse *mf*.

deal[2] [diːl] *n* (*wood*) sapin *m*.

dean [diːn] *n Rel Univ* doyen *m*.

dear [dɪər] *a* (**-er, -est**) (*loved, precious, expensive*) cher; (*price*) élevé; **D. Sir** (*in letter*) *Com* Monsieur; **D. Uncle** (mon) cher oncle; **oh d.!** oh là là!, oh mon Dieu!; – *n* **(my) d.** (*darling*) (mon) chéri, (ma) chérie; (*friend*) mon cher, ma chère; **she's a d.** c'est un amour; **be a d.!** sois un ange!; – *adv* (*to cost, pay*) cher. ◆**—ly** *adv* tendrement; (*very much*) beaucoup; **to pay d. for sth** payer qch cher.

dearth [dɜːθ] *n* manque *m*, pénurie *f*.

death [deθ] *n* mort *f*; **to put to d.** mettre à mort; **to be bored to d.** s'ennuyer à mourir; **to be burnt to d.** mourir carbonisé; **to be sick to d.** en avoir vraiment marre; **many deaths** (*people killed*) de nombreux morts *mpl*; – *a* (*march*) funèbre; (*mask*) mortuaire; **d. certificate** acte *m* de décès; **d. duty** droits *mpl* de succession; **d. penalty** *or* **sentence** peine *f* de mort; **d. rate** mortalité *f*; **it's a d. trap** il y a danger de mort. ◆**deathbed** *n* lit *m* de mort. ◆**deathblow** *n* coup *m* mortel. ◆**deathly** *a* mortel, de mort; – *adv* **d. pale** d'une pâleur mortelle.

debar [dɪ'bɑːr] *vt* (**-rr-**) exclure; **to d. from doing** interdire de faire.

debase [dɪ'beɪs] *vt* (*person*) avilir; (*reputation, talents*) galvauder; (*coinage*) altérer.

debat/e [dɪ'beɪt] *vti* discuter; **to d. (with oneself) whether to leave**/*etc* se demander si on doit partir/*etc*; – *n* débat *m*, discussion *f*. ◆**—able** *a* discutable, contestable.

debauch [dɪ'bɔːtʃ] *vt* corrompre, débaucher. ◆**debauchery** *n* débauche *f*.

debilitate [dɪ'bɪlɪteɪt] *vt* débiliter. ◆**debility** *n* faiblesse *f*, débilité *f*.

debit ['debɪt] *n* débit *m*; **in d.** (*account*) débiteur; – *a* (*balance*) *Fin* débiteur; – *vt* débiter (**s.o. with sth** qn de qch).

debonair [debə'neər] *a* jovial; (*charming*) charmant; (*polite*) poli.

debris ['debriː] *n* débris *mpl*.

debt [det] *n* dette *f*; **to be in d.** avoir des dettes; **to be £50 in d.** devoir 50 livres; **to run** *or* **get into d.** faire des dettes. ◆**debtor** *n* débiteur, -trice *mf*.

debunk [diː'bʌŋk] *vt Fam* démystifier.

debut ['debjuː] *n Th* début *m*.

decade ['dekeɪd] *n* décennie *f*.

decadent ['dekədənt] *a* décadent. ◆**decadence** *n* décadence *f*.

decaffeinated [diː'kæfɪneɪtɪd] *a* décaféiné.

decal ['diːkæl] *n Am* décalcomanie *f*.

decant [dɪ'kænt] *vt* (*wine*) décanter. ◆**—er** *n* carafe *f*.

decapitate [dɪ'kæpɪteɪt] *vt* décapiter.

decathlon [dɪ'kæθlɒn] *n Sp* décathlon *m*.

decay [dɪ'keɪ] *vi* (*go bad*) se gâter; (*rot*) pourrir; (*of tooth*) se carier, se gâter; (*of building*) tomber en ruine; (*decline*) *Fig* décliner; – *n* pourriture *f*; *Archit* délabrement *m*; (*of tooth*) carie(s) *f(pl)*; (*of nation*) décadence *f*; **to fall into d.** (*of building*) tomber en ruine. ◆**—ing** *a* (*nation*) décadent; (*meat, fruit etc*) pourrissant.

deceased [dɪ'siːst] *a* décédé, défunt; – *n* **the d.** le défunt, la défunte; *pl* les défunt(e)s.

deceit [dɪ'siːt] *n* tromperie *f*. ◆**deceitful** *a*

trompeur. ◆**deceitfully** *adv* avec duplicité.
deceive [dɪ'siːv] *vti* tromper; **to d. oneself** se faire des illusions.
December [dɪ'sembər] *n* décembre *m*.
decent ['diːsənt] *a* (*respectable*) convenable, décent; (*good*) *Fam* bon; (*kind*) *Fam* gentil; **that was d. (of you)** c'était chic de ta part. ◆**decency** *n* décence *f*; (*kindness*) *Fam* gentillesse *f*. ◆**decently** *adv* décemment.
decentralize [diː'sentrəlaɪz] *vt* décentraliser. ◆**decentrali'zation** *n* décentralisation *f*.
deception [dɪ'sepʃ(ə)n] *n* tromperie *f*. ◆**deceptive** *a* trompeur.
decibel ['desɪbel] *n* décibel *m*.
decid/e [dɪ'saɪd] *vt* (*question etc*) régler, décider; (*s.o.'s career, fate etc*) décider de; **to d. to do** décider de faire; **to d. that** décider que; **to d. s.o. to do** décider qn à faire; – *vi* (*make decisions*) décider; (*make up one's mind*) se décider (**on doing** à faire); **to d. on sth** décider de qch, se décider à qch; (*choose*) se décider pour qch. ◆**—ed** *a* (*firm*) décidé, résolu; (*clear*) net. ◆**—edly** *adv* résolument; nettement. ◆**—ing** *a* (*factor etc*) décisif.
decimal ['desɪməl] *a* décimal; **d. point** virgule *f*; – *n* décimale *f*. ◆**decimali'zation** *n* décimalisation *f*.
decimate ['desɪmeɪt] *vt* décimer.
decipher [dɪ'saɪfər] *vt* déchiffrer.
decision [dɪ'sɪʒ(ə)n] *n* décision *f*. ◆**decisive** [dɪ'saɪsɪv] *a* (*defeat, tone etc*) décisif; (*victory*) net, incontestable. ◆**decisively** *adv* (*to state*) avec décision; (*to win*) nettement, incontestablement.
deck [dek] **1** *n Nau* pont *m*; **top d.** (*of bus*) impériale *f*. **2** *n* **d. of cards** jeu *m* de cartes. **3** *n* (*of record player*) platine *f*. **4** *vt* **to d. (out)** (*adorn*) orner. ◆**deckchair** *n* chaise *f* longue.
declare [dɪ'kleər] *vt* déclarer (**that** que); (*verdict, result*) proclamer. ◆**decla'ration** *n* déclaration *f*; proclamation *f*.
declin/e [dɪ'klaɪn] **1** *vi* (*deteriorate*) décliner; (*of birthrate, price etc*) baisser; **to d. in importance** perdre de l'importance; – *n* déclin *m*; (*fall*) baisse *f*. **2** *vt* refuser, décliner; **to d. to do** refuser de faire. ◆**—ing** *a* **one's d. years** ses dernières années.
decode [diː'kəud] *vt* (*message*) décoder.
decompose [diːkəm'pəuz] *vt* décomposer; – *vi* se décomposer. ◆**decompo'sition** *n* décomposition *f*.
decompression [diːkəm'preʃ(ə)n] *n* décompression *f*.
decontaminate [diːkən'tæmɪneɪt] *vt* décontaminer.
decor ['deɪkɔːr] *n* décor *m*.
decorat/e ['dekəreɪt] *vt* (*cake, house, soldier*) décorer (**with** de); (*paint etc*) peindre (et tapisser); (*hat, skirt etc*) orner (**with** de). ◆**—ing** *n* **interior d.** décoration *f* d'intérieurs. ◆**deco'ration** *n* décoration *f*. ◆**decorative** *a* décoratif. ◆**decorator** *n* (*house painter etc*) peintre *m* décorateur; (**interior**) **d.** ensemblier *m*, décorateur, -trice *mf*.
decorum [dɪ'kɔːrəm] *n* bienséances *fpl*.
decoy ['diːkɔɪ] *n* (*artificial bird*) appeau *m*; (**police**) **d.** policier *m* en civil.
decreas/e [dɪ'kriːs] *vti* diminuer; – ['diːkriːs] *n* diminution *f* (**in** de). ◆**—ing** *a* (*number etc*) décroissant. ◆**—ingly** *adv* de moins en moins.
decree [dɪ'kriː] *n Pol Rel* décret *m*; *Jur* jugement *m*; (*municipal*) arrêté *m*; – *vt* (*pt & pp* **decreed**) décréter.
decrepit [dɪ'krepɪt] *a* (*building*) en ruine; (*person*) décrépit.
decry [dɪ'kraɪ] *vt* décrier.
dedicat/e ['dedɪkeɪt] *vt* (*devote*) consacrer (**to** à); (*book*) dédier (**to** à); **to d. oneself to** se consacrer à. ◆**dedi'cation** *n* (*in book*) dédicace *f*; (*devotion*) dévouement *m*.
deduce [dɪ'djuːs] *vt* (*conclude*) déduire (**from** de, **that** que).
deduct [dɪ'dʌkt] *vt* (*subtract*) déduire, retrancher (**from** de); (*from wage, account*) prélever (**from** sur). ◆**deductible** *a* à déduire (**from** de); (*expenses*) déductible. ◆**deduction** *n* (*inference*) & *Com* déduction *f*.
deed [diːd] *n* action *f*, acte *m*; (*feat*) exploit *m*; *Jur* acte *m* (notarié).
deem [diːm] *vt* juger, estimer.
deep [diːp] *a* (**-er, -est**) profond; (*snow*) épais; (*voice*) grave; (*note*) *Mus* bas; (*person*) insondable; **to be six metres/***etc* **d.** avoir six mètres/*etc* de profondeur; **d. in thought** absorbé *or* plongé dans ses pensées; **the d. end** (*in swimming pool*) le grand bain; **d. red** rouge foncé; – *adv* (*to breathe*) profondément; **d. into the night** tard dans la nuit; – *n* **the d.** l'océan *m*. ◆**—ly** *adv* (*grateful, to regret etc*) profondément. ◆**deep-'freeze** *vt* surgeler; – *n* congélateur *m*. ◆**d.-'fryer** *n* friteuse *f*. ◆**d.-'rooted** *a*, ◆**d.-'seated** *a* bien ancré, profond. ◆**d.-'set** *a* (*eyes*) enfoncés.

deepen ['diːpən] *vt* approfondir; (*increase*) augmenter; – *vi* devenir plus profond; (*of mystery*) s'épaissir. ◆**—ing** *a* grandissant.
deer [dɪər] *n inv* cerf *m*.
deface [dɪ'feɪs] *vt* (*damage*) dégrader; (*daub*) barbouiller.
defamation [defə'meɪʃ(ə)n] *n* diffamation *f*. ◆**de'famatory** *a* diffamatoire.
default [dɪ'fɔːlt] *n* **by d.** *Jur* par défaut; **to win by d.** gagner par forfait; – *vi Jur* faire défaut; **to d. on one's payments** *Fin* être en rupture de paiement.
defeat [dɪ'fiːt] *vt* battre, vaincre; (*plan*) faire échouer; – *n* défaite *f*; (*of plan*) échec *m*. ◆**defeatism** *n* défaitisme *m*.
defect 1 ['diːfekt] *n* défaut *m*. **2** [dɪ'fekt] *vi Pol* déserter, faire défection; **to d. to** (*the West, the enemy*) passer à. ◆**de'fection** *n* défection *f*. ◆**de'fective** *a* défectueux; *Med* déficient. ◆**de'fector** *n* transfuge *mf*.
defence [dɪ'fens] (*Am* **defense**) *n* défense *f*; **the body's defences** la défense de l'organisme (**against** contre); **in his d.** *Jur* à sa décharge, pour le défendre. ◆**defenceless** *a* sans défense. ◆**defensible** *a* défendable. ◆**defensive** *a* défensif; – *n* **on the d.** sur la défensive.
defend [dɪ'fend] *vt* défendre. ◆**defendant** *n* (*accused*) *Jur* prévenu, -ue *mf*. ◆**defender** *n* défenseur *m*; (*of title*) *Sp* détenteur, -trice *mf*.
defer [dɪ'fɜːr] **1** *vt* (**-rr-**) (*postpone*) différer, reporter. **2** *vi* (**-rr-**) **to d. to** (*yield*) déférer à. ◆**—ment** *n* report *m*.
deference ['defərəns] *n* déférence *f*. ◆**defe'rential** *a* déférent, plein de déférence.
defiant [dɪ'faɪənt] *a* (*tone etc*) de défi; (*person*) rebelle. ◆**defiance** *n* (*resistance*) défi *m* (**of** à); **in d. of** (*contempt*) au mépris de. ◆**defiantly** *adv* d'un air de défi.
deficient [dɪ'fɪʃənt] *a* insuffisant; *Med* déficient; **to be d. in** manquer de. ◆**deficiency** *n* manque *m*; (*flaw*) défaut *m*; *Med* carence *f*; (*mental*) déficience *f*.
deficit ['defɪsɪt] *n* déficit *m*.
defile [dɪ'faɪl] *vt* souiller, salir.
define [dɪ'faɪn] *vt* définir. ◆**defi'nition** *n* définition *f*.
definite ['defɪnɪt] *a* (*date, plan*) précis, déterminé; (*obvious*) net, évident; (*firm*) ferme; (*certain*) certain; **d. article** *Gram* article *m* défini. ◆**—ly** *adv* certainement; (*appreciably*) nettement; (*to say*) catégoriquement.
definitive [dɪ'fɪnɪtɪv] *a* définitif.
deflate [dɪ'fleɪt] *vt* (*tyre*) dégonfler. ◆**deflation** *n* dégonflement *m*; *Econ* déflation *f*.
deflect [dɪ'flekt] *vt* faire dévier; – *vi* dévier.
deform [dɪ'fɔːm] *vt* déformer. ◆**—ed** *a* (*body*) difforme. ◆**deformity** *n* difformité *f*.
defraud [dɪ'frɔːd] *vt* (*customs, State etc*) frauder; **to d. s.o. of sth** escroquer qch à qn.
defray [dɪ'freɪ] *vt* (*expenses*) payer.
defrost [diː'frɒst] *vt* (*fridge*) dégivrer; (*food*) décongeler.
deft [deft] *a* adroit (**with** de). ◆**—ness** *n* adresse *f*.
defunct [dɪ'fʌŋkt] *a* défunt.
defuse [diː'fjuːz] *vt* (*bomb, conflict*) désamorcer.
defy [dɪ'faɪ] *vt* (*person, death etc*) défier; (*effort, description*) résister à; **to d. s.o. to do** défier qn de faire.
degenerate [dɪ'dʒenəreɪt] *vi* dégénérer (**into** en); – [dɪ'dʒenərət] *a* & *n* dégénéré, -ée (*mf*). ◆**degene'ration** *n* dégénérescence *f*.
degrade [dɪ'greɪd] *vt* dégrader. ◆**degradation** [degrə'deɪʃ(ə)n] *n Mil Ch* dégradation *f*; (*of person*) déchéance *f*.
degree [dɪ'griː] *n* **1** degré *m*; **not in the slightest d.** pas du tout; **to such a d.** à tel point (**that** que). **2** *Univ* diplôme *m*; (*Bachelor's*) licence *f*; (*Master's*) maîtrise *f*; (*PhD*) doctorat *m*.
dehumanize [diː'hjuːmənaɪz] *vt* déshumaniser.
dehydrate [diːhaɪ'dreɪt] *vt* déshydrater.
de-ice [diː'aɪs] *vt Av Aut* dégivrer.
deign [deɪn] *vt* daigner (**to do** faire).
deity ['diːɪtɪ] *n* dieu *m*.
dejected [dɪ'dʒektɪd] *a* abattu, découragé. ◆**dejection** *n* abattement *m*.
dekko ['dekəʊ] *n Sl* coup *m* d'œil.
delay [dɪ'leɪ] *vt* retarder; (*payment*) différer; – *vi* (*be slow*) tarder (**doing** à faire); (*linger*) s'attarder; – *n* (*lateness*) retard *m*; (*waiting period*) délai *m*; **without d.** sans tarder. ◆**delayed-'action** *a* (*bomb*) à retardement. ◆**delaying** *a* **d. tactics** moyens *mpl* dilatoires.
delectable [dɪ'lektəb(ə)l] *a* délectable.
delegate 1 ['delɪgeɪt] *vt* déléguer (**to** à). **2** ['delɪgət] *n* délégué, -ée *mf*. ◆**dele'gation** *n* délégation *f*.
delete [dɪ'liːt] *vt* rayer, supprimer. ◆**deletion** *n* (*thing deleted*) rature *f*; (*act*) suppression *f*.
deleterious [delɪ'tɪərɪəs] *a* néfaste.
deliberate¹ [dɪ'lɪbəreɪt] *vi* délibérer; – *vt* délibérer sur.
deliberate² [dɪ'lɪbərət] *a* (*intentional*) délibéré; (*cautious*) réfléchi; (*slow*) mesuré.

◆—**ly** *adv* (*intentionally*) exprès, délibérément; (*to walk*) avec mesure. ◆**delibe'ration** *n* délibération *f*.

delicate ['delɪkət] *a* délicat. ◆**delicacy** *n* délicatesse *f*; *Culin* mets *m* délicat, gourmandise *f*. ◆**delicately** *adv* délicatement. ◆**delica'tessen** *n* (*shop*) épicerie *f* fine, traiteur *m*.

delicious [dɪ'lɪʃəs] *a* délicieux.

delight [dɪ'laɪt] *n* délice *m*, grand plaisir *m*, joie *f*; *pl* (*pleasures, things*) délices *fpl*; **to be the d. of** faire les délices de; **to take d. in sth/in doing** se délecter de qch/à faire; – *vt* réjouir; – *vi* se délecter (**in doing** à faire). ◆—**ed** *a* ravi, enchanté (**with sth** de qch, **to do** de faire, **that** que). ◆**delightful** *a* charmant; (*meal, perfume, sensation*) délicieux. ◆**delightfully** *adv* avec beaucoup de charme; (*wonderfully*) merveilleusement.

delineate [dɪ'lɪnɪeɪt] *vt* (*outline*) esquisser; (*portray*) décrire.

delinquent [dɪ'lɪŋkwənt] *a* & *n* délinquant, -ante (*mf*). ◆**delinquency** *n* délinquance *f*.

delirious [dɪ'lɪərɪəs] *a* délirant; **to be d.** avoir le délire, délirer. ◆**delirium** *n Med* délire *m*.

deliver [dɪ'lɪvər] *vt* **1** (*goods, milk etc*) livrer; (*letters*) distribuer; (*hand over*) remettre (**to** à). **2** (*rescue*) délivrer (**from** de). **3** (*give birth to*) mettre au monde, accoucher de; **to d. a woman('s baby)** accoucher une femme. **4** (*speech*) prononcer; (*ultimatum, warning*) lancer; (*blow*) porter. ◆**deliverance** *n* délivrance *f*. ◆**delivery** *n* **1** livraison *f*; distribution *f*; remise *f*. **2** *Med* accouchement *m*. **3** (*speaking*) débit *m*. ◆**deliveryman** *n* (*pl* **-men**) livreur *m*.

delta ['deltə] *n* (*of river*) delta *m*.

delude [dɪ'luːd] *vt* tromper; **to d. oneself** se faire des illusions. ◆**delusion** *n* illusion *f*; *Psy* aberration *f* mentale.

deluge ['deljuːdʒ] *n* (*of water, questions etc*) déluge *m*; – *vt* inonder (**with** de).

de luxe [dɪ'lʌks] *a* de luxe.

delve [delv] *vi* **to d. into** (*question, past*) fouiller; (*books*) fouiller dans.

demagogue ['deməgɒg] *n* démagogue *mf*.

demand [dɪ'mɑːnd] *vt* exiger (**sth from s.o.** qch de qn), réclamer (**sth from s.o.** qch à qn); (*rights, more pay*) revendiquer; **to d. that** exiger que; **to d. to know** insister pour savoir; – *n* exigence *f*; (*claim*) revendication *f*, réclamation *f*; (*request*) & *Econ* demande *f*; **in great d.** très demandé; **to make demands on s.o.** exiger beaucoup de qn. ◆—**ing** *a* exigeant.

demarcation [diːmɑː'keɪʃ(ə)n] *n* démarcation *f*.

demean [dɪ'miːn] *vt* **to d. oneself** s'abaisser, s'avilir.

demeanour [dɪ'miːnər] *n* (*behaviour*) comportement *m*.

demented [dɪ'mentɪd] *a* dément.

demerara [demə'reərə] *n* **d. (sugar)** cassonade *f*, sucre *m* roux.

demise [dɪ'maɪz] *n* (*death*) décès *m*; *Fig* disparition *f*.

demo ['deməʊ] *n* (*pl* **-os**) (*demonstration*) *Fam* manif *f*.

demobilize [diː'məʊbɪlaɪz] *vt* démobiliser.

democracy [dɪ'mɒkrəsɪ] *n* démocratie *f*. ◆**democrat** ['deməkræt] *n* démocrate *mf*. ◆**demo'cratic** *a* démocratique; (*person*) démocrate.

demography [dɪ'mɒgrəfɪ] *n* démographie *f*.

demolish [dɪ'mɒlɪʃ] *vt* démolir. ◆**demo'lition** *n* démolition *f*.

demon ['diːmən] *n* démon *m*.

demonstrate ['demənstreɪt] *vt* démontrer; (*machine*) faire une démonstration de; – *vi Pol* manifester. ◆**demon'stration** *n* démonstration *f*; *Pol* manifestation *f*. ◆**de'monstrative** *a* démonstratif. ◆**demonstrator** *n Pol* manifestant, -ante *mf*; (*in shop etc*) démonstrateur, -trice *mf*.

demoralize [dɪ'mɒrəlaɪz] *vt* démoraliser.

demote [dɪ'məʊt] *vt* rétrograder.

demure [dɪ'mjʊər] *a* sage, réservé.

den [den] *n* antre *m*, tanière *f*.

denationalize [diː'næʃ(ə)nəlaɪz] *vt* dénationaliser.

denial [dɪ'naɪəl] *n* (*of truth etc*) dénégation *f*; (*of rumour*) démenti *m*; (*of authority*) rejet *m*; **to issue a d.** publier un démenti.

denigrate ['denɪgreɪt] *vt* dénigrer.

denim ['denɪm] *n* (toile *f* de) coton *m*; *pl* (*jeans*) (blue-)jean *m*.

denizen ['denɪz(ə)n] *n* habitant, -ante *mf*.

Denmark ['denmɑːk] *n* Danemark *m*.

denomination [dɪnɒmɪ'neɪʃ(ə)n] *n* confession *f*, religion *f*; (*sect*) secte *m*; (*of coin, banknote*) valeur *f*; *Math* unité *f*. ◆**denominational** *a* (*school*) confessionnel.

denote [dɪ'nəʊt] *vt* dénoter.

denounce [dɪ'naʊns] *vt* (*person, injustice etc*) dénoncer (**to** à); **to d. s.o. as a spy/etc** accuser qn publiquement d'être un espion/*etc*. ◆**denunci'ation** *n* dénonciation *f*; accusation *f* publique.

dense [dens] *a* (**-er, -est**) dense; (*stupid*)

Fam lourd, bête. ◆**—ly** *adv* **d. populated/***etc* très peuplé/*etc.* ◆**density** *n* densité *f.*

dent [dent] *n* (*in metal*) bosselure *f*; (*in car*) bosse *f*, gnon *m*; **full of dents** (*car*) cabossé; **to make a d. in one's savings** taper dans ses économies; – *vt* cabosser, bosseler.

dental ['dent(ə)l] *a* dentaire; **d. surgeon** chirurgien *m* dentiste. ◆**dentist** *n* dentiste *mf.* ◆**dentistry** *n* médecine *f* dentaire; **school of d.** école *f* dentaire. ◆**dentures** *npl* dentier *m.*

deny [dɪ'naɪ] *vt* nier (**doing** avoir fait, **that** que); (*rumour*) démentir; (*authority*) rejeter; (*disown*) renier; **to d. s.o. sth** refuser qch à qn.

deodorant [diː'əʊdərənt] *n* déodorant *m.*

depart [dɪ'pɑːt] *vi* partir; (*deviate*) s'écarter (**from** de); – *vt* **to d. this world** *Lit* quitter ce monde. ◆**—ed** *a* & *n* (*dead*) défunt, -unte (*mf*). ◆**departure** *n* départ *m*; **a d. from** (*custom, rule*) un écart par rapport à, une entorse à; **to be a new d. for** constituer une nouvelle voie pour.

department [dɪ'pɑːtmənt] *n* département *m*; (*in office*) service *m*; (*in shop*) rayon *m*; *Univ* section *f*, département *m*; **that's your d.** (*sphere*) c'est ton rayon; **d. store** grand magasin *m.* ◆**depart'mental** *a* **d. manager** (*office*) chef *m* de service; (*shop*) chef *m* de rayon.

depend [dɪ'pend] *vi* dépendre (**on, upon** de); **to d. (up)on** (*rely on*) compter sur (**for sth** pour qch); **you can d. on it!** tu peux en être sûr! ◆**—able** *a* (*person, information etc*) sûr; (*machine*) fiable, sûr. ◆**dependant** *n* personne *f* à charge. ◆**dependence** *n* dépendance *f.* ◆**dependency** *n* (*country*) dépendance *f.* ◆**dependent** *a* dépendant (**on, upon** de); (*relative*) à charge; **to be d. (up)on** dépendre de.

depict [dɪ'pɪkt] *vt* (*describe*) dépeindre; (*pictorially*) représenter. ◆**depiction** *n* peinture *f*; représentation *f.*

deplete [dɪ'pliːt] *vt* (*use up*) épuiser; (*reduce*) réduire. ◆**depletion** *n* épuisement *m*; réduction *f.*

deplor/e [dɪ'plɔːr] *vt* déplorer. ◆**—able** *a* déplorable.

deploy [dɪ'plɔɪ] *vt* (*troops etc*) déployer.

depopulate [diː'pɒpjʊleɪt] *vt* dépeupler. ◆**depopu'lation** *n* dépeuplement *m.*

deport [dɪ'pɔːt] *vt Pol Jur* expulser; (*to concentration camp etc*) *Hist* déporter. ◆**depor'tation** *n* expulsion *f*; déportation *f.*

deportment [dɪ'pɔːtmənt] *n* maintien *m.*

depose [dɪ'pəʊz] *vt* (*king etc*) déposer.

deposit [dɪ'pɒzɪt] *vt* (*object, money etc*) déposer; – *n* (*in bank, wine*) & *Ch* dépôt *m*; (*part payment*) acompte *m*; (*against damage*) caution *f*; (*on bottle*) consigne *f*; **d. account** *Fin* compte *m* d'épargne. ◆**—or** *n* déposant, -ante *mf*, épargnant, -ante *mf.*

depot ['depəʊ, *Am* 'diːpəʊ] *n* dépôt *m*; (*station*) *Rail Am* gare *f*; **(bus) d.** *Am* gare *f* routière.

deprave [dɪ'preɪv] *vt* dépraver. ◆**depravity** *n* dépravation *f.*

deprecate ['deprɪkeɪt] *vt* désapprouver.

depreciate [dɪ'priːʃɪeɪt] *vt* (*reduce in value*) déprécier; – *vi* se déprécier. ◆**depreci'ation** *n* dépréciation *f.*

depress [dɪ'pres] *vt* (*discourage*) déprimer; (*push down*) appuyer sur. ◆**—ed** *a* déprimé; (*in decline*) en déclin; (*in crisis*) en crise; **to get d.** se décourager. ◆**depression** *n* dépression *f.*

depriv/e [dɪ'praɪv] *vt* priver (**of** de). ◆**—ed** *a* (*child etc*) déshérité. ◆**depri'vation** *n* privation *f*; (*loss*) perte *f.*

depth [depθ] *n* profondeur *f*; (*of snow*) épaisseur *f*; (*of interest*) intensité *f*; **in the depths of** (*forest, despair*) au plus profond de; (*winter*) au cœur de; **to get out of one's d.** *Fig* perdre pied, nager; **in d.** en profondeur.

deputize ['depjʊtaɪz] *vi* assurer l'intérim (**for** de); – *vt* députer (**s.o. to do** qn pour faire). ◆**depu'tation** *n* députation *f.* ◆**deputy** *n* (*replacement*) suppléant, -ante *mf*; (*assistant*) adjoint, -ointe *mf*; **d. (sheriff)** *Am* shérif *m* adjoint; **d. chairman** vice-président, -ente *mf.*

derailed [dɪ'reɪld] *a* **to be d.** (*of train*) dérailler. ◆**derailment** *n* déraillement *m.*

deranged [dɪ'reɪndʒd] *a* (*person, mind*) dérangé.

derelict ['derɪlɪkt] *a* à l'abandon, abandonné.

deride [dɪ'raɪd] *vt* tourner en dérision. ◆**derision** *n* dérision *f.* ◆**derisive** *a* (*laughter etc*) moqueur; (*amount*) dérisoire. ◆**derisory** *a* dérisoire.

derive [dɪ'raɪv] *vt* **to d. from** (*pleasure, profit etc*) tirer de; *Ling* dériver de; **to be derived from** dériver de, provenir de; – *vi* **to d. from** dériver de. ◆**deri'vation** *n Ling* dérivation *f.* ◆**derivative** *a* & *n Ling Ch* dérivé (*m*).

dermatology [dɜːmə'tɒlədʒɪ] *n* dermatologie *f.*

derogatory [dɪ'rɒgət(ə)rɪ] *a* (*word*) péjoratif; (*remark*) désobligeant (**to** pour).

derrick ['derɪk] *n* (*over oil well*) derrick *m*.
derv [dɜːv] *n* gazole *m*, gas-oil *m*.
descend [dɪ'send] *vi* descendre (**from** de); (*of rain*) tomber; **to d. upon** (*attack*) faire une descente sur, tomber sur; (*of tourists*) envahir; – *vt* (*stairs*) descendre; **to be descended from** descendre de. ◆**—ing** *a* (*order*) décroissant. ◆**descendant** *n* descendant,. -ante *mf*. ◆**descent** *n* **1** descente *f*; (*into crime*) chute *f*. **2** (*ancestry*) souche *f*, origine *f*.
describe [dɪ'skraɪb] *vt* décrire. ◆**description** *n* description *f*; (*on passport*) signalement *m*; **of every d.** de toutes sortes. ◆**descriptive** *a* descriptif.
desecrate ['desɪkreɪt] *vt* profaner. ◆**dese'cration** *n* profanation *f*.
desegregate [diː'segrɪgeɪt] *vt* supprimer la ségrégation raciale dans. ◆**desegre'gation** *n* déségrégation *f*.
desert[1] ['dezət] *n* désert *m*; – *a* désertique; **d. island** île *f* déserte.
desert[2] [dɪ'zɜːt] *vt* déserter, abandonner; **to d. s.o.** (*of luck etc*) abandonner qn; – *vi Mil* déserter. ◆**—ed** *a* (*place*) désert. ◆**—er** *n Mil* déserteur *m*. ◆**desertion** *n* désertion *f*; (*by spouse*) abandon *m* (du domicile conjugal).
deserts [dɪ'zɜːts] *n* **one's just d.** ce qu'on mérite.
deserv/e [dɪ'zɜːv] *vt* mériter (**to do** de faire). ◆**—ing** *a* (*person*) méritant; (*act, cause*) louable, méritoire; **d. of** digne de. ◆**—edly** [-ɪdlɪ] *adv* à juste titre.
desiccated ['desɪkeɪtɪd] *a* (des)séché.
design [dɪ'zaɪn] *vt* (*car, furniture etc*) dessiner; (*dress*) créer, dessiner; (*devise*) concevoir (**for s.o.** pour qn, **to do** pour faire); **well designed** bien conçu; – *n* (*aim*) dessein *m*, intention *f*; (*sketch*) plan *m*, dessin *m*; (*of dress, car*) modèle *m*; (*planning*) conception *f*, création *f*; (*pattern*) motif *m*, dessin *m*; **industrial d.** dessin *m* industriel; **by d.** intentionellement; **to have designs on** avoir des desseins sur. ◆**—er** *n* dessinateur, -trice *mf*; **d. clothes** vêtements *mpl* griffés.
designate ['dezɪgneɪt] *vt* désigner. ◆**desig'nation** *n* désignation *f*.
desir/e [dɪ'zaɪər] *n* désir *m*; **I've no d. to** je n'ai aucune envie de; – *vt* désirer (**to do** faire). ◆**—able** *a* désirable; **d. property**/*etc* (*in advertising*) (très) belle propriété/*etc*.
desk [desk] *n Sch* pupitre *m*; (*in office*) bureau *m*; (*in shop*) caisse *f*; (**reception**) **d.** réception *f*; **the news d.** *Journ* le service des informations; – *a* (*job*) de bureau; **d. clerk** (*in hotel*) *Am* réceptionniste *mf*.
desolate ['desələt] *a* (*deserted*) désolé; (*in ruins*) dévasté; (*dreary, bleak*) morne, triste. ◆**deso'lation** *n* (*ruin*) dévastation *f*; (*emptiness*) solitude *f*.
despair [dɪ'speər] *n* désespoir *m*; **to drive s.o. to d.** désespérer qn; **in d.** au désespoir; – *vi* désespérer (**of s.o.** de qn, **of doing** de faire). ◆**—ing** *a* désespéré. ◆**'desperate** *a* désespéré; (*criminal*) capable de tout; (*serious*) grave; **to be d. for** (*money, love etc*) avoir désespérément besoin de; (*a cigarette, baby etc*) mourir d'envie d'avoir. ◆**'desperately** *adv* (*ill*) gravement; (*in love*) éperdument. ◆**despe'ration** *n* désespoir *m*; **in d.** (*as a last resort*) en désespoir de cause.
despatch [dɪ'spætʃ] *see* **dispatch**.
desperado [despə'rɑːdəʊ] *n* (*pl* **-oes** *or* **-os**) criminel *m*.
despise [dɪ'spaɪz] *vt* mépriser. ◆**despicable** *a* ignoble, méprisable.
despite [dɪ'spaɪt] *prep* malgré.
despondent [dɪ'spɒndənt] *a* découragé. ◆**despondency** *n* découragement *m*.
despot ['despɒt] *n* despote *m*. ◆**despotism** *n* despotisme *m*.
dessert [dɪ'zɜːt] *n* dessert *m*. ◆**dessertspoon** *n* cuiller *f* à dessert.
destabilize [diː'steɪbəlaɪz] *vt* déstabiliser.
destination [destɪ'neɪʃ(ə)n] *n* destination *f*.
destine ['destɪn] *vt* destiner (**for** à, **to do** à faire); **it was destined to happen** ça devait arriver. ◆**destiny** *n* destin *m*; (*fate of individual*) destinée *f*.
destitute ['destɪtjuːt] *a* (*poor*) indigent; **d. of** (*lacking in*) dénué de. ◆**desti'tution** *n* dénuement *m*.
destroy [dɪ'strɔɪ] *vt* détruire; (*horse etc*) abattre. ◆**—er** *n* (*person*) destructeur, -trice *mf*; (*ship*) contre-torpilleur *m*. ◆**destruct** *vt Mil* détruire. ◆**destruction** *n* destruction *f*. ◆**destructive** *a* (*person, war*) destructeur; (*power*) destructif.
detach [dɪ'tætʃ] *vt* détacher (**from** de). ◆**—ed** *a* (*indifferent*) détaché; (*view*) désintéressé; **d. house** maison *f* individuelle. ◆**—able** *a* (*lining*) amovible. ◆**—ment** *n* (*attitude*) & *Mil* détachement *m*; **the d. of** (*action*) la séparation de.
detail ['diːteɪl, *Am* dɪ'teɪl] **1** *n* détail *m*; **in d.** en détail; – *vt* raconter *or* exposer en détail *or* par le menu, détailler. **2** *vt Mil* détacher (**to do** pour faire); – *n* détachement *m*. ◆**—ed** *a* (*account etc*) détaillé.
detain [dɪ'teɪn] *vt* retenir; (*imprison*) détenir.

◆**detai'nee** *n Pol Jur* détenu, -ue *mf.* ◆**detention** *n Jur* détention *f*; *Sch* retenue *f.*

detect [dɪ'tekt] *vt* découvrir; (*perceive*) distinguer; (*identify*) identifier; (*mine*) détecter; (*illness*) dépister. ◆**detection** *n* découverte *f*; identification *f*; détection *f*; dépistage *m.* ◆**detector** *n* détecteur *m.*

detective [dɪ'tektɪv] *n* agent *m* de la Sûreté, policier *m* (en civil); (*private*) détective *m*; – *a* (*film etc*) policier; **d. story** roman *m* policier; **d. constable** = inspecteur *m* de police.

deter [dɪ'tɜːr] *vt* (-rr-) **to d. s.o.** dissuader *or* décourager qn (**from doing** de faire, **from** sth de qch).

detergent [dɪ'tɜːdʒənt] *n* détergent *m.*

deteriorate [dɪ'tɪərɪəreɪt] *vi* se détériorer; (*of morals*) dégénérer. ◆**deterio'ration** *n* détérioration *f*; dégénérescence *f.*

determin/e [dɪ'tɜːmɪn] *vt* déterminer; (*price*) fixer; **to d. s.o. to do** décider qn à faire; **to d. that** décider que; **to d. to do** se déterminer à faire. ◆**—ed** *a* (*look, quantity*) déterminé; **d. to do** *or* **on doing** décidé à faire; **I'm d. she'll succeed** je suis bien décidé à ce qu'elle réussisse.

deterrent [dɪ'terənt, *Am* dɪ'tɜːrənt] *n Mil* force *f* de dissuasion; **to be a d.** *Fig* être dissuasif.

detest [dɪ'test] *vt* détester (**doing** faire). ◆**—able** *a* détestable.

detonate ['detəneɪt] *vt* faire détoner *or* exploser; – *vi* détoner. ◆**deto'nation** *n* détonation *f.* ◆**detonator** *n* détonateur *m.*

detour ['diːtʊər] *n* détour *m.*

detract [dɪ'trækt] *vi* **to d. from** (*make less*) diminuer. ◆**detractor** *n* détracteur, -trice *mf.*

detriment ['detrɪmənt] *n* détriment *m.* ◆**detri'mental** *a* préjudiciable (to à).

devalue [diː'væljuː] *vt* (*money*) & *Fig* dévaluer. ◆**devalu'ation** *n* dévaluation *f.*

devastat/e ['devəsteɪt] *vt* (*lay waste*) dévaster; (*opponent*) anéantir; (*person*) *Fig* foudroyer. ◆**—ing** *a* (*storm etc*) dévastateur; (*overwhelming*) confondant, accablant; (*charm*) irrésistible.

develop [dɪ'veləp] *vt* développer; (*area, land*) mettre en valeur; (*habit, illness*) contracter; (*talent*) manifester; *Phot* développer; **to d. a liking for** prendre goût à; – *vi* se développer; (*of event*) se produire; **to d. into** devenir. ◆**—ing** *a* (*country*) en voie de développement; – *n Phot* développement *m.* ◆**—er** *n* (**property**) **d.** promoteur *m* (de construction). ◆**—ment** *n* développement *m*; (*of land*) mise *f* en valeur; (**housing**) **d.** lotissement *m*; (*large*) grand ensemble *m*; **a (new) d.** (*in situation*) un fait nouveau.

deviate ['diːvɪeɪt] *vi* dévier (**from** de); **to d. from the norm** s'écarter de la norme. ◆**deviant** *a* anormal. ◆**devi'ation** *n* déviation *f.*

device [dɪ'vaɪs] *n* dispositif *m*, engin *m*; (*scheme*) procédé *m*; **left to one's own devices** livré à soi-même.

devil ['dev(ə)l] *n* diable *m*; **a** *or* **the d. of a problem** *Fam* un problème épouvantable; **a** *or* **the d. of a noise** *Fam* un bruit infernal; **I had a** *or* **the d. of a job** *Fam* j'ai eu un mal fou (**doing, to do** à faire); **what/where/why the d.?** *Fam* que/où/pourquoi diable?; **like the d.** (*to run etc*) comme un fou. ◆**devilish** *a* diabolique. ◆**devilry** *n* (*mischief*) diablerie *f.*

devious ['diːvɪəs] *a* (*mind, behaviour*) tortueux; **he's d.** il a l'esprit tortueux. ◆**—ness** *n* (*of person*) esprit *m* tortueux.

devise [dɪ'vaɪz] *vt* (*plan*) combiner; (*plot*) tramer; (*invent*) inventer.

devitalize [diː'vaɪtəlaɪz] *vt* rendre exsangue, affaiblir.

devoid [dɪ'vɔɪd] *a* **d. of** dénué *or* dépourvu de; (*guilt*) exempt de.

devolution [diːvə'luːʃ(ə)n] *n Pol* décentralisation *f*; **the d. of** (*power*) la délégation de.

devolve [dɪ'vɒlv] *vi* **to d. upon** incomber à.

devot/e [dɪ'vəʊt] *vt* consacrer (**to** à). ◆**—ed** *a* dévoué; (*admirer*) fervent. ◆**—edly** *adv* avec dévouement. ◆**devo'tee** *n Sp Mus* passionné, -ée *mf.* ◆**devotion** *n* dévouement *m*; (*religious*) dévotion *f*; *pl* (*prayers*) dévotions *fpl.*

devour [dɪ'vaʊər] *vt* (*eat, engulf, read etc*) dévorer.

devout [dɪ'vaʊt] *a* dévot, pieux; (*supporter, prayer*) fervent.

dew [djuː] *n* rosée *f.* ◆**dewdrop** *n* goutte *f* de rosée.

dext(e)rous ['dekst(ə)rəs] *a* adroit, habile. ◆**dex'terity** *n* adresse *f*, dextérité *f.*

diabetes [daɪə'biːtiːz] *n Med* diabète *m.* ◆**diabetic** *a* & *n* diabétique (*mf*).

diabolical [daɪə'bɒlɪk(ə)l] *a* diabolique; (*bad*) épouvantable.

diadem ['daɪədem] *n* diadème *m.*

diagnosis, *pl* **-oses** [daɪəg'nəʊsɪs, -əʊsiːz] *n* diagnostic *m.* ◆**'diagnose** *vt* diagnostiquer.

diagonal [daɪ'ægən(ə)l] *a* diagonal; – *n* (*line*) diagonale *f.* ◆**—ly** *adv* en diagonale.

diagram ['daɪəgræm] *n* schéma *m*,

diagramme *m*; *Geom* figure *f*. ◆**dia·gra'mmatic** *a* schématique.

dial ['daɪəl] *n* cadran *m*; – *vt* (-**ll**-, *Am* -**l**-) (*number*) *Tel* faire, composer; (*person*) appeler; **to d. s.o. direct** appeler qn par l'automatique; **d. tone** *Am* tonalité *f*. ◆**dialling** *a* **d. code** indicatif *m*; **d. tone** tonalité *f*.

dialect ['daɪəlekt] *n* (*regional*) dialecte *m*; (*rural*) patois *m*.

dialogue ['daɪəlɒg] (*Am* **dialog**) *n* dialogue *m*.

dialysis, *pl* **-yses** [daɪ'ælɪsɪs, -ɪsiːz] *n* *Med* dialyse *f*.

diameter [daɪ'æmɪtər] *n* diamètre *m*. ◆**dia'metrically** *adv* (*opposed*) diamétralement.

diamond ['daɪəmənd] **1** *n* (*stone*) diamant *m*; (*shape*) losange *m*; **(baseball) d.** *Am* terrain *m* (de baseball); **d. necklace/***etc* rivière *f*/*etc* de diamants. **2** *n* & *npl* *Cards* carreau *m*.

diaper ['daɪəpər] *n* (*for baby*) *Am* couche *f*.

diaphragm ['daɪəfræm] *n* diaphragme *m*.

diarrh(o)ea [daɪə'riːə] *n* diarrhée *f*.

diary ['daɪərɪ] *n* (*calendar*) agenda *m*; (*private*) journal *m* (intime).

dice [daɪs] *n inv* dé *m* (à jouer); – *vt* *Culin* couper en dés.

dicey ['daɪsɪ] *a* (-**ier**, -**iest**) *Fam* risqué.

dichotomy [daɪ'kɒtəmɪ] *n* dichotomie *f*.

dickens ['dɪkɪnz] *n* **where/why/what the d.?** *Fam* où/pourquoi/que diable?

dictate [dɪk'teɪt] *vt* dicter (**to** à); – *vi* dicter; **to d. to s.o.** (*order around*) régenter qn. ◆**dictation** *n* dictée *f*. ◆**'dictaphone®** *n* dictaphone® *m*.

dictates ['dɪkteɪts] *npl* préceptes *mpl*; **the d. of conscience** la voix de la conscience.

dictator [dɪk'teɪtər] *n* dictateur *m*. ◆**dicta'torial** *a* dictatorial. ◆**dictatorship** *n* dictature *f*.

diction ['dɪkʃ(ə)n] *n* langage *m*; (*way of speaking*) diction *f*.

dictionary ['dɪkʃənərɪ] *n* dictionnaire *m*.

dictum ['dɪktəm] *n* dicton *m*.

did [dɪd] *see* **do**.

diddle ['dɪd(ə)l] *vt* *Sl* rouler; **to d. s.o. out of sth** carotter qch à qn; **to get diddled out of sth** se faire refaire de qch.

die [daɪ] **1** *vi* (*pt* & *pp* **died**, *pres p* **dying**) mourir (**of, from** de); **to be dying to do** *Fam* mourir d'envie de faire; **to be dying for sth** *Fam* avoir une envie folle de qch; **to d. away** (*of noise*) mourir; **to d. down** (*of fire*) mourir; (*of storm*) se calmer; **to d. off** mourir (les uns après les autres); **to d. out** (*of custom*) mourir. **2** *n* (*in engraving*) coin *m*; *Tech* matrice *f*; **the d. is cast** *Fig* les dés sont jetés.

diehard ['daɪhɑːd] *n* réactionnaire *mf*.

diesel ['diːzəl] *a* & *n* **d. (engine)** (moteur *m*) diesel *m*; **d. (oil)** gazole *m*.

diet ['daɪət] *n* (*for slimming etc*) régime *m*; (*usual food*) alimentation *f*; **to go on a d.** faire un régime; – *vi* suivre un régime. ◆**dietary** *a* diététique; **d. fibre** fibre(s) *f*(*pl*) alimentaire(s). ◆**die'tician** *n* diététicien, -ienne *mf*.

differ ['dɪfər] *vi* différer (**from** de); (*disagree*) ne pas être d'accord (**from** avec). ◆**difference** *n* différence *f* (**in** de); (*in age, weight etc*) écart *m*, différence *f*; **d. (of opinion)** différend *m*; **it makes no d.** ça n'a pas d'importance; **it makes no d. to me** ça m'est égal; **to make a d. in sth** changer qch. ◆**different** *a* différent (**from, to** de); (*another*) autre; (*various*) différents, divers. ◆**diffe'rential** *a* différentiel; – *npl* *Econ* écarts *mpl* salariaux. ◆**diffe'rentiate** *vt* différencier (**from** de); **to d. (between)** faire la différence entre. ◆**differently** *adv* différemment (**from, to** de), autrement (**from, to** que).

difficult ['dɪfɪkəlt] *a* difficile (**to do** à faire); **it's d. for us to . . .** il nous est difficile de . . . ; **the d. thing is to . . .** le plus difficile est de . . . . ◆**difficulty** *n* difficulté *f*; **to have d. doing** avoir du mal à faire; **to be in d.** avoir des difficultés; **d. with** des ennuis *mpl* avec.

diffident ['dɪfɪdənt] *a* (*person*) qui manque d'assurance; (*smile, tone*) mal assuré. ◆**diffidence** *n* manque *m* d'assurance.

diffuse [dɪ'fjuːz] *vt* (*spread*) diffuser; – [dɪ'fjuːs] *a* (*spread out, wordy*) diffus. ◆**diffusion** *n* diffusion *f*.

dig [dɪg] *vt* (*pt* & *pp* **dug**, *pres p* **digging**) (*ground*) bêcher; (*hole, grave etc*) creuser; (*understand*) *Sl* piger; (*appreciate*) *Sl* aimer; **to d. sth into** (*thrust*) enfoncer qch dans; **to d. out** (*animal, fact*) déterrer; (*accident victim*) dégager; (*find*) *Fam* dénicher; **to d. up** déterrer; (*weed*) arracher; (*earth*) retourner; (*street*) piocher; – *vi* creuser; (*of pig*) fouiller; **to d. (oneself) in** *Mil* se retrancher; **to d. in** (*eat*) *Fam* manger; **to d. into** (*s.o.'s past*) fouiller dans; (*meal*) *Fam* attaquer; – *n* (*with spade*) coup *m* de bêche; (*push*) coup *m* de poing *or* de coude; (*remark*) *Fam* coup *m* de griffe. ◆**digger** *n* (*machine*) pelleteuse *f*.

digest [daɪ'dʒest] *vti* digérer; – ['daɪdʒest] *n* *Journ* condensé *m*. ◆**digestible** *a* digeste.

◆**digestion** *n* digestion *f*. ◆**digestive** *a* digestif.

digit ['dɪdʒɪt] *n* (*number*) chiffre *m*. ◆**digital** *a* (*watch, keyboard etc*) numérique.

dignified ['dɪgnɪfaɪd] *a* digne, qui a de la dignité. ◆**dignify** *vt* donner de la dignité à; **to d. with the name of** honorer du nom de. ◆**dignitary** *n* dignitaire *m*. ◆**dignity** *n* dignité *f*.

digress [daɪ'gres] *vi* faire une digression; **to d. from** s'écarter de. ◆**digression** *n* digression *f*.

digs [dɪgz] *npl Fam* chambre *f* (meublée), logement *m*.

dilapidated [dɪ'læpɪdeɪtɪd] *a* (*house*) délabré. ◆**dilapi'dation** *n* délabrement *m*.

dilate [daɪ'leɪt] *vt* dilater; – *vi* se dilater. ◆**dilation** *n* dilatation *f*.

dilemma [daɪ'lemə] *n* dilemme *m*.

dilettante [dɪlɪ'tæntɪ] *n* dilettante *mf*.

diligent ['dɪlɪdʒənt] *a* assidu, appliqué; **to be d. in doing sth** faire qch avec zèle. ◆**diligence** *n* zèle *m*, assiduité *f*.

dilly-dally [dɪlɪ'dælɪ] *vi Fam* (*dawdle*) lambiner, lanterner; (*hesitate*) tergiverser.

dilute [daɪ'luːt] *vt* diluer; – *a* dilué.

dim [dɪm] *a* (**dimmer, dimmest**) (*feeble*) faible; (*colour*) terne; (*room*) sombre; (*memory, outline*) vague; (*person*) stupide; – *vt* (**-mm-**) (*light*) baisser, réduire; (*glory*) ternir; (*memory*) estomper. ◆**—ly** *adv* faiblement; (*vaguely*) vaguement. ◆**—ness** *n* faiblesse *f*; (*of memory etc*) vague *m*; (*of room*) pénombre *f*. ◆**dimwit** *n* idiot, -ote *mf*. ◆**dim'witted** *a* idiot.

dime [daɪm] *n* (*US & Can coin*) (pièce *f* de) dix cents *mpl*; **a d. store** = un Prisunic®, un Monoprix®.

dimension [daɪ'menʃ(ə)n] *n* dimension *f*; (*extent*) *Fig* étendue *f*. ◆**dimensional** *a* **two-d.** à deux dimensions.

diminish [dɪ'mɪnɪʃ] *vti* diminuer. ◆**—ing** *a* qui diminue.

diminutive [dɪ'mɪnjʊtɪv] **1** *a* (*tiny*) minuscule. **2** *a & n Gram* diminutif (*m*).

dimple ['dɪmp(ə)l] *n* fossette *f*. ◆**dimpled** *a* (*chin, cheek*) à fossettes.

din [dɪn] **1** *n* (*noise*) vacarme *m*. **2** *vt* (**-nn-**) **to d. into s.o. that** rabâcher à qn que.

din/e [daɪn] *vi* dîner (**off, on** de); **to d. out** dîner en ville. ◆**—ing** *a* **d. car** *Rail* wagon-restaurant *m*; **d. room** salle *f* à manger. ◆**—er** *n* dîneur, -euse *mf*; *Rail* wagon-restaurant *m*; (*short-order restaurant*) *Am* petit restaurant *m*.

ding(dong)! ['dɪŋ(dɒŋ)] *int* (*of bell*) dring!, ding (dong)!

dinghy ['dɪŋgɪ] *n* petit canot *m*, youyou *m*; (**rubber**) **d.** canot *m* pneumatique.

dingy ['dɪndʒɪ] *a* (**-ier, -iest**) (*dirty*) malpropre; (*colour*) terne. ◆**dinginess** *n* malpropreté *f*.

dinner ['dɪnər] *n* (*evening meal*) dîner *m*; (*lunch*) déjeuner *m*; (*for dog, cat*) pâtée *f*; **to have d.** dîner; **to have s.o. to d.** avoir qn à dîner; **d. dance** dîner-dansant *m*; **d. jacket** smoking *m*; **d. party** dîner *m* (à la maison); **d. plate** grande assiette *f*; **d. service, d. set** service *m* de table.

dinosaur ['daɪnəsɔːr] *n* dinosaure *m*.

dint [dɪnt] *n* **by d. of** à force de.

diocese ['daɪəsɪs] *n Rel* diocèse *m*.

dip [dɪp] *vt* (**-pp-**) plonger; (*into liquid*) tremper, plonger; **to d. one's headlights** se mettre en code; – *vi* (*of sun etc*) baisser; (*of road*) plonger; **to d. into** (*pocket, savings*) puiser dans; (*book*) feuilleter; – *n* (*in road*) déclivité *f*; **to go for a d.** faire trempette.

diphtheria [dɪp'θɪərɪə] *n* diphtérie *f*.

diphthong ['dɪfθɒŋ] *n Ling* diphtongue *f*.

diploma [dɪ'pləʊmə] *n* diplôme *m*.

diplomacy [dɪ'pləʊməsɪ] *n* (*tact*) & *Pol* diplomatie *f*. ◆**'diplomat** *n* diplomate *mf*. ◆**diplo'matic** *a* diplomatique; **to be d.** (*tactful*) *Fig* être diplomate.

dipper ['dɪpər] *n* **the big d.** (*at fairground*) les montagnes *fpl* russes.

dire ['daɪər] *a* affreux; (*poverty, need*) extrême.

direct [daɪ'rekt] **1** *a* (*result, flight, person etc*) direct; (*danger*) immédiat; – *adv* directement. **2** *vt* (*work, one's steps, one's attention*) diriger; (*letter, remark*) adresser (**to** à); (*efforts*) orienter (**to, towards** vers); (*film*) réaliser; (*play*) mettre en scène; **to d. s.o. to** (*place*) indiquer à qn le chemin de; **to d. s.o. to do** charger qn de faire. ◆**direction** *n* direction *f*, sens *m*; (*management*) direction *f*; (*of film*) réalisation *f*; (*of play*) mise *f* en scène; *pl* (*orders*) indications *fpl*; **directions (for use)** mode *m* d'emploi; **in the opposite d.** en sens inverse. ◆**directive** [dɪ'rektɪv] *n* directive *f*. ◆**directly** *adv* (*without detour*) directement; (*at once*) tout de suite; (*to speak*) franchement; – *conj Fam* aussitôt que. ◆**directness** *n* (*of reply*) franchise *f*. ◆**director** *n* directeur, -trice *mf*; (*of film*) réalisateur, -trice *mf*; (*of play*) metteur *m* en scène. ◆**directorship** *n Com* poste *m* de directeur.

directory [daɪ'rektərɪ] *n Tel* annuaire *m*; (*of*

streets) guide *m*; (*of addresses*) répertoire *m*; **d. enquiries** *Tel* renseignements *mpl*.
dirge [dɜːdʒ] *n* chant *m* funèbre.
dirt [dɜːt] *n* saleté *f*; (*filth*) ordure *f*; (*mud*) boue *f*; (*earth*) terre *f*; (*talk*) *Fig* obscénité(s) *f*(*pl*); **d. cheap** *Fam* très bon marché; **d. road** chemin *m* de terre; **d. track** *Sp* cendrée *f*. **◆dirty** *a* (**-ier, -iest**) sale; (*job*) salissant; (*obscene, unpleasant*) sale; (*word*) grossier, obscène; **to get d.** se salir; **to get sth d.** salir qch; **a d. joke** une histoire cochonne; **a d. trick** un sale tour; **a d. old man** un vieux cochon; – *adv* (*to fight*) déloyalement; – *vt* salir; (*machine*) encrasser; – *vi* se salir.
disabl/e [dɪ'seɪb(ə)l] *vt* rendre infirme; (*maim*) mutiler. **◆—ed** *a* infirme, handicapé; (*maimed*) mutilé; – *n* **the d.** les infirmes *mpl*, les handicapés *mpl*. **◆disa'bility** *n* infirmité *f*; *Fig* désavantage *m*.
disadvantage [dɪsəd'vɑːntɪdʒ] *n* désavantage *m*; – *vt* désavantager.
disaffected [dɪsə'fektɪd] *a* mécontent. **◆disaffection** *n* désaffection *f* (**for** pour).
disagree [dɪsə'griː] *vi* ne pas être d'accord, être en désaccord (**with** avec); (*of figures*) ne pas concorder; **to d. with** (*of food etc*) ne pas réussir à. **◆—able** *a* désagréable. **◆—ment** *n* désaccord *m*; (*quarrel*) différend *m*.
disallow [dɪsə'laʊ] *vt* rejeter.
disappear [dɪsə'pɪər] *vi* disparaître. **◆disappearance** *n* disparition *f*.
disappoint [dɪsə'pɔɪnt] *vt* décevoir; **I'm disappointed with it** ça m'a déçu. **◆—ing** *a* décevant. **◆—ment** *n* déception *f*.
disapprov/e [dɪsə'pruːv] *vi* **to d. of s.o./sth** désapprouver qn/qch; **I d.** je suis contre. **◆—ing** *a* (*look etc*) désapprobateur. **◆disapproval** *n* désapprobation *f*.
disarm [dɪs'ɑːm] *vti* désarmer. **◆disarmament** *n* désarmement *m*.
disarray [dɪsə'reɪ] *n* (*disorder*) désordre *m*; (*distress*) désarroi *m*.
disaster [dɪ'zɑːstər] *n* désastre *m*, catastrophe *f*; **d. area** région *f* sinistrée. **◆d.-stricken** *a* sinistré. **◆disastrous** *a* désastreux.
disband [dɪs'bænd] *vt* disperser; – *vi* se disperser.
disbelief [dɪsbə'liːf] *n* incrédulité *f*.
disc [dɪsk] (*Am* **disk**) *n* disque *m*; **identity d.** plaque *f* d'identité; **d. jockey** animateur, -trice *mf* (de variétés *etc*), disc-jockey *m*.
discard [dɪs'kɑːd] *vt* (*get rid of*) se débarrasser de; (*plan, hope etc*) *Fig* abandonner.
discern [dɪ'sɜːn] *vt* discerner. **◆—ing** *a* (*person*) averti, sagace. **◆—ible** *a* perceptible. **◆—ment** *n* discernement *m*.
discharge [dɪs'tʃɑːdʒ] *vt* (*gun, accused person*) décharger; (*liquid*) déverser; (*patient, employee*) renvoyer; (*soldier*) libérer; (*unfit soldier*) réformer; (*one's duty*) accomplir; – *vi* (*of wound*) suppurer; – ['dɪstʃɑːdʒ] *n* (*of gun*) & *El* décharge *f*; (*of liquid*) & *Med* écoulement *m*; (*dismissal*) renvoi *m*; (*freeing*) libération *f*; (*of unfit soldier*) réforme *f*.
disciple [dɪ'saɪp(ə)l] *n* disciple *m*.
discipline ['dɪsɪplɪn] *n* (*behaviour, subject*) discipline *f*; – *vt* (*control*) discipliner; (*punish*) punir. **◆discipli'narian** *n* partisan, -ane *mf* de la discipline; **to be a (strict) d.** être très à cheval sur la discipline. **◆disci'plinary** *a* disciplinaire.
disclaim [dɪs'kleɪm] *vt* désavouer; (*responsibility*) (dé)nier.
disclose [dɪs'kləʊz] *vt* révéler, divulguer. **◆disclosure** *n* révélation *f*.
disco ['dɪskəʊ] *n* (*pl* **-os**) *Fam* disco(thèque) *f*.
discolour [dɪs'kʌlər] *vt* décolorer; (*teeth*) jaunir; – *vi* se décolorer; jaunir. **◆discolo(u)'ration** *n* décoloration *f*; jaunissement *m*.
discomfort [dɪs'kʌmfət] *n* (*physical, mental*) malaise *m*, gêne *f*; (*hardship*) inconvénient *m*.
disconcert [dɪskən'sɜːt] *vt* déconcerter.
disconnect [dɪskə'nekt] *vt* (*unfasten etc*) détacher; (*unplug*) débrancher; (*wires*) *El* déconnecter; (*gas, telephone etc*) couper. **◆—ed** *a* (*speech*) décousu.
discontent [dɪskən'tent] *n* mécontentement *m*. **◆discontented** *a* mécontent.
discontinu/e [dɪskən'tɪnjuː] *vt* cesser, interrompre. **◆—ed** *a* (*article*) *Com* qui ne se fait plus.
discord ['dɪskɔːd] *n* discorde *f*; *Mus* dissonance *f*.
discotheque ['dɪskətek] *n* (*club*) discothèque *f*.
discount 1 ['dɪskaʊnt] *n* (*on article*) remise *f*; (*on account paid early*) escompte *m*; **at a d.** (*to buy, sell*) au rabais; **d. store** solderie *f*. **2** [dɪs'kaʊnt] *vt* (*story etc*) ne pas tenir compte de.
discourage [dɪs'kʌrɪdʒ] *vt* décourager; **to get discouraged** se décourager. **◆—ment** *n* découragement *m*.
discourse ['dɪskɔːs] *n* discours *m*.
discourteous [dɪs'kɜːtɪəs] *a* impoli, discourtois. **◆discourtesy** *n* impolitesse *f*.
discover [dɪs'kʌvər] *vt* découvrir. **◆discovery** *n* découverte *f*.

discredit [dɪs'kredɪt] *vt* (*cast slur on*) discréditer; (*refuse to believe*) ne pas croire; – *n* discrédit *m*. ◆**—able** *a* indigne.

discreet [dɪ'skriːt] *a* (*careful*) prudent, avisé; (*unassuming, reserved etc*) discret. ◆**discretion** *n* prudence *f*; discrétion *f*; **I'll use my own d.** je ferai comme bon me semblera. ◆**discretionary** *a* discrétionnaire.

discrepancy [dɪ'skrepənsɪ] *n* divergence *f*, contradiction *f* (**between** entre).

discriminat/e [dɪ'skrɪmɪneɪt] *vi* **to d. between** distinguer entre; **to d. against** établir une discrimination contre; – *vt* **to d. sth/s.o. from** distinguer qch/qn de. ◆**—ing** *a* (*person*) averti, sagace; (*ear*) fin. ◆**discrimi'nation** *n* (*judgement*) discernement *m*; (*distinction*) distinction *f*; (*partiality*) discrimination *f*. ◆**discriminatory** [-ətərɪ] *a* discriminatoire.

discus ['dɪskəs] *n Sp* disque *m*.

discuss [dɪ'skʌs] *vt* (*talk about*) discuter de; (*examine in detail*) discuter. ◆**discussion** *n* discussion *f*; **under d.** (*matter etc*) en question, en discussion.

disdain [dɪs'deɪn] *vt* dédaigner; – *n* dédain *m*. ◆**disdainful** *a* dédaigneux; **to be d. of** dédaigner.

disease [dɪ'ziːz] *n* maladie *f*. ◆**diseased** *a* malade.

disembark [dɪsɪm'bɑːk] *vti* débarquer. ◆**disembar'kation** *n* débarquement *m*.

disembodied [dɪsɪm'bɒdɪd] *a* désincarné.

disembowel [dɪsɪm'baʊəl] *vt* (**-ll-**, *Am* **-l-**) éventrer.

disenchant [dɪsɪn'tʃɑːnt] *vt* désenchanter. ◆**—ment** *n* désenchantement *m*.

disengage [dɪsɪn'geɪdʒ] *vt* (*object*) dégager; (*troops*) désengager.

disentangle [dɪsɪn'tæŋg(ə)l] *vt* démêler; **to d. oneself from** se dégager de.

disfavour [dɪs'feɪvər] *n* défaveur *f*.

disfigure [dɪs'fɪgər] *vt* défigurer. ◆**—ment** *n* défigurement *m*.

disgorge [dɪs'gɔːdʒ] *vt* (*food*) vomir.

disgrac/e [dɪs'greɪs] *n* (*shame*) honte *f* (**to** à); (*disfavour*) disgrâce *f*; – *vt* déshonorer, faire honte à. ◆**—ed** *a* (*politician etc*) disgracié. ◆**disgraceful** *a* honteux (**of s.o.** de la part de qn). ◆**disgracefully** *adv* honteusement.

disgruntled [dɪs'grʌnt(ə)ld] *a* mécontent.

disguise [dɪs'gaɪz] *vt* déguiser (**as** en); – *n* déguisement *m*; **in d.** déguisé.

disgust [dɪs'gʌst] *n* dégoût *m* (**for, at, with** de); **in d.** dégoûté; – *vt* dégoûter, écœurer. ◆**—ed** *a* dégoûté (**at, by, with** de); **to be d. with s.o.** (*annoyed*) être fâché contre qn; **d. to hear that . . .** indigné d'apprendre que . . . . ◆**—ing** *a* dégoûtant, écœurant. ◆**—ingly** *adv* d'une façon dégoûtante.

dish [dɪʃ] **1** *n* (*container*) plat *m*; (*food*) mets *m*, plat *m*; **the dishes** la vaisselle; **she's a (real) d.** *Sl* c'est un beau brin de fille. **2** *vt* **to d. out** distribuer; **to d. out** *or* **up** (*food*) servir. ◆**dishcloth** *n* (*for washing*) lavette *f*; (*for drying*) torchon *m*. ◆**dishpan** *n Am* bassine *f* (à vaisselle). ◆**dishwasher** *n* lave-vaisselle *m inv*.

disharmony [dɪs'hɑːmənɪ] *n* désaccord *m*; *Mus* dissonance *f*.

dishearten [dɪs'hɑːt(ə)n] *vt* décourager.

dishevelled [dɪ'ʃevəld] *a* hirsute, échevelé.

dishonest [dɪs'ɒnɪst] *a* malhonnête; (*insincere*) de mauvaise foi. ◆**dishonesty** *n* malhonnêteté *f*; mauvaise foi *f*.

dishonour [dɪs'ɒnər] *n* déshonneur *m*; – *vt* déshonorer; (*cheque*) refuser d'honorer. ◆**—able** *a* peu honorable. ◆**—ably** *adv* avec déshonneur.

dishy ['dɪʃɪ] *a* (**-ier, -iest**) (*woman, man*) *Sl* beau, sexy, qui a du chien.

disillusion [dɪsɪ'luːʒ(ə)n] *vt* désillusionner; – *n* désillusion *f*. ◆**—ment** *n* désillusion *f*.

disincentive [dɪsɪn'sentɪv] *n* mesure *f* dissuasive; **to be a d. to s.o.** décourager qn; **it's a d. to work/invest/***etc* cela n'encourage pas à travailler/investir/*etc*.

disinclined [dɪsɪŋ'klaɪnd] *a* peu disposé (**to** à). ◆**disincli'nation** *n* répugnance *f*.

disinfect [dɪsɪn'fekt] *vt* désinfecter. ◆**disinfectant** *a* & *n* désinfectant (*m*). ◆**disinfection** *n* désinfection *f*.

disinherit [dɪsɪn'herɪt] *vt* déshériter.

disintegrate [dɪs'ɪntɪgreɪt] *vi* se désintégrer; – *vt* désintégrer. ◆**disinte'gration** *n* désintégration *f*.

disinterested [dɪs'ɪntrɪstɪd] *a* (*impartial*) désintéressé; (*uninterested*) *Fam* indifférent (**in** à).

disjointed [dɪs'dʒɔɪntɪd] *a* décousu.

disk [dɪsk] *n* **1** *Am* = **disc. 2 (magnetic) d.** (*of computer*) disque *m* (magnétique).

dislike [dɪs'laɪk] *vt* ne pas aimer (**doing** faire); **he doesn't d. it** ça ne lui déplaît pas; – *n* aversion *f* (**for, of** pour); **to take a d. to** (*person, thing*) prendre en grippe; **our likes and dislikes** nos goûts et dégoûts *mpl*.

dislocate ['dɪsləkeɪt] *vt* (*limb*) disloquer; *Fig* désorganiser. ◆**dislo'cation** *n* dislocation *f*.

dislodge [dɪs'lɒdʒ] *vt* faire bouger, déplacer; (*enemy*) déloger.

disloyal [dɪs'lɔɪəl] *a* déloyal. ◆**disloyalty** *n* déloyauté *f*.

dismal ['dɪzməl] *a* morne, triste. ◆**—ly** *adv* (*to fail, behave*) lamentablement.

dismantle [dɪs'mænt(ə)l] *vt* (*machine etc*) démonter; (*organization*) démanteler.

dismay [dɪs'meɪ] *vt* consterner; – *n* consternation *f*.

dismember [dɪs'membər] *vt* (*country etc*) démembrer.

dismiss [dɪs'mɪs] *vt* congédier, renvoyer (**from** de); (*official*) destituer; (*appeal*) *Jur* rejeter; (*thought etc*) *Fig* écarter; **d.!** *Mil* rompez!; (**class**) **d.!** *Sch* vous pouvez partir. ◆**dismissal** *n* renvoi *m*; destitution *f*.

dismount [dɪs'maʊnt] *vi* descendre (**from** de); – *vt* (*rider*) démonter, désarçonner.

disobey [dɪsə'beɪ] *vt* désobéir à; – *vi* désobéir. ◆**disobedience** *n* désobéissance *f*. ◆**disobedient** *a* désobéissant.

disorder [dɪs'ɔːdər] *n* (*confusion*) désordre *m*; (*riots*) désordres *mpl*; **disorder(s)** *Med* troubles *mpl*. ◆**disorderly** *a* (*meeting etc*) désordonné.

disorganize [dɪs'ɔːgənaɪz] *vt* désorganiser.

disorientate [dɪs'ɔːrɪənteɪt] (*Am* **disorient** [dɪs'ɔːrɪənt]) *vt* désorienter.

disown [dɪs'əʊn] *vt* désavouer, renier.

disparag/e [dɪs'pærɪdʒ] *vt* dénigrer. ◆**—ing** *a* peu flatteur.

disparate ['dɪspərət] *a* disparate. ◆**dis'parity** *n* disparité *f* (**between** entre, de).

dispassionate [dɪs'pæʃənət] *a* (*unemotional*) calme; (*not biased*) impartial.

dispatch [dɪs'pætʃ] *vt* (*letter, work*) expédier; (*troops, messenger*) envoyer; – *n* expédition *f* (**of** de); *Journ Mil* dépêche *f*; **d. rider** *Mil etc* courrier *m*.

dispel [dɪs'pel] *vt* (**-ll-**) dissiper.

dispensary [dɪs'pensərɪ] *n* (*in hospital*) pharmacie *f*; (*in chemist's shop*) officine *f*.

dispense [dɪs'pens] **1** *vt* (*give out*) distribuer; (*justice*) administrer; (*medicine*) préparer. **2** *vi* **to d. with** (*do without*) se passer de; **to d. with the need for** rendre superflu. ◆**dispen'sation** *n* distribution *f*; **special d.** (*exemption*) dérogation *f*. ◆**dispenser** *n* (*device*) distributeur *m*; **cash d.** distributeur *m* de billets.

disperse [dɪ'spɜːs] *vt* disperser; – *vi* se disperser. ◆**dispersal** *n*, ◆**dispersion** *n* dispersion *f*.

dispirited [dɪ'spɪrɪtɪd] *a* découragé.

displace [dɪs'pleɪs] *vt* (*bone, furniture, refugees*) déplacer; (*replace*) supplanter.

display [dɪ'spleɪ] *vt* montrer; (*notice, electronic data etc*) afficher; (*painting, goods*) exposer; (*courage etc*) faire preuve de; – *n* (*in shop*) étalage *m*; (*of force*) déploiement *m*; (*of anger etc*) manifestation *f*; (*of paintings*) exposition *f*; (*of luxury*) étalage *m*; *Mil* parade *f*; (*of electronic data*) affichage *m*; **d. (unit)** (*of computer*) moniteur *m*; **on d.** exposé; **air d.** fête *f* aéronautique.

displeas/e [dɪs'pliːz] *vt* déplaire à. ◆**—ed** *a* mécontent (**with** de). ◆**—ing** *a* désagréable. ◆**displeasure** *n* mécontentement *m*.

dispos/e [dɪ'spəʊz] *vt* disposer (**s.o. to do** qn à faire); – *vi* **to d. of** (*get rid of*) se débarrasser de; (*one's time, money*) disposer de; (*sell*) vendre; (*matter*) expédier, liquider; (*kill*) liquider. ◆**—ed** *a* disposé (**to do** à faire); **well-d. towards** bien disposé envers. ◆**—able** *a* (*plate etc*) à jeter, jetable; (*income*) disponible. ◆**disposal** *n* (*sale*) vente *f*; (*of waste*) évacuation *f*; **at the d. of** à la disposition de. ◆**dispo'sition** *n* (*placing*) disposition *f*; (*character*) naturel *m*; (*readiness*) inclination *f*.

dispossess [dɪspə'zes] *vt* déposséder (**of** de).

disproportion [dɪsprə'pɔːʃ(ə)n] *n* disproportion *f*. ◆**disproportionate** *a* disproportionné.

disprove [dɪs'pruːv] *vt* réfuter.

dispute [dɪ'spjuːt] *n* discussion *f*; (*quarrel*) dispute *f*; *Pol* conflit *m*; *Jur* litige *m*; **beyond d.** incontestable; **in d.** (*matter*) en litige; (*territory*) contesté; – *vt* (*claim etc*) contester; (*discuss*) discuter.

disqualify [dɪs'kwɒlɪfaɪ] *vt* (*make unfit*) rendre inapte (**from** à); *Sp* disqualifier; **to d. from driving** retirer le permis à. ◆**disqualifi'cation** *n* *Sp* disqualification *f*.

disquiet [dɪs'kwaɪət] *n* inquiétude *f*; – *vt* inquiéter.

disregard [dɪsrɪ'gɑːd] *vt* ne tenir aucun compte de; – *n* indifférence *f* (**for** à); (*law*) désobéissance *f* (**for** à).

disrepair [dɪsrɪ'peər] *n* **in (a state of) d.** en mauvais état.

disreputable [dɪs'repjʊtəb(ə)l] *a* peu recommandable; (*behaviour*) honteux.

disrepute [dɪsrɪ'pjuːt] *n* discrédit *m*; **to bring into d.** jeter le discrédit sur.

disrespect [dɪsrɪ'spekt] *n* manque *m* de respect. ◆**disrespectful** *a* irrespectueux (**to** envers).

disrupt [dɪs'rʌpt] *vt* perturber; (*communications*) interrompre; (*plan*) déranger. ◆**disruption** *n* perturbation *f*; interruption *f*;

dérangement *m.* ◆**disruptive** *a* (*element etc*) perturbateur.

dissatisfied [dɪ'sætɪsfaɪd] *a* mécontent (with de). ◆**dissatis'faction** *n* mécontentement *m.*

dissect [daɪ'sekt] *vt* disséquer. ◆**dissection** *n* dissection *f.*

disseminate [dɪ'semɪneɪt] *vt* disséminer.

dissension [dɪ'senʃ(ə)n] *n* dissension *f.*

dissent [dɪ'sent] *vi* différer (d'opinion) (from sth à l'égard de qch); – *n* dissentiment *m.* ◆**—ing** *a* dissident.

dissertation [dɪsə'teɪʃ(ə)n] *n Univ* mémoire *m.*

dissident ['dɪsɪdənt] *a* & *n* dissident, -ente (*mf*). ◆**dissidence** *n* dissidence *f.*

dissimilar [dɪ'sɪmɪlər] *a* dissemblable (to à).

dissipate ['dɪsɪpeɪt] *vt* dissiper; (*energy*) gaspiller. ◆**dissi'pation** *n* dissipation *f*; gaspillage *m.*

dissociate [dɪ'səʊʃɪeɪt] *vt* dissocier (from de).

dissolute ['dɪsəluːt] *a* (*life, person*) dissolu.

dissolve [dɪ'zɒlv] *vt* dissoudre; – *vi* se dissoudre. ◆**disso'lution** *n* dissolution *f.*

dissuade [dɪ'sweɪd] *vt* dissuader (from doing de faire); to d. s.o. from sth détourner qn de qch. ◆**dissuasion** *n* dissuasion *f.*

distance ['dɪstəns] *n* distance *f*; **in the d.** au loin; **from a d.** de loin; **at a d.** à quelque distance; **it's within walking d.** on peut y aller à pied; **to keep one's d.** garder ses distances. ◆**distant** *a* éloigné, lointain; (*relative*) éloigné; (*reserved*) distant; **5 km d. from** à (une distance de) 5 km de. ◆**distantly** *adv* **we're d. related** nous sommes parents éloignés.

distaste [dɪs'teɪst] *n* aversion *f* (for pour). ◆**distasteful** *a* désagréable, déplaisant.

distemper [dɪ'stempər] **1** *n* (*paint*) badigeon *m*; – *vt* badigeonner. **2** *n* (*in dogs*) maladie *f.*

distend [dɪ'stend] *vt* distendre; – *vi* se distendre.

distil [dɪ'stɪl] *vt* (-ll-) distiller. ◆**disti'llation** *n* distillation *f.* ◆**distillery** *n* distillerie *f.*

distinct [dɪ'stɪŋkt] *a* **1** (*voice, light etc*) distinct; (*definite, marked*) net, marqué; (*promise*) formel. **2** (*different*) distinct (from de). ◆**distinction** *n* distinction *f*; *Univ* mention *f* très bien; **of d.** (*singer, writer etc*) de marque. ◆**distinctive** *a* distinctif. ◆**distinctively** *adv* distinctement; (*to stipulate, forbid*) formellement; (*noticeably*) nettement, sensiblement; **d. possible** tout à fait possible.

distinguish [dɪ'stɪŋgwɪʃ] *vti* distinguer (from de, between entre); **to d. oneself** se distinguer (as en tant que). ◆**—ed** *a* distingué. ◆**—ing** *a* **d. mark** signe *m* particulier. ◆**—able** *a* qu'on peut distinguer; (*discernible*) visible.

distort [dɪ'stɔːt] *vt* déformer. ◆**—ed** *a* (*false*) faux. ◆**distortion** *n El Med* distorsion *f*; (*of truth*) déformation *f.*

distract [dɪ'strækt] *vt* distraire (from de). ◆**—ed** *a* (*troubled*) préoccupé; (*mad with worry*) éperdu. ◆**—ing** *a* (*noise etc*) gênant. ◆**distraction** *n* (*lack of attention, amusement*) distraction *f*; **to drive to d.** rendre fou.

distraught [dɪ'strɔːt] *a* éperdu, affolé.

distress [dɪ'stres] *n* (*pain*) douleur *f*; (*anguish*) chagrin *m*; (*misfortune, danger*) détresse *f*; **in d.** (*ship, soul*) en détresse; **in (great) d.** (*poverty*) dans la détresse; – *vt* affliger, peiner. ◆**—ing** *a* affligeant, pénible.

distribute [dɪ'strɪbjuːt] *vt* distribuer; (*spread evenly*) répartir. ◆**distri'bution** *n* distribution *f*; répartition *f.* ◆**distributor** *n Aut Cin* distributeur *m*; (*of goods*) *Com* concessionnaire *mf.*

district ['dɪstrɪkt] *n* région *f*; (*of town*) quartier *m*; (*administrative*) arrondissement *m*; **d. attorney** *Am* = procureur *m* (de la République); **d. nurse** infirmière *f* visiteuse.

distrust [dɪs'trʌst] *vt* se méfier de; – *n* méfiance *f* (of de). ◆**distrustful** *a* méfiant; **to be d. of** se méfier de.

disturb [dɪ'stɜːb] *vt* (*sleep, water*) troubler; (*papers, belongings*) déranger; **to d. s.o.** (*bother*) déranger qn; (*alarm, worry*) troubler qn. ◆**—ed** *a* (*person etc*) *Psy* troublé. ◆**—ing** *a* (*worrying*) inquiétant; (*annoying, irksome*) gênant. ◆**disturbance** *n* (*noise*) tapage *m*; *pl Pol* troubles *mpl.*

disunity [dɪs'juːnɪtɪ] *n* désunion *f.*

disuse [dɪs'juːs] *n* **to fall into d.** tomber en désuétude. ◆**disused** [-'juːzd] *a* désaffecté.

ditch [dɪtʃ] **1** *n* fossé *m.* **2** *vt Fam* se débarrasser de.

dither ['dɪðər] *vi Fam* hésiter, tergiverser; **to d. (around)** (*waste time*) tourner en rond.

ditto ['dɪtəʊ] *adv* idem.

divan [dɪ'væn] *n* divan *m.*

div/e [daɪv] **1** *vi* (*pt* **dived**, *Am* **dove** [dəʊv]) plonger; (*rush*) se précipiter, se jeter; **to d. for** (*pearls*) pêcher; – *n* plongeon *m*; (*of submarine*) plongée *f*; (*of aircraft*) piqué *m.* **2** *n* (*bar, club*) *Pej* boui-boui *m.* ◆**—ing** *n* (*underwater*) plongée *f* sous-marine; **d. suit** scaphandre *m*; **d. board** plongeoir *m*. ◆**—er** *n* plongeur, -euse *mf*; (*in suit*) scaphandrier *m*.

diverge [daɪ'vɜːdʒ] *vi* diverger (**from** de). ◆**divergence** *n* divergence *f*. ◆**divergent** *a* divergent.

diverse [daɪ'vɜːs] *a* divers. ◆**diversify** *vt* diversifier; – *vi Econ* se diversifier. ◆**diversity** *n* diversité *f*.

divert [daɪ'vɜːt] *vt* détourner (**from** de); (*traffic*) dévier; (*aircraft*) dérouter; (*amuse*) divertir. ◆**diversion** *n Aut* déviation *f*; (*amusement*) divertissement *m*; *Mil* diversion *f*.

divest [daɪ'vest] *vt* **to d. of** (*power, rights*) priver de.

divid/e [dɪ'vaɪd] *vt* diviser (**into** en); **to d. (off) from** séparer de; **to d. up** (*money*) partager; **to d. one's time between** partager son temps entre; – *vi* se diviser. ◆**—ed** *a* (*opinion*) partagé. ◆**—ing** *a* **d. line** ligne *f* de démarcation.

dividend ['dɪvɪdend] *n Math Fin* dividende *m*.

divine [dɪ'vaɪn] *a* divin. ◆**divinity** *n* (*quality, deity*) divinité *f*; (*study*) théologie *f*.

division [dɪ'vɪʒ(ə)n] *n* division *f*; (*dividing object*) séparation *f*. ◆**divisible** *a* divisible. ◆**divisive** [-'vaɪsɪv] *a* qui sème la zizanie.

divorc/e [dɪ'vɔːs] *n* divorce *m*; – *vt* (*spouse*) divorcer d'avec; *Fig* séparer; – *vi* divorcer. ◆**—ed** *a* divorcé (**from** d'avec); **to get d.** divorcer. ◆**divorcee** [dɪvɔː'siː, *Am* dɪvɔː'seɪ] *n* divorcé, -ée *mf*.

divulge [dɪ'vʌldʒ] *vt* divulguer.

DIY [diːaɪ'waɪ] *n abbr* (*do-it-yourself*) bricolage *m*.

dizzy ['dɪzɪ] *a* (**-ier, -iest**) (*heights*) vertigineux; **to feel d.** avoir le vertige; **to make s.o. (feel) d.** donner le vertige à qn. ◆**dizziness** *n* vertige *m*.

DJ [diː'dʒeɪ] *abbr* = **disc jockey**.

do [duː] **1** *v aux* (*3rd person sing pres t* **does**; *pt* **did**; *pp* **done**; *pres p* **doing**) **do you know?** savez-vous?, est-ce que vous savez?; **I do not** *or* **don't see** je ne vois pas; **he** *did* **say so** (*emphasis*) il l'a bien dit; **do stay** reste donc; **you know him, don't you?** tu le connais, n'est-ce pas?; **better than I do** mieux que je ne le fais; **neither do I** moi non plus; **so do I** moi aussi; **oh, does he?** (*surprise*) ah oui?; **don't!** non! **2** *vt* faire; **to do nothing but sleep** ne faire que dormir; **what does she do?** (*in general*), **what is she doing?** (*now*) qu'est-ce qu'elle fait?, que fait-elle?; **what have you done (with)...?** qu'as-tu fait (de)...?; **well done** (*congratulations*) bravo!; *Culin* bien cuit; **it's over and done (with)** c'est fini; **that'll do me** (*suit*) ça fera mon affaire; **I've been done** (*cheated*) *Fam* je me suis fait avoir; **I'll do you!** *Fam* je t'aurai!; **to do s.o. out of sth** escroquer qch à qn; **he's hard done by** on le traite durement; **I'm done (in)** (*tired*) *Sl* je suis claqué *or* vanné; **he's done for** *Fam* il est fichu; **to do in** (*kill*) *Sl* supprimer; **to do out** (*clean*) nettoyer; **to do over** (*redecorate*) refaire; **to do up** (*coat, button*) boutonner; (*zip*) fermer; (*house*) refaire; (*goods*) emballer; **do yourself up (well)!** (*wrap up*) couvre-toi (bien)! **3** *vi* (*get along*) aller, marcher; (*suit*) faire l'affaire, convenir; (*be enough*) suffire; (*finish*) finir; **how do you do?** (*introduction*) enchanté; (*greeting*) bonjour; **he did well** *or* **right to leave** il a bien fait de partir; **do as I do** fais comme moi; **to make do** se débrouiller; **to do away with sth/s.o.** supprimer qch/qn; **I could do with** (*need, want*) j'aimerais bien (avoir *or* prendre); **to do without sth/s.o.** se passer de qch/qn; **to have to do with** (*relate to*) avoir à voir avec; (*concern*) concerner; **anything doing?** *Fam* est-ce qu'il se passe quelque chose? **4** *n* (*pl* **dos** *or* **do's**) (*party*) soirée *f*, fête *f*; **the do's and don'ts** ce qu'il faut faire ou ne pas faire.

docile ['dəʊsaɪl] *a* docile.

dock [dɒk] **1** *n Nau* dock *m*; – *vi* (*in port*) relâcher; (*at quayside*) se mettre à quai; (*of spacecraft*) s'arrimer. **2** *n Jur* banc *m* des accusés. **3** *vt* (*wages*) rogner; **to d. sth from** (*wages*) retenir qch sur. ◆**—er** *n* docker *m*. ◆**dockyard** *n* chantier *m* naval.

docket ['dɒkɪt] *n* fiche *f*, bordereau *m*.

doctor ['dɒktər] **1** *n Med* médecin *m*, docteur *m*; *Univ* docteur *m*. **2** *vt* (*text, food*) altérer; (*cat*) *Fam* châtrer. ◆**doctorate** *n* doctorat *m* (**in** ès, en).

doctrine ['dɒktrɪn] *n* doctrine *f*. ◆**doctri'naire** *a* & *n Pej* doctrinaire (*mf*).

document ['dɒkjʊmənt] *n* document *m*; – ['dɒkjʊment] *vt* (*inform*) documenter; (*report in detail*) *TV Journ* accorder une large place à. ◆**docu'mentary** *a* & *n* documentaire (*m*).

doddering ['dɒdərɪŋ] *a* (*senile*) gâteux; (*shaky*) branlant.

dodge [dɒdʒ] *vt* (*question, acquaintance etc*) esquiver; (*pursuer*) échapper à; (*tax*) éviter de payer; – *vi* faire un saut (de côté); **to d. out of sight** s'esquiver; **to d. through**

(*crowd*) se faufiler dans; – *n* mouvement *m* de côté; (*trick*) *Fig* truc *m*, tour *m*.
dodgems ['dɒdʒəmz] *npl* autos *fpl* tamponneuses.
dodgy ['dɒdʒɪ] *a* (**-ier, -iest**) *Fam* (*tricky*) délicat; (*dubious*) douteux; (*unreliable*) peu sûr.
doe [dəʊ] *n* (*deer*) biche *f*.
doer ['duːər] *n Fam* personne *f* dynamique.
does [dʌz] *see* **do.**
dog [dɒg] **1** *n* chien *m*; (*person*) *Pej* type *m*; **d. biscuit** biscuit *m or* croquette *f* pour chien; **d. collar** *Fam* col *m* de pasteur; **d. days** canicule *f*. **2** *vt* (**-gg-**) (*follow*) poursuivre. ◆**d.-eared** *a* (*page etc*) écorné. ◆**d.-'tired** *a Fam* claqué, crevé. ◆**doggy** *n Fam* toutou *m*; **d. bag** (*in restaurant*) *Am* petit sac *m* pour emporter les restes.
dogged ['dɒgɪd] *a* obstiné. ◆**–ly** *adv* obstinément.
dogma ['dɒgmə] *n* dogme *m*. ◆**dog'matic** *a* dogmatique. ◆**dogmatism** *n* dogmatisme *m*.
dogsbody ['dɒgzbɒdɪ] *n Pej* factotum *m*, sous-fifre *m*.
doily ['dɔɪlɪ] *n* napperon *m*.
doing ['duːɪŋ] *n* **that's your d.** c'est toi qui as fait ça; **doings** *Fam* activités *fpl*, occupations *fpl*.
do-it-yourself [duːɪtjə'self] *n* bricolage *m*; – *a* (*store, book*) de bricolage.
doldrums ['dɒldrəmz] *npl* **to be in the d.** (*of person*) avoir le cafard; (*of business*) être en plein marasme.
dole [dəʊl] **1** *n* **d. (money)** allocation *f* de chômage; **to go on the d.** s'inscrire au chômage. **2** *vt* **to d. out** distribuer au compte-gouttes.
doleful ['dəʊlfʊl] *a* morne, triste.
doll [dɒl] **1** *n* poupée *f*; (*girl*) *Fam* nana *f*; **doll's house,** *Am* **dollhouse** maison *f* de poupée. **2** *vt* **to d. up** *Fam* bichonner.
dollar ['dɒlər] *n* dollar *m*.
dollop ['dɒləp] *n* (*of food*) *Pej* gros morceau *m*.
dolphin ['dɒlfɪn] *n* (*sea animal*) dauphin *m*.
domain [dəʊ'meɪn] *n* (*land, sphere*) domaine *m*.
dome [dəʊm] *n* dôme *m*, coupole *f*.
domestic [də'mestɪk] *a* familial, domestique; (*animal*) domestique; (*trade, flight*) intérieur; (*product*) national; **d. science** arts *mpl* ménagers; **d. servant** domestique *mf*. ◆**domesticated** *a* habitué à la vie du foyer; (*animal*) domestiqué.
domicile ['dɒmɪsaɪl] *n* domicile *m*.
dominant ['dɒmɪnənt] *a* dominant; (*person*) dominateur. ◆**dominance** *n* prédominance *f*. ◆**dominate** *vti* dominer. ◆**domi'nation** *n* domination *f*. ◆**domi'neering** *a* dominateur.
dominion [də'mɪnjən] *n* domination *f*; (*land*) territoire *m*; *Br Pol* dominion *m*.
domino ['dɒmɪnəʊ] *n* (*pl* **-oes**) domino *m*; *pl* (*game*) dominos *mpl*.
don [dɒn] **1** *n Br Univ* professeur *m*. **2** *vt* (**-nn-**) revêtir.
donate [dəʊ'neɪt] *vt* faire don de; (*blood*) donner; – *vi* donner. ◆**donation** *n* don *m*.
done [dʌn] *see* **do.**
donkey ['dɒŋkɪ] *n* âne *m*; **for d.'s years** *Fam* depuis belle lurette, depuis un siècle; **d. work** travail *m* ingrat.
donor ['dəʊnər] *n* (*of blood, organ*) donneur, -euse *mf*.
doodle ['duːd(ə)l] *vi* griffonner.
doom [duːm] *n* ruine *f*; (*fate*) destin *m*; (*gloom*) *Fam* tristesse *f*; – *vt* condamner, destiner (**to** à); **to be doomed (to failure)** être voué à l'échec.
door [dɔːr] *n* porte *f*; (*of vehicle, train*) portière *f*, porte *f*; **out of doors** dehors; **d.-to-door salesman** démarcheur *m*. ◆**doorbell** *n* sonnette *f*. ◆**doorknob** *n* poignée *f* de porte. ◆**doorknocker** *n* marteau *m*. ◆**doorman** *n* (*pl* **-men**) (*of hotel etc*) portier *m*, concierge *m*. ◆**doormat** *n* paillasson *m*. ◆**doorstep** *n* seuil *m*. ◆**doorstop(per)** *n* butoir *m* (de porte). ◆**doorway** *n* **in the d.** dans l'encadrement de la porte.
dope [dəʊp] **1** *n Fam* drogue *f*; (*for horse, athlete*) doping *m*; – *vt* doper. **2** *n* (*information*) *Fam* tuyaux *mpl*. **3** *n* (*idiot*) *Fam* imbécile *mf*. ◆**dopey** *a* (**-ier, -iest**) *Fam* (*stupid*) abruti; (*sleepy*) endormi; (*drugged*) drogué, camé.
dormant ['dɔːmənt] *a* (*volcano, matter*) en sommeil; (*passion*) endormi.
dormer ['dɔːmər] *n* **d. (window)** lucarne *f*.
dormitory ['dɔːmɪtrɪ, *Am* 'dɔːmɪtɔːrɪ] *n* dortoir *m*; *Am* résidence *f* (universitaire).
dormouse, *pl* **-mice** ['dɔːmaʊs, -maɪs] *n* loir *m*.
dos/e [dəʊs] *n* dose *f*; (*of hard work*) *Fig* période *f*; (*of illness*) attaque *f*; – *vt* **to d. oneself (up)** se bourrer de médicaments. ◆**–age** *n* (*amount*) dose *f*.
dosshouse ['dɒshaʊs] *n Sl* asile *m* (de nuit).
dossier ['dɒsɪeɪ] *n* (*papers*) dossier *m*.
dot [dɒt] *n* point *m*; **polka d.** pois *m*; **on the d.** *Fam* à l'heure pile; – *vt* (**-tt-**) (*an i*)

mettre un point sur. ◆**dotted** *a* **d. line** pointillé *m*; **d. with** parsemé de.

dot/e [dəʊt] *vt* **to d. on** être gaga de. ◆**—ing** *a* affectueux; **her d. husband/father** son mari/père qui lui passe tout.

dotty ['dɒtɪ] *a* (**-ier, -iest**) *Fam* cinglé, toqué.

double ['dʌb(ə)l] *a* double; **a d. bed** un grand lit; **a d. room** une chambre pour deux personnes; **d. 's'** deux 's'; **d. six** deux fois six; **d. three four two** (*phone number*) trente-trois quarante-deux; – *adv* deux fois; (*to fold*) en deux; **he earns d. what I earn** il gagne le double de moi *or* deux fois plus que moi; **to see d.** voir double; – *n* double *m*; (*person*) double *m*, sosie *m*; (*stand-in*) *Cin* doublure *f*; **on** *or* **at the d.** au pas de course; – *vt* doubler; **to d. back** *or* **over** replier; – *vi* doubler; **to d. back** (*of person*) revenir en arrière; **to d. up** (*with pain, laughter*) être plié en deux. ◆**d.-'barrelled** *a* (*gun*) à deux canons; (*name*) à rallonges. ◆**d.-'bass** *n Mus* contrebasse *f*. ◆**d.-'breasted** *a* (*jacket*) croisé. ◆**d.-'cross** *vt* tromper. ◆**d.-'dealing** *n* double jeu *m*. ◆**d.-'decker (bus)** *n* autobus *m* à impériale. ◆**d.-'door** *n* porte *f* à deux battants. ◆**d.-'dutch** *n Fam* baragouin *m*. ◆**d.-'glazing** *n* (*window*) double vitrage *m*, double(s) fenêtre(s) *f(pl)*. ◆**d.-'parking** *n* stationnement *m* en double file. ◆**d.-'quick** *adv* en vitesse.

doubly ['dʌblɪ] *adv* doublement.

doubt [daʊt] *n* doute *m*; **to be in d. about** avoir des doutes sur; **I have no d. about it** je n'en doute pas; **no d.** (*probably*) sans doute; **in d.** (*result, career etc*) dans la balance; – *vt* douter de; **to d. whether** *or* **that** *or* **if** douter que (+ *sub*). ◆**doubtful** *a* douteux; **to be d. about sth** avoir des doutes sur qch; **it's d. whether** *or* **that** il est douteux que (+ *sub*). ◆**doubtless** *adv* sans doute.

dough [dəʊ] *n* pâte *f*; (*money*) *Fam* fric *m*, blé *m*. ◆**doughnut** *n* beignet *m* (rond).

dour ['dʊər] *a* austère.

douse [daʊs] *vt* arroser, tremper; (*light*) *Fam* éteindre.

dove[1] [dʌv] *n* colombe *f*. ◆**dovecote** [-kɒt] *n* colombier *m*.

dove[2] [dəʊv] *Am see* **dive 1.**

Dover ['dəʊvər] *n* Douvres *m or f*.

dovetail ['dʌvteɪl] **1** *n Carp* queue *f* d'aronde. **2** *vi* (*fit*) *Fig* concorder.

dowdy ['daʊdɪ] *a* (**-ier, -iest**) peu élégant, sans chic.

down[1] [daʊn] *adv* en bas; (*to the ground*) par terre, à terre; (*of sun*) couché; (*of blind, temperature*) baissé; (*out of bed*) descendu; (*of tyre*) dégonflé, (*worn*) usé; **d. (in writing)** inscrit; **(lie) d.!** (*to dog*) couché!; **to come** *or* **go d.** descendre; **to come d. from** (*place*) arriver de; **to fall d.** tomber (par terre); **d. there** *or* **here** en bas; **d. with traitors/***etc*! à bas les traîtres/*etc*!; **d. with (the) flu** grippé; **to feel d.** (*depressed*) *Fam* avoir le cafard; **d. to** (*in series, numbers, dates etc*) jusqu'à; **d. payment** acompte *m*; **d. under** aux antipodes, en Australie; **d. at heel,** *Am* **d. at the heels** miteux; – *prep* (*at bottom of*) en bas de; (*from top to bottom of*) du haut en bas de; (*along*) le long de; **to go d.** (*hill etc*) descendre; **to live d. the street** habiter plus loin dans la rue; – *vt* (*shoot down*) abattre; (*knock down*) terrasser; **to d. a drink** vider un verre. ◆**down-and-'out** *a* sur le pavé; – *n* clochard, -arde *mf*. ◆**downbeat** *a* (*gloomy*) *Fam* pessimiste. ◆**downcast** *a* découragé. ◆**downfall** *n* chute *f*. ◆**downgrade** *vt* (*job etc*) déclasser; (*person*) rétrograder. ◆**down'hearted** *a* découragé. ◆**down'hill** *adv* en pente; **to go d.** descendre; *Fig* être sur le déclin. ◆**downmarket** *a Com* bas de gamme. ◆**downpour** *n* averse *f*, pluie *f* torrentielle. ◆**downright** *a* (*rogue etc*) véritable; (*refusal etc*) catégorique; **a d. nerve** *or* **cheek** un sacré culot; – *adv* (*rude etc*) franchement. ◆**'downstairs** *a* (*room, neighbours*) d'en bas; (*on the ground floor*) du rez-de-chaussée; – [daʊn'steəz] *adv* en bas; au rez-de-chaussée; **to come** *or* **go d.** descendre l'escalier. ◆**down'stream** *adv* en aval. ◆**down-to-'earth** *a* terre-à-terre *inv*. ◆**down'town** *adv* en ville; **d. Chicago/***etc* le centre de Chicago/*etc*. ◆**downtrodden** *a* opprimé. ◆**downward** *a* vers le bas; (*path*) qui descend; (*trend*) à la baisse. ◆**downward(s)** *adv* vers le bas.

down[2] [daʊn] *n* (*on bird, person etc*) duvet *m*.

downs [daʊnz] *npl* collines *fpl*.

dowry ['daʊərɪ] *n* dot *f*.

doze [dəʊz] *n* petit somme *m*; – *vi* sommeiller; **to d. off** s'assoupir. ◆**dozy** *a* (**-ier, -iest**) assoupi; (*silly*) *Fam* bête, gourde.

dozen ['dʌz(ə)n] *n* douzaine *f*; **a d.** (*eggs, books etc*) une douzaine de; **dozens of** *Fig* des dizaines de.

Dr *abbr* (*Doctor*) Docteur.

drab [dræb] *a* terne; (*weather*) gris. ◆**—ness** *n* caractère *m* terne; (*of weather*) grisaille *f*.

draconian [drə'kəʊnɪən] *a* draconien.

draft [drɑːft] **1** *n* (*outline*) ébauche *f*; (*of letter etc*) brouillon *m*; (*bill*) *Com* traite *f*; – *vt* to **d. (out)** (*sketch out*) faire le brouillon de; (*write out*) rédiger. **2** *n Mil Am* conscription *f*; (*men*) contingent *m*; – *vt* (*conscript*) appeler (sous les drapeaux). **3** *n Am* = **draught.**
draftsman ['drɑːftsmən] *n* = **draughtsman.**
drag [dræg] *vt* (-gg-) traîner, tirer; (*river*) draguer; **to d. sth from s.o.** (*confession etc*) arracher qch à qn; **to d. along** (en)traîner; **to d. s.o. away from** arracher qn à; **to d. s.o. into** entraîner qn dans; – *vi* traîner; **to d. on** *or* **out** (*last a long time*) se prolonger; – *n Fam* (*tedium*) corvée *f*; (*person*) raseur, -euse *mf*; (*on cigarette*) bouffée *f* (**on** de); **in d.** (*clothing*) en travesti.
dragon ['drægən] *n* dragon *m*. ◆**dragonfly** *n* libellule *f*.
drain [dreɪn] *n* (*sewer*) égout *m*; (*pipe, channel*) canal *m*; (*outside house*) puisard *m*; (*in street*) bouche *f* d'égout; **it's (gone) down the d.** (*wasted*) *Fam* c'est fichu; **to be a d. on** (*resources, patience*) épuiser; – *vt* (*land*) drainer; (*glass, tank*) vider; (*vegetables*) égoutter; (*resources*) épuiser; **to d. (off)** (*liquid*) faire écouler; **to d. of** (*deprive of*) priver de; – *vi* **to d. (off)** (*of liquid*) s'écouler; **to d. away** (*of strength*) s'épuiser; **draining board** paillasse *f*. ◆**—age** *n* (*act*) drainage *m*; (*sewers*) système *m* d'égouts. ◆**—er** *n* (*board*) paillasse *f*; (*rack, basket*) égouttoir *m*. ◆**drainboard** *n Am* paillasse *f*. ◆**drainpipe** *n* tuyau *m* d'évacuation.
drake [dreɪk] *n* canard *m* (mâle).
dram [dræm] *n* (*drink*) *Fam* goutte *f*.
drama ['drɑːmə] *n* (*event*) drame *m*; (*dramatic art*) théâtre *m*; **d. critic** critique *m* dramatique. ◆**dra'matic** *a* dramatique; (*very great, striking*) spectaculaire. ◆**dra'matically** *adv* (*to change, drop etc*) de façon spectaculaire. ◆**dra'matics** *n* théâtre *m*. ◆**dramatist** ['dræmətɪst] *n* dramaturge *m*. ◆**dramatize** *vt* (*exaggerate*) dramatiser; (*novel etc*) adapter (pour la scène *or* l'écran).
drank [dræŋk] *see* **drink.**
drap/e [dreɪp] *vt* draper (**with** de); (*wall*) tapisser (de tentures); – *npl* tentures *fpl*; (*heavy curtains*) *Am* rideaux *mpl*. ◆**—er** *n* marchand, -ande *mf* de nouveautés.
drastic ['dræstɪk] *a* radical, sévère; (*reduction*) massif. ◆**drastically** *adv* radicalement.
draught [drɑːft] *n* courant *m* d'air; (*for fire*) tirage *m*; *pl* (*game*) dames *fpl*; – *a* (*horse*) de trait; (*beer*) (à la) pression; **d. excluder** bourrelet *m* (*de porte, de fenêtre*). ◆**draughtboard** *n* damier *m*. ◆**draughty** *a* (**-ier, -iest**) (*room*) plein de courants d'air.
draughtsman ['drɑːftsmən] *n* (*pl* **-men**) dessinateur, -trice *mf* (industriel(le) *or* technique).
draw[1] [drɔː] *n* (*of lottery*) tirage *m* au sort; *Sp* match *m* nul; (*attraction*) attraction *f*; – *vt* (*pt* **drew**, *pp* **drawn**) (*pull*) tirer; (*pass*) passer (**over** sur, **into** dans); (*prize*) gagner; (*applause*) provoquer; (*money from bank*) retirer (**from, out of** de); (*salary*) toucher; (*attract*) attirer; (*well-water, comfort*) puiser (**from** dans); **to d. a smile** faire sourire (**from s.o.** qn); **to d. a bath** faire couler un bain; **to d. sth to a close** mettre fin à qch; **to d. a match** *Sp* faire match nul; **to d. in** (*claws*) rentrer; **to d. out** (*money*) retirer; (*meeting*) prolonger; **to d. up** (*chair*) approcher; (*contract, list, plan*) dresser, rédiger; **to d. (up)on** (*savings*) puiser dans; – *vi* (*enter*) entrer (**into** dans); (*arrive*) arriver; **to d. near (to)** s'approcher (de); (*of time*) approcher (de); **to d. to a close** tirer à sa fin; **to d. aside** (*step aside*) s'écarter; **to d. away** (*go away*) s'éloigner; **to d. back** (*recoil*) reculer; **to d. in** (*of days*) diminuer; **to d. on** (*of time*) s'avancer; **to d. up** (*of vehicle*) s'arrêter. ◆**drawback** *n* inconvénient *m*. ◆**drawbridge** *n* pont-levis *m*.
draw[2] [drɔː] *vt* (*pt* **drew**, *pp* **drawn**) (*picture*) dessiner; (*circle*) tracer; (*parallel, distinction*) *Fig* faire (**between** entre); – *vi* (*as artist*) dessiner. ◆**—ing** *n* dessin *m*; **d. board** planche *f* à dessin; **d. pin** punaise *f*; **d. room** salon *m*.
drawer [drɔːr] **1** *n* (*in furniture*) tiroir *m*. **2** *npl* (*women's knickers*) culotte *f*.
drawl [drɔːl] *vi* parler d'une voix traînante; – *n* voix *f* traînante.
drawn [drɔːn] *see* **draw**[1,2]; – *a* (*face*) tiré, crispé; **d. match** *or* **game** match *m* nul.
dread [dred] *vt* redouter (**doing** de faire); – *n* crainte *f*, terreur *f*. ◆**dreadful** *a* épouvantable; (*child*) insupportable; (*ill*) malade; **I feel d. (about it)** j'ai vraiment honte. ◆**dreadfully** *adv* terriblement; **to be** *or* **feel d. sorry** regretter infiniment.
dream [driːm] *vti* (*pt* & *pp* **dreamed** *or* **dreamt** [dremt]) rêver; (*imagine*) songer (**of** à, **that** que); **I wouldn't d. of it!** (il n'en est pas question!; **to d. sth up** imaginer qch; – *n* rêve *m*; (*wonderful thing or person*) *Fam* merveille *f*; **to have a d.** faire un rêve (**about** de); **to have dreams of** rêver de; **a d. house**/*etc* une maison/*etc* de rêve; **a d.**

world un monde imaginaire. ◆**—er** *n* rêveur, -euse *mf.* ◆**dreamy** *a* (-ier, -iest) rêveur.

dreary ['drɪərɪ] *a* (-ier, -iest) (*gloomy*) morne; (*monotonous*) monotone; (*boring*) ennuyeux.

dredg/e [dredʒ] *vt* (*river etc*) draguer; – *n* drague *f.* ◆**—er** *n* **1** (*ship*) dragueur *m.* **2** *Culin* saupoudreuse *f.*

dregs [dregz] *npl* **the d.** (*in liquid, of society*) la lie.

drench [drentʃ] *vt* tremper; **to get drenched** se faire tremper (jusqu'aux os).

dress [dres] **1** *n* (*woman's garment*) robe *f*; (*style of dressing*) tenue *f*; **d. circle** *Th* (premier) balcon *m*; **d. designer** dessinateur, -trice *mf* de mode; (*well-known*) couturier *m*; **d. rehearsal** (répétition *f*) générale *f*; **d. shirt** chemise *f* de soirée. **2** *vt* (*clothe*) habiller; (*adorn*) orner; (*salad*) assaisonner; (*wound*) panser; (*skins, chicken*) préparer; **to get dressed** s'habiller; **dressed for tennis/***etc* en tenue de tennis/*etc*; – *vi* s'habiller; **to d. up** (*smartly*) bien s'habiller; (*in disguise*) se déguiser (**as** en). ◆**—ing** *n Med* pansement *m*; (*seasoning*) *Culin* assaisonnement *m*; **to give s.o. a d.-down** passer un savon à qn; **d. gown** robe *f* de chambre; (*of boxer*) peignoir *m*; **d. room** *Th* loge *f*; **d. table** coiffeuse *f.* ◆**—er** *n* **1** (*furniture*) vaisselier *m*; *Am* coiffeuse *f.* **2 she's a good d.** elle s'habille toujours bien. ◆**dressmaker** *n* couturière *f.* ◆**dressmaking** *n* couture *f.*

dressy ['dresɪ] *a* (-ier, -iest) (*smart*) chic *inv*; (**too**) **d.** trop habillé.

drew [druː] *see* **draw** [1,2].

dribble ['drɪb(ə)l] *vi* (*of baby*) baver; (*of liquid*) tomber goutte à goutte; *Sp* dribbler; – *vt* laisser tomber goutte à goutte; (*ball*) *Sp* dribbler.

dribs [drɪbz] *npl* **in d. and drabs** par petites quantités; (*to arrive*) par petits groupes.

dried [draɪd] *a* (*fruit*) sec; (*milk*) en poudre; (*flowers*) séché.

drier ['draɪər] *n* = **dryer.**

drift [drɪft] *vi* être emporté par le vent *or* le courant; (*of ship*) dériver; *Fig* aller à la dérive; (*of snow*) s'amonceler; **to d. about** (**aimlessly**) se promener sans but, traînailler; **to d. apart** (*of husband and wife*) devenir des étrangers l'un pour l'autre; to **d. into/towards** glisser dans/vers; – *n* mouvement *m*; (*direction*) sens *m*; (*of events*) cours *m*; (*of snow*) amoncellement *m*, congère *f*; (*meaning*) sens *m* général. ◆**—er** *n* (*aimless person*) paumé, -ée *mf.* ◆**driftwood** *n* bois *m* flotté.

drill [drɪl] **1** *n* (*tool*) perceuse *f*; (*bit*) mèche *f*; (*for rock*) foreuse *f*; (*for tooth*) fraise *f*; (*pneumatic*) marteau *m* pneumatique; – *vt* percer; (*tooth*) fraiser; (*oil well*) forer; – *vi* **to d. for oil** faire de la recherche pétrolière. **2** *n Mil Sch* exercice(s) *m*(*pl*); (*procedure*) *Fig* marche *f* à suivre; – *vi* faire l'exercice; – *vt* faire faire l'exercice à.

drink [drɪŋk] *n* boisson *f*; (*glass of sth*) verre *m*; **to give s.o. a d.** donner (quelque chose) à boire à qn; – *vt* (*pt* **drank**, *pp* **drunk**) boire; **to d. oneself to death** se tuer à force de boire; **to d. down** *or* **up** boire; – *vi* boire (**out of dans**); **to d. up** finir son verre; **to d. to** boire à la santé de. ◆**—ing** *a* (*water*) potable; (*song*) à boire; **d. bout** beuverie *f*; **d. fountain** fontaine *f* publique, borne-fontaine *f*; **d. trough** abreuvoir *m.* ◆**—able** *a* (*fit for drinking*) potable; (*palatable*) buvable. ◆**—er** *n* buveur, -euse *mf.*

drip [drɪp] *vi* (**-pp-**) dégouliner, dégoutter; (*of washing, vegetables*) s'égoutter; (*of tap*) fuir; – *vt* (*paint etc*) laisser couler; – *n* (*drop*) goutte *f*; (*sound*) bruit *m* (de goutte); (*fool*) *Fam* nouille *f.* ◆**d.-dry** *a* (*shirt etc*) sans repassage. ◆**dripping** *n* (*Am* **drippings**) *Culin* graisse *f*; – *a* & *adv* **d.** (**wet**) dégoulinant.

driv/e [draɪv] *n* promenade *f* en voiture; (*energy*) énergie *f*; *Psy* instinct *m*; *Pol* campagne *f*; (*road to private house*) allée *f*; **an hour's d.** une heure de voiture; **left-hand d.** *Aut* (véhicule *m* à) conduite *f* à gauche; **front-wheel d.** *Aut* traction *f* avant; – *vt* (*pt* **drove**, *pp* **driven**) (*vehicle, train, passenger*) conduire; (*machine*) actionner; **to d. (away** *or* **out)** (*chase away*) chasser; **to d. s.o. to do** pousser qn à faire; **to d. to despair** réduire au désespoir; **to d. mad** *or* **crazy** rendre fou; **to d. the rain/smoke against** (*of wind*) rabattre la pluie/fumée contre; **to d. back** (*enemy etc*) repousser; (*passenger*) *Aut* ramener (en voiture); **to d. in** (*thrust*) enfoncer; **to d. s.o. hard** surmener qn; **he drives a Ford** il a une Ford; – *vi* (*drive a car*) conduire; **to d. (along)** (*go, run*) *Aut* rouler; **to d. on the left** rouler à gauche; **to d. away** *or* **off** *Aut* partir; **to d. back** *Aut* revenir; **to d. on** *Aut* continuer; **to d. to** *Aut* aller (en voiture) à; **to d. up** *Aut* arriver; **what are you driving at?** *Fig* où veux-tu en venir? ◆**—ing 1** *n* conduite *f*; **d. lesson** leçon *f* de conduite; **d. licence**, **d. test** permis *m* de conduire; **d. school** auto-école *f.* **2** *a* (*forceful*) **d. force** force *f* agissante; **d. rain** pluie *f* battante. ◆**—er** *n* (*of car*) conducteur, -trice *mf*; (*of taxi, lorry*) chauffeur *m*, conducteur, -trice *mf*; **(train) d.** mécanicien *m*; **she's a good d.** elle conduit bien; **driver's license** *Am* permis *m* de conduire.

drivel ['drɪv(ə)l] *vi* (**-ll-**, *Am* **-l-**) radoter; – *n* radotage *m*.

drizzle ['drɪz(ə)l] *n* bruine *f*, crachin *m*; – *vi* bruiner. ◆**drizzly** *a* (*weather*) de bruine; **it's d.** il bruine.

droll [drəʊl] *a* drôle, comique.

dromedary ['drɒmədərɪ, *Am* 'drɒmɪderɪ] *n* dromadaire *m*.

drone [drəʊn] **1** *n* (*bee*) abeille *f* mâle. **2** *n* (*hum*) bourdonnement *m*; (*purr*) ronronnement *m*; *Fig* débit *m* monotone; – *vi* (*of bee*) bourdonner; (*of engine*) ronronner; **to d. (on)** *Fig* parler d'une voix monotone.

drool [druːl] *vi* (*slaver*) baver; *Fig* radoter; **to d. over** *Fig* s'extasier devant.

droop [druːp] *vi* (*of head*) pencher; (*of eyelid*) tomber; (*of flower*) se faner.

drop [drɒp] **1** *n* (*of liquid*) goutte *f*. **2** *n* (*fall*) baisse *f*, chute *f* (**in** de); (*slope*) descente *f*; (*distance of fall*) hauteur *f* (de chute); (*jump*) *Av* saut *m*; – *vt* (**-pp-**) laisser tomber; (*price, voice*) baisser; (*bomb*) larguer; (*passenger, goods*) *Aut* déposer; *Nau* débarquer; (*letter*) envoyer (**to** à); (*put*) mettre; (*omit*) omettre; (*remark*) laisser échapper; (*get rid of*) supprimer; (*habit*) abandonner; (*team member*) *Sp* écarter; **to d. s.o. off** *Aut* déposer qn; **to d. a line** écrire un petit mot (**to** à); **to d. a hint** faire une allusion; **to d. a hint that** laisser entendre que; **to d. one's h's** ne pas aspirer les h; **to d. a word in s.o.'s ear** glisser un mot à l'oreille de qn; – *vi* (*fall*) tomber; (*of person*) (se laisser) tomber; (*of price*) baisser; (*of conversation*) cesser; **he's ready to d.** *Fam* il tombe de fatigue; **let it d.!** *Fam* laisse tomber!; **to d. across** *or* **in** passer (chez qn); **to d. away** (*diminish*) diminuer; **to d. back** *or* **behind** rester en arrière, se laisser distancer; **to d. off** (*fall asleep*) s'endormir; (*fall off*) tomber; (*of interest, sales etc*) diminuer. ◆**d.-off** *n* (*decrease*) diminution *f* (**in** de); **to d. out** (*fall out*) tomber; (*withdraw*) se retirer; (*socially*) se mettre en marge de la société; *Sch Univ* laisser tomber ses études. ◆**d.-out** *n* marginal, -ale *mf*; *Univ* étudiant, -ante *mf* qui abandonne ses études. ◆**droppings** *npl* (*of animal*) crottes *fpl*; (*of bird*) fiente *f*.

dross [drɒs] *n* déchets *mpl*.

drought [draʊt] *n* sécheresse *f*.

drove [drəʊv] *see* **drive**.

droves [drəʊvz] *npl* (*of people*) foules *fpl*; **in d.** en foule.

drown [draʊn] *vi* se noyer; – *vt* noyer; **to d. oneself, be drowned** se noyer. ◆**—ing** *a* qui se noie; – *n* (*death*) noyade *f*.

drowse [draʊz] *vi* somnoler. ◆**drows/y** *a* (**-ier, -iest**) somnolent; **to feel d.** avoir sommeil; **to make s.o. (feel) d.** assoupir qn. ◆**—ily** *adv* d'un air somnolent. ◆**—iness** *n* somnolence *f*.

drubbing ['drʌbɪŋ] *n* (*beating*) raclée *f*.

drudge [drʌdʒ] *n* bête *f* de somme, esclave *mf* du travail; – *vi* trimer. ◆**drudgery** *n* corvée(s) *f(pl)*, travail *m* ingrat.

drug [drʌg] *n Med* médicament *m*, drogue *f*; (*narcotic*) stupéfiant *m*, drogue *f*; *Fig* drogue *f*; **drugs** (*dope in general*) la drogue; **to be on drugs, take drugs** se droguer; **d. addict** drogué, -ée *mf*; **d. addiction** toxicomanie *f*; **d. taking** usage *m* de la drogue; – *vt* (**-gg-**) droguer; (*drink*) mêler un somnifère à. ◆**druggist** *n Am* pharmacien, -ienne *mf*, droguiste *mf*. ◆**drugstore** *n Am* drugstore *m*.

drum [drʌm] *n Mus* tambour *m*; (*for oil*) bidon *m*; **the big d.** *Mus* la grosse caisse; **the drums** *Mus* la batterie; – *vi* (**-mm-**) *Mil* battre du tambour; (*with fingers*) tambouriner; – *vt* **to d. sth into s.o.** *Fig* rabâcher qch à qn; **to d. up** (*support, interest*) susciter; **to d. up business** *or* **custom** attirer les clients. ◆**drummer** *n* (joueur, -euse *mf* de) tambour *m*; (*in pop or jazz group*) batteur *m*. ◆**drumstick** *n Mus* baguette *f* de tambour; (*of chicken*) pilon *m*, cuisse *f*.

drunk [drʌŋk] *see* **drink**; – *a* ivre; **d. with** *Fig* ivre de; **to get d.** s'enivrer; – *n* ivrogne *mf*, pochard, -arde *mf*. ◆**drunkard** *n* ivrogne *mf*. ◆**drunken** *a* (*quarrel*) d'ivrogne; (*person*) ivrogne; (*driver*) ivre; **d. driving** conduite *f* en état d'ivresse. ◆**drunkenness** *n* (*state*) ivresse *f*; (*habit*) ivrognerie *f*.

dry [draɪ] *a* (**drier, driest**) sec; (*well, river*) à sec; (*day*) sans pluie; (*toast*) sans beurre; (*wit*) caustique; (*subject, book*) aride; **on d. land** sur la terre ferme; **to keep sth d.** tenir qch au sec; **to wipe d.** essuyer; **to run d.** se tarir; **to feel** *or* **be d.** *Fam* avoir soif; **d. dock** cale *f* sèche; **d. goods store** *Am* magasin *m* de nouveautés; – *vt* sécher; (*dishes etc*) essuyer; **to d. off** *or* **up** sécher; – *vi* sécher; **to d. off** sécher; **to d. up** sécher; (*run dry*) se tarir; **d. up!** *Fam* tais-toi! ◆**—ing** *n* séchage *m*; essuyage *m*. ◆**—er** *n* (*for hair,* *clothes*) sèchoir *m*; (*helmet-style for hair*) casque *m*. ◆**—ness** *n* sécheresse *f*; (*of wit*) causticité *f*; (*of book etc*) aridité *f*. ◆**dry-'clean** *vt* nettoyer à sec. ◆**dry-'cleaner** *n* teinturier, -ière *mf*.

dual ['djuːəl] *a* double; **d. carriageway** route *f* à deux voies (séparées). ◆**du'ality** *n* dualité *f*.

dub [dʌb] *vt* (**-bb-**) **1** (*film*) doubler. **2** (*nickname*) surnommer. ◆**dubbing** *n Cin* doublage *m*.

dubious ['djuːbɪəs] *a* (*offer, person etc*) douteux; **I'm d. about going** *or* **whether to go** je me demande si je dois y aller; **to be d. about sth** douter de qch.

duchess ['dʌtʃɪs] *n* duchesse *f*. ◆**duchy** *n* duché *m*.

duck [dʌk] **1** *n* canard *m*. **2** *vi* se baisser (vivement); – *vt* (*head*) baisser; **to d. s.o.** plonger qn dans l'eau. ◆**—ing** *n* bain *m* forcé. ◆**duckling** *n* caneton *m*.

duct [dʌkt] *n Anat Tech* conduit *m*.

dud [dʌd] *a Fam* (*bomb*) non éclaté; (*coin*) faux; (*cheque*) en bois; (*watch etc*) qui ne marche pas; – *n* (*person*) zéro *m*, type *m* nul.

dude [duːd] *n Am Fam* dandy *m*; **d. ranch** ranch(-hôtel) *m*.

due[1] [djuː] *a* (*money, sum*) dû (**to** à); (*rent, bill*) à payer; (*respect*) qu'on doit (**to** à); (*fitting*) qui convient; **to fall d.** échoir; **she's d. for** (*a rise etc*) elle doit *or* devrait recevoir; **he's d. (to arrive)** (*is awaited*) il doit arriver, il est attendu; **I'm d. there** je dois être là-bas; **in d. course** (*at proper time*) en temps utile; (*finally*) à la longue; **d. to** (*attributable to*) dû à; (*because of*) à cause de; (*thanks to*) grâce à; – *n* dû *m*; *pl* (*of club*) cotisation *f*; (*official charges*) droits *mpl*; **to give s.o. his d.** admettre que qn a raison.

due[2] [djuː] *adv* (tout) droit; **d. north/south** plein nord/sud.

duel ['djuːəl] *n* duel *m*; – *vi* (**-ll-**, *Am* **-l-**) se battre en duel.

duet [djuː'et] *n* duo *m*.

duffel, duffle ['dʌf(ə)l] *a* **d. bag** sac *m* de marin; **d. coat** duffel-coat *m*.

dug [dʌg] *see* **dig**. ◆**dugout** *n* **1** *Mil* abri *m* souterrain. **2** (*canoe*) pirogue *f*.

duke [djuːk] *n* duc *m*.

dull [dʌl] *a* (**-er, -est**) (*boring*) ennuyeux; (*colour, character*) terne; (*weather*) maussade; (*mind*) lourd, borné; (*sound, ache*) sourd; (*edge, blade*) émoussé; (*hearing, sight*) faible; – *vt* (*senses*) émousser; (*sound, pain*) amortir; (*colour*) ternir; (*mind*) engourdir. ◆**—ness** *n* (*of mind*) lourdeur *f* d'esprit; (*tedium*) monotonie *f*; (*of colour*) manque *m* d'éclat.

duly ['djuːlɪ] *adv* (*properly*) comme il convient (convenait *etc*); (*in fact*) en effet; (*in due time*) en temps utile.

dumb [dʌm] *a* (**-er, -est**) muet; (*stupid*) *Fam* idiot, bête. ◆**—ness** *n* mutisme *m*; bêtise *f*. ◆**dumbbell** *n* (*weight*) haltère *m*. ◆**dumb'waiter** *n* (*lift for food*) monte-plats *m inv*.

dumbfound [dʌm'faʊnd] *vt* sidérer, ahurir.

dummy ['dʌmɪ] **1** *n* (*of baby*) sucette *f*; (*of dressmaker*) mannequin *m*; (*of book*) maquette *f*; (*of ventriloquist*) pantin *m*; (*fool*) *Fam* idiot, -ote *mf*. **2** *a* factice, faux; **d. run** (*on car etc*) essai *m*.

dump [dʌmp] *vt* (*rubbish*) déposer; **to d. (down)** déposer; **to d. s.o.** (*ditch*) *Fam* plaquer qn; – *n* (*for ammunition*) *Mil* dépôt *m*; (*dirty or dull town*) *Fam* trou *m*; (*house, slum*) *Fam* baraque *f*; **(rubbish) d.** tas *m* d'ordures; (*place*) dépôt *m* d'ordures, décharge *f*; **to be (down) in the dumps** *Fam* avoir le cafard; **d. truck = dumper.** ◆**—er** *n* **d. (truck)** camion *m* à benne basculante.

dumpling ['dʌmplɪŋ] *n Culin* boulette *f* (de pâte).

dumpy ['dʌmpɪ] *a* (**-ier, -iest**) (*person*) boulot, gros et court.

dunce [dʌns] *n* cancre *m*, âne *m*.

dune [djuːn] *n* dune *f*.

dung [dʌŋ] *n* crotte *f*; (*of cattle*) bouse *f*; (*manure*) fumier *m*.

dungarees [dʌŋgə'riːz] *npl* (*of child, workman*) salopette *f*; (*jeans*) *Am* jean *m*.

dungeon ['dʌndʒən] *n* cachot *m*.

dunk [dʌŋk] *vt* (*bread, biscuit etc*) tremper.

dupe [djuːp] *vt* duper; – *n* dupe *f*.

duplex ['duːpleks] *n* (*apartment*) *Am* duplex *m*.

duplicate ['djuːplɪkeɪt] *vt* (*key, map*) faire un double de; (*on machine*) polycopier; – ['djuːplɪkət] *n* double *m*; **in d.** en deux exemplaires; **a d. copy/***etc* une copie/*etc* en double; **a d. key** un double de la clef. ◆**dupli'cation** *n* (*on machine*) polycopie *f*; (*of effort*) répétition *f*. ◆**duplicator** *n* duplicateur *m*.

duplicity [djuː'plɪsɪtɪ] *n* duplicité *f*.

durable ['djʊərəb(ə)l] *a* (*shoes etc*) résistant; (*friendship, love*) durable. ◆**dura'bility** *n* résistance *f*; durabilité *f*.

duration [djʊə'reɪʃ(ə)n] *n* durée *f*.

duress [djʊ'res] *n* **under d.** sous la contrainte.

during ['djʊərɪŋ] *prep* pendant, durant.

dusk [dʌsk] *n* (*twilight*) crépuscule *m*.
dusky ['dʌskɪ] *a* (**-ier, -iest**) (*complexion*) foncé.
dust [dʌst] *n* poussière *f*; **d. cover** (*for furniture*) housse *f*; (*for book*) jaquette *f*; **d. jacket** jaquette *f*; – *vt* épousseter; (*sprinkle*) saupoudrer (**with** de). ◆**—er** *n* chiffon *m*. ◆**dustbin** *n* poubelle *f*. ◆**dustcart** *n* camion-benne *m*. ◆**dustman** *n* (*pl* **-men**) éboueur *m*, boueux *m*. ◆**dustpan** *n* petite pelle *f* (à poussière).
dusty ['dʌstɪ] *a* (**-ier, -iest**) poussiéreux.
Dutch [dʌtʃ] *a* néerlandais, hollandais; **D. cheese** hollande *m*; **to go D.** partager les frais (**with** avec); – *n* (*language*) hollandais *m*. ◆**Dutchman** *n* (*pl* **-men**) Hollandais *m*. ◆**Dutchwoman** *n* (*pl* **-women**) Hollandaise *f*.
duty ['djuːtɪ] *n* devoir *m*; (*tax*) droit *m*; *pl* (*responsibilities*) fonctions *fpl*; **on d.** *Mil* de service; (*doctor etc*) de garde; *Sch* de permanence; **off d.** libre. ◆**d.-'free** *a* (*goods, shop*) hors-taxe *inv*. ◆**dutiful** *a* respectueux, obéissant; (*worker*) consciencieux.
dwarf [dwɔːf] *n* nain *m*, naine *f*; – *vt* (*of building, person etc*) rapetisser, écraser.
dwell [dwel] *vi* (*pt & pp* **dwelt**) demeurer; **to d. (up)on** (*think about*) penser sans cesse à; (*speak about*) parler sans cesse de, s'étendre sur; (*insist on*) appuyer sur. ◆**—ing** *n* habitation *f*. ◆**—er** *n* habitant, -ante *mf*.
dwindl/e ['dwɪnd(ə)l] *vi* diminuer (peu à peu). ◆**—ing** *a* (*interest etc*) décroissant.
dye [daɪ] *n* teinture *f*; – *vt* teindre; **to d. green/etc** teindre en vert/*etc*. ◆**dyeing** *n* teinture *f*; (*industry*) teinturerie *f*. ◆**dyer** *n* teinturier, -ière *mf*.
dying ['daɪɪŋ] *see* **die 1**; – *a* mourant, moribond; (*custom*) qui se perd; (*day, words*) dernier; – *n* (*death*) mort *f*.
dyke [daɪk] *n* (*wall*) digue *f*; (*ditch*) fossé *m*.
dynamic [daɪ'næmɪk] *a* dynamique. ◆**'dynamism** *n* dynamisme *m*.
dynamite ['daɪnəmaɪt] *n* dynamite *f*; – *vt* dynamiter.
dynamo ['daɪnəməʊ] *n* (*pl* **-os**) dynamo *f*.
dynasty ['dɪnəstɪ, *Am* 'daɪnəstɪ] *n* dynastie *f*.
dysentery ['dɪsəntrɪ] *n* *Med* dysenterie *f*.
dyslexic [dɪs'leksɪk] *a & n* dyslexique (*mf*).

E

E, e [iː] *n* E, e *m*.
each [iːtʃ] *a* chaque; – *pron* chacun, -une; **e. one** chacun, -une; **e. other** l'un(e) l'autre, *pl* les un(e)s les autres; **to see e. other** se voir (l'un(e) l'autre); **e. of us** chacun, -une d'entre nous.
eager ['iːgər] *a* impatient (**to do** de faire); (*enthusiastic*) ardent, passionné; **to be e. for** désirer vivement; **e. for** (*money*) avide de; **e. to help** empressé (à aider); **to be e. to do** (*want*) avoir envie de faire. ◆**—ly** *adv* (*to await*) avec impatience; (*to work, serve*) avec empressement. ◆**—ness** *n* impatience *f* (**to do** de faire); (*zeal*) empressement *m* (**to do** à faire); (*greed*) avidité *f*.
eagle ['iːg(ə)l] *n* aigle *m*. ◆**e.-'eyed** *a* au regard d'aigle.
ear¹ [ɪər] *n* oreille *f*; **all ears** *Fam* tout ouïe; **up to one's ears in work** débordé de travail; **to play it by e.** *Fam* agir selon la situation; **thick e.** *Fam* gifle *f*. ◆**earache** *n* mal *m* d'oreille. ◆**eardrum** *n* tympan *m*. ◆**earmuffs** *npl* serre-tête *m inv* (*pour protéger les oreilles*), protège-oreilles *m inv*. ◆**earphones** *npl* casque *m*. ◆**earpiece** *n* écouteur *m*. ◆**earplug** *n* (*to keep out noise*) boule *f* Quiès®. ◆**earring** *n* boucle *f* d'oreille. ◆**earshot** *n* **within e.** à portée de voix. ◆**ear-splitting** *a* assourdissant.
ear² [ɪər] *n* (*of corn*) épi *m*.
earl [ɜːl] *n* comte *m*.
early ['ɜːlɪ] *a* (**-ier, -iest**) (*first*) premier; (*fruit, season*) précoce; (*death*) prématuré; (*age*) jeune; (*painting, work*) de jeunesse; (*reply*) rapide; (*return, retirement*) anticipé; (*ancient*) ancien; **it's e.** (*looking at time*) il est tôt; (*referring to appointment etc*) c'est tôt; **it's too e. to get up/etc** il est trop tôt pour se lever/*etc*; **to be e.** (*ahead of time*) arriver de bonne heure *or* tôt, être en avance; (*in getting up*) être matinal; **in e. times** jadis; **in e. summer** au début de l'été; **one's e. life** sa jeunesse; – *adv* tôt, de bonne heure; (*ahead of time*) en avance; (*to die*) prématurément; **as e. as possible** le plus tôt possible; **earlier (on)** plus tôt; **at**

the earliest au plus tôt; as e. as yesterday déjà hier. ◆e.-'warning system *n* dispositif *m* de première alerte.

earmark ['ɪəmɑːk] *vt* (*funds*) assigner (**for** à).

earn [ɜːn] *vt* gagner; (*interest*) *Fin* rapporter. ◆**—ings** *npl* (*wages*) rémunérations *fpl*; (*profits*) bénéfices *mpl*.

earnest ['ɜːnɪst] *a* sérieux; (*sincere*) sincère; – *n* **in e.** sérieusement; **it's raining in e.** il pleut pour de bon; **he's in e.** il est sérieux. ◆**—ness** *n* sérieux *m*; sincérité *f*.

earth [ɜːθ] *n* (*world, ground*) terre *f*; *El* terre *f*, masse *f*; **to fall to e.** tomber à *or* par terre; **nothing/nobody on e.** rien/personne au monde; **where/what on e.?** où/que diable? ◆**earthly** *a* (*possessions etc*) terrestre; **not an e. chance** *Fam* pas la moindre chance; **for no e. reason** *Fam* sans la moindre raison. ◆**earthy** *a* terreux; (*person*) *Fig* terre-à-terre *inv*. ◆**earthquake** *n* tremblement *m* de terre. ◆**earthworks** *npl* (*excavations*) terrassements *mpl*. ◆**earthworm** *n* ver *m* de terre.

earthenware ['ɜːθənweər] *n* faïence *f*; – *a* en faïence.

earwig ['ɪəwɪg] *n* (*insect*) perce-oreille *m*.

ease [iːz] **1** *n* (*physical*) bien-être *m*; (*mental*) tranquillité *f*; (*facility*) facilité *f*; **(ill) at e.** (*in situation*) (mal) à l'aise; **at e.** (*of mind*) tranquille; **(stand) at e.!** *Mil* repos!; **with e.** facilement. **2** *vt* (*pain*) soulager; (*mind*) calmer; (*tension*) diminuer; (*loosen*) relâcher; **to e. off/along** enlever/déplacer doucement; **to e. oneself through** se glisser par; – *vi* **to e. (off** *or* **up)** (*of situation*) se détendre; (*of pressure*) diminuer; (*of demand*) baisser; (*of pain*) se calmer; (*not work so hard*) se relâcher. ◆**easily** *adv* facilement; **e. the best/*etc*** de loin le meilleur/*etc*; **that could e. be** ça pourrait bien être. ◆**easiness** *n* aisance *f*.

easel ['iːz(ə)l] *n* chevalet *m*.

east [iːst] *n* est *m*; **Middle/Far E.** Moyen-/Extrême-Orient *m*; – *a* (*coast*) est *inv*; (*wind*) d'est; **E. Africa** Afrique *f* orientale; **E. Germany** Allemagne *f* de l'Est; – *adv* à l'est, vers l'est. ◆**eastbound** *a* (*carriageway*) est *inv*; (*traffic*) en direction de l'est. ◆**easterly** *a* (*point*) est *inv*; (*direction*) de l'est; (*wind*) d'est. ◆**eastern** *a* (*coast*) est *inv*; **E. France** l'Est *m* de la France; **E. Europe** Europe *f* de l'Est. ◆**easterner** *n* habitant, -ante *mf* de l'Est. ◆**eastward(s)** *a* & *adv* vers l'est.

Easter ['iːstər] *n* Pâques *m sing or fpl*; **E. week** semaine *f* pascale; **Happy E.!** joyeuses Pâques!

easy ['iːzɪ] *a* (**-ier, -iest**) facile; (*manners*) naturel; (*life*) tranquille; (*pace*) modéré; **to feel e. in one's mind** être tranquille; **to be an e. first** *Sp* être bon premier; **I'm e.** *Fam* ça m'est égal; **e. chair** fauteuil *m* (rembourré); – *adv* doucement; **go e. on** (*sugar etc*) vas-y doucement *or* mollo avec; (*person*) ne sois pas trop dur avec *or* envers; **take it e.** (*rest*) repose-toi; (*work less*) ne te fatigue pas; (*calm down*) calme-toi; (*go slow*) ne te presse pas. ◆**easy'going** *a* (*carefree*) insouciant; (*easy to get on with*) traitable.

eat [iːt] *vt* (*pt* **ate** [et, *Am* eɪt], *pp* **eaten** ['iːt(ə)n]) manger; (*meal*) prendre; (*one's words*) *Fig* ravaler; **to e. breakfast** *or* **lunch** déjeuner; **what's eating you?** *Sl* qu'est-ce qui te tracasse?; **to e. up** (*finish*) finir; **eaten up with** (*envy*) dévoré de; – *vi* manger; **to e. into** (*of acid*) ronger; **to e. out** (*lunch*) déjeuner dehors; (*dinner*) dîner dehors. ◆**—ing** *a* **e. apple** pomme *f* à couteau; **e. place** restaurant *m*. ◆**—able** *a* mangeable. ◆**—er** *n* **big e.** gros mangeur *m*, grosse mangeuse *f*.

eau de Cologne [əudəkə'ləun] *n* eau *f* de Cologne.

eaves [iːvz] *npl* avant-toit *m*. ◆**eavesdrop** *vt* (**-pp-**) **to e. (on)** écouter (de façon indiscrète). ◆**eavesdropper** *n* oreille *f* indiscrète.

ebb [eb] *n* reflux *m*; **e. and flow** le flux et le reflux; **e. tide** marée *f* descendante; **at a low e.** *Fig* très bas; – *vi* refluer; **to e. (away)** (*of strength etc*) *Fig* décliner.

ebony ['ebənɪ] *n* (*wood*) ébène *f*.

ebullient [ɪ'bʌlɪənt] *a* exubérant.

eccentric [ɪk'sentrɪk] *a* & *n* excentrique (*mf*). ◆**eccen'tricity** *n* excentricité *f*.

ecclesiastic [ɪkliːzɪ'æstɪk] *a* & *n* ecclésiastique (*m*). ◆**ecclesiastical** *a* ecclésiastique.

echelon ['eʃəlɒn] *n* (*of organization*) échelon *m*.

echo ['ekəu] *n* (*pl* **-oes**) écho *m*; – *vt* (*sound*) répercuter; (*repeat*) *Fig* répéter; – *vi* **the explosion/*etc* echoed** l'écho de l'explosion/*etc* se répercuta; **to e. with the sound of** résonner de l'écho de.

éclair [eɪ'kleər] *n* (*cake*) éclair *m*.

eclectic [ɪ'klektɪk] *a* éclectique.

eclipse [ɪ'klɪps] *n* (*of sun etc*) & *Fig* éclipse *f*; – *vt* éclipser.

ecology [ɪ'kɒlədʒɪ] *n* écologie *f*. ◆**eco'logical** *a* écologique.

economic [iːkə'nɒmɪk] *a* économique; (*profitable*) rentable. ◆**economical** *a* économique; (*thrifty*) économe. ◆**economically** *adv* économiquement. ◆**economics** *n* (science *f*) économique *f*; (*profitability*) aspect *m* financier.

economy [ɪ'kɒnəmɪ] *n* (*saving, system, thrift*) économie *f*; **e. class** *Av* classe *f* touriste. ◆**economist** *n* économiste *mf*. ◆**economize** *vti* économiser (**on** sur).

ecstasy ['ekstəsɪ] *n* extase *f*. ◆**ec'static** *a* extasié; **to be e. about** s'extasier sur. ◆**ec'statically** *adv* avec extase.

ecumenical [iːkjʊ'menɪk(ə)l] *a* œcuménique.

eczema ['eksɪmə] *n Med* eczéma *m*.

eddy ['edɪ] *n* tourbillon *m*, remous *m*.

edg/e [edʒ] *n* bord *m*; (*of forest*) lisière *f*; (*of town*) abords *mpl*; (*of page*) marge *f*; (*of knife etc*) tranchant *m*, fil *m*; **on e.** (*person*) énervé; (*nerves*) tendu; **to set s.o.'s teeth on e.** (*irritate s.o.*) crisper qn, faire grincer les dents à qn; **to have the e.** *or* **a slight e.** *Fig* être légèrement supérieur (**over, on** à); — *vt* (*clothing etc*) border (**with** de); — *vti* **to e. (oneself) into** (*move*) se glisser dans; **to e. (oneself) forward** avancer doucement. ◆**—ing** *n* (*border*) bordure *f*. ◆**edgeways** *adv* de côté; **to get a word in e.** *Fam* placer un mot.

edgy ['edʒɪ] *a* (**-ier, -iest**) énervé. ◆**edginess** *n* nervosité *f*.

edible ['edɪb(ə)l] *a* (*mushroom, berry etc*) comestible; (*meal, food*) mangeable.

edict ['iːdɪkt] *n* décret *m*; *Hist* édit *m*.

edifice ['edɪfɪs] *n* (*building, organization*) édifice *m*.

edify ['edɪfaɪ] *vt* (*improve the mind of*) édifier.

Edinburgh ['edɪnb(ə)rə] *n* Édimbourg *m or f*.

edit ['edɪt] *vt* (*newspaper etc*) diriger; (*article etc*) mettre au point; (*film*) monter; (*annotate*) éditer; (*compile*) rédiger; **to e. (out)** (*cut out*) couper. ◆**editor** *n* (*of review*) directeur, -trice *mf*; (*compiler*) rédacteur, -trice *mf*; *TV Rad* réalisateur, -trice *mf*; **sports e.** *Journ* rédacteur *m* sportif, rédactrice *f* sportive; **the e. (in chief)** (*of newspaper*) le rédacteur *m* en chef. ◆**edi'torial** *a* de la rédaction; **e. staff** rédaction *f*; — *n* éditorial *m*.

edition [ɪ'dɪʃ(ə)n] *n* édition *f*.

educat/e ['edjʊkeɪt] *vt* (*family, children*) éduquer; (*pupil*) instruire; (*mind*) former, éduquer; **to be educated at** faire ses études à. ◆**—ed** *a* (*voice*) cultivé; (**well-**)**e.** (*person*) instruit. ◆**edu'cation** *n* éducation *f*; (*teaching*) instruction *f*, enseignement *m*; (*training*) formation *f*; (*subject*) *Univ* pédagogie *f*. ◆**edu'cational** *a* (*establishment*) d'enseignement; (*method*) pédagogique; (*game*) éducatif; (*supplies*) scolaire. ◆**edu'cationally** *adv* du point de vue de l'éducation. ◆**educator** *n* éducateur, -trice *mf*.

EEC [iːiː'siː] *n abbr* (*European Economic Community*) CEE *f*.

eel [iːl] *n* anguille *f*.

eerie ['ɪərɪ] *a* (**-ier, -iest**) sinistre, étrange.

efface [ɪ'feɪs] *vt* effacer.

effect [ɪ'fekt] **1** *n* (*result, impression*) effet *m* (**on** sur); *pl* (*goods*) biens *mpl*; **to no e.** en vain; **in e.** en fait; **to put into e.** mettre en application, faire entrer en vigueur; **to come into e., take e.** entrer en vigueur; **to take e.** (*of drug etc*) agir; **to have an e.** (*of medicine etc*) faire de l'effet; **to have no e.** rester sans effet; **to this e.** (*in this meaning*) dans ce sens; **to the e. that** (*saying that*) comme quoi. **2** *vt* (*carry out*) effectuer, réaliser.

effective [ɪ'fektɪv] *a* (*efficient*) efficace; (*actual*) effectif; (*striking*) frappant; **to become e.** (*of law*) prendre effet. ◆**—ly** *adv* efficacement; (*in effect*) effectivement. ◆**—ness** *n* efficacité *f*; (*quality*) effet *m* frappant.

effeminate [ɪ'femɪnɪt] *a* efféminé.

effervescent [efə'ves(ə)nt] *a* (*mixture, youth*) effervescent; (*drink*) gazeux. ◆**effervesce** *vi* (*of drink*) pétiller. ◆**effervescence** *n* (*excitement*) & *Ch* effervescence *f*; pétillement *m*.

effete [ɪ'fiːt] *a* (*feeble*) mou, faible; (*decadent*) décadent.

efficient [ɪ'fɪʃ(ə)nt] *a* (*method*) efficace; (*person*) compétent, efficace; (*organization*) efficace, performant; (*machine*) performant, à haut rendement. ◆**efficiency** *n* efficacité *f*; compétence *f*; performances *fpl*. ◆**efficiently** *adv* efficacement; avec compétence; **to work e.** (*of machine*) bien fonctionner.

effigy ['efɪdʒɪ] *n* effigie *f*.

effort ['efət] *n* effort *m*; **to make an e.** faire un effort (**to** pour); **it isn't worth the e.** ça ne *or* n'en vaut pas la peine; **his** *or* **her latest e.** *Fam* ses dernières tentatives. ◆**—less** *a* (*victory etc*) facile. ◆**—lessly** *adv* facilement, sans effort.

effrontery [ɪ'frʌntərɪ] *n* effronterie *f*.

effusive [ɪ'fjuːsɪv] *a* (*person*) expansif; (*thanks, excuses*) sans fin. ◆**—ly** *adv* avec effusion.

e.g. [iːˈdʒiː] *abbr* (*exempli gratia*) par exemple.

egalitarian [ɪgælɪˈteərɪən] *a* (*society etc*) égalitaire.

egg[1] [eg] *n* œuf *m*; **e. timer** sablier *m*; **e. whisk** fouet *m* (à œufs). ◆**eggcup** *n* coquetier *m*. ◆**egghead** *n Pej* intellectuel, -elle *mf*. ◆**eggplant** *n* aubergine *f*. ◆**eggshell** *n* coquille *f*.

egg[2] [eg] *vt* **to e. on** (*encourage*) inciter (to do à faire).

ego [ˈiːgəʊ] *n* (*pl* **-os**) **the e.** *Psy* le moi. ◆**egoˈcentric** *a* égocentrique. ◆**egoism** *n* égoïsme *m*. ◆**egoist** *n* égoïste *mf*. ◆**egoˈistic(al)** *a* égoïste. ◆**egotism** *n* égotisme *m*.

Egypt [ˈiːdʒɪpt] *n* Égypte *f*. ◆**Eˈgyptian** *a & n* égyptien, -ienne (*mf*).

eh? [eɪ] *int Fam* hein?

eiderdown [ˈaɪdədaʊn] *n* édredon *m*.

eight [eɪt] *a & n* huit (*m*). ◆**eighˈteen** *a & n* dix-huit (*m*). ◆**eighˈteenth** *a & n* dix-huitième (*mf*). ◆**eighth** *a & n* huitième (*mf*); **an e.** un huitième. ◆**eightieth** *a & n* quatre-vingtième (*mf*). ◆**eighty** *a & n* quatre-vingts (*m*); **e.-one** quatre-vingt-un.

Eire [ˈeərə] *n* République *f* d'Irlande.

either [ˈaɪðər] **1** *a & pron* (*one or other*) l'un(e) ou l'autre; (*with negative*) ni l'un(e) ni l'autre; (*each*) chaque; **on e. side** de chaque côté, des deux côtés. **2** *adv* **she can't swim e.** elle ne sait pas nager non plus; **I don't e.** (ni) moi non plus; **not so far off e.** (*moreover*) pas si loin d'ailleurs. **3** *conj* **e. . . . or** ou (bien) . . . ou (bien), soit . . . soit; (*with negative*) ni . . . ni.

eject [ɪˈdʒekt] *vt* expulser; *Tech* éjecter. ◆**ejector** *a* **e. seat** *Av* siège *m* éjectable.

eke [iːk] *vt* **to e. out** (*income etc*) faire durer; **to e. out a living** gagner (difficilement) sa vie.

elaborate [ɪˈlæbərət] *a* compliqué, détaillé; (*preparation*) minutieux; (*style*) recherché; (*meal*) raffiné; – [ɪˈlæbəreɪt] *vt* (*theory etc*) élaborer; – *vi* entrer dans les détails (on de). ◆**—ly** *adv* (*to plan*) minutieusement; (*to decorate*) avec recherche. ◆**elaboˈration** *n* élaboration *f*.

elapse [ɪˈlæps] *vi* s'écouler.

elastic [ɪˈlæstɪk] *a* (*object, character*) élastique; **e. band** élastique *m*; – *n* (*fabric*) élastique *m*. ◆**elaˈsticity** *n* élasticité *f*.

elated [ɪˈleɪtɪd] *a* transporté de joie. ◆**elation** *n* exaltation *f*.

elbow [ˈelbəʊ] *n* coude *m*; **e. grease** *Fam* huile *f* de coude; **to have enough e. room** avoir assez de place; – *vt* **to e. one's way** se frayer un chemin (à coups de coude) (**through** à travers).

elder[1] [ˈeldər] *a & n* (*of two people*) aîné, -ée (*mf*). ◆**elderly** *a* assez âgé, entre deux âges. ◆**eldest** *a & n* aîné, -ée (*mf*); **his** *or* **her e. brother** l'aîné de ses frères.

elder[2] [ˈeldər] *n* (*tree*) sureau *m*.

elect [ɪˈlekt] *vt Pol* élire (to à); **to e. to do** choisir de faire; – *a* **the president/***etc* **e.** le président/*etc* désigné. ◆**election** *n* élection *f*; **general e.** élections *fpl* législatives; – *a* (*campaign*) électoral; (*day, results*) du scrutin, des élections. ◆**electioˈneering** *n* campagne *f* électorale. ◆**elective** *a* (*course*) *Am* facultatif. ◆**electoral** *a* électoral. ◆**electorate** *n* électorat *m*.

electric [ɪˈlektrɪk] *a* électrique; **e. blanket** couverture *f* chauffante; **e. shock** décharge *f* électrique; **e. shock treatment** électrochoc *m*. ◆**electrical** *a* électrique; **e. engineer** ingénieur *m* électricien. ◆**elecˈtrician** *n* électricien *m*. ◆**elecˈtricity** *n* électricité *f*. ◆**electrify** *vt Rail* électrifier; (*excite*) *Fig* électriser. ◆**electrocute** *vt* électrocuter.

electrode [ɪˈlektrəʊd] *n El* électrode *f*.

electron [ɪˈlektrɒn] *n* électron *m*; – *a* (*microscope*) électronique. ◆**elecˈtronic** *a* électronique. ◆**elecˈtronics** *n* électronique *f*.

elegant [ˈelɪgənt] *a* élégant. ◆**elegance** *n* élégance *f*. ◆**elegantly** *adv* avec élégance, élégamment.

elegy [ˈelədʒɪ] *n* élégie *f*.

element [ˈeləmənt] *n* (*component, environment*) élément *m*; (*of heater*) résistance *f*; **an e. of truth** un grain *or* une part de vérité; **the human/chance e.** le facteur humain/chance; **in one's e.** dans son élément. ◆**eleˈmental** *a* élémentaire. ◆**eleˈmentary** *a* élémentaire; (*school*) *Am* primaire; **e. courtesy** la courtoisie la plus élémentaire.

elephant [ˈelɪfənt] *n* éléphant *m*. ◆**elephantine** [elɪˈfæntaɪn] *a* (*large*) éléphantesque; (*clumsy*) gauche.

elevate [ˈelɪveɪt] *vt* élever (to à). ◆**eleˈvation** *n* élévation *f* (**of** de); (*height*) altitude *f*. ◆**elevator** *n Am* ascenseur *m*.

eleven [ɪˈlev(ə)n] *a & n* onze (*m*). ◆**elevenses** [ɪˈlev(ə)nzɪz] *n Fam* pause-café *f* (*vers onze heures du matin*). ◆**eleventh** *a & n* onzième (*mf*).

elf [elf] *n* (*pl* **elves**) lutin *m*.

elicit [ɪˈlɪsɪt] *vt* tirer, obtenir (**from** de).

elide [ɪˈlaɪd] *vt Ling* élider. ◆**elision** *n* élision *f*.

eligible ['elɪdʒəb(ə)l] *a* (*for post etc*) admissible (**for** à); (*for political office*) éligible (**for** à); **to be e. for** (*entitled to*) avoir droit à; **an e. young man** (*suitable as husband*) un beau parti. ◆**eligi'bility** *n* admissibilité *f*; *Pol* éligibilité *f*.
eliminate [ɪ'lɪmɪneɪt] *vt* éliminer (**from** de). ◆**elimi'nation** *n* élimination *f*.
elite [eɪ'liːt] *n* élite *f* (**of** de).
elk [elk] *n* (*animal*) élan *m*.
ellipse [ɪ'lɪps] *n Geom* ellipse *f*. ◆**elliptical** *a* elliptique.
elm [elm] *n* (*tree, wood*) orme *m*.
elocution [elə'kjuːʃ(ə)n] *n* élocution *f*.
elongate ['iːlɒŋgeɪt] *vt* allonger. ◆**elon'gation** *n* allongement *m*.
elope [ɪ'ləʊp] *vi* (*of lovers*) s'enfuir (**with** avec). ◆**—ment** *n* fugue *f* (amoureuse).
eloquent ['eləkwənt] *a* éloquent. ◆**eloquence** *n* éloquence *f*.
else [els] *adv* d'autre; **someone e.** quelqu'un d'autre; **everybody e.** tout le monde à part moi, vous *etc*, tous les autres; **nobody/nothing e.** personne/rien d'autre; **something e.** autre chose; **something** *or* **anything e.?** encore quelque chose?; **somewhere e.** ailleurs, autre part; **who e.?** qui encore?, qui d'autre?; **how e.?** de quelle autre façon?; **or e.** ou bien, sinon. ◆**elsewhere** *adv* ailleurs; **e. in the town** dans une autre partie de la ville.
elucidate [ɪ'luːsɪdeɪt] *vt* élucider.
elude [ɪ'luːd] *vt* (*enemy*) échapper à; (*question*) éluder; (*obligation*) se dérober à; (*blow*) esquiver. ◆**elusive** *a* (*enemy, aims*) insaisissable; (*reply*) évasif.
emaciated [ɪ'meɪsɪeɪtɪd] *a* émacié.
emanate ['eməneɪt] *vi* émaner (**from** de).
emancipate [ɪ'mænsɪpeɪt] *vt* (*women*) émanciper. ◆**emanci'pation** *n* émancipation *f*.
embalm [ɪm'bɑːm] *vt* (*dead body*) embaumer.
embankment [ɪm'bæŋkmənt] *n* (*of path etc*) talus *m*; (*of river*) berge *f*.
embargo [ɪm'bɑːgəʊ] *n* (*pl* **-oes**) embargo *m*.
embark [ɪm'bɑːk] *vt* embarquer; – *vi* (s')embarquer; **to e. on** (*start*) commencer, entamer; (*launch into*) se lancer dans, s'embarquer dans. ◆**embar'kation** *n* embarquement *m*.
embarrass [ɪm'bærəs] *vt* embarrasser, gêner. ◆**—ing** *a* (*question etc*) embarrassant. ◆**—ment** *n* embarras *m*, gêne *f*; (*financial*) embarras *mpl*.
embassy ['embəsɪ] *n* ambassade *f*.
embattled [ɪm'bæt(ə)ld] *a* (*political party, person etc*) assiégé de toutes parts; (*attitude*) belliqueux.
embedded [ɪm'bedɪd] *a* (*stick, bullet*) enfoncé; (*jewel*) & *Ling* enchâssé; (*in one's memory*) gravé; (*in stone*) scellé.
embellish [ɪm'belɪʃ] *vt* embellir. ◆**—ment** *n* embellissement *m*.
embers ['embəz] *npl* braise *f*, charbons *mpl* ardents.
embezzl/e [ɪm'bez(ə)l] *vt* (*money*) détourner. ◆**—ement** *n* détournement *m* de fonds. ◆**—er** *n* escroc *m*, voleur *m*.
embitter [ɪm'bɪtər] *vt* (*person*) aigrir; (*situation*) envenimer.
emblem ['embləm] *n* emblème *m*.
embody [ɪm'bɒdɪ] *vt* (*express*) exprimer; (*represent*) incarner; (*include*) réunir. ◆**embodiment** *n* incarnation *f* (**of** de).
emboss [ɪm'bɒs] *vt* (*metal*) emboutir; (*paper*) gaufrer, emboutir. ◆**—ed** *a* en relief.
embrace [ɪm'breɪs] *vt* étreindre, embrasser; (*include, adopt*) embrasser; – *vi* s'étreindre, s'embrasser; – *n* étreinte *f*.
embroider [ɪm'brɔɪdər] *vt* (*cloth*) broder; (*story, facts*) *Fig* enjoliver. ◆**embroidery** *n* broderie *f*.
embroil [ɪm'brɔɪl] *vt* **to e. s.o. in** mêler qn à.
embryo ['embrɪəʊ] *n* (*pl* **-os**) embryon *m*. ◆**embry'onic** *a Med & Fig* embryonnaire.
emcee [em'siː] *n Am* présentateur, -trice *mf*.
emend [ɪ'mend] *vt* (*text*) corriger.
emerald ['emərəld] *n* émeraude *f*.
emerge [ɪ'mɜːdʒ] *vi* apparaître (**from** de); (*from hole etc*) sortir; (*of truth, from water*) émerger; (*of nation*) naître; **it emerges that** il apparaît que. ◆**emergence** *n* apparition *f*.
emergency [ɪ'mɜːdʒənsɪ] *n* (*case*) urgence *f*; (*crisis*) crise *f*; (*contingency*) éventualité *f*; **in an e.** en cas d'urgence; – *a* (*measure etc*) d'urgence; (*exit, brake*) de secours; (*ward, services*) *Med* des urgences; **e. landing** atterrissage *m* forcé; **e. powers** *Pol* pouvoirs *mpl* extraordinaires.
emery ['emərɪ] *a* **e. cloth** toile *f* (d')émeri.
emigrant ['emɪgrənt] *n* émigrant, -ante *mf*. ◆**emigrate** *vi* émigrer. ◆**emi'gration** *n* émigration *f*.
eminent ['emɪnənt] *a* éminent. ◆**eminence** *n* distinction *f*; **his E.** *Rel* son Éminence. ◆**eminently** *adv* hautement, remarquablement.
emissary ['emɪsərɪ] *n* émissaire *m*.
emit [ɪ'mɪt] *vt* (**-tt-**) (*light, heat etc*) émettre;

(*smell*) dégager. ◆**emission** *n* émission *f*; dégagement *m*.

emotion [ɪ'məʊʃ(ə)n] *n* (*strength of feeling*) émotion *f*; (*joy, love etc*) sentiment *m*. ◆**emotional** *a* (*person, reaction*) émotif; (*story, speech*) émouvant; (*moment*) d'émotion intense; (*state*) *Psy* émotionnel. ◆**emotionally** *adv* (*to say*) avec émotion; **to be e. unstable** avoir des troubles émotifs. ◆**emotive** *a* (*person*) émotif; (*word*) affectif; **an e. issue** une question sensible.

emperor ['empərər] *n* empereur *m*.

emphasize ['emfəsaɪz] *vt* souligner (**that** que); (*word, fact*) appuyer *or* insister sur, souligner. ◆**emphasis** *n Ling* accent *m* (tonique); (*insistence*) insistance *f*; **to lay** *or* **put e. on** mettre l'accent sur. ◆**em'phatic** *a* (*person, refusal*) catégorique; (*forceful*) énergique; **to be e. about** insister sur. ◆**em'phatically** *adv* catégoriquement; énergiquement; **e. no!** absolument pas!

empire ['empaɪər] *n* empire *m*.

empirical [em'pɪrɪk(ə)l] *a* empirique. ◆**empiricism** *n* empirisme *m*.

employ [ɪm'plɔɪ] *vt* (*person, means*) employer; – *n* **in the e. of** employé par. ◆**employee** [ɪm'plɔɪiː, emplɔɪ'iː] *n* employé, -ée *mf*. ◆**employer** *n* patron, -onne *mf*. ◆**employment** *n* emploi *m*; **place of e.** lieu *m* de travail; **in the e. of** employé par; **e. agency** bureau *m* de placement.

empower [ɪm'paʊər] *vt* autoriser (**to do** à faire).

empress ['emprɪs] *n* impératrice *f*.

empt/y ['emptɪ] *a* (**-ier, -iest**) vide; (*threat, promise etc*) vain; (*stomach*) creux; **on an e. stomach** à jeun; **to return/***etc* **e.-handed** revenir/*etc* les mains vides; – *npl* (*bottles*) bouteilles *fpl* vides; – *vt* **to e. (out)** (*box, pocket, liquid etc*) vider; (*vehicle*) décharger; (*objects in box etc*) sortir (**from, out of** de); – *vi* se vider; (*of river*) se jeter (**into** dans). ◆**—iness** *n* vide *m*.

emulate ['emjʊleɪt] *vt* imiter. ◆**emu'lation** *n* émulation *f*.

emulsion [ɪ'mʌlʃ(ə)n] *n* (*paint*) peinture *f* (mate); *Phot* émulsion *f*.

enable [ɪ'neɪb(ə)l] *vt* **to e. s.o. to do** permettre à qn de faire.

enact [ɪn'ækt] *vt* (*law*) promulguer; (*part of play*) jouer.

enamel [ɪ'næm(ə)l] *n* émail *m*; – *a* en émail; – *vt* (**-ll-**, *Am* **-l-**) émailler.

enamoured [ɪn'æməd] *a* **e. of** (*thing*) séduit par; (*person*) amoureux de.

encamp [ɪn'kæmp] *vi* camper. ◆**—ment** *n* campement *m*.

encapsulate [ɪn'kæpsjʊleɪt] *vt Fig* résumer.

encase [ɪn'keɪs] *vt* recouvrir (**in** de).

enchant [ɪn'tʃɑːnt] *vt* enchanter. ◆**—ing** *a* enchanteur. ◆**—ment** *n* enchantement *m*.

encircle [ɪn'sɜːk(ə)l] *vt* entourer; *Mil* encercler. ◆**—ment** *n* encerclement *m*.

enclave ['enkleɪv] *n* enclave *f*.

enclos/e [ɪn'kləʊz] *vt* (*send with letter*) joindre (**in, with** à); (*fence off*) clôturer; **to e. with** (*a fence, wall*) entourer de. ◆**—ed** *a* (*space*) clos; (*cheque etc*) ci-joint; (*market*) couvert. ◆**enclosure** *n Com* pièce *f* jointe; (*fence, place*) enceinte *f*.

encompass [ɪn'kʌmpəs] *vt* (*surround*) entourer; (*include*) inclure.

encore ['ɒŋkɔːr] *int* & *n* bis (*m*); – *vt* bisser.

encounter [ɪn'kaʊntər] *vt* rencontrer; – *n* rencontre *f*.

encourage [ɪn'kʌrɪdʒ] *vt* encourager (**to do** à faire). ◆**—ment** *n* encouragement *m*.

encroach [ɪn'krəʊtʃ] *vi* empiéter (**on, upon** sur); **to e. on the land** (*of sea*) gagner du terrain. ◆**—ment** *n* empiètement *m*.

encumber [ɪn'kʌmbər] *vt* encombrer (**with** de). ◆**encum'brance** *n* embarras *m*.

encyclical [ɪn'sɪklɪk(ə)l] *n Rel* encyclique *f*.

encyclop(a)edia [ɪnsaɪklə'piːdɪə] *n* encyclopédie *f*. ◆**encyclop(a)edic** *a* encyclopédique.

end [end] *n* (*of street, object etc*) bout *m*, extrémité *f*; (*of time, meeting, book etc*) fin *f*; (*purpose*) fin *f*, but *m*; **at an e.** (*discussion etc*) fini; (*period*) écoulé; (*patience*) à bout; **in the e.** à la fin; **to come to an e.** prendre fin; **to put an e. to, bring to an e.** mettre fin à; **there's no e. to it** ça n'en finit plus; **no e. of** *Fam* beaucoup de; **six days on e.** six jours d'affilée; **for days on e.** pendant des jours (et des jours); **(standing) on e.** (*box etc*) debout; (*hair*) hérissé; – *a* (*row, house*) dernier; **e. product** *Com* produit *m* fini; *Fig* résultat *m*; – *vt* finir, terminer, achever (**with** par); (*rumour, speculation*) mettre fin à; – *vi* finir, se terminer, s'achever; **to e. in failure** se solder par un échec; **to e. in a point** finir en pointe; **to e. up doing** finir par faire; **to e. up in** (*London etc*) se retrouver à; **he ended up in prison/a doctor** il a fini en prison/par devenir médecin.

endanger [ɪn'deɪndʒər] *vt* mettre en danger.

endear [ɪn'dɪər] *vt* faire aimer *or* apprécier (**to** de); **that's what endears him to me** c'est cela qui me plaît en lui. ◆**—ing** *a* attachant, sympathique. ◆**—ment** *n* parole *f* tendre; **term of e.** terme *m* d'affection.

endeavour [ɪn'devər] *vi* s'efforcer (**to do** de faire); – *n* effort *m* (**to do** pour faire).

ending ['endɪŋ] *n* fin *f*; (*outcome*) issue *f*; *Ling* terminaison *f*. ◆**endless** *a* (*speech, series etc*) interminable; (*patience*) infini; (*countless*) innombrable. ◆**endlessly** *adv* interminablement.

endive ['endɪv, *Am* 'endaɪv] *n Bot Culin* (*curly*) chicorée *f*; (*smooth*) endive *f*.

endorse [ɪn'dɔːs] *vt* (*cheque etc*) endosser; (*action*) approuver; (*claim*) appuyer. ◆**—ment** *n* (*on driving licence*) contravention *f*.

endow [ɪn'daʊ] *vt* (*institution*) doter (**with** de); (*chair, hospital bed*) fonder; **endowed with** (*person*) *Fig* doté de. ◆**—ment** *n* dotation *f*; fondation *f*.

endur/e [ɪn'djʊər] **1** *vt* (*bear*) supporter (**doing** de faire). **2** *vi* (*last*) durer. ◆**—ing** *a* durable. ◆**—able** *a* supportable. ◆**endurance** *n* endurance *f*, résistance *f*.

enemy ['enəmɪ] *n* ennemi, -ie *mf*; – *a* (*army, tank etc*) ennemi.

energy ['enədʒɪ] *n* énergie *f*; – *a* (*crisis, resources etc*) énergétique. ◆**ener'getic** *a* énergique; **to feel e.** se sentir en pleine forme. ◆**ener'getically** *adv* énergiquement.

enforc/e [ɪn'fɔːs] *vt* (*law*) faire respecter; (*discipline*) imposer (**on** à). ◆**—ed** *a* (*rest, silence etc*) forcé.

engag/e [ɪn'geɪdʒ] *vt* (*take on*) engager, prendre; **to e. s.o. in conversation** engager la conversation avec qn; **to e. the clutch** *Aut* embrayer; – *vi* **to e. in** (*launch into*) se lancer dans; (*be involved in*) être mêlé à. ◆**—ed** *a* **1** (*person, toilet*) & *Tel* occupé; **e. in doing** occupé à faire; **to be e. in business/***etc* être dans les affaires/*etc*. **2** (*betrothed*) fiancé; **to get e.** se fiancer. ◆**—ing** *a* (*smile*) engageant. ◆**—ement** *n* (*agreement to marry*) fiançailles *fpl*; (*meeting*) rendez-vous *m inv*; (*undertaking*) engagement *m*; **to have a prior e.** (*be busy*) être déjà pris, ne pas être libre; **e. ring** bague *f* de fiançailles.

engender [ɪn'dʒendər] *vt* (*produce*) engendrer.

engine ['endʒɪn] *n Aut* moteur *m*; *Rail* locomotive *f*; *Nau* machine *f*; **e. driver** mécanicien *m*.

engineer [endʒɪ'nɪər] **1** *n* ingénieur *m*; (*repairer*) dépanneur *m*; *Rail Am* mécanicien *m*; **civil e.** ingénieur *m* des travaux publics; **mechanical e.** ingénieur *m* mécanicien. **2** *vt* (*arrange secretly*) machiner. ◆**—ing** *n* ingénierie *f*; (**civil**) **e.** génie *m* civil, travaux *mpl* publics; (**mechanical**) **e.** mécanique *f*; **e. factory** atelier *m* de construction mécanique.

England ['ɪŋglənd] *n* Angleterre *f*. ◆**English** *a* anglais; **the E. Channel** la Manche; **the E.** les Anglais *mpl*; – *n* (*language*) anglais *m*. ◆**Englishman** *n* (*pl* **-men**) Anglais *m*. ◆**English-speaking** *a* anglophone. ◆**Englishwoman** *n* (*pl* **-women**) Anglaise *f*.

engrav/e [ɪn'greɪv] *vt* graver. ◆**—ing** *n* gravure *f*. ◆**—er** *n* graveur *m*.

engrossed [ɪn'grəʊst] *a* absorbé (**in** par).

engulf [ɪn'gʌlf] *vt* engloutir.

enhance [ɪn'hɑːns] *vt* (*beauty etc*) rehausser; (*value*) augmenter.

enigma [ɪ'nɪgmə] *n* énigme *f*. ◆**enig'matic** *a* énigmatique.

enjoy [ɪn'dʒɔɪ] *vt* aimer (**doing** faire); (*meal*) apprécier; (*income, standard of living etc*) jouir de; **to e. the evening** passer une bonne soirée; **to e. oneself** s'amuser; **to e. being in London/***etc* se plaire à Londres/*etc*. ◆**—able** *a* agréable. ◆**—ably** *adv* agréablement. ◆**—ment** *n* plaisir *m*.

enlarge [ɪn'lɑːdʒ] *vt* agrandir; – *vi* s'agrandir; **to e. (up)on** (*say more about*) s'étendre sur. ◆**—ment** *n* agrandissement *m*.

enlighten [ɪn'laɪt(ə)n] *vt* éclairer (**s.o. on** *or* **about sth** qn sur qch). ◆**—ing** *a* instructif. ◆**—ment** *n* (*explanations*) éclaircissements *mpl*; **an age of e.** une époque éclairée.

enlist [ɪn'lɪst] *vi* (*in the army etc*) s'engager; – *vt* (*recruit*) engager; (*supporter*) recruter; (*support*) obtenir. ◆**—ment** *n* engagement *m*; recrutement *m*.

enliven [ɪn'laɪv(ə)n] *vt* (*meeting, people etc*) égayer, animer.

enmeshed [ɪn'meʃt] *a* empêtré (**in** dans).

enmity ['enmɪtɪ] *n* inimitié *f* (**between** entre).

enormous [ɪ'nɔːməs] *a* énorme; (*explosion*) terrible; (*success*) fou. ◆**enormity** *n* (*vastness, extent*) énormité *f*; (*atrocity*) atrocité *f*. ◆**enormously** *adv* (*very much*) énormément; (*very*) extrêmement.

enough [ɪ'nʌf] *a* & *n* assez (de); **e. time/cups/***etc* assez de temps/de tasses/*etc*; **to have e. to live on** avoir de quoi vivre; **to have e. to drink** avoir assez à boire; **to have had e. of** *Pej* en avoir assez de; **it's e. for me to see that . . .** il me suffit de voir que . . . ; **that's e.** ça suffit, c'est assez; – *adv* assez,

suffisamment (to pour); **strangely e., he left** chose curieuse, il est parti.
enquire [ɪn'kwaɪər] *vi* = **inquire.**
enquiry [ɪn'kwaɪərɪ] *n* = **inquiry.**
enrage [ɪn'reɪdʒ] *vt* mettre en rage.
enrapture [ɪn'ræptʃər] *vt* ravir.
enrich [ɪn'rɪtʃ] *vt* enrichir; (*soil*) fertiliser. ◆**—ment** *n* enrichissement *m.*
enrol [ɪn'rəʊl] (*Am* **enroll**) *vi* (**-ll-**) s'inscrire (**in, for** à); – *vt* inscrire. ◆**—ment** *n* inscription *f*; (*people enrolled*) effectif *m.*
ensconced [ɪn'skɒnst] *a* bien installé (**in** dans).
ensemble [ɒn'sɒmb(ə)l] *n* (*clothes*) & *Mus* ensemble *m.*
ensign ['ensən] *n* (*flag*) pavillon *m*; (*rank*) *Am Nau* enseigne *m* de vaisseau.
enslave [ɪn'sleɪv] *vt* asservir.
ensu/e [ɪn'sjuː] *vi* s'ensuivre. ◆**—ing** *a* (*day, year etc*) suivant; (*event*) qui s'ensuit.
ensure [ɪn'ʃʊər] *vt* assurer; **to e. that** (*make sure*) s'assurer que.
entail [ɪn'teɪl] *vt* (*imply, involve*) entraîner, impliquer.
entangle [ɪn'tæŋg(ə)l] *vt* emmêler, enchevêtrer; **to get entangled** s'empêtrer. ◆**—ment** *n* enchevêtrement *m*; **an e. with** (*police*) des démêlés *mpl* avec.
enter ['entər] *vt* (*room, vehicle, army etc*) entrer dans; (*road*) s'engager dans; (*university*) s'inscrire à; (*write down*) inscrire (**in** dans, **on** sur); (*in ledger*) porter (**in** sur); **to e. s.o. for** (*exam*) présenter qn à; **to e. a painting/***etc* **in** (*competition*) présenter un tableau/*etc* à; **it didn't e. my head** ça ne m'est pas venu à l'esprit (**that** que); – *vi* entrer; **to e. for** (*race, exam*) s'inscrire pour; **to e. into** (*plans*) entrer dans; (*conversation, relations*) entrer en; **you don't e. into it** tu n'y es pour rien; **to e. into** *or* **upon** (*career*) entrer dans; (*negotiations*) entamer; (*agreement*) conclure.
enterpris/e ['entəpraɪz] *n* (*undertaking, firm*) entreprise *f*; (*spirit*) *Fig* initiative *f.* ◆**—ing** *a* (*person*) plein d'initiative; (*attempt*) hardi.
entertain [entə'teɪn] *vt* amuser, distraire; (*guest*) recevoir; (*idea, possibility*) envisager; (*hope*) chérir; **to e. s.o. to a meal** recevoir qn à dîner; – *vi* (*receive guests*) recevoir. ◆**—ing** *a* amusant. ◆**—er** *n* artiste *mf.* ◆**—ment** *n* amusement *m*, distraction *f*; (*show*) spectacle *m.*
enthral(l) [ɪn'θrɔːl] *vt* (**-ll-**) (*delight*) captiver.
enthuse [ɪn'θjuːz] *vi* **to e. over** *Fam* s'emballer pour. ◆**enthusiasm** *n* enthousiasme *m.* ◆**enthusiast** *n* enthousiaste *mf*; **jazz/***etc* **e.** passionné, -ée *mf* du jazz/*etc.* ◆**enthusi'astic** *a* enthousiaste; (*golfer etc*) passionné; **to be e. about** (*hobby*) être passionné de; **he was e. about** *or* **over** (*gift etc*) il a été emballé par; **to get e.** s'emballer (**about** pour). ◆**enthusi'astically** *adv* avec enthousiasme.
entic/e [ɪn'taɪs] *vt* attirer (par la ruse); **to e. to do** entraîner (par la ruse) à faire. ◆**—ing** *a* séduisant, alléchant. ◆**—ement** *n* (*bait*) attrait *m.*
entire [ɪn'taɪər] *a* entier. ◆**—ly** *adv* tout à fait, entièrement. ◆**entirety** [ɪn'taɪərətɪ] *n* intégralité *f*; **in its e.** en entier.
entitl/e [ɪn'taɪt(ə)l] *vt* **to e. s.o. to do** donner à qn le droit de faire; **to e. s.o. to sth** donner à qn (le) droit à qch; **that entitles me to believe that . . .** ça m'autorise à croire que . . . . ◆**—ed** *a* (*book*) intitulé; **to be e. to do** avoir le droit de faire; **to be e. to sth** avoir droit à qch. ◆**—ement** *n* **one's e.** son dû.
entity ['entɪtɪ] *n* entité *f.*
entourage ['ɒntʊrɑːʒ] *n* entourage *m.*
entrails ['entreɪlz] *npl* entrailles *fpl.*
entrance 1 ['entrəns] *n* entrée *f* (**to** de); (*to university etc*) admission *f* (**to** à); **e. examination** examen *m* d'entrée. **2** [ɪn'trɑːns] *vt* *Fig* transporter, ravir.
entrant ['entrənt] *n* (*in race*) concurrent, -ente *mf*; (*for exam*) candidat, -ate *mf.*
entreat [ɪn'triːt] *vt* supplier, implorer (**to do** de faire). ◆**entreaty** *n* supplication *f.*
entrée ['ɒntreɪ] *n* *Culin* entrée *f*; (*main dish*) *Am* plat *m* principal.
entrench [ɪn'trentʃ] *vt* **to e. oneself** *Mil* & *Fig* se retrancher.
entrust [ɪn'trʌst] *vt* confier (**to** à); **to e. s.o. with sth** confier qch à qn.
entry ['entrɪ] *n* (*way in, action*) entrée *f*; (*in ledger*) écriture *f*; (*term in dictionary or logbook*) entrée *f*; (*competitor*) *Sp* concurrent, -ente *mf*; (*thing to be judged in competition*) objet *m* (*or* œuvre *f* *or* projet *m*) soumis à un jury; **e. form** feuille *f* d'inscription; **'no e.'** (*on door etc*) 'entrée interdite'; (*road sign*) 'sens interdit'.
entwine [ɪn'twaɪn] *vt* entrelacer.
enumerate [ɪ'njuːməreɪt] *vt* énumérer. ◆**enume'ration** *n* énumération *f.*
enunciate [ɪ'nʌnsɪeɪt] *vt* (*word*) articuler; (*theory*) énoncer. ◆**enunci'ation** *n* articulation *f*; énonciation *f.*
envelop [ɪn'veləp] *vt* envelopper (**in fog/mystery/***etc* de brouillard/mystère/*etc*).
envelope ['envələʊp] *n* enveloppe *f.*
envious ['envɪəs] *a* envieux (**of sth** de qch);

e. of s.o. jaloux de qn. ◆**enviable** *a* enviable. ◆**enviously** *adv* avec envie.
environment [ɪn'vaɪərənmənt] *n* milieu *m*; (*cultural, natural*) environnement *m*. ◆**environ'mental** *a* du milieu; de l'environnement. ◆**environ'mentalist** *n* écologiste *mf*.
envisage [ɪn'vɪzɪdʒ] *vt* (*imagine*) envisager; (*foresee*) prévoir.
envision [ɪn'vɪʒ(ə)n] *vt Am* = **envisage**.
envoy ['envɔɪ] *n Pol* envoyé, -ée *mf*.
envy ['envɪ] *n* envie *f*; – *vt* envier (**s.o. sth** qch à qn).
ephemeral [ɪ'femərəl] *a* éphémère.
epic ['epɪk] *a* épique; – *n* épopée *f*; (**screen**) **e. film** *m* à grand spectacle.
epidemic [epɪ'demɪk] *n* épidémie *f*; – *a* épidémique.
epilepsy ['epɪlepsɪ] *n* épilepsie *f*. ◆**epi'leptic** *a* & *n* épileptique (*mf*).
epilogue ['epɪlɒg] *n* épilogue *m*.
episode ['epɪsəʊd] *n* épisode *m*. ◆**epi'sodic** [epɪ'sɒdɪk] *a* épisodique.
epistle [ɪ'pɪs(ə)l] *n* épître *f*.
epitaph ['epɪtɑːf] *n* épitaphe *f*.
epithet ['epɪθet] *n* épithète *f*.
epitome [ɪ'pɪtəmɪ] *n* **the e. of** l'exemple même de, l'incarnation de. ◆**epitomize** *vt* incarner.
epoch ['iːpɒk] *n* époque *f*. ◆**e.-making** *a* (*event*) qui fait date.
equal ['iːkwəl] *a* égal (**to** à); **with e. hostility** avec la même hostilité; **on an e. footing** sur un pied d'égalité (**with** avec); **to be e. to** égaler; **e. to** (*task, situation*) *Fig* à la hauteur de; – *n* égal, -ale *mf*; **to treat s.o. as an e.** traiter qn en égal *or* d'égal à égal; **he doesn't have his e.** il n'a pas son pareil; – *vt* (**-ll-**, *Am* **-l-**) égaler (**in beauty**/*etc* en beauté/*etc*); **equals sign** *Math* signe *m* d'égalité. ◆**e'quality** *n* égalité *f*. ◆**equalize** *vt* égaliser; – *vi Sp* égaliser. ◆**equally** *adv* (*to an equal degree, also*) également; (*to divide*) en parts égales; **he's e. stupid** (*just as*) il est tout aussi bête.
equanimity [ekwə'nɪmɪtɪ] *n* égalité *f* d'humeur.
equate [ɪ'kweɪt] *vt* mettre sur le même pied (**with** que), assimiler (**with** à).
equation [ɪ'kweɪʒ(ə)n] *n Math* équation *f*.
equator [ɪ'kweɪtər] *n* équateur *m*; **at** *or* **on the e.** sous l'équateur. ◆**equatorial** [ekwə'tɔːrɪəl] *a* équatorial.
equestrian [ɪ'kwestrɪən] *a* équestre.
equilibrium [iːkwɪ'lɪbrɪəm] *n* équilibre *m*.
equinox ['iːkwɪnɒks] *n* équinoxe *m*.
equip [ɪ'kwɪp] *vt* (**-pp-**) équiper (**with** de); (**well-**)**equipped with** pourvu de; (**well-**)**equipped to do** compétent pour faire. ◆**—ment** *n* équipement *m*, matériel *m*.
equity ['ekwɪtɪ] *n* (*fairness*) équité *f*; *pl Com* actions *fpl*. ◆**equitable** *a* équitable.
equivalent [ɪ'kwɪvələnt] *a* & *n* équivalent (*m*). ◆**equivalence** *n* équivalence *f*.
equivocal [ɪ'kwɪvək(ə)l] *a* équivoque.
era ['ɪərə, *Am* 'erə] *n* époque *f*; (*historical, geological*) ère *f*.
eradicate [ɪ'rædɪkeɪt] *vt* supprimer; (*evil, prejudice*) extirper.
erase [ɪ'reɪz, *Am* ɪ'reɪs] *vt* effacer. ◆**eraser** *n* (*rubber*) gomme *f*. ◆**erasure** *n* rature *f*.
erect [ɪ'rekt] **1** *a* (*upright*) (bien) droit. **2** *vt* (*build*) construire; (*statue, monument*) ériger; (*scaffolding*) monter; (*tent*) dresser. ◆**erection** *n* construction *f*; érection *f*; montage *m*; dressage *m*.
ermine ['ɜːmɪn] *n* (*animal, fur*) hermine *f*.
erode [ɪ'rəʊd] *vt* éroder; (*confidence etc*) *Fig* miner, ronger. ◆**erosion** *n* érosion *f*.
erotic [ɪ'rɒtɪk] *a* érotique. ◆**eroticism** *n* érotisme *m*.
err [ɜːr] *vi* (*be wrong*) se tromper; (*sin*) pécher.
errand ['erənd] *n* commission *f*, course *f*; **e. boy** garçon *m* de courses.
erratic [ɪ'rætɪk] *a* (*conduct etc*) irrégulier; (*person*) lunatique.
error ['erər] *n* (*mistake*) erreur *f*, faute *f*; (*wrongdoing*) erreur *f*; **in e.** par erreur. ◆**erroneous** [ɪ'rəʊnɪəs] *a* erroné.
erudite ['eruːdaɪt, *Am* 'erjʊdaɪt] *a* érudit, savant. ◆**eru'dition** *n* érudition *f*.
erupt [ɪ'rʌpt] *vi* (*of volcano*) entrer en éruption; (*of pimples*) apparaître; (*of war, violence*) éclater. ◆**eruption** *n* (*of volcano, pimples, anger*) éruption *f* (**of** de); (*of violence*) flambée *f*.
escalate ['eskəleɪt] *vi* (*of war, violence*) s'intensifier; (*of prices*) monter en flèche; – *vt* intensifier. ◆**esca'lation** *n* escalade *f*.
escalator ['eskəleɪtər] *n* escalier *m* roulant.
escapade ['eskəpeɪd] *n* (*prank*) frasque *f*.
escape [ɪ'skeɪp] *vi* (*of gas, animal etc*) s'échapper; (*of prisoner*) s'évader, s'échapper; **to e. from** (*person*) échapper à; (*place, object*) s'échapper de; **escaped prisoner** évadé, -ée *mf*; – *vt* (*death*) échapper à; (*punishment*) éviter; **that name escapes me** ce nom m'échappe; **to e. notice** passer inaperçu; – *n* (*of gas etc*) fuite *f*; (*of person*) évasion *f*, fuite *f*; **to have a lucky** *or* **narrow e.** l'échapper belle. ◆**escapism** *n* évasion *f* (hors de la réalité). ◆**escapist** *a* (*film etc*) d'évasion.

eschew [ɪ'stʃuː] *vt* éviter, fuir.
escort ['eskɔːt] *n Mil Nau* escorte *f*; (*of woman*) cavalier *m*; – [ɪ'skɔːt] *vt* escorter.
Eskimo ['eskɪməʊ] *n* (*pl* -os) Esquimau, -aude *mf*; – *a* esquimau.
esoteric [esəʊ'terɪk] *a* obscur, ésotérique.
especial [ɪ'speʃəl] *a* particulier. ◆**—ly** *adv* (*in particular*) particulièrement; (*for particular purpose*) (tout) exprès; **e. as** d'autant plus que.
espionage ['espɪənɑːʒ] *n* espionnage *m*.
esplanade ['esplәneɪd] *n* esplanade *f*.
espouse [ɪ'spaʊz] *vt* (*a cause*) épouser.
espresso [e'spresəʊ] *n* (*pl* -os) (café *m*) express *m*.
Esq [ɪ'skwaɪər] *abbr* (**esquire**) **J. Smith Esq** (*on envelope*) Monsieur J. Smith.
essay ['eseɪ] *n* (*attempt*) & *Liter* essai *m*; *Sch* rédaction *f*; *Univ* dissertation *f*.
essence ['esəns] *n Phil Ch* essence *f*; *Culin* extrait *m*, essence *f*; (*main point*) essentiel *m* (**of** de); **in e.** essentiellement.
essential [ɪ'senʃ(ə)l] *a* (*principal*) essentiel; (*necessary*) indispensable, essentiel; **it's e. that** il est indispensable que (+ *sub*); – *npl* **the essentials** l'essentiel *m* (**of** de); (*of grammar*) les éléments *mpl*. ◆**—ly** *adv* essentiellement.
establish [ɪ'stæblɪʃ] *vt* établir; (*state, society*) fonder. ◆**—ed** *a* (**well-**)**e.** (*firm*) solide; (*fact*) reconnu; (*reputation*) établi; **she's (well-)e.** elle a une réputation établie. ◆**—ment** *n* (*institution, firm*) établissement *m*; **the e. of** l'établissement de; la fondation de; **the E.** les classes *fpl* dirigeantes.
estate [ɪ'steɪt] *n* (*land*) terre(s) *f*(*pl*), propriété *f*; (*possessions*) *Jur* fortune *f*; (*of deceased person*) succession *f*; **housing e.** lotissement *m*; (*workers'*) cité *f* (ouvrière); **industrial e.** complexe *m* industriel; **e. agency** agence *f* immobilière; **e. agent** agent *m* immobilier; **e. car** break *m*; **e. tax** *Am* droits *mpl* de succession.
esteem [ɪ'stiːm] *vt* estimer; **highly esteemed** très estimé; – *n* estime *f*.
esthetic [es'θetɪk] *a Am* esthétique.
estimate ['estɪmeɪt] *vt* (*value*) estimer, évaluer; (*consider*) estimer (**that** que); – ['estɪmət] *n* (*assessment*) évaluation *f*, estimation *f*; (*judgement*) évaluation *f*; (*price for work to be done*) devis *m*; **rough e.** chiffre *m* approximatif. ◆**esti'mation** *n* jugement *m*; (*esteem*) estime *f*; **in my e.** à mon avis.
estranged [ɪ'streɪndʒd] *a* **to become e.** (*of couple*) se séparer.
estuary ['estjʊərɪ] *n* estuaire *m*.
etc [et'setərə] *adv* etc.
etch [etʃ] *vti* graver à l'eau forte. ◆**—ing** *n* (*picture*) eau-forte *f*.
eternal [ɪ'tɜːn(ə)l] *a* éternel. ◆**eternally** *adv* éternellement. ◆**eternity** *n* éternité *f*.
ether ['iːθər] *n* éther *m*. ◆**e'thereal** *a* éthéré.
ethic ['eθɪk] *n* éthique *f*. ◆**ethics** *n* (*moral standards*) moralité *f*; (*study*) *Phil* éthique *f*. ◆**ethical** *a* moral, éthique.
Ethiopia [iːθɪ'əʊpɪə] *n* Éthiopie *f*. ◆**Ethiopian** *a* & *n* éthiopien, -ienne (*mf*).
ethnic ['eθnɪk] *a* ethnique.
ethos ['iːθɒs] *n* génie *m*.
etiquette ['etɪket] *n* (*rules*) bienséances *fpl*; (**diplomatic**) **e.** protocole *m*, étiquette *f*; **professional e.** déontologie *f*.
etymology [etɪ'mɒlədʒɪ] *n* étymologie *f*.
eucalyptus [juːkə'lɪptəs] *n* (*tree*) eucalyptus *m*.
eulogy ['juːlədʒɪ] *n* panégyrique *m*, éloge *m*.
euphemism ['juːfəmɪz(ə)m] *n* euphémisme *m*.
euphoria [juː'fɔːrɪə] *n* euphorie *f*. ◆**euphoric** *a* euphorique.
Euro- ['jʊərəʊ] *pref* euro-.
Europe ['jʊərəp] *n* Europe *f*. ◆**Euro'pean** *a* & *n* européen, -éenne (*mf*).
euthanasia [juːθə'neɪzɪə] *n* euthanasie *f*.
evacuate [ɪ'vækjʊeɪt] *vt* évacuer. ◆**evacu'ation** *n* évacuation *f*.
evade [ɪ'veɪd] *vt* éviter, esquiver; (*pursuer, tax*) échapper à; (*law, question*) éluder.
evaluate [ɪ'væljʊeɪt] *vt* évaluer (**at** à). ◆**evalu'ation** *n* évaluation *f*.
evangelical [iːvæn'dʒelɪk(ə)l] *a Rel* évangélique.
evaporat/e [ɪ'væpəreɪt] *vi* s'évaporer; (*of hopes*) s'évanouir. ◆**—ed** *a* **e. milk** lait *m* concentré. ◆**evapo'ration** *n* évaporation *f*.
evasion [ɪ'veɪʒ(ə)n] *n* **e. of** (*pursuer etc*) fuite *f* devant; (*question*) esquive *f* de; **tax e.** évasion *f* fiscale. ◆**evasive** *a* évasif.
eve [iːv] *n* **the e. of** la veille de.
even ['iːv(ə)n] **1** *a* (*flat*) uni, égal, lisse; (*equal*) égal; (*regular*) régulier; (*number*) pair; **to get e. with** se venger de; **I'll get e. with him (for that)** je lui revaudrai ça; **we're e.** (*quits*) nous sommes quittes; (*in score*) nous sommes à égalité; **to break e.** *Fin* s'y retrouver; – *vt* **to e. (out** *or* **up)** égaliser. **2** *adv* même; **e. better/more** encore mieux/plus; **e. if** *or* **though** même si; **e. so** quand même. ◆**—ly** *adv* de manière égale; (*regularly*) régulièrement. ◆**—ness** *n* (*of*

surface, temper) égalité *f*; (*of movement etc*) régularité *f*. ◆**even-'tempered** *a* de caractère égal.

evening ['iːvnɪŋ] *n* soir *m*; (*duration of evening, event*) soirée *f*; **in the e.**, *Am* **evenings** le soir; **at seven in the e.** à sept heures du soir; **every Tuesday e.** tous les mardis soir; **all e. (long)** toute la soirée; – *a* (*newspaper etc*) du soir; **e. performance** *Th* soirée *f*; **e. dress** tenue *f* de soirée; (*of woman*) robe *f* du soir *or* de soirée.

event [ɪ'vent] *n* événement *m*; *Sp* épreuve *f*; **in the e. of death** en cas de décès; **in any e.** en tout cas; **after the e.** après coup. ◆**eventful** *a* (*journey etc*) mouvementé; (*occasion*) mémorable.

eventual [ɪ'ventʃʊəl] *a* final, définitif. ◆**eventu'ality** *n* éventualité *f*. ◆**eventually** *adv* finalement, à la fin; (*some day or other*) un jour ou l'autre; (*after all*) en fin de compte.

ever ['evər] *adv* jamais; **has he e. seen it?** l'a-t-il jamais vu?; **more than e.** plus que jamais; **nothing e.** jamais rien; **hardly e.** presque jamais; **e. ready** toujours prêt; **the first e.** le tout premier; **e. since** (*that event etc*) depuis; **e. since then** depuis lors, dès lors; **for e.** (*for always*) pour toujours; (*continually*) sans cesse; **the best son e.** le meilleur fils du monde; **e. so sorry/happy/***etc* *Fam* vraiment désolé/heureux/*etc*; **thank you e. so much** *Fam* merci mille fois; **it's e. such a pity** *Fam* c'est vraiment dommage; **why e. not?** pourquoi pas donc? ◆**evergreen** *n* arbre *m* à feuilles persistantes. ◆**ever'lasting** *a* éternel. ◆**ever'more** *adv* **for e.** à (tout) jamais.

every ['evrɪ] *a* chaque; **e. child** chaque enfant, tous les enfants; **e. time** chaque fois (**that** que); **e. one** chacun; **e. single one** tous (sans exception); **to have e. confidence in** avoir pleine confiance en; **e. second** *or* **other day** tous les deux jours; **her e. gesture** ses moindres gestes; **e. bit as big** tout aussi grand (**as** que); **e. so often, e. now and then** de temps en temps. ◆**everybody** *pron* tout le monde; **e. in turn** chacun à son tour. ◆**everyday** *a* (*happening, life etc*) de tous les jours; (*banal*) banal; **in e. use** d'usage courant. ◆**everyone** *pron* = **everybody**. ◆**everyplace** *adv* *Am* = **everywhere**. ◆**everything** *pron* tout; **e. I have** tout ce que j'ai. ◆**everywhere** *adv* partout; **e. she goes** où qu'elle aille, partout où elle va.

evict [ɪ'vɪkt] *vt* expulser (**from** de). ◆**eviction** *n* expulsion *f*.

evidence ['evɪdəns] *n* (*proof*) preuve(s) *f(pl)*; (*testimony*) témoignage *m*; (*obviousness*) évidence *f*; **to give e.** témoigner (**against** contre); **e. of** (*wear etc*) des signes *mpl* de; **in e.** (*noticeable*) (bien) en vue. ◆**evident** *a* évident (**that** que); **it is e. from . . .** il apparaît de . . . (**that** que). ◆**evidently** *adv* (*obviously*) évidemment; (*apparently*) apparemment.

evil ['iːv(ə)l] *a* (*spell, influence, person*) malfaisant; (*deed, advice, system*) mauvais; (*consequence*) funeste; – *n* mal *m*; **to speak e.** dire du mal (**about, of** de).

evince [ɪ'vɪns] *vt* manifester.

evoke [ɪ'vəʊk] *vt* (*recall, conjure up*) évoquer; (*admiration*) susciter. ◆**evocative** *a* évocateur.

evolution [iːvə'luːʃ(ə)n] *n* évolution *f*. ◆**evolve** *vi* (*of society, idea etc*) évoluer; (*of plan*) se développer; – *vt* (*system etc*) développer.

ewe [juː] *n* brebis *f*.

ex [eks] *n* (*former spouse*) *Fam* ex *mf*.

ex- [eks] *pref* ex-; **ex-wife** ex-femme *f*.

exacerbate [ɪk'sæsəbeɪt] *vt* (*pain*) exacerber.

exact [ɪg'zækt] **1** *a* (*accurate, precise etc*) exact; **to be (more) e. about** préciser. **2** *vt* (*demand*) exiger (**from** de); (*money*) extorquer (**from** à). ◆**—ing** *a* exigeant. ◆**—ly** *adv* exactement; **it's e. 5 o'clock** il est 5 heures juste. ◆**—ness** *n* exactitude *f*.

exaggerate [ɪg'zædʒəreɪt] *vt* exagérer; (*in one's own mind*) s'exagérer; – *vi* exagérer. ◆**exagge'ration** *n* exagération *f*.

exalt [ɪg'zɔːlt] *vt* (*praise*) exalter. ◆**—ed** *a* (*position, rank*) élevé. ◆**exal'tation** *n* exaltation *f*.

exam [ɪg'zæm] *n* *Univ Sch Fam* examen *m*.

examine [ɪg'zæmɪn] *vt* examiner; (*accounts, luggage*) vérifier; (*passport*) contrôler; (*orally*) interroger (*témoin, élève*). ◆**exami'nation** *n* (*inspection*) & *Univ Sch* examen *m*; (*of accounts etc*) vérification *f*; (*of passport*) contrôle *m*; **class e.** *Sch* composition *f*. ◆**examiner** *n* *Sch* examinateur, -trice *mf*.

example [ɪg'zɑːmp(ə)l] *n* exemple *m*; **for e.** par exemple; **to set a good/bad e.** donner le bon/mauvais exemple (**to** à); **to make an e. of** punir pour l'exemple.

exasperate [ɪg'zɑːspəreɪt] *vt* exaspérer; **to get exasperated** s'exaspérer (**at** de). ◆**exaspe'ration** *n* exaspération *f*.

excavate ['ekskəveɪt] *vt* (*dig*) creuser; (*for relics etc*) fouiller; (*uncover*) déterrer. ◆**exca'vation** *n* *Tech* creusement *m*; (*archeological*) fouille *f*.

exceed [ɪk'siːd] *vt* dépasser, excéder. **◆—ingly** *adv* extrêmement.

excel [ɪk'sel] *vi* (-ll-) exceller (in sth en qch, in doing à faire); – *vt* surpasser.

Excellency ['eksələnsɪ] *n* (*title*) Excellence *f*.

excellent ['eksələnt] *a* excellent. **◆excellence** *n* excellence *f*. **◆excellently** *adv* parfaitement, admirablement.

except [ɪk'sept] *prep* sauf, excepté; **e. for** à part; **e. that** à part le fait que, sauf que; **e. if** sauf si; **to do nothing e. wait** ne rien faire sinon attendre; – *vt* excepter. **◆exception** *n* exception *f*; **with the e. of** à l'exception de; **to take e. to** (*object to*) désapprouver; (*be hurt by*) s'offenser de. **◆exceptional** *a* exceptionnel. **◆exceptionally** *adv* exceptionnellement.

excerpt ['eksɜːpt] *n* (*from film, book etc*) extrait *m*.

excess ['ekses] *n* excès *m*; (*surplus*) *Com* excédent *m*; **one's excesses** ses excès *mpl*; **to e.** à l'excès; **an e. of** (*details*) un luxe de; – *a* (*weight etc*) excédentaire, en trop; **e. fare** supplément *m* (de billet); **e. luggage** excédent *m* de bagages. **◆ex'cessive** *a* excessif. **◆ex'cessively** *adv* (*too, too much*) excessivement; (*very*) extrêmement.

exchange [ɪks'tʃeɪndʒ] *vt* (*addresses, blows etc*) échanger (**for** contre); – *n* échange *m*; *Fin* change *m*; (**telephone**) **e.** central *m* (téléphonique); **in e.** en échange (**for** de).

Exchequer [ɪks'tʃekər] *n* **Chancellor of the E.** = ministre *m* des Finances.

excise ['eksaɪz] *n* taxe *f* (**on** sur).

excit/e [ɪk'saɪt] *vt* (*agitate, provoke, stimulate*) exciter; (*enthuse*) passionner, exciter. **◆—ed** *a* excité; (*laughter*) énervé; **to get e.** (*nervous, angry, enthusiastic*) s'exciter; **to be e. about** (*new car, news*) se réjouir de; **to be e. about the holidays** être surexcité à l'idée de partir en vacances. **◆—ing** *a* (*book, adventure*) passionnant. **◆—able** *a* excitable. **◆—edly** *adv* avec agitation; (*to wait, jump about*) dans un état de surexcitation. **◆—ement** *n* agitation *f*, excitation *f*, fièvre *f*; (*emotion*) vive émotion *f*; (*adventure*) aventure *f*; **great e.** surexcitation *f*.

exclaim [ɪk'skleɪm] *vti* s'exclamer, s'écrier (**that** que). **◆excla'mation** *n* exclamation *f*; **e. mark** *or Am* **point** point *m* d'exclamation.

exclude [ɪks'kluːd] *vt* exclure (**from** de); (*name from list*) écarter (**from** de). **◆exclusion** *n* exclusion *f*. **◆exclusive** *a* (*right, interest, design*) exclusif; (*club, group*) fermé; (*interview*) en exclusivité; **e. of wine/etc** vin/etc non compris. **◆exclusively** *adv* exclusivement.

excommunicate [ekskə'mjuːnɪkeɪt] *vt* excommunier.

excrement ['ekskrəmənt] *n* excrément(s) *m(pl)*.

excruciating [ɪk'skruːʃɪeɪtɪŋ] *a* insupportable, atroce.

excursion [ɪk'skɜːʃ(ə)n] *n* excursion *f*.

excuse [ɪk'skjuːz] *vt* (*justify, forgive*) excuser (**s.o. for doing** qn d'avoir fait, qn de faire); (*exempt*) dispenser (**from** de); **e. me for asking** permettez-moi de demander; **e. me!** excusez-moi!, pardon!; **you're excused** tu peux t'en aller *or* sortir; – [ɪk'skjuːs] *n* excuse *f*; **it was an e. for** cela a servi de prétexte à.

ex-directory [eksdaɪ'rektərɪ] *a* *Tel* sur la liste rouge.

execute ['eksɪkjuːt] *vt* (*criminal, order, plan etc*) exécuter. **◆exe'cution** *n* exécution *f*. **◆exe'cutioner** *n* bourreau *m*.

executive [ɪg'zekjʊtɪv] *a* (*power*) exécutif; (*ability*) d'exécution; (*job*) de cadre; (*car, plane*) de direction; – *n* (*person*) cadre *m*; (*board, committee*) bureau *m*; **the e.** *Pol* l'exécutif *m*; (**senior**) **e.** cadre *m* supérieur; **junior e.** jeune cadre *m*; **business e.** directeur *m* commercial.

exemplary [ɪg'zemplərɪ] *a* exemplaire. **◆exemplify** *vt* illustrer.

exempt [ɪg'zempt] *a* exempt (**from** de); – *vt* exempter (**from** de). **◆exemption** *n* exemption *f*.

exercise ['eksəsaɪz] *n* (*of power etc*) & *Sch Sp Mil* exercice *m*; *pl Univ Am* cérémonies *fpl*; **e. book** cahier *m*; – *vt* exercer; (*troops*) faire faire l'exercice à; (*dog, horse etc*) promener; (*tact, judgement etc*) faire preuve de; (*rights*) faire valoir, exercer; – *vi* (*take exercise*) prendre de l'exercice.

exert [ɪg'zɜːt] *vt* exercer; (*force*) employer; **to e. oneself** (*physically*) se dépenser; **he never exerts himself** (*takes the trouble*) il ne se fatigue jamais; **to e. oneself to do** (*try hard*) s'efforcer de faire. **◆exertion** *n* effort *m*; (*of force*) emploi *m*.

exhale [eks'heɪl] *vt* (*breathe out*) expirer; (*give off*) exhaler; – *vi* expirer.

exhaust [ɪg'zɔːst] **1** *vt* (*use up, tire*) épuiser; **to become exhausted** s'épuiser. **2** *n* **e.** (**pipe**) *Aut* pot *m* *or* tuyau *m* d'échappement. **◆—ing** *a* épuisant. **◆exhaustion** *n* épuisement *m*. **◆exhaustive** *a* (*study etc*) complet; (*research*) approfondi.

exhibit [ɪg'zɪbɪt] *vt* (*put on display*) exposer; (*ticket, courage etc*) montrer; – *n* objet *m* exposé; *Jur* pièce *f* à conviction. ◆**exhi'bition** *n* exposition *f*; **an e. of** (*display*) une démonstration de; **to make an e. of oneself** se donner en spectacle. ◆**exhi'bitionist** *n* exhibitionniste *mf*. ◆**exhibitor** *n* exposant, -ante *mf*.

exhilarate [ɪg'zɪləreɪt] *vt* stimuler; (*of air*) vivifier; (*elate*) rendre fou de joie. ◆**exhila'ration** *n* liesse *f*, joie *f*.

exhort [ɪg'zɔːt] *vt* exhorter (**to do** à faire, **to sth** à qch).

exhume [eks'hjuːm] *vt* exhumer.

exile ['egzaɪl] *vt* exiler; – *n* (*absence*) exil *m*; (*person*) exilé, -ée *mf*.

exist [ɪg'zɪst] *vi* exister; (*live*) vivre (**on** de); (**to continue**) **to e.** subsister; **the notion exists that . . .** il existe une notion selon laquelle . . . . ◆**—ing** *a* (*law*) existant; (*circumstances*) actuel. ◆**existence** *n* existence *f*; **to come into e.** être créé; **to be in e.** exister. ◆**exi'stentialism** *n* existentialisme *m*.

exit ['eksɪt, 'egzɪt] *n* (*action*) sortie *f*; (*door, window*) sortie *f*, issue *f*; – *vi Th* sortir.

exodus ['eksədəs] *n inv* exode *m*.

exonerate [ɪg'zɒnəreɪt] *vt* (*from blame*) disculper (**from** de).

exorbitant [ɪg'zɔːbɪtənt] *a* exorbitant. ◆**—ly** *adv* démesurément.

exorcize ['eksɔːsaɪz] *vt* exorciser. ◆**exorcism** *n* exorcisme *m*.

exotic [ɪg'zɒtɪk] *a* exotique.

expand [ɪk'spænd] *vt* (*one's fortune, knowledge etc*) étendre; (*trade, ideas*) développer; (*production*) augmenter; (*gas, metal*) dilater; – *vi* s'étendre; se développer; augmenter; se dilater; **to e. on** développer ses idées sur; (**fast** *or* **rapidly**) **expanding sector/***etc* *Com* secteur/*etc* en (pleine) expansion. ◆**expansion** *n Com Phys Pol* expansion *f*; développement *m*; augmentation *f*. ◆**expansionism** *n* expansionnisme *m*.

expanse [ɪk'spæns] *n* étendue *f*.

expansive [ɪk'spænsɪv] *a* expansif. ◆**—ly** *adv* avec effusion.

expatriate [eks'pætrɪət, *Am* eks'peɪtrɪət] *a* & *n* expatrié, -ée (*mf*).

expect [ɪk'spekt] *vt* (*anticipate*) s'attendre à, attendre, escompter; (*think*) penser (**that** que); (*suppose*) supposer (**that** que); (*await*) attendre; **to e. sth from s.o./sth** attendre qch de qn/qch; **to e. to do** compter faire; **to e. that** (*anticipate*) s'attendre à ce que (+ *sub*); **I e. you to come** (*want*) je te demande de venir; **it was expected** c'était prévu (**that** que); **she's expecting a baby** elle attend un bébé. ◆**expectancy** *n* attente *f*; **life e.** espérance *f* de vie. ◆**expectant** *a* (*crowd*) qui attend; **e. mother** future mère *f*. ◆**expec'tation** *n* attente *f*; **to come up to s.o.'s expectations** répondre à l'attente de qn.

expedient [ɪks'piːdɪənt] *a* avantageux; (*suitable*) opportun; – *n* (*resource*) expédient *m*.

expedite ['ekspədaɪt] *vt* (*hasten*) accélérer; (*task*) expédier.

expedition [ekspɪ'dɪʃ(ə)n] *n* expédition *f*.

expel [ɪk'spel] *vt* (**-ll-**) expulser (**from** de); (*from school*) renvoyer; (*enemy*) chasser.

expend [ɪk'spend] *vt* (*energy, money*) dépenser; (*resources*) épuiser. ◆**—able** *a* (*object*) remplaçable; (*soldiers*) sacrifiable. ◆**expenditure** *n* (*money spent*) dépenses *fpl*; **an e. of** (*time, money*) une dépense de.

expense [ɪk'spens] *n* frais *mpl*, dépense *f*; *pl Fin* frais *mpl*; **business/travelling expenses** frais *mpl* généraux/de déplacement; **to go to some e.** faire des frais; **at s.o.'s e.** aux dépens de qn; **an** *or* **one's e. account** une *or* sa note de frais (professionnels).

expensive [ɪk'spensɪv] *a* (*goods etc*) cher, coûteux; (*hotel etc*) cher; (*tastes*) dispendieux; **to be e.** coûter cher; **an e. mistake** une faute qui coûte cher. ◆**—ly** *adv* à grands frais.

experienc/e [ɪk'spɪərɪəns] *n* (*knowledge, skill, event*) expérience *f*; **from** *or* **by e.** par expérience; **he's had e. of** (*work etc*) il a déjà fait; (*grief etc*) il a déjà éprouvé; **I've had e. of driving** j'ai déjà conduit; **terrible experiences** de rudes épreuves *fpl*; **unforgettable e.** moment *m* inoubliable; – *vt* (*undergo*) connaître, subir; (*remorse, difficulty*) éprouver; (*joy*) ressentir. ◆**—ed** *a* (*person*) expérimenté; (*eye, ear*) exercé; **to be e. in** s'y connaître en (matière de).

experiment [ɪk'sperɪmənt] *n* expérience *f*; – [ɪk'sperɪment] *vi* faire une expérience *or* des expériences; **to e. with sth** *Phys Ch* expérimenter qch. ◆**experi'mental** *a* expérimental; **e. period** période *f* d'expérimentation.

expert ['ekspɜːt] *n* expert *m* (**on, in** en), spécialiste *mf* (**on, in** de); – *a* expert (**in sth** en qch, **in** *or* **at doing** à faire); (*advice*) d'un expert, d'expert; (*eye*) connaisseur; **e. touch** doigté *m*, grande habileté *f*. ◆**exper'tise** *n* compétence *f* (**in** en). ◆**expertly** *adv* habilement.

expiate ['ekspɪeɪt] *vt* (*sins*) expier.

expir/e [ɪk'spaɪər] *vi* expirer. ◆**—ed** *a*

(*ticket, passport etc*) périmé. ◆**expi'ration** *n Am.* ◆**expiry** *n* expiration *f.*

explain [ɪk'spleɪn] *vt* expliquer (to à, that que); (*reasons*) exposer; (*mystery*) éclaircir; **e. yourself!** explique-toi!; **to e. away** justifier. ◆**—able** *a* explicable. ◆**expla'nation** *n* explication *f.* ◆**explanatory** *a* explicatif.

expletive [ɪk'spliːtɪv, *Am* 'eksplətɪv] *n* (*oath*) juron *m.*

explicit [ɪk'splɪsɪt] *a* explicite. ◆**—ly** *adv* explicitement.

explode [ɪk'spləud] *vi* exploser; **to e. with laughter** *Fig* éclater de rire; – *vt* faire exploser; (*theory*) *Fig* démythifier, discréditer.

exploit 1 [ɪk'splɔɪt] *vt* (*person, land etc*) exploiter. **2** ['eksplɔɪt] *n* (*feat*) exploit *m.* ◆**exploi'tation** *n* exploitation *f.*

explore [ɪk'splɔːr] *vt* explorer; (*possibilities*) examiner. ◆**explo'ration** *n* exploration *f.* ◆**exploratory** *a* d'exploration; (*talks, step etc*) préliminaire, exploratoire; **e. operation** *Med* sondage *m.* ◆**explorer** *n* explorateur, -trice *mf.*

explosion [ɪk'spləuʒ(ə)n] *n* explosion *f.* ◆**explosive** *a* (*weapon, question*) explosif; (*mixture, gas*) détonant; – *n* explosif *m.*

exponent [ɪk'spəunənt] *n* (*of opinion, theory etc*) interprète *m* (of de).

export ['ekspɔːt] *n* exportation *f*; – *a* (*goods etc*) d'exportation; – [ɪk'spɔːt] *vt* exporter (to vers, from de). ◆**expor'tation** *n* exportation *f.* ◆**ex'porter** *n* exportateur, -trice *mf*; (*country*) pays *m* exportateur.

expose [ɪk'spəuz] *vt* (*leave uncovered, describe*) & *Phot* exposer; (*wire*) dénuder; (*plot, scandal etc*) révéler, dévoiler; (*crook etc*) démasquer; **to e. to** (*subject to*) exposer à; **to e. oneself** *Jur* commettre un attentat à la pudeur. ◆**expo'sition** *n* exposition *f.* ◆**exposure** *n* exposition *f* (to à); (*of plot etc*) révélation *f*; (*of house etc*) exposition *f*; *Phot* pose *f*; **to die of e.** mourir de froid.

expound [ɪk'spaund] *vt* (*theory etc*) exposer.

express [ɪk'spres] **1** *vt* exprimer; (*proposition*) énoncer; **to e. oneself** s'exprimer. **2** *a* (*order*) exprès, formel; (*intention*) explicite; (*purpose*) seul; (*letter, delivery*) exprès *inv*; (*train*) rapide, express *inv*; – *adv* (*to send*) par exprès; – *n* (*train*) rapide *m*, express *m inv.* ◆**expression** *n* (*phrase, look etc*) expression *f*; **an e. of** (*gratitude, affection etc*) un témoignage de. ◆**expressive** *a* expressif. ◆**expressly** *adv* expressément. ◆**expressway** *n Am* autoroute *f.*

expulsion [ɪk'spʌlʃ(ə)n] *n* expulsion *f*; (*from school*) renvoi *m.*

expurgate ['ekspəgeɪt] *vt* expurger.

exquisite [ɪk'skwɪzɪt] *a* exquis. ◆**—ly** *adv* d'une façon exquise.

ex-serviceman [eks'sɜːvɪsmən] *n* (*pl* **-men**) ancien combattant *m.*

extant ['ekstənt, ek'stænt] *a* existant.

extend [ɪk'stend] *vt* (*arm, business*) étendre; (*line, visit, meeting*) prolonger (by de); (*hand*) tendre (to s.o. à qn); (*house*) agrandir; (*knowledge*) élargir; (*time limit*) reculer; (*help, thanks*) offrir (to à); **to e. an invitation to** faire une invitation à; – *vi* (*of wall, plain etc*) s'étendre (to jusqu'à); (*in time*) se prolonger; **to e. to s.o.** (*of joy etc*) gagner qn. ◆**extension** *n* (*in space*) prolongement *m*; (*in time*) prolongation *f*; (*of powers, measure, meaning, strike*) extension *f*; (*for table, wire*) rallonge *f*; (*to building*) agrandissement(s) *m(pl)*; (*of telephone*) appareil *m* supplémentaire; (*of office telephone*) poste *m*; **an e. (of time)** un délai. ◆**extensive** *a* étendu, vaste; (*repairs, damage*) important; (*use*) courant. ◆**extensively** *adv* (*very much*) beaucoup, considérablement; **e. used** largement répandu.

extent [ɪk'stent] *n* (*scope*) étendue *f*; (*size*) importance *f*; (*degree*) mesure *f*; **to a large/certain e.** dans une large/certaine mesure; **to such an e. that** à tel point que.

extenuating [ɪk'stenjueɪtɪŋ] *a* **e. circumstances** circonstances *fpl* atténuantes.

exterior [ɪks'tɪərɪər] *a* & *n* extérieur (*m*).

exterminate [ɪk'stɜːmɪneɪt] *vt* (*people etc*) exterminer; (*disease*) supprimer; (*evil*) extirper. ◆**extermi'nation** *n* extermination *f*; suppression *f.*

external [ek'stɜːn(ə)l] *a* (*influence, trade etc*) extérieur; **for e. use** (*medicine*) à usage externe; **e. affairs** *Pol* affaires *fpl* étrangères. ◆**—ly** *adv* extérieurement.

extinct [ɪk'stɪŋkt] *a* (*volcano, love*) éteint; (*species, animal*) disparu. ◆**extinction** *n* extinction *f*; disparition *f.*

extinguish [ɪk'stɪŋgwɪʃ] *vt* éteindre. ◆**—er** *n* **(fire) e.** extincteur *m.*

extol [ɪk'stəul] *vt* (**-ll-**) exalter, louer.

extort [ɪk'stɔːt] *vt* (*money*) extorquer (**from** à); (*consent*) arracher (**from** à). ◆**extortion** *n Jur* extorsion *f* de fonds; **it's (sheer) e.!** c'est du vol! ◆**extortionate** *a* exorbitant.

extra ['ekstrə] *a* (*additional*) supplémentaire; **one e. glass** un verre de *or* en plus, encore un verre; **(any) e. bread?**

encore du pain?; to be e. (*spare*) être en trop; (*cost more*) être en supplément; (*of postage*) être en sus; **wine is 3 francs e.** il y a un supplément de 3F pour le vin; **e. care** un soin tout particulier; **e. charge** *or* **portion** supplément *m*; **e. time** *Fb* prolongation *f*; – *adv* **e. big**/*etc* plus grand/*etc* que d'habitude; – *n* (*perk*) à-côté *m*; *Cin Th* figurant, -ante *mf*; *pl* (*expenses*) frais *mpl* supplémentaires; **an optional e.** (*for car etc*) un accessoire en option.

extra- ['ekstrə] *pref* extra-. ◆**e.-'dry** *a* (*champagne*) brut. ◆**e.-'fine** *a* extra-fin. ◆**e.-'strong** *a* extra-fort.

extract [ɪk'strækt] *vt* extraire (**from** de); (*tooth*) arracher, extraire; (*promise*) arracher, soutirer (**from** à); (*money*) soutirer (**from** à); – ['ekstrækt] *n* (*of book etc*) & *Culin Ch* extrait *m*. ◆**ex'traction** *n* extraction *f*; arrachement *m*; (*descent*) origine *f*.

extra-curricular [ekstrəkə'rɪkjʊlər] *a* (*activities etc*) en dehors des heures de cours, extrascolaire.

extradite ['ekstrədaɪt] *vt* extrader. ◆**extra'dition** *n* extradition *f*.

extramarital [ekstrə'mærɪt(ə)l] *a* en dehors du mariage, extra-conjugal.

extramural [ekstrə'mjʊərəl] *a* (*studies*) hors faculté.

extraneous [ɪk'streɪnɪəs] *a* (*detail etc*) accessoire.

extraordinary [ɪk'strɔːdən(ə)rɪ] *a* (*strange, exceptional*) extraordinaire.

extra-special [ekstrə'speʃəl] *a* (*occasion*) très spécial; (*care*) tout particulier.

extravagant [ɪk'strævəgənt] *a* (*behaviour, idea etc*) extravagant; (*claim*) exagéré; (*wasteful with money*) dépensier, prodigue. ◆**extravagance** *n* extravagance *f*; prodigalité *f*; (*thing bought*) folle dépense *f*.

extravaganza [ɪkstrævə'gænzə] *n Mus Liter & Fig* fantaisie *f*.

extreme [ɪk'striːm] *a* (*exceptional, furthest*) extrême; (*danger, poverty*) très grand; (*praise*) outré; **at the e. end** à l'extrémité; **of e. importance** de première importance; – *n* (*furthest degree*) extrême *m*; **to carry** *or* **take to extremes** pousser à l'extrême; **extremes of temperature** températures *fpl* extrêmes; **extremes of climate** excès *mpl* du climat. ◆**extremely** *adv* extrêmement. ◆**extremist** *a* & *n* extrémiste (*mf*). ◆**extremity** [ɪk'stremɪtɪ] *n* extrémité *f*.

extricate ['ekstrɪkeɪt] *vt* dégager (**from** de); **to e. oneself from** (*difficulty*) se tirer de.

extrovert ['ekstrəvɜːt] *n* extraverti, -ie *mf*.

exuberant [ɪg'z(j)uːbərənt] *a* exubérant. ◆**exuberance** *n* exubérance *f*.

exude [ɪg'zjuːd] *vt* (*charm, honesty etc*) *Fig* respirer.

exultation [egzʌl'teɪʃ(ə)n] *n* exultation *f*.

eye[1] [aɪ] *n* œil *m* (*pl* yeux); **before my very eyes** sous mes yeux; **to be all eyes** être tout yeux; **as far as the e. can see** à perte de vue; **up to one's eyes in debt** endetté jusqu'au cou; **up to one's eyes in work** débordé de travail; **to have an e. on** (*house, car*) avoir en vue; **to keep an e. on** surveiller; **to make eyes at** *Fam* faire de l'œil à; **to lay** *or* **set eyes on** voir, apercevoir; **to take one's eyes off s.o./sth** quitter qn/qch des yeux; **to catch the e.** attirer l'œil, accrocher le regard; **keep an e. out!, keep your eyes open!** ouvre l'œil!, sois vigilant!; **we don't see e. to e.** nous n'avons pas le même point de vue; **e. shadow** fard *m* à paupières; **to be an e.-opener for s.o.** *Fam* être une révélation pour qn. ◆**eyeball** *n* globe *m* oculaire. ◆**eyebrow** *n* sourcil *m*. ◆**eye-catching** *a* (*title etc*) accrocheur. ◆**eyeglass** *n* monocle *m*. ◆**eyeglasses** *npl* (*spectacles*) *Am* lunettes *fpl*. ◆**eyelash** *n* cil *m*. ◆**eyelid** *n* paupière *f*. ◆**eyeliner** *n* eye-liner *m*. ◆**eyesight** *n* vue *f*. ◆**eyesore** *n* (*building etc*) horreur *f*. ◆**eyestrain** *n* **to have e.** avoir les yeux qui tirent. ◆**eyewash** *n* (*nonsense*) *Fam* sottises *fpl*. ◆**eyewitness** *n* témoin *m* oculaire.

eye[2] [aɪ] *vt* reluquer, regarder.

F

F, f [ef] *n* F, f *m*.

fable ['feɪb(ə)l] *n* fable *f*.

fabric ['fæbrɪk] *n* (*cloth*) tissu *m*, étoffe *f*; (*of building*) structure *f*; **the f. of society** le tissu social.

fabricate ['fæbrɪkeɪt] *vt* (*invent, make*) fabriquer. ◆**fabri'cation** *n* fabrication *f*.

fabulous ['fæbjʊləs] *a* (*incredible, legendary*) fabuleux; (*wonderful*) *Fam* formidable.

façade [fə'sɑːd] *n Archit & Fig* façade *f*.

face [feɪs] *n* visage *m*, figure *f*; (*expression*) mine *f*; (*of clock*) cadran *m*; (*of building*) façade *f*; (*of cliff*) paroi *f*; (*of the earth*) surface *f*; **she laughed in my f.** elle m'a ri au nez; **to show one's f.** se montrer; **f. down(wards)** (*person*) face contre terre; (*thing*) tourné à l'envers; **f. to f.** face à face; **in the f. of** devant; (*despite*) en dépit de; **to save/lose f.** sauver/perdre la face; **to make** *or* **pull faces** faire des grimaces; **to tell s.o. sth to his f.** dire qch à qn tout cru; **f. powder** poudre *f* de riz; **f. value** (*of stamp etc*) valeur *f*; **to take sth at f. value** prendre qch au pied de la lettre; – *vt* (*danger, enemy etc*) faire face à; (*accept*) accepter; (*look in the face*) regarder (*qn*) bien en face; **to f., be facing** (*be opposite*) être en face de; (*of window etc*) donner sur; **faced with** (*prospect, problem*) face à, devant; (*defeat*) menacé par; (*bill*) contraint à payer; **he can't f. leaving** il n'a pas le courage de partir; – *vi* (*of house*) être orienté (**north/***etc* au nord/*etc*); (*of person*) se tourner (**towards** vers); **to f. up to** (*danger*) faire face à; (*fact*) accepter; **about f.!** *Am Mil* demi-tour! ◆**facecloth** *n* gant *m* de toilette. ◆**facelift** *n Med* lifting *m*; (*of building*) ravalement *m*.

faceless ['feɪsləs] *a* anonyme.

facet ['fæsɪt] *n* (*of problem, diamond etc*) facette *f*.

facetious [fə'siːʃəs] *a* (*person*) facétieux; (*remark*) plaisant.

facial ['feɪʃ(ə)l] *a* du visage; *Med* facial; – *n* soin *m* du visage.

facile ['fæsaɪl, *Am* 'fæs(ə)l] *a* facile, superficiel.

facilitate [fə'sɪlɪteɪt] *vt* faciliter. ◆**facility** *n* (*ease*) facilité *f*; *pl* (*possibilities*) facilités *fpl*; (*for sports*) équipements *mpl*; (*in harbour, airport etc*) installations *fpl*; (*means*) moyens *mpl*, ressources *fpl*; **special facilities** (*conditions*) conditions *fpl* spéciales (**for** pour).

facing ['feɪsɪŋ] *n* (*of dress etc*) parement *m*.

fact [fækt] *n* fait *m*; **as a matter of f., in f.** en fait; **the facts of life** les choses *fpl* de la vie; **is that a f.?** c'est vrai?; **f. and fiction** le réel et l'imaginaire.

faction ['fækʃ(ə)n] *n* (*group*) *Pol* faction *f*.

factor ['fæktər] *n* (*element*) facteur *m*.

factory ['fækt(ə)rɪ] *n* (*large*) usine *f*; (*small*) fabrique *f*; **arms/porcelain f.** manufacture *f* d'armes/de porcelaine.

factual ['fæktʃʊəl] *a* objectif, basé sur les faits, factuel; (*error*) de fait.

faculty ['fækəltɪ] *n* (*aptitude*) & *Univ* faculté *f*.

fad [fæd] *n* (*personal habit*) marotte *f*; (*fashion*) folie *f*, mode *f* (**for** de).

fade [feɪd] *vi* (*of flower*) se faner; (*of light*) baisser; (*of colour*) passer; (*of fabric*) se décolorer; **to f. (away)** (*of memory, smile*) s'effacer; (*of sound*) s'affaiblir; (*of person*) dépérir; – *vt* (*fabric*) décolorer.

fag [fæg] *n* **1** (*cigarette*) *Fam* clope *m*, tige *f*; **f. end** mégot *m*. **2** (*male homosexual*) *Am Sl* pédé *m*.

fagged [fægd] *a* **f. (out)** (*tired*) *Sl* claqué.

faggot ['fægət] *n* **1** *Culin* boulette *f* (de viande). **2** (*male homosexual*) *Am Sl* pédé *m*.

fail [feɪl] *vi* (*of person, plan etc*) échouer; (*of business*) faire faillite; (*of light, health, sight*) baisser; (*of memory, strength*) défaillir; (*of brakes*) *Aut* lâcher; (*run short*) manquer; (*of gas, electricity*) être coupé; (*of engine*) tomber en panne; **to f. in** (*one's duty*) manquer à; (*exam*) échouer à; – *vt* (*exam*) échouer à; (*candidate*) refuser, recaler; **to f. s.o.** (*let down*) laisser tomber qn, décevoir qn; (*of words*) manquer à qn, faire défaut à qn; **to f. to do** (*omit*) manquer de faire; (*not be able*) ne pas arriver à faire; **I f. to see** je ne vois pas; – *n* **without f.** à coup sûr, sans faute. ◆**—ed** *a* (*attempt, poet*) manqué. ◆**—ing** *n* (*fault*) défaut *m*; – *prep* à défaut de; **f. this, f. that** à défaut. ◆**failure** *n* échec *m*; (*of business*) faillite *f*; (*of engine, machine*) panne *f*; (*of gas etc*) coupure *f*, panne *f*; (*person*) raté, -ée *mf*; **f. to do** (*inability*) incapacité *f* de faire; **her f. to leave** le fait qu'elle n'est pas partie; **to end in f.** se solder par un échec; **heart f.** arrêt *m* du cœur.

faint [feɪnt] **1** *a* (**-er, -est**) léger; (*voice*) faible; (*colour*) pâle; (*idea*) vague; **I haven't the faintest idea** je n'en ai pas la moindre idée. **2** *a Med* défaillant (**with** de); **to feel f.** se trouver mal, défaillir; – *vi* s'évanouir (**from** de); **fainting fit** évanouissement *m*. ◆**—ly** *adv* (*weakly*) faiblement; (*slightly*) légèrement. ◆**—ness** *n* légèreté *f*; faiblesse *f*. ◆**faint-'hearted** *a* timoré, timide.

fair[1] [feər] *n* foire *f*; (*for charity*) fête *f*; (*funfair*) fête *f* foraine; (*larger*) parc *m* d'attractions. ◆**fairground** *n* champ *m* de foire.

fair² [feər] **1** *a* (**-er, -est**) (*equitable*) juste, équitable; (*game, fight*) loyal; **f. (and square)** honnête(ment); **f. play** fair-play *m inv*; **that's not f. play!** ce n'est pas du jeu!; **that's not f. to him** ce n'est pas juste pour lui; **f. enough!** très bien!; – *adv* (*to play*) loyalement. **2** *a* (*rather good*) passable, assez bon; (*amount, warning*) raisonnable; **a f. amount (of)** pas mal (de); **f. copy** copie *f* au propre. **3** *a* (*wind*) favorable; (*weather*) beau. ◆**—ly** *adv* **1** (*to treat*) équitablement; (*to get*) loyalement. **2** (*rather*) assez, plutôt; **f. sure** presque sûr. ◆**—ness¹** *n* justice *f*; (*of decision*) équité *f*; **in all f.** en toute justice. ◆**fair-'minded** *a* impartial. ◆**fair-'sized** *a* assez grand.

fair³ [feər] *a* (*hair, person*) blond; (*complexion, skin*) clair. ◆**—ness²** *n* (*of hair*) blond *m*; (*of skin*) blancheur *f*. ◆**fair-'haired** *a* blond. ◆**fair-'skinned** *a* à la peau claire.

fairy ['feərɪ] *n* fée *f*; **f. lights** guirlande *f* multicolore; **f. tale** conte *m* de fées.

faith [feɪθ] *n* foi *f*; **to have f. in s.o.** avoir confiance en qn; **to put one's f. in** (*justice, medicine etc*) se fier à; **in good/bad f.** de bonne/mauvaise foi; **f. healer** guérisseur, -euse *mf*. ◆**faithful** *a* fidèle. ◆**faithfully** *adv* fidèlement; **yours f.** (*in letter*) *Com* veuillez agréer l'expression de mes salutations distinguées. ◆**faithfulness** *n* fidélité *f*. ◆**faithless** *a* déloyal, infidèle.

fake [feɪk] *n* (*painting, document etc*) faux *m*; (*person*) imposteur *m*; – *vt* (*document, signature etc*) falsifier, maquiller; (*election*) truquer; **to f. death** faire semblant d'être mort; – *vi* (*pretend*) faire semblant; – *a* faux; (*elections*) truqué.

falcon ['fɔːlkən] *n* faucon *m*.

fall [fɔːl] *n* chute *f*; (*in price, demand etc*) baisse *f*; *pl* (*waterfall*) chutes *fpl* (d'eau); **the f.** *Am* l'automne *m*; – *vi* (*pt* **fell**, *pp* **fallen**) tomber; (*of building*) s'effondrer; **her face fell** *Fig* son visage se rembrunit; **to f. into** tomber dans; (*habit*) *Fig* prendre; **to f. off a bicycle/***etc* tomber d'une bicyclette/*etc*; **to f. off** *or* **down a ladder** tomber (en bas) d'une échelle; **to fall on s.o.** (*of onus*) retomber sur qn; **to f. on a Monday/***etc* (*of event*) tomber un lundi/*etc*; **to f. over sth** tomber en butant contre qch; **to f. short of** (*expectation*) ne pas répondre à; **to f. short of being** être loin d'être; **to f. victim** devenir victime (**to** de); **to f. asleep** s'endormir; **to f. ill** tomber malade; **to f. due** échoir. ■ **to f. apart** (*of mechanism*) tomber en morceaux; *Fig* se désagréger; **to f. away** (*come off*) se détacher, tomber; (*of numbers*) diminuer; **to f. back on** (*as last resort*) se rabattre sur; **to f. behind** rester en arrière; (*in work*) prendre du retard; **to f. down** tomber; (*of building*) s'effondrer; **to f. for** *Fam* (*person*) tomber amoureux de; (*trick*) se laisser prendre à; **to f. in** (*collapse*) s'écrouler; **to f. in with** (*tally with*) cadrer avec; (*agree to*) accepter; **to f. off** (*come off*) se détacher, tomber; (*of numbers*) diminuer. ◆**falling-'off** *n* diminution *f*; **to f. out with** (*quarrel with*) se brouiller avec; **to f. over** tomber; (*of table, vase*) se renverser; **to f. through** (*of plan*) tomber à l'eau, échouer. ◆**fallen** *a* tombé; (*angel, woman*) déchu; **f. leaf** feuille *f* morte. ◆**fallout** *n* (*radioactive*) retombées *fpl*.

fallacious [fə'leɪʃəs] *a* faux. ◆**fallacy** ['fæləsɪ] *n* erreur *f*; *Phil* faux raisonnement *m*.

fallible ['fæləb(ə)l] *a* faillible.

fallow ['fæləʊ] *a* (*land*) en jachère.

false [fɔːls] *a* faux; **a f. bottom** un double fond. ◆**falsehood** *n* mensonge *m*; **truth and f.** le vrai et le faux. ◆**falseness** *n* fausseté *f*. ◆**falsify** *vt* falsifier.

falter ['fɔːltər] *vi* (*of step, resolution*) chanceler; (*of voice, speaker*) hésiter; (*of courage*) vaciller.

fame [feɪm] *n* renommée *f*; (*glory*) gloire *f*. ◆**famed** *a* renommé.

familiar [fə'mɪljər] *a* (*task, atmosphere etc*) familier; (*event*) habituel; **f. with s.o.** (*too friendly*) familier avec qn; **to be f. with** (*know*) connaître; **I'm f. with her voice** je connais bien sa voix, sa voix m'est familière; **to make oneself f. with** se familiariser avec; **he looks f. (to me)** je l'ai déjà vu (quelque part). ◆**famili'arity** *n* familiarité *f* (**with** avec); (*of event, sight etc*) caractère *m* familier. ◆**familiarize** *vt* familiariser (**with** avec); **to f. oneself with** se familiariser avec.

family ['fæmɪlɪ] *n* famille *f*; – *a* (*name, doctor etc*) de famille; (*planning, problem*) familial; (*tree*) généalogique; **f. man** père *m* de famille.

famine ['fæmɪn] *n* famine *f*.

famished ['fæmɪʃt] *a* affamé.

famous ['feɪməs] *a* célèbre (**for** par, pour). ◆**—ly** *adv* (*very well*) *Fam* rudement bien.

fan [fæn] **1** *n* (*hand-held*) éventail *m*; (*mechanical*) ventilateur *m*; **f. heater** radiateur *m* soufflant; – *vt* (**-nn-**) (*person etc*) éventer; (*fire, quarrel*) attiser. **2** *n* (*of person*) admirateur, -trice *mf*, fan *m*; *Sp* supporter *m*; **to be a jazz/sports f.** être passionné *or* mordu de jazz/de sport.

fanatic [fə'nætɪk] *n* fanatique *mf*. ◆**fanatical** *a* fanatique. ◆**fanaticism** *n* fanatisme *m*.

fancy ['fænsɪ] **1** *n* (*whim, imagination*) fantaisie *f*; (*liking*) goût *m*; **to take a f. to s.o.** se prendre d'affection pour qn; **I took a f. to it, it took my f.** j'en ai eu envie; **when the f. takes me** quand ça me chante; – *a* (*hat, button etc*) fantaisie *inv*; (*idea*) fantaisiste; (*price*) exorbitant; (*car*) de luxe; (*house, restaurant*) chic; **f. dress** (*costume*) travesti *m*; **f.-dress ball** bal *m* masqué. **2** *vt* (*imagine*) se figurer (**that** que); (*think*) croire (**that** que); (*want*) avoir envie de; (*like*) aimer; **f. that!** tiens (donc)!; **he fancies her** *Fam* elle lui plaît; **to f. oneself as** se prendre pour; **she fancies herself!** elle se prend pour qn! ◆**fancier** *n* **horse/etc f.** amateur *m* de chevaux/*etc*. ◆**fanciful** *a* fantaisiste.

fanfare ['fænfeər] *n* (*of trumpets*) fanfare *f*.

fang [fæŋ] *n* (*of dog etc*) croc *m*; (*of snake*) crochet *m*.

fantastic [fæn'tæstɪk] *a* fantastique; **a f. idea** (*absurd*) une idée aberrante.

fantasy ['fæntəsɪ] *n* (*imagination*) fantaisie *f*; *Psy* fantasme *m*. ◆**fantasize** *vi* fantasmer (**about** sur).

far [fɑːr] *adv* (**farther** *or* **further, farthest** *or* **furthest**) (*distance*) loin; **f. bigger/more expensive/etc** (*much*) beaucoup plus grand/plus cher/*etc* (**than** que); **f. more** beaucoup plus; **f. advanced** très avancé; **how f. is it to . . . ?** combien y a-t-il d'ici à . . . ?; **is it f. to . . . ?** sommes-nous, suis-je *etc* loin de . . . ?; **how f. are you going?** jusqu'où vas-tu?; **how f. has he got with?** (*plans, work etc*) où en est-il de?; **so f.** (*time*) jusqu'ici; (*place*) jusque-là; **as f. as** (*place*) jusqu'à; **as f.** *or* **so f. as I know** autant que je sache; **as f.** *or* **so f. as I'm concerned** en ce qui me concerne; **as f. back as 1820** dès 1820; **f. from doing** loin de faire; **f. from it!** loin de là!; **f. away** *or* **off** au loin; **to be (too) f. away** être (trop) loin (**from** de); **f. and wide** partout; **by f.** de loin; **f. into the night** très avant dans la nuit; – *a* (*side, end*) autre; **it's a f. cry from** on est loin de. ◆**faraway** *a* lointain; (*look*) distrait, dans le vague. ◆**far-'fetched** *a* forcé, exagéré. ◆**f.-'flung** *a* (*widespread*) vaste. ◆**f.-'off** *a* lointain. ◆**f.-'reaching** *a* de grande portée. ◆**f.-'sighted** *a* clairvoyant.

farce [fɑːs] *n* farce *f*. ◆**farcical** *a* grotesque, ridicule.

fare [feər] **1** *n* (*price*) prix *m* du billet; (*ticket*) billet *m*; (*taxi passenger*) client, -ente *mf*. **2** *n* (*food*) chère *f*, nourriture *f*; **prison f.** régime *m* de prison; **bill of f.** menu *m*. **3** *vi* (*manage*) se débrouiller; **how did she f.?** comment ça s'est passé (pour elle)?

farewell [feə'wel] *n* & *int* adieu (*m*); – *a* (*party etc*) d'adieu.

farm [fɑːm] *n* ferme *f*; – *a* (*worker, produce etc*) agricole; **f. land** terres *fpl* cultivées; – *vt* cultiver; – *vi* être agriculteur. ◆**—ing** *n* agriculture *f*; (*breeding*) élevage *m*; **dairy f.** industrie *f* laitière. ◆**—er** *n* fermier, -ière *mf*, agriculteur *m*. ◆**farmhand** *n* ouvrier, -ière *mf* agricole. ◆**farmhouse** *n* ferme *f*. ◆**farmyard** *n* basse-cour *f*.

farther ['fɑːðər] *adv* plus loin; **nothing is f. from** (*my mind, the truth etc*) rien n'est plus éloigné de; **f. forward** plus avancé; **to get f. away** s'éloigner; – *a* (*end*) autre. ◆**farthest** *a* le plus éloigné; – *adv* le plus loin.

fascinate ['fæsɪneɪt] *vt* fasciner. ◆**fasci'nation** *n* fascination *f*.

fascism ['fæʃɪz(ə)m] *n* fascisme *m*. ◆**fascist** *a* & *n* fasciste (*mf*).

fashion ['fæʃ(ə)n] **1** *n* (*style in clothes etc*) mode *f*; **in f.** à la mode; **out of f.** démodé; **f. designer** (grand) couturier *m*; **f. house** maison *f* de couture; **f. show** présentation *f* de collections. **2** *n* (*manner*) façon *f*; (*custom*) habitude *f*; **after a f.** tant bien que mal, plus au moins. **3** *vt* (*make*) façonner. ◆**—able** *a* à la mode; (*place*) chic *inv*; **it's f. to do** il est de bon ton de faire. ◆**—ably** *adv* (*dressed etc*) à la mode.

fast [fɑːst] **1** *a* (**-er, -est**) rapide; **to be f.** (*of clock*) avancer (**by** de); **f. colour** couleur *f* grand teint *inv*; **f. living** vie *f* dissolue; – *adv* (*quickly*) vite; (*firmly*) ferme, bien; **how f.?** à quelle vitesse?; **f. asleep** profondément endormi. **2** *vi* (*go without food*) jeûner; – *n* jeûne *m*.

fasten ['fɑːs(ə)n] *vt* attacher (**to** à); (*door, window*) fermer (bien); **to f. down** *or* **up** attacher; – *vi* (*of dress etc*) s'attacher; (*of door, window*) se fermer. ◆**—er** *n*, ◆**—ing** *n* (*clip*) attache *f*; (*of garment*) fermeture *f*; (*of bag*) fermoir *m*; (*hook*) agrafe *f*.

fastidious [fə'stɪdɪəs] *a* difficile (à contenter), exigeant.

fat [fæt] **1** *n* graisse *f*; (*on meat*) gras *m*; **vegetable f.** huile *f* végétale. **2** *a* (**fatter, fattest**) gras; (*cheek, salary, volume*) gros; **to get f.** grossir; **that's a f. lot of good** *or* **use!** *Iron*

Fam ça va vraiment servir (à quelque chose)! ◆**fathead** *n* imbécile *mf.*

fatal ['feɪt(ə)l] *a* mortel; (*error, blow etc*) *Fig* fatal. ◆**—ly** *adv* (*wounded*) mortellement.

fatality [fə'tælɪtɪ] *n* **1** (*person killed*) victime *f.* **2** (*of event*) fatalité *f.*

fate [feɪt] *n* destin *m,* sort *m;* **one's f.** son sort. ◆**fated** *a* **f. to do** destiné à faire; **our meeting/his death/***etc* **was f.** notre rencontre/sa mort/*etc* devait arriver. ◆**fateful** *a* (*important*) fatal, décisif; (*prophetic*) fatidique; (*disastrous*) néfaste.

father ['fɑːðər] *n* père *m;* – *vt* engendrer; (*idea*) *Fig* inventer. ◆**f.-in-law** *n* (*pl* **fathers-in-law**) beau-père *m.* ◆**fatherhood** *n* paternité *f.* ◆**fatherland** *n* patrie *f.* ◆**fatherly** *a* paternel.

fathom ['fæðəm] **1** *n Nau* brasse *f* (= *1,8 m*). **2** *vt* **to f. (out)** (*understand*) comprendre.

fatigue [fə'tiːg] **1** *n* fatigue *f;* – *vt* fatiguer. **2** *n* **f. (duty)** *Mil* corvée *f.*

fatness ['fætnɪs] *n* corpulence *f.* ◆**fatten** *vt* engraisser. ◆**fattening** *a* qui fait grossir. ◆**fatty** *a* (**-ier, -iest**) (*food*) gras; (*tissue*) *Med* adipeux; – *n* (*person*) *Fam* gros lard *m.*

fatuous ['fætʃuəs] *a* stupide.

faucet ['fɔːsɪt] *n* (*tap*) *Am* robinet *m.*

fault [fɔːlt] *n* (*blame*) faute *f;* (*failing, defect*) défaut *m;* (*mistake*) erreur *f; Geol* faille *f;* **to find f. (with)** critiquer; **he's at f.** c'est sa faute, il est fautif; **his** *or* **her memory is at f.** sa mémoire lui fait défaut; – *vt* **to f. s.o./sth** trouver des défauts chez qn/à qch. ◆**f.-finding** *a* critique, chicanier. ◆**faultless** *a* irréprochable. ◆**faulty** *a* (**-ier, -iest**) défectueux.

fauna ['fɔːnə] *n* (*animals*) faune *f.*

favour ['feɪvər] *n* (*approval, advantage*) faveur *f;* (*act of kindness*) service *m;* **to do s.o. a f.** rendre service à qn; **in f.** (*person*) bien vu; (*fashion*) en vogue; **it's in her f. to do** elle a intérêt à faire; **in f. of** (*for the sake of*) au profit de, en faveur de; **to be in f. of** (*support*) être pour, être partisan de; (*prefer*) préférer; – *vt* (*encourage*) favoriser; (*support*) être partisan de; (*prefer*) préférer; **he favoured me with a visit** il a eu la gentillesse de me rendre visite. ◆**—able** *a* favorable (**to** à). ◆**favourite** *a* favori, préféré; – *n* favori, -ite *mf.* ◆**favouritism** *n* favoritisme *m.*

fawn [fɔːn] **1** *n* (*deer*) faon *m;* – *a* & *n* (*colour*) fauve (*m*). **2** *vi* **to f. (up)on** flatter, flagorner.

fear [fɪər] *n* crainte *f,* peur *f;* **for f. of** de peur de; **for f. that** de peur que (+ ne + *sub*); **there's no f. of his going** il ne risque pas d'y aller; **there are fears (that) he might leave** on craint qu'il ne parte; – *vt* craindre; **I f. (that) he might leave** je crains qu'il ne parte; **to f. for** (*one's life etc*) craindre pour. ◆**fearful** *a* (*frightful*) affreux; (*timid*) peureux. ◆**fearless** *a* intrépide. ◆**fearlessness** *n* intrépidité *f.* ◆**fearsome** *a* redoutable.

feasible ['fiːzəb(ə)l] *a* (*practicable*) faisable; (*theory, explanation etc*) plausible. ◆**feasi'bility** *n* possibilité *f* (**of doing** de faire); plausibilité *f.*

feast [fiːst] *n* festin *m,* banquet *m; Rel* fête *f;* – *vi* banqueter; **to f. on** (*cakes etc*) se régaler de.

feat [fiːt] *n* exploit *m,* tour *m* de force; **f. of skill** tour *m* d'adresse.

feather ['feðər] **1** *n* plume *f;* **f. duster** plumeau *m.* **2** *vt* **to f. one's nest** (*enrich oneself*) faire sa pelote.

feature ['fiːtʃər] **1** *n* (*of face, person*) trait *m;* (*of thing, place, machine*) caractéristique *f;* **f. (article)** article *m* de fond; **f. (film)** grand film *m;* **to be a regular f.** (*in newspaper*) paraître régulièrement. **2** *vt* représenter (as comme); *Journ Cin* présenter; **a film featuring Chaplin** un film avec Charlot en vedette; – *vi* (*appear*) figurer (**in** dans).

February ['februərɪ] *n* février *m.*

fed [fed] *see* **feed;** – *a* **to be f. up** *Fam* en avoir marre (**with** de).

federal ['fedərəl] *a* fédéral. ◆**federate** *vt* fédérer. ◆**fede'ration** *n* fédération *f.*

fee [fiː] *n* (*price*) prix *m;* (*sum*) somme *f;* **fee(s)** (*professional*) honoraires *mpl;* (*of artist*) cachet *m;* (*for registration*) droits *mpl;* **tuition fees** frais *mpl* de scolarité; **entrance f.** droit *m* d'entrée; **membership fee(s)** cotisation *f;* **f.-paying school** école *f* privée.

feeble ['fiːb(ə)l] *a* (**-er, -est**) faible; (*excuse*) pauvre. ◆**f.-'minded** *a* imbécile.

feed [fiːd] *n* (*food*) nourriture *f;* (*baby's breast feed*) tétée *f;* (*baby's bottle feed*) biberon *m;* – *vt* (*pt & pp* **fed**) donner à manger à, nourrir; (*breast-feed*) allaiter (*un bébé*); (*bottle-feed*) donner le biberon à (*un bébé*); (*machine*) *Fig* alimenter; – *vi* (*eat*) manger; **to f. on** se nourrir de. ◆**—ing** *n* alimentation *f.* ◆**feedback** *n* réaction(s) *f*(*pl*).

feel [fiːl] *n* (*touch*) toucher *m;* (*sensation*) sensation *f;* – *vt* (*pt & pp* **felt**) (*be aware of*) sentir; (*experience*) éprouver, ressentir; (*touch*) tâter, palper; (*think*) avoir l'impression (**that** que); **to f. one's way**

avancer à tâtons; – *vi* (*tired, old etc*) se sentir; **to f. (about)** (*grope*) tâtonner; (*in pocket etc*) fouiller; **it feels hard** c'est dur (au toucher); **I f. sure** je suis sûr (**that** que); **I f. hot/sleepy/hungry** j'ai chaud/ sommeil/faim; **she feels better** elle va mieux; **to f. like** (*want*) avoir envie de; **to f. as if** avoir l'impression que; **it feels like cotton** on dirait du coton; **what do you f. about . . . ?** que pensez-vous de . . . ?; **I f. bad about it** ça m'ennuie, ça me fait de la peine; **what does it f. like?** quelle impression ça (te) fait?; **to f. for** (*look for*) chercher; (*pity*) éprouver de la pitié pour; **to f. up to doing** être (assez) en forme pour faire. ◆**—ing** *n* (*emotion, impression*) sentiment *m*; (*physical*) sensation *f*; **a f. for** (*person*) de la sympathie pour; (*music*) une appréciation de; **bad f.** animosité *f*. ◆**—er** *n* (*of snail etc*) antenne *f*; **to put out a f.** *Fig* lancer un ballon d'essai.

feet [fiːt] *see* **foot**[1].

feign [feɪn] *vt* feindre, simuler.

feint [feɪnt] *n Mil Boxing* feinte *f*.

feisty ['faɪstɪ] *a* (**-ier, -iest**) (*lively*) *Am Fam* plein d'entrain.

felicitous [fə'lɪsɪtəs] *a* heureux.

feline ['fiːlaɪn] *a* félin.

fell [fel] **1** *see* **fall. 2** *vt* (*tree etc*) abattre.

fellow ['feləʊ] *n* **1** (*man, boy*) garçon *m*, type *m*; **an old f.** un vieux; **poor f.!** pauvre malheureux! **2** (*comrade*) compagnon *m*, compagne *f*; **f. being** *or* **man** semblable *m*; **f. countryman, f. countrywoman** compatriote *mf*; **f. passenger** compagnon *m* de voyage, compagne *f* de voyage. **3** (*of society*) membre *m*. ◆**fellowship** *n* camaraderie *f*; (*group*) association *f*; (*membership*) qualité *f* de membre; (*grant*) bourse *f* universitaire.

felony ['felənɪ] *n* crime *m*.

felt[1] [felt] *see* **feel.**

felt[2] [felt] *n* feutre *m*; **f.-tip(ped) pen** crayon *m* feutre.

female ['fiːmeɪl] *a* (*animal etc*) femelle; (*quality, name, voice etc*) féminin; (*vote*) des femmes; **f. student** étudiante *f*; – *n* (*woman*) femme *f*; (*animal*) femelle *f*.

feminine ['femɪnɪn] *a* féminin. ◆**femi'ninity** *n* féminité *f*. ◆**feminist** *a* & *n* féministe (*mf*).

fenc/e [fens] **1** *n* barrière *f*, clôture *f*; *Sp* obstacle *m*; – *vt* **to f. (in)** clôturer. **2** *vi* (*with sword*) *Sp* faire de l'escrime. **3** *n* (*criminal*) *Fam* receleur, -euse *mf*. ◆**—ing** *n Sp* escrime *f*.

fend [fend] **1** *vi* **to f. for oneself** se débrouiller. **2** *vt* **to f. off** (*blow etc*) parer, éviter. ◆**—er** *n* **1** (*for fire*) garde-feu *m inv*. **2** (*on car*) *Am* aile *f*.

fennel ['fen(ə)l] *n Bot Culin* fenouil *m*.

ferment ['fɜːment] *n* ferment *m*; *Fig* effervescence *f*; – [fə'ment] *vi* fermenter. ◆**fermen'tation** *n* fermentation *f*.

fern [fɜːn] *n* fougère *f*.

ferocious [fə'rəʊʃəs] *a* féroce. ◆**ferocity** *n* férocité *f*.

ferret ['ferɪt] *n* (*animal*) furet *m*; – *vi* **to f. about** (*pry*) fureter; – *vt* **to f. out** dénicher.

Ferris wheel ['ferɪswiːl] *n* (*at funfair*) grande roue *f*.

ferry ['ferɪ] *n* ferry-boat *m*; (*small, for river*) bac *m*; – *vt* transporter.

fertile ['fɜːtaɪl, *Am* 'fɜːt(ə)l] *a* (*land, imagination*) fertile; (*person, creature*) fécond. ◆**fer'tility** *n* fertilité *f*; fécondité *f*. ◆**fertilize** *vt* (*land*) fertiliser; (*egg, animal etc*) féconder. ◆**fertilizer** *n* engrais *m*

fervent ['fɜːv(ə)nt] *a* fervent. ◆**fervour** *n* ferveur *f*.

fester ['festər] *vi* (*of wound*) suppurer; (*of anger etc*) *Fig* couver.

festival ['festɪv(ə)l] *n Mus Cin* festival *m*; *Rel* fête *f*. ◆**festive** *a* (*atmosphere, clothes*) de fête; (*mood*) joyeux; **f. season** période *f* des fêtes. ◆**fe'stivities** *npl* réjouissances *fpl*, festivités *fpl*.

festoon [fe'stuːn] *vt* **to f. with** orner de.

fetch [fetʃ] *vt* **1** (*person*) amener; (*object*) apporter; **to (go and) f.** aller chercher; **to f. in** rentrer; **to f. out** sortir. **2** (*be sold for*) rapporter (**ten pounds/*etc*** dix livres/*etc*); (*price*) atteindre. ◆**—ing** *a* (*smile etc*) charmant, séduisant.

fête [feɪt] *n* fête *f*; – *vt* fêter.

fetid ['fetɪd] *a* fétide.

fetish ['fetɪʃ] *n* (*magical object*) fétiche *m*; **to make a f. of** *Fig* être obsédé par.

fetter ['fetər] *vt* (*hinder*) entraver.

fettle ['fet(ə)l] *n* **in fine f.** en pleine forme.

fetus ['fiːtəs] *n Am* fœtus *m*.

feud [fjuːd] *n* querelle *f*, dissension *f*.

feudal ['fjuːd(ə)l] *a* féodal.

fever ['fiːvər] *n* fièvre *f*; **to have a f.** (*temperature*) avoir de la fièvre. ◆**feverish** *a* (*person, activity*) fiévreux.

few [fjuː] *a* & *pron* peu (de); **f. towns/*etc*** peu de villes/*etc*; **a f. towns/*etc*** quelques villes/*etc*; **f. of them** peu d'entre eux; **a f.** quelques-un(e)s (**of** de); **a f. of us** quelques-uns d'entre nous; **one of the f. books** l'un des rares livres; **quite a f., a good f.** bon nombre (de); **a f. more books/*etc*** encore quelques livres/*etc*; **f. and far between** rares (et espacés); **f. came** peu sont venus; **to be f.** être peu nombreux; **every f. days** tous les trois ou quatre jours. ◆**fewer** *a & pron* moins (de) (**than** que); **to be f.** être moins nombreux (**than** que); **no f. than** pas moins de. ◆**fewest** *a & pron* le moins (de).

fiancé(e) [fɪ'ɒnseɪ] *n* fiancé, -ée *mf*.

fiasco [fɪ'æskəʊ] *n* (*pl* **-os**, *Am* **-oes**) fiasco *m*.

fib [fɪb] *n Fam* blague *f*, bobard *m*; – *vi* (**-bb-**) *Fam* raconter des blagues. ◆**fibber** *n Fam* blagueur, -euse *mf*.

fibre ['faɪbər] *n* fibre *f*; *Fig* caractère *m*. ◆**fibreglass** *n* fibre *f* de verre.

fickle ['fɪk(ə)l] *a* inconstant.

fiction ['fɪkʃ(ə)n] *n* fiction *f*; (**works of**) **f.** romans *mpl*. ◆**fictional** *a*, ◆**fic'titious** *a* fictif.

fiddl/e ['fɪd(ə)l] **1** *n* (*violin*) *Fam* violon *m*; – *vi Fam* jouer du violon. **2** *vi Fam* **to f. about** (*waste time*) traînailler, glandouiller; **to f. (about) with** (*watch, pen etc*) tripoter; (*cars etc*) bricoler. **3** *n* (*dishonesty*) *Fam* combine *f*, fraude *f*; – *vi* (*swindle*) *Fam* faire de la fraude; – *vt* (*accounts etc*) *Fam* falsifier. ◆**—ing** *a* (*petty*) insignifiant. ◆**—er** *n* **1** *Fam* joueur, -euse *mf* de violon. **2** (*swindler*) *Sl* combinard, -arde *mf*. ◆**fiddly** *a* (*task*) délicat.

fidelity [fɪ'delɪtɪ] *n* fidélité *f* (**to** à).

fidget ['fɪdʒɪt] *vi* **to f. (about)** gigoter, se trémousser; **to f. (about) with** tripoter; – *n* personne *f* qui ne tient pas en place. ◆**fidgety** *a* agité, remuant.

field [fiːld] *n* champ *m*; *Sp* terrain *m*; (*sphere*) domaine *m*; **to have a f. day** (*a good day*) s'en donner à cœur joie; **f. glasses** jumelles *fpl*; **f. marshal** maréchal *m*.

fiend [fiːnd] *n* démon *m*; **a jazz/***etc* **f.** *Fam* un(e) passionné, -ée de jazz/*etc*; (**sex**) **f.** *Fam* satyre *m*. ◆**fiendish** *a* diabolique.

fierce [fɪəs] *a* (**-er, -est**) féroce; (*wind, attack*) furieux. ◆**—ness** *n* férocité *f*; fureur *f*.

fiery ['faɪərɪ] *a* (**-ier, -iest**) (*person, speech*) fougueux; (*sun, eyes*) ardent.

fiesta [fɪ'estə] *n* fiesta *f*.

fifteen [fɪf'tiːn] *a & n* quinze (*m*). ◆**fifteenth** *a & n* quinzième (*mf*). ◆**fifth** *a & n* cinquième (*mf*); **a f.** un cinquième. ◆**'fiftieth** *a & n* cinquantième (*mf*). ◆**'fifty** *a & n* cinquante (*m*).

fig [fɪg] *n* figue *f*; **f. tree** figuier *m*.

fight [faɪt] *n* bagarre *f*, rixe *f*; *Mil Boxing* combat *m*; (*struggle*) lutte *f*; (*quarrel*) dispute *f*; (*spirit*) combativité *f*; **to put up a (good) f.** bien se défendre; – *vi* (*pt & pp* **fought**) se battre (**against** contre); *Mil* se battre, combattre; (*struggle*) lutter; (*quarrel*) se disputer; **to f. back** se défendre; **to f. over sth** se disputer qch; – *vt* se battre avec (s.o. qn); (*evil*) lutter contre, combattre; **to f. a battle** livrer bataille; **to f. back** (*tears*) refouler; **to f. off** (*attacker, attack*) repousser; (*illness*) lutter contre; **to f. it out** se bagarrer. ◆**—ing** *n Mil* combat(s) *m*(*pl*); – *a* (*person*) combatif; (*troops*) de combat. ◆**—er** *n* combattant, -ante *mf*; *Boxing* boxeur *m*; *Fig* battant *m*, lutteur, -euse *mf*; (*aircraft*) chasseur *m*.

figment ['fɪgmənt] *n* **a f. of one's imagination** une création de son esprit.

figurative ['fɪgjʊrətɪv] *a* (*meaning*) figuré; (*art*) figuratif. ◆**—ly** *adv* au figuré.

figure¹ ['fɪgər, *Am* 'fɪgjər] *n* **1** (*numeral*) chiffre *m*; (*price*) prix *m*; *pl* (*arithmetic*) calcul *m*. **2** (*shape*) forme *f*; (*outlined shape*) silhouette *f*; (*of woman*) ligne *f*; **she has a nice f.** elle est bien faite. **3** (*diagram*) & *Liter* figure *f*; **a f. of speech** une figure de rhétorique; *Fig* une façon de parler; **f. of eight**, *Am* **f. eight** huit *m*; **f. skating** patinage *m* artistique. **4** (*important person*) figure *f*, personnage *m*. ◆**figurehead** *n Nau* figure *f* de proue; (*person*) *Fig* potiche *f*.

figure² ['fɪgər, *Am* 'fɪgjər] **1** *vt* (*imagine*) (s')imaginer; (*guess*) penser (**that** que); **to f. out** arriver à comprendre; (*problem*) résoudre; – *vi* (*make sense*) s'expliquer; **to f. on doing** *Am* compter faire. **2** *vi* (*appear*) figurer (**on** sur).

filament ['fɪləmənt] *n* filament *m*.

filch [fɪltʃ] *vt* (*steal*) voler (**from** à).

fil/e [faɪl] **1** *n* (*tool*) lime *f*; – *vt* **to f. (down)** limer. **2** *n* (*folder, information*) dossier *m*; (*loose-leaf*) classeur *m*; (*for card index, computer data*) fichier *m*; – *vt* (*claim, application*) déposer; **to f. (away)** classer. **3** *n* **in single f.** en file; – *vi* **to f. in/out** entrer/sortir à la queue leu leu; **to f. past** (*coffin etc*) défiler devant. ◆**—ing 1** *a* **f. clerk** documentaliste *mf*; **f. cabinet** classeur *m*. **2** *npl* (*particles*) limaille *f*.

fill [fɪl] *vt* remplir (**with** de); (*tooth*) plomber; (*sail*) gonfler; (*need*) répondre à; **to f. in** (*form*) remplir; (*hole*) combler; (*door*) condamner; **to f. s.o. in on** *Fam* mettre qn au courant de; **to f. up** (*glass etc*) remplir; **to f. up** *or* **out** (*form*) remplir; – *vi* **to f. (up)** se remplir; **to f. out** (*get fatter*) grossir, se remplumer; **to f. up** *Aut* faire le plein; – *n* **to eat one's f.** manger à sa faim; **to have had one's f. of** *Pej* en avoir assez de. ◆**—ing** *a*

(*meal etc*) substantiel, nourrissant; – *n* (*in tooth*) plombage *m*; *Culin* garniture *f*; **f. station** poste *m* d'essence. ◆**—er** *n* (*for cracks in wood*) mastic *m*.
fillet ['fɪlɪt, *Am* fɪ'leɪ] *n Culin* filet *m*; – *vt* (*pt* & *pp Am* [fɪ'leɪd]) (*fish*) découper en filets; (*meat*) désosser.
fillip ['fɪlɪp] *n* (*stimulus*) coup *m* de fouet.
filly ['fɪlɪ] *n* (*horse*) pouliche *f*.
film [fɪlm] *n* film *m*; (*layer*) & *Phot* pellicule *f*; – *a* (*festival*) du film; (*studio, technician, critic*) de cinéma; **f. fan** *or* **buff** cinéphile *mf*; **f. library** cinémathèque *f*; **f. star** vedette *f* (de cinéma); – *vt* filmer.
filter ['fɪltər] *n* filtre *m*; (*traffic sign*) flèche *f*; **f. lane** *Aut* couloir *m* (pour tourner); **f. tip** (bout *m*) filtre *m*; **f.-tipped cigarette** cigarette *f* (à bout) filtre; – *vt* filtrer; – *vi* filtrer (**through sth** à travers qch); **to f. through** filtrer.
filth [fɪlθ] *n* saleté *f*; (*obscenities*) *Fig* saletés *fpl*. ◆**filthy** *a* (**-ier, -iest**) (*hands etc*) sale; (*language*) obscène; (*habit*) dégoûtant; **f. weather** un temps infect, un sale temps.
fin [fɪn] *n* (*of fish, seal*) nageoire *f*; (*of shark*) aileron *m*.
final ['faɪn(ə)l] *a* dernier; (*decision*) définitif; (*cause*) final; – *n Sp* finale *f*; *pl Univ* examens *mpl* de dernière année. ◆**finalist** *n Sp* finaliste *mf*. ◆**finalize** *vt* (*plan*) mettre au point; (*date*) fixer (définitivement). ◆**finally** *adv* (*lastly*) enfin, en dernier lieu; (*eventually*) finalement, enfin; (*once and for all*) définitivement.
finale [fɪ'nɑːlɪ] *n Mus* finale *m*.
finance ['faɪnæns] *n* finance *f*; – *a* (*company, page*) financier; – *vt* financer. ◆**fi'nancial** *a* financier; **f. year** année *f* budgétaire. ◆**fi'nancially** *adv* financièrement. ◆**fi'nancier** *n* (grand) financier *m*.
find [faɪnd] *n* (*discovery*) trouvaille *f*; – *vt* (*pt* & *pp* **found**) trouver; (*sth or s.o. lost*) retrouver; (*difficulty*) éprouver, trouver (**in doing** à faire); **I f. that** je trouve que; **£20 all found** 20 livres logé et nourri; **to f. s.o. guilty** *Jur* prononcer qn coupable; **to f. one's feet** (*settle in*) s'adapter; **to f. oneself** (*to be*) se trouver. ■ **to f. out** *vt* (*information etc*) découvrir; (*person*) démasquer; – *vi* (*enquire*) se renseigner (**about** sur); **to f. out about** (*discover*) découvrir. ◆**—ings** *npl* conclusions *fpl*.
fine[1] [faɪn] *n* (*money*) amende *f*; *Aut* contravention *f*; – *vt* **to f. s.o.** (**£10**/*etc*) infliger une amende (de dix livres/*etc*) à qn.
fine[2] [faɪn] **1** *a* (**-er, -est**) (*thin, small, not coarse*) fin; (*gold*) pur; (*feeling*) délicat; (*distinction*) subtil; – *adv* (*to cut, write*) menu. **2** *a* (**-er, -est**) (*beautiful*) beau; (*good*) bon; (*excellent*) excellent; **to be f.** (*in good health*) aller bien; – *adv* (*well*) très bien. ◆**—ly** *adv* (*dressed*) magnifiquement; (*chopped*) menu; (*embroidered, ground*) finement.
finery ['faɪnərɪ] *n* (*clothes*) parure *f*, belle toilette *f*.
finesse [fɪ'nes] *n* (*skill, tact*) doigté *m*; (*refinement*) finesse *f*.
finger ['fɪŋgər] *n* doigt *m*; **little f.** auriculaire *m*, petit doigt *m*; **middle f.** majeur *m*; **f. mark** trace *f* de doigt; – *vt* toucher (des doigts), palper. ◆**—ing** *n Mus* doigté *m*. ◆**fingernail** *n* ongle *m*. ◆**fingerprint** *n* empreinte *f* digitale. ◆**fingerstall** *n* doigtier *m*. ◆**fingertip** *n* bout *m* du doigt.
finicky ['fɪnɪkɪ] *a* (*precise*) méticuleux; (*difficult*) difficile (**about** sur).
finish ['fɪnɪʃ] *n* (*end*) fin *f*; *Sp* arrivée *f*; (*of article, car etc*) finition *f*; **paint with a matt f.** peinture *f* mate; – *vt* **to f.** (**off** *or* **up**) finir, terminer; **to f. doing** finir de faire; **to f. s.o. off** (*kill*) achever qn; – *vi* (*of meeting etc*) finir, se terminer; (*of person*) finir, terminer; **to f. first** terminer premier; (*in race*) arriver premier; **to have finished with** (*object*) ne plus avoir besoin de; (*situation, person*) en avoir fini avec; **to f. off** *or* **up** (*of person*) finir, terminer; **to f. up in** (*end up in*) se retrouver à; **to f. up doing** finir par faire; **finishing school** institution *f* pour jeunes filles; **finishing touch** touche *f* finale. ◆**—ed** *a* (*ended, done for*) fini.
finite ['faɪnaɪt] *a* fini.
Finland ['fɪnlənd] *n* Finlande *f*. ◆**Finn** *n* Finlandais, -aise *mf*, Finnois, -oise *mf*. ◆**Finnish** *a* finlandais, finnois; – *n* (*language*) finnois *m*.
fir [fɜːr] *n* (*tree, wood*) sapin *m*.
fire[1] ['faɪər] *n* feu *m*; (*accidental*) incendie *m*; (*electric*) radiateur *m*; **on f.** en feu; (**there's a**) **f.!** au feu!; **f.!** *Mil* feu!; **f. alarm** avertisseur *m* d'incendie; **f. brigade**, *Am* **f. department** pompiers *mpl*; **f. engine** (*vehicle*) voiture *f* de pompiers; (*machine*) pompe *f* à incendie; **f. escape** escalier *m* de secours; **f. station** caserne *f* de pompiers. ◆**firearm** *n* arme *f* à feu. ◆**firebug** *n* pyromane *mf*. ◆**firecracker** *n Am* pétard *m*. ◆**fireguard** *n* garde-feu *m inv*. ◆**fireman** *n* (*pl* **-men**) (sapeur-)pompier *m*. ◆**fireplace** *n* cheminée *f*. ◆**fireproof** *a* (*door*) ignifugé, anti-incendie. ◆**fireside** *n* coin *m* du feu; **f. chair** fauteuil *m*. ◆**firewood** *n* bois *m* de chauffage.

◆**firework** *n* feu *m* d'artifice; **a f. display, fireworks,** un feu d'artifice.

fire² ['faɪər] *vt* (*cannon*) tirer; (*pottery*) cuire; (*imagination*) enflammer; **to f. a gun** tirer un coup de fusil; **to f. questions at** bombarder de questions; **to f. s.o.** (*dismiss*) *Fam* renvoyer qn; – *vi* tirer (**at** sur); **f. away!** *Fam* vas-y, parle!; **firing squad** peloton *m* d'exécution; **in** *or Am* **on the firing line** en butte aux attaques.

firm [fɜːm] **1** *n Com* maison *f*, firme *f*. **2** *a* (**-er, -est**) (*earth, decision etc*) ferme; (*strict*) ferme (**with** avec); (*faith*) solide; (*character*) résolu. ◆**—ly** *adv* fermement; (*to speak*) d'une voix ferme. ◆**—ness** *n* fermeté *f*; (*of faith*) solidité *f*.

first [fɜːst] *a* premier; **I'll do it f. thing in the morning** je le ferai dès le matin, sans faute; **f. cousin** cousin, -ine *mf* germain(e); – *adv* d'abord, premièrement; (*for the first time*) pour la première fois; **f. of all** tout d'abord; **at f.** d'abord; **to come f.** (*in race*) arriver premier; (*in exam*) être le premier; – *n* premier, -ière *mf*; *Univ* = licence *f* avec mention très bien; **from the f.** dès le début; **f. aid** premiers soins *mpl or* secours *mpl*; **f. (gear)** *Aut* première *f*. ◆**f.-'class** *a* (*ticket etc*) de première (classe); (*mail*) ordinaire; – *adv* (*to travel*) en première. ◆**f.-'hand** *a & adv* de première main; **to have (had) f.-hand experience of** avoir fait l'expérience personnelle de. ◆**f.-'rate** *a* excellent. ◆**firstly** *adv* premièrement.

fiscal ['fɪsk(ə)l] *a* fiscal.

fish [fɪʃ] *n* (*pl inv or* **-es** [-ɪz]) poisson *m*; **f. market** marché *m* aux poissons; **f. bone** arête *f*; **f. bowl** bocal *m*; **f. fingers,** *Am* **f. sticks** *Culin* bâtonnets *mpl* de poisson; **f. shop** poissonnerie *f*; – *vi* pêcher; **to f. for** (*salmon etc*) pêcher; (*compliment etc*) *Fig* chercher; – *vt* **to f. out** (*from water*) repêcher; (*from pocket etc*) *Fig* sortir. ◆**—ing** *n* pêche *f*; **to go f.** aller à la pêche; **f. net** (*of fisherman*) filet *m* (de pêche); (*of angler*) épuisette *f*; **f. rod** canne *f* à pêche. ◆**fisherman** *n* (*pl* **-men**) pêcheur *m*. ◆**fishmonger** *n* poissonnier, -ière *mf*. ◆**fishy** *a* (**-ier, -iest**) (*smell*) de poisson; *Fig Pej* louche.

fission ['fɪʃ(ə)n] *n Phys* fission *f*.

fissure ['fɪʃər] *n* fissure *f*.

fist [fɪst] *n* poing *m*. ◆**fistful** *n* poignée *f*.

fit¹ [fɪt] **1** *a* (**fitter, fittest**) (*suited*) propre, bon (**for** à); (*fitting*) convenable; (*worthy*) digne (**for** de); (*able*) capable (**for** de, **to do** de faire); (*healthy*) en bonne santé; **f. to eat** bon à manger, mangeable; **to see f. to do** juger à propos de faire; **as you see f.** comme bon vous semble; **f. to drop** *Fam* prêt à tomber; **to keep f.** se maintenir en forme. **2** *vt* (**-tt-**) (*of coat etc*) aller (bien) à (*qn*), être à la taille de (*qn*); (*match*) répondre à; (*equal*) égaler; **to f. sth on s.o.** (*garment*) ajuster qch à qn; **to f. sth (on) to sth** (*put*) poser qch sur qch; (*adjust*) adapter qch à qch; (*fix*) fixer qch à qch; **to f. (out or up) with** (*house, ship etc*) équiper de; **to f. (in)** (*window*) poser; **to f. in** (*object*) faire entrer; (*patient, customer*) prendre; **to f. (in) the lock** (*of key*) aller dans la serrure; – *vi* (*of clothes*) aller (bien) (*à qn*); **this shirt fits** (*fits me*) cette chemise me va (bien); **to f. (in)** (*go in*) entrer, aller; (*of facts, plans*) s'accorder, cadrer (**with** avec); **he doesn't f. in** il ne peut pas s'intégrer; – *n* **a good f.** (*dress etc*) à la bonne taille; **a close** *or* **tight f.** ajusté. ◆**fitted** *a* (*cupboard*) encastré; (*garment*) ajusté; **f. carpet** moquette *f*; **f. (kitchen) units** éléments *mpl* de cuisine. ◆**fitting 1** *a* (*suitable*) convenable. **2** *n* (*of clothes*) essayage *m*; **f. room** salon *m* d'essayage; (*booth*) cabine *f* d'essayage. **3** *npl* (*in house etc*) installations *fpl*. ◆**fitment** *n* (*furniture*) meuble *m* encastré; (*accessory*) *Tech* accessoire *m*. ◆**fitness** *n* (*of remark etc*) à-propos *m*; (*for job*) aptitudes *fpl* (**for** pour); *Med* santé *f*. ◆**fitter** *n Tech* monteur, -euse *mf*.

fit² [fɪt] *n Med & Fig* accès *m*, crise *f*; **in fits and starts** par à-coups. ◆**fitful** *a* (*sleep*) agité.

five [faɪv] *a & n* cinq (*m*). ◆**fiver** *n Fam* billet *m* de cinq livres.

fix [fɪks] **1** *vt* (*make firm, decide*) fixer; (*tie with rope*) attacher; (*mend*) réparer; (*deal with*) arranger; (*prepare, cook*) *Am* préparer, faire; (*in s.o.'s mind*) graver (**in** dans); (*conduct fraudulently*) *Fam* truquer; (*bribe*) *Fam* acheter; (*hopes, ambitions*) mettre (**on** en); **to f. s.o.** (*punish*) *Fam* régler son compte à qn; **to f. (on)** (*lid etc*) mettre en place; **to f. up** arranger; **to f. s.o. up with sth** (*job etc*) procurer qch à qn. **2** *n Av Nau* position *f*; (*injection*) *Sl* piqûre *f*; **in a f.** *Fam* dans le pétrin. ◆**—ed** *a* (*idea, price etc*) fixe; (*resolution*) inébranlable; **how's he f. for ...?** *Fam* (*cash etc*) a-t-il assez de ...?; (*tomorrow etc*) qu'est-ce qu'il fait pour ...? ◆**fixings** *npl Culin Am* garniture *f*. ◆**fix'ation** *n* fixation *f*. ◆**fixer** *n* (*schemer*) *Fam* combinard, -arde *mf*. ◆**fixture 1** *n Sp* match *m* (prévu). **2** *npl* (*in house*) meubles *mpl* fixes, installations *fpl*.

fizz [fɪz] *vi* (*of champagne*) pétiller; (*of gas*) siffler. ◆**fizzy** *a* (-ier, -iest) pétillant.
fizzle ['fɪz(ə)l] *vi* (*hiss*) siffler; (*of liquid*) pétiller; **to f. out** (*of firework*) rater, faire long feu; (*of plan*) *Fig* tomber à l'eau; (*of custom*) disparaître.
flabbergasted ['flæbəgɑːstɪd] *a Fam* sidéré.
flabby ['flæbɪ] *a* (-ier, -iest) (*skin, character, person*) mou, flasque.
flag [flæg] **1** *n* drapeau *m*; *Nau* pavillon *m*; (*for charity*) insigne *m*; **f. stop** *Am* arrêt *m* facultatif; – *vt* (-gg-) **to f. down** (*taxi*) faire signe à. **2** *vi* (-gg-) (*of plant*) dépérir; (*of conversation*) languir; (*of worker*) fléchir. ◆**flagpole** *n* mât *m*.
flagrant ['fleɪgrənt] *a* flagrant.
flagstone ['flægstəʊn] *n* dalle *f*.
flair [fleər] *n* (*intuition*) flair *m*; **to have a f. for** (*natural talent*) avoir un don pour.
flake [fleɪk] *n* (*of snow etc*) flocon *m*; (*of metal, soap*) paillette *f*; – *vi* **to f. (off)** (*of paint*) s'écailler. ◆**flaky** *a* **f. pastry** pâte *f* feuilletée.
flamboyant [flæm'bɔɪənt] *a* (*person, manner*) extravagant.
flam/e [fleɪm] *n* flamme *f*; **to go up in flames** s'enflammer; – *vi* **to f. (up)** (*of fire, house*) flamber. ◆**—ing** *a* **1** (*sun*) flamboyant. **2** (*damn*) *Fam* fichu.
flamingo [flə'mɪŋgəʊ] *n* (*pl* -os *or* -oes) (*bird*) flamant *m*.
flammable ['flæməb(ə)l] *a* inflammable.
flan [flæn] *n* tarte *f*.
flank [flæŋk] *n* flanc *m*; – *vt* flanquer (**with** de).
flannel ['flænəl] *n* (*cloth*) flanelle *f*; (**face**) **f.** gant *m* de toilette, carré-éponge *m*. ◆**flanne'lette** *n* pilou *m*, finette *f*.
flap [flæp] **1** *vi* (-pp-) (*of wings, sail, shutter etc*) battre; – *vt* **to f. its wings** (*of bird*) battre des ailes; – *n* battement *m*. **2** *n* (*of pocket, envelope*) rabat *m*; (*of table*) abattant *m*; (*of door*) battant *m*.
flare [fleər] *n* (*light*) éclat *m*; *Mil* fusée *f* éclairante; (*for runway*) balise *f*; – *vi* (*blaze*) flamber; (*shine*) briller; **to f. up** (*of fire*) s'enflammer; (*of region*) *Fig* s'embraser; (*of war*) éclater; (*get angry*) s'emporter. ◆**f.-up** *n* (*of violence, fire*) flambée *f*; (*of region*) embrasement *m*. ◆**flared** *a* (*skirt*) évasé; (*trousers*) à pattes d'éléphant.
flash [flæʃ] *n* (*of light*) éclat *m*; (*of anger, genius*) éclair *m*; *Phot* flash *m*; **f. of lightning** éclair *m*; **news f.** flash *m*; **in a f.** en un clin d'œil; – *vi* (*shine*) briller; (*on and off*) clignoter; **to f. past** (*rush*) *Fig* passer comme un éclair; – *vt* (*aim*) diriger (**on, at** sur); (*a light*) projeter; (*a glance*) jeter; **to f. (around)** (*flaunt*) étaler; **to f. one's headlights** faire un appel de phares. ◆**flashback** *n* retour *m* en arrière. ◆**flashlight** *n* lampe *f* électrique *or* de poche; *Phot* flash *m*.
flashy ['flæʃɪ] *a* (-ier, -iest) *a* voyant, tape-à-l'œil *inv*.
flask [flɑːsk] *n* thermos® *m or f inv*; *Ch* flacon *m*; (*phial*) fiole *f*.
flat[1] [flæt] *a* (**flatter, flattest**) plat; (*tyre, battery*) à plat; (*nose*) aplati; (*beer*) éventé; (*refusal*) net; (*rate, fare*) fixe; (*voice*) *Mus* faux; (*razed to the ground*) rasé; **to put sth (down) f.** mettre qch à plat; **f. (on one's face)** à plat ventre; **to fall f.** *Fig* tomber à plat; **to be f.-footed** avoir les pieds plats; – *adv* (*to say*) carrément; (*to sing*) faux; **f. broke** *Fam* complètement fauché; **in two minutes f.** en deux minutes pile; **f. out** (*to work*) d'arrache-pied; (*to run*) à toute vitesse; – *n* (*of hand*) plat *m*; (*puncture*) *Aut* crevaison *f*; *Mus* bémol *m*. ◆**—ly** *adv* (*to deny etc*) catégoriquement. ◆**—ness** *n* (*of surface*) égalité *f*. ◆**flatten** *vt* (*crops*) coucher; (*town*) raser; **to f. (out)** (*metal etc*) aplatir.
flat[2] [flæt] *n* (*rooms*) appartement *m*.
flatter ['flætər] *vt* flatter; (*of clothes*) avantager (*qn*). ◆**—ing** *a* flatteur; (*clothes*) avantageux. ◆**—er** *n* flatteur, -euse *mf*. ◆**flattery** *n* flatterie *f*.
flatulence ['flætjʊləns] *n* **to have f.** avoir des gaz.
flaunt [flɔːnt] *vt* (*show off*) faire étalage de; (*defy*) *Am* narguer, défier.
flautist ['flɔːtɪst] *n* flûtiste *mf*.
flavour ['fleɪvər] *n* (*taste*) goût *m*, saveur *f*; (*of ice cream, sweet etc*) parfum *m*; – *vt* (*food*) assaisonner; (*sauce*) relever; (*ice cream etc*) parfumer (**with** à). ◆**—ing** *n* assaisonnement *m*; (*in cake*) parfum *m*.
flaw [flɔː] *n* défaut *m*. ◆**flawed** *a* imparfait. ◆**flawless** *a* parfait.
flax [flæks] *n* lin *m*. ◆**flaxen** *a* de lin.
flay [fleɪ] *vt* (*animal*) écorcher; (*criticize*) *Fig* éreinter.
flea [fliː] *n* puce *f*; **f. market** marché *m* aux puces. ◆**fleapit** *n Fam* cinéma *m* miteux.
fleck [flek] *n* (*mark*) petite tache *f*.
fledgling ['fledʒlɪŋ] *n* (*novice*) blanc-bec *m*.
flee [fliː] *vi* (*pt & pp* **fled**) fuir, s'enfuir, se sauver; – *vt* (*place*) s'enfuir de; (*danger etc*) fuir.
fleece [fliːs] **1** *n* (*sheep's coat*) toison *f*. **2** *vt* (*rob*) voler.

fleet [fliːt] *n* (*of ships*) flotte *f*; **a f. of cars** un parc automobile.
fleeting ['fliːtɪŋ] *a* (*visit, moment*) bref; (*beauty*) éphémère.
Flemish ['flemɪʃ] *a* flamand; – *n* (*language*) flamand *m*.
flesh [fleʃ] *n* chair *f*; **her (own) f. and blood** la chair de sa chair; **in the f.** en chair et en os; **f. wound** blessure *f* superficielle. ◆**fleshy** *a* (**-ier, -iest**) charnu.
flew [fluː] *see* **fly**².
flex [fleks] **1** *vt* (*limb*) fléchir; (*muscle*) faire jouer, bander. **2** *n* (*wire*) fil *m* (souple); (*for telephone*) cordon *m*.
flexible ['fleksɪb(ə)l] *a* flexible, souple. ◆**flexi'bility** *n* flexibilité *f*.
flick [flɪk] *vt* donner un petit coup à; **to f. off** (*remove*) enlever (d'une chiquenaude); – *vi* **to f. over** *or* **through** (*pages*) feuilleter; – *n* petit coup *m*; (*with finger*) chiquenaude *f*; **f. knife** couteau *m* à cran d'arrêt.
flicker ['flɪkər] *vi* (*of flame, light*) vaciller; (*of needle*) osciller; – *n* vacillement *m*; **f. of light** lueur *f*.
flier ['flaɪər] *n* **1** (*person*) aviateur, -trice *mf*. **2** (*handbill*) *Am* prospectus *m*, *Pol* tract *m*.
flies [flaɪz] *npl* (*on trousers*) braguette *f*.
flight [flaɪt] *n* **1** (*of bird, aircraft etc*) vol *m*; (*of bullet*) trajectoire *f*; (*of imagination*) élan *m*; (*floor, storey*) étage *m*; **f. of stairs** escalier *m*; **f. deck** cabine *f* de pilotage. **2** (*fleeing*) fuite *f* (**from** de); **to take f.** prendre la fuite.
flighty ['flaɪtɪ] *a* (**-ier, -iest**) inconstant, volage.
flimsy ['flɪmzɪ] *a* (**-ier, -iest**) (*cloth, structure etc*) (trop) léger *or* mince; (*excuse*) mince, frivole.
flinch [flɪntʃ] *vi* (*with pain*) tressaillir; **to f. from** (*duty etc*) se dérober à; **without flinching** (*complaining*) sans broncher.
fling [flɪŋ] **1** *vt* (*pt & pp* **flung**) jeter, lancer; **to f. open** (*door etc*) ouvrir brutalement. **2** *n* **to have one's** *or* **a f.** (*indulge oneself*) s'en donner à cœur joie.
flint [flɪnt] *n* silex *m*; (*for cigarette lighter*) pierre *f*.
flip [flɪp] **1** *vt* (**-pp-**) (*with finger*) donner une chiquenaude à; – *vi* **to f. through** (*book etc*) feuilleter; – *n* chiquenaude *f*; **the f. side** (*of record*) la face deux. **2** *a* (*cheeky*) *Am Fam* effronté.
flip-flops ['flɪpflɒps] *npl* tongs *fpl*.
flippant ['flɪpənt] *a* irrévérencieux; (*offhand*) désinvolte.
flipper ['flɪpər] *n* (*of seal*) nageoire *f*; (*of swimmer*) palme *f*.
flipping ['flɪpɪŋ] *a Fam* sacré; – *adv Fam* sacrément, bougrement.
flirt [flɜːt] *vi* flirter (**with** avec); – *n* flirteur, -euse *mf*. ◆**flir'tation** *n* flirt *m*. ◆**flir'tatious** *a* flirteur.
flit [flɪt] *vi* (**-tt-**) (*fly*) voltiger; **to f. in and out** (*of person*) *Fig* entrer et sortir (rapidement).
float [fləʊt] *n Fishing* flotteur *m*; (*in parade*) char *m*; – *vi* flotter (**on** sur); **to f. down the river** descendre la rivière; – *vt* (*boat, currency*) faire flotter; (*loan*) *Com* émettre. ◆**—ing** *a* (*wood, debt etc*) flottant; (*population*) instable; (*voters*) indécis.
flock [flɒk] *n* (*of sheep etc*) troupeau *m*; (*of birds*) volée *f*; *Rel Hum* ouailles *fpl*; (*of tourists etc*) foule *f*; – *vi* venir en foule; **to f. round s.o.** s'attrouper autour de qn.
floe [fləʊ] *n* (**ice**) **f.** banquise *f*.
flog [flɒg] *vt* (**-gg-**) **1** (*beat*) flageller. **2** (*sell*) *Sl* vendre. ◆**flogging** *n* flagellation *f*.
flood [flʌd] *n* inondation *f*; (*of letters, tears etc*) *Fig* flot *m*, déluge *m*, torrent *m*; – *vt* (*field etc*) inonder (**with** de); (*river*) faire déborder; **to f. (out)** (*house*) inonder; – *vi* (*of building*) être inondé; (*of river*) déborder; (*of people, money*) affluer; **to f. into** (*of tourists etc*) envahir. ◆**—ing** *n* inondation *f*. ◆**floodgate** *n* (*in water*) vanne *f*.
floodlight ['flʌdlaɪt] *n* projecteur *m*; – *vt* (*pt & pp* **floodlit**) illuminer; **floodlit match** *Sp* (match *m* en) nocturne *m*.
floor [flɔːr] **1** *n* (*ground*) sol *m*; (*wooden etc in building*) plancher *m*; (*storey*) étage *m*; (**dance**) **f.** piste *f* (de danse); **on the f.** par terre; **first f.** premier étage *m*; (*ground floor*) *Am* rez-de-chaussée *m inv*; **f. polish** encaustique *f*; **f. show** spectacle *m* (de cabaret). **2** *vt* (*knock down*) terrasser; (*puzzle*) stupéfier. ◆**floorboard** *n* planche *f*.
flop [flɒp] **1** *vi* (**-pp-**) **to f. down** (*collapse*) s'effondrer; **to f. about** s'agiter mollement. **2** *vi* (**-pp-**) *Fam* échouer; (*of play, film etc*) faire un four; – *n Fam* échec *m*, fiasco *m*; *Th Cin* four *m*.
floppy ['flɒpɪ] *a* (**-ier, -iest**) (*soft*) mou; (*clothes*) (trop) large; (*ears*) pendant; **f. disk** (*of computer*) disquette *f*.
flora ['flɔːrə] *n* (*plants*) flore *f*. ◆**floral** *a* floral; (*material*) à fleurs.
florid ['flɒrɪd] *a* (*style*) fleuri; (*complexion*) rougeaud, fleuri.
florist ['flɒrɪst] *n* fleuriste *mf*.
floss [flɒs] *n* (**dental**) **f.** fil *m* (de soie) dentaire.
flotilla [flə'tɪlə] *n Nau* flottille *f*.

flounce [flaʊns] *n* (*frill on dress etc*) volant *m*.

flounder ['flaʊndər] **1** *vi* (*in water etc*) patauger (avec effort), se débattre; (*in speech*) hésiter, patauger. **2** *n* (*fish*) carrelet *m*.

flour ['flaʊər] *n* farine *f*.

flourish ['flʌrɪʃ] **1** *vi* (*of person, business, plant etc*) prospérer; (*of the arts*) fleurir. **2** *vt* (*wave*) brandir. **3** *n* (*decoration*) fioriture *f*; *Mus* fanfare *f*. ◆**—ing** *a* prospère, florissant.

flout [flaʊt] *vt* narguer, braver.

flow [fləʊ] *vi* couler; (*of current*) *El* circuler; (*of hair, clothes*) flotter; (*of traffic*) s'écouler; **to f. in** (*of people, money*) affluer; **to f. back** refluer; **to f. into the sea** se jeter dans la mer; – *n* (*of river*) courant *m*; (*of tide*) flux *m*; (*of blood*) & *El* circulation *f*; (*of traffic, liquid*) écoulement *m*; (*of words*) *Fig* flot *m*. ◆**—ing** *a* (*movement*) gracieux; (*style*) coulant; (*beard*) flottant.

flower ['flaʊər] *n* fleur *f*; **f. bed** plate-bande *f*; **f. shop** (boutique *f* de) fleuriste *mf*; **f. show** floralies *fpl*; – *vi* fleurir. ◆**—ed** *a* (*dress*) à fleurs. ◆**—ing** *n* floraison *f*; – *a* (*in bloom*) en fleurs; (*with flowers*) à fleurs. ◆**flowery** *a* (*style etc*) fleuri; (*material*) à fleurs.

flown [fləʊn] *see* fly².

flu [fluː] *n* (*influenza*) *Fam* grippe *f*.

fluctuate ['flʌktʃʊeɪt] *vi* varier. ◆**fluctu'ation(s)** *n*(*pl*) (*in prices etc*) fluctuations *fpl* (in de).

flue [fluː] *n* (*of chimney*) conduit *m*.

fluent ['fluːənt] *a* (*style*) aisé; **to be f., be a f. speaker** s'exprimer avec facilité; **he's f. in Russian, his Russian is f.** il parle couramment le russe. ◆**fluency** *n* facilité *f*. ◆**fluently** *adv* avec facilité; (*to speak*) *Ling* couramment.

fluff [flʌf] **1** *n* (*down*) duvet *m*; (*of material*) peluche(s) *f*(*pl*); (*on floor*) moutons *mpl*. **2** *vt* (*bungle*) *Fam* rater. ◆**fluffy** *a* (-ier, -iest) (*bird etc*) duveteux; (*material*) pelucheux; (*toy*) en peluche; (*hair*) bouffant.

fluid ['fluːɪd] *a* fluide; (*plans*) flexible, non arrêté; – *n* fluide *m*, liquide *m*.

fluke [fluːk] *n Fam* coup *m* de chance; **by a f.** par raccroc.

flummox ['flʌməks] *vt Fam* désorienter, dérouter.

flung [flʌŋ] *see* **fling 1**.

flunk [flʌŋk] *vi* (*in exam*) *Am Fam* être collé; – *vt Am Fam* (*pupil*) coller; (*exam*) être collé à; (*school*) laisser tomber.

flunk(e)y ['flʌŋkɪ] *n Pej* larbin *m*.

fluorescent [fluə'res(ə)nt] *a* fluorescent.

fluoride ['fluəraɪd] *n* (*in water, toothpaste*) fluor *m*.

flurry ['flʌrɪ] *n* **1** (*of activity*) poussée *f*. **2** (*of snow*) rafale *f*.

flush [flʌʃ] **1** *n* (*of blood*) flux *m*; (*blush*) rougeur *f*; (*of youth, beauty*) éclat *m*; (*of victory*) ivresse *f*; – *vi* (*blush*) rougir. **2** *vt* to **f.** (**out**) (*clean*) nettoyer à grande eau; **to f. the pan** *or* **the toilet** tirer la chasse d'eau; **to f. s.o. out** (*chase away*) faire sortir qn (from de). **3** *a* (*level*) de niveau (**with** de); **f.** (**with money**) *Fam* bourré de fric. ◆**—ed** *a* (*cheeks etc*) rouge; **f. with** (*success*) ivre de.

fluster ['flʌstər] *vt* énerver; **to get flustered** s'énerver.

flute [fluːt] *n* flûte *f*. ◆**flutist** *n Am* flûtiste *mf*.

flutter ['flʌtər] **1** *vi* voltiger; (*of wing*) battre; (*of flag*) flotter (mollement); (*of heart*) palpiter; **to f. about** (*of person*) papillonner; – *vt* **to f. its wings** battre des ailes. **2** *n* **to have a f.** (*bet*) *Fam* parier.

flux [flʌks] *n* changement *m* continuel.

fly¹ [flaɪ] *n* (*insect*) mouche *f*; **f. swatter** (*instrument*) tapette *f*. ◆**flypaper** *n* papier *m* tue-mouches.

fly² [flaɪ] *vi* (*pt* **flew**, *pp* **flown**) (*of bird, aircraft etc*) voler; (*of passenger*) aller en avion; (*of time*) passer vite; (*of flag*) flotter; (*flee*) fuir; **to f. away** *or* **off** s'envoler; **to f. out** *Av* partir en avion; (*from room*) sortir à toute vitesse; **I must f.!** il faut que je file!; **to f. at s.o.** (*attack*) sauter sur qn; – *vt* (*aircraft*) piloter; (*passengers*) transporter (par avion); (*airline*) voyager par; (*flag*) arborer; (*kite*) faire voler; **to f. the French flag** battre pavillon français; **to f. across** *or* **over** survoler. ◆**—ing** *n* (*flight*) vol *m*; (*air travel*) aviation *f*; **to like f.** aimer l'avion; – *a* (*personnel, saucer etc*) volant; (*visit*) éclair *inv*; **with f. colours** (*to succeed*) haut la main; **a f. start** un très bon départ; **f. time** (*length*) *Av* durée *f* du vol; **ten hours'/***etc* **f. time** dix heures/*etc* de vol. ◆**—er** *n* = **flier**. ◆**flyby** *n Av Am* défilé *m* aérien. ◆**fly-by-night** *a* (*firm*) véreux. ◆**flyover** *n* (*bridge*) toboggan *m*. ◆**flypast** *n Av* défilé *m* aérien.

fly³ [flaɪ] *n* (*on trousers*) braguette *f*.

foal [fəʊl] *n* poulain *m*.

foam [fəʊm] *n* (*on sea, mouth*) écume *f*; (*on beer*) mousse *f*; **f. rubber** caoutchouc *m* mousse; **f.** (**rubber**) **mattress/***etc* matelas *m*/*etc* mousse; – *vi* (*of sea, mouth*) écumer; (*of beer, soap*) mousser.

fob [fɒb] *vt* (-bb-) **to f. sth off on s.o., f. s.o. off with sth,** refiler qch à qn.
focal ['fəʊk(ə)l] *a* focal; **f. point** point *m* central. ◆**focus** *n* foyer *m*; (*of attention, interest*) centre *m*; **in f.** au point; – *vt Phot* mettre au point; (*light*) faire converger; (*efforts, attention*) concentrer (**on** sur); – *vi* (*converge*) converger (**on** sur); **to f. (one's eyes) on** fixer les yeux sur; **to f. on** (*direct one's attention to*) se concentrer sur.
fodder ['fɒdər] *n* fourrage *m*.
foe [fəʊ] *n* ennemi, -ie *mf*.
foetus ['fiːtəs] *n* fœtus *m*.
fog [fɒg] *n* brouillard *m*, brume *f*; – *vt* (-gg-) (*issue*) *Fig* embrouiller. ◆**fogbound** *a* bloqué par le brouillard. ◆**foghorn** *n* corne *f* de brume; (*voice*) *Pej* voix *f* tonitruante. ◆**foglamp** *n* (phare *m*) anti-brouillard *m*. ◆**foggy** *a* (-ier, -iest) (*day*) de brouillard; **it's f.** il fait du brouillard; **f. weather** brouillard *m*; **she hasn't the foggiest (idea)** *Fam* elle n'en a pas la moindre idée.
fog(e)y ['fəʊgɪ] *n* **old f.** vieille baderne *f*.
foible ['fɔɪb(ə)l] *n* petit défaut *m*.
foil [fɔɪl] **1** *n* feuille *f* de métal; *Culin* papier *m* alu(minium). **2** *n* (*contrasting person*) repoussoir *m*. **3** *vt* (*plans etc*) déjouer.
foist [fɔɪst] *vt* **to f. sth on s.o.** (*fob off*) refiler qch à qn; **to f. oneself on s.o.** s'imposer à qn.
fold[1] [fəʊld] *n* pli *m*; – *vt* plier; (*wrap*) envelopper (**in** dans); **to f. away** *or* **down** *or* **up** plier; **to f. back** *or* **over** replier; **to f. one's arms** (se) croiser les bras; – *vi* (*of chair etc*) se plier; (*of business*) *Fam* s'écrouler; **to f. away** *or* **down** *or* **up** (*of chair etc*) se plier; **to f. back** *or* **over** (*of blanket etc*) se replier. ◆**—ing** *a* (*chair etc*) pliant. ◆**—er** *n* (*file holder*) chemise *f*; (*pamphlet*) dépliant *m*.
fold[2] [fəʊld] *n* (*for sheep*) parc *m* à moutons; *Rel Fig* bercail *m*.
-fold [fəʊld] *suffix* **tenfold** *a* par dix; – *adv* dix fois.
foliage ['fəʊlɪɪdʒ] *n* feuillage *m*.
folk [fəʊk] **1** *n* gens *mpl or fpl*; *pl* gens *mpl or fpl*; (*parents*) *Fam* parents *mpl*; **hello folks!** *Fam* salut tout le monde!; **old f. like it** les vieux l'apprécient. **2** *a* (*dance etc*) folklorique; **f. music** (*contemporary*) (musique *f*) folk *m*. ◆**folklore** *n* folklore *m*.
follow ['fɒləʊ] *vt* suivre; (*career*) poursuivre; **followed by** suivi de; **to f. suit** *Fig* en faire autant; **to f. s.o. around** suivre qn partout; **to f. through** (*idea etc*) poursuivre jusqu'au bout; **to f. up** (*suggestion, case*) suivre; (*advantage*) exploiter; (*letter*) donner suite à; (*remark*) faire suivre (**with** de); – *vi* **to f. (on)** suivre; **it follows that** il s'ensuit que; **that doesn't f.** ce n'est pas logique. ◆**—ing 1** *a* suivant; – *prep* à la suite de. **2** *n* (*supporters*) partisans *mpl*; **to have a large f.** avoir de nombreux partisans; (*of serial, fashion*) être très suivi. ◆**—er** *n* partisan *m*. ◆**follow-up** *n* suite *f*; (*letter*) rappel *m*.
folly ['fɒlɪ] *n* folie *f*, sottise *f*.
foment [fəʊ'ment] *vt* (*revolt etc*) fomenter.
fond [fɒnd] *a* (-er, -est) (*loving*) tendre, affectueux; (*doting*) indulgent; (*wish, ambition*) naïf; **to be (very) f. of** aimer (beaucoup). ◆**—ly** *adv* tendrement. ◆**—ness** *n* (*for things*) prédilection *f* (**for** pour); (*for people*) affection *f* (**for** pour).
fondle ['fɒnd(ə)l] *vt* caresser.
food [fuːd] *n* nourriture *f*; (*particular substance*) aliment *m*; (*cooking*) cuisine *f*; (*for cats, pigs*) pâtée *f*; (*for plants*) engrais *m*; *pl* (*foodstuffs*) aliments *mpl*; – *a* (*needs etc*) alimentaire; **a fast f. shop** un fast-food; **f. poisoning** intoxication *f* alimentaire; **f. value** valeur *f* nutritive. ◆**foodstuffs** *npl* denrées *fpl or* produits *mpl* alimentaires.
fool [fuːl] *n* imbécile *mf*, idiot, -ote *mf*; **(you) silly f.!** espèce d'imbécile!; **to make a f. of** (*ridicule*) ridiculiser; (*trick*) duper; **to be f. enough to do** être assez stupide pour faire; **to play the f.** faire l'imbécile; – *vt* (*trick*) duper; – *vi* **to f. (about** *or* **around)** faire l'imbécile; (*waste time*) perdre son temps; **to f. around** (*make love*) *Am Fam* faire l'amour (**with** avec). ◆**foolish** *a* bête, idiot. ◆**foolishly** *adv* bêtement. ◆**foolishness** *n* bêtise *f*, sottise *f*. ◆**foolproof** *a* (*scheme etc*) infaillible.
foolhardy ['fuːlhɑːdɪ] *a* téméraire. ◆**foolhardiness** *n* témérité *f*.
foot[1], *pl* **feet** [fʊt, fiːt] *n* pied *m*; (*of animal*) patte *f*; (*measure*) pied *m* (= *30,48 cm*); **at the f. of** (*page, stairs*) au bas de; (*table*) au bout de; **on f.** à pied; **on one's feet** (*standing*) debout; (*recovered*) *Med* sur pied; **f. brake** *Aut* frein *m* au plancher; **f.-and-mouth disease** fièvre *f* aphteuse. ◆**footbridge** *n* passerelle *f*. ◆**foothills** *npl* contreforts *mpl*. ◆**foothold** *n* prise *f* (de pied); *Fig* position *f*; **to gain a f.** prendre pied. ◆**footlights** *npl Th* rampe *f*. ◆**footloose** *a* libre de toute attache. ◆**footman** *n* (*pl* -men) valet *m* de pied. ◆**footmark** *n* empreinte *f* (de pied). ◆**footnote** *n* note *f* au bas de la page; *Fig*

post-scriptum *m*. ◆**footpath** *n* sentier *m*; (*at roadside*) chemin *m* (piétonnier). ◆**footstep** *n* pas *m*; **to follow in s.o.'s footsteps** suivre les traces de qn. ◆**footwear** *n* chaussures *fpl*.

foot² [fʊt] *vt* (*bill*) payer.

football ['fʊtbɔːl] *n* (*game*) football *m*; (*ball*) ballon *m*. ◆**footballer** *n* joueur, -euse *mf* de football.

footing ['fʊtɪŋ] *n* prise *f* (de pied); *Fig* position *f*; **on a war f.** sur le pied de guerre; **on an equal f.** sur un pied d'égalité.

for [fɔr, *unstressed* fər] **1** *prep* pour; (*in exchange for*) contre; (*for a distance of*) pendant; (*in spite of*) malgré; **f. you/me/etc** pour toi/moi/*etc*; **what f.?** pourquoi?; **what's it f.?** ça sert à quoi?; **f. example** par exemple; **f. love** par amour; **f. sale** à vendre; **to swim f.** (*towards*) nager vers; **a train f.** un train à destination de *or* en direction de; **the road f. London** la route (en direction) de Londres; **fit f. eating** bon à manger; **eager f.** avide de; **to look f.** chercher; **to come f. dinner** venir dîner; **to sell f. £7** vendre sept livres; **what's the Russian f. 'book'?** comment dit-on 'livre' en russe?; **but f. her** sans elle; **he was away f. a month** (*throughout*) il a été absent pendant un mois; **he won't be back f. a month** il ne sera pas de retour avant un mois; **he's been here f. a month** (*he's still here*) il est ici depuis un mois; **I haven't seen him f. ten years** voilà dix ans que je ne l'ai vu; **it's easy f. her to do it** il lui est facile de le faire; **it's f. you to say** c'est à toi de dire; **f. that to be done** pour que ça soit fait. **2** *conj* (*because*) car.

forage ['fɒrɪdʒ] *vi* **to f. (about)** fourrager (**for** pour trouver).

foray ['fɒreɪ] *n* incursion *f*.

forbearance [fɔːˈbeərəns] *n* patience *f*.

forbid [fəˈbɪd] *vt* (*pt* **forbad(e)**, *pp* **forbidden**, *pres p* **forbidding**) interdire, défendre (**s.o. to do** à qn de faire); **to f. s.o. sth** interdire *or* défendre qch à qn. ◆**forbidden** *a* (*fruit etc*) défendu; **she is f. to leave** il lui est interdit de partir. ◆**forbidding** *a* menaçant, sinistre.

force [fɔːs] *n* force *f*; **the (armed) forces** *Mil* les forces armées; **by (sheer) f.** de force; **in f.** (*rule*) en vigueur; (*in great numbers*) en grand nombre, en force; – *vt* contraindre, forcer (**to do** à faire); (*impose*) imposer (**on** à); (*push*) pousser; (*lock*) forcer; (*confession*) arracher (**from** à); **to f. back** (*enemy etc*) faire reculer; (*repress*) refouler; **to f. down** (*aircraft*) forcer à atterrir; **to f. out** faire sortir de force. ◆**forced** *a* forcé (**to do** de faire); **a f. smile** un sourire forcé. ◆**force-feed** *vt* (*pt & pp* **f.-fed**) nourrir de force. ◆**forceful** *a* énergique, puissant. ◆**forcefully** *adv* avec force, énergiquement. ◆**forcible** *a* de force; (*forceful*) énergique. ◆**forcibly** *adv* (*by force*) de force.

forceps ['fɔːseps] *n* forceps *m*.

ford [fɔːd] *n* gué *m*; – *vt* (*river etc*) passer à gué.

fore [fɔːr] *n* **to come to the f.** se mettre en évidence.

forearm ['fɔːrɑːm] *n* avant-bras *m inv*.

forebod/e [fɔːˈbəʊd] *vt* (*be a warning of*) présager. ◆**—ing** *n* (*feeling*) pressentiment *m*.

forecast ['fɔːkɑːst] *vt* (*pt & pp* **forecast**) prévoir; – *n* prévision *f*; *Met* prévisions *fpl*; *Sp* pronostic *m*.

forecourt ['fɔːkɔːt] *n* avant-cour *f*; (*of filling station*) aire *f* (de service), devant *m*.

forefathers ['fɔːfɑːðəz] *npl* aïeux *mpl*.

forefinger ['fɔːfɪŋgər] *n* index *m*.

forefront ['fɔːfrʌnt] *n* **in the f. of** au premier rang de.

forego [fɔːˈgəʊ] *vt* (*pp* **foregone**) renoncer à. ◆**'foregone** *a* **it's a f. conclusion** c'est couru d'avance.

foregoing [fɔːˈgəʊɪŋ] *a* précédent.

foreground ['fɔːgraʊnd] *n* premier plan *m*.

forehead ['fɒrɪd, 'fɔːhed] *n* (*brow*) front *m*.

foreign ['fɒrən] *a* étranger; (*trade*) extérieur; (*travel, correspondent*) à l'étranger; (*produce*) de l'étranger; **F. Minister** ministre *m* des Affaires étrangères. ◆**foreigner** *n* étranger, -ère *mf*.

foreman ['fɔːmən] *n* (*pl* **-men**) (*worker*) contremaître *m*; (*of jury*) président *m*.

foremost ['fɔːməʊst] **1** *a* principal. **2** *adv* **first and f.** tout d'abord.

forensic [fəˈrensɪk] *a* (*medicine*) légal; (*laboratory*) médico-légal.

forerunner ['fɔːrʌnər] *n* précurseur *m*.

foresee [fɔːˈsiː] *vt* (*pt* **foresaw**, *pp* **foreseen**) prévoir. ◆**—able** *a* prévisible.

foreshadow [fɔːˈʃædəʊ] *vt* présager.

foresight ['fɔːsaɪt] *n* prévoyance *f*.

forest ['fɒrɪst] *n* forêt *f*. ◆**forester** *n* (garde *m*) forestier *m*.

forestall [fɔːˈstɔːl] *vt* devancer.

foretaste ['fɔːteɪst] *n* avant-goût *m*.

foretell [fɔːˈtel] *vt* (*pt & pp* **foretold**) prédire.

forethought ['fɔːθɔːt] *n* prévoyance *f*.

forever [fəˈrevər] *adv* (*for always*) pour toujours; (*continually*) sans cesse.

forewarn [fɔːˈwɔːn] *vt* avertir.

foreword ['fɔːwɜːd] *n* avant-propos *m inv.*
forfeit ['fɔːfɪt] *vt* (*lose*) perdre; – *n* (*penalty*) peine *f*; (*in game*) gage *m*.
forg/e [fɔːdʒ] **1** *vt* (*signature, money*) contrefaire; (*document*) falsifier. **2** *vt* (*friendship, bond*) forger. **3** *vi* **to f. ahead** (*progress*) aller de l'avant. **4** *vt* (*metal*) forger; – *n* forge *f*. ◆**—er** *n* (*of banknotes etc*) faussaire *m*. ◆**forgery** *n* faux *m*, contrefaçon *f*.
forget [fə'get] *vt* (*pt* **forgot**, *pp* **forgotten**, *pres p* **forgetting**) oublier (**to do** de faire); **f. it!** *Fam* (*when thanked*) pas de quoi!; (*it doesn't matter*) peu importe!; **to f. oneself** s'oublier; – *vi* oublier; **to f. about** oublier. ◆**f.-me-not** *n Bot* myosotis *m*. ◆**forgetful** *a* **to be f. (of)** oublier, être oublieux (de). ◆**forgetfulness** *n* manque *m* de mémoire; (*carelessness*) négligence *f*; **in a moment of f.** dans un moment d'oubli.
forgiv/e [fə'gɪv] *vt* (*pt* **forgave**, *pp* **forgiven**) pardonner (**s.o. sth** qch à qn). ◆**—ing** *a* indulgent. ◆**forgiveness** *n* pardon *m*; (*compassion*) clémence *f*.
forgo [fɔː'gəʊ] *vt* (*pp* **forgone**) renoncer à.
fork [fɔːk] **1** *n* (*for eating*) fourchette *f*; (*for garden etc*) fourche *f*. **2** *vi* (*of road*) bifurquer; **to f. left** (*in vehicle*) prendre à gauche; – *n* bifurcation *f*, fourche *f*. **3** *vt* **to f. out** (*money*) *Fam* allonger; – *vi* **to f. out** (*pay*) *Fam* casquer. ◆**—ed** *a* fourchu. ◆**forklift truck** *n* chariot *m* élévateur.
forlorn [fə'lɔːn] *a* (*forsaken*) abandonné; (*unhappy*) triste, affligé.
form [fɔːm] *n* (*shape, type, style*) forme *f*; (*document*) formulaire *m*; *Sch* classe *f*; **it's good f.** c'est ce qui se fait; **in the f. of** en forme de; **a f. of speech** une façon de parler; **on f., in good f.** en (pleine) forme; – *vt* (*group, character etc*) former; (*clay*) façonner; (*habit*) contracter; (*an opinion*) se former; (*constitute*) constituer, former; **to f. part of** faire partie de; – *vi* (*appear*) se former. ◆**for'mation** *n* formation *f*. ◆**formative** *a* formateur.
formal ['fɔːm(ə)l] *a* (*person, tone etc*) cérémonieux; (*stuffy*) *Pej* compassé; (*official*) officiel; (*in due form*) en bonne et due forme; (*denial, structure, logic*) formel; (*resemblance*) extérieur; **f. dress** tenue *f or* habit *m* de cérémonie; **f. education** éducation *f* scolaire. ◆**for'mality** *n* cérémonie *f*; (*requirement*) formalité *f*. ◆**formally** *adv* (*to declare etc*) officiellement; **f. dressed** en tenue de cérémonie.
format ['fɔːmæt] *n* format *m*.
former ['fɔːmər] **1** *a* (*previous*) ancien; (*situation*) antérieur; **her f. husband** son ex-mari *m*; **in f. days** autrefois. **2** *a* (*of two*) premier; – *pron* **the f.** celui-là, celle-là, le premier, la première. ◆**—ly** *adv* autrefois.
formidable ['fɔːmɪdəb(ə)l] *a* effroyable, terrible.
formula ['fɔːmjʊlə] *n* **1** (*pl* **-as** *or* **-ae** [-iː]) formule *f*. **2** (*pl* **-as**) (*baby's feed*) *Am* mélange *m* lacté. ◆**formulate** *vt* formuler. ◆**formu'lation** *n* formulation *f*.
forsake [fə'seɪk] *vt* (*pt* **forsook**, *pp* **forsaken**) abandonner.
fort [fɔːt] *n Hist Mil* fort *m*; **to hold the f.** (*in s.o.'s absence*) *Fam* prendre la relève.
forte ['fɔːteɪ, *Am* fɔːt] *n* (*strong point*) fort *m*.
forth [fɔːθ] *adv* en avant; **from this day f.** désormais; **and so f.** et ainsi de suite.
forthcoming [fɔːθ'kʌmɪŋ] *a* **1** (*event*) à venir; (*book, film*) qui va sortir; **my f. book** mon prochain livre. **2** (*available*) disponible. **3** (*open*) communicatif; (*helpful*) serviable.
forthright ['fɔːθraɪt] *a* direct, franc.
forthwith [fɔːθ'wɪð] *adv* sur-le-champ.
fortieth ['fɔːtɪəθ] *a* & *n* quarantième (*mf*).
fortify ['fɔːtɪfaɪ] *vt* (*strengthen*) fortifier; **to f. s.o.** (*of food, drink*) réconforter qn, remonter qn. ◆**fortifi'cation** *n* fortification *f*.
fortitude ['fɔːtɪtjuːd] *n* courage *m* (moral).
fortnight ['fɔːtnaɪt] *n* quinze jours *mpl*, quinzaine *f*. ◆**—ly** *adv* bimensuel; – *adv* tous les quinze jours.
fortress ['fɔːtrɪs] *n* forteresse *f*.
fortuitous [fɔː'tjuːɪtəs] *a* fortuit.
fortunate ['fɔːtʃənɪt] *a* (*choice, event etc*) heureux; **to be f.** (*of person*) avoir de la chance; **it's f. (for her) that** c'est heureux (pour elle) que. ◆**—ly** *adv* heureusement.
fortune ['fɔːtʃuːn] *n* (*wealth*) fortune *f*; (*luck*) chance *f*; (*chance*) sort *m*, hasard *m*, fortune *f*; **to have the good f. to** avoir la chance *or* le bonheur de; **to tell s.o.'s f.** dire la bonne aventure à qn; **to make one's f.** faire fortune. ◆**f.-teller** *n* diseur, -euse *mf* de bonne aventure.
forty ['fɔːtɪ] *a* & *n* quarante (*m*).
forum ['fɔːrəm] *n* forum *m*.
forward ['fɔːwəd] *adv* **forward(s)** en avant; **to go f.** avancer; **from this time f.** désormais; – *a* (*movement*) en avant; (*gears*) *Aut* avant *inv*; (*child*) *Fig* précoce; (*pert*) effronté; – *n Fb* avant *m*; – *vt* (*letter*) faire suivre; (*goods*) expédier. ◆**—ness** *n* précocité *f*; effronterie *f*. ◆**forward-looking** *a* tourné vers l'avenir.
fossil ['fɒs(ə)l] *n* & *a* fossile (*m*).

foster ['fɒstər] **1** *vt* encourager; (*hope*) nourrir. **2** *vt* (*child*) élever; – *a* (*child, family*) adoptif.

fought [fɔːt] *see* **fight**.

foul [faʊl] **1** *a* (**-er, -est**) infect; (*air*) vicié; (*breath*) fétide; (*language*) grossier; (*action, place*) immonde; **to be f.-mouthed** avoir un langage grossier. **2** *n Sp* coup *m* irrégulier; *Fb* faute *f*; – *a* **f. play** *Sp* jeu *m* irrégulier; *Jur* acte *m* criminel. **3** *vt* **to f. (up)** salir; (*air*) vicier; (*drain*) encrasser; **to f. up** (*life, plans*) *Fam* gâcher. ◆**f.-up** *n* (*in system*) *Fam* raté *m*.

found[1] [faʊnd] *see* **find**.

found[2] [faʊnd] *vt* (*town, opinion etc*) fonder (**on** sur). ◆**—er**[1] *n* fondateur, -trice *mf*. ◆**foun'dation** *n* fondation *f*; (*basis*) *Fig* base *f*, fondement *m*; **without f.** sans fondement; **f. cream** fond *m* de teint.

founder[2] ['faʊndər] *vi* (*of ship*) sombrer.

foundry ['faʊndrɪ] *n* fonderie *f*.

fountain ['faʊntɪn] *n* fontaine *f*; **f. pen** stylo(-plume) *m*.

four [fɔːr] *a* & *n* quatre (*m*); **on all fours** à quatre pattes; **the Big F.** *Pol* les quatre Grands; **f.-letter word** = mot *m* de cinq lettres. ◆**fourfold** *a* quadruple; – *adv* au quadruple. ◆**foursome** *n* deux couples *mpl*. ◆**four'teen** *a* & *n* quatorze (*m*). ◆**fourth** *a* & *n* quatrième (*mf*).

fowl [faʊl] *n* (*hens*) volaille *f*; **a f.** une volaille.

fox [fɒks] **1** *n* renard *m*. **2** *vt* (*puzzle*) mystifier; (*trick*) tromper. ◆**foxy** *a* (*sly*) rusé, futé.

foxglove ['fɒksglʌv] *n Bot* digitale *f*.

foyer ['fɔɪeɪ] *n Th* foyer *m*; (*in hotel*) hall *m*.

fraction ['frækʃ(ə)n] *n* fraction *f*. ◆**fractionally** *adv* un tout petit peu.

fractious ['frækʃəs] *a* grincheux.

fracture ['fræktʃər] *n* fracture *f*; – *vt* fracturer; **to f. one's leg/***etc* se fracturer la jambe/*etc*; – *vi* se fracturer.

fragile ['frædʒaɪl, *Am* 'frædʒ(ə)l] *a* fragile. ◆**fra'gility** *n* fragilité *f*.

fragment ['frægmənt] *n* fragment *m*, morceau *m*. ◆**frag'mented** *a*, ◆**fragmentary** *a* fragmentaire.

fragrant ['freɪgrənt] *a* parfumé. ◆**fragrance** *n* parfum *m*.

frail [freɪl] *a* (**-er, -est**) (*person*) frêle, fragile; (*hope, health*) fragile. ◆**frailty** *n* fragilité *f*.

frame [freɪm] **1** *n* (*of person, building*) charpente *f*; (*of picture, bicycle*) cadre *m*; (*of window, car*) châssis *m*; (*of spectacles*) monture *f*; **f. of mind** humeur *f*; – *vt* (*picture*) encadrer; (*proposals etc*) *Fig* formuler. **2** *vt* **to f. s.o.** *Fam* monter un coup contre qn. ◆**f.-up** *n Fam* coup *m* monté. ◆**framework** *n* structure *f*; **(with)in the f. of** (*context*) dans le cadre de.

franc [fræŋk] *n* franc *m*.

France [frɑːns] *n* France *f*.

franchise ['fræntʃaɪz] *n* **1** *Pol* droit *m* de vote. **2** (*right to sell product*) *Com* franchise *f*.

Franco- ['fræŋkəʊ] *pref* franco-.

frank [fræŋk] **1** *a* (**-er, -est**) (*honest*) franc. **2** *vt* (*letter*) affranchir. ◆**—ly** *adv* franchement. ◆**—ness** *n* franchise *f*.

frankfurter ['fræŋkfɜːtər] *n* saucisse *f* de Francfort.

frantic ['fræntɪk] *a* (*activity, shout*) frénétique; (*rush, desire*) effréné; (*person*) hors de soi; **f. with joy** fou de joie. ◆**frantically** *adv* comme un fou.

fraternal [frə'tɜːn(ə)l] *a* fraternel. ◆**fraternity** *n* (*bond*) fraternité *f*; (*society*) & *Univ Am* confrérie *f*. ◆**fraternize** ['frætənaɪz] *vi* fraterniser (**with** avec).

fraud [frɔːd] *n* **1** *Jur* fraude *f*. **2** (*person*) imposteur *m*. ◆**fraudulent** *a* frauduleux.

fraught [frɔːt] *a* **f. with** plein de, chargé de; **to be f.** (*of situation*) être tendu; (*of person*) *Fam* être contrarié.

fray [freɪ] **1** *vt* (*garment*) effilocher; (*rope*) user; – *vi* s'effilocher; s'user. **2** *n* (*fight*) rixe *f*. ◆**—ed** *a* (*nerves*) *Fig* tendu.

freak [friːk] *n* (*person*) phénomène *m*, monstre *m*; **a jazz/***etc* **f.** *Fam* un(e) fana de jazz/*etc*; – *a* (*result, weather etc*) anormal. ◆**freakish** *a* anormal.

freckle ['frek(ə)l] *n* tache *f* de rousseur. ◆**freckled** *a* couvert de taches de rousseur.

free [friː] *a* (**freer, freest**) (*at liberty, not occupied*) libre; (*gratis*) gratuit; (*lavish*) généreux (**with** de); **to get f.** se libérer; **f. to do** libre de faire; **to let s.o. go f.** relâcher qn; **f. of charge** gratuit; **f. of** (*without*) sans; **f. of s.o.** (*rid of*) débarrassé de qn; **to have a f. hand** *Fig* avoir carte blanche (**to do** pour faire); **f. and easy** décontracté; **f. trade** libre-échange *m*; **f. speech** liberté *f* d'expression; **f. kick** *Fb* coup *m* franc; **f.-range egg** œuf *m* de ferme; – *adv* **f. (of charge)** gratuitement; – *vt* (*pt* & *pp* **freed**) (*prisoner etc*) libérer; (*trapped person, road*) dégager; (*country*) affranchir, libérer; (*untie*) détacher. ◆**Freefone®** *Tel* = numéro *m* vert. ◆**free-for-'all** *n* mêlée *f* générale. ◆**freehold** *n* propriété *f* foncière libre. ◆**freelance** *a* indépendant; – *n* collaborateur, -trice *mf* indépendant(e). ◆**freeloader** *n* (*sponger*) *Am* parasite *m*. ◆**Freemason** *n* franc-maçon *m*. ◆**Freemasonry** *n* franc-maçonnerie *f*. ◆**freestyle** *n* *Swimming* nage *f* libre. ◆**free'thinker** *n* libre penseur, -euse *mf*. ◆**freeway** *n Am* autoroute *f*.

freedom ['friːdəm] *n* liberté *f*; **f. from** (*worry, responsibility*) absence *f* de.

freely ['friːli] *adv* (*to speak, circulate etc*) librement; (*to give*) libéralement.

freez/e [friːz] *vi* (*pt* **froze**, *pp* **frozen**) geler; (*of smile*) *Fig* se figer; *Culin* se congeler; **to f. to death** mourir de froid; **to f. up** *or* **over** geler; (*of windscreen*) se givrer; – *vt Culin* congeler, surgeler; (*credits, river*) geler; (*prices, wages*) bloquer; **frozen food** surgelés *mpl*; – *n Met* gel *m*; (*of prices etc*) blocage *m*. ◆**—ing** *a* (*weather etc*) glacial; (*hands, person*) gelé; **it's f.** on gèle; – *n* **below f.** au-dessous de zéro. ◆**—er** *n* (*deep-freeze*) congélateur *m*; (*in fridge*) freezer *m*.

freight [freɪt] *n* (*goods, price*) fret *m*; (*transport*) transport *m*; **f. train** *Am* train *m* de marchandises; – *vt* (*ship*) affréter. ◆**—er** *n* (*ship*) cargo *m*.

French [frentʃ] *a* français; (*teacher*) de français; (*embassy*) de France; **F. fries** *Am* frites *fpl*; **the F.** les Français *mpl*; – *n* (*language*) français *m*. ◆**Frenchman** *n* (*pl* **-men**) Français *m*. ◆**French-speaking** *a* francophone. ◆**Frenchwoman** *n* (*pl* **-women**) Française *f*.

frenzy ['frenzi] *n* frénésie *f*. ◆**frenzied** *a* (*shouts etc*) frénétique; (*person*) effréné; (*attack*) violent.

frequent ['friːkwənt] *a* fréquent; **f. visitor** habitué, -ée *mf* (to de); – [frɪ'kwent] *vt* fréquenter. ◆**frequency** *n* fréquence *f*. ◆**frequently** *adv* fréquemment.

fresco ['freskəʊ] *n* (*pl* **-oes** *or* **-os**) fresque *f*.

fresh [freʃ] **1** *a* (**-er, -est**) frais; (*new*) nouveau; (*impudent*) *Fam* culotté; **to get some f. air** prendre le frais; **f. water** eau *f* douce. **2** *adv* **f. from** fraîchement arrivé de; **f. out of, f. from** (*university*) frais émoulu de. ◆**freshen 1** *vi* (*of wind*) fraîchir. **2** *vi* **to f. up** faire un brin de toilette; – *vt* **to f. up** (*house etc*) retaper; **to f. s.o. up** (*of bath*) rafraîchir qn. ◆**freshener** *n* **air f.** désodorisant *m*. ◆**freshman** *n* (*pl* **-men**) étudiant, -ante *mf* de première année. ◆**freshness** *n* fraîcheur *f*; (*cheek*) *Fam* culot *m*.

fret [fret] *vi* (**-tt-**) (*worry*) se faire du souci, s'en faire; (*of baby*) pleurer. ◆**fretful** *a* (*baby etc*) grognon.

friar ['fraɪər] *n* frère *m*, moine *m*.

friction ['frɪkʃ(ə)n] *n* friction *f*.

Friday ['fraɪdɪ] *n* vendredi *m*.

fridge [frɪdʒ] *n Fam* frigo *m*.

fried [fraɪd] *pt & pp of* **fry 1**; – *a* (*fish etc*) frit; **f. egg** œuf *m* sur le plat. ◆**frier** *n* (*pan*) friteuse *f*.

friend [frend] *n* ami, -ie *mf*; (*from school, work*) camarade *mf*; **to be friends with** être ami avec; **to make friends** se lier (**with** avec). ◆**friendly** *a* (**-ier, -iest**) amical; (*child, animal*) gentil, affectueux; (*kind*) gentil; **some f. advice** un conseil d'ami; **to be f. with** être ami avec. ◆**friendship** *n* amitié *f*.

frieze [friːz] *n Archit* frise *f*.

frigate ['frɪgət] *n* (*ship*) frégate *f*.

fright [fraɪt] *n* peur *f*; (*person, hat etc*) *Fig Fam* horreur *f*; **to have a f.** avoir peur; **to give s.o. a f.** faire peur à qn. ◆**frighten** *vt* effrayer, faire peur à; **to f. away** *or* **off** (*animal*) effaroucher; (*person*) chasser. ◆**frightened** *a* effrayé; **to be f.** avoir peur (**of** de). ◆**frightening** *a* effrayant. ◆**frightful** *a* affreux. ◆**frightfully** *adv* (*ugly, late*) affreusement; (*kind, glad*) terriblement.

frigid ['frɪdʒɪd] *a* (*air, greeting etc*) froid; *Psy* frigide.

frill [frɪl] *n Tex* volant *m*; *pl* (*fuss*) *Fig* manières *fpl*, chichis *mpl*; (*useless embellishments*) fioritures *fpl*, superflu *m*; **no frills** (*spartan*) spartiate.

fringe [frɪndʒ] **1** *n* (*of hair, clothes etc*) frange *f*. **2** *n* (*of forest*) lisière *f*; **on the fringe(s) of society** en marge de la société; – *a* (*group, theatre*) marginal; **f. benefits** avantages *mpl* divers.

frisk [frɪsk] **1** *vt* (*search*) fouiller (au corps). **2** *vi* **to f. (about)** gambader. ◆**frisky** *a* (**-ier, -iest**) *a* vif.

fritter ['frɪtər] **1** *vt* **to f. away** (*waste*) gaspiller. **2** *n Culin* beignet *m*.

frivolous ['frɪvələs] *a* frivole. ◆**fri'volity** *n* frivolité *f*.

frizzy ['frɪzɪ] *a* (*hair*) crépu.

fro [frəʊ] *adv* **to go to and f.** aller et venir.

frock [frɒk] *n* (*dress*) robe *f*; (*of monk*) froc *m*.

frog [frɒg] *n* grenouille *f*; **a f. in one's throat** *Fig* un chat dans la gorge. ◆**frogman** *n* (*pl* **-men**) homme-grenouille *m*.

frolic ['frɒlɪk] *vi* (*pt & pp* **frolicked**) **to f. (about)** gambader; – *npl* (*capers*) ébats *mpl*; (*pranks*) gamineries *fpl*.

from [frɒm, *unstressed* frəm] *prep* **1** de; **a letter f.** une lettre de; **to suffer f.** souffrir de;

where are you f.? d'où êtes-vous?; **a train f.** un train en provenance de; **to be ten metres (away) f. the house** être à dix mètres de la maison. **2** (*time onwards*) à partir de, dès, depuis; **f. today (on), as f. today** à partir d'aujourd'hui, dès aujourd'hui; **f. her childhood** dès *or* depuis son enfance. **3** (*numbers, prices onwards*) à partir de; **f. five francs** à partir de cinq francs. **4** (*away from*) à; **to take/hide/borrow f.** prendre/cacher/emprunter à. **5** (*out of*) dans; sur; **to take f.** (*box*) prendre dans; (*table*) prendre sur; **to drink f. a cup/***etc* boire dans une tasse/*etc*; **to drink (straight) f. the bottle** boire à (même) la bouteille. **6** (*according to*) d'après; **f. what I saw** d'après ce que j'ai vu. **7** (*cause*) par; **f. conviction/habit/***etc* par conviction/habitude/*etc*. **8** (*on the part of, on behalf of*) de la part de; **tell her f. me** dis-lui de ma part.

front [frʌnt] *n* (*of garment, building*) devant *m*; (*of boat, car*) avant *m*; (*of crowd*) premier rang *m*; (*of book*) début *m*; *Mil Pol Met* front *m*; (*beach*) front *m* de mer; (*appearance*) *Fig* façade *f*; **in f. (of)** devant; **in f.** (*ahead*) en avant; *Sp* en tête; **in the f.** (*of vehicle*) à l'avant; (*of house*) devant; – *a* (*tooth etc*) de devant; (*part, wheel, car seat*) avant *inv*; (*row, page*) premier; (*view*) de face; **f. door** porte *f* d'entrée; **f. line** *Mil* front *m*; **f. room** (*lounge*) salon *m*; **f. runner** *Fig* favori, -ite *mf*; **f.-wheel drive** (*on vehicle*) traction *f* avant; – *vi* **to f. on to** (*of windows etc*) donner sur. ◆**frontage** *n* façade *f*. ◆**frontal** *a* (*attack*) de front.

frontier ['frʌntɪər] *n* frontière *f*; – *a* (*town, post*) frontière *inv*.

frost [frɒst] *n* gel *m*, gelée *f*; (*frozen drops on glass, grass etc*) gelée *f* blanche, givre *m*; – *vi* **to f. up** (*of windscreen etc*) se givrer. ◆**frostbite** *n* gelure *f*. ◆**frostbitten** *a* gelé. ◆**frosty** *a* (-ier, -iest) glacial; (*window*) givré; **it's f.** il gèle.

frosted ['frɒstɪd] *a* (*glass*) dépoli.

frosting ['frɒstɪŋ] *n* (*icing*) *Culin* glaçage *m*.

froth [frɒθ] *n* mousse *f*; – *vi* mousser. ◆**frothy** *a* (-ier, -iest) (*beer etc*) mousseux.

frown [fraʊn] *n* froncement *m* de sourcils; – *vi* froncer les sourcils; **to f. (up)on** *Fig* désapprouver.

froze, frozen [frəʊz, 'frəʊz(ə)n] *see* **freeze**.

frugal ['fruːg(ə)l] *a* (*meal*) frugal; (*thrifty*) parcimonieux. ◆**—ly** *adv* parcimonieusement.

fruit [fruːt] *n* fruit *m*; **(some) f.** (*one item*) un fruit; (*more than one*) des fruits; – *a* (*basket*) à fruits; (*drink*) aux fruits; (*salad*) de fruits; **f. tree** arbre *m* fruitier. ◆**fruitcake** *n* cake *m*. ◆**fruiterer** *n* fruitier, -ière *mf*. ◆**fruitful** *a* (*meeting, career etc*) fructueux, fécond. ◆**fruitless** *a* stérile. ◆**fruity** *a* (-ier, -iest) *a* fruité, de fruit; (*joke*) *Fig Fam* corsé.

fruition [fruː'ɪʃ(ə)n] *n* **to come to f.** se réaliser.

frumpish ['frʌmpɪʃ] *a*, **frumpy** ['frʌmpɪ] *a* *Fam* (mal) fagoté.

frustrat/e [frʌ'streɪt] *vt* (*person*) frustrer; (*plans*) faire échouer. ◆**—ed** *a* (*mentally, sexually*) frustré; (*effort*) vain. ◆**—ing** *a* irritant. ◆**fru'stration** *n* frustration *f*; (*disappointment*) déception *f*.

fry [fraɪ] **1** *vt* (faire) frire; – *vi* frire. **2** *n* **small f.** menu fretin *m*. ◆**—ing** *n* friture *f*; **f. pan** poêle *f* (à frire). ◆**—er** *n* (*pan*) friteuse *f*.

ft *abbr* (*measure*) = **foot, feet**.

fuddled ['fʌd(ə)ld] *a* (*drunk*) gris; (*confused*) embrouillé.

fuddy-duddy ['fʌdɪdʌdɪ] *n* **he's an old f.-duddy** *Fam* il est vieux jeu.

fudge [fʌdʒ] **1** *n* (*sweet*) caramel *m* mou. **2** *vt* **to f. the issue** refuser d'aborder le problème.

fuel [fjʊəl] *n* combustible *m*; *Aut* carburant *m*; **f. (oil)** mazout *m*; – *vt* (-ll-, *Am* -l-) (*stove*) alimenter; (*ship*) ravitailler (en combustible); (*s.o.'s anger etc*) attiser.

fugitive ['fjuːdʒɪtɪv] *n* fugitif, -ive *mf*.

fugue [fjuːg] *n* *Mus* fugue *f*.

fulfil, *Am* **fulfill** [fʊl'fɪl] *vt* (-ll-) (*ambition, dream*) accomplir, réaliser; (*condition, duty*) remplir; (*desire*) satisfaire; **to f. oneself** s'épanouir. ◆**fulfilling** *a* satisfaisant. ◆**fulfilment** *n*, *Am* ◆**fulfillment** *n* accomplissement *m*, réalisation *f*; (*feeling*) satisfaction *f*.

full [fʊl] *a* (-er, -est) plein (of de); (*bus, theatre, meal*) complet; (*life, day*) (bien) rempli; (*skirt*) ample; (*hour*) entier; (*member*) à part entière; **the f. price** le prix fort; **to pay (the) f. fare** payer plein tarif; **to be f. (up)** (*of person*) *Culin* n'avoir plus faim; (*of hotel*) être complet; **the f. facts** tous les faits; **at f. speed** à toute vitesse; **f. name** (*on form*) nom et prénom; **f. stop** *Gram* point *m*; – *adv* **to know f. well** savoir fort bien; **f. in the face** (*to hit etc*) en pleine figure; – *n* **in f.** (*text*) intégral; (*to publish, read*) intégralement; (*to write one's name*) en toutes lettres; **to the f.** (*completely*) tout à fait. ◆**fullness** *n* (*of details*) abondance *f*; (*of dress*) ampleur *f*. ◆**fully** *adv* entièrement; (*at least*) au moins.

full-back ['fulbæk] *n Fb* arrière *m*. ◆**f.-'grown** *a* adulte; (*foetus*) arrivé à terme. ◆**f.-'length** *a* (*film*) de long métrage; (*portrait*) en pied; (*dress*) long. ◆**f.-'scale** *a* (*model etc*) grandeur nature *inv*; (*operation etc*) *Fig* de grande envergure. ◆**f.-'sized** *a* (*model*) grandeur nature *inv*. ◆**f.-'time** *a* & *adv* à plein temps.

fully-fledged, *Am* **full-fledged** [ful(ɪ)'fledʒd] *a* (*engineer etc*) diplômé; (*member*) à part entière. ◆**f.-formed** *a* (*baby etc*) formé. ◆**f.-grown** *a* = **full-grown.**

fulsome ['fulsəm] *a* (*praise etc*) excessif.

fumble ['fʌmb(ə)l] *vi* **to f. (about)** (*grope*) tâtonner; (*search*) fouiller (**for** pour trouver); **to f. (about) with** tripoter.

fume [fjuːm] *vi* (*give off fumes*) fumer; (*of person*) *Fig* rager; – *npl* émanations *fpl*; (*from car exhaust*) gaz *m inv*.

fumigate ['fjuːmɪgeɪt] *vt* désinfecter (par fumigation).

fun [fʌn] *n* amusement *m*; **to be (good) f.** être très amusant; **to have (some) f.** s'amuser; **to make f. of, poke f. at** se moquer de; **for f., for the f. of it** pour le plaisir.

function ['fʌŋkʃ(ə)n] **1** *n* (*role, duty*) & *Math* fonction *f*; (*meeting*) réunion *f*; (*ceremony*) cérémonie *f* (publique). **2** *vi* (*work*) fonctionner. ◆**functional** *a* fonctionnel.

fund [fʌnd] *n* (*for pension, relief etc*) *Fin* caisse *f*; (*of knowledge etc*) *Fig* fond *m*; *pl* (*money resources*) fonds *mpl*; (*for special purpose*) crédits *mpl*; – *vt* (*with money*) fournir des fonds *or* des crédits à.

fundamental [fʌndə'ment(ə)l] *a* fondamental; – *npl* principes *mpl* essentiels.

funeral ['fjuːnərəl] *n* enterrement *m*; (*grandiose*) funérailles *fpl*; – *a* (*service, march*) funèbre; (*expenses, parlour*) funéraire.

funfair ['fʌnfeər] *n* fête *f* foraine; (*larger*) parc *m* d'attractions.

fungus, *pl* **-gi** ['fʌŋgəs, -gaɪ] *n Bot* champignon *m*; (*mould*) moisissure *f*.

funicular [fjʊ'nɪkjulər] *n* funiculaire *m*.

funk [fʌŋk] *n* **to be in a f.** (*afraid*) *Fam* avoir la frousse; (*depressed, sulking*) *Am Fam* faire la gueule.

funnel ['fʌn(ə)l] *n* **1** (*of ship*) cheminée *f*. **2** (*tube for pouring*) entonnoir *m*.

funny ['fʌnɪ] *a* (**-ier, -iest**) (*amusing*) drôle; (*strange*) bizarre; **a f. idea** une drôle d'idée; **there's some f. business going on** il y a quelque chose de louche; **to feel f.** ne pas se sentir très bien. ◆**funnily** *adv* drôlement; bizarrement; **f. enough . . .** chose bizarre . . . .

fur [fɜːr] **1** *n* (*of animal*) poil *m*, pelage *m*; (*for wearing etc*) fourrure *f*. **2** *n* (*in kettle*) dépôt *m* (de tartre); – *vi* (**-rr-**) **to f. (up)** s'entartrer.

furious ['fjuərɪəs] *a* (*violent, angry*) furieux (**with, at** contre); (*pace, speed*) fou. ◆**—ly** *adv* furieusement; (*to drive, rush*) à une allure folle.

furnace ['fɜːnɪs] *n* (*forge*) fourneau *m*; (*room etc*) *Fig* fournaise *f*.

furnish ['fɜːnɪʃ] *vt* **1** (*room*) meubler. **2** (*supply*) fournir (s.o. **with sth** qch à qn). ◆**—ings** *npl* ameublement *m*.

furniture ['fɜːnɪtʃər] *n* meubles *mpl*; **a piece of f.** un meuble.

furrier ['fʌrɪər] *n* fourreur *m*.

furrow ['fʌrəu] *n* (*on brow*) & *Agr* sillon *m*.

furry ['fɜːrɪ] *a* (*animal*) à poil; (*toy*) en peluche.

further ['fɜːðər] **1** *adv* & *a* = **farther. 2** *adv* (*more*) davantage, plus; (*besides*) en outre; – *a* (*additional*) supplémentaire; (*education*) post-scolaire; **f. details** de plus amples détails; **a f. case**/*etc* (*another*) un autre cas/*etc*; **without f. delay** sans plus attendre. **3** *vt* (*cause, research etc*) promouvoir. ◆**furthermore** *adv* en outre. ◆**furthest** *a* & *adv* = **farthest.**

furtive ['fɜːtɪv] *a* furtif.

fury ['fjuərɪ] *n* (*violence, anger*) fureur *f*.

fuse [fjuːz] **1** *vti* (*melt*) *Tech* fondre; *Fig* fusionner. **2** *vt* **to f. the lights** *etc* faire sauter les plombs; – *vi* **the lights** *etc* **have fused** les plombs ont sauté; – *n* (*wire*) *El* fusible *m*, plomb *m*. **3** *n* (*of bomb*) amorce *f*. ◆**fused** *a* (*plug*) *El* avec fusible incorporé. ◆**fusion** *n* (*union*) & *Phys Biol* fusion *f*.

fuselage ['fjuːzəlɑːʒ] *n Av* fuselage *m*.

fuss [fʌs] *n* façons *fpl*, histoires *fpl*, chichis *mpl*; (*noise*) agitation *f*; **what a (lot of) f.!** quelle histoire!; **to kick up** *or* **make a f.** faire des histoires; **to make a f. of** être aux petits soins pour; – *vi* faire des chichis; (*worry*) se tracasser (**about** pour); (*rush about*) s'agiter; **to f. over s.o.** être aux petits soins pour qn. ◆**fusspot** *n*, *Am* ◆**fussbudget** *n Fam* enquiquineur, -euse *mf*. ◆**fussy** *a* (**-ier, -iest**) méticuleux; (*difficult*) difficile (**about** sur).

fusty ['fʌstɪ] *a* (**-ier, -iest**) (*smell*) de renfermé.

futile ['fjuːtaɪl, *Am* 'fjuːt(ə)l] *a* futile, vain. ◆**fu'tility** *n* futilité *f*.

future ['fjuːtʃər] *n* avenir *m*; *Gram* futur *m*; **in f.** (*from now on*) à l'avenir; **in the f.** (*one day*) un jour (futur); – *a* futur, à venir; (*date*) ultérieur.

fuzz [fʌz] *n* **1** (*down*) *Fam* duvet *m*. **2 the f.** (*police*) *Sl* les flics *mpl*. ◆**fuzzy** *a* (**-ier, -iest**) (*hair*) crépu; (*picture, idea*) flou.

G

G, g [dʒiː] *n* G, g *m*. ◆**G.-string** *n* (*cloth*) cache-sexe *m inv*.

gab [gæb] *n* **to have the gift of the g.** *Fam* avoir du bagou(t).

gabardine [gæbə'diːn] *n* (*material, coat*) gabardine *f*.

gabble ['gæb(ə)l] *vi* (*chatter*) jacasser; (*indistinctly*) bredouiller; – *n* baragouin *m*.

gable ['geɪb(ə)l] *n Archit* pignon *m*.

gad ['gæd] *vi* (**-dd-**) **to g. about** se balader, vadrouiller.

gadget ['gædʒɪt] *n* gadget *m*.

Gaelic ['geɪlɪk, 'gælɪk] *a & n* gaélique (*m*).

gaffe [gæf] *n* (*blunder*) gaffe *f*, bévue *f*.

gag [gæg] **1** *n* (*over mouth*) bâillon *m*; – *vt* (**-gg-**) (*victim, press etc*) bâillonner. **2** *n* (*joke*) plaisanterie *f*; *Cin Th* gag *m*. **3** *vi* (**-gg-**) (*choke*) *Am* s'étouffer (on avec).

gaggle ['gæg(ə)l] *n* (*of geese*) troupeau *m*.

gaiety ['geɪətɪ] *n* gaieté *f*; (*of colour*) éclat *m*. ◆**gaily** *adv* gaiement.

gain [geɪn] *vt* (*obtain, win*) gagner; (*objective*) atteindre; (*experience, reputation*) acquérir; (*popularity*) gagner en; **to g. speed/weight** prendre de la vitesse/du poids; – *vi* (*of watch*) avancer; **to g. in strength** gagner en force; **to g. on** (*catch up with*) rattraper; – *n* (*increase*) augmentation *f* (in de); (*profit*) *Com* bénéfice *m*, gain *m*; *Fig* avantage *m*. ◆**gainful** *a* profitable; (*employment*) rémunéré.

gainsay [geɪn'seɪ] *vt* (*pt & pp* **gainsaid** [-sed]) (*person*) contredire; (*facts*) nier.

gait [geɪt] *n* (*walk*) démarche *f*.

gala ['gɑːlə, 'geɪlə] *n* gala *m*, fête *f*; **swimming g.** concours *m* de natation.

galaxy ['gæləksɪ] *n* galaxie *f*.

gale [geɪl] *n* grand vent *m*, rafale *f* (de vent).

gall [gɔːl] **1** *n Med* bile *f*; (*bitterness*) *Fig* fiel *m*; (*cheek*) *Fam* effronterie *f*; **g. bladder** vésicule *f* biliaire. **2** *vt* (*vex*) blesser, froisser.

gallant ['gælənt] *a* (*brave*) courageux; (*splendid*) magnifique; (*chivalrous*) galant. ◆**gallantry** *n* (*bravery*) courage *m*.

galleon ['gælɪən] *n* (*ship*) *Hist* galion *m*.

gallery ['gælərɪ] *n* (*room etc*) galerie *f*; (*for public, press*) tribune *f*; **art g.** (*private*) galerie *f* d'art; (*public*) musée *m* d'art.

galley ['gælɪ] *n* (*ship*) *Hist* galère *f*; (*kitchen*) *Nau Av* cuisine *f*.

Gallic ['gælɪk] *a* (*French*) français. ◆**gallicism** *n* (*word etc*) gallicisme *m*.

gallivant ['gælɪvænt] *vi* **to g. (about)** *Fam* courir, vadrouiller.

gallon ['gælən] *n* gallon *m* (*Br* = *4,5 litres, Am* = *3,8 litres*).

gallop ['gæləp] *n* galop *m*; – *vi* galoper; **to g. away** (*rush*) *Fig* partir au galop *or* en vitesse. ◆**—ing** *a* (*inflation etc*) *Fig* galopant.

gallows ['gæləʊz] *npl* potence *f*.

gallstone ['gɔːlstəʊn] *n Med* calcul *m* biliaire.

galore [gə'lɔːr] *adv* à gogo, en abondance.

galoshes [gə'lɒʃɪz] *npl* (*shoes*) caoutchoucs *mpl*.

galvanize ['gælvənaɪz] *vt* (*metal*) & *Fig* galvaniser.

gambit ['gæmbɪt] *n* **opening g.** *Fig* manœuvre *f* stratégique.

gambl/e ['gæmb(ə)l] *vi* jouer (on sur, **with** avec); **to g. on** (*count on*) miser sur; – *vt* (*wager*) jouer; **to g. (away)** (*lose*) perdre (au jeu); – *n* (*bet*) & *Fig* coup *m* risqué. ◆**—ing** *n* jeu *m*. ◆**—er** *n* joueur, -euse *mf*.

game¹ [geɪm] **1** *n* jeu *m*; (*of football, cricket etc*) match *m*; (*of tennis, chess, cards*) partie *f*; **to have a g. of** jouer un match de; faire une partie de; **games** *Sch* le sport; **games teacher** professeur *m* d'éducation physique. **2** *n* (*animals, birds*) gibier *m*; **to be fair g. for** *Fig* être une proie idéale pour. **3** *a* (*brave*) courageux; **g. for** (*willing*) prêt à. **4** *a* (*leg*) estropié; **to have a g. leg** être boiteux. ◆**gamekeeper** *n* garde-chasse *m*.

gammon ['gæmən] *n* (*ham*) jambon *m* fumé.

gammy ['gæmɪ] *a Fam* = **game 4**.

gamut ['gæmət] *n Mus & Fig* gamme *f*.

gang [gæŋ] *n* bande *f*; (*of workers*) équipe *f*; (*of crooks*) gang *m*; – *vi* **to g. up on** *or* against se liguer contre. ◆**gangster** *n* gangster *m*.

gangling ['gæŋglɪŋ] *a* dégingandé.

gangrene ['gæŋgriːn] *n* gangrène *f*.

gangway ['gæŋweɪ] *n* passage *m*; (*in train*) couloir *m*; (*in bus, cinema, theatre*) allée *f*; (*footbridge*) *Av Nau* passerelle *f*; **g.!** dégagez!

gaol [dʒeɪl] *n* & *vt* = **jail**.

gap [gæp] *n* (*empty space*) trou *m*, vide *m*; (*breach*) trou *m*; (*in time*) intervalle *m*; (*in knowledge*) lacune *f*; **the g. between** (*divergence*) l'écart *m* entre.

gap/e [geɪp] *vi* (*stare*) rester *or* être bouche bée; **to g. at** regarder bouche bée. ◆**—ing** *a* (*chasm, wound*) béant.

garage ['gærɑː(d)ʒ, 'gærɪdʒ, *Am* gə'rɑːʒ] *n* garage *m*; – *vt* mettre au garage.

garb [gɑːb] *n* (*clothes*) costume *m*.

garbage ['gɑːbɪdʒ] *n* ordures *fpl*; **g. can** *Am* poubelle *f*; **g. collector** *or* **man** *Am* éboueur *m*; **g. truck** *Am* camion-benne *m*.

garble ['gɑːb(ə)l] *vt* (*words etc*) déformer, embrouiller.

garden ['gɑːd(ə)n] *n* jardin *m*; **the gardens** (*park*) le parc; **g. centre** (*store*) jardinerie *f*; (*nursery*) pépinière *f*; **g. party** garden-party *f*; **g. produce** produits *mpl* maraîchers; – *vi* **to be gardening** jardiner. ◆**—ing** *n* jardinage *m*. ◆**—er** *n* jardinier, -ière *mf*.

gargle ['gɑːg(ə)l] *vi* se gargariser; – *n* gargarisme *m*.

gargoyle ['gɑːgɔɪl] *n Archit* gargouille *f*.

garish ['geərɪʃ, *Am* 'gærɪʃ] *a* voyant, criard.

garland ['gɑːlənd] *n* guirlande *f*.

garlic ['gɑːlɪk] *n* ail *m*; **g. sausage** saucisson *m* à l'ail.

garment ['gɑːmənt] *n* vêtement *m*.

garnish ['gɑːnɪʃ] *vt* garnir (**with** de); – *n* garniture *f*.

garret ['gærət] *n* mansarde *f*.

garrison ['gærɪsən] *n Mil* garnison *f*.

garrulous ['gærələs] *a* (*talkative*) loquace.

garter ['gɑːtər] *n* (*round leg*) jarretière *f*; (*attached to belt*) *Am* jarretelle *f*; (*for men*) fixe-chaussette *m*.

gas [gæs] **1** *n* gaz *m inv*; (*gasoline*) *Am* essence *f*; *Med Fam* anesthésie *f* au masque; – *a* (*meter, mask, chamber*) à gaz; (*pipe*) de gaz; (*industry*) du gaz; (*heating*) au gaz; **g. fire** *or* **heater** appareil *m* de chauffage à gaz; **g. station** *Am* poste *m* d'essence; **g. stove** (*portable*) réchaud *m* à gaz; (*large*) cuisinière *f* à gaz; – *vt* (**-ss-**) (*poison*) asphyxier; *Mil* gazer. **2** *vi* (**-ss-**) (*talk*) *Fam* bavarder; – *n* **for a g.** (*fun*) *Am Fam* pour rire. ◆**gasbag** *n Fam* commère *f*. ◆**gasman** *n* (*pl* **-men**) employé *m* du gaz. ◆**gasoline** *n Am* essence *f*. ◆**gasworks** *n* usine *f* à gaz.

gash [gæʃ] *n* entaille *f*; – *vt* entailler.

gasp [gɑːsp] **1** *vi* **to g.** (**for breath**) haleter; – *n* halètement *m*. **2** *vi* **to g. with** *or* **in surprise/***etc* avoir le souffle coupé de surprise/*etc*; – *vt* (*say gasping*) hoqueter; – *n* **a g. of surprise/***etc* un hoquet de surprise/*etc*.

gassy ['gæsɪ] *a* (**-ier, -iest**) (*drink*) gazeux.

gastric ['gæstrɪk] *a* (*juices, ulcer*) gastrique. ◆**ga'stronomy** *n* gastronomie *f*.

gate [geɪt] *n* (*of castle, airport etc*) porte *f*; (*at level crossing, field etc*) barrière *f*; (*metal*) grille *f*; (*in Paris Metro*) portillon *m*. ◆**gateway** *n* **the g. to success/***etc* le chemin du succès/*etc*.

gâteau, *pl* **-eaux** ['gætəʊ, -əʊz] *n Culin* gros gâteau *m* à la crème.

gatecrash ['geɪtkræʃ] *vti* **to g.** (**a party**) s'inviter de force (à une réception).

gather ['gæðər] *vt* (*people, objects*) rassembler; (*pick up*) ramasser; (*flowers*) cueillir; (*information*) recueillir; (*understand*) comprendre; (*skirt, material*) froncer; **I g. that...** (*infer*) je crois comprendre que...; **to g. speed** prendre de la vitesse; **to g. in** (*crops, harvest*) rentrer; (*essays, exam papers*) ramasser; **to g. up** (*strength*) rassembler; (*papers*) ramasser; – *vi* (*of people*) se rassembler, s'assembler, s'amasser; (*of clouds*) se former; (*of dust*) s'accumuler; **to g. round** s'approcher; **to g. round s.o.** entourer qn. ◆**—ing** *n* (*group*) réunion *f*.

gaudy ['gɔːdɪ] *a* (**-ier, -iest**) voyant, criard.

gauge [geɪdʒ] *n* (*instrument*) jauge *f*, indicateur *m*; *Rail* écartement *m*; **to be a g. of sth** *Fig* permettre de jauger qch; – *vt* (*measure*) mesurer; (*estimate*) évaluer, jauger.

gaunt [gɔːnt] *a* (*thin*) décharné.

gauntlet ['gɔːntlɪt] *n* gant *m*; **to run the g. of** *Fig* essuyer (le feu de).

gauze [gɔːz] *n* (*fabric*) gaze *f*.

gave [geɪv] *see* **give**.

gawk [gɔːk] *vi* **to g.** (**at**) regarder bouche bée.

gawp [gɔːp] *vi* = **gawk**.

gay [geɪ] *a* (**-er, -est**) **1** (*cheerful*) gai, joyeux; (*colour*) vif, gai. **2** *Fam* homo(sexuel), gay *inv*.

gaze [geɪz] *n* regard *m* (fixe); – *vi* regarder; **to g. at** regarder (fixement).

gazelle [gə'zel] *n* (*animal*) gazelle *f*.

gazette [gə'zet] *n* journal *m* officiel.

GB [dʒiːˈbiː] *abbr* (*Great Britain*) Grande-Bretagne *f*.
GCSE [dʒiːsiːesˈiː] *abbr* (*General Certificate of Secondary Education*) = baccalauréat *m*.
gear [gɪər] **1** *n* matériel *m*, équipement *m*; (*belongings*) affaires *fpl*; (*clothes*) *Fam* vêtements *mpl* (à la mode); (*toothed wheels*) *Tech* engrenage *m*; (*speed*) *Aut* vitesse *f*; **in g.** *Aut* en prise; **not in g.** *Aut* au point mort; **g. lever,** *Am* **g. shift** levier *m* de (changement de) vitesse. **2** *vt* (*adapt*) adapter (to à); **geared (up) to do** prêt à faire; **to g. oneself up for** se préparer pour. ◆**gearbox** *n* boîte *f* de vitesses.
gee! [dʒiː] *int Am Fam* ça alors!
geese [giːs] *see* **goose.**
geezer [ˈgiːzər] *n Hum Sl* type *m*.
Geiger counter [ˈgaɪgəkaʊntər] *n* compteur *m* Geiger.
gel [dʒel] *n* (*substance*) gel *m*.
gelatin(e) [ˈdʒelətiːn, *Am* -tən] *n* gélatine *f*.
gelignite [ˈdʒelɪgnaɪt] *n* dynamite *f* (au nitrate de soude).
gem [dʒem] *n* pierre *f* précieuse; (*person or thing of value*) *Fig* perle *f*; (*error*) *Iron* perle *f*.
Gemini [ˈdʒemɪnaɪ] *n* (*sign*) les Gémeaux *mpl*.
gen [dʒen] *n* (*information*) *Sl* coordonnées *fpl*; – *vi* (**-nn-**) **to g. up on** *Sl* se rancarder sur.
gender [ˈdʒendər] *n Gram* genre *m*; (*of person*) sexe *m*.
gene [dʒiːn] *n Biol* gène *m*.
genealogy [dʒiːnɪˈælədʒɪ] *n* généalogie *f*.
general [ˈdʒenərəl] **1** *a* général; **in g.** en général; **the g. public** le (grand) public; **for g. use** à l'usage du public; **a g. favourite** aimé *or* apprécié de tous; **g. delivery** *Am* poste *f* restante; **to be g.** (*widespread*) être très répandu. **2** *n* (*officer*) *Mil* général *m*. ◆**geneˈrality** *n* généralité *f*. ◆**generaliˈzation** *n* généralisation *f*. ◆**generalize** *vti* généraliser. ◆**generally** *adv* généralement; **g. speaking** en général, généralement parlant.
generate [ˈdʒenəreɪt] *vt* (*heat*) produire; (*fear, hope etc*) & *Ling* engendrer. ◆**geneˈration** *n* génération *f*; **the g. of** (*heat*) la production de; **g. gap** conflit *m* des générations. ◆**generator** *n El* groupe *m* électrogène, génératrice *f*.
generous [ˈdʒenərəs] *a* généreux (**with** de); (*helping, meal etc*) copieux. ◆**geneˈrosity** *n* générosité *f*. ◆**generously** *adv* généreusement; (*to serve s.o.*) copieusement.
genesis [ˈdʒenəsɪs] *n* genèse *f*.
genetic [dʒɪˈnetɪk] *a* génétique. ◆**genetics** *n* génétique *f*.
Geneva [dʒɪˈniːvə] *n* Genève *m or f*.
genial [ˈdʒiːnɪəl] *a* (*kind*) affable; (*cheerful*) jovial.
genie [ˈdʒiːnɪ] *n* (*goblin*) génie *m*.
genital [ˈdʒenɪt(ə)l] *a* génital; – *npl* organes *mpl* génitaux.
genius [ˈdʒiːnɪəs] *n* (*ability, person*) génie *m*; **to have a g. for doing/for sth** avoir le génie pour faire/de qch.
genocide [ˈdʒenəsaɪd] *n* génocide *m*.
gent [dʒent] *n Fam* monsieur *m*; **gents' shoes** *Com* chaussures *fpl* pour hommes; **the gents** *Fam* les toilettes *fpl* (pour hommes).
genteel [dʒenˈtiːl] *a Iron* distingué.
gentle [ˈdʒent(ə)l] *a* (**-er, -est**) (*person, sound, slope etc*) doux; (*hint, reminder*) discret; (*touch*) léger; (*pace*) mesuré; (*exercise, progress*) modéré; (*birth*) noble. ◆**gentleman** *n* (*pl* **-men**) monsieur *m*; (*well-bred*) gentleman *m*, monsieur *m* bien élevé. ◆**gentlemanly** *a* distingué, bien élevé. ◆**gentleness** *n* douceur *f*. ◆**gently** *adv* doucement; (*to remind*) discrètement; (*smoothly*) en douceur.
genuine [ˈdʒenjʊɪn] *a* (*authentic*) véritable, authentique; (*sincere*) sincère, vrai. ◆**—ly** *adv* authentiquement; sincèrement. ◆**—ness** *n* authenticité *f*; sincérité *f*.
geography [dʒɪˈɒgrəfɪ] *n* géographie *f*. ◆**geoˈgraphical** *a* géographique.
geology [dʒɪˈɒlədʒɪ] *n* géologie *f*. ◆**geoˈlogical** *a* géologique. ◆**geologist** *n* géologue *mf*.
geometry [dʒɪˈɒmɪtrɪ] *n* géométrie *f*. ◆**geoˈmetric(al)** *a* géométrique.
geranium [dʒɪˈreɪnɪəm] *n Bot* géranium *m*.
geriatric [dʒerɪˈætrɪk] *a* (*hospital*) du troisième âge; **g. ward** service *m* de gériatrie.
germ [dʒɜːm] *n Biol* & *Fig* germe *m*; *Med* microbe *m*; **g. warfare** guerre *f* bactériologique.
German [ˈdʒɜːmən] *a* & *n* allemand, -ande (*mf*); **G. measles** *Med* rubéole *f*; **G. shepherd** (*dog*) *Am* berger *m* allemand; – *n* (*language*) allemand *m*. ◆**Gerˈmanic** *a* germanique.
Germany [ˈdʒɜːmənɪ] *n* Allemagne *f*; **West G.** Allemagne de l'Ouest.
germinate [ˈdʒɜːmɪneɪt] *vi Bot* & *Fig* germer.
gestation [dʒeˈsteɪʃ(ə)n] *n* gestation *f*.
gesture [ˈdʒestʃər] *n* geste *m*; – *vi* **to g. to**

s.o. to do faire signe à qn de faire. ◆**ge'sticulate** *vi* gesticuler.

get [get] **1** *vt* (*pt & pp* **got,** *pp Am* **gotten,** *pres p* **getting**) (*obtain*) obtenir, avoir; (*find*) trouver; (*buy*) acheter, prendre; (*receive*) recevoir, avoir; (*catch*) attraper, prendre; (*seize*) prendre, saisir; (*fetch*) aller chercher (*qn, qch*); (*put*) mettre; (*derive*) tirer (**from** de); (*understand*) comprendre, saisir; (*prepare*) préparer; (*lead*) mener; (*target*) atteindre, avoir; (*reputation*) se faire; (*annoy*) *Fam* ennuyer; **I have got,** *Am* **I have gotten** j'ai; **to g. s.o. to do sth** faire faire qch à qn; **to g. sth built/***etc* faire construire/*etc* qch; **to g. things going** *or* **started** faire démarrer les choses. **2** *vi* (*go*) aller; (*arrive*) arriver (**to** à); (*become*) devenir, se faire; **to g. caught/run over/***etc* se faire prendre/écraser/*etc*; **to g. married** se marier; **to g. dressed/washed** s'habiller/se laver; **where have you got** *or Am* **gotten to?** où en es-tu?; **you've got to stay** (*must*) tu dois rester; **to g. to do** (*succeed in doing*) parvenir à faire; **to g. working** se mettre à travailler. ■ **to g. about** *or* **(a)round** *vi* se déplacer; (*of news*) circuler; **to g. across** *vt* (*road*) traverser; (*person*) faire traverser; (*message*) communiquer; – *vi* traverser; (*of speaker*) se faire comprendre (**to** de); **to g. across to s.o. that** faire comprendre à qn que; **to g. along** *vi* (*leave*) se sauver; (*manage*) se débrouiller; (*progress*) avancer; (*be on good terms*) s'entendre (**with** avec); **to g. at** *vt* (*reach*) parvenir à, atteindre; (*taunt*) s'en prendre à; **what is he getting at?** où veut-il en venir?; **to g. away** *vi* (*leave*) partir, s'en aller; (*escape*) s'échapper; **there's no getting away from it** il faut le reconnaître, c'est comme ça. ◆**getaway** *n* (*escape*) fuite *f*; **to g. back** *vt* (*recover*) récupérer; (*replace*) remettre; – *vi* (*return*) revenir, retourner; **to g. back at, g. one's own back at** (*punish*) se venger de; **g. back!** (*move back*) reculez!; **to g. by** *vi* (*pass*) passer; (*manage*) se débrouiller; **to g. down** *vi* (*go down*) descendre (**from** de); – *vt* (*bring down*) descendre (**from** de); (*write*) noter; (*depress*) *Fam* déprimer; **to g. down to** (*task, work*) se mettre à; **to g. in** *vt* (*bicycle, washing etc*) rentrer; (*buy*) acheter; (*summon*) faire venir; **to g. in a car/***etc* monter dans une voiture/*etc*; – *vi* (*enter*) entrer; (*come home*) rentrer; (*enter vehicle or train*) monter; (*of plane, train*) arriver; (*of candidate*) *Pol* être élu; **to g. into** *vt* entrer dans; (*vehicle, train*) monter dans; (*habit*) prendre; **to g. into bed/a rage** se mettre au lit/en colère; **to g. into trouble** avoir des ennuis; **to g. off** *vi* (*leave*) partir; (*from vehicle or train*) descendre (**from** de); (*escape*) s'en tirer; (*finish work*) sortir; (*be acquitted*) *Jur* être acquitté; – *vt* (*remove*) enlever; (*despatch*) expédier; *Jur* faire acquitter (*qn*); **to g. off (from) a chair** se lever d'une chaise; **to g. off doing** *Fam* se dispenser de faire; **to g. on** *vt* (*shoes, clothes*) mettre; (*bus, train*) monter dans; – *vi* (*progress*) marcher, avancer; (*continue*) continuer; (*succeed*) réussir; (*enter bus or train*) monter; (*be on good terms*) s'entendre (**with** avec); **how are you getting on?** comment ça va?; **to g. on to s.o.** (*telephone*) toucher qn, contacter qn; **to g. on with** (*task*) continuer; **to g. out** *vi* sortir; (*from vehicle or train*) descendre (**from, of** de); **to g. out of** (*obligation*) échapper à; (*trouble*) se tirer de; (*habit*) perdre; – *vt* (*remove*) enlever; (*bring out*) sortir (*qch*), faire sortir (*qn*); **to g. over** *vt* (*road*) traverser; (*obstacle*) surmonter; (*fence*) franchir; (*illness*) se remettre de; (*surprise*) revenir de; (*ideas*) communiquer; **let's g. it over with** finissons-en; – *vi* (*cross*) traverser; **to g. round** *vt* (*obstacle*) contourner; (*person*) entortiller; – *vi* **to g. round to doing** en venir à faire; **to g. through** *vi* (*pass*) passer; (*finish*) finir; (*pass exam*) être reçu; **to g. through to s.o.** se faire comprendre de qn; (*on the telephone*) contacter qn; – *vt* (*hole etc*) passer par; (*task, meal*) venir à bout de; (*exam*) être reçu à; **g. me through to your boss** (*on the telephone*) passe-moi ton patron; **to g. together** *vi* (*of people*) se rassembler. ◆**g.-together** *n* réunion *f*; **to g. up** *vi* (*rise*) se lever (**from** de); **to g. up to** (*in book*) en arriver à; (*mischief, trouble etc*) faire; – *vt* (*ladder, stairs etc*) monter; (*party, group*) organiser; **to g. sth up** (*bring up*) monter qch. ◆**g.-up** *n* (*clothes*) *Fam* accoutrement *m*.

geyser ['giːzər] *n* **1** (*water heater*) chauffe-eau *m inv*. **2** *Geol* geyser *m*.

Ghana ['gɑːnə] *n* Ghana *m*.

ghastly ['gɑːstlɪ] *a* (**-ier, -iest**) (*pale*) blême, pâle; (*horrible*) affreux.

gherkin ['gɜːkɪn] *n* cornichon *m*.

ghetto ['getəʊ] *n* (*pl* **-os**) ghetto *m*.

ghost [gəʊst] *n* fantôme *m*; **not the g. of a chance** pas l'ombre d'une chance; – *a* (*story*) de fantômes; (*ship*) fantôme; (*town*) mort. ◆**—ly** *a* spectral.

ghoulish ['guːlɪʃ] *a* morbide.

giant ['dʒaɪənt] *n* géant *m*; – *a* géant, gigantesque; (*steps*) de géant; (*packet etc*) *Com* géant.
gibberish ['dʒɪbərɪʃ] *n* baragouin *m*.
gibe [dʒaɪb] *vi* railler; **to g. at** railler; – *n* raillerie *f*.
giblets ['dʒɪblɪts] *npl* (*of fowl*) abats *mpl*.
giddy ['gɪdɪ] *a* (-**ier, -iest**) (*heights*) vertigineux; **to feel g.** avoir le vertige; **to make g.** donner le vertige à. ◆**giddiness** *n* vertige *m*.
gift ['gɪft] *n* cadeau *m*; (*talent*) & *Jur* don *m*; **g. voucher** chèque-cadeau *m*. ◆**gifted** *a* doué (**with** de, **for** pour). ◆**giftwrapped** *a* en paquet-cadeau.
gig [gɪg] *n Mus Fam* engagement *m*, séance *f*.
gigantic [dʒaɪ'gæntɪk] *a* gigantesque.
giggle ['gɪg(ə)l] *vi* rire (sottement); – *n* petit rire *m* sot; **to have the giggles** avoir le fou rire.
gild [gɪld] *vt* dorer. ◆**gilt** *a* doré; – *n* dorure *f*.
gills [gɪlz] *npl* (*of fish*) ouïes *fpl*.
gimmick ['gɪmɪk] *n* (*trick, object*) truc *m*.
gin [dʒɪn] *n* (*drink*) gin *m*.
ginger ['dʒɪndʒər] **1** *a* (*hair*) roux. **2** *n Bot Culin* gingembre *m*; **g. beer** boisson *f* gazeuse au gingembre. ◆**gingerbread** *n* pain *m* d'épice.
gingerly ['dʒɪndʒəlɪ] *adv* avec précaution.
gipsy ['dʒɪpsɪ] *n* bohémien, -ienne *mf*; (*Central European*) Tsigane *mf*; – *a* (*music*) tsigane.
giraffe [dʒɪ'rɑːf, dʒɪ'ræf] *n* girafe *f*.
girder ['gɜːdər] *n* (*metal beam*) poutre *f*.
girdle ['gɜːd(ə)l] *n* (*belt*) ceinture *f*; (*corset*) gaine *f*.
girl ['gɜːl] *n* (jeune) fille *f*; (*daughter*) fille *f*; (*servant*) bonne *f*; (*sweetheart*) *Fam* petite amie *f*; **English g.** jeune Anglaise *f*; **g. guide** éclaireuse *f*. ◆**girlfriend** *n* amie *f*; (*of boy*) petite amie *f*. ◆**girlish** *a* de (jeune) fille.
girth [gɜːθ] *n* (*measure*) circonférence *f*; (*of waist*) tour *m*.
gist [dʒɪst] *n* **to get the g. of** comprendre l'essentiel de.
give [gɪv] *vt* (*pt* **gave**, *pp* **given**) donner (**to** à); (*help, support*) prêter; (*gesture, pleasure*) faire; (*a sigh*) pousser; (*a look*) jeter; (*a blow*) porter; **g. me York 234** passez-moi le 234 à York; **she doesn't g. a damn** *Fam* elle s'en fiche; **to g. way** (*yield, break*) céder (**to** à); (*collapse*) s'effondrer; *Aut* céder la priorité (**to** à); – *n* (*in fabric etc*) élasticité *f*. ■ **to g. away** *vt* (*prize*) distribuer; (*money*) donner; (*facts*) révéler; (*betray*) trahir (*qn*); **to g. back** *vt* (*return*) rendre; **to g. in** *vi* (*surrender*) céder (**to** à); – *vt* (*hand in*) remettre; **to g. off** *vt* (*smell, heat*) dégager; **to g. out** *vt* distribuer; – *vi* (*of supplies, patience*) s'épuiser; (*of engine*) rendre l'âme; **to g. over** *vt* (*devote*) donner, consacrer (**to** à); **to g. oneself over to** s'adonner à; – *vi* **g. over!** (*stop*) *Fam* arrête!; **to g. up** *vi* abandonner, renoncer; – *vt* abandonner, renoncer à; (*seat*) céder (**to** à); (*prisoner*) livrer (**to** à); (*patient*) condamner; **to g. up smoking** cesser de fumer. ◆**given** *a* (*fixed*) donné; **to be g. to doing** (*prone to do*) avoir l'habitude de faire; **g. your age** (*in view of*) étant donné votre âge; **g. that** étant donné que. ◆**giver** *n* donateur, -trice *mf*.
glacier ['glæsɪər, *Am* 'gleɪʃər] *n* glacier *m*.
glad [glæd] *a* (*person*) content (**of, about** de). ◆**gladden** *vt* réjouir. ◆**gladly** *adv* (*willingly*) volontiers.
glade [gleɪd] *n* clairière *f*.
gladiolus, *pl* **-i** [glædɪ'əʊləs, -aɪ] *n Bot* glaïeul *m*.
glamour ['glæmər] *n* (*charm*) enchantement *m*; (*splendour*) éclat *m*. ◆**glamorize** *vt* montrer sous un jour séduisant. ◆**glamorous** *a* séduisant.
glance [glɑːns] **1** *n* coup *m* d'œil; – *vi* jeter un coup d'œil (**at** à, **sur**). **2** *vt* **to g. off sth** (*of bullet*) ricocher sur qch.
gland [glænd] *n* glande *f*. ◆**glandular** *a* **g. fever** *Med* mononucléose *f* infectieuse.
glar/e [gleər] **1** *vi* **to g. at s.o.** foudroyer qn (du regard); – *n* regard *m* furieux. **2** *vi* (*of sun*) briller d'un éclat aveuglant; – *n* éclat *m* aveuglant. ◆**—ing** *a* (*sun*) aveuglant; (*eyes*) furieux; (*injustice*) flagrant; **a g. mistake** une faute grossière.
glass [glɑːs] *n* verre *m*; (*mirror*) miroir *m*, glace *f*; *pl* (*spectacles*) lunettes *fpl*; **a pane of g.** une vitre, un carreau; – *a* (*door*) vitré; (*industry*) du verre. ◆**glassful** *n* (plein) verre *m*.
glaze [gleɪz] *vt* (*door*) vitrer; (*pottery*) vernisser; (*paper*) glacer; – *n* (*on pottery*) vernis *m*; (*on paper*) glacé *m*. ◆**glazier** *n* vitrier *m*.
gleam [gliːm] *n* lueur *f*; – *vi* (re)luire.
glean [gliːn] *vt* (*grain, information etc*) glaner.
glee [gliː] *n* joie *f*. ◆**gleeful** *a* joyeux.
glen [glen] *n* vallon *m*.
glib [glɪb] *a* (*person*) qui a la parole facile; (*speech*) facile, peu sincère. ◆**—ly** *adv* (*to say*) peu sincèrement.
glid/e [glaɪd] *vi* glisser; (*of vehicle*) avancer

silencieusement; (*of aircraft, bird*) planer. ◆**—ing** *n Av Sp* vol *m* à voile. ◆**—er** *n Av* planeur *m*.

glimmer ['glɪmər] *vi* luire (faiblement); – *n* (*light, of hope etc*) (faible) lueur *f*.

glimpse [glɪmps] *n* aperçu *m*; **to catch** *or* **get a g. of** entrevoir.

glint [glɪnt] *vi* (*shine with flashes*) briller; – *n* éclair *m*; (*in eye*) étincelle *f*.

glisten ['glɪs(ə)n] *vi* (*of wet surface*) briller; (*of water*) miroiter.

glitter ['glɪtər] *vi* scintiller, briller; – *n* scintillement *m*.

gloat [gləʊt] *vi* jubiler (**over** à la vue de).

globe [gləʊb] *n* globe *m*. ◆**global** *a* (*comprehensive*) global; (*universal*) universel, mondial.

gloom [gluːm] *n* (*darkness*) obscurité *f*; (*sadness*) *Fig* tristesse *f*. ◆**gloomy** *a* (**-ier, -iest**) (*dark, dismal*) sombre, triste; (*sad*) *Fig* triste; (*pessimistic*) pessimiste.

glory ['glɔːrɪ] *n* gloire *f*; **in all one's g.** *Fig* dans toute sa splendeur; **to be in one's g.** (*very happy*) *Fam* être à son affaire; – *vi* **to g. in** se glorifier de. ◆**glorify** *vt* (*praise*) glorifier; **it's a glorified barn/***etc* ce n'est guère plus qu'une grange/*etc*. ◆**glorious** *a* (*full of glory*) glorieux; (*splendid, enjoyable*) magnifique.

gloss [glɒs] **1** *n* (*shine*) brillant *m*; **g. paint** peinture *f* brillante; **g. finish** brillant *m*. **2** *n* (*note*) glose *f*, commentaire *m*. **3** *vt* **to g. over** (*minimize*) glisser sur; (*conceal*) dissimuler. ◆**glossy** *a* (**-ier, -iest**) brillant; (*paper*) glacé; (*magazine*) de luxe.

glossary ['glɒsərɪ] *n* glossaire *m*.

glove [glʌv] *n* gant *m*; **g. compartment** *Aut* (*shelf*) vide-poches *m inv*; (*enclosed*) boîte *f* à gants. ◆**gloved** *a* **a g. hand** une main gantée.

glow [gləʊ] *vi* (*of sky, fire*) rougeoyer; (*of lamp*) luire; (*of eyes, person*) *Fig* rayonner (**with** de); – *n* rougeoiement *m*; (*of colour*) éclat *m*; (*of lamp*) lueur *f*. ◆**—ing** *a* (*account, terms etc*) très favorable, enthousiaste. ◆**glow-worm** *n* ver *m* luisant.

glucose ['gluːkəʊs] *n* glucose *m*.

glue [gluː] *n* colle *f*; – *vt* coller (**to, on** à). ◆**glued** *a* **g. to** (*eyes*) *Fam* fixés *or* rivés sur; **to be g. to** (*television*) *Fam* être cloué devant.

glum [glʌm] *a* (**glummer, glummest**) triste.

glut [glʌt] *vt* (**-tt-**) (*overfill*) rassasier; (*market*) *Com* surcharger (**with** de); – *n* (*of produce, oil etc*) *Com* surplus *m* (**of** de).

glutton ['glʌt(ə)n] *n* glouton, -onne *mf*; **g. for work** bourreau *m* de travail; **g. for punishment** masochiste *mf*. ◆**gluttony** *n* gloutonnerie *f*.

glycerin(e) ['glɪsərɪːn] *n* glycérine *f*.

GMT [dʒiːem'tiː] *abbr* (*Greenwich Mean Time*) GMT.

gnarled [nɑːld] *a* noueux.

gnash [næʃ] *vt* **to g. one's teeth** grincer des dents.

gnat [næt] *n* (*insect*) cousin *m*.

gnaw [nɔː] *vti* **to g. (at)** ronger.

gnome [nəʊm] *n* (*little man*) gnome *m*.

go [gəʊ] **1** *vi* (*3rd person sing pres t* **goes**; *pt* **went**; *pp* **gone**; *pres p* **going**) aller (**to** à, **from** de); (*depart*) partir, s'en aller; (*disappear*) disparaître; (*be sold*) se vendre; (*function*) marcher, fonctionner; (*progress*) aller, marcher; (*become*) devenir; (*be*) être; (*of time*) passer; (*of hearing, strength*) baisser; (*of rope*) céder; (*of fuse*) sauter; (*of material*) s'user; **to go well/badly** (*of event*) se passer bien/mal; **she's going to do** (*is about to, intends to*) elle va faire; **it's all gone** (*finished*) il n'y en a plus; **to go and get** (*fetch*) aller chercher; **to go and see** aller voir; **to go riding/sailing/on a trip/***etc* faire du cheval/de la voile/un voyage/*etc*; **to let go of** lâcher; **to go to** (*doctor, lawyer etc*) aller voir; **to get things going** faire démarrer les choses; **is there any beer going?** (*available*) y a-t-il de la bière?; **it goes to show that . . .** ça sert à montrer que . . . ; **two hours/***etc* **to go** (*still left*) encore deux heures/*etc*. **2** *n* (*pl* **goes**) (*energy*) dynamisme *m*; (*attempt*) coup *m*; **to have a go at (doing) sth** essayer (de faire) qch; **at one go** d'un seul coup; **on the go** en mouvement, actif; **to make a go of** (*make a success of*) réussir. ■ **to go about** *or* **(a)round** *vi* se déplacer; (*of news, rumour*) circuler; **to go about** *vt* (*one's duties etc*) s'occuper de; **to know how to go about it** savoir s'y prendre; **to go across** *vt* traverser; – *vi* (*cross*) traverser; (*go*) aller (**to** à); **to go across to s.o.('s)** faire un saut chez qn; **to go after** *vt* (*follow*) suivre; (*job*) viser; **to go against** *vt* (*of result*) être défavorable à; (*s.o.'s wishes*) aller contre; (*harm*) nuire à; **to go ahead** *vi* aller de l'avant; **to go ahead with** (*plan etc*) poursuivre; **go ahead!** allez-y! ◆**go-ahead** *a* dynamique; – *n* **to get the go-ahead** avoir le feu vert; **to go along** *vi* aller, avancer; **to go along with** (*agree*) être d'accord avec; **to go away** *vi* partir, s'en aller; **to go back** *vi* retourner, revenir; (*in time*) remonter; (*retreat, step back*) reculer; **to go back on** (*promise*) revenir sur; **to go by** *vi* passer; – *vt* (*act according to*) se fonder sur; (*judge from*) juger d'après; (*instruction*) suivre; **to go down** *vi* descendre; (*fall down*) tomber; (*of ship*) couler; (*of sun*) se coucher; (*of storm*) s'apaiser; (*of temperature, price etc*) baisser; (*of tyre*) se dégonfler; **to go down well** (*of speech etc*) être bien reçu; **to go down with** (*illness*) attraper; – *vt* **to go down the stairs/street** descendre l'escalier/la rue; **to go for** *vt* (*fetch*) aller chercher; (*attack*) attaquer; (*like*) *Fam* aimer beaucoup; **to go forward(s)** *vi* avancer; **to go in** *vi* (r)entrer; (*of sun*) se cacher; **to go in for** (*exam*) se présenter à; (*hobby, sport*) faire; (*career*) entrer dans; (*like*) *Fam* aimer beaucoup; – *vt* **to go in a room/***etc* entrer dans une pièce/*etc*; **to go into** *vt* (*room etc*) entrer dans; (*question*) examiner; **to go off** *vi* (*leave*) partir; (*go bad*) se gâter; (*of effect*) passer; (*of alarm*) se déclencher; (*of event*) se passer; – *vt* (*one's food*) perdre le goût de; **to go on** *vi* continuer (**doing** à faire); (*travel*) poursuivre sa route; (*happen*) se passer; (*last*) durer; (*of time*) passer; **to go on at** (*nag*) *Fam* s'en prendre à; **to go on about** *Fam* parler sans cesse de; **to go out** *vi* sortir; (*of light, fire*) s'éteindre; (*of tide*) descendre; (*of newspaper, product*) être distribué (**to** à); (*depart*) partir; **to go out to work** travailler (au dehors); **to go over** *vi* (*go*) aller (**to** à); (*cross over*) traverser; (*to enemy*) passer (**to** à); **to go over to s.o.('s)** faire un saut chez qn; – *vt* examiner; (*speech*) revoir; (*in one's mind*) repasser; (*touch up*) retoucher; (*overhaul*) réviser (*véhicule, montre*); **to go round** *vi* (*turn*) tourner; (*make a detour*) faire le tour; (*be sufficient*) suffire; **to go round to s.o.('s)** passer chez qn, faire un saut chez qn; **enough to go round** assez pour tout le monde; – *vt* **to go round a corner** tourner un coin; **to go through** *vi* passer; (*of deal*) être conclu; – *vt* (*undergo, endure*) subir; (*examine*) examiner; (*search*) fouiller; (*spend*) dépenser; (*wear out*) user; (*perform*) accomplir; **to go through with** (*carry out*) réaliser, aller jusqu'au bout de; **to go under** *vi* (*of ship, person, firm*) couler; **to go up** *vi* monter; (*explode*) sauter; – *vt* **to go up the stairs/street** monter l'escalier/la rue; **to go without** *vi* se passer de.

goad [gəʊd] *n* aiguillon *m*; – *vt* **to g. (on)** aiguillonner.

goal [gəʊl] *n* but *m*. ◆**goalkeeper** *n Fb* gardien *m* de but, goal *m*. ◆**goalpost** *n Fb* poteau *m* de but.

goat [gəʊt] *n* chèvre *f*; **to get s.o.'s g.** *Fam* énerver qn. ◆**goa'tee** *n* (*beard*) barbiche *f*.

gobble ['gɒb(ə)l] *vt* **to g. (up)** engloutir, engouffrer.

go-between ['gəʊbɪtwiːn] *n* intermédiaire *mf*.

goblet ['gɒblɪt] *n* verre *m* à pied.

goblin ['gɒblɪn] *n* (*evil spirit*) lutin *m*.

god [gɒd] *n* dieu *m*; **G.** Dieu *m*; **the gods** *Th Fam* le poulailler. ◆**g.-fearing** *a* croyant. ◆**g.-forsaken** *a* (*place*) perdu, misérable. ◆**goddess** *n* déesse *f*. ◆**godly** *a* dévot.

godchild ['gɒdtʃaɪld] *n* (*pl* **-children**) filleul, -eule *mf*. ◆**goddaughter** *n* filleule *f*. ◆**godfather** *n* parrain *m*. ◆**godmother** *n* marraine *f*. ◆**godson** *n* filleul *m*.

goddam(n) ['gɒdæm] *a Am Fam* foutu.

godsend ['gɒdsend] *n* aubaine *f*.

goes [gəʊz] *see* **go 1**.

goggle ['gɒg(ə)l] **1** *vi* **to g. at** regarder en roulant de gros yeux. **2** *npl* (*spectacles*) lunettes *fpl* (protectrices). ◆**g.-'eyed** *a* aux yeux saillants.

going ['gəʊɪŋ] **1** *n* (*departure*) départ *m*; (*speed*) allure *f*; (*conditions*) conditions *fpl*; **it's hard g.** c'est difficile. **2** *a* **the g. price** le prix pratiqué (**for** pour); **a g. concern** une entreprise qui marche bien. ◆**goings-'on** *npl Pej* activités *fpl*.

go-kart ['gəʊkɑːt] *n Sp* kart *m*.

gold [gəʊld] *n* or *m*; – *a* (*watch etc*) en or; (*coin, dust*) d'or. ◆**golden** *a* (*made of gold*) d'or; (*in colour*) doré, d'or; (*opportunity*) excellent. ◆**goldmine** *n* mine *f* d'or. ◆**gold-'plated** *a* plaqué or. ◆**goldsmith** *n* orfèvre *m*.

goldfinch ['gəʊldfɪntʃ] *n* (*bird*) chardonneret *m*.

goldfish ['gəʊldfɪʃ] *n* poisson *m* rouge.

golf [gɒlf] *n* golf *m*. ◆**golfer** *n* golfeur, -euse *mf*.

golly! ['gɒlɪ] *int* **(by) g.!** *Fam* mince (alors)!

gondola ['gɒndələ] *n* (*boat*) gondole *f*. ◆**gondo'lier** *n* gondolier *m*.

gone [gɒn] see **go 1**; – *a* **it's g. two** *Fam* il est plus de deux heures. ◆**goner** *n* **to be a g.** *Sl* être fichu.

gong [gɒŋ] *n* gong *m*.

good [gʊd] *a* (**better, best**) bon; (*kind*) gentil; (*weather*) beau; (*pleasant*) bon, agréable; (*well-behaved*) sage; **be g. enough to . . .** ayez la gentillesse de . . . ; **my g. friend** mon cher ami; **a g. chap** *or* **fellow** un brave type; **g. and strong** bien fort; **a g. (long) walk** une bonne promenade, **ery g.!** (*all right*) très bien!; **that's g. of you** c'est gentil de ta part; **to feel g.** se sentir bien;

that isn't g. enough (*bad*) ça ne va pas; (*not sufficient*) ça ne suffit pas; **it's g. for us** ça nous fait du bien; **g. at** (*French etc*) *Sch* bon *or* fort en; **to be g. with** (*children*) savoir s'y prendre avec; **it's a g. thing (that)**... heureusement que...; **a g. many, a g. deal (of)** beaucoup (de); **as g. as** (*almost*) pratiquement; **g. afternoon, g. morning** bonjour; (*on leaving someone*) au revoir; **g. evening** bonsoir; **g. night** bonsoir; (*before going to bed*) bonne nuit; **to make g.** *vi* (*succeed*) réussir; – *vt* (*loss*) compenser; (*damage*) réparer; **G. Friday** Vendredi *m* Saint; – *n* (*virtue*) bien *m*; **for her g.** pour son bien; **there's some g. in him** il a du bon; **it's no g. crying/shouting/***etc* ça ne sert à rien de pleurer/crier/*etc*; **that's no g.** (*worthless*) ça ne vaut rien; (*bad*) ça ne va pas; **what's the g.?** à quoi bon?; **for g.** (*to leave, give up etc*) pour de bon. ◆**g.-for-nothing** *a* & *n* propre à rien (*mf*). ◆**g.-'humoured** *a* de bonne humeur. ◆**g.-'looking** *a* beau. ◆**goodness** *n* bonté *f*; **my g.!** mon Dieu! ◆**good'will** *n* bonne volonté *f*; (*zeal*) zèle *m*.

goodbye [gʊd'baɪ] *int* & *n* au revoir (*m inv*).

goodly ['gʊdlɪ] *a* (*size, number*) grand.

goods [gʊdz] *npl* marchandises *fpl*; (*articles for sale*) articles *mpl*.

gooey ['guːɪ] *a Fam* gluant, poisseux.

goof [guːf] *vi* **to g. (up)** (*blunder*) *Am* faire une gaffe.

goon [guːn] *n Fam* idiot, -ote *mf*.

goose, *pl* **geese** [guːs, giːs] *n* oie *f*; **g. pimples** *or* **bumps** chair *f* de poule. ◆**gooseflesh** *n* chair *f* de poule.

gooseberry ['gʊzbərɪ, *Am* 'guːsbərɪ] *n* groseille *f* à maquereau.

gorge [gɔːdʒ] **1** *n* (*ravine*) gorge *f*. **2** *vt* (*food*) engloutir; **to g. oneself** s'empiffrer (**on** de).

gorgeous ['gɔːdʒəs] *a* magnifique.

gorilla [gə'rɪlə] *n* gorille *m*.

gormless ['gɔːmləs] *a Fam* stupide.

gorse [gɔːs] *n inv* ajonc(s) *m*(*pl*).

gory ['gɔːrɪ] *a* (**-ier, -iest**) (*bloody*) sanglant; (*details*) *Fig* horrible.

gosh! [gɒʃ] *int Fam* mince (alors)!

go-slow [gəʊ'sləʊ] *n* (*strike*) grève *f* perlée.

gospel ['gɒspəl] *n* évangile *m*.

gossip ['gɒsɪp] *n* (*talk*) bavardage(s) *m*(*pl*); (*malicious*) cancan(s) *m*(*pl*); (*person*) commère *f*; **g. column** *Journ* échos *mpl*; – *vi* bavarder; (*maliciously*) cancaner. ◆**—ing** *a*, ◆**gossipy** *a* bavard, cancanier.

got, *Am* **gotten** [gɒt, 'gɒt(ə)n] *see* **get**.

Gothic ['gɒθɪk] *a* & *n* gothique (*m*).

gouge [gaʊdʒ] *vt* **to g. out** (*eye*) crever.

goulash ['guːlæʃ] *n Culin* goulasch *f*.

gourmet ['gʊəmeɪ] *n* gourmet *m*.

gout [gaʊt] *n Med* goutte *f*.

govern ['gʌvən] *vt* (*rule*) gouverner; (*city*) administrer; (*business*) gérer; (*emotion*) maîtriser, gouverner; (*influence*) déterminer; – *vi Pol* gouverner; **governing body** conseil *m* d'administration. ◆**governess** *n* gouvernante *f*. ◆**government** *n* gouvernement *m*; (*local*) administration *f*; – *a* (*department, policy etc*) gouvernemental; (*loan*) d'État. ◆**govern'mental** *a* gouvernemental. ◆**governor** *n* gouverneur *m*; (*of school*) administrateur, -trice *mf*; (*of prison*) directeur, -trice *mf*.

gown [gaʊn] *n* (*dress*) robe *f*; (*of judge, lecturer*) toge *f*.

GP [dʒiː'piː] *n abbr* (*general practitioner*) (médecin *m*) généraliste *m*.

GPO [dʒiːpiː'əʊ] *abbr* (*General Post Office*) = PTT *fpl*.

grab [græb] *vt* (**-bb-**) **to g. (hold of)** saisir, agripper; **to g. sth from s.o.** arracher qch à qn.

grace [greɪs] **1** *n* (*charm, goodwill etc*) *Rel* grâce *f*; (*extension of time*) délai *m* de grâce; **to say g.** dire le bénédicité. **2** *vt* (*adorn*) orner; (*honour*) honorer (**with** de). ◆**graceful** *a* gracieux. ◆**gracious** *a* (*kind*) aimable, gracieux (**to** envers); (*elegant*) élégant; **good g.!** *Fam* bonté divine!

gradation [grə'deɪʃ(ə)n, *Am* greɪ'deɪʃ(ə)n] *n* gradation *f*.

grade [greɪd] *n* catégorie *f*; *Mil Math* grade *m*; (*of milk*) qualité *f*; (*of eggs*) calibre *m*; (*level*) niveau *m*; (*mark*) *Sch Univ* note *f*; (*class*) *Am Sch* classe *f*; **g. school** *Am* école *f* primaire; **g. crossing** *Am* passage *m* à niveau; – *vt* (*classify*) classer; (*colours etc*) graduer; (*paper*) *Sch Univ* noter.

gradient ['greɪdɪənt] *n* (*slope*) inclinaison *f*.

gradual ['grædʒʊəl] *a* progressif, graduel; (*slope*) doux. ◆**—ly** *adv* progressivement, peu à peu.

graduat/e ['grædʒʊeɪt] *vi Univ* obtenir son diplôme; *Am Sch* obtenir son baccalauréat; **to g. from** sortir de; – *vt* (*mark with degrees*) graduer; – ['grædʒʊət] *n* diplômé, -ée *mf*, licencié, -ée *mf*. ◆**—ed** *a* (*tube etc*) gradué; **to be g.** *Am Sch Univ* = **to graduate** *vi*. ◆**gradu'ation** *n Univ* remise *f* des diplômes.

graffiti [grə'fiːtɪ] *npl* graffiti *mpl*.

graft [grɑːft] *n Med Bot* greffe *f*; – *vt* greffer (**on to** à).

grain [greɪn] *n* (*seed, particle*) grain *m*;

(*seeds*) grain(s) *m*(*pl*); (*in cloth*) fil *m*; (*in wood*) fibre *f*; (*in leather, paper*) grain *m*; (*of truth*) *Fig* once *f*.

gram(me) [græm] *n* gramme *m*.

grammar ['græmər] *n* grammaire *f*; **g. school** lycée *m*. ◆**gra'mmatical** *a* grammatical.

gramophone ['græməfəʊn] *n* phonographe *m*.

granary ['grænərɪ] *n Agr* grenier *m*; **g. loaf** pain *m* complet.

grand [grænd] **1** *a* (**-er, -est**) magnifique, grand; (*style*) grandiose; (*concert, duke*) grand; (*piano*) à queue; (*wonderful*) *Fam* magnifique. **2** *n inv Am Sl* mille dollars *mpl*; *Br Sl* mille livres *fpl*. ◆**grandeur** ['grændʒər] *n* magnificence *f*; (*of person, country*) grandeur *f*.

grandchild ['græntʃaɪld] *n* (*pl* **-children**) petit(e)-enfant *mf*. ◆**grand(d)ad** *n Fam* pépé *m*, papi *m*. ◆**granddaughter** *n* petite-fille *f*. ◆**grandfather** *n* grand-père *m*. ◆**grandmother** *n* grand-mère *f*. ◆**grandparents** *npl* grands-parents *mpl*. ◆**grandson** *n* petit-fils *m*.

grandstand ['grændstænd] *n Sp* tribune *f*.

grange [greɪndʒ] *n* (*house*) manoir *m*.

granite ['grænɪt] *n* granit(e) *m*.

granny ['grænɪ] *n Fam* mamie *f*.

grant [grɑːnt] **1** *vt* accorder (**to** à); (*request*) accéder à; (*prayer*) exaucer; (*admit*) admettre (**that** que); **to take for granted** (*event*) considérer comme allant de soi; (*person*) considérer comme faisant partie du décor; **I take (it) for granted that . . .** je présume que . . . . **2** *n* subvention *f*, allocation *f*; *Univ* bourse *f*.

granule ['grænjuːl] *n* granule *m*. ◆**granulated** *a* **g. sugar** sucre *m* cristallisé.

grape [greɪp] *n* grain *m* de raisin; *pl* le raisin, les raisins *mpl*; **to eat grapes** manger du raisin *or* des raisins; **g. harvest** vendange *f*. ◆**grapefruit** *n* pamplemousse *m*. ◆**grapevine** *n* **on the g.** *Fig* par le téléphone arabe.

graph [græf, grɑːf] *n* graphique *m*, courbe *f*; **g. paper** papier *m* millimétré.

graphic ['græfɪk] *a* graphique; (*description*) *Fig* explicite, vivant. ◆**graphically** *adv* (*to describe*) explicitement.

grapple ['græp(ə)l] *vi* **to g. with** (*person, problem etc*) se colleter avec.

grasp [grɑːsp] *vt* (*seize, understand*) saisir; – *n* (*firm hold*) prise *f*; (*understanding*) compréhension *f*; (*knowledge*) connaissance *f*; **to have a strong g.** (*strength of hand*) avoir de la poigne; **within s.o.'s g.** (*reach*) à la portée de qn. ◆**—ing** *a* (*greedy*) rapace.

grass [grɑːs] *n* herbe *f*; (*lawn*) gazon *m*; **the g. roots** *Pol* la base. ◆**grasshopper** *n* sauterelle *f*. ◆**grassland** *n* prairie *f*. ◆**grassy** *a* herbeux.

grat/e [greɪt] **1** *n* (*for fireplace*) grille *f* de foyer. **2** *vt Culin* râper. **3** *vi* (*of sound*) grincer (**on sur**); **to g. on the ears** écorcher les oreilles; **to g. on s.o.'s nerves** taper sur les nerfs de qn. ◆**—ing 1** *a* (*sound*) grinçant; *Fig* irritant. **2** *n* (*bars*) grille *f*. ◆**—er** *n Culin* râpe *f*.

grateful ['greɪtfʊl] *a* reconnaissant (**to** à, **for** de); (*words, letter*) de remerciement; (*friend, attitude*) plein de reconnaissance; **I'm g. (to you) for your help** je vous suis reconnaissant de votre aide; **I'd be g. if you'd be quieter** j'aimerais bien que tu fasses moins de bruit; **g. thanks** mes sincères remerciements. ◆**—ly** *adv* avec reconnaissance.

gratif/y ['grætɪfaɪ] *vt* (*whim*) satisfaire; **to g. s.o.** faire plaisir à qn. ◆**—ied** *a* très content (**with** *or* **at sth** de qch, **to do** de faire). ◆**—ying** *a* très satisfaisant; **it's g. to . . .** ça fait plaisir de . . . . ◆**gratifi'cation** *n* satisfaction *f*.

gratis ['grætɪs, 'greɪtɪs] *adv* gratis.

gratitude ['grætɪtjuːd] *n* reconnaissance *f*, gratitude *f* (**for** de).

gratuitous [grə'tjuːɪtəs] *a* (*act etc*) gratuit.

gratuity [grə'tjuːɪtɪ] *n* (*tip*) pourboire *m*.

grave[1] [greɪv] *n* tombe *f*; **g. digger** fossoyeur *m*. ◆**gravestone** *n* pierre *f* tombale. ◆**graveyard** *n* cimetière *m*; **auto g.** *Am Fam* cimetière *m* de voitures.

grave[2] [greɪv] *a* (**-er, -est**) (*serious*) grave. ◆**—ly** *adv* gravement; (*concerned, displeased*) extrêmement.

gravel ['græv(ə)l] *n* gravier *m*.

gravitate ['grævɪteɪt] *vi* **to g. towards** (*be drawn towards*) être attiré vers; (*move towards*) se diriger vers. ◆**gravi'tation** *n* gravitation *f*.

gravity ['grævɪtɪ] *n* **1** (*seriousness*) gravité *f*. **2** *Phys* pesanteur *f*, gravité *f*.

gravy ['greɪvɪ] *n* jus *m* de viande.

gray [greɪ] *Am* = grey.

graze [greɪz] **1** *vi* (*of cattle*) paître. **2** *vt* (*scrape*) écorcher; (*touch lightly*) frôler, effleurer; – *n* (*wound*) écorchure *f*.

grease [griːs] *n* graisse *f*; – *vt* graisser. ◆**greaseproof** *a* & *n* **g. (paper)** papier *m* sulfurisé. ◆**greasy** *a* (**-ier, -iest**) graisseux; (*hair*) gras; (*road*) glissant.

great [greɪt] *a* (**-er, -est**) grand; (*effort, heat,* *parcel*) gros, grand; (*excellent*) magnifique, merveilleux; **g. at** (*English, tennis etc*) doué pour; **a g. deal** *or* **number (of), a g. many** beaucoup (de); **a g. opinion of** une haute opinion de; **a very g. age** un âge très avancé; **the greatest team/***etc* (*best*) la meilleure équipe/*etc*; **Greater London** le grand Londres. ◆**g.-'grandfather** *n* arrière-grand-père *m*. ◆**g.-'grandmother** *n* arrière-grand-mère *f*. ◆**greatly** *adv* (*much*) beaucoup; (*very*) très, bien; **I g. prefer** je préfère de beaucoup. ◆**greatness** *n* (*in size, importance*) grandeur *f*; (*in degree*) intensité *f*.

Great Britain [greɪt'brɪt(ə)n] *n* Grande-Bretagne *f*.

Greece [griːs] *n* Grèce *f*. ◆**Greek** *a* grec; – *n* Grec *m*, Greque *f*; (*language*) grec *m*.

greed [griːd] *n* avidité *f* (**for** de); (*for food*) gourmandise *f*. ◆**greed/y** *a* (**-ier, -iest**) avide (**for** de); (*for food*) glouton, gourmand. ◆**—ily** *adv* avidement; (*to eat*) gloutonnement. ◆**—iness** *n* = **greed**.

green [griːn] *a* (**-er, -est**) vert; (*pale*) blême, vert; (*immature*) *Fig* inexpérimenté, naïf; **to turn** *or* **go g.** verdir; **the g. belt** (*land*) la ceinture verte; **the g. light** *Fig* le (feu) vert; **to have g. fingers** *or Am* **a g. thumb** avoir la main verte; **g. with envy** *Fig* vert de jalousie; – *n* (*colour*) vert *m*; (*lawn*) pelouse *f*; (*village square*) place *f* gazonnée; *pl Culin* légumes *mpl* verts. ◆**greenery** *n* (*plants, leaves*) verdure *f*. ◆**greenfly** *n* puceron *m* (des plantes). ◆**greengrocer** *n* marchand, -ande *mf* de légumes. ◆**greenhouse** *n* serre *f*. ◆**greenish** *a* verdâtre. ◆**greenness** *n* (*colour*) vert *m*; (*greenery*) verdure *f*.

greengage ['griːngeɪdʒ] *n* (*plum*) reine-claude *f*.

Greenland ['griːnlənd] *n* Groenland *m*.

greet [griːt] *vt* saluer, accueillir; **to g. s.o.** (*of sight*) s'offrir aux regards de qn. ◆**—ing** *n* salutation *f*; (*welcome*) accueil *m*; *pl* (*for birthday, festival*) vœux *mpl*; **send my greetings to . . .** envoie mon bon souvenir à . . . ; **greetings card** carte *f* de vœux.

gregarious [grɪ'geərɪəs] *a* (*person*) sociable; (*instinct*) grégaire.

gremlin ['gremlɪn] *n Fam* petit diable *m*.

grenade [grə'neɪd] *n* (*bomb*) grenade *f*.

grew [gruː] *see* **grow**.

grey [greɪ] *a* (**-er, -est**) gris; (*outlook*) *Fig* sombre; **to be going g.** grisonner; – *vi* **to be greying** être grisonnant. ◆**g.-'haired** *a* aux cheveux gris. ◆**greyhound** *n* lévrier *m*. ◆**greyish** *a* grisâtre.

grid [grɪd] *n* (*grating*) grille *f*; (*system*) *El* réseau *m*; *Culin* gril *m*. ◆**gridiron** *n Culin* gril *m*.

griddle ['grɪd(ə)l] *n* (*on stove*) plaque *f* à griller.

grief [griːf] *n* chagrin *m*, douleur *f*; **to come to g.** avoir des ennuis; (*of driver, pilot etc*) avoir un accident; (*of plan*) échouer; **good g.!** ciel!, bon sang!

grieve [griːv] *vt* peiner, affliger; – *vi* s'affliger (**over** de); **to g. for s.o.** pleurer qn. ◆**grievance** *n* grief *m*; *pl* (*complaints*) doléances *fpl*.

grievous ['griːvəs] *a* (*serious*) très grave.

grill [grɪl] **1** *n* (*utensil*) gril *m*; (*dish*) grillade *f*; – *vti* griller. **2** *vt* (*question*) *Fam* cuisiner.

grille [grɪl] *n* (*metal bars*) grille *f*; (**radiator**) **g.** *Aut* calandre *f*.

grim [grɪm] *a* (**grimmer, grimmest**) sinistre; (*face*) sévère; (*truth*) brutal; (*bad*) *Fam* (plutôt) affreux; **a g. determination** une volonté inflexible. ◆**—ly** *adv* (*to look at*) sévèrement.

grimace ['grɪməs] *n* grimace *f*; – *vi* grimacer.

grime [graɪm] *n* saleté *f*. ◆**grimy** *a* (**-ier, -iest**) sale.

grin [grɪn] *vi* (**-nn-**) avoir un large sourire; (*with pain*) avoir un rictus; – *n* large sourire *m*; rictus *m*.

grind [graɪnd] **1** *vt* (*pt & pp* **ground**) moudre; (*blade, tool*) aiguiser; (*handle*) tourner; (*oppress*) *Fig* écraser; **to g. one's teeth** grincer des dents; – *vi* **to g. to a halt** s'arrêter (progressivement). **2** *n Fam* corvée *f*, travail *m* long et monotone. ◆**—ing** *a* **g. poverty** la misère noire. ◆**—er** *n* **coffee g.** moulin *m* à café.

grip [grɪp] *vt* (**-pp-**) (*seize*) saisir; (*hold*) tenir serré; (*of story*) *Fig* empoigner (*qn*); **to g. the road** (*of tyres*) adhérer à la route; – *vi* (*of brakes*) mordre; – *n* (*hold*) prise *f*; (*hand clasp*) poigne *f*; **get a g. on yourself!** secoue-toi!; **to get to grips with** (*problem*) s'attaquer à; **in the g. of** en proie à. ◆**gripping** *a* (*book, film etc*) prenant.

gripe [graɪp] *vi* (*complain*) *Sl* rouspéter.

grisly ['grɪzlɪ] *a* (*gruesome*) horrible.

gristle ['grɪs(ə)l] *n Culin* cartilage *m*.

grit [grɪt] **1** *n* (*sand*) sable *m*; (*gravel*) gravillon *m*; – *vt* (**-tt-**) (*road*) sabler. **2** *n* (*pluck*) *Fam* cran *m*. **3** *vt* (**-tt-**) **to g. one's teeth** serrer les dents.

grizzle ['grɪz(ə)l] *vi Fam* pleurnicher. ◆**grizzly** *a* **1** (*child*) *Fam* pleurnicheur. **2** (*bear*) gris.

groan [grəʊn] *vi* (*with pain*) gémir;

(*complain*) grogner, gémir; – *n* gémissement *m*; grognement *m*.

grocer ['grəʊsər] *n* épicier, -ière *mf*; **grocer's (shop)** épicerie *f*. ◆**grocery** *n* (*shop*) épicerie *f*; *pl* (*food*) épicerie *f*.

grog [grɒg] *n* (*drink*) grog *m*.

groggy ['grɒgɪ] *a* (**-ier, -iest**) (*weak*) faible; (*shaky on one's feet*) pas solide sur les jambes.

groin [grɔɪn] *n Anat* aine *f*.

groom [gruːm] **1** *n* (*bridegroom*) marié *m*. **2** *n* (*for horses*) lad *m*; – *vt* (*horse*) panser; **to g. s.o. for** (*job*) *Fig* préparer qn pour; **well groomed** (*person*) très soigné.

groove [gruːv] *n* (*for sliding door etc*) rainure *f*; (*in record*) sillon *m*.

grope [grəʊp] *vi* **to g. (about)** tâtonner; **to g. for** chercher à tâtons.

gross [grəʊs] **1** *a* (**-er, -est**) (*coarse*) grossier; (*error*) gros, grossier; (*injustice*) flagrant. **2** *a* (*weight, income*) *Com* brut; – *vt* faire une recette brute de. **3** *n* (*number*) grosse *f*. ◆**—ly** *adv* grossièrement; (*very*) énormément, extrêmement.

grotesque [grəʊ'tesk] *a* (*ludicrous, strange*) grotesque; (*frightening*) monstrueux.

grotto ['grɒtəʊ] *n* (*pl* **-oes** *or* **-os**) grotte *f*.

grotty ['grɒtɪ] *a* (**-ier, -iest**) *Fam* affreux, moche.

ground[1] [graʊnd] **1** *n* terre *f*, sol *m*; (*area for camping, football etc*) & *Fig* terrain *m*; (*estate*) terres *fpl*; (*earth*) *El Am* terre *f*, masse *f*; (*background*) fond *m*; *pl* (*reasons*) raisons *fpl*, motifs *mpl*; (*gardens*) parc *m*; **on the g.** (*lying etc*) par terre; **to lose g.** perdre du terrain; **g. floor** rez-de-chaussée *m inv*; **g. frost** gelée *f* blanche. **2** *vt* (*aircraft*) bloquer *or* retenir au sol. ◆**—ing** *n* connaissances *fpl* (de fond) (in en). ◆**groundless** *a* sans fondement. ◆**groundnut** *n* arachide *f*. ◆**groundsheet** *n* tapis *m* de sol. ◆**groundswell** *n* lame *f* de fond. ◆**groundwork** *n* préparation *f*.

ground[2] [graʊnd] *see* **grind 1**; – *a* (*coffee*) moulu; – *npl* **(coffee) grounds** marc *m* (de café).

group [gruːp] *n* groupe *m*; – *vt* **to g. (together)** grouper; – *vi* se grouper. ◆**—ing** *n* (*group*) groupe *m*.

grouse [graʊs] **1** *n inv* (*bird*) coq *m* de bruyère. **2** *vi* (*complain*) *Fam* rouspéter.

grove [grəʊv] *n* bocage *m*.

grovel ['grɒv(ə)l] *vi* (**-ll-**, *Am* **-l-**) *Pej* ramper, s'aplatir (**to s.o.** devant qn).

grow [grəʊ] *vi* (*pt* **grew**, *pp* **grown**) (*of person*) grandir; (*of plant, hair*) pousser; (*increase*) augmenter, grandir, croître; (*expand*) s'agrandir; **to g. fat(ter)** grossir; **to g. to like** finir par aimer; **to g. into** devenir; **to g. on s.o.** (*of book, music etc*) plaire progressivement à qn; **to g. out of** (*one's clothes*) devenir trop grand pour; (*a habit*) perdre; **to g. up** devenir adulte; **when I g. up** quand je serai grand; – *vt* (*plant, crops*) cultiver, faire pousser; (*beard, hair*) laisser pousser. ◆**—ing** *a* (*child*) qui grandit; (*number*) grandissant. ◆**grown** *a* (*full-grown*) adulte. ◆**grown-up** *n* grande personne *f*, adulte *mf*; – *a* (*ideas etc*) d'adulte. ◆**grower** *n* (*person*) cultivateur, -trice *mf*.

growl [graʊl] *vi* grogner (**at** contre); – *n* grognement *m*.

growth [grəʊθ] *n* croissance *f*; (*increase*) augmentation *f* (**in** de); (*of hair*) pousse *f*; (*beard*) barbe *f*; *Med* tumeur *f* (**on** à).

grub [grʌb] *n* (*food*) *Fam* bouffe *f*.

grubby ['grʌbɪ] *a* (**-ier, -iest**) sale.

grudg/e [grʌdʒ] **1** *vt* (*give*) donner à contrecœur; (*reproach*) reprocher (**s.o. sth** qch à qn); **to g. doing** faire à contrecœur. **2** *n* rancune *f*; **to have a g. against** en vouloir à. ◆**—ing** *a* peu généreux. ◆**—ingly** *adv* (*to give etc*) à contrecœur.

gruelling, *Am* **grueling** ['gruəlɪŋ] *a* (*day, detail etc*) éprouvant, atroce.

gruesome ['gruːsəm] *a* horrible.

gruff [grʌf] *a* (**-er, -est**) (*voice, person*) bourru.

grumble ['grʌmb(ə)l] *vi* (*complain*) grogner (**about, at** contre), se plaindre (**about, at** de).

grumpy ['grʌmpɪ] *a* (**-ier, -iest**) grincheux.

grunt [grʌnt] *vti* grogner; – *n* grognement *m*.

guarantee [gærən'tiː] *n* garantie *f*; – *vt* garantir (**against** contre); (*vouch for*) se porter garant de; **to g. (s.o.) that** certifier *or* garantir (à qn) que. ◆**guarantor** *n* garant, -ante *mf*.

guard [gɑːd] *n* (*vigilance, group of soldiers etc*) garde *f*; (*individual person*) garde *m*; *Rail* chef *m* de train; **to keep a g. on** surveiller; **under g.** sous surveillance; **on one's g.** sur ses gardes; **to catch s.o. off his g.** prendre qn au dépourvu; **on g. (duty)** de garde; **to stand g.** monter la garde; – *vt* (*protect*) protéger (**against** contre); (*watch over*) surveiller, garder; – *vi* **to g. against** (*protect oneself*) se prémunir contre; (*prevent*) empêcher; **to g. against doing** se garder de faire. ◆**—ed** *a* (*cautious*) prudent.

◆**guardian** *n* gardien, -ienne *mf*; (*of child*) *Jur* tuteur, -trice *mf*.

guerrilla [gə'rɪlə] *n* (*person*) guérillero *m*; **g. warfare** guérilla *f*.

guess [ges] *n* conjecture *f*; (*intuition*) intuition *f*; (*estimate*) estimation *f*; **to make a g.** (essayer de) deviner; **an educated** *or* **informed g.** une conjecture fondée; **at a g.** au jugé, à vue de nez; – *vt* deviner (**that** que); (*estimate*) estimer; (*suppose*) *Am* supposer (**that** que); (*think*) *Am* croire (**that** que); – *vi* deviner; **I g. (so)** *Am* je suppose; je crois. ◆**guesswork** *n* hypothèse *f*; **by g.** au jugé.

guest [gest] *n* invité, -ée *mf*; (*in hotel*) client, -ente *mf*; (*at meal*) convive *mf*; – *a* (*speaker, singer etc*) invité. ◆**guesthouse** *n* pension *f* de famille. ◆**guestroom** *n* chambre *f* d'ami.

guffaw [gə'fɔː] *vi* rire bruyamment.

guidance ['gaɪdəns] *n* (*advice*) conseils *mpl*.

guid/e [gaɪd] *n* (*person, book etc*) guide *m*; (*indication*) indication *f*; (**girl**) **g.** éclaireuse *f*; **g. dog** chien *m* d'aveugle; **g. book** guide *m*; – *vt* (*lead*) guider. ◆**—ed** *a* (*missile, rocket*) téléguidé; **g. tour** visite *f* guidée. ◆**—ing** *a* (*principle*) directeur. ◆**guidelines** *npl* lignes *fpl* directrices, indications *fpl* à suivre.

guild [gɪld] *n* association *f*; *Hist* corporation *f*.

guile [gaɪl] *n* (*deceit*) ruse *f*.

guillotine ['gɪlətiːn] *n* guillotine *f*; (*for paper*) massicot *m*.

guilt [gɪlt] *n* culpabilité *f*. ◆**guilty** *a* (-**ier**, -**iest**) coupable; **g. person** coupable *mf*; **to find s.o. g.** déclarer qn coupable.

guinea pig ['gɪnɪpɪg] *n* (*animal*) & *Fig* cobaye *m*.

guise [gaɪz] *n* **under the g. of** sous l'apparence de.

guitar [gɪ'tɑːr] *n* guitare *f*. ◆**guitarist** *n* guitariste *mf*.

gulf [gʌlf] *n* (*in sea*) golfe *m*; (*chasm*) gouffre *m*; **a g. between** *Fig* un abîme entre.

gull [gʌl] *n* (*bird*) mouette *f*.

gullet ['gʌlɪt] *n* gosier *m*.

gullible ['gʌlɪb(ə)l] *a* crédule.

gully ['gʌlɪ] *n* (*valley*) ravine *f*; (*drain*) rigole *f*.

gulp [gʌlp] **1** *vt* **to g. (down)** avaler (vite); – *n* (*of drink*) gorgée *f*, lampée *f*; **in** *or* **at one g.** d'une seule gorgée. **2** *vi* (*with emotion*) avoir la gorge serrée; – *n* serrement *m* de gorge.

gum¹ [gʌm] *n* *Anat* gencive *f*. ◆**gumboil** *n* abcès *m* (dentaire).

gum² [gʌm] **1** *n* (*glue from tree*) gomme *f*; (*any glue*) colle *f*; – *vt* (-**mm**-) coller. **2** *n* (*for chewing*) chewing-gum *m*.

gumption ['gʌmpʃ(ə)n] *n* *Fam* (*courage*) initiative *f*; (*commonsense*) jugeote *f*.

gun [gʌn] *n* pistolet *m*, revolver *m*; (*cannon*) canon *m*; – *vt* (-**nn**-) **to g. down** abattre. ◆**gunfight** *n* échange *m* de coups de feu. ◆**gunfire** *n* coups *mpl* de feu; *Mil* tir *m* d'artillerie. ◆**gunman** *n* (*pl* -**men**) bandit *m* armé. ◆**gunner** *n* *Mil* artilleur *m*. ◆**gunpoint** *n* **at g.** sous la menace d'un pistolet *or* d'une arme. ◆**gunpowder** *n* poudre *f* à canon. ◆**gunshot** *n* coup *m* de feu; **g. wound** blessure *f* par balle.

gurgle ['gɜːg(ə)l] *vi* (*of water*) glouglouter; – *n* glouglou *m*.

guru ['gʊruː] *n* (*leader*) *Fam* gourou *m*.

gush [gʌʃ] *vi* jaillir (**out of** de); – *n* jaillissement *m*.

gust [gʌst] *n* (*of smoke*) bouffée *f*; **g. (of wind)** rafale *f* (de vent). ◆**gusty** *a* (-**ier**, -**iest**) (*weather*) venteux; (*day*) de vent.

gusto ['gʌstəʊ] *n* **with g.** avec entrain.

gut [gʌt] **1** *n* *Anat* intestin *m*; (*catgut*) boyau *m*; *pl* *Fam* (*innards*) ventre *m*, tripes *fpl*; (*pluck*) cran *m*, tripes *fpl*; **he hates your guts** *Fam* il ne peut pas te sentir. **2** *vt* (-**tt**-) (*of fire*) dévaster.

gutter ['gʌtər] *n* (*on roof*) gouttière *f*; (*in street*) caniveau *m*.

guttural ['gʌtərəl] *a* guttural.

guy [gaɪ] *n* (*fellow*) *Fam* type *m*.

guzzle ['gʌz(ə)l] *vi* (*eat*) bâfrer; – *vt* (*eat*) engloutir; (*drink*) siffler.

gym [dʒɪm] *n* gym(nastique) *f*; (*gymnasium*) gymnase *m*; **g. shoes** tennis *fpl*. ◆**gym'nasium** *n* gymnase *m*. ◆**gymnast** *n* gymnaste *mf*. ◆**gym'nastics** *n* gymnastique *f*.

gynaecology, *Am* **gynecology** [gaɪnɪ'kɒlədʒɪ] *n* gynécologie *f*. ◆**gynaecologist** *n*, *Am* ◆**gynecologist** *n* gynécologue *mf*.

gypsy ['dʒɪpsɪ] = **gipsy**.

gyrate [dʒaɪ'reɪt] *vi* tournoyer.

H

H, h [eɪtʃ] *n* H, h *m*; **H bomb** bombe *f* H.

haberdasher ['hæbədæʃər] *n* mercier, -ière *mf*; (*men's outfitter*) *Am* chemisier *m*. ◆**haberdashery** *n* mercerie *f*; *Am* chemiserie *f*.

habit ['hæbɪt] *n* **1** habitude *f*; **to be in/get into the h. of doing** avoir/prendre l'habitude de faire; **to make a h. of doing** avoir pour habitude de faire. **2** (*addiction*) *Med* accoutumance *f*; **a h.-forming drug** une drogue qui crée une accoutumance. **3** (*costume*) *Rel* habit *m*. ◆**ha'bitual** *a* habituel; (*smoker, drinker etc*) invétéré. ◆**ha'bitually** *adv* habituellement.

habitable ['hæbɪtəb(ə)l] *a* habitable. ◆**habitat** *n* (*of animal, plant*) habitat *m*. ◆**habi'tation** *n* habitation *f*; **fit for h.** habitable.

hack [hæk] **1** *vt* (*cut*) tailler, hacher. **2** *n* (*old horse*) rosse *f*; (*hired*) cheval *m* de louage; **h. (writer)** *Pej* écrivaillon *m*.

hackney ['hæknɪ] *a* **h. carriage** *Hist* fiacre *m*.

hackneyed ['hæknɪd] *a* (*saying*) rebattu, banal.

had [hæd] *see* **have**.

haddock ['hædək] *n* (*fish*) aiglefin *m*; **smoked h.** haddock *m*.

haemorrhage ['hemərɪdʒ] *n Med* hémorragie *f*.

haemorrhoids ['hemərɔɪdz] *npl* hémorroïdes *fpl*.

hag [hæg] *n* (*woman*) *Pej* (vieille) sorcière *f*.

haggard ['hægəd] *a* (*person, face*) hâve, émacié.

haggl/e ['hæg(ə)l] *vi* marchander; **to h. over** (*thing*) marchander; (*price*) débattre, discuter. ◆**—ing** *n* marchandage *m*.

Hague (The) [ðə'heɪg] *n* La Haye.

ha-ha! [hɑː'hɑː] *int* (*laughter*) ha, ha!

hail[1] [heɪl] *n Met & Fig* grêle *f*; – *v imp Met* grêler; **it's hailing** il grêle. ◆**hailstone** *n* grêlon *m*.

hail[2] [heɪl] **1** *vt* (*greet*) saluer; (*taxi*) héler. **2** *vi* **to h. from** (*of person*) être originaire de; (*of ship etc*) être en provenance de.

hair [heər] *n* (*on head*) cheveux *mpl*; (*on body, of animal*) poils *mpl*; **a h.** (*on head*) un cheveu; (*on body, of animal*) un poil; **by a hair's breadth** de justesse; **long-/red-/***etc* **haired** aux cheveux longs/roux/*etc*; **h. cream** brillantine *f*; **h. dryer** sèche-cheveux *m inv*; **h. spray** (bombe *f* de) laque *f*. ◆**hairbrush** *n* brosse *f* à cheveux. ◆**haircut** *n* coupe *f* de cheveux; **to have a h.** se faire couper les cheveux. ◆**hairdo** *n* (*pl* **-dos**) *Fam* coiffure *f*. ◆**hairdresser** *n* coiffeur, -euse *mf*. ◆**hairgrip** *n* pince *f* à cheveux. ◆**hairnet** *n* résille *f*. ◆**hairpiece** *n* postiche *m*. ◆**hairpin** *n* épingle *f* à cheveux; **h. bend** *Aut* virage *m* en épingle à cheveux. ◆**hair-raising** *a* à faire dresser les cheveux sur la tête. ◆**hair-splitting** *n* ergotage *m*. ◆**hairstyle** *n* coiffure *f*.

hairy ['heərɪ] *a* (**-ier, -iest**) (*person, animal, body*) poilu; (*unpleasant, frightening*) *Fam* effroyable.

hake [heɪk] *n* (*fish*) colin *m*.

hale [heɪl] *a* **h. and hearty** vigoureux.

half [hɑːf] *n* (*pl* **halves**) moitié *f*, demi, -ie *mf*; (*of match*) *Sp* mi-temps *f*; **h. (of) the apple/***etc* la moitié de la pomme/*etc*; **ten and a h.** dix et demi; **ten and a h. weeks** dix semaines et demie; **to cut in h.** couper en deux; **to go halves with** partager les frais avec; – *a* demi; **h. a day, a h.-day** une demi-journée; **at h. price** à moitié prix; **h. man h. beast** mi-homme mi-bête; **h. sleeves** manches *fpl* mi-longues; – *adv* (*dressed, full etc*) à demi, à moitié; (*almost*) presque; **h. asleep** à moitié endormi; **h. past one** une heure et demie; **he isn't h. lazy/***etc* *Fam* il est rudement paresseux/*etc*; **h. as much as** moitié moins que; **h. as much again** moitié plus.

half-back ['hɑːfbæk] *n Fb* demi *m*. ◆**h.-'baked** *a* (*idea*) *Fam* à la manque, à la noix. ◆**h.-breed** *n*, ◆**h.-caste** *n Pej* métis, -isse *mf*. ◆**h.-(a-)'dozen** *n* demi-douzaine *f*. ◆**h.-'hearted** *a* (*person, manner*) peu enthousiaste; (*effort*) timide. ◆**h.-'hour** *n* demi-heure *f*. ◆**h.-light** *n* demi-jour *m*. ◆**h.-'mast** *n* **at h.-mast** (*flag*) en berne. ◆**h.-'open** *a* entrouvert. ◆**h.-'term** *n Sch* petites vacances *fpl*, congé *m* de demi-trimestre. ◆**h.-'time** *n Sp* mi-temps *f*. ◆**half'way** *adv* (*between places*) à mi-chemin (**between** entre); **to fill/***etc* **h.** remplir/*etc* à moitié; **h. through**

(*book*) à la moitié de. ◆**h.-wit** *n*, ◆**h.-'witted** *a* imbécile (*mf*).
halibut ['hælıbət] *n* (*fish*) flétan *m*.
hall [hɔːl] *n* (*room*) salle *f*; (*house entrance*) entrée *f*, vestibule *m*; (*of hotel*) hall *m*; (*mansion*) manoir *m*; (*for meals*) *Univ* réfectoire *m*; **h. of residence** *Univ* pavillon *m* universitaire; **halls of residence** cité *f* universitaire; **lecture h.** *Univ* amphithéâtre *m*. ◆**hallmark** *n* (*on silver or gold*) poinçon *m*; *Fig* sceau *m*. ◆**hallstand** *n* portemanteau *m*. ◆**hallway** *n* entrée *f*, vestibule *m*.
hallelujah [hælı'luːjə] *n & int* alléluia (*m*).
hallo! [hə'ləʊ] *int* (*greeting*) bonjour!; *Tel* allô!; (*surprise*) tiens!
hallow ['hæləʊ] *vt* sanctifier.
Hallowe'en [hæləʊ'iːn] *n* la veille de la Toussaint.
hallucination [həluːsı'neıʃ(ə)n] *n* hallucination *f*.
halo ['heıləʊ] *n* (*pl* **-oes** *or* **-os**) auréole *f*, halo *m*.
halt [hɔːlt] *n* halte *f*; **to call a h. to** mettre fin à; **to come to a h.** s'arrêter; – *vi* faire halte; – *int Mil* halte! ◆**—ing** *a* (*voice*) hésitant.
halve [hɑːv] *vt* (*time, expense*) réduire de moitié; (*cake, number etc*) diviser en deux.
ham [hæm] *n* **1** jambon *m*; **h. and eggs** œufs *mpl* au jambon. **2** (*actor*) *Th Pej* cabotin, -ine *mf*. ◆**h.-'fisted** *a Fam* maladroit.
hamburger ['hæmbɜːgər] *n* hamburger *m*.
hamlet ['hæmlıt] *n* hameau *m*.
hammer ['hæmər] *n* marteau *m*; – *vt* (*metal, table*) marteler; (*nail*) enfoncer (**into** dans); (*defeat*) *Fam* battre à plate(s) couture(s); (*criticize*) *Fam* démolir; **to h. out** (*agreement*) mettre au point; – *vi* frapper (au marteau). ◆**—ing** *n* (*defeat*) *Fam* raclée *f*, défaite *f*.
hammock ['hæmək] *n* hamac *m*.
hamper ['hæmpər] **1** *vt* gêner. **2** *n* (*basket*) panier *m*; (*laundry basket*) *Am* panier *m* à linge.
hamster ['hæmstər] *n* hamster *m*.
hand[1] [hænd] **1** *n* main *f*; **to hold in one's h.** tenir à la main; **by h.** (*to deliver etc*) à la main; **at** *or* **to h.** (*within reach*) sous la main, à portée de la main; **(close) at h.** (*person etc*) tout près; (*day etc*) proche; **in h.** (*situation*) bien en main; (*matter*) en question; (*money*) disponible; **on h.** (*ready for use*) disponible; **to have s.o. on one's hands** *Fig* avoir qn sur les bras; **on the right h.** du côté droit (**of** de); **on the one h.** . . . d'une part . . . : **on the other h.** . . . d'autre part . . . ; **hands up!** (*in attack*) haut les mains!; *Sch* levez la main!; **hands off!** pas touche!, bas les pattes!; **my hands are full** *Fig* je suis très occupé; **to give s.o. a (helping) h.** donner un coup de main à qn; **to get out of h.** (*of person*) devenir impossible; (*of situation*) devenir incontrôlable; **h. in h.** la main dans la main; **h. in h. with** (*together with*) *Fig* de pair avec; **at first h.** de première main; **to win hands down** gagner haut la main; – *a* (*luggage etc*) à main. **2** *n* (*worker*) ouvrier, -ière *mf*; (*of clock*) aiguille *f*; *Cards* jeu *m*; (*writing*) écriture *f*. ◆**handbag** *n* sac *m* à main. ◆**handbook** *n* (*manual*) manuel *m*; (*guide*) guide *m*. ◆**handbrake** *n* frein *m* à main. ◆**handbrush** *n* balayette *f*. ◆**handcuff** *vt* passer les menottes à. ◆**handcuffs** *npl* menottes *fpl*. ◆**hand'made** *a* fait à la main. ◆**hand'picked** *a Fig* trié sur le volet. ◆**handrail** *n* (*on stairs*) rampe *f*. ◆**handshake** *n* poignée *f* de main. ◆**handwriting** *n* écriture *f*. ◆**hand'written** *a* écrit à la main.
hand[2] [hænd] *vt* (*give*) donner (**to** à); **to h. down** (*bring down*) descendre; (*knowledge, heirloom*) transmettre (**to** à); **to h. in** remettre; **to h. out** distribuer; **to h. over** remettre; (*power*) transmettre; **to h. round** (*cakes*) passer. ◆**handout** *n* (*leaflet*) prospectus *m*; (*money*) aumône *f*.
handful ['hændfʊl] *n* (*bunch, group*) poignée *f*; **(quite) a h.** (*difficult*) *Fig* difficile.
handicap ['hændıkæp] *n* (*disadvantage*) & *Sp* handicap *m*; – *vt* (**-pp-**) handicaper. ◆**handicapped** *a* (*disabled*) handicapé.
handicraft ['hændıkrɑːft] *n* artisanat *m* d'art. ◆**handiwork** *n* artisanat *m* d'art; (*action*) *Fig* ouvrage *m*.
handkerchief ['hæŋkətʃıf] *n* (*pl* **-fs**) mouchoir *m*; (*for neck*) foulard *m*.
handle ['hænd(ə)l] **1** *n* (*of door*) poignée *f*; (*of knife*) manche *m*; (*of bucket*) anse *f*; (*of saucepan*) queue *f*; (*of pump*) bras *m*. **2** *vt* (*manipulate*) manier; (*touch*) toucher à; (*ship, vehicle*) manœuvrer; (*deal with*) s'occuper de; (*difficult child etc*) s'y prendre avec; – *vi* **to h. well** (*of machine*) être facile à manier.
handlebars ['hænd(ə)lbɑːz] *npl* guidon *m*.
handsome ['hænsəm] *a* (*person, building etc*) beau; (*gift*) généreux; (*profit, sum*) considérable. ◆**—ly** *adv* (*generously*) généreusement.
handy ['hændı] *a* (**-ier, -iest**) (*convenient, practical*) commode, pratique; (*skilful*) habile (**at doing** à faire); (*useful*) utile; (*near*) proche, accessible; **to come in h.** se

révéler utile; **to keep h.** avoir sous la main. **◆handyman** *n* (*pl* **-men**) (*DIY enthusiast*) bricoleur *m*.

hang¹ [hæŋ] **1** *vt* (*pt & pp* **hung**) suspendre (**on, from** à); (*on hook*) accrocher (**on, from** à), suspendre; (*wallpaper*) poser; (*let dangle*) laisser pendre (**from, out of** de); **to h. with** (*decorate with*) orner de; **to h. out** (*washing*) étendre; (*flag*) arborer; **to h. up** (*picture etc*) accrocher; – *vi* (*dangle*) pendre; (*of threat*) planer; (*of fog, smoke*) flotter; **to h. about** (*loiter*) traîner, rôder; (*wait*) *Fam* attendre; **to h. down** (*dangle*) pendre; (*of hair*) tomber; **to h. on** (*hold out*) résister; (*wait*) *Fam* attendre; **to h. on to** (*cling to*) ne pas lâcher; (*keep*) garder; **to h. out** (*of tongue, shirt*) pendre; (*live*) *Sl* crécher; **to h. together** (*of facts*) se tenir; (*of plan*) tenir debout; **to h. up** *Tel* raccrocher. **2** *n* **to get the h. of sth** *Fam* arriver à comprendre qch; **to get the h. of doing** *Fam* trouver le truc pour faire. **◆—ing¹** *n* suspension *f*; – *a* suspendu (**from** à); (*leg, arm*) pendant; **h. on** (*wall*) accroché à. **◆hang-glider** *n* delta-plane® *m*. **◆hang-gliding** *n* vol *m* libre. **◆hangnail** *n* petites peaux *fpl*. **◆hangover** *n Fam* gueule *f* de bois. **◆hangup** *n Fam* complexe *m*.

hang² [hæŋ] *vt* (*pt & pp* **hanged**) (*criminal*) pendre (**for** pour); – *vi* (*of criminal*) être pendu. **◆—ing²** *n Jur* pendaison *f*. **◆hangman** *n* (*pl* **-men**) bourreau *m*.

hangar ['hæŋər] *n Av* hangar *m*.

hanger ['hæŋər] *n* (**coat**) **h.** cintre *m*. **◆hanger-'on** *n* (*pl* **hangers-on**) (*person*) *Pej* parasite *m*.

hanker ['hæŋkər] *vi* **to h. after** *or* **for** avoir envie de. **◆—ing** *n* (forte) envie *f*, (vif) désir *m*.

hankie, hanky ['hæŋkı] *n Fam* mouchoir *m*.

hanky-panky [hæŋkı'pæŋkı] *n inv Fam* (*deceit*) manigances *fpl*, magouilles *fpl*; (*sexual behaviour*) papouilles *fpl*, pelotage *m*.

haphazard [hæp'hæzəd] *a* au hasard, au petit bonheur; (*selection, arrangement*) aléatoire. **◆—ly** *adv* au hasard.

hapless ['hæplıs] *a Lit* infortuné.

happen ['hæpən] *vi* arriver, se passer, se produire; **to h. to s.o./sth** arriver à qn/qch; **it (so) happens that I know, I h. to know** il se trouve que je le sais; **do you h. to have . . . ?** est-ce que par hasard vous avez . . . ?; **whatever happens** quoi qu'il arrive. **◆—ing** *n* événement *m*.

happy ['hæpı] *a* (**-ier, -iest**) heureux (**to do** de faire, **about sth** de qch); **I'm not (too** *or* **very) h. about (doing) it** ça ne me plaît pas beaucoup (de le faire); **H. New Year!** bonne année!; **H. Christmas!** joyeux Noël! **◆h.-go-'lucky** *a* insouciant. **◆happily** *adv* (*contentedly*) tranquillement; (*joyously*) joyeusement; (*fortunately*) heureusement. **◆happiness** *n* bonheur *m*.

harass ['hærəs, *Am* hə'ræs] *vt* harceler. **◆—ment** *n* harcèlement *m*.

harbour ['hɑːbər] **1** *n* port *m*. **2** *vt* (*shelter*) héberger; (*criminal*) cacher, abriter; (*fear, secret*) nourrir.

hard [hɑːd] *a* (**-er, -est**) (*not soft, severe*) dur; (*difficult*) difficile, dur; (*study*) assidu; (*fact*) brutal; (*drink*) alcoolisé; (*water*) calcaire; **h. drinker/worker** gros buveur *m*/travailleur *m*; **a h. frost** une forte gelée; **to be h. on** *or* **to s.o.** être dur avec qn; **to find it h. to sleep/***etc* avoir du mal à dormir/*etc*; **h. labour** *Jur* travaux *mpl* forcés; **h. cash** espèces *fpl*; **h. core** (*group*) noyau *m*; **h. of hearing** malentendant; **h. up** (*broke*) *Fam* fauché; **to be h. up for** manquer de; – *adv* (**-er, -est**) (*to work*) dur; (*to pull*) fort; (*to hit, freeze*) dur, fort; (*to study*) assidûment, (*to think*) sérieusement; (*to rain*) à verse; (*badly*) mal; **h. by** tout près; **h. done by** traité injustement.

hard-and-fast [hɑːdən(d)'fɑːst] *a* (*rule*) strict. **◆'hardback** *n* livre *m* relié. **◆'hardboard** *n* Isorel® *m*. **◆hard-'boiled** *a* (*egg*) dur. **◆hard-'core** *a* (*rigid*) *Pej* inflexible. **◆hard'headed** *a* réaliste. **◆hard'wearing** *a* résistant. **◆hard-'working** *a* travailleur.

harden ['hɑːd(ə)n] *vti* durcir; **to h. oneself to** s'endurcir à. **◆—ed** *a* (*criminal*) endurci.

hardly ['hɑːdlı] *adv* à peine; **he h. talks** il parle à peine, il ne parle guère; **h. ever** presque jamais.

hardness ['hɑːdnıs] *n* dureté *f*.

hardship ['hɑːdʃıp] *n* (*ordeal*) épreuve(s) *f*(*pl*); (*deprivation*) privation(s) *f*(*pl*).

hardware ['hɑːdweər] *n inv* quincaillerie *f*; (*of computer*) & *Mil* matériel *m*.

hardy ['hɑːdı] *a* (**-ier, -iest**) (*person, plant*) résistant.

hare [heər] *n* lièvre *m*. **◆h.-brained** *a* (*person*) écervelé; (*scheme*) insensé.

harem [hɑː'riːm] *n* harem *m*.

hark [hɑːk] *vi Lit* écouter; **to h. back to** (*subject etc*) *Fam* revenir sur.

harm [hɑːm] *n* (*hurt*) mal *m*; (*prejudice*) tort *m*; **he means (us) no h.** il ne nous veut pas de mal; **she'll come to no h.** il ne lui arrivera rien; – *vt* (*hurt*) faire du mal à; (*prejudice*) nuire à, faire du tort à; (*object*) endommager, abîmer. ◆**harmful** *a* nuisible. ◆**harmless** *a* (*person, treatment*) inoffensif; (*hobby, act*) innocent; (*gas, fumes etc*) qui n'est pas nuisible, inoffensif.

harmonica [hɑːˈmɒnɪkə] *n* harmonica *m*.

harmony [ˈhɑːmənɪ] *n* harmonie *f*. ◆**har'monic** *a* & *n Mus* harmonique (*m*). ◆**har'monious** *a* harmonieux. ◆**har'monium** *n Mus* harmonium *m*. ◆**harmonize** *vt* harmoniser; – *vi* s'harmoniser.

harness [ˈhɑːnɪs] *n* (*for horse, baby*) harnais *m*; – *vt* (*horse*) harnacher; (*energy etc*) *Fig* exploiter.

harp [hɑːp] **1** *n Mus* harpe *f*. **2** *vt* **to h. on (about) sth** *Fam* rabâcher qch. ◆**harpist** *n* harpiste *mf*.

harpoon [hɑːˈpuːn] *n* harpon *m*; – *vt* (*whale*) harponner.

harpsichord [ˈhɑːpsɪkɔːd] *n Mus* clavecin *m*.

harrowing [ˈhærəʊɪŋ] *a* (*tale, memory*) poignant; (*cry, sight*) déchirant.

harsh [hɑːʃ] *a* (**-er, -est**) (*severe*) dur, sévère; (*sound, taste*) âpre; (*surface*) rugueux; (*fabric*) rêche. ◆**—ly** *adv* durement, sévèrement. ◆**—ness** *n* dureté *f*, sévérité *f*; âpreté *f*; rugosité *f*.

harvest [ˈhɑːvɪst] *n* moisson *f*, récolte *f*; (*of people, objects*) *Fig* ribambelle *f*; – *vt* moissonner, récolter.

has [hæz] *see* **have**. ◆**has-been** *n Fam* personne *f* finie.

hash [hæʃ] **1** *n Culin* hachis *m*; – *vt* **to h. (up)** hacher. **2** *n* (*mess*) *Fam* gâchis *m*. **3** *n* (*hashish*) *Sl* hasch *m*, H *m*.

hashish [ˈhæʃiːʃ] *n* haschisch *m*.

hassle [ˈhæs(ə)l] *n Fam* (*trouble*) histoires *fpl*; (*bother*) mal *m*, peine *f*.

haste [heɪst] *n* hâte *f*; **in h.** à la hâte; **to make h.** se hâter. ◆**hasten** *vi* se hâter (**to do** de faire); – *vt* hâter. ◆**hasty** *a* (**-ier, -iest**) (*sudden*) précipité; (*visit*) rapide; (*decision, work*) hâtif. ◆**hastily** *adv* (*quickly*) en hâte; (*too quickly*) hâtivement.

hat [hæt] *n* chapeau *m*; **that's old h.** *Fam* (*old-fashioned*) c'est vieux jeu; (*stale*) c'est vieux comme les rues; **to score** *or* **get a h. trick** *Sp* réussir trois coups consécutifs.

hatch [hætʃ] **1** *vi* (*of chick, egg*) éclore; – *vt* faire éclore; (*plot*) *Fig* tramer. **2** *n* (*in kitchen wall*) passe-plats *m inv*.

hatchback [ˈhætʃbæk] *n* (*door*) hayon *m*; (*car*) trois-portes *f inv*, cinq-portes *f inv*.

hatchet [ˈhætʃɪt] *n* hachette *f*.

hate [heɪt] *vt* détester, haïr; **to h. doing** *or* **to do** détester faire; **I h. to say it** ça me gêne de le dire; – *n* haine *f*; **pet h.** *Fam* bête *f* noire. ◆**hateful** *a* haïssable. ◆**hatred** *n* haine *f*.

haughty [ˈhɔːtɪ] *a* (**-ier, -iest**) hautain. ◆**haughtily** *adv* avec hauteur.

haul [hɔːl] **1** *vt* (*pull*) tirer, traîner; (*goods*) camionner. **2** *n* (*fish*) prise *f*; (*of thief*) butin *m*; **a long h.** (*trip*) un long voyage. ◆**haulage** *n* camionnage *m*. ◆**hauler** *n Am*, ◆**haulier** *n* transporteur *m* routier.

haunt [hɔːnt] **1** *vt* hanter. **2** *n* endroit *m* favori; (*of criminal*) repaire *m*. ◆**—ing** *a* (*music, memory*) obsédant.

have [hæv] **1** (*3rd person sing pres t* **has**; *pt* & *pp* **had**; *pres p* **having**) *vt* avoir; (*get*) recevoir, avoir; (*meal, shower etc*) prendre; **he has got, he has** il a; **to h. a walk/dream/***etc* faire une promenade/un rêve/*etc*; **to h. a drink** prendre *or* boire un verre; **to h. a wash** se laver; **to h. a holiday** (*spend*) passer des vacances; **will you h. . . . ?** (*a cake, some tea etc*) est-ce que tu veux . . . ?; **to let s.o. h. sth** donner qch à qn; **to h. it from s.o. that** tenir de qn que; **he had me by the hair** il me tenait par les cheveux; **I won't h. this** (*allow*) je ne tolérerai pas ça; **you've had it!** *Fam* tu es fichu!; **to h. on** (*clothes*) porter; **to have sth on** (*be busy*) être pris; **to h. s.o. over** inviter qn chez soi. **2** *v aux* avoir; (*with monter, sortir etc* & *pronominal verbs*) être; **to h. decided/been** avoir décidé/été; **to h. gone** être allé; **to h. cut oneself** s'être coupé; **I've just done it** je viens de le faire; **to h. to do** (*must*) devoir faire; **I've got to go, I h. to go** je dois partir, je suis obligé de partir, il faut que je parte; **I don't h. to go** je ne suis pas obligé de partir; **to h. sth done** (*get sth done*) faire faire qch; **he's had his suitcase brought up** il a fait monter sa valise; **I've had my car stolen** on m'a volé mon auto; **she's had her hair cut** elle s'est fait couper les cheveux; **I've been doing it for months** je le fais depuis des mois; **haven't I?, hasn't she?** *etc* n'est-ce pas?; **no I haven't!** non!; **yes I h.!** si!; **after he had eaten, he left** après avoir mangé, il partit. **3** *npl* **the haves and (the) have-nots** les riches *mpl* et les pauvres *mpl*.

haven [ˈheɪv(ə)n] *n* refuge *m*, havre *m*.

haversack [ˈhævəsæk] *n* (*shoulder bag*) musette *f*.

havoc [ˈhævək] *n* ravages *mpl*.

hawk [hɔːk] **1** *n* (*bird*) & *Pol* faucon *m*. **2** *vt* (*goods*) colporter. ◆**—er** *n* colporteur, -euse *mf*.

hawthorn [ˈhɔːθɔːn] *n* aubépine *f*.

hay [heɪ] *n* foin *m*; **h. fever** rhume *m* des foins. ◆**haystack** *n* meule *f* de foin.

haywire ['heɪwaɪər] *a* **to go h.** (*of machine*) se détraquer; (*of scheme, plan*) mal tourner.

hazard ['hæzəd] *n* risque *m*; **health h.** risque *m* pour la santé; **it's a fire h.** ça risque de provoquer un incendie; – *vt* (*guess, remark etc*) hasarder, risquer. ◆**hazardous** *a* hasardeux.

haze [heɪz] *n* brume *f*; **in a h.** (*person*) *Fig* dans le brouillard. ◆**hazy** *a* (**-ier, -iest**) (*weather*) brumeux; (*sun*) voilé; (*photo, idea*) flou; **I'm h. about my plans** je ne suis pas sûr de mes projets.

hazel ['heɪz(ə)l] *n* (*bush*) noisetier *m*; – *a* (*eyes*) noisette *inv*. ◆**hazelnut** *n* noisette *f*.

he [hiː] *pron* il; (*stressed*) lui; **he wants** il veut; **he's a happy man** c'est un homme heureux; **if I were he** si j'étais lui; **he and I** lui et moi; – *n* **mâle** *m*; **he-bear** ours *m* mâle.

head [hed] **1** *n* (*of person, hammer etc*) tête *f*; (*of page*) haut *m*; (*of bed*) chevet *m*, tête *f*; (*of arrow*) pointe *f*; (*of beer*) mousse *f*; (*leader*) chef *m*; (*subject heading*) rubrique *f*; **h. of hair** chevelure *f*; **h. cold** rhume *m* de cerveau; **it didn't enter my h.** ça ne m'est pas venu à l'esprit (**that** que); **to take it into one's h. to do** se mettre en tête de faire; **the h.** *Sch* = **the headmaster**; = **the headmistress**; **to shout one's h. off** *Fam* crier à tue-tête; **to have a good h. for business** avoir le sens des affaires; **at the h. of** (*in charge of*) à la tête de; **at the h. of the table** au haut bout de la table; **at the h. of the list** en tête de liste; **it's above my h.** ça me dépasse; **to keep one's h.** garder son sang-froid; **to go off one's h.** devenir fou; **it's coming to a h.** (*of situation*) ça devient critique; **heads or tails?** pile ou face?; **per h., a h.** (*each*) par personne. **2** *a* principal; (*gardener*) en chef; **h. waiter** maître *m* d'hôtel; **a h. start** une grosse avance. **3** *vt* (*group, firm*) être à la tête de; (*list, poll*) être en tête de; (*vehicle*) diriger (**towards** vers); **to h. the ball** *Fb* faire une tête; **to h. off** (*person*) détourner de son chemin; (*prevent*) empêcher; **to be headed for** *Am* = **to h. for**; – *vi* **to h. for, be heading for** (*place*) se diriger vers; (*ruin etc*) *Fig* aller à. ◆**—ed** *a* (*paper*) à en-tête. ◆**—ing** *n* (*of chapter, page etc*) titre *m*; (*of subject*) rubrique *f*; (*printed on letter etc*) en-tête *m*. ◆**—er** *n Fb* coup *m* de tête.

headache ['hedeɪk] *n* mal *m* de tête; (*difficulty, person*) *Fig* problème *m*. ◆**headdress** *n* (*ornamental*) coiffe *f*. ◆**headlamp** *n*, ◆**headlight** *n Aut* phare *m*. ◆**headline** *n* (*of newspaper*) manchette *f*; *pl* (gros) titres *mpl*; *Rad TV* (grands) titres *mpl*. ◆**headlong** *adv* (*to fall*) la tête la première; (*to rush*) tête baissée. ◆**head'master** *n Sch* directeur *m*; (*of lycée*) proviseur *m*. ◆**head'mistress** *n Sch* directrice *f*; (*of lycée*) proviseur *m*. ◆**head-'on** *adv* & *a* (*to collide, collision*) de plein fouet. ◆**headphones** *npl* casque *m* (à écouteurs). ◆**headquarters** *npl Com Pol* siège *m* (central); *Mil* quartier *m* général. ◆**headrest** *n* appuie-tête *m inv*. ◆**headscarf** *n* (*pl* **-scarves**) foulard *m*. ◆**headstrong** *a* têtu. ◆**headway** *n* progrès *mpl*.

heady ['hedɪ] *a* (**-ier, -iest**) (*wine etc*) capiteux; (*action, speech*) emporté.

heal [hiːl] *vi* **to h. (up)** (*of wound*) se cicatriser; – *vt* (*wound*) cicatriser, guérir; (*person, sorrow*) guérir. ◆**—er** *n* guérisseur, -euse *mf*.

health [helθ] *n* santé *f*; **h. food** aliment *m* naturel; **h. food shop** *or Am* **store** magasin *m* diététique; **h. resort** station *f* climatique; **the H. Service** = la Sécurité Sociale. ◆**healthful** *a* (*climate*) sain. ◆**healthy** *a* (**-ier, -iest**) (*person*) en bonne santé, sain; (*food, attitude etc*) sain; (*appetite*) bon, robuste.

heap [hiːp] *n* tas *m*; **heaps of** *Fam* des tas de; **to have heaps of time** *Fam* avoir largement le temps; – *vt* entasser, empiler; **to h. on s.o.** (*gifts, praise*) couvrir qn de; (*work*) accabler qn de. ◆**—ed** *a* **h. spoonful** grosse cuillerée *f*. ◆**—ing** *a* **h. spoonful** *Am* grosse cuillerée *f*.

hear [hɪər] *vt* (*pt & pp* **heard** [hɜːd]) entendre; (*listen to*) écouter; (*learn*) apprendre (**that** que); **I heard him coming** je l'ai entendu venir; **to h. it said that** entendre dire que; **have you heard the news?** connais-tu la nouvelle?; **I've heard that . . .** on m'a dit que . . . , j'ai appris que . . . ; **to h. out** écouter jusqu'au bout; **h., h.!** bravo!; – *vi* entendre; (*get news*) recevoir *or* avoir des nouvelles (**from** de); **I've heard of** *or* **about him** j'ai entendu parler de lui; **she wouldn't h. of it** elle ne voulait pas en entendre parler; **I wouldn't h. of it!** pas question! ◆**—ing** *n* (*sense*) ouïe *f*; *Jur* audition *f*; **h. aid** appareil *m* auditif. ◆**hearsay** *n* ouï-dire *m inv*.

hearse [hɜːs] *n* corbillard *m*.

heart [hɑːt] *n* cœur *m*; *pl Cards* cœur *m*; **(off) by h.** par cœur; **to lose h.** perdre courage; **to one's h.'s content** tout son saoul *or* content; **at h.** au fond; **his h. is set on it** il le veut à tout prix, il y tient; **his h. is set on doing it** il veut le faire à tout prix, il tient à le faire; **h. disease** maladie *f* de cœur; **h. attack** crise *f* cardiaque. ◆**heartache** *n* chagrin *m*. ◆**heartbeat** *n* battement *m* de cœur. ◆**heartbreaking** *a* navrant. ◆**heartbroken** *a* navré, au cœur brisé. ◆**heartburn** *n Med* brûlures *fpl* d'estomac. ◆**heartthrob** *n* (*man*) *Fam* idole *f*.

hearten ['hɑːt(ə)n] *vt* encourager. ◆**—ing** *a* encourageant.

hearth [hɑːθ] *n* foyer *m*.

hearty ['hɑːtɪ] *a* (**-ier, -iest**) (*meal, appetite*) gros. ◆**heartily** *adv* (*to eat*) avec appétit; (*to laugh*) de tout son cœur; (*absolutely*) absolument.

heat [hiːt] **1** *n* chaleur *f*; (*of oven*) température *f*; (*heating*) chauffage *m*; **in the h. of** (*argument etc*) dans le feu de; (*the day*) au plus chaud de; **at low h., on a low h.** *Culin* à feu doux; **h. wave** vague *f* de chaleur; – *vti* **to h. (up)** chauffer. **2** *n* (*in race, competition*) éliminatoire *f*; **it was a dead h.** ils sont arrivés ex aequo. ◆**—ed** *a* (*swimming pool*) chauffé; (*argument*) passionné. ◆**—edly** *adv* avec passion. ◆**—ing** *n* chauffage *m*. ◆**—er** *n* radiateur *m*, appareil *m* de chauffage; **water h.** chauffe-eau *m inv*.

heath [hiːθ] *n* (*place, land*) lande *f*.

heathen ['hiːð(ə)n] *a* & *n* païen, -enne (*mf*).

heather ['heðər] *n* (*plant*) bruyère *f*.

heave [hiːv] *vt* (*lift*) soulever; (*pull*) tirer; (*drag*) traîner; (*throw*) *Fam* lancer; (*a sigh*) pousser; – *vi* (*of stomach, chest*) se soulever; (*retch*) *Fam* avoir des haut-le-cœur; – *n* (*effort*) effort *m* (*pour soulever etc*).

heaven ['hev(ə)n] *n* ciel *m*, paradis *m*; **h. knows when** *Fam* Dieu sait quand; **good heavens!** *Fam* mon Dieu!; **it was h.** *Fam* c'était divin. ◆**—ly** *a* céleste; (*pleasing*) *Fam* divin.

heavy ['hevɪ] *a* (**-ier, -iest**) lourd; (*weight etc*) lourd, pesant; (*work, cold etc*) gros; (*blow*) violent; (*concentration, rain*) fort; (*traffic*) dense; (*smoker, drinker*) grand; (*film, text*) difficile; **a h. day** une journée chargée; **h. casualties** de nombreuses victimes; **to be h. on petrol** *or Am* **gas** *Aut* consommer beaucoup; **it's h. going** c'est difficile. ◆**heavily** *adv* (*to walk, tax etc*) lourdement; (*to breathe*) péniblement; (*to smoke, drink*) beaucoup; (*underlined*) fortement; (*involved*) très; **to rain h.** pleuvoir à verse. ◆**heaviness** *n* pesanteur *f*, lourdeur *f*. ◆**heavyweight** *n Boxing* poids *m* lourd; *Fig* personnage *m* important.

Hebrew ['hiːbruː] *a* hébreu (*m only*), hébraïque; – *n* (*language*) hébreu *m*.

heck [hek] *int Fam* zut!; – *n* = **hell** *in expressions*.

heckl/e ['hek(ə)l] *vt* interpeller, interrompre. ◆**—ing** *n* interpellations *fpl*. ◆**—er** *n* interpellateur, -trice *mf*.

hectic ['hektɪk] *a* (*activity*) fiévreux; (*period*) très agité; (*trip*) mouvementé; **h. life** vie *f* trépidante.

hedge [hedʒ] **1** *n Bot* haie *f*. **2** *vi* (*answer evasively*) ne pas se mouiller, éviter de se compromettre. ◆**hedgerow** *n Bot* haie *f*.

hedgehog ['hedʒhɒg] *n* (*animal*) hérisson *m*.

heed [hiːd] *vt* faire attention à; – *n* **to pay h. to** faire attention à. ◆**—less** *a* **h. of** (*danger etc*) inattentif à.

heel [hiːl] *n* **1** talon *m*; **down at h.**, *Am* **down at the heels** (*shabby*) miteux; **h. bar** cordonnerie *f* express; (*on sign*) 'talon minute'. **2** (*person*) *Am Fam* salaud *m*.

hefty ['heftɪ] *a* (**-ier, -iest**) (*large, heavy*) gros; (*person*) costaud.

heifer ['hefər] *n* (*cow*) génisse *f*.

height [haɪt] *n* hauteur *f*; (*of person*) taille *f*; (*of mountain*) altitude *f*; **the h. of** (*glory, success, fame*) le sommet de, l'apogée *m* de; (*folly, pain*) le comble de; **at the h. of** (*summer, storm*) au cœur de. ◆**heighten** *vt* (*raise*) rehausser; (*tension, interest*) *Fig* augmenter.

heinous ['heɪnəs] *a* (*crime etc*) atroce.

heir [eər] *n* héritier *m*. ◆**heiress** *n* héritière *f*. ◆**heirloom** *n* héritage *m*, bijou *m or* meuble *m* de famille.

heist [haɪst] *n Am Sl* hold-up *m inv*.

held [held] *see* **hold**.

helicopter ['helɪkɒptər] *n* hélicoptère *m*. ◆**heliport** *n* héliport *m*.

hell [hel] *n* enfer *m*; **a h. of a lot** (*very much*) *Fam* énormément, vachement; **a h. of a lot of** (*very many, very much*) *Fam* énormément de; **a h. of a nice guy** *Fam* un type super; **what the h. are you doing?** *Fam* qu'est-ce que tu fous?; **to h. with him** *Fam* qu'il aille se faire voir; **h.!** *Fam* zut!; **to be h.-bent on** *Fam* être acharné à. ◆**hellish** *a* diabolique.

hello! [hə'ləʊ] *int* = **hallo**.

helm [helm] *n Nau* barre *f*.

helmet ['helmɪt] *n* casque *m*.

help [help] *n* aide *f*, secours *m*; (*cleaning woman*) femme *f* de ménage; (*office or shop workers*) employés, -ées *mfpl*; **with the h. of**

(*stick etc*) à l'aide de; **to cry** *or* **shout for h.** crier au secours; **h.!** au secours!; – *vt* aider (**do, to do** à faire); **to h. s.o. to soup**/*etc* (*serve*) servir du potage/*etc* à qn; **to h. out** aider; **to h. up** aider à monter; **to h. oneself** se servir (to de); **I can't h. laughing**/*etc* je ne peux m'empêcher de rire/*etc*; **he can't h. being blind**/*etc* ce n'est pas sa faute s'il est aveugle/*etc*; **it can't be helped** on n'y peut rien; – *vi* **to h. (out)** aider. ◆**—ing** *n* (*serving*) portion *f*. ◆**—er** *n* assistant, -ante *mf*. ◆**helpful** *a* (*useful*) utile; (*obliging*) serviable. ◆**helpless** *a* (*powerless*) impuissant; (*baby*) désarmé; (*disabled*) impotent. ◆**helplessly** *adv* (*to struggle*) en vain.

helter-skelter [heltə'skeltər] **1** *adv* à la débandade. **2** *n* (*slide*) toboggan *m*.

hem [hem] *n* ourlet *m*; – *vt* (**-mm-**) (*garment*) ourler; **to h. in** *Fig* enfermer, cerner.

hemisphere ['hemɪsfɪər] *n* hémisphère *m*.

hemorrhage ['hemərɪdʒ] *n Med* hémorragie *f*.

hemorrhoids ['hemərɔɪdz] *npl* hémorroïdes *fpl*.

hemp [hemp] *n* chanvre *m*.

hen [hen] *n* poule *f*; **h. bird** oiseau *m* femelle. ◆**henpecked** *a* (*husband*) harcelé *or* dominé par sa femme.

hence [hens] *adv* **1** (*therefore*) d'où. **2** (*from now*) **ten years**/*etc* **h.** d'ici dix ans/*etc*. ◆**henceforth** *adv* désormais.

henchman ['hentʃmən] *n* (*pl* **-men**) *Pej* acolyte *m*.

hepatitis [hepə'taɪtɪs] *n* hépatite *f*.

her [hɜːr] **1** *pron* la, l'; (*after prep etc*) elle; **(to) h.** (*indirect*) lui; **I see h.** je la vois; **I saw h.** je l'ai vue; **I give (to) h.** je lui donne; **with h.** avec elle. **2** *poss a* son, sa, *pl* ses.

herald ['herəld] *vt* annoncer.

heraldry ['herəldrɪ] *n* héraldique *f*.

herb [hɜːb, *Am* ɜːb] *n* herbe *f*; *pl Culin* fines herbes *fpl*. ◆**herbal** *a* **h. tea** infusion *f* (d'herbes).

Hercules ['hɜːkjʊliːz] *n* (*strong man*) hercule *m*.

herd [hɜːd] *n* troupeau *m*; – *vti* **to h. together** (se) rassembler (en troupeau).

here [hɪər] **1** *adv* ici; (*then*) alors; **h. is, h. are** voici; **h. he is** le voici; **h. she is** la voici; **this man h.** cet homme-ci; **I won't be h. tomorrow** je ne serai pas là demain; **h. and there** çà et là; **h. you are!** (*take this*) tenez!; **h.'s to you!** (*toast*) à la tienne! **2** *int* (*calling s.o.'s attention*) holà!, écoutez!; (*giving s.o. sth*) tenez! ◆**herea'bouts** *adv* par ici. ◆**here'after** *adv* après; (*in book*) ci-après. ◆**here'by** *adv* (*to declare*) par le présent acte. ◆**here'with** *adv* (*with letter*) *Com* ci-joint.

heredity [hɪ'redɪtɪ] *n* hérédité *f*. ◆**hereditary** *a* héréditaire.

heresy ['herəsɪ] *n* hérésie *f*. ◆**heretic** *n* hérétique *mf*. ◆**he'retical** *a* hérétique.

heritage ['herɪtɪdʒ] *n* héritage *m*.

hermetically [hɜː'metɪklɪ] *adv* hermétiquement.

hermit ['hɜːmɪt] *n* solitaire *mf*, ermite *m*.

hernia ['hɜːnɪə] *n Med* hernie *f*.

hero ['hɪərəʊ] *n* (*pl* **-oes**) héros *m*. ◆**he'roic** *a* héroïque. ◆**he'roics** *npl Pej* grandiloquence *f*. ◆**heroine** ['herəʊɪn] *n* héroïne *f*. ◆**heroism** ['herəʊɪz(ə)m] *n* héroïsme *m*.

heroin ['herəʊɪn] *n* (*drug*) héroïne *f*.

heron ['herən] *n* (*bird*) héron *m*.

herring ['herɪŋ] *n* hareng *m*; **a red h.** *Fig* une diversion.

hers [hɜːz] *poss pron* le sien, la sienne, *pl* les sien(ne)s; **this hat is h.** ce chapeau est à elle *or* est le sien; **a friend of h.** une amie à elle. ◆**her'self** *pron* elle-même; (*reflexive*) se, s'; (*after prep*) elle; **she cut h.** elle s'est coupée; **she thinks of h.** elle pense à elle.

hesitate ['hezɪteɪt] *vi* hésiter (**over, about** sur; **to do** à faire). ◆**hesitant** *a* hésitant. ◆**hesitantly** *adv* avec hésitation. ◆**hesi'tation** *n* hésitation *f*.

hessian ['hesɪən] *n* toile *f* de jute.

heterogeneous [het(ə)rəʊ'dʒiːnɪəs] *a* hétérogène.

het up [het'ʌp] *a Fam* énervé.

hew [hjuː] *vt* (*pp* **hewn** *or* **hewed**) tailler.

hexagon ['heksəgən] *n* hexagone *m*. ◆**hex'agonal** *a* hexagonal.

hey! [heɪ] *int* hé!, holà!

heyday ['heɪdeɪ] *n* (*of person*) apogée *m*, zénith *m*; (*of thing*) âge *m* d'or.

hi! [haɪ] *int Am Fam* salut!

hiatus [haɪ'eɪtəs] *n* (*gap*) hiatus *m*.

hibernate ['haɪbəneɪt] *vi* hiberner. ◆**hiber'nation** *n* hibernation *f*.

hiccough, hiccup ['hɪkʌp] *n* hoquet *m*; **(the) hiccoughs, (the) hiccups** le hoquet; – *vi* hoqueter.

hick [hɪk] *n* (*peasant*) *Am Sl Pej* plouc *mf*.

hide[1] [haɪd] *vt* (*pt* **hid**, *pp* **hidden**) cacher, dissimuler (**from** à); – *vi* **to h. (away** *or* **out)** se cacher (**from** de). ◆**h.-and-'seek** *n* cache-cache *m inv*. ◆**h.-out** *n* cachette *f*. ◆**hiding** *n* **1 to go into h.** se cacher; **h. place** cachette *f*. **2 a good h.** (*thrashing*) *Fam* une bonne volée *or* correction.

hide[2] [haɪd] *n* (*skin*) peau *f*.

hideous ['hɪdɪəs] *a* horrible; (*person, sight, crime*) hideux. ◆**—ly** *adv* (*badly, very*) horriblement.

hierarchy ['haɪərɑːkɪ] *n* hiérarchie *f*.

hi-fi ['haɪfaɪ] *n* hi-fi *f inv*; (*system*) chaîne *f* hi-fi; – *a* hi-fi *inv*.

high [haɪ] *a* (**-er, -est**) haut; (*speed*) grand; (*price*) élevé; (*fever*) fort, gros; (*colour, complexion*) vif; (*idea, number*) grand, élevé; (*meat, game*) faisandé; (*on drugs*) *Fam* défoncé; **to be five metres h.** être haut de cinq mètres, avoir cinq mètres de haut; **it is h. time that** il est grand temps que (+ *sub*); **h. jump** *Sp* saut *m* en hauteur; **h. noon** plein midi *m*; **h. priest** grand prêtre *m*; **h. school** *Am* = collège *m* d'enseignement secondaire; **h. spirits** entrain *m*; **h. spot** (*of visit, day*) point *m* culminant; (*of show*) clou *m*; **h. street** grand-rue *f*; **h. summer** le cœur de l'été; **h. table** table *f* d'honneur; **h. and mighty** arrogant; **to leave s.o. h. and dry** *Fam* laisser qn en plan; – *adv* **h. (up)** (*to fly, throw etc*) haut; **to aim h.** viser haut; – *n* **on h.** en haut; **a new h., an all-time h.** (*peak*) *Fig* un nouveau record. ◆**—er** *a* supérieur (**than** à). ◆**—ly** *adv* hautement, fortement; (*interesting*) très; (*paid*) très bien; (*to recommend*) chaudement; **to speak h. of** dire beaucoup de bien de; **h. strung** nerveux. ◆**—ness** *n* **H.** (*title*) Altesse *f*.

highbrow ['haɪbraʊ] *a* & *n* intellectuel, -elle (*mf*).

high-chair ['haɪtʃeər] *n* chaise *f* haute. ◆**h.-'class** *a* (*service*) de premier ordre; (*building*) de luxe; (*person*) raffiné. ◆**h.-'flown** *a* (*language*) ampoulé. ◆**h.-'handed** *a* tyrannique. ◆**h.-'minded** *a* à l'âme noble. ◆**h.-'pitched** *a* (*sound*) aigu. ◆**h.-'powered** *a* (*person*) très dynamique. ◆**h.-rise** *a* **h.-rise flats** tour *f*. ◆**h.-'speed** *a* ultra-rapide. ◆**h.-'strung** *a Am* nerveux. ◆**h.-'up** *a* (*person*) haut placé.

highlands ['haɪləndz] *npl* régions *fpl* montagneuses.

highlight ['haɪlaɪt] *n* (*of visit, day*) point *m* culminant; (*of show*) clou *m*; (*in hair*) reflet *m*; – *vt* souligner.

highroad ['haɪrəʊd] *n* grand-route *f*.

highway ['haɪweɪ] *n* grande route *f*; *Am* autoroute *f*; **public h.** voie *f* publique; **h. code** code *m* de la route.

hijack ['haɪdʒæk] *vt* (*aircraft, vehicle*) détourner; – *n* détournement *m*. ◆**—ing** *n* (*air piracy*) piraterie *f* aérienne; (*hijack*) détournement *m*. ◆**—er** *n Av* pirate *m* de l'air.

hik/e [haɪk] **1** *n* excursion *f* à pied; – *vi* marcher à pied. **2** *vt* (*price*) *Am Fam* augmenter; – *n Am Fam* hausse *f*. ◆**—er** *n* excursionniste *mf*.

hilarious [hɪ'leərɪəs] *a* (*funny*) désopilant.

hill [hɪl] *n* colline *f*; (*small*) coteau *m*; (*slope*) pente *f*. ◆**hillbilly** *n Am Fam* péquenaud, -aude *mf*. ◆**hillside** *n* coteau *m*; **on the h.** à flanc de coteau. ◆**hilly** *a* (**-ier, -iest**) accidenté.

hilt [hɪlt] *n* (*of sword*) poignée *f*; **to the h.** *Fig* au maximum.

him [hɪm] *pron* le, l'; (*after prep etc*) lui; **(to) h.** (*indirect*) lui; **I see h.** je le vois; **I saw h.** je l'ai vu; **I give (to) h.** je lui donne; **with h.** avec lui. ◆**him'self** *pron* lui-même; (*reflexive*) se, s'; (*after prep*) lui; **he cut h.** il s'est coupé; **he thinks of h.** il pense à lui.

hind [haɪnd] *a* de derrière, postérieur. ◆**hindquarters** *npl* arrière-train *m*.

hinder ['hɪndər] *vt* (*obstruct*) gêner; (*prevent*) empêcher (**from doing** de faire). ◆**hindrance** *n* gêne *f*.

hindsight ['haɪndsaɪt] *n* **with h.** rétrospectivement.

Hindu ['hɪnduː] *a* & *n* hindou, -oue (*mf*).

hing/e [hɪndʒ] **1** *n* (*of box, stamp*) charnière *f*; (*of door*) gond *m*, charnière *f*. **2** *vi* **to h. on** (*depend on*) dépendre de. ◆**—ed** *a* à charnière(s).

hint [hɪnt] *n* indication *f*; (*insinuation*) allusion *f*; (*trace*) trace *f*; *pl* (*advice*) conseils *mpl*; **to drop a h.** faire une allusion; – *vt* laisser entendre (**that** que); – *vi* **to h. at** faire allusion à.

hip [hɪp] *n Anat* hanche *f*.

hippie ['hɪpɪ] *n* hippie *mf*.

hippopotamus [hɪpə'pɒtəməs] *n* hippopotame *m*.

hire ['haɪər] *vt* (*vehicle etc*) louer; (*person*) engager; **to h. out** donner en location, louer; – *n* location *f*; (*of boat, horse*) louage *m*; **for h.** à louer; **on h.** en location; **h. purchase** vente *f* à crédit, location-vente *f*; **on h. purchase** à crédit.

his [hɪz] **1** *poss a* son, sa, *pl* ses. **2** *poss pron* le sien, la sienne, *pl* les sien(ne)s; **this hat is h.** ce chapeau est à lui *or* est le sien; **a friend of h.** un ami à lui.

Hispanic [hɪs'pænɪk] *a* & *n Am* hispano-américain, -aine (*mf*).

hiss [hɪs] *vti* siffler; – *n* sifflement *m*; *pl Th* sifflets *mpl*. ◆**—ing** *n* sifflement(s) *m*(*pl*).

history ['hɪstərɪ] *n* (*study, events*) histoire *f*; **it will make h.** *or* **go down in h.** ça va faire date; **your medical h.** vos antécédents médicaux. ◆**hi'storian** *n* historien, -ienne *mf*. ◆**hi'storic(al)** *a* historique.

histrionic [hɪstrɪ'ɒnɪk] *a Pej* théâtral; – *npl* attitudes *fpl* théâtrales.

hit [hɪt] *vti* (*pt & pp* **hit,** *pres p* **hitting**) (*strike*) frapper; (*knock against*) & *Aut* heurter; (*reach*) atteindre; (*affect*) toucher, affecter; (*find*) trouver, rencontrer; **to h. the headlines** *Fam* faire les gros titres; **to h. back** rendre coup pour coup; (*verbally, militarily etc*) riposter; **to h. it off** *Fam* s'entendre bien (**with** avec); **to h. out (at)** *Fam* attaquer; **to h. (up)on** (*find*) tomber sur; – *n* (*blow*) coup *m*; (*success*) coup *m* réussi; *Th* succès *m*; **h. (song)** chanson *f* à succès; **to make a h. with** *Fam* avoir un succès avec; **h.-and-run driver** chauffard *m* (*qui prend la fuite*). ◆**h.-or-'miss** *a* (*chancy, random*) aléatoire.

hitch [hɪtʃ] **1** *n* (*snag*) anicroche *f*, os *m*, problème *m*. **2** *vt* (*fasten*) accrocher (**to** à). **3** *vti* **to h. (a lift** *or* **a ride)** *Fam* faire du stop (**to** jusqu'à). ◆**hitchhike** *vi* faire de l'auto-stop (**to** jusqu'à). ◆**hitchhiking** *n* auto-stop *m*. ◆**hitchhiker** *n* auto-stoppeur, -euse *mf*.

hitherto [hɪðə'tuː] *adv* jusqu'ici.

hive [haɪv] **1** *n* ruche *f*. **2** *vt* **to h. off** (*industry*) dénationaliser.

hoard [hɔːd] *n* réserve *f*; (*of money*) trésor *m*; – *vt* amasser. ◆**—ing** *n* (*fence*) panneau *m* d'affichage.

hoarfrost ['hɔːfrɒst] *n* givre *m*.

hoarse [hɔːs] *a* (**-er, -est**) (*person, voice*) enroué. ◆**—ness** *n* enrouement *m*.

hoax [həʊks] *n* canular *m*; – *vt* faire un canular à, mystifier.

hob [hɒb] *n* (*on stove*) plaque *f* chauffante.

hobble ['hɒb(ə)l] *vi* (*walk*) clopiner.

hobby ['hɒbɪ] *n* passe-temps *m inv*; **my h.** mon passe-temps favori. ◆**hobbyhorse** *n* (*favourite subject*) dada *m*.

hobnob ['hɒbnɒb] *vi* (**-bb-**) **to h. with** frayer avec.

hobo ['həʊbəʊ] *n* (*pl* **-oes** *or* **-os**) *Am* vagabond *m*.

hock [hɒk] *vt* (*pawn*) *Fam* mettre au clou; – *n* **in h.** *Fam* au clou.

hockey ['hɒkɪ] *n* hockey *m*; **ice h.** hockey sur glace.

hocus-pocus [həʊkəs'pəʊkəs] *n* (*talk*) charabia *m*; (*deception*) tromperie *f*.

hodgepodge ['hɒdʒpɒdʒ] *n* fatras *m*.

hoe [həʊ] *n* binette *f*, houe *f*; – *vt* biner.

hog [hɒg] **1** *n* (*pig*) cochon *m*, porc *m*; **road h.** *Fig* chauffard *m*. **2** *n* **to go the whole h.** *Fam* aller jusqu'au bout. **3** *vt* (**-gg-**) *Fam* monopoliser, garder pour soi.

hoist [hɔɪst] *vt* hisser; – *n Tech* palan *m*.

hold [həʊld] *n* (*grip*) prise *f*; (*of ship*) cale *f*; (*of aircraft*) soute *f*; **to get h. of** (*grab*) saisir; (*contact*) joindre; (*find*) trouver; **to get a h. of oneself** se maîtriser; – *vt* (*pt & pp* **held**) tenir; (*breath, interest, heat, attention*) retenir; (*a post*) occuper; (*a record*) détenir; (*weight*) supporter; (*possess*) posséder; (*contain*) contenir; (*maintain, believe*) maintenir (**that** que); (*ceremony, mass*) célébrer; (*keep*) garder; **to h. hands** se tenir par la main; **to h. one's own** se débrouiller; (*of sick person*) se maintenir; **h. the line!** *Tel* ne quittez pas!; **h. it!** (*stay still*) ne bouge pas!; **to be held** (*of event*) avoir lieu; **to h. back** (*crowd, tears*) contenir; (*hide*) cacher (**from** à); **to h. down** (*job*) occuper, (*keep*) garder; (*person on ground*) maintenir au sol; **to h. in** (*stomach*) rentrer; **to h. off** (*enemy*) tenir à distance; **to h. on** (*keep in place*) tenir en place (*son chapeau etc*); **to h. out** (*offer*) offrir; (*arm*) étendre; **to h. over** (*postpone*) remettre; **to h. together** (*nation, group*) assurer l'union de; **to h. up** (*raise*) lever; (*support*) soutenir; (*delay*) retarder; (*bank*) attaquer (à main armée); – *vi* (*of nail, rope*) tenir; (*of weather*) se maintenir; **to h. (good)** (*of argument*) valoir (**for** pour); **to h. forth** (*talk*) *Pej* disserter; **if the rain holds off** s'il ne pleut pas; **to h. on** (*endure*) tenir bon; (*wait*) attendre; **h. on!** *Tel* ne quittez pas!; **to h. onto** (*cling to*) tenir bien; (*keep*) garder; **h. on (tight)!** tenez bon!; **to h. out** (*resist*) résister; (*last*) durer. ◆**holdall** *n* (*bag*) fourre-tout *m inv*. ◆**holdup** *n* (*attack*) hold-up *m inv*; (*traffic jam*) bouchon *m*; (*delay*) retard *m*.

holder ['həʊldər] *n* (*of post, passport*) titulaire *mf*; (*of record, card*) détenteur, -trice *mf*; (*container*) support *m*.

holdings ['həʊldɪŋz] *npl Fin* possessions *fpl*.

hole [həʊl] *n* trou *m*; (*town etc*) *Fam* bled *m*, trou *m*; (*room*) *Fam* baraque *f*; – *vt* trouer; – *vi* **to h. up** (*hide*) *Fam* se terrer.

holiday ['hɒlɪdeɪ] *n* (*rest*) vacances *fpl*; **holiday(s)** (*from work, school etc*) vacances *fpl*; **a h.** (*day off*) un congé; **a (public** *or* **bank) h.**, *Am* **a legal h.** un jour férié; **on h.** en vacances; **holidays with pay** congés *mpl* payés; – *a* (*camp, clothes etc*) de vacances; **in h. mood** d'humeur folâtre. ◆**holidaymaker** *n* vacancier, -ière *mf*.

holiness ['həʊlɪnəs] *n* sainteté *f*.

Holland ['hɒlənd] *n* Hollande *f*.

hollow ['hɒləʊ] *a* creux; (*victory*) faux; (*promise*) vain; – *n* creux *m*; – *vt* **to h. out** creuser.
holly ['hɒlɪ] *n* houx *m*.
holocaust ['hɒləkɔːst] *n* (*massacre*) holocauste *m*.
holster ['həʊlstər] *n* étui *m* de revolver.
holy ['həʊlɪ] *a* (**-ier, -iest**) saint; (*bread, water*) bénit; (*ground*) sacré.
homage ['hɒmɪdʒ] *n* hommage *m*.
home[1] [həʊm] *n* maison *f*; (*country*) pays *m* (natal); (*for soldiers*) foyer *m*; **(at) h.** à la maison, chez soi; **to feel at h.** se sentir à l'aise; **to play at h.** *Fb* jouer à domicile; **far from h.** loin de chez soi; **a broken h.** un foyer désuni; **a good h.** une bonne famille; **to make one's h. in** s'installer à *or* en; **my h. is here** j'habite ici; – *adv* à la maison, chez soi; **to go** *or* **come h.** rentrer; **to be h.** être rentré; **to drive h.** ramener (*qn*) (en voiture); (*nail*) enfoncer; **to bring sth h. to s.o.** *Fig* faire voir qch à qn; – *a* (*life, pleasures etc*) de famille; *Pol* national; (*cooking, help*) familial; (*visit, match*) à domicile; **h. economics** économie *f* domestique; **h. town** (*birth place*) ville *f* natale; **h. rule** *Pol* autonomie *f*; **H. Office** = ministère *m* de l'Intérieur; **H. Secretary** = ministre *m* de l'Intérieur. ◆**homecoming** *n* retour *m* au foyer. ◆**home'grown** *a Bot* du jardin; *Pol* du pays. ◆**homeland** *n* patrie *f*. ◆**homeloving** *a* casanier. ◆**home'made** *a* (fait à la) maison *inv*. ◆**homework** *n Sch* devoir(s) *m(pl)*.
home[2] [həʊm] *vi* **to h. in on** se diriger automatiquement sur.
homeless ['həʊmlɪs] *a* sans abri; – *n* **the h.** les sans-abri *m inv*.
homely ['həʊmlɪ] *a* (**-ier, -iest**) (*simple*) simple; (*comfortable*) accueillant; (*ugly*) *Am* laid.
homesick ['həʊmsɪk] *a* nostalgique; **to be h.** avoir le mal du pays. ◆**—ness** *n* nostalgie *f*, mal *m* du pays.
homeward ['həʊmwəd] *a* (*trip*) de retour; – *adv* **h. bound** sur le chemin de retour.
homey ['həʊmɪ] *a* (**-ier, -iest**) *Am Fam* accueillant.
homicide ['hɒmɪsaɪd] *n* homicide *m*.
homily ['hɒmɪlɪ] *n* homélie *f*.
homogeneous [həʊmə'dʒiːnɪəs] *a* homogène.
homosexual [həʊmə'sekʃʊəl] *a* & *n* homosexuel, -elle (*mf*). ◆**homosexu'ality** *n* homosexualité *f*.
honest ['ɒnɪst] *a* honnête; (*frank*) franc (**with** avec); (*profit, money*) honnêtement gagné; **the h. truth** la pure vérité; **to be (quite) h. . . .** pour être franc. . . . ◆**honesty** *n* honnêteté *f*; franchise *f*; (*of report, text*) exactitude *f*.
honey ['hʌnɪ] *n* miel *m*; (*person*) *Fam* chéri, -ie *mf*. ◆**honeycomb** *n* rayon *m* de miel. ◆**honeymoon** *n* (*occasion*) lune *f* de miel; (*trip*) voyage *m* de noces. ◆**honeysuckle** *n Bot* chèvrefeuille *f*.
honk [hɒŋk] *vi Aut* klaxonner; – *n* coup *m* de klaxon®.
honour ['ɒnər] *n* honneur *m*; **in h. of** en l'honneur de; **an honours degree** *Univ* = une licence; – *vt* honorer (**with** de). ◆**honorary** *a* (*member*) honoraire; (*title*) honorifique. ◆**honourable** *a* honorable.
hood [hʊd] *n* **1** capuchon *m*; (*mask of robber*) cagoule *f*; (*soft car or pram roof*) capote *f*; (*bonnet*) *Aut Am* capot *m*; (*above stove*) hotte *f*. **2** (*hoodlum*) *Am Sl* gangster *m*. ◆**hooded** *a* (*person*) encapuchonné; (*coat*) à capuchon.
hoodlum ['huːdləm] *n Fam* (*hooligan*) voyou *m*; (*gangster*) gangster *m*.
hoodwink ['hʊdwɪŋk] *vt* tromper, duper.
hoof, *pl* **-fs, -ves** [huːf, -fs, -vz] (*Am* [hʊf, -fs, huːvz]) *n* sabot *m*.
hoo-ha ['huːhɑː] *n Fam* tumulte *m*.
hook [hʊk] *n* crochet *m*; (*on clothes*) agrafe *f*; *Fishing* hameçon *m*; **off the h.** (*phone*) décroché; **to let** *or* **get s.o. off the h.** tirer qn d'affaire; – *vt* **to h. (on** *or* **up)** accrocher (to à). ◆**—ed** *a* (*nose, beak*) recourbé, crochu; (*end, object*) recourbé; **h. on** *Fam* (*chess etc*) enragé de; (*person*) entiché de; **to be h. on drugs** *Fam* ne plus pouvoir se passer de la drogue. ◆**—er** *n Am Sl* prostituée *f*.
hook(e)y ['hʊkɪ] *n* **to play h.** *Am Fam* faire l'école buissonnière.
hooligan ['huːlɪgən] *n* vandale *m*, voyou *m*. ◆**hooliganism** *n* vandalisme *m*.
hoop [huːp] *n* cerceau *m*; (*of barrel*) cercle *m*.
hoot [huːt] **1** *vi Aut* klaxonner; (*of train*) siffler; (*of owl*) hululer; – *n Aut* coup *m* de klaxon®. **2** *vti* (*jeer*) huer; – *n* huée *f*. ◆**—er** *n Aut* klaxon® *m*; (*of factory*) sirène *f*.
hoover® ['huːvər] *n* aspirateur *m*; – *vt Fam* passer à l'aspirateur.
hop [hɒp] *vi* (**-pp-**) (*of person*) sauter (à cloche-pied); (*of animal*) sauter; (*of bird*) sautiller; **h. in!** (*in car*) montez!; **to h. on a bus** monter dans un autobus; **to h. on a plane** attraper un vol; – *vt* **h. it!** *Fam* fiche le camp!; – *n* (*leap*) saut *m*; *Av* étape *f*.
hope [həʊp] *n* espoir *m*, espérance *f*; – *vi*

espérer; **to h. for** (*desire*) espérer; (*expect*) attendre; **I h. so/not** j'espère que oui/non; – *vt* espérer (**to** do faire, **that** que). ◆**hopeful** *a* (*person*) optimiste, plein d'espoir; (*promising*) prometteur; (*encouraging*) encourageant; **to be h. that** avoir bon espoir que. ◆**hopefully** *adv* avec optimisme; (*one hopes*) on espère (que). ◆**hopeless** *a* désespéré, sans espoir; (*useless, bad*) nul; (*liar*) invétéré. ◆**hopelessly** *adv* sans espoir; (*extremely*) complètement; (*in love*) éperdument.

hops [hɒps] *npl Bot* houblon *m*.

hopscotch ['hɒpskɒtʃ] *n* (*game*) marelle *f*.

horde [hɔːd] *n* horde *f*, foule *f*.

horizon [hə'raɪz(ə)n] *n* horizon *m*; **on the h.** à l'horizon.

horizontal [hɒrɪ'zɒnt(ə)l] *a* horizontal. ◆**—ly** *adv* horizontalement.

hormone ['hɔːməʊn] *n* hormone *f*.

horn [hɔːn] **1** *n* (*of animal*) corne *f*; *Mus* cor *m*; *Aut* klaxon® *m*. **2** *vi* **to h. in** *Am Fam* dire son mot, interrompre.

hornet ['hɔːnɪt] *n* (*insect*) frelon *m*.

horoscope ['hɒrəskəʊp] *n* horoscope *m*.

horror ['hɒrər] *n* horreur *f*; **(little) h.** (*child*) *Fam* petit monstre *m*; – *a* (*film etc*) d'épouvante, d'horreur. ◆**ho'rrendous** *a* horrible. ◆**horrible** *a* horrible, affreux. ◆**horribly** *adv* horriblement. ◆**horrid** *a* horrible; (*child*) épouvantable, méchant. ◆**ho'rrific** *a* horrible, horrifiant. ◆**horrify** *vt* horrifier.

hors-d'œuvre [ɔː'dɜːv] *n* hors-d'œuvre *m inv*.

horse [hɔːs] *n* **1** cheval *m*; **to go h. riding** faire du cheval; **h. show** concours *m* hippique. **2 h. chestnut** marron *m* (d'Inde). ◆**horseback** *n* **on h.** à cheval. ◆**horseman** *n* (*pl* **-men**) cavalier *m*. ◆**horseplay** *n* jeux *mpl* brutaux. ◆**horsepower** *n* cheval *m* (vapeur). ◆**horseracing** *n* courses *fpl*. ◆**horseradish** *n* radis *m* noir, raifort *m*. ◆**horseshoe** *n* fer *m* à cheval. ◆**horsewoman** *n* (*pl* **-women**) cavalière *f*.

horticulture ['hɔːtɪkʌltʃər] *n* horticulture *f*. ◆**horti'cultural** *a* horticole.

hose [həʊz] *n* (*tube*) tuyau *m*; – *vt* (*garden etc*) arroser. ◆**hosepipe** *n* tuyau *m*.

hosiery ['həʊzɪərɪ, *Am* 'həʊʒərɪ] *n* bonneterie *f*.

hospice ['hɒspɪs] *n* (*for dying people*) hospice *m* (pour incurables).

hospitable [hɒ'spɪtəb(ə)l] *a* hospitalier. ◆**hospitably** *adv* avec hospitalité. ◆**hospi'tality** *n* hospitalité *f*.

hospital ['hɒspɪt(ə)l] *n* hôpital *m*; **in h.**, *Am* **in the h.** à l'hôpital; – *a* (*bed etc*) d'hôpital; (*staff, services*) hospitalier. ◆**hospitalize** *vt* hospitaliser.

host [həʊst] *n* **1** (*man who receives guests*) hôte *m*. **2 a h. of** (*many*) une foule de. **3** *Rel* hostie *f*. ◆**hostess** *n* (*in house, aircraft, nightclub*) hôtesse *f*.

hostage ['hɒstɪdʒ] *n* otage *m*; **to take s.o. h.** prendre qn en otage.

hostel ['hɒst(ə)l] *n* foyer *m*; **youth h.** auberge *f* de jeunesse.

hostile ['hɒstaɪl, *Am* 'hɒst(ə)l] *a* hostile (**to, towards** à). ◆**ho'stility** *n* hostilité *f* (**to, towards** envers); *pl Mil* hostilités *fpl*.

hot[1] [hɒt] *a* (**hotter, hottest**) chaud; (*spice*) fort; (*temperament*) passionné; (*news*) *Fam* dernier; (*favourite*) *Sp* grand; **to be** *or* **feel h.** avoir chaud; **it's h.** il fait chaud; **not so h. at** (*good at*) *Fam* pas très calé en; **not so h.** (*bad*) *Fam* pas fameux; **h. dog** (*sausage*) hot-dog *m*. ◆**hotbed** *n Pej* foyer *m* (**of** de). ◆**hot-'blooded** *a* ardent. ◆**hothead** *n* tête *f* brûlée. ◆**hot'headed** *a* impétueux. ◆**hothouse** *n* serre *f* (chaude). ◆**hotplate** *n* chauffe-plats *m inv*; (*on stove*) plaque *f* chauffante. ◆**hot-'tempered** *a* emporté. ◆**hot-'water bottle** *n* bouillotte *f*.

hot[2] [hɒt] *vi* (**-tt-**) **to h. up** (*increase*) s'intensifier; (*become dangerous or excited*) chauffer.

hotchpotch ['hɒtʃpɒtʃ] *n* fatras *m*.

hotel [həʊ'tel] *n* hôtel *m*; – *a* (*industry*) hôtelier. ◆**hotelier** [həʊ'telɪeɪ] *n* hôtelier, -ière *mf*.

hotly ['hɒtlɪ] *adv* passionnément.

hound [haʊnd] **1** *n* (*dog*) chien *m* courant. **2** *vt* (*pursue*) poursuivre avec acharnement; (*worry*) harceler.

hour ['aʊər] *n* heure *f*; **half an h., a half-h.** une demi-heure; **a quarter of an h.** un quart d'heure; **paid ten francs an h.** payé dix francs (de) l'heure; **ten miles an h.** dix miles à l'heure; **open all hours** ouvert à toute heure; **h. hand** (*of watch, clock*) petite aiguille *f*. ◆**—ly** *a* (*rate, pay*) horaire; **an h. bus/train/***etc* un bus/train/*etc* toutes les heures; – *adv* toutes les heures; **h. paid, paid h.** payé à l'heure.

house[1], *pl* **-ses** [haʊs, -zɪz] *n* maison *f*; (*audience*) *Th* salle *f*, auditoire *m*; (*performance*) *Th* séance *f*; **the H.** *Pol* la Chambre; **the Houses of Parliament** le Parlement; **at** *or* **to my h.** chez moi; **on the h.** (*free of charge*) aux frais de la maison; **h. prices** prix *mpl* immobiliers. ◆**housebound** *a* confiné chez soi. ◆**house-**

breaking *n Jur* cambriolage *m.* ◆**house-broken** *a* (*dog etc*) *Am* propre. ◆**household** *n* ménage *m*, maison *f*, famille *f*; **h. duties** soins *mpl* du ménage; **a h. name** un nom très connu. ◆**householder** *n* (*owner*) propriétaire *mf*; (*family head*) chef *m* de famille. ◆**housekeeper** *n* (*employee*) gouvernante *f*; (*housewife*) ménagère *f.* ◆**housekeeping** *n* ménage *m.* ◆**houseman** *n* (*pl* **-men**) interne *mf* (des hôpitaux). ◆**houseproud** *a* qui s'occupe méticuleusement de sa maison. ◆**housetrained** *a* (*dog etc*) propre. ◆**housewarming** *n* & *a* **to have a h.-warming (party)** pendre la crémaillère. ◆**housewife** *n* (*pl* **-wives**) ménagère *f.* ◆**housework** *n* (travaux *mpl* de) ménage *m.*

hous/e² [haʊz] *vt* loger; (*of building*) abriter; **it is housed in** (*kept*) on le garde dans. ◆**—ing** *n* logement *m*; (*houses*) logements *mpl*; – *a* (*crisis etc*) du logement.

hovel ['hɒv(ə)l] *n* (*slum*) taudis *m.*

hover ['hɒvər] *vi* (*of bird, aircraft, danger etc*) planer; (*of person*) rôder, traîner. ◆**hovercraft** *n* aéroglisseur *m.*

how [haʊ] *adv* comment; **h.'s that?, h. so?, h. come?** *Fam* comment ça?; **h. kind!** comme c'est gentil!; **h. do you do?** (*greeting*) bonjour; **h. long/high is . . . ?** quelle est la longueur/hauteur de . . . ?; **h. much?, h. many?** combien?; **h. much time/*etc*?** combien de temps/*etc*?; **h. many apples/*etc*?** combien de pommes/*etc*?; **h. about a walk?** si on faisait une promenade?; **h. about some coffee?** (si on prenait) du café?; **h. about me?** et moi?

howdy! ['haʊdɪ] *int Am Fam* salut!

however [haʊ'evər] **1** *adv* **h. big he may be** quelque *or* si grand qu'il soit; **h. she may do it** de quelque manière qu'elle le fasse; **h. that may be** quoi qu'il en soit. **2** *conj* cependant.

howl [haʊl] *vi* hurler; (*of baby*) brailler; (*of wind*) mugir; – *n* hurlement *m*; braillement *m*; mugissement *m*; (*of laughter*) éclat *m.*

howler ['haʊlər] *n* (*mistake*) *Fam* gaffe *f.*

HP [eɪtʃ'piː] *abbr* = **hire purchase.**

hp *abbr* (*horsepower*) CV.

HQ [eɪtʃ'kjuː] *abbr* = **headquarters.**

hub [hʌb] *n* (*of wheel*) moyeu *m*; *Fig* centre *m.* ◆**hubcap** *n Aut* enjoliveur *m.*

hubbub ['hʌbʌb] *n* vacarme *m.*

huckleberry ['hʌk(ə)lbərɪ] *n Bot Am* myrtille *f.*

huddle ['hʌd(ə)l] *vi* **to h. (together)** se blottir (les uns contre les autres).

hue [hjuː] *n* (*colour*) teinte *f.*

huff [hʌf] *n* **in a h.** (*offended*) *Fam* fâché.

hug [hʌg] *vt* (**-gg-**) (*person*) serrer dans ses bras, étreindre; **to h. the kerb/coast** (*stay near*) serrer le trottoir/la côte; – *n* (*embrace*) étreinte *f.*

huge [hjuːdʒ] *a* énorme. ◆**—ly** *adv* énormément. ◆**—ness** *n* énormité *f.*

hulk [hʌlk] *n* (*person*) lourdaud, -aude *mf.*

hull [hʌl] *n* (*of ship*) coque *f.*

hullabaloo [hʌləbə'luː] *n Fam* (*noise*) vacarme *m*; (*fuss*) histoire(s) *f(pl)*.

hullo! [hʌ'ləʊ] *int* = **hallo.**

hum [hʌm] *vi* (**-mm-**) (*of insect*) bourdonner; (*of person*) fredonner; (*of top, radio*) ronfler; (*of engine*) vrombir; – *vt* (*tune*) fredonner; – *n* (*of insect*) bourdonnement *m.*

human ['hjuːmən] *a* humain; **h. being** être *m* humain; – *npl* humains *mpl.* ◆**hu'mane** *a* (*kind*) humain. ◆**hu'manely** *adv* humainement. ◆**humani'tarian** *a* & *n* humanitaire (*mf*). ◆**hu'manity** *n* (*human beings, kindness*) humanité *f.* ◆**humanly** *adv* (*possible etc*) humainement.

humble ['hʌmb(ə)l] *a* humble; – *vt* humilier. ◆**humbly** *adv* humblement.

humbug ['hʌmbʌg] *n* (*talk*) fumisterie *f*; (*person*) fumiste *mf.*

humdrum ['hʌmdrʌm] *a* monotone.

humid ['hjuːmɪd] *a* humide. ◆**hu'midify** *vt* humidifier. ◆**hu'midity** *n* humidité *f.*

humiliate [hjuː'mɪlɪeɪt] *vt* humilier. ◆**humili'ation** *n* humiliation *f.* ◆**humility** *n* humilité *f.*

humour ['hjuːmər] **1** *n* (*fun*) humour *m*; (*temper*) humeur *f*; **to have a sense of h.** avoir le sens de l'humour; **in a good h.** de bonne humeur. **2** *vt* **to h. s.o.** faire plaisir à qn, ménager qn. ◆**humorist** *n* humoriste *mf.* ◆**humorous** *a* (*book etc*) humoristique; (*person*) plein d'humour. ◆**humorously** *adv* avec humour.

hump [hʌmp] **1** *n* (*lump, mound*) bosse *f*; – *vt* (*one's back*) voûter. **2** *n* **to have the h.** *Fam* (*depression*) avoir le cafard; (*bad temper*) être en rogne. ◆**humpback** *a* **h. bridge** *Aut* pont *m* en dos d'âne.

hunch [hʌntʃ] **1** *vt* (*one's shoulders*) voûter. **2** *n* (*idea*) *Fam* intuition *f*, idée *f.* ◆**hunchback** *n* bossu, -ue *mf.*

hundred ['hʌndrəd] *a* & *n* cent (*m*); **a h. pages** cent pages; **two h. pages** deux cents pages; **hundreds of** des centaines de.

◆**hundredfold** *a* centuple; – *adv* au centuple. ◆**hundredth** *a* & *n* centième (*mf*). ◆**hundredweight** *n* 112 livres (= *50,8 kg*); *Am* 100 livres (= *45,3 kg*).
hung [hʌŋ] *see* **hang**[1].
Hungary ['hʌŋgərɪ] *n* Hongrie *f*. ◆**Hun'garian** *a* & *n* hongrois, -oise (*mf*); – *n* (*language*) hongrois *m*.
hunger ['hʌŋgər] *n* faim *f*. ◆**hungry** *a* (-**ier**, -**iest**) **to be** *or* **feel h.** avoir faim; **to go h.** souffrir de la faim; **to make h.** donner faim à; **h. for** (*news etc*) avide de. ◆**hungrily** *adv* avidement.
hunk [hʌŋk] *n* (gros) morceau *m*.
hunt [hʌnt] *n Sp* chasse *f*; (*search*) recherche *f* (for de); – *vt Sp* chasser; (*pursue*) poursuivre; (*seek*) chercher; **to h. down** (*fugitive etc*) traquer; **to h. out** (*information etc*) dénicher; – *vi Sp* chasser; **to h. for sth** (re)chercher qch. ◆**—ing** *n Sp* chasse *f*. ◆**—er** *n* (*person*) chasseur *m*.
hurdle ['hɜːd(ə)l] *n* (*fence*) *Sp* haie *f*; *Fig* obstacle *m*.
hurl [hɜːl] *vt* (*throw*) jeter, lancer; (*abuse*) lancer; **to h. oneself at s.o.** se ruer sur qn.
hurly-burly ['hɜːlɪbɜːlɪ] *n* tumulte *m*.
hurray! [hʊ'reɪ] *int* hourra!
hurricane ['hʌrɪkən, *Am* 'hʌrɪkeɪn] *n* ouragan *m*.
hurry ['hʌrɪ] *n* hâte *f*; **in a h.** à la hâte, en hâte; **to be in a h.** être pressé; **to be in a h. to do** avoir hâte de faire; **there's no h.** rien ne presse; – *vi* se dépêcher, se presser (**to do** de faire); **to h. out** sortir à la hâte; **to h. along** *or* **on** *or* **up** se dépêcher; – *vt* (*person*) bousculer, presser; (*pace*) presser; **to h. one's meal** manger à toute vitesse; **to h. s.o. out** faire sortir qn à la hâte. ◆**hurried** *a* (*steps, decision etc*) précipité; (*travail*) fait à la hâte; (*visit*) éclair *inv*; **to be h.** (*in a hurry*) être pressé.
hurt [hɜːt] *vt* (*pt & pp* **hurt**) (*physically*) faire du mal à, blesser; (*emotionally*) faire de la peine à; (*offend*) blesser; (*prejudice, damage*) nuire à; **to h. s.o.'s feelings** blesser qn; **his arm hurts (him)** son bras lui fait mal; – *vi* faire mal; – *n* mal *m*; – *a* (*injured*) blessé. ◆**hurtful** *a* (*remark*) blessant.
hurtle ['hɜːt(ə)l] *vi* **to h. along** aller à toute vitesse; **to h. down** dégringoler.
husband ['hʌzbənd] *n* mari *m*.
hush [hʌʃ] *int* chut!; – *n* silence *m*; – *vt* (*person*) faire taire; (*baby*) calmer; **to h. up** (*scandal*) *Fig* étouffer. ◆**—ed** *a* (*voice*) étouffé; (*silence*) profond. ◆**hush-hush** *a Fam* ultra-secret.
husk [hʌsk] *n* (*of rice, grain*) enveloppe *f*.
husky ['hʌskɪ] *a* (-**ier**, -**iest**) (*voice*) enroué, voilé.
hussy ['hʌsɪ] *n Pej* friponne *f*, coquine *f*.
hustings ['hʌstɪŋz] *npl* campagne *f* électorale, élections *fpl*.
hustle ['hʌs(ə)l] **1** *vt* (*shove, rush*) bousculer (*qn*); – *vi* (*work busily*) *Am* se démener (**to get sth** pour avoir qch). **2** *n* **h. and bustle** agitation *f*, activité *f*, tourbillon *m*.
hut [hʌt] *n* cabane *f*, hutte *f*.
hutch [hʌtʃ] *n* (*for rabbit*) clapier *m*.
hyacinth ['haɪəsɪnθ] *n* jacinthe *f*.
hybrid ['haɪbrɪd] *a* & *n* hybride (*m*).
hydrangea [haɪ'dreɪndʒə] *n* (*shrub*) hortensia *m*.
hydrant ['haɪdrənt] *n* (**fire**) **h.** bouche *f* d'incendie.
hydraulic [haɪ'drɔːlɪk] *a* hydraulique.
hydroelectric [haɪdrəʊɪ'lektrɪk] *a* hydroélectrique.
hydrogen ['haɪdrədʒən] *n Ch* hydrogène *m*.
hyena [haɪ'iːnə] *n* (*animal*) hyène *f*.
hygiene ['haɪdʒiːn] *n* hygiène *f*. ◆**hy'gienic** *a* hygiénique.
hymn [hɪm] *n Rel* cantique *m*, hymne *m*.
hyper- ['haɪpər] *pref* hyper-.
hypermarket ['haɪpəmɑːkɪt] *n* hypermarché *m*.
hyphen ['haɪf(ə)n] *n* trait *m* d'union. ◆**hyphenat/e** *vt* mettre un trait d'union à. ◆**—ed** *a* (*word*) à trait d'union.
hypnosis [hɪp'nəʊsɪs] *n* hypnose *f*. ◆**hypnotic** *a* hypnotique. ◆**'hypnotism** *n* hypnotisme *m*. ◆**'hypnotist** *n* hypnotiseur *m*. ◆**'hypnotize** *vt* hypnotiser.
hypochondriac [haɪpə'kɒndrɪæk] *n* malade *mf* imaginaire.
hypocrisy [hɪ'pɒkrɪsɪ] *n* hypocrisie *f*. ◆**'hypocrite** *n* hypocrite *mf*. ◆**hypo'critical** *a* hypocrite.
hypodermic [haɪpə'dɜːmɪk] *a* hypodermique.
hypothesis, *pl* **-eses** [haɪ'pɒθɪsɪs, -ɪsiːz] *n* hypothèse *f*. ◆**hypo'thetical** *a* hypothétique.
hysteria [hɪ'stɪərɪə] *n* hystérie *f*. ◆**hysterical** *a* hystérique; (*funny*) *Fam* désopilant; **to be** *or* **become h.** (*wildly upset*) avoir une crise de nerfs. ◆**hysterically** *adv* (*to cry*) sans pouvoir s'arrêter; **to laugh h.** rire aux larmes. ◆**hysterics** *npl* (*tears etc*) crise *f* de nerfs; (*laughter*) crise *f* de rire.

I

I, i [aɪ] *n* I, i *m*.

I [aɪ] *pron* je, j'; (*stressed*) moi; **I want** je veux; **she and I** elle et moi.

ic/e¹ [aɪs] *n* glace *f*; (*on road*) verglas *m*; **i. (cream)** glace *f*; **black i.** (*on road*) verglas *m*; **i. cube** glaçon *m*; – *vi* **to i. (over)** (*of lake*) geler; (*of windscreen*) givrer. ◆**—ed** *a* (*tea*) glacé. ◆**iceberg** *n* iceberg *m* ◆**icebox** *n* (*box*) & *Fig* glacière *f*; *Am* réfrigérateur *m*. ◆**ice-'cold** *a* glacial; (*drink*) glacé. ◆**ice-skating** *n* patinage *m* (sur glace). ◆**icicle** *n* glaçon *m*.

ic/e² [aɪs] *vt* (*cake*) glacer. ◆**—ing** *n* (*on cake etc*) glaçage *m*.

Iceland ['aɪslənd] *n* Islande *f*. ◆**Ice'landic** *a* islandais.

icon ['aɪkɒn] *n Rel* icône *f*.

icy ['aɪsɪ] *a* (**-ier, -iest**) (*water, hands, room*) glacé; (*manner, weather*) glacial; (*road etc*) verglacé.

idea [aɪ'dɪə] *n* idée *f* (**of** de); **I have an i. that . . .** j'ai l'impression que . . . ; **that's my i. of rest** c'est ce que j'appelle du repos; **that's the i.!** *Fam* c'est ça!; **not the slightest** *or* **foggiest i.** pas la moindre idée.

ideal [aɪ'dɪəl] *a* idéal; – *n* (*aspiration*) idéal *m*; *pl* (*spiritual etc*) idéal *m*. ◆**idealism** *n* idéalisme *m*. ◆**idealist** *n* idéaliste *mf*. ◆**idea'listic** *a* idéaliste. ◆**idealize** *vt* idéaliser. ◆**ideally** *adv* idéalement; **i. we should stay** l'idéal, ce serait de rester *or* que nous restions.

identical [aɪ'dentɪk(ə)l] *a* identique (**to, with** à). ◆**identifi'cation** *n* identification *f*; **I have (some) i.** j'ai une pièce d'identité. ◆**identify** *vt* identifier; **to i. (oneself) with** s'identifier avec. ◆**identikit** *n* portrait-robot *m*. ◆**identity** *n* identité *f*; **i. card** carte *f* d'identité.

ideology [aɪdɪ'ɒlədʒɪ] *n* idéologie *f*. ◆**ideo'logical** *a* idéologique.

idiom ['ɪdɪəm] *n* expression *f* idiomatique; (*language*) idiome *m*. ◆**idio'matic** *a* idiomatique.

idiosyncrasy [ɪdɪə'sɪŋkrəsɪ] *n* particularité *f*.

idiot ['ɪdɪət] *n* idiot, -ote *mf*. ◆**idiocy** *n* idiotie *f*. ◆**idi'otic** *a* idiot, bête. ◆**idi'otically** *adv* idiotement.

idle ['aɪd(ə)l] *a* (*unoccupied*) désœuvré, oisif; (*lazy*) paresseux; (*unemployed*) en chômage; (*moment*) de loisir; (*machine*) au repos; (*promise*) vain; (*pleasure, question*) futile; (*rumour*) sans fondement; – *vi* (*laze about*) paresser; (*of machine, engine*) tourner au ralenti; – *vt* **to i. away** (*time*) gaspiller. ◆**—ness** *n* oisiveté *f*; (*laziness*) paresse *f*. ◆**idler** *n* paresseux, -euse *mf*. ◆**idly** *adv* paresseusement; (*to suggest, say*) négligemment.

idol ['aɪd(ə)l] *n* idole *f*. ◆**idolize** *vt* idolâtrer.

idyllic [aɪ'dɪlɪk] *a* idyllique.

i.e. [aɪ'iː] *abbr* (*id est*) c'est-à-dire.

if [ɪf] *conj* si; **if he comes** s'il vient; **even if** même si; **if so** dans ce cas, si c'est le cas; **if not for pleasure** sinon pour le plaisir; **if only I were rich** si seulement j'étais riche; **if only to look** ne serait-ce que pour regarder; **as if** comme si; **as if nothing had happened** comme si de rien n'était; **as if to say** comme pour dire; **if necessary** s'il le faut.

igloo ['ɪgluː] *n* igloo *m*.

ignite [ɪg'naɪt] *vt* mettre le feu à; – *vi* prendre feu. ◆**ignition** *n Aut* allumage *m*; **to switch on the i.** mettre le contact.

ignominious [ɪgnə'mɪnɪəs] *a* déshonorant, ignominieux.

ignoramus [ɪgnə'reɪməs] *n* ignare *mf*.

ignorance ['ɪgnərəns] *n* ignorance *f* (**of** de). ◆**ignorant** *a* ignorant (**of** de). ◆**ignorantly** *adv* par ignorance.

ignore [ɪg'nɔːr] *vt* ne prêter aucune attention à, ne tenir aucun compte de; (*duty*) méconnaître; (*pretend not to recognize*) faire semblant de ne pas reconnaître.

ilk [ɪlk] *n* **of that i.** (*kind*) de cet acabit.

ill [ɪl] *a* (*sick*) malade; (*bad*) mauvais; **i. will** malveillance *f*; – *npl* (*misfortunes*) maux *mpl*, malheurs *mpl*; – *adv* mal; **to speak i. of** dire du mal de. ◆**ill-ad'vised** *a* malavisé, peu judicieux. ◆**ill-'fated** *a* malheureux. ◆**ill-'gotten** *a* mal acquis. ◆**ill-in'formed** *a* mal renseigné. ◆**ill-'mannered** *a* mal élevé. ◆**ill-'natured** *a* (*mean, unkind*) désagréable. ◆**ill-'timed** *a* inopportun. ◆**ill-'treat** *vt* maltraiter.

illegal [ɪ'liːg(ə)l] *a* illégal. ◆**ille'gality** *n* illégalité *f*.

illegible [ɪ'ledʒəb(ə)l] *a* illisible.

illegitimate [ɪlɪ'dʒɪtɪmət] *a* (*child, claim*) illégitime. ◆**illegitimacy** *n* illégitimité *f*.
illicit [ɪ'lɪsɪt] *a* illicite.
illiterate [ɪ'lɪtərət] *a* & *n* illettré, -ée (*mf*), analphabète (*mf*). ◆**illiteracy** *n* analphabétisme *m*.
illness ['ɪlnɪs] *n* maladie *f*.
illogical [ɪ'lɒdʒɪk(ə)l] *a* illogique.
illuminate [ɪ'luːmɪneɪt] *vt* (*street, question etc*) éclairer; (*monument etc for special occasion*) illuminer. ◆**illumi'nation** *n* éclairage *m*; illumination *f*.
illusion [ɪ'luːʒ(ə)n] *n* illusion *f* (**about** sur); **I'm not under any i.** je ne me fais aucune illusion (**about** sur, quant à). ◆**illusive** *a*, ◆**illusory** *a* illusoire.
illustrate ['ɪləstreɪt] *vt* (*with pictures, examples*) illustrer (**with** de). ◆**illu'stration** *n* illustration *f*. ◆**i'llustrative** *a* (*example*) explicatif.
illustrious [ɪ'lʌstrɪəs] *a* illustre.
image ['ɪmɪdʒ] *n* image *f*; **(public) i.** (*of firm etc*) image *f* de marque; **he's the (living** *or* **spitting** *or* **very) i. of his brother** c'est (tout) le portrait de son frère. ◆**imagery** *n* images *fpl*.
imagin/e [ɪ'mædʒɪn] *vt* (*picture to oneself*) (s')imaginer, se figurer (**that** que); (*suppose*) imaginer (**that** que); **i. that . . .** imaginez que . . . ; **you're imagining (things)!** tu te fais des illusions! ◆**—ings** *npl* (*dreams*) imaginations *fpl*. ◆**—able** *a* imaginable; **the worst thing i.** le pire que l'on puisse imaginer. ◆**imaginary** *a* imaginaire. ◆**imagi'nation** *n* imagination *f*. ◆**imaginative** *a* plein d'imagination, imaginatif.
imbalance [ɪm'bæləns] *n* déséquilibre *m*.
imbecile ['ɪmbəsiːl, *Am* 'ɪmbəs(ə)l] *a* & *n* imbécile (*mf*). ◆**imbe'cility** *n* imbécillité *f*.
imbibe [ɪm'baɪb] *vt* absorber.
imbued [ɪm'bjuːd] *a* **i. with** (*ideas*) imprégné de; (*feelings*) pénétré de, imbu de.
imitate ['ɪmɪteɪt] *vt* imiter. ◆**imi'tation** *n* imitation *f*; – *a* (*jewels*) artificiel; **i. leather** imitation *f* cuir. ◆**imitative** *a* imitateur. ◆**imitator** *n* imitateur, -trice *mf*.
immaculate [ɪ'mækjʊlət] *a* (*person, appearance, shirt etc*) impeccable.
immaterial [ɪmə'tɪərɪəl] *a* peu important (**to** pour).
immature [ɪmə'tʃʊər] *a* (*fruit*) vert; (*animal*) jeune; (*person*) qui manque de maturité.
immeasurable [ɪ'meʒərəb(ə)l] *a* incommensurable.
immediate [ɪ'miːdɪət] *a* immédiat. ◆**immediacy** *n* caractère *m* immédiat. ◆**immediately** *adv* (*at once*) tout de suite, immédiatement; (*to concern, affect*) directement; – *conj* (*as soon as*) dès que.
immense [ɪ'mens] *a* immense. ◆**immensely** *adv* (*rich etc*) immensément; **to enjoy oneself i.** s'amuser énormément. ◆**immensity** *n* immensité *f*.
immerse [ɪ'mɜːs] *vt* plonger, immerger; **immersed in work** plongé dans le travail. ◆**immersion** *n* immersion *f*; **i. heater** chauffe-eau *m inv* électrique.
immigrate ['ɪmɪgreɪt] *vi* immigrer. ◆**immigrant** *n* immigrant, -ante *mf*; (*long-established*) immigré, -ée *mf*; – *a* immigré. ◆**immi'gration** *n* immigration *f*.
imminent ['ɪmɪnənt] *a* imminent. ◆**imminence** *n* imminence *f*.
immobile [ɪ'məʊbaɪl, *Am* ɪ'məʊb(ə)l] *a* immobile. ◆**immo'bility** *n* immobilité *f*. ◆**immobilize** *vt* immobiliser.
immoderate [ɪ'mɒdərət] *a* immodéré.
immodest [ɪ'mɒdɪst] *a* impudique.
immoral [ɪ'mɒrəl] *a* immoral. ◆**immo'rality** *n* immoralité *f*.
immortal [ɪ'mɔːt(ə)l] *a* immortel. ◆**immor'tality** *n* immortalité *f*. ◆**immortalize** *vt* immortaliser.
immune [ɪ'mjuːn] *a Med & Fig* immunisé (**to, from** contre). ◆**immunity** *n* immunité *f*. ◆**'immunize** *vt* immuniser (**against** contre).
immutable [ɪ'mjuːtəb(ə)l] *a* immuable.
imp [ɪmp] *n* diablotin *m*, lutin *m*.
impact ['ɪmpækt] *n* impact *m* (**on** sur).
impair [ɪm'peər] *vt* détériorer; (*hearing, health*) abîmer.
impale [ɪm'peɪl] *vt* empaler.
impart [ɪm'pɑːt] *vt* communiquer (**to** à).
impartial [ɪm'pɑːʃ(ə)l] *a* impartial. ◆**imparti'ality** *n* impartialité *f*.
impassable [ɪm'pɑːsəb(ə)l] *a* (*road*) impraticable; (*river*) infranchissable.
impasse ['æmpɑːs, *Am* 'ɪmpæs] *n* (*situation*) impasse *f*.
impassioned [ɪm'pæʃ(ə)nd] *a* (*speech etc*) enflammé, passionné.
impassive [ɪm'pæsɪv] *a* impassible. ◆**—ness** *n* impassibilité *f*.
impatient [ɪm'peɪʃ(ə)nt] *a* impatient (**to do** de faire); **i. of** *or* **with** intolérant à l'égard de. ◆**impatience** *n* impatience *f*. ◆**impatiently** *adv* impatiemment.
impeccab/le [ɪm'pekəb(ə)l] *a* impeccable. ◆**—ly** *adv* impeccablement.

impecunious [ɪmpɪ'kjuːnɪəs] *a Hum* sans le sou, impécunieux.

impede [ɪm'piːd] *vt* (*hamper*) gêner; **to i. s.o. from doing** (*prevent*) empêcher qn de faire.

impediment [ɪm'pedɪmənt] *n* obstacle *m*; (*of speech*) défaut *m* d'élocution.

impel [ɪm'pel] *vt* (**-ll-**) (*drive*) pousser; (*force*) obliger (**to do** à faire).

impending [ɪm'pendɪŋ] *a* imminent.

impenetrable [ɪm'penɪtrəb(ə)l] *a* (*forest, mystery etc*) impénétrable.

imperative [ɪm'perətɪv] *a* (*need, tone*) impérieux; (*necessary*) essentiel; **it is i. that you come** il faut absolument que *or* il est indispensable que tu viennes; – *n Gram* impératif *m*.

imperceptible [ɪmpə'septəb(ə)l] *a* imperceptible (**to** à).

imperfect [ɪm'pɜːfɪkt] **1** *a* imparfait; (*goods*) défectueux. **2** *n* (*tense*) *Gram* imparfait *m*. ◆**imper'fection** *n* imperfection *f*.

imperial [ɪm'pɪərɪəl] *a* impérial; (*majestic*) majestueux; (*measure*) *Br* légal. ◆**imperialism** *n* impérialisme *m*.

imperil [ɪm'perɪl] *vt* (**-ll-**, *Am* **-l-**) mettre en péril.

imperious [ɪm'pɪərɪəs] *a* impérieux.

impersonal [ɪm'pɜːsən(ə)l] *a* impersonnel.

impersonate [ɪm'pɜːsəneɪt] *vt* (*mimic*) imiter; (*pretend to be*) se faire passer pour. ◆**imperso'nation** *n* imitation *f*. ◆**impersonator** *n* imitateur, -trice *mf*.

impertinent [ɪm'pɜːtɪnənt] *a* impertinent (**to** envers). ◆**impertinence** *n* impertinence *f*. ◆**impertinently** *adv* avec impertinence.

impervious [ɪm'pɜːvɪəs] *a* imperméable (**to** à).

impetuous [ɪm'petjʊəs] *a* impétueux. ◆**impetu'osity** *n* impétuosité *f*.

impetus ['ɪmpɪtəs] *n* impulsion *f*.

impinge [ɪm'pɪndʒ] *vi* **to i. on** (*affect*) affecter; (*encroach on*) empiéter sur.

impish ['ɪmpɪʃ] *a* (*naughty*) espiègle.

implacable [ɪm'plækəb(ə)l] *a* implacable.

implant [ɪm'plɑːnt] *vt* (*ideas*) inculquer (**in** à).

implement[1] ['ɪmplɪmənt] *n* (*tool*) instrument *m*; (*utensil*) *Culin* ustensile *m*; *pl Agr* matériel *m*.

implement[2] ['ɪmplɪment] *vt* (*carry out*) mettre en œuvre, exécuter. ◆**implemen'tation** *n* mise *f* en œuvre, exécution *f*.

implicate ['ɪmplɪkeɪt] *vt* impliquer (**in** dans). ◆**impli'cation** *n* (*consequence, involvement*) implication *f*; (*innuendo*) insinuation *f*; (*impact*) portée *f*; **by i.** implicitement.

implicit [ɪm'plɪsɪt] *a* (*implied*) implicite; (*belief, obedience etc*) absolu. ◆**—ly** *adv* implicitement.

implore [ɪm'plɔːr] *vt* implorer (**s.o. to do** qn de faire).

imply [ɪm'plaɪ] *vt* (*assume*) impliquer, supposer (**that** que); (*suggest*) laisser entendre (**that** que); (*insinuate*) *Pej* insinuer (**that** que). ◆**implied** *a* implicite.

impolite [ɪmpə'laɪt] *a* impoli. ◆**—ness** *n* impolitesse *f*.

import 1 [ɪm'pɔːt] *vt* (*goods etc*) importer (**from** de); – ['ɪmpɔːt] *n* (*object, action*) importation *f*. **2** ['ɪmpɔːt] *n* (*meaning*) sens *m*. ◆**im'porter** *n* importateur, -trice *mf*.

importance [ɪm'pɔːtəns] *n* importance *f*; **to be of i.** avoir de l'importance; **of no i.** sans importance. ◆**important** *a* (*significant*) important. ◆**importantly** *adv* **more i.** ce qui est plus important.

impose [ɪm'pəʊz] *vt* imposer (**on** à); (*fine, punishment*) infliger (**on** à); **to i. (oneself) on s.o.** s'imposer à qn; – *vi* s'imposer. ◆**impo'sition** *n* imposition *f* (**of** de); (*inconvenience*) dérangement *m*.

impossible [ɪm'pɒsəb(ə)l] *a* impossible (**to do** à faire); **it is i. (for us) to do** il (nous) est impossible de faire; **it is i. that** il est impossible que (+ *sub*); **to make it i. for s.o. to do** mettre qn dans l'impossibilité de faire; – *n* **to do the i.** faire l'impossible. ◆**impossi'bility** *n* impossibilité *f*. ◆**impossibly** *adv* (*late, hard*) incroyablement.

impostor [ɪm'pɒstər] *n* imposteur *m*.

impotent ['ɪmpətənt] *a Med* impuissant. ◆**impotence** *n Med* impuissance *f*.

impound [ɪm'paʊnd] *vt* (*of police*) saisir, confisquer; (*vehicle*) emmener à la fourrière.

impoverish [ɪm'pɒvərɪʃ] *vt* appauvrir.

impracticable [ɪm'præktɪkəb(ə)l] *a* irréalisable, impraticable.

impractical [ɪm'præktɪk(ə)l] *a* peu réaliste.

imprecise [ɪmprɪ'saɪs] *a* imprécis.

impregnable [ɪm'pregnəb(ə)l] *a Mil* imprenable; (*argument*) *Fig* inattaquable.

impregnate ['ɪmpregneɪt] *vt* (*imbue*) imprégner (**with** de); (*fertilize*) féconder.

impresario [ɪmprɪ'sɑːrɪəʊ] *n* (*pl* **-os**) impresario *m*.

impress [ɪm'pres] *vt* impressionner (*qn*); (*mark*) imprimer; **to i. sth on s.o.** faire comprendre qch à qn. ◆**impression** *n* impression *f*; **to be under** *or* **have the i. that** avoir l'impression que; **to make a good i. on s.o.** faire une bonne impression à qn. ◆**impressionable** *a* (*person*) impression-

nable; (*age*) où l'on est impressionnable. ◆**impressive** *a* impressionnant.
imprint [ɪm'prɪnt] *vt* imprimer; – ['ɪmprɪnt] *n* empreinte *f*.
imprison [ɪm'prɪz(ə)n] *vt* emprisonner. ◆**—ment** *n* emprisonnement *m*; **life i.** la prison à vie.
improbable [ɪm'prɒbəb(ə)l] *a* improbable; (*story, excuse*) invraisemblable. ◆**impro ba'bility** *n* improbabilité *f*; invraisemblance *f*.
impromptu [ɪm'prɒmptjuː] *a* & *adv* impromptu.
improper [ɪm'prɒpər] *a* (*indecent*) inconvenant, indécent; (*wrong*) incorrect. ◆**impropriety** [ɪmprə'praɪətɪ] *n* inconvenance *f*; (*wrong use*) *Ling* impropriété *f*.
improve [ɪm'pruːv] *vt* améliorer; (*mind*) cultiver, développer; **to i. one's English** se perfectionner en anglais; **to i. s.o.'s looks** embellir qn; **to i. oneself** se cultiver; – *vi* s'améliorer; (*of business*) aller de mieux en mieux, reprendre; **to i. on** (*do better than*) faire mieux que. ◆**—ment** *n* amélioration *f*; (*of mind*) développement *m*; (*progress*) progrès *m*(*pl*); **there has been some** *or* **an i.** il y a du mieux.
improvise ['ɪmprəvaɪz] *vti* improviser. ◆**improvi'sation** *n* improvisation *f*.
impudent ['ɪmpjʊdənt] *a* impudent. ◆**impudence** *n* impudence *f*.
impulse ['ɪmpʌls] *n* impulsion *f*; **on i.** sur un coup de tête. ◆**im'pulsive** *a* (*person, act*) impulsif, irréfléchi; (*remark*) irréfléchi. ◆**im'pulsively** *adv* de manière impulsive.
impunity [ɪm'pjuːnɪtɪ] *n* **with i.** impunément.
impure [ɪm'pjʊər] *a* impur. ◆**impurity** *n* impureté *f*.
in [ɪn] *prep* **1** dans; **in the box/the school/***etc* dans la boîte/l'école/*etc*; **in an hour('s time)** dans une heure; **in so far as** dans la mesure où. **2** à; **in school** à l'école; **in the garden** dans le jardin, au jardin; **in Paris** à Paris; **in the USA** aux USA; **in Portugal** au Portugal; **in fashion** à la mode; **in pencil** au crayon; **in my opinion** à mon avis. **3** en; **in summer/secret/French** en été/secret/français; **in Spain** en Espagne; **in May** en mai, au mois de mai; **in season** en saison; **in an hour** (*during the period of an hour*) en une heure; **in doing** en faisant; **dressed in black** habillé en noir; **in all** en tout. **4** de; **in a soft voice** d'une voix douce; **the best in the class** le meilleur de la classe. **5 in the rain** sous la pluie; **in the morning** le matin; **he hasn't done it in years** ça fait des années qu'il ne l'a pas fait; **in an hour** (*at the end of an hour*) au bout d'une heure; **one in ten** un sur dix; **in thousands** par milliers; **in here** ici; **in there** là-dedans. **6** *adv* **to be in** (*home*) être là, être à la maison; (*of train*) être arrivé; (*in fashion*) être en vogue; (*in season*) être en saison; (*in power*) *Pol* être au pouvoir; **day in day out** jour après jour; **in on** (*a secret*) au courant de; **we're in for some rain/trouble/***etc* on va avoir de la pluie/des ennuis/*etc*; **it's the in thing** *Fam* c'est dans le vent. **7** *npl* **the ins and outs of** les moindres détails de.
inability [ɪnə'bɪlɪtɪ] *n* incapacité *f* (**to do** de faire).
inaccessible [ɪnək'sesəb(ə)l] *a* inaccessible.
inaccurate [ɪn'ækjʊrət] *a* inexact. ◆**inaccuracy** *n* inexactitude *f*.
inaction [ɪn'ækʃ(ə)n] *n* inaction *f*.
inactive [ɪn'æktɪv] *a* inactif; (*mind*) inerte. ◆**inac'tivity** *n* inactivité *f*, inaction *f*.
inadequate [ɪn'ædɪkwət] *a* (*quantity*) insuffisant; (*person*) pas à la hauteur, insuffisant; (*work*) médiocre. ◆**inadequacy** *n* insuffisance *f*. ◆**inadequately** *adv* insuffisamment.
inadmissible [ɪnəd'mɪsəb(ə)l] *a* inadmissible.
inadvertently [ɪnəd'vɜːtəntlɪ] *adv* par inadvertance.
inadvisable [ɪnəd'vaɪzəb(ə)l] *a* (*action*) à déconseiller; **it is i. to** il est déconseillé de.
inane [ɪ'neɪn] *a* (*absurd*) inepte.
inanimate [ɪn'ænɪmət] *a* inanimé.
inappropriate [ɪnə'prəʊprɪət] *a* (*unsuitable*) peu approprié, inadéquat; (*untimely*) inopportun.
inarticulate [ɪnɑː'tɪkjʊlət] *a* (*person*) incapable de s'exprimer; (*sound*) inarticulé.
inasmuch as [ɪnəz'mʌtʃəz] *adv* (*because*) vu que; (*to the extent that*) en ce sens que.
inattentive [ɪnə'tentɪv] *a* inattentif (**to** à).
inaudible [ɪn'ɔːdəb(ə)l] *a* inaudible.
inaugural [ɪ'nɔːgjʊrəl] *a* inaugural. ◆**inaugurate** *vt* (*policy, building*) inaugurer; (*official*) installer (dans ses fonctions). ◆**inaugu'ration** *n* inauguration *f*; investiture *f*.
inauspicious [ɪnɔː'spɪʃəs] *a* peu propice.
inborn [ɪn'bɔːn] *a* inné.
inbred [ɪn'bred] *a* (*quality etc*) inné.
Inc *abbr* (*Incorporated*) *Am Com* SA, SARL.
incalculable [ɪn'kælkjʊləb(ə)l] *a* incalculable.
incandescent [ɪnkæn'des(ə)nt] *a* incandescent.
incapable [ɪn'keɪpəb(ə)l] *a* incapable (**of**

doing de faire); **i. of** (*pity etc*) inaccessible à.

incapacitate [ɪnkəˈpæsɪteɪt] *vt Med* rendre incapable (*de travailler etc*). ◆**incapacity** *n* (*inability*) *Med* incapacité *f*.

incarcerate [ɪnˈkɑːsəreɪt] *vt* incarcérer. ◆**incarceˈration** *n* incarcération *f*.

incarnate [ɪnˈkɑːnət] *a* incarné; – [ɪnˈkɑːneɪt] *vt* incarner. ◆**incarˈnation** *n* incarnation *f*.

incendiary [ɪnˈsendɪərɪ] *a* (*bomb*) incendiaire.

incense 1 [ɪnˈsens] *vt* mettre en colère. **2** [ˈɪnsens] *n* (*substance*) encens *m*.

incentive [ɪnˈsentɪv] *n* encouragement *m*, motivation *f*; **to give s.o. an i. to work/***etc* encourager qn à travailler/*etc*.

inception [ɪnˈsepʃ(ə)n] *n* début *m*.

incessant [ɪnˈses(ə)nt] *a* incessant. ◆**—ly** *adv* sans cesse.

incest [ˈɪnsest] *n* inceste *m*. ◆**inˈcestuous** *a* incestueux.

inch [ɪntʃ] *n* pouce *m* (= *2,54 cm*); (*loosely*) *Fig* centimètre *m*; **within an i. of** (*success*) à deux doigts de; **i. by i.** petit à petit; – *vti* to **i. (one's way) forward** avancer petit à petit.

incidence [ˈɪnsɪdəns] *n* fréquence *f*.

incident [ˈɪnsɪdənt] *n* incident *m*; (*in book, film etc*) épisode *m*.

incidental [ɪnsɪˈdent(ə)l] *a* accessoire, secondaire; (*music*) de fond; **i. expenses** frais *mpl* accessoires. ◆**—ly** *adv* accessoirement; (*by the way*) à propos.

incinerate [ɪnˈsɪnəreɪt] *vt* (*refuse, leaves etc*) incinérer. ◆**incinerator** *n* incinérateur *m*.

incipient [ɪnˈsɪpɪənt] *a* naissant.

incision [ɪnˈsɪʒ(ə)n] *n* incision *f*.

incisive [ɪnˈsaɪsɪv] *a* incisif.

incisor [ɪnˈsaɪzər] *n* (*tooth*) incisive *f*.

incite [ɪnˈsaɪt] *vt* inciter (**to do** à faire). ◆**—ment** *n* incitation *f* (**to do** à faire).

incline 1 [ɪnˈklaɪn] *vt* (*tilt, bend*) incliner; **to i. s.o. to do** incliner qn à faire; **to be inclined to do** (*feel a wish to*) être enclin à faire; (*tend to*) avoir tendance à faire; – *vi* **to i.** *or* **be inclined towards** (*indulgence etc*) incliner à. **2** [ˈɪnklaɪn] *n* (*slope*) inclinaison *f*. ◆**incliˈnation** *n* inclination *f*; **to have no i. to do** n'avoir aucune envie de faire.

includ/e [ɪnˈkluːd] *vt* (*contain*) comprendre, englober; (*refer to*) s'appliquer à; **my invitation includes you** mon invitation s'adresse aussi à vous; **to be included** être compris; (*on list*) être inclus. ◆**—ing** *prep* y compris; **i. service** service *m* compris. ◆**inclusion** *n* inclusion *f*. ◆**inclusive** *a* inclus; **from the fourth to the tenth of May i.** du quatre jusqu'au dix mai inclus(ivement); **to be i. of** comprendre; **i. charge** prix *m* global.

incognito [ɪnkɒgˈniːtəʊ] *adv* incognito.

incoherent [ɪnkəʊˈhɪərənt] *a* incohérent. ◆**—ly** *adv* sans cohérence.

income [ˈɪŋkʌm] *n* revenu *m*; **private i.** rentes *fpl*; **i. tax** impôt *m* sur le revenu.

incoming [ˈɪnkʌmɪŋ] *a* (*tenant, president*) nouveau; **i. tide** marée *f* montante; **i. calls** *Tel* appels *mpl* de l'extérieur.

incommunicado [ɪnkəmjuːnɪˈkɑːdəʊ] *a* (tenu) au secret.

incomparable [ɪnˈkɒmpərəb(ə)l] *a* incomparable.

incompatible [ɪnkəmˈpætəb(ə)l] *a* incompatible (**with** avec). ◆**incompatiˈbility** *n* incompatibilité *f*.

incompetent [ɪnˈkɒmpɪtənt] *a* incompétent. ◆**incompetence** *n* incompétence *f*.

incomplete [ɪnkəmˈpliːt] *a* incomplet.

incomprehensible [ɪnkɒmprɪˈhensəb(ə)l] *a* incompréhensible.

inconceivable [ɪnkənˈsiːvəb(ə)l] *a* inconcevable.

inconclusive [ɪnkənˈkluːsɪv] *a* peu concluant.

incongruous [ɪnˈkɒŋgrʊəs] *a* (*building, colours*) qui jure(nt) (**with** avec); (*remark, attitude*) incongru; (*absurd*) absurde.

inconsequential [ɪnkɒnsɪˈkwenʃ(ə)l] *a* sans importance.

inconsiderate [ɪnkənˈsɪdərət] *a* (*action, remark*) irréfléchi, inconsidéré; **to be i.** (*of person*) manquer d'égards (**towards** envers).

inconsistent [ɪnkənˈsɪstənt] *a* inconséquent, incohérent; (*reports etc at variance*) contradictoire; **i. with** incompatible avec. ◆**inconsistency** *n* inconséquence *f*, incohérence *f*.

inconsolable [ɪnkənˈsəʊləb(ə)l] *a* inconsolable.

inconspicuous [ɪnkənˈspɪkjʊəs] *a* peu en évidence, qui passe inaperçu. ◆**—ly** *adv* discrètement.

incontinent [ɪnˈkɒntɪnənt] *a* incontinent.

inconvenient [ɪnkənˈviːnɪənt] *a* (*room, situation*) incommode; (*time*) inopportun; **it's i. (for me) to . . .** ça me dérange de . . . ; **that's very i.** c'est très gênant. ◆**inconvenience** *n* (*bother*) dérangement *m*; (*disadvantage*) inconvénient *m*; – *vt* déranger, gêner.

incorporate [ɪnˈkɔːpəreɪt] *vt* (*introduce*) incorporer (**into** dans); (*contain*) contenir;

incorporated society *Am* société *f* anonyme, société *f* à responsabilité limitée.

incorrect [ɪnkə'rekt] *a* incorrect, inexact; **you're i.** vous avez tort.

incorrigible [ɪn'kɒrɪdʒəb(ə)l] *a* incorrigible.

incorruptible [ɪnkə'rʌptəb(ə)l] *a* incorruptible.

increas/e [ɪn'kriːs] *vi* augmenter; (*of effort, noise*) s'intensifier; **to i. in weight** prendre du poids; – *vt* augmenter; intensifier; – ['ɪnkriːs] *n* augmentation *f* (**in, of** de); intensification *f* (**in, of** de); **on the i.** en hausse. **◆–ing** *a* (*amount etc*) croissant. **◆–ingly** *adv* de plus en plus.

incredib/le [ɪn'kredəb(ə)l] *a* incroyable. **◆–ly** *adv* incroyablement.

incredulous [ɪn'kredjʊləs] *a* incrédule. **◆incre'dulity** *n* incrédulité *f*.

increment ['ɪŋkrəmənt]] *n* augmentation *f*.

incriminat/e [ɪn'krɪmɪneɪt] *vt* incriminer. **◆–ing** *a* compromettant.

incubate ['ɪŋkjʊbeɪt] *vt* (*eggs*) couver. **◆incu'bation** *n* incubation *f*. **◆incubator** *n* (*for baby, eggs*) couveuse *f*.

inculcate ['ɪnkʌlkeɪt] *vt* inculquer (**in** à).

incumbent [ɪn'kʌmbənt] *a* **it is i. upon him** *or* **her to** il lui incombe de; – *n Rel Pol* titulaire *mf*.

incur [ɪn'kɜːr] *vt* (**-rr-**) (*debt*) contracter; (*expenses*) faire; (*criticism, danger*) s'attirer.

incurable [ɪn'kjʊərəb(ə)l] *a* incurable.

incursion [ɪn'kɜːʃ(ə)n] *n* incursion *f* (**into** dans).

indebted [ɪn'detɪd] *a* **i. to s.o. for sth/for doing sth** redevable à qn de qch/d'avoir fait qch. **◆–ness** *n* dette *f*.

indecent [ɪn'diːs(ə)nt] *a* (*offensive*) indécent; (*unsuitable*) peu approprié. **◆indecency** *n* indécence *f*; (*crime*) *Jur* outrage *m* à la pudeur. **◆indecently** *adv* indécemment.

indecisive [ɪndɪ'saɪsɪv] *a* (*person, answer*) indécis. **◆indecision** *n*, **◆indecisiveness** *n* indécision *f*.

indeed [ɪn'diːd] *adv* en effet; **very good/***etc* **i.** vraiment très bon/*etc*; **yes i.!** bien sûr!; **thank you very much i.!** merci mille fois!

indefensible [ɪndɪ'fensəb(ə)l] *a* indéfendable.

indefinable [ɪndɪ'faɪnəb(ə)l] *a* indéfinissable.

indefinite [ɪn'defɪnət] *a* (*feeling, duration etc*) indéfini; (*plan*) mal déterminé. **◆–ly** *adv* indéfiniment.

indelible [ɪn'deləb(ə)l] *a* (*ink, memory*) indélébile; **i. pencil** crayon *m* à marquer.

indelicate [ɪn'delɪkət] *a* (*coarse*) indélicat.

indemnify [ɪn'demnɪfaɪ] *vt* indemniser (**for** de). **◆indemnity** *n* indemnité *f*.

indented [ɪn'dentɪd] *a* (*edge*) dentelé, découpé; (*line*) *Typ* renfoncé. **◆inden'tation** *n* dentelure *f*, découpure *f*; *Typ* renfoncement *m*.

independent [ɪndɪ'pendənt] *a* indépendant (**of** de); (*opinions, reports*) de sources différentes. **◆independence** *n* indépendance *f*. **◆independently** *adv* de façon indépendante; **i. of** indépendamment de.

indescribable [ɪndɪ'skraɪbəb(ə)l] *a* indescriptible.

indestructible [ɪndɪ'strʌktəb(ə)l] *a* indestructible.

indeterminate [ɪndɪ'tɜːmɪnət] *a* indéterminé.

index ['ɪndeks] *n* (*in book etc*) index *m*; (*in library*) catalogue *m*; (*number, sign*) indice *m*; **i. card** fiche *f*; **i. finger** index *m*; – *vt* (*classify*) classer. **◆i.-'linked** *a Econ* indexé (**to** sur).

India ['ɪndɪə] *n* Inde *f*. **◆Indian** *a* & *n* indien, -ienne (*mf*).

indicate ['ɪndɪkeɪt] *vt* indiquer (**that** que); **I was indicating right** *Aut* j'avais mis mon clignotant droit. **◆indi'cation** *n* (*sign*) indice *m*, indication *f*; (*idea*) idée *f*. **◆in'dicative** *a* indicatif (**of** de); – *n* (*mood*) *Gram* indicatif *m*. **◆indicator** *n* (*instrument*) indicateur *m*; (*sign*) indication *f* (**of** de); *Aut* clignotant *m*; (*display board*) tableau *m* (indicateur).

indict [ɪn'daɪt] *vt* inculper (**for** de). **◆–ment** *n* inculpation *f*.

Indies ['ɪndɪz] *npl* **the West I.** les Antilles *fpl*.

indifferent [ɪn'dɪf(ə)rənt] *a* indifférent (**to** à); (*mediocre*) *Pej* médiocre. **◆indifference** *n* indifférence *f* (**to** à). **◆indifferently** *adv* indifféremment.

indigenous [ɪn'dɪdʒɪnəs] *a* indigène.

indigestion [ɪndɪ'dʒestʃ(ə)n] *n* dyspepsie *f*; (**an attack of**) **i.** une indigestion, une crise de foie. **◆indigestible** *a* indigeste.

indignant [ɪn'dɪgnənt] *a* indigné (**at** de, **with** contre); **to become i.** s'indigner. **◆indignantly** *adv* avec indignation. **◆indig'nation** *n* indignation *f*.

indignity [ɪn'dɪgnɪtɪ] *n* indignité *f*.

indigo ['ɪndɪgəʊ] *n* & *a* (*colour*) indigo *m* & *a inv*.

indirect [ɪndaɪ'rekt] *a* indirect. **◆–ly** *adv* indirectement.

indiscreet [ɪndɪ'skriːt] *a* indiscret. **◆indis'cretion** *n* indiscrétion *f*.

indiscriminate [ɪndɪ'skrɪmɪnət] *a* (*person*)

qui manque de discernement; (*random*) fait, donné *etc* au hasard. ◆**—ly** *adv* (*at random*) au hasard; (*without discrimination*) sans discernement.

indispensable [ɪndɪ'spensəb(ə)l] *a* indispensable (to à).

indisposed [ɪndɪ'spəʊzd] *a* (*unwell*) indisposé. ◆**indispo'sition** *n* indisposition *f*.

indisputable [ɪndɪ'spjuːtəb(ə)l] *a* incontestable.

indistinct [ɪndɪ'stɪŋkt] *a* indistinct.

indistinguishable [ɪndɪ'stɪŋgwɪʃəb(ə)l] *a* indifférenciable (**from** de).

individual [ɪndɪ'vɪdʒʊəl] *a* individuel; (*unusual, striking*) singulier, particulier; – *n* (*person*) individu *m*. ◆**individualist** *n* individualiste *mf*. ◆**individua'listic** *a* individualiste. ◆**individu'ality** *n* (*distinctiveness*) individualité *f*. ◆**individually** *adv* (*separately*) individuellement; (*unusually*) de façon (très) personnelle.

indivisible [ɪndɪ'vɪzəb(ə)l] *a* indivisible.

Indo-China [ɪndəʊ'tʃaɪnə] *n* Indochine *f*.

indoctrinate [ɪn'dɒktrɪneɪt] *vt Pej* endoctriner. ◆**indoctri'nation** *n* endoctrinement *m*.

indolent ['ɪndələnt] *a* indolent. ◆**indolence** *n* indolence *f*.

indomitable [ɪn'dɒmɪtəb(ə)l] *a* (*will, energy*) indomptable.

Indonesia [ɪndəʊ'niːʒə] *n* Indonésie *f*.

indoor ['ɪndɔːr] *a* (*games, shoes etc*) d'intérieur; (*swimming pool etc*) couvert. ◆**in'doors** *adv* à l'intérieur; **to go** *or* **come i.** rentrer.

induce [ɪn'djuːs] *vt* (*persuade*) persuader (**to do** de faire); (*cause*) provoquer; **to i. labour** *Med* déclencher le travail. ◆**—ment** *n* encouragement *m* (**to do** à faire).

indulge [ɪn'dʌldʒ] *vt* (*s.o.'s desires*) satisfaire; (*child etc*) gâter, tout passer à; **to i. oneself** se gâter; – *vi* **to i. in** (*action*) s'adonner à; (*ice cream etc*) se permettre. ◆**indulgence** *n* indulgence *f*. ◆**indulgent** *a* indulgent (**to** envers, **with** avec).

industrial [ɪn'dʌstrɪəl] *a* industriel; (*conflict, legislation*) du travail; **i. action** action *f* revendicative; **i. park** *Am* complexe *m* industriel. ◆**industrialist** *n* industriel, -ielle *mf*. ◆**industrialized** *a* industrialisé.

industrious [ɪn'dʌstrɪəs] *a* travailleur.

industry ['ɪndəstrɪ] *n* industrie *f*; (*hard work*) application *f*.

inedible [ɪn'edəb(ə)l] *a* immangeable.

ineffective [ɪnɪ'fektɪv] *a* (*measure etc*) sans effet, inefficace; (*person*) incapable. ◆**—ness** *n* inefficacité *f*.

ineffectual [ɪnɪ'fektʃʊəl] *a* (*measure etc*) inefficace; (*person*) incompétent.

inefficient [ɪnɪ'fɪʃ(ə)nt] *a* (*person, measure etc*) inefficace; (*machine*) peu performant. ◆**inefficiency** *n* inefficacité *f*.

ineligible [ɪn'elɪdʒəb(ə)l] *a* (*candidate*) inéligible; **to be i. for** ne pas avoir droit à.

inept [ɪ'nept] *a* (*foolish*) inepte; (*unskilled*) peu habile (**at sth** à qch); (*incompetent*) incapable, inapte. ◆**ineptitude** *n* (*incapacity*) inaptitude *f*.

inequality [ɪnɪ'kwɒlɪtɪ] *n* inégalité *f*.

inert [ɪ'nɜːt] *a* inerte. ◆**inertia** [ɪ'nɜːʃə] *n* inertie *f*.

inescapable [ɪnɪ'skeɪpəb(ə)l] *a* inéluctable.

inevitable [ɪn'evɪtəb(ə)l] *a* inévitable. ◆**inevitably** *adv* inévitablement.

inexcusable [ɪnɪk'skjuːzəb(ə)l] *a* inexcusable.

inexhaustible [ɪnɪg'zɔːstəb(ə)l] *a* inépuisable.

inexorable [ɪn'eksərəb(ə)l] *a* inexorable.

inexpensive [ɪnɪk'spensɪv] *a* bon marché *inv*.

inexperience [ɪnɪk'spɪərɪəns] *n* inexpérience *f*. ◆**inexperienced** *a* inexpérimenté.

inexplicable [ɪnɪk'splɪkəb(ə)l] *a* inexplicable.

inexpressible [ɪnɪk'spresəb(ə)l] *a* inexprimable.

inextricable [ɪnɪk'strɪkəb(ə)l] *a* inextricable.

infallible [ɪn'fæləb(ə)l] *a* infaillible. ◆**infalli'bility** *n* infaillibilité *f*.

infamous ['ɪnfəməs] *a* (*evil*) infâme. ◆**infamy** *n* infamie *f*.

infant ['ɪnfənt] *n* (*child*) petit(e) enfant *mf*; (*baby*) nourrisson *m*; **i. school** classes *fpl* préparatoires. ◆**infancy** *n* petite enfance *f*; **to be in its i.** (*of art, technique etc*) en être à ses premiers balbutiements. ◆**infantile** *a* (*illness, reaction etc*) infantile.

infantry ['ɪnfəntrɪ] *n* infanterie *f*.

infatuated [ɪn'fætʃʊeɪtɪd] *a* amoureux; **i. with** (*person*) amoureux de, engoué de; (*sport etc*) engoué de. ◆**infatu'ation** *n* engouement *m* (**for, with** pour).

infect [ɪn'fekt] *vt* (*contaminate*) *Med* infecter; **to become infected** s'infecter; **to i. s.o. with sth** communiquer qch à qn. ◆**infection** *n* infection *f*. ◆**infectious** *a* (*disease*) infectieux, contagieux; (*person, laughter etc*) contagieux.

infer [ɪn'fɜːr] *vt* (**-rr-**) déduire (**from** de, **that** que). ◆**'inference** *n* déduction *f*, conclusion *f*.

inferior [ɪn'fɪərɪər] *a* inférieur (to à); (*goods, work*) de qualité inférieure; – *n* (*person*) *Pej* inférieur, -eure *mf*. ◆**inferi'ority** *n* infériorité *f*.

infernal [ɪn'fɜːn(ə)l] *a* infernal. ◆**—ly** *adv Fam* épouvantablement.

inferno [ɪn'fɜːnəʊ] *n* (*pl* **-os**) (*blaze*) brasier *m*, incendie *m*; (*hell*) enfer *m*.

infertile [ɪn'fɜːtaɪl, *Am* ɪn'fɜːt(ə)l] *a* (*person, land*) stérile.

infest [ɪn'fest] *vt* infester (with de).

infidelity [ɪnfɪ'delɪtɪ] *n* infidélité *f*.

infighting ['ɪnfaɪtɪŋ] *n* (*within group*) luttes *fpl* intestines.

infiltrate ['ɪnfɪltreɪt] *vi* s'infiltrer (into dans); – *vt* (*group etc*) s'infiltrer dans. ◆**infil'tration** *n* infiltration *f*; *Pol* noyautage *m*.

infinite ['ɪnfɪnɪt] *a* & *n* infini (*m*). ◆**infinitely** *adv* infiniment. ◆**in'finity** *n Math Phot* infini *m*; to i. *Math* à l'infini.

infinitive [ɪn'fɪnɪtɪv] *n Gram* infinitif *m*.

infirm [ɪn'fɜːm] *a* infirme. ◆**infirmary** *n* (*sickbay*) infirmerie *f*; (*hospital*) hôpital *m*. ◆**infirmity** *n* (*disability*) infirmité *f*.

inflame [ɪn'fleɪm] *vt* enflammer. ◆**inflammable** *a* inflammable. ◆**infla'mmation** *n Med* inflammation *f*. ◆**inflammatory** *a* (*remark*) incendiaire.

inflate [ɪn'fleɪt] *vt* (*tyre, prices etc*) gonfler. ◆**inflatable** *a* gonflable. ◆**inflation** *n Econ* inflation *f*. ◆**inflationary** *a Econ* inflationniste.

inflection [ɪn'flekʃ(ə)n] *n Gram* flexion *f*; (*of voice*) inflexion *f*.

inflexible [ɪn'fleksəb(ə)l] *a* inflexible.

inflexion [ɪn'flekʃ(ə)n] *n* = **inflection**.

inflict [ɪn'flɪkt] *vt* infliger (on à); (*wound*) occasionner (on à).

influence ['ɪnflʊəns] *n* influence *f*; **under the i. of** (*anger, drugs*) sous l'effet de; **under the i. of drink** *or* **alcohol** *Jur* en état d'ébriété; – *vt* influencer. ◆**influ'ential** *a* influent.

influenza [ɪnflʊ'enzə] *n Med* grippe *f*.

influx ['ɪnflʌks] *n* flot *m*, afflux *m*.

info ['ɪnfəʊ] *n Sl* tuyaux *mpl*, renseignements *mpl* (on sur).

inform [ɪn'fɔːm] *vt* informer (of de, that que); – *vi* **to i. on** dénoncer. ◆**—ed** *a* informé; **to keep s.o. i. of** tenir qn au courant de. ◆**informant** *n* informateur, -trice *mf*. ◆**informative** *a* instructif. ◆**informer** *n* (police) i. indicateur, -trice *mf*.

informal [ɪn'fɔːm(ə)l] *a* (*without fuss*) simple, sans façon; (*occasion*) dénué de formalité; (*tone, expression*) familier; (*announcement*) officieux; (*meeting*) non-officiel. ◆**infor'mality** *n* simplicité *f*; (*of tone etc*) familiarité *f*. ◆**informally** *adv* (*without fuss*) sans cérémonie; (*to meet*) officieusement; (*to dress*) simplement.

information [ɪnfə'meɪʃ(ə)n] *n* (*facts*) renseignements *mpl* (about, on sur); (*knowledge*) & *Math* information *f*; **a piece of i.** un renseignement, une information; **to get some i.** se renseigner.

infrared [ɪnfrə'red] *a* infrarouge.

infrequent [ɪn'friːkwənt] *a* peu fréquent.

infringe [ɪn'frɪndʒ] *vt* (*rule*) contrevenir à; – *vi* **to i. upon** (*encroach on*) empiéter sur. ◆**—ment** *n* infraction *f* (of à).

infuriat/e [ɪn'fjʊərɪeɪt] *vt* exaspérer. ◆**—ing** *a* exaspérant.

infuse [ɪn'fjuːz] *vt* (*tea*) (faire) infuser. ◆**infusion** *n* infusion *f*.

ingenious [ɪn'dʒiːnɪəs] *a* ingénieux. ◆**inge'nuity** *n* ingéniosité *f*.

ingot ['ɪŋgət] *n* lingot *m*.

ingrained [ɪn'greɪnd] *a* (*prejudice*) enraciné; **i. dirt** crasse *f*.

ingratiat/e [ɪn'greɪʃɪeɪt] *vt* **to i. oneself with** s'insinuer dans les bonnes grâces de. ◆**—ing** *a* (*person, smile*) insinuant.

ingratitude [ɪn'grætɪtjuːd] *n* ingratitude *f*.

ingredient [ɪn'griːdɪənt] *n* ingrédient *m*.

ingrown [ɪn'grəʊn] *a* (*nail*) incarné.

inhabit [ɪn'hæbɪt] *vt* habiter. ◆**—able** *a* habitable. ◆**inhabitant** *n* habitant, -ante *mf*.

inhale [ɪn'heɪl] *vt* aspirer; **to i. the smoke** (*of smoker*) avaler la fumée. ◆**inha'lation** *n* inhalation *f*. ◆**inhaler** *n Med* inhalateur *m*.

inherent [ɪn'hɪərənt] *a* inhérent (in à). ◆**—ly** *adv* intrinsèquement, en soi.

inherit [ɪn'herɪt] *vt* hériter (de); (*title*) succéder à. ◆**inheritance** *n* héritage *m*; (*process*) *Jur* succession *f*; (*cultural*) patrimoine *m*.

inhibit [ɪn'hɪbɪt] *vt* (*hinder*) gêner; (*control*) maîtriser; (*prevent*) empêcher (from de); **to be inhibited** être inhibé, avoir des inhibitions. ◆**inhi'bition** *n* inhibition *f*.

inhospitable [ɪnhɒ'spɪtəb(ə)l] *a* inhospitalier.

inhuman [ɪn'hjuːmən] *a* (*not human, cruel*) inhumain. ◆**inhu'mane** *a* (*not kind*) inhumain. ◆**inhu'manity** *n* brutalité *f*, cruauté *f*.

inimitable [ɪ'nɪmɪtəb(ə)l] *a* inimitable.

iniquitous [ɪ'nɪkwɪtəs] *a* inique. ◆**iniquity** *n* iniquité *f*.

initial [ɪ'nɪʃ(ə)l] *a* initial, premier; – *n* (*letter*) initiale *f*; (*signature*) paraphe *m*; –

vt (-ll-, *Am* -l-) parapher. ◆**—ly** *adv* initialement, au début.

initiate [ɪ'nɪʃɪeɪt] *vt* (*reforms*) amorcer; (*schemes*) inaugurer; **to i. s.o. into** initier qn à; **the initiated** les initiés *mpl*. ◆**initi'ation** *n* amorce *f*; inauguration *f*; initiation *f*. ◆**initiator** *n* initiateur, -trice *mf*.

initiative [ɪ'nɪʃətɪv] *n* initiative *f*.

inject [ɪn'dʒekt] *vt* injecter (**into** à); (*new life etc*) *Fig* insuffler (**into** à). ◆**injection** *n Med* injection *f*, piqûre *f*.

injunction [ɪn'dʒʌŋkʃ(ə)n] *n Jur* ordonnance *f*.

injur/e ['ɪndʒər] *vt* (*physically*) blesser; (*prejudice, damage*) nuire à; (*one's chances*) compromettre; **to i. one's foot/*etc*** se blesser au pied/*etc*. ◆**—ed** *a* blessé; – *n* **the i.** les blessés *mpl*. ◆**injury** *n* (*to flesh*) blessure *f*; (*fracture*) fracture *f*; (*sprain*) foulure *f*; (*bruise*) contusion *f*; (*wrong*) *Fig* préjudice *m*.

injurious [ɪn'dʒʊərɪəs] *a* préjudiciable (**to** à).

injustice [ɪn'dʒʌstɪs] *n* injustice *f*.

ink [ɪŋk] *n* encre *f*; **Indian i.** encre *f* de Chine. ◆**inkpot** *n*, ◆**inkwell** *n* encrier *m*. ◆**inky** *a* couvert d'encre.

inkling ['ɪŋklɪŋ] *n* (petite) idée *f*; **to have some** *or* **an i. of sth** soupçonner qch, avoir une (petite) idée de qch.

inlaid [ɪn'leɪd] *a* (*marble etc*) incrusté (**with** de); (*wood*) marqueté.

inland ['ɪnlənd, 'ɪnlænd] *a* intérieur; **the I. Revenue** le fisc; – [ɪn'lænd] *adv* à l'intérieur (*des terres*).

in-laws ['ɪnlɔːz] *npl* belle-famille *f*.

inlet ['ɪnlet] *n* (*of sea*) crique *f*; **i. pipe** tuyau *m* d'arrivée.

inmate ['ɪnmeɪt] *n* résident, -ente *mf*; (*of asylum*) interné, -ée *mf*; (*of prison*) détenu, -ue *mf*.

inmost ['ɪnməʊst] *a* le plus profond.

inn [ɪn] *n* auberge *f*. ◆**innkeeper** *n* aubergiste *mf*.

innards ['ɪnədz] *npl Fam* entrailles *fpl*.

innate [ɪ'neɪt] *a* inné.

inner ['ɪnər] *a* intérieur; (*ear*) interne; (*feelings*) intime, profond; **the i. city** le cœur de la ville; **an i. circle** (*group of people*) un cercle restreint; **the i. circle** le saint des saints; **i. tube** (*of tyre*) chambre *f* à air. ◆**innermost** *a* le plus profond.

inning ['ɪnɪŋ] *n Baseball* tour *m* de batte. ◆**innings** *n inv Cricket* tour *m* de batte; **a good i.** *Fig* une vie longue.

innocent ['ɪnəs(ə)nt] *a* innocent. ◆**innocence** *n* innocence *f*. ◆**innocently** *adv* innocemment.

innocuous [ɪ'nɒkjʊəs] *a* inoffensif.

innovate ['ɪnəveɪt] *vi* innover. ◆**inno'vation** *n* innovation *f*. ◆**innovator** *n* innovateur, -trice *mf*.

innuendo [ɪnjʊ'endəʊ] *n* (*pl* -oes *or* -os) insinuation *f*.

innumerable [ɪ'njuːmərəb(ə)l] *a* innombrable.

inoculate [ɪ'nɒkjʊleɪt] *vt* vacciner (**against** contre). ◆**inocu'lation** *n* inoculation *f*.

inoffensive [ɪnə'fensɪv] *a* inoffensif.

inoperative [ɪn'ɒpərətɪv] *a* (*without effect*) inopérant.

inopportune [ɪn'ɒpətjuːn] *a* inopportun.

inordinate [ɪ'nɔːdɪnət] *a* excessif. ◆**—ly** *adv* excessivement.

in-patient ['ɪnpeɪʃ(ə)nt] *n* malade *mf* hospitalisé(e).

input ['ɪnpʊt] *n* (*computer operation*) entrée *f*; (*data*) données *fpl*; (*current*) *El* énergie *f*.

inquest ['ɪnkwest] *n* enquête *f*.

inquir/e [ɪn'kwaɪər] *vi* se renseigner (**about** sur); **to i. after** s'informer de; **to i. into** examiner, faire une enquête sur; – *vt* demander; **to i. how to get** to demander le chemin de. ◆**—ing** *a* (*mind, look*) curieux. ◆**inquiry** *n* (*question*) question *f*; (*request for information*) demande *f* de renseignements; (*information*) renseignements *mpl*; *Jur* enquête *f*; **to make inquiries** demander des renseignements; (*of police*) enquêter.

inquisitive [ɪn'kwɪzɪtɪv] *a* curieux. ◆**inquisitively** *adv* avec curiosité. ◆**inqui'sition** *n* (*inquiry*) & *Rel* inquisition *f*.

inroads ['ɪnrəʊdz] *npl* (*attacks*) incursions *fpl* (**into** dans); **to make i. into** (*start on*) *Fig* entamer.

insane [ɪn'seɪn] *a* fou, dément. ◆**insanely** *adv* comme un fou. ◆**insanity** *n* folie *f*, démence *f*.

insanitary [ɪn'sænɪt(ə)rɪ] *a* insalubre.

insatiable [ɪn'seɪʃəb(ə)l] *a* insatiable.

inscribe [ɪn'skraɪb] *vt* inscrire; (*book*) dédicacer (**to** à). ◆**inscription** *n* inscription *f*; dédicace *f*.

inscrutable [ɪn'skruːtəb(ə)l] *a* impénétrable.

insect ['ɪnsekt] *n* insecte *m*; – *a* (*powder, spray*) insecticide; **i. repellant** crème *f* anti-insecte. ◆**in'secticide** *n* insecticide *m*.

insecure [ɪnsɪ'kjʊər] *a* (*not fixed*) peu solide; (*furniture, ladder*) branlant, bancal; (*window*) mal fermé; (*uncertain*) incertain;

(*unsafe*) peu sûr; (*person*) qui manque d'assurance. ◆**insecurity** *n* (*of person, situation*) insécurité *f*.

insemination [ɪnsemɪ'neɪʃ(ə)n] *n Med* insémination *f*.

insensible [ɪn'sensəb(ə)l] *a Med* inconscient.

insensitive [ɪn'sensɪtɪv] *a* insensible (**to** à). ◆**insensi'tivity** *n* insensibilité *f*.

inseparable [ɪn'sep(ə)rəb(ə)l] *a* inséparable (**from** de).

insert [ɪn'sɜːt] *vt* inserer (**in, into** dans). ◆**insertion** *n* insertion *f*.

inshore ['ɪnʃɔːr] *a* côtier.

inside [ɪn'saɪd] *adv* dedans, à l'intérieur; **come i.!** entrez!; – *prep* à l'intérieur de, dans; (*time*) en moins de; – *n* dedans *m*, intérieur *m*; *pl* (*stomach*) *Fam* ventre *m*; **on the i.** à l'intérieur (**of** de); **i. out** (*coat, socks etc*) à l'envers; (*to know, study etc*) à fond; **to turn everything i. out** *Fig* tout chambouler; – *a* intérieur; (*information*) obtenu à la source; **the i. lane** *Aut* la voie de gauche, *Am* la voie de droite.

insidious [ɪn'sɪdɪəs] *a* insidieux.

insight ['ɪnsaɪt] *n* perspicacité *f*; **to give an i. into** (*s.o.'s character*) permettre de comprendre, éclairer; (*question*) donner un aperçu de.

insignia [ɪn'sɪgnɪə] *npl* (*of important person*) insignes *mpl*.

insignificant [ɪnsɪg'nɪfɪkənt] *a* insignifiant. ◆**insignificance** *n* insignifiance *f*.

insincere [ɪnsɪn'sɪər] *a* peu sincère. ◆**insincerity** *n* manque *m* de sincérité.

insinuate [ɪn'sɪnjʊeɪt] *vt* **1** *Pej* insinuer (**that** que). **2 to i. oneself into** s'insinuer dans. ◆**insinu'ation** *n* insinuation *f*.

insipid [ɪn'sɪpɪd] *a* insipide.

insist [ɪn'sɪst] *vi* insister (**on doing** pour faire); **to i. on sth** (*demand*) exiger qch; (*assert*) affirmer qch; – *vt* (*order*) insister (**that** pour que); (*declare firmly*) affirmer (**that** que); **I i. that you come** *or* **on your coming** j'insiste pour que tu viennes. ◆**insistence** *n* insistance *f*; **her i. on seeing me** l'insistance qu'elle met à vouloir me voir. ◆**insistent** *a* insistant; **I was i. (about it)** j'ai été pressant. ◆**insistently** *adv* avec insistance.

insolent ['ɪnsələnt] *a* insolent. ◆**insolence** *n* insolence *f*. ◆**insolently** *adv* insolemment.

insoluble [ɪn'sɒljʊb(ə)l] *a* insoluble.

insolvent [ɪn'sɒlvənt] *a Fin* insolvable.

insomnia [ɪn'sɒmnɪə] *n* insomnie *f*. ◆**insomniac** *n* insomniaque *mf*.

insomuch as [ɪnsəʊ'mʌtʃəz] *adv* = **inasmuch as**.

inspect [ɪn'spekt] *vt* inspecter; (*tickets*) contrôler; (*troops*) passer en revue. ◆**inspection** *n* inspection *f*; contrôle *m*; revue *f*. ◆**inspector** *n* inspecteur, -trice *mf*; (*on bus*) contrôleur, -euse *mf*.

inspir/e [ɪn'spaɪər] *vt* inspirer (**s.o. with sth** qch à qn); **to be inspired to do** avoir l'inspiration de faire. ◆**—ed** *a* inspiré. ◆**—ing** *a* qui inspire. ◆**inspi'ration** *n* inspiration *f*; (*person*) source *f* d'inspiration.

instability [ɪnstə'bɪlɪtɪ] *n* instabilité *f*.

install [ɪn'stɔːl] *vt* installer. ◆**insta'llation** *n* installation *f*.

instalment [ɪn'stɔːlmənt] (*Am* **installment**) *n* (*of money*) acompte *m*, versement *m* (partiel); (*of serial*) épisode *m*; (*of publication*) fascicule *m*; **to buy on the i. plan** *Am* acheter à crédit.

instance ['ɪnstəns] *n* (*example*) exemple *m*; (*case*) cas *m*; (*occasion*) circonstance *f*; **for i.** par exemple; **in the first i.** en premier lieu.

instant ['ɪnstənt] *a* immédiat; **i. coffee** café *m* soluble *or* instantané, nescafé® *m*; **of the 3rd i.** (*in letter*) *Com* du 3 courant; – *n* (*moment*) instant *m*; **this (very) i.** (*at once*) à l'instant; **the i. that** (*as soon as*) dès que. ◆**instan'taneous** *a* instantané. ◆**instantly** *adv* immédiatement.

instead [ɪn'sted] *adv* (*as alternative*) au lieu de cela, plutôt; **i. of** au lieu de; **i. of s.o.** à la place de qn; **i. (of him** *or* **her)** à sa place.

instep ['ɪnstep] *n* (*of foot*) cou-de-pied *m*; (*of shoe*) cambrure *f*.

instigate ['ɪnstɪgeɪt] *vt* provoquer. ◆**insti'gation** *n* instigation *f*. ◆**instigator** *n* instigateur, -trice *mf*.

instil [ɪn'stɪl] *vt* (**-ll-**) (*idea*) inculquer (**into** à); (*courage*) insuffler (**into** à).

instinct ['ɪnstɪŋkt] *n* instinct *m*; **by i.** d'instinct. ◆**in'stinctive** *a* instinctif. ◆**in'stinctively** *adv* instinctivement.

institute ['ɪnstɪtjuːt] **1** *vt* (*rule, practice*) instituer; (*inquiry, proceedings*) *Jur* entamer, intenter. **2** *n* institut *m*. ◆**insti'tution** *n* (*custom, private or charitable organization etc*) institution *f*; (*school, hospital*) établissement *m*; (*home*) *Med* asile *m*. ◆**insti'tutional** *a* institutionnel.

instruct [ɪn'strʌkt] *vt* (*teach*) enseigner (**s.o. in sth** qch à qn); **to i. s.o. about sth** (*inform*) instruire qn de qch; **to i. s.o. to do** (*order*) charger qn de faire. ◆**instruction** *n* (*teaching*) instruction *f*; *pl* (*orders*) instructions *fpl*; **instructions (for use)** mode *m* d'emploi. ◆**Instructive** *a* instructif. ◆**Instructor** *n* professeur *m*; *Sp* moniteur, -trice *mf*; *Mil* instructeur *m*; *Univ Am* maître-assistant, -ante *mf*; **driving i.** moniteur, -trice *mf* de conduite.

Instrument ['ɪnstrumənt] *n* instrument *m*. ◆**Instru'mental** *a Mus* instrumental; **to be i. in sth/in doing sth** contribuer à qch/à faire qch. ◆**Instru'mentalist** *n Mus* instrumentaliste *mf*. ◆**Instrumen'tation** *n Mus* orchestration *f*.

Insubordinate [ɪnsə'bɔːdɪnət] *a* indiscipliné. ◆**Insubordi'nation** *n* indiscipline *f*.

Insubstantial [ɪnsəb'stænʃ(ə)l] *a* (*argument, evidence*) peu solide.

Insufferable [ɪn'sʌfərəb(ə)l] *a* intolérable.

Insufficient [ɪnsə'fɪʃənt] *a* insuffisant. ◆**—ly** *adv* insuffisamment.

Insular ['ɪnsjulər] *a* (*climate*) insulaire; (*views*) *Pej* étroit, borné.

Insulate ['ɪnsjuleɪt] *vt* (*against cold etc*) & *El* isoler; (*against sound*) insonoriser; **to i. s.o. from** *Fig* protéger qn de; **insulating tape** chatterton *m*. ◆**Insu'lation** *n* isolation *f*; insonorisation *f*; (*material*) isolant *m*.

Insulin ['ɪnsjulɪn] *n Med* insuline *f*.

Insult [ɪn'sʌlt] *vt* insulter; – ['ɪnsʌlt] *n* insulte *f* (**to** à).

Insuperable [ɪn'suːpərəb(ə)l] *a* insurmontable.

Insure [ɪn'ʃuər] *vt* **1** (*protect against damage etc*) assurer (**against** contre). **2** *Am* = ensure. ◆**Insurance** *n* assurance *f*; **i. company** compagnie *f*, d'assurances; **i. policy** police *f* d'assurance.

Insurgent [ɪn'sɜːdʒənt] *a* & *n* insurgé, -ée (*mf*).

Insurmountable [ɪnsə'mauntəb(ə)l] *a* insurmontable.

Insurrection [ɪnsə'rekʃ(ə)n] *n* insurrection *f*.

Intact [ɪn'tækt] *a* intact.

Intake ['ɪnteɪk] *n* (*of food*) consommation *f*; *Sch Univ* admissions *fpl*; *Tech* admission *f*.

Intangible [ɪn'tændʒəb(ə)l] *a* intangible.

Integral ['ɪntɪgrəl] *a* intégral; **to be an i. part of** faire partie intégrante de.

Integrate ['ɪntɪgreɪt] *vt* intégrer (**into** dans); – *vi* s'intégrer (**into** dans); (**racially**) **integrated** (*school etc*) *Am* où se pratique la déségrégation raciale. ◆**Integration** *n* intégration *f*; (**racial**) **i.** déségrégation *f* raciale.

Integrity [ɪn'tegrɪtɪ] *n* intégrité *f*.

Intellect ['ɪntɪlekt] *n* (*faculty*) intellect *m*, intelligence *f*; (*cleverness, person*) intelligence *f*. ◆**Inte'llectual** *a* & *n* intellectuel, -elle (*mf*).

Intelligence [ɪn'telɪdʒəns] *n* intelligence *f*; *Mil* renseignements *mpl*. ◆**Intelligent** *a* intelligent. ◆**Intelligently** *adv* intelligemment. ◆**Intelli'gentsia** *n* intelligentsia *f*.

Intelligible [ɪn'telɪdʒəb(ə)l] *a* intelligible. ◆**Intelligi'bility** *n* intelligibilité *f*.

Intemperance [ɪn'tempərəns] *n* intempérance *f*.

Intend [ɪn'tend] *vt* (*gift, remark etc*) destiner (**for** à); **to i. to do** avoir l'intention de faire; **I i. you to stay** mon intention est que vous restiez. ◆**—ed** *a* (*deliberate*) intentionnel, voulu; (*planned*) projeté; **i. to be** (*meant*) destiné à être. ◆**Intention** *n* intention *f* (**of doing** de faire). ◆**Intentional** *a* intentionnel; **it wasn't i.** ce n'était pas fait exprès. ◆**Intentionally** *adv* intentionnellement, exprès.

Intense [ɪn'tens] *a* intense; (*interest*) vif; (*person*) passionné. ◆**Intensely** *adv* intensément; *Fig* extrêmement. ◆**Intensifi'cation** *n* intensification *f*. ◆**Intensify** *vt* intensifier; – *vi* s'intensifier. ◆**Intensity** *n* intensité *f*. ◆**Intensive** *a* intensif; **in i. care** *Med* en réanimation.

Intent [ɪn'tent] **1** *a* (*look*) attentif; **i. on** (*task*) absorbé par; **i. on doing** résolu à faire. **2** *n* intention *f*; **to all intents and purposes** en fait, essentiellement.

Inter [ɪn'tɜːr] *vt* (**-rr-**) enterrer.

Inter- ['ɪntə(r)] *pref* inter-.

Interact [ɪntə'rækt] *vi* (*of ideas etc*) être interdépendants; (*of people*) agir conjointement; *Ch* interagir. ◆**Interaction** *n* interaction *f*.

Intercede [ɪntə'siːd] *vi* intercéder (**with** auprès de).

Intercept [ɪntə'sept] *vt* intercepter. ◆**Interception** *n* interception *f*.

Interchange ['ɪntətʃeɪndʒ] *n Aut* échangeur *m*. ◆**Inter'changeable** *a* interchangeable.

Intercom ['ɪntəkɒm] *n* interphone *m*.

Interconnect/ed [ɪntəkə'nektɪd] *a* (*facts etc*) liés. ◆**—ing** *a* **i. rooms** pièces *fpl* communicantes.

Intercontinental [ɪntəkɒntɪ'nent(ə)l] *a* intercontinental.

Intercourse ['ɪntəkɔːs] *n* (*sexual, social*) rapports *mpl*.

Interdependent [ɪntədɪ'pendənt] *a* interdépendant; (*parts of machine*) solidaire.

Interest ['ɪnt(ə)rɪst, 'ɪntrəst] *n* intérêt *m*; *Fin* intérêts *mpl*; **an i. in** (*stake*) *Com* des intérêts dans; **his *or* her i. is** (*hobby etc*) ce qui l'intéresse c'est; **to take an i. in** s'intéresser à; **to be of i. to s.o.** intéresser qn; – *vt* intéresser. **◆—ed** *a* (*involved*) intéressé; (*look*) d'intérêt; **to seem i.** sembler intéressé (**in** par); **to be i. in sth/s.o.** s'intéresser à qch/qn; **I'm i. in doing** ça m'intéresse de faire; **are you i.?** ça vous intéresse? **◆—ing** *a* intéressant. **◆—ingly** *adv* **i. (enough), she . . .** curieusement, elle . . . .

interface ['ɪntəfeɪs] *n Tech* interface *f.*

interfer/e [ɪntə'fɪər] *vi* se mêler des affaires d'autrui; **to i. in** s'ingérer dans; **to i. with** (*upset*) déranger; (*touch*) toucher (à). **◆—ing** *a* (*person*) importun. **◆interference** *n* ingérence *f*; *Rad* parasites *mpl.*

interim ['ɪntərɪm] *n* intérim *m*; **in the i.** pendant l'intérim; – *a* (*measure etc*) provisoire; (*post*) intérimaire.

interior [ɪn'tɪərɪər] *a* intérieur; – *n* intérieur *m*; **Department of the I.** *Am* ministère *m* de l'Intérieur.

interjection [ɪntə'dʒekʃ(ə)n] *n* interjection *f.*

interlock [ɪntə'lɒk] *vi Tech* s'emboîter.

interloper ['ɪntələʊpər] *n* intrus, -use *mf.*

interlude ['ɪntəluːd] *n* intervalle *m*; *Th* intermède *m*; *Mus TV* interlude *m.*

intermarry [ɪntə'mærɪ] *vi* se marier (entre eux). **◆intermarriage** *n* mariage *m* (*entre personnes de races etc différentes*).

intermediary [ɪntə'miːdɪərɪ] *a* & *n* intermédiare (*mf*).

intermediate [ɪntə'miːdɪət] *a* intermédiaire; (*course*) *Sch* moyen.

interminable [ɪn'tɜːmɪnəb(ə)l] *a* interminable.

intermingle [ɪntə'mɪŋg(ə)l] *vi* se mélanger.

intermission [ɪntə'mɪʃ(ə)n] *n Cin Th* entracte *m.*

intermittent [ɪntə'mɪtənt] *a* intermittent. **◆—ly** *adv* par intermittence.

intern 1 [ɪn'tɜːn] *vt Pol* interner. **2** ['ɪntɜːn] *n Med Am* interne *mf* (des hôpitaux). **◆inter'nee** *n* interné, -ée *mf.* **◆in'ternment** *n Pol* internement *m.*

internal [ɪn'tɜːn(ə)l] *a* interne; (*policy, flight*) intérieur; **i. combustion engine** moteur *m* à explosion; **the I. Revenue Service** *Am* le fisc. **◆—ly** *adv* intérieurement.

international [ɪntə'næʃ(ə)nəl] *a* international; (*fame, reputation*) mondial; – *n* (*match*) rencontre *f* internationale; (*player*) international *m.* **◆—ly** *adv* (*renowned etc*) mondialement.

interplanetary [ɪntə'plænɪt(ə)rɪ] *a* interplanétaire.

interplay ['ɪntəpleɪ] *n* interaction *f*, jeu *m.*

interpolate [ɪn'tɜːpəleɪt] *vt* interpoler.

interpret [ɪn'tɜːprɪt] *vt* interpréter; – *vi Ling* faire l'interprète. **◆interpre'tation** *n* interprétation *f.* **◆interpreter** *n* interprète *mf.*

interrelated [ɪntərɪ'leɪtɪd] *a* en corrélation. **◆interrelation** *n* corrélation *f.*

interrogate [ɪn'terəgeɪt] *vt* (*question closely*) interroger. **◆interro'gation** *n* interrogation *f*; *Jur* interrogatoire *m.* **◆interrogator** *n* (*questioner*) interrogateur, -trice *mf.*

interrogative [ɪntə'rɒgətɪv] *a* & *n Gram* interrogatif (*m*).

interrupt [ɪntə'rʌpt] *vt* interrompre. **◆interruption** *n* interruption *f.*

intersect [ɪntə'sekt] *vt* couper; – *vi* s'entrecouper, se couper. **◆intersection** *n* (*crossroads*) croisement *m*; (*of lines etc*) intersection *f.*

intersperse [ɪntə'spɜːs] *vt* parsemer (**with** de).

intertwine [ɪntə'twaɪn] *vt* entrelacer.

interval ['ɪntəv(ə)l] *n* intervalle *m*; *Th* entracte *m*; **at intervals** (*time*) de temps à autre; (*space*) par intervalles; **bright intervals** *Met* éclaircies *fpl.*

intervene [ɪntə'viːn] *vi* intervenir; (*of event*) survenir; **ten years intervened** dix années s'écoulèrent; **if nothing intervenes** s'il n'arrive rien entre-temps. **◆intervention** *n* intervention *f.*

interview ['ɪntəvjuː] *n* entrevue *f*, entretien *m* (**with** avec); *Journ TV* interview *f*; **to call for (an) i.** convoquer; – *vt* avoir une entrevue avec; *Journ TV* interviewer. **◆—er** *n Journ TV* interviewer *m*; *Com Pol* enquêteur, -euse *mf.*

intestine [ɪn'testɪn] *n* intestin *m.*

intimate[1] ['ɪntɪmət] *a* intime; (*friendship*) profond; (*knowledge, analysis*) approfondi. **◆intimacy** *n* intimité *f.* **◆intimately** *adv* intimement.

intimate[2] ['ɪntɪmeɪt] *vt* (*hint*) suggérer (**that** que). **◆inti'mation** *n* (*announcement*) annonce *f*; (*hint*) suggestion *f*; (*sign*) indication *f.*

intimidate [ɪn'tɪmɪdeɪt] *vt* intimider. **◆intimi'dation** *n* intimidation *f.*

into ['ɪntuː, *unstressed* 'ɪntə] *prep* **1** dans; **to put i.** mettre dans; **to go i.** (*room, detail*) entrer dans. **2** en; **to translate i.** traduire en; **to change i.** transformer *or* changer en; **to go i. town** aller en ville; **i. pieces** (*to break etc*) en morceaux. **3 to be i. yoga**/*etc Fam* être à fond dans le yoga/*etc.*

intolerable [ɪn'tɒlərəb(ə)l] *a* intolérable

(that que (+ *sub*)). ◆**intolerably** *adv* insupportablement. ◆**intolerance** *n* intolérance *f*. ◆**intolerant** *a* intolérant (of de). ◆**intolerantly** *adv* avec intolérance.

intonation [ɪntə'neɪʃ(ə)n] *n Ling* intonation *f*.

intoxicate [ɪn'tɒksɪkeɪt] *vt* enivrer. ◆**intoxicated** *a* ivre. ◆**intoxi'cation** *n* ivresse *f*.

intra- ['ɪntrə] *pref* intra-.

intransigent [ɪn'trænsɪdʒənt] *a* intransigeant. ◆**intransigence** *n* intransigeance *f*.

intransitive [ɪn'trænsɪtɪv] *a & n Gram* intransitif (*m*).

intravenous [ɪntrə'viːnəs] *a Med* intraveineux.

intrepid [ɪn'trepɪd] *a* intrépide.

intricate ['ɪntrɪkət] *a* complexe, compliqué. ◆**intricacy** *n* complexité *f*. ◆**intricately** *adv* de façon complexe.

intrigu/e 1 [ɪn'triːg] *vt* (*interest*) intriguer; **I'm intrigued to know . . .** je suis curieux de savoir . . . . **2** ['ɪntriːg] *n* (*plot*) intrigue *f*. ◆**—ing** *a* (*news etc*) curieux.

intrinsic [ɪn'trɪnsɪk] *a* intrinsèque. ◆**intrinsically** *adv* intrinsèquement.

introduce [ɪntrə'djuːs] *vt* (*insert, bring in*) introduire (**into** dans); (*programme, subject*) présenter; **to i. s.o. to s.o.** présenter qn à qn; **to i. s.o. to Dickens/geography/***etc* faire découvrir Dickens/la géographie/*etc* à qn. ◆**introduction** *n* introduction *f*; présentation *f*; (*book title*) initiation *f*; **her i. to** (*life abroad etc*) son premier contact avec. ◆**introductory** *a* (*words*) d'introduction; (*speech*) de présentation; (*course*) d'initiation.

introspective [ɪntrə'spektɪv] *a* introspectif. ◆**introspection** *n* introspection *f*.

introvert ['ɪntrəvɜːt] *n* introverti, -ie *mf*.

intrude [ɪn'truːd] *vi* (*of person*) s'imposer (**on s.o.** à qn), déranger (**on s.o.** qn); **to i. on** (*s.o.'s time etc*) abuser de. ◆**intruder** *n* intrus, -use *mf*. ◆**intrusion** *n* intrusion *f* (**into** dans); **forgive my i.** pardonnez-moi de vous avoir dérangé.

intuition [ɪntjuː'ɪʃ(ə)n] *n* intuition *f*. ◆**in'tuitive** *a* intuitif.

inundate ['ɪnʌndeɪt] *vt* inonder (**with** de); **inundated with work** submergé de travail. ◆**inun'dation** *n* inondation *f*.

invad/e [ɪn'veɪd] *vt* envahir; (*privacy*) violer. ◆**—er** *n* envahisseur, -euse *mf*.

invalid[1] ['ɪnvəlɪd] *a & n* malade (*mf*); (*through injury*) infirme (*mf*); **i. car** voiture *f* d'infirme.

invalid[2] [ɪn'vælɪd] *a* non valable. ◆**invalidate** *vt* invalider, annuler.

invaluable [ɪn'væljuəb(ə)l] *a* (*help etc*) inestimable.

invariab/le [ɪn'veərɪəb(ə)l] *a* invariable. ◆**—ly** *adv* invariablement.

invasion [ɪn'veɪʒ(ə)n] *n* invasion *f*; **i. of s.o.'s privacy** intrusion *f* dans la vie privée de qn.

invective [ɪn'vektɪv] *n* invective *f*.

inveigh [ɪn'veɪ] *vi* **to i. against** invectiver contre.

inveigle [ɪn'veɪg(ə)l] *vt* **to i. s.o. into doing** amener qn à faire par la ruse.

invent [ɪn'vent] *vt* inventer. ◆**invention** *n* invention *f*. ◆**inventive** *a* inventif. ◆**inventiveness** *n* esprit *m* d'invention. ◆**inventor** *n* inventeur, -trice *mf*.

inventory ['ɪnvənt(ə)rɪ] *n* inventaire *m*.

inverse [ɪn'vɜːs] *a & n Math* inverse (*m*).

invert [ɪn'vɜːt] *vt* intervertir; **inverted commas** guillemets *mpl*. ◆**inversion** *n* interversion *f*; *Gram Anat etc* inversion *f*.

invest [ɪn'vest] *vt* (*funds*) investir (**in** dans); (*money*) placer, investir; (*time, effort*) consacrer (**in** à); **to i. s.o. with** (*endow*) investir qn de; – *vi* **to i. in** (*project*) placer son argent dans; (*firm*) investir dans; (*house, radio etc*) *Fig* se payer. ◆**investiture** *n* (*of bishop etc*) investiture *f*. ◆**investment** *n* investissement *m*, placement *m*. ◆**investor** *n* (*shareholder*) actionnaire *mf*; (*saver*) épargnant, -ante *mf*.

investigate [ɪn'vestɪgeɪt] *vt* (*examine*) examiner, étudier; (*crime*) enquêter sur. ◆**investi'gation** *n* examen *m*, étude *f*; (*by police*) enquête *f* (**of** sur); (*inquiry*) enquête *f*, investigation *f*. ◆**investigator** *n* (*detective*) enquêteur, -euse *mf*.

inveterate [ɪn'vetərət] *a* invétéré.

invidious [ɪn'vɪdɪəs] *a* qui suscite la jalousie; (*hurtful*) blessant; (*odious*) odieux.

invigilate [ɪn'vɪdʒɪleɪt] *vi* être de surveillance (*à un examen*). ◆**invigilator** *n* surveillant, -ante *mf*.

invigorat/e [ɪn'vɪgəreɪt] *vt* revigorer. ◆**—ing** *a* stimulant.

invincible [ɪn'vɪnsəb(ə)l] *a* invincible.

invisible [ɪn'vɪzəb(ə)l] *a* invisible; **i. ink** encre *f* sympathique.

invit/e [ɪn'vaɪt] *vt* inviter (**to do** à faire); (*ask for*) demander; (*lead to, give occasion for*) appeler; (*trouble*) chercher; **to i. out** inviter (à sortir); **to i. over** inviter (à venir); – ['ɪnvaɪt] *n Fam* invitation *f*. ◆**—ing** *a* engageant, invitant; (*food*) appétissant. ◆**invi'tation** *n* invitation *f*.

invoice ['ɪnvɔɪs] *n* facture *f*; – *vt* facturer.

invoke [ɪn'vəʊk] *vt* invoquer.

involuntar/y [ɪn'vɒləntərɪ] *a* involontaire. ◆**—ily** *adv* involontairement.

involv/e [ɪn'vɒlv] *vt* (*include*) mêler (*qn*) (in à), impliquer (*qn*) (in dans); (*associate*) associer (*qn*) (in à); (*entail*) entraîner; **to i. oneself, get involved** (*commit oneself*) s'engager (in dans); **to i. s.o. in expense** entraîner qn à des dépenses; **the job involves going abroad** le poste nécessite des déplacements à l'étranger. ◆**—ed** *a* (*complicated*) compliqué; **the factors/***etc* **i.** (*at stake*) les facteurs/*etc* en jeu; **the person i.** la personne en question; **i. with s.o.** mêlé aux affaires de qn; **personally i.** concerné; **emotionally i. with** amoureux de; **to become i.** (*of police*) intervenir. ◆**—ement** *n* participation *f* (in à), implication *f* (in dans); (*commitment*) engagement *m* (in dans); (*problem*) difficulté *f*; **emotional i.** liaison *f*.

invulnerable [ɪn'vʌln(ə)rəb(ə)l] *a* invulnérable.

inward ['ɪnwəd] *a & adv* (*movement, to move*) vers l'intérieur; – *a* (*inner*) intérieur. ◆**i.-looking** *a* replié sur soi. ◆**inwardly** *adv* (*inside*) à l'intérieur; (*to laugh, curse etc*) intérieurement. ◆**inwards** *adv* vers l'intérieur.

iodine ['aɪədiːn, *Am* 'aɪədaɪn] *n Med* teinture *f* d'iode.

iota [aɪ'əʊtə] *n* (*of truth etc*) grain *m*; (*in text*) iota *m*.

IOU [aɪəʊ'juː] *n abbr* (*I owe you*) reconnaissance *f* de dette.

IQ [aɪ'kjuː] *n abbr* (*intelligence quotient*) QI *m inv*.

Iran [ɪ'rɑːn] *n* Iran *m*. ◆**Iranian** [ɪ'reɪnɪən] *a & n* iranien, -ienne (*mf*).

Iraq [ɪ'rɑːk] *n* Irak *m*. ◆**Iraqi** *a & n* irakien, -ienne (*mf*).

irascible [ɪ'ræsəb(ə)l] *a* irascible.

ire ['aɪər] *n Lit* courroux *m*. ◆**i'rate** *a* furieux.

Ireland ['aɪələnd] *n* Irlande *f*. ◆**Irish** *a* irlandais; – *n* (*language*) irlandais *m*. ◆**Irishman** *n* (*pl* -men) Irlandais *m*. ◆**Irishwoman** *n* (*pl* -women) Irlandaise *f*.

iris ['aɪərɪs] *n Anat Bot* iris *m*.

irk [ɜːk] *vt* ennuyer. ◆**irksome** *a* ennuyeux.

iron ['aɪən] *n* fer *m*; (*for clothes*) fer *m* (à repasser); **old i., scrap i.** ferraille *f*; **i. and steel industry** sidérurgie *f*; **the I. Curtain** *Pol* le rideau de fer; – *vt* (*clothes*) repasser; **to i. out** (*difficulties*) *Fig* aplanir. ◆**—ing** *n* repassage *m*; **i. board** planche *f* à repasser. ◆**ironmonger** *n* quincaillier *m*. ◆**ironmongery** *n* quincaillerie *f*. ◆**ironwork** *n* ferronnerie *f*.

irony ['aɪərənɪ] *n* ironie *f*. ◆**i'ronic(al)** *a* ironique.

irradiate [ɪ'reɪdɪeɪt] *vt* irradier.

irrational [ɪ'ræʃən(ə)l] *a* (*act*) irrationnel; (*fear*) irraisonné; (*person*) peu rationnel, illogique.

irreconcilable [ɪrekən'saɪləb(ə)l] *a* irréconciliable, inconciliable; (*views, laws etc*) inconciliable.

irrefutable [ɪrɪ'fjuːtəb(ə)l] *a* irréfutable.

irregular [ɪ'regjʊlər] *a* irrégulier. ◆**irregu'larity** *n* irrégularité *f*.

irrelevant [ɪ'reləvənt] *a* (*remark*) non pertinent; (*course*) peu utile; **i. to** sans rapport avec; **that's i.** ça n'a rien à voir. ◆**irrelevance** *n* manque *m* de rapport.

irreparable [ɪ'rep(ə)rəb(ə)l] *a* (*harm, loss*) irréparable.

irreplaceable [ɪrɪ'pleɪsəb(ə)l] *a* irremplaçable.

irrepressible [ɪrɪ'presəb(ə)l] *a* (*laughter etc*) irrépressible.

irresistible [ɪrɪ'zɪstəb(ə)l] *a* (*person, charm etc*) irrésistible.

irresolute [ɪ'rezəluːt] *a* irrésolu, indécis.

irrespective of [ɪrɪ'spektɪvəv] *prep* sans tenir compte de.

irresponsible [ɪrɪ'spɒnsəb(ə)l] *a* (*act*) irréfléchi; (*person*) irresponsable.

irretrievable [ɪrɪ'triːvəb(ə)l] *a* irréparable.

irreverent [ɪ'revərənt] *a* irrévérencieux.

irreversible [ɪrɪ'vɜːsəb(ə)l] *a* (*process*) irréversible; (*decision*) irrévocable.

irrevocable [ɪ'revəkəb(ə)l] *a* irrévocable.

irrigate ['ɪrɪgeɪt] *vt* irriguer. ◆**irri'gation** *n* irrigation *f*.

irritat/e ['ɪrɪteɪt] *vt* irriter. ◆**—ing** *a* irritant. ◆**irritable** *a* (*easily annoyed*) irritable. ◆**irritant** *n* irritant *m*. ◆**irri'tation** *n* (*anger*) & *Med* irritation *f*.

is [ɪz] *see* **be**.

Islam ['ɪzlɑːm] *n* islam *m*. ◆**Islamic** [ɪz'læmɪk] *a* islamique.

island ['aɪlənd] *n* île *f*; **traffic i.** refuge *m*; – *a* insulaire. ◆**islander** *n* insulaire *mf*. ◆**isle** [aɪl] *n* île *f*; **the British Isles** les îles Britanniques.

isolate ['aɪsəleɪt] *vt* isoler (from de). ◆**isolated** *a* (*remote, unique*) isolé. ◆**iso'lation** *n* isolement *m*; **in i.** isolément.

Israel ['ɪzreɪl] *n* Israël *m*. ◆**Is'raeli** *a & n* israélien, -ienne (*mf*).

issue ['ɪʃuː] *vt* (*book etc*) publier; (*an order*) donner; (*tickets*) distribuer; (*passport*) délivrer; (*stamps, banknotes*) émettre;

(*warning*) lancer; (*supply*) fournir (**with** de, **to** à); – *vi* **to i. from** (*of smell*) se dégager de; (*stem from*) provenir de; – *n* (*matter*) question *f*; (*problem*) problème *m*; (*outcome*) résultat *m*; (*of text*) publication *f*; (*of stamps etc*) émission *f*; (*newspaper*) numéro *m*; **at i.** (*at stake*) en cause; **to make an i. of** faire toute une affaire de.

isthmus ['ɪsməs] *n Geog* isthme *m*.

it [ɪt] *pron* **1** (*subject*) il, elle; (*object*) le, la, l'; (**to**) **it** (*indirect object*) lui; **it bites** (*dog*) il mord; **I've done it** je l'ai fait. **2** (*impersonal*) il; **it's snowing** il neige; **it's hot** il fait chaud. **3** (*non specific*) ce, cela, ça; **it's good** c'est bon; **it was pleasant** c'était agréable; **who is it?** qui est-ce?; **that's it!** (*I agree*) c'est ça!; (*it's done*) ça y est!; **to consider it wise to do** juger prudent de faire; **it was Paul who . . .** c'est Paul qui . . . ; **she's got it in her to succeed** elle est capable de réussir; **to have it in for s.o.** en vouloir à qn. **4 of it, from it, about it** en; **in it, to it, at it** y; **on it** dessus; **under it** dessous.

italic [ɪ'tælɪk] *a Typ* italique; – *npl* italique *m*.

Italy ['ɪtəlɪ] *n* Italie *f*. ◆**I'talian** *a* & *n* italien, -ienne (*mf*); – *n* (*language*) italien *m*.

itch [ɪtʃ] *n* démangeaison(s) *f*(*pl*); **to have an i. to do** avoir une envie folle de faire; – *vi* démanger; **his arm itches** son bras le *or* lui démange; **I'm itching to do** *Fig* ça me démange de faire. ◆**–ing** *n* démangeaison(s) *f*(*pl*). ◆**itchy** *a* **an i. hand** une main qui me démange.

item ['aɪtəm] *n Com Journ* article *m*; (*matter*) question *f*; (*on entertainment programme*) numéro *m*; **a news i.** une information. ◆**itemize** *vt* détailler.

itinerant [aɪ'tɪnərənt] *a* (*musician, actor*) ambulant; (*judge, preacher*) itinérant.

itinerary [aɪ'tɪnərərɪ] *n* itinéraire *m*.

its [ɪts] *poss a* son, sa, *pl* ses. ◆**it'self** *pron* lui-même, elle-même; (*reflexive*) se, s'; **goodness i.** la bonté même; **by i.** tout seul.

IUD [aɪjuː'diː] *n abbr* (*intrauterine device*) stérilet *m*.

ivory ['aɪvərɪ] *n* ivoire *m*.

ivy ['aɪvɪ] *n* lierre *m*.

J

J, j [dʒeɪ] *n* J, j *m*.

jab [dʒæb] *vt* (**-bb-**) (*thrust*) enfoncer (**into** dans); (*prick*) piquer (*qn*) (**with sth** du bout de qch); – *n* coup *m* (sec); (*injection*) *Med Fam* piqûre *f*.

jabber ['dʒæbər] *vi* bavarder, jaser; – *vt* bredouiller. ◆**–ing** *n* bavardage *m*.

jack [dʒæk] **1** *n Aut* cric *m*; – *vt* **to j. up** soulever (*avec un cric*); (*price*) *Fig* augmenter. **2** *n Cards* valet *m*. **3** *vt* **to j. (in)** (*job etc*) *Fam* plaquer. **4** *n* **j. of all trades** homme *m* à tout faire. ◆**j.-in-the-box** *n* diable *m* (à ressort).

jackal ['dʒæk(ə)l] *n* (*animal*) chacal *m*.

jackass ['dʒækæs] *n* (*fool*) idiot, -ote *mf*.

jackdaw ['dʒækdɔː] *n* (*bird*) choucas *m*.

jacket ['dʒækɪt] *n* (*short coat*) veste *f*; (*of man's suit*) veston *m*; (*of woman*) veste *f*, jaquette *f*; (*bulletproof*) gilet *m*; (**dust**) **j.** (*of book*) jaquette *f*; **in their jackets** (*potatoes*) en robe des champs.

jack-knife ['dʒæknaɪf] **1** *n* couteau *m* de poche. **2** *vi* (*of lorry, truck*) se mettre en travers de la route.

jackpot ['dʒækpɒt] *n* gros lot *m*.

jacks [dʒæks] *npl* (jeu *m* d')osselets *mpl*.

jacuzzi [dʒə'kuːzɪ] *n* (*bath, pool*) jacousi *m*.

jade [dʒeɪd] *n* **1** (*stone*) jade *m*. **2** (*horse*) rosse *f*, canasson *m*.

jaded ['dʒeɪdɪd] *a* blasé.

jagged ['dʒægɪd] *a* déchiqueté.

jaguar ['dʒægjʊər] *n* (*animal*) jaguar *m*.

jail [dʒeɪl] *n* prison *f*; – *vt* emprisonner (**for theft**/*etc* pour vol/*etc*); **to j. for life** condamner à perpétuité. ◆**jailbreak** *n* évasion *f* (de prison). ◆**jailer** *n* geôlier, -ière *mf*.

jalopy [dʒə'lɒpɪ] *n* (*car*) *Fam* vieux tacot *m*.

jam[1] [dʒæm] *n Culin* confiture *f*. ◆**jamjar** *n* pot *m* à confiture.

jam[2] [dʒæm] **1** *n* (**traffic**) **j.** embouteillage *m*; **in a j.** (*trouble*) *Fig Fam* dans le pétrin. **2** *vt* (**-mm-**) (*squeeze, make stuck*) coincer, bloquer; (*gun*) enrayer; (*street, corridor etc*) encombrer; (*building*) envahir; *Rad* brouiller; **to j. sth into** (*pack, cram*) (en)tasser qch dans; (*thrust, put*) enfoncer *or* fourrer qch dans; **to j. on** (*brakes*) bloquer; – *vi* (*get stuck*) se coincer, se bloquer; (*of gun*) s'enrayer; **to j. into** (*of crowd*) s'entasser dans. ◆**jammed** *a* (*machine etc*) coincé, bloqué; (*street etc*) encombré. ◆**jam-'packed** *a* (*hall etc*) bourré de monde.

Jamaica [dʒə'meɪkə] *n* Jamaïque *f.*

jangl/e ['dʒæŋg(ə)l] *vi* cliqueter; – *n* cliquetis *m.* ◆**—ing** *a* (*noise*) discordant.

janitor ['dʒænɪtər] *n* concierge *m.*

January ['dʒænjʊərɪ] *n* janvier *m.*

Japan [dʒə'pæn] *n* Japon *m.* ◆**Japa'nese** *a & n* japonais, -aise (*mf*); – *n* (*language*) japonais *m.*

jar [dʒɑːr] **1** *n* (*vessel*) pot *m*; (*large, glass*) bocal *m.* **2** *n* (*jolt*) choc *m*; – *vt* (**-rr-**) (*shake*) ébranler. **3** *vi* (**-rr-**) (*of noise*) grincer; (*of note*) *Mus* détonner; (*of colours, words*) jurer (**with** avec); **to j. on** (*s.o.'s nerves*) porter sur; (*s.o.'s ears*) écorcher. ◆**jarring** *a* (*note*) discordant.

jargon ['dʒɑːgən] *n* jargon *m.*

jasmine ['dʒæzmɪn] *n* *Bot* jasmin *m.*

jaundice ['dʒɔːndɪs] *n* *Med* jaunisse *f.* ◆**jaundiced** *a* (*bitter*) *Fig* aigri; **to take a j. view of** voir d'un mauvais œil.

jaunt [dʒɔːnt] *n* (*journey*) balade *f.*

jaunt/y ['dʒɔːntɪ] *a* (**-ier, -iest**) (*carefree*) insouciant; (*cheerful, lively*) allègre; (*hat etc*) coquet, chic. ◆**—ily** *adv* avec insouciance; allègrement.

javelin ['dʒævlɪn] *n* javelot *m.*

jaw [dʒɔː] **1** *n* *Anat* mâchoire *f.* **2** *vi* (*talk*) *Pej Fam* papoter; – *n* **to have a j.** *Pej Fam* tailler une bavette.

jay [dʒeɪ] *n* (*bird*) geai *m.*

jaywalker ['dʒeɪwɔːkər] *n* piéton *m* imprudent.

jazz [dʒæz] *n* jazz *m*; – *vt* **to j. up** *Fam* (*music*) jazzifier; (*enliven*) animer; (*clothes, room*) égayer.

jealous ['dʒeləs] *a* jaloux (**of** de). ◆**jealousy** *n* jalousie *f.*

jeans [dʒiːnz] *npl* (blue-)jean *m.*

jeep [dʒiːp] *n* jeep *f.*

jeer [dʒɪər] *vti* **to j. (at)** (*mock*) railler; (*boo*) huer; – *n* raillerie *f*; *pl* (*boos*) huées *fpl.* ◆**—ing** *a* railleur; – *n* railleries *fpl*; (*of crowd*) huées *fpl.*

jell [dʒel] *vi* (*of ideas etc*) *Fam* prendre tournure.

jello® ['dʒeləʊ] *n inv* *Culin* *Am* gelée *f.* ◆**jellied** *a* *Culin* en gelée. ◆**jelly** *n* *Culin* gelée *f.* ◆**jellyfish** *n* méduse *f.*

jeopardy ['dʒepədɪ] *n* danger *m*, péril *m.* ◆**jeopardize** *vt* mettre en danger *or* en péril.

jerk [dʒɜːk] **1** *vt* donner une secousse à (*pour tirer, pousser etc*); – *n* secousse *f*, saccade *f.* **2** *n* (*person*) *Pej Fam* pauvre type *m*; (*stupid*) j. crétin, -ine *mf.* ◆**jerk/y** *a* (**-ier, -iest**) **1** saccadé. **2** (*stupid*) *Am Fam* stupide, bête. ◆**—ily** *adv* par saccades.

jersey ['dʒɜːzɪ] *n* (*cloth*) jersey *m*; (*garment*) & *Fb* maillot *m.*

Jersey ['dʒɜːzɪ] *n* Jersey *f.*

jest [dʒest] *n* plaisanterie *f*; **in j.** pour rire; – *vi* plaisanter. ◆**—er** *n* *Hist* bouffon *m.*

Jesus ['dʒiːzəs] *n* Jésus *m*; **J. Christ** Jésus-Christ *m.*

jet [dʒet] **1** *n* (*of liquid, steam etc*) jet *m.* **2** *n* *Av* avion *m* à réaction; – *a* (*engine*) à réaction; **j. lag** fatigue *f* (due au décalage horaire). ◆**jet-lagged** *a* *Fam* qui souffre du décalage horaire.

jet-black [dʒet'blæk] *a* noir comme (du) jais, (noir) de jais.

jettison ['dʒetɪs(ə)n] *vt* *Nau* jeter à la mer; (*fuel*) *Av* larguer; *Fig* abandonner.

jetty ['dʒetɪ] *n* jetée *f*; (*landing-place*) embarcadère *m.*

Jew [dʒuː] *n* (*man*) Juif *m*; (*woman*) Juive *f.* ◆**Jewess** *n* Juive *f.* ◆**Jewish** *a* juif.

jewel ['dʒuːəl] *n* bijou *m*; (*in watch*) rubis *m.* ◆**jewelled** *a* orné de bijoux. ◆**jeweller** *n* bijoutier, -ière *mf.* ◆**jewellery** *n*, *Am* ◆**jewelry** *n* bijoux *mpl.*

jib [dʒɪb] *vi* (**-bb-**) regimber (**at** devant); **to j. at doing** se refuser à faire.

jibe [dʒaɪb] *vi & n* = **gibe.**

jiffy ['dʒɪfɪ] *n* *Fam* instant *m.*

jig [dʒɪg] *n* (*dance, music*) gigue *f.*

jigsaw ['dʒɪgsɔː] *n* **j. (puzzle)** puzzle *m.*

jilt [dʒɪlt] *vt* (*lover*) laisser tomber.

jingle ['dʒɪŋg(ə)l] *vi* (*of keys, bell etc*) tinter; – *vt* faire tinter; – *n* tintement *m.*

jinx [dʒɪŋks] *n* (*person, object*) porte-malheur *m inv*; (*spell, curse*) (mauvais) sort *m*, poisse *f.*

jitters ['dʒɪtəz] *npl* **to have the j.** *Fam* avoir la frousse. ◆**jittery** *a* **to be j.** *Fam* avoir la frousse.

job [dʒɒb] *n* (*task*) travail *m*; (*post*) poste *m*, situation *f*; (*crime*) *Fam* coup *m*; **to have a j. doing** *or* **to do** (*much trouble*) avoir du mal à faire; **to have the j. of doing** (*unpleasant task*) être obligé de faire; (*for a living etc*) être chargé de faire; **it's a good j. (that)** *Fam* heureusement que; **that's just the j.** *Fam* c'est juste ce qu'il faut; **out of a j.** au chômage. ◆**jobcentre** *n* agence *f* nationale pour l'emploi. ◆**jobless** *a* au chômage.

jockey ['dʒɒkɪ] *n* jockey *m*; – *vi* **to j. for** (*position, job*) manœuvrer pour obtenir.

jocular ['dʒɒkjʊlər] *a* jovial, amusant.

jog [dʒɒg] **1** *n* (*jolt*) secousse *f*; (*nudge*) coup *m* de coude; – *vt* (-gg-) (*shake*) secouer; (*elbow*) pousser; (*memory*) *Fig* rafraîchir. **2** *vi* (-gg-) **to j. along** (*of vehicle*) cahoter; (*of work*) aller tant bien que mal; (*of person*) faire son petit bonhomme de chemin. **3** *vi* (-gg-) *Sp* faire du jogging. ◆**jogging** *n Sp* jogging *m*.

john [dʒɒn] *n* (*toilet*) *Am Sl* cabinets *mpl*.

join [dʒɔɪn] **1** *vt* (*unite*) joindre, réunir; (*link*) relier; (*wires, pipes*) raccorder; **to j. s.o.** (*catch up with, meet*) rejoindre qn; (*associate oneself with, go with*) se joindre à qn (**in doing** pour faire); **to j. the sea** (*of river*) rejoindre la mer; **to j. hands** se donner la main; **to j. together** *or* **up** (*objects*) joindre; – *vi* (*of roads, rivers etc*) se rejoindre; **to j. (together** *or* **up)** (*of objects*) se joindre (**with** à); **to j. in** participer; **to j. in a game** prendre part à un jeu; – *n* raccord *m*, joint *m*. **2** *vt* (*become a member of*) s'inscrire à (*club, parti*); (*army*) s'engager dans; (*queue, line*) se mettre à; – *vi* (*become a member*) devenir membre; **to j. up** *Mil* s'engager.

joiner ['dʒɔɪnər] *n* menuisier *m*.

joint [dʒɔɪnt] **1** *n Anat* articulation *f*; *Culin* rôti *m*; *Tech* joint *m*; **out of j.** *Med* démis. **2** *n* (*nightclub etc*) *Sl* boîte *f*. **3** *a* (*account, statement etc*) commun; (*effort*) conjugué; **j. author** coauteur *m*. ◆**—ly** *adv* conjointement.

jok/e [dʒəʊk] *n* plaisanterie *f*; (*trick*) tour *m*; **it's no j.** (*it's unpleasant*) ce n'est pas drôle (**doing** de faire); – *vi* plaisanter (**about** sur). ◆**—er** *n* plaisantin *m*; (*fellow*) *Fam* type *m*; *Cards* joker *m*. ◆**—ingly** *adv* en plaisantant.

jolly ['dʒɒlɪ] **1** *a* (**-ier, -iest**) (*happy*) gai; (*drunk*) *Fam* éméché. **2** *adv* (*very*) *Fam* rudement. ◆**jollifi'cation** *n* (*merry-making*) réjouissances *fpl*. ◆**jollity** *n* jovialité *f*; (*merry-making*) réjouissances *fpl*.

jolt [dʒɒlt] *vt* **to j. s.o.** (*of vehicle*) cahoter qn; (*shake*) *Fig* secouer qn; – *vi* **to j. (along)** (*of vehicle*) cahoter; – *n* cahot *m*, secousse *f*; (*shock*) *Fig* secousse *f*.

Jordan ['dʒɔːd(ə)n] *n* Jordanie *f*.

jostle ['dʒɒs(ə)l] *vt* (*push*) bousculer; – *vi* (*push each other*) se bousculer (**for** pour obtenir); **don't j.!** ne bousculez pas!

jot [dʒɒt] *vt* (-tt-) **to j. down** noter. ◆**jotter** *n* (*notepad*) bloc-notes *m*.

journal ['dʒɜːn(ə)l] *n* (*periodical*) revue *f*, journal *m*. ◆**journa'lese** *n* jargon *m* journalistique. ◆**journalism** *n* journalisme *m*. ◆**journalist** *n* journaliste *mf*.

journey ['dʒɜːnɪ] *n* (*trip*) voyage *m*; (*distance*) trajet *m*; **to go on a j.** partir en voyage; – *vi* voyager.

jovial ['dʒəʊvɪəl] *a* jovial.

joy [dʒɔɪ] *n* joie *f*; *pl* (*of countryside, motherhood etc*) plaisirs *mpl* (**of** de). ◆**joyful** *a*, ◆**joyous** *a* joyeux. ◆**joyride** *n* virée *f* (*dans une voiture volée*).

joystick ['dʒɔɪstɪk] *n* (*of aircraft, computer*) manche *m* à balai.

JP [dʒeɪ'piː] *abbr* = **Justice of the Peace**.

jubilant ['dʒuːbɪlənt] *a* **to be j.** jubiler. ◆**jubi'lation** *n* jubilation *f*.

jubilee ['dʒuːbɪliː] *n* (**golden**) **j.** jubilé *m*.

Judaism ['dʒuːdeɪɪz(ə)m] *n* judaïsme *m*.

judder ['dʒʌdər] *vi* (*shake*) vibrer; – *n* vibration *f*.

judg/e [dʒʌdʒ] *n* juge *m*; – *vti* juger; **judging by** à en juger par. ◆**—(e)ment** *n* jugement *m*.

judicial [dʒuː'dɪʃ(ə)l] *a* judiciaire. ◆**judiciary** *n* magistrature *f*. ◆**judicious** *a* judicieux.

judo ['dʒuːdəʊ] *n* judo *m*.

jug [dʒʌg] *n* cruche *f*; (*for milk*) pot *m*.

juggernaut ['dʒʌgənɔːt] *n* (*truck*) poids *m* lourd, mastodonte *m*.

juggl/e ['dʒʌg(ə)l] *vi* jongler; – *vt* jongler avec. ◆**—er** *n* jongleur, -euse *mf*.

Jugoslavia [juːgəʊ'slɑːvɪə] *n* Yougoslavie *f*. ◆**Jugoslav** *a* & *n* yougoslave (*mf*).

juice [dʒuːs] *n* jus *m*; (*in stomach*) suc *m*. ◆**juicy** *a* (**-ier, -iest**) (*fruit*) juteux; (*meat*) succulent; (*story*) *Fig* savoureux.

jukebox ['dʒuːkbɒks] *n* juke-box *m*.

July [dʒuː'laɪ] *n* juillet *m*.

jumble ['dʒʌmb(ə)l] *vt* **to j. (up)** (*objects, facts etc*) brouiller, mélanger; – *n* fouillis *m*; **j. sale** (*used clothes etc*) vente *f* de charité.

jumbo ['dʒʌmbəʊ] *a* géant; – *a* & *n* (*pl* **-os**) **j. (jet)** jumbo-jet *m*, gros-porteur *m*.

jump [dʒʌmp] *n* (*leap*) saut *m*, bond *m*; (*start*) sursaut *m*; (*increase*) hausse *f*; – *vi* sauter (**at** sur); (*start*) sursauter; (*of price, heart*) faire un bond; **to j. about** sautiller; **to j. across sth** traverser qch d'un bond; **to j. to conclusions** tirer des conclusions hâtives; **j. in** *or* **on!** *Aut* montez!; **to j. on** (*bus*) sauter dans; **to j. off** *or* **out** sauter; **to j. off sth, j. out of sth** sauter de qch; **to j. out of the window** sauter par la fenêtre; **to j. up** se lever d'un bond; – *vt* sauter; **to j. the lights** *Aut* griller un feu rouge; **to j. the rails** (*of train*) dérailler; **to j. the queue** resquiller.

jumper ['dʒʌmpər] *n* pull(-over) *m*; (*dress*) *Am* robe *f* chasuble.

jumpy ['dʒʌmpɪ] *a* (**-ier, -iest**) nerveux.

junction [ˈdʒʌŋkʃ(ə)n] *n* (*joining*) jonction *f*; (*crossroads*) carrefour *m*.
juncture [ˈdʒʌŋktʃər] *n* **at this j.** (*critical point in time*) en ce moment même.
June [dʒuːn] *n* juin *m*.
jungle [ˈdʒʌŋg(ə)l] *n* jungle *f*.
junior [ˈdʒuːnɪər] *a* (*younger*) plus jeune; (*in rank, status etc*) subalterne; (*teacher, doctor*) jeune; **to be j. to s.o., be s.o.'s j.** être plus jeune que qn; (*in rank, status*) être au-dessous de qn; **Smith j.** Smith fils *or* junior; **j. school** école *f* primaire; **j. high school** *Am* = collège *m* d'enseignement secondaire; – *n* cadet, -ette *mf*; *Sch* petit, -ite *mf*, petit(e) élève *mf*; *Sp* junior *mf*, cadet, -ette *mf*.
junk [dʒʌŋk] **1** *n* (*objects*) bric-à-brac *m inv*; (*metal*) ferraille *f*; (*goods*) *Pej* camelote *f*; (*film, book etc*) *Pej* idiotie *f*; (*nonsense*) idioties *fpl*; **j. shop** (boutique *f* de) brocanteur *m*. **2** *vt* (*get rid of*) *Am Fam* balancer.
junkie [ˈdʒʌŋkɪ] *n Fam* drogué, -ée *mf*.
junta [ˈdʒʌntə] *n Pol* junte *f*.
jurisdiction [dʒʊərɪsˈdɪkʃ(ə)n] *n* juridiction *f*.
jury [ˈdʒʊərɪ] *n* (*in competition*) & *Jur* jury *m*. ◆**juror** *n Jur* juré *m*.
just [dʒʌst] **1** *adv* (*exactly, slightly*) juste; (*only*) juste, seulement; (*simply*) (tout) simplement; **it's j. as I thought** c'est bien ce que je pensais; **j. at that time** à cet instant même; **she has/had j. left** elle vient/venait de partir; **I've j. come from** j'arrive de; **I'm j. coming!** j'arrive!; **he'll (only) j. catch the bus** il aura son bus de justesse; **he j. missed it** il l'a manqué de peu; **j. as big/light/***etc* tout aussi grand/léger/*etc* (**as** que); **j. listen!** écoute donc!; **j. a moment!** un instant!; **j. over ten** un peu plus de dix; **j. one** un(e) seul(e) (**of** de); **j. about** (*approximately*) à peu près; (*almost*) presque; **j. about to do** sur le point de faire. **2** *a* (*fair*) juste (**to** envers). ◆**—ly** *adv* avec justice. ◆**—ness** *n* (*of cause etc*) justice *f*.
justice [ˈdʒʌstɪs] *n* justice *f*; (*judge*) juge *m*; **to do j. to** (*meal*) faire honneur à; **it doesn't do you j.** (*hat, photo*) cela ne vous avantage pas; (*attitude*) cela ne vous fait pas honneur; **J. of the Peace** juge *m* de paix.
justify [ˈdʒʌstɪfaɪ] *vt* justifier; **to be justified in doing** (*have right*) être en droit de faire; (*have reason*) avoir toutes les bonnes raisons de faire. ◆**justiˈfiable** *a* justifiable. ◆**justiˈfiably** *adv* légitimement. ◆**justifiˈcation** *n* justification *f*.
jut [dʒʌt] *vi* (**-tt-**) **to j. out** faire saillie; **to j. out over sth** (*overhang*) surplomber qch.
jute [dʒuːt] *n* (*fibre*) jute *m*.
juvenile [ˈdʒuːvənaɪl] *n* adolescent, -ente *mf*; – *a* (*court, book etc*) pour enfants; (*delinquent*) jeune; (*behaviour*) *Pej* puéril.
juxtapose [dʒʌkstəˈpəʊz] *vt* juxtaposer. ◆**juxtapoˈsition** *n* juxtaposition *f*.

K

K, k [keɪ] *n* K, k *m*.
kaleidoscope [kəˈlaɪdəskəʊp] *n* kaléidoscope *m*.
kangaroo [kæŋgəˈruː] *n* kangourou *m*.
kaput [kəˈpʊt] *a* (*broken, ruined*) *Sl* fichu.
karate [kəˈrɑːtɪ] *n Sp* karaté *m*.
keel [kiːl] *n Nau* quille *f*; – *vi* **to k. over** (*of boat*) chavirer.
keen [kiːn] *a* (*edge, appetite*) aiguisé; (*interest, feeling*) vif; (*mind*) pénétrant; (*wind*) coupant, piquant; (*enthusiastic*) enthousiaste; **a k. sportsman** un passionné de sport; **to be k. to do** *or* **on doing** tenir (beaucoup) à faire; **to be k. on** (*music, sport etc*) être passionné de; **he is k. on her/the idea** elle/l'idée lui plaît beaucoup. ◆**—ly** *adv* (*to work etc*) avec enthousiasme; (*to feel, interest*) vivement. ◆**—ness** *n* enthousiasme *m*; (*of mind*) pénétration *f*; (*of interest*) intensité *f*; **k. to do** empressement *m* à faire.
keep[1] [kiːp] *vt* (*pt & pp* **kept**) garder; (*shop, car*) avoir; (*diary, promise*) tenir; (*family*) entretenir; (*rule*) observer, respecter; (*feast day*) célébrer; (*birthday*) fêter; (*detain, delay*) retenir; (*put*) mettre; **to k. (on) doing** (*continue*) continuer à faire; **to k. clean** tenir *or* garder propre; **to k. from** (*conceal*) cacher à; **to k. s.o. from doing** (*prevent*) empêcher qn de faire; **to k. s.o. waiting/working** faire attendre/travailler qn; **to k. sth going** (*engine, machine*) laisser qch en marche; **to k. s.o. in whisky/***etc* fournir qn en whisky/*etc*; **to k. an appointment** se rendre à un rendez-vous; **to k. back** (*withhold, delay*) retenir; (*conceal*) cacher (**from**

à); **to k. down** (*control*) maîtriser; (*restrict*) limiter; (*costs, price*) maintenir bas; **to k. in** empêcher de sortir; (*pupil*) *Sch* consigner; **to k. off** *or* **away** (*person*) éloigner (**from** de); **'k. off the grass'** 'ne pas marcher sur les pelouses'; **k. your hands off!** n'y touche(z) pas!; **to k. on** (*hat, employee*) garder; **to k. out** empêcher d'entrer; **to k. up** (*continue, maintain*) continuer (**doing sth** à faire qch); (*road, building*) entretenir; – *vi* (*continue*) continuer; (*remain*) rester; (*of food*) se garder, se conserver; (*wait*) attendre; **how is he keeping?** comment va-t-il?; **to k. still** rester *or* se tenir tranquille; **to k. from doing** (*refrain*) s'abstenir de faire; **to k. going** (*continue*) continuer; **to k. at it** (*keep doing it*) continuer à le faire; **to k. away** *or* **off** *or* **back** ne pas s'approcher (**from** de); **if the rain keeps off** s'il ne pleut pas; **to k. on at s.o.** harceler qn; **to k. out** rester en dehors (**of** de); **to k. to** (*subject, path*) ne pas s'écarter de; (*room*) garder; **to k. to the left** tenir la gauche; **to k. to oneself** se tenir à l'écart; **to k. up** (*continue*) continuer; (*follow*) suivre; **to k. up with s.o** (*follow*) suivre qn; (*in quality of work etc*) se maintenir à la hauteur de qn; – *n* (*food*) subsistance *f*; **to have one's k.** être logé et nourri; **for keeps** *Fam* pour toujours. ◆**—ing** *n* (*care*) garde *f*; **in k. with** en rapport avec. ◆**—er** *n* gardien, -ienne *mf*.

keep² [kiːp] *n* (*tower*) *Hist* donjon *m*.

keepsake ['kiːpseɪk] *n* (*object*) souvenir *m*.

keg [keg] *n* tonnelet *m*.

kennel ['ken(ə)l] *n* niche *f*; (*for boarding*) chenil *m*.

Kenya ['kiːnjə, 'kenjə] *n* Kenya *m*.

kept [kept] *see* **keep¹**; – *a* **well** *or* **nicely k.** (*house etc*) bien tenu.

kerb [kɜːb] *n* bord *m* du trottoir.

kernel ['kɜːn(ə)l] *n* (*of nut*) amande *f*.

kerosene ['kerəsiːn] *n* (*aviation fuel*) kérosène *m*; (*paraffin*) *Am* pétrole *m* (lampant).

ketchup ['ketʃəp] *n* (*sauce*) ketchup *m*.

kettle ['ket(ə)l] *n* bouilloire *f*; **the k. is boiling** l'eau bout.

key [kiː] *n* clef *f*, clé *f*; (*of piano, typewriter, computer*) touche *f*; – *a* (*industry, post etc*) clef (*f inv*), clé (*f inv*); **k. man** pivot *m*; **k. ring** porte-clefs *m inv*. ◆**keyboard** *n* clavier *m*. ◆**keyhole** *n* trou *m* de (la) serrure. ◆**keynote** *n* (*of speech*) note *f* dominante. ◆**keystone** *n* (*of policy etc*) & *Archit* clef *f* de voûte.

keyed [kiːd] *a* **to be k. up** avoir les nerfs tendus.

khaki ['kɑːkɪ] *a* & *n* kaki *a inv* & *m*.

kibbutz [kɪ'bʊts] *n* kibboutz *m*.

kick [kɪk] *n* coup *m* de pied; (*of horse*) ruade *f*; **to get a k. out of doing** (*thrill*) *Fam* prendre un malin plaisir à faire; **for kicks** *Pej Fam* pour le plaisir; – *vt* donner un coup de pied à; (*of horse*) lancer une ruade à; **to k. back** (*ball*) renvoyer (*du pied*); **to k. down** *or* **in** démolir à coups de pied; **to k. out** (*eject*) *Fam* flanquer dehors; **to k. up** (*fuss, row*) *Fam* faire; – *vi* donner des coups de pied; (*of horse*) ruer; **to k. off** *Fb* donner le coup d'envoi; (*start*) *Fig* démarrer. ◆**k.-off** *n Fb* coup *m* d'envoi.

kid [kɪd] **1** *n* (*goat*) chevreau *m*. **2** *n* (*child*) *Fam* gosse *mf*; **his** *or* **her k. brother** *Am Fam* son petit frère. **3** *vti* (**-dd-**) (*joke, tease*) *Fam* blaguer; **to k. oneself** se faire des illusions.

kidnap ['kɪdnæp] *vt* (**-pp-**) kidnapper. ◆**kidnapping** *n* enlèvement *m*. ◆**kidnapper** *n* kidnappeur, -euse *mf*.

kidney ['kɪdnɪ] *n Anat* rein *m*; *Culin* rognon *m*; **on a k. machine** sous rein artificiel; **k. bean** haricot *m* rouge.

kill [kɪl] *vt* tuer; (*bill*) *Pol* repousser, faire échouer; (*chances*) détruire; (*rumour*) étouffer; (*story*) *Fam* supprimer; (*engine*) *Fam* arrêter; **my feet are killing me** *Fam* je ne sens plus mes pieds, j'ai les pieds en compote; **to k. off** (*person etc*) & *Fig* détruire; – *vi* tuer; – *n* mise *f* à mort; (*prey*) animaux *mpl* tués. ◆**—ing 1** *n* (*of person*) meurtre *m*; (*of group*) massacre *m*; (*of animal*) mise *f* à mort; **to make a k.** *Fin* réussir un beau coup. **2** *a* (*tiring*) *Fam* tuant. ◆**—er** *n* tueur, -euse *mf*. ◆**killjoy** *n* rabat-joie *m inv*.

kiln [kɪln] *n* (*for pottery*) four *m*.

kilo ['kiːləʊ] *n* (*pl* **-os**) kilo *m*. ◆**kilogramme** ['kɪləʊgræm] *n* kilogramme *m*.

kilometre [kɪ'lɒmɪtər] *n* kilomètre *m*.

kilowatt ['kɪləʊwɒt] *n* kilowatt *m*.

kilt [kɪlt] *n* kilt *m*.

kimono [kɪ'məʊnəʊ] *n* (*pl* **-os**) kimono *m*.

kin [kɪn] *n* (*relatives*) parents *mpl*; **one's next of k.** son plus proche parent.

kind [kaɪnd] **1** *n* (*sort, type*) genre *m*; **a k. of** une sorte *or* une espèce de; **to pay in k.** payer en nature; **what k. of drink/etc is it?** qu'est-ce que c'est comme boisson/*etc*?; **that's the k. of man he is** il est comme ça; **nothing of the k.!** absolument pas!; **k. of worried/sad/etc** (*somewhat*) plutôt inquiet/triste/*etc*; **k. of fascinated** (*as if*) *Fam* comme fasciné; **in a k. of way** d'une certaine façon; **it's the only one of its k., it's one of a k.** c'est unique en son genre; **we are**

two of a k. nous nous ressemblons. **2** *a* (**-er, -est**) (*helpful, pleasant*) gentil (to avec, pour), bon (to pour); **that's k. of you** c'est gentil *or* aimable à vous. ◆**k.-'hearted** *a* qui a bon cœur. ◆**kindly** *adv* avec bonté; **k. wait/***etc* ayez la bonté d'attendre/*etc*; **not to take k. to sth** ne pas apprécier qch; – *a* (*person*) bienveillant. ◆**kindness** *n* bonté *f*, gentillesse *f*.

kindergarten ['kɪndəgɑːt(ə)n] *n* jardin *m* d'enfants.

kindle ['kɪnd(ə)l] *vt* allumer; – *vi* s'allumer.

kindred ['kɪndrɪd] *n* (*relationship*) parenté *f*; (*relatives*) parents *mpl*; **k. spirit** semblable *mf*, âme *f* sœur.

king [kɪŋ] *n* roi *m*. ◆**k.-size(d)** *a* géant; (*cigarette*) long. ◆**kingdom** *n* royaume *m*; **animal/plant k.** règne *m* animal/végétal. ◆**kingly** *a* royal.

kingfisher ['kɪŋfɪʃər] *n* (*bird*) martin-pêcheur *m*.

kink [kɪŋk] *n* (*in rope*) entortillement *m*.

kinky ['kɪŋkɪ] *a* (**-ier, -iest**) (*person*) *Psy Pej* vicieux; (*clothes etc*) bizarre.

kinship ['kɪnʃɪp] *n* parenté *f*.

kiosk ['kiːɒsk] *n* kiosque *m*; (**telephone**) **k.** cabine *f* (téléphonique).

kip [kɪp] *vi* (**-pp-**) (*sleep*) *Sl* roupiller.

kipper ['kɪpər] *n* (*herring*) kipper *m*.

kiss [kɪs] *n* baiser *m*, bise *f*; **the k. of life** *Med* le bouche-à-bouche; – *vt* (*person*) embrasser; **to k. s.o.'s hand** baiser la main de qn; – *vi* s'embrasser.

kit [kɪt] *n* équipement *m*, matériel *m*; (*set of articles*) trousse *f*; **gym k.** (*belongings*) affaires *fpl* de gym; **tool k.** trousse *f* à outils; (**do-it-yourself**) **k.** kit *m*; **in k. form** en kit; **k. bag** sac *m* (*de soldat etc*); – *vt* (**-tt-**) **to k. out** équiper (**with** de).

kitchen ['kɪtʃɪn] *n* cuisine *f*; **k. cabinet** buffet *m* de cuisine; **k. garden** jardin *m* potager; **k. sink** évier *m*. ◆**kitche'nette** *n* kitchenette *f*, coin-cuisine *m*.

kite [kaɪt] *n* (*toy*) cerf-volant *m*.

kith [kɪθ] *n* **k. and kin** amis *mpl* et parents *mpl*.

kitten ['kɪt(ə)n] *n* chaton *m*, petit chat *m*.

kitty ['kɪtɪ] *n* (*fund*) cagnotte *f*.

km *abbr* (*kilometre*) km.

knack [næk] *n* (*skill*) coup *m* (de main), truc *m* (**of doing** pour faire); **to have a** *or* **the k. of doing** (*aptitude, tendency*) avoir le don de faire.

knackered ['nækəd] *a* (*tired*) *Sl* vanné.

knapsack ['næpsæk] *n* sac *m* à dos.

knead [niːd] *vt* (*dough*) pétrir.

knee [niː] *n* genou *m*; **to go down on one's knees** se mettre à genoux; **k. pad** *Sp* genouillère *f*. ◆**kneecap** *n Anat* rotule *f*. ◆**knees-up** *n Sl* soirée *f* dansante, sauterie *f*.

kneel [niːl] *vi* (*pt & pp* **knelt** *or* **kneeled**) **to k. (down)** s'agenouiller; **to be kneeling (down)** être à genoux.

knell [nel] *n* glas *m*.

knew [njuː] *see* **know**.

knickers ['nɪkəz] *npl* (*woman's undergarment*) culotte *f*, slip *m*.

knick-knack ['nɪknæk] *n* babiole *f*.

knife [naɪf] *n* (*pl* **knives**) couteau *m*; (*penknife*) canif *m*; – *vt* poignarder.

knight [naɪt] *n Hist & Br Pol* chevalier *m*; *Chess* cavalier *m*; – *vt* (*of monarch*) *Br Pol* faire (*qn*) chevalier. ◆**knighthood** *n* titre *m* de chevalier.

knit [nɪt] *vt* (**-tt-**) tricoter; **to k. together** *Fig* souder; **to k. one's brow** froncer les sourcils; – *vi* tricoter; **to k. (together)** (*of bones*) se souder. ◆**knitting** *n* tricot *m*; **k. needle** aiguille *f* à tricoter. ◆**knitwear** *n* tricots *mpl*.

knob [nɒb] *n* (*on door etc*) bouton *m*; (*on stick*) pommeau *m*; (*of butter*) noix *f*.

knock [nɒk] *vt* (*strike*) frapper; (*collide with*) heurter; (*criticize*) *Fam* critiquer; **to k. one's head on** se cogner la tête contre; **to k. senseless** (*stun*) assommer; **to k. to the ground** jeter à terre; **to k. about** (*ill-treat*) malmener; **to k. back** (*drink, glass etc*) *Fam* s'envoyer (derrière la cravate), siffler; **to k. down** (*vase, pedestrian etc*) renverser; (*house, tree, wall etc*) abattre; (*price*) baisser, casser; **to k. in** (*nail*) enfoncer; **to k. off** (*person, object*) faire tomber (**from** de); (*do quickly*) *Fam* expédier; (*steal*) *Fam* piquer; **to k. £5 off (the price)** baisser le prix de cinq livres, faire cinq livres sur le prix; **to k. out** (*stun*) assommer; (*beat in competition*) éliminer; **to k. oneself out** (*tire*) *Fam* s'esquinter (**doing** à faire); **to k. over** (*pedestrian, vase etc*) renverser; **to k. up** (*meal*) *Fam* préparer à la hâte; – *vi* (*strike*) frapper; **to k. against** *or* **into** (*bump into*) heurter; **to k. about** (*travel*) *Fam* bourlinguer; (*lie around, stand around*) traîner; **to k. off** (*stop work*) *Fam* s'arrêter de travailler; – *n* (*blow*) coup *m*; (*collision*) heurt *m*; **there's a k. at the door** quelqu'un frappe; **I heard a k.** j'ai entendu frapper. ◆**knockdown** *a* **k. price** prix *m* imbattable. ◆**knock-'kneed** *a* cagneux. ◆**knock-out** *n Boxing* knock-out *m*; **to be a k.-out** (*of person, film etc*) *Fam* être formidable.

knocker ['nɒkər] *n* (*for door*) marteau *m*.

knot [nɒt] **1** *n* (*in rope etc*) nœud *m*; – *vt* (**-tt-**) nouer. **2** *n* (*unit of speed*) *Nau* nœud *m*. ◆**knotty** *a* (**-ier**, **-iest**) (*wood etc*) noueux; (*problem*) *Fig* épineux.

know [nəʊ] *vt* (*pt* **knew**, *pp* **known**) (*facts, language etc*) savoir; (*person, place etc*) connaître; (*recognize*) reconnaître (**by** à); **to k. that** savoir que; **to k. how to do** savoir faire; **for all I k.** (autant) que je sache; **I'll let you k.** je te le ferai savoir; **I'll have you k. that . . .** sachez que . . . ; **to k. (a lot) about** (*person, event*) en savoir long sur; (*cars, sewing etc*) s'y connaître en; **I've never known him to complain** je ne l'ai jamais vu se plaindre; **to get to k. (about) sth** apprendre qch; **to get to k. s.o.** (*meet*) faire la connaissance de qn; – *vi* savoir; **I k.** je (le) sais; **I wouldn't k., I k. nothing about it** je n'en sais rien; **I k. about that** je sais ça, je suis au courant; **to k. of** (*have heard of*) avoir entendu parler de; **do you k. of?** (*a good tailor etc*) connais-tu?; **you (should) k. better than to do that** tu es trop intelligent pour faire ça; **you should have known better** tu aurais dû réfléchir; – *n* **in the k.** *Fam* au courant. ◆**–ing** *a* (*smile, look*) entendu. ◆**–ingly** *adv* (*consciously*) sciemment. ◆**known** *a* connu; **a k. expert** un expert reconnu; **well k.** (bien) connu (**that** que); **she is k. to be . . .** on sait qu'elle est . . . . ◆**know-all** *n*, *Am* ◆**know-it-all** *n* je-sais-tout *mf inv*. ◆**know-how** *n* (*skill*) compétence *f* (**to do** pour faire), savoir-faire *m inv*.

knowledge ['nɒlɪdʒ] *n* connaissance *f* (**of** de); (*learning*) connaissances *fpl*, savoir *m*; **to (the best of) my k.** à ma connaissance; **without the k. of** à l'insu de; **to have no k. of** ignorer; **general k.** culture *f* générale. ◆**knowledgeable** *a* bien informé (**about** sur).

knuckle ['nʌk(ə)l] **1** *n* articulation *f* du doigt. **2** *vi* **to k. down to** (*task*) *Fam* s'atteler à; **to k. under** céder.

Koran [kə'rɑːn] *n Rel* Coran *m*.

kosher ['kəʊʃər] *a Rel* kascher *inv*.

kowtow [kaʊ'taʊ] *vi* se prosterner (**to** devant).

kudos ['kjuːdɒs] *n* (*glory*) gloire *f*.

L

L, l [el] L, l *m*.

lab [læb] *n Fam* labo *m*. ◆**laboratory** [lə'bɒrət(ə)rɪ, *Am* 'læbrətɔːrɪ] *n* laboratoire *m*; **language l.** laboratoire *m* de langues.

label ['leɪb(ə)l] *n* étiquette *f*; – *vt* (**-ll-**, *Am* **-l-**) (*goods, person*) étiqueter (**as** comme).

laborious [lə'bɔːrɪəs] *a* laborieux.

labour ['leɪbər] *n* (*work, childbirth*) travail *m*; (*workers*) main-d'œuvre *f*; **L.** *Br Pol* les travaillistes *mpl*; **in l.** *Med* au travail; – *a* (*market, situation*) du travail; (*conflict, dispute*) ouvrier; (*relations*) ouvriers-patronat *inv*; **l. force** main-d'œuvre *f*; **l. union** *Am* syndicat *m*; – *vi* (*toil*) peiner; – *vt* **to l. a point** insister sur un point. ◆**–ed** *a* (*style*) laborieux. ◆**–er** *n* (*on roads etc*) manœuvre *m*; *Agr* ouvrier *m* agricole.

laburnum [lə'bɜːnəm] *n Bot* cytise *f*.

labyrinth ['læbɪrɪnθ] *n* labyrinthe *m*.

lace [leɪs] **1** *n* (*cloth*) dentelle *f*. **2** *n* (*of shoe*) lacet *m*; – *vt* **to l. (up)** (*tie up*) lacer. **3** *vt* (*drink*) additionner, arroser (**with** de).

lacerate ['læsəreɪt] *vt* (*flesh etc*) lacérer.

lack [læk] *n* manque *m*; **for l. of** à défaut de; – *vt* manquer de; – *vi* **to be lacking** manquer (**in, for** de).

lackey ['lækɪ] *n Hist & Fig* laquais *m*.

laconic [lə'kɒnɪk] *a* laconique.

lacquer ['lækər] *n* laque *f*; – *vt* laquer.

lad [læd] *n* gars *m*, garçon *m*; **when I was a l.** quand j'étais gosse.

ladder ['lædər] *n* échelle *f*; (*in stocking*) maille *f* filée; – *vti* (*stocking*) filer.

laden ['leɪd(ə)n] *a* chargé (**with** de).

ladle ['leɪd(ə)l] *n* louche *f*.

lady ['leɪdɪ] *n* dame *f*; **a young l.** une jeune fille; (*married*) une jeune femme; **the l. of the house** la maîtresse de maison; **Ladies and Gentlemen!** Mesdames, Mesdemoiselles, Messieurs!; **l. doctor** femme *f* médecin; **l. friend** amie *f*; **ladies' room** *Fig* toilettes *fpl*. ◆**l.-in-'waiting** *n* (*pl* **ladies-in-waiting**) dame *f* d'honneur. ◆**ladybird** *n*, *Am* ◆**ladybug** *n* coccinelle *f*. ◆**ladylike** *a* (*manner*) distingué; **she's (very) l.** elle est très grande dame.

lag [læg] **1** *vi* (**-gg-**) **to l. behind** (*in progress, work*) avoir du retard; (*dawdle*) traîner; **to l. behind s.o.** avoir du retard sur qn; – *n*

time l. (*between events*) décalage *m*; (*between countries*) décalage *m* horaire. **2** *vt* (**-gg-**) (*pipe*) calorifuger.

lager ['lɑːgər] *n* bière *f* blonde.

lagoon [lə'guːn] *n* lagune *f*; (*small, coral*) lagon *m*.

laid [leɪd] *see* **lay**[2]. ◆**l.-'back** *a Fam* relax.

lain [leɪn] *see* **lie**[1].

lair [leər] *n* tanière *f*.

laity ['leɪɪtɪ] *n* **the l.** les laïcs *mpl*.

lake [leɪk] *n* lac *m*.

lamb [læm] *n* agneau *m*. ◆**lambswool** *n* laine *f* d'agneau.

lame [leɪm] *a* (**-er, -est**) (*person, argument*) boiteux; (*excuse*) piètre; **to be l.** boiter. ◆**—ness** *n Med* claudication *f*; (*of excuse*) *Fig* faiblesse *f*.

lament [lə'ment] *n* lamentation *f*; – *vt* **to l. (over)** se lamenter sur. ◆**lamentable** *a* lamentable. ◆**lamen'tation** *n* lamentation *f*.

laminated ['læmɪneɪtɪd] *a* (*metal*) laminé.

lamp [læmp] *n* lampe *f*; (*bulb*) ampoule *f*; *Aut* feu *m*. ◆**lamppost** *n* réverbère *m*. ◆**lampshade** *n* abat-jour *m inv*.

lance [lɑːns] **1** *n* (*weapon*) lance *f*. **2** *vt Med* inciser.

land [lænd] **1** *n* terre *f*; (*country*) pays *m*; **(plot of) l.** terrain *m*; **on dry l.** sur la terre ferme; **no man's l.** *Mil & Fig* no man's land *m inv*; – *a* (*flora, transport etc*) terrestre; (*reform, law*) agraire; (*owner, tax*) foncier. **2** *vi* (*of aircraft*) atterrir, se poser; (*of ship*) mouiller, relâcher; (*of passengers*) débarquer; (*of bomb etc*) (re)tomber; **to l. up** (*end up*) se retrouver; – *vt* (*passengers, cargo*) débarquer; (*aircraft*) poser; (*blow*) *Fig* flanquer (**on** à); (*job, prize etc*) *Fam* décrocher; **to l. s.o. in trouble** *Fam* mettre-qn dans le pétrin; **to be landed with** *Fam* (*person*) avoir sur les bras; (*fine*) ramasser, écoper de. ◆**—ed** *a* (*owning land*) terrien. ◆**—ing** *n* **1** *Av* atterrissage *m*; *Nau* débarquement *m*; **forced l.** atterrissage *m* forcé; **l. stage** débarcadère *m*. **2** *n* (*at top of stairs*) palier *m*; (*floor*) étage *m*. ◆**landlady** *n* logeuse *f*, propriétaire *f*. ◆**landlocked** *a* sans accès à la mer. ◆**landlord** *n* propriétaire *m*; (*of pub*) patron *m*. ◆**landmark** *n* point *m* de repère. ◆**landslide** *n Geol* glissement *m* de terrain, éboulement *m*; *Pol* raz-de-marée *m inv* électoral.

landscape ['lændskeɪp] *n* paysage *m*.

lane [leɪn] *n* (*in country*) chemin *m*; (*in town*) ruelle *f*; (*division of road*) voie *f*; (*line of traffic*) file *f*; *Av Nau Sp* couloir *m*; **bus l.** couloir *m* (*réservé aux autobus*).

language ['læŋgwɪdʒ] *n* (*faculty, style*) langage *m*; (*national tongue*) langue *f*; **computer l.** langage *m* machine; – *a* (*laboratory*) de langues; (*teacher, studies*) de langue(s).

languid ['læŋgwɪd] *a* languissant. ◆**languish** *vi* languir (**for, after** après).

lank [læŋk] *a* (*hair*) plat et terne.

lanky ['læŋkɪ] *a* (**-ier, -iest**) dégingandé.

lantern ['læntən] *n* lanterne *f*; **Chinese l.** lampion *m*.

lap [læp] **1** *n* (*of person*) genoux *mpl*; **the l. of luxury** le plus grand luxe. **2** *n Sp* tour *m* (de piste). **3** *vt* (**-pp-**) **to l. up** (*drink*) laper; (*like very much*) *Fam* adorer; (*believe*) *Fam* gober; – *vi* (*of waves*) clapoter. **4** *vi* (**-pp-**) **to l. over** (*overlap*) se chevaucher.

lapel [lə'pel] *n* (*of jacket etc*) revers *m*.

lapse [læps] **1** *n* (*fault*) faute *f*; (*weakness*) défaillance *f*; **a l. of memory** un trou de mémoire; **a l. in behaviour** un écart de conduite; – *vi* (*err*) commettre une faute; **to l. into** retomber dans. **2** *n* (*interval*) intervalle *m*; **a l. of time** un intervalle (**between** entre). **3** *vi* (*expire*) se périmer, expirer; (*of subscription*) prendre fin.

larceny ['lɑːsənɪ] *n* vol *m* simple.

lard [lɑːd] *n* saindoux *m*.

larder ['lɑːdər] *n* (*cupboard*) garde-manger *m inv*.

large [lɑːdʒ] *a* (**-er, -est**) (*in size or extent*) grand; (*in volume, bulkiness*) gros; (*quantity*) grand, important; **to become** *or* **grow** *or* **get l.** grossir, grandir; **to a l. extent** en grande mesure; **at l.** (*of prisoner, animal*) en liberté; (*as a whole*) en général; **by and l.** dans l'ensemble, généralement. ◆**l.-scale** *a* (*reform*) (fait) sur une grande échelle. ◆**largely** *adv* (*to a great extent*) en grande mesure. ◆**largeness** *n* grandeur *f*; grosseur *f*.

largesse [lɑː'ʒes] *n* largesse *f*.

lark [lɑːk] **1** *n* (*bird*) alouette *f*. **2** *n* (*joke*) *Fam* rigolade *f*, blague *f*; – *vi* **to l. about** *Fam* s'amuser.

larva, *pl* **-vae** ['lɑːvə, -viː] *n* (*of insect*) larve *f*.

larynx ['lærɪŋks] *n Anat* larynx *m*. ◆**laryn'gitis** *n Med* laryngite *f*.

lascivious [lə'sɪvɪəs] *a* lascif.

laser ['leɪzər] *n* laser *m*.

lash[1] [læʃ] *n* (*with whip*) coup *m* de fouet; – *vt* (*strike*) fouetter; (*tie*) attacher (**to** à); **the dog lashed its tail** le chien donna un coup de queue; – *vi* **to l. out** (*spend wildly*) *Fam* claquer son argent; **to l. out at** envoyer des coups à; (*abuse*) *Fig* invectiver; (*criticize*) *Fig* fustiger. ◆**—ings** *npl* **l. of** *Culin Fam* des masses de, une montagne de.

lash[2] [læʃ] *n* (*eyelash*) cil *m*.

lass [læs] *n* jeune fille *f*.

lassitude ['læsɪtjuːd] *n* lassitude *f*.

lasso [læ'suː] *n* (*pl* **-os**) lasso *m*; – *vt* attraper au lasso.

last[1] [lɑːst] *a* dernier; **the l. ten lines** les dix dernières lignes; **l. but one** avant-dernier; **l. night** (*evening*) hier soir; (*during night*) cette nuit; **the day before l.** avant-hier; – *adv* (*lastly*) en dernier lieu, enfin; (*on the last occasion*) (pour) la dernière fois; **to leave l.** sortir le dernier *or* en dernier; – *n* (*person, object*) dernier, -ière *mf*; (*end*) fin *f*; **the l. of the beer/***etc* (*remainder*) le reste de la bière/*etc*; **at (long) l.** enfin. ◆**l.-ditch** *a* désespéré. ◆**l.-minute** *a* de dernière minute. ◆**lastly** *adv* en dernier lieu, enfin.

last[2] [lɑːst] *vi* durer; **to l. (out)** (*endure, resist*) tenir; (*of money, supplies*) durer; **it lasted me ten years** ça m'a duré *or* fait dix ans. ◆**—ing** *a* durable.

latch [lætʃ] **1** *n* loquet *m*; **the door is on the l.** la porte n'est pas fermée à clef. **2** *vi* **to l. on to** *Fam* (*grab*) s'accrocher à; (*understand*) saisir.

late[1] [leɪt] *a* **(-er, -est)** (*not on time*) en retard **(for** à); (*former*) ancien; (*meal, fruit, season, hour*) tardif; (*stage*) avancé; (*edition*) dernier; **to be l.** (*of person, train etc*) être en retard, avoir du retard; **to be l. (in) coming** arriver en retard; **he's an hour l.** il a une heure de retard; **to make s.o. l.** mettre qn en retard; **it's l.** il est tard; **Easter/***etc* **is l.** Pâques/*etc* est tard; **in l. June/***etc* fin juin/*etc*; **a later edition/***etc* (*more recent*) une édition/*etc* plus récente; **the latest edition/***etc* (*last*) la dernière édition/*etc*; **in later life** plus tard dans la vie; **to take a later train** prendre un train plus tard; **at a later date** à une date ultérieure; **the latest date** la date limite; **at the latest** au plus tard; **of l.** dernièrement; – *adv* (*in the day, season etc*) tard; (*not on time*) en retard; **it's getting l.** il se fait tard; **later (on)** plus tard; **not** *or* **no later than** pas plus tard que. ◆**latecomer** *n* retardataire *mf*. ◆**lately** *adv* dernièrement. ◆**lateness** *n* (*of person, train etc*) retard *m*; **constant l.** des retards continuels; **the l. of the hour** l'heure tardive.

late[2] [leɪt] *a* **the l. Mr Smith/***etc* (*deceased*) feu Monsieur Smith/*etc*; **our l. friend** notre regretté ami.

latent ['leɪtənt] *a* latent.

lateral ['lætərəl] *a* latéral.

lathe [leɪð] *n Tech* tour *m*.

lather ['lɑːðər] *n* mousse *f*; – *vt* savonner; – *vi* mousser.

Latin ['lætɪn] *a* latin; **L. America** Amérique *f* latine; **L. American** d'Amérique latine; – *n* (*person*) Latin, -ine *mf*; (*language*) latin *m*.

latitude ['lætɪtjuːd] *n Geog* & *Fig* latitude *f*.

latrines [lə'triːnz] *npl* latrines *fpl*.

latter ['lætər] *a* (*later, last-named*) dernier; (*second*) deuxième; – *n* dernier, -ière *mf*; second, -onde *mf*. ◆**—ly** *adv* dernièrement; (*late in life*) sur le tard.

lattice ['lætɪs] *n* treillis *m*.

laudable ['lɔːdəb(ə)l] *a* louable.

laugh [lɑːf] *n* rire *m*; **to have a good l.** bien rire; – *vi* rire **(at, about** de); **to l. to oneself** rire en soi-même; – *vt* **to l. off** tourner en plaisanterie. ◆**—ing** *a* riant; **it's no l. matter** il n'y a pas de quoi rire; **to be the l.-stock of** être la risée de. ◆**—able** *a* ridicule. ◆**laughter** *n* rire(s) *m(pl)*; **to roar with l.** rire aux éclats.

launch [lɔːntʃ] **1** *n* (*motor boat*) vedette *f*; (*pleasure boat*) bateau *m* de plaisance. **2** *vt* (*rocket, boat, fashion etc*) lancer; – *vi* **to l. (out) into** (*begin*) se lancer dans; – *n* lancement *m*. ◆**—ing** *n* lancement *m*.

launder ['lɔːndər] *vt* (*clothes*) blanchir; (*money from drugs etc*) *Fig* blanchir. ◆**—ing** *n* blanchissage *m*. ◆**launde'rette** *n*, *Am* ◆**laundromat** *n* laverie *f* automatique. ◆**laundry** *n* (*place*) blanchisserie *f*; (*clothes*) linge *m*.

laurel ['lɒrəl] *n Bot* laurier *m*.

lava ['lɑːvə] *n Geol* lave *f*.

lavatory ['lævətrɪ] *n* cabinets *mpl*.

lavender ['lævɪndər] *n* lavande *f*.

lavish ['lævɪʃ] *a* prodigue **(with** de); (*helping, meal*) généreux; (*decor, house etc*) somptueux; (*expenditure*) excessif; – *vt* prodiguer **(sth on s.o.** qch à qn). ◆**—ly** *adv* (*to give*) généreusement; (*to furnish*) somptueusement.

law [lɔː] *n* (*rule, rules*) loi *f*; (*study, profession, system*) droit *m*; **court of l., l. court** cour *f* de justice; **l. and order** l'ordre public. ◆**l.-abiding** *a* respectueux des lois. ◆**lawful** *a* (*action*) légal; (*child, wife etc*) légitime. ◆**lawfully** *adv* légalement. ◆**lawless** *a* (*country*) anarchique. ◆**lawlessness** *n* anarchie *f*. ◆**lawsuit** *n* procès *m*.

lawn [lɔːn] *n* pelouse *f*, gazon *m*; **l. mower** tondeuse *f* (à gazon); **l. tennis** tennis *m* (sur gazon).

lawyer ['lɔːjər] *n* (*in court*) avocat *m*; (*author,* *legal expert*) juriste *m*; (*for wills, sales*) notaire *m*.

lax [læks] *a* (*person*) négligent; (*discipline, behaviour*) relâché; **to be l. in doing** faire avec négligence. ◆**laxity** *n*, ◆**laxness** *n* négligence *f*; relâchement *m*.

laxative ['læksətɪv] *n* & *a Med* laxatif (*m*).

lay[1] [leɪ] *a* (*non-religious*) laïque; (*non-specialized*) d'un profane; **l. person** profane *mf*. ◆**layman** *n* (*pl* **-men**) (*non-specialist*) profane *mf*.

lay[2] [leɪ] (*pt & pp* **laid**) **1** *vt* (*put down, place*) poser; (*table*) mettre; (*blanket*) étendre (over sur); (*trap*) tendre; (*money*) miser (on sur); (*accusation*) porter; (*ghost*) exorciser; **to l. a bet** parier; **to l. bare** mettre à nu; **to l. waste** ravager; **to l. s.o. open to** exposer qn à; **to l. one's hands on** mettre la main sur; **to l. a hand** *or* **a finger on s.o.** lever la main sur qn; **to l. down** poser; (*arms*) déposer; (*condition*) (im)poser; **to l. down the law** faire la loi (to à); **to l. s.o. off** (*worker*) licencier qn; **to l. on** (*install*) mettre, installer; (*supply*) fournir; **to l. it on (thick)** *Fam* y aller un peu fort; **to l. out** (*garden*) dessiner; (*house*) concevoir; (*prepare*) préparer; (*display*) disposer; (*money*) *Fam* dépenser (on pour); **to be laid up** (*in bed*) *Med* être alité; – *vi* **to l. into** *Fam* attaquer; **to l. off** (*stop*) *Fam* arrêter; **to l. off s.o.** (*leave alone*) *Fam* laisser qn tranquille; **l. off!** (*don't touch*) *Fam* pas touche!; **to l. out** *Fam* payer. **2** *vt* (*egg*) pondre; – *vi* (*of bird etc*) pondre. ◆**layabout** *n Fam* fainéant, -ante *mf*. ◆**lay-by** *n* (*pl* **-bys**) *Aut* aire *f* de stationnement *or* de repos. ◆**lay-off** *n* (*of worker*) licenciement *m*. **layout** *n* disposition *f*; *Typ* mise *f* en pages. ◆**lay-over** *n Am* halte *f*.

lay[3] [leɪ] *see* **lie**[1].

layer ['leɪər] *n* couche *f*.

laze [leɪz] *vi* **to l. (about** *or* **around)** paresser. ◆**lazy** *a* (**-ier, -iest**) (*person etc*) paresseux; (*holiday*) passé à ne rien faire. ◆**lazybones** *n Fam* paresseux, -euse *mf*.

lb *abbr* (*libra*) = **pound** (*weight*).

lead[1] [liːd] *vt* (*pt & pp* **led**) (*conduct*) mener, conduire (to à); (*team, government etc*) diriger; (*regiment*) commander; (*life*) mener; **to l. s.o. in/out/***etc* faire entrer/sortir/*etc* qn; **to l. s.o. to do** (*induce*) amener qn à faire; **to l. the way** montrer le chemin; **to l. the world** tenir le premier rang mondial; **easily led** influençable; **to l. away** *or* **off** emmener; **to l. back** ramener; **to l. on** (*tease*) faire marcher; – *vi* (*of street etc*) mener, conduire (to à); (*in match*) mener; (*in race*) être en tête; (*go ahead*) aller devant; **to l. to** (*result in*) aboutir à; (*cause*) causer, amener; **to l. up to** (*of street*) conduire à, mener à; (*precede*) précéder; (*approach gradually*) en venir à; – *n* (*distance or time ahead*) *Sp* avance *f* (**over** sur); (*example*) exemple *m*, initiative *f*; (*clue*) piste *f*, indice *m*; (*star part*) *Th* rôle *m* principal; (*leash*) laisse *f*; (*wire*) *El* fil *m*; **to take the l.** *Sp* prendre la tête; **to be in the l.** (*in race*) être en tête; (*in match*) mener. ◆**leading** *a* (*main*) principal; (*important*) important; (*front*) de tête; **the l. author** l'auteur principal *or* le plus important; **a l. figure** un personnage marquant; **the l. lady** *Cin* la vedette féminine; **l. article** *Journ* éditorial *m*. ◆**leader** *n* chef *m*; *Pol* dirigeant, -ante *mf*; (*of strike, riot*) meneur, -euse *mf*; (*guide*) guide *m*; (*article*) *Journ* éditorial *m*. ◆**leadership** *n* direction *f*; (*qualities*) qualités *fpl* de chef; (*leaders*) *Pol* dirigeants *mpl*.

lead[2] [led] *n* (*metal*) plomb *m*; (*of pencil*) mine *f*; **l. pencil** crayon *m* à mine de plomb. ◆**leaden** *a* (*sky*) de plomb.

leaf [liːf] **1** *n* (*pl* **leaves**) *Bot* feuille *f*; (*of book*) feuillet *m*; (*of table*) rallonge *f*. **2** *vi* **to l. through** (*book*) feuilleter. ◆**leaflet** *n* prospectus *m*; (*containing instructions*) notice *f*. ◆**leafy** *a* (**-ier, -iest**) (*tree*) feuillu.

league [liːg] *n* **1** (*alliance*) ligue *f*; *Sp* championnat *m*; **in l. with** *Pej* de connivence avec. **2** (*measure*) *Hist* lieue *f*.

leak [liːk] *n* (*in pipe, information etc*) fuite *f*; (*in boat*) voie *f* d'eau; – *vi* (*of liquid, pipe, tap etc*) fuir; (*of ship*) faire eau; **to l. out** (*of information*) *Fig* être divulgué; – *vt* (*liquid*) répandre; (*information*) *Fig* divulguer. ◆**–age** *n* fuite *f*; (*amount lost*) perte *f*. ◆**leaky** *a* (**-ier, -iest**) *a* (*kettle etc*) qui fuit.

lean[1] [liːn] *a* (**-er, -est**) (*thin*) maigre; (*year*) difficile. ◆**–ness** *n* maigreur *f*.

lean[2] [liːn] *vi* (*pt & pp* **leaned** *or* **leant** [lent]) (*of object*) pencher; (*of person*) se pencher; **to l. against/on** (*of person*) s'appuyer contre/sur; **to l. back against** s'adosser à; **to l. on s.o.** (*influence*) *Fam* faire pression sur qn (**to do** pour faire); **to l. forward** *or* **over** (*of person*) se pencher (en avant); **to l. over** (*of object*) pencher; – *vt* appuyer (**against** contre); **to l. one's head on/out of** pencher la tête sur/par. ◆**–ing 1** *a* penché; **l. against** (*resting*) appuyé contre. **2** *npl* tendances *fpl* (**towards** à). ◆**lean-to** *n* (*pl* **-tos**) (*building*) appentis *m*.

leap [liːp] *n* (*jump*) bond *m*, saut *m*; (*change, increase etc*) *Fig* bond *m*; **l. year** année *f* bissextile; **in leaps and bounds** à pas de géant; – *vi* (*pt & pp* **leaped** *or* **leapt** [lept]) bondir, sauter; (*of flames*) jaillir; (*of profits*) faire un bond; **to l. to one's feet, l. up** se lever d'un bond. ◆**leapfrog** *n* saute-mouton *m inv*.

learn [lɜːn] *vt* (*pt & pp* **learned** *or* **learnt**) apprendre (**that** que); **to l. (how) to do** apprendre à faire; – *vi* apprendre; **to l. about** (*study*) étudier; (*hear about*) apprendre. ◆**—ed** [-ɪd] *a* savant. ◆**—ing** *n* érudition *f*, savoir *m*; (*of language*) apprentissage *m* (**of** de). ◆**—er** *n* débutant, -ante *mf*.

lease [liːs] *n Jur* bail *m*; **a new l. of life** *or Am* **on life** un regain de vie, une nouvelle vie; – *vt* (*house etc*) louer à bail. ◆**leasehold** *n* propriété *f* louée à bail.

leash [liːʃ] *n* laisse *f*; **on a l.** en laisse.

least [liːst] *a* **the l.** (*smallest amount of*) le moins de; (*slightest*) le *or* la moindre; **he has (the) l. talent** il a le moins de talent (**of all** de tous); **the l. effort/noise/***etc* le moindre effort/bruit/*etc*; – *n* **the l.** le moins; **at l.** (*with quantity*) au moins; **at l. that's what she says** du moins c'est ce qu'elle dit; **not in the l.** pas du tout; – *adv* (*to work, eat etc*) le moins; (*with adjective*) le *or* la moins; **l. of all** (*especially not*) surtout pas.

leather ['leðər] *n* cuir *m*; **(wash) l.** peau *f* de chamois.

leave [liːv] **1** *n* (*holiday*) congé *m*; (*consent*) & *Mil* permission *f*; **l. of absence** congé *m* exceptionnel; **to take (one's) l. of** prendre congé de. **2** *vt* (*pt & pp* **left**) (*allow to remain, forget*) laisser; (*depart from*) quitter; (*room*) sortir de, quitter; **to l. the table** sortir de table; **to l. s.o. in charge of s.o./sth** laisser à qn la garde de qn/qch; **to l. sth with s.o.** (*entrust, give*) laisser qch à qn; **to be left (over)** rester; **there's no hope/bread/***etc* **left** il ne reste plus d'espoir/de pain/*etc*; **l. it to me!** laisse-moi faire!; **I'll l. it (up) to you** je m'en remets à toi; **to l. go (of)** (*release*) lâcher; **to l. behind** laisser; (*surpass*) dépasser; (*in race*) *Sp* distancer; **to l. off** (*lid*) ne pas (re)mettre; **to l. off doing** (*stop*) *Fam* arrêter de faire; **to l. on** (*hat, gloves*) garder; **to l. out** (*forget*) omettre; (*exclude*) exclure; – *vi* (*depart*) partir (**from** de, **for** pour); **to l. off** (*stop*) *Fam* s'arrêter. ◆**leavings** *npl* restes *mpl*.

Lebanon ['lebənən] *n* Liban *m*. ◆**Leba'nese** *a* & *n* libanais, -aise (*mf*).

lecher ['letʃər] *n* débauché *m*. ◆**lecherous** *a* lubrique, luxurieux.

lectern ['lektən] *n* (*for giving speeches*) pupitre *m*; *Rel* lutrin *m*.

lecture ['lektʃər] **1** *n* (*public speech*) conférence *f*; (*as part of series*) *Univ* cours *m* (magistral); – *vi* faire une conférence *or* un cours; **I l. in chemistry** je suis professeur de chimie. **2** *vt* (*scold*) *Fig* faire la morale à, sermonner; – *n* (*scolding*) sermon *m*. ◆**lecturer** *n* conférencier, -ière *mf*; *Univ* enseignant, -ante *mf*. ◆**lectureship** *n* poste *m* à l'université.

led [led] *see* **lead**[1].

ledge [ledʒ] *n* rebord *m*; (*on mountain*) saillie *f*.

ledger ['ledʒər] *n Com* registre *m*, grand livre *m*.

leech [liːtʃ] *n* (*worm, person*) sangsue *f*.

leek [liːk] *n* poireau *m*.

leer [lɪər] *vi* **to l. (at)** lorgner; – *n* regard *m* sournois.

leeway ['liːweɪ] *n* (*freedom*) liberté *f* d'action; (*safety margin*) marge *f* de sécurité.

left[1] [left] *see* **leave 2**; – *a* **l. luggage office** consigne *f*. ◆**leftovers** *npl* restes *mpl*.

left[2] [left] *a* (*side, hand etc*) gauche; – *adv* à gauche; – *n* gauche *f*; **on** *or* **to the l.** à gauche (**of** de). ◆**l.-hand** *a* à *or* de gauche; **on the l.-hand side** à gauche (**of** de). ◆**l.-'handed** *a* (*person*) gaucher. ◆**l.-wing** *a Pol* de gauche. ◆**leftist** *n* & *a Pol* gauchiste (*mf*).

leg [leg] *n* jambe *f*; (*of bird, dog etc*) patte *f*; (*of lamb*) *Culin* gigot *m*; (*of chicken*) *Culin* cuisse *f*; (*of table*) pied *m*; (*of journey*) étape *f*; **to pull s.o.'s l.** (*make fun of*) mettre qn en boîte; **on its last legs** (*machine etc*) *Fam* prêt à claquer; **to be on one's last legs** *Fam* avoir un pied dans la tombe. ◆**l.-room** *n* place *f* pour les jambes. ◆**leggy** *a* (**-ier, -iest**) (*person*) aux longues jambes, tout en jambes.

legacy ['legəsɪ] *n Jur & Fig* legs *m*.

legal ['liːg(ə)l] *a* (*lawful*) légal; (*mind, affairs, adviser*) juridique; (*aid, error*) judiciaire; **l. expert** juriste *m*; **l. proceedings** procès *m*. ◆**le'gality** *n* légalité *f*. ◆**legalize** *vt* légaliser. ◆**legally** *adv* légalement.

legation [lɪ'geɪʃ(ə)n] *n Pol* légation *f*.

legend ['ledʒənd] *n* (*story, inscription etc*) légende *f*. ◆**legendary** *a* légendaire.

leggings ['legɪŋz] *npl* jambières *fpl*.

legible ['ledʒəb(ə)l] *a* lisible. ◆**legi'bility** *n* lisibilité *f*. ◆**legibly** *adv* lisiblement.

legion ['liːdʒən] *n Mil & Fig* légion *f*.

legislate ['ledʒɪsleɪt] *vi* légiférer. ◆**legis-**

'lation *n* (*laws*) législation *f*; (*action*) élaboration *f* des lois; (**piece of**) **l.** loi *f*. ◆**legislative** *a* législatif.

legitimate [lɪ'dʒɪtɪmət] *a* (*reason, child etc*) légitime. ◆**legitimacy** *n* légitimité *f*.

legless ['legləs] *a* (*drunk*) *Fam* (complètement) bourré.

leisure ['leʒər, *Am* 'liːʒər] *n* **l.** (**time**) loisirs *mpl*; **l. activities** loisirs *mpl*; **moment of l.** moment *m* de loisir; **at (one's) l.** à tête reposée. ◆**—ly** *a* (*walk, occupation*) peu fatigant; (*meal, life*) calme; **at a l. pace, in a l. way** sans se presser.

lemon ['lemən] *n* citron *m*; **l. drink, l. squash** citronnade *f*; **l. tea** thé *m* au citron. ◆**lemo'nade** *n* (*fizzy*) limonade *f*; (*still*) *Am* citronnade *f*.

lend [lend] *vt* (*pt & pp* **lent**) prêter (**to** à); (*charm, colour etc*) *Fig* donner (**to** à); **to l. credence to** ajouter foi à. ◆**—ing** *n* prêt *m*. ◆**—er** *n* prêteur, -euse *mf*.

length [leŋθ] *n* longueur *f*; (*section of pipe etc*) morceau *m*; (*of road*) tronçon *m*; (*of cloth*) métrage *m*; (*of horse, swimming pool*) *Sp* longueur *f*; (*duration*) durée *f*; **l. of time** temps *m*; **at l.** (*at last*) enfin; **at (great) l.** (*in detail*) dans le détail; (*for a long time*) longuement; **to go to great lengths** se donner beaucoup de mal (**to do** pour faire). ◆**lengthen** *vt* allonger; (*in time*) prolonger. ◆**lengthwise** *adv* dans le sens de la longueur. ◆**lengthy** *a* (**-ier, -iest**) long.

lenient ['liːnɪənt] *a* indulgent (**to** envers). ◆**leniency** *n* indulgence *f*. ◆**leniently** *adv* avec indulgence.

lens [lenz] *n* lentille *f*; (*in spectacles*) verre *m*; *Phot* objectif *m*.

Lent [lent] *n Rel* Carême *m*.

lentil ['lent(ə)l] *n Bot Culin* lentille *f*.

leopard ['lepəd] *n* léopard *m*.

leotard ['liːətɑːd] *n* collant *m* (*de danse*).

leper ['lepər] *n* lépreux, -euse *mf*. ◆**leprosy** *n* lèpre *f*.

lesbian ['lezbɪən] *n & a* lesbienne (*f*).

lesion ['liːʒ(ə)n] *n Med* lésion *f*.

less [les] *a & n* moins (de) (**than** que); **l. time/***etc* moins de temps/*etc*; **she has l. (than you)** elle en a moins (que toi); **l. than a kilo/ten/***etc* (*with quantity, number*) moins d'un kilo/de dix/*etc*; – *adv* (*to sleep, know etc*) moins (**than** que); **l. (often)** moins souvent; **l. and l.** de moins en moins; **one l.** un(e) de moins; – *prep* moins; **l. six francs** moins six francs. ◆**lessen** *vti* diminuer. ◆**lessening** *n* diminution *f*. ◆**lesser** *a* moindre; – *n* **the l. of** le *or* la moindre de.

-less [ləs] *suffix* sans; **childless** sans enfants.

lesson ['les(ə)n] *n* leçon *f*; **an English l.** une leçon *or* un cours d'anglais; **I have lessons now** j'ai cours maintenant.

lest [lest] *conj Lit* de peur que (+ ne + *sub*).

let[1] [let] **1** *vt* (*pt & pp* **let**, *pres p* **letting**) (*allow*) laisser (**s.o. do** qn faire); **to l. s.o. have sth** donner qch à qn; **to l. away** (*allow to leave*) laisser partir; **to l. down** (*lower*) baisser; (*hair*) dénouer; (*dress*) rallonger; (*tyre*) dégonfler; **to l. s.o. down** (*disappoint*) décevoir qn; **don't l. me down** je compte sur toi; **the car l. me down** la voiture est tombée en panne. ◆**letdown** *n* déception *f*; **to l. in** (*person, dog*) faire entrer; (*noise, light*) laisser entrer; **to l. in the clutch** *Aut* embrayer; **to l. s.o. in on** *Fig* mettre qn au courant de; **to l. oneself in for** (*expense*) se laisser entraîner à; (*trouble*) s'attirer; **to l. off** (*bomb*) faire éclater; (*firework, gun*) faire partir; **to l. s.o. off** laisser partir qn; (*not punish*) ne pas punir qn; (*clear*) *Jur* disculper qn; **to be l. off with** (*a fine etc*) s'en tirer avec; **to l. s.o. off doing** dispenser qn de faire; **to l. on that** *Fam* (*admit*) avouer que; (*reveal*) dire que; **to l. out** faire *or* laisser sortir; (*prisoner*) relâcher; (*cry, secret*) laisser échapper; (*skirt*) élargir; **to l. s.o. out (of the house)** ouvrir la porte à qn; **to l. out the clutch** *Aut* débrayer; – *vi* **not to l. on** *Fam* ne rien dire, garder la bouche cousue; **to l. up** (*of rain, person etc*) s'arrêter. ◆**letup** *n* arrêt *m*, répit *m*. **2** *v aux* **l. us eat/go/***etc*, **l.'s eat/go/***etc* mangeons/partons/*etc*; **l.'s go for a stroll** allons nous promener; **l. him come** qu'il vienne.

let[2] [let] *vt* (*pt & pp* **let**, *pres p* **letting**) **to l. (off** *or* **out)** (*house, room etc*) louer. ◆**letting** *n* (*renting*) location *f*.

lethal ['liːθ(ə)l] *a* mortel; (*weapon*) meurtrier.

lethargy ['leθədʒɪ] *n* léthargie *f*. ◆**le'thargic** *a* léthargique.

letter ['letər] *n* (*missive, character*) lettre *f*; **man of letters** homme *m* de lettres; **l. bomb** lettre *f* piégée; **l. writer** correspondant, -ante *mf*. ◆**letterbox** *n* boîte *f* aux *or* à lettres. ◆**letterhead** *n* en-tête *m*. ◆**lettering** *n* (*letters*) lettres *fpl*; (*on tomb*) inscription *f*.

lettuce ['letɪs] *n* laitue *f*, salade *f*.

leuk(a)emia [luː'kiːmɪə] *n* leucémie *f*.

level ['lev(ə)l] **1** *n* niveau *m*; **on the l.** (*speed*) en palier; – *a* (*surface*) plat, uni; (*object on surface*) horizontal; (*spoonful*) ras; (*equal in score*) à égalité (**with** avec); (*in height*) au même niveau, à la même hauteur (**with** que); **l. crossing** *Rail* passage *m* à niveau; – *vt* (**-ll-**, *Am* **-l-**) (*surface, differences*) niveler, aplanir; (*plane down*) raboter; (*building*) raser; (*gun*) braquer; (*accusation*) lancer (**at** contre); – *vi* **to l. off** *or* **out** (*stabilize*) *Fig* se stabiliser. **2** *n* **on the l.** *Fam* (*honest*) honnête, franc; (*frankly*) honnêtement, franchement; – *vi* (**-ll-**, *Am* **-l-**) **to l. with** *Fam* être franc avec. ◆**l.-'headed** *a* équilibré.

lever ['liːvər, *Am* 'levər] *n* levier *m*. ◆**leverage** *n* (*power*) influence *f*.

levity ['levɪtɪ] *n* légèreté *f*.

levy ['levɪ] *vt* (*tax, troops*) lever; – *n* (*tax*) impôt *m*.

lewd [luːd] *a* (**-er, -est**) obscène.

liable ['laɪəb(ə)l] *a* **l. to** (*dizziness etc*) sujet à; (*fine, tax*) passible de; **he's l. to do** il est susceptible de faire, il pourrait faire; **l. for** (*responsible*) responsable de. ◆**lia'bility** *n* responsabilité *f* (**for** de); (*disadvantage*) handicap *m*; *pl* (*debts*) dettes *fpl*.

liaise [lɪ'eɪz] *vi* travailler en liaison (**with** avec). ◆**liaison** *n* (*association*) & *Mil* liaison *f*.

liar ['laɪər] *n* menteur, -euse *mf*.

libel ['laɪb(ə)l] *vt* (**-ll-**, *Am* **-l-**) diffamer (par écrit); – *n* diffamation *f*.

liberal ['lɪbərəl] *a* (*open-minded*) & *Pol* libéral; (*generous*) généreux (**with** de); – *n* *Pol* libéral, -ale *mf*. ◆**liberalism** *n* libéralisme *m*.

liberate ['lɪbəreɪt] *vt* libérer. ◆**libe'ration** *n* libération *f*. ◆**liberator** *n* libérateur, -trice *mf*.

liberty ['lɪbətɪ] *n* liberté *f*; **at l. to do** libre de faire; **what a l.!** (*cheek*) *Fam* quel culot!; **to take liberties with s.o.** se permettre des familiarités avec qn.

Libra ['liːbrə] *n* (*sign*) la Balance.

library ['laɪbrərɪ] *n* bibliothèque *f*. ◆**li'brarian** *n* bibliothécaire *mf*.

libretto [lɪ'bretəʊ] *n* (*pl* **-os**) *Mus* livret *m*.

Libya ['lɪbjə] *n* Libye *f*. ◆**Libyan** *a* & *n* libyen, -enne (*mf*).

lice [laɪs] *see* **louse**.

licence, *Am* **license** ['laɪsəns] *n* **1** permis *m*, autorisation *f*; (*for driving*) permis *m*; *Com* licence *f*; **pilot's l.** brevet *m* de pilote; **l. fee** *Rad TV* redevance *f*; **l. plate/number** *Aut* plaque *f*/numéro *m* d'immatriculation. **2** (*freedom*) licence *f*.

license ['laɪsəns] *vt* accorder une licence à, autoriser; **licensed premises** établissement *m* qui a une licence de débit de boissons.

licit ['lɪsɪt] *a* licite.

lick [lɪk] *vt* lécher; (*defeat*) *Fam* écraser; (*beat physically*) *Fam* rosser; **to be licked** (*by problem etc*) *Fam* être dépassé; – *n* coup *m* de langue; **a l. of paint** un coup de peinture. ◆**—ing** *n* *Fam* (*defeat*) déculottée *f*; (*beating*) rossée *f*.

licorice ['lɪkərɪʃ, -rɪs] *n* *Am* réglisse *f*.

lid [lɪd] *n* **1** (*of box etc*) couvercle *m*. **2** (*of eye*) paupière *f*.

lido ['liːdəʊ] *n* (*pl* **-os**) piscine *f* (découverte).

lie[1] [laɪ] *vi* (*pt* **lay**, *pp* **lain**, *pres p* **lying**) (*in flat position*) s'allonger, s'étendre; (*remain*) rester; (*be*) être; (*in grave*) reposer; **to be lying** (*on the grass etc*) être allongé *or* étendu; **he lay asleep** il dormait; **here lies** (*on tomb*) ci-gît; **the problem lies in** le problème réside dans; **to l. heavy on** (*of meal etc*) & *Fig* peser sur; **to l. low** (*hide*) se cacher; (*be inconspicuous*) se faire tout petit; **to l. about** *or* **around** (*of objects, person*) traîner; **to l. down, to have a l.-down** s'allonger, se coucher; **lying down** (*resting*) allongé, couché; **to l. in, to have a l.-in** *Fam* faire la grasse matinée.

lie[2] [laɪ] *vi* (*pt* & *pp* **lied**, *pres p* **lying**) (*tell lies*) mentir; – *n* mensonge *m*; **to give the l. to** (*show as untrue*) démentir.

lieu [luː] *n* **in l. of** au lieu de.

lieutenant [lef'tenənt, *Am* luː'tenənt] *n* lieutenant *m*.

life [laɪf] *n* (*pl* **lives**) vie *f*; (*of battery, machine*) durée *f* (de vie); **to come to l.** (*of street, party etc*) s'animer; **at your time of l.** à ton âge; **loss of l.** perte *f* en vies humaines; **true to l.** conforme à la réalité; **to take one's (own) l.** se donner la mort; **bird l.** les oiseaux *mpl*; – *a* (*cycle, style*) de vie; (*belt, raft*) de sauvetage; (*force*) vital; **l. annuity** rente *f* viagère; **l. blood** *Fig* âme *f*; **l. insurance** assurance-vie *f*; **l. jacket** gilet *m* de sauvetage; **l. peer** pair *m* à vie. ◆**lifeboat** *n* canot *m* de sauvetage. ◆**lifebuoy** *n* bouée *f* de sauvetage. ◆**lifeguard** *n* maître-nageur *m* sauveteur. ◆**lifeless** *a* sans vie. ◆**lifelike** *a* qui semble vivant. ◆**lifelong** *a* de toute sa vie; (*friend*) de toujours. ◆**lifesaving** *n* sauvetage *m*. ◆**lifesize(d)** *a* grandeur nature *inv*. ◆**lifetime** *n* vie *f*; *Fig* éternité *f*; **in my l.** de mon vivant; **a once-in-a-l. experience/*etc*** l'expérience/*etc* de votre vie.

lift [lɪft] *vt* lever; (*sth heavy*) (sou)lever; (*ban, siege*) *Fig* lever; (*idea etc*) *Fig* voler, prendre (**from** à); **to l. down** *or* **off** (*take down*) descendre (**from** de); **to l. out** (*take out*) sortir; **to l. up** (*arm, eyes*) lever; (*object*) (sou)lever; – *vi* (*of fog*) se lever; **to l. off** (*of space vehicle*) décoller; – *n* (*elevator*) ascenseur *m*; **to give s.o. a l.** emmener *or* accompagner qn (en voiture) (**to** à). ◆**l.-off** *n Av* décollage *m*.

ligament ['lɪgəmənt] *n* ligament *m*.

light[1] [laɪt] **1** *n* lumière *f*; (*daylight*) jour *m*, lumière *f*; (*on vehicle*) feu *m*, (*headlight*) phare *m*; **by the l. of** à la lumière de; **in the l. of** (*considering*) à la lumière de; **in that l.** *Fig* sous ce jour *or* cet éclairage; **against the l.** à contre-jour; **to bring to l.** mettre en lumière; **to come to l.** être découvert; **to throw l. on** (*matter*) éclaircir; **do you have a l.?** (*for cigarette*) est-ce que vous avez du feu?; **to set l. to** mettre le feu à; **leading l.** (*person*) *Fig* phare *m*, sommité *f*, lumière *f*; **l. bulb** ampoule *f* (électrique); – *vt* (*pt & pp* **lit** *or* **lighted**) (*candle etc*) allumer; (*match*) gratter; **to l. (up)** (*room*) éclairer; – *vi* **to l. up** (*of window*) s'allumer. **2** *a* (*bright, not dark*) clair; **a l. green jacket** une veste vert clair. ◆**—ing** *n El* éclairage *m*; **the l. of** (*candle etc*) l'allumage *m* de. ◆**lighten**[1] *vt* (*light up*) éclairer; (*colour, hair*) éclaircir. ◆**lighter** *n* (*for cigarettes etc*) briquet *m*; *Culin* allume-gaz *m inv*. ◆**lighthouse** *n* phare *m*. ◆**lightness**[1] *n* clarté *f*.

light[2] [laɪt] *a* (*in weight, quantity, strength etc*) léger; (*task*) facile; **l. rain** pluie *f* fine; **to travel l.** voyager avec peu de bagages. ◆**l.-'fingered** *a* chapardeur. ◆**l.-'headed** *a* (*giddy, foolish*) étourdi. ◆**l.-'hearted** *a* gai. ◆**lighten**[2] *vt* (*a load*) alléger. ◆**lightly** *adv* légèrement. ◆**lightness**[2] *n* légèreté *f*.

light[3] [laɪt] *vi* (*pt & pp* **lit** *or* **lighted**) **to l. upon** trouver par hasard.

lightning ['laɪtnɪŋ] *n Met* (*light*) éclair *m*; (*charge*) foudre *f*; **(flash of) l.** éclair *m*; – *a* (*speed*) foudroyant; (*visit*) éclair *inv*; **l. conductor** paratonnerre *m*.

lightweight ['laɪtweɪt] *a* (*cloth etc*) léger; (*not serious*) pas sérieux, léger.

like[1] [laɪk] *a* (*alike*) semblable, pareil; – *prep* comme; **l. this** comme ça; **what's he l.?** (*physically, as character*) comment est-il?; **to be** *or* **look l.** ressembler à; **what was the book l.?** comment as-tu trouvé le livre?; **I have one l. it** j'en ai un pareil; – *adv* **nothing l. as big**/*etc* loin d'être aussi grand/*etc*; – *conj* (*as*) *Fam* comme; **it's l. I say** c'est comme je vous le dis; – *n* **... and the l.** ... et ainsi de suite; **the l. of which we shan't see again** comme on n'en reverra plus; **the likes of you** des gens de ton acabit.

lik/e[2] [laɪk] *vt* aimer (bien) (**to do, doing** faire); **I l. him** je l'aime bien, il me plaît; **she likes it here** elle se plaît ici; **to l. best** préférer; **I'd l. to come** (*want*) je voudrais (bien) *or* j'aimerais (bien) venir; **I'd l. a kilo of apples** je voudrais un kilo de pommes; **would you l. a cigar?** voulez-vous un cigare?; **if you l.** si vous voulez; **(how) would you l. to come?** ça te plairait *or* te dirait de venir?; – *npl* **one's likes** nos goûts *mpl*. ◆**—ing** *n* **a l. for** (*person*) de la sympathie pour; (*thing*) du goût pour; **to my l.** à mon goût. ◆**likeable** *a* sympathique.

likely ['laɪklɪ] *a* (**-ier, -iest**) (*event, result etc*) probable; (*excuse*) vraisemblable; (*place*) propice; (*candidate*) prometteur; **a l. excuse!** *Iron* belle excuse!; **it's l. (that) she'll come** il est probable qu'elle viendra; **he's l. to come** il viendra probablement; **he's not l. to come** il ne risque pas de venir; – *adv* **very l.** très probablement; **not l.!** pas question! ◆**likelihood** *n* probabilité *f*; **there's little l. that** il y a peu de chances que (+ *sub*).

liken ['laɪkən] *vt* comparer (**to** à).

likeness ['laɪknɪs] *n* ressemblance *f*; **a family l.** un air de famille; **it's a good l.** c'est très ressemblant.

likewise ['laɪkwaɪz] *adv* (*similarly*) de même, pareillement.

lilac ['laɪlək] *n* lilas *m*; – *a* (*colour*) lilas *inv*.

Lilo® ['laɪləʊ] *n* (*pl* **-os**) matelas *m* pneumatique.

lilt [lɪlt] *n Mus* cadence *f*.

lily ['lɪlɪ] *n* lis *m*, lys *m*; **l. of the valley** muguet *m*.

limb [lɪm] *n Anat* membre *m*; **to be out on a l.** *Fig* être le seul de son opinion.

limber ['lɪmbər] *vi* **to l. up** faire des exercices d'assouplissement.

limbo (in) [ɪn'lɪmbəʊ] *adv* (*uncertain, waiting*) dans l'expectative.

lime [laɪm] *n* **1** (*tree*) tilleul *m*. **2** (*substance*) chaux *f*. **3** (*fruit*) lime *f*, citron *m* vert; **l. juice** jus *m* de citron vert.

limelight ['laɪmlaɪt] *n* **in the l.** (*glare of publicity*) en vedette.

limit ['lɪmɪt] *n* limite *f*; (*restriction*) limitation *f* (**of** de); **that's the l.!** *Fam* c'est le comble!; **within limits** dans une certaine limite; – *vt* limiter (**to** à); **to l. oneself to doing** se borner à faire. ◆**—ed** *a* (*restricted*) limité; (*mind*) borné; (*edition*) à tirage limité; **l. company** *Com* société *f* à responsabilité limitée; **(public) l. company** (*with shareholders*) société *f* anonyme; **to a**

l. degree jusqu'à un certain point. ◆**limi'tation** *n* limitation *f*. ◆**limitless** *a* illimité.

limousine [lɪmə'ziːn] *n* (*car*) limousine *f*; (*airport etc shuttle*) *Am* voiture-navette *f*.

limp [lɪmp] **1** *vi* (*of person*) boiter; (*of vehicle etc*) *Fig* avancer tant bien que mal; – *n* **to have a l.** boiter. **2** *a* (**-er, -est**) (*soft*) mou; (*flabby*) flasque; (*person, hat*) avachi.

limpid ['lɪmpɪd] *a* (*liquid*) *Lit* limpide.

linchpin ['lɪntʃpɪn] *n* (*person*) pivot *m*.

linctus ['lɪŋktəs] *n Med* sirop *m* (contre la toux).

line[1] [laɪn] *n* ligne *f*; (*stroke*) trait *m*, ligne *f*; (*of poem*) vers *m*; (*wrinkle*) ride *f*; (*track*) voie *f*; (*rope*) corde *f*; (*row*) rangée *f*, ligne *f*; (*of vehicles*) file *f*; (*queue*) *Am* file *f*, queue *f*; (*family*) lignée *f*; (*business*) métier *m*, rayon *m*; (*article*) *Com* article *m*; **one's lines** (*of actor*) son texte *m*; **on the l.** *Tel* (*speaking*) au téléphone; (*at other end of line*) au bout du fil; **to be on the l.** (*at risk*) être en danger; **hold the l.!** *Tel* ne quittez pas!; **the hot l.** *Tel* le téléphone rouge; **to stand in l.** *Am* faire la queue; **to step** *or* **get out of l.** *Fig* refuser de se conformer; (*misbehave*) faire une incartade; **out of l. with** (*ideas etc*) en désaccord avec; **in l. with** conforme à; **he's in l. for** (*promotion etc*) il doit recevoir; **to take a hard l.** adopter une attitude ferme; **along the same lines** (*to work, think*) de la même façon; **sth along those lines** qch dans ce genre-là; **to drop a l.** *Fam* envoyer un mot (to à); **where do we draw the l.?** où fixer les limites?; – *vt* (*paper*) régler; (*face*) rider; **to l. the street** (*of trees*) border la rue; (*of people*) faire la haie le long de la rue; **to l. up** (*children, objects*) aligner; (*arrange*) organiser; (*get ready*) préparer; **to have sth lined up** (*in mind*) avoir qch en vue; – *vi* **to l. up** s'aligner; (*queue*) *Am* faire la queue. ◆**l.-up** *n* (*row*) file *f*; *Pol* front *m*; *TV* programme(s) *m*(*pl*).

line[2] [laɪn] *vt* (*clothes*) doubler; (*pockets*) *Fig* se remplir. ◆**lining** *n* (*of clothes*) doublure *f*; (*of brakes*) garniture *f*.

lineage ['lɪnɪɪdʒ] *n* lignée *f*.

linear ['lɪnɪər] *a* linéaire.

linen ['lɪnɪn] *n* (*sheets etc*) linge *m*; (*material*) (toile *f* de) lin *m*, fil *m*.

liner ['laɪnər] *n* **1** (*ship*) paquebot *m*. **2** **(dust)bin l.** sac *m* poubelle.

linesman ['laɪnzmən] *n* (*pl* **-men**) *Fb etc* juge *m* de touche.

linger ['lɪŋgər] *vi* **to l. (on)** (*of person*) s'attarder; (*of smell, memory*) persister; (*of doubt*) subsister. ◆**—ing** *a* (*death*) lent.

lingo ['lɪŋgəʊ] *n* (*pl* **-os**) *Hum Fam* jargon *m*.

linguist ['lɪŋgwɪst] *n* linguiste *mf*. ◆**lin'guistic** *a* linguistique. ◆**lin'guistics** *n* linguistique *f*.

liniment ['lɪnɪmənt] *n* onguent *m*, pommade *f*.

link [lɪŋk] *vt* (*connect*) relier (**to** à); (*relate, associate*) lier (**to** à); **to l. up** *Tel* relier; – *vi* **to l. up** (*of roads*) se rejoindre; – *n* (*connection*) lien *m*; (*of chain*) maillon *m*; (*by road, rail*) liaison *f*. ◆**l.-up** *n TV Rad* liaison *f*; (*of spacecraft*) jonction *f*.

lino ['laɪnəʊ] *n* (*pl* **-os**) lino *m*. ◆**linoleum** [lɪ'nəʊlɪəm] *n* linoléum *m*.

linseed ['lɪnsiːd] *n* **l. oil** huile *f* de lin.

lint [lɪnt] *n Med* tissu *m* ouaté; (*fluff*) peluche(s) *f*(*pl*).

lion ['laɪən] *n* lion *m*; **l. cub** lionceau *m*. ◆**lioness** *n* lionne *f*.

lip [lɪp] *n Anat* lèvre *f*; (*rim*) bord *m*; (*cheek*) *Sl* culot *m*. ◆**l.-read** *vi* (*pt & pp* **-read** [red]) lire sur les lèvres. ◆**lipstick** *n* (*material*) rouge *m* à lèvres; (*stick*) tube *m* de rouge.

liqueur [lɪ'kjʊər] *n* liqueur *f*.

liquid ['lɪkwɪd] *n* & *a* liquide (*m*). ◆**liquefy** *vt* liquéfier; – *vi* se liquéfier. ◆**liquidizer** *n Culin* (*for fruit juices*) centrifugeuse *f*; (*for purées etc*) robot *m*, moulinette® *f*.

liquidate ['lɪkwɪdeɪt] *vt* (*debt, person*) liquider. ◆**liqui'dation** *n* liquidation *f*.

liquor ['lɪkər] *n* alcool *m*, spiritueux *m*; **l. store** *Am* magasin *m* de vins et de spiritueux.

liquorice ['lɪkərɪʃ, -rɪs] *n* réglisse *f*.

lira, *pl* **lire** ['lɪərə, 'lɪəreɪ] *n* (*currency*) lire *f*.

lisp [lɪsp] *vi* zézayer; – *n* **to have a l.** zézayer.

list [lɪst] **1** *n* liste *f*; – *vt* (*one's possessions etc*) faire la liste de; (*names*) mettre sur la liste; (*enumerate*) énumérer; (*catalogue*) cataloguer. **2** *vi* (*of ship*) gîter. ◆**—ed** *a* (*monument etc*) classé.

listen ['lɪsən] *vi* écouter; **to l. to** écouter; **to l. (out) for** (*telephone, person etc*) tendre l'oreille pour, guetter; **to l. in (to)** *Rad* écouter. ◆**—ing** *n* écoute *f* (**to** de). ◆**—er** *n Rad* auditeur, -trice *mf*; **to be a good l.** (*pay attention*) savoir écouter.

listless ['lɪstləs] *a* apathique, indolent. ◆**—ness** *n* apathie *f*.

lit [lɪt] *see* **light**[1] **1.**

litany ['lɪtənɪ] *n Rel* litanies *fpl*.

literal ['lɪtərəl] *a* littéral; (*not exaggerated*) réel. ◆**—ly** *adv* littéralement; (*really*) réellement; **he took it l.** il l'a pris au pied de la lettre.

literate ['lɪtərət] *a* qui sait lire et écrire;

highly l. (*person*) très instruit. ◆**literacy** *n* capacité *f* de lire et d'écrire; (*of country*) degré *m* d'alphabétisation.

literature ['lɪt(ə)rɪtʃər] *n* littérature *f*; (*pamphlets etc*) documentation *f*. ◆**literary** *a* littéraire.

lithe [laɪð] *a* agile, souple.

litigation [lɪtɪ'geɪʃ(ə)n] *n Jur* litige *m*.

litre ['liːtər] *n* litre *m*.

litter ['lɪtər] **1** *n* (*rubbish*) détritus *m*; (*papers*) papiers *mpl*; (*bedding for animals*) litière *f*; (*confusion*) *Fig* fouillis *m*; **l. basket** *or* **bin** boîte *f* à ordures; – *vt* **to l. (with papers** *or* **rubbish)** (*street etc*) laisser traîner des papiers *or* des détritus dans; **a street littered with** une rue jonchée de. **2** *n* (*young animals*) portée *f*.

little ['lɪt(ə)l] **1** *a* (*small*) petit; **the l. ones** les petits. **2** *a* & *n* (*not much*) peu (de); **l. time/money/***etc* peu de temps/d'argent/*etc*; **I've l. left** il m'en reste peu; **she eats l.** elle mange peu; **to have l. to say** avoir peu de chose à dire; **as l. as possible** le moins possible; **a l. money/time/***etc* (*some*) un peu d'argent/de temps/*etc*; **I have a l.** (*some*) j'en ai un peu; **the l. that I have** le peu que j'ai; – *adv* (*somewhat, rather*) peu; **a l. heavy/***etc* un peu lourd/*etc*; **to work/***etc* **a l.** travailler/*etc* un peu; **it's l. better** (*hardly*) ce n'est guère mieux; **l. by l.** peu à peu.

liturgy ['lɪtədʒɪ] *n* liturgie *f*.

live¹ [lɪv] *vi* vivre; (*reside*) habiter, vivre; **where do you l.?** où habitez-vous?; **to l. in Paris** habiter (à) Paris; **to l. off** *or* **on** (*eat*) vivre de; (*sponge on*) *Pej* vivre aux crochets *or* aux dépens de (*qn*); **to l. on** (*of memory etc*) survivre, se perpétuer; **to l. through** (*experience*) vivre; (*survive*) survivre à; **to l. up to** (*one's principles*) vivre selon; (*s.o.'s expectations*) se montrer à la hauteur de; – *vt* (*life*) vivre, mener; (*one's faith etc*) vivre pleinement; **to l. down** faire oublier (avec le temps); **to l. it up** *Fam* mener la grande vie.

live² [laɪv] **1** *a* (*alive, lively*) vivant; (*coal*) ardent; (*bomb*) non explosé; (*ammunition*) réel, de combat; (*wire*) *El* sous tension; (*switch*) *El* mal isolé; (*plugged in*) *El* branché; **a real l. king/***etc* un roi/*etc* en chair et en os. **2** *a* & *adv Rad TV* en direct; **a l. broadcast** une émission en direct; **a l. audience** le *or* un public; **a l. recording** un enregistrement public.

livelihood ['laɪvlɪhʊd] *n* moyens *mpl* de subsistance; **my l.** mon gagne-pain; **to earn one's** *or* **a l.** gagner sa vie.

livel/y ['laɪvlɪ] *a* (**-ier, -iest**) (*person, style*) vif, vivant; (*street, story*) vivant; (*interest, mind, colour*) vif; (*day*) movementé; (*forceful*) vigoureux; (*conversation, discussion*) animé. ◆**—iness** *n* vivacité *f*.

liven ['laɪv(ə)n] *vt* **to l. up** (*person*) égayer; (*party*) animer; – *vi* **to l. up** (*of person, party*) s'animer.

liver ['lɪvər] *n* foie *m*.

livery ['lɪvərɪ] *n* (*uniform*) livrée *f*.

livestock ['laɪvstɒk] *n* bétail *m*.

livid ['lɪvɪd] *a* (*blue-grey*) livide; (*angry*) *Fig* furieux; **l. with cold** blême de froid.

living ['lɪvɪŋ] **1** *a* (*alive*) vivant; **not a l. soul** (*nobody*) personne, pas âme qui vive; **within l. memory** de mémoire d'homme; **l. or dead** mort ou vif; **the l.** les vivants *mpl*. **2** *n* (*livelihood*) vie *f*; **to make a** *or* **one's l.** gagner sa vie; **to work for a l.** travailler pour vivre; **the cost of l.** le coût de la vie; – *a* (*standard, conditions*) de vie; (*wage*) qui permet de vivre; **l. room** salle *f* de séjour.

lizard ['lɪzəd] *n* lézard *m*.

llama ['lɑːmə] *n* (*animal*) lama *m*.

load [ləʊd] *n* (*object carried, burden*) charge *f*; (*freight*) chargement *m*, charge *f*; (*strain, weight*) poids *m*; **a l. of, loads of** (*people, money etc*) *Fam* un tas de, énormément de; **to take a l. off s.o.'s mind** ôter un grand poids à qn; – *vt* charger; **to l. down** *or* **up** charger (**with** de); – *vi* **to l. (up)** charger la voiture, le navire *etc*. ◆**—ed** *a* (*gun, vehicle etc*) chargé; (*dice*) pipé; (*rich*) *Fam* plein aux as; **a l. question** une question piège; **l. (down) with** (*debts*) accablé de.

loaf [ləʊf] **1** *n* (*pl* **loaves**) pain *m*; **French l.** baguette *f*. **2** *vi* **to l. (about)** fainéanter. ◆**—er** *n* fainéant, -ante *mf*.

loam [ləʊm] *n* (*soil*) terreau *m*.

loan [ləʊn] *n* (*money lent*) prêt *m*; (*money borrowed*) emprunt *m*; **on l. from** prêté par; **(out) on l.** (*book*) sorti; **may I have the l. of . . . ?** puis-je emprunter . . . ?; – *vt* (*lend*) prêter (**to** à).

loath [ləʊθ] *a* **l. to do** *Lit* peu disposé à faire.

loath/e [ləʊð] *vt* détester (**doing** faire). ◆**—ing** *n* dégoût *m*. ◆**loathsome** *a* détestable.

lobby ['lɒbɪ] **1** *n* (*of hotel*) vestibule *m*, hall *m*; *Th* foyer *m*. **2** *n Pol* groupe *m* de pression, lobby *m*; – *vt* faire pression sur.

lobe [ləʊb] *n Anat* lobe *m*.

lobster ['lɒbstər] *n* homard *m*; (*spiny*) langouste *f*.

local ['ləʊk(ə)l] *a* local; (*of the neighbourhood*) du *or* de quartier; (*regional*) du pays; **are you l.?** êtes-vous du coin *or* d'ici?; **the doctor is l.** le médecin est tout près d'ici; **a l. phone call** (*within town*) une communication urbaine; – *n* (*pub*) *Fam* bistrot *m* du coin, pub *m*; **she's a l.** elle est du coin; **the locals** (*people*) les gens du coin. ◆**lo'cality** *n* (*neighbourhood*) environs *mpl*; (*region*) région *f*; (*place*) lieu *m*; (*site*) emplacement *m*. ◆**localize** *vt* (*confine*) localiser. ◆**locally** *adv* dans les environs, dans le coin; (*around here*) par ici; (*in precise place*) localement.

locate [ləʊ'keɪt] *vt* (*find*) repérer; (*pain, noise, leak*) localiser; (*situate*) situer; (*build*) construire. ◆**location** *n* (*site*) emplacement *m*; (*act*) repérage *m*; localisation *f*; **on l.** *Cin* en extérieur.

lock [lɒk] **1** *vt* **to l. (up)** fermer à clef; **to l. the wheels** *Aut* bloquer les roues; **to l. s.o. in** enfermer qn; **to l. s.o. in sth** enfermer qn dans qch; **to l. s.o. out** (*accidentally*) enfermer qn dehors; **to l. away** *or* **up** (*prisoner*) enfermer; (*jewels etc*) mettre sous clef, enfermer; – *vi* **to l. (up)** fermer à clef; – *n* (*on door, chest etc*) serrure *f*; (*of gun*) cran *m* de sûreté; (*turning circle*) *Aut* rayon *m* de braquage; **(anti-theft) l.** *Aut* antivol *m*; **under l. and key** sous clef. **2** *n* (*on canal*) écluse *f*. **3** *n* (*of hair*) mèche *f*. ◆**locker** *n* casier *m*; (*for luggage*) *Rail* casier *m* de consigne automatique; (*for clothes*) vestiaire *m* (métallique); **l. room** *Sp Am* vestiaire *m*. ◆**lockout** *n* (*industrial*) lock-out *m inv*. ◆**locksmith** *n* serrurier *m*.

locket ['lɒkɪt] *n* (*jewel*) médaillon *m*.

loco ['ləʊkəʊ] *a Sl* cinglé, fou.

locomotion [ləʊkə'məʊʃ(ə)n] *n* locomotion *f*. ◆**locomotive** *n* locomotive *f*.

locum ['ləʊkəm] *n* (*doctor*) remplaçant, -ante *mf*.

locust ['ləʊkəst] *n* criquet *m*, sauterelle *f*.

lodg/e [lɒdʒ] **1** *vt* (*person*) loger; (*valuables*) déposer (**with** chez); **to l. a complaint** porter plainte; – *vi* (*of bullet*) se loger (**in** dans); **to be lodging** (*accommodated*) être logé (**with** chez). **2** *n* (*house*) pavillon *m* de gardien *or* de chasse; (*of porter*) loge *f*. ◆**—ing** *n* (*accommodation*) logement *m*; *pl* (*flat*) logement *m*; (*room*) chambre *f*; **in lodgings** en meublé. ◆**—er** *n* (*room and meals*) pensionnaire *mf*; (*room only*) locataire *mf*.

loft [lɒft] *n* (*attic*) grenier *m*.

loft/y ['lɒftɪ] *a* **(-ier, -iest)** (*high, noble*) élevé; (*haughty*) hautain. ◆**—iness** *n* hauteur *f*.

log [lɒg] **1** *n* (*tree trunk*) rondin *m*; (*for fire*) bûche *f*, rondin *m*; **l. fire** feu *m* de bois. **2** *vt* **(-gg-)** (*facts*) noter; **to l. (up)** (*distance*) faire, couvrir. ◆**logbook** *n Nau Av* journal *m* de bord.

logarithm ['lɒgərɪðəm] *n* logarithme *m*.

loggerheads (at) [æt'lɒgəhedz] *adv* en désaccord (**with** avec).

logic ['lɒdʒɪk] *n* logique *f*. ◆**logical** *a* logique. ◆**logically** *adv* logiquement.

logistics [lə'dʒɪstɪks] *n* logistique *f*.

logo ['ləʊgəʊ] *n* (*pl* **-os**) logo *m*.

loin [lɔɪn] *n* (*meat*) filet *m*.

loins [lɔɪnz] *npl Anat* reins *mpl*.

loiter ['lɔɪtər] *vi* traîner.

loll [lɒl] *vi* (*in armchair etc*) se prélasser.

lollipop ['lɒlɪpɒp] *n* (*sweet on stick*) sucette *f*; (*ice on stick*) esquimau *m*. ◆**lolly** *n Fam* sucette *f*; (*money*) *Sl* fric *m*; **(ice) l.** *Fam* esquimau *m*.

London ['lʌndən] *n* Londres *m or f*; – *a* (*taxi etc*) londonien. ◆**Londoner** *n* Londonien, -ienne *mf*.

lone [ləʊn] *a* solitaire; **l. wolf** *Fig* solitaire *mf*. ◆**loneliness** *n* solitude *f*. ◆**lonely** *a* **(-ier, -iest)** (*road, house, life etc*) solitaire; (*person*) seul, solitaire. ◆**loner** *n* solitaire *mf*. ◆**lonesome** *a* solitaire.

long[1] [lɒŋ] **1** *a* **(-er, -est)** long; **to be ten metres l.** être long de dix mètres, avoir dix mètres de long; **to be six weeks l.** durer six semaines; **how l. is . . .** quelle est la longueur de . . . ?; (*time*) quelle est la durée de . . . ?; **a l. time** longtemps; **in the l. run** à la longue; **a l. face** une grimace; **a l. memory** une bonne mémoire; **l. jump** *Sp* saut *m* en longueur. **2** *adv* (*a long time*) longtemps; **l. before** longtemps avant; **has he been here l.?** il y a longtemps qu'il est ici?, il est ici depuis longtemps?; **how l. (ago)?** (il y a) combien de temps?; **not l. ago** il y a peu de temps; **before l.** sous *or* avant peu; **no longer** ne plus; **she no longer swims** elle ne nage plus; **a bit longer** (*to wait etc*) encore un peu; **I won't be l.** je n'en ai pas pour longtemps; **at the longest** (tout) au plus; **all summer l.** tout l'été; **l. live the queen**/*etc* vive la reine/*etc*; **as l. as, so l. as** (*provided that*) pourvu que (+ *sub*); **as l. as I live** tant que je vivrai.

long[2] [lɒŋ] *vi* **to l. for sth** avoir très envie de qch; **to l. for s.o.** languir après qn; **to l. to do** avoir très envie de faire. ◆**—ing** *n* désir *m*, envie *f*.

long-distance [lɒŋ'dɪstəns] *a* (*race*) de fond; (*phone call*) interurbain; (*flight*) long-courrier. ◆**long-drawn-'out** *a* interminable. ◆**long'haired** *a* aux cheveux longs. ◆**'longhand** *n* écriture *f* normale. ◆**long-'playing** *a* **l.-playing record** 33 tours *m inv*. ◆**'long-range** *a* (*forecast*) à long terme. ◆**long'sighted** *a Med* presbyte. ◆**long'standing** *a* de longue date. ◆**long'suffering** *a* très patient. ◆**long-'term** *a* à long terme. ◆**long-'winded** *a* (*speech, speaker*) verbeux.

longevity [lɒn'dʒevɪtɪ] *n* longévité *f*.

longitude ['lɒndʒɪtjuːd] *n* longitude *f*.

longways ['lɒŋweɪz] *adv* en longueur.

loo [luː] *n* (*toilet*) *Fam* cabinets *mpl*.

look [lʊk] *n* regard *m*; (*appearance*) air *m*, allure *f*; **(good) looks** la beauté, un beau physique; **to have a l. (at)** jeter un coup d'œil (à), regarder; **to have a l. (for)** chercher; **to have a l. (a)round** regarder; (*walk*) faire un tour; **let me have a l.** fais voir; **I like the l. of him** il me fait bonne impression, il me plaît; – *vti* regarder; **to l. s.o. in the face** regarder qn dans les yeux; **to l. tired/happy/***etc* (*seem*) sembler *or* avoir l'air fatigué/heureux/*etc*; **to l. pretty/ugly** (*be*) être joli/laid; **to l. one's age** faire son âge; **l. here!** dites donc!; **you l. like** *or* **as if you're tired** tu as l'air fatigué, on dirait que tu es fatigué; **it looks like** *or* **as if she won't leave** elle n'a pas l'air de vouloir partir; **it looks like it!** c'est probable; **to l. like a child** avoir l'air d'un enfant; **to l. like an apple** avoir l'air d'être une pomme; **you l. like my brother** (*resemble*) tu ressembles à mon frère; **it looks like rain (to me)** il me semble *or* on dirait qu'il va pleuvoir; **what does he l. like?** (*describe him*) comment est-il?; **to l. well** *or* **good** (*of person*) avoir bonne mine; **you l. good in that hat/***etc* ce chapeau/*etc* te va très bien; **that looks bad** (*action etc*) ça fait mauvais effet. ■ **to l. after** *vt* (*deal with*) s'occuper de; (*patient, hair*) soigner; (*keep safely*) garder **(for s.o.** pour qn); **to l. after oneself** (*keep healthy*) faire bien attention à soi; **I can l. after myself** (*cope*) je suis assez grand pour me débrouiller; **to l. around** *vt* (*visit*) visiter; – *vi* (*have a look*) regarder; (*walk round*) faire un tour; **to l. at** *vt* regarder; (*consider*) considérer, voir; (*check*) vérifier; **to l. away** *vi* détourner les yeux; **to l. back** *vi* regarder derrière soi; (*in time*) regarder en arrière; **to l. down** *vi* baisser les yeux; (*from height*) regarder en bas; **to l. down on** (*consider scornfully*) mépriser, regarder de haut; **to l. for** *vt* (*seek*) chercher; **to l. forward to** *vt* (*event*) attendre avec impatience; **to l. in** *vi* regarder (à l'intérieur); **to l. in on s.o.** *Fam* passer voir qn; **to l. into** *vt* (*examine*) examiner; (*find out about*) se renseigner sur; **to l. on** *vi* regarder; – *vt* (*consider*) considérer; **to l. out** *vi* (*be careful*) faire attention **(for** à); **to l. out for** (*seek*) chercher; (*watch*) guetter; **to l. (out) on to** (*of window, house etc*) donner sur; **to l. over** *or* **through** *vt* (*examine fully*) examiner, regarder de près; (*briefly*) parcourir; (*region, town*) parcourir, visiter; **to l. round** *vt* (*visit*) visiter; – *vi* (*have a look*) regarder; (*walk round*) faire un tour; (*look back*) se retourner; **to l. round for** (*seek*) chercher; **to l. up** *vi* (*of person*) lever les yeux; (*into the air or sky*) regarder en l'air; (*improve*) s'améliorer; **to l. up to s.o.** *Fig* respecter qn; – *vt* (*word*) chercher; **to l. s.o. up** (*visit*) passer voir qn. ◆**-looking** *suffix* **pleasant-/tired-/***etc* **l.** à l'air agréable/fatigué/*etc*. ◆**looking-glass** *n* glace *f*, miroir *m*.

lookout ['lʊkaʊt] *n* (*soldier*) guetteur *m*; (*sailor*) vigie *f*; **l. (post)** poste *m* de guet; (*on ship*) vigie *f*; **to be on the l.** faire le guet; **to be on the l. for** guetter.

loom [luːm] **1** *vi* **to l. (up)** (*of mountain etc*) apparaître indistinctement; *Fig* paraître imminent. **2** *n Tex* métier *m* à tisser.

loony ['luːnɪ] *n* & *a Sl* imbécile (*mf*).

loop [luːp] *n* (*in river etc*) & *Av* boucle *f*; (*contraceptive device*) stérilet *m*; – *vt* **to l. the loop** *Av* boucler la boucle. ◆**loophole** *n* (*in rules*) point *m* faible, lacune *f*; (*way out*) échappatoire *f*.

loose [luːs] *a* **(-er, -est)** (*screw, belt, knot*) desserré; (*tooth, stone*) branlant; (*page*) détaché; (*animal*) libre, (*set loose*) lâché; (*clothes*) flottant; (*hair*) dénoué; (*flesh*) flasque; (*wording, translation*) approximatif, vague; (*link*) vague; (*discipline*) relâché; (*articles*) *Com* en vrac; (*cheese, tea etc*) *Com* au poids; (*woman*) *Pej* facile; **l. change** petite monnaie *f*; **l. covers** housses *fpl*; **l. living** vie *f* dissolue; **to get l.** (*of dog, page*) se détacher; **to set** *or* **turn l.** (*dog etc*) libérer, lâcher; **he's at a l. end** *or Am* **at l. ends** il ne sait pas trop quoi faire; – *n* **on the l.** (*prisoner etc*) en liberté; – *vt* (*animal*) lâcher. ◆**loosely** *adv* (*to hang*) lâchement; (*to hold, tie*) sans serrer; (*to translate*) librement; (*to link*) vaguement. ◆**loosen** *vt* (*knot, belt, screw*) desserrer; (*rope*) détendre; (*grip*) relâcher; – *vi* **to l. up** *Sp* faire des exercices d'assouplissement. ◆**looseness** *n* (*of screw, machine parts*) jeu *m*.

loot [luːt] *n* butin *m*; (*money*) *Sl* fric *m*; – *vt* piller. ◆**—ing** *n* pillage *m*. ◆**—er** *n* pillard, -arde *mf*.

lop [lɒp] *vt* **(-pp-)** **to l. (off)** couper.

lop-sided [lɒp'saɪdɪd] *a* (*crooked*) de travers; **to walk l.-sided** (*limp*) se déhancher.

loquacious [ləʊ'kweɪʃəs] *a* loquace.

lord [lɔːd] *n* seigneur *m*; (*title*) *Br* lord *m*; **good L.!** *Fam* bon sang!; **oh L.!** *Fam* mince!; **the House of Lords** *Pol* la Chambre des Lords; – *vt* **to l. it over s.o.** *Fam* dominer qn. ◆**lordly** *a* digne d'un grand seigneur; (*arrogant*) hautain. ◆**lordship** *n* **Your L.** (*to judge*) Monsieur le juge.

lore [lɔːr] *n* traditions *fpl*.

lorry ['lɒrɪ] *n* camion *m*; (*heavy*) poids *m* lourd; **l. driver** camionneur *m*; **long-distance l. driver** routier *m*.

los/e [luːz] *vt* (*pt & pp* **lost**) perdre; **to get lost** (*of person*) se perdre; **the ticket/***etc* **got lost** on a perdu le billet/*etc*; **get lost!** *Fam* fiche le camp!; **to l. s.o. sth** faire perdre qch à qn; **to l. interest in** se désintéresser de; **I've lost my bearings** je suis désorienté; **the clock loses six minutes a day** la pendule retarde de six minutes par jour; **to l. one's life** trouver la mort (**in** dans); – *vi* perdre; **to l. out** être perdant; **to l. to** *Sp* être battu par. ◆**—ing** *a* perdant; **a l. battle** *Fig* une bataille perdue d'avance. ◆**—er** *n* perdant, -ante *mf*; (*failure in life*) *Fam* paumé, -ée *mf*; **to be a good l.** être bon *or* beau joueur.

loss [lɒs] *n* perte *f*; **at a l.** (*confused*) perplexe; **to sell at a l.** *Com* vendre à perte; **at a l. to do** incapable de faire. ◆**lost** *a* perdu; **l. property,** *Am* **l. and found** objets *mpl* trouvés.

lot [lɒt] *n* **1** (*destiny*) sort *m*; (*batch, land*) lot *m*; **to draw lots** tirer au sort; **parking l.** *Am* parking *m*; **a bad l.** (*person*) *Fam* un mauvais sujet. **2 the l.** (*everything*) (le) tout; **the l. of you** vous tous; **a l. of, lots of** beaucoup de; **a l.** beaucoup; **quite a l.** pas mal (**of** de); **such a l.** tellement (**of** de), tant (**of** de); **what a l. of flowers/water/***etc*! que de fleurs/d'eau/*etc*!; **what a l.!** quelle quantité!; **what a l. of flowers/***etc* **you have!** que vous avez (beaucoup) de fleurs/*etc*!

lotion ['ləʊʃ(ə)n] *n* lotion *f*.

lottery ['lɒtərɪ] *n* loterie *f*.

lotto ['lɒtəʊ] *n* (*game*) loto *m*.

loud [laʊd] *a* (**-er, -est**) bruyant; (*voice, radio*) fort; (*noise, cry*) grand; (*gaudy*) voyant; – *adv* (*to shout etc*) fort; **out l.** tout haut. ◆**—ly** *adv* (*to speak, laugh etc*) bruyamment, fort; (*to shout*) fort. ◆**—ness** *n* (*of voice etc*) force *f*; (*noise*) bruit *m*. ◆**loud'hailer** *n* mégaphone *m*. ◆**loudmouth** *n* (*person*) *Fam* grande gueule *f*. ◆**loud'speaker** *n* haut-parleur *m*; (*of hi-fi unit*) enceinte *f*.

lounge [laʊndʒ] **1** *n* salon *m*; **l. suit** complet *m* veston. **2** *vi* (*loll*) se prélasser; **to l. about** (*idle*) paresser; (*stroll*) flâner.

louse, *pl* **lice** [laʊs, laɪs] **1** *n* (*insect*) pou *m*. **2** *n* (*person*) *Pej Sl* salaud *m*. **3** *vt* **to l. up** (*mess up*) *Sl* gâcher.

lousy ['laʊzɪ] *a* (**-ier, -iest**) (*bad*) *Fam* infect; **l. with** (*crammed, loaded*) *Sl* bourré de.

lout [laʊt] *n* rustre *m*. ◆**loutish** *a* (*attitude*) de rustre.

lov/e [lʌv] *n* amour *m*; *Tennis* zéro *m*; **in l.** amoureux (**with** de); **they're in l.** ils s'aiment; **art is his** *or* **her l.** l'art est sa passion; **yes, my l.** oui mon amour; – *vt* aimer; (*like very much*) adorer, aimer (beaucoup) (**to do, doing** faire); **give him** *or* **her my l.** (*greeting*) dis-lui bien des choses de ma part; **l. affair** liaison *f* (amoureuse). ◆**—ing** *a* affectueux, aimant. ◆**—able** *a* adorable. ◆**—er** *n* (*man*) amant *m*; (*woman*) maîtresse *f*; **a l. of** (*art, music etc*) un amateur de; **a nature l.** un amoureux de la nature. ◆**lovesick** *a* amoureux.

lovely ['lʌvlɪ] *a* (**-ier, -iest**) (*pleasing*) agréable, bon; (*excellent*) excellent; (*pretty*) joli; (*charming*) charmant; (*kind*) gentil; **the weather's l.** il fait beau; **l. to see you!** je suis ravi de te voir; **l. and hot/dry/***etc* bien chaud/sec/*etc*.

low[1] [ləʊ] *a* (**-er, -est**) bas; (*speed, income, intelligence*) faible; (*opinion, quality*) mauvais; **she's l. on** (*money etc*) elle n'a plus beaucoup de; **to feel l.** (*depressed*) être déprimé; **in a l. voice** à voix basse; **lower** inférieur; – *adv* (**-er, -est**) bas; **to turn (down) l.** mettre plus bas; **to run l.** (*of supplies*) s'épuiser; – *n Met* dépression *f*; **to reach a new l.** *or* **an all-time l.** (*of prices etc*) atteindre leur niveau le plus bas. ◆**low-'calorie** *a* (*diet*) (à) basses calories. ◆**low-'cost** *a* bon marché *inv*. ◆**low-cut** *a* décolleté. ◆**low-down** *a* méprisable. ◆**lowdown** *n* (*facts*) *Fam* tuyaux *mpl*. ◆**low-'fat** *a* (*milk*) écrémé; (*cheese*) de régime. ◆**low-'key** *a* (*discreet*) discret. ◆**lowland(s)** *n* plaine *f*. ◆**low-level** *a* bas. ◆**low-paid** *a* mal payé. ◆**low-'salt** *a* (*food*) à faible teneur en sel.

low[2] [ləʊ] *vi* (*of cattle*) meugler.

lower ['ləʊər] *vt* baisser; **to l. s.o./sth** (*by rope*) descendre qn/qch; **to l. oneself** *Fig* s'abaisser. ◆**—ing** *n* (*drop*) baisse *f*.

lowly ['ləʊlɪ] *a* (**-ier, -iest**) humble.

loyal ['lɔɪəl] *a* loyal (**to** envers), fidèle (**to** à). ◆**loyalty** *n* loyauté *f*, fidélité *f*.

lozenge ['lɒzɪndʒ] *n* (*sweet*) *Med* pastille *f*; (*shape*) *Geom* losange *m*.

LP [el'piː] *abbr* = **long-playing record.**

L-plates ['elpleɪts] *npl Aut* plaques *fpl* d'apprenti conducteur.
Ltd *abbr* (*Limited*) *Com* SARL.
lubricate ['luːbrɪkeɪt] *vt* lubrifier; *Aut* graisser. ◆**lubricant** *n* lubrifiant *m*. ◆**lubri'cation** *n Aut* graissage *m*.
lucid ['luːsɪd] *a* lucide. ◆**lu'cidity** *n* lucidité *f*.
luck [lʌk] *n* (*chance*) chance *f*; (*good fortune*) (bonne) chance *f*, bonheur *m*; (*fate*) hasard *m*, fortune *f*; **bad l.** malchance *f*, malheur *m*; **hard l.!, tough l.!** pas de chance!; **worse l.** (*unfortunately*) malheureusement. ◆**luckily** *adv* heureusement. ◆**lucky** *a* (**-ier, -iest**) (*person*) chanceux, heureux; (*guess, event*) heureux; **to be l.** (*of person*) avoir de la chance (**to do** de faire); **I've had a l. day** j'ai eu de la chance aujourd'hui; **l. charm** porte-bonheur *m inv*; **l. number**/*etc* chiffre *m*/*etc* porte-bonheur; **how l.!** quelle chance!
lucrative ['luːkrətɪv] *a* lucratif.
ludicrous ['luːdɪkrəs] *a* ridicule.
ludo ['luːdəʊ] *n* jeu *m* des petits chevaux.
lug [lʌg] *vt* (**-gg-**) (*pull*) traîner; **to l. around** trimbaler.
luggage ['lʌgɪdʒ] *n* bagages *mpl*.
lugubrious [luː'guːbrɪəs] *a* lugubre.
lukewarm ['luːkwɔːm] *a* tiède.
lull [lʌl] **1** *n* arrêt *m*; (*in storm*) accalmie *f*. **2** *vt* (**-ll-**) apaiser; **to l. to sleep** endormir.
lullaby ['lʌləbaɪ] *n* berceuse *f*.
lumbago [lʌm'beɪgəʊ] *n* lumbago *m*.
lumber[1] ['lʌmbər] *n* (*timber*) bois *m* de charpente; (*junk*) bric-à-brac *m inv*. ◆**lumberjack** *n Am Can* bûcheron *m*. ◆**lumberjacket** *n* blouson *m*. ◆**lumber-room** *n* débarras *m*.
lumber[2] ['lʌmbər] *vt* **to l. s.o. with sth/s.o.** *Fam* coller qch/qn à qn; **he got lumbered with the chore** il s'est appuyé la corvée.
luminous ['luːmɪnəs] *a* (*dial etc*) lumineux.
lump [lʌmp] *n* morceau *m*; (*in soup*) grumeau *m*; (*bump*) bosse *f*; (*swelling*) *Med* grosseur *f*; **l. sum** somme *f* forfaitaire; – *vt* **to l. together** réunir; *Fig Pej* mettre dans le même sac. ◆**lumpy** *a* (**-ier, -iest**) (*soup etc*) grumeleux; (*surface*) bosselé.
lunar ['luːnər] *a* lunaire.
lunatic ['luːnətɪk] *a* fou, dément; – *n* fou *m*, folle *f*. ◆**lunacy** *n* folie *f*, démence *f*.
lunch [lʌntʃ] *n* déjeuner *m*; **to have l.** déjeuner; **l. break, l. hour, l. time** heure *f* du déjeuner; – *vi* déjeuner (**on, off** de). ◆**luncheon** *n* déjeuner *m*; **l. meat** mortadelle *f*, saucisson *m*; **l. voucher** chèque-déjeuner *m*.
lung [lʌŋ] *n* poumon *m*; **l. cancer** cancer *m* du poumon.
lunge [lʌndʒ] *n* coup *m* en avant; – *vi* **to l. at s.o.** se ruer sur qn.
lurch [lɜːtʃ] **1** *vi* (*of person*) tituber; (*of ship*) faire une embardée. **2** *n* **to leave s.o. in the l.** *Fam* laisser qn en plan, laisser tomber qn.
lure [lʊər] *vt* attirer (par la ruse) (**into** dans); – *n* (*attraction*) attrait *m*.
lurid ['lʊərɪd] *a* (*horrifying*) horrible, affreux; (*sensational*) à sensation; (*gaudy*) voyant; (*colour, sunset*) sanglant.
lurk [lɜːk] *vi* (*hide*) se cacher (**in** dans); (*prowl*) rôder; (*of suspicion, fear etc*) persister.
luscious ['lʌʃəs] *a* (*food etc*) appétissant.
lush [lʌʃ] **1** *a* (*vegetation*) luxuriant; (*wealthy*) *Fam* opulent. **2** *n Am Sl* ivrogne *mf*.
lust [lʌst] *n* (*for person, object*) convoitise *f* (**for** de); (*for power, knowledge*) soif *f* (**for** de); – *vi* **to l. after** (*object, person*) convoiter; (*power, knowledge*) avoir soif de.
lustre ['lʌstər] *n* (*gloss*) lustre *m*.
lusty [lʌstɪ] *a* (**-ier, -iest**) vigoureux.
lute [luːt] *n Mus* luth *m*.
Luxembourg ['lʌksəmbɜːg] *n* Luxembourg *m*.
luxuriant [lʌg'ʒʊərɪənt] *a* luxuriant. ◆**luxuriate** *vi* (*laze about*) paresser (**in bed**/*etc* au lit/*etc*).
luxury ['lʌkʃərɪ] *n* luxe *m*; – *a* (*goods, flat etc*) de luxe. ◆**luxurious** [lʌg'ʒʊərɪəs] *a* luxueux.
lying ['laɪɪŋ] *see* **lie**[1,2]; – *n* le mensonge; – *a* (*account*) mensonger; (*person*) menteur.
lynch [lɪntʃ] *vt* lyncher. ◆**—ing** *n* lynchage *m*.
lynx [lɪŋks] *n* (*animal*) lynx *m*.
lyre ['laɪər] *n Mus Hist* lyre *f*.
lyric ['lɪrɪk] *a* lyrique; – *npl* (*of song*) paroles *fpl*. ◆**lyrical** *a* (*effusive*) lyrique. ◆**lyricism** *n* lyrisme *m*.

M

M, m [em] *n* M, m *m*.
m *abbr* **1** (*metre*) mètre *m*. **2** (*mile*) mile *m*.
MA *abbr* = **Master of Arts.**
ma'am [mæm] *n* madame *f*.
mac [mæk] *n* (*raincoat*) *Fam* imper *m*.
macabre [mə'kɑːbrə] *a* macabre.
macaroni [mækə'rəʊnɪ] *n* macaroni(s) *m*(*pl*).
macaroon [mækə'ruːn] *n* (*cake*) macaron *m*.
mace [meɪs] *n* (*staff, rod*) masse *f*.
Machiavellian [mækɪə'velɪən] *a* machiavélique.
machination [mækɪ'neɪʃ(ə)n] *n* machination *f*.
machine [mə'ʃiːn] *n* (*apparatus, car, system etc*) machine *f*. ◆**machinegun** *n* mitrailleuse *f*; – *vt* (**-nn-**) mitrailler. ◆**machinery** *n* (*machines*) machines *fpl*; (*works*) mécanisme *m*; *Fig* rouages *mpl*. ◆**machinist** *n* (*on sewing machine*) piqueur, -euse *mf*.
macho ['mætʃəʊ] *n* (*pl* **-os**) macho *m*; – *a* (*attitude etc*) macho (*f inv*).
mackerel ['mækrəl] *n inv* (*fish*) maquereau *m*.
mackintosh ['mækɪntɒʃ] *n* imperméable *m*.
mad [mæd] *a* (**madder, maddest**) fou; (*dog*) enragé; (*bull*) furieux; **m. (at)** (*angry*) *Fam* furieux (contre); **to be m. (keen) on** *Fam* (*person*) être fou de; (*films etc*) se passionner *or* s'emballer pour; **to drive m.** rendre fou; (*irritate*) énerver; **he drove me m. to go** *Fam* il m'a cassé les pieds pour que j'y aille; **like m.** comme un fou. ◆**maddening** *a* exaspérant. ◆**madhouse** *n Fam* maison *f* de fous. ◆**madly** *adv* (*in love, to spend money etc*) follement; (*desperately*) désespérément. ◆**madman** *n* (*pl* **-men**) fou *m*. ◆**madness** *n* folie *f*.
Madagascar [mædə'gæskər] *n* Madagascar *f*.
madam ['mædəm] *n* (*married*) madame *f*; (*unmarried*) mademoiselle *f*.
made [meɪd] *see* **make.**
Madeira [mə'dɪərə] *n* (*wine*) madère *m*.
madonna [mə'dɒnə] *n Rel* madone *f*.
maestro ['maɪstrəʊ] *n* (*pl* **-os**) *Mus* maestro *m*.
Mafia ['mæfɪə] *n* maf(f)ia *f*.
magazine [mægə'ziːn] *n* (*periodical*) magazine *m*, revue *f*; (*of gun, camera*) magasin *m*.
maggot ['mægət] *n* ver *m*, asticot *m*. ◆**maggoty** *a* véreux.
magic ['mædʒɪk] *n* magie *f*; – *a* (*word, wand*) magique. ◆**magical** *a* (*evening etc*) magique. ◆**ma'gician** *n* magicien, -ienne *mf*.
magistrate ['mædʒɪstreɪt] *n* magistrat *m*.
magnanimous [mæg'nænɪməs] *a* magnanime.
magnate ['mægneɪt] *n* (*tycoon*) magnat *m*.
magnesium [mæg'niːzɪəm] *n* magnésium *m*.
magnet ['mægnɪt] *n* aimant *m*. ◆**mag'netic** *a* magnétique. ◆**magnetism** *n* magnétisme *m*. ◆**magnetize** *vt* magnétiser.
magnificent [mæg'nɪfɪsənt] *a* magnifique. ◆**magnificence** *n* magnificence *f*. ◆**magnificently** *adv* magnifiquement.
magnify ['mægnɪfaɪ] *vt* (*image*) & *Fig* grossir; (*sound*) amplifier; **magnifying glass** loupe *f*. ◆**magnifi'cation** *n* grossissement *m*; amplification *f*. ◆**magnitude** *n* ampleur *f*.
magnolia [mæg'nəʊlɪə] *n* (*tree*) magnolia *m*.
magpie ['mægpaɪ] *n* (*bird*) pie *f*.
mahogany [mə'hɒgənɪ] *n* acajou *m*.
maid [meɪd] *n* (*servant*) bonne *f*; **old m.** *Pej* vieille fille *f*. ◆**maiden** *n Old-fashioned* jeune fille *f*; – *a* (*speech etc*) premier; (*flight*) inaugural; **m. name** nom *m* de jeune fille. ◆**maidenly** *a* virginal.
mail [meɪl] *n* (*system*) poste *f*; (*letters*) courrier *m*; – *a* (*van, bag etc*) postal; **m. order** vente *f* par correspondance; – *vt* mettre à la poste; **mailing list** liste *f* d'adresses. ◆**mailbox** *n Am* boîte *f* à *or* aux lettres. ◆**mailman** *n* (*pl* **-men**) *Am* facteur *m*.
maim [meɪm] *vt* mutiler, estropier.
main [meɪn] **1** *a* principal; **the m. thing is to . . .** l'essentiel est de . . . ; **m. line** *Rail* grande ligne *f*; **m. road** grande route *f*; **in the m.** (*mostly*) en gros, dans l'ensemble. **2** *n* **water/gas m.** conduite *f* d'eau/de gaz; **the mains** *El* le secteur; **a mains radio** une radio secteur. ◆**—ly** *adv* principalement, surtout. ◆**mainland** *n* continent *m*. ◆**main-**

stay *n* (*of family etc*) soutien *m*; (*of organization, policy*) pilier *m*. ◆**mainstream** *n* tendance *f* dominante.

maintain [meɪn'teɪn] *vt* (*continue, assert*) maintenir (**that** que); (*vehicle, family etc*) entretenir; (*silence*) garder. ◆**maintenance** *n* (*of vehicle, road etc*) entretien *m*; (*of prices, order, position etc*) maintien *m*; (*alimony*) pension *f* alimentaire.

maisonette [meɪzə'net] *n* duplex *m*.

maize [meɪz] *n* (*cereal*) maïs *m*.

majesty ['mædʒəstɪ] *n* majesté *f*; **Your M.** (*title*) Votre Majesté. ◆**ma'jestic** *a* majestueux.

major ['meɪdʒər] **1** *a* (*main, great*) & *Mus* majeur; **a m. road** une grande route. **2** *n Mil* commandant *m*. **3** *n* (*subject*) *Univ Am* dominante *f*; – *vi* **to m. in** se spécialiser en. ◆**majo'rette** *n* (**drum**) **m.** majorette *f*.

Majorca [mə'jɔːkə] *n* Majorque *f*.

majority [mə'dʒɒrɪtɪ] *n* majorité *f* (**of** de); **in the** *or* **a m.** en majorité, majoritaire; **the m. of people** la plupart des gens; – *a* (*vote etc*) majoritaire.

make [meɪk] *vt* (*pt & pp* **made**) faire; (*tool, vehicle etc*) fabriquer; (*decision*) prendre; (*friends, wage*) se faire; (*points*) *Sp* marquer; (*destination*) arriver à; **to m. happy/tired/***etc* rendre heureux/fatigué/*etc*; **he made ten francs on it** *Com* ça lui a rapporté dix francs; **she made the train** (*did not miss*) elle a eu le train; **to m. s.o. do sth** faire faire qch à qn, obliger qn à faire qch; **to m. oneself heard** se faire entendre; **to m. oneself at home** se mettre à l'aise; **to m. ready** préparer; **to m. yellow** jaunir; **she made him her husband** elle en a fait son mari; **to m. do** (*manage*) se débrouiller (**with** avec); **to m. do with** (*be satisfied with*) se contenter de; **to m. it** (*arrive*) arriver; (*succeed*) réussir; (*say*) dire; **I m. it five o'clock** j'ai cinq heures; **what do you m. of it?** qu'en penses-tu?; **I can't m. anything of it** je n'y comprends rien; **to m. a living** gagner sa vie; **you're made (for life)** ton avenir est assuré; **to m. believe** (*pretend*) faire semblant (**that one is** d'être); (*n*) **it's m.-believe** (*story etc*) c'est pure invention; **to live in a world of m.-believe** se bercer d'illusions; – *vi* **to m. as if to** (*appear to*) faire mine de; **to m. for** (*go towards*) aller vers; – *n* (*brand*) marque *f*; **of French/***etc* **m.** de fabrication française/*etc*. ■ **to m. off** *vi* (*run away*) se sauver; **to m. out** *vt* (*see*) distinguer; (*understand*) comprendre; (*decipher*) déchiffrer; (*draw up*) faire (*chèque, liste*); (*claim*) prétendre (**that** que); **you made me out to be silly** tu m'as fait passer pour un idiot; – *vi* (*manage*) *Fam* se débrouiller; **to m. over** *vt* (*transfer*) céder; (*change*) transformer (**into** en); **to m. up** *vt* (*story*) inventer; (*put together*) faire (*collection, liste, lit etc*); (*prepare*) préparer; (*form*) former, composer; (*loss*) compenser; (*quantity*) compléter; (*quarrel*) régler; (*one's face*) maquiller; – *vi* (*of friends*) se réconcilier; **to m. up for** (*loss, damage, fault*) compenser; (*lost time, mistake*) rattraper. ◆**m.-up** *n* (*of object etc*) constitution *f*; (*of person*) caractère *m*; (*for face*) maquillage *m*. ◆**making** *n* (*manufacture*) fabrication *f*; (*of dress*) confection *f*; **history in the m.** l'histoire en train de se faire; **the makings of** les éléments *mpl* (essentiels) de; **to have the makings of a pianist/***etc* avoir l'étoffe d'un pianiste/*etc*. ◆**maker** *n Com* fabricant *m*. ◆**makeshift** *n* expédient *m*; – *a* (*arrangement etc*) de fortune, provisoire.

maladjusted [mælə'dʒʌstɪd] *a* inadapté.

malaise [mæ'leɪz] *n* malaise *m*.

malaria [mə'leərɪə] *n* malaria *f*.

Malaysia [mə'leɪzɪə] *n* Malaisie *f*.

male [meɪl] *a Biol Bot etc* mâle; (*clothes, sex*) masculin; – *n* (*man, animal*) mâle *m*.

malevolent [mə'levələnt] *a* malveillant. ◆**malevolence** *n* malveillance *f*.

malfunction [mæl'fʌŋkʃ(ə)n] *n* mauvais fonctionnement *m*; – *vi* fonctionner mal.

malice ['mælɪs] *n* méchanceté *f*; **to bear s.o. m.** vouloir du mal à qn. ◆**ma'licious** *a* malveillant. ◆**ma'liciously** *adv* avec malveillance.

malign [mə'laɪn] *vt* (*slander*) calomnier.

malignant [mə'lɪgnənt] *a* (*person etc*) malfaisant; **m. tumour** *Med* tumeur *f* maligne. ◆**malignancy** *n Med* malignité *f*.

malingerer [mə'lɪŋgərər] *n* (*pretending illness*) simulateur, -euse *mf*.

mall [mɔːl] *n* (**shopping**) **m.** (*covered*) galerie *f* marchande; (*street*) rue *f* piétonnière.

malleable ['mælɪəb(ə)l] *a* malléable.

mallet ['mælɪt] *n* (*tool*) maillet *m*.

malnutrition [mælnjuː'trɪʃ(ə)n] *n* malnutrition *f*, sous-alimentation *f*.

malpractice [mæl'præktɪs] *n Med Jur* faute *f* professionnelle.

malt [mɔːlt] *n* malt *m*.

Malta ['mɔːltə] *n* Malte *f*. ◆**Mal'tese** *a & n* maltais, -aise (*mf*).

mammal ['mæm(ə)l] *n* mammifère *m*.

mammoth ['mæməθ] *a* (*large*) immense; – *n* (*extinct animal*) mammouth *m*.

man [mæn] *n* (*pl* **men** [men]) homme *m*; (*player*) *Sp* joueur *m*; (*chess piece*) pièce *f*; **a golf m.** (*enthusiast*) un amateur de golf; **he's a Bristol m.** (*by birth*) il est de Bristol; **to be m. and wife** être mari et femme; **my old m.** *Fam* (*father*) mon père; (*husband*) mon homme; **yes old m.!** *Fam* oui mon vieux!; **the m. in the street** l'homme de la rue; – *vt* (**-nn-**) (*ship*) pourvoir d'un équipage; (*fortress*) armer; (*guns*) servir; (*be on duty at*) être de service à; **manned spacecraft** engin *m* spatial habité. ◆**manhood** *n* (*period*) âge *m* d'homme. ◆**manhunt** *n* chasse *f* à l'homme. ◆**manlike** *a* (*quality*) d'homme viril. ◆**manly** *a* (**-ier, -iest**) viril. ◆**man-'made** *a* artificiel; (*fibre*) synthétique. ◆**manservant** *n* (*pl* **menservants**) domestique *m*. ◆**man-to-'man** *a* & *adv* d'homme à homme.

manacle ['mænɪk(ə)l] *n* menotte *f*.

manag/e ['mænɪdʒ] *vt* (*run*) diriger; (*affairs etc*) *Com* gérer; (*handle*) manier; (*take*) *Fam* prendre; (*eat*) *Fam* manger; (*contribute*) *Fam* donner; **to m. to do** (*succeed*) réussir *or* arriver à faire; (*contrive*) se débrouiller pour faire; **I'll m. it** j'y arriverai; – *vi* (*succeed*) y arriver; (*make do*) se débrouiller (**with** avec); **to m. without** sth se passer de qch. ◆**—ing** *a* **m. director** directeur *m* général; **the m. director** le PDG. ◆**—eable** *a* (*parcel, person etc*) maniable; (*feasible*) faisable. ◆**—ement** *n* direction *f*; (*of property etc*) gestion *f*; (*executive staff*) cadres *mpl*. ◆**—er** *n* directeur *m*; (*of shop, café*) gérant *m*; (**business**) **m.** (*of actor, boxer etc*) manager *m*. ◆**manage'ress** *n* directrice *f*; gérante *f*. ◆**managerial** [mænə'dʒɪərɪəl] *a* directorial; **the m. class** *or* **staff** les cadres *mpl*.

mandarin ['mændərɪn] **1** *n* (*high-ranking official*) haut fonctionnaire *m*; (*in political party*) bonze *m*; (*in university*) *Pej* mandarin *m*. **2** *a* & *n* **m. (orange)** mandarine *f*.

mandate ['mændeɪt] *n* mandat *m*. ◆**mandatory** *a* obligatoire.

mane [meɪn] *n* crinière *f*.

maneuver [mə'nuːvər] *n* & *vti Am* = **manoeuvre**.

mangle ['mæŋg(ə)l] **1** *n* (*for wringing*) essoreuse *f*; – *vt* (*clothes*) essorer. **2** *vt* (*damage*) mutiler.

mango ['mæŋgəʊ] *n* (*pl* **-oes** *or* **-os**) (*fruit*) mangue *f*.

mangy ['meɪndʒɪ] *a* (*animal*) galeux.

manhandle [mæn'hænd(ə)l] *vt* maltraiter.

manhole ['mænhəʊl] *n* trou *m* d'homme; **m. cover** plaque *f* d'égout.

mania ['meɪnɪə] *n* manie *f*. ◆**maniac** *n* fou *m*, folle *f*; *Psy Med* maniaque *mf*; **sex m.** obsédé *m* sexuel.

manicure ['mænɪkjʊər] *n* soin *m* des mains; – *vt* (*person*) manucurer; (*s.o.'s nails*) faire. ◆**manicurist** *n* manucure *mf*.

manifest ['mænɪfest] **1** *a* (*plain*) manifeste. **2** *vt* (*show*) manifester.

manifesto [mænɪ'festəʊ] *n* (*pl* **-os** *or* **-oes**) *Pol* manifeste *m*.

manifold ['mænɪfəʊld] *a* multiple.

manipulate [mə'nɪpjʊleɪt] *vt* manœuvrer; (*facts, electors etc*) *Pej* manipuler. ◆**manipu'lation** *n* manœuvre *f*; *Pej* manipulation *f* (**of** de).

mankind [mæn'kaɪnd] *n* (*humanity*) le genre humain.

manner ['mænər] *n* (*way*) manière *f*; (*behaviour*) attitude *f*, comportement *m*; *pl* (*social habits*) manières *fpl*; **in this m.** (*like this*) de cette manière; **all m. of** toutes sortes de. ◆**mannered** *a* (*affected*) maniéré; **well-/bad-m.** bien/mal élevé. ◆**mannerism** *n Pej* tic *m*.

manoeuvre [mə'nuːvər] *n* manœuvre *f*; – *vti* manœuvrer. ◆**manoeuvra'bility** *n* (*of vehicle etc*) maniabilité *f*.

manor ['mænər] *n* **m. (house)** manoir *m*.

manpower ['mænpaʊər] *n* (*labour*) main-d'œuvre *f*; *Mil* effectifs *mpl*; (*effort*) force *f*.

mansion ['mænʃ(ə)n] *n* hôtel *m* particulier; (*in country*) manoir *m*.

manslaughter ['mænslɔːtər] *n Jur* homicide *m* involontaire.

mantelpiece ['mænt(ə)lpiːs] *n* (*shelf*) cheminée *f*.

mantle ['mænt(ə)l] *n* (*cloak*) cape *f*.

manual ['mænjʊəl] **1** *a* (*work etc*) manuel. **2** *n* (*book*) manuel *m*.

manufactur/e [mænjʊ'fæktʃər] *vt* fabriquer; – *n* fabrication *f*. ◆**—er** *n* fabricant, -ante *mf*.

manure [mə'njʊər] *n* fumier *m*, engrais *m*.

manuscript ['mænjʊskrɪpt] *n* manuscrit *m*.

many ['menɪ] *a* & *n* beaucoup (de); **m. things** beaucoup de choses; **m. came** beaucoup sont venus; **very m., a good** *or* **great m.** un très grand nombre (de); **(a good** *or* **great) m. of** un (très) grand nombre de; **m. of them** un grand nombre d'entre eux; **m. times, m. a time** bien des fois; **m. kinds** toutes sortes (**of** de); **how m.?** combien (de)?; **too m.** trop (de); **one too m.** un de trop; **there are too m. of them** ils sont trop nombreux; **so m.** tant (de); **as m. books/***etc* as autant de livres/*etc* que; **as m. as** (*up to*) jusqu'à.

map [mæp] *n* (*of country etc*) carte *f*; (*plan*) plan *m*; – *vt* (**-pp-**) faire la carte *or* le plan de; **to m. out** (*road*) faire le tracé de; (*one's day etc*) *Fig* organiser.

maple ['meɪp(ə)l] *n* (*tree, wood*) érable *m*.

mar [mɑːr] *vt* (**-rr-**) gâter.

marathon ['mærəθən] *n* marathon *m*.

maraud [mə'rɔːd] *vi* piller. ◆**—ing** *a* pillard. ◆**—er** *n* pillard, -arde *mf*.

marble ['mɑːb(ə)l] *n* (*substance*) marbre *m*; (*toy ball*) bille *f*.

march [mɑːtʃ] *n* *Mil* marche *f*; – *vi* *Mil* marcher (au pas); **to m. in/out/***etc* *Fig* entrer/sortir/*etc* d'un pas décidé; **to m. past** défiler; – *vt* **to m. s.o. off** *or* **away** emmener qn. ◆**m.-past** *n* défilé *m*.

March [mɑːtʃ] *n* mars *m*.

mare [meər] *n* jument *f*.

margarine [mɑːdʒə'riːn] *n* margarine *f*.

margin ['mɑːdʒɪn] *n* (*of page etc*) marge *f*; **by a narrow m.** (*to win*) de justesse. ◆**marginal** *a* marginal; **m. seat** *Pol* siège *m* disputé. ◆**marginally** *adv* très légèrement.

marguerite [mɑːgə'riːt] *n* (*daisy*) marguerite *f*.

marigold ['mærɪgəʊld] *n* (*flower*) souci *m*.

marijuana [mærɪ'wɑːnə] *n* marijuana *f*.

marina [mə'riːnə] *n* marina *f*.

marinate ['mærɪneɪt] *vti* *Culin* mariner.

marine [mə'riːn] **1** *a* (*life, flora etc*) marin. **2** *n* (*soldier*) fusilier *m* marin, *Am* marine *m*.

marionette [mærɪə'net] *n* marionnette *f*.

marital ['mærɪt(ə)l] *a* matrimonial; (*relations*) conjugal; **m. status** situation *f* de famille.

maritime ['mærɪtaɪm] *a* (*province, climate etc*) maritime.

marjoram ['mɑːdʒərəm] *n* (*spice*) marjolaine *f*.

mark[1] [mɑːk] *n* (*symbol*) marque *f*; (*stain, trace*) trace *f*, tache *f*, marque *f*; (*token, sign*) *Fig* signe *m*; (*for exercise etc*) *Sch* note *f*; (*target*) but *m*; (*model*) *Tech* série *f*; **to make one's m.** *Fig* s'imposer; **up to the m.** (*person, work*) à la hauteur; – *vt* marquer; (*exam etc*) *Sch* corriger, noter; (*pay attention to*) faire attention à; **to m. time** *Mil* marquer le pas; *Fig* piétiner; **m. you . . . !** remarquez que . . . !; **to m. down** (*price*) baisser; **to m. off** (*separate*) séparer; (*on list*) cocher; **to m. out** (*area*) délimiter; **to m. s.o. out for** désigner qn pour; **to m. up** (*increase*) augmenter. ◆**—ed** *a* (*noticeable*) marqué. ◆**—edly** [-ɪdlɪ] *adv* visiblement. ◆**—ing(s)** *n*(*pl*) (*on animal etc*) marques *fpl*; (*on road*) signalisation *f* horizontale. ◆**—er** *n* (*flag etc*) marque *f*; (*pen*) feutre *m*, marqueur *m*.

mark[2] [mɑːk] *n* (*currency*) mark *m*.

market ['mɑːkɪt] *n* marché *m*; **on the open m.** en vente libre; **on the black m.** au marché noir; **the Common M.** le Marché commun; **m. value** valeur *f* marchande; **m. price** prix *m* courant; **m. gardener** maraîcher, -ère *mf*; – *vt* (*sell*) vendre; (*launch*) commercialiser. ◆**—ing** *n* marketing *m*, vente *f*. ◆**—able** *a* vendable.

marksman ['mɑːksmən] *n* (*pl* **-men**) tireur *m* d'élite.

marmalade ['mɑːməleɪd] *n* confiture *f* d'oranges.

maroon [mə'ruːn] *a* (*colour*) bordeaux *inv*.

marooned [mə'ruːnd] *a* abandonné; (*in snowstorm etc*) bloqué (**by** par).

marquee [mɑː'kiː] *n* (*for concerts, garden parties etc*) chapiteau *m*; (*awning*) *Am* marquise *f*.

marquis ['mɑːkwɪs] *n* marquis *m*.

marrow ['mærəʊ] *n* **1** (*of bone*) moelle *f*. **2** (*vegetable*) courge *f*.

marr/y ['mærɪ] *vt* épouser, se marier avec; **to m. (off)** (*of priest etc*) marier; – *vi* se marier. ◆**—ied** *a* marié; (*life, state*) conjugal; **m. name** nom *m* de femme mariée; **to get m.** se marier. ◆**marriage** *n* mariage *m*; **to be related by m. to** être parent par alliance de; – *a* (*bond*) conjugal; (*certificate*) de mariage; **m. bureau** agence *f* matrimoniale. ◆**marriageable** *a* en état de se marier.

marsh [mɑːʃ] *n* marais *m*, marécage *m*. ◆**marshland** *n* marécages *mpl*. ◆**marsh'mallow** *n* *Bot* *Culin* guimauve *f*.

marshal ['mɑːʃ(ə)l] **1** *n* (*in army*) maréchal *m*; (*in airforce*) général *m*; (*at public event*) membre *m* du service d'ordre; *Jur* *Am* shérif *m*. **2** *vt* (**-ll-**, *Am* **-l-**) (*gather*) rassembler; (*lead*) mener cérémonieusement.

martial ['mɑːʃ(ə)l] *a* martial; **m. law** loi *f* martiale.

Martian ['mɑːʃ(ə)n] *n* & *a* martien, -ienne (*mf*).

martyr ['mɑːtər] *n* martyr, -yre *mf*; – *vt* *Rel* martyriser. ◆**martyrdom** *n* martyre *m*.

marvel ['mɑːv(ə)l] *n* (*wonder*) merveille *f*; (*miracle*) miracle *m*; – *vi* (**-ll-**, *Am* **-l-**) s'émerveiller (**at** de); – *vt* **to m. that** s'étonner de ce que (+ *sub or indic*). ◆**marvellous** *a* merveilleux.

Marxism ['mɑːksɪz(ə)m] *n* marxisme *m*. ◆**Marxist** *a* & *n* marxiste (*mf*).

marzipan ['mɑːzɪpæn] *n* pâte *f* d'amandes.
mascara [mæ'skɑːrə] *n* mascara *m*.
mascot ['mæskɒt] *n* mascotte *f*.
masculine ['mæskjʊlɪn] *a* masculin. ◆**mascu'linity** *n* masculinité *f*.
mash [mæʃ] *n* (*for poultry etc*) pâtée *f*; (*potatoes*) *Culin* purée *f*; – *vt* **to m. (up)** (*crush*) & *Culin* écraser; **mashed potatoes** purée *f* (de pommes de terre).
mask [mɑːsk] *n* masque *m*; – *vt* (*cover, hide*) masquer (**from** à).
masochism ['mæsəkɪz(ə)m] *n* masochisme *m*. ◆**masochist** *n* masochiste *mf*. ◆**maso'chistic** *a* masochiste.
mason ['meɪs(ə)n] *n* maçon *m*. ◆**masonry** *n* maçonnerie *f*.
masquerade [mɑːskə'reɪd] *n* (*gathering, disguise*) mascarade *f*; – *vi* **to m. as** se faire passer pour.
mass[1] [mæs] *n* masse *f*; **a m. of** (*many*) une multitude de; (*pile*) un tas de, une masse de; **to be a m. of bruises** *Fam* être couvert de bleus; **masses of** *Fam* des masses de; **the masses** (*people*) les masses *fpl*; – *a* (*education*) des masses; (*culture, demonstration*) de masse; (*protests, departure*) en masse; (*production*) en série, en masse; (*hysteria*) collectif; **m. grave** fosse *f* commune; **m. media** mass media *mpl*; – *vi* (*of troops, people*) se masser. ◆**m.-pro'duce** *vt* fabriquer en série.
mass[2] [mæs] *n Rel* messe *f*.
massacre ['mæsəkər] *n* massacre *m*; – *vt* massacrer.
massage ['mæsɑːʒ] *n* massage *m*; – *vt* masser. ◆**ma'sseur** *n* masseur *m*. ◆**ma'sseuse** *n* masseuse *f*.
massive ['mæsɪv] *a* (*solid*) massif; (*huge*) énorme, considérable. ◆**—ly** *adv* (*to increase, reduce etc*) considérablement.
mast [mɑːst] *n Nau* mât *m*; *Rad TV* pylône *m*.
master ['mɑːstər] *n* maître *m*; (*in secondary school*) professeur *m*; **a m.'s degree** une maîtrise (**in** de); **M. of Arts/Science** (*person*) *Univ* Maître *m* ès lettres/sciences; **m. of ceremonies** (*presenter*) *Am* animateur, -trice *mf*; **m. card** carte *f* maîtresse; **m. stroke** coup *m* de maître; **m. key** passe-partout *m inv*; **old m.** (*painting*) tableau *m* de maître; **I'm my own m.** je ne dépends que de moi; – *vt* (*control*) maîtriser; (*subject, situation*) dominer; **she has mastered Latin** elle possède le latin. ◆**masterly** *a* magistral. ◆**mastery** *n* maîtrise *f* (**of** de).
mastermind ['mɑːstəmaɪnd] *n* (*person*) cerveau *m*; – *vt* organiser.
masterpiece ['mɑːstəpiːs] *n* chef-d'œuvre *m*.
mastic ['mæstɪk] *n* mastic *m* (silicone).
masturbate ['mæstəbeɪt] *vi* se masturber. ◆**mastur'bation** *n* masturbation *f*.
mat [mæt] **1** *n* tapis *m*, natte *f*; (*at door*) paillasson *m*; (**table**) **m.** (*of fabric*) napperon *m*; (*hard*) dessous-de-plat *m inv*; (**place**) **m.** set *m* (de table). **2** *a* (*paint, paper*) mat.
match[1] [mætʃ] *n* allumette *f*; **book of matches** pochette *f* d'allumettes. ◆**matchbox** *n* boîte *f* à allumettes. ◆**matchstick** *n* allumette *f*.
match[2] [mætʃ] *n* (*game*) *Sp* match *m*; (*equal*) égal, -ale *mf*; (*marriage*) mariage *m*; **to be a good m.** (*of colours, people etc*) être bien assortis; **he's a good m.** (*man to marry*) c'est un bon parti; – *vt* (*of clothes*) aller (bien) avec; **to m. (up to)** (*equal*) égaler; **to m. (up)** (*plates etc*) assortir; **to be well-matched** (*of colours, people etc*) être (bien) assortis, aller (bien) ensemble; – *vi* (*go with each other*) être assortis, aller (bien) ensemble. ◆**—ing** *a* (*dress etc*) assorti.
mate [meɪt] **1** *n* (*friend*) camarade *mf*; (*of animal*) mâle *m*, femelle *f*; **builder's/electrician's/***etc* **m.** aide-maçon/-électricien/*etc m*. **2** *vi* (*of animals*) s'accoupler (**with** avec). **3** *n Chess* mat *m*; – *vt* faire *or* mettre mat.
material [mə'tɪərɪəl] **1** *a* matériel; (*important*) important. **2** *n* (*substance*) matière *f*; (*cloth*) tissu *m*; (*for book*) matériaux *mpl*; **material(s)** (*equipment*) matériel *m*; **building material(s)** matériaux *mpl* de construction. ◆**materialism** *n* matérialisme *m*. ◆**materialist** *n* matérialiste *mf*. ◆**materia'listic** *a* matérialiste. ◆**materialize** *vi* se matérialiser. ◆**materially** *adv* matériellement; (*well-off etc*) sur le plan matériel.
maternal [mə'tɜːn(ə)l] *a* maternel. ◆**maternity** *n* maternité *f*; **m. hospital, m. unit** maternité *f*; – *a* (*clothes*) de grossesse; (*allowance, leave*) de maternité.
mathematical [mæθə'mætɪk(ə)l] *a* mathématique; **to have a m. brain** être doué pour les maths. ◆**mathema'tician** *n* mathématicien, -ienne *mf*. ◆**mathematics** *n* mathématiques *fpl*. ◆**maths** *n*, *Am* ◆**math** *n Fam* maths *fpl*.
matinée ['mætɪneɪ] *n Th* matinée *f*.

matriculation [mətrɪkjʊ'leɪʃ(ə)n] *n Univ* inscription *f.*

matrimony ['mætrɪmənɪ] *n* mariage *m.* ◆**matri'monial** *a* matrimonial.

matrix, *pl* **-ices** ['meɪtrɪks, -ɪsiːz] *n Tech* matrice *f.*

matron ['meɪtrən] *n Lit* mère *f* de famille, dame *f* âgée; (*nurse*) infirmière *f* (en) chef. ◆**matronly** *a* (*air etc*) de mère de famille; (*mature*) mûr; (*portly*) corpulent.

matt [mæt] *a* (*paint, paper*) mat.

matted ['mætɪd] *a* **m. hair** cheveux *mpl* emmêlés.

matter[1] ['mætər] *n* matière *f*; (*affair*) affaire *f*, question *f*; (*thing*) chose *f*; **no m.!** (*no importance*) peu importe!; **no m. what she does** quoi qu'elle fasse; **no m. where you go** où que tu ailles; **no m. who you are** qui que vous soyez; **no m. when** quel que soit le moment; **what's the m.?** qu'est-ce qu'il y a?; **what's the m. with you?** qu'est-ce que tu as?; **there's sth the m.** il y a qch qui ne va pas; **there's sth the m. with my leg** j'ai qch à la jambe; **there's nothing the m. with him** il n'a rien; – *vi* (*be important*) importer (**to** à); **it doesn't m. if/when/who/***etc* peu importe si/quand/qui/*etc*; **it doesn't m.!** ça ne fait rien!, peu importe! ◆**m.-of-'fact** *a* (*person, manner*) terre à terre; (*voice*) neutre.

matter[2] ['mætər] *n* (*pus*) *Med* pus *m.*

matting ['mætɪŋ] *n* (*material*) nattage *m*; **a piece of m., some m.** une natte.

mattress ['mætrəs] *n* matelas *m.*

mature [mə'tʃʊər] *a* mûr; (*cheese*) fait; – *vt* (*person, plan*) (faire) mûrir; – *vi* mûrir; (*of cheese*) se faire. ◆**maturity** *n* maturité *f.*

maul [mɔːl] *vt* (*of animal*) mutiler; (*of person*) *Fig* malmener.

mausoleum [mɔːsə'lɪəm] *n* mausolée *m.*

mauve [məʊv] *a* & *n* (*colour*) mauve (*m*).

maverick ['mævərɪk] *n* & *a Pol* dissident, -ente (*mf*).

mawkish ['mɔːkɪʃ] *a* d'une sensiblerie excessive, mièvre.

maxim ['mæksɪm] *n* maxime *f.*

maximum ['mæksɪməm] *n* (*pl* **-ima** [-ɪmə] *or* **-imums**) maximum *m*; – *a* maximum (*f inv*), maximal. ◆**maximize** *vt* porter au maximum.

may [meɪ] *v aux* (*pt* **might**) **1** (*possibility*) **he m. come** il peut arriver; **he might come** il pourrait arriver; **I m.** *or* **might be wrong** il se peut que je me trompe, je me trompe peut-être; **you m.** *or* **might have** tu aurais pu; **I m.** *or* **might have forgotten it** je l'ai peut-être oublié; **we m.** *or* **might as well go** nous ferions aussi bien de partir; **she fears I m.** *or* **might get lost** elle a peur que je ne me perde. **2** (*permission*) **m. I stay?** puis-je rester?; **m. I?** vous permettez?; **you m. go** tu peux partir. **3** (*wish*) **m. you be happy** (que tu) sois heureux. ◆**maybe** *adv* peut-être.

May [meɪ] *n* mai *m.*

mayhem ['meɪhem] *n* (*chaos*) pagaïe *f*; (*havoc*) ravages *mpl.*

mayonnaise [meɪə'neɪz] *n* mayonnaise *f.*

mayor [meər] *n* (*man, woman*) maire *m.* ◆**mayoress** *n* femme *f* du maire.

maze [meɪz] *n* labyrinthe *m.*

MC [em'siː] *abbr* = **master of ceremonies.**

me [miː] *pron* me, m'; (*after prep etc*) moi; **(to) me** (*indirect*) me, m'; **she knows me** elle me connaît; **he helps me** il m'aide; **he gives (to) me** il me donne; **with me** avec moi.

meadow ['medəʊ] *n* pré *m*, prairie *f.*

meagre ['miːgər] *a* maigre.

meal [miːl] *n* **1** (*food*) repas *m.* **2** (*flour*) farine *f.*

mealy-mouthed [miːlɪ'maʊðd] *a* mielleux.

mean[1] [miːn] *vt* (*pt* & *pp* **meant** [ment]) (*signify*) vouloir dire, signifier; (*destine*) destiner (**for** à); (*entail*) entraîner; (*represent*) représenter; (*refer to*) faire allusion à; **to m. to do** (*intend*) avoir l'intention de faire, vouloir faire; **I m. it, I m. what I say** je suis sérieux; **to m. sth to s.o.** (*matter*) avoir de l'importance pour qn; **it means sth to me** (*name, face*) ça me dit qch; **I didn't m. to!** je ne l'ai pas fait exprès!; **you were meant to come** vous étiez censé venir. ◆**—ing** *n* sens *m*, signification *f.* ◆**meaningful** *a* significatif. ◆**meaningless** *a* qui n'a pas de sens; (*absurd*) *Fig* insensé.

mean[2] [miːn] *a* (**-er, -est**) (*stingy*) avare, mesquin; (*petty*) mesquin; (*nasty*) méchant; (*inferior*) misérable. ◆**—ness** *n* (*greed*) avarice *f*; (*nastiness*) méchanceté *f.*

mean[3] [miːn] *a* (*distance*) moyen; – *n* (*middle position*) milieu *m*; (*average*) *Math* moyenne *f*; **the happy m.** le juste milieu.

meander [mɪ'ændər] *vi* (*of river*) faire des méandres.

means [miːnz] *n*(*pl*) (*method*) moyen(s) *m*(*pl*) (**to do, of doing** de faire); (*wealth*) moyens *mpl*; **by m. of** (*stick etc*) au moyen de; (*work, concentration*) à force de; **by all m.!** très certainement!; **by no m.** nullement; **independent** *or* **private m.** fortune *f* personnelle.

meant [ment] *see* **mean**[1].

meantime ['miːntaɪm] *adv* & *n* **(in the) m.** entre-temps. ◆**meanwhile** *adv* entre-temps.

measles ['miːz(ə)lz] *n* rougeole *f*.
measly ['miːzlɪ] *a* (*contemptible*) *Fam* minable.
measur/e ['meʒər] *n* mesure *f*; (*ruler*) règle *f*; **made to m.** fait sur mesure; – *vt* mesurer; (*strength etc*) *Fig* estimer, mesurer; (*adjust, adapt*) adapter (**to** à); **to m. up** mesurer; – *vi* **to m. up to** être à la hauteur de. ◆**—ed** *a* (*careful*) mesuré. ◆**—ement** *n* (*of chest, waist etc*) tour *m*; *pl* (*dimensions*) mesures *fpl*; **your hip m.** ton tour de hanches.
meat [miːt] *n* viande *f*; (*of crab, lobster etc*) chair *f*; *Fig* substance *f*; **m. diet** régime *m* carné. ◆**meaty** *a* (**-ier, -iest**) (*fleshy*) charnu; (*flavour*) de viande; *Fig* substantiel.
mechanic [mɪ'kænɪk] *n* mécanicien, -ienne *mf*. ◆**mechanical** *a* mécanique; (*reply etc*) *Fig* machinal. ◆**mechanics** *n* (*science*) mécanique *f*; *pl* (*workings*) mécanisme *m*. ◆**'mechanism** *n* mécanisme *m*. ◆**'mechanize** *vt* mécaniser.
medal ['med(ə)l] *n* médaille *f*. ◆**me'dallion** *n* (*ornament, jewel*) médaillon *m*. ◆**medallist** *n* médaillé, -ée *mf*; **to be a gold/silver m.** *Sp* être médaillé d'or/d'argent.
meddle ['med(ə)l] *vi* (*interfere*) se mêler (**in** de); (*tamper*) toucher (**with** à). ◆**meddlesome** *a* qui se mêle de tout.
media ['miːdɪə] *npl* **1 the (mass) m.** les médias *mpl*. **2** *see* **medium 2.**
mediaeval [medɪ'iːv(ə)l] *a* médiéval.
median ['miːdɪən] *a* **m. strip** *Aut Am* bande *f* médiane.
mediate ['miːdɪeɪt] *vi* servir d'intermédiaire (**between** entre). ◆**medi'ation** *n* médiation *f*. ◆**mediator** *n* médiateur, -trice *mf*.
medical ['medɪk(ə)l] *a* médical; (*school, studies*) de médecine; (*student*) en médecine; – *n* (*in school, army*) visite *f* médicale; (*private*) examen *m* médical. ◆**medicated** *a* (*shampoo*) médical. ◆**medi'cation** *n* médicaments *mpl*. ◆**me'dicinal** *a* médicinal. ◆**medicine** *n* médecine *f*; (*substance*) médicament *m*; **m. cabinet, m. chest** pharmacie *f*.
medieval [medɪ'iːv(ə)l] *a* médiéval.
mediocre [miːdɪ'əʊkər] *a* médiocre. ◆**mediocrity** *n* médiocrité *f*.
meditate ['medɪteɪt] *vi* méditer (**on** sur). ◆**medi'tation** *n* méditation *f*. ◆**meditative** *a* méditatif.
Mediterranean [medɪtə'reɪnɪən] *a* méditerranéen; – *n* **the M.** la Méditerranée.
medium ['miːdɪəm] **1** *a* (*average, middle*) moyen. **2** *n* (*pl* **media** ['miːdɪə]) *Phys* véhicule *m*; *Biol* milieu *m*; (*for conveying data or publicity*) support *m*; **through the m. of** par l'intermédiaire de; **the happy m.** le juste milieu. **3** *n* (*person*) médium *m*. ◆**m.-sized** *a* moyen, de taille moyenne.
medley ['medlɪ] *n* mélange *m*; *Mus* pot-pourri *m*.
meek [miːk] *a* (**-er, -est**) doux.
meet [miːt] *vt* (*pt & pp* **met**) (*encounter*) rencontrer; (*see again, join*) retrouver; (*pass in street, road etc*) croiser; (*fetch*) (aller *or* venir) chercher; (*wait for*) attendre; (*debt, enemy, danger*) faire face à; (*need*) combler; (*be introduced to*) faire la connaissance de; **to arrange to m. s.o.** donner rendez-vous à qn; – *vi* (*of people, teams, rivers, looks*) se rencontrer; (*of people by arrangement*) se retrouver; (*be introduced*) se connaître; (*of society*) se réunir; (*of trains, vehicles*) se croiser; **to m. up with** rencontrer; (*by arrangement*) retrouver; **to m. up** se rencontrer; se retrouver; **to m. with** (*accident, problem*) avoir; (*loss, refusal*) essuyer; (*obstacle, difficulty*) rencontrer; **to m. with s.o.** *Am* rencontrer qn; retrouver qn; – *n Sp Am* réunion *f*; **to make a m. with** *Fam* donner rendez-vous à. ◆**—ing** *n* réunion *f*; (*large*) assemblée *f*; (*between two people*) rencontre *f*, (*prearranged*) rendez-vous *m inv*; **in a m.** en conférence.
megalomania [megələʊ'meɪnɪə] *n* mégalomanie *f*. ◆**megalomaniac** *n* mégalomane *mf*.
megaphone ['megəfəʊn] *n* porte-voix *m inv*.
melancholy ['melənkəlɪ] *n* mélancolie *f*; – *a* mélancolique.
mellow ['meləʊ] *a* (**-er, -est**) (*fruit*) mûr; (*colour, voice, wine*) moelleux; (*character*) mûri par l'expérience; – *vi* (*of person*) s'adoucir.
melodrama ['melədrɑːmə] *n* mélodrame *m*. ◆**melodra'matic** *a* mélodramatique.
melody ['melədɪ] *n* mélodie *f*. ◆**me'lodic** *a* mélodique. ◆**me'lodious** *a* mélodieux.
melon ['melən] *n* (*fruit*) melon *m*.
melt [melt] *vi* fondre; **to m. into** (*merge*) *Fig* se fondre dans; – *vt* (faire) fondre; **to m. down** (*metal object*) fondre; **melting point** point *m* de fusion; **melting pot** *Fig* creuset *m*.
member ['membər] *n* membre *m*; **M. of Parliament** député *m*. ◆**membership** *n* adhésion *f* (**of** à); (*number*) nombre *m* de(s) membres; (*members*) membres *mpl*; **m.** (**fee**) cotisation *f*.

membrane ['membreɪn] *n* membrane *f*.
memento [mə'mentəʊ] *n* (*pl* **-os** *or* **-oes**) (*object*) souvenir *m*.
memo ['meməʊ] *n* (*pl* **-os**) note *f*; **m. pad** bloc-notes *m*. ◆**memo'randum** *n* note *f*; *Pol Com* mémorandum *m*.
memoirs ['memwɑːz] *npl* (*essays*) mémoires *mpl*.
memory ['memərɪ] *n* mémoire *f*; (*recollection*) souvenir *m*; **to the** *or* **in m. of** à la mémoire de. ◆**memorable** *a* mémorable. ◆**me'morial** *a* (*plaque etc*) commémoratif; – *n* monument *m*, mémorial *m*. ◆**memorize** *vt* apprendre par cœur.
men [men] *see* **man.** ◆**menfolk** *n Fam* hommes *mpl*.
menac/e ['menɪs] *n* danger *m*; (*nuisance*) *Fam* plaie *f*; (*threat*) menace *f*; – *vt* menacer. ◆**–ingly** *adv* (*to say*) d'un ton menaçant; (*to do*) d'une manière menaçante.
menagerie [mɪ'nædʒərɪ] *n* ménagerie *f*.
mend [mend] *vt* (*repair*) réparer; (*clothes*) raccommoder; **to m. one's ways** se corriger, s'amender; – *n* raccommodage *m*; **to be on the m.** (*after illness*) aller mieux.
menial ['miːnɪəl] *a* inférieur.
meningitis [menɪn'dʒaɪtɪs] *n Med* méningite *f*.
menopause ['menəpɔːz] *n* ménopause *f*.
menstruation [menstrʊ'eɪʃ(ə)n] *n* menstruation *f*.
mental ['ment(ə)l] *a* mental; (*hospital*) psychiatrique; (*mad*) *Sl* fou; **m. strain** tension *f* nerveuse. ◆**men'tality** *n* mentalité *f*. ◆**mentally** *adv* mentalement; **he's m. handicapped** c'est un handicapé mental; **she's m. ill** c'est une malade mentale.
mention ['menʃ(ə)n] *vt* mentionner, faire mention de; **not to m. . . .** sans parler de . . . , sans compter . . . ; **don't m. it!** il n'y a pas de quoi!; **no savings/***etc* **worth mentioning** pratiquement pas d'économies/*etc*; – *n* mention *f*.
mentor ['mentɔːr] *n* (*adviser*) mentor *m*.
menu ['menjuː] *n* menu *m*.
mercantile ['mɜːkəntaɪl] *a* (*activity etc*) commercial; (*ship*) marchand; (*nation*) commerçant.
mercenary ['mɜːsɪnərɪ] *a* & *n* mercenaire (*m*).
merchandise ['mɜːtʃəndaɪz] *n* (*articles*) marchandises *fpl*; (*total stock*) marchandise *f*.
merchant ['mɜːtʃ(ə)nt] *n* (*trader*) *Fin* négociant, -ante *mf*; (**retail**) **m.** commerçant *m* (en détail); **wine m.** négociant, -ante *mf* en vins; (*shopkeeper*) marchand *m* de vins; – *a* (*vessel, navy*) marchand; (*seaman*) de la marine marchande; **m. bank** banque *f* de commerce.
mercury ['mɜːkjʊrɪ] *n* mercure *m*.
mercy ['mɜːsɪ] *n* pitié *f*; *Rel* miséricorde *f*; **to beg for m.** demander grâce; **at the m. of** à la merci de; **it's a m. that . . .** (*stroke of luck*) c'est une chance que . . . . ◆**merciful** *a* miséricordieux. ◆**mercifully** *adv* (*fortunately*) *Fam* heureusement. ◆**merciless** *a* impitoyable.
mere [mɪər] *a* simple; (*only*) ne . . . que; **she's a m. child** ce n'est qu'une enfant; **it's a m. kilometre** ça ne fait qu'un kilomètre; **by m. chance** par pur hasard; **the m. sight of her** *or* **him** sa seule vue. ◆**–ly** *adv* (tout) simplement.
merg/e [mɜːdʒ] *vi* (*blend*) se mêler (**with** à); (*of roads*) se (re)joindre; (*of firms*) *Com* fusionner; – *vt* (*unify*) *Pol* unifier; *Com* fusionner. ◆**–er** *n Com* fusion *f*.
meridian [mə'rɪdɪən] *n* méridien *m*.
meringue [mə'ræŋ] *n* (*cake*) meringue *f*.
merit ['merɪt] *n* mérite *m*; **on its merits** (*to consider sth etc*) objectivement; – *vt* mériter.
mermaid ['mɜːmeɪd] *n* (*woman*) sirène *f*.
merry ['merɪ] *a* (**-ier, -iest**) gai; (*drunk*) *Fam* éméché. ◆**m.-go-round** *n* (*at funfair etc*) manège *m*. ◆**m.-making** *n* réjouissances *fpl*. ◆**merrily** *adv* gaiement. ◆**merriment** *n* gaieté *f*, rires *mpl*.
mesh [meʃ] *n* (*of net etc*) maille *f*; (*fabric*) tissu *m* à mailles; (*of intrigue etc*) *Fig* réseau *m*; (*of circumstances*) *Fig* engrenage *m*; **wire m.** grillage *m*.
mesmerize ['mezməraɪz] *vt* hypnotiser.
mess[1] [mes] **1** *n* (*confusion*) désordre *m*, pagaïe *f*; (*muddle*) gâchis *m*; (*dirt*) saleté *f*; **in a m.** en désordre; (*trouble*) *Fam* dans le pétrin; (*pitiful state*) dans un triste état; **to make a m. of** (*spoil*) gâcher. **2** *vt* **to m. s.o. about** (*bother, treat badly*) *Fam* déranger qn, embêter qn; **to m. up** (*spoil*) gâcher; (*dirty*) salir; (*room*) mettre en désordre; – *vi* **to m. about** (*have fun, idle*) s'amuser; (*play the fool*) faire l'idiot; **to m. about with** (*fiddle with*) s'amuser avec. ◆**m.-up** *n* (*disorder*) *Fam* gâchis *m*. ◆**messy** *a* (**-ier, -iest**) (*untidy*) en désordre; (*dirty*) sale; (*confused*) *Fig* embrouillé, confus.
mess[2] [mes] *n Mil* mess *m inv*.
message ['mesɪdʒ] *n* message *m*. ◆**messenger** *n* messager, -ère *mf*; (*in office, hotel*) coursier, -ière *mf*.
Messiah [mɪ'saɪə] *n* Messie *m*.

Messrs ['mesəz] *npl* **M. Brown** Messieurs *or* MM Brown.
met [met] *see* **meet.**
metal ['met(ə)l] *n* métal *m.* ◆**me'tallic** *a* métallique; (*paint*) métallisé. ◆**metalwork** *n* (*objects*) ferronnerie *f*; (*study, craft*) travail *m* des métaux.
metamorphosis, *pl* **-oses** [metə'mɔːfəsɪs, -əsiːz] *n* métamorphose *f*.
metaphor ['metəfər] *n* métaphore *f.* ◆**meta'phorical** *a* métaphorique.
metaphysical [metə'fɪzɪk(ə)l] *a* métaphysique.
mete [miːt] *vt* **to m. out** (*justice*) rendre; (*punishment*) infliger.
meteor ['miːtɪər] *n* météore *m.* ◆**mete'oric** *a* **m. rise** *Fig* ascension *f* fulgurante. ◆**meteorite** *n* météorite *m.*
meteorological [miːtɪərə'lɒdʒɪk(ə)l] *a* météorologique. ◆**meteo'rology** *n* météorologie *f*.
meter ['miːtər] *n* (*device*) compteur *m*; **(parking) m.** parcmètre *m*; **m. maid** *Am Fam* contractuelle *f*.
method ['meθəd] *n* méthode *f.* ◆**me'thodical** *a* méthodique.
Methodist ['meθədɪst] *a* & *n Rel* méthodiste (*mf*).
methylated ['meθɪleɪtɪd] *a* **m. spirit(s)** alcool *m* à brûler. ◆**meths** *n Fam* = **methylated spirits.**
meticulous [mɪ'tɪkjʊləs] *a* méticuleux. ◆**—ness** *n* soin *m* méticuleux.
metre ['miːtər] *n* mètre *m.* ◆**metric** ['metrɪk] *a* métrique.
metropolis [mə'trɒpəlɪs] *n* (*chief city*) métropole *f.* ◆**metro'politan** *a* métropolitain.
mettle ['met(ə)l] *n* courage *m*, fougue *f*.
mew [mjuː] *vi* (*of cat*) miauler.
mews [mjuːz] *n* (*street*) ruelle *f*; **m. flat** appartement *m* chic (*aménagé dans une ancienne écurie*).
Mexico ['meksɪkəʊ] *n* Mexique *m.* ◆**Mexican** *a* & *n* mexicain, -aine (*mf*).
mezzanine ['mezəniːn] *n* **m. (floor)** entresol *m.*
miaow [miː'aʊ] *vi* (*of cat*) miauler; – *n* miaulement *m*; – *int* miaou.
mice [maɪs] *see* **mouse.**
mickey ['mɪkɪ] *n* **to take the m. out of s.o.** *Sl* charrier qn.
micro- ['maɪkrəʊ] *pref* micro-.
microbe ['maɪkrəʊb] *n* microbe *m.*
microchip ['maɪkrəʊtʃɪp] *n* puce *f*.
microcosm ['maɪkrəʊkɒz(ə)m] *n* microcosme *m.*
microfilm ['maɪkrəʊfɪlm] *n* microfilm *m.*
microphone ['maɪkrəfəʊn] *n* microphone *m.*
microscope ['maɪkrəskəʊp] *n* microscope *m.* ◆**micro'scopic** *a* microscopique.
microwave ['maɪkrəʊweɪv] *n* micro-onde *f*; **m. oven** four *m* à micro-ondes.
mid [mɪd] *a* **(in) m.-June** (à) la mi-juin; **(in) m. morning** au milieu de la matinée; **in m. air** en plein ciel; **to be in one's m.-twenties** avoir environ vingt-cinq ans.
midday [mɪd'deɪ] *n* midi *m*; – *a* de midi.
middle ['mɪd(ə)l] *n* milieu *m*; (*waist*) *Fam* taille *f*; **(right) in the m. of** au (beau) milieu de; **in the m. of work** en plein travail; **in the m. of saying/working/***etc* en train de dire/travailler/*etc*; – *a* (*central*) du milieu; (*class, ear, quality*) moyen; (*name*) deuxième. ◆**m.-'aged** *a* d'un certain âge. ◆**m.-'class** *a* bourgeois. ◆**m.-of-the-'road** *a* (*politics, views*) modéré; (*music, tastes*) sage.
middling ['mɪdlɪŋ] *a* moyen, passable.
midge [mɪdʒ] *n* (*fly*) moucheron *m.*
midget ['mɪdʒɪt] *n* nain *m*, naine *f*; – *a* minuscule.
Midlands ['mɪdləndz] *npl* **the M.** les comtés *mpl* du centre de l'Angleterre.
midnight ['mɪdnaɪt] *n* minuit *f*.
midriff ['mɪdrɪf] *n Anat* diaphragme *m*; (*belly*) *Fam* ventre *m.*
midst [mɪdst] *n* **in the m. of** (*middle*) au milieu de; **in our/their m.** parmi nous/eux.
midsummer [mɪd'sʌmər] *n* milieu *m* de l'été; (*solstice*) solstice *m* d'été. ◆**midwinter** *n* milieu *m* de l'hiver; solstice *m* d'hiver.
midterm ['mɪdtɜːm] *a* **m. holidays** *Sch* petites vacances *fpl*.
midway [mɪd'weɪ] *a* & *adv* à mi-chemin.
midweek [mɪd'wiːk] *n* milieu *m* de la semaine.
midwife ['mɪdwaɪf] *n* (*pl* **-wives**) sage-femme *f*.
might [maɪt] **1** *see* **may. 2** *n* (*strength*) force *f*. ◆**mighty** *a* **(-ier, -iest)** puissant; (*ocean*) vaste; (*very great*) *Fam* sacré; – *adv* (*very*) *Fam* rudement.
migraine ['miːgreɪn, 'maɪgreɪn] *n Med* migraine *f*.
migrate [maɪ'greɪt] *vi* émigrer. ◆**'migrant** *a* & *n* **m. (worker)** migrant, -ante (*mf*). ◆**migration** *n* migration *f*.
mike [maɪk] *n Fam* micro *m.*
mild [maɪld] *a* **(-er, -est)** (*person, weather, taste etc*) doux; (*beer, punishment*) léger; (*medicine, illness*) bénin. ◆**—ly** *adv* douce-

ment; (*slightly*) légèrement; **to put it m.** pour ne pas dire plus. ◆**—ness** *n* douceur *f*; légèreté *f*; caractère *m* bénin.

mildew ['mɪldjuː] *n* (*on cheese etc*) moisissure *f*.

mile [maɪl] *n* mile *m*, mille *m* (= *1,6 km*); *pl* (*loosely*) = kilomètres *mpl*; **to walk for miles** marcher pendant des kilomètres; **miles better** (*much*) *Fam* bien mieux. ◆**mileage** *n* = kilométrage *m*; **m. (per gallon)** = consommation *f* aux cent kilomètres. ◆**milestone** *n* = borne *f* kilométrique; *Fig* jalon *m*.

militant ['mɪlɪtənt] *a* & *n* militant, -ante (*mf*). ◆**military** *a* militaire; – *n* **the m.** (*soldiers*) les militaires *mpl*; (*army*) l'armée *f*. ◆**militate** *vi* (*of arguments etc*) militer (**in favour of** pour).

militia [mə'lɪʃə] *n* milice *f*. ◆**militiaman** *n* (*pl* **-men**) milicien *m*.

milk [mɪlk] *n* lait *m*; **evaporated m.** lait *m* concentré; – *a* (*chocolate*) au lait; (*bottle, can*) à lait; (*diet*) lacté; (*produce*) laitier; **m. float** voiture *f* de laitier; **m. shake** milk-shake *m*; – *vt* (*cow*) traire; (*extract*) *Fig* soutirer (**s.o. of sth** qch à qn); (*exploit*) *Fig* exploiter. ◆**—ing** *n* traite *f*. ◆**milkman** *n* (*pl* **-men**) laitier *m*. ◆**milky** *a* (**-ier, -iest**) (*diet*) lacté; (*coffee, tea*) au lait; (*colour*) laiteux; **the M. Way** la Voie lactée.

mill [mɪl] **1** *n* moulin *m*; (*factory*) usine *f*; **cotton m.** filature *f* de coton; **paper m.** papeterie *f*; – *vt* (*grind*) moudre. **2** *vi* **to m. around** (*of crowd*) grouiller. ◆**miller** *n* meunier, -ière *mf*. ◆**millstone** *n* (*burden*) boulet *m* (**round one's neck** qu'on traîne).

millennium, *pl* **-nia** [mɪ'lenɪəm, -nɪə] *n* millénaire *m*.

millet ['mɪlɪt] *n Bot* millet *m*.

milli- [mɪlɪ] *pref* milli-.

millimetre ['mɪlɪmiːtər] *n* millimètre *m*.

million ['mɪljən] *n* million *m*; **a m. men/***etc* un million d'hommes/*etc*; **two m.** deux millions. ◆**millio'naire** *n* millionnaire *mf*. ◆**millionth** *a* & *n* millionième (*mf*).

mime [maɪm] *n* (*actor*) mime *mf*; (*art*) mime *m*; – *vti* mimer.

mimeograph® ['mɪmɪəgræf] *vt* polycopier.

mimic ['mɪmɪk] *vt* (**-ck-**) imiter; – *n* imitateur, -trice *mf*. ◆**mimicking** *n*, ◆**mimicry** *n* imitation *f*.

mimosa [mɪ'məʊzə] *n Bot* mimosa *m*.

minaret [mɪnə'ret] *n* (*of mosque*) minaret *m*.

mince [mɪns] *n* (*meat*) hachis *m* (de viande); *Am* = **mincemeat**; – *vt* hacher; **not to m. matters** *or* **one's words** ne pas mâcher ses mots. ◆**mincemeat** *n* (*dried fruit*) mélange *m* de fruits secs. ◆**mincer** *n* (*machine*) hachoir *m*.

mind [maɪnd] **1** *n* esprit *m*; (*sanity*) raison *f*; (*memory*) mémoire *f*; (*opinion*) avis *m*, idée *f*; (*thought*) pensée *f*; (*head*) tête *f*; **to change one's m.** changer d'avis; **to my m.** à mon avis; **in two minds** (*undecided*) irrésolu; **to make up one's m.** se décider; **to be on s.o.'s m.** (*worry*) préoccuper qn; **out of one's m.** (*mad*) fou; **to bring to m.** (*recall*) rappeler; **to bear** *or* **keep in m.** (*remember*) se souvenir de; **to have in m.** (*person, plan*) avoir en vue; **to have a good m. to do** avoir bien envie de faire. **2** *vti* (*heed*) faire attention à; (*look after*) garder, s'occuper de; (*noise, dirt etc*) être gêné par; (*one's language*) surveiller; **m. you don't fall** (*beware*) prends garde de ne pas tomber; **m. you do it** n'oublie pas de le faire; **do you m. if?** (*I smoke etc*) ça vous gêne si?; (*I leave, help etc*) ça ne vous fait rien si?; **I don't m. the sun** le soleil ne me gêne pas, je ne suis pas gêné par le soleil; **I don't m.** (*care*) ça m'est égal; **I wouldn't m. a cup of tea** (*would like*) j'aimerais bien une tasse de thé; **I m. that . . .** ça m'ennuie *or* me gêne que . . . ; **never m.!** (*it doesn't matter*) ça ne fait rien!, tant pis!; (*don't worry*) ne vous en faites pas!; **m. (out)!** (*watch out*) attention!; **m. you . . .** remarquez (que) . . . ; **m. your own business!, never you m.!** mêlez-vous de ce qui vous regarde! ◆**—ed** *suffix* **fair-m.** *a* impartial; **like-m.** *a* de même opinion. ◆**—er** *n* (*for children*) gardien, -ienne *mf*, (*nurse*) nourrice *f*; (*bodyguard*) *Fam* gorille *m*. ◆**mind-boggling** *a* stupéfiant, qui confond l'imagination. ◆**mindful** *a* **m. of sth/doing** attentif à qch/à faire. ◆**mindless** *a* stupide.

mine[1] [maɪn] *poss pron* le mien, la mienne, *pl* les mien(ne)s; **this hat is m.** ce chapeau est à moi *or* est le mien; **a friend of m.** un ami à moi.

min/e[2] [maɪn] **1** *n* (*for coal, gold etc*) & *Fig* mine *f*; – *vt* **to m. (for)** (*coal etc*) extraire. **2** *n* (*explosive*) mine *f*; – *vt* (*beach, bridge etc*) miner. ◆**—ing** *n* exploitation *f* minière; – *a* (*industry*) minier. ◆**—er** *n* mineur *m*.

mineral ['mɪnərəl] *a* & *n* minéral (*m*).

mingle ['mɪŋg(ə)l] *vi* se mêler (**with** à); **to m. with** (*socially*) fréquenter.

mingy ['mɪndʒɪ] *a* (**-ier, -iest**) (*mean*) *Fam* radin.

mini ['mɪnɪ] *pref* mini-.

miniature ['mɪnɪtʃər] *n* miniature *f*; – *a* (*train etc*) miniature *inv*; (*tiny*) minuscule.

minibus ['mɪnɪbʌs] *n* minibus *m.* ◆**mini-cab** *n* (radio-)taxi *m.*
minim ['mɪnɪm] *n Mus* blanche *f.*
minimum ['mɪnɪməm] *n* (*pl* **-ima** [-ɪmə] *or* **-imums**) minimum *m*; – *a* minimum (*f inv*), minimal. ◆**minimal** *a* minimal. ◆**minimize** *vt* minimiser.
minister ['mɪnɪstər] *n Pol Rel* ministre *m.* ◆**mini'sterial** *a* ministériel. ◆**ministry** *n* ministère *m.*
mink [mɪŋk] *n* (*animal, fur*) vison *m.*
minor ['maɪnər] *a* (*small*) *Jur Mus* mineur; (*detail, operation*) petit; – *n Jur* mineur, -eure *mf.*
Minorca [mɪ'nɔːkə] *n* Minorque *f.*
minority [maɪ'nɒrɪtɪ] *n* minorité *f*; **in the** *or* **a m.** en minorité, minoritaire; – *a* minoritaire.
mint [mɪnt] **1** *n* (*place*) Hôtel *m* de la Monnaie; **a m. (of money)** *Fig* une petite fortune; – *vt* (*money*) frapper; – *a* (*stamp*) neuf; **in m. condition** à l'état neuf. **2** *n Bot Culin* menthe *f*; (*sweet*) pastille *f* de menthe; – *a* à la menthe.
minus ['maɪnəs] *prep Math* moins; (*without*) *Fam* sans; **it's m. ten (degrees)** il fait moins dix (degrès); – *n* **m. (sign)** (signe *m*) moins *m.*
minute[1] ['mɪnɪt] **1** *n* minute *f*; **this (very) m.** (*now*) à la minute; **any m. (now)** d'une minute à l'autre; **m. hand** (*of clock*) grande aiguille *f.* **2** *npl* (*of meeting*) procès-verbal *m.*
minute[2] [maɪ'njuːt] *a* (*tiny*) minuscule; (*careful, exact*) minutieux.
minx [mɪŋks] *n* (*girl*) *Pej* diablesse *f*, chipie *f.*
miracle ['mɪrək(ə)l] *n* miracle *m.* ◆**mi'raculous** *a* miraculeux.
mirage ['mɪrɑːʒ] *n* mirage *m.*
mire [maɪər] *n Lit* fange *f.*
mirror ['mɪrər] *n* miroir *m*, glace *f*; *Fig* miroir *m*; **(rear view) m.** *Aut* rétroviseur *m*; – *vt* refléter.
mirth [mɜːθ] *n Lit* gaieté *f*, hilarité *f.*
misadventure [mɪsəd'ventʃər] *n* mésaventure *f.*
misanthropist [mɪ'zænθrəpɪst] *n* misanthrope *mf.*
misapprehend [mɪsæprɪ'hend] *vt* mal comprendre. ◆**misapprehension** *n* malentendu *m.*
misappropriate [mɪsə'prəʊprɪeɪt] *vt* (*money*) détourner.
misbehave [mɪsbɪ'heɪv] *vi* se conduire mal; (*of child*) faire des sottises.
miscalculate [mɪs'kælkjʊleɪt] *vt* mal calculer; – *vi Fig* se tromper. ◆**miscalcu'lation** *n* erreur *f* de calcul.
miscarriage [mɪs'kærɪdʒ] *n* **to have a m.** *Med* faire une fausse couche; **m. of justice** erreur *f* judiciaire. ◆**miscarry** *vi Med* faire une fausse couche; (*of plan*) *Fig* échouer.
miscellaneous [mɪsɪ'leɪnɪəs] *a* divers.
mischief ['mɪstʃɪf] *n* espièglerie *f*; (*maliciousness*) méchanceté *f*; **to get into m.** faire des bêtises; **full of m. = mischievous; to make m. for** (*trouble*) créer des ennuis à; **to do s.o. a m.** (*harm*) faire mal à qn; **a little m.** (*child*) un petit démon. ◆**mischievous** *a* (*playful, naughty*) espiègle, malicieux; (*malicious*) méchant.
misconception [mɪskən'sepʃ(ə)n] *n* idée *f* fausse.
misconduct [mɪs'kɒndʌkt] *n* mauvaise conduite *f*; *Com* mauvaise gestion *f.*
misconstrue [mɪskən'struː] *vt* mal interpréter.
misdeed [mɪs'diːd] *n* méfait *m.*
misdemeanor [mɪsdɪ'miːnər] *n Jur* délit *m.*
misdirect [mɪsdɪ'rekt] *vt* (*letter*) mal adresser; (*energies*) mal diriger; (*person*) mal renseigner.
miser ['maɪzər] *n* avare *mf.* ◆**—ly** *a* avare.
misery ['mɪzərɪ] *n* (*suffering*) souffrances *fpl*; (*sadness*) tristesse *f*; (*sad person*) *Fam* grincheux, -euse *mf*; *pl* (*troubles*) misères *fpl*; **his life is a m.** il est malheureux. ◆**miserable** *a* (*wretched*) misérable; (*unhappy*) malheureux; (*awful*) affreux; (*derisory*) dérisoire. ◆**miserably** *adv* misérablement; (*to fail*) lamentablement.
misfire [mɪs'faɪər] *vi* (*of engine*) avoir des ratés; (*of plan*) *Fig* rater.
misfit ['mɪsfɪt] *n Pej* inadapté, -ée *mf.*
misfortune [mɪs'fɔːtʃuːn] *n* malheur *m*, infortune *f.*
misgivings [mɪs'gɪvɪŋz] *npl* (*doubts*) doutes *mpl*; (*fears*) craintes *fpl.*
misguided [mɪs'gaɪdɪd] *a* (*action etc*) imprudent; **to be m.** (*of person*) se tromper.
mishandle [mɪs'hænd(ə)l] *vt* (*affair, situation*) traiter avec maladresse; (*person*) s'y prendre mal avec.
mishap ['mɪshæp] *n* (*accident*) mésaventure *f*; (*hitch*) contretemps *m.*
misinform [mɪsɪn'fɔːm] *vt* mal renseigner.
misinterpret [mɪsɪn'tɜːprɪt] *vt* mal interpréter.
misjudge [mɪs'dʒʌdʒ] *vt* (*person, distance etc*) mal juger.
mislay [mɪs'leɪ] *vt* (*pt & pp* **mislaid**) égarer.
mislead [mɪs'liːd] *vt* (*pt & pp* **misled**) tromper. ◆**—ing** *a* trompeur.

mismanage [mɪsˈmænɪdʒ] *vt* mal administrer. ◆**—ment** *n* mauvaise administration *f*.
misnomer [mɪsˈnəʊmər] *n* (*name*) nom *m or* terme *m* impropre.
misogynist [mɪˈsɒdʒɪnɪst] *n* misogyne *mf*.
misplac/e [mɪsˈpleɪs] *vt* (*trust etc*) mal placer; (*lose*) égarer. ◆**—ed** *a* (*remark etc*) déplacé.
misprint [ˈmɪsprɪnt] *n* faute *f* d'impression, coquille *f*.
mispronounce [mɪsprəˈnaʊns] *vt* mal prononcer.
misquote [mɪsˈkwəʊt] *vt* citer inexactement.
misrepresent [mɪsreprɪˈzent] *vt* présenter sous un faux jour.
miss[1] [mɪs] *vt* (*train, target, opportunity etc*) manquer, rater; (*not see*) ne pas voir; (*not understand*) ne pas comprendre; (*one's youth, deceased person etc*) regretter; (*sth just lost*) remarquer l'absence de; **he misses Paris/her** Paris/elle lui manque; **I m. you** tu me manques; **don't m. seeing this play** (*don't fail to*) ne manque pas de voir cette pièce; **to m. out** (*omit*) sauter; – *vi* manquer, rater; **to m. out** (*lose a chance*) rater l'occasion; **to m. out on** (*opportunity etc*) rater, laisser passer; – *n* coup *m* manqué; **that was** *or* **we had a near m.** on l'a échappé belle; **I'll give it a m.** *Fam* (*not go*) je n'y irai pas; (*not take or drink or eat*) je n'en prendrai pas. ◆**—ing** *a* (*absent*) absent; (*in war, after disaster*) disparu; (*object*) manquant; **there are two cups/students m.** il manque deux tasses/deux étudiants.
miss[2] [mɪs] *n* mademoiselle *f*; **Miss Brown** Mademoiselle *or* Mlle Brown.
misshapen [mɪsˈʃeɪp(ə)n] *a* difforme.
missile [ˈmɪsaɪl, *Am* ˈmɪs(ə)l] *n* (*rocket*) *Mil* missile *m*; (*object thrown*) projectile *m*.
mission [ˈmɪʃ(ə)n] *n* mission *f*. ◆**missionary** *n* missionnaire *m*.
missive [ˈmɪsɪv] *n* (*letter*) missive *f*.
misspell [mɪsˈspel] *vt* (*pt & pp* **-ed** *or* **misspelt**) mal écrire.
mist [mɪst] *n* (*fog*) brume *f*; (*on glass*) buée *f*; – *vi* **to m. over** *or* **up** s'embuer.
mistake [mɪˈsteɪk] *n* erreur *f*, faute *f*; **to make a m.** se tromper, faire (une) erreur; **by m.** par erreur; – *vt* (*pt* **mistook**, *pp* **mistaken**) (*meaning, intention etc*) se tromper sur; **to m. the date/place/***etc* se tromper de date/de lieu/*etc*; **you can't m., there's no mistaking** (*his face, my car etc*) il est impossible de ne pas reconnaître; **to m. s.o./sth for** prendre qn/qch pour. ◆**mistaken** *a* (*idea etc*) erroné; **to be m.** se tromper. ◆**mistakenly** *adv* par erreur.
mister [ˈmɪstər] *n Fam* monsieur *m*.
mistletoe [ˈmɪs(ə)ltəʊ] *n Bot* gui *m*.
mistreat [mɪsˈtriːt] *vt* maltraiter.
mistress [ˈmɪstrɪs] *n* maîtresse *f*; (*in secondary school*) professeur *m*.
mistrust [mɪsˈtrʌst] *n* méfiance *f*; – *vt* se méfier de. ◆**mistrustful** *a* méfiant.
misty [ˈmɪstɪ] *a* (**-ier, -iest**) (*foggy*) brumeux; (*glass*) embué.
misunderstand [mɪsʌndəˈstænd] *vt* (*pt & pp* **-stood**) mal comprendre. ◆**misunderstanding** *n* (*disagreement*) malentendu *m*; (*mistake*) erreur *f*. ◆**misunderstood** *a* (*person*) incompris.
misuse [mɪsˈjuːz] *vt* (*word, tool*) mal employer; (*power etc*) abuser de; – [mɪsˈjuːs] *n* (*of word*) emploi *m* abusif; (*of tool*) usage *m* abusif; (*of power etc*) abus *m*.
mite [maɪt] *n* **1** (*insect*) mite *f*. **2** **(poor) m.** (*child*) (pauvre) petit, -ite *mf*. **3** **a m.** (*somewhat*) *Fam* un petit peu.
mitigate [ˈmɪtɪgeɪt] *vt* atténuer.
mitt(en) [mɪt, ˈmɪt(ə)n] *n* (*glove*) moufle *f*.
mix [mɪks] *vt* mélanger, mêler; (*cement, cake*) préparer; (*salad*) remuer; **to m. up** mélanger; (*perplex*) embrouiller (*qn*); (*confuse, mistake*) confondre (**with** avec); **to be mixed up with s.o.** (*involved*) être mêlé aux affaires de qn; **to m. up in** (*involve*) mêler à; – *vi* se mêler; (*of colours*) s'allier; **to m. with** (*socially*) fréquenter; **she doesn't m. (in)** elle n'est pas sociable; – *n* (*mixture*) mélange *m*. ◆**—ed** *a* (*school, marriage*) mixte; (*society*) mêlé; (*feelings*) mitigés, mêlés; (*results*) divers; (*nuts, chocolates etc*) assortis; **to be (all) m. up** (*of person*) être désorienté; (*of facts, account etc*) être embrouillé. ◆**—ing** *n* mélange *m*. ◆**—er** *n Culin El* mixe(u)r *m*; (*for mortar*) *Tech* malaxeur *m*; **to be a good m.** (*of person*) être sociable. ◆**mixture** *n* mélange *m*; (*for cough*) sirop *m*. ◆**mix-up** *n Fam* confusion *f*.
mm *abbr* (*millimetre*) mm.
moan [məʊn] *vi* (*groan*) gémir; (*complain*) se plaindre (**to** à, **about** de, **that** que); – *n* gémissement *m*; plainte *f*.
moat [məʊt] *n* douve(s) *f*(*pl*).
mob [mɒb] *n* (*crowd*) cohue *f*, foule *f*; (*gang*) bande *f*; **the m.** (*masses*) la populace; (*Mafia*) *Am Sl* la mafia; – *vt* (**-bb-**) assiéger. ◆**mobster** *n Am Sl* gangster *m*.
mobile [ˈməʊbaɪl, *Am* ˈməʊb(ə)l] *a* mobile; (*having a car etc*) *Fam* motorisé; **m. home**

mobil-home *m*; **m. library** bibliobus *m*; – *n* (*Am* ['məʊbiːl]) (*ornament*) mobile *m*. ◆**mo'bility** *n* mobilité *f*. ◆**mobili'zation** *n* mobilisation *f*. ◆**mobilize** *vti* mobiliser.

moccasin ['mɒkəsɪn] *n* (*shoe*) mocassin *m*.

mocha ['məʊkə] *n* (*coffee*) moka *m*.

mock [mɒk] **1** *vt* se moquer de; (*mimic*) singer; – *vi* se moquer (**at** de). **2** *a* (*false*) simulé; (*exam*) blanc. ◆**—ing** *n* moquerie *f*; – *a* moqueur. ◆**mockery** *n* (*act*) moquerie *f*; (*parody*) parodie *f*; **to make a m. of** tourner en ridicule.

mock-up ['mɒkʌp] *n* (*model*) maquette *f*.

mod cons [mɒd'kɒnz] *abbr Fam* = **modern conveniences.**

mode [məʊd] *n* (*manner, way*) mode *m*; (*fashion, vogue*) mode *f*.

model ['mɒd(ə)l] *n* (*example, person etc*) modèle *m*; **(fashion) m.** mannequin *m*; **(scale) m.** modèle *m* (réduit); – *a* (*behaviour, factory etc*) modèle; (*car, plane*) modèle réduit *inv*; **m. railway** train *n* miniature; – *vt* modeler (**on** sur); (*hats*) présenter (les modèles de); – *vi* (*for fashion*) être mannequin; (*pose for artist*) poser. ◆**modelling** *n* (*of statues etc*) modelage *m*.

moderate[1] ['mɒdərət] *a* modéré; (*in speech*) mesuré; (*result*) passable; – *n Pol* modéré, -ée *mf*. ◆**—ly** *adv* (*in moderation*) modérément; (*averagely*) moyennement.

moderate[2] ['mɒdəreɪt] *vt* (*diminish, tone down*) modérer. ◆**mode'ration** *n* modération *f*; **in m.** avec modération.

modern ['mɒd(ə)n] *a* moderne; **m. languages** langues *fpl* vivantes; **m. conveniences** tout le confort moderne. ◆**modernism** *n* modernisme *m*. ◆**moderni'zation** *n* modernisation *f*. ◆**modernize** *vt* moderniser.

modest ['mɒdɪst] *a* modeste. ◆**modesty** *n* (*quality*) modestie *f*; (*moderation*) modération *f*; (*of salary etc*) modicité *f*.

modicum ['mɒdɪkəm] *n* **a m. of** un soupçon de, un petit peu de.

modify ['mɒdɪfaɪ] *vt* (*alter*) modifier; (*tone down*) modérer. ◆**modifi'cation** *n* modification *f*.

modulate ['mɒdjʊleɪt] *vt* moduler. ◆**modu'lation** *n* modulation *f*.

module ['mɒdjuːl] *n* module *m*.

mogul ['məʊg(ə)l] *n* magnat *m*, manitou *m*.

mohair ['məʊheər] *n* mohair *m*.

moist [mɔɪst] *a* (**-er, -est**) humide; (*clammy, sticky*) moite. ◆**moisten** *vt* humecter. ◆**moisture** *n* humidité *f*; (*on glass*) buée *f*. ◆**moisturiz/e** *vt* (*skin*) hydrater. ◆**—er** *n* (*cream*) crème *f* hydratante.

molar ['məʊlər] *n* (*tooth*) molaire *f*.

molasses [mə'læsɪz] *n* (*treacle*) *Am* mélasse *f*.

mold [məʊld] *Am* = **mould.**

mole [məʊl] *n* **1** (*on skin*) grain *m* de beauté. **2** (*animal, spy*) taupe *f*.

molecule ['mɒlɪkjuːl] *n* molécule *f*.

molest [mə'lest] *vt* (*annoy*) importuner; (*child, woman*) *Jur* attenter à la pudeur de.

mollusc ['mɒləsk] *n* mollusque *m*.

mollycoddle ['mɒlɪkɒd(ə)l] *vt* dorloter.

molt [məʊlt] *Am* = **moult.**

molten ['məʊlt(ə)n] *a* (*metal*) en fusion.

mom [mɒm] *n Am Fam* maman *f*.

moment ['məʊmənt] *n* moment *m*, instant *m*; **this (very) m.** (*now*) à l'instant; **the m. she leaves** dès qu'elle partira; **any m. (now)** d'un moment *or* d'un instant à l'autre. ◆**momentarily** (*Am* [məʊmən'terɪlɪ]) *adv* (*temporarily*) momentanément; (*soon*) *Am* tout à l'heure. ◆**momentary** *a* momentané.

momentous [məʊ'mentəs] *a* important.

momentum [məʊ'mentəm] *n* (*speed*) élan *m*; **to gather** *or* **gain m.** (*of ideas etc*) *Fig* gagner du terrain.

mommy ['mɒmɪ] *n Am Fam* maman *f*.

Monaco ['mɒnəkəʊ] *n* Monaco *f*.

monarch ['mɒnək] *n* monarque *m*. ◆**monarchy** *n* monarchie *f*.

monastery ['mɒnəst(ə)rɪ] *n* monastère *m*.

Monday ['mʌndɪ] *n* lundi *m*.

monetary ['mʌnɪt(ə)rɪ] *a* monétaire.

money ['mʌnɪ] *n* argent *m*; **paper m.** papier-monnaie *m*, billets *mpl*; **to get one's m.'s worth** en avoir pour son argent; **he gets** *or* **earns good m.** il gagne bien (sa vie); **to be in the m.** *Fam* rouler sur l'or; **m. order** mandat *m*. ◆**moneybags** *n Pej Fam* richard, -arde *mf*. ◆**moneybox** *n* tirelire *f*. ◆**moneychanger** *n* changeur *m*. ◆**moneylender** *n* prêteur, -euse *mf* sur gages. ◆**moneymaking** *a* lucratif. ◆**money-spinner** *n* (*source of wealth*) *Fam* mine *f* d'or.

mongol ['mɒŋg(ə)l] *n* & *a Med* mongolien, -ienne (*mf*).

mongrel ['mʌŋgrəl] *n* (*dog*) bâtard *m*.

monitor ['mɒnɪtər] **1** *n* (*pupil*) chef *m* de classe. **2** *n* (*screen*) *Tech* moniteur *m*. **3** *vt* (*a broadcast*) *Rad* écouter; (*check*) *Fig* contrôler.

monk [mʌŋk] *n* moine *m*, religieux *m*.

monkey ['mʌŋkɪ] *n* singe *m*; **little m.** (*child*) *Fam* polisson, -onne *mf*; **m. business** *Fam*

singeries *fpl*; – *vi* **to m. about** *Fam* faire l'idiot.
mono ['mɒnəʊ] *a* (*record etc*) mono *inv*.
mono- ['mɒnəʊ] *pref* mono-.
monocle ['mɒnək(ə)l] *n* monocle *m*.
monogram ['mɒnəgræm] *n* monogramme *m*.
monologue ['mɒnəlɒg] *n* monologue *m*.
monopoly [mə'nɒpəli] *n* monopole *m*. ◆**monopolize** *vt* monopoliser.
monosyllable ['mɒnəsɪləb(ə)l] *n* monosyllabe *m*. ◆**monosy'llabic** *a* monosyllabique.
monotone ['mɒnətəʊn] *n* **in a m.** sur un ton monocorde.
monotony [mə'nɒtəni] *n* monotonie *f*. ◆**monotonous** *a* monotone.
monsoon [mɒn'suːn] *n* (*wind, rain*) mousson *f*.
monster ['mɒnstər] *n* monstre *m*. ◆**mon'strosity** *n* (*horror*) monstruosité *f*. ◆**monstrous** *a* (*abominable, enormous*) monstrueux.
month [mʌnθ] *n* mois *m*. ◆**monthly** *a* mensuel; **m. payment** mensualité *f*; – *n* (*periodical*) mensuel *m*; – *adv* (*every month*) mensuellement.
Montreal [mɒntrɪ'ɔːl] *n* Montréal *m or f*.
monument ['mɒnjʊmənt] *n* monument *m*. ◆**monu'mental** *a* monumental; **m. mason** marbrier *m*.
moo [muː] *vi* meugler; – *n* meuglement *m*.
mooch [muːtʃ] **1** *vi* **to m. around** *Fam* flâner. **2** *vt* **to m. sth off s.o.** (*cadge*) *Am Sl* taper qch à qn.
mood [muːd] *n* (*of person*) humeur *f*; (*of country*) état *m* d'esprit; *Gram* mode *m*; **in a good/bad m.** de bonne/mauvaise humeur; **to be in the m. to do** *or* **for doing** être d'humeur à faire, avoir envie de faire. ◆**moody** *a* (**-ier, -iest**) (*changeable*) d'humeur changeante; (*bad-tempered*) de mauvaise humeur.
moon [muːn] *n* lune *f*; **once in a blue m.** (*rarely*) *Fam* tous les trente-six du mois; **over the m.** (*delighted*) *Fam* ravi (**about** de). ◆**moonlight 1** *n* clair *m* de lune. **2** *vi Fam* travailler au noir. ◆**moonshine** *n* (*talk*) *Fam* balivernes *fpl*.
moor [mʊər] **1** *vt Nau* amarrer; – *vi* mouiller. **2** *n* (*open land*) lande *f*. ◆**—ings** *npl Nau* (*ropes etc*) amarres *fpl*; (*place*) mouillage *m*.
moose [muːs] *n inv* (*animal*) orignac *m*, élan *m*.
moot [muːt] **1** *a* (*point*) discutable. **2** *vt* (*question*) soulever, suggérer.
mop [mɒp] **1** *n* balai *m* (à laver), balai *m* éponge; **dish m.** lavette *f*; **m. of hair** tignasse *f*. **2** *vt* (**-pp-**) **to m. (up)** (*wipe*) essuyer; **to m. one's brow** s'essuyer le front.
mope [məʊp] *vi* **to m. (about)** être déprimé, avoir le cafard.
moped ['məʊped] *n* cyclomoteur *m*, mobylette® *f*.
moral ['mɒrəl] *a* moral; – *n* (*of story etc*) morale *f*; *pl* (*standards*) moralité *f*, morale *f*. ◆**morale** [mə'rɑːl, *Am* mə'ræl] *n* moral *m*. ◆**moralist** *n* moraliste *mf*. ◆**mo'rality** *n* (*morals*) moralité *f*. ◆**moralize** *vi* moraliser. ◆**morally** *adv* moralement.
morass [mə'ræs] *n* (*land*) marais *m*; (*mess*) *Fig* bourbier *m*.
moratorium [mɒrə'tɔːrɪəm] *n* moratoire *m*.
morbid ['mɔːbɪd] *a* morbide.
more [mɔːr] *a* & *n* plus (de) (**than** que); (*other*) d'autres; **m. cars/***etc* plus de voitures/*etc*; **he has m. (than you)** il en a plus (que toi); **a few m. months** encore quelques mois, quelques mois de plus; **(some) m. tea/***etc* encore du thé/*etc*; **(some) m. details** d'autres détails; **m. than a kilo/ten/***etc* (*with quantity, number*) plus d'un kilo/de dix/*etc*; – *adv* (*tired, rapidly etc*) plus (**than** que); **m. and m.** de plus en plus; **m. or less** plus ou moins; **the m. he shouts the m. hoarse he gets** plus il crie plus il s'enroue; **she hasn't any m.** elle n'en a plus. ◆**mo'reover** *adv* de plus, d'ailleurs.
moreish ['mɔːrɪʃ] *a Fam* qui a un goût de revenez-y.
mores ['mɔːreɪz] *npl* mœurs *fpl*.
morgue [mɔːg] *n* (*mortuary*) morgue *f*.
moribund ['mɒrɪbʌnd] *a* moribond.
morning ['mɔːnɪŋ] *n* matin *m*; (*duration of morning*) matinée *f*; **in the m.** (*every morning*) le matin; (*during the morning*) pendant la matinée; (*tomorrow*) demain matin; **at seven in the m.** à sept heures du matin; **every Tuesday m.** tous les mardis matin; **in the early m.** au petit matin; – *a* du matin, matinal. ◆**mornings** *adv Am* le matin.
Morocco [mə'rɒkəʊ] *n* Maroc *m*. ◆**Moroccan** *a* & *n* marocain, -aine (*mf*).
moron ['mɔːrɒn] *n* crétin, -ine *mf*.
morose [mə'rəʊs] *a* morose.
morphine ['mɔːfiːn] *n* morphine *f*.
Morse [mɔːs] *n* & *a* **M. (code)** morse *m*.
morsel ['mɔːs(ə)l] *n* (*of food*) petite bouchée *f*.
mortal ['mɔːt(ə)l] *a* & *n* mortel, -elle (*mf*). ◆**mor'tality** *n* (*death rate*) mortalité *f*.
mortar ['mɔːtər] *n* mortier *m*.

mortgage ['mɔːgɪdʒ] *n* prêt-logement *m*; – *vt* (*house, future*) hypothéquer.
mortician [mɔː'tɪʃ(ə)n] *n Am* entrepreneur *m* de pompes funèbres.
mortify ['mɔːtɪfaɪ] *vt* mortifier.
mortuary ['mɔːtʃʊəri] *n* morgue *f*.
mosaic [məʊ'zeɪɪk] *n* mosaïque *f*.
Moscow ['mɒskəʊ, *Am* 'mɒskaʊ] *n* Moscou *m or f*.
Moses ['məʊzɪz] *a* **M. basket** couffin *m*.
Moslem ['mɒzlɪm] *a* & *n* musulman, -ane (*mf*).
mosque [mɒsk] *n* mosquée *f*.
mosquito [mɒ'skiːtəʊ] *n* (*pl* **-oes**) moustique *m*; **m. net** moustiquaire *f*.
moss [mɒs] *n Bot* mousse *f*. ◆**mossy** *a* moussu.
most [məʊst] *a* & *n* **the m.** (*greatest in amount etc*) le plus (de); **I have (the) m. books** j'ai le plus de livres; **I have (the) m.** j'en ai le plus; **m. (of the) books/***etc* la plupart des livres/*etc*; **m. of the cake/***etc* la plus grande partie du gâteau/*etc*; **m. of them** la plupart d'entre eux; **m. of it** la plus grande partie; **at (the very) m.** tout au plus; **to make the m. of** profiter (au maximum) de; – *adv* (le) plus; (*very*) fort, très; **the m. beautiful** le plus beau, la plus belle (**in, of** de); **to talk (the) m.** parler le plus; **m. of all** (*especially*) surtout. ◆**—ly** *adv* surtout, pour la plupart.
motel [məʊ'tel] *n* motel *m*.
moth [mɒθ] *n* papillon *m* de nuit; (**clothes**) **m.** mite *f*. ◆**m.-eaten** *a* mité. ◆**mothball** *n* boule *f* de naphtaline.
mother ['mʌðər] *n* mère *f*; **M.'s Day** la fête des Mères; **m. tongue** langue *f* maternelle; – *vt* (*care for*) materner. ◆**motherhood** *n* maternité *f*. ◆**motherly** *a* maternel.
mother-in-law ['mʌðərɪnlɔː] *n* (*pl* **mothers-in-law**) belle-mère *f*. ◆**m.-of-pearl** *n* (*substance*) nacre *f*. ◆**m.-to-'be** *n* (*pl* **mothers-to-be**) future mère *f*.
motion ['məʊʃ(ə)n] *n* mouvement *m*; *Pol* motion *f*; **m. picture** film *m*; – *vti* **to m. (to) s.o. to do** faire signe à qn de faire. ◆**—less** *a* immobile.
motive ['məʊtɪv] *n* motif *m* (**for, of** de); *Jur* mobile *m* (**for** de). ◆**motivate** *vt* (*person, decision etc*) motiver. ◆**moti'vation** *n* motivation *f*; (*incentive*) encouragement *m*.
motley ['mɒtlɪ] *a* (*coloured*) bigarré; (*collection*) hétéroclite.
motor ['məʊtər] *n* (*engine*) moteur *m*; (*car*) *Fam* auto *f*; – *a* (*industry, vehicle etc*) automobile; (*accident*) d'auto; **m. boat** canot *m* automobile; **m. mechanic** mécanicien-auto *m*; **m. mower** tondeuse *f* à moteur; – *vi* (*drive*) rouler en auto. ◆**—ing** *n Sp* automobilisme *m*; **school of m.** auto-école *f*. ◆**motorbike** *n Fam* moto *f*. ◆**motorcade** *n* cortège *m* (officiel) (*de voitures*). ◆**motorcar** *n* automobile *f*. ◆**motorcycle** *n* moto *f*, motocyclette *f*. ◆**motorcyclist** *n* motocycliste *mf*. ◆**motorist** *n* automobiliste *mf*. ◆**motorized** *a* motorisé. ◆**motorway** *n* autoroute *f*.
mottled ['mɒt(ə)ld] *a* tacheté.
motto ['mɒtəʊ] *n* (*pl* **-oes**) devise *f*.
mould [məʊld] **1** *n* (*shape*) moule *m*; – *vt* (*clay etc*) mouler; (*statue, character*) modeler. **2** *n* (*growth, mildew*) moisissure *f*. ◆**mouldy** *a* (**-ier, -iest**) moisi; **to go m.** moisir.
moult [məʊlt] *vi* muer. ◆**—ing** *n* mue *f*.
mound [maʊnd] *n* (*of earth*) tertre *m*; (*pile*) *Fig* monceau *m*.
mount [maʊnt] **1** *n* (*mountain*) *Lit* mont *m*. **2** *n* (*horse*) monture *f*; (*frame for photo or slide*) cadre *m*; (*stamp hinge*) charnière *f*; – *vt* (*horse, hill, jewel, photo, demonstration etc*) monter; (*ladder, tree etc*) monter sur, grimper à; (*stamp*) coller (dans un album); – *vi* **to m. (up)** (*on horse*) se mettre en selle. **3** *vi* (*increase*) monter; **to m. up** (*add up*) chiffrer (**to** à); (*accumulate*) s'accumuler.
mountain ['maʊntɪn] *n* montagne *f*; – *a* (*people, life*) montagnard. ◆**mountai'neer** *n* alpiniste *mf*. ◆**mountai'neering** *n* alpinisme *m*. ◆**mountainous** *a* montagneux.
mourn [mɔːn] *vti* **to m. (for)** pleurer. ◆**—ing** *n* deuil *m*; **in m.** en deuil. ◆**—er** *n* parent, -ente *mf or* ami, -ie *mf* du défunt *or* de la défunte. ◆**mournful** *a* triste.
mouse, *pl* mice [maʊs, maɪs] *n* souris *f*. ◆**mousetrap** *n* souricière *f*.
mousse [muːs] *n Culin* mousse *f*.
moustache [mə'stɑːʃ, *Am* 'mʌstæʃ] *n* moustache *f*.
mousy ['maʊsɪ] *a* (**-ier, -iest**) (*hair*) *Pej* châtain terne; (*shy*) *Fig* timide.
mouth [maʊθ] *n* (*pl* **-s** [maʊðz]) bouche *f*; (*of dog, lion etc*) gueule *f*; (*of river*) embouchure *f*; (*of cave, harbour*) entrée *f*; – [maʊð] *vt Pej* dire. ◆**mouthful** *n* (*of food*) bouchée *f*; (*of liquid*) gorgée *f*. ◆**mouthorgan** *n* harmonica *m*. ◆**mouthpiece** *n Mus* embouchure *f*; (*spokesman*) *Fig* porte-parole *m inv*. ◆**mouthwash** *n* bain *m* de bouche. ◆**mouth-watering** *a* appétissant.
mov/e [muːv] *n* mouvement *m*; (*change of*

house etc) déménagement *m*; (*change of job*) changement *m* d'emploi; (*transfer of employee*) mutation *f*; (*in game*) coup *m*, (*one's turn*) tour *m*; (*act*) *Fig* démarche *f*; (*step*) pas *m*; (*attempt*) tentative *f*; **to make a m.** (*leave*) se préparer à partir; (*act*) *Fig* passer à l'action; **to get a m. on** *Fam* se dépêcher; **on the m.** en marche; – *vt* déplacer, remuer, bouger; (*arm, leg*) remuer; (*crowd*) faire partir; (*put*) mettre; (*transport*) transporter; (*piece in game*) jouer; (*propose*) *Pol* proposer; **to m. s.o.** (*incite*) pousser qn (**to do** à faire); (*emotionally*) émouvoir qn; (*transfer in job*) muter qn; **to m. house** déménager; **to m. sth back** reculer qch; **to m. sth down** descendre qch; **to m. sth forward** avancer qch; **to m. sth over** pousser qch; – *vi* bouger, remuer; (*go*) aller (**to** à); (*pass*) passer (**to** à); (*leave*) partir; (*change seats*) changer de place; (*progress*) avancer; (*act*) agir; (*play*) jouer; **to m. (out)** (*of house etc*) déménager; **to m. to** (*a new region etc*) aller habiter; **to m. about** se déplacer; (*fidget*) remuer; **to m. along** *or* **forward** *or* **on** avancer; **to m. away** *or* **off** (*go away*) s'éloigner; **to m. back** (*withdraw*) reculer; (*return*) retourner; **to m. in** (*to house*) emménager; **to m. into** (*house*) emménager dans; **m. on!** circulez!; **to m. over** *or* **up** se pousser. ◆**—ing** *a* en mouvement; (*part*) *Tech* mobile; (*stairs*) mécanique; (*touching*) émouvant. ◆**mov(e)able** *a* mobile. ◆**movement** *n* (*action, group etc*) & *Mus* mouvement *m*.

movie ['muːvɪ] *n Fam* film *m*; **the movies** (*cinema*) le cinéma; **m. camera** caméra *f*. ◆**moviegoer** *n* cinéphile *mf*.

mow [məʊ] *vt* (*pp* **mown** *or* **mowed**) (*field*) faucher; **to m. the lawn** tondre le gazon; **to m. down** (*kill etc*) *Fig* faucher. ◆**—er** *n* (**lawn**) **m.** tondeuse *f* (à gazon).

MP [em'piː] *n abbr* (*Member of Parliament*) député *m*.

Mrs ['mɪsɪz] *n* (*married woman*) **Mrs Brown** Madame *or* Mme Brown.

Ms [mɪz] *n* (*married or unmarried woman*) **Ms Brown** Madame *or* Mme Brown.

MSc, *Am* **MS** *abbr* = **Master of Science.**

much [mʌtʃ] *a* & *n* beaucoup (de); **not m. time/money/***etc* pas beaucoup de temps/d'argent/*etc*; **not m.** pas beaucoup; **m. of** (*a good deal of*) une bonne partie de; **as m. as** (*to do, know etc*) autant que; **as m. wine/***etc* **as** autant de vin/*etc* que; **as m. as you like** autant que tu veux; **twice as m.** deux fois plus (de); **how m.?** combien (de)?; **too m.** trop (de); **so m.** tant (de), tellement (de); **I know/I shall do this m.** je sais/je ferai ceci (du moins); **this m. wine** ça de vin; **it's not m. of a garden** ce n'est pas merveilleux comme jardin; **m. the same** presque le même; – *adv* **very m.** beaucoup; **not (very) m.** pas beaucoup; **she doesn't say very m.** elle ne dit pas grand-chose.

muck [mʌk] **1** *n* (*manure*) fumier *m*; (*filth*) *Fig* saleté *f*. **2** *vi* **to m. about** *Fam* (*have fun, idle*) s'amuser; (*play the fool*) faire l'idiot; **to m. about with** *Fam* (*fiddle with*) s'amuser avec; (*alter*) changer (*texte etc*); **to m. in** (*join in*) *Fam* participer, contribuer; – *vt* **to m. s.o. about** *Fam* embêter qn, déranger qn; **to m. up** (*spoil*) *Fam* gâcher, ruiner. ◆**m.-up** *n Fam* gâchis *m*. ◆**mucky** *a* (**-ier, -iest**) sale.

mucus ['mjuːkəs] *n* mucosités *fpl*.

mud [mʌd] *n* boue *f*. ◆**muddy** *a* (**-ier, -iest**) (*water*) boueux; (*hands etc*) couvert de boue. ◆**mudguard** *n* garde-boue *m inv*.

muddle ['mʌd(ə)l] *n* (*mess*) désordre *m*; (*mix-up*) confusion *f*; **in a m.** (*room etc*) sens dessus dessous, en désordre; (*person*) désorienté; (*mind, ideas*) embrouillé; – *vt* (*person, facts etc*) embrouiller; (*papers*) mélanger; – *vi* **to m. through** *Fam* se débrouiller tant bien que mal.

muff [mʌf] *n* (*for hands*) manchon *m*.

muffin ['mʌfɪn] *n* petit pain *m* brioché.

muffl/e ['mʌf(ə)l] *vt* (*noise*) assourdir. ◆**—ed** *a* (*noise*) sourd. ◆**—er** *n* (*scarf*) cache-col *m inv*; *Aut Am* silencieux *m*.

mug [mʌg] **1** *n* grande tasse *f*; (*of metal or plastic*) gobelet *m*; (**beer**) **m.** chope *f*. **2** *n* (*face*) *Sl* gueule *f*; **m. shot** *Pej* photo *f* (d'identité). **3** *n* (*fool*) *Fam* niais, -aise *mf*. **4** *vt* (**-gg-**) (*attack*) agresser. ◆**mugger** *n* agresseur *m*. ◆**mugging** *n* agression *f*.

muggy ['mʌgɪ] *a* (**-ier, -iest**) (*weather*) lourd.

mulberry ['mʌlbərɪ] *n* (*fruit*) mûre *f*.

mule [mjuːl] *n* (*male*) mulet *m*; (*female*) mule *f*.

mull [mʌl] **1** *vt* (*wine*) chauffer. **2** *vi* **to m. over** (*think over*) ruminer.

mullet ['mʌlɪt] *n* (*fish*) mulet *m*; (**red**) **m.** rouget *m*.

multi- ['mʌltɪ] *pref* multi-.

multicoloured ['mʌltɪkʌləd] *a* multicolore.

multifarious [mʌltɪ'feərɪəs] *a* divers.

multimillionaire [mʌltɪmɪljə'neər] *n* milliardaire *mf*.

multinational [mʌltɪ'naeʃ(ə)nəl] *n* multinationale *f*.

multiple ['mʌltɪp(ə)l] *a* multiple; – *n Math* multiple *m*. ◆**multipli'cation** *n* multiplication *f*. ◆**multi'plicity** *n* multiplicité *f*. ◆**multiply** *vt* multiplier; – *vi* (*reproduce*) se multiplier.

multistorey [mʌltɪ'stɔːrɪ] (*Am* **multistoried**) *a* à étages.

multitude ['mʌltɪtjuːd] *n* multitude *f*.

mum [mʌm] **1** *n Fam* maman *f*. **2** *a* **to keep m.** garder le silence.

mumble ['mʌmb(ə)l] *vti* marmotter.

mumbo-jumbo [mʌmbəʊ'dʒʌmbəʊ] *n* (*words*) charabia *m*.

mummy ['mʌmɪ] *n* **1** *Fam* maman *f*. **2** (*body*) momie *f*.

mumps [mʌmps] *n* oreillons *mpl*.

munch [mʌntʃ] *vti* (*chew*) mastiquer; **to m. (on)** (*eat*) *Fam* bouffer.

mundane [mʌn'deɪn] *a* banal.

municipal [mjuː'nɪsɪp(ə)l] *a* municipal. ◆**munici'pality** *n* municipalité *f*.

munitions [mjuː'nɪʃ(ə)nz] *npl* munitions *fpl*.

mural ['mjʊərəl] *a* mural; – *n* fresque *f*, peinture *f* murale.

murder ['mɜːdər] *n* meurtre *m*, assassinat *m*; **it's m.** (*dreadful*) *Fam* c'est affreux; – *vt* (*kill*) assassiner; (*spoil*) *Fig* massacrer. ◆**—er** *n* meurtrier, -ière *mf*, assassin *m*. ◆**murderous** *a* meurtrier.

murky ['mɜːkɪ] *a* (**-ier, -iest**) obscur; (*water, business, past*) trouble; (*weather*) nuageux.

murmur ['mɜːmər] *n* murmure *m*; (*of traffic*) bourdonnement *m*; – *vti* murmurer.

muscle ['mʌs(ə)l] *n* muscle *m*; – *vi* **to m. in on** (*group*) *Sl* s'introduire par la force à. ◆**muscular** *a* (*tissue etc*) musculaire; (*brawny*) musclé.

muse [mjuːz] *vi* méditer (**on** sur).

museum [mjuː'zɪəm] *n* musée *m*.

mush [mʌʃ] *n* (*soft mass*) bouillie *f*; *Fig* sentimentalité *f*. ◆**mushy** *a* (**-ier, -iest**) (*food etc*) en bouillie; *Fig* sentimental.

mushroom ['mʌʃrum] **1** *n* champignon *m*. **2** *vi* (*grow*) pousser comme des champignons; (*spread*) se multiplier.

music ['mjuːzɪk] *n* musique *f*; **m. centre** chaîne *f* stéréo compacte; **m. critic** critique *m* musical; **m. hall** music-hall *m*; **m. lover** mélomane *mf*; **canned m.** musique *f* (de fond) enregistrée. ◆**musical** *a* musical; (*instrument*) de musique; **to be (very) m.** être (très) musicien; – *n* (*film, play*) comédie *f* musicale. ◆**mu'sician** *n* musicien, -ienne *mf*.

musk [mʌsk] *n* (*scent*) musc *m*.

Muslim ['muzlɪm] *a* & *n* musulman, -ane (*mf*).

muslin ['mʌzlɪn] *n* (*cotton*) mousseline *f*.

mussel ['mʌs(ə)l] *n* (*mollusc*) moule *f*.

must [mʌst] *v aux* **1** (*necessity*) **you m. obey** tu dois obéir, il faut que tu obéisses. **2** (*certainty*) **she m. be clever** elle doit être intelligente; **I m. have seen it** j'ai dû le voir; – *n* **this is a m.** ceci est (absolument) indispensable.

mustache ['mʌstæʃ] *n Am* moustache *f*.

mustard ['mʌstəd] *n* moutarde *f*.

muster ['mʌstər] *vt* (*gather*) rassembler; (*sum*) réunir; – *vi* se rassembler.

musty ['mʌstɪ] *a* (**-ier, -iest**) (*smell*) de moisi; **it smells m., it's m.** ça sent le moisi.

mutation [mjuː'teɪʃ(ə)n] *n Biol* mutation *f*.

mut/e [mjuːt] *a* (*silent*) & *Gram* muet; – *vt* (*sound, colour*) assourdir. ◆**—ed** *a* (*criticism*) voilé.

mutilate ['mjuːtɪleɪt] *vt* mutiler. ◆**muti'lation** *n* mutilation *f*.

mutiny ['mjuːtɪnɪ] *n* mutinerie *f*; – *vi* se mutiner. ◆**mutinous** *a* (*troops*) mutiné.

mutter ['mʌtər] *vti* marmonner.

mutton ['mʌt(ə)n] *n* (*meat*) mouton *m*.

mutual ['mjuːtʃʊəl] *a* (*help, love etc*) mutuel, réciproque; (*common, shared*) commun; **m. fund** *Fin Am* fonds *m* commun de placement. ◆**—ly** *adv* mutuellement.

muzzle ['mʌz(ə)l] *n* (*snout*) museau *m*; (*device*) muselière *f*; (*of gun*) gueule *f*; – *vt* (*animal, press etc*) museler.

my [maɪ] *poss a* mon, ma, *pl* mes. ◆**my'self** *pron* moi-même; (*reflexive*) me, m'; (*after prep*) moi; **I wash m.** je me lave; **I think of m.** je pense à moi.

mystery ['mɪstərɪ] *n* mystère *m*. ◆**my'sterious** *a* mystérieux.

mystic ['mɪstɪk] *a* *n* mystique (*mf*). ◆**mystical** *a* mystique. ◆**mysticism** *n* mysticisme *m*. ◆**my'stique** *n* (*mystery, power*) mystique *f* (**of** de).

mystify ['mɪstɪfaɪ] *vt* (*bewilder*) laisser perplexe; (*fool*) mystifier. ◆**mystifi'cation** *n* (*bewilderment*) perplexité *f*.

myth [mɪθ] *n* mythe *m*. ◆**mythical** *a* mythique. ◆**mytho'logical** *a* mythologique. ◆**my'thology** *n* mythologie *f*.

N

N, n [en] *n* N, n *m*; **the nth time** la énième fois.
nab [næb] *vt* **(-bb-)** *(catch, arrest) Fam* épingler.
nag [næg] *vti* **(-gg-)** *(criticize)* critiquer; **to n. (at) s.o.** *(pester)* harceler *or* embêter qn (to do pour qu'il fasse). ◆**nagging** *a (doubt, headache)* qui subsiste; – *n* critiques *fpl.*
nail [neɪl] **1** *n (of finger, toe)* ongle *m*; – *a (polish, file etc)* à ongles. **2** *n (metal)* clou *m*; – *vt* clouer; **to n. s.o.** *(nab) Fam* épingler qn; **to n. down** *(lid etc)* clouer.
naïve [naɪ'iːv] *a* naïf. ◆**naïveté** *n* naïveté *f.*
naked ['neɪkɪd] *a (person)* (tout) nu; *(eye, flame)* nu; **to see with the n. eye** voir à l'œil nu. ◆**—ness** *n* nudité *f.*
name [neɪm] *n* nom *m*; *(reputation) Fig* réputation *f*; **my n. is . . .** je m'appelle . . . ; **in the n. of** au nom de; **to put one's n. down for** *(school, course)* s'inscrire à; *(job, house)* demander, faire une demande pour avoir; **to call s.o. names** injurier qn; **first n., given n.** prénom *m*; **last n.** nom *m* de famille; **a good/bad n.** *Fig* une bonne/mauvaise réputation; **n. plate** plaque *f*; – *vt* nommer; *(ship, street)* baptiser; *(designate)* désigner, nommer; *(date, price)* fixer; **he was named after** *or Am* **for . . .** il a reçu le nom de . . . . ◆**—less** *a* sans nom, anonyme. ◆**—ly** *adv (that is)* à savoir. ◆**namesake** *n (person)* homonyme *m.*
nanny ['nænɪ] *n* nurse *f*, bonne *f* d'enfants; *(grandmother) Fam* mamie *f.*
nanny-goat ['nænɪgəʊt] *n* chèvre *f.*
nap [næp] *n (sleep)* petit somme *m*; **to have** *or* **take a n.** faire un petit somme; *(after lunch)* faire la sieste; – *vi* **(-pp-) to be napping** sommeiller; **to catch napping** *Fig* prendre au dépourvu.
nape [neɪp] *n* **n. (of the neck)** nuque *f.*
napkin ['næpkɪn] *n (at table)* serviette *f*; *(for baby)* couche *f.* ◆**nappy** *n (for baby)* couche *f.* ◆**nappy-liner** *n* protège-couche *m.*
narcotic [nɑː'kɒtɪk] *a & n* narcotique *(m).*
narrate [nə'reɪt] *vt* raconter. ◆**narration** *n*, ◆**'narrative** *n (story)* récit *m*, narration *f*; *(art, act)* narration *f.* ◆**narrator** *n* narrateur, -trice *mf.*
narrow ['nærəʊ] *a* **(-er, -est)** étroit; *(majority)* faible, petit; – *vi (of path)* se rétrécir; **to n. down** *(of choice etc)* se limiter (to à); – *vt* **to n. (down)** *(limit)* limiter. ◆**—ly** *adv (to miss etc)* de justesse; *(strictly)* strictement; **he n. escaped** *or* **missed being killed/***etc* il a failli être tué/*etc.* ◆**—ness** *n* étroitesse *f.*
narow-minded [nærəʊ'maɪndɪd] *a* borné. ◆**—ness** *n* étroitesse *f* (d'esprit).
nasal ['neɪz(ə)l] *a* nasal; *(voice)* nasillard.
nasty ['nɑːstɪ] *a* **(-ier, -iest)** *(bad)* mauvais, vilain; *(spiteful)* méchant, désagréable **(to, towards** avec); **a n. mess** *or* **muddle** un gâchis. ◆**nastily** *adv (to act)* méchamment; *(to rain)* horriblement. ◆**nastiness** *n (malice)* méchanceté *f*; **the n. of the weather/taste/***etc* le mauvais temps/goût/*etc.*
nation ['neɪʃ(ə)n] *n* nation *f*; **the United Nations** les Nations Unies. ◆**n.-wide** *a & adv* dans le pays (tout) entier. ◆**national** *a* national; **n. anthem** hymne *m* national; **N. Health Service** = Sécurité *f* Sociale; **n. insurance** = assurances *fpl* sociales; – *n (citizen)* ressortissant, -ante *mf.* ◆**nationalist** *n* nationaliste *mf.* ◆**nationa'listic** *a Pej* nationaliste. ◆**natio'nality** *n* nationalité *f.* ◆**nationalize** *vt* nationaliser. ◆**nationally** *adv (to travel, be known etc)* dans le pays (tout) entier.
native ['neɪtɪv] *a (country)* natal; *(habits, costume)* du pays; *(tribe, plant)* indigène; *(charm, ability)* inné; **n. language** langue *f* maternelle; **to be an English n. speaker** parler l'anglais comme langue maternelle; – *n (person)* autochtone *mf*; *(non-European in colony)* indigène *mf*; **to be a n. of** être originaire *or* natif de.
nativity [nə'tɪvɪtɪ] *n Rel* nativité *f.*
NATO ['neɪtəʊ] *n abbr (North Atlantic Treaty Organization)* OTAN *f.*
natter ['nætər] *vi Fam* bavarder; – *n Fam* **to have a n.** bavarder.
natural ['nætʃ(ə)rəl] *a* naturel; *(actor, gardener etc)* né; – *n* **to be a n. for** *(job etc) Fam* être celui qu'il faut pour, être fait pour. ◆**naturalist** *n* naturaliste *mf.* ◆**naturally** *adv (as normal, of course)* naturellement; *(by nature)* de nature; *(with naturalness)* avec naturel. ◆**naturalness** *n* naturel *m.*

naturalize ['nætʃ(ə)rəlaɪz] *vt* (*person*) *Pol* naturaliser. ◆**naturali'zation** *n* naturalisation *f*.

nature ['neɪtʃər] *n* (*natural world, basic quality*) nature *f*; (*disposition*) naturel *m*; **by n.** de nature; **n. study** sciences *fpl* naturelles.

naught [nɔːt] *n* **1** *Math* zéro *m*. **2** (*nothing*) *Lit* rien *m*.

naught/y ['nɔːtɪ] *a* (**-ier, -iest**) (*child*) vilain, malicieux; (*joke, story*) osé, grivois. ◆**—ily** *adv* (*to behave*) mal; (*to say*) avec malice. ◆**—iness** *n* mauvaise conduite *f*.

nausea ['nɔːzɪə] *n* nausée *f*. ◆**nauseate** *vt* écœurer. ◆**nauseous** *a* (*smell etc*) nauséabond; **to feel n.** *Am* (*sick*) avoir envie de vomir; (*disgusted*) *Fig* être écœuré.

nautical ['nɔːtɪk(ə)l] *a* nautique.

naval ['neɪv(ə)l] *a* naval; (*power, hospital*) maritime; (*officer*) de marine.

nave [neɪv] *n* (*of church*) nef *f*.

navel ['neɪv(ə)l] *n Anat* nombril *m*.

navigate ['nævɪgeɪt] *vi* naviguer; – *vt* (*boat*) diriger, piloter; (*river*) naviguer sur. ◆**navigable** *a* (*river*) navigable; (*seaworthy*) en état de naviguer. ◆**navi'gation** *n* navigation *f*. ◆**navigator** *n Av* navigateur *m*.

navvy ['nævɪ] *n* (*labourer*) terrassier *m*.

navy ['neɪvɪ] *n* marine *f*; – *a* **n. (blue)** bleu marine *inv*.

Nazi ['nɑːtsɪ] *a* & *n Pol Hist* nazi, -ie (*mf*).

near [nɪər] *adv* (**-er, -est**) près; **quite n., n. at hand** tout près; **to draw n.** (s')approcher (**to** de); (*of date*) approcher; **n. to** près de; **to come n. to being killed/***etc* faillir être tué/*etc*; **n. enough** (*more or less*) *Fam* plus ou moins; – *prep* (**-er, -est**) **n. (to)** près de; **n. the bed** près du lit; **to be n. (to) victory/death** frôler la victoire/la mort; **n. the end** vers la fin; **to come n. s.o.** s'approcher de qn; – *a* (**-er, -est**) proche; (*likeness*) fidèle; **the nearest hospital** l'hôpital le plus proche; **the nearest way** la route la plus directe; **in the n. future** dans un avenir proche; **to the nearest franc** (*to calculate*) à un franc près; (*to round up or down*) au franc supérieur *or* inférieur; **n. side** *Aut* côté *m* gauche, *Am* côté *m* droit; – *vt* (*approach*) approcher de; **nearing completion** près d'être achevé. ◆**near'by** *adv* tout près; – ['nɪəbaɪ] *a* proche. ◆**nearness** *n* (*in space, time*) proximité *f*.

nearly ['nɪəlɪ] *adv* presque; **she (very) n. fell** elle a failli tomber; **not n. as clever/***etc* **as** loin d'être aussi intelligent/*etc* que.

neat [niːt] *a* (**-er, -est**) (*clothes, work*) soigné, propre, net; (*room*) ordonné, bien rangé; (*style*) élégant; (*pretty*) *Fam* joli, beau; (*pleasant*) *Fam* agréable; **to drink one's whisky/***etc* **n.** prendre son whisky/*etc* sec. ◆**—ly** *adv* avec soin; (*skilfully*) habilement. ◆**—ness** *n* netteté *f*; (*of room*) ordre *m*.

necessary ['nesɪs(ə)rɪ] *a* nécessaire; **it's n. to do** il est nécessaire de faire, il faut faire; **to make it n. for s.o. to do** mettre qn dans la nécessité de faire; **to do what's n.** *or* **the n.** *Fam* faire le nécessaire (**for** pour); – *npl* **the necessaries** (*food etc*) l'indispensable *m*. ◆**nece'ssarily** *adv* nécessairement.

necessity [nɪ'sesɪtɪ] *n* (*obligation, need*) nécessité *f*; (*poverty*) indigence *f*; **there's no n. for you to do that** tu n'es pas obligé de faire cela; **of n.** nécessairement; **to be a n.** être indispensable; **the (bare) necessities** le (strict) nécessaire. ◆**necessitate** *vt* nécessiter.

neck[1] [nek] *n Anat* cou *m*; (*of dress, horse*) encolure *f*; (*of bottle*) col *m*; **low n.** (*of dress*) décolleté *m*; **n. and n.** *Sp* à égalité. ◆**necklace** *n* collier *m*. ◆**neckline** *n* encolure *f*. ◆**necktie** *n* cravate *f*.

neck[2] [nek] *vi* (*kiss etc*) *Fam* se peloter.

nectarine ['nektəriːn] *n* (*fruit*) nectarine *f*, brugnon *m*.

née [neɪ] *adv* **n. Dupont** née Dupont.

need [niːd] **1** *n* (*necessity, want, poverty*) besoin *m*; **in n.** dans le besoin; **to be in n. of** avoir besoin de; **there's no n. (for you) to do** tu n'as pas besoin de faire; **if n. be** si besoin est, s'il le faut; – *vt* avoir besoin de; **you n. it** tu en as besoin, il te le faut; **it needs an army to do, an army is needed to do** il faut une armée pour faire; **this sport needs patience** ce sport demande de la patience; **her hair needs cutting** il faut qu'elle se fasse couper les cheveux. **2** *v aux* **n. he wait?** est-il obligé d'attendre?, a-t-il besoin d'attendre?; **I needn't have rushed** ce n'était pas la peine de me presser; **I n. hardly say that . . .** je n'ai guère besoin de dire que . . . . ◆**needless** *a* inutile. ◆**needlessly** *adv* inutilement. ◆**needy** *a* (**-ier, -iest**) *a* nécessiteux.

needle ['niːd(ə)l] **1** *n* aiguille *f*; (*of record player*) saphir *m*. **2** *vt* (*irritate*) *Fam* agacer. ◆**needlework** *n* couture *f*, travaux *mpl* d'aiguille; (*object*) ouvrage *m*.

negate [nɪ'geɪt] *vt* (*nullify*) annuler; (*deny*) nier. ◆**negation** *n* (*denial*) & *Gram* négation *f*.

negative ['negətɪv] *a* négatif; – *n Phot* négatif *m*; (*word*) *Gram* négation *f*; (*form*)

Gram forme *f* négative; **to answer in the n.** répondre par la négative.

neglect [nɪ'glekt] *vt* (*person, health, work etc*) négliger; (*garden, car etc*) ne pas s'occuper de; (*duty*) manquer à; (*rule*) désobéir à, méconnaître; **to n. to do** négliger de faire; – *n* (*of person*) manque *m* de soins (**of** envers); (*of rule*) désobéissance *f* (**of** à); (*of duty*) manquement *m* (**of** à); (*carelessness*) négligence *f*; **in a state of n.** (*garden, house etc*) mal tenu. ◆**neglected** *a* (*appearance, person*) négligé; (*garden, house etc*) mal tenu; **to feel n.** sentir qu'on vous néglige. ◆**neglectful** *a* négligent; **to be n. of** négliger.

negligent ['neglɪdʒənt] *a* négligent. ◆**negligence** *n* négligence *f*. ◆**negligently** *adv* négligemment.

negligible ['neglɪdʒəb(ə)l] *a* négligeable.

negotiate [nɪ'gəʊʃɪeɪt] **1** *vti Fin Pol* négocier. **2** *vt* (*fence, obstacle*) franchir; (*bend*) *Aut* négocier. ◆**negotiable** *a Fin* négociable. ◆**negoti'ation** *n* négociation *f*; **in n. with** en pourparlers avec. ◆**negotiator** *n* négociateur, -trice *mf*.

Negro ['niːgrəʊ] *n* (*pl* **-oes**) (*man*) Noir *m*; (*woman*) Noire *f*; – *a* noir; (*art, sculpture etc*) nègre. ◆**Negress** *n* Noire *f*.

neigh [neɪ] *vi* (*of horse*) hennir; – *n* hennissement *m*.

neighbour ['neɪbər] *n* voisin, -ine *mf*. ◆**neighbourhood** *n* (*neighbours*) voisinage *m*; (*district*) quartier *m*, voisinage *m*; (*region*) région *f*; **in the n. of ten pounds** dans les dix livres. ◆**neighbouring** *a* avoisinant. ◆**neighbourly** *a* (*feeling etc*) de bon voisinage, amical; **they're n.** (**people**) ils sont bons voisins.

neither ['naɪðər, *Am* 'niːðər] *adv* ni; **n. . . . nor** ni . . . ni; **n. you nor me** ni toi ni moi; **he n. sings nor dances** il ne chante ni ne danse; – *conj* (*not either*) (ne) . . . non plus; **n. shall I go** je n'y irai pas non plus; **n. do I, n. can I** *etc* (ni) moi non plus; – *a* **n. boy (came)** aucun des deux garçons (n'est venu); **on n. side** ni d'un côté ni de l'autre; – *pron* **n. (of them)** ni l'un(e) ni l'autre, aucun(e) (des deux).

neo- ['niːəʊ] *pref* néo-.

neon ['niːɒn] *n* (*gas*) néon *m*; – *a* (*lighting etc*) au néon.

nephew ['nevjuː, 'nefjuː] *n* neveu *m*.

nepotism ['nepətɪz(ə)m] *n* népotisme *m*.

nerve [nɜːv] *n* nerf *m*; (*courage*) *Fig* courage *m* (**to do** de faire); (*confidence*) assurance *f*; (*calm*) sang-froid *m*; (*cheek*) *Fam* culot *m* (**to do** de faire); **you get on my nerves** *Fam* tu me portes *or* me tapes sur les nerfs; **to have (an attack of) nerves** (*fear, anxiety*) avoir le trac; **a bundle** *or* **mass** *or* **bag of nerves** (*person*) *Fam* un paquet de nerfs; **to have bad nerves** être nerveux; – *a* (*cell, centre*) nerveux. ◆**n.-racking** *a* éprouvant pour les nerfs. ◆**nervous** *a* (*tense*) & *Anat* nerveux; (*worried*) inquiet (**about** de); **to be** *or* **feel n.** (*ill-at-ease*) se sentir mal à l'aise; (*before exam etc*) avoir le trac. ◆**nervously** *adv* nerveusement; (*worriedly*) avec inquiétude. ◆**nervousness** *n* nervosité *f*; (*fear*) trac *m*. ◆**nervy** *a* (**-ier, -iest**) *Fam* (*anxious*) nerveux; (*brash*) *Am* culotté.

nest [nest] *n* nid *m*; **n. egg** (*money saved*) pécule *m*; **n. of tables** table *f* gigogne; – *vi* (*of bird*) (se) nicher.

nestle ['nes(ə)l] *vi* se pelotonner (**up to** contre); **a village nestling in** (*forest, valley etc*) un village niché dans.

net [net] **1** *n* filet *m*; **n. curtain** voilage *m*; – *vt* (**-tt-**) (*fish*) prendre au filet. **2** *a* (*profit, weight etc*) net *inv*; – *vt* (**-tt-**) (*of person, firm etc*) gagner net; **this venture netted him** *or* **her . . .** cette entreprise lui a rapporté . . . . ◆**netting** *n* (*nets*) filets *mpl*; (*mesh*) mailles *fpl*; (*fabric*) voile *m*; (**wire**) **n.** treillis *m*.

Netherlands (the) [ðə'neðələndz] *npl* les Pays-Bas *mpl*.

nettle ['net(ə)l] *n Bot* ortie *f*.

network ['netwɜːk] *n* réseau *m*.

neurosis, *pl* **-oses** [njʊə'rəʊsɪs, -əʊsiːz] *n* névrose *f*. ◆**neurotic** *a* & *n* névrosé, -ée (*mf*).

neuter ['njuːtər] **1** *a* & *n Gram* neutre (*m*). **2** *vt* (*cat etc*) châtrer.

neutral ['njuːtrəl] *a* neutre; (*policy*) de neutralité; – *n El* neutre *m*; **in n. (gear)** *Aut* au point mort. ◆**neu'trality** *n* neutralité *f*. ◆**neutralize** *vt* neutraliser.

never ['nevər] *adv* **1** (*not ever*) (ne) . . . jamais; **she n. lies** elle ne ment jamais; **n. in (all) my life** jamais de ma vie; **n. again** plus jamais. **2** (*certainly not*) *Fam* **I n. did it** je ne l'ai pas fait. ◆**n.-'ending** *a* interminable.

nevertheless [nevəðə'les] *adv* néanmoins, quand même.

new [njuː] *a* (**-er, -est**) nouveau; (*brand-new*) neuf; **to be n. to** (*job*) être nouveau dans; (*city*) être un nouveau-venu dans, être fraîchement installé dans; **a n. boy** *Sch* un nouveau; **what's n.?** *Fam* quoi de neuf?; **a n. glass/pen/***etc* (*different*) un autre verre/stylo/*etc*; **to break n. ground** innover; **n. look** style *m* nouveau; **as good as**

n. comme neuf; **a n.-laid egg** un œuf du jour; **a n.-born baby** un nouveau-né, une nouveau-née. ◆**newcomer** *n* nouveau-venu *m*, nouvelle-venue *f*. ◆**new-'fangled** *a Pej* moderne. ◆**new-found** *a* nouveau. ◆**newly** *adv* (*recently*) nouvellement, fraîchement; **the n.-weds** les nouveaux mariés. ◆**newness** *n* (*condition*) état *m* neuf; (*novelty*) nouveauté *f*.

news [njuːz] *n* nouvelle(s) *f*(*pl*); *Journ Rad TV* informations *fpl*, actualités *fpl*; **sports/etc n.** (*newspaper column*) chronique *f or* rubrique *f* sportive/*etc*; **a piece of n., some n.** une nouvelle; *Journ Rad TV* une information; **n. headlines** titres *mpl* de l'actualité; **n. flash** flash *m*. ◆**newsagent** *n* marchand, -ande *mf* de journaux. ◆**newsboy** *n* vendeur *m* de journaux. ◆**newscaster** *n* présentateur, -trice *mf*. ◆**newsletter** *n* (*of club, group etc*) bulletin *m*. ◆**newspaper** *n* journal *m*. ◆**newsreader** *n* présentateur, -trice *mf*. ◆**newsreel** *n Cin* actualités *fpl*. ◆**newsworthy** *a* digne de faire l'objet d'un reportage. ◆**newsy** *a* (**-ier, -iest**) *Fam* plein de nouvelles.

newt [njuːt] *n* (*animal*) triton *m*.

New Zealand [njuː'ziːlənd] *n* Nouvelle-Zélande *f*; – *a* néo-zélandais. ◆**New Zealander** *n* Néo-Zélandais, -aise *mf*.

next [nekst] *a* prochain; (*room, house*) d'à-côté, voisin; (*following*) suivant; **n. month** (*in the future*) le mois prochain; **he returned the n. month** (*in the past*) il revint le mois suivant; **the n. day** le lendemain; **the n. morning** le lendemain matin; **within the n. ten days** d'ici (à) dix jours, dans un délai de dix jours; **(by) this time n. week** d'ici (à) la semaine prochaine; **from one year to the n.** d'une année à l'autre; **you're n.** c'est ton tour; **n. (please)!** (au) suivant!; **the n. thing to do is . . .** ce qu'il faut faire ensuite c'est . . . ; **the n. size (up)** la taille au-dessus; **to live/etc n. door** habiter/*etc* à côté (**to** de); **n.-door neighbour/room** voisin *m*/pièce *f* d'à-côté; – *n* (*in series etc*) suivant, -ante *mf*; – *adv* (*afterwards*) ensuite, après; (*now*) maintenant; **when you come n.** la prochaine fois que tu viendras; **the n. best solution** la seconde solution; – *prep* **n. to** (*beside*) à côté de; **n. to nothing** presque rien.

NHS [eneɪtʃ'es] *abbr* = **National Health Service.**

nib [nɪb] *n* (*of pen*) plume *f*, bec *m*.

nibble ['nɪb(ə)l] *vti* (*eat*) grignoter; (*bite*) mordiller.

nice [naɪs] *a* (**-er, -est**) (*pleasant*) agréable; (*charming*) charmant, gentil; (*good*) bon; (*fine*) beau; (*pretty*) joli; (*kind*) gentil (**to** avec); (*respectable*) bien *inv*; (*subtle*) délicat; **it's n. here** c'est bien ici; **n. and easy/warm/etc** (*very*) bien facile/chaud/*etc*. ◆**n.-'looking** *a* beau, joli. ◆**nicely** *adv* agréablement; (*kindly*) gentiment; (*well*) bien. ◆**niceties** ['naɪsətɪz] *npl* (*pleasant things*) agréments *mpl*; (*subtleties*) subtilités *fpl*.

niche [niːʃ, nɪtʃ] *n* **1** (*recess*) niche *f*. **2** (*job*) (bonne) situation *f*; (*direction*) voie *f*; **to make a n. for oneself** faire son trou.

nick [nɪk] **1** *n* (*on skin, wood*) entaille *f*; (*in blade, crockery*) brèche *f*. **2** *n* (*prison*) *Sl* taule *f*; – *vt* (*steal, arrest*) *Sl* piquer. **3** *n* **in the n. of time** juste à temps; **in good n.** *Sl* en bon état.

nickel ['nɪk(ə)l] *n* (*metal*) nickel *m*; (*coin*) *Am* pièce *f* de cinq cents.

nickname ['nɪkneɪm] *n* (*informal name*) surnom *m*; (*short form*) diminutif *m*; – *vt* surnommer.

nicotine ['nɪkətiːn] *n* nicotine *f*.

niece [niːs] *n* nièce *f*.

nifty ['nɪftɪ] *a* (**-ier, -iest**) (*stylish*) chic *inv*; (*skilful*) habile; (*fast*) rapide.

Nigeria [naɪ'dʒɪərɪə] *n* Nigéria *m or f*. ◆**Nigerian** *a* & *n* nigérian, -ane (*mf*).

niggardly ['nɪgədlɪ] *a* (*person*) avare; (*amount*) mesquin.

niggling ['nɪglɪŋ] *a* (*trifling*) insignifiant; (*irksome*) irritant; (*doubt*) persistant.

night [naɪt] *n* nuit *f*; (*evening*) soir *m*; *Th* soirée *f*; **last n.** (*evening*) hier soir; (*night*) la nuit dernière; **to have an early/late n.** se coucher tôt/tard; **to have a good n.** (*sleep well*) bien dormir; **first n.** *Th* première *f*; – *a* (*work etc*) de nuit; (*life*) nocturne; **n. school** cours *mpl* du soir; **n. watchman** veilleur *m* de nuit. ◆**nightcap** *n* (*drink*) boisson *f* (*alcoolisée ou chaude prise avant de se coucher*). ◆**nightclub** *n* boîte *f* de nuit. ◆**nightdress** *n*, ◆**nightgown** *n*, *Fam* ◆**nightie** *n* (*woman's*) chemise *f* de nuit. ◆**nightfall** *n* **at n.** à la tombée de la nuit. ◆**nightlight** *n* veilleuse *f*. ◆**nighttime** *n* nuit *f*.

nightingale ['naɪtɪŋgeɪl] *n* rossignol *m*.

nightly ['naɪtlɪ] *adv* chaque nuit *or* soir; – *a* de chaque nuit *or* soir.

nil [nɪl] *n* (*nothing*) & *Sp* zéro *m*; **the risk/result/etc is n.** le risque/résultat/*etc* est nul.

nimble ['nɪmb(ə)l] *a* (**-er, -est**) agile.

nincompoop ['nɪŋkəmpuːp] *n Fam* imbécile *mf.*

nine [naɪn] *a & n* neuf (*m*). ◆**nine'teen** *a & n* dix-neuf (*m*). ◆**nine'teenth** *a & n* dix-neuvième (*mf*). ◆**ninetieth** *a & n* quatre-vingt-dixième (*mf*). ◆**ninety** *a & n* quatre-vingt-dix (*m*). ◆**ninth** *a & n* neuvième (*mf*); **a n.** un neuvième.

nip [nɪp] **1** *vt* (**-pp-**) (*pinch, bite*) pincer; **to n. in the bud** *Fig* étouffer dans l'œuf; – *n* pinçon *m*; **there's a n. in the air** ça pince. **2** *vi* (**-pp-**) (*dash*) *Fam* **to n. round to s.o.** courir *or* faire un saut chez qn; **to n. in/out** entrer/sortir un instant.

nipper ['nɪpər] *n* (*child*) *Fam* gosse *mf.*

nipple ['nɪp(ə)l] *n* bout *m* de sein, mamelon *m*; (*teat on bottle*) *Am* tétine *f.*

nippy ['nɪpɪ] *a* **1** (**-ier, -iest**) (*chilly*) frais; **it's n.** (*weather*) ça pince. **2 to be n. (about it)** (*quick*) *Fam* faire vite.

nit [nɪt] *n* **1** (*fool*) *Fam* idiot, -ote *mf.* **2** (*of louse*) lente *f.* ◆**nitwit** *n* (*fool*) *Fam* idiot, -ote *mf.*

nitrogen ['naɪtrədʒən] *n* azote *m.*

nitty-gritty [nɪtɪ'grɪtɪ] *n* **to get down to the n.-gritty** *Fam* en venir au fond du problème.

no [nəʊ] *adv & n* non (*m inv*); **no!** non!; **no more than ten/a kilo/***etc* pas plus de dix/d'un kilo/*etc*; **no more time/***etc* plus de temps/*etc*; **I have no more time** je n'ai plus de temps; **no more than you** pas plus que vous; **you can do no better** tu ne peux pas faire mieux; **the noes** *Pol* les non; – *a* aucun(e); pas de; **I've (got)** *or* **I have no idea** je n'ai aucune idée; **no child came** aucun enfant n'est venu; **I've (got)** *or* **I have no time/***etc* je n'ai pas de temps/*etc*; **of no importance/value/***etc* sans importance/valeur/*etc*; **with no gloves/***etc* **on** sans gants/*etc*; **there's no knowing . . .** impossible de savoir . . . ; **'no smoking'** 'défense de fumer'; **no way!** *Am Fam* pas question!; **no one = nobody.**

noble ['nəʊb(ə)l] *a* (**-er, -est**) noble; (*building*) majestueux. ◆**nobleman** *n* (*pl* **-men**) noble *m.* ◆**noblewoman** *n* (*pl* **-women**) noble *f.* ◆**no'bility** *n* (*character, class*) noblesse *f.*

nobody ['nəʊbɒdɪ] *pron* (ne) . . . personne; **n. came** personne n'est venu; **he knows n.** il ne connaît personne; **n.!** personne!; – *n* **a n.** une nullité.

nocturnal [nɒk'tɜːn(ə)l] *a* nocturne.

nod [nɒd] **1** *vti* (**-dd-**) **to n. (one's head)** incliner la tête, faire un signe de tête; – *n* inclination *f or* signe *m* de tête. **2** *vi* (**-dd-**) **to n. off** (*go to sleep*) s'assoupir.

noise [nɔɪz] *n* bruit *m*; (*of bell, drum*) son *m*; **to make a n.** faire du bruit. ◆**noisily** *adv* bruyamment. ◆**noisy** *a* (**-ier, -iest**) (*person, street etc*) bruyant.

nomad ['nəʊmæd] *n* nomade *mf.* ◆**no'madic** *a* nomade.

nominal ['nɒmɪn(ə)l] *a* (*value, fee etc*) nominal; (*head, ruler*) de nom.

nominate ['nɒmɪneɪt] *vt Pol* désigner, proposer (**for** comme candidat à); (*appoint*) désigner, nommer. ◆**nomi'nation** *n* désignation *f or* proposition *f* de candidat; (*appointment*) nomination *f.* ◆**nomi'nee** *n* (*candidate*) candidat *m.*

non- [nɒn] *pref* non-.

nonchalant ['nɒnʃələnt] *a* nonchalant.

noncommissioned [nɒnkə'mɪʃ(ə)nd] *a* **n. officer** *Mil* sous-officier *m.*

non-committal [nɒnkə'mɪt(ə)l] *a* (*answer, person*) évasif.

nonconformist [nɒnkən'fɔːmɪst] *a & n* non-conformiste (*mf*).

nondescript ['nɒndɪskrɪpt] *a* indéfinissable; *Pej* médiocre.

none [nʌn] *pron* aucun(e) *mf*; (*in filling a form*) néant; **n. of them** aucun d'eux; **she has n. (at all)** elle n'en a pas (du tout); **n. (at all) came** pas un(e) seul(e) n'est venu(e); **n. can tell** personne ne peut le dire; **n. of the cake/***etc* pas une seule partie du gâteau/*etc*; **n. of the trees/***etc* aucun arbre/*etc*, aucun des arbres/*etc*; **n. of it** *or* **this** rien (de ceci); – *adv* **n. too hot/***etc* pas tellement chaud/*etc*; **he's n. the happier/wiser/***etc* il n'en est pas plus heureux/sage/*etc*; **n. the less** néanmoins. ◆**nonethe'less** *adv* néanmoins.

nonentity [nɒ'nentɪtɪ] *n* (*person*) nullité *f.*

non-existent [nɒnɪg'zɪstənt] *a* inexistant.

non-fiction [nɒn'fɪkʃ(ə)n] *n* littérature *f* non-romanesque; (*in library*) ouvrages *mpl* généraux.

non-flammable [nɒn'flæməb(ə)l] *a* ininflammable.

nonplus [nɒn'plʌs] *vt* (**-ss-**) dérouter.

nonsense ['nɒnsəns] *n* absurdités *fpl*; **that's n.** c'est absurde. ◆**non'sensical** *a* absurde.

non-smoker [nɒn'sməʊkər] *n* (*person*) non-fumeur, -euse *mf*; (*compartment*) *Rail* compartiment *m* non-fumeurs.

non-stick [nɒn'stɪk] *a* (*pan*) anti-adhésif, qui n'attache pas.

non-stop [nɒn'stɒp] *a* sans arrêt; (*train,*

flight) direct; – *adv* (*to work etc*) sans arrêt; (*to fly*) sans escale.
noodles ['nuːd(ə)lz] *npl* nouilles *fpl*; (*in soup*) vermicelle(s) *m*(*pl*).
nook [nʊk] *n* coin *m*; **in every n. and cranny** dans tous les coins (et recoins).
noon [nuːn] *n* midi *m*; **at n.** à midi; – *a* (*sun etc*) de midi.
noose [nuːs] *n* (*loop*) nœud *m* coulant; (*of hangman*) corde *f*.
nor [nɔːr] *conj* ni; **neither you n. me** ni toi ni moi; **she neither drinks n. smokes** elle ne fume ni ne boit; **n. do I, n. can I** *etc* (ni) moi non plus; **n. will I (go)** je n'y irai pas non plus.
norm [nɔːm] *n* norme *f*.
normal ['nɔːm(ə)l] *a* normal; – *n* **above n.** au-dessus de la normale. ◆**nor'mality** *n* normalité *f*. ◆**normalize** *vt* normaliser. ◆**normally** *adv* normalement.
Norman ['nɔːmən] *a* normand.
north [nɔːθ] *n* nord *m*; – *a* (*coast*) nord *inv*; (*wind*) du nord; **to be n. of** être au nord de; **N. America/Africa** Amérique *f*/Afrique *f* du Nord; **N. American** *a* & *n* nord-américain, -aine (*mf*); – *adv* au nord, vers le nord. ◆**northbound** *a* (*carriageway*) nord *inv*; (*traffic*) en direction du nord. ◆**north-'east** *n* & *a* nord-est *m* & *a inv*. ◆**northerly** *a* (*point*) nord *inv*; (*direction, wind*) du nord. ◆**northern** *a* (*coast*) nord *inv*; (*town*) du nord; **N. France** le Nord de la France; **N. Europe** Europe *f* du Nord; **N. Ireland** Irlande *f* du Nord. ◆**northerner** *n* habitant, -ante *mf* du Nord. ◆**northward(s)** *a* & *adv* vers le nord. ◆**north-'west** *n* & *a* nord-ouest *m* & *a inv*.
Norway ['nɔːweɪ] *n* Norvège *f*. ◆**Nor'wegian** *a* & *n* norvégien, -ienne (*mf*); – *n* (*language*) norvégien *m*.
nose [nəʊz] *n* nez *m*; **her n. is bleeding** elle saigne du nez; **to turn one's n. up** *Fig* faire le dégoûté (**at** devant); – *vi* **to n. about** (*pry*) *Fam* fouiner. ◆**nosebleed** *n* saignement *m* de nez. ◆**nosedive** *n Av* piqué *m*; (*in prices*) chute *f*.
nos(e)y ['nəʊzɪ] *a* (**-ier, -iest**) fouineur, indiscret; **n. parker** fouineur, -euse *mf*.
nosh [nɒʃ] *vi Fam* (*eat heavily*) bouffer; (*nibble*) grignoter (entre les repas); – *n* (*food*) *Fam* bouffe *f*.
nostalgia [nɒ'stældʒɪə] *n* nostalgie *f*. ◆**nostalgic** *a* nostalgique.
nostril ['nɒstr(ə)l] *n* (*of person*) narine *f*; (*of horse*) naseau *m*.
not [nɒt] *adv* **1** (ne) . . . pas; **he's n. there, he isn't there** il n'est pas là; **n. yet** pas encore; **why n.?** pourquoi pas?; **n. one reply**/*etc* pas une seule réponse/*etc*; **n. at all** pas du tout; (*after 'thank you'*) je vous en prie. **2** non; **I think/hope n.** je pense/j'espère que non; **n. guilty** non coupable; **isn't she?, don't you?** *etc* non?
notable ['nəʊtəb(ə)l] *a* (*remarkable*) notable; – *n* (*person*) notable *m*. ◆**notably** *adv* (*noticeably*) notablement; (*particularly*) notamment.
notary ['nəʊtərɪ] *n* notaire *m*.
notation [nəʊ'teɪʃ(ə)n] *n* notation *f*.
notch [nɒtʃ] **1** *n* (*in wood etc*) entaille *f*, encoche *f*; (*in belt, wheel*) cran *m*. **2** *vt* **to n. up** (*a score*) marquer; (*a victory*) enregistrer.
note [nəʊt] *n* (*written comment, tone etc*) & *Mus* note *f*; (*summary, preface*) notice *f*; (*banknote*) billet *m*; (*piano key*) touche *f*; (*message, letter*) petit mot *m*; **to take (a) n. of, make a n. of** prendre note de; **of n.** (*athlete, actor etc*) éminent; – *vt* (*take note of*) noter; (*notice*) remarquer, noter; **to n. down** noter. ◆**notebook** *n* carnet *m*; *Sch* cahier *m*; (*pad*) bloc-notes *m*. ◆**notepad** *n* bloc-notes *m*. ◆**notepaper** *n* papier *m* à lettres.
noted ['nəʊtɪd] *a* (*author etc*) éminent; **to be n. for** être connu pour.
noteworthy ['nəʊtwɜːðɪ] *a* notable.
nothing ['nʌθɪŋ] *pron* (ne) . . . rien; **he knows n.** il ne sait rien; **n. to do/eat/***etc* rien à faire/manger/*etc*; **n. big/***etc* rien de grand/*etc*; **n. much** pas grand-chose; **I've got n. to do with it** je n'y suis pour rien; **I can do n. (about it)** je n'y peux rien; **to come to n.** (*of effort etc*) ne rien donner; **there's n. like it** il n'y a rien de tel; **for n.** (*in vain, free of charge*) pour rien; – *adv* **to look n. like s.o.** ne ressembler nullement à qn; **n. like as large/***etc* loin d'être aussi grand/*etc*; – *n* **a (mere) n.** (*person*) une nullité; (*thing*) un rien. ◆**—ness** *n* (*void*) néant *m*.
notice ['nəʊtɪs] *n* (*notification*) avis *m*; *Journ* annonce *f*; (*sign*) pancarte *f*, écriteau *m*; (*poster*) affiche *f*; (*review of film etc*) critique *f*; (*attention*) attention *f*; (*knowledge*) connaissance *f*; **(advance) n.** (*of departure etc*) préavis *m*; **n. (to quit), n. (of dismissal)** congé *m*; **to give (in) one's n.** (*resignation*) donner sa démission; **to give s.o. n. of** (*inform of*) avertir qn de; **to take n.** faire attention (**of à**); **to bring sth to s.o.'s n.** porter qch à la connaissance de qn; **until further n.** jusqu'à nouvel ordre; **at short n.** à

bref délai; **n. board** tableau *m* d'affichage; – *vt* (*perceive*) remarquer (*qn*); (*fact, trick, danger*) s'apercevoir de, remarquer; **I n. that** je m'aperçois que. ◆**—able** *a* visible, perceptible; **that's n.** ça se voit; **she's n.** elle se fait remarquer.

notify ['nəʊtɪfaɪ] *vt* (*inform*) aviser (**s.o. of sth** qn de qch); (*announce*) notifier (**to** à). ◆**notifi'cation** *n* annonce *f*, avis *m*.

notion ['nəʊʃ(ə)n] **1** *n* (*thought*) idée *f*; (*awareness*) notion *f*; **some n. of** (*knowledge*) quelques notions de. **2** *npl* (*sewing articles*) *Am* mercerie *f*.

notorious [nəʊ'tɔːrɪəs] *a* (*event, person etc*) tristement célèbre; (*stupidity, criminal*) notoire. ◆**notoriety** [-ə'raɪətɪ] *n* (triste) notoriété *f*.

notwithstanding [nɒtwɪð'stændɪŋ] *prep* malgré; – *adv* tout de même.

nougat ['nuːgɑː, 'nʌgət] *n* nougat *m*.

nought [nɔːt] *n Math* zéro *m*.

noun [naʊn] *n Gram* nom *m*.

nourish ['nʌrɪʃ] *vt* nourrir. ◆**—ing** *a* nourrissant. ◆**—ment** *n* nourriture *f*.

novel ['nɒv(ə)l] **1** *n Liter* roman *m*. **2** *a* (*new*) nouveau, original. ◆**novelist** *n* romancier, -ière *mf*. ◆**novelty** *n* (*newness, object, idea*) nouveauté *f*.

November [nəʊ'vembər] *n* novembre *m*.

novice ['nɒvɪs] *n* novice *mf* (**at** en).

now [naʊ] *adv* maintenant; **just n., right n.** en ce moment; **I saw her just n.** je l'ai vue à l'instant; **for n.** pour le moment; **even n.** encore maintenant; **from n. on** désormais, à partir de maintenant; **until n., up to n.** jusqu'ici; **before n.** avant; **n. and then** de temps à autre; **n. hot, n. cold** tantôt chaud, tantôt froid; **n. (then)!** bon!, alors!; (*telling s.o. off*) allons!; **n. it happened that . . .** or il advint que . . . ; – *conj* **n. (that)** maintenant que. ◆**nowadays** *adv* aujourd'hui, de nos jours.

noway ['nəʊweɪ] *adv Am* nullement.

nowhere ['nəʊweər] *adv* nulle part; **n. else** nulle part ailleurs; **it's n. I know** ce n'est pas un endroit que je connais; **n. near the house** loin de la maison; **n. near enough** loin d'être assez.

nozzle ['nɒz(ə)l] *n* (*of hose*) jet *m*, lance *f* (à eau); (*of syringe, tube*) embout *m*.

nth [enθ] *a* nième.

nuance ['njuːɑːns] *n* (*of meaning, colour etc*) nuance *f*.

nub [nʌb] *n* (*of problem*) cœur *m*.

nuclear ['njuːklɪər] *a* nucléaire; **n. scientist** spécialiste *mf* du nucléaire, atomiste *mf*.

nucleus, *pl* **-clei** ['njuːklɪəs, -klɪaɪ] *n* noyau *m*.

nude [njuːd] *a* nu; – *n* (*female or male figure*) nu *m*; **in the n.** (tout) nu. ◆**nudism** *n* nudisme *m*, naturisme *m*. ◆**nudist** *n* nudiste *mf*, naturiste *mf*; – *a* (*camp*) de nudistes, de naturistes. ◆**nudity** *n* nudité *f*.

nudge [nʌdʒ] *vt* pousser du coude; – *n* coup *m* de coude.

nugget ['nʌgɪt] *n* (*of gold etc*) pépite *f*.

nuisance ['njuːs(ə)ns] *n* (*annoyance*) embêtement *m*; (*person*) peste *f*; **that's a n.** c'est embêtant; **he's being a n., he's making a n. of himself** il nous embête, il m'embête *etc*.

null [nʌl] *a* **n. (and void)** nul (et non avenu). ◆**nullify** *vt* infirmer.

numb [nʌm] *a* (*stiff*) engourdi; *Fig* paralysé; – *vt* engourdir; *Fig* paralyser.

number ['nʌmbər] *n* nombre *m*; (*of page, house, newspaper etc*) numéro *m*; **a dance/song n.** un numéro de danse/de chant; **a/any n. of** un certain/grand nombre de; **n. plate** (*of vehicle*) plaque *f* d'immatriculation; – *vt* (*page etc*) numéroter; (*include, count*) compter; **they n. eight** ils sont au nombre de huit. ◆**—ing** *n* numérotage *m*.

numeral ['njuːm(ə)rəl] *n* chiffre *m*; – *a* numéral. ◆**nu'merical** *a* numérique. ◆**numerous** *a* nombreux.

numerate ['njuːm(ə)rət] *a* (*person*) qui sait compter.

nun [nʌn] *n* religieuse *f*.

nurs/e [nɜːs] **1** *n* infirmière *f*; (*nanny*) nurse *f*; **(male) n.** infirmier *m*. **2** *vt* (*look after*) soigner; (*cradle*) bercer; (*suckle*) nourrir; (*a grudge etc*) *Fig* nourrir; (*support, encourage*) *Fig* épauler (*qn*). ◆**—ing** *a* (*mother*) qui allaite; **the n. staff** le personnel infirmier; – *n* (*care*) soins *mpl*; (*job*) profession *f* d'infirmière *or* d'infirmier; **n. home** clinique *f*. ◆**nursemaid** *n* bonne *f* d'enfants.

nursery ['nɜːsərɪ] *n* (*room*) chambre *f* d'enfants; (*for plants, trees*) pépinière *f*; **(day) n.** (*school etc*) crèche *f*, garderie *f*; **n. rhyme** chanson *f* enfantine; **n. school** école *f* maternelle.

nurture ['nɜːtʃər] *vt* (*educate*) éduquer.

nut¹ [nʌt] *n* (*fruit*) fruit *m* à coque; (*walnut*) noix *f*; (*hazelnut*) noisette *f*; (*peanut*) cacah(o)uète *f*; **Brazil/cashew n.** noix *f* du Brésil/de cajou. ◆**nutcracker(s)** *n(pl)* casse-noix *m inv*. ◆**nutshell** *n* coquille *f* de noix; **in a n.** *Fig* en un mot.

nut² [nʌt] *n* **1** (*for bolt*) *Tech* écrou *m*. **2**

(*head*) *Sl* caboche *f*. **3** (*person*) *Sl* cinglé, -ée *mf*; **to be nuts** *Sl* être cinglé. ◆**nutcase** *n* cinglé, -ée *mf*. ◆**nutty** *a* (**-ier, -iest**) *Sl* cinglé.

nutmeg ['nʌtmeg] *n* muscade *f*.

nutritious [njuː'trɪʃəs] *a* nutritif. ◆**'nutrient** *n* élément *m* nutritif. ◆**nutrition** *n* nutrition *f*.

nylon ['naɪlɒn] *n* nylon *m*; *pl* (*stockings*) bas *mpl* nylon.

nymph [nɪmf] *n* nymphe *f*. ◆**nympho'maniac** *n Pej* nymphomane *f*.

O

O, o [əʊ] *n* O, o *m*.

oaf [əʊf] *n* rustre *m*. ◆**oafish** *a* (*behaviour*) de rustre.

oak [əʊk] *n* (*tree, wood*) chêne *m*.

OAP [əʊeɪ'piː] *n abbr* (*old age pensioner*) retraité, -ée *mf*.

oar [ɔːr] *n* aviron *m*, rame *f*.

oasis, *pl* **oases** [əʊ'eɪsɪs, əʊ'eɪsiːz] *n* oasis *f*.

oath [əʊθ] *n* (*pl* **-s** [əʊðz]) (*promise*) serment *m*; (*profanity*) juron *m*; **to take an o. to do** faire le serment de faire.

oats [əʊts] *npl* avoine *f*. ◆**oatmeal** *n* flocons *mpl* d'avoine.

obedient [ə'biːdɪənt] *a* obéissant. ◆**obedience** *n* obéissance *f* (**to** à). ◆**obediently** *adv* docilement.

obelisk ['ɒbəlɪsk] *n* (*monument*) obélisque *m*.

obese [əʊ'biːs] *a* obèse. ◆**obesity** *n* obésité *f*.

obey [ə'beɪ] *vt* obéir à; **to be obeyed** être obéi; – *vi* obéir.

obituary [ə'bɪtʃʊərɪ] *n* nécrologie *f*.

object[1] ['ɒbdʒɪkt] *n* (*thing*) objet *m*; (*aim*) but *m*, objet *m*; *Gram* complément *m* (d'objet); **with the o. of** dans le but de; **that's no o.** (*no problem*) ça ne pose pas de problème; **price no o.** prix *m* indifférent.

object[2] [əb'dʒekt] *vi* **to o. to sth/s.o.** désapprouver qch/qn; **I o. to you(r) doing that** ça me gêne que tu fasses ça; **I o.!** je proteste!; **she didn't o. when . . .** elle n'a fait aucune objection quand . . . ; – *vt* **to o. that** objecter que. ◆**objection** *n* objection *f*; **I've got no o.** ça ne me gêne pas, je n'y vois pas d'objection *or* d'inconvénient. ◆**objectionable** *a* très désagréable. ◆**objector** *n* opposant, -ante *mf* (**to** à); **conscientious o.** objecteur *m* de conscience.

objective [əb'dʒektɪv] **1** *a* (*opinion etc*) objectif. **2** *n* (*aim, target*) objectif *m*. ◆**objectively** *adv* objectivement. ◆**objec'tivity** *n* objectivité *f*.

obligate ['ɒblɪgeɪt] *vt* contraindre (**to do** à faire). ◆**obli'gation** *n* obligation *f*; (*debt*) dette *f*; **under an o. to do** dans l'obligation de faire; **under an o. to s.o.** redevable à qn (**for** de). ◆**o'bligatory** *a* (*compulsory*) obligatoire; (*imposed by custom*) de rigueur.

oblig/e [ə'blaɪdʒ] *vt* **1** (*compel*) obliger (**s.o. to do** qn à faire); **obliged to do** obligé de faire. **2** (*help*) rendre service à, faire plaisir à; **obliged to s.o.** reconnaissant à qn (**for** de); **much obliged!** merci infiniment! ◆**—ing** *a* (*kind*) obligeant. ◆**—ingly** *adv* obligeamment.

oblique [ə'bliːk] *a* oblique; (*reference*) *Fig* indirect.

obliterate [ə'blɪtəreɪt] *vt* effacer. ◆**oblite'ration** *n* effacement *m*.

oblivion [ə'blɪvɪən] *n* oubli *m*. ◆**oblivious** *a* inconscient (**to, of** de).

oblong ['ɒblɒŋ] *a* (*elongated*) oblong; (*rectangular*) rectangulaire; – *n* rectangle *m*.

obnoxious [əb'nɒkʃəs] *a* odieux; (*smell*) nauséabond.

oboe ['əʊbəʊ] *n Mus* hautbois *m*.

obscene [əb'siːn] *a* obscène. ◆**obscenity** *n* obscénité *f*.

obscure [əb'skjʊər] *a* (*reason, word, actor, life etc*) obscur; – *vt* (*hide*) cacher; (*confuse*) embrouiller, obscurcir. ◆**obscurely** *adv* obscurément. ◆**obscurity** *n* obscurité *f*.

obsequious [əb'siːkwɪəs] *a* obséquieux.

observe [əb'zɜːv] *vt* (*notice, watch, respect*) observer; (*say*) (faire) remarquer (**that** que); **to o. the speed limit** respecter la limitation de vitesse. ◆**observance** *n* (*of rule etc*) observation *f*. ◆**observant** *a* observateur. ◆**obser'vation** *n* (*observing, remark*) observation *f*; (*by police*) surveillance *f*; **under o.** (*hospital patient*) en observation. ◆**observatory** *n* observatoire *m*. ◆**observer** *n* observateur, -trice *mf*.

obsess [əb'ses] *vt* obséder. ◆**obsession** *n* obsession *f*; **to have an o. with** *or* **about** avoir l'obsession de. ◆**obsessive** *a* (*memory, idea*) obsédant; (*fear*) obsessif; (*neurotic*) *Psy* obsessionnel; **to be o. about** avoir l'obsession de.

obsolete ['ɒbsəliːt] *a* (*out of date, superseded*) désuet, dépassé; (*ticket*) périmé; (*machinery*) archaïque. ◆**obso'lescent** *a* quelque peu désuet; (*word*) vieilli.

obstacle ['ɒbstək(ə)l] *n* obstacle *m*.

obstetrics [əb'stetrɪks] *n Med* obstétrique *f*. ◆**obste'trician** *n* médecin *m* accoucheur.

obstinate ['ɒbstɪnət] *a* (*person, resistance etc*) obstiné, opiniâtre; (*disease, pain*) rebelle, opiniâtre. ◆**obstinacy** *n* obstination *f*. ◆**obstinately** *adv* obstinément.

obstreperous [əb'strepərəs] *a* turbulent.

obstruct [əb'strʌkt] *vt* (*block*) boucher; (*hinder*) entraver; (*traffic*) entraver, bloquer. ◆**obstruction** *n* (*act, state*) & *Med Pol Sp* obstruction *f*; (*obstacle*) obstacle *m*; (*in pipe*) bouchon *m*; (*traffic jam*) embouteillage *m*. ◆**obstructive** *a* **to be o.** faire de l'obstruction.

obtain [əb'teɪn] **1** *vt* obtenir. **2** *vi* (*of practice etc*) avoir cours. ◆**—able** *a* (*available*) disponible; (*on sale*) en vente.

obtrusive [əb'truːsɪv] *a* (*person*) importun; (*building etc*) trop en évidence.

obtuse [əb'tjuːs] *a* (*angle, mind*) obtus.

obviate ['ɒbvɪeɪt] *vt* (*necessity*) éviter.

obvious ['ɒbvɪəs] *a* évident; **he's the o. man to see** c'est évidemment l'homme qu'il faut voir. ◆**—ly** *adv* (*evidently, of course*) évidemment; (*conspicuously*) visiblement.

occasion [ə'keɪʒ(ə)n] **1** *n* (*time, opportunity*) occasion *f*; (*event, ceremony*) événement *m*; **on the o. of** à l'occasion de; **on o.** à l'occasion; **on several occasions** à plusieurs reprises *or* occasions. **2** *n* (*cause*) raison *f*, occasion *f*; – *vt* occasionner. ◆**occasional** *a* (*event*) qui a lieu de temps en temps; (*rain, showers*) intermittent; **she drinks the o. whisky** elle boit un whisky de temps en temps. ◆**occasionally** *adv* de temps en temps; **very o.** très peu souvent, rarement.

occult [ə'kʌlt] *a* occulte.

occupy ['ɒkjʊpaɪ] *vt* (*house, time, space, post etc*) occuper; **to keep oneself occupied** s'occuper (**doing** à faire). ◆**occupant** *n* (*inhabitant*) occupant, -ante *mf*. ◆**occu'pation** *n* (*activity*) occupation *f*; (*job*) emploi *m*; (*trade*) métier *m*; (*profession*) profession *f*; **the o. of** (*action*) l'occupation *f* de; **fit for o.** (*house*) habitable. ◆**occu'pational** *a* (*hazard*) du métier; (*disease*) du travail. ◆**occupier** *n* (*of house*) occupant, -ante *mf*; *Mil* occupant *m*.

occur [ə'kɜːr] *vi* (-rr-) (*happen*) avoir lieu; (*be found*) se rencontrer; (*arise*) se présenter; **it occurs to me that . . .** il me vient à l'esprit que . . . ; **the idea occurred to her to . . .** l'idée lui est venue de . . . . ◆**occurrence** [ə'kʌrəns] *n* (*event*) événement *m*; (*existence*) existence *f*; (*of word*) *Ling* occurrence *f*.

ocean ['əʊʃ(ə)n] *n* océan *m*. ◆**oce'anic** *a* océanique.

o'clock [ə'klɒk] *adv* **(it's) three o'c./***etc* (il est) trois heures/*etc*.

octagon ['ɒktəgən] *n* octogone *m*. ◆**oc'tagonal** *a* octogonal.

octave ['ɒktɪv, 'ɒkteɪv] *n Mus* octave *f*.

October [ɒk'təʊbər] *n* octobre *m*.

octogenarian [ɒktəʊdʒɪ'neərɪən] *n* octogénaire *mf*.

octopus ['ɒktəpəs] *n* pieuvre *f*.

odd [ɒd] *a* **1** (*strange*) bizarre, curieux; **an o. size** une taille peu courante. **2** (*number*) impair. **3** (*left over*) **I have an o. penny** il me reste un penny; **a few o. stamps** quelques timbres (qui restent); **the o. man out, the o. one out** l'exception *f*; **sixty o.** soixante et quelques; **an o. glove/book/***etc* un gant/livre/*etc* dépareillé. **4** (*occasional*) qu'on fait, voit *etc* de temps en temps; **to find the o. mistake** trouver de temps en temps une (petite) erreur; **at o. moments** de temps en temps; **o. jobs** (*around house*) menus travaux *mpl*; **o. job man** homme *m* à tout faire. ◆**oddity** *n* (*person*) personne *f* bizarre; (*object*) curiosité *f*; *pl* (*of language, situation*) bizarreries *fpl*. ◆**oddly** *adv* bizarrement; **o. (enough), he was . . .** chose curieuse, il était . . . . ◆**oddment** *n Com* fin *f* de série. ◆**oddness** *n* bizarrerie *f*.

odds [ɒdz] *npl* **1** (*in betting*) cote *f*; (*chances*) chances *fpl*; **we have heavy o. against us** nous avons très peu de chances de réussir. **2 it makes no o.** (*no difference*) *Fam* ça ne fait rien. **3 at o.** (*in disagreement*) en désaccord (**with** avec). **4 o. and ends** des petites choses.

ode [əʊd] *n* (*poem*) ode *f*.

odious ['əʊdɪəs] *a* détestable, odieux.

odour ['əʊdər] *n* odeur *f*. ◆**—less** *a* inodore.

oecumenical [iːkjʊ'menɪk(ə)l] *a Rel* œcuménique.

of [əv, *stressed* ɒv] *prep* de; **of the table** de la table; **of the boy** du garçon; **of the boys** des garçons; **of a book** d'un livre; **of it, of them** en; **she has a lot of it** *or* **of them** elle en a beaucoup; **a friend of his** un ami à lui; **there are ten of us** nous sommes dix; **that's nice of you** c'est gentil de ta part; **of no value/interest/***etc* sans valeur/intérêt/*etc*; **of late** ces derniers temps; **a man of fifty** un homme de cinquante ans; **the fifth of June** le cinq juin.

off [ɒf] **1** *adv* (*absent*) absent, parti; (*light, gas, radio etc*) éteint, fermé; (*tap*) fermé; (*switched off at mains*) coupé; (*detached*) détaché; (*removed*) enlevé; (*cancelled*) annulé; (*not fit to eat or drink*) mauvais; (*milk, meat*) tourné; **2 km o.** à 2 km (d'ici *or* de là), éloigné de 2 km; **to be** *ou* **go o.** (*leave*) partir; **where are you o. to?** où vas-tu?; **he has his hat o.** il a enlevé son chapeau; **with his, my** *etc* **gloves o.** sans gants; **a day o.** (*holiday*) un jour de congé; **I'm o. today, I have today o.** j'ai congé aujourd'hui; **the strike's o.** il n'y aura pas de grève, la grève est annulée; **5% o.** une réduction de 5%; **on and o., o. and on** (*sometimes*) de temps à autre; **to be better o.** (*wealthier, in a better position*) être mieux. **2** *prep* (*from*) de; (*distant*) éloigné de; **to fall/***etc* **o. the wall/ladder/***etc* tomber/*etc* du mur/de l'échelle/*etc*; **to get o. the bus/***etc* descendre du bus/*etc*; **to take sth o. the table/***etc* prendre qch sur la table/*etc*; **to eat o. a plate** manger dans une assiette; **to keep** *or* **stay o. the grass** ne pas marcher sur les pelouses; **she's o. her food** elle ne mange plus rien; **o. Dover/***etc* *Nau* au large de Douvres/*etc*; **o. limits** interdit; **the o. side** *Aut* le côté droit, *Am* le côté gauche. ◆**off'beat** *a* excentrique. ◆**off-'colour** *a* (*ill*) patraque; (*indecent*) scabreux. ◆**off'hand** *a* désinvolte; – *adv* impromptu. ◆**off'handedness** *n* désinvolture *f*. ◆**off-licence** *n* magasin *m* de vins et de spiritueux. ◆**off-'load** *vt* (*vehicle etc*) décharger; **to o.-load sth onto s.o.** (*task etc*) se décharger de qch sur qn. ◆**off-'peak** *a* (*crowds, traffic*) aux heures creuses; (*rate, price*) heures creuses *inv*; **o.-peak hours** heures *fpl* creuses. ◆**off-putting** *a Fam* rebutant. ◆**off'side** *a* **to be o.** *Fb* être hors jeu. ◆**off'stage** *a & adv* dans les coulisses. ◆**off-'white** *a* blanc cassé *inv*.

offal ['ɒf(ə)l] *n Culin* abats *mpl*.

offence [ə'fens] *n Jur* délit *m*; **to take o.** s'offenser (at de); **to give o.** offenser.

offend [ə'fend] *vt* froisser, offenser; (*eye*) *Fig* choquer; **to be offended (at)** se froisser (de), s'offenser (de). ◆**—ing** *a* (*object, remark*) incriminé. ◆**offender** *n Jur* délinquant, -ante *mf*; (*habitual*) récidiviste *mf*.

offensive [ə'fensɪv] **1** *a* (*unpleasant*) choquant, repoussant; (*insulting*) insultant, offensant; (*weapon*) offensif. **2** *n Mil* offensive *f*.

offer ['ɒfər] *n* offre *f*; **on (special) o.** *Com* en promotion, en réclame; **o. of marriage** demande *f* en mariage; – *vt* offrir; (*opinion, remark*) proposer; **to o. to do** offrir *or* proposer de faire. ◆**—ing** *n* (*gift*) offrande *f*; (*act*) offre *f*; **peace o.** cadeau *m* de réconciliation.

office ['ɒfɪs] *n* **1** bureau *m*; (*of doctor*) *Am* cabinet *m*; (*of lawyer*) étude *f*; **head o.** siège *m* central; **o. block** immeuble *m* de bureaux; **o. worker** employé, -ée *mf* de bureau. **2** (*post*) fonction *f*; (*duty*) fonctions *fpl*; **to be in o.** (*of party etc*) *Pol* être au pouvoir. **3 one's good offices** (*help*) ses bons offices *mpl*.

officer ['ɒfɪsər] *n* (*in army, navy etc*) officier *m*; (*of company*) *Com* directeur, -trice *mf*; **(police) o.** agent *m* (de police).

official [ə'fɪʃ(ə)l] *a* officiel; (*uniform*) réglementaire; – *n* (*person of authority*) officiel *m*; (*civil servant*) fonctionnaire *mf*; (*employee*) employé, -ée *mf*. ◆**officialdom** *n* bureaucratie *f*. ◆**officially** *adv* officiellement. ◆**officiate** *vi* faire fonction d'officiel (**at** à); (*preside*) présider; *Rel* officier.

officious [ə'fɪʃəs] *a Pej* empressé.

offing ['ɒfɪŋ] *n* **in the o.** en perspective.

offset ['ɒfset, ɒf'set] *vt* (*pt & pp* **offset**, *pres p* **offsetting**) (*compensate for*) compenser; (*s.o.'s beauty etc by contrast*) faire ressortir.

offshoot ['ɒfʃuːt] *n* (*of firm*) ramification *f*; (*consequence*) conséquence *f*.

offspring ['ɒfsprɪŋ] *n* progéniture *f*.

often ['ɒf(t)ən] *adv* souvent; **how o.?** combien de fois?; **how o. do they run?** (*trains, buses etc*) il y en a tous les combien?; **once too o.** une fois de trop; **every so o.** de temps en temps.

ogle ['əʊg(ə)l] *vt Pej* reluquer.

ogre ['əʊgər] *n* ogre *m*.

oh! [əʊ] *int* oh!, ah!; (*pain*) aïe!; **oh yes?** ah oui?, ah bon?

oil [ɔɪl] *n* (*for machine, in cooking etc*) huile *f*; (*mineral*) pétrole *m*; (*fuel oil*) mazout *m*; **to paint in oils** faire de la peinture à l'huile; – *a* (*industry, product*) pétrolier; (*painting, paints*) à l'huile; **o. lamp** lampe *f* à pétrole *or* à huile; **o. change** *Aut* vidange *f*; – *vt* graisser, huiler. ◆**oilcan** *n* burette *f.* ◆**oilfield** *n* gisement *m* pétrolifère. ◆**oil-fired** *a* au mazout. ◆**oilskin(s)** *n(pl)* (*garment*) ciré *m.* ◆**oily** *a* (**-ier, -iest**) (*substance, skin*) huileux; (*hands*) graisseux; (*food*) gras.

ointment ['ɔɪntmənt] *n* pommade *f.*

OK [əʊ'keɪ] *int* (*approval, exasperation*) ça va!; (*agreement*) d'accord!, entendu!, OK!; – *a* (*satisfactory*) bien *inv*; (*unharmed*) sain et sauf; (*undamaged*) intact; (*without worries*) tranquille; **it's OK now** (*fixed*) ça marche maintenant; **I'm OK** (*healthy*) je vais bien; – *adv* (*to work etc*) bien; – *vt* (*pt & pp* **OKed,** *pres p* **OKing**) approuver.

okay [əʊ'keɪ] = OK.

old [əʊld] *a* (**-er, -est**) vieux; (*former*) ancien; **how o. is he?** quel âge a-t-il?; **he's ten years o.** il a dix ans, il est âgé de dix ans; **he's older than** il est plus âgé que; **an older son** un fils aîné; **the oldest son** le fils aîné; **o. enough to do** assez grand pour faire; **o. enough to marry/vote** en âge de se marier/de voter; **an o. man** un vieillard, un vieil homme; **an o. woman** une vieille (femme); **to get** *or* **grow old(er)** vieillir; **o. age** vieillesse *f*; **the O. Testament** l'Ancien Testament; **the O. World** l'Ancien Monde; **any o. how** *Fam* n'importe comment; – *n* **the o.** (*people*) les vieux *mpl.* ◆**o.-'fashioned** *a* (*customs etc*) d'autrefois; (*idea, attitude*) *Pej* vieux jeu *inv*; (*person*) de la vieille école, *Pej* vieux jeu *inv.* ◆**o.-'timer** *n* (*old man*) *Fam* vieillard *m.*

olden ['əʊld(ə)n] *a* **in o. days** jadis.

olive ['ɒlɪv] *n* (*fruit*) olive *f*; – *a* **o. (green)** (vert) olive *inv*; **o. oil** huile *f* d'olive; **o. tree** olivier *m.*

Olympic [ə'lɪmpɪk] *a* olympique.

ombudsman ['ɒmbʊdzmən] *n* (*pl* **-men**) *Pol* médiateur *m.*

omelet(te) ['ɒmlɪt] *n* omelette *f*; **cheese/etc o.** omelette au fromage/*etc.*

omen ['əʊmən] *n* augure *m.* ◆**ominous** *a* de mauvais augure; (*tone*) menaçant; (*noise*) sinistre.

omit [əʊ'mɪt] *vt* (**-tt-**) omettre (**to do** de faire). ◆**omission** *n* omission *f.*

omni- ['ɒmnɪ] *prep* omni-. ◆**om'nipotent** *a* omnipotent.

on [ɒn] *prep* **1** (*position*) sur; **on the chair** sur la chaise; **to put on (to)** mettre sur; **to look out on to** donner sur. **2** (*concerning, about*) sur; **an article on** un article sur; **to speak** *or* **talk on Dickens/*etc*** parler sur Dickens/*etc.* **3** (*manner, means*) à; **on foot** à pied; **on the blackboard** au tableau; **on the radio** à la radio; **on the train/plane/*etc*** dans le train/avion/*etc*; **on holiday,** *Am* **on vacation** en vacances; **to be on** (*course*) suivre; (*project*) travailler à; (*salary*) toucher; (*team, committee*) être membre de, faire partie de; **to keep** *or* **stay on** (*road, path etc*) suivre; **it's on me!** (*I'll pay*) *Fam* c'est moi qui paie! **4** (*time*) **on Monday** lundi; **on Mondays** le lundi; **on May 3rd** le 3 mai; **on the evening of May 3rd** le 3 mai au soir; **on my arrival** à mon arrivée. **5** (+ *present participle*) en; **on learning that...** en apprenant que...; **on seeing this** en voyant ceci. **6** *adv* (*ahead*) en avant; (*in progress*) en cours; (*started*) commencé; (*lid, brake*) mis; (*light, radio*) allumé; (*gas, tap*) ouvert; (*machine*) en marche; **on (and on)** sans cesse; **to play/*etc* on** continuer à jouer/*etc*; **she has her hat on** elle a mis *or* elle porte son chapeau; **he has sth/nothing on** il est habillé/tout nu; **I've got sth on** (*I'm busy*) je suis pris; **the strike's on** la grève aura lieu; **what's on?** *TV* qu'y a-t-il à la télé?; *Cin Th* qu'est-ce qu'on joue?; **there's a film on** on passe un film; **to be on at s.o.** (*pester*) *Fam* être après qn; **I've been on to him** *Tel* je l'ai eu au bout du fil; **to be on to s.o.** (*of police etc*) être sur la piste de qn; **from then on** à partir de là. ◆**on-coming** *a* (*vehicle*) qui vient en sens inverse. ◆**on-going** *a* (*project*) en cours.

once [wʌns] *adv* (*on one occasion*) une fois; (*formerly*) autrefois; **o. a month/*etc*** une fois par mois/*etc*; **o. again, o. more** encore une fois; **at o.** (*immediately*) tout de suite; **all at o.** (*suddenly*) tout à coup; (*at the same time*) à la fois; **o. and for all** une fois pour toutes; – *conj* une fois que. ◆**o.-over** *n* **to give sth the o.-over** (*quick look*) *Fam* regarder qch d'un coup d'œil.

one [wʌn] *a* **1** un, une; **o. man** un homme; **o. woman** une femme; **twenty-o.** vingt-et-un. **2** (*sole*) seul; **my o. (and only) aim** mon seul (et unique) but. **3** (*same*) même; **in the o. bus** dans le même bus; – *pron* **1** un, une; **do you want o.?** en veux-tu (un)?; **he's o. of us** il est des nôtres; **o. of them** l'un d'eux, l'une d'elles; **a big/small/*etc* o.** un grand/petit/*etc*; **this book is o. that I've read** ce livre est parmi ceux que j'ai lus; **she's o.** (*a teacher, gardener etc*) elle l'est; **this o.** celui-ci, celle-ci; **that o.** celui-là, celle-là; **the o. who** *or* **which** celui *or* celle qui; **it's Paul's o.** *Fam* c'est celui de Paul; **it's my o.** *Fam* c'est à moi; **another o.** un(e) autre; **I for o.** pour ma part. **2** (*impersonal*) on; **o. knows** on sait; **it helps o.** ça nous *or* vous aide; **one's**

family sa famille. ◆**one-'armed** *a* (*person*) manchot. ◆**one-'eyed** *a* borgne. ◆**one-'off** *a*, *Am* **one-of-a-'kind** *a Fam* unique, exceptionnel. ◆**one-'sided** *a* (*judgement etc*) partial; (*contest*) inégal; (*decision*) unilatéral. ◆**one-time** *a* (*former*) ancien. ◆**one-'way** *a* (*street*) à sens unique; (*traffic*) en sens unique; (*ticket*) *Am* simple.

oneself [wʌn'self] *pron* soi-même; (*reflexive*) se, s'; **to cut o.** se couper.

onion ['ʌnjən] *n* oignon *m*.

onlooker ['ɒnlʊkər] *n* spectateur, -trice *mf*.

only ['əʊnlɪ] *a* seul; **the o. house/***etc* la seule maison/*etc*; **the o. one** le seul, la seule; **an o. son** un fils unique; – *adv* seulement, ne . . . que; **I o. have ten, I have ten o.** je n'en ai que dix, j'en ai dix seulement; **if o.** si seulement; **not o.** non seulement; **I have o. just seen it** je viens tout juste de le voir; **o. he knows** lui seul le sait; – *conj* (*but*) *Fam* seulement; **o. I can't** seulement je ne peux pas.

onset ['ɒnset] *n* (*of disease*) début *m*; (*of old age*) approche *m*.

onslaught ['ɒnslɔːt] *n* attaque *f*.

onto ['ɒntuː] *prep* = **on to.**

onus ['əʊnəs] *n inv* **the o. is on you/***etc* c'est votre/*etc* responsabilité (**to do** de faire).

onward(s) ['ɒnwəd(z)] *adv* en avant; **from that time o.** à partir de là.

onyx ['ɒnɪks] *n* (*precious stone*) onyx *m*.

ooze [uːz] *vi* **to o. (out)** suinter; – *vt* (*blood etc*) laisser couler.

opal ['əʊp(ə)l] *n* (*precious stone*) opale *f*.

opaque [əʊ'peɪk] *a* opaque; (*unclear*) *Fig* obscur.

open ['əʊpən] *a* ouvert; (*site, view, road*) dégagé; (*car*) décapoté, découvert; (*meeting*) public; (*competition*) ouvert à tous; (*post*) vacant; (*attempt, envy*) manifeste; (*question*) non résolu; (*result*) indécis; (*ticket*) *Av* open *inv*; **wide o.** grand ouvert; **in the o. air** en plein air; **in (the) o. country** en rase campagne; **the o. spaces** les grands espaces; **it's o. to doubt** c'est douteux; **o. to** (*criticism, attack*) exposé à; (*ideas, suggestions*) ouvert à; **I've got an o. mind on it** je n'ai pas d'opinion arrêtée là-dessus; **to leave o.** (*date*) ne pas préciser; – *n* **(out) in the o.** (*outside*) en plein air; **to sleep (out) in the o.** dormir à la belle étoile; **to bring (out) into the o.** (*reveal*) divulguer; – *vt* ouvrir; (*conversation*) entamer; (*legs*) écarter; **to o. out** *or* **up** ouvrir; – *vi* (*of flower, eyes etc*) s'ouvrir; (*of shop, office etc*) ouvrir; (*of play*) débuter; (*of film*) sortir; **the door opens** (*is opened*) la porte s'ouvre; (*can open*) la porte ouvre; **to o. on to** (*of window etc*) donner sur; **to o. out** *or* **up** s'ouvrir; **to o. out** (*widen*) s'élargir; **to o. up** (*open a or the door*) ouvrir. ◆**—ing** *n* ouverture *f*; (*of flower*) éclosion *f*; (*career prospect, trade outlet*) débouché *m*; – *a* (*time, speech*) d'ouverture; **o. night** *Th* première *f*. ◆**—ly** *adv* (*not secretly, frankly*) ouvertement; (*publicly*) publiquement. ◆**—ness** *n* (*frankness*) franchise *f*; **o. of mind** ouverture *f* d'esprit.

open-air [əʊpən'eər] *a* (*pool etc*) en plein air. ◆**o.-'heart** *a* (*operation*) *Med* à cœur ouvert. ◆**o.-'necked** *a* (*shirt*) sans cravate. ◆**o.-'plan** *a Archit* sans cloisons.

opera ['ɒprə] *n* opéra *m*; **o. glasses** jumelles *fpl* de théâtre. ◆**ope'ratic** *a* d'opéra. ◆**ope'retta** *n* opérette *f*.

operat/e ['ɒpəreɪt] **1** *vi* (*of machine etc*) fonctionner; (*proceed*) opérer; – *vt* faire fonctionner; (*business*) gérer. **2** *vi* (*of surgeon*) opérer (**on s.o.** qn, **for** de). ◆**—ing** *a* **o. costs** frais *mpl* d'exploitation; **o. theatre**, *Am* **o. room** *Med* salle *f* d'opération; **o. wing** *Med* bloc *m* opératoire. ◆**ope'ration** *n* (*working*) fonctionnement *m*; *Med Mil Math etc* opération *f*; **in o.** (*machine*) en service; (*plan*) *Fig* en vigueur. ◆**ope'rational** *a* opérationnel. ◆**operative** *a Med* opératoire; (*law, measure etc*) en vigueur; – *n* ouvrier, -ière *mf*. ◆**operator** *n Tel* standardiste *mf*; (*on machine*) opérateur, -trice *mf*; (*criminal*) escroc *m*; **tour o.** organisateur, -trice *mf* de voyages, voyagiste *m*.

opinion [ə'pɪnjən] *n* opinion *f*, avis *m*; **in my o.** à mon avis. ◆**opinionated** *a* dogmatique.

opium ['əʊpɪəm] *n* opium *m*.

opponent [ə'pəʊnənt] *n* adversaire *mf*.

opportune ['ɒpətjuːn] *a* opportun. ◆**oppor'tunism** *n* opportunisme *m*.

opportunity [ɒpə'tjuːnɪtɪ] *n* occasion *f* (**to do** de faire); *pl* (*prospects*) perspectives *fpl*; **equal opportunities** des chances *fpl* égales.

oppos/e [ə'pəʊz] *vt* (*person, measure etc*) s'opposer à; (*law, motion*) *Pol* faire opposition à. ◆**—ed** *a* opposé (**to** à); **as o. to** par opposition à. ◆**—ing** *a* (*team, interests*) opposé. ◆**oppo'sition** *n* opposition *f* (**to** à); **the o.** (*rival camp*) *Fam* l'adversaire *m*.

opposite ['ɒpəzɪt] *a* (*side etc*) opposé; (*house*) d'en face; **one's o. number** (*counterpart*) son homologue *mf*; – *adv* (*to sit etc*) en face; – *prep* **o. (to)** en face de; – *n* **the o.** le contraire, l'opposé *m*.

oppress [ə'pres] *vt* (*tyrannize*) opprimer; (*of heat, anguish*) oppresser; **the oppressed** les opprimés *mpl*. ◆**oppression** *n* oppression *f*. ◆**oppressive** *a* (*ruler etc*) oppressif; (*heat*) oppressant; (*régime*) tyrannique. ◆**oppressor** *n* oppresseur *m*.

opt [ɒpt] *vi* **to o. for** opter pour; **to o. to do** choisir de faire; **to o. out** *Fam* refuser de participer (**of** à). ◆**option** *n* option *f*; (*subject*) *Sch* matière *f* à option; **she has no o.** elle n'a pas le choix. ◆**optional** *a* facultatif; **o. extra** (*on car etc*) option *f*, accessoire *m* en option.

optical ['ɒptɪk(ə)l] *a* (*glass*) optique; (*illusion, instrument etc*) d'optique. ◆**op'tician** *n* opticien, -ienne *mf*.

optimism ['ɒptɪmiz(ə)m] *n* optimisme *m*. ◆**optimist** *n* optimiste *mf*. ◆**opti'mistic** *a* optimiste. ◆**opti'mistically** *adv* avec optimisme.

optimum ['ɒptɪməm] *a* & *n* optimum (*m*); **the o. temperature** la température optimum. ◆**optimal** *a* optimal.

opulent ['ɒpjʊlənt] *a* opulent. ◆**opulence** *n* opulence *f*.

or [ɔːr] *conj* ou; **one or two** un ou deux; **he doesn't drink or smoke** il ne boit ni ne fume; **ten or so** environ dix.

oracle ['ɒrək(ə)l] *n* oracle *m*.

oral ['ɔːrəl] *a* oral; – *n* (*examination*) *Sch* oral *m*.

orange ['ɒrɪndʒ] **1** *n* (*fruit*) orange *f*; – *a* (*drink*) à l'orange; **o. tree** oranger *m*. **2** *a* & *n* (*colour*) orange *a* & *m inv*. ◆**orangeade** *n* orangeade *f*.

orang-outang [ɔːræŋuː'tæŋ] *n* orang-outan(g) *m*.

oration [ɔː'reɪʃ(ə)n] *n* **funeral o.** oraison *f* funèbre.

oratory ['ɒrətərɪ] *n* (*words*) *Pej* rhétorique *f*.

orbit ['ɔːbɪt] *n* (*of planet etc*) & *Fig* orbite *f*; – *vt* (*sun etc*) graviter autour de.

orchard ['ɔːtʃəd] *n* verger *m*.

orchestra ['ɔːkɪstrə] *n* (*classical*) orchestre *m*. ◆**or'chestral** *a* (*music*) orchestral; (*concert*) symphonique. ◆**orchestrate** *vt* (*organize*) & *Mus* orchestrer.

orchid ['ɔːkɪd] *n* orchidée *f*.

ordain [ɔː'deɪn] *vt* (*priest*) ordonner; **to o. that** décréter que.

ordeal [ɔː'diːl] *n* épreuve *f*, supplice *m*.

order ['ɔːdər] *n* (*command, structure, association etc*) ordre *m*; (*purchase*) *Com* commande *f*; **in o** (*drawer, room etc*) en ordre; (*passport etc*) en règle; **in (numerical) o.** dans l'ordre numérique; **in working o.** en état de marche; **in o. of age** par ordre d'âge; **in o. to do** pour faire; **in o. that** pour que (+ *sub*); **it's in o. to smoke/***etc* (*allowed*) il est permis de fumer/*etc*; **out of o.** (*machine*) en panne; (*telephone*) en dérangement; **to make** *or* **place an o.** *Com* passer une commande; **on o.** *Com* commandé; **money o.** mandat *m*; **postal o.** mandat *m* postal; – *vt* (*command*) ordonner (**s.o. to do** à qn de faire); (*meal, goods etc*) commander; (*taxi*) appeler; **to o. s.o. around** commander qn, régenter qn; – *vi* (*in café etc*) commander. ◆**—ly 1** *a* (*tidy*) ordonné; (*mind*) méthodique; (*crowd*) discipliné. **2** *n Mil* planton *m*; (*in hospital*) garçon *m* de salle.

ordinal ['ɔːdɪnəl] *a* (*number*) ordinal.

ordinary ['ɔːd(ə)nrɪ] *a* (*usual*) ordinaire; (*average*) moyen; (*mediocre*) médiocre, ordinaire; **an o. individual** un simple particulier; **in o. use** d'usage courant; **in the o. course of events** en temps normal; **in the o. way** normalement; **it's out of the o.** ça sort de l'ordinaire.

ordination [ɔːdɪ'neɪʃ(ə)n] *n Rel* ordination *f*.

ordnance ['ɔːdnəns] *n* (*guns*) *Mil* artillerie *f*.

ore [ɔːr] *n* minerai *m*.

organ ['ɔːgən] *n* **1** *Anat* & *Fig* organe *m*. **2** *Mus* orgue *m*, orgues *fpl*; **barrel o.** orgue *m* de Barbarie. ◆**organist** *n* organiste *mf*.

organic [ɔː'gænɪk] *a* organique. ◆**'organism** *n* organisme *m*.

organization [ɔːgənaɪ'zeɪʃ(ə)n] *n* (*arrangement, association*) organisation *f*.

organiz/e ['ɔːgənaɪz] *vt* organiser. ◆**—ed** *a* (*mind, group etc*) organisé. ◆**—er** *n* organisateur, -trice *mf*.

orgasm ['ɔːgæz(ə)m] *n* orgasme *m*.

orgy ['ɔːdʒɪ] *n* orgie *f*.

orient ['ɔːrɪənt] *vt Am* = **orientate**. ◆**orientate** *vt* orienter.

Orient ['ɔːrɪənt] *n* **the O.** l'Orient *m*. ◆**ori'ental** *a* & *n* oriental, -ale (*mf*).

orifice ['ɒrɪfɪs] *n* orifice *m*.

origin ['ɒrɪdʒɪn] *n* origine *f*.

original [ə'rɪdʒɪn(ə)l] *a* (*first*) premier, originel, primitif; (*novel, unusual*) original; (*sin*) originel; (*copy, version*) original; – *n* (*document etc*) original *m*. ◆**origi'nality** *n* originalité *f*. ◆**originally** *adv* (*at first*) à l'origine; (*in a novel way*) originalement; **she comes o. from** elle est originaire de. ◆**originate** *vi* (*begin*) prendre naissance (**in** dans); **to o. from** (*of idea etc*) émaner de; (*of person*) être originaire de; – *vt* être l'auteur de ◆**originator** *n* auteur *m* (**of** de).

ornament ['ɔːnəmənt] *n* (*decoration*) ornement *m*; *pl* (*vases etc*) bibelots *mpl*. ◆**orna'mental** *a* ornemental. ◆**ornamen'tation** *n* ornementation *f*. ◆**or'nate** *a* (*style etc*) (très) orné. ◆**or'nately** *adv* (*decorated etc*) de façon surchargée, à outrance.

orphan ['ɔːf(ə)n] *n* orphelin, -ine *mf*; – *a* orphelin. ◆**orphaned** *a* orphelin; **he was o. by the accident** l'accident l'a rendu orphelin. ◆**orphanage** *n* orphelinat *m*.

orthodox ['ɔːθədɒks] *a* orthodoxe. ◆**orthodoxy** *n* orthodoxie *f*.

orthop(a)edics [ɔːθə'piːdɪks] *n* orthopédie *f*.

Oscar ['ɒskər] *n Cin* oscar *m*.

oscillate ['ɒsɪleɪt] *vi* osciller.

ostensibly [ɒ'stensɪblɪ] *adv* apparemment, en apparence.

ostentation [ɒsten'teɪʃ(ə)n] *n* ostentation *f*. ◆**ostentatious** *a* plein d'ostentation, prétentieux.

ostracism ['ɒstrəsɪz(ə)m] *n* ostracisme *m*. ◆**ostracize** *vt* proscrire, frapper d'ostracisme.

ostrich ['ɒstrɪtʃ] *n* autruche *f*.

other ['ʌðər] *a* autre; **o. people** d'autres; **the o. one** l'autre *mf*; **I have no o. gloves than these** je n'ai pas d'autres gants que ceux-ci; – *pron* autre; **(some) others** d'autres; **some do, others don't** les uns le font, les autres ne le font pas; **none o. than, no o. than** nul autre que; – *adv* **o. than** autrement que. ◆**otherwise** *adv* autrement; – *a* (*different*) (tout) autre.

otter ['ɒtər] *n* loutre *f*.

ouch! [aʊtʃ] *int* aïe!, ouille!

ought [ɔːt] *v aux* **1** (*obligation, desirability*) **you o. to leave** tu devrais partir; **I o. to have done it** j'aurais dû le faire; **he said he o. to stay** il a dit qu'il devait rester. **2** (*probability*) **it o. to be ready** ça devrait être prêt.

ounce [aʊns] *n* (*measure*) & *Fig* once *f* (= *28,35 g*).

our [aʊər] *poss a* notre, *pl* nos. ◆**ours** *pron* le nôtre, la nôtre, *pl* les nôtres; **this book is o.** ce livre est à nous *or* est le nôtre; **a friend of o.** un ami à nous. ◆**our'selves** *pron* nous-mêmes; (*reflexive & after prep etc*) nous; **we wash o.** nous nous lavons.

oust [aʊst] *vt* évincer (**from** de).

out [aʊt] *adv* (*outside*) dehors; (*not at home etc*) sorti; (*light, fire*) éteint; (*news, secret*) connu, révélé; (*flower*) ouvert; (*book*) publié, sorti; (*finished*) fini; **to be** *or* **go o. a lot** sortir beaucoup; **he's o. in Italy** il est (parti) en Italie; **o. there** là-bas; **to have a day o.** sortir pour la journée; **5 km o.** *Nau* à 5 km du rivage; **the sun's o.** il fait (du) soleil; **the tide's o.** la marée est basse; **you're o.** (*wrong*) tu t'es trompé; (*in game etc*) tu es éliminé (**of** de); **the trip** *or* **journey o.** l'aller *m*; **to be o. to win** être résolu à gagner; – *prep* **o. of** (*outside*) en dehors de; (*danger, breath, reach, water*) hors de; (*without*) sans; **o. of pity/love/***etc* par pitié/amour/*etc*; **to look/jump/***etc* **o. of** (*window etc*) regarder/sauter/*etc* par; **to drink/take/copy o. of** boire/prendre/copier dans; **made o. of** (*wood etc*) fait en; **to make sth o. of a box/rag/***etc* faire qch avec une boîte/un chiffon/*etc*; **a page o. of** une page de; **she's o. of town** elle n'est pas en ville; **5 km o. of** (*away from*) à 5 km de; **four o. of five** quatre sur cinq; **o. of the blue** de manière inattendue; **to feel o. of it** *or* **of things** se sentir hors du coup. ◆**'out-and-out** *a* (*cheat, liar etc*) achevé; (*believer*) à tout crin. ◆**o.-of-'date** *a* (*expired*) périmé; (*old-fashioned*) démodé. ◆**o.-of-'doors** *adv* dehors. ◆**o.-of-the-'way** *a* (*place*) écarté.

outbid [aʊt'bɪd] *vt* (*pt & pp* **outbid**, *pres p* **outbidding**) **to o. s.o.** (sur)enchérir sur qn.

outboard ['aʊtbɔːd] *a* **o. motor** *Nau* moteur *m* hors-bord *inv*.

outbreak ['aʊtbreɪk] *n* (*of war*) début *m*; (*of violence, pimples*) éruption *f*; (*of fever*) accès *m*; (*of hostilities*) ouverture *f*.

outbuilding ['aʊtbɪldɪŋ] *n* (*of mansion, farm*) dépendance *f*.

outburst ['aʊtbɜːst] *n* (*of anger, joy*) explosion *f*; (*of violence*) flambée *f*; (*of laughter*) éclat *m*.

outcast ['aʊtkɑːst] *n* **(social) o.** paria *m*.

outcome ['aʊtkʌm] *n* résultat *m*, issue *f*.

outcry ['aʊtkraɪ] *n* tollé *m*.

outdated [aʊt'deɪtɪd] *a* démodé.

outdistance [aʊt'dɪstəns] *vt* distancer.

outdo [aʊt'duː] *vt* (*pt* **outdid**, *pp* **outdone**) surpasser (**in** en).

outdoor ['aʊtdɔːr] *a* (*game*) de plein air; (*pool, life*) en plein air; **o. clothes** tenue *f* pour sortir. ◆**out'doors** *adv* dehors.

outer ['aʊtər] *a* extérieur; **o. space** l'espace *m* (cosmique); **the o. suburbs** la grande banlieue.

outfit ['aʊtfɪt] *n* équipement *m*; (*kit*) trousse *f*; (*toy*) panoplie *f* (*de pompier, cow-boy etc*); (*clothes*) costume *m*; (*for woman*) toilette *f*; (*group, gang*) *Fam* bande *f*; (*firm*) *Fam* boîte *f*; **sports/ski o.** tenue *f* de sport/de ski. ◆**outfitter** *n* chemisier *m*.

outgoing ['aʊtgəʊɪŋ] **1** *a* (*minister etc*)

sortant; (*mail, ship*) en partance. **2** *a* (*sociable*) liant, ouvert. **3** *npl* (*expenses*) dépenses *fpl.*

outgrow [aut'grəʊ] *vt* (*pt* **outgrew**, *pp* **outgrown**) (*clothes*) devenir trop grand pour; (*habit*) perdre (en grandissant); **to o. s.o.** (*grow more than*) grandir plus vite que qn.

outhouse ['authaus] *n* (*of mansion, farm*) dépendance *f*; (*lavatory*) *Am* cabinets *mpl* extérieurs.

outing ['aʊtɪŋ] *n* sortie *f*, excursion *f*.

outlandish [aut'lændɪʃ] *a* (*weird*) bizarre; (*barbaric*) barbare.

outlast [aut'lɑːst] *vt* durer plus longtemps que; (*survive*) survivre à.

outlaw ['aʊtlɔː] *n* hors-la-loi *m inv*; – *vt* (*ban*) proscrire.

outlay ['aʊtleɪ] *n* (*money*) dépense(s) *f(pl).*

outlet ['aʊtlet] *n* (*for liquid, of tunnel etc*) sortie *f*; *El* prise *f* de courant; (*market for goods*) *Com* débouché *m*; (*for feelings, energy*) moyen *m* d'exprimer, exutoire *m*; **retail o.** *Com* point *m* de vente, magasin *m.*

outline ['aʊtlaɪn] *n* (*shape*) contour *m*, profil *m*; **(rough) o.** (*of article, plan etc*) esquisse *f*; **the broad** *or* **general** *or* **main outline(s)** (*chief features*) les grandes lignes; – *vt* (*plan, situation*) décrire à grands traits, esquisser; (*book, speech*) résumer; **to be outlined against** (*of tree etc*) se profiler sur.

outlive [aut'lɪv] *vt* survivre à.

outlook ['aʊtlʊk] *n inv* (*for future*) perspective(s) *f(pl)*; (*point of view*) perspective *f* (on sur), attitude *f* (on à l'égard de); *Met* prévisions *fpl.*

outlying ['aʊtlaɪɪŋ] *a* (*remote*) isolé; (*neighbourhood*) périphérique.

outmoded [aut'məʊdɪd] *a* démodé.

outnumber [aut'nʌmbər] *vt* être plus nombreux que.

outpatient ['aʊtpeɪʃ(ə)nt] *n* malade *mf* en consultation externe.

outpost ['aʊtpəʊst] *n* avant-poste *m.*

output ['aʊtpʊt] *n* rendement *m*, production *f*; (*computer process*) sortie *f*; (*computer data*) donnée(s) *f(pl)* de sortie.

outrage ['aʊtreɪdʒ] *n* atrocité *f*, crime *m*; (*indignity*) indignité *f*; (*scandal*) scandale *m*; (*indignation*) indignation *f*; **bomb o.** attentat *m* à la bombe; – *vt* (*morals*) outrager; **outraged by sth** indigné de qch. ◆**out'rageous** *a* (*atrocious*) atroce; (*shocking*) scandaleux; (*dress, hat etc*) grotesque.

outright [aut'raɪt] *adv* (*completely*) complètement; (*to say, tell*) franchement; (*to be killed*) sur le coup; **to buy o.** (*for cash*) acheter au comptant; – ['aʊtraɪt] *a* (*complete*) complet; (*lie, folly*) pur; (*refusal, rejection etc*) catégorique, net; (*winner*) incontesté.

outset ['aʊtset] *n* **at the o.** au début; **from the o.** dès le départ.

outside [aut'saɪd] *adv* (au) dehors, à l'extérieur; **to go o.** sortir; – *prep* à l'extérieur de, en dehors de; (*beyond*) *Fig* en dehors de; **o. my room** *or* **door** à la porte de ma chambre; – *n* extérieur *m*, dehors *m*; – ['aʊtsaɪd] *a* extérieur; (*bus or train seat etc*) côté couloir *inv*; (*maximum*) *Fig* maximum; **the o. lane** *Aut* la voie de droite, *Am* la voie de gauche; **an o. chance** une faible chance. ◆**out'sider** *n* (*stranger*) étranger, -ère *mf*; *Sp* outsider *m.*

outsize ['aʊtsaɪz] *a* (*clothes*) grande taille *inv.*

outskirts ['aʊtskɜːts] *npl* banlieue *f.*

outsmart [aut'smɑːt] *vt* être plus malin que.

outspoken [aut'spəʊk(ə)n] *a* (*frank*) franc.

outstanding [aut'stændɪŋ] *a* remarquable, exceptionnel; (*problem, business*) non réglé, en suspens; (*debt*) impayé; **work o.** travail *m* à faire.

outstay [aut'steɪ] *vt* **to o. one's welcome** abuser de l'hospitalité de son hôte, s'incruster.

outstretched [aut'stretʃt] *a* (*arm*) tendu.

outstrip [aut'strɪp] *vt* (**-pp-**) devancer.

outward ['aʊtwəd] *a* (*look, movement*) vers l'extérieur; (*sign, appearance*) extérieur; **o. journey** *or* **trip** aller *m.* ◆**outward(s)** *adv* vers l'extérieur.

outweigh [aut'weɪ] *vt* (*be more important than*) l'emporter sur.

outwit [aut'wɪt] *vt* (**-tt-**) être plus malin que.

oval ['əʊv(ə)l] *a & n* ovale (*m*).

ovary ['əʊvərɪ] *n* *Anat* ovaire *m.*

ovation [əʊ'veɪʃ(ə)n] *n* **(standing) o.** ovation *f.*

oven ['ʌv(ə)n] *n* four *m*; (*hot place*) *Fig* fournaise *f*; **o. glove** gant *m* isolant.

over ['əʊvər] *prep* (*on*) sur; (*above*) au-dessus de; (*on the other side of*) de l'autre côté de; **bridge o. the river** pont *m* sur le fleuve; **to jump/look/*etc* o. sth** sauter/regarder/*etc* par-dessus qch; **to fall o. the balcony/*etc*** tomber du balcon/*etc*; **she fell o. it** elle en est tombée; **o. it** (*on*) dessus; (*above*) au-dessus; (*to jump etc*) par-dessus; **to criticize/*etc* o. sth** (*about*) critiquer/*etc* à propos de qch; **an advantage o.** un avantage sur *or* par rapport à; **o. the radio** (*on*) à la radio; **o. the phone** au téléphone; **o. the holidays** (*during*) pendant les vacances; **o. ten days** (*more than*) plus de dix jours; **men o. sixty** les hommes de plus de soixante ans; **o. and above** en plus de; **he's o. his flu** (*recovered from*) il est remis de sa grippe; **all o. Spain** (*everywhere in*) dans toute l'Espagne, partout en Espagne; **all o. the carpet** (*everywhere on*) partout sur le tapis; – *adv* (*above*) (par-)dessus; (*finished*) fini; (*danger*) passé; (*again*) encore; (*too*) trop; **jump o.!** sautez par-dessus!; **o. here** ici; **o. there** là-bas; **to be** *or* **come** *or* **go o.** (*visit*) passer; **he's o. in Italy** il est (parti) en Italie; **she's o. from Paris** elle est venue de Paris; **all o.** (*everywhere*) partout; **wet all o.** tout mouillé; **it's (all) o.!** (*finished*) c'est fini!; **she's o.** (*fallen*) elle est tombée; **a kilo or o.** (*more*) un kilo ou plus; **I have ten o.** (*left*) il m'en reste dix; **there's some bread o.** il reste du pain; **o. and o. (again)** (*often*) à plusieurs reprises; **to start all o. (again)** recommencer à zéro; **o. pleased/***etc* trop content/*etc*. **◆o.-a'bundant** *a* surabondant. **◆o.-de'veloped** *a* trop développé. **◆o.-fa'miliar** *a* trop familier. **◆o.-in'dulge** *vt* (*one's desires etc*) céder trop facilement à; (*person*) trop gâter. **◆o.-sub'scribed** *a* (*course*) ayant trop d'inscrits.

overall 1 [əʊvər'ɔːl] *a* (*measurement, length, etc*) total; (*result, effort etc*) global; – *adv* globalement. **2** ['əʊvərɔːl] *n* blouse *f* (de travail); *pl* bleus *mpl* de travail.

overawe [əʊvər'ɔː] *vt* intimider.

overbalance [əʊvə'bæləns] *vi* basculer.

overbearing [əʊvə'beərɪŋ] *a* autoritaire.

overboard ['əʊvəbɔːd] *adv* à la mer.

overburden [əʊvə'bɜːd(ə)n] *vt* surcharger.

overcast [əʊvə'kɑːst] *a* (*sky*) couvert.

overcharge [əʊvə'tʃɑːdʒ] *vt* **to o. s.o. for sth** faire payer qch trop cher à qn.

overcoat ['əʊvəkəʊt] *n* pardessus *m*.

overcome [əʊvə'kʌm] *vt* (*pt* **overcame**, *pp* **overcome**) (*enemy, shyness etc*) vaincre; (*disgust, problem*) surmonter; **to be o. by** (*fatigue, grief*) être accablé par; (*fumes, temptation*) succomber à; **he was o. by emotion** l'émotion eut raison de lui.

overcrowded [əʊvə'kraʊdɪd] *a* (*house, country*) surpeuplé; (*bus, train*) bondé. **◆overcrowding** *n* surpeuplement *m*.

overdo [əʊvə'duː] *vt* (*pt* **overdid**, *pp* **overdone**) exagérer; *Culin* cuire trop; **to o. it** (*exaggerate*) exagérer; (*work too much*) se surmener; *Iron* se fatiguer.

overdose ['əʊvədəʊs] *n* overdose *f*, dose *f* excessive (*de barbituriques etc*).

overdraft ['əʊvədrɑːft] *n Fin* découvert *m*. **◆over'draw** *vt* (*pt* **overdrew**, *pp* **overdrawn**) (*account*) mettre à découvert.

overdress [əʊvə'dres] *vi* s'habiller avec trop de recherche.

overdue [əʊvə'djuː] *a* (*train etc*) en retard; (*debt*) arriéré; (*apology, thanks*) tardif.

overeat [əʊvər'iːt] *vi* manger trop.

overestimate [əʊvər'estɪmeɪt] *vt* surestimer.

overexcited [əʊvərɪk'saɪtɪd] *a* surexcité.

overfeed [əʊvə'fiːd] *vt* (*pt & pp* **overfed**) suralimenter.

overflow 1 ['əʊvəfləʊ] *n* (*outlet*) trop-plein *m*; (*of people, objects*) *Fig* excédent *m*. **2** [əʊvə'fləʊ] *vi* déborder (**with** de); **to be overflowing with** (*of town, shop, house etc*) regorger de (*visiteurs, livres etc*).

overgrown [əʊvə'grəʊn] *a* envahi par la végétation; **o. with** (*weeds etc*) envahi par; **you're an o. schoolgirl** *Fig Pej* tu as la mentalité d'une écolière.

overhang [əʊvə'hæŋ] *vi* (*pt & pp* **overhung**) faire saillie; – *vt* surplomber.

overhaul [əʊvə'hɔːl] *vt* (*vehicle, doctrine etc*) réviser; – ['əʊvəhɔːl] *n* révision *f*.

overhead [əʊvə'hed] *adv* au-dessus; – ['əʊvəhed] **1** *a* (*railway etc*) aérien. **2** *npl* (*expenses*) frais *mpl* généraux.

overhear [əʊvə'hɪər] *vt* (*pt & pp* **overheard**) surprendre, entendre.

overheat [əʊvə'hiːt] *vt* surchauffer; – *vi* (*of engine*) chauffer.

overjoyed [əʊvə'dʒɔɪd] *a* ravi, enchanté.

overland ['əʊvəlænd] *a & adv* par voie de terre.

overlap [əʊvə'læp] *vi* (**-pp-**) se chevaucher; – *vt* chevaucher; – ['əʊvəlæp] *n* chevauchement *m*.

overleaf [əʊvə'liːf] *adv* au verso.

overload [əʊvə'ləʊd] *vt* surcharger.

overlook [əʊvə'lʊk] *vt* **1** (*not notice*) ne pas remarquer; (*forget*) oublier; (*disregard, ignore*) passer sur. **2** (*of window, house etc*) donner sur; (*of tower, fort*) dominer.

overly ['əʊvəlɪ] *adv* excessivement.

overmuch [əʊvə'mʌtʃ] *adv* trop, excessivement.

overnight [əʊvə'naɪt] *adv* (*during the night*) (pendant) la nuit; (*all night*) toute la nuit; (*suddenly*) *Fig* du jour au lendemain; **to stay o.** passer la nuit; – ['əʊvənaɪt] *a* (*stay*) d'une nuit; (*clothes*) pour une nuit; (*trip*) de nuit.

overpass ['əʊvəpæs] *n* (*bridge*) *Am* toboggan *m*.

overpopulated [əʊvə'pɒpjʊleɪtɪd] *a* surpeuplé.

overpower [əʊvə'paʊər] *vt* (*physically*) maîtriser; (*defeat*) vaincre; *Fig* accabler. **◆—ing** *a* (*charm etc*) irrésistible; (*heat etc*) accablant.

overrat/e [əʊvə'reɪt] *vt* surestimer. **◆—ed** *a* surfait.

overreach [əʊvə'riːtʃ] *vt* **to o. oneself** trop entreprendre.

overreact [əʊvərɪ'ækt] *vi* réagir excessivement.

overrid/e [əʊvə'raɪd] *vt* (*pt* **overrode,** *pp* **overridden**) (*invalidate*) annuler; (*take no notice of*) passer outre à; (*be more important than*) l'emporter sur. **◆—ing** *a* (*passion*) prédominant; (*importance*) primordial.

overrule [əʊvə'ruːl] *vt* (*reject*) rejeter.

overrun [əʊvə'rʌn] *vt* (*pt* **overran,** *pp* **overrun,** *pres p* **overrunning**) **1** (*invade*) envahir. **2** (*go beyond*) aller au-delà de.

overseas [əʊvə'siːz] *adv* (*Africa etc*) outre-mer; (*abroad*) à l'étranger; – ['əʊvəsiːz] *a* (*visitor, market etc*) d'outre-mer; étranger; (*trade*) extérieur.

overse/e [əʊvə'siː] *vt* (*pt* **oversaw,** *pp* **overseen**) surveiller. **◆—er** ['əʊvəsiːər] *n* (*foreman*) contremaître *m*.

overshadow [əʊvə'ʃædəʊ] *vt* (*make less important*) éclipser; (*make gloomy*) assombrir.

overshoot [əʊvə'ʃuːt] *vt* (*pt* & *pp* **overshot**) (*of aircraft*) & *Fig* dépasser.

oversight ['əʊvəsaɪt] *n* omission *f*, oubli *m*; (*mistake*) erreur *f*.

oversimplify [əʊvə'sɪmplɪfaɪ] *vti* trop simplifier.

oversize(d) ['əʊvəsaɪz(d)] *a* trop grand.

oversleep [əʊvə'sliːp] *vi* (*pt* & *pp* **overslept**) dormir trop longtemps, oublier de se réveiller.

overspend [əʊvə'spend] *vi* dépenser trop.

overstaffed [əʊvə'stɑːft] *a* au personnel pléthorique.

overstay [əʊvə'steɪ] *vt* **to o. one's welcome** abuser de l'hospitalité de son hôte, s'incruster.

overstep [əʊvə'step] *vt* (**-pp-**) dépasser.

overt ['əʊvɜːt] *a* manifeste.

overtake [əʊvə'teɪk] *vt* (*pt* **overtook,** *pp* **overtaken**) dépasser; (*vehicle*) doubler, dépasser; **overtaken by** (*nightfall, storm*) surpris par; – *vi Aut* doubler, dépasser.

overtax [əʊvə'tæks] *vt* **1** (*strength*) excéder; (*brain*) fatiguer. **2** (*taxpayer*) surimposer.

overthrow [əʊvə'θrəʊ] *vt* (*pt* **overthrew,** *pp* **overthrown**) *Pol* renverser; – ['əʊvəθrəʊ] *n* renversement *m*.

overtime ['əʊvətaɪm] *n* heures *fpl* supplémentaires; – *adv* **to work o.** faire des heures supplémentaires.

overtones ['əʊvətəʊnz] *npl Fig* note *f*, nuance *f* (**of** de).

overture ['əʊvətjʊər] *n Mus* & *Fig* ouverture *f*.

overturn [əʊvə'tɜːn] *vt* (*chair, table etc*) renverser; (*car, boat*) retourner; (*decision etc*) *Fig* annuler; – *vi* (*of car, boat*) se retourner.

overweight [əʊvə'weɪt] *a* **to be o.** (*of suitcase etc*) peser trop; (*of person*) avoir des kilos en trop.

overwhelm [əʊvə'welm] *vt* (*of feelings, heat etc*) accabler; (*defeat*) écraser; (*amaze*) bouleverser. **◆—ed** *a* (*overjoyed*) ravi (**by, with** de); **o. with** (*grief, work etc*) accablé de; (*offers*) submergé par; **o. by** (*kindness, gift etc*) vivement touché par. **◆—ing** *a* (*heat, grief etc*) accablant; (*majority*) écrasant; (*desire*) irrésistible; (*impression*) dominant. **◆—ingly** *adv* (*to vote, reject etc*) en masse; (*utterly*) carrément.

overwork [əʊvə'wɜːk] *n* surmenage *m*; – *vi* se surmener; – *vt* surmener.

overwrought [əʊvə'rɔːt] *a* (*tense*) tendu.

owe [əʊ] *vt* devoir (**to** à); **I'll o. it (to) you, I'll o. you (for) it** (*money*) je te le devrai; **to o. it to oneself to do** se devoir de faire. **◆owing 1** *a* (*money etc*) dû, qu'on doit. **2** *prep* **o. to** à cause de.

owl [aʊl] *n* hibou *m*.

own [əʊn] **1** *a* propre; **my o. house** ma propre maison; – *pron* **it's my (very) o.** c'est à moi (tout seul); **a house of his o.** sa propre maison, sa maison à lui; **(all) on one's o.** (*alone*) tout seul; **to get one's o. back** prendre sa revanche (**on** sur, **for** de); **to come into one's o.** (*fulfil oneself*) s'épanouir. **2** *vt* (*possess*) posséder; **who owns this ball/***etc*? à qui appartient cette balle/*etc*? **3** *vi* **to o. up** (*confess*) avouer; **to o. up to sth** avouer qch. **◆owner** *n* propriétaire *mf*. **◆ownership** *n* possession *f*; **home o.** accession *f* à la propriété; **public o.** *Econ* nationalisation *f*.

ox, *pl* **oxen** [ɒks, 'ɒks(ə)n] *n* bœuf *m*.

oxide ['ɒksaɪd] *n Ch* oxide *m*. **◆oxidize** *vi* s'oxyder; – *vt* oxyder.

oxygen ['ɒksɪdʒ(ə)n] *n* oxygène *m*; – *a* (*mask, tent*) à oxygène.

oyster ['ɔɪstər] *n* huître *f*.

P

P, p [piː] *n* P, p *m*.
p [piː] *abbr* = **penny, pence.**
pa [pɑː] *n* (*father*) *Fam* papa *m*.
pace [peɪs] *n* (*speed*) pas *m*, allure *f*; (*measure*) pas *m*; **to keep p. with** (*follow*) suivre; (*in work, progress*) se maintenir à la hauteur de; – *vi* **to p. up and down** faire les cent pas; – *vt* (*room etc*) arpenter. ◆**pacemaker** *n* (*device*) stimulateur *m* cardiaque.
Pacific [pə'sɪfɪk] *a* (*coast etc*) pacifique; – *n* **the P.** le Pacifique.
pacify ['pæsɪfaɪ] *vt* (*country*) pacifier; (*calm, soothe*) apaiser. ◆**pacifier** *n* (*dummy*) *Am* sucette *f*, tétine *f*. ◆**pacifist** *n* & *a* pacifiste (*mf*).
pack [pæk] **1** *n* (*bundle, packet*) paquet *m*; (*bale*) balle *f*; (*of animal*) charge *f*; (*rucksack*) sac *m* (à dos); *Mil* paquetage *m*; (*of hounds, wolves*) meute *f*; (*of runners*) *Sp* peloton *m*; (*of thieves*) bande *f*; (*of cards*) jeu *m*; (*of lies*) tissu *m*. **2** *vt* (*fill*) remplir (**with** de); (*excessively*) bourrer; (*suitcase*) faire; (*object into box etc*) emballer; (*object into suitcase*) mettre dans sa valise; (*make into package*) empaqueter; **to p. into** (*cram*) entasser dans; (*put*) mettre dans; **to p. away** (*tidy away*) ranger; **to p. (down)** (*compress, crush*) tasser; **to p. off** (*person*) *Fam* expédier; **to p. up** (*put into box*) emballer; (*put into case*) mettre dans sa valise; (*give up*) *Fam* laisser tomber; – *vi* (*fill one's bags*) faire ses valises; **to p. into** (*of people*) s'entasser dans; **to p. in** *or* **up** (*of machine, vehicle*) *Fam* tomber en panne; **to p. up** (*stop*) *Fam* s'arrêter; (*leave*) plier bagage. ◆**—ed** *a* (*bus, cinema etc*) bourré; **p. lunch** panier-repas *m*; **p. out** (*crowded*) *Fam* bourré. ◆**—ing** *n* (*material, action*) emballage *m*; **p. case** caisse *f* d'emballage.
packag/e ['pækɪdʒ] *n* paquet *m*; (*computer programs*) progiciel *m*; **p. deal** *Com* contrat *m* global, train *m* de propositions; **p. tour** voyage *m* organisé; – *vt* emballer, empaqueter. ◆**—ing** *n* (*material, action*) emballage *m*.
packet ['pækɪt] *n* paquet *m*; (*of sweets*) sachet *m*, paquet *m*; **to make/cost a p.** *Fam* faire/coûter beaucoup d'argent.
pact [pækt] *n* pacte *m*.
pad [pæd] *n* (*wad, plug*) tampon *m*; (*for writing, notes etc*) bloc *m*; (*on leg*) *Sp* jambière *f*; (*on knee*) *Sp* genouillère *f*; (*room*) *Sl* piaule *f*; **launch(ing) p.** rampe *f* de lancement; **ink(ing) p.** tampon *m* encreur; – *vt* (**-dd-**) (*stuff*) rembourrer, matelasser; **to p. out** (*speech, text*) délayer. ◆**padding** *n* rembourrage *m*; (*of speech, text*) délayage *m*.
paddle ['pæd(ə)l] **1** *vi* (*splash about*) barboter; (*dip one's feet*) se mouiller les pieds; – *n* **to have a (little) p.** se mouiller les pieds. **2** *n* (*pole*) pagaie *f*; **p. boat, p. steamer** bateau *m* à roues; – *vt* **to p. a canoe** pagayer.
paddock ['pædək] *n* enclos *m*; (*at racecourse*) paddock *m*.
paddy ['pædɪ] *n* **p. (field)** rizière *f*.
padlock ['pædlɒk] *n* (*on door etc*) cadenas *m*; (*on bicycle, moped*) antivol *m*; – *vt* (*door etc*) cadenasser.
p(a)ediatrician [piːdɪə'trɪʃ(ə)n] *n* *Med* pédiatre *mf*.
pagan ['peɪgən] *a* & *n* païen, -enne (*mf*). ◆**paganism** *n* paganisme *m*.
page [peɪdʒ] **1** *n* (*of book etc*) page *f*. **2** *n* **p. (boy)** (*in hotel etc*) chasseur *m*; (*at court*) *Hist* page *m*; – *vt* **to p. s.o.** faire appeler qn.
pageant ['pædʒənt] *n* grand spectacle *m* historique. ◆**pageantry** *n* pompe *f*, apparat *m*.
pagoda [pə'gəʊdə] *n* pagode *f*.
paid [peɪd] *see* **pay**; – *a* (*assassin etc*) à gages; **to put p. to** (*hopes, plans*) anéantir; **to put p. to s.o.** (*ruin*) couler qn.
pail [peɪl] *n* seau *m*.
pain [peɪn] *n* (*physical*) douleur *f*; (*grief*) peine *f*; *pl* (*efforts*) efforts *mpl*; **to have a p. in one's arm** avoir mal *or* une douleur au bras; **to be in p.** souffrir; **to go to** *or* **take (great) pains to do** (*exert oneself*) se donner du mal à faire; **to go to** *or* **take (great) pains not to do** (*be careful*) prendre bien soin de ne pas faire; **to be a p. (in the neck)** (*of person*) *Fam* être casse-pieds; – *vt* (*grieve*) peiner. ◆**p.-killer** *n* analgésique *m*, calmant *m*. ◆**painful** *a* (*illness, operation*) douloureux; (*arm, leg*) qui fait mal, douloureux; (*distressing*) douloureux, pénible; (*difficult*) pénible; (*bad*) *Fam*

affreux. ◆**painless** *a* sans douleur; (*illness, operation*) indolore; (*easy*) *Fam* facile. ◆**painstaking** *a* (*person*) soigneux; (*work*) soigné.

paint [peɪnt] *n* peinture *f*; *pl* (*in box, tube*) couleurs *fpl*; – *vt* (*colour, describe*) peindre; **to p. blue/***etc* peindre en bleu/*etc*; – *vi* peindre. ◆**—ing** *n* (*activity*) peinture *f*; (*picture*) tableau *m*, peinture *f*. ◆**—er** *n* peintre *m*. ◆**paintbrush** *n* pinceau *m*. ◆**paintwork** *n* peinture(s) *f*(*pl*).

pair [peər] *n* paire *f*; (*man and woman*) couple *m*; **a p. of shorts** un short; **the p. of you** *Fam* vous deux; – *vi* **to p. off** (*of people*) former un couple; – *vt* (*marry*) marier.

pajama(s) [pə'dʒɑːmə(z)] *a* & *npl Am* = pyjama(s).

Pakistan [pɑːkɪ'stɑːn] *n* Pakistan *m*. ◆**Pakistani** *a* & *n* pakistanais, -aise (*mf*).

pal [pæl] *n Fam* copain *m*, copine *f*; – *vi* (**-ll-**) **to p. up** devenir copains; **to p. up with** devenir copain avec.

palace ['pælɪs] *n* (*building*) palais *m*. ◆**palatial** [pə'leɪʃ(ə)l] *a* comme un palais.

palatable ['pælətəb(ə)l] *a* (*food*) agréable; (*fact, idea etc*) acceptable.

palate ['pælɪt] *n Anat* palais *m*.

palaver [pə'lɑːvər] *n Fam* (*fuss*) histoire(s) *f*(*pl*); (*talk*) palabres *mpl*.

pale [peɪl] *a* (**-er, -est**) (*face, colour etc*) pâle; **p. ale** bière *f* blonde; – *vi* pâlir. ◆**—ness** *n* pâleur *f*.

palette ['pælɪt] *n* (*of artist*) palette *f*.

paling ['peɪlɪŋ] *n* (*fence*) palissade *f*.

pall [pɔːl] **1** *vi* devenir insipide *or* ennuyeux (**on** pour). **2** *n* (*of smoke*) voile *m*.

pallbearer ['pɔːlbeərər] *n* personne *f* qui aide à porter un cercueil.

pallid ['pælɪd] *a* pâle. ◆**pallor** *n* pâleur *f*.

pally ['pælɪ] *a* (**-ier, -iest**) *Fam* copain *am*, copine *af* (**with** avec).

palm [pɑːm] **1** *n* (*of hand*) paume *f*. **2** *n* (*symbol*) palme *f*; **p. (tree)** palmier *m*; **p. (leaf)** palme *f*; **P. Sunday** les Rameaux *mpl*. **3** *vt Fam* **to p. sth off** (*pass off*) refiler qch (**on** à), coller qch (**on** à); **to p. s.o. off on s.o.** coller qn à qn.

palmist ['pɑːmɪst] *n* chiromancien, -ienne *mf*. ◆**palmistry** *n* chiromancie *f*.

palpable ['pælpəb(ə)l] *a* (*obvious*) manifeste.

palpitate ['pælpɪteɪt] *vi* (*of heart*) palpiter. ◆**palpi'tation** *n* palpitation *f*.

paltry ['pɔːltrɪ] *a* (**-ier, -iest**) misérable, dérisoire.

pamper ['pæmpər] *vt* dorloter.

pamphlet ['pæmflɪt] *n* brochure *f*.

pan [pæn] **1** *n* casserole *f*; (*for frying*) poêle *f* (à frire); (*of lavatory*) cuvette *f*. **2** *vt* (**-nn-**) (*criticize*) *Fam* éreinter. **3** *vi* (**-nn-**) **to p. out** (*succeed*) aboutir.

Pan- [pæn] *pref* pan-.

panacea [pænə'sɪə] *n* panacée *f*.

panache [pə'næʃ] *n* (*showy manner*) panache *m*.

pancake ['pænkeɪk] *n* crêpe *f*.

pancreas ['pæŋkrɪəs] *n Anat* pancréas *m*.

panda ['pændə] *n* (*animal*) panda *m*; **P. car** = voiture *f* pie *inv* (de la police).

pandemonium [pændɪ'məʊnɪəm] *n* (*chaos*) chaos *m*; (*uproar*) tumulte *m*; (*place*) bazar *m*.

pander ['pændər] *vi* **to p. to** (*tastes, fashion etc*) sacrifier à; **to p. to s.o.** *or* **to s.o.'s desires** se plier aux désirs de qn.

pane [peɪn] *n* vitre *f*, carreau *m*.

panel ['pæn(ə)l] *n* **1** (*of door etc*) panneau *m*; **(control) p.** *Tech El* console *f*; **(instrument) p.** *Av Aut* tableau *m* de bord. **2** (*of judges*) jury *m*; (*of experts*) groupe *m*; (*of candidates*) équipe *f*; **a p. of guests** des invités; **a p. game** *TV Rad* un jeu par équipes. ◆**panelled** *a* (*room etc*) lambrissé. ◆**panelling** *n* lambris *m*. ◆**panellist** *n TV Rad* (*guest*) invité, -ée *mf*; (*expert*) expert *m*; (*candidate*) candidat, -ate *mf*.

pangs [pæŋz] *npl* **p. of conscience** remords *mpl* (de conscience); **p. of hunger/death** les affres *fpl* de la faim/de la mort.

panic ['pænɪk] *n* panique *f*; **to get into a p.** paniquer; – *vi* (**-ck-**) s'affoler, paniquer. ◆**p.-stricken** *a* affolé. ◆**panicky** (*person*) *a Fam* qui s'affole facilement; **to get p.** s'affoler.

panorama [pænə'rɑːmə] *n* panorama *m*. ◆**panoramic** *a* panoramique.

pansy ['pænzɪ] *n Bot* pensée *f*.

pant [pænt] *vi* (*gasp*) haleter.

panther ['pænθər] *n* (*animal*) panthère *f*.

panties ['pæntɪz] *npl* (*female underwear*) slip *m*.

pantomime ['pæntəmaɪm] *n* (*show*) spectacle *m* de Noël.

pantry ['pæntrɪ] *n* (*larder*) garde-manger *m inv*; (*storeroom in hotel etc*) office *m or f*.

pants [pænts] *npl* (*male underwear*) slip *m*; (*loose, long*) caleçon *m*; (*female underwear*) slip *m*; (*trousers*) *Am* pantalon *m*.

pantyhose ['pæntɪhəʊz] *n* (*tights*) *Am* collant(s) *m*(*pl*).

papacy ['peɪpəsɪ] *n* papauté *f*. ◆**papal** *a* papal.

paper ['peɪpər] *n* papier *m*; (*newspaper*) journal *m*; (*wallpaper*) papier *m* peint;

(*exam*) épreuve *f* (écrite); (*student's exercise*) *Sch* copie *f*; (*learned article*) exposé *m*, communication *f*; **brown p.** papier *m* d'emballage; **to put down on p.** mettre par écrit; – *a* (*bag etc*) en papier; (*cup, plate*) en carton; **p. clip** trombone *m*; **p. knife** coupe-papier *m inv*; **p. mill** papeterie *f*; **p. shop** marchand *m* de journaux; – *vt* (*room, wall*) tapisser. ◆**paperback** *n* (*book*) livre *m* de poche. ◆**paperboy** *n* livreur *m* de journaux. ◆**paperweight** *n* presse-papiers *m inv*. ◆**paperwork** *n Com* écritures *fpl*; (*red tape*) *Pej* paperasserie *f*.

paprika ['pæprɪkə] *n* paprika *m*.

par [pɑːr] *n* **on a p.** au même niveau (**with** que); **below p.** (*unwell*) *Fam* pas en forme.

para- ['pærə] *pref* para-.

parable ['pærəb(ə)l] *n* (*story*) parabole *f*.

parachute ['pærəʃuːt] *n* parachute *f*; **to drop by p.** (*men, supplies*) parachuter; – *vi* descendre en parachute; – *vt* parachuter. ◆**parachutist** *n* parachutiste *mf*.

parade [pə'reɪd] **1** *n Mil* (*ceremony*) parade *f*; (*procession*) défilé *m*; **fashion p.** défilé *m* de mode *or* de mannequins; **p. ground** *Mil* terrain *m* de manœuvres; **to make a p. of** faire étalage de; – *vi Mil* défiler; **to p. about** (*walk about*) se balader; – *vt* faire étalage de. **2** *n* (*street*) avenue *f*.

paradise ['pærədaɪs] *n* paradis *m*.

paradox ['pærədɒks] *n* paradoxe *m*. ◆**para'doxically** *adv* paradoxalement.

paraffin ['pærəfɪn] *n* pétrole *m* (lampant); (*wax*) *Am* paraffine *f*; **p. lamp** lampe *f* à pétrole.

paragon ['pærəg(ə)n] *n* **p. of virtue** modèle *m* de vertu.

paragraph ['pærəgrɑːf] *n* paragraphe *m*; **'new p.'** 'à la ligne'.

parakeet ['pærəkiːt] *n* perruche *f*.

parallel ['pærəlel] *a* (*comparable*) & *Math* parallèle (**with, to** à); **to run p. to** *or* **with** être parallèle à; – *n* (*comparison*) & *Geog* parallèle *m*; (*line*) *Math* parallèle *f*; – *vt* être semblable à.

paralysis [pə'ræləsɪs] *n* paralysie *f*. ◆**'paralyse** *vt* (*Am* **-lyze**) paralyser. ◆**para'lytic** *a* & *n* paralytique (*mf*).

parameter [pə'ræmɪtər] *n* paramètre *m*.

paramount ['pærəmaunt] *a* **of p. importance** de la plus haute importance.

paranoia [pærə'nɔɪə] *n* paranoïa *f*. ◆**'paranoid** *a* & *n* paranoïaque (*mf*).

parapet ['pærəpɪt] *n* parapet *m*.

paraphernalia [pærəfə'neɪlɪə] *n* attirail *m*.

paraphrase ['pærəfreɪz] *n* paraphrase *f*; – *vt* paraphraser.

parasite ['pærəsaɪt] *n* (*person, organism*) parasite *m*.

parasol ['pærəsɒl] *n* (*over table, on beach*) parasol *m*; (*lady's*) ombrelle *f*.

paratrooper ['pærətruːpər] *n Mil* parachutiste *m*. ◆**paratroops** *npl Mil* parachutistes *mpl*.

parboil [pɑː'bɔɪl] *vt Culin* faire bouillir à demi.

parcel ['pɑːs(ə)l] **1** *n* colis *m*, paquet *m*; **to be part and p. of** faire partie intégrante de. **2** *vt* (**-ll-**, *Am* **-l-**) **to p. out** (*divide*) partager; **to p. up** faire un paquet de.

parch [pɑːtʃ] *vt* dessécher; **to be parched** (*thirsty*) être assoiffé; **to make parched** (*thirsty*) donner très soif à.

parchment ['pɑːtʃmənt] *n* parchemin *m*.

pardon ['pɑːd(ə)n] *n* pardon *m*; *Jur* grâce *f*; **general p.** amnistie *f*; **I beg your p.** (*apologize*) je vous prie de m'excuser; (*not hearing*) vous dites?; **p.?** (*not hearing*) comment?; **p. (me)!** (*sorry*) pardon!; – *vt* pardonner (**s.o. for sth** qch à qn); **to p. s.o.** pardonner (à) qn; *Jur* gracier qn.

pare [peər] *vt* (*trim*) rogner; (*peel*) éplucher; **to p. down** *Fig* réduire, rogner.

parent ['peərənt] *n* père *m*, mère *f*; **one's parents** ses parent *mpl*, son père et sa mère; **p. firm, p. company** *Com* maison *f* mère. ◆**parentage** *n* (*origin*) origine *f*. ◆**pa'rental** *a* des parents, parental. ◆**parenthood** *n* paternité *f*, maternité *f*.

parenthesis, *pl* **-eses** [pə'renθəsɪs, -əsiːz] *n* parenthèse *f*.

Paris ['pærɪs] *n* Paris *m or f*. ◆**Parisian** [pə'rɪzɪən, *Am* pə'riːʒən] *a* & *n* parisien, -ienne (*mf*).

parish ['pærɪʃ] *n Rel* paroisse *f*; (*civil*) commune *f*; – *a* (*church, register*) paroissial; **p. council** conseil *m* municipal. ◆**pa'rishioner** *n* paroissien, -ienne *mf*.

parity ['pærɪtɪ] *n* parité *f*.

park [pɑːk] **1** *n* (*garden*) parc *m*. **2** *vt* (*vehicle*) garer; (*put*) *Fam* mettre, poser; – *vi Aut* se garer; (*remain parked*) stationner. ◆**—ing** *n* stationnement *m*; **'no p.'** 'défense de stationner'; **p. bay** aire *f* de stationnement; **p. lot** *Am* parking *m*; **p. meter** parcmètre *m*; **p. place** endroit *m* pour se garer; **p. ticket** contravention *f*.

parka ['pɑːkə] *n* (*coat*) parka *m*.

parkway ['pɑːkweɪ] *n Am* avenue *f*.

parliament ['pɑːləmənt] *n* parlement *m*; **P.** *Br* Parlement *m*. ◆**parlia'mentary** *a* parlementaire. ◆**parliamen'tarian** *n* parlementaire *mf* (expérimenté(e)).

parlour ['pɑːlər] *n* (*in mansion*) (petit) salon

m; **ice-cream p.** *Am* salon de glaces; **p. game** jeu *m* de société.

parochial [pə'rəʊkɪəl] *a* (*mentality, quarrel*) *Pej* de clocher; (*person*) *Pej* provincial, borné; *Rel* paroissial.

parody ['pærədɪ] *n* parodie *f*; – *vt* parodier.

parole [pə'rəʊl] *n* **on p.** *Jur* en liberté conditionnelle.

parquet ['pɑːkeɪ] *n* **p. (floor)** parquet *m*.

parrot ['pærət] *n* perroquet *m*; **p. fashion** *Pej* comme un perroquet.

parry ['pærɪ] *vt* (*blow*) parer; (*question*) éluder; – *n Sp* parade *f*.

parsimonious [pɑːsɪ'məʊnɪəs] *a* parcimonieux. ◆**–ly** *adv* avec parcimonie.

parsley ['pɑːslɪ] *n* persil *m*.

parsnip ['pɑːsnɪp] *n* panais *m*.

parson ['pɑːs(ə)n] *n* pasteur *m*; **p.'s nose** (*of chicken*) croupion *m*.

part [pɑːt] **1** *n* partie *f*; (*of machine*) pièce *f*; (*of periodical*) livraison *f*; (*of serial*) épisode *m*; (*in play, film, activity*) rôle *m*; (*division*) *Culin* mesure *f*; (*in hair*) *Am* raie *f*; **to take p.** participer (**in** à); **to take s.o.'s p.** (*side*) prendre parti pour qn; **in p.** en partie; **for the most p.** dans l'ensemble; **to be a p. of** faire partie de; **on the p. of** (*on behalf of*) de la part de; **for my p.** pour ma part; **in these parts** dans ces parages; **p. exchange** reprise *f*; **to take in p. exchange** reprendre; **p. owner** copropriétaire *mf*; **p. payment** paiement *m* partiel; – *adv* en partie; **p. American** en partie américain. **2** *vt* (*separate*) séparer; (*crowd*) diviser; **to p. one's hair** se faire une raie; **to p. company with** (*leave*) quitter; – *vi* (*of friends etc*) se quitter; (*of married couple*) se séparer; **to p. with** (*get rid of*) se séparer de. ◆**–ing 1** *n* séparation *f*; – *a* (*gift, words*) d'adieu. **2** *n* (*in hair*) raie *f*.

partake [pɑː'teɪk] *vi* (*pt* **partook**, *pp* **partaken**) **to p. in** participer à; **to p. of** (*meal, food*) prendre, manger.

partial ['pɑːʃəl] *a* partiel; (*biased*) partial (**towards** envers); **to be p. to** (*fond of*) *Fam* avoir un faible pour. ◆**parti'ality** *n* (*bias*) partialité *f*; (*liking*) prédilection *f*.

participate [pɑː'tɪsɪpeɪt] *vi* participer (**in** à). ◆**participant** *n* participant, -ante *mf*. ◆**partici'pation** *n* participation *f*.

participle [pɑː'tɪsɪp(ə)l] *n* participe *m*.

particle ['pɑːtɪk(ə)l] *n* (*of atom, dust, name*) particule *f*; (*of truth*) grain *m*.

particular [pə'tɪkjʊlər] **1** *a* (*specific, special*) particulier; (*fastidious, fussy*) difficile (**about** sur); (*meticulous*) méticuleux; **this p. book** ce livre-ci en particulier; **in p.** en particulier; **to be p. about** faire très attention à. **2** *n* (*detail*) détail *m*; **s.o.'s particulars** le nom et l'adresse de qn; (*description*) le signalement de qn. ◆**–ly** *adv* particulièrement.

partisan [pɑːtɪ'zæn, *Am* 'pɑːtɪz(ə)n] *n* partisan *m*.

partition [pɑː'tɪʃ(ə)n] **1** *n* (*of room*) cloison *f*; – *vt* **to p. off** cloisonner. **2** *n* (*of country*) *Pol* partition *f*, partage *m*; – *vt Pol* partager.

partly ['pɑːtlɪ] *adv* en partie; **p. English p. French** moitié anglais moitié français.

partner ['pɑːtnər] *n Com* associé, -ée *mf*; (*lover, spouse*) & *Sp Pol* partenaire *mf*; (*of racing driver etc*) coéquipier, -ière *mf*; (**dancing**) **p.** cavalier, -ière *mf*. ◆**partnership** *n* association *f*; **to take into p.** prendre comme associé(e); **in p. with** en association avec.

partridge ['pɑːtrɪdʒ] *n* perdrix *f*.

part-time [pɑːt'taɪm] *a* & *adv* à temps partiel; (*half-time*) à mi-temps.

party ['pɑːtɪ] *n* **1** (*group*) groupe *m*; *Pol* parti *m*; (*in contract, lawsuit*) *Jur* partie *f*; *Mil* détachement *m*; *Tel* correspondant, -ante *mf*; **rescue p.** équipe *f* de sauveteurs *or* de secours; **third p.** *Jur* tiers *m*; **innocent p.** innocent, -ente *mf*; **to be (a) p. to** (*crime*) être complice de; **p. line** *Tel* ligne *f* partagée; *Pol* ligne *f* du parti; **p. ticket** billet *m* collectif. **2** (*gathering*) réception *f*; (*informal*) surprise-partie *f*; (*for birthday*) fête *f*; **cocktail p.** cocktail *m*; **dinner p.** dîner *m*; **tea p.** thé *m*.

pass [pɑːs] **1** *n* (*entry permit*) laissez-passer *m inv*; (*free ticket*) *Th* billet *m* de faveur; (*season ticket*) carte *f* d'abonnement; (*over mountains*) *Geog* col *m*; *Fb etc* passe *f*; (*in exam*) mention *f* passable (**in French/***etc* en français/*etc*); **to make a p. at** faire des avances à; **p. mark** (*in exam*) moyenne *f*, barre *f* d'admissibilité; **p. key** passe-partout *m inv*. **2** *vi* (*go, come, disappear*) passer (**to** à, **through** par); (*overtake*) *Aut* dépasser; (*in exam*) être reçu (**in French/***etc* en français/*etc*); (*take place*) se passer; **that'll p.** (*be acceptable*) ça ira; **he can p. for thirty** on lui donnerait trente ans; **to p. along** *or* **through** passer; **to p. away** *or* **on** (*die*) mourir; **to p. by** passer (à côté); **to p. off** (*happen*) se passer; **to p. on to** (*move on to*) passer à; **to p. out** (*faint*) s'évanouir; – *vt* (*move, spend, give etc*) passer (**to** à); (*go past*) passer devant (*immeuble etc*); (*vehicle*) dépasser; (*exam*) être reçu à; (*candidate*) recevoir; (*judgement, opinion*) prononcer (**on** sur); (*remark*) faire; (*allow*) autoriser; (*bill, law*) *Pol* voter; **to p. (by) s.o.** (*in street*) croiser qn; **to p. by** (*building*) passer devant; **to p. oneself off** as se faire passer pour; **to p. sth off on** (*fob off on*) refiler qch à; **to p. on** (*message, title, illness etc*) transmettre (to à); **to p. out** *or* **round** (*hand out*) distribuer; **to p. over** (*ignore*) passer sur, oublier; **to p. round** (*cigarettes, sweets etc*) faire passer; **to p. up** (*chance etc*) laisser passer. ◆**—ing** *a* (*vehicle etc*) qui passe; (*beauty*) passager; – *n* (*of visitor, vehicle etc*) passage *m*; (*of time*) écoulement *m*; (*death*) disparition *f*.

passable ['pɑːsəb(ə)l] *a* (*not bad*) passable; (*road*) praticable; (*river*) franchissable.

passage ['pæsɪdʒ] *n* (*passing, way through, of text, of speech etc*) passage *m*; (*of time*) écoulement *m*; (*corridor*) couloir *m*; *Nau* traversée *f*, passage *m*. ◆**passageway** *n* (*way through*) passage *m*; (*corridor*) couloir *m*.

passbook ['pɑːsbʊk] *n* livret *m* de caisse d'épargne.

passenger ['pæsɪndʒər] *n* passager, -ère *mf*; *Rail* voyageur, -euse *mf*.

passer-by [pɑːsə'baɪ] *n* (*pl* **passers-by**) passant, -ante *mf*.

passion ['pæʃ(ə)n] *n* passion *f*; **to have a p. for** (*cars etc*) avoir la passion de, adorer. ◆**passionate** *a* passionné. ◆**passionately** *adv* passionnément.

passive ['pæsɪv] *a* (*not active*) passif; – *n* *Gram* passif *m*. ◆**—ness** *n* passivité *f*.

Passover ['pɑːsəʊvər] *n* *Rel* Pâque *f*.

passport ['pɑːspɔːt] *n* passeport *m*.

password ['pɑːswɜːd] *n* mot *m* de passe.

past [pɑːst] **1** *n* (*time, history*) passé *m*; **in the p.** (*formerly*) dans le temps; **it's a thing of the p.** ça n'existe plus; – *a* (*gone by*) passé; (*former*) ancien; **these p. months** ces derniers mois; **that's all p.** c'est du passé; **in the p. tense** *Gram* au passé. **2** *prep* (*in front of*) devant; (*after*) après; (*further than*) plus loin que; (*too old for*) *Fig* trop vieux pour; **p. four o'clock** quatre heures passées, plus de quatre heures; **to be p. fifty** avoir cinquante ans passés; **it's p. belief** c'est incroyable; **I wouldn't put it p. him** ça ne m'étonnerait pas de lui, il en est bien capable; – *adv* devant; **to go p.** passer.

pasta ['pæstə] *n* *Culin* pâtes *fpl* (alimentaires).

paste [peɪst] **1** *n* (*of meat*) pâté *m*; (*of anchovy etc*) beurre *m*; (*dough*) pâte *f*. **2** *n* (*glue*) colle *f* (blanche); – *vt* coller; **to p. up** (*notice etc*) afficher.

pastel ['pæstəl, *Am* pæ'stel] *n* pastel *m*; – *a* (*shade*) pastel *inv*; (*drawing*) au pastel.

pasteurized ['pæstəraɪzd] *a* (*milk*) pasteurisé.

pastiche [pæ'stiːʃ] *n* pastiche *m*.

pastille ['pæstɪl, *Am* pæ'stiːl] *n* pastille *f*.

pastime ['pɑːstaɪm] *n* passe-temps *m inv*.

pastor ['pɑːstər] *n* *Rel* pasteur *m*. ◆**pastoral** *a* pastoral.

pastry ['peɪstrɪ] *n* (*dough*) pâte *f*; (*cake*) pâtisserie *f*; **puff p.** pâte *f* feuilletée. ◆**pastrycook** *n* pâtissier, -ière *mf*.

pasture ['pɑːstʃər] *n* pâturage *m*.

pasty 1 ['peɪstɪ] *a* (**-ier, -iest**) (*complexion*) terreux. **2** ['pæstɪ] *n* *Culin* petit pâté *m* (en croûte).

pat [pæt] **1** *vt* (**-tt-**) (*cheek, table etc*) tapoter; (*animal*) caresser; – *n* petite tape; caresse *f*. **2** *adv* **to answer p.** avoir la réponse toute prête; **to know sth off p.** savoir qch sur le bout du doigt.

patch [pætʃ] *n* (*for clothes*) pièce *f*; (*over eye*) bandeau *m*; (*for bicycle tyre*) rustine® *f*; (*of colour*) tache *f*; (*of sky*) morceau *m*; (*of fog*) nappe *f*; (*of ice*) plaque *f*; **a cabbage/*etc* p.** un carré de choux/*etc*; **a bad p.** *Fig* une mauvaise passe; **not to be a p. on** (*not as good as*) *Fam* ne pas arriver à la cheville de; – *vt* **to p. (up)** (*clothing*) rapiécer; **to p. up** (*quarrel*) régler; (*marriage*) replâtrer. ◆**patchwork** *n* patchwork *m*. ◆**patchy** *a* (**-ier, -iest**) inégal.

patent 1 ['peɪtənt] *a* patent, manifeste; **p. leather** cuir *m* verni. **2** ['peɪtənt, 'pætənt] *n* brevet *m* (d'invention); – *vt* (faire) breveter. ◆**—ly** *adv* manifestement.

paternal [pə'tɜːn(ə)l] *a* paternel. ◆**paternity** *n* paternité *f*.

path [pɑːθ] *n* (*pl* **-s** [pɑːðz]) sentier *m*, chemin *m*; (*in park*) allée *f*; (*of river*) cours *m*; (*of bullet, planet*) trajectoire *f*. ◆**pathway** *n* sentier *m*, chemin *m*.

pathetic [pə'θetɪk] *a* pitoyable.

pathology [pə'θɒlədʒɪ] *n* pathologie *f*. ◆**patho'logical** *a* pathologique.

pathos ['peɪθɒs] *n* pathétique *m*.

patient ['peɪʃ(ə)nt] **1** *a* patient. **2** *n* (*in hospital*) malade *mf*, patient, -ente *mf*; (*on doctor's or dentist's list*) patient, -ente *mf*. ◆**patience** *n* patience *f*; **to have p.** prendre patience; **to lose p.** perdre patience; **I have no p. with him** il m'impatiente; **to play p.** *Cards* faire des réussites. ◆**patiently** *adv* patiemment.

patio ['pætɪəʊ] *n* (*pl* **-os**) patio *m*.

patriarch ['peɪtrɪɑːk] *n* patriarche *m*.

patriot ['pætrɪət, 'peɪtrɪət] *n* patriote *mf.* ◆**patri'otic** *a* (*views, speech etc*) patriotique; (*person*) patriote. ◆**patriotism** *n* patriotisme *m.*

patrol [pə'trəʊl] *n* patrouille *f*; **p. boat** patrouilleur *m*; **police p. car** voiture *f* de police; **p. wagon** *Am* fourgon *m* cellulaire; – *vi* (**-ll-**) patrouiller; – *vt* patrouiller dans. ◆**patrolman** *n* (*pl* **-men**) *Am* agent *m* de police; (*repair man*) *Aut* dépanneur *m.*

patron ['peɪtrən] *n* (*of artist*) protecteur, -trice *mf*; (*customer*) *Com* client, -ente *mf*; (*of cinema, theatre*) habitué, -ée *mf*; **p. saint** patron, -onne *mf.* ◆**patronage** *n* (*support*) patronage *m*; (*of the arts*) protection *f*; (*custom*) *Com* clientèle *f.* ◆**patroniz/e** ['pætrənaɪz, *Am* 'peɪtrənaɪz] *vt* **1** *Com* accorder sa clientèle à. **2** (*person*) *Pej* traiter avec condescendance. ◆**—ing** *a* condescendant.

patter ['pætər] **1** *n* (*of footsteps*) petit bruit *m*; (*of rain, hail*) crépitement *m*; – *vi* (*of rain, hail*) crépiter, tambouriner. **2** *n* (*talk*) baratin *m.*

pattern ['pæt(ə)n] *n* dessin *m*, motif *m*; (*paper model for garment*) patron *m*; (*fabric sample*) échantillon *m*; *Fig* modèle *m*; (*plan*) plan *m*; (*method*) formule *f*; (*of a crime*) scénario *m.* ◆**patterned** *a* (*dress, cloth*) à motifs.

paucity ['pɔːsɪtɪ] *n* pénurie *f.*

paunch [pɔːntʃ] *n* panse *f*, bedon *m.* ◆**paunchy** *a* (**-ier, -iest**) bedonnant.

pauper ['pɔːpər] *n* pauvre *mf*, indigent, -ente *mf.*

pause [pɔːz] *n* pause *f*; (*in conversation*) silence *m*; – *vi* (*stop*) faire une pause; (*hesitate*) hésiter.

pav/e [peɪv] *vt* paver; **to p. the way for** *Fig* ouvrir la voie à. ◆**—ing** *n* (*surface*) pavage *m*, dallage *m*; **p. stone** pavé *m.* ◆**pavement** *n* trottoir *m*; (*roadway*) *Am* chaussée *f*; (*stone*) pavé *m.*

pavilion [pə'vɪljən] *n* (*building*) pavillon *m.*

paw [pɔː] **1** *n* patte *f*; – *vt* (*of animal*) donner des coups de patte à. **2** *vt* (*touch improperly*) tripoter.

pawn [pɔːn] **1** *n Chess* pion *m.* **2** *vt* mettre en gage; – *n* **in p.** en gage. ◆**pawnbroker** *n* prêteur, -euse *mf* sur gages. ◆**pawnshop** *n* mont-de-piété *m.*

pay [peɪ] *n* salaire *m*; (*of workman*) paie *f*, salaire *m*; *Mil* solde *f*, paie *f*; **p. phone** téléphone *m* public; **p. day** jour *m* de paie; **p. slip** bulletin *m or* fiche *f* de paie; – *vt* (*pt & pp* **paid**) (*person, sum*) payer; (*deposit*) verser; (*yield*) *Com* rapporter; (*compliment, attention, visit*) faire; **to p. s.o. to do** *or* **for doing** payer qn pour faire; **to p. s.o. for sth** payer qch à qn; **to p. money into one's account** *or* **the bank** verser de l'argent sur son compte; **it pays (one) to be cautious** on a intérêt à être prudent; **to p. homage** *or* **tribute** to rendre hommage à; **to p. back** (*creditor, loan etc*) rembourser; **I'll p. you back for this!** je te revaudrai ça!; **to p. in** (*cheque*) verser (**to one's account** sur son compte); **to p. off** (*debt, creditor etc*) rembourser; (*in instalments*) rembourser par acomptes; (*staff, worker*) licencier; **to p. off an old score** *or* **a grudge** *Fig* régler un vieux compte; **to p. out** (*spend*) dépenser; **to p. up** payer; – *vi* payer; **to p. for sth** payer qch; **to p. a lot (for)** payer cher; **to p. off** (*be successful*) être payant; **to p. up** payer. ◆**—ing** *a* (*guest*) payant; (*profitable*) rentable. ◆**—able** *a* (*due*) payable; **a cheque p. to** un chèque à l'ordre de. ◆**—ment** *n* paiement *m*; (*of deposit*) versement *m*; (*reward*) récompense *f*; **on p. of 20 francs** moyennant 20 francs. ◆**payoff** *n Fam* (*reward*) récompense *f*; (*revenge*) règlement *m* de comptes. ◆**payroll** *n* **to be on the p. of** (*firm, factory*) être employé par; **to have twenty workers on the p.** employer vingt ouvriers.

pea [piː] *n* pois *m*; **garden** *or* **green peas** petits pois *mpl*; **p. soup** soupe *f* aux pois.

peace [piːs] *n* paix *f*; **p. of mind** tranquillité *f* d'esprit; **in p.** en paix; **at p.** en paix (**with** avec); **to have (some) p. and quiet** avoir la paix; **to disturb the p.** troubler l'ordre public; **to hold one's p.** garder le silence. ◆**p.-keeping** *a* (*force*) de maintien de la paix; (*measure*) de pacification. ◆**p.-loving** *a* pacifique. ◆**peaceable** *a* paisible, pacifique. ◆**peaceful** *a* paisible, calme; (*coexistence, purpose, demonstration*) pacifique. ◆**peacefulness** *n* paix *f.*

peach [piːtʃ] *n* (*fruit*) pêche *f*; (*tree*) pêcher *m*; – *a* (*colour*) pêche *inv.*

peacock ['piːkɒk] *n* paon *m.*

peak [piːk] *n* (*mountain top*) sommet *m*; (*mountain itself*) pic *m*; (*of cap*) visière *f*; (*of fame etc*) *Fig* sommet *m*, apogée *m*; **the traffic has reached** *or* **is at its p.** la circulation est à son maximum; – *a* (*hours, period*) de pointe; (*demand, production*) maximum; – *vi* (*of sales etc*) atteindre son maximum. ◆**peaked** *a* **p. cap** casquette *f.*

peaky ['piːkɪ] *a* (**-ier, -iest**) *Fam* (*ill*) patraque; (*pale*) pâlot.

peal [piːl] **1** *n* (*of laughter*) éclat *m*; (*of thun-*

der) roulement *m*. **2** *n* **p. of bells** carillon *m*; – *vi* **to p. (out)** (*of bells*) carillonner.

peanut ['piːnʌt] *n* cacah(o)uète *f*; (*plant*) arachide *f*; **to earn/***etc* **peanuts** (*little money*) *Fam* gagner/*etc* des clopinettes.

pear [peər] *n* poire *f*; **p. tree** poirier *m*.

pearl [pɜːl] *n* perle *f*; (*mother-of-pearl*) nacre *f*. ◆**pearly** *a* (**-ier, -iest**) (*colour*) nacré.

peasant ['pezənt] *n* & *a* paysan, -anne (*mf*).

peashooter ['piːʃuːtər] *n* sarbacane *f*.

peat [piːt] *n* tourbe *f*.

pebble ['peb(ə)l] *n* (*stone*) caillou *m*; (*on beach*) galet *m*. ◆**pebbly** *a* (*beach*) (couvert) de galets.

pecan ['piːkæn] *n* (*nut*) *Am* pacane *f*.

peck [pek] *vti* **to p. (at)** (*of bird*) picorer (*du pain etc*); (*person*) *Fig* donner un coup de bec à; **to p. at one's food** (*of person*) manger du bout des dents; – *n* coup *m* de bec; (*kiss*) *Fam* bécot *m*.

peckish ['pekɪʃ] *a* **to be p.** (*hungry*) *Fam* avoir un petit creux.

peculiar [pɪ'kjuːlɪər] *a* (*strange*) bizarre; (*characteristic, special*) particulier (**to** à). ◆**peculi'arity** *n* (*feature*) particularité *f*; (*oddity*) bizarrerie *f*. ◆**peculiarly** *adv* bizarrement; (*specially*) particulièrement.

pedal ['ped(ə)l] *n* pédale *f*; **p. boat** pédalo *m*; – *vi* (**-ll-**, *Am* **-l-**) pédaler; – *vt* (*bicycle etc*) actionner les pédales de. ◆**pedalbin** *n* poubelle *f* à pédale.

pedant ['pedənt] *n* pédant, -ante *mf*. ◆**pe'dantic** *a* pédant. ◆**pedantry** *n* pédantisme *m*.

peddl/e ['ped(ə)l] *vt* colporter; (*drugs*) faire le trafic de; – *vi* faire du colportage. ◆**–er** *n Am* (*door-to-door*) colporteur, -euse *mf*; (*in street*) camelot *m*; **drug p.** revendeur, -euse *mf* de drogues.

pedestal ['pedɪst(ə)l] *n Archit* & *Fig* piédestal *m*.

pedestrian [pə'destrɪən] **1** *n* piéton *m*; **p. crossing** passage *m* pour piétons; **p. precinct** zone *f* piétonnière. **2** *a* (*speech, style*) prosaïque. ◆**pedestrianize** *vt* (*street etc*) rendre piétonnier.

pedigree ['pedɪgriː] *n* (*of dog, horse etc*) pedigree *m*; (*of person*) ascendance *f*; – *a* (*dog, horse etc*) de race.

pedlar ['pedlər] *n* (*door-to-door*) colporteur, -euse *mf*; (*in street*) camelot *m*.

pee [piː] *n* **to go for a p.** *Fam* faire pipi.

peek [piːk] *n* coup *m* d'œil (furtif); – *vi* jeter un coup d'œil (furtif) (**at** à).

peel [piːl] *n* (*of vegetable, fruit*) pelure(s) *f*(*pl*), épluchure(s) *f*(*pl*); (*of orange skin*) écorce *f*; (*in food, drink*) zeste *m*; **a piece of p.** une pelure, une épluchure; – *vt* (*fruit, vegetable*) peler, éplucher; **to keep one's eyes peeled** *Fam* être vigilant; **to p. off** (*label etc*) décoller; – *vi* (*of sunburnt skin*) peler; (*of paint*) s'écailler; **to p. easily** (*of fruit*) se peler facilement. ◆**–ings** *npl* pelures *fpl*, épluchures *fpl*. ◆**–er** *n* (*knife etc*) éplucheur *m*.

peep [piːp] **1** *n* coup *m* d'œil (furtif); – *vi* **to p. (at)** regarder furtivement; **to p. out** se montrer; **peeping Tom** voyeur, -euse *mf*. **2** *vi* (*of bird*) pépier. ◆**peephole** *n* judas *m*.

peer [pɪər] **1** *n* (*equal*) pair *m*, égal, -ale *mf*; (*noble*) pair *m*. **2** *vi* **to p. (at)** regarder attentivement (*comme pour mieux voir*); **to p. into** (*darkness*) scruter. ◆**peerage** *n* (*rank*) pairie *f*.

peeved [piːvd] *a Fam* irrité.

peevish ['piːvɪʃ] *a* grincheux, irritable.

peg [peg] **1** *n* (*wooden*) *Tech* cheville *f*; (*metal*) *Tech* fiche *f*; (*for tent*) piquet *m*; (*for clothes*) pince *f* (à linge); (*for coat, hat etc*) patère *f*; **to buy off the p.** acheter en prêt-à-porter. **2** *vt* (**-gg-**) (*prices*) stabiliser.

pejorative [pɪ'dʒɒrətɪv] *a* péjoratif.

pekin(g)ese [piːkɪ'niːz] *n* (*dog*) pékinois *m*.

pelican ['pelɪk(ə)n] *n* (*bird*) pélican *m*.

pellet ['pelɪt] *n* (*of paper etc*) boulette *f*; (*for gun*) (grain *m* de) plomb *m*.

pelt [pelt] **1** *n* (*skin*) peau *f*; (*fur*) fourrure *f*. **2** *vt* **to p. s.o. with** (*stones etc*) bombarder qn de. **3** *vi* **it's pelting (down)** (*raining*) il pleut à verse. **4** *vi* **to p. along** (*run, dash*) *Fam* foncer, courir.

pelvis [pelvɪs] *n Anat* bassin *m*.

pen [pen] **1** *n* (*dipped in ink*) porte-plume *m inv*; (*fountain pen*) stylo *m* (à encre *or* à plume); (*ballpoint*) stylo *m* à bille, stylo(-)bille *m*; **to live by one's p.** *Fig* vivre de sa plume; **p. friend, p. pal** correspondant, -ante *mf*; **p. name** pseudonyme *m*; **p. nib** (bec *m* de) plume *f*; **p. pusher** *Pej* gratte-papier *m inv*; – *vt* (**-nn-**) (*write*) écrire. **2** *n* (*enclosure for baby or sheep or cattle*) parc *m*.

penal ['piːn(ə)l] *a* (*law, code etc*) pénal; (*colony*) pénitentiaire. ◆**penalize** *vt Sp Jur* pénaliser (**for** pour); (*handicap*) désavantager.

penalty ['pen(ə)ltɪ] *n Jur* peine *f*; (*fine*) amende *f*; *Sp* pénalisation *f*; *Fb* penalty *m*; *Rugby* pénalité *f*; **to pay the p.** *Fig* subir les conséquences.

penance ['penəns] *n* pénitence *f*.

pence [pens] *see* **penny**.

pencil ['pens(ə)l] *n* crayon *m*; **in p.** au crayon; **p. box** plumier *m*; **p. sharpener**

taille-crayon(s) *m inv*; – *vt* (**-ll-**, *Am* **-l-**) crayonner; **to p. in** *Fig* noter provisoirement.

pendant ['pendənt] *n* pendentif *m*; (*on earring, chandelier*) pendeloque *f*.

pending ['pendɪŋ] **1** *a* (*matter*) en suspens. **2** *prep* (*until*) en attendant.

pendulum ['pendjʊləm] *n* (*of clock*) balancier *m*, pendule *m*; *Fig* pendule *m*.

penetrat/e ['penɪtreɪt] *vt* (*substance, mystery etc*) percer; (*plan, secret etc*) découvrir; – *vti* **to p. (into)** (*forest, group etc*) pénétrer dans. ◆**—ing** *a* (*mind, cold etc*) pénétrant. ◆**pene'tration** *n* pénétration *f*.

penguin ['peŋgwɪn] *n* manchot *m*, pingouin *m*.

penicillin [penɪ'sɪlɪn] *n* pénicilline *f*.

peninsula [pə'nɪnsjʊlə] *n* presqu'île *f*, péninsule *f*. ◆**pensinsular** *a* péninsulaire.

penis ['piːnɪs] *n* pénis *m*.

penitent ['penɪtənt] *a* & *n* pénitent, -ente (*mf*). ◆**penitence** *n* pénitence *f*.

penitentiary [penɪ'tenʃərɪ] *n* *Am* prison *f* (centrale).

penknife ['pennaɪf] *n* (*pl* **-knives**) canif *m*.

pennant ['penənt] *n* (*flag*) flamme *f*, banderole *f*.

penny ['penɪ] *n* **1** (*pl* **pennies**) (*coin*) penny *m*; *Am Can* cent *m*; **I don't have a p.** *Fig* je n'ai pas le sou. **2** (*pl* **pence** [pens]) (*value, currency*) penny *m*. ◆**p.-pinching** *a* (*miserly*) *Fam* avare. ◆**penniless** *a* sans le sou.

pension ['penʃ(ə)n] *n* pension *f*; **retirement p.** (pension *f* de) retraite *f*; (*private*) retraite *f* complémentaire; – *vt* **to p. off** mettre à la retraite. ◆**—able** *a* (*age*) de la retraite; (*job*) qui donne droit à une retraite. ◆**—er** *n* pensionné, -ée *mf*; **(old age) p.** retraité, -ée *mf*.

pensive ['pensɪv] *a* pensif.

pentagon ['pentəgən] *n* **the P.** *Am Pol* le Pentagone.

pentathlon [pen'tæθlən] *n Sp* pentathlon *m*.

Pentecost ['pentɪkɒst] *n* (*Whitsun*) *Am* Pentecôte *f*.

penthouse ['penthaus] *n* appartement *m* de luxe (*construit sur le toit d'un immeuble*).

pent-up [pent'ʌp] *a* (*feelings*) refoulé.

penultimate [pɪ'nʌltɪmət] *a* avant-dernier.

peony ['pɪənɪ] *n Bot* pivoine *f*.

people ['piːp(ə)l] *npl* (*in general*) gens *mpl or fpl*; (*specific persons*) personnes *fpl*; (*of region, town*) habitants *mpl*, gens *mpl or fpl*; **the p.** (*citizens*) *Pol* le peuple; **old p.** les personnes *fpl* âgées; **old people's home** hospice *m* de vieillards; (*private*) maison *f* de retraite; **two p.** deux personnes; **English p.** les Anglais *mpl*, le peuple anglais; **a lot of p.** beaucoup de monde *or* de gens; **p. think that . . .** on pense que . . . ; – *n* (*nation*) peuple *m*; – *vt* (*populate*) peupler (**with** de).

pep [pep] *n* entrain *m*; **p. talk** *Fam* petit laïus d'encouragement; – *vt* (**-pp-**) **to p. up** (*perk up*) ragaillardir.

pepper ['pepər] *n* poivre *m*; (*vegetable*) poivron *m*; – *vt* poivrer. ◆**peppercorn** *n* grain *m* de poivre. ◆**peppermint** *n* (*plant*) menthe *f* poivrée; (*sweet*) pastille *f* de menthe. ◆**peppery** *a Culin* poivré.

per [pɜːr] *prep* par; **p. annum** par an; **p. head, p. person** par personne; **p. cent** pour cent; **50 pence p. kilo** 50 pence le kilo; **40 km p. hour** 40 km à l'heure. ◆**per'centage** *n* pourcentage *m*.

perceive [pə'siːv] *vt* (*see, hear*) percevoir; (*notice*) remarquer (**that** que). ◆**perceptible** *a* perceptible. ◆**perception** *n* perception *f* (**of** de); (*intuition*) intuition *f*. ◆**perceptive** *a* (*person*) perspicace; (*study, remark*) pénétrant.

perch [pɜːtʃ] **1** *n* perchoir *m*; – *vi* (*of bird*) (se) percher; (*of person*) *Fig* se percher, se jucher; – *vt* (*put*) percher. **2** *n* (*fish*) perche *f*.

percolate ['pɜːkəleɪt] *vi* (*of liquid*) filtrer, passer (**through** par); – *vt* (*coffee*) faire dans une cafetière; **percolated coffee** du vrai café. ◆**percolator** *n* cafetière *f*; (*in café or restaurant*) percolateur *m*.

percussion [pə'kʌʃ(ə)n] *n Mus* percussion *f*.

peremptory [pə'remptərɪ] *a* péremptoire.

perennial [pə'renɪəl] **1** *a* (*complaint, subject etc*) perpétuel. **2** *a* (*plant*) vivace; – *n* plante *f* vivace.

perfect ['pɜːfɪkt] *a* parfait; – *a* & *n* **p. (tense)** *Gram* parfait *m*; – [pə'fekt] *vt* (*book, piece of work etc*) parachever, parfaire; (*process, technique*) mettre au point; (*one's French etc*) parfaire ses connaissances en. ◆**per'fection** *n* perfection *f*; (*act*) parachèvement *m* (**of** de); mise *f* au point (**of** de); **to p.** à la perfection. ◆**per'fectionist** *n* perfectionniste *mf*. ◆**'perfectly** *adv* parfaitement.

perfidious [pə'fɪdɪəs] *a Lit* perfide.

perforate ['pɜːfəreɪt] *vt* perforer. ◆**perfo'ration** *n* perforation *f*.

perform [pə'fɔːm] *vt* (*task, miracle*) accomplir; (*a function, one's duty*) remplir; (*rite*) célébrer; (*operation*) *Med* pratiquer (**on**

sur); (*a play, symphony*) jouer; (*sonata*) interpréter; – *vi* (*play*) jouer; (*sing*) chanter; (*dance*) danser; (*of circus animal*) faire un numéro; (*function*) fonctionner; (*behave*) se comporter; **you performed very well!** tu as très bien fait! ◆**—ing** *a* (*animal*) savant. ◆**performance** *n* **1** (*show*) *Th* représentation *f*, séance *f*; *Cin Mus* séance *f*. **2** (*of athlete, machine etc*) performance *f*; (*of actor, musician etc*) interprétation *f*; (*circus act*) numéro *m*; (*fuss*) *Fam* histoire(s) *f*(*pl*); **the p. of one's duties** l'exercice *m* de ses fonctions. ◆**performer** *n* interprète *mf* (**of** de); (*entertainer*) artiste *mf*.

perfume ['pɜːfjuːm] *n* parfum *m*; – [pə'fjuːm] *vt* parfumer.

perfunctory [pə'fʌŋktərɪ] *a* (*action*) superficiel; (*smile etc*) de commande.

perhaps [pə'hæps] *adv* peut-être; **p. not** peut-être que non.

peril ['perɪl] *n* péril *m*, danger *m*; **at your p.** à vos risques et péril. ◆**perilous** *a* périlleux.

perimeter [pə'rɪmɪtər] *n* périmètre *m*.

period ['pɪərɪəd] **1** *n* (*length of time, moment in time*) période *f*; (*historical*) époque *f*; (*time limit*) délai *m*; (*lesson*) *Sch* leçon *f*; (*full stop*) *Gram* point *m*; **in the p. of a month** en l'espace d'un mois; **I refuse, p.!** *Am* je refuse, un point c'est tout!; – *a* (*furniture etc*) d'époque; (*costume*) de l'époque. **2** *n* (*menstruation*) règles *fpl*. ◆**peri'odic** *a* périodique. ◆**peri'odical** *n* (*magazine*) périodique *m*. ◆**peri'odically** *adv* périodiquement.

periphery [pə'rɪfərɪ] *n* périphérie *f*. ◆**peripheral** *a* (*question*) sans rapport direct (**to** avec); (*interest*) accessoire; (*neighbourhood*) périphérique.

periscope ['perɪskəʊp] *n* périscope *m*.

perish ['perɪʃ] *vi* (*die*) périr; (*of food, substance*) se détériorer; **to be perished** *or* **perishing** (*of person*) *Fam* être frigorifié. ◆**—ing** *a* (*cold, weather*) *Fam* glacial. ◆**—able** *a* (*food*) périssable; – *npl* denrées *fpl* périssables.

perjure ['pɜːdʒər] *vt* **to p. oneself** se parjurer. ◆**perjurer** *n* (*person*) parjure *mf*. ◆**perjury** *n* parjure *m*; **to commit p.** se parjurer.

perk [pɜːk] **1** *vi* **to p. up** (*buck up*) se ragaillardir; – *vt* **to p. s.o. up** remonter qn, ragaillardir qn. **2** *n* (*advantage*) avantage *m*; (*extra profit*) à-côté *m*. ◆**perky** *a* (**-ier, -iest**) (*cheerful*) guilleret, plein d'entrain.

perm [pɜːm] *n* (*of hair*) permanente *f*; – *vt* **to have one's hair permed** se faire faire une permanente.

permanent ['pɜːmənənt] *a* permanent; (*address*) fixe; **she's p. here** elle est ici à titre permanent. ◆**permanence** *n* permanence *f*. ◆**permanently** *adv* à titre permanent.

permeate ['pɜːmɪeɪt] *vt* (*of ideas etc*) se répandre dans; **to p. (through)** (*of liquid etc*) pénétrer. ◆**permeable** *a* perméable.

permit [pə'mɪt] *vt* (**-tt-**) permettre (**s.o. to do** à qn de faire); **weather permitting** si le temps le permet; – ['pɜːmɪt] *n* (*licence*) permis *m*; (*entrance pass*) laissez-passer *m inv*. ◆**per'missible** *a* permis. ◆**per'mission** *n* permission *f*, autorisation *f* (**to do** de faire); **to ask (for)/give p.** demander/donner la permission. ◆**per'missive** *a* (trop) tolérant, laxiste. ◆**per'missiveness** *n* laxisme *m*.

permutation [pɜːmjʊ'teɪʃ(ə)n] *n* permutation *f*.

pernicious [pə'nɪʃəs] *a* (*harmful*) & *Med* pernicieux.

pernickety [pə'nɪkətɪ] *a Fam* (*precise*) pointilleux; (*demanding*) difficile (**about** sur).

peroxide [pə'rɒksaɪd] *n* (*bleach*) eau *f* oxygénée; – *a* (*hair, blond*) oxygéné.

perpendicular [pɜːpən'dɪkjʊlər] *a* & *n* perpendiculaire (*f*).

perpetrate ['pɜːpɪtreɪt] *vt* (*crime*) perpétrer. ◆**perpetrator** *n* auteur *m*.

perpetual [pə'petʃʊəl] *a* perpétuel. ◆**perpetually** *adv* perpétuellement. ◆**perpetuate** *vt* perpétuer. ◆**perpetuity** [pɜːpɪ'tjuːɪtɪ] *n* perpétuité *f*.

perplex [pə'pleks] *vt* rendre perplexe, dérouter. ◆**—ed** *a* perplexe. ◆**—ing** *a* déroutant. ◆**perplexity** *n* perplexité *f*; (*complexity*) complexité *f*.

persecute ['pɜːsɪkjuːt] *vt* persécuter. ◆**perse'cution** *n* persécution *f*.

persever/e [pɜːsɪ'vɪər] *vi* persévérer (**in** dans). ◆**—ing** *a* (*persistent*) persévérant. ◆**perseverance** *n* persévérance *f*.

Persian ['pɜːʃ(ə)n, 'pɜːʒ(ə)n] *a* (*language, cat, carpet*) persan; – *n* (*language*) persan *m*.

persist [pə'sɪst] *vi* persister (**in doing** à faire, **in sth** dans qch). ◆**persistence** *n* persistance *f*. ◆**persistent** *a* (*fever, smell etc*) persistant; (*person*) obstiné; (*attempts, noise etc*) continuel. ◆**persistently** *adv* (*stubbornly*) obstinément; (*continually*) continuellement.

person ['pɜːs(ə)n] *n* personne *f*; **in p.** en personne; **a p. to p. call** *Tel* une communi-

cation avec préavis. ◆**personable** *a* avenant, qui présente bien.
personal ['pɜːsən(ə)l] *a* personnel; (*application*) en personne; (*hygiene, friend*) intime; (*life*) privé; (*indiscreet*) indiscret; **p. assistant, p. secretary** secrétaire *m* particulier, secrétaire *f* particulière. ◆**perso'nality** *n* (*character, famous person*) personnalité *f*; **a television p.** une vedette de la télévision. ◆**personalize** *vt* personnaliser. ◆**personally** *adv* personnellement; (*in person*) en personne.
personify [pə'sɒnɪfaɪ] *vt* personnifier. ◆**personifi'cation** *n* personnification *f*.
personnel [pɜːsə'nel] *n* (*staff*) personnel *m*; (*department*) service *m* du personnel.
perspective [pə'spektɪv] *n* (*artistic & viewpoint*) perspective *f*; **in (its true) p.** *Fig* sous son vrai jour.
perspire [pə'spaɪər] *vi* transpirer. ◆**perspi'ration** *n* transpiration *f*, sueur *f*.
persuade [pə'sweɪd] *vt* persuader (**s.o. to do** qn de faire). ◆**persuasion** *n* persuasion *f*; *Rel* religion *f*. ◆**persuasive** *a* (*person, argument etc*) persuasif. ◆**persuasively** *adv* de façon persuasive.
pert [pɜːt] *a* (*impertinent*) impertinent; (*lively*) gai, plein d'entrain; (*hat etc*) coquet, chic. ◆**—ly** *adv* avec impertinence.
pertain [pə'teɪn] *vt* **to p. to** (*relate*) se rapporter à; (*belong*) appartenir à.
pertinent ['pɜːtɪnənt] *a* pertinent. ◆**—ly** *adv* pertinemment.
perturb [pə'tɜːb] *vt* troubler, perturber.
Peru [pə'ruː] *n* Pérou *m*. ◆**Peruvian** *a & n* péruvien, -ienne (*mf*).
peruse [pə'ruːz] *vt* lire (attentivement); (*skim through*) parcourir. ◆**perusal** *n* lecture *f*.
pervade [pə'veɪd] *vt* se répandre dans. ◆**pervasive** *a* qui se répand partout, envahissant.
perverse [pə'vɜːs] *a* (*awkward*) contrariant; (*obstinate*) entêté; (*wicked*) pervers. ◆**perversion** *n* perversion *f*; (*of justice, truth*) travestissement *m*. ◆**perversity** *n* esprit *m* de contradiction; (*obstinacy*) entêtement *m*; (*wickedness*) perversité *f*.
pervert [pə'vɜːt] *vt* pervertir; (*mind*) corrompre; (*justice, truth*) travestir; – ['pɜːvɜːt] *n* perverti, -ie *mf*.
pesky ['peskɪ] *a* (**-ier, -iest**) (*troublesome*) *Am Fam* embêtant.
pessimism ['pesɪmɪz(ə)m] *n* pessimisme *m*. ◆**pessimist** *n* pessimiste *mf*. ◆**pessi'mistic** *a* pessimiste. ◆**pessi'mistically** *adv* avec pessimisme.
pest [pest] *n* animal *m or* insecte *m* nuisible; (*person*) *Fam* casse-pieds *mf inv*, peste *f*. ◆**pesticide** *n* pesticide *m*.
pester ['pestər] *vt* (*harass*) harceler (**with questions** de questions); **to p. s.o. to do sth/for sth** harceler *or* tarabuster qn pour qu'il fasse qch/jusqu'à ce qu'il donne qch.
pet [pet] **1** *n* animal *m* (domestique); (*favourite person*) chouchou, -oute *mf*; **yes (my) p.** *Fam* oui mon chou; **to have** *or* **keep a p.** avoir un animal chez soi; – *a* (*dog etc*) domestique; (*tiger etc*) apprivoisé; (*favourite*) favori; **p. shop** magasin *m* d'animaux; **p. hate** bête *f* noire; **p. name** petit nom *m* (d'amitié); **p. subject** dada *m*. **2** *vt* (**-tt-**) (*fondle*) caresser; (*sexually*) *Fam* peloter; – *vi Fam* se peloter.
petal ['pet(ə)l] *n* pétale *m*.
peter ['piːtər] *vi* **to p. out** (*run out*) s'épuiser; (*dry up*) se tarir; (*die out*) mourir; (*disappear*) disparaître.
petite [pə'tiːt] *a* (*woman*) petite et mince, menue.
petition [pə'tɪʃ(ə)n] *n* (*signatures*) pétition *f*; (*request*) *Jur* requête *f*; **p. for divorce** demande *f* en divorce; – *vt* adresser une pétition *or* une requête à (**for sth** pour demander qch).
petrify ['petrɪfaɪ] *vt* (*frighten*) pétrifier de terreur.
petrol ['petrəl] *n* essence *f*; **I've run out of p.** je suis tombé en panne d'essence; **p. engine** moteur *m* à essence; **p. station** poste *m* d'essence, station-service *f*.
petroleum [pə'trəʊlɪəm] *n* pétrole *m*.
petticoat ['petɪkəʊt] *n* jupon *m*.
petty ['petɪ] *a* (**-ier, -iest**) (*small*) petit; (*trivial*) insignifiant, menu, petit; (*mean*) mesquin; **p. cash** *Com* petite caisse *f*, menue monnaie *f*. ◆**pettiness** *n* petitesse *f*; insignifiance *f*; mesquinerie *f*.
petulant ['petjʊlənt] *a* irritable. ◆**petulance** *n* irritabilité *f*.
petunia [pɪ'tjuːnɪə] *n Bot* pétunia *m*.
pew [pjuː] *n* banc *m* d'église; **take a p.!** *Hum* assieds-toi!
pewter ['pjuːtər] *n* étain *m*.
phallic ['fælɪk] *a* phallique.
phantom ['fæntəm] *n* fantôme *m*.
pharmacy ['fɑːməsɪ] *n* pharmacie *f*. ◆**pharmaceutical** [-'sjuːtɪk(ə)l] *a* pharmaceutique. ◆**pharmacist** *n* pharmacien, -ienne *mf*.
pharynx ['færɪŋks] *n Anat* pharynx *m*. ◆**pharyn'gitis** *n Med* pharyngite *f*.
phase [feɪz] *n* (*stage*) phase *f*; – *vt* **to p.**

in/out introduire/supprimer progressivement. ◆**phased** *a* (*changes etc*) progressif.

PhD [piːeɪtʃ'diː] *n abbr* (*Doctor of Philosophy*) (*degree*) *Univ* doctorat *m*.

pheasant ['fezənt] *n* (*bird*) faisan *m*.

phenomenon, *pl* **-ena** [fɪ'nɒmɪnən, -ɪnə] *n* phénomène *m*. ◆**phenomenal** *a* phénoménal.

phew! [fjuː] *int* (*relief*) ouf!

philanderer [fɪ'lændərər] *n* coureur *m* de jupons.

philanthropist [fɪ'lænθrəpɪst] *n* philanthrope *mf*. ◆**philan'thropic** *a* philanthropique.

philately [fɪ'lætəlɪ] *n* philatélie. ◆**phila'telic** *a* philatélique. ◆**philatelist** *n* philatéliste *mf*.

philharmonic [fɪlə'mɒnɪk] *a* philharmonique.

Philippines ['fɪlɪpiːnz] *npl* **the P.** les Philippines *fpl*.

philistine ['fɪlɪstaɪn] *n* béotien, -ienne *mf*, philistin *m*.

philosophy [fɪ'lɒsəfɪ] *n* philosophie *f*. ◆**philosopher** *n* philosophe *mf*. ◆**philo'sophical** *a* philosophique; (*stoical, resigned*) *Fig* philosophe. ◆**philo'sophically** *adv* (*to say etc*) avec philosophie. ◆**philosophize** *vi* philosopher.

phlegm [flem] *n Med* glaires *fpl*; (*calmness*) *Fig* flegme *m*. ◆**phleg'matic** *a* flegmatique.

phobia ['fəʊbɪə] *n* phobie *f*.

phone [fəʊn] *n* téléphone *m*; **on the p.** (*speaking here*) au téléphone; (*at other end*) au bout du fil; **to be on the p.** (*as subscriber*) avoir le téléphone; **p. call** coup *m* de fil *or* de téléphone; **to make a p. call** téléphoner (**to** à); **p. book** annuaire *m*; **p. box, p. booth** cabine *f* téléphonique; **p. number** numéro *m* de téléphone; – *vt* (*message*) téléphoner (**to** à); **to p. s.o. (up)** téléphoner à qn; – *vi* **to p. (up)** téléphoner; **to p. back** rappeler. ◆**phonecard** *n* télécarte *f*.

phonetic [fə'netɪk] *a* phonétique. ◆**phonetics** *n* (*science*) phonétique *f*.

phoney ['fəʊnɪ] *a* (**-ier, -iest**) *Fam* (*jewels, writer etc*) faux; (*attack, firm*) bidon *inv*; (*attitude*) fumiste; – *n Fam* (*impostor*) imposteur *m*; (*joker, shirker*) fumiste *mf*; **it's a p.** (*jewel, coin etc*) c'est du faux.

phonograph ['fəʊnəgræf] *n Am* électrophone *m*.

phosphate ['fɒsfeɪt] *n Ch* phosphate *m*.

phosphorus ['fɒsfərəs] *n Ch* phosphore *m*.

photo ['fəʊtəʊ] *n* (*pl* **-os**) photo *f*; **to have one's p. taken** se faire photographier. ◆**photocopier** *n* (*machine*) photocopieur *m*. ◆**photocopy** *n* photocopie *f*; – *vt* photocopier. ◆**photo'genic** *a* photogénique. ◆**photograph** *n* photographie *f*; – *vt* photographier; – *vi* **to p. well** être photogénique. ◆**photographer** [fə'tɒgrəfər] *n* photographe *mf*. ◆**photo'graphic** *a* photographique. ◆**photography** [fə'tɒgrəfɪ] *n* (*activity*) photographie *f*. ◆**photostat®** = **photocopy**.

phras/e [freɪz] *n* (*saying*) expression *f*; (*idiom*) & *Gram* locution *f*; – *vt* (*express*) exprimer; (*letter*) rédiger. ◆**—ing** *n* (*wording*) termes *mpl*. ◆**phrasebook** *n* (*for tourists*) manuel *m* de conversation.

physical ['fɪzɪk(ə)l] *a* physique; (*object, world*) matériel; **p. examination** *Med* examen *m* médical; **p. education, p. training** éducation *f* physique. ◆**physically** *adv* physiquement; **p. impossible** matériellement impossible.

physician [fɪ'zɪʃ(ə)n] *n* médecin *m*.

physics ['fɪzɪks] *n* (*science*) physique *f*. ◆**physicist** *n* physicien, -ienne *mf*.

physiology [fɪzɪ'ɒlədʒɪ] *n* physiologie *f*. ◆**physio'logical** *a* physiologique.

physiotherapy [fɪzɪəʊ'θerəpɪ] *n* kinésithérapie *f*. ◆**physiotherapist** *n* kinésithérapeute *mf*.

physique [fɪ'ziːk] *n* (*appearance*) physique *m*; (*constitution*) constitution *f*.

piano [pɪ'ænəʊ] *n* (*pl* **-os**) piano *m*. ◆**'pianist** *n* pianiste *mf*.

piazza [pɪ'ætsə] *n* (*square*) place *f*; (*covered*) passage *m* couvert.

picayune [pɪkə'juːn] *a* (*petty*) *Am Fam* mesquin.

pick [pɪk] *n* (*choice*) choix *m*; **the p. of** (*best*) le meilleur de; **the p. of the bunch** le dessus du panier; **to take one's p.** faire son choix, choisir; – *vt* (*choose*) choisir; (*flower, fruit etc*) cueillir; (*hole*) faire (**in** dans); (*lock*) crocheter; **to p. one's nose** se mettre les doigts dans le nez; **to p. one's teeth** se curer les dents; **to p. a fight** chercher la bagarre (**with** avec); **to p. holes in** *Fig* relever les défauts de; **to p. (off)** (*remove*) enlever; **to p. out** (*choose*) choisir; (*identify*) reconnaître, distinguer; **to p. up** (*sth dropped*) ramasser; (*fallen person or chair*) relever; (*person into air, weight*) soulever; (*cold, money*) *Fig* ramasser; (*habit, accent, speed*) prendre; (*fetch, collect*) (passer) prendre; (*find*) trouver; (*baby*) prendre dans ses bras; (*programme etc*) *Rad* capter; (*survivor*) recueillir; (*arrest*) arrêter, ramasser; (*learn*) apprendre; – *vi* **to p. and choose** choisir avec soin; **to p. on** (*nag*) harceler; (*blame*) accuser; **why p. on me?** pourquoi moi?; **to p. up** (*improve*) s'améliorer; (*of business, trade*) reprendre; *Med* aller mieux; (*resume*) continuer. ◆**—ing 1** *n* (*choosing*) choix *m* (of de); (*of flower, fruit etc*) cueillette *f*. **2** *npl* (*leftovers*) restes *mpl*; *Com* profits *mpl*. ◆**pick-me-up** *n* (*drink*) *Fam* remontant *m*. ◆**pick-up** *n* (*of record player*) (bras *m* de) pick-up *m*; (*person*) *Pej Fam* partenaire *mf* de rencontre; **p.-up (truck)** pick-up *m*.

pick(axe) (*Am* (**-ax**)) ['pɪk(æks)] *n* (*tool*) pioche *f*; **ice pick** pic *m* à glace.

picket ['pɪkɪt] **1** *n* (*striker*) gréviste *mf*; **p. (line)** piquet *m* (de grève); – *vt* (*factory*) installer des piquets de grève aux portes de. **2** *n* (*stake*) piquet *m*.

pickle ['pɪk(ə)l] **1** *n* (*brine*) saumure *f*; (*vinegar*) vinaigre *m*; *pl* (*vegetables*) pickles *mpl*; *Am* concombres *mpl*, cornichons *mpl*; – *vt* mariner. **2** *n* **in a p.** (*trouble*) *Fam* dans le pétrin.

pickpocket ['pɪkpɒkɪt] *n* (*thief*) pickpocket *m*.

picky ['pɪkɪ] *a* (**-ier, -iest**) (*choosey*) *Am* difficile.

picnic ['pɪknɪk] *n* pique-nique *m*; – *vi* (**-ck-**) pique-niquer.

pictorial [pɪk'tɔːrɪəl] *a* (*in pictures*) en images; (*periodical*) illustré.

picture ['pɪktʃər] **1** *n* image *f*; (*painting*) tableau *m*, peinture *f*; (*drawing*) dessin *m*; (*photo*) photo *f*; (*film*) film *m*; (*scene*) *Fig* tableau *m*; **the pictures** *Cin* le cinéma; **to put s.o. in the p.** *Fig* mettre qn au courant; **p. frame** cadre *m*. **2** *vt* (*imagine*) s'imaginer (**that** que); (*remember*) revoir; (*depict*) décrire.

picturesque [pɪktʃə'resk] *a* pittoresque.

piddling ['pɪdlɪŋ] *a Pej* dérisoire.

pidgin ['pɪdʒɪn] *n* **p. (English)** pidgin *m*.

pie [paɪ] *n* (*of meat, vegetable*) tourte *f*; (*of fruit*) tarte *f*, tourte *f*; (*compact filling*) pâté *m* en croûte; **cottage p.** hachis *m* Parmentier.

piebald ['paɪbɔːld] *a* pie *inv*.

piece [piːs] *n* morceau *m*; (*of bread, paper, chocolate, etc*) bout *m*, morceau *m*; (*of fabric, machine, game, artillery*) pièce *f*; (*coin*) pièce *f*; **bits and pieces** des petites choses; **in pieces** en morceaux, en pièces; **to smash to pieces** briser en morceaux; **to take to pieces** (*machine etc*) démonter; **to come to pieces** se démonter; **to go to pieces** (*of person*) *Fig* craquer; **a p. of luck/news/***etc* une chance/nouvelle/*etc*; **in one p.** (*object*) intact; (*person*) indemne; – *vt* **to p. together** (*facts*) reconstituer; (*one's life*) refaire. ◆**piecemeal** *adv* petit à petit; – *a* (*unsystematic*) peu méthodique. ◆**piecework** *n* travail *m* à la tâche *or* à la pièce.

pier [pɪər] *n* (*promenade*) jetée *f*; (*for landing*) appontement *m*.

pierc/e [pɪəs] *vt* percer; (*of cold, sword, bullet*) transpercer (*qn*). ◆**—ing** *a* (*voice, look etc*) perçant; (*wind etc*) glacial.

piety ['paɪətɪ] *n* piété *f*.

piffling ['pɪflɪŋ] *a Fam* insignifiant.

pig [pɪg] *n* cochon *m*, porc *m*; (*evil person*) *Pej* cochon *m*; (*glutton*) *Pej* goinfre *m*. ◆**piggish** *a Pej* (*dirty*) sale; (*greedy*) goinfre. ◆**piggy** *a* (*greedy*) *Fam* goinfre. ◆**piggybank** *n* tirelire *f* (*en forme de cochon*).

pigeon ['pɪdʒɪn] *n* pigeon *m*. ◆**pigeonhole** *n* casier *m*; – *vt* classer; (*shelve*) mettre en suspens.

piggyback ['pɪgɪbæk] *n* **to give s.o. a p.** porter qn sur le dos.

pigheaded [pɪg'hedɪd] *a* obstiné.

pigment ['pɪgmənt] *n* pigment *m*. ◆**pigmen'tation** *n* pigmentation *f*.

pigsty ['pɪgstaɪ] *n* porcherie *f*.

pigtail ['pɪgteɪl] *n* (*hair*) natte *f*.

pike [paɪk] *n* **1** (*fish*) brochet *m*. **2** (*weapon*) pique *f*.

pilchard ['pɪltʃəd] *n* pilchard *m*, sardine *f*.

pile¹ [paɪl] *n* pile *f*; (*fortune*) *Fam* fortune *f*; **piles of, a p. of** *Fam* beaucoup de, un tas de; – *vt* **to p. (up)** (*stack up*) empiler; – *vi* **to p. into** (*of people*) s'entasser dans; **to p. up** (*accumulate*) s'accumuler, s'amonceler. ◆**p.-up** *n Aut* collision *f* en chaîne, carambolage *m*.

pile² [paɪl] *n* (*of carpet*) poils *mpl*.

piles [paɪlz] *npl Med* hémorroïdes *fpl*.

pilfer ['pɪlfər] *vt* (*steal*) chaparder (**from s.o.** à qn). ◆**—ing** *n*, ◆**—age** *n* chapardage *m*.

pilgrim ['pɪlgrɪm] *n* pèlerin *m*. ◆**pilgrimage** *n* pèlerinage *m*.

pill [pɪl] *n* pilule *f*; **to be on the p.** (*of woman*) prendre la pilule; **to go on/off the p.** se mettre à/arrêter la pilule.

pillage ['pɪlɪdʒ] *vti* piller; – *n* pillage *m*.

pillar ['pɪlər] *n* pilier *m*; (*of smoke*) *Fig* colonne *f*. ◆**p.-box** *n* boîte *f* à *or* aux lettres (*située sur le trottoir*).

pillion ['pɪljən] *adv* **to ride p.** (*on motorbike*) monter derrière.

pillory ['pɪlərɪ] *vt* (*ridicule, scorn*) mettre au pilori.

pillow ['pɪləʊ] *n* oreiller *m*. ◆**pillowcase** *n*, ◆**pillowslip** *n* taie *f* d'oreiller.

pilot ['paɪlət] **1** *n* (*of aircraft, ship*) pilote *m*; – *vt* piloter; – *a* **p. light** (*on appliance*) voyant *m*. **2** *a* (*experimental*) (-)pilote; **p. scheme** projet(-)pilote *m*.

pimento [pɪ'mentəʊ] *n* (*pl* **-os**) piment *m*.

pimp [pɪmp] *n* souteneur *m*.

pimple ['pɪmp(ə)l] *n* bouton *m*. ◆**pimply** *a* (**-ier, iest**) boutonneux.

pin [pɪn] *n* épingle *f*; (*drawing pin*) punaise *f*; *Tech* goupille *f*, fiche *f*; **to have pins and needles** *Med Fam* avoir des fourmis (**in** dans); **p. money** argent *m* de poche; – *vt* (**-nn-**) **to p. (on)** (*attach*) épingler (**to** sur, à); (*to wall*) punaiser (**to, on** à); **to p. one's hopes on** mettre tous ses espoirs dans; **to p. on (to) s.o.** (*crime, action*) accuser qn de; **to p. down** (*immobilize*) immobiliser; (*fix*) fixer; (*enemy*) clouer; **to p. s.o. down** *Fig* forcer qn à préciser ses idées; **to p. up** (*notice*) afficher. ◆**pincushion** *n* pelote *f* (à épingles). ◆**pinhead** *n* tête *f* d'épingle.

pinafore ['pɪnəfɔːr] *n* (*apron*) tablier *m*; (*dress*) robe *f* chasuble.

pinball ['pɪnbɔːl] *a* **p. machine** flipper *m*.

pincers ['pɪnsəz] *npl* tenailles *fpl*.

pinch [pɪntʃ] **1** *n* (*mark*) pinçon *m*; (*of salt*) pincée *f*; **to give s.o. a p.** pincer qn; **at a p., Am in a p.** (*if necessary*) au besoin; **to feel the p.** *Fig* souffrir (*du manque d'argent etc*); – *vt* pincer; – *vi* (*of shoes*) faire mal. **2** *vt Fam* (*steal*) piquer (**from** à); (*arrest*) pincer.

pine [paɪn] **1** *n* (*tree, wood*) pin *m*; **p. forest** pinède *f*. **2** *vi* **to p. for** désirer vivement (retrouver), languir après; **to p. away** dépérir.

pineapple ['paɪnæp(ə)l] *n* ananas *m*.

ping [pɪŋ] *n* bruit *m* métallique. ◆**pinger** *n* (*on appliance*) signal *m* sonore.

ping-pong ['pɪŋpɒŋ] *n* ping-pong *m*.

pink [pɪŋk] *a* & *n* (*colour*) rose (*m*).

pinkie ['pɪŋkɪ] *n Am* petit doigt *m*.

pinnacle ['pɪnək(ə)l] *n* (*highest point*) *Fig* apogée *m*.

pinpoint ['pɪnpɔɪnt] *vt* (*locate*) repérer; (*define*) définir.

pinstripe ['pɪnstraɪp] *a* (*suit*) rayé.

pint [paɪnt] *n* pinte *f* (*Br* = *0,57 litre, Am* = *0,47 litre*); **a p. of beer** = un demi.

pinup ['pɪnʌp] *n* (*girl*) pin-up *f inv*.

pioneer [paɪə'nɪər] *n* pionnier, -ière *mf*; – *vt* (*research, study*) entreprendre pour la première fois.

pious ['paɪəs] *a* (*person, deed*) pieux.

pip [pɪp] **1** *n* (*of fruit*) pépin *m*. **2** *n* (*on uniform*) *Mil* galon *m*, sardine *f*. **3** *npl* **the pips** (*sound*) *Tel* le bip-bip.

pip/e [paɪp] **1** *n* tuyau *m*; (*of smoker*) pipe *f*; (*instrument*) *Mus* pipeau *m*; **the pipes** (*bagpipes*) *Mus* la cornemuse; **(peace) p.** calumet *m* de la paix; **to smoke a p.** fumer la pipe; **p. cleaner** cure-pipe *m*; **p. dream** chimère *f*; – *vt* (*water etc*) transporter par tuyaux *or* par canalisation; **piped music** musique *f* (de fond) enregistrée. **2** *vi* **to p. down** (*shut up*) *Fam* la boucler, se taire. ◆**—ing** *n* (*system of pipes*) canalisations *fpl*, tuyaux *mpl*; **length of p.** tuyau *m*; – *adv* **it's p. hot** (*soup etc*) c'est très chaud. ◆**pipeline** *n* pipeline *m*; **it's in the p.** *Fig* c'est en route.

pirate ['paɪərət] *n* pirate *m*; – *a* (*radio, ship*) pirate. ◆**piracy** *n* piraterie *f*. ◆**pirated** *a* (*book, record etc*) pirate.

Pisces ['paɪsiːz] *npl* (*sign*) les Poissons *mpl*.

pistachio [pɪ'stæʃɪəʊ] *n* (*pl* **-os**) (*fruit, flavour*) pistache *f*.

pistol ['pɪstəl] *n* pistolet *m*.

piston ['pɪst(ə)n] *n Aut* piston *m*.

pit [pɪt] **1** *n* (*hole*) trou *m*; (*mine*) mine *f*; (*quarry*) carrière *f*; (*of stomach*) creux *m*; *Th* orchestre *m*; *Sp Aut* stand *m* de ravitaillement. **2** *vt* (**-tt-**) **to p. oneself** *or* **one's wits against** se mesurer à. **3** *n* (*stone of fruit*) *Am* noyau *m*. ◆**pitted** *a* **1** (*face*) grêlé; **p. with rust** piqué de rouille. **2** (*fruit*) *Am* dénoyauté.

pitch[1] [pɪtʃ] **1** *n Sp* terrain *m*; (*in market*) place *f*. **2** *n* (*degree*) degré *m*; (*of voice*) hauteur *f*; *Mus* ton *m*. **3** *vt* (*ball*) lancer; (*camp*) établir; (*tent*) dresser; **a pitched battle** *Mil* une bataille rangée; *Fig* une belle bagarre. **4** *vi* (*of ship*) tanguer. **5** *vi* **to p. in** (*cooperate*) *Fam* se mettre de la partie; **to p. into s.o.** attaquer qn.

pitch[2] [pɪtʃ] *n* (*tar*) poix *f*. ◆**p.-'black** *a*, ◆**p.-'dark** *a* noir comme dans un four.

pitcher ['pɪtʃər] *n* cruche *f*, broc *m*.

pitchfork ['pɪtʃfɔːk] *n* fourche *f* (à foin).

pitfall ['pɪtfɔːl] *n* (*trap*) piège *m*.

pith [pɪθ] *n* (*of orange*) peau *f* blanche; (*essence*) *Fig* moelle *f*. ◆**pithy** *a* (**-ier, -iest**) (*remark etc*) piquant et concis.

pitiful ['pɪtɪfəl] *a* pitoyable. ◆**pitiless** *a* impitoyable.

pittance ['pɪtəns] *n* (*income*) revenu *m or* salaire *m* misérable; (*sum*) somme *f* dérisoire.

pitter-patter ['pɪtəpætər] *n* = **patter 1.**

pity [pɪtɪ] *n* pitié *f*; **(what) a p.!** (quel) dommage!; **it's a p.** c'est dommage (**that**

que (+ *sub*), **to do** de faire); **to have** *or* **take p.** on avoir pitié de; – *vt* plaindre.
pivot ['pɪvət] *n* pivot *m*; – *vi* pivoter.
pixie ['pɪksɪ] *n* (*fairy*) lutin *m*.
pizza ['piːtsə] *n* pizza *f*.
placard ['plækɑːd] *n* (*notice*) affiche *f*.
placate [plə'keɪt, *Am* 'pleɪkeɪt] *vt* calmer.
place [pleɪs] *n* endroit *m*; (*specific*) lieu *m*; (*house*) maison *f*; (*premises*) locaux *mpl*; (*seat, position, rank*) place *f*; **in the first p.** (*firstly*) en premier lieu; **to take p.** (*happen*) avoir lieu; **p. of work** lieu *m* de travail; **market p.** (*square*) place *f* du marché; **at my p., to my p.** *Fam* chez moi; **some p.** (*somewhere*) *Am* quelque part; **no p.** (*nowhere*) *Am* nulle part; **all over the p.** partout; **to lose one's p.** perdre sa place; (*in book etc*) perdre sa page; **p. setting** couvert *m*; **to lay three places** (*at the table*) mettre trois couverts; **to take the p. of** remplacer; **in p. of** à la place de; **out of p.** (*remark, object*) déplacé; (*person*) dépaysé; **p. mat** set *m* (de table); – *vt* (*put, situate, invest*) & *Sp* placer; (*an order*) *Com* passer (**with s.o.** à qn); (*remember*) se rappeler; (*identify*) reconnaître. ◆**placing** *n* (*of money*) placement *m*.
placid ['plæsɪd] *a* placide.
plagiarize ['pleɪdʒəraɪz] *vt* plagier. ◆**plagiarism** *n* plagiat *m*.
plague [pleɪg] **1** *n* (*disease*) peste *f*; (*nuisance*) *Fam* plaie *f*. **2** *vt* (*harass, pester*) harceler (**with** de).
plaice [pleɪs] *n* (*fish*) carrelet *m*, plie *f*.
plaid [plæd] *n* (*fabric*) tissu *m* écossais.
plain[1] [pleɪn] **1** *a* (**-er, -est**) (*clear, obvious*) clair; (*outspoken*) franc; (*simple*) simple; (*not patterned*) uni; (*woman, man*) sans beauté; (*sheer*) pur; **in p. clothes** en civil; **to make it p. to s.o. that** faire comprendre à qn que; **p. speaking** franc-parler *m*; – *adv* (*tired etc*) tout bonnement. ◆**—ly** *adv* clairement; franchement. ◆**—ness** *n* clarté *f*; simplicité *f*; manque *m* de beauté.
plain[2] [pleɪn] *n* *Geog* plaine *f*.
plaintiff ['pleɪntɪf] *n* *Jur* plaignant, -ante *mf*.
plait [plæt] *n* tresse *f*, natte *f*; – *vt* tresser, natter.
plan [plæn] *n* projet *m*; (*elaborate*) plan *m*; (*of house, book etc*) & *Pol Econ* plan *m*; **the best p. would be to...** le mieux serait de...; **according to p.** comme prévu; **to have no plans** (*be free*) n'avoir rien de prévu; **to change one's plans** (*decide differently*) changer d'idée; **master p.** stratégie *f* d'ensemble; – *vt* (**-nn-**) (*envisage, decide on*) prévoir, projeter; (*organize*) organiser; (*prepare*) préparer; (*design*) concevoir; *Econ* planifier; **to p. to do** (*intend*) avoir l'intention de faire; **as planned** comme prévu; – *vi* faire des projets; **to p. for** (*rain, disaster*) prévoir. ◆**planning** *n* *Econ* planification *f*; (*industrial, commercial*) planning *m*; **family p.** planning *m* familial; **town p.** urbanisme *m*. ◆**planner** *n* **town p.** urbaniste *mf*.
plane [pleɪn] *n* **1** (*aircraft*) avion *m*. **2** *Carp* rabot *m*. **3** (*tree*) platane *m*. **4** (*level*) & *Fig* plan *m*.
planet ['plænɪt] *n* planète *f*. ◆**plane'tarium** *n* planétarium *m*. ◆**planetary** *a* planétaire.
plank [plæŋk] *n* planche *f*.
plant [plɑːnt] **1** *n* plante *f*; **house p.** plante d'appartement; – *vt* planter (**with** en, de); (*bomb*) *Fig* (dé)poser; **to p. sth on s.o.** (*hide*) cacher qch sur qn. **2** *n* (*machinery*) matériel *m*; (*fixtures*) installation *f*; (*factory*) usine *f*. ◆**plan'tation** *n* (*land, trees etc*) plantation *f*.
plaque [plæk] *n* **1** (*commemorative plate*) plaque *f*. **2** (*on teeth*) plaque *f* dentaire.
plasma ['plæzmə] *n* *Med* plasma *m*.
plaster ['plɑːstər] *n* (*substance*) plâtre *m*; (**sticking**) **p.** sparadrap *m*; **p. of Paris** plâtre *m* à mouler; **in p.** *Med* dans le plâtre; **p. cast** *Med* plâtre *m*; – *vt* plâtrer; **to p. down** (*hair*) plaquer; **to p. with** (*cover*) couvrir de. ◆**—er** *n* plâtrier *m*.
plastic ['plæstɪk] *a* (*substance, art*) plastique; (*object*) en plastique; **p. explosive** plastic *m*; **p. surgery** chirurgie *f* esthétique; – *n* plastique *m*, matière *f* plastique.
plasticine® ['plæstɪsiːn] *n* pâte *f* à modeler.
plate [pleɪt] *n* (*dish*) assiette *f*; (*metal sheet on door, on vehicle etc*) plaque *f*; (*book illustration*) gravure *f*; (*dental*) dentier *m*; **gold/silver p.** vaisselle *f* d'or/d'argent; **a lot on one's p.** (*work*) *Fig* du pain sur la planche; **p. glass** verre *m* à vitre; – *vt* (*jewellery, metal*) plaquer (**with** de). ◆**plateful** *n* assiettée *f*, assiette *f*.
plateau ['plætəʊ] *n* *Geog* (*pl* **-s** *or* **-x**) plateau *m*.
platform ['plætfɔːm] *n* estrade *f*; (*for speaker*) tribune *f*; (*on bus*) & *Pol* plate-forme *f*; *Rail* quai *m*; **p. shoes** chaussures *fpl* à semelles compensées.
platinum ['plætɪnəm] *n* (*metal*) platine *m*; – *a* **p.** *or* **p.-blond(e) hair** cheveux *mpl* platinés.
platitude ['plætɪtjuːd] *n* platitude *f*.
platonic [plə'tɒnɪk] *a* (*love etc*) platonique.
platoon [plə'tuːn] *n* *Mil* section *f*.

platter ['plætər] *n Culin* plat *m*.

plaudits ['plɔːdɪts] *npl* applaudissements *mpl*.

plausible ['plɔːzəb(ə)l] *a* (*argument etc*) plausible; (*speaker etc*) convaincant.

play [pleɪ] *n* (*amusement, looseness*) jeu *m*; *Th* pièce *f* (de théâtre), spectacle *m*; **a p. on words** un jeu de mots; **to come into p.** entrer en jeu; **to call into p.** faire entrer en jeu; – *vt* (*card, part, tune etc*) jouer; (*game*) jouer à; (*instrument*) jouer de; (*match*) disputer (**with** avec); (*team, opponent*) jouer contre; (*record*) passer; (*radio*) faire marcher; **to p. ball with** *Fig* coopérer avec; **to p. the fool** faire l'idiot; **to p. a part in doing/in sth** contribuer à faire/à qch; **to p. it cool** *Fam* garder son sang-froid; **to p. back** (*tape*) réécouter; **to p. down** minimiser; **to p. s.o. up** *Fam* (*of bad back etc*) tracasser qn; (*of child etc*) faire enrager qn; **played out** *Fam* (*tired*) épuisé; (*idea, method*) périmé, vieux jeu *inv*; – *vi* jouer (**with** avec, **at** à); (*of record player, tape recorder*) marcher; **what are you playing at?** *Fam* qu'est-ce que tu fais?; **to p. about** *or* **around** jouer, s'amuser; **to p. on** (*piano etc*) jouer de; (*s.o.'s emotions etc*) jouer sur; **to p. up** (*of child, machine etc*) *Fam* faire des siennes; **to p. up to s.o.** faire de la lèche à qn. ◆**—ing** *n* jeu *m*; **p. card** carte *f* à jouer; **p. field** terrain *m* de jeu. ◆**—er** *n Sp* joueur, -euse *mf*; *Th* acteur *m*, actrice *f*; **clarinette/***etc* **p.** joueur, -euse *mf* de clarinette/*etc*; **cassette p.** lecteur *m* de cassettes.

play-act ['pleɪækt] *vi* jouer la comédie. ◆**playboy** *n* playboy *m*. ◆**playgoer** *n* amateur *m* de théâtre. ◆**playground** *n Sch* cour *f* de récréation. ◆**playgroup** *n* = **playschool**. ◆**playmate** *n* camarade *mf*. ◆**playpen** *n* parc *m* (pour enfants). ◆**playroom** *n* (*in house*) salle *f* de jeux. ◆**playschool** *n* garderie *f* (d'enfants). ◆**plaything** *n* (*person*) *Fig* jouet *m*. ◆**playtime** *n Sch* récréation *f*. ◆**playwright** *n* dramaturge *mf*.

playful ['pleɪfəl] *a* enjoué; (*child*) joueur. ◆**—ly** *adv* (*to say*) en badinant. ◆**—ness** *n* enjouement *m*.

plc [piːel'siː] *abbr* (*public limited company*) SA.

plea [pliː] *n* (*request*) appel *m*; (*excuse*) excuse *f*; **to make a p. of guilty** *Jur* plaider coupable. ◆**plead** *vi Jur* plaider; **to p. with s.o. to do** implorer qn de faire; **to p. for** (*help etc*) implorer; – *vt Jur* plaider; (*as excuse*) alléguer. ◆**pleading** *n* (*requests*) prières *fpl*.

pleasant ['plezənt] *a* agréable; (*polite*) aimable. ◆**—ly** *adv* agréablement. ◆**—ness** *n* (*charm*) charme *m*; (*of person*) amabilité *f*. ◆**pleasantries** *npl* (*jokes*) plaisanteries *fpl*; (*polite remarks*) civilités *fpl*.

pleas/e [pliːz] *adv* s'il vous plaît, s'il te plaît; **p. sit down** asseyez-vous, je vous prie; **p. do!** bien sûr!, je vous en prie!; **'no smoking p.'** 'prière de ne pas fumer'; – *vt* plaire à; (*satisfy*) contenter; **hard to p.** difficile (à contenter), exigeant; **p. yourself!** comme tu veux!; – *vi* plaire; **do as you p.** fais comme tu veux; **as much** *or* **as many as you p.** autant qu'il vous plaira. ◆**—ed** *a* content (**with** de, **that** que (+ *sub*), **to do** de faire); **p. to meet you!** enchanté!; **I'd be p. to!** avec plaisir! ◆**—ing** *a* agréable, plaisant.

pleasure ['pleʒər] *n* plaisir *m*; **p. boat** bateau *m* de plaisance. ◆**pleasurable** *a* très agréable.

pleat [pliːt] *n* (*fold*) pli *m*; – *vt* plisser.

plebiscite ['plebɪsɪt, -saɪt] *n* plébiscite *m*.

pledge [pledʒ] **1** *n* (*promise*) promesse *f*, engagement *m* (**to do** de faire); – *vt* promettre (**to do** de faire). **2** *n* (*token, object*) gage *m*; – *vt* (*pawn*) engager.

plenty ['plentɪ] *n* abondance *f*; **in p.** en abondance; **p. of** beaucoup de; **that's p.** (*enough*) c'est assez, ça suffit. ◆**plentiful** *a* abondant.

plethora ['pleθərə] *n* pléthore *f*.

pleurisy ['pluərɪsɪ] *n Med* pleurésie *f*.

pliable ['plaɪəb(ə)l] *a* souple.

pliers ['plaɪəz] *npl* (*tool*) pince(s) *f(pl)*.

plight [plaɪt] *n* (*crisis*) situation *f* critique; (**sorry**) **p.** triste situation *f*.

plimsoll ['plɪmsəul] *n* chaussure *f* de tennis, tennis *f*.

plinth [plɪnθ] *n* socle *m*.

plod [plɒd] *vi* (**-dd-**) **to p.** (**along**) avancer *or* travailler laborieusement; **to p. through** (*book*) lire laborieusement. ◆**plodding** *a* (*slow*) lent; (*step*) pesant. ◆**plodder** *n* (*steady worker*) bûcheur, -euse *mf*.

plonk [plɒŋk] **1** *int* (*splash*) plouf! **2** *vt* **to p.** (**down**) (*drop*) *Fam* poser (bruyamment). **3** *n* (*wine*) *Pej Sl* pinard *m*.

plot [plɒt] **1** *n* (*conspiracy*) complot *m* (**against** contre); *Cin Th Liter* intrigue *f*; – *vti* (**-tt-**) comploter (**to do** de faire). **2** *n* **p.** (**of land**) terrain *m*; (*patch in garden*) carré *m* de terre; **building p.** terrain *m* à bâtir. **3** *vt* (**-tt-**) **to p.** (**out**) déterminer; (*graph, diagram*) tracer; (*one's position*) relever. ◆**plotting** *n* (*conspiracies*) complots *mpl*.

plough [plau] *n* charrue *f*; – *vt* labourer; to

p. back into (*money*) *Fig* réinvestir dans; – *vi* labourer; **to p. into** (*crash into*) percuter; **to p. through** (*snow etc*) avancer péniblement dans; (*fence, wall*) défoncer. ◆**ploughman** *n* (*pl* **-men**) laboureur *m*; **p.'s lunch** *Culin* assiette *f* composée (*de crudités et fromage*).

plow [plaʊ] *Am* = **plough.**

ploy [plɔɪ] *n* stratagème *m*.

pluck [plʌk] **1** *n* courage *m*; – *vt* **to p. up courage** s'armer de courage. **2** *vt* (*fowl*) plumer; (*eyebrows*) épiler; (*string*) *Mus* pincer; (*flower*) cueillir. ◆**plucky** *a* (**-ier, -iest**) courageux.

plug [plʌg] **1** *n* (*of cotton wool, wood etc*) tampon *m*, bouchon *m*; (*for sink etc drainage*) bonde *f*; – *vt* (**-gg-**) **to p. (up)** (*stop up*) boucher. **2** *n El* fiche *f*, prise *f* (mâle); – *vt* (**-gg-**) **to p. in** brancher. **3** *n Aut* bougie *f*. **4** *n* (*publicity*) *Fam* battage *m* publicitaire; – *vt* (**-gg-**) *Fam* faire du battage publicitaire pour. **5** *vi* (**-gg-**) **to p. away** (*work*) *Fam* bosser (**at** à). ◆**plughole** *n* trou *m* (du lavabo *etc*), vidange *f*.

plum [plʌm] *n* prune *f*; **a p. job** *Fam* un travail en or, un bon fromage.

plumage ['pluːmɪdʒ] *n* plumage *m*.

plumb [plʌm] **1** *vt* (*probe, understand*) sonder. **2** *adv* (*crazy etc*) *Am Fam* complètement; **p. in the middle** en plein milieu.

plumber ['plʌmər] *n* plombier *m*. ◆**plumbing** *n* plomberie *f*.

plume [pluːm] *n* (*feather*) plume *f*; (*on hat etc*) plumet *m*; **a p. of smoke** un panache de fumée.

plummet ['plʌmɪt] *vi* (*of aircraft etc*) plonger; (*of prices*) dégringoler.

plump [plʌmp] **1** *a* (**-er, -est**) (*person*) grassouillet; (*arm, chicken*) dodu; (*cushion, cheek*) rebondi. **2** *vi* **to p. for** (*choose*) se décider pour, choisir. ◆**—ness** *n* rondeur *f*.

plunder ['plʌndər] *vt* piller; – *n* (*act*) pillage *m*; (*goods*) butin *m*.

plung/e [plʌndʒ] *vt* (*thrust*) plonger (**into** dans); – *vi* (*dive*) plonger (**into** dans); (*fall*) tomber (**from** de); (*rush*) se lancer; – *n* (*dive*) plongeon *m*; (*fall*) chute *f*; **to take the p.** *Fig* se jeter à l'eau. ◆**—ing** *a* (*neckline*) plongeant. ◆**—er** *n* ventouse *f* (*pour déboucher un tuyau*), déboucheur *m*.

plural ['plʊərəl] *a* (*form*) pluriel; (*noun*) au pluriel; – *n* pluriel *m*; **in the p.** au pluriel.

plus [plʌs] *prep* plus; – *a* (*factor etc*) & *El* positif; **twenty p.** vingt et quelques; – *n* **p.** (*sign*) *Math* (signe *m*) plus *m*; **it's a p.** c'est un (avantage en) plus.

plush [plʌʃ] *a* (**-er, -est**) (*splendid*) somptueux.

plutonium [pluː'təʊnɪəm] *n* plutonium *m*.

ply [plaɪ] **1** *vt* (*trade*) exercer; (*oar, tool*) *Lit* manier. **2** *vi* **to p. between** (*travel*) faire la navette entre. **3** *vt* **to p. s.o. with** (*whisky etc*) faire boire continuellement à qn; (*questions*) bombarder qn de.

p.m. [piː'em] *adv* (*afternoon*) de l'après-midi; (*evening*) du soir.

PM [piː'em] *n abbr* (*Prime Minister*) Premier ministre *m*.

pneumatic [njuː'mætɪk] *a* **p. drill** marteau-piqueur *m*, marteau *m* pneumatique.

pneumonia [njuː'məʊnɪə] *n* pneumonie *f*.

poach [pəʊtʃ] **1** *vt* (*egg*) pocher. **2** *vi* (*hunt, steal*) braconner; – *vt* (*employee from rival firm*) débaucher, piquer. ◆**—ing** *n* braconnage *m*. ◆**—er** *n* **1** (*person*) braconnier *m*. **2** (**egg**) **p.** pocheuse *f*.

PO Box [piːəʊ'bɒks] *abbr* (*Post Office Box*) BP.

pocket ['pɒkɪt] *n* poche *f*; (*area*) *Fig* petite zone *f*; (*of resistance*) poche *f*, îlot *m*; **I'm $5 out of p.** j'ai perdu 5 dollars; – *a* (*money, book etc*) de poche; – *vt* (*gain, steal*) empocher. ◆**pocketbook** *n* (*notebook*) carnet *m*; (*woman's handbag*) *Am* sac *m* à main. ◆**pocketful** *n* **a p. of** une pleine poche de.

pockmarked ['pɒkmɑːkt] *a* (*face*) grêlé.

pod [pɒd] *n* cosse *f*.

podgy ['pɒdʒɪ] *a* (**-ier, -iest**) (*arm etc*) dodu; (*person*) rondelet.

podium ['pəʊdɪəm] *n* podium *m*.

poem ['pəʊɪm] *n* poème *m*. ◆**poet** *n* poète *m*. ◆**po'etic** *a* poétique. ◆**poetry** *n* poésie *f*.

poignant ['pɔɪnjənt] *a* poignant.

point [pɔɪnt] **1** *n* (*of knife etc*) pointe *f*; *pl Rail* aiguillage *m*; (**power**) **p.** *El* prise *f* (de courant). **2** *n* (*dot, position, question, degree, score etc*) point *m*; (*decimal*) virgule *f*; (*meaning*) *Fig* sens *m*; (*importance*) intérêt *m*; (*remark*) remarque *f*; **p. of view** point *m* de vue; **at this p. in time** en ce moment; **on the p. of doing** sur le point de faire; **what's the p.?** à quoi bon? (**of waiting/***etc* attendre/*etc*); **there's no p. (in) staying/***etc* ça ne sert à rien de rester/*etc*; **that's not the p.** il ne s'agit pas de ça; **it's beside the p.** c'est à côté de la question; **to the p.** (*relevant*) pertinent; **get to the p.!** au fait!; **to make a p. of doing** prendre garde de faire; **his good**

points ses qualités *fpl*; **his bad points** ses défauts *mpl*. **3** *vt* (*aim*) pointer (**at** sur); (*vehicle*) tourner (**towards** vers); **to p. the way** indiquer le chemin (**to** à); *Fig* montrer la voie (**to** à); **to p. one's finger at** indiquer du doit, pointer son doigt vers; **to p. out** (*show*) indiquer; (*mention*) signaler (**that** que); – *vi* **to p.** (**at** *or* **to s.o.**) indiquer (qn) du doigt; **to p. to, be pointing to** (*show*) indiquer; **to p. east** indiquer l'est; **to be pointing** (*of vehicle*) être tourné (**towards** vers); (*of gun*) être braqué (**at** sur). ◆**—ed** *a* pointu; (*beard*) en pointe; (*remark, criticism*) *Fig* pertinent; (*incisive*) mordant. ◆**—edly** *adv* (*to the point*) avec pertinence; (*incisively*) d'un ton mordant. ◆**—er** *n* (*on dial etc*) index *m*; (*advice*) conseil *m*; (*clue*) indice *m*; **to be a p. to** (*possible solution etc*) laisser entrevoir. ◆**—less** *a* inutile, futile. ◆**—lessly** *adv* inutilement.

point-blank [pɔɪnt'blæŋk] *adv & a* (*to shoot, a shot*) à bout portant; (*to refuse, a refusal*) *Fig* (tout) net; (*to request, a request*) de but en blanc.

pois/e [pɔɪz] *n* (*balance*) équilibre *m*; (*of body*) port *m*; (*grace*) grâce *f*; (*confidence*) assurance *f*, calme *m*; – *vt* tenir en équilibre. ◆**—ed** *a* en équilibre; (*hanging*) suspendu; (*composed*) calme; **p. to attack**/*etc* (*ready*) prêt à attaquer/*etc*.

poison ['pɔɪz(ə)n] *n* poison *m*; (*of snake*) venin *m*; **p. gas** gaz *m* toxique; – *vt* empoisonner; **to p. s.o.'s mind** corrompre qn. ◆**poisoning** *n* empoisonnement *m*. ◆**poisonous** *a* (*fumes, substance*) toxique; (*snake*) venimeux; (*plant*) vénéneux.

pok/e [pəʊk] *vt* (*push*) pousser (*avec un bâton etc*); (*touch*) toucher; (*fire*) tisonner; **to p. sth into** (*put, thrust*) fourrer *or* enfoncer qch dans; **to p. one's finger at** pointer son doigt vers; **to p. one's nose into** fourrer le nez dans; **to p. a hole in** faire un trou dans; **to p. one's head out of the window** passer la tête par la fenêtre; **to p. out s.o.'s eye** crever un œil à qn; – *vi* pousser; **to p. about** *or* **around in** fouiner dans; – *n* (*jab*) (petit) coup *m*; (*shove*) poussée *f*, coup *m*. ◆**—er** *n* **1** (*for fire*) tisonnier *m*. **2** *Cards* poker *m*.

poky ['pəʊkɪ] *a* (**-ier, -iest**) (*small*) exigu et misérable, rikiki; (*slow*) *Am* lent.

Poland ['pəʊlənd] *n* Pologne *f*. ◆**Pole** *n* Polonais, -aise *mf*.

polarize ['pəʊləraɪz] *vt* polariser.

pole [pəʊl] *n* **1** (*rod*) perche *f*; (*fixed*) poteau *m*; (*for flag*) mât *m*. **2** *Geog* pôle *m*; **North/South P.** pôle Nord/Sud. ◆**polar** *a* polaire; **p. bear** ours *m* blanc.

polemic [pə'lemɪk] *n* polémique *f*. ◆**polemical** *a* polémique.

police [pə'liːs] *n* police *f*; **more** *or* **extra p.** des renforts *mpl* de police; – *a* (*inquiry etc*) de la police; (*state, dog*) policier; **p. cadet** agent *m* de police stagiaire; **p. car** voiture *f* de police; **p. force** police *f*; – *vt* (*city etc*) maintenir l'ordre *or* la paix dans; (*frontier*) contrôler. ◆**policeman** *n* (*pl* **-men**) agent *m* de police. ◆**policewoman** *n* (*pl* **-women**) femme-agent *f*.

policy ['pɒlɪsɪ] *n* **1** *Pol Econ etc* politique *f*; (*individual course of action*) règle *f*, façon *f* d'agir; *pl* (*ways of governing*) *Pol* politique *f*; **matter of p.** question *f* de principe. **2** (**insurance**) **p.** police *f* (d'assurance); **p. holder** assuré, -ée *mf*.

polio(myelitis) ['pəʊlɪəʊ(maɪə'laɪtɪs)] *n* polio(myélite) *f*; **p. victim** polio *mf*.

polish ['pɒlɪʃ] *vt* (*floor, table, shoes etc*) cirer; (*metal*) astiquer; (*rough surface*) polir; (*manners*) *Fig* raffiner; (*style*) *Fig* polir; **to p. up** (*one's French etc*) travailler; **to p. off** (*food, work etc*) *Fam* liquider, finir (en vitesse); – *n* (*for shoes*) cirage *m*; (*for floor, furniture*) cire *f*; (*shine*) vernis *m*; *Fig* raffinement *m*; (**nail**) **p.** vernis *m* (à ongles); **to give sth a p.** faire briller qch.

Polish ['pəʊlɪʃ] *a* polonais; – *n* (*language*) polonais *m*.

polite [pə'laɪt] *a* (**-er, -est**) poli (**to, with** avec); **in p. society** dans la bonne société. ◆**—ly** *adv* poliment. ◆**—ness** *n* politesse *f*.

political [pə'lɪtɪk(ə)l] *a* politique. ◆**poli'tician** *n* homme *m or* femme *f* politique. ◆**politicize** *vt* politiser. ◆**'politics** *n* politique *f*.

polka ['pɒlkə, *Am* 'pəʊlkə] *n* (*dance*) polka *f*; **p. dot** pois *m*.

poll [pəʊl] *n* (*voting*) scrutin *m*, élection *f*; (*vote*) vote *m*; (*turnout*) participation *f* électorale; (*list*) liste *f* électorale; **to go to the polls** aller aux urnes; (**opinion**) **p.** sondage *m* (d'opinion); **50% of the p.** 50% des votants; – *vt* (*votes*) obtenir; (*people*) sonder l'opinion de. ◆**—ing** *n* (*election*) élections *fpl*; **p. booth** isoloir *m*; **p. station** bureau *m* de vote.

pollen ['pɒlən] *n* pollen *m*.

pollute [pə'luːt] *vt* polluer. ◆**pollutant** *n* polluant *m*. ◆**pollution** *n* pollution *f*.

polo ['pəʊləʊ] *n Sp* polo *m*; **p. neck** (*sweater, neckline*) col *m* roulé.

polyester [pɒlɪ'estər] *n* polyester *m*.

Polynesia [pɒlɪ'niːʒə] *n* Polynésie *f*.
polytechnic [pɒlɪ'teknɪk] *n* institut *m* universitaire de technologie.
polythene ['pɒlɪθiːn] *n* polyéthylène *m*; **p. bag** sac *m* en plastique.
pomegranate ['pɒmɪgrænɪt] *n* (*fruit*) grenade *f*.
pomp [pɒmp] *n* pompe *f*. ◆**pom'posity** *n* emphase *f*, solennité *f*. ◆**pompous** *a* pompeux.
pompon ['pɒmpɒn] *n* (*ornament*) pompon *m*.
pond [pɒnd] *n* étang *m*; (*stagnant*) mare *f*:(*artificial*) bassin *m*.
ponder ['pɒndər] *vt* **to p. (over)** réfléchir à; – *vi* réfléchir.
ponderous ['pɒndərəs] *a* (*heavy, slow*) pesant.
pong [pɒŋ] *n Sl* mauvaise odeur *f*; – *vi* (*stink*) *Sl* schlinguer.
pontificate [pɒn'tɪfɪkeɪt] *vi* (*speak*) *Pej* pontifier (**about** sur).
pony ['pəʊnɪ] *n* poney *m*. ◆**ponytail** *n* (*hair*) queue *f* de cheval.
poodle ['puːd(ə)l] *n* caniche *m*.
poof [puf] *n* (*homosexual*) *Pej Sl* pédé *m*.
pooh! [puː] *int* bah!; (*bad smell*) ça pue!
pooh-pooh [puː'puː] *vt* (*scorn*) dédaigner; (*dismiss*) se moquer de.
pool [puːl] **1** *n* (*puddle*) flaque *f*; (*of blood*) mare *f*; (*pond*) étang *m*; (*for swimming*) piscine *f*. **2** *n* (*of experience, talent*) réservoir *m*; (*of advisers etc*) équipe *f*; (*of typists*) *Com* pool *m*; (*kitty*) cagnotte *f*; (**football**) **pools** prognostics *mpl* (*sur les matchs de football*); – *vt* (*share*) mettre en commun; (*combine*) unir. **3** *n Sp* billard *m* américain.
pooped [puːpt] *a* (*exhausted*) *Am Fam* vanné, crevé.
poor [pʊər] *a* (**-er, -est**) (*not rich, deserving pity*) pauvre; (*bad*) mauvais; (*inferior*) médiocre; (*meagre*) maigre; (*weak*) faible; **p. thing!** le *or* la pauvre!; – *n* **the p.** les pauvres *mpl*. ◆**—ly 1** *adv* (*badly*) mal; (*clothed, furnished*) pauvrement. **2** *a* (*ill*) malade.
pop[1] [pɒp] **1** *int* pan! – *n* (*noise*) bruit *m* sec; **to go p.** faire pan; (*of champagne bottle*) faire pop; – *vt* (**-pp-**) (*balloon etc*) crever; (*bottle top, button*) faire sauter; – *vi* (*burst*) crever; (*come off*) sauter; (*of ears*) se déboucher. **2** *vt* (*put*) *Fam* mettre; – *vi Fam* **to p. in** (*go in*) entrer (en passant); **to p. off** (*leave*) partir; **to p. out** sortir (un instant); **to p. over** *or* **round** faire un saut (**to** chez); **to p. up** (*of person*) surgir, réapparaître; (*of question etc*) surgir. ◆**p.-'eyed** *a* aux yeux exorbités. ◆**p.-up book** *n* livre *m* en relief.
pop[2] [pɒp] **1** *n* (*music*) pop *m*; – *a* (*concert, singer etc*) pop *inv*. **2** *n* (*father*) *Am Fam* papa *m*. **3** *n* (**soda**) **p.** (*drink*) *Am* soda *m*.
popcorn ['pɒpkɔːn] *n* pop-corn *m*.
pope [pəʊp] *n* pape *m*; **p.'s nose** (*of chicken*) croupion *m*.
poplar ['pɒplər] *n* (*tree, wood*) peuplier *m*.
poppy ['pɒpɪ] *n* (*cultivated*) pavot *m*; (*red, wild*) coquelicot *m*.
poppycock ['pɒpɪkɒk] *n Fam* fadaises *fpl*.
popsicle® ['pɒpsɪk(ə)l] *n* (*ice lolly*) *Am* esquimau *m*.
popular ['pɒpjʊlər] *a* (*person, song, vote, science etc*) populaire; (*fashionable*) à la mode; **to be p. with** plaire beaucoup à. ◆**popu'larity** *n* popularité *f* (**with** auprès de). ◆**popularize** *vt* populariser; (*science, knowledge*) vulgariser. ◆**popularly** *adv* communément.
populat/e ['pɒpjʊleɪt] *vt* peupler. ◆**—ed** *a* peuplé (**with** de). ◆**popu'lation** *n* population *f*. ◆**populous** *a* (*crowded*) populeux.
porcelain ['pɔːsəlɪn] *n* porcelaine *f*.
porch [pɔːtʃ] *n* porche *m*; (*veranda*) *Am* véranda *f*.
porcupine ['pɔːkjʊpaɪn] *n* (*animal*) porc-épic *m*.
pore [pɔːr] **1** *n* (*of skin*) pore *m*. **2** *vi* **to p. over** (*book, question etc*) étudier de près. ◆**porous** *a* poreux.
pork [pɔːk] *n* (*meat*) porc *m*; **p. butcher** charcutier, -ière *mf*.
pornography [pɔː'nɒgrəfɪ] *n* (*Fam* **porn**) pornographie *f*. ◆**porno'graphic** *a* pornographique, porno (*f inv*).
porpoise ['pɔːpəs] *n* (*sea animal*) marsouin *m*.
porridge ['pɒrɪdʒ] *n* porridge *m*; **p. oats** flocons *mpl* d'avoine.
port [pɔːt] **1** *n* (*harbour*) port *m*; **p. of call** escale *f*; – *a* (*authorities, installations etc*) portuaire. **2** *n* **p. (side)** (*left*) *Nau Av* bâbord *m*; – *a* de bâbord. **3** *n* (*wine*) porto *m*.
portable ['pɔːtəb(ə)l] *a* portatif, portable.
portal ['pɔːt(ə)l] *n* portail *m*.
porter ['pɔːtər] *n* (*for luggage*) porteur *m*; (*doorman*) portier *m*; (*caretaker*) concierge *m*, (*of public building*) gardien, -ienne *mf*.
portfolio [pɔːt'fəʊlɪəʊ] *n* (*pl* **-os**) *Com Pol* portefeuille *m*.
porthole ['pɔːthəʊl] *n Nau Av* hublot *m*.
portico ['pɔːtɪkəʊ] *n* (*pl* **-oes** *or* **-os**) *Archit* portique *m*; (*of house*) porche *m*.
portion ['pɔːʃ(ə)n] *n* (*share, helping*) portion

f; (*of train, book etc*) partie *f*; – *vt* **to p. out** répartir.

portly ['pɔːtlɪ] *a* (**-ier, -iest**) corpulent.

portrait ['pɔːtrɪt, 'pɔːtreɪt] *n* portrait *m*; **p. painter** portraitiste *mf*.

portray [pɔː'treɪ] *vt* (*describe*) représenter. ◆**portrayal** *n* portrait *m*, représentation *f*.

Portugal ['pɔːtjʊg(ə)l] *n* Portugal. ◆**Portu'guese** *a* & *n inv* portugais, -aise (*mf*); – *n* (*language*) portugais *m*.

pose [pəʊz] **1** *n* (*in art or photography*) & *Fig* pose *f*; – *vi* (*of model etc*) poser (**for** pour); **to p. as a lawyer/etc** se faire passer pour un avocat/*etc*. **2** *vt* (*question*) poser. ◆**poser** *n* **1** (*question*) *Fam* colle *f*. **2** = **poseur**. ◆**poseur** [-'zɜːr] *n Pej* poseur, -euse *mf*.

posh [pɒʃ] *a Pej Fam* (*smart*) chic *inv*; (*snobbish*) snob (*f inv*).

position [pə'zɪʃ(ə)n] *n* (*place, posture, opinion etc*) position *f*; (*of building, town*) emplacement *m*, position *f*; (*job, circumstances*) situation *f*; (*customer window in bank etc*) guichet *m*; **in a p. to do** en mesure *or* en position de faire; **in a good p. to do** bien placé pour faire; **in p.** en place, en position; – *vt* (*camera, machine etc*) mettre en position; (*put*) placer.

positive ['pɒzɪtɪv] *a* positif; (*order*) catégorique; (*progress, change*) réel; (*tone*) assuré; (*sure*) sûr, certain (**of** de, **that** que); **a p. genius** *Fam* un vrai génie. ◆**—ly** *adv* (*for certain*) & *El* positivement; (*undeniably*) indéniablement; (*completely*) complètement; (*categorically*) catégoriquement.

possess [pə'zes] *vt* posséder. ◆**possession** *n* possession *f*; **in p. of** en possession de; **to take p. of** prendre possession de. ◆**possessive** *a* (*adjective, person etc*) possessif; – *n Gram* possessif *m*. ◆**possessor** *n* possesseur *m*.

possible ['pɒsəb(ə)l] *a* possible (**to do** à faire); **it is p. (for us) to do it** il (nous) est possible de le faire; **it is p. that** il est possible que (+ *sub*); **as far as p.** dans la mesure du possible; **if p.** si possible; **as much** *or* **as many as p.** autant que possible; – *n* (*person, object*) *Fam* choix *m* possible. ◆**possi'bility** *n* possibilité; **some p. of** quelques chances *fpl* de; **there's some p. that** il est (tout juste) possible que (+ *sub*); **she has possibilities** elle promet; **it's a distinct p.** c'est bien possible. ◆**possibly** *adv* **1** (*with can, could etc*) **if you p. can** si cela t'est possible; **to do all one p. can** faire tout son possible (**to do** pour faire); **he cannot p. stay** il ne peut absolument pas rester. **2** (*perhaps*) peut-être.

post[1] [pəʊst] *n* (*postal system*) poste *f*; (*letters*) courrier *m*; **by p.** par la poste; **to catch/miss the p.** avoir/manquer la levée; – *a* (*bag, code etc*) postal; **p. office** (bureau *m* de) poste *f*; **P. Office** (*administration*) (service *m* des) postes *fpl*; – *vt* (*put in postbox*) poster, mettre à la poste; (*send*) envoyer; **to keep s.o. posted** *Fig* tenir qn au courant. ◆**postage** *n* tarif *m* (postal), tarifs *mpl* (postaux) (**to** pour); **p. stamp** timbre-poste *m*. ◆**postal** *a* (*district etc*) postal; (*inquiries*) par la poste; (*clerk*) des postes; (*vote*) par correspondance. ◆**postbox** *n* boîte *f* à *or* aux lettres. ◆**postcard** *n* carte *f* postale. ◆**postcode** *n* code *m* postal. ◆**post-'free** *adv*, ◆**post'paid** *adv* franco.

post[2] [pəʊst] *n* (*job, place*) & *Mil* poste *m*; – *vt* (*sentry, guard*) poster; (*employee*) affecter (**to** à). ◆**—ing** *n* (*appointment*) affectation *f*.

post[3] [pəʊst] *n* (*pole*) poteau *m*; (*of bed, door*) montant *m*; **finishing** *or* **winning p.** *Sp* poteau *m* d'arrivée; – *vt* **to p. (up)** (*notice etc*) afficher.

post- [pəʊst] *pref* post-; **p.-1800** après 1800.

postdate [pəʊst'deɪt] *vt* postdater.

poster ['pəʊstər] *n* affiche *f*; (*for decoration*) poster *m*.

posterior [pɒ'stɪərɪər] *n* (*buttocks*) *Hum* postérieur *m*.

posterity [pɒ'sterɪtɪ] *n* postérité *f*.

postgraduate [pəʊst'grædʒʊət] *a* (*studies etc*) *Univ* de troisième cycle; – *n* étudiant, -ante *mf* de troisième cycle.

posthumous ['pɒstjʊməs] *a* posthume. ◆**—ly** *adv* à titre posthume.

postman ['pəʊstmən] *n* (*pl* **-men**) facteur *m*. ◆**postmark** *n* cachet *m* de la poste; – *vt* oblitérer. ◆**postmaster** *n* receveur *m* (des postes).

post-mortem [pəʊst'mɔːtəm] *n* **p.-mortem (examination)** autopsie *f* (**on** de).

postpone [pəʊ'spəʊn] *vt* remettre (**for** de), renvoyer (à plus tard). ◆**—ment** *n* remise *f*, renvoi *m*.

postscript ['pəʊstskrɪpt] *n* post-scriptum *m inv*.

postulate ['pɒstjʊleɪt] *vt* postuler.

posture ['pɒstʃər] *n* posture *f*; *Fig* attitude *f*; – *vi* (*for effect*) *Pej* poser.

postwar ['pəʊstwɔːr] *a* d'après-guerre.

posy ['pəʊzɪ] *n* petit bouquet *m* (de fleurs).

pot [pɒt] **1** *n* pot *m*; (*for cooking*) marmite *f*; **pots and pans** casseroles *fpl*; **jam p.** pot *m* à confiture; **to take p. luck** tenter sa chance; (*with food*) manger à la fortune du pot; **to go to p.** *Fam* aller à la ruine; **gone to p.** (*person, plans etc*) *Fam* fichu; – *vt* (**-tt-**) mettre en pot. **2** *n* (*marijuana*) *Sl* marie-jeanne *f*; (*hashish*) *Sl* haschisch *m*. ◆**potted** *a* **1** (*plant*) en pot; (*jam, meat*) en bocaux. **2** (*version etc*) abrégé, condensé.

potato [pə'teɪtəʊ] *n* (*pl* **-oes**) pomme *f* de terre; **p. peeler** (*knife*) couteau *m* à éplucher, éplucheur *m*; **p. crisps,** *Am* **p. chips** pommes *fpl* chips.

potbelly ['pɒtbelɪ] *n* bedaine *f*. ◆**potbellied** *a* ventru.

potent ['pəʊtənt] *a* puissant; (*drink*) fort; (*man*) viril. ◆**potency** *n* puissance *f*; (*of man*) virilité *f*.

potential [pə'tenʃ(ə)l] *a* (*danger, resources*) potentiel; (*client, sales*) éventuel; (*leader, hero etc*) en puissance; – *n* potentiel *m*; *Fig* (perspectives *fpl* d')avenir *m*; **to have p.** avoir de l'avenir. ◆**potenti'ality** *n* potentialité *f*; *pl Fig* (perspectives *fpl* d')avenir *m*. ◆**potentially** *adv* potentiellement.

pothole ['pɒthəʊl] *n* (*in road*) nid *m* de poules; (*in rock*) gouffre *m*; (*cave*) caverne *f*. ◆**potholing** *n* spéléologie *f*.

potion ['pəʊʃ(ə)n] *n* breuvage *m* magique; *Med* potion *f*.

potshot ['pɒtʃɒt] *n* **to take a p.** faire un carton (**at** sur).

potter ['pɒtər] **1** *n* (*person*) potier *m*. **2** *vi* **to p. (about)** bricoler. ◆**pottery** *n* (*art*) poterie *f*; (*objects*) poteries *fpl*; **a piece of p.** une poterie.

potty ['pɒtɪ] *a* **1** (**-ier, -iest**) (*mad*) *Fam* toqué. **2** *n* pot *m* (de bébé).

pouch [paʊtʃ] *n* petit sac *m*; (*of kangaroo, under eyes*) poche *f*; (*for tobacco*) blague *f*.

pouf(fe) [puːf] *n* (*seat*) pouf *m*.

poultice ['pəʊltɪs] *n Med* cataplasme *m*.

poultry ['pəʊltrɪ] *n* volaille *f*. ◆**poulterer** *n* volailler *m*.

pounce [paʊns] *vi* (*leap*) bondir, sauter (**on** sur); **to p. on** (*idea*) *Fig* sauter sur; – *n* bond *m*.

pound [paʊnd] **1** *n* (*weight*) livre *f* (= *453,6 grammes*); **p. (sterling)** livre *f* (sterling). **2** *n* (*for cars, dogs*) fourrière *f*. **3** *vt* (*spices, nuts etc*) piler; (*meat*) attendrir; (*bombard*) *Mil* pilonner; **to p. (on)** (*thump*) *Fig* taper sur, marteler; (*of sea*) battre; – *vi* (*of heart*) battre à tout rompre; (*walk heavily*) marcher à pas pesants.

pour [pɔːr] *vt* (*liquid*) verser; (*wax*) couler; **to p. money into** investir beaucoup d'argent dans; **to p. away** *or* **off** (*empty*) vider; **to p. out** verser; (*empty*) vider; (*feelings*) épancher (**to** devant); – *vi* **to p. (out)** (*of liquid*) couler *or* sortir à flots; **to p. in** (*of liquid, sunshine*) entrer à flots; (*of people, money*) *Fig* affluer; **to p. out** (*of people*) sortir en masse (**from** de); (*of smoke*) s'échapper (**from** de); **it's pouring (down)** il pleut à verse; **pouring rain** pluie *f* torrentielle.

pout [paʊt] *vti* **to p. (one's lips)** faire la moue; – *n* moue *f*.

poverty ['pɒvətɪ] *n* pauvreté *f*; **(grinding** *or* **extreme) p.** misère *f*. ◆**p.-stricken** *a* (*person*) indigent; (*conditions*) misérable.

powder ['paʊdər] *n* poudre *f*; **p. keg** (*place*) *Fig* poudrière *f*; **p. puff** houppette *f*; **p. room** toilettes *fpl* (*pour dames*); – *vt* (*hair, skin*) poudrer; **to p. one's face** *or* **nose** se poudrer. ◆**—ed** *a* (*milk, eggs*) en poudre. ◆**powdery** *a* (*snow*) poudreux; (*face*) couvert de poudre.

power ['paʊər] *n* (*ability, authority*) pouvoir *m*; (*strength, nation*) & *Math Tech* puissance *f*; (*energy*) *Phys Tech* énergie *f*; (*current*) *El* courant *m*; **he's a p. within the firm** c'est un homme de poids au sein de l'entreprise; **in p.** *Pol* au pouvoir; **in one's p.** en son pouvoir; **the p. of speech** la faculté de la parole; **p. cut** coupure *f* de courant; **p. station,** *Am* **p. plant** *El* centrale *f* (électrique); – *vt* **to be powered by** être actionné *or* propulsé par; (*gas, oil etc*) fonctionnant à. ◆**powerful** *a* puissant. ◆**powerfully** *adv* puissamment. ◆**powerless** *a* impuissant (**to do** à faire).

practicable ['præktɪkəb(ə)l] *a* (*project, road etc*) praticable.

practical ['præktɪk(ə)l] *a* (*knowledge, person, tool etc*) pratique; **p. joke** farce *f*. ◆**practi'cality** *n* (*of scheme etc*) aspect *m* pratique; (*of person*) sens *m* pratique; (*detail*) détail *m* pratique.

practically ['præktɪk(ə)lɪ] *adv* (*almost*) pratiquement.

practice ['præktɪs] *n* (*exercise, proceeding*) pratique *f*; (*habit*) habitude *f*; *Sp* entraînement *m*; (*rehearsal*) répétition *f*; (*of profession*) exercice *m* (**of** de); (*clients*) clientèle *f*; **to put into p.** mettre en pratique; **in p.** (*in reality*) en pratique; **to be in p.** (*have skill etc*) être en forme; (*of doctor, lawyer*) exercer; **to be in general p.** (*of doctor*) faire de la médecine générale; **to be out of p.** avoir perdu la pratique. ◆**practis/e** *vt* (*put into practice*) pratiquer; (*medicine, law etc*) exercer; (*flute,* *piano etc*) s'exercer à; (*language*) (s'exercer à) parler (**on** avec); (*work at*) travailler; (*do*) faire; – *vi Mus Sp* s'exercer; (*of doctor, lawyer*) exercer; – *n Am* = **practice.** ◆**—ed** *a* (*experienced*) chevronné; (*ear, eye*) exercé. ◆**—ing** *a Rel* pratiquant; (*doctor, lawyer*) exerçant.

practitioner [præk'tɪʃ(ə)nər] *n* praticien, -ienne *mf*; **general p.** (médecin *m*) généraliste *m*.

pragmatic [præg'mætɪk] *a* pragmatique.

prairie(s) ['preərɪ(z)] *n*(*pl*) (*in North America*) Prairies *fpl*.

praise [preɪz] *vt* louer (**for sth** de qch); **to p. s.o. for doing** *or* **having done** louer qn d'avoir fait; – *n* louange(s) *f*(*pl*), éloge(s) *m*(*pl*); **in p. of** à la louange de. ◆**praiseworthy** *a* digne d'éloges.

pram [præm] *n* landau *m*, voiture *f* d'enfant.

prance [prɑːns] *vi* **to p. about** (*of dancer etc*) caracoler; (*strut*) se pavaner; (*go about*) *Fam* se balader.

prank [præŋk] *n* (*trick*) farce *f*, tour *m*; (*escape*) frasque *f*.

prattle ['præt(ə)l] *vi* jacasser.

prawn [prɔːn] *n* crevette *f* (rose), bouquet *m*.

pray [preɪ] *vt Lit* prier (**that** que (+ *sub*), **s.o. to do** qn de faire); – *vi Rel* prier; **to p. (to God) for sth** prier Dieu pour qu'il nous accorde qch. ◆**prayer** [preər] *n* prière *f*.

pre- [priː] *pref* **p.-1800** avant 1800.

preach [priːtʃ] *vti* prêcher; (*sermon*) faire; **to p. to s.o.** *Rel & Fig* prêcher qn. ◆**—ing** *n* prédication *f*. ◆**—er** *n* prédicateur *m*.

preamble [priː'æmb(ə)l] *n* préambule *m*.

prearrange [priːə'reɪndʒ] *vt* arranger à l'avance.

precarious [prɪ'keərɪəs] *a* précaire.

precaution [prɪ'kɔːʃ(ə)n] *n* précaution *f* (**of doing** de faire); **as a p.** par précaution.

preced/e [prɪ'siːd] *vti* précéder; **to p. sth by sth** faire précéder qch de qch. ◆**—ing** *a* précédent.

precedence ['presɪdəns] *n* (*in rank*) préséance *f*; (*importance*) priorité *f*; **to take p. over** avoir la préséance sur; avoir la priorité sur. ◆**precedent** *n* précédent *m*.

precept ['priːsept] *n* précept *m*.

precinct ['priːsɪŋkt] *n* (*of convent etc*) enceinte *f*; (*boundary*) limite *f*; (*of town*) *Am Pol* circonscription *f*; (*for shopping*) zone *f* (piétonnière).

precious ['preʃəs] **1** *a* précieux; **her p. little bike** *Iron* son cher petit vélo. **2** *adv* **p. few, p. little** *Fam* très peu (de).

precipice ['presɪpɪs] *n* (*sheer face*) *Geog* à-pic *m inv*; (*chasm*) *Fig* précipice *m*.

precipitate [prɪ'sɪpɪteɪt] *vt* (*hasten, throw*) & *Ch* précipiter; (*trouble, reaction etc*) provoquer, déclencher. ◆**precipi'tation** *n* (*haste*) & *Ch* précipitation *f*; (*rainfall*) précipitations *fpl*.

précis ['preɪsiː, *pl* 'preɪsiːz] *n inv* précis *m*.

precise [prɪ'saɪs] *a* précis; (*person*) minutieux. ◆**—ly** *adv* (*accurately, exactly*) précisément; **at 3 o'clock p.** à 3 heures précises; **p. nothing** absolument rien. ◆**precision** *n* précision *f*.

preclude [prɪ'kluːd] *vt* (*prevent*) empêcher (**from doing** de faire); (*possibility*) exclure.

precocious [prɪ'kəʊʃəs] *a* (*child etc*) précoce. ◆**—ness** *n* précocité *f*.

preconceived [priːkən'siːvd] *a* préconçu. ◆**preconception** *n* préconception *f*.

precondition [priːkən'dɪʃ(ə)n] *n* préalable *m*.

precursor [priː'kɜːsər] *n* précurseur *m*.

predate [priː'deɪt] *vt* (*precede*) précéder; (*cheque etc*) antidater.

predator ['predətər] *n* (*animal*) prédateur *m*. ◆**predatory** *a* (*animal, person*) rapace.

predecessor ['priːdɪsesər] *n* prédécesseur *m*.

predicament [prɪ'dɪkəmənt] *n* situation *f* fâcheuse.

predict [prɪ'dɪkt] *vt* prédire. ◆**predictable** *a* prévisible. ◆**prediction** *n* prédiction *f*.

predispose [priːdɪ'spəʊz] *vt* prédisposer (**to do** à faire). ◆**predispo'sition** *n* prédisposition *f*.

predominant [prɪ'dɒmɪnənt] *a* prédominant. ◆**predominance** *n* prédominance *f*. ◆**predominantly** *adv* (*almost all*) pour la plupart, en majorité. ◆**predominate** *vi* prédominer (**over** sur).

preeminent [priː'emɪnənt] *a* prééminent.

preempt [priː'empt] *vt* (*decision, plans etc*) devancer.

preen [priːn] *vt* (*feathers*) lisser; **she's preening herself** *Fig* elle se bichonne.

prefab ['priːfæb] *n Fam* maison *f* préfabriquée. ◆**pre'fabricate** *vt* préfabriquer.

preface ['prefɪs] *n* préface *f*; – *vt* (*speech etc*) faire précéder (**with** de).

prefect ['priːfekt] *n Sch* élève *mf* chargé(e) de la discipline; (*French official*) préfet *m*.

prefer [prɪ'fɜːr] *vt* (**-rr-**) préférer (**to** à), aimer mieux (**to** que); **to p. to do** préférer faire, aimer mieux faire; **to p. charges** *Jur* porter plainte (**against** contre). ◆**'preferable** *a* préférable (**to** à). ◆**'preferably** *adv* de préférence. ◆**'preference** *n* préférence *f* (**for** pour); **in p. to** de préférence à. ◆**prefe'rential** *a* préférentiel.

prefix ['pri:fɪks] *n* préfixe *m*.

pregnant ['pregnənt] *a* (*woman*) enceinte; (*animal*) pleine; **five months p.** enceinte de cinq mois. ◆**pregnancy** *n* (*of woman*) grossesse *f*.

prehistoric [pri:hɪ'stɒrɪk] *a* préhistorique.

prejudge [pri:'dʒʌdʒ] *vt* (*question*) préjuger de; (*person*) juger d'avance.

prejudic/e ['predʒədɪs] *n* (*bias*) préjugé *m*, parti *m* pris; (*attitude*) préjugés *mpl*; *Jur* préjudice *m*; – *vt* (*person*) prévenir (**against** contre); (*success, chances etc*) porter préjudice à, nuire à. ◆**—ed** *a* (*idea*) partial; **she's p.** elle a des préjugés *or* un préjugé (**against** contre); (*on an issue*) elle est de parti pris. ◆**preju'dicial** *a Jur* préjudiciable.

preliminary [prɪ'lɪmɪnərɪ] *a* (*initial*) initial; (*speech, inquiry, exam*) préliminaire; – *npl* préliminaires *mpl*.

prelude ['prelju:d] *n* prélude *m*; – *vt* préluder à.

premarital [pri:'mærɪt(ə)l] *a* avant le mariage.

premature ['premətʃʊər, *Am* pri:mə'tʃʊər] *a* prématuré. ◆**—ly** *adv* prématurément; (*born*) avant terme.

premeditate [pri:'medɪteɪt] *vt* préméditer. ◆**premedi'tation** *n* préméditation *f*.

premier ['premɪər, *Am* prɪ'mɪər] *n* Premier ministre *m*.

première ['premɪeər, *Am* prɪ'mjeər] *n Th Cin* première *f*.

premise ['premɪs] *n Phil* prémisse *f*.

premises ['premɪsɪz] *npl* locaux *mpl*; **on the p.** sur les lieux; **off the p.** hors des lieux.

premium ['pri:mɪəm] *n Fin* prime *f*; (**insurance**) **p.** prime *f* (d'assurance); **to be at a p.** (*rare*) être (une) denrée rare, faire prime; **p. bond** bon *m* à lots.

premonition [premə'nɪʃ(ə)n, *Am* pri:mə-'nɪʃ(ə)n] *n* prémonition *f*, pressentiment *m*.

prenatal [pri:'neɪt(ə)l] *a Am* prénatal.

preoccupy [pri:'ɒkjʊpaɪ] *vt* (*worry*) préoccuper (**with** de). ◆**preoccu'pation** *n* préoccupation *f*; **a p. with** (*money etc*) une obsession de.

prep [prep] *a* **p. school** école *f* primaire privée; *Am* école *f* secondaire privée; – *n* (*homework*) *Sch* devoirs *mpl*.

prepaid [pri:'peɪd] *a* (*reply*) payé.

prepar/e [prɪ'peər] *vt* préparer (**sth for s.o.** qch à qn, **s.o. for sth** qn à qch); **to p. to do** se préparer à faire; – *vi* **to p. for** (*journey, occasion*) faire des préparatifs pour; (*get dressed up for*) se préparer pour; (*exam*) préparer. ◆**—ed** *a* (*ready*) prêt, disposé (**to** do à faire); **to be p. for** (*expect*) s'attendre à. ◆**prepa'ration** *n* préparation *f*; *pl* préparatifs *mpl* (**for** de). ◆**pre'paratory** *a* préparatoire; **p. school** = **prep school**.

preposition [prepə'zɪʃ(ə)n] *n* préposition *f*.

prepossessing [pri:pə'zesɪŋ] *a* avenant, sympathique.

preposterous [prɪ'pɒstərəs] *a* absurde.

prerecorded [pri:rɪ'kɔ:dɪd] *a* (*message etc*) enregistré à l'avance; **p. broadcast** *Rad TV* émission *f* en différé.

prerequisite [pri:'rekwɪzɪt] *n* (condition *f*) préalable *m*.

prerogative [prɪ'rɒgətɪv] *n* prérogative *f*.

Presbyterian [prezbɪ'tɪərɪən] *a & n Rel* presbytérien, -ienne (*mf*).

preschool ['pri:sku:l] *a* (*age etc*) préscolaire.

prescrib/e [prɪ'skraɪb] *vt* prescrire. ◆**—ed** *a* (*textbook*) (inscrit) au programme. ◆**prescription** *n* (*order*) prescription *f*; *Med* ordonnance *f*; **on p.** sur ordonnance.

presence ['prezəns] *n* présence *f*; **in the p. of** en présence de; **p. of mind** présence *f* d'esprit.

present[1] ['prezənt] **1** *a* (*not absent*) présent (**at** à, **in** dans); **those p.** les personnes présentes. **2** *a* (*year, state etc*) présent, actuel; (*being considered*) présent; (*job, house etc*) actuel; – *n* (*time*) présent *m*; **for the p.** pour le moment; **at p.** à présent. **3** *n* (*gift*) cadeau *m*. ◆**—ly** *adv* (*soon*) tout à l'heure; (*now*) à présent. ◆**present-'day** *a* actuel.

present[2] [prɪ'zent] *vt* (*show, introduce, compere etc*) présenter (**to** à); (*concert etc*) donner; (*proof*) fournir; **to p. s.o. with** (*gift*) offrir à qn; (*prize*) remettre à qn. ◆**—able** *a* présentable. ◆**—er** *n* présentateur, -trice *mf*. ◆**presen'tation** *n* présentation *f*; (*of prize*) remise *f*.

preserve [prɪ'zɜ:v] **1** *vt* (*keep, maintain*) conserver; (*fruit etc*) *Culin* mettre en conserve; **to p. from** (*protect*) préserver de. **2** *n* (*sphere*) domaine *m*. **3** *n & npl* (*fruit etc*) *Culin* confiture *f*. ◆**preser'vation** *n* conservation *f*. ◆**preservative** *n* (*in food*) agent *m* de conservation. ◆**preserver** *n* **life p.** *Am* gilet *m* de sauvetage.

preside [prɪ'zaɪd] *vi* présider; **to p. over** *or* **at** (*meeting*) présider.

president ['prezɪdənt] *n* président, -ente *mf*. ◆**presidency** *n* présidence *f*. ◆**presi'dential** *a* présidentiel.

press[1] [pres] **1** *n* (*newspapers*) presse *f*; (*printing firm*) imprimerie *f*; (**printing**) **p.** presse *f*; – *a* (*conference etc*) de presse. **2** *n* (*machine for trousers, gluing etc*) presse *f*; (*for making wine*) pressoir *m*.

press² [pres] *vt* (*button, doorbell etc*) appuyer sur; (*tube, lemon, creditor*) presser; (*hand*) serrer; (*clothes*) repasser; (*demand, insist on*) insister sur; (*claim*) renouveler; **to p. s.o. to do** (*urge*) presser qn de faire; **to p. down** (*button etc*) appuyer sur; **to p. charges** *Jur* engager des poursuites (**against** contre); – *vi* (*with finger*) appuyer (**on** sur); (*of weight*) faire pression (**on** sur); (*of time*) presser; **to p. for sth** faire des démarches pour obtenir qch; (*insist*) insister pour obtenir qch; **to p. on** (*continue*) continuer (**with sth** qch); – *n* **to give sth a p.** (*trousers etc*) repasser qch. ◆**—ed** *a* (**hard**) **p.** (*busy*) débordé; **to be hard p.** (*in difficulties*) être en difficultés; **to be (hard) p. for** (*time, money*) être à court de. ◆**—ing 1** *a* (*urgent*) pressant. **2** *n* (*ironing*) repassage *m*.

pressgang ['presgæŋ] *vt* **to p. s.o.** faire pression sur qn (**into doing** pour qu'il fasse). ◆**press-stud** *n* (bouton-)pression *m*. ◆**press-up** *n Sp* pompe *f*.

pressure ['preʃər] *n* pression *f*; **the p. of work** le surmenage; **p. cooker** cocotte-minute *f*; **p. group** groupe *m* de pression; **under p.** (*duress*) sous la contrainte; (*hurriedly, forcibly*) sous pression; – *vt* **to p. s.o.** faire pression sur qn (**into doing** pour qu'il fasse). ◆**pressurize** *vt Av* pressuriser; **to p. s.o.** faire pression sur qn (**into doing** pour qu'il fasse).

prestige [pre'stiːʒ] *n* prestige *m*. ◆**prestigious** [pre'stɪdʒəs, *Am* -'stiːdʒəs] *a* prestigieux.

presume [prɪ'zjuːm] *vt* (*suppose*) présumer (**that** que); **to p. to do** se permettre de faire. ◆**presumably** *adv* (*you'll come etc*) je présume que. ◆**presumption** *n* (*supposition, bold attitude*) présomption *f*. ◆**presumptuous** *a* présomptueux.

presuppose [priːsə'pəʊz] *vt* présupposer (**that** que).

pretence [prɪ'tens] *n* feinte *f*; (*claim, affectation*) prétention *f*; (*pretext*) prétexte *m*; **to make a p. of sth/of doing** feindre qch/de faire; **on** *or* **under false pretences** sous des prétextes fallacieux. ◆**pretend** *vt* (*make believe*) faire semblant (**to do** de faire, **that** que); (*claim, maintain*) prétendre (**to do** faire, **that** que); – *vi* faire semblant; **to p. to** (*throne, title*) prétendre à.

pretension [prɪ'tenʃ(ə)n] *n* (*claim, vanity*) prétention *f*. ◆**pre'tentious** *a* prétentieux.

pretext ['priːtekst] *n* prétexte *m*; **on the p. of/that** sous prétexte de/que.

pretty ['prɪtɪ] **1** *a* (**-ier, -iest**) joli. **2** *adv Fam* (*rather, quite*) assez; **p. well, p. much, p. nearly** (*almost*) pratiquement, à peu de chose près.

prevail [prɪ'veɪl] *vi* (*be prevalent*) prédominer; (*win*) prévaloir (**against** contre); **to p. (up)on s.o.** (*persuade*) persuader qn (**to do** de faire). ◆**—ing** *a* (*most common*) courant; (*most important*) prédominant; (*situation*) actuel; (*wind*) dominant.

prevalent ['prevələnt] *a* courant, répandu. ◆**prevalence** *n* fréquence *f*; (*predominance*) prédominance *f*.

prevaricate [prɪ'værɪkeɪt] *vi* user de faux-fuyants.

prevent [prɪ'vent] *vt* empêcher (**from doing** de faire). ◆**preventable** *a* évitable. ◆**prevention** *n* prévention *f*. ◆**preventive** *a* préventif.

preview ['priːvjuː] *n* (*of film, painting*) avant-première *f*; (*survey*) *Fig* aperçu *m*.

previous ['priːvɪəs] *a* précédent, antérieur; (*experience*) préalable; **she's had a p. job** elle a déjà eu un emploi; **p. to** avant. ◆**—ly** *adv* avant, précédemment.

prewar ['priːwɔːr] *a* d'avant-guerre.

prey [preɪ] *n* proie *f*; **to be (a) p. to** être en proie à; **bird of p.** rapace *m*, oiseau *m* de proie; – *vi* **to p. on** faire sa proie de; **to p. on s.o.** *or* **s.o.'s mind** *Fig* tracasser qn.

price [praɪs] *n* (*of object, success etc*) prix *m*; **to pay a high p. for sth** payer cher qch; *Fig* payer chèrement qch; **he wouldn't do it at any p.** il ne le ferait à aucun prix; – *a* (*control, war, rise etc*) des prix; **p. list** tarif *m*; – *vt* mettre un prix à; **it's priced at £5** ça coûte cinq livres. ◆**priceless** *a* (*jewel, help etc*) inestimable; (*amusing*) *Fam* impayable. ◆**pricey** *a* (**-ier, -iest**) *Fam* coûteux.

prick [prɪk] *vt* piquer (**with** avec); (*burst*) crever; **to p. up one's ears** dresser l'oreille; – *n* (*act, mark, pain*) piqûre *f*.

prickle ['prɪk(ə)l] *n* (*of animal*) piquant *m*; (*of plant*) épine *f*, piquant *m*. ◆**prickly** *a* (**-ier, -iest**) (*plant*) épineux; (*animal*) hérissé; (*subject*) *Fig* épineux; (*person*) *Fig* irritable.

pride [praɪd] *n* (*satisfaction*) fierté *f*; (*self-esteem*) amour-propre *m*, orgueil *m*; (*arrogance*) orgueil *m*; **to take p. in** (*person, work etc*) être fier de; (*look after*) prendre soin de; **to take p. in doing** mettre (toute) sa fierté à faire; **to be s.o.'s p. and joy** être la fierté de qn; **to have p. of place** avoir la

place d'honneur; – *vt* to p. oneself on s'enorgueillir de.
priest [priːst] *n* prêtre *m*. ◆**priesthood** *n* (*function*) sacerdoce *m*. ◆**priestly** *a* sacerdotal.
prig [prɪg] *n* hypocrite *mf*, pharisien, -ienne *mf*. ◆**priggish** *a* hypocrite, suffisant.
prim [prɪm] *a* (**primmer, primmest**) p. (**and proper**) (*affected*) guindé; (*seemly*) convenable; (*neat*) impeccable.
primacy ['praɪməsɪ] *n* primauté *f*.
primary ['praɪmərɪ] *a Sch Pol Geol etc* primaire; (*main, basic*) principal, premier; **of p. importance** de première importance; – *n* (*election*) *Am* primaire *f*. ◆**primarily** [*Am* praɪ'merɪlɪ] *adv* essentiellement.
prime [praɪm] **1** *a* (*reason etc*) principal; (*importance*) primordial; (*quality, number*) premier; (*meat*) de premier choix; (*example, condition*) excellent, parfait; **P. Minister** Premier ministre *m*. **2** *n* **the p. of life** la force de l'âge. **3** *vt* (*gun, pump*) amorcer; (*surface*) apprêter. ◆**primer** *n* **1** (*book*) *Sch* premier livre *m*. **2** (*paint*) apprêt *m*.
primeval [praɪ'miːv(ə)l] *a* primitif.
primitive ['prɪmɪtɪv] *a* (*art, society, conditions etc*) primitif. ◆**—ly** *adv* (*to live*) dans des conditions primitives.
primrose ['prɪmrəʊz] *n Bot* primevère *f* (jaune).
prince [prɪns] *n* prince *m*. ◆**princely** *a* princier. ◆**prin'cess** *n* princesse *f*. ◆**princi'pality** *n* principauté *f*.
principal ['prɪnsɪp(ə)l] **1** *a* (*main*) principal. **2** *n* (*of school*) directeur, -trice *mf*. ◆**—ly** *adv* principalement.
principle ['prɪnsɪp(ə)l] *n* principe *m*; **in p.** en principe; **on p.** par principe.
print [prɪnt] *n* (*of finger, foot etc*) empreinte *f*; (*letters*) caractères *mpl*; (*engraving*) estampe *f*, gravure *f*; (*fabric, textile design*) imprimé *m*; *Phot* épreuve *f*; (*ink*) encre *m*; **in p.** (*book*) disponible (en librairie); **out of p.** (*book*) épuisé; – *vt Typ* imprimer; *Phot* tirer; (*write*) écrire en caractères d'imprimerie; **to p. 100 copies of** (*book etc*) tirer à 100 exemplaires; **to p. out** (*of computer*) imprimer. ◆**—ed** *a* imprimé; **p. matter** *or* **papers** imprimés *mpl*; **to have a book p.** publier un livre. ◆**—ing** *n* (*action*) *Typ* impression *f*; (*technique, art*) *Typ* imprimerie *f*; *Phot* tirage *m*; **p. press** *Typ* presse *f*. ◆**—able** *a* **not p.** (*word etc*) *Fig* obscène. ◆**—er** *n* (*person*) imprimeur *m*; (*of computer*) imprimante *f*. ◆**print-out** *n* (*of computer*) sortie *f* sur imprimante.
prior ['praɪər] *a* précédent, antérieur; (*experience*) préalable; **p. to sth/to doing** avant qch/de faire.
priority [praɪ'ɒrɪtɪ] *n* priorité *f* (**over** sur).
priory ['praɪərɪ] *n Rel* prieuré *m*.
prise [praɪz] *vt* **to p. open/off** (*box, lid*) ouvrir/enlever (en faisant levier).
prism ['prɪz(ə)m] *n* prisme *m*.
prison ['prɪz(ə)n] *n* prison *f*; **in p.** en prison; – *a* (*system, life etc*) pénitentiaire; (*camp*) de prisonniers; **p. officer** gardien, -ienne *mf* de prison. ◆**prisoner** *n* prisonnier, -ière *mf*; **to take s.o. p.** faire qn prisonnier.
prissy ['prɪsɪ] *a* (**-ier, -iest**) bégueule.
pristine ['prɪstiːn] *a* (*condition*) parfait; (*primitive*) primitif.
privacy ['praɪvəsɪ, 'prɪvəsɪ] *n* intimité *f*, solitude *f*; (*quiet place*) coin *m* retiré; (*secrecy*) secret *m*; **to give s.o. some p.** laisser qn seul. ◆**private** **1** *a* privé; (*lesson, car etc*) particulier; (*confidential*) confidentiel; (*personal*) personnel; (*wedding etc*) intime; **a p. citizen** un simple particulier; **p. detective, p. investigator,** *Fam* **p. eye** détective *m* privé; **p. parts** parties *fpl* génitales; **p. place** coin *m* retiré; **p. tutor** précepteur *m*; **to be a very p. person** aimer la solitude; – *n* **in p.** (*not publicly*) en privé; (*ceremony*) dans l'intimité. **2** *n Mil* (simple) soldat *m*. ◆**privately** *adv* en privé; (*inwardly*) intérieurement; (*personally*) à titre personnel; (*to marry, dine etc*) dans l'intimité; **p. owned** appartenant à un particulier.
privet ['prɪvɪt] *n* (*bush*) troène *m*.
privilege ['prɪvɪlɪdʒ] *n* privilège *m*. ◆**privileged** *a* privilégié; **to be p. to do** avoir le privilège de faire.
privy ['prɪvɪ] *a* **p. to** (*knowledge etc*) au courant de.
prize[1] [praɪz] *n* prix *m*; (*in lottery*) lot *m*; **the first p.** (*in lottery*) le gros lot; – *a* (*essay, animal etc*) primé; **a p. fool/***etc Fig Hum* un parfait idiot/*etc*. ◆**p.-giving** *n* distribution *f* des prix. ◆**p.-winner** *n* lauréat, -ate *mf*; (*in lottery*) gagnant, -ante *mf*. ◆**p.-winning** *a* (*essay, animal etc*) primé; (*ticket*) gagnant.
priz/e[2] [praɪz] *vt* (*value*) priser. ◆**—ed** *a* (*possession etc*) précieux.
prize[3] [praɪz] *vt* = **prise**.
pro [prəʊ] *n* (*professional*) *Fam* pro *mf*.
pro- [prəʊ] *pref* pro-.
probable ['prɒbəb(ə)l] *a* probable (**that** que); (*plausible*) vraisemblable. ◆**proba'bility** *n* probabilité *f*; **in all p.** selon toute probabilité. ◆**probably** *adv* probablement, vraisemblablement.
probation [prə'beɪʃ(ə)n] *n* **on p.** *Jur* en

liberté surveillée, sous contrôle judiciaire; (*in job*) à l'essai; **p. officer** responsable *mf* des délinquants mis en liberté surveillée. ◆**probationary** *a* (*period*) d'essai, *Jur* de liberté surveillée.

prob/e [prəʊb] *n* (*device*) sonde *f*; *Journ* enquête *f* (**into** dans); – *vt* (*investigate*) & *Med* sonder; (*examine*) examiner; – *vi* (*investigate*) faire des recherches; *Pej* fouiner; **to p. into** (*origins etc*) sonder. ◆**—ing** *a* (*question etc*) pénétrant.

problem ['prɒbləm] *n* problème *m*; **he's got a drug/a drink p.** c'est un drogué/un alcoolique; **you've got a smoking p.** tu fumes beaucoup trop; **no p.!** *Am Fam* pas de problème!; **to have a p. doing** avoir du mal à faire; – *a* (*child*) difficile, caractériel. ◆**proble'matic** *a* problématique; **it's p. whether** il est douteux que (+ *sub*).

procedure [prə'siːdʒər] *n* procédure *f*.

proceed [prə'siːd] *vi* (*go*) avancer, aller; (*act*) procéder; (*continue*) continuer; (*of debate*) se poursuivre; **to p. to** (*next question etc*) passer à; **to p. with** (*task etc*) continuer; **to p. to do** (*start*) se mettre à faire. ◆**—ing** *n* (*course of action*) procédé *m*; *pl* (*events*) événements *mpl*; (*meeting*) séance *f*; (*discussions*) débats *mpl*; (*minutes*) actes *mpl*; **to take (legal) proceedings** intenter un procès (**against** contre).

proceeds ['prəʊsiːdz] *npl* (*profits*) produit *m*, bénéfices *mpl*.

process ['prəʊses] **1** *n* (*operation, action*) processus *m*; (*method*) procédé *m* (**for** *or* **of doing** pour faire); **in p.** (*work etc*) en cours; **in the p. of doing** en train de faire. **2** *vt* (*food, data etc*) traiter; (*examine*) examiner; *Phot* développer; **processed cheese** fromage *m* fondu. ◆**—ing** *n* traitement *m*; *Phot* développement *m*; **data** *or* **information p.** informatique *f*. ◆**processor** *n* (*in computer*) processeur *m*; **food p.** robot *m* (ménager); **word p.** machine *f* de traitement de texte.

procession [prə'seʃ(ə)n] *n* cortège *m*, défilé *m*.

proclaim [prə'kleɪm] *vt* proclamer (**that** que); **to p. king** proclamer roi. ◆**procla'mation** *n* proclamation *f*.

procrastinate [prə'kræstɪneɪt] *vi* temporiser, tergiverser.

procreate ['prəʊkrɪeɪt] *vt* procréer. ◆**procre'ation** *n* procréation *f*.

procure [prə'kjʊər] *vt* obtenir; **to p. sth (for oneself)** se procurer qch; **to p. sth for s.o.** procurer qch à qn.

prod [prɒd] *vti* (**-dd-**) **to p. (at)** pousser (*du coude, avec un bâton etc*); **to p. s.o. into doing** *Fig* pousser qn à faire; – *n* (petit) coup *m*; (*shove*) poussée *f*.

prodigal ['prɒdɪg(ə)l] *a* (*son etc*) prodigue.

prodigious [prə'dɪdʒəs] *a* prodigieux.

prodigy ['prɒdɪdʒɪ] *n* prodige *m*; **infant p., child p.** enfant *mf* prodige.

produce [prə'djuːs] *vt* (*manufacture, yield etc*) produire; (*bring out, show*) sortir (*pistolet, mouchoir etc*); (*passport, proof*) présenter; (*profit*) rapporter; (*cause*) provoquer, produire; (*publish*) publier; (*play*) *Th TV* mettre en scène; (*film*) *Cin* produire; *Rad* réaliser; (*baby*) donner naissance à; **oil-producing country** pays *m* producteur de pétrole; – *vi* (*of factory etc*) produire; – ['prɒdjuːs] *n* (*agricultural etc*) produits *mpl*. ◆**pro'ducer** *n* (*of goods*) & *Cin* producteur, -trice *mf*; *Th TV* metteur *m* en scène; *Rad* réalisateur, -trice *mf*.

product ['prɒdʌkt] *n* produit *m*.

production [prə'dʌkʃ(ə)n] *n* production *f*; *Th TV* mise *f* en scène; *Rad* réalisation *f*; **to work on the p. line** travailler à la chaîne. ◆**productive** *a* (*land, meeting, efforts*) productif. ◆**produc'tivity** *n* productivité *f*.

profane [prə'feɪn] *a* (*sacrilegious*) sacrilège; (*secular*) profane; – *vt* (*dishonour*) profaner. ◆**profanities** *npl* (*oaths*) blasphèmes *mpl*.

profess [prə'fes] *vt* professer; **to p. to be** prétendre être. ◆**—ed** *a* (*anarchist etc*) déclaré.

profession [prə'feʃ(ə)n] *n* profession *f*; **by p.** de profession. ◆**professional** *a* professionnel; (*man, woman*) qui exerce une profession libérale; (*army*) de métier; (*diplomat*) de carrière; (*piece of work*) de professionnel; – *n* professionnel, -elle *mf*; (*executive, lawyer etc*) membre *m* des professions libérales. ◆**professionalism** *n* professionnalisme *m*. ◆**professionally** *adv* professionnellement; (*to perform, play*) en professionnel; (*to meet s.o.*) dans le cadre de son travail.

professor [prə'fesər] *n Univ* professeur *m* (titulaire d'une chaire). ◆**profe'ssorial** *a* professoral.

proffer ['prɒfər] *vt* offrir.

proficient [prə'fɪʃ(ə)nt] *a* compétent (**in** en). ◆**proficiency** *n* compétence *f*.

profile ['prəʊfaɪl] *n* (*of person, object*) profil *m*; **in p.** de profil; **to keep a low p.** *Fig* garder un profil bas. ◆**profiled** *a* **to be p. against** se profiler sur.

profit ['prɒfɪt] *n* profit *m*, bénéfice *m*; **to sell**

at a p. vendre à profit; **p. margin** marge *f* bénéficiaire; **p. motive** recherche *f* du profit; – *vi* to p. by *or* from tirer profit de. ◆**p.-making** *a* à but lucratif. ◆**profita'bility** *n Com* rentabilité *f*. ◆**profitable** *a Com* rentable; (*worthwhile*) *Fig* rentable, profitable. ◆**profitably** *adv* avec profit. ◆**profi'teer** *n Pej* profiteur, -euse *mf*; – *vi Pej* faire des profits malhonnêtes.

profound [prə'faʊnd] *a* (*silence, remark etc*) profond. ◆**profoundly** *adv* profondément. ◆**profundity** *n* profondeur *f*.

profuse [prə'fjuːs] *a* abondant; **p. in** (*praise etc*) prodigue de. ◆**profusely** *adv* (*to flow, grow*) à profusion; (*to bleed*) abondamment; (*to thank*) avec effusion; **to apologize p.** se répandre en excuses. ◆**profusion** *n* profusion *f*; **in p.** à profusion.

progeny ['prɒdʒɪnɪ] *n* progéniture *f*.

program[1] ['prəʊgræm] *n* (*of computer*) programme *m*; – *vt* (-mm-) (*computer*) programmer. ◆**programming** *n* programmation *f*. ◆**programmer** *n* (**computer**) **p.** programmeur, -euse *mf*.

programme, *Am* **program**[2] ['prəʊgræm] *n* programme *m*; (*broadcast*) émission *f*; – *vt* (*arrange*) programmer.

progress ['prəʊgres] *n* progrès *m*(*pl*); **to make (good) p.** faire des progrès; (*in walking, driving etc*) bien avancer; **in p.** en cours; – [prə'gres] *vi* (*advance, improve*) progresser; (*of story, meeting*) se dérouler. ◆**pro'gression** *n* progression *f*. ◆**pro'gressive** *a* (*gradual*) progressif; (*party*) *Pol* progressiste; (*firm, ideas*) moderniste. ◆**pro'gressively** *adv* progressivement.

prohibit [prə'hɪbɪt] *vt* interdire (**s.o. from doing** à qn de faire); **we're prohibited from leaving/***etc* il nous est interdit de partir/*etc*. ◆**prohi'bition** *n* prohibition *f*. ◆**prohibitive** *a* (*price, measure etc*) prohibitif.

project 1 ['prɒdʒekt] *n* (*plan*) projet *m* (**for sth** pour qch; **to do, for doing** pour faire); (*undertaking*) entreprise *f*; (*study*) étude *f*; (**housing**) **p.** (*for workers*) *Am* cité *f* (ouvrière). **2** [prə'dʒekt] *vt* (*throw, show etc*) projeter; – *vi* (*jut out*) faire saillie. ◆**—ed** *a* (*planned*) prévu. ◆**pro'jection** *n* projection *f*; (*projecting object*) saillie *f*. ◆**pro'jectionist** *n Cin* projectionniste *mf*. ◆**pro'jector** *n Cin* projecteur *m*.

proletarian [prəʊlə'teərɪən] *n* prolétaire *mf*; – *a* (*class*) prolétarien; (*outlook*) de prolétaire. ◆**proletariat** *n* prolétariat *m*.

proliferate [prə'lɪfəreɪt] *vi* proliférer. ◆**prolife'ration** *n* prolifération *f*.

prolific [prə'lɪfɪk] *a* prolifique.

prologue ['prəʊlɒg] *n* prologue *m* (**to** de, à).

prolong [prə'lɒŋ] *vt* prolonger.

promenade [prɒmə'nɑːd] *n* (*place, walk*) promenade *f*; (*gallery*) *Th* promenoir *m*.

prominent ['prɒmɪnənt] *a* (*nose*) proéminent; (*chin, tooth*) saillant; (*striking*) *Fig* frappant, remarquable; (*role*) majeur; (*politician*) marquant; (*conspicuous*) (bien) en vue. ◆**prominence** *n* (*importance*) importance *f*. ◆**prominently** *adv* (*displayed, placed*) bien en vue.

promiscuous [prə'mɪskjʊəs] *a* (*person*) de mœurs faciles; (*behaviour*) immoral. ◆**promi'scuity** *n* liberté *f* de mœurs; immoralité *f*.

promis/e ['prɒmɪs] *n* promesse *f*; **to show great p., be full of p.** (*hope*) être très prometteur; – *vt* promettre (**s.o. sth, sth to s.o.** qch à qn; **to do** de faire; **that** que); – *vi* **I p.!** je te le promets!; **p.?** promis? ◆**—ing** *a* (*start etc*) prometteur; (*person*) qui promet; **that looks p.** ça s'annonce bien.

promote [prə'məʊt] *vt* (*product, research*) promouvoir; (*good health, awareness*) favoriser; **to p. s.o.** promouvoir qn (**to** à); **promoted (to) manager/general/***etc* promu directeur/général/*etc*. ◆**promoter** *n Sp* organisateur, -trice *mf*; (*instigator*) promoteur, -trice *mf*. ◆**promotion** *n* (*of person*) avancement *m*, promotion *f*; (*of sales, research etc*) promotion *f*.

prompt [prɒmpt] **1** *a* (*speedy*) rapide; (*punctual*) à l'heure, ponctuel; **p. to act** prompt à agir; – *adv* **at 8 o'clock p.** à 8 heures pile. **2** *vt* (*urge*) inciter, pousser (**to do** à faire); (*cause*) provoquer. **3** *vt* (*person*) *Th* souffler (son rôle) à. ◆**—ing** *n* (*urging*) incitation *f*. ◆**—er** *n Th* souffleur, -euse *mf*. ◆**—ness** *n* rapidité *f*; (*readiness to act*) promptitude *f*.

prone [prəʊn] *a* **1 p. to sth** (*liable*) prédisposé à qch; **to be p. to do** avoir tendance à faire. **2** (*lying flat*) sur le ventre.

prong [prɒŋ] *n* (*of fork*) dent *f*.

pronoun ['prəʊnaʊn] *n Gram* pronom *m*. ◆**pro'nominal** *a* pronominal.

pronounce [prə'naʊns] *vt* (*articulate, declare*) prononcer; – *vi* (*articulate*) prononcer; (*give judgment*) se prononcer (**on** sur). ◆**pronouncement** *n* déclaration *f*. ◆**pronunci'ation** *n* prononciation *f*.

pronto ['prɒntəʊ] *adv* (*at once*) *Fam* illico.

proof [pruːf] **1** *n* (*evidence*) preuve *f*; (*of book, photo*) épreuve *f*; (*of drink*) teneur *f* en alcool. **2** *a* **p. against** (*material*) à l'épreuve de (*feu, acide etc*). ◆**proofreader** *n Typ* correcteur, -trice *mf*.

prop [prɒp] **1** *n Archit* support *m*, étai *m*; (*for clothes line*) perche *f*; (*person*) *Fig* soutien *m*; – *vt* (**-pp-**) **to p. up** (*ladder etc*) appuyer (**against** contre); (*one's head*) caler; (*wall*) étayer; (*help*) *Fig* soutenir. **2** *n* **prop(s)** *Th* accessoire(s) *m(pl)*.

propaganda [prɒpə'gændə] *n* propagande *f*. ◆**propagandist** *n* propagandiste *mf*.

propagate ['prɒpəgeɪt] *vt* propager; – *vi* se propager.

propel [prə'pel] *vt* (**-ll-**) (*drive, hurl*) propulser. ◆**propeller** *n Av Nau* hélice *f*.

propensity [prə'pensɪtɪ] *n* propension *f* (**for** sth à qch, **to do** à faire).

proper ['prɒpər] *a* (*suitable, seemly*) convenable; (*correct*) correct; (*right*) bon; (*real, downright*) véritable; (*noun, meaning*) propre; **in the p. way** comme il faut; **the village/***etc* **p.** le village/*etc* proprement dit. ◆**—ly** *adv* comme il faut, convenablement, correctement; (*completely*) *Fam* vraiment; **very p.** (*quite rightly*) à juste titre.

property ['prɒpətɪ] **1** *n* (*building etc*) propriété *f*; (*possessions*) biens *mpl*, propriété *f*; – *a* (*crisis, market etc*) immobilier; (*owner, tax*) foncier. **2** *n* (*of substance etc*) propriété *f*. ◆**propertied** *a* possédant.

prophecy ['prɒfɪsɪ] *n* prophétie *f*. ◆**prophesy** [-ɪsaɪ] *vti* prophétiser; **to p. that** prédire que.

prophet ['prɒfɪt] *n* prophète *m*. ◆**pro'phetic** *a* prophétique.

proponent [prə'pəʊnənt] *n* (*of cause etc*) défenseur *m*, partisan, -ane *mf*.

proportion [prə'pɔːʃ(ə)n] *n* (*ratio*) proportion *f*; (*portion*) partie *f*; (*amount*) pourcentage *m*; *pl* (*size*) proportions *fpl*; **in p.** en proportion (**to** de); **out of p.** hors de proportion (**to** avec); – *vt* proportionner (**to** à); **well** *or* **nicely proportioned** bien proportionné. ◆**proportional** *a*, ◆**proportionate** *a* proportionnel (**to** à).

propose [prə'pəʊz] *vt* (*suggest*) proposer (**to** à, **that** que (+ *sub*)); **to p. to do, p. doing** (*intend*) se proposer de faire; – *vi* faire une demande (en mariage) (**to** à). ◆**proposal** *n* proposition *f*; (*of marriage*) demande *f* (en mariage). ◆**propo'sition** *n* proposition *f*; (*matter*) *Fig* affaire *f*.

propound [prə'paʊnd] *vt* proposer.

proprietor [prə'praɪətər] *n* propriétaire *mf*. ◆**proprietary** *a* (*article*) *Com* de marque déposée; **p. name** marque *f* déposée.

propriety [prə'praɪətɪ] *n* (*behaviour*) bienséance *f*; (*of conduct, remark*) justesse *f*.

propulsion [prə'pʌlʃ(ə)n] *n* propulsion *f*.

pros [prəʊz] *npl* **the p. and cons** le pour et le contre.

prosaic [prəʊ'zeɪɪk] *a* prosaïque.

proscribe [prəʊ'skraɪb] *vt* proscrire.

prose [prəʊz] *n* prose *f*; (*translation*) *Sch* thème *m*.

prosecute ['prɒsɪkjuːt] *vt* poursuivre (en justice) (**for stealing/***etc* pour vol/*etc*). ◆**prose'cution** *n Jur* poursuites *fpl*; **the p.** (*lawyers*) = le ministère public. ◆**prosecutor** *n* (**public**) **p.** *Jur* procureur *m*.

prospect[1] ['prɒspekt] *n* (*idea, outlook*) perspective *f* (**of doing** de faire); (*possibility*) possibilité *f* (**of sth** de **qch**); (**future**) **prospects** perspectives *fpl* d'avenir; **it has prospects** c'est prometteur; **she has prospects** elle a de l'avenir. ◆**pro'spective** *a* (*possible*) éventuel; (*future*) futur.

prospect[2] [prə'spekt] *vt* (*land*) prospecter; – *vi* **to p. for** (*gold etc*) chercher. ◆**—ing** *n* prospection *f*. ◆**prospector** *n* prospecteur, -trice *mf*.

prospectus [prə'spektəs] *n* (*publicity leaflet*) prospectus *m*; *Univ* guide *m* (de l'étudiant).

prosper ['prɒspər] *vi* prospérer. ◆**pro'sperity** *n* prospérité *f*. ◆**prosperous** *a* (*thriving*) prospère; (*wealthy*) riche, prospère.

prostate ['prɒsteɪt] *n* **p. (gland)** *Anat* prostate *f*.

prostitute ['prɒstɪtjuːt] *n* (*woman*) prostituée *f*; – *vt* prostituer. ◆**prosti'tution** *n* prostitution *f*.

prostrate ['prɒstreɪt] *a* (*prone*) sur le ventre; (*worshipper*) prosterné; (*submissive*) soumis; (*exhausted*) prostré; – [prɒ'streɪt] *vt* **to p. oneself** se prosterner (**before** devant).

protagonist [prəʊ'tægənɪst] *n* protagoniste *mf*.

protect [prə'tekt] *vt* protéger (**from** de, **against** contre); (*interests*) sauvegarder. ◆**protection** *n* protection *f*. ◆**protective** *a* (*tone etc*) & *Econ* protecteur; (*screen, clothes etc*) de protection. ◆**protector** *n* protecteur, -trice *mf*.

protein ['prəʊtiːn] *n* protéine *f*.

protest ['prəʊtest] *n* protestation *f* (**against** contre); **under p.** contre son gré; – [prə'test] *vt* protester (**that** que); (*one's innocence*) protester de; – *vi* protester (**against** contre); (*in the streets etc*) *Pol* contester. ◆**—er** *n Pol* contestataire *mf*.

Protestant ['prɒtɪstənt] *a* & *n* protestant.

-ante (*mf*). ◆**Protestantism** *n* protestantisme *m*.

protocol ['prəutəkɒl] *n* protocole *m*.

prototype ['prəutəutaɪp] *n* prototype *m*.

protract [prə'trækt] *vt* prolonger.

protractor [prə'træktər] *n* (*instrument*) *Geom* rapporteur *m*.

protrud/e [prə'truːd] *vi* dépasser; (*of balcony, cliff etc*) faire saillie; (*of tooth*) avancer. ◆**—ing** *a* saillant; (*of tooth*) qui avance.

proud [praud] *a* (**-er, -est**) (*honoured, pleased*) fier (**of** de, **to do** de faire); (*arrogant*) orgueilleux. ◆**—ly** *adv* fièrement; orgueilleusement.

prove [pruːv] *vt* prouver (**that** que); **to p. oneself** faire ses preuves; – *vi* **to p. (to be) difficult/***etc* s'avérer difficile/*etc*. ◆**proven** *a* (*method etc*) éprouvé.

proverb ['prɒvɜːb] *n* proverbe *m*. ◆**pro'verbial** *a* proverbial.

provid/e [prə'vaɪd] *vt* (*supply*) fournir (s.o. **with sth** qch à qn); (*give*) donner, offrir (**to** à); **to p. s.o. with** (*equip*) pourvoir qn de; **to p. that** *Jur* stipuler que; – *vi* **to p. for s.o.** (*s.o.'s needs*) pourvoir aux besoins de qn; (*s.o.'s future*) assurer l'avenir de qn; **to p. for sth** (*make allowance for*) prévoir qch. ◆**—ed** *conj* **p. (that)** pourvu que (+ *sub*). ◆**—ing** *conj* **p. (that)** pourvu que (+ *sub*).

providence ['prɒvɪdəns] *n* providence *f*.

provident ['prɒvɪdənt] *a* (*society*) de prévoyance; (*person*) prévoyant.

province ['prɒvɪns] *n* province *f*; *Fig* domaine *m*, compétence *f*; **the provinces** la province; **in the provinces** en province. ◆**pro'vincial** *a* & *n* provincial, -ale (*mf*).

provision [prə'vɪʒ(ə)n] *n* (*supply*) provision *f*; (*clause*) disposition *f*; **the p. of** (*supplying*) la fourniture de; **to make p. for** = **to provide for**.

provisional [prə'vɪʒən(ə)l] *a* provisoire. ◆**—ly** *adv* provisoirement.

proviso [prə'vaɪzəu] *n* (*pl* **-os**) stipulation *f*.

provok/e [prə'vəuk] *vt* (*rouse, challenge*) provoquer (**to do, into doing** à faire); (*annoy*) agacer; (*cause*) provoquer (*accident, réaction etc*). ◆**—ing** *a* (*annoying*) agaçant. ◆**provo'cation** *n* provocation *f*. ◆**provocative** *a* (*person, remark etc*) provocant; (*thought-provoking*) qui donne à penser.

prow [prau] *n Nau* proue *f*.

prowess ['prauɛs] *n* (*bravery*) courage *m*; (*skill*) talent *m*.

prowl [praul] *vi* **to p. (around)** rôder; – *n* **to be on the p.** rôder. ◆**—er** *n* rôdeur, -euse *mf*.

proximity [prɒk'sɪmɪtɪ] *n* proximité *f*.

proxy ['prɒksɪ] *n* **by p.** par procuration.

prude [pruːd] *n* prude *f*. ◆**prudery** *n* pruderie *f*. ◆**prudish** *a* prude.

prudent ['pruːdənt] *a* prudent. ◆**prudence** *n* prudence *f*. ◆**prudently** *adv* prudemment.

prun/e [pruːn] **1** *n* (*dried plum*) pruneau *m*. **2** *vt* (*cut*) *Bot* tailler, élaguer; (*speech etc*) *Fig* élaguer. ◆**—ing** *n Bot* taille *f*.

pry [praɪ] **1** *vi* être indiscret; **to p. into** (*meddle*) se mêler de; (*s.o.'s reasons etc*) chercher à découvrir. **2** *vt* **to p. open** *Am* forcer (en faisant levier). ◆**—ing** *a* indiscret.

PS [piː'es] *abbr* (*postscript*) P.-S.

psalm [sɑːm] *n* psaume *m*.

pseud [sjuːd] *n Fam* bêcheur, -euse *mf*.

pseudo- ['sjuːdəu] *pref* pseudo-.

pseudonym ['sjuːdənɪm] *n* pseudonyme *m*.

psychiatry [saɪ'kaɪətrɪ] *n* psychiatrie *f*. ◆**psychi'atric** *a* psychiatrique. ◆**psychiatrist** *n* psychiatre *mf*.

psychic ['saɪkɪk] *a* (méta)psychique; **I'm not p.** *Fam* je ne suis pas devin; – *n* (*person*) médium *m*.

psycho- ['saɪkəu] *pref* psycho-. ◆**psycho-a'nalysis** *n* psychanalyse *f*. ◆**psycho-'analyst** *n* psychanalyste *mf*.

psychology [saɪ'kɒlədʒɪ] *n* psychologie *f*. ◆**psycho'logical** *a* psychologique. ◆**psychologist** *n* psychologue *mf*.

psychopath ['saɪkəupæθ] *n* psychopathe *mf*.

psychosis, *pl* **-oses** [saɪ'kəusɪs, -əusiːz] *n* psychose *f*.

PTO [piːtiː'əu] *abbr* (*please turn over*) TSVP.

pub [pʌb] *n* pub *m*.

puberty ['pjuːbətɪ] *n* puberté *f*.

public ['pʌblɪk] *a* public; (*baths, library*) municipal; **to make a p. protest** protester publiquement; **in the p. eye** très en vue; **p. building** édifice *m* public; **p. company** société *f* par actions; **p. corporation** société *f* nationalisée; **p. figure** personnalité *f* connue; **p. house** pub *m*; **p. life** les affaires *fpl* publiques; **to be p.-spirited** avoir le sens civique; – *n* public *m*; **in p.** en public; **a member of the p.** un simple particulier; **the sporting/***etc* **p.** les amateurs *mpl* de sport/*etc*. ◆**—ly** *adv* publiquement; **p. owned** (*nationalized*) *Com* nationalisé.

publican ['pʌblɪk(ə)n] *n* patron, -onne *mf* d'un pub.

publication [pʌblɪ'keɪʃ(ə)n] *n* (*publishing, book etc*) publication *f*. **publicity** [pʌb'lɪsɪtɪ] *n* publicité *f*. ◆**'publicize** *vt* rendre public; (*advertise*) *Com* faire de la publicité pour.

publish ['pʌblɪʃ] *vt* publier; (*book*) éditer, publier; **to p. s.o.** éditer qn; **'published weekly'** 'paraît toutes les semaines'. ◆**—ing** *n* publication *f* (**of** de); (*profession*) édition *f*. ◆**—er** *n* éditeur, -trice *mf*.

puck [pʌk] *n* (*in ice hockey*) palet *m*.

pucker ['pʌkər] *vt* **to p. (up)** (*brow, lips*) plisser; – *vi* **to p. (up)** se plisser.

pudding ['pʊdɪŋ] *n* dessert *m*, gâteau *m*; **(plum) p.** pudding *m*; **rice p.** riz *m* au lait.

puddle ['pʌd(ə)l] *n* flaque *f* (d'eau).

pudgy ['pʌdʒɪ] *a* **(-ier, -iest)** = **podgy**.

puerile ['pjʊəraɪl] *a* puérile.

puff [pʌf] *n* (*of smoke*) bouffée *f*; (*of wind, air*) bouffée *f*, souffle *m*; **to have run out of p.** *Fam* être à bout de souffle; – *vi* (*blow, pant*) souffler; **to p. at** (*cigar*) tirer sur; – *vt* (*smoke etc*) souffler (**into** dans); **to p. out** (*cheeks etc*) gonfler. ◆**puffy** *a* **(-ier, -iest)** (*swollen*) gonflé.

puke [pjuːk] *vi* (*vomit*) *Sl* dégueuler.

pukka ['pʌkə] *a Fam* authentique.

pull [pʊl] *n* (*attraction*) attraction *f*; (*force*) force *f*; (*influence*) influence *f*; **to give sth a p.** tirer qch; – *vt* (*draw, tug*) tirer; (*tooth*) arracher; (*stopper*) enlever; (*trigger*) appuyer sur; (*muscle*) se claquer; **to p. apart** *or* **to bits** *or* **to pieces** mettre en pièces; **to p. a face** faire la moue; **to (get s.o. to) p. strings** *Fig* se faire pistonner; – *vi* (*tug*) tirer; (*go, move*) aller; **to p. at** *or* **on** tirer (sur). ■ **to p. along** *vt* (*drag*) traîner (**to** jusqu'à); **to p. away** *vt* (*move*) éloigner; (*snatch*) arracher (**from** à); – *vi Aut* démarrer; **to p. away from** s'éloigner de; **to p. back** *vi* (*withdraw*) *Mil* se retirer; – *vt* retirer; (*curtains*) ouvrir; **to p. down** *vt* (*lower*) baisser; (*knock down*) faire tomber; (*demolish*) démolir, abattre; **to p. in** *vt* (*rope*) ramener; (*drag into room etc*) faire entrer; (*stomach*) rentrer; (*crowd*) attirer; – *vi* (*arrive*) *Aut* arriver; (*stop*) *Aut* se garer; **to p. into the station** (*of train*) entrer en gare; **to p. off** *vt* enlever; (*plan, deal*) *Fig* mener à bien; **to p. it off** *Fig* réussir son coup; **to p. on** *vt* (*boots etc*) mettre; **to p. out** *vt* (*extract*) arracher (**from** à); (*remove*) enlever (**from** de); (*from pocket, bag etc*) tirer, sortir (**from** de); (*troops*) retirer; – *vi* (*depart*) *Aut* démarrer; (*move out*) *Aut* déboîter; **to p. out from** (*negotiations etc*) se retirer de; **to p. over** *vt* (*drag*) traîner (**to** jusqu'à); (*knock down*) faire tomber; – *vi Aut* se ranger (sur le côté); **to p. round** *vi Med* se remettre; **to p. through** *vi* s'en tirer; **to p. oneself together** *vt* se ressaisir; **to p. up** *vt* (*socks, bucket etc*) remonter; (*haul up*) hisser; (*uproot*) arracher; (*stop*) arrêter; – *vi Aut* s'arrêter. ◆**p.-up** *n Sp* traction *f*.

pulley ['pʊlɪ] *n* poulie *f*.

pullout ['pʊlaʊt] *n* (*in newspaper etc*) supplément *m* détachable.

pullover ['pʊləʊvər] *n* pull(-over) *m*.

pulp [pʌlp] *n* (*of fruit etc*) pulpe *f*; (*for paper*) pâte *f* à papier; **in a p.** *Fig* en bouillie.

pulpit ['pʊlpɪt] *n Rel* chaire *f*.

pulsate [pʌl'seɪt] *vi* produire des pulsations, battre. ◆**pulsation** *n* (*heartbeat etc*) pulsation *f*.

pulse [pʌls] *n Med* pouls *m*.

pulverize ['pʌlvəraɪz] *vt* (*grind, defeat*) pulvériser.

pumice ['pʌmɪs] *n* **p. (stone)** pierre *f* ponce.

pump [pʌmp] **1** *n* pompe *f*; **(petrol) p. attendant** pompiste *mf*; – *vt* pomper; (*blood*) *Med* faire circuler; (*money*) *Fig* injecter (**into** dans); **to p. s.o. (for information)** tirer les vers du nez à qn; **to p. in** refouler (*à l'aide d'une pompe*); **to p. out** pomper (**of** de); **to p. air into, p. up** (*tyre*) gonfler; – *vi* pomper; (*of heart*) battre. **2** *n* (*for dancing*) escarpin *m*; (*plimsoll*) tennis *f*.

pumpkin ['pʌmpkɪn] *n* potiron *m*.

pun [pʌn] *n* calembour *m*.

punch[1] [pʌntʃ] *n* (*blow*) coup *m* de poing; (*force*) *Fig* punch *m*; **to pack a p.** *Boxing & Fig* avoir du punch; **p. line** (*of joke*) astuce *f* finale; – *vt* (*person*) donner un coup de poing à; (*ball etc*) frapper d'un coup de poing. ◆**p.-up** *n Fam* bagarre *f*.

punch[2] [pʌntʃ] **1** *n* (*for tickets*) poinçonneuse *f*; (*for paper*) perforeuse *f*; **p. card** carte *f* perforée; – *vt* (*ticket*) poinçonner, (*with date*) composter; (*card, paper*) perforer; **to p. a hole in** faire un trou dans. **2** *n* (*drink*) punch *m*.

punctilious [pʌŋk'tɪlɪəs] *a* pointilleux.

punctual ['pʌŋktʃʊəl] *a* (*arriving on time*) à l'heure; (*regularly on time*) ponctuel, exact. ◆**punctu'ality** *n* ponctualité *f*, exactitude *f*. ◆**punctually** *adv* à l'heure; (*habitually*) ponctuellement.

punctuate ['pʌŋktʃʊeɪt] *vt* ponctuer (**with** de). ◆**punctu'ation** *n* ponctuation *f*; **p. mark** signe *m* de ponctuation.

puncture ['pʌŋktʃər] *n* (*in tyre*) crevaison *f*;

to have a p. crever; – *vt* (*burst*) crever; (*pierce*) piquer; – *vi* (*of tyre*) crever.

pundit ['pʌndɪt] *n* expert *m*, ponte *m*.

pungent ['pʌndʒənt] *a* âcre, piquant. ◆**pungency** *n* âcreté *f*.

punish ['pʌnɪʃ] *vt* punir (**for sth** de qch, **for doing** *or* **having done** pour avoir fait); (*treat roughly*) *Fig* malmener. ◆**—ing** *n* punition *f*; – *a* (*tiring*) éreintant. ◆**—able** *a* punissable (**by** de). ◆**—ment** *n* punition *f*, châtiment *m*; **capital p.** peine *f* capitale; **to take a (lot of) p.** (*damage*) *Fig* en encaisser.

punitive ['pju:nɪtɪv] *a* (*measure etc*) punitif.

punk [pʌŋk] **1** *n* (*music*) punk *m*; (*fan*) punk *mf*; – *a* punk *inv*. **2** *n* (*hoodlum*) *Am Fam* voyou *m*.

punt [pʌnt] **1** *n* barque *f* (à fond plat). **2** *vi* (*bet*) *Fam* parier. ◆**—ing** *n* canotage *m*. ◆**—er** *n* **1** (*gambler*) parieur, -euse *mf*. **2** (*customer*) *Sl* client, -ente *mf*.

puny ['pju:nɪ] *a* (**-ier, -iest**) (*sickly*) chétif; (*small*) petit; (*effort*) faible.

pup ['pʌp] *n* (*dog*) chiot *m*.

pupil ['pju:p(ə)l] *n* **1** (*person*) élève *mf*. **2** (*of eye*) pupille *f*.

puppet ['pʌpɪt] *n* marionnette *f*; – *a* (*government, leader*) fantoche.

puppy ['pʌpɪ] *n* (*dog*) chiot *m*.

purchas/e ['pɜ:tʃɪs] *n* (*bought article, buying*) achat *m*; – *vt* acheter (**from s.o.** à qn, **for s.o.** à *or* pour qn). ◆**—er** *n* acheteur, -euse *mf*.

pure [pjʊər] *a* (**-er, -est**) pur. ◆**purely** *adv* purement. ◆**purifi'cation** *n* purification *f*. ◆**purify** *vt* purifier. ◆**purity** *n* pureté *f*.

purée ['pjʊəreɪ] *n* purée *f*.

purgatory ['pɜ:gətrɪ] *n* purgatoire *m*.

purge [pɜ:dʒ] *n Pol Med* purge *f*; – *vt* (*rid*) purger (**of** de); (*group*) *Pol* épurer.

purist ['pjʊərɪst] *n* puriste *mf*.

puritan ['pjʊərɪt(ə)n] *n* & *a* puritain, -aine (*mf*). ◆**puri'tanical** *a* puritain.

purl [pɜ:l] *n* (*knitting stitch*) maille *f* à l'envers.

purple ['pɜ:p(ə)l] *a* & *n* violet (*m*); **to go p.** (*with anger*) devenir pourpre; (*with shame*) devenir cramoisi.

purport [pɜ:'pɔ:t] *vt* **to p. to be** (*claim*) prétendre être.

purpose ['pɜ:pəs] *n* **1** (*aim*) but *m*; **for this p.** dans ce but; **on p.** exprès; **to no p.** inutilement; **to serve no p.** ne servir à rien; **for (the) purposes of** pour les besoins de. **2** (*determination, willpower*) résolution *f*; **to have a sense of p.** être résolu. ◆**p.-'built** *a* construit spécialement. ◆**purposeful** *a* (*determined*) résolu. ◆**purposefully** *adv* dans un but précis; (*resolutely*) résolument. ◆**purposely** *adv* exprès.

purr [pɜ:r] *vi* ronronner; – *n* ronron(nement) *m*.

purse [pɜ:s] **1** *n* (*for coins*) porte-monnaie *m inv*; (*handbag*) *Am* sac *m* à main. **2** *vt* **to p. one's lips** pincer les lèvres.

purser ['pɜ:sər] *n Nau* commissaire *m* du bord.

pursue [pə'sju:] *vt* (*chase, hound, seek, continue*) poursuivre; (*fame, pleasure*) rechercher; (*course of action*) suivre. ◆**pursuer** *n* poursuivant, -ante *mf*. ◆**pursuit** *n* (*of person, glory etc*) poursuite *f*; (*activity, pastime*) occupation *f*; **to go in p. of** se mettre à la poursuite de.

purveyor [pə'veɪər] *n Com* fournisseur *m*.

pus [pʌs] *n* pus *m*.

push [pʊʃ] *n* (*shove*) poussée *f*; (*energy*) *Fig* dynamisme *m*; (*help*) coup *m* de pouce; (*campaign*) campagne *f*; **to give s.o./sth a p.** pousser qn/qch; **to give s.o. the p.** (*dismiss*) *Fam* flanquer qn à la porte; – *vt* pousser (**to, as far as** jusqu'à); (*product*) *Com* pousser la vente de; (*drugs*) *Fam* revendre; **to p. (down)** (*button*) appuyer sur; (*lever*) abaisser; **to p. (forward)** (*views etc*) mettre en avant; **to p. sth into/between** (*thrust*) enfoncer *or* fourrer qch dans/entre; **to p. s.o. into doing** (*urge*) pousser qn à faire; **to p. sth off the table** faire tomber qch de la table (en le poussant); **to p. s.o. off a cliff** pousser qn du haut d'une falaise; **to be pushing forty/***etc* *Fam* friser la quarantaine/*etc*; – *vi* pousser; **to p. for** faire pression pour obtenir. ■ **to p. about** *or* **around** *vt* (*bully*) *Fam* marcher sur les pieds à; **to p. aside** *vt* (*person, objection etc*) écarter; **to p. away** *or* **back** *vt* repousser; (*curtains*) ouvrir; **to p. in** *vi* (*in queue*) *Fam* resquiller; **to p. off** *vi* (*leave*) *Fam* filer; **p. off!** *Fam* fiche le camp!; **to p. on** *vi* continuer (**with sth** qch); (*in journey*) poursuivre sa route; **to p. over** *vt* (*topple*) renverser; **to p. through** *vt* (*law*) faire adopter; – *vti* **to p. (one's way) through** se frayer un chemin (**a crowd/***etc* à travers une foule/*etc*); **to p. up** *vt* (*lever etc*) relever; (*increase*) *Fam* augmenter, relever. ◆**pushed** *a* **to be p. (for time)** (*rushed, busy*) être très bousculé. ◆**pusher** *n* (*of drugs*) revendeur, -euse *mf* (de drogue).

pushbike ['pʊʃbaɪk] *n Fam* vélo *m*. ◆**push-button** *n* poussoir *m*; – *a* (*radio etc*) à poussoir. ◆**pushchair** *n* poussette *f* (pliante). ◆**pushover** *n* **to be a p.** (*easy*)

Fam être facile, être du gâteau. ◆**push-up** *n Sp Am* pompe *f*.
pushy ['pʊʃɪ] *a* (**-ier, -iest**) *Pej* entreprenant; (*in job*) arriviste.
puss(y) ['pʊs(ɪ)] *n* (*cat*) minet *m*, minou *m*.
put [pʊt] *vt* (*pt & pp* **put**, *pres p* **putting**) mettre; (*savings, money*) placer (**into** dans); (*pressure, mark*) faire (**on** sur); (*problem, argument*) présenter (**to** à); (*question*) poser (**to** à); (*say*) dire; (*estimate*) évaluer (**at** à); **to p. it bluntly** pour parler franc. ■ **to p. across** *vt* (*idea etc*) communiquer (**to** à); **to p. away** *vt* (*in its place*) ranger (*livre, voiture etc*); **to p. s.o. away** (*criminal*) mettre qn en prison; (*insane person*) enfermer qn; **to p. back** *vt* remettre; (*receiver*) *Tel* raccrocher; (*progress, clock*) retarder; **to p. by** *vt* (*money*) mettre de côté; **to p. down** *vt* (*on floor, table etc*) poser; (*passenger*) déposer; (*deposit*) *Fin* verser; (*revolt*) réprimer; (*write down*) inscrire; (*assign*) attribuer (**to** à); (*kill*) faire piquer (*chien etc*); **to p. forward** *vt* (*argument, clock, meeting*) avancer; (*opinion*) exprimer; (*candidate*) proposer (**for** à); **to p. in** *vt* (*insert*) introduire; (*add*) ajouter; (*present*) présenter; (*request, application*) faire; (*enrol*) inscrire (**for** à); (*spend*) passer (*une heure etc*) (**doing** à faire); – *vi* **to p. in for** (*job etc*) faire une demande de; **to p. in at** (*of ship etc*) faire escale à; **to p. off** *vt* (*postpone*) renvoyer (à plus tard); (*passenger*) déposer; (*gas, radio*) fermer; (*dismay*) déconcerter; **to p. s.o. off** (*dissuade*) dissuader qn (**doing** de faire); **to p. s.o. off** (*disgust*) dégoûter qn (**sth** de qch); **to p. s.o. off doing** (*disgust*) ôter à qn l'envie de faire; **to p. on** *vt* (*clothes, shoe etc*) mettre; (*weight, accent*) prendre; (*film*) jouer; (*gas, radio*) mettre, allumer; (*record, cassette*) passer; (*clock*) avancer; **to p. s.o. on** (*tease*) *Am* faire marcher qn; **she p. me on to you** elle m'a donné votre adresse; **p. me on to him!** *Tel* passez-le-moi!; **to p. out** *vt* (*take outside*) sortir; (*arm, leg*) étendre; (*hand*) tendre; (*tongue*) tirer; (*gas, light*) éteindre, fermer; (*inconvenience*) déranger; (*upset*) déconcerter; (*issue*) publier; (*dislocate*) démettre; **to p. through** *vt Tel* passer (**to** à); **to p. together** *vt* (*assemble*) assembler; (*compose*) composer; (*prepare*) préparer; (*collection*) faire; **to p. up** *vi* (*lodge*) descendre (**at a hotel** dans un hôtel); **to p. up with** (*tolerate*) supporter; – *vt* (*lift*) lever; (*window*) remonter; (*tent, statue, barrier, ladder*) dresser; (*flag*) hisser; (*building*) construire; (*umbrella*) ouvrir; (*picture, poster*) mettre; (*price, sales, numbers*) augmenter; (*resistance, plea, suggestion*) offrir; (*candidate*) proposer (**for** à); (*guest*) loger; **p.-up job** *Fam* coup *m* monté. ◆**p.-you-up** *n* canapé-lit *m*, convertible *m*.
putrid ['pjuːtrɪd] *a* putride. ◆**putrify** *vi* se putréfier.
putt [pʌt] *n Golf* putt *m*. ◆**putting** *n Golf* putting *m*; **p. green** green *m*.
putter ['pʌtər] *vi* **to p. around** *Am* bricoler.
putty ['pʌtɪ] *n* (*pour fixer une vitre*) mastic *m*.
puzzl/e ['pʌz(ə)l] *n* mystère *m*, énigme *f*; (*game*) casse-tête *m inv*; (*jigsaw*) puzzle *m*; – *vt* laisser perplexe; **to p. out why/when/***etc* essayer de comprendre pourquoi/quand/*etc*; – *vi* **to p. over** (*problem, event*) se creuser la tête sur. ◆**—ed** *a* perplexe. ◆**—ing** *a* mystérieux, surprenant.
PVC [piːviː'siː] *n* (*plastic*) PVC *m*.
pygmy ['pɪgmɪ] *n* pygmée *m*.
pyjama [pɪ'dʒɑːmə] *a* (*jacket etc*) de pyjama. ◆**pyjamas** *npl* pyjama *m*; **a pair of p.** un pyjama.
pylon ['paɪlən] *n* pylône *m*.
pyramid ['pɪrəmɪd] *n* pyramide *f*.
Pyrenees [pɪrə'niːz] *npl* **the P.** les Pyrénées *fpl*.
python ['paɪθən] *n* (*snake*) python *m*.

Q

Q, q [kjuː] *n* Q, q *m*.
quack [kwæk] **1** *n* (*of duck*) coin-coin *m inv*. **2** *a & n* **q. (doctor)** charlatan *m*.
quad(rangle) ['kwɒd(ræŋg(ə)l)] *n* (*of college*) cour *f*.
quadruped ['kwɒdrʊped] *n* quadrupède *m*.
quadruple [kwɒ'druːp(ə)l] *vt* quadrupler.
quadruplets [kwɒ'druːplɪts] (*Fam* **quads** [kwɒdz]) *npl* quadruplés, -ées *mfpl*.
quaff [kwɒf] *vt* (*drink*) avaler.
quagmire ['kwægmaɪər] *n* bourbier *m*.
quail [kweɪl] *n* (*bird*) caille *f*.

quaint [kweɪnt] *a* (**-er, -est**) (*picturesque*) pittoresque; (*antiquated*) vieillot; (*odd*) bizarre. ◆**—ness** *n* pittoresque *m*; caractère *m* vieillot; bizarrerie *f*.
quake [kweɪk] *vi* trembler (**with** de); – *n Fam* tremblement *m* de terre.
Quaker ['kweɪkər] *n* quaker, -eresse *mf*.
qualification [kwɒlɪfɪ'keɪʃ(ə)n] *n* **1** (*competence*) compétence *f* (**for** pour, **to do** pour faire); (*diploma*) diplôme *m*; *pl* (*requirements*) conditions *fpl* requises. **2** (*reservation*) réserve *f*.
qualify ['kwɒlɪfaɪ] **1** *vt* (*make competent*) & *Sp* qualifier (**for sth** pour qch, **to do** pour faire); – *vi* obtenir son diplôme (**as a doctor/***etc* de médecin/*etc*); *Sp* se qualifier (**for** pour); **to q. for** (*post*) remplir les conditions requises pour. **2** *vt* (*modify*) faire des réserves à; (*opinion*) nuancer; *Gram* qualifier. ◆**qualified** *a* (*able*) qualifié (**to do** pour faire); (*doctor etc*) diplômé; (*success*) limité; (*opinion*) nuancé; (*support*) conditionnel. ◆**qualifying** *a* (*exam*) d'entrée; **q. round** *Sp* (épreuve *f*) éliminatoire *f*.
quality ['kwɒlɪtɪ] *n* qualité *f*; – *a* (*product*) de qualité. ◆**qualitative** *a* qualitatif.
qualms [kwɑːmz] *npl* (*scruples*) scrupules *mpl*; (*anxieties*) inquiétudes *fpl*.
quandary ['kwɒndrɪ] *n* **in a q.** bien embarrassé; **to be in a q. about what to do** ne pas savoir quoi faire.
quantity ['kwɒntɪtɪ] *n* quantité *f*; **in q.** (*to purchase etc*) en grande(s) quantité(s). ◆**quantify** *vt* quantifier. ◆**quantitative** *a* quantitatif.
quarantine ['kwɒrəntiːn] *n Med* quarantaine *f*; – *vt* mettre en quarantaine.
quarrel ['kwɒrəl] *n* querelle *f*, dispute *f*; **to pick a q.** chercher querelle (**with s.o.** à qn); – *vi* (**-ll-**, *Am* **-l-**) se disputer, se quereller (**with** avec); **to q. with sth** trouver à redire à qch. ◆**quarrelling** *n*, *Am* ◆**quarreling** *n* (*quarrels*) querelles *fpl*. ◆**quarrelsome** *a* querelleur.
quarry ['kwɒrɪ] *n* **1** (*excavation*) carrière *f*. **2** (*prey*) proie *f*.
quart [kwɔːt] *n* litre *m* (*mesure approximative*) (*Br* = *1,14 litres, Am* = *0,95 litre*).
quarter ['kwɔːtər] **1** *n* quart *m*; (*of year*) trimestre *m*; (*money*) *Am Can* quart *m* de dollar; (*of moon, fruit*) quartier *m*; **to divide into quarters** diviser en quatre; **q. (of a) pound** quart *m* de livre; **a q. past nine,** *Am* **a q. after nine** neuf heures et *or* un quart; **a q. to nine** neuf heures moins le quart; **from all quarters** de toutes parts. **2** *n* (*district*) quartier *m*; *pl* (*circles*) milieux *mpl*; (**living**) **quarters** logement(s) *m*(*pl*); *Mil* quartier(s) *m*(*pl*); – *vt* (*troops*) *Mil* cantonner. ◆**—ly** *a* trimestriel; – *adv* trimestriellement; – *n* publication *f* trimestrielle.
quarterfinal [kwɔːtə'faɪn(ə)l] *n Sp* quart *m* de finale.
quartet(te) [kwɔː'tet] *n Mus* quatuor *m*; (**jazz**) **q.** quartette *m*.
quartz [kwɔːts] *n* quartz *m*; – *a* (*clock etc*) à quartz.
quash [kwɒʃ] *vt* (*rebellion etc*) réprimer; (*verdict*) *Jur* casser.
quaver ['kweɪvər] **1** *vi* chevroter; – *n* chevrotement *m*. **2** *n Mus* croche *f*.
quay [kiː] *n Nau* quai *m*. ◆**quayside** *n* **on the q.** sur les quais.
queas/y ['kwiːzɪ] *a* (**-ier, -iest**) **to feel** *or* **be q.** avoir mal au cœur. ◆**—iness** *n* mal *m* au cœur.
Quebec [kwɪ'bek] *n* le Québec.
queen [kwiːn] *n* reine *f*; *Chess Cards* dame *f*; **the q. mother** la reine mère.
queer ['kwɪər] *a* (**-er, -est**) (*odd*) bizarre; (*dubious*) louche; (*ill*) *Fam* patraque; – *n* (*homosexual*) *Pej Fam* pédé *m*.
quell [kwel] *vt* (*revolt etc*) réprimer.
quench [kwentʃ] *vt* (*fire*) éteindre; **to q. one's thirst** se désaltérer.
querulous ['kwerʊləs] *a* (*complaining*) grognon.
query ['kwɪərɪ] *n* question *f*; (*doubt*) doute *m*; – *vt* mettre en question.
quest [kwest] *n* quête *f* (**for** de); **in q. of** en quête de.
question ['kwestʃ(ə)n] *n* question *f*; **there's some q. of it** il en est question; **there's no q. of it, it's out of the q.** il n'en est pas question, c'est hors de question; **without q.** incontestable(ment); **in q.** en question, dont il s'agit; **q. mark** point *m* d'interrogation; **q. master** *TV Rad* animateur, -trice *mf*; – *vt* interroger (**about** sur); (*doubt*) mettre en question; **to q. whether** douter que (+ *sub*). ◆**—ing** *a* (*look etc*) interrogateur; – *n* interrogation *f*. ◆**—able** *a* douteux. ◆**questio'nnaire** *n* questionnaire *m*.
queue [kjuː] *n* (*of people*) queue *f*; (*of cars*) file *f*; **to stand in a q., form a q.** faire la queue; – *vi* **to q. (up)** faire la queue.
quibbl/e ['kwɪb(ə)l] *vi* ergoter, discuter (**over** sur). ◆**—ing** *n* ergotage *m*.
quiche [kiːʃ] *n* (*tart*) quiche *f*.
quick [kwɪk] **1** *a* (**-er, -est**) rapide; **q. to react** prompt à réagir; **to be q.** faire vite; **to have a q. shave/meal/***etc* se raser/manger/*etc* en

vitesse; to be a q. worker travailler vite; – *adv* (-er, -est) vite; as q. as a flash en un clin d'œil. 2 *n* to cut to the q. blesser au vif. ◆**q.-'tempered** *a* irascible. ◆**q.-'witted** *a* à l'esprit vif. ◆**quicken** *vt* accélérer; – *vi* s'accélérer. ◆**quickie** *n* (*drink*) *Fam* pot *m* (*pris en vitesse*). ◆**quickly** *adv* vite. ◆**quicksands** *npl* sables *mpl* mouvants.

quid [kwɪd] *n inv Fam* livre *f* (sterling).

quiet [kwaɪət] *a* (-er, -est) (*silent, still, peaceful*) tranquille, calme; (*machine, vehicle, temperament*) silencieux; (*gentle*) doux; (*voice*) bas, doux; (*sound*) léger, doux; (*private*) intime; (*colour*) discret; to be *or* keep q. (*shut up*) se taire; (*make no noise*) ne pas faire de bruit; q.! silence!; to keep q. about sth, keep sth q. ne pas parler de qch; on the q. (*secretly*) *Fam* en cachette; – *vt* = quieten. ◆**quieten** *vti* to q. (down) (se) calmer. ◆**quietly** *adv* tranquillement; (*gently, not loudly*) doucement; (*silently*) silencieusement; (*secretly*) en cachette; (*discreetly*) discrètement. ◆**quietness** *n* tranquillité *f*.

quill [kwɪl] *n* (*pen*) plume *f* (d'oie).

quilt [kwɪlt] *n* édredon *m*; (continental) q. couette *f*; – *vt* (*stitch*) piquer; (*pad*) matelasser.

quintessence [kwɪn'tesəns] *n* quintessence *f*.

quintet(te) [kwɪn'tet] *n* quintette *m*.

quintuplets [kwɪn'tjuːplɪts] (*Fam* quins [kwɪnz]) *npl* quintuplés, -ées *mfpl*.

quip [kwɪp] *n* (*remark*) boutade *f*; – *vi* (-pp-) faire des boutades; – *vt* dire sur le ton de la boutade.

quirk [kwɜːk] *n* bizarrerie *f*; (*of fate*) caprice *m*.

quit [kwɪt] *vt* (*pt & pp* quit *or* quitted, *pres p* quitting) (*leave*) quitter; to q. doing arrêter de faire; – *vi* (*give up*) abandonner; (*resign*) démissionner.

quite [kwaɪt] *adv* (*entirely*) tout à fait; (*really*) vraiment; (*rather*) assez; q. another matter une tout autre affaire *or* question; q. a genius un véritable génie; q. good (*not bad*) pas mal (du tout); q. (so)! exactement!; I q. understand je comprends très bien; q. a lot pas mal (of de); q. a (long) time ago il y a pas mal de temps.

quits [kwɪts] *a* quitte (with envers); to call it q. en rester là.

quiver ['kwɪvər] *vi* frémir (with de); (*of voice*) trembler, frémir; (*of flame*) vaciller, trembler.

quiz [kwɪz] *n* (*pl* quizzes) (*riddle*) devinette *f*; (*test*) test *m*; q. (programme) *TV Rad* jeu(-concours) *m*; – *vt* (-zz-) questionner. ◆**quizmaster** *n TV Rad* animateur, -trice *mf*.

quizzical ['kwɪzɪk(ə)l] *a* (*mocking*) narquois; (*perplexed*) perplexe.

quorum ['kwɔːrəm] *n* quorum *m*.

quota ['kwəʊtə] *n* quota *m*.

quote [kwəʊt] *vt* citer; (*reference number*) *Com* rappeler; (*price*) indiquer; (*price on Stock Exchange*) coter; – *vi* to q. from (*author, book*) citer; – *n Fam* = quotation; in quotes entre guillemets. ◆**quo'tation** *n* citation *f*; (*estimate*) *Com* devis *m*; (*on Stock Exchange*) cote *f*; q. marks guillemets *mpl*; in q. marks entre guillemets.

quotient ['kwəʊʃ(ə)nt] *n* quotient *m*.

R

R, r [ɑːr] *n* R, r *m*.

rabbi ['ræbaɪ] *n* rabbin *m*; chief r. grand rabbin.

rabbit ['ræbɪt] *n* lapin *m*.

rabble ['ræb(ə)l] *n* (*crowd*) cohue *f*; the r. *Pej* la populace.

rabies ['reɪbiːz] *n Med* rage *f*. ◆**rabid** ['ræbɪd] *a* (*dog*) enragé; (*person*) *Fig* fanatique.

raccoon [rə'kuːn] *n* (*animal*) raton *m* laveur.

rac/e[1] [reɪs] *n Sp & Fig* course *f*; – *vt* (*horse*) faire courir; (*engine*) emballer; to r. (against *or* with) s.o. faire une course avec qn; – *vi* (*run*) courir; (*of engine*) s'emballer; (*of pulse*) battre à tout rompre. ◆**—ing** *n* courses *fpl*; – *a* (*car, bicycle etc*) de course; r. driver coureur *m* automobile. ◆**racecourse** *n* champ *m* de courses. ◆**racegoer** *n* turfiste *mf*. ◆**racehorse** *n* cheval *m* de course. ◆**racetrack** *n* piste *f*; (*for horses*) *Am* champ *m* de courses.

race[2] [reɪs] *n* (*group*) race *f*; – *a* (*prejudice etc*) racial; r. relations rapports *mpl* entre les races. ◆**racial** *a* racial. ◆**racialism** *n* racisme *m.* ◆**racism** *n* racisme *m.* ◆**racist** *a* & *n* raciste (*mf*).

rack [ræk] **1** *n* (*shelf*) étagère *f*; (*for bottles etc*) casier *m*; (*for drying dishes*) égouttoir *m*; **(luggage) r.** (*on bicycle*) porte-bagages *m inv*; (*on bus, train etc*) filet *m* à bagages; **(roof) r.** (*of car*) galerie *f*. **2** *vt* **to r. one's brains** se creuser la cervelle. **3** *n* **to go to r. and ruin** (*of person*) aller à la ruine; (*of building*) tomber en ruine; (*of health*) se délabrer.

racket ['rækɪt] *n* **1** (*for tennis etc*) raquette *f*. **2** (*din*) vacarme *m*. **3** (*crime*) racket *m*; (*scheme*) combine *f*; **the drug(s) r.** le trafic *m* de (la) drogue. ◆**racke'teer** *n* racketteur *m*. ◆**racke'teering** *n* racket *m*.

racoon [rə'kuːn] *n* (*animal*) raton *m* laveur.

racy ['reɪsɪ] *a* (**-ier, -iest**) piquant; (*suggestive*) osé.

radar ['reɪdɑːr] *n* radar *m*; – *a* (*control, trap etc*) radar *inv*; **r. operator** radariste *mf*.

radiant ['reɪdɪənt] *a* (*person*) rayonnant (**with** de), radieux. ◆**radiance** *n* éclat *m*, rayonnement *m*. ◆**radiantly** *adv* (*to shine*) avec éclat; **r. happy** rayonnant de joie.

radiate ['reɪdɪeɪt] *vt* (*emit*) dégager; (*joy*) *Fig* rayonner de; – *vi* (*of heat, lines*) rayonner (**from** de). ◆**radia'tion** *n* (*of heat etc*) rayonnement *m* (**of** de); (*radioactivity*) *Phys* radiation *f*; (*rays*) irradiation *f*; **r. sickness** mal *m* des rayons.

radiator ['reɪdɪeɪtər] *n* radiateur *m*.

radical ['rædɪk(ə)l] *a* radical; – *n* (*person*) *Pol* radical, -ale *mf*.

radio ['reɪdɪəʊ] *n* (*pl* **-os**) radio *f*; **on the r.** à la radio; **car r.** autoradio *m*; **r. set** poste *m* (de) radio; **r. operator** radio *m*; **r. wave** onde *f* hertzienne; – *vt* (*message*) transmettre (par radio) (**to** à); **to r. s.o.** appeler qn par radio. ◆**r.-con'trolled** *a* radioguidé. ◆**radio'active** *a* radioactif. ◆**radioac'tivity** *n* radioactivité *f*.

radiographer [reɪdɪ'ɒgrəfər] *n* (*technician*) radiologue *mf*. ◆**radiography** *n* radiographie *f*. ◆**radiologist** *n* (*doctor*) radiologue *mf*. ◆**radiology** *n* radiologie *f*.

radish ['rædɪʃ] *n* radis *m*.

radius, *pl* **-dii** ['reɪdɪəs, -dɪaɪ] *n* (*of circle*) rayon *m*; **within a r. of** dans un rayon de.

RAF [ɑːreɪ'ef] *n abbr* (*Royal Air Force*) armée *f* de l'air (britannique).

raffia ['ræfɪə] *n* raphia *m*.

raffle ['ræf(ə)l] *n* tombola *f*.

raft [rɑːft] *n* (*boat*) radeau *m*.

rafter ['rɑːftər] *n* (*beam*) chevron *m*.

rag [ræg] *n* **1** (*old garment*) loque *f*, haillon *m*; (*for dusting etc*) chiffon *m*; **in rags** (*clothes*) en loques; (*person*) en haillons; **r.-and-bone man** chiffonnier *m*. **2** (*newspaper*) torchon *m*. **3** (*procession*) *Univ* carnaval *m* (*au profit d'œuvres de charité*). ◆**ragged** ['rægɪd] *a* (*clothes*) en loques; (*person*) en haillons; (*edge*) irrégulier. ◆**ragman** *n* (*pl* **-men**) chiffonnier *m*.

ragamuffin ['rægəmʌfɪn] *n* va-nu-pieds *m inv*.

rag/e [reɪdʒ] *n* rage *f*; (*of sea*) furie *f*; **to fly into a r.** se mettre en rage; **to be all the r.** (*of fashion etc*) faire fureur; – *vi* (*be angry*) rager; (*of storm, battle*) faire rage. ◆**—ing** *a* (*storm, fever*) violent; **a r. fire** un grand incendie; **in a r. temper** furieux.

raid [reɪd] *n Mil* raid *m*; (*by police*) descente *f*; (*by thieves*) hold-up *m*; **air r.** raid *m* aérien, attaque *f* aérienne; – *vt* faire un raid *or* une descente *or* un hold-up dans; *Av* attaquer; (*larder, fridge etc*) *Fam* dévaliser. ◆**raider** *n* (*criminal*) malfaiteur *m*; *pl Mil* commando *m*.

rail [reɪl] **1** *n* (*for train*) rail *m*; **by r.** (*to travel*) par le train; (*to send*) par chemin de fer; **to go off the rails** (*of train*) dérailler; – *a* ferroviaire; (*strike*) des cheminots. **2** *n* (*rod on balcony*) balustrade *f*; (*on stairs, for spotlight*) rampe *f*; (*for curtain*) tringle *f*; **(towel) r.** porte-serviettes *m inv*. ◆**railing** *n* (*of balcony*) balustrade *f*; *pl* (*fence*) grille *f*. ◆**railroad** *n Am* = **railway; r. track** voie *f* ferrée. ◆**railway** *n* (*system*) chemin *m* de fer; (*track*) voie *f* ferrée; – *a* (*ticket*) de chemin de fer; (*network*) ferroviaire; **r. line** (*route*) ligne *f* de chemin de fer; (*track*) voie *f* ferrée; **r. station** gare *f*. ◆**railwayman** *n* (*pl* **-men**) cheminot *m*.

rain [reɪn] *n* pluie *f*; **in the r.** sous la pluie; **I'll give you a r. check** (*for invitation*) *Am Fam* j'accepterai volontiers à une date ultérieure; – *vi* pleuvoir; **to r. (down)** (*of blows, bullets*) pleuvoir; **it's raining** il pleut. ◆**rainbow** *n* arc-en-ciel *m*. ◆**raincoat** *n* imper(méable) *m*. ◆**raindrop** *n* goutte *f* de pluie. ◆**rainfall** *n* (*shower*) chute *f* de pluie; (*amount*) précipitations *fpl*. ◆**rainstorm** *n* trombe *f* d'eau. ◆**rainwater** *n* eau *f* de pluie. ◆**rainy** *a* (**-ier, -iest**) pluvieux; **the r. season** la saison des pluies.

raise [reɪz] *vt* (*lift*) lever; (*sth heavy*) (sou)lever; (*child, animal, voice, statue*) élever; (*crops*) cultiver; (*salary, price*) augmenter, relever; (*temperature*) faire monter; (*question, protest*) soulever; (*taxes, blockade*) lever; **to r. a smile/a laugh** (*in others*) faire sourire/rire; **to r. s.o.'s hopes**

faire naître les espérances de qn; **to r. money** réunir des fonds; – *n* (*pay rise*) *Am* augmentation *f* (de salaire).
raisin ['reɪz(ə)n] *n* raison *m* sec.
rake [reɪk] *n* râteau *m*; – *vt* (*garden*) ratisser; (*search*) fouiller dans; **to r. (up)** (*leaves*) ramasser (avec un râteau); **to r. in** (*money*) *Fam* ramasser à la pelle; **to r. up** (*the past*) remuer. ◆**r.-off** *n* *Fam* pot-de-vin *m*, ristourne *f*.
rally ['rælɪ] *vt* (*unite, win over*) rallier (**to** à); (*one's strength*) *Fig* reprendre; – *vi* se rallier (**to** à); (*recover*) se remettre (**from** de); **to r. round** (*help*) venir en aide (**s.o.** à qn); – *n* *Mil* ralliement *m*; *Pol* rassemblement *m*; *Sp Aut* rallye *m*.
ram [ræm] **1** *n* (*animal*) bélier *m*. **2** *vt* (**-mm-**) (*ship*) heurter; (*vehicle*) emboutir; **to r. sth into** (*thrust*) enfoncer qch dans.
rambl/e ['ræmb(ə)l] **1** *n* (*hike*) randonnée *f*; – *vi* faire une randonnée *or* des randonnées. **2** *vi* **to r. on** (*talk*) *Pej* discourir. ◆**—ing 1** *a* (*house*) construit sans plan; (*spread out*) vaste; (*rose etc*) grimpant. **2** *a* (*speech*) décousu; – *npl* divagations *fpl*. ◆**—er** *n* promeneur, -euse *mf*.
ramification [ræmɪfɪ'keɪʃ(ə)n] *n* ramification *f*.
ramp [ræmp] *n* (*slope*) rampe *f*; (*in garage*) *Tech* pont *m* (de graissage); *Av* passerelle *f*; **'r.'** *Aut* 'dénivellation'.
rampage ['ræmpeɪdʒ] *n* **to go on the r.** (*of crowd*) se déchaîner; (*loot*) se livrer au pillage.
rampant ['ræmpənt] *a* **to be r.** (*of crime, disease etc*) sévir.
rampart ['ræmpɑːt] *n* rempart *m*.
ramshackle ['ræmʃæk(ə)l] *a* délabré.
ran [ræn] *see* **run**.
ranch [rɑːntʃ] *n* *Am* ranch *m*; **r. house** maison *f* genre bungalow (sur sous-sol).
rancid ['rænsɪd] *a* rance.
rancour ['ræŋkər] *n* rancœur *f*.
random ['rændəm] *n* **at r.** au hasard; – *a* (*choice*) fait au hasard; (*sample*) prélevé au hasard; (*pattern*) irrégulier.
randy ['rændɪ] *a* (**-ier, -iest**) *Fam* sensuel, lascif.
rang [ræŋ] *see* **ring**[2].
range [reɪndʒ] **1** *n* (*of gun, voice etc*) portée *f*; (*of aircraft, ship*) rayon *m* d'action; (*series*) gamme *f*; (*choice*) choix *m*; (*of prices*) éventail *m*; (*of voice*) *Mus* étendue *f*; (*of temperature*) variations *fpl*; (*sphere*) *Fig* champ *m*, étendue *f*; – *vi* (*vary*) varier; (*extend*) s'étendre; (*roam*) errer, rôder. **2** *n* (*of mountains*) chaîne *f*; (*grassland*) *Am* prairie *f*. **3** *n* (*stove*) *Am* cuisinière *f*. **4** *n* (**shooting** *or* **rifle**) **r.** (*at funfair*) stand *m* de tir; (*outdoors*) champ *m* de tir.
ranger ['reɪndʒər] *n* (**forest**) **r.** *Am* garde *m* forestier.
rank [ræŋk] **1** *n* (*position, class*) rang *m*; (*grade*) *Mil* grade *m*, rang *m*; **the r. and file** (*workers etc*) *Pol* la base; **the ranks** (*men in army, numbers*) les rangs *mpl* (**of** de); **taxi r.** station *f* de taxi; – *vti* **to r. among** compter parmi. **2** *a* (**-er, -est**) (*smell*) fétide; (*vegetation*) luxuriant; *Fig* absolu.
rankle ['ræŋk(ə)l] *vi* **it rankles (with me)** je l'ai sur le cœur.
ransack ['rænsæk] *vt* (*search*) fouiller; (*plunder*) saccager.
ransom ['ræns(ə)m] *n* rançon *f*; **to hold to r.** rançonner; – *vt* (*redeem*) racheter.
rant [rænt] *vi* **to r. (and rave)** tempêter (**at** contre).
rap [ræp] *n* petit coup *m* sec; – *vi* (**-pp-**) frapper (**at** à); – *vt* **to r. s.o. over the knuckles** taper sur les doigts de qn.
rapacious [rə'peɪʃəs] *a* (*greedy*) rapace.
rape [reɪp] *vt* violer; – *n* viol *m*. ◆**rapist** *n* violeur *m*.
rapid ['ræpɪd] **1** *a* rapide. **2** *n & npl* (*of river*) rapide(s) *m*(*pl*). ◆**ra'pidity** *n* rapidité *f*. ◆**rapidly** *adv* rapidement.
rapport [ræ'pɔːr] *n* (*understanding*) rapport *m*.
rapt [ræpt] *a* (*attention*) profond.
rapture ['ræptʃər] *n* extase *f*; **to go into raptures** s'extasier (**about** sur). ◆**rapturous** *a* (*welcome, applause*) enthousiaste.
rare [reər] *a* (**-er, -est**) rare; (*meat*) *Culin* saignant; (*first-rate*) *Fam* fameux; **it's r. for her to do it** il est rare qu'elle le fasse. ◆**—ly** *adv* rarement. ◆**—ness** *n* rareté *f*. ◆**rarity** *n* (*quality, object*) rareté *f*.
rarefied ['reərɪfaɪd] *a* raréfié.
raring ['reərɪŋ] *a* **r. to start/***etc* impatient de commencer/*etc*.
rascal ['rɑːsk(ə)l] *n* coquin, -ine *mf*. ◆**rascally** *a* (*child etc*) coquin; (*habit, trick etc*) de coquin.
rash [ræʃ] **1** *n* *Med* éruption *f*. **2** *a* (**-er, -est**) irréfléchi. ◆**—ly** *adv* sans réfléchir. ◆**—ness** *n* irréflexion *f*.
rasher ['ræʃər] *n* tranche *f* de lard.
rasp [rɑːsp] *n* (*file*) râpe *f*.
raspberry ['rɑːzbərɪ] *n* (*fruit*) framboise *f*; (*bush*) framboisier *m*.
rasping ['rɑːspɪŋ] *a* (*voice*) âpre.
rat [ræt] **1** *n* rat *m*; **r. poison** mort-aux-rats *f*; **the r. race** *Fig* la course au bifteck, la jungle. **2** *vi* (**-tt-**) **to r. on** (*desert*) lâcher;

(*denounce*) cafarder sur; (*promise etc*) manquer à.

rate [reɪt] **1** *n* (*percentage, level*) taux *m*; (*speed*) vitesse *f*; (*price*) tarif *m*; *pl* (*on housing*) impôts *mpl* locaux; **insurance rates** primes *fpl* d'assurance; **r. of flow** débit *m*; **postage** *or* **postal r.** tarif *m* postal; **at the r. of** à une vitesse de; (*amount*) à raison de; **at this r.** (*slow speed*) à ce train-là; **at any r.** en tout cas; **the success r.** (*chances*) les chances *fpl* de succès; (*candidates*) le pourcentage de reçus. **2** *vt* (*evaluate*) évaluer; (*regard*) considérer (**as** comme); (*deserve*) mériter; **to r. highly** apprécier (beaucoup); **to be highly rated** être très apprécié. ◆**rateable** *a* **r. value** valeur *f* locative nette. ◆**ratepayer** *n* contribuable *mf*.

rather ['rɑːðər] *adv* (*preferably, fairly*) plutôt; **I'd r. stay** j'aimerais mieux *or* je préférerais rester (**than** que); **I'd r. you came** je préférerais que vous veniez; **r. than leave**/*etc* plutôt que de partir/*etc*; **r. more tired**/*etc* un peu plus fatigué/*etc* (**than** que); **it's r. nice** c'est bien.

ratify ['rætɪfaɪ] *vt* ratifier. ◆**ratifi'cation** *n* ratification *f*.

rating ['reɪtɪŋ] *n* (*classification*) classement *m*; (*wage etc level*) indice *m*; **credit r.** *Fin* réputation *f* de solvabilité; **the ratings** *TV* l'indice *m* d'écoute.

ratio ['reɪʃɪəʊ] *n* (*pl* **-os**) proportion *f*.

ration ['ræʃ(ə)n, *Am* 'reɪʃ(ə)n] *n* ration *f*; *pl* (*food*) vivres *mpl*; – *vt* rationner; **I was rationed to . . .** ma ration était . . . .

rational ['ræʃən(ə)l] *a* (*method, thought etc*) rationnel; (*person*) raisonnable. ◆**rationalize** *vt* (*organize*) rationaliser; (*explain*) justifier. ◆**rationally** *adv* raisonnablement.

rattle ['ræt(ə)l] **1** *n* (*baby's toy*) hochet *m*; (*of sports fan*) crécelle *f*. **2** *n* petit bruit *m* (sec); cliquetis *m*; crépitement *m*; – *vi* faire du bruit; (*of bottles*) cliqueter; (*of gunfire*) crépiter; (*of window*) trembler; – *vt* (*shake*) agiter; (*window*) faire trembler; (*keys*) faire cliqueter. **3** *vt* **to r. s.o.** (*make nervous*) *Fam* ébranler qn; **to r. off** (*poem etc*) *Fam* débiter (à toute vitesse). ◆**rattlesnake** *n* serpent *m* à sonnette.

ratty ['rætɪ] *a* (**-ier, -iest**) **1** (*shabby*) *Am Fam* minable. **2 to get r.** (*annoyed*) *Fam* prendre la mouche.

raucous ['rɔːkəs] *a* rauque.

raunchy ['rɔːntʃɪ] *a* (**-ier, -iest**) (*joke etc*) *Am Fam* grivois.

ravage ['rævɪdʒ] *vt* ravager; – *npl* ravages *mpl*.

rav/e [reɪv] *vi* (*talk nonsense*) divaguer; (*rage*) tempêter (**at** contre); **to r. about** (*enthuse*) ne pas se tarir d'éloges sur; – *a* **r. review** *Fam* critique *f* dithyrambique. ◆**—ing** *a* **to be r. mad** être fou furieux; – *npl* (*wild talk*) divagations *fpl*.

raven ['reɪv(ə)n] *n* corbeau *m*.

ravenous ['rævənəs] *a* vorace; **I'm r.** *Fam* j'ai une faim de loup.

ravine [rə'viːn] *n* ravin *m*.

ravioli [rævɪ'əʊlɪ] *n* ravioli *mpl*.

ravish ['rævɪʃ] *vt* (*rape*) *Lit* violenter. ◆**—ing** *a* (*beautiful*) ravissant. ◆**—ingly** *adv* **r. beautiful** d'une beauté ravissante.

raw [rɔː] *a* (**-er, -est**) (*vegetable etc*) cru; (*sugar*) brut; (*immature*) inexpérimenté; (*wound*) à vif; (*skin*) écorché; (*weather*) rigoureux; **r. edge** bord *m* coupé; **r. material** matière *f* première; **to get a r. deal** *Fam* être mal traité.

Rawlplug® ['rɔːlplʌg] *n* cheville *f*, tampon *m*.

ray [reɪ] *n* (*of light, sun etc*) & *Phys* rayon *m*; (*of hope*) *Fig* lueur *f*.

raze [reɪz] *vt* **to r. (to the ground)** (*destroy*) raser.

razor ['reɪzər] *n* rasoir *m*.

re [riː] *prep Com* en référence à.

re- [riː] *pref* ré-, re-, r-.

reach [riːtʃ] *vt* (*place, aim etc*) atteindre, arriver à; (*gain access to*) accéder à; (*of letter*) parvenir à (*qn*); (*contact*) joindre (*qn*); **to r. s.o. (over) sth** (*hand over*) passer qch à qn; **to r. out** (*one's arm*) (é)tendre; – *vi* (*extend*) s'étendre (**to** à); (*of voice*) porter; **to r. (out)** (é)tendre le bras (**for** pour prendre); – *n* portée *f*; *Boxing* allonge *f*; **within r. of** à portée de; (*near*) à proximité de; **within easy r.** (*object*) à portée de main; (*shops*) facilement accessible.

react [rɪ'ækt] *vi* réagir. ◆**reaction** *n* réaction *f*. ◆**reactionary** *a* & *n* réactionnaire (*mf*).

reactor [rɪ'æktər] *n* réacteur *m*.

read [riːd] *vt* (*pt* & *pp* **read** [red]) lire; (*study*) *Univ* faire des études de; (*meter*) relever; (*of instrument*) indiquer; **to r. back** *or* **over** relire; **to r. out** lire (à haute voix); **to r. through** (*skim*) parcourir; **to r. up (on)** (*study*) étudier; – *vi* lire; **to r. well** (*of text*) se lire bien; **to r. to s.o.** faire la lecture à qn; **to r. about** (*s.o., sth*) lire qch sur; **to r. for** (*degree*) *Univ* préparer; – *n* **to have a r.** *Fam* faire un peu de lecture; **this book's a**

good r. *Fam* ce livre est agréable à lire. ◆**—ing** *n* lecture *f*; (*of meter*) relevé *m*; (*by instrument*) indication *f*; (*variant*) variante *f*; – *a* (*room*) de lecture; **r. matter** choses *fpl* à lire; **r. lamp** lampe *f* de bureau *or* de chevet. ◆**—able** *a* lisible. ◆**—er** *n* lecteur, -trice *mf*; (*book*) livre *m* de lecture. ◆**readership** *n* lecteurs *mpl*, public *m*.

readdress [riːəˈdres] *vt* (*letter*) faire suivre.

readjust [riːəˈdʒʌst] *vt* (*instrument*) régler; (*salary*) réajuster; – *vi* se réadapter (to à). ◆**—ment** *n* réglage *m*; réajustement *m*; réadaptation *f*.

readily [ˈredɪlɪ] *adv* (*willingly*) volontiers; (*easily*) facilement. ◆**readiness** *n* empressement *m* (**to do** à faire); **in r. for** prêt pour.

ready [ˈredɪ] *a* (**-ier, -iest**) prêt (**to do** à faire, **for sth** à *or* pour qch); (*quick*) *Fig* prompt (**to do** à faire); **to get sth r.** préparer qch; **to get r.** se préparer (**for sth** à qch, **to do** à faire); **r. cash, r. money** argent *m* liquide; – *n* **at the r.** tout prêt. ◆**r.-ˈcooked** *a* tout cuit. ◆**r.-ˈmade** *a* tout fait; **r.-made clothes** prêt-à-porter *m inv*.

real [rɪəl] *a* vrai, véritable; (*life, world etc*) réel; **it's the r. thing** *Fam* c'est du vrai de vrai; **r. estate** *Am* immobilier *m*; – *adv* *Fam* vraiment; **r. stupid** vraiment bête; – *n* **for r.** *Fam* pour de vrai. ◆**realism** *n* réalisme *m*. ◆**realist** *n* réaliste *mf*. ◆**reaˈlistic** *a* réaliste. ◆**reaˈlistically** *adv* avec réalisme.

reality [rɪˈælətɪ] *n* réalité *f*; **in r.** en réalité.

realize [ˈrɪəlaɪz] *vt* **1** (*know*) se rendre compte de, réaliser; (*understand*) comprendre (**that** que); **to r. that** (*know*) se rendre compte que. **2** (*carry out, convert into cash*) réaliser; (*price*) atteindre. ◆**realiˈzation** *n* **1** (prise *f* de) conscience *f*. **2** (*of aim, assets*) réalisation *f*.

really [ˈrɪəlɪ] *adv* vraiment; **is it r. true?** est-ce bien vrai?

realm [relm] *n* (*kingdom*) royaume *m*; (*of dreams etc*) *Fig* monde *m*.

realtor [ˈrɪəltər] *n Am* agent *m* immobilier.

reap [riːp] *vt* (*field, crop*) moissonner; *Fig* récolter.

reappear [riːəˈpɪər] *vi* réapparaître.

reappraisal [riːəˈpreɪz(ə)l] *n* réévaluation *f*.

rear [rɪər] **1** *n* (*back part*) arrière *m*; (*of column*) queue *f*; **in** *or* **at the r.** à l'arrière (**of** de); **from the r.** par derrière; – *a* arrière *inv*, de derrière; **r.-view mirror** rétroviseur *m*. **2** *vt* (*family, animals etc*) élever; (*one's head*) relever. **3** *vi* **to r. (up)** (*of horse*) se cabrer. ◆**rearguard** *n* arrière-garde *f*.

rearrange [riːəˈreɪndʒ] *vt* réarranger.

reason [ˈriːz(ə)n] *n* (*cause, sense*) raison *f*; **the r. for/why** *or* **that . . .** la raison de/pour laquelle . . . ; **for no r.** sans raison; **that stands to r.** cela va sans dire, c'est logique; **within r.** avec modération; **to do everything within r. to . . .** faire tout ce qu'il est raisonnable de faire pour . . . ; **to have every r. to believe/***etc* avoir tout lieu de croire/*etc*; – *vi* raisonner; **to r. with s.o.** raisonner qn; – *vt* **to r. that** calculer que. ◆**—ing** *n* raisonnement *m*. ◆**—able** *a* raisonnable. ◆**—ably** *adv* raisonnablement; (*fairly, rather*) assez; **r. fit** en assez bonne forme.

reassur/e [riːəˈʃʊər] *vt* rassurer. ◆**—ing** *a* rassurant. ◆**reassurance** *n* réconfort *m*.

reawaken [riːəˈweɪk(ə)n] *vt* (*interest etc*) réveiller. ◆**—ing** *n* réveil *m*.

rebate [ˈriːbeɪt] *n* (*discount on purchase*) ristourne *f*; (*refund*) remboursement *m* (partiel).

rebel [ˈreb(ə)l] *a* & *n* rebelle (*mf*); – [rɪˈbel] *vi* (**-ll-**) se rebeller (**against** contre). ◆**reˈbellion** *n* rébellion *f*. ◆**reˈbellious** *a* rebelle.

rebirth [ˈriːbɜːθ] *n* renaissance *f*.

rebound [rɪˈbaʊnd] *vi* (*of ball*) rebondir; (*of stone*) ricocher; (*of lies, action etc*) *Fig* retomber (**on** sur); – [ˈriːbaʊnd] *n* rebond *m*; ricochet *m*; **on the r.** (*to marry s.o. etc*) par dépit.

rebuff [rɪˈbʌf] *vt* repousser; – *n* rebuffade *f*.

rebuild [riːˈbɪld] *vt* (*pt* & *pp* **rebuilt**) reconstruire.

rebuke [rɪˈbjuːk] *vt* réprimander; – *n* réprimande *f*.

rebuttal [rɪˈbʌt(ə)l] *n* réfutation *f*.

recalcitrant [rɪˈkælsɪtrənt] *a* récalcitrant.

recall [rɪˈkɔːl] *vt* (*call back*) rappeler; (*remember*) se rappeler (**that** que, **doing** avoir fait); **to r. sth to s.o.** rappeler qch à qn; – *n* rappel *m*; **beyond r.** irrévocable.

recant [rɪˈkænt] *vi* se rétracter.

recap [riːˈkæp] *vti* (**-pp-**) récapituler; – *n* récapitulation *f*. ◆**recaˈpitulate** *vti* récapituler. ◆**recapituˈlation** *n* récapitulation *f*.

recapture [riːˈkæptʃər] *vt* (*prisoner etc*) reprendre; (*rediscover*) retrouver; (*recreate*) recréer; – *n* (*of prisoner*) arrestation *f*.

reced/e [rɪˈsiːd] *vi* (*into the distance*) s'éloigner; (*of floods*) baisser. ◆**—ing** *a* (*forehead*) fuyant; **his hair(line) is r.** son front se dégarnit.

receipt [rɪˈsiːt] *n* (*for payment*) reçu *m* (**for** de); (*for letter, parcel*) récépissé *m*, accusé *m* de réception; *pl* (*takings*) recettes *fpl*; to **acknowledge r.** accuser réception (**of** de); **on r. of** dès réception de.

receiv/e [rɪ'siːv] *vt* recevoir; (*stolen goods*) *Jur* receler. ◆**—ing** *n Jur* recel *m*. ◆**—er** *n Tel* combiné *m*; *Rad* récepteur *m*; (*of stolen goods*) *Jur* receleur, -euse *mf*; **to pick up** *or* **lift the r.** *Tel* décrocher.

recent ['riːsənt] *a* récent; **in r. months** ces mois-ci. ◆**—ly** *adv* récemment; **as r. as** pas plus tard que.

receptacle [rɪ'septək(ə)l] *n* récipient *m*.

reception [rɪ'sepʃ(ə)n] *n* (*receiving, welcome, party etc*) & *Rad* réception *f*; **r. desk** réception *f*; **r. room** salle *f* de séjour. ◆**receptionist** *n* réceptionniste *mf*. ◆**receptive** *a* réceptif (**to an idea/***etc* à une idée/*etc*); **r. to s.o.** compréhensif envers qn.

recess [rɪ'ses, 'riːses] *n* **1** (*holiday*) vacances *fpl*; *Sch Am* récréation *f*. **2** (*alcove*) renfoncement *m*; (*nook*) & *Fig* recoin *m*.

recession [rɪ'seʃ(ə)n] *n Econ* récession *f*.

recharge [riː'tʃɑːdʒ] *vt* (*battery*) recharger.

recipe ['resɪpɪ] *n Culin* & *Fig* recette *f* (**for** de).

recipient [rɪ'sɪpɪənt] *n* (*of award, honour*) récipiendaire *m*.

reciprocal [rɪ'sɪprək(ə)l] *a* réciproque. ◆**reciprocate** *vt* (*compliment*) retourner; (*gesture*) faire à son tour; — *vi* (*do the same*) en faire autant.

recital [rɪ'saɪt(ə)l] *n Mus* récital *m*.

recite [rɪ'saɪt] *vt* (*poem etc*) réciter; (*list*) énumérer. ◆**reci'tation** *n* récitation *f*.

reckless ['rekləs] *a* (*rash*) imprudent. ◆**—ly** *adv* imprudemment.

reckon ['rek(ə)n] *vt* (*count*) compter; (*calculate*) calculer; (*consider*) considérer; (*think*) *Fam* penser (**that** que); — *vi* compter; calculer; **to r. with** (*take into account*) compter avec; (*deal with*) avoir affaire à; **to r. on/without** compter sur/sans; **to r. on doing** *Fam* compter *or* penser faire. ◆**—ing** *n* calcul(s) *m(pl)*.

reclaim [rɪ'kleɪm] *vt* **1** (*land*) mettre en valeur; (*from sea*) assécher. **2** (*ask for back*) réclamer; (*luggage at airport*) récupérer.

reclin/e [rɪ'klaɪn] *vi* (*of person*) être allongé; (*of head*) être appuyé; — *vt* (*head*) appuyer (**on** sur). ◆**—ing** *a* (*seat*) à dossier inclinable *or* réglable.

recluse [rɪ'kluːs] *n* reclus, -use *mf*.

recognize ['rekəgnaɪz] *vt* reconnaître (**by** à, **that** que). ◆**recog'nition** *n* reconnaissance *f*; **to change beyond** *or* **out of all r.** devenir méconnaissable; **to gain r.** être reconnu. ◆**recognizable** *a* reconnaissable.

recoil [rɪ'kɔɪl] *vi* reculer (**from doing** à l'idée de faire).

recollect [rekə'lekt] *vt* se souvenir de; **to r. that** se souvenir que; — *vi* se souvenir. ◆**recollection** *n* souvenir *m*.

recommend [rekə'mend] *vt* (*praise, support, advise*) recommander (**to** à, **for** pour); **to r. s.o. to do** recommander à qn de faire. ◆**recommen'dation** *n* recommandation *f*.

recompense ['rekəmpens] *vt* (*reward*) récompenser; — *n* récompense *f*.

reconcile ['rekənsaɪl] *vt* (*person*) réconcilier (**with, to** avec); (*opinion*) concilier (**with** avec); **to r. oneself to sth** se résigner à qch. ◆**reconcili'ation** *n* réconciliation *f*.

reconditioned [riːkən'dɪʃ(ə)nd] *a* (*engine*) refait (à neuf).

reconnaissance [rɪ'kɒnɪsəns] *n Mil* reconnaissance *f*. ◆**reconnoitre** [rekə'nɔɪtər] *vt Mil* reconnaître.

reconsider [riːkən'sɪdər] *vt* reconsidérer; — *vi* revenir sur sa décision.

reconstruct [riːkən'strʌkt] *vt* (*crime*) reconstituer.

record 1 ['rekɔːd] *n* (*disc*) disque *m*; **r. library** discothèque *f*; **r. player** électrophone *m*. **2** *n Sp* & *Fig* record *m*; — *a* (*attendance, time etc*) record *inv*. **3** *n* (*report*) rapport *m*; (*register*) registre *m*; (*recording on tape etc*) enregistrement *m*; (*mention*) mention *f*; (*note*) note *f*; (*background*) antécédents *mpl*; (*case history*) dossier *m*; **(police) r.** casier *m* judiciaire; **(public) records** archives *fpl*; **to make** *or* **keep a r. of** noter; **on r.** (*fact, event*) attesté; **off the r.** à titre confidentiel; **their safety r.** leurs résultats *mpl* en matière de sécurité. **4** [rɪ'kɔːd] *vt* (*on tape etc, in register etc*) enregistrer; (*in diary*) noter; (*relate*) rapporter (**that** que); — *vi* (*on tape etc*) enregistrer. ◆**—ed** *a* enregistré; (*prerecorded*) *TV* en différé; (*fact*) attesté; **letter sent (by) r. delivery** = lettre *f* avec avis de réception. ◆**—ing** *n* enregistrement *m*. ◆**—er** *n Mus* flûte *f* à bec; **(tape) r.** magnétophone *m*.

recount 1 [rɪ'kaʊnt] *vt* (*relate*) raconter. **2** ['riːkaʊnt] *n Pol* nouveau dépouillement *m* du scrutin.

recoup [rɪ'kuːp] *vt* (*loss*) récupérer.

recourse ['riːkɔːs] *n* recours *m*; **to have r. to** avoir recours à.

recover [rɪ'kʌvər] **1** *vt* (*get back*) retrouver, récupérer. **2** *vi* (*from shock etc*) se remettre; (*get better*) *Med* se remettre (**from** de); (*of*

economy, country) se redresser; (*of currency*) remonter. ◆**recovery** *n* **1** *Econ* redressement *m*. **2 the r. of sth** (*getting back*) la récupération de qch.
recreate [riːkrɪ'eɪt] *vt* recréer.
recreation [rekrɪ'eɪʃ(ə)n] *n* récréation *f*. ◆**recreational** *a* (*activity etc*) de loisir.
recrimination [rɪkrɪmɪ'neɪʃ(ə)n] *n Jur* contre-accusation *f*.
recruit [rɪ'kruːt] *n* recrue *f*; – *vt* recruter; **to r. s.o. to do** (*persuade*) *Fig* embaucher qn pour faire. ◆**—ment** *n* recrutement *m*.
rectangle ['rektæŋg(ə)l] *n* rectangle *m*. ◆**rec'tangular** *a* rectangulaire.
rectify ['rektɪfaɪ] *vt* rectifier. ◆**rectifi'cation** *n* rectification *f*.
rector ['rektər] *n Rel* curé *m*; *Univ* président *m*.
recuperate [rɪ'kuːpəreɪt] *vi* récupérer (ses forces); – *vt* récupérer.
recur [rɪ'kɜːr] *vi* (**-rr-**) (*of theme*) revenir; (*of event*) se reproduire; (*of illness*) réapparaître. ◆**recurrence** [rɪ'kʌrəns] *n* répétition *f*; (*of illness*) réapparition *f*. ◆**recurrent** *a* fréquent.
recycle [riː'saɪk(ə)l] *vt* (*material*) recycler.
red [red] *a* (**redder, reddest**) rouge; (*hair*) roux; **to turn** *or* **go r.** rougir; **r. light** (*traffic light*) feu *m* rouge; **R. Cross** Croix-Rouge *f*; **R. Indian** Peau-Rouge *mf*; **r. tape** bureaucratie *f*; – *n* (*colour*) rouge *m*; **R.** (*person*) *Pol* rouge *mf*; **in the r.** (*firm, account*) en déficit; (*person*) à découvert. ◆**r.-'faced** *a Fig* rouge de confusion. ◆**r.-'handed** *adv* **caught r.-handed** pris en flagrant délit. ◆**r.-'hot** *a* brûlant. ◆**redden** *vti* rougir. ◆**reddish** *a* rougeâtre; (*hair*) carotte. ◆**redness** *n* rougeur *f*; (*of hair*) rousseur *f*.
redcurrant [red'kʌrənt] *n* groseille *f*.
redecorate [riː'dekəreɪt] *vt* (*room etc*) refaire; – *vi* refaire la peinture et les papiers.
redeem [rɪ'diːm] *vt* (*restore to favour, free, pay off*) racheter; (*convert into cash*) réaliser; **redeeming feature** point *m* favorable. ◆**redemption** *n* rachat *m*; réalisation *f*; *Rel* rédemption *f*.
redeploy [riːdɪ'plɔɪ] *vt* (*staff*) réorganiser; (*troops*) redéployer.
redhead ['redhed] *n* roux *m*, rousse *f*.
redirect [riːdaɪ'rekt] *vt* (*mail*) faire suivre.
redo [riː'duː] *vt* (*pt* **redid**, *pp* **redone**) refaire.
redress [rɪ'dres] *n* **to seek r.** demander réparation (**for** de).
reduce [rɪ'djuːs] *vt* réduire (**to** à, **by** de); (*temperature*) faire baisser; **at a reduced price** (*ticket*) à prix réduit; (*goods*) au rabais. ◆**reduction** *n* réduction *f*; (*of temperature*) baisse *f*; (*discount*) rabais *m*.
redundant [rɪ'dʌndənt] *a* (*not needed*) superflu, de trop; **to make r.** (*workers*) mettre en chômage, licencier. ◆**redundancy** *n* (*of workers*) licenciement *m*; **r. pay(ment)** indemnité *f* de licenciement.
re-echo [riː'ekəu] *vi* résonner; – *vt* (*sound*) répercuter; *Fig* répéter.
reed [riːd] *n* **1** *Bot* roseau *m*. **2** *Mus* anche *f*; – *a* (*instrument*) à anche.
re-educate [riː'edjukeɪt] *vt* (*criminal, limb*) rééduquer.
reef [riːf] *n* récif *m*, écueil *m*.
reek [riːk] *vi* puer; **to r. of** (*smell*) & *Fig* puer; – *n* puanteur *f*.
reel [riːl] **1** *n* (*of thread, film*) bobine *f*; (*film itself*) *Cin* bande *f*; (*of hose*) dévidoir *m*; (*for fishing line*) moulinet *m*. **2** *vi* (*stagger*) chanceler; (*of mind*) chavirer; (*of head*) tourner. **3** *vt* **to r. off** (*rattle off*) débiter (à toute vitesse).
re-elect [riːɪ'lekt] *vt* réélire.
re-entry [riː'entrɪ] *n* (*of spacecraft*) rentrée *f*.
re-establish [riːɪ'stæblɪʃ] *vt* rétablir.
ref [ref] *n Sp Fam* arbitre *m*.
refectory [rɪ'fektərɪ] *n* réfectoire *m*.
refer [rɪ'fɜːr] *vi* (**-rr-**) **to r. to** (*allude to*) faire allusion à; (*speak of*) parler de; (*apply to*) s'appliquer à; (*consult*) se reporter à; – *vt* **to r. sth to** (*submit*) soumettre qch à; **to r. s.o. to** (*office, article etc*) renvoyer qn à. ◆**refe'ree** *n Sp* arbitre *m*; (*for job etc*) répondant, -ante *mf*; – *vt Sp* arbitrer. ◆**'reference** *n* (*in book, recommendation*) référence *f*; (*allusion*) allusion *f* (**to** à); (*mention*) mention *f* (**to** de); (*connection*) rapport *m* (**to** avec); **in** *or* **with r. to** concernant; *Com* suite à; **terms of r.** (*of person, investigating body*) compétence *f*; (*of law*) étendue *f*; **r. book** livre *m* de référence.
referendum [refə'rendəm] *n* référendum *m*.
refill [riː'fɪl] *vt* remplir (à nouveau); (*lighter, pen etc*) recharger; – ['riːfɪl] *n* recharge *f*; **a r.** (*drink*) *Fam* un autre verre.
refine [rɪ'faɪn] *vt* (*oil, sugar, manners*) raffiner; (*metal, ore*) affiner; (*technique, machine*) perfectionner; – *vi* **to r. upon** raffiner sur. ◆**refinement** *n* (*of person*) raffinement *m*; (*of sugar, oil*) raffinage *m*; (*of technique*) perfectionnement *m*; *pl* (*improvements*) *Tech* améliorations *fpl*. ◆**refinery** *n* raffinerie *f*.
refit [riː'fɪt] *vt* (**-tt-**) (*ship*) remettre en état.
reflate [riː'fleɪt] *vt* (*economy*) relancer.

reflect [rɪ'flekt] **1** *vt* (*light*) & *Fig* refléter; (*of mirror*) réfléchir, refléter; **to r. sth on s.o.** (*credit, honour*) faire rejaillir qch sur qn; – *vi* **to r. on s.o., be reflected on s.o.** (*rebound*) rejaillir sur qn. **2** *vi* (*think*) réfléchir (**on** à); – *vt* **to r. that** penser que. ◆**reflection** *n* **1** (*thought, criticism*) réflexion (**on** sur); **on r.** tout bien réfléchi. **2** (*image*) & *Fig* reflet *m*; (*reflecting*) réflexion *f* (**of** de). ◆**reflector** *n* réflecteur *m*. ◆**reflexion** *n* = **reflection.** ◆**reflexive** *a* (*verb*) *Gram* réfléchi.

reflex ['riːfleks] *n* & *a* réflexe (*m*); **r. action** réflexe *m*.

refloat [riː'fləʊt] *vt* (*ship*) & *Com* renflouer.

reform [rɪ'fɔːm] *n* réforme *f*; – *vt* réformer; (*person, conduct*) corriger; – *vi* (*of person*) se réformer. ◆**—er** *n* réformateur, -trice *mf*.

refrain [rɪ'freɪn] **1** *vi* s'abstenir (**from doing** de faire). **2** *n Mus* & *Fig* refrain *m*.

refresh [rɪ'freʃ] *vt* (*of bath, drink*) rafraîchir; (*of sleep, rest*) délasser; **to r. oneself** (*drink*) se rafraîchir; **to r. one's memory** se rafraîchir la mémoire. ◆**—ing** *a* rafraîchissant; (*sleep*) réparateur; (*pleasant*) agréable; (*original*) nouveau. ◆**—er** *a* (*course*) de recyclage. ◆**—ments** *npl* (*drinks*) rafraîchissements *mpl*; (*snacks*) collation *f*.

refrigerate [rɪ'frɪdʒəreɪt] *vt* réfrigérer. ◆**refrigerator** *n* réfrigérateur *m*.

refuel [riː'fjʊəl] *vi* (**-ll-**, *Am* **-l-**) *Av* se ravitailler; – *vt Av* ravitailler.

refuge ['refjuːdʒ] *n* refuge *m*; **to take r.** se réfugier (**in** dans). ◆**refu'gee** *n* réfugié, -ée *mf*.

refund [rɪ'fʌnd] *vt* rembourser; – ['riːfʌnd] *n* remboursement *m*.

refurbish [riː'fɜːbɪʃ] *vt* remettre à neuf.

refuse[1] [rɪ'fjuːz] *vt* refuser (**s.o. sth** qch à qn, **to do** de faire); – *vi* refuser. ◆**refusal** *n* refus *m*.

refuse[2] ['refjuːs] *n* (*rubbish*) ordures *fpl*, détritus *m*; (*waste materials*) déchets *mpl*; **r. collector** éboueur *m*; **r. dump** dépôt *m* d'ordures.

refute [rɪ'fjuːt] *vt* réfuter.

regain [rɪ'geɪn] *vt* (*favour, lost ground*) regagner; (*strength*) récupérer, retrouver, reprendre; (*health, sight*) retrouver; (*consciousness*) reprendre.

regal ['riːg(ə)l] *a* royal, majestueux.

regalia [rɪ'geɪlɪə] *npl* insignes *mpl* (royaux).

regard [rɪ'gɑːd] *vt* (*consider*) considérer, regarder; (*concern*) regarder; **as regards** en ce qui concerne; – *n* considération *f* (**for** pour); **to have (a) great r. for** avoir de l'estime pour; **without r. to** sans égard pour; **with r. to** en ce qui concerne; **to give** *or* **send one's regards to** (*greetings*) faire ses hommages à. ◆**—ing** *prep* en ce qui concerne. ◆**—less 1** *a* **r. of** sans tenir compte de. **2** *adv* (*all the same*) *Fam* quand même.

regatta [rɪ'gætə] *n* régates *fpl*.

regency ['riːdʒənsɪ] *n* régence *f*.

regenerate [rɪ'dʒenəreɪt] *vt* régénérer.

reggae ['regeɪ] *n* (*music*) reggae *m*; – *a* (*group etc*) reggae *inv*.

régime [reɪ'ʒiːm] *n Pol* régime *m*.

regiment ['redʒɪmənt] *n* régiment *m*. ◆**regi'mental** *a* régimentaire, du régiment. ◆**regimen'tation** *n* discipline *f* excessive.

region ['riːdʒ(ə)n] *n* région *f*; **in the r. of** (*about*) *Fig* environ; **in the r. of £500** dans les 500 livres. ◆**regional** *a* régional.

register ['redʒɪstər] *n* registre *m*; *Sch* cahier *m* d'appel; **electoral r.** liste *f* électorale; – *vt* (*record, note*) enregistrer; (*birth, death*) déclarer; (*vehicle*) immatriculer; (*express*) exprimer; (*indicate*) indiquer; (*letter*) recommander; (*realize*) *Fam* réaliser; – *vi* (*enrol*) s'inscrire; (*in hotel*) signer le registre; **it hasn't registered (with me)** *Fam* je n'ai pas encore réalisé ça. ◆**—ed** *a* (*member*) inscrit; (*letter*) recommandé; **r. trademark** marque *f* déposée. ◆**regi'strar** *n* officier *m* de l'état civil; *Univ* secrétaire *m* général. ◆**regi'stration** *n* enregistrement *m*; (*enrolment*) inscription *f*; **r. (number)** *Aut* numéro *m* d'immatriculation; **r. document** *Aut* = carte *f* grise. ◆**registry** *a* & *n* **r. (office)** bureau *m* de l'état civil.

regress [rɪ'gres] *vi* régresser.

regret [rɪ'gret] *vt* (**-tt-**) regretter (**doing, to do** de faire; **that** que (+ *sub*)); **I r. to hear that ...** je suis désolé d'apprendre que ...; – *n* regret *m*. ◆**regretfully** *adv* **r., I ...** à mon grand regret, je .... ◆**regrettable** *a* regrettable (**that** que (+ *sub*)). ◆**regrettably** *adv* malheureusement; (*poor, ill etc*) fâcheusement.

regroup [riː'gruːp] *vi* se regrouper; – *vt* regrouper.

regular ['regjʊlər] *a* (*steady, even*) régulier; (*surface*) uni; (*usual*) habituel; (*price, size*) normal; (*reader, listener*) fidèle; (*staff*) permanent; (*fool, slave etc*) *Fam* vrai; **a r. guy** *Am Fam* un chic type; – *n* (*in bar etc*) habitué, -ée *mf*; *Mil* régulier *m*. ◆**regu'larity** *n* régularité *f*. ◆**regularly** *adv* régulièrement.

regulate ['regjʊleɪt] *vt* régler. ◆**regu-**

'lation 1 *n* (*rule*) règlement *m*; – *a* (*uniform etc*) réglementaire. **2** *n* (*regulating*) réglage *m*.

rehabilitate [riːhə'bɪlɪteɪt] *vt* (*in public esteem*) réhabiliter; (*wounded soldier etc*) réadapter.

rehash [riː'hæʃ] *vt* (*text*) *Pej* remanier; *Culin* réchauffer; – ['riːhæʃ] *n* **a r.** *Culin & Fig* du réchauffé.

rehearse [rɪ'hɜːs] *vt Th* répéter; (*prepare*) *Fig* préparer; – *vi Th* répéter. ◆**rehearsal** *n Th* répétition *f*.

reign [reɪn] *n* règne *m*; **in** *or* **during the r. of** sous le règne de; – *vi* régner (**over** sur).

reimburse [riːɪm'bɜːs] *vt* rembourser (**for** de). ◆**—ment** *n* remboursement *m*.

rein [reɪn] *n* **reins** rênes *fpl*; **to give free r. to** *Fig* donner libre cours à.

reindeer ['reɪndɪər] *n inv* renne *m*.

reinforce [riːɪn'fɔːs] *vt* renforcer (**with** de); **reinforced concrete** béton *m* armé. ◆**—ment** *n* renforcement *m* (**of** de); *pl Mil* renforts *mpl*.

reinstate [riːɪn'steɪt] *vt* réintégrer. ◆**—ment** *n* réintégration *f*.

reissue [riː'ɪʃjuː] *vt* (*book*) rééditer.

reiterate [riː'ɪtəreɪt] *vt* (*say again*) réitérer.

reject [rɪ'dʒekt] *vt* (*refuse to accept*) rejeter; (*as useless*) refuser; – ['riːdʒekt] *n Com* article *m* de rebut; – *a* (*article*) de deuxième choix; **r. shop** solderie *f*. ◆**re'jection** *n* rejet *m*; (*of candidate etc*) refus *m*.

rejoic/e [rɪ'dʒɔɪs] *vi* se réjouir (**over** *or* **at sth** de qch, **in doing** de faire). ◆**—ing(s)** *n*(*pl*) réjouissance(s) *f*(*pl*).

rejoin [rɪ'dʒɔɪn] **1** *vt* (*join up with*) rejoindre. **2** *vi* (*retort*) répliquer.

rejuvenate [rɪ'dʒuːvəneɪt] *vt* rajeunir.

rekindle [riː'kɪnd(ə)l] *vt* rallumer.

relapse [rɪ'læps] *n Med* rechute *f*; – *vi Med* rechuter; **to r. into** *Fig* retomber dans.

relat/e [rɪ'leɪt] **1** *vt* (*narrate*) raconter (**that** que); (*report*) rapporter (**that** que). **2** *vt* (*connect*) établir un rapport entre (*faits etc*); **to r. sth to** (*link*) rattacher qch à; – *vi* **to r. to** (*apply to*) se rapporter à; (*get on with*) communiquer *or* s'entendre avec. ◆**—ed** *a* (*linked*) lié (**to** à); (*languages, styles*) apparentés; **to be r. to** (*by family*) être parent de.

relation [rɪ'leɪʃ(ə)n] *n* (*relative*) parent, -ente *mf*; (*relationship*) rapport *m*, relation *f* (**between** entre, **with** avec); **what r. are you to him?** quel est ton lien de parenté avec lui?; **international**/*etc* **relations** relations *fpl* internationales/*etc*. ◆**relationship** *n* (*kinship*) lien(s) *m*(*pl*) de parenté; (*relations*) relations *fpl*, rapports *mpl*; (*connection*) rapport *m*; **in r. to** relativement à.

relative ['relətɪv] *n* (*person*) parent, -ente *mf*; – *a* relatif (**to** à); (*respective*) respectif; **r. to** (*compared to*) relativement à; **to be r. to** (*depend on*) être fonction de. ◆**rela'tively** *adv* relativement.

relax [rɪ'læks] **1** *vt* (*person, mind*) détendre; – *vi* se détendre; **r.!** (*calm down*) *Fam* du calme! **2** *vt* (*grip, pressure etc*) relâcher; (*restrictions, principles, control*) assouplir. ◆**—ed** *a* (*person, atmosphere*) décontracté, détendu. ◆**—ing** *a* (*bath etc*) délassant. ◆**rela'xation** *n* **1** (*rest, recreation*) détente *f*; (*of body*) décontraction *f*. **2** (*of grip etc*) relâchement *m*; (*of restrictions etc*) assouplissement *m*.

relay ['riːleɪ] *n* relais *m*; **r. race** course *f* de relais; – *vt* (*message etc*) *Rad* retransmettre, *Fig* transmettre (**to** à).

release [rɪ'liːs] *vt* (*free*) libérer (**from** de); (*bomb, s.o.'s hand*) lâcher; (*spring*) déclencher; (*brake*) desserrer; (*film, record*) sortir; (*news, facts*) publier; (*smoke, trapped person*) dégager; (*tension*) éliminer; – *n* libération *f*; (*of film, book*) sortie *f* (**of** de); (*record*) nouveau disque *m*; (*film*) nouveau film *m*; (*relief*) *Fig* délivrance *f*; *Psy* défoulement *m*; **press r.** communiqué *m* de presse; **to be on general r.** (*of film*) passer dans toutes les salles.

relegate ['relɪgeɪt] *vt* reléguer (**to** à).

relent [rɪ'lent] *vi* (*be swayed*) se laisser fléchir; (*change one's mind*) revenir sur sa décision. ◆**—less** *a* implacable.

relevant ['reləvənt] *a* (*apt*) pertinent (**to** à); (*fitting*) approprié; (*useful*) utile; (*significant*) important; **that's not r.** ça n'a rien à voir. ◆**relevance** *n* pertinence *f* (**to** à); (*significance*) intérêt *m*; (*connection*) rapport *m* (**to** avec).

reliable [rɪ'laɪəb(ə)l] *a* (*person, information, firm*) sérieux, sûr, fiable; (*machine*) fiable. ◆**relia'bility** *n* (*of person*) sérieux *m*, fiabilité *f*; (*of machine, information, firm*) fiabilité *f*. ◆**reliably** *adv* **to be r. informed that** apprendre de source sûre que.

reliance [rɪ'laɪəns] *n* (*trust*) confiance *f* (**on** en); (*dependence*) dépendance *f* (**on** de). ◆**reliant** *a* **to be r. on** (*dependent*) dépendre de; (*trusting*) avoir confiance en.

relic ['relɪk] *n* relique *f*; *pl* (*of the past*) vestiges *mpl*.

relief [rɪ'liːf] *n* (*from pain etc*) soulagement *m* (**from** à); (*help, supplies*) secours *m*; (*in art*) & *Geog* relief *m*; **tax r.** dégrèvement *m*; **to be on r.** *Am* recevoir l'aide sociale; – *a* (*train etc*) supplémentaire; (*work etc*) de secours; **r. road** route *f* de délestage. ◆**relieve** *vt* (*pain etc*) soulager; (*boredom*) dissiper; (*situation*) remédier à; (*take over from*) relayer (*qn*); (*help*) secourir, soulager; **to r. s.o. of** (*rid*) débarrasser qn de; **to r. s.o. of his post** relever qn de ses fonctions; **to r. congestion in** *Aut* décongestionner; **to r. oneself** (*go to the lavatory*) *Hum Fam* se soulager.

religion [rɪ'lɪdʒ(ə)n] *n* religion *f*. ◆**religious** *a* religieux; (*war, book*) de religion. ◆**religiously** *adv* religieusement.

relinquish [rɪ'lɪŋkwɪʃ] *vt* (*give up*) abandonner; (*let go*) lâcher.

relish ['relɪʃ] *n* (*liking, taste*) goût *m* (**for** pour); (*pleasure*) plaisir *m*; (*seasoning*) assaisonnement *m*; **to eat with r.** manger de bon appétit; – *vt* (*food etc*) savourer; (*like*) aimer (**doing** faire).

relocate [riːləʊ'keɪt] *vi* (*move to new place*) déménager; **to r. in** *or* **to** s'installer à.

reluctant [rɪ'lʌktənt] *a* (*greeting, gift, promise*) accordé à contrecœur; **to be r. to do** être peu disposé à faire; **a r. teacher/***etc* un professeur/*etc* malgré lui. ◆**reluctance** *n* répugnance *f* (**to do** à faire). ◆**reluctantly** *adv* à contrecœur.

rely [rɪ'laɪ] *vi* **to r. on** (*count on*) compter sur; (*be dependent upon*) dépendre de.

remain [rɪ'meɪn] **1** *vi* rester. **2** *npl* restes *mpl*; **mortal r.** dépouille *f* mortelle. ◆**—ing** *a* qui reste(nt). ◆**remainder** *n* **1** reste *m*; **the r.** (*remaining people*) les autres *mfpl*; **the r. of the girls** les autres filles. **2** (*book*) invendu *m* soldé.

remand [rɪ'mɑːnd] *vt* **to r. (in custody)** *Jur* placer en détention préventive; – *n* **on r.** en détention préventive.

remark [rɪ'mɑːk] *n* remarque *f*; – *vt* (faire) remarquer (**that** que); – *vi* **to r. on** faire des remarques sur. ◆**—able** *a* remarquable (**for** par). ◆**—ably** *adv* remarquablement.

remarry [riː'mærɪ] *vi* se remarier.

remedial [rɪ'miːdɪəl] *a* (*class*) *Sch* de rattrapage; (*measure*) de redressement; (*treatment*) *Med* thérapeutique.

remedy ['remɪdɪ] *vt* remédier à; – *n* remède *m* (**for** contre, à, de).

remember [rɪ'membər] *vt* se souvenir de, se rappeler; (*commemorate*) commémorer; **to r. that/doing** se rappeler que/d'avoir fait; **to r. to do** (*not forget to do*) penser à faire; **r. me to him** *or* **her!** rappelle-moi à son bon souvenir!; – *vi* se souvenir, se rappeler. ◆**remembrance** *n* (*memory*) souvenir *m*; **in r. of** en souvenir de.

remind [rɪ'maɪnd] *vt* rappeler (**s.o. of sth** qch à qn, **s.o. that** à qn que); **to r. s.o. to do** faire penser à qn à faire; **that** *or* **which reminds me!** à propos! ◆**—er** *n* (*of event & letter*) rappel *m*; (*note to do sth*) pense-bête *m*; **it's a r. (for him** *or* **her) that . . .** c'est pour lui rappeler que. . . .

reminisce [remɪ'nɪs] *vi* raconter *or* se rappeler ses souvenirs (**about** de). ◆**reminiscences** *npl* réminiscences *fpl*. ◆**reminiscent** *a* **r. of** qui rappelle.

remiss [rɪ'mɪs] *a* négligent.

remit [rɪ'mɪt] *vt* (**-tt-**) (*money*) envoyer. ◆**remission** *n Jur* remise *f* (de peine); *Med Rel* rémission *f*. ◆**remittance** *n* (*sum*) paiement *m*.

remnant ['remnənt] *n* (*remaining part*) reste *m*; (*trace*) vestige *m*; (*of fabric*) coupon *m*; (*oddment*) fin *f* de série.

remodel [riː'mɒd(ə)l] *vt* (**-ll-**, *Am* **-l-**) remodeler.

remonstrate ['remənstreɪt] *vi* **to r. with s.o.** faire des remontrances à qn.

remorse [rɪ'mɔːs] *n* remords *m(pl)* (**for** pour); **without r.** sans pitié. ◆**—less** *a* implacable. ◆**—lessly** *adv* (*to hit etc*) implacablement.

remote [rɪ'məʊt] *a* (**-er, -est**) **1** (*far-off*) lointain, éloigné; (*isolated*) isolé; (*aloof*) distant; **r. from** loin de; **r. control** télécommande *f*. **2** (*slight*) petit, vague; **not the remotest idea** pas la moindre idée. ◆**—ly** *adv* (*slightly*) vaguement, un peu; (*situated*) au loin; **not r. aware/***etc* nullement conscient/*etc*. ◆**—ness** *n* éloignement *m*; isolement *m*; *Fig* attitude *f* distante.

remould ['riːməʊld] *n* pneu *m* rechapé.

remove [rɪ'muːv] *vt* (*clothes, stain etc*) enlever (**from s.o.** à qn, **from sth** de qch); (*withdraw*) retirer; (*lead away*) emmener (**to** à); (*furniture*) déménager; (*obstacle, threat, word*) supprimer; (*fear, doubt*) dissiper; (*employee*) renvoyer; **(far) removed from** loin de. ◆**removable** *a* (*lining etc*) amovible. ◆**removal** *n* enlèvement *m*; déménagement *m*; suppression *f*; **r. man** déménageur *m*; **r. van** camion *m* de déménagement. ◆**remover** *n* (*for make-up*) démaquillant *m*; (*for nail polish*) dissolvant *m*; (*for paint*) décapant *m*; (*for stains*) détachant *m*.

remunerate [rɪ'mjuːnəreɪt] *vt* rémunérer. ◆**remune'ration** *n* rémunération *f*.

renaissance [rə'neɪsəns] *n* (*in art etc*) renaissance *f*.

rename [riː'neɪm] *vt* (*street etc*) rebaptiser.

render ['rendər] *vt* (*give, make*) rendre; *Mus*

interpréter; (*help*) prêter. ◆**—ing** *n Mus* interprétation *f*; (*translation*) traduction *f*.
rendez-vous ['rɒndɪvuː, *pl* -vuːz] *n inv* rendez-vous *m inv*.
renegade ['renɪgeɪd] *n* renégat, -ate *mf*.
reneg(u)e [rɪ'niːg] *vi* **to r. on** (*promise etc*) revenir sur.
renew [rɪ'njuː] *vt* renouveler; (*resume*) reprendre; (*library book*) renouveler le prêt de. ◆**—ed** *a* (*efforts*) renouvelés; (*attempt*) nouveau; **with r. vigour/***etc* avec un regain de vigueur/*etc*. ◆**renewable** *a* renouvelable. ◆**renewal** *n* renouvellement *m*; (*resumption*) reprise *f*; (*of strength etc*) regain *m*.
renounce [rɪ'naʊns] *vt* (*give up*) renoncer à; (*disown*) renier.
renovate ['renəveɪt] *vt* (*house*) rénover, restaurer; (*painting*) restaurer. ◆**reno'vation** *n* rénovation *f*; restauration *f*.
renown [rɪ'naʊn] *n* renommée *f*. ◆**renowned** *a* renommé (**for** pour).
rent [rent] *n* loyer *m*; (*of television*) (prix *m* de) location *f*; **r. collector** encaisseur *m* de loyers; – *vt* louer; **to r. out** louer; – *vi* (*of house etc*) se louer. ◆**r.-'free** *adv* sans payer de loyer; – *a* gratuit. ◆**rental** *n* (*of television*) (prix *m* de) location *f*; (*of telephone*) abonnement *m*.
renunciation [rɪnʌnsɪ'eɪʃ(ə)n] *n* (*giving up*) renonciation *f* (**of** à); (*disowning*) reniement *m* (**of** de).
reopen [riː'əʊpən] *vti* rouvrir. ◆**—ing** *n* réouverture *f*.
reorganize [riː'ɔːgənaɪz] *vt* réorganiser.
rep [rep] *n Fam* représentant, -ante *mf* de commerce.
repaid [riː'peɪd] *see* **repay**.
repair [rɪ'peər] *vt* réparer; – *n* réparation *f*; **beyond r.** irréparable; **in good/bad r.** en bon/mauvais état; **'road under r.'** *Aut* 'travaux'; **r. man** réparateur *m*; **r. woman** réparatrice *f*.
reparation [repə'reɪʃ(ə)n] *n* réparation *f* (**for** de); *pl Mil Hist* réparations *fpl*.
repartee [repɑː'tiː] *n* (*sharp reply*) repartie *f*.
repatriate [riː'pætrɪeɪt] *vt* rapatrier.
repay [riː'peɪ] *vt* (*pt & pp* **repaid**) (*pay back*) rembourser; (*kindness*) payer de retour; (*reward*) récompenser (**for** de). ◆**—ment** *n* remboursement *m*; récompense *f*.
repeal [rɪ'piːl] *vt* (*law*) abroger; – *n* abrogation *f*.
repeat [rɪ'piːt] *vt* répéter (**that** que); (*promise, threat*) réitérer; (*class*) *Sch* redoubler; **to r. oneself** *or* **itself** se répéter; – *vi* répéter; **to r. on s.o.** (*of food*) *Fam* revenir à qn; – *n TV Rad* rediffusion *f*; – *a* (*performance*) deuxième. ◆**—ed** *a* répété; (*efforts*) renouvelés. ◆**—edly** *adv* à maintes reprises.
repel [rɪ'pel] *vt* (**-ll-**) repousser. ◆**repellent** *a* repoussant; **insect r.** insectifuge *m*.
repent [rɪ'pent] *vi* se repentir (**of** de). ◆**repentance** *n* repentir *m*. ◆**repentant** *a* repentant.
repercussion [riːpə'kʌʃ(ə)n] *n* répercussion *f*.
repertoire ['repətwɑːr] *n Th & Fig* répertoire *m*. ◆**repertory** *n Th & Fig* répertoire *m*; **r. (theatre)** théâtre *m* de répertoire.
repetition [repɪ'tɪʃ(ə)n] *n* répétition *f*. ◆**repetitious** *a*, ◆**re'petitive** *a* (*speech etc*) répétitif.
replace [rɪ'pleɪs] *vt* (*take the place of*) remplacer (**by, with** par); (*put back*) remettre, replacer; (*receiver*) *Tel* raccrocher. ◆**—ment** *n* remplacement *m* (**of** de); (*person*) remplaçant, -ante *mf*; (*machine part*) pièce *f* de rechange.
replay ['riːpleɪ] *n Sp* match *m* rejoué; (**instant** *or* **action**) **r.** *TV* répétition *f* immédiate (au ralenti).
replenish [rɪ'plenɪʃ] *vt* (*refill*) remplir (de nouveau) (**with** de); (*renew*) renouveler.
replete [rɪ'pliːt] *a* **r. with** rempli de; **r. (with food)** rassasié.
replica ['replɪkə] *n* copie *f* exacte.
reply [rɪ'plaɪ] *vti* répondre; – *n* réponse *f*; **in r.** en réponse (**to** à).
report [rɪ'pɔːt] *n* (*account*) rapport *m*; (*of meeting*) compte rendu *m*; *Journ TV Rad* reportage *m*; *Pol* enquête *f*; *Sch Met* bulletin *m*; (*rumour*) rumeur *f*; (*of gun*) détonation *f*; – *vt* (*give account of*) rapporter, rendre compte de; (*announce*) annoncer (**that** que); (*notify*) signaler (**to** à); (*denounce*) dénoncer (**to** à); (*event*) *Journ* faire un reportage sur; – *vi* faire un rapport *or Journ* un reportage (**on** sur); (*go*) se présenter (**to** à, **to s.o.** chez qn, **for work** au travail). ◆**—ed** *a* (*speech*) *Gram* indirect; **it is r. that** on dit que; **r. missing** porté disparu. ◆**—edly** *adv* à ce qu'on dit. ◆**—ing** *n Journ* reportage *m*. ◆**—er** *n* reporter *m*.
repose [rɪ'pəʊz] *n Lit* repos *m*.
repossess [riːpə'zes] *vt Jur* reprendre possession de.
reprehensible [reprɪ'hensəb(ə)l] *a* répréhensible.
represent [reprɪ'zent] *vt* représenter. ◆**represen'tation** *n* représentation *f*; *pl* (*complaints*) remontrances *fpl*. ◆**repre-**

sentative *a* représentatif (**of** de); – *n* représentant, -ante *mf*; *Pol Am* député *m*.

repress [rɪ'pres] *vt* réprimer; (*feeling*) refouler. ◆**repressive** *a* répressif.

reprieve [rɪ'priːv] *n Jur* sursis *m*; *Fig* répit *m*, sursis *m*; – *vt* accorder un sursis *or Fig* un répit à.

reprimand ['reprɪmɑːnd] *n* réprimande *f*; – *vt* réprimander.

reprint ['riːprɪnt] *n* (*reissue*) réimpression *f*; – *vt* réimprimer.

reprisal [rɪ'praɪz(ə)l] *n* **reprisals** représailles *fpl*; **in r. for** en représailles de.

reproach [rɪ'prəʊtʃ] *n* (*blame*) reproche *m*; (*shame*) honte *f*; **beyond r.** sans reproche; – *vt* reprocher (**s.o. for sth** qch à qn). ◆**reproachful** *a* réprobateur. ◆**reproachfully** *adv* d'un ton *or* d'un air réprobateur.

reproduce [riːprə'djuːs] *vt* reproduire; – *vi Biol Bot* se reproduire. ◆**reproduction** *n* (*of sound etc*) & *Biol Bot* reproduction *f*. ◆**reproductive** *a* reproducteur.

reptile ['reptaɪl] *n* reptile *m*.

republic [rɪ'pʌblɪk] *n* république *f*. ◆**republican** *a* & *n* républicain, -aine (*mf*).

repudiate [rɪ'pjuːdɪeɪt] *vt* (*offer*) repousser; (*accusation*) rejeter; (*spouse, idea*) répudier.

repugnant [rɪ'pʌgnənt] *a* répugnant; **he's r. to me** il me répugne. ◆**repugnance** *n* répugnance *f* (**for** pour).

repulse [rɪ'pʌls] *vt* repousser. ◆**repulsion** *n* répulsion *f*. ◆**repulsive** *a* repoussant.

reputable ['repjʊtəb(ə)l] *a* de bonne réputation. ◆**re'pute** *n* réputation *f*; **of r.** de bonne réputation. ◆**re'puted** *a* réputé (**to be** pour être). ◆**re'putedly** *adv* à ce qu'on dit.

reputation [repjʊ'teɪʃ(ə)n] *n* réputation *f*; **to have a r. for frankness**/*etc* avoir la réputation d'être franc/*etc*.

request [rɪ'kwest] *n* demande *f* (**for** de); **on r.** sur demande; **on s.o.'s r.** à la demande de qn; **by popular r.** à la demande générale; **r. stop** (*for bus*) arrêt *m* facultatif; – *vt* demander (**from** *or* **of s.o.** à qn, **s.o. to do** à qn de faire).

requiem ['rekwɪəm] *n* requiem *m inv*.

requir/e [rɪ'kwaɪər] *vt* (*necessitate*) demander; (*demand*) exiger; (*of person*) avoir besoin de (*qch, qn*); (*staff*) rechercher; **to r. sth of s.o.** (*order*) exiger qch de qn; **to r. s.o. to do** exiger de qn qu'il fasse; (*ask*) demander à qn de faire; **if required** s'il le faut. ◆**—ed** *a* requis, exigé. ◆**—ement** *n* (*need*) exigence *f*; (*condition*) condition *f* (requise).

requisite ['rekwɪzɪt] **1** *a* nécessaire. **2** *n* (*for travel etc*) article *m*; **toilet requisites** articles *mpl or* nécessaire *m* de toilette.

requisition [rekwɪ'zɪʃ(ə)n] *vt* réquisitionner; – *n* réquisition *f*.

reroute [riː'ruːt] *vt* (*aircraft etc*) dérouter.

rerun ['riːrʌn] *n Cin* reprise *f*; *TV* rediffusion *f*.

resale ['riːseɪl] *n* revente *f*.

resat [riː'sæt] *see* **resit**.

rescind [rɪ'sɪnd] *vt Jur* annuler; (*law*) abroger.

rescu/e ['reskjuː] *vt* (*save*) sauver; (*set free*) délivrer (**from** de); – *n* (*action*) sauvetage *m* (**of** de); (*help, troops etc*) secours *mpl*; **to go**/*etc* **to s.o.'s r.** aller/*etc* au secours de qn; **to the r.** à la rescousse; – *a* (*team, operation*) de sauvetage. ◆**—er** *n* sauveteur *m*.

research [rɪ'sɜːtʃ] *n* recherches *fpl* (**on, into** sur); **some r.** de la recherche; **a piece of r.** (**work**) un travail de recherche; – *vi* faire des recherches (**on, into** sur). ◆**—er** *n* chercheur, -euse *mf*.

resemble [rɪ'zemb(ə)l] *vt* ressembler à. ◆**resemblance** *n* ressemblance *f* (**to** avec).

resent [rɪ'zent] *vt* (*anger*) s'indigner de, ne pas aimer; (*bitterness*) éprouver de l'amertume à l'égard de; **I r. that** ça m'indigne. ◆**resentful** *a* **to be r.** éprouver de l'amertume. ◆**resentment** *n* amertume *f*, ressentiment *m*.

reserv/e [rɪ'zɜːv] **1** *vt* (*room, decision etc*) réserver; (*right*) se réserver; (*one's strength*) ménager; – *n* (*reticence*) réserve *f*. **2** *n* (*stock, land*) réserve *f*; **r.** (**player**) *Sp* remplaçant, -ante *mf*; **the r.** *Mil* la réserve; **the reserves** (*troops*) *Mil* les réserves *fpl*; **nature r.** réserve *f* naturelle; **in r.** en réserve; **r. tank** *Av Aut* réservoir *m* de secours. ◆**—ed** *a* (*person, room*) réservé. ◆**reser'vation** *n* **1** (*doubt etc*) réserve *f*; (*booking*) réservation *f*. **2** (*land*) *Am* réserve *f*; **central r.** (*on road*) terre-plein *m*.

reservoir ['rezəvwɑːr] *n* réservoir *m*.

resettle [riː'set(ə)l] *vt* (*refugees*) implanter.

reshape [riː'ʃeɪp] *vt* (*industry etc*) réorganiser.

reshuffle [riː'ʃʌf(ə)l] *n* (**cabinet**) **r.** *Pol* remaniement *m* (ministériel); – *vt Pol* remanier.

reside [rɪ'zaɪd] *vi* résider. ◆**'residence** *n* (*home*) résidence *f*; (*of students*) foyer *m*; **in r.** (*doctor*) sur place; (*students on campus*) sur le campus, (*in halls of residence*) rentrés. ◆'**resident** *n* habitant, -ante *mf*; (*of hotel*) pensionnaire *mf*; (*foreigner*) résident, -ente *mf*; – *a* résidant, qui habite sur place; (*population*) fixe; (*correspondent*) permanent; **to be r. in London** résider à Londres. ◆**resi'dential** *a* (*neighbourhood*) résidentiel.

residue ['rezɪdjuː] *n* résidu *m*. ◆**re'sidual** *a* résiduel.

resign [rɪ'zaɪn] *vt* (*right, claim*) abandonner; **to r. (from) one's job** démissionner; **to r. oneself to sth/to doing** se résigner à qch/à faire; – *vi* démissionner (**from** de). ◆**—ed** *a* résigné. ◆**resig'nation** *n* (*from job*) démission *f*; (*attitude*) résignation *f*.

resilient [rɪ'zɪlɪənt] *a* élastique; (*person*) *Fig* résistant. ◆**resilience** *n* élasticité *f*; *Fig* résistance *f*.

resin ['rezɪn] *n* résine *f*.

resist [rɪ'zɪst] *vt* (*attack etc*) résister à; **to r. doing sth** s'empêcher de faire qch; **she can't r. cakes** elle ne peut pas résister devant des gâteaux; **he can't r. her** (*indulgence*) il ne peut rien lui refuser; (*charm*) il ne peut pas résister à son charme; – *vi* résister. ◆**resistance** *n* résistance *f* (**to** à). ◆**resistant** *a* résistant (**to** à); **r. to** *Med* rebelle à.

resit [riː'sɪt] *vt* (*pt & pp* **resat**, *pres p* **resitting**) (*exam*) repasser.

resolute ['rezəluːt] *a* résolu. ◆**—ly** *adv* résolument. ◆**reso'lution** *n* résolution *f*.

resolv/e [rɪ'zɒlv] *vt* résoudre (**to do** de faire, **that** que); – *n* résolution *f*. ◆**—ed** *a* résolu (**to do** à faire).

resonant ['rezənənt] *a* (*voice*) résonnant; **to be r. with** résonner de. ◆**resonance** *n* résonance *f*.

resort [rɪ'zɔːt] **1** *n* (*recourse*) recours *m* (**to** à); **as a last r.** en dernier ressort; – *vi* **to r. to s.o.** avoir recours à qn; **to r. to doing** en venir à faire; **to r. to drink** se rabattre sur la boisson. **2** *n* (**holiday**) **r.** station *f* de vacances; **seaside/ski r.** station *f* balnéaire/de ski.

resound [rɪ'zaʊnd] *vi* résonner (**with** de); *Fig* avoir du retentissement. ◆**—ing** *a* (*success, noise*) retentissant.

resource [rɪ'sɔːs, rɪ'zɔːs] *n* (*expedient, recourse*) ressource *f*; *pl* (*wealth etc*) ressources *fpl*. ◆**resourceful** *a* (*person, scheme*) ingénieux. ◆**resourcefulness** *n* ingéniosité *f*, ressource *f*.

respect [rɪ'spekt] *n* respect *m* (**for** pour, de); (*aspect*) égard *m*; **in r. of, with r. to** en ce qui concerne; **with all due r.** sans vouloir vous vexer; – *vt* respecter. ◆**respecta'bility** *n* respectabilité *f*. ◆**respectable** *a* (*honourable, sizeable*) respectable; (*satisfying*) honnête; (*clothes, behaviour*) convenable. ◆**respectably** *adv* (*to dress etc*) convenablement; (*rather well*) passablement. ◆**respectful** *a* respectueux (**to** envers, **of** de). ◆**respectfully** *adv* respectueusement.

respective [rɪ'spektɪv] *a* respectif. ◆**—ly** *adv* respectivement.

respiration [respɪ'reɪʃ(ə)n] *n* respiration *f*.

respite ['respaɪt] *n* répit *m*.

respond [rɪ'spɒnd] *vi* répondre (**to** à); **to r. to treatment** *Med* réagir positivement au traitement. ◆**response** *n* réponse *f*; **in r. to** en réponse à.

responsible [rɪ'spɒnsəb(ə)l] *a* responsable (**for** de, **to s.o.** devant qn); (*job*) à responsabilités; **who's r. for ...?** qui est (le) responsable de ...? ◆**responsi'bility** *n* responsabilité *f*. ◆**responsibly** *adv* de façon responsable.

responsive [rɪ'spɒnsɪv] *a* (*reacting*) qui réagit bien; (*alert*) éveillé; (*attentive*) qui fait attention; **r. to** (*kindness*) sensible à; (*suggestion*) réceptif à. ◆**—ness** *n* (bonne) réaction *f*.

rest[1] [rest] *n* (*repose*) repos *m*; (*support*) support *m*; **to have** *or* **take a r.** se reposer; **to set** *or* **put s.o.'s mind at r.** tranquilliser qn; **to come to r.** (*of ball etc*) s'immobiliser; (*of bird, eyes*) se poser (**on** sur); **r. home** maison *f* de repos; **r. room** *Am* toilettes *fpl*; – *vi* (*relax*) se reposer; (*be buried*) reposer; **to r. on** (*of roof, argument*) reposer sur; **I won't r. till** je n'aurai de repos que (+ *sub*); **to be resting on** (*of hand etc*) être posé sur; **a resting place** un lieu de repos; – *vt* (*eyes etc*) reposer; (*horse etc*) laisser reposer; (*lean*) poser, appuyer (**on** sur); (*base*) fonder. ◆**restful** *a* reposant.

rest[2] [rest] *n* (*remainder*) reste *m* (**of** de); **the r.** (*others*) les autres *mfpl*; **the r. of the men/***etc* les autres hommes/*etc*; – *vi* (*remain*) **it rests with you to do** il vous incombe de faire; **r. assured** soyez assuré (**that** que).

restaurant ['restərɒnt] *n* restaurant *m*.

restitution [restɪ'tjuːʃ(ə)n] *n* (*for damage*) *Jur* réparation *f*; **to make r. of** restituer.

restive ['restɪv] *a* (*person, horse*) rétif.

restless ['restləs] *a* agité. ◆**—ly** *adv* avec agitation. ◆**—ness** *n* agitation *f*.

restore [rɪ'stɔːr] *vt* (*give back*) rendre (**to** à); (*order, right*) *Jur* rétablir; (*building, painting*) restaurer; (*to life or power*) ramener (*qn*) (**to** à).

restrain [rɪ'streɪn] *vt* (*person, emotions*) retenir, maîtriser; (*crowd*) contenir; (*limit*) limiter; **to r. s.o. from doing** retenir qn de faire; **to r. oneself** se maîtriser. ◆**—ed** *a* (*feelings*) contenu; (*tone*) mesuré. ◆**restraint** *n* (*moderation*) retenue *f*, mesure *f*; (*restriction*) contrainte *f*.

restrict [rɪ'strɪkt] *vt* limiter, restreindre (to à). ◆**—ed** *a* (*space, use*) restreint; (*sale*) contrôlé. ◆**restriction** *n* restriction *f*, limitation *f*. ◆**restrictive** *a* restrictif.

result [rɪ'zʌlt] *n* (*outcome, success*) résultat *m*; **as a r.** en conséquence; **as a r. of** par suite de; – *vi* résulter (**from** de); **to r. in** aboutir à.

resume [rɪ'zjuːm] *vti* (*begin or take again*) reprendre; **to r. doing** se remettre à faire. ◆**resumption** *n* reprise *f*.

résumé ['rezjʊmeɪ] *n* (*summary*) résumé *m*; *Am* curriculum vitae *m inv*.

resurface [riː'sɜːfɪs] *vt* (*road*) refaire le revêtement de.

resurgence [rɪ'sɜːdʒəns] *n* réapparition *f*.

resurrect [rezə'rekt] *vt* (*custom, hero*) *Pej* ressusciter. ◆**resurrection** *n* résurrection *f*.

resuscitate [rɪ'sʌsɪteɪt] *vt Med* réanimer.

retail ['riːteɪl] *n* (vente *f* au) détail *m*; – *a* (*price, shop etc*) de détail; – *vi* se vendre (au détail); – *vt* vendre (au détail), détailler; – *adv* (*to sell*) au détail. ◆**—er** *n* détaillant, -ante *mf*.

retain [rɪ'teɪn] *vt* (*hold back, remember*) retenir; (*freshness, hope etc*) conserver. ◆**retainer** *n* (*fee*) avance *f*, acompte *m*. ◆**retention** *n* (*memory*) mémoire *f*. ◆**retentive** *a* (*memory*) fidèle.

retaliate [rɪ'tælɪeɪt] *vi* riposter (**against s.o.** contre qn, **against an attack** à une attaque). ◆**retali'ation** *n* riposte *f*, représailles *fpl*; **in r. for** en représailles de.

retarded [rɪ'tɑːdɪd] *a* (**mentally**) **r.** arriéré.

retch [retʃ] *vi* avoir un *or* des haut-le-cœur.

rethink [riː'θɪŋk] *vt* (*pt & pp* **rethought**) repenser.

reticent ['retɪsənt] *a* réticent. ◆**reticence** *n* réticence *f*.

retina ['retɪnə] *n Anat* rétine *f*.

retir/e [rɪ'taɪər] **1** *vi* (*from work*) prendre sa retraite; – *vt* mettre à la retraite. **2** *vi* (*withdraw*) se retirer (**from** de, **to** à); (*go to bed*) aller se coucher. ◆**—ed** *a* (*having stopped working*) retraité. ◆**—ing** *a* **1** (*age*) de la retraite. **2** (*reserved*) réservé. ◆**retirement** *n* retraite *f*; **r. age** âge *m* de la retraite.

retort [rɪ'tɔːt] *vt* rétorquer; – *n* réplique *f*.

retrace [riː'treɪs] *vt* (*past event*) se remémorer, reconstituer; **to r. one's steps** revenir sur ses pas, rebrousser chemin.

retract [rɪ'trækt] *vt* (*statement etc*) rétracter; – *vi* (*of person*) se rétracter. ◆**retraction** *n* (*of statement*) rétractation *f*.

retrain [riː'treɪn] *vi* se recycler; – *vt* recycler. ◆**—ing** *n* recyclage *m*.

retread ['riːtred] *n* pneu *m* rechapé.

retreat [rɪ'triːt] *n* (*withdrawal*) retraite *f*; (*place*) refuge *m*; – *vi* se retirer (**from** de); *Mil* battre en retraite.

retrial [riː'traɪəl] *n Jur* nouveau procès *m*.

retribution [retrɪ'bjuːʃ(ə)n] *n* châtiment *m*.

retrieve [rɪ'triːv] *vt* (*recover*) récupérer; (*rescue*) sauver (**from** de); (*loss, error*) réparer; (*honour*) rétablir. ◆**retrieval** *n* récupération *f*; **information r.** recherche *f* documentaire. ◆**retriever** *n* (*dog*) chien *m* d'arrêt.

retro- ['retrəʊ] *pref* rétro-. ◆**retro'active** *a* rétroactif.

retrograde ['retrəgreɪd] *a* rétrograde.

retrospect ['retrəspekt] *n* **in r.** rétrospectivement. ◆**retro'spective** **1** *a* (*law, effect*) rétroactif. **2** *n* (*of film director, artist*) rétrospective *f*.

return [rɪ'tɜːn] *vi* (*come back*) revenir; (*go back*) retourner; (*go back home*) rentrer; **to r. to** (*subject*) revenir à; – *vt* (*give back*) rendre; (*put back*) remettre; (*bring back*) & *Fin* rapporter; (*send back*) renvoyer; (*greeting*) répondre à; (*candidate*) *Pol* élire; – *n* retour *m*; (*yield*) *Fin* rapport *m*; *pl* (*profits*) *Fin* bénéfices *mpl*: **the r. to school** la rentrée (des classes); **r. (ticket)** (billet *m* d')aller et retour *m*; **tax r.** déclaration *f* de revenus; **many happy returns (of the day)!** bon anniversaire!; **in r.** (*exchange*) en échange (**for** de); – *a* (*trip, flight etc*) (de) retour; **r. match** match *m* retour. ◆**—able** *a* (*bottle*) consigné.

reunion [riː'juːnɪən] *n* réunion *f*. ◆**reu'nite** *vt* réunir.

rev [rev] *n Aut Fam* tour *m*; **r. counter** compte-tours *m inv*; – *vt* (**-vv-**) **to r. (up)** (*engine*) *Fam* faire ronfler.

revamp [riː'væmp] *vt* (*method, play etc*) *Fam* remanier.

reveal [rɪ'viːl] *vt* (*make known*) révéler (**that** que); (*make visible*) laisser voir. ◆**—ing** *a* (*sign etc*) révélateur.

revel ['rev(ə)l] *vi* (**-ll-**) faire la fête; **to r. in sth** se délecter de qch. ◆**revelling** *n*, ◆**revelry** *n* festivités *fpl*. ◆**reveller** *n* noceur, -euse *mf*.

revenge [rɪ'vendʒ] *n* vengeance *f*; *Sp* revanche *f*; **to have** *or* **get one's r.** se venger

(**on s.o.** de qn. **on s.o. for sth** de qch sur qn); **in r.** pour se venger; – *vt* venger.
revenue ['revənjuː] *n* revenu *m*.
reverberate [rɪ'vɜːbəreɪt] *vi* (*of sound*) se répercuter.
revere [rɪ'vɪər] *vt* révérer. ◆**'reverence** *n* révérence *f*. ◆**'reverend** *a* (*father*) *Rel* révérend; – *n* **R. Smith** (*Anglican*) le révérend Smith; (*Catholic*) l'abbé *m* Smith; (*Jewish*) le rabbin Smith. ◆**'reverent** *a* respectueux.
reverse [rɪ'vɜːs] *a* contraire; (*order, image*) inverse; **r. side** (*of coin etc*) revers *m*; (*of paper*) verso *m*; – *n* contraire *m*; (*of coin, fabric etc*) revers *m*; (*of paper*) verso *m*; **in r. (gear)** *Aut* en marche arrière; – *vt* (*situation*) renverser; (*order, policy*) inverser; (*decision*) annuler; (*bucket etc*) retourner; **to r. the charges** *Tel* téléphoner en PCV; – *vti* **to r. (the car)** faire marche arrière; **to r. in/out** rentrer/sortir en marche arrière; **reversing light** phare *m* de recul. ◆**reversal** *n* renversement *m*; (*of policy, situation, opinion*) revirement *m*; (*of fortune*) revers *m*. ◆**reversible** *a* (*fabric etc*) réversible.
revert [rɪ'vɜːt] *vi* **to r.** to revenir à.
review [rɪ'vjuː] **1** *vt* (*troops, one's life*) passer en revue; (*situation*) réexaminer; (*book*) faire la critique de; – *n* revue *f*; (*of book*) critique *f*. **2** *n* (*magazine*) revue *f*. ◆**—er** *n* critique *m*.
revile [rɪ'vaɪl] *vt* injurier.
revise [rɪ'vaɪz] *vt* (*opinion, notes, text*), réviser; – *vi* (*for exam*) réviser (**for** pour). ◆**revision** *n* révision *f*.
revitalize [riː'vaɪt(ə)laɪz] *vt* revitaliser.
revive [rɪ'vaɪv] *vt* (*unconscious person, memory, conversation*) ranimer; (*dying person*) réanimer; (*custom, plan, fashion*) ressusciter; (*hope, interest*) faire renaître; – *vi* (*of unconscious person*) reprendre connaissance; (*of country, dying person*) ressusciter; (*of hope, interest*) renaître. ◆**revival** *n* (*of custom, business, play*) reprise *f*; (*of country*) essor *m*; (*of faith, fashion, theatre*) renouveau *m*.
revoke [rɪ'vəʊk] *vt* (*decision*) annuler; (*contract*) *Jur* révoquer.
revolt [rɪ'vəʊlt] *n* révolte *f*; – *vt* (*disgust*) révolter; – *vi* (*rebel*) se révolter (**against** contre). ◆**—ing** *a* dégoûtant; (*injustice*) révoltant.
revolution [revə'luːʃ(ə)n] *n* révolution *f*. ◆**revolutionary** *a* & *n* révolutionnaire (*mf*). ◆**revolutionize** *vt* révolutionner.
revolv/e [rɪ'vɒlv] *vi* tourner (**around** autour de). ◆**—ing** *a* **r. chair** fauteuil *m* pivotant; **r. door(s)** (porte *f* à) tambour *m*.
revolver [rɪ'vɒlvər] *n* revolver *m*.
revue [rɪ'vjuː] *n* (*satirical*) *Th* revue *f*.
revulsion [rɪ'vʌlʃ(ə)n] *n* **1** (*disgust*) dégoût *m*. **2** (*change*) revirement *m*.
reward [rɪ'wɔːd] *n* récompense *f* (**for** de): – *vt* récompenser (**s.o. for sth** qn de *or* pour qch). ◆**—ing** *a* qui (en) vaut la peine; (*satisfying*) satisfaisant; (*financially*) rémunérateur.
rewind [riː'waɪnd] *vt* (*pt* & *pp* **rewound**) (*tape*) rèembobiner.
rewire [riː'waɪər] *vt* (*house*) refaire l'installation électrique de.
rewrite [riː'raɪt] *vt* (*pt* **rewrote**, *pp* **rewritten**) récrire; (*edit*) réécrire.
rhapsody ['ræpsədɪ] *n* rhapsodie *f*.
rhetoric ['retərɪk] *n* rhétorique *f*. ◆**rhe'torical** *a* (*question*) de pure forme.
rheumatism ['ruːmətɪz(ə)m] *n Med* rhumatisme *m*; **to have r.** avoir des rhumatismes. ◆**rheu'matic** *a* (*pain*) rhumatismal; (*person*) rhumatisant.
rhinoceros [raɪ'nɒsərəs] *n* rhinocéros *m*.
rhubarb ['ruːbɑːb] *n* rhubarbe *f*.
rhyme [raɪm] *n* rime *f*; (*poem*) vers *mpl*; – *vi* rimer.
rhythm ['rɪð(ə)m] *n* rythme *m*. ◆**rhythmic(al)** *a* rythmique.
rib [rɪb] *n Anat* côte *f*.
ribald ['rɪb(ə)ld] *a Lit* grivois.
ribbon ['rɪbən] *n* ruban *m*; **to tear to ribbons** mettre en lambeaux.
rice [raɪs] *n* riz *m*. ◆**ricefield** *n* rizière *f*.
rich [rɪtʃ] *a* (**-er, -est**) riche (**in** en); (*profits*) gros; – *n* **the r.** les riches *mpl*. ◆**riches** *npl* richesses *fpl*. ◆**richly** *adv* (*dressed, illustrated etc*) richement; (*deserved*) amplement. ◆**richness** *n* richesse *f*.
rick [rɪk] *vt* **to r. one's back** se tordre le dos.
rickety ['rɪkɪtɪ] *a* (*furniture*) branlant.
ricochet ['rɪkəʃeɪ] *vi* ricocher; – *n* ricochet *m*.
rid [rɪd] *vt* (*pt* & *pp* **rid**, *pres p* **ridding**) débarrasser (**of** de); **to get r. of, r. oneself of** se débarrasser de. ◆**riddance** *n* **good r.!** *Fam* bon débarras!
ridden ['rɪd(ə)n] *see* **ride**.
-ridden ['rɪd(ə)n] *suffix* **debt-r.** criblé de dettes; **disease-r.** en proie à la maladie.
riddle ['rɪd(ə)l] **1** *n* (*puzzle*) énigme *f*. **2** *vt* cribler (**with** de); **riddled with** (*bullets, holes, mistakes*) criblé de; (*criminals*) plein de; (*corruption*) en proie à.
rid/e [raɪd] *n* (*on bicycle, by car etc*) promenade *f*; (*distance*) trajet *m*; (*in taxi*) course

f; (*on merry-go-round*) tour *m*; **to go for a (car) r.** faire une promenade (en voiture); **to give s.o. a r.** *Aut* emmener qn en voiture; **to have a r. on** (*bicycle*) monter sur; **to take s.o. for a r.** (*deceive*) *Fam* mener qn en bateau; – *vi* (*pt* **rode**, *pp* **ridden**) aller (à bicyclette, à moto, à cheval *etc*) (to à); (*on horse*) *Sp* monter (à cheval); **to be riding in a car** être en voiture; **to r. up** (*of skirt*) remonter; – *vt* (*a particular horse*) monter; (*distance*) faire (à cheval *etc*); **to r. a horse** *or* **horses** (*go riding*) *Sp* monter à cheval; **I was riding (on) a bike/donkey** j'étais à bicyclette/à dos d'âne; **to know how to r. a bike** savoir faire de la bicyclette; **to r. a bike to** aller à bicylette à; **may I r. your bike?** puis-je monter sur ta bicyclette?; **to r. s.o.** (*annoy*) *Am Fam* harceler qn. ◆**–ing** *n* **(horse) r.** équitation *f*; **r. boots** bottes *fpl* de cheval. ◆**–er** *n* **1** (*on horse*) cavalier, -ière *mf*; (*cyclist*) cycliste *mf*. **2** (*to document*) *Jur* annexe *f*.

ridge [rɪdʒ] *n* (*of roof, mountain*) arête *f*, crête *f*.

ridicule [ˈrɪdɪkjuːl] *n* ridicule *m*; **to hold up to r.** tourner en ridicule; **object of r.** objet *m* de risée; – *vt* tourner en ridicule, ridiculiser. ◆**ri'diculous** *a* ridicule.

rife [raɪf] *a* (*widespread*) répandu.

riffraff [ˈrɪfræf] *n* racaille *f*.

rifle [ˈraɪf(ə)l] **1** *n* fusil *m*, carabine *f*. **2** *vt* (*drawers, pockets etc*) vider.

rift [rɪft] *n* (*crack*) fissure *f*; (*in party*) *Pol* scission *f*; (*disagreement*) désaccord *m*.

rig [rɪg] **1** *n* **(oil) r.** derrick *m*; (*at sea*) plate-forme *f* pétrolière. **2** *vt* **(-gg-)** (*result, election etc*) *Pej* truquer; **to r. up** (*equipment*) installer; (*meeting etc*) *Fam* arranger. **3** *vt* **(-gg-) to r. out** (*dress*) *Fam* habiller. ◆**r.-out** *n Fam* tenue *f*.

right[1] [raɪt] **1** *a* (*correct*) bon, exact, juste; (*fair*) juste; (*angle*) droit; **to be r.** (*of person*) avoir raison (to do de faire); **it's the r. road** c'est la bonne route, c'est bien la route; **the r. time** l'heure exacte; **the clock's r.** la pendule est à l'heure; **at the r. time** au bon moment; **he's the r. man** c'est l'homme qu'il faut; **the r. thing to do** la meilleure chose à faire; **it's not r. to steal** ce n'est pas bien de voler; **it doesn't look r.** ça ne va pas; **to put r.** (*error*) rectifier; (*fix*) arranger; **to put s.o. r.** (*inform*) éclairer qn, détromper qn; **r.!** bien!; **that's r.** c'est ça, c'est bien, c'est exact; – *adv* (*straight*) (tout) droit; (*completely*) tout à fait; (*correctly*) juste; (*well*) bien; **she did r.** elle a bien fait; **r. round** tout autour (sth de qch); **r. behind** juste derrière; **r. here** ici même; **r. away, r. now** tout de suite; **R. Honourable** *Pol* Très Honorable; – *n* **to be in the r.** avoir raison; **r. and wrong** le bien et le mal; – *vt* (*error, wrong, car*) redresser. **2 all r.** *a* (*satisfactory*) bien *inv*; (*unharmed*) sain et sauf; (*undamaged*) intact; (*without worries*) tranquille; **it's all r.** ça va; **it's all r. now** (*fixed*) ça marche maintenant; **I'm all r.** (*healthy*) je vais bien, ça va; – *adv* (*well*) bien; **all r.!, r. you are!** (*yes*) d'accord!; **I got your letter all r.** j'ai bien reçu ta lettre. ◆**rightly** *adv* bien, correctement; (*justifiably*) à juste titre; **r. or wrongly** à tort ou à raison.

right[2] [raɪt] *a* (*hand, side etc*) droit; – *adv* à droite; – *n* droite *f*; **on** *or* **to the r.** à droite (of de). ◆**r.-hand** *a* à *or* de droite; **on the r.-hand side** à droite (of de); **r.-hand man** bras *m* droit. ◆**r.-'handed** *a* (*person*) droitier. ◆**r.-wing** *a Pol* de droite.

right[3] [raɪt] *n* (*claim, entitlement*) droit *m* (to do de faire); **to have a r. to sth** avoir droit à qch; **he's famous in his own r.** il est lui-même célèbre; **r. of way** *Aut* priorité *f*; **human rights** les droits de l'homme.

righteous [ˈraɪtʃəs] *a* (*person*) vertueux; (*cause, indignation*) juste.

rightful [ˈraɪtfəl] *a* légitime. ◆**–ly** *adv* légitimement.

rigid [ˈrɪdʒɪd] *a* rigide. ◆**ri'gidity** *n* rigidité *f*. ◆**rigidly** *adv* (*opposed*) rigoureusement (to à).

rigmarole [ˈrɪgmərəʊl] *n* (*process*) procédure *f* compliquée.

rigour [ˈrɪgər] *n* rigueur *f*. ◆**rigorous** *a* rigoureux.

rile [raɪl] *vt* (*annoy*) *Fam* agacer.

rim [rɪm] *n* (*of cup etc*) bord *m*; (*of wheel*) jante *f*.

rind [raɪnd] *n* (*of cheese*) croûte *f*; (*of melon, lemon*) écorce *f*; (*of bacon*) couenne *f*.

ring[1] [rɪŋ] *n* anneau *m*; (*on finger*) anneau *m*, (*with stone*) bague *f*; (*of people, chairs*) cercle *m*; (*of smoke, for napkin*) rond *m*; (*gang*) bande *f*; (*at circus*) piste *f*; *Boxing* ring *m*; (*burner on stove*) brûleur *m*; **diamond r.** bague *f* de diamants; **to have rings under one's eyes** avoir les yeux cernés; **r. road** route *f* de ceinture; (*motorway*) périphérique *m*; – *vt* **to r. (round)** (*surround*) entourer (with de); (*item on list etc*) entourer d'un cercle. ◆**ringleader** *n Pej* (*of gang*) chef *m* de bande; (*of rebellion etc*) meneur, -euse *mf*.

ring[2] [rɪŋ] *n* (*sound*) sonnerie *f*; **there's a r.** on sonne; **to give s.o. a r.** (*phone call*) passer un coup de fil à qn; **a r. of** (*truth*) *Fig* l'accent *m* de; – *vi* (*pt* **rang**, *pp* **rung**) (*of bell, person etc*) sonner; (*of sound, words*) retentir; **to r. (up)** *Tel* téléphoner; **to r. back** *Tel* rappeler; **to r. for s.o.** sonner qn; **to r. off** *Tel* raccrocher; **to r. out** (*of bell*) sonner; (*of sound*) retentir; – *vt* sonner; **to r. s.o. (up)** *Tel* téléphoner à qn; **to r. s.o. back** *Tel* rappeler qn; **to r. the bell** sonner; **to r. the doorbell** sonner à la porte; **that rings a bell** *Fam* ça me rappelle quelque chose; **to r. in** (*the New Year*) carillonner. ◆**—ing** *a* **r. tone** *Tel* tonalité *f*; – *n* (*of bell*) sonnerie *f*; **a r. in one's ears** un bourdonnement dans les oreilles.

ringlet ['rɪŋlɪt] *n* (*curl*) anglaise *f*.

rink [rɪŋk] *n* (*ice-skating*) patinoire *f*; (*roller-skating*) skating *m*.

rinse [rɪns] *vt* rincer; **to r. one's hands** se passer les mains à l'eau; (*remove soap*) se rincer les mains; **to r. out** rincer; – *n* rinçage *m*; (*hair colouring*) shampooing *m* colorant; **to give sth a r.** rincer qch.

riot ['raɪət] *n* (*uprising*) émeute *f*; (*demonstration*) manifestation *f* violente; **a r. of colour** *Fig* une orgie de couleurs; **to run r.** (*of crowd*) se déchaîner; **the r. police** = les CRS *mpl*; – *vi* (*rise up*) faire une émeute; (*fight*) se bagarrer. ◆**—ing** *n* émeutes *fpl*; bagarres *fpl*. ◆**—er** *n* émeutier, -ière *mf*; (*demonstrator*) manifestant, -ante *mf* violent(e). ◆**riotous** *a* (*crowd etc*) tapageur; **r. living** vie *f* dissolue.

rip [rɪp] *vt* (**-pp-**) déchirer; **to r. off** *or* **out** arracher; **to r. off** *Fam* (*deceive*) rouler; (*steal*) *Am* voler; **to r. up** déchirer; – *vi* (*of fabric*) se déchirer; – *n* déchirure *f*; **it's a r.-off** *Fam* c'est du vol organisé.

ripe [raɪp] *a* (**-er, -est**) mûr; (*cheese*) fait. ◆**ripen** *vti* mûrir. ◆**ripeness** *n* maturité *f*.

ripple ['rɪp(ə)l] *n* (*on water*) ride *f*; (*of laughter*) *Fig* cascade *f*; – *vi* (*of water*) se rider.

ris/e [raɪz] *vi* (*pt* **rose**, *pp* **risen**) (*get up from chair or bed*) se lever; (*of temperature, balloon, price etc*) monter, s'élever; (*in society*) s'élever; (*of hope*) grandir; (*of sun, curtain, wind*) se lever; (*of dough*) lever; **to r. in price** augmenter de prix; **to r. to the surface** remonter à la surface; **the river rises in . . .** le fleuve prend sa source dans . . . ; **to r. (up)** (*rebel*) se soulever (**against** contre); **to r. to power** accéder au pouvoir; **to r. from the dead** ressusciter; – *n* (*of sun, curtain*) lever *m*; (*in pressure, price etc*) hausse *f* (**in** de); (*in river*) crue *f*; (*of leader*) *Fig* ascension *f*; (*of industry, technology*) essor *m*; (*to power*) accession *f*; (*slope in ground*) éminence *f*; **(pay) r.** augmentation *f* (de salaire); **to give r. to** donner lieu à. ◆**—ing** *n* (*of curtain*) lever *m*; (*of river*) crue *f*; (*revolt*) soulèvement *m*; – *a* (*sun*) levant; (*number*) croissant; (*tide*) montant; (*artist etc*) d'avenir; **the r. generation** la nouvelle génération; **r. prices** la hausse des prix. ◆**—er** *n* **early r.** lève-tôt *mf inv*; **late r.** lève-tard *mf inv*.

risk [rɪsk] *n* risque *m* (**of doing** de faire); **at r.** (*person*) en danger; (*job*) menacé; **at your own r.** à tes risques et périls; – *vt* (*one's life, an accident etc*) risquer; **she won't r. leaving** (*take the risk*) elle ne se risquera pas à partir; **let's r. it** risquons le coup. ◆**riskiness** *n* risques *mpl*. ◆**risky** *a* (**-ier, -iest**) (*full of risk*) risqué.

rissole ['rɪsəʊl] *n* *Culin* croquette *f*.

rite [raɪt] *n* rite *m*; **the last rites** *Rel* les derniers sacrements *mpl*. ◆**ritual** *a* & *n* rituel (*m*).

ritzy ['rɪtsɪ] *a* (**-ier, -iest**) *Fam* luxueux, classe *inv*.

rival ['raɪv(ə)l] *a* (*firm etc*) rival; (*forces, claim etc*) opposé; – *n* rival, -ale *mf*; – *vt* (**-ll-**, *Am* **-l-**) (*compete with*) rivaliser avec (**in** de); (*equal*) égaler (**in** en). ◆**rivalry** *n* rivalité *f* (**between** entre).

river ['rɪvər] *n* (*small*) rivière *f*; (*major, flowing into sea*) & *Fig* fleuve *m*; **the R. Thames** la Tamise; – *a* (*port etc*) fluvial; **r. bank** rive *f*. ◆**riverside** *a* & *n* **(by the) r.** au bord de l'eau.

rivet ['rɪvɪt] *n* (*pin*) rivet *m*; – *vt* riveter; (*eyes*) *Fig* fixer. ◆**—ing** *a* (*story etc*) fascinant.

Riviera [rɪvɪ'eərə] *n* **the (French) R.** la Côte d'Azur.

road [rəʊd] *n* route *f* (**to** qui va à); (*small*) chemin *m*; (*in town*) rue *f*; (*roadway*) chaussée *f*; (*path*) *Fig* voie *f*, chemin *m*, route *f* (**to** de); **the Paris r.** la route de Paris; **across** *or* **over the r.** (*building etc*) en face; **by r.** par la route; **get out of the r.!** ne reste pas sur la chaussée!; – *a* (*map, safety*) routier; (*accident*) de la route; (*sense*) de la conduite; **r. hog** *Fam* chauffard *m*; **r. sign** panneau *m* (routier *or* de signalisation); **r. works** travaux *mpl*. ◆**roadblock** *n* barrage *m* routier. ◆**roadside** *a* & *n* **(by the) r.** au bord de la route. ◆**roadway** *n* chaussée *f*. ◆**roadworthy** *a* (*vehicle*) en état de marche.

roam [rəʊm] *vt* parcourir; – *vi* errer, rôder; **to r. (about) the streets** (*of child etc*) traîner dans les rues.

roar [rɔːr] *vi* hurler; (*of lion, wind, engine*) rugir; (*of thunder*) gronder; **to r. with laughter** éclater de rire; **to r. past** (*of truck etc*) passer dans un bruit de tonnerre; – *vt* **to r. (out)** hurler; – *n* hurlement *m*; rugissement *m*; grondement *m*. ◆**—ing** *n* = **roar** *n*; – *a* **a r. fire** une belle flambée; **a r. success** un succès fou; **to do a r. trade** vendre beaucoup (**in** de).

roast [rəʊst] *vt* rôtir; (*coffee*) griller; – *vi* (*of meat*) rôtir; **we're roasting here** *Fam* on rôtit ici; – *n* (*meat*) rôti *m*; – *a* (*chicken etc*) rôti; **r. beef** rosbif *m*.

rob [rɒb] *vt* (**-bb-**) (*person*) voler; (*bank, house*) dévaliser; **to r. s.o. of sth** voler qch à qn; (*deprive*) priver qn de qch. ◆**robber** *n* voleur, -euse *mf*. ◆**robbery** *n* vol *m*; **it's daylight r.!** c'est du vol organisé; **armed r.** vol *m* à main armée.

robe [rəʊb] *n* (*of priest, judge etc*) robe *f*; (*dressing gown*) peignoir *m*.

robin ['rɒbɪn] *n* (*bird*) rouge-gorge *m*.

robot ['rəʊbɒt] *n* robot *m*.

robust [rəʊ'bʌst] *a* robuste.

rock[1] [rɒk] **1** *vt* (*baby, boat*) bercer, balancer; (*cradle, branch*) balancer; (*violently*) secouer; – *vi* (*sway*) se balancer; (*of building, ground*) trembler. **2** *n Mus* rock *m*. ◆**—ing** *a* (*horse, chair*) à bascule. ◆**rocky**[1] *a* (**-ier, -iest**) (*furniture etc*) branlant.

rock[2] [rɒk] *n* (*substance*) roche *f*; (*boulder, rock face*) rocher *m*; (*stone*) *Am* pierre *f*; **a stick of r.** (*sweet*) un bâton de sucre d'orge; **r. face** paroi *f* rocheuse; **on the rocks** (*whisky*) avec des glaçons; (*marriage*) en pleine débâcle. ◆**r.-'bottom** *n* point *m* le plus bas; – *a* (*prices*) les plus bas, très bas. ◆**r.-climbing** *n* varappe *f*. ◆**rockery** *n* (*in garden*) rocaille *f*. ◆**rocky**[2] *a* (**-ier, -iest**) (*road*) rocailleux; (*hill*) rocheux.

rocket ['rɒkɪt] *n* fusée *f*; – *vi* (*of prices*) *Fig* monter en flèche.

rod [rɒd] *n* (*wooden*) baguette *f*; (*metal*) tige *f*; (*of curtain*) tringle *f*; (*for fishing*) canne *f* à pêche.

rode [rəʊd] *see* **ride**.

rodent ['rəʊdənt] *n* (*animal*) rongeur *m*.

rodeo ['rəʊdɪəʊ] *n* (*pl* **-os**) *Am* rodéo *m*.

roe [rəʊ] *n* **1** (*eggs*) œufs *mpl* de poisson. **2 r. (deer)** chevreuil *m*.

rogue [rəʊg] *n* (*dishonest*) crapule *f*; (*mischievous*) coquin, -ine *mf*. ◆**roguish** *a* (*smile etc*) coquin.

role [rəʊl] *n* rôle *m*.

roll [rəʊl] *n* (*of paper, film etc*) rouleau *m*; (*of bread*) petit pain *m*; (*of fat, flesh*) bourrelet *m*; (*of drum, thunder*) roulement *m*; (*of ship*) roulis *m*; (*list*) liste *f*; **to have a r. call** faire l'appel; **r. neck** (*neckline, sweater*) col *m* roulé; – *vi* (*of ball, ship etc*) rouler; (*of person, animal*) se rouler; **to be rolling in money** *or* **in it** *Fam* rouler sur l'or; **r. on tonight!** *Fam* vivement ce soir!; **to r. in** *Fam* (*flow in*) affluer; (*of person*) s'amener; **to r. over** (*many times*) se rouler; (*once*) se retourner; **to r. up** (*arrive*) *Fam* s'amener; **to r. (up) into a ball** (*of animal*) se rouler en boule; – *vt* rouler; **to r. down** (*blind*) baisser; (*slope*) descendre (en roulant); **to r. on** (*paint, stocking*) mettre; **to r. out** (*dough*) étaler; **to r. up** (*map, cloth*) rouler; (*sleeve, trousers*) retrousser. ◆**—ing** *a* (*ground, gait*) onduleux; **r. pin** rouleau *m* à pâtisserie. ◆**—er** *n* (*for hair, painting etc*) rouleau *m*; **r. coaster** (*at funfair*) montagnes *fpl* russes. ◆**roller-skate** *n* patin *m* à roulettes; – *vi* faire du patin à roulettes.

rollicking ['rɒlɪkɪŋ] *a* joyeux (et bruyant).

roly-poly [rəʊlɪ'pəʊlɪ] *a Fam* grassouillet.

Roman ['rəʊmən] **1** *a & n* romain, -aine *mf*. **2 R. Catholic** *a & n* catholique (*mf*).

romance [rəʊ'mæns] **1** *n* (*story*) histoire *f* or roman *m* d'amour; (*love*) amour *m*; (*affair*) aventure *f* amoureuse; (*charm*) poésie *f*. **2** *a* **R. language** langue *f* romane. ◆**romantic** *a* (*of love, tenderness etc*) romantique; (*fanciful, imaginary*) romanesque; – *n* (*person*) romantique *mf*. ◆**romantically** *adv* (*to behave*) de façon romantique. ◆**romanticism** *n* romantisme *m*.

Romania [rəʊ'meɪnɪə] *n* Roumanie *f*. ◆**Romanian** *a & n* roumain, -aine *mf*; – *n* (*language*) roumain *m*.

romp [rɒmp] *vi* s'ébattre (bruyamment); **to r. through** (*exam*) *Fig* avoir les doigts dans le nez; – *n* ébats *mpl*.

rompers ['rɒmpəz] *npl* (*for baby*) barboteuse *f*.

roof [ruːf] *n* (*of building, vehicle*) toit *m*; (*of tunnel, cave*) plafond *m*; **r. of the mouth** voûte *f* du palais; **r. rack** (*of car*) galerie *f*. ◆**—ing** *n* toiture *f*. ◆**rooftop** *n* toit *m*.

rook [rʊk] *n* **1** (*bird*) corneille *f*. **2** *Chess* tour *f*.

rookie ['rʊkɪ] *n* (*new recruit*) *Mil Fam* bleu *m*.

room [ruːm, rʊm] *n* **1** (*in house etc*) pièce *f*; (*bedroom*) chambre *f*; (*large, public*) salle *f*; **one's rooms** son appartement *m*; **in rooms** en meublé; **men's r., ladies' r.** *Am* toilettes *fpl*. **2** (*space*) place *f* (**for** pour); **(some) r.** de la place; **there's r. for doubt** le doute est permis; **no r. for doubt** aucun doute possible. ◆**rooming house** *n Am* maison *f* de rapport. ◆**roommate** *n* camarade *mf* de chambre. ◆**roomy** *a* (**-ier, -iest**) spacieux; (*clothes*) ample.

roost [ruːst] *vi* (*of bird*) percher; – *n* perchoir *m*.

rooster ['ruːstər] *n* coq *m*.

root [ruːt] **1** *n* (*of plant, person etc*) & *Math* racine *f*; *Fig* cause *f*, origine *f*; **to pull up by the root(s)** déraciner; **to take r.** (*of plant*) & *Fig* prendre racine; **to put down (new) roots** *Fig* s'enraciner; **r. cause** cause *f* première; – *vt* to **r. out** (*destroy*) extirper. **2** *vi* (*of plant cutting*) s'enraciner; **to r. about for** fouiller pour trouver. **3** *vi* **to r. for** (*cheer, support*) *Fam* encourager. ◆**—ed** *a* **deeply r.** bien enraciné (**in** dans); **r. to the spot** (*immobile*) cloué sur place. ◆**—less** *a* sans racines.

rope [rəʊp] *n* corde *f*; *Nau* cordage *m*; **to know the ropes** *Fam* être au courant; – *vt* (*tie*) lier; **to r. s.o. in** (*force to help*) *Fam* embrigader qn (**to do** pour faire); **to r. off** séparer (par une corde).

rop(e)y ['rəʊpɪ] *a* (**-ier, -iest**) *Fam* (*thing*) minable; (*person*) patraque.

rosary ['rəʊzərɪ] *n Rel* chapelet *m*.

rose[1] [rəʊz] *n* **1** (*flower*) rose *f*; (*colour*) rose *m*; **r. bush** rosier *m*. **2** (*of watering can*) pomme *f*. ◆**ro'sette** *n Sp* cocarde *f*; (*rose-shaped*) rosette *f*. ◆**rosy** *a* (**-ier, -iest**) (*pink*) rose; (*future*) *Fig* tout en rose.

rose[2] [rəʊz] *see* **rise**.

rosé ['rəʊzeɪ] *n* (*wine*) rosé *m*.

rosemary ['rəʊzmərɪ] *n Bot Culin* romarin *m*.

roster ['rɒstər] *n* (**duty**) **r.** liste *f* (de service).

rostrum ['rɒstrəm] *n* tribune *f*; *Sp* podium *m*.

rot [rɒt] *n* pourriture *f*; (*nonsense*) *Fam* inepties *fpl*; – *vti* (**-tt-**) **to r.** (**away**) pourrir.

rota ['rəʊtə] *n* liste *f* (de service).

rotate [rəʊ'teɪt] *vi* tourner; – *vt* faire tourner; (*crops*) alterner. ◆**'rotary** *a* rotatif; **r. airer** (*washing line*) séchoir *m* parapluie; – *n* (*roundabout*) *Aut Am* sens *m* giratoire. ◆**rotation** *n* rotation *f*; **in r.** à tour de rôle.

rote [rəʊt] *n* **by r.** machinalement.

rotten ['rɒt(ə)n] *a* (*decayed, corrupt*) pourri; (*bad*) *Fam* moche; (*filthy*) *Fam* sale; **to feel r.** (*ill*) être mal fichu. ◆**rottenness** *n* pourriture *f*. ◆**rotting** *a* (*meat, fruit etc*) qui pourrit.

rotund [rəʊ'tʌnd] *a* (*round*) rond; (*plump*) rondelet.

rouble ['ruːb(ə)l] *n* (*currency*) rouble *m*.

rouge [ruːʒ] *n* rouge *m* (à joues).

rough[1] [rʌf] *a* (**-er, -est**) (*surface, task, manners*) rude; (*ground*) inégal, accidenté; (*rocky*) rocailleux; (*plank, bark*) rugueux; (*sound*) âpre, rude; (*coarse*) grossier; (*brutal*) brutal; (*weather, neighbourhood*) mauvais; (*sea*) agité; (*justice*) sommaire; (*diamond*) brut; **a r. child** (*unruly*) un enfant dur; **to feel r.** (*ill*) *Fam* être mal fichu; **r. and ready** (*conditions, solution*) grossier (mais adéquat); – *adv* (*to sleep, live*) à la dure; (*to play*) brutalement; – *n* (*violent man*) *Fam* voyou *m*; – *vt* **to r. it** *Fam* vivre à la dure; **to r. up** (*hair*) ébouriffer; (*person*) *Fam* malmener. ◆**r.-and-'tumble** *n* (*fight*) mêlée *f*; (*of s.o.'s life*) remue-ménage *m inv*. ◆**roughen** *vt* rendre rude. ◆**roughly**[1] *adv* (*not gently*) rudement; (*coarsely*) grossièrement; (*brutally*) brutalement. ◆**roughness** *n* rudesse *f*; inégalité *f*; grossièreté *f*; brutalité *f*.

rough[2] [rʌf] *a* (**-er, -est**) (*calculation, figure, terms etc*) approximatif; **r. copy, r. draft** brouillon *m*; **r. paper** du papier brouillon; **r. guess, r. estimate** approximation *f*; **a r. plan** l'ébauche *f* d'un projet; – *vt* **to r. out** (*plan*) ébaucher. ◆**—ly**[2] *adv* (*approximately*) à peu (de choses) près.

roughage ['rʌfɪdʒ] *n* (*in food*) fibres *fpl* (alimentaires).

roulette [ruː'let] *n* roulette *f*.

round [raʊnd] **1** *adv* autour; **all r., right r.** tout autour; **to go r. to s.o.** passer chez qn; **to ask r.** inviter chez soi; **he'll be r.** il passera; **r. here** par ici; **the long way r.** le chemin le plus long; – *prep* autour de; **r. about** (*house etc*) autour de; (*approximately*) environ; **r.** (**about**) **midday** vers midi; **to go r.** (*world*) faire le tour de; (*corner*) tourner. **2** *a* (**-er, -est**) rond; **a r. trip** *Am* un (voyage) aller et retour. **3** *n* (*slice*) *Culin* tranche *f*; *Sp Pol* manche *f*; (*of golf*) partie *f*; *Boxing* round *m*; (*of talks*) série *f*; (*of drinks, visits*) tournée *f*; **one's round(s)** (*of milkman etc*) sa tournée; (*of doctor*) ses visites *fpl*; (*of policeman*) sa ronde; **delivery r.** livraisons *fpl*, tournée *f*; **r. of applause** salve *f* d'applaudissements; **r. of ammunition** cartouche *f*, balle *f*; – *vt* **to r. a corner** (*in car*) prendre un virage; **to r. off** (*finish*) terminer; **to r. up** (*gather*) rassembler; (*figure*) arrondir au chiffre supérieur. ◆**r.-'shouldered** *a* voûté, aux épaules rondes. ◆**rounded** *a* arrondi. ◆**rounders** *npl Sp sorte de baseball.* ◆**roundness** *n* rondeur *f*. ◆**roundup** *n* (*of criminals*) rafle *f*.

roundabout ['raʊndəbaʊt] **1** *a* indirect, détourné. **2** *n* (*at funfair*) manège *m*; (*junction*) *Aut* rond-point *m* (à sens giratoire).

rous/e [raʊz] *vt* éveiller; **roused (to anger)** en colère; **to r. to action** inciter à agir. ◆**—ing** *a* (*welcome*) enthousiaste; (*speech*) vibrant; (*music*) allègre.

rout [raʊt] *n* (*defeat*) déen déroute *f*; – *vt* mettre route.

route 1 [ruːt] *n* itinéraire *m*; (*of aircraft*) route *f*; **sea r.** route *f* maritime; **bus r.** ligne *f* d'autobus; – *vt* (*train etc*) fixer l'itinéraire de. **2** [raʊt] *n* (*delivery round*) *Am* tournée *f*.

routine [ruːˈtiːn] *n* routine *f*; **one's daily r.** (*in office etc*) son travail journalier; **the daily r.** (*monotony*) le train-train quotidien; – *a* (*inquiry, work etc*) de routine; *Pej* routinier.

rov/e [rəʊv] *vi* errer; – *vt* parcourir. ◆**—ing** *a* (*life*) nomade; (*ambassador*) itinérant.

row[1] [rəʊ] **1** *n* (*line*) rang *m*, rangée *f*; (*of cars*) file *f*; **two days in a r.** deux jours de suite *or* d'affilée. **2** *vi* (*in boat*) ramer; – *vt* (*boat*) faire aller à la rame; (*person*) transporter en canot; – *n* **to go for a r.** canoter; **r. boat** *Am* bateau *m* à rames. ◆**—ing** *n* canotage *m*; *Sp* aviron *m*; **r. boat** bateau *m* à rames.

row[2] [raʊ] *n Fam* (*noise*) vacarme *m*; (*quarrel*) querelle *f*; – *vi Fam* se quereller (**with** avec).

rowdy ['raʊdɪ] *a* (**-ier, -iest**) chahuteur (et brutal); – *n* (*person*) *Fam* voyou *m*.

royal ['rɔɪəl] *a* royal; – *npl* **the royals** *Fam* la famille royale. ◆**royalist** *a* & *n* royaliste (*mf*). ◆**royally** *adv* (*to treat*) royalement. ◆**royalty 1** *n* (*persons*) personnages *mpl* royaux. **2** *npl* (*from book*) droits *mpl* d'auteur; (*on oil, from patent*) royalties *fpl*.

rub [rʌb] *vt* (**-bb-**) frotter; (*polish*) astiquer; **to r. shoulders with** *Fig* coudoyer, côtoyer; **to r. away** (*mark*) effacer; (*tears*) essuyer; **to r. down** (*person*) frictionner; (*wood, with sandpaper*) poncer; **to r. in** (*cream*) *Med* faire pénétrer (en massant); **to r. it in** *Pej Fam* retourner le couteau dans la plaie; **to r. off** *or* **out** (*mark*) effacer; **rubbing alcohol** *Am* alcool *m* à 90°; – *vi* frotter; **to r. off** (*of mark*) partir; (*of manners etc*) déteindre (**on s.o.** sur qn); – *n* (*massage*) friction *f*; **to give sth a r.** frotter qch; (*polish*) astiquer qch.

rubber ['rʌbər] *n* (*substance*) caoutchouc *m*; (*eraser*) gomme *f*; (*contraceptive*) *Am Sl* capote *f*; **r. stamp** tampon *m*. ◆**r.-'stamp** *vt Pej* approuver (sans discuter). ◆**rubbery** *a* caoutchouteux.

rubbish ['rʌbɪʃ] **1** *n* (*refuse*) ordures *fpl*, détritus *mpl*; (*waste*) déchets *mpl*; (*junk*) saleté(s) *f*(*pl*); (*nonsense*) *Fig* absurdités *fpl*; **that's r.** (*absurd*) c'est absurde; (*worthless*) ça ne vaut rien; **r. bin** poubelle *f*; **r. dump** dépôt *m* d'ordures, décharge *f* (publique); (*in garden*) tas *m* d'ordures. **2** *vt* **to r. s.o./sth** (*criticize*) *Fam* dénigrer qn/qch. ◆**rubbishy** *a* (*book etc*) sans valeur; (*goods*) de mauvaise qualité.

rubble ['rʌb(ə)l] *n* décombres *mpl*.

ruble ['ruːb(ə)l] *n* (*currency*) rouble *m*.

ruby ['ruːbɪ] *n* (*gem*) rubis *m*.

rucksack ['rʌksæk] *n* sac *m* à dos.

ruckus ['rʌkəs] *n* (*uproar*) *Fam* chahut *m*.

rudder ['rʌdər] *n* gouvernail *m*.

ruddy [rʌdɪ] *a* (**-ier, -iest**) **1** (*complexion*) coloré. **2** (*bloody*) *Sl* fichu.

rude [ruːd] *a* (**-er, -est**) (*impolite*) impoli (**to** envers); (*coarse*) grossier; (*indecent*) indécent, obscène; (*shock*) violent. ◆**—ly** *adv* impoliment; grossièrement. ◆**—ness** *n* impolitesse *f*; grossièreté *f*.

rudiments ['ruːdɪmənts] *npl* rudiments *mpl*. ◆**rudi'mentary** *a* rudimentaire.

ruffian ['rʌfɪən] *n* voyou *m*.

ruffle ['rʌf(ə)l] **1** *vt* (*hair*) ébouriffer; (*water*) troubler; **to r. s.o.** (*offend*) froisser qn. **2** *n* (*frill*) ruche *f*.

rug [rʌg] *n* carpette *f*, petit tapis *m*; (*over knees*) plaid *m*; **(bedside) r.** descente *f* de lit.

rugby ['rʌgbɪ] *n* **r. (football)** rugby *m*. ◆**rugger** *n Fam* rugby *m*.

rugged ['rʌgɪd] *a* (*surface*) rugueux, rude; (*terrain, coast*) accidenté; (*person, features, manners*) rude; (*determination*) *Fig* farouche.

ruin ['ruːɪn] *n* (*destruction, rubble, building etc*) ruine *f*; **in ruins** (*building*) en ruine; – *vt* (*health, country, person etc*) ruiner; (*clothes*) abîmer; (*spoil*) gâter. ◆**—ed** *a* (*person, country etc*) ruiné; (*building*) en ruine. ◆**ruinous** *a* ruineux.

rul/e [ruːl] **1** *n* (*principle*) règle *f*; (*regulation*) règlement *m*; (*custom*) coutume *f*; (*authority*) autorité *f*; *Pol* gouvernement *m*; **against the rules** contraire à la règle; **as a (general) r.** en règle générale; **it's the** *or* **a r. that** il est de règle que (+ *sub*); – *vt* (*country*) *Pol* gouverner; (*decide*) *Jur Sp* décider (**that** que); **to r. s.o.** (*dominate*) mener qn; **to r. out** (*exclude*) exclure; – *vi* (*of monarch*) régner (**over** sur); (*of judge*) statuer (**against** contre, **on** sur). **2** *n* (*for measuring*) règle *f*. ◆**—ed** *a* (*paper*) réglé, ligné. ◆**—ing** *a* (*passion*) dominant;

(*class*) dirigeant; (*party*) *Pol* au pouvoir; – *n Jur Sp* décision *f*. ◆**ruler** *n* **1** (*of country*) *Pol* dirigeant, -ante *mf*; (*sovereign*) souverain, -aine *mf*. **2** (*measure*) règle *f*.

rum [rʌm] *n* rhum *m*.

Rumania [ruːˈmeɪnɪə] *see* **Romania.**

rumble [ˈrʌmb(ə)l] *vi* (*of train, thunder, gun*) gronder; (*of stomach*) gargouiller; – *n* grondement *m*; gargouillement *m*.

ruminate [ˈruːmɪneɪt] *vi* **to r. over** (*scheme etc*) ruminer.

rummage [ˈrʌmɪdʒ] *vi* **to r. (about)** farfouiller; **r. sale** (*used clothes etc*) *Am* vente *f* de charité.

rumour [ˈruːmər] *n* rumeur *f*, bruit *m*. ◆**rumoured** *a* **it is r. that** on dit que.

rump [rʌmp] *n* (*of horse*) croupe *f*; (*of fowl*) croupion *m*; **r. steak** rumsteck *m*.

rumple [ˈrʌmp(ə)l] *vt* (*clothes*) chiffonner.

run [rʌn] *n* (*running*) course *f*; (*outing*) tour *m*; (*journey*) parcours *m*, trajet *m*; (*series*) série *f*; (*period*) période *f*; *Cards* suite *f*; (*rush*) ruée *f* (**on** sur); (*trend*) tendance *f*; (*for skiing*) piste *f*; (*in cricket*) point *m*; **to go for a r.** courir, faire une course à pied; **on the r.** (*prisoner etc*) en fuite; **to have the r. of** (*house etc*) avoir à sa disposition; **in the long r.** avec le temps, à la longue; **the runs** *Med Fam* la diarrhée; – *vi* (*pt* **ran**, *pp* **run**, *pres p* **running**) courir; (*flee*) fuir; (*of curtain*) glisser; (*of river, nose, pen, tap*) couler; (*of colour in washing*) déteindre; (*of ink*) baver; (*melt*) fondre; (*of play, film*) se jouer; (*of contract*) être valide; (*last*) durer; (*pass*) passer; (*function*) marcher; (*tick over*) *Aut* tourner; (*of stocking*) filer; **to r. down/in/***etc* descendre/entrer/*etc* en courant; **to r. for president** être candidat à la présidence; **to r. with blood** ruisseler de sang; **to r. between** (*of bus*) faire le service entre; **to go running** *Sp* faire du jogging; **the road runs to . . .** la route va à . . . ; **the river runs into the sea** le fleuve se jette dans la mer; **it runs into a hundred pounds** ça va chercher dans les cent livres; **it runs in the family** ça tient de famille; – *vt* (*race, risk*) courir; (*horse*) faire courir; (*temperature, errand*) faire; (*blockade*) forcer; (*machine*) faire fonctionner; (*engine*) *Aut* faire tourner; (*drive*) *Aut* conduire; (*furniture, goods*) transporter (**to** à); (*business, country etc*) diriger; (*courses, events*) organiser; (*film, play*) présenter; (*house*) tenir; (*article*) publier (**on** sur); (*bath*) faire couler; **to r. one's hand over** passer la main sur; **to r. one's eye over** jeter un coup d'œil à *or* sur; **to r. its course** (*of illness etc*) suivre son cours; **to r. 5 km** *Sp* faire 5 km de course à pied; **to r. a car** avoir une voiture. ■ **to r. about** *vi* courir çà et là; (*gallivant*) se balader; **to r. across** *vt* (*meet*) tomber sur; **to r. along** *vi* **r. along!** filez!; **to r. away** *vi* (*flee*) s'enfuir, se sauver (**from** de); **to r. back** *vt* (*person*) *Aut* ramener (**to** à); **to r. down** *vt* (*pedestrian*) *Aut* renverser; (*belittle*) dénigrer; (*restrict*) limiter peu à peu. ◆**r.-ˈdown** *a* (*weak, tired*) *Med* à plat; (*district etc*) miteux; **to r. in** *vt* (*vehicle*) roder; **to r. s.o. in** (*of police*) *Fam* arrêter qn; **to r. into** *vt* (*meet*) tomber sur; (*crash into*) *Aut* percuter; **to r. into debt** s'endetter; **to r. off** *vt* (*print*) tirer; – *vi* (*flee*) s'enfuir; **to r. out** *vi* (*of stocks*) s'épuiser; (*of lease*) expirer; (*of time*) manquer; **to r. out of** (*time, money*) manquer de; **we've r. out of coffee** on n'a plus de café; – *vt* **to r. s.o. out of** (*chase*) chasser qn de; **to r. over** *vi* (*of liquid*) déborder; – *vt* (*kill pedestrian*) *Aut* écraser; (*knock down pedestrian*) *Aut* renverser; (*notes, text*) revoir; **to r. round** *vt* (*surround*) entourer; **to r. through** *vt* (*recap*) revoir; **to r. up** *vt* (*bill, debts*) laisser s'accumuler. ◆**r.-up** *n* **the r.-up to** (*elections etc*) la période qui précède. ◆**running** *n* course *f*; (*of machine*) fonctionnement *m*; (*of firm, country*) direction *f*; **to be in/out of the r.** être/ne plus être dans la course; – *a* (*commentary*) suivi; (*battle*) continuel; **r. water** eau *f* courante; **six days/***etc* **r.** six jours/*etc* de suite; **r. costs** (*of factory*) frais *mpl* d'exploitation; (*of car*) dépenses *fpl* courantes. ◆**runner** *n Sp etc* coureur *m*; **r. bean** haricot *m* (grimpant). ◆**runner-ˈup** *n Sp* second, -onde *mf*. ◆**runny** *a* (**-ier, -iest**) *a* liquide; (*nose*) qui coule.

runaway [ˈrʌnəweɪ] *n* fugitif, -ive *mf*; – *a* (*car, horse*) emballé; (*lorry*) fou; (*wedding*) clandestin; (*victory*) qu'on remporte haut la main; (*inflation*) galopant.

rung[1] [rʌŋ] *n* (*of ladder*) barreau *m*.

rung[2] [rʌŋ] *see* **ring**[2].

run-of-the-mill [rʌnəvðəˈmɪl] *a* ordinaire.

runway [ˈrʌnweɪ] *n Av* piste *f*.

rupture [ˈrʌptʃər] *n Med* hernie *f*; **the r. of** (*breaking*) la rupture de; – *vt* rompre; **to r. oneself** se donner une hernie.

rural [ˈrʊərəl] *a* rural.

ruse [ruːz] *n* (*trick*) ruse *f*.

rush[1] [rʌʃ] *vi* (*move fast, throw oneself*) se précipiter, se ruer (**at** sur, **towards** vers); (*of blood*) affluer (**to** à); (*hurry*) se dépêcher (**to do** de faire); (*of vehicle*) foncer; **to r. out** partir en vitesse; – *vt* (*attack*) *Mil* foncer sur; **to r. s.o.** bousculer qn; **to r. s.o. to hospital** transporter qn d'urgence à l'hôpital; **to r. (through) sth** (*job, meal, order etc*) faire, manger, envoyer *etc* qch en vitesse; **to be rushed into** (*decision, answer etc*) être forcé à prendre, donner *etc*; – *n* ruée *f* (**for** vers, **on** sur); (*confusion*) bousculade *f*; (*hurry*) hâte *f*; (*of orders*) avalanche *f*; **to be in a r.** être pressé (**to do** de faire); **to leave/***etc* **in a r.** partir/*etc* en vitesse; **the gold r.** la ruée vers l'or; **the r. hour** l'heure *f* d'affluence; **a r. job** un travail d'urgence.

rush[2] [rʌʃ] *n* (*plant*) jonc *m*.

rusk [rʌsk] *n* biscotte *f*.

russet ['rʌsɪt] *a* roux, roussâtre.

Russia ['rʌʃə] *n* Russie *f*. ◆**Russian** *a* & *n* russe (*mf*); – *n* (*language*) russe *m*.

rust [rʌst] *n* rouille *f*; – *vi* (se) rouiller. ◆**rustproof** *a* inoxydable. ◆**rusty** *a* (**-ier, -iest**) (*metal, athlete, memory etc*) rouillé.

rustic ['rʌstɪk] *a* rustique.

rustle ['rʌs(ə)l] **1** *vi* (*of leaves*) bruire; (*of skirt*) froufrouter; – *n* bruissement *m*; frou-frou *m*. **2** *vt* **to r. up** *Fam* (*prepare*) préparer; (*find*) trouver.

rut [rʌt] *n* ornière *f*; **to be in a r.** *Fig* être encroûté.

rutabaga [ruːtə'beɪgə] *n* (*swede*) *Am* rutabaga *m*.

ruthless ['ruːθləs] *a* (*attack, person etc*) impitoyable, cruel; (*in taking decisions*) très ferme. ◆**—ness** *n* cruauté *f*.

rye [raɪ] *n* seigle *m*; **r. bread** pain *m* de seigle.

S

S, s [es] *n* S, s *m*.

Sabbath ['sæbəθ] *n* (*Jewish*) sabbat *m*; (*Christian*) dimanche *m*. ◆**sa'bbatical** *a* (*year etc*) *Univ* sabbatique.

sabotage ['sæbətɑːʒ] *n* sabotage *m*; – *vt* saboter. ◆**saboteur** [-'tɜːr] *n* saboteur, -euse *mf*.

sabre ['seɪbər] *n* (*sword*) sabre *m*.

saccharin ['sækərɪn] *n* saccharine *f*.

sachet ['sæʃeɪ] *n* (*of lavender etc*) sachet *m*; (*of shampoo*) dosette *f*.

sack [sæk] **1** *n* (*bag*) sac *m*. **2** *vt* (*dismiss*) *Fam* virer, renvoyer; – *n Fam* **to get the s.** se faire virer; **to give s.o. the s.** virer qn. **3** *vt* (*town etc*) saccager, mettre à sac. ◆**—ing** *n* **1** (*cloth*) toile *f* à sac. **2** (*dismissal*) *Fam* renvoi *m*.

sacrament ['sækrəmənt] *n Rel* sacrement *m*.

sacred ['seɪkrɪd] *a* (*holy*) sacré.

sacrifice ['sækrɪfaɪs] *n* sacrifice *m*; – *vt* sacrifier (**to** à, **for sth/s.o.** pour qch/qn).

sacrilege ['sækrɪlɪdʒ] *n* sacrilège *m*. ◆**sacri'legious** *a* sacrilège.

sacrosanct ['sækrəʊsæŋkt] *a Iron* sacro-saint.

sad [sæd] *a* (**sadder, saddest**) triste. ◆**sadden** *vt* attrister. ◆**sadly** *adv* tristement; (*unfortunately*) malheureusement; (*very*) très. ◆**sadness** *n* tristesse *f*.

saddle ['sæd(ə)l] *n* selle *f*; **to be in the s.** (*in control*) *Fig* tenir les rênes; – *vt* (*horse*) seller; **to s. s.o. with** (*chore, person*) *Fam* coller à qn.

sadism ['seɪdɪz(ə)m] *n* sadisme *m*. ◆**sadist** *n* sadique *mf*. ◆**sa'distic** *a* sadique.

sae [eseɪ'iː] *abbr* = **stamped addressed envelope.**

safari [sə'fɑːrɪ] *n* safari *m*; **to be** *or* **go on s.** faire un safari.

safe[1] [seɪf] *a* (**-er, -est**) (*person*) en sécurité; (*equipment, toy, animal*) sans danger; (*place, investment, method*) sûr; (*bridge, ladder*) solide; (*prudent*) prudent; (*winner*) assuré, garanti; **s. (and sound)** sain et sauf; **it's s. to go out** on peut sortir sans danger; **the safest thing (to do) is . . .** le plus sûr est de . . . ; **s. from** à l'abri de; **to be on the s. side** pour plus de sûreté; **in s. hands** en mains sûres; **s. journey!** bon voyage! ◆**s.-'conduct** *n* sauf-conduit *m*. ◆**safe-'keeping** *n* **for s.** à garder en sécurité. ◆**safely** *adv* (*without mishap*) sans accident; (*securely*) en sûreté; (*without risk*) sans risque, sans danger. ◆**safety** *n* sécurité *f*; (*solidity*) solidité *f*; (*salvation*) salut *m*; – *a* (*belt, device, screen, margin*) de sécurité; (*pin, razor, chain, valve*) de sûreté; **s. precaution** mesure *f* de sécurité.

safe[2] [seɪf] *n* (*for money etc*) coffre-fort *m*.

safeguard ['seɪfgɑːd] *n* sauvegarde *f* (**against** contre); – *vt* sauvegarder.

saffron ['sæfrən] *n* safran *m.*

sag [sæg] *vi* **(-gg-)** (*of roof, ground*) s'affaisser; (*of cheeks*) pendre; (*of prices, knees*) fléchir. ◆**sagging** *a* (*roof, breasts*) affaissé.

saga ['sɑːgə] *n Liter* saga *f*; (*bad sequence of events*) *Fig* feuilleton *m.*

sage [seɪdʒ] *n* **1** *Bot Culin* sauge *f.* **2** (*wise man*) sage *m.*

Sagittarius [sædʒɪ'teərɪəs] *n* (*sign*) le Sagittaire.

sago ['seɪgəʊ] *n* (*cereal*) sagou *m.*

Sahara [sə'hɑːrə] *n* **the S. (desert)** le Sahara.

said [sed] *see* **say.**

sail [seɪl] *vi* (*navigate*) naviguer; (*leave*) partir; *Sp* faire de la voile; (*glide*) *Fig* glisser; **to s. into port** entrer au port; **to s. round** (*world, island etc*) faire le tour de en bateau; **to s. through** (*exam etc*) *Fig* réussir haut la main; – *vt* (*boat*) piloter; (*seas*) parcourir; – *n* voile *f*; (*trip*) tour *m* en bateau; **to set s.** (*of boat*) partir (**for** à destination de). ◆**—ing** *n* navigation *f*; *Sp* voile *f*; (*departure*) départ *m*; (*crossing*) traversée *f*; **s. boat** voilier *m.* ◆**sailboard** *n* planche *f* (à voile). ◆**sailboat** *n Am* voilier *m.* ◆**sailor** *n* marin *m,* matelot *m.*

saint [seɪnt] *n* saint *m,* sainte *f*; **S. John** saint Jean; **s.'s day** *Rel* fête *f* (de saint). ◆**saintly** *a* **(-ier, -iest)** saint.

sake [seɪk] *n* **for my/your s.** pour moi/toi; **for your father's s.** pour (l'amour de) ton père; **(just) for the s. of eating/***etc* simplement pour manger/*etc*; **for heaven's** *or* **God's s.** pour l'amour de Dieu.

salacious [sə'leɪʃəs] *a* obscène.

salad ['sæləd] *n* (*dish of vegetables, fruit etc*) salade *f*; **s. bowl** saladier *m*; **s. cream** mayonnaise *f*; **s. dressing** vinaigrette *f.*

salamander ['sæləmændər] *n* (*lizard*) salamandre *f.*

salami [sə'lɑːmɪ] *n* salami *m.*

salary ['sælərɪ] *n* (*professional*) traitement *m*; (*wage*) salaire *m.* ◆**salaried** *a* (*person*) qui perçoit un traitement.

sale [seɪl] *n* vente *f*; **sale(s)** (*at reduced prices*) *Com* soldes *mpl*; **in a** *or* **the s.,** *Am* **on s.** (*cheaply*) en solde; **on s.** (*available*) en vente; **(up) for s.** à vendre; **to put up for s.** mettre en vente; **s. price** *Com* prix *m* de solde; **sales check** *or* **slip** *Am* reçu *m.* ◆**saleable** *a Com* vendable. ◆**salesclerk** *n Am* vendeur, -euse *mf.* ◆**salesman** *n* (*pl* **-men**) (*in shop*) vendeur *m*; **(travelling) s.** représentant *m* (de commerce). ◆**saleswoman** *n* (*pl* **-women**) vendeuse *f*; représentante *f* (de commerce).

salient ['seɪlɪənt] *a* (*point, fact*) marquant.

saliva [sə'laɪvə] *n* salive *f.* ◆**'salivate** *vi* saliver.

sallow ['sæləʊ] *a* **(-er, -est)** jaunâtre.

sally ['sælɪ] *n Mil* sortie *f*; – *vi* **to s. forth** *Fig* sortir allègrement.

salmon ['sæmən] *n* saumon *m.*

salmonella [sælmə'nelə] *n* (*poisoning*) salmonellose *f.*

salon ['sælɒn] *n* **beauty/hairdressing s.** salon *m* de beauté/de coiffure.

saloon [sə'luːn] *n Nau* salon *m*; (*car*) berline *f*; (*bar*) *Am* bar *m*; **s. bar** (*of pub*) salle *f* chic.

salt [sɔːlt] *n* sel *m*; **bath salts** sels *mpl* de bain; – *a* (*water, beef etc*) salé; (*mine*) de sel; **s. free** sans sel; – *vt* saler. ◆**saltcellar** *n, Am* ◆**saltshaker** *n* salière *f.* ◆**salty** *a* **(-ier, -iest)** *a* salé.

salubrious [sə'luːbrɪəs] *a* salubre.

salutary ['sæljʊtərɪ] *a* salutaire.

salute [sə'luːt] *n Mil* salut *m*; (*of guns*) salve *f*; – *vt* (*greet*) & *Mil* saluer; – *vi Mil* faire un salut.

salvage ['sælvɪdʒ] *n* sauvetage *m* (**of** de); récupération *f* (**of** de); (*saved goods*) objets *mpl* sauvés; – *vt* (*save*) sauver (**from** de); (*old iron etc to be used again*) récupérer.

salvation [sæl'veɪʃ(ə)n] *n* salut *m.*

same [seɪm] *a* même; **the (very) s. house as** (exactement) la même maison que; – *pron* **the s.** le même, la même; **the s. (thing)** la même chose; **it's all the s. to me** ça m'est égal; **all** *or* **just the s.** tout de même; **to do the s.** en faire autant. ◆**—ness** *n* identité *f*; *Pej* monotonie *f.*

sampl/e ['sɑːmp(ə)l] *n* échantillon *m*; (*of blood*) prélèvement *m*; – *vt* (*wine, cheese etc*) déguster, goûter; (*product, recipe etc*) essayer; (*army life etc*) goûter de. ◆**—ing** *n* (*of wine*) dégustation *f.*

sanatorium [sænə'tɔːrɪəm] *n* sanatorium *m.*

sanctify ['sæŋktɪfaɪ] *vt* sanctifier. ◆**sanctity** *n* sainteté *f.* ◆**sanctuary** *n Rel* sanctuaire *m*; (*refuge*) & *Pol* asile *m*; (*for animals*) réserve *f.*

sanctimonious [sæŋktɪ'məʊnɪəs] *a* (*person, manner*) tartuffe.

sanction ['sæŋkʃ(ə)n] *n* (*approval, punishment*) sanction *f*; – *vt* (*approve*) sanctionner.

sand [sænd] *n* sable *m*; **the sands** (*beach*) la plage; – *vt* (*road*) sabler; **to s. (down)** (*wood etc*) poncer. ◆**sandbag** *n* sac *m* de sable. ◆**sandcastle** *n* château *m* de sable. ◆**sander** *n* (*machine*) ponceuse *f.* ◆**sandpaper** *n* papier *m* de verre; – *vt* poncer. ◆**sandstone** *n* (*rock*) grès *m*. ◆**sandy** *a* **1** (**-ier, -iest**) (*beach*) de sable; (*road, ground*) sablonneux; (*water*) sableux. **2** (*hair*) blond roux *inv*.

sandal ['sænd(ə)l] *n* sandale *f*.

sandwich ['sænwɪdʒ] **1** *n* sandwich *m*; **cheese/***etc* **s.** sandwich au fromage/*etc*. **2** *vt* **to s. (in)** (*fit in*) intercaler; **sandwiched in between** (*caught*) coincé entre.

sane [seɪn] *a* (**-er, -est**) (*person*) sain (d'esprit); (*idea, attitude*) raisonnable.

sang [sæŋ] *see* **sing**.

sanguine ['sæŋgwɪn] *a* (*hopeful*) optimiste.

sanitarium [sænɪ'teərɪəm] *n Am* sanatorium *m*.

sanitary ['sænɪtərɪ] *a* (*fittings, conditions*) sanitaire; (*clean*) hygiénique. ◆**sani'tation** *n* hygiène *f* (publique); (*plumbing etc*) installations *fpl* sanitaires.

sanity ['sænɪtɪ] *n* santé *f* mentale; (*reason*) raison *f*.

sank [sæŋk] *see* **sink**[2].

Santa Claus ['sæntəklɔːz] *n* le père Noël.

sap [sæp] **1** *n Bot & Fig* sève *f*. **2** *vt* (**-pp-**) (*weaken*) miner (*énergie etc*).

sapphire ['sæfaɪər] *n* (*jewel, needle*) saphir *m*.

sarcasm ['sɑːkæz(ə)m] *n* sarcasme *m*. ◆**sar'castic** *a* sarcastique.

sardine [sɑː'diːn] *n* sardine *f*.

Sardinia [sɑː'dɪnɪə] *n* Sardaigne *f*.

sardonic [sɑː'dɒnɪk] *a* sardonique.

sash [sæʃ] *n* **1** (*on dress*) ceinture *f*; (*of mayor etc*) écharpe *f*. **2 s. window** fenêtre *f* à guillotine.

sat [sæt] *see* **sit**.

Satan ['seɪt(ə)n] *n* Satan *m*. ◆**sa'tanic** *a* satanique.

satchel ['sætʃ(ə)l] *n* cartable *m*.

satellite ['sætəlaɪt] *n* satellite *m*; **s. (country)** *Pol* pays *m* satellite.

satiate ['seɪʃɪeɪt] *vt* rassasier.

satin ['sætɪn] *n* satin *m*.

satire ['sætaɪər] *n* satire *f* (**on** contre). ◆**sa'tirical** *a* satirique. ◆**satirist** *n* écrivain *m* satirique. ◆**satirize** *vt* faire la satire de.

satisfaction [sætɪs'fækʃ(ə)n] *n* satisfaction *f*. ◆**satisfactory** *a* satisfaisant. ◆**'satisfy** *vt* satisfaire; (*persuade, convince*) persuader (**that** que); (*demand, condition*) satisfaire à; **to s. oneself as to/that** s'assurer de/que; **satisfied with** satisfait de; – *vi* donner satisfaction. ◆**'satisfying** *a* satisfaisant; (*food, meal*) substantiel.

satsuma [sæt'suːmə] *n* (*fruit*) mandarine *f*.

saturate ['sætʃəreɪt] *vt* (*fill*) saturer (**with** de); (*soak*) tremper. ◆**satu'ration** *n* saturation *f*.

Saturday ['sætədɪ] *n* samedi *m*.

sauce [sɔːs] *n* **1** sauce *f*; **tomato s.** sauce tomate; **s. boat** saucière *f*. **2** (*cheek*) *Fam* toupet *m*. ◆**saucy** *a* (**-ier, -iest**) (*cheeky*) impertinent; (*smart*) *Fam* coquet.

saucepan ['sɔːspən] *n* casserole *f*.

saucer ['sɔːsər] *n* soucoupe *f*.

Saudi Arabia [saudɪə'reɪbɪə, *Am* sɔːdɪə'reɪbɪə] *n* Arabie *f* Séoudite.

sauna ['sɔːnə] *n* sauna *m*.

saunter ['sɔːntər] *vi* flâner.

sausage ['sɒsɪdʒ] *n* (*cooked, for cooking*) saucisse *f*; (*precooked, dried*) saucisson *m*.

sauté ['səʊteɪ] *a Culin* sauté.

savage ['sævɪdʒ] *a* (*primitive*) sauvage; (*fierce*) féroce; (*brutal, cruel*) brutal, sauvage; – *n* (*brute*) sauvage *mf*; – *vt* (*of animal, critic etc*) attaquer (férocement). ◆**savagery** *n* (*cruelty*) sauvagerie *f*.

sav/e [seɪv] **1** *vt* sauver (**from** de); (*keep*) garder, réserver; (*money, time*) économiser, épargner; (*stamps*) collectionner; (*prevent*) empêcher (**from** de); (*problems, trouble*) éviter; **that will s. him** *or* **her (the bother of) going** ça lui évitera d'y aller; **to s. up** (*money*) économiser; – *vi* **to s. (up)** faire des économies (**for sth, to buy sth** pour (s')acheter qch); – *n Fb* arrêt *m*. **2** *prep* (*except*) sauf. ◆**—ing** *n* (*of time, money*) économie *f*, épargne *f* (**of** de); (*rescue*) sauvetage *m*; (*thrifty habit*) l'épargne *f*; *pl* (*money*) économies *fpl*; **savings bank** caisse *f* d'épargne. ◆**saviour** *n* sauveur *m*.

saveloy ['sævəlɔɪ] *n* cervelas *m*.

savour ['seɪvər] *n* (*taste, interest*) saveur *f*; – *vt* savourer. ◆**savoury** *a* (*tasty*) savoureux; (*not sweet*) *Culin* salé; **not very s.** (*neighbourhood*) *Fig* peu recommandable.

saw[1] [sɔː] *n* scie *f*; – *vt* (*pt* **sawed**, *pp* **sawn** *or* **sawed**) scier; **to s. off** scier; **a sawn-off** *or Am* **sawed-off shotgun** un fusil à canon scié. ◆**sawdust** *n* sciure *f*. ◆**sawmill** *n* scierie *f*.

saw[2] [sɔː] *see* **see**[1].

saxophone ['sæksəfəʊn] *n* saxophone *m*.

say [seɪ] *vt* (*pt & pp* **said** [sed]) dire (**to** à, **that** que); (*prayer*) faire, dire; (*of dial etc*) marquer; **to s. again** répéter; **it is said that . . .** on dit que . . . ; **what do you s. to a walk?** que dirais-tu d'une promenade?; **(let's) s. tomorrow** disons demain; **to s. the least** c'est le moins que l'on puisse dire; **to s. nothing of . . .** sans parler de . . . ; **that's to s.** c'est-à-dire; – *vi* dire; **you don't s.!**

Fam sans blague!; **I s.!** dites donc!; **s.!** *Am Fam* dis donc!; – *n* **to have one's s.** dire ce que l'on a à dire, s'exprimer; **to have a lot of s.** avoir beaucoup d'influence; **to have no s.** ne pas avoir voix au chapitre (**in** pour). ◆**—ing** *n* proverbe *m*.

scab [skæb] *n* **1** *Med* croûte *f*. **2** (*blackleg*) *Fam* jaune *m*.

scaffold ['skæfəld] *n* échafaudage *m*; (*gallows*) échafaud *m*. ◆**—ing** *n* échafaudage *m*.

scald [skɔːld] *vt* (*burn, cleanse*) ébouillanter; (*sterilize*) stériliser; – *n* brûlure *f*.

scale [skeɪl] **1** *n* (*of map, wages etc*) échelle *f*; (*of numbers*) série *f*; *Mus* gamme *f*; **on a small/large s.** sur une petite/grande échelle; – *a* (*drawing*) à l'échelle; **s. model** modèle *m* réduit; – *vt* **to s. down** réduire (proportionnellement). **2** *n* (*on fish*) écaille *f*; (*dead skin*) *Med* squame *f*; (*on teeth*) tartre *m*; – *vt* (*teeth*) détartrer. **3** *vt* (*wall*) escalader.

scales [skeɪlz] *npl* (*for weighing*) balance *f*; (**bathroom**) **s.** pèse-personne *m*; (**baby**) **s.** pèse-bébé *m*.

scallion ['skæljən] *n* (*onion*) *Am* ciboule *f*.

scallop ['skɒləp] *n* coquille *f* Saint-Jacques.

scalp [skælp] *n Med* cuir *m* chevelu; – *vt* (*cut off too much hair from*) *Fig Hum* tondre (*qn*).

scalpel ['skælp(ə)l] *n* bistouri *m*, scalpel *m*.

scam [skæm] *n* (*swindle*) *Am Fam* escroquerie *f*.

scamp [skæmp] *n* coquin, -ine *mf*.

scamper ['skæmpər] *vi* **to s. off** *or* **away** détaler.

scampi ['skæmpɪ] *npl* gambas *fpl*.

scan [skæn] **1** *vt* (**-nn-**) (*look at briefly*) parcourir (des yeux); (*scrutinize*) scruter; (*poetry*) scander; (*of radar*) balayer. **2** *n* **to have a s.** (*of pregnant woman*) passer une échographie.

scandal ['skænd(ə)l] *n* (*disgrace*) scandale *m*; (*gossip*) médisances *fpl*; **to cause a s.** (*of film, book etc*) causer un scandale; (*of attitude, conduct*) faire (du) scandale. ◆**scandalize** *vt* scandaliser. ◆**scandalous** *a* scandaleux.

Scandinavia [skændɪ'neɪvɪə] *n* Scandinavie *f*. ◆**Scandinavian** *a* & *n* scandinave (*mf*).

scanner ['skænər] *n* (*device*) *Med* scanner *m*.

scant [skænt] *a* (*meal, amount*) insuffisant; **s. attention/regard** peu d'attention/de cas. ◆**scantily** *adv* insuffisamment; **s. dressed** à peine vêtu. ◆**scanty** *a* (**-ier, -iest**) insuffisant; (*bikini*) minuscule.

scapegoat ['skeɪpgəʊt] *n* bouc *m* émissaire.

scar [skɑːr] *n* cicatrice *f*; – *vt* (**-rr-**) marquer d'une cicatrice; *Fig* marquer.

scarce [skeəs] *a* (**-er, -est**) (*food, people, book etc*) rare; **to make oneself s.** se tenir à l'écart. ◆**scarcely** *adv* à peine. ◆**scarceness** *n*, ◆**scarcity** *n* (*shortage*) pénurie *f*; (*rarity*) rareté *f*.

scare [skeər] *n* peur *f*; **to give s.o. a s.** faire peur à qn; **bomb s.** alerte *f* à la bombe; – *vt* faire peur à; **to s. off** (*person*) faire fuir; (*animal*) effaroucher. ◆**scared** *a* effrayé; **to be s.** (**stiff**) avoir (très) peur. ◆**scarecrow** *n* épouvantail *m*. ◆**scaremonger** *n* alarmiste *mf*. ◆**scary** *a* (**-ier, -iest**) *Fam* qui fait peur.

scarf [skɑːf] *n* (*pl* **scarves**) (*long*) écharpe *f*; (*square, for women*) foulard *m*.

scarlet ['skɑːlət] *a* écarlate; **s. fever** scarlatine *f*.

scathing ['skeɪðɪŋ] *a* (*remark etc*) acerbe; **to be s. about** critiquer de façon acerbe.

scatter ['skætər] *vt* (*disperse*) disperser (*foule, nuages etc*); (*dot or throw about*) éparpiller; (*spread*) répandre; – *vi* (*of crowd*) se disperser. ◆**—ing** *n* **a s. of houses/***etc* quelques maisons/*etc* dispersées. ◆**scatterbrain** *n* écervelé, -ée *mf*. ◆**scatty** *a* (**-ier, -iest**) *Fam* écervelé, farfelu.

scaveng/e ['skævɪndʒ] *vi* fouiller dans les ordures (**for** pour trouver). ◆**—er** *n Pej* clochard, -arde *mf* (qui fait les poubelles).

scenario [sɪ'nɑːrɪəʊ] *n* (*pl* **-os**) *Cin* & *Fig* scénario *m*.

scene [siːn] *n* (*setting, fuss*) & *Th* scène *f*; (*of crime, accident etc*) lieu *m*; (*situation*) situation *f*; (*incident*) incident *m*; (*view*) vue *f*; **behind the scenes** *Th* & *Fig* dans les coulisses; **on the s.** sur les lieux; **to make** *or* **create a s.** faire une scène (à qn). ◆**scenery** *n* paysage *m*, décor *m*; *Th* décor(s) *m*(*pl*). ◆**scenic** *a* (*beauty etc*) pittoresque.

scent [sent] *n* (*fragrance, perfume*) parfum *m*; (*animal's track*) & *Fig* piste *f*; – *vt* parfumer (**with** de); (*smell, sense*) flairer.

sceptic ['skeptɪk] *a* & *n* sceptique (*mf*). ◆**sceptical** *a* sceptique. ◆**scepticism** *n* scepticisme *m*.

sceptre ['septər] *n* sceptre *m*.

schedul/e ['ʃedjuːl, *Am* 'skedjʊl] *n* (*of work etc*) programme *m*; (*timetable*) horaire *m*; (*list*) liste *f*; **to be behind s.** (*of person, train*) avoir du retard; **to be on s.** (*on time*) être à l'heure; (*up to date*) être à jour; **ahead of s.** en avance; **according to s.** comme prévu; –

vt (*plan*) prévoir; (*event*) fixer le programme *or* l'horaire de. ◆**—ed** *a* (*planned*) prévu; (*service, flight*) régulier; **she's s. to leave at 8** elle doit partir à 8 h.

schem/e [skiːm] *n* plan *m* (**to do** pour faire); (*idea*) idée *f*; (*dishonest trick*) combine *f*, manœuvre *f*; (*arrangement*) arrangement *m*; – *vi* manœuvrer. ◆**—ing** *a* intrigant; – *npl Pej* machinations *fpl*. ◆**—er** *n* intrigant, -ante *mf*.

schizophrenic [skɪtsəʊ'frenɪk] *a* & *n* schizophrène (*mf*).

scholar ['skɒlər] *n* érudit, -ite *mf*; (*specialist*) spécialiste *mf*; (*grant holder*) boursier, -ière *mf*. ◆**scholarly** *a* érudit. ◆**scholarship** *n* érudition *f*; (*grant*) bourse *f* (d'études). ◆**scho'lastic** *a* scolaire.

school [skuːl] *n* école *f*; (*teaching, lessons*) classe *f*; *Univ Am* faculté *f*; (*within university*) institut *m*, département *m*; **in** *or* **at s.** à l'école; **secondary s.**, *Am* **high s.** collège *m*, lycée *m*; **public s.** école *f* privée; *Am* école publique; **s. of motoring** auto-école *f*; **summer s.** cours *mpl* d'été *or* de vacances; – *a* (*year, equipment etc*) scolaire; (*hours*) de classe; **s. fees** frais *mpl* de scolarité. ◆**—ing** *n* (*learning*) instruction *f*; (*attendance*) scolarité *f*. ◆**schoolboy** *n* écolier *m*. ◆**schooldays** *npl* années *fpl* d'école. ◆**schoolgirl** *n* écolière *f*. ◆**schoolhouse** *n* école *f*. ◆**school-'leaver** *n* jeune *mf* qui a terminé ses études secondaires. ◆**schoolmaster** *n* (*primary*) instituteur *m*; (*secondary*) professeur *m*. ◆**schoolmate** *n* camarade *mf* de classe. ◆**schoolmistress** *n* institutrice *f*; professeur *m*. ◆**schoolteacher** *n* (*primary*) instituteur, -trice *mf*; (*secondary*) professeur *m*.

schooner ['skuːnər] *n Nau* goélette *f*.

science ['saɪəns] *n* science *f*; **to study s.** étudier les sciences; – *a* (*subject*) scientifique; (*teacher*) de sciences; **s. fiction** science-fiction *f*. ◆**scien'tific** *a* scientifique. ◆**scientist** *n* scientifique *mf*.

scintillating ['sɪntɪleɪtɪŋ] *a* (*conversation, wit*) brillant.

scissors ['sɪzəz] *npl* ciseaux *mpl*; **a pair of s.** une paire de ciseaux.

sclerosis [sklɪ'rəʊsɪs] *n Med* sclérose *f*; **multiple s.** sclérose en plaques.

scoff [skɒf] **1** *vt* **to s. at** se moquer de. **2** *vti* (*eat*) *Fam* bouffer.

scold [skəʊld] *vt* gronder, réprimander (**for doing** pour avoir fait). ◆**—ing** *n* réprimande *f*.

scone [skəʊn, skɒn] *n* petit pain *m* au lait.

scoop [skuːp] *n* (*shovel*) pelle *f* (à main); (*spoon-shaped*) *Culin* cuiller *f*; *Journ* exclusivité *f*; **at one s.** d'un seul coup; – *vt* (*prizes*) rafler; **to s. out** (*hollow out*) (é)vider; **to s. up** ramasser (avec une pelle *or* une cuiller).

scoot [skuːt] *vi* (*rush, leave*) *Fam* filer.

scooter ['skuːtər] *n* (*child's*) trottinette *f*; (*motorcycle*) scooter *m*.

scope [skəʊp] *n* (*range*) étendue *f*; (*of mind*) envergure *f*; (*competence*) compétence(s) *f*(*pl*); (*limits*) limites *fpl*; **s. for sth/for doing** (*opportunity*) des possibilités *fpl* de qch/de faire; **the s. of one's activity** le champ de ses activités.

scorch [skɔːtʃ] *vt* (*linen, grass etc*) roussir; – *n* **s. (mark)** brûlure *f* légère. ◆**—ing** *a* (*day*) torride; (*sun, sand*) brûlant. ◆**—er** *n Fam* journée *f* torride.

score[1] [skɔːr] *n Sp* score *m*; *Cards* marque *f*; *Mus* partition *f*; (*of film*) musique *f*; **a s. to settle** *Fig* un compte à régler; **on that s.** (*in that respect*) à cet égard; – *vt* (*point, goal*) marquer; (*exam mark*) avoir; (*success*) remporter; *Mus* orchestrer; – *vi* marquer un point *or* un but; (*keep score*) marquer les points. ◆**scoreboard** *n Sp* tableau *m* d'affichage. ◆**scorer** *n Sp* marqueur *m*.

score[2] [skɔːr] *n* (*twenty*) vingt; **a s. of** une vingtaine de; **scores of** *Fig* un grand nombre de.

score[3] [skɔːr] *vt* (*cut*) rayer; (*paper*) marquer.

scorn [skɔːn] *vt* mépriser; – *n* mépris *m*. ◆**scornful** *a* méprisant; **to be s. of** mépriser. ◆**scornfully** *adv* avec mépris.

Scorpio ['skɔːpɪəʊ] *n* (*sign*) le Scorpion.

scorpion ['skɔːpɪən] *n* scorpion *m*.

Scot [skɒt] *n* Écossais, -aise *mf*. ◆**Scotland** *n* Écosse *f*. ◆**Scotsman** *n* (*pl* **-men**) Écossais *m*. ◆**Scotswoman** *n* (*pl* **-women**) Écossaise *f*. ◆**Scottish** *a* écossais.

scotch [skɒtʃ] **1** *a* **s. tape®** *Am* scotch® *m*. **2** *vt* (*rumour*) étouffer; (*attempt*) faire échouer.

Scotch [skɒtʃ] *n* (*whisky*) scotch *m*.

scot-free [skɒt'friː] *adv* sans être puni.

scoundrel ['skaʊndr(ə)l] *n* vaurien *m*.

scour ['skaʊər] *vt* (*pan*) récurer; (*streets etc*) *Fig* parcourir (**for** à la recherche de). ◆**—er** *n* tampon *m* à récurer.

scourge [skɜːdʒ] *n* fléau *m*.

scout [skaʊt] **1** *n* (*soldier*) éclaireur *m*; (**boy**) **s.** scout *m*, éclaireur *m*; **girl s.** *Am* éclaireuse *f*; **s. camp** camp *m* scout. **2** *vi* **to**

s. round for (*look for*) chercher. ◆—**ing** *n* scoutisme *m*.

scowl [skaʊl] *vi* se renfrogner; **to s. at s.o.** regarder qn d'un air mauvais. ◆—**ing** *a* renfrogné.

scraggy ['skrægɪ] *a* (**-ier, -iest**) (*bony*) osseux, maigrichon; (*unkempt*) débraillé.

scram [skræm] *vi* (**-mm-**) *Fam* filer.

scramble ['skræmb(ə)l] **1** *vi* **to s. for** se ruer vers; **to s. up** (*climb*) grimper; **to s. through** traverser avec difficulté; – *n* ruée *f* (**for** vers). **2** *vt* (*egg, message*) brouiller.

scrap [skræp] **1** *n* (*piece*) petit morceau *m* (**of** de); (*of information, news*) fragment *m*; *pl* (*food*) restes *mpl*; **not a s. of** (*truth etc*) pas un brin de; **s. paper** (papier *m*) brouillon *m*. **2** *n* (*metal*) ferraille *f*; **to sell for s.** vendre à la casse; – *a* (*yard, heap*) de ferraille; **s. dealer, s. merchant** marchand *m* de ferraille; **s. iron** ferraille *f*; **on the s. heap** *Fig* au rebut; – *vt* (**-pp-**) envoyer à la ferraille; (*unwanted object, idea, plan*) *Fig* mettre au rancart. **3** *n* (*fight*) *Fam* bagarre *f*. ◆**scrapbook** *n* album *m* (*pour collages etc*).

scrap/e [skreɪp] *vt* racler, gratter; (*skin*) *Med* érafler; **to s. away** *or* **off** (*mud etc*) racler; **to s. together** (*money, people*) réunir (difficilement); – *vi* **to s. against** frotter contre; **to s. along** *Fig* se débrouiller; **to s. through** (*in exam*) réussir de justesse; – *n* raclement *m*; éraflure *f*; **to get into a s.** *Fam* s'attirer des ennuis. ◆—**ings** *npl* raclures *fpl*. ◆—**er** *n* racloir *m*.

scratch [skrætʃ] *n* (*mark, injury*) éraflure *f*; (*on glass*) rayure *f*; **to have a s.** (*scratch oneself*) *Fam* se gratter; **to start from s.** (re)partir de zéro; **to be/come up to s.** être/se montrer à la hauteur; – *vt* (*to relieve an itch*) gratter; (*skin, wall etc*) érafler; (*glass*) rayer; (*with claw*) griffer; (*one's name*) graver (**on** sur); – *vi* (*relieve an itch*) se gratter; (*of cat etc*) griffer; (*of pen*) gratter, accrocher.

scrawl [skrɔːl] *vt* gribouiller; – *n* gribouillis *m*.

scrawny ['skrɔːnɪ] *a* (**-ier, -iest**) (*bony*) osseux, maigrichon.

scream [skriːm] *vti* crier, hurler; **to s. at s.o.** crier après qn; **to s. with pain/***etc* hurler de douleur/*etc*; – *n* cri *m* (perçant).

screech [skriːtʃ] *vi* crier, hurler; (*of brakes*) hurler; – *n* cri *m*; hurlement *m*.

screen [skriːn] **1** *n* écran *m*; *Fig* masque *m*; **(folding) s.** paravent *m*. **2** *vt* (*hide*) cacher (**from s.o.** à qn); (*protect*) protéger (**from** de); (*a film*) projeter; (*visitors, documents*) filtrer; (*for cancer etc*) *Med* faire subir un test de dépistage à (*qn*) (**for** pour). ◆—**ing** *n* (*of film*) projection *f*; (*selection*) tri *m*; (*medical examination*) (test *m* de) dépistage *m*. ◆**screenplay** *n* *Cin* scénario *m*.

screw [skruː] *n* vis *f*; – *vt* visser (**to** à); **to s. down** *or* **on** visser; **to s. off** dévisser; **to s. up** (*paper*) chiffonner; (*eyes*) plisser; (*mess up*) *Sl* gâcher; **to s. one's face up** grimacer. ◆**screwball** *n* & *a* *Am Fam* cinglé, -ée (*mf*). ◆**screwdriver** *n* tournevis *m*. ◆**screwy** *a* (**-ier, -iest**) (*idea, person etc*) farfelu.

scribble ['skrɪb(ə)l] *vti* griffonner; – *n* griffonnage *m*.

scribe [skraɪb] *n* scribe *m*.

scrimmage ['skrɪmɪdʒ] *n* *Fb Am* mêlée *f*.

script [skrɪpt] *n* (*of film*) scénario *m*; (*of play*) texte *m*; (*in exam*) copie *f*. ◆**scriptwriter** *n* *Cin* scénariste *mf*, dialoguiste *mf*; *TV Rad* dialoguiste *mf*.

Scripture ['skrɪptʃər] *n* *Rel* Écriture *f* (sainte).

scroll [skrəʊl] *n* rouleau *m* (de parchemin); (*book*) manuscrit *m*.

scrooge [skruːdʒ] *n* (*miser*) harpagon *m*.

scroung/e [skraʊndʒ] *vt* (*meal*) se faire payer (**off** *or* **from s.o.** par qn); (*steal*) piquer (**off** *or* **from s.o.** à qn); **to s. money off** *or* **from** taper; – *vi* vivre en parasite; (*beg*) quémander; **to s. around for** *Pej* chercher. ◆—**er** *n* parasite *m*.

scrub [skrʌb] **1** *vt* (**-bb-**) frotter, nettoyer (à la brosse); (*pan*) récurer; (*cancel*) *Fig* annuler; **to s. out** (*erase*) *Fig* effacer; – *vi* (*scrub floors*) frotter les planchers; **scrubbing brush** brosse *f* dure; – *n* **to give sth a s.** frotter qch; **s. brush** *Am* brosse *f* dure. **2** *n* (*land*) broussailles *fpl*.

scruff [skrʌf] *n* **1 by the s. of the neck** par la peau du cou. **2** (*person*) *Fam* individu *m* débraillé. ◆**scruffy** *a* (**-ier, -iest**) (*untidy*) négligé; (*dirty*) malpropre.

scrum [skrʌm] *n* *Rugby* mêlée *f*.

scrumptious ['skrʌmpʃəs] *a* *Fam* super bon, succulent.

scruple ['skruːp(ə)l] *n* scrupule *m*. ◆**scrupulous** *a* scrupuleux. ◆**scrupulously** *adv* (*conscientiously*) scrupuleusement; (*completely*) absolument.

scrutinize ['skruːtɪnaɪz] *vt* scruter. ◆**scrutiny** *n* examen *m* minutieux.

scuba ['skjuːbə, *Am* 'skuːbə] *n* scaphandre *m* autonome; **s. diving** la plongée sous-marine.

scuff [skʌf] *vt* **to s. (up)** (*scrape*) érafler.

scuffle ['skʌf(ə)l] *n* bagarre *f*.

scullery ['skʌlərɪ] *n* arrière-cuisine *f.* ·
sculpt [skʌlpt] *vti* sculpter. ◆**sculptor** *n* sculpteur *m.* ◆**sculpture** *n* (*art, object*) sculpture *f*; – *vti* sculpter.
scum [skʌm] *n* **1** (*on liquid*) écume *f.* **2** *Pej* (*people*) racaille *f*; (*person*) salaud *m*; **the s. of** (*society etc*) la lie de.
scupper ['skʌpər] *vt* (*plan*) *Fam* saboter.
scurf [skɜːf] *n* pellicules *fpl.*
scurrilous ['skʌrɪləs] *a* (*criticism, attack*) haineux, violent et grossier.
scurry ['skʌrɪ] *vi* (*rush*) se précipiter, courir; **to s. off** décamper.
scuttle ['skʌt(ə)l] **1** *vt* (*ship*) saborder. **2** *vi* **to s. off** filer.
scythe [saɪð] *n* faux *f.*
sea [siː] *n* mer *f*; **(out) at s.** en mer; **by s.** par mer; **by** *or* **beside the s.** au bord de la mer; **to be all at s.** *Fig* nager complètement; – *a* (*level, breeze*) de la mer; (*water, fish*) de mer; (*air, salt*) marin; (*battle, power*) naval; (*route*) maritime; **s. bed, s. floor** fond *m* de la mer; **s. lion** (*animal*) otarie *f* ◆**seaboard** *n* littoral *m.* ◆**seafarer** *n* marin *m.* ◆**seafood** *n* fruits *mpl* de mer. ◆**seafront** *n* front *m* de mer. ◆**seagull** *n* mouette *f.* ◆**seaman** *n* (*pl* **-men**) marin *m.* ◆**seaplane** *n* hydravion *m.* ◆**seaport** *n* port *m* de mer. ◆**seashell** *n* coquillage *m.* ◆**seashore** *n* bord *m* de la mer. ◆**seasick** *a* **to be s.** avoir le mal de mer. ◆**seasickness** *n* mal *m* de mer. ◆**seaside** *n* bord *m* de la mer; – *a* (*town, holiday*) au bord de la mer. ◆**seaway** *n* route *f* maritime. ◆**seaweed** *n* algue(s) *f(pl).* ◆**seaworthy** *a* (*ship*) en état de naviguer.
seal [siːl] **1** *n* (*animal*) phoque *m.* **2** *n* (*mark, design*) sceau *m*; (*on letter*) cachet *m* (de cire); (*putty for sealing*) joint *m*; – *vt* (*document, container*) sceller; (*with wax*) cacheter; (*stick down*) coller; (*with putty*) boucher; (*s.o.'s fate*) *Fig* décider de; **to s. off** (*room etc*) interdire l'accès de; **to s. off a house/district** (*of police, troops*) boucler une maison/un quartier.
seam [siːm] *n* (*in cloth etc*) couture *f*; (*of coal, quartz etc*) veine *f.*
seamy ['siːmɪ] *a* (**-ier, -iest**) **the s. side** le côté peu reluisant (**of** de).
séance ['seɪɑːns] *n* séance *f* de spiritisme.
search [sɜːtʃ] *n* (*quest*) recherche *f* (**for** de); (*of person, place*) fouille *f*; **in s. of** à la recherche de; **s. party** équipe *f* de secours; – *vt* (*person, place*) fouiller (**for** pour trouver); (*study*) examiner (*documents etc*); **to s. (through) one's papers/***etc* **for sth** chercher qch dans ses papiers/*etc*; – *vi* chercher; **to s. for sth** chercher qch. ◆**—ing** *a* (*look*) pénétrant; (*examination*) minutieux. ◆**searchlight** *n* projecteur *m.*
season ['siːz(ə)n] **1** *n* saison *f*; **the festive s.** la période des fêtes; **in the peak s., in (the) high s.** en pleine *or* haute saison; **in the low** *or* **off s.** en basse saison; **a Truffaut s.** *Cin* une rétrospective Truffaut; **s. ticket** carte *f* d'abonnement. **2** *vt* (*food*) assaisonner; **highly seasoned** (*dish*) relevé. ◆**—ed** *a* (*worker*) expérimenté; (*soldier*) aguerri ◆**—ing** *n* *Culin* assaisonnement *m.* ◆**seasonable** *a* (*weather*) de saison. ◆**seasonal** *a* saisonnier.
seat [siːt] *n* (*for sitting, centre*) & *Pol* siège *m*; (*on train, bus*) banquette *f*; *Cin Th* fauteuil *m*; (*place*) place *f*; (*of trousers*) fond *m*; **to take** *or* **have a s.** s'asseoir; **in the hot s.** (*in difficult position*) *Fig* sur la sellette; **s. belt** ceinture *f* de sécurité; – *vt* (*at table*) placer (*qn*); (*on one's lap*) asseoir (*qn*); **the room seats 50** la salle a 50 places (assises); **be seated!** asseyez-vous! ◆**—ed** *a* (*sitting*) assis. ◆**—ing** *n* **s. (room)** (*seats*) places *fpl* assises; **the s. arrangements** la disposition des places; **s. capacity** nombre *m* de places assises. ◆**—er** *a* & *n* **two-s. (car)** voiture *f* à deux places.
secateurs [sekə'tɜːz] *npl* sécateur *m.*
secede [sɪ'siːd] *vi* faire sécession. ◆**secession** *n* sécession *f.*
secluded [sɪ'kluːdɪd] *a* (*remote*) isolé. ◆**seclusion** *n* solitude *f.*
second[1] ['sekənd] *a* deuxième, second; **every s. week** une semaine sur deux; **in s. (gear)** *Aut* en seconde; **s. to none** sans pareil; **s. in command** second *m*; *Mil* commandant *m* en second; – *adv* (*to say*) deuxièmement; **to come s.** *Sp* se classer deuxième; **the s. biggest** le deuxième en ordre de grandeur; **the s. richest country** le deuxième pays le plus riche; **my s. best** (*choice*) mon deuxième choix; – *n* (*person, object*) deuxième *mf*, second, -onde *mf*; **Louis the S.** Louis Deux; *pl* (*goods*) *Com* articles *mpl* de second choix; – *vt* (*motion*) appuyer. ◆**s.-'class** *a* (*product*) de qualité inférieure; (*ticket*) *Rail* de seconde (classe); (*mail*) non urgent. ◆**s.-'rate** *a* médiocre. ◆**secondly** *adv* deuxièmement.
second[2] ['sekənd] *n* (*unit of time*) seconde *f*; **s. hand** (*of clock, watch*) trotteuse *f.*
second[3] [sɪ'kɒnd] *vt* (*employee*) détacher (**to** à). ◆**—ment** *n* détachement *m*; **on s.** en (position de) détachement (**to** à).
secondary ['sekəndərɪ] *a* secondaire.
secondhand [sekənd'hænd] **1** *a* & *adv* (*not

new) d'occasion. **2** *a* (*report, news*) de seconde main.

secret ['siːkrɪt] *a* secret; – *n* secret *m*; **in s.** en secret; **an open s.** le secret de Polichinelle. ◆**secrecy** *n* (*discretion, silence*) secret *m*; **in s.** en secret. ◆**secretive** *a* (*person*) cachottier; (*organization*) qui a le goût du secret; **to be s. about** faire un mystère de; (*organization*) être très discret sur. ◆**secretively** *adv* en catimini.

secretary ['sekrət(ə)rɪ] *n* secrétaire *mf*; **Foreign S.**, *Am* **S. of State** = ministre *m* des Affaires étrangères. ◆**secre'tarial** *a* (*work*) de secrétaire, de secrétariat; (*school*) de secrétariat. ◆**secre'tariat** *n* (*in international organization*) secrétariat *m*.

secrete [sɪ'kriːt] *vt Med Biol* sécréter. ◆**sec'retion** *n* sécrétion *f*.

sect [sekt] *n* secte *f*. ◆**sec'tarian** *a* & *n Pej* sectaire (*mf*).

section ['sekʃ(ə)n] *n* (*of road, book, wood etc*) section *f*; (*of town, country*) partie *f*; (*of machine, furniture*) élément *m*; (*department*) section *f*; (*in store*) rayon *m*; **the sports/***etc* **s.** (*of newspaper*) la page des sports/*etc*; – *vt* **to s. off** (*separate*) séparer.

sector ['sektər] *n* secteur *m*.

secular ['sekjʊlər] *a* (*teaching etc*) laïque; (*music, art*) profane.

secure [sɪ'kjʊər] **1** *a* (*person, valuables*) en sûreté, en sécurité; (*in one's mind*) tranquille; (*place*) sûr; (*solid, firm*) solide; (*door, window*) bien fermé; (*certain*) assuré; **s. from** à l'abri de; **(emotionally) s.** sécurisé; – *vt* (*fasten*) attacher; (*window etc*) bien fermer; (*success, future etc*) assurer; **to s. against** protéger de. **2** *vt* (*obtain*) procurer (**sth for s.o.** qch à qn); **to s. sth (for oneself)** se procurer qch. ◆**securely** *adv* (*firmly*) solidement; (*safely*) en sûreté. ◆**security** *n* sécurité *f*; (*for loan, bail*) caution *f*; **s. firm** société *f* de surveillance; **s. guard** agent *m* de sécurité; (*transferring money*) convoyeur *m* de fonds.

sedan [sɪ'dæn] *n* (*saloon*) *Aut Am* berline *f*.

sedate [sɪ'deɪt] **1** *a* calme. **2** *vt* mettre sous calmants. ◆**sedation** *n* **under s.** sous calmants. ◆**'sedative** *n* calmant *m*.

sedentary ['sedəntərɪ] *a* sédentaire.

sediment ['sedɪmənt] *n* sédiment *m*.

sedition [sə'dɪʃ(ə)n] *n* sédition *f*. ◆**seditious** *a* séditieux.

seduce [sɪ'djuːs] *vt* séduire. ◆**seducer** *n* séducteur, -trice *mf*. ◆**seduction** *n* séduction *f*. ◆**seductive** *a* (*person, offer*) séduisant.

see[1] [siː] *vti* (*pt* **saw**, *pp* **seen**) voir; **we'll s.** on verra (bien); **I s.!** je vois!; **I can s. (clearly)** j'y vois clair; **I saw him run(ning)** je l'ai vu courir; **to s. reason** entendre raison; **to s. the joke** comprendre la plaisanterie; **s. who it is** va voir qui c'est; **s. you (later)!** à tout à l'heure!; **s. you (soon)!** à bientôt!; **to s. about** (*deal with*) s'occuper de; (*consider*) songer à; **to s. in the New Year** fêter la Nouvelle Année; **to s. s.o. off** accompagner qn (*à la gare etc*); **to s. s.o. out** raccompagner qn; **to s. through** (*task*) mener à bonne fin; **to s. s.o. through** (*be enough for*) suffire à qn; **to s. through s.o.** deviner le jeu de qn; **to s. to** (*deal with*) s'occuper de; (*mend*) réparer; **to s. (to it) that** (*attend*) veiller à ce que (+ *sub*); (*check*) s'assurer que; **to s. s.o. to** (*accompany*) raccompagner qn à. ◆**s.-through** *a* (*dress etc*) transparent.

see[2] [siː] *n* (*of bishop*) siège *m* (épiscopal).

seed [fɪd] *n Agr* graine *f*; (*in grape*) pépin *m*; (*source*) *Fig* germe; *Tennis* tête *f* de série; **seed(s)** (*for sowing*) *Agr* graines *fpl*; **to go to s.** (*of lettuce etc*) monter en graine. ◆**seedbed** *n Bot* semis *m*; (*of rebellion etc*) *Fig* foyer *m* (**of** de). ◆**seedling** *n* (*plant*) semis *m*.

seedy ['siːdɪ] *a* (**-ier, -iest**) miteux. ◆**seediness** *n* aspect *m* miteux.

seeing ['siːɪŋ] *conj* **s. (that)** vu que.

seek [siːk] *vt* (*pt* & *pp* **sought**) chercher (**to do** à faire); (*ask for*) demander (**from** à); **to s. (after)** rechercher; **to s. out** aller trouver.

seem [siːm] *vi* sembler (**to do** faire); **it seems that . . .** (*impression*) il semble que . . . (+ *sub or indic*); (*rumour*) il paraît que . . . ; **it seems to me that . . .** il me semble que . . . ; **we s. to know each other** il me semble qu'on se connaît; **I can't s. to do it** je n'arrive pas à le faire. ◆**—ing** *a* apparent. ◆**—ingly** *adv* apparemment.

seemly ['siːmlɪ] *a* convenable.

seen [siːn] *see* **see**[1].

seep [siːp] *vi* (*ooze*) suinter; **to s. into** s'infiltrer dans. ◆**—age** *n* suintement *m*; infiltration(s) *f(pl)* (**into** dans); (*leak*) fuite *f*.

seesaw ['siːsɔː] *n* (jeu *m* de) bascule *f*.

seethe [siːð] *vi* **to s. with anger** bouillir de colère; **to s. with people** grouiller de monde.

segment ['segmənt] *n* segment *m*; (*of orange*) quartier *m*.

segregate ['segrɪgeɪt] *vt* séparer; **(racially)**

segregated (*school*) où se pratique la ségrégation raciale. ◆**segre'gation** *n* ségrégation *f*.

seize [siːz] **1** *vt* saisir; (*power, land*) s'emparer de; – *vi* **to s. on** (*offer etc*) saisir. **2** *vi* **to s. up** (*of engine*) (se) gripper. ◆**seizure** [-ʒər] *n* (*of goods etc*) saisie *f*; *Mil* prise *f*; *Med* crise *f*.

seldom ['seldəm] *adv* rarement.

select [sɪ'lekt] *vt* choisir (**from** parmi); (*candidates, pupils etc*) & *Sp* sélectionner; – *a* (*chosen*) choisi; (*exclusive*) sélect, chic *inv*. ◆**selection** *n* sélection *f*. ◆**selective** *a* (*memory, recruitment etc*) sélectif; (*person*) qui opère un choix; (*choosey*) difficile.

self [self] *n* (*pl* **selves**) **the s.** *Phil* le moi; **he's back to his old s.** *Fam* il est redevenu lui-même. ◆**s.-a'ssurance** *n* assurance *f*. ◆**s.-a'ssured** *a* sûr de soi. ◆**s.-'catering** *a* où l'on fait la cuisine soi-même. ◆**s.-'centred** *a* égocentrique. ◆**s.-'cleaning** *a* (*oven*) autonettoyant. ◆**s.-con'fessed** *a* (*liar*) de son propre aveu. ◆**s.-'confident** *a* sûr de soi. ◆**s.-'conscious** *a* gêné. ◆**s.-'consciousness** *n* gêne *f*. ◆**s.-con'tained** *a* (*flat*) indépendant. ◆**s.-con'trol** *n* maîtrise *f* de soi. ◆**s.-de'feating** *a* qui a un effet contraire à celui qui est recherché. ◆**s.-de'fence** *n Jur* légitime défense *f*. ◆**s.-de'nial** *n* abnégation *f*. ◆**s.-determi'nation** *n* autodétermination *f*. ◆**s.-'discipline** *n* autodiscipline *f*. ◆**s.-em'ployed** *a* qui travaille à son compte. ◆**s.-es'teem** *n* amour-propre *m*. ◆**s.-'evident** *a* évident, qui va de soi. ◆**s.-ex'planatory** *a* qui tombe sous le sens, qui se passe d'explication. ◆**s.-'governing** *a* autonome. ◆**s.-im'portant** *a* suffisant. ◆**s.-in'dulgent** *a* qui ne se refuse rien. ◆**s.-'interest** *n* intérêt *m* (personnel). ◆**s.-o'pinionated** *a* entêté. ◆**s.-'pity** *n* **to feel** s.-pity s'apitoyer sur son propre sort. ◆**s.-'portrait** *n* autoportrait *m*. ◆**s.-po'ssessed** *a* assuré. ◆**s.-raising** *or Am* **s.-rising 'flour** *n* farine *f* à levure. ◆**s.-re'liant** *a* indépendant. ◆**s.-re'spect** *n* amour-propre *m*. ◆**s.-re'specting** *a* qui se respecte. ◆**s.-'righteous** *a* pharisaïque. ◆**s.-'sacrifice** *n* abnégation *f*. ◆**s.-'satisfied** *a* content de soi. ◆**s.-'service** *n* & *a* libre-service (*m inv*). ◆**s.-'styled** *a* soi-disant. ◆**s.-su'fficient** *a* indépendant, qui a son indépendance. ◆**s.-su'pporting** *a* financièrement indépendant. ◆**s.-'taught** *a* autodidacte.

selfish ['selfɪʃ] *a* égoïste; (*motive*) intéressé. ◆**selfless** *a* désintéressé. ◆**selfishness** *n* égoïsme *m*.

selfsame ['selfseɪm] *a* même.

sell [sel] *vt* (*pt* & *pp* **sold**) vendre; (*idea etc*) *Fig* faire accepter; **she sold me it for twenty pounds** elle me l'a vendu vingt livres; **to s. back** revendre; **to s. off** liquider; **to have** *or* **be sold out of** (*cheese etc*) n'avoir plus de; **this book is sold out** ce livre est épuisé; – *vi* se vendre; (*of idea etc*) *Fig* être accepté; **to s. up** vendre sa maison; *Com* vendre son affaire; **selling price** prix *m* de vente. ◆**seller** *n* vendeur, -euse *mf*. ◆**sellout** *n* **1** (*betrayal*) trahison *f*. **2 it was a s.** *Th Cin* tous les billets ont été vendus.

sellotape® ['seləteɪp] *n* scotch® *m*; – *vt* scotcher.

semantic [sɪ'mæntɪk] *a* sémantique. ◆**semantics** *n* sémantique *f*.

semaphore ['seməfɔːr] *n* (*device*) *Rail Nau* sémaphore *m*; (*system*) signaux *mpl* à bras.

semblance ['sembləns] *n* semblant *m*.

semen ['siːmən] *n* sperme *m*.

semester [sɪ'mestər] *n Univ* semestre *m*.

semi- ['semɪ] *pref* demi-, semi-. ◆**semiauto'matic** *a* semi-automatique. ◆**semibreve** [-briːv] *n Mus* ronde *f*. ◆**semicircle** *n* demi-cercle *m*. ◆**semi'circular** *a* semi-circulaire. ◆**semi'colon** *n* point-virgule *m*. ◆**semi-'conscious** *a* à demi conscient. ◆**semide'tached** *a* **s. house** maison *f* jumelle. ◆**semi'final** *n Sp* demi-finale *f*.

seminar ['semɪnɑːr] *n Univ* séminaire *m*.

seminary ['semɪnərɪ] *n Rel* séminaire *m*.

Semite ['siːmaɪt, *Am* 'semaɪt] *n* Sémite *mf*. ◆**Se'mitic** *a* sémite; (*language*) sémitique.

semolina [semə'liːnə] *n* semoule *f*.

senate ['senɪt] *n Pol* sénat *m*. ◆**senator** *n Pol* sénateur *m*.

send [send] *vt* (*pt* & *pp* **sent**) envoyer (**to** à); **to s. s.o. for sth/s.o.** envoyer qn chercher qch/qn; **to s. s.o. crazy** *or* **mad** rendre qn fou; **to s. s.o. packing** *Fam* envoyer promener qn; **to s. away** *or* **off** envoyer (**to** à); (*dismiss*) renvoyer; **to s. back** renvoyer; **to s. in** (*form*) envoyer; (*person*) faire entrer; **to s. on** (*letter, luggage*) faire suivre; **to s. out** (*invitation etc*) envoyer; (*heat*) émettre; (*from room etc*) faire sortir (*qn*); **to s. up** (*balloon, rocket*) lancer; (*price, luggage*) faire monter; (*mock*) *Fam* parodier; – *vi* **to s. away** *or* **off for** commander (par courrier); **to s. for** (*doctor etc*) faire venir, envoyer chercher; **to s. (out) for** (*meal, groceries*) envoyer chercher. ◆**s.-off** *n* **to give s.o. a s.-off** *Fam* faire des adieux chaleureux à qn. ◆**s.-up** *n Fam* parodie *f*. ◆**sender** *n* expéditeur, -trice *mf*.

senile ['siːnaɪl] *a* gâteux, sénile. ◆**se'nility** *n* gâtisme *m*, sénilité *f*.

senior ['siːnɪər] *a* (*older*) plus âgé; (*position, executive, rank*) supérieur; (*teacher, partner*) principal; **to be s. to s.o., be s.o.'s s.** être plus âgé que qn; (*in rank*) être au-dessus de qn; **Brown s.** Brown père; **s. citizen** personne *f* âgée; **s. year** *Sch Univ Am* dernière année *f*; – *n* aîné, -ée *mf*; *Sch* grand, -ande *mf*; *Sch Univ Am* étudiant, -ante *mf* de dernière année; *Sp* senior *mf*. ◆**seni'ority** *n* priorité *f* d'âge; (*in service*) ancienneté *f*; (*in rank*) supériorité *f*.

sensation [sen'seɪʃ(ə)n] *n* sensation *f*. ◆**sensational** *a* (*event*) qui fait sensation; (*newspaper, film*) à sensation; (*terrific*) *Fam* sensationnel.

sense [sens] *n* (*faculty, awareness, meaning*) sens *m*; **a s. of hearing** (le sens de) l'ouïe *f*; **to have (good) s.** avoir du bon sens; **a s. of** (*physical*) une sensation de (*chaleur etc*); (*mental*) un sentiment de (*honte etc*); **a s. of humour/direction** le sens de l'humour/de l'orientation; **a s. of time** la notion de l'heure; **to bring s.o. to his senses** ramener qn à la raison; **to make s.** (*of story, action etc*) avoir du sens; **to make s. of** comprendre; – *vt* sentir (intuitivement) (**that** que); (*have a forebdoing of*) pressentir. ◆**—less** *a* (*stupid, meaningless*) insensé; (*unconscious*) sans connaissance. ◆**—lessness** *n* stupidité *f*.

sensibility [sensɪ'bɪlətɪ] *n* sensibilité *f*; *pl* (*touchiness*) susceptibilité *f*.

sensible ['sensəb(ə)l] *a* (*wise*) raisonnable, sensé; (*clothes*) pratique.

sensitive ['sensɪtɪv] *a* (*responsive, painful*) sensible (**to** à); (*delicate*) délicat (*peau, question etc*); (*touchy*) susceptible (**about** à propos de). ◆**sensi'tivity** *n* sensibilité *f*; (*touchiness*) susceptibilité *f*.

sensory ['sensərɪ] *a* sensoriel.

sensual ['senʃʊəl] *a* (*bodily, sexual*) sensuel. ◆**sensu'ality** *n* sensualité *f*. ◆**sensuous** *a* (*pleasing, refined*) sensuel. ◆**sensuously** *adv* avec sensualité. ◆**sensuousness** *n* sensualité *f*.

sent [sent] *see* **send**.

sentence ['sentəns] **1** *n Gram* phrase *f*. **2** *n Jur* condamnation *f*; (*punishment*) peine *f*; **to pass s.** prononcer une condamnation (**on s.o.** contre qn); **to serve a s.** purger une peine; – *vt Jur* prononcer une condamnation contre; **to s. to** condamner à.

sentiment ['sentɪmənt] *n* sentiment *m*. ◆**senti'mental** *a* sentimental. ◆**sentimen'tality** *n* sentimentalité *f*.

sentry ['sentrɪ] *n* sentinelle *f*; **s. box** guérite *f*.

separate ['sepərət] *a* (*distinct*) séparé; (*independent*) indépendant; (*different*) différent; (*individual*) particulier; – ['sepəreɪt] *vt* séparer (**from** de); – *vi* se séparer (**from** de). ◆**'separately** *adv* séparément. ◆**sepa'ration** *n* séparation *f*.

separates ['sepərəts] *npl* (*garments*) coordonnés *mpl*.

September [sep'tembər] *n* septembre *m*.

septic ['septɪk] *a* (*wound*) infecté; **s. tank** fosse *f* septique.

sequel ['siːkw(ə)l] *n* suite *f*.

sequence ['siːkwəns] *n* (*order*) ordre *m*; (*series*) succession *f*; *Mus Cards* séquence *f*; **film s.** séquence de film; **in s.** dans l'ordre, successivement.

sequin ['siːkwɪn] *n* paillette *f*.

serenade [serə'neɪd] *n* sérénade *f*; – *vt* donner une *or* la sérénade à.

serene [sə'riːn] *a* serein ◆**serenity** *n* sérénité *f*.

sergeant ['sɑːdʒənt] *n Mil* sergent *m*; (*in police force*) brigadier *m*.

serial ['sɪərɪəl] *n* (*story, film*) feuilleton *m*; **s. number** (*of banknote, TV set etc*) numéro de série. ◆**serialize** *vt* publier en feuilleton; *TV Rad* adapter en feuilleton.

series ['sɪəriːz] *n inv* série *f*; (*book collection*) collection *f*.

serious ['sɪərɪəs] *a* sérieux; (*illness, mistake, tone*) grave, sérieux; (*damage*) important. ◆**—ly** *adv* sérieusement; (*ill, damaged*) gravement; **to take s.** prendre au sérieux. ◆**—ness** *n* sérieux *m*; (*of illness etc*) gravité *f*; (*of damage*) importance *f*; **in all s.** sérieusement.

sermon ['sɜːmən] *n* sermon *m*.

serpent ['sɜːpənt] *n* serpent *m*.

serrated [sə'reɪtɪd] *a* (*knife*) à dents (de scie).

serum ['sɪərəm] *n* sérum *m*.

servant ['sɜːvənt] *n* (*in house etc*) domestique *mf*; (*person who serves*) serviteur *m*; **public s.** fonctionnaire *mf*.

serve [sɜːv] *vt* servir (**to s.o.** à qn, **s.o. with sth** qch à qn); (*of train, bus etc*) desservir (*un village, un quartier etc*); (*supply*) *El* alimenter; (*apprenticeship*) faire; (*summons*) *Jur* remettre (**on** à); **it serves its**

purpose ça fait l'affaire; **(it) serves you right!** *Fam* ça t'apprendra!; **to s. up** *or* **out** servir; – *vi* servir (**as** de); **to s. on** (*jury, committee*) être membre de; **to s. to show/***etc* servir à montrer/*etc*; – *n Tennis* service *m*.

servic/e ['sɜːvɪs] *n* (*serving*) & *Mil Rel Tennis* service *m*; (*machine or vehicle repair*) révision *f*; **to be of s. to** être utile à, rendre service à; **the (armed) services** les forces *fpl* armées; **s. (charge)** (*tip*) service *m*; **s. department** (*workshop*) atelier *m*; **s. area** (*on motorway*) aire *f* de service; **s. station** station-service *f*; – *vt* (*machine, vehicle*) réviser. ◆**—ing** *n Tech Aut* révision *f*. ◆**serviceable** *a* (*usable*) utilisable; (*useful*) commode; (*durable*) solide. ◆**serviceman** *n* (*pl* **-men**) *n* militaire *m*.

serviette [sɜːvɪ'et] *n* serviette *f* (de table).

servile ['sɜːvaɪl] *a* servile.

session ['seʃ(ə)n] *n* séance *f*; *Jur Pol* session *f*, séance *f*; *Univ* année *f or* trimestre *m* universitaire; *Univ Am* semestre *m* universitaire.

set [set] **1** *n* (*of keys, needles, tools*) jeu *m*; (*of stamps, numbers*) série *f*; (*of people*) groupe *m*; (*of facts*) & *Math* ensemble *m*; (*of books*) collection *f*; (*of plates*) service *m*; (*of tyres*) train *m*; (*kit*) trousse *f*; (*stage*) *Th Cin* plateau *m*; (*scenery*) *Th Cin* décor *m*, scène *f*; (*hairstyle*) mise *f* en plis; *Tennis* set *m*; **television s.** téléviseur *m*; **radio s.** poste *m* de radio; **tea s.** service *m* à thé; **chess s.** (*box*) jeu *m* d'échecs; **a s. of teeth** une rangée de dents, une denture; **the skiing/racing s.** le monde du ski/des courses. **2** *a* (*time etc*) fixe; (*lunch*) à prix fixe; (*book etc*) *Sch* au programme; (*speech*) préparé à l'avance; (*in one's habits*) régulier; (*situated*) situé; **s. phrase** expression *f* consacrée; **a s. purpose** un but déterminé; **the s. menu** le plat du jour; **dead s. against** absolument opposé à; **s. on doing** résolu à faire; **to be s. on sth** vouloir qch à tout prix; **all s.** (*ready*) prêt (**to do** pour faire); **to be s. back from** (*of house etc*) être en retrait de (*route etc*). **3** *vt* (*pt & pp* **set**, *pres p.* **setting**) (*put*) mettre, poser; (*date, limit etc*) fixer; (*record*) *Sp* établir; (*adjust*) *Tech* régler; (*arm etc in plaster*) *Med* plâtrer; (*task*) donner (**for s.o.** à qn); (*problem*) poser; (*diamond*) monter; (*precedent*) créer; **to have one's hair s.** se faire faire une mise en plis; **to s. (loose)** (*dog*) lâcher (**on** contre); **to s. s.o. (off) crying/***etc* faire pleurer/*etc* qn; **to s. back** (*in time*) retarder; (*cost*) *Fam* coûter; **to s. down** déposer; **to s. off** (*bomb*) faire exploser; (*activity, mechanism*) déclencher; (*complexion, beauty*) rehausser; **to s. out** (*display, explain*) exposer (**to** à); (*arrange*) disposer; **to s. up** (*furniture*) installer; (*statue, tent*) dresser; (*school*) fonder; (*government*) établir; (*business*) créer; (*inquiry*) ouvrir; **to s. s.o. up in business** lancer qn dans les affaires; – *vi* (*of sun*) se coucher; (*of jelly*) prendre; (*of bone*) *Med* se ressoudre; **to s. about** (*job*) se mettre à; **to s. about doing** se mettre à faire; **to s. in** (*start*) commencer; (*arise*) surgir; **to s. off** *or* **out** (*leave*) partir; **to s. out do do** entreprendre de faire; **to s. up in business** monter une affaire; **to s. upon** (*attack*) attaquer (*qn*). ◆**setting** *n* (*surroundings*) cadre *m*; (*of sun*) coucher *m*; (*of diamond*) monture *f*. ◆**setter** *n* chien *m* couchant.

setback ['setbæk] *n* revers *m*; *Med* rechute *f*.

setsquare ['setskweər] *n Math* équerre *f*.

settee [se'tiː] *n* canapé *m*.

settle ['set(ə)l] *vt* (*decide, arrange, pay*) régler; (*date*) fixer; (*place in position*) placer; (*person*) installer (*dans son lit etc*); (*nerves*) calmer; (*land*) coloniser; **let's s. things** arrangeons les choses; **that's (all) settled** (*decided*) c'est décidé; – *vi* (*live*) s'installer, s'établir; (*of dust*) se déposer; (*of bird*) se poser; (*of snow*) tenir; **to s. (down) into** (*armchair*) s'installer dans; (*job*) s'habituer à; **to s. (up) with s.o.** régler qn; **to s. for** se contenter de, accepter; **to s. down** (*in chair or house*) s'installer; (*of nerves*) se calmer; (*in one's lifestyle*) se ranger; (*marry*) se caser; **to s. down to** (*get used to*) s'habituer à; (*work, task*) se mettre à. ◆**settled** *a* (*weather, period*) stable; (*habits*) régulier. ◆**settlement** *n* (*of account etc*) règlement *m*; (*agreement*) accord *m*; (*colony*) colonie *f*. ◆**settler** *n* colon *m*.

set-to [set'tuː] *n* (*quarrel*) *Fam* prise *f* de bec.

setup ['setʌp] *n Fam* situation *f*.

seven ['sev(ə)n] *a & n* sept (*m*). ◆**seven'teen** *a & n* dix-sept (*m*). ◆**seven'teenth** *a & n* dix-septième (*mf*). ◆**seventh** *a & n* septième (*mf*). ◆**seventieth** *a & n* soixante-dixième (*mf*). ◆**seventy** *a & n* soixante-dix (*m*); **s.-one** soixante et onze.

sever ['sevər] *vt* sectionner, couper; (*relations*) *Fig* rompre. ◆**severing** *n*, ◆**severance** *n* (*of relations*) rupture *f*.

several ['sev(ə)rəl] *a & pron* plusieurs (**of** d'entre).

severe [sə'vɪər] *a* (*judge, tone etc*) sévère; (*winter, training*) rigoureux; (*test*) dur; (*injury*) grave; (*blow, pain*) violent; (*cold, frost*) intense; (*overwork*) excessif; **a s. cold** *Med* un gros rhume; **s. to** *or* **with s.o.** sévère envers qn. ◆**severely** *adv* sévèrement; (*wounded*) gravement. ◆**se'verity** *n* sévérité *f*; rigueur *f*; gravité *f*; violence *f*.

sew [səʊ] *vti* (*pt* **sewed**, *pp* **sewn** [səʊn] *or* **sewed**) coudre; **to s. on** (*button*) (re)coudre; **to s. up** (*tear*) (re)coudre. ◆**—ing** *n* couture *f*; **s. machine** machine *f* à coudre.

sewage ['suːɪdʒ] *n* eaux *fpl* usées *or* d'égout. ◆**sewer** *n* égout *m*.

sewn [səʊn] *see* **sew**.

sex [seks] *n* (*gender, sexuality*) sexe *m*; (*activity*) relations *fpl* sexuelles; **the opposite s.** l'autre sexe; **to have s. with** coucher avec; – *a* (*education, act etc*) sexuel; **s. maniac** obsédé, -ée *mf* sexuel(le). ◆**sexist** *a* & *n* sexiste (*mf*). ◆**sexual** *a* sexuel. ◆**sexu'ality** *n* sexualité *f*. ◆**sexy** *a* (**-ier, -iest**) (*book, garment, person*) sexy *inv*; (*aroused*) qui a envie (de faire l'amour).

sextet [sek'stet] *n* sextuor *m*.

sh! [ʃ] *int* chut!

shabby ['ʃæbɪ] *a* (**-ier, -iest**) (*town, room etc*) miteux; (*person*) pauvrement vêtu; (*mean*) *Fig* mesquin. ◆**shabbily** *adv* (*dressed*) pauvrement. ◆**shabbiness** *n* aspect *m* miteux; mesquinerie *f*.

shack [ʃæk] **1** *n* cabane *f*. **2** *vi* **to s. up with** *Pej Fam* se coller avec.

shackles ['ʃæk(ə)lz] *npl* chaînes *fpl*.

shade [ʃeɪd] *n* ombre *f*; (*of colour*) ton *m*, nuance *f*; (*of opinion, meaning*) nuance *f*; (*of lamp*) abat-jour *m inv*; (*blind*) store *m*; **in the s.** à l'ombre; **a s. faster/taller/***etc* (*slightly*) un rien plus vite/plus grand/*etc*; – *vt* (*of tree*) ombrager; (*protect*) abriter (**from** de); **to s. in** (*drawing*) ombrer. ◆**shady** *a* (**-ier, -iest**) (*place*) ombragé; (*person etc*) *Fig* louche.

shadow ['ʃædəʊ] **1** *n* ombre *f*. **2** *a* (*cabinet*) *Pol* fantôme. **3** *vt* **to s. s.o.** (*follow*) filer qn. ◆**shadowy** *a* (**-ier, -iest**) (*form etc*) obscur, vague.

shaft [ʃɑːft] *n* **1** (*of tool*) manche *m*; (*in machine*) arbre *m*; **s. of light** trait *m* de lumière. **2** (*of mine*) puits *m*; (*of lift*) cage *f*.

shaggy ['ʃægɪ] *a* (**-ier, -iest**) (*hair, beard*) broussailleux; (*dog etc*) à longs poils.

shake [ʃeɪk] *vt* (*pt* **shook**, *pp* **shaken**) (*move up and down*) secouer; (*bottle*) agiter; (*belief, resolution etc*) *Fig* ébranler; (*upset*) bouleverser, secouer; **to s. the windows** (*of shock*) ébranler les vitres; **to s. one's head** (*say no*) secouer la tête; **to s. hands with** serrer la main à; **we shook hands** nous nous sommes serré la main; **to s. off** (*dust etc*) secouer; (*cough, infection, pursuer*) *Fig* se débarrasser de; **to s. s.o. up** (*disturb, rouse*) secouer qn; **to s. sth out of sth** (*remove*) secouer qch de qch; **s. yourself out of it!** secoue-toi!; – *vi* trembler (**with** de); – *n* secousse *f*; **to give sth a s.** secouer qch; **with a s. of his** *or* **her head** en secouant la tête; **in two shakes** (*soon*) *Fam* dans une minute. ◆**s.-up** *n Fig* réorganisation *f*.

shaky ['ʃeɪkɪ] *a* (**-ier, -iest**) (*trembling*) tremblant; (*ladder etc*) branlant; (*memory, health*) chancelant; (*on one's legs, in a language*) mal assuré.

shall [ʃæl, *unstressed* ʃəl] *v aux* **1** (*future*) **I s. come, I'll come** je viendrai; **we s. not come, we shan't come** nous ne viendrons pas. **2** (*question*) **s. I leave?** veux-tu que je parte?; **s. we leave?** on part? **3** (*order*) **he s. do it if I order it** il devra le faire si je l'ordonne.

shallot [ʃə'lɒt] *n* (*onion*) échalote *f*.

shallow ['ʃæləʊ] *a* (**-er, -est**) peu profond; *Fig Pej* superficiel; – *npl* (*of river*) bas-fond *m*. ◆**—ness** *n* manque *m* de profondeur; *Fig Pej* caractère *m* superficiel.

sham [ʃæm] *n* (*pretence*) comédie *f*, feinte *f*; (*person*) imposteur *m*; (*jewels*) imitation *f*; – *a* (*false*) faux; (*illness, emotion*) feint; – *vt* (**-mm-**) feindre.

shambles ['ʃæmb(ə)lz] *n* désordre *m*, pagaïe *f*; **to be a s.** être en pagaïe; **to make a s. of** gâcher.

shame [ʃeɪm] *n* (*feeling, disgrace*) honte *f*; **it's a s.** c'est dommage (**to do** de faire); **it's a s. (that)** c'est dommage que (+ *sub*); **what a s.!** (quel) dommage!; **to put to s.** faire honte à; – *vt* (*disgrace, make ashamed*) faire honte à. ◆**shamefaced** *a* honteux; (*bashful*) timide. ◆**shameful** *a* honteux. ◆**shamefully** *adv* honteusement. ◆**shameless** *a* (*brazen*) effronté; (*indecent*) impudique.

shammy ['ʃæmɪ] *n* **s. (leather)** *Fam* peau *f* de chamois.

shampoo [ʃæm'puː] *n* shampooing *m*; – *vt* (*carpet*) shampooiner; **to s. s.o.'s hair** faire un shampooing à qn.

shandy ['ʃændɪ] *n* (*beer*) panaché *m*.

shan't [ʃɑːnt] = **shall not**.

shanty[1] ['ʃæntɪ] *n* (*hut*) baraque *f*. ◆**shantytown** *n* bidonville *f*.

shanty[2] ['ʃæntɪ] *n* **sea s.** chanson *f* de marins.

shap/e [ʃeɪp] *n* forme *f*; **in (good) s.** (*fit*) en forme; **to be in good/bad s.** (*of vehicle,* *house etc*) être en bon/mauvais état; (*of business*) marcher bien/mal; **to take s.** prendre forme; **in the s. of a pear** en forme de poire; – *vt* (*fashion*) façonner (**into** en); (*one's life*) *Fig* déterminer; – *vi* **to s. up** (*of plans*) prendre (bonne) tournure, s'annoncer bien; (*of pupil, wrongdoer*) s'y mettre, s'appliquer; (*of patient*) faire des progrès. ◆**–ed** *suffix* **pear-s./***etc* en forme de poire/*etc.* ◆**shapeless** *a* informe. ◆**shapely** *a* (**-ier, -iest**) (*woman, legs*) bien tourné.

share [ʃeər] *n* part *f* (**of, in** de); (*in company*) *Fin* action *f*; **one's (fair) s. of** sa part de; **to do one's (fair) s.** fournir sa part d'efforts; **stocks and shares** *Fin* valeurs *fpl* (boursières); – *vt* (*meal, joy, opinion etc*) partager (**with** avec); (*characteristic*) avoir en commun; **to s. out** (*distribute*) partager; – *vi* **to s. (in)** partager. ◆**shareholder** *n Fin* actionnaire *mf*.

shark [ʃɑːk] *n* (*fish*) & *Fig* requin *m*.

sharp [ʃɑːp] **1** *a* (**-er, -est**) (*knife, blade etc*) tranchant; (*pointed*) pointu; (*point, voice*) aigu; (*pace, mind*) vif; (*pain*) aigu, vif; (*change, bend*) brusque; (*taste*) piquant; (*words, wind, tone*) âpre; (*eyesight, cry*) perçant; (*distinct*) net; (*lawyer etc*) *Pej* peu scrupuleux; **s. practice** *Pej* procédé(s) *m(pl)* malhonnête(s); – *adv* (*to stop*) net; **five o'clock/***etc* **s.** cinq heures/*etc* pile; **s. right/left** tout de suite à droite/à gauche. **2** *n Mus* dièse *m*. ◆**sharpen** *vt* (*knife*) aiguiser; (*pencil*) tailler. ◆**sharpener** *n* (*for pencils*) taille-crayon(s) *m inv*; (*for blades*) aiguisoir *m*. ◆**sharply** *adv* (*suddenly*) brusquement; (*harshly*) vivement; (*clearly*) nettement. ◆**sharpness** *n* (*of blade*) tranchant *m*; (*of picture*) netteté *f*. ◆**sharpshooter** *n* tireur *m* d'élite.

shatter [ˈʃætər] *vt* (*smash*) fracasser; (*glass*) faire voler en éclats; (*career, health*) briser; (*person, hopes*) anéantir; – *vi* (*smash*) se fracasser; (*of glass*) voler en éclats. ◆**–ed** *a* (*exhausted*) anéanti. ◆**–ing** *a* (*defeat*) accablant; (*news, experience*) bouleversant.

shav/e [ʃeɪv] *vt* (*person, head*) raser; **to s. off one's beard/***etc* se raser la barbe/*etc*; – *vi* se raser; – *n* **to have a s.** se raser, se faire la barbe; **to have a close s.** *Fig Fam* l'échapper belle. ◆**–ing** *n* rasage *m*; (*strip of wood*) copeau *m*; **s. brush** blaireau *m*; **s. cream, s. foam** crème *f* à raser. ◆**shaven** *a* rasé (de près). ◆**shaver** *n* rasoir *m* électrique.

shawl [ʃɔːl] *n* châle *m*.

she [ʃiː] *pron* elle; **s. wants** elle veut; **she's a happy woman** c'est une femme heureuse; **if I were s.** si j'étais elle; – *n* femelle *f*; **s.-bear** ourse *f*.

sheaf [ʃiːf] *n* (*pl* **sheaves**) (*of corn*) gerbe *f*.

shear [ʃɪər] *vt* tondre; – *npl* cisaille(s) *f(pl)*; **pruning shears** sécateur *m*. ◆**–ing** *n* tonte *f*.

sheath [ʃiːθ] *n* (*pl* **-s** [ʃiːðz]) (*container*) gaine *f*, fourreau *m*; (*contraceptive*) préservatif *m*.

shed [ʃed] **1** *n* (*in garden etc*) remise *f*; (*for goods or machines*) hangar *m*. **2** *vt* (*pt & pp* **shed**, *pres p* **shedding**) (*lose*) perdre; (*tears, warmth etc*) répandre; (*get rid of*) se défaire de; (*clothes*) enlever; **to s. light on** *Fig* éclairer.

sheen [ʃiːn] *n* lustre *m*.

sheep [ʃiːp] *n inv* mouton *m*. ◆**sheepdog** *n* chien *m* de berger. ◆**sheepskin** *n* peau *f* de mouton.

sheepish [ˈʃiːpɪʃ] *a* penaud. ◆**–ly** *adv* d'un air penaud.

sheer [ʃɪər] **1** *a* (*luck, madness etc*) pur; (*impossibility etc*) absolu; **it's s. hard work** ça demande du travail; **by s. determination/hard work** à force de détermination/de travail. **2** *a* (*cliff*) à pic; – *adv* (*to rise*) à pic. **3** *a* (*fabric*) très fin.

sheet [ʃiːt] *n* (*on bed*) drap *m*; (*of paper, wood etc*) feuille *f*; (*of glass, ice*) plaque *f*; (*dust cover*) housse *f*; (*canvas*) bâche *f*; **s. metal** tôle *f*.

sheikh [ʃeɪk] *n* scheik *m*, cheik *m*.

shelf [ʃelf] *n* (*pl* **shelves**) rayon *m*, étagère *f*; (*in shop*) rayon *m*; (*on cliff*) saillie *f*; **to be (left) on the s.** (*not married*) *Fam* être toujours célibataire.

shell [ʃel] **1** *n* coquille *f*; (*of tortoise*) carapace *f*; (*seashell*) coquillage *m*; (*of peas*) cosse *f*; (*of building*) carcasse *f*; – *vt* (*peas*) écosser; (*nut, shrimp*) décortiquer. **2** *n* (*explosive*) *Mil* obus *m*; – *vt* (*town etc*) *Mil* bombarder. ◆**–ing** *n Mil* bombardement *m*. ◆**shellfish** *n inv Culin* (*oysters etc*) fruits *mpl* de mer.

shelter [ˈʃeltər] *n* (*place, protection*) abri *m*; **to take s.** se mettre à l'abri (**from** de); **to seek s.** chercher un abri; – *vt* abriter (**from** de); (*criminal*) protéger; – *vi* s'abriter. ◆**–ed** *a* (*place*) abrité; (*life*) très protégé.

shelve [ʃelv] *vt* (*postpone*) laisser en suspens.

shelving [ˈʃelvɪŋ] *n* (*shelves*) rayonnage(s) *m(pl)*; **s. unit** (*set of shelves*) étagère *f*.

shepherd [ˈʃepəd] **1** *n* berger *m*; **s.'s pie** hachis *m* Parmentier. **2** *vt* **to s. in** faire entrer: **to s. s.o. around** piloter qn. ◆**shepherdess** *n* bergère *f*.

sherbet ['ʃɜːbət] *n* (*powder*) poudre *f* acidulée: (*water ice*) *Am* sorbet *m*.

sheriff ['ʃerɪf] *n Am* shérif *m*.

sherry ['ʃerɪ] *n* xérès *m*, sherry *m*.

shh! [ʃ] *int* chut!

shield [ʃiːld] *n* bouclier *m*; (*on coat of arms*) écu *m*; (*screen*) *Tech* écran *m*; – *vt* protéger (**from** de).

shift [ʃɪft] *n* (*change*) changement *m* (**of, in** de); (*period of work*) poste *m*; (*workers*) équipe *f*; **gear s.** *Aut Am* levier *m* de vitesse; **s. work** travail *m* en équipe; – *vt* (*move*) déplacer, bouger; (*limb*) bouger; (*employee*) muter (**to** à); (*scenery*) *Th* changer; (*blame*) rejeter (**on to** sur); **to s. places** changer de place; **to s. gear(s)** *Aut Am* changer de vitesse; – *vi* bouger; (*of heavy object*) se déplacer; (*of views*) changer; (*pass*) passer (**to** à); (*go*) aller (**to** à); **to s. to** (*new town*) déménager à; **to s. along** avancer; **to s. over** *or* **up** se pousser. ◆**—ing** *a* (*views*) changeant.

shiftless ['ʃɪftləs] *a* velléitaire, paresseux.

shifty ['ʃɪftɪ] *a* (**-ier, -iest**) (*sly*) sournois; (*dubious*) louche.

shilling ['ʃɪlɪŋ] *n* shilling *m*.

shilly-shally ['ʃɪlɪʃælɪ] *vi* hésiter, tergiverser.

shimmer ['ʃɪmər] *vi* chatoyer, miroiter; – *n* chatoiement *m*, miroitement *m*.

shin [ʃɪn] *n* tibia *m*; **s. pad** *n Sp* jambière *f*.

shindig ['ʃɪndɪg] *n Fam* réunion *f* bruyante.

shin/e [ʃaɪn] *vi* (*pt & pp* **shone** [ʃɒn, *Am* ʃəʊn]) briller; **to s. with** (*happiness etc*) rayonner de; – *vt* (*polish*) faire briller; **to s. a light** *or* **a torch** éclairer (**on sth** qch); – *n* éclat *m*; (*on shoes, cloth*) brillant *m*. ◆**—ing** *a* (*bright, polished*) brillant; **a shining example of** un bel exemple de. ◆**shiny** *a* (**-ier, -iest**) (*bright, polished*) brillant; (*clothes, through wear*) lustré.

shingle ['ʃɪŋg(ə)l] *n* (*on beach*) galets *mpl*; (*on roof*) bardeau *m*.

shingles ['ʃɪŋg(ə)lz] *n Med* zona *m*.

ship [ʃɪp] *n* navire *m*, bateau *m*; **by s.** en bateau; **s. owner** armateur *m*; – *vt* (**-pp-**) (*send*) expédier; (*transport*) transporter; (*load up*) embarquer (**on to** sur). ◆**shipping** *n* (*traffic*) navigation *f*; (*ships*) navires *mpl*; – *a* (*agent*) maritime; **s. line** compagnie *f* de navigation. ◆**shipbuilding** *n* construction *f* navale. ◆**shipmate** *n* camarade *m* de bord. ◆**shipment** *n* (*goods*) chargement *m*, cargaison *f*. ◆**shipshape** *a & adv* en ordre. ◆**shipwreck** *n* naufrage *m*. ◆**shipwrecked** *a* naufragé; **to be s.** faire naufrage. ◆**shipyard** *n* chantier *m* naval.

shirk [ʃɜːk] *vt* (*duty*) se dérober à; (*work*) éviter de faire; – *vi* tirer au flanc. ◆**—er** *n* tire-au-flanc *m inv*.

shirt [ʃɜːt] *n* chemise *f*; (*of woman*) chemisier *m*. ◆**shirtfront** *n* plastron *m*. ◆**shirtsleeves** *npl* **in (one's) s.** en bras de chemise.

shiver ['ʃɪvər] *vi* frissonner (**with** de); – *n* frisson *m*.

shoal [ʃəʊl] *n* (*of fish*) banc *m*.

shock [ʃɒk] *n* (*moral blow*) choc *m*; (*impact*) & *Med* choc *m*; (*of explosion*) secousse *f*; **(electric) s.** décharge *f* (électrique) (**from sth** en touchant qch); **a feeling of s.** un sentiment d'horreur; **suffering from s., in a state of s.** en état de choc; **to come as a s. to s.o.** stupéfier qn; – *a* (*tactics, wave*) de choc; (*effect, image etc*) -choc *inv*; **s. absorber** amortisseur *m*; – *vt* (*offend*) choquer; (*surprise*) stupéfier; (*disgust*) dégoûter. ◆**—ing** *a* affreux; (*outrageous*) scandaleux; (*indecent*) choquant. ◆**—ingly** *adv* affreusement. ◆**—er** *n* **to be a s.** *Fam* être affreux *or* horrible. ◆**shockproof** *a* résistant au choc.

shoddy ['ʃɒdɪ] *a* (**-ier, -iest**) (*goods etc*) de mauvaise qualité. ◆**shoddily** *adv* (*made, done*) mal.

shoe [ʃuː] *n* chaussure *f*, soulier *m*; (*for horse*) fer *m*; *Aut* sabot *m* (de frein); **in your shoes** *Fig* à ta place; **s. polish** cirage *m*; – *vt* (*pt & pp* **shod**) (*horse*) ferrer. ◆**shoehorn** *n* chausse-pied *m*. ◆**shoelace** *n* lacet *m*. ◆**shoemaker** *n* fabricant *m* de chaussures; (*cobbler*) cordonnier *m*. ◆**shoestring** *n* **on a s.** *Fig* avec peu d'argent (en poche).

shone [ʃɒn, *Am* ʃəʊn] *see* **shine**.

shoo [ʃuː] *vt* **to s. (away)** chasser; – *int* ouste!

shook [ʃʊk] *see* **shake**.

shoot[1] [ʃuːt] *vt* (*pt & pp* **shot**) (*kill*) tuer (d'un coup de feu), abattre; (*wound*) blesser (d'un coup de feu); (*execute*) fusiller; (*hunt*) chasser; (*gun*) tirer un coup de; (*bullet*) tirer; (*missile, glance, questions*) lancer (**at** à); (*film*) tourner; (*person*) *Phot* prendre; **to s. down** (*aircraft*) abattre; – *vi* (*with gun, bow etc*) tirer (**at** sur); **to s. ahead/off** avancer/partir à toute vitesse; **to s. up** (*grow*) pousser vite; (*rise, spurt*) jaillir; (*of price*) monter en flèche. ◆**—ing** *n* (*gunfire, execution*) fusillade *f*; (*shots*) coups *mpl* de feu; (*murder*) meurtre *m*; (*of* *film*) tournage *m*; (*hunting*) chasse *f*. ◆**shoot-out** *n Fam* fusillade *f*.

shoot² [ʃuːt] *n* (*on plant*) pousse *f*.

shop [ʃɒp] **1** *n* magasin *m*; (*small*) boutique *f*; (*workshop*) atelier *m*; **at the baker's s.** à la boulangerie, chez le boulanger; **s. assistant** vendeur, -euse *mf*; **s. floor** (*workers*) ouvriers *mpl*; **s. steward** délégué, -ée *mf* syndical(e); **s. window** vitrine *f*; – *vi* (**-pp-**) faire ses courses (**at** chez); **to s. around** comparer les prix. **2** *vt* (**-pp-**) **to s. s.o.** *Fam* dénoncer qn (*à la police etc*). ◆**shopping** *n* (*goods*) achats *mpl*; **to go s.** faire des courses; **to do one's s.** faire ses courses; – *a* (*street, district*) commerçant; (*bag*) à provisions; **s. centre** centre *m* commercial. ◆**shopper** *n* (*buyer*) acheteur, -euse *mf*; (*customer*) client, -ente *mf*; (*bag*) sac *m* à provisions.

shopkeeper [ˈʃɒpkiːpər] *n* commerçant, -ante *mf*. ◆**shoplifter** *n* voleur, -euse *mf* à l'étalage. ◆**shoplifting** *n* vol *m* à l'étalage. ◆**shopsoiled** *a*, *Am* ◆**shopworn** *a* abîmé.

shore [ʃɔːr] **1** *n* (*of sea, lake*) rivage *m*; (*coast*) côte *f*, bord *m* de (la) mer; (*beach*) plage *f*; **on s.** (*passenger*) *Nau* à terre. **2** *vt* **to s. up** (*prop up*) étayer.

shorn [ʃɔːn] *a* (*head*) tondu; **s. of** (*stripped of*) *Lit* dénué de.

short [ʃɔːt] *a* (**-er, -est**) court; (*person, distance*) petit; (*syllable*) bref; (*curt, impatient*) brusque; **a s. time** *or* **while ago** il y a peu de temps; **s. cut** raccourci *m*; **to be s. of money/time** être à court d'argent/de temps; **we're s. of ten men** il nous manque dix hommes; **money/time is s.** l'argent/le temps manque; **not far s. of** pas loin de; **s. of** (*except*) sauf; **to be s. for** (*of name*) être l'abréviation *or* le diminutif de; **in s.** bref; **s. circuit** *El* court-circuit *m*; **s. list** liste *f* de candidats choisis; – *adv* **to cut s.** (*visit etc*) abréger; (*person*) couper la parole à; **to go** *or* **get** *or* **run s. of** manquer de; **to get** *or* **run s.** manquer; **to stop s.** s'arrêter net; – *n El* court-circuit *m*; **(a pair of) shorts** un short. ◆**shorten** *vt* (*visit, line, dress etc*) raccourcir. ◆**shortly** *adv* (*soon*) bientôt; **s. after** peu après. ◆**shortness** *n* (*of person*) petitesse *f*; (*of hair, stick, legs*) manque *m* de longueur.

shortage [ˈʃɔːtɪdʒ] *n* manque *m*, pénurie *f*; (*crisis*) crise *f*.

shortbread [ˈʃɔːtbred] *n* sablé *m*. ◆**short-ˈchange** *vt* (*buyer*) ne pas rendre juste à. ◆**short-ˈcircuit** *vt El & Fig* court-circuiter. ◆**shortcoming** *n* défaut *m*. ◆**shortfall** *n* manque *m*. ◆**shorthand** *n* sténo *f*; **s. typist** sténodactylo *f*. ◆**short-ˈhanded** *a* à court de personnel. ◆**short-ˈlived** *a* éphémère. ◆**shortˈsighted** *a* myope; *Fig* imprévoyant. ◆**short-ˈsightedness** *n* myopie *f*; imprévoyance *f*. ◆**short-ˈsleeved** *a* à manches courtes. ◆**short-ˈstaffed** *a* à court de personnel. ◆**short-ˈterm** *a* à court terme.

shortening [ˈʃɔːt(ə)nɪŋ] *n Culin* matière *f* grasse.

shot [ʃɒt] *see* **shoot¹**; – *n* coup *m*; (*bullet*) balle *f*; *Cin Phot* prise *f* de vues; (*injection*) *Med* piqûre *f*; **a good s.** (*person*) un bon tireur; **to have a s. at (doing) sth** essayer de faire qch; **a long s.** (*attempt*) un coup à tenter; **big s.** *Fam* gros bonnet *m*; **like a s.** (*at once*) tout de suite; **to be s. of** (*rid of*) *Fam* être débarrassé de. ◆**shotgun** *n* fusil *m* de chasse.

should [ʃʊd, *unstressed* ʃəd] *v aux* **1** (= *ought to*) **you s. do it** vous devriez le faire; **I s. have stayed** j'aurais dû rester; **that s. be Pauline** ça doit être Pauline. **2** (= *would*) **I s. like to** j'aimerais bien; **it's strange she s. say no** il est étrange qu'elle dise non. **3** (*possibility*) **if he s. come** s'il vient; **s. I be free** si je suis libre.

shoulder [ˈʃəʊldər] **1** *n* épaule *f*; **to have round shoulders** avoir le dos voûté, être voûté; **(hard) s.** (*of motorway*) accotement *m* stabilisé; **s. bag** sac *m* à bandoulière; **s. blade** omoplate *f*; **s.-length hair** cheveux *mpl* mi-longs. **2** *vt* (*responsibility*) endosser, assumer.

shout [ʃaʊt] *n* cri *m*; **to give s.o. a s.** appeler qn; – *vi* **to s. (out)** crier; **to s. to** *or* **at s.o. to do** crier à qn de faire; **to s. at s.o.** (*scold*) crier après qn; – *vt* **to s. (out)** (*insult etc*) crier; **to s. down** (*speaker*) huer. ◆**—ing** *n* (*shouts*) cris *mpl*.

shove [ʃʌv] *n* poussée *f*; **to give a s. (to)** pousser; – *vt* pousser; (*put*) *Fam* fourrer; **to s. sth into** (*thrust*) enfoncer *or* fourrer qch dans; **to s. s.o. around** *Fam* régenter qn; – *vi* pousser; **to s. off** (*leave*) *Fam* ficher le camp, filer; **to s. over** (*move over*) *Fam* se pousser.

shovel [ˈʃʌv(ə)l] *n* pelle *f*; – *vt* (**-ll-**, *Am* **-l-**) (*grain etc*) pelleter; **to s. up** *or* **away** (*remove*) enlever à la pelle; **to s. sth into** (*thrust*) *Fam* fourrer qch dans.

show [ʃəʊ] *n* (*of joy, force*) démonstration *f* (**of** de); (*semblance*) semblant *m* (**of** de); (*ostentation*) parade *f*; (*sight*) & *Th* spectacle *m*; (*performance*) *Cin* séance *f*; (*exhibition*) exposition *f*; **the Boat/Motor S.** le

Salon de la Navigation/de l'Automobile; **horse s.** concours *m* hippique; **to give a good s.** *Sp Mus Th* jouer bien; **good s.!** bravo!; **(just) for s.** pour l'effet; **on s.** (*painting etc*) exposé; **s. business** le monde du spectacle; **s. flat** appartement *m* témoin; – *vt* (*pt* **showed**, *pp* **shown**) montrer (to à, **that** que); (*exhibit*) exposer; (*film*) passer, donner; (*indicate*) indiquer, montrer; **to s. s.o. to the door** reconduire qn; **it (just) goes to s. that...** ça (dé)montre (bien) que...; **I'll s. him** *or* **her!** *Fam* je lui apprendrai!; – *vi* (*be visible*) se voir; (*of film*) passer; **'now showing'** *Cin* 'à l'affiche' (**at** à). ■ **to s. (a)round** *vt* faire visiter; **he** *or* **she was shown (a)round the house** on lui a fait visiter la maison; **to s. in** *vt* faire entrer; **to s. off** *vt Pej* étaler; (*highlight*) faire valoir; – *vi Pej* crâner. ◆**s.-off** *n Pej* crâneur, -euse *mf*; **to s. out** *vt* (*visitor*) reconduire; **to s. up** *vt* (*fault*) faire ressortir; (*humiliate*) faire honte à; – *vi* ressortir (**against** sur); (*of error*) être visible; (*of person*) *Fam* arriver, s'amener. ◆**showing** *n* (*of film*) projection *f* (**of** de); (*performance*) *Cin* séance *f*; (*of team, player*) performance *f*.

showcase ['ʃəʊkeɪs] *n* vitrine *f*. ◆**showdown** *n* confrontation *f*, conflit *m*. ◆**showgirl** *n* (*in chorus etc*) girl *f*. ◆**showjumping** *n Sp* jumping *m*. ◆**showmanship** *n* art *m* de la mise en scène. ◆**showpiece** *n* modèle *m* du genre. ◆**showroom** *n* (*for cars etc*) salle *f* d'exposition.

shower ['ʃaʊər] *n* (*of rain*) averse *f*; (*of blows*) déluge *m*; (*bath*) douche *f*; (*party*) *Am* réception *f* (*pour la remise de cadeaux*); – *vt* **to s. s.o. with** (*gifts, abuse*) couvrir qn de. ◆**showery** *a* pluvieux.

shown [ʃəʊn] *see* **show**.

showy ['ʃəʊɪ] *a* (**-ier, -iest**) (*colour, hat*) voyant; (*person*) prétentieux.

shrank [ʃræŋk] *see* **shrink 1**.

shrapnel ['ʃræpn(ə)l] *n* éclats *mpl* d'obus.

shred [ʃred] *n* lambeau *m*; (*of truth*) *Fig* grain *m*; **not a s. of evidence** pas la moindre preuve; – *vt* (**-dd-**) mettre en lambeaux; (*cabbage, carrots*) râper. ◆**shredder** *n Culin* râpe *f*.

shrew [ʃruː] *n* (*woman*) *Pej* mégère *f*.

shrewd [ʃruːd] *a* (**-er, -est**) (*person, plan*) astucieux. ◆**—ly** *adv* astucieusement. ◆**—ness** *n* astuce *f*.

shriek [ʃriːk] *n* cri *m* (aigu); – *vti* crier; **to s. with pain/laughter** hurler de douleur/de rire.

shrift [ʃrɪft] *n* **to get short s.** être traité sans ménagement.

shrill [ʃrɪl] *a* (**-er, -est**) aigu, strident.

shrimp [ʃrɪmp] *n* crevette *f*; (*person*) *Pej* nabot, -ote *mf*; (*child*) *Pej* puce *f*.

shrine [ʃraɪn] *n* lieu *m* saint; (*tomb*) châsse *f*.

shrink [ʃrɪŋk] **1** *vi* (*pt* **shrank**, *pp* **shrunk** *or* **shrunken**) (*of clothes*) rétrécir; (*of aging person*) se tasser; (*of amount, audience etc*) diminuer; **to s. from** reculer devant (**doing** l'idée de faire); – *vt* rétrécir. **2** *n* (*person*) *Am Hum* psy(chiatre) *m*. ◆**—age** *n* rétrécissement *m*; diminution *f*.

shrivel ['ʃrɪv(ə)l] *vi* (**-ll-**, *Am* **-l-**) **to s. (up)** se ratatiner; – *vt* **to s. (up)** ratatiner.

shroud [ʃraʊd] *n* linceul *m*; (*of mystery*) *Fig* voile *m*; – *vt* **shrouded in mist** enseveli *or* enveloppé sous la brume; **shrouded in mystery** enveloppé de mystère.

Shrove Tuesday [ʃrəʊv'tjuːzdɪ] *n* Mardi *m* gras.

shrub [ʃrʌb] *n* arbrisseau *m*.

shrug [ʃrʌg] *vt* (**-gg-**) **to s. one's shoulders** hausser les épaules; **to s. off** (*dismiss*) écarter (dédaigneusement); – *n* haussement *m* d'épaules.

shrunk(en) ['ʃrʌŋk(ən)] *see* **shrink 1**.

shudder ['ʃʌdər] *vi* frémir (**with** de); (*of machine etc*) vibrer; – *n* frémissement *m*; vibration *f*.

shuffle ['ʃʌf(ə)l] **1** *vti* **to s. (one's feet)** traîner les pieds. **2** *vt* (*cards*) battre.

shun [ʃʌn] *vt* (**-nn-**) fuir, éviter; **to s. doing** éviter de faire.

shunt [ʃʌnt] *vt* (*train, conversation*) aiguiller (**on to** sur); **we were shunted (to and fro)** *Fam* on nous a baladés (**from office to office/***etc* de bureau en bureau/*etc*).

shush! [ʃʊʃ] *int* chut!

shut [ʃʌt] *vt* (*pt* & *pp* **shut**, *pp* **shutting**) fermer; **to s. one's finger in** (*door etc*) se prendre le doigt dans; **to s. away** *or* **in** (*lock away or in*) enfermer; **to s. down** fermer; **to s. off** fermer; (*engine*) arrêter; (*isolate*) isoler; **to s. out** (*light*) empêcher d'entrer; (*view*) boucher; (*exclude*) exclure (**of, from** de); **to s. s.o. out** (*lock out accidentally*) enfermer qn dehors; **to s. up** fermer; (*lock up*) enfermer (*personne, objet précieux etc*); (*silence*) *Fam* faire taire; – *vi* (*of door etc*) se fermer; (*of shop, museum etc*) fermer; **the door doesn't s.** la porte ne ferme pas; **to s. down** fermer (définitivement); **to s. up** (*be quiet*) *Fam* se taire. ◆**shutdown** *n* fermeture *f*.

shutter ['ʃʌtər] *n* volet *m*; (*of camera*) obturateur *m*.

shuttle ['ʃʌt(ə)l] *n* (*bus, spacecraft etc*) navette *f*; **s. service** navette; – *vi* faire la navette; – *vt* (*in vehicle etc*) transporter. ◆**shuttlecock** *n* (*in badminton*) volant *m*.

shy [ʃaɪ] *a* (**-er, -est**) timide; **to be s. of doing** avoir peur de faire; – *vi* **to s. away** reculer (**from s.o.** devant qn, **from doing** à l'idée de faire). ◆**—ness** *n* timidité *f*.

Siamese [saɪə'miːz] *a* siamois; **S. twins** frères *mpl* siamois, sœurs *fpl* siamoises.

sibling ['sɪblɪŋ] *n* frère *m*, sœur *f*.

Sicily ['sɪsɪlɪ] *n* Sicile *f*.

sick [sɪk] *a* (**-er, -est**) (*ill*) malade; (*mind*) malsain; (*humour*) noir; (*cruel*) sadique; **to be s.** (*vomit*) vomir; **to be off** *or* **away s., be on s. leave** être en congé de maladie; **to feel s.** avoir mal au cœur; **to be s. (and tired) of** *Fam* en avoir marre de; **he makes me s.** *Fam* il m'écœure; – *n* **the s.** les malades *mpl*; – *vi* (*vomit*) *Fam* vomir; – *vt* **to s. sth up** *Fam* vomir qch. ◆**sickbay** *n* infirmerie *f*. ◆**sickbed** *n* lit *m* de malade. ◆**sickly** *a* (**-ier, -iest**) maladif; (*pale, faint*) pâle; (*taste*) écœurant. ◆**sickness** *n* maladie *f*; (*vomiting*) vomissement(s) *m*(*pl*); **motion s.** *Aut* mal *m* de la route.

sicken ['sɪkən] **1** *vt* écœurer. **2** *vi* **to be sickening for** (*illness*) couver. ◆**—ing** *a* écœurant.

side [saɪd] *n* côté *m*; (*of hill, animal*) flanc *m*; (*of road, river*) bord *m*; (*of beef*) quartier *m*; (*of question*) aspect *m*; (*of character*) facette *f*, aspect *m*; *Sp* équipe *f*; *Pol* parti *m*; **the right s.** (*of fabric*) l'endroit *m*; **the wrong s.** (*of fabric*) l'envers *m*; **by the s. of** (*nearby*) à côté de; **at** *or* **by my s.** à côté de moi, à mes côtés; **s. by s.** l'un à côté de l'autre; **to move to one s.** s'écarter; **on this s.** de ce côté; **on the other s.** de l'autre côté; **the other s.** *TV Fam* l'autre chaîne *f*; **on the big/***etc* **s.** *Fam* plutôt grand/*etc*; **to take sides with** se ranger du côté de; **on our s.** de notre côté, avec nous; **on the s.** *Fam* (*secretly*) en catimini; (*to make money*) en plus; – *a* (*lateral*) latéral; (*effect, issue*) secondaire; (*glance, view*) de côté; (*street*) transversal; – *vi* **to s. with** se ranger du côté de. ◆**-sided** *suffix* **ten-s.** à dix côtés. ◆**sideboard 1** *n* buffet *m*. **2** *npl* (*hair*) pattes *fpl*. ◆**sideburns** *npl* (*hair*) *Am* pattes *fpl*. ◆**sidecar** *n* side-car *m*. ◆**sidekick** *n Fam* associé, -ée *mf*. ◆**sidelight** *n Aut* feu *m* de position. ◆**sideline** *n* activité *f* secondaire. ◆**sidesaddle** *adv* (*to ride*) en amazone. ◆**sidestep** *vt* (**-pp-**) éviter. ◆**sidetrack** *vt* **to get sidetracked** s'écarter du sujet. ◆**sidewalk** *n Am* trottoir *m*. ◆**sideways** *adv* & *a* de côté.

siding ['saɪdɪŋ] *n Rail* voie *f* de garage.

sidle ['saɪd(ə)l] *vi* **to s. up to s.o.** s'approcher furtivement de qn.

siege [siːdʒ] *n Mil* siège *m*.

siesta [sɪ'estə] *n* sieste *f*.

sieve [sɪv] *n* tamis *m*; (*for liquids*) *Culin* passoire *f*; – *vt* tamiser. ◆**sift** *vt* tamiser; **to s. out** (*truth*) *Fig* dégager; – *vi* **to s. through** (*papers etc*) examiner (à la loupe).

sigh [saɪ] *n* soupir *m*; – *vti* soupirer.

sight [saɪt] *n* vue *f*; (*spectacle*) spectacle *m*; (*on gun*) mire *f*; **to lose s. of** perdre de vue; **to catch s. of** apercevoir; **to come into s.** apparaître; **at first s.** à première vue; **by s.** de vue; **on** *or* **at s.** à vue; **in s.** (*target, end, date etc*) en vue; **keep out of s.!** ne te montre pas!; **he hates the s. of me** il ne peut pas me voir; **it's a lovely s.** c'est beau à voir; **the (tourist) sights** les attractions *fpl* touristiques; **to set one's sights on** (*job etc*) viser; **a s. longer/***etc Fam* bien plus long/*etc*; – *vt* (*land*) apercevoir. ◆**—ed** *a* qui voit, clairvoyant. ◆**—ing** *n* **to make a s. of** voir. ◆**sightseer** *n* touriste *mf*. ◆**sightseeing** *n* tourisme *m*.

sightly ['saɪtlɪ] *a* **not very s.** laid.

sign [saɪn] **1** *n* signe *m*; (*notice*) panneau *m*; (*over shop, inn*) enseigne *f*; **no s. of** aucune trace de; **to use s. language** parler par signes. **2** *vt* (*put signature to*) signer; **to s. away** *or* **over** céder (**to** à); **to s. on** *or* **up** (*worker, soldier*) engager; – *vi* signer; **to s. for** (*letter*) signer le reçu de; **to s. in** signer le registre; **to s. off** dire au revoir; **to s. on** (*on the dole*) s'inscrire au chômage; **to s. on** *or* **up** (*of soldier, worker*) s'engager; (*for course*) s'inscrire. ◆**signpost** *n* poteau *m* indicateur; – *vt* flécher.

signal ['sɪgnəl] *n* signal *m*; **traffic signals** feux *mpl* de circulation; **s. box,** *Am* **s. tower** *Rail* poste *m* d'aiguillage; – *vt* (**-ll-**, *Am* **-l-**) (*message*) communiquer (**to** à); (*arrival etc*) signaler (**to** à); – *vi* faire des signaux; **to s. (to) s.o. to do** faire signe à qn de faire. ◆**signalman** *n* (*pl* **-men**) *Rail* aiguilleur *m*.

signature ['sɪgnətʃər] *n* signature *f*; **s. tune** indicatif *m* (musical). ◆**signatory** *n* signataire *mf*.

signet ring ['sɪgnɪtrɪŋ] *n* chevalière *f*.

significant [sɪg'nɪfɪkənt] *a* (*meaningful*) significatif; (*important, large*) important. ◆**significance** *n* (*meaning*) signification *f*; (*importance*) importance *f*. ◆**significantly** *adv* (*appreciably*) sensiblement; **s.,**

he . . . fait significatif. il . . . ◆**'signify** *vt* (*mean*) signifier (**that** que); (*make known*) indiquer, signifier (**to** à).
silence ['saɪləns] *n* silence *m*; **in s.** en silence; – *vt* faire taire. ◆**silencer** *n* (*on car, gun*) silencieux *m*. ◆**silent** *a* silencieux; (*film, anger*) muet; **to keep** *or* **be s.** garder le silence (**about** sur). ◆**silently** *adv* silencieusement.
silhouette [sɪluːˈet] *n* silhouette *f*. ◆**silhouetted** *a* **to be s. against** se profiler contre.
silicon ['sɪlɪkən] *n* silicium *m*; **s. chip** puce *f* de silicium. ◆**silicone** ['sɪlɪkəʊn] *n* silicone *f*.
silk [sɪlk] *n* soie *f*. ◆**silky** *a* (**-ier, -iest**) soyeux.
sill [sɪl] *n* (*of window etc*) rebord *m*.
silly ['sɪlɪ] *a* (**-ier, -iest**) idiot, bête; **to do sth s.** faire une bêtise; **s. fool,** *Fam* **s. billy** idiot, -ote *mf*; – *adv* (*to act, behave*) bêtement.
silo ['saɪləʊ] *n* (*pl* **-os**) silo *m*.
silt [sɪlt] *n* vase *f*.
silver ['sɪlvər] *n* argent *m*; (*silverware*) argenterie *f*; **£5 in s.** 5 livres en pièces d'argent; – *a* (*spoon etc*) en argent, d'argent; (*hair, colour*) argenté; **s. jubilee** vingt-cinquième anniversaire *m* (*d'un événement*); **s. paper** papier *m* d'argent; **s. plate** argenterie *f*. ◆**s.-'plated** *a* plaqué argent. ◆**silversmith** *n* orfèvre *m*. ◆**silverware** *n* argenterie *f*. ◆**silvery** *a* (*colour*) argenté.
similar ['sɪmɪlər] *a* semblable (**to** à). ◆**simi'larity** *n* ressemblance *f* (**between** entre, **to** avec). ◆**similarly** *adv* de la même façon; (*likewise*) de même.
simile ['sɪmɪlɪ] *n Liter* comparaison *f*
simmer ['sɪmər] *vi Culin* mijoter, cuire à feu doux; (*of water*) frémir; (*of revolt, hatred etc*) couver; **to s. with** (*rage*) bouillir de; **to s. down** (*calm down*) *Fam* se calmer; – *vt* faire cuire à feu doux; (*water*) laisser frémir.
simper ['sɪmpər] *vi* minauder.
simple ['sɪmp(ə)l] *a* (**-er, -est**) (*plain, uncomplicated, basic etc*) simple. ◆**s.-'minded** *a* simple d'esprit. ◆**s.-'mindedness** *n* simplicité *f* d'esprit. ◆**simpleton** *n* nigaud, -aude *mf*. ◆**sim'plicity** *n* simplicité *f*. ◆**simplifi'cation** *n* simplification *f*. ◆**simplify** *vt* simplifier. ◆**sim'plistic** *a* simpliste. ◆**simply** *adv* (*plainly, merely*) simplement; (*absolutely*) absolument.
simulate ['sɪmjʊleɪt] *vt* simuler.
simultaneous [sɪməl'teɪnɪəs, *Am* saɪməl'teɪnɪəs] *a* simultané. ◆**—ly** *adv* simultanément.
sin [sɪn] *n* péché *m*; – *vi* (**-nn-**) pécher.
since [sɪns] **1** *prep* (*in time*) depuis; **s. my departure** depuis mon départ; – *conj* depuis que; **s. she's been here** depuis qu'elle est ici; **it's a year s. I saw him** ça fait un an que je ne l'ai pas vu; – *adv* (**ever**) **s.** depuis. **2** *conj* (*because*) puisque.
sincere [sɪn'sɪər] *a* sincère. ◆**sincerely** *adv* sincèrement; **yours s.** (*in letter*) *Com* veuillez croire à mes sentiments dévoués. ◆**sin'cerity** *n* sincérité *f*.
sinew ['sɪnjuː] *n Anat* tendon *m*.
sinful ['sɪnfəl] *a* (*guilt-provoking*) coupable; (*shocking*) scandaleux; **he's s.** c'est un pécheur; **that's s.** c'est un péché.
sing [sɪŋ] *vti* (*pt* **sang,** *pp* **sung**) chanter; **to s. up** chanter plus fort. ◆**—ing** *n* (*of bird & musical technique*) chant *m*; (*way of singing*) façon *f* de chanter; – *a* (*lesson, teacher*) de chant. ◆**—er** *n* chanteur, -euse *mf*.
singe [sɪndʒ] *vt* (*cloth*) roussir; (*hair*) brûler; **to s. s.o.'s hair** (*at hairdresser's*) faire un brûlage à qn.
single [sɪŋg(ə)l] *a* (*only one*) seul; (*room, bed*) pour une personne; (*unmarried*) célibataire; **s. ticket** billet *m* simple; **every s. day** tous les jours sans exception; **s. party** *Pol* parti *m* unique; – *n* (*ticket*) aller *m* (simple); (*record*) 45 tours *m inv*; *pl Tennis* simples *mpl*; **singles bar** bar *m* pour célibataires; – *vt* **to s. out** (*choose*) choisir. ◆**s.-'breasted** *a* (*jacket*) droit. ◆**s.-'decker** *n* (*bus*) autobus *m* sans impériale. ◆**s.-'handed** *a* sans aide. ◆**s.-'minded** *a* (*person*) résolu, qui n'a qu'une idée en tête. ◆**singly** *adv* (*one by on*) un à un.
singlet ['sɪŋglɪt] *n* (*garment*) maillot *m* de corps.
singsong ['sɪŋsɒŋ] *n* **to get together for a s.** se réunir pour chanter.
singular ['sɪŋgjʊlər] **1** *a* (*unusual*) singulier **2** *a Gram* (*form*) singulier; (*noun*) au singulier; – *n Gram* singulier *m*; **in the s.** au singulier.
sinister ['sɪnɪstər] *a* sinistre.
sink[1] [sɪŋk] *n* (*in kitchen*) évier *m*; (*washbasin*) lavabo *m*.
sink[2] [sɪŋk] *vi* (*pt* **sank,** *pp* **sunk**) (*of ship, person etc*) couler; (*of sun, price, water level*) baisser; (*collapse, subside*) s'affaisser; **to s.** (**down**) **into** (*mud etc*) s'enfoncer dans; (*armchair etc*) s'affaler dans; **to s. in** (*of ink etc*) pénétrer; (*of fact etc*) *Fam* rentrer

(dans le crâne); **has that sunk in?** *Fam* as-tu compris ça?; – *vt* (*ship*) couler; (*well*) creuser; **to s. into** (*thrust*) enfoncer dans; (*money*) *Com* investir dans; **a sinking feeling** un serrement de cœur.

sinner ['sɪnər] *n* pècheur *m*, pécheresse *f*.

sinuous ['sɪnjʊəs] *a* sinueux.

sinus [saɪnəs] *n Anat* sinus *m inv*.

sip [sɪp] *vi* (**-pp-**) boire à petites gorgées; – *n* (*mouthful*) petite gorgée *f*; (*drop*) goutte *f*.

siphon ['saɪfən] *n* siphon *m*; – *vt* **to s. off** (*petrol*) siphonner; (*money*) *Fig* détourner.

sir [sɜːr] *n* monsieur *m*; **S. Walter Raleigh** (*title*) sir Walter Raleigh.

siren ['saɪərən] *n* (*of factory etc*) sirène *f*.

sirloin ['sɜːlɔɪn] *n* (*steak*) faux-filet *m*; (*joint*) aloyau *m*.

sissy ['sɪsɪ] *n* (*boy, man*) *Fam* femmelette *f*.

sister ['sɪstər] *n* sœur *f*; (*nurse*) infirmière *f* en chef. ◆**s.-in-law** *n* (*pl* **sisters-in-law**) belle-sœur *f*. ◆**sisterly** *a* fraternel.

sit [sɪt] *vi* (*pp* & *pp* **sat**, *pres p* **sitting**) s'asseoir; (*for artist*) poser (**for** pour); (*remain*) rester; (*of assembly etc*) siéger, être en séance; **to be sitting** (*of person, cat etc*) être assis; (*of bird*) être perché; **she sat** *or* **was sitting reading** elle était assise à lire; **to s. around** (*do nothing*) ne rien faire; **to s. back** (*in chair*) se caler; (*rest*) se reposer; (*do nothing*) ne rien faire; **to s. down** s'asseoir; **s.-down strike** grève *f* sur le tas; **to s. in on** (*lecture etc*) assister à; **to s. on** (*jury etc*) être membre de; (*fact etc*) *Fam* garder pour soi; **to s. through** *or* **out** (*film etc*) rester jusqu'au bout de; **to s. up (straight)** s'asseoir (bien droit); **to s. up waiting for s.o.** (*at night*) ne pas se coucher en attendant qn; – *vt* **to s. s.o. (down)** asseoir qn; **to s. (for)** (*exam*) se présenter à; **to s. out** (*event, dance*) ne pas prendre part à. ◆**sitting** *n* séance *f*; (*for one's portrait*) séance *f* de pose; (*in restaurant*) service *m*; – *a* (*committee etc*) en séance; **s. duck** *Fam* victime *f* facile; **s. tenant** locataire *mf* en possession des lieux. ◆**sitting room** *n* salon *m*.

site [saɪt] *n* emplacement *m*; (*archaeological*) site *m*; (**building**) **s.** chantier *m*; **launching s.** aire *f* de lancement; – *vt* (*building*) placer.

sit-in ['sɪtɪn] *n Pol* sit-in *m inv*.

sitter ['sɪtər] *n* (*for child*) baby-sitter *mf*.

situate ['sɪtʃʊeɪt] *vt* situer; **to be situated** être situé. ◆**situ'ation** *n* situation *f*.

six [sɪks] *a* & *n* six (*m*). ◆**six'teen** *a* & *n* seize (*m*). ◆**six'teenth** *a* & *n* seizième (*mf*). ◆**sixth** *a* & *n* sixième (*mf*); (**lower**) **s. form** *Sch* = classe *f* de première; (**upper**) **s. form** *Sch* = classe *f* terminale; **a s.** (*fraction*) un sixième. ◆**sixtieth** *a* & *n* soixantième (*mf*). ◆**sixty** *a* & *n* soixante (*m*).

size [saɪz] **1** *n* (*of person, animal, garment etc*) taille *f*; (*measurements*) dimensions *fpl*; (*of egg, packet*) grosseur *f*; (*of book*) grandeur *f*, format *m*; (*of problem, town, damage*) importance *f*, étendue *f*; (*of sum*) montant *m*, importance *f*; (*of shoes, gloves*) pointure *f*; (*of shirt*) encolure *f*; **hip/chest s.** tour *m* de hanches/de poitrine; **it's the s. of** . . . c'est grand comme . . . . **2** *n* (*glue*) colle *f*. **3** *vt* **to s. up** (*person*) jauger; (*situation*) évaluer. ◆**sizeable** *a* assez grand *or* gros.

sizzl/e ['sɪz(ə)l] *vi* grésiller. ◆**—ing** *a* **s. (hot)** brûlant.

skat/e[1] [skeɪt] *n* patin *m*; – *vi* patiner. ◆**—ing** *n* patinage *m*; **to go s.** faire du patinage; **s. rink** (*ice*) patinoire *f*; (*roller*) skating *m*. ◆**skateboard** *n* skateboard *m*. ◆**skater** *n* patineur, -euse *mf*.

skate[2] [skeɪt] *n* (*fish*) raie *f*.

skedaddle [skɪ'dæd(ə)l] *vi Fam* déguerpir.

skein [skeɪn] *n* (*of yarn*) écheveau *m*.

skeleton ['skelɪt(ə)n] *n* squelette *m*; – *a* (*crew, staff*) (réduit au) minimum; **s. key** passe-partout *m inv*.

skeptic ['skeptɪk] *Am* = **sceptic**.

sketch [sketʃ] *n* (*drawing*) croquis *m*, esquisse *f*; *Th* sketch *m*; **a rough s. of** (*plan*) *Fig* une esquisse de; – *vt* **to s. (out)** (*view, idea etc*) esquisser; **to s. in** (*details*) ajouter; – *vi* faire un *or* des croquis. ◆**sketchy** *a* (**-ier, -iest**) incomplet, superficiel.

skew [skjuː] *n* **on the s.** de travers.

skewer ['skjʊər] *n* (*for meat etc*) broche *f*; (*for kebab*) brochette *f*.

ski [skiː] *n* (*pl* **skis**) ski *m*; **s. lift** télésiège *m*; **s. pants** fuseau *m*; **s. run** piste *f* de ski; **s. tow** téléski *m*; – *vi* (*pt* **skied** [skiːd], *pres p* **skiing**) faire du ski. ◆**—ing** *n Sp* ski *m*; – *a* (*school, clothes*) de ski. ◆**—er** *n* skieur, -euse *mf*.

skid [skɪd] **1** *vi* (**-dd-**) *Aut* déraper; **to s. into** déraper et heurter; – *n* dérapage *m*. **2** *a* **s. row** *Am* quartier *m* de clochards *or* de squats.

skill [skɪl] *n* habileté *f*, adresse *f* (**at** à); (*technique*) technique *f*; **one's skills** (*aptitudes*) ses compétences *fpl*. ◆**skilful** *a*, *Am* ◆**skillful** *a* habile (**at doing** à faire, **at sth** à qch). ◆**skilled** *a* habile (**at doing** à faire, **at sth** à qch); (*worker*) qualifié; (*work*) de spécialiste, de professionnel.

skillet ['skɪlɪt] *n Am* poêle *f* (à frire).

skim [skɪm] **1** *vt* (**-mm-**) (*milk*) écrémer;

(*soup*) écumer. **2** *vti* (**-mm-**) **to s. (over)** (*surface*) effleurer; **to s. through** (*book*) parcourir.

skimp [skɪmp] *vi* (*on fabric, food etc*) lésiner (on sur). ◆**skimpy** *a* (**-ier, -iest**) (*clothes*) étriqué; (*meal*) insuffisant.

skin [skɪn] *n* peau *f*; **he has thick s.** *Fig* c'est un dur; **s. diving** plongée *f* sous-marine; **s. test** cuti(-réaction) *f*; – *vt* (**-nn-**) (*animal*) écorcher; (*fruit*) peler. ◆**s.-'deep** *a* superficiel. ◆**s.-'tight** *a* moulant, collant.

skinflint ['skɪnflɪnt] *n* avare *mf*.

skinhead ['skɪnhed] *n* skinhead *m*, jeune voyou *m*.

skinny ['skɪnɪ] *a* (**-ier, -iest**) maigre.

skint [skɪnt] *a* (*penniless*) *Fam* fauché.

skip¹ [skɪp] **1** *vi* (**-pp-**) (*jump*) sauter; (*hop about*) sautiller; (*with rope*) sauter à la corde; **to s. off** (*leave*) *Fam* filer; **skipping rope** corde *f* à sauter; – *n* petit saut *m*. **2** *vt* (**-pp-**) (*omit, miss*) sauter; **to s. classes** sécher les cours; **s. it!** (*forget it*) *Fam* laisse tomber!

skip² [skɪp] *n* (*container for debris*) benne *f*.

skipper ['skɪpər] *n Nau Sp* capitaine *m*.

skirmish ['skɜːmɪʃ] *n* accrochage *m*.

skirt [skɜːt] **1** *n* jupe *f*. **2** *vt* **to s. round** contourner; **skirting board** (*on wall*) plinthe *f*.

skit [skɪt] *n Th* pièce *f* satirique; **a s. on** une parodie de.

skittle ['skɪt(ə)l] *n* quille *f*; *pl* (*game*) jeu *m* de quilles.

skiv/e [skaɪv] *vi* (*skirk*) *Fam* tirer au flanc; **to s. off** (*slip away*) *Fam* se défiler. ◆**—er** *n Fam* tire-au-flanc *m inv*.

skivvy ['skɪvɪ] *n Pej Fam* bonne *f* à tout faire, bon(n)iche *f*.

skulk [skʌlk] *vi* rôder (furtivement).

skull [skʌl] *n* crâne *m*. ◆**skullcap** *n* calotte *f*.

skunk [skʌŋk] *n* (*animal*) mouffette *f*; (*person*) *Pej* salaud *m*.

sky [skaɪ] *n* ciel *m*. ◆**skydiving** *n* parachutisme *m* (en chute libre). ◆**sky-'high** *a* (*prices*) exorbitant. ◆**skylight** *n* lucarne *f*. ◆**skyline** *n* (*outline of buildings*) ligne *f* d'horizon. ◆**skyrocket** *vi* (*of prices*) *Fam* monter en flèche. ◆**skyscraper** *n* gratte-ciel *m inv*.

slab [slæb] *n* (*of concrete etc*) bloc *m*; (*thin, flat*) plaque *f*; (*of chocolate*) tablette *f*, plaque *f*; (*paving stone*) dalle *f*.

slack [slæk] *a* (**-er, -est**) (*knot, spring*) lâche; (*discipline, security*) relâché, lâche; (*trade, grip*) faible, mou; (*negligent*) négligent; (*worker, student*) peu sérieux; **s. periods** (*weeks etc*) périodes *fpl* creuses; (*hours*) heures *fpl* creuses; **to be s.** (*of rope*) avoir du mou; – *vi* **to s. off** (*in effort*) se relâcher. ◆**slacken** *vi* **to s. (off)** (*in effort*) se relâcher; (*of production, speed, zeal*) diminuer; – *vt* **to s. (off)** (*rope*) relâcher; (*pace, effort*) ralentir. ◆**slacker** *n* (*person*) *Fam* flemmard, -arde *mf*. ◆**slackly** *adv* (*loosely*) lâchement. ◆**slackness** *n* négligence *f*; (*of discipline*) relâchement *m*; (*of rope*) mou *m*; *Com* stagnation *f*.

slacks [slæks] *npl* pantalon *m*.

slag [slæg] *n* (*immoral woman*) *Sl* salope *f*, traînée *f*.

slagheap ['slæghiːp] *n* terril *m*.

slake [sleɪk] *vt* (*thirst*) *Lit* étancher.

slalom ['slɑːləm] *n Sp* slalom *m*.

slam [slæm] **1** *vt* (**-mm-**) (*door, lid*) claquer; (*hit*) frapper violemment; **to s. (down)** (*put down*) poser violemment; **to s. on the brakes** écraser le frein, freiner à bloc; – *vi* (*of door*) claquer; – *n* claquement *m*. **2** *vt* (**-mm-**) (*criticize*) *Fam* critiquer (avec virulence).

slander ['slɑːndər] *n* diffamation *f*, calomnie *f*; – *vt* diffamer, calomnier.

slang [slæŋ] *n* argot *m*; – *a* (*word etc*) d'argot, argotique. ◆**slanging match** *n Fam* engueulade *f*.

slant [slɑːnt] *n* inclinaison *f*; (*point of view*) *Fig* angle *m* (**on** sur); (*bias*) *Fig* parti-pris *m*; **on a s.** penché; (*roof*) en pente; – *vi* (*of writing*) pencher; (*of roof*) être en pente; – *vt* (*writing*) faire pencher; (*news*) *Fig* présenter de façon partiale. ◆**—ed** *a*, ◆**—ing** *a* penché; (*roof*) en pente.

slap [slæp] **1** *n* tape *f*, claque *f*; (*on face*) gifle *f*; – *vt* (**-pp-**) donner une tape à; **to s. s.o.'s face** gifler qn; **to s. s.o.'s bottom** donner une fessée à qn. **2** *vt* (**-pp-**) (*put*) mettre, flanquer; **to s. on** (*apply*) appliquer à la va-vite; (*add*) ajouter. **3** *adv* **s. in the middle** *Fam* en plein milieu. ◆**slapdash** *a* (*person*) négligent; (*task*) fait à la va-vite; – *adv* à la va-vite. ◆**slaphappy** *a Fam* (*carefree*) insouciant; (*negligent*) négligent. ◆**slapstick** *a* & *n* **s. (comedy)** grosse farce *f*. ◆**slap-up 'meal** *n Fam* gueuleton *m*.

slash [slæʃ] **1** *vt* (*cut with blade etc*) entailler, taillader; (*sever*) trancher; – *n* entaille *f*, taillade *f*. **2** *vt* (*reduce*) réduire radicalement; (*prices*) *Com* écraser.

slat [slæt] *n* (*in blind*) lamelle *f*.

slate [sleɪt] **1** *n* ardoise *f*. **2** *vt* (*book etc*) *Fam* critiquer, démolir.

slaughter ['slɔːtər] *vt* (*people*) massacrer;

(*animal*) abattre; – *n* massacre *m*; abattage *m*. ◆**slaughterhouse** *n* abattoir *m*.

Slav [slɑːv] *a* & *n* slave (*mf*). ◆**Sla'vonic** *a* (*language*) slave.

slave [sleɪv] *n* esclave *mf*; **the s. trade** *Hist* la traite des noirs; **s. driver** *Fig Pej* négrier *m*; – *vi* **to s. (away)** se crever (au travail), bosser comme une bête; **to s. away doing** s'escrimer à faire. ◆**slavery** *n* esclavage *m*. ◆**slavish** *a* servile.

slaver ['slævər] *vi* (*dribble*) baver (**over** sur); – *n* bave *f*.

slay [sleɪ] *vt* (*pt* **slew**, *pp* **slain**) *Lit* tuer.

sleazy ['sliːzɪ] *a* (**-ier, -iest**) *Fam* sordide, immonde.

sledge [sledʒ] (*Am* **sled** [sled]) *n* luge *f*; (*horse-drawn*) traîneau *m*.

sledgehammer ['sledʒhæmər] *n* masse *f*.

sleek [sliːk] *a* (**-er, -est**) lisse, brillant; (*manner*) onctueux.

sleep [sliːp] *n* sommeil *m*; **to have a s., get some s.** dormir; **to send to s.** endormir; **to go** *or* **get to s.** s'endormir; **to go to s.** (*of arm, foot*) *Fam* s'engourdir; – *vi* (*pt* & *pp* **slept**) dormir; (*spend the night*) coucher; **s. tight** *or* **well!** dors bien!; **I'll s. on it** *Fig* je déciderai demain, la nuit portera conseil; – *vt* **this room sleeps six** on peut coucher *or* loger six personnes dans cette chambre; **to s. it off** *Fam*, **s. off a hangover** cuver son vin. ◆**—ing** *a* (*asleep*) endormi; **s. bag** sac *m* de couchage; **s. car** wagon-lit *m*; **s. pill** somnifère *m*; **s. quarters** chambre(s) *f*(*pl*), dortoir *m*. ◆**sleeper** *n* **1 to be a light/sound s.** avoir le sommeil léger/lourd. **2** *Rail* (*on track*) traverse *f*; (*berth*) couchette *f*; (*train*) train *m* couchettes. ◆**sleepiness** *n* torpeur *f*. ◆**sleepless** *a* (*hours*) sans sommeil; (*night*) d'insomnie. ◆**sleepwalker** *n* somnambule *mf*. ◆**sleepwalking** *n* somnambulisme *m*. ◆**sleepy** *a* (**-ier, -iest**) (*town, voice*) endormi; **to be s.** (*of person*) avoir sommeil.

sleet [sliːt] *n* neige *f* fondue; (*sheet of ice*) *Am* verglas *m*; – *vi* **it's sleeting** il tombe de la neige fondue.

sleeve [sliːv] *n* (*of shirt etc*) manche *f*; (*of record*) pochette *f*; **up one's s.** (*surprise, idea etc*) *Fig* en réserve; **long-/short-sleeved** à manches longues/courtes.

sleigh [sleɪ] *n* traîneau *m*.

sleight [slaɪt] *n* **s. of hand** prestidigitation *f*.

slender ['slendər] *a* (*person*) mince, svelte; (*neck, hand*) fin; (*feeble, small*) *Fig* faible.

slept [slept] *see* **sleep**.

sleuth [sluːθ] *n* (*detective*) *Hum* (fin) limier *m*.

slew [sluː] *n* **a s. of** *Am Fam* un tas de, une tapée de.

slice [slaɪs] *n* tranche *f*; (*portion*) *Fig* partie *f*, part *f*; – *vt* **to s. (up)** couper (en tranches); **to s. off** (*cut off*) couper.

slick [slɪk] **1** *a* (**-er, -est**) (*glib*) qui a la parole facile;. (*manner*) mielleux; (*cunning*) astucieux; (*smooth, slippery*) lisse. **2** *n* **oil s.** nappe *f* de pétrole; (*large*) marée *f* noire.

slid/e [slaɪd] *n* (*act*) glissade *f*; (*in value etc*) *Fig* (légère) baisse *f*; (*in playground*) toboggan *m*; (*on ice*) glissoire *f*; (*for hair*) barrette *f*; *Phot* diapositive *f*; (*of microscope*) lamelle *f*, lame *f*; **s. rule** règle *f* à calcul; – *vi* (*pt* & *pp* **slid**) glisser; **to s. into** (*room etc*) se glisser dans; – *vt* (*letter etc*) glisser (**into** dans); (*table etc*) faire glisser. ◆**—ing** *a* (*door, panel*) à glissière; (*roof*) ouvrant; **s. scale** *Com* échelle *f* mobile

slight [slaɪt] **1** *a* (**-er, -est**) (*slim*) mince; (*frail*) frêle; (*intelligence*) faible; **the slightest thing** la moindre chose; **not in the slightest** pas le moins du monde. **2** *vt* (*offend*) offenser; (*ignore*) bouder; – *n* affront *m* (**on** à). ◆**—ly** *adv* légèrement, un peu; **s. built** fluet.

slim [slɪm] *a* (**slimmer, slimmest**) mince; – *vi* (**-mm-**) maigrir. ◆**slimming** *a* (*diet*) amaigrissant; (*food*) qui ne fait pas grossir. ◆**slimness** *n* minceur *f*.

slime [slaɪm] *n* boue *f* (visqueuse); (*of snail*) bave *f*. ◆**slimy** *a* (**-ier, -iest**) (*muddy*) boueux; (*sticky, smarmy*) visqueux.

sling [slɪŋ] **1** *n* (*weapon*) fronde *f*; (*toy*) lance-pierres *m inv*; (*for arm*) *Med* écharpe *f*; **in a s.** en écharpe. **2** *vt* (*pt* & *pp* **slung**) (*throw*) jeter, lancer; (*hang*) suspendre; **to s. away** *or* **out** (*throw out*) *Fam* balancer. ◆**slingshot** *n Am* lance-pierres *m inv*.

slip [slɪp] **1** *n* (*mistake*) erreur *f*; (*woman's undergarment*) combinaison *f*; (*of paper for filing*) fiche *f*; **a s. of paper** (*bit*) un bout de papier; **a s. (of the tongue)** un lapsus; **to give s.o. the s.** fausser compagnie à qn; **s. road** *Aut* bretelle *f*. **2** *vi* (**-pp-**) glisser; **to s. into** (*go, get*) se glisser dans; (*habit*) prendre; (*garment*) mettre; **to let s.** (*chance, oath, secret*) laisser échapper; **to s. through** (*crowd*) se faufiler parmi; **to s. along** *or* **over to** faire un saut chez; **to s. away** (*escape*) s'esquiver; **to s. back/in** retourner/entrer furtivement; **to s. out** sortir furtivement; (*pop out*) sortir (un instant); (*of secret*) s'éventer; **to s. past** (*guards*) passer sans être vu de; **to s. up** (*make a *mistake*) *Fam* gaffer; – *vt* (*slide*) glisser (to à, into dans); **it slipped his** *or* **her notice** ça lui a échappé; **it slipped his** *or* **her mind** ça lui est sorti de l'esprit; **to s. off** (*garment etc*) enlever; **to s. on** (*garment etc*) mettre. ◆**s.-up** *n Fam* gaffe *f*, erreur *f*.

slipcover ['slɪpkʌvər] *n Am* housse *f*.

slipper ['slɪpər] *n* pantoufle *f*.

slippery ['slɪpərɪ] *a* glissant.

slipshod ['slɪpʃɒd] *a* (*negligent*) négligent; (*slovenly*) négligé.

slit [slɪt] *n* (*opening*) fente *f*; (*cut*) coupure *f*; – *vt* (*pt & pp* **slit**, *pres p* **slitting**) (*cut*) couper; (*tear*) déchirer; **to s. open** (*sack*) éventrer.

slither ['slɪðər] *vi* glisser; (*of snake*) se couler.

sliver ['slɪvər] *n* (*of apple etc*) lichette *f*; (*of wood*) éclat *m*.

slob [slɒb] *n Fam* malotru *m*, goujat *m*.

slobber ['slɒbər] *vi* (*of dog etc*) baver (**over** sur); – *n* bave *f*.

slog [slɒg] **1** *n* **a (hard) s.** (*effort*) un gros effort; (*work*) un travail dur; – *vi* (**-gg-**) **to s. (away)** bosser, trimer. **2** *vt* (**-gg-**) (*hit*) donner un grand coup à.

slogan ['sləʊgən] *n* slogan *m*.

slop [slɒp] *n* **slops** eaux *fpl* sales; – *vi* (**-pp-**) **to s. (over)** (*spill*) se répandre; – *vt* répandre.

slop/e [sləʊp] *n* pente *f*; (*of mountain*) flanc *m*; (*slant*) inclinaison *f*; – *vi* être en pente; (*of handwriting*) pencher; **to s. down** descendre en pente. ◆**—ing** *a* en pente; (*handwriting*) penché.

sloppy ['slɒpɪ] *a* (**-ier, -iest**) (*work, appearance*) négligé; (*person*) négligent; (*mawkish*) sentimental; (*wet*) détrempé; (*watery*) liquide.

slosh [slɒʃ] *vt* (*pour*) *Fam* répandre. ◆**—ed** *a* (*drunk*) *Fam* bourré.

slot [slɒt] *n* (*slit*) fente *f*; (*groove*) rainure *f*; (*in programme*) *Rad TV* créneau *m*; **s. machine** (*vending*) distributeur *m* automatique; (*gambling*) machine *f* à sous; – *vt* (**-tt-**) (*insert*) insérer (**into** dans); – *vi* s'insérer (**into** dans).

sloth [sləʊθ] *n Lit* paresse *f*.

slouch [slaʊtʃ] **1** *vi* ne pas se tenir droit; (*have stoop*) avoir le dos voûté; (*in chair*) se vautrer (**in** dans); **slouching over** (*desk etc*) penché sur; – *n* mauvaise tenue *f*; **with a s.** (*to walk*) en se tenant mal; le dos voûté. **2** *n Fam* (*person*) lourdaud, -aude *mf*; (*lazy*) paresseux, -euse *mf*.

slovenly ['slʌvənlɪ] *a* négligé. ◆**slovenliness** *n* (*of dress*) négligé *m*; (*carelessness*) négligence *f*.

slow [sləʊ] *a* (**-er, -est**) lent; (*business*) calme; (*party, event*) ennuyeux; **at (a) s. speed** à vitesse réduite; **to be a s. walker** marcher lentement; **to be s.** (*of clock, watch*) retarder; **to be five minutes s.** retarder de cinq minutes; **to be s. to act** *or* **in acting** être lent à agir; **in s. motion** au ralenti; – *adv* lentement; – *vt* **to s. down** *or* **up** ralentir; (*delay*) retarder; – *vi* **to s. down** *or* **up** ralentir. ◆**—ly** *adv* lentement; (*bit by bit*) peu à peu. ◆**—ness** *n* lenteur *f*.

slowcoach ['sləʊkəʊtʃ] *n Fam* lambin, -ine *mf*. ◆**slow-down** *n* ralentissement *m*; **s.-down (strike)** *Am* grève *f* perlée. ◆**slow-'moving** *a* (*vehicle etc*) lent. ◆**slowpoke** *n Am Fam* lambin, -ine *mf*.

sludge [slʌdʒ] *n* gadoue *f*.

slue [sluː] *n Am Fam* = **slew**.

slug [slʌg] **1** *n* (*mollusc*) limace *f*. **2** *n* (*bullet*) *Am Sl* pruneau *m*. **3** *vt* (**-gg-**) (*hit*) *Am Fam* frapper; – *n* coup *m*, marron *m*.

sluggish ['slʌgɪʃ] *a* lent, mou.

sluice [sluːs] *n* **s. (gate)** vanne *f*.

slum [slʌm] *n* (*house*) taudis *m*; **the slums** les quartiers *mpl* pauvres; – *a* (*district*) pauvre; – *vt* (**-mm-**) **to s. it** *Fam* manger de la vache enragée. ◆**slummy** *a* (**-ier, -iest**) sordide, pauvre.

slumber ['slʌmbər] *n Lit* sommeil *m*.

slump [slʌmp] *n* baisse *f* soudaine (**in** de); (*in prices*) effrondement *m*; *Econ* crise *f*; – *vi* (*decrease*) baisser; (*of prices*) s'effondrer; **to s. into** (*armchair etc*) s'affaisser dans.

slung [slʌŋ] *see* **sling 2**.

slur [slɜːr] **1** *vt* (**-rr-**) prononcer indistinctement; **to s. one's words** manger ses mots. **2** *n* **to cast a s. on** (*reputation etc*) porter atteinte à. ◆**slurred** *a* (*speech*) indistinct.

slush [slʌʃ] *n* (*snow*) neige *f* fondue; (*mud*) gadoue *f*. ◆**slushy** *a* (**-ier, -iest**) (*road*) couvert de neige fondue.

slut [slʌt] *n Pej* (*immoral*) salope *f*, traînée *f*; (*untidy*) souillon *f*.

sly [slaɪ] *a* (**-er, -est**) (*deceitful*) sournois; (*crafty*) rusé; – *n* **on the s.** en cachette. ◆**—ly** *adv* sournoisement; (*in secret*) en cachette.

smack [smæk] **1** *n* claque *f*; gifle *f*; fessée *f*; – *vt* donner une claque à; **to s. s.o.'s face** gifler qn; **to s. s.o.('s bottom)** donner une fessée à qn. **2** *adv* **s. in the middle** *Fam* en plein milieu. **3** *vi* **to s. of** (*be suggestive of*) avoir des relents de. ◆**—ing** *n* fessée *f*.

small [smɔːl] *a* (**-er, -est**) petit; **in the s. hours** au petit matin; **s. talk** menus propos *mpl*; – *adv* (*to cut, chop*) menu; – *n* **the s. of the back** le creux *m* des reins. ◆**—ness** *n* petitesse *f*. ◆**smallholding** *n* petite ferme *f*. ◆**small-scale** *a Fig* peu important. ◆**small-time** *a* (*crook, dealer etc*) petit, sans grande envergure.

smallpox ['smɔːlpɒks] *n* petite vérole *f*.

smarmy ['smɑːmɪ] *a* (**-ier, -iest**) *Pej Fam* visqueux, obséquieux.

smart[1] ['smɑːt] *a* (**-er, -est**) (*in appearance*) élégant; (*astute*) astucieux; (*clever*) intelligent; (*quick*) rapide; **s. aleck** *Fam* je-sais-tout *mf inv*. ◆**smarten** *vt* **to s. up** (*room etc*) embellir; – *vti* **to s. (oneself) up** (*make oneself spruce*) se faire beau, s'arranger. ◆**smartly** *adv* élégamment; (*quickly*) en vitesse; (*astutely*) astucieusement. ◆**smartness** *n* élégance *f*.

smart[2] [smɑːt] *vi* (*sting*) brûler, faire mal.

smash [smæʃ] *vt* (*break*) briser; (*shatter*) fracasser; (*enemy*) écraser; (*record*) pulvériser; **to s. s.o.'s face (in)** *Fam* casser la gueule à qn; **to s. down** *or* **in** (*door*) fracasser; **to s. up** (*car*) esquinter; (*room*) démolir; – *vi* se briser; **to s. into** (*of car*) se fracasser contre; – *n* (*noise*) fracas *m*; (*blow*) coup *m*; (*accident*) collision *f*; **s. hit** *Fam* succès *m* fou. ◆**s.-up** *n* collision *f*.

smashing ['smæʃɪŋ] *a* (*wonderful*) *Fam* formidable. ◆**smasher** *n* **to be a (real) s.** *Fam* être formidable.

smattering ['smætərɪŋ] *n* **a s. of** (*French etc*) quelques notions *fpl* de.

smear [smɪər] *vt* (*coat*) enduire (**with** de); (*stain*) tacher (**with** de); (*smudge*) faire une trace sur; – *n* (*mark*) trace *f*; (*stain*) tache *f*; *Med* frottis *m*; **a s. on** (*attack*) *Fig* une atteinte à; **s. campaign** campagne *f* de diffamation.

smell [smel] *n* odeur *f*; (**sense of**) **s.** odorat *m*; – *vt* (*pt & pp* **smelled** *or* **smelt**) sentir; (*of animal*) flairer; – *vi* (*stink*) sentir (mauvais); (*have smell*) avoir une odeur; **to s. of smoke/***etc* sentir la fumée/*etc*; **smelling salts** sels *mpl*. ◆**smelly** *a* (**-ier, -iest**) **to be s.** sentir (mauvais).

smelt[1] [smelt] *see* **smell**.

smelt[2] [smelt] *vt* (*ore*) fondre; **smelting works** fonderie *f*.

smidgen ['smɪdʒən] *n* **a s.** (*a little*) *Am Fam* un brin (**of** de).

smil/e [smaɪl] *n* sourire *m*; – *vi* sourire (**at s.o.** à qn, **at sth** de qch). ◆**—ing** *a* souriant.

smirk [smɜːk] *n* (*smug*) sourire *m* suffisant; (*scornful*) sourire *m* goguenard.

smith [smɪθ] *n* (*blacksmith*) forgeron *m*.

smithereens [smɪðə'riːnz] *npl* **to smash to s.** briser en mille morceaux.

smitten ['smɪt(ə)n] *a* **s. with** *Hum* (*desire, remorse*) pris de: (*in love with*) épris de.

smock [smɒk] *n* blouse *f*.

smog [smɒg] *n* brouillard *m* épais, smog *m*.

smoke [sməʊk] *n* fumée *f*; **to have a s.** fumer une cigarette *etc*; – *vt* (*cigarette, salmon etc*) fumer; **to s. out** (*room etc*) enfumer; – *vi* fumer; **'no smoking'** 'défense de fumer'; **smoking compartment** *Rail* compartiment *m* fumeurs. ◆**smokeless** *a* **s. fuel** combustible *m* non polluant. ◆**smoker** *n* fumeur, -euse *mf*; *Rail* compartiment *m* fumeurs. ◆**smoky** *a* (**-ier, -iest**) (*air*) enfumé; (*wall*) noirci de fumée; **it's s. here** il y a de la fumée ici.

smooth [smuːð] *a* (**-er, -est**) (*surface, skin etc*) lisse; (*road*) à la surface égale; (*movement*) régulier, sans à-coups; (*flight*) agréable; (*cream, manners*) onctueux; (*person*) doucereux; (*sea*) calme; **the s. running** la bonne marche (**of** de); – *vt* **to s. down** *or* **out** lisser; **to s. out** *or* **over** (*problems etc*) *Fig* aplanir. ◆**—ly** *adv* (*to land, pass off*) en douceur. ◆**—ness** *n* aspect *m* lisse; (*of road*) surface *f* égale.

smother ['smʌðər] *vt* (*stifle*) étouffer; **to s. with** (*kisses etc*) *Fig* couvrir de.

smoulder ['sməʊldər] *vi* (*of fire, passion etc*) couver.

smudge [smʌdʒ] *n* tache *f*, bavure *f*; – *vt* (*paper etc*) faire des taches sur, salir.

smug [smʌg] *a* (**smugger, smuggest**) (*smile etc*) béat; (*person*) content de soi, suffisant. ◆**—ly** *adv* avec suffisance.

smuggl/e ['smʌg(ə)l] *vt* passer (en fraude); **smuggled goods** contrebande *f*. ◆**—ing** *n* contrebande *f*. ◆**—er** *n* contrebandier, -ière *mf*.

smut [smʌt] *n inv* (*obscenity*) saleté(s) *f(pl)*. ◆**smutty** *a* (**-ier, -iest**) (*joke etc*) cochon.

snack [snæk] *n* casse-croûte *m inv*; **s. bar** snack(-bar) *m*.

snafu [snæ'fuː] *n Sl* embrouillamini *m*.

snag [snæg] *n* **1** (*hitch*) inconvénient *m*, os *m*. **2** (*in cloth*) accroc *m*.

snail [sneɪl] *n* escargot *m*; **at a s.'s pace** comme une tortue.

snake [sneɪk] *n* (*reptile*) serpent *m*; – *vi* (*of river*) serpenter.

snap [snæp] **1** *vt* (**-pp-**) casser (avec un bruit sec); (*fingers, whip*) faire claquer; **to s. up a bargain** sauter sur une occasion; – *vi* se casser net; (*of whip*) claquer; (*of person*) *Fig* parler sèchement (**at** à); **s. out of it!** *Fam* secoue-toi!; – *n* claquement *m*, bruit *m* sec; *Phot* photo *f*; (*fastener*) *Am* bouton-pression *m*; **cold s.** *Met* coup *m* de froid. **2** *a* soudain, brusque; **to make a s. decision** décider sans réfléchir. ◆**snapshot** *n* photo *f*, instantané *m*.

snappy ['snæpɪ] *a* (**-ier, -iest**) (*pace*) vif; **make it s.!** *Fam* dépêche-toi!

snare [sneər] *n* piège *m*.

snarl [snɑːl] *vi* gronder (en montrant les dents); – *n* grondement *m*. ◆**s.-up** *n Aut Fam* embouteillage *m*.

snatch [snætʃ] *vt* saisir (*d'un geste vif*); (*some rest etc*) *Fig* (réussir à) prendre; **to s. sth from s.o.** arracher qch à qn; – *n* (*theft*) vol *m* (à l'arraché).

snatches ['snætʃɪz] *npl* (*bits*) fragments *mpl* (of de).

snazzy ['snæzɪ] *a* (**-ier, -iest**) *Fam* (*flashy*) tapageur; (*smart*) élégant.

sneak [sniːk] **1** *vi* **to s. in/out** entrer/sortir furtivement; **to s. off** s'esquiver; – *a* (*attack, visit*) furtif. **2** *n* (*telltale*) *Sch Fam* rapporteur, -euse *mf*; – *vi* **to s. on** *Sch Fam* dénoncer. ◆**sneaking** *a* (*suspicion*) vague; (*desire*) secret. ◆**sneaky** *a* (**-ier, -iest**) (*sly*) *Fam* sournois.

sneaker ['sniːkər] *n* (*shoe*) tennis *f*.

sneer [snɪər] *n* ricanement *m*; – *vi* ricaner; **to s. at** se moquer de.

sneeze [sniːz] *n* éternuement *m*; – *vi* éternuer.

snicker ['snɪkər] *n & vi Am* = **snigger**.

snide [snaɪd] *a* (*remark etc*) sarcastique.

sniff [snɪf] *n* reniflement *m*; – *vt* renifler; (*of dog*) flairer, renifler; **to s. out** (*bargain*) *Fig* renifler; – *vi* **to s. (at)** renifler. ◆**sniffle** *vi* renifler; – *n* **a s., the sniffles** *Fam* un petit rhume.

snigger ['snɪgər] *n* (petit) ricanement *m*; – *vi* ricaner. ◆**—ing** *n* ricanement(s) *m*(*pl*).

snip [snɪp] *n* (*piece*) petit bout *m* (coupé); (*bargain*) *Fam* bonne affaire *f*; **to make a s.** couper; – *vt* (**-pp-**) couper.

sniper ['snaɪpər] *n Mil* tireur *m* embusqué.

snippet ['snɪpɪt] *n* (*of conversation etc*) bribe *f*.

snivel ['snɪv(ə)l] *vi* (**-ll-**, *Am* **-l-**) pleurnicher. ◆**snivelling** *a* pleurnicheur.

snob [snɒb] *n* snob *mf*. ◆**snobbery** *n* snobisme *m*. ◆**snobbish** *a* snob *inv*.

snook [snuːk] *n* **to cock a s.** faire un pied de nez (**at** à).

snooker ['snuːkər] *n* snooker *m*, *sorte de jeu de billard*.

snoop [snuːp] *vi* fourrer son nez partout; **to s. on s.o.** (*spy on*) espionner qn.

snooty ['snuːtɪ] *a* (**-ier, -iest**) *Fam* snob *inv*.

snooze [snuːz] *n* petit somme *m*; – *vi* faire un petit somme.

snor/e [snɔːr] *vi* ronfler; – *n* ronflement *m*. ◆**—ing** *n* ronflements *mpl*.

snorkel ['snɔːk(ə)l] *n Sp Nau* tuba *m*.

snort [snɔːt] *vi* (*grunt*) grogner; (*sniff*) renifler; (*of horse*) renâcler; – *n* (*grunt*) grognement *m*.

snot [snɒt] *n Pej Fam* morve *f*. ◆**snotty** *a* (**-ier, -iest**) *Fam* (*nose*) qui coule; (*child*) morveux. ◆**snotty-nosed** *a Fam* morveux.

snout [snaʊt] *n* museau *m*.

snow [snəʊ] *n* neige *f*; – *vi* neiger; – *vt* **to be snowed in** être bloqué par la neige; **to be s. under with** (*work etc*) être submergé de. ◆**snowball** *n* boule *f* de neige; – *vi* (*increase*) faire boule de neige. ◆**snowbound** *a* bloqué par la neige. ◆**snow-capped** *a* (*mountain*) enneigé. ◆**snowdrift** *n* congère *f*. ◆**snowdrop** *n Bot* perce-neige *m or f inv*. ◆**snowfall** *n* chute *f* de neige. ◆**snowflake** *n* flocon *m* de neige. ◆**snowman** *n* (*pl* **-men**) bonhomme *m* de neige. ◆**snowmobile** *n* motoneige *f*. ◆**snowplough** *n*, *Am* ◆**snowplow** *n* chasse-neige *m inv*. ◆**snowstorm** *n* tempête *f* de neige. ◆**snowy** *a* (**-ier, -iest**) (*weather, hills, day etc*) neigeux.

snub [snʌb] **1** *n* rebuffade *f*; – *vt* (**-bb-**) (*offer etc*) rejeter; **to s. s.o.** snober qn. **2** *a* (*nose*) retroussé.

snuff [snʌf] **1** *n* tabac *m* à priser. **2** *vt* **to s. (out)** (*candle*) moucher. ◆**snuffbox** *n* tabatière *f*.

snuffle ['snʌf(ə)l] *vi & n* = **sniffle**.

snug [snʌg] *a* (**snugger, snuggest**) (*house etc*) confortable, douillet; (*garment*) bien ajusté; **we're s.** (*in chair etc*) on est bien; **s. in bed** bien au chaud dans son lit.

snuggle ['snʌg(ə)l] *vi* **to s. up to** se pelotonner contre.

so [səʊ] **1** *adv* (*to such a degree*) si, tellement (**that** que); (*thus*) ainsi, comme ça; **so that** (*purpose*) pour que (+ *sub*); (*result*) si bien que; **so as to do** pour faire; **I think so** je le pense, je pense que oui; **do so!** faites-le!; **if so** si oui; **is that so?** c'est vrai?; **so am I, so do I** *etc* moi aussi; **so much** (*to work etc*) tant, tellement (**that** que); **so much courage/***etc* tant *or* tellement de courage/*etc* (**that** que); **so many** tant, tellement; **so many books/***etc* tant *or* tellement de livres/*etc* (**that** que); **so very fast/***etc* vraiment si vite/*etc*; **ten or so** environ dix; **so long!** *Fam* au revoir!; **and so on** et ainsi de suite. **2** *conj* (*therefore*) donc; (*in that case*) alors; **so what?** et alors? ◆**So-and-so** *n* **Mr So-and-so** Monsieur Un tel. ◆**so-'called** *a* soi-disant *inv*. ◆**so-so** *a Fam* comme ci comme ça.

soak [səʊk] *vt* (*drench*) tremper; (*washing, food*) faire tremper; **to s. up** absorber; – *vi* (*of washing etc*) tremper; **to s. in** (*of liquid*) s'infiltrer; – *n* **to give sth a s.** faire tremper qch. ◆**—ed** *a* **s. (through)** trempé (jusqu'aux os). ◆**—ing** *a & adv* **s. (wet)** trempé; – *n* trempage *m*.

soap [səʊp] *n* savon *m*; **s. opera** téléroman *m*; **s. powder** lessive *f*; – *vt* savonner. ◆**soapflakes** *npl* savon *m* en paillettes. ◆**soapsuds** *npl* mousse *f* de savon. ◆**soapy** *a* (**-ier, -iest**) *a* savonneux.

soar [sɔːr] *vi* (*of bird etc*) s'élever; (*of price*) monter (en flèche); (*of hope*) *Fig* grandir.

sob [sɒb] *n* sanglot *m*; – *vi* (**-bb-**) sangloter. ◆**sobbing** *n* (*sobs*) sanglots *mpl*.

sober ['səʊbər] **1** *a* **he's s.** (*not drunk*) il n'est pas ivre; – *vti* **to s. up** dessoûler. **2** *a* (*serious*) sérieux, sensé; (*meal, style*) sobre. ◆**—ly** *adv* sobrement.

soccer ['sɒkər] *n* football *m*.

sociable ['səʊʃəb(ə)l] *a* (*person*) sociable; (*evening*) amical. ◆**sociably** *adv* (*to act, reply*) aimablement.

social ['səʊʃəl] *a* social; (*life, gathering*) mondain; **s. club** foyer *m*; **s. science(s)** sciences *fpl* humaines; **s. security** (*aid*) aide *f* sociale; (*retirement pension*) *Am* pension *f* de retraite; **s. services** = sécurité *f* sociale; **s. worker** assistant *m* social; – *n* (*gathering*) réunion *f* (amicale). ◆**socialism** *n* socialisme *m*. ◆**socialist** *a & n* socialiste (*mf*). ◆**socialite** *n* mondain, -aine *mf*. ◆**socialize** *vi* (*mix*) se mêler aux autres; (*talk*) bavarder (**with** avec). ◆**socially** *adv* socialement; (*to meet s.o., behave*) en société.

society [sə'saɪətɪ] *n* (*community, club, companionship etc*) société *f*; *Univ Sch* club *m*; – *a* (*wedding etc*) mondain.

sociology [səʊsɪ'ɒlədʒɪ] *n* sociologie *f*. ◆**socio'logical** *a* sociologique. ◆**soci'ologist** *n* sociologue *mf*.

sock [sɒk] **1** *n* chaussette *f*. **2** *vt* (*hit*) *Sl* flanquer un marron à.

socket ['sɒkɪt] *n* (*of bone*) cavité *f*; (*of eye*) orbite *f*; (*power point*) *El* prise *f* de courant; (*of lamp*) douille *f*.

sod [sɒd] *n* (*turf*) *Am* gazon *m*.

soda ['səʊdə] *n* **1** *Ch* soude *f*; **washing s.** cristaux *mpl* de soude. **2** (*water*) eau *f* de Seltz; **s. (pop)** *Am* soda *m*.

sodden ['sɒd(ə)n] *a* (*ground*) détrempé.

sodium ['səʊdɪəm] *n Ch* sodium *m*.

sofa ['səʊfə] *n* canapé *m*, divan *m*; **s. bed** canapé-lit *m*.

soft [sɒft] *a* (**-er, -est**) (*smooth, gentle, supple*) doux; (*butter, ground, snow*) mou; (*wood, heart, paste, colour*) tendre; (*flabby*) flasque, mou; (*easy*) facile; (*indulgent*) indulgent; (*cowardly*) *Fam* poltron; (*stupid*) *Fam* ramolli; **it's too s.** (*radio etc*) ce n'est pas assez fort; **s. drink** boisson *f* non alcoolisée. ◆**s.-'boiled** *a* (*egg*) à la coque. ◆**soften** ['sɒf(ə)n] *vt* (*object*) ramollir; (*voice, pain, colour*) adoucir; – *vi* se ramollir; s'adoucir. ◆**softie** *n Fam* sentimental, -ale *mf*; (*weakling*) mauviette *f*. ◆**softly** *adv* doucement. ◆**softness** *n* douceur *f*; (*of butter, ground, snow*) mollesse *f*.

software ['sɒftweər] *n inv* (*of computer*) logiciel *m*.

soggy ['sɒgɪ] *a* (**-ier, -iest**) (*ground*) détrempé; (*biscuit, bread*) ramolli.

soil [sɔɪl] **1** *n* (*earth*) sol *m*, terre *f*. **2** *vt* (*dirty*) salir; – *vi* se salir.

solar ['səʊlər] *a* solaire.

sold [səʊld] *see* **sell**.

solder ['sɒldər, *Am* 'sɒdər] *vt* souder; – *n* soudure *f*.

soldier ['səʊldʒər] **1** *n* soldat *m*, militaire *m*. **2** *vi* **to s. on** persévérer.

sole [səʊl] **1** *n* (*of shoe*) semelle *f*; (*of foot*) plante *f*; – *vt* ressemeler **2** *a* (*only*) seul, unique; (*rights, representative*) *Com* exclusif. **3** *n* (*fish*) sole *f*. ◆**—ly** *adv* uniquement; **you're s. to blame** tu es seul coupable.

solemn ['sɒləm] *a* (*formal*) solennel; (*serious*) grave. ◆**so'lemnity** *n* solennité *f*; gravité *f*. ◆**solemnly** *adv* (*to promise*) solennellement; (*to say*) gravement.

solicit [sə'lɪsɪt] *vt* (*seek*) solliciter; – *vi* (*of prostitute*) racoler. ◆**solicitor** *n* (*for wills etc*) notaire *m*.

solid ['sɒlɪd] *a* (*car, character, meal etc*) & *Ch* solide; (*wall, line, ball*) plein; (*gold, rock*) massif; (*crowd, mass*) compact; **frozen s.** entièrement gelé; **ten days s.** dix jours d'affilée; – *n Ch* solide *m*; *pl Culin* aliments *mpl* solides. ◆**so'lidify** *vi* se solidifier. ◆**so'lidity** *n* solidité *f*. ◆**solidly** *adv* (*built etc*) solidement; (*to support, vote*) en masse.

solidarity [sɒlɪ'dærətɪ] *n* solidarité *f* (**with** avec).

soliloquy [sə'lɪləkwɪ] *n* monologue *m*.

solitary ['sɒlɪtərɪ] *a* (*lonely, alone*) solitaire;

(*only*) seul; **s. confinement** *Jur* isolement *m* (cellulaire). ◆**solitude** *n* solitude *f*.

solo ['səʊləʊ] *n* (*pl* **-os**) *Mus* solo *m*; – *a* solo *inv*; – *adv Mus* en solo; (*to fly*) en solitaire. ◆**soloist** *n Mus* soliste *mf*.

solstice ['sɒlstɪs] *n* solstice *m*.

soluble ['sɒljʊb(ə)l] *a* (*substance, problem*) soluble.

solution [sə'luːʃ(ə)n] *n* (*to problem etc*) & *Ch* solution *f* (**to** de).

solv/e [sɒlv] *vt* (*problem etc*) résoudre. ◆**—able** *a* soluble.

solvent ['sɒlvənt] **1** *a* (*financially*) solvable. **2** *n Ch* (dis)solvant *m*. ◆**solvency** *n Fin* solvabilité *f*.

sombre ['sɒmbər] *a* sombre, triste.

some [sʌm] *a* **1** (*amount, number*) **s. wine** du vin; **s. glue** de la colle; **s. water** de l'eau; **s. dogs** des chiens; **s. pretty flowers** de jolies fleurs. **2** (*unspecified*) un, une; **s. man (or other)** un homme (quelconque); **s. charm** (*a certain amount of*) un certain charme; **s. other way** quelque autre *or* un autre moyen; **that's s. book!** *Fam* ça, c'est un livre! **3** (*a few*) quelques, certains; (*a little*) un peu de; – *pron* **1** (*number*) quelques-un(e)s, certain(e)s (**of** de, d'entre). **2** (*a certain quantity*) en; **I want s.** j'en veux; **do you have s.?** en as-tu?; **s. of it is over** il en reste un peu *or* une partie; – *adv* (*about*) quelque; **s. ten years** quelque dix ans.

somebody ['sʌmbɒdɪ] *pron* = **someone**. ◆**someday** *adv* un jour. ◆**somehow** *adv* (*in some way*) d'une manière ou d'une autre; (*for some reason*) on ne sait pourquoi. ◆**someone** *pron* quelqu'un; **at s.'s house** chez qn; **s. small/***etc* quelqu'un de petit/*etc*. ◆**someplace** *adv Am* quelque part. ◆**something** *pron* quelque chose; **s. awful/***etc* quelque chose d'affreux/*etc*; **s. of a liar/***etc* un peu menteur/*etc*; – *adv* **she plays s. like . . .** elle joue un peu comme . . . ; **it was s. awful** c'était vraiment affreux. ◆**sometime 1** *adv* un jour; **s. in May/***etc* au cours du mois de mai/*etc*; **s. before his departure** avant son départ. **2** *a* (*former*) ancien. ◆**sometimes** *adv* quelquefois, parfois. ◆**somewhat** *adv* quelque peu, assez. ◆**somewhere** *adv* quelque part; **s. about fifteen** (*approximately*) environ quinze.

somersault ['sʌməsɔːlt] *n* culbute *f*; (*in air*) saut *m* périlleux; – *vi* faire la *or* une culbute.

son [sʌn] *n* fils *m*. ◆**s.-in-law** *n* (*pl* **sons-in-law**) beau-fils *m*, gendre *m*.

sonar ['səʊnɑːr] *n* sonar *m*.

sonata [sə'nɑːtə] *n Mus* sonate *f*.

song [sɒŋ] *n* chanson *f*; (*of bird*) chant *m*. ◆**songbook** *n* recueil *m* de chansons.

sonic ['sɒnɪk] *a* **s. boom** bang *m* (supersonique).

sonnet ['sɒnɪt] *n* (*poem*) sonnet *m*.

soon [suːn] *adv* (**-er, -est**) (*in a short time*) bientôt; (*quickly*) vite; (*early*) tôt; **s. after** peu après; **as s. as she leaves** aussitôt qu'elle partira; **no sooner had he spoken than** à peine avait-il parlé que; **I'd sooner leave** je préférerais partir; **I'd just as s. leave** j'aimerais autant partir; **sooner or later** tôt ou tard.

soot [sʊt] *n* suie *f*. ◆**sooty** *a* (**-ier, -iest**) couvert de suie.

sooth/e [suːð] *vt* (*pain, nerves*) calmer; *Fig* rassurer. ◆**—ing** *a* (*ointment, words*) calmant.

sophisticated [sə'fɪstɪkeɪtɪd] *a* (*person, taste*) raffiné; (*machine, method, beauty*) sophistiqué.

sophomore ['sɒfəmɔːr] *n Am* étudiant, -ante *mf* de seconde année.

soporific [sɒpə'rɪfɪk] *a* (*substance, speech etc*) soporifique.

sopping [sɒpɪŋ] *a* & *adv* **s. (wet)** trempé.

soppy ['sɒpɪ] *a* (**-ier, -iest**) *Fam* (*silly*) idiot, bête; (*sentimental*) sentimental.

soprano [sə'prɑːnəʊ] *n* (*pl* **-os**) *Mus* (*singer*) soprano *mf*; (*voice*) soprano *m*.

sorbet ['sɔːbeɪ] *n* (*water ice*) sorbet *m*.

sorcerer ['sɔːsərər] *n* sorcier *m*.

sordid ['sɔːdɪd] *a* (*act, street etc*) sordide.

sore [sɔːr] *a* (**-er, -est**) (*painful*) douloureux; (*angry*) *Am* fâché (**at** contre); **a s. point** *Fig* un sujet délicat; **she has a s. thumb** elle a mal au pouce; **he's still s.** *Med* il a encore mal; – *n Med* plaie *f*. ◆**—ly** *adv* (*tempted, regretted*) très; **s. needed** dont on a grand besoin. ◆**—ness** *n* (*pain*) douleur *f*.

sorrow ['sɒrəʊ] *n* chagrin *m*, peine *f*. ◆**sorrowful** *a* triste.

sorry ['sɒrɪ] *a* (**-ier, -iest**) (*sight, state etc*) triste; **to be s.** (*regret*) être désolé, regretter (**to do** de faire); **I'm s. she can't come** je regrette qu'elle ne puisse pas venir; **I'm s. about the delay** je m'excuse pour ce retard; **s.!** pardon!; **to say s.** demander pardon (**to** à); **to feel** *or* **be s. for** plaindre.

sort [sɔːt] **1** *n* genre *m*, espèce *f*, sorte *f*; **a s. of** une sorte *or* espèce de; **a good s.** (*person*) *Fam* un brave type; **s. of sad/***etc* plutôt triste/*etc*. **2** *vt* (*letters*) trier; **to s. out** (*classify, select*) trier; (*separate*) séparer (**from** de); (*arrange*) arranger; (*tidy*) ranger; (*problem*) régler; **to s. s.o. out** (*punish*) *Fam*

faire voir à qn; – *vi* **to s. through** (*letters etc*) trier; **sorting office** centre *m* de tri. ◆**—er** *n* (*person*) trieur, -euse *mf*.
soufflé ['suːfleɪ] *n Culin* soufflé *m*.
sought [sɔːt] *see* **seek**.
soul [səʊl] *n* âme *f*; **not a living s.** (*nobody*) personne, pas âme qui vive; **a good s.** *Fig* un brave type; **s. mate** âme *f* sœur. ◆**s.-destroying** *a* abrutissant. ◆**s.-searching** *n* examen *m* de conscience.
sound[1] [saʊnd] *n* son *m*; (*noise*) bruit *m*; **I don't like the s. of it** ça ne me plaît pas du tout; – *a* (*wave, film*) sonore; (*engineer*) du son; **s. archives** phonothèque *f*; **s. barrier** mur *m* du son; **s. effects** bruitage *m*; – *vt* (*bell, alarm etc*) sonner; (*bugle*) sonner de; (*letter*) *Gram* prononcer; **to s. one's horn** *Aut* klaxonner; – *vi* retentir, sonner; (*seem*) sembler; **to s. like** sembler être; (*resemble*) ressembler à; **it sounds like** *or* **as if** il semble que (+ *sub or indic*); **to s. off about** *Pej* (*boast*) se vanter de; (*complain*) rouspéter à propos de. ◆**soundproof** *a* insonorisé; – *vt* insonoriser. ◆**soundtrack** *n* (*of film etc*) bande *f* sonore.
sound[2] [saʊnd] *a* (**-er, -est**) (*healthy*) sain; (*sturdy, reliable*) solide; (*instinct*) sûr; (*advice*) sensé; (*beating, sense*) bon; – *adv* **s. asleep** profondément endormi. ◆**—ly** *adv* (*asleep*) profondément; (*reasoned*) solidement; (*beaten*) complètement. ◆**—ness** *n* (*of mind*) santé *f*; (*of argument*) solidité *f*.
sound[3] [saʊnd] *vt* (*test, measure*) sonder; **to s. s.o. out** sonder qn (**about** sur).
soup [suːp] *n* soupe *f*, potage *m*; **in the s.** (*in trouble*) *Fam* dans le pétrin.
sour ['saʊər] *a* (**-er, -est**) aigre; **to turn s.** (*of wine*) s'aigrir; (*of milk*) tourner; (*of friendship*) se détériorer; (*of conversation*) tourner au vinaigre; – *vi* (*of temper*) s'aigrir.
source [sɔːs] *n* (*origin*) source *f*; **s. of energy** source d'énergie.
south [saʊθ] *n* sud *m*; – *a* (*coast*) sud *inv*; (*wind*) du sud; **to be s. of** être au sud de; **S. America/Africa** Amérique *f*/Afrique *f* du Sud; **S. American** *a* & *n* sud-américain, -aine (*mf*); **S. African** *a* & *n* sud-africain, -aine (*mf*); – *adv* au sud, vers le sud. ◆**southbound** *a* (*carriageway*) sud *inv*; (*traffic*) en direction du sud. ◆**south-'east** *n* & *a* sud-est *m* & *a inv*. ◆**southerly** ['sʌðəlɪ] *a* (*point*) sud *inv*; (*direction, wind*) du sud. ◆**southern** ['sʌðən] *a* (*town*) du sud; (*coast*) sud *inv*; **S. Italy** le Sud de l'Italie; **S. Africa** Afrique *f* australe. ◆**southerner** ['sʌðənər] *n* habitant, -ante *mf* du Sud. ◆**southward(s)** *a* & *adv* vers le sud. ◆**south-'west** *n* & *a* sud-ouest *m* & *a inv*.
souvenir [suːvə'nɪər] *n* (*object*) souvenir *m*.
sovereign ['sɒvrɪn] *n* souverain, -aine *mf*; – *a* (*State, authority*) souverain; (*rights*) de souveraineté. ◆**sovereignty** *n* souveraineté *f*.
Soviet ['səʊvɪət] *a* soviétique; **the S. Union** l'Union *f* soviétique.
sow[1] [saʊ] *n* (*pig*) truie *f*.
sow[2] [səʊ] *vt* (*pt* **sowed**, *pp* **sowed** *or* **sown**) (*seeds, doubt etc*) semer; (*land*) ensemencer (**with** de).
soya ['sɔɪə] *n* **s. (bean)** graine *f* de soja. ◆**soybean** *n Am* graine *f* de soja.
sozzled ['sɒz(ə)ld] *a* (*drunk*) *Sl* bourré.
spa [spɑː] *n* (*town*) station *f* thermale; (*spring*) source *f* minérale.
space [speɪs] *n* (*gap, emptiness*) espace *m*; (*period*) période *f*; **blank s.** espace *m*, blanc *m*; **(outer) s.** l'espace (cosmique); **to take up s.** (*room*) prendre de la place; **in the s. of** en l'espace de; **s. heater** (*electric*) radiateur *m*; – *a* (*voyage etc*) spatial; – *vt* **to s. out** espacer; **double/single spacing** (*on typewriter*) double/simple interligne *m*. ◆**spaceman** *n* (*pl* **-men**) astronaute *m*. ◆**spaceship** *n*, ◆**spacecraft** *n inv* engin *m* spatial. ◆**spacesuit** *n* scaphandre *m* (de cosmonaute).
spacious ['speɪʃəs] *a* spacieux, grand. ◆**—ness** *n* grandeur *f*.
spade [speɪd] *n* **1** (*for garden*) bêche *f*; (*of child*) pelle *f*. **2** *Cards* pique *m*. ◆**spadework** *n Fig* travail *m* préparatoire; (*around problem or case*) débroussaillage *m*.
spaghetti [spə'getɪ] *n* spaghetti(s) *mpl*.
Spain [speɪn] *n* Espagne *f*.
span [spæn] *n* (*of arch*) portée *f*; (*of wings*) envergure *f*; (*of life*) *Fig* durée *f*; – *vt* (**-nn-**) (*of bridge etc*) enjamber (*rivière etc*); *Fig* couvrir, embrasser.
Spaniard ['spænjəd] *n* Espagnol, -ole *mf*. ◆**Spanish** *a* espagnol; – *n* (*language*) espagnol *m*. ◆**Spanish-A'merican** *a* hispano-américain.
spaniel ['spænjəl] *n* épagneul *m*.
spank [spæŋk] *vt* fesser, donner une fessée à; – *n* **to give s.o. a s.** fesser qn. ◆**—ing** *n* fessée *f*.
spanner ['spænər] *n* (*tool*) clé *f* (à écrous); **adjustable s.** clé *f* à molette.
spar/e[1] [speər] **1** *a* (*extra, surplus*) de *or* en

trop; (*clothes, tyre*) de rechange; (*wheel*) de secours; (*available*) disponible; (*bed, room*) d'ami; **s. time** loisirs *mpl*; – *n* **s. (part)** *Tech Aut* pièce *f* détachée. **2** *vt* (*do without*) se passer de; (*s.o.'s life*) épargner; (*efforts, s.o.'s feelings*) ménager; **to s. s.o.** (*not kill*) épargner qn; (*grief, details etc*) épargner à qn; (*time*) accorder à qn; (*money*) donner à qn; **I can't s. the time** je n'ai pas le temps; **five to s.** cinq de trop. **◆—ing** *a* (*use*) modéré; **to be s. with** (*butter etc*) ménager.

spare² [speər] *a* (*lean*) maigre.

spark [spɑːk] **1** *n* étincelle *f*. **2** *vi* **to s. off** (*cause*) provoquer. **◆spark(ing) plug** *n* *Aut* bougie *f*.

sparkl/e ['spɑːk(ə)l] *vi* étinceler, scintiller; – *n* éclat *m*. **◆—ing** *a* (*wine, water*) pétillant.

sparrow ['spærəʊ] *n* moineau *m*.

sparse [spɑːs] *a* clairsemé. **◆—ly** *adv* (*populated etc*) peu.

spartan ['spɑːtən] *a* spartiate, austère.

spasm ['spæzəm] *n* (*of muscle*) spasme *m*; (*of coughing etc*) *Fig* accès *m*. **◆spas'modic** *a* (*pain etc*) spasmodique; *Fig* irrégulier.

spastic ['spæstɪk] *n* handicapé, -ée *mf* moteur.

spat [spæt] *see* **spit 1**.

spate [speɪt] *n* **a s. of** (*orders etc*) une avalanche de.

spatter ['spætər] *vt* (*clothes, person etc*) éclabousser (**with** de); – *vi* **to s. over s.o.** (*of mud etc*) éclabousser qn.

spatula ['spætjʊlə] *n* spatule *f*.

spawn [spɔːn] *n* (*of fish etc*) frai *m*; – *vi* frayer; – *vt* pondre; *Fig* engendrer.

speak [spiːk] *vi* (*pt* **spoke**, *pp* **spoken**) parler; (*formally, in assembly*) prendre la parole; **so to s.** pour ainsi dire; **that speaks for itself** c'est évident; **to s. well of** dire du bien de; **nothing to s. of** pas grand-chose; **Bob speaking** *Tel* Bob à l'appareil; **that's spoken for** c'est pris *or* réservé; **to s. out** *or* **up** (*boldly*) parler (franchement); **to s. up** (*more loudly*) parler plus fort; – *vt* (*language*) parler; (*say*) dire; **to s. one's mind** dire ce que l'on pense. **◆—ing** *n* **public s.** art *m* oratoire; – *a* **to be on s. terms with** parler à; **English-/French-speaking** anglophone/francophone. **◆—er** *n* (*public*) orateur *m*; (*in dialogue*) interlocuteur, -trice *mf*; (*loudspeaker*) *El* haut-parleur *m*; (*of hi-fi*) enceinte *f*; **to be a Spanish/a bad/***etc* **s.** parler espagnol/mal/*etc*.

spear [spɪər] *n* lance *f*. **◆spearhead** *vt* (*attack*) être le fer de lance de; (*campaign*) mener.

spearmint ['spɪəmɪnt] *n* *Bot* menthe *f* (verte); – *a* à la menthe; (*chewing-gum*) mentholé.

spec [spek] *n* **on s.** (*as a gamble*) *Fam* à tout hasard.

special ['speʃ(ə)l] *a* spécial; (*care, attention*) (tout) particulier; (*measures*) *Pol* extraordinaire; (*favourite*) préféré; **by s. delivery** (*letter etc*) par exprès; – *n* **today's s.** (*in restaurant*) le plat du jour. **◆specialist** *n* spécialiste *mf* (**in** de); – *a* (*dictionary, knowledge*) technique, spécialisé. **◆speci'ality** *n* spécialité *f*. **◆specialize** *vi* se spécialiser (**in** dans). **◆specialized** *a* spécialisé. **◆specially** *adv* (*specifically*) spécialement; (*on purpose*) (tout) spécialement. **◆specialty** *n* *Am* spécialité *f*.

species ['spiːʃiːz] *n inv* espèce *f*.

specific [spə'sɪfɪk] *a* précis, explicite; *Phys Ch* spécifique. **◆specifically** *adv* (*expressly*) expressément; (*exactly*) précisément.

specify ['spesɪfaɪ] *vt* spécifier (**that** que). **◆specifi'cation** *n* spécification*f*; *pl* (*of car, machine etc*) caractéristiques *fpl*.

specimen ['spesɪmɪn] *n* (*example, person*) spécimen *m*; (*of blood*) prélèvement *m*; (*of urine*) échantillon *m*; **s. signature** spécimen *m* de signature; **s. copy** (*of book etc*) spécimen *m*.

specious ['spiːʃəs] *a* spécieux.

speck [spek] *n* (*stain*) petite tache *f*; (*of dust*) grain *m*; (*dot*) point *m*.

speckled ['spek(ə)ld] *a* tacheté.

specs [speks] *npl Fam* lunettes *fpl*.

spectacle ['spektək(ə)l] **1** *n* (*sight*) spectacle *m*. **2** *npl* (*glasses*) lunettes *fpl*. **◆spec'tacular** *a* spectaculaire. **◆spec'tator** *n* *Sp etc* spectateur, -trice *mf*.

spectre ['spektər] *n* (*menacing image*) spectre *m* (**of** de).

spectrum, *pl* **-tra** ['spektrəm, -trə] *n* *Phys* spectre *m*; (*range*) *Fig* gamme *f*.

speculate ['spekjʊleɪt] *vi* *Fin Phil* spéculer; **to s. about** (*s.o.'s motives etc*) s'interroger sur; – *vt* **to s. that** (*guess*) conjecturer que. **◆specu'lation** *n* *Fin Phil* spéculation *f*; (*guessing*) conjectures *fpl* (**about** sur). **◆speculator** *n* spéculateur, -trice *mf*. **◆speculative** *a* *Fin Phil* spéculatif; **that's s.** (*guesswork*) c'est (très) hypothétique.

sped [sped] *see* **speed 1**.

speech [spiːtʃ] *n* (*talk, address*) & *Gram* discours *m* (**on** sur); (*faculty*) parole *f*;

(*diction*) élocution *f*; (*of group*) langage *m*; **a short s.** une allocution *f*; **freedom of s.** liberté *f* d'expression; **part of s.** *Gram* catégorie *f* grammaticale. ◆**—less** *a* muet (**with** de).

speed [spiːd] **1** *n* (*rate of movement*) vitesse *f*; (*swiftness*) rapidité *f*; **s. limit** *Aut* limitation *f* de vitesse; – *vt* (*pt & pp* **sped**) **to s. up** accélérer; – *vi* **to s. up** (*of person*) aller plus vite; (*of pace*) s'accélérer; **to s. past** passer à toute vitesse (**sth** devant qch). **2** *vi* (*pt & pp* **speeded**) (*drive too fast*) aller trop vite. ◆**—ing** *n Jur* excès *m* de vitesse. ◆**speedboat** *n* vedette *f*. ◆**spee'dometer** *n Aut* compteur *m* (de vitesse). ◆**speedway** *n Sp* piste *f* de vitesse pour motos; *Sp Aut Am* autodrome *m*.

speed/y ['spiːdɪ] *a* (**-ier, -iest**) rapide. ◆**—ily** *adv* rapidement.

spell¹ [spel] *n* (*magic*) charme *m*, sortilège *m*; (*curse*) sort *m*; *Fig* charme *m*; **under a s.** envoûté. ◆**spellbound** *a* (*audience etc*) captivé.

spell² [spel] *n* (*period*) (courte) période *f*; (*moment, while*) moment *m*; **s. of duty** tour *m* de service.

spell³ [spel] *vt* (*pt & pp* **spelled** *or* **spelt**) (*write*) écrire; (*say aloud*) épeler; (*of letters*) former (*mot*); (*mean*) *Fig* signifier; **to be able to s.** savoir l'orthographe; **how is it spelt?** comment cela s'écrit-il?; **to s. out** (*aloud*) épeler; *Fig* expliquer très clairement. ◆**—ing** *n* orthographe *f*.

spend [spend] **1** *vt* (*pt & pp* **spent**) (*money*) dépenser (**on** pour); – *vi* dépenser. **2** *vt* (*pt & pp* **spent**) (*time, holiday etc*) passer (**on sth** sur qch, **doing** à faire); (*energy, care etc*) consacrer (**on sth** à qch, **doing** à faire). ◆**—ing** *n* dépenses *fpl*; – *a* (*money*) de poche. ◆**—er** *n* **to be a big s.** dépenser beaucoup. ◆**spendthrift** *n* **to be a s.** être dépensier.

spent [spent] *see* **spend**; – *a* (*used*) utilisé; (*energy*) épuisé.

sperm [spɜːm] *n* (*pl* **sperm** *or* **sperms**) sperme *m*.

spew [spjuː] *vt* vomir.

sphere [sfɪər] *n* (*of influence, action etc*) & *Geom Pol* sphère *f*; (*of music, poetry etc*) domaine *m*; **the social s.** le domaine social. ◆**spherical** ['sferɪk(ə)l] *a* sphérique.

sphinx [sfɪŋks] *n* sphinx *m*.

spice [spaɪs] *n Culin* épice *f*; (*interest etc*) *Fig* piment *m*; – *vt* épicer. ◆**spicy** *a* (**-ier, -iest**) épicé; (*story*) *Fig* pimenté.

spick-and-span [spɪkən'spæn] *a* (*clean*) impeccable.

spider ['spaɪdər] *n* araignée *f*.

spiel [ʃpiːl] *n Fam* baratin *m*.

spike [spaɪk] *n* (*of metal*) pointe *f*; – *vt* (*pierce*) transpercer. ◆**spiky** *a* (**-ier, -iest**) *a* garni de pointes.

spill [spɪl] *vt* (*pt & pp* **spilled** *or* **spilt**) (*liquid*) répandre, renverser (**on, over** sur); **to s. the beans** *Fam* vendre la mèche; – *vi* **to s. (out)** se répandre; **to s. over** déborder.

spin [spɪn] *n* (*motion*) tour *m*; (*car ride*) petit tour *m*; (*on washing machine*) essorage *m*; **s. dryer** essoreuse *f*; – *vt* (*pt & pp* **spun**, *pres p* **spinning**) (*web, yarn, wool etc*) filer (**into** en); (*wheel, top*) faire tourner; (*washing*) essorer; (*story*) *Fig* débiter; **to s. out** (*speech etc*) faire durer; – *vi* (*of spinner, spider*) filer; **to s. (round)** (*of dancer, top, planet etc*) tourner; (*of head, room*) *Fig* tourner; (*of vehicle*) faire un tête-à-queue. ◆**spinning** *n* (*by hand*) filage *m*; (*process*) *Tech* filature *f*; **s. top** toupie *f*; **s. wheel** rouet *m*. ◆**spin-'dry** *vt* essorer. ◆**spin-off** *n* avantage *m* inattendu; (*of process, book etc*) dérivé *m*.

spinach ['spɪnɪdʒ] *n* (*plant*) épinard *m*; (*leaves*) *Culin* épinards *mpl*.

spindle ['spɪnd(ə)l] *n Tex* fuseau *m*. ◆**spindly** *a* (**-ier, -iest**) (*legs, arms*) grêle.

spine [spaɪn] *n Anat* colonne *f* vertébrale; (*spike of animal or plant*) épine *f*. ◆**spinal** *a* (*column*) vertébral; **s. cord** moelle *f* épinière. ◆**spineless** *a Fig* mou, faible.

spinster ['spɪnstər] *n* célibataire *f*; *Pej* vieille fille *f*.

spiral ['spaɪərəl] **1** *n* spirale *f*; – *a* en spirale; (*staircase*) en colimaçon. **2** *vi* (**-ll-**, *Am* **-l-**) (*of prices*) monter en flèche.

spire ['spaɪər] *n* (*of church*) flèche *f*.

spirit ['spɪrɪt] **1** *n* (*soul, ghost etc*) esprit *m*; (*courage*) *Fig* courage *m*, vigueur *f*; *pl* (*drink*) alcool *m*, spiritueux *mpl*; **spirit(s)** (*morale*) moral *m*; *Ch* alcool *m*; **in good spirits** de bonne humeur; **the right s.** l'attitude *f* qu'il faut; – *a* (*lamp*) à alcool; **s. level** niveau *m* à bulle (d'air). **2** *vt* **to s. away** (*person*) faire disparaître mystérieusement; (*steal*) *Hum* subtiliser. ◆**—ed** *a* (*person, remark*) fougueux; (*campaign*) vigoureux.

spiritual ['spɪrɪtʃʊəl] *a Phil Rel* spirituel; – *n* (**Negro**) **s.** (negro-)spiritual *m*. ◆**spiritualism** *n* spiritisme *m*. ◆**spiritualist** *n* spirite *mf*.

spit [spɪt] **1** *n* crachat *m*; – *vi* (*pt & pp* **spat** *or* **spit**, *pres p* **spitting**) cracher; (*splutter*) *Fig* crépiter; – *vt* cracher; **to s. out** (**re**)**cracher**; **the spitting image of s.o.** le portrait (tout craché) de qn. **2** *n* (*for meat*) broche *f*.

spite [spaɪt] **1** *n* **in s. of** malgré; **in s. of the fact that** (*although*) bien que (+ *sub*). **2** *n* (*dislike*) rancune *f*; – *vt* (*annoy*) contrarier. ◆**spiteful** *a* méchant. ◆**spitefully** *adv* méchamment.

spittle ['spɪt(ə)l] *n* salive *f*, crachat(s) *m*(*pl*).

splash [splæʃ] *vt* (*spatter*) éclabousser (**with** de, **over** sur); (*spill*) répandre; – *vi* (*of mud, ink etc*) faire des éclaboussures; (*of waves*) clapoter, déferler; **to s. over sth/s.o.** éclabousser qch/qn; **to s. (about)** (*in river, mud*) patauger; (*in bath*) barboter; **to s. out** (*spend money*) *Fam* claquer de l'argent; – *n* (*splashing*) éclaboussement *m*; (*of colour*) *Fig* tache *f*; **s. (mark)** éclaboussure *f*; **s.!** plouf!

spleen [spliːn] *n Anat* rate *f*.

splendid ['splendɪd] *a* (*wonderful, rich, beautiful*) splendide. ◆**splendour** *n* splendeur *f*.

splint [splɪnt] *n Med* éclisse *f*.

splinter ['splɪntər] *n* (*of wood etc*) éclat *m*; (*in finger*) écharde *f*; **s. group** *Pol* groupe *m* dissident.

split [splɪt] *n* fente *f*; (*tear*) déchirure *f*; (*of couple*) rupture *f*; *Pol* scission *f*; **to do the splits** (*in gymnastics*) faire le grand écart; **one's s.** (*share*) *Fam* sa part; – *a* **a s. second** une fraction de seconde; – *vt* (*pt & pp* **split**, *pres p* **splitting**) (*break apart*) fendre; (*tear*) déchirer; **to s. (up)** (*group*) diviser; (*money, work*) partager (**between** entre); **to s. one's head open** s'ouvrir la tête; **to s. one's sides (laughing)** se tordre (de rire); **to s. hairs** *Fig* couper les cheveux en quatre; **s.-level apartment** duplex *m*; – *vi* se fendre; (*tear*) se déchirer; **to s. (up)** (*of group*) éclater; (*of couple*) rompre, se séparer; **to s. off** (*become loose*) se détacher (**from** de); **to s. up** (*of crowd*) se disperser. ◆**splitting** *a* (*headache*) atroce. ◆**split-up** *n* (*of couple*) rupture *f*.

splodge [splɒdʒ] *n*, **splotch** [splɒtʃ] *n* (*mark*) tache *f*.

splurge [splɜːdʒ] *vi* (*spend money*) *Fam* claquer de l'argent.

splutter ['splʌtər] *vi* (*of sparks, fat*) crépiter; (*stammer*) bredouiller.

spoil [spɔɪl] *vt* (*pt & pp* **spoilt** *or* **spoiled**) (*pamper, make unpleasant or less good*) gâter; (*damage, ruin*) abîmer; (*pleasure, life*) gâcher, gâter. ◆**spoilsport** *n* rabat-joie *m inv*.

spoils [spɔɪlz] *npl* (*rewards*) butin *m*.

spoke[1] [spəʊk] *n* (*of wheel*) rayon *m*.

spoke[2] [spəʊk] *see* **speak**. ◆**spoken** *see* **speak**; – *a* (*language etc*) parlé; **softly s.** (*person*) à la voix douce. ◆**spokesman** *n* (*pl* **-men**) porte-parole *m inv* (**for, of** de).

sponge [spʌndʒ] **1** *n* éponge *f*; **s. bag** trousse *f* de toilette; **s. cake** gâteau *m* de Savoie; – *vt* **to s. down/off** laver/enlever à l'éponge. **2** *vi* **to s. off** *or* **on s.o.** *Fam* vivre aux crochets de qn; – *vt* **to s. sth off s.o.** *Fam* taper qn de qch. ◆**sponger** *n Fam* parasite *m*. ◆**spongy** *a* (**-ier, -iest**) spongieux.

sponsor ['spɒnsər] *n* (*of appeal, advertiser etc*) personne *f* assurant le patronage (**of** de); (*for membership*) parrain *m*, marraine *f*; *Jur* garant, -ante *mf*; *Sp* sponsor *m*; – *vt* (*appeal etc*) patronner; (*member, firm*) parrainer. ◆**sponsorship** *n* patronage *m*; parrainage *m*.

spontaneous [spɒn'teɪnɪəs] *a* spontané. ◆**spontaneity** [spɒntə'neɪətɪ] *n* spontanéité *f*. ◆**spontaneously** *adv* spontanément.

spoof [spuːf] *n Fam* parodie *f* (**on** de).

spooky ['spuːkɪ] *a* (**-ier, -iest**) *Fam* qui donne le frisson.

spool [spuːl] *n* bobine *f*.

spoon [spuːn] *n* cuiller *f*. ◆**spoonfeed** *vt* (*pt & pp* **spoonfed**) (*help*) *Fig* mâcher le travail à. ◆**spoonful** *n* cuillerée *f*.

sporadic [spə'rædɪk] *a* sporadique; **s. fighting** échauffourées *fpl*. ◆**sporadically** *adv* sporadiquement.

sport [spɔːt] **1** *n* sport *m*; **a (good) s.** (*person*) *Fam* un chic type; **to play s.** *or Am* **sports** faire du sport; **sports club** club *m* sportif; **sports car/jacket** voiture *f*/veste *f* de sport; **sports results** résultats *mpl* sportifs. **2** *vt* (*wear*) arborer. ◆**—ing** *a* (*conduct, attitude, person etc*) sportif; **that's s. of you** *Fig* c'est chic de ta part. ◆**sportsman** *n* (*pl* **-men**) sportif *m*. ◆**sportsmanlike** *a* sportif. ◆**sportsmanship** *n* sportivité *f*. ◆**sportswear** *n* vêtements *mpl* de sport. ◆**sportswoman** *n* (*pl* **-women**) sportive *f*. ◆**sporty** *a* (**-ier, -iest**) sportif.

spot[1] [spɒt] *n* (*stain, mark*) tache *f*; (*dot*) point *m*; (*polka dot*) pois *m*; (*pimple*) bouton *m*; (*place*) endroit *m*, coin *m*; (*act*) *Th* numéro *m*; (*drop*) goutte *f*; **a s. of** (*bit*) *Fam* un peu de; **a soft s. for** un faible pour; **on the s.** sur place, sur les lieux; (*at once*) sur le coup; **in a (tight) s.** (*difficulty*) dans le pétrin; **(accident) black s.** *Aut* point *m* noir; **s. cash** argent *m* comptant; **s. check** contrôle *m* au hasard *or* l'improviste. ◆**spotless** *a* (*clean*) impeccable. ◆**spot-**

lessly *adv* s. clean impeccable. ◆**spotlight** *n* (*lamp*) *Th* projecteur *m*; (*for photography etc*) spot *m*; **in the s.** *Th* sous le feu des projecteurs. ◆**spot-'on** *a Fam* tout à fait exact. ◆**spotted** *a* (*fur*) tacheté; (*dress etc*) à pois; (*stained*) taché. ◆**spotty** *a* (**-ier, -iest**) **1** (*face etc*) boutonneux. **2** (*patchy*) *Am* inégal.

spot² [spɒt] *vt* (**-tt-**) (*notice*) apercevoir, remarquer.

spouse [spaus, spauz] *n* époux *m*, épouse *f*.

spout [spaut] **1** *n* (*of jug etc*) bec *m*; **up the s.** (*hope etc*) *Sl* fichu. **2** *vi* **to s. (out)** jaillir. **3** *vt* (*say*) *Pej* débiter.

sprain [spreɪn] *n* entorse *f*, foulure *f*; **to s. one's ankle/wrist** se fouler la cheville/le poignet.

sprang [spræŋ] *see* **spring¹**.

sprawl [sprɔːl] *vi* (*of town, person*) s'étaler; **to be sprawling** être étalé; – *n* **the urban s.** les banlieues *fpl* tentaculaires. ◆**–ing** *a* (*city*) tentaculaire.

spray [spreɪ] **1** *n* (*water drops*) (nuage *m* de) gouttelettes *fpl*; (*from sea*) embruns *mpl*; (*can, device*) bombe *f*, vaporisateur *m*; **hair s.** laque *f* à cheveux; – *vt* (*liquid, surface*) vaporiser; (*crops, plant*) arroser, traiter; (*car etc*) peindre à la bombe. **2** *n* (*of flowers*) petit bouquet *m*.

spread [spred] *vt* (*pt & pp* **spread**) (*stretch, open out*) étendre; (*legs, fingers*) écarter; (*strew*) répandre, étaler (**over** sur); (*paint, payment, cards, visits*) étaler; (*people*) disperser; (*fear, news*) répandre; (*illness*) propager; **to s. out** étendre; écarter; étaler; – *vi* (*of fire, town, fog*) s'étendre; (*of news, fear*) se répandre; **to s. out** (*of people*) se disperser; – *n* (*of fire, illness, ideas*) propagation *f*; (*of wealth*) répartition *f*; (*paste*) *Culin* pâte *f* (à tartiner); (*meal*) festin *m*; **cheese s.** fromage *m* à tartiner. ◆**s.-'eagled** *a* bras et jambes écartés.

spree [spriː] *n* **to go on a spending s.** faire des achats extravagants.

sprig [sprɪg] *n* (*branch of heather etc*) brin *m*; (*of parsley*) bouquet *m*.

sprightl/y ['spraɪtlɪ] *a* (**-ier, -iest**) alerte. ◆**–iness** *n* vivacité *f*.

spring¹ [sprɪŋ] *n* (*metal device*) ressort *m*; (*leap*) bond *m*; – *vi* (*pt* **sprang**, *pp* **sprung**) (*leap*) bondir; **to s. to mind** venir à l'esprit; **to s. into action** passer à l'action; **to s. from** (*stem from*) provenir de; **to s. up** (*appear*) surgir; – *vt* (*news*) annoncer brusquement (**on** à); (*surprise*) faire (**on** à); **to s. a leak** (*of boat*) commencer à faire eau. ◆**springboard** *n* tremplin *m*. ◆**springy** *a* (**-ier, -iest**) élastique.

spring² [sprɪŋ] *n* (*season*) printemps *m*; **in (the) s.** au printemps; **s. onion** ciboule *f*. ◆**s.-'cleaning** *n* nettoyage *m* de printemps. ◆**springlike** *a* printanier. ◆**springtime** *n* printemps *m*.

spring³ [sprɪŋ] *n* (*of water*) source *f*; **s. water** eau *f* de source.

sprinkl/e ['sprɪŋk(ə)l] *vt* (*sand etc*) répandre (**on, over** sur); **to s. with water, s. water on** asperger d'eau, arroser; **to s. with** (*sugar, salt, flour*) saupoudrer de. ◆**–ing** *n* **a s. of** (*a few*) quelques. ◆**–er** *n* (*in garden*) arroseur *m*.

sprint [sprɪnt] *n Sp* sprint *m*; – *vi* sprinter. ◆**–er** *n* sprinter *m*, sprinteuse *f*.

sprite [spraɪt] *n* (*fairy*) lutin *m*.

sprout [spraut] **1** *vi* (*of seed, bulb etc*) germer, pousser; **to s. up** (*grow*) pousser vite; (*appear*) surgir; – *vt* (*leaves*) pousser; (*beard*) *Fig* laisser pousser. **2** *n* (**Brussels**) **s.** chou *m* de Bruxelles.

spruce [spruːs] *a* (**-er, -est**) (*neat*) pimpant, net; – *vt* **to s. oneself up** se faire beau.

sprung [sprʌŋ] *see* **spring¹**; – *a* (*mattress, seat*) à ressorts.

spry [spraɪ] *a* (**spryer, spryest**) (*old person etc*) alerte.

spud [spʌd] *n* (*potato*) *Fam* patate *f*.

spun [spʌn] *see* **spin**.

spur [spɜːr] *n* (*of horse rider etc*) éperon *m*; (*stimulus*) *Fig* aiguillon *m*; **on the s. of the moment** sur un coup de tête; – *vt* (**-rr-**) **to s. (on)** (*urge on*) éperonner.

spurious ['spjʊərɪəs] *a* faux.

spurn [spɜːn] *vt* rejeter (avec mépris).

spurt [spɜːt] *vi* (*gush out*) jaillir; (*rush*) foncer; **to s. out** jaillir; – *n* jaillissement *m*; (*of energy*) sursaut *m*; **to put on a s.** (*rush*) foncer.

spy [spaɪ] *n* espion, -onne *mf*; – *a* (*story etc*) d'espionnage; **s. hole** (*peephole*) judas *m*; **s. ring** réseau *m* d'espionnage; – *vi* espionner; **to s. on s.o.** espionner qn; – *vt* (*notice*) *Lit* apercevoir. ◆**–ing** *n* espionnage *m*.

squabbl/e ['skwɒb(ə)l] *vi* se chamailler (**over** à propos de). – *n* chamaillerie *f*. ◆**–ing** *n* chamailleries *fpl*.

squad [skwɒd] *n* (*group*) & *Mil* escouade *f*; (*team*) *Sp* équipe *f*; **s. car** voiture *f* de police.

squadron ['skwɒdrən] *n Mil* escadron *m*; *Nau Av* escadrille *f*.

squalid ['skwɒlɪd] *a* sordide. ◆**squalor** *n* conditions *fpl* sordides.

squall [skwɔːl] *n* (*of wind*) rafale *f*.

squander ['skwɒndər] *vt* (*money, time etc*) gaspiller (**on** en).
square ['skweər] *n* carré *m*; (*on chessboard, graph paper*) case *f*; (*in town*) place *f*; (*drawing implement*) *Tech* équerre *f*; **to be back to s. one** repartir à zéro; – *a* carré; (*in order, settled*) *Fig* en ordre; (*honest*) honnête; (*meal*) solide; (**all**) **s.** (*quits*) quitte (**with** envers); – *vt* (*settle*) mettre en ordre, régler; (*arrange*) arranger; *Math* carrer; (*reconcile*) faire cadrer; – *vi* (*tally*) cadrer (**with** avec); **to s. up to** faire face à. ◆**—ly** *adv* (*honestly*) honnêtement; (*exactly*) tout à fait; **s. in the face** bien en face.
squash [skwɒʃ] **1** *vt* (*crush*) écraser; (*squeeze*) serrer; – *n* **lemon/orange s.** (*concentrated*) sirop *m* de citron/d'orange; (*diluted*) citronnade *f*/orangeade *f*. **2** *n* (*game*) squash *m*. **3** *n* (*vegetable*) *Am* courge *f*. ◆**squashy** *a* (**-ier, -iest**) (*soft*) mou.
squat [skwɒt] **1** *a* (*short and thick*) trapu. **2** *vi* (**-tt-**) **to s. (down)** s'accroupir. **3** *n* (*house*) squat *m*. ◆**squatting** *a* accroupi. ◆**squatter** *n* squatter *m*.
squawk [skwɔːk] *vi* pousser des cris rauques; – *n* cri *m* rauque.
squeak [skwiːk] *vi* (*of door*) grincer; (*of shoe*) craquer; (*of mouse*) faire couic; – *n* grincement *m*; craquement *m*; couic *m*. ◆**squeaky** *a* (**-ier, -iest**) (*door*) grinçant; (*shoe*) qui craque.
squeal [skwiːl] *vi* pousser des cris aigus; (*of tyres*) crisser; – *n* cri *m* aigu; crissement *m*. **2** *vi* **to s. on s.o.** (*inform on*) *Fam* balancer qn.
squeamish ['skwiːmɪʃ] *a* bien délicat, facilement dégoûté.
squeegee ['skwiːdʒiː] *n* raclette *f* (à vitres).
squeez/e [skwiːz] *vt* (*press*) presser; (*hand, arm*) serrer; **to s. sth out of s.o.** (*information*) soutirer qch à qn; **to s. sth into** faire rentrer qch dans; **to s. (out)** (*extract*) exprimer (**from** de); – *vi* **to s. through/into/***etc* (*force oneself*) se glisser par/dans/ *etc*; **to s. in** trouver un peu de place; – *n* pression *f*; **to give sth a s.** presser qch; **it's a tight s.** il y a peu de place; **credit s.** *Fin* restrictions *fpl* de crédit. ◆**—er** *n* **lemon s.** presse-citron *m inv*.
squelch [skweltʃ] **1** *vi* patauger (*en faisant floc-floc*). **2** *vt* (*silence*) *Fam* réduire au silence.
squid [skwɪd] *n* (*mollusc*) calmar *m*.
squiggle ['skwɪg(ə)l] *n* ligne *f* onduleuse, gribouillis *m*.
squint [skwɪnt] *n* *Med* strabisme *m*; **to have a s.** loucher; – *vi* loucher; (*in the sunlight etc*) plisser les yeux.
squire ['skwaɪər] *n* propriétaire *m* terrien.
squirm [skwɜːm] *vi* (*wriggle*) se tortiller; **to s. in pain** se tordre de douleur.
squirrel ['skwɪrəl, *Am* 'skwɜːrəl] *n* écureuil *m*.
squirt [skwɜːt] **1** *vt* (*liquid*) faire gicler; – *vi* gicler; – *n* giclée *f*, jet *m*. **2** *n* **little s.** (*person*) *Fam* petit morveux *m*.
stab [stæb] *vt* (**-bb-**) (*with knife etc*) poignarder; – *n* coup *m* (de couteau *or* de poignard). ◆**stabbing** *n* **there was a s.** quelqu'un a été poignardé; – *a* (*pain*) lancinant.
stable[1] ['steɪb(ə)l] *a* (**-er, -est**) stable; **mentally s.** (*person*) bien équilibré. ◆**sta'bility** *n* stabilité *f*; **mental s.** équilibre *m*. ◆**stabilize** *vt* stabiliser; – *vi* se stabiliser. ◆**stabilizer** *n* stabilisateur *m*.
stable[2] ['steɪb(ə)l] *n* écurie *f*; **s. boy** lad *m*.
stack [stæk] **1** *n* (*heap*) tas *m*; **stacks of** (*lots of*) *Fam* un *or* des tas de; – *vt* **to s. (up)** entasser. **2** *npl* (*in library*) réserve *f*.
stadium ['steɪdɪəm] *n* *Sp* stade *m*.
staff [stɑːf] **1** *n* personnel *m*; *Sch* professeurs *mpl*; *Mil* état-major *m*; **s. meeting** *Sch Univ* conseil *m* des professeurs; **s. room** *Sch Univ* salle *f* des professeurs; – *vt* pourvoir en personnel. **2** *n* (*stick*) *Lit* bâton *m*.
stag [stæg] *n* cerf *m*; **s. party** réunion *f* entre hommes.
stage[1] [steɪdʒ] *n* (*platform*) *Th* scène *f*; **the s.** (*profession*) le théâtre; **on s.** sur (la) scène; **s. door** entrée *f* des artistes; **s. fright** le trac; – *vt* (*play*) *Th* monter; *Fig* organiser, effectuer; **it was staged** (*not real*) c'était un coup monté. ◆**s.-hand** *n* machiniste *m*. ◆**s.-manager** *n* régisseur *m*.
stage[2] [steɪdʒ] *n* (*phase*) stade *m*, étape *f*; (*of journey*) étape *f*; (*of track, road*) section *f*; **in (easy) stages** par étapes; **at an early s.** au début.
stagecoach ['steɪdʒkəʊtʃ] *n* *Hist* diligence *f*.
stagger ['stægər] **1** *vi* (*reel*) chanceler. **2** *vt* (*holidays etc*) étaler, échelonner. **3** *vt* **to s. s.o.** (*shock, amaze*) stupéfier qn. ◆**—ing** *a* stupéfiant.
stagnant ['stægnənt] *a* stagnant. ◆**stag'nate** *vi* stagner. ◆**stag'nation** *n* stagnation *f*.
staid [steɪd] *a* posé, sérieux.
stain [steɪn] **1** *vt* (*mark, dirty*) tacher (**with**

de); – *n* tache *f*. **2** *vt* (*colour*) teinter (*du bois*); **stained glass window** vitrail *m*; – *n* (*colouring for wood*) teinture *f*. ◆**–less** *a* (*steel*) inoxydable; **s.-steel knife/***etc* couteau *m*/*etc* inoxydable.

stair [steər] *n* **a s.** (*step*) une marche; **the stairs** (*staircase*) l'escalier *m*; – *a* (*carpet etc*) d'escalier. ◆**staircase** *n*, ◆**stairway** *n* escalier *m*.

stake [steɪk] **1** *n* (*post*) pieu *m*; (*for plant*) tuteur *m*; *Hist* bûcher *m*; – *vt* **to s. (out)** (*land*) jalonner, délimiter; **to s. one's claim** to revendiquer. **2** *n* (*betting*) enjeu *m*; (*investment*) *Fin* investissement *m*; (*interest*) *Fin* intérêts *mpl*; **at s.** en jeu; – *vt* (*bet*) jouer (**on** sur).

stale [steɪl] *a* (**-er, -est**) (*food*) pas frais; (*bread*) rassis; (*beer*) éventé; (*air*) vicié; (*smell*) de renfermé; (*news*) *Fig* vieux; (*joke*) usé, vieux; (*artist*) manquant d'invention. ◆**—ness** *n* (*of food*) manque *m* de fraîcheur.

stalemate ['steɪlmeɪt] *n Chess* pat *m*; *Fig* impasse *f*.

stalk [stɔːk] **1** *n* (*of plant*) tige *f*, queue *f*; (*of fruit*) queue *f*. **2** *vt* (*animal, criminal*) traquer. **3** *vi* **to s. out** (*walk*) partir avec raideur *or* en marchant à grands pas.

stall [stɔːl] **1** *n* (*in market*) étal *m*, éventaire *m*; (*for newspapers, flowers*) kiosque *m*; (*in stable*) stalle *f*; **the stalls** *Cin* l'orchestre *m*. **2** *vti Aut* caler. **3** *vi* **to s. (for time)** chercher à gagner du temps.

stallion ['stæljən] *n* (*horse*) étalon *m*.

stalwart ['stɔːlwət] *a* (*suppporter*) brave, fidèle; – *n* (*follower*) fidèle *mf*.

stamina ['stæmɪnə] *n* vigueur *f*, résistance *f*.

stammer ['stæmər] *vti* bégayer; – *n* bégaiement *m*; **to have a s.** être bègue.

stamp [stæmp] **1** *n* (*for postage, implement*) timbre *m*; (*mark*) cachet *m*, timbre *m*; **the s. of** *Fig* la marque de; **men of your s.** les hommes de votre trempe; **s. collecting** philatélie *f*; – *vt* (*mark*) tamponner, timbrer; (*letter*) timbrer; (*metal*) estamper; **to s. sth on sth** (*affix*) apposer qch sur qch; **to s. out** (*rebellion, evil*) écraser; (*disease*) supprimer; **stamped addressed envelope** enveloppe *f* timbrée à votre adresse. **2** *vti* **to s. (one's feet)** taper *or* frapper des pieds; **stamping ground** *Fam* lieu *m* favori.

stampede [stæm'piːd] *n* fuite *f* précipitée; (*rush*) ruée *f*; – *vi* fuir en désordre; (*rush*) se ruer.

stance [stɑːns] *n* position *f*.

stand [stænd] *n* (*position*) position *f*; (*support*) support *m*; (*at exhibition*) stand *m*; (*for spectators*) *Sp* tribune *f*; **(witness) s.** *Jur Am* barre *f*; **to make a s., take one's s.** prendre position (**against** contre); **news/flower s.** (*in street*) kiosque *m* à journaux/à fleurs; **hat s.** porte-chapeaux *m inv*; **music s.** pupitre *m* à musique; – *vt* (*pt & pp* **stood**) (*pain, journey, person etc*) supporter; **to s. (up)** (*put straight*) mettre (debout); **to s. s.o. sth** (*pay for*) payer qch à qn; **to s. a chance** avoir une chance; **to s. s.o. up** *Fam* poser un lapin à qn; – *vi* être *or* se tenir (debout); (*rise*) se lever; (*remain*) rester (debout); (*be situated*) se trouver; (*be*) être; (*of object, argument*) reposer (**on** sur); **to leave to s.** (*liquid*) laisser reposer; **to s. to lose** risquer de perdre; **to s. around** (*in street etc*) traîner; **to s. aside** s'écarter; **to s. back** reculer; **to s. by** (*do nothing*) rester là (sans rien faire); (*be ready*) être prêt (à partir *or* à intervenir); (*one's opinion etc*) s'en tenir à; (*friend etc*) rester fidèle à; **to s. down** (*withdraw*) se désister; **to s. for** (*represent*) représenter; *Pol* être candidat à; (*put up with*) supporter; **to s. in for** (*replace*) remplacer; **to s. out** (*be visible or conspicuous*) ressortir (**against** sur); **to s. over s.o.** (*watch closely*) surveiller qn; **to s. up** (*rise*) se lever; **to s. up for** (*defend*) défendre; **to s. up to** (*resist*) résister à. ◆**—ing** *a* debout *inv*; (*committee, offer, army*) permanent; **s. room** places *fpl* debout; **s. joke** plaisanterie *f* classique; – *n* (*reputation*) réputation *f*; (*social, professional*) rang *m*; (*financial*) situation *f*; **of six years' s.** (*duration*) qui dure depuis six ans; **of long s.** de longue date. ◆**standby** *n* (*pl* **-bys**) **on s.** prêt à partir *or* à intervenir; – *a* (*battery etc*) de réserve; (*ticket*) *Av* sans garantie. ◆**stand-in** *n* remplaçant, -ante *mf* (**for** de); *Th* doublure *f* (**for** de).

standard ['stændəd] **1** *n* (*norm*) norme *f*, critère *m*; (*level*) niveau *m*; (*of weight, gold*) étalon *m*; *pl* (*morals*) principes *mpl*; **s. of living** niveau *m* de vie; **to be** *or* **come up to s.** (*of person*) être à la hauteur; (*of work etc*) être au niveau; – *a* (*average*) ordinaire, courant; (*model, size*) *Com* standard *inv*; (*weight*) étalon *inv*; (*dictionary, book*) classique; **s. lamp** lampadaire *m*. **2** *n* (*flag*) étendard *m*. ◆**standardize** *vt* standardiser.

stand-offish [stænd'ɒfɪʃ] *a* (*person*) distant, froid.

standpoint ['stændpɔɪnt] *n* point *m* de vue.

standstill ['stændstɪl] *n* **to bring to a s.** immobiliser; **to come to a s.** s'immobiliser;

at a s. immobile; (*industry, negotiations*) paralysé.

stank [stæŋk] *see* **stink.**

stanza ['stænzə] *n* strophe *f*.

stapl/e ['steɪp(ə)l] **1** *a* (*basic*) de base; **s. food** *or* **diet** nourriture *f* de base. **2** *n* (*for paper etc*) agrafe *f*; – *vt* agrafer. ◆**—er** *n* (*for paper etc*) agrafeuse *f*.

star [stɑːr] *n* étoile *f*; (*person*) *Cin* vedette *f*; **shooting s.** étoile *f* filante; **s. part** rôle *m* principal; **the Stars and Stripes, the S.-Spangled Banner** *Am* la bannière étoilée; **two-s. (petrol)** de l'ordinaire *m*; **four-s. (petrol)** du super; – *vi* (**-rr-**) (*of actor*) être la vedette (**in** de); – *vt* (*of film*) avoir pour vedette. ◆**stardom** *n* célébrité *f*. ◆**starfish** *n* étoile *f* de mer. ◆**starlit** *a* (*night*) étoilé.

starboard ['stɑːbəd] *n Nau Av* tribord *m*.

starch [stɑːtʃ] *n* (*for stiffening*) amidon *m*; *pl* (*foods*) féculents *mpl*; – *vt* amidonner. ◆**starchy** *a* (**-ier, -iest**) (*food*) féculent; (*formal*) *Fig* guindé.

stare [steər] *n* regard *m* (fixe); – *vi* **to s. at** fixer (du regard); – *vt* **to s. s.o. in the face** dévisager qn.

stark [stɑːk] *a* (**-er, -est**) (*place*) désolé; (*austere*) austère; (*fact, reality*) brutal; **the s. truth** la vérité toute nue; – *adv* **s. naked** complètement nu. ◆**starkers** *a Sl* complèment nu, à poil.

starling ['stɑːlɪŋ] *n* étourneau *m*.

starry ['stɑːrɪ] *a* (**-ier, -iest**) (*sky*) étoilé. ◆**s.-'eyed** *a* (*naïve*) ingénu, naïf.

start[1] [stɑːt] *n* commencement *m*, début *m*; (*of race*) départ *m*; (*lead*) *Sp & Fig* avance *f* (**on** sur); **to make a s.** commencer; **for a s.** pour commencer; **from the s.** dès le début; – *vt* commencer; (*bottle*) entamer, commencer; (*fashion*) lancer; **to s. a war** provoquer une guerre; **to s. a fire** (*in grate*) allumer un feu; (*accidentally*) provoquer un incendie; **to s. s.o. (off) on** (*career*) lancer qn dans; **to s. (up)** (*engine, vehicle*) mettre en marche; **to s. doing** *or* **to do** commencer *or* se mettre à faire; – *vi* commencer (**with sth** par qch, **by doing** par faire); **to s. on sth** commencer qch; **to s. (up)** commencer; (*of vehicle*) démarrer; **to s. (off** *or* **out)** (*leave*) partir (**for** pour); (*in job*) débuter; **to s. back** (*return*) repartir; **to s. with** (*firstly*) pour commencer. ◆**—ing** *n* (*point, line*) de départ; **s. post** *Sp* ligne *f* de départ; **s. from** à partir de. ◆**—er** *n* (*runner*) partant *m*; (*official*) *Sp* starter *m*; (*device*) *Aut* démarreur *m*; *pl Culin* hors-d'œuvre *m inv*; **for starters** (*first*) pour commencer.

start[2] [stɑːt] *vi* (*be startled, jump*) sursauter; – *n* sursaut *m*; **to give s.o. a s.** faire sursauter qn.

startle ['stɑːt(ə)l] *vt* (*make jump*) faire sursauter; (*alarm*) *Fig* alarmer; (*surprise*) surprendre.

starve [stɑːv] *vi* (*die*) mourir de faim; (*suffer*) souffrir de la faim; **I'm starving** *Fig* je meurs de faim; – *vt* (*kill*) laisser mourir de faim; (*make suffer*) faire souffrir de la faim; (*deprive*) *Fig* priver (**of** de). ◆**star'vation** *n* faim *f*; – *a* (*wage, ration*) de famine; **on a s. diet** à la diète.

stash [stæʃ] *vt* **to s. away** (*hide*) cacher; (*save up*) mettre de côté.

state[1] [steɪt] **1** *n* (*condition*) état *m*; (*pomp*) apparat *m*; **not in a (fit) s. to, in no (fit) s. to** hors d'état de; **to lie in s.** (*of body*) être exposé. **2** *n* **S.** (*nation etc*) État *m*; **the States** *Geog Fam* les États-Unis *mpl*; – *a* (*secret, document*) d'État; (*control, security*) de l'État; (*school, education*) public; **s. visit** voyage *m* officiel; **S. Department** *Pol Am* Département *m* d'État. ◆**stateless** *a* apatride; **s. person** apatride *mf*. ◆**state-'owned** *a* étatisé. ◆**statesman** *n* (*pl* **-men**) homme *m* d'État. ◆**statesmanship** *n* diplomatie *f*.

state[2] [steɪt] *vt* déclarer (**that** que); (*opinion*) formuler; (*problem*) exposer; (*time, date*) fixer. ◆**statement** *n* déclaration *f*; *Jur* déposition *f*; **bank s., s. of account** *Fin* relevé *m* de compte.

stately ['steɪtlɪ] *a* (**-ier, -iest**) majestueux; **s. home** château *m*.

static ['stætɪk] *a* statique; – *n* (*noise*) *Rad* parasites *mpl*.

station ['steɪʃ(ə)n] *n Rail* gare *f*; (*underground*) station *f*; (*position*) & *Mil* poste *m*; (*social*) rang *m*; **(police) s.** commissariat *m* *or* poste *m* (de police); **space/observation/radio/***etc* **s.** station *f* spatiale/d'observation/de radio/*etc*; **bus** *or* **coach s.** gare *f* routière; **s. wagon** *Aut Am* break *m*; – *vt* (*position*) placer, poster. ◆**stationmaster** *n Rail* chef *m* de gare.

stationary ['steɪʃən(ə)rɪ] *a* (*motionless*) stationnaire; (*vehicle*) à l'arrêt.

stationer ['steɪʃ(ə)nər] *n* papetier, -ière *mf*; **s.'s (shop)** papeterie *f*. ◆**stationery** *n* (*paper*) papier *m*; (*articles*) papeterie *f*.

statistic [stə'tɪstɪk] *n* (*fact*) statistique *f*; *pl* (*science*) la statistique. ◆**statistical** *a* statistique.

statue ['stætʃuː] *n* statue *f*. ◆**statu'esque** *a* (*beauty etc*) sculptural.

stature ['stætʃər] *n* stature *f*.

status ['steɪtəs] *n* (*position*) situation *f*; *Jur* statut *m*; (*prestige*) standing *m*, prestige *m*; **s. symbol** marque *f* de standing; **s. quo** statu quo *m inv*.

statute ['stætʃuːt] *n* (*law*) loi *f*; *pl* (*of club, institution*) statuts *mpl*. ◆**statutory** *a* (*right etc*) statutaire; **s. holiday** fête *f* légale.

staunch [stɔːntʃ] *a* (**-er, -est**) loyal, fidèle. ◆**—ly** *adv* loyalement.

stave [steɪv] **1** *vt* **to s. off** (*danger, disaster*) conjurer; (*hunger*) tromper. **2** *n Mus* portée *f*.

stay [steɪ] **1** *n* (*visit*) séjour *m*; – *vi* (*remain*) rester; (*reside*) loger; (*visit*) séjourner; **to s. put** ne pas bouger; **to s. with** (*plan, idea*) ne pas lâcher; **to s. away** (*keep one's distance*) ne pas s'approcher (**from** de); **to s. away from** (*school, meeting etc*) ne pas aller à; **to s. in** (*at home*) rester à la maison; (*of nail, tooth etc*) tenir; **to s. out** (*outside*) rester dehors; (*not come home*) ne pas rentrer; **to s. out of sth** (*not interfere in*) ne pas se mêler de qch; (*avoid*) éviter qch; **to s. up** (*at night*) ne pas se coucher; (*of fence etc*) tenir; **to s. up late** se coucher tard; **staying power** endurance *f*. **2** *vt* (*hunger*) tromper. ◆**s.-at-home** *n* & *a Pej* casanier, -ière (*mf*).

St Bernard [sənt'bɜːnəd, *Am* seɪntbə'nɑːd] *n* (*dog*) saint-bernard *m*.

stead [sted] *n* **to stand s.o. in good s.** être bien utile à qn; **in s.o.'s s.** à la place de qn.

steadfast ['stedfɑːst] *a* (*intention etc*) ferme.

steady ['stedɪ] *a* (**-ier, -iest**) (*firm, stable*) stable; (*hand*) sûr, assuré; (*progress, speed, demand*) régulier, constant; (*nerves*) solide; (*staid*) sérieux; **a s. boyfriend** un petit ami; **s. (on one's feet)** solide sur ses jambes; – *adv* **to go s. with** *Fam* sortir avec; – *vt* (*chair etc*) maintenir (en place); (*hand*) assurer; (*nerves*) calmer; (*wedge, prop up*) caler; **to s. oneself** (*stop oneself falling*) reprendre son aplomb. ◆**steadily** *adv* (*to walk*) d'un pas assuré; (*regularly*) régulièrement; (*gradually*) progressivement; (*continuously*) sans arrêt. ◆**steadiness** *n* stabilité *f*; régularité *f*.

steak [steɪk] *n* steak *m*, bifteck *m*. ◆**steakhouse** *n* grill(-room) *m*.

steal[1] [stiːl] *vti* (*pt* **stole**, *pp* **stolen**) voler (**from s.o.** à qn).

steal[2] [stiːl] *vi* (*pt* **stole**, *pp* **stolen**) **to s. in/out** entrer/sortir furtivement. ◆**stealth** [stelθ] *n* **by s.** furtivement. ◆**stealthy** *a* (**-ier, -iest**) furtif.

steam [stiːm] *n* vapeur *f*; (*on glass*) buée *f*; **to let off s.** (*unwind*) *Fam* se défouler, décompresser; **s. engine/iron** locomotive *f*/fer *m* à vapeur; – *vt Culin* cuire à la vapeur; **to get steamed up** (*of glass*) se couvrir de buée; *Fig Fam* s'énerver; – *vi* (*of kettle etc*) fumer; **to s. up** (*of glass*) se couvrir de buée. ◆**steamer** *n*, ◆**steamship** *n* (bateau *m* à) vapeur *m*; (*liner*) paquebot *m*. ◆**steamroller** *n* rouleau *m* compresseur. ◆**steamy** *a* (**-ier, -iest**) humide; (*window*) embué; (*love affair etc*) brûlant.

steel [stiːl] **1** *n* acier *m*; **s. industry** sidérurgie *f*. **2** *vt* **to s. oneself** s'endurcir (**against** contre). ◆**steelworks** *n* aciérie *f*.

steep [stiːp] **1** *a* (**-er, -est**) (*stairs, slope etc*) raide; (*hill*) escarpé; (*price*) *Fig* excessif. **2** *vt* (*soak*) tremper (**in** dans); **steeped in** *Fig* imprégné de. ◆**—ly** *adv* (*to rise*) en pente raide, (*of prices*) *Fig* excessivement.

steeple ['stiːp(ə)l] *n* clocher *m*.

steeplechase ['stiːp(ə)ltʃeɪs] *n* (*race*) steeple(-chase) *m*.

steer [stɪər] *vt* (*vehicle, person*) diriger, piloter; (*ship*) diriger, gouverner; – *vi* (*of person*) *Nau* tenir le gouvernail, gouverner; **to s. towards** faire route vers; **to s. clear of** éviter. ◆**—ing** *n Aut* direction *f*; **s. wheel** volant *m*.

stem [stem] **1** *n* (*of plant etc*) tige *f*; (*of glass*) pied *m*. **2** *vt* (**-mm-**) **to s. (the flow of)** (*stop*) arrêter, contenir. **3** *vi* (**-mm-**) **to s. from** provenir de.

stench [stentʃ] *n* puanteur *f*.

stencil ['stens(ə)l] *n* (*metal, plastic*) pochoir *m*; (*paper, for typing*) stencil *m*; – *vt* (**-ll-**, *Am* **-l-**) (*notes etc*) polycopier.

stenographer [stə'nɒgrəfər] *n Am* sténodactylo *f*.

step [step] *n* (*movement, sound*) pas *m*; (*stair*) marche *f*; (*on train, bus*) marchepied *m*; (*doorstep*) pas *m* de la porte; (*action*) *Fig* mesure *f*; **(flight of) steps** (*indoors*) escalier *m*; (*outdoors*) perron *m*; **(pair of) steps** (*ladder*) escabeau *m*; **s. by s.** pas à pas; **to keep in s.** marcher au pas; **in s. with** *Fig* en accord avec; – *vi* (**-pp-**) (*walk*) marcher (**on** sur); **s. this way!** (venez) par ici!; **to s. aside** s'écarter; **to s. back** reculer; **to s. down** descendre (**from** de); (*withdraw*) *Fig* se retirer; **to s. forward** faire un pas en avant; **to s. in** entrer; (*intervene*) *Fig* intervenir; **to s. into** (*car etc*) monter dans; **to s. off** (*chair etc*) descendre de; **to s. out of** (*car etc*) descendre de; **to s. over** (*obstacle*) enjamber; – *vt* **to s. up** (*increase*) augmenter, intensifier; (*speed up*) activer. ◆**stepladder** *n* escabeau *m*. ◆**stepping-stone** *n* *Fig* tremplin *m* (to pour arriver à).

stepbrother ['stepbrʌðər] *n* demi-frère *m*. ◆**stepdaughter** *n* belle-fille *f*. ◆**stepfather** *n* beau-père *m*. ◆**stepmother** *n* belle-mère *f*. ◆**stepsister** *n* demi-sœur *f*. ◆**stepson** *n* beau-fils *m*.

stereo ['sterɪəʊ] *n* (*pl* **-os**) (*sound*) stéréo(phonie) *f*; (*record player*) chaîne *f* (stéréo *inv*); – *a* (*record etc*) stéréo *inv*; (*broadcast*) en stéréo. ◆**stereo'phonic** *a* stéréophonique.

stereotype ['sterɪətaɪp] *n* stéréotype *m*. ◆**stereotyped** *a* stéréotypé.

sterile ['steraɪl, *Am* 'sterəl] *a* stérile. ◆**ste'rility** *n* stérilité *f*. ◆**sterili'zation** *n* stérilisation *f*. ◆**sterilize** *vt* stériliser.

sterling ['stɜːlɪŋ] *n* (*currency*) livre(s) *f(pl)* sterling *inv*; – *a* (*pound*) sterling *inv*; (*silver*) fin; (*quality, person*) *Fig* sûr.

stern [stɜːn] **1** *a* (**-er, -est**) sévère. **2** *n* (*of ship*) arrière *m*.

stethoscope ['steθəskəʊp] *n* stéthoscope *m*.

stetson ['stetsən] *n* *Am* chapeau *m* à larges bords.

stevedore ['stiːvədɔːr] *n* docker *m*.

stew [stjuː] *n* ragoût *m*; **in a s.** *Fig* dans le pétrin; **s. pan, s. pot** cocotte *f*; – *vt* (*meat*) faire *or* cuire en ragoût; (*fruit*) faire cuire; **stewed fruit** compote *f*; – *vi* cuire. ◆**—ing** *a* (*pears etc*) à cuire.

steward ['stjuːəd] *n* *Av Nau* steward *m*; (*in college, club etc*) intendant *m* (*préposé au ravitaillement*); **shop s.** délégué, -ée *mf* syndical(e). ◆**stewar'dess** *n* *Av* hôtesse *f*.

stick[1] [stɪk] *n* (*piece of wood, chalk, dynamite*) bâton *m*; (*branch*) branche *f*; (*for walking*) canne *f*; **the sticks** *Pej Fam* la campagne, la cambrousse; **to give s.o. some s.** (*scold*) *Fam* engueuler qn.

stick[2] [stɪk] *vt* (*pt & pp* **stuck**) (*glue*) coller; (*put*) *Fam* mettre, planter; (*tolerate*) *Fam* supporter; **to s. sth into** (*thrust*) planter *or* enfoncer qch dans; **to s. down** (*envelope*) coller; (*put down*) *Fam* poser; **to s. on** (*stamp*) coller; (*hat etc*) mettre, planter; **to s. out** (*tongue*) tirer; (*head*) *Fam* sortir; **to s. it out** (*resist*) *Fam* tenir le coup; **to s. up** (*notice*) afficher; (*hand*) *Fam* lever; – *vi* coller, adhérer (**to** à); (*of food in pan*) attacher; (*remain*) *Fam* rester; (*of drawer etc*) être bloqué *or* coincé; **to s. by s.o.** rester fidèle à qn; **to s. to the facts** (*confine oneself to*) s'en tenir aux faits; **to s. around** *Fam* rester dans les parages; **to s. out** (*of petticoat etc*) dépasser; (*of tooth*) avancer; **to s. up for** (*defend*) défendre; **sticking plaster** sparadrap *m*. ◆**sticker** *n* (*label*) autocollant *m*. ◆**stick-on** *a* (*label*) adhésif. ◆**stick-up** *n* *Fam* hold-up *m inv*.

stickler ['stɪklər] *n* **a s. for** (*rules, discipline, details*) intransigeant sur.

sticky ['stɪkɪ] *a* (**-ier, -iest**) collant, poisseux; (*label*) adhésif; (*problem*) *Fig* difficile.

stiff [stɪf] *a* (**-er, -est**) raide; (*joint, leg etc*) ankylosé; (*brush, paste*) dur; (*person*) *Fig* froid, guindé; (*difficult*) difficile; (*price*) élevé; (*whisky*) bien tassé; **to have a s. neck** avoir le torticolis; **to feel s.** être courbaturé; **to be bored s.** *Fam* s'ennuyer à mourir; **frozen s.** *Fam* complètement gelé. ◆**stiffen** *vt* raidir; – *vi* se raidir. ◆**stiffly** *adv* (*coldly*) *Fig* froidement. ◆**stiffness** *n* raideur *f*; (*hardness*) dureté *f*.

stifle ['staɪf(ə)l] *vt* (*feeling, person etc*) étouffer; – *vi* **it's stifling** on étouffe.

stigma ['stɪgmə] *n* (*moral stain*) flétrissure *f*. ◆**stigmatize** *vt* (*denounce*) stigmatiser.

stile [staɪl] *n* (*between fields etc*) échalier *m*.

stiletto [stɪ'letəʊ] *a* **s. heel** talon *m* aiguille.

still[1] [stɪl] *adv* encore, toujours; (*even*) encore; (*nevertheless*) tout de même; **better s., s. better** encore mieux.

still[2] [stɪl] *a* (**-er, -est**) (*motionless*) immobile; (*calm*) calme, tranquille; (*drink*) non gazeux; **to keep** *or* **lie** *or* **stand s.** rester tranquille; **s. life** nature *f* morte; – *n* (*of night*) silence *m*; *Cin* photo *f*. ◆**stillborn** *a* mort-né. ◆**stillness** *n* immobilité *f*; calme *m*.

still[3] [stɪl] *n* (*for making alcohol*) alambic *m*.

stilt [stɪlt] *n* (*pole*) échasse *f*.

stilted ['stɪltɪd] *a* guindé.

stimulate ['stɪmjʊleɪt] *vt* stimuler. ◆**stimulant** *n* *Med* stimulant *m*. ◆**stimu'lation** *n* stimulation *f*. ◆**stimulus,** *pl* **-li** [-laɪ] *n* (*encouragement*) stimulant *m*; (*physiological*) stimulus *m*.

sting [stɪŋ] *vt* (*pt & pp* **stung**) (*of insect, ointment, wind etc*) piquer; (*of remark*) *Fig* blesser; – *vi* piquer; – *n* piqûre *f*; (*insect's organ*) dard *m*. ◆**—ing** *a* (*pain, remark*) cuisant.

sting/y ['stɪndʒɪ] *a* (**-ier, -iest**) avare, mesquin; **s. with** (*money, praise*) avare de; (*food, wine*) mesquin sur. ◆**—iness** *n* avarice *f*.

stink [stɪŋk] *n* puanteur *f*; **to cause** *or* **make a s.** (*trouble*) *Fam* faire du foin; – *vi* (*pt* **stank** *or* **stunk**, *pp* **stunk**) puer; (*of book, film etc*)

Fam être infect; to s. of smoke/*etc* empester la fumée/*etc*; – *vt* to s. out (*room etc*) empester. ◆**—ing** *a Fam* infect, sale. ◆**—er** *n Fam* (*person*) sale type *m*; (*question, task etc*) vacherie *f*.

stint [stɪnt] **1** *n* (*share*) part *f* de travail; (*period*) période *f* de travail. **2** *vi* to s. on lésiner sur.

stipend ['staɪpend] *n Rel* traitement *n*.

stipulate ['stɪpjʊleɪt] *vt* stipuler (that que). ◆**stipu'lation** *n* stipulation *f*

stir [stɜːr] *n* agitation *f*; to give sth a s. remuer qch; to cause a s. *Fig* faire du bruit; – *vt* (-rr-) (*coffee, leaves etc*) remuer; (*excite*) *Fig* exciter; (*incite*) inciter (to do à faire); to s. oneself (*make an effort*) se secouer; to s. up (*trouble*) provoquer; (*memory*) réveiller; – *vi* remuer, bouger. ◆**stirring** *a* (*speech etc*) excitant, émouvant.

stirrup ['stɪrəp] *n* étrier *m*.

stitch [stɪtʃ] *n* point *m*; (*in knitting*) maille *f*; *Med* point *m* de suture; a s. (in one's side) (*pain*) un point de côté; to be in stitches *Fam* se tordre (de rire); – *vt* to s. (up) (*sew up*) coudre; *Med* suturer.

stoat [stəʊt] *n* (*animal*) hermine *f*.

stock [stɒk] *n* (*supply*) provision *f*, stock *m*, réserve *f*; (*of knowledge, jokes*) fonds *m*, mine *f*; *Fin* valeurs *fpl*, titres *mpl*; (*descent, family*) souche *f*; (*soup*) bouillon *m*; (*cattle*) bétail *m*; the stocks *Hist* le pilori; in s. (*goods*) en magasin, disponible; out of s. (*goods*) épuisé, non disponible; to take s. *Fig* faire le point (of de); s. reply/size réponse *f*/taille *f* courante; s. phrase expression *f* toute faite; the S. Exchange *or* Market la Bourse; – *vt* (*sell*) vendre; (*keep in store*) stocker; to s. (up) (*shop, larder*) approvisionner; well-stocked bien approvisionné; – *vi* to s. up s'approvisionner (with de, en). ◆**stockbroker** *n* agent *m* de change. ◆**stockcar** *n* stock-car *m*. ◆**stockholder** *n Fin* actionnaire *mf* ◆**stockist** *n* dépositaire *mf*, stockiste *m*. ◆**stockpile** *vt* stocker, amasser. ◆**stockroom** *n* réserve *f*, magasin *m*. ◆**stocktaking** *n Com* inventaire *m*.

stocking ['stɒkɪŋ] *n* (*garment*) bas *m*.

stocky ['stɒkɪ] *a* (-ier, -iest) trapu.

stodge [stɒdʒ] *n* (*food*) *Fam* étouffe-chrétien *m inv*. ◆**stodgy** *a* (-ier, -iest) *Fam* lourd, indigeste, (*person, style*) compassé.

stoic ['stəʊɪk] *a* & *n* stoïque (*mf*). ◆**stoical** *a* stoïque. ◆**stoicism** *n* stoïcisme *m*.

stok/e [stəʊk] *vt* (*fire*) entretenir; (*engine*) chauffer. ◆**—er** *n Rail* chauffeur *m*.

stole[1] [stəʊl] *n* (*shawl*) étole *f*.

stole[2], **stolen** [stəʊl, 'stəʊl(ə)n] *see* **steal**[1,2].

stolid ['stɒlɪd] *a* (*manner, person*) impassible.

stomach ['stʌmək] **1** *n Anat* estomac *m*; (*abdomen*) ventre *m*; – *vt* (*put up with*) *Fig* supporter. ◆**stomachache** *n* mal *m* de ventre; to have a s. avoir mal au ventre.

stone [stəʊn] *n* pierre *f*; (*pebble*) caillou *m*; (*in fruit*) noyau *m*; (*in kidney*) *Med* calcul *m*; (*weight*) = 6,348 kg; a stone's throw away *Fig* à deux pas d'ici; – *vt* lancer des pierres sur, lapider; (*fruit*) dénoyauter. ◆**stonemason** *n* tailleur *m* de pierre, maçon *m*. ◆**stony** *a* **1** (-ier, -iest) (*path etc*) pierreux, caillouteux. **2** s. broke (*penniless*) *Sl* fauché.

stone- [stəʊn] *pref* complètement. ◆**s.-'broke** *a Am Sl* fauché. ◆**s.-'cold** *a* complètement froid. ◆**s.-'dead** *a* raide mort. ◆**s.-'deaf** *a* sourd comme un pot.

stoned [stəʊnd] *a* (*high on drugs*) *Fam* camé.

stooge [stuːdʒ] *n* (*actor*) comparse *mf*; (*flunkey*) *Pej* larbin *m*; (*dupe*) *Pej* pigeon *m*.

stood [stʊd] *see* **stand**.

stool [stuːl] *n* tabouret *m*.

stoop [stuːp] **1** *n* to have a s. être voûté; – *vi* se baisser; to s. to doing/to sth *Fig* s'abaisser à faire/à qch. **2** *n* (*in front of house*) *Am* perron *m*.

stop [stɒp] *n* (*place, halt*) arrêt *m*, halte *f*; *Av Nau* escale *f*; *Gram* point *m*; bus s. arrêt *m* d'autobus; to put a s. to mettre fin à; to bring to a s. arrêter; to come to a s. s'arrêter; without a s. sans arrêt; s. light (*on vehicle*) stop *m*; s. sign (*road sign*) stop *m*; – *vt* (-pp-) arrêter; (*end*) mettre fin à; (*prevent*) empêcher (from doing de faire); (*cheque*) faire opposition à; to s. up (*sink, pipe, leak etc*) boucher; – *vi* s'arrêter (*of pain, conversation etc*) cesser; (*stay*) rester; to s. eating/*etc* s'arrêter de manger/*etc*; to s. snowing/*etc* cesser de neiger/*etc*; to s. by passer (s.o.'s chez qn); to s. off *or* over (*on journey*) s'arrêter. ◆**stoppage** *n* arrêt *m*; (*in pay*) retenue *f*; (*in work*) arrêt *m* de travail; (*strike*) débrayage *m*; (*blockage*) obstruction *f* ◆**stopper** *n* bouchon *m*.

stopcock [stɒpkɒk] *n* robinet *m* d'arrêt. ◆**stopgap** *n* bouche-trou *m*; – *a* intérimaire. ◆**stopoff** *n*, ◆**stopover** *n* halte *f* ◆**stopwatch** *n* chronomètre *m*.

store [stɔːr] *n* (*supply*) provision *f*; (*of information, jokes etc*) *Fig* fonds *m*; (*depot, warehouse*) entrepôt *m*; (*shop*) grand magasin *m*, *Am* magasin *m*; (*computer memory*) mémoire *f*; **to have sth in s. for s.o.** (*surprise*) réserver qch à qn; **to keep in s.** garder en réserve; **to set great s. by** attacher une grande importance à; – *vt* **to s. (up)** (*in warehouse etc*) emmagasiner; (*for future use*) mettre en réserve; **to s. (away)** (*furniture*) entreposer. ◆**storage** *n* emmagasinage *m*; (*for future use*) mise *f* en réserve; **s. space** *or* **room** espace *m* de rangement. ◆**storekeeper** *n* magasinier *m*; (*shopkeeper*) *Am* commerçant, -ante *mf*. ◆**storeroom** *n* réserve *f*.

storey ['stɔːrɪ] *n* étage *m*.

stork [stɔːk] *n* cigogne *f*.

storm [stɔːm] **1** *n* (*weather*) & *Fig* tempête *f*; (*thunderstorm*) orage *m*; **s. cloud** nuage *m* orageux. **2** *vt* (*attack*) *Mil* prendre d'assaut. **3** *vi* **to s. out** (*angrily*) sortir comme une furie. ◆**stormy** *a* (**-ier, -iest**) (*weather, meeting etc*) orageux; (*wind*) d'orage.

story ['stɔːrɪ] *n* **1** histoire *f*; (*newspaper article*) article *m*; **s. (line)** *Cin Th* intrigue *f*; **short s.** *Liter* nouvelle *f*, conte *m*; **fairy s.** conte *m* de fées. **2** (*storey*) *Am* étage *m*. ◆**storyteller** *n* conteur, -euse *mf*; (*liar*) *Fam* menteur, -euse *mf*.

stout [staʊt] **1** *a* (**-er, -est**) (*person*) gros, corpulent; (*stick, volume*) gros, épais; (*shoes*) solide. **2** *n* (*beer*) bière *f* brune. ◆**—ness** *n* corpulence *f*.

stove [stəʊv] *n* (*for cooking*) cuisinière *f*; (*solid fuel*) fourneau *m*; (*small*) réchaud *m*; (*for heating*) poêle *m*.

stow [stəʊ] **1** *vt* (*cargo*) arrimer; **to s. away** (*put away*) ranger. **2** *vi* **to s. away** *Nau* voyager clandestinement. ◆**stowaway** *n* *Nau* passager, -ère *mf* clandestin(e).

straddle ['stræd(ə)l] *vt* (*chair, fence*) se mettre *or* être à califourchon sur; (*step over, span*) enjamber; (*line in road*) *Aut* chevaucher.

straggl/e ['stræg(ə)l] *vi* (*stretch*) s'étendre (en désordre); (*trail*) traîner (en désordre); **to s. in** entrer par petits groupes. ◆**—er** *n* traînard, -arde *mf*.

straight [streɪt] *a* (**-er, -est**) droit; (*hair*) raide; (*route*) direct; (*tidy*) en ordre; (*frank*) franc; (*refusal*) net; (*actor, role*) sérieux; **I want to get this s.** comprenons-nous bien; **to keep a s. face** garder son sérieux; **to put** *or* **set s.** (*tidy*) ranger; – *n* **the s.** *Sp* la ligne droite; – *adv* (*to walk etc*) droit; (*directly*) tout droit, directement; (*to drink gin, whisky etc*) sec; **s. away** (*at once*) tout de suite; **s. out, s. off** sans hésiter; **s. opposite** juste en face; **s. ahead** *or* **on** (*to walk etc*) tout droit; **s. ahead** (*to look*) droit devant soi. ◆**straighta'way** *adv* tout de suite. ◆**straighten** *vt* **to s. (up)** redresser; (*tie, room*) arranger; **to s. things out** *Fig* arranger les choses. ◆**straight'forward** *a* (*frank*) franc; (*easy*) simple.

strain [streɪn] **1** *n* tension *f*; (*tiredness*) fatigue *f*; (*stress*) *Med* tension *f* nerveuse; (*effort*) effort *m*; – *vt* (*rope, wire*) tendre excessivement; (*muscle*) *Med* froisser; (*ankle, wrist*) fouler; (*eyes*) fatiguer; (*voice*) forcer; *Fig* mettre à l'épreuve; **to s. one's ears** (*to hear*) tendre l'oreille; **to s. oneself** (*hurt oneself*) se faire mal; (*tire oneself*) se fatiguer; – *vi* fournir un effort (**to do** pour faire). **2** *vt* (*soup etc*) passer; (*vegetables*) égoutter. **3** *n* (*breed*) lignée *f*; (*of virus*) souche *f*; (*streak*) tendance *f*. **4** *npl* *Mus* accents *mpl* (of de). ◆**—ed** *a* (*relations*) tendu; (*laugh*) forcé; (*ankle, wrist*) foulé. ◆**—er** *n* passoire *f*.

strait [streɪt] **1** *n* & *npl* *Geog* détroit *m*. **2** *npl* **in financial straits** dans l'embarras. ◆**straitjacket** *n* camisole *f* de force. ◆**strait'laced** *a* collet monté *inv*.

strand [strænd] *n* (*of wool etc*) brin *m*; (*of hair*) mèche *f*; (*of story*) *Fig* fil *m*.

stranded ['strændɪd] *a* (*person, vehicle*) en rade.

strange [streɪndʒ] *a* (**-er, -est**) (*odd*) étrange, bizarre; (*unknown*) inconnu; (*new*) nouveau; **to feel s.** (*in a new place*) se sentir dépaysé. ◆**strangely** *adv* étrangement; **s. (enough) she . . .** chose étrange, elle . . . . ◆**strangeness** *n* étrangeté *f*. ◆**stranger** *n* (*unknown*) inconnu, -ue *mf*; (*outsider*) étranger, -ère *mf*; **he's a s. here** il n'est pas d'ici; **she's a s. to me** elle m'est inconnue.

strangle ['stræŋg(ə)l] *vt* étrangler. ◆**strangler** *n* étrangleur, -euse *mf*. ◆**stranglehold** *n* emprise *f* totale (**on** sur).

strap [stræp] *n* courroie *f*, sangle *f*; (*on dress*) bretelle *f*; (*on watch*) bracelet *m*; (*on sandal*) lanière *f*; – *vt* (**-pp-**) **to s. (down** *or* **in)** attacher (avec une courroie).

strapping ['stræpɪŋ] *a* (*well-built*) robuste.

stratagem ['strætədʒəm] *n* stratagème *m*.

strategy ['strætədʒɪ] *n* stratégie *f*. ◆**stra'tegic** *a* stratégique.

stratum, *pl* **-ta** ['strɑːtəm, -tə] *n* couche *f*.

straw [strɔː] *n* paille *f*; **a (drinking) s.** une paille; **that's the last s.!** c'est le comble!

strawberry ['strɔːbərɪ] *n* fraise *f*; – *a*

(*flavour, ice cream*) à la fraise; (*jam*) de fraises; (*tart*) aux fraises.

stray [streɪ] *a* (*lost*) perdu; **a s. car/***etc* une voiture/*etc* isolée; **a few s. cars/***etc* quelques rares voitures/*etc*; – *n* animal *m* perdu; – *vi* s'égarer; **to s. from** (*subject, path*) s'écarter de.

streak [striːk] *n* (*line*) raie *f*; (*of light*) filet *m*; (*of colour*) strie *f*; (*trace*) *Fig* trace *f*; (*tendency*) tendance *f*; **grey/***etc* **streaks** (*in hair*) mèches *fpl* grises/*etc*; **a mad s.** une tendance à la folie; **my literary s.** ma fibre littéraire. ◆**streaked** *a* (*marked*) strié, zébré; (*stained*) taché **(with** de). ◆**streaky** *a* **(-ier, -iest)** strié; (*bacon*) pas trop maigre.

stream [striːm] *n* (*brook*) ruisseau *m*; (*current*) courant *m*; (*flow*) & *Fig* flot *m*; *Sch* classe *f* (de niveau); – *vi* ruisseler **(with** de); **to s. in** (*of sunlight, people etc*) *Fig* entrer à flots.

streamer ['striːmər] *n* (*paper*) serpentin *m*; (*banner*) banderole *f*.

streamlin/e ['striːmlaɪn] *vt* (*work, method etc*) rationaliser. ◆**—ed** *a* (*shape*) aérodynamique.

street [striːt] *n* rue *f*; **s. door** porte *f* d'entrée; **s. lamp, s. light** réverbère *m*; **s. map, s. plan** plan *m* des rues; **up my s.** *Fig Fam* dans mes cordes; **streets ahead** *Fam* très en avance **(of** sur). ◆**streetcar** *n* (*tram*) *Am* tramway *m*.

strength [streŋθ] *n* force *f*; (*health, energy*) forces *fpl*; (*of wood, fabric*) solidité *f*; **on the s. of** *Fig* en vertu de; **in full s.** au (grand) complet. ◆**strengthen** *vt* (*building, position etc*) renforcer, consolider; (*body, soul, limb*) fortifier.

strenuous ['strenjʊəs] *a* (*effort etc*) vigoureux, énergique; (*work*) ardu; (*active*) actif; (*tiring*) fatigant. ◆**—ly** *adv* énergiquement.

strep [strep] *a* **s. throat** *Med Am* angine *f*.

stress [stres] *n* (*pressure*) pression *f*; *Med Psy* tension *f* (nerveuse), stress *m*; (*emphasis*) & *Gram* accent *m*; *Tech* tension *f*; **under s.** *Med Psy* sous pression, stressé; – *vt* insister sur; (*word*) accentuer; **to s. that** souligner que. ◆**stressful** *a* stressant.

stretch [stretʃ] *vt* (*rope, neck*) tendre; (*shoe, rubber*) étirer; (*meaning*) *Fig* forcer; **to s. (out)** (*arm, leg*) étendre, allonger; **to s. (out) one's arm** (*reach out*) tendre le bras **(to take** pour prendre); **to s. one's legs** *Fig* se dégourdir les jambes; **to s. s.o.** *Fig* exiger un effort de qn; **to be (fully) stretched** (*of budget etc*) être tiré au maximum; **to s. out** (*visit*) prolonger; – *vi* (*of person, elastic*) s'étirer; (*of influence etc*) s'étendre; **to s. (out)** (*of rope, plain*) s'étendre; – *n* (*area, duration*) étendue *f*; (*of road*) tronçon *m*, partie *f*; (*route, trip*) trajet *m*; **at a s.** d'une (seule) traite; **ten/***etc* **hours at a s.** dix/*etc* heures d'affilée; **s. socks/***etc* chaussettes *fpl*/*etc* extensibles; **s. nylon** nylon *m* stretch *inv*. ◆**stretchmarks** *npl* (*on body*) vergetures *fpl*.

stretcher ['stretʃər] *n* brancard *m*.

strew [struː] *vt* (*pt* **strewed**, *pp* **strewed** *or* **strewn**) (*scatter*) répandre; **strewn with** (*covered*) jonché de.

stricken ['strɪk(ə)n] *a* **s. with** (*illness*) atteint de; (*panic*) frappé de.

strict [strɪkt] *a* **(-er, -est)** (*severe, absolute*) strict. ◆**—ly** *adv* strictement; **s. forbidden** formellement interdit. ◆**—ness** *n* sévérité *f*.

stride [straɪd] *n* (grand) pas *m*, enjambée *f*; **to make great strides** *Fig* faire de grands progrès; – *vi* (*pt* **strode) to s. across** *or* **over** enjamber; **to s. up and down a room** arpenter une pièce.

strident ['straɪdənt] *a* strident.

strife [straɪf] *n inv* conflit(s) *m*(*pl*).

strik/e [straɪk] **1** *n* (*attack*) *Mil* raid *m* (aérien); (*of oil etc*) découverte *f*; – *vt* (*pt* & *pp* **struck**) (*hit, impress*) frapper; (*collide with*) heurter; (*beat*) battre; (*a blow*) donner; (*a match*) frotter; (*gold, problem*) trouver; (*coin*) frapper; (*of clock*) sonner; **to s. a bargain** conclure un accord; **to s. a balance** trouver l'équilibre; **to s. (off)** (*from list*) rayer **(from** de); **to be struck off** (*of doctor*) être radié; **it strikes me as/that** il me semble être/que; **how did it s. you?** quelle impression ça t'a fait?; **to s. down** (*of illness etc*) terrasser (*qn*); **to s. up a friendship** lier amitié **(with** avec); – *vi* **to s. (at)** (*attack*) attaquer; **to s. back** (*retaliate*) riposter; **to s. out** donner des coups. **2** *n* (*of workers*) grève *f*; **to go (out) on s.** se mettre en grève **(for** pour obtenir, **against** pour protester contre); – *vi* (*pt* & *pp* **struck**) (*of workers*) faire grève. ◆**—ing** *a* (*impressive*) frappant. ◆**—ingly** *adv* (*beautiful etc*) extraordinairement. ◆**—er** *n* gréviste *mf*; *Fb* buteur *m*.

string [strɪŋ] *n* ficelle *f*; (*of anorak, apron*) cordon *m*; (*of violin, racket etc*) corde *f*; (*of pearls, beads*) rang *m*; (*of onions, insults*) chapelet *m*; (*of people, vehicles*) file *f*; (*of questions etc*) série *f*; **to pull strings** *Fig* faire jouer ses relations; – *a* (*instrument, quartet*) *Mus* à cordes, **s. bean** haricot *m* vert; – *vt* (*pt* & *pp* **strung**) (*beads*) enfiler; **to s. up**

(*hang up*) suspendre; – *vi* **to s. along (with)** *Fam* suivre. ◆**—ed** *a* (*instrument*) *Mus* à cordes. ◆**stringy** *a* (**-ier, -iest**) (*meat etc*) filandreux.

stringent ['strɪndʒ(ə)nt] *a* rigoureux. ◆**stringency** *n* rigueur *f*.

strip [strɪp] **1** *n* (*piece*) bande *f*; (*of water*) bras *m*; (**thin**) **s.** (*of metal etc*) lamelle *f*; **landing s.** piste *f or* terrain *m* d'atterrissage; **s. cartoon, comic s.** bande *f* dessinée. **2** *vt* (**-pp-**) (*undress*) déshabiller; (*bed*) défaire; (*deprive*) dépouiller (**of** de); **to s. (down)** (*machine*) démonter; **to s. off** (*remove*) enlever; – *vi* **to s. (off)** (*undress*) se déshabiller. ◆**stripper** *n* (*woman*) strip-teaseuse *f*; (**paint**) **s.** décapant *m*. ◆**strip-'tease** *n* strip-tease *m*.

stripe [straɪp] *n* rayure *f*; *Mil* galon *m*. ◆**striped** *a* rayé (**with** de). ◆**stripy** *a* rayé.

strive [straɪv] *vi* (*pt* **strove**, *pp* **striven**) s'efforcer (**to do** de faire, **for** d'obtenir).

strode [strəʊd] *see* **stride**.

stroke [strəʊk] *n* (*movement*) coup *m*; (*of pen, genius*) trait *m*; (*of brush*) touche *f*; (*on clock*) coup *m*; (*caress*) caresse *f*; *Med* coup *m* de sang; (*swimming style*) nage *f*; **at a s.** d'un coup; **a s. of luck** un coup de chance; **you haven't done a s. (of work)** tu n'as rien fait; **heat s.** (*sunstroke*) insolation *f*; **four-s. engine** moteur *m* à quatre temps; – *vt* (*beard, cat etc*) caresser.

stroll [strəʊl] *n* promenade *f*; – *vi* se promener, flâner; **to s. in/***etc* entrer/*etc* sans se presser. ◆**—ing** *a* (*musician etc*) ambulant.

stroller ['strəʊlər] *n* (*pushchair*) *Am* poussette *f*.

strong [strɒŋ] *a* (**-er, -est**) fort; (*shoes, nerves*) solide; (*interest*) vif; (*measures*) énergique; (*supporter*) ardent; **sixty s.** au nombre de soixante; – *adv* **to be going s.** aller toujours bien. ◆**—ly** *adv* (*to protest, defend*) énergiquement; (*to desire, advise, remind*) fortement; (*to feel*) profondément; **s. built** solide. ◆**strongarm** *a* brutal. ◆**strongbox** *n* coffre-fort *m*. ◆**stronghold** *n* bastion *m*. ◆**strong-'willed** *a* résolu.

strove [strəʊv] *see* **strive**.

struck [strʌk] *see* **strike 1,2**.

structure ['strʌktʃər] *n* structure *f*; (*of building*) armature *f*; (*building itself*) construction *f*. ◆**structural** *a* structural; (*fault*) *Archit* de construction.

struggle ['strʌg(ə)l] *n* (*fight*) lutte *f* (**to do** pour faire); (*effort*) effort *m*; **to put up a s.** résister; **to have a s. doing** *or* **to do** avoir du mal à faire; – *vi* (*fight*) lutter, se battre (**with** avec); (*resist*) résister; (*thrash about wildly*) se débattre; **to s. to do** (*try hard*) s'efforcer de faire; **to s. out of** sortir péniblement de; **to s. along** *or* **on** se débrouiller; **a struggling lawyer/***etc* un avocat/*etc* qui a du mal à débuter.

strum [strʌm] *vt* (**-mm-**) (*guitar etc*) gratter de.

strung [strʌŋ] *see* **string**; – *a* **s. out** (*things, people*) espacés; (*washing*) étendu.

strut [strʌt] **1** *vi* (**-tt-**) **to s. (about** *or* **around)** se pavaner. **2** *n* (*support*) *Tech* étai *m*.

stub [stʌb] **1** *n* (*of pencil, cigarette etc*) bout *m*; (*counterfoil of cheque etc*) talon *m*; – *vt* (**-bb-**) **to s. out** (*cigarette*) écraser. **2** *vt* (**-bb-**) **to s. one's toe** se cogner le doigt de pied (**on, against** contre).

stubble ['stʌb(ə)l] *n* barbe *f* de plusieurs jours.

stubborn ['stʌbən] *a* (*person*) entêté, opiniâtre; (*cough, efforts, manner etc*) opiniâtre. ◆**—ly** *adv* opiniâtrement. ◆**—ness** *n* entêtement *m*; opiniâtreté *f*.

stubby ['stʌbɪ] *a* (**-ier, -iest**) (*finger etc*) gros et court, épais; (*person*) trapu.

stuck [stʌk] *see* **stick**[2]; – *a* (*caught, jammed*) coincé; **s. in bed/indoors** cloué au lit/chez soi; **to be s.** (*unable to do sth*) ne pas savoir quoi faire; **I'm s. (for an answer)** je ne sais que répondre; **to be s. with sth/s.o.** se farcir qch/qn. ◆**s.-'up** *a Fam* prétentieux, snob *inv*.

stud [stʌd] *n* **1** (*nail*) clou *m* (à grosse tête); (*for collar*) bouton *m* de col. **2** (*farm*) haras *m*; (*horses*) écurie *f*; (*stallion*) étalon *m*; (*virile man*) *Sl* mâle *m*. ◆**studded** *a* (*boots, tyres*) clouté; **s. with** (*covered*) *Fig* constellé de, parsemé de.

student ['stju:dənt] *n Univ* étudiant, -ante *mf*; *Sch Am* élève *mf*; **music/***etc* **s.** étudiant, -ante en musique/*etc*; – *a* (*life, protest*) étudiant; (*restaurant, residence, grant*) universitaire.

studio ['stju:dɪəʊ] *n* (*pl* **-os**) (*of painter etc*) & *Cin TV* studio *m*; **s. flat** *or Am* **apartment** studio *m*.

studious ['stju:dɪəs] *a* (*person*) studieux. ◆**—ly** *adv* (*carefully*) avec soin. ◆**—ness** *n* application *f*.

study ['stʌdɪ] *n* étude *f*; (*office*) bureau *m*; – *vt* (*learn, observe*) étudier; – *vi* étudier; **to s. to be a doctor/***etc* faire des études pour devenir médecin/*etc*; **to s. for** (*exam*) préparer. ◆**studied** *a* (*deliberate*) étudié.

stuff [stʌf] **1** *n* (*thing*) truc *m*, chose *f*;

(*substance*) substance *f*; (*things*) trucs *mpl*, choses *fpl*; (*possessions*) affaires *fpl*; (*nonsense*) sottises *fpl*; **this s.'s good, it's good s.** c'est bon (ça). **2** *vt* (*chair, cushion etc*) rembourrer (**with** avec); (*animal*) empailler; (*cram, fill*) bourrer (**with** de); (*put, thrust*) fourrer (**into** dans); (*chicken etc*) *Culin* farcir; **to s. (up)** (*hole etc*) colmater; **my nose is stuffed (up)** j'ai le nez bouché. ◆**—ing** *n* (*padding*) bourre *f*; *Culin* farce *f*.

stuffy ['stʌfɪ] *a* (**-ier, -iest**) (*room etc*) mal aéré; (*formal*) *Fig* compassé; (*old-fashioned*) vieux jeu *inv*; **it smells s.** ça sent le renfermé.

stumble ['stʌmb(ə)l] *vi* trébucher (**over** sur, **against** contre); **to s. across** *or* **on** (*find*) tomber sur; **stumbling block** pierre *f* d'achoppement.

stump [stʌmp] *n* (*of tree*) souche *f*; (*of limb*) moignon *m*; (*of pencil*) bout *m*; *Cricket* piquet *m*.

stumped ['stʌmpt] *a* **to be s. by sth** (*baffled*) ne pas savoir que penser de qch.

stun [stʌn] *vt* (**-nn-**) (*daze*) étourdir; (*animal*) assommer; (*amaze*) *Fig* stupéfier. ◆**stunned** *a Fig* stupéfait (**by** par). ◆**stunning** *a* (*blow*) étourdissant; (*news*) stupéfiant; (*terrific*) *Fam* sensationnel.

stung [stʌŋ] *see* **sting**.

stunk [stʌŋk] *see* **stink**.

stunt [stʌnt] **1** *n* (*feat*) tour *m* (de force); *Cin* cascade *f*; (*ruse, trick*) truc *m*; **s. man** *Cin* cascadeur *m*; **s. woman** *Cin* cascadeuse *f*. **2** *vt* (*growth*) retarder. ◆**—ed** *a* (*person*) rabougri.

stupefy ['stju:pɪfaɪ] *vt* (*of drink etc*) abrutir; (*amaze*) *Fig* stupéfier.

stupendous [stju:'pendəs] *a* prodigieux.

stupid ['stju:pɪd] *a* stupide, bête; **a s. thing** une sottise; **s. fool, s. idiot** idiot, -ote *mf*. ◆**stu'pidity** *n* stupidité *f*. ◆**stupidly** *adv* stupidement, bêtement.

stupor ['stju:pər] *n* (*daze*) stupeur *f*.

sturdy ['stɜ:dɪ] *a* (**-ier, -iest**) (*person, shoe etc*) robuste. ◆**sturdiness** *n* robustesse *f*.

sturgeon ['stɜ:dʒ(ə)n] *n* (*fish*) esturgeon *m*.

stutter ['stʌtər] *n* bégaiement *m*; **to have a s.** être bègue; – *vi* bégayer.

sty [staɪ] *n* (*pigsty*) porcherie *f*.

sty(e) [staɪ] *n* (*on eye*) orgelet *m*.

style [staɪl] *n* style *m*; (*fashion*) mode *f*; (*design of dress etc*) modèle *m*; (*of hair*) coiffure *f*; (*sort*) genre *m*; **to have s.** avoir de la classe; **in s.** (*in superior manner*) de la meilleure façon possible; (*to live, travel*) dans le luxe; – *vt* (*design*) créer; **he styles himself...** *Pej* il se fait appeler...; **to s. s.o.'s hair** coiffer qn. ◆**styling** *n* (*cutting of hair*) coupe *f*. ◆**stylish** *a* chic, élégant. ◆**stylishly** *adv* élégamment. ◆**stylist** *n* (**hair**) **s.** coiffeur, -euse *mf*. ◆**sty'listic** *a* de style, stylistique. ◆**stylized** *a* stylisé.

stylus ['staɪləs] *n* (*of record player*) pointe *f* de lecture.

suave [swɑ:v] *a* (**-er, -est**) (*urbane*) courtois; *Pej* doucereux.

sub- [sʌb] *pref* sous-, sub-.

subconscious [sʌb'kɒnʃəs] *a & n* subconscient (*m*). ◆**—ly** *adv* inconsciemment.

subcontract [sʌbkən'trækt] *vt* sous-traiter. ◆**subcontractor** *n* sous-traitant *m*.

subdivide [sʌbdɪ'vaɪd] *vt* subdiviser (**into** en). ◆**subdivision** *n* subdivision *f*.

subdu/e [səb'dju:] *vt* (*country*) asservir; (*feelings*) maîtriser. ◆**—ed** *a* (*light*) atténué; (*voice*) bas; (*reaction*) faible; (*person*) qui manque d'entrain.

subheading ['sʌbhedɪŋ] *n* sous-titre *m*.

subject[1] ['sʌbdʒɪkt] *n* **1** (*matter*) & *Gram* sujet *m*; *Sch Univ* matière *f*; **s. matter** (*topic*) sujet *m*; (*content*) contenu *m*. **2** (*citizen*) ressortissant, -ante *mf*; (*of monarch, monarchy*) sujet, -ette *mf*; (*person etc in experiment*) sujet *m*.

subject[2] ['sʌbdʒekt] *a* (*tribe etc*) soumis; **s. to** (*prone to*) sujet à (*maladie etc*); (*ruled by*) soumis à (*loi, règle etc*); (*conditional upon*) sous réserve de; **prices are s. to change** les prix peuvent être modifiés; – [səb'dʒekt] *vt* soumettre (**to** à); (*expose*) exposer (**to** à). ◆**sub'jection** *n* soumission *f* (**to** à).

subjective [səb'dʒektɪv] *a* subjectif. ◆**—ly** *adv* subjectivement. ◆**subjec'tivity** *n* subjectivité *f*.

subjugate ['sʌbdʒʊgeɪt] *vt* subjuguer.

subjunctive [səb'dʒʌŋktɪv] *n Gram* subjonctif *m*.

sublet [sʌb'let] *vt* (*pt & pp* **sublet**, *pres p* **subletting**) sous-louer.

sublimate ['sʌblɪmeɪt] *vt Psy* sublimer.

sublime [sə'blaɪm] *a* sublime; (*indifference, stupidity*) suprême; – *n* sublime *m*.

submachine-gun [sʌbmə'ʃi:ngʌn] *n* mitraillette *f*.

submarine ['sʌbməri:n] *n* sous-marin *m*.

submerge [səb'mɜ:dʒ] *vt* (*flood, overwhelm*) submerger; (*immerse*) immerger (**in** dans); – *vi* (*of submarine*) s'immerger.

submit [səb'mɪt] *vt* (**-tt-**) soumettre (**to** à); **to s. that** *Jur* suggérer que; – *vi* se soumettre (**to** à). ◆**submission** *n* soumission *f* (**to** à). ◆**submissive** *a* soumis. ◆**submissively** *adv* avec soumission.

subnormal [sʌb'nɔːm(ə)l] *a* au-dessous de la normale; (*mentally*) arriéré.

subordinate [sə'bɔːdɪnət] *a* subalterne; *Gram* subordonné; – *n* subordonné, -ée *mf*; – [sə'bɔːdɪneɪt] *vt* subordonner (**to** à). ◆**subordi'nation** *n* subordination *f* (**to** à).

subpoena [səb'piːnə] *vt Jur* citer; – *n Jur* citation *f*.

subscribe [səb'skraɪb] *vt* (*money*) donner (**to** à); – *vi* cotiser; **to s. to** (*take out subscription*) s'abonner à (*journal etc*); (*be a subscriber*) être abonné à (*journal etc*); (*fund, idea*) souscrire à. ◆**subscriber** *n Journ Tel* abonné, -ée *mf*. ◆**subscription** *n* (*to newspaper etc*) abonnement *m*; (*to fund, idea*) & *Fin* souscription *f*; (*to club etc*) cotisation *f*.

subsequent ['sʌbsɪkwənt] *a* postérieur (**to** à); **our s. problems** les problèmes que nous avons eus par la suite; **s. to** (*as a result of*) consécutif à. ◆**—ly** *adv* par la suite.

subservient [səb'sɜːvɪənt] *a* obséquieux; **to be s. to** (*a slave to*) être asservi à.

subside [səb'saɪd] *vi* (*of building, land*) s'affaisser; (*of wind, flood*) baisser. ◆**'subsidence** *n* affaissement *m*.

subsidiary [səb'sɪdɪərɪ] *a* accessoire; (*subject*) *Univ* secondaire; – *n* (*company*) *Com* filiale *f*.

subsidize ['sʌbsɪdaɪz] *vt* subventionner. ◆**subsidy** *n* subvention *f*.

subsist [səb'sɪst] *vi* (*of person, doubts etc*) subsister. ◆**subsistence** *n* subsistance *f*.

substance ['sʌbstəns] *n* substance *f*; (*firmness*) solidité *f*; **a man of s.** un homme riche. ◆**substantial** [səb'stænʃ(ə)l] *a* important, considérable; (*meal*) substantiel. ◆**sub'stantially** *adv* considérablement, beaucoup; **s. true**/*etc* (*to a great extent*) en grande partie vrai/*etc*; **s. different** très différent.

substandard [sʌb'stændəd] *a* de qualité inférieure.

substantiate [səb'stænʃɪeɪt] *vt* prouver, justifier.

substitute ['sʌbstɪtjuːt] *n* (*thing*) produit *m* de remplacement; (*person*) remplaçant, -ante *mf* (**for** de); **there's no s. for . . .** rien ne peut remplacer . . . ; – *vt* substituer (**for** à); – *vi* **to s. for** remplacer; (*deputize for in job*) se substituer à. ◆**substi'tution** *n* substitution *f*.

subtitle ['sʌbtaɪt(ə)l] *n* sous-titre *m*; – *vt* sous-titrer.

subtle ['sʌt(ə)l] *a* (**-er, -est**) subtil. ◆**subtlety** *n* subtilité *f*. ◆**subtly** *adv* subtilement.

subtotal [sʌb'təʊt(ə)l] *n* total *m* partiel, sous-total *m*.

subtract [səb'trækt] *vt* soustraire (**from** de). ◆**subtraction** *n* soustraction *f*.

suburb ['sʌbɜːb] *n* banlieue *f*; **the suburbs** la banlieue; **in the suburbs** en banlieue. ◆**su'burban** *a* (*train*) de banlieue; (*accent*) de la banlieue. ◆**su'burbia** *n* la banlieue.

subversive [səb'vɜːsɪv] *a* subversif. ◆**subversion** *n* subversion *f*. ◆**subvert** *vt* (*system etc*) bouleverser; (*person*) corrompre.

subway ['sʌbweɪ] *n* passage *m* souterrain; *Rail Am* métro *m*.

succeed [sək'siːd] **1** *vi* réussir (**in doing** à faire, **in sth** dans qch). **2** *vt* **to s. s.o.** (*follow*) succéder à qn; – *vi* **to s. to the throne** succéder à la couronne. ◆**—ing** *a* (*in past*) suivant; (*in future*) futur; (*consecutive*) consécutif.

success [sək'ses] *n* succès *m*, réussite *f*; **to make a s. of sth** réussir qch; **he was a s.** il a eu du succès; **his** *or* **her s. in the exam** sa réussite à l'examen; **s. story** réussite *f* complète *or* exemplaire. ◆**successful** *a* (*venture etc*) couronné de succès, réussi; (*outcome*) heureux; (*firm*) prospère; (*candidate in exam*) admis, reçu; (*in election*) élu; (*writer, film etc*) à succès; **to be s.** réussir (**in** dans, **in an exam** à un examen, **in doing** à faire). ◆**successfully** *adv* avec succès.

succession [sək'seʃ(ə)n] *n* succesion *f*; **in s.** successivement; **ten days in s.** dix jours consécutifs; **in rapid s.** coup sur coup. ◆**successive** *a* successif; **ten s. days** dix jours consécutifs. ◆**successor** *n* successeur *m* (**of, to** de).

succinct [sək'sɪŋkt] *a* succinct.

succulent ['sʌkjʊlənt] *a* succulent.

succumb [sə'kʌm] *vi* (*yield*) succomber (**to** à).

such [sʌtʃ] *a* tel; **s. a car**/*etc* une telle voiture/*etc*; **s. happiness**/*etc* (*so much*) tant *or* tellement de bonheur/*etc*; **there's no s. thing** ça n'existe pas; **I said no s. thing** je n'ai rien dit de tel; **s. as** comme, tel que; **s. and s.** tel ou tel; – *adv* (*so very*) si; (*in comparisons*) aussi; **s. a kind woman as you** une femme aussi gentille que vous; **s. long trips** de si longs voyages; **s. a large helping** une si grosse portion; – *pron* **happiness**/*etc* **as s.** le bonheur/*etc* en tant que tel; **s. was**

my idea telle était mon idée. ◆**suchlike** *n* . . . **and s.** *Fam* . . . et autres.

suck [sʌk] *vt* sucer; (*of baby*) têter (*lait, biberon etc*); **to s. (up)** (*with straw, pump*) aspirer; **to s. up** *or* **in** (*absorb*) absorber; – *vi* (*of baby*) têter; **to s. at** sucer. ◆**—er** *n* **1** (*fool*) *Fam* pigeon *m*, dupe *f*. **2** (*pad*) ventouse *f*.

suckle ['sʌk(ə)l] *vt* (*of woman*) allaiter; (*of baby*) têter.

suction ['sʌkʃ(ə)n] *n* succion *f*; **s. disc, s. pad** ventouse *f*.

Sudan [suː'dɑːn] *n* Soudan *m*.

sudden ['sʌd(ə)n] *a* soudain, subit; **all of a s.** tout à coup. ◆**—ly** *adv* subitement. ◆**—ness** *n* soudaineté *f*.

suds [sʌdz] *npl* mousse *f* de savon.

sue [suː] *vt* poursuivre (en justice); – *vi* engager des poursuites (judiciaires).

suede [sweɪd] *n* daim *m*; – *a* de daim.

suet ['suːɪt] *n* graisse *f* de rognon.

suffer ['sʌfər] *vi* souffrir (**from** de); **to s. from pimples/the flu** avoir des boutons/la grippe; **your work/*etc* will s.** ton travail/*etc* s'en ressentira; – *vt* (*attack, loss etc*) subir; (*pain*) ressentir; (*tolerate*) souffrir. ◆**—ing** *n* souffrance(s) *f*(*pl*). ◆**—er** *n Med* malade *mf*; (*from misfortune*) victime *f*.

suffice [sə'faɪs] *vi* suffire.

sufficient [sə'fɪʃ(ə)nt] *a* (*quantity, number*) suffisant; **s. money/*etc*** (*enough*) suffisamment d'argent/*etc*; **to have s.** en avoir suffisamment. ◆**—ly** *adv* suffisamment.

suffix ['sʌfɪks] *n Gram* suffixe *m*.

suffocate ['sʌfəkeɪt] *vti* étouffer, suffoquer. ◆**suffo'cation** *n* (*of industry, mind etc*) & *Med* étouffement *m*, asphyxie *f*.

suffrage ['sʌfrɪdʒ] *n* (*right to vote*) *Pol* suffrage *m*.

suffused [sə'fjuːzd] *a* **s. with** (*light, tears*) baigné de.

sugar ['ʃʊgər] *n* sucre *m*; – *a* (*cane, tongs*) à sucre; (*industry*) sucrier; **s. bowl** sucrier *m*; – *vt* sucrer. ◆**sugary** *a* (*taste, tone*) sucré.

suggest [sə'dʒest] *vt* (*propose*) suggérer, proposer (**to** à, **that** que (+ *sub*)); (*evoke, imply*) suggérer; (*hint*) *Pej* insinuer. ◆**suggestion** *n* suggestion *f*, proposition *f*; (*evocation*) suggestion *f*; *Pej* insinuation *f*. ◆**suggestive** *a* suggestif; **to be s. of** suggérer.

suicide ['suːɪsaɪd] *n* suicide *m*; **to commit s.** se suicider. ◆**sui'cidal** *a* suicidaire.

suit [suːt] **1** *n* (*man's*) complet *m*, costume *m*; (*woman's*) tailleur *m*; (*of pilot, diver etc*) combinaison *f*. **2** *n* (*lawsuit*) *Jur* procès *m*. **3** *n Cards* couleur *f*. **4** *vt* (*satisfy, be appropriate to*) convenir à; (*of dress, colour etc*) aller (bien) à; (*adapt*) adapter (**to** à); **it suits me to stay** ça m'arrange de rester; **s. yourself!** comme tu voudras!; **suited to** (*made for*) fait pour; (*appropriate to*) approprié à; **well suited** (*couple etc*) bien assorti. ◆**suita'bility** *n* (*of remark etc*) à-propos *m*; (*of person*) aptitudes *fpl* (**for** pour); **I'm not sure of the s. of it** (*date etc*) je ne sais pas si ça convient. ◆**suitable** *a* qui convient (**for** à); (*dress, colour*) qui va (bien); (*example*) approprié; (*socially*) convenable. ◆**suitably** *adv* convenablement.

suitcase ['suːtkeɪs] *n* valise *f*.

suite [swiːt] *n* (*rooms*) suite *f*; (*furniture*) mobilier *m*; **bedroom s.** (*furniture*) chambre *f* à coucher.

suitor ['suːtər] *n* soupirant *m*.

sulfur ['sʌlfər] *n Am* soufre *m*.

sulk [sʌlk] *vi* bouder. ◆**sulky** *a* (**-ier, -iest**) boudeur.

sullen ['sʌlən] *a* maussade. ◆**—ly** *adv* d'un air maussade.

sully ['sʌlɪ] *vt Lit* souiller.

sulphur ['sʌlfər] *n* soufre *m*.

sultan ['sʌltən] *n* sultan *m*.

sultana [sʌl'tɑːnə] *n* raisin *m* de Smyrne.

sultry ['sʌltrɪ] *a* (**-ier, -iest**) (*heat*) étouffant; *Fig* sensuel.

sum [sʌm] **1** *n* (*amount, total*) somme *f*; *Math* calcul *m*; *pl* (*arithmetic*) le calcul; **s. total** résultat *m*. **2** *vt* (**-mm-**) **to s. up** (*facts etc*) récapituler, résumer; (*text*) résumer; (*situation*) évaluer; (*person*) jauger; – *vi* **to s. up** récapituler. ◆**summing-'up** *n* (*pl* **summings-up**) résumé *m*.

summarize ['sʌməraɪz] *vt* résumer. ◆**summary** *n* résumé *m*; – *a* (*brief*) sommaire.

summer ['sʌmər] *n* été *m*; **in (the) s.** en été; **Indian s.** été indien *or* de la Saint-Martin; – *a* d'été; **s. holidays** grandes vacances *fpl*. ◆**summerhouse** *n* pavillon *m* (de jardien). ◆**summertime** *n* été *m*; **in (the) s.** en été. ◆**summery** *a* (*weather etc*) estival; (*dress*) d'été.

summit ['sʌmɪt] *n* (*of mountain, power etc*) sommet *m*; **s. conference/meeting** *Pol* conférence *f*/rencontre *f* au sommet.

summon ['sʌmən] *vt* (*call*) appeler; (*meeting, s.o. to meeting*) convoquer (**to** à); **to s. s.o. to do** sommer qn de faire; **to s. up** (*courage, strength*) rassembler.

summons ['sʌmənz] *n Jur* assignation *f*; – *vt Jur* assigner.

sumptuous ['sʌmptʃʊəs] *a* somptueux. ◆**—ness** *n* somptuosité *f*.

sun [sʌn] *n* soleil *m*; **in the s.** au soleil; **the**

sun's shining il fait (du) soleil; – *a* (*cream, filter etc*) solaire; **s. lounge** solarium *m*; – *vt* (**-nn-**) **to s. oneself** se chauffer au soleil. ◆**sunbaked** *a* brûlé par le soleil. ◆**sunbathe** *vi* prendre un bain de soleil. ◆**sunbeam** *n* rayon *m* de soleil. ◆**sunburn** *n* (*tan*) bronzage *m*; *Med* coup *m* de soleil. ◆**sunburnt** *a* bronzé; *Med* brûlé par le soleil. ◆**sundial** *n* cadran *m* solaire. ◆**sundown** *n* coucher *m* du soleil. ◆**sundrenched** *a* brûlé par le soleil. ◆**sunflower** *n* tournesol *m*. ◆**sunglasses** *npl* lunettes *fpl* de soleil. ◆**sunlamp** *n* lampe *f* à rayons ultraviolets. ◆**sunlight** *n* (lumière *f* du) soleil *m*. ◆**sunlit** *a* ensoleillé. ◆**sunrise** *n* lever *m* du soleil. ◆**sunroof** *n Aut* toit *m* ouvrant. ◆**sunset** *n* coucher *m* du soleil. ◆**sunshade** *n* (*on table*) parasol *m*; (*portable*) ombrelle *f*. ◆**sunshine** *n* soleil *m*. ◆**sunstroke** *n* insolation *f*. ◆**suntan** *n* bronzage *m*; – *a* (*lotion, oil*) solaire. ◆**suntanned** *a* bronzé. ◆**sunup** *n Am* lever *m* du soleil.

sundae ['sʌndeɪ] *n* glace *f* aux fruits.

Sunday ['sʌndɪ] *n* dimanche *m*.

sundry ['sʌndrɪ] *a* divers; **all and s.** tout le monde; – *npl Com* articles *mpl* divers.

sung [sʌŋ] *see* **sing**.

sunk [sʌŋk] *see* **sink**[2]; – *a* **I'm s.** *Fam* je suis fichu. ◆**sunken** *a* (*rock etc*) submergé; (*eyes*) cave.

sunny ['sʌnɪ] *a* (**-ier, -iest**) ensoleillé; **it's s.** il fait (du) soleil; **s. period** *Met* éclaircie *f*.

super ['suːpər] *a Fam* sensationnel.

super- ['suːpər] *pref* super-.

superannuation [suːpərænjʊ'eɪʃ(ə)n] *n* (*amount*) cotisations *fpl* (pour la) retraite.

superb [suː'pɜːb] *a* superbe.

supercilious [suːpə'sɪlɪəs] *a* hautain.

superficial [suːpə'fɪʃ(ə)l] *a* superficiel. ◆**—ly** *adv* superficiellement.

superfluous [suː'pɜːflʊəs] *a* superflu.

superhuman [suːpə'hjuːmən] *a* surhumain.

superimpose [suːpərɪm'pəʊz] *vt* superposer (**on** à).

superintendent [suːpərɪn'tendənt] *n* directeur, -trice *mf*; (**police**) **s.** commissaire *m* (de police).

superior [su'pɪərɪər] *a* supérieur (**to** à); (*goods*) de qualité supérieure; – *n* (*person*) supérieur, -eure *mf*. ◆**superi'ority** *n* supériorité *f*.

superlative [suː'pɜːlətɪv] *a* sans pareil; – *a* & *n Gram* superlatif (*m*).

superman ['suːpəmæn] *n* (*pl* **-men**) surhomme *m*.

supermarket ['suːpəmɑːkɪt] *n* supermarché *m*.

supernatural [suːpə'nætʃ(ə)rəl] *a* & *n* surnaturel (*m*).

superpower ['suːpəpaʊər] *n Pol* superpuissance *f*.

supersede [suːpə'siːd] *vt* remplacer, supplanter.

supersonic [suːpə'sɒnɪk] *a* supersonique.

superstition [suːpə'stɪʃ(ə)n] *n* superstition *f*. ◆**superstitious** *a* superstitieux.

supertanker ['suːpətæŋkər] *n* pétrolier *m* géant.

supervise ['suːpəvaɪz] *vt* (*person, work*) surveiller; (*office, research*) diriger. ◆**super'vision** *n* surveillance *f*; direction *f*. ◆**supervisor** *n* surveillant, -ante *mf*; (*in office*) chef *m* de service; (*shop*) chef *m* de rayon. ◆**super'visory** *a* (*post*) de surveillant(e).

supper ['sʌpər] *n* dîner *m*; (*late-night*) souper *m*.

supple ['sʌp(ə)l] *a* souple. ◆**—ness** *n* souplesse *f*.

supplement ['sʌplɪmənt] *n* (*addition*) & *Journ* supplément *m* (**to** à); – ['sʌplɪment] *vt* compléter; **to s. one's income** arrondir ses fins de mois. ◆**supple'mentary** *a* supplémentaire.

supply [sə'plaɪ] *vt* (*provide*) fournir; (*feed*) alimenter (**with** en); (*equip*) équiper, pourvoir (**with** de); **to s. a need** subvenir à un besoin; **to s. s.o. with sth, s. sth to s.o.** (*facts etc*) fournir qch à qn; – *n* (*stock*) provision *f*, réserve *f*; (*equipment*) matériel *m*; **the s. of** (*act*) la fourniture de; **the s. of gas/electricity to** l'alimentation *f* en gaz/électricité de; (**food**) **supplies** vivres *mpl*; (**office**) **supplies** fournitures *fpl* (de bureau); **s. and demand** l'offre *f* et la demande; **to be in short s.** manquer; – *a* (*ship, train*) ravitailleur; **s. teacher** suppléant, -ante *mf*. ◆**—ing** *n* (*provision*) fourniture *f*; (*feeding*) alimentation *f*. ◆**supplier** *n Com* fournisseur *m*.

support [sə'pɔːt] *vt* (*bear weight of*) soutenir, supporter; (*help, encourage*) soutenir, appuyer; (*theory, idea*) appuyer; (*be in favour of*) être en faveur de; (*family, wife etc*) assurer la subsistance de; (*endure*) supporter; – *n* (*help, encouragement*) appui *m*, soutien *m*; *Tech* support *m*; **means of s.** moyens *mpl* de subsistance; **in s. of** en faveur de; (*evidence, theory*) à l'appui de. ◆**—ing** *a* (*role*) *Th Cin* secondaire; (*actor*) qui a un rôle secondaire. ◆**supporter** *n* partisan, -ane *mf*; *Fb* supporter *m*. ◆**supportive** *a* to be s. prêter son appui (of, to à).

suppos/e [sə'pəʊz] *vti* supposer (that que); I'm supposed to work *or* be working (*ought*) je suis censé travailler; he's s. to be rich on le dit riche; I s. (so) je pense; I don't s. so, I s. not je ne pense pas; you're tired, I s. vous êtes fatigué, je suppose; s. *or* supposing we go (*suggestion*) si nous partions; s. *or* supposing (that) you're right supposons que tu aies raison. ◆**—ed** *a* soi-disant. ◆**—edly** [-ɪdlɪ] *adv* soi-disant. ◆**suppo'sition** *n* supposition *f*.

suppository [sə'pɒzɪtərɪ] *n Med* suppositoire *m*.

suppress [sə'pres] *vt* (*put an end to*) supprimer; (*feelings*) réprimer; (*scandal, yawn etc*) étouffer. ◆**suppression** *n* suppression *f*; répression *f*. ◆**suppressor** *n El* dispositif *m* antiparasite.

supreme [suː'priːm] *a* suprême. ◆**supremacy** *n* suprématie *f* (over sur).

supremo [suː'priːməʊ] *n* (*pl* -os) *Fam* grand chef *m*.

surcharge ['sɜːtʃɑːdʒ] *n* (*extra charge*) supplément *m*; (*on stamp*) surcharge *f*; (*tax*) surtaxe *f*.

sure [ʃʊər] *a* (-er, -est) sûr (of de, that que); she's s. to accept il est sûr qu'elle acceptera; it's s. to snow il va sûrement neiger; to make s. of s'assurer de; for s. à coup sûr, pour sûr; s.!, *Fam* s. thing! bien sûr!; s. enough (*in effect*) en effet; it s. is cold *Am* il fait vraiment froid; be s. to do it! ne manquez pas de le faire! ◆**surefire** *a* infaillible. ◆**surely** *adv* (*certainly*) sûrement; s. he didn't refuse? (*I think, I hope*) il n'a tout de même pas refusé.

surety ['ʃʊərətɪ] *n* caution *f*.

surf [sɜːf] *n* (*foam*) ressac *m*. ◆**surfboard** *n* planche *f* (de surf). ◆**surfing** *n Sp* surf *m*.

surface ['sɜːfɪs] *n* surface *f*; s. area superficie *f*; s. mail courrier *m* par voie(s) de surface; on the s. (*to all appearances*) *Fig* en apparence; – *vt* (*road*) revêtir; – *vi* (*of swimmer etc*) remonter à la surface; (*of ideas, person etc*) *Fam* apparaître.

surfeit ['sɜːfɪt] *n* (*excess*) excès *m* (of de).

surge [sɜːdʒ] *n* (*of sea, enthusiasm*) vague *f*; (*rise*) montée *f*; – *vi* (*of crowd, hatred*) déferler; (*rise*) monter; to s. forward se lancer en avant.

surgeon ['sɜːdʒ(ə)n] *n* chirurgien *m*. ◆**surgery** *n* (*science*) chirurgie *f*; (*doctor's office*) cabinet *m*; (*sitting, period*) consultation *f*; to undergo s. subir une intervention. ◆**surgical** *a* chirurgical; (*appliance*) orthopédique; s. spirit alcool *m* à 90°.

surly ['sɜːlɪ] *a* (-ier, -iest) bourru. ◆**surliness** *n* air *m* bourru.

surmise [sə'maɪz] *vt* conjecturer (that que).

surmount [sə'maʊnt] *vt* (*overcome, be on top of*) surmonter.

surname ['sɜːneɪm] *n* nom *m* de famille.

surpass [sə'pɑːs] *vt* surpasser (in en).

surplus ['sɜːpləs] *n* surplus *m*; – *a* (*goods*) en surplus; some s. material/*etc* (*left over*) un surplus de tissu/*etc*; s. stock surplus *mpl*.

surpris/e [sə'praɪz] *n* surprise *f*; to give s.o. a s. faire une surprise à qn; to take s.o. by s. prendre qn au dépourvu; – *a* (*visit, result etc*) inattendu; – *vt* (*astonish*) étonner, surprendre; (*come upon*) surprendre. ◆**—ed** *a* surpris (that que (+ *sub*), at sth de qch, at seeing/*etc* de voir/*etc*); I'm s. at his *or* her stupidity sa bêtise m'étonne *or* me surprend. ◆**—ing** *a* surprenant. ◆**—ingly** *adv* étonnamment; s. (enough) he . . . chose étonnante, il . . . .

surrealistic [sərɪə'lɪstɪk] *a* (*strange*) *Fig* surréaliste.

surrender [sə'rendər] 1 *vi* (*give oneself up*) se rendre (to à); to s. to (*police*) se livrer à; – *n Mil* reddition *f*, capitulation *f*. 2 *vt* (*hand over*) remettre, rendre (to à); (*right, claim*) renoncer à.

surreptitious [sʌrəp'tɪʃəs] *a* subreptice.

surrogate ['sʌrəgət] *n* substitut *m*; s. mother mère *f* porteuse.

surround [sə'raʊnd] *vt* entourer (with de); *Mil* encercler; surrounded by entouré de. ◆**—ing** *a* environnant. ◆**—ings** *npl* environs *mpl*; (*setting*) cadre *m*.

surveillance [sɜː'veɪləns] *n* (*of prisoner etc*) surveillance *f*.

survey [sə'veɪ] *vt* (*look at*) regarder; (*review*) passer en revue; (*house etc*) inspecter; (*land*) arpenter; – ['sɜːveɪ] *n* (*investigation*) enquête *f*; (*of house etc*) inspection *f*; (*of opinion*) sondage *m*; a (general) s. of une vue générale de. ◆**sur'veying** *n* arpentage *m*. ◆**sur'veyor** *n* (arpenteur *m*) géomètre *m*; (*of house etc*) expert *m*.

survive [sə'vaɪv] *vi* (*of person, custom etc*) survivre; – *vt* survivre à. ◆**survival** *n* (*act*) survie *f*; (*relic*) vestige *m*. ◆**survivor** *n* survivant, -ante *mf*.

susceptible [sə'septəb(ə)l] *a* (*sensitive*) sensible (to à); s. to colds/*etc* (*prone to*) prédisposé aux rhumes/*etc*. ◆**suscepti'bility** *n* sensibilité *f*; prédisposition *f*; *pl* susceptibilité *f*.

suspect ['sʌspekt] *n* & *a* suspect, -ecte (*mf*); – [sə'spekt] *vt* soupçonner (**that** que, **of sth** de qch, **of doing** d'avoir fait); (*think questionable*) suspecter, douter de; **yes, I s.** oui, j'imagine.

suspend [sə'spend] *vt* **1** (*hang*) suspendre (**from** à). **2** (*stop, postpone, dismiss*) suspendre; (*passport etc*) retirer (provisoirement); (*pupil*) *Sch* renvoyer; **suspended sentence** *Jur* condamnation *f* avec sursis. ◆**suspender** *n* (*for stocking*) jarretelle *f*; *pl* (*braces*) *Am* bretelles *fpl*; **s. belt** porte-jarretelles *m inv*. ◆**suspension** *n* **1** (*stopping*) suspension *f*; (*of passport etc*) retrait *m* (provisoire). **2** (*of vehicle etc*) suspension *f*; **s. bridge** pont *m* suspendu.

suspense [sə'spens] *n* attente *f* (angoissée); (*in film, book etc*) suspense *m*; **in s.** (*person, matter*) en suspens.

suspicion [sə'spɪʃ(ə)n] *n* soupçon *m*; **to arouse s.** éveiller les soupçons; **with s.** (*distrust*) avec méfiance; **under s.** considéré comme suspect. ◆**suspicious** *a* (*person*) soupçonneux, méfiant; (*behaviour*) suspect; **s.(-looking)** (*suspect*) suspect; **to be s. of** *or* **about** (*distrust*) se méfier de. ◆**suspiciously** *adv* (*to behave etc*) d'une manière suspecte; (*to consider etc*) avec méfiance.

sustain [sə'steɪn] *vt* (*effort, theory*) soutenir; (*weight*) supporter; (*with food*) nourrir; (*life*) maintenir; (*damage, attack*) subir; (*injury*) recevoir. ◆**sustenance** *n* (*food*) nourriture *f*; (*quality*) valeur *f* nutritive.

swab [swɒb] *n* (*pad*) *Med* tampon *m*; (*specimen*) *Med* prélèvement *m*.

swagger ['swægər] *vi* (*walk*) parader; – *n* démarche *f* fanfaronne.

swallow ['swɒləʊ] **1** *vt* avaler; **to s. down** *or* **up** avaler; **to s. up** *Fig* engloutir; – *vi* avaler. **2** *n* (*bird*) hirondelle *f*.

swam [swæm] *see* **swim**.

swamp [swɒmp] *n* marais *m*, marécage *m*; – *vt* (*flood, overwhelm*) submerger (**with** de). ◆**swampy** *a* (**-ier, -iest**) marécageux.

swan [swɒn] *n* cygne *m*.

swank [swæŋk] *vi* (*show off*) *Fam* crâner, fanfaronner.

swap [swɒp] *n* échange *m*; *pl* (*stamps etc*) doubles *mpl*; – *vt* (**-pp-**) échanger (**for** contre); **to s. seats** changer de place; – *vi* échanger.

swarm [swɔːm] *n* (*of bees, people etc*) essaim *m*; – *vi* (*of streets, insects, people etc*) fourmiller (**with** de); **to s. in** (*of people*) entrer en foule.

swarthy ['swɔːðɪ] *a* (**-ier, -iest**) (*dark*) basané.

swastika ['swɒstɪkə] *n* (*Nazi emblem*) croix *f* gammée.

swat [swɒt] *vt* (**-tt-**) (*fly etc*) écraser.

sway [sweɪ] *vi* se balancer, osciller; – *vt* balancer; *Fig* influencer; – *n* balancement *m*; *Fig* influence *f*.

swear ['sweər] *vt* (*pt* **swore**, *pp* **sworn**) jurer (**to do** de faire, **that** que); **to s. an oath** prêter serment; **to s. s.o. to secrecy** faire jurer le silence à qn; **sworn enemies** ennemis *mpl* jurés; – *vi* (*take an oath*) jurer (**to sth** de qch); (*curse*) jurer, pester (**at** contre); **she swears by this lotion** elle ne jure que par cette lotion. ◆**swearword** *n* gros mot *m*, juron *m*.

sweat [swet] *n* sueur *f*; **s. shirt** sweat-shirt *m*; – *vi* (*of person, wall etc*) suer (**with** de); – *vt* **to s. out** (*cold*) *Med* se débarrasser de (*en transpirant*). ◆**sweater** *n* (*garment*) pull *m*. ◆**sweaty** *a* (**-ier, -iest**) (*shirt etc*) plein de sueur; (*hand*) moite; (*person*) (tout) en sueur, (tout) en nage.

swede [swiːd] *n* (*vegetable*) rutabaga *m*.

Swede [swiːd] *n* Suédois, -oise *mf*. ◆**Sweden** *n* Suède *f*. ◆**Swedish** *a* suédois; – *n* (*language*) suédois *m*.

sweep [swiːp] *n* coup *m* de balai; (*movement*) *Fig* (large) mouvement *m*; (*curve*) courbe *f*; **to make a clean s.** (*removal*) faire table rase (**of** de); (*victory*) remporter une victoire totale; – *vt* (*pt* & *pp* **swept**) (*with broom*) balayer; (*chimney*) ramoner; (*river*) draguer; **to s. away** *or* **out** *or* **up** balayer; **to s. away** *or* **along** (*carry off*) emporter; **to s. aside** (*dismiss*) écarter; – *vi* **to s. (up)** balayer; **to s. in** (*of person*) *Fig* entrer rapidement *or* majestueusement; **to s. through** (*of fear etc*) saisir (*groupe etc*); (*of disease etc*) ravager (*pays etc*). ◆**—ing** *a* (*gesture*) large; (*change*) radical; (*statement*) trop général. ◆**sweepstake** *n* (*lottery*) sweepstake *m*.

sweet [swiːt] *a* (**-er, -est**) (*not sour*) doux; (*agreeable*) agréable, doux; (*tea, coffee etc*) sucré; (*person, house, kitchen*) mignon, gentil; **to have a s. tooth** aimer les sucreries; **to be s.-smelling** sentir bon; **s. corn** maïs *m*; **s. pea** *Bot* pois *m* de senteur; **s. potato** patate *f* douce; **s. shop** confiserie *f*; **s. talk** *Fam* cajoleries *fpl*, douceurs *fpl*; – *n* (*candy*) bonbon *m*; (*dessert*) dessert *m*; **my s.!** (*darling*) mon ange! ◆**sweeten** *vt* (*tea etc*) sucrer; *Fig* adoucir. ◆**sweetener** *n* saccharine *f*. ◆**sweetie** *n* (*darling*) *Fam* chéri, -ie *mf*. ◆**sweetly** *adv* (*kindly*) genti-

ment; (*softly*) doucement. ◆**sweetness** *n* douceur *f*; (*taste*) goût *m* sucré.
sweetbread ['swiːtbred] *n* ris *m* de veau *or* d'agneau.
sweetheart ['swiːthɑːt] *n* (*lover*) ami, -ie *mf*; my s.! (*darling*) mon ange!
swell [swel] **1** *n* (*of sea*) houle *f*. **2** *a* (*very good*) *Am Fam* formidable. **3** *vi* (*pt* **swelled**, *pp* **swollen** *or* **swelled**) se gonfler; (*of river, numbers*) grossir; **to s. (up)** *Med* enfler, gonfler; – *vt* (*river, numbers*) grossir. ◆**—ing** *n Med* enflure *f*.
swelter ['sweltər] *vi* étouffer. ◆**—ing** *a* étouffant; **it's s.** on étouffe.
swept [swept] *see* **sweep**.
swerve [swɜːv] *vi* (*while running etc*) faire un écart; (*of vehicle*) faire une embardée.
swift [swɪft] **1** *a* (**-er, -est**) rapide; **s. to act** prompt à agir. **2** *n* (*bird*) martinet *m*. ◆**—ly** *adv* rapidement. ◆**—ness** *n* rapidité *f*.
swig [swɪg] *n* (*of beer etc*) lampée *f*.
swill [swɪl] *vt* **to s. (out** *or* **down)** laver (à grande eau).
swim [swɪm] *n* baignade *f*; **to go for a s.** se baigner, nager; – *vi* (*pt* **swam**, *pp* **swum**, *pres p* **swimming**) nager; *Sp* faire de la natation; (*of head, room*) *Fig* tourner; **to go swimming** aller nager; **to s. away** se sauver (à la nage); – *vt* (*river*) traverser à la nage; (*length, crawl etc*) nager. ◆**swimming** *n* natation *f*; **s. costume** maillot *m* de bain; **s. pool, s. baths** piscine *f*; **s. trunks** slip *m* or caleçon *m* de bain. ◆**swimmer** *n* nageur, -euse *mf*. ◆**swimsuit** *n* maillot *m* de bain.
swindl/e ['swɪnd(ə)l] *n* escroquerie *f*; – *vt* escroquer; **to s. s.o. out of money** escroquer de l'argent à qn. ◆**—er** *n* escroc *m*.
swine [swaɪn] *n inv* (*person*) *Pej* salaud *m*.
swing [swɪŋ] *n* (*seat*) balançoire *f*; (*movement*) balancement *m*; (*of pendulum*) oscillation *f*; (*in opinion*) revirement *m*; (*rhythm*) rythme *m*; **to be in full s.** battre son plein; **to be in the s. of things** *Fam* être dans le bain; **s. door** porte *f* de saloon; – *vi* (*pt & pp* **swung**) (*sway*) se balancer; (*of pendulum*) osciller; (*turn*) virer; **to s. round** (*turn suddenly*) virer, tourner; (*of person*) se retourner (vivement); (*of vehicle in collision etc*) faire un tête-à-queue; **to s. into action** passer à l'action; – *vt* (*arms etc*) balancer; (*axe*) brandir; (*influence*) *Fam* influencer; **to s. round** (*car etc*) faire tourner. ◆**—ing** *a Fam* (*trendy*) dans le vent; (*lively*) plein de vie; (*music*) entraînant.
swingeing ['swɪndʒɪŋ] *a* **s. cuts** des réductions *fpl* draconiennes.
swipe [swaɪp] *vt Fam* (*hit*) frapper dur; (*steal*) piquer (**from s.o.** à qn): – *n Fam* grand coup *m*.
swirl [swɜːl] *n* tourbillon *m*; – *vi* tourbillonner.
swish [swɪʃ] **1** *a* (*posh*) *Fam* rupin, chic. **2** *vi* (*of whip etc*) siffler; (*of fabric*) froufrouter; – *n* sifflement *m*; froufrou *m*.
Swiss [swɪs] *a* suisse; – *n inv* Suisse *m*, Suissesse *f*; **the S.** les Suisses *mpl*.
switch [swɪtʃ] *n El* bouton *m* (électrique), interrupteur *m*; (*change*) changement *m* (**in** de); (*reversal*) revirement *m* (**in** de); – *vt* (*money, employee etc*) transférer (**to** à); (*affection, support*) reporter (**to** sur, **from** de); (*exchange*) échanger (**for** contre); **to s. buses/***etc* changer de bus/*etc*; **to s. places** *or* **seats** changer de place; **to s. off** (*lamp, gas, radio etc*) éteindre; (*engine*) arrêter; **to s. itself off** (*of heating etc*) s'éteindre tout seul; **to s. on** (*lamp, gas, radio etc*) mettre, allumer; (*engine*) mettre en marche; – *vi* **to s. (over) to** passer à; **to s. off** (*switch off light, radio etc*) éteindre; **to s. on** (*switch on light, radio etc*) allumer. ◆**switchback** *n* (*at funfair*) montagnes *fpl* russes. ◆**switchblade** *n Am* couteau *m* à cran d'arrêt. ◆**switchboard** *n Tel* standard *m*; **s. operator** standardiste *mf*.
Switzerland ['swɪtsələnd] *n* Suisse *f*.
swivel ['swɪv(ə)l] *vi* (**-ll-**, *Am* **-l-**) **to s. (round)** (*of chair etc*) pivoter; – *a* **s. chair** fauteuil *m* pivotant.
swollen ['swəʊl(ə)n] *see* **swell 3**; – *a* (*leg etc*) enflé.
swoon [swuːn] *vi Lit* se pâmer.
swoop [swuːp] **1** *vi* **to s. (down) on** (*of bird*) fondre sur. **2** *n* (*of police*) descente *f*; – *vi* faire une descente (**on** dans).
swop [swɒp] *n, vt & vi* = **swap**.
sword [sɔːd] *n* épée *f*. ◆**swordfish** *n* espadon *m*.
swore, sworn [swɔːr, swɔːn] *see* **swear**.
swot [swɒt] *vti* (**-tt-**) **to s. (up)** (*study*) *Fam* potasser; **to s. (up) for** (*exam*), **to s. up on** (*subject*) *Fam* potasser; – *n Pej Fam* bûcheur, -euse *mf*.
swum [swʌm] *see* **swim**.
swung [swʌŋ] *see* **swing**.
sycamore ['sɪkəmɔːr] *n* (*maple*) sycomore *m*; (*plane*) *Am* platane *m*.
sycophant ['sɪkəfænt] *n* flagorneur, -euse *mf*.
syllable ['sɪləb(ə)l] *n* syllabe *f*.
syllabus ['sɪləbəs] *n Sch Univ* programme *m*.
symbol ['sɪmb(ə)l] *n* symbole *m*. ◆**sym-**

'bolic *a* symbolique. ◆**symbolism** *n* symbolisme *m.* ◆**symbolize** *vt* symboliser.

symmetry ['sɪmətrɪ] *n* symétrie *f.* ◆**sy'mmetrical** *a* symétrique.

sympathy ['sɪmpəθɪ] *n* (*pity*) compassion *f*; (*understanding*) compréhension *f*; (*condolences*) condoléances *fpl*; (*solidarity*) solidarité *f* (**for** avec); **to be in s. with** (*workers in dispute*) être du côté de; (*s.o.'s opinion etc*) comprendre, être en accord avec. ◆**sympa'thetic** *a* (*showing pity*) compatissant; (*understanding*) compréhensif; **s. to** (*favourable*) bien disposé à l'égard de. ◆**sympa'thetically** *adv* avec compassion; avec compréhension. ◆**sympathize** *vi* **I s. (with you)** (*pity*) je compatis (à votre sort); (*understanding*) je vous comprends. ◆**sympathizer** *n Pol* sympathisant, -ante *mf.*

symphony ['sɪmfənɪ] *n* symphonie *f*; – *a* (*orchestra, concert*) symphonique. ◆**sym'phonic** *a* symphonique.

symposium [sɪm'pəʊzɪəm] *n* symposium *m.*

symptom ['sɪmptəm] *n* symptôme *m.* ◆**sympto'matic** *a* symptomatique (**of** de).

synagogue ['sɪnəgɒg] *n* synagogue *f.*

synchronize ['sɪŋkrənaɪz] *vt* synchroniser.

syndicate ['sɪndɪkət] *n* (*of businessmen, criminals*) syndicat *m.*

syndrome ['sɪndrəʊm] *n Med & Fig* syndrome *m.*

synod ['sɪnəd] *n Rel* synode *m.*

synonym ['sɪnənɪm] *n* synonyme *m.* ◆**sy'nonymous** *a* synonyme (**with** de).

synopsis, *pl* **-opses** [sɪ'nɒpsɪs, -ɒpsiːz] *n* résumé *m,* synopsis *m*; (*of film*) synopsis *m.*

syntax ['sɪntæks] *n Gram* syntaxe *f.*

synthesis, *pl* **-theses** ['sɪnθəsɪs, -θəsiːz] *n* synthèse *f.*

synthetic [sɪn'θetɪk] *a* synthétique.

syphilis ['sɪfɪlɪs] *n* syphilis *f.*

Syria ['sɪrɪə] *n* Syrie *f.* ◆**Syrian** *a & n* syrien, -ienne (*mf*).

syringe [sɪ'rɪndʒ] *n* seringue *f.*

syrup ['sɪrəp] *n* sirop *m*; **(golden) s.** (*treacle*) mélasse *f* (raffinée). ◆**syrupy** *a* sirupeux.

system ['sɪstəm] *n* (*structure, plan, network etc*) & *Anat* système *m*; (*human body*) organisme *m*; (*order*) méthode *f*; **systems analyst** analyste-programmeur *mf.* ◆**syste'matic** *a* systématique. ◆**syste'matically** *adv* systématiquement.

T

T, t [tiː] *n* T, t *m.* ◆**T-junction** *n Aut* intersection *f* en T. ◆**T-shirt** *n* tee-shirt *m,* T-shirt *m.*

ta! [tɑː] *int Sl* merci!

tab [tæb] *n* (*label*) étiquette *f*; (*tongue*) patte *f*; (*loop*) attache *f*; (*bill*) *Am* addition *f*; **to keep tabs on** *Fam* surveiller (de près).

tabby ['tæbɪ] *a* **t. cat** chat, chatte *mf* tigré(e).

table[1] ['teɪb(ə)l] *n* **1** (*furniture*) table *f*; **bedside/card/operating t.** table de nuit/de jeu/d'opération; **to lay** *or* **set/clear the t.** mettre/débarrasser la table; **(sitting) at the t.** à table; **t. top** dessus *m* de table. **2** (*list*) table *f*; **t. of contents** table des matières. ◆**tablecloth** *n* nappe *f.* ◆**tablemat** *n* (*of fabric*) napperon *m*; (*hard*) dessous-de-plat *m inv* ◆**tablespoon** *n* = cuiller *f* à soupe. ◆**tablespoonful** *n* = cuillerée *f* à soupe.

table[2] ['teɪb(ə)l] *vt* (*motion etc*) *Pol* présenter; (*postpone*) *Am* ajourner.

tablet ['tæblɪt] *n* **1** (*pill*) *Med* comprimé *m.* **2** (*inscribed stone*) plaque *f.*

tabloid ['tæblɔɪd] *n* (*newspaper*) quotidien *m* populaire.

taboo [tə'buː] *a & n* tabou (*m*).

tabulator ['tæbjʊleɪtər] *n* (*of typewriter*) tabulateur *m.*

tacit ['tæsɪt] *a* tacite. ◆**—ly** *adv* tacitement.

taciturn ['tæsɪtɜːn] *a* taciturne.

tack [tæk] **1** *n* (*nail*) semence *f*; (*thumbtack*) *Am* punaise *f*; **to get down to brass tacks** *Fig* en venir aux faits; – *vt* **to t. (down)** clouer. **2** *n* (*stitch*) *Tex* point *m* de bâti; – *vt* **to t. (down** *or* **on)** bâtir; **to t. on** (*add*) *Fig* (r)ajouter. **3** *vi* (*of ship*) louvoyer; – *n* (*course of action*) *Fig* voie *f.*

tackle ['tæk(ə)l] **1** *n* (*gear*) matériel *m,* équipement *m.* **2** *vt* (*task, problem etc*) s'attaquer à; (*thief etc*) saisir; *Sp* plaquer; – *n Sp* plaquage *m.*

tacky ['tækɪ] *a* (**-ier, -iest**) **1** (*wet, sticky*) collant, pas sec. **2** (*clothes, attitude etc*) *Am Fam* moche.

tact [tækt] *n* tact *m.* ◆**tactful** *a* (*remark etc*) plein de tact, diplomatique; **she's t.** elle a du tact. ◆**tactfully** *adv* avec tact. ◆**tactless** *a* qui manque de tact. ◆**tactlessly** *adv* sans tact.

tactic ['tæktɪk] *n* **a t.** une tactique; **tactics** la tactique. ◆**tactical** *a* tactique.

tactile ['tæktaɪl] *a* tactile.

tadpole ['tædpəʊl] *n* têtard *m*.

taffy ['tæfɪ] *n* (*toffee*) *Am* caramel *m* (*dur*).

tag [tæg] **1** *n* (*label*) étiquette *f*; (*end piece*) bout *m*; – *vt* (**-gg-**) **to t. on** (*add*) *Fam* rajouter (**to** à). **2** *vi* (**-gg-**) **to t. along** (*follow*) suivre.

Tahiti [tɑːˈhiːtɪ] *n* Tahiti *m*.

tail [teɪl] **1** *n* (*of animal*) queue *f*; (*of shirt*) pan *m*; *pl* (*outfit*) habit *m*, queue-de-pie *f*; **t. end** fin *f*, bout *m*; **heads or tails?** pile ou face? **2** *vt* (*follow*) suivre, filer. **3** *vi* **to t. off** (*lessen*) diminuer. ◆**tailback** *n* (*of traffic*) bouchon *m*. ◆**tailcoat** *n* queue-de-pie *f*. ◆**taillight** *n Aut Am* feu *m* arrière *inv*.

tailor ['teɪlər] *n* (*person*) tailleur *m*; – *vt* (*garment*) façonner; *Fig* adapter (**to, to suit** à). ◆**t.-'made** *a* fait sur mesure; **t.-made for** (*specially designed*) conçu pour; (*suited*) fait pour.

tainted ['teɪntɪd] *a* (*air*) pollué; (*food*) gâté; *Fig* souillé.

take [teɪk] *vt* (*pt* **took**, *pp* **taken**) prendre; (*choice*) faire; (*prize*) remporter; (*exam*) passer; (*contain*) contenir; *Math* soustraire (**from** de); (*tolerate*) supporter; (*bring*) apporter (*qch*) (**to** à), (*person*) amener (**to** à), (*person by car*) conduire (**to** à); (*escort*) accompagner (**to** à); (*lead away*) emmener; (*of road*) mener (*qn*): **to t. sth to s.o.** (ap)porter qch à qn; **to t. s.o. (out) to** (*theatre etc*) emmener qn à; **to t. sth with one** emporter qch; **to t. over** *or* **round** *or* **along** (*object*) apporter; (*person*) amener; **to t. s.o. home** (*on foot, by car etc*) ramener qn; **it takes an army/courage/***etc* (*requires*) il faut une armée/du courage/*etc* (**to do** pour faire); **I took an hour to do it** *or* **over it** j'ai mis une heure à le faire, ça m'a pris une heure pour le faire; **I t. it that** je présume que; – *n Cin* prise *f* de vue(s); – *vi* (*of fire*) prendre. ■ **to t. after** *vi* (*be like*) ressembler à; **to t. apart** *vt* (*machine*) démonter; **to t. away** *vt* (*thing*) emporter; (*person*) emmener; (*remove*) enlever (**from** à); *Math* soustraire (**from** de). ◆**t.-away** *a* (*meal*) à emporter; – *n* café *m or* restaurant *m* qui fait des plats à emporter; (*meal*) plat *m* à emporter; **to t. back** *vt* reprendre; (*return*) rapporter, (*statement*) retirer; **to t. down** *vt* (*object*) descendre; (*notes*) prendre; **to t. in** *vt* (*chair, car etc*) rentrer; (*orphan*) recueillir; (*skirt*) reprendre; (*include*) englober; (*distance*) couvrir; (*understand*) comprendre; (*deceive*) *Fam* rouler; **to t. off** *vt* (*remove*) enlever; (*train, bus*) supprimer; (*lead away*) emmener; (*mimic*) imiter; *Math* déduire (**from** de); – *vi* (*of aircraft*) décoller. ◆**takeoff** *n* (*of aircraft*) décollage *m*; **to t. on** *vt* (*work, employee, passenger, shape*) prendre; **to t. out** *vt* (*from pocket etc*) sortir; (*stain*) enlever; (*tooth*) arracher; (*licence, insurance*) prendre; **to t. it out on** *Fam* passer sa colère sur. ◆**t.-out** *a* & *n Am* = **t.-away**; **to t. over** *vt* (*be responsible for the running of*) prendre la direction de; (*overrun*) envahir; (*buy out*) *Com* racheter (*compagnie*); **to t. over s.o.'s job** remplacer qn; – *vi Mil Pol* prendre le pouvoir; (*relieve*) prendre la relève (**from** de); (*succeed*) prendre la succession (**from** de). ◆**t.-over** *n Com* rachat *m*; *Pol* prise *f* de pouvoir; **to t. round** *vt* (*distribute*) distribuer; (*visitor*) faire visiter; **to t. to** *vi* **to t. to doing** se mettre à faire; **I didn't t. to him/it** il/ça ne m'a pas plu; **to t. up** *vt* (*carry up*) monter; (*hem*) raccourcir; (*continue*) reprendre; (*occupy*) prendre; (*hobby*) se mettre à; – *vi* **to t. up with** se lier avec. ◆**taken** *a* (*seat*) pris; (*impressed*) impressionné (**with, by** par); **to be t. ill** tomber malade. ◆**taking** *n* (*capture*) *Mil* prise *f*; *pl* (*money*) *Com* recette *f*.

talcum ['tælkəm] *a* **t. powder** talc *m*.

tale [teɪl] *n* (*story*) conte *m*; (*account, report*) récit *m*; (*lie*) histoire *f*; **to tell tales** rapporter (**on** sur).

talent ['tælənt] *n* talent *m*; (*talented people*) talents *mpl*; **to have a t. for** avoir du talent pour. ◆**talented** *a* doué, talentueux.

talk [tɔːk] *n* (*words*) propos *mpl*; (*gossip*) bavardage(s) *m(pl)*; (*conversation*) conversation *f* (**about** à propos de); (*interview*) entretien *m*; (*lecture*) exposé *m* (**on** sur); (*informal*) causerie *f* (**on** sur); *pl* (*negotiations*) pourparlers *mpl*; **to have a t. with** parler avec; **there's t. of** on parle de; – *vi* parler (**to** à; **with** avec; **about, of** de); (*chat*) bavarder; **to t. down to s.o.** parler à qn comme à un inférieur; – *vt* (*nonsense*) dire; **to t. politics** parler politique; **to t. s.o. into doing/out of doing** persuader qn de faire/de ne pas faire; **to t. over** discuter (de); **to t. s.o. round** persuader qn. ◆**—ing** *a* (*film*) parlant; **to give s.o. a talking-to** *Fam* passer un savon à qn. ◆**talkative** *a* bavard. ◆**talker** *n* causeur, -euse *mf*; **she's a good t.** elle parle bien.

tall [tɔːl] *a* (**-er, -est**) (*person*) grand; (*tree,* *house etc*) haut; **how t. are you?** combien mesures-tu?; **a t. story** *Fig* une histoire invraisemblable *or* à dormir debout. ◆**tallboy** *n* grande commode *f*. ◆**tallness** *n* (*of person*) grande taille *f*; (*of building etc*) hauteur *f*.

tally ['tælɪ] *vi* correspondre (**with** à).

tambourine [tæmbə'riːn] *n* tambourin *m*.

tame [teɪm] *a* (**-er, -est**) (*animal, bird*) apprivoisé; (*person*) *Fig* docile; (*book, play*) fade. – *vt* (*animal, bird*) apprivoiser; (*lion, passion*) dompter.

tamper ['tæmpər] *vi* **to t. with** (*lock, car etc*) toucher à; (*text*) altérer.

tampon ['tæmpɒn] *n* tampon *m* hygiénique.

tan [tæn] **1** *n* (*suntan*) bronzage *m*; – *vti* (**-nn-**) bronzer. **2** *a* (*colour*) marron clair *inv*. **3** *vt* (**-nn-**) (*hide*) tanner.

tandem ['tændəm] *n* **1** (*bicycle*) tandem *m*. **2 in t.** (*to work etc*) en tandem.

tang [tæŋ] *n* (*taste*) saveur *f* piquante; (*smell*) odeur *f* piquante. ◆**tangy** *a* (**-ier, -iest**) piquant.

tangerine [tændʒə'riːn] *n* mandarine *f*.

tangible ['tændʒəb(ə)l] *a* tangible.

tangl/e ['tæŋg(ə)l] *n* enchevêtrement *m*; **to get into a t.** (*of rope*) s'enchevêtrer; (*of hair*) s'emmêler; (*of person*) *Fig* se mettre dans une situation pas possible. ◆**—ed** *a* enchevêtré; (*hair*) emmêlé; **to get t. = to get into a tangle.**

tank [tæŋk] *n* **1** (*for storage of water, fuel etc*) réservoir *m*; (*vat*) cuve *f*; **(fish) t.** aquarium *m*. **2** (*vehicle*) *Mil* char *m*, tank *m*.

tankard ['tæŋkəd] *n* (*beer mug*) chope *f*.

tanker ['tæŋkər] *n* (*truck*) *Aut* camion-citerne *m*; **(oil) t.** (*ship*) pétrolier *m*.

tantalizing ['tæntəlaɪzɪŋ] *a* (irrésistiblement) tentant. ◆**—ly** *adv* d'une manière tentante.

tantamount ['tæntəmaʊnt] *a* **it's t. to** cela équivaut à.

tantrum ['tæntrəm] *n* accès *m* de colère.

tap [tæp] **1** *n* (*for water*) robinet *m*; **on t.** *Fig* disponible. **2** *vti* (**-pp-**) frapper légèrement, tapoter; – *n* petit coup *m*; **t. dancing** claquettes *fpl*. **3** *vt* (**-pp-**) (*phone*) placer sur table d'écoute. **4** *vt* (**-pp-**) (*resources*) exploiter.

tape [teɪp] **1** *n* ruban *m*; **(sticky) t.** ruban adhésif; **t. measure** mètre *m* (à) ruban; – *vt* (*stick*) coller (*avec du ruban adhésif*). **2** *n* (*for sound recording*) bande *f* (magnétique); **(video) t.** bande (vidéo); **t. recorder** magnétophone *m*; – *vt* enregistrer.

taper ['teɪpər] **1** *vi* (*of fingers etc*) s'effiler; **to t. off** *Fig* diminuer. **2** *n* (*candle*) *Rel* cierge *m*. ◆**—ed** *a*, ◆**—ing** *a* (*fingers*) fuselé; (*trousers*) à bas étroits.

tapestry ['tæpəstrɪ] *n* tapisserie *f*.

tapioca [tæpɪ'əʊkə] *n* tapioca *m*.

tar [tɑːr] *n* goudron *m*; – *vt* (**-rr-**) goudronner.

tardy ['tɑːdɪ] *a* (**-ier, -iest**) (*belated*) tardif; (*slow*) lent.

target ['tɑːgɪt] *n* cible *f*; *Fig* objectif *m*; **t. date** date *f* fixée; – *vt* (*aim*) *Fig* destiner (**at** à); (*aim at*) *Fig* viser.

tariff ['tærɪf] *n* (*tax*) tarif *m* douanier; (*prices*) tarif *m*.

tarmac ['tɑːmæk] *n* macadam *m* (goudronné); (*runway*) piste *f*.

tarnish ['tɑːnɪʃ] *vt* ternir.

tarpaulin [tɑː'pɔːlɪn] *n* bâche *f* (goudronnée).

tarragon ['tærəgən] *n* *Bot Culin* estragon *m*.

tarry ['tærɪ] *vi* (*remain*) *Lit* rester.

tart [tɑːt] **1** *n* (*pie*) tarte *f*. **2** *a* (**-er, -est**) (*taste, remark*) aigre. **3** *n* (*prostitute*) *Pej Fam* poule *f*. **4** *vt* **to t. up** *Pej Fam* (*decorate*) embellir; (*dress*) attifer. ◆**—ness** *n* aigreur *f*.

tartan ['tɑːt(ə)n] *n* tartan *m*; – *a* écossais.

tartar ['tɑːtər] **1** *n* (*on teeth*) tartre *m*. **2** *a* **t. sauce** sauce *f* tartare.

task [tɑːsk] *n* tâche *f*; **to take to t.** prendre à partie; **t. force** *Mil* détachement *m* spécial; *Pol* commission *f* spéciale.

tassel ['tas(ə)l] *n* (*on clothes etc*) gland *m*.

taste [teɪst] *n* goût *m*; **to get a t. for** prendre goût à; **in good/bad t.** de bon/mauvais goût; **to have a t. of** goûter; goûter à; goûter de; – *vt* (*eat, enjoy*) goûter; (*try, sample*) goûter à; (*make out the taste of*) sentir (le goût de); (*experience*) goûter de; – *vi* **to t. of** *or* **like** avoir un goût de; **to t. delicious/***etc* avoir un goût délicieux/*etc*; **how does it t.?** comment le trouves-tu?; – *a* **t. bud** papille *f* gustative. ◆**tasteful** *a* de bon goût. ◆**tastefully** *adv* avec goût. ◆**tasteless** *a* (*food etc*) sans goût; (*joke etc*) *Fig* de mauvais goût. ◆**tasty** *a* (**-ier, -iest**) savoureux.

tat [tæt] *see* **tit 2**.

ta-ta! [tæ'tɑː] *int Sl* au revoir!

tattered ['tætəd] *a* (*clothes*) en lambeaux; (*person*) déguenillé. ◆**tatters** *npl* **in t.** en lambeaux.

tattoo [tæ'tuː] **1** *n* (*pl* **-oos**) (*on body*) tatouage *m*; – *vt* tatouer. **2** *n* (*pl* **-oos**) *Mil* spectacle *m* militaire.

tatty ['tætɪ] *a* (**-ier, -iest**) (*clothes etc*) *Fam* miteux.

taught [tɔːt] *see* **teach**.

taunt [tɔːnt] *vt* railler; – *n* raillerie *f*. ◆**—ing** *a* railleur.
Taurus ['tɔːrəs] *n* (*sign*) le Taureau.
taut [tɔːt] *a* (*rope, person etc*) tendu.
tavern ['tævən] *n* taverne *f*.
tawdry ['tɔːdrɪ] *a* (**-ier, -iest**) *Pej* tape-à-l'œil *inv*.
tawny ['tɔːnɪ] *a* (*colour*) fauve; (*port*) ambré.
tax[1] [tæks] *n* taxe *f*, impôt *m*; (**income**) **t.** impôts *mpl* (sur le revenu); – *a* fiscal; **t. collector** percepteur *m*; **t. relief** dégrèvement *m* (d'impôt); – *vt* (*person, goods*) imposer. ◆**taxable** *a* imposable. ◆**tax'ation** *n* (*act*) imposition *f*; (*taxes*) impôts *mpl*. ◆**tax-free** *a* exempt d'impôts. ◆**taxman** *n* (*pl* **-men**) *Fam* percepteur *m*. ◆**taxpayer** *n* contribuable *mf*.
tax[2] [tæks] *vt* (*patience etc*) mettre à l'épreuve; (*tire*) fatiguer. ◆**—ing** *a* (*journey etc*) éprouvant.
taxi ['tæksɪ] **1** *n* taxi *m*; **t. cab** taxi *m*; **t. rank**, *Am* **t. stand** station *f* de taxis. **2** *vi* (*of aircraft*) rouler au sol.
tea [tiː] *n* thé *m*; (*snack*) goûter *m*; **high t.** goûter *m* (dînatoire); **to have t.** prendre le thé; (*afternoon snack*) goûter; **t. break** pause-thé *f*; **t. chest** caisse *f* (à thé); **t. cloth** (*for drying dishes*) torchon *m*; **t. set** service *m* à thé; **t. towel** torchon *m*. ◆**teabag** *n* sachet *m* de thé. ◆**teacup** *n* tasse *f* à thé. ◆**tealeaf** *n* (*pl* **-leaves**) feuille *f* de thé. ◆**teapot** *n* théière *f*. ◆**tearoom** *n* salon *m* de thé. ◆**teaspoon** *n* petite cuiller *f*. ◆**teaspoonful** *n* cuillerée *f* à café. ◆**teatime** *n* l'heure *f* du thé.
teach [tiːtʃ] *vt* (*pt & pp* **taught**) apprendre (**s.o. sth** qch à qn, **that** que); (*in school etc*) enseigner (**s.o. sth** qch à qn); **to t. s.o. (how) to do** apprendre à qn à faire; **to t. school** *Am* enseigner; **to t. oneself sth** apprendre qch tout seul; – *vi* enseigner. ◆**—ing** *n* enseignement *m*; – *a* (*staff*) enseignant; (*method, material*) pédagogique; **t. profession** enseignement *m*; (*teachers*) enseignants *mpl*; **t. qualification** diplôme *m* permettant d'enseigner. ◆**—er** *n* professeur *m*; (*in primary school*) instituteur, -trice *mf*.
teak [tiːk] *n* (*wood*) teck *m*.
team [tiːm] *n Sp* équipe *f*; (*of oxen*) attelage *m*; **t. mate** coéquipier, -ière *mf*; – *vi* **to t. up** faire équipe (**with** avec). ◆**teamster** *n Am* routier *m*. ◆**teamwork** *n* collaboration *f*.
tear[1] [teər] **1** *n* déchirure *f*; – *vt* (*pt* **tore**, *pp* **torn**) (*rip*) déchirer; (*snatch*) arracher (**from s.o.** à qn); **torn between** *Fig* tiraillé entre; **to t. down** (*house etc*) démolir; **to t. away** *or* **off** *or* **out** (*forcefully*) arracher; (*stub, receipt, stamp etc*) détacher; **to t. up** déchirer; – *vi* (*of cloth etc*) se déchirer. **2** *vi* (*pt* **tore**, *pp* **torn**) **to t. along** (*rush*) aller à toute vitesse.
tear[2] [tɪər] *n* larme *f*; **in tears** en larmes; **close to** *or* **near (to) tears** au bord des larmes. ◆**tearful** *a* (*eyes, voice*) larmoyant; (*person*) en larmes. ◆**tearfully** *adv* en pleurant. ◆**teargas** *n* gaz *m* lacrymogène.
tearaway ['teərəweɪ] *n Fam* petit voyou *m*.
teas/e [tiːz] *vt* taquiner; (*harshly*) tourmenter; – *n* (*person*) taquin, -ine *mf*. ◆**—ing** *a* (*remark etc*) taquin. ◆**—er** *n* **1** (*person*) taquin, -ine *mf*. **2** (*question*) *Fam* colle *f*.
teat [tiːt] *n* (*of bottle, animal*) tétine *f*.
technical ['teknɪk(ə)l] *a* technique. ◆**techni'cality** *n* (*detail*) détail *m* technique. ◆**technically** *adv* techniquement; *Fig* théoriquement. ◆**tech'nician** *n* technicien, -ienne *mf*. ◆**tech'nique** *n* technique *f*. ◆**technocrat** *n* technocrate *m*. ◆**techno'logical** *a* technologique. ◆**tech'nology** *n* technologie *f*.
teddy ['tedɪ] *n* **t. (bear)** ours *m* (en peluche).
tedious ['tiːdɪəs] *a* fastidieux. ◆**tediousness** *n*. ◆**tedium** *n* ennui *m*.
teem [tiːm] *vi* **1** (*swarm*) grouiller (**with** de). **2 to t. (with rain)** pleuvoir à torrents. ◆**—ing** *a* **1** (*crowd, street etc*) grouillant. **2 t. rain** pluie *f* torrentielle.
teenage ['tiːneɪdʒ] *a* (*person, behaviour*) adolescent; (*fashion*) pour adolescents. ◆**teenager** *n* adolescent, -ente *mf*. ◆**teens** *npl* **in one's t.** adolescent.
teeny (weeny) ['tiːnɪ('wiːnɪ)] *a* (*tiny*) *Fam* minuscule.
tee-shirt ['tiːʃɜːt] *n* tee-shirt *m*.
teeter ['tiːtər] *vi* chanceler.
teeth [tiːθ] *see* **tooth**. ◆**teeth/e** [tiːð] *vi* faire ses dents. ◆**—ing** *n* dentition *f*; **t. ring** anneau *m* de dentition; **t. troubles** *Fig* difficultés *fpl* de mise en route.
teetotal [tiː'təʊt(ə)l] *a*. ◆**teetotaller** *n* (personne *f*) qui ne boit pas d'alcool.
tele- ['telɪ] *pref* télé-.
telecommunications [telɪkəmjuːnɪ'keɪʃ(ə)nz] *npl* télécommunications *fpl*.
telegram ['telɪgræm] *n* télégramme *m*.
telegraph ['telɪgrɑːf] *n* télégraphe *m*; – *a* (*wire etc*) télégraphique; **t. pole** poteau *m* télégraphique.
telepathy [tə'lepəθɪ] *n* télépathie *f*.
telephone ['telɪfəʊn] *n* téléphone *m*; **on the t.** (*speaking*) au téléphone; – *a* (*call, line etc*) téléphonique; (*directory*) du télé-

phone; (*number*) de téléphone; **t. booth, t. box** cabine *f* téléphonique; – *vi* téléphoner; – *vt* (*message*) téléphoner (to à); **to t. s.o.** téléphoner à qn. ◆**te'lephonist** *n* téléphoniste *mf.*

teleprinter ['telɪprɪntər] *n* téléscripteur *m.*

telescope ['telɪskəʊp] *n* télescope *m.* ◆**tele'scopic** *a* (*pictures, aerial, umbrella*) télescopique.

teletypewriter [telɪ'taɪpraɪtər] *n Am* téléscripteur *m.*

televise ['telɪvaɪz] *vt* téléviser. ◆**tele'vision** *n* télévision *f*; **on (the) t.** à la télévision; **to watch (the) t.** regarder la télévision; – *a* (*programme etc*) de télévision; (*serial, report*) télévisé.

telex ['teleks] *n* (*service, message*) télex *m*; – *vt* envoyer par télex.

tell [tel] *vt* (*pt & pp* **told**) dire (**s.o. sth** qch à qn, **that** que); (*story*) raconter; (*future*) prédire; (*distinguish*) distinguer (**from** de); (*know*) savoir; **to t. s.o. to do** dire à qn de faire; **to know how to t. the time** savoir lire l'heure; **to t. the difference** voir la différence (**between** entre); **to t. off** (*scold*) *Fam* gronder; – *vi* dire; (*have an effect*) avoir un effet; (*know*) savoir; **to t. of** *or* **about sth** parler de qch; **to t. on s.o.** *Fam* rapporter sur qn. ◆**—ing** *a* (*smile etc*) révélateur; (*blow*) efficace. ◆**telltale** *n Fam* rapporteur, -euse *mf.*

teller ['telər] *n* **(bank) t.** caissier, -ière *mf.*

telly ['telɪ] *n Fam* télé *f.*

temerity [tə'merɪtɪ] *n* témérité *f.*

temp [temp] *n* (*secretary etc*) *Fam* intérimaire *mf.*

temper ['tempər] **1** *n* (*mood, nature*) humeur *f*; (*anger*) colère *f*; **to lose one's t.** se mettre en colère; **in a bad t.** de mauvaise humeur; **to have a (bad** *or* **an awful) t.** avoir un caractère de cochon. **2** *vt* (*steel*) tremper; *Fig* tempérer.

temperament ['temp(ə)rəmənt] *n* tempérament *m.* ◆**tempera'mental** *a* (*person, machine etc*) capricieux; (*inborn*) inné.

temperance ['temp(ə)rəns] *n* (*in drink*) tempérance *f.*

temperate ['tempərət] *a* (*climate etc*) tempéré.

temperature ['temp(ə)rətʃər] *n* température *f*; **to have a t.** *Med* avoir *or* faire de la température.

tempest ['tempɪst] *n Lit* tempête *f.* ◆**tem'pestuous** *a* (*meeting etc*) orageux.

template ['templət] *n* (*of plastic, metal etc*) *Tex* patron *m*; *Math* trace-courbes *m inv.*

temple ['temp(ə)l] *n* **1** *Rel* temple *m.* **2** *Anat* tempe *f.*

tempo ['tempəʊ] *n* (*pl* **-os**) tempo *m.*

temporal ['temp(ə)rəl] *a* temporel.

temporary ['temp(ə)rərɪ] *a* provisoire; (*job, worker*) temporaire; (*secretary*) intérimaire.

tempt [tempt] *vt* tenter; **tempted to do** tenté de faire; **to t. s.o. to do** persuader qn de faire. ◆**—ing** *a* tentant. ◆**—ingly** *adv* d'une manière tentante. ◆**temp'tation** *n* tentation *f.*

ten [ten] *a & n* dix (*m*). ◆**tenfold** *a* **t. increase** augmentation *f* par dix; – *adv* **to increase t.** (se) multiplier par dix.

tenable ['tenəb(ə)l] *a* (*argument*) défendable; (*post*) qui peut etre occupé.

tenacious [tə'neɪʃəs] *a* tenace. ◆**tenacity** *n* ténacité *f.*

tenant ['tenənt] *n* locataire *nmf.* ◆**tenancy** *n* (*lease*) location *f*; (*period*) occupation *f.*

tend [tend] **1** *vt* (*look after*) s'occuper de. **2** *vi* **to t. to do** avoir tendance à faire; **to t. towards** incliner vers. ◆**tendency** *n* tendance *f* (**to do** à faire).

tendentious [ten'denʃəs] *a Pej* tendancieux.

tender¹ ['tendər] *a* (*delicate, soft, loving*) tendre; (*painful, sore*) sensible. ◆**—ly** *adv* tendrement. ◆**—ness** *n* tendresse *f*; (*soreness*) sensibilité *f*; (*of meat*) tendreté *f.*

tender² ['tendər] **1** *vt* (*offer*) offrir; **to t. one's resignation** donner sa démission. **2** *n* **to be legal t.** (*of money*) avoir cours. **3** *n* (*for services etc*) *Com* soumission *f* (**for** pour).

tendon ['tendən] *n Anat* tendon *m.*

tenement ['tenəmənt] *n* immeuble *m* (de rapport) (*Am dans un quartier pauvre*).

tenet ['tenɪt] *n* principe *m.*

tenner ['tenər] *n Fam* billet *m* de dix livres.

tennis ['tenɪs] *n* tennis *m*; **table t.** tennis de table; **t. court** court *m* (de tennis), tennis *m.*

tenor ['tenər] *n* **1** (*sense, course*) sens *m* général. **2** *Mus* ténor *m.*

tenpin ['tenpɪn] *a* **t. bowling** bowling *m.* ◆**tenpins** *n Am* bowling *m.*

tense [tens] **1** *a* (**-er, -est**) (*person, muscle, situation*) tendu; – *vt* tendre, crisper; – *vi* **to t. (up)** (*of person, face*) se crisper. **2** *n Gram* temps *m.* ◆**tenseness** *n* tension *f.* ◆**tension** *n* tension *f.*

tent [tent] *n* tente *f.*

tentacle ['tentək(ə)l] *n* tentacule *m.*

tentative ['tentətɪv] *a* (*not definite*) provisoire; (*hesitant*) timide. ◆**—ly** *adv* provisoirement; timidement.

tenterhooks ['tentəhʊks] *npl* **on t.** (*anxious*) sur des charbons ardents.

tenth [tenθ] *a* & *n* dixième (*mf*); **a t.** un dixième.

tenuous ['tenjuəs] *a* (*link, suspicion etc*) ténu.

tenure ['tenjər] *n* (*in job*) période *f* de jouissance; (*job security*) *Am* titularisation *f*.

tepid ['tepɪd] *a* (*liquid*) & *Fig* tiède.

term [tɜːm] *n* (*word, limit*) terme *m*; (*period*) période *f*; *Sch Univ* trimestre *m*; (*semester*) *Am* semestre *m*; *pl* (*conditions*) conditions *fpl*; (*prices*) *Com* prix *mpl*; **t. (of office)** *Pol* mandat *m*; **easy terms** *Fin* facilités *fpl* de paiement; **on good/bad terms** en bons/mauvais termes (**with s.o.** avec qn); **to be on close terms** être intime (**with** avec); **in terms of** (*speaking of*) sur le plan de; **in real terms** dans la pratique; **to come to terms with** (*person*) tomber d'accord avec; (*situation etc*) *Fig* faire face à; **in the long/short t.** à long/court terme; **at (full) t.** (*baby*) à terme; – *vt* (*name, call*) appeler.

terminal ['tɜːmɪn(ə)l] **1** *n* (*of computer*) terminal *m*; *El* borne *f*; **(air) t.** aérogare *f*; **(oil) t.** terminal *m* (pétrolier). **2** *a* (*patient, illness*) incurable; (*stage*) terminal. ◆**—ly** *adv* **t. ill** (*patient*) incurable.

terminate ['tɜːmɪneɪt] *vt* mettre fin à; (*contract*) résilier; (*pregnancy*) interrompre; – *vi* se terminer. ◆**termi'nation** *n* fin *f*; résiliation *f*; interruption *f*.

terminology [tɜːmɪ'nɒlədʒɪ] *n* terminologie *f*.

terminus ['tɜːmɪnəs] *n* terminus *m*.

termite ['tɜːmaɪt] *n* (*insect*) termite *m*.

terrace ['terɪs] *n* terrace *f*; (*houses*) maisons *fpl* en bande; **the terraces** *Sp* les gradins *mpl*. ◆**terraced** *a* **t. house** maison *f* attenante aux maisons voisines.

terracota [terə'kɒtə] *n* terre *f* cuite.

terrain [tə'reɪn] *n* *Mil Geol* terrain *m*.

terrestrial [tə'restrɪəl] *a* terrestre.

terrible ['terəb(ə)l] *a* affreux, terrible. ◆**terribly** *adv* (*badly*) affreusement; (*very*) terriblement.

terrier ['terɪər] *n* (*dog*) terrier *m*.

terrific [tə'rɪfɪk] *a* *Fam* (*extreme*) terrible; (*excellent*) formidable, terrible. ◆**terrifically** *adv* *Fam* (*extremely*) terriblement; (*extremely well*) terriblement bien.

terrify ['terɪfaɪ] *vt* terrifier; **to be terrified of** avoir très peur de. ◆**—ing** *a* terrifiant. ◆**—ingly** *adv* épouvantablement.

territory ['terɪtərɪ] *n* territoire *m*. ◆**terri'torial** *a* territorial.

terror ['terər] *n* terreur *f*; (*child*) *Fam* polisson, -onne *mf*. ◆**terrorism** *n* terrorisme *m*. ◆**terrorist** *n* & *a* terroriste (*mf*). ◆**terrorize** *vt* terroriser.

terry(cloth) ['terɪ(klɒθ)] *n* tissu-éponge *m*.

terse [tɜːs] *a* laconique.

tertiary ['tɜːʃərɪ] *a* tertiaire.

Terylene® ['terəliːn] *n* tergal® *m*.

test [test] *vt* (*try*) essayer; (*examine*) examiner; (*analyse*) analyser; (*product, intelligence*) tester; (*pupil*) *Sch* faire subir une interrogation à; (*nerves, courage etc*) *Fig* éprouver; – *n* (*trial*) test *m*, essai *m*; examen *m*; analyse *f*; *Sch* interrogation *f*, test *m*; (*of courage etc*) *Fig* épreuve *f*; **driving t.** (examen *m* du) permis *m* de conduire; – *a* (*pilot, flight*) d'essai; **t. case** *Jur* affaire-test *f*; **t. match** *Sp* match *m* international; **t. tube** éprouvette *f*; **t. tube baby** bébé *m* éprouvette.

testament ['testəmənt] *n* testament *m*; (*proof, tribute*) témoignage *m*; **Old/New T.** *Rel* Ancien/Nouveau Testament.

testicle ['testɪk(ə)l] *n* *Anat* testicule *m*.

testify ['testɪfaɪ] *vi* *Jur* témoigner (**against** contre); **to t. to sth** (*of person, event etc*) témoigner de qch; – *vt* **to t. that** *Jur* témoigner que. ◆**testi'monial** *n* références *fpl*, recommandation *f*. ◆**testimony** *n* témoignage *m*.

testy ['testɪ] *a* (**-ier, -iest**) irritable.

tetanus ['tetənəs] *n* *Med* tétanos *m*.

tête-à-tête [teɪtɑː'teɪt] *n* tête-à-tête *m inv*.

tether ['teðər] **1** *vt* (*fasten*) attacher. **2** *n* **at the end of one's t.** à bout de nerfs.

text [tekst] *n* texte *m*. ◆**textbook** *n* manuel *m*.

textile ['tekstaɪl] *a* & *n* textile (*m*).

texture ['tekstʃər] *n* (*of fabric, cake etc*) texture *f*; (*of paper, wood*) grain *n*.

Thames [temz] *n* **the T.** la Tamise *f*.

than [ðən, *stressed* ðæn] *conj* **1** que; **happier t.** plus heureux que; **he has more t. you** il en a plus que toi; **fewer oranges t. plums** moins d'oranges que de prunes. **2** (*with numbers*) de; **more t. six** plus de six.

thank [θæŋk] *vt* remercier (**for sth** de qch, **for doing** d'avoir fait); **t. you** merci (**for sth** pour *or* de qch, **for doing** d'avoir fait); **no, t. you** (non) merci; **t. God, t. heavens, t. goodness** Dieu merci; – *npl* remerciements *mpl*; **thanks to** (*because of*) grâce à; **(many) thanks!** merci (beaucoup)! ◆**thankful** *a* reconnaissant (**for** de); **t. that** bien heureux que (+ *sub*). ◆**thankfully** *adv* (*gratefully*) avec reconnaissance; (*happily*) heureusement. ◆**thankless** *a* ingrat. ◆**Thanks'giving** *n* **T. (day)** (*holiday*) *Am* jour *m* d'action de grâce(s).

that [ðət, *stressed* ðæt] **1** *conj* que; **to say t.** dire que. **2** *rel pron* (*subject*) qui; (*object*) que; **the boy t. left** le garçon qui est parti; **the book t. I read** le livre que j'ai lu; **the carpet t. I put it on** (*with prep*) le tapis sur lequel je l'ai mis; **the house t. she told me about** la maison dont elle m'a parlé; **the day/morning t. she arrived** le jour/matin où elle est arrivée. **3** *dem a* (*pl see* **those**) ce, cet (*before vowel or mute h*), cette; (*opposed to 'this'*) ... + -là; **t. day** ce jour; ce jour-là; **t. man** cet homme; cet homme-là; **t. girl** cette fille; cette fille-là. **4** *dem pron* (*pl see* **those**) ça, cela; ce; **t. (one)** celui-là *m*, celle-là *f*; **give me t.** donne-moi ça *or* cela; **I prefer t. (one)** je préfère celui-là; **before t.** avant ça *or* cela; **t.'s right** c'est juste; **who's t.?** qui est-ce?; **t.'s the house** c'est la maison; (*pointing*) voilà la maison; **what do you mean by t.?** qu'entends-tu par là; **t. is (to say)...** c'est-à-dire.... **5** *adv* (*so*) *Fam* si; **not t. good** pas si bon; **t. high** (*pointing*) haut comme ça; **t. much** (*to cost, earn etc*) (au)tant que ça.

thatch [θætʃ] *n* chaume *m*. ◆**thatched** *a* (*roof*) de chaume; **t. cottage** chaumière *f*.

thaw [θɔː] *n* dégel *m*; – *vi* dégeler; (*of snow*) fondre; **it's thawing** *Met* ça dégèle; **to t. (out)** (*of person*) *Fig* se dégeler; – *vt* (*ice*) dégeler, faire fondre; (*food*) faire dégeler; (*snow*) faire fondre.

the [ðə, *before vowel* ðɪ, *stressed* ðiː] *def art* le, l', la, *pl* les; **t. roof** le toit; **t. man** l'homme; **t. moon** la lune; **t. orange** l'orange; **t. boxes** les boîtes; **the smallest** le plus petit; **of t., from t.** du, de l', de la, *pl* des; **to t., at t.** au, à l', à la, *pl* aux; **Elizabeth t. Second** Élisabeth deux; **all t. better** d'autant mieux.

theatre ['θɪətər] *n* (*place, art*) & *Mil* théâtre *m*. ◆**theatregoer** *n* amateur *m* de théâtre. ◆**the'atrical** *a* théâtral; **t. company** troupe *f* de théâtre.

theft [θeft] *n* vol *m*.

their [ðeər] *poss a* leur, *pl* leurs; **t. house** leur maison *f*. ◆**theirs** [ðeəz] *poss pron* le leur, la leur, *pl* les leurs; **this book is t.** ce livre est à eux *or* est le leur; **a friend of t.** un ami à eux.

them [ðəm, *stressed* ðem] *pron* les; (*after prep etc*) eux *mpl*, elles *fpl*; **(to) t.** (*indirect*) leur; **I see t.** je les vois; **I give (to) t.** je leur donne; **with t.** avec eux, avec elles; **ten of t.** dix d'entre eux, dix d'entre elles; **all of t.** tous, toutes. ◆**them'selves** *pron* eux-mêmes *mpl*, elles-mêmes *fpl*; (*reflexive*) se, s'; (*after prep etc*) eux *mpl*, elles *fpl*; **they wash t.** ils se lavent, elles se lavent; **they think of t.** ils pensent à eux, elles pensent à elles.

theme [θiːm] *n* thème *m*; **t. song** *or* **tune** *Cin TV* chanson *f* principale.

then [ðen] **1** *adv* (*at that time*) alors, à ce moment-là; (*next*) ensuite, puis; **from t. on** dès lors; **before t.** avant cela; **until t.** jusque-là, jusqu'alors; – *a* **the t. mayor/***etc* le maire/*etc* d'alors. **2** *conj* (*therefore*) donc, alors.

theology [θɪ'ɒlədʒɪ] *n* théologie *f*. ◆**theo'logical** *a* théologique. ◆**theo'logian** *n* théologien *m*.

theorem ['θɪərəm] *n* théorème *m*.

theory ['θɪərɪ] *n* théorie *f*; **in t.** en théorie. ◆**theo'retical** *a* théorique. ◆**theo'retically** *adv* théoriquement. ◆**theorist** *n* théoricien, -ienne *mf*.

therapy ['θerəpɪ] *n* thérapeutique *f*. ◆**thera'peutic** *a* thérapeutique.

there [ðeər] *adv* là; **(down** *or* **over) t.** là-bas; **on t.** là-dessus; **she'll be t.** elle sera là, elle y sera; **t. is, t. are** il y a; (*pointing*) voilà; **t. he is** le voilà; **t. she is** la voilà; **t. they are** les voilà; **that man t.** cet homme-là; **t. (you are)!** (*take this*) tenez!; **t., (t.,) don't cry!** allons, allons, ne pleure pas! ◆**therea'bout(s)** *adv* par là; (*in amount*) à peu près. ◆**there'after** *adv* après cela. ◆**thereby** *adv* de ce fait. ◆**therefore** *adv* donc. ◆**thereu'pon** *adv* sur ce.

thermal ['θɜːm(ə)l] *a* (*energy, unit*) thermique; (*springs*) thermal; (*underwear*) tribo-électrique, en thermolactyl®.

thermometer [θə'mɒmɪtər] *n* thermomètre *m*.

thermonuclear [θɜːməʊ'njuːklɪər] *a* thermonucléaire.

Thermos® ['θɜːməs] *n* **T. (flask)** thermos® *m or f*.

thermostat ['θɜːməstæt] *n* thermostat *m*.

thesaurus [θɪ'sɔːrəs] *n* dictionnaire *m* de synonymes.

these [ðiːz] **1** *dem a* (*sing see* **this**) ces; (*opposed to 'those'*) ... + -ci; **t. men** ces hommes; ces hommes-ci. **2** *dem pron* (*sing see* **this**) **t. (ones)** ceux-ci *mpl*, celles-ci *fpl*; **t. are my friends** ce sont mes amis.

thesis, *pl* **theses** ['θiːsɪs, 'θiːsiːz] *n* thèse *f*.

they [ðeɪ] *pron* **1** ils *mpl*, elles *fpl*; (*stressed*) eux *mpl*, elles *fpl*; **t. go** ils vont, elles vont; **t. are doctors** ce sont des médecins. **2** (*people in general*) on; **t. say** on dit.

thick [θɪk] *a* (**-er, -est**) épais; (*stupid*) *Fam* lourd; **to be t.** (*of friends*) *Fam* être très liés; – *adv* (*to grow*) dru; (*to spread*) en couche épaisse; – *n* **in the t. of** (*battle etc*) au plus gros de. ◆**thicken** *vt* épaissir; – *vi* s'épaissir. ◆**thickly** *adv* (*to grow, fall*) dru; (*to spread*) en couche épaisse; (*populated, wooded*) très. ◆**thickness** *n* épaisseur *f*.

thicket ['θɪkɪt] *n* (*trees*) fourré *m*.

thickset [θɪk'set] *a* (*person*) trapu. ◆**thick-skinned** *a* (*person*) dur, peu sensible.

thief [θiːf] *n* (*pl* **thieves**) voleur, -euse *mf*. ◆**thiev/e** *vti* voler. ◆**—ing** *a* voleur; – *n* vol *m*.

thigh [θaɪ] *n* cuisse *f*. ◆**thighbone** *n* fémur *m*.

thimble ['θɪmb(ə)l] *n* dé *m* (à coudre).

thin [θɪn] *a* (**thinner, thinnest**) (*slice, paper etc*) mince; (*person, leg*) maigre, mince; (*soup*) peu épais; (*hair, audience*) clairsemé; (*powder*) fin; (*excuse, profit*) *Fig* maigre, mince; – *adv* (*to spread*) en couche mince; – *vt* (**-nn-**) **to t. (down)** (*paint etc*) délayer; – *vi* **to t. out** (*of crowd, mist*) s'éclaircir. ◆**—ly** *adv* (*to spread*) en couche mince; (*populated, wooded*) peu; (*disguised*) à peine. ◆**—ness** *n* minceur *f*; maigreur *f*.

thing [θɪŋ] *n* chose *f*; **one's things** (*belongings, clothes*) ses affaires *fpl*; **it's a funny t.** c'est drôle; **poor little t.!** pauvre petit!; **that's (just) the t.** voilà (exactement) ce qu'il faut; **how are things?**, *Fam* **how's things?** comment (ça) va?; **I'll think things over** j'y réfléchirai; **for one t. . . . , and for another t.** d'abord . . . et ensuite; **tea things** (*set*) service *m* à thé; (*dishes*) vaisselle *f*. ◆**thingummy** *n Fam* truc *m*, machin *m*.

think [θɪŋk] *vi* (*pt & pp* **thought**) penser (**about, of** à); **to t. (carefully)** réfléchir (**about, of** à); **to t. of doing** penser *or* songer à faire; **to t. highly of, t. a lot of** penser beaucoup de bien de; **she doesn't t. much of it** ça ne lui dit pas grand-chose; **to t. better of it** se raviser; **I can't t. of it** je n'arrive pas à m'en souvenir; – *vt* penser (**that** que); **I t. so** je pense *or* crois que oui; **what do you t. of him?** que penses-tu de lui?; **I thought it difficult** je l'ai trouvé difficile; **to t. out** *or* **through** (*reply etc*) réfléchir sérieusement à, peser; **to t. over** réfléchir à; **to t. up** (*invent*) inventer, avoir l'idée de; – *n* **to have a t.** *Fam* réfléchir (**about** à); – *a* **t. tank** comité *m* d'experts. ◆**—ing** *a* (*person*) intelligent; – *n* (*opinion*) opinion *f*; **to my t.** à mon avis. ◆**—er** *n* penseur, -euse *mf*.

thin-skinned [θɪn'skɪnd] *a* (*person*) susceptible.

third [θɜːd] *a* troisième; **t. person** *or* **party** tiers *m*; **t.-party insurance** assurance *f* au tiers; **T. World** Tiers-Monde *m*; – *n* troisième *mf*; **a t.** (*fraction*) un tiers; – *adv* (*in race*) troisième. ◆**—ly** *adv* troisièmement.

third-class [θɜːd'klɑːs] *a* de troisième classe. ◆**t.-rate** *a* (très) inférieur.

thirst [θɜːst] *n* soif *f* (**for** de). ◆**thirsty** *a* (**-ier, -iest**) *a* **to be** *or* **feel t.** avoir soif; **to make t.** donner soif à; **t. for** (*power etc*) *Fig* assoiffé de.

thirteen [θɜː'tiːn] *a & n* treize (*m*). ◆**thirteenth** *a & n* treizième (*mf*). ◆**'thirtieth** *a & n* trentième (*mf*). ◆**'thirty** *a & n* trente (*m*).

this [ðɪs] **1** *dem a* (*pl see* **these**) ce, cet (*before vowel or mute h*), cette; (*opposed to 'that'*) . . . + -ci; **t. book** ce livre; ce livre-ci; **t. man** cet homme; cet homme-ci; **t. photo** cette photo; cette photo-ci. **2** *dem pron* (*pl see* **these**) ceci; ce; **t. (one)** celui-ci *m*, celle-ci *f*; **give me t.** donne-moi ceci; **I prefer t. (one)** je préfère celui-ci; **before t.** avant ceci; **who's t.?** qui est-ce?; **t. is Paul** c'est Paul; **t. is the house** voici la maison. **3** *adv* (*so*) *Fam* si; **t. high** (*pointing*) haut comme ceci; **t. far** (*until now*) jusqu'ici.

thistle ['θɪs(ə)l] *n* chardon *m*.

thorn [θɔːn] *n* épine *f*. ◆**thorny** *a* (**-ier, -iest**) (*bush, problem etc*) épineux.

thorough ['θʌrə] *a* (*painstaking, careful*) minutieux, consciencieux; (*knowledge, examination*) approfondi; (*rogue, liar*) fieffé; (*disaster*) complet; **to give sth a t. washing** laver qch à fond. ◆**—ly** *adv* (*completely*) tout à fait; (*painstakingly*) avec minutie; (*to know, clean, wash*) à fond. ◆**—ness** *n* minutie *f*; (*depth*) profondeur *f*.

thoroughbred ['θʌrəbred] *n* (*horse*) pur-sang *m inv*.

thoroughfare ['θʌrəfeər] *n* (*street*) rue *f*; **'no t.'** 'passage interdit'.

those [ðəʊz] **1** *dem a* (*sing see* **that**) ces; (*opposed to 'these'*) . . . + -là; **t. men** ces hommes; ces hommes-là. **2** *dem pron* (*sing see* **that**) **t. (ones)** ceux-là *mpl*, celles-là *fpl*; **t. are my friends** ce sont mes amis.

though [ðəʊ] **1** *conj* (**even**) **t.** bien que (+ *sub*); **as t.** comme si; **strange t. it may seem** si étrange que cela puisse paraître. **2** *adv* (*nevertheless*) cependant, quand même.

thought [θɔːt] *see* **think**; – *n* pensée *f*; (*idea*) idée *f*, pensée *f*; **(careful) t.** réflexion *f*; **without (a) t. for** sans penser à; **to have second thoughts** changer d'avis; **on second thoughts**, *Am* **on second t.** à la réflexion. ◆**thoughtful** *a* (*pensive*) pensif; (*serious*) sérieux; (*considerate, kind*) gentil, prévenant. ◆**thoughtfully** *adv* (*considerately*) gentiment. ◆**thoughtfulness** *n* gentillesse *f*, prévenance *f*. ◆**thoughtless** *a* (*towards others*) désinvolte; (*careless*) étourdi. ◆**thoughtlessly** *adv* (*carelessly*) étourdiment; (*inconsiderately*) avec désinvolture.

thousand ['θauzənd] *a & n* mille *a & m inv*; **a t. pages** mille pages; **two t. pages** deux mille pages; **thousands of** des milliers de.

thrash [θræʃ] **1** *vt* **to t. s.o.** rouer qn de coups; (*defeat*) écraser qn; **to t. out** (*plan etc*) élaborer (à force de discussions). **2** *vi* **to t. about** (*struggle*) se débattre. ◆**—ing** *n* (*beating*) correction *f*.

thread [θred] *n* (*yarn*) & *Fig* fil *m*; (*of screw*) pas *m*; – *vt* (*needle, beads*) enfiler; **to t. one's way** *Fig* se faufiler (**through the crowd/***etc* parmi la foule/*etc*). ◆**threadbare** *a* élimé, râpé.

threat [θret] *n* menace *f* (to à). ◆**threaten** *vi* menacer; – *vt* menacer (**to do** de faire, **with sth** de qch). ◆**threatening** *a* menaçant. ◆**threateningly** *adv* (*to say*) d'un ton menaçant.

three [θriː] *a & n* trois (*m*); **t.-piece suite** canapé *m* et deux fauteuils. ◆**threefold** *a* triple; – *adv* **to increase t.** tripler. ◆**three-'wheeler** *n* (*tricycle*) tricycle *m*; (*car*) voiture *f* à trois roues.

thresh [θreʃ] *vt Agr* battre.

threshold ['θreʃhəuld] *n* seuil *m*.

threw [θruː] *see* **throw**.

thrift [θrɪft] *n* (*virtue*) économie *f*. ◆**thrifty** *a* (**-ier, -iest**) économe.

thrill [θrɪl] *n* émotion *f*, frisson *m*; **to get a t. out of doing** prendre plaisir à faire; – *vt* (*delight*) réjouir; (*excite*) faire frissonner. ◆**—ed** *a* ravi (**with sth** de qch, **to do** de faire). ◆**—ing** *a* passionnant. ◆**—er** *n* film *m or* roman *m* à suspense.

thriv/e [θraɪv] *vi* (*of business, person, plant etc*) prospérer; **he** *or* **she thrives on hard work** le travail lui profite. ◆**—ing** *a* prospère, florissant.

throat [θrəut] *n* gorge *f*; **to have a sore t.** avoir mal à la gorge. ◆**throaty** *a* (*voice*) rauque; (*person*) à la voix rauque.

throb [θrɒb] *vi* (**-bb-**) (*of heart*) palpiter; (*of engine*) vrombir; *Fig* vibrer; **my finger is throbbing** mon doigt me fait des élancements; – *n* palpitation *f*; vrombissement *m*; élancement *m*.

throes [θrəuz] *npl* **in the t. of** au milieu de; (*illness, crisis*) en proie à; **in the t. of doing** en train de faire.

thrombosis [θrɒm'bəusɪs] *n* (*coronary*) *Med* infarctus *m*.

throne [θrəun] *n* trône *m*.

throng [θrɒŋ] *n* foule *f*; – *vi* (*rush*) affluer; – *vt* (*street, station etc*) se presser dans; **thronged with people** noir de monde.

throttle ['θrɒt(ə)l] **1** *n Aut* accélérateur *m*. **2** *vt* (*strangle*) étrangler.

through [θruː] *prep* (*place*) à travers; (*time*) pendant; (*means*) par; (*thanks to*) grâce à; **to go** *or* **get t.** (*forest etc*) traverser; (*hole etc*) passer par; **t. the window/door** par la fenêtre/porte; **to speak t. one's nose** parler du nez; **Tuesday t. Saturday** *Am* de mardi à samedi; – *adv* à travers; **to go t.** (*cross*) traverser; (*pass*) passer; **to let t.** laisser passer; **all** *or* **right t.** (*to the end*) jusqu'au bout; **French t. and t.** français jusqu'au bout des ongles; **to be t.** (*finished*) *Am Fam* avoir fini; **we're t.** *Am Fam* c'est fini entre nous; **I'm t. with the book** *Am Fam* je n'ai plus besoin du livre; **t. to** *or* **till** jusqu'à; **I'll put you t. (to him)** *Tel* je vous le passe; – *a* (*train, traffic, ticket*) direct; **'no t. road'** (*no exit*) 'voie sans issue'. ◆**through'out** *prep* **t. the neighbourhood/***etc* dans tout le quartier/*etc*; **t. the day/***etc* (*time*) pendant toute la journée/*etc*; – *adv* (*everywhere*) partout; (*all the time*) tout le temps. ◆**throughway** *n Am* autoroute *f*.

throw [θrəu] *n* (*of stone etc*) jet *m*; *Sp* lancer *m*; (*of dice*) coup *m*; (*turn*) tour *m*; – *vt* (*pt* **threw**, *pp* **thrown**) jeter (**to, at** à); (*stone, ball*) lancer, jeter; (*hurl*) projeter; (*of horse*) désarçonner (*qn*); (*party, reception*) donner; (*baffle*) *Fam* dérouter; **to t. away** (*discard*) jeter; (*ruin, waste*) *Fig* gâcher; **to t. back** (*ball*) renvoyer (**to** à); (*one's head*) rejeter en arrière; **to t. in** (*include as extra*) *Fam* donner en prime; **to t. off** (*get rid of*) se débarrasser de; **to t. out** (*discard*) jeter; (*suggestion*) repousser; (*expel*) mettre (*qn*) à la porte; (*distort*) fausser (*calcul etc*); **to t. over** abandonner; **to t. up** (*job*) *Fam* laisser tomber; – *vi* **to t. up** (*vomit*) *Sl* dégobiller. ◆**throwaway** *a* (*disposable*) à jeter, jetable.

thrush [θrʌʃ] *n* (*bird*) grive *f*.

thrust [θrʌst] *n* (*push*) poussée *f*; (*stab*) coup *m*; (*of argument*) poids *m*; (*dynamism*) allant *m*; – *vt* (*pt & pp* **thrust**) (*push*) pousser; (*put*) mettre (**into** dans); **to t. sth into sth** (*stick, knife, pin*) enfoncer qch dans qch; **to t. sth/s.o. upon s.o.** *Fig* imposer qch/qn à qn.

thud [θʌd] *n* bruit *m* sourd.

thug [θʌg] *n* voyou *m*.

thumb [θʌm] *n* pouce *m*; **with a t. index** (*book*) à onglets; – *vt* **to t. (through)** (*book etc*) feuilleter; **to t. a lift** *or* **a ride** *Fam* faire du stop. ◆**thumbtack** *n Am* punaise *f*.

thump [θʌmp] *vt* (*person*) frapper, cogner sur; (*table*) taper sur; **to t. one's head** (*on door etc*) se cogner la tête (**on** contre); – *vi* frapper, cogner (**on** sur); (*of heart*) battre à grands coups; – *n* (grand) coup *m*; (*noise*) bruit *m* sourd. ◆**—ing** *a* (*huge, great*) *Fam* énorme.

thunder ['θʌndər] *n* tonnerre *m*; – *vi* (*of weather, person, guns*) tonner; **it's thundering** *Met* il tonne; **to t. past** passer (vite) dans un bruit de tonnerre. ◆**thunderbolt** *n* (*event*) *Fig* coup *m* de tonnerre. ◆**thunderclap** *n* coup *m* de tonnerre. ◆**thunderstorm** *n* orage *m*. ◆**thunderstruck** *a* abasourdi.

Thursday ['θɜːzdɪ] *n* jeudi *m*.

thus [ðʌs] *adv* ainsi.

thwart [θwɔːt] *vt* (*plan, person*) contrecarrer.

thyme [taɪm] *n Bot Culin* thym *m*.

thyroid ['θaɪrɔɪd] *a* & *n Anat* thyroïde (*f*).

tiara [tɪ'ɑːrə] *n* (*of woman*) diadème *m*.

tic [tɪk] *n* (*in face, limbs*) tic *m*.

tick [tɪk] **1** *n* (*of clock*) tic-tac *m*; – *vi* faire tic-tac; **to t. over** (*of engine, factory, business*) tourner au ralenti. **2** *n* (*on list*) coche *f*, trait *m*; – *vt* **to t. (off)** cocher; **to t. off** (*reprimand*) *Fam* passer un savon à. **3** *n* (*moment*) *Fam* instant *m*. **4** *n* (*insect*) tique *f*. **5** *adv* **on t.** (*on credit*) *Fam* à crédit. ◆**—ing** *n* (*of clock*) tic-tac *m*; **to give s.o. a t.-off** *Fam* passer un savon à qn.

ticket ['tɪkɪt] *n* billet *m*; (*for tube, bus, cloakroom*) ticket *m*; (*for library*) carte *f*; (*fine*) *Aut Fam* contravention *f*, contredanse *f*; *Pol Am* liste *f*; **(price) t.** étiquette *f*; **t. collector** contrôleur, -euse *mf*; **t. holder** personne *f* munie d'un billet; **t. office** guichet *m*.

tickle ['tɪk(ə)l] *vt* chatouiller; (*amuse*) *Fig* amuser; – *n* chatouillement *m*. ◆**ticklish** *a* (*person*) chatouilleux; (*fabric*) qui chatouille; (*problem*) *Fig* délicat.

tidbit ['tɪdbɪt] *n* (*food*) *Am* bon morceau *m*.

tiddlywinks ['tɪdlɪwɪŋks] *n* jeu *m* de puce.

tide [taɪd] **1** *n* marée *f*; **against the t.** *Nau* & *Fig* à contre-courant; **the rising t. of discontent** le mécontentement grandissant. **2** *vt* **to t. s.o. over** (*help out*) dépanner qn. ◆**tidal** *a* (*river*) qui a une marée; **t. wave** raz-de-marée *m inv*; (*in public opinion etc*) *Fig* vague *f* de fond. ◆**tidemark** *n Fig Hum* ligne *f* de crasse.

tidings ['taɪdɪŋz] *npl Lit* nouvelles *fpl*.

tidy ['taɪdɪ] *a* (**-ier, -iest**) (*place, toys etc*) bien rangé; (*clothes, looks*) soigné; (*methodical*) ordonné; (*amount, sum*) *Fam* joli, bon; **to make t.** ranger; – *vt* **to t. (up** *or* **away)** ranger; **to t. oneself (up)** s'arranger; **to t. out** (*cupbaord etc*) vider; – *vi* **to t. up** ranger. ◆**tidily** *adv* avec soin. ◆**tidiness** *n* (bon) ordre *m*; (*care*) soin *m*.

tie [taɪ] *n* (*string, strap etc*) & *Fig* lien *m*, attache *f*; (*necktie*) cravate *f*; (*sleeper*) *Rail Am* traverse *f*; *Sp* égalité *f* de points; (*match*) match *m* nul; – *vt* (*fasten*) attacher, lier (**to** à); (*a knot*) faire (**in** à); (*shoe*) lacer; (*link*) lier (**to** à); **to t. down** attacher; **to t. s.o. down to** (*date, place etc*) obliger qn à accepter; **to t. up** attacher; (*money*) *Fig* immobiliser; **to be tied up** (*linked*) être lié (**with** avec); (*busy*) *Fam* être occupé; – *vi Sp* finir à égalité de points; *Fb* faire match nul; (*in race*) être ex aequo; **to t. in with** (*tally with*) se rapporter à. ◆**t.-up** *n* (*link*) lien *m*; (*traffic jam*) *Am Fam* bouchon *m*.

tier [tɪər] *n* (*seats*) *Sp Th* gradin *m*; (*of cake*) étage *m*.

tiff [tɪf] *n* petite querelle *f*.

tiger ['taɪgər] *n* tigre *m*. ◆**tigress** *n* tigresse *f*.

tight [taɪt] *a* (**-er, -est**) (*rope etc*) raide; (*closely-fitting clothing*) ajusté, (*fitting too closely*) (trop) étroit, (trop) serré; (*drawer, lid*) dur; (*control*) strict; (*schedule, credit*) serré; (*drunk*) *Fam* gris; (*with money*) *Fam* avare; **a t. spot** *or* **corner** *Fam* une situation difficile; **it's a t. squeeze** il y a juste la place; – *adv* (*to hold, shut, sleep*) bien; (*to squeeze*) fort; **to sit t.** ne pas bouger. ◆**tighten** *vt* **to t. (up)** (*rope*) tendre; (*bolt etc*) (res)serrer; (*security*) *Fig* renforcer; – *vi* **to t. up on** se montrer plus strict à l'égard de. ◆**tightly** *adv* (*to hold*) bien; (*to squeeze*) fort; **t. knit** (*close*) très uni. ◆**tightness** *n* (*of garment*) étroitesse *f*; (*of control*) rigueur *f*; (*of rope*) tension *f*.

tight-fitting [taɪt'fɪtɪŋ] *a* (*garment*) ajusté. ◆**tightfisted** *a* avare. ◆**'tightrope** *n* corde *f* raide. ◆**'tightwad** *n* (*miser*) *Am Fam* grippe-sou *m*.

tights [taɪts] *npl* (*garment*) collant *m*; (*for dancer etc*) justaucorps *m*.

til/e [taɪl] *n* (*on roof*) tuile *f*; (*on wall or floor*) carreau *m*; – *vt* (*wall, floor*) carreler. ◆**—ed** *a* (*roof*) de tuiles; (*wall, floor*) carrelé.

till [tɪl] **1** *prep & conj* = **until**. **2** *n* (*for money*) caisse *f* (enregistreuse). **3** *vt* (*land*) *Agr* cultiver.

tilt [tɪlt] *vti* pencher; – *n* inclinaison *f*; **(at) full t.** à toute vitesse.

timber ['tɪmbər] *n* bois *m* (de construction); (*trees*) arbres *mpl*; – *a* de *or* en bois. ◆**timberyard** *n* entrepôt *m* de bois.

time [taɪm] *n* temps *m*; (*point in time*) moment *m*; (*epoch*) époque *f*; (*on clock*) heure *f*; (*occasion*) fois *f*; *Mus* mesure *f*; **in (the course of) t., with (the passage of) t.** avec le temps; **some of the t.** (*not always*) une partie du temps; **most of the t.** la plupart du temps; **in a year's t.** dans un an; **a long t.** longtemps; **a short t.** peu de temps, un petit moment; **full-t.** à plein temps; **part-t.** à temps partiel; **to have a good** *or* **a nice t.** (*fun*) s'amuser (bien); **to have a hard t. doing** avoir du mal à faire; **t. off** du temps libre; **in no t. (at all)** en un rien de temps; **(just) in t.** (*to arrive*) à temps (**for sth** pour qch, **to do** pour faire); **in my t.** (*formerly*) de mon temps; **from t. to t.** de temps en temps; **what t. is it?** quelle heure est-il?; **the right** *or* **exact t.** l'heure *f* exacte; **on t.** à l'heure; **at the same t.** en même temps (**as** que); (*simultaneously*) à la fois; **for the t. being** pour le moment; **at the t.** à ce moment-là; **at the present t.** à l'heure actuelle; **at times** par moments, parfois; **at one t.** à un moment donné; **this t. tomorrow** demain à cette heure-ci; **(the) next t. you come** la prochaine fois que tu viendras; **(the) last t.** la dernière fois; **one at a t.** un à un; **t. and again** maintes fois; **ten times ten** dix fois dix; **t. bomb** bombe *f* à retardement; **t. lag** décalage *m*; **t. limit** délai *m*; **t. zone** fuseau *m* horaire; – *vt* (*sportsman, worker etc*) chronométrer; (*programme, operation*) minuter; (*choose the time of*) choisir le moment de; (*to plan*) prévoir. ◆**timing** *n* chronométrage *m*; minutage *m*; (*judgement of artist etc*) rythme *m*; **the t. of** (*time*) le moment choisi pour. ◆**time-consuming** *a* qui prend du temps. ◆**time-honoured** *a* consacré (par l'usage).

timeless ['taɪmləs] *a* éternel.

timely ['taɪmlɪ] *a* à propos. ◆**timeliness** *n* à-propos *m*.

timer ['taɪmər] *n* *Culin* minuteur *m*, compte-minutes *m inv*; (*sand-filled*) sablier *m*; (*on machine*) minuteur *m*; (*to control lighting*) minuterie *f*.

timetable ['taɪmteɪb(ə)l] *n* horaire *m*; (*in school*) emploi *m* du temps.

timid ['tɪmɪd] *a* (*shy*) timide; (*fearful*) timoré. ◆**—ly** *adv* timidement.

tin [tɪn] *n* étain *m*; (*tinplate*) fer-blanc *m*; (*can*) boîte *f*; (*for baking*) moule *m*; **t. can** boîte *f* (en fer-blanc); **t. opener** ouvre-boîtes *m inv*; **t. soldier** soldat *m* de plomb. ◆**tinfoil** *n* papier *m* d'aluminium, papier alu. ◆**tinned** *a* en boîte. ◆**tinplate** *n* fer-blanc *m*.

tinge [tɪndʒ] *n* teinte *f*. ◆**tinged** *a* **t. with** (*pink etc*) teinté de; (*jealousy etc*) *Fig* empreint de.

tingle ['tɪŋg(ə)l] *vi* picoter; **it's tingling** ça me picote. ◆**tingly** *a* (*feeling*) de picotement.

tinker ['tɪŋkər] *vi* **to t. (about) with** bricoler.

tinkle ['tɪŋk(ə)l] *vi* tinter; – *n* tintement *m*; **to give s.o. a t.** (*phone s.o.*) *Fam* passer un coup de fil à qn.

tinny ['tɪnɪ] *a* **(-ier, -iest)** (*sound*) métallique; (*vehicle, machine*) de mauvaise qualité.

tinsel ['tɪns(ə)l] *n* clinquant *m*, guirlandes *fpl* de Noël.

tint [tɪnt] *n* teinte *f*; (*for hair*) shampooing *m* colorant; – *vt* (*paper, glass*) teinter.

tiny ['taɪnɪ] *a* **(-ier, -iest)** tout petit.

tip [tɪp] **1** *n* (*end*) bout *m*; (*pointed*) pointe *f*. **2** *n* (*money*) pourboire *m*; – *vt* **(-pp-)** donner un pourboire à. **3** *n* (*advice*) conseil *m*; (*information*) & *Sp* tuyau *m*; **to get a t.-off** se faire tuyauter; – *vt* **(-pp-) to t. a horse/***etc* donner un cheval/*etc* gagnant; **to t. off** (*police*) prévenir. **4** *n* (*for rubbish*) décharge *f*; – *vt* **(-pp-) to t. (up** *or* **over)** (*tilt*) incliner, pencher; (*overturn*) faire basculer; **to t. (out)** (*liquid, load*) déverser (**into** dans); – *vi* **to t. (up** *or* **over)** (*tilt*) pencher; (*overturn*) basculer.

tipped [tɪpt] *a* **t. cigarette** cigarette *f* (à bout) filtre.

tipple ['tɪp(ə)l] *vi* (*drink*) *Fam* picoler.

tipsy ['tɪpsɪ] *a* **(-ier, -iest)** (*drunk*) gai, pompette.

tiptoe ['tɪptəʊ] *n* **on t.** sur la pointe des pieds; – *vi* marcher sur la pointe des pieds.

tiptop ['tɪptɒp] *a* *Fam* excellent.

tirade [taɪ'reɪd] *n* diatribe *f*.

tir/e[1] ['taɪər] *vt* fatiguer; **to t. out** (*exhaust*) épuiser; – *vi* se fatiguer. ◆**—ed** *a* fatigué; **to be t. of sth/s.o./doing** en avoir assez de qch/de qn/de faire; **to get t. of doing** se lasser de faire. ◆**—ing** *a* fatigant. ◆**tiredness** *n* fatigue *f*. ◆**tireless** *a* infatigable. ◆**tiresome** *a* ennuyeux.

tire[2] ['taɪər] *n* *Am* pneu *m*.

tissue ['tɪʃuː] *n* *Biol* tissu *m*; (*handkerchief*) mouchoir *m* en papier, kleenex® *m*; **t. (paper)** papier *m* de soie.

tit [tɪt] *n* **1** (*bird*) mésange *f*. **2 to give t. for tat** rendre coup pour coup.

titbit ['tɪtbɪt] *n* (*food*) bon morceau *m*.

titillate ['tɪtɪleɪt] *vt* exciter.
titl/e ['taɪt(ə)l] *n (name, claim)* & *Sp* titre *m*; **t. deed** titre *m* de propriété; **t. role** *Th Cin* rôle *m* principal; – *vt (film)* intituler, titrer. ◆**–ed** *a (person)* titré.
titter ['tɪtər] *vi* rire bêtement.
tittle-tattle ['tɪt(ə)ltæt(ə)l] *n Fam* commérages *mpl.*
to [tə, *stressed* tuː] **1** *prep* à; *(towards)* vers; *(of feelings, attitude)* envers; *(right up to)* jusqu'à; *(of)* de; **give it to him** *or* **her** donne-le-lui; **to town** en ville; **to France** en France; **to Portugal** au Portugal; **to the butcher('s)**/*etc* chez le boucher/*etc*; **the road to** la route de; **the train to** le train pour; **well-disposed to** bien disposé envers; **kind to** gentil envers *or* avec *or* pour; **from bad to worse** de mal en pis; **ten to one** *(proportion)* dix contre un; **it's ten (minutes) to one** il est une heure moins dix; **one person to a room** une personne par chambre; **to say/to remember**/*etc (with inf)* dire/se souvenir/*etc*; **she tried to** elle a essayé; **wife**/*etc*-**to-be** future femme *f*/*etc.* **2** *adv* **to push to** *(door)* fermer; **to go** *or* **walk to and fro** aller et venir. ◆**to-do** [tə'duː] *n (fuss) Fam* histoire *f.*
toad [təʊd] *n* crapaud *m.*
toadstool ['təʊdstuːl] *n* champignon *m* (vénéneux).
toast [təʊst] **1** *n Culin* pain *m* grillé, toast *m*; – *vt (bread)* (faire) griller. **2** *n (drink)* toast *m*; – *vt (person)* porter un toast à; *(success, event)* arroser. ◆**toaster** *n* grille-pain *m inv.*
tobacco [tə'bækəʊ] *n (pl* **-os)** tabac *m.* ◆**tobacconist** *n* buraliste *mf*; **t., tobacconist's (shop)** (bureau *m* de) tabac *m.*
toboggan [tə'bɒgən] *n* luge *f,* toboggan *m.*
today [tə'deɪ] *adv* & *n* aujourd'hui *(m).*
toddle ['tɒd(ə)l] *vi* **to t. off** *(leave) Hum Fam* se sauver.
toddler ['tɒdlər] *n* petit(e) enfant *mf.*
toddy ['tɒdɪ] *n* **(hot) t.** grog *m.*
toe [təʊ] **1** *n* orteil *m*; **on one's toes** *Fig* vigilant. **2** *vt* **to t. the line** se conformer; **to t. the party line** respecter la ligne du parti. ◆**toenail** *n* ongle *m* du pied.
toffee ['tɒfɪ] *n (sweet)* caramel *m (dur)*; **t. apple** pomme *f* d'amour.
together [tə'geðər] *adv* ensemble; *(at the same time)* en même temps; **t. with** avec. ◆**–ness** *n (of group)* camaraderie *f*; *(of husband and wife)* intimité *f.*
togs [tɒgz] *npl (clothes) Sl* nippes *fpl.*
toil [tɔɪl] *n* labeur *m*; – *vi* travailler dur.
toilet ['tɔɪlɪt] *n (room)* toilettes *fpl,* cabinets *mpl*; *(bowl, seat)* cuvette *f or* siège *m* des cabinets; **to go to the t.** aller aux toilettes; – *a (articles)* de toilette; **t. paper** papier *m* hygiénique; **t. roll** rouleau *m* de papier hygiénique; **t. water** *(perfume)* eau *f* de toilette. ◆**toiletries** *npl* articles *mpl* de toilette.
token ['təʊkən] *n (symbol, sign)* témoignage *m*; *(metal disc)* jeton *m*; *(voucher)* bon *m*; **gift t.** chèque-cadeau *m*; **book t.** chèque-livre *m*; **record t.** chèque-disque *m*; – *a* symbolique.
told [təʊld] *see* **tell**; – *adv* **all t.** *(taken together)* en tout.
tolerable ['tɒlərəb(ə)l] *a (bearable)* tolérable; *(fairly good)* passable. ◆**tolerably** *adv (fairly, fairly well)* passablement. ◆**tolerance** *n* tolérance *f.* ◆**tolerant** *a* tolérant (of à l'égard de). ◆**tolerantly** *adv* avec tolérance. ◆**tolerate** *vt* tolérer.
toll [təʊl] **1** *n* péage *m*; – *a (road)* à péage. **2** *n* **the death t.** le nombre de morts, le bilan en vies humaines; **to take a heavy t.** *(of accident etc)* faire beaucoup de victimes. **3** *vi (of bell)* sonner. ◆**tollfree** *a* **t. number** *Tel Am* numéro *m* vert.
tomato [tə'mɑːtəʊ, *Am* tə'meɪtəʊ] *n (pl* **-oes)** tomate *f.*
tomb [tuːm] *n* tombeau *m.* ◆**tombstone** *n* pierre *f* tombale.
tomboy ['tɒmbɔɪ] *n (girl)* garçon *m* manqué.
tomcat ['tɒmkæt] *n* matou *m.*
tome [təʊm] *n (book)* tome *m.*
tomfoolery [tɒm'fuːlərɪ] *n* niaiserie(s) *f(pl).*
tomorrow [tə'mɒrəʊ] *adv* & *n* demain *(m)*; **t. morning/evening** demain matin/soir; **the day after t.** après-demain.
ton [tʌn] *n* tonne *f (Br = 1016 kg, Am = 907 kg)*; **metric t.** tonne *f (= 1000 kg)*; **tons of** *(lots of) Fam* des tonnes de.
tone [təʊn] *n* ton *m*; *(of radio, telephone)* tonalité *f*; **in that t.** sur ce ton; **to set the t.** donner le ton; **she's t.-deaf** elle n'a pas d'oreille; – *vt* **to t. down** atténuer; **to t. up** *(muscles, skin)* tonifier; – *vi* **to t. in** s'harmoniser (**with** avec).
tongs [tɒŋz] *npl* pinces *fpl*; *(for sugar)* pince *f*; **(curling) t.** fer *m* à friser.
tongue [tʌŋ] *n* langue *f*; **t. in cheek** ironique(ment). ◆**t.-tied** *a* muet (et gêné).
tonic ['tɒnɪk] *a* & *n* tonique *(m)*; **gin and t.** gin-tonic *m.*
tonight [tə'naɪt] *adv* & *n (this evening)* ce soir *(m)*; *(during the night)* cette nuit *(f).*
tonne [tʌn] *n (metric)* tonne *f.* ◆**tonnage** *n* tonnage *m.*
tonsil ['tɒns(ə)l] *n* amygdale *f.* ◆**tonsil'l-**

lectomy *n* opération *f* des amygdales. ◆**tonsillitis** [tɒnsəˈlaɪtəs] *n* **to have t.** avoir une angine.

too [tuː] *adv* **1** (*excessively*) trop; **t. tired to play** trop fatigué pour jouer; **t. hard to solve** trop difficile à résoudre; **it's only t. true** ce n'est que trop vrai. **2** (*also*) aussi; (*moreover*) en plus.

took [tʊk] *see* **take.**

tool [tuːl] *n* outil *m*; **t. bag, t. kit** trousse *f* à outils.

toot [tuːt] *vti* **to t. (the horn)** *Aut* klaxonner.

tooth, *pl* **teeth** [tuːθ, tiːθ] *n* dent *f*; **front t.** dent de devant; **back t.** molaire *f*; **milk/wisdom t.** dent de lait/de sagesse; **t. decay** carie *f* dentaire; **to have a sweet t.** aimer les sucreries; **long in the t.** (*old*) *Hum* chenu, vieux. ◆**toothache** *n* mal *m* de dents. ◆**toothbrush** *n* brosse *f* à dents. ◆**toothcomb** *n* peigne *m* fin. ◆**toothpaste** *n* dentifrice *m*. ◆**toothpick** *n* cure-dent *m*.

top[1] [tɒp] *n* (*of mountain, tower, tree*) sommet *m*; (*of wall, dress, ladder, page*) haut *m*; (*of box, table, surface*) dessus *m*; (*of list*) tête *f*; (*of water*) surface *f*; (*of car*) toit *m*; (*of bottle, tube*) bouchon *m*; (*bottle cap*) capsule *f*; (*of saucepan*) couvercle *m*; (*of pen*) capuchon *m*; **pyjama t.** veste *f* de pyjama; **(at the) t. of the class** le premier de la classe; **on t. of** sur; (*in addition to*) *Fig* en plus de; **on t.** (*in bus etc*) en haut; **from t. to bottom** de fond en comble; **the big t.** (*circus*) le chapiteau; – *a* (*drawer, shelf*) du haut, premier; (*step, layer, storey*) dernier; (*upper*) supérieur; (*in rank, exam*) premier; (*chief*) principal; (*best*) meilleur; (*great, distinguished*) éminent; (*maximum*) maximum; **in t. gear** *Aut* en quatrième vitesse; **at t. speed** à toute vitesse; **t. hat** (chapeau *m*) haut-de-forme *m*. ◆**t.-ˈflight** *a Fam* excellent. ◆**t.-ˈheavy** *a* trop lourd du haut. ◆**t.-level** *a* (*talks etc*) au sommet. ◆**t.-ˈnotch** *a Fam* excellent. ◆**t.-ˈranking** *a* (*official*) haut placé. ◆**t.-ˈsecret** *a* ultra-secret.

top[2] [tɒp] *vt* (**-pp-**) (*exceed*) dépasser; **to t. up** (*glass etc*) remplir (de nouveau); (*coffee, oil etc*) rajouter; **and to t. it all . . .** et pour comble . . . ; **topped with** *Culin* nappé de.

top[3] [tɒp] *n* (*toy*) toupie *f*.

topaz [ˈtəʊpæz] *n* (*gem*) topaze *f*.

topic [ˈtɒpɪk] *n* sujet *m*. ◆**topical** *a* d'actualité. ◆**topiˈcality** *n* actualité *f*.

topless [ˈtɒpləs] *a* (*woman*) aux seins nus.

topography [təˈpɒgrəfɪ] *n* topographie *f*.

topple [ˈtɒp(ə)l] *vi* **to t. (over)** tomber; – *vt* **to t. (over)** faire tomber.

topsy-turvy [tɒpsɪˈtɜːvɪ] *a & adv* sens dessus dessous.

torch [tɔːtʃ] *n* (*burning*) torche *f*, flambeau *m*; (*electric*) lampe *f* électrique. ◆**torchlight** *n & a* **by t.** à la lumière des flambeaux; **t. procession** retraite *f* aux flambeaux.

tore [tɔːr] *see* **tear**[1].

torment [tɔːˈment] *vt* (*make suffer*) tourmenter; (*annoy*) agacer; – [ˈtɔːment] *n* tourment *m*.

tornado [tɔːˈneɪdəʊ] *n* (*pl* **-oes**) tornade *f*.

torpedo [tɔːˈpiːdəʊ] *n* (*pl* **-oes**) torpille *f*; **t. boat** torpilleur *m*; – *vt* torpiller.

torrent [ˈtɒrənt] *n* torrent *m*. ◆**torrential** [təˈrenʃ(ə)l] *a* torrentiel.

torrid [ˈtɒrɪd] *a* (*love affair etc*) brûlant, passionné; (*climate, weather*) torride.

torso [ˈtɔːsəʊ] *n* (*pl* **-os**) torse *m*.

tortoise [ˈtɔːtəs] *n* tortue *f*. ◆**tortoiseshell** *a* (*comb etc*) en écaille; (*spectacles*) à monture d'écaille.

tortuous [ˈtɔːtʃʊəs] *a* tortueux.

tortur/e [ˈtɔːtʃər] *n* torture *f*; – *vt* torturer. ◆**—er** *n* tortionnaire *m*.

Tory [ˈtɔːrɪ] *n* tory *m*; – *a* tory *inv*.

toss [tɒs] *vt* (*throw*) jeter, lancer (**to** à); **to t. s.o. (about)** (*of boat, vehicle*) ballotter qn, faire tressauter qn; **to t. a coin** jouer à pile ou à face; **to t. back** (*one's head*) rejeter en arrière; – *vi* **to t. (about), t. and turn** (*in one's sleep etc*) se tourner et se retourner; **we'll t. (up) for it, we'll t. up** on va jouer à pile ou à face; – *n* **with a t. of the head** d'un mouvement brusque de la tête. ◆**t.-up** *n* **it's a t.-up whether he leaves or stays** *Sl* il y a autant de chances pour qu'il parte ou pour qu'il reste.

tot [tɒt] **1** *n* **(tiny) t.** petit(e) enfant *mf*. **2** *vt* (**-tt-**) **to t. up** (*total*) *Fam* additionner.

total [ˈtəʊt(ə)l] *a* total; **the t. sales** le total des ventes; – *n* total *m*; **in t.** au total; – *vt* (**-ll-**, *Am* **-l-**) (*of debt, invoice*) s'élever à; **to t. (up)** (*find the total of*) totaliser; **that totals $9** ça fait neuf dollars en tout. ◆**—ly** *adv* totalement.

totalitarian [təʊtælɪˈteərɪən] *a Pol* totalitaire.

tote [təʊt] **1** *n Sp Fam* pari *m* mutuel. **2** *vt* (*gun*) porter.

totter [ˈtɒtər] *vi* chanceler.

touch [tʌtʃ] *n* (*contact*) contact *m*, toucher *m*; (*sense*) toucher *m*; (*of painter*) & *Fb Rugby* touche *f*; **a t. of** (*small amount*) un petit peu de, un soupçon de; **the finishing**

touches la dernière touche; **in t. with** (*person*) en contact avec; (*events*) au courant de; **to be out of t. with** ne plus être en contact avec; (*events*) ne plus être au courant de; **to get in t.** se mettre en contact (**with** avec); **we lost t.** on s'est perdu de vue; – *vt* toucher; (*lay a finger on, tamper with, eat*) toucher à; (*move emotionally*) toucher; (*equal*) *Fig* égaler; **to t. up** retoucher; **I don't t. the stuff** (*beer etc*) je n'en bois jamais; – *vi* (*of lines, ends etc*) se toucher; **don't t.!** n'y *or* ne touche pas!; **he's always touching** c'est un touche-à-tout; **to t. down** (*of aircraft*) atterrir; **to t. on** (*subject*) toucher à. ◆**—ed** *a* (*emotionally*) touché (**by** de); (*crazy*) *Fam* cinglé. ◆**—ing** *a* (*story etc*) touchant. ◆**touch-and-'go** *a* (*uncertain*) *Fam* douteux. ◆**touchdown** *n* *Av* atterrissage *m*. ◆**touchline** *n Fb Rugby* (ligne *f* de) touche *f*.

touchy ['tʌtʃɪ] *a* (**-ier, -iest**) (*sensitive*) susceptible (**about** à propos de).

tough [tʌf] *a* (**-er, -est**) (*hard*) dur; (*meat, businessman*) coriace; (*sturdy*) solide; (*strong*) fort; (*relentless*) acharné; (*difficult*) difficile, dur; **t. guy** dur *m*; **t. luck!** *Fam* pas de chance!, quelle déveine!; – *n* (*tough guy*) *Fam* dur *m*. ◆**toughen** *vt* (*body, person*) endurcir; (*reinforce*) renforcer. ◆**toughness** *n* dureté *f*; solidité *f*; force *f*.

toupee ['tuːpeɪ] *n* postiche *m*.

tour [tʊər] *n* (*journey*) voyage *m*; (*visit*) visite *f*; (*by artist, team etc*) tournée *f*; (*on bicycle, on foot*) randonnée *f*; **on t.** en voyage; en tournée; **a t. of** (*France*) un voyage en; une tournée en; une randonnée en; – *vt* visiter; (*of artist etc*) être en tournée en *or* dans *etc*. ◆**—ing** *n* tourisme *m*; **to go t.** faire du tourisme. ◆**tourism** *n* tourisme *m*. ◆**tourist** *n* touriste *mf*; – *a* touristique; (*class*) touriste *inv*; **t. office** syndicat *m* d'initiative. ◆**touristy** *a Pej Fam* (trop) touristique.

tournament ['tʊənəmənt] *n Sp & Hist* tournoi *m*.

tousled ['taʊz(ə)ld] *a* (*hair*) ébouriffé.

tout [taʊt] *vi* racoler; **to t. for** (*customers*) racoler; – *n* racoleur, -euse *mf*; **ticket t.** revendeur, -euse *mf* (en fraude) de billets.

tow [təʊ] *vt* (*car, boat*) remorquer; (*caravan, trailer*) tracter; **to t. away** (*vehicle*) *Jur* emmener à la fourrière; – *n* **'on t.'** 'en remorque'; **t. truck** (*breakdown lorry*) *Am* dépanneuse *f*. ◆**towpath** *n* chemin *m* de halage. ◆**towrope** *n* (câble *m* de) remorque *f*.

toward(s) [tə'wɔːd(z), *Am* tɔːd(z)] *prep* vers; (*of feelings*) envers; **money t.** de l'argent pour (acheter).

towel ['taʊəl] *n* serviette *f* (de toilette); (*for dishes*) torchon *m*; **t. rail** porte-serviettes *m inv*. ◆**towelling** *n*, *Am* ◆**toweling** *n* tissu-éponge *m*; (**kitchen**) **t.** *Am* essuie-tout *m inv*.

tower ['taʊər] *n* tour *f*; **t. block** tour *f*, immeuble *m*; **ivory t.** *Fig* tour *f* d'ivoire; – *vi* **to t. above** *or* **over** dominer. ◆**—ing** *a* très haut.

town [taʊn] *n* ville *f*; **in t., (in)to t.** en ville; **out of t.** en province; **country t.** bourg *m*; **t. centre** centre-ville *m*; **t. clerk** secrétaire *mf* de mairie; **t. council** conseil *m* municipal; **t. hall** mairie *f*; **t. planner** urbaniste *mf*; **t. planning** urbanisme *m*. ◆**township** *n* (*in South Africa*) commune *f* (noire).

toxic ['tɒksɪk] *a* toxique. ◆**toxin** *n* toxine *f*.

toy [tɔɪ] *n* jouet *m*; **soft t.** (jouet *m* en) peluche *f*; – *a* (*gun*) d'enfant; (*house, car, train*) miniature; – *vi* **to t. with** jouer avec. ◆**toyshop** *n* magasin *m* de jouets.

trac/e [treɪs] *n* trace *f* (**of** de); **to vanish** *or* **disappear without (a) t.** disparaître sans laisser de traces; – *vt* (*draw*) tracer; (*with tracing paper*) (dé)calquer; (*locate*) retrouver (la trace de), dépister; (*follow*) suivre (la piste de) (**to** à); (*relate*) retracer; **to t. (back) to** (*one's family*) faire remonter jusqu'à. ◆**—ing** *n* (*drawing*) calque *m*; **t. paper** papier-calque *m inv*.

track [træk] *n* trace *f*; (*of bullet, rocket*) trajectoire *f*; (*of person, animal, tape recorder*) & *Sp* piste *f*; (*of record*) plage *f*; *Rail* voie *f*; (*path*) piste *f*, chemin *m*; *Sch Am* classe *f* (de niveau); **to keep t. of** suivre; **to lose t. of** (*friend*) perdre de vue; (*argument*) perdre le fil de; **to make tracks** *Fam* se sauver; **the right t.** la bonne voie *or* piste; **t. event** *Sp* épreuve *f* sur piste; **t. record** (*of person, firm etc*) *Fig* antécédents *mpl*; – *vt* **to t. (down)** (*locate*) retrouver, dépister; (*pursue*) traquer. ◆**—er** *a* **t. dog** chien *m* policier. ◆**tracksuit** *n Sp* survêtement *m*.

tract [trækt] *n* (*stretch of land*) étendue *f*.

traction ['trækʃ(ə)n] *n Tech* traction *f*.

tractor ['træktər] *n* tracteur *m*.

trade [treɪd] *n* commerce *m*; (*job*) métier *m*; (*exchange*) échange *m*; – *a* (*fair, balance, route*) commercial; (*price*) de (demi-)gros; (*secret*) de fabrication; (*barrier*) douanier; **t. union** syndicat *m*; **t. unionist** syndicaliste *mf*; – *vi* faire du commerce (**with** avec); **to t. in** (*sugar etc*) faire le commerce de; – *vt* (*exchange*) échanger (**for** contre); **to t. sth in** (*old article*) faire reprendre qch. ◆**t.-in** *n*

Com reprise *f.* ◆**t.-off** *n* échange *m.* ◆**trading** *n* commerce *m*; – *a* (*activity, port etc*) commercial; (*nation*) commerçant; **t. estate** zone *f* industrielle. ◆**trader** *n* commerçant, -ante *mf*; **(street) t.** vendeur, -euse *mf* de rue. ◆**tradesman** *n* (*pl* **-men**) commerçant *m.*

trademark ['treɪdmɑːk] *n* marque *f* de fabrique; **(registered) t.** marque déposée.

tradition [trə'dɪʃ(ə)n] *n* tradition *f.* ◆**tra'ditional** *a* traditionnel. ◆**traditionally** *adv* traditionnellement.

traffic ['træfɪk] **1** *n* (*on road*) circulation *f*; *Av Nau Rail* trafic *m*; **busy** *or* **heavy t.** beaucoup de circulation; **heavy t.** (*vehicles*) poids *mpl* lourds; **t. circle** *Am* rond-point *m*; **t. cone** cône *m* de chantier; **t. jam** embouteillage *m*; **t. lights** feux *mpl* (de signalisation); (*when red*) feu *m* rouge; **t. sign** panneau *m* de signalisation. **2** *n* (*trade*) *Pej* trafic *m* **(in** de); – *vi* **(-ck-)** trafiquer **(in** de). ◆**trafficker** *n Pej* trafiquant, -ante *mf.*

tragedy ['trædʒədɪ] *n Th & Fig* tragédie *f.* ◆**tragic** *a* tragique. ◆**tragically** *adv* tragiquement.

trail [treɪl] *n* (*of powder, smoke, blood etc*) traînée *f*; (*track*) piste *f,* trace *f*; (*path*) sentier *m*; **in its t.** (*wake*) dans son sillage; – *vt* (*drag*) traîner; (*caravan*) tracter; (*follow*) suivre (la piste de); – *vi* (*on the ground etc*) traîner; (*of plant*) ramper; **to t. behind** (*lag behind*) traîner. ◆**—er** *n* **1** *Aut* remorque *f*; *Am* caravane *f.* **2** *Cin* bande *f* annonce.

train [treɪn] **1** *n* (*engine, transport, game*) train *m*; (*underground*) rame *f*; (*procession*) *Fig* file *f*; (*of events*) suite *f*; (*of dress*) traîne *f*; **my t. of thought** le fil de ma pensée; **t. set** train *m* électrique. **2** *vt* (*teach, develop*) former **(to do** à faire); *Sp* entraîner; (*animal, child*) dresser **(to do** à faire); (*ear*) exercer; **to t. oneself to do** s'entraîner à faire; **to t. sth on** (*aim*) braquer qch sur; – *vi* recevoir une formation **(as a doctor/***etc* de médecin/*etc*); *Sp* s'entraîner. ◆**—ed** *a* (*having professional skill*) qualifié; (*nurse etc*) diplômé; (*animal*) dressé; (*ear*) exercé. ◆**—ing** *n* formation *f*; *Sp* entraînement *m*; (*of animal*) dressage *m*; **to be in t.** *Sp* s'entraîner; **(teachers') t. college** école *f* normale. ◆**trai'nee** *n & a* stagiaire (*mf*). ◆**trainer** *n* (*of athlete, racehorse*) entraîneur *m*; (*of dog, lion etc*) dresseur *m*; (*running shoe*) jogging *m,* chaussure *f* de sport.

traipse [treɪps] *vi Fam* (*tiredly*) traîner les pieds; **to t. (about)** (*wander*) se balader.

trait [treɪt] *n* (*of character*) trait *m.*

traitor ['treɪtər] *n* traître *m.*

trajectory [trə'dʒektərɪ] *n* trajectoire *f.*

tram [træm] *n* tram(way) *m.*

tramp [træmp] **1** *n* (*vagrant*) clochard, -arde *mf*; (*woman*) *Pej Am* traînée *f.* **2** *vi* (*walk*) marcher d'un pas lourd; (*hike*) marcher à pied; – *vt* (*streets etc*) parcourir; – *n* (*sound*) pas lourds *mpl*; (*hike*) randonnée *f.*

trample ['træmp(ə)l] *vti* **to t. sth (underfoot), t. on sth** piétiner qch.

trampoline [træmpə'liːn] *n* trampoline *m.*

trance [trɑːns] *n* **in a t.** (*mystic*) en transe.

tranquil ['træŋkwɪl] *a* tranquille. ◆**tran'quillity** *n* tranquillité *f.* ◆**tranquillizer** *n Med* tranquillisant *m.*

trans- [træns, trænz] *pref* trans-.

transact [træn'zækt] *vt* (*business*) traiter. ◆**transaction** *n* (*in bank etc*) opération *f*; (*on Stock Market*) transaction *f*; **the t. of** (*business*) la conduite de.

transatlantic [trænzət'læntɪk] *a* transatlantique.

transcend [træn'send] *vt* transcender. ◆**transcendent** *a* transcendant.

transcribe [træn'skraɪb] *vt* transcrire. ◆**'transcript** *n* (*document*) transcription *f.* ◆**transcription** *n* transcription *f.*

transfer [træns'fɜːr] *vt* **(-rr-)** (*person, goods etc*) transférer **(to** à); (*power*) *Pol* faire passer **(to** à); **to t. the charges** téléphoner en PCV; – *vi* être transféré **(to** à); – ['trænsfɜːr] *n* transfert *m* **(to** à); (*of power*) *Pol* passation *f*; (*image*) décalcomanie *f*; **bank** *or* **credit t.** virement *m* (bancaire). ◆**trans'ferable** *a* **not t.** (*on ticket*) strictement personnel.

transform [træns'fɔːm] *vt* transformer **(into** en). ◆**transfor'mation** *n* transformation *f.* ◆**transformer** *n El* transformateur *m.*

transfusion [træns'fjuːʒ(ə)n] *n* **(blood) t.** transfusion *f* (sanguine).

transient ['trænzɪənt] *a* (*ephemeral*) transitoire.

transistor [træn'zɪstər] *n* (*device*) transistor *m*; **t. (radio)** transistor *m.*

transit ['trænzɪt] *n* transit *m*; **in t.** en transit.

transition [træn'zɪʃ(ə)n] *n* transition *f.* ◆**transitional** *a* de transition, transitoire.

transitive ['trænsɪtɪv] *a Gram* transitif.

transitory ['trænzɪtərɪ] *a* transitoire.

translate [træns'leɪt] *vt* traduire **(from** de, **into** en). ◆**translation** *n* traduction *f*; (*into mother tongue*) *Sch* version *f*; (*from mother tongue*) *Sch* thème *m.* ◆**translator** *n* traducteur, -trice *mf.*

transmit [trænz'mɪt] *vt* **(-tt-)** (*send, pass*)

transmettre; – *vti* (*broadcast*) émettre. ◆**transmission** *n* transmission *f*; (*broadcast*) émission *f*. ◆**transmitter** *n Rad TV* émetteur *m*.

transparent [træns'pærənt] *a* transparent. ◆**transparency** *n* transparence *f*; (*slide*) *Phot* diapositive *f*.

transpire [træn'spaɪər] *vi* (*of secret etc*) s'ébruiter; (*happen*) *Fam* arriver; **it transpired that . . .** il s'est avéré que . . . .

transplant [træns'plɑːnt] *vt* (*plant*) transplanter; (*organ*) *Med* greffer, transplanter; – ['trænsplɑːnt] *n Med* greffe *f*, transplantation *f*.

transport [træn'spɔːt] *vt* transporter; – ['trænspɔːt] *n* transport *m*; **public t.** les transports en commun; **do you have t.?** es-tu motorisé?; **t. café** routier *m*. ◆**transpor'tation** *n* transport *m*.

transpose [træns'pəʊz] *vt* transposer.

transvestite [trænz'vestaɪt] *n* travesti *m*.

trap [træp] *n* piège *m*; (*mouth*) *Pej Sl* gueule *f*; **t. door** trappe *f*; – *vt* (**-pp-**) (*snare*) prendre (au piège); (*jam, corner*) coincer, bloquer; (*cut off by snow etc*) bloquer (**by** par); **to t. one's finger** se coincer le doigt. ◆**trapper** *n* (*hunter*) trappeur *m*.

trapeze [trə'piːz] *n* (*in circus*) trapèze *m*; **t. artist** trapéziste *mf*.

trappings ['træpɪŋz] *npl* signes *mpl* extérieurs.

trash [træʃ] *n* (*nonsense*) sottises *fpl*; (*junk*) saleté(s) *f(pl)*; (*waste*) *Am* ordures *fpl*; (*riffraff*) *Am* racaille *f*. ◆**trashcan** *n Am* poubelle *f*. ◆**trashy** *a* (**-ier, -iest**) (*book etc*) moche, sans valeur; (*goods*) de camelote.

trauma ['trɔːmə, 'traʊmə] *n* (*shock*) traumatisme *m*. ◆**trau'matic** *a* traumatisant. ◆**traumatize** *vt* traumatiser.

travel ['trævəl] *vi* (**-ll-**, *Am* **-l-**) voyager; (*move*) aller, se déplacer; – *vt* (*country, distance, road*) parcourir; – *n* & *npl* voyages *mpl*; **on one's travels** en voyage; – *a* (*agency, book*) de voyages; **t. brochure** dépliant *m* touristique. ◆**travelled** *a* **to be well** *or* **widely t.** avoir beaucoup voyagé. ◆**travelling** *n* voyages *mpl*; – *a* (*bag etc*) de voyage; (*expenses*) de déplacement; (*circus, musician*) ambulant. ◆**traveller** *n* voyageur, -euse *mf*; **traveller's cheque**, *Am* **traveler's check** chèque *m* de voyage. ◆**travelogue** *n*, *Am* ◆**travelog** *n* (*book*) récit *m* de voyages. ◆**travelsickness** *n* (*in car*) mal *m* de la route; (*in aircraft*) mal *m* de l'air.

travesty ['trævəstɪ] *n* parodie *f*.

travolator ['trævəleɪtər] *n* trottoir *m* roulant.

trawler ['trɔːlər] *n* (*ship*) chalutier *m*.

tray [treɪ] *n* plateau *m*; (*for office correspondence etc*) corbeille *f*.

treacherous ['tretʃ(ə)rəs] *a* (*person, action, road, journey etc*) traître. ◆**treacherously** *adv* traîtreusement; (*dangerously*) dangereusement. ◆**treachery** *n* traîtrise *f*.

treacle ['triːk(ə)l] *n* mélasse *f*.

tread [tred] *vi* (*pt* **trod**, *pp* **trodden**) (*walk*) marcher (**on** sur); (*proceed*) *Fig* avancer; – *vt* (*path*) parcourir; (*soil*) *Fig* fouler; **to t. sth into a carpet** étaler qch (avec les pieds) sur un tapis; – *n* (*step*) pas *m*; (*of tyre*) chape *f*. ◆**treadmill** *n Pej Fig* routine *f*.

treason ['triːz(ə)n] *n* trahison *f*.

treasure ['treʒər] *n* trésor *m*; **a real t.** (*person*) *Fig* une vraie perle; **t. hunt** chasse *f* au trésor; – *vt* (*value*) tenir à, priser; (*keep*) conserver (précieusement). ◆**treasurer** *n* trésorier, -ière *mf*. ◆**Treasury** *n* **the T.** *Pol* = le ministère des Finances.

treat [triːt] **1** *vt* (*person, product etc*) & *Med* traiter; (*consider*) considérer (**as** comme); **to t. with care** prendre soin de; **to t. s.o. to sth** offrir qch à qn. **2** *n* (*pleasure*) plaisir *m* (spécial); (*present*) cadeau-surprise *m*; (*meal*) régal *m*; **it was a t. (for me) to do it** ça m'a fait plaisir de le faire. ◆**treatment** *n* (*behaviour*) & *Med* traitement *m*; **his t. of her** la façon dont il la traite; **rough t.** mauvais traitements *mpl*.

treatise ['triːtɪz] *n* (*book*) traité *m* (**on** de).

treaty ['triːtɪ] *n Pol* traité *m*.

treble ['treb(ə)l] *a* triple; – *vti* tripler; – *n* le triple; **it's t. the price** c'est le triple du prix.

tree [triː] *n* arbre *m*; **Christmas t.** sapin *m* de Noël; **family t.** arbre *m* généalogique. ◆**t.-lined** *a* bordé d'arbres. ◆**t.-top** *n* cime *f* (d'un arbre). ◆**t.-trunk** *n* tronc *m* d'arbre.

trek [trek] *vi* (**-kk-**) cheminer *or* voyager (péniblement); *Sp* marcher à pied; (*go*) *Fam* traîner; – *n* voyage *m* (pénible); *Sp* randonnée *f*; (*distance*) *Fam* tirée *f*.

trellis ['trelɪs] *n* treillage *m*.

tremble ['tremb(ə)l] *vi* trembler (**with** de). ◆**tremor** *n* tremblement *m*; (**earth**) **t.** secousse *f* (sismique).

tremendous [trə'mendəs] *a* (*huge*) énorme; (*dreadful*) terrible; (*wonderful*) formidable, terrible. ◆**—ly** *adv* terriblement.

trench [trentʃ] *n* tranchée *f*.

trend [trend] *n* tendance *f* (**towards** à); **the t.** (*fashion*) la mode; **to set a** *or* **the t.** donner le ton, lancer une *or* la mode. ◆**trendy** *a* (**-ier, -iest**) (*person, clothes, topic etc*) *Fam* à la mode, dans le vent.

trepidation [trepɪ'deɪʃ(ə)n] *n* inquiétude *f*.

trespass ['trespəs] *vi* s'introduire sans autorisation (**on, upon** dans); **'no trespassing'** 'entrée interdite'.

tresses ['tresɪz] *npl Lit* chevelure *f*.

trestle ['tres(ə)l] *n* tréteau *m*.

trial ['traɪəl] *n Jur* procès *m*; (*test*) essai *m*; (*ordeal*) épreuve *f*; **t. of strength** épreuve de force; **to go** *or* **be on t., stand t.** passer en jugement; **to put s.o. on t.** juger qn; **by t. and error** par tâtonnements; – *a* (*period, flight etc*) d'essai; (*offer*) à l'essai; **t. run** (*of new product etc*) période *f* d'essai.

triangle ['traɪæŋg(ə)l] *n* triangle *m*; (*setsquare*) *Math Am* équerre *f*. ◆**tri'angular** *a* triangulaire.

tribe [traɪb] *n* tribu *f*. ◆**tribal** *a* tribal.

tribulations [trɪbjʊ'leɪʃ(ə)nz] *npl* (**trials and**) **t.** tribulations *fpl*.

tribunal [traɪ'bjuːn(ə)l] *n* commission *f*, tribunal *m*; *Mil* tribunal *m*.

tributary ['trɪbjʊtərɪ] *n* affluent *m*.

tribute ['trɪbjuːt] *n* hommage *m*, tribut *m*; **to pay t. to** rendre hommage à.

trick [trɪk] *n* (*joke, deception & of conjurer etc*) tour *m*; (*ruse*) astuce *f*; (*habit*) manie *f*; **to play a t. on s.o.** jouer un tour à qn; **card t.** tour *m* de cartes; **that will do the t.** *Fam* ça fera l'affaire; **t. photo** photo *f* truquée; **t. question** question-piège *f*; – *vt* (*deceive*) tromper, attraper; **to t. s.o. into doing sth** amener qn à faire qch par la ruse. ◆**trickery** *n* ruse *f*. ◆**tricky** *a* (**-ier, -iest**) (*problem etc*) difficile, délicat; (*person*) rusé.

trickle ['trɪk(ə)l] *n* (*of liquid*) filet *m*; **a t. of** (*letters, people etc*) *Fig* un petit nombre de; – *vi* (*flow*) dégouliner, couler (lentement); **to t. in** (*of letters, people etc*) *Fig* arriver en petit nombre.

tricycle ['traɪsɪk(ə)l] *n* tricycle *m*.

trier ['traɪər] *n* **to be a t.** être persévérant.

trifl/e ['traɪf(ə)l] *n* (*article, money*) bagatelle *f*; (*dessert*) diplomate *m*; – *adv* **a t. small/too much/***etc* un tantinet petit/trop/*etc*; – *vi* **to t. with** (*s.o.'s feelings*) jouer avec; (*person*) plaisanter avec. ◆**—ing** *a* insignifiant.

trigger ['trɪgər] *n* (*of gun*) gâchette *f*; – *vt* **to t.** (**off**) (*start, cause*) déclencher.

trilogy ['trɪlədʒɪ] *n* trilogie *f*.

trim [trɪm] **1** *a* (**trimmer, trimmest**) (*neat*) soigné, net; (*slim*) svelte; – *n* **in t.** (*fit*) en (bonne) forme. **2** *n* (*cut*) légère coupe *f*; (*haircut*) coupe *f* de rafraîchissement; **to have a t.** se faire rafraîchir les cheveux; – *vt* (**-mm-**) couper (légèrement); (*finger nail, edge*) rogner; (*hair*) rafraîchir. **3** *n* (*on garment*) garniture *f*; (*on car*) garnitures *fpl*; – *vt* (**-mm-**) **to t. with** (*lace etc*) orner de. ◆**trimmings** *npl* garniture(s) *f(pl)*; (*extras*) *Fig* accessoires *mpl*.

Trinity ['trɪnɪtɪ] *n* **the T.** (*union*) *Rel* la Trinité.

trinket ['trɪŋkɪt] *n* colifichet *m*.

trio ['triːəʊ] *n* (*pl* **-os**) (*group*) & *Mus* trio *m*.

trip [trɪp] **1** *n* (*journey*) voyage *m*; (*outing*) excursion *f*; **to take a t. to** (*cinema, shops etc*) aller à. **2** *n* (*stumble*) faux pas *m*; – *vi* (**-pp-**) **to t.** (**over** *or* **up**) trébucher; **to t. over sth** trébucher contre qch; – *vt* **to t. s.o. up** faire trébucher qn. **3** *vi* (**-pp-**) (*walk gently*) marcher d'un pas léger. ◆**tripper** *n* **day t.** excursionniste *mf*.

tripe [traɪp] *n Culin* tripes *fpl*; (*nonsense*) *Fam* bêtises *fpl*.

triple ['trɪp(ə)l] *a* triple; – *vti* tripler. ◆**triplets** *npl* (*children*) triplés, -ées *mfpl*.

triplicate ['trɪplɪkət] *n* **in t.** en trois exemplaires.

tripod ['traɪpɒd] *n* trépied *m*.

trite [traɪt] *a* banal. ◆**—ness** *n* banalité *f*.

triumph ['traɪʌmf] *n* triomphe *m* (**over** sur); – *vi* triompher (**over** de). ◆**tri'umphal** *a* triomphal. ◆**tri'umphant** *a* (*team, army, gesture*) triomphant; (*success, welcome, return*) triomphal. ◆**tri'umphantly** *adv* triomphalement.

trivia ['trɪvɪə] *npl* vétilles *fpl*. ◆**trivial** *a* (*unimportant*) insignifiant; (*trite*) banal. ◆**trivi'ality** *n* insignifiance *f*; banalité *f*; *pl* banalités *fpl*.

trod, trodden [trɒd, 'trɒd(ə)n] *see* **tread**.

trolley ['trɒlɪ] *n* (*for luggage*) chariot *m*; (*for shopping*) poussette *f* (de marché); (*in supermarket*) caddie® *m*; (*trolleybus*) trolley *m*; (**tea**) **t.** table *f* roulante; (*for tea urn*) chariot *m*; **t.** (**car**) *Am* tramway *m*. ◆**trolleybus** *n* trolleybus *m*.

trombone [trɒm'bəʊn] *n Mus* trombone *m*.

troop [truːp] *n* bande *f*; *Mil* troupe *f*; **the troops** (*army, soldiers*) les troupes, la troupe; – *vi* **to t. in/out/***etc* entrer/sortir/*etc* en masse. ◆**—ing** *n* **t. the colour** le salut du drapeau. ◆**—er** *n* (**state**) **t.** *Am* membre *m* de la police montée.

trophy ['trəʊfɪ] *n* trophée *m*.

tropic ['trɒpɪk] *n* tropique *m*. ◆**tropical** *a* tropical.

trot [trɒt] *n* (*of horse*) trot *m*; **on the t.** (*one after another*) *Fam* de suite; – *vi* (**-tt-**) trotter; **to t. off** *or* **along** (*leave*) *Hum Fam* se sauver; – *vt* **to t. out** (*say*) *Fam* débiter.

troubl/e ['trʌb(ə)l] *n* (*difficulty*) ennui(s) *m(pl)*; (*bother, effort*) peine *f*, mal *m*; **trouble(s)** (*social unrest etc*) & *Med* troubles *mpl*; **to be in t.** avoir des ennuis; **to get into t.** s'attirer des ennuis (**with** avec); **the t. (with you) is . . .** l'ennui (avec toi) c'est que . . . ; **to go to the t. of doing, take the t. to do** se donner la peine *or* le mal de faire; **I didn't put her to any t.** je ne l'ai pas dérangée; **to find the t.** trouver le problème; **a spot of t.** un petit problème; **a t. spot** *Pol* un point chaud; – *vt* (*inconvenience*) déranger, ennuyer; (*worry, annoy*) ennuyer; (*hurt*) faire mal à; (*grieve*) peiner; **to t. to do** se donner la peine de faire; – *vi* **to t. (oneself)** se déranger. ◆**—ed** *a* (*worried*) inquiet; (*period*) agité. ◆**trouble-free** *a* (*machine, vehicle*) qui ne tombe jamais en panne, fiable. ◆**troublemaker** *n* fauteur *m* de troubles. ◆**troubleshooter** *n Tech* dépanneur *m*, expert *m*; *Pol* conciliateur, -trice *mf*.

troublesome ['trʌb(ə)ls(ə)m] *a* ennuyeux, gênant; (*leg etc*) qui fait mal.

trough [trɒf] *n* (*for drinking*) abreuvoir *m*; (*for feeding*) auge *f*; **t. of low pressure** *Met* dépression *f*.

trounce [trauns] *vt* (*defeat*) écraser.

troupe [truːp] *n Th* troupe *f*.

trousers ['trauzəz] *npl* pantalon *m*; **a pair of t., some t.** un pantalon; **(short) t.** culottes *fpl* courtes.

trousseau ['truːsəu] *n* (*of bride*) trousseau *m*.

trout [traut] *n* truite *f*.

trowel ['trauəl] *n* (*for cement or plaster*) truelle *f*; (*for plants*) déplantoir *m*.

truant ['truːənt] *n* (*pupil, shirker*) absentéiste *mf*; **to play t.** faire l'école buissonnière. ◆**truancy** *n Sch* absentéisme *m* scolaire.

truce [truːs] *n Mil* trêve *f*.

truck [trʌk] *n* **1** (*lorry*) camion *m*; *Rail* wagon *m* plat; **t. driver** camionneur *m*; (*long-distance*) routier *m*; **t. stop** (*restaurant*) routier *m*. **2 t. farmer** *Am* maraîcher, -ère *mf*. ◆**trucker** *n Am* (*haulier*) transporteur *m* routier; (*driver*) camionneur *m*, routier *m*.

truculent ['trʌkjulənt] *a* agressif.

trudge [trʌdʒ] *vi* marcher d'un pas pesant.

true [truː] *a* (**-er, -est**) vrai; (*accurate*) exact; (*genuine*) vrai, véritable; **t. to** (*person, promise etc*) fidèle à; **t. to life** conforme à la réalité; **to come t.** se réaliser; **to hold t.** (*of argument etc*) valoir (**for** pour); **too t.!** *Fam* ah, ça oui! ◆**truly** *adv* vraiment; (*faithfully*) fidèlement; **well and t.** bel et bien.

truffle ['trʌf(ə)l] *n* (*mushroom*) truffe *f*.

truism ['truːɪz(ə)m] *n* lapalissade *f*.

trump [trʌmp] **1** *n Cards* atout *m*; **t. card** (*advantage*) *Fig* atout *m*. **2** *vt* **to t. up** (*charge, reason*) inventer.

trumpet ['trʌmpɪt] *n* trompette *f*; **t. player** trompettiste *mf*.

truncate [trʌŋ'keɪt] *vt* tronquer.

truncheon ['trʌntʃ(ə)n] *n* matraque *f*.

trundle ['trʌnd(ə)l] *vti* **to t. along** rouler bruyamment.

trunk [trʌŋk] *n* (*of tree, body*) tronc *m*; (*of elephant*) trompe *f*; (*case*) malle *f*; (*of vehicle*) *Am* coffre *m*; *pl* (*for swimming*) slip *m* *or* caleçon *m* de bain; **t. call** *Tel* communication *f* interurbaine; **t. road** route *f* nationale.

truss [trʌs] *vt* **to t. (up)** (*prisoner*) ligoter.

trust [trʌst] *n* (*faith*) confiance *f* (**in** en); (*group*) *Fin* trust *m*; *Jur* fidéicommis *m*; **to take on t.** accepter de confiance; – *vt* (*person, judgement*) avoir confiance en, se fier à; (*instinct, promise*) se fier à; **to t. s.o. with sth, t. sth to s.o.** confier qch à qn; **to t. s.o. to do** (*rely on, expect*) compter sur qn pour faire; **I t. that** (*hope*) j'espère que; – *vi* **to t. in s.o.** se fier à qn; **to t. to luck** *or* **chance** se fier au hasard. ◆**—ed** *a* (*friend, method etc*) éprouvé. ◆**—ing** *a* confiant. ◆**trus'tee** *n* (*of school*) administrateur -trice *mf*. ◆**trustworthy** *a* sûr, digne de confiance.

truth [truːθ] *n* (*pl* -s [truːðz]) vérité *f*; **there's some t. in . . .** il y a du vrai dans . . . . ◆**truthful** *a* (*statement etc*) véridique, vrai; (*person*) sincère. ◆**truthfully** *adv* sincèrement.

try [traɪ] **1** *vt* essayer (**to do, doing** de faire); (*s.o.'s patience etc*) mettre à l'épreuve; **to t. one's hand at** s'essayer à; **to t. one's luck** tenter sa chance; **to t. (out)** (*car, method etc*) essayer; (*employee etc*) mettre à l'essai; **to t. on** (*clothes, shoes*) essayer; – *vi* essayer (**for sth** d'obtenir qch); **to t. hard** faire un gros effort; **t. and come!** essaie de venir!; – *n* (*attempt*) & *Rugby* essai *m*; **to have a t.** essayer; **at (the) first t.** du premier coup. **2** *vt* (*person*) *Jur* juger (**for theft/***etc* pour vol/*etc*). ◆**—ing** *a* pénible, éprouvant.

tsar [zɑːr] *n* tsar *m*.

tub [tʌb] *n* (*for washing clothes etc*) baquet *m*; (*bath*) baignoire *f*; (*for ice cream etc*) pot *m*.

tuba ['tjuːbə] *n Mus* tuba *m*.

tubby ['tʌbɪ] *a* (**-ier, -iest**) *Fam* dodu.

tube [tjuːb] *n* tube *m*. *Rail Fam* métro *m*; (*of tyre*) chambre *f* à air. ◆**tubing** *n* (*tubes*) tubes *mpl*. ◆**tubular** *a* tubulaire.

tuberculosis [tjuːbɜːkjʊˈləʊsɪs] *n* tuberculose *f*.

tuck [tʌk] **1** *n* (*fold in garment*) rempli *m*; – *vt* (*put*) mettre; **to t. away** ranger; (*hide*) cacher; **to t. in** (*shirt*) rentrer; (*person in bed, a blanket*) border; **to t. up** (*skirt*) remonter. **2** *vi* **to t. in** (*eat*) *Fam* manger; **to t. into** (*meal*) *Fam* attaquer; – *n* **t. shop** *Sch* boutique *f* à provisions.

Tuesday [ˈtjuːzdɪ] *n* mardi *m*.

tuft [tʌft] *n* (*of hair, grass*) touffe *f*.

tug [tʌg] **1** *vt* (**-gg-**) (*pull*) tirer; – *vi* tirer (**at, on** sur); – *n* **to give sth a t.** tirer (sur) qch. **2** *n* (*boat*) remorqueur *m*.

tuition [tjuːˈɪʃ(ə)n] *n* (*teaching*) enseignement *m*; (*lessons*) leçons *fpl*; (*fee*) frais *mpl* de scolarité.

tulip [ˈtjuːlɪp] *n* tulipe *f*.

tumble [ˈtʌmb(ə)l] *vi* **to t. (over)** (*fall*) dégringoler; (*backwards*) tomber à la renverse; **to t. to sth** (*understand*) *Sl* réaliser qch; – *n* (*fall*) dégringolade *f*; **t. drier** sèche-linge *m inv*.

tumbledown [ˈtʌmb(ə)ldaʊn] *a* délabré.

tumbler [ˈtʌmblər] *n* (*drinking glass*) gobelet *m*.

tummy [ˈtʌmɪ] *n* *Fam* ventre *m*.

tumour [ˈtjuːmər] *n* tumeur *f*.

tumult [ˈtjuːmʌlt] *n* tumulte *m*. ◆**tuˈmultuous** *a* tumultueux.

tuna [ˈtjuːnə] *n* **t. (fish)** thon *m*.

tun/e [tjuːn] *n* (*melody*) air *m*; **to be** *or* **sing in t./out of t.** chanter juste/faux; **in t.** (*instrument*) accordé; **out of t.** (*instrument*) désaccordé; **in t. with** (*harmony*) *Fig* en accord avec; **to the t. of £50** d'un montant de 50 livres, dans les 50 livres; – *vt* **to t. (up)** *Mus* accorder; *Aut* régler; – *vi* **to t. in (to)** *Rad TV* se mettre à l'écoute (de), écouter. ◆**—ing** *n* *Aut* réglage *m*; **t. fork** *Mus* diapason *m*. ◆**tuneful** *a* mélodieux.

tunic [ˈtjuːnɪk] *n* tunique *f*.

Tunisia [tjuːˈnɪzɪə] *n* Tunisie *f*. ◆**Tunisian** *a & n* tunisien, -ienne (*mf*).

tunnel [ˈtʌn(ə)l] *n* tunnel *m*; (*in mine*) galerie *f*; – *vi* (**-ll-**, *Am* **-l-**) percer un tunnel (**into** dans).

turban [ˈtɜːbən] *n* turban *m*.

turbine [ˈtɜːbaɪn, *Am* ˈtɜːbɪn] *n* turbine *f*.

turbulence [ˈtɜːbjʊləns] *n* *Phys Av* turbulences *fpl*.

turbulent [ˈtɜːbjʊlənt] *a* (*person etc*) turbulent.

tureen [tjʊˈriːn, təˈriːn] *n* **(soup) t.** soupière *f*.

turf [tɜːf] **1** *n* (*grass*) gazon *m*; **the t.** *Sp* le turf; **t. accountant** bookmaker *m*. **2** *vt* **to t. out** (*get rid of*) *Fam* jeter dehors.

turgid [ˈtɜːdʒɪd] *a* (*style, language*) boursouflé.

turkey [ˈtɜːkɪ] *n* dindon *m*, dinde *f*; (*as food*) dinde *f*.

Turkey [ˈtɜːkɪ] *n* Turquie *f*. ◆**Turk** *n* Turc *m*, Turque *f*. ◆**Turkish** *a* turc; **T. delight** (*sweet*) loukoum *m*; – *n* (*language*) turc *m*.

turmoil [ˈtɜːmɔɪl] *n* confusion *f*, trouble *m*. **in t.** en ébullition.

turn [tɜːn] *n* (*movement, action & in game etc*) tour *m*; (*in road*) tournant *m*; (*of events, mind*) tournure *f*; *Med* crise *f*; *Psy* choc *m*; (*act*) *Th* numéro *m*; **t. of phrase** tour *m* *or* tournure *f* (de phrase); **to take turns** se relayer; **in t.** à tour de rôle; **by turns** tour à tour; **in (one's) t.** à son tour; **it's your t. to play** c'est à toi de jouer; **to do s.o. a good t.** rendre service à qn; **the t. of the century** le début du siècle; – *vt* tourner; (*mechanically*) faire tourner; (*mattress, pancake*) retourner; **to turn s.o./sth into** (*change*) changer *or* transformer qn/qch en; **to t. sth red/yellow** rougir/jaunir qch; **to t. sth on s.o.** (*aim*) braquer qch sur qn; **she's turned twenty** elle a vingt ans passés; **it's turned seven** il est sept heures passées; **it turns my stomach** cela me soulève le cœur; – *vi* (*of wheel, driver etc*) tourner; (*turn head or body*) se (re)tourner (**towards** vers); (*become*) devenir; **to t. to** (*question, adviser etc*) se tourner vers; **to t. against** se retourner contre; **to t. into** (*change*) se changer *or* se transformer en. ■ **to t. around** *vi* (*of person*) se retourner; **to t. away** *vt* (*avert*) détourner (**from** de); (*refuse*) renvoyer (*qn*); – *vi* (*stop facing*) détourner les yeux, se détourner; **to t. back** *vt* (*bed sheet, corner of page*) replier; (*person*) renvoyer; (*clock*) reculer (**to** jusqu'à); – *vi* (*return*) retourner (sur ses pas); **to t. down** *vt* (*fold down*) rabattre; (*gas, radio etc*) baisser; (*refuse*) refuser (*qn, offre etc*); **to t. in** *vt* (*hand in*) rendre (**to** à); (*prisoner etc*) *Fam* livrer (à la police); – *vi* (*go to bed*) *Fam* se coucher; **to t. off** *vt* (*light, radio etc*) éteindre; (*tap*) fermer; (*machine*) arrêter; – *vi* (*in vehicle*) tourner; **to t. on** *vt* (*light, radio etc*) mettre, allumer; (*tap*) ouvrir; (*machine*) mettre en marche; **to t. s.o. on** (*sexually*) *Fam* exciter qn; – *vi* **to t. on s.o.** (*attack*) attaquer qn; **to t. out** *vt* (*light*) éteindre; (*contents of box etc*) vider (**from** de); (*produce*) produire; – *vi* (*of crowds*) venir; (*happen*) se passer; **it turns out that** il s'avère que; **she turned out to be . . .** elle s'est révélée être . . . ; **to t. over** *vt* (*page*) tourner; – *vi* (*of vehicle, person etc*) se retourner; (*of car engine*) tourner au ralenti; **to t. round** *vt* (*head, object*) tourner; (*vehicle*) faire faire demi-tour à; – *vi* (*of person*) se retourner; **to t. up** *vt* (*radio, light etc*) mettre plus fort; (*collar*) remonter; (*unearth, find*) déterrer; **a turned-up nose** un nez retroussé; – *vi* (*arrive*) arriver; (*be found*) être (re)trouvé. ◆**turning** *n* (*street*) petite rue *f*; (*bend in road*) tournant *m*; **t. circle** *Aut* rayon *m* de braquage; **t. point** (*in time*) tournant *m*. ◆**turner** *n* (*workman*) tourneur *m*.

turncoat ['tɜːnkəʊt] *n* renégat, -ate *mf*. ◆**turn-off** *n* (*in road*) embranchement *m*. ◆**turnout** *n* (*people*) assistance *f*; (*at polls*) participation *f*. ◆**turnover** *n* (*money*) *Com* chiffre *m* d'affaires; (*of stock*) *Com* rotation *f*; **staff t.** (*starting and leaving*) la rotation du personnel; **apple t.** chausson *m* (aux pommes). ◆**turnup** *n* (*on trousers*) revers *m*.

turnip ['tɜːnɪp] *n* navet *m*.

turnpike ['tɜːnpaɪk] *n Am* autoroute *f* à péage.

turnstile ['tɜːnstaɪl] *n* (*gate*) tourniquet *m*.

turntable ['tɜːnteɪb(ə)l] *n* (*of record player*) platine *f*.

turpentine ['tɜːpəntaɪn] (*Fam* **turps** [tɜːps]) *n* térébenthine *f*.

turquoise ['tɜːkwɔɪz] *a* turquoise *inv*.

turret ['tʌrɪt] *n* tourelle *f*.

turtle ['tɜːt(ə)l] *n* tortue *f* de mer; *Am* tortue *f*. ◆**turtleneck** *a* (*sweater*) à col roulé; – *n* col *m* roulé.

tusk [tʌsk] *n* (*of elephant*) défense *f*.

tussle ['tʌs(ə)l] *n* bagarre *f*.

tutor ['tjuːtər] *n* précepteur, -trice *mf*; *Univ* directeur, -trice *mf* d'études; *Univ Am* assistant, -ante *mf*; – *vt* donner des cours particuliers à. ◆**tu'torial** *n Univ* travaux *mpl* dirigés.

tut-tut! [tʌt'tʌt] *int* allons donc!

tuxedo [tʌk'siːdəʊ] *n* (*pl* **-os**) *Am* smoking *m*.

TV [tiː'viː] *n* télé *f*.

twaddle ['twɒd(ə)l] *n* fadaises *fpl*.

twang [twæŋ] *n* son *m* vibrant; **(nasal) t.** nasillement *m*; – *vi* (*of wire etc*) vibrer.

twee [twiː] *a* (*fussy*) maniéré.

tweed [twiːd] *n* tweed *m*.

tweezers ['twiːzəz] *npl* pince *f* (à épiler).

twelve [twelv] *a* & *n* douze (*m*). ◆**twelfth** *a* & *n* douzième (*mf*).

twenty ['twentɪ] *a* & *n* vingt (*m*). ◆**twentieth** *a* & *n* vingtième (*mf*).

twerp [twɜːp] *n Sl* crétin, -ine *mf*.

twice [twaɪs] *adv* deux fois; **t. as heavy/***etc* deux fois plus lourd/*etc*; **t. a month/***etc*, **t. monthly/***etc* deux fois par mois/*etc*.

twiddle ['twɪd(ə)l] *vti* **to t. (with) sth** (*pencil, knob etc*) tripoter qch; **to t. one's thumbs** se tourner les pouces.

twig [twɪg] **1** *n* (*of branch*) brindille *f*. **2** *vti* (**-gg-**) (*understand*) *Sl* piger.

twilight ['twaɪlaɪt] *n* crépuscule *m*; – *a* crépusculaire.

twin [twɪn] *n* jumeau *m*, jumelle *f*; **identical t.** vrai jumeau; **t. brother** frère *m* jumeau; **t. beds** lits *mpl* jumeaux; **t. town** ville *f* jumelée; – *vt* (**-nn-**) (*town*) jumeler. ◆**twinning** *n* jumelage *m*.

twine [twaɪn] **1** *n* (*string*) ficelle *f*. **2** *vi* (*twist*) s'enlacer (**round** autour de).

twinge [twɪndʒ] *n* **a t. (of pain)** un élancement; **a t. of remorse** un pincement de remords.

twinkle ['twɪŋk(ə)l] *vi* (*of star*) scintiller; (*of eye*) pétiller; – *n* scintillement *m*; pétillement *m*.

twirl [twɜːl] *vi* tournoyer; – *vt* faire tournoyer; (*moustache*) tortiller.

twist [twɪst] *vt* (*wine, arm etc*) tordre; (*roll round*) enrouler; (*weave together*) entortiller; (*knob*) tourner; (*truth etc*) *Fig* déformer; **to t. s.o.'s arm** *Fig* forcer la main à qn; – *vi* (*wind*) s'entortiller (**round sth** autour de qch); (*of road, river*) serpenter; – *n* torsion *f*; (*turn*) tour *m*; (*in rope*) entortillement *m*; (*bend in road*) tournant *m*; (*in story*) coup *m* de théâtre; (*in event*) tournure *f*; (*of lemon*) zeste *m*; **a road full of twists** une route qui fait des zigzags. ◆**—ed** *a* (*ankle, wire, mind*) tordu. ◆**—er** *n* **tongue t.** mot *m* or expression *f* imprononçable.

twit [twɪt] *n Fam* idiot, -ote *mf*.

twitch [twɪtʃ] **1** *n* (*nervous*) tic *m*; – *vi* (*of person*) avoir un tic; (*of muscle*) se convulser. **2** *n* (*jerk*) secousse *f*.

twitter ['twɪtər] *vi* (*of bird*) pépier.

two [tuː] *a* & *n* deux (*m*). ◆**t.-cycle** *n Am* = **t.-stroke**. ◆**t.-'faced** *a Fig* hypocrite. ◆**t.-'legged** *a* bipède. ◆**t.-piece** *n* (*garment*) deux-pièces *m inv*. ◆**t.-'seater** *n Aut* voiture *f* à deux places. ◆**t.-stroke** *n* **t.-stroke (engine)** deux-temps *m inv*. ◆**t.-way** *a* (*traffic*) dans les deux sens; **t.-way radio** émetteur-récepteur *m*.

twofold ['tu:fəuld] *a* double; – *adv* to increase t. doubler.
twosome ['tu:səm] *n* couple *m*.
tycoon [taɪ'ku:n] *n* magnat *m*.
type[1] [taɪp] *n* **1** (*example, person*) type *m*; (*sort*) genre *m*, sorte *f*, type *m*; **blood t.** groupe *m* sanguin. **2** (*print*) *Typ* caractères *mpl*; **in large t.** en gros caractères. ◆**typesetter** *n* compositeur, -trice *mf*.
typ/e[2] [taɪp] *vti* (*write*) taper (à la machine). ◆**—ing** *n* dactylo(graphie) *f*; **a page of t.** une page dactylographiée; **t. error** faute *f* de frappe. ◆**typewriter** *n* machine *f* à écrire. ◆**typewritten** *a* dactylographié. ◆**typist** *n* dactylo *f*.
typhoid ['taɪfɔɪd] *n* **t. (fever)** *Med* typhoïde *f*.
typhoon [taɪ'fu:n] *n Met* typhon *m*.
typical ['tɪpɪk(ə)l] *a* typique (**of** de); (*customary*) habituel; **that's t. (of him)!** c'est bien lui! ◆**typically** *adv* typiquement; (*as usual*) comme d'habitude. ◆**typify** *vt* être typique de; (*symbolize*) représenter.
tyranny ['tɪrənɪ] *n* tyrannie *f*. ◆**ty'rannical** *a* tyrannique. ◆**tyrant** ['taɪərənt] *n* tyran *m*.
tyre ['taɪər] *n* pneu *m*.

U

U, u [ju:] *n* U, u *m*. ◆**U-turn** *n Aut* demi-tour *m*; *Fig Pej* volte-face *f inv*.
ubiquitous [ju:'bɪkwɪtəs] *a* omniprésent.
udder ['ʌdər] *n* (*of cow etc*) pis *m*.
ugh! [ɜ:(h)] *int* pouah!
ugly ['ʌglɪ] *a* (**-ier, -iest**) laid, vilain. ◆**ugliness** *n* laideur *f*.
UK [ju:'keɪ] *abbr* = **United Kingdom.**
ulcer ['ʌlsər] *n* ulcère *m*.
ulterior [ʌl'tɪərɪər] *a* **u. motive** arrière-pensée *f*.
ultimate ['ʌltɪmət] *a* (*final, last*) ultime; (*definitive*) définitif; (*basic*) fondamental; (*authority*) suprême. ◆**—ly** *adv* (*finally*) à la fin; (*fundamentally*) en fin de compte; (*subsequently*) à une date ultérieure.
ultimatum [ʌltɪ'meɪtəm] *n* ultimatum *m*.
ultra- ['ʌltrə] *pref* ultra-.
ultramodern [ʌltrə'mɒdən] *a* ultramoderne.
ultraviolet [ʌltrə'vaɪələt] *a* ultraviolet.
umbilical [ʌm'bɪlɪk(ə)l] *a* **u. cord** cordon *m* ombilical.
umbrage ['ʌmbrɪdʒ] *n* **to take u.** se froisser (**at** de).
umbrella [ʌm'brelə] *n* parapluie *m*; **u. stand** porte-parapluies *m inv*.
umpire ['ʌmpaɪər] *n Sp* arbitre *m*; – *vt* arbitrer.
umpteen [ʌmp'ti:n] *a* (*many*) *Fam* je ne sais combien de. ◆**umpteenth** *a Fam* énième.
un- [ʌn] *pref* in-, peu, non, sans.
UN [ju:'en] *abbr* = **United Nations.**
unabashed [ʌnə'bæʃt] *a* nullement décontenancé.
unabated [ʌnə'beɪtɪd] *a* aussi fort qu'avant.
unable [ʌn'eɪb(ə)l] *a* **to be u. to do** être incapable de faire; **he's u. to swim** il ne sait pas nager.
unabridged [ʌnə'brɪdʒd] *a* intégral.
unacceptable [ʌnək'septəb(ə)l] *a* inacceptable.
unaccompanied [ʌnə'kʌmpənɪd] *a* (*person*) non accompagné; (*singing*) sans accompagnement.
unaccountab/le [ʌnə'kauntəb(ə)l] *a* inexplicable. ◆**—ly** *adv* inexplicablement.
unaccounted [ʌnə'kauntɪd] *a* **to be (still) u. for** rester introuvable.
unaccustomed [ʌnə'kʌstəmd] *a* inaccoutumé; **to be u. to sth/to doing** ne pas être habitué à qch/à faire.
unadulterated [ʌnə'dʌltəreɪtɪd] *a* pur.
unaided [ʌn'eɪdɪd] *a* sans aide.
unanimity [ju:nə'nɪmɪtɪ] *n* unanimité *f*. ◆**u'nanimous** *a* unanime. ◆**u'nanimously** *adv* à l'unanimité.
unappetizing [ʌn'æpɪtaɪzɪŋ] *a* peu appétissant.
unapproachable [ʌnə'prəutʃəb(ə)l] *a* (*person*) inabordable.
unarmed [ʌn'ɑ:md] *a* (*person*) non armé; (*combat*) à mains nues.
unashamed [ʌnə'ʃeɪmd] *a* éhonté; **she's u. about it** elle n'en a pas honte. ◆**—ly** [-ɪdlɪ] *adv* sans vergogne.
unassailable [ʌnə'seɪləb(ə)l] *a* (*argument, reputation*) inattaquable.
unassuming [ʌnə'sju:mɪŋ] *a* modeste.
unattached [ʌnə'tætʃt] *a* (*independent, not married*) libre.
unattainable [ʌnə'teɪnəb(ə)l] *a* (*goal, aim*) inaccessible.

unattended [ʌnə'tendɪd] *a* sans surveillance.
unattractive [ʌnə'træktɪv] *a* (*idea, appearance etc*) peu attrayant; (*character*) peu sympathique; (*ugly*) laid.
unauthorized [ʌn'ɔːθəraɪzd] *a* non autorisé.
unavailable [ʌnə'veɪləb(ə)l] *a* (*person, funds*) indisponible; (*article*) *Com* épuisé.
unavoidab/le [ʌnə'vɔɪdəb(ə)l] *a* inévitable. ◆**—ly** *adv* inévitablement; (*delayed*) pour une raison indépendante de sa volonté.
unaware [ʌnə'weər] *a* **to be u. of** ignorer; **to be u. that** ignorer que. ◆**unawares** *adv* **to catch s.o. u.** prendre qn au dépourvu.
unbalanced [ʌn'bælənst] *a* (*mind, person*) déséquilibré.
unbearab/le [ʌn'beərəb(ə)l] *a* insupportable. ◆**—ly** *adv* insupportablement.
unbeatable [ʌn'biːtəb(ə)l] *a* imbattable. ◆**unbeaten** *a* (*player*) invaincu; (*record*) non battu.
unbeknown(st) [ʌnbɪ'nəʊn(st)] *a* **u. to** à l'insu de.
unbelievable [ʌnbɪ'liːvəb(ə)l] *a* incroyable. ◆**unbelieving** *a* incrédule.
unbend [ʌn'bend] *vi* (*pt & pp* **unbent**) (*relax*) se détendre. ◆**—ing** *a* inflexible.
unbias(s)ed [ʌn'baɪəst] *a* impartial.
unblock [ʌn'blɒk] *vt* (*sink etc*) déboucher.
unborn [ʌn'bɔːn] *a* (*child*) à naître.
unbounded [ʌn'baʊndɪd] *a* illimité.
unbreakable [ʌn'breɪkəb(ə)l] *a* incassable. ◆**unbroken** *a* (*continuous*) continu; (*intact*) intact; (*record*) non battu.
unbridled [ʌn'braɪd(ə)ld] *a* *Fig* débridé.
unburden [ʌn'bɜːd(ə)n] *vt* **to u. oneself** *Fig* s'épancher (to auprès de, avec).
unbutton [ʌn'bʌt(ə)n] *vt* déboutonner.
uncalled-for [ʌn'kɔːldfɔːr] *a* déplacé, injustifié.
uncanny [ʌn'kænɪ] *a* (**-ier, -iest**) étrange, mystérieux.
unceasing [ʌn'siːsɪŋ] *a* incessant. ◆**—ly** *adv* sans cesse.
unceremoniously [ʌnserɪ'məʊnɪəslɪ] *adv* (*to treat*) sans ménagement; (*to show out*) brusquement.
uncertain [ʌn'sɜːt(ə)n] *a* incertain (**about, of** de); **it's** *or* **he's u. whether** *or* **that** il n'est pas certain que (+ *sub*). ◆**uncertainty** *n* incertitude *f*.
unchanged [ʌn'tʃeɪndʒd] *a* inchangé. ◆**unchanging** *a* immuable.
uncharitable [ʌn'tʃærɪtəb(ə)l] *a* peu charitable.
unchecked [ʌn'tʃekt] *adv* sans opposition.
uncivil [ʌn'sɪv(ə)l] *a* impoli, incivil.
uncivilized [ʌn'sɪvɪlaɪzd] *a* barbare.
uncle ['ʌŋk(ə)l] *n* oncle *m*.
unclear [ʌn'klɪər] *a* (*meaning*) qui n'est pas clair; (*result*) incertain; **it's u. whether . . .** on ne sait pas très bien si . . . .
uncomfortable [ʌn'kʌmftəb(ə)l] *a* (*house, chair etc*) inconfortable; (*heat, experience*) désagréable; (*feeling*) troublant; **she is** *or* **feels u.** (*uneasy*) elle est mal à l'aise.
uncommon [ʌn'kɒmən] *a* rare. ◆**—ly** *adv* (*very*) extraordinairement; **not u.** (*fairly often*) assez souvent.
uncommunicative [ʌnkə'mjuːnɪkətɪv] *a* peu communicatif.
uncomplicated [ʌn'kɒmplɪkeɪtɪd] *a* simple.
uncompromising [ʌn'kɒmprəmaɪzɪŋ] *a* intransigeant.
unconcerned [ʌnkən'sɜːnd] *a* (*not anxious*) imperturbable; (*indifferent*) indifférent (**by, with** à).
unconditional [ʌnkən'dɪʃ(ə)nəl] *a* inconditionnel; (*surrender*) sans condition.
unconfirmed [ʌnkən'fɜːmd] *a* non confirmé.
uncongenial [ʌnkən'dʒiːnɪəl] *a* peu agréable; (*person*) antipathique.
unconnected [ʌnkə'nektɪd] *a* (*events, facts etc*) sans rapport (**with** avec).
unconscious [ʌn'kɒnʃəs] *a* *Med* sans connaissance; (*desire*) inconscient; **u. of** (*unaware of*) inconscient de; – *n* *Psy* inconscient *m*. ◆**—ly** *adv* inconsciemment.
uncontrollable [ʌnkən'trəʊləb(ə)l] *a* (*emotion, laughter*) irrépressible.
unconventional [ʌnkən'venʃ(ə)nəl] *a* peu conventionnel.
unconvinced [ʌnkən'vɪnst] *a* **to be** *or* **remain u.** ne pas être convaincu (**of** de). ◆**unconvincing** *a* peu convaincant.
uncooperative [ʌnkəʊ'ɒp(ə)rətɪv] *a* peu coopératif.
uncork [ʌn'kɔːk] *vt* (*bottle*) déboucher.
uncouple [ʌn'kʌp(ə)l] *vt* (*carriages*) *Rail* dételer.
uncouth [ʌn'kuːθ] *a* grossier.
uncover [ʌn'kʌvər] *vt* (*saucepan, conspiracy etc*) découvrir.
unctuous ['ʌŋktʃʊəs] *a* (*insincere*) onctueux.
uncut [ʌn'kʌt] *a* (*film, play*) intégral; (*diamond*) brut.
undamaged [ʌn'dæmɪdʒd] *a* (*goods*) en bon état.
undaunted [ʌn'dɔːntɪd] *a* nullement découragé.
undecided [ʌndɪ'saɪdɪd] *a* (*person*) indécis

(about sur); **I'm u. whether to do it or not** je n'ai pas décidé si je le ferai ou non.
undefeated [ʌndɪ'fiːtɪd] *a* invaincu.
undeniable [ʌndɪ'naɪəb(ə)l] *a* incontestable.
under ['ʌndər] *prep* sous; (*less than*) moins de; (*according to*) selon; **children u. nine** les enfants de moins de *or* enfants au-dessous de neuf ans; **u. the circumstances** dans les circonstances; **u. there** là-dessous; **u. it** dessous; **u. (the command of) s.o.** sous les ordres de qn; **u. age** mineur; **u. discussion/repair** en discussion/réparation; **u. way** (*in progress*) en cours; (*on the way*) en route; **to be u. the impression that** avoir l'impression que; – *adv* au-dessous.
under- ['ʌndər] *pref* sous-.
undercarriage ['ʌndəkærɪdʒ] *n* (*of aircraft*) train *m* d'atterrissage.
undercharge [ʌndə'tʃɑːdʒ] *vt* **I undercharged him (for it)** je ne (le) lui ai pas fait payer assez.
underclothes ['ʌndəkləuðz] *npl* sous-vêtements *mpl*.
undercoat ['ʌndəkəut] *n* (*of paint*) couche *f* de fond.
undercooked [ʌndə'kukt] *a* pas assez cuit.
undercover [ʌndə'kʌvər] *a* (*agent, operation*) secret.
undercurrent ['ʌndəkʌrənt] *n* (*in sea*) courant *m* (sous-marin); **an u. of** *Fig* un courant profond de.
undercut [ʌndə'kʌt] *vt* (*pt & pp* **undercut**, *pres p* **undercutting**) *Com* vendre moins cher que.
underdeveloped [ʌndədɪ'veləpt] *a* (*country*) sous-développé.
underdog ['ʌndədɒg] *n* (*politically, socially*) opprimé, -ée *mf*; (*likely loser*) perdant, -ante *mf* probable.
underdone [ʌndə'dʌn] *a* *Culin* pas assez cuit; (*steak*) saignant.
underestimate [ʌndər'estɪmeɪt] *vt* sous-estimer.
underfed [ʌndə'fed] *a* sous-alimenté.
underfoot [ʌndə'fut] *adv* sous les pieds.
undergo [ʌndə'gəu] *vt* (*pt* **underwent**, *pp* **undergone**) subir.
undergraduate [ʌndə'grædʒuət] *n* étudiant, -ante *mf* (qui prépare la licence).
underground ['ʌndəgraund] *a* souterrain; (*secret*) *Fig* clandestin; – *n* *Rail* métro *m*; (*organization*) *Pol* résistance *f*; – [ʌndə'graund] *adv* sous terre; **to go u.** (*of fugitive etc*) *Fig* passer dans la clandestinité.
undergrowth ['ʌndəgrəuθ] *n* sous-bois *m inv*.
underhand [ʌndə'hænd] *a* (*dishonest*) sournois.
underlie [ʌndə'laɪ] *vt* (*pt* **underlay**, *pp* **underlain**, *pres p* **underlying**) sous-tendre. ◆**underlying** *a* (*basic*) fondamental; (*hidden*) profond.
underline [ʌndə'laɪn] *vt* (*text, idea etc*) souligner.
undermanned [ʌndə'mænd] *a* (*office etc*) à court de personnel.
undermine [ʌndə'maɪn] *vt* (*building, strength, society etc*) miner, saper.
underneath [ʌndə'niːθ] *prep* sous; – *adv* (en) dessous; **the book u.** le livre d'en dessous; – *n* dessous *m*.
undernourished [ʌndə'nʌrɪʃt] *a* sous-alimenté.
underpants ['ʌndəpænts] *npl* (*male underwear*) slip *m*; (*loose, long*) caleçon *m*.
underpass ['ʌndəpɑːs] *n* (*for cars or pedestrians*) passage *m* souterrain.
underpay [ʌndə'peɪ] *vt* sous-payer. ◆**underpaid** *a* sous-payé.
underpriced [ʌndə'praɪst] *a* **it's u.** le prix est trop bas, c'est bradé.
underprivileged [ʌndə'prɪvɪlɪdʒd] *a* défavorisé.
underrate [ʌndə'reɪt] *vt* sous-estimer.
undershirt ['ʌndəʃɜːt] *n* *Am* tricot *m* *or* maillot *m* de corps.
underside ['ʌndəsaɪd] *n* dessous *m*.
undersigned ['ʌndəsaɪnd] *a* soussigné; **I the u.** je soussigné(e).
undersized [ʌndə'saɪzd] *a* trop petit.
underskirt ['ʌndəskɜːt] *n* jupon *m*.
understaffed [ʌndə'stɑːft] *a* à court de personnel.
understand [ʌndə'stænd] *vti* (*pt & pp* **understood**) comprendre; **I u. that** (*hear*) je crois comprendre que, il paraît que; **I've been given to u. that** on m'a fait comprendre que. ◆**—ing** *n* (*act, faculty*) compréhension *f*; (*agreement*) accord *m*, entente *f*; (*sympathy*) entente *f*; **on the u. that** à condition que (+ *sub*); – *a* (*person*) compréhensif. ◆**understood** *a* (*agreed*) entendu; (*implied*) sous-entendu. ◆**understandable** *a* compréhensible. ◆**understandably** *adv* naturellement.
understatement ['ʌndəsteɪtmənt] *n* euphémisme *m*.
understudy ['ʌndəstʌdɪ] *n* *Th* doublure *f*.
undertak/e [ʌndə'teɪk] *vt* (*pt* **undertook**, *pp* **undertaken**) (*task*) entreprendre; (*responsibility*) assumer; **to u. to do** se charger de faire. ◆**—ing** *n* (*task*) entreprise *f*; (*prom-

ise) promesse *f*; **to give an u.** promettre (**that** que).

undertaker ['ʌndəteɪkər] *n* entrepreneur *m* de pompes funèbres.

undertone ['ʌndətəʊn] *n* **in an u.** à mi-voix; **an u. of** (*criticism, sadness etc*) *Fig* une note de.

undervalue [ʌndə'væljuː] *vt* sous-évaluer; **it's undervalued at ten pounds** ça vaut plus que dix livres.

underwater [ʌndə'wɔːtər] *a* sous-marin; – *adv* sous l'eau.

underwear ['ʌndəweər] *n* sous-vêtements *mpl.*

underweight [ʌndə'weɪt] *a* (*person*) qui ne pèse pas assez; (*goods*) d'un poids insuffisant.

underworld ['ʌndəwɜːld] *n* **the u.** (*criminals*) le milieu, la pègre.

undesirable [ʌndɪ'zaɪərəb(ə)l] *a* peu souhaitable (**that** que (+ *sub*)); (*person*) indésirable; – *n* (*person*) indésirable *mf.*

undetected [ʌndɪ'tektɪd] *a* non découvert; **to go u.** passer inaperçu.

undies ['ʌndɪz] *npl* (*female underwear*) *Fam* dessous *mpl.*

undignified [ʌn'dɪgnɪfaɪd] *a* qui manque de dignité.

undisciplined [ʌn'dɪsɪplɪnd] *a* indiscipliné.

undiscovered [ʌndɪ'skʌvəd] *a* **to remain u.** ne pas être découvert.

undisputed [ʌndɪ'spjuːtɪd] *a* incontesté.

undistinguished [ʌndɪ'stɪŋgwɪʃt] *a* médiocre.

undivided [ʌndɪ'vaɪdɪd] *a* **my u. attention** toute mon attention.

undo [ʌn'duː] *vt* (*pt* **undid**, *pp* **undone**) défaire; (*bound person, hands*) détacher, délier; (*a wrong*) réparer. ◆**—ing** *n* (*downfall*) perte *f*, ruine *f*. ◆**undone** *a* **to leave u.** (*work etc*) ne pas faire; **to come u.** (*of knot etc*) se défaire.

undoubted [ʌn'daʊtɪd] *a* indubitable. ◆**—ly** *adv* indubitablement.

undreamt-of [ʌn'dremtɒv] *a* insoupçonné.

undress [ʌn'dres] *vi* se déshabiller; – *vt* déshabiller; **to get undressed** se déshabiller.

undue [ʌn'djuː] *a* excessif. ◆**unduly** *adv* excessivement.

undulating ['ʌndjʊleɪtɪŋ] *a* (*movement*) onduleux; (*countryside*) vallonné.

undying [ʌn'daɪɪŋ] *a* éternel.

unearned [ʌn'ɜːnd] *a* **u. income** rentes *fpl.*

unearth [ʌn'ɜːθ] *vt* (*from ground*) déterrer; (*discover*) *Fig* dénicher, déterrer.

unearthly [ʌn'ɜːθlɪ] *a* sinistre, mystérieux; **u. hour** *Fam* heure *f* indue.

uneasy [ʌn'iːzɪ] *a* (*peace, situation*) précaire; (*silence*) gêné; **to be** *or* **feel u.** (*ill at ease*) être mal à l'aise, être gêné; (*worried*) être inquiet.

uneconomic(al) [ʌniːkə'nɒmɪk((ə)l)] *a* peu économique.

uneducated [ʌn'edʒʊkeɪtɪd] *a* (*person*) inculte; (*accent*) populaire.

unemployed [ʌnɪm'plɔɪd] *a* sans travail, en chômage; – *n* **the u.** les chômeurs *mpl.* ◆**unemployment** *n* chômage *m.*

unending [ʌn'endɪŋ] *a* interminable.

unenthusiastic [ʌnɪnθjuːzɪ'æstɪk] *a* peu enthousiaste.

unenviable [ʌn'envɪəb(ə)l] *a* peu enviable.

unequal [ʌn'iːkwəl] *a* inégal; **to be u. to** (*task*) ne pas être à la hauteur de. ◆**unequalled** *a* (*incomparable*) inégalé.

unequivocal [ʌnɪ'kwɪvək(ə)l] *a* sans équivoque.

unerring [ʌn'ɜːrɪŋ] *a* infaillible.

unethical [ʌn'eθɪk(ə)l] *a* immoral.

uneven [ʌn'iːv(ə)n] *a* inégal.

uneventful [ʌnɪ'ventfəl] *a* (*journey, life etc*) sans histoires.

unexceptionable [ʌnɪk'sepʃ(ə)nəb(ə)l] *a* irréprochable.

unexpected [ʌnɪk'spektɪd] *a* inattendu. ◆**—ly** *adv* à l'improviste; (*suddenly*) subitement; (*unusually*) exceptionnellement.

unexplained [ʌnɪk'spleɪnd] *a* inexpliqué.

unfailing [ʌn'feɪlɪŋ] *a* (*optimism, courage, support etc*) inébranlable; (*supply*) inépuisable.

unfair [ʌn'feər] *a* injuste (**to s.o.** envers qn); (*competition*) déloyal. ◆**—ly** *adv* injustement. ◆**—ness** *n* injustice *f*.

unfaithful [ʌn'feɪθfəl] *a* infidèle (**to** à).

unfamiliar [ʌnfə'mɪlɪər] *a* inconnu, peu familier; **to be u. with** ne pas connaître.

unfashionable [ʌn'fæʃ(ə)nəb(ə)l] *a* (*subject etc*) démodé; (*district etc*) peu chic *inv*, ringard; **it's u. to do** il n'est pas de bon ton de faire.

unfasten [ʌn'fɑːs(ə)n] *vt* défaire.

unfavourable [ʌn'feɪv(ə)rəb(ə)l] *a* défavorable.

unfeeling [ʌn'fiːlɪŋ] *a* insensible.

unfinished [ʌn'fɪnɪʃt] *a* inachevé; **to have some u. business** avoir une affaire à régler.

unfit [ʌn'fɪt] *a* (*unwell*) mal fichu; (*unsuited*) inapte (**for sth** à qch, **to do** à faire); (*unworthy*) indigne (**for sth** de qch, **to do** de faire);

to **be u. to do** (*incapable*) ne pas être en état de faire.
unflagging [ʌn'flægɪŋ] *a* (*zeal*) inlassable; (*interest*) soutenu.
unflappable [ʌn'flæpəb(ə)l] *a Fam* imperturbable.
unflattering [ʌn'flæt(ə)rɪŋ] *a* peu flatteur
unflinching [ʌn'flɪntʃɪŋ] *a* (*fearless*) intrépide.
unfold [ʌn'fəʊld] *vt* déplier; (*wings*) déployer; (*ideas, plan*) *Fig* exposer; – *vi* (*of story, view*) se dérouler.
unforeseeable [ʌnfɔː'siːəb(ə)l] *a* imprévisible. ◆**unforeseen** *a* imprévu.
unforgettable [ʌnfə'getəb(ə)l] *a* inoubliable.
unforgivable [ʌnfə'gɪvəb(ə)l] *a* impardonnable.
unfortunate [ʌn'fɔːtʃ(ə)nət] *a* malheureux; (*event*) fâcheux; **you were u.** tu n'as pas eu de chance. ◆**—ly** *adv* malheureusement.
unfounded [ʌn'faʊndɪd] *a* (*rumour etc*) sans fondement.
unfriendly [ʌn'frendlɪ] *a* peu amical, froid. ◆**unfriendliness** *n* froideur *f*.
unfulfilled [ʌnfʊl'fɪld] *a* (*desire*) insatisfait; (*plan*) non réalisé; (*condition*) non rempli.
unfurl [ʌn'fɜːl] *vt* (*flag etc*) déployer.
unfurnished [ʌn'fɜːnɪʃt] *a* non meublé.
ungainly [ʌn'geɪnlɪ] *a* (*clumsy*) gauche.
ungodly [ʌn'gɒdlɪ] *a* impie; **u. hour** *Fam* heure *f* indue.
ungrammatical [ʌngrə'mætɪk(ə)l] *a* non grammatical.
ungrateful [ʌn'greɪtfəl] *a* ingrat.
unguarded [ʌn'gɑːdɪd] *a* **in an u. moment** dans un moment d'inattention.
unhappy [ʌn'hæpɪ] *a* (**-ier, -iest**) (*sad*) malheureux, triste; (*worried*) inquiet; **u. with** (*not pleased*) mécontent de; **he's u. about doing it** ça le dérange de le faire. ◆**unhappily** *adv* (*unfortunately*) malheureusement. ◆**unhappiness** *n* tristesse *f*.
unharmed [ʌn'hɑːmd] *a* indemne, sain et sauf.
unhealthy [ʌn'helθɪ] *a* (**-ier, -iest**) (*person*) en mauvaise santé; (*climate, place, job*) malsain; (*lungs*) malade.
unheard-of [ʌn'hɜːdɒv] *a* (*unprecedented*) inouï.
unheeded [ʌn'hiːdɪd] *a* **it went u.** on n'en a pas tenu compte.
unhelpful [ʌn'helpfəl] *a* (*person*) peu obligeant *or* serviable; (*advice*) peu utile.
unhinge [ʌn'hɪndʒ] *vt* (*person, mind*) déséquilibrer.
unholy [ʌn'həʊlɪ] *a* (**-ier, -iest**) impie; (*din*) *Fam* de tous les diables.
unhook [ʌn'hʊk] *vt* (*picture, curtain*) décrocher; (*dress*) dégrafer.
unhoped-for [ʌn'həʊptfɔːr] *a* inespéré.
unhurried [ʌn'hʌrɪd] *a* (*movement*) lent; (*stroll, journey*) fait sans hâte.
unhurt [ʌn'hɜːt] *a* indemne, sain et sauf.
unhygienic [ʌnhaɪ'dʒiːnɪk] *a* pas très hygiénique.
unicorn ['juːnɪkɔːn] *n* licorne *f*.
uniform ['juːnɪfɔːm] **1** *n* uniforme *m*. **2** *a* (*regular*) uniforme; (*temperature*) constant. ◆**uniformed** *a* en uniforme. ◆**uni'formity** *n* uniformité *f*. ◆**uniformly** *adv* uniformément.
unify ['juːnɪfaɪ] *vt* unifier. ◆**unifi'cation** *n* unification *f*.
unilateral [juːnɪ'læt(ə)rəl] *a* unilatéral.
unimaginable [ʌnɪ'mædʒɪnəb(ə)l] *a* inimaginable. ◆**unimaginative** *a* (*person, plan etc*) qui manque d'imagination.
unimpaired [ʌnɪm'peəd] *a* intact.
unimportant [ʌnɪm'pɔːtənt] *a* peu important.
uninhabitable [ʌnɪn'hæbɪtəb(ə)l] *a* inhabitable. ◆**uninhabited** *a* inhabité.
uninhibited [ʌnɪn'hɪbɪtɪd] *a* (*person*) sans complexes.
uninitiated [ʌnɪ'nɪʃɪeɪtɪd] *n* **the u.** les profanes *mpl*, les non-initiés.
uninjured [ʌn'ɪndʒəd] *a* indemne.
uninspiring [ʌnɪn'spaɪərɪŋ] *a* (*subject etc*) pas très inspirant.
unintelligible [ʌnɪn'telɪdʒəb(ə)l] *a* inintelligible.
unintentional [ʌnɪn'tenʃ(ə)nəl] *a* involontaire.
uninterested [ʌn'ɪntrɪstɪd] *a* indifférent (**in** à). ◆**uninteresting** *a* (*book etc*) inintéressant; (*person*) fastidieux.
uninterrupted [ʌnɪntə'rʌptɪd] *a* ininterrompu.
uninvited [ʌnɪn'vaɪtɪd] *a* (*to arrive*) sans invitation. ◆**uninviting** *a* peu attrayant.
union ['juːnɪən] *n* union *f*; (*trade union*) syndicat *m*; – *a* syndical; **(trade) u. member** syndiqué, -ée *mf*; **U. Jack** drapeau *m* britannique. ◆**unionist** *n* **trade u.** syndicaliste *mf*. ◆**unionize** *vt* syndiquer.
unique [juː'niːk] *a* unique. ◆**—ly** *adv* exceptionnellement.
unisex ['juːnɪseks] *a* (*clothes etc*) unisexe *inv*.
unison ['juːnɪs(ə)n] *n* **in u.** à l'unisson (**with** de).
unit ['juːnɪt] *n* unité *f*; (*of furniture etc*) élément *m*; (*system*) bloc *m*; (*group, team*)

groupe *m*; **u. trust** *Fin* fonds *m* commun de placement.

unite [juːˈnaɪt] *vt* unir; (*country, party*) unifier; **United Kingdom** Royaume-Uni *m*; **United Nations** (Organisation *f* des) Nations unies *fpl*; **United States (of America)** États-Unis *mpl* (d'Amérique); – *vi* s'unir. ◆**unity** *n* (*cohesion*) unité *f*; (*harmony*) *Fig* harmonie *f*.

universal [juːnɪˈvɜːs(ə)l] *a* universel. ◆**—ly** *adv* universellement.

universe [ˈjuːnɪvɜːs] *n* univers *m*.

university [juːnɪˈvɜːsɪtɪ] *n* université *f*; **at u.** à l'université; – *a* universitaire; (*student, teacher*) d'université.

unjust [ʌnˈdʒʌst] *a* injuste.

unjustified [ʌnˈdʒʌstɪfaɪd] *a* injustifié.

unkempt [ʌnˈkempt] *a* (*appearance*) négligé; (*hair*) mal peigné.

unkind [ʌnˈkaɪnd] *a* peu aimable (**to s.o.** avec qn); (*nasty*) méchant (**to s.o.** avec qn). ◆**—ly** *adv* méchamment.

unknowingly [ʌnˈnəʊɪŋlɪ] *adv* inconsciemment.

unknown [ʌnˈnəʊn] *a* inconnu; **u. to me, he'd left** il était parti, ce que j'ignorais; – *n* (*person*) inconnu, -ue *mf*; **the u.** *Phil* l'inconnu *m*; **u. (quantity)** *Math & Fig* inconnue *f*.

unlawful [ʌnˈlɔːfəl] *a* illégal.

unleaded [ʌnˈledɪd] *a* (*gasoline*) *Am* sans plomb.

unleash [ʌnˈliːʃ] *vt* (*force etc*) déchaîner.

unless [ʌnˈles] *conj* à moins que; **u. she comes** à moins qu'elle ne vienne; **u. you work harder, you'll fail** à moins de travailler plus dur, vous échouerez.

unlike [ʌnˈlaɪk] *a* différent; – *prep* **u. me, she** . . . à la différence de moi *or* contrairement à moi, elle . . . ; **he's very u. his father** il n'est pas du tout comme son père; **that's u. him** ça ne lui ressemble pas.

unlikely [ʌnˈlaɪklɪ] *a* improbable; (*implausible*) invraisemblable; **she's u. to win** il est peu probable qu'elle gagne. ◆**unlikelihood** *n* improbabilité *f*.

unlimited [ʌnˈlɪmɪtɪd] *a* illimité.

unlisted [ʌnˈlɪstɪd] *a* (*phone number*) *Am* qui ne figure pas à l'annuaire.

unload [ʌnˈləʊd] *vt* décharger.

unlock [ʌnˈlɒk] *vt* ouvrir (*avec une clef*).

unlucky [ʌnˈlʌkɪ] *a* (**-ier, -iest**) (*person*) malchanceux; (*colour, number etc*) qui porte malheur; **you're u.** tu n'as pas de chance. ◆**unluckily** *adv* malheureusement.

unmade [ʌnˈmeɪd] *a* (*bed*) défait.

unmanageable [ʌnˈmænɪdʒəb(ə)l] *a* (*child*) difficile; (*hair*) difficile à coiffer; (*packet, size*) peu maniable.

unmanned [ʌnˈmænd] *a* (*ship*) sans équipage; (*spacecraft*) inhabité.

unmarked [ʌnˈmɑːkt] *a* (*not blemished*) sans marque; **u. police car** voiture *f* banalisée.

unmarried [ʌnˈmærɪd] *a* célibataire.

unmask [ʌnˈmɑːsk] *vt* démasquer.

unmentionable [ʌnˈmenʃ(ə)nəb(ə)l] *a* dont il ne faut pas parler; (*unpleasant*) innommable.

unmercifully [ʌnˈmɜːsɪf(ə)lɪ] *adv* sans pitié.

unmistakable [ʌnmɪˈsteɪkəb(ə)l] *a* (*obvious*) indubitable; (*face, voice etc*) facilement reconnaissable.

unmitigated [ʌnˈmɪtɪgeɪtɪd] *a* (*disaster*) absolu; (*folly*) pur.

unmoved [ʌnˈmuːvd] *a* **to be u.** (*feel no emotion*) ne pas être ému (**by** par); (*be unconcerned*) être indifférent (**by** à).

unnatural [ʌnˈnætʃ(ə)rəl] *a* (*not normal*) pas naturel; (*crime*) contre nature; (*affected*) qui manque de naturel. ◆**—ly** *adv* **not u.** naturellement.

unnecessary [ʌnˈnesəs(ə)rɪ] *a* inutile; (*superfluous*) superflu.

unnerve [ʌnˈnɜːv] *vt* désarçonner, déconcerter.

unnoticed [ʌnˈnəʊtɪst] *a* inaperçu.

unobstructed [ʌnəbˈstrʌktɪd] *a* (*road, view*) dégagé.

unobtainable [ʌnəbˈteɪnəb(ə)l] *a* impossible à obtenir.

unobtrusive [ʌnəbˈtruːsɪv] *a* discret.

unoccupied [ʌnˈɒkjʊpaɪd] *a* (*person, house*) inoccupé; (*seat*) libre.

unofficial [ʌnəˈfɪʃ(ə)l] *a* officieux; (*visit*) privé; (*strike*) sauvage. ◆**—ly** *adv* à titre officieux.

unorthodox [ʌnˈɔːθədɒks] *a* peu orthodoxe.

unpack [ʌnˈpæk] *vt* (*case*) défaire; (*goods, belongings, contents*) déballer; **to u. a comb/*etc* from** sortir un peigne/*etc* de; – *vi* défaire sa valise; (*take out goods*) déballer.

unpaid [ʌnˈpeɪd] *a* (*bill, sum*) impayé; (*work, worker*) bénévole; (*leave*) non payé.

unpalatable [ʌnˈpælətəb(ə)l] *a* désagréable, déplaisant.

unparalleled [ʌnˈpærəleld] *a* sans égal.

unperturbed [ʌnpəˈtɜːbd] *a* nullement déconcerté.

unplanned [ʌnˈplænd] *a* (*visit, baby etc*) imprévu.

unpleasant [ʌnˈplezənt] *a* désagréable (**to s.o.** avec qn). ◆**—ness** *n* caractère *m* désagréable (**of** de); (*quarrel*) petite querelle *f.*

unplug [ʌn'plʌg] *vt* (**-gg-**) *El* débrancher; (*unblock*) déboucher.

unpopular [ʌn'pɒpjʊlər] *a* impopulaire; **to be u. with** ne pas plaire à.

unprecedented [ʌn'presɪdentɪd] *a* sans précédent.

unpredictable [ʌnprɪ'dɪktəb(ə)l] *a* imprévisible; (*weather*) indécis.

unprepared [ʌnprɪ'peəd] *a* non préparé; (*speech*) improvisé; **to be u. for** (*not expect*) ne pas s'attendre à.

unprepossessing [ʌnpriːpə'zesɪŋ] *a* peu avenant.

unpretentious [ʌnprɪ'tenʃəs] *a* sans prétention.

unprincipled [ʌn'prɪnsɪp(ə)ld] *a* sans scrupules.

unprofessional [ʌnprə'feʃ(ə)nəl] *a* (*unethical*) contraire aux règles de sa profession.

unpublished [ʌn'pʌblɪʃt] *a* (*text, writer*) inédit.

unpunished [ʌn'pʌnɪʃt] *a* **to go u.** rester impuni.

unqualified [ʌn'kwɒlɪfaɪd] *a* **1** (*teacher etc*) non diplômé; **he's u. to do** il n'est pas qualifié pour faire. **2** (*support*) sans réserve; (*success, rogue*) parfait.

unquestionab/le [ʌn'kwestʃ(ə)nəb(ə)l] *a* incontestable. ◆**—ly** *adv* incontestablement.

unravel [ʌn'ræv(ə)l] *vt* (**-ll-**, *Am* **-l-**) (*threads etc*) démêler; (*mystery*) *Fig* éclaircir.

unreal [ʌn'rɪəl] *a* irréel. ◆**unrea'listic** *a* peu réaliste.

unreasonable [ʌn'riːz(ə)nəb(ə)l] *a* qui n'est pas raisonnable; (*price*) excessif.

unrecognizable [ʌnrekəg'naɪzəb(ə)l] *a* méconnaissable.

unrelated [ʌnrɪ'leɪtɪd] *a* (*facts etc*) sans rapport (**to** avec); **we're u.** il n'y a aucun lien de parenté entre nous.

unrelenting [ʌnrɪ'lentɪŋ] *a* (*person*) implacable; (*effort*) acharné.

unreliable [ʌnrɪ'laɪəb(ə)l] *a* (*person*) peu sérieux, peu sûr; (*machine*) peu fiable.

unrelieved [ʌnrɪ'liːvd] *a* (*constant*) constant; (*colour*) uniforme.

unremarkable [ʌnrɪ'mɑːkəb(ə)l] *a* médiocre.

unrepeatable [ʌnrɪ'piːtəb(ə)l] *a* (*offer*) unique.

unrepentant [ʌnrɪ'pentənt] *a* impénitent.

unreservedly [ʌnrɪ'zɜːvɪdlɪ] *adv* sans réserve.

unrest [ʌn'rest] *n* troubles *mpl*, agitation *f.*

unrestricted [ʌnrɪ'strɪktɪd] *a* illimité; (*access*) libre.

unrewarding [ʌnrɪ'wɔːdɪŋ] *a* ingrat; (*financially*) peu rémunérateur.

unripe [ʌn'raɪp] *a* (*fruit*) vert, pas mûr.

unroll [ʌn'rəʊl] *vt* dérouler; – *vi* se dérouler.

unruffled [ʌn'rʌf(ə)ld] *a* (*person*) calme.

unruly [ʌn'ruːlɪ] *a* (**-ier, -iest**) indiscipliné.

unsafe [ʌn'seɪf] *a* (*place, machine etc*) dangereux; (*person*) en danger.

unsaid [ʌn'sed] *a* **to leave sth u.** passer qch sous silence.

unsaleable [ʌn'seɪləb(ə)l] *a* invendable.

unsatisfactory [ʌnsætɪs'fækt(ə)rɪ] *a* peu satisfaisant. ◆**un'satisfied** *a* insatisfait; **u. with** peu satisfait de.

unsavoury [ʌn'seɪv(ə)rɪ] *a* (*person, place etc*) répugnant.

unscathed [ʌn'skeɪðd] *a* indemne.

unscrew [ʌn'skruː] *vt* dévisser.

unscrupulous [ʌn'skruːpjʊləs] *a* (*person, act*) peu scrupuleux.

unseemly [ʌn'siːmlɪ] *a* inconvenant.

unseen [ʌn'siːn] **1** *a* inaperçu. **2** *n* (*translation*) *Sch* version *f.*

unselfish [ʌn'selfɪʃ] *a* (*person, motive etc*) désintéressé.

unsettl/e [ʌn'set(ə)l] *vt* (*person*) troubler. ◆**—ed** *a* (*weather, situation*) instable; (*in one's mind*) troublé; (*in a job*) mal à l'aise.

unshakeable [ʌn'ʃeɪkəb(ə)l] *a* (*person, faith*) inébranlable.

unshaven [ʌn'ʃeɪv(ə)n] *a* pas rasé.

unsightly [ʌn'saɪtlɪ] *a* laid, disgracieux.

unskilled [ʌn'skɪld] *a* inexpert; (*work*) de manœuvre; **u. worker** manœuvre *m*, ouvrier, -ière *mf* non qualifié(e).

unsociable [ʌn'səʊʃəb(ə)l] *a* insociable.

unsocial [ʌn'səʊʃəl] *a* **to work u. hours** travailler en dehors des heures de bureau.

unsolved [ʌn'sɒlvd] *a* (*problem*) non résolu; (*mystery*) inexpliqué; (*crime*) dont l'auteur n'est pas connu.

unsophisticated [ʌnsə'fɪstɪkeɪtɪd] *a* simple.

unsound [ʌn'saʊnd] *a* (*construction etc*) peu solide; (*method*) peu sûr; (*decision*) peu judicieux; **he is of u. mind** il n'a pas toute sa raison.

unspeakable [ʌn'spiːkəb(ə)l] *a* (*horrible*) innommable.

unspecified [ʌn'spesɪfaɪd] *a* indéterminé.

unsporting [ʌn'spɔːtɪŋ] *a* déloyal.

unstable [ʌn'steɪb(ə)l] *a* instable.

unsteady [ʌn'stedɪ] *a* (*hand, voice, step etc*) mal assuré; (*table, ladder etc*) instable. ◆**unsteadily** *adv* (*to walk*) d'un pas mal assuré.

unstinting [ʌn'stɪntɪŋ] *a* (*generosity*) sans bornes.

unstoppable [ʌn'stɒpəb(ə)l] *a* qu'on ne peut (pas) arrêter.

unstuck [ʌn'stʌk] *a* **to come u.** (*of stamp etc*) se décoller; (*fail*) *Fam* se planter.

unsuccessful [ʌnsək'sesfəl] *a* (*attempt etc*) infructueux; (*outcome, candidate*) malheureux; (*application*) non retenu; **to be u.** ne pas réussir (**in doing** à faire); (*of book, artist*) ne pas avoir de succès. ◆**—ly** *adv* en vain, sans succès.

unsuitable [ʌn'suːtəb(ə)l] *a* qui ne convient pas (**for** à); (*example*) peu approprié; (*manners, clothes*) peu convenable. ◆**unsuited** *a* **u. to** impropre à; **they're u.** ils ne sont pas compatibles.

unsure [ʌn'ʃʊər] *a* incertain (**of, about** de).

unsuspecting [ʌnsə'spektɪŋ] *a* qui ne se doute de rien.

unswerving [ʌn'swɜːvɪŋ] *a* (*loyalty etc*) inébranlable.

unsympathetic [ʌnsɪmpə'θetɪk] *a* incompréhensif; **u. to** indifférent à.

untangle [ʌn'tæŋg(ə)l] *vt* (*rope etc*) démêler.

untapped [ʌn'tæpt] *a* inexploité.

untenable [ʌn'tenəb(ə)l] *a* (*position*) intenable.

unthinkable [ʌn'θɪŋkəb(ə)l] *a* impensable, inconcevable.

untidy [ʌn'taɪdɪ] *a* (**-ier, -iest**) (*appearance, hair*) peu soigné; (*room*) en désordre; (*unmethodical*) désordonné. ◆**untidily** *adv* sans soin.

untie [ʌn'taɪ] *vt* (*person, hands*) détacher; (*knot, parcel*) défaire.

until [ʌn'tɪl] *prep* jusqu'à; **u. then** jusque-là; **not u. tomorrow/***etc* (*in the future*) pas avant demain/*etc*; **I didn't come u. Monday** (*in the past*) je ne suis venu que lundi; – *conj* **u. she comes** jusqu'à ce qu'elle vienne, en attendant qu'elle vienne; **do nothing u. I come** (*before*) ne fais rien avant que j'arrive.

untimely [ʌn'taɪmlɪ] *a* inopportun; (*death*) prématuré.

untiring [ʌn'taɪ(ə)rɪŋ] *a* infatigable.

untold [ʌn'təʊld] *a* (*quantity, wealth*) incalculable.

untoward [ʌntə'wɔːd] *a* malencontreux.

untranslatable [ʌntræn'leɪtəb(ə)l] *a* intraduisible.

untroubled [ʌn'trʌb(ə)ld] *a* (*calm*) calme.

untrue [ʌn'truː] *a* faux. ◆**untruth** *n* contre-vérité *f*. ◆**untruthful** *a* (*person*) menteur; (*statement*) mensonger.

unused 1 [ʌn'juːzd] *a* (*new*) neuf; (*not in use*) inutilisé. **2** [ʌn'juːst] *a* **u. to sth/to doing** peu habitué à qch/à faire.

unusual [ʌn'juːʒʊəl] *a* exceptionnel, rare; (*strange*) étrange. ◆**—ly** *adv* exceptionnellement.

unveil [ʌn'veɪl] *vt* dévoiler. ◆**—ing** *n* (*ceremony*) inauguration *f*.

unwanted [ʌn'wɒntɪd] *a* (*useless*) superflu, dont on n'a pas besoin; (*child*) non désiré.

unwarranted [ʌn'wɒrəntɪd] *a* injustifié.

unwavering [ʌn'weɪv(ə)rɪŋ] *a* (*belief etc*) inébranlable.

unwelcome [ʌn'welkəm] *a* (*news, fact*) fâcheux; (*gift, visit*) inopportun; (*person*) importun.

unwell [ʌn'wel] *a* indisposé.

unwieldy [ʌn'wiːldɪ] *a* (*package etc*) encombrant.

unwilling [ʌn'wɪlɪŋ] *a* **he's u. to do** il ne veut pas faire, il est peu disposé à faire. ◆**—ly** *adv* à contrecœur.

unwind [ʌn'waɪnd] **1** *vt* (*thread etc*) dérouler; – *vi* se dérouler. **2** *vi* (*relax*) *Fam* décompresser.

unwise [ʌn'waɪz] *a* imprudent. ◆**—ly** *adv* imprudemment.

unwitting [ʌn'wɪtɪŋ] *a* involontaire. ◆**—ly** *adv* involontairement.

unworkable [ʌn'wɜːkəb(ə)l] *a* (*idea etc*) impraticable.

unworthy [ʌn'wɜːðɪ] *a* indigne (**of** de).

unwrap [ʌn'ræp] *vt* (**-pp-**) ouvrir, défaire.

unwritten [ʌn'rɪt(ə)n] *a* (*agreement*) verbal, tacite.

unyielding [ʌn'jiːldɪŋ] *a* (*person*) inflexible.

unzip [ʌn'zɪp] *vt* (**-pp-**) ouvrir (la fermeture éclair® de).

up [ʌp] *adv* en haut; (*in the air*) en l'air; (*of sun, hand*) levé; (*out of bed*) levé, debout; (*of road*) en travaux; (*of building*) construit; (*finished*) fini; **to come** *or* **go up** monter; **to be up** (*of price, level etc*) être monté (**by** de); **up there** là-haut; **up above** au-dessus; **up on** (*roof etc*) sur; **further** *or* **higher up** plus haut; **up to** (*as far as*) jusqu'à; (*task*) *Fig* à la hauteur de; **to be up to doing** (*capable*) être de taille à faire; (*in a position to*) être à même de faire; **it's up to you to do it** c'est à toi de le faire; **it's up to you** ça dépend de toi; **where are you up to?** (*in book etc*) où en es-tu?; **what are you up to?** *Fam* que fais-tu?; **what's up?** (*what's the matter?*) *Fam* qu'est-ce qu'il y a?; **time's up** c'est l'heure; **halfway up** (*on hill etc*) à mi-chemin; **to walk up and down** marcher de long en large; **to be well up in** (*versed in*) *Fam* s'y connaître en; **to be up against**

(*confront*) être confronté à; **up (with) the workers/*etc*!** *Fam* vive(nt) les travailleurs/*etc*!; – *prep* (*a hill*) en haut de; (*a tree*) dans; (*a ladder*) sur; **to go up** (*hill, stairs*) monter; **to live up the street** habiter plus loin dans la rue; – *npl* **to have ups and downs** avoir des hauts et des bas; – *vt* (**-pp-**) (*increase*) *Fam* augmenter. ◆**up-and-'coming** *a* plein d'avenir. ◆**upbeat** *a* (*cheerful*) *Am Fam* optimiste. ◆**upbringing** *n* éducation *f*. ◆**upcoming** *a Am* imminent. ◆**up'date** *vt* mettre à jour. ◆**up'grade** *vt* (*job*) revaloriser; (*person*) promouvoir. ◆**up'hill 1** *adv* **to go u.** monter. **2** ['ʌphɪl] *a* (*struggle, task*) pénible. ◆**up'hold** *vt* (*pt & pp* **upheld**) maintenir. ◆**upkeep** *n* entretien *m*. ◆**uplift** [ʌp'lɪft] *vt* élever; – ['ʌplɪft] *n* élévation *f* spirituelle. ◆**upmarket** *a Com* haut de gamme. ◆**upright 1** *a & adv* (*erect*) droit; – *n* (*post*) montant *m*. **2** *a* (*honest*) droit. ◆**uprising** *n* insurrection *f*. ◆**up'root** *vt* (*plant, person*) déraciner. ◆**upside 'down** *adv* à l'envers; **to turn u. down** (*room, plans etc*) *Fig* chambouler. ◆**up'stairs** *adv* en haut; **to go u.** monter (l'escalier); – ['ʌpsteəz] *a* (*people, room*) du dessus. ◆**up'stream** *adv* en amont. ◆**upsurge** *n* (*of interest*) recrudescence *f*; (*of anger*) accès *m*. ◆**uptake** *n* **to be quick on the u.** comprendre vite. ◆**up'tight** *a Fam* (*tense*) crispé; (*angry*) en colère. ◆**up-to-'date** *a* moderne; (*information*) à jour; (*well-informed*) au courant (**on** de). ◆**upturn** *n* (*improvement*) amélioration *f* (**in** de); (*rise*) hausse *f* (**in** de). ◆**up'turned** *a* (*nose*) retroussé. ◆**upward** *a* (*movement*) ascendant; (*path*) qui monte; (*trend*) à la hausse. ◆**upwards** *adv* vers le haut; **from five francs u.** à partir de cinq francs; **u. of fifty** cinquante et plus.

upheaval [ʌp'hiːv(ə)l] *n* bouleversement *m*.

upholster [ʌp'həʊlstər] *vt* (*pad*) rembourrer; (*cover*) recouvrir. ◆**upholsterer** *n* tapissier *m*. ◆**upholstery** *n* (*activity*) réfection *f* de sièges; (*in car*) sièges *mpl*.

upon [ə'pɒn] *prep* sur.

upper ['ʌpər] **1** *a* supérieur; **u. class** aristocratie *f*; **to have/get the u. hand** avoir/prendre le dessus. **2** *n* (*of shoe*) empeigne *f*, dessus *m*. ◆**u.-'class** *a* aristocratique. ◆**uppermost** *a* (*highest*) le plus haut; **to be u.** (*on top*) être en dessus.

uproar ['ʌprɔːr] *n* tumulte *m*.

upset [ʌp'set] *vt* (*pt & pp* **upset**, *pres p* **upsetting**) (*knock over*) renverser; (*plans, stomach, routine etc*) déranger; **to u. s.o.** (*grieve*) peiner qn; (*offend*) vexer qn; (*annoy*) contrarier qn; – *a* vexé; contrarié; (*stomach*) dérangé; – ['ʌpset] *n* (*in plans etc*) dérangement *m* (**in** de); (*grief*) peine *f*; **to have a stomach u.** avoir l'estomac dérangé.

upshot ['ʌpʃɒt] *n* résultat *m*.

upstart ['ʌpstɑːt] *n Pej* parvenu, -ue *mf*.

uranium [jʊ'reɪnɪəm] *n* uranium *m*.

urban ['ɜːbən] *a* urbain.

urbane [ɜː'beɪn] *a* courtois, urbain.

urchin ['ɜːtʃɪn] *n* polisson, -onne *mf*.

urge [ɜːdʒ] *vt* **to u. s.o. to do** (*advise*) conseiller vivement à qn de faire; **to u. on** (*person, team*) encourager; – *n* forte envie *f*, besoin *m*.

urgency ['ɜːdʒənsɪ] *n* urgence *f*; (*of request, tone*) insistance *f*. ◆**urgent** *a* urgent, pressant; (*tone*) insistant; (*letter*) urgent. ◆**urgently** *adv* d'urgence; (*insistently*) avec insistance.

urinal [jʊ'raɪn(ə)l] *n* urinoir *m*.

urine ['jʊ(ə)rɪn] *n* urine *f*. ◆**urinate** *vi* uriner.

urn [ɜːn] *n* urne *f*; (*for coffee or tea*) fontaine *f*.

us [əs, *stressed* ʌs] *pron* nous; **(to) us** (*indirect*) nous; **she sees us** elle nous voit; **he gives (to) us** il nous donne; **with us** avec nous; **all of us** nous tous; **let's** *or* **let us eat!** mangeons!

US [juː'es] *abbr* = **United States**.

USA [juːes'eɪ] *abbr* = **United States of America**.

usage ['juːsɪdʒ] *n* (*custom*) & *Ling* usage *m*.

use [juːs] *n* usage *m*, emploi *m*; (*way of using*) emploi *m*; **to have the u. of** avoir l'usage de; **to make u. of** se servir de; **in u.** en usage; **out of u.** hors d'usage; **ready for u.** prêt à l'emploi; **to be of u.** servir, être utile; **it's no u. crying/*etc*** ça ne sert à rien de pleurer/*etc*; **what's the u. of worrying/*etc*?** à quoi bon s'inquiéter/*etc*?, à quoi ça sert de s'inquiéter/*etc*?; **I have no u. for it** je n'en ai pas l'usage, qu'est-ce que je ferais de ça?; **he's no u.** (*hopeless*) il est nul; – [juːz] *vt* se servir de, utiliser, employer (**as** comme; **to do, for doing** pour faire); **it's used to do** *or* **for doing** ça sert à faire; **it's used as** ça sert de; **I u. it to clean** je m'en sers pour nettoyer, ça me sert à nettoyer; **to u. (up)** (*fuel etc*) consommer; (*supplies*) épuiser; (*money*) dépenser. ◆**used 1** [juːzd] *a* (*second-hand*) d'occasion; (*stamp*) oblitéré. **2** [juːst] *v aux* **I u. to do** avant, je faisais; – *a* **u. to sth/to doing** (*accustomed*) habitué à qch/à faire; **to get u. to** s'habituer à. ◆**useful** ['juːsfəl] *a* utile; **to**

come **in u.** être utile; **to make oneself u.** se rendre utile. ◆**usefulness** *n* utilité *f*. ◆**useless** ['juːsləs] *a* inutile; (*unusable*) inutilisable; (*person*) nul, incompétent. ◆**user** ['juːzər] *n* (*of road, dictionary etc*) usager *m*; (*of machine*) utilisateur, -trice *mf*.

usher ['ʌʃər] *n* (*in church or theatre*) placeur *m*; (*in law court*) huissier *m*; – *vt* **to u. in** faire entrer; (*period etc*) *Fig* inaugurer. ◆**ushe'rette** *n Cin* ouvreuse *f*.

USSR [juːeses'ɑːr] *n abbr* (*Union of Soviet Socialist Republics*) URSS *f*.

usual ['juːʒʊəl] *a* habituel, normal; **as u.** comme d'habitude; **it's her u. practice** c'est son habitude; – *n* **the u.** (*food, excuse etc*) *Fam* la même chose que d'habitude. ◆**—ly** *adv* d'habitude.

usurer ['juːʒərər] *n* usurier, -ière *mf*.

usurp [juː'zɜːp] *vt* usurper.

utensil [juː'tens(ə)l] *n* ustensile *m*.

uterus ['juːt(ə)rəs] *n Anat* utérus *m*.

utilitarian [juːtɪlɪ'teərɪən] *a* utilitaire. ◆**u'tility** *n* (**public**) **u.** service *m* public; – *a* (*goods vehicle*) utilitaire.

utilize ['juːtɪlaɪz] *vt* utiliser. ◆**utili'zation** *n* utilisation *f*.

utmost ['ʌtməʊst] *a* **the u. ease**/*etc* (*greatest*) la plus grande facilité/*etc*; **the u. danger/limit**/*etc* (*extreme*) un danger/une limite/*etc* extrême; – *n* **to do one's u.** faire tout son possible (**to do** pour faire).

utopia [juː'təʊpɪə] *n* (*perfect state*) utopie *f*. ◆**utopian** *a* utopique.

utter ['ʌtər] **1** *a* complet, total; (*folly*) pur; (*idiot*) parfait; **it's u. nonsense** c'est complètement absurde. **2** *vt* (*say, express*) proférer; (*a cry, sigh*) pousser. ◆**utterance** *n* (*remark etc*) déclaration *f*; **to give u. to** exprimer. ◆**utterly** *adv* complètement.

V

V, v [viː] *n* V, v *m*. ◆**V.-neck(ed)** *a* (*pullover etc*) à col en V.

vacant ['veɪkənt] *a* (*post*) vacant; (*room, seat*) libre; (*look*) vague, dans le vide. ◆**vacancy** *n* (*post*) poste *m* vacant; (*room*) chambre *f* disponible; **'no vacancies'** (*in hotel*) 'complet'. ◆**vacantly** *adv* **to gaze v.** regarder dans le vide.

vacate [və'keɪt, *Am* 'veɪkeɪt] *vt* quitter.

vacation [veɪ'keɪʃ(ə)n] *n Am* vacances *fpl*; **on v.** en vacances. ◆**—er** *n Am* vacancier, -ière *mf*.

vaccinate ['væksɪneɪt] *vt* vacciner. ◆**vacci'nation** *n* vaccination *f*. ◆**vaccine** [-iːn] *n* vaccin *m*.

vacillate ['væsɪleɪt] *vi* (*hesitate*) hésiter.

vacuum ['vækjʊ(ə)m] *n* vide *m*; **v. cleaner** aspirateur *m*; **v. flask** thermos® *m or f*; – *vt* (*carpet etc*) passer à l'aspirateur. ◆**v.-packed** *a* emballé sous vide.

vagabond ['vægəbɒnd] *n* vagabond, -onde *mf*.

vagary ['veɪgərɪ] *n* caprice *m*.

vagina [və'dʒaɪnə] *n* vagin *m*.

vagrant ['veɪgrənt] *n Jur* vagabond, -onde *mf*.

vague [veɪg] *a* (**-er, -est**) vague; (*memory, outline, photo*) flou; **the vaguest idea** la moindre idée; **he was v. (about it)** il est resté vague. ◆**—ly** *adv* vaguement.

vain [veɪn] *a* (**-er, -est**) **1** (*attempt, hope*) vain; **in v.** en vain; **his** *or* **her efforts were in v.** ses efforts ont été inutiles. **2** (*conceited*) vaniteux. ◆**—ly** *adv* (*in vain*) vainement.

valentine ['væləntaɪn] *n* (*card*) carte *f* de la Saint-Valentin.

valet ['vælɪt, 'væleɪ] *n* valet *m* de chambre.

valiant ['væljənt] *a* courageux. ◆**valour** *n* bravoure *f*.

valid ['vælɪd] *a* (*ticket, motive etc*) valable. ◆**validate** *vt* valider. ◆**va'lidity** *n* validité *f*; (*of argument*) justesse *f*.

valley ['vælɪ] *n* vallée *f*.

valuable ['væljʊəb(ə)l] *a* (*object*) de (grande) valeur; (*help, time etc*) *Fig* précieux; – *npl* objets *mpl* de valeur.

value ['væljuː] *n* valeur *f*; **to be of great/little v.** (*of object*) valoir cher/peu (cher); **it's good v.** c'est très avantageux; **v. added tax** taxe *f* à la valeur ajoutée; – *vt* (*appraise*) évaluer; (*appreciate*) attacher de la valeur à. ◆**valu'ation** *n* évaluation *f*; (*by expert*) expertise *f*. ◆**valuer** *n* expert *m*.

valve [vælv] *n* (*of machine*) soupape *f*; (*in radio*) lampe *f*; (*of tyre*) valve *f*; (*of heart*) valvule *f*.

vampire ['væmpaɪər] *n* vampire *m*.

van [væn] *n* (*small*) camionnette *f*; (*large*) camion *m*; *Rail* fourgon *m*.

vandal ['vænd(ə)l] *n* vandale *mf*. ◆**vandal-**

ism *n* vandalisme *m*. ◆**vandalize** *vt* saccager, détériorer.
vanguard ['vængɑːd] *n* (*of army, progress etc*) avant-garde *f*.
vanilla [və'nɪlə] *n* vanille *f*; – *a* (*ice cream*) à la vanille.
vanish ['vænɪʃ] *vi* disparaître.
vanity ['vænɪtɪ] *n* vanité *f*; **v. case** vanity *m inv*.
vanquish ['væŋkwɪʃ] *vt* vaincre.
vantage point ['vɑːntɪdʒpɔɪnt] *n* (*place, point of view*) (bon) point *m* de vue.
vapour ['veɪpər] *n* vapeur *f*; (*on glass*) buée *f*.
variable ['veərɪəb(ə)l] *a* variable. ◆**variance** *n* **at v.** en désaccord (**with** avec). ◆**variant** *a* différent; – *n* variante *f*. ◆**vari'ation** *n* variation *f*.
varicose ['værɪkəʊs] *a* **v. veins** varices *fpl*.
variety [və'raɪətɪ] *n* **1** (*diversity*) variété *f*; **a v. of opinions/reasons/***etc* (*many*) diverses opinions/raisons/*etc*; **a v. of** (*articles*) *Com* une gamme de. **2** *Th* variétés *fpl*; **v. show** spectacle *m* de variétés.
various ['veərɪəs] *a* divers. ◆**—ly** *adv* diversement.
varnish ['vɑːnɪʃ] *vt* vernir; – *n* vernis *m*.
vary ['veərɪ] *vti* varier (**from** de). ◆**varied** *a* varié. ◆**varying** *a* variable.
vase [vɑːz, *Am* veɪs] *n* vase *m*.
Vaseline® ['væsəliːn] *n* vaseline *f*.
vast [vɑːst] *a* vaste, immense. ◆**—ly** *adv* (*very*) infiniment, extrêmement. ◆**—ness** *n* immensité *f*.
vat [væt] *n* cuve *f*.
VAT [viːiː'tiː, væt] *n abbr* (*value added tax*) TVA *f*.
Vatican ['vætɪkən] *n* Vatican *m*.
vaudeville ['vɔːdəvɪl] *n Th Am* variétés *fpl*.
vault [vɔːlt] **1** *n* (*cellar*) cave *f*; (*tomb*) caveau *m*; (*in bank*) chambre *f* forte, coffres *mpl*; (*roof*) voûte *f*. **2** *vti* (*jump*) sauter.
veal [viːl] *n* (*meat*) veau *m*.
veer [vɪər] *vi* (*of wind*) tourner; (*of car, road*) virer; **to v. off the road** quitter la route.
vegan ['viːgən] *n* végétaliste *mf*.
vegetable ['vedʒtəb(ə)l] *n* légume *m*; – *a* (*kingdom, oil*) végétal; **v. garden** (jardin *m*) potager *m*. ◆**vege'tarian** *a* & *n* végétarien, -ienne (*mf*). ◆**vege'tation** *n* végétation *f*.
vegetate ['vedʒɪteɪt] *vi* (*of person*) *Pej* végéter.
vehement ['vɪəmənt] *a* (*feeling, speech*) véhément; (*attack*) violent. ◆**—ly** *adv* avec véhémence; violemment.
vehicle ['viːɪk(ə)l] *n* véhicule *m*; **heavy goods v.** (*lorry*) poids *m* lourd.
veil [veɪl] *n* (*covering*) & *Fig* voile *m*; – *vt* (*face, truth etc*) voiler.
vein [veɪn] *n* (*in body or rock*) veine *f*; (*in leaf*) nervure *f*; (*mood*) *Fig* esprit *m*.
vellum ['veləm] *n* (*paper, skin*) vélin *m*.
velocity [və'lɒsɪtɪ] *n* vélocité *f*.
velvet ['velvɪt] *n* velours *m*; – *a* de velours. ◆**velvety** *a* velouté.
vendetta [ven'detə] *n* vendetta *f*.
vending machine ['vendɪŋməʃiːn] *n* distributeur *m* automatique.
vendor ['vendər] *n* vendeur, -euse *mf*.
veneer [və'nɪər] *n* (*wood*) placage *m*; (*appearance*) *Fig* vernis *m*.
venerable ['ven(ə)rəb(ə)l] *a* vénérable. ◆**venerate** *vt* vénérer.
venereal [və'nɪərɪəl] *a* (*disease etc*) vénérien.
venetian [və'niːʃ(ə)n] *a* **v. blind** store *m* vénitien.
vengeance ['vendʒəns] *n* vengeance *f*; **with a v.** (*to work, study etc*) furieusement; (*to rain, catch up etc*) pour de bon.
venison ['venɪs(ə)n] *n* venaison *f*.
venom ['venəm] *n* (*substance*) & *Fig* venin *m*. ◆**venomous** *a* (*speech, snake etc*) venimeux.
vent [vent] **1** *n* (*hole*) orifice *m*; (*for air*) bouche *f* d'aération; (*in jacket*) fente *f*. **2** *n* **to give v. to** (*feeling etc*) donner libre cours à; – *vt* (*anger*) décharger (**on** sur).
ventilate ['ventɪleɪt] *vt* ventiler. ◆**venti'lation** *n* ventilation *f*. ◆**ventilator** *n* (*in wall etc*) ventilateur *m*.
ventriloquist [ven'trɪləkwɪst] *n* ventriloque *mf*.
venture ['ventʃər] *n* entreprise *f* (risquée); **my v. into** mon incursion *f* dans; – *vt* (*opinion, fortune*) hasarder; **to v. to do** (*dare*) oser faire; – *vi* s'aventurer, se risquer (**into** dans).
venue ['venjuː] *n* lieu *m* de rencontre *or* de rendez-vous.
veranda(h) [və'rændə] *n* véranda *f*.
verb [vɜːb] *n* verbe *m*. ◆**verbal** *a* (*promise, skill etc*) verbal. ◆**verbatim** [vɜː'beɪtɪm] *a* & *adv* mot pour mot.
verbose [vɜː'bəʊs] *a* (*wordy*) verbeux.
verdict ['vɜːdɪkt] *n* verdict *m*.
verdigris ['vɜːdɪgrɪs] *n* vert-de-gris *m inv*.
verge [vɜːdʒ] *n* (*of road*) accotement *m*, bord *m*; **on the v. of** *Fig* (*ruin, tears etc*) au bord de; (*discovery*) à la veille de; **on the v. of doing** sur le point de faire; – *vi* **to v. on** friser, frôler; (*of colour*) tirer sur.
verger ['vɜːdʒər] *n Rel* bedeau *m*.

verify ['verɪfaɪ] *vt* vérifier. ◆**verifi'cation** *n* vérification *f*.
veritable ['verɪtəb(ə)l] *a* véritable.
vermicelli [vɜːmɪ'selɪ] *n Culin* vermicelle(s) *m(pl)*.
vermin ['vɜːmɪn] *n* (*animals*) animaux *mpl* nuisibles; (*insects, people*) vermine *f*.
vermouth ['vɜːməθ] *n* vermouth *m*.
vernacular [və'nækjʊlər] *n* (*of region*) dialecte *m*.
versatile ['vɜːsətaɪl, *Am* 'vɜːsət(ə)l] *a* (*mind*) souple; (*material, tool, computer*) polyvalent; **he's v.** il a des talents variés, il est polyvalent. ◆**versa'tility** *n* souplesse *f*; **his v.** la variété de ses talents.
verse [vɜːs] *n* (*stanza*) strophe *f*; (*poetry*) vers *mpl*; (*of Bible*) verset *m*.
versed [vɜːst] *a* (**well**) **v. in** versé dans.
version ['vɜːʃ(ə)n] *n* version *f*.
versus ['vɜːsəs] *prep* contre.
vertebra, *pl* **-ae** ['vɜːtɪbrə, -iː] *n* vertèbre *f*.
vertical ['vɜːtɪk(ə)l] *a* vertical; – *n* verticale *f*. ◆**—ly** *adv* verticalement.
vertigo ['vɜːtɪgəʊ] *n* (*fear of falling*) vertige *m*.
verve [vɜːv] *n* fougue *f*.
very ['verɪ] **1** *adv* très; **I'm v. hot** j'ai très chaud; **v. much** beaucoup; **the v. first** le tout premier; **at the v. least/most** tout au moins/plus; **at the v. latest** au plus tard. **2** *a* (*actual*) même; **his** *or* **her v. brother** son frère même; **at the v. end** (*of play etc*) tout à la fin; **to the v. end** jusqu'au bout.
vespers ['vespəz] *npl Rel* vêpres *fpl*.
vessel ['ves(ə)l] *n Anat Bot Nau* vaisseau *m*; (*receptacle*) récipient *m*.
vest [vest] *n* tricot *m or* maillot *m* de corps; (*woman's*) chemise *f* (américaine); (*waistcoat*) *Am* gilet *m*.
vested ['vestɪd] *a* **v. interests** *Com* droits *mpl* acquis; **she's got a v. interest in** *Fig* elle est directement intéressée dans.
vestige ['vestɪdʒ] *n* vestige *m*; **not a v. of truth/good sense** pas un grain de vérité/de bon sens.
vestry ['vestrɪ] *n* sacristie *f*.
vet [vet] **1** *n* vétérinaire *mf*. **2** *vt* (**-tt-**) (*document*) examiner de près; (*candidate*) se renseigner à fond sur. ◆**veteri'narian** *n Am* vétérinaire *mf*. ◆**veterinary** *a* vétérinaire; **v. surgeon** vétérinaire *mf*.
veteran ['vet(ə)rən] *n* vétéran *m*; (**war**) **v.** ancien combattant *m*; – *a* **v. golfer/***etc* golfeur/*etc* expérimenté.
veto ['viːtəʊ] *n* (*pl* **-oes**) (*refusal*) veto *m inv*; (*power*) droit *m* de veto; – *vt* mettre *or* opposer son veto à.
vex [veks] *vt* contrarier, fâcher; **vexed question** question *f* controversée.
via ['vaɪə] *prep* via, par.
viable ['vaɪəb(ə)l] *a* (*baby, firm, plan etc*) viable. ◆**via'bility** *n* viabilité *f*.
viaduct ['vaɪədʌkt] *n* viaduc *m*.
vibrate [vaɪ'breɪt] *vi* vibrer. ◆**'vibrant** *a* vibrant. ◆**vibration** *n* vibration *f*. ◆**vibrator** *n* vibromasseur *m*.
vicar ['vɪkər] *n* (*in Church of England*) pasteur *m*. ◆**vicarage** *n* presbytère *m*.
vicarious [vɪ'keərɪəs] *a* (*emotion*) ressenti indirectement. ◆**—ly** *adv* (*to experience*) indirectement.
vice [vaɪs] *n* **1** (*depravity*) vice *m*; (*fault*) défaut *m*; **v. squad** brigade *f* des mœurs. **2** (*tool*) étau *m*.
vice- [vaɪs] *pref* vice-. ◆**v.-'chancellor** *n Univ* président *m*.
vice versa [vaɪs(ɪ)'vɜːsə] *adv* vice versa.
vicinity [və'sɪnɪtɪ] *n* environs *mpl*; **in the v. of** (*place, amount*) aux environs de.
vicious ['vɪʃəs] *a* (*spiteful*) méchant; (*violent*) brutal; **v. circle** cercle *m* vicieux. ◆**—ly** *adv* méchamment; brutalement. ◆**—ness** *n* méchanceté *f*; brutalité *f*.
vicissitudes [vɪ'sɪsɪtjuːdz] *npl* vicissitudes *fpl*.
victim ['vɪktɪm] *n* victime *f*; **to be the v. of** être victime de. ◆**victimize** *vt* persécuter. ◆**victimi'zation** *n* persécution *f*.
Victorian [vɪk'tɔːrɪən] *a* & *n* victorien, -ienne (*mf*).
victory ['vɪktərɪ] *n* victoire *f*. ◆**victor** *n* vainqueur *m*. ◆**vic'torious** *a* victorieux.
video ['vɪdɪəʊ] *a* vidéo *inv*; – *n* **v.** (**cassette**) vidéocassette *f*; **v.** (**recorder**) magnétoscope *m*; **on v.** sur cassette; **to make a v. of** faire une cassette de; – *vt* (*programme etc*) enregistrer au magnétoscope. ◆**videotape** *n* bande *f* vidéo.
vie [vaɪ] *vi* (*pres p* **vying**) rivaliser (**with** avec).
Vietnam [vjet'næm, *Am* -'nɑːm] *n* Viêt-nam *m*. ◆**Vietna'mese** *a* & *n* vietnamien, -ienne (*mf*).
view [vjuː] *n* vue *f*; **to come into v.** apparaître; **in full v. of everyone** à la vue de tous; **in my v.** (*opinion*) à mon avis; **on v.** (*exhibit*) exposé; **in v. of** (*considering*) étant donné (**the fact that** que); **with a v. to doing** afin de faire; – *vt* (*regard*) considérer; (*house*) visiter. ◆**—er** *n* **1** *TV* téléspectateur, -trice *mf*. **2** (*for slides*) visionneuse *f*. ◆**viewfinder** *n Phot* viseur *m*. ◆**viewpoint** *n* point *m* de vue.

vigil ['vɪdʒɪl] *n* veille *f*; (*over sick person or corpse*) veillée *f*.
vigilant ['vɪdʒɪlənt] *a* vigilant. ◆**vigilance** *n* vigilance *f*.
vigilante [vɪdʒɪ'læntɪ] *n Pej* membre *m* d'une milice privée.
vigour ['vɪgər] *n* vigueur *f*. ◆**vigorous** *a* (*person, speech etc*) vigoureux.
vile [vaɪl] *a* (-er, -est) (*base*) infâme, vil; (*unpleasant*) abominable.
vilify ['vɪlɪfaɪ] *vt* diffamer
villa ['vɪlə] *n* (*in country*) grande maison *f* de campagne.
village ['vɪlɪdʒ] *n* village *m*. ◆**villager** *n* villageois, -oise *mf*.
villain ['vɪlən] *n* scélérat, -ate *mf*; (*in story or play*) traître *m*. ◆**villainy** *n* infamie *f*.
vindicate ['vɪndɪkeɪt] *vt* justifier. ◆**vindi'cation** *n* justification *f*.
vindictive [vɪn'dɪktɪv] *a* vindicatif, rancunier.
vine [vaɪn] *n* (*grapevine*) vigne *f*; **v. grower** viticulteur *m*. ◆**vineyard** ['vɪnjəd] *n* vignoble *m*.
vinegar ['vɪnɪgər] *n* vinaigre *m*.
vintage ['vɪntɪdʒ] **1** *n* (*year*) année *f*. **2** *a* (*wine*) de grand cru; (*car*) d'époque; (*film*) classique; (*good*) *Fig* bon; **v. Shaw/*etc*** du meilleur Shaw/*etc*.
vinyl ['vaɪn(ə)l] *n* vinyle *m*.
viola [vɪ'əʊlə] *n* (*instrument*) *Mus* alto *m*.
violate ['vaɪəleɪt] *vt* violer. ◆**vio'lation** *n* violation *f*.
violence ['vaɪələns] *n* violence *f*. ◆**violent** *a* violent; **a v. dislike** une aversion vive. ◆**violently** *adv* violemment; **to be v. sick** (*vomit*) vomir.
violet ['vaɪələt] **1** *a & n* (*colour*) violet (*m*). **2** *n* (*plant*) violette *f*.
violin [vaɪə'lɪn] *n* violon *m*; – *a* (*concerto etc*) pour violon. ◆**violinist** *n* violoniste *mf*.
VIP [viːaɪ'piː] *n abbr* (*very important person*) personnage *m* de marque.
viper ['vaɪpər] *n* vipère *f*.
virgin ['vɜːdʒɪn] *n* vierge *f*; **to be a v.** (*of woman, man*) être vierge; – *a* (*woman, snow etc*) vierge. ◆**vir'ginity** *n* virginité *f*.
Virgo ['vɜːgəʊ] *n* (*sign*) la Vierge.
virile ['vɪraɪl, *Am* 'vɪrəl] *a* viril. ◆**vi'rility** *n* virilité *f*.
virtual ['vɜːtʃʊəl] *a* **it was a v. failure/*etc*** ce fut en fait un échec/*etc*. ◆**—ly** *adv* (*in fact*) en fait; (*almost*) pratiquement.
virtue ['vɜːtʃuː] *n* **1** (*goodness, chastity*) vertu *f*; (*advantage*) mérite *m*, avantage *m*. **2 by or in v. of** en raison de. ◆**virtuous** *a* vertueux.
virtuoso, *pl* **-si** [vɜːtʃʊ'əʊsəʊ, -siː] *n* virtuose *mf*. ◆**virtuosity** [-'ɒsɪtɪ] *n* virtuosité *f*.
virulent ['vɪrʊlənt] *a* virulent. ◆**virulence** *n* virulence *f*.
virus ['vaɪ(ə)rəs] *n* virus *m*.
visa ['viːzə] *n* visa *m*.
vis-à-vis [viːzə'viː] *prep* vis-à-vis de.
viscount ['vaɪkaʊnt] *n* vicomte *m*. ◆**viscountess** *n* vicomtesse *f*.
viscous ['vɪskəs] *a* visqueux.
vise [vaɪs] *n* (*tool*) *Am* étau *m*.
visible ['vɪzəb(ə)l] *a* visible. ◆**visi'bility** *n* visibilité *f*. ◆**visibly** *adv* visiblement.
vision ['vɪʒ(ə)n] *n* vision *f*; **a man/a woman of v.** *Fig* un homme/une femme qui voit loin. ◆**visionary** *a & n* visionnaire (*mf*).
visit ['vɪzɪt] *n* (*call, tour*) visite *f*; (*stay*) séjour *m*; – *vt* (*place*) visiter; **to visit s.o.** (*call on*) rendre visite à qn; (*stay with*) faire un séjour chez qn; – *vi* être en visite (*Am* **with** chez). ◆**—ing** *a* (*card, hours*) de visite. ◆**visitor** *n* visiteur, -euse *mf*; (*guest*) invité, -ée *mf*; (*in hotel*) client, -ente *mf*.
visor ['vaɪzər] *n* (*of helmet*) visière *f*.
vista ['vɪstə] *n* (*view of place etc*) vue *f*; (*of future*) *Fig* perspective *f*.
visual ['vɪʒʊəl] *a* visuel; **v. aid** (*in teaching*) support *m* visuel. ◆**visualize** *vt* (*imagine*) se représenter; (*foresee*) envisager.
vital ['vaɪt(ə)l] *a* vital; **of v. importance** d'importance capitale; **v. statistics** (*of woman*) *Fam* mensurations *fpl*. ◆**—ly** *adv* extrêmement.
vitality [vaɪ'tælɪtɪ] *n* vitalité *f*.
vitamin ['vɪtəmɪn, *Am* 'vaɪtəmɪn] *n* vitamine *f*.
vitriol ['vɪtrɪəl] *n Ch Fig* vitriol *m*. ◆**vitri'olic** *a* (*attack, speech etc*) au vitriol.
vivacious [vɪ'veɪʃəs] *a* plein d'entrain.
vivid ['vɪvɪd] *a* (*imagination, recollection etc*) vif; (*description*) vivant. ◆**—ly** *adv* (*to describe*) de façon vivante; **to remember sth v.** avoir un vif souvenir de qch.
vivisection [vɪvɪ'sekʃ(ə)n] *n* vivisection *f*.
vocabulary [və'kæbjʊlərɪ] *n* vocabulaire *m*.
vocal ['vəʊk(ə)l] *a* (*cords, music*) vocal; (*outspoken, noisy, critical*) qui se fait entendre. ◆**vocalist** *n* chanteur, -euse *mf*.
vocation [vəʊ'keɪʃ(ə)n] *n* vocation *f*. ◆**vocational** *a* professionnel.
vociferous [və'sɪf(ə)rəs] *a* bruyant.
vodka ['vɒdkə] *n* vodka *f*.
vogue [vəʊg] *n* vogue *f*; **in v.** en vogue.
voice [vɔɪs] *n* voix *f*; **at the top of one's v.** à

tue-tête; – *vt* (*feeling, opinion etc*) formuler, exprimer.
void [vɔɪd] **1** *n* vide *m*; – *a* **v. of** (*lacking in*) dépourvu de. **2** *a* (*not valid*) *Jur* nul.
volatile ['vɒlətaɪl, *Am* 'vɒlət(ə)l] *a* (*person*) versatile, changeant; (*situation*) explosif.
volcano [vɒl'keɪnəʊ] *n* (*pl* **-oes**) volcan *m*. ◆**volcanic** [-'kænɪk] *a* volcanique.
volition [və'lɪʃ(ə)n] *n* **of one's own v.** de son propre gré.
volley ['vɒlɪ] *n* (*of blows*) volée *f*; (*gunfire*) salve *f*; (*of insults*) *Fig* bordée *f*. ◆**volleyball** *n Sp* volley(-ball) *m*.
volt [vəʊlt] *n El* volt *m*. ◆**voltage** *n* voltage *m*.
volume ['vɒljuːm] *n* (*book, capacity, loudness*) volume *m*. ◆**voluminous** [və'luːmɪnəs] *a* volumineux.
voluntary ['vɒlənt(ə)rɪ] *a* volontaire; (*unpaid*) bénévole. ◆**voluntarily** [*Am* vɒlən'terɪlɪ] *adv* volontairement; bénévolement. ◆**volun'teer** *n* volontaire *mf*; – *vi* se proposer (**for sth** pour qch, **to do** pour faire); *Mil* s'engager comme volontaire (**for** dans); – *vt* offrir (spontanément).
voluptuous [və'lʌptʃʊəs] *a* voluptueux, sensuel.
vomit ['vɒmɪt] *vti* vomir; – *n* (*matter*) vomi *m*.
voracious [və'reɪʃəs] *a* (*appetite, reader etc*) vorace.
vot/e [vəʊt] *n* vote *m*; (*right to vote*) droit *m* de vote; **to win votes** gagner des voix; **v. of censure** *or* **no confidence** motion *f* de censure; **v. of thanks** discours *m* de remerciement; – *vt* (*bill, funds etc*) voter; (*person*) élire; – *vi* voter; **to v. Conservative** voter conservateur *or* pour les conservateurs. ◆**—ing** *n* vote *m* (**of** de); (*polling*) scrutin *m*. ◆**—er** *n Pol* électeur, -trice *mf*.
vouch [vaʊtʃ] *vi* **to v. for** répondre de.
voucher ['vaʊtʃər] *n* (*for meals etc*) bon *m*, chèque *m*.
vow [vaʊ] *n* vœu *m*; – *vt* (*obedience etc*) jurer (**to** à); **to v. to do** jurer de faire, faire le vœu de faire.
vowel ['vaʊəl] *n* voyelle *f*.
voyage ['vɔɪɪdʒ] *n* voyage *m* (par mer).
vulgar ['vʌlgər] *a* vulgaire. ◆**vul'garity** *n* vulgarité *f*.
vulnerable ['vʌln(ə)rəb(ə)l] *a* vulnérable. ◆**vulnera'bility** *n* vulnérabilité *f*.
vulture ['vʌltʃər] *n* vautour *m*.

W

W, w ['dʌb(ə)ljuː] *n* W, w *m*.
wacky ['wækɪ] *a* (**-ier, -iest**) *Am Fam* farfelu.
wad [wɒd] *n* (*of banknotes, papers etc*) liasse *f*; (*of cotton wool, cloth*) tampon *m*.
waddle ['wɒd(ə)l] *vi* se dandiner.
wade [weɪd] *vi* **to w. through** (*mud, water etc*) patauger dans; (*book etc*) *Fig* venir péniblement à bout de; **I'm wading through this book** j'avance péniblement dans ce livre.
wafer ['weɪfər] *n* (*biscuit*) gaufrette *f*; *Rel* hostie *f*.
waffle ['wɒf(ə)l] **1** *n* (*talk*) *Fam* verbiage *m*, blabla *m*; – *vi Fam* parler pour ne rien dire, blablater. **2** *n* (*cake*) gaufre *f*.
waft [wɒft] *vi* (*of smell etc*) flotter.
wag [wæg] **1** *vt* (**-gg-**) (*tail, finger*) agiter, remuer; – *vi* remuer; **tongues are wagging** *Pej* on en jase, les langues vont bon train. **2** *n* (*joker*) farceur, -euse *mf*.
wage [weɪdʒ] **1** *n* **wage(s)** salaire *m*, paie *f*; **w. claim** *or* **demand** revendication *f* salariale; **w. earner** salarié, -ée *mf*; (*breadwinner*) soutien *m* de famille; **w. freeze** blocage *m* des salaires; **w. increase** *or* **rise** augmentation *f* de salaire. **2** *vt* (*campaign*) mener; **to w. war** faire la guerre (**on** à).
wager ['weɪdʒər] *n* pari *m*; – *vt* parier (**that** que).
waggle ['wæg(ə)l] *vti* remuer.
wag(g)on ['wægən] *n* (*cart*) chariot *m*; *Rail* wagon *m* (de marchandises); **on the w.** (*abstinent*) *Fam* au régime sec.
waif [weɪf] *n* enfant *mf* abandonné(e).
wail [weɪl] *vi* (*cry out, complain*) gémir; (*of siren*) hurler; – *n* gémissement *m*; (*of siren*) hurlement *m*.
waist [weɪst] *n* taille *f*; **stripped to the w.** nu jusqu'à la ceinture. ◆**waistband** *n* (*part of garment*) ceinture *f*. ◆**waistcoat** ['weɪskəʊt] *n* gilet *m*. ◆**waistline** *n* taille *f*.
wait [weɪt] **1** *n* attente *f*; **to lie in w. (for)** guetter; – *vi* attendre; **to w. for** attendre; **w. until I've gone, w. for me to go** attends que je sois parti; **to keep s.o. waiting** faire attendre qn; **w. and see!** attends voir!; **I can't w.**

to do it j'ai hâte de le faire; **to w. about (for)** attendre; **to w. behind** rester; **to w. up** veiller; **to w. up for s.o.** attendre le retour de qn avant de se coucher. **2** *vi* (*serve*) **to w. at table** servir à table; **to w. on s.o.** servir qn. **◆—ing** *n* attente *f*; **'no w.'** *Aut* 'arrêt interdit'; – *a* **w. list/room** liste *f*/salle *f* d'attente. **◆waiter** *n* garçon *m* (de café), serveur *m*; **w.!** garçon! **◆waitress** *n* serveuse *f*; **w.!** mademoiselle!

waive [weɪv] *vt* renoncer à, abandonner.

wake[1] [weɪk] *vi* (*pt* **woke**, *pp* **woken**) **to w. (up)** se réveiller; **to w. up to** (*fact etc*) *Fig* prendre conscience de; – *vt* **to w. (up)** réveiller; **to spend one's waking hours working/***etc* passer ses journées à travailler/*etc*. **◆waken** *vt* éveiller, réveiller; – *vi* s'éveiller, se réveiller.

wake[2] [weɪk] *n* (*of ship*) & *Fig* sillage *m*; **in the w. of** *Fig* dans le sillage de, à la suite de.

Wales [weɪlz] *n* pays *m* de Galles.

walk [wɔːk] *n* promenade *f*; (*short*) (petit) tour *m*; (*gait*) démarche *f*; (*pace*) marche *f*, pas *m*; (*path*) allée *f*, chemin *m*; **to go for a w.** faire une promenade; (*shorter*) faire un (petit) tour; **to take for a w.** (*child etc*) emmener se promener; (*baby, dog*) promener; **five minutes' w. (away)** à cinq minutes à pied; **walks of life** *Fig* conditions sociales *fpl*; – *vi* marcher; (*stroll*) se promener; (*go on foot*) aller à pied; **w.!** (*don't run*) ne cours pas!; **to w. away** *or* **off** s'éloigner, partir **(from** de); **to w. away** *or* **off with** (*steal*) *Fam* faucher; **to w. in** entrer; **to w. into** (*tree etc*) rentrer dans; (*trap*) tomber dans; **to w. out** (*leave*) partir; (*of workers*) se mettre en grève; **to w. out on s.o.** (*desert*) *Fam* laisser tomber qn; **to w. over to** (*go up to*) s'approcher de; – *vt* (*distance*) faire à pied; (*streets*) (par)courir; (*take for a walk*) promener (*bébé, chien*); **to w. s.o. to** (*station etc*) accompagner qn à. **◆—ing** *n* marche *f* (à pied); – *a* **a w. corpse/dictionary** (*person*) *Fig* un cadavre/dictionnaire ambulant; **at a w. pace** au pas; **w. stick** canne *f*. **◆walker** *n* marcheur, -euse *mf*; (*for pleasure*) promeneur, -euse *mf*. **◆walkout** *n* (*strike*) grève *f* surprise; (*from meeting*) départ *m* (en signe de protestation). **◆walkover** *n* (*in contest etc*) victoire *f* facile. **◆walkway** *n* **moving w.** trottoir *m* roulant.

walkie-talkie [wɔːkɪ'tɔːkɪ] *n* talkie-walkie *m*.

Walkman® ['wɔːkmən] *n* (*pl* **Walkmans**) baladeur *m*.

wall [wɔːl] *n* mur *m*; (*of cabin, tunnel, stomach etc*) paroi *f*; (*of ice*) *Fig* muraille *f*; (*of smoke*) *Fig* rideau *m*; **to go to the w.** (*of firm*) *Fig* faire faillite; – *a* mural; – *vt* **to w. up** (*door etc*) murer; **walled city** ville *f* fortifiée. **◆wallflower** *n Bot* giroflée *f*; **to be a w.** (*at dance*) faire tapisserie. **◆wallpaper** *n* papier *m* peint; – *vt* tapisser. **◆wall-to-wall 'carpet(ing)** *n* moquette *f*.

wallet ['wɒlɪt] *n* portefeuille *m*.

wallop ['wɒləp] *vt* (*hit*) *Fam* taper sur; – *n* (*blow*) *Fam* grand coup *m*.

wallow ['wɒləʊ] *vi* **to w. in** (*mud, vice etc*) se vautrer dans.

wally ['wɒlɪ] *n* (*idiot*) *Fam* andouille *f*, imbécile *mf*.

walnut ['wɔːlnʌt] *n* (*nut*) noix *f*; (*tree, wood*) noyer *m*.

walrus ['wɔːlrəs] *n* (*animal*) morse *m*.

waltz [wɔːls, *Am* wɒlts] *n* valse *f*; – *vi* valser.

wan [wɒn] *a* (*pale*) *Lit* pâle.

wand [wɒnd] *n* baguette *f* (magique).

wander ['wɒndər] *vi* (*of thoughts*) vagabonder; **to w. (about** *or* **around)** (*roam*) errer, vagabonder; (*stroll*) flâner; **to w. from** *or* **off** (*path, subject*) s'écarter de; **to w. off** (*go away*) s'éloigner; **my mind's wandering** je suis distrait; – *vt* **to w. the streets** errer dans les rues. **◆—ing** *a* (*life, tribe*) vagabond, nomade; – *npl* vagabondages *mpl*. **◆—er** *n* vagabond, -onde *mf*.

wane [weɪn] *vi* (*of moon, fame, strength etc*) décroître; – *n* **to be on the w.** décroître, être en déclin.

wangle ['wæŋg(ə)l] *vt Fam* (*obtain*) se débrouiller pour obtenir; (*avoiding payment*) carotter **(from** à).

want [wɒnt] *vt* vouloir **(to do** faire); (*ask for*) demander; (*need*) avoir besoin de; **I w. him to go** je veux qu'il parte; **you w. to try** (*should*) tu devrais essayer; **you're wanted on the phone** on vous demande au téléphone; – *vi* **not to w. for** (*not lack*) ne pas manquer de; – *n* (*lack*) manque *m* **(of** de); (*poverty*) besoin *m*; **for w. of** par manque de; **for w. of money/time** faute d'argent/de temps; **for w. of anything better** faute de mieux; **your wants** (*needs*) tes besoins *mpl*. **◆—ed** *a* (*man, criminal*) recherché par la police; **to feel w.** sentir qu'on vous aime. **◆—ing** *a* (*inadequate*) insuffisant; **to be w.** manquer **(in** de).

wanton ['wɒntən] *a* (*gratuitous*) gratuit; (*immoral*) impudique.

war [wɔːr] *n* guerre *f*; **at w.** en guerre **(with** avec); **to go to w.** entrer en guerre **(with** avec); **to declare w.** déclarer la guerre **(on** à); – *a* (*wound, criminal etc*) de guerre; **w.**

memorial monument *m* aux morts. ◆**warfare** *n* guerre *f*. ◆**warhead** *n* (*of missile*) ogive *f*. ◆**warlike** *a* guerrier. ◆**warmonger** *n* fauteur *m* de guerre. ◆**warpath** *n* **to be on the w.** (*angry*) *Fam* être d'humeur massacrante. ◆**warring** *a* (*countries etc*) en guerre; (*ideologies etc*) *Fig* en conflit. ◆**warship** *n* navire *m* de guerre. ◆**wartime** *n* **in w.** en temps de guerre.

warble ['wɔːb(ə)l] *vi* (*of bird*) gazouiller.

ward[1] [wɔːd] *n* **1** (*in hospital*) salle *f*. **2** (*child*) *Jur* pupille *mf*. **3** (*electoral division*) circonscription *f* électorale.

ward[2] [wɔːd] *vt* **to w. off** (*blow, anger*) détourner; (*danger*) éviter.

warden ['wɔːd(ə)n] *n* (*of institution, Am of prison*) directeur, -trice *mf*; (*of park*) gardien, -ienne *mf*; **(traffic) w.** contractuel, -elle *mf*.

warder ['wɔːdər] *n* gardien *m* (de prison).

wardrobe ['wɔːdrəʊb] *n* (*cupboard*) penderie *f*; (*clothes*) garde-robe *f*.

warehouse, *pl* **-ses** ['weəhaʊs, -zɪz] *n* entrepôt *m*.

wares [weəz] *npl* marchandises *fpl*.

warily ['weərɪlɪ] *adv* avec précaution.

warm [wɔːm] *a* **(-er, -est)** chaud; (*iron, oven*) moyen; (*welcome, thanks etc*) chaleureux; **to be** *or* **feel w.** avoir chaud; **it's (nice and) w.** (*of weather*) il fait (agréablement) chaud; **to get w.** (*of person, room etc*) se réchauffer; (*of food, water*) chauffer; – *vt* **to w. (up)** (*person, food etc*) réchauffer; – *vi* **to w. up** (*of person, room, engine*) se réchauffer; (*of food, water*) chauffer; (*of discussion*) s'échauffer; **to w. to s.o.** *Fig* se prendre de sympathie pour qn. ◆**warm-'hearted** *a* chaleureux. ◆**warmly** *adv* (*to wrap up*) chaudement; (*to welcome, thank etc*) chaleureusement. ◆**warmth** *n* chaleur *f*.

warn [wɔːn] *vt* avertir, prévenir (**that** que); **to w. s.o. against** *or* **off sth** mettre qn en garde contre qch; **to w. s.o. against doing** conseiller à qn de ne pas faire. ◆**—ing** *n* avertissement *m*; (*advance notice*) (pré)avis *m*; *Met* avis *m*; (*alarm*) alerte *f*; **without w.** sans prévenir; **a note** *or* **word of w.** une mise en garde; **w. light** (*on appliance etc*) voyant *m* lumineux; **hazard w. lights** *Aut* feux *mpl* de détresse.

warp [wɔːp] **1** *vt* (*wood etc*) voiler; (*judgment, person etc*) *Fig* pervertir; **a warped mind** un esprit tordu; **a warped account** un récit déformé; – *vi* se voiler. **2** *n* *Tex* chaîne *f*.

warrant ['wɒrənt] **1** *n Jur* mandat *m*; **a w. for your arrest** un mandat d'arrêt contre vous. **2** *vt* (*justify*) justifier; **I w. you that...** (*declare confidently*) je t'assure que.... ◆**warranty** *n Com* garantie *f*.

warren ['wɒrən] *n* **(rabbit) w.** garenne *f*.

warrior ['wɒrɪər] *n* guerrier, -ière *mf*.

wart [wɔːt] *n* verrue *f*.

wary ['weərɪ] *a* **(-ier, -iest)** prudent; **to be w. of s.o./sth** se méfier de qn/qch; **to be w. of doing** hésiter beaucoup à faire.

was [wəz, *stressed* wɒz] *see* **be.**

wash [wɒʃ] *n* (*clothes*) lessive *f*; (*of ship*) sillage *m*; **to have a w.** se laver; **to give sth a w.** laver qch; **to do the w.** faire la lessive; **in the w.** à la lessive; – *vt* laver; (*flow over*) baigner; **to w. one's hands** se laver les mains (*Fig* **of sth** de qch); **to w. (away)** (*of sea etc*) emporter (*qch, qn*); **to w. away** *or* **off** *or* **out** (*stain*) faire partir (en lavant); **to w. down** (*vehicle, deck*) laver à grande eau; (*food*) arroser (**with** de); **to w. out** (*bowl etc*) laver; – *vi* se laver; (*do the dishes*) laver la vaisselle; **to w. away** *or* **off** *or* **out** (*of stain*) partir (au lavage); **to w. up** (*do the dishes*) faire la vaisselle; (*have a wash*) *Am* se laver. ◆**washed-'out** *a* (*tired*) lessivé. ◆**washed-'up** *a* **(all) w.-up** (*person, plan*) *Sl* fichu. ◆**washable** *a* lavable. ◆**washbasin** *n* lavabo *m*. ◆**washcloth** *n Am* gant *m* de toilette. ◆**washout** *n Sl* (*event etc*) fiasco *m*; (*person*) nullité *f*. ◆**washroom** *n Am* toilettes *fpl*.

washer ['wɒʃər] *n* (*ring*) rondelle *f*, joint *m*.

washing ['wɒʃɪŋ] *n* (*act*) lavage *m*; (*clothes*) lessive *f*, linge *m*; **to do the w.** faire la lessive; **w. line** corde *f* à linge; **w. machine** machine *f* à laver; **w. powder** lessive *f*. ◆**w.-'up** *n* vaisselle *f*; **to do the w.-up** faire la vaisselle; **w.-up liquid** produit *m* pour la vaisselle.

wasp [wɒsp] *n* guêpe *f*.

wast/e [weɪst] *n* gaspillage *m*; (*of time*) perte *f*; (*rubbish*) déchets *mpl*; *pl* (*land*) étendue *f* déserte; **w. disposal unit** broyeur *m* d'ordures; – *a* **w. material** *or* **products** déchets *mpl*; **w. land** (*uncultivated*) terres *fpl* incultes; (*in town*) terrain *m* vague; **w. paper** vieux papiers *mpl*; **w. pipe** tuyau *m* d'évacuation; – *vt* (*money, food etc*) gaspiller; (*time, opportunity*) perdre; **to w. one's time on frivolities/***etc* gaspiller son temps en frivolités/*etc*, perdre son temps à des frivolités/*etc*; **to w. one's life** gâcher sa vie; – *vi* **to w. away** dépérir. ◆**—ed** *a* (*effort*) inutile; (*body etc*) émacié. ◆**wastage** *n* gaspillage *m*; (*losses*) pertes *fpl*; **some w.** (*of goods, staff etc*) du déchet. ◆**wastebin** *n* (*in kitchen*) poubelle *f*. ◆**wastepaper basket** *n* corbeille *f* (à papier).

wasteful ['weɪstfəl] *a* (*person*) gaspilleur; (*process*) peu économique.

watch [wɒtʃ] **1** *n* (*small clock*) montre *f*. **2** *n* (*over suspect, baby etc*) surveillance *f*; *Nau* quart *m*; **to keep (a) w. on** *or* **over** surveiller; **to keep w.** faire le guet; **to be on the w. (for)** guetter; – *vt* regarder; (*observe*) observer; (*suspect, baby etc*) surveiller; (*be careful of*) faire attention à; – *vi* regarder; **to w. (out) for** (*be on the lookout for*) guetter; **to w. out** (*take care*) faire attention (**for** à); **w. out!** attention!; **to w. over** surveiller. ◆**watchdog** *n* chien *m* de garde. ◆**watchmaker** *n* horloger, -ère *mf*. ◆**watchman** *n* (*pl* **-men**) **night w.** veilleur *m* de nuit. ◆**watchstrap** *n* bracelet *m* de montre. ◆**watchtower** *n* tour *f* de guet.

watchful ['wɒtʃfəl] *a* vigilant.

water ['wɔːtər] *n* eau *f*; **by w.** en bateau; **under w.** (*road, field etc*) inondé; (*to swim*) sous l'eau; **at high w.** à marée haute; **it doesn't hold w.** (*of theory etc*) *Fig* ça ne tient pas debout; **in hot w.** *Fig* dans le pétrin; **w. cannon** lance *f* à eau; **w. ice** sorbet *m*; **w. lily** nénuphar *m*; **w. pistol** pistolet *m* à eau; **w. polo** *Sp* water-polo *m*; **w. power** énergie *f* hydraulique; **w. rates** taxes *fpl* sur l'eau; **w. skiing** ski *m* nautique; **w. tank** réservoir *m* d'eau; **w. tower** château *m* d'eau; – *vt* (*plant etc*) arroser; **to w. down** (*wine etc*) couper (d'eau); (*text etc*) édulcorer; – *vi* (*of eyes*) larmoyer; **it makes his** *or* **her mouth w.** ça lui fait venir l'eau à la bouche. ◆**—ing** *n* (*of plant etc*) arrosage *m*; **w. can** arrosoir *m*. ◆**watery** *a* (*colour*) délavé; (*soup*) *Pej* trop liquide; (*eyes*) larmoyant; **w. tea** *or* **coffee** de la lavasse.

watercolour ['wɔːtəkʌlər] *n* (*picture*) aquarelle *f*; (*paint*) couleur *f* pour aquarelle. ◆**watercress** *n* cresson *m* (de fontaine). ◆**waterfall** *n* chute *f* d'eau. ◆**waterhole** *n* (*in desert*) point *m* d'eau. ◆**waterline** *n* (*on ship*) ligne *f* de flottaison. ◆**waterlogged** *a* délavé. ◆**watermark** *n* (*in paper*) filigrane *m*. ◆**watermelon** *n* pastèque *f*. ◆**waterproof** *a* (*material*) imperméable. ◆**watershed** *n* (*turning point*) tournant *m* (décisif). ◆**watertight** *a* (*container etc*) étanche. ◆**waterway** *n* voie *f* navigable. ◆**waterworks** *n* (*place*) station *f* hydraulique.

watt [wɒt] *n El* watt *m*.

wave [weɪv] *n* (*of sea*) & *Fig* vague *f*; (*in hair*) ondulation *f*; *Rad* onde *f*; (*sign*) signe *m* (de la main); **long/medium/short w.** *Rad* ondes *fpl* longues/moyennes/courtes; – *vi* (*with hand*) faire signe (de la main); (*of flag*) flotter; **to w. to** (*greet*) saluer de la main; – *vt* (*arm, flag etc*) agiter; (*hair*) onduler; **to w. s.o. on** faire signe à qn d'avancer; **to w. aside** (*objection etc*) écarter. ◆**waveband** *n Rad* bande *f* de fréquence. ◆**wavelength** *n Rad* & *Fig* longueur *f* d'ondes.

waver ['weɪvər] *vi* (*of flame, person etc*) vaciller.

wavy ['weɪvɪ] *a* (**-ier, -iest**) (*line*) onduleux; (*hair*) ondulé.

wax [wæks] **1** *n* cire *f*; (*for ski*) fart *m*; – *vt* cirer; (*ski*) farter; (*car*) lustrer; – *a* (*candle, doll etc*) de cire; **w. paper** *Culin Am* papier *m* paraffiné. **2** *vi* (*of moon*) croître. **3** *vi* **to w. lyrical/merry** (*become*) se faire lyrique/gai. ◆**waxworks** *npl* (*place*) musée *m* de cire; (*dummies*) figures *fpl* de cire.

way [weɪ] **1** *n* (*path, road*) chemin *m* (**to** de); (*direction*) sens *m*, direction *f*; (*distance*) distance *f*; **all the w., the whole w.** (*to talk etc*) pendant tout le chemin; **this w.** par ici; **that way** par là; **which w.?** par où?; **to lose one's w.** se perdre; **I'm on my w.** (*coming*) j'arrive; (*going*) je pars; **he made his w. out/home** il est sorti/rentré; **the w. there** l'aller *m*; **the w. back** le retour; **the w. in** l'entrée *f*; **the w. out** la sortie; **a w. out of** (*problem etc*) *Fig* une solution à; **the w. is clear** *Fig* la voie est libre; **across the w.** en face; **on the w.** en route (**to** pour); **by w. of** (*via*) par; (*as*) *Fig* comme; **out of the w.** (*isolated*) isolé; **to go out of one's w. to do** se donner du mal pour faire; **by the w. . . .** *Fig* à propos . . . ; **to be** *or* **stand in the w.** barrer le passage; **she's in my w.** (*hindrance*) *Fig* elle me gêne; **to get out of the w., make w.** s'écarter; **to give w.** céder; *Aut* céder le passage *or* la priorité; **a long w. (away** *or* **off)** très loin; **it's the wrong w. up** c'est dans le mauvais sens; **do it the other w. round** fais le contraire; **to get under w.** (*of campaign etc*) démarrer; – *adv* (*behind etc*) très loin; **w. ahead** très en avance (**of** sur). **2** *n* (*manner*) façon *f*; (*means*) moyen *m*; (*condition*) état *m*; (*habit*) habitude *f*; (*particular*) égard *m*; **one's ways** (*behaviour*) ses manières *fpl*; **to get one's own w.** obtenir ce qu'on veut; **(in) this w.** de cette façon; **in a way** (*to some extent*) dans un certain sens; **w. of life** façon *f* de vivre, mode *m* de vie; **no w.!** (*certainly not*) *Fam* pas question! ◆**wayfarer** *n* voyageur, -euse *mf*. ◆**way-'out** *a Fam* extraordinaire. ◆**wayside** *n* **by the w.** au bord de la route.

waylay [weɪ'leɪ] *vt* (*pt & pp* **-laid**) (*attack*) attaquer par surprise; (*stop*) *Fig* arrêter au passage.

wayward ['weɪwəd] *a* rebelle, capricieux.

WC [dʌb(ə)ljuː'siː] *n* w-c *mpl*, waters *mpl*.

we [wiː] *pron* nous; **we go** nous allons; **we teachers** nous autres professeurs; **we never know** (*indefinite*) on ne sait jamais.

weak [wiːk] *a* (**-er, -est**) faible; (*tea, coffee*) léger; (*health, stomach*) fragile. ◆**w.-'willed** *a* faible. ◆**weaken** *vt* affaiblir; – *vi* faiblir. ◆**weakling** *n* (*in body*) mauviette *f*; (*in character*) faible *mf*. ◆**weakly** *adv* faiblement. ◆**weakness** *n* faiblesse *f*; (*of health, stomach*) fragilité *f*; (*fault*) point *m* faible; **a w. for** (*liking*) un faible pour.

weal [wiːl] *n* (*wound on skin*) marque *f*, zébrure *f*.

wealth [welθ] *n* (*money, natural resources*) richesse(s) *f*(*pl*); **a w. of** (*abundance*) *Fig* une profusion de. ◆**wealthy** *a* (**-ier, -iest**) riche; – *n* **the w.** les riches *mpl*.

wean [wiːn] *vt* (*baby*) sevrer.

weapon ['wepən] *n* arme *f*. ◆**weaponry** *n* armements *mpl*.

wear [weər] **1** *vt* (*pt* **wore**, *pp* **worn**) (*have on body*) porter; (*look, smile*) avoir; (*put on*) mettre; **to have nothing to w.** n'avoir rien à se mettre; – *n* **men's/sports w.** vêtements *mpl* pour hommes/de sport; **evening w.** tenue *f* de soirée. **2** *vt* (*pt* **wore**, *pp* **worn**) **to w. (away** *or* **down** *or* **out)** (*material, patience etc*) user; **to w. s.o. out** (*exhaust*) épuiser qn; **to w. oneself out** s'épuiser (**doing** à faire); – *vi* (*last*) faire de l'usage, durer; **to w. (out)** (*of clothes etc*) s'user; **to w. off** (*of colour, pain etc*) passer, disparaître; **to w. on** (*of time*) passer; **to w. out** (*of patience*) s'épuiser; – *n* (*use*) usage *m*; **w. (and tear)** usure *f*. ◆**—ing** *a* (*tiring*) épuisant. ◆**—er** *n* **the w. of** (*hat, glasses etc*) la personne qui porte.

weary ['wɪərɪ] *a* (**-ier, -iest**) (*tired*) fatigué, las (**of doing** de faire); (*tiring*) fatigant; (*look, smile*) las; – *vi* **to w. of** se lasser de. ◆**wearily** *adv* avec lassitude. ◆**weariness** *n* lassitude *f*.

weasel ['wiːz(ə)l] *n* belette *f*.

weather ['weðər] *n* temps *m*; **what's the w. like?** quel temps fait-il?; **in (the) hot w.** par temps chaud; **under the w.** (*not well*) *Fig* patraque; – *a* (*chart etc*) météorologique; **w. forecast, w. report** prévisions *fpl* météorologiques, météo *f*; **w. vane** girouette *f*; – *vt* (*storm, hurricane*) essuyer; (*crisis*) *Fig* surmonter. ◆**weather-beaten** *a* (*face, person*) tanné, hâlé. ◆**weathercock** *n* girouette *f*. ◆**weatherman** *n* (*pl* **-men**) *TV Rad Fam* monsieur *m* météo.

weav/e [wiːv] *vt* (*pt* **wove**, *pp* **woven**) (*cloth, plot*) tisser; (*basket, garland*) tresser; – *vi Tex* tisser; **to w. in and out of** (*crowd, cars etc*) *Fig* se faufiler entre; – *n* (*style*) tissage *m*. ◆**—ing** *n* tissage *m*. ◆**—er** *n* tisserand, -ande *mf*.

web [web] *n* (*of spider*) toile *f*; (*of lies*) *Fig* tissu *m*. ◆**webbed** *a* (*foot*) palmé. ◆**webbing** *n* (*in chair*) sangles *fpl*.

wed [wed] *vt* (**-dd-**) (*marry*) épouser; (*qualities etc*) *Fig* allier (**to** à); – *vi* se marier. ◆**wedded** *a* (*bliss, life*) conjugal. ◆**wedding** *n* mariage *m*; **golden/silver w.** noces *fpl* d'or/d'argent; – *a* (*cake*) de noces; (*anniversary, present*) de mariage; (*dress*) de mariée; **his** *or* **her w. day** le jour de son mariage; **w. ring**, *Am* **w. band** alliance *f*. ◆**wedlock** *n* **born out of w.** illégitime.

wedge [wedʒ] *n* (*for splitting*) coin *m*; (*under wheel, table etc*) cale *f*; **w. heel** (*of shoe*) semelle *f* compensée; – *vt* (*wheel, table etc*) caler; (*push*) enfoncer (**into** dans); **wedged (in) between** (*caught, trapped*) coincé entre.

Wednesday ['wenzdɪ] *n* mercredi *m*.

wee [wiː] *a* (*tiny*) *Fam* tout petit.

weed [wiːd] *n* (*plant*) mauvaise herbe *f*; (*weak person*) *Fam* mauviette *f*; **w. killer** désherbant *m*; – *vti* désherber; – *vt* **to w. out** *Fig* éliminer (**from** de). ◆**weedy** *a* (**-ier, -iest**) (*person*) *Fam* maigre et chétif.

week [wiːk] *n* semaine *f*; **the w. before last** pas la semaine dernière, celle d'avant; **the w. after next** pas la semaine prochaine, celle d'après; **tomorrow w., a w. tomorrow** demain en huit. ◆**weekday** *n* jour *m* de semaine. ◆**week'end** *n* week-end *m*; **at** *or* **on** *or* **over the w.** ce week-end, pendant le week-end. ◆**weekly** *a* hebdomadaire; – *adv* toutes les semaines; – *n* (*magazine*) hebdomadaire *m*.

weep [wiːp] *vi* (*pt & pp* **wept**) pleurer; (*of wound*) suinter; **to w. for s.o.** pleurer qn; – *vt* (*tears*) pleurer; **weeping willow** saule *m* pleureur.

weft [weft] *n Tex* trame *f*.

weigh [weɪ] *vt* peser; **to w. down** (*with load etc*) surcharger (**with** de); (*bend*) faire plier; **to w. up** (*goods, chances etc*) peser; – *vi* peser; **it's weighing on my mind** ça me tracasse; **to w. down on s.o.** (*of worries etc*) accabler qn. ◆**weighing-machine** *n* balance *f*.

weight [weɪt] *n* poids *m*; **to put on w.** grossir; **to lose w.** maigrir; **to carry w.** (*of argument etc*) *Fig* avoir du poids (**with** pour); **to pull one's w.** (*do one's share*) *Fig* faire sa part du travail; **w. lifter** haltérophile *mf*; **w. lifting** haltérophilie *f*; – *vt* **to w. (down)** (*light object*) maintenir avec un poids; **to w. down with** (*overload*) surcharger de. ◆**weightlessness** *n* apesanteur *f*. ◆**weighty** *a* (**-ier, -iest**) lourd; (*argument, subject*) *Fig* de poids.

weighting ['weɪtɪŋ] *n* (*on salary*) indemnité *f* de résidence.

weir [wɪər] *n* (*across river*) barrage *m*.

weird [wɪəd] *a* (**-er, -est**) (*odd*) bizarre; (*eerie*) mystérieux.

welcome ['welkəm] *a* (*pleasant*) agréable; (*timely*) opportun; **to be w.** (*of person, people*) être le bienvenu *or* la bienvenue *or* les bienvenu(e)s; **w.!** soyez le bienvenu *or* la bienvenue *or* les bienvenu(e)s!; **to make s.o. (feel) w.** faire bon accueil à qn; **you're w.!** (*after 'thank you'*) il n'y a pas de quoi!; **w. to do** (*free*) libre de faire; **you're w. to (take *or* use) my bike** mon vélo est à ta disposition; **you're w. to it!** *Iron* grand bien vous fasse!; – *n* accueil *m*; **to extend a w. to** (*greet*) souhaiter la bienvenue à; – *vt* accueillir; (*warmly*) faire bon accueil à; (*be glad of*) se réjouir de; **I w. you!** je vous souhaite la bienvenue! ◆**welcoming** *a* (*smile etc*) accueillant; (*speech, words*) d'accueil.

weld [weld] *vt* **to w. (together)** souder; (*groups etc*) *Fig* unir; – *n* (*joint*) soudure *f*. ◆**—ing** *n* soudure *f*. ◆**—er** *n* soudeur *m*.

welfare ['welfeər] *n* (*physical, material*) bien-être *m*; (*spiritual*) santé *f*; (*public aid*) aide *f* sociale; **public w.** (*good*) le bien public; **the w. state** (*in Great Britain*) l'État-providence *m*; **w. work** assistance *f* sociale.

well[1] [wel] **1** *n* (*for water*) puits *m*; (*of stairs, lift*) cage *f*; **(oil) w.** puits de pétrole. **2** *vi* **to w. up** (*rise*) monter.

well[2] [wel] *adv* (**better, best**) bien; **to do w.** (*succeed*) réussir; **you'd do w. to refuse** tu ferais bien de refuser; **w. done!** bravo!; **I, you, she** *etc* **might (just) as w. have left** il valait mieux partir, autant valait partir; **it's just as w. that** (*lucky*) heureusement que . . . ; **as w.** (*also*) aussi; **as w. as** aussi bien que; **as w. as two cats, he has . . .** en plus de deux chats, il a . . . ; – *a* bien *inv*; **she's w.** (*healthy*) elle va bien; **not a w. man** un homme malade; **to get w.** se remettre; **that's all very w., but . . .** tout ça c'est très joli, mais . . . ; – *int* eh bien!; **w., w.!** (*surprise*) tiens, tiens!; **enormous, w., quite big** énorme, enfin, assez grand.

well-behaved [welbɪ'heɪvd] *a* sage. ◆**w.-'being** *n* bien-être *m*. ◆**w.-'built** *a* (*person, car*) solide. ◆**w.-'founded** *a* bien fondé. ◆**w.-'heeled** *a* (*rich*) *Fam* nanti. ◆**w.-in'formed** *a* (*person, newspaper*) bien informé. ◆**w.-'known** *a* (bien) connu. ◆**w.-'meaning** *a* bien intentionné. ◆**'w.-nigh** *adv* presque. ◆**w.-'off** *a* aisé, riche. ◆**w.-'read** *a* instruit. ◆**w.-'spoken** *a* (*person*) qui a un accent cultivé, qui parle bien. ◆**w.-'thought-of** *a* hautement considéré. ◆**w.-'timed** *a* opportun. ◆**w.-to-'do** *a* aisé, riche. ◆**w.-'tried** *a* (*method*) éprouvé. ◆**w.-'trodden** *a* (*path*) battu. ◆**'w.-wishers** *npl* admirateurs, -trices *mfpl*. ◆**w.-'worn** *a* (*clothes, carpet*) usagé.

wellington ['welɪŋtən] *n* botte *f* de caoutchouc.

welsh [welʃ] *vi* **to w. on** (*debt, promise*) ne pas honorer.

Welsh [welʃ] *a* gallois; **W. rabbit** *Culin* toast *m* au fromage; – *n* (*language*) gallois *m*. ◆**Welshman** *n* (*pl* **-men**) Gallois *m*. ◆**Welshwoman** *n* (*pl* **-women**) Galloise *f*.

wench [wentʃ] *n Hum* jeune fille *f*.

wend [wend] *vt* **to w. one's way** s'acheminer (**to** vers).

went [went] *see* **go 1**.

wept [wept] *see* **weep**.

were [wər, *stressed* wɜːr] *see* **be**.

werewolf ['weəwulf] *n* (*pl* **-wolves**) loup-garou *m*.

west [west] *n* ouest *m*; – *a* (*coast*) ouest *inv*; (*wind*) d'ouest; **W. Africa** Afrique *f* occidentale; **W. Indian** *a* & *n* antillais, -aise (*mf*); **the W. Indies** les Antilles *fpl*; – *adv* à l'ouest, vers l'ouest. ◆**westbound** *a* (*carriageway*) ouest *inv*; (*traffic*) en direction de l'ouest. ◆**westerly** *a* (*point*) ouest *inv*; (*direction*) de l'ouest; (*wind*) d'ouest. ◆**western** *a* (*coast*) ouest *inv*; (*culture*) *Pol* occidental; **W. Europe** Europe *f* de l'Ouest; – *n* (*film*) western *m*. ◆**westerner** *n* habitant, -ante *mf* de l'Ouest; *Pol* occidental, -ale *mf*. ◆**westernize** *vt* occidentaliser. ◆**westward(s)** *a* & *adv* vers l'ouest.

wet [wet] *a* (**wetter, wettest**) mouillé; (*damp, rainy*) humide; (*day, month*) de pluie; **w. paint/ink** peinture *f*/encre *f* fraîche; **w. through** trempé; **to get w.** se mouiller; **it's w.** (*raining*) il pleut; **he's w.** (*weak-willed*)

Fam c'est une lavette; **w. blanket** *Fig* rabat-joie *m inv*; **w. nurse** nourrice *f*; **w. suit** combinaison *f* de plongée; – *n* **the w.** (*rain*) la pluie; (*damp*) l'humidité *f*; – *vt* (**-tt-**) mouiller. ◆**—ness** *n* humidité *f*.

whack [wæk] *n* (*blow*) grand coup *m*; – *vt* donner un grand coup à. ◆**—ed** *a* **w. (out)** (*tired*) *Fam* claqué. ◆**—ing** *a* (*big*) *Fam* énorme.

whale [weɪl] *n* baleine *f*. ◆**whaling** *n* pêche *f* à la baleine.

wham! [wæm] *int* vlan!

wharf [wɔːf] *n* (*pl* **wharfs** *or* **wharves**) (*for ships*) quai *m*.

what [wɒt] **1** *a* quel, quelle, *pl* quel(le)s; **w. book?** quel livre?; **w. one?** *Fam* lequel?, laquelle?; **w. a fool/***etc***!** quel idiot/*etc*!; **I know w. book it is** je sais quel livre c'est; **w. (little) she has** le peu qu'elle a. **2** *pron* (*in questions*) qu'est-ce qui; (*object*) (qu'est-ce) que; (*after prep*) quoi; **w.'s happening?** qu'est-ce qui se passe?; **w. does he do?** qu'est-ce qu'il fait?, que fait-il?; **w. is it?** qu'est-ce que c'est?; **w.'s that book?** quel est ce livre?; **w.!** (*surprise*) quoi!, comment!; **w.'s it called?** comment ça s'appelle?; **w. for?** pourquoi?; **w. about me/***etc***?** et moi/*etc*?; **w. about leaving/***etc***?** si on partait/*etc*? **3** *pron* (*indirect, relative*) ce qui; (*object*) ce que; **I know w. will happen/w. she'll do** je sais ce qui arrivera/ce qu'elle fera; **w. happens is . . .** ce qui arrive c'est que . . . ; **w. I need** ce dont j'ai besoin. ◆**what'ever** *a* **w. (the) mistake/***etc* (*no matter what*) quelle que soit l'erreur/*etc*; **of w. size** de n'importe quelle taille; **no chance w.** pas la moindre chance; **nothing w.** rien du tout; – *pron* (*no matter what*) quoi que (+ *sub*); **w. happens** quoi qu'il arrive; **w. you do** quoi que tu fasses; **w. is important** tout ce qui est important; **w. you want** tout ce que tu veux. ◆**what's-it** *n* (*thing*) *Fam* machin *m*. ◆**whatso'ever** *a* & *pron* = **whatever**.

wheat [wiːt] *n* blé *m*, froment *m*. ◆**wheatgerm** *n* germes *mpl* de blé.

wheedle ['wiːd(ə)l] *vt* **to w. s.o.** enjôler qn (**into doing** pour qu'il fasse); **to w. sth out of s.o.** obtenir qch de qn par la flatterie.

wheel [wiːl] **1** *n* roue *f*; **at the w.** *Aut* au volant; *Nau* au gouvernail; – *vt* (*push*) pousser; – *vi* (*turn*) tourner. **2** *vi* **to w. and deal** *Fam* faire des combines. ◆**wheelbarrow** *n* brouette *f*. ◆**wheelchair** *n* fauteuil *m* roulant.

wheeze [wiːz] **1** *vi* respirer bruyamment. **2** *n* (*scheme*) *Fam* combine *f*. ◆**wheezy** *a* (**-ier, -iest**) poussif.

whelk [welk] *n* (*mollusc*) buccin *m*.

when [wen] *adv* quand; – *conj* quand, lorsque; (*whereas*) alors que; **w. I finish, w. I've finished** quand j'aurai fini; **w. I saw him** *or* **w. I'd seen him, I left** après l'avoir vu, je suis parti; **the day/moment w.** le jour/moment où; **I talked about w. . . .** j'ai parlé de l'époque où . . . . ◆**when'ever** *conj* (*at whatever time*) quand; (*each time that*) chaque fois que.

where [weər] *adv* où; **w. are you from?** d'où êtes-vous?; – *conj* où; (*whereas*) alors que; **that's w. you'll find it** c'est là que tu le trouveras; **I found it w. she'd left it** je l'ai trouvé là où elle l'avait laissé; **I went to w. he was** je suis allé à l'endroit où il était. ◆**whereabouts** *adv* où (donc); – *n* **his w.** l'endroit *m* où il est. ◆**where'as** *conj* alors que. ◆**where'by** *adv* par quoi. ◆**where'upon** *adv* sur quoi. ◆**wher'ever** *conj* **w. you go** (*everywhere*) partout où tu iras, où que tu ailles; **I'll go w. you like** (*anywhere*) j'irai (là) où vous voudrez.

whet [wet] *vt* (**-tt-**) (*appetite, desire etc*) aiguiser.

whether ['weðər] *conj* si; **I don't know w. to leave** je ne sais pas si je dois partir; **w. she does it or not** qu'elle le fasse ou non; **w. now or tomorrow** que ce soit maintenant ou demain; **it's doubtful w.** il est douteux que (+ *sub*).

which [wɪtʃ] **1** *a* (*in questions etc*) quel, quelle, *pl* quel(le)s; **w. hat?** quel chapeau?; **in w. case** auquel cas. **2** *rel pron* qui; (*object*) que; (*after prep*) lequel, laquelle, *pl* lesquel(le)s; **the house w. is . . .** la maison qui est . . . ; **the book w. I like** le livre que j'aime; **the film of w. . . .** le film dont *or* duquel . . . ; **she's ill, w. is sad** elle est malade, ce qui est triste; **he lies, w. I don't like** il ment, ce que je n'aime pas; **after w.** (*whereupon*) après quoi. **3** *pron* **w. (one)** (*in questions*) lequel, laquelle, *pl* lesquel(le)s; **w. (one) of us?** lequel *or* laquelle d'entre nous?; **w. (ones) are the best of the books** quels sont les meilleurs de ces livres? **4** *pron* **w. (one)** (*the one that*) celui qui, celle qui, *pl* ceux qui, celles qui; (*object*) celui *etc* que; **show me w. (one) is red** montrez-moi celui *or* celle qui est rouge; **I know w. (ones) you want** je sais ceux *or* celles que vous désirez. ◆**which'ever** *a* & *pron* **w. book/***etc* *or* **w. of the books/***etc* **you buy** quel que soit le livre/*etc* que tu achètes; **take w. books** *or* **w. of the books interest you** prenez les livres qui vous intéressent; **take w. (one) you like** prends celui *or* celle que tu veux; **w. (ones) remain** ceux *or* celles qui restent.

whiff [wɪf] *n* (*puff*) bouffée *f*; (*smell*) odeur *f*.

while [waɪl] *conj* (*when*) pendant que; (*although*) bien que (+ *sub*); (*as long as*) tant que; (*whereas*) tandis que; **w. doing** (*in the course of*) en faisant; – *n* **a w.** un moment, quelque temps; **all the w.** tout le temps; – *vt* **to w. away** (*time*) passer. ◆**whilst** [waɪlst] *conj* = **while.**

whim [wɪm] *n* caprice *m*.

whimper ['wɪmpər] *vi* (*of dog, person*) gémir faiblement; (*snivel*) *Pej* pleurnicher; – *n* faible gémissement *m*; **without a w.** (*complaint*) *Fig* sans se plaindre.

whimsical ['wɪmzɪk(ə)l] *a* (*look, idea*) bizarre; (*person*) fantasque, capricieux.

whine [waɪn] *vi* gémir; (*complain*) *Fig* se plaindre; – *n* gémissement *m*; plainte *f*.

whip [wɪp] *n* fouet *m*; – *vt* (**-pp-**) (*person, cream etc*) fouetter; (*defeat*) *Fam* dérouiller; **to w. off** (*take off*) enlever brusquement; **to w. out** (*from pocket etc*) sortir brusquement (**from** de); **to w. up** (*interest*) susciter; (*meal*) *Fam* préparer rapidement; – *vi* (*move*) aller à toute vitesse; **to w. round to s.o.'s** faire un saut chez qn. ◆**whip-round** *n Fam* collecte *f*.

whirl [wɜːl] *vi* tourbillonner, tournoyer; – *vt* faire tourbillonner; – *n* tourbillon *m*. ◆**whirlpool** *n* tourbillon *m*; **w. bath** *Am* bain *m* à remous. ◆**whirlwind** *n* tourbillon *m* (de vent).

whirr [wɜːr] *vi* (*of engine*) vrombir; (*of top*) ronronner.

whisk [wɪsk] **1** *n Culin* fouet *m*; – *vt* fouetter. **2** *vt* **to w. away** *or* **off** (*tablecloth etc*) enlever rapidement; (*person*) emmener rapidement; (*chase away*) chasser.

whiskers ['wɪskəz] *npl* (*of animal*) moustaches *fpl*; (*beard*) barbe *f*; (*moustache*) moustache *f*; **(side) w.** favoris *mpl*.

whisky, *Am* **whiskey** ['wɪskɪ] *n* whisky *m*.

whisper ['wɪspər] *vti* chuchoter; **w. to me!** chuchote à mon oreille!; – *n* chuchotement *m*; (*rumour*) *Fig* rumeur *f*, bruit *m*.

whistle ['wɪs(ə)l] *n* sifflement *m*; (*object*) sifflet *m*; **to blow** *or* **give a w.** siffler; – *vti* siffler; **to w. at** (*girl*) siffler; **to w. for** (*dog, taxi*) siffler.

Whit [wɪt] *a* **W. Sunday** dimanche *m* de Pentecôte.

white [waɪt] *a* (**-er, -est**) blanc; **to go** *or* **turn w.** blanchir; **w. coffee** café *m* au lait; **w. elephant** *Fig* objet *m or* projet *m etc* inutile; **w. lie** pieux mensonge *m*; **w. man** blanc *m*; **w. woman** blanche *f*; – *n* (*colour, of egg, of eye*) blanc *m*; (*person*) blanc *m*, blanche *f*. ◆**white-collar 'worker** *n* employé, -ée *mf* de bureau. ◆**whiten** *vti* blanchir. ◆**whiteness** *n* blancheur *f*. ◆**whitewash** *n* (*for walls etc*) blanc *m* de chaux; – *vt* blanchir à la chaux; (*person*) *Fig* blanchir; (*faults*) justifier.

whiting ['waɪtɪŋ] *n* (*fish*) merlan *m*.

Whitsun ['wɪts(ə)n] *n* la Pentecôte.

whittle ['wɪt(ə)l] *vt* **to w. down** (*wood*) tailler; (*price etc*) *Fig* rogner.

whizz [wɪz] **1** *vi* (*rush*) aller à toute vitesse; **to w. past** passer à toute vitesse; **to w. through the air** fendre l'air. **2** *a* **w. kid** *Fam* petit prodige *m*.

who [huː] *pron* qui; **w. did it?** qui (est-ce qui) a fait ça?; **the woman w.** la femme qui; **w. did you see** tu as vu qui? ◆**who'ever** *pron* (*no matter who*) qui que ce soit qui; (*object*) qui que ce soit que; **w. has travelled** (*anyone who*) quiconque a *or* celui qui a voyagé; **w. you are** qui que vous soyez; **this man, w. he is** cet homme, quel qu'il soit; **w. did that?** qui donc a fait ça?

whodunit [huː'dʌnɪt] *n* (*detective story*) *Fam* polar *m*.

whole [həʊl] *a* entier; (*intact*) intact; **the w. time** tout le temps; **the w. apple** toute la pomme, la pomme (tout) entière; **the w. truth** toute la vérité; **the w. world** le monde entier; **the w. lot** le tout; **to swallow sth w.** avaler qch tout rond; – *n* (*unit*) tout *m*; (*total*) totalité *f*; **the w. of the village** le village (tout) entier, tout le village; **the w. of the night** toute la nuit; **on the w., as a w.** dans l'ensemble. ◆**whole-'hearted** *a*, ◆**whole-'heartedly** *adv* sans réserve. ◆**wholemeal** *a*, *Am* ◆**wholewheat** *a* (*bread*) complet. ◆**wholly** *adv* entièrement.

wholesale ['həʊlseɪl] *n Com* gros *m*; – *a* (*firm*) de gros; (*destruction etc*) *Fig* en masse; – *adv* (*in bulk*) en gros; (*to buy or sell one article*) au prix de gros; (*to destroy etc*) *Fig* en masse. ◆**wholesaler** *n* grossiste *mf*.

wholesome ['həʊlsəm] *a* (*food, climate etc*) sain.

whom [huːm] *pron* (*object*) que; (*in questions and after prep*) qui; **w. did she see?** qui a-t-elle vu?; **the man w. you know** l'homme que tu connais; **with w.** avec qui; **of w.** dont.

whooping cough ['huːpɪŋkɒf] *n* coqueluche *f*.

whoops! [wups] *int* (*apology etc*) oups!

whopping ['wɒpɪŋ] *a* (*big*) *Fam* énorme. **◆whopper** *n Fam* chose *f* énorme.

whore [hɔːr] *n* (*prostitute*) putain *f*.

whose [huːz] *poss pron & a* à qui, de qui; **w. book is this?, w. is this book?** à qui est ce livre?; **w. daughter are you?** de qui es-tu la fille?; **the woman w. book I have** la femme dont *or* de qui j'ai le livre; **the man w. mother I spoke to** l'homme à la mère de qui j'ai parlé.

why [waɪ] **1** *adv* pourquoi; **w. not?** pourquoi pas?; – *conj* **the reason w. they ...** la raison pour laquelle ils ...; – *npl* **the whys and wherefores** le pourquoi et le comment. **2** *int* (*surprise*) eh bien!, tiens!

wick [wɪk] *n* (*of candle, lamp*) mèche *f*.

wicked ['wɪkɪd] *a* (*evil*) méchant, vilain; (*mischievous*) malicieux. **◆—ly** *adv* méchamment; malicieusement. **◆—ness** *n* méchanceté *f*.

wicker ['wɪkər] *n* osier *m*; – *a* (*chair etc*) en osier, d'osier. **◆wickerwork** *n* (*objects*) vannerie *f*.

wicket ['wɪkɪt] *n* (*cricket stumps*) guichet *m*.

wide [waɪd] *a* (**-er, -est**) large; (*desert, ocean*) vaste; (*choice, knowledge, variety*) grand; **to be three metres w.** avoir trois mètres de large; – *adv* (*to fall, shoot*) loin du but; (*to open*) tout grand. **◆wide-'awake** *a* (*alert, not sleeping*) éveillé. **◆widely** *adv* (*to broadcast, spread*) largement; (*to travel*) beaucoup; **w. different** très différent; **it's w. thought** *or* **believed that ...** on pense généralement que .... **◆widen** *vt* élargir; – *vi* s'élargir. **◆wideness** *n* largeur *f*.

widespread ['waɪdspred] *a* (très) répandu.

widow ['wɪdəʊ] *n* veuve *f*. **◆widowed** *a* (*man*) veuf; (*woman*) veuve; **to be w.** (*become a widower or widow*) devenir veuf *or* veuve. **◆widower** *n* veuf *m*.

width [wɪdθ] *n* largeur *f*.

wield [wiːld] *vt* (*handle*) manier; (*brandish*) brandir; (*power*) *Fig* exercer.

wife [waɪf] *n* (*pl* **wives**) femme *f*, épouse *f*.

wig [wɪg] *n* perruque *f*.

wiggle ['wɪg(ə)l] *vt* agiter; **to w. one's hips** tortiller des hanches; – *vi* (*of worm etc*) se tortiller; (*of tail*) remuer.

wild [waɪld] *a* (**-er, -est**) (*animal, flower, region etc*) sauvage; (*enthusiasm, sea*) déchaîné; (*idea, life*) fou; (*look*) farouche; (*angry*) furieux (**with** contre); **w. with** (*joy, anger etc*) fou de; **I'm not w. about it** (*plan etc*) *Fam* ça ne m'emballe pas; **to be w. about s.o.** (*very fond of*) être dingue de qn; **to grow w.** (*of plant*) pousser à l'état sauvage; **to run w.** (*of animals*) courir en liberté; (*of crowd*) se déchaîner; **the W. West** *Am* le Far West; – *npl* régions *fpl* sauvages. **◆wildcat 'strike** *n* grève *f* sauvage. **◆wild-'goose chase** *n* fausse piste *f*. **◆wildlife** *n* animaux *mpl* sauvages, faune *f*.

wilderness ['wɪldənəs] *n* désert *m*.

wildly ['waɪldlɪ] *adv* (*madly*) follement; (*violently*) violemment.

wile [waɪl] *n* ruse *f*, artifice *m*.

wilful ['wɪlfəl] *a* (*Am* **willful**) (*intentional, obstinate*) volontaire. **◆—ly** *adv* volontairement.

will[1] [wɪl] *v aux* **he will come, he'll come** (*future tense*) il viendra (**won't he?** n'est-ce pas?); **you will not come, you won't come** tu ne viendras pas (**will you?** n'est-ce pas?); **w. you have a tea?** veux-tu prendre un thé?; **w. you be quiet!** veux-tu te taire!; **I w.!** (*yes*) oui!; **it won't open** ça ne s'ouvre pas, ça ne veut pas s'ouvrir.

will[2] [wɪl] **1** *vt* (*wish, intend*) vouloir (**that** que (+ *sub*)); **to w. oneself to do** faire un effort de volonté pour faire; – *n* volonté *f*; **against one's w.** à contrecœur; **at w.** (*to depart etc*) quand on veut; (*to choose*) à volonté. **2** *n* (*legal document*) testament *m*. **◆willpower** *n* volonté *f*.

willing ['wɪlɪŋ] *a* (*helper, worker*) de bonne volonté; (*help etc*) spontané; **to be w. to do** être disposé *or* prêt à faire, vouloir bien faire; – *n* **to show w.** faire preuve de bonne volonté. **◆—ly** *adv* (*with pleasure*) volontiers; (*voluntarily*) volontairement. **◆—ness** *n* (*goodwill*) bonne volonté *f*; **his** *or* **her w. to do** (*enthusiasm*) son empressement *m* à faire.

willow ['wɪləʊ] *n* (*tree, wood*) saule *m*. **◆willowy** *a* (*person*) svelte.

willy-nilly [wɪlɪ'nɪlɪ] *adv* bon gré mal gré, de gré ou de force.

wilt [wɪlt] *vi* (*of plant*) dépérir; (*of enthusiasm etc*) *Fig* décliner.

wily ['waɪlɪ] *a* (**-ier, -iest**) rusé.

wimp [wɪmp] *n* (*weakling*) *Fam* mauviette *f*.

win [wɪn] *n* (*victory*) victoire *f*; – *vi* (*pt & pp* **won**, *pres p* **winning**) gagner; – *vt* (*money, race etc*) gagner; (*victory, prize*) remporter; (*fame*) acquérir; (*friends*) se faire; **to w. s.o. over** gagner qn (**to** à). **◆winning** *a* (*number, horse etc*) gagnant; (*team*) victorieux; (*goal*) décisif; (*smile*) engageant; – *npl* gains *mpl*.

wince [wɪns] *vi* (*flinch*) tressaillir; (*pull a face*) grimacer; **without wincing** sans sourciller.

winch [wɪntʃ] *n* treuil *m*; – *vt* **to w. (up)** hisser au treuil.

wind[1] [wɪnd] *n* vent *m*; (*breath*) souffle *m*; **to have w.** *Med* avoir des gaz; **to get w. of** *Fig* avoir vent de; **in the w.** *Fig* dans l'air; **w. instrument** *Mus* instrument *m* à vent; – *vt* **to w. s.o.** (*of blow etc*) couper le souffle à qn. ◆**windbreak** *n* (*fence, trees*) brise-vent *m inv*. ◆**windcheater** *n*, *Am* ◆**windbreaker** *n* blouson *m*, coupe-vent *m inv*. ◆**windfall** *n* (*piece of fruit*) fruit *m* abattu par le vent; (*unexpected money*) *Fig* aubaine *f*. ◆**windmill** *n* moulin *m* à vent. ◆**windpipe** *n* *Anat* trachée *f*. ◆**windscreen** *n*, *Am* ◆**windshield** *n* *Aut* pare-brise *m inv*; **w. wiper** essuie-glace *m inv*. ◆**windsurfing** *n* **to go w.** faire de la planche à voile. ◆**windswept** *a* (*street etc*) balayé par les vents. ◆**windy** *a* (**-ier, -iest**) venteux, venté; **it's w.** (*of weather*) il y a du vent.

wind[2] [waɪnd] *vt* (*pt & pp* **wound**) (*roll*) enrouler; **to w. (up)** (*clock*) remonter; **to w. up** (*meeting*) terminer; (*firm*) liquider; – *vi* (*of river, road*) serpenter; **to w. down** (*relax*) se détendre; **to w. up** (*end up*) finir (**doing** par faire); **to w. up with sth** se retrouver avec qch. ◆**—ing** *a* (*road etc*) sinueux; (*staircase*) tournant. ◆**—er** *n* (*of watch*) remontoir *m*.

window ['wɪndəʊ] *n* fenêtre *f*; (*pane*) vitre *f*, carreau *m*; (*in vehicle or train*) vitre *f*; (*in shop*) vitrine *f*; (*counter*) guichet *m*; **French w.** porte-fenêtre *f*; **w. box** jardinière *f*; **w. cleaner** *or Am* **washer** laveur, -euse *mf* de carreaux; **w. dresser** étalagiste *mf*; **w. ledge** = **windowsill**; **to go w. shopping** faire du lèche-vitrines. ◆**windowpane** *n* vitre *f*, carreau *m*. ◆**windowsill** *n* (*inside*) appui *m* de (la) fenêtre; (*outside*) rebord *m* de (la) fenêtre.

wine [waɪn] *n* vin *m*; – *a* (*bottle, cask*) à vin; **w. cellar** cave *f* (à vin); **w. grower** viticulteur *m*; **w. list** carte *f* des vins; **w. taster** dégustateur, -trice *mf* de vins; **w. tasting** dégustation *f* de vins; **w. waiter** sommelier *m*; – *vt* **to w. and dine s.o.** offrir à dîner et à boire à qn. ◆**wineglass** *n* verre *m* à vin. ◆**wine-growing** *a* viticole.

wing [wɪŋ] *n* aile *f*; **the wings** *Th* les coulisses *fpl*; **under one's w.** *Fig* sous son aile. ◆**winged** *a* ailé. ◆**winger** *n* *Sp* ailier *m*. ◆**wingspan** *n* envergure *f*.

wink [wɪŋk] *vi* faire un clin d'œil (**at, to** à); (*of light*) clignoter; – *n* clin *m* d'œil.

winkle ['wɪŋk(ə)l] *n* (*sea animal*) bigorneau *m*.

winner ['wɪnər] *n* (*of contest etc*) gagnant, -ante *mf*; (*of argument, fight*) vainqueur *m*; **that idea/***etc* **is a w.** *Fam* c'est une idée/*etc* en or.

winter ['wɪntər] *n* hiver *m*; – *a* d'hiver; **in (the) w.** en hiver. ◆**wintertime** *n* hiver *m*. ◆**wintry** *a* hivernal.

wip/e [waɪp] *vt* essuyer; **to w. one's feet/hands** s'essuyer les pieds/les mains; **to w. away** *or* **off** *or* **up** (*liquid*) essuyer; **to w. out** (*clean*) essuyer; (*erase*) effacer; (*destroy*) anéantir; – *vi* **to w. up** (*dry the dishes*) essuyer la vaisselle; – *n* coup *m* de torchon *or* d'éponge. ◆**—er** *n* *Aut* essuie-glace *m inv*.

wir/e ['waɪər] *n* fil *m*; (*telegram*) télégramme *m*; **w. netting** grillage *m*; – *vt* **to w. (up)** (*house*) *El* faire l'installation électrique de; **to w. s.o.** (*telegraph*) télégraphier à qn. ◆**—ing** *n* *El* installation *f* électrique. ◆**wirecutters** *npl* pince *f* coupante.

wireless ['waɪələs] *n* (*set*) TSF *f*, radio *f*; **by w.** (*to send a message*) par sans-fil.

wiry ['waɪərɪ] *a* (**-ier, -iest**) maigre et nerveux.

wisdom ['wɪzdəm] *n* sagesse *f*.

wise [waɪz] *a* (**-er, -est**) (*prudent*) sage, prudent; (*learned*) savant; **to put s.o. w./be w. to** *Fam* mettre qn/être au courant de; **w. guy** *Fam* gros malin *m*. ◆**wisecrack** *n* *Fam* (*joke*) astuce *f*; (*sarcastic remark*) sarcasme *m*. ◆**wisely** *adv* prudemment.

-wise [waɪz] *suffix* (*with regard to*) **money/***etc***-wise** question argent/*etc*.

wish [wɪʃ] *vt* souhaiter, vouloir (**to do** faire); **I w. (that) you could help me/could have helped me** je voudrais que/j'aurais voulu que vous m'aidiez; **I w. I hadn't done that** je regrette d'avoir fait ça; **if you w.** si tu veux; **I w. you well** *or* **luck** je vous souhaite bonne chance; **I wished him** *or* **her (a) happy birthday** je lui ai souhaité bon anniversaire; **I w. I could** si seulement je pouvais; – *vi* **to w. for sth** souhaiter qch; – *n* (*specific*) souhait *m*, vœu *m*; (*general*) désir *m*; **the w. for sth/to do** le désir de qch/de faire; **best wishes** (*on greeting card*) meilleurs vœux *mpl*; (*in letter*) amitiés *fpl*, bien amicalement; **send him** *or* **her my best wishes** fais-lui mes amitiés. ◆**wishbone** *n* bréchet *m*. ◆**wishful** *a* **it's w. thinking (on your part)** tu te fais des illusions, tu prends tes désirs pour la réalité.

wishy-washy ['wɪʃɪwɒʃɪ] *a* (*taste, colour*) fade.

wisp [wɪsp] *n* (*of smoke*) volute *f*; (*of hair*)

fine mèche *f*; **a (mere) w. of a girl** une fillette toute menue.

wisteria [wɪ'stɪərɪə] *n Bot* glycine *f*.

wistful ['wɪstfəl] *a* mélancolique et rêveur. ◆**—ly** *adv* avec mélancolie.

wit [wɪt] *n* **1** (*humour*) esprit *m*; (*person*) homme *m or* femme *f* d'esprit. **2 wit(s)** (*intelligence*) intelligence *f* (**to do** de faire); **to be at one's wits' or wit's end** ne plus savoir que faire.

witch [wɪtʃ] *n* sorcière *f*. ◆**witchcraft** *n* sorcellerie *f*. ◆**witch-hunt** *n Pol* chasse *f* aux sorcières.

with [wɪð] *prep* **1** avec; **come w. me** viens avec moi; **w. no hat** sans chapeau; **I'll be right w. you** je suis à vous dans une minute; **I'm w. you** (*I understand*) *Fam* je te suis; **w. it** (*up-to-date*) *Fam* dans le vent. **2** (*at the house, flat etc of*) chez; **she's staying w. me** elle loge chez moi; **it's a habit w. me** c'est une habitude chez moi. **3** (*cause*) de; **to jump w. joy** sauter de joie. **4** (*instrument, means*) avec, de; **to write w. a pen** écrire avec un stylo; **to fill w.** remplir de; **satisfied w.** satisfait de; **w. my own eyes** de mes propres yeux. **5** (*description*) à; **w. blue eyes** aux yeux bleus. **6** (*despite*) malgré.

withdraw [wɪð'drɔː] *vt* (*pt* **withdrew,** *pp* **withdrawn**) retirer (**from** de); – *vi* se retirer (**from** de). ◆**withdrawn** *a* (*person*) renfermé. ◆**withdrawal** *n* retrait *m*; **to suffer from w. symptoms** (*of drug addict etc*) être en manque.

wither ['wɪðər] *vi* (*of plant etc*) se flétrir; – *vt* flétrir. ◆**—ed** *a* (*limb*) atrophié. ◆**—ing** *a* (*look*) foudroyant; (*remark*) cinglant.

withhold [wɪð'həʊld] *vt* (*pt & pp* **withheld**) (*help, permission etc*) refuser (**from** à); (*decision*) différer; (*money*) retenir (**from** de); (*information etc*) cacher (**from** à).

within [wɪ'ðɪn] *adv* à l'intérieur; – *prep* (*place, container etc*) à l'intérieur de, dans; **w. a kilometre of** à moins d'un kilomètre de; **w. a month** (*to return etc*) avant un mois; (*to finish sth*) en moins d'un mois; (*to pay*) sous un mois; **w. my means** dans (les limites de) mes moyens; **w. sight** en vue.

without [wɪ'ðaʊt] *prep* sans; **w. a tie**/*etc* sans cravate/*etc*; **w. doing** sans faire.

withstand [wɪð'stænd] *vt* (*pt & pp* **withstood**) résister à.

witness ['wɪtnɪs] *n* (*person*) témoin *m*; (*evidence*) *Jur* témoignage *m*; **to bear w. to** témoigner de; – *vt* être (le) témoin de, voir; (*document*) signer (pour attester l'authenticité de).

witty ['wɪtɪ] *a* (**-ier, -iest**) spirituel. ◆**witticism** *n* bon mot *m*, mot *m* d'esprit. ◆**wittiness** *n* esprit *m*.

wives [waɪvz] *see* **wife.**

wizard ['wɪzəd] *n* magicien *m*; (*genius*) *Fig* génie *m*, as *m*.

wizened ['wɪz(ə)nd] *a* ratatiné.

wobble ['wɒb(ə)l] *vi* (*of chair etc*) branler, boiter; (*of cyclist, pile etc*) osciller; (*of jelly, leg*) trembler; (*of wheel*) tourner de façon irrégulière. ◆**wobbly** *a* (*table etc*) bancal, boiteux; **to be w. = to wobble.**

woe [wəʊ] *n* malheur *m*. ◆**woeful** *a* triste.

woke, woken [wəʊk, 'wəʊkən] *see* **wake**[1].

wolf [wʊlf] **1** *n* (*pl* **wolves**) loup *m*; **w. whistle** sifflement *m* admiratif. **2** *vt* **to w. (down)** (*food*) engloutir.

woman, *pl* **women** ['wʊmən, 'wɪmɪn] *n* femme *f*; **she's a London w.** c'est une Londonienne; **w. doctor** femme *f* médecin; **women drivers** les femmes *fpl* au volant; **w. friend** amie *f*; **w. teacher** professeur *m* femme; **women's** (*attitudes, clothes etc*) féminin. ◆**womanhood** *n* (*quality*) féminité *f*; **to reach w.** devenir femme. ◆**womanizer** *n Pej* coureur *m* (de femmes *or* de jupons). ◆**womanly** *a* féminin.

womb [wuːm] *n* utérus *m*.

women ['wɪmɪn] *see* **woman.**

won [wʌn] *see* **win.**

wonder ['wʌndər] **1** *n* (*marvel*) merveille *f*, miracle *m*; (*sense, feeling*) émerveillement *m*; **in w.** (*to watch etc*) émerveillé; **(it's) no w.** ce n'est pas étonnant (**that** que (+ *sub*)); – *vi* (*marvel*) s'étonner (**at** de); – *vt* **I w. that** je *or* ça m'étonne que (+ *sub*). **2** *vt* (*ask oneself*) se demander (**if** si, **why** pourquoi); – *vi* (*reflect*) songer (**about** à). ◆**wonderful** *a* (*excellent, astonishing*) merveilleux. ◆**wonderfully** *adv* (*beautiful, hot etc*) merveilleusement; (*to do, work etc*) à merveille.

wonky ['wɒŋkɪ] *a* (**-ier, -iest**) *Fam* (*table etc*) bancal; (*hat, picture*) de travers.

won't [wəʊnt] = **will not.**

woo [wuː] *vt* (*woman*) faire la cour à, courtiser; (*try to please*) *Fig* chercher à plaire à.

wood [wʊd] *n* (*material, forest*) bois *m*. ◆**woodcut** *n* gravure *f* sur bois. ◆**wooded** *a* (*valley etc*) boisé. ◆**wooden** *a* de *or* en bois; (*manner, dancer etc*) *Fig* raide. ◆**woodland** *n* région *f* boisée. ◆**woodpecker** *n* (*bird*) pic *m*. ◆**woodwind** *n* (*instruments*) *Mus* bois *mpl*. ◆**woodwork** *n* (*craft, objects*) menuiserie *f*. ◆**woodworm** *n* (*larvae*) vers *mpl* (du bois); **it has w.** c'est vermoulu. ◆**woody** *a*

(-ier, -iest) (*hill etc*) boisé; (*stem etc*) ligneux.

wool [wʊl] *n* laine *f*; – *a* de laine; (*industry*) lainier. ◆**woollen** *a* de laine; (*industry*) lainier; – *npl* (*garments*) lainages *mpl*. ◆**woolly** *a* (-ier, -iest) laineux; (*unclear*) *Fig* nébuleux; – *n* (*garment*) *Fam* lainage *m*.

word [wɜːd] *n* mot *m*; (*spoken*) parole *f*, mot *m*; (*promise*) parole *f*; (*command*) ordre *m*; *pl* (*of song etc*) paroles *fpl*; **by w. of mouth** de vive voix; **to have a w. with s.o.** (*speak to*) parler à qn; (*advise, lecture*) avoir un mot avec qn; **in other words** autrement dit; **I have no w. from** (*news*) je suis sans nouvelles de; **to send w. that . . .** faire savoir que . . . ; **to leave w. that . . .** dire que . . . ; **the last w. in** (*latest development*) le dernier cri en matière de; **w. processing** traitement *m* de texte; – *vt* (*express*) rédiger, formuler. ◆**wording** *n* termes *mpl*. ◆**wordy** *a* (-ier, -iest) verbeux.

wore [wɔːr] *see* **wear 1,2**.

work [wɜːk] *n* travail *m*; (*product*) & *Liter* œuvre *f*, ouvrage *m*; (*building or repair work*) travaux *mpl*; **to be at w.** travailler; **farm w.** travaux *mpl* agricoles; **out of w.** au *or* en chômage; **a day off w.** un jour de congé *or* de repos; **he's off w.** il n'est pas allé travailler; **the works** (*mechanism*) le mécanisme; **a gas works** (*factory*) une usine à gaz; **w. force** main-d'œuvre *f*; **a heavy w. load** beaucoup de travail; – *vi* travailler; (*of machine etc*) marcher, fonctionner; (*of drug*) agir; **to w. on** (*book etc*) travailler à; (*principle*) se baser sur; **to w. at** *or* **on sth** (*improve*) travailler qch; **to w. loose** (*of knot, screw*) se desserrer; (*of tooth*) se mettre à branler; **to w. towards** (*result, agreement, aim*) travailler à; **to w. out** (*succeed*) marcher; (*train*) *Sp* s'entraîner; **it works out at £5** ça fait cinq livres; **it works up to** (*climax*) ça tend vers; **to w. up to sth** (*in speech etc*) en venir à qch; – *vt* (*person*) faire travailler; (*machine*) faire marcher; (*mine*) exploiter; (*miracle*) faire; (*metal, wood etc*) travailler; **to get worked up** s'exciter; **to w. in** (*reference, bolt*) introduire; **to w. off** (*debt*) payer en travaillant; (*excess fat*) se débarrasser de (par l'exercice); (*anger*) passer, assouvir; **to w. out** (*solve*) résoudre; (*calculate*) calculer; (*scheme, plan*) élaborer; **to w. up an appetite** s'ouvrir l'appétit; **to w. up enthusiasm** s'enthousiasmer; **to w. one's way up** (*rise socially etc*) faire du chemin. ◆**working** *a* (*day, clothes etc*) de travail; (*population*) actif; **Monday's a w. day** on travaille le lundi, lundi est un jour ouvré; **w. class** class *f* ouvrière; **in w. order** en état de marche; – *npl* (*mechanism*) mécanisme *m*. ◆**workable** *a* (*plan*) praticable. ◆**worker** *n* travailleur, -euse *mf*; (*manual*) ouvrier, -ière *mf*; (*employee, clerk*) employé, -ée *mf*; **blue-collar w.** col *m* bleu.

workaholic [wɜːkəˈhɒlɪk] *n Fam* bourreau *m* de travail. ◆**'workbench** *n* établi *m*. ◆**working-'class** *a* ouvrier. ◆**'workman** *n* (*pl* -men) ouvrier *m*. ◆**'workmanship** *n* maîtrise *f*, travail *m*. ◆**'workmate** *n* camarade *mf* de travail. ◆**'workout** *n Sp* (séance *f*) d'entraînement *m*. ◆**'workroom** *n* salle *f* de travail. ◆**'workshop** *n* atelier *m*. ◆**'work-shy** *a* peu enclin au travail. ◆**work-to-'rule** *n* grève *f* du zèle.

world [wɜːld] *n* monde *m*; **all over the w.** dans le monde entier; **the richest/*etc* in the world** le *or* la plus riche/*etc* du monde; **a w. of** (*a lot of*) énormément de; **to think the w. of** penser énormément de bien de; **why in the w. . . . ?** pourquoi diable . . . ?; **out of this w.** (*wonderful*) *Fam* formidable; – *a* (*war etc*) mondial; (*champion, cup, record*) du monde. ◆**world-'famous** *a* de renommée mondiale. ◆**worldly** *a* (*pleasures*) de ce monde; (*person*) qui a l'expérience du monde. ◆**world'wide** *a* universel.

worm [wɜːm] **1** *n* ver *m*. **2** *vt* **to w. one's way into** s'insinuer dans; **to w. sth out of s.o.** soutirer qch à qn. ◆**worm-eaten** *a* (*wood*) vermoulu; (*fruit*) véreux.

worn [wɔːn] *see* **wear 1,2**; – *a* (*tyre etc*) usé. ◆**worn-'out** *a* (*object*) complètement usé; (*person*) épuisé.

worry [ˈwʌrɪ] *n* souci *m*; – *vi* s'inquiéter (**about sth** de qch, **about s.o.** pour qn); – *vt* inquiéter; **to be worried** être inquiet; **to be worried sick** se ronger les sangs. ◆**—ing** *a* (*news etc*) inquiétant. ◆**worrier** *n* anxieux, -euse *mf*. ◆**worryguts** *n*, *Am* ◆**worrywart** *n Fam* anxieux, -euse *mf*.

worse [wɜːs] *a* pire, plus mauvais (**than** que); **to get w.** se détériorer; **he's getting w.** (*in health*) il va de plus en plus mal; (*in behaviour*) il se conduit de plus en plus mal; – *adv* plus mal (**than** que); **I could do w.** je pourrais faire pire; **to hate/*etc* w. than** détester/*etc* plus que; **to be w. off** (*financially*) aller moins bien financièrement; – *n* **there's w. (to come)** il y a pire encore; **a change for the w.** une détérioration. ◆**worsen** *vti* empirer.

worship [ˈwɜːʃɪp] *n* culte *m*; **his W. the Mayor** Monsieur le Maire; – *vt* (-pp-)

(*person*) & *Rel* adorer; (*money etc*) *Pej* avoir le culte de; – *vi Rel* faire ses dévotions (**at** à). ◆**worshipper** *n* adorateur, -trice *mf*; (*in church*) fidèle *mf*.

worst [wɜːst] *a* pire, plus mauvais; – *adv* (**the**) **w.** le plus mal; **to come off w.** (*in struggle etc*) avoir le dessous; – *n* **the w.** (**one**) (*object, person*) le *or* la pire, le *or* la plus mauvais(e); **the w.** (**thing**) **is that . . .** le pire c'est que . . . ; **at** (**the**) **w.** au pis aller; **at its w.** (*crisis*) à son plus mauvais point *or* moment; **to get the w. of it** (*in struggle etc*) avoir le dessous; **the w. is yet to come** on n'a pas encore vu le pire.

worsted ['wʊstɪd] *n* laine *f* peignée.

worth [wɜːθ] *n* valeur *f*; **to buy 50 pence w. of chocolates** acheter pour cinquante pence de chocolats; – *a* **to be w.** valoir; **how much** *or* **what is it w.?** ça vaut combien?; **the film's w. seeing** le film vaut la peine *or* le coup d'être vu; **it's w.** (**one's**) **while** ça (en) vaut la peine *or* le coup; **it's w.** (**while**) **waiting** ça vaut la peine d'attendre. ◆**worthless** *a* qui ne vaut rien. ◆**worth'while** *a* (*book, film etc*) qui vaut la peine d'être lu, vu *etc*; (*activity*) qui (en) vaut la peine; (*contribution, plan*) valable; (*cause*) louable; (*satisfying*) qui donne des satisfactions.

worthy ['wɜːðɪ] *a* (**-ier, -iest**) digne (**of** de); (*laudable*) louable; – *n* (*person*) notable *m*.

would [wʊd, *unstressed* wəd] *v aux* **I w. stay, I'd stay** (*conditional tense*) je resterais; **he w. have done it** il l'aurait fait; **w. you help me, please?** voulez-vous m'aider, s'il vous plaît?; **w. you like some tea?** voudriez-vous (prendre) du thé?; **I w. see her every day** (*used to*) je la voyais chaque jour. ◆**would-be** *a* (*musician etc*) soi-disant.

wound[1] [wuːnd] *vt* (*hurt*) blesser; **the wounded** les blessés *mpl*; – *n* blessure *f*.

wound[2] [waʊnd] *see* **wind**[2].

wove, woven [wəʊv, 'wəʊv(ə)n] *see* **weave**.

wow! [waʊ] *int Fam* (c'est) formidable!

wrangle ['ræŋg(ə)l] *n* dispute *f*; – *vi* se disputer.

wrap [ræp] *vt* (**-pp-**) **to w.** (**up**) envelopper; **to w.** (**oneself**) **up** (*dress warmly*) se couvrir; **wrapped up in** (*engrossed*) *Fig* absorbé par; – *n* (*shawl*) châle *m*; (*cape*) pèlerine *f*; **plastic w.** *Am* scel-o-frais® *m*. ◆**wrapping** *n* (*action, material*) emballage *m*; **w. paper** papier *m* d'emballage. ◆**wrapper** *n* (*of sweet*) papier *m*; (*of book*) jaquette *f*.

wrath [rɒθ] *n Lit* courroux *m*.

wreak [riːk] *vt* **to w. vengeance on** se venger de; **to w. havoc on** ravager.

wreath [riːθ] *n* (*pl* **-s** [riːðz]) (*on head, for funeral*) couronne *f*.

wreck [rek] *n* (*ship*) épave *f*; (*sinking*) naufrage *m*; (*train etc*) train *m etc* accidenté; (*person*) épave *f* (humaine); **to be a nervous w.** être à bout de nerfs; – *vt* détruire; (*ship*) provoquer le naufrage de; (*career, hopes etc*) *Fig* briser, détruire. ◆**—age** *n* (*fragments*) débris *mpl*. ◆**—er** *n* (*breakdown truck*) *Am* dépanneuse *f*.

wren [ren] *n* (*bird*) roitelet *m*.

wrench [rentʃ] *vt* (*tug at*) tirer sur; (*twist*) tordre; **to w. sth from s.o.** arracher qch à qn; – *n* mouvement *m* de torsion; (*tool*) clé *f* (à écrous), *Am* clé *f* à mollette; (*distress*) *Fig* déchirement *m*.

wrest [rest] *vt* **to w. sth from s.o.** arracher qch à qn.

wrestl/e ['res(ə)l] *vi* lutter (**with s.o.** contre qn); **to w. with** (*problem etc*) *Fig* se débattre avec. ◆**—ing** *n Sp* lutte *f*; (**all-in**) **w.** catch *m*. ◆**—er** *n* lutteur, -euse *mf*; catcheur, -euse *mf*.

wretch [retʃ] *n* (*unfortunate person*) malheureux, -euse *mf*; (*rascal*) misérable *mf*. ◆**wretched** [-ɪd] *a* (*poor, pitiful*) misérable; (*dreadful*) affreux; (*annoying*) maudit.

wriggle ['rɪg(ə)l] *vi* **to w.** (**about**) se tortiller; (*of fish*) frétiller; **to w. out of** (*difficulty, task etc*) esquiver; – *vt* (*fingers, toes*) tortiller.

wring [rɪŋ] *vt* (*pt & pp* **wrung**) (*neck*) tordre; **to w.** (**out**) (*clothes*) essorer; (*water*) faire sortir; **to w. sth out of s.o.** *Fig* arracher qch à qn; **wringing wet** (trempé) à tordre.

wrinkle ['rɪŋk(ə)l] *n* (*on skin*) ride *f*; (*in cloth or paper*) pli *m*; – *vt* (*skin*) rider; (*cloth, paper*) plisser; – *vi* se rider; faire des plis.

wrist [rɪst] *n* poignet *m*. ◆**wristwatch** *n* montre-bracelet *f*.

writ [rɪt] *n* acte *m* judiciaire; **to issue a w. against s.o.** assigner qn (en justice).

write [raɪt] *vt* (*pt* **wrote**, *pp* **written**) écrire; **to w. down** noter; **to w. off** (*debt*) passer aux profits et pertes; **to w. out** écrire; (*copy*) recopier; **to w. up** (*from notes*) rédiger; (*diary, notes*) mettre à jour; – *vi* écrire; **to w. away** *or* **off** *or* **up for** (*details etc*) écrire pour demander; **to w. back** répondre; **to w. in** *Rad TV* écrire (**for information/***etc* pour demander des renseignements/*etc*). ◆**w.-off** *n* **a** (**complete**) **w.-off** (*car*) une véritable épave. ◆**w.-up** *n* (*report*) *Journ* compte rendu *m*. ◆**writing** *n* (*handwriting*) écriture *f*; (*literature*) littérature *f*; **to put** (**down**) **in w.** mettre par écrit; **some w.** (*on page*) quelque chose d'écrit; **his** *or* **her**

writing(s) (*works*) ses écrits *mpl*; **w. desk** secrétaire *m*; **w. pad** bloc *m* de papier à lettres; **w. paper** papier *m* à lettres. ◆**writer** *n* auteur *m* (**of** de); (*literary*) écrivain *m*.

writhe [raɪð] *vi* (*in pain etc*) se tordre.

written ['rɪt(ə)n] *see* **write.**

wrong [rɒŋ] *a* (*sum, idea etc*) faux, erroné; (*direction, time etc*) mauvais; (*unfair*) injuste; **to be w.** (*of person*) avoir tort (**to do** de faire); (*mistaken*) se tromper; **it's w. to swear**/*etc* (*morally*) c'est mal de jurer/*etc*; **it's the w. road** ce n'est pas la bonne route; **you're the w. man** (*for job etc*) tu n'es pas l'homme qu'il faut; **the clock's w.** la pendule n'est pas à l'heure; **something's w.** quelque chose ne va pas; **something's w. with the phone** le téléphone ne marche pas bien; **something's w. with her arm** elle a quelque chose au bras; **nothing's w.** tout va bien; **what's w. with you?** qu'est-ce que tu as?; **the w. way round** *or* **up** à l'envers; – *adv* mal; **to go w.** (*err*) se tromper; (*of plan*) mal tourner; (*of vehicle, machine*) tomber en panne; – *n* (*injustice*) injustice *f*; (*evil*) mal *m*; **to be in the w.** avoir tort; **right and w.** le bien et le mal; – *vt* faire (du) tort à. ◆**wrongdoer** *n* (*criminal*) malfaiteur *m*. ◆**wrongful** *a* injustifié; (*arrest*) arbitraire. ◆**wrongfully** *adv* à tort. ◆**wrongly** *adv* incorrectement; (*to inform, translate*) mal; (*to suspect etc*) à tort.

wrote [rəʊt] *see* **write.**

wrought [rɔːt] *a* **w. iron** fer *m* forgé. ◆**w.-'iron** *a* en fer forgé.

wrung [rʌŋ] *see* **wring.**

wry [raɪ] *a* (**wryer, wryest**) (*comment*) ironique; (*smile*) forcé; **to pull a w. face** grimacer.

X

X, x [eks] *n* X, x *m*. ◆**X-ray** *n* (*beam*) rayon *m* X; (*photo*) radio(graphie) *f*; **to have an X-ray** passer une radio; **X-ray examination** examen *m* radioscopique; – *vt* radiographier.

xenophobia [zenə'fəʊbɪə] *n* xénophobie *f*.

Xerox® ['zɪərɒks] *n* photocopie *f*; – *vt* photocopier.

Xmas ['krɪsməs] *n Fam* Noël *m*.

xylophone ['zaɪləfəʊn] *n* xylophone *m*.

Y

Y, y [waɪ] *n* Y, y *m*.

yacht [jɒt] *n* yacht *m*. ◆**—ing** *n* yachting *m*.

yank [jæŋk] *vt Fam* tirer d'un coup sec; **to y. off** *or* **out** arracher; – *n* coup *m* sec.

Yank(ee) ['jæŋk(ɪ)] *n Fam* Ricain, -aine *mf*, *Pej* Amerloque *mf*.

yap [jæp] *vi* (**-pp-**) (*of dog*) japper; (*jabber*) *Fam* jacasser.

yard [jɑːd] *n* **1** (*of house etc*) cour *f*; (*for storage*) dépôt *m*, chantier *m*; (*garden*) *Am* jardin *m* (*à l'arrière de la maison*); **builder's y.** chantier *m* de construction. **2** (*measure*) yard *m* (*= 91,44 cm*). ◆**yardstick** *n* (*criterion*) mesure *f*.

yarn [jɑːn] *n* **1** (*thread*) fil *m*. **2** (*tale*) *Fam* longue histoire *f*.

yawn [jɔːn] *vi* bâiller; – *n* bâillement *m*. ◆**—ing** *a* (*gulf etc*) béant.

yeah [jeə] *adv* (*yes*) *Fam* ouais.

year [jɪər] *n* an *m*, année *f*; (*of wine*) année *f*; **school/tax/***etc* **y.** année *f* scolaire/fiscale/*etc*; **this y.** cette année; **in the y. 1990** en (l'an) 1990; **he's ten years old** il a dix ans; **New Y.** Nouvel An, Nouvelle Année; **New Year's Day** le jour de l'An; **New Year's Eve** la Saint-Sylvestre. ◆**yearbook** *n* annuaire *m*. ◆**yearly** *a* annuel; – *adv* annuellement.

yearn [jɜːn] *vi* **to y. for s.o.** languir après qn; **to y. for sth** avoir très envie de qch; **to y. to do** avoir très envie de faire. ◆**—ing** *n* grande envie *f* (**for** de, **to do** de faire); (*nostalgia*) nostalgie *f*.

yeast [jiːst] *n* levure *f*.

yell [jel] *vti* **to y. (out)** hurler; **to y. at s.o.** (*scold*) crier après qn; – *n* hurlement *m*.

yellow ['jeləʊ] **1** *a & n (colour)* jaune (*m*); – *vi* jaunir. **2** *a (cowardly) Fam* froussard. ◆**yellowish** *a* jaunâtre.
yelp [jelp] *vi (of dog)* japper; – *n* jappement *m*.
yen [jen] *n (desire)* grande envie *f* (**for** de, **to** do de faire).
yes [jes] *adv* oui; *(contradicting negative question)* si; – *n* oui *m inv*.
yesterday ['jestədɪ] *adv & n* hier (*m*); **y. morning/evening** hier matin/soir; **the day before y.** avant-hier.
yet [jet] **1** *adv* encore; *(already)* déjà; **she hasn't come (as) y.** elle n'est pas encore venue; **has he come y.?** est-il déjà arrivé?; **the best y.** le meilleur jusqu'ici; **y. more complicated** *(even more)* encore plus compliqué; **not (just) y., not y. awhile** pas pour l'instant. **2** *conj (nevertheless)* pourtant.
yew [juː] *n (tree, wood)* if *m*.
Yiddish ['jɪdɪʃ] *n & a* yiddish (*m*).
yield [jiːld] *n* rendement *m*; *(profit)* rapport *m*; – *vt (produce)* produire, rendre; *(profit)* rapporter; *(give up)* céder (**to** à); – *vi (surrender, give way)* céder (**to** à); *(of tree, land etc)* rendre; '**y.**' *(road sign) Am* 'cédez la priorité'.
yob(bo) ['jɒb(əʊ)] *n (pl* **yob(bo)s**) *Sl* loubar(d) *m*.
yoga ['jəʊgə] *n* yoga *m*.
yog(h)urt ['jɒgət, *Am* 'jəʊgɜːt] *n* yaourt *m*.
yoke [jəʊk] *n (for oxen) & Fig* joug *m*.
yokel ['jəʊk(ə)l] *n Pej* plouc *m*.
yolk [jəʊk] *n* jaune *m* (d'œuf).
yonder ['jɒndər] *adv Lit* là-bas.
you [juː] *pron* **1** *(polite form singular)* vous; *(familiar form singular)* tu; *(polite and familar form plural)* vous; *(object)* vous; te, t'; *pl* vous; *(after prep & stressed)* vous; toi; *pl* vous; **(to) y.** *(indirect)* vous; te, t'; *pl* vous; **y. are** vous êtes; tu es; **I see y.** je vous vois; je te vois; **I give it to y.** je vous le donne; je te le donne; **with y.** avec vous; avec toi; **y. teachers** vous autres professeurs; **y. idiot!** espèce d'imbécile! **2** *(indefinite)* on; *(object)* vous; te, t'; *pl* vous; **y. never know** on ne sait jamais.
young [jʌŋ] *a* (**-er, -est**) jeune; **my young(er) brother** mon (frère) cadet; **his** *or* **her youngest brother** le cadet de ses frères; **the youngest son** le cadet; – *n (of animals)* petits *mpl*; **the y.** *(people)* les jeunes *mpl*. ◆**young-looking** *a* qui a l'air jeune. ◆**youngster** *n* jeune *mf*.
your [jɔːr] *poss a (polite form singular, polite and familiar form plural)* votre, *pl* vos; *(familiar form singular)* ton, ta, *pl* tes; *(one's)* son, sa, *pl* ses. ◆**yours** *poss pron* le vôtre, la vôtre, *pl* les vôtres; *(familiar form singular)* le tien, la tienne, *pl* les tien(ne)s; **this book is y.** ce livre est à vous *or* est le vôtre; ce livre est à toi *or* est le tien; **a friend of y.** un ami à vous; un ami à toi. ◆**your'self** *pron (polite form)* vous-même; *(familiar form)* toi-même; *(reflexive)* vous; te, t'; *(after prep)* vous; toi; **you wash y.** vous vous lavez; tu te laves. ◆**your'selves** *pron pl* vous-mêmes; *(reflexive & after prep)* vous.
youth [juːθ] *n (pl* **-s** [juːðz]) *(age, young people)* jeunesse *f*; *(young man)* jeune *m*; **y. club** maison *f* des jeunes. ◆**youthful** *a (person)* jeune; *(quality, smile etc)* juvénile, jeune. ◆**youthfulness** *n* jeunesse *f*.
yoyo ['jəʊjəʊ] *n (pl* **-os**) yo-yo *m inv*.
yucky ['jʌkɪ] *a Sl* dégueulasse.
Yugoslav ['juːgəʊslɑːv] *a & n* yougoslave (*mf*). ◆**Yugo'slavia** *n* Yougoslavie *f*.
yummy ['jʌmɪ] *a* (**-ier, -iest**) *Sl* délicieux.
yuppie ['jʌpɪ] *n* jeune cadre *m* ambitieux, jeune loup *m*, NAP *mf*.

Z

Z, z [zed, *Am* ziː] *n* Z, z *m*.
zany ['zeɪnɪ] *a* (**-ier, -iest**) farfelu.
zeal [ziːl] *n* zèle *m*. ◆**zealous** ['zeləs] *a* zélé. ◆**zealously** *adv* avec zèle.
zebra ['ziːbrə, 'zebrə] *n* zèbre *m*; **z. crossing** passage *m* pour piétons.
zenith ['zenɪθ] *n* zénith *m*.
zero ['zɪərəʊ] *n (pl* **-os**) zéro *m*; **z. hour** *Mil & Fig* l'heure H.
zest [zest] *n* **1** *(gusto)* entrain *m*; *(spice) Fig* piquant *m*; **z. for living** appétit *m* de vivre. **2** *(of lemon, orange)* zeste *m*.
zigzag ['zɪgzæg] *n* zigzag *m*; – *a & adv* en zigzag; – *vi* (**-gg-**) zigzaguer.
zinc [zɪŋk] *n (metal)* zinc *m*.
zip [zɪp] **1** *n* **z. (fastener)** fermeture *f* éclair®; – *vt* (**-pp-**) **to z. (up)** fermer (avec une fermeture éclair®). **2** *n (vigour) Fam*

entrain *m*; – *vi* (-pp-) (*go quickly*) aller comme l'éclair. **3** *a* **z. code** *Am* code *m* postal. ◆**zipper** *n Am* fermeture *f* éclair®.

zit [zɪt] *n* (*pimple*) *Am Fam* bouton *m*.

zither ['zɪðər] *n* cithare *f*.

zodiac ['zəʊdɪæk] *n* zodiaque *m*.

zombie ['zɒmbɪ] *n* (*spiritless person*) *Fam* robot *m*, zombie *m*.

zone [zəʊn] *n* zone *f*; (*division of city*) secteur *m*.

zoo [zuː] *n* zoo *m*. ◆**zoological** [zuːə'lɒdʒɪk(ə)l] *a* zoologique. ◆**zoology** [zuː'ɒlədʒɪ] *n* zoologie *f*.

zoom [zuːm] **1** *vi* (*rush*) se précipiter; **to z. past** passer comme un éclair. **2** *n* **z. lens** zoom *m*; – *vi* **to z. in** *Cin* faire un zoom, zoomer (**on** sur).

zucchini [zuː'kiːnɪ] *n* (*pl* **-ni** *or* **-nis**) *Am* courgette *f*.

zwieback ['zwiːbæk] *n* (*rusk*) *Am* biscotte *f*